LABELS AND ABBREVIATIONS

JEWEL.	jewelry
JOURN.	journalism
LAW	law
LING.	linguistics
LIT.	literature
LOG.	logic
m.	masculine
MACH.	machinery
MARIT.	maritime, nautical
MAS.	masonry
MATH.	mathematics
MECH.	mechanics
MED.	medicine
METAL.	metallurgy
METEOROL.	meteorology
MEX.	Mexico
MIL.	military
MIN.	mining, mineralogy
MUS.	music
MYTH.	mythology
NEOL.	neologism
neut.	neuter
NIC.	Nicaragua
NUMIS.	numismatics
OPHTHAL.	ophthalmology
OPT.	optics
ORNITH.	ornithology
PAINT.	painting
PALEON.	paleontology
PAN.	Panama
PAR.	Paraguay
past part.	past participle
pers.	person, personal
PERU	Peru
PHARM.	pharmaceutics
PHILAT.	philately
PHILIP.	Philippines
PHILOL.	philology
PHILOS.	philosophy
PHONET.	phonetics
PHOTO.	photography
PHYS.	physics
PHYSIOL.	physiology
pl.	plural
POET.	poetry, poetic
POL.	politics
poss.	possessive

prep.	preposition
pres.	present
pres. part.	present participle
pret.	preterite
P. RICO	Puerto Rico
PRINT.	printing
pron.	pronoun
PSYCH.	psychology
RAD.	radio
RAIL.	railway
RARE	rare
reflex.	reflexive
REG.	regional
rel.	relative
RELIG.	religion
RHET.	rhetoric
SALV.	El Salvador
S. AMER.	South America
SCI.	science
SCULP.	sculpture
SEW.	sewing
sing.	singular
SL.	slang
SOCIOL.	sociology
SP.	Spain
SPORT.	sports
subj.	subjunctive
superl.	superlative
SURG.	surgery
SURV.	surveying
TAUR.	tauromachy
TECH.	technical
TELEC.	telecommunications
TELEV.	television
TEX.	textiles
THEAT.	theater
THEOL.	theology
TOP.	topography
tr.	transitive
URUG.	Uruguay
U.S.	United States
var.	variant
VEN.	Venezuela
VET.	veterinary
VULG.	vulgarism
ZOOL.	zoology

THE AMERICAN HERITAGE LAROUSSE SPANISH DICTIONARY

SPANISH/ENGLISH
ENGLISH/SPANISH

 Houghton Mifflin Company Boston

Library of Congress Cataloging-in-Publication Data

The American heritage Larousse Spanish dictionary.

"Spanish-English/English-Spanish"—Pref.

1. Spanish language—Dictionaries—English. 2. English language—Dictionaries—Spanish. I. Title: Larousse Spanish dictionary.

PC4640.A54   1986   463'.21   86-7202
ISBN 0-395-32429-7

Manufactured in the United States of America

TABLE OF CONTENTS

ÍNDICE

STAFF

Librairie Larousse

Project Editor
Françoise Dubois-Charlier, Ph.D.

Editors

Diane Traynor Senerth   J. Mauricio Sola

**Editorial Director,
Development Stage**
Philip M. Rideout

Houghton Mifflin Company

Editor
David R. Pritchard

**Director of Editorial
Operations**
Margery S. Berube

Publisher
Howard R. Webber

Executive Editor
Anne H. Soukhanov

Compilers

Gerardo Chang
Andrew Gordon
Hugo Halbrich
Laurie Anne Kaplis
Rafael Marcos
Esmeralda Martínez-Tapia

Beth Pfannl
Fernando Pfannl
Antonio Prieto
Robert Schmieder
Ralph Tachuk
Susan Wald

Editorial Consultants

Edmund L. King, Ph.D.
Princeton University

Rodolfo Cardona, Ph.D.
Boston University

Consultant in Lexicography
Roger J. Steiner, Ph.D.
University of Delaware

Assistant Editors
Lois Grossman
Roberto S. Miranda

Editorial Assistants
Janet Risheill Kelsen
Maria Christina Panos

Editorial Assistance
Flavia Radulescu

Pronunciation Editor
Anne D. Steinhardt

Proofreaders
Roy McCoy
Douglas Pauley
David Weeks

Special Consultant
Bernice Randall

Production Manager
Christopher Leonesio

Production Coordinator
Donna L. Muise

Editorial Production Assistant
Patricia McTiernan

Composition Keyboarding
Brenda Bregoli-Sturtevant
Celester Jackson
Ron Perkins

PREFACE

Houghton Mifflin's *American Heritage Dictionary* is the most innovative, and the most imitated, of American dictionaries to be published in recent decades. Its overwhelming critical and popular success has been testimony to the achievement of its principal goal of faithfully recording modern American English in an accessible and understandable way.

In the Spanish-speaking world, the name of Larousse has long enjoyed special distinction due to the recognized authority and wide circulation of its *Pequeño Larousse ilustrado*. Thoroughly revised and updated in recent years, this work is particularly noted for the currency of its lexicon and for the extensive inclusion of Latin American vocabulary and usage.

Now Houghton Mifflin and Larousse have joined forces to produce the first major new bilingual dictionary in many years, *The American Heritage Larousse Spanish Dictionary,* based upon the *American Heritage Dictionary* and the *Pequeño Larousse*.

This new work is distinguished from others of its kind in several ways. The English usage on both sides is that of the United States, with careful indication of the various levels of propriety. Peculiarly British forms and senses (always so noted) that the average reader is likely to encounter are also included. On the Spanish side, a corresponding effort has been made to represent both "pan-Hispanic" usage and the diverse special forms and senses found in Spanish America.

It would be rash to claim that any dictionary is without error. Nevertheless, in compiling *The American Heritage Larousse Spanish Dictionary,* the lexicographers have been at some pains to correct errors that have been passed down from one generation of dictionaries to another. And because the ease with which a dictionary is used depends not only on the words it contains but on those it omits, the compilers have generally omitted words that are not more or less current, and the space vacated by such obsolete forms is filled with a generous quota of technical and commercial words more serviceable in the contemporary world.

Because accuracy depends as much on the user of the dictionary as on its compilers, in multiple-sense entries synonyms for each sense are given in the language of the entry word. Entries are keyed to appropriate grammar references in the introductory matter, all entries are syllabicated, and the gender of Spanish nouns is noted on the English side.

In sum, Houghton Mifflin and Larousse offer here a new lexical base, an emphasis on U.S. and Latin American usage, greater accuracy, up-to-dateness, and a sensitivity to the practical needs of the user.

Edmund L. King, Ph.D.
Walter S. Carpenter, Jr., Professor in the Language, Literature, and Civilization of Spain, Emeritus; Professor of Romance Languages and Literatures, Emeritus
Princeton University

Rodolfo Cardona, Ph.D.
University Professor and Professor of Spanish and Comparative Literature
Boston University

EXPLANATORY DIAGRAM

equivalent

gra·má·ti·ca I. f. *(arte o texto)* grammar ♦ **andar a la g.** COLL. to look out for oneself • **g. parda** COLL. cleverness, shrewdness II. adj. see **gramático, –ca.** ← **related entry words**
gra·ma·ti·cal adj. grammatical.
gra·má·ti·co, –ca I. adj. grammatical II. m.f. grammarian —f. see **gramática.**
gra·mi·lla f. *(para agramar)* bed of a brake *or* scutcher; ARG., BOT. grass, lawn.
gra·mo m. gram, gramme (G.B.). ← **British variant**
gra·mó·fo·no m. gramophone, phonograph.
gra·mo·la f. phonograph.
gran §G21 adj. [contr. of **grande** used before sing. nouns] ← **grammatical information** great, grand *<una gran aventura* a great adventure> —see **grande.**

homographs →
gra·na¹ f. *(acción)* seeding; *(época)* seeding time; *(semilla)* seed ♦ **dar g.** to go to seed.
gra·na² f. ENTOM. cochineal insect; *(materia colorante)* cochineal; *(color)* scarlet; *(tela)* fine scarlet cloth ♦ **g. de Paraíso** BOT. cardamom • **ponerse rojo como la g.** to turn as red as a beet.

inflected entry word →
ha·ri·ne·ro, –ra I. adj. flour, of flour *<molino h.* flour mill> ← **example phrase** II. m. *(persona)* flour dealer; *(receptáculo)* flour bin.
ha·ri·no·so, –sa adj. *(que tiene harina)* floury, farinose; *(farináceo)* farinaceous.
har·mo·ni·a f. var. of **armonía.** ← **variant cross-reference**
har·ne·ro m. sieve, sifter.
har·pi·lle·ra f. burlap, sackcloth.
har·tar tr. *(saciar el apetito)* to fill, stuff; FIG. *(satisfacer)* to ← **sense discriminations** satisfy; *(fastidiar)* to annoy; *(aburrir)* to bore; *(cansar)* to tire, weary.
har·taz·go m. fill, bellyfull ♦ **darse un h. de** *(comer mucho)* to eat one's fill of; FIG. to have had one's fill of *<me di un h. de estudiar* I have had my fill of studying>.

past participle reference
har·to, –ta I. past part. of **hartar** II. adj. *(saciado)* full, satiated; *(cansado)* tired, fed up III. adv. *(bastante)* ← **parts of speech** enough; *(muy)* very.
har·tu·ra f. *(hartazgo)* bellyful, fill; POET. *(abundancia)* ← **usage label** abundance, wealth; FIG. *(logro)* gratification, fulfillment.

grammar reference
has·ta §G46 I. prep. until *<estudiamos h. las seis* we studied until six o'clock>; up to, as far as *<caminaron h. la biblioteca* they walked as far as the library> ♦ **h. la vista** *or* ← **example sentence** **h. luego** see you, so long • **h. mañana** see you tomorrow • **h. que** until II. adv. even *<h. los criados lo sabían* even the servants knew about it>.

irregular verb table reference
has·tiar §30 tr. *(cansar)* to tire, bore; *(asquear)* to disgust, sicken; *(fastidiar)* to annoy, bother.
has·tí·o m. *(repugnancia)* repugnance, revulsion (to food); ← **elaboration of equivalent** FIG. *(fastidio)* annoyance; *(tedio)* boredom, tedium.
ha·te·ar intr. *(recoger)* to gather (one's things together), pack up; AGR. *(dar hatería)* to give provisions (to shepherds).
ha·ti·llo m. small bundle (of one's belongings) ♦ **tomar el h.** FIG., COLL. to leave.
ha·to¹ m. *(porción de ganado)* herd *or* flock; *(cabaña de pastores)* pastor's hut; *(hatería)* provisions, supplies; FIG. *(banda)* gang, band; *(montón)* lot, bunch; CUBA, VEN. ← **regional labels** *(hacienda)* cattle ranch.
ha·to² m. everyday clothes, belongings ♦ **liar uno el h.** COLL. to pack one's things.

combined parts of speech
ha·wai·a·no, –na adj. & m.f. Hawaiian.
hay, haya see **haber².** ← **irregular verb forms**
Ha·ya f. ♦ **La H.** The Hague.

field label
haz¹ m. [pl. **ha·ces**] *(fardo)* bundle, bunch; *(de leña)* fagot; PHYS. pencil (of light rays) ♦ **haces de rectas** MATH. pencil of lines.

irregular plural
haz² f. [pl. **ha·ces**] *(cara)* face, countenance; FIG. *(de tela)* right side (of cloth) ♦ **a dos haces** FIG. with an ulterior motive • **h. de la tierra** face of the earth • **ser uno de dos** ← **idioms and phrases** **haces** FIG. to be two-faced.
haz³ see **hacer.**

GUIDE TO USING THE DICTIONARY

General Design

The American Heritage Larousse Spanish Dictionary has been specially designed for clarity, precision, and ease of use. The aim has been to provide the user with a precise equivalent for a word or phrase without having to turn back and forth between the sides to verify that choice. A combination of features in both English and Spanish is included within the entry in order to achieve this aim, and clear typographic distinctions have been observed in organizing the various elements of an entry into an easily usable form.

The diagram on the facing page identifies the chief organizational features of the Dictionary and indicates their position within the entry. Note that a distinction is maintained throughout the entry between the Spanish and English elements. The entry word, along with any idioms or phrases in which it is used, is in boldface type. Spanish words used to discriminate the various senses are in italic, as are example sentences that illustrate usage. All English elements, including equivalents, labels, and translations of example sentences, are in roman type. The entries are structured so as to enable the user to quickly scan a large amount of information for the particular item being sought.

Guide Words

As an aid to finding the page on which an entry appears, a pair of guide words is printed at the top of each page:

flotar	**fondo**	**252**

The word to the left of the vertical bar is the first of the sequence of entries on that page of the Dictionary. The word to the right of the bar is the last entry on the page. Thus **flotar** and **fondo** and all entries that fall between them alphabetically are entered on page 252.

Entry Words

Entry words are entered in alphabetical order in boldface type. Entry words are divided into syllables using boldface centered dots. For the criteria followed in syllabicating Spanish words, see the section on Spanish Orthography below (page xxix).

Homographs. Words which are identical in spelling but which constitute separate entries are entered with superscript numbers (Diagram: **grana¹** and **grana²**).

Inflected entry words. Nouns and adjectives that inflect for gender are entered under the masculine form. The syllable containing the feminine ending is separated from the masculine form by a comma and is preceded by a dash (Diagram: **harinero, –ra**).

Cross-references

Variants. When variant spellings of an entry word fall close to each other in alphabetical order, they are entered together and combined by *or:*

> **gra·de·rí·a** f. *or* **gra·de·rí·o** m. . . .

Otherwise they are entered as a cross-reference to the main entry (Diagram: **harmonía**).

Masculine and feminine nouns. Feminine noun forms are entered at their own place in the alphabetical order wherever appropriate. Entry words whose masculine and feminine forms are treated in separate entries are fully referenced to each other (Diagram: **gramática** and **gramático, –ca**).

Past participles. When an entry word functions as a past participle as well as an adjective or noun, this information is noted at the beginning of the entry along with a reference to the infinitive form (Diagram: **harto, –ta**). Only the most common adjectival meanings are given for such words, since adjectival usages are easily derived from the various senses listed at the infinitive.

Irregular verbs. All irregular verbs are referenced to the Spanish Verb Table (pp. xviii–xxv) by means of a boldface section number immediately following the entry word (Diagram: **hastiar**). The number corresponds to the appropriate model verb in the Table. Thus the irregular conjugations for **hastiar** will be found at section 30 in the Table, under the model verb **enviar.**

Representative inflected forms of irregular verbs are entered in the Dictionary whenever these forms fall more than five lines away from their infinitive in alphabetical order. Such forms are cross-referenced to their infinitive (Diagram: **hay, haya**).

Grammar references. Entry words that are treated at length in the Notes on Grammar and Usage (pp. ix–xvii) are referenced to the appropriate section by a boldface number following the entry word (Diagram: **hasta**). Note that references to the numbered sections of the Notes on Grammar and Usage are preceded by a boldface **G** to distinguish them from irregular verb numbers.

Grammatical Information

Additional information regarding the formation of irregular plurals, contractions, and similar grammatical items is provided in square brackets following the part-of-speech label wherever appropriate (Diagram: **gran** and **haz²**).

Labels

Wherever possible, the labels used in the Dictionary have been styled to be intelligible to both English and Spanish speakers. A full list of the labels used in the Spanish-English side is printed on the front endpaper.

Parts of speech. Part-of-speech labels are given in roman type following the entry word. Nouns are identified by their gender, while verbs are listed as transitive, intransitive, or reflexive.

When an entry word functions as more than one part of speech, boldface roman numerals are used to separate the parts of the entry (Diagram: **harto, –ta**). An exception is made when two parts of speech yield the same equivalent, in which case the labels are joined by an ampersand without the use of roman numerals (Diagram: **hawaiano, –na**).

Field, usage, and region. Labels used to identify special fields, levels of usage, and geographic regions are given in small capital letters at the beginning of the sense to which they apply (Diagram: **haz¹, hartura, hato¹**). As a general rule, labeled senses will appear after unlabeled ones. When several senses require the same label, they are grouped together in the entry and the label is not repeated. Regional meanings are placed after all other senses for a particular part of speech and are grouped by general region first, then specific countries. Note that field, usage, and regional labels used in the main body of the entry do not apply to the idioms and phrases that follow the bold diamond.

Discrimination of Senses

When a word is defined with more than one sense for a particular part of speech, the various senses are distinguished by means of an identifying word or phrase in Spanish known as a discrimination. Discriminations are in italic type in parentheses immediately preceding the sense to which they apply (Diagram: **hartar**).

In many cases a discrimination will simply be an approximate synonym of the entry word. However, discriminations may also take the form of a prepositional phrase or, for verbs, a common subject or object which identifies the sense being defined.

Equivalents

As is customary in bilingual dictionaries, words are translated wherever possible by a direct equivalent rather than a lengthy definition (Diagram: **gramática**). In many cases two synonymous equivalents, separated by a comma, are provided for a particular sense. Different senses are separated by a semicolon and are distinguished by a combination of italic discriminations or small capital labels.

Equivalents are given in the appropriate part of speech and reflect the same level of usage as the sense they define. British variants are labeled in

parentheses (Diagram: **gramo**). An italic *or* is used to indicate a variation in the phrasing of an equivalent in which one or more words are not repeated but are assumed to apply to both phrasings (Diagram: **gramilla**).

Elaboration of Equivalent

Additional information about an equivalent is provided, when appropriate, in parentheses immediately following the equivalent (Diagram: **hastío, hatear**). Elaborations are of three general types:

- Optional words or phrases that offer a fuller version of the equivalent:

ma·jal m. shoal, school (of fish).

- Appropriate objects for transitive verbs or subjects for intransitive verbs:

de·ci·dir tr. *(resolver)* to decide, resolve (a matter); . . .

mos·car·de·ar intr. to lay eggs (queen bee); . . .

- Explanations of obscure equivalents:

gua·ji·ro, –ra . . . —f. MUS. guajira (peasant song).

Examples

Thousands of example sentences and phrases have been included throughout the Dictionary to illustrate the idiomatic use of entry words. Examples and their translations are enclosed within angle brackets following the sense to which they apply (Diagram: **harinero, –ra** and **hasta**).

Note that when the entry word appears in the example exactly as it is entered, it is abbreviated to its initial letter. Otherwise it is spelled out in full. Words of only two letters, such as *si* or *no*, are not abbreviated.

Idioms and Phrases

Common idioms and phrases containing the entry word are listed as run-on entries at the appropriate part of speech. The first run-on is introduced by a bold diamond (♦) (Diagram: **haz²**). Additional items follow in alphabetical order and are separated by bold bullets (•). As with examples, the entry word is abbreviated to its initial letter unless there is any variation in spelling, in which case it is written in full. Two-letter entry words are not abbreviated.

Run-ons are printed in boldface type and use all the features that apply to the main body of the entry, including labels, italic discriminations, elaborations, and example sentences. As a general rule an idiom or phrase will be listed under its first significant term, though a number of the more common idioms are entered at more than one place as a convenience to the user. For example, the idiom *buscarle tres pies al gato* is listed at both **pie** and **gato.**

Usage Notes

Brief notes are occasionally provided at the end of an entry to explain a point of grammar or usage. Usage notes are introduced by a bold triangle (▲) and follow the entire entry regardless of the part of speech to which they refer.

NOTES ON GRAMMAR AND USAGE

THE VERB

G1 The Infinitive

The infinitive sometimes functions as a verbal noun and, as such, may be used as a subject <*el viajar por avión es más rápido* traveling by air is faster>. It may also be used as the object of a verb <*él quería marcharse* he wanted to leave>, or as the object of a preposition <*se fue sin darles nada* he left without giving them anything>.

G2 The Present Indicative

The present indicative tense in Spanish translates not only the simple English present, but the English progressive and emphatic forms as well <*ella habla español* she speaks Spanish, she does speak Spanish, *or* she is speaking Spanish>. The present indicative may be substituted in both English and Spanish for the future <*mañana voy a La Paz* tomorrow I am going to La Paz>.

G3 The Imperfect Indicative

The imperfect indicative tense denotes that an action or a state was continuing or being repeated in past time. As the name implies, the tense gives an impression of incompleteness <*los pájaros cantaban* the birds were singing>. It is commonly used to indicate that an action was going on when something else happened <*comíamos cuando nos llamó* we were eating when he called us>. It is also appropriate for descriptions and for expressing mental and physical states in past time <*ellos no eran felices* they were not happy>.

G4 The Preterit Indicative

The preterit is a past tense which implies that an act was completed at a definite time in the past. It is the tense commonly used in narration to denote happenings and events <*Ana entró en la sala* Anna entered the room>. The preterit stands in contrast to the imperfect which provides the circumstances or setting in which the events of the preterit occur <*hablaban de la política cuando Ana entró en la sala* they were talking about politics when Anna entered the room>.

G5 The Future Indicative

Simple future time is expressed most directly by the future indicative <*vendrán mañana* they will come tomorrow>. The future tense may also express present probability <*serán las diez* it must be about ten o'clock>.

G6 The Conditional Indicative

As in English, the conditional is used in indirect discourse <*dijo que iría* he said that he would go> and in the main clause of a contrary-to-fact statement <*si fuera rico, lo compraría* if I were rich, I would buy it>. The conditional may also express probability in past time <*serían las dos cuando llegó a casa* it must have been about two o'clock when he came home>.

G7 The Imperative Mood

The imperative mood is used to express affirmative commands in the second person. Its use is limited to familiar speech <*Juan, vuelve a casa* John, go back home>. Since object pronouns are attached to the imperative, a written accent is often necessary <*siéntate, chico* sit down, little one>. Commands in the first and third persons and negative second person commands are formed using the subjunctive mood.

G8 The Subjunctive Mood

The subjunctive is used to express commands in the first and third persons, for which there exist no forms in the imperative mood <*que hable ella* let her speak>. The form *usted* is considered a third person form <*escriba usted la carta en seguida* write the letter at once>. When the object pronoun *nos* follows the first person plural of the subjunctive, the final *s* of the verb is dropped <*sentémonos* let's sit down>. The subjunctive is used to express negative commands in the second person <*no hables así* don't talk like that>.

The subjunctive mood deals with the realms of subjectivity and uncertainty and is primarily used in subordinate clauses.

The subjunctive is used in noun clauses when the verb of the main clause expresses volition <*no quiero que nadie le maltrate* I don't want anyone to hurt him>. It is also used when the verb of the main clause expresses an emotion <*temía que le mataran* she was afraid that they would kill her>. When doubt or denial is implied by the main clause verb, the subjunctive is used in the subordinate clause <*es dudoso que lleguen a tiempo* it is doubtful that they will arrive on time>.

The subjunctive is used in the adverb clause with temporal conjunctions that imply indefiniteness or future intention <*esperaremos hasta que vuelvan* we will wait until they return>. Other temporal conjunctions that may require the subjunctive are: *así que* (as soon as), *antes de que* (before), *cuando* (when), *después de que* (after), *en cuanto* (as soon as), *hasta que* (until), *luego que* (as soon as), *mientras* (while), and *tan pronto como* (as soon as). The subjunctive is also used when the conjunction indicates purpose or proviso <*haga usted la letra clara para que la leamos fácilmente* make the writing clear so that we may read it easily>. Some conjunctions that indicate purpose or proviso and thus may require the subjunctive are: *a fin de que* (so that), *a menos que* (unless), *aunque* (although), *con tal que* (provided that), *de manera que* (so that), *de modo que* (so that), *en caso de que* (in case), *para que* (in order that), and *sin que* (without).

The subjunctive is used in adjective clauses if the antecedent is indefinite or negative <*busco un cuarto que no sea demasiado pequeño* I am looking for a room which is not too small> <*no hay nadie que pueda ayudarnos* there is no one who can help us>.

Contrary-to-fact statements require a subjunctive verb in the subordinate clause <*si yo fuera usted, vendría en seguida* if I were you, I would come at once>. The conditional tense is used in the main clause.

The tense of the subjunctive depends on the tense of the main clause verb. The present and perfect tenses of the subjunctive are used in a dependent clause after present or future tenses in the main clause <*siento que usted esté enfermo* I am sorry that you are sick>. After any past tense in the main clause, the imperfect or the pluperfect subjunctive is used in the dependent clause <*queríamos que ella nos acompañara* we wanted her to accompany us>.

There are two forms of the imperfect subjunctive. The *–ra* form is more commonly used in Spanish America and northern Spain, while both the *–ra* and *–se* forms are used in central and southern Spain. Both forms are fully conjugated in the Spanish Verb Table (pp. xviii–xxv).

G9 The Present Participle

The present participle is invariable in form. In dependent constructions, it denotes action going on at the time or immediately before the time of the main verb <*llegando tarde, no encontré a nadie* arriving late, I found no one>. The present participle is used with the verb *estar* to form progressive constructions <*el señor está esperando* the gentleman is waiting>. The idea of verbal continuity of the action can also be conveyed by the verbs *ir* (to go), *seguir* (to continue), *andar* (to go), and *venir* (to come) <*ellos seguían leyendo* they continued reading>.

G10 The Past Participle

The past participle is an adjective that expresses the verbal idea in a completed state. It agrees in number and gender with the substantive to which it refers, except when used after the verb *haber* to form the perfect tenses <*todos estaban dormidos* all were asleep>.

For each simple tense of the Spanish verb there is a perfect tense formed by the corresponding simple tense of *haber* and the past participle of the main verb. The past participle used with *haber* is invariable in form. In general, the perfect tenses in Spanish have the same relation to the simple tenses as they have in English:

• Present Perfect <*ella me ha escrito una carta* she has written me a letter>
• Pluperfect <*sabíamos que usted había llegado* we knew that you had arrived>
• Future Perfect <*se habrá marchado cuando usted llegue* he will have gone when you arrive>
• Preterit Perfect <*apenas hubo llegado cuando vino a verme* he had hardly arrived when he came to see me>

Note that the preterit perfect is a rare tense used in literary style after conjunctions that express immediate priority of time such as *apenas* (hardly), *así que* (as soon as), and *luego que* (as soon as).

G11 The Passive Voice

The true passive voice, in which the subject is acted upon, is formed by the auxiliary *ser* with the past participle, which agrees in gender and number with the subject <*la oveja fue devorada por el lobo* the sheep was devoured by the wolf>. Note that the agent, when expressed, is introduced by the preposition *por*. The passive voice is not used often in Spanish, except when the agent is expressed. The English passive voice is frequently translated into Spanish by a reflexive construction <*aquí se habla español* Spanish is spoken here>.

The verb *estar* is used with a past participle to express, not a passive act, but a passive state <*la ventana está rota* the window is broken>.

G12 Reflexive Verbs

A verb is reflexive when both its subject and pronoun object (direct or indirect) refer to the same person or thing <*María se miró en el espejo* Mary looked at herself in the mirror>. In English only transitive verbs are used reflexively. In Spanish the reflexive construction is extended to intransitive verbs <*me quedaré aquí* I will stay here>. Impersonal and general statements may be expressed in Spanish by the reflexive <*se dice que ella es rica* it is said that she is rich>.

G13 Ser and Estar

Ser is used to express a quality or characteristic of the subject <*Pablo es alto y guapo* Paul is tall and handsome>, the origin of the subject <*estos zapatos son de Italia* these shoes are from Italy>, and in expressing time and dates <*son las dos* it is two o'clock>. Impersonal expressions are also formed with the verb *ser* <*es importante estudiar* it is important to study>. The passive voice is formed with *ser* and the past participle <*la novela fue escrita por Rulfo* the novel was written by Rulfo>.

Estar is used to indicate a state or condition of the subject <*nosotros estamos cansados* we are tired>. It is also used to express location or position <*Felipe estaba en la biblioteca* Philip was in the library>. The progressive tenses are formed with *estar* and the present participle <*los chicos están jugando* the boys are playing>. The verb *estar* is also used to express a passive state <*la ventana está cerrada* the window is closed>.

Some adjectives may be used with either *ser* or *estar*. In those cases, use of *estar* indicates a personal reaction to something whereas *ser* refers to what is considered a characteristic of the subject by relatively objective standards <*ella es joven* she is young> <*ella está joven* she looks young>.

THE NOUN

G14 Gender of Nouns

In Spanish all nouns are either of masculine or feminine gender.

Feminine: Nouns that refer to female beings or that end in –*a* are usually feminine. Some nouns ending in –*a*, particularly those of Greek origin, are masculine <*el clima* the climate, *el día* the day>. Nouns ending in –*dad*, –*tad*, –*tud*, –*ión*, –*umbre*, and –*ie* are generally feminine <*la ciudad* the city, *la voluntad* the will, *la virtud* the virtue, *la nación* the nation, *la muchedumbre* the crowd, *la serie* the series>. The most notable exception is *el avión* (the airplane). The letters of the alphabet are also feminine.

Masculine: Nouns that refer to male beings or that end in –*o* are usually masculine. Note the exceptions <*la mano* the hand, *la radio* the radio>. Days of the week, months of the year, and the names of rivers are all masculine. The infinitive used as a noun is also masculine <*el esquiar es difícil* skiing is difficult>.

Masculine nouns ending in –*o* change to –*a* to form the feminine <*el hijo* the son, *la hija* the daughter>. Masculine nouns that refer to people and that end in –*or*, –*és*, or –*n* add –*a* to form the feminine <*el autor* the author, *la autora* the authoress>. A few masculine nouns that end in –*e* change to –*a* to form the feminine <*el monje* the monk, *la monja* the nun>. A few titles add –*sa* or –*esa* in their feminine form <*el conde* the count, *la condesa* the countess>.

Many animate nouns have the same form for both genders <*el artista, la artista* the artist>. Some nouns are either masculine or feminine, depending on their meaning <*el justicia* the magistrate, *la justicia* justice>. The masculine plural form frequently refers to both sexes <*los padres* the parents (both father and mother)>.

G15 Plural of Nouns
Nouns ending in a vowel form the plural by adding –*s* <*el hombre* the man, *los hombres* the men>. Nouns ending in a consonant other than –*s* add –*es* in the plural <*el león* the lion, *los leones* the lions>. Nouns ending in –*s* that are not accented in the last syllable remain unchanged in the plural <*el paraguas* the umbrella, *los paraguas* the umbrellas>. In forming the plural, the usual rules of accentuation and spelling must be observed <*la luz* the light, *las luces* the lights><*el avión* the airplane, *los aviones* the airplanes>.

THE ARTICLE

G16 The Definite Article

	Masculine	Feminine	Neuter
Singular	el	la	lo
Plural	los	las	

The definite article agrees in number and gender with its noun <*el hombre* the man, *las niñas* the girls>. Before feminine singular nouns beginning with a stressed *a* or *ha*, the definite article *el* is used instead of *la* <*el agua* the water>.

Note the contractions *de* + *el* = *del* and *a* + *el* = *al*.

The neuter article *lo* combines with the masculine singular form of the adjective to form an expression equivalent to an abstract noun <*lo bueno* the good>. *Lo* combines with an adjective of any number and gender in a relative clause <*no se daban cuenta de lo enfermas que estaban* they did not realize how sick they were>.

The definite article may be used as a demonstrative pronoun. It is regularly found before the preposition *de* or the relative pronoun *que* <*el verde de las hojas, y el de la hierba* the green of the leaves and that of the grass>. The definite article is also used with an adjective of any number or gender to form a noun <*las ancianas* the old women>.

The definite article is used in Spanish but not in English:

• with a general noun representing an entire class of persons or objects <*¿te gusta la música?* do you like music?>
• with names of languages, except after the prepositions *de* or *en* and immediately after the verb *hablar* <*el inglés* English> <*hablan francés* they speak French>
• before titles not used in direct address <*el general Patton* General Patton> <*está bien, señor Azorín* very well, Mr. Azorín>
• before parts of the body and personal possessions <*llevaba el sombrero* he was wearing his hat>
• before names of the seasons except after *de* or *en* <*la primavera pasó rápidamente* spring passed quickly>
• when the name of a country is modified <*la Grecia antigua* ancient Greece>
• with the time of day <*son las dos* it is two o'clock>
• with days of the week except after the verb *ser* <*voy al teatro los viernes* I go to the theater on Fridays>
• before infinitives used as nouns <*el mentir es un vicio* lying is a vice>

The definite article is omitted in Spanish:

• before nouns in apposition <*Madrid, capital de España* Madrid, the capital of Spain>
• before numerals in the titles of sovereigns <*Carlos Quinto* Charles the Fifth>
• in certain set expressions <*en nombre de Dios* in the name of God>

G17 The Indefinite Article

	Masculine	Feminine
Singular	un	una
Plural	unos	unas

The indefinite article agrees in number and gender with its noun <*una mesa* a table, *unos libros* some books>. Before a feminine noun beginning with a stressed *a* or *ha*, the indefinite article *un* is used instead of *una* <*no quedó ni un alma viviente* not a soul remained alive>.

The indefinite article is regularly repeated before nouns of clearly different meaning, whereas in English the indefinite article is used only once

<*unos libros y unos papeles están en el escritorio* some books and papers are on the desk>.

The indefinite article is omitted in Spanish:

- before predicate nouns denoting a class or group <*es soldado* he is a soldier>; if the noun is modified, the article is retained <*es un buen soldado* he is a good soldier>
- after *de* and *como* corresponding to English 'as' or 'as a' <*servía de consejero* he served as an advisor>
- after *qué* in exclamations <*¡qué desastre!* what a disaster!>
- before certain adjectives such as *ciento* (hundred), *cierto* (certain), *medio* (half), *mil* (thousand), and *otro* (other) <*compré mil lápices* I bought a thousand pencils>

THE ADJECTIVE

G18 Agreement of Adjectives

Adjectives agree in gender and number with the nouns they modify <*una niña bonita* a pretty child, *libros interesantes* interesting books>.

When an adjective modifies two nouns that refer to persons of both sexes or to things of both genders it takes the masculine plural form <*Carlos y María se encontraban solos* Charles and Mary found themselves alone>. When nouns of different genders refer to things, a preceding adjective regularly agrees with the nearest noun <*muchos lápices y plumas* many pencils and pens>.

G19 Feminine Form of Adjectives

Adjectives ending in –*o* in the masculine form the feminine by changing the –*o* to –*a* <*seco, seca* dry>. Many adjectives ending in –*or*, –*on*, –*an* and adjectives of nationality form the feminine by adding –*a*. Note that the rules for accentuation must be observed <*holgazán, holgazana* lazy>. Adjectives that end in –*e* have the same form in the masculine and feminine, as do most adjectives that end in other vowels or consonants <*grande* big, *feliz* happy, *popular* popular, *agrícola* agricultural>.

G20 Plural of Adjectives

Adjectives form the plural by adding –*s* to a singular ending in a vowel, and –*es* to one ending in a consonant <*rico, ricos* rich, *hablador, habladores* talkative>.

G21 Apocopation of Adjectives

The following adjectives drop their final –*o* when they precede a masculine singular noun:

alguno <*algún día* some day>
bueno <*un buen caballo* a good horse>
malo <*un mal año* a bad year>
ninguno <*ningún dinero* no money>
postrero <*el postrer suspiro* the last sigh>
primero <*el primer capítulo* the first chapter>
tercero <*el tercer piso* the third floor>
uno <*un poema* a poem>

Ciento becomes *cien* when it precedes a noun or a numeral larger than itself <*cien mil soldados* a hundred thousand soldiers, *cien casas* a hundred houses>.

Grande usually becomes *gran* before a singular noun of either gender <*un gran hombre* a great man, *gran felicidad* great happiness>.

Santo becomes *San* when used before the name of a saint <*San Pablo* Saint Paul> except *Santo Domingo* and *Santo Tomás*.

G22 Position of Adjectives

An adjective follows the noun when it is used to describe a noun objectively, to emphasize a special characteristic, or to differentiate the noun from other members of its group <*arte italiano* Italian art>. An adjective precedes the noun when it denotes a usual or inherent characteristic <*la blanca nieve* the white snow>.

With many adjectives the meaning is more literal and emphatic when the adjective follows the noun, and more rhetorical when the adjective precedes the noun <*mis zapatos viejos* my old shoes, *mi viejo amigo* my old friend>. Some adjectives have developed distinct meanings for each position <*una casa grande* a big house, *un gran hombre* a great man>.

Limiting adjectives precede the noun. These include numerals <*dos cartas* two letters>; possessive adjectives <*nuestra casa* our house>; demonstrative adjectives <*esta mesa* this table>; and indefinite adjectives such as *alguno* (some), *cada* (each), *ninguno* (none), *otro* (other, another), and *todo* (all) <*otro ejemplo* another example>.

G23 Adjectives used as Nouns

In Spanish, the adjective is used substantively much more freely than in English <*el anciano* the old man>. The neuter article *lo* combines with the masculine singular form of the adjective to form an abstract noun <*lo bueno* the good>.

G24 Comparison of Adjectives

The comparative degree is formed by placing *más* (more) or *menos* (less) before the positive form of the adjective <*más pobre* poorer, *menos feliz* less happy>.

The following adjectives have irregular comparative forms:

mucho much, *más* more
poco little, *menos* less
bueno good, *mejor* better
malo bad, *peor* worse
grande big, *mayor* larger
pequeño small, *menor* smaller

The nearest equivalent to the English superlative degree is the use of the definite article or a possessive adjective before the comparative <*el más pobre* the poorest one, *mi mejor amigo* my best friend>. To express a high degree of quality without making a comparison, –*ísimo* is added to the positive form of the adjective <*una niña lindísima* a very pretty little girl>.

G25 Possessive Adjectives

The possessives agree in person with the possessor and in number and gender with the thing possessed <*nuestra tía* our aunt, *nuestros libros* our books>.

The possessive is repeated before each noun <*su casa y su coche* his house and his car>, except when two or more nouns refer to identical persons or ideas.

Since *su, sus* have many possible meanings, a phrase such as *de él* (of his) or *de ustedes* (of yours) may be used for clarification <*los padres de ella* her parents>.

Used before the noun						
	Singular			Plural		
	Masculine	Feminine		Masculine	Feminine	
1st Person	mi(s)	mi(s)	my	nuestro(s)	nuestras(s)	our
2nd Person	tu(s)	tu(s)	your (familiar)	vuestro(s)	vuestra(s)	your
3rd Person	su(s)	su(s)	his, her, its your (formal)	su(s)	su(s)	their, your

Used after the noun						
	Singular			Plural		
	Masculine	Feminine		Masculine	Feminine	
1st Person	mío(s)	mía(s)	my, of mine	nuestro(s)	nuestra(s)	our, of ours
2nd Person	tuyo(s)	tuya(s)	your, of yours	vuestro(s)	vuestra(s)	your, of yours
3rd Person	suyo(s)	suya(s)	his, of his, her, of hers, its, your, of yours	suyo(s)	suya(s)	their, of theirs, your, of yours

G26 Demonstrative Adjectives

	masculine	feminine	
singular	este	esta	this
plural	estos	estas	these
singular	ese	esa	that
plural	esos	esas	those
singular	aquel	aquella	that (distant)
plural	aquellos	aquellas	those (distant)

The adjective *este* and its corresponding feminine and plural forms refer to that which is near to or associated with the speaker in place, time, or thought <*estos zapatos que llevo son italianos* these shoes that I am wearing are Italian>.

The adjective *ese* and its corresponding forms refer to that which is near to or in some way connected with the person spoken to <*déme ese lápiz que tiene en la mano* give me that pencil that you have in your hand>.

The adjective *aquel* and its corresponding forms refer to what is distant in place, time, or mental association from both the speaker and the person addressed <*el imperio romano floreció durante aquel siglo* the Roman Empire flourished during that century>.

THE ADVERB

G27 Formation of Adverbs

Adverbs may be formed from adjectives by adding –*mente* (–ly) to the feminine singular form

<*nuevo, nuevamente* new, newly>. An accent on the adjective is retained <*cortés, cortésmente* courteous, courteously>. When two adjectives of this type are used together and are to be transformed into adverbs, the ending –*mente* is joined to the second adjective only <*ella escribió clara y rápidamente* she wrote clearly and rapidly>.

G28 Position of Adverbs

Short adverbs follow the verbs as closely as possible <*Juan trata mal a su hermana* John treats his sister badly>. Longer adverbs or adverbial phrases may occur in other positions <*saludó a la profesora cortésmente, saludó a la profesora con cortesía* he greeted the professor courteously>. An adverb modifying an adjective or adverb immediately precedes it <*no corrió tan rápido como yo* he didn't run as fast as I did> <*Juana es muy rica* Jane is very rich>.

G29 Comparison of Adverbs

The comparative degree is formed by placing *más* (more) or *menos* (less) before the positive form of the adverb <*más temprano* earlier, *menos rápidamente* less rapidly>. The superlative of adverbs is formed with the neuter article *lo* <*lo más rápidamente* most rapidly>. The following adverbs have irregular comparative and superlative forms:

mucho much, *más* more, *lo más* the most *poco* little, *menos* less, *lo menos* the least *bien* well, *mejor* better, *lo mejor* the best *mal* badly, *peor* worse, *lo peor* the worst

THE PRONOUN

G30 Personal Pronouns

SUBJECT	OBJECT		AFTER PREPOSITION	REFLEXIVE
	direct	indirect		
Singular				
yo (I)	**me** (me)	**me**	**mí** (me)	**me** (myself)
tú (you)	**te** (you)	**te**	**ti** (you)	**te** (yourself)
él (he)	**le, lo** (him)		**él** (him)	himself
ella (she)	**la** (her)	**le**	**ella** (her)	**se** (herself), **sí** (after prep.)
ello (neuter: it)	**lo** (it)		**ello** (it)	itself
Plural				
nosotros, as (we)	**nos** (us)	**nos**	**nosotros, as** (us)	**nos** (ourselves)
vosotros, as (you)	**os** (you)	**os**	**vosotros, as** (you)	**os** (yourselves)
ellos (they)	**los** (them)	**les**	**ellos** (them)	**se** (themselves), **sí** (after prep.)
ellas (they)	**las** (them)		**ellas** (them)	

Note: for **usted, ustedes,** see G32; for **le, les** as direct object, see G35.

G31 Subject Personal Pronouns

Since the Spanish verb has distinctive forms for the first and second persons, the subject personal pronouns are normally omitted for those forms <*estoy enferma* I am ill, *estamos enfermos* we are ill>. They may be used for emphasis <*yo pago la comida si tú pagas la propina* I will pay for the meal if *you* leave the tip>. Since the third person endings may be used to refer to several possible subjects (you, he, she, it), the subject pronoun is often included for clarity <*ella tiene hambre* she is hungry>.

G32 Usted

Usted and *ustedes* are the pronouns of address used in formal speech. They have lost all feeling of class distinction that they had long ago as the shortened forms of *vuestra merced* and *vuestras mercedes.* Now they are used to address people whom one respects or strangers.

Usted is not omitted as a subject pronoun <*usted puede entrar ahora* you can come in now>; but it need not be repeated in the same sentence <*usted no pide, manda como reina* you do not request, you command like a queen>.

Usted may be abbreviated to *Ud.* or *Vd.* and *ustedes* to *Uds.* or *Vds.*

G33 Tú, Vosotros, and Vos

The second person pronouns *tú* and *vosotros* are used in familiar discourse—in family life, among friends, and in addressing children or animals. The second person familiar should not be used as a sign of inferiority: a beggar is addressed as *usted;* servants are addressed in the second person only when they are felt to be members of the family.

Vosotros is the plural form of the second person and may be used by a speaker to address his audience, or by an author to address his readers.

Vos is used instead of *usted* in poetic style to address God or an eminent person. In many parts of Latin America *vos* has replaced *tú* as the second person singular pronoun and, as such, is used to address one's family members or friends.

G34 After a Preposition

The forms of the personal pronoun used after prepositions are the same as those used as the subject of a verb (*él, ella, usted, nosotros, vosotros, ellos, ellas, ustedes*) except in the cases of *mí, ti* and *sí* <*lo compré para ti* I bought it for you>. When the preposition is *con* (with), the syllable *–go* is added and the accent is dropped <*conmigo, contigo, consigo*>.

G35 Third Person Object Pronouns

There is much individual and regional variation in the use of third person object pronouns.

As indirect objects, *le* and *les* are the preferable forms.

As direct object in the masculine gender, *le* or *les* is preferred for persons and *lo* or *los* for things. It is also acceptable to use *lo* or *los* to refer to persons as direct objects. The feminine direct objects are *la* and *las.*

G36 Position of Object Pronouns

An object pronoun generally precedes the verb <*me dio el libro* he gave me the book>. Exceptions:

When a conjugated verb is used with an infinitive or present participle, the object pronouns can either precede the conjugated verb or be attached to the infinitive or participle <*voy a leerlo, lo voy a leer* I am going to read it> <*estoy leyéndolo, lo estoy leyendo* I am reading it>.

In affirmative commands, the object pronoun must follow the verb and is attached to it <*léalo a su madre* read it to your mother>.

When an indirect object and a direct object pronoun are used together, the indirect precedes the direct object pronoun <*no te lo doy* I won't give it to you> <*léamelo* read it to me>.

If both pronouns are of the third person, *se* is used instead of the indirect object *le* or *les* <*se lo di* I gave it to him>. This *se* is not to be confused with the reflexive *se* <*se las lavaron* they washed them>.

G37 Repetition of Personal Pronoun

The direct and indirect object forms of the personal pronoun can never be stressed or emphatic. If emphasis is needed, the prepositional form is used in addition to the object pronoun <*a mí me dan miedo* they frighten *me*>. When the reference of an object pronoun is not sufficiently clear, it is made explicit by adding the prepositional form <*a ella le debo esta ansia* I owe this anxiety to her>. In the example, *le* could refer to any number of people (*a él, a ella, a usted*), and the *a ella* clarifies its meaning.

G38 Reflexive Pronouns

When the subject and the object (direct or indirect) of a sentence are the same person or thing, a reflexive form is used. For the first and second persons it is the same as the object pronoun form. *Se* is used for the third person <*Elena se miró en el espejo* Ellen looked at herself in the mirror>.

The reflexive pronoun also serves for the reciprocal construction which is equivalent to 'each other' or 'one another' <*se pegaron* they hit each other>. When the reciprocal action is not clear from the context, it is explained by adding a phrase such as *uno a otro* or *unos a otros* <*se mataron unos a otros* they killed each other (as opposed to committing suicide)>.

The pronoun *sí* can also be used to express a reflexive action <*lo dijo para sí* he said it to himself> or a reciprocal situation <*cambiaron una mirada entre sí* they gave each other a look>.

G39 Neuter Personal Pronouns

Since all nouns in Spanish have a gender, the neuter personal pronouns are used only to refer to an idea or to an unidentified object in the singular. The pronoun *ello* is rarely found, but *lo* is frequently used <*no lo sabe nadie* no one knows it>.

G40 Possessive Pronouns

el mío, la mía, los míos, las mías, lo mío	mine
el tuyo, la tuya, los tuyos, las tuyas, lo tuyo	yours (familiar sing.)
el nuestro, la nuestra, los nuestros, las nuestras, lo nuestro	ours
el vuestro, la vuestra, los vuestros, las vuestras, lo vuestro	yours (familiar pl.)
el suyo, la suya, los suyos, las suyas, lo suyo	his, hers, its, theirs, yours (formal)

The possessive pronoun agrees in gender and number with the thing possessed <*él tiene sus guantes pero yo no tengo los míos* he has his gloves but I don't have mine>. Since *suyo* covers many cases, a phrase such as *la de usted* (yours) or *los de ella* (hers) may be substituted for *suyo* for clarity <*mis amigos y los de usted* my friends and yours>.

The neuter of the possessive pronouns is used to denote one's belongings in a general sense <*todo lo mío* all that is mine>.

G41 Demonstrative Pronouns

	masculine	feminine	neuter	
singular	éste	ésta	esto	this, this one
plural	éstos	éstas		these
singular	ése	ésa	eso	that, that one
plural	ésos	ésas		those
singular	aquél	aquélla	aquello	that, that one (distant)
plural	aquéllos	aquéllas		those (distant)

The pronoun *éste* refers to that which is near or associated with the speaker in time, place, or thought <*éste es el libro a que me refiero* this is the book to which I am referring>.

The pronoun *ése* refers to that which is near or in some way connected with the person spoken to <*no quiero ésa que tienes* I do not want that one that you have>.

The pronoun *aquél* refers to that which is distant in place, time, or mental association from both the speaker and the person addressed <*compré aquélla que vi en el escaparate el año pasado* I bought that one that I saw in the window last year>.

The neuter forms (*esto, eso, aquello*) are used to refer to an idea or to an object not yet identified <*¿qué es eso?* what is that?>.

G42 Relative Pronouns

A relative pronoun introduces a subordinate clause and joins it to the preceding noun or pronoun that is its antecedent.

Que (who, whom, that, which) is the most commonly used of the relative pronouns. It is invariable in form. As a subject or object of a verb it may refer to persons or things <*el libro que leyó* the book that he read> <*el hombre que habla* the man who is speaking>. As the object of a preposition it can refer only to things, and is usually found after the prepositions *a* (to), *con* (with), *de* (from), or *en* (in) <*la pluma con que escribo* the pen with which I am writing>.

Quien, quienes (who, whom) can refer only to a person, with whom it agrees in number <*el hombre con quien hablé* the man with whom I spoke> <*las chicas de quienes hablamos* the girls of whom we are speaking>. *Quien* may include its antecedent in a use equivalent to the English 'he who' <*quien estudia siempre aprenderá* he who studies will always learn>.

The relatives *el cual, la cual, los cuales, las cuales* and *el que, la que, los que, las que* are practically synonymous in their use. They are used instead of *que* to refer to persons or things after prepositions other than *a, con, de,* or *en* <*la muchacha detrás de la cual estaba sentado* the girl behind whom I was sitting> <*la casa dentro de la que se celebró la fiesta* the house in which the party was held>. They are also used to refer to the more distant of two possible antecedents when other relative pronouns would be ambiguous <*la madre de Juan, la cual está visitándonos* John's mother, who is visiting us>.

Cuanto, a neuter pronoun form, is invariable and is equivalent to 'all' or 'everything' <*cuanto usted me ha contado parece increíble* all that you have told me seems incredible>. The relative *cuanto, cuanta, cuantos, cuantas* is used to refer to quantity <*comeré cuanto usted me dé* I will eat as much as you give me>.

Cuyo, cuya, cuyos, cuyas (whose) is a relative possessive pronoun used mainly to refer to people. It agrees in number and gender with the thing possessed <*es una mujer cuyo nombre es bien conocido* she is a woman whose name is well known>.

G43 Interrogative Pronouns

The interrogative pronouns are:

¿qué? what?
¿quién?, ¿quiénes? who?, whom?
¿cuál?, ¿cuáles? which?, which one(s)?
¿cuánto?, ¿cuánta?, ¿cuántos?, ¿cuántas? how much?, how many?

¿Quién?, ¿quiénes? refer only to persons and *¿qué?* refers only to things <*¿quién es ese chico?* who is that boy?> <*¿qué es esto?* what is this?>.

As a pronoun, *¿qué?* is used in asking for a description, definition, or explanation <*¿qué es un archivador?* what is a file cabinet?>. In contrast, *¿cuál?, ¿cuáles?* are used when asking for a choice or selection <*¿cuál prefieres?* which one do you prefer?>.

¿Cuánto?, ¿cuánta?, ¿cuántos?, ¿cuántas? are used to form a question of quantity <*¿cuánto tienes?* how much do you have?>.

Note that *¿qué?* and *¿cuánto(s)?, ¿cuánta(s)?* are also used as interrogative adjectives <*¿qué libro desea usted?* what book do you want?> <*¿cuántos lápices necesitan?* how many pencils do they need?>.

G44 The Personal *a*

The preposition *a* should be used before a direct object that belongs to any of the following groups:

- proper names of persons and animals <*voy a buscar a Blanca* I am going to look for Blanche> but not things <*voy a buscar un libro* I am going to look for a book>
- geographical names <*he visitado a Madrid muchas veces* I have visited Madrid many times> but not those that require the definite article <*he visitado el Perú muchas veces* I have visited Peru many times>
- common nouns that refer to persons <*mataron a nuestro hermano* they killed our brother> but not those that refer to things <*mataron un gallo* they killed a rooster>
- things personified <*al anochecer insultaba a la luna* at nightfall he would insult the moon> but not things considered in their ordinary state <*al anochecer miraba la luna* at nightfall he would look at the moon>
- pets or personified animals <*María quiere a su perro* Mary loves her dog> but not animals in a general sense <*María vio un elefante en el jardín zoológico* Mary saw an elephant at the zoo>.

G45 Negation

Negation in Spanish is expressed by the use of *no* which precedes the verb <*no comprendo* I don't understand>, and can be separated from it only by object personal pronouns <*no te comprendo* I don't understand you>.

The negative adverbs, adjectives and pronouns are: *jamás* (never), *nada* (nothing), *nadie* (no one), *ni* (neither, nor), *ningún, ninguno(a)* (no, none, not any), *no* (no), *nunca* (never), and *tampoco* (neither, nor). These negatives usually follow the verb <*no lo sabe nadie* no one knows it>. When, for emphasis or any other reason, a negative other than *no* precedes the verb, *no* is omitted <*nadie lo sabe* no one knows it>.

G46 Conjunctions

The most frequently used simple coordinating conjunctions are *y* (and), *o* (or), *pero* (but), *mas* (but), *sino* (but), and *ni* (nor).

Before a word beginning with *i* or *hi, y* is replaced by *e* <*padre e hijo* father and son>.

Before a word beginning with *o* or *ho, o* is replaced by *u* <*setenta u ochenta* seventy or eighty>.

Pero (and less frequently *mas*) is the usual conjunction that translates the English 'but' <*quería venir, pero no pude* I wanted to come, but I couldn't>.

Sino is used after a negative statement in the sense of 'but on the contrary' <*no es fácil, sino muy difícil* it's not easy, but very difficult>.

Ni is regularly used in double negation <*no tiene ni amigos ni dinero* he has neither friends nor money>.

Many complex conjunctions are formed by adding *que* to an adverb or to a preposition: *hasta que* (until), *sin que* (without), *aunque* (although), *porque* (because), *puesto que* (since).

G47 Titles of Address and Family Names

The titles *don* and *doña* have no equivalent in English. *Don* is used only before a given name <*Don Carlos*>. Its use does not imply extreme familiarity. It is used between friends of age and dignity, as a term of familiarity mingled with respect by the young to their elders, and by people of humble station to those whom they consider their superiors. In formal address, *don* is used after *señor* when both given and family names are used <*Señor Don Eduardo Sanchez y Robles*>. The abbreviations are *D.* and *Da.*

The titles *señor* (Mr.), *señora* (Mrs.), and *señorita* (Miss) are used before family names <*Señor Gonzalez* Mr. Gonzalez>. The abbreviated forms are *Sr., Sra.,* and *Srta.*

Spanish-speaking people use two family names. Frequently, though not always, these two last names are connected by the conjunction *y*. The first one is the father's family name, which descends continuously down the male line; the second one is the mother's family name, which is lost in the second generation or by a daughter at marriage. A married woman uses her father's family name followed by the preposition *de* and the first or even both family names of the husband. Thus *la señorita Rodríguez y Castro* marries *el señor Molino y Guerra*. She becomes by her marriage *la señora Rodríguez de Molino*. Her son Pablo is addressed formally as *Señor Don Pablo Molino y Rodríguez*. Many people prefer to use only the first family name in daily life; thus the woman above would be called *la señorita Rodríguez* (before her marriage) and her son would be called *el señor Molino*. The second family name should never be used alone, although it is sometimes used by an author as his or her pen name.

SPANISH VERB TABLE

The following Table presents model conjugations for all regular and irregular Spanish verbs. Section §01 outlines the full conjugation of all tenses for regular –ar, –er, and –ir verbs. Regular verbs included as entries in the Dictionary are not specifically referenced to the Table. Sections §02 to §85 contain model conjugations for irregular Spanish verbs. These models include only those tenses in which an irregular conjugation occurs, with the irregular forms within each tense highlighted in boldface type. Irregular verbs included as entries in the Dictionary are referenced by number to the appropriate model in the Table.

Note that two forms are offered for the imperfect subjunctive tense. The –ra form is more commonly used in Spanish America and northern Spain, while both the –ra and –se forms are used in central and southern Spain. Representative inflected forms entered in the Dictionary are in the –ra form only. Since all imperative forms are derived from the present subjunctive with the exception of the affirmative familiar imperative, only this latter form is given in the Table.

MODEL SPANISH VERBS

§01 Regular Verb Conjugations

amar:

Present
amo
amas
ama
amamos
amáis
aman

Imperfect
amaba
amabas
amaba
amábamos
amabais
amaban

Preterit
amé
amaste
amó
amamos
amasteis
amaron

Future
amaré
amarás
amará
amaremos
amaréis
amarán

Conditional
amaría
amarías
amaría
amaríamos
amaríais
amarían

Present Subjunctive
ame
ames
ame
amemos
améis
amen

Imperfect Subjunctive
amara *or* amase
amaras *or* amases
amara *or* amase
amáramos *or* amásemos
amarais *or* amaseis
amaran *or* amasen

Imperative
ama
amad

Present Participle
amando

Past Participle
amado

vender:

Present
vendo
vendes
vende
vendemos
vendéis
venden

Imperfect
vendía
vendías
vendía
vendíamos
vendíais
vendían

Preterit
vendí
vendiste
vendió
vendimos
vendisteis
vendieron

Future
venderé
venderás
venderá
venderemos
venderéis
venderán

Conditional
vendería
venderías
vendería
venderíamos
venderíais
venderían

Present Subjunctive
venda
vendas
venda
vendamos
vendáis
vendan

Imperfect Subjunctive
vendiera *or* vendiese
vendieras *or* vendieses
vendiera *or* vendiese
vendiéramos *or* vendiésemos
vendierais *or* vendieseis
vendieran *or* vendiesen

Imperative
vende
vended

Present Participle
vendiendo

Past Participle
vendido

partir:

Present
parto
partes
parte
partimos
partís
parten

Imperfect
partía
partías
partía
partíamos
partíais
partían

Preterit
partí
partiste
partió
partimos
partisteis
partieron

Future
partiré
partirás
partirá
partiremos
partiréis
partirán

Conditional
partiría
partirías
partiría
partiríamos
partiríais
partirían

Present Subjunctive
parta
partas
parta
partamos
partáis
partan

Imperfect Subjunctive
partiera *or* partiese
partieras *or* partieses
partiera *or* partiese
partiéramos *or* partiésemos
partierais *or* partieseis
partieran *or* partiesen

Imperative
parte
partid

Present Participle
partiendo

Past Participle
partido

§02 adquirir
Present: **adquiero, adquieres, adquiere,** adquirimos, adquirís, **adquieren**
Pres. Subj.: **adquiera, adquieras, adquiera,** adquiramos, adquiráis, **adquieran**
Imperative: **adquiere,** adquirid

§03 agorar
Present: **agüero, agüeras, agüera,** agoramos, agoráis, **agüeran**
Pres. Subj.: **agüere, agüeres, agüere,** agoremos, agoréis, **agüeren**
Imperative: **agüera,** agorad

§04 alzar
Preterit: **alcé,** alzaste, alzó, alzamos, alzasteis, alzaron
Pres. Subj.: **alce, alces, alce, alcemos, alcéis, alcen**

§05 andar
Preterit: **anduve, anduviste, anduvo, anduvimos, anduvisteis, anduvieron**
Imp. Subj.: **anduviera, anduvieras, anduviera, anduviéramos, anduvierais, anduvieran**
or: **anduviese, anduvieses, anduviese, anduviésemos, anduvieseis, anduviesen**

§06 arcaizar
Present: **arcaízo, arcaízas, arcaíza,** arcaizamos, arcaizáis, **arcaízan**
Preterit: **arcaicé,** arcaizaste, arcaizó, arcaizamos, arcaizasteis, arcaizaron
Pres. Subj.: **arcaíce, arcaíces, arcaíce, arcaicemos, arcaicéis, arcaícen**
Imperative: **arcaíza,** arcaizad

§07 argüir
Present: **arguyo, arguyes, arguye,** argüimos, argüís, **arguyen**
Preterit: argüí, argüiste, **arguyó,** argüimos, argüisteis, **arguyeron**
Pres. Subj.: **arguya, arguyas, arguya, arguyamos, arguyáis, arguyan**
Imp. Subj.: **arguyera, arguyeras, arguyera, arguyéramos, arguyerais, arguyeran**
or: **arguyese, arguyeses, arguyese, arguyésemos, arguyeseis, arguyesen**
Imperative: **arguye,** argüid
Pres. Participle: **arguyendo**

§08 asir
Present: **asgo,** ases, ase, asimos, asís, asen
Pres. Subj.: **asga, asgas, asga, asgamos, asgáis, asgan**

§09 avergonzar
Present: **avergüenzo, avergüenzas, avergüenza,** avergonzamos, avergonzáis, **avergüenzan**
Preterit: **avergoncé,** avergonzaste, avergonzó, avergonzamos, avergonzasteis, avergonzaron
Pres. Subj.: **avergüence, avergüences, avergüence, avergoncemos, avergoncéis, avergüencen**
Imperative: **avergüenza,** avergonzad

§10 averiguar
Preterit: **averigüé,** averiguaste, averiguó, averiguamos, averiguasteis, averiguaron
Pres. Subj.: **averigüe, averigües, averigüe, averigüemos, averigüéis, averigüen**

§11 bendecir
Present: **bendigo,** bendices, bendice, bendecimos, bendecís, **bendicen**
Preterit: **bendije, bendijiste, bendijo, bendijimos, bendijisteis, bendijeron**
Pres. Subj.: **bendiga, bendigas, bendiga, bendigamos, bendigáis, bendigan**
Imp. Subj.: **bendijera, bendijeras, bendijera, bendijéramos, bendijerais, bendijeran**
or: **bendijese, bendijeses, bendijese, bendijésemos, bendijeseis, bendijesen**
Imperative: **bendice,** bendecid
Pres. Participle: **bendiciendo**

§12 bruñir
Preterit: bruñí, bruñiste, **bruñó,** bruñimos, bruñisteis, **bruñeron**
Imp. Subj.: **bruñera, bruñeras, bruñera, bruñéramos, bruñerais, bruñeran**
or: **bruñese, bruñeses, bruñese, bruñésemos, bruñeseis, bruñesen**
Pres. Participle: **bruñendo**

§13 bullir
Preterit: bullí, bulliste, **bulló,** bullimos, bullisteis, **bulleron**
Imp. Subj.: **bullera, bulleras, bullera, bulléramos, bullerais, bulleran**
or: **bullese, bulleses, bullese, bullésemos, bulleseis, bullesen**
Pres. Participle: **bullendo**

§14 caber
Present: **quepo,** cabes, cabe, cabemos, cabéis, caben
Preterit: **cupe, cupiste, cupo, cupimos, cupisteis, cupieron**
Future: **cabré, cabrás, cabrá, cabremos, cabréis, cabrán**
Conditional: **cabría, cabrías, cabría, cabríamos, cabríais, cabrían**
Pres. Subj.: **quepa, quepas, quepa, quepamos, quepáis, quepan**
Imp. Subj.: **cupiera, cupieras, cupiera, cupiéramos, cupierais, cupieran**
or: **cupiese, cupieses, cupiese, cupiésemos, cupieseis, cupiesen**

§15 caer
Present: **caigo,** caes, cae, caemos, caéis, caen
Preterit: caí, **caíste,** cayó, **caímos, caísteis, cayeron**
Pres. Subj.: **caiga, caigas, caiga, caigamos, caigáis, caigan**
Imp. Subj.: **cayera, cayeras, cayera, cayéramos, cayerais, cayeran**
or: **cayese, cayeses, cayese, cayésemos, cayeseis, cayesen**
Pres. Participle: **cayendo**
Past Participle: **caído**

§16 colgar
Present: **cuelgo, cuelgas, cuelga,** colgamos, colgáis, **cuelgan**
Preterit: **colgué,** colgaste, colgó, colgamos, colgasteis, colgaron
Pres. Subj.: **cuelgue, cuelgues, cuelgue, colguemos, colguéis, cuelguen**
Imperative: **cuelga,** colgad

§17 conocer
Present: **conozco,** conoces, conoce, conocemos, conocéis, conocen
Pres. Subj.: **conozca, conozcas, conozca, conozcamos, conozcáis, conozcan**

§18 construir
Present: **construyo, construyes, construye,** construimos, construís, **construyen**
Preterit: construí, construiste, **construyó,** construimos, construisteis, **construyeron**
Pres. Subj.: **construya, construyas, construya, construyamos, construyáis, construyan**
Imp. Subj.: **construyera, construyeras, construyera, construyéramos, construyerais, construyeran**
or: **construyese, construyeses, construyese, construyésemos, construyeseis, construyesen**
Imperative: **construye,** construid
Pres. Participle: **construyendo**

§19 contar
Present: **cuento, cuentas, cuenta,** contamos, contáis, **cuentan**
Pres. Subj.: **cuente, cuentes, cuente,** contemos, contéis, **cuenten**
Imperative: **cuenta,** contad

§20 dar
Present: **doy,** das, da, damos, dais, dan
Preterit: **di, diste, dio, dimos, disteis, dieron**
Pres. Subj.: **dé,** des, **dé,** demos, deis, den
Imp. Subj.: **diera, dieras, diera, diéramos, dierais, dieran**
or: **diese, dieses, diese, diésemos, dieseis, diesen**

§21 decir
Present **digo, dices, dice,** decimos, decís, **dicen**
Preterit: **dije, dijiste, dijo, dijimos, dijisteis, dijeron**
Future: **diré, dirás, dirá, diremos, diréis, dirán**
Conditional: **diría, dirías, diría, diríamos, diríais, dirían**
Pres. Subj.: **diga, digas, diga, digamos, digáis, digan**
Imp. Subj.: **dijera, dijeras, dijera, dijéramos, dijerais, dijeran**
or: **dijese, dijeses, dijese, dijésemos, dijeseis, dijesen**
Imperative: **di,** decid
Pres. Participle: **diciendo**
Past Participle: **dicho**

§22 deducir
Present: **deduzco,** deduces, deduce, deducimos, deducís, deducen
Preterit: **deduje, dedujiste, dedujo, dedujimos, dedujisteis, dedujeron**
Pres. Subj.: **deduzca, deduzcas, deduzca, deduzcamos, deduzcáis, deduzcan**
Imp. Subj.: **dedujera, dedujeras, dedujera, dedujéramos, dedujerais, dedujeran**
or: **dedujese, dedujeses, dedujese, dedujésemos, dedujeseis, dedujesen**

§23 delinquir
Present: **delinco,** delinques, delinque, delinquimos, delinquís, delinquen
Pres. Subj.: **delinca, delincas, delinca, delincamos, delincáis, delincan**

§24 desosar
Present: **deshueso, deshuesas, deshuesa,** desosamos, desosáis, **deshuesan**
Pres. Subj.: **deshuese, deshueses, deshuese,** desosemos, desoséis, **deshuesen**
Imperative: **deshuesa,** desosad

§25 discernir
Present: **discierno, disciernes, discierne,** discernimos, discernís, **disciernen**
Pres. Subj.: **discierna, disciernas, discierna,** discernamos, discernáis, **disciernan**
Imperative: **discierne,** discernid

§26 distinguir
Present: **distingo,** distingues, distingue, distinguimos, distinguís, distinguen
Pres. Subj.: **distinga, distingas, distinga, distingamos, distingáis, distingan**

§27 dormir
Present: **duermo, duermes, duerme,** dormimos, dormís, **duermen**
Preterit: dormí, dormiste, **durmió,** dormimos, dormisteis, **durmieron**
Pres. Subj.: **duerma, duermas, duerma, durmamos, durmáis, duerman**
Imp. Subj.: **durmiera, durmieras, durmiera, durmiéramos, durmierais, durmieran**
or: **durmiese, durmieses, durmiese, durmiésemos, durmieseis, durmiesen**
Imperative: **duerme,** dormid
Pres. Participle: **durmiendo**

§28 empeller
Preterit: empellí, empelliste, **empelló,** empellimos, empellisteis, **empelleron**
Imp. Subj.: **empellera, empelleras, empellera, empelléramos, empellerais, empelleran**
or: **empellese, empelleses, empellese, empellésemos, empelleseis, empellesen**
Pres. Participle: **empellendo**

§29 empezar
Present: **empiezo, empiezas, empieza,** empezamos, empezáis, **empiezan**
Preterit: **empecé,** empezaste, empezó, empezamos, empezasteis, empezaron
Pres. Subj.: **empiece, empieces, empiece, empecemos, empecéis, empiecen**
Imperative: **empieza,** empezad

§30 enviar
Present: **envío, envías, envía,** enviamos, enviáis, **envían**
Pres. Subj.:   **envíe, envíes, envíe,** enviemos, enviéis, **envíen**
Imperative: **envía,** enviad

§31 erguir
Present: **irgo, irgues, irgue,** erguimos, erguís, **irguen**
or: **yergo, yergues, yergue,** erguimos, erguís, **yerguen**
Preterit: erguí, erguiste, **irguió,** erguimos, erguisteis, **irguieron**
Pres. Subj.:   **irga, irgas, irga, irgamos, irgáis, irgan**
or: **yerga, yergas, yerga, yergamos, yergáis, yergan**
Imp. Subj.:   **irguiera, irguieras, irguiera, irguiéramos, irguierais, irguieran**
or: **irguiese, irguieses, irguiese, irguiésemos, irguieseis, irguiesen**
Imperative: **irgue** *or* **yergue,** erguid
Pres. Participle: **irguiendo**

§32 erigir
Present: **erijo,** eriges, erige, erigimos, erigís, erigen
Pres. Subj.:   **erija, erijas, erija, erijamos, erijáis, erijan**

§33 errar
Present: **yerro, yerras, yerra,** erramos, erráis, **yerran**
Pres. Subj.:   **yerre, yerres, yerre,** erremos, erréis, **yerren**
Imperative: **yerra,** errad

§34 escoger
Present: **escojo,** escoges, escoge, escogemos, escogéis, escogen
Pres. Subj.:   **escoja, escojas, escoja, escojamos, escojáis, escojan**

§35 esparcir
Present: **esparzo,** esparces, esparce, esparcimos, esparcís, esparcen
Pres. Subj.:   **esparza, esparzas, esparza, esparzamos, esparzáis, esparzan**

§36 estar
Present: **estoy, estás, está,** estamos, estáis, **están**
Preterit: **estuve, estuviste, estuvo, estuvimos, estuvisteis, estuvieron**
Pres. Subj.:   **esté, estés, esté,** estemos, estéis, **estén**
Imp. Subj.:   **estuviera, estuvieras, estuviera, estuviéramos, estuvierais, estuvieran**
or: **estuviese, estuvieses, estuviese, estuviésemos, estuvieseis, estuviesen**
Imperative: **está,** estad

§37 forzar
Present: **fuerzo, fuerzas, fuerza,** forzamos, forzáis, **fuerzan**
Preterit: **forcé,** forzaste, forzó, forzamos, forzasteis, forzaron
Pres. Subj.:   **fuerce, fuerces, fuerce, forcemos, forcéis, fuercen**
Imperative: **fuerza,** forzad

§38 garantir [defective]
Present: –, –, –, garantimos, garantís, –
Pres. Subj.:   –, –, –, –, –, –
Imperative: –, garantid

§39 haber
Present: **he, has, ha, hemos,** habéis, **han**
Preterit: **hube, hubiste, hubo, hubimos, hubisteis, hubieron**
Future: **habré, habrás, habrá, habremos, habréis, habrán**
Conditional: **habría, habrías, habría, habríamos, habríais, habrían**
Pres. Subj.:   **haya, hayas, haya, hayamos, hayáis, hayan**
Imp. Subj.:   **hubiera, hubieras, hubiera, hubiéramos, hubierais, hubieran**
or: **hubiese, hubieses, hubiese, hubiésemos, hubieseis, hubiesen**
Imperative: **hé,** habed

§40 hacer
Present: **hago,** haces, hace, hacemos, hacéis, hacen
Preterit: **hice, hiciste, hizo, hicimos, hicisteis, hicieron**
Future: **haré, harás, hará, haremos, haréis, harán**
Conditional: **haría, harías, haría, haríamos, haríais, harían**
Pres. Subj.:   **haga, hagas, haga, hagamos, hagáis, hagan**
Imp. Subj.:   **hiciera, hicieras, hiciera, hiciéramos, hicierais, hicieran**
or: **hiciese, hicieses, hiciese, hiciésemos, hicieseis, hiciesen**
Imperative: **haz,** haced
Past Participle: **hecho**

§41 ir
Present: **voy, vas, va, vamos, vais, van**
Imperfect: **iba, ibas, iba, íbamos, ibais, iban**
Preterit: **fui, fuiste, fue, fuimos, fuisteis, fueron**
Pres. Subj.:   **vaya, vayas, vaya, vayamos, vayáis, vayan**
Imp. Subj.:   **fuera, fueras, fuera, fuéramos, fuerais, fueran**
or: **fuese, fueses, fuese, fuésemos, fueseis, fuesen**
Imperative: **ve,** id
Pres. Participle: **yendo**

§42 jugar
Present: **juego, juegas, juega,** jugamos, jugáis, **juegan**
Preterit: **jugué,** jugaste, jugó, jugamos, jugasteis, jugaron

§42 jugar (*continued*)

Pres Subj.:	**juegue, juegues, juegue, juguemos, juguéis, jueguen**
Imperative:	**juega,** jugad

§43 leer

Preterit:	leí, **leíste, leyó, leímos, leísteis, leyeron**
Imp. Subj.:	**leyera, leyeras, leyera, leyéramos, leyerais, leyeran**
or:	**leyese, leyeses, leyese, leyésemos, leyeseis, leyesen**
Pres. Participle:	**leyendo**

§44 lucir

Present:	**luzco,** luces, luce, lucimos, lucís, lucen
Pres. Subj.:	**luzca, luzcas, luzca, luzcamos, luzcáis, luzcan**

§45 oír

Present:	**oigo, oyes, oye, oímos,** oís, **oyen**
Preterit:	oí, **oíste, oyó, oímos, oísteis, oyeron**
Pres. Subj.:	**oiga, oigas, oiga, oigamos, oigáis, oigan**
Imp. Subj.:	**oyera, oyeras, oyera, oyéramos, oyerais, oyeran**
or:	**oyese, oyeses, oyese, oyésemos, oyeseis, oyesen**
Imperative:	**oye,** oíd
Pres. Participle:	**oyendo**
Past Participle:	**oído**

§46 oler

Present:	**huelo, hueles, huele,** olemos, oléis, **huelen**
Pres. Subj.:	**huela, huelas, huela,** olamos, oláis, **huelan**
Imperative:	**huele,** oled

§47 pagar

Preterit:	**pagué,** pagaste, pagó, pagamos, pagasteis, pagaron
Pres. Subj.:	**pague, pagues, pague, paguemos, paguéis, paguen**

§48 pedir

Present:	**pido, pides, pide,** pedimos, pedís, **piden**
Preterit:	pedí, pediste, **pidió,** pedimos, pedisteis, **pidieron**
Pres. Subj.:	**pida, pidas, pida, pidamos, pidáis, pidan**
Imp. Subj.:	**pidiera, pidieras, pidiera, pidiéramos, pidierais, pidieran**
or:	**pidiese, pidieses, pidiese, pidiésemos, pidieseis, pidiesen**
Imperative:	**pide,** pedid
Pres. Participle:	**pidiendo**

§49 pensar

Present:	**pienso, piensas, piensa,** pensamos, pensáis, **piensan**
Pres. Subj.:	**piense, pienses, piense,** pensemos, penséis, **piensen**
Imperative:	**piensa,** pensad

§50 perder

Present:	**pierdo, pierdes, pierde,** perdemos, perdéis, **pierden**
Pres. Subj.:	**pierda, pierdas, pierda,** perdamos, perdáis, **pierdan**
Imperative:	**pierde,** perded

§51 placer

Present:	**plazco,** places, place, placemos, placéis, placen
Preterit:	plací, placiste, plació *or* **plugo,** placimos, placisteis, placieron *or* **pluguieron**
Pres. Subj.:	**plazca, plazcas, plazca** *or* **plega** *or* **plegue, plazcamos, plazcáis, plazcan**
Imp. Subj.:	placiera, placieras, placiera *or* **pluguiera,** placiéramos, placierais, placieran
or:	placiese, placieses, placiese *or* **pluguiese,** placiésemos, placieseis, placiesen

§52 plegar

Present:	**pliego, pliegas, pliega,** plegamos, plegáis, **pliegan**
Preterit:	**plegué,** plegaste, plegó, plegamos, plegasteis, plegaron
Pres. Subj.:	**pliegue, pliegues, pliegue, pleguemos, pleguéis, plieguen**
Imperative:	**pliega,** plegad

§53 poder

Present:	**puedo, puedes, puede,** podemos, podéis, **pueden**
Preterit:	**pude, pudiste, pudo, pudimos, pudisteis, pudieron**
Future:	**podré, podrás, podrá, podremos, podréis, podrán**
Conditional:	**podría, podrías, podría, podríamos, podríais, podrían**
Pres. Subj.:	**pueda, puedas, pueda,** podamos, podáis, **puedan**
Imp. Subj.:	**pudiera, pudieras, pudiera, pudiéramos, pudierais, pudieran**
or:	**pudiese, pudieses, pudiese, pudiésemos, pudieseis, pudiesen**
Imperative:	**puede**
Pres. Participle:	**pudiendo**

§54 poner

Present:	**pongo,** pones, pone, ponemos, ponéis, ponen
Preterit:	**puse, pusiste, puso, pusimos, pusisteis, pusieron**
Future:	**pondré, pondrás, pondrá, pondremos, pondréis, pondrán**
Conditional:	**pondría, pondrías, pondría, pondríamos, pondríais, pondrían**
Pres. Subj.:	**ponga, pongas, ponga, pongamos, pongáis, pongan**
Imp. Subj.:	**pusiera, pusieras, pusiera, pusiéramos, pusierais, pusieran**
or:	**pusiese, pusieses, pusiese, pusiésemos, pusieseis, pusiesen**
Imperative:	**pon,** poned
Past Participle:	**puesto**

§55 querer
Present: **quiero, quieres, quiere,** queremos, queréis, **quieren**
Preterit: **quise, quisiste, quiso, quisimos, quisisteis, quisieron**
Future: **querré, querrás, querrá, querremos, querréis, querrán**
Conditional: **querría, querrías, querría, querríamos, querríais, querrían**
Pres. Subj.: **quiera, quieras, quiera,** queramos, queráis, **quieran**
Imp. Subj.: **quisiera, quisieras, quisiera, quisiéramos, quisierais, quisieran**
  or: **quisiese, quisieses, quisiese, quisiésemos, quisieseis, quisiesen**
Imperative: **quiere,** quered

§56 raer
Present: **raigo** *or* **rayo,** raes, rae, raemos, raéis, raen
Preterit: raí, **raíste, rayó, raímos, raísteis, rayeron**
Pres. Subj.: **raiga** *or* **raya, raigas, raiga, raigamos, raigáis, raigan**
Imp. Subj.: **rayera, rayeras, rayera, rayéramos, rayerais, rayeran**
  or: **rayese, rayeses, rayese, rayésemos, rayeseis, rayesen**
Pres. Participle: **rayendo**
Past Participle: **raído**

§57 regir
Present: **rijo, riges, rige,** regimos, regís, **rigen**
Preterit: regí, registe, **rigió,** regimos, registeis, **rigieron**
Pres. Subj.: **rija, rijas, rija, rijamos, rijáis, rijan**
Imp. Subj.: **rigiera, rigieras, rigiera, rigiéramos, rigierais, rigieran**
  or: **rigiese, rigieses, rigiese, rigiésemos, rigieseis, rigiesen**
Imperative: **rige,** regid
Pres. Participle: **rigiendo**

§58 reír
Present: **río, ríes, ríe, reímos,** reís, **ríen**
Preterit: reí, **reíste, rió, reímos, reísteis,** rieron
Pres. Subj.: **ría, rías, ría, riamos, riáis, rían**
Imp. Subj.: **riera, rieras, riera, riéramos, rierais, rieran**
  or: **riese, rieses, riese, riésemos, rieseis, riesen**
Imperative: **ríe,** reíd
Pres. Participle: **riendo**
Past Participle: **reído**

§59 reñir
Present: **riño, riñes, riñe,** reñimos, reñís, **riñen**
Preterit: reñí, reñiste, **riñó,** reñimos, reñisteis, **riñeron**
Pres. Subj.: **riña, riñas, riña, riñamos, riñáis, riñan**
Imp. Subj.: **riñera, riñeras, riñera, riñéramos, riñerais, riñeran**
  or: **riñese, riñeses, riñese, riñésemos, riñeseis, riñesen**
Imperative: **riñe,** reñid
Pres. Participle: **riñendo**

§60 reunir
Present: **reúno, reúnes, reúne,** reunimos, reunís, **reúnen**
Pres. Subj.: **reúna, reúnas, reúna,** reunamos, reunáis, **reúnan**
Imperative: **reúne,** reunid

§61 roer
Present: **roo** *or* **roigo** *or* **royo,** roes, roe, roemos, roéis, roen
Preterit: roí, **roíste, royó, roímos, roísteis, royeron**
Pres. Subj.: **roa** *or* **roiga** *or* **roya, roas, roa, roamos, roáis, roan**
Imp. Subj.: **royera, royeras, royera, royéramos, royerais, royeran**
  or: **royese, royeses, royese, royésemos, royeseis, royesen**
Pres. Participle: **royendo**
Past Participle: **roído**

§62 saber
Present: **sé,** sabes, sabe, sabemos, sabéis, saben
Preterit: **supe, supiste, supo, supimos, supisteis, supieron**
Future: **sabré, sabrás, sabrá, sabremos, sabréis, sabrán**
Conditional: **sabría, sabrías, sabría, sabríamos, sabríais, sabrían**
Pres. Subj.: **sepa, sepas, sepa, sepamos, sepáis, sepan**
Imp. Subj.: **supiera, supieras, supiera, supiéramos, supierais, supieran**
  or: **supiese, supieses, supiese, supiésemos, supieseis, supiesen**

§63 salir
Present: **salgo,** sales, sale, salimos, salís, salen
Future: **saldré, saldrás, saldrá, saldremos, saldréis, saldrán**
Conditional: **saldría, saldrías, saldría, saldríamos, saldríais, saldrían**
Pres. Subj.: **salga, salgas, salga, salgamos, salgáis, salgan**
Imperative: **sal,** salid

§64 seguir
Present: **sigo, sigues, sigue,** seguimos, seguís, **siguen**
Preterit: seguí, seguiste, **siguió,** seguimos, seguisteis, **siguieron**
Pres. Subj.: **siga, sigas, siga, sigamos, sigáis, sigan**
Imp. Subj.: **siguiera, siguieras, siguiera, siguiéramos, siguierais, siguieran**
  or: **siguiese, siguieses, siguiese, siguiésemos, siguieseis, siguiesen**
Imperative: **sigue,** seguid
Pres. Participle: **siguiendo**

§65 sentir

Present:	**siento, sientes, siente,** sentimos, sentís, **sienten**
Preterit:	sentí, sentiste, **sintió,** sentimos, sentisteis, **sintieron**
Pres. Subj.:	**sienta, sientas, sienta, sintamos, sintáis, sientan**
Imp. Subj.:	**sintiera, sintieras, sintiera, sintiéramos, sintierais, sintieran**
or:	**sintiese, sintieses, sintiese, sintiésemos, sintieseis, sintiesen**
Imperative:	**siente,** sentid
Pres. Participle:	**sintiendo**

§66 ser

Present:	**soy, eres, es, somos, sois, son**
Imperfect:	**era, eras, era, éramos, erais, eran**
Preterit:	**fui, fuiste, fue, fuimos, fuisteis, fueron**
Pres. Subj.:	**sea, seas, sea, seamos, seáis, sean**
Imp. Subj.:	**fuera, fueras, fuera, fuéramos, fuerais, fueran**
or:	**fuese, fueses, fuese, fuésemos, fueseis, fuesen**
Imperative:	**sé,** sed

§67 situar

Present:	**sitúo, sitúas, sitúa,** situamos, situáis, **sitúan**
Pres. Subj.:	**sitúe, sitúes, sitúe,** situemos, situéis, **sitúen**
Imperative:	**sitúa,** situad

§68 tañer

Preterit:	tañí, tañiste, **tañó,** tañimos, tañisteis, **tañeron**
Imp. Subj.:	**tañera, tañeras, tañera, tañéramos, tañerais, tañeran**
or:	**tañese, tañeses, tañese, tañésemos, tañeseis, tañesen**
Pres. Participle:	**tañendo**

§69 tener

Present:	**tengo, tienes, tiene,** tenemos, tenéis, **tienen**
Preterit:	**tuve, tuviste, tuvo, tuvimos, tuvisteis, tuvieron**
Future:	**tendré, tendrás, tendrá, tendremos, tendréis, tendrán**
Conditional:	**tendría, tendrías, tendría, tendríamos, tendríais, tendrían**
Pres. Subj.:	**tenga, tengas, tenga, tengamos, tengáis, tengan**
Imp. Subj.:	**tuviera, tuvieras, tuviera, tuviéramos, tuvierais, tuvieran**
or:	**tuviese, tuvieses, tuviese, tuviésemos, tuvieseis, tuviesen**
Imperative:	**ten,** tened

§70 tocar

Preterit:	**toqué,** tocaste, tocó, tocamos, tocasteis, tocaron
Pres. Subj.:	**toque, toques, toque, toquemos, toquéis, toquen**

§71 torcer

Present:	**tuerzo, tuerces, tuerce,** torcemos, torcéis, **tuercen**
Pres. Subj.:	**tuerza, tuerzas, tuerza, torzamos, torzáis, tuerzan**
Imperative:	**tuerce,** torced

§72 traer

Present:	**traigo,** traes, trae, traemos, traéis, traen
Preterit:	**traje, trajiste, trajo, trajimos, trajisteis, trajeron**
Pres. Subj.:	**traiga, traigas, traiga, traigamos, traigáis, traigan**
Imp. Subj.:	**trajera, trajeras, trajera, trajéramos, trajerais, trajeran**
or:	**trajese, trajeses, trajese, trajésemos, trajeseis, trajesen**
Pres. Participle:	**trayendo**
Past Participle:	**traído**

§73 trocar

Present:	**trueco, truecas, trueca,** trocamos, trocáis, **truecan**
Preterit:	**troqué,** trocaste, trocó, trocamos, trocasteis, trocaron
Pres. Subj.:	**trueque, trueques, trueque, troquemos, troquéis, truequen**
Imperative:	**trueca,** trocad

§74 valer

Present:	**valgo,** vales, vale, valemos, valéis, valen
Future:	**valdré, valdrás, valdrá, valdremos, valdréis, valdrán**
Conditional:	**valdría, valdrías, valdría, valdríamos, valdríais, valdrían**
Pres. Subj.:	**valga, valgas, valga, valgamos, valgáis, valgan**

§75 vencer

Present:	**venzo,** vences, vence, vencemos, vencéis, vencen
Pres. Subj.:	**venza, venzas, venza, venzamos, venzáis, venzan**

§76 venir

Present:	**vengo, vienes, viene,** venimos, venís, **vienen**
Preterit:	**vine, viniste, vino, vinimos, vinisteis, vinieron**
Future:	**vendré, vendrás, vendrá, vendremos, vendréis, vendrán**
Conditional:	**vendría, vendrías, vendría, vendríamos, vendríais, vendrían**
Pres. Subj.:	**venga, vengas, venga, vengamos, vengáis, vengan**
Imp. Subj.:	**viniera, vinieras, viniera, viniéramos, vinierais, vinieran**
or:	**viniese, vinieses, viniese, viniésemos, vinieseis, viniesen**
Imperative:	**ven,** venid
Pres. Participle:	**viniendo**

§77 ver
Present:	**veo,** ves, ve, vemos, veis, ven
Imperfect:	**veía, veías, veía, veíamos, veíais, veían**
Preterit:	**vi,** viste, **vio,** vimos, visteis, vieron
Pres. Subj.:	**vea, veas, vea, veamos, veáis, vean**
Past Participle:	**visto**

§78 volver
Present:	**vuelvo, vuelves, vuelve,** volvemos, volvéis, **vuelven**
Pres. Subj.:	**vuelva, vuelvas, vuelva,** volvamos, volváis, **vuelvan**
Imperative:	**vuelve,** volved
Past Participle:	**vuelto**

§79 yacer
Present:	**yazco** *or* **yazgo** *or* **yago,** yaces, yace, yacemos, yacéis, yacen
Pres. Subj.:	**yazca** *or* **yazga** *or* **yaga, yazcas, yazca, yazcamos, yazcáis, yazcan**
Imperative:	yace *or* **yaz,** yaced

§80 ahincar
Present:	**ahínco, ahíncas, ahínca,** ahincamos, ahincáis, **ahíncan**
Preterit:	**ahinqué,** ahincaste, ahincó, ahincamos, ahincasteis, ahincaron
Pres. Subj.:	**ahínque, ahínques, ahínque, ahinquemos, ahinquéis, ahínquen**
Imperative:	**ahínca,** ahincad

§81 aislar
Present:	**aíslo, aíslas, aísla,** aislamos, aisláis, **aíslan**
Pres. Subj.:	**aísle, aísles, aísle,** aislemos, aisléis, **aíslen**
Imperative:	**aísla,** aislad

§82 aunar
Present:	**aúno, aúnas, aúna,** aunamos, aunáis, **aúnan**
Pres. Subj.:	**aúne, aúnes, aúne,** aunemos, aunéis, **aúnen**
Imperative:	**aúna,** aunad

§83 embaír
Present:	–, –, –, **embaímos,** embaís, –
Preterit:	embaí, **embaíste, embayó, embaímos, embaísteis, embayeron**
Pres. Subj.:	–, –, –, –, –, –
Imp. Subj.:	**embayera, embayeras, embayera, embayéramos, embayerais, embayeran**
or:	**embayese, embayeses, embayese, embayésemos, embayeseis, embayesan**
Imperative:	–, embaíd
Pres. Participle:	**embayendo**
Past Participle:	**embaído**

§84 podrir *or* pudrir
All forms are on root **pud–,** except for the infinitive, the preterit, the future, the conditional, and the imperative plural, which have both **pod–** or **pud–** forms; for example, preterit: **pudrí** *or* **podrí.** The past participle is **podrido.**

§85 Irregular Past Participles
In addition to verbs already mentioned in this section, the following verbs have irregular past participles. Note that combined forms of these verbs have similar irregularities. Thus the past participle of **transcribir** is **transcrito** based on the irregularity reflected in the verb **escribir.**

abrir	abierto	imprimir	impreso
cubrir	cubierto	morir	muerto
escribir	escrito	romper	roto
freír	frito	resolver	resuelto

NUMERALS, WEIGHTS, AND MEASURES

	Cardinal	Ordinal		Cardinal	Ordinal
0	cero		15	quince	decimoquinto, ta
1	uno, una	primero, ra	16	dieciséis	decimosexto, ta
2	dos	segundo, da	17	diecisiete	decimoséptimo, ma
3	tres	tercero, ra	18	dieciocho	decimoctavo, va
4	cuatro	cuarto, ta	19	diecinueve	decimonoveno, na
5	cinco	quinto, ta	20	veinte	vigésimo, ma
6	seis	sexto, ta	21	veintiuno, na	vigésimo (-ma) primero, ra
7	siete	séptimo, ma	22	veintidós	vigésimo (-ma) segundo, da
8	ocho	octavo, va	30	treinta	trigésimo, ma
9	nueve	noveno, na	40	cuarenta	cuadragésimo, ma
10	diez	décimo, ma	50	cincuenta	quincuagésimo, ma
11	once	undécimo, ma	60	sesenta	sexagésimo, ma
12	doce	duodécimo, ma	70	setenta	septuagésimo, ma
13	trece	decimotercero, ra	80	ochenta	octogésimo, ma
14	catorce	decimocuarto, ta	90	noventa	nonagésimo, ma

	Cardinal	Ordinal
100	cien or ciento	centésimo, ma
101	ciento uno	centésimo (-ma) primero, ra
134	ciento treinta y cuatro	centésimo (-ma) trigésimo (-ma) cuarto, ta
200	doscientos, tas	ducentésimo, ma
300	trescientos, tas	tricentésimo, ma
400	cuatrocientos, tas	cuadringentésimo, ma
500	quinientos, tas	quingentésimo, ma
600	seiscientos, tas	sexcentésimo, ma
700	setecientos, tas	septingentésimo, ma
800	ochocientos, tas	octingentésimo, ma
900	novecientos, tas	noningentésimo, ma
1000	mil	milésimo, ma
1001	mil uno	milésimo (-ma) primero, ra
1 000 000	un millón	millonésimo, ma
1 000 000 000	mil millones	mil millonésimo, ma
1 000 000 000 000	un billón	billonésimo, ma

METRIC CONVERSION TABLE

Multiply	by	to find	Multiply	by	to find
Length					
centímetros	0.4	pulgadas	pulgadas	2.5	centímetros
metros	3.3	pies	pies	30.5	centímetros
metros	1.1	yardas	yardas	0.9	metros
kilómetros	0.6	millas	millas	1.6	kilómetros
Area					
$centímetros^2$	0.16	$pulgadas^2$	$pulgadas^2$	6.5	$centímetros^2$
$metros^2$	1.2	$yardas^2$	$yardas^2$	0.8	$metros^2$
$kilómetros^2$	0.4	$millas^2$	$millas^2$	2.6	$kilómetros^2$
hectáreas	2.5	acres	acres	0.4	hectáreas
Mass and Weight					
gramos	0.035	onzas	onzas	28.3	gramos
kilogramos	2.2	libras	libras	0.45	kilogramos
toneladas (1000 kg)	1.1	toneladas (cortas)	toneladas (2000 lbs)	0.9	toneladas (métricas)
Volume					
mililitros	0.03	onzas líquidas	onzas líquidas	30	mililitros
litros	1.06	cuartos (de galón)	cuartos (de gálon)	0.95	litros
litros	0.26	galones	galones	3.8	litros
$metros^3$	35	$pies^3$	$pies^3$	0.03	$metros^3$

COMMON SPANISH
ABBREVIATIONS

á. área.
(a) alias.
A. 1. Alteza **2.** *Educ.* aprobado.
AA. 1. Autores **2.** Altezas.
ab. abad.
abr. *or* **ab.ˡ** abril.
a.c. año corriente.
a/c 1. al cuidado de **2.** a cuenta.
A.C. *or* **A. de C.** Año de Cristo.
acr. acreedor.
a. de J.C. antes de Jesucristo.
admón. administración.
admor. *or* **adm.ᵒʳ** administrador.
a/f. a favor.
afmo. *or* **af.ᵐᵒ** afectísimo.
af.ᵗᵒ afecto.
ago. *or* **ag.ᵗᵒ** agosto.
a la v/ a la vista.
alc.ᵈᵉ alcalde.
alt. altitud.
a.m. ante meridiem.
ap. 1. aparte **2.** apóstol.
aplica., aplico. *or* **ap.ᵃ, ap.ᵒ** apostólica, apostólico.
apdo. apartado (de correos).
apóst. apóstol.
art. *or* **art.ᵒ** artículo.
arz. *or* **arzbpo.** arzobispo.
atto. *or* **att.ᵒ** atento.
Aud.ᵃ Audiencia.
Av. *or* **Avda.** Avenida.
a/v. a vista.

B. 1. Beato **2.** *Educ.* bueno.
bca. barrica.
B.I.D. Banco Interamericano de Desarrollo.
B.ᵐᵒ P.ᵉ Beatísimo Padre.
Br. *or* **br.** bachiller.
Bs. As. Buenos Aires.
bto. 1. bulto **2.** bruto.

c/ 1. cargo **2.** contra.
c. *or* **cap.** capítulo.
c.ᵃ compañía.
C.A. corriente alterna.
cap. *or* **cap.ⁿ** capitán.
capp.ⁿ capellán.
Card.ˡ Cardenal.
c.c. *or* **c/c** cuenta corriente.
C.C. corriente continua.
c/d en casa de.
C.D. corriente directa.
C. de J. Compañía de Jesús.
cénts. céntimos.
cf. compárese.
cf. *or* **conf.** *or* **confr.** confesor.
cg. centigramo, centigramos.
C.ᶦᵃ *or* **Cía.** Compañía.
cje. corretaje.
cl. centilitro, centilitros.
cllo. cuartillo.
cm. centímetro, centímetros.
Cnel. coronel.
Co. Compañía.
col. *or* **col.ᵃ 1.** columna **2.** colonia.
comis.ᵒ comisario.
comp. compárese.
cons.ᵒ consejo.
Const. Constitución.
const.ˡ constitucional.
conv.ᵗᵉ conveniente.
corr.ᵗᵉ corriente.

C.P. contestación pagada.
C.P.T. Contador Público Titulado.
cs. 1. cuartos **2.** centavos **3.** céntimos.
c.s.f. costo, seguro y flete.
cta. *or* **c.ᵗᵃ** cuenta.
cta. cte. cuenta corriente.
cte. corriente.
c/u cado uno.
cuad. cuadrado.
C.V. caballos de vapor.
c/vta. cuenta de venta.

D. Don.
Da *or* **D.ᵃ** Doña.
dcha. derecha.
DD. doctores.
d. de J.C. después de Jesucristo.
der. *or* **der.ᵃ, der.ᵒ** derecha, derecho.
descto. descuento.
d/f días fecha.
D.F. *Mex.* Distrito Federal.
dg. decigramo, decigramos.
Dg. decagramo, decagramos.
D.G.T. Dirección General de Turismo.
dha., dho. dicha, dicho.
dic. *or* **dic.ᵉ** diciembre.
dl. decilitro, decilitros.
Dl. decalitro, decalitros.
dls. dólares.
dm. decímetro, decímetros.
Dm. decámetro, decámetros.
D.ⁿ *or* **d.ⁿ** don.
dna. docena.
doc. 1. documento **2.** docena.
docum.ᵗᵒ documento.
dom.ᵒ domingo.
d/p. días plazo.
dpto. *or* **dto.** departamento.
D.ʳ *or* **Dr.** Doctor.
dra., dro. derecha, derecho.
dup. *or* **dup.ᵈᵒ** duplicado.
d/v días vista.

E. este, oriente.
EE. UU. Estados Unidos.
ej. ejemplo.
E.M. 1. Estado Mayor **2.** Edad Media.
Em.ᵃ Eminencia.
E.M.G. Estado Mayor General.
Em.ᵐᵒ *or* **Emmo.** Eminentísimo.
ene *or* **en.ᵒ** enero.
ENE. estenordeste.
E.P.D. En paz descanse.
E.P.M. en propia mano.
esc.ᵒ escudo.
escrit.ᵃ escritura.
escrnía. escribanía.
escrno. escribano.
escs. escudos.
ESE. estesudeste.
etc. etcétera.
E.U., E.U.A. U.S., U.S.A.
Evang.ᵗᵃ Evangelista.
Exc.ᵃ Excelencia.
Excma, Excmo. *or* **Exc.ᵐᵃ, Exc.ᵐᵒ** Excelentísima, Excelentísimo.

f/ fardo, fardos.
f.a.b. *or* **FAB** franco a bordo.
fact.ᵃ factura.
F.C. *or* **f.c.** ferrocarril.
fcos. francos.
feb. *or* **feb.ᵒ** febrero.

F.E.M. fuerza electromotriz.
fha., fho. fecha, fecho.
F.M.I. Fondo Monetario Internacional.
fol. *or* **fo.ᵒ** folio.
Fr. Fray.
fra. factura.
F.ˢ *or* **f.ˢ** francos.
fund. fundador.
fut. futuro.

g. gramo, gramos.
g/ giro.
G. gracia.
gue. *or* **g.ᵈᵉ** guarde.
Gen.ˡ General (*title*).
gnte. gerente.
gob.ᵒ gobierno.
gob.ʳ gobernador.
g.p. giro postal.
gr. gramo, gramos.
gral. general.
gte. gerente.

h. hijo.
H. 1. *Com.* haber **2.** hectáreas.
hect. hectárea, hectáreas.
Hg. hectogramo, hectogramos.
Hl. hectolitro, hectolitros.
Hm. hectómetro, hectómetros.
Hno., Hnos. Hermano, Hermanos.
HP *or* **H.P.** caballo(s) de vapor.

ib. *Lat.* ibídem.
íd. *Lat.* ídem.
igl.ᵃ iglesia.
Il.ᵉ Ilustre.
inq.ʳ inquisidor.
intend.ᵗᵉ intendente.
ít. *Lat.* ítem.
izq.ᵃ, izq.ᵒ *or* **izq.ᵈᵃ, izq.ᵈᵒ** izquierda, izquierdo.

J.C. Jesucristo.
Jhs. Jesús.
juev. *or* **jue.** jueves.
jul. julio.
jun. junio.

k/c. kilociclos.
Kg. *or* **kg.** kilogramo, kilogramos.
Kl. *or* **kl.** kilolitro, kilolitros.
Km. *or* **km.** kilómetro, kilómetros.
kms./h. kilómetros por hora.
kv. *or* **k.w.** kilovatio, kilovatios.
kv/h. kilovatios-hora.

l. 1. ley **2.** libro **3.** litro, litros.
L/ letra.
L. *or* **L.ᵈᵒ** *or* **l.ᵈᵒ** Licenciado.
lb. libra.
lín. línea.
líq.ⁿ liquidación.
líq.ᵒ líquido.
Ltda. limitada.
lun. lunes.

m. 1. minuto, minutos **2.** metro, metros.
m/ 1. mes **2.** mi, mis **3.** mío, míos.
mar. marzo.
mart. martes.
may.ᵐᵒ mayordomo.
mcos. marcos.
m/cta. mi cuenta.

M.º Madre, religiosa.
meng. menguante.
merc. mercaderías.
m/f mi favor.
M.F. modulación de frecuencia.
mg. miligramo, miligramos.
miérc. miércoles.
milés.ª milésimas.
min.º ministro.
m/L. mi letra.
ml. mililitros.
mm. *or* **m/m** milímetro, milímetros.
m/n. moneda nacional.
m/o mi orden.
m/ o m/ más o menos.
monast.º monasterio.
Mons. Monseñor.
Mr. 1. Monsieur 2. Mister.
mrd. merced.
Mro. Maestro.
M.ª marcos.
M.S. manuscrito.
M.ª a.ª muchos años.
M.SS. manuscritos.

n. noche.
n/ nuestro, nuestra.
N. norte.
nac. nacional.
N.ª S.ª Nuestra Señora.
N.B. *Lat.* Nota bene.
n/cta. nuestra cuenta.
N. de la R. nota de la redacción.
NE. nordeste.
n/f. nuestro favor.
NNE. nornordeste.
NNO. nornoroeste.
n.º número.
n/o. nuestra orden.
NO. noroeste.
nov. *or* **nov.º** noviembre.
Nov. Recop. Novísima Recopilación.
N. Recop. Nueva Recopilación.
nra., nro. *or* **ntra., ntro.** nuestra, nuestro.
N.U. Naciones Unidas.
núm. *or* **núm.º** número.
N.S. Nuestro Señor.
N.S.J.C. Nuestro Señor Jesucristo.
nto. neto.

o/ orden.
O. oeste.
ob. *or* **obpo.** obispo.
oct. *or* **oct.º** octubre.
ONO. oesnoroeste.
O.N.U. Organización de Naciones Unidas.
onz. onza.
orn. orden.
OSO. oessudoeste.
OTAN Organización del Tratado del Atlántico Norte.
OVNI objeto volante no identificado.

P. 1. Papa (*pope*) 2. padre 3. pregunta.
p.ª para.
p. A. 1. por ausencia 2. por autorización.
pág., págs. página, páginas.
PBAI proyectil balístico de alcance intermedio.
PBI proyectil balístico intercontinental.
p.bro *or* **presb.** presbítero.
p.c. por cien, por ciento.
P.C. Partido Comunista.
Pcia. provincia.
P.D. posdata.
P.º Padre.
p. ej. por ejemplo.
penit. penitente.

perg. *or* **pno.** pergamino.
Pf., Pfs. peso fuerte, pesos fuertes.
p.m. post meridiem.
P.M. Padre Maestro.
pmo. próximo.
P.O. *or* **p.o.** por orden.
p.º pero.
P.P. 1. porte pagado 2. por poder.
ppdo. *or* **p.p.do** próximo pasado.
p.r por.
P.R. Puerto Rico.
pral. principal.
pralte. principalmente.
priv. privilegio.
proc. procesión.
prof. 1. profesor 2. profeta.
prom. promedio.
pror. procurador.
prov.or provisor.
próx.º próximo.
P.S. *Lat.* post scriptum.
P.S.M. por su mandato.
ps. pesos.
pta., ptas. peseta, pesetas.
Pta. *Geog.* punta.
p.te parte.
pza. pieza.

q. *or* **q.º** que.
q.e.g.e. que en gloria esté.
q.e.p.d. que en paz descanse.
q.e.s.m. que estrecha su mano.
q.q. quintales.

R. 1. Reverendo 2. reverencia 3. respuesta 4. *Educ.* reprobado.
R). Responde o respuesta.
R.A.U. República Árabe Unida.
Rbí. Recibí.
R.D. Real Decreto.
Rda. M. *or* **R.M.** Reverenda Madre.
Rdo. Reverendo.
Rdo. P. *or* **R.P.** Reverendo Padre.
R.º Récipe.
Rep. República.
Resp. *Com.* responsabilidad.
r.l real (*royal*).
Rmo. Reverendísimo.
R.O. Real Orden.
r.p.m. revoluciones por minuto.
R.S. Real Servicio.
rte. remite, remitente.
rúst. rústica.

s/ 1. su, sus 2. sobre.
S. 1. San, Santo 2. sur 3. *Educ.* sobresaliente.
S.ª Señora.
S.A. 1. Su Alteza 2. Sociedad Anónima 3. Sud América.
sáb. sábado.
S.A.I. Su Alteza Imperial.
S.A.R. Su Alteza Real.
s/c. su cuenta.
S.C. *or* **s.c.** su casa.
s/cta. su cuenta.
S.D. se despide.
S.D.M. Su Divina Majestad.
SE. sudeste.
secret.ª secretaría.
sept. *or* **sept.º** septiembre.
serv.º servicio.
serv.or servidor.
set.º septiembre.
s.e.u.o. salvo error u omisión.
s/f. su favor.
sig.te siguiente.
S.M. Su Majestad.
S.M.A. Su Majestad Apostólica.
S.M.B. Su Majestad Británica.
S.M.I. Su Majestad Imperial.
S.n San.

S.N. Servicio Nacional.
s/o. su orden.
SO. sudoeste.
Soc. Com. por Acc. Sociedad en Comandita por Acciones.
Sor. Señor.
Sores. Señores.
spre. siempre.
Sr. *or* **S.r** Señor.
Sra., Sras. Señora, Señoras.
Sres. *or* **S.res** Señores.
Sría. Secretaría.
S.ria, S.rio *or* **sria., srio.** secretaria, secretario.
S.R.L. Sociedad de Responsabilidad Limitada.
S.R.M. Su Real Majestad.
Srta. Señorita.
s.s. *or* **ss.** seguro servidor.
S.S. Su Santidad.
S.S.ª Su Señoría.
SSE. sudsudeste.
SS. MM. Sus Majestades.
SS.mo Santísimo.
SS.mo P. Santísimo Padre.
SS.no escribano.
SSO. sudsudoeste.
S.S.S. *or* **s.s.s.** su seguro servidor.
Sta. 1. Santa 2. Señorita.
Sto. Santo.
sup. suplica.
supert.te superintendente.
supl.te suplente.
sup.te suplicante.

t. 1. tarde 2. tonelada.
tel. *or* **teléf.** teléfono.
ten.te teniente.
test.mto testamento.
test.º testigo.
tít. *or* **tít.º** título.
Tm. tonelada métrica.
tpo. tiempo.
trib.l tribunal.
t.º *or* **tom.** tomo.
Tte. teniente.
Tte. Cnel. teniente coronel.

U. *or* **Ud.** usted.
Uds. *or* **UU.** ustedes.
U.R.S.S. U.S.S.R.

V. 1. usted 2. venerable 3. véase.
V. versículo.
V.A. Vuestra Alteza.
V.A.R. Vuestra Alteza Real.
Vd. usted.
Vda. de viuda de.
Vds. ustedes.
V.E. Vuestra Excelencia, Vuecencia.
vencim.to vencimiento.
vers.º versículo.
vg. 1. verbigracia 2. virgen.
v.g. *or* **v.gr.** verbigracia.
vier. viernes.
V.M. Vuestra Majestad.
Vm. *or* **Vmd.** 1. Vuestra Merced 2. Usted.
vn. vellón.
V.º B.º visto bueno.
vol. 1. volumen 2. voluntad.
vols. volúmenes.
vra., vro. vuestra, vuestro.
vras., vros. vuestras, vuestros.
vs. *or* **v.ª** varas.
V.S. Vueseñoría, Usía.
V.S.I. Vueseñoría (*or* Usía) Ilustrísima.
v.ta, v.to vuelta, vuelto.
V.V. *or* **VV.** ustedes.

SPANISH ORTHOGRAPHY

The Spanish Alphabet

The Spanish alphabet has 30 letters: the 26 letters of the English alphabet plus *ch, ll, ñ,* and *rr,* which form separate letters in the alphabetical order. The letters *k* and *w* are used only in words of foreign origin.

a	a	j	jota	r	ere
b	be	k	ka	rr	erre
c	ce	l	ele	s	ese
ch	che	ll	elle	t	te
d	de	m	eme	u	u
e	e	n	ene	v	ve, uve
f	efe	ñ	eñe	w	doble u
g	ge	o	o	x	equis
h	hache	p	pe	y	i griega
i	i	q	cu	z	zeta

Stress and Accentuation

Words ending in a vowel or the consonants *–n* or *–s* are stressed on the next to last syllable *<cerrado, comieron, naranjas>*. Words ending in any other consonant are stressed on the last syllable *<cerrar, estoy, ferrocarril>*. Exceptions to these rules are marked with a written accent over the vowel of the stressed syllable *<rubí, noción, francés, árbol, pájaro>*. When a diphthong or triphthong requires an accent, it is placed over the strong vowel *<cantáis, evaluéis>*.

Stress remains on the same syllable in the singular and plural forms. If necessary the written accent is added or dropped to preserve stress *<nación, naciones>*. The first element of a compound word drops the accent *<décimo, decimocuarto>*. Adjectives retain the accent when adding *–mente* to form the adverb even though the stress shifts to the next to the last syllable *<útil, útilmente>*.

The written accent is used with the weak vowels (*i, u*) in cases when they do not form diphthongs *<hacía, baúl>*. It is no longer used with mono-syllabic verbs according to rules set by the Spanish Academy in 1952 *<dio, fue, vio>*.

Capitalization and Punctuation

Capitalization is used less frequently in Spanish than in English. Capital letters are not used with days of the week or months of the year *<lunes Monday>* *<marzo March>*. The subject pronoun *<yo I>* is not capitalized. Names of countries are capitalized but adjectives of nationality and names of languages are not *<el rey francés the French king>* *<estudio español I study Spanish>*.

Spanish punctuation differs from English in the use of inverted exclamation and question marks at the start of the exclamation or question *<¿qué es esto? what is this?>* *<¡qué lástima! what a pity!>*. Dialogue is set off by the use of dashes (—). In numbers, Spanish uses a comma for the English decimal point and a period for the English comma. Thus the English 6,482.83 would be 6.482,83 in Spanish.

Syllabication

Single consonants between vowels join the following vowel *<pa·re·ci·do>*. The letters *ch, ll,* and *rr* are never separated *<te·cho, si·lla, pe·rro>*. The letter *y* is considered a consonant when followed by a vowel *<o·ye·ra>* but as a vowel in other cases.

Two consonants between vowels are divided *<lec·ción, ges·to, gim·na·sia>* unless the second consonant is an *l* or *r* *<a·blan·dar, a·pro·bar>*. When more than two consonants occur between vowels, the last consonant joins the following vowel *<trans·pa·ren·te>* unless it is an *l* or *r* *<sor·pren·der>*.

Two adjacent strong vowels (*a, e, o*) split into two syllables *<ca·er, ro·er>*. Diphthongs count as one syllable *<tien·da, vue·lo, ra·cio·nal>*. An accent over the weak vowel (*i, u*) makes it strong *<ca·í·da, re·ú·ne>*. Triphthongs always form one syllable *<a·pre·ciáis>*.

SPANISH PRONUNCIATION GUIDE

1 = Spanish letter; 2 = Spanish examples; 3 = English word with similar sound; 4 = description.

1	2	3	4
a	año, pata	father	
b	boca, embargo	bib	Initial in the word or with *m,* similar to English *b*
	labio, tabla		Between vowels or before *l* or *r,* more like the *v* in *lever*
c	cedro, civil	cedar	*c* before *e* or *i*: in most of Spain, similar to the *th* in *thick;* in southern Spain and Spanish America, similar to the English *s*
	cable, cobre	cat	The hard *c* in Spanish is not aspirated as it is in English
ch	chiste, muchacho	church	
d	dar, falda	deed	Initial in the word or after *n* or *l,* similar to English *d,* but not aspirated
	lodo, padre		In all other positions, similar to the *th* in *rather*
e	denso, espada	pet	When the syllable ends in a consonant, similar to the *e* in *pet*
	me, pero	café	When the syllable ends in a vowel, similar to the *e* in *café*

1	2	3	4
f	fuerte, sofa	fat	
g	general, gitano		Before *e* or *i*, similar to the strongly aspirated *h* in *ha!*
	gato, grupo		The hard *g* is not aspirated as it is in English
h	honor, ahora		Is always silent
i	silla, grito	machine	
j	jugo, pájaro		Similar to the strongly aspirated *h* in *ha!*
k	kilo, kimono	kick	Not aspirated as it is in English
l	listo, oler	lid	
ll	llamar, olla		In most of Spain, similar to the *lli* in *million;* in southern Spain and most of Spanish America, similar to the *j* in *jar;* in Argentina and Uruguay, similar to the *s* in *vision*
m	masa, amargo	mum	
n	sin, nota, tono	no	
	rencor, fango		Before hard *c* or *g*, sounds like the *ng* of *thing*
ñ	riña		Sounds like the *ny* in *canyon*
o	sordo, toldo	cord	When the syllable ends in a consonant, sounds like the *o* in *cord*
	lodo, ocupar	note	When the syllable ends in a vowel, sounds like the *o* in *note*
p	parte, capa	pot	Not aspirated as it is in English
q	quinto, níquel	pique	Pronounced like an unaspirated *k*
r	raya, enredo		Initial in the word or after *l, n,* or *s,* it is strongly trilled
	caro, contar		Elsewhere, pronounced with a flap of the tongue like the *dd* in *ladder*
rr	carro		Is strongly trilled
s	cosa, sino	salty	
t	tonto, matar	tight	Not aspirated as it is in English
u	luto, útil	rude	
	quince, guerra		Silent when preceded by *q* or in *gui* and *gue,* unless marked by dieresis
	agüero, güiro		When marked by dieresis, sounds like the *u* in Guinevere
v	vino, vista		Initial in the word, sounds like the *b* in *bib*
	lavar, salvo		In all other positions it is softer, more like the *v* in *lever*
w	wat, water		Pronounced like either the English *v* or *w*
x	éxito, exacto		Pronounced like either the *x* of *exit* or the *gs* of *eggs*
	mixta, experto		Sometimes softened to the sound of an *s*
	México		In *México* and *mexicano,* sounds like the aspirated *h* in *ha!*
y	yeso, suyo	young	Initial in the word or between vowels, is like the *y* in *young;* in Argentina and Uruguay sounds like the *s* in *vision* between vowels
	y, carey		As a word, or final in the word, is like the *i* in *machine*
z	zona, trazar		In most of Spain, is like the *th* in *thick;* in southern Spain and Spanish America, is like the English *s*
Diphthongs			
ai, ay	baile, vaya		Like the *i* in *wide*
au	causa		Like the *ou* in *round*
ei, ey	peinar, rey		Like the *ey* in *they*
eu	deuda		Like the combined vowel sounds of *hey, you!*
ia, ya	estudiar, haya		Like the *ya* in *yarn*
ie, ye	sierra, yermo		Like the *ye* in *yes*
io, yo	porción, yodo		Like the *yo* in *yoke*
iu, yu	viudo, yugo		Like the *yu* in *yule*
oi, oy	oigo, voy		Like the *oi* in *voice*
ua	cuanto		Like the *wa* in *wand*
ue	cuento		Like the *we* in *went*
ui	cuidar		Like the *wee* in *weed*
uo	cuota		Like the *uo* in *quote*
Triphthongs			
iai	estudiáis		Like the *yi* in *yipes*
iau	miau		Like the *eow* in *meow*
iei	confiéis		Like *yea*
uai, uay	continuáis, Uruguay		Like the *wi* in *wire*
uau	guau		Like *wow*
uei, uey	continuéis, buey		Like the *wei* in *weight*

A

a, A f. first letter of the Spanish alphabet ♦ **a por a y be por be** point by point.

a prep. □ DIRECTION to <*voy a la biblioteca* I am going to the library>; into <*se lanzó al agua* he threw himself into the water> □ DESTINATION in, at <*llegó a Londres* she arrived in London> □ ORIENTATION to, toward <*mira al sur* look to the south> □ LOCATION at <*están a la puerta* they are at the door>; on <*comieron a bordo* they ate on board>; to <*ella vive al oeste de la ciudad* she lives to the west of the city> □ DISTANCE to <*de aquí a Santiago* from here to Santiago>; up to <*a la rodilla* up to the knee> □ TIME at <*a las doce* at twelve o'clock>; on <*a 3 de abril* on April 3>; after, in <*a poco* after a while> □ METHOD on <*a pie* on foot>; in <*a la española* in the Spanish style>; by <*a mano* by hand>; with <*a balazos* with bullets>; according to <*a lo que dice* according to what he says> □ RATE at <*a cinco dólares la hora* at five dollars an hour>; per, a <*tres veces al año* three times a year>; by <*poco a poco* little by little> □ WITH SOME INFINITIVES to <*comenzamos a correr* we began to run>; if <*a saberlo yo* if I had known it>; on, upon <*al llegar* upon arriving>; let's <*¡a comer!* let's eat! □ WITH AN INDIRECT OBJECT to <*se las di a ella* I gave them to her>; from <*se lo quité a la niña* I took it away from the child> □ WITH A DIRECT OBJECT §G44 <*vimos a los estudiantes* we saw the students>.

a·ba·ba f. *or* **a·ba·bol** m. BOT. poppy; COLL. (*simplón*) fool, simpleton.

a·ba·cá m. BOT. abaca; TEX. Manila hemp.

a·ba·ce·rí·a f. grocery store.

á·ba·co m. (*tablero*) abacus; ARCHIT. abacus; MIN. washing trough.

a·bad m. RELIG. abbot; ENTOM. blister beetle.

a·ba·de·jo m. ICHTH. cod, codfish; ORNITH. kinglet; ENTOM. blister beetle, Spanish fly.

a·ba·de·sa f. RELIG. abbess.

a·ba·dí·a f. RELIG. (*convento*) abbey; (*dignidad o territorio*) abbacy.

a·ba·je·ño, –ña *or* **a·ba·je·ro, –ra** AMER. I. adj. lowland II. m.f. lowlander.

a·ba·jo I. adv. (*dirección*) down; (*en una casa*) downstairs; (*posición*) below, beneath, underneath ♦ **echar a.** to destroy, demolish; POL. to overthrow • **hacia a.** downward(s) • **más a.** farther down II. interj. down with <*¡abajo el rey!* down with the king!>.

a·ba·lan·zar §04 tr. (*equilibrar*) to balance; (*lanzar*) to fling, hurl —reflex. (*arrojarse*) to hurl *or* throw oneself; ARG. to rear (horses).

a·ba·laus·tra·do, –da adj. balustered.

a·bal·do·nar tr. (*degradar*) to degrade, debase; (*ofender*) to offend, affront.

a·ba·le·ar tr. AGR. to separate grain from chaff; AMER. (*tirotear*) to shoot at, fire on; (*herir*) to wound.

a·ba·le·o m. AGR. (*acción de abalear*) separation of grain from chaff; (*escoba*) broom.

a·ba·li·zar §04 MARIT. tr. to buoy, mark with buoys —reflex. to take bearings.

a·ba·lo·rio m. (*cuentas de vidrio*) glass beads; (*cuenta*) bead.

a·ba·lles·tar tr. MARIT. to haul (a cable or rope).

a·ban·de·ra·do I. past part. see **abanderar** II. m. MIL. standard-bearer; FIG. (*adherente*) advocate, adherent.

a·ban·de·ra·mien·to m. MARIT. registration (of a ship); POL. joining a cause.

a·ban·de·rar tr. MARIT. to register (a ship); POL. (*unirse a*) to join (a cause).

a·ban·de·ri·zar §04 tr. to divide into factions —reflex. to join (a cause).

a·ban·do·na·do, –da I. past part. see **abandonar** II. adj. (*dejado*) abandoned; (*descuidado*) careless, negligent; (*desaliñado*) slovenly, untidy; PERU depraved.

a·ban·do·nar tr. (*dejar*) to abandon, desert, forsake <*el padre abandonó a sus hijos* the father deserted his children>; (*desertar*) to leave <*abandonó la casa paterna* he left his father's house>; (*renunciar*) to give up <*abandonó la idea*

he gave up the idea>; (*descuidar*) to neglect <*abandonaron sus deberes* they neglected their duties> —intr. to resign (in chess) —reflex. (*entregarse a*) to surrender oneself to, yield to <*abandonarse al dolor* to yield to sorrow>; (*desesperarse*) to despair, give up; (*descuidarse*) to let oneself go, become slovenly.

a·ban·do·no m. (*deserción*) abandonment, desertion; (*descuido*) neglect, slovenliness; (*desenfrenamiento*) abandon, unrestraint; LAW (*incumplimiento*) abandonment.

a·ba·ni·car §70 tr. to fan —reflex. to fan oneself.

a·ba·ni·ca·zo m. blow *or* swat given with a fan.

a·ba·ni·co m. fan <*un abanico pintado a mano* a handpainted fan>; FIG. (*gama*) range; MARIT. capstan, winch.

a·ba·ni·que·o m. (*acción de abanicar*) fanning; FIG. (*gesticulación*) excessive gesticulation.

a·ba·no m. ceiling fan, hanging fan.

a·ba·ña·dor, –do·ra I. adj. sifting, sorting (of grain) II. m.f. sifter, sorter (of grain).

a·ba·ñar tr. to sift, sort (grain).

a·ba·ra·jar tr. ARG., PAR., URUG. (*parar*) to block, parry (a blow); (*agarrar*) to catch (in flight).

a·ba·ra·ta·mien·to m. cheapening, reduction (in price).

a·ba·ra·tar tr. (*depreciar*) to cheapen; (*reducir*) to reduce, lower (prices) —reflex. to get *or* become cheaper.

a·bar·ca·dor, –do·ra I. adj. (*abrazador*) embracing; FIG. (*comprensivo*) comprehensive, all-encompassing II. m.f. gatherer; AMER. (*acaparador*) hoarder, stockpiler.

a·bar·ca·du·ra f. *or* **a·bar·ca·mien·to** m. (*abrazamiento*) embracing, surrounding; FIG. (*inclusión*) inclusion, encompassment; AMER. hoarding, stockpiling.

a·bar·car §70 tr. (*contener*) embrace, cover <*este libro abarca toda la materia* this book covers the whole subject>; (*abrazar*) to embrace; (*divisar*) to take in (with the eyes); FIG. (*encargarse de*) to undertake (too much at once); AMER. to stockpile, corner (the market); ECUAD., COLL. to hatch (eggs).

a·bar·qui·llar tr. to roll up, curl —reflex. to wrap.

a·ba·rra·car §70 intr. MIL. to set up camp, bivouac.

a·ba·rra·ga·nar·se reflex. to cohabit, live together.

a·ba·rra·jar tr. (*atropellar*) to attack, overwhelm; AMER. (*tirar*) to hurl, throw —reflex. PERU (*tropezarse*) to trip, fall; (*depravarse*) to become corrupt.

a·ba·rra·jo m. PERU fall, stumble.

a·ba·rra·mien·to m. (*lanzamiento*) hurling, hurtling; (*sacudimiento*) shaking.

a·ba·rran·ca·de·ro m. (*abismo*) precipice; FIG. (*aprieto*) difficult situation.

a·ba·rran·car §70 tr. to form gulleys *or* ditches in —intr. MARIT. (*varar*) to run aground —reflex. (*caerse*) to fall into a ditch *or* ravine; FIG. (*atascarse*) to get into a fix *or* a jam.

a·ba·rra·qué, abarraque see **abarracar**.

a·ba·rrar tr. (*lanzar*) to hurl, hurtle; (*sacudir*) to shake.

a·ba·rro·ta·do, –da I. past part. see **abarrotar** II. adj. full, crowded III. m. CHILE grocery store.

a·ba·rro·tar tr. (*fortalecer*) to bar up, strengthen with bars; MARIT. (*cargar*) to stow (*cargo*); (*llenar*) to fill up, pack; AMER. (*acaparar*) to monopolize, buy up —reflex. AMER. to become cheap (because of abundance).

a·ba·rro·te m. MARIT. bundle ♦ **abarrotes** AMER. (*comestibles*) groceries; (*tienda*) grocery store.

a·ba·rro·te·rí·a f. C. AMER. hardware store.

a·ba·rro·te·ro, –ra m.f. AMER. general storekeeper, hardware storekeeper.

a·bas·tar tr. to supply, provision —intr. to be enough *or* sufficient —reflex. to satisfy *or* content oneself.

a·bas·tar·dar tr. to bastardize —intr. to degenerate.

a·bas·te·ce·dor, –do·ra I. adj. supplying II. m.f. supplier.

a·bas·te·cer §17 tr. to supply, provide <*la tienda nos abasteció de azúcar* the store provided us with sugar>.

a·bas·te·ci·do, –da I. past part. see **abastecer** II. adj. supplied, stocked <*una tienda bien a.* a well-stocked store>.

a·bas·te·ci·mien·to m. (*provisión*) supply; (*aprovisionamiento*) supplying, provisioning.

a·bas·tio·nar tr. to fortify *or* protect with bastions.

a·bas·to m. (*aprovisionamiento*) supplying, provisioning; AMER. (*matadero*) slaughterhouse ♦ **abastos** supplies,

provisions • **dar a.** to produce to capacity • **no dar a. (a)** not to be able to keep up (with).

a·ba·ta·nar tr. *(batir el paño)* to full (cloth); FIG. *(golpear)* to beat, hit.

a·ba·ta·tar tr. to frighten, scare —reflex. *(acobardarse)* to become frightened *or* intimidated; *(avergonzarse)* to become embarrassed.

a·ba·ti·ble adj. collapsible, folding *<asiento a.* folding chair>.

a·ba·ti·da·men·te adv. dejectedly, despondently.

a·ba·ti·do, –da I. past part. see **abatir II.** adj. *(desanimado)* dejected, despondent; *(vil)* low, despicable, abject; COM. depreciated.

a·ba·ti·mien·to m. *(desaliento)* dejection, low spirits; *(vileza)* baseness, abjection; *(bajada)* lowering; *(armas)* dismantling (of weapons); MARIT. drift, leeway.

a·ba·tir tr. *(derribar)* to knock down, demolish; *(bajar)* to lower, bring down *<a. la bandera* to lower the flag>; *(desanimar)* to depress, discourage; *(descomponer)* to take apart, dismantle (weapons); *(humillar)* to humble, humiliate —intr. MARIT. to drift off course —reflex. *(desanimarse)* to become discouraged *or* depressed; *(humillarse)* to humiliate oneself; *(aves)* to swoop, dive (birds).

ab·di·ca·ción f. abdication.

ab·di·car §70 tr. *(resignar)* to abdicate *<el rey abdicó el trono* the king abdicated the throne>; *(renunciar)* to renounce, give up *<abdicó sus principios* he gave up his principles>* —intr. to abdicate.

ab·do·men m. ANAT., ZOOL. abdomen.

ab·do·mi·nal adj. abdominal.

ab·duc·ción f. abduction.

ab·duc·tor I. adj. ANAT. abducent **II.** m. abductor.

a·be·cé m. *(alfabeto)* alphabet; FIG. *(rudimentos)* rudiments.

a·be·ce·da·rio m. *(alfabeto)* alphabet; *(libro)* primer.

a·be·dul m. BOT. *(árbol)* birch; *(madera)* birchwood.

a·be·ja f. ENTOM. bee.

a·be·jar m. apiary, beehive.

a·be·jo·ne·ar intr. COL., DOM. REP. to whisper, murmur.

a·be·jo·rro m. ENTOM. bumblebee; FIG. *(pesado)* boring person, pest.

a·be·lla·car §70 tr. to make villainous —reflex. to become villainous.

a·be·mo·lar tr. MUS. to put into a minor key; *(dulcificar)* to soften, lower (voice).

a·be·rra·ción f. aberration, abnormality.

a·be·rran·te adj. aberrant, abnormal.

a·be·rre·ar tr. PERU to anger —reflex. to become angry.

a·ber·tu·ra f. *(apertura)* opening; *(hendidura)* crack, fissure, cleft; FIG. *(franqueza)* openness, frankness; GEOG. valley; OPT., PHOTOG. aperture.

a·bes·tiar·se reflex. to become brutish *or* animal-like.

a·be·te m. BOT. fir (tree and wood).

a·be·to m. BOT. fir (tree).

a·be·tu·na·do, –da I. past part. see **abetunar II.** adj. *(como brea)* pitch-like, tar-like; *(embreado)* tarred.

a·be·tu·nar tr. *(embrear)* to tar, cover with pitch *or* tar; *(los zapatos)* to apply polish to.

a·bier·ta·men·te adv. openly, frankly.

a·bier·to, –ta I. past part. see **abrir II.** adj. open *<con los ojos abiertos* with open eyes>; *(raso)* open, clear *<campo a.* open country>; *(libre de limitaciones)* open *<un puerto a.* an open port>; *(franco)* open, candid *<tiene un carácter a.* she has an open nature>; *(sincero)* open, sincere *<un rostro a.* an open face>; S. AMER. generous **III.** m. COL. clearing, cleared land.

a·bi·ga·rra·do, –da I. past part. see **abigarrar II.** adj. *(multicolor)* variegated, multicolored; *(heterogéneo)* heterogeneous.

a·bi·ga·rrar tr. to mottle, variegate.

a·bi·ge·a·to m. LAW cattle stealing *or* rustling.

a·bi·go·ta·do, –da adj. mustachioed, having a thick, large mustache.

ab in·tes·ta·to adv. *(intestado)* intestate; FIG. *(negligentemente)* negligently, neglectfully; *(descuidadamente)* carelessly.

a·bi·sa·grar tr. to hinge.

a·bi·se·lar tr. to bevel.

a·bis·mal adj. abysmal.

a·bis·mar tr. *(hundir)* to throw into an abyss; *(abatir)* to overwhelm, depress; *(humillar)* to humble —reflex. AMER. to be amazed; DOM. REP. to be ruined ♦ **abismarse en** FIG. to yield to, give oneself up to (grief, pain).

a·bis·má·ti·co, –ca adj. deep, profound.

a·bis·mo m. *(sima)* abyss, chasm; FIG. abyss *<un a. de dolor* an abyss of sadness>; RELIG. hell ♦ **estar al borde del a.** to be on the brink of disaster.

ab·ju·ra·ción f. abjuration, renunciation.

ab·ju·rar tr. to abjure, renounce.

a·bla·ción f. SURG. ablation.

a·blan·da·bre·vas m.f. [pl. **-vas**] COLL. good-for-nothing.

a·blan·da·dor, –do·ra adj. softening.

a·blan·da·mien·to m. *(acción de ablandar)* softening; *(suavizamiento)* mollification, easing; FIG. *(mitigación)* mitigation, moderation.

a·blan·dar tr. *(reblandecer)* to soften; *(suavizar)* to mollify, calm; FIG. *(mitigar)* to mitigate, moderate —intr. *(el viento)* to calm down (wind); *(la nieve)* to thaw —reflex. *(reblandecerse)* to soften; *(calmarse)* to calm down; *(el tiempo)* to calm down (the weather).

a·blan·de m. ARG. set of wheels (of an automobile).

a·blan·de·cer §17 tr. to soften.

a·bla·ti·vo m. GRAM. ablative.

a·blu·ción f. RELIG. ablution, washing.

ab·ne·ga·ción f. abnegation, self-denial.

ab·ne·ga·da·men·te adv. unselfishly, altruistically.

ab·ne·ga·do, –da I. past part. see **abnegar II.** adj. unselfish, altruistic.

ab·ne·gar §52 tr. to abnegate, renounce —reflex. to deny oneself.

a·bo·ba·do, –da I. past part. see **abobar II.** adj. stupid, dim-witted.

a·bo·ba·mien·to m. *(tontería)* stupidity, silliness; *(asombro)* stupefaction, bewilderment.

a·bo·bar tr. *(entontecer)* to make stupid; *(asombrar)* to stupefy, bewilder —reflex. to become stupid.

a·bo·ca·do, –da I. past part. see **abocar II.** adj. *(agradable)* mild, smooth (wine); ARG., PAR., URUG. involved, engaged.

a·bo·ca·mien·to m. *(acción de asir)* biting; *(acercamiento)* approaching, drawing near; *(reunión)* meeting, appointment; MARIT. entering.

a·bo·car §70 tr. *(asir)* to seize with the mouth; *(escanciar)* to decant, pour; *(acercar)* to bring near —intr. MARIT. to enter a channel *or* strait —reflex. *(reunirse)* to meet by appointment, confer; *(approximarse)* to approach; ARG. to engage in.

a·bo·car·da·do, –da I. past part. see **abocardar II.** adj. bell-mouthed, flared (said of firearms).

a·bo·car·dar tr. to widen, ream (the opening of a tube or hole).

a·bo·ce·tar tr. to sketch.

a·bo·ci·nar tr. to shape like a trumpet —intr. COLL. to fall on one's face.

a·bo·chor·na·do, –da I. past part. see **abochornar II.** adj. *(sofocante)* stifling, suffocating; FIG. *(avergonzado)* embarrassed, ashamed.

a·bo·chor·nar tr. *(sofocar)* to stiffle, suffocate (from heat); FIG. *(avergonzar)* to embarrass, shame; *(hacer sonrojar)* to make blush —reflex. *(avergonzarse)* to become embarrassed; *(sonrojarse)* to blush; AGR. to parch, become parched.

a·bo·fe·te·ar tr. to slap.

a·bo·ga·cí·a f. law (profession).

a·bo·ga·di·llo m. DEROG. quack lawyer, shyster.

a·bo·ga·do, –da m.f. lawyer, attorney; FIG. *(mediador)* mediator ♦ **a. del diablo** devil's advocate • **a. de pobres** public defender • **a. de secano** FIG. quack lawyer, shyster.

a·bo·gar §47 intr. *(defender)* to advocate, plead; FIG. *(interceder)* to intercede.

a·bo·len·go m. *(ascendencia)* ancestry, lineage; LAW *(patrimonio)* patrimony, inheritance ♦ **de a.** of noble lineage.

a·bo·li·ción f. abolition, repeal.

a·bo·li·cio·nis·ta m.f. abolitionist.

a·bo·lir §38 tr. to abolish, repeal.

a·bol·sar·se reflex. *(formar bolsas)* to form pockets; *(la ropa)* to bag, become baggy; *(la piel)* to sag.

a·bo·lla·do, –da I. past part. see **abollar II.** adj. *(mellado)* dented, crushed; FIG., COLL. *(sin dinero)* penniless, broke **III.** m. embossment.

a·bo·lla·du·ra f. dent.

a·bo·llar tr. *(mellar)* to dent, crush; *(grabar en relieve)* to emboss —reflex. to become dented.

a·bo·llo·nar tr. to emboss.

a·bom·ba·do, –da I. past part. see **abombar II.** adj. *(convexo)* convex; FIG., COLL. *(aturdido)* stunned, stupefied; AMER. bad, spoiled (food); CHILE drunk, bombed.

a·bom·bar tr. *(dar forma convexa)* to make convex; FIG., COLL. *(aturdir)* to stun, stupefy —reflex. AMER. *(corromperse)* to spoil, go bad; CHILE to get drunk *or* bombed.

a·bo·mi·na·ble adj. *(detestable)* abominable, detestable; *(desagradable)* abominable, disagreeable <un gusto a. a disagreeable taste>.

a·bo·mi·na·ción f. abomination.

a·bo·mi·nar tr. to abominate, detest.

a·bo·na·ble adj. payable, due.

a·bo·na·do, –da I. past part. see **abonar II.** adj. *(fiable)* reliable, trustworthy; *(dispuesto)* inclined, apt; AGR. *(fértil)* rich (soil) **III.** m.f. subscriber, season ticket holder; *(viajero)* commuter.

a·bo·na·dor, –do·ra m.f. *(garante)* guarantor, bondsman —m. *(barrena)* auger.

a·bo·nan·zar §04 intr. METEOROL. *(aclararse)* to grow calm, clear up; FIG. *(serenarse)* to clear up (a situation).

a·bo·nar tr. *(acreditar)* to vouch for, guarantee; AGR. *(estercolar)* to fertilize, apply fertilizer; *(subscribir)* to subscribe to; *(pagar)* to pay —intr. to become calm (weather) ♦ **a. a cuenta** COM. to pay in installments —reflex. to subscribe, buy a season ticket.

a·bo·na·ré m. promissory note, IOU.

a·bo·no m. *(garantía)* guarantee, security; *(estiércol)* fertilizer, manure; *(billete)* subscription, season ticket; AMER. payment, installment.

a·bo·qué, aboque see **abocar.**

a·bor·da·ble adj. approachable, accessible; MARIT. boardable.

a·bor·da·je m. MARIT. boarding.

a·bor·dar tr. MARIT. *(atacar)* to board, broach (a ship); *(acostar)* to dock; FIG. *(acercar)* to approach; *(emprender)* to undertake, tackle (a problem) —intr. MARIT. to put into port, dock.

a·bo·ri·gen I. adj. aboriginal, indigenous **II.** m.f. aborigine, aboriginal.

a·bo·rras·car·se §70 reflex. to become stormy *or* cloudy.

a·bo·rre·cer §17 tr. *(odiar)* to hate, abhor, loathe; *(abandonar)* to desert, abandon (animals, their young); *(aburrir)* to bore, weary.

a·bo·rre·ci·ble adj. hateful, abhorrent, loathsome.

a·bo·rre·ci·mien·to m. *(odio)* hatred, abhorrence, loathing; *(aburrimiento)* boredom.

a·bo·rre·ga·do, –da I. past part. see **aborregarse II.** adj. FIG. lacking initiative, sheepish.

a·bo·rre·gar·se §47 reflex. METEOROL. to become covered with fleecy clouds; AMER. *(acobardarse)* to turn cowardly.

a·bo·rrez·ca, aborezco see **aborrecer.**

a·bor·tar intr. PHYSIOL. to abort, miscarry; FIG. *(fracasar)* to fail, go awry ♦ **hacerse a.** MED. to have an abortion.

a·bor·ti·vo, –va adj. abortive.

a·bor·to m. PHYSIOL. miscarriage; *(voluntario)* abortion; FIG. *(fracaso)* failure; COLL. *(feo)* ugly person.

a·bo·ru·jar tr. to make lumpy —reflex. to wrap oneself up, bundle up.

a·bo·ta·gar·se §47 *or* **a·bo·tar·gar·se §47** reflex. to swell (up).

a·bo·to·na·dor m. buttonhook.

a·bo·to·na·du·ra f. buttoning, fastening.

a·bo·to·nar tr. to button (up) —intr. to bud —reflex. to button up.

a·bo·ve·da·do, –da I. past part. see **abovedar II.** adj. arched, vaulted **III.** m. ARCHIT. vaulting.

a·bo·ve·dar tr. ARCHIT. to arch, vault.

a·bo·yar tr. MARIT. to mark with buoys —intr. to float.

a·bo·za·lar tr. to muzzle, put a muzzle on.

a·bra f. *(bahía)* bay, cove; *(valle)* valley, dale; *(grieta)* fissure, crack; AMER. *(de una puerta)* leaf; *(de una ventana)* pane; *(en un bosque)* clearing (in a wood).

a·bra·ca·da·bra m. abracadabra.

a·bra·cé, abrace see **abrazar.**

a·bra·sa·do, –da I. past part. see **abrasar II.** adj. burned, scorched.

a·bra·sa·dor, –do·ra *or* **a·bra·san·te** adj. burning, scorching.

a·bra·sar tr. *(quemar)* to burn, set fire to; *(secar)* to dry; *(calentar en exceso)* to overheat; FIG. *(malgastar)* to consume, squander; FIG. *(avergonzar)* to shame, humiliate —intr. to burn up —reflex. to burn up ♦ **abrasarse de** *or* **en** FIG. to be consumed with (passion, rage).

a·bra·sión f. abrasion; GEOL. erosion.

a·bra·si·vo, –va adj. & m. abrasive.

a·bra·za·de·ra f. *(zuncho)* clamp, bracket; PRINT. *(en la imprenta)* bracket.

a·bra·za·dor, –do·ra adj. embracing, hugging.

a·bra·zar §04 tr. to embrace, hug <abrazó a su madre he hugged his mother>; *(ceñir)* to clasp; *(adoptar)* to adopt, embrace <a. la religión católica to embrace the Catholic religion>; FIG. *(rodear)* to surround, encompass <a. mucho terreno to encompass a lot of territory>; *(incluir)* to include, encompass; *(encargarse de)* to take charge of <a. una empresa to take charge of an enterprise> —reflex. to embrace *or* hug each other.

a·bra·zo m. *(acción)* embracing; *(apretón)* embrace, hug.

a·bre·bo·ca m.f. ARG. absent-minded person, featherbrain.

a·bre·car·tas m. [pl. -tas] letter opener.

á·bre·go m. south wind.

a·bre·la·tas m. [pl. -tas] can opener.

a·bre·va·de·ro m. watering place, drinking trough.

a·bre·var tr. to water (livestock); *(pieles)* to soak (in tanning); *(dar de beber a)* to give a drink to; *(mojar)* to wet, water; *(satisfacer)* to slake (thirst).

a·bre·via·ción f. abbreviation, shortening; *(libros)* abridgement.

a·bre·via·do, –da I. past part. see **abreviar II.** adj. *(breve)* brief, short; *(libros)* abridged, shortened.

a·bre·via·dor, –do·ra I. adj. abbreviating, shortening **II.** m.f. abbreviator, abridger.

a·bre·viar tr. *(reducir)* to abbreviate; *(libros)* to abridge, shorten; *(acortar)* to shorten, cut short; *(acelerar)* to shorten, hasten <el trabajo abrevia las horas work shortens the hours> —reflex. C. AMER. to hurry, make haste.

a·bre·via·tu·ra f. abbreviation; *(compendio)* compendium, résumé ♦ **en a.** COLL. *(en breve)* in brief; *(con prisa)* hastily.

a·bri·bo·nar·se reflex. to become a rogue *or* rascal.

a·bri·dor, –do·ra I. adj. opening **II.** m. *(abrelatas)* can opener; BOT. freestone peach; AGR. grafting knife; ECUAD. large-toothed comb.

a·bri·ga·de·ro m. *(sitio protegido)* sheltered place; MARIT. shelter, den, lair.

a·bri·ga·do, –da I. past part. see **abrigar II.** adj. sheltered, protected **III.** m. *or* f. sheltered place.

a·bri·gar §47 tr. *(proteger)* to shelter, protect; *(cubrir)* to cover up, keep warm; FIG. *(ayudar)* to aid, assist; *(guardar)* to harbor <a. sospechas to harbor suspicions> —reflex. *(resguardarse)* to take shelter; *(cubrirse)* to wrap *or* cover oneself up.

a·bri·go m. *(protección)* shelter, protection, cover; *(sobretodo)* overcoat, wrap; FIG. *(ayuda)* aid, protection; MARIT. harbor, haven; ARG. blanket, quilt ♦ **a. antiaéreo** bomb shelter • **al a. de** sheltered *or* protected by.

a·bril m. *(mes)* April; FIG. *(juventud)* early youth ♦ **estar hecho un a.** FIG., COLL. to be all dressed up • **tener quince abriles** to be fifteen years old.

a·bri·llan·ta·dor m. *(obrero)* lapidary (gem cutter and polisher); *(instrumento para abrillantar)* instrument for cutting and polishing gems.

a·bri·llan·tar tr. *(labrar)* to cut (precious stones); *(pulir)* to polish; FIG. *(realzar)* to enhance <la educación abrillanta los dotes naturales education enhances one's natural talents>; AMER. to glaze (fruit).

a·brir §85 tr. to open <ella abrió la caja she opened the box>; *(desplegar)* to spread out; *(empezar)* to open, begin

<a. la licitación to open the bidding>; (cortar) to open, cut <a. un libro to open a book>; (encabezar) to lead, head <a. la procesión to lead the procession>; (horadar) to dig; FIG. (hacer accesible) to open <a. la casa a alguien to open one's home to someone>; (dar principio a) to open, begin <a. la sesión to open the session>; PRINT. (grabar) to engrave; AMER. to clear (land) ◆ a. el apetito to whet the appetite • a. con llave to unlock • a. una cuenta to open an account • a. la mano FIG. to extend one's hand • a. los ojos a alguien FIG. to open someone's eyes • a. paso to make way • en un a. y cerrar de ojos FIG. in the twinkling of an eye —reflex. to open <la puerta se abre fácilmente the door opens easily>; (aclarar) to clear up (weather); (florecer) to blossom; (hender) to split, crack; (esparcirse) to spread out, scatter (objects); AMER. (largarse) to leave, clear out; (retirarse) to back out, withdraw; (desviarse) to swerve ◆ abrirse con to confide in, open up to.

a·bro·cha·dor m. (abotonador) buttonhook; S. AMER. stapler.

a·bro·cha·mien·to m. (con botones) buttoning; (con broches) fastening.

a·bro·char tr. (con botones) to button (up); (con broches) to fasten; (zapatos) to lace, tie; AMER. to seize, apprehend; S. AMER. to staple.

a·bro·ga·ble adj. repealable, revokable.

a·bro·ga·ción f. abrogation, repeal.

a·bro·gar §47 tr. LAW to abrogate, repeal —reflex. AMER. to assume, take upon oneself.

a·bro·jo m. BOT. thistle, caltrop; MIL. caltrop; AMER. prickly or thorny plant ◆ abrojos MARIT. (peñas) reefs, sharp rocks; FIG., COLL. (dolores) sorrows, grief.

a·bron·car §70 tr. (disgustar) to disgust, annoy; (avergonzar) to embarrass, shame; (echar una bronca) to tell off, reprimand.

a·bro·que·lar tr. (proteger) to protect, shield; MARIT. to boxhaul, veer sharply —reflex. to shield or protect oneself.

a·bru·ma·do, –da I. past part. see abrumar II. adj. (agobiado) overwhelmed, crushed; FIG. (molestado) bothered, annoyed.

a·bru·ma·dor, –do·ra I. adj. overwhelming, oppressive II. m.f. oppressor.

a·bru·mar tr. (agobiar) to overwhelm, crush; (oprimir) to oppress; FIG. (molestar) to bother, annoy —reflex. METEOROL. to become cloudy or foggy.

a·brup·to, –ta adj. (escarpado) craggy, rugged <tierra a. craggy ground>; (precipitoso) steep, abrupt <una montaña a. a steep mountain>; FIG. (áspero) abrupt, curt <una respuesta a. an abrupt response>.

a·bru·ta·do, –da adj. brutish, uncouth.

abs·ce·so m. MED. abscess.

ab·sen·tis·mo m. absenteeism.

ab·sen·tis·ta adj. & m.f. absentee.

ab·so·lu·ción f. RELIG. absolution; LAW acquittal.

ab·so·lu·ta I. f. (proposición) dogmatic assertion; MIL. discharge II. adj. see **absoluto, –ta.**

ab·so·lu·ta·men·te adv. (completamente) absolutely, completely; (de ninguna manera) not at all, by no means.

ab·so·lu·tis·mo m. absolutism, despotism.

ab·so·lu·to, –ta I. adj. (completo) absolute, complete; (incondicional) absolute, unconditional <poder a. absolute power>; (despótico) absolute, despotic; (sin mezcla) pure (alcohol); FIG., COLL. (imperioso) imperious, dominant ◆ en a. absolutely not, not at all • lo a. the absolute II. f. see absoluta.

ab·so·lu·to·rio, –ria adj. absolutory, absolving.

ab·sol·ver §78 tr. (perdonar) to absolve; LAW (exculpar) to acquit; (liberar) to release.

ab·sor·ben·te I. adj. absorbent <algodón a. absorbent cotton>; FIG. (cautivante) absorbing <trabajo a. absorbing work> II. m. absorbent.

ab·sor·ber tr. (embeber) to absorb; FIG. (consumir) to absorb, engross <sus estudios le absorben his studies engross him> —reflex. to become absorbed or engrossed.

ab·sor·bi·ble adj. absorbable.

ab·sor·bi·mien·to m. or **ab·sor·ción** f. absorption.

ab·sor·tar tr. to engross, entrance —reflex. to be engrossed or entranced.

ab·sor·to, –ta adj. engrossed, entranced.

abs·te·mio, –mia I. adj. abstemious, teetotaling II. m.f. teetotaler, non-drinker.

abs·ten·ción f. abstention.

abs·ten·cio·nis·mo m. abstentionism.

abs·te·ner·se §69 reflex. to abstain, refrain.

abs·ti·nen·cia f. (privación) abstinence; RELIG. (ayuno) abstinence, fasting.

abs·ti·nen·te adj. abstinent.

abs·trac·ción f. abstraction; FIG. (preocupación) preoccupation.

abs·trac·to, –ta I. adj. abstract ◆ en a. in the abstract II. m. abstract.

abs·tra·er §72 tr. to abstract, consider apart ◆ a. de to do without —reflex. to become withdrawn or lost in thought.

abs·tra·í·do, –da I. past part. see abstraer II. adj. (distraído) engrossed, absorbed, preoccupied; (retirado) withdrawn.

abs·tru·so, –sa adj. abstruse, obscure.

abs·tu·vie·ra, abstuvo see abstenerse.

ab·suel·to past part. see absolver.

ab·suel·va, absuelve see absolver.

ab·sur·di·dad f. absurdity.

ab·sur·do, –da I. adj. absurd, ridiculous II. m. absurdity.

a·bu·che·ar tr. to boo, hiss.

a·bu·che·o m. booing, hissing.

a·bue·la f. grandmother; FIG. (vieja) old woman.

a·bue·lo m. grandfather; FIG. (viejo) old man ◆ abuelos grandparents; (ascendientes) ancestors.

a·bu·lia f. abulia, lack of will power.

a·bul·ta·do, –da I. past part. see abultar II. adj. (grande) large, bulky; FIG. (exagerado) exaggerated.

a·bul·ta·mien·to m. (aumento) increase, enlarging; (bulto) bulkiness; (hinchazón) swelling; FIG. (exageración) exaggeration.

a·bul·tar tr. (engrosar) to enlarge, make large; (hinchar) to swell; FIG. (exagerar) to exaggerate —intr. to be bulky or large.

a·bun·dan·cia f. (profusión) abundance; (riqueza) wealth, plenty.

a·bun·dan·te adj. abundant, plentiful.

a·bun·dan·te·men·te adv. abundantly.

a·bun·dar intr. (pulular) to be abundant, abound <el trigo abunda en esta región wheat is abundant in this area>; (convenir) to agree <a. en un dictamen to agree with a dictum>.

a·bur·gue·sa·mien·to m. becoming bourgeois.

a·bur·gue·sar·se reflex. to become bourgeois.

a·bu·rri·do, –da I. past part. see aburrir II. adj. (cansado) bored; (fastidiado) annoyed; (tedioso) boring, tiresome.

a·bu·rri·dor, –do·ra adj. boring, tedious.

a·bu·rri·mien·to m. boredom, tedium.

a·bu·rrir tr. (cansar) to bore, weary; (fastidiar) to annoy; (abandonar) to leave, abandon <a. a la familia to abandon one's family>; COLL. (gastar) to spend, waste <a. una tarde to waste an afternoon> —reflex. to become bored or wearied ◆ aburrirse como una ostra to be bored to death.

a·bu·sa·dor, –do·ra adj. abusive.

a·bu·sar intr. to go too far, exceed ◆ a. de to abuse, misuse.

a·bu·sión f. (abuso) abuse; (absurdo) absurdity; (superstición) superstition, omen.

a·bu·so m. (exceso) abuse, excess; (injusticia) injustice.

ab·yec·ción f. abjection, abjectness.

ab·yec·to, –ta adj. (vil) abject, low; (abatido) wretched, miserable.

a·cá adv. here, over here ◆ a. y allá here and there, everywhere • de a. para allá from here to there • más a. closer • por a. around here.

a·ca·ba·ble adj. that can be finished.

a·ca·ba·da·men·te adv. completely, perfectly.

a·ca·ba·do, –da I. past part. see acabar II. adj. (terminado) finished; (perfecto) complete, consummate; (arrui-

nado) ruined, finished <*su salud está a.* his health is ruined> **III. m.** ARTS finish <*a. satinado* satin finish>.

a·ca·ba·dor, –do·ra m.f. finisher, dresser.

a·ca·ba·lar tr. to finish, complete.

a·ca·ba·lla·de·ro m. stud farm.

a·ca·ba·lla·do, –da adj. horselike, horsy.

a·ca·ba·llar tr. to cover (a mare).

a·ca·ba·mien·to m. *(fin)* finishing, completion, end; FIG. *(muerte)* death.

a·ca·bar tr. *(terminar)* to finish, complete, conclude; *(perfeccionar)* to put the finishing touches on; *(pulir)* to give a finish to; *(consumir)* to finish *or* use up <*a. las provisiones* to use up the provisions>; ECUAD., COLL. to slander —intr. *(terminar)* to end, stop <*la palabra acaba con la letra o* the word ends in an o>; *(morir)* to die ◆ **¡acabáramos!** finally!, at last! • **a. con** to put an end to, destroy • **a. de** to have just <*acaban de salir* they have just left> • **a. mal** to end badly • **a. por** to end up <*él acabó por perderlo* he ended up losing it> —reflex. *(terminarse)* to end, terminate; *(extinguirse)* to become extinct; to run out of <*se me acabó el tiempo* I ran out of time> ◆ **¡se acabó!** that's the end of that!

a·ca·bil·dar tr. to call together, organize into a group.

a·ca·cia f. BOT. acacia.

a·ca·che·te·ar tr. to slap, hit.

a·ca·de·mia f. *(sociedad)* academy <*una a. literaria* a literary academy>; *(escuela)* school; PAINT. nude study.

a·ca·dé·mi·co, –ca I. adj. academic II. m.f. academician.

a·ca·de·mis·ta m.f. academician.

a·ca·de·mi·zar §04 tr. to academize.

a·ca·e·cer §17 intr. to happen, occur.

a·ca·e·ci·mien·to m. happening, occurrence.

a·ca·lam·brar·se reflex. to cramp up, get cramps.

a·ca·lo·ra·da·men·te adv. *(con ardor)* heatedly, vehemently; *(ávidamente)* enthusiastically, passionately.

a·ca·lo·ra·do, –da I. past part. see **acalorar** II. adj. *(caliente)* heated, hot; *(cansado)* tired; FIG. *(entusiasmado)* enthusiastic, passionate <*partidarios acalorados* enthusiastic supporters>; *(enardecido)* heated, animated <*discusión a.* heated discussion>.

a·ca·lo·ra·mien·to m. *(ardor)* ardor, heat; FIG. *(entusiasmo)* vehemence, passion.

a·ca·lo·rar tr. *(calentar)* to heat *or* warm up; *(cansar)* to tire <*esta labor me acalora* this work tires me>; FIG. *(alentar)* to inspire, encourage; *(incitar)* to arouse, excite —reflex. *(calentarse)* to get hot, heat up; *(hacerse vivo)* to heat up, get heated <*el debate se acaloró* the debate got heated>; FIG. *(irritarse)* to get excited *or* upset.

a·ca·lo·ro m. var. of **acaloramiento**.

a·ca·llar tr. *(hacer callar)* to hush, quiet; FIG. *(aplacar)* to placate, calm.

a·cam·pa·dor, –do·ra m.f. camper.

a·cam·pa·mien·to m. *(acción)* camping; *(lugar)* camp, encampment.

a·cam·pa·na·do, –da I. past part. see **acampanar** II. adj. bell-shaped.

a·cam·pa·nar tr. to shape like a bell.

a·cam·par tr., intr., & reflex. to camp, encamp.

á·ca·na m.f. acana (hard reddish Cuban wood).

a·ca·na·la·do, –da I. past part. see **acanalar** II. adj. *(encañonado)* channeled; *(estriado)* fluted, striated.

a·ca·na·la·du·ra f. groove, fluting.

a·ca·na·lar tr. *(estriar)* to striate, flute; *(encañonar)* to channel, form a channel.

a·ca·na·llar tr. to corrupt, deprave —reflex. to become corrupted *or* depraved.

a·can·ti·la·do, –da I. adj. *(abrupto)* steep; *(escalonado)* shelved (coastline) II. m. cliff.

a·ca·ño·ne·ar tr. MIL. to cannonade, bombard.

a·can·to·nar tr. to quarter, billet —reflex. MIL. to be quartered *or* billeted; *(limitarse)* to confine *or* limit oneself <*acantonarse en las ciencias* to limit oneself to the sciences>.

a·ca·pa·ra·dor, –do·ra I. adj. hoarding II. m.f. *(acumulador)* stockpiler, hoarder; FIG. *(monopolizador)* monopolizer.

a·ca·pa·ra·mien·to m. *(acumulación)* stockpiling, hoarding; FIG. *(posesión exclusiva)* monopolizing, monopoly.

a·ca·pa·rar tr. *(acumular)* to stockpile, hoard; FIG. *(monopolizar)* to monopolize <*a. el poder* to monopolize power>.

a·cá·pi·te m. S. AMER. *(párrafo)* paragraph; *(subtítulo)* subheading.

a·ca·ra·co·la·do, –da adj. spiral-shaped, shaped like a shell.

a·ca·ra·me·la·do, –da I. past part. see **acaramelar** II. adj. *(bañado de caramelo)* caramelized; *(de color de caramelo)* caramel-colored; FIG. *(melifluo)* sugary, very sweet.

a·ca·ra·me·lar tr. to caramelize, cover with caramel —reflex. FIG. to be *or* become extremely sweet.

a·car·de·na·lar tr. to bruise, make black-and-blue —reflex. to turn black-and-blue.

a·ca·re·ar tr. to confront, face.

a·ca·ri·cia·dor, –do·ra I. adj. caressing II. m.f. caresser, fondler.

a·ca·ri·ciar tr. *(abrazar)* to caress, fondle; *(rozar)* to caress, brush <*la brisa acarició su rostro* the breeze caressed his face>; FIG. *(abrigar)* to cherish, hold dear <*a. vanas esperanzas* to cherish vain hopes>.

a·ca·ri·ñar tr. AMER. var. of **acariciar**.

a·ca·rra·la·du·ra f. CHILE, PERU run, runner (in stockings).

a·ca·rre·a·dor, –do·ra I. adj. carting, transporting II. m.f. carrier, transporter.

a·ca·rre·ar tr. *(transportar)* to cart, transport; *(ocasionar)* to occasion, cause <*a. una desgracia* to cause a disgrace> —reflex. to incur.

a·ca·rre·o m. cartage, transportation.

a·ca·rro·ñar·se reflex. AMER., COLL. *(acobardarse)* to get scared, chicken out; ARCH. to rot, decay.

a·car·to·nar tr. to give the appearance of cardboard —reflex. *(ponerse como cartón)* to become like cardboard; FIG., COLL. *(enjutarse)* to become withered (with age).

a·ca·so I. m. chance, accident II. adv. *(por casualidad)* by chance, by accident; *(quizás)* perhaps, maybe ◆ **al a.** by chance, at random • **por si a.** just in case.

a·ca·ta·dor, –do·ra adj. respectful.

a·ca·ta·mien·to m. *(respeto)* respect, reverence; *(sumisión)* observance, compliance.

a·ca·tar tr. *(respetar)* to respect, revere; *(obedecer)* to observe, comply with <*a. la ley* to observe the law>; AMER. *(notar)* to notice, realize.

a·ca·ta·rrar·se reflex. *(resfriarse)* to catch a cold; AMER., COLL. to get tipsy *or* drunk.

a·ca·to m. respect, reverence.

a·ca·tó·li·co, –ca adj. non-Catholic.

a·cau·da·la·do, –da adj. wealthy, rich.

a·cau·da·lar tr. to accumulate, amass.

a·cau·di·lla·dor, –do·ra I. adj. leading, commanding II. m.f. leader, commander.

a·cau·di·lla·mien·to m. leadership, command.

a·cau·di·llar tr. to lead, command.

ac·ce·der intr. *(consentir)* to agree, consent; *(al trono)* to accede.

ac·ce·si·bi·li·dad f. accessibility.

ac·ce·si·ble adj. *(alcanzable)* accessible, attainable; *(tratable)* approachable, accessible <*un rey muy a.* a very accessible king>.

ac·ce·sión f. *(consentimiento)* agreement, consent; *(al trono)* accession; *(entrada)* access, entry; MED. attack.

ac·ce·so m. *(entrada)* access, entry, admittance; *(accesibilidad)* accessibility; *(arrebato)* outburst, fit <*un a. de rabia* an outburst of anger>; MED. attack, fit <*a. de tos* a coughing fit>.

ac·ce·so·ria I. f. annex ◆ **accesorias** street level apartments II. adj. see **accesorio, –ria**.

ac·ce·so·ria·men·te adv. accessorily.

ac·ce·so·rio, –ria I. adj. accessory II. m. *(utensilio auxiliar)* accessory; *(en el teatro)* prop —f. see **accesoria**.

ac·ci·den·ta·do, –da I. past part. see **accidentar** II. adj. *(escarpado)* rough, uneven <*terreno a.* rough terrain>; *(agitado)* agitated, troubled III. m.f. accident victim.

ac·ci·den·tal I. adj. *(imprevisto)* accidental <*una muerte a.* an accidental death>; *(casual)* accidental, chance <*un encuentro a.* a chance meeting>; *(ocasional)* temporary, acting <*un director a.* an acting director> II. m. MUS. accidental.

ac·ci·den·tal·men·te adv. accidentally.

ac·ci·den·tar tr. to cause (an accident) —reflex. to have an accident.

ac·ci·den·te m. *(contratiempo)* accident, mishap <*un a. de trabajo* an occupational accident>; *(casualidad)* accident, chance; *(del terreno)* accident, unevenness (of terrain); MED. fit, spell; GRAM. accidence, inflection; MUS. accidental ♦ **por a.** by accident or chance.

ac·ción f. action <*un hombre de a.* a man of action>; *(hecho)* act, deed; *(efecto)* effect, influence <*la a. de un veneno* the effect of a poison>; *(judicial)* legal action, lawsuit; MIL. action, battle; COM. share, stock; ARTS pose; LIT., THEAT. action, plot; THEAT. gesture; PERU raffle or lottery ticket ♦ **a. de gracias** thanksgiving • **a. ordinaria** or **primitiva** COM. common stock • **a. preferida** COM. preferred stock • **a. refleja** PHYSIOL. reflex action • **mala a.** evil deed.

ac·cio·na·mien·to m. MECH. driving, propelling.

ac·cio·nar tr. *(poner en movimiento)* to put in motion; MECH. to drive, propel —intr. *(gesticular)* to gesticulate, gesture; AMER., LAW to bring a suit.

ac·cio·na·rio, -ria COM. I. adj. stock, of shares of stock II. m.f. stockholder, shareholder.

ac·cio·nis·ta m.f. shareholder, stockholder.

a·ce·cé, acece see **acezar.**

a·ce·ci·nar tr. to cure (meat) —reflex. FIG. to wizen, wither (with age).

a·ce·cha·dor, -do·ra I. adj. *(observador)* watching, observing; *(al acecho)* ambushing II. m.f. *(observador)* watcher, observer; *(emboscador)* ambusher; *(espía)* spy.

a·ce·char tr. *(observar)* to watch; *(emboscar)* to ambush, lie in wait for; *(espiar)* to spy on.

a·ce·cho m. *(observación)* watching, observing; *(emboscada)* ambush.

a·ce·dar tr. *(poner agrio)* to make sour; FIG. *(agriar)* to sour (someone); *(disgustar)* to annoy, displease —reflex. *(ponerse agrio)* to become sour; *(las plantas)* to fade, wilt.

a·ce·dí·a f. acidity, sourness; MED. heartburn, acid indigestion; FIG. *(del carácter)* rudeness, uncouthness; ICHTH. flounder, plaice.

a·ce·do, -da adj. *(agrio)* acid, sour; FIG. *(áspero)* rude, uncouth.

a·cé·fa·lo, -la adj. *(sin cabeza)* acephalous, headless; FIG. *(sin jefe)* leaderless.

a·cei·tar tr. to oil, lubricate.

a·cei·te m. oil <*a. de oliva* olive oil>; *(perfume)* attar <*a. de rosas* attar of roses> ♦ **a. combustible** or **de quemar** fuel oil • **a. de ballena** whale oil • **a. de fusel** fusel oil • **a. de hígado de bacalao** cod-liver oil • **a. de ricino** castor oil • **a. de vitriolo** sulphuric acid • **a. esencial** or **volátil** essence, attar • **a. fijo** CHEM. fixed oil • **a. mineral** mineral oil; *(petróleo)* petroleum • **a. secante** or **de linaza** linseed oil • **a. vegetal** vegetable oil • **a. virgen** virgin olive oil.

a·cei·te·ra I. f. *(alcuza)* oil cruet; ENTOM. oil beetle ♦ **aceiteras** oil and vinegar cruets II. adj. see **aceitero, -ra.**

a·cei·te·rí·a f. oil shop.

a·cei·te·ro, -ra I. adj. oil II. m.f. oil vendor —f. see **aceitera.**

a·cei·to·so, -sa adj. oily.

a·cei·tu·na f. olive.

a·cei·tu·na·do, -da adj. olive-green (complexion).

a·cei·tu·ne·ro, -ra m.f. *(labrador)* olive picker, olive harvester; *(vendedor)* olive seller —m. *(almacén)* olive storehouse.

a·cei·tu·no, -na I. m. BOT. olive tree II. adj. AMER. olive, olive-colored.

a·ce·le·ra·ción f. acceleration.

a·ce·le·ra·da I. f. AUTO. acceleration II. adj. see **acelerado, -da.**

a·ce·le·ra·da·men·te adv. acceleratedly.

a·ce·le·ra·do, -da I. adj. accelerated II. m. CINEM. quick motion —f. see **acelerada.**

a·ce·le·ra·dor, -do·ra I. adj. accelerating II. m. accelerator.

a·ce·le·ra·mien·to m. var. of **aceleración.**

a·ce·le·rar tr. *(hacer más rapido)* to accelerate, speed up; *(anticipar)* to speed up, expedite ♦ **a. el paso** to hurry,

hasten —intr. *(precipitarse)* to hurry, hasten; *(motores)* to race.

a·cel·ga f. BOT. chard, beet.

a·cé·mi·la f. *(mula)* (pack) mule; FIG., COLL. *(tonto)* boor, brute.

a·ce·mi·le·ro, -ra I. adj. pertaining to mules II. m. muleteer, mule driver.

a·ce·mi·ta f. CUL. bran bread.

a·ce·mi·te m. CUL. *(rollón)* whole-meal flour, bran mixed with flour; *(potaje)* porridge.

a·cen·dra·do, -da adj. pure, stainless.

a·cen·drar tr. METAL. to refine, purify; FIG. *(purificar)* to purify, make pure.

a·cen·suar §67 or **a·cen·sar** tr. *(imponer censo)* to take a census; *(gravar)* to tax.

a·cen·to m. accent <*a. tónico* tonic accent>; *(signo)* accent mark; *(pronunciación particular)* accent <*habla con a. gallego* he speaks with a Galician accent>; *(tono)* tone, inflection ♦ **a. ortográfico** GRAM. written accent.

a·cen·tua·ble adj. GRAM. that should be accentuated.

a·cen·tua·ción f. accentuation.

a·cen·tua·da·men·te adv. FIG. *(señaladamente)* markedly, noticeably; *(con acento escrito)* with a written accent.

a·cen·tua·do, -da I. past part. see **acentuar** II. adj. *(que lleva acento)* accented, stressed; *(sobresaliente)* accentuated.

a·cen·tual adj. GRAM. accentual.

a·cen·tuar §67 tr. *(poner acento)* to accent, stress; FIG. *(hacer resaltar)* to accentuate, emphasize —reflex. FIG. *(sobresalir)* to stand out, become noticeable.

a·ce·ña f. water wheel, water mill.

a·ce·par intr. to take root.

a·cep·ción f. *(significación)* meaning, acceptation; *(de personas)* preference, favoritism.

a·ce·pi·lla·do·ra f. CARP. planing machine, surfacer.

a·ce·pi·lla·du·ra f. CARP. *(allanamiento)* planing; *(viruta)* shavings (of wood or metal).

a·ce·pi·llar tr. *(limpiar)* to brush; CARP. *(allanar)* to plane; FIG. *(pulir)* to polish.

a·cep·ta·bi·li·dad f. acceptability.

a·cep·ta·ble adj. acceptable.

a·cep·ta·ción f. acceptance <*la a. de una donación* the acceptance of a donation>; *(aprobación)* approval, approbation; *(de personas)* favoritism, preference.

a·cep·ta·dor, -do·ra I. adj. accepting II. m.f. acceptor.

a·cep·tar tr. *(recibir)* to accept; *(admitir)* to accept, believe in; *(aprobar)* to approve of, sanction; COM. to accept, honor.

a·cep·to, -ta adj. acceptable, agreeable.

a·cep·tor m. acceptor.

a·ce·quia f. *(reguera)* irrigation ditch; AMER. *(arroyo)* stream.

a·ce·quiar intr. to construct or dig irrigation ditches or channels.

a·ce·ra f. *(vereda)* sidewalk; *(fila de casas)* row of houses; ARCHIT. *(paramento)* facing.

a·ce·ra·do, -da I. past part. see **acerar** II. adj. *(de acero)* steel, steely; BOT. barbed, spiky; FIG. *(fuerte)* strong; *(mordaz)* biting, mordant.

a·ce·rar tr. *(cubrir)* to steel, cover with steel; *(convertir)* to turn into steel; *(poner aceras)* to pave; FIG. *(fortalecer)* to strengthen, steel; *(volver acerbo)* to make mordant —reflex. FIG. to steel or strengthen oneself.

a·cer·ba·men·te adv. cruelly, harshly.

a·cer·bi·dad f. *(sabor)* bitterness, sourness; *(severidad)* cruelty, harshness.

a·cer·bo, -ba adj. *(agrio)* bitter, sour; *(severo)* cruel, harsh.

a·cer·ca de prep. about, concerning.

a·cer·ca·mien·to m. approach; POL. rapprochement.

a·cer·car §70 tr. to bring near —reflex. to approach, draw near; POL. to make a rapprochement.

a·ce·rí·a f. steel mill.

a·ce·ri·co m. *(almohada pequeña)* small pillow, cushion; *(almohadilla para alfileres)* pincushion.

a·ce·ris·ta m. steel manufacturer.

a·ce·ro m. METAL. steel; FIG. blade, sword ♦ **a. colado** or **fundido** cast steel • **a. inoxidable** stainless steel • **aceros** *(valentía)* courage; *(apetito)* appetite.

a·ce·ro·la f. BOT. haw (fruit).
a·cer·qué, acerque see **acercar.**
a·cé·rri·mo, –ma adj. FIG. staunch, stalwart.
a·ce·rro·jar tr. to bolt, lock.
a·cer·ta·da·men·te adv. correctly, accurately.
a·cer·ta·do, –da I. past part. see **acertar** II. adj. *(correcto)* correct, accurate; *(al caso)* to the point; *(apropiado)* appropriate, fitting <*una respuesta a.* an appropriate answer>.
a·cer·tan·te I. adj. winning II. m.f. *(ganador)* winner; *(el que resuelve un problema)* solver.
a·cer·tar §49 tr. *(adivinar)* to guess correctly; *(encontrar)* to find, hit upon —intr. *(tener razón)* to hit the mark, be correct; *(lograr)* succeed; AGR. to thrive, flourish ♦ **a.** a to happen to <*acertó a llegar en ese momento* he happened to arrive just then> • **a. con** to come upon *or* across <*acertó con la casa* he came upon the house>.
a·cer·ti·jo m. riddle.
a·cer·vo m. *(montón)* pile, heap; *(propiedad común)* common property; *(valores culturales)* cultural background; FIG. *(riquezas)* wealth, riches.
a·ces·cen·cia f. slight sourness.
a·ces·cen·te adj. slightly sour.
a·ce·ta·to m. acetate.
a·cé·ti·co, –ca adj. acetic.
a·ce·ti·fi·ca·ción f. acetification.
a·ce·ti·fi·car §70 tr. to acetify.
a·ce·ti·le·no m. CHEM. acetylene.
a·ce·ti·lo m. CHEM. acetyl.
a·ce·to·na f. CHEM. acetone.
a·ce·to·so, –sa adj. acetous.
a·ce·tre m. *(caldero)* water bucket; RELIG. font.
a·ce·tri·nar tr. to make sallow.
a·ce·zar §04 intr. to pant, gasp.
a·ce·zo m. pant, panting.
a·cia·go, –ga adj. fateful, unlucky.
a·cial m. *(para ganado)* barnacle (for livestock); ECUAD., GUAT. whip, switch.
a·cí·bar m. BOT. aloes; FIG. *(amargura)* sourness, bitterness.
a·ci·ba·rar tr. *(agregar acíbar)* to add bitter aloes to; FIG. *(amargar)* to embitter.
a·ci·be·rar tr. to pulverize, grind very fine.
a·ci·ca·la·do, –da I. past part. see **acicalar** II. adj. dressed up, spruced up; *(pulido)* polished, burnished III. m. polishing.
a·ci·ca·la·dor, –do·ra I. adj. polishing, burnishing II. m.f. polisher, burnisher.
a·ci·ca·lar tr. *(aderezar)* to dress *or* spruce up; *(pulir)* to polish, burnish; ARCHIT. to finish, put a finish on —reflex. to dress *or* spruce up.
a·ci·ca·te m. *(espuela)* spur; FIG. *(incentivo)* spur, incentive.
a·ci·ca·te·ar tr. to spur, incite.
a·ci·cu·lar adj. *(en forma de aguja)* needle-shaped, spiny; MIN. aciculate.
a·ci·dez f. acidity.
a·ci·dia f. laziness, indolence.
a·ci·dí·fe·ro, –ra adj. CHEM. acidiferous, acid-containing.
a·ci·di·fi·ca·ble adj. acidifiable.
a·ci·di·fi·ca·ción f. CHEM. acidification.
a·ci·di·fi·can·te adj. acidifying.
a·ci·di·fi·car §70 tr. to acidify —reflex. to become acidic.
á·ci·do, –da I. adj. CHEM. acid; *(agrio)* sour, tart; FIG. *(amargo)* sour *(disposition)* II. m. CHEM. acid; COLL. L.S.D. ♦ **a. bórico** boric acid • **a. carbónico** carbonic acid • **a. clorhídrico** hydrochloric acid • **a. gálico** gallic acid • **a. graso** fatty acid • **a. nítrico** nitric acid • **a. sulfúrico** sulfuric acid.
a·ci·du·lar tr. to acidulate.
a·cí·du·lo, –la adj. acidulous, sour.
a·cier·te, acierto see **acertar.**
a·cier·to m. *(logro)* good shot, hit; *(éxito)* success; *(cordura)* good judgment *or* sense; *(coincidencia)* coincidence; FIG. *(habilidad)* skill, dexterity, knack ♦ **con a.** *(con éxito)* successfully; *(con destreza)* skillfully.
a·ci·gua·ta·do, –da adj. *(pálido)* jaundiced, yellowish; C. RICA listless, bored.

a·ci·je m. CHEM. copperas, ferrous sulfate.
á·ci·mo adj. unleavened (bread).
a·ci·mut m. [pl. **-mut** *or* **-muts**] azimuth.
a·ción f. stirrup, strap.
a·ci·ra·te m. *(lindero)* boundary, landmark; *(caballón)* ridge of earth (between plots); *(paseo)* path (between rows).
a·ci·ta·ra f. *(tabique)* partition, wall; *(pretil de puente)* bridge railing; *(cobertura de silla)* chair cover; *(cobertura de silla de montar)* saddle cover.
a·cla·ma·ción f. acclamation, acclaim.
a·cla·ma·dor, –do·ra I. adj. acclamatory, acclaiming II. m.f. acclaimer.
a·cla·mar tr. to acclaim, hail.
a·cla·ra·ción f. clarification, explanation.
a·cla·ra·do I. past part. see **aclarar** II. m. rinse, rinsing.
a·cla·rar tr. *(líquidos)* to clarify, make clear; FIG. *(explicar)* to clarify, explain; *(aguar)* to thin (sauces); *(entresacar)* to thin out (trees, plants); *(volver a lavar)* to rinse; MIN. to wash ♦ **a. la voz** to clear one's throat —intr. *(clarear)* to clear up (weather); *(amanecer)* to dawn —reflex. *(hacerse inteligible)* to become clear; *(clarear)* to clear up (weather); *(abrirse)* to reveal a secret; AMER. to be clarified *or* purified (liquids).
a·cla·ra·to·rio, –ria adj. clarifying, explanatory.
a·cla·re·cer §17 var. of **aclarar.**
a·cli·ma·ta·ble adj. able to acclimatize.
a·cli·ma·ta·ción f. acclimatization.
a·cli·ma·tar tr. to acclimatize, acclimate —reflex. to become acclimatized *or* acclimated.
a·clo·car §73 tr. to brood (hens) —reflex. *(extenderse)* to stretch out, lie down; *(gallinas)* to become broody (hens).
ac·né f. MED. acne.
a·co·bar·da·mien·to m. cowardice, cowardliness.
a·co·bar·dar tr. to intimidate, frighten —reflex. to become intimidated *or* frightened.
a·co·bra·do, –da adj. copper-colored.
a·co·ce·a·dor, –do·ra adj. kicking.
a·co·ce·ar tr. *(dar coces)* to kick; FIG., COLL. *(maltratar)* to treat badly, mistreat.
a·co·chi·nar tr. COLL. to murder, bump off.
a·co·da·do, –da I. past part. see **acodar** II. adj. *(doblado)* elbowed, bent in the form of an elbow; *(en los codos)* leaning on one's elbow.
a·co·da·du·ra f. *(apoyo)* leaning on one's elbows; AGR. layering; CARP. squaring.
a·co·da·lar tr. ARCHIT. to prop *or* shore up.
a·co·dar tr. *(apoyar)* to lean, rest (arm, elbow); AGR. to layer (vines); CARP. to square —reflex. *(apoyarse)* to lean *or* rest one's elbows on <*acodarse en la mesa* to lean one's elbows on the table>.
a·co·de·rar tr. MARIT. to anchor broadside on.
a·co·di·ciar tr. to covet, long for —reflex. to yearn, be covetous.
a·co·do m. BOT. shoot.
a·co·ge·di·zo, –za I. adj. easily and indiscriminately adaptable II. m.f. one who adapts easily and indiscriminately.
a·co·ge·dor, –do·ra I. adj. *(cordial)* welcoming; *(cómodo)* inviting, cozy <*una sala a.* a cozy room>; *(protector)* sheltering II. m.f. protector.
a·co·ger §34 tr. *(dar bienvenida)* to receive, welcome; *(amparar)* to shelter, give refuge to; FIG. *(aceptar)* to accept <*acogieron la proposición* they accepted the proposition> —reflex. *(refugiarse)* to take refuge <*se acogió en casa de un amigo* he took refuge in a friend's house>; AGR. *(apacentar)* to pasture (animals); FIG. *(recurrir a)* to resort to ♦ **acogerse a la ley** to have recourse in the law.
a·co·gi·da f. *(recibimiento)* reception, welcome <*una a calurosa* a warm welcome>; *(amparo)* shelter, refuge, protection; *(asilo)* asylum, haven; *(afluencia)* confluence (of waters); COM. acceptance ♦ **tener buena a.** to be well received.
a·co·gi·do, –da I. past part. see **acoger** II. m.f. *(pobre)* poorhouse resident —m. AGR. pasturing fee —f. see **acogida.**
a·co·go·llar tr. AGR. to protect, cover (plants) —intr. BOT. to bud.
a·co·go·tar tr. *(matar)* to kill (with a blow to the back of the

head); COLL. *(derribar)* to knock down (with a blow to the back of the head); FIG. *(dominar)* to dominate, intimidate.

a·co·ja, acojo see **acoger.**

a·co·ji·nar tr. to stuff, pad —reflex. MECH. to cushion.

a·co·la·da f. accolade.

a·co·lar tr. HER. *(juntar dos escudos)* to unite two coats of arms under one crown; *(adornar un escudo)* to adorn a coat of arms with special marks of distinction.

a·col·cha·do, –da I. past part. see **acolchar** II. adj. padded, quilted III. m. *(relleno)* padding; ARG. bedspread.

a·col·char tr. *(rellenar)* to stuff, pad (a quilt); *(muebles)* to upholster.

a·có·li·to m. RELIG. acolyte; *(monaguillo)* altar boy; FIG. *(discípulo)* disciple, follower.

a·co·lla·dor m. MARIT. lanyard.

a·co·llar §19 tr. AGR. to cover with earth; MARIT. *(calafatear)* to caulk; *(tensar)* to make taut, tighten (ropes).

a·co·lla·ra·do, –da I. past part. see **acollarar** II. adj. ZOOL. ring-necked <*paloma a.* ring-necked dove>.

a·co·lla·rar tr. *(poner collar)* to put a collar on (an animal); *(uncir)* to yoke; ARG., CHILE to tie together —reflex. *(asirse)* to hold each other by the neck; ARG., URUG., COLL. to get hitched *or* married.

a·com·bar tr. to bend, curve.

a·co·me·di·do, –da I. past part. see **acomedirse** II. adj. AMER. accommodating, obliging.

a·co·me·dir·se §48 reflex. AMER. to oblige, volunteer.

a·co·me·te·dor, –do·ra I. adj. aggressive, attacking II. m.f. aggressor, attacker.

a·co·me·ter tr. *(atacar)* to attack; *(intentar)* to undertake, attempt <*a. un trabajo* to undertake a job>; *(dominar)* to overcome, come over <*me acometió el sueño* sleep overcame me>; TECH. *(desembocar)* to converge, join (conduits).

a·co·me·ti·da f. *(ataque)* attack, assault; TECH. *(de cañerías)* connection, link-up (of conduits).

a·co·me·ti·mien·to m. *(acción de atacar)* attacking, assaulting; *(ataque)* attack, assault; TECH. *(cañería)* connection (of conduits).

a·co·mi·da, acomido see **acomedirse.**

a·co·mi·die·ra, acomidió see **acomedirse.**

a·co·mo·da·ble adj. accommodating, adaptable.

a·co·mo·da·ción f. accommodation, adaptation.

a·co·mo·da·da·men·te adv. *(convenientemente)* conveniently; *(confortablemente)* comfortably.

a·co·mo·da·di·zo, –za adj. accommodating, obliging.

a·co·mo·da·do, –da I. past part. see **acomodar** II. adj. *(conveniente)* suitable; *(rico)* prosperous, well-off; *(comodón)* comfort-loving; *(moderado)* moderate, reasonable <*un precio a.* a reasonable price>.

a·co·mo·da·dor, –do·ra I. adj. accommodating II. m. usher —f. usherette.

a·co·mo·da·mien·to m. *(transacción)* accommodation; *(convenio)* arrangement; *(coveniencia)* convenience, suitability.

a·co·mo·dar tr. *(arreglar)* to arrange, put in order; *(adaptar)* to adapt, adjust; *(colocar)* to accommodate, find a place for; *(conciliar)* to reconcile; *(emplear)* to employ, find employment for; *(proveer)* to provide, furnish —intr. to suit, be suitable —reflex. *(colocarse)* to find a place for oneself, settle down; ARG., CHILE *(arreglarse)* to set oneself up (through connections); *(casarse)* to marry well ♦ **acomodarse a** to adapt oneself to, conform with • **acomodarse con** to reconcile oneself with.

a·co·mo·da·ti·cio, –cia adj. *(acomodadizo)* accommodating, obliging; *(conveniente)* suitable; DEROG. pliant, noncommital.

a·co·mo·do m. *(empleo)* job, position, employment; *(alojamiento)* lodgings, accommodations; AMER. *(soborno)* bribe; *(convenio)* secret agreement, fix.

a·com·pa·ña·do, –da I. past part. see **acompañar** II. adj. accompanied; *(concurrido)* busy, frequented <*un sitio a.* a busy place>; CUBA drunk III. m.f. *(compañero)* companion —m. COL. culvert, sewage pipe.

a·com·pa·ña·dor, –do·ra I. adj. accompanying II. m.f. *(compañero)* companion; *(escolta)* escort, attendant; MUS. accompanist.

a·com·pa·ña·mien·to m. *(complemento)* accompaniment;

(comitiva) escort, retinue; THEAT. extra; MUS. accompaniment.

a·com·pa·ñan·te, –ta I. adj. accompanying II. m.f. *(compañero)* companion; MUS. accompanist —m. *(escolta)* escort —f. *(dueña)* chaperon.

a·com·pa·ñar tr. *(ir con)* to accompany; *(escoltar)* to escort, attend; *(agregar)* to enclose, attach <*le acompaño una copia del documento* I am enclosing a copy of the document> ♦ **a. a uno en sentimiento** to express one's condolences —reflex. to be accompanied by ♦ **acompañarse con** *o* **en** MUS. to accompany oneself on.

a·com·pa·sa·da·men·te adv. *(rítmicamente)* rhythmically; *(lentamente)* slowly, deliberately.

a·com·pa·sa·do, –da I. past part. see **acompasar** II. adj. *(rítmico)* rhythmic; FIG. *(pausado)* leisurely, slow-paced.

a·com·pa·sar tr. MUS. to measure (with a metronome); *(dar cadencia)* to give rhythm to.

a·com·ple·ja·do, –da I. past part. see **acomplejar** II. adj. suffering from complexes III. m.f. person who suffers from complexes.

a·com·ple·jar tr. to give a complex to —reflex. to get a complex.

a·co·mu·nar·se reflex. to unite, join forces.

a·con·cha·ba·mien·to m. banding together.

a·con·cha·bar·se reflex. COLL. to gang up, band together.

a·con·char tr. *(proteger)* to push to safety; MARIT. to beach (a boat) —reflex. *(arrimarse)* to back against <*aconcharse a una pared* to back against a wall>; MARIT. to run aground; CHILE to settle (sediment).

a·con·di·cio·na·do, –da I. past part. see **acondicionar** II. adj. conditioned ♦ **aire a.** air-conditioned • **bien a.** in good condition • **mal a.** in bad condition.

a·con·di·cio·na·dor m. conditioner ♦ **a. de aire** air conditioner.

a·con·di·cio·na·mien·to m. conditioning.

a·con·di·cio·nar tr. *(disponer)* to condition, prepare; *(reparar)* to repair, renovate <*a. un barco* to repair a boat>; *(el aire)* to air-condition —reflex. to be conditioned.

a·con·go·ja·da·men·te adv. distressfully, with anguish.

a·con·go·jar tr. to distress, afflict —reflex. to be distressed *or* afflicted.

a·con·se·ja·ble adj. advisable.

a·con·se·ja·do, –da I. past part. see **aconsejar** II. adj. sensible, prudent ♦ **mal a.** imprudent, ill-advised.

a·con·se·ja·dor, –do·ra I. adj. advising, counseling II. m.f. advisor, counselor.

a·con·se·jar tr. to advise, counsel —reflex. to take advice ♦ **aconsejarse con** *o* **de** to consult with, get advice from.

a·con·so·nan·tar intr. to rhyme (two words) —tr. to make two words rhyme.

a·con·te·cer §17 intr. to happen, occur.

a·con·te·ci·do, –da I. past part. see **acontecer** II. adj. sad, depressed.

a·con·te·ci·mien·to m. event, occurrence.

a·co·pa·do, –da I. past part. see **acopar** II. adj. cuplike, cupped.

a·co·par intr. to form a crown (trees) —tr. *(árbol)* to trim, shape (crown of tree); MARIT. to shape (plank of wood).

a·co·pas adv. MEX. unexpectedly, without warning.

a·co·pia·dor, –do·ra I. adj. gathering, collecting II. m.f. gatherer, collector.

a·co·piar tr. *(recoger)* to gather, collect; *(amontonar)* to store.

a·co·pio m. *(recogimiento)* gathering, collecting; *(amontonamiento)* storing; *(provisiones)* store, stock; *(abundancia)* abundance.

a·co·pla·do, –da I. past part. see **acoplar** II. adj. coupled, joined III. m. AMER. trailer.

a·co·pla·du·ra f. *or* **a·co·pla·mien·to** m. coupling, joint, connection.

a·co·plar tr. *(unir)* to couple, join, connect; *(uncir)* to yoke, hitch; *(aparear)* to pair, mate (animals); FIG. *(conciliar)* to reconcile (differences); ARG. to hitch (a trailer) —reflex. FIG., COLL. *(aparearse)* to mate; FIG. *(conciliarse)* to be reconciled.

a·co·ra·za·do, –da I. past part. see **acorazar** II. adj. *(blindado)* armored, amor-plated; FIG. *(endurecido)* hardened, inured III. m. battleship.

a·co·ra·zar §04 tr. to armor —reflex. FIG. to steel or harden oneself.

a·cor·da·da I. f. LAW (orden) decree, order; (documento) authorization II. adj. see **acordado, –da.**

a·cor·da·da·men·te adv. (de común acuerdo) unanimously, by common consent; (con reflexión) prudently, sensibly.

a·cor·da·do, –da I. past part. see **acordar** II. adj. (hecho con acuerdo) agreed, agreed upon; (prudente) prudent, sensible ♦ **lo a.** that which has been agreed upon III. f. see **acordada.**

a·cor·dar §19 tr. (concordar) to agree <acordaron que lo harían they agreed that they would do it>; (decidir) to decide, resolve; (conciliar) to reconcile, integrate; (recordar) to remind; MUS. to tune (one voice or instrument with another); PAINT. to harmonize, blend (colors); AMER. to grant, accord —intr. to harmonize, go together —reflex. (recordar) to remember, recollect <ella no se acuerda de eso she doesn't remember that>; (ponerse de acuerdo) to agree, come to an agreement <no se acuerdan con nosotros they don't agree with us> ♦ **si mal no me acuerdo** if I remember correctly, if my memory serves me right.

a·cor·de I. adj. (conforme) agreed, in agreement; (con armonía) harmonious, in tune II. m. MUS. chord.

a·cor·de·lar tr. (medir) to measure with a string; (señalar) to mark off with a cord (perimeter, boundary).

a·cor·de·ón m. accordion.

a·cor·de·o·nis·ta m.f. accordionist.

a·cor·do·na·do, –da I. past part. see **acordonar** II. adj. (rodeado) cordoned off, surrounded; (como un cordón) cord-like; (atado) laced up; (monedas) milled (coins); MEX. (cenceño) thin, lean.

a·cor·do·na·mien·to m. (rodeo) cordoning off, surrounding; (zapatos) lacing; (las monedas) milling (coins).

a·cor·do·nar tr. (rodear) to cordon off, surround; (monedas) to mill (coins); (atar) to tie or lace (up); C. AMER., CUBA (cultivar) to till.

a·cor·nar or **a·cor·ne·ar** §19 tr. to butt, gore.

a·co·rra·la·mien·to m. (encierro) penning, corralling (animals); (arrinconamiento) cornering.

a·co·rra·lar tr. (encerrar) to corral, pen; FIG. (atrapar) to corner, trap; (intimidar) to intimidate, scare.

a·cor·tar tr. to shorten, reduce —reflex. (disminuirse) to shrink, get shorter; (intimidarse) to be shy or bashful; (los caballos) to shy, draw back (horses).

a·co·sa·dor, –do·ra I. adj. pursuing, harassing II. m.f. pursuer, harasser.

a·co·sa·mien·to m. dogged pursuit, harassment.

a·co·sar tr. (perseguir) to pursue doggedly, harass; (un caballo) to spur (a horse).

a·cos·ta·do, –da I. past part. see **acostar** II. adj. in bed, lying down.

a·cos·tar §19 tr. (tender en la cama) to put to bed, lay down; MARIT. to bring alongside —intr. (llegar) to reach shore —reflex. (tenderse en la cama) to go to bed, lie down; (inclinarse) to list, lean; MARIT. (arrimarse) to go alongside; FIG. (adherirse) to adhere; C. AMER., MEX. to give birth ♦ **acostarse con** COLL. to sleep with, make love to • **acostarse con las gallinas** COLL. to go to bed early.

a·cos·tum·bra·da·men·te adv. (según costumbre) customarily; (habitualmente) habitually.

a·cos·tum·bra·do, –da adj. (habituado) accustomed or used to; (habitual) habitual, customary.

a·cos·tum·brar tr. to accustom —intr. to be accustomed to —reflex. to accustom oneself, get accustomed.

a·co·ta·ción f. annotation; (nota) remark, note; THEAT. stage direction; GEOG. elevation mark ♦ **a. al margen** marginal note.

a·co·ta·da f. enclosed ground (for cultivation).

a·co·ta·mien·to m. (acción de limitar) demarcation; (señal) boundary mark; (acotación) annotation; GEOG. elevation mark.

a·co·tar tr. (amojonar) to survey, stake out; (reservar) to reserve, preserve (land); (fijar) to fix, set limits on; (anotar) to annotate <a. un texto to annotate a text>; (notar) to remark, note; (admitir) to admit; (elegir) to choose, select; (cortar) to prune (trees); (en los mapas) to indicate elevations on (a map) —reflex. to seek refuge.

a·co·ti·llo m. sledgehammer.

a·cra·cia f. anarchy.

á·cra·ta m.f. anarchist.

a·cre[1] m. acre.

a·cre[2] adj. (picante) acrid, pungent; (agrio) bitter, sour; FIG. (mordaz) caustic, biting.

a·cre·cen·cia f. (aumento) growth, increase; LAW (recibo de bienes) accretion.

a·cre·cen·ta·dor, –do·ra adj. increasing, growing.

a·cre·cen·ta·mien·to m. increase, growth.

a·cre·cen·tar §49 tr. (aumentar) to increase, grow; (avanzar) to promote, advance (in a job) —reflex. to increase, grow.

a·cre·cer §17 tr. to augment, increase —reflex. to increase, grow.

a·cre·ci·mien·to m. (aumento) increase, growth; LAW (acrecencia) accretion.

a·cre·di·ta·ción f. accreditation.

a·cre·di·ta·do, –da I. past part. see **acreditar** II. adj. (con crédito) accredited; (ilustre) reputable.

a·cre·di·tar tr. (hacer digno de crédito) to grant credit to; (afamar) to make famous; (asegurar) guarantee, vouch for; COM. to credit —reflex. (hacerse famoso) to become famous; to develop a reputation <se acreditan de necios they are developing a reputation as fools>.

a·cre·di·ta·ti·vo, –va adj. accrediting.

a·cre·e·dor, –do·ra I. adj. worthy, deserving II. m.f. creditor.

a·cre·en·cia f. AMER. credit.

a·crez·ca, acrezco see **acrecer.**

a·cri·ba·du·ra f. sifting, sieving ♦ **acribaduras** siftings.

a·cri·bar tr. (pasar por criba) to sift, sieve; (agujerear) to perforate, riddle (with holes); FIG. (molestar) to hound, harass.

a·cri·bi·llar tr. (agujerear) to riddle, pepper (with holes); FIG. (molestar) to hound, harass <le acribillan los acreedores his creditors are hounding him> ♦ **a. a tiros** or **a balazos** to shoot full of holes, riddle with bullets.

a·crí·li·co, –ca adj. & m.f. CHEM. acrylic.

a·cri·mi·na·dor, –do·ra I. adj. incriminating, accusing II. m.f. accuser.

a·cri·mi·nar tr. to accuse, incriminate —reflex. CHILE to disgrace oneself.

a·cri·mo·nia f. (aspereza) acridity, pungency; (sabor) bitterness, sourness; FIG. (mordacidad) acrimony, severity.

a·cri·mo·nio·so, –sa adj. acrimonious, sarcastic.

a·crio·lla·do, –da I. past part. see **acriollarse** II. adj. Hispanicized.

a·crio·llar·se reflex. AMER. to adopt native ways.

a·cri·so·la·do, –da I. past part. see **acrisolar** II. adj. (honrado) upright, honest; (probado) proven, tested; AMER. indisputable.

a·cri·so·lar tr. METAL. to refine, purify; (aclarar) to clarify; (probar) to prove, test (the truth).

a·cro·ba·cia f. acrobatics.

a·cró·ba·ta m.f. acrobat.

a·cro·bá·ti·co, –ca adj. acrobatic.

a·cro·ma·do, –da adj. chrome-like.

a·cro·má·ti·co, –ca adj. achromatic, colorless.

a·cro·ma·top·sia f. MED. color blindness, achromatopsia.

a·cró·po·lis f. acropolis, citadel, fortress.

a·crós·ti·co, –ca adj. & m. acrostic.

ac·ta f. (informe) record; (minutas) minutes; (certificado) certificate; S. AMER. act, law ♦ **a. notarial** affidavit • **actas de un santo** life or deeds of a saint • **levantar una a.** to draw up a certificate • **tomar a. de** ARG. to take note of.

ac·ti·nio m. CHEM. actinium.

ac·ti·tud f. (postura) attitude, pose; FIG. (disposición) attitude.

ac·ti·va·ción f. activation.

ac·ti·va·dor m. activator.

ac·ti·va·men·te adv. actively.

ac·ti·var tr. (hacer más activo) to activate; (acelerar) to hasten, accelerate —reflex. to become activated.

ac·ti·vi·dad f. (acción) activity, action; (diligencia) action, energy; (profesión) profession, career ♦ **en (plena) a.** in (full) operation.

ac·ti·vis·mo m. activism.

ac·ti·vis·ta adj. & m.f. activist.

ac·ti·vo, –va I. adj. active; *(diligente)* energetic II. m. COM. assets.

ac·to m. *(hecho)* act <*a. de caridad* act of charity>; *(acción)* action, movement <*a. reflejo* reflex action>; *(ceremonia)* act, ceremony; EDUC. thesis; THEAT. act ♦ **a. continuo** *or* **seguido** immediately after • **a. de presencia** token appearance • **Actos de los Apóstoles** BIBL. Acts (of the Apostles) • **en el a.** at once, immediately.

ac·tor, –to·ra I. m. THEAT. actor, performer —m.f. LAW plaintiff II. adj. acting.

ac·triz f. [pl. **-tri·ces**] actress.

ac·tua·ción f. *(acción)* action, behavior; THEAT. performance (of a part) ♦ **actuaciones** LAW proceedings.

ac·tual adj. present-day, current.

ac·tua·li·cé, actualice see **actualizar.**

ac·tua·li·dad f. *(ahora)* present (time); *(estado presente)* current situation ♦ **en la a.** at the present time, nowadays • **actualidades** news, current events.

c·tua·li·za·ción f. *(modernización)* modernization; PHILOS. actualization.

ac·tua·li·zar §04 tr. *(modernizar)* to modernize; PHILOS. to actualize.

ac·tual·men·te adv. at present, nowadays.

ac·tuan·te I. adj. acting II. m.f. student who defends a thesis.

ac·tuar §67 tr. to operate, activate —intr. *(obrar)* to act; *(defenderse)* to defend a thesis; LAW *(formar autos)* to perform judicial acts ♦ **a. de** to act as —reflex. LAW to instruct oneself.

ac·tua·rial adj. actuarial.

a·cua·dri·llar tr. *(juntar)* to band together; *(encabezar)* to lead (a band); CHILE to gang up on —reflex. to band together, form a band.

a·cua·re·la f. water color.

a·cua·re·lis·ta m.f. water colorist.

a·cua·rio m. aquarium ♦ **A.** ASTROL. Aquarius.

a·cuar·te·la·do, –da I. past part. see **acuartelar** II. adj. MIL. quartered, billeted; *(escudo)* quartered.

a·cuar·te·lar tr. MIL. to quarter, billet; *(dividir)* to quarter, divide into quarters *or* plots —reflex. to withdraw to quarters.

a·cuá·ti·co, –ca *or* **a·cuá·til** adj. aquatic.

a·cua·ti·za·je m. AER. landing on water.

a·cua·ti·zar §04 intr. AER. to land on water.

a·cu·cia·mien·to m. *(estimulación)* hastening, goading; *(anhelo)* desiring, desire.

a·cu·ciar tr. *(estimular)* to hasten, goad; *(anhelar)* to desire, long *or* yearn for.

a·cu·cio·sa·men·te adv. *(con solicitud)* diligently; *(con deseo vehemente)* eagerly.

a·cu·cio·si·dad f. diligence, meticulousness.

a·cu·cio·so, –sa adj. *(diligente)* diligent, meticulous; *(deseoso)* desirous, eager.

a·cu·cli·llar·se reflex. to squat, crouch down.

a·cu·cha·ma·do, –da adj. VEN. downcast, dejected.

a·cu·char tr. COL. to harass, pursue.

a·cu·cha·ra·do, –da adj. spoonlike, spoon-shaped.

a·cu·chi·lla·do, –da I. past part. see **acuchillar** II. adj. *(herido)* knifed, slashed; SEW. *(vestidos)* slashed, gored; FIG. *(experimentado)* experienced III. m. CARP. floor scraping, floor planing.

a·cu·chi·lla·dor, –do·ra I. adj. slashing, stabbing; *(reñidor)* quarrelsome II. m.f. *(apuñalador)* stabber, slasher; *(abusador)* quarrelsome person, bully; CARP. floor-scraper, floor-planer.

a·cu·chi·lla·mien·to m. *(apuñalamiento)* stabbing, slashing; CARP. surfacing (of wood).

a·cu·chi·llar tr. *(apuñalar)* to slash, cut; *(herir)* to knife, stab; SEW. *(vestidos)* to slash, gore; CARP. to plane, scrape; AGR. to thin out (plants) —reflex. to fight with knives.

a·cu·chi·lle·ar tr. CHILE to knife, stab.

a·cu·di·mien·to m. aid, assistance.

a·cu·dir intr. *(presentarse)* to go, come <*a. a la puerta* to come to the door>; *(valerse)* to appeal, to have recourse <*a. a la ley* to have recourse to the law>; *(asistir)* to attend, show up <*a. a la cita* to show up for the appointment>; *(frecuentar)* to go often; *(socorrer)* to go to the aid of <*acudió en su ayuda* she went to his aid>; *(replicar)* to

respond, reply; AGR. to be fruitful (land); EQUIT. to obey, respond (horses).

a·cue·duc·to m. ARCHIT., ANAT. aqueduct.

a·cue·lle, acuello see **acollar.**

a·cuer·de, acuerdo see **acordar.**

a·cuer·do m. *(convenio)* agreement, accord; *(pacto)* pact, resolution; *(armonía)* harmony, understanding <*vivir en perfecto a.* to live in absolute harmony>; *(cordura)* good sense, prudence; *(recuerdo)* remembrance, memory; *(dictamen)* opinion, ruling; ARG. cabinet meeting ♦ **de a. con** in agreement *or* accordance with • **de** *or* **por común a.** of common accord • **estar de a.** to be in agreement.

a·cuer·ne, acuerno see **acornar.**

a·cues·te, acuesto see **acostar.**

a·cui·dad f. acuity, sharpness.

a·cuí·fe·ro, –ra adj. aquiferous, water-bearing.

a·cuil·mar·se reflex. C. AMER. to falter, lose one's nerve.

a·cui·tar tr. to distress, afflict —reflex. to grieve, be grieved.

a·cu·lar tr. *(arrimar)* to put *or* place against; COLL. *(arrinconar)* to corner, keep at bay —reflex. MARIT. to run aground.

a·cul·tu·ra·ción f. acculturation.

a·cu·llá adv. (over) there, yonder.

a·cu·mu·la·ble adj. accumulable, gatherable.

a·cu·mu·la·ción f. *or* **a·cu·mu·la·mien·to** m. accumulation, gathering.

a·cu·mu·la·dor, –do·ra I. adj. accumulative, amassing II. m. ELEC. storage battery, accumulator (G.B.).

a·cu·mu·lar tr. *(juntar)* to accumulate, gather; LAW *(juzgar)* to dispose of jointly; *(imputar)* to impute.

a·cu·mu·la·ti·vo, –va adj. accumulative, joint.

a·cu·nar tr. to rock, cradle (a child).

a·cu·ñar tr. *(amonedar)* to coin, mint; *(meter cuñas)* to wedge, key —reflex. VEN. to struggle to finish.

a·cuo·si·dad f. wateriness.

a·cuo·so, –sa adj. watery, aqueous.

a·cu·pun·tu·ra f. acupuncture.

a·cu·rru·car·se §70 reflex. *(encogerse)* to cuddle *or* curl up; FIG. *(agacharse)* to cower, crouch.

a·cu·sa·ble adj. chargeable, liable to accusation.

a·cu·sa·ción f. accusation, charge.

a·cu·sa·do, –da I. past part. see **acusar** II. m.f. accused III. adj. accused.

a·cu·sa·dor, –do·ra I. adj. accusing II. m.f. accuser.

a·cu·san·te adj. accusing, accusatory.

a·cu·sar tr. *(imputar)* to accuse, charge; *(denunciar)* to denounce, give away <*las apariencias le acusaban* appearances gave him away>; *(indicar)* to acknowledge (receipt); *(naipes)* to lay down, declare (cards) —reflex. to confess.

a·cu·sa·ti·vo m. GRAM. accusative.

a·cu·sa·to·rio, –ria adj. accusatory, accusing.

a·cu·se m. *(aviso)* acknowledgment; *(en los naipes)* revealing certain cards (in games) ♦ **a. de recibo** acknowledgment of receipt.

a·cu·són, –so·na I. m.f. tattler, gossip II. adj. gossipy.

a·cús·ti·co, –ca I. adj. acoustic, acoustical II. f. acoustics.

a·cha·ba·ca·nar tr. to cheapen, make vulgar *or* crude.

a·cha·car §70 tr. to attribute, to impute.

a·cha·co·si·dad f. sickliness, frailty.

a·cha·co·so, –sa adj. *(enfermizo)* sickly, frail; *(indispuesto)* indisposed.

a·cha·fla·nar tr. to chamfer, bevel.

a·cham·par·se reflex. *(apropiarse)* to retain another's property; *(arraigar)* to settle, establish roots.

a·chan·char tr. to block a doublet (in dominoes); CHILE to jump (in checkers); ARG., URUG. *(engordar)* to fatten —reflex. AMER. *(apoltronarse)* to get lazy; *(debilitarse)* to become weak; ARG., URUG. *(engordarse)* to get fat.

a·chan·tar·se reflex. COLL. *(acobardarse)* to become afraid, lose one's nerve; *(esconderse)* to hide (from danger); *(conformarse)* to conform.

a·cha·pa·rra·do, –da I. past part. see **achaparrarse** II. adj. BOT. small and spreading, stumpy; FIG. *(regordete)* short and stocky, stubby.

a·cha·pa·rrar·se reflex. BOT. to grow thick and stunted; FIG. *(ponerse gordo)* to get chubby.

a·cha·que m. *(enfermedad)* ailment, illness; *(indisposición)*

indisposition; COLL. *(menstruación)* (menstrual) period; FIG. *(embarazo)* pregnancy; *(asunto)* matter, subject; *(excusa)* excuse, pretext; *(motivo)* motive, cause; *(vicio)* vice; *(reputación)* reputation ♦ **achaques** C. AMER. morning sickness • **achaques de la edad** aches and pains, ailments of old age.
a·cha·qué, achaque see achacar.
a·cha·ro·la·do, –da I. past part. see acharolar II. adj. resembling patent leather, varnished.
a·cha·ro·lar tr. *(barnizar)* to varnish, enamel; *(dar brillo)* to polish.
a·cha·ta·do, –da I. past part. see achatar II. adj. flat, flattened <*nariz a.* flat nose>; ARG., FIG. crushed, overwhelmed.
a·cha·ta·mien·to m. flattening; ARG. overwhelming.
a·cha·tar tr. to flatten, level, squash —reflex. to become flat; ARG. to be overwhelmed *or* crushed.
a·chi·ca·do, –da I. past part. see achicar II. adj. childish.
a·chi·ca·du·ra f. *or* **a·chi·ca·mien·to** m. *(disminución)* reduction, diminution; MARIT. bailing.
a·chi·car §70 tr. *(disminuir)* to reduce, diminish; *(humillar)* to humiliate, put in one's place; SEW. *(ropa)* to take in; MARIT. *(extraer)* to bail (water); FIG. *(humillar)* to humble, belittle; COL. to kill —reflex. *(disminuirse)* to get smaller, shrink; *(humillarse)* to humble oneself, minimize one's own importance; *(acobardarse)* to become intimidated, shrink back.
a·chi·co·ria f. BOT. chicory.
a·chi·cha·rran·te adj. *(quemante)* burning, scorching; *(bochornoso)* sweltering.
a·chi·cha·rrar tr. *(quemar)* to scorch, burn; *(calentar demasiado)* to overheat; FIG. *(molestar)* to plague, bother; AMER. to squash —reflex. *(quemarse)* to burn, get burned (food); *(calentarse demasiado)* to swelter, get overheated.
a·chi·guar·se §10 reflex. ARG. to bulge, sag; *(ponerse gordo)* to put on weight (a person).
a·chi·me·ro, –ra m.f. C. AMER. peddler, hawker.
a·chi·mes m.pl. C. AMER. peddler's wares.
a·chín, –chi·na m.f. HOND. peddler, hawker.
a·chi·na·do, –da I. past part. see achinar II. adj. AMER. Oriental, having Oriental features; ARG. *(rojizo)* reddish-brown, russet; FIG. *(aplebeyado)* vulgar, coarse.
a·chi·nar tr. COLL. to frighten, intimidate —reflex. ARG., URUG. to become coarse *or* common.
a·chi·qué, achique see achicar.
a·chi·qui·lla·do, –da adj. MEX. childish.
a·chi·qui·tar tr. AMER., COLL. to diminish, make smaller —reflex. to get scared, become frightened.
a·chis·pa·do, –da I. past part. see achispar II. adj. tipsy, slightly drunk.
a·chis·par tr. COLL. to make tipsy —reflex. to get tipsy.
a·cho·car §70 tr. *(tirar)* to throw against the wall *or* floor; *(herir)* to hit, strike; FIG., COLL. *(guardar)* to hoard, stash away —intr. DOM. REP., P. RICO to faint, lose consciousness.
a·cho·char·se reflex. to begin to dote, become senile.
a·cho·la·do, –da I. past part. see acholar II. adj. AMER. *(mestizo)* half-breed, half-Indian; FIG. *(avergonzado)* ashamed, red in the face.
a·cho·lar tr. AMER. to embarrass, make blush —reflex. AMER. *(acriollarse)* to adopt mestizo ways; *(avergonzarse)* to be ashamed; *(aterrarse)* to be frightened; ARG. to suffer sunstroke.
a·cho·qué, achoque see achocar.
a·cho·te m. BOT. annatto tree.
a·chu·bas·car·se §70 reflex. to become threatening *or* overcast (the sky).
a·chu·cu·tar·se *or* **a·chu·cu·yar·se** reflex. C. AMER. *(abatirse)* to be disheartened; *(humillarse)* to humble oneself; GUAT. *(marchitarse)* to wither, become faded.
a·chu·cha·do, –da I. past part. see achuchar II. adj. COLL. hard, difficult.
a·chu·char COLL. tr. *(aplastar)* to crush, squash; *(empujar)* to push, jostle; *(azuzar)* to excite, entice.
a·chu·cha·rrar tr. AMER. to crush, squash —reflex. MEX. to be disheartened *or* discouraged.
a·chu·la·do, –da adj. COLL. *(chulo)* jaunty, cocky; *(grosero)* coarse, vulgar.

a·chu·ra f. ARG. offal, cattle gut.
a·chu·rar *or* **a·chu·re·ar** tr. ARG. to gut, disembowel; COLL. *(matar)* to stab to death.
a·chu·rrus·car §70 tr. CHILE to crush, squash —reflex. COL., ECUAD. to be disheartened *or* discouraged.
a·da·gio m. *(refrán)* proverb, saying, adage; MUS. adagio.
a·da·lid m. MIL. military leader, commander; FIG. *(jefe)* leader, head (of a party).
a·da·man·ti·no, –na adj. adamantine, diamond-like.
a·da·mar tr. to court, woo —reflex. *(adelgazarse)* to become thin *or* delicate (a man); *(afeminarse)* to become effeminate; GUAT. to live together, cohabit.
a·da·mas·car §70 tr. to damask.
a·dán m. FIG., COLL. *(desaseado)* ragamuffin, scruffy fellow; *(perezoso)* lazy, slovenly fellow ♦ **Adán** Adam • **ir en traje de Adán** to be naked, be in one's birthday suit • **ir hecho un a.** to be slovenly dressed, go about in rags • **manzana de Adán** Adam's apple.
a·dap·ta·bi·li·dad f. adaptability.
a·dap·ta·ble adj. adaptable, adjustable.
a·dap·ta·ción f. adaptation, adjustment.
a·dap·ta·dor, –do·ra m.f. adaptable person —m. MECH. adapter.
a·dap·tar tr. & reflex. to adapt (oneself), adjust (oneself).
a·dar·gar §47 tr. *(proteger)* to protect with a shield; FIG. *(defender)* to defend, protect.
a·dar·me m. ARCH. *(medida)* dram; FIG., COLL. *(pizca)* grain, trace ♦ **por adarmes** stingily, in dribs and drabs.
a·dar·var¹ tr. *(pasmar)* to amaze, astonish.
a·dar·var² tr. *(fortificar)* to fortify with parapet walks.
a·da·tar tr. COM. to enter <*a. los costos en los libros de contabilidad* to enter the costs into the accounting books>.
a·de·ce·nar tr. to divide into groups of ten.
a·de·cen·tar tr. to tidy up, clean up —reflex. to make oneself look decent.
a·de·cua·ción f. fitting, adjustment.
a·de·cua·da·men·te adv. *(apropiadamente)* appropriately, suitably; *(suficientemente)* sufficiently, adequately.
a·de·cua·do, –da I. past part. see adecuar II. adj. *(apropiado)* appropriate, suitable; *(suficiente)* adequate, sufficient.
a·de·cuar tr. to make suitable, adapt.
a·de·fe·sio m. COLL. *(disparate)* absurdity, nonsense; *(persona)* mess, sight; *(traje)* ridiculous *or* gaudy outfit.
a·de·ha·la f. bonus, tip.
a·de·he·sa·mien·to m. *(pradera)* pasturage, pasture land; *(acción)* converting into pasturage.
a·de·he·sar tr. to convert into pasture.
a·de·lan·ta·da·men·te adv. in advance, beforehand.
a·de·lan·ta·do, –da I. past part. see adelantar II. adj. *(precoz)* precocious, advanced <*este niño es muy a.* this child is very precocious>; fast <*mi reloj anda a.* my watch is fast>; FIG. *(atrevido)* forward, impudent ♦ **por a.** in advance III. m. ARCH. governor, captain general.
a·de·lan·ta·dor, –do·ra adj. advancing.
a·de·lan·tar tr. *(avanzar)* to advance, move forward; *(acelerar)* to speed up, hasten <*a. el paso* to speed up the pace>; *(anticipar)* to advance <*a. la paga* to advance one's salary>; *(aventajar)* to outdo, surpass; AUTO. to overtake, pass; *(relojes)* to set ahead *or* forward (clocks); FIG. *(mejorar)* to promote, advance —intr. *(avanzar)* to advance, go forward; *(relojes)* to be fast, gain time (clocks); FIG. *(progresar)* to make progress, improve <*este alumno adelantó mucho* this student made a lot of progress> —reflex. to go forward, get ahead ♦ **adelantarse a** to get ahead of.
a·de·lan·te adv. forward, ahead ♦ **¡adelante!** come in!, come on ahead! • **de aquí en a.** from now on, henceforth • **más a.** farther on.
a·de·lan·to m. *(de paga)* advance (of salary); FIG. *(progreso)* advance, progress ♦ **a. en cuenta corriente** overdraft.
a·del·ga·za·dor, –do·ra adj. slenderizing, slimming.
a·del·ga·za·mien·to m. *(acción)* slimming; *(delgadez)* slimness.
a·del·ga·zar §04 tr. *(enflaquecer)* to make slim *or* thin; FIG. *(purificar)* to purify, refine; *(discurrir sutilmente)* to discuss subtly —intr. & reflex. to lose weight, become slim.
a·de·mán m. expression, look, gesture ♦ **ademanes** *(moda-*

les) manners; *(señales)* signs • **en a. de** as if about to • **hacer a. de** to make a move to.
a·de·mar tr. MIN. to shore.
a·de·más adv. besides, in addition <*a. de lo dicho* in addition to what has been said>.
a·den·te·llar tr. *(hincar los dientes)* to bite; ARCHIT. to leave toothing stones in a wall.
a·den·trar tr. & reflex. to probe.
a·den·tro I. adv. within, inside ◊ ¡**adentro!** come in!, enter! • **ser de tierra a.** AMER. to be from the interior • **ser muy de a.** to be one of the family II. m.pl. **adentros** the innermost self.
a·dep·to, -ta I. adj. *(partidario)* supportive; *(iniciado)* initiated II. m.f. *(partidario)* supporter, follower; *(iniciado)* initiate.
a·de·re·zar §04 tr. CUL. *(condimentar)* to season, flavor, dress; *(adornar)* to adorn, embellish; *(arreglar)* to prepare, get ready <*a. la comida* to prepare the meal>; *(reparar)* to repair, mend; TEX. *(las telas)* to treat (fabrics) —reflex. to get dressed, get ready.
a·de·re·zo m. CUL. *(condimento)* seasoning, flavoring, dressing; *(adorno)* adornment, embellishment; *(arreglo)* preparation; *(reparo)* repair; TEX. *(para las telas)* starch, gum; set <*a. de diamantes* set of diamonds>; *(arreos)* harness, trappings; *(en armas blancas)* ornamentation (on swords).
a·des·trar §49 tr. var. of **adiestrar.**
a·deu·dar tr. *(deber)* to owe, be liable for; ACC., COM. to debit <*a. los costos de depreciación* to debit depreciation costs> —intr. to become related —reflex. to get into debt.
a·deu·do m. *(deuda)* debt; *(aduanas)* duty, tariff; COM. debit.
ad·he·ren·cia f. *(cohesión)* adherence, adhesion; *(añadido)* addition; MED. adhesion; FIG. *(enlace)* bond, connection.
ad·he·ren·te I. adj. adherent, adhesive II. m.f. *(partidario)* adherent, follower —m. *(requisito)* requirement.
ad·he·rir §65 tr. to affix, stick on —intr. & reflex. *(pegarse)* to stick, adhere; FIG. *(consentir)* to support, adhere <*él se adhiere al dictamen* he supports the ruling>.
ad·he·sión f. *(cohesión)* adhesion; FIG. *(apoyo)* adherence, support.
ad·he·si·vo, -va adj. & m. adhesive.
a·dia·man·ta·do, -da adj. diamond-like, adamantine.
a·diar §30 tr. to fix, appoint (day).
a·di·ción f. *(agregación)* addition, adding; *(nota)* explanatory note; MATH. addition; AMER. bill, check ◊ **a. de una herencia** LAW acceptance of a bequest.
a·di·cio·nal adj. additional, added.
a·di·cio·nar tr. *(añadir)* to add <*a. un cuarto a la casa* to add a room to the house>; *(alargar)* to extend, prolong; MATH. to add.
a·dic·to, -ta I. adj. *(a las drogas)* addicted; *(dedicado)* fond, attached II. m.f. *(a las drogas)* addict; *(partidario)* follower, supporter.
a·dies·tra·ble adj. trainable.
a·dies·tra·do, -da I. past part. see **adiestrar** II. adj. trained, able.
a·dies·tra·dor, -do·ra I. adj. training, instructing II. m.f. trainer, coach.
a·dies·tra·mien·to m. training, instruction.
a·dies·trar tr. *(instruir)* to train, coach; *(guiar)* to guide, lead —reflex. to teach *or* coach oneself <*adiestrarse a montar bicicleta* to teach oneself to ride a bicycle>.
a·dies·tre, adiestro see **adestrar.**
a·die·tar tr. to put on a diet —reflex. to diet, go on a diet.
a·di·fés I. adv. VEN. on purpose, purposely <*hacer algo a.* to do something purposely> II. adj. GUAT. difficult, costly; MEX. without method *or* logic.
a·di·ná·mi·co, -ca adj. & m.f. adynamic.
a·di·ne·ra·do, -da I. past part. see **adinerarse** II. adj. wealthy, affluent III. m.f. wealthy *or* affluent person.
a·di·ne·rar·se reflex. COLL. to get rich.
a·diós I. interj. good-by II. m. parting, farewell.
a·di·po·si·dad f. adiposity.
a·di·po·so, -sa adj. adipose, fatty <*tejido a.* fatty tissue>; *(gordo)* obese, overweight.

a·di·ta·men·to m. *(añadidura)* addition; *(accesorio)* attachment ◊ **por a.** in addition.
a·di·ti·vo, -va adj. & m. additive.
a·di·vi·na·ble adj. which can be guessed.
a·di·vi·na·ción f. *(predicción)* prophecy, prediction; *(conjetura)* guessing ◊ **a. del pensamiento** mind reading.
a·di·vi·na·dor, -do·ra I. adj. prophetic, divinatory II. m.f. diviner.
a·di·vi·nan·za f. riddle, puzzle.
a·di·vi·nar tr. *(predecir)* to prophesy, predict <*a. el porvenir* to predict the future>; *(conjeturar)* to guess, divine; *(penetrar)* to read <*a. el pensamiento de otro* to read someone's mind>; *(resolver)* to solve <*a. un acertijo* to solve a riddle> ◊ **dejar a. algo** to hint at something.
a·di·vi·na·to·rio, -ria adj. divinatory.
a·di·vi·no, -na m.f. prophet, diviner.
ad·je·ti·va·ción f. use as an adjective.
ad·je·ti·va·do, -da I. past part. see **adjetivar** II. adj. used as an adjective.
ad·je·ti·var tr. GRAM. *(poner adjetivos)* to qualify (nouns); *(usar como adjetivo)* to use as an adjective; *(calificar)* to name, describe —reflex. GRAM. to be used as an adjective.
ad·je·ti·vo, -va GRAM. I. adj. adjectival II. m. adjective.
ad·ju·di·ca·ción f. adjudication, awarding.
ad·ju·di·ca·dor, -do·ra I. adj. adjudging II. m.f. awarder, adjudger.
ad·ju·di·car §70 tr. to adjudge, award —reflex. to appropriate (for oneself) <*él se adjudicó el uso exclusivo del jardín* he appropriated the exclusive use of the garden for himself>.
ad·ju·di·ca·ta·rio, -ria m.f. awardee.
ad·jun·ción f. *(añadidura)* addition, adjoining; LAW adjunction; LIT., RHET. zeugma.
ad·jun·tar tr. to attach, enclose.
ad·jun·to, -ta I. adj. *(a un texto)* attached, enclosed; *(persona)* assistant, adjunct II. m.f. *(asistente)* assistant, helper —m. *(añadidura)* addition; GRAM. adjunct.
ad·ju·tor, -to·ra I. adj. helping, assisting II. m.f. helper, assistant.
ad·mi·ní·cu·lo m. *(ayuda)* support, aid; LAW adminicle; *(utensilio)* instrument, utensil ◊ **adminículos** emergency equipment.
ad·mi·nis·tra·ble adj. administrable.
ad·mi·nis·tra·ción f. *(dirección)* administration, management; *(oficina)* administration office ◊ **en a.** in trust • **por a.** officially.
ad·mi·nis·tra·do, -da I. past part. see **administrar** II. adj. under administration III. m.f. person under administration.
ad·mi·nis·tra·dor, -do·ra I. adj. administrative II. m.f. administrator, manager ◊ **a. de correos** postmaster • **a. judicial** administrator (of an estate).
ad·mi·nis·trar tr. *(dirigir)* to administer, manage; *(conferir)* to administer, confer, give <*a. un medicamento* to administer a medication>; COLL. *(dar)* to give, deal <*le administré un puntapié* I gave him a kick>.
ad·mi·nis·tra·ti·vo, -va I. adj. administrative, managerial II. m.f. administrator.
ad·mi·ra·ble adj. admirable.
ad·mi·ra·ble·men·te adv. admirably.
ad·mi·ra·ción f. admiration; *(sorpresa)* surprise, wonder; GRAM. exclamation point.
ad·mi·ra·dor, -do·ra I. adj. admiring II. m.f. admirer.
ad·mi·rar tr. to admire <*admiramos su talento* we admire his talent>; *(sorprender)* to surprise, amaze, astonish <*su inteligencia admiraba a todo el mundo* his intelligence astonished everyone> —reflex. to be surprised, amazed, marvel at <*me admiro de tu franqueza* I'm amazed by your frankness>.
ad·mi·ra·ti·vo, -va adj. admiring <*una mirada a.* an admiring look>; *(admirable)* admirable.
ad·mi·si·ble adj. admissible <*evidencia a.* admissible evidence>; *(aceptable)* acceptable, allowable <*una excusa a.* an acceptable excuse>.
ad·mi·sión f. *(acción de admitir)* admission; *(aceptación)* acceptance; ENGIN. induction, intake.
ad·mi·tir tr. *(dar entrada)* to admit, receive; *(aceptar)* to

accept, allow <*a. una explicación* to accept an explanation>; *(reconocer)* to acknowledge, recognize; to hold, accommodate <*este autobús admite 40 pasajeros* this bus holds 40 passengers> ♦ **admitamos que** supposing • **esto no admite demora** this allows no delay.

ad·mo·ni·ción f. admonition, warning.

ad·mo·ni·tor, –to·ra m.f. admonisher, monitor.

ad·mo·ni·to·rio, –ria adj. warning <*voz a.* warning voice>.

a·do·ba·do, –da I. past part. see **adobar** II. m. marinated meat.

a·do·ba·dor, –do·ra I. adj. *(sazonador)* seasoning; *(curtiente)* tanning II. m.f. *(reparador)* repairer, mender; *(curtidor)* tanner.

a·do·ba·du·ra f. *or* **a·do·ba·mien·to** m. CUL. *(aderezamiento)* seasoning, flavoring, marinade; *(reparo)* repair; *(curtimiento)* tanning, dressing (of hides).

a·do·bar tr. CUL. *(aderezar)* to season, flavor, marinate; *(preservar)* to pickle, preserve (meat); *(reparar)* to repair, mend; *(zurrar)* to tan, dress (hides); *(mejorar)* to improve, fortify (wines).

a·do·be m. *(ladrillo)* adobe, sun-dried brick; *(grilletes)* shackles, irons; ARG., COLL. big foot.

a·do·be·rí·a f. *(de adobes)* adobe brick factory; *(tenería)* tannery.

a·do·bo m. CUL. *(aderezamiento)* seasoning, marinade; *(reparo)* repair; *(aderezo)* dressing (for hides); *(cosmética)* cosmetic.

a·do·ce·na·do, –da I. past part. see **adocenar** II. adj. common, ordinary.

a·do·ce·nar tr. *(dividir)* to divide into dozens; *(menospreciar)* to consider common *or* ordinary —reflex. to become common *or* ordinary.

a·doc·tri·na·mien·to m. indoctrination, instruction.

a·doc·tri·nar tr. to indoctrinate, instruct.

a·do·le·cer §17 intr. *(caer enfermo)* to become sick, fall ill; FIG. *(padecer)* to suffer from, have <*a. de pereza* to suffer from laziness> —reflex. to condole, sympathize.

a·do·les·cen·cia f. adolescence, youth.

a·do·les·cen·te adj. & m.f. adolescent, youth.

a·do·lo·rar tr. to afflict, distress.

a·don·de conj. where <*el lugar a. voy está muy lejos* the place where I am going is very far away>.

a·dón·de I. adv. where <*¿a. vas?* where are you going?> II. conj. where <*dígame usted a. va* tell me where you are going>.

▲ *Adónde* and *adonde* mean literally "to where" or "whither," and are used when motion toward a place or thing is expressed. *Dónde* and *donde* mean simply "where" and stand for the place where something is located.

a·don·de·quie·ra adv. wherever, anywhere <*a. que vayas, lo encontrarás* wherever you go, you'll find it>.

a·do·nis m. [pl. **-nis**] Adonis, adonis (beautiful youth).

a·do·ni·zar·se §04 reflex. to adorn *or* beautify oneself.

a·dop·ción f. adoption.

a·dop·ta·ble adj. adoptable.

a·dop·tan·te I. adj. adopting II. m.f. adopter, adoptive parent.

a·dop·tar tr. *(prohijar)* to adopt <*a. a un niño* to adopt a child>; FIG. *(aceptar)* to adopt, espouse <*a. un nuevo sistema* to adopt a new system>; LAW to adopt, pass <*a. una ley* to pass a law>.

a·dop·ti·vo, –va adj. adoptive, adopted <*un hijo a.* an adopted son>.

a·do·quín m. *(piedra)* paving stone; FIG., COLL. *(tonto)* dunce, idiot; ARG. wooden paving block.

a·do·qui·na·do I. past part. see **adoquinar** II. m. *(pavimento)* pavement; *(acción)* paving.

a·do·qui·nar tr. to pave.

a·do·ra·ble adj. adorable.

a·do·ra·ción f. *(amor)* adoration, idolization; RELIG. worship.

a·do·ra·dor, –do·ra I. adj. *(amante)* adoring, idolizing; RELIG. worshiping II. m.f. *(amante)* adorer, idolizer; RELIG. worshiper.

a·do·rar tr. *(amar)* to adore, idolize; RELIG. to worship —intr. to worship.

a·dor·me·ce·dor, –do·ra adj. soporific.

a·dor·me·cer §17 tr. *(dar sueño)* to induce sleep, lull; FIG.

(calmar) to calm, soothe —reflex. *(dormirse)* to doze off; *(amodorrarse)* to become sleepy *or* drowsy; *(entorpecerse)* to become numb ♦ **adormecerse en** to surrender *or* yield to (vices).

a·dor·me·ci·do, –da I. past part. see **adormecer** II. adj. *(soñoliento)* sleepy, drowsy; *(un miembro)* numb, asleep.

a·dor·me·ci·mien·to m. *(acción)* dozing off; *(sueño)* sleepiness; *(modorra)* drowsiness.

a·dor·mi·lar·se *or* **a·dor·mi·tar·se** reflex. to doze, drowse.

a·dor·na·do I. past part. see **adornar** II. m. adornment, decoration, ornament.

a·dor·na·dor, –do·ra I. adj. adorning, beautifying II. m.f. adorner, decorator.

a·dor·na·mien·to m. adornment, decoration.

a·dor·nar tr. *(ornamentar)* to adorn, decorate; SEW. *(guarnecer)* to trim; CUL. to garnish; FIG. *(elaborar)* to elaborate on, embellish <*a. una historia* to embellish a story>; *(dotar)* to endow, grace <*le adornan mil virtudes* he is endowed with many virtues> —reflex. to adorn oneself.

a·dor·nis·ta m. decorator.

a·dor·no m. *(ornamento)* adornment, decoration; SEW. *(orladura)* trimming; CUL. garnish; TAUR. bullfighter's gesture ♦ **adornos** BOT. balsam • **de a.** decorative.

a·do·sar tr. *(arrimar)* to place along *or* against <*a. las sillas a la pared* to place the chairs along the wall>; *(apoyar)* to rest *or* lean against <*a. la tabla a la pared* to lean the board against the wall>; S. AMER. *(unir)* to join firmly; *(agregar)* to attach, enclose (with a letter).

ad·quie·ra, adquiero see **adquirir**.

ad·qui·ri·ble adj. acquirable, obtainable.

ad·qui·ri·do, –da I. past part. see **adquirir** II. adj. acquired <*hábito a.* acquired habit> ♦ **mal a.** ill-gotten.

ad·qui·ri·dor, –do·ra I. adj. acquiring; *(comprador)* buying II. m.f. acquirer; *(comprador)* buyer.

ad·qui·rir §02 tr. *(conseguir)* to acquire; *(comprar)* to buy.

ad·qui·si·ción f. *(acción de adquirir)* acquisition; *(compra)* purchase.

ad·qui·si·dor, –do·ra adj. var. of **adquiridor, –do·ra**.

ad·qui·si·ti·vo, –va adj. acquisitive, purchasing <*poder a.* purchasing power>.

a·dre·de adv. on purpose, deliberately.

a·dre·na·li·na f. BIOCHEM. adrenaline.

a·drián m. MED. bunion.

A·driá·ti·co m. Adriatic (sea).

a·dri·zar §04 tr. MARIT. to right (a ship) —reflex. to right itself (a ship).

ads·cri·bir §85 tr. *(atribuir)* to attribute, ascribe; *(designar)* to assign, appoint.

ads·crip·ción f. *(atribución)* attribution, ascription; *(designación)* assignment, appointment.

ads·crip·to, –ta *or* **ads·cri·to, –ta** I. past part. see **adscribir** II. adj. *(atribuido)* attributed, ascribed; *(designado)* assigned, appointed.

ad·sor·ción f. CHEM. adsorption.

a·dua·na f. *(administración)* customs; *(oficina)* customs house.

a·dua·ne·ro, –ra I. adj. customs II. m. customs officer.

a·duc·ción f. ZOOL. adduction.

a·du·cir §22 tr. to adduce, cite.

a·due·ñar·se reflex. to take over *or* possession, appropriate.

a·du·fe m. tambourine.

a·du·la·ción f. adulation, flattery.

a·du·la·dor, –do·ra I. adj. adulating, flattering II. m.f. adulator, flatterer.

a·du·lar tr. to adulate, flatter.

a·du·la·to·rio, –ria adj. adulating, flattering.

a·dul·cé, adulce see **adulzar**.

a·du·lón, –lo·na COLL. I. adj. fawning, flattering II. m.f. flatterer, fawner.

a·dul·te·ra·ción f. adulteration.

a·dul·te·ra·dor, –do·ra I. adj. adulterating II. m.f. adulterator.

a·dul·te·ran·te adj. adulterant, adulterating.

a·dul·te·rar tr. to adulterate —intr. to commit adultery.

a·dul·te·ri·no, –na adj. *(procedente de adulterio)* adulterine; FIG. *(falso)* false, spurious.

a·dul·te·rio m. adultery.

a·dúl·te·ro, –ra I. adj. *(infiel)* adulterous; FIG. *(corrompido)* corrupt **II.** m. adulterer —f. adulteress
a·dul·to, –ta adj. & m.f. adult.
a·dul·zar §04 tr. METAL. to soften, make pliable (metals); *(dulcificar)* to sweeten.
a·dul·zo·rar tr. *(suavizar)* to soften; *(dulcificar)* to sweeten —reflex. to become sweet-tempered.
a·dum·brar tr. PAINT. to adumbrate, shadow.
a·du·nar tr. to unite, join (together).
a·dus·tez f. austerity, harshness.
a·dus·to, –ta adj. *(quemado)* scorching, burning hot; FIG. *(austero)* austere, severe; VEN. stubborn, inflexible.
a·duz·ca, aduzco see aducir.
ad·ve·ne·di·zo, –za I. adj. foreign, alien **II.** m.f. *(extranjero)* immigrant, foreigner; *(nuevo rico)* parvenu, upstart.
ad·ve·ni·mien·to m. *(venida)* advent, arrival; *(accesión)* accession (to a throne).
ad·ve·nir §76 intr. to come, arrive.
ad·ven·ti·cio, –cia adj. *(occasional)* accidental, adventitious; BOT. adventitious.
ad·ven·tis·mo m. RELIG. Adventism.
ad·ven·tis·ta adj. & m.f. RELIG. Adventist.
ad·ve·rar tr. to certify, authenticate.
ad·ver·bial adj. GRAM. adverbial.
ad·ver·bio m. GRAM. adverb.
ad·ver·sa·men·te adv. adversely, unfavorably.
ad·ver·sa·rio, –ria m.f. adversary, opponent.
ad·ver·si·dad f. adversity, misfortune.
ad·ver·so, –sa adj. *(desfavorable)* adverse, unfavorable; *(opuesto)* opposing, opposite.
ad·ver·ten·cia f. *(admonición)* warning; *(consejo)* advice; *(noticia)* notice; *(prefacio)* preface, foreword.
ad·ver·ti·da·men·te adv. knowingly.
ad·ver·ti·do, –da I. past part. see advertir **II.** adj. *(avisado)* informed, warned; *(capaz)* capable, skillful.
ad·ver·tir §65 tr. *(fijar)* to notice, note; *(avisar)* to warn, notify; *(aconsejar)* to counsel, advise —intr. to realize, notice.
ad·vie·ne see advenir.
ad·vien·to m. RELIG. Advent.
ad·vi·nie·ra, advino see advenir.
ad·ya·cen·cia f. adjacency, contiguity.
ad·ya·cen·te adj. adjacent.
a·é·re·o, –a adj. air, aerial; FIG. *(leve)* light.
a·e·ro·bús m. airbus.
a·e·ro·di·ná·mi·co, –ca I. adj. aerodynamic, aerodynamical **II.** f. aerodynamics.
a·e·ro·di·na·mis·mo m. aerodynamism.
a·e·ró·dro·mo m. airdrome, aerodrome (G.B.).
a·e·ró·fo·bo, –ba adj. aerophobic.
a·e·ro·fo·to·gra·fí·a f. *(fotografía)* aerial photography; *(foto)* aerial photograph.
a·e·ro·gra·fí·a f. aerography.
a·e·ro·gra·ma f. aerogram, air letter.
a·e·ro·lí·ne·a f. airline.
a·e·ro·li·to m. ASTRON. aerolite, meteorite.
a·e·ro·lo·gí·a f. aerology.
a·e·ro·man·cia f. aeromancy.
a·e·ro·ma·rí·ti·mo, –ma adj. aeromarine.
a·e·ro·mo·de·lis·mo m. airplane modeling.
a·e·ro·mo·zo, –za m.f. flight attendant —m. steward —f. stewardess.
a·e·ro·nau·ta m.f. aeronaut.
a·e·ro·náu·ti·co, –ca I. adj. aeronautic, aeronautical **II.** f. aeronautics.
a·e·ro·na·val adj. air and sea.
a·e·ro·na·ve f. airship.
a·e·ro·pla·no m. airplane.
a·e·ro·pos·tal adj. airmail.
a·e·ro·puer·to m. airport.
a·e·ro·sol m. aerosol.
a·e·ros·pa·cial adj. aerospace.
a·e·ros·ta·ción f. aerostation.
a·e·ros·tá·ti·co, –ca I. adj. aerostatic, aerostatical **II.** f. aerostatics.
a·e·ro·tec·nia or **a·e·ro·téc·ni·ca** f. aerotechnology.
a·e·ro·te·rres·tre adj. MIL. air-land, air-to-ground.
a·e·ro·trans·por·ta·do, –da adj. airborne, airlifted.

a·e·ro·ví·a f. airway, air lane.
a·fa·bi·li·dad f. affability, geniality.
a·fa·ble adj. affable, genial.
a·fa·ble·men·te adv. affably, genially.
a·fa·ce·ta·do, –da adj. faceted.
a·fa·ma·do, –da I. past part. see afamar **II.** adj. famous, renowned.
a·fa·mar tr. to make famous.
a·fán m. *(fervor)* eagerness, zeal <*trabajar con a.* to work with zeal>; *(anhelo)* urge, desire <*a. de victoria* desire to win>; *(trabajo)* hard work, manual labor.
a·fa·na·da·men·te adj. eagerly, zealously.
a·fa·na·do, –da I. past part. see afanar **II.** adj. *(fervoroso)* eager, zealous; *(trabajador)* hard-working, diligent; COLL. *(hurtado)* stolen, pilfered.
a·fa·na·dor, –do·ra I. adj. *(fervoroso)* eager, zealous; *(trabajador)* hard-working, diligent **II.** m.f. hard worker; ARG. thief; MEX. manual laborer.
a·fa·nar intr. *(trabajar)* to work hard, work zealously; *(fatigar)* to grow tired —tr. *(insistir)* to urge, press; COLL. *(hurtar)* to pilfer; AMER. to earn —reflex. *(trabajar)* to work hard, toil; *(consagrarse)* to strive <*afanarse por ganar dinero* to strive to earn money>.
a·fa·no·sa·men·te adv. eagerly, zealously.
a·fa·no·so, –sa adj. *(fervoroso)* eager, zealous; *(trabajador)* hard-working, diligent; *(difícil)* hard, laborious <*trabajo a.* hard work>; *(agitado)* hectic, feverish <*una búsqueda a.* a hectic search>.
a·fa·ro·lar·se reflex. AMER., COLL. to get excited, get worked up.
a·fa·sia f. MED. aphasia.
a·fe·a·mien·to m. *(deformación)* defacing, deformation; *(censura)* censure, condemnation.
a·fe·ar tr. *(hacer feo)* to make ugly, deform; *(tachar)* censure, condemn.
a·fec·ción f. *(cariño)* affection, fondness; *(impresión)* impression, affect; MED. illness, disease.
a·fec·cio·nar·se reflex. to become attached (to), grow fond (of).
a·fec·ta·ble adj. impressionable.
a·fec·ta·ción f. affectation.
a·fec·ta·do, –da I. past part. see afectar **II.** adj. *(amanerado)* affected, mannered; *(influido)* affected, influenced <*a. por el anuncio* affected by the announcement>; *(dañado)* afflicted; *(fingido)* affected, feigned <*ignorancia a.* feigned ignorance>.
a·fec·tar tr. *(fingir)* to affect, feign <*a. ignorancia* to feign ignorance>; *(impresionar)* to affect, move <*su muerte nos afectó mucho* his death moved us greatly>; *(influir)* to have an effect on, influence; *(dañar)* to afflict, injure; LAW *(anexar)* to encumber, distrain; S. AMER. to set aside (funds) —reflex. *(impresionarse)* to be moved or affected; S. AMER. to fall ill, be afflicted.
a·fec·ti·vi·dad f. affectivity, emotions.
a·fec·ti·vo, –va adj. affective, emotional.
a·fec·to, –ta I. adj. *(cariñoso)* affectionate; *(gravado)* encumbered; *(afligido)* afflicted; *(destinado)* destined **II.** m. *(cariño)* affection, fondness; MED. affliction, disease.
a·fec·tuo·sa·men·te adv. affectionately.
a·fec·tuo·si·dad f. affection.
a·fec·tuo·so, –sa adj. affectionate, loving.
a·fei·ta·do, –da I. past part. see afeitar **II.** adj. shaved **III.** m. *(rasura)* shave; TAUR. blunting, shaving (of the bull's horns) —f. AMER. shave, shaving.
a·fei·ta·do·ra f. electric razor or shaver.
a·fei·tar tr. *(rasurar)* to shave; *(maquillar)* to make up, put make-up on; TAUR. to blunt, shave (a bull's horns); FIG., COLL. *(rozar)* to graze, brush (against) —reflex. *(rasurarse)* to shave oneself; *(maquillarse)* to put on make-up, make oneself up.
a·fei·te m. *(aderezo)* ornament, adornment; *(cosmético)* make-up, cosmetics.
a·fel·pa·do, –da I. past part. see afelpar **II.** adj. plush, velvety **III.** m. doormat.
a·fel·par tr. to make velvety or plush.
a·fe·mi·na·ción f. effeminacy.
a·fe·mi·na·do, –da I. past part. see afeminar **II.** adj. effeminate **III.** m. sissy.

a·fe·mi·nar tr. to make effeminate —reflex. to become effeminate.

a·fe·rra·da·men·te adv. tenaciously, persistently.

a·fe·rra·do, –da I. past part. see **aferrar** II. adj. tenacious, persistent.

a·fe·rra·mien·to m. *(asimiento)* grasping, seizing; *(insistencia)* insistence, persistence; MARIT. *(enrollamiento)* furling; *(agarro)* grappling; *(anclaje)* anchoring.

a·fe·rrar §49 tr. *(asir)* to grasp, seize; MARIT. *(plegar)* to furl; *(agarrar)* to hook, grapple; *(amarrar)* to moor —intr. *(insistir)* to persist, insist; MARIT. to anchor, moor —reflex. to grapple, grasp one another; *(insistir)* to persist ♦ **aferrarse a** to cling to, persist in (opinions).

Af·ga·nis·tán m. Afghanistan.

af·ga·no, –na adj. & m.f. Afghan, Afghani.

a·fian·za·mien·to m. *(garantía)* guarantee, security; *(aseguramiento)* securing, strengthening; FIG. *(sostenimiento)* support, backing.

a·fian·zar §04 tr. *(garantizar)* to guarantee; *(asegurar)* to secure, strengthen <*a. un tablero* to secure a bulletin board>; *(agarrar)* to grasp, seize; FIG. *(sostener)* to back, support <*a. la monarquía* to support the monarchy> —reflex. *(asegurarse)* to make oneself secure, steady oneself <*afianzarse en los estribos* to steady oneself in the stirrups>; *(establecerse)* to establish oneself.

a·fi·ción f. *(inclinación)* liking, inclination, fondness; *(aficionados)* fans, enthusiasts ♦ **tener a. a** to have a liking for, be a fan of.

a·fi·cio·na·do, –da I. past part. see **aficionar** II. adj. *(entusiástico)* enthusiastic, keen; *(novicio)* amateur III. m.f. *(diletante)* fan, enthusiast; *(novicio)* amateur.

a·fi·cio·nar tr. to inspire a liking or fondness —reflex. to become fond or enthusiastic.

a·fie·bra·do, –da I. past part. see **afiebrarse** II. adj. feverish.

a·fie·brar·se reflex. AMER. to become feverish, have a fever.

a·fie·rra, afierro see **aferrar**.

a·fi·la·do, –da I. past part. see **afilar** II. adj. *(punzante)* sharp, sharpened; *(cenceño)* slender, thin (features); FIG. *(perspicaz)* sharp, keen III. m. sharpening, honing.

a·fi·la·dor, –do·ra I. adj. sharpening II. m. *(persona)* sharpener, grinder; *(correa)* strop; *(aguzador)* sharpening or grinding machine.

a·fi·la·lá·pi·ces m. [pl. -ces] pencil sharpener.

a·fi·la·mien·to m. fineness, sharpness (of features).

a·fi·lar tr. *(aguzar)* to sharpen <*a. un cuchillo* to sharpen a knife>; *(una navaja)* to strop, sharpen; FIG. *(afinar)* to sharpen, refine; AMER., COLL. *(requebrar)* to court, woo; AMER. *(halagar)* to flatter; ECUAD. to be or get ready —reflex. *(adelgazarse)* to grow or become thin; AMER. to get ready.

a·fi·lia·ción f. affiliation.

a·fi·lia·do, –da I. past part. see **afiliar** II. adj. affiliated III. m.f. affiliate, member.

a·fi·liar tr. to affiliate —reflex. to become affiliated, become a member ♦ **afiliarse a** to become affiliated with, join.

a·fi·li·gra·na·do, –da I. past part. see **afiligranar** II. adj. *(de filigrana)* filigreed; FIG. *(delicado)* delicate, dainty.

a·fi·li·gra·nar tr. *(hacer filigrana)* to filigree; FIG. *(pulir)* to polish; *(hermosear)* to adorn, embellish.

a·fi·lón m. *(chaira)* knife sharpener; *(correa)* strop.

a·fín I. adj. *(próximo)* nearby, adjacent <*campos afines* adjacent fields>; *(parecido)* related, similar <*ideas afines* related ideas> II. m.f. relative, relation (by marriage).

a·fi·na·ción f. *(perfeccionamiento)* completion; *(depuración)* refining; FIG. *(de una persona)* refining, polishing (of a person); MUS. tuning.

a·fi·na·dor, –do·ra I. adj. refining, finishing II. m.f. tuner (person) —m. *(para el piano o el arpa)* tuning key.

a·fi·nar tr. *(perfeccionar)* to perfect, refine; *(purificar)* to refine (metals); FIG. *(una persona)* to refine, polish (a person); MUS. to tune (an instrument) —intr. MUS. *(cantar)* to sing in tune; *(tocar)* to play in tune —reflex. FIG. *(refinarse)* to become refined or polished.

a·fin·car §70 intr. to acquire property or real estate —reflex. to settle down, establish oneself.

a·fi·ni·dad f. *(semejanza)* affinity, similarity; BOT., CHEM., MATH. affinity ♦ **por a.** by marriage.

a·fir·ma·ción f. affirmation.

a·fir·ma·do, –da I. past part. see **afirmar** II. m. roadbed.

a·fir·ma·dor, –do·ra I. adj. affirming II. m.f. affirmer.

a·fir·man·te adj. affirming.

a·fir·mar tr. *(declarar)* to affirm; *(fortificar)* to make firm or fast, secure; CHILE to whip, beat —reflex. *(asegurarse)* to insure or assure oneself, make sure; *(apoyarse)* to steady oneself, make oneself steady or secure.

a·fir·ma·ti·va·men·te adv. affirmatively.

a·fir·ma·ti·vo, –va I. adj. affirmative II. f. affirmative answer or statement.

a·flau·ta·do, –da adj. high-pitched (tone or voice).

a·fle·cha·do, –da adj. arrow-shaped.

a·flic·ción f. affliction.

a·flic·ti·vo, –va adj. distressing, afflictive.

a·fli·gen·te adj. distressing, afflictive.

a·fli·gi·do, –da I. past part. see **afligir** II. adj. *(desconsolado)* afflicted, distressed; *(por la muerte)* bereaved, griefstricken.

a·fli·gir §32 tr. *(apenar)* to afflict, cause pain; *(pesar)* to trouble, distress —reflex. to be troubled or distressed ♦ **afligirse con, de,** or **por** to be distressed or troubled by.

a·flo·ja·mien·to m. *(soltura)* slackening, loosening; *(de disciplina)* relaxing, relaxation; *(disminución)* lessening, abatement.

a·flo·jar tr. *(soltar)* to loosen, slacken; FIG., COLL. *(entregar)* to give up, hand over —intr. *(perder fuerza)* to diminish, lessen; *(ceder)* to grow lax, slack —reflex. to become loose or slack <*el cabo se aflojó* the cable became loose>; *(debilitarse)* to weaken.

a·flo·ra·mien·to m. MIN. outcrop; FIG. *(surgimiento)* emergence.

a·flo·rar intr. GEOL. to outcrop; FIG. *(aparecer)* to appear, arise —tr. to sieve, sift.

a·fluen·cia f. *(multitud)* crowd, crowding; *(abundancia)* abundance, affluence; FIG. *(facundia)* eloquence, loquacity; *(de sangre)* flow.

a·fluen·te I. adj. flowing; FIG. *(facundo)* eloquent, loquacious II. m. tributary.

a·fluir §18 intr. *(manar)* to flow; *(acudir)* to flock, crowd <*los turistas afluyen a Roma* the tourists flock to Rome>.

a·fo·far·se reflex. to become soft, fluffy, or spongy.

a·fo·ga·rar tr. CUL. to overcook, burn.

a·fo·llar tr. *(soplar)* to blow with a bellows; *(plegar)* to pleat —reflex. to blister, form bubbles (said of walls).

a·fon·dar tr. to sink, submerge —intr. to sink, go under.

a·fo·ní·a f. MED. aphonia (loss of voice).

a·fó·ni·co, –ca or **á·fo·no, –na** adj. MED. aphonic, hoarse; PHONET. voiceless, silent.

a·fo·ra·do, –da I. past part. see **aforar** II. adj. privileged III. m.f. holder of a privilege.

a·fo·ra·dor m. estimator, appraiser.

a·fo·ra·mien·to m. *(medición)* measuring, gauging; *(evaluación)* appraisal, assessment; *(fuero)* privilege, license.

a·fo·rar §19 tr. *(medir)* to measure, gauge; COM. *(valorar)* to appraise, assess; *(ortogar)* to grant (privileges or license) —intr. THEAT. to highlight center-stage.

a·fo·ris·mo m. aphorism.

a·fo·ro m. *(medida)* measurement, gauging; COM. *(valoración)* appraisal, assessment; THEAT. *(capacidad)* seating capacity.

a·fo·rrar tr. to line, sheathe —reflex. *(ponerse ropa)* to put on heavy underclothing; FIG., COLL. *(comer y beber)* to stuff oneself, gorge.

a·for·tu·na·da·men·te adv. fortunately, luckily.

a·for·tu·na·do, –da I. past part. see **afortunar** II. adj. *(oportuno)* fortunate, lucky; *(dichoso)* happy, blessed; MARIT. *(tempestuoso)* stormy III. m.f. lucky sort, fortunate person.

a·for·tu·nar tr. to make happy.

a·fos·car·se §70 reflex. MARIT. to become foggy or misty.

a·fre·cho m. AGR. bran.

a·fren·ta f. *(ofensa)* affront, insult; *(deshonor)* disgrace, dishonor.

a·fren·tar tr. *(ofender)* to affront, insult; *(humillar)* to humiliate, disgrace —reflex. to be ashamed, humiliated.

a·fren·to·so, –sa adj. insolent, offensive.

Á·fri·ca f. Africa.

a·fri·ca·nis·mo m. Africanism.

a·fri·ca·nis·ta m.f. Africanist.

a·fri·ca·no, –na adj. & m.f. African.

a·fro·di·sia·co, –ca adj. & m. aphrodisiac.

a·fron·ta·do, –da I. past part. see **afrontar II.** adj. HER. facing, face-to-face.

a·fron·ta·mien·to m. (accion de afrontar) facing, confronting; (confrontación) confrontation.

a·fron·tar tr. (confrontar) to face (up to), confront; (carear) to bring face to face.

af·ta f. MED. aphtha, canker sore.

a·fue·ra I. adv. out, outside <salgamos a. let's go outside>; (en público) in public **II.** interj. (¡mueva!) out of the way!; (¡salga!) get out of here! **III.** f.pl. **afueras** (alrededores) suburbs, outskirts; MIL. embankment (around a fortress).

a·fue·re, afuero see **aforar.**

a·fu·sión f. affusion, shower.

a·ga·cha·da f. COLL. (astucia) trick, ruse; (acción de agacharse) stooping, crouching.

a·ga·cha·par·se reflex. SP. to stoop, crouch.

a·ga·char tr. (inclinar) to bow or bend <a. la cabeza to bow one's head> ♦ **a. las orejas** to hang one's head, be crestfallen —reflex. (ponerse en cuclillas) to crouch, squat; FIG. (aguantarse) to grin and bear it, cope; (retirarse) to lie low, hide out; AMER. to give in, yield; ARG. to get ready; MEX. to keep quiet.

a·gal·ba·na·do, –da adj. lazy, idle.

a·ga·lla f. ANAT. tonsil; ICHTH. gill; BOT. nutgall; COL. greed ♦ **agallas** MED. quinsy, angina; FIG., COLL. guts, courage.

a·ga·llón m. (de collar) silver bead; RELIG. rosary bead; ARCHIT. echinus; BOT. COL. gallnut ♦ **agallones** MED. ARG., COL. parotitis.

a·gan·gre·nar·se reflex. to become gangrenous.

á·ga·pe m. (amor) agape; (banquete) banquet.

a·ga·rra·ba·do, –da adj. hook-shaped, hooked.

a·gar·ba·do, –da adj. graceful.

a·gá·ri·co m. BOT. agaric, mushroom ♦ **a. mineral** agaric mineral.

a·ga·rra·da I. f. COLL. quarrel, row **II.** adj. see **agarrado, –da.**

a·ga·rra·de·ra f. AMER. handle, holder ♦ **agarraderas** COLL. pull, influence.

a·ga·rra·de·ro m. (mango) handle, holder; FIG., COLL. (amparo) protection; MARIT. anchorage.

a·ga·rra·do, –da I. past part. see **agarrar II.** adj. COLL. (mezquino) stingy, tight; (en los bailes) cheek-to-cheek **III.** m.f. COLL. cheapskate, tightwad —f. see **agarrada.**

a·ga·rrar tr. (asir) to seize, grab, grasp; COLL. to get, catch <a. un resfriado to catch a cold>; to get, wangle <agarraron lo que querían they got what they wanted>; AMER. (tomar) to get, take <agarró el autobús he took the bus> —intr. (pegarse) to take hold, stick; (arraigar) to root, take root ♦ **a. para** S. AMER. to head for (a place) —reflex. to cling, hold on <¡agárrate bien! hold on tight!>; (pelearse) to grapple, come to blows ♦ **agarrársela con alguien** S. AMER. to pick on someone • **se le agarró la fiebre** he came down with a fever.

a·ga·rre m. (asimiento) grabbing, grasping; FIG. (valor) guts, toughness; AMER., COLL. influence, pull; COL. handle.

a·ga·rrón m. AMER. (tirón) pull, tug; (altercado) scrap, fight.

a·ga·rro·ta·do, –da I. past part. see **agarrotar II.** adj. MECH. seized up; FIG. (rígido) stiff, tense.

a·ga·rro·ta·mien·to m. (estrangulación) garroting, strangulation; (acción de atar) tightly binding or tying up; (compresión) compression, tightening; FIG. (opresión) oppression, harassment; (rigidez) stiffness, tenseness.

a·ga·rro·tar tr. (estrangular) to garrote, strangle; (atar) to tightly bind or tie; (comprimir) to compress, tighten; FIG. (oprimir) to oppress, harass —reflex. (ponerse rígido) to become stiff or tense; MECH. to seize up.

a·ga·sa·ja·dor, –do·ra I. m.f. (acogedor) welcomer, host; (festejador) entertainer **II.** adj. (acogedor) welcoming,

hospitable; (festejante) entertaining, hosting; (obsequiante) attentive.

a·ga·sa·jar tr. (acoger) to greet, welcome; (festejar) to entertain, fete; (regalar) to lavish gifts or attention on.

a·ga·sa·jo m. (acogida) welcome, reception; (festejo) fete, entertainment; (regalo) present, attention; (refresco) refreshment.

á·ga·ta f. MIN. agate.

a·ga·vi·llar tr. AGR. to bind, sheave <a. la cebada to sheave the barley> —reflex. to band together.

a·ga·za·par tr. COLL. to nab, seize —reflex. (agacharse) to crouch, squat; (esconderse) to hide out, lay low.

a·gen·cia f. agency <a. de viajes travel agency>; (oficina) office, bureau; (diligencia) diligence; CHILE pawnshop ♦ **a. de publicidad** advertising agency.

a·gen·ciar tr. (promover) to solicit, go after; (obtener) to obtain, acquire —reflex. to manage, succeed in.

a·gen·cio·so –sa adj. diligent, industrious.

a·gen·da f. (cuaderno) appointment or memoranda book; (orden del día) agenda.

a·gen·te m. agent ♦ **a. de bolsa** stockbroker, broker • **a. de cambio** moneychanger • **a. de policía** policeman.

a·gi·bí·li·bus m. [pl. **-bus**] COLL. know-how, savvy.

a·gi·gan·ta·do, –da I. past part. see **agigantar II.** adj. (gigantesco) huge, gigantic; (sobresaliente) extraordinary, uncommon.

a·gi·gan·tar tr. (aumentar) to enlarge, aggrandize; FIG. (exagerar) to exaggerate.

á·gil adj. agile, nimble.

a·gi·li·dad f. agility, nimbleness.

a·gi·li·tar tr. (hacer ágil) to render agile or nimble; AMER. to activate, hasten.

a·gi·li·zar §04 tr. to make agile or nimble.

á·gil·men·te adv. agilely, nimbly.

a·gio m. COM. (beneficio) agio, exchange premium; (especulación) agiotage, currency speculation.

a·gio·ta·dor m. COM. speculator.

a·gio·tis·ta m.f. moneychanger, bill-broker.

a·gi·ta·ción f. agitation, shaking; FIG. (alboroto) upset, disturbance; MARIT. (tempestad) roughness, choppiness.

a·gi·ta·dor, –do·ra I. adj. agitating **II.** m.f. (provocador) agitator —m. CHEM. stirring rod.

a·gi·tar tr. (sacudir) to wave, shake; FIG. (alborotar) to agitate, excite —reflex. (sacudirse) to wave, flutter; FIG. (perturbarse) to be agitated or excited; MARIT. to be rough or choppy.

a·glo·me·ra·ción f. (acumulación) agglomeration, amassing; (gentío) crowd, throng.

a·glo·me·ra·do I. past part. see **aglomerar II.** m. (agregación) agglomerate; (combustible) coal briquette.

a·glo·me·ran·te I. adj. agglomerative **II.** m. PRINT. binding material.

a·glo·me·rar tr. to agglomerate, amass —reflex. (amontonarse) to be amassed or heaped together; FIG. (apiñarse) to crowd, press together.

a·glu·ti·na·ción f. agglutination.

a·glu·ti·nan·te adj. & m. agglutinant.

a·glu·ti·nar tr. to agglutinate, bind.

ag·na·ción f. agnation.

ag·nos·ti·cis·mo m. RELIG. agnosticism.

ag·nós·ti·co, –ca RELIG. adj. & m.f. agnostic.

a·go·bia·do, –da I. past part. see **agobiar II.** adj. (cargado de espaldas) bent over, stooped; (fatigado) exhausted, weary.

a·go·bia·dor, –do·ra adj. (bochornoso) oppressive, stifling <calor a. stifling heat>; (agotador) exhausting, backbreaking <trabajo a. backbreaking work>; (abrumador) overwhelming, crushing <problemas agobiadores overwhelming problems>.

a·go·bian·te adj. (agotador) backbreaking, overwhelming; (sofocante) stifling, suffocating (heat).

a·go·biar tr. (cargar) to weigh down, burden; FIG. (cansar) to exhaust, weary; (humillar) to oppress, overwhelm; (deprimir) to depress, dispirit —reflex. to bend, stoop.

a·go·bio m. (carga) load, burden; (fatiga) fatigue, exhaustion.

a·gol·pa·mien·to m. (amontonamiento) accumulation, pile; (apretamiento) crowding, thronging.

a·gol·par·se reflex. *(apiñarse)* to throng, rush; FIG. *(venirse encima)* to come in one fell swoop.
a·go·ní·a f. *(condición moribunda)* death-throes, deathknell; FIG. *(aflicción)* agony, distress; *(deseo)* desire, yearning —m.pl. **agonías** COLL. cowardly, pessimistic sort.
a·gó·ni·co, –ca adj. *(moribundo)* moribund, dying; *(angustiado)* agonizing, in agony.
a·go·ni·zan·te I. adj. *(moribundo)* dying; FIG. in agony II. m.f. dying person.
a·go·ni·zar §04 intr. *(estar moribundo)* to be at death's door; FIG. *(sufrir)* to be in agony; *(extinguirse)* to fade, dim ♦ **a. por** FIG. to be dying or yearning to <*agonizan por ir* they are dying to go> —tr. *(ayudar a bien morir)* to minister (to the dying); FIG., COLL. *(molestar)* to plague, bother.
a·go·rar §03 tr. to augur, foretell.
a·go·re·ro, –ra I. m.f. *(adivino)* soothsayer, fortune teller; *(profeta de mal agüero)* prophet of doom II. adj. *(augural)* divinatory, augural; *(ominoso)* ominous, foreboding.
a·gor·go·jar·se reflex. to become infested with weevils.
a·gos·tar tr. *(secar)* to wither, parch; *(arar)* to plow in the summer —intr. to graze in the summer.
a·gos·to m. August; *(cosecha)* harvest ♦ **hacer su a.** FIG., COLL. to feather one's nest, make hay while the sun shines.
a·go·ta·ble adj. exhaustible.
a·go·ta·do, –da I. past part. see **agotar** II. adj. *(acabado)* exhausted, used up; *(cansado)* exhausted, tired; *(fuera de publicación)* out-of-print; COM. sold-out; AMER. dead (battery).
a·go·ta·dor, –do·ra adj. exhausting, tiring.
a·go·ta·mien·to m. *(abatimiento)* exhaustion; *(disminución)* depletion.
a·go·tar tr. FIG. *(acabar)* to exhaust, use up <*agotaron las provisiones* they used up the provisions>; *(desaguar)* to drain <*a. una cisterna* to drain a tank> —reflex. *(acabarse)* to be used up or depleted; *(cansarse)* to be exhausted or worn out; *(libros)* to be out of print.
a·gra·cé, agrace see **agrazar.**
a·gra·ce·ño, –ña adj. sour, tart.
a·gra·cia·da·men·te adv. gracefully, genteelly.
a·gra·cia·do, –da I. past part. see **agraciar** II. adj. *(gentil)* graceful, genteel; *(hermoso)* good-looking, attractive; *(premiado)* prize-winning III. m.f. *(premiado)* prize-winner.
a·gra·ciar tr. *(embellecer)* to embellish, adorn; *(favorecer)* to grace, favor; *(premiar)* to award, reward; *(perdonar)* to pardon <*a. a un condenado* to pardon a criminal>.
a·gra·da·ble adj. agreeable, pleasant, pleasing.
a·gra·da·ble·men·te adv. agreeably, pleasantly.
a·gra·dar intr. to be pleasing or agreeable —reflex. to be pleased or satisfied (with) <*me agrada la novedad* I am pleased with the news>; *(gustarse)* to like one another.
a·gra·de·cer §17 tr. *(dar gracias)* to thank; *(sentir gratitud)* to be grateful for.
a·gra·de·ci·da·men·te adv. gratefully, thankfully.
a·gra·de·ci·do, –da I. past part. see **agradecer** II. adj. grateful, thankful ♦ **muy a.** much obliged III. m.f. grateful or thankful person.
a·gra·de·ci·mien·to m. gratitude, thanks.
a·gra·dez·ca, agradezco see **agradecer.**
a·gra·do m. *(gracia)* grace, affability; *(gusto)* taste, liking <*no es de su a.* it is not to his liking>.
a·gra·mar tr. AGR. to scutch, brake (hemp, flax); COLL. *(golpear)* to beat, flog.
a·gran·da·mien·to m. *(aumento)* enlargement, increase; *(exageración)* exaggeration, aggrandizement.
a·gran·dar tr. *(aumentar)* to enlarge, increase; *(exagerar)* to exaggerate, aggrandize —reflex. to increase, grow larger.
a·gra·nu·ja·do, –da adj. *(granular)* granular; *(granujiento)* pimply <*piel a.* pimply skin>; *(pícaro)* roguish.
a·gra·rio, –ria adj. agrarian, agricultural.
a·gra·va·ción f. var. of **agravamiento.**
a·gra·va·dor, –do·ra I. adj. aggravating, worsening II. m.f. aggravator.
a·gra·va·mien·to m. aggravation, worsening.
a·gra·van·te I. adj. aggravating II. m. aggravating circumstance.

a·gra·var tr. to aggravate —reflex. to become worse.
a·gra·via·dor, –do·ra I. adj. insulting, offensive II. m.f. offender, wrongdoer.
a·gra·vian·te I. adj. offensive, insulting II. m.f. offender, wrongdoer.
a·gra·viar tr. *(ofender)* to offend, insult; *(perjudicar)* to injure, harm —reflex. *(ofenderse)* to take offense, be offended; *(empeorarse)* to worsen (illness).
a·gra·vio m. *(ofensa)* offense, insult; *(perjuicio)* injury, harm.
a·gra·vio·so, –sa adj. insulting, offensive.
a·graz m. [pl. **-ces**] BOT. *(uva)* unripe grape; *(zumo)* verjuice, sour grape juice; *(marojo)* mistletoe; *(calderilla)* alpine currant; FIG., COLL. *(disgusto)* annoyance, displeasure ♦ **en a.** prematurely.
a·gra·zar §04 intr. to be sour or tart —tr. FIG. *(amargar)* to embitter; *(disgustar)* to vex. annoy.
a·gre·di·do, –da I. past part. see **agredir** II. adj. assaulted, attacked III. m.f. assault or attack victim.
a·gre·dir §38 tr. to attack, assault.
a·gre·ga·ción f. *(combinación)* aggregation, sum; *(incorporación)* attachment, addition; *(designación)* appointment, nomination.
a·gre·ga·do, –da I. past part. see **agregar** II. adj. aggregate III. m. *(compuesto)* aggregate; *(añadidura)* addition; AMER. newcomer; ARG., URUG., PAR., DEROG. freeloader; COL., VEN. sharecropper, tenant farmer; P. RICO day laborer ♦ **a. militar** military attaché.
a·gre·gar §47 tr. *(añadir)* to add, attach; *(unir)* to gather, collect; *(designar)* to appoint, nominate —reflex. to join.
a·gre·mia·ción f. INDUS. union meeting.
a·gre·miar intr. INDUS. to form a union, unionize.
a·gre·sión f. *(provocación)* aggression, provocation; *(ataque)* attack, assault.
a·gre·si·va·men·te adv. aggressively, hostilely.
a·gre·si·vi·dad f. aggressiveness.
a·gre·si·vo, –va adj. aggressive, hostile.
a·gre·sor, –so·ra I. m.f. *(provocador)* aggressor, provoker; *(acometedor)* attacker, assailant II. adj. *(hostil)* aggressive, hostile; *(acometedor)* attacking, assailing.
a·gres·te adj. *(campestre)* rural, rustic; FIG. *(tosco)* rude, uncouth.
a·gria·men·te adv. *(ásperamente)* sourly, harshly; FIG. *(amargamente)* acrimoniously, bitterly.
a·griar tr. *(acedar)* to (make) sour; FIG. *(amargar)* to embitter; *(irritar)* to exasperate, annoy —reflex. to become sour.
a·grí·co·la I. adj. agricultural, farming II. m.f. agriculturist, farmer.
a·gri·cul·tor, –to·ra I. m.f. farmer, agriculturist II. adj. farming, agricultural.
a·gri·cul·tu·ra f. agriculture, farming.
a·gri·dul·ce adj. CUL. bittersweet, sweet-and-sour; FIG. bittersweet.
a·grie·ta·mien·to m. *(grieta)* cracking; GEOL. fissure, crack.
a·grie·tar tr. to crack, split —reflex. to be cracked or split.
a·gri·men·sor, –so·ra m.f. surveyor.
a·gri·men·su·ra f. surveying.
a·grio, –gria I. adj. *(ácido)* acrid, sour <*fruta a.* sour fruit>; *(chocante)* garish, discordant <*coloridos agrios* garish colors>; FIG. *(áspero)* rough, uneven <*terreno a.* rough terrain>; *(desabrido)* rude, disagreeable <*una respuesta a.* a rude response>; *(frágil)* brittle II. m. *(sabor)* sourness, acidity; *(zumo)* sour juice ♦ **agrios** citrus fruits.
a·grio·so, –sa adj. *(agrio)* sour, bitter; CUBA bittersweet.
a·gro m. agriculture, farming.
a·gro·no·mí·a f. agronomy, agronomics.
a·gro·nó·mi·co, –ca adj. agronomical.
a·gró·no·mo, –ma I. adj. agronomical II. m. agronomist.
a·gro·pe·cua·rio, –ria adj. ♦ **la industria a.** agriculture and livestock industry.
a·gror m. sourness, bitterness.
a·gru·mar tr. to curdle, clot —reflex. to clot, coagulate.
a·gru·pa·ción f. or **a·gru·pa·mien·to** m. *(combinación)* grouping, gathering; *(grupo)* group, assemblage; *(manojo)* cluster, bunch; ARG. political group.
a·gru·pa·dor, –do·ra adj. grouping, assembling.
a·gru·par tr. *(acumular)* to group, gather; *(apiñar)* to clus-

ter, bunch —reflex. *(acumularse)* to form a group, assemble; *(apiñarse)* to crowd or cluster together.

a·gru·ra f. *(agror)* sourness; *(acidez)* acidity ♦ **agruras** citrus fruits.

a·gua f. *(líquido)* water; *(lluvia)* rain; ARCHIT. *(vertiente)* slope, pitch; MARIT. *abertura)* leak; *(marea)* tide; PERU COLL. money ♦ **a. bendita** RELIG. holy water • **a. corriente** running water • **a. de borrajas** or **de cerrajas** FIG. nothing, trifle • **a. de cepas** COLL. wine • **a. de colonia** eau de cologne, toilet water • **a. fuerte** CHEM. nitric acid • **a. nieve** sleet • **a. oxigenada** CHEM. hydrogen peroxide • **a. salobre** or **salada** salt water • **a. viento** rainstorm • **aguas** *(reflejos)* wavy pattern; *(destellos)* glimmer, sparkle; *(orina)* urine; waters, springs *<aguas termales* hot springs>; *(mares)* seas; *(corrientes)* currents (of water); MARIT. course, route • **aguas abajo** downstream • **aguas arriba** upstream • **aguas llenas** high tide • **aguas muertas** neap tide • **claro como a.** crystal-clear • **como a.** in abundance • **con el a. al cuello** in hot water, in trouble • **entre dos aguas** in doubt, undecided • **hacer a.** to leak • **hacerse a. en la boca** to melt in one's mouth • **hacérsele a. la boca** COLL. to make one's mouth water • **sin decir a. va ni a. viene** suddenly, unexpectedly.

a·gua·cal m. whitewash.

a·gua·ca·te m. BOT. avocado (fruit and tree);˙ JEWEL. *(esmeralda)* pear-shaped emerald; AMER. weakling, milksop ♦ **ser a. con pan** MEX., FIG. to be dull or boring.

a·gua·cé, aguace see **aguazar.**

a·gua·ce·ro m. METEOROL. cloudburst, downpour; FIG. *(desgracia)* misfortune, misery; CUBA, ENTOM. glowworm, firefly.

a·gua·cil m. var. of **alguacil.**

a·gua·char tr. *(enaguachar)* to flood; CHILE *(amansar)* to tame; ARG. *(apartar)* to separate a calf or lamb from its mother —reflex. ARG. *(engordar)* to get fat (horses); CHILE *(encariñarse)* to become fond of or attached to.

a·gua·chen·to, -ta adj. AMER. moist, sodden.

a·gua·chir·le f. FIG. *(aguapié)* dishwater *<este café es a.* this coffee is like dishwater>; *(nadería)* trifle, mere nothing.

a·gua·cho·so, -sa adj. COL., P. RICO watery.

a·gua·da I. f. *(sitio)* watering place; MARIT. water supply; *(inundación)* flood, flooding (in a mine); PAINT. water color; AMER. watering hole, watering trough II. adj. see **aguado, -da.**

a·gua·de·ro, -ra I. adj. waterproof II. m. watering trough or hole —f. wing feather.

a·gua·do, -da I. past part. see **aguar** II. adj. *(con agua)* diluted, watered-down; *(abstemio)* abstemious; FIG. *(malogrado)* spoiled, marred; VEN. tasteless (fruit); GUAT. weak, spent; C. RICA dull, boring III. f. see **aguada.**

a·gua·dor, -do·ra m.f. water vendor.

a·gua·du·cho m. *(inundación)* freshet; *(puesto)* refreshment stand; *(acueducto)* aqueduct; *(noria)* waterwheel, noria.

a·gua·fies·tas m.f. [pl. **-tas**] killjoy, spoilsport.

a·gua·fuer·te m.f. ARTS etching (print or plate).

a·guai·tar tr. AMER. *(acechar)* to lie in wait for, spy on; *(mirar)* to look at.

a·gua·je m. *(abrevadero)* watering place, water hole; MARIT. *(marea)* tide, tidal water; *(aguada)* water supply; *(estela)* wake; *(corriente)* current; COL., GUAT., HOND. reprimand, telling off; ECUAD., GUAT. downpour.

a·gua·ma·la f. ZOOL. jellyfish.

a·gua·ma·nil m. *(jarro)* water jug; *(palangana)* washbowl, washbasin; *(lavamanos)* ewer; AMER. sink.

a·gua·ma·ri·na f. MIN. aquamarine.

a·gua·miel f. *(hidromel)* mead, hydromel; MEX. agave juice; VEN. sugar-cane spirits.

a·gua·nie·ve f. METEOROL. sleet ♦ **aguanieves** ORNITH. wagtail.

a·gua·no·so, -sa adj. *(húmedo)* watery, moist; *(empapado)* sodden, waterlogged (ground); ECUAD. *(jugoso)* juicy; AMER. *(insípido)* watery, tasteless (fruit).

a·guan·ta·ble adj. bearable, tolerable.

a·guan·ta·do, -da I. past part. see **aguantar** II. adj. COL. stingy.

a·guan·ta·dor, -do·ra adj. AMER., COLL. patient, enduring.

a·guan·tar tr. *(resistir)* to endure, stand *<¿puedes a. el dolor?*

can you stand the pain?>; *(tolerar)* to tolerate, put up with *<no puedo a. a los novelistas malos* I cannot tolerate bad novelists>; *(sostener)* to hold up, sustain; *(contener)* to hold *<a. el aliento* to hold one's breath>; MARIT. to tense, tauten —intr. TAUR. to stand firm —reflex. to control or contain oneself.

a·guan·te m. *(paciencia)* patience, tolerance; *(fuerza)* stamina, endurance.

a·guar §10 tr. *(diluir)* to water down, dilute *<a. el vino* to water down wine>; FIG. *(malograr)* to spoil, mar *<a. la fiesta* to spoil the party>; *(moderar)* to water down; *(atenuar)* to attenuate, ease (troubles); *(echar al agua)* to throw into water; C. AMER., CHILE to water (livestock) —reflex. to become diluted; *(llenarse de agua)* to flood.

a·guar·da·da f. wait, waiting.

a·guar·dar tr. to wait for, await —intr. to wait, hold on —reflex. to stop, halt.

a·guar·dien·te m. spirits, liquor ♦ **a. de caña** rum.

a·gua·rrás m. turpentine oil.

a·gua·sal f. pickling brine.

a·gua·te·ro m. AMER. water carrier.

a·gua·vien·to m. squall, downpour.

a·gua·zal m. pool, puddle (of standing water).

a·gua·zar §04 tr. & reflex. to flood.

a·gua·zo m. PAINT. gouache.

a·gu·cé, aguce see **aguzar.**

a·gu·da·men·te adv. *(sutilmente)* acutely, keenly; FIG. *(ingeniosamente)* wittily.

a·gu·de·za f. *(filo)* sharpness; *(acuidad)* acuteness, acuity; FIG. *(ingenio)* wit, wittiness; *(dicho)* witticism, witty saying.

a·gu·di·za·ción f. *(agravación)* worsening, aggravation; *(aumento)* increase, intensification.

a·gu·di·zar §04 tr. *(afilar)* to sharpen, make sharp; *(empeorar)* to make more acute, worsen —reflex. to become serious or acute *<la enfermedad se agudiza* the illness is becoming serious>.

a·gu·do, -da adj. *(afilado)* sharp, pointed; *(chillón)* shrill *<un sonido a.* a shrill sound>; *(picante)* pungent *<un olor a.* a pungent odor>; *(serio)* acute, serious *<una enfermedad a.* an acute illness>; FIG. *(perspicaz)* keen, sharp *<vista a.* keen sight>; *(vivaz)* witty, clever *<dicho a.* a witty remark>; *(vivo)* lively, quick; MUS. high-pitched; GRAM. acute (accent); GEOM. acute (angle).

a·güe, agüe see **aguar.**

a·güe·ra f. drainage ditch (for rainwater).

a·güe·re, agüero see **agorar.**

a·güe·ro m. *(presagio)* augury, prediction; *(señal)* sign, omen.

a·gue·rri·do, -da I. past part. see **aguerrir** II. adj. MIL. *(cursado)* trained, drilled; FIG. *(probado)* experienced, seasoned.

a·gue·rrir §38 tr. to harden, accustom to war —intr. to become hardened or accustomed to war.

a·gui·ja·da f. goad.

a·gui·ja·dor, -do·ra I. adj. goading, inciting II. m.f. goader, inciter.

a·gui·jar tr. *(espolear)* to spur, goad; FIG. *(estimular)* to incite, urge —intr. to hurry or scurry along.

a·gui·jón m. ENTOM. sting; BOT. thorn, pricker; *(punta)* goad; FIG. *(estímulo)* stimulus, spur.

a·gui·jo·na·mien·to m. *(aguijadura)* goading, spurring; FIG. *(estimulación)* inciting, urging on.

·a·gui·jo·na·zo m. sting, prick.

a·gui·jo·ne·a·dor, -do·ra I. adj. *(estimulante)* goading, inciting; *(punzante)* pricking, stinging II. m.f. goader, provoker.

a·gui·jo·ne·ar tr. *(torturar)* to torment, torture; *(picar)* to sting, prick; FIG. *(estimular)* to goad, arouse *<a. la curiosidad* to arouse curiosity>.

á·gui·la f. ORNITH. eagle; FIG. *(condecoración)* emblem; FIG. *(astuto)* astute person ♦ **a. calva** bald eagle • **a. grande** spread eagle (in skating) • **a. pescadora** osprey • **a. real** or **caudal** golden eagle. —m. NUMIS. eagle; ICHTH. eagle ray; CHILE, COLL. swindler, cheat.

a·gui·le·ño, -ña adj. aquiline, hook-nosed.

a·gui·lón m. MECH. jib, arm; ARCHIT. *(de un techo)* gable; *(caño)* clay drainpipe; *(teja)* beveled tile; ORNITH. *(águila)* large eagle; HER. *(blasón)* eagle without beak or talons; ECUAD., COL. slow horse.

a·gui·nal·do m. *(regalo)* Christmas gift *or* tip; *(villancico)* Christmas carol, noël; CUBA, BOT. aguinaldo.

a·gu·ja f. *(varilla)* needle; *(alfiler para sombreros)* hatpin; *(del reloj)* hand (of a clock); ARCHIT. spire, steeple; RAIL. *(riel)* switch rail; CARP. brad, nail; ICHTH. needlefish; AGR. graft; BOT. needle; AMER. fence post, stake ♦ **a. capotera** darning needle • **a. de gancho** crochet hook • **a. de marear** *or* **a. magnética** compass • **a. de media** knitting needle • **agujas** ZOOL. front ribs.

a·gu·ja·dor m. CHILE pincushion.

a·gu·je·rar *or* **a·gu·je·re·ar** tr. to pierce, prick, perforate —reflex. to be pierced *or* perforated.

a·gu·je·ro m. *(abertura)* hole; *(alfiletero)* pincushion.

a·gu·je·ta f. *(cinta)* lace, cord; VEN. hatpin ♦ **agujetas** MED. soreness, stiffness (from exercise); MEX. shoelaces.

a·gu·jue·la f. brad.

a·guo·so, –sa adj. watery, aqueous.

a·gu·sa·nar·se reflex. to become worm-eaten *or* worm-ridden.

A·gus·tín Augustine.

a·gus·ti·nia·no, –na adj. Augustinian, of Saint Augustine.

a·gus·ti·no, –na adj. & m.f. RELIG. Augustinian.

a·gu·za·do, –da I. past part. see **aguzar** II. adj. sharpened.

a·gu·za·dor, –do·ra I. adj. sharpening II. m.f. sharpener (person) III. f. whetstone.

a·gu·za·du·ra f. *or* **a·gu·za·mien·to** m. sharpening, whetting.

a·gu·zar §04 tr. *(sacar punta)* to sharpen, make pointed; *(afilar)* to sharpen, whet; FIG. *(estimular)* to sharpen, excite; *(afinar)* to sharpen, make keen ♦ **a. los dientes** *or* **el apetito** to whet one's appetite • **a. el ingenio** to sharpen one's wit • **a. las orejas** *or* **los oídos** to prick up one's ears.

¡ah! interj. ah!, ha!

a·he·bra·do, –da adj. fibrous, stringy.

a·he·cha·de·ro m. place where grain is sifted.

a·he·cha·dor, –do·ra I. adj. sifting, winnowing II. m.f. sifter, winnower.

a·he·cha·du·ras f.pl. chaff, siftings.

a·he·char tr. to sift, winnow.

a·he·cho m. sifting, winnowing.

a·he·le·ar tr. *(amargar)* to make bitter; FIG. *(entristecer)* to sadden, embitter —intr. to taste bitter.

a·he·rro·ja·mien·to m. *(encadenamiento)* shackling, putting in chains; FIG. *(subyugación)* subjugation, bondage.

a·he·rro·jar tr. *(encadenar)* to shackle, put in chains; FIG. *(subyugar)* to subjugate, oppress.

a·he·rrum·brar tr. *(dar color)* to give a rusty-red color to; *(dar sabor)* to give a rusty taste to —reflex. *(oxidarse)* to rust, get rusty; *(color)* to get rusty-red; *(sabor)* to taste of rust.

a·her·vo·rar·se reflex. to heat up, become heated (grain in granary).

a·hí adv. there ♦ **a.** *or* **de a.** therefore, hence • **a. no más** ARG. right over there • **por a.** thereabouts.

a·hi·ja·do, –da I. past part. see **ahijar** II. m.f. godchild; *(hijo adoptivo)* adopted child; FIG. *(favorecido)* protegé, favorite —m. godson —f. goddaughter.

a·hi·jar §81 tr. *(adoptar)* to adopt; FIG. *(imputar)* to impute, attribute to —intr. *(procrear)* to procreate, reproduce; AGR. to bud, send out shoots (plants).

a·hi·la·do, –da I. past part. see **ahilar** II. adj. *(suave)* gentle, soft (breeze); *(tenue)* faint (voice).

a·hi·lar §81 tr. to line up, put in line —intr. to go in single file —reflex. *(desmayarse)* to faint; *(hacer hebra)* to spoil, go bad (food); *(adelgazarse)* to become thin *or* drawn; BOT. to grow tall and slender; CUBA to go away, leave.

a·hi·lo m. faintness, weakness.

a·hin·ca·da·men·te adv. earnestly, zealously.

a·hin·ca·do, –da I. past part. see **ahincar** II. adj. earnest, zealous.

a·hin·car §80 intr. to urge, press —reflex. to hurry, rush.

a·hín·co m. eagerness, zeal, determination.

a·hi·tar §81 tr. to give indigestion, upset one's stomach <*la carne le ha ahitado* the meat has upset his stomach>; *(poner hitos)* to stake *or* mark out —reflex. *(hartarse)* to

gorge *or* stuff oneself; *(indigestarse)* to have indigestion *or* an upset stomach.

a·hí·to, –ta I. adj. *(repleto)* stuffed, gorged; FIG. *(harto)* disgusted, fed up II. m. indigestion *or* upset stomach.

a·ho·ci·car §70 intr. MARIT. *(cabecear)* to pitch, dip (prow of boat in water); *(caer de bruces)* to fall flat on one's face; COLL. *(ceder)* to give in, admit defeat —tr. COLL. *(vencer)* to win out.

a·ho·ga·di·zo, –za adj. *(que se puede ahogar)* easily drowned *or* suffocated; *(áspero)* sharp, hard to swallow (fruit); *(pesado)* heavy, non-floating (wood); *(mortecino)* tainted (meat).

a·ho·ga·do, –da I. past part. see **ahogar** II. adj. *(sofocante)* close, stifling; S. AMER. stewed III. m.f. *(muerto)* drowned *or* suffocated person; FIG. *(pobre)* needy person —m. S. AMER. sauce.

a·ho·ga·dor, –ra I. adj. choking, suffocating II. m. *(collar)* choker, necklace; AMER. *(correa)* throatlatch (horse's harness).

a·ho·ga·mien·to m. *(asfixia)* suffocation, asphyxiation; *(en agua)* drowning; FIG. *(aprieto)* tight spot, hard time.

a·ho·gan·te adj. *(en agua)* drowning; *(sofocante)* stifling, suffocating.

a·ho·gar §47 tr. *(sofocar)* to suffocate, choke, smother; *(en agua)* to drown; *(extinguir)* to extinguish, put out <*a. la lumbre* to put out the fire>; *(en el ajedrez)* to stalemate (in chess); FIG. *(oprimir)* to oppress, overwhelm; AGR. to drown, soak (plants); S. AMER. to stew —reflex. *(sentir sofocación)* to suffocate, choke; *(en agua)* to drown; FIG. to feel oppressed *or* overwhelmed ♦ **ahogarse en un vaso de agua** FIG. to make a mountain out of a molehill.

a·ho·go m. *(falta de aliento)* shortness of breath; FIG. *(angustia)* anguish, distress; *(aprieto)* difficulty, tight spot; *(falta de recursos)* need, poverty; COL. stewing sauce.

a·hom·bra·do, –da I. past part. see **ahombrarse** II. adj. COLL. manly, mannish.

a·hom·brar·se reflex. COLL. to become mannish *or* masculine.

a·hon·da·mien·to m. *(profundización)* deepening, digging; FIG. *(investigación)* investigation, probe.

a·hon·dar tr. *(profundizar)* to dig, deepen; FIG. *(investigar)* to investigate, probe —intr. *(penetrar)* to go deep, penetrate; FIG. *(investigar)* to study thoroughly —reflex. to go deep, penetrate.

a·ho·ra I. adv. *(actualmente)* now; *(pronto)* soon, very soon <*a. le llamaré* I will call him very soon>; FIG. *(hace poco)* just now, a few minutes ago <*a. me lo han dicho* they told me about it just now> ♦ **a. bien** *or* **a. pues** well, now then • **a. mismo** right now • **hasta ahora** until now • **por a.** for the time being II. conj. now then, well then ♦ **a. que** however, but <*el sueldo es escaso, a. que no hay que trabajar mucho* the salary is low, but you don't have to work hard>.

a·hor·ca·do, –da I. past part. see **ahorcar** II. m.f. hanged person.

a·hor·ca·du·ra f. hanging.

a·hor·ca·jar·se reflex. to sit astride, straddle.

a·hor·car §70 tr. *(estrangular)* to hang, kill by hanging; FIG. *(dejar)* to give up, abandon <*a. los estudios* to abandon one's studies> —reflex *(colgarse)* to hang oneself.

a·ho·ri·ta adv. COLL. right now, this minute.

a·hor·mar tr. *(ajustar)* to mold, fit; *(usar)* to break in (clothes, shoes); FIG. *(amoldar)* to mold (a person's character); TAUR. to bring into position for the kill.

a·hor·na·gar·se §47 reflex. *(secarse)* to become parched, dry out (land); *(marchitarse)* to wither (vegetation).

a·hor·nar tr. to put in the oven —reflex. to bake *or* burn on the outside only.

a·hor·qué, ahorque see **ahorcar.**

a·hor·qui·llar tr. AGR. to stay *or* prop up (with forks); *(dar forma de horquilla)* to shape like a fork.

a·ho·rra·do, –da I. past part. see **ahorrar** II. adj. *(libre)* free; *(económico)* thrifty, economical.

a·ho·rra·dor, –do·ra I. m.f. economizer, saver II. adj. economizing, thrifty.

a·ho·rrar tr. *(guardar)* save, put aside <*a. dinero* to save money>; FIG. *(evitar)* to save, spare <*a. palabras* to save words>; *(liberar)* to emancipate, free —reflex. to save *or* spare oneself <*ahorrarse molestias* to save oneself the trouble>; AMER. to fail; ECUAD. to shirk, refuse work.

a·ho·rra·ti·vo, –va adj. *(frugal)* thrifty, frugal; *(mezquino)* stingy, miserly.

a·ho·rro m. *(accion)* saving; *(economía)* economy, thrift ♦ **ahorros** savings.

a·ho·ya·du·ra f. *(acción de cavar)* excavation, digging holes; *(hoyo)* hole (in ground).

a·ho·yar intr. to dig holes.

a·hu·cha·dor, –do·ra I. adj. hoarding II. m.f. hoarder.

a·hu·char §82 tr. *(guardar)* to hoard; FIG. *(conservar en sitio seguro)* to keep in a safe place; AMER. *(azuzar)* to sic, set the dogs on (someone); *(incitar)* to incite.

a·hue·ca·do, –da I. past part. see **ahuecar** II. adj. *(vacío)* hollow, empty; *(mullido)* fluffed up, loosened; *(la voz)* deep.

a·hue·ca·mien·to m. *(el dejar hueco)* hollowing-out; *(el mullir)* fluffing-up (pillow, wool); FIG. *(engreimiento)* conceit, vanity.

a·hue·car §70 tr. *(vaciar)* to hollow out, empty; *(mullir)* to fluff up, loosen <*a. la lana* to fluff up wool>; FIG. *(la voz)* to make deep *or* pompous (the voice) —intr. ♦ **a. el ala** COLL. to beat it, split —reflex. FIG., COLL. to put on airs, become puffed up.

a·hue·sa·do, –da I. past part. see **ahuesarse** II. adj. *(amarillento)* bone-colored; *(duro)* bony, bone-like.

a·hue·sar·se reflex. AMER., COM. to become useless *or* worthless (goods); GUAT. to become very thin.

a·hue·va·do, –da I. past part. see **ahuevar** II. adj. eggshaped III. m. egg-shaped ornament.

a·hue·var tr. *(dar forma)* to make egg-shaped; *(clarificar)* to clarify (wine) with egg white.

a·hu·ma·do, –da I. past part. see **ahumar** II. adj. *(lleno de humo)* smoky, smoke-filled; *(color)* smoke-colored; CUL. *(acecinado)* smoked, cured III. m. CUL. smoking, curing —f. smoke signal.

a·hu·mar tr. CUL. to smoke, cure; *(llenar de humo)* to fill with smoke, make smoky —intr. to fume, smoke —reflex. CUL. to be smoked *or* cured; *(llenarse de humo)* to be smoky; *(ennegrecerse)* to be blackened by smoke; COLL. *(embriagarse)* to get drunk ♦ **ahumársele a uno el pescado** FIG., COLL. to get all steamed up *or* annoyed.

a·hu·sa·mien·to m. tapering.

a·hu·sar tr. & reflex. to taper.

a·hu·yen·ta·dor, –do·ra I. adj. scary II. m.f. scarecrow.

a·hu·yen·tar tr. *(hacer huir)* to drive *or* scare away; FIG. *(desechar)* to banish, dismiss <*a. un pensamiento* to dismiss a thought> —reflex. to flee, turn away.

ai·ma·rá I. adj. Aymaran II. m.f. Aymara (South American Indian).

ain·dia·do, –da adj. Indian-like, having American Indian features.

ai·ra·da·men·te adv. angrily, irately.

ai·ra·do, –da I. past part. see **airar** II. adj. *(enfadado)* angry, irate; FIG. *(depravado)* loose, depraved.

ai·rar §81 tr. to anger, annoy.

ai·re m. air; *(viento)* wind; *(atmósfera)* atmosphere; *(de los caballos)* gait, pace (of horses); FIG. *(apariencia)* air, appearance, aura; *(gracia)* grace, elegance; *(vanidad)* vanity; MUS. air, tune; MED., COLL. crick, stiff neck; PARA. paralysis ♦ **a. acondicionado** air conditioning • **al a. libre** in the open air • **darse aires** to put on airs • **darse un a. a** to resemble • **de buen a.** in a good mood • **de mal a.** in a bad mood • **estar en el a.** RAD., TELEV. to be on the air; FIG. to be up in the air • **tomar el a.** FIG. to take a stroll.

ai·re·a·ción f. ventilation, air circulation.

ai·re·a·do, –da I. past part. see **airear** II. adj. *(ventilado)* ventilated, aired out; CUL. *(agrio)* sour, bitter.

ai·re·ar tr. *(ventilar)* to ventilate, aerate; *(discutir)* to discuss, air out —reflex. *(refrescarse)* to take in the air; MED. to come down with *or* catch a cold.

ai·re·o m. airing, ventilation.

ai·rón m. ORNITH. crested heron; *(penacho)* crest, tuft (on birds); *(adorno)* panache, crest (on hat, helmet); *(pozo)* very deep well ♦ **al a.** CUBA at a gallop.

ai·ro·sa·men·te adv. gracefully, elegantly.

ai·ro·si·dad f. grace, elegance.

ai·ro·so, –sa adj. *(ventoso)* airy, windy; FIG. *(gentil)* graceful, elegant; *(ingenioso)* neat, clever.

ais·la·ble adj. isolable, isolatable; ELEC. insulatable.

ais·la·cio·nis·mo m. POL. isolationism.

ais·la·cio·nis·ta adj. & m.f. POL. isolationist.

ais·la·do, –da I. past part. see **aislar** II. adj. *(independiente)* isolated, separated <*un caso a.* an isolated case>; *(solo)* alone, in isolation <*vivir a.* to live alone>; *(apartado)* isolated, remote <*una región a.* an isolated area>; ELEC. insulated.

ais·la·dor, –do·ra I. m. ELEC., PHYS. insulator, isolator II. adj. *(apartador)* isolating, separating; ELEC., PHYS. insulating, isolating.

ais·la·mien·to m. *(apartamiento)* isolation, insulation; FIG. *(retiro)* isolation, seclusion <*vivir en a.* to live in isolation>.

ais·lan·te I. m.f. insulator, isolator II. adj. insulating, isolating.

ais·lar §81 tr. *(apartar)* to isolate, set apart; FIG. *(retirar)* to isolate, seclude; ELEC., PHYS. *(insular)* to insulate, isolate; *(cercar de agua)* to surround with water —reflex. to isolate oneself, withdraw.

¡a·já! interj. *(para expresar aprobación)* sure!, great!; *(para expresar sorpresa)* aha!

a·ja·mo·nar·se reflex. COLL. to run to fat, get middle-age spread.

a·jar tr. *(arrugar)* to crumple, wrinkle; *(deslucir)* to fade, dull; FIG. *(injuriar)* to abuse, insult —reflex. *(arrugarse)* to get crumpled *or* wrinkled; FIG. *(ofenderse)* to be insulted; BOT. to wither, fade.

a·je·dre·cis·ta I. m.f. chess player II. adj. (pertaining to) chess.

a·je·drez m. *(juego)* chess; *(conjunto de piezas)* chess set; MARIT. netting, grating.

a·jen·jo m. BOT. absinthe, wormwood; *(bebida)* absinthe.

a·je·no, –na adj. *(de otro)* another's, someone else's <*los bienes ajenos* someone else's property>; *(extraño)* foreign, alien; *(diverso)* different, distinct; FIG. *(libre)* free, devoid <*a. de cuidados* free from care>; *(impropio)* inappropriate, unsuitable ♦ **a. de sí** detached, aloof.

a·je·tre·ar tr. & reflex. *(apresurar)* to rush, hurry; *(fatigar)* to tire.

a·je·tre·o m. *(prisa)* bustle, rush; *(cansancio)* fatigue, weariness.

a·jí m. [pl. **a·jí·es**] BOT. chili pepper; CUL. *(salsa)* chili sauce; CUBA uproar, commotion ♦ **ponerse como a.** AMER. to turn as red as a beet, blush.

a·ji·li·mo·je *or* **a·ji·li·mó·ji·li** m. pepper, garlic, and vinegar sauce ♦ **ajilimójilis** COLL. bits and pieces • **con todos sus ajilimójilis** with all the trimmings *or* the works.

a·ji·llo m. BOT. young garlic ♦ **al a.** CUL. highly seasoned with garlic.

a·ji·se·co m. PERU dried red pepper.

a·jo m. *(planta)* garlic; *(diente)* garlic clove; *(salsa)* garlic sauce; FIG., COLL. *(negocio)* secret deal ♦ **andar** *or* **estar en el a.** FIG. to be in the know • **revolver el a.** FIG. to stir up trouble • **soltar ajos y cebollas** FIG. to curse, swear.

a·jo·bar tr. to carry on one's back.

a·jo·bo m. *(acción de ajobar)* carrying on one's back; *(carga)* burden, load; FIG. *(trabajo)* burden, chore.

a·jon·jo·lí m. [pl. **-lí·es**] BOT. sesame (plant *or* seed).

a·jor·ca f. JEWEL. bracelet, anklet.

a·jor·na·lar tr. to hire by the day.

a·jo·tar tr. C. AMER. to torment, harass.

a·juar m. *(muebles)* furnishings, household furniture; *(de la novia)* trousseau.

a·jui·cia·do, –da I. past part. see **ajuiciar** II. adj. wise, sensible.

a·jui·ciar tr. *(hacer juicioso)* to make wise *or* sensible; *(enjuiciar)* to judge.

a·jus·ta·do, –da I. past part. see **ajustar** II. adj. *(justo)* just, fair; *(apretado)* tight.

a·jus·ta·mien·to m. adjustment; COM. settlement.

a·jus·tar tr. *(modificar)* to alter, fit <*el sastre ajustó el vestido* the tailor altered the dress>; *(adaptar)* to adapt, adjust; *(arreglar)* to arrange <*a. un matrimonio* to arrange a marriage>; *(reconciliar)* to reconcile <*a. a los contrincantes* to reconcile the opponents>; *(precios)* to fix (prices); *(contra-*

tar) to contract, hire <*a. a un criado* to hire a servant>; COM. (*liquidar*) to settle (accounts); (*asestar*) to deal, give <*le ajustaron un golpe* they dealt him a blow>; PRINT. (*justificar*) to justify (type); MECH. (*encajar*) to fit; AMER. to catch, come down with (an illness); COL. to scrimp ♦ **a. las cuentas** to settle accounts —intr. to be tight —reflex. (*conformarse*) to adjust, conform; (*ponerse de acuerdo*) to come to an agreement.

a·jus·te m. adjustment; (*modificación*) alteration; (*adaptación*) adaptation; (*arreglo*) arrangement, agreement; (*conciliación*) reconciliation; COM. settlement; PRINT. justification; MECH. (*encaje*) fitting; GUAT., SALV. tip, gratuity.

a·jus·ti·cia·do, –da I. past part. see **ajusticiar** II. m.f. executed criminal.

a·jus·ti·cia·mien·to m. execution, death by capital punishment.

a·jus·ti·ciar tr. to execute (a criminal), inflict capital punishment on.

al §G16 [contr. of **a** and **el**] to the <*voy al museo* I am going to the museum>; at the <*al final* at the end>; on, upon <*al entrar* upon entering> ♦ **al momento** immediately, at once.

a·la f. ORNITH. wing; (*parte lateral*) wing <*el a. de un avión* the wing of a plane>; (*fila*) row, line; (*del sombrero*) brim; FIG. (*amparo*) protection, wing; ARCHIT. (*alero*) eave; POL. wing, faction <*a. derecha* right wing>; MARIT. sail; MECH. (*hélice*) blade; SPORT. (*en los deportes*) wing; ANAT. ala ♦ **a. del corazón** ANAT. auricle • **caérsele las alas** FIG. to lose one's nerve • **cortarle las alas** FIG. to discourage, clip someone's wings • **dar alas a** FIG. to encourage • **tomar alas** FIG. to try one's wings.

A·lá m. RELIG. Allah.

a·la·ba·dor, –do·ra I. adj. praising, laudatory II. m.f. praiser, lauder.

a·la·ban·ce·ro, –ra COLL. I. adj. flattering II. m.f. flatterer.

a·la·ban·cio·so, –sa adj. COLL. boastful, bragging.

a·la·ban·za f. (*encomio*) praise; (*elogio*) eulogy ♦ **cantar las alabanzas de** to sing the praises of.

a·la·bar tr. to praise, laud —intr. C. AMER., RELIG. to sing the dawn or "Alabado" hymn —reflex. (*contentarse*) to be glad or pleased; (*jactarse*) to boast, brag.

a·la·bas·tro m. MIN. alabaster; FIG. (*blancura*) alabaster, whiteness.

a·la·be·ar tr. & reflex. to warp (wood).

a·la·ce·na f. cupboard, closet.

a·la·crán m. ZOOL. scorpion, arachnid; SEW. (*asilla*) button hook or extender; EQUIT. (*anillo*) bridle ring; ARG. gossipmonger.

a·la·cri·dad f. alacrity, eagerness.

a·la·da I. f. fluttering of the wing (in birds) II. adj. see **alado, –da.**

a·la·da·res m.pl. locks of hair falling over the temples.

a·la·do, –da I. adj. ORINTH., ZOOL. winged, flying <*un insecto a.* a winged insect>; FIG. (*rápido*) swift, quick; BOT. (*con forma de alas*) alate, wing-shaped II. f. see **alada.**

a·la·gar·ta·do, –da adj. motley, variegated.

a·la·mar m. (*presilla*) frog, clasp; (*cairel*) fringe, trimming.

a·lam·bi·ca·do, –da I. past part. see **alambicar** II. adj. FIG. (*dado con escasez*) doled out, given sparingly; (*sutil*) precious, subtle.

a·lam·bi·ca·mien·to m. (*destilación*) distillation; FIG. (*sutileza*) excessive subtlety.

a·lam·bi·car §70 tr. (*destilar*) to distill; FIG. (*volver demasiado sutil*) to overrefine; (*examinar*) to scrutinize; (*los precios*) to slash (prices).

a·lam·bi·que m. CUL. still, alembic ♦ **pasar por el a.** FIG. to scrutinize, go over with a fine-toothed comb • **por a.** sparingly.

a·lam·bra·da f. wire netting.

a·lam·bra·do I. past part. see **alambrar** II. m. (*alambrera*) wire-mesh screen; (*cerco*) wire fence or fencing.

a·lam·brar tr. (*guarnecer*) to wire; (*cercar*) to fence in or surround with wire.

a·lam·bre m. wire, metallic thread or cable ♦ **a. de púas** barbed wire.

a·lam·bris·ta m.f. tightrope walker, high-wire acrobat.

a·la·me·da f. BOT. poplar grove; (*paseo*) boulevard, tree-lined avenue.

á·la·mo m. BOT. poplar.

a·lan·ce·a·do, –da I. past part. see **alancear** II. adj. (*herido*) wounded, speared; BOT. lanceolate.

a·lan·ce·ar tr. (*dar lanzadas*) to spear; (*zaherir*) to criticize, reproach.

a·lan·zar §04 tr. to spear, wound.

a·lar m. ARCHIT. (*del tejado*) eave; COL. sidewalk.

a·lar·de m. MIL. review, parade; FIG. (*ostentación*) show, display ♦ **hacer a. de** to make a show or display of.

a·lar·de·ar intr. to boast, brag.

a·lar·de·o m. boasting bragging.

a·lar·do·so, –sa adj. boastful, ostentatious, showy.

a·lar·ga·dor, –do·ra adj. lengthening, extending.

a·lar·ga·mien·to m. (*acción de alargar*) lengthening; (*extensión*) length, extension.

a·lar·gar §47 tr. (*dar más longitud*) to lengthen, make longer; (*extender*) to extend, prolong <*a. la vida* to prolong life>; (*estirar*) to stretch (out); (*entregar*) to hand, pass <*alárgame el libro* pass me the book>; (*soltar poco a poco*) to play out (rope); FIG. (*aumentar*) to increase, augment <*a. el sueldo* to increase one's salary> —reflex. to lengthen, get longer <*las noches se alargan* the nights are getting longer>; (*apartarse*) to go away, leave; FIG. (*ampliar*) to elaborate, enlarge upon.

a·la·ri·do m. yell, howl ♦ **dar alaridos** to yell, howl.

a·la·ri·fe m. (*maestro*) master builder; MIN. bricklayer; ARG. clever or crafty person.

a·lar·ma f. (*rebato*) alarm; MIL. call to arms; (*inquietud*) fright, anxiety ♦ **a. aérea** air-raid warning • **a. de incendios** fire alarm • **dar la a.** to give or sound the alarm.

a·lar·ma·dor, –do·ra or **a·lar·man·te** adj. alarming.

a·lar·mar tr. (*alertar*) to alarm, alert; MIL. to call to arms, rouse; (*asustar*) to frighten, alarm —reflex. to become alarmed or frightened.

a·lar·mis·mo m. alarmism.

a·lar·mis·ta adj. & m.f. alarmist.

a·la·zán, –za·na adj. & m.f. sorrel, chestnut.

al·ba I. f. (*amanecer*) dawn, daybreak; RELIG. alb ♦ **al a.** at dawn • **al romper el a.** at daybreak or dawn II. adj. see **albo, –ba.**

al·ba·ce·a m. LAW executor —f. executrix.

al·ba·ne·ga f. (*redecilla*) hair net; (*caza*) rabbit net.

al·ba·nés, –ne·sa adj. & m.f. Albanian —m. (*idioma*) Albanian.

Al·ba·nia f. Albania.

al·ba·ñal m. (*alcantarilla*) sewer, drain; (*letrina*) cesspool; FIG. (*suciedad*) filth ♦ **salir por el a.** FIG., COLL. to turn out badly.

al·ba·ñil m. bricklayer, mason.

al·ba·ñi·le·rí·a f. (*arte*) bricklaying; (*producto*) brickwork, masonry.

al·bar I. adj. white II. m. dry whitish land.

al·ba·ra·za·do, –da adj. MED. leprous; (*blanquecino*) whitish; MEX. of Chinese-Indian descent.

al·ba·ra·zo m. MED. white leprosy.

al·bar·da f. (*de una caballería*) packsaddle; (*de tocino*) strip of bacon; AMER. (*silla de montar*) saddle.

al·bar·di·lla f. (*silla de montar*) training saddle; (*almohadilla*) small cushion; (*en un huerto o un camino*) ridge (of earth); (*tejadillo*) coping; (*de tocino*) strip of fatback.

al·ba·ri·co·que m. apricot (tree and fruit).

al·ba·ri·zo m. FIG. whitish II. m. white earth.

al·ba·rra·da f. (*pared*) dry stone wall; (*parata*) earthen terrace; (*cerca*) earthwork, barricade; (*alcarraza*) clay bottle.

al·ba·tros m. [pl. **-tros**] ORNITH. albatross.

al·ba·yal·de m. CHEM. white lead.

al·be·ar intr. (*blanquear*) to whiten; ARG. to get up early.

al·be·drí·o m. will <*libre a.* free will>; (*capricho*) whim, fancy; (*costumbre*) unwritten law or precedent ♦ **al a. de uno** at one's pleasure, to suit oneself • **rendir el a.** to submit, give in.

al·ber·ca f. (*tanque*) reservoir, tank; (*poza para cáñamo*) retting pit or vat; MEX. swimming pool.

al·ber·gar §47 tr. (*alojar*) to lodge, give shelter to, house <*el colegio alberga a cincuenta estudiantes* the dormitory houses fifty students>; FIG. *(una esperanza)* to harbor, cherish; *(una duda)* to harbor —intr. & reflex. *(alojarse)* to stay, take lodgings; *(refugiarse)* to take shelter.

al·ber·gue m. *(alojamiento)* lodgings; *(refugio)* shelter, refuge; *(de un animal)* den, lair ♦ **a. de jóvenes** youth hostel.

al·ber·gue·rí·a f. *(posada)* inn; *(asilo)* poorhouse.

al·bi·can·te adj. whitening, bleaching.

al·bi·nis·mo m. MED. albinism.

al·bi·no, –na I. adj. albino II. m.f. MED. albino; MEX. half-breed; DOM. REP. half-caste, light-skinned Black.

al·bo, –ba I. adj. POET. white II. f. see **alba.**

al·bón·di·ga f. meatball.

al·bor m. *(blancura)* whiteness; *(alba)* dawn, daybreak; FIG. *(principio)* beginning ♦ **a.** *or* **albores de la vida** FIG. infancy, youth • **a los albores** at dawn.

al·bo·ra·da f. *(alba)* dawn; MIL. *(ataque)* dawn attack; *(toque)* reveille; POET., MUS. aubade, dawn song.

al·bo·re·ar intr. to dawn.

al·bor·noz m. [pl. **-no·ces**] *(capa)* burnoose (hooded woolen cap); *(bata)* bathrobe.

al·bo·ro·cé, alboroce see **alborozar.**

al·bo·ro·ta·da·men·te adv. *(agitadamente)* excitedly; *(ruidosamente)* noisily, boisterously.

al·bo·ro·ta·do, –da adj. *(agitado)* excited, agitated; *(ruidoso)* noisy, rowdy; *(atolondrado)* impetuous, rash; *(amotinado)* riotous, mutinous; *(el mar)* rough, choppy.

al·bo·ro·ta·dor, –do·ra I. adj. *(rebelde)* rebellious; *(ruidoso)* noisy, rowdy II. m.f. *(instigador)* agitator, troublemaker; *(amotinador)* rioter, mutineer; *(niño)* unruly child.

al·bo·ro·ta·pue·blos m.f. *(alborotador)* agitator, rabblerouser; COLL. *(persona bullanguera)* life of the party.

al·bo·ro·tar tr. *(agitar)* to excite, agitate; *(incitar)* to incite; ARG. *(causar curiosidad)* to excite *or* arouse the curiosity of; *(enredar)* to involve —intr. to make noise *or* racket —reflex. *(agitarse)* to get excited *or* agitated; *(rebelarse)* to riot, mutiny; *(el mar)* to become rough *or* choppy; C. AMER. to become amorous; ARG., CHILE to rear up (horses).

al·bo·ro·to m. *(jaleo)* uproar; *(ruido)* racket, din; *(motín)* riot, brawl; *(susto)* scare, fright; MEX. *(alegría)* joy, jubilation ♦ **alborotos** C. AMER. popcorn.

al·bo·ro·za·da·men·te adv. joyfully, jubilantly.

al·bo·ro·za·do, –da I. past part. see **alborozar** II. adj. jubilant, overjoyed.

al·bo·ro·za·dor, –do·ra I. adj. cheering, heartening II. m.f. one who brings cheer *or* joy.

al·bo·ro·zar §04 tr. to delight, gladden —reflex. to be overjoyed *or* elated, rejoice.

al·bo·ro·zo m. joy, jubilation.

al·bri·cias I. interj. great!, congratulations! II. f.pl. *(regalo)* gift; *(premio)* reward (for bringing good news); AMER., METAL. air vents (in casting mold) ♦ **dar a.** to congratulate.

al·bu·fe·ra f. lagoon.

al·bu·he·ra f. *(albufera)* lagoon; *(estanque)* reservoir, pool.

ál·bum m. [pl. **-bums** *or* **-bu·mes**] album ♦ **a. de recortes** scrapbook.

al·bu·men m. BIOL. albumen; *(clara)* egg white.

al·bú·mi·na f. CHEM. albumin.

al·bur m. FIG. *(riesgo)* risk, hazard; *(naipes)* first two draws (in monte); ICHTH. bleak; MEX. pun; P. RICO lie ♦ **albures** lansquenet (card game) • **jugar** *or* **correr un a.** to take a risk.

al·bu·ra f. *(blancura)* whiteness; *(clara)* egg white; BOT. alburnam, sapwood.

al·ca·cho·fa f. BOT. artichoke (plant and fruit); *(de ducha, de regadera)* nozzle, head; *(pan)* sandwich bread; MECH. filter, strainer.

al·ca·hue·te, –ta m.f. FIG., COLL. *(chismoso)* gossip; *(encubridor)* fence, receiver of stolen goods; AMER. informer —m. *(proxeneta)* procurer, pimp; THEAT. intermission curtain —f. procuress, madam.

al·ca·hue·te·ar tr. to procure —intr. *(servir de alcahuete)* to procure, pimp; *(chismear)* to gossip; *(encubrir)* to be a receiver of stolen goods.

al·ca·hue·te·rí·a f. *(acción de alcahuetear)* procuring, pimping; FIG., COLL. *(triquiñela)* trick, scheme.

al·cai·ce·rí·a f. silk district *or* exchange.

al·ca·lá m. ARCH. citadel, fortress.

al·cal·de m. *(oficial)* mayor; *(naipes)* card game; S. AMER. procurer, pimp ♦ **a. de monterilla** small-town mayor • **a. mayor** magistrate • **tener el padre a.** FIG. to have influence.

al·cal·dí·a f. *(cargo)* mayoralty, mayorship; *(casa)* mayoral residence; *(oficina)* mayor's office.

ál·ca·li m. CHEM. alkali ♦ **a. volátil** ammonia.

al·ca·li·ni·dad f. CHEM. alkalinity.

al·ca·li·no, –na adj. CHEM. alkaline.

al·ca·loi·de m. CHEM. alkaloid.

al·can·ce m. *(distancia)* reach, arm's length <*el vaso no está a mi a.* the glass is not within my reach>; *(extensión)* range, scope <*el a. de un cañón* the range of a cannon>; *(persecución)* pursuit, chase; *(novedades)* latest news; *(talento)* talent, ability <*ella es una mujer de mucho a.* she is a woman of much talent>; PRINT. typesetting copy; SP. special delivery, express ♦ **a.** accessible • **al a. de** within reach of • **al a. del oído** within earshot • **dar a. a** to catch up with • **de gran a.** FIG. far-reaching • **tener alcances** to have ability.

al·can·cé, alcance see **alcanzar.**

al·can·cí·a f. *(hucha)* coin bank, piggy bank; AMER., RELIG. collection box.

al·can·for m. camphor.

al·can·fo·rar tr. to camphorate —reflex. AMER. to disappear, vanish.

al·can·ta·ri·lla f. *(cloaca)* sewer, drain; *(en un camino)* culvert; *(puentecillo)* small bridge; MEX. *(depósito)* water tank; MEX., VEN. *(fuente)* fountain.

al·can·ta·ri·lla·do I. past part. see **alcantarillar** II. m. sewers, drains.

al·can·ta·ri·llar tr. to lay sewers in (a street), provide (a building, neighborhood) with drains *or* sewers.

al·can·za·do, –da I. past part. see **alcanzar** II. adj. *(adeudado)* in debt, in arrears; *(falto)* needy, short of money; COL. wearied, fatigued.

al·can·zar §04 tr. *(llegar hasta)* to reach, overtake <*alcanzó al general* he overtook the general>; *(tomar)* to take hold of, grasp <*alcancé el plato* I took hold of the plate>; *(estirar)* to reach up to <*a. el techo* to reach up to the ceiling>; FIG. *(conseguir)* to attain, obtain <*a. su deseo* to attain one's goal>; *(comprender)* to understand, grasp <*no alcanzo lo que me dices* I don't understand what you are telling me>; to catch up with <*a. a uno en los estudios* to catch up with someone in one's studies>; *(percibir)* to take in, reach (with the senses); AMER. to pass, hand over —intr. *(llegar hasta)* to reach; FIG. *(gastar)* to be sufficient *or* enough <*las provisiones alcanzarán* the provisions will be sufficient> ♦ **a. a** to manage to, be able to <*no alcanzo a verlo* I am not able to see it>.

al·ca·pa·rra f. BOT. caper (plant and fruit).

al·ca·pa·rra·do, –da adj. dressed with capers.

al·ca·ra·ve·a m. BOT. caraway.

al·ca·rra·za f. clay water jug.

al·ca·traz m. [pl. **-tra·ces**] ORNITH. gannet, pelican; BOT. arum.

al·cau·cil m. BOT. artichoke.

al·cá·zar m. *(fortaleza)* castle, fortress; *(palacio)* royal palace; MARIT. quarter-deck.

al·ce[1] m. ZOOL. elk, moose.

al·ce[2] m. *(en los naipes)* cut (in cards) ♦ **no dar alce a alguien** ARG. to give someone no rest.

al·cé, alce see **alzar.**

al·cis·ta FIN. I. m.f. bull (in the stock market) II. adj. bull, bullish <*mercado a.* bull market>.

al·co·ba f. *(dormitorio)* bedroom; *(muebles)* bedroom suite; *(de una balanza)* pointer case.

al·co·fa f. wicker basket.

al·co·hol m. CHEM. alcohol <*a. metílico* methyl alcohol>; *(aguardiente)* alcohol, spirits; *(polvo)* kohl; MIN. galena ♦ **a. de grano** grain alcohol • **a. etílico** ethyl alcohol.

al·co·ho·li·cé, alcoholice see **alcoholizar.**

al·co·hó·li·co, –ca adj. & m.f. alcoholic.

al·co·ho·lí·me·tro m. alcoholometer.

al·co·ho·lis·mo m. alcoholism.

al·co·ho·li·za·ción f. alcoholization.

al·co·ho·li·za·do, –da I. past part. see **alcoholizar** II. adj. suffering from alcoholism III. m.f. alcoholic.

al·co·ho·li·zar §04 tr. to alcoholize —reflex. to become an alcoholic.

al·cor m. hill.

al·cor·no·que m. BOT. cork oak; FIG. *(necio)* blockhead, dummy.

al·cor·zar §04 tr. to frost, ice (a cake).

al·co·ta·na f. pickaxe.

al·cu·bi·lla f. tank, reservoir.

al·cu·ce·ro, –ra I. adj. FIG., COLL. greedy, gluttonous II. m.f. oil seller.

al·cur·nia f. ancestry, lineage ♦ **de noble a.** of noble birth.

al·cu·za f. *(vasija)* oil bottle *or* container; S. AMER. cruet.

al·da·ba f. *(picaporte)* (door) knocker; *(barra)* crossbar, bolt; *(de caballería)* hitching ring ♦ **tener buenas aldabas** FIG., COLL. to have influence, have pull.

al·da·ba·da f. *(toque)* knock; FIG. *(susto)* fright, scare ♦ **dar aldabadas** to knock.

al·da·ba·zo m. knock, knocking.

al·da·be·ar intr. to knock at *or* on the door.

al·da·be·o m. knocking, rapping.

al·da·bi·lla f. latch, catch.

al·da·bón m. *(picaporte)* large knocker (of a door); *(asa)* large handle.

al·da·bo·na·zo m. loud knock (on a door).

al·de·a f. village, hamlet.

al·de·a·no, –na I. adj. village <*costumbres aldeanas* village customs>; FIG. *(campesino)* rustic, peasant II. m.f. *(habitante)* villager; FIG. *(campesino)* peasant.

al·de·rre·dor adv. var. of **alrededor.**

a·le m. ale.

¡a·le! interj. come on!, let's go!

a·le·a·ción f. METAL. alloy.

a·le·ar¹ intr. ORNITH. to flap, flutter; FIG. *(recobrar)* to get better, convalesce.

a·le·ar² tr. METAL. to alloy.

a·le·a·to·rio, –ria adj. aleatory, contingent <*un contrato a.* an aleatory contract>; *(incierto)* uncertain.

a·le·brar·se reflex. *(agazaparse)* to throw oneself on the ground; FIG. *(acobardarse)* to become frightened.

a·lec·cio·na·dor, –do·ra adj. instructive, enlightening.

a·lec·cio·na·mien·to m. instruction, training.

a·lec·cio·nar tr. *(enseñar)* to instruct, teach; *(amaestrar)* to train.

a·le·da·ño, –ña I. adj. bordering, adjoining II. m. boundary, border ♦ **aledaños** outskirts.

a·le·ga·ble adj. allegeable.

a·le·ga·ción f. allegation; AMER. argument.

a·le·gar §47 tr. *(citar)* to allege, contend; *(aseverar)* to affirm, claim; AMER. to dispute —intr. to argue (a case).

a·le·ga·to m. *(de un abogado)* argument; *(razonamiento)* allegation, argument; AMER. argument.

a·le·go·rí·a f. allegory.

a·le·gó·ri·ca·men·te adv. allegorically.

a·le·gó·ri·co, –ca adj. allegorical, allegoric.

a·le·grar tr. *(regocijar)* to cheer, gladden <*su visita nos alegró* his visit cheered us>; FIG. *(avivar)* to enliven, brighten <*el sol alegra las calles* the sun brightens the streets>; MARIT. to loosen (cables); TAUR. to incite —reflex. *(sentir alegría)* to be cheered *or* gladdened <*alegrarse por una noticia* to be cheered by the news>; to be happy, be glad <*me alegro de oírlo* I am happy to hear it>; FIG., COLL. *(achisparse)* to get tipsy *or* lit.

a·le·gre adj. *(regocijado)* happy, glad; *(jovial)* cheerful, sunny (disposition); FIG., COLL. *(vivo)* lively, bright (colors); *(achispado)* tipsy, lit; risqué, racy <*un cuento a.* a racy story>; *(ligero)* daring, bold, reckless.

a·le·gre·men·te adv. happily, cheerfully.

a·le·gre·to m. MUS. allegretto.

a·le·grí·a f. *(regocijo)* happiness, gladness; *(jovialidad)* cheerfulness, joy; FIG., COLL. *(ligereza)* daring, boldness, recklessness; BOT. sesame ♦ **alegrías** *(regocijos)* festivities; *(baile)* flamenco dance.

a·le·gro m. MUS. allegro.

a·le·grón, –gro·na I. adj. AMER. *(alegre)* merry, cheerful; *(coquetón)* flirtatious II. m. COLL. *(alegría)* sudden joy; *(llamarada)* flare-up, burst of flame; MEX. fall corn har-

vest —f. AMER. *(coquetona)* flirt; *(prostituta)* prostitute, whore.

a·le·gué, alegue see **alegar.**

a·le·ja·do, –da I. past part. see **alejar** II. adj. distant, remote.

a·le·ja·mien·to m. *(acción de alejar)* removal; *(acción de alejarse)* withdrawal, going away; *(enajenación)* estrangement; *(distancia)* distance, remoteness.

A·le·jan·drí·a f. Alexandria.

a·le·jan·dri·no adj. & m. POET. alexandrine, Alexandrine.

a·le·jar tr. FIG. *(poner lejos)* to put farther away; *(enajenar)* to estrange, alienate —reflex. *(irse)* to move away, go away; *(apartarse)* to withdraw, retreat.

a·le·la·do, –da I. past part. see **alelar** II. adj. stupefied, bewildered.

a·le·lar tr. to stupefy, bewilder —reflex. to be stupefied *or* bewildered.

a·le·lí m. [pl. **-lí·es**] BOT. wallflower, stock.

¡a·le·lu·ya! interj. alleluia!, hallelujah!

a·le·mán, –ma·na adj. & m.f. German —m. *(idioma)* German.

A·le·ma·na, República Democrática f. German Democratic Republic.

A·le·ma·nia f. Germany ♦ **A. Occidental** West Germany • **A. Oriental** East Germany.

A·le·ma·nia, República Federal de f. Federal Republic of Germany.

a·len·ta·do, –da I. past part. see **alentar** II. adj. *(animoso)* brave, gallant; *(soberbio)* proud, haughty; AMER. *(robusto)* healthy; *(aliviado)* recovered (from an illness) III. f. long breath.

a·len·ta·dor, –do·ra adj. encouraging.

a·len·tar §49 intr. to breathe —tr. *(animar)* to encourage, inspire; COL., ECUAD. *(palmotear)* to applaud; C. AMER., COL. *(dar a luz)* to give birth to —reflex. *(animarse)* to be encouraged; *(reponerse)* to recover (from an illness).

a·le·o·na·do, –da adj. tawny.

a·ler·gia f. allergy.

a·lér·gi·co, –ca I. adj. allergic ♦ **ser a. a** to be allergic to II. m.f. allergy sufferer.

a·le·ro m. *(tejado)* eaves; *(carruaje)* fender.

a·le·rón m. AVIA. aileron.

a·ler·ta I. adv. alertly, vigilantly ♦ **¡alerta!** watch out! • **estar a.** to be on the alert II. f. alert, warning III. adj. see **alerto, –ta.**

a·ler·ta·men·te adv. alertly, vigilantly.

a·ler·tar tr. to alert, warn.

a·ler·to, –ta I. adj. watchful, careful II. f. see **alerta.**

a·les·na f. awl.

a·le·ta f. ICHTH. fin, flipper; *(hélice)* blade (of a propeller); MECH. leaf (of a hinge); ARCHIT. alette, wing; ANAT. ala, wing (of the nose).

a·le·ta·da f. beating *or* flapping of wings.

a·le·tar·ga·mien·to m. lethargy, drowsiness.

a·le·tar·gar §47 tr. to lethargize, make drowsy.

a·le·te·ar intr. ICHTH., ORINTH. to flutter, flap (fins or wings); FIG. *(agitar los brazos)* to wave *or* flap one's arms.

a·le·te·o m. ORNITH., ICHTH. fluttering, flapping (of fins or wings); FIG. *(latido)* palpitation, throbbing.

a·le·ve adj. treacherous, perfidious.

a·le·vo·sa·men·te adv. treacherously, perfidiously.

a·le·vo·sí·a f. treachery, perfidy.

a·le·vo·so, –sa I. adj. treacherous, perfidious II. m. traitor —f. traitor, traitress.

al·fa f. alpha (Greek letter) ♦ **a. y omega** FIG. alpha and omega.

al·fa·be·ti·cé, alfabetice see **alfabetizar.**

al·fa·bé·ti·co, –ca adj. alphabetical.

al·fa·be·ti·za·ción f. alphabetization; EDUC. literacy instruction.

al·fa·be·ti·za·do, –da I. past part. see **alfabetizar** II. adj. literate III. m.f. literate person.

al·fa·be·ti·zar §04 tr. *(ordenar)* to alphabetize, arrange in alphabetical order; EDUC. to make literate, teach literacy skills to.

al·fa·be·to m. *(abecedario)* alphabet; *(código)* code <*a. telegráfico* telegraphic code> ♦ **a. Morse** Morse code.

al·fal·fa f. BOT. alfalfa.

al·fa·nu·mé·ri·co, –ca adj. alphanumeric.
al·fa·que m. sand bar, shoal.
al·fa·quí m. ulema (Moslem scholar of law and religion).
al·fa·re·rí·a f. CERAM. *(arte)* pottery, ceramics; *(taller)* pottery shop *or* factory.
al·fa·re·ro, –ra m.f. CERAM. potter, ceramist.
al·far·jí·a f. CARP. door *or* window frame.
al·féi·zar m. ARCHIT. *(hueco)* door *or* window embrasure; *(borde biselado)* window sill.
al·fe·ñi·car·se §70 reflex. FIG., COLL. *(adelgazarse)* to become very thin, lose a lot of weight; *(remilgarse)* to put on prim and proper airs.
al·fe·ñi·que m. CUL. *(almendrado)* sweetened almond paste; FIG., COLL. *(persona delicada)* weakling; *(remilgo)* primness, affectation.
al·fe·re·cí·a f. MED. epilepsy, grand *or* petit mal.
al·fé·rez m. [pl. **-re·ces**] MIL. ensign, second lieutenant.
al·fil m. bishop (in chess).
al·fi·ler m. *(clavillo)* pin; *(adorno)* pin, brooch ♦ **alfileres** pin money • **a. de gancho** AMER. safety pin • **de veinticinco alfileres** FIG., COLL. dressed up, dressed to kill • **no caber un a.** COLL. to be filled to the brim • **pegado** *or* **prendido con alfileres** COLL. shaky, jerrybuilt.
al·fi·le·rar tr. SEW. to pin.
al·fi·le·ra·zo m. *(punzada)* pinprick; FIG. *(pulla)* gibe, dig.
al·fi·le·te·ro m. pincushion.
al·fo·lí m. *(granero)* granary; *(de la sal)* salt warehouse.
al·fom·bra f. *(tapiz)* carpet <*a. oriental*> Oriental carpet; *(tapete)* rug, mat; FIG. *(capa)* covering, carpet <*a. de flores* a carpet of flowers>; MED. German measles ♦ **a. de baño** bath mat • **a. voladora** flying carpet.
al·fom·bra·do, –da I. past part. see **alfombrar** II. adj. carpeted III. m. carpets, carpeting.
al·fom·brar tr. to carpet.
al·for·ja f. *(talega)* knapsack, saddle bag; *(provisión)* provisions, supplies.
al·for·za f. SEW. *(pliegue)* pleat, tuck; FIG., COLL. *(cicatriz)* scar, mark.
al·for·zar §04 tr. SEW. to pleat, tuck.
al·ga f. BOT. alga, seaweed.
al·gai·da f. *(bosque)* thicket, brush; *(duna)* sand dune.
al·ga·lia f. *(perfume)* civet; BOT. abelmosk; MED. catheter.
al·ga·ra f. *(tropa)* raiding party; *(telilla)* thin skin (of onion).
al·ga·ra·bí·a f. *(árabe)* Arabic (language); FIG., COLL. *(garabatos)* scribble, scrawl; *(jerigonza)* gibberish, babbling; *(jaleo)* uproar, din; BOT. broom.
al·ga·ra·da f. *(tropa)* raiding party; *(ataque)* raid, attack; *(jaleo)* uproar, din.
al·ga·rro·ba f. BOT. *(planta)* vetch; *(fruto)* carob bean.
al·ga·rro·bo m. BOT. carob tree, locust tree ♦ **a. loco** Judas tree.
ál·ge·bra f. MATH. algebra; MED. bonesetting.
al·ge·brai·co, –ca adj. MATH. algebraic.
al·gi·dez f. algidity, coldness.
ál·gi·do, –da adj. *(frío)* icy, cold; MED. algid, chilly.
al·go I. indef. pron. something <*hay a. que no entiendo* there is something that I do not understand>; [in negative and interrogative sentences] anything <*¿hay a. para mí?* is there anything for me?>; *(cantidad indeterminada)* some ♦ **a. es a.** something is better than nothing • **por a.** for some reason II. adv. somewhat, a little <*esto es a. difícil* this is somewhat difficult> III. m. COL. snack, refreshment.
al·go·dón m. BOT. cotton (plant and cloth) ♦ **a. de azúcar** cotton candy • **a. en rama** raw cotton • **a. hidrófilo** absorbent cotton • **a. pólvora** guncotton (explosive).
al·go·do·nal m. AGR. cotton plantation *or* field.
al·go·do·ne·ro, –ra I. adj. cotton II. m.f. *(obrero)* cotton worker; *(comerciante)* cotton dealer *or* trader —m. BOT. cotton plant.
al·go·do·no·so, –sa adj. cottony.
al·go·rít·mi·co adj. ♦ **lenguaje a.** COMPUT. ALGOL.
al·go·rín m. olive bin.
al·go·rit·mo m. MATH. algorithm.
al·gua·cil m. *(oficial)* sheriff, constable; *(ganzúa)* skeleton key; ENTOM. spider; ARG., URUG. dragonfly.
al·gua·ci·laz·go m. post of sheriff *or* constable.

al·guien indef. pron. someone, somebody <*hay a. en la sala de espera* there is someone in the waiting room>; [in negative and interrogative sentences] anyone, anybody <*¿has visto a a.?* have you seen anybody?>.
al·gún adj. [apocopation of **alguno** used before m. sing. nouns] some <*algún día* someday> —see **alguno**.
al·gu·no, –na §G21 I. adj. some <*algunos hombres* some men>; some, reasonable <*de a. duración* of a reasonable length>; [in negative and interrogative sentences] any <*no tengo duda a.* I don't have any doubt> ♦ **a. vez** sometime II. indef. pron. someone <*¿ha llegado a.?* has someone arrived?> ♦ **a. que otro** a few, one or two • **algunos** some <*compremos algunos* let's buy some>.
al·ha·ja f. *(joya)* jewel, gem; *(preciosidad)* exquisite object *or* furnishing; FIG. *(tesoro)* treasure, gem ♦ **buena a.** FIG., DEROG. good-for-nothing.
al·ha·jar tr. *(amueblar)* to decorate, furnish (a house); *(adornar)* to bedeck with jewels.
al·ha·je·ra f. *or* **al·ha·je·ro** m. AMER. jewelry box.
al·ha·ra·ca f. fuss, ado.
al·he·lí m. [pl. **-lí·es**] BOT. wallflower, stock.
al·he·ña f. BOT. henna; *(polvo)* powdered henna; AGR. blight, mildew.
al·he·ñar tr. to dye with henna —reflex. AGR. to become blighted *or* mildewed (grain).
al·hu·ce·ma f. BOT. lavender.
a·lia·do, –da I. past part. see **aliar** II. m.f. ally, confederate ♦ **los Aliados** the Allies III. adj. allied, confederate.
a·lian·za f. *(unión)* alliance, confederacy; *(anillo)* wedding ring.
a·liar §30 tr. to ally, join —reflex. to become allies, form an alliance.
a·lias I. adv. alias, also known as II. m. alias, assumed name.
a·li·bí m. LAW alibi; COLL. *(disculpa)* alibi, excuse.
a·li·ble adj. alible, nourishing.
a·li·ca·í·do, –da adj. ORNITH. with drooping wings; FIG., COLL. *(débil)* weak, haggard; *(deprimido)* depressed, sad.
a·li·ca·ta·do I. past part. see **alicatar** II. m. glazed tiling.
a·li·ca·tar tr. to tile.
a·li·ca·tes m.pl. pliers, pincers ♦ **a. de uñas** nail clippers.
a·li·cien·te m. *(incentivo)* inducement, incentive <*les ofrecí un a. para que lo completaran a tiempo* I offered them an incentive to complete it on time>; *(atractivo)* attraction, lure <*el a. de la juventud* the attraction of youth>.
a·lie·na·ble adj. alienable.
a·lie·na·ción f. LAW *(transmisión)* alienation, transfer (of property); MED. insanity, mental derangement.
a·lie·na·do, –da I. past part. see **alienar** II. adj. MED. insane, mentally deranged III. m.f. MED. insane *or* mentally deranged person.
a·lie·na·dor, –do·ra *or* **a·lie·nan·te** adj. oppressive.
a·lie·nar tr. LAW *(transmitir)* to alienate, transfer (property); MED. to drive mad *or* insane.
a·lien·te, aliento see **alentar.**
a·lien·to m. *(soplo)* breath; *(respiración)* breathing, respiration; FIG. *(valor)* strength, courage ♦ **dar a. a** FIG. to encourage • **de un a.** FIG. in one breath, without stopping • **cobrar a.** FIG. to take heart • **sin a.** breathless.
a·lí·fe·ro, –ra adj. winged.
a·li·ga·ción f. *or* **a·li·ga·mien·to** m. *(liga)* bond, tie; *(aleación)* alloy, mixture.
a·li·ga·tor m. alligator.
a·li·ge·ra·mien·to m. *(de una carga)* lightening; *(alivio)* alleviation, easing; *(prisa)* hastening, hurrying.
a·li·ge·rar tr. *(hacer menos pesado)* to lighten, make less heavy <*a. la carga* to lighten the load>; *(acelerar)* to hasten, quicken; FIG. *(templar)* to alleviate, ease <*a. el dolor* to ease the pain> —reflex. to become lighter ♦ **aligerarse de ropa** to slip into something lighter *or* more comfortable.
a·lí·ge·ro, –ra adj. POET. *(alado)* winged; FIG. *(rápido)* fleet.
a·li·ja·dor, –do·ra I. adj. unloading II. m. *(lanchón)* lighter, barge; *(trabajador)* stevedore, dockworker.
a·li·jar¹ m. untilled *or* barren land ♦ **alijares** common pasture *or* land.
a·li·jar² tr. MARIT. *(alijerar)* to lighten, unload (a vessel);

(descargar) to unload (cargo); TEX. to gin (cotton); *(alisar)* to sandpaper.

a·li·ma·ña f. *(animal perjudicial)* pest, vermin; *(animal grande)* large animal, beast.

a·li·men·ta·ción f. *(acción de alimentar)* feeding, nourishing; *(comida)* food, nourishment; *(manutención)* support; MECH. feed, stoking • **a. deficiente** malnutrition.

a·li·men·tar tr. *(nutrir)* to feed, nourish; *(mantener)* to support (a family); FIG. *(fomentar)* to nurture, encourage *<el estudio alimenta el espíritu* study nurtures the spirit*>*; MECH. to feed, stoke *<a. un motor* to fuel a motor*>* —reflex. to take nourishment ♦ **alimentarse con** to feed on.

a·li·men·ta·rio, –ria adj. alimentary, nutritional.

a·li·men·ti·cio, –cia adj. nourishing, nutritious.

a·li·men·to m. *(comida)* food, nourishment; FIG. *(aliento)* encouragement; MECH. fuel ♦ **alimentos** alimony, support.

a·lin·da·do, –da I. past part. see **alindar** II. adj. dandified, foppish.

a·lin·da·mien·to m. setting of boundaries *or* limits.

a·lin·dar[1] tr. *(poner lindes a)* to establish *or* set boundaries to —intr. to be contiguous *or* adjacent.

a·lin·dar[2] tr. *(embellecer)* to embellish, adorn.

a·li·ne·a·ción f. *(línea)* alignment; *(colocación en línea)* aligning, lining up; SPORT. *(rol de equipo)* line-up, team roster.

a·li·ne·a·do, –da I. past part. see **alinear** II. adj. *(puesto en línea)* aligned, lined up; POL. *(apoyador)* seconding, supporting ♦ **no a.** POL. nonaligned, neutral.

a·li·ne·a·mien·to m. alignment ♦ **no a.** POL. nonalignment, neutrality.

a·li·ne·ar tr. *(enfilar)* to align, line up; *(componer)* to make up, form (a team) —reflex. to line up; MIL. to fall in.

a·li·ña·do, –da I. past part. see **aliñar** II. adj. *(aseado)* neat, tidy; CUL. prepared, spiced III. m. CUBA brandy.

a·li·ña·dor, –do·ra I. adj. fixing II. m.f. *(persona que arregla)* fixer; CHILE, MED. bonesetter.

a·li·ña·mien·to m. seasoning, dressing.

a·li·ñar tr. *(arreglar)* to straighten, tidy; *(adornar)* to adorn, embellish; *(administrar)* to administrate, organize; CUL. to season, flavor, dress; CHILE, MED. to set (a bone) —reflex. to primp, preen.

a·li·ño m. *(aseo)* neatness, tidiness; *(adorno)* adornment, embellishment; *(preparación)* preparation, readiness; CUL. seasoning, flavoring, dressing.

a·li·que·bra·do, –da adj. FIG. crestfallen, dejected.

a·li·sar tr. *(allanar)* to smooth, make smooth; *(el pelo)* to slick, smooth (hair).

a·li·sios adj. MARIT. trade *<vientos a.* trade winds*>*.

a·lis·ta·do, –da I. past part. see **alistar** II. adj. *(listado)* listed; *(inscrito)* enlisted, enrolled.

a·lis·ta·mien·to m. *(acción de alistar)* listing; *(registro)* enrollment, listing; MIL. *(enganche)* enlistment, recruitment; *(recluta)* levy, draft.

a·lis·tar tr. *(escribir en lista)* to list, put on a list; *(preparar)* to prepare, get *or* make ready; MIL. *(enganchar)* to recruit —reflex. MIL. to enlist, sign up (for the service); AMER. to get ready, get dressed.

a·li·te·ra·ción f. RHET. *(repetición)* alliteration; *(paronomasia)* paronomasia.

a·li·via·de·ro m. overflow channel, spillway.

a·li·via·dor, –do·ra I. adj. comforting, consoling II. m.f. *(persona)* consoler —m. *(palanca)* lever which raises or lowers a millstone.

a·li·via·nar tr. & reflex. AMER. var. of **aliviar**.

a·li·viar tr. *(disminuir)* to alleviate, ease *<a. el dolor* to ease the pain*>*; *(aligerar)* to lighten, make lighter *<a. la carga* to lighten the load*>*; *(confortar)* to comfort, console *<su visita me alivió* his visit comforted me*>*; FIG. *(acelerar)* to quicken, speed up *<alivió el paso* he quickened his step*>* —reflex. *(ser confortado)* to be relieved; *(recuperarse)* to recover, get better.

a·li·vio m. *(disminución)* easing, alleviation; *(aligeramiento)* lightening, *(consuelo)* comfort, consolation; MED. relief.

al·jez m. MIN. gypsum.

al·ji·be m. *(cisterna)* cistern, water tank; MARIT. tanker; COL. spring, fountain; PERU dungeon, prison.

al·jó·far m. *(perla)* seed pearl; *(conjunto de perlas)* pearls; FIG. *(gota)* pearl, drop.

al·ma f. *(espíritu)* soul, spirit, heart; FIG. *(individuo)* human being, soul *<no había un a. allí* there was not a soul around*>*; *(centro)* core, crux *<el a. del movimiento* the core of the movement*>*; TECH. core, center; CONST. web, stem; ARTIL. bore; MUS. soundpost ♦ **a. de caballo** COLL. blackguard • **a. de Caín** *or* **de Judas** fiend, villain • **a. de cántaro** fool • **a. de Dios** COLL. good soul • **a. mía** dearest, darling • **caérsele el a. a los pies** FIG. to be disheartened • **con toda el a.** with all one's heart • **entregar el a.** FIG. to give up the ghost, die • **no tener a.** FIG. to be heartless • **partir** *or* **romper el a. a** FIG. to break someone's heart • **tener el a. en un hilo** FIG. to have one's heart in one's mouth, be afraid.

al·ma·cén m. *(tienda)* store, shop; *(depósito)* storehouse, warehouse; ARTIL. magazine; S. AMER. grocery store.

al·ma·ce·na·je m. COM. *(gasto)* storage *or* warehouse charge; *(almacenamiento)* warehousing, storage ♦ **a. frigorífico** cold storage.

al·ma·ce·na·mien·to m. *(acción)* storing; *(estado)* storage; *(conjunto)* stock, stored goods.

al·ma·ce·nar tr. COM. *(guardar)* to store, warehouse; FIG. *(amontonar)* to hoard, hold on to.

al·ma·ce·ne·ro m. COM. warehouseman; AMER. *(comerciante)* merchant, storekeeper; *(abacero)* grocer.

al·má·ci·ga f. *(resina)* mastic (resin); *(masilla)* putty; AGR. nursery, seedbed.

al·má·ci·go m. BOT. mastic tree, lentiscus; *(semilla)* nursery seed; AGR. *(semillero)* nursery, seedbed.

al·ma·de·na *or* **al·má·da·na** f. sledgehammer.

al·ma·dre·ña f. clog, wooden shoe.

al·ma·gre m. red ocher.

al·mai·zal *or* **al·mai·zar** m. *(toca)* gauze veil; RELIG. humeral veil.

al·ma·ja·ne·que m. MIL. battering ram.

al·ma·na·que m. *(pronóstico)* almanac; *(calendario)* calendar.

al·más·ti·ga f. mastic.

al·ma·za·ra f. oil mill.

al·me·ja f. ICHTH. clam, edible shellfish.

al·me·na·ra f. *(fuego)* beacon, signal fire; *(candelero)* candelabrum, candelabra.

al·men·dra f. *(nuez)* almond; *(semilla)* kernel, stone ♦ **a. garrapiñada** praline • **a. de la media a.** COLL. finicky, fussy.

al·men·dra·do, –da I. adj. almond-shaped II. m. CUL. *(pasta)* almond paste; *(macarrón)* macaroon; PERU prepared dish in almond sauce —f. CUL. almond milk.

al·men·dri·lla f. *(lima)* round file; *(grava)* fine gravel.

al·men·dro m. BOT. almond tree.

al·me·te m. helmet.

al·mí·bar m. CUL. syrup; FIG., COLL. *(persona amable)* sweet person, sweetheart ♦ **almíbares** CUL. preserved fruit.

al·mi·ba·ra·do, –da I. past part. see **almibarar** II. adj. CUL. *(muy dulce)* sugary, sweet; *(bañado en almíbar)* syrupy, honeyed; FIG., COLL. *(meloso)* sugary, syrupy (of words); *(afeminado)* effeminate, dainty.

al·mi·ba·rar tr. CUL. *(cubrir)* to coat with syrup, glaze; *(confitar)* to preserve in syrup; FIG. *(lisonjear)* to sweet-talk, coax.

al·mi·dón m. BOT. starch; AMER. paste (for gluing) ♦ **dar a.** to starch.

al·mi·do·na·do, –da I. past part. see **almidonar** II. adj. starched *<una camisa a.* a starched shirt*>*; FIG. *(muy compuesto)* smart, dapper III. m. starching.

al·mi·do·nar tr. to starch.

al·mi·nar m. minaret.

al·mi·ran·taz·go m. MIL. *(tribunal)* admiralty (court); *(jurisdicción)* admiralty, admiralship.

al·mi·ran·te m. MIL. admiral.

al·miz·cle m. musk.

al·mo·ha·da f. *(cabezal)* pillow, cushion; *(funda)* pillowcase ARCHIT. *(de un sillar)* bolster ♦ **consultar con la a.** to sleep on it.

al·mo·ha·da·do, –da adj. ARCHIT. cushioned, bolstered; *(acolchado)* padded, stuffed.

al·mo·ha·di·lla f. *(cojincillo)* small cushion, pad; *(saquito)* silk handkerchief pouch; ARCHIT. *(de sillares)* bolster, boss; *(de sellos)* inkpad; AMER. pincushion.

al·mo·ha·di·llar tr. *(acolchar)* to pad, stuff; ARCHIT. *(labrar con collarinos)* to decorate with bolsters *or* cushions.

al·mo·ha·dón *(cojín)* (large) cushion; ARCHIT. *(collarino)* springer, annulet.

al·mo·ne·da f. *(subasta)* auction; *(a bajo precio)* clearance sale; *(antigüedades)* antiques.

al·mo·rra·nas f.pl. MED. hemorrhoids, piles.

al·mor·zar §37 intr. to eat lunch, lunch —tr. to eat (something) for lunch, lunch on.

al·muer·zo m. *(comida)* lunch; *(vajilla)* luncheon set.

al·mu·nia f. fruit *or* vegetable garden.

al·na·do, –da m. stepson —f. stepdaughter ♦ **alnados** stepchildren.

¡a·ló! *or* **¡a·ló!** interj. hello! (in answering the telephone).

a·lo·ca·da·men·te adv. *(locamente)* crazily; *(sin reflexionar)* thoughtlessly, rashly.

a·lo·ca·do, –da I. past part. see **alocar** II. adj. *(loco)* crazy, insane; *(de poco juicio)* thoughtless, rash.

a·lo·car §70 tr. to drive crazy *or* insane —reflex. *(volverse loco)* to go crazy *or* insane; FIG. *(desquiciarse)* to lose one's head.

a·lo·cu·ción f. allocution, address.

á·lo·e *or* **a·lo·e** m. BOT. aloe; MED. aloes.

a·ló·ge·no, –na adj. of a different race.

a·lo·ja·do, –da I. past part. see **alojar** II. m.f. AMER. guest, lodger —m. *(soldado)* billeted soldier.

a·lo·ja·mien·to m. lodging, boarding; *(vivienda)* lodgings, accommodations; MIL. *(acuartelamiento)* billeting, quartering; *(cuartel)* billet, quarters; *(campamento)* camp.

a·lo·jar tr. *(hospedar)* to lodge, house; *(albergar)* to accommodate, house; *(meter)* to lodge <*una bala alojada en la espalda* a bullet lodged in one's shoulder>; MIL. *(acuartelar)* to billet, quarter —reflex. *(hospedarse)* to lodge oneself, be lodged; MIL. *(acuartelarse)* to be billeted *or* quartered; *(situarse)* to take up a position.

a·lo·jo m. AMER. var. of **alojamiento**.

a·lo·ma·do, –da I. past. part. see **alomar** II. adj. ZOOL. high-backed; ARCHIT. ridged, arched.

a·lo·mar tr. AGR. to plow in furrows, ridge.

a·lon·dra f. ORNITH. lark.

a·lon·gar §16 tr. *(prolongar)* to prolong, extend; *(estirar)* to lengthen, stretch; *(alejar)* to remove, make distant —reflex. to move *or* go away.

a·lo·pa·tí·a f. MED. allopathy.

a·lo·qué, aloque see **alocar**.

al·pa·ca f. ZOOL. alpaca (animal and skin); *(tejido)* alpaca; METAL. German *or* nickel silver.

al·par·ga·ta f. sandal, espadrille.

al·par·ga·ti·lla m.f. FIG., COLL. crafty *or* cunning person.

al·pe·chín m. *(de las aceitunas)* foul-smelling liquid which oozes from heaped olives; AMER. sour fruit juice.

al·pen·de *or* **al·pen·dre** m. tool shed.

Al·pes m.pl. Alps.

al·pes·tre adj. alpine.

al·pi·nis·mo m. mountain climbing, mountaineering.

al·pi·nis·ta m.f. mountain climber, mountaineer.

al·pi·no, –na adj. alpine.

al·pis·te m. BOT. alpist, canary grass; *(comida para pájaros)* birdseed; FIG., COLL. *(aguardiente)* alcohol, drink.

al·que·rí·a f. *(cortijo)* farmhouse, grange; *(aldea)* hamlet.

al·qui·la·ble adj. rentable, leasable.

al·qui·la·di·zo, –za I. adj. *(que se alquila)* to rent, for let; *(persona)* for hire II. m.f. hireling.

al·qui·la·dor, –do·ra m.f. *(arrendatario)* renter, tenant; *(arrendador)* landlord, lessor.

al·qui·la·mien·to m. renting, leasing.

al·qui·lar tr. *(arrendar)* to rent, lease; *(personas)* to hire —reflex. to hire oneself out, be for hire ♦ **se alquila** to let, for hire.

al·qui·ler m. *(acción)* renting, hiring; *(renta)* rent ♦ **de a.** for hire, for rent.

al·qui·lón, –lo·na DEROG. I. adj. mercenary II. m.f. mercenary, hireling.

al·qui·mia f. alchemy.

al·qui·mi·co, –ca adj. alchemic, alchemical.

al·qui·mis·ta m. alchemist.

al·qui·ta·ra f. still, distillery.

al·qui·ta·rar tr. *(destilar)* to distill; FIG. *(sutilizar)* to overrefine.

al·qui·trán m. tar, pitch.

al·qui·tra·na·do, –da I. past part. see **alquitranar** II. adj. tarred III. m. MARIT. tarpaulin; *(acción)* tarring.

al·qui·tra·nar tr. to tar, cover with tar *or* pitch.

al·re·de·dor I. adv. *(en torno)* around <*mirar a. de sí* to look around oneself>; about, approximately <*a. de 100 dólares* about 100 dollars> II. m.pl. **alrededores** *(cercanías)* surroundings; *(afueras)* outskirts, environs.

Al·sa·cia f. Alsace.

Al·sa·cia Lo·re·na f. Alsace-Lorraine.

al·sa·cia·no, –na adj. & m.f. Alsatian.

al·ta I. f. MED. discharge (of patients); *(ingreso)* entry, admittance (to the military, a profession) ♦ **dar de a.** MIL. to admit; MED. to discharge (patients) • **darse de a.** to join, become a member II. adj. see **alto, –ta**.

al·ta·men·te adv. highly, extremely <*a. satisfecho* highly satisfied>.

al·ta·ne·ra·men·te adv. arrogantly, haughtily.

al·ta·ne·rí·a f. *(caza)* falconry; *(de pájaros)* high flight; FIG. *(orgullo)* arrogance, haughtiness.

al·ta·ne·ro, –ra adj. ORNITH. high-flying; FIG. *(orgulloso)* arrogant, haughty.

al·tar m. *(ara)* altar; MIN. fire, flue, *or* furnace bridge ♦ **a. mayor** high *or* main altar.

al·ta·voz m. [pl. **-vo·ces**] loudspeaker.

al·te·ra·bi·li·dad f. alterability.

al·te·ra·ble adj. alterable.

al·te·ra·ción f. *(variación)* alteration, change; *(inquietud)* worry, irritation; *(alboroto)* disturbance, commotion; *(disputa)* altercation, fight; *(desarreglo)* irregularity <*a. del pulso* irregularity of the pulse>.

al·te·ra·di·zo, –za adj. *(alterable)* changeable, alterable; *(caprichoso)* fickle.

al·te·ra·do, –da I. past part. see **alterar** II. adj. *(modificado)* altered, changed; *(perturbado)* disturbed, upset; *(enfadado)* angry, annoyed.

al·te·ra·dor, –do·ra adj. *(variante)* altering; *(perturbador)* disturbing.

al·te·rar tr. *(variar)* to alter, change <*a. la verdad* to alter the truth>; *(perturbar)* to disturb, upset; *(enfadar)* to anger, annoy —reflex. *(variarse)* to undergo change, alter; *(perturbarse)* to become disturbed *or* upset; *(enojarse)* to become angry *or* annoyed; COL. *(tener sed)* to be thirsty.

al·te·ra·ti·vo, –va adj. alterative.

al·ter·ca·ción f. *or* **al·ter·ca·do** m. altercation, argument.

al·ter·ca·dor, –do·ra I. adj. argumentative, quarrelsome II. m.f. argumentative *or* quarrelsome person.

al·ter·car §70 intr. to argue, quarrel.

al·ter·na·ción f. alternation.

al·ter·na·da·men·te adv. alternately.

al·ter·na·do, –da I. past part. see **alternar** II. adj. alternate.

al·ter·na·dor m. ELEC. alternator.

al·ter·nan·te adj. alternating.

al·ter·nar tr. to alternate —intr. to alternate, take turns ♦ **a. con** to socialize *or* associate with.

al·ter·na·ti·va I. f. *(opción)* alternative, choice; *(sucesión)* alternation; AGR. rotation (of crops) ♦ **tomar la a.** TAUR. to receive formal recognition as a matador • **tomar una a.** to make a decision II. adj. see **alternativo, –va**.

al·ter·na·ti·va·men·te adv. alternately.

al·ter·na·ti·vo, –va I. adj. alternating, alternate II. f. see **alternativa**.

al·ter·no, –na adj. *(alternativo)* alternating; ELEC. alternating; GEOM., BOT. alternate.

al·ter·qué, alterque see **altercar**.

al·te·za f. *(elevación)* elevation, sublimity; *(título)* Highness; *(altura)* height.

al·ti·ba·jo m. downward thrust (in fencing) ♦ **altibajos** *(terreno)* undulating land; FIG., COLL. *(vicisitudes)* ups and downs (of life).

al·ti·lo·cuen·cia f. grandiloquence.

al·ti·lo·cuen·te *or* **al·ti·lo·cuo, –cua** adj. grandiloquent.

al·ti·llo m. *(colina)* hill, hillock; S. AMER. *(desván)* attic; PERU *(entresuelo)* mezzanine.

al·ti·me·trí·a f. AER. altimetry.

al·tí·me·tro, –tra AER. I. adj. altimetrical II. m. altimeter ♦ **a. aneroide** aneroid altimeter • **a. barométrico** barometric altimeter.

al·ti·pla·ni·cie f. high plateau, altiplano.

al·ti·pla·no m. AMER. var. of **altiplanicie.**

al·tí·si·mo, –ma adj. very high, most high ♦ **El A.** God, the Almighty.

al·ti·so·nan·cia f. grandiloquence, bombast.

al·ti·so·nan·te or **al·tí·so·no, –na** adj. high-sounding, grandiloquent.

al·ti·tud f. altitude, height.

al·ti·va·men·te adv. haughtily, proudly.

al·ti·var·se reflex. to put on airs.

al·ti·ve·cer·se §17 reflex. var. of **altivarse.**

al·ti·vez or **al·ti·ve·za** f. haughtiness, pride.

al·ti·vo, –va adj. haughty, proud.

al·to, –ta I. adj. high <*montañas altas* high mountains>; *(estatura)* tall <*una mujer a.* a tall woman>; upper <*piso a.* upper floor>; loud <*en voz a.* in a loud voice>; *(crecido)* swollen <*río a.* swollen river>; *(elevado)* lofty <*altos ideales* lofty ideals>; *(grave)* high, serious <*a. traición* high treason>; FIG. *(caro)* high <*precio a.* high price> ♦ **a. atmósfera** upper atmosphere • **a. cocina** haute cuisine • **a. costura** haute couture • **a. fidelidad** high fidelity • **a. frecuencia** high frequency • **a. horno** blast furnace • **a. mar** high seas • **a. relieve** high relief • **a. sociedad** high society • **altas horas** late hours • **altos y bajos** ups and downs • **en a.** on high II. m. *(altura)* height, elevation; *(colina)* hill; MUS. alto; MIL. halt, stop; AMER. pile, heap ♦ **altos** AMER. upper floor • **de a.** high <*seis pies de a.* six feet high> • **de lo a.** from on high, from above • **hacer a.** to stop, come to a stop • **hacer a. a** MIL. to halt, stop (someone) —f. see **alta** III. adv. *(arriba)* up high, above; *(en voz fuerte)* aloud, loudly ♦ **pasar por a.** to overlook, omit IV. interj. MIL. halt!, stop! ♦ **¡a. el fuego!** cease fire!

al·to·cú·mu·lo m. METEOROL. altocumulus.

al·to·par·lan·te m. AMER. loudspeaker.

al·tor m. height.

Al·to Vol·ta m. Upper Volta.

al·to·vol·tai·co, –ca adj. Voltaic, of the Upper Volta.

al·truis·mo m. altruism.

al·truis·ta I. adj. altruistic II. m.f. altruist.

al·tu·ra f. *(elevación)* height, altitude; *(cumbre)* summit, top; *(nivel)* level, height <*a la misma a.* at the same level>; FIG. *(alteza)* loftiness ♦ **a estas alturas** FIG. at this point *or* stage • **alturas** the heavens, Heaven • **estar a la a. de las circunstancias** FIG. to be worthy of the occasion, be equal to the challenge.

a·lu·bia f. BOT. French *or* kidney bean.

a·lu·ci·na·ción f. hallucination.

a·lu·ci·na·da·men·te adv. hallucinatorily.

a·lu·ci·na·do, –da I. past part. see **alucinar** II. adj. hallucinating III. m.f. person who hallucinates.

a·lu·ci·na·dor, –do·ra I. adj. hallucinatory II. m. hallucinogen.

a·lu·ci·na·mien·to m. hallucination, illusion.

a·lu·ci·nan·te adj. hallucinating; *(extraordinario)* extraordinary.

a·lu·ci·nar tr. to hallucinate; FIG. *(engañar)* to delude, deceive —reflex. to hallucinate.

a·lu·ci·na·to·rio, –ria adj. hallucinatory.

a·lu·ci·no·gé·ni·co, –ca adj. hallucinogenic.

a·lu·ci·nó·ge·no, –na I. adj. hallucinogenic II. m. hallucinogen.

a·lud m. avalanche.

a·lu·di·do, –da I. past part. see **aludir** II. adj. abovementioned, referred to.

a·lu·dir intr. ♦ **a. a** to allude *or* refer to.

a·lu·do, –da I. adj. having large wings II. f. ENTOM. winged ant.

a·luen·go, aluengue see **alongar.**

a·lum·bra·do, –da I. past part. see **alumbrar** II. adj. *(encendido)* lighted, lit; COLL. *(achispado)* tipsy, lit; CHEM. aluminiferous III. m. *(iluminación)* lighting; HIST., RELIG. illuminist ♦ **los Alumbrados** HIST. the Illuminati.

a·lum·bra·mien·to m. *(iluminación)* illumination, lighting; *(parto)* childbirth.

a·lum·brar tr. *(iluminar)* to light (up), illuminate <*a. la sala*

to light up the room>; *(acompañar con luz)* to light the way for; *(dar vista a)* to give *or* restore sight to (the blind); FIG. *(ilustrar)* to enlighten, illuminate —intr. *(dar luz)* to give light <*esta lámpara alumbra bien* this lamp gives good light>; *(dar a luz)* to give birth —reflex. COLL. to get tipsy *or* lit.

a·lum·bre f. CHEM. alum.

a·lu·mi·nio m. CHEM. aluminum, aluminium (G.B.).

a·lu·mi·no·so, –sa adj. aluminous.

a·lum·na·do m. student body.

a·lum·no, –na m.f. pupil, student.

a·lu·na·do, –da I. past part. see **alunarse** II. adj. *(loco)* crazy, insane; VET. spastic (horses).

a·lu·na·ra·do, –da adj. spotted, dotted.

a·lu·nar·se reflex. *(herida)* to fester; *(corromperse)* to spoil, rot; COLL., VEN to become sore *or* chafed.

a·lu·ni·za·je m. lunar landing.

a·lu·ni·zar §04 intr. to land on the moon.

a·lu·sión f. *(acción de aludir)* allusion; *(mención)* mention, reference.

a·lu·si·vo, –va adj. allusive.

a·lu·ta·ción f. MIN. gold nugget.

a·lu·vial adj. alluvial.

a·lu·vión m. *(inundación)* flood; *(sedimento)* alluvium, sediment (left by a flood); FIG. *(cantidad grande)* flood, deluge <*un a. de improperios* a flood of insults>.

al·ve·o·lar adj. ANAT., PHONET. alveolar.

al·ve·o·lo or **al·vé·o·lo** m. ANAT., ENTOM. alveolus.

al·ver·ja f. BOT. vetch; AMER. pea.

al·ver·ji·lla f. AMER., BOT. sweet pea.

al·vi·no, –na adj. MED. alvine, intestinal.

al·za f. *(aumento)* rise, increase <*el a. de los precios* the rise in prices>; ARTIL. backsight; PRINT. *(imprenta)* overlay ♦ **en a.** rising, on the rise.

al·za·cue·llo m. clerical collar.

al·za·da I. f. *(altura)* height (of horses); *(apelación)* appeal II. adj. see **alzado, –da.**

al·za·da·men·te adv. for a lump sum.

al·za·do, –da I. past part. see **alzar** II. adj. *(elevado)* raised, elevated; FIN. *(quebrado)* fraudulently bankrupt; *(estipulado)* fixed, settled <*un precio a.* a fixed price>; AMER. *(montaraz)* wild, feral (animal); *(en celo)* in heat (animal); *(insolente)* arrogant, insolent; *(rebelde)* rebellious, mutinous; MEX. crude, unpolished; COL. drunk III. m. *(elevación)* raising, elevating; *(altura)* height; ARCHIT. front elevation —f. see **alzada.**

al·za·mien·to m. *(elevación)* raising, lifting; *(aumento)* rise, increase; *(en un remate)* bid (at auctions); POL. uprising, rebellion; FIN. *(quiebra)* fraudulent bankruptcy.

al·za·pri·ma f. *(palanca)* crowbar, lever; *(cuña)* wedge; ARG. timber cart.

al·zar §04 tr. *(levantar)* to raise, lift (up) <*a. la mano* to raise one's hand>; *(recoger)* to gather (up) <*a. los frutos* to gather fruit>; MARIT. to raise, hoist (sails); RELIG. to elevate (the host); PRINT. to collate ♦ **a. cabeza** FIG. to recover, get back on one's feet • **a. el codo** FIG. to have a lot to drink —reflex. *(levantarse)* to rise, get up; POL. to rebel, rise up; FIN. to go bankrupt fraudulently; *(apelar)* to appeal (to a higher court); AMER. to run wild (animals); COL. to get drunk ♦ **alzarse con** COLL. to make off with, steal.

a·llá adv. *(allí)* there, over there; *(en tiempo remoto)* way back <*a. en mi niñez* way back in my childhood> ♦ **a. tú** that's your business, it's up to you • **el más a.** the (great) beyond • **más a.** farther • **más a. de** beyond • **por a.** over there, thereabouts.

a·lla·na·dor, –do·ra I. adj. leveling II. m.f. *(nivelador)* leveler; *(ladrón)* burglar.

a·lla·na·mien·to m. *(nivelación)* leveling, flattening; *(invasión)* raid, forced entry; LAW *(conformidad)* acceptance (of a decision) ♦ **a. de morada** search of premises (by police).

a·lla·nar tr. *(nivelar)* to level, flatten; *(invadir)* to raid; FIG. *(superar)* to overcome <*a. los obstáculos* to overcome obstacles>; *(pacificar)* to pacify, subdue <*a. la revuelta* to subdue the rebellion> —reflex. *(nivelarse)* to level out, become level; to submit, acquiesce <*se allana a todo* he submits to everything>.

a·lle·ga·di·zo, –za adj. added indiscriminately, thrown in (to increase the number).

a·lle·ga·do, –da I. past part. see **allegar** II. adj. *(cercano)* near, close; *(emparentado)* related III. m.f. *(pariente)* relative, relation; *(partidario)* supporter, adherent; ARG., COL. freeloader.

a·lle·ga·dor, –do·ra I. adj. gathering, collecting II. m.f. *(persona que allega)* gatherer, collector —m. *(rastro)* rake; *(hurgón)* poker.

a·lle·gar §47 tr. *(arrimar)* to place near; *(añadir)* to add; AGR. to reap, gather —intr. to arrive —reflex. *(acercarse)* to approach, draw near; *(adherirse)* to adhere, conform.

a·lle·ga·mien·to m. gathering, collecting.

A·lle·gha·nys m. Alleghenies, Allegheny Mountains.

a·llen·de I. adv. *(de la parte de allá)* beyond, on the other side; *(además)* moreover, furthermore ♦ **de a. los mares** beyond the seas, overseas II. prep. *(más allá de)* on the other side of <a. el río on the other side of the river>; *(fuera de)* besides, in addition to.

a·llí adv. *(en aquel lugar)* there; *(entonces)* then, at that time.

a·ma f. *(señora)* lady of the house, mistress; *(dueña)* proprietess ♦ **a. de brazos** AMER. nursemaid • **a. de cría** or **de leche** wet nurse • **a. de llaves** housekeeper.

a·ma·bi·li·dad f. affability, amiability.

a·ma·bi·lí·si·mo, –ma adj. very affable or amiable.

a·ma·ble adj. affable, amiable.

a·ma·ble·men·te adv. affably, amiably.

a·ma·ción f. mystic or spiritual love.

a·ma·chim·brar·se or **a·ma·chi·nar·se** reflex. AMER. to live together, cohabit.

a·ma·do, –da I. past part. see **amar** II. adj. beloved, dear III. m.f. beloved, loved one.

a·ma·dor, –do·ra I. adj. loving, fond II. m.f. lover <él es a. de la poesía he is a lover of poetry>.

a·ma·dri·gar §47 tr. FIG. to welcome, receive well —reflex. *(un animal)* to burrow, hide; FIG. *(retraerse)* to withdraw, seclude oneself.

a·ma·dri·nar tr. *(uncir)* to yoke, couple; FIG. *(apadrinar)* to sponsor; AMER. to train (horses) to follow the lead.

a·ma·es·tra·do, –da I. past part. see **amaestrar** II. adj. trained, skilled.

a·ma·es·tra·dor, –do·ra I. adj. training II. m.f. trainer.

a·ma·es·tra·mien·to m. training.

a·ma·es·trar tr. to train, teach.

a·ma·gar §47 tr. *(amenazar)* to threaten; *(fingir)* to feign, simulate <a. una retirada to feign a retreat> —intr. *(ser inminente)* to be imminent <amaga un motín an uprising is imminent> ♦ **a. a** to threaten to, show signs of <el enemigo amagaba a atacar the enemy threatened to attack> —reflex. COLL. to hide.

a·ma·go m. *(amenaza)* threat; *(señal)* sign, indication; *(ataque simulado)* feigned or mock attack.

a·mai·nar tr. MARIT. to take in, lower (the sails) —intr. *(aflojar)* to die down, subside <el viento amaina the wind is dying down>; FIG. *(ceder)* to give or let up; *(tener paciencia)* to be patient.

a·mai·ne m. MARIT. lowering, shortening (sails); *(aflojamiento)* lessening, subsiding.

a·mal·ga·ma f. CHEM. amalgam; FIG. *(mezcla)* amalgam, mixture <una a. de colores an amalgam of colors>.

a·mal·ga·ma·ción f. or **a·mal·ga·ma·mien·to** m. CHEM. amalgamation; FIG. *(mezcla)* amalgamation, combination.

a·mal·ga·mar tr. CHEM. to amalgamate; FIG. *(mezclar)* to amalgamate, mix —reflex. FIG. *(mezclar)* to amalgamate, mix.

a·ma·man·ta·dor, –do·ra I. adj. suckling II. f. suckler, nursing mother.

a·ma·man·ta·mien·to m. suckling, nursing.

a·ma·man·tar tr. to suckle, nurse.

a·man·ce·ba·mien·to m. cohabitation.

a·man·ce·bar·se reflex. to cohabit, live together.

a·ma·ne·cer §17 I. intr. to dawn <amanece temprano en la primavera it dawns early in the spring>; *(llegar)* to arrive at dawn or daybreak; *(despertar)* to wake up at dawn or daybreak; FIG. *(aparecer)* to appear, begin to show II. m. dawn, daybreak ♦ **al a.** at dawn or daybreak.

a·ma·ne·ci·da f. dawn, daybreak.

a·ma·ne·ra·da·men·te adv. affectedly.

a·ma·ne·ra·do, –da I. past part. see **amanerarse** II. adj. mannered, affected.

a·ma·ne·ra·mien·to m. affectation.

a·ma·ne·rar·se reflex. to become affected or mannered.

a·ma·nez·ca see **amanecer**.

a·ma·no·jar tr. to bundle, bunch.

a·man·sa·dor, –do·ra I. adj. taming, soothing II. m.f. *(domador)* tamer, soother; AMER. *(de caballos)* horsebreaker —f. ARG. public waiting room.

a·man·sa·mien·to m. *(domadura)* taming; *(del caballo)* breaking; *(efecto)* tameness; FIG. *(apaciguamiento)* easing, soothing.

a·man·sar tr. *(domar)* to tame <a. un animal to tame an animal>; *(un caballo)* to break (a horse); FIG. *(sosegar)* to ease, soothe —reflex. to calm down.

a·man·te I. adj. fond, loving II. m.f. *(enamorado)* lover; FIG. *(aficionado)* lover, fan —m. MARIT. *(cabo)* runner.

a·ma·nuen·se m.f. *(secretario)* amanuensis, clerk; *(escribiente)* copyist, transcriber.

a·ma·ña·do, –da I. past part. see **amañar** II. adj. *(falsificado)* fixed, falsified; *(diestro)* clever, skillful.

a·ma·ñar tr. DEROG. to fix, arrange, falsify —reflex. *(lograr)* to manage <amañarse a escribir to manage to write>; *(acostumbrarse)* to adapt oneself.

a·ma·ño m. *(maña)* skill, ability; *(arreglo)* scheme, ruse ♦ **amaños** tools, instruments.

a·ma·po·la f. BOT. poppy.

a·mar tr. to love.

a·ma·ra·je m. AER., AVIA. landing on water.

a·ma·ran·to m. BOT. amaranth.

a·ma·rar intr. AER., AVIA. to land on water.

a·mar·fi·la·do, –da adj. *(semejante al marfil)* ivory-like; *(color)* ivory.

a·mar·ga·do, –da I. past part. see **amargar** II. adj. bitter, embittered.

a·mar·ga·men·te adv. bitterly.

a·mar·gar §47 tr. FIG. to make bitter, embitter —intr. to be or taste bitter —reflex. FIG. to become bitter or embittered.

a·mar·go, –ga I. adj. *(acerbo)* bitter <almendra a. bitter almond>; FIG. bitter, painful <un recuerdo a. a painful memory>; *(afligido)* bitter, embittered <él se puso muy a. he became very bitter>; ARG. cowardly II. m. *(amargor)* bitterness; *(licor)* bitters; AMER. sugarless maté.

a·mar·gor m. or **a·mar·gu·ra** f. *(sabor)* bitterness; FIG. *(pena)* bitterness, pain.

a·mar·gué, amargue see **amargar**.

a·mar·gu·ra f. *(sabor)* bitterness; FIG. bitterness, grief ♦ **¡qué a.!** what a pity!

a·ma·ri·lla I. f. FIG., COLL. *(moneda)* gold coin; VET. liver disease of sheep II. adj. see **amarillo, –lla**.

a·ma·ri·lle·ar intr. *(ser amarillo)* to be yellow; *(amarillecer)* to yellow, turn yellow; *(palidecer)* to pale, turn pale.

a·ma·ri·llen·to, –ta adj. *(que tira a amarillo)* yellowish; *(de tez)* yellow.

a·ma·ri·llo, –lla adj. & m. yellow —f. see **amarilla**.

a·ma·ro·mar tr. to moor, tie up.

a·ma·rra f. *(cable)* mooring line or rope; *(para caballos)* martingale ♦ **amarras** FIG. protection, support.

a·ma·rra·de·ro m. *(poste)* hitching post; *(argolla)* hitching ring; MARIT. *(poste)* bollard; *(argolla)* mooring ring; *(sitio)* mooring.

a·ma·rra·do, –da I. past part. see **amarrar** II. adj. *(atado)* tied down, moored; AMER. *(tacaño)* stingy, mean; CUBA, CHILE *(torpe)* stupid, slow.

a·ma·rra·du·ra f. mooring, tying.

a·ma·rra·je m. MARIT. mooring charge.

a·ma·rrar tr. *(atar)* to tie (up), fasten; MARIT. to moor, make fast; FIG. *(en los juegos de naipes)* to stack (the deck) —reflex. COLL. to make sure ♦ **amarrársela** C. AMER., COL. to get drunk.

a·ma·rre m. *(atado)* tying, fastening; MARIT. mooring; *(fullería)* stacking (of the deck).

a·ma·rre·te adj. ARG., PERU stingy, mean.

a·mar·te·la·da·men·te adv. lovingly.

a·mar·te·la·mien·to m. *(enamoramiento)* infatuation; *(galanteo)* courting, wooing.

a·mar·te·lar tr. *(atormentar)* to drive crazy with love *or* jealousy; *(enamorar)* to enamor, inspire love —reflex. to fall madly *or* deeply in love.

a·mar·ti·llar tr. *(martillar)* to hammer; *(un arma)* to cock (a gun); FIG., COLL. *(asegurar)* to secure.

a·ma·sa·de·ra f. kneading bowl.

a·ma·sa·dor, –do·ra I. adj. kneading II. m.f. *(persona que amasa)* kneader; *(panadero)* baker.

a·ma·sa·du·ra f. *(acción de amasar)* kneading; *(amasijo)* dough.

a·ma·sar tr. to knead <*a. el pan* to knead the bread>; *(dar masajes)* to give a massage, massage; FIG. *(acumular)* to amass <*a. una fortuna* to amass a fortune>; FIG., COLL. *(tramar)* to cook up, concoct.

a·ma·si·jo m. CUL. dough; *(amasamiento)* kneading; FIG. *(tarea)* task; FIG., COLL. *(revoltijo)* hodgepodge, potpourri; *(convenio)* plot, scheme; ARG., COLL. thrashing, beating; VEN. wheat bread.

a·ma·teur adj. & m.f. amateur.

a·ma·teu·ris·mo m. amateurism.

a·ma·tis·ta f. MIN. amethyst.

a·ma·ti·vo, –va adj. amorous.

a·ma·to·rio, –ria adj. amatory, love <*cartas amatorias* love letters>.

a·mau·ro·sis f. [pl. **-sis**] MED. amaurosis ♦ **a. fugax** AVIA., MED. flight blindness.

a·ma·za·co·ta·do, –da adj. *(pesado)* heavy, lumpy; FIG. *(confuso)* jumbled, incoherent (of literature).

a·ma·zo·na f. MYTH. Amazon; FIG. *(mujer varonil)* amazon; *(caballista)* horsewoman: *(traje)* woman's riding clothes; ORNITH. amazon (parrot).

A·ma·zo·nas m. Amazon (River).

a·ma·zó·ni·co, –ca adj. Amazonian.

am·ba·ges m.pl. FIG. circumlocution ♦ **hablar sin a.** to speak plainly, not beat around the bush.

ám·bar m. MIN. amber; *(perfume)* perfume ♦ **a. gris** ambergris.

am·ba·ri·no, –na adj. amber.

Am·be·res Antwerp.

am·bi·ción f. ambition.

am·bi·cio·nar tr. to aspire to, strive for.

am·bi·cio·sa·men·te adv. ambitiously.

am·bi·cio·so, –sa I. adj. ambitious II. m.f. ambitious person.

am·bi·dex·tro, –tra *or* **am·bi·dies·tro, –tra** adj. ambidextrous.

am·bien·ta·ción f. *(ambiente)* atmosphere; *(acción)* creating an atmosphere; *(ajuste)* adjustment (to surroundings or situation); LIT. setting, scene.

am·bien·tal adj. environmental.

am·bien·tar tr. to give atmosphere to; LIT. to set —reflex. to adjust *or* orientate oneself.

am·bien·te I. adj. surrounding, ambient ♦ **el medio a.** the environment II. m. *(aire)* atmosphere; FIG. *(atmósfera)* atmosphere, ambiance <*este café tiene un a. elegante* this café has an elegant ambiance>; ARG., CHILE, URUG. room.

am·bi·gua·men·te adv. ambiguously.

am·bi·güe·dad f. ambiguity, uncertainty.

am·bi·guo, –gua adj. *(de doble sentido)* ambiguous <*lenguaje a.* ambiguous language>; *(incierto)* ambiguous, uncertain; GRAM. of either gender.

ám·bi·to m. *(perímetro)* boundary, limit; *(recinto)* enclosure; *(esfera)* scope, extent; *(campo)* field <*el a. musical* the field of music>.

am·bi·va·len·cia f. ambivalence.

am·bi·va·len·te adj. ambivalent.

am·bos, –bas adj. & indef. pron. both.

am·bro·sí·a f. MYTH. ambrosia; FIG. *(cosa o comida exquisita)* ambrosia; BOT. ambrosia, ragweed.

am·bro·sia·co, –ca adj. ambrosial.

am·bu·lan·cia f. *(vehículo)* ambulance; *(hospital móvil)* field hospital *or* ambulance.

am·bu·lan·te I. adj. *(viajero)* traveling <*vendedor a.* traveling salesman>; *(itinerante)* itinerant, walking II. m. AMER. peddler; MEX. ambulance driver.

am·bu·lar intr. to ambulate, amble, stroll.

am·bu·la·to·rio, –ria I. adj. ambulatory II. m. health clinic.

a·me·ba f. ZOOL. amoeba.

a·me·dren·ta·dor, –do·ra I. adj. scary, frightening II. m.f. scarer, frightener.

a·me·dren·tar tr. to scare, frighten —reflex. to become scared *or* frightened.

a·mel·gar §47 tr. AGR. to furrow.

a·mén I. m. amen ♦ **decir a. a todo** FIG., COLL. to agree to everything • **en un decir a.** FIG. in an instant II. adv. ♦ **a. de** *(además)* besides, in addition to; *(excepto)* except for, aside from.

a·me·na·men·te adv. pleasantly, agreeably.

a·me·na·za f. threat, menace.

a·me·na·za·dor, –do·ra *or* **a·me·na·zan·te** adj. threatening, menacing.

a·me·na·zar §04 tr. to threaten, menace —intr. to threaten, be imminent <*amenaza tormenta* a storm is threatening>.

a·men·gua·dor, –do·ra adj. *(reductor)* reducing, diminishing; *(deshonrador)* denigrating, belittling.

a·men·gua·mien·to m. *(reducción)* reduction, diminution; *(denigración)* denigration, belittling.

a·men·guar §10 tr. *(reducir)* to reduce, diminish; FIG. *(deshonrar)* to denigrate, belittle.

a·me·ni·dad f. amenity, pleasantness.

a·me·ni·zar §04 tr. *(hacer ameno)* to make pleasant *or* charming; FIG. *(avivar)* to enliven, brighten up <*su música amenizó la fiesta* their music enlivened the party>.

a·me·no, –na adj. pleasant, agreeable.

a·me·rar tr. to mix with water —reflex. to soak through, seep.

A·mé·ri·ca f. America ♦ **A. Central** Central America • **A. del Norte** North America • **A. del Sur** South America • **A. Latina** Latin America • **las Américas** the Americas.

a·me·ri·ca·na f. *(chaqueta)* jacket, coat; *(faetón)* phaeton, carriage II. adj. see **americano, –na.**

a·me·ri·ca·nis·mo m. *(algo de Hispanoamérica)* Spanish-American word, custom, *or* trait; AMER. liking for North American ways.

a·me·ri·ca·ni·za·ción f. Americanization.

a·me·ri·ca·ni·zar §04 tr. to Americanize (to make culturally North American or Spanish-American) —reflex. to become Americanized (made culturally North American or Spanish-American).

a·me·ri·ca·no, –na adj. & m.f. American —f. see **americana.**

a·me·ri·cio m. CHEM. americium.

a·me·rin·dio, –dia I. adj. Amerindian II. m.f. Amerind, Amerindian.

a·mes·ti·za·do, –da adj. mestizo-like, having mestizo features.

a·me·ta·la·do, –da adj. metallic.

a·me·tra·lla·dor, –do·ra I. m.f. *(operador)* machine gunner II. adj. machine-gun.

a·me·tra·lla·do·ra I. f. machine gun II. adj. see **ametrallador, –dora.**

a·me·tra·lla·mien·to m. MIL. machine-gunning; FIG. *(matanza)* slaughter.

a·me·tra·llar tr. to machine-gun.

a·mian·ti·na f. asbestos fabric.

a·mian·to m. MIN. amianthus, asbestos.

a·mi·cal adj. friendly.

a·mi·ga·bi·li·dad f. amicability, friendliness.

a·mi·ga·ble adj. *(amistoso)* amicable, friendly; FIG. *(armonioso)* harmonious, concordant.

a·mi·ga·ble·men·te adv. amicably.

a·mi·gar §47 tr. *(amistar)* to bring (people) together; *(reconciliar)* to reconcile —reflex. *(amistarse)* to make friends, become friendly; *(reconciliarse)* to make up, reconcile; *(cohabitar)* to cohabit, live together.

a·mi·ga·zo, –za COLL. I. adj. close (friend) II. m.f. *(amigo)* buddy, pal; ARG., DEROG. pal.

a·míg·da·la f. ANAT. tonsil, amygdala.

a·mig·da·li·tis f. [pl. **-tis**] MED. tonsilitis.

a·mi·go, –ga I. m.f. friend ♦ **a. íntimo** *or* **del alma** close friend, bosom buddy • **a. de lo ajeno** COLL. thief • **hacerse a. de** to make friends with • **hacerse amigos** to become friends **II.** adj. *(amistoso)* friendly; FIG. *(aficionado)* fond of <*ser a. de comer mucho* to be fond of eating a lot>.

a·mi·go·te m.f. COLL. great friend, pal; ARG., DEROG. pal.

a·mi·gué, amigue see **amigar.**

a·mi·gui·si·mo, –ma adj. very friendly.

a·mi·la·na·do, –da I. past part. see **amilanar II.** adj. *(acobardado)* cowardly; *(pusilánime)* pusillanimous.

a·mi·la·nar tr. *(asustar)* to frighten, intimidate; FIG. *(desanimar)* to dishearten, discourage —reflex. *(asustarse)* to become frightened *or* intimidated; *(desanimarse)* to become disheartened *or* discouraged.

a·mi·lla·rar tr. to assess a tax on, assess for taxes.

a·mi·no·á·ci·do m. CHEM. amino acid.

a·mi·no·rar tr. to reduce, diminish ♦ **a. el paso** to walk more slowly.

a·mis·tad f. *(afección)* friendship; *(afinidad)* affinity ♦ **amistades** friends, acquaintances • **trabar** *or* **estrechar a.** to make friends • **hacer las amistades** to reconcile, make up • **romper las amistades** to quarrel.

a·mis·tar tr. *(amigar)* to make friends with; *(reconciliar)* to reconcile —reflex. *(estrechar amistad)* to become friends; *(reconciliarse)* to become reconciled, make up.

a·mis·to·sa·men·te adv. amicably, in a friendly way.

a·mis·to·so, –sa adj. amicable, friendly.

a·mi·to m. RELIG. amice.

am·ne·sia f. MED. amnesia ♦ **a. temporal** blackout.

am·né·si·co, –ca adj. & m.f. MED. amnesiac, amnesic.

am·nió·ti·co, –ca adj. ANAT. amniotic.

am·nis·tí·a f. amnesty.

am·nis·tia·do, –da I. past part. see **amnistiar II.** adj. amnestied **III.** m.f. amnestied person.

am·nis·tiar §30 tr. to amnesty, grant amnesty to.

a·mo m. *(señor)* master; *(dueño)* owner, proprietor; *(jefe)* boss, employer ♦ **ser el a. del cotarro** COLL. to rule the roost.

a·mo·blar §19 tr. var. of **amueblar.**

a·mo·do·rra·mien·to m. drowsiness, sleepiness.

a·mo·do·rra·do, –da I. past part. see **amodorrarse II.** adj. drowsy, sleepy.

a·mo·do·rrar·se reflex. *(caer en modorra)* to become drowsy *or* sleepy; *(adormecerse)* to doze.

a·mo·hi·nar §81 tr. to irritate, annoy —reflex. to become irritated *or* annoyed.

a·mo·jo·nar tr. to mark with boundaries, delimit.

a·mo·la·dor I. m. *(afilador)* grinder, sharpener; *(molestia)* nuisance **II.** adj. FIG., COLL. tedious, bothersome.

a·mo·la·du·ra f. grinding, sharpening ♦ **amoladuras** grindstone dust.

a·mo·lar §19 tr. *(afilar)* to grind, sharpen; FIG. *(molestar)* to irritate, annoy; *(adelgazar)* to lose weight —reflex. ARG., MEX., URUG. to become irritated *or* annoyed.

a·mol·da·ble adj. moldable, malleable.

a·mol·da·mien·to m. *(acción)* fitting, molding; *(ajuste)* adjusting; FIG. *(adaptación)* adaptation.

a·mol·dar tr. *(ajustar al molde)* to mold, model; FIG. *(adaptar)* to adapt, adjust —reflex. to adapt oneself, conform.

a·mo·ne·dar tr. to mint, coin.

a·mo·nes·ta·ción f. *(represión)* admonition, reprimand; *(advertencia)* warning ♦ **correr las amonestaciones** RELIG. to publish the marriage banns.

a·mo·nes·tar tr. *(reprender)* to admonish, reprimand; *(advertir)* to warn; RELIG. to publish (marriage banns).

a·mo·nia·co *or* **a·mo·ní·a·co** m. CHEM. *(gas)* ammonia; *(goma)* gum resin.

a·mo·nia·co, –ca adj. ammoniac, ammoniacal.

a·mon·to·na·mien·to m. *(acción de apilar)* heaping, piling up; *(acción de acumular)* gathering; *(montón)* heap, pile, accumulation; *(de tráfico)* traffic jam; *(de gente)* crowding.

a·mon·to·nar tr. *(apilar)* to heap *or* pile (up); *(acumular)* to accumulate, gather; *(riquezas)* to hoard; ECUAD. to insult —reflex. *(apilarse)* to pile up; *(acumularse)* to crowd (together); *(coches)* to jam; *(enfadarse)* to get angry; FIG., COLL. *(amancebarse)* to cohabit.

a·mor m. *(adoración)* love; *(afecto)* affection; *(querido)* darling, beloved ♦ **al a. de** close to • **a. patrio** love of country, patriotism • **a. propio** pride • **amores** *(amoríos)* love affairs, romances; *(requiebros)* endearments; BOT. hedgehog parsley • **con** *or* **de mil amores** COLL. gladly, with pleasure • **hacer el a.** to make love • **¡por a. a Dios!** for goodness sake! • **sin a.** loveless.

a·mo·ral adj. amoral.

a·mo·ra·li·dad f. amorality.

a·mo·ra·ta·do, –da I. past part. see **amoratar II.** adj. *(morado)* purplish, blue; AMER. black-and-blue, bruised ♦ **a. de frío** blue with cold.

a·mo·ra·tar tr. *(poner morado)* to make blue *or* purple; AMER. to bruise —reflex. *(ponerse morado)* to turn blue *or* purple; *(magullarse)* to bruise, turn black-and-blue.

a·mor·ci·llo m. *(enamoramiento)* flirtation, fling; *(figura)* cupid.

a·mor·da·zar §04 tr. *(una persona)* to gag; *(un perro)* to muzzle; FIG. *(callar)* to silence, gag.

a·mor·fia f. *or* **a·mor·fis·mo** m. *(falta de forma regular)* amorphism, amorphousness; MED. amorphy, organic deformity.

a·mor·fo, –fa adj. *(sin forma regular)* amorphous, shapeless; FIG., COLL. *(insulso)* dull.

a·mo·rí·o m. fling, love affair.

a·mo·ris·ca·do, –da adj. Moorish, Moorish-looking.

a·mo·ro·sa·men·te adv. lovingly, affectionately.

a·mo·ro·so, –sa adj. *(afectuoso)* loving, affectionate <*un padre a.* a loving father>; *(enamoradizo)* amorous <*miradas amorosas* amorous glances>; FIG. *(tierra)* workable (land); *(tiempo)* pleasant, mild (weather); AMER. charming.

a·mo·rri·ñar·se reflex. to become sad and sullen.

a·mor·ta·ja·mien·to m. shrouding.

a·mor·ta·jar tr. *(poner la mortaja a)* to shroud; TECH. to join (tenon and mortise); FIG. *(cubrir)* to cover, conceal.

a·mor·te·cer §17 tr. *(golpes)* to cushion, absorb; *(ruidos)* to muffle, deaden; *(luces)* to dim; *(colores, música)* to tone down, soften —reflex. *(ruidos)* to be deadened *or* muffled; *(desmayarse)* to faint.

a·mor·ti·cé, amortice see **amortizar.**

a·mor·ti·gua·ción f. var. of **amortiguamiento.**

a·mor·ti·gua·dor, –do·ra I. adj. *(de golpes)* cushioning, softening; *(de ruidos)* deadening, muffling; *(de luces)* dimming; *(de colores, música)* softening **II.** m. AUTO. shock absorber; *(parachoques)* bumper ♦ **a. de luz** dimmer • **a. de ruido** silencer, muffler • **a. de sonido** sound absorber.

a·mor·ti·gua·mien·to m. *(de golpes)* cushioning, softening; *(de ruidos)* deadening, muffling; *(de luces)* dimming; *(de colores, música)* toning down, softening; MED. *(desmayo)* fainting.

a·mor·ti·guar §10 tr. *(golpes)* to cushion, absorb; *(ruidos)* to muffle, deaden; *(luces)* to dim; *(colores, música)* to tone down, soften; *(fuegos)* to dampen; FIG. *(mitigar)* to mitigate, alleviate —reflex. *(ruidos)* to be deadened *or* muffled; ARG., BOT. to wither; FIG. *(desanimarse)* to get depressed.

a·mor·ti·za·ble adj. LAW amortizable; FIN. *(como un bono)* redeemable; *(como una deuda)* repayable.

a·mor·ti·za·ción f. LAW amortization; *(de una plaza)* elimination (of a position); FIN. *(de un bono)* redemption; *(de una deuda)* repayment.

a·mor·ti·zar §04 tr. LAW to amortize; *(una plaza)* to eliminate (a position); FIN. *(un bono)* to redeem; *(el capital)* to recuperate (invested capital); *(una deuda)* to repay, pay off —intr. to depreciate.

a·mos·car·se §70 reflex. COLL. *(irritarse)* to get angry; CUBA to blush.

a·mos·ta·zar §04 tr. COLL. to irritate, annoy —reflex. *(irritarse)* to get irritated *or* annoyed; AMER. to become embarrassed.

a·mo·ti·na·do, –da I. past part. see **amotinar II.** adj. *(insurrecto)* riotous, rebellious; MIL. mutinous **III.** m.f. *(insurrecto)* rebel, rioter; MIL. mutineer.

a·mo·ti·na·mien·to m. *(motín)* riot, uprising; MIL. mutiny.

a·mo·ti·nar tr. *(sublevar)* to agitate, to incite (to riot) —reflex. *(sublevarse)* to riot, rebel; MIL. to mutiny.

a·mo·ver §78 tr. to remove *or* dismiss (from a job).

a·mo·vi·ble adj. removable, detachable.

a·mo·vi·li·dad f. removability, detachability.

am·pa·rar tr. *(proteger)* to shelter, protect; *(defender)* to defend, aid —reflex. *(protegerse)* to shelter *or* protect oneself; *(acogerse)* to seek protection *or* sanctuary.

am·pa·ro m. *(protección)* shelter, protection; *(defensa)* defense, aid.

am·pe·ra·je m. ELEC. amperage.

am·pe·rí·me·tro m. ELEC. ammeter, amperemeter.

am·pe·rio m. ELEC. ampere ♦ **a. hora** ampere-hour.

am·plia·ble adj. extendible, expandable.

am·plia·ción f. *(extensión)* extension, expansion; *(desarrollo)* elaboration; PHOTOG. enlargement.

am·plia·dor, –do·ra I. adj. extending, expanding II. f. PHOTOG. enlarger.

am·plia·men·te adv. amply, fully.

am·pliar §30 tr. *(extender)* to extend, expand; *(desarrollar)* to develop, elaborate on; *(aumentar)* to increase; *(ensanchar)* to widen; PHOTOG. to enlarge.

am·plia·ti·vo, –va adj. amplifying, enlarging.

am·pli·fi·ca·ción f. *(aumento)* amplification, magnification; PHOTOG. enlargement.

am·pli·fi·ca·dor, –do·ra I. adj. amplifying II. m. ELEC. magnifier, amplifier; RAD. amplifier; *(altavoz)* loudspeaker.

am·pli·fi·car §70 tr. *(aumentar)* to amplify; *(con microscopio)* to magnify; PHOTOG. to enlarge.

am·plio, –plia adj. *(espacioso)* spacious, roomy; *(extenso)* ample, broad, extensive; *(ancho)* full, wide.

am·pli·tud f. *(anchura)* amplitude, fullness; *(extensión)* extent, size; *(de una pieza)* room, spaciousness ♦ **a. de miras** broad-mindedness • **de gran a.** far-reaching, of large scope.

am·po·lla f. *(vejiga)* blister; *(frasco)* bottle, flask; MED. ampoule; *(burbuja)* bubble (in boiling water); RELIG. cruet, ampulla.

am·po·llar tr. & reflex. to blister.

am·po·lle·ta f. hourglass.

am·pu·lo·sa·men·te adv. pompously, bombastically.

am·pu·lo·si·dad f. pomposity, bombast (of style).

am·pu·lo·so, –sa adj. pompous, bombastic.

am·pu·ta·ción f. SURG. amputation.

am·pu·ta·do, –da I. past part. see **amputar** II. adj. amputated III. m.f. amputee.

am·pu·tar tr. to amputate, cut off.

a·mu·cha·cha·do, –da adj. childish.

a·mue·blar tr. to furnish.

a·mue·ble, amueblo see **amoblar** *or* **amueblar.**

a·mue·le, amuelo see **amolar.**

a·mue·va, amuevo see **amover.**

a·mu·je·ra·do, –da adj. effeminate, womanish.

a·mu·la·ta·do, –da adj. mulatto-like, mulatto-colored.

a·mu·le·to m. amulet, charm.

a·mu·ni·cio·nar tr. to supply with ammunition.

a·mu·ñe·ca·do, –da adj. doll-like.

a·mu·ra·lla·do, –da I. past part. see **amurallar** II. adj. walled, fortified with walls *<una ciudad a.* a walled city>.

a·mu·ra·llar tr. to wall, fortify with walls.

a·mu·rrar·se reflex. AMER. to get depressed, feel low.

a·mu·rriar·se reflex. var. of **amurrarse.**

a·mus·gar §47 tr. *(tirar hacia atrás)* to lay back (the ears, said of an animal about to attack); *(entrecerrar los ojos)* to squint —reflex. HOND. to become embarrassed; ARG. to give up, concede.

a·mus·tiar tr. & reflex. to wither.

a·na·bap·tis·mo m. RELIG. Anabaptism.

a·na·bap·tis·ta adj. & m.f. RELIG. Anabaptist.

a·na·bo·lis·mo m. BIOL. anabolism.

a·na·ca·ra·do, –da adj. pearly, mother-of-pearl.

a·na·car·do m. BOT. cashew (nut and tree).

a·na·con·da f. ZOOL. anaconda.

a·na·co·ré·ti·co, –ca adj. anchoritic, anchoretic.

a·na·cre·ón·ti·co, –ca adj. POET. Anacreontic.

a·na·cró·ni·co, –ca adj. anachronistic, dated.

a·na·cro·nis·mo m. anachronism.

á·na·de m.f. duck ♦ **á. silvestre** *or* **real** mallard duck.

a·na·de·ar intr. to waddle.

a·na·e·ro·bio BIOL. I. adj. aneorobic, aneorobical II. m. aneorobe.

a·ná·fo·ra f. RHET. anaphora, repetition.

a·na·fre m. portable oven.

a·na·fro·di·sia f. MED. anaphrodisia (absence of sexual desire).

a·na·gra·ma m. anagram.

a·nal adj. ANAT. anal.

a·na·les m.pl. annals.

a·nal·fa·be·tis·mo m. illiteracy.

a·nal·fa·be·to, –ta adj. & m.f. illiterate.

a·nal·ge·sia f. MED. analgesia.

a·nal·gé·si·co, –ca MED. adj. & m. analgesic.

a·na·li·cé, analice see **analizar.**

a·ná·li·sis m. [pl. **-sis**] analysis ♦ **a. de Fourier** MATH. Fourier analysis • **a. de orina** urinalysis • **a. de sangre** blood test.

a·na·lis·ta m.f. *(persona que hace análisis)* analyst; *(historiador)* annalist, historian; RAD., TELEV. commentator.

a·na·lí·ti·ca·men·te adv. analytically.

a·na·lí·ti·co, –ca I. adj. analytical II. f. analytics.

a·na·li·za·ble adj. analyzable.

a·na·li·zar §04 tr. to analyze, examine.

a·ná·lo·ga·men·te adv. analogously, similarly.

a·na·lo·gí·a f. *(relación)* analogy; *(semejanza)* analogy, similarity; GRAM. analogy ♦ **por a.** by analogy.

a·na·ló·gi·co, –ca adj. analogical.

a·na·lo·gis·mo m. LOG. analogism.

a·ná·lo·go, –ga adj. analogous, similar.

a·nam·ne·sia *or* **a·nam·ne·sis** f. MED. anamnesis, case history.

a·na·ná *or* **a·na·nás** m. [pl. **-na·es** *or* **-na·ses**] BOT. pineapple (plant and fruit).

a·na·plas·tia f. SURG. anaplasty, plastic surgery.

a·na·quel m. shelf.

a·na·ran·ja·do, –da adj. & m. *(color)* orange.

a·nar·quí·a f. anarchy.

a·nár·qui·co, –ca adj. anarchic, anarchical.

a·nar·quis·mo m. anarchism.

a·nar·quis·ta I. m.f. anarchist II. adj. anarchistic.

a·nar·qui·zar §04 tr. to make anarchic —intr. to propagate anarchism.

a·na·te·ma m. anathema.

a·na·te·ma·ti·zar §04 tr. RELIG. to anathematize, excommunicate; *(maldecir)* to curse, condemn.

a·na·to·mí·a f. *(ciencia)* anatomy; *(disección)* dissection.

a·na·tó·mi·co, –ca I. adj. anatomic, anatomical II. m.f. anatomist.

a·na·to·mi·zar §04 tr. *(disecar)* to anatomize, dissect; ARTS. to delineate (muscles).

an·ca f. *(cacha)* haunch; *(grupa)* croup, rump; *(nalga)* rump, buttock ♦ **ancas de rana** frogs' legs • **en ancas** COLL. accompanying, as a side effect • **llevar a las ancas** FIG. to support someone at one's expense • **montar** *or* **llevar en ancas** to ride (*or* carry) behind another person.

an·ces·tral adj. ancestral.

an·cia·ni·dad f. old age.

an·cia·no, –na I. adj. old, elderly II. m. old *or* elderly man; RELIG. elder —f. old *or* elderly woman.

an·cla f. anchor ♦ **a. de la esperanza** *or* **de salvación** MARIT. sheet anchor; FIG. *(última esperanza)* last hope.

an·clar intr. MARIT. to anchor, drop *or* cast anchor.

an·cón m. *(ensenada)* cove, inlet; ARCHIT. ancon, bracket; MEX. corner; P. RICO raft.

án·co·ra f. anchor.

an·co·ra·je m. MARIT. anchoring.

an·co·rar intr. MARIT. to anchor, drop anchor.

an·char tr. & intr. to widen, broaden.

an·cho, –cha I. adj. *(extenso)* wide, broad *<una calle a.* a wide street>; *(holgado)* loose, full (clothes) ♦ **de a.** wide *<tres metros de a.* three meters wide> • **estar** *or* **ponerse muy a.** FIG., COLL. to boast, become conceited • **quedarse tan a.** FIG. to be at ease, remain unworried II. m. width, breadth ♦ **a sus anchas** FIG. as one pleases, comfortably.

an·cho·a f. anchovy.

an·chu·ra f. *(latitud)* width, breadth; *(amplitud)* fullness; FIG. *(soltura)* laxity, freedom.

an·chu·ro·so, –sa adj. var. of **ancho, –cha.**

an·da·da I. f. *(pan)* thin, crisp bread; *(caminata)* long walk ♦ **andadas** HUNT. tracks • **volver a las andadas** FIG., COLL. to be up to one's old tricks II. adj. see **andado, –da.**

an·da·de·ras f.pl. walker, go-cart (to teach children to walk).

an·da·de·ro, –ra adj. passable (on foot).

an·da·do, –da I. past part. see **andar¹** II. adj. *(animado)* busy, well-traveled; *(común)* common, ordinary; *(usado)* worn, used III. f. see **andada**.

an·da·dor, –do·ra I. adj. *(veloz)* quick, fast-walking; *(andariego)* wandering, roving II. m.f. *(caminante)* walker (person); *(andariego)* wanderer, rover; LAW *(mensajero)* court messenger, courier ♦ **andadores** straps (to support an infant learning to walk).

an·da·du·ra f. *(acción de andar)* walking; *(manera de andar)* gait, pace.

An·da·lu·cí·a f. Andalusia.

an·da·luz, –lu·za adj. & m.f. [m.pl. **-lu·ces**] Andalusian.

an·da·mio m. *(armazón)* scaffold, scaffolding; *(tablado)* stage, platform ♦ **a. colgado, colgante,** *or* **suspendido** hanging scaffold.

an·da·na f. *(fila)* row, tier; *(estantes)* shelves ♦ **llamarse uno Andana** COLL. *(desentenderse de un asunto)* to wash one's hands of a matter; *(desdecirse de lo que se prometió)* to go back on one's word.

an·da·na·da f. MARIT. broadside; *(gradería)* covered grandstand ♦ **por andanadas** ARG. in abundance • **soltar una a.** FIG., COLL. to scold, reprimand.

¡an·dan·do! interj. *(¡en seguida!)* right away, immediately; *(¡vamos!)* let's go.

an·dan·te I. adj. walking, traveling ♦ **caballero a.** knight errant II. m. & adv. MUS. andante.

an·dan·za m. *(suceso)* occurrence, event; *(aventura)* adventure ♦ **buena a.** good luck *or* fortune • **mala a.** bad luck *or* fortune • **volver a las andanzas** to be up to one's old tricks.

an·dar¹ §05, §G9 intr. *(caminar)* to walk; *(marchar)* to go, move; *(funcionar)* to work, function; *(transcurrir)* to go by, elapse; FIG. *(estar)* to be <*andan escribiendo* they are writing>; *(sentirse)* to be, feel <*a. alegre* to be happy> ♦ **¡anda!** *(como exhortación)* get going! move along!; *(expresando admiración)* no kidding! • **¡ándale!** COLL. hurry up! • **a. a** to go on <*a. a caballo* to go on horseback> • **a. con cuidado** *or* **con pies de plomo** to be careful, tread cautiously • **a. de broma** to be joking • **a. en** *(envolverse)* to be mixed up *or* engaged in <*a. en pleitos* to be engaged in lawsuits>; *(escudriñar)* rummage through, search <*a. en los cajones* to rummage through the drawers>; to be going on, be about <*ella a. en los 30 años* she is about 30 years old> • **a. por las nubes** FIG. to be absent-minded • **a. tras** FIG. to go after, pursue • **¿cómo andas de . . . ?** how is your . . . ? <*¿cómo andas de salud?* how is your health?> —tr. *(viajar)* to travel, go <*a. tres millas* to travel three miles> —reflex. to leave, go away ♦ **andarse en** to be mixed up in • **andarse por las ramas** FIG. to beat around the bush.

an·dar² m. walk, pace, gait ♦ **a. largo a.** in due course • **a más** *or* **todo a.** at full speed • **a un a.** on the same level.

an·da·rie·go, –ga I. adj. wandering, roving II. m.f. wanderer, rover.

an·da·rín, –ri·na I. adj. walking II. m.f. walker.

an·da·ri·vel m. *(balsa)* cable ferry; *(maroma)* ferry cable; MARIT. lifeline, safety ropes.

an·das f.pl. *(parihuelas)* stretcher; *(litera)* litter, sedan chair; *(féretro)* bier; *(plataforma)* portable platform.

an·dén m. *(plataforma)* station *or* railway platform; *(de una carretera)* shoulder, side of the road; *(muelle)* wharf, dock; *(acera)* sidewalk, pavement, *(parapeto)* parapet, railing ♦ **andenes** AMER. cultivation terraces.

An·des m.pl. Andes (Mountains).

an·di·nis·mo m. AMER. mountain climbing, mountaineering.

an·di·nis·ta m.f. mountain climber, mountaineer.

an·di·no, –na adj. Andean.

An·do·rra f. Andorra.

an·do·rra·no, –na adj. & m.f. Andorran.

an·do·rre·ro, –ra I. adj. roving, roaming II. m.f. rover, roamer.

an·dra·jo m. *(jirón)* tatter, rag; DEROG. wretch.

an·dra·jo·sa·men·te adv. raggedly.

an·dra·jo·so, –sa adj. tattered, ragged.

an·dro·cé·fa·lo, –la adj. ANAT. androcephalous.

an·dro·ce·o m. BOT. androecium.

an·dro·cra·cia f. SOCIOL. male supremacy.

an·dro·fo·bia f. MED. androphobia.

an·dró·gi·no, –na I. adj. BIOL., ZOOL. androgynous, hermaphroditic; BOT. androgynous II. m.f. BIOL., ZOOL. androgyne, hermaphrodite.

an·droi·de m. android.

an·dro·mor·fo, –fa adj. andromorphous.

an·du·llo m. *(hoja de tabaco)* rolled tobacco leaf; MARIT. fender; ARG., CUBA plug of chewing tobacco; DOM. REP. chewing tobacco.

an·du·rria·les m.pl. COLL. out-of-the-way places, boondocks.

an·du·vie·ra, anduvo see **andar¹**.

a·ne·ar tr. to measure by ells.

a·néc·do·ta f. anecdote.

a·nec·do·ta·rio m. anecdotage, collection of anecdotes.

a·nec·dó·ti·co, –ca adj. anecdotal.

a·nec·do·tis·ta m.f. anecdotist.

a·ne·ga·ble adj. floodable, subject to flooding.

a·ne·ga·ción f. *(muerte)* drowning; *(inundación)* flooding, inundation.

a·ne·ga·di·zo, –za adj. frequently flooded, subject to flooding.

a·ne·ga·mien·to m. *(inundación)* flooding, inundation; *(ahogo)* drowning.

a·ne·gar §47 tr. *(ahogar)* to drown; *(inundar)* to flood, inundate —reflex. *(ahogarse)* to drown; *(inundarse)* to flood, be inundated; MARIT. *(hundirse)* to sink, founder ♦ **anegarse en llanto** to dissolve into *or* be overwhelmed by tears.

a·ne·jar tr. to join, attach.

a·ne·jín *or* **a·ne·jir** m. rhymed popular proverb which can be sung.

a·ne·jo, –ja I. adj. *(anexo)* attached, annexed; *(dependiente)* dependent II. m. *(suplemento)* annex; LIT. *(apéndice)* annex, appendix.

a·ne·mia f. MED. anemia.

a·né·mi·co, –ca I. adj. anemic II. m.f. MED. anemic person; COLL. *(persona débil)* weakling.

a·ne·mó·me·tro m. anemometer, wind gauge.

a·né·mo·na *or* **a·ne·mo·ne** f. BOT. anemone; ZOOL. sea anemone.

a·nes·te·sia f. MED. anesthesia.

a·nes·te·siar tr. MED. to anesthetize, give an anesthetic to.

a·nes·té·si·co, –ca adj. & m. MED. anesthetic.

a·nes·te·sió·lo·go, –ga m.f. MED. anesthesiologist.

a·nes·te·sis·ta m.f. MED. anesthetist.

a·neu·ris·ma m. MED. aneurysm, aneurism.

a·ne·xar tr. *(unir)* to annex, join; *(documentos)* to annex, append.

a·ne·xión f. annexation.

a·ne·xio·nar tr. var. of **anexar**.

a·ne·xio·nis·mo m. annexationism.

a·ne·xio·nis·ta adj. & m.f. annexationist.

a·ne·xo, –xa I. adj. *(unido)* annexed, joined; *(documento)* annexed, appended II. m. *(suplemento)* annex; *(apéndice)* annex, appendix.

an·fe·ta·mi·na f. PHARM. amphetamine.

an·fi·bio, –bia I. adj. amphibious, amphibian II. m. ZOOL. amphibian ♦ **anfibios** Amphibia.

an·fi·bo·lo·gí·a f. RHET. amphibology, amphiboly.

an·fi·tea·tro m. *(edificio)* amphitheater; THEAT. balcony ♦ **a. anatómico** dissecting room.

an·fi·trión, –trio·na m. host —f. hostess.

án·fo·ra f. *(cántaro)* amphora; AMER. ballot box.

an·frac·tuo·si·dad f. *(desigualdad)* roughness, cragginess; *(cavidad)* cavity, depression; ANAT. depression separating the convolutions of the brain.

an·frac·tuo·so, –sa adj. twisting, winding.

an·ga·ri·llas f.pl *(andas)* stretcher; *(camilla)* packsaddle with panniers; *(vinagreras)* cruet stand.

án·gel m. angel ♦ **a. custodio** *or* **de la guardia** guardian angel • **a. malo** *or* **de las tinieblas** devil • **tener a.** FIG. to have grace *or* charm.

an·gé·li·co, –ca *or* **an·ge·li·cal** adj. angelic, angelical.

an·ge·li·to m. *(ángel)* little angel, cherub; FIG., COLL. *(niño)* cherub, small child.
an·ge·lo·te m. COLL. *(estatua)* large figure of an angel; FIG. *(niño)* chubby child; *(persona sencilla)* good sort (of person); ICHTH. angelfish.
an·gi·na f. MED. angina.
an·gio·gra·fí·a f. MED. angiography.
an·gli·ca·nis·mo m. RELIG. Anglicanism.
an·gli·ca·ni·za·do, –da adj. Anglicized.
an·gli·ca·no, –na adj. & m.f. RELIG. Anglican.
an·gli·cis·mo m. Anglicism.
an·gli·cis·ta m.f. Anglicist.
an·gló·fi·lo, –la I. adj. Anglophilic II. m.f. Anglophile.
an·glo·fo·bia f. Anglophobia.
an·gló·fo·bo, –ba adj. & m.f. Anglophobe.
an·glo·par·lan·te adj. English-speaking.
an·glo·sa·jón, –jo·na adj. & m.f. Anglo-Saxon —m. *(idioma)* Anglo-Saxon.
An·go·la f. Angola.
an·go·le·ño, –ña adj. & m.f. Angolan.
an·go·ra adj. & m. Angora, angora (goat, cat, rabbit).
an·gos·tar tr., intr., & reflex. to narrow.
an·gos·to, –ta adj. narrow, tight.
an·gos·tu·ra f. *(calidad de angosto)* narrowness; GEOG. *(paso estrecho)* narrow passage *or* place; MARIT. *(estrecho)* narrows, strait; BOT., CUL. angostura (bark *or* bitters).
an·gra f. cove, bay.
an·gui·la f. ICHTH. eel.
an·gu·lar adj. angular.
an·gu·le·ma f. hemp cloth ♦ **angulemas** COLL. flattery • **hacer** *or* **venir con angulemas** COLL. to butter up, softsoap (someone).
án·gu·lo m. GEOM. angle; *(esquina)* corner, angle ♦ **á. agudo** acute angle • **á. obtuso** obtuse angle • **á. recto** right angle • **de á. ancho** PHOTOG. wide-angle • **en á.** at an angle.
an·gu·lo·si·dad f. angularity.
an·gu·lo·so, –sa adj. angular, sharp.
an·gu·rria f. MED., COLL. strangury; AMER. *(hambre)* hunger; *(avaricia)* greed, avarice.
an·gu·rrien·to, –ta AMER. adj. *(avaro)* greedy, avaricious; *(hambriento)* hungry, starved.
an·gus·tia f. anguish, torment.
an·gus·tia·do, –da I. past part. see **angustiar** II. adj. *(afligido)* anguished, tormented; *(estrecho)* narrow; FIG. *(codicioso)* greedy, covetous; *(miserable)* miserable, wretched.
an·gus·tiar tr. to anguish, cause anguish —reflex. *(afligirse)* to become anguished *or* distressed; *(inquietarse)* to worry, become *or* get worried.
an·gus·tio·sa·men·te adv. *(con angustia)* distressfully, in an anguished way; *(que angustia)* distressingly.
an·gus·tio·so, –sa adj. *(afligido)* distressed, anguished; *(penoso)* distressing, agonizing.
an·he·la·ción f. FIG. *(ansia)* yearning, longing; *(jadeo)* gasping, panting.
an·he·lan·te adj. FIG. *(ansioso)* yearning, longing; *(jadeante)* gasping, panting.
an·he·lar intr. FIG. *(ansiar)* to yearn *or* long to; *(jadear)* to gasp, pant —tr. FIG. *(ansiar)* to yearn *or* long for.
an·he·lo m. FIG. yearning, longing, desire.
an·he·lo·sa·men·te adv. FIG. yearningly, longingly.
an·he·lo·so, –sa adj. FIG. longing.
an·hí·dri·do m. CHEM. anhydride ♦ **a. carbónico** carbon dioxide • **a. nítrico** nitric oxide • **a. sulfúrico** sulfur dioxide.
an·hi·dro·sis f. [pl. **-sis**] MED. anhidrosis.
a·ni·dar intr. ORNITH. to nest, make a nest; FIG. *(habitar)* to live, make one's home —tr. FIG. to shelter, take in —reflex. to nest, make one's nest.
a·ni·li·na f. CHEM. aniline, anilin.
a·ni·lla f. *(argolla)* ring; *(de cortina)* curtain ring ♦ **anillas** SPORT. rings.
a·ni·lla·do, –da I. past part. see **anillar** II. adj. *(rizado)* curly, wavy; *(de forma de anillo)* ring, ring-shaped; ZOOL. annelid III. m. ZOOL. annelid (worm).
a·ni·llar tr. *(dar forma de anillo)* to form *or* shape into a ring; *(sujetar)* to fasten with rings.
a·ni·llo m. *(aro)* ring <*un a. de metal* a metal ring>; *(sortija)*

ring <*un a. de compromiso* an engagement ring>; ARCHIT. annulet (molding); ZOOL., ANAT. annulus, ring ♦ **a. de boda** wedding ring • **a. pastoral** bishop's ring • **de a.** honorary • **caer** *or* **venir como a. al dedo** COLL. to be just right, come just at the right time.
á·ni·ma f. *(alma)* soul, spirit; ARTIL. *(de las armas)* bore (of a gun).
a·ni·ma·ción f. *(viveza)* animation, liveliness; *(movimiento)* animation, movement.
a·ni·ma·da·men·te adv. animatedly, in a lively way.
a·ni·ma·do, –da I. past part. see **animar** II. adj. *(vivo)* animated, lively <*una fiesta a.* a lively party>; *(activo)* animated, bustling <*una calle a.* a bustling street>; FIG. *(movido)* moved, motivated <*a. de buenas intenciones* motivated by good intentions>; ZOOL. *(vivo)* animate; AMER. improved, better (of health).
a·ni·ma·dor, –do·ra I. adj. *(excitador)* animating, enlivening; *(alentador)* encouraging, inspiring II. m.f. *(maestro de ceremonias)* emcee, master of ceremonies; *(artista)* entertainer; S. AMER. cheerleader.
a·ni·mad·ver·sión f. *(enemistad)* ill will, malice; *(crítica)* animadversion, censure.
a·ni·mal I. adj. ZOOL. animal; FIG. *(estúpido)* stupid II. m. ZOOL. animal; FIG. *(idiota)* idiot, fool; *(bestia)* brute, beast.
a·ni·ma·la·da f. COLL. *(estupidez)* stupidity, foolishness; *(borricada)* foolish *or* silly thing.
a·ni·ma·li·dad f. animality.
a·ni·ma·lu·cho m. ugly beast.
a·ní·mi·co, –ca adj. psychic.
a·ni·mar tr. *(dar vida a)* to give life to, vitalize; FIG. *(avivar)* to animate, enliven; *(estimular)* to animate, stimulate <*a. la conversación* to stimulate the conversation>; *(alentar)* to encourage, inspire <*a. al ejército* to encourage the army>; *(alegrar)* to cheer up —reflex. *(avivarse)* to become animated *or* lively; *(atreverse)* to feel encouraged ♦ **animarse a.** to decide to, get in the mood to.
a·ni·mis·mo m. PHILOS., RELIG. animism.
á·ni·mo m. *(alma)* spirit; *(energía)* energy, vitality <*trabajar con á.* to work with energy>; *(intención)* purpose, will ♦ **¡ánimo!** courage! • **caerse los ánimos** to lose heart, become discouraged • **dar á. a** to encourage • **estar** *or* **tener ánimos para** to be in the mood to, decide to.
a·ni·mo·sa·men·te adv. spiritedly, courageously.
a·ni·mo·si·dad f. animosity, enmity.
a·ni·mo·so, –sa adj. spirited, courageous.
a·ni·ña·da·men·te adv. childishly.
a·ni·ña·do, –da adj. *(pueril)* childlike <*un rostro a.* a childlike face>; *(infantil)* childish.
a·ni·ñar·se reflex. to be childish.
a·ni·qui·la·ción f. annihilation, destruction.
a·ni·qui·la·mien·to m. var. of **aniquilación**.
a·ni·qui·lar tr. *(destruir)* to annihilate, destroy; FIG. *(apocar)* to overwhelm, overcome —reflex. *(ser destruido)* to be annihilated *or* destroyed; FIG. *(apocarse)* to be overwhelmed *or* overcome; *(la salud)* to decline, deteriorate.
a·nís m. BOT. anise; *(grano)* aniseed; *(aguardiente)* anisette.
a·ni·sa·do m. anisette.
a·ni·ver·sa·rio, –ria I. adj. anniversary II. m. *(conmemoración)* anniversary; *(misa)* memorial service.
a·no m. ANAT. anus.
a·no·che adv. last night, yesterday evening.
a·no·che·ce·dor, –do·ra I. adj. staying up late II. m.f. night owl, person who stays up late.
a·no·che·cer¹ §17 intr. *(oscurecer)* to get dark, fall (night); *(llegar)* to arrive at nightfall.
a·no·che·cer² m. nightfall, dusk ♦ **al a.** at dusk, at nightfall.
a·no·che·ci·da f. nightfall, dusk.
a·no·di·no, –na I. adj. MED. anodyne; *(insignificante)* insignificant, insubstantial; FIG. *(insípido)* insipid, vapid II. m. MED. anodyne.
a·no·do m. ELEC., PHYS. anode.
a·no·fe·les [pl. **-les**] ENTOM. I. adj. anopheline II. m. anopheles (mosquito genus).
a·no·ma·lí·a f. anomaly.
a·nó·ma·lo, –la adj. anomalous.

a·no·na·da·ción f. *(aniquilación)* annihilation, destruction; *(depresión)* depression, dejection.

a·no·na·da·dor, –do·ra adj. *(destructivo)* annihilating, destroying; FIG. *(aplastante)* crushing, overwhelming.

a·no·na·da·mien·to m. var. of **anonadación.**

a·no·na·dar tr. *(aniquilar)* to annihilate, destroy; FIG. *(aplastar)* to overwhelm, overcome <*me anonadó la noticia* the news overwhelmed me>; *(deprimir)* to depress, dishearten —reflex. *(ser aniquilado)* to be annihilated or destroyed; *(apocarse)* to be overwhelmed or overcome; *(deprimirse)* to be depressed or disheartened.

a·nó·ni·ma·men·te adv. anonymously.

a·no·ni·ma·to m. anonymity.

a·nó·ni·mo, –ma I. adj. anonymous II. m. *(persona)* anonymous person; *(anonimato)* anonymity; *(seudónimo)* pseudonym; *(carta)* anonymous letter.

a·no·re·xia f. MED. anorexia.

a·nor·mal adj. abnormal, irregular.

a·nor·ma·li·dad f. abnormality, irregularity.

a·nor·mal·men·te adv. abnormally.

a·no·ta·ción f. *(acción de anotar)* noting; *(nota)* note, annotation.

a·no·ta·dor, –do·ra I. adj. annotating, noting II. m.f. annotator.

a·no·tar tr. *(poner notas)* to annotate; *(notar)* to note, make note of.

a·no·ve·la·do, –da adj. novelistic.

an·qui·lo·sa·mien·to m. MED. stiffening; FIG. paralysis <*la guerra causó un a. del comercio* the war caused a paralysis of trade>.

an·qui·lo·sar tr. MED. to stiffen —reflex. MED. to become stiff; FIG. *(paralizarse)* to be paralyzed.

an·qui·los·to·ma m. MED. hookworm.

án·sar m. ORNITH. goose.

an·sa·ri·no, –na ZOOL. I. adj. anserine II. m. gosling.

an·sia f. *(inquietud)* anxiety, worry; *(angustia)* anguish; *(anhelo)* yearning, longing; *(tortura)* torture, torment ♦ **ansias** nausea.

an·sia·da·men·te adv. *(con inquietud)* anxiously; *(anhelosamente)* longingly, yearningly.

an·siar §30 tr. to yearn or long for.

an·sie·dad f. anxiety, worry.

an·sio·sa·men·te adv. *(con inquietud)* anxiously, worriedly; *(con anhelo)* eagerly.

an·sio·so, –sa adj. *(preocupado)* anxious, worried; *(codicioso)* greedy; *(deseoso)* eager; COL. nauseous.

an·ta f. ZOOL. elk, moose; AMER., ZOOL. tapir.

an·ta·gó·ni·co, –ca adj. antagonistic.

an·ta·go·nis·mo m. antagonism.

an·ta·go·nis·ta I. adj. antagonist, antagonistic II. m.f. antagonist, rival.

an·ta·ño adv. *(en tiempo antiguo)* long ago, in days gone by; *(en el año pasado)* last year.

an·ta·ñón, –ño·na adj. COLL. very old.

an·ta·ra f. PERU panpipe.

An·tár·ti·da f. Antarctica ♦ **la A.** the Antarctic.

an·tár·ti·co, –ca adj. Antarctic.

an·te¹ m. ZOOL. *(anta)* elk, moose; *(búfalo)* African antelope; *(piel)* buckskin, suede.

an·te² prep. *(delante de)* before, in front of <*presentarse a. el juez* to appear before the judge>; in view of, regarding <*a. esta situación* in view of this situation> ♦ **a. todo** above all.

an·te·a·do, –da adj. *(amarillento)* buff-colored; MEX. damaged, unsalable.

an·te·al·tar m. chancel, choir.

an·te·a·no·che adv. the night before last, two nights ago.

an·te·a·yer adv. the day before yesterday, two days ago.

an·te·bra·zo m. ANAT. forearm; ZOOL. shoulder.

an·te·cá·ma·ra f. antechamber, anteroom.

an·te·ce·den·te I. adj. preceding, prior II. m. *(precedente)* antecedent; GRAM. antecedent ♦ **antecedentes** record, history, background.

an·te·ce·der tr. & intr. to precede, antecede.

an·te·ce·sor, –so·ra I. adj. preceding, former II. m.f. *(predecesor)* predecessor; *(antepasado)* ancestor, forebear.

an·te·da·ta f. antedate.

an·te·da·tar tr. to antedate, backdate.

an·te·de·cir §11 tr. to foretell, predict.

an·te·di·cho, –cha adj. aforesaid, aforementioned.

an·te·di·lu·via·no, –na adj. antediluvian, before the flood.

an·te·fir·ma f. *(fórmula)* closing (of a letter); *(título)* title (of the signer).

an·te·fo·so m. outer moat.

an·te·la·ción f. priority, advance ♦ **con a.** in advance, beforehand • **con a. a** before, prior to.

an·te·lar tr. CHILE to anticipate.

an·te·ma·no adv. ♦ **de a.** in advance, beforehand <*lo averiguó de a.* he verified it beforehand>.

an·te·na f. ZOOL. antenna; RAD., TELEV. antenna, aerial; MARIT. lateen yard.

an·te·no·che adv. var. of **anteanoche.**

an·te·nom·bre m. title before a name.

an·te·o·je·ra f. eyeglass case ♦ **anteojeras** blinkers, blinders.

an·te·o·jo m. *(catalejo)* telescope, spyglass; *(anteojera)* blinker, blinder ♦ **a. de larga vista** binoculars, field glasses • **anteojos** *(gafas)* eyeglasses, spectacles; INDUS., SPORT. goggles.

an·te·pa·gar §47 tr. to prepay, pay in advance.

an·te·pa·sa·do, –da I. past part. see **antepasar** II. adj. before last <*el año a.* the year before last> III. m.f. ancestor, forebear.

an·te·pa·sar tr. to precede.

an·te·pe·cho m. *(baranda)* rail, railing; *(alféizar)* sill; *(reborde)* ledge; EQUIT. breast collar (of a harness); MIN. stratum, layer.

an·te·pe·núl·ti·mo, –ma adj. antepenultimate, second from the last.

an·te·po·ner §54 tr. *(poner delante)* to precede, place in front of; FIG. *(dar prioridad)* to put before.

an·te·por·ta·da f. PRINT. half title.

an·te·por·tal m. porch.

an·te·pro·yec·to m. *(trabajo preliminar)* draft, preliminary plan; ARCHIT., ENG. blueprint ♦ **a. de ley** draft bill.

an·te·puer·ta f. *(cortina)* portière; FORT. inner gate.

an·te·pues·to, –ta see **anteponer.**

an·te·pu·sie·ra, antepuso see **anteponer.**

an·te·rior adj. previous, before <*el día a.* the previous day>; ANAT., ZOOL. front, fore ♦ **a. a** before, prior to <*el viaje a. a éste* the trip prior to this one>.

an·te·rio·ri·dad f. *(precedencia)* precedence, anteriority; *(prioridad)* priority ♦ **con a.** beforehand, in advance • **con a. a** prior to.

an·te·rior·men·te adv. *(antes)* previously, before; *(con antelación)* beforehand, in advance ♦ **véase a.** see above.

an·tes I. adv. before <*lo he dicho a.* I have said it before>; *(antiguamente)* previously, formerly <*a. viví en Caracas* previously I lived in Caracas>; *(más bien)* rather <*a. muerto que traidor* sooner dead than a traitor> ♦ **a. de** before, previous to <*a. de comer* before eating>; rather than <*me mataría a. de casarme con él* I would kill myself rather than marry him> • **a. de ayer** the day before yesterday • **a. que** before <*a. que te vayas* before you go>; rather than <*prefiero jugar a. que hacer los quehaceres* I prefer to play rather than to do chores> II. adj. before <*la noche a.* the night before> III. conj. rather, on the contrary <*ellos no se entregaron, a. prefirieron morir* they did not surrender, but rather they preferred to die>.

an·te·sa·la f. anteroom, lobby ♦ **hacer a.** FIG. to wait to be received, cool one's heels.

an·te·úl·ti·mo, –ma adj. penultimate, next to the last.

an·te·vís·pe·ra f. day before yesterday.

an·ti·á·ci·do, –da adj. & m. PHARM. antacid.

an·ti·a·é·re·o, –a I. adj. antiaircraft II. m. S. AMER. antiaircraft gun.

an·tial·co·hó·li·co, –ca I. adj. antialcoholic, teetotaling II. m.f. teetotaler.

an·tia·me·ri·ca·no, –ca adj. & m.f. anti-American.

an·tias·má·ti·co, –ca adj. PHARM. antiasthmatic.

an·tia·tó·mi·co, –ca adj. antinuclear.

an·ti·bió·ti·co, –ca adj. & m. PHARM. antibiotic.

an·ti·can·ce·ro·so, –sa adj. PHARM. anticarcinogenic, anticancerous.

an·ti·ca·pi·ta·lis·ta adj. & m.f. anticapitalist.

an·ti·ca·tó·li·co, –ca adj. & m.f. anti-Catholic.

an·ti·ci·clón m. METEROL. anticyclone.

an·ti·cien·tí·fi·co, –ca adj. antiscientific.

an·ti·ci·pa·ción f. anticipation ♦ con a. in advance.

an·ti·ci·pa·da I. f. unexpected thrust (in fencing) II. adj. see anticipado, –da.

an·ti·ci·pa·da·men·te adv. in advance, beforehand.

an·ti·ci·pa·do, –da I. past part. see anticipar II. adj. advance, advanced ♦ por a. in advance, ahead of time III. f. see anticipada.

an·ti·ci·pa·dor, –do·ra I. anticipatory II. m.f. anticipator.

an·ti·ci·par tr. to advance, move forward <anticipó la fecha de la fiesta he advanced the date of the party>; (prestar) to advance, lend (money); S. AMER. to foresee, anticipate ♦ a. agradecimientos to thank in advance —reflex. to be or arrive early <las nieves se han anticipado este año the snows have arrived early this year>; (adelantarse) to get ahead.

an·ti·ci·po m. (adelanto) anticipation; (dinero) advance (payment).

an·ti·cle·ri·cal adj. & m.f. anticlerical.

an·ti·cle·ri·ca·lis·mo m. anticlericalism.

an·ti·cli·nal m. GEOL. anticline.

an·ti·co·a·gu·lan·te adj. & m. anticoagulant.

an·ti·co·lo·nia·lis·mo m. anticolonialism.

an·ti·co·lo·nia·lis·ta adj. & m.f. anticolonialist.

an·ti·com·bus·ti·ble adj. & m. noncombustible.

an·ti·co·mu·nis·mo m. anticommunism.

an·ti·co·mu·nis·ta adj. & m.f. anticommunist.

an·ti·con·cep·ti·vo, –va I. adj. contraceptive, birth-control II. m. contraceptive, birth-control device.

an·ti·con·for·mis·mo m. nonconformism.

an·ti·con·for·mis·ta adj. & m.f. nonconformist.

an·ti·con·ge·lan·te I. adj antifreezing II. m. AUTO. (de radiador) antifreeze; (de parabrisas) deicer.

an·ti·cons·ti·tu·cio·nal adj. unconstitutional.

an·ti·cons·ti·tu·cio·nal·men·te adv. unconstitutionally.

an·ti·cre·sis f. [pl. -sis] antichresis.

an·ti·cris·tia·no, –na adj. anti-Christian.

an·ti·cris·to m. Antichrist.

an·ti·cua·do, –da adj. (en desuso) antiquated, obsolete; (pasado de moda) old-fashioned, out-of-date.

an·ti·cuar tr. to antiquate, consider obsolete or old-fashioned —reflex. to become antiquated or old-fashioned.

an·ti·cua·rio, –ria I. adj. antiquarian II. m. (arqueólogo) antiquarian, antiquary; (vendedor) antique dealer; (tienda) antique shop.

an·ti·cuer·po m. antibody.

an·ti·de·mo·crá·ti·co, –ca adj. undemocratic.

an·ti·de·pre·si·vo, –va adj. & m. PHARM. antidepressant.

an·ti·di·lu·via·no, –na adj. var. of antediluviano.

an·tí·do·to m. antidote.

an·tie·co·nó·mi·co, –ca adj. (no económico) uneconomical; (caro) expensive.

an·ties·té·ti·co, –ca adj. unaesthetic, unsightly.

an·ti·fas·cis·ta adj. & m.f. antifascist.

an·ti·faz m. [pl. -fa·ces] (máscara) mask; (velo) veil.

an·ti·gás adj. (against) gas <careta a. gas mask>.

an·ti·ge·no m. MED. antigen.

an·ti·gua·lla f. (antigüedad) antique; COLL. (reliquia) relic, old-fashioned item.

an·ti·gua·men·te adv. formerly, once <a. trabajó en esa oficina he formerly worked in that office>; (en tiempos remotos) in ancient times.

an·ti·guar §10 intr. to acquire seniority —reflex. to become old-fashioned.

an·ti·güe·dad f. (vejez) old age; (época) antiquity, ancient times; (en el empleo) seniority ♦ antigüedades antiques.

an·ti·gu·ber·na·men·tal adj. antigovernmental.

an·ti·guo, –gua I. adj. ancient, old <un hombre a. an old man>; former <mi a. profesor my former professor> ♦ a la a. in the old-fashioned way • de a. from time immemorial II. m. veteran, old-timer ♦ los antiguos the ancients.

an·ti·he·mo·rroi·dal adj. MED. antihemorrhoidal.

an·ti·hi·gié·ni·co, –ca adj. unhygienic, unsanitary.

an·ti·im·pe·ria·lis·mo m. anti-imperialism.

an·ti·im·pe·ria·lis·ta adj. & m.f. anti-imperialist.

an·ti·in·fla·cio·nis·ta adj. anti-inflationary.

an·ti·ju·rí·di·co, –ca adj. illegal, unlawful.

an·tí·lo·pe m. ZOOL. antelope.

an·ti·lla·no, –na adj. & m.f. West Indian, Antillean.

An·ti·llas f.pl. Antilles, West Indies ♦ A. Mayores Greater Antilles • A. Menores Lesser Antilles.

an·ti·ma·só·ni·co, –ca adj. antimasonic.

an·ti·ma·te·ria f. antimatter.

an·ti·mi·li·ta·ris·mo m. antimilitarism.

an·ti·mi·li·ta·ris·ta adj. & m.f. antimilitarist.

an·ti·mo·nár·qui·co, –ca adj. antimonarchical, antimonarchist.

an·ti·mo·nio m. CHEM. antimony.

an·ti·na·cio·nal adj. antinational.

an·ti·na·tu·ral adj. unnatural.

an·ti·no·mia f. LAW antinomy.

an·ti·nu·cle·ar adj. antinuclear.

An·tio·quí·a f. Antioch.

an·ti·pa·lú·di·co, –ca adj. PHARM. antimalarial.

an·ti·pa·pis·ta adj. & m.f. antipapal.

an·ti·pa·ra f. (biombo) screen; (polaina) gaiter.

an·ti·pa·rá·si·to or an·ti·pa·ra·si·ta·rio adj. & m. RAD., TELEV. suppressor.

an·ti·par·la·men·ta·rio, –ria I. adj. antiparliamentary II. m.f. antiparliamentarian.

an·ti·par·tí·cu·la f. PHYS. antiparticle.

an·ti·pa·tí·a f. antipathy, dislike.

an·ti·pá·ti·co, –ca adj. disagreeable, unpleasant.

an·ti·pa·ti·zar §04 intr. AMER. to dislike someone or something.

an·ti·pa·trió·ti·co, –ca adj. unpatriotic.

an·ti·pe·da·gó·gi·co, –ca adj. antipedagogical.

an·tí·po·da m. antipodes.

an·ti·po·li·lla m. moth killer.

an·ti·pro·tec·cio·nis·mo m. antiprotectionism.

an·ti·pro·tec·cio·nis·ta adj. & m.f. antiprotectionist.

an·ti·rrá·bi·co, –ca adj. MED. antirabies, antirabic.

an·ti·rra·cis·mo m. antiracism.

an·ti·rra·cis·ta adj. & m.f. antiracist.

an·ti·rre·pu·bli·ca·no, –na adj. & m.f. antirepublican.

an·ti·rreu·má·ti·co, –ca adj. & m. PHARM. antirheumatic.

an·ti·rre·vo·lu·cio·na·rio, –ria adj. & m.f. antirevolutionary.

an·ti·se·mi·ta I. adj. anti-Semitic II. m.f. anti-Semite.

an·ti·se·mí·ti·co, –ca adj. anti-Semitic.

an·ti·se·mi·tis·mo m. anti-Semitism.

an·ti·sép·ti·co, –ca adj. & m. MED. antiseptic.

an·ti·so·cia·ble adj. antisocial, unsociable.

an·ti·so·cial adj. antisocial.

an·tis·tro·fa f. POET. antistrophe.

an·ti·sub·ma·ri·no, –na adj. MIL. antisubmarine.

an·ti·su·do·ral adj. & m. deodorant, antiperspirant.

an·ti·tan·que adj. MIL. antitank.

an·ti·te·rro·ris·mo m. antiterrorism.

an·ti·te·rro·ris·ta adj. antiterrorist.

an·tí·te·sis f. [pl. -sis] antithesis.

an·ti·te·tá·ni·co, –ca adj. PHARM. antitetanic.

an·ti·té·ti·co, –ca adj. antithetical, antithetic.

an·ti·tó·xi·co, –ca adj. antitoxic.

an·ti·to·xi·na f. antitoxin, antibody.

an·to·ja·di·zo, –za adj. (caprichoso) capricious, whimsical; (cambiadizo) unpredictable, fickle.

an·to·jar·se reflex. (gustar) to fancy, feel like <no hace más que lo que se le antoja he does only what he feels like doing>; (parecer) to seem, appear <se me antoja que va a llover it seems to me that it's going to rain>.

an·to·jo m. (capricho) fancy, whim; (de una mujer preñada) craving; (lunar) birthmark, mole ♦ a su a. as one pleases • no morirse de a. ARG. to be unwilling • tener antojos AMER., COLL. to be pregnant.

an·to·lo·gí·a f. anthology ♦ de a. COLL. fantastic, great <consiguió un trabajo de a. she got a fantastic job>.

an·to·ló·gi·co, –ca adj. anthological.

an·to·ni·mia f. RHET. antonymy.

an·tó·ni·mo, –ma GRAM. I. m. antonym II. adj. antonymous.

an·to·no·ma·sia f. RHET. antonomasia.

an·to·no·más·ti·co, –ca adj. antonomastic.

an·tor·cha f. (hacha) torch; FIG. (guía) guide, guiding light ♦ a. a soplete blowtorch • a. soldadura welding torch.

an·tra·ci·ta I. f. anthracite, hard coal II. adj. dark-gray.

án·trax m. [pl. **-trax**] MED. anthrax.

an·tro m. *(cueva)* cavern, grotto; FIG. *(guarida)* den, lair; ANAT. anthrum <*a. timpánico* tympanic anthrum> ♦ **a. de corrupción** den of iniquity.

an·tro·po·cen·tris·mo m. anthropocentrism.

an·tro·pó·fa·go, –ga I. adj. anthropophagous, cannibalistic II. m.f. anthropophagus, cannibal.

an·tro·po·gra·fí·a f. anthropography.

an·tro·poi·de adj. & m. ZOOL. anthropoid.

an·tro·po·lo·gí·a f. anthropology.

an·tro·po·ló·gi·co, –ca adj. anthropologic, anthropological.

an·tro·pó·lo·go, –ga m.f. anthropologist.

an·tro·po·me·trí·a f. anthropometry.

an·tro·po·mór·fi·co, –ca adj. anthropomorphic.

an·tro·po·mor·fis·mo m. anthropomorphism.

an·tro·po·mor·fo, –fa ZOOL. I. adj. anthropomorphous II. m.f. anthropomorph.

an·true·jo m. carnival (before Lent).

a·nual adj. *(añal)* annual, yearly <*la cosecha a.* the annual harvest>; per annum, a year <*mil dólares anuales* one thousand dollars a year>.

a·nua·li·dad f. *(acontecimiento)* annual occurrence; *(pago)* annuity, annual payment.

a·nual·men·te adv. annually, yearly.

a·nua·rio m. yearbook, annual ♦ **a. telefónico** telephone directory.

a·nu·ba·rra·do, –da adj. cloudy, overcast.

a·nu·blar tr. *(ocultar)* to cloud; FIG. *(empañar)* to darken, tarnish <*a. la reputación de alguien* to tarnish another's reputation> —reflex. METEOROL. to become cloudy *or* overcast; FIG. *(empañarse)* to be tarnished; *(desvanecerse)* to fade away, disappear; BOT. to be withered *or* wilted.

a·nu·blo m. AGR. blight, mildew.

a·nu·da·du·ra f. *or* **a·nu·da·mien·to** m. knotting, tying.

a·nu·dar tr. *(hacer nudos)* to knot, tie in knots <*a. una cinta* to knot a sash>; *(atar)* to tie together <*a. dos cables* to tie two cables together>; FIG. *(unir)* to unite, join; *(continuar)* to continue, resume —reflex. to become stunted ♦ **anudarse la lengua** FIG. to become tongue-tied.

a·nuen·cia f. consent, agreement.

a·nuen·te adj. consenting, agreeing.

a·nu·la·ble adj. annullable, revocable.

a·nu·la·ción f. annulment, nullification ♦ **a. del juicio** LAW mistrial.

a·nu·la·dor, –do·ra I. adj. annulling II. m.f. annuller.

a·nu·lar¹ I. adj. annular, ring-shaped II. m. ring finger.

a·nu·lar² tr. *(abolir)* to annul, nullify; *(cancelar)* to cancel (a reservation); FIG. *(desautorizar)* to remove from power —reflex. to be removed from power.

a·nu·la·ti·vo, –va adj. nullifying.

a·nu·lo·so, –sa adj. *(formado de anillos)* annulate, annulose; *(en forma de anillo)* annular, ring-shaped.

a·nun·cia·ción f. announcement ♦ **Anunciación** RELIG. Annunciation.

a·nun·cia·dor, –do·ra I. adj. *(declarativo)* announcing; *(publicitario)* advertising II. m.f. announcer; *(en un periódico)* advertiser —m. ELEC. annunciator.

a·nun·cian·te I. adj. advertising II. m.f. advertiser.

a·nun·ciar tr. *(declarar)* to announce, declare; *(publicar)* to publicize, advertise; *(presagiar)* to foreshadow, presage.

a·nun·cio m. *(aviso)* announcement; *(cartel)* placard, poster; *(señal)* omen, sign; COM. advertisement, notice ♦ **anuncios clasificados** *or* **por palabras** classified advertisements.

a·nuo, –nua adj. annual <*planta a.* annual plant>.

an·ver·so m. *(de una moneda)* obverse.

an·zue·lo m. *(arponcillo)* fishhook, hook; FIG. *(aliciente)* bait, lure ♦ **echar el a.** to offer an inducement • **picar** *or* **tragarse el a.** FIG., COLL. to swallow the bait, be taken in.

a·ña·di·do I. past part. see **añadir** II. m. *(postizo)* toupee, hairpiece; *(adición)* addition; *(de una mesa)* leaf.

a·ña·di·du·ra f. addition ♦ **de a.** for good measure • **por a.** moreover, in addition.

a·ña·dir tr. *(agregar)* to add; *(aumentar)* to increase; *(conferir)* to lend, add.

a·ña·ga·za f. *(señuelo)* bird decoy, lure; FIG. *(ardid)* ruse, scheme.

a·ñe·ja·mien·to m. aging, maturing.

a·ñe·jar tr. to age, mature —reflex. *(mejorarse)* to age, mature; COLL. *(deteriorarse)* to become stale.

a·ñe·jo, –ja adj. *(viejo)* aged, mature <*vino a.* a mature wine>; COLL. *(pasado)* stale, old <*noticia a.* old news>.

a·ñi·cos m.pl. bits, pieces ♦ **hacerse a.** *(romper)* to break into pieces; FIG. *(cansarse)* to wear oneself out.

a·ñil I. m. BOT. indigo; *(pasta del lavado)* bluing II. adj. indigo, blue.

a·ñi·lar tr. to dye indigo *or* blue.

a·ñi·nos m.pl. *(piel)* lambskins; *(lana)* lambswool.

a·ño m. year ♦ **a. bisiesto** leap year • **a. civil** calendar year • **a. económico** fiscal year • **a. escolar** school year • **a. en curso** current year • **a. luz** light-year • **de buen a.** in good health • **el a. verde** ARG., PAR., VEN., COLL. never • **en el a. de la nana** COLL. in the year one, way back • **entrado en años** advanced in years, elderly • **¡Feliz Año Nuevo!** Happy New Year! • **tener . . . años** to be . . . years old <*¿cuántos años tiene usted?* how old are you?>.

a·ño·jo, –ja m.f. yearling.

a·ño·ran·za f. yearning, longing, nostalgia.

a·ño·rar tr. *(desear)* to long for; *(llorar la pérdida de)* to grieve for —intr. *(desear)* to feel nostalgic, yearn; *(acongojarse)* to sorrow, grieve.

a·ño·so, –sa adj. old, aged.

a·ñus·gar §47 intr. *(atragantarse)* to choke; FIG. *(enfadarse)* to get angry.

a·o·ja·dor, –do·ra I. adj. casting the evil eye II. m.f. person who casts the evil eye.

a·o·ja·du·ra f. *or* **a·o·ja·mien·to** m. evil eye, jinx.

a·o·jar tr. *(hacer mal de ojo)* to give the evil eye to, jinx; FIG. *(malograr)* to spoil.

a·o·jo m. evil eye, spell, jinx.

a·or·ta f. ANAT. aorta.

a·o·va·do, –da I. past part. see **aovar** II. adj. *(oval)* oval, egg-shaped; BOT. ovate.

a·o·var intr. to lay eggs. —tr. to make egg-shaped.

a·o·vi·llar·se reflex. to curl up, roll up into a ball.

a·pa·bi·lar tr. to trim (a wick).

a·pa·bu·lla·mien·to m. var. of **apabullo**.

a·pa·bu·llar tr. COLL. *(estrujar)* to crush, squash; FIG. *(callar)* to silence, squelch.

a·pa·bu·llo m. COLL. *(estrujamiento)* crushing, squashing; FIG. *(aquietamiento)* silencing, squelching.

a·pa·cen·ta·de·ro m. pasture.

a·pa·cen·ta·dor, –do·ra I. adj. grazing II. m. shepherd —f. shepherdess.

a·pa·cen·ta·mien·to m. AGR. *(acción)* grazing, pasturing; *(pasto)* pasture, grass.

a·pa·cen·tar §49 tr. *(dar pasto a)* to graze, pasture; FIG. *(enseñar)* to instruct, teach; PERU to pacify —reflex. to graze, feed.

a·pa·ci·bi·li·dad f. calmness, gentleness.

a·pa·ci·ble adj. calm, gentle.

a·pa·ci·ble·men·te adv. calmly, gently.

a·pa·ci·gua·dor, –do·ra I. adj. appeasing, pacifying II. m.f. appeaser, pacifier.

a·pa·ci·gua·mien·to m. appeasement, pacifying.

a·pa·ci·guar §10 tr. *(sosegar)* to appease, pacify; *(un dolor)* to relieve, soothe —reflex. to calm down, grow calm.

a·pa·che m.f. *(indio)* Apache; FIG. *(malhechor)* thug, bandit —m. MEX. raincoat.

a·pa·chu·gar·se §47 reflex. CHILE to lie down flat.

a·pa·chu·rrar tr. to crush, squash.

a·pa·dri·na·mien·to m. *(patrocinio)* sponsorship, backing; *(a un niño)* acting as godfather to; *(en una boda)* acting as best man for; *(en un desafío)* seconding.

a·pa·dri·nar tr. *(patrocinar)* to sponsor, back; *(apoyar)* to support, defend; *(a un niño)* to be godfather to; *(en una boda)* to be best man for; *(en un desafío)* to act as second for; EQUIT. to ride alongside (to train an unbroken horse).

a·pa·ga·ble adj. extinguishable.

a·pa·ga·di·zo, –za adj. slow to burn.

a·pa·ga·do, –da I. past part. see **apagar** II. adj. *(extinguido)* extinguished; *(apocado)* timid, shy; FIG. *(amortiguado)* dull, subdued (colors).

a·pa·ga·dor, –do·ra I. adj. extinguishing II. m. *(apagavelas)* snuffer; MUS. damper.

a·pa·ga·mien·to m. extinguishment.

a·pa·gar §47 tr. *(el fuego)* to put out, extinguish (a fire); *(la luz)* to turn out, switch off (a light); *(la cal)* to slake (lime); *(el ruido)* to silence, deaden (a noise); *(el color)* to tone down, soften; FIG. *(aplacar)* to placate, soothe <*el tiempo apaga los rencores* time soothes ill feelings> —reflex. to go out, fade.

a·pa·ga·ve·las m. [pl. -las] candle snuffer.

a·pa·gón, –go·na I. m. blackout, power failure II. adj. CUBA, GUAT., MEX. slow to burn.

a·pa·la·brar tr. to agree to; *(arreglar de antemano)* to arrange *or* discuss beforehand; COLL. *(dar trabajo a)* to take on, hire <*a. un criado* to hire a servant> —reflex. to come to an agreement.

A·pa·la·ches m.pl. Appalachians, Appalachian Mountains.

a·pa·lan·ca·mien·to m. levering, leverage.

a·pa·lan·car §70 tr. *(levantar)* to lever, move with a lever; *(abrir)* to pry open.

a·pa·le·a·dor I. adj. *(de una persona)* beating, thrashing; AGR. threshing, winnowing II. m.f. *(de una persona)* beater, thrasher; AGR. thresher, winnower.

a·pa·le·a·mien·to m. *(tunda)* beating, thrashing; AGR. threshing, winnowing.

a·pa·le·ar tr. *(pegar)* to beat, thrash; AGR. to thresh, winnow ♦ **a. oro** *or* **plata** to be rolling in money.

a·pa·le·o m. COLL. *(tunda)* beating, thrashing; AGR. *(de trigo)* winnowing, threshing.

a·pa·na·la·do, –da adj. honeycombed.

a·pa·nar tr. PERU to bread, coat with breadcrumbs.

a·pan·dar tr. COLL. to lift, swipe.

a·pan·di·llar tr. to form into a gang —reflex. to form a gang, band together.

a·pa·ña·dor, –do·ra I. adj. *(que prepara)* preparing, getting ready; *(que roba)* seizing, pilfering II. m.f. *(preparador)* preparer; *(ladrón)* pilferer, thief.

a·pa·ña·du·ra f. *or* **a·pa·ña·mien·to** m. *(asimiento)* seizing, grasping; *(preparación)* preparation, getting ready; *(reparo)* repairing, mending.

a·pa·ñar tr. *(asir)* to seize, grasp; *(apoderarse de)* to take, seize; *(aderezar)* to season, dress; COLL. *(abrigar)* to wrap up; *(reparar)* to repair, mend; ARG., PERU to cover up for, protect; MEX. to excuse, forgive —reflex. *(darse maña)* to be skillful, manage; ARG. to manage to get one's hands on <*ellos se apañaron un negocio lucrativo* they managed to get their hands on a lucrative deal> ♦ **apañárselas** AMER. to set oneself up, manage for oneself.

a·pa·ño m. *(acción de asir)* seizing, grasping; COLL. *(remiendo)* repair, patch; *(habilidad)* skill, knack; *(lío)* mess, trouble; *(amante)* lover.

a·pa·ñus·car §70 tr. COLL. *(ajar)* to crumple; *(asir)* to swipe, snatch.

a·pa·ra·dor m. *(armario)* sideboard, cupboard; *(taller)* workshop, studio; *(escaparate)* show *or* display window; HOND. banquet, buffet.

a·pa·rar tr. *(preparar)* to prepare, touch up; to stretch out *or* open (the hands, an apron) in order to catch something.

a·pa·ra·to m. *(máquina)* apparatus, device; COLL. *(avión)* airplane; FIG. *(ceremonia)* pomp, show; ANAT., ZOOL. system <*a. digestivo* digestive system>; MED. *(vendaje)* bandage, dressing; *(síntomas)* symptoms, syndrome ♦ **a. auditivo** hearing aid • **a. de seguridad** safety device • **a. de televisión, de radio** television, radio set • **aparatos de mando** controls.

a·pa·ra·to·si·dad f. showiness, ostentation.

a·pa·ra·to·so, –sa adj. *(pomposo)* pompous, ostentatious; *(espectacular)* spectacular, captivating.

a·par·ca·mien·to m. *(acción)* parking; *(garaje)* parking lot, garage.

a·par·car §70 tr. MIL. *(depositar)* to deposit (arms); AUTO. *(estacionar)* to park.

a·par·ce·rí·a f. AGR. sharecropping.

a·par·ce·ro, –ra m.f. AGR. sharecropper; AMER. companion, comrade.

a·pa·re·a·mien·to m. *(acoplamiento)* pairing off, matching up; ZOOL. mating, breeding.

a·pa·re·ar tr. *(igualar)* to equalize, make equal *or* uniform; *(acoplar)* to match up, pair off; ZOOL. to mate, breed.

a·pa·re·cer §17 intr. & reflex. *(manifestarse)* to appear <*su nombre no aparece en la lista* his name does not appear on the list>; *(mostrarse)* to show up, turn up <*por fin apareció el libro* the book finally turned up>.

a·pa·re·ci·do, –da I. past part. see **aparecer** II. m. ghost, phantom.

a·pa·re·ci·mien·to m. appearance.

a·pa·re·ja·do, –da I. past part. see **aparejar** II. adj. apt, fit ♦ **ir a. con** to go hand in hand with • **traer a.** to mean, involve <*el no cumplimiento trae a. una multa* noncompliance involves a fine>.

a·pa·re·ja·dor, –do·ra I. adj. preparing, readying II. m.f. *(preparador)* preparer —m. ARCHIT. quantity surveyor; CONSTR. building foreman.

a·pa·re·jar tr. *(preparar)* to prepare, make ready; *(los caballos)* to harness, saddle; PAINT. to prime, size; MARIT. to rig, fit out —reflex. *(prepararse)* to get ready <*aparejarse para un viaje* to get ready for a trip>; C. AMER. to mate, pair off.

a·pa·re·jo m. *(preparación)* preparation; *(arreo)* harness; *(poleas)* tackle, derrick; MARIT. rigging, tackle; PAINT. priming, sizing; CONST. bond, bonding; AMER. saddle ♦ **aparejos** equipment, tools, instruments.

a·pa·ren·ta·dor, –do·ra adj. pretended, feigned.

a·pa·ren·tar tr. *(fingir)* to pretend, feign <*a. alegría* to feign happiness>; *(parecer)* to seem, look <*él no aparenta la edad que tiene* he does not look his age>.

a·pa·ren·te adj. *(presumible)* apparent, seeming <*un éxito a.* an apparent success>; *(visible)* apparent, visible <*manifestaciones aparentes* visible symptoms>; *(conveniente)* apt, suitable.

a·pa·ren·te·men·te adv. apparently.

a·pa·rez·ca, aparezco see **aparecer.**

a·pa·ri·ción f. *(acción de aparecer)* appearance, apparition; *(fantasma)* apparition, specter.

a·pa·rien·cia f. *(aspecto)* appearance, look; *(verosimilitud)* likelihood, probability ♦ **en a.** apparently, seemingly • **salvar las apariencias** FIG. to keep up appearances, save face.

a·par·qué, aparque see **aparcar.**

a·pa·rra·do, –da adj. *(un árbol)* spreading sideways (said of trees); FIG. *(achaparrrado)* short and stubby.

a·pa·rro·quia·do, –da I. past part. see **aparroquiar** II. adj. established in a parish.

a·pa·rro·quiar tr. RELIG. to get parishioners; *(procurar clientes)* to get customers *or* clients —reflex. to become a parishioner.

a·par·ta·da·men·te adv. separately.

a·par·ta·de·ro m. RAIL. sidetrack, siding; *(al lado del camino)* grazing field (on roadside); *(para los animales)* pen, corral ♦ **a. muerto** RAIL. dead-end siding.

a·par·ta·do, –da I. past part. see **apartar** II. adj. *(retirado)* remote, isolated <*un pueblo a.* a remote town>; *(diferente)* different, distinct III. m. *(aposento)* side room; *(casilla postal)* post office box, box number; *(párrafo)* paragraph, section.

a·par·ta·dor m. *(separador)* sorter, selecter; ECUAD. goad.

a·par·ta·men·to m. apartment, flat (G.B.).

a·par·ta·mien·to m. *(separación)* separation; *(aislamiento)* remoteness, isolation; *(lugar)* remote area, secluded spot; *(piso)* apartment, flat (G.B.).

a·par·tar tr. *(separar)* to separate, divide; *(llevar aparte)* to take aside; *(alejar)* to remove, put aside; FIG. *(disuadir)* to dissuade, divert —reflex. *(retirarse)* to withdraw, move away; *(divorciarse)* to get divorced.

a·par·te I. adv. *(por separado)* apart, separate <*ésa es cuestión a.* that is a separate question>; *(a un lado)* aside, to one side <*dejar los sentimientos a.* to leave one's feelings aside> ♦ **a. de** besides, apart from <*a. de algunos casos* apart from a few cases> II. m. *(párrafo)* new *or* separate paragraph; THEAT. *(monólogo)* aside.

a·par·theid m. apartheid.

a·par·ti·jo m. small share *or* portion.

a·par·var tr. AGR. to heap (grain) for threshing.

a·pa·sio·na·da·men·te adv. enthusiastically, intensely.

a·pa·sio·na·do, –da I. past part. see **apasionar** II. enthusiastic, intense.

a·pa·sio·na·mien·to m. enthusiasm, excitement.

a·pa·sio·nan·te adj. exciting, thrilling.

a·pa·sio·nar tr. to enthuse, excite —reflex. to become enthused or excited.

a·pa·tí·a f. apathy, indifference.

a·pá·ti·co, –ca adj. apathetic, indifferent.

a·pá·tri·da I. adj. stateless, without a country II. m.f. stateless person, one without a country.

a·pe·a·de·ro m. (poyo) mounting block; (fonda) inn; RAIL. (estación secundaria) way station.

a·pe·a·dor, –do·ra I. adj. surveying II. m.f. surveyor.

a·pe·a·mien·to m. (de un caballo) dismounting; (de un vehículo) alighting, getting down or out; ARCHIT. (apuntalamiento) propping, shoring, bracing; SURV. (amojonamiento) surveying.

a·pe·ar tr. (bajar) to bring down, lower; to fell <apeó el árbol he felled the tree>; (maniatar) to fetter, hobble (a horse); (calzar) to scotch, chock (a wheel); (amojonar) to survey, measure; FIG. (vencer) to overcome, surmount; COLL. (disuadir) to dissuade <no puedo apearle de su opinión I cannot dissuade him from his opinion>; ARCHIT. (apuntalar) to shore or prop up; C. AMER. to tell off, reprimand ♦ **a. el tratamiento** to address informally —reflex. (de un caballo) to dismount; (de un vehículo) to get down or out of, alight; AMER. to stay, lodge.

a·pe·chu·gar §47 intr. to push or shove with one's chest —tr. AMER. to seize, take hold of ♦ **a. con** FIG., COLL. to put up with, face <tendremos que a. con lo que venga we'll have to face what's coming>.

a·pe·da·zar §04 tr. (despedazar) to tear (to pieces), shred; (remendar) to patch, repair.

a·pe·dre·a·mien·to m. (lanzamiento) stone-throwing, (matanza) stoning; (tormenta) hailstorm, hail; (daño) hail damage.

a·pe·dre·ar tr. (lanzar) to hurl stones at, stone; (matar) to stone to death —intr. METEOROL. to hail —reflex. to suffer damage from hail.

a·pe·dre·o m. var. of **apedreamiento**.

a·pe·gar·se §47 reflex. FIG. (aficionarse) to become attached or fond; ECUAD. to approach, draw near.

a·pe·go m. FIG. (afición) attachment, fondness ♦ **cobrar a. a** to become attached to or fond of.

a·pe·la·ble adj. LAW appealable.

a·pe·la·ción f. LAW (petición) appeal; (recurso) remedy, recourse; COLL. (consulta) consultation ♦ **desamparar la a.** to abandon the appeal • **interponer a.** to (file an) appeal • **sin a.** FIG. hopeless, without recourse.

a·pe·lar intr. to appeal <a. una sentencia to appeal a verdict> ♦ **a. a or ante** FIG. to appeal to, call on.

a·pe·la·ti·vo, –va I. adj. GRAM. appellative II. m. AMER., COLL. last name, surname.

a·pel·ma·za·do, –da I. past part. see **apelmazar** II. adj. FIG. (pesado) dull, stodgy; (compacto) compact, compressed.

a·pel·ma·zar §04 tr. to compress, compact.

a·pe·lo·to·nar tr. to form into balls or tufts —reflex. (hacer bolitas) to form balls or tufts; FIG. (apiñarse) to cluster, throng.

a·pe·lli·dar tr. (llamar por apellido) to call by the last name or surname; (nombrar) to call, name —reflex. to be called or named.

a·pe·lli·do m. (nombre de familia) last name, surname; (apodo) nickname, sobriquet; (clasificación) tag, label ♦ **a. de soltera** maiden name.

a·pe·nar tr. to grieve, pain —reflex. (afligirse) to be grieved or pained; AMER. to be shy or embarrassed.

a·pe·nas §G10 adv. (casi no) scarcely, hardly <a. tiene ocho años he is scarcely eight years old>; (con dificultad) hardly, with difficulty <pudo levantarse a. he could hardly get up>; (luego que) as soon as <la vi a. entré I saw her as soon as I came in>.

a·pen·dec·to·mí·a f. SURG. appendectomy.

a·pén·di·ce m. (añadidura) appendage, adjunct; (de un libro) appendix; COLL. (compinche) sidekick; ANAT. appendix; BIOL., ZOOL. appendage.

a·pen·di·ci·tis f. MED. appendicitis.

A·pe·ni·nos m.pl. Apennines.

a·pe·o m. (demarcación) surveying, setting landmarks; (tala) felling, timber removal; ARCHIT. (apuntalamiento) propping, shoring; (puntal) prop, shore.

a·pep·sia f. MED. indigestion.

a·pe·ra·dor, –do·ra m.f. (ruedero) wheelwright; (capataz) overseer, foreman.

a·pe·rar tr. (fabricar o reparar) to make or repair farm equipment; AMER. to supply, furnish; ARG., VEN. to saddle, harness.

a·per·ci·bi·mien·to m. (preparación) preparation; (advertencia) warning, advice; (observación) perception, observation.

a·per·ci·bir tr. (disponer) to prepare, make ready; (advertir) to warn, advise; (observar) to perceive, observe —reflex. (prepararse) to prepare oneself <apercibirse para un viaje to prepare oneself for a trip>.

a·per·co·llar §19 tr. COLL. (coger) to collar, grab by the neck; (acogotar) to kill with a rabbit punch; FIG., COLL. (hurtar) to swipe, snatch.

a·per·ga·mi·na·do, –da I. past part. see **apergaminarse** II. adj. (como el pergamino) parchment-like; FIG. (seco) wizened, dried-up.

a·per·ga·mi·nar·se reflex. FIG., COLL. to become wizened, dry up.

a·pe·ri·ti·vo, –va I. adj. CUL. appetizing; MED. aperient, aperitive II. m. CUL. apéritif, appetizer; MED. aperient, aperitive.

a·pe·ro m. (utensilios) equipment, gear; AGR. draft animals; AMER. riding gear, trappings.

a·pe·rre·a·do, –da I. past part. see **aperrear** II. adj. lousy, rotten <una vida a. a lousy life>.

a·pe·rre·ar tr. (echar a uno los perros) to set the dogs on; FIG., COLL. (cansar) to tire, weary; (molestar) to annoy, bother —reflex. FIG. to dig in one's heels, be stubborn.

a·pe·rre·o m. FIG., COLL. (molestia) nuisance; (trabajo) chore.

a·per·so·nar·se reflex. to appear (in person), present oneself.

a·per·tu·ra f. (principio) opening, commencement; (entrada) opening, entrance; LAW (de un testamento) reading (of a will); (ajedrez) opening move; POL. conciliatory move or step.

a·pe·sa·dum·brar tr. to grieve, distress —reflex. to be grieved or distressed ♦ **apesadumbrarse de or por** to be grieved or upset by.

a·pe·sa·rar tr. to grieve, trouble —reflex. CHILE to repent, regret.

a·pes·tar tr. (contaminar) to infect (with the plague); FIG. (corromper) to corrupt, spoil; (fastidiar) to annoy, irritate —intr. to stink, smell —reflex. (ser contaminado) to be infected with the plague; COL., PERU to catch cold.

a·pes·to·so, –sa adj. (fétido) stinking, foul-smelling; COLL. (fastidioso) annoying, irritating.

a·pe·te·ce·dor, –do·ra adj. appetizing, tempting.

a·pe·te·cer §17 tr. (ansiar) to long for, crave; FIG. (desear) to desire <a. la fama to desire fame> —intr. to be appealing or attractive <esa idea no me apetece that idea is not appealing to me>.

a·pe·te·ci·ble adj. appealing, appetizing.

a·pe·ten·cia f. (hambre) appetite, hunger; (deseo) longing, desire.

a·pe·ti·to m. (hambre) appetite, hunger; FIG. (ambición) appetite, longing ♦ **abrir, dar, or despertar el a.** to whet one's appetite.

a·pe·ti·to·so, –sa adj. (apetecedor) appetizing, tempting; (sabroso) tasty, delicious.

a·pe·zo·na·do, –da adj. mammillate, nipple-shaped.

a·pia·dar tr. to move to pity —reflex. to (have) pity ♦ **apiadarse de** to take pity on.

a·pia·nar tr. to soften, lower (the voice).

a·pi·ca·rar·se reflex. to become a rogue.

á·pi·ce m. (cima) apex, top, pinnacle; FIG. (nonada) iota, whit; (punto crítico) crux, root <el a. del problema the crux of the problem> ♦ **estar en los ápices de** FIG. to be on top of, know all about • **ni un a.** nothing, not a bit • **no ceder un a.** to not give an inch.

a·pi·cul·tor, –to·ra m.f. beekeeper, apiculturist.

a·pi·cul·tu·ra f. beekeeping, apiculture.

a·pi·lar tr. to pile *or* heap.

a·pim·po·llar·se reflex. BOT. to bud, sprout; FIG. *(aderezarse)* to spruce *or* smarten up.

a·pi·ña·do, –da I. past part. see **apiñar** II. adj. *(de figura de piña)* cone-shaped, conical; *(apretado)* crammed *or* packed together.

a·pi·ña·mien·to m. *(apretamiento)* crowding, cramming; *(aprieto)* crowd, crush.

a·pi·ñar tr. to cram *or* pack together —reflex. to crowd, cram together.

a·pio m. BOT. celery.

a·pio·lar tr. *(un halcón)* to fetter (a hawk); *(un animal)* to tie the legs (of a dead animal); FIG., COLL. *(prender)* to capture, arrest; *(matar)* to kill.

a·pi·so·na·do·ra f. *(aplastador)* leveler, flattener; *(de carretera)* steamroller; *(de tierra)* rammer, tamper.

a·pi·so·na·mien·to m. *(aplastamiento)* leveling, flattening; *(de tierra)* ramming, tamping, packing down; *(de carretera)* steamrolling, leveling.

a·pi·so·nar tr. *(tierra)* to ram, pack down; *(carretera)* to steamroller, level.

a·pi·to·nar intr. ZOOL. to sprout *or* begin to grow horns; BOT. to bud, sprout —reflex. FIG., COLL. to insult one another.

a·pla·ca·ble adj. placable.

a·pla·ca·dor, –do·ra adj. placating, soothing.

a·pla·ca·mien·to m. appeasement, placation, calming.

a·pla·car §70 tr. to appease, placate, calm.

a·pla·cé, aplace see **aplazar.**

a·pla·cer §51 tr. & intr. to please, satisfy.

a·pla·na·de·ra f. *(apisonadora)* leveler, flattener; *(de carretera)* steamroller; *(de tierra)* rammer, tamper.

a·pla·na·dor, –do·ra I. adj. *(allanador)* leveling, flattening, collapsing; *(abrumador)* disheartening, discouraging II. m.f. *(apisonadora)* leveler, flattener —m. *(de tierra)* tamper, rammer; *(de carretera)* steamroller.

a·pla·na·mien·to m. *(apisonamiento)* leveling, flattening; *(derrumbamiento)* collapse, crumbling; FIG., COLL. *(desaliento)* discouragement, disheartenment.

a·pla·nar tr. *(allanar)* to level, make even, flatten; FIG., COLL. *(pasmar)* to stun, astonish —reflex. *(venirse abajo)* to collapse, cave in; FIG. *(desanimarse)* to lose heart, become discouraged.

a·pla·qué, aplaque see **aplacar.**

a·plas·ta·mien·to m. crushing, squashing.

a·plas·tan·te adj. *(agobiador)* overwhelming, crushing; FIG. *(cansador)* exhausting, tiring.

a·plas·tar tr. *(estrujar)* to crush, squash; FIG. *(vencer)* to overwhelm, crush; FIG., COLL. *(apabullar)* to stun, astound; ARG. to exhaust, tire —reflex. ARG. *(desanimarse)* to become discouraged; *(cansarse)* to become exhausted, get tired.

a·plau·di·dor, –do·ra I. adj. applauding II. m.f. applauder.

a·plau·dir tr. *(palmotear)* to applaud <*aplaudieron el espectáculo* they applauded the spectacle>; FIG. *(aprobar)* to applaud, commend <*aplaudo tu decisión* I applaud your decision>.

a·plau·so m. *(palmas)* applause, clapping; FIG. *(aprobación)* applause, praise.

a·pla·za·ble adj. deferrable, postponable.

a·pla·za·mien·to m. *(demora)* postponement; *(emplazamiento)* convocation, summons.

a·pla·zar §04 tr. *(diferir)* to postpone, put off; *(emplazar)* to call, convene; AMER. to fail, flunk (an examination).

a·plaz·ca, aplazco see **aplacer.**

a·ple·be·yar tr. to degrade, debase.

a·pli·ca·ble adj. applicable, appropriate.

a·pli·ca·ción f. *(superposición)* application; *(adorno)* appliqué; FIG. *(esmero)* diligence, assiduity; AMER. request, application.

a·pli·ca·do, –da I. past part. see **aplicar** II. adj. FIG. diligent, assiduous.

a·pli·car §70 tr. *(superponer)* to apply, put on; *(atribuir)* to impute, attribute; *(designar)* to assign, devote; FIG. *(usar)* to use, employ <*a. un remedio* to use a remedy>; LAW *(adjudicar)* to adjudge —reflex. to apply oneself.

a·pli·que m. *(lámpara)* wall lamp *or* light; THEAT. *(bastidor)* wing, side flat.

a·plo·ma·do, –da I. past part. see **aplomar** II. adj. *(sereno)* poised, self-assured; *(color)* lead-colored.

a·plo·mar tr. CONST. to plumb up, make vertical; CHILE to embarrass —intr. CONST. to be plumb *or* vertical <*la pared aploma* the wall is plumb> —reflex. *(caerse)* to collapse, fall down; *(cobrar aplomo)* to become poised; CHILE to get embarrassed.

a·plo·mo m. *(serenidad)* aplomb, poise, self-assurance; *(verticalidad)* vertical alignment; *(de caballos)* alignment of legs.

a·po·ca·do, –da I. past part. see **apocar** II. adj. FIG. *(tímido)* diffident, timid; *(vil)* base, lowly.

A·po·ca·lip·sis m. BIBL. Apocalypse.

a·po·ca·líp·ti·co, –ca adj. BIBL. apocalyptic, apocalyptical; FIG. *(enigmático)* enigmatic, mysterious; *(terrorífico)* terrifying, frightening.

a·po·ca·mien·to m. *(timidez)* timidity, timidness; FIG. *(desánimo)* depression, low spirits.

a·po·car §70 tr. *(reducir)* to lessen, diminish; *(restringir)* to restrict, contract —reflex. to be humiliated, humble oneself.

a·po·co·par tr. GRAM., PHONET. to apocopate, elide.

a·pó·co·pe f. GRAM., PHONET. apocope, elision.

a·pó·cri·fo, –fa adj. *(supuesto)* apocryphal, supposed; *(falso)* false, counterfeit ♦ **libros apócrifos** BIBL. Apocrypha.

a·po·dar tr. to nickname.

a·po·de·ra·do, –da I. past part. see **apoderar** II. adj. empowered, authorized III. m.f. COM. proxy, representative, agent; LAW *(poderhabiente)* attorney, proxy; SPORT. *(empresario)* manager, agent ♦ **constituir a.** LAW to grant power of attorney, appoint a proxy.

a·po·de·ra·mien·to m. *(autorización)* empowering, authorization; *(apropiación)* appropriation, seizure.

a·po·de·rar tr. *(autorizar)* to empower, authorize; LAW *(constituir apoderado a)* to grant power of attorney to —reflex. ♦ **apoderarse de** *(apropiar)* to seize, take possession of; FIG. *(dominar)* to take hold of, overwhelm.

a·po·do m. nickname.

á·po·do, –da adj. ZOOL. apodal, having no feet.

a·po·ge·o m. ASTRON. apogee; FIG. *(cumbre)* height, acme.

a·po·li·lla·mien·to m. damage done by moths.

a·po·li·llar tr. to eat, infest (said of moths) —intr. AMER., COLL. to snooze, doze —reflex. to be moth-eaten.

a·po·lí·ti·co, –ca I. adj. apolitical, nonpolitical II. m.f. nonpolitical person.

A·po·lo m. MYTH. Apollo.

a·po·lo·gé·ti·co, –ca I. adj. apologetic, defensive II. f. THEOL. apologetics.

a·po·lo·gí·a f. *(defensa)* apologia, formal defense; *(elogio)* eulogy, praise.

a·po·lo·gis·ta m.f. apologist, defender.

a·pó·lo·go m. apologue.

a·pol·tro·na·do, –da I. past part. see **apoltronarse** II. adj. lazy, idle.

a·pol·tro·nar·se reflex. *(hacerse poltrón)* to get lazy; *(arrellanarse)* to laze *or* loll around.

a·po·neu·ro·sis f. [pl. **-sis**] ANAT. aponeurosis.

a·po·ple·jí·a f. MED. apoplexy.

a·po·qué, apoque see **apocar.**

a·por·car §73 tr. AGR. to hill, earth up (plants).

a·po·rrar intr. COLL. to be struck dumb, be left speechless.

a·po·rre·a·do, –da I. past part. see **aporrear** II. adj. wretched, miserable <*vida a.* wretched life> III. m. CUBA, CUL. beef stew.

a·po·rre·ar tr. *(golpear)* to club, beat; to pound, bang on <*a. el piano* to bang on the piano>; FIG. *(machacar)* to annoy, harp on ♦ **aporrearle a uno los oídos** FIG., COLL. to talk *or* chew one's ear off —reflex. FIG. to slave, break one's back.

a·po·rre·o m. *(golpeo)* beating, clubbing; FIG. *(molestia)* bother, annoyance; *(trabajo)* drudgery, toil.

a·por·ta·ción f. *(contribución)* contribution; *(dote)* dowry, marriage portion.

a·por·tar intr. MARIT. to make port, arrive; *(llegar)* to arrive, reach; FIG. *(llegar por casualidad)* to arrive *or* end up by chance —tr. *(traer)* to bring, carry; *(contribuir)* to contribute, furnish; *(en el casamiento)* to bring into marriage —reflex. CHILE to show up, arrive.

a·por·te m. AMER. contribution, donation.

a·por·ti·llar tr. *(un muro)* to breach (a wall); *(romper)* to break —reflex. to collapse, fall down (said of a wall).

a·po·sen·tar tr. to lodge, put up —reflex. to lodge, stay.

a·po·sen·to m. *(habitación)* room, chamber; *(hospedaje)* lodging, quarters; ARCHIT., THEAT. *(palco)* box; CUBA, P. RICO master bedroom ♦ **tomar a.** to put up, stay.

a·po·si·ción f. GRAM. apposition.

a·pos·ta or **a·pos·ta·da·men·te** adv. on purpose, deliberately.

a·pos·ta·de·ro m. *(paraje)* post, station; MARIT., MIL. *(base)* naval base or station.

a·pos·tar §19 tr. *(jugar)* to bet, wager; *(colocar)* to post, station —reflex. *(colocarse)* to position or station oneself; *(competir)* to compete, be rivals.

a·pós·ta·ta adj. & m.f. RELIG. apostate, renegade.

a·pos·ta·tar intr. to apostatize; FIG. *(cambiar de opinión)* to change one's opinions and beliefs.

a·pos·ti·lla f. marginal note, annotation.

a·pós·tol m.f. RELIG. apostle; FIG. *(propagador)* champion, apostle.

a·pos·to·la·do m. RELIG. *(misión)* apostolate, apostleship; *(pontificado)* papacy, pontificate; FIG. *(diseminación)* dissemination of new ideas.

a·pos·tó·li·ca·men·te adv. RELIG. apostolically; COLL. *(pobremente)* poorly, simply.

a·pos·tó·li·co, -ca adj. RELIG. *(de los apóstoles)* apostolic; *(del papa)* papal, pontific.

a·pós·tro·fe m.f. RHET. apostrophe, digression; FIG. *(insulto)* insult.

a·pós·tro·fo m. GRAM. apostrophe.

a·pos·tu·ra f. *(aspecto)* looks, bearing; *(gentileza)* gracefulness, pleasantness.

a·po·te·ca·rio, -ria I. adj. pharmaceutical II. m.f. apothecary.

a·po·teg·ma m. apothegm, maxim.

a·po·te·ó·si·co, -ca adj. *(glorificador)* glorifying, deifying; *(glorioso)* glorious, tremendous.

a·po·te·o·sis f. [pl. **-sis**] *(deificación)* apotheosis, deification; FIG. *(ensalzamiento)* glorification, extolment.

a·po·te·ó·ti·co, -ca adj. glorious, magnificent.

a·po·yar tr. *(estribar)* to lean, rest *<a. el codo en la mesa* to lean one's elbow on the table>; *(ayudar)* to aid, support *<a. una facción* to support a faction>; *(confirmar)* to confirm, uphold *<apoyó su posición con citas* he upheld his position with references>; MIL. to reinforce —intr. to lean, rest *<la columna apoya sobre el pedestal* the column rests on the pedestal> —reflex. to lean, rest; FIG. *(fiarse)* to rely on.

a·po·ya·tu·ra f. MUS. appoggiatura, grace note; FIG. *(fundamento)* basis, foundation.

a·po·yo m. *(soporte)* support; *(fundamento)* basis, foundation; FIG. *(protección)* aid, protection.

a·pre·cia·ble adj. COM. appreciable, assessable; FIG. *(estimable)* worthy, estimable.

a·pre·cia·ción f. COM. appraisal, assessment, valuation; FIG. *(consideración)* consideration, evaluation.

a·pre·cia·dor, -do·ra I. adj. *(que estima)* appreciative; *(que valora)* appraising II. m.f. estimator, appraiser.

a·pre·ciar tr. COM. to appraise, assess, value; FIG. *(estimar)* to appreciate, esteem *<aprecio mucho a este amigo* I appreciate this friend a great deal>; *(considerar)* to consider, evaluate *<debes a. la magnitud del problema* you must consider the magnitude of the problem>.

a·pre·cia·ti·vo, -va adj. appraising *<una mirada a.* an appraising look>.

a·pre·cio m. COM. appraisal, valuation; FIG. *(estima)* appreciation, esteem; MEX. attention ♦ **no hacer a. a** MEX. not to pay attention to.

a·pre·hen·der tr. *(apresar)* to apprehend, arrest *<a. a un criminal* to apprehend a criminal>; *(confiscar)* to seize, confiscate; *(concebir)* to apprehend, conceive of; *(temer)* to fear, feel apprehension about.

a·pre·hen·sión f. *(apresamiento)* apprehension, capture;

(embargo) seizure, confiscation; *(comprensión)* comprehension, conception; *(miedo)* fear, apprehension.

a·pre·hen·si·vo, -va adj. apprehensive.

a·pre·mia·dor, -do·ra I. adj. urgent, compelling II. m.f. compeller, coercer.

a·pre·mian·te adj. pressing, urgent.

a·pre·miar tr. *(acelerar)* to hurry, press; *(oprimir)* to oppress; LAW *(compeler)* to compel, oblige.

a·pre·mio m. *(urgencia)* pressure, urgency; LAW *(orden judicial)* judicial order, judgment.

a·pren·der tr. to learn ♦ **a. a** to learn to *<aprendió a nadar* she learned to swim>.

a·pren·diz, -di·za m.f. *(meritorio)* apprentice, trainee; *(principiante)* novice, beginner ♦ **ser a. de todo y oficial de nada** to be a Jack of all trades and a master of none.

a·pren·di·za·je m. *(adiestramiento)* apprenticeship, traineeship; FIG. *(primeros ensayos)* initiation, first lessons ♦ **pagar el a.** COLL. to pay for one's inexperience, pay one's dues.

a·pren·sión f. *(miedo)* apprehension, dread; *(sospecha)* suspicion, misgiving; *(delicadeza)* good manners, courtesy; *(aprehensión)* capture, seizure.

a·pren·si·vo, -va adj. apprehensive, timid, fearful.

a·pre·sa·dor, -do·ra I. adj. capturing, seizing II. m.f. captor —m. privateer.

a·pre·sa·mien·to m. *(detención)* arrest, capture; ZOOL. *(asimiento)* clutch, hold; MARIT. *(toma)* capture, seizure.

a·pre·sar tr. *(aprisionar)* to take prisoner, capture; ZOOL. *(agarrar)* to grasp, seize (with claws, teeth); MARIT. *(tomar)* to capture, seize.

a·pres·tar tr. *(preparar)* to make ready, prepare; TEX. *(engomar)* to size, prime (fabrics) —reflex. to get ready, prepare oneself.

a·pres·to m. *(preparación)* preparation, making ready; TEX. *(cola)* sizing, size; *(procedimiento)* sizing.

a·pre·su·ra·da·men·te adv. hurriedly, hastily, in a hurry.

a·pre·su·ra·do, -da I. past part. see **apresurar** II. adj. hurried, hasty.

a·pre·su·ra·mien·to m. *(prisa)* hurry, haste; *(aceleración)* hurrying, hastening.

a·pre·su·rar tr. to hurry, hasten —reflex. to hurry, make haste ♦ **apresurarse a** or **por** to hurry or make haste to.

a·pre·ta·da·men·te adv. tightly, closely.

a·pre·ta·de·ra f. strap, tie ♦ **apretaderas** FIG., COLL. urging, insistence.

a·pre·ta·di·zo, -za adj. compressible.

a·pre·ta·do, -da I. past part. see **apretar** II. adj. *(comprimido)* cramped, tight; FIG. *(arduo)* difficult, tricky *<un asunto a.* a tricky matter>; FIG., COLL. *(mezquino)* stingy, tight ♦ **estar muy a.** FIG., COLL. *(tener problemas)* to be in a jam or a tight spot; *(dinero)* to be hard up, be short of money • **estar a. de trabajo** to be up to one's neck in work.

a·pre·ta·dor, -do·ra I. adj. tightening II. m. *(instrumento)* tightener; *(almilla)* bodice, jerkin; *(cotilla de niños)* harness (for infants); *(faja de niños)* bellyband.

a·pre·ta·du·ra f. tightening, compression.

a·pre·ta·mien·to m. var. of **aprieto**.

a·pre·tar §49 tr. to tighten *<a. un nudo* to tighten a knot>; *(estrujar)* to squeeze, squash; *(comprimir)* to compress, press down; *(abrazar)* to hug, squeeze; *(afligir)* to distress, trouble; to tighten up *<a. la disciplina* to tighten up discipline>; *(apremiar)* to press, urge ♦ **a. la mano** to shake hands; FIG. *(aumentar el rigor)* to tighten the reins; *(ser tacaño)* to be stingy • **a. los dientes** to grit or clench one's teeth —intr. *(los zapatos)* to pinch; *(la ropa)* to be too tight; *(empeorar)* to worsen, get worse ♦ **a. a correr** COLL. to start to run, break into a run • **a. con** to come to grips with —reflex. to cram or press in.

a·pre·tón m. *(estrujón)* grip, squeeze; *(dolor)* cramp, sharp pain; *(aprieto)* jam, crush (of people); FIG., COLL. *(lío)* jam, fix; COLL *(carrera)* dash, sprint.

a·pre·tu·jar tr. COLL. *(apretar)* to squeeze, press hard; *(apiñar)* to crowd, cram.

a·pre·tu·jón m. COLL. *(estrujón)* squeeze, crush; *(aprieto)* jam, crush (of people).

a·prie·te, aprieto see **apretar**.

a·prie·to m. *(opresión)* jam, crush (of people); FIG. *(lío)* jam, fix ♦ **poner a alguien en un a.** to put someone on the spot.

a·prio·ris·mo m. apriority.

a·pri·sa adv. quickly, swiftly.

a·pris·co m. fold, pen.

a·pri·sio·na·mien·to m. (*encarcelamiento*) incarceration, imprisonment; FIG. (*restricción*) constraint, restraint.

a·pri·sio·nar tr. (*encarcelar*) to incarcerate, imprison; FIG. (*atar*) to tie down, bind.

a·pro·ba·ción f. (*consentimiento*) approval, approbation; LAW (*adopción*) adoption, ratification; (*de una prueba*) passing grade.

a·pro·ba·do, –da I. past part. see **aprobar** II. adj. approved III. m. (*nota*) pass, passing grade.

a·pro·ba·dor, –do·ra I. adj. approving II. m.f. approver.

a·pro·bar §19 tr. (*consentir*) to approve of, agree with; LAW (*adoptar*) to pass, ratify; to pass <*aprobé el examen* I passed the test> —intr. to pass an examination.

a·pro·ba·to·rio, –ria adj. approbatory, approbative, approving.

a·pron·tar tr. (*prevenir*) to quickly prepare or have ready; (*entregar*) to pay or deliver at once —intr. URUG. to turn up, arrive unexpectedly.

a·pron·te m. ARG., CHILE trial (race); FIG. (*preparación*) dry run.

a·pro·pia·ción f. (*confiscación*) appropriation, taking possession; (*acomodación*) fitting, adapting.

a·pro·pia·da·men·te adv. appropriately, suitably.

a·pro·pia·do, –da I. past part. see **apropiar** II. adj. appropriate, suitable.

a·pro·piar tr. (*adaptar*) to adapt, fit; AMER., FIN. to appropriate, earmark —reflex. to take possession ♦ **apropiarse de** to take possession of, seize.

a·pro·pin·cuar·se reflex. to approach, draw near.

a·pro·ve·cha·ble adj. useful, usable.

a·pro·ve·cha·da·men·te adv. for one's own benefit or profit.

a·pro·ve·cha·do, –da I. past part. see **aprovechar** II. adj. (*oportunista*) opportunistic; (*aplicado*) diligent, industrious.

a·pro·ve·cha·dor, –do·ra I. adj. opportunistic II. m.f. opportunist.

a·pro·ve·cha·mien·to m. use, utilization.

a·pro·ve·char intr. (*servir*) to be useful, be of use; (*adelantar*) to progress, improve —tr. to make good use of, take advantage of —reflex. ♦ **aprovecharse de** to take advantage of, avail oneself of.

a·pro·vi·sio·na·mien·to m. (*acción de abastecer*) supplying, provisioning; (*provisiones*) supplies, provisions.

a·pro·vi·sio·nar tr. to supply, provision.

a·pro·xi·ma·ción f. (*proximidad*) nearness, closeness; (*estimación*) approximation.

a·pro·xi·ma·da·men·te adv. approximately, about.

a·pro·xi·ma·do, –da I. past part. see **aproximar** II. adj. approximate, close.

a·pro·xi·mar tr. to approximate, bring near —reflex. to draw near.

a·prue·be, apruebo see **aprobar.**

ap·ti·tud f. (*capacidad*) aptitude, ability; (*conformidad*) aptness, suitability ♦ **aptitudes** gift, talent.

ap·to, –ta adj. (*hábil*) able, competent; (*conveniente*) apt, fit.

a·puer·que, apuerco see **aporcar.**

a·pues·ta I. f. bet, wager ♦ **apuestas mutuas** pari-mutuel (betting system) II. adj. see **apuesto, –ta.**

a·pues·ta·men·te adv. smartly, elegantly.

a·pues·te, apuesto see **apostar.**

a·pues·to, –ta I. adj. smart, elegant II. f. see **apuesta.**

a·pul·ga·rar·se reflex. to mildew, become mildewed (said of linen).

a·pu·nar·se reflex. AMER., MED. to be overcome by altitude sickness.

a·pun·ta·do, –da I. past part. see **apuntar** II. adj. pointed, sharp.

a·pun·ta·dor, –do·ra I. adj. observing, noting II. m.f. (*observador*) observer, noter; THEAT. (*traspunte*) prompter; MIL. pointer, gunner.

a·pun·ta·la·mien·to m. propping, shoring, bracing.

a·pun·ta·lar tr. to prop up, shore up.

a·pun·ta·mien·to m. (*anotación*) noting, taking down; (*afiladura*) sharpening; (*asestadura*) pointing, aiming; LAW case summary.

a·pun·tar tr. (*asestar un arma*) to aim, point (guns); (*señalar*) to point to or at, indicate; (*tomar nota*) to note, make a note of; (*sugerir*) to cue, clue; (*sacar punta a*) to sharpen, point; FIG. (*insinuar*) to hint at, suggest; THEAT. to prompt —intr. to begin to show <*le apuntaba la barba* his beard was beginning to show> —reflex. (*agriarse*) to begin to sour; COLL. (*embriagarse*) to begin to get tipsy.

a·pun·te m. (*nota*) note, notation; (*apuesta*) stake (in cards); COLL. (*pícaro*) rogue, rascal; COM. entry; THEAT. (*señal*) cue; (*apuntador*) prompter ♦ **apuntes** notes • **llevar el a.** ARG., CHILE, COLL. to pay attention; (*en el galanteo*) to accept someone's attentions.

a·pu·ña·la·do, –da I. past part. see **apuñalar** II. adj. shaped like a dagger.

a·pu·ña·lar tr. to stab, knife ♦ **a. a alguien con la mirada** to look daggers at someone • **a. a alguien por la espalda** to stab someone in the back.

apu·ñar tr. to seize in one's fist.

a·pu·ñe·ar or **a·pu·ñe·te·ar** tr. COLL. to punch, pummel.

a·pu·ra·ca·bos m. [pl. **-bos**] save-all (candleholder).

a·pu·ra·ción f. (*purificación*) purification; (*acabamiento*) completion, finishing; FIG. (*aclaración*) clarification.

a·pu·ra·da·men·te adv. COLL. exactly, precisely.

a·pu·ra·do, –da I. past part. see **apurar** II. adj. AMER. in a hurry; (*pobre*) poor, needy; (*peligroso*) dangerous, difficult; (*exacto*) exact, precise.

a·pu·ra·dor, –do·ra I. adj. (*agotador*) tiring, exhausting; (*purificador*) purifying, refining II. m.f. (*purificador*) purifier —m. (*apuracabos*) save-all.

a·pu·ra·mien·to m. (*purificación*) purification; (*agotamiento*) exhaustion; FIG. (*aclaración*) clarification.

a·pu·rar tr. AMER. to hurry, press; (*purificar*) to purify, refine <*a. el oro* to refine gold>; (*agotar*) to use or finish up, exhaust; (*terminar*) to finish, end; FIG. (*averiguar*) to verify, check <*a. una historia* to verify a story>; (*enfadar*) to annoy, irritate —reflex. (*preocuparse*) to worry, fret; AMER. to hurry, make haste.

a·pu·ro m. (*pobreza*) poverty, need; (*dificultad*) difficulty, jam; (*prisa*) hurry, haste ♦ **estar en apuros** to be hard up (for money).

a·que·jar tr. to afflict, distress.

a·quel, a·que·lla §G26 dem. adj. [pl. **a·que·llos, a·que·llas**] that (. . . over there) <*a. hombre* that man over there> ♦ **aquellas** or **aquellos** those <*aquellos chicos* those boys>.

a·quél, aqué·lla §G41 I. dem. pron. [pl. **a·qué·llos, a·qué·llas**] that one (over there) <*a. no funciona* that one (over there) is not working>; (*el primero*) the former ♦ **aquéllas** or **aquéllos** those II. m. COLL. charm, appeal <*ese chico tiene mucho a.* that boy has a lot of charm>.

a·que·llo §G41 neut. dem. pron. that, that matter ♦ **a. de** that business about <*a. de mi hermano fue un disparate* that business about my brother was nonsense>.

a·que·ren·cia·do, –da I. past part. see **aquerenciarse** II. adj. MEX. in love, enamored.

a·que·ren·ciar·se reflex. ♦ **a. a** to become fond of or attached to.

a·quí adv. (*en este lugar*) here <*ella no está a.* she isn't here>; (*ahora*) now <*a. empieza lo difícil* now comes the hard part>; (*entonces*) then, at that point <*a. no pudo seguir más* at that point he could not go on> ♦ **de a. en adelante** from now on, from here on in • **por a.** hereabouts, around here; this way <*venga por a.* come this way>.

a·quies·cen·cia f. acquiescence, assent.

a·quies·cen·te adj. acquiescent, assenting.

a·quie·tar tr. to calm, soothe —reflex. to calm down, become calm or quiet.

a·qui·la·tar tr. JEWEL. (*ensayar*) to appraise, assay; FIG. (*apreciar*) to appreciate, esteem —reflex. ARG., FIG. to improve.

a·qui·li·no, –na adj. aquiline.

a·qui·lón m. north wind.

a·qui·lla·do, –da adj. keel-shaped.

A·qui·ta·nia f. Aquitaine.

a·quis·tar tr. to get, obtain.

a·ra f. *(altar)* (sacrificial) altar; *(piedra)* altar stone —m. ORNITH. macaw, ara ♦ **en aras de** in honor of.

á·ra·be I. adj. Arab, Arabian II. m.f. Arab —m. *(idioma)* Arabic.

á·ra·be sau·di·ta adj. & m.f. Saudi Arabian, Saudi.

A·ra·bia f. Arabia.

A·ra·bia Sau·di·ta f. Saudi Arabia.

a·rá·bi·co, -ca *or* **a·rá·bi·go, -ga** I. adj. Arabic, Arabian ♦ **número a.** Arabic numeral II. m. *(idioma)* Arabic.

a·ra·bis·mo m. Arabic word *or* expression.

a·ra·bis·ta m.f. Arabist.

a·ra·ble adj. AGR. arable, cultivatable.

a·rác·ni·dos m.pl. ENTOM. arachnids.

a·ra·da f. *(acción de arar)* plowing; *(tierra arada)* plowed land; *(labranza)* farming; *(jornal)* day's plowing.

a·ra·do AGR. I. past part. see **arar** II. m. *(instrumento)* plow; *(acción)* plowing; COL. *(tierra cultivada)* plowed field, orchard.

A·ra·gón m. Aragon.

a·ra·go·nés, -ne·sa adj. & m.f. Aragonese ♦ **los aragoneses** the Aragonese.

a·ran·cel m. tariff, duty.

a·ran·ce·la·rio, -ria adj. pertaining to tariffs or customs.

a·ran·de·la f. MECH. washer; *(de un candelero)* rim (of a candlestick); *(candelabro)* candelabrum; ARM. hand guard (on a lance); MARIT. hatch; AMER. frills, flounce (on a shirt).

a·ra·ne·ro, -ra *or* **a·ra·no·so, -sa** I. adj. deceitful, tricky II. m.f. trickster, swindler.

a·ra·ña f. ENTOM. spider; *(candelabro)* chandelier; BOT. love-in-the-mist; ICHTH. stingbull, weaver; MARIT. crowfoot, rigging; S. AMER. prostitute, whore ♦ **a. de mar** spider crab.

a·ra·ñar tr. *(rasgar)* to scratch, scrape; FIG., COLL. *(recoger)* to scrape together (money) —reflex. to scratch oneself, scratch.

a·ra·ña·zo m. scratch, scrape.

a·rar tr. AGR. to plow; FIG. *(caminar)* to plow through (snow); *(arrugar)* to furrow, wrinkle.

a·rau·ca·no, -na adj. & m.f. Araucanian.

ar·bi·tra·dor, -do·ra I. adj. arbitrating II. m.f. arbitrator, arbiter.

ar·bi·tra·je m. *(juicio)* arbitration; COM. arbitrage.

ar·bi·tral adj. LAW arbitral <*juicio a.* arbitral decision>.

ar·bi·trar tr. *(juzgar)* to arbitrate; SPORT. to referee, umpire; *(allegar)* to gather <*a. recursos* to gather resources>; *(proceder libremente)* to act freely —intr. to arbitrate —reflex. to get along, manage.

ar·bi·tra·ria·men·te adv. arbitrarily.

ar·bi·tra·rie·dad f. *(calidad de arbitrario)* arbitrariness; *(ilegalidad)* arbitrary act, outrage.

ar·bi·tra·rio, -ria adj. arbitrary.

ar·bi·trio m. *(voluntad)* will <*libre a.* free will>; *(recurso)* means, way; *(juicio)* judgment, decision ♦ **arbitrios** taxes.

ar·bi·tris·ta m.f. utopian, idealist.

ár·bi·tro m. LAW *(juez)* arbiter, arbitrator; FIG. *(dueño absoluto)* absolute *or* sole judge; SPORT. *(en los deportes)* umpire, referee.

ár·bol m. BOT. tree; MECH. axle, spindle; MARIT. mast; ARCHIT. crown post; CHILE clothes rack ♦ **á. de levas** MECH. camshaft • **á de la ciencia** FIG. tree of knowledge • **á. de Navidad** Christmas tree • **á. motor** MECH. drive shaft.

ar·bo·la·do, -da I. past part. see **arbolar** II. adj. wooded, tree-covered III. m. wood, grove.

ar·bo·lar tr. *(enarbolar)* to hoist, raise <*a. la bandera* to raise the flag>; MARIT. to rig; *(arrimar derecho)* to set upright —reflex. to rear (said of a horse).

ar·bo·le·cer §17 intr. to grow into a tree (said of a sapling).

ar·bo·le·da f. grove, wood.

ar·bo·lis·ta m.f. arborist.

ar·bó·re·o, -a adj. arboreal.

ar·bo·re·to m. arboretum.

ar·bo·ri·cul·tu·ra f. BOT. arboriculture, tree cultivation.

ar·bo·ri·za·ción f. MIN. arborization.

ar·bo·ri·za·do, -da I. past part. see **arborizar** II. adj. MIN. arborized.

ar·bo·ri·zar §04 tr. to forest, plant with trees.

ar·bus·to m. BOT. bush, shrub.

ar·ca f. *(cofre)* chest; *(horno)* tempering oven (in glassmaking) ♦ **a. cerrada** FIG., COLL. reticent person, clam • **a. de agua** reservoir, water tank • **a. de la Alianza** BIBL. Ark of the Covenant • **a. de Noé** BIBL. Noah's Ark; ICHTH. *(molusco)* arkshell • **arcas** coffers, treasury boxes; ANAT. hollows (under the ribs).

ar·ca·buz m. [pl. **-bu·ces**] *(arma)* harquebus; *(arcabucero)* harquebusier.

ar·ca·da f. ARCHIT. arcade; *(de un puente)* arch, span; *(basca)* retch.

ar·ca·duz m. [pl. **-du·ces**] *(caño)* pipe, conduit; *(de noria)* bucket (of a water wheel); FIG., COLL. *(medio)* means, way.

ar·cai·co, -ca adj. archaic, old-fashioned.

ar·ca·ís·mo m. archaism.

ar·ca·ís·ta m.f. archaist.

ar·cai·zan·te adj. archaizing.

ar·cai·zar §06 intr. & tr. to archaize.

ar·cán·gel m. archangel.

ar·ca·no, -na I. adj. arcane, secret II. m. secret, mystery.

ar·ce m. BOT. maple (tree).

ar·ce·dia·no m. archdeacon.

ar·ci·lla f. clay ♦ **a. figulina** potter's clay.

ar·ci·llar tr. AGR. to loam, clay.

ar·ci·llo·so, -sa adj. clay-like, clayey.

ar·ci·pres·te m. archpriest.

ar·co m. GEOM. arc; ARCHIT. arch, archway; ARM., MUS. bow; ANAT. arch; SPORT. *(portería)* goal; *(aro)* hoop (of barrels) ♦ **a. iris** rainbow • **a. voltaico** ELEC. arc lamp • **arcos caídos** ANAT. fallen arches.

ar·chi·du·que m. archduke.

ar·chi·du·que·sa f. archduchess.

ar·chi·la·úd m. MUS. large lute.

ar·chi·mi·llo·na·rio, -ria m. multimillionaire —f. multimillionairess.

ar·chi·pám·pa·no m. COLL. muckamuck, honcho.

ar·chi·pié·la·go m. archipelago.

ar·chi·va·dor, -do·ra I. adj. archiving, filing II. m.f. *(registrador)* archivist; *(oficinista)* filing clerk —m. *(mueble)* filing cabinet.

ar·chi·var tr. *(guardar)* to archive, put into archives; *(clasificar)* to file, put into a file; FIG., COLL. *(dar carpetazo)* to shelve, file away <*a una idea* to shelve an idea>.

ar·chi·ve·ro, -ra *or* **ar·chi·vis·ta** m.f. archivist.

ar·chi·vo m. *(registro)* archives, records; *(sitio)* archives; *(de una oficina)* files; FIG. *(persona fiable)* soul of discretion, trustworthy person; *(persona inteligente)* mine, fountain of information.

ar·den·tí·a f. MED. pyrosis, heartburn.

ar·der intr. *(quemarse)* to burn, blaze; FIG. to glow, blaze <*el acero arde* the steel is glowing>; AGR. to ferment (manure) ♦ **a. de** *or* **en** FIG. to rage *or* be ablaze with <*a. de ira* to be ablaze with anger> —tr. to burn, char —reflex. *(quemarse)* to burn up; AGR. to spoil, rot (from excessive heat).

ar·did m. ruse, scheme.

ar·di·do, -da I. past part. see **arder** II. adj. *(valiente)* brave, courageous; S. AMER. angry, irritated.

ar·dien·te adj. *(quemante)* burning, blazing; FIG. *(fogoso)* ardent, fervent, fiery; *(al rojo)* glowing.

ar·dien·te·men·te adv. ardently, fervently.

ar·di·lla f. ZOOL. squirrel; S. AMER., COLL. go-getter ♦ **a. listada** *or* **rayada** ZOOL. chipmunk.

ar·di·te m. old Spanish coin of little value ♦ **no valer un a.** COLL. not to be worth a cent.

ar·dor m. *(calor)* heat; FIG. *(anhelo)* zeal, eagerness; *(valor)* courage, valor; *(enardecimiento)* heat <*en el a. de la disputa* in the heat of the argument>.

ar·do·ro·sa·men·te adv. FIG. ardently, fervently.

ar·do·ro·so, -sa adj. *(encendido)* hot, fiery <*sol a.* hot sun>; FIG. *(apasionado)* ardent, fervent.

ar·dua·men·te adv. arduously, with great difficulty.

ar·duo, -dua adj. arduous, difficult.

á·re·a f. *(superficie)* area <*el a. de un campo* the area of a field>; GEOM. area; *(de juego)* playground.

a·re·na f. sand <*hay a. blanca en esa playa* there is white sand on that beach>; *(metal en polvo)* filings, dust; *(redondel)* ring, bullring; FIG. *(campo de batalla)* arena, battlefield ♦ **arenas** MED. gallstones • **arenas movedizas** quicksand • **sembrar en a.** FIG. to labor in vain.

a·re·nal m. *(terreno arenoso)* sandy ground; *(arena movediza)* quicksand).

a·re·nar tr. *(enarenar)* to sand, cover with sand; *(frotar)* to sand, rub or clean with sand.

a·re·ne·ro, –ra m.f. *(vendedor)* sand merchant —m. RAIL. sandbox; TAUR. sand boy (who smooths the surface of the bullring).

a·ren·ga f. *(perorata)* harangue; FIG., COLL. *(discurso)* sermon; CHILE quarrel, argument.

a·ren·gar §47 tr. & intr. to harangue.

a·re·ní·fe·ro, –ra adj. containing sand.

a·re·ni·lla MED. stone, calculus; *(polvo)* blotting powder, pounce ♦ **arenillas** ARM. granulated saltpeter.

a·re·nis·co, –ca I. adj. sandy II. f. sandstone.

a·re·no·so, –sa adj. sandy.

a·ren·que m. ICHTH. herring.

a·re·o·la f. ANAT., BOT., MED. areola.

a·re·o·lar adj. areolar.

a·re·o·me·trí·a f. hydrometry.

a·re·o·me·tro m. PHYS. hydrometer.

a·re·te m. *(aro)* hoop, ring; *(pendiente)* earring.

ar·far intr. MARIT. to pitch.

ar·ga·di·jo or **ar·ga·di·llo** m. *(devanadera)* spool, reel; FIG., COLL. *(persona bulliciosa)* noisy and blustering person.

ar·ga·lle·ra f. saw for cutting grooves.

ar·ga·man·del m. rag, tatter.

ar·ga·ma·sa f. mortar, plaster.

ar·ga·ma·sar intr. to make or mix mortar —tr. to mortar, plaster.

ár·ga·na f. MECH. crane ♦ **árganas** wicker baskets (hung from a saddle).

ar·ga·vie·so m. short sudden downpour.

ar·ga·yo m. landslide.

Ar·gel m. Algiers.

Ar·ge·lia f. Algeria.

ar·ge·li·no, –na adj. & m.f. Algerian.

ar·gen·ta·do, –da I. past part. see **argentar** II. adj. *(bañado de plata)* silvered, silver-plated; *(de color de plata)* silver, silvery.

ar·gen·tar tr. *(platear)* to silver, silver-plate; *(decorar)* to decorate with silver; FIG. *(dar brillo)* to make shine like silver <*la luna argentaba el paisaje* the moon made the landscape shine like silver>.

ar·gen·ta·rio m. silversmith.

ar·gén·te·o, –a adj. *(de plata)* silver; *(bañado de plata)* silver-plated; FIG. *(brillante)* shiny, silvery.

ar·gen·te·rí·a f. gold or silver embroidery.

Ar·gen·ti·na f. Argentina.

ar·gen·ti·nis·mo m. Argentine word or expression.

ar·gen·ti·no, –na I. adj. *(de Argentina)* Argentine, Argentinian; *(de plata)* silvery, argentine; FIG. silvery, clear <*una voz a.* a silvery voice> II. m.f. Argentine, Argentinian.

ar·gen·to m. POET. silver ♦ **a. vivo** quicksilver.

ar·go·lla f. *(aro)* ring, hoop; *(juego)* croquet; FIG. *(sujeción)* shackles; S. AMER. *(anillo)* wedding or engagement ring; AMER. *(alianza)* alliance; MEX., COLL. luck ♦ **formar a.** C. AMER., COLL. to form a monopoly.

ar·gón m. CHEM. argon.

ar·go·nau·ta m. MYTH. Argonaut; ICHTH. *(molusco)* argonaut, paper nautilus.

ar·gos m. FIG. *(persona vigilante)* Argus, vigilant person; ORNITH. argus pheasant.

ar·got m. slang, jargon.

ar·gu·cia f. *(sutileza)* subtlety; *(sofisma)* sophistry, sophism.

ar·güir §07 intr. to argue —tr. *(deducir)* to deduce, infer <*de sus acciones puedo a. su verdadera intención* from his actions I can deduce his true intention>; *(probar)* to prove; *(acusar)* to reproach, accuse.

ar·gu·men·ta·ción f. *(acción)* arguing, argumentation; *(argumento)* argument.

ar·gu·men·ta·dor, –do·ra I. adj. arguing, argumentative II. m.f. arguer.

ar·gu·men·ta·ti·vo, –va adj. argumentative.

ar·gu·men·tar intr. to argue.

ar·gu·men·tis·ta m.f. *(argumentador)* arguer; CINEM. *(escritor)* script writer.

ar·gu·men·to m. *(razonamiento)* argument, line of reasoning; *(trama)* plot; *(sumario)* summary, synopsis; S. AMER. argument, dispute.

ar·gu·ya, arguyo see **argüir.**

ar·gu·yen·te adj. arguing, opposing.

ar·gu·ye·ra, arguyó see **argüir.**

a·ria I. f. MUS. aria II. adj. see **ario, –ria.**

a·ri·dez f. aridity, aridness.

á·ri·do, –da I. adj. *(seco)* arid, dry; FIG. *(trillado)* dry, dull <*estudios áridos* dull studies> II. m.pl. **áridos** dry goods.

A·ries m. Aries.

a·rie·te m. MIL., HIST. battering ram; MARIT. ram (armored steamship); *(fútbol)* center forward ♦ **a. hidráulico** MECH. hydraulic ram.

a·rio, –ria adj. & m.f. Aryan —f. see **aria.**

a·ris·co, –ca adj. *(desabrido)* unfriendly, surly; *(salvaje)* vicious, wild; CUBA shy, timid.

a·ris·ta f. GEOM. edge (between two planes); BOT. beard, awn; ARCHIT. arris.

a·ris·ta·do, –da adj. BOT. bearded, awned; *(con borde)* edged, with edges.

a·ris·to·cra·cia f. aristocracy.

a·ris·tó·cra·ta m.f. aristocrat.

a·ris·to·crá·ti·ca·men·te adv. aristocratically.

a·ris·to·crá·ti·co, –ca adj. *(noble)* aristocratic; *(distinguido)* distinguished.

A·ris·tó·te·les Aristotle.

a·ris·to·té·li·co, –ca adj. & m.f. PHILOS. Aristotelian.

a·rit·mé·ti·co, –ca I. adj. arithmetical, arithmetic II. m.f. arithmetician —f. *(ciencia)* arithmetic; *(libro)* arithmetic book.

a·rit·mó·gra·fo m. adding machine.

a·ri·to m. COL., GUAT. earring.

ar·le·quín m. *(payaso)* harlequin, clown; *(bufón)* buffoon, clown; *(sorbete)* Neapolitan ice cream.

ar·le·qui·na·da f. clowning, buffoonery.

ar·le·qui·nes·co, –ca adj. THEAT. harlequinesque; *(ridículo)* ridiculous, buffoonish.

ar·ma f. *(instrumento)* weapon, arm; MIL. division, arm <*a. de infantería* infantry division> ♦ **¡a las armas!** to arms! • **alzarse en armas** to rise up in arms, rebel • **a. arrojadiza** missile, projectile • **a. blanca** bladed weapon • **a. de fuego** firearm • **a. negra** fencing foil • **armas** *(instrumentos)* arms, weapons; *(ejército)* troops, army; FIG. *(medios)* means; HER. coat of arms, escutcheon • **de armas tomar** resolute, of action <*él es un hombre de armas tomar* he is a man of action> • **pasar por las armas** to shoot • **presentar armas** to present arms • **rendir las armas** to present arms.

ar·ma·da I. f. *(flota de guerra)* armada, (naval) fleet; *(escuadra)* squadron; S. AMER. lasso ♦ **la Armada Invencible** the Spanish Armada II. adj. see **armado, –da.**

ar·ma·di·llo m. ZOOL. armadillo.

ar·ma·do, –da I. past part. see **armar** II. adj. *(provisto de armas)* armed; CONSTR. reinforced (with metal) <*cemento a.* reinforced cement>; MEX., P. RICO stubborn, obstinate III. m. ICHTH. catfish; GUAT. armadillo; ARG. hand-rolled cigarette; CHILE armor —f. see **armada.**

ar·ma·du·ra f. MIL. armor; *(armazón)* frame, framework; ELEC. armature; ANAT. skeleton, frame; ARCHIT. frame, shell; MUS. key signature ♦ **a. de la cama** bedstead, bed frame • **a. volada** cantilever truss.

ar·ma·men·tis·ta adj. MIL. arms, armaments <*carrera a.* arms race>.

ar·ma·men·to m. *(accion de armar)* armament; *(armas)* armaments, weapons.

ar·mar tr. *(dar armas)* to arm, provide with arms; *(aprestar)* to prime (weapons); *(montar)* to assemble, put together; *(dar fuerza)* to strengthen, reinforce; *(fundar)* to base, found; MARIT. to provision, equip; FIG., COLL. to cause, create <*a. un jaleo* to cause a fuss>; *(disponer)* to arrange, organize; ARG. to roll (a cigarette) ♦ **a. caballero** to knight, dub (someone) a knight • **armarla** to cause a scandal —reflex. to arm oneself <*la nación se armó* the nation armed itself>; FIG. to arm oneself <*armarse de paciencia* to arm oneself with patience>; C. AMER., MEX. *(los animales)* to balk, shy; *(personas)* to balk, refuse, be obstinate; S. AMER. to strike it rich, get lucky ♦ ¡**te vas a.!** ARG., IRON. lots of luck!

ar·ma·rio m. closet, wardrobe.

ar·ma·tos·te m. *(mueble tosco)* monstrosity; FIG. *(palurdo)* slob, big oaf.

ar·ma·zón f. *(estructura)* framework, frame; *(bastidor)* chassis; *(esqueleto)* skeleton, frame —m. AMER. *(anaquelería)* shelving, shelves; *(estantería)* bookshelves.

ar·me·lla f. eyebolt.

Ar·me·nia f. GEOG. Armenia.

ar·me·nio, -nia adj. & m.f. Armenian.

ar·me·rí·a f. *(deposito)* armory; *(museo)* military museum; *(tienda)* gunsmith's shop; *(fabricación)* gunsmithing.

ar·me·ro m. *(fabricante de armas)* gunsmith; *(aparato)* gun rack.

ar·mi·lar adj. armillary <*esfera a.* armillary sphere>.

ar·mi·ño m. ZOOL. ermine (animal and skin).

ar·mis·ti·cio m. armistice.

ar·mo·ní·a f. MUS. harmony; FIG. *(amistad)* harmony <*vivir en a.* to live in harmony>.

ar·mó·ni·ca I. f. harmonica II. adj. see **armónico, -ca**.

ar·mó·ni·ca·men·te adv. harmonically, harmoniously.

ar·mo·ni·cé, armonice see **armonizar**.

ar·mó·ni·co, -ca I. adj. MUS. harmonic, harmonious II. m. MUS. harmonic —f. see **armónica**.

ar·mo·nio m. MUS. harmonium.

ar·mo·nio·sa·men·te adv. harmoniously, in harmony.

ar·mo·nio·so, -sa adj. harmonious.

ar·mo·ni·za·ble adj. harmonizable.

ar·mo·ni·za·ción f. MUS. harmonizing, harmonization; *(reconciliación)* harmonizing, reconciliation; *(de colores)* matching, coordinating.

ar·mo·ni·za·dor, -do·ra I. adj. harmonious II. m.f. harmonizer.

ar·mo·ni·zar §04 tr. MUS. to harmonize, provide harmony for; *(reconciliar)* to harmonize, make harmonious —intr. to harmonize, be harmonious.

ar·nés m. armor ♦ **arneses** EQUIT. harness; FIG. *(necesidades)* tools, equipment.

a·ro m. *(círculo)* hoop, ring; *(servilletero)* napkin ring; SPORT. quoit; BOT. arum; AMER. wedding ring; ARG., CHILE earring ♦ **a. de Etiopía** BOT. calla lily • **a. del émbolo** MECH. piston ring • **entrar por el a.** COLL. to have no choice, yield unwillingly.

a·ro·ma m. *(olor)* aroma, scent; *(del vino)* bouquet —f. BOT. aroma, huisache flower.

a·ro·mar tr. to perfume, scent.

a·ro·má·ti·co, -ca adj. aromatic.

a·ro·ma·ti·za·ción f. perfuming, scenting.

a·ro·ma·ti·za·dor m. AMER. vaporizer, atomizer.

a·ro·ma·ti·zan·te adj. perfuming.

a·ro·ma·ti·zar §04 tr. *(perfumar)* to perfume, scent; CUL. *(dar sabor)* to flavor.

a·ro·mo·so, -sa adj. aromatic, fragrant.

ar·pa f. MUS. harp ♦ **a. eolia** Aeolian harp.

ar·pa·do, -da I. past part. see **arpar** II. adj. *(serrado)* serrated, jagged; POET. *(armonioso)* melodious, sweet-voiced.

ar·pa·du·ra f. scratch.

ar·par tr. *(arañar)* to scratch; *(hacer tiras)* to tear, tear to shreds.

ar·pí·a f. ORNITH. harpy; FIG., COLL. *(mujer codiciosa)* harpy, shrew; *(mujer vieja)* hag.

ar·pi·llar tr. MEX. to cover with burlap *or* sackcloth.

ar·pi·lle·ra f. burlap, sackcloth.

ar·pis·ta m.f. MUS. harpist.

ar·pón m. *(dardo)* harpoon; ARCHIT. *(grapa)* clamp.

ar·po·nar *or* **ar·po·ne·ar** tr. to harpoon.

ar·que·a·da f. MUS. bowing; *(nausea)* retching, nausea.

ar·que·a·je *or* **ar·que·a·mien·to** m. MARIT. *(medida)* gauging; *(cabida)* tonnage.

ar·que·ar tr. *(dar figura de arco)* to arch, curve; *(medir)* to gauge (the capacity of a ship); *(la lana)* to beat (wool) —intr. COLL. *(nausear)* to retch; AMER. *(hacer el arqueo)* to audit, do the books —reflex. to curve, arch.

ar·que·o m. *(acción de arquear)* arching, curving; MARIT.

(acción de medir capacidad) gauging; *(cabida)* tonnage, capacity; *(de lana)* beating; COM. audit, examination of accounts ♦ **a. bruto** MARIT. gross tonnage • **a. de registro** MARIT. registered tonnage.

ar·que·o·lí·ti·co, -ca adj. Stone-Age.

ar·que·o·lo·gí·a f. archaeology.

ar·que·o·ló·gi·co, -ca adj. archaeological.

ar·que·ó·lo·go, -ga m.f. archaeologist.

ar·que·rí·a f. arcade, series of arches.

ar·que·ro m. *(soldado)* archer; COLL. *(cajero)* cashier; *(tonelero)* cooper; S. AMER., SPORT. goalkeeper, goalie.

ar·que·ti·po m. archetype.

ar·qui·dió·ce·sis f. [pl. **-sis**] archdiocese.

Ar·quí·me·des Archimedes.

ar·qui·tec·to, -ta m.f. architect.

ar·qui·tec·tó·ni·co, -ca adj. architectonic, architectural.

ar·qui·tec·tu·ra f. architecture.

ar·qui·tec·tu·ral adj. architectural.

a·rra·bal m. *(barrio)* suburb; S. AMER. slum ♦ **arrabales** outskirts.

a·rra·ba·le·ro, -ra I. m.f. *(habitante)* suburbanite; FIG., COLL. *(persona vulgar)* common, coarse person II. adj. *(de las afueras)* suburban; FIG., COLL. *(vulgar)* coarse, common.

a·rra·bio m. METAL. cast iron.

a·rra·ca·da f. drop *or* pendant earring.

a·rra·ci·ma·do, -da I. past part. see **arracimarse** II. adj. clustered, bunched.

a·rra·ci·mar·se reflex. to cluster together, form a bunch.

a·rrai·ga·do, -da I. past part. see **arraigar** II. adj. landed, property-owning III. m. MARIT. lashing, mooring.

a·rrai·ga·mien·to m. var. of **arraigo**.

a·rrai·gar §47 intr. BOT. to root, take root; LAW *(afianzar)* to post bail *or* bond —tr. *(fijar)* to fix, establish; AMER. LAW. to limit *or* restrict movement —reflex. BOT. to take root; FIG. *(establecerse)* to settle down, establish oneself; to take hold, become deeply rooted <*los vicios se arraigan muy rápidamente* vices take hold very quickly>.

a·rrai·go m. BOT. rooting; *(establecimiento)* settling down; *(bienes raíces)* real estate ♦ **tener a.** to have a sense of belonging.

a·rram·blar tr. *(cubrir de arena)* to cover with sand (receding waters); FIG. *(arrastrar)* to sweep away; COLL. *(arrebatar)* to make off with <*arrambló con la plata* he made off with the money> —reflex. to become covered with sand (after flooding).

a·rram·plar tr. COLL. to make off with, steal.

a·rran·ca·cla·vos m. [pl. **-vos**] claw (of a hammer).

a·rran·ca·da f. I. f. *(arranque)* sudden start <*la a. de un automóvil* the sudden start of a car>; *(sacudida)* jolt, jerk II. adj. see **arrancado, -da**.

a·rran·ca·de·ra f. large cowbell.

a·rran·ca·de·ro m. starting point.

a·rran·ca·do, -da I. past part. see **arrancar** II. adj. FIG., COLL. broke, penniless III. f. see **arrancada**.

a·rran·ca·dor, -do·ra I. adj. starting II. m. AUTO. starter —f. AGR. lifter, picker.

a·rran·ca·du·ra f. *(desarraigo)* pulling up, uprooting; *(extracción)* pulling out, extraction.

a·rran·car §70 tr. *(sacar de raíz)* to uproot, pull up; *(sacar con violencia)* to pull out, tear out *or* away <*a. un clavo* to pull out a nail>; FIG. to obtain, seize <*a. la victoria* to seize victory>; *(separar)* to pull away, snatch <*nos arrancaron de la fiesta* they pulled us away from the party> —intr. *(salir)* to set out, get started; FIG. *(provenir)* to originate, stem <*esta idea arranca de una teoría antigua* this idea stems from an old theory>; AUTO. to start (up); RAIL. to pull out; MARIT. to set sail.

a·rran·ciar·se reflex. to become rancid *or* stale.

a·rran·char tr. MARIT. *(acercarse)* to skirt, pass close to (coastline); *(bracear)* to brace (sails); AMER. *(arrebatar)* to seize, snatch.

a·rran·que m. *(acción de arrancar)* pulling out, uprooting; *(toma)* seizure, snatching; *(principio)* outset, start; FIG. *(arrebato)* fit, outburst; *(prontitud)* sudden jolt *or* start; *(ocurrencia)* witticism, witty remark; AUTO. starter.

a·rran·qué, arranque see **arrancar**.

a·rra·pie·zo m. *(harapo)* rag, tatter; FIG., COLL. *(granuja)* urchin, young scallywag.

a·rras f.pl. *(prenda)* pledge, security (for a contract); *(monedas)* coins given by bridegroom to bride as token.

a·rra·sa·do, –da I. past part. see **arrasar** II. adj. satiny, satin-like.

a·rra·sa·du·ra f. leveling, smoothing.

a·rra·sar tr. *(allanar)* to level, smooth <*a. un campo* to level a field>; *(arruinar)* to raze, destroy <*a. los muros* to destroy the walls>; *(llenar)* to fill to the brim —intr. & reflex. *(despejarse)* to clear (the sky) ♦ **arrasarse en** or **de lágrimas** to fill with tears.

a·rras·tra·de·ro m. *(camino)* log path over which timber is dragged; TAUR. *(sitio)* place where dead bull is dragged after bullfight; MEX. *(garito)* gambling den.

a·rras·tra·di·zo, –za adj. *(a rastras)* dragging, trailing; *(trillado)* beaten, frequented <*un camino a.* a beaten path>.

a·rras·tra·do, –da I. past part. see **arrastrar** II. adj. FIG., COLL. *(pobre)* miserable, wretched <*una vida a.* a wretched life>; *(pícaro)* roguish, mischievous III. m.f. rogue, rascal.

a·rras·tra·mien·to m. dragging, towing.

a·rras·trar tr. *(tirar)* to pull, drag; to drag, shuffle <*a. los pies* to drag one's feet>; FIG. *(convencer)* to convince, win over <*su discurso arrastró a la multitud* his speech won over the crowd>; *(atraer)* to attract, draw —intr. *(tirarse)* to creep, crawl; *(colgar)* to trail, hang down —reflex. *(tirarse)* to drag oneself, crawl; *(colgar)* to trail, hang down <*la falda se arrastra* the skirt is hanging down>; FIG. *(humillarse)* to crawl, grovel; *(ser tedioso)* to drag on <*su estilo se arrastra* his style drags on>.

a·rras·tre m. *(acción)* pulling, dragging; *(costo)* haulage; MIN. slope (of an adit); AMER., FIG. influence, pull; MEX. silver mill ♦ **estar para el a.** FIG., COLL. to be useless, be washed-up.

a·rra·yán m. BOT. myrtle.

¡a·rre! interj. giddyap!, get up!

a·rre·ar tr. *(espolear)* to drive, herd; *(estimular)* to urge on, hurry; *(poner arreos)* to harness <*a. una mula* to harness a mule>; COLL. to let fly, strike <*a. una bofetada* to strike a blow>; AMER. to steal, rustle —intr. to hurry, move along ♦ **¡arrea!** hurry up!, move along!

a·rre·ba·ta·da·men·te adv. *(precipitadamente)* impetuously, hastily; *(inconsideradamente)* thoughtlessly, carelessly.

a·rre·ba·ta·di·zo, –za adj. FIG. excitable, impetuous.

a·rre·ba·ta·do, –da I. past part. see **arrebatar** II. adj. FIG. *(precipitado)* excitable, impetuous; *(sonrojado)* flushed.

a·rre·ba·ta·dor, –do·ra adj. *(cautivante)* captivating, charming; *(excitante)* exciting, stirring; *(violento)* violent.

a·rre·ba·tar tr. *(arrancar)* to snatch, seize <*le arrebató la carta* he snatched the letter from her>; FIG. *(conmover)* to move, stir; AGR. to parch, dry up; AMER. to knock down —reflex. FIG. *(enfurecerse)* to get carried away, be seized by; AGR. to become parched or dry; CUL. to burn, overcook.

a·rre·ba·ti·ña f. scramble, scuffle.

a·rre·ba·to m. *(arranque)* fit, seizure; FIG. *(furor)* fury, rage; *(éxtasis)* rapture, ecstasy.

a·rre·bol m. *(color rojo)* red glow; *(afeite)* rouge; *(rubor)* rosiness, ruddiness.

a·rre·bo·lar tr. to redden, make red —reflex. *(ruborizarse)* to redden, turn red; *(maquillarse)* to put on rouge.

a·rre·bo·zar §04 tr. *(cubrir)* to cover, coat; *(rebozar)* to muffle or cover up (the face); FIG. *(esconder)* to hide, conceal —reflex. *(cubrirse)* to muffle or cover up one's face; *(insectos)* to swarm.

a·rre·bu·jar tr. to leave in a heap or jumble —reflex. to wrap or bundle oneself up.

a·rre·ciar intr. *(empeorarse)* to worsen, get worse <*la calentura arreciaba* the fever got worse>; *(el tiempo)* to blow or rain harder <*el viento arrecia* the wind is blowing harder> —reflex. *(empeorarse)* to worsen, get worse; *(cobrar fuerzas)* to get stronger.

a·rre·ci·fe m. MARIT. reef.

a·rre·cir·se §38 reflex. to become numb from cold.

a·rre·chu·cho m. COLL. *(arranque)* fit, attack <*un a. de cólera* a fit of anger>; *(indisposición)* bad turn, sudden indisposition.

a·rre·drar tr. *(apartar)* to move away, remove; FIG. *(atemorizar)* to scare or frighten away —reflex. *(apartarse)* to move away, draw back; *(asustarse)* to be scared or frightened.

a·rre·ga·za·do, –da I. past part. see **arregazar** II. adj. *(nariz)* turned-up (nose); *(falda)* tucked up, hiked up (skirt).

a·rre·ga·zar §04 tr. to tuck up, gather towards one's lap —reflex. to become hiked up (skirt).

a·rre·gla·da·men·te adv. *(con regularidad)* regularly; *(con orden)* in an orderly fashion.

a·rre·gla·do, –da I. past part. see **arreglar** II. adj. *(ordenado)* orderly, neat; FIG. *(conveniente)* reasonable, moderate <*un precio a.* a reasonable price>.

a·rre·glar tr. *(componer)* to arrange <*a. la fiesta* to arrange the party>; *(ordenar)* put in order; *(ajustar)* adjust, fix up; *(reparar)* to repair, mend <*a. un mueble roto* to repair a broken piece of furniture>; *(solucionar)* to resolve, settle; *(acomodar)* to fix up, tidy up <*a. la casa* to fix up the house>; MUS. to arrange; ARG., MEX. to settle (a debt); AMER. to castrate (an animal) ♦ **¡ya te arreglaré yo!** I'll fix you! —reflex. *(conformarse)* to conform, adjust; *(ataviarse)* to get dressed (up), tidy oneself up ♦ **arreglárselas** COLL. to manage.

a·rre·glo m. *(acción)* arrangement; *(orden)* order, orderliness; *(conciliación)* agreement, understanding; *(compostura)* repair, mending; COLL. *(concubinato)* cohabitation; MUS. arrangement ♦ **con a. a** according to, in accordance with.

a·rre·ja·car §70 tr. AGR. to harrow.

a·rre·lla·nar·se reflex. to lounge, loll; FIG. *(gustar de su trabajo)* to enjoy one's work.

a·rre·man·ga·do, –da I. past part. see **arremangar** II. adj. turned-up <*una nariz a.* a turned-up nose>.

a·rre·man·gar §47 tr. *(levantar)* to lift or tuck up <*a. la falda* to tuck up one's skirt>; *(recoger)* to roll up <*a. las mangas* to roll up one's sleeves> —reflex. COLL. to become determined, show determination.

a·rre·me·dar tr. to imitate, copy.

a·rre·me·te·dor, –do·ra FIG., COLL. I. adj. determined, resolute II. m.f. determined or resolute person.

a·rre·me·ter tr. *(atacar)* to attack, assault; *(un caballo)* to spur on (a horse); FIG., COLL. *(emprender)* to attack, go at —intr. *(arrojarse)* to rush, attack <*a. al enemigo* to rush at the enemy>; FIG., COLL. *(chocar)* to shock, offend.

a·rre·me·ti·da f. *(ataque)* attack, assault; *(empujón)* push, shove.

a·rre·mo·li·nar·se reflex. FIG. *(apiñarse)* to mill or crowd about; *(el agua)* to swirl, eddy.

a·rren·da·ble adj. rentable, leasable.

a·rren·da·dor, –do·ra m.f. *(propietario)* landlord, lessor; *(inquilino)* tenant, lessee.

a·rren·da·jo m. ORNITH. jay; FIG. *(remedador)* mimic.

a·rren·da·mien·to m. *(acción)* rental, leasing; *(alquiler)* rent, rental; *(contrato)* contract, lease.

a·rren·dar §49 tr. *(alquilar)* to rent, let, lease; *(atar)* to tie up, hitch (horses); *(enseñar)* to train (horses); *(remedar)* to ape, mimic.

a·rren·da·ta·rio, –ria I. adj. leasing, renting <*una compañía a.* a leasing company> II. m.f. tenant, lessee.

a·rre·o m. *(adorno)* ornament, adornment; AMER. *(recua)* herd, drove ♦ **arreos** harness, trappings (of a horse); *(accesorios)* accessories, equipment.

a·rre·pá·pa·lo m. fritter.

a·rre·pen·ti·mien·to m. *(remordimiento)* repentance; *(arte)* alteration, correction (in painting).

a·rre·pen·tir·se §65 reflex. *(lamentar)* to repent, be repentant <*a. del pecado* to repent one's sins>; *(sentir)* to be sorry, regret.

a·rre·que·so·nar·se reflex. to curdle, go sour.

a·rre·qui·ve m. decorative border (on a dress) ♦ **arrequives** COLL. *(vestidos)* finery, best clothes; *(circunstancias)* circumstances; *(requisitos)* requirements.

a·rres·ta·do, –da I. past part. see **arrestar** II. adj. *(detenido)* arrested, apprehended; *(audaz)* bold, daring.

a·rres·tar tr. to arrest, place under arrest —reflex. to rush boldly at danger <*arrestarse a un peligro* to rush boldly at danger>.

a·rres·to m. *(detención)* arrest; *(reclusión)* imprisonment; *(audacia)* boldness, daring.

a·rre·za·gar §47 tr. *(arremangar)* to roll up, tuck up <*a. las mangas* to roll up one's sleeves>; *(alzar)* to raise, put up <*a. el brazo* to raise one's arm>.

a·rria f. drove, team of pack animals.

a·rria·nis·mo m. RELIG. Arianism, Arian heresy.

a·rria·no, –na adj. & m.f. RELIG. Arian.

a·rriar §30 tr. *(bajar)* to haul down, lower <*a. las velas* to lower the sails>; *(aflojar)* to slacken <*a. un cable* to slacken a rope>; *(inundar)* to flood, swamp —reflex. to become flooded *or* swamped.

a·rria·ta f. *or* **a·rria·te** m. *(terreno)* flower bed, flower border; *(camino)* road.

a·rri·ba adv. *(en lugar más alto)* above; *(en una casa)* upstairs; *(en lo alto)* overhead, on high; MARIT. aloft ♦ ¡**arriba!** *(para animar)* get up!, come on!; up with . . . !, hurrah for . . . ! <¡*arriba el rey!* hurrah for the king!> • **a. citado** abovementioned • **de a.** from above, from on high; AMER., COLL. free, gratis • **de a. abajo** COLL. *(de cabo a rabo)* from top to bottom; *(desde el principio al fin)* from beginning to end; up and down, from head to foot <*mirar a alguien de a. abajo* to look someone up and down> • **más a.** higher *or* farther up • **para a.** upwards, up <*de quince pesos para a.* from fifteen pesos up>.

a·rri·ba·da f. MARIT. *(llegada)* arrival, entry into port; *(bordada)* leeward tack.

a·rri·bar intr. *(llegar)* to arrive by boat, land; FIG. *(mejorar)* to improve, recover ♦ **a. a** to manage to <*a. a comprender* to manage to understand>.

a·rri·be·ño, –na I. adj. AMER. highland II. m.f. AMER. highlander; ARG., PAR. stranger, transient.

a·rri·bis·mo m. *(ambición)* ambition; *(oportunismo)* opportunism; *(ambición social)* social climbing.

a·rri·bis·ta I. adj. social-climbing II. m.f. parvenu, social climber.

a·rri·bo m. MARIT. arrival.

a·rrien·de, arriendo see arrendar.

a·rrien·do m. *(acción de arrendar)* renting, leasing; *(precio)* rent; *(contrato)* lease.

a·rrie·ro m. *(muletero)* muleteer, mule skinner; ORNITH. Cuban cuckoo; C. RICA carrier.

a·rries·ga·da·men·te adv. *(con riesgo)* riskily, dangerously; *(con valor)* boldly, daringly.

a·rries·ga·do, –da I. past part. see arriesgar II. adj. *(peligroso)* risky, dangerous; *(audaz)* bold, daring.

a·rries·gar §47 tr. to risk, venture ♦ **a. el pellejo** to risk one's neck —reflex. to risk, take a risk.

a·rri·ma·di·zo, –za I. adj. sycophantic, parasitic II. m.f. sycophant, parasite, hanger-on.

a·rri·mar tr. *(acercar)* to bring *or* draw near; FIG. *(abandonar)* to put aside, shelve <*a. un plan* to shelve a plan>; *(arrinconar)* to ignore, push aside <*se cansaron de él y le arrimaron* they got tired of him and pushed him aside>; MARIT. to stow ♦ **a. el hombro** to pitch in, lend a hand —reflex. *(apoyarse)* to lean, rest <*arrimarse a la pared* to lean against the wall>; FIG *(juntarse)* to join together; *(ampararse)* to seek protection; *(acercarse)* to approach <*arrimarse al punto de la dificultad* to approach the trouble spot>; COLL. *(vivir juntos)* to shack up, live together ♦ **arrimarse al sol que más calienta** FIG., COLL. to know which side one's bread is buttered on.

a·rri·mo m. *(sostén)* support; *(pared)* partition, dividing wall; FIG. *(apoyo)* aid, protection; *(apego)* attachment, fondness.

a·rri·món m. loafer, loiterer ♦ **estar de a.** to hang about, wait around.

a·rrin·co·na·do, –da I. past part. see arrinconar II. adj. *(apartado)* distant, out of the way; FIG. *(desatendido)* neglected, abandoned.

a·rrin·co·nar tr. *(poner en un rincón)* to put in a corner, put away; FIG. *(perseguir)* to corner, pursue; FIG., COLL. *(abandonar)* to neglect, abandon <*a. a un amigo* to abandon a friend> —reflex. to withdraw, retreat.

a·rris·ca·do, –da I. past part. see arriscar II. adj. *(atrevido)* daring, bold; *(ágil)* agile; *(gallardo)* gallant, dashing; *(peñascoso)* craggy, rough.

a·rris·ca·mien·to m. daring, boldness.

a·rris·car §70 tr. *(arriesgar)* to risk, dare; AMER. *(arremangar)* to turn up, fold up <*a. el ala del sombrero* to turn up

the brim of a hat> —intr. COL. to come to <*no arrisca a cien pesos* it doesn't come to 100 pesos> —reflex. *(engreírse)* to become conceited; *(despeñarse)* to plunge over a cliff (cattle); FIG. *(irritarse)* to get irritated, angry; AMER. *(vestirse)* to dress up, dress elegantly.

a·rrit·mia f. *(falta de ritmo)* lack of rhythm; MED. arrhythmia.

a·rrít·mi·co, –ca adj. arrhythmic, arrhythmical.

a·rro·ba f. arroba (Spanish dry or liquid measure).

a·rro·ba·do, –da I. past. part. see arrobar II. adj. *(con placer)* ecstatic, enraptured; *(en trance)* entranced.

a·rro·ba·mien·to m. ecstasy, rapture, enchantment.

a·rro·bar tr. *(dar placer)* to enchant, enrapture; *(poner en trance)* to entrance —reflex. *(extasiarse)* to be enchanted *or* enraptured; *(entrar en trance)* to be entranced.

a·rro·bo m. *(placer)* ecstasy, rapture; *(trance)* trance.

a·rro·ce·ro, –ra I. adj. rice <*la industria a.* the rice industry> II. m.f. *(cultivador)* rice grower; *(vendedor)* rice dealer.

a·rro·ci·na·do, –da I. past part. see arrocinar II. adj. naglike, broken-down.

a·rro·ci·nar tr. *(embrutecer)* to brutalize; ARG., URUG. *(amansar)* to tame, break (a colt) —reflex. FIG., COLL. to fall madly in love.

a·rro·di·lla·mien·to m. *(acción de arodillar)* kneeling; FIG. *(humillación)* humiliation, humbling.

a·rro·di·llar tr. to make (someone) kneel —reflex. *(ponerse de rodillas)* to kneel (down); FIG. *(humillarse)* to be humiliated *or* embarrassed.

a·rro·ga·ción f. arrogation.

a·rro·gan·cia f. *(soberbia)* arrogance, haughtiness; *(valor)* bravery, gallantry.

a·rro·gan·te adj. *(soberbio)* arrogant, haughty; *(valiente)* brave, gallant.

a·rro·gan·te·men·te adv. *(con soberbia)* arrogantly, haughtily; *(con valor)* bravely, gallantly.

a·rro·gar §47 tr. *(atribuir)* to arrogate, assume; *(adoptar)* to adopt —reflex. to arrogate to oneself, claim.

a·rro·ja·da·men·te adv. FIG. *(atrevidamente)* daringly, boldly; *(con resolución)* resolutely.

a·rro·ja·do, –da I. past part. see arrojar II. adj. FIG. *(atrevido)* rash, bold, daring; *(resuelto)* resolute.

a·rro·jar tr. *(lanzar)* to throw, hurl, fling; *(emitir)* to emit, shed (light); COLL. *(vomitar)* to vomit, throw up; COM. to show <*a. déficit* to show a deficit> —reflex. *(lanzarse)* to throw *or* hurl oneself; FIG. *(resolverse)* to rush, venture <*arrojarse a pelear* to rush to fight> ♦ **arrojarse sobre** to rush at, attack.

a·rro·jo m. FIG. *(atrevimiento)* rashness, boldness, daring; *(resolución)* resolution, resoluteness.

a·rro·lla·ble adj. rollable.

a·rro·lla·dor, –do·ra adj. *(grande)* great, sweeping <*un éxito a.* a great success>; *(aplastante)* crushing, overwhelming.

a·rro·llar tr. *(envolver)* to roll up, coil, wind <*a. un mapa* to roll up a map>; *(llevar)* to sweep *or* carry away <*el agua arrolla la arena* the water sweeps away the sand>; *(atropellar)* to trample, run over; FIG. *(derrotar)* to defeat, crush; *(confundir)* to confuse, confound; *(mecer)* to rock, cradle (a child).

a·rro·ma·di·zar·se §04 reflex. to catch a cold.

a·rro·pa·mien·to m. wrapping up, bundling up.

a·rro·par tr. *(cubrir)* to clothe, wrap with clothes; *(acostar)* to tuck in (to bed); FIG. *(proteger)* to protect —reflex. *(cubrirse)* to wrap up *or* clothe oneself; *(acostarse)* to tuck oneself in.

a·rro·pe m. *(mosto cocido)* boiled must; *(jarabe)* syrup.

a·rro·rró *or* **a·rru·rrú** m. AMER., COLL. lullaby.

a·rros·trar tr. to face (up to), confront —reflex. to face (up to), stand up to.

a·rro·ya·da f. *(valle)* valley (through which a stream runs); *(surco)* gulley, channel; *(inundación)* flood, freshet.

a·rro·yar tr. to channel, form channels in (rain on ground) —reflex. *(formarse arroyos)* to become hollowed out, channeled (ground); BOT. to become mildewed (plants).

a·rro·yo m. *(riachuelo)* stream, brook; *(cauce)* bed, watercourse; *(cuneta)* gutter; FIG. *(afluencia)* afflux, affluence; S. AMER. small river ♦ **estar en el a.** to be on the street • **plantar** *or* **poner en el a.** to put on the street, turn out of the house • **sacar del a.** to lift from the gutter • **ser del a.** to be an orphan.

a·rroz m. rice ♦ **a. con leche** rice pudding • **haber a. y gallo muerto** FIG. to have a feast.

a·rro·zal m. rice field or paddy.

a·rruar intr. to grunt.

a·rru·ga f. (en la piel) wrinkle, line; (en la ropa) wrinkle, crease; GEOL. ruga, fold; ECUAD., PERU trick, swindle.

a·rru·ga·do, –da I. past part. see **arrugar** II. adj. (piel) wrinkled, lined; (ropa) wrinkled, creased.

a·rru·gar §47 tr. (fruncir) to wrinkle, line; (hacer arrugas) to wrinkle, crease; (apañuscar) to crumple <a. el papel to crumple paper>; AMER. to annoy, bother ♦ **a. el entrecejo** to frown, knit one's brow • **a. la cara** to screw up one's face —reflex. to wrinkle, become wrinkled; (plegarse) to become wrinkled or creased; (apañuscarse) to become crumpled (up); (encogerse) to shrink; MEX. to get scared.

a·rrui·nar tr. (asolar) to ruin; FIG. (destruir) to destroy —reflex. (destruirse) to be ruined, go to wrack and ruin; (caerse) to fall (down), fall into ruin.

a·rru·llar tr. (adormecer) to lull or sing to sleep; FIG., COLL. (enamorar) to court.

a·rru·lla·dor, –do·ra I. adj. (calmante) lulling, soothing; FIG. (lisonjero) cajoling, coaxing II. m.f. (apaciguador) luller, soother; FIG. (zalamero) flatterer, cajoler.

a·rru·llo m. ORNITH. cooing; MUS. lullaby.

a·rru·ma f. MARIT. partition in hold of ship (for stowing cargo); CHILE pile, heap.

a·rru·ma·co m. (abrazo) caress; (zalamería) flattery, cajolery; COLL. (adorno) frill, trinket ♦ **arrumacos** endearments, show of affection • **andar con arrumacos** to flatter.

a·rru·ma·je m. MARIT. (distribución) stowage (of cargo); (nublado) bank of clouds (on horizon).

a·rru·mar tr. MARIT. (cargar) to stow (cargo); COL., CHILE (amontonar) to pile up, heap together —reflex. MARIT. to become overcast or cloudy.

a·rrum·ba·dor, –do·ra I. adj. navigating, steering II. m.f. MARIT. navigator —m. worker in a wine cellar.

a·rrum·ba·mien·to m. MARIT. course.

a·rrum·bar tr. (desechar) to cast or put aside; FIG. (arrinconar) to neglect, abandon <a. a un amigo to abandon a friend>; to overwhelm, leave speechless <arrumbó a su rival he left his rival speechless> —intr. MARIT. to set a course —reflex. to get seasick.

a·rru·rruz m. arrowroot (starch).

ar·se·nal m. MARIT. navy yard, shipyard; MIL. arsenal; FIG. (depósito) storehouse, arsenal <a. de datos storehouse of information>.

ar·sé·ni·co m. CHEM. arsenic.

ar·te m.f. art <el a. moderno modern art>; (habilidad) art, skill; (astucia) cleverness, cunning; (en la pesca) fishing tackle ♦ **bellas artes** fine arts • **con a.** skillfully, cleverly • **no tener ni a. ni parte** to have nothing to do with • **por amor al a.** free, gratis • **por a. de magia** as if by magic • **sin a.** clumsily, artlessly.

ar·te·fac·to m. (aparato) device, appliance; ARCHEOL. artifact ♦ **a. de alumbrado** light fixture.

ar·te·ra·men·te adv. craftily, cunningly, slyly.

ar·te·ria f. artery.

ar·te·rí·a f. artfulness, cunning.

ar·te·rial adj. ANAT. arterial.

ar·te·rios·cle·ro·sis f. MED. arteriosclerosis.

ar·te·ro, –ra adj. crafty, cunning, sly.

ar·te·sa f. trough, kneading trough.

ar·te·sa·na·do m. (artesanos) craftsmen; (arte) artisanship, artisanry.

ar·te·sa·nal adj. artisan, pertaining to craftsmen or artisans.

ar·te·sa·ní·a f. (habilidad) craftsmanship, artisanry; (producto) handicrafts, crafts.

ar·te·sa·no, –na m.f. artisan, craftsman —f. craftswoman.

ar·te·sia·no, –na adj. artesian (well).

ar·te·si·lla f. small trough (of a well).

ar·te·són m. (artesa) washtub; ARCHIT. (adorno) coffer, molding; (techo) coffered ceiling.

ar·te·so·nar tr. ARCHIT. to apply coffers to.

ár·ti·co, –ca adj. & m. Arctic.

ar·ti·cu·la·ción f. ANAT. articulation, joint; MECH. joint; (separación) separation, division; (pronunciación) enunciation; CHILE, LAW question ♦ **a. esférica** ball-and-socket joint • **a. giratoria** swivel joint • **a. universal** universal joint.

ar·ti·cu·la·da·men·te adv. PHONET. articulately, distinctly.

ar·ti·cu·la·do, –da I. past part. see **articular²** II. adj. (lenguaje) articulated, articulate; ANAT. articulate, jointed III. m. articles (of a law, treaty).

ar·ti·cu·lar¹ adj. ANAT. articular, of the joints.

ar·ti·cu·lar² tr. (pronunciar) to articulate, enunciate; (dividir) to divide into articles; MECH. to join, joint; LAW (interrogar) to interrogate, question —intr. CHILE to argue, quarrel.

ar·ti·cu·lis·ta m.f. JOURN. article writer, feature writer.

ar·tí·cu·lo m. (cosa) article, item, thing; (escrito) article, essay; (en un diccionario) entry; GRAM. article; ANAT. articulation, joint; LAW (de una ley) article, section ♦ **a. adicional** adjunct, addendum • **a. de comercio** commodity • **a. de fe** RELIG. article of faith • **a. de fondo** JOURN. editorial • **a. de primera necesidad** basic commodity • **a. definido** or **determinado** GRAM. definite article • **a. indefinido** or **indeterminado** GRAM. indefinite article • **artículos** COM. commodities, goods • **artículos de consumo** consumer goods • **artículos de tocador** toiletries • **artículos de novedad** novelties.

ar·ti·fi·ce m.f. (hacedor) maker, artisan; FIG. (estafador) schemer; (causa) author, architect.

ar·ti·fi·cial adj. artificial.

ar·ti·fi·cia·li·dad f. artificiality.

ar·ti·fi·cial·men·te adv. artificially.

ar·ti·fi·cio m. (habilidad) skill, ability; (aparato) device, contrivance; (pirotecnia) firework; FIG. (ardid) trick, artifice.

ar·ti·fi·cio·sa·men·te adv. (habilmente) skillfully, ingeniously; FIG. (arteramente) cunningly, craftily.

ar·ti·fi·cio·so, –sa adj. (hábil) skillful, ingenious; FIG. (disimulado) cunning, crafty.

ar·ti·lu·gio m. (aparato) gadget, contraption; FIG. (trampa) gimmick, trick.

ar·ti·lle·rí·a f. artillery ♦ **a. de batalla** or **de campo** field artillery • **a. de sitio** siege artillery.

ar·ti·lle·ro m. MIL. artillery soldier.

ar·ti·ma·ña f. (trampa) trick, ruse; COLL. (astucia) cunning.

ar·tis·ta I. m.f. artist <Goya era un a. famoso Goya was a famous artist>; (actor, actriz) actor, actress ♦ **a. invitado** guest artist II. adj. artistic.

ar·tís·ti·ca·men·te adv. artistically.

ar·tís·ti·co, –ca adj. artistic.

ar·trí·ti·co, –ca adj. & m.f. MED. arthritic.

ar·tri·tis f. MED. arthritis.

ar·tró·po·dos m.pl. ZOOL. arthropods.

ar·ve·ja f. BOT. (algarroba) (spring) vetch, tare; AMER. green pea ♦ **a. silvestre** BOT. yellow vetch, meadow or everlasting pea.

ar·ve·jo m. BOT. green pea.

ar·zo·bis·pa·do m. RELIG. archbishopric.

ar·zo·bis·po m. archbishop.

as m. (naipe) ace; (dado) ace; FIG. (experto) ace, star <a. del tenis star tennis player>; HIST. (moneda) as (Roman coin).

a·sa f. (asidero) handle, grip; FIG. (pretexto) pretext, excuse; BOT. juice, sap ♦ **a. fétida** asafetida • **en asas** akimbo • **ser del a.** to be on good terms.

a·sá or **a·sa·o** adv. COLL. thus, so.

a·sa·do, –da I. past part. see **asar** II. m. (carne) roasted meat; AMER. barbecued meat; (comida) cookout, barbecue.

a·sa·dor m. (varilla) spit; (aparato) roaster, grill.

a·sa·du·ra f. (hígado) liver; (bofes) lungs; COLL. (pesadez) sluggishness, laziness; (pelma) bore, boring person ♦ **asaduras** innards, entrails • **echar las asaduras** COLL. to bust a gut (working).

a·sa·e·te·a·dor I. adj. piercing, wounding II. m. bowman, archer.

a·sa·e·te·ar tr. (disparar) to shoot, hit (with arrows); FIG. (molestar) to annoy, bother.

a·sa·la·ria·do, –da I. past part. see **asalariar** II. adj. salaried **III.** m.f. *(trabajador)* salaried worker, wage earner; DEROG. *(mercenario)* mercenary, hireling.

a·sa·la·riar tr. *(fijar)* to set a salary for; *(dar trabajo)* to hire, take on; *(pagar)* to pay a salary to.

a·sal·ta·dor, –do·ra or **a·sal·tan·te I.** adj. assaulting, attacking **II.** m.f. assailant, attacker.

a·sal·tar tr. *(atacar)* to attack, assault; FIG. *(sobrevenir)* to strike suddenly, overtake <*me asaltó una duda* a doubt overtook me>.

a·sal·to m. *(ataque)* attack, assault; COLL. *(fiesta)* surprise party; *(en el boxeo)* round (in boxing); FENC. *(en la esgrima)* bout.

a·sam·ble·a f. *(reunión)* assembly, meeting; *(congreso)* congress, conference ♦ **a. de accionistas** stockholders' meeting • **A. General** U.N. General Assembly • **a. plenaria** plenary session.

a·sam·ble·ís·ta m.f. member of an assembly.

a·sar tr. CUL. to roast; FIG. *(importunar)* to grill <*me asaron con mil preguntas* they grilled me with a thousand questions> ♦ **a. al horno** to bake • **a. a la parrilla** to broil, grill —reflex. FIG. to feel very hot, roast ♦ **asarse vivo** FIG. to be roasted alive.

as·bes·to m. MIN. asbestos.

as·ca·lo·nia f. BOT. shallot.

as·cen·den·cia f. *(linaje)* ancestry, origin; FIG. *(influencia)* influence, ascendancy.

as·cen·den·te I. adj. ascending, upward **II.** m. ASTROL. ascendant.

as·cen·der §50 intr. *(subir)* to rise, ascend; *(adelantarse)* to be promoted <*García ascenderá a gerente el mes próximo* García will be promoted to manager next month> ♦ **a.** to amount to, reach —tr. *(adelantar)* to promote <*lo ascendieron a la jefatura* they promoted him to the directorship>.

as·cen·dien·te I. adj. ascending, upward **II.** m.f. *(antepasado)* ancestor, ascendant —m. FIG. influence, ascendancy.

as·cen·sión f. ascension, rise. ♦ **A.** RELIG. Ascension.

as·cen·so m. *(adelanto)* promotion; *(subida)* ascent, rise ♦ **a. muerto** MARIT. dead rise.

as·cen·sor m. elevator, lift (G.B.) ♦ **a. de carga** freight elevator.

as·cen·so·ris·ta m.f. elevator operator.

as·ce·ta m.f. ascetic.

as·cé·ti·co, –ca I. adj. ascetic **II.** f. asceticism.

as·ce·tis·mo m. asceticism.

as·cien·da, asciendo see **ascender.**

as·co m. *(repugnancia)* disgust, revulsion; *(cosa)* disgusting or revolting thing; FIG., COLL. *(miedo)* fear ♦ **cobrar** or **coger a. a** FIG., COLL. to become sick of • **dar a.** FIG., COLL. to sicken or disgust • **estar hecho un a.** FIG., COLL. to be filthy • **hacer ascos** FIG., COLL. to turn up one's nose at • **poner a alguien de a.** MEX., FIG., COLL. to call someone names • **ser un a.** FIG., COLL. to be disgusting or worthless.

as·cua f. ember, live coal ♦ **arrimar el a. a su sardina** FIG., COLL. to look out for number one • **a. de oro** FIG. glittering object • **estar en ascuas** FIG., COLL. to be on edge • **sacar el a. con la mano del gato** or **con mano ajena** FIG. to get someone else to do the dirty work.

a·se·a·do, –da adj. *(limpio)* clean; *(ordenado)* neat, tidy.

a·se·ar tr. *(lavar)* to wash; *(limpiar)* to clean; *(ordenar)* to tidy (up) —reflex. *(lavarse)* to wash (up); *(limpiarse)* to clean (up); *(ordenarse)* to tidy (up).

a·se·cha·dor, –do·ra I. adj. trapping, deceiving **II.** m.f. trapper, deceiver.

a·se·cha·mien·to m. trap, snare.

a·se·chan·za f. trap, snare ♦ **armar una a.** to set a trap.

a·se·char tr. to trap, snare.

a·se·dar tr. to make silky, make smooth.

a·se·dia·dor, –do·ra I. adj. *(sitiador)* besieging; FIG. *(importuno)* annoying, harassing **II.** m.f. *(sitiador)* besieger; *(persona que importuna)* annoyer, pest.

a·se·diar tr. *(sitiar)* to besiege, lay siege to; FIG. *(importunar)* to pester, bother.

a·se·dio m. *(cerco)* siege, blockade; FIG. *(molestia)* nuisance, annoyance.

a·se·gun·dar tr. to repeat immediately (an action).

a·se·gu·ra·ción f. insurance, insurance policy.

a·se·gu·ra·do, –da I. past part. see **asegurar II.** adj. insured **III.** m.f. insured (person), policyholder.

a·se·gu·ra·dor, –do·ra I. adj. insuring, assuring **II.** m. *(empresa)* insurer, insurance company —m.f. *(persona)* insurance agent.

a·se·gu·ra·mien·to m. *(acción de fijar)* fastening, securing; *(afirmación)* assurance, guarantee; *(seguro)* insurance.

a·se·gu·rar tr. *(consolidar)* to secure, make secure <*a. el edificio* to secure the building>; *(garantizar)* to insure, guarantee, safeguard; *(tranquilizar)* to assure, reassure <*te aseguro que todo irá bien* I assure you that everything will be fine>; COM. to insure —reflex. *(cerciorarse)* to make sure <*asegúrate de la veracidad de las noticias* make sure that the news is true>; COM. to insure oneself, take out insurance.

a·se·me·jar tr. *(hacer semejante)* to make alike or similar; *(comparar)* to liken, compare —reflex. to resemble, be similar to ♦ **asemejarse a** to be like, resemble.

a·sen·de·re·ar tr. *(abrir camino)* to open paths through; FIG. *(perseguir)* to pursue, harry (someone).

a·sen·so m. assent, approbation.

a·sen·ta·da f. sitting, session ♦ **de una a.** at one sitting.

a·sen·ta·de·ras f.pl. COLL. behind, buttocks.

a·sen·ta·do, –da I. past part. see **asentar II.** adj. *(juicioso)* sensible, judicious; FIG. *(estable)* stable, established.

a·sen·ta·dor m. *(mercader)* wholesale dealer; *(formón)* turning chisel; *(suavizador)* razor strop; MEX., PRINT. planer.

a·sen·ta·mien·to m. *(acción de sentarse)* sitting, sitting down; *(establecimiento)* settlement, establishment (persons); MIL. *(emplazamiento)* emplacement; FIG. *(juicio)* common sense, wisdom.

a·sen·tar §49 tr. *(anotar)* to note, write down, record; *(fundar)* to found, establish <*asentaron el pueblo en el valle* they founded the town in the valley>; *(ajustar)* to establish, agree on <*a. un tratado* to settle a treaty>; *(colocar)* to set, place; *(afirmar)* to affirm, confirm; *(dar)* to give, deal <*a. golpes* to deal blows>; *(aplanar)* to smooth, level; *(afinar)* to hone, sharpen; COM. to enter <*a. el debe* to enter a debit>; MEX. to afflict, sadden; ARG. to iron, press —intr. to suit, be suitable —reflex. *(establecerse)* to settle down, establish oneself; *(las aves)* to perch, alight; *(los líquidos)* to settle (liquids); ARCHIT. to settle (buildings).

a·sen·ti·mien·to m. consent, assent.

a·sen·tir §65 intr. to assent, agree ♦ **a. a** to agree, approve • **a. con la cabeza** to nod (one's approval).

a·sen·tis·ta m.f. *(contratista)* contractor; *(abastecedor)* supplier.

a·se·o m. *(limpieza)* cleanliness; *(orden)* neatness, tidiness; *(baño)* rest room, washroom ♦ **aseos** (public) bathrooms.

a·sép·ti·co, –ca adj. MED. aseptic.

a·se·qui·ble adj. *(accesible)* accessible; *(posible)* attainable, feasible; *(comprensible)* understandable, comprehensible; reasonable <*un precio a.* a reasonable price>.

a·ser·ción f. assertion, affirmation.

a·se·rra·de·ro m. sawmill.

a·se·rra·do, –da I. past part. see **aserrar II.** adj. serrated **III.** m. sawing.

a·se·rra·dor, –do·ra I. adj. sawing **II.** m. sawyer, sawer.

a·se·rra·du·ra f. cut (of a saw) ♦ **aserraduras** sawdust.

a·se·rrar §49 tr. to saw.

a·se·rrín m. sawdust.

a·ser·ti·vo, –va adj. positive, affirmative.

a·ser·to m. assertion, affirmation.

a·se·si·nar tr. *(matar)* to murder; POL. to assassinate.

a·se·si·na·to m. murder; POL. assassination.

a·se·si·no, –na I. adj. murderous **II.** m.f. *(matador)* killer, murderer; POL. assassin.

a·se·sor, –so·ra I. adj. advising, advisory **II.** m.f. adviser, counselor.

a·se·so·ra·mien·to m. *(acción)* advising; *(consejo)* advice, counsel.

a·se·so·rar tr. to advise, counsel —reflex. to seek advice, consult ♦ **a. de una situación** to take stock of or evaluate a situation.

a·se·so·rí·a f. *(acción)* advising, counseling; *(estipendio)* consultant's fee; *(oficina)* consultant's office.

a·ses·tar tr. *(dirigir)* to aim, point; *(descargar)* to fire, shoot; FIG. *(golpear)* to deal, deliver (a blow).

a·se·ve·ra·ción f. asseveration, assertion.

a·se·ve·rar tr. to asseverate, assert.

a·se·ve·ra·ti·vo, -va adj. assertive, affirmative.

a·se·xua·do, -da *or* **a·se·xual** adj. asexual.

as·fal·ta·do, -da I. past part. see **asfaltar** II. adj. covered with asphalt, paved III. m. *(acción)* asphalting, paving; *(pavimiento)* asphalt, asphalt pavement.

as·fal·tar tr. to asphalt.

as·fal·to m. asphalt.

as·fi·xia f. MED. asphyxia, suffocation.

as·fi·xiar tr. to asphyxiate, smother —reflex. to suffocate, be asphyxiated.

as·ga, asgo see **asir.**

a·sí I. adv. *(de esta manera)* so, thus, this way <*ellos lo hicieron a.* they did it this way>; *(de esa manera)* that way, like that <*no seas a.* don't be like that>; *(tanto)* so, in such a way <*a. corrió que no pudimos alcanzarlo* he ran in such a way that we couldn't catch up with him>; as well, both <*a. yo como usted* both you and I> ♦ **a. a.** so-so, fair • **a. como** as soon as • **a. como a.** anyway, anyhow • **a. de** so <*a. de grande* so big> • **a. nada más** *or* **a. no más** just like that • **a. o asá** COLL. either way, one way or the other • **a. sea** so be it • **a. y todo** even so, just the same • **o algo a.** or thereabouts, or something like that <*ella tiene seis años o algo a.* she is six years old or something like that> • **y a.** thus, and so • **y a. sucesivamente** and so on, and so forth II. §G10 conj. *(en consecuencia)* therefore, thus; *(aunque)* even if, even though <*no nos lo dirá, a. le paguemos* he will not tell us, even if we pay him> ♦ **a. pues** therefore, and so III. adj. such <*una situación a. es muy peligrosa* such a situation is very dangerous>.

A·sia f. Asia ♦ **A. Mayor** Asia Major • **A. Menor** Asia Minor.

a·siá·ti·co, -ca adj. & m.f. Asiatic, Asian.

a·si·de·ro m. *(asa)* handle; FIG. *(pretexto)* pretext, excuse; ARG. basis, support.

a·si·dua·men·te adv. *(persistentemente)* assiduously, diligently; *(frecuentemente)* frequently, regularly.

a·si·dui·dad f. *(persistencia)* assiduousness, assiduity; *(frecuencia)* frequency, regularity.

a·si·duo, -dua adj. *(persistente)* assiduous, diligent; *(frecuente)* frequent, regular.

a·sien·ta, asiente, asiento see **asentar** *or* **asentir.**

a·sien·to m. *(silla)* seat, chair; *(puesto)* seat (in congress, parliament); *(sitio)* site, location; *(poso)* sediment; *(del freno)* bit; COLL. *(empacho)* indigestion; SL. *(trasero)* bottom, seat, behind; FIG. *(estabilidad)* stability, permanence; *(cordura)* good sense, judgment; ARCHIT. settling; COM. entry; AMER. mining district *or* area.

a·sie·rre, asierro see **aserrar.**

a·sig·na·ción f. *(distribución)* assignation, allotment; *(cita)* appointment; *(salario)* salary, allowance.

a·sig·nar tr. *(señalar)* to assign, allot; *(nombrar)* to appoint.

a·sig·na·tu·ra f. subject, course (in school) ♦ **aprobar una a.** to pass a subject • **suspender una a.** to fail a subject.

a·si·la·do, -da I. past part. see **asilar** II. m.f. *(acogido)* political refugee; *(preso)* inmate.

a·si·lar tr. *(albergar)* to place in an asylum *or* institution; *(refugiar)* to give shelter; to give political asylum —reflex. *(albergarse)* to enter an asylum *or* institution; *(refugiarse)* to take refuge *or* shelter; *(buscar asilo)* to seek political asylum.

a·si·lo m. *(santuario)* asylum, sanctuary; *(establecimiento)* home, institution; FIG. *(refugio)* shelter, refuge ♦ **a. de ancianos** old folks' home • **a. de huérfanos** orphanage • **a. de locos** insane asylum • **a. de pobres** poorhouse • **buscar** *or* **pedir a.** to seek asylum • **dar a.** to shelter.

a·si·me·tría f. asymmetry.

a·si·mé·tri·co, -ca adj. asymmetric, asymmetrical.

a·si·mien·to m. *(acción de asir)* grasping, holding; FIG. *(afecto)* attachment.

a·si·mi·la·ble adj. assimilable.

a·si·mi·la·ción f. assimilation.

a·si·mi·lar tr. to assimilate —reflex. to be similar.

a·si·mis·mo adj. *(igualmente)* likewise, in like manner; *(también)* also, too.

a·sin·cro·nis·mo m. asynchronism.

a·sin·tie·ra, asintió see **asentir.**

a·sir §08 tr. to grasp, seize —intr. BOT. to take root —reflex. *(agarrarse)* to grab on; FIG. *(reñir)* to fight, come to blows ♦ **asirse de** to take advantage of, avail oneself of.

A·si·ria f. Assyria.

a·si·rio, -ria adj. & m.f. Assyrian.

a·si·rio·lo·gí·a f. Assyriology.

a·sis·ten·cia f. *(concurrencia)* attendance, presence; *(ayuda)* aid, assistance; MEX. parlor; COL. guest house ♦ **a. pública** health clinic.

a·sis·ten·cial adj. assisting, relief <*agencia a.* relief agency>.

a·sis·ten·te, -ta I. adj. attending, assisting II. m.f. *(ayudante)* attendant, assistant —m. MIL. aide —f. *(criada)* maid.

a·sis·tir intr. *(concurrir)* to attend, be present; *(en los naipes)* to follow suit (in cards) —tr. *(acompañar)* to accompany; *(ayudar)* to aid, assist; *(cuidar)* to care for, nurse; to be on the side of <*la razón le asiste* right is on his side>; S. AMER., LAW to represent.

a·sis·tó·li·co, -ca adj. MED. asystolic.

as·ma f. MED. asthma.

as·má·ti·co, -ca adj. & m.f. asthmatic.

as·na f. ZOOL. she-ass, jenny ♦ **asnas** CARP. rafters.

as·na·da f. FIG., COLL. stupidity, foolishness, asininity.

as·nal·men·te adv. COLL. *(montado)* riding a donkey *or* ass; *(brutalmente)* brutishly, bestially; *(estúpidamente)* stupidly, foolishly.

as·ni·lla f. prop, stanchion.

as·no m. ZOOL. ass, donkey; FIG., COLL. *(imbécil)* fool, jackass; *(grosero)* pig, slob ♦ **caer uno de su a.** FIG. to back down, give in.

a·so·cia·ble adj. associable.

a·so·cia·ción f. *(ligamiento)* connecting, joining; *(grupo)* association, league, partnership ♦ **a. gremial** COM. trade union • **a. sindical** COM. labor union.

a·so·cia·do, -da I. past part. see **asociar** II. adj. associated III. m.f. *(miembro)* associate, member; COM. *(socio)* associate, partner.

a·so·ciar tr. *(ligar)* to associate, connect; *(combinar)* to combine, pool —reflex. to become partners, enter into partnership ♦ **asociarse a** *or* **con** to join, team up with.

a·so·cia·ti·vo, -va adj. associative.

a·so·la·dor, -do·ra I. adj. *(destructor)* ravaging, destroying; *(allanador)* razing, leveling II. m.f. *(destruidor)* destroyer, ravager; *(allanador)* leveler.

a·so·la·nar tr. AGR. to spoil, damage (said of the east wind) —reflex. to become spoiled *or* damaged <*la cosecha se asolanó* the crop was damaged (by the east wind)>.

a·so·la·par tr. to overlap (tiles or shingles).

a·so·lar¹ tr. AGR. to scorch, parch.

a·so·lar² §19 tr. *(destruir)* to ravage, destroy; *(arrasar)* to raze, level —reflex. CHEM. to settle, clarify.

a·sol·dar §19 tr. to hire.

a·so·le·a·mien·to m. sunstroke.

a·so·le·ar tr. to put in the sun, insolate —reflex. *(tomar el sol)* to bask in the sun, sun oneself; *(tostarse)* to become tanned, get a tan; VET. *(sofocar)* to suffer sunstroke *or* heat suffocation; AMER. to work, slave.

a·so·le·o n. *(insolación)* sunning, insolation; VET. *(sofocación)* heat suffocation.

a·so·ma·da f. *(aparición)* brief appearance, apparition; *(atalaya)* vantage point, lookout.

a·so·mar intr. to appear, begin to show <*los brotes asoman en la primavera* the buds appear in the spring> —tr. to show <*a. la cara* to show one's face> —reflex. *(mostrarse)* to show oneself, appear; to look *or* lean out, stick one's head out <*asomarse a la ventana* to lean out the window>; COLL. *(embriagarse)* to get tipsy.

a·som·bra·dor, -do·ra adj. amazing, astonishing.

a·som·brar tr. FIG. *(sorprender)* to amaze, astonish; FIG. *(asustar)* to frighten, scare; *(hacer sombra)* to shade, shadow; *(oscurecer)* to darken, make darker (colors) —reflex. FIG. *(sorprenderse)* to be amazed *or* astonished; *(asustarse)* to be frightened *or* scared.

a·som·bro m. *(sorpresa)* amazement, astonishment; *(susto)* fright, fear; *(maravilla)* marvel, wonder.

a·som·bro·sa·men·te adv. amazingly, astonishingly.

a·som·bro·so, –sa adj. amazing, astonishing.

a·so·mo m. *(mirada)* look, peek; *(señal)* clue, hint, sign; *(sospecha)* suspicion, conjecture ♦ **ni asomos** *or* **un a. de** not a trace of, not the least bit of • **ni por a.** not by a long shot, no way.

a·so·na·da f. riot.

a·so·nan·cia f. POET., RHET. assonance; PHONET. consonance, harmony; FIG. *(correspondencia)* relation, correspondence.

a·so·nan·te adj. & m.f. PHONET. assonant.

a·sor·dar tr. to deafen.

a·so·ro·char·se reflex. AMER. to get altitude sickness; CHILE, SL. to blush.

as·pa f. *(cruz)* X-shaped cross; *(devanadera)* spool, reel; *(de molinos)* vane, blade (of a windmill); *(signo)* multiplication sign; ARG., VEN. horn (of an animal) ♦ **en a.** crosswise.

as·pa·do, –da I. past part. see **aspar** II. adj. *(que tiene forma de cruz)* shaped like a cross; *(con los brazos extendidos)* with arms extended; FIG., COLL. *(llevando ropa estrecha)* hobbled (by tight clothing) III. m.f. penitent with arms tied to a bar in the shape of a cross.

as·pa·dor, –do·ra I. adj. reeling, winding II. m.f. *(persona)* reeler, winder; *(aparato)* reel, spool.

as·par tr. *(hilo)* to reel, wind; *(crucificar)* to crucify; FIG., COLL. *(mortificar)* to mortify; *(vejar)* to vex, annoy ♦ **que me aspen si lo hago** I'll be damned if I'll do it —reflex. FIG. to writhe (in pain).

as·pa·ven·tar §49 tr. to frighten, scare.

as·pa·ven·te·ro, –ra *or* **as·pa·ven·to·so, –sa** adj. effusive, theatrical, dramatic.

as·pa·vien·tar·se reflex. C. AMER. *(asustarse)* to become frightened *or* scared; *(alarmarse)* to become alarmed.

as·pa·vien·to m. exaggerated behavior, theatricality ♦ **hacer aspavientos** to make a fuss *or* a scene.

as·pec·to m. aspect; *(apariencia)* appearance, looks ♦ **a primer a.** at first glance.

ás·pe·ra·men·te adv. gruffly, harshly, roughly.

as·pe·re·te m. tartness, sourness.

as·pe·re·za f. *(escabrosidad)* roughness, ruggedness; FIG. *(desabrimiento)* harshness, asperity; *(brusquedad)* gruffness, surliness.

as·per·ges m. [pl. **-ges**] RELIG. *(canto)* liturgical chant; *(aspersión)* asperges, sprinkling.

as·pe·rie·go, –ga adj. sour (apple).

as·pe·ri·llo m. tartness, sourness.

as·per·jar tr. *(rociar)* to sprinkle; RELIG. to sprinkle with holy water.

ás·pe·ro, –ra adj. *(rugoso)* rough, asperous (surface); *(escabroso)* rugged, scabrous (terrain); FIG. *(desapacible)* harsh, rough; *(brusco)* gruff, surly.

as·pe·rón m. sandstone.

as·per·sión f. sprinkling ♦ **sistema de a. automática** (automatic) sprinkling system.

as·per·sor m. sprinkler.

as·per·so·rio m. sprinkler.

ás·pid *or* **ás·pi·de** m. ZOOL. asp; ARTIL. *(cañón)* culverin.

as·pi·lle·ra f. MIL. loophole, embrasure.

as·pi·ra·ción f. PHYSIOL. inhalation, breathing in; MECH. *(succión)* suction, draft; FIG. *(anhelo)* aspiration, desire; PHONET. aspiration, rough mute; MUS. short pause ♦ **aspiraciones** pretensions, lofty claims.

as·pi·ra·do, –da I. past part. see **aspirar** II. adj. PHONET. aspirated.

as·pi·ra·dor, –do·ra I. adj. PHYSIOL. inhaling, aspirating; MECH. sucking, suction II. m. MECH., MED. aspirator; MECH. suction pump —f. MECH. *(de polvo)* vacuum cleaner.

as·pi·ran·te I. adj. PHYSIOL. inhaling, aspirating; MECH. *(de succión)* suction, sucking; FIG. *(ambicioso)* aspiring, ambitious II. m.f. aspirant, candidate.

as·pi·rar tr. PHYSIOL. to inhale, breathe in; MECH. *(atraer)* to suck, draw in; PHONET. *(pronunciar)* to aspirate ♦ **a. a** to aspire to, yearn for.

as·pi·ra·to·rio, –ria adj. aspiratory.

as·pi·ri·na f. PHARM. aspirin.

as·que·a·do, –da I. past part. see **asquear** II. adj. *(repugnante)* sickening, disgusting; FIG. *(aburrido)* bothersome, annoying.

as·que·ar tr. to nauseate, disgust —intr. to be sickening *or* disgusting.

as·que·ro·sa·men·te adv. disgustingly, repulsively.

as·que·ro·si·dad f. *(suciedad)* filth, foulness; *(vileza)* vileness, loathsomeness.

as·que·ro·so, –sa adj. *(repugnante)* sickening, repulsive; *(sucio)* filthy, foul; *(nauseabundo)* squeamish, nauseous.

as·ta f. *(lanza)* lance, spear; *(palo de una lanza)* shaft; *(palo de una bandera)* flagpole, flagstaff; *(mango)* handle; *(cuerno)* horn, antler ♦ **a media a.** *(la bandera)* at half-mast, at half-staff; C. RICA, FIG. tipsy, half-drunk.

as·te·ris·co m. asterisk.

as·te·roi·de I. m. ASTRON. asteroid, planetoid II. adj. asteroidal, starlike.

as·tig·má·ti·co, –ca adj. OPHTHAL. astigmatic.

as·tig·ma·tis·mo m. OPHTHAL. astigmatism.

as·til m. *(de herramienta)* handle; *(de flecha)* shaft (of an arrow); *(de balanza)* arm, beam (of a scale); *(de pluma)* quill.

as·ti·lla f. splinter, fragment, chip ♦ **astillas** kindling • **hacer astillas** to chip, splinter • **sacar a.** COLL. to get a cut *or* a piece of the action.

as·ti·llar tr. *(fragmentar)* to chip, splinter; *(destruir)* to destroy, break into pieces.

as·ti·lle·ro m. MARIT. *(taller)* shipyard, dockyard; ARM. *(percha)* spear *or* lance rack; COM. *(almacén)* lumberyard; MEX. lumbering site.

as·ti·llo·so, –sa adj. splintery.

as·tra·cán m. astrakhan, astrachan (pelt *or* cloth).

as·trá·ga·lo m. BOT. tragacanth; ARCHIT. astragal; ANAT. astragalus.

as·tral adj. ASTRON. astral.

as·tre·ñir §59 tr. to constrict, bind.

as·tric·ción f. *(astringencia)* astringency; *(sujeción)* astriction.

as·tric·ti·vo, –va adj. astrictive, astringent.

a·stric·to, –ta I. past part. see **astringir** II. adj. FIG. obligated, bound.

as·trin·gen·cia f. astringency; *(constricción)* astriction, constriction.

as·trin·gen·te adj. & m. astringent.

as·trin·gir §32 tr. ANAT. to astringe, contract; FIG. *(sujetar)* to bind, constrain.

as·tri·ña, astriño see **astreñir**.

as·tro m. ASTRON. heavenly body, star; FIG. *(celebridad)* star, celebrity.

as·tro·fí·si·co, –ca I. adj. astrophysical II. m.f. astrophysicist —f. astrophysics.

as·tro·lo·gí·a f. astrology.

as·tro·ló·gi·co, –ca adj. astrological.

as·tró·lo·go, –ga I. m.f. astrologist II. adj. astrological.

as·tro·nau·ta m.f. astronaut, cosmonaut.

as·tro·náu·ti·ca f. astronautics.

as·tro·na·ve f. ASTRONAUT. spaceship, spacecraft.

as·tro·no·mí·a f. astronomy.

as·tro·nó·mi·co, –ca adj. astronomic; FIG. *(enorme)* astronomical, enormous.

as·tró·no·mo, –ma m.f. astronomer.

as·tro·so, –sa adj. *(desastrado)* shabby, untidy; *(sucio)* dirty; *(despreciable)* despicable, vile.

as·tu·cia f. *(listeza)* astuteness, cleverness; *(artimaña)* craftiness, slyness; *(ardid)* trick, ruse.

as·tu·ria·no, –na adj. & m.f. Asturian.

As·tu·rias f. Asturias.

as·tu·to, –ta adj. *(listo)* astute, clever; *(mañoso)* crafty, shrewd.

a·suel·de, asueldo see **asoldar**.

a·sue·le, asuelo see **asolar²**.

a·sue·to m. holiday ♦ **día de a.** day off, holiday.

a·su·mir tr. to assume, take on.

a·sun·ción f. assumption ♦ **Asunción** RELIG. Assumption.

A·sun·ción f. GEOG. Asunción; RELIG. Assumption.

a·sun·tar intr. DOM. REP. to pay attention; C. AMER. to investigate, pry.

a·sun·to m. *(tópico)* matter, topic; ARTS, LIT. *(tema)* theme, subject matter; LIT. *(argumento)* plot; *(preocupación)* affair, concern; COLL. *(amorío)* love affair ♦ **a. pendiente** pending business, unresolved matter • **asuntos** *(efectos)* property, possessions; affairs, business <*tengo asuntos que liquidar* I have some business to settle> • **asuntos exteriores** *or* **extranjeros** POL. foreign affairs *or* relations • **el a. es que . . .** the fact is that . . . • **ir al a.** to get down to business *or* to the matter at hand • **poner el a.** AMER. to watch one's step, pay attention • **tener muchos asuntos entre manos** FIG. to have many matters to deal with.

a·su·rar tr. CUL. to burn, scorch (meats); AGR. to scorch crops; FIG. *(inquietar)* to worry, trouble —reflex. CUL. to be burned *or* scorched (meats); AGR. to be scorched (crops); FIG. *(inquietarse)* to worry, be troubled.

a·sur·ca·do, –da adj. furrowed, grooved.

a·sus·ta·di·zo, –za adj. easily frightened, skittish.

a·sus·ta·dor, –do·ra *or* **a·sus·tón, –to·na** adj. AMER. scary, frightening.

a·sus·tar tr. to frighten, scare —reflex. to be frightened *or* scared ♦ **a. de, por,** *or* **con** to be frightened of *or* by.

a·ta·ba·ca·do, –da adj. tobacco-colored; BOL. clumsy, awkward.

a·ta·be m. pipe vent.

a·ta·blar tr. AGR. to level (freshly sown ground).

a·ta·ca·ble adj. vulnerable, susceptible to attack.

a·ta·ca·do, –da I. past part. see **atacar II.** adj. FIG., COLL. *(irresoluto)* wishy-washy; *(mesquino)* stingy, tightfisted.

a·ta·ca·dor, –do·ra *or* **a·ta·can·te I.** adj. attacking, assaulting **II.** m.f. *(agresor)* attacker, assailant —m. ARTIL. ramrod.

a·ta·ca·du·ra f. *or* **a·ta·ca·mien·to** m. fastening, buttoning.

a·ta·can·te adj. attacking, assaulting.

a·ta·car §70 tr. *(acometer)* to attack, assault; *(abrochar)* to fasten, attach; FIG. *(contradecir)* to refute, contradict; to attack, overcome <*le atacó la fiebre* the fever overcame him>; *(iniciar)* to start work on, attack <*atacaron el proyecto* they attacked the project>; ARM. to pack *or* tamp down; CHEM. to corrode, eat away —reflex. to fasten, button up.

a·ta·de·ras f.pl. COLL. garters.

a·ta·de·ro m. *(lo que ata)* tie fastener; *(lo que se ata)* hook, loop ♦ **no tener a.** FIG. not to hang together, not to make sense.

a·ta·di·jo m. COLL. awkward bundle.

a·ta·do, –da I. past part. see **atar II.** adj. FIG. timid, inhibited **III.** m. *(manojo)* bundle; ARG. cigarette pack.

a·ta·dor, –do·ra I. adj. tying, binding **II.** m.f. *(persona)* binder —f. *(máquina)* sheaf binder.

a·ta·du·ra f. *(acción)* tying, binding; *(cuerda)* cord, string; FIG. *(enlace)* bond, tie; *(traba)* restriction, hindrance.

a·ta·fa·gar §47 tr. *(sofocar)* to suffocate, stifle; FIG., COLL. *(molestar)* to pester.

a·ta·guí·a f. CONSTR. cofferdam.

a·tai·re m. CARP. molding.

a·ta·ja·da f. CHILE interception, heading off; AMER., SPORT. catch, block.

a·ta·ja·di·zo m. *(tabique)* partition; *(terreno)* segment, parcel (of land).

a·ta·ja·dor, –do·ra I. adj. barring, obstructing **II.** m.f. *(obstructor)* obstructor —m. MEX. cattle driver.

a·ta·jar tr. *(detener)* to intercept, head off; *(separar)* to fence, partition; FIG. *(impedir)* to stop, halt; *(interrumpir)* to interrupt, cut off; AMER. *(contener)* to hold back (from a fight); *(tomar)* to catch (in midair) ♦ **a un golpe** AMER. to parry a blow —reflex. FIG. *(avergonzarse)* to be embarrassed *or* ashamed; SP. to get drunk; ARG., PAR. to contain oneself, keep one's temper —intr. to take a short cut.

a·ta·jo m. *(senda)* short cut; *(división)* division, segment; FIG. *(procedimiento rápido)* short cut, quick method; *(conjunto)* pack, group <*un a. de mentiras* a pack of lies>.

a·ta·la·jar tr. to harness (a horse).

a·ta·la·je m. ARTIL. team of draft horses; *(arreos)* harness; FIG., COLL. *(equipo)* outfit, equipment.

a·ta·lan·tar tr. *(agradar)* to please, suit; *(aturdir)* to stun, shock.

a·ta·la·ya f. *(torre)* watchtower, observation tower; *(altura)* vantage point, lookout —m. *(centinela)* guard, lookout.

a·ta·la·ya·dor, –do·ra I. adj. watching, observing **II.** m.f. *(observador)* watcher, observer; FIG., COLL. *(averiguador)* investigator, inquirer.

a·ta·la·yar tr. *(vigilar)* to watch, observe; FIG. *(espiar)* to spy on.

a·ta·la·ye·ro m. MIL. sentry, lookout.

a·ta·lu·dar *or* **a·ta·lu·zar** §04 tr. to slope, slant.

a·ta·mien·to m. FIG., COLL. meekness, shyness.

a·ta·nor m. water tube *or* pipe.

a·tan·quí·a f. *(depilatorio)* depilatory cream; *(seda)* coarse silk.

a·ta·ñer §68 intr. to concern, pertain <*eso no nos atañe* that doesn't pertain to us>.

a·ta·que m. *(asalto)* attack, assault; FIG. attack, fit <*un a. de tos* a coughing fit>; *(disputa)* dispute, attack ♦ **a. aéreo** air raid • **a. por sorpresa** surprise attack.

a·ta·qué, ataque see **atacar.**

a·tar tr. *(unir)* to tie, bind, lace <*a. por la cintura* to tie at the waist>; *(sujetar)* to tie up, bind; FIG. *(maniatar)* to bind, restrict; *(relacionar)* reconcile, relate (one thing to another) ♦ **a. cabos** FIG. to put two and two together —reflex. FIG. *(embarazarse)* to get flustered; to stick <*atarse a una opinión* to stick to an opinion> ♦ **atarse a la letra** FIG. to stick to the letter of the law.

a·ta·ra·cé, atarace see **atarazar.**

a·ta·ra·ce·a f. marquetry, inlay.

a·ta·ran·ta·do, –da I. past part. see **atarantar II.** adj. *(picado de la tarántula)* bitten by a tarantula; FIG., COLL. *(bullicioso)* restless; *(aturdido)* stunned, dazed; *(espantado)* terrified, frightened.

a·ta·ran·tar tr. to daze, stun —reflex. COL., CHILE to rush, dash; GUAT., MEX. to get tipsy.

a·ta·ra·xia f. ataraxia, tranquility.

a·ta·ra·za·na f. *(astillero)* shipyard; *(taller del cordelero)* ropemaker's workshop.

a·ta·ra·zar §04 tr. to bite, chomp.

a·tar·de·cer §17 **I.** intr. to draw toward evening, get dark <*atardecía* it was getting dark> **II.** m. late afternoon, dusk ♦ **al a.** at dusk.

a·ta·re·ar tr. to assign work to —reflex. to busy *or* occupy oneself.

a·tar·je·a f. *(cañería)* piping, pipeline; *(alcantarilla)* culvert, drain; PERU water supply.

a·tar·qui·nar tr. to cover with mud.

a·ta·rra·ya f. casting net.

a·ta·ru·ga·mien·to m. *(aseguramiento)* pegging, pinning; *(tapamiento)* plugging; FIG., COLL. *(confusión)* confusion, embarrassment; *(atestamiento)* stuffing, cramming; *(acción de atracarse)* stuffing, gorging.

a·ta·ru·gar §47 tr. *(asegurar)* to peg, pin; *(tapar)* to plug; FIG., COLL. *(hacer callar)* to shut up, squelch; *(llenar)* to stuff, cram —reflex. FIG., COLL. to stuff *or* gorge oneself.

a·ta·sa·jar tr. to jerk (beef).

a·tas·ca·de·ro m. *(ciénaga)* bog, mire; FIG. *(estorbo)* stumbling block.

a·tas·ca·mien·to m. *(obstrucción)* blockage, obstruction; FIG. *(impedimento)* obstacle, barrier.

a·tas·car §70 tr. *(obstruir)* to stop up, clog; MARIT. *(calafatear)* to calk; FIG. *(impedir)* to hamper, impede —reflex. *(estancarse)* to get stuck *or* clogged; FIG. *(embrollarse)* to become bogged down.

a·tas·co m. *(obstrucción)* blockage, obstruction; FIG. *(impedimento)* obstacle, barrier.

a·ta·úd m. coffin, casket.

a·ta·viar §30 tr. to adorn, deck out.

a·tá·vi·co, –ca adj. atavistic.

a·ta·ví·o m. *(adorno)* decoration, adornment; FIG. *(vestido)* dress, attire ♦ **atavíos** finery, trappings, accouterments.

a·ta·vis·mo m. atavism, intermittent heredity.

a·ta·xia f. MED. ataxia, ataxy ♦ **a. locomotriz progresiva** MED. locomotor ataxia.

a·te·cé, atece see **atezar.**

a·te·ís·mo m. atheism.

a·te·la·je m. ARTIL. team of draft horses; *(arreos)* harness.

a·te·mo·ri·zar §04 tr. to frighten, terrify —reflex. to be frightened *or* terrified ♦ **a. de** *or* **por** to be frightened of *or* by.

a·tem·pe·ra·ción f. tempering, moderation.

a·tem·pe·ra·dor, –do·ra I. adj. tempering, moderating II. m. PHYS. moderator.

a·tem·pe·rar tr. *(moderar)* to temper, moderate; *(acomodar)* to adjust, accommodate.

a·te·na·ce·ar *or* **a·te·na·zar** §04 tr. *(atormentar)* to torture by tearing off the flesh with pincers; *(sujetar)* to secure, immobilize; FIG. *(afligir)* to torture, torment (physically).

A·te·nas f. Athens.

a·ten·ción f. attention ♦ **atenciones** *(negocios)* duties, responsibilities; *(cortesías)* courtesies • **en a.** a bearing in mind • **llamar la a.** *(atraer)* to attract one's attention, catch the eye; *(reprender)* to reprimand • **prestar a.** to pay attention.

a·ten·der §50 tr. *(hacer caso de)* to pay attention to; *(tener en cuenta)* keep in mind; *(cuidar)* to attend to, take care of; *(obedecer)* to comply with, heed; *(esperar)* to await, wait for; COM. to wait on, serve —intr. to pay attention, attend.

a·ten·di·ble adj. considerable, worthy of consideration.

a·te·ne·o m. athenaeum.

a·te·ner·se §69 reflex. ♦ **a. a** *(adherirse a)* to depend *or* rely on; *(sujetarse)* to abide by, adhere to <**a. a una orden** to abide by an order> ♦ **no saber a qué a.** FIG. not to know which way to turn.

a·te·nien·se adj. & m.f. Athenian.

a·ten·ta·do, –da I. past part. see **atentar** II. adj. prudent, cautious, moderate III. m. *(crimen)* illegal act, crime; *(ataque)* assault, attempt (on someone's life).

a·ten·ta·men·te adv. attentively.

a·ten·tar §49 tr. to attempt to commit —intr. to make an attempt <**atentó contra la vida del presidente** he made an attempt on the president's life> —reflex. to control *or* contain oneself.

a·ten·ta·to·rio, –ria adj. which constitutes an attempt *or* threat.

a·ten·to, –ta I. past part. see **atender** II. adj. *(observador)* attentive, observant; *(cortés)* courteous, considerate ♦ **a. a** in view of, considering.

a·te·nua·ción f. *(disminución)* attenuation, diminishing; RHET. litotes.

a·te·nua·dor, –do·ra I. adj. attenuating II. m. ELEC. attenuator.

a·te·nuan·te adj. attenuating, palliative; LAW *(mitigante)* extenuating, mitigating.

a·te·nuar §67 tr. *(disminuir)* to attenuate, diminish; LAW *(aliviar)* to extenuate, mitigate.

a·te·o, –a I. adj. atheistic II. m.f. atheist.

a·ter·cio·pe·la·do, –da adj. velvety, velour-like.

a·te·ri·do, –da I. past part. see **aterirse** II. adj. frozen (stiff), numb with cold.

a·te·rir·se §38 reflex. to be frozen (stiff), numb with cold.

a·te·rra·dor, –do·ra adj. terrifying, frightening.

a·te·rra·jar tr. MECH. to thread, tap.

a·te·rra·je m. AVIA. landing; MARIT. approaching land, landfall.

a·te·rrar¹ §49 tr. *(echar por tierra)* to knock down; *(derribar)* to destroy, demolish; *(cubrir)* to cover with earth —intr. AVIA. to land; MARIT. to stand inshore —reflex. MARIT. to approach land.

a·te·rrar² tr. *(asustar)* to terrify, frighten; *(abatir)* to knock down, demolish.

a·te·rri·za·je m. AVIA. landing, touchdown; MARIT. landfall ♦ **a. a ciegas** AVIA. blind *or* instrument landing • **a. for·zoso** forced landing.

a·te·rri·zar §04 intr. AVIA. to land, touch down.

a·te·rro·ri·za·dor, –do·ra adj. terrifying, frightening.

a·te·rro·ri·zar §04 tr. to frighten, terrorize.

a·te·so·ra·mien·to m. hoarding, amassing.

a·te·so·rar tr. *(ahorrar)* to store up, hoard; FIG. *(tener)* to possess (virtues).

a·tes·ta·ción f. LAW affidavit *or* deposition.

a·tes·ta·do I. m. affidavit, sworn statement ♦ **atestados** testimonials II. adj. see **atestado, –da.**

a·tes·ta·do, –da I. past part. see **atestar¹,²** II. adj. *(testa-*

---

rudo) stubborn, obstinate; *(lleno)* full to the rim, chock-full.

a·tes·ta·du·ra f. *or* **a·tes·ta·mien·to** m. stuffing, cramming.

a·tes·tar¹ §49 tr. *(llenar)* to stuff, pack; FIG., COLL. *(atracar)* to stuff, gorge.

a·tes·tar² tr. to attest, witness.

a·tes·ti·gua·ción f. *or* **a·tes·ti·gua·mien·to** m. LAW attestation, providing testimony.

a·tes·ti·guar §10 tr. to attest, witness.

a·te·tar tr. to suckle, nurse.

a·te·za·do, –da I. past part. see **atezar** II. adj. *(bronceado)* suntanned, bronzed; *(negro)* black.

a·te·za·mien·to m. *(pulimento)* smoothing, polishing; *(bronceadura)* tanning, bronzing; *(ennegrecimiento)* blackening.

a·te·zar §04 tr. *(pulir)* to polish, smooth; *(broncear)* to brown, tan; *(ennegrecer)* to blacken —reflex. to tan, get brown.

a·ti·bo·rra·mien·to m. packing, stuffing.

a·ti·bo·rrar tr. *(llenar)* to cram, pack; FIG., COLL. *(hartar)* to gorge, stuff —reflex. FIG., COLL. to gorge *or* stuff oneself.

Á·ti·ca Attica.

a·ti·cé, atice see **atizar.**

á·ti·co, –ca I. adj. HIST., LIT. Attic II. m.f. HIST. *(persona)* Attic —m. *(idioma)* Attic (Greek); ARCHIT. attic, garret.

a·tien·da, atiendo see **atender.**

a·tie·ne see **atenerse.**

a·tien·te, atiento see **atentar.**

a·tie·rre m. MIN. cave-in; C. AMER., MEX. filling with earth.

a·tie·rre, atierro see **aterrar¹.**

a·tie·sar tr. to stiffen, harden.

a·ties·te, atiesto see **atestar¹.**

a·ti·gra·do, –da I. adj. tiger-striped, marked like a tiger II. m.f. tabby (cat).

a·til·da·do, –da I. past part. see **atildar** II. adj. neat, spruce.

a·til·da·du·ra f. *or* **a·til·da·mien·to** m. *(acción de poner tildes)* putting tildes on letters; *(crítica)* criticism, censure; FIG. *(del vestido)* neatness, smartness.

a·til·dar tr. GRAM. to write a tilde over (the letter "n"); FIG. *(censurar)* to censure, criticize; *(asear)* to primp, spruce up —reflex. to spruce up, preen.

a·ti·na·da·men·te adv. prudently, sensibly.

a·ti·nar tr. *(encontrar)* to find, locate; *(acertar)* to hit upon, discover ♦ **a. a** to manage to, succeed in • **a. al blanco** to hit the mark • **a. con** to find, come upon.

a·ti·nen·te adj. relevant, pertinent.

a·ti·pla·do, –da I. past part. see **atiplar** II. adj. high-pitched, shrill.

a·ti·plar tr. MUS. to raise the pitch of (an instrument) —reflex. to rise in pitch.

a·ti·ran·tar tr. to tighten, make taut; ARCHIT. *(jabalconar)* to stay, brace with ties.

a·tis·ba·dor, –do·ra adj. watching, observing.

a·tis·bar tr. *(mirar)* to watch, observe.

a·tis·bo m. *(acecho)* watching, observation; *(indicio)* sign, hint, glimmer <**un a. de inteligencia** a glimmer of intelligence>.

¡a·ti·za! interj. my goodness!, you don't say!

a·ti·za·dor, –do·ra I. adj. rousing, stirring up II. m.f. *(incitador)* inciter —m. *(hurgón)* poker (fire tool).

a·ti·zar §04 tr. *(el fuego)* to stir, poke (a fire); *(despabilar)* to snuff, trim (a wick); *(avivar)* to excite, arouse (emotions); FIG., COLL. *(pegar)* to strike, land (a blow).

a·ti·zo·nar tr. CONSTR. *(un muro)* to bond (a wall); *(un madero)* to embed (a beam in a wall) —reflex. AGR. to blight, become blighted.

At·lán·ti·co m. Atlantic (Ocean).

At·lán·ti·da f. Atlantis.

at·las m. [pl. **-las**] GEOG. atlas, book of maps; *(ilustraciones)* set of illustrations, charts; ANAT. atlas, first cervical vertebra.

at·le·ta m.f. athlete; *(gimnasta)* gymnast; FIG. *(defensor)* stalwart, staunch defender.

at·lé·ti·co, –ca adj. athletic.

at·le·tis·mo m. athletics.

at·mós·fe·ra f. atmosphere; *(aire)* air; FIG. *(influencia)*

sphere of influence, clout; *(entorno)* atmosphere, environment; PHYS. *(unidad)* atmosphere, unit of pressure.
at·mos·fé·ri·co, –ca adj. atmospheric.
a·to·ar tr. MARIT. to tow.
a·to·ci·na·do, –da I. past part. see **atocinar** II. adj. FIG., COLL. fat, obese.
a·to·ci·nar tr. *(partir un cerdo)* to cut up (a pig); *(hacer tocino)* to make into bacon; FIG., COLL. *(asesinar)* to murder.
a·to·cha f. BOT. esparto grass.
a·to·char tr. *(llenar de esparto)* to fill with esparto; *(rellenar)* to stuff, pack.
a·tol m. GEOG. atoll.
a·to·lon·dra·da·men·te adv. impulsively, recklessly; *(confusamente)* bewilderedly, confusedly.
a·to·lon·dra·do, –da I. past part. see **atolondrar** II. adj. *(impulsivo)* impulsive, reckless; *(turbado)* bewildered, confused.
a·to·lon·dra·mien·to m. *(irreflexión)* recklessness, rashness; *(aturdimiento)* bewilderment, confusion.
a·to·lon·drar tr. to bewilder, confuse —reflex. to be bewildered *or* confused.
a·to·lla·de·ro m. *(atascadero)* bog, mire; FIG. *(impedimento)* obstruction, handicap; *(callejón)* impasse, dead end ♦ **estar en un a.** to be in a fix *or* jam.
a·to·llar intr. to get bogged down *or* get stuck in the mud —reflex. FIG., COLL. to be bogged down, be stuck in a situation.
a·to·mi·cé, atomice see **atomizar.**
a·tó·mi·co, –ca adj. CHEM., PHYS. atomic.
a·to·mis·mo m. PHILOS. atomism.
a·to·mis·ta m.f. PHILOS. atomist; PHYS. atomic physicist.
a·to·mi·za·ción f. atomization, atomizing.
a·to·mi·za·dor m. atomizer, sprayer.
a·to·mi·zar §04 tr. to atomize, pulverize.
á·to·mo m. CHEM., PHYS. atom; FIG. *(partícula)* iota, speck ♦ **á. activo** PHYS. hot atom • **á. fisionado** PHYS. split atom.
a·to·nal adj. MUS. atonal.
a·to·na·li·dad f. MUS. atonality, tonelessness.
a·to·ní·a f. MED. atony.
a·tó·ni·to, –ta adj. astonished, amazed.
á·to·no, –na adj. MED., PHONET. atonic.
a·ton·ta·da·men·te adv. foolishly, stupidly.
a·ton·ta·mien·to m. *(embrutecimiento)* stupefaction, dullness; *(aturdimiento)* confusion, bewilderment.
a·ton·tar tr. *(embrutecer)* to stun, stupefy; *(aturdir)* to confuse, bewilder.
a·to·ra·mien·to m. obstruction, blockage.
a·to·rar tr. to obstruct, clog —reflex. to choke, have something stuck in the throat.
a·tor·men·ta·da·men·te adv. tormentedly, distressedly.
a·tor·men·ta·dor, –do·ra I. adj. *(afligente)* tormenting, persecuting; *(preocupante)* troubling, worrisome II. m.f. *(perseguidor)* tormentor, persecutor; *(torcionario)* torturer.
a·tor·men·tan·te adj. tormenting, distressing.
a·tor·men·tar tr. *(causar dolor)* to torment, cause pain; *(dar tormenta a)* to torture; FIG. *(acongojar)* to plague, torment —reflex. to torment oneself, worry ♦ **no atormentarse por nada** not to worry about a thing.
a·tor·ni·llar tr. MECH. to screw in *or* on; AMER. to needle, harass.
a·to·ro m. blockage, obstruction.
a·to·rran·te ARG. I. adj. loafing, lazy II. m.f. loafer, bum.
a·tor·to·lar tr. COLL. to shake up, confuse —reflex. ARG. to fall in love.
a·tor·tu·jar tr. to flatten, squash.
a·to·si·ga·dor, –do·ra adj. poisonous, toxic.
a·to·si·ga·mien·to m. *(envenenamiento)* poisoning; FIG. *(apremio)* urging, pressing.
a·to·si·gar §47 tr. *(envenenar)* to poison; FIG. *(dar prisa a)* to press, rush —reflex. to get flustered.
a·tó·xi·co, –ca adj. nontoxic.
a·tra·ban·car §70 tr. *(hacer de prisa)* to do in a hurry; SP. to stuff, fill —reflex. to be broke.
a·tra·ban·co m. hurrying, rushing.

a·tra·bi·lia·rio, –ria adj. MED. atrabilious; COLL. *(desabrido)* cranky, peevish.
a·tra·bi·lis f. [pl. **-lis**] PHYSIOL. black bile; FIG. *(mal genio)* bad temper.
a·tra·ca·da f. MARIT. *(al lado de una embarcación)* coming alongside, drawing near; *(en un muelle)* docking, berthing; AMER. feast.
a·tra·ca·de·ro m. MARIT. pier, dock.
a·tra·car §70 tr. *(asaltar)* to hold up, waylay; COLL. *(hartar)* to cram, stuff (with food); MARIT. to bring alongside; CHILE, MEX. to beat, hit —intr. MARIT. to moor, tie up, dock —reflex. *(hartarse)* to stuff *or* gorge oneself; ARG., P. RICO, COLL. *(acercarse)* to approach, come near; CUBA, P. RICO *(pelear)* to fight, quarrel.
a·trac·ción f. attraction ♦ **atracciones** entertainment, amusements • **atracción universal** PHYS. gravity • **sentir atracción por** to feel attracted to.
a·tra·co m. holdup, robbery.
a·tra·cón m. COLL. *(comida)* big feed, spread; AMER. brawl, fight; CHILE, P. RICO push, shove.
a·trac·ti·vo, –va I. adj. *(atrayente)* attractive; *(placentero)* pleasing, charming II. m. *(encanto)* charm, grace; *(aliciente)* lure, attraction.
a·tra·er §72 tr. to attract, draw; *(inducir)* to attract, lure.
a·tra·fa·gar §47 intr. to toil, labor.
a·tra·gan·ta·mien·to m. choking, gagging.
a·tra·gan·tar tr. to choke, to stick (in one's throat) —intr. to gag, swallow with difficulty —reflex. to choke, have something stuck in one's throat; FIG., COLL. *(turbarse)* to get mixed up *or* tongue-tied.
a·tra·í·ble adj. attractable.
a·trai·ga, atraigo see **atraer.**
a·trai·llar §81 tr. *(los perros)* to leash; FIG. *(dominar)* to hold in check.
a·trai·mien·to m. attraction, attracting.
a·tra·je·ra, atrajo see **atraer.**
a·tram·par·se reflex. *(en una trampa)* to fall into a trap; *(un conducto)* to become clogged; *(un pestillo)* to stick, jam; FIG., COLL. *(detenerse)* to get hung up.
a·tran·car §70 tr. *(cerrar)* to bar, bolt (a door); *(obstruir)* to obstruct, block —intr. COLL. *(caminar)* to stride, take big steps; FIG., COLL. *(leer)* to scan, read quickly —reflex. MEX. to be stubborn; ARG., CHILE to be constipated.
a·tran·co *or* **a·tran·que** m. *(atasco)* obstruction, blockage; FIG. *(apuro)* tight spot, jam.
a·tra·pa·mos·cas f. [pl. **-cas**] BOT. Venus's-flytrap.
a·tra·par tr. COLL. *(asir)* to catch, trap; FIG., COLL. *(conseguir)* to land, get <a. un empleo to land a job>; *(engañar)* to fool, take in.
a·tra·que m. MARIT. *(amarre)* mooring; *(muelle)* berth, mooring; ASTRONAUT. docking, link-up; ARM. packing (of an explosive); PERU traffic jam.
a·tra·qué, atraque see **atracar.**
a·trás adv. *(detrás)* back, behind <quedarse a. to remain behind>; *(antes)* back, ago <días a. days ago> ♦ **¡atrás!** back!, stand back! • **dar marcha a.** AUTO. to go in reverse, back up • **ir hacia a.** to go backward.
a·tra·sa·do, –da I. past part. see **atrasar** II. adj. *(relojes)* slow (clocks); *(tarde)* late, delayed; overdue, in arrears <esta cuenta está a. this account is in arrears>; *(pobre)* short of funds, poor; back <número a. back issue>; *(subdesarrollado)* backward, underdeveloped ♦ **a. de noticias** behind the times (in news).
a·tra·sar tr. *(retardar)* to retard, delay; *(relojes)* to slow down, set back (clocks) —intr. to be slow <mi reloj atrasa my watch is slow> —reflex. *(quedarse atrás)* to be late; CHILE *(no crecer)* to be stunted; *(estar encinta)* to be pregnant.
a·tra·so m. delay; *(retraso)* slowness, tardiness ♦ **a. mental** mental retardation • **atrasos** arrears.
a·tra·ve·sa·do, –da I. past part. see **atravesar** II. adj. *(bizco)* cross-eyed, cock-eyed; FIG. *(malo)* evil, wicked; ZOOL. crossbred, mongrel; ECUAD. broad, wide.
a·tra·ve·sa·ño m. crosspiece.
a·tra·ve·sar §49 tr. *(pasar)* to cross, go across, cross over <a. las montañas to go across the mountains>; to put *or* lay across <a. un tronco en el camino to put a log across the road>; *(traspasar)* to pierce, run through; COLL. *(ao-*

jar) to give the evil eye, cast a spell on; MARIT. to lie to; AMER. to hoard, buy up —reflex. *(obstruir)* to be in the way, block <*se me atravesó un venado en la ruta* a deer blocked my route>; FIG. *(mezclarse)* to interfere, butt in; *(reñir)* to quarrel, argue; *(apostar)* to bet, wager; *(ocurrir)* to arise, come up ♦ **atravesársele a uno una persona** to run up against someone, have a running battle with someone.

a·tra·yen·do see atraer.

a·tra·yen·te adj. attractive.

a·tre·gua·do, -da I. past part. see atreguar II. adj. *(lunático)* mad, deranged.

a·tre·guar §10 tr. to grant (a truce).

a·tre·ver·se reflex. to dare ♦ **a. a** to dare to <*no se atreven a hacerlo* they don't dare to do it> • **a. con** or **contra** *(descararse)* to be disrespectful to, insult; to take on, oppose <*me atrevo contigo* I'll take you on>.

a·tre·vi·da·men·te adv. *(osadamente)* daringly, boldly; *(descaradamente)* impudently, brazenly.

a·tre·vi·do, -da I. past part. see atreverse II. adj. *(osado)* daring, bold; *(descarado)* impudent, forward III. m.f. *(temerario)* daredevil, bold person; *(caradura)* brazen or insolent person.

a·tre·vi·mien·to m. *(osadía)* daring, boldness; *(insolencia)* impudence, rudeness.

a·tri·bu·ción f. attribution; *(función)* duty, function ♦ **atribuciones** authority, jurisdiction.

a·tri·bui·ble adj. attributable.

a·tri·buir §18 tr. *(aplicar)* to attribute, credit; FIG. *(imputar)* to confer, grant —reflex. to claim, take credit for.

a·tri·bu·la·ción f. tribulation.

a·tri·bu·lar tr. to distress, afflict —reflex. to become distressed.

a·tri·bu·ti·vo, -va adj. attributive.

a·tri·bu·to m. attribute, characteristic; *(símbolo)* symbol; GRAM., LOG. *(predicado)* predicate; HOND., RELIG. processional stand for artifacts.

a·tri·bu·ya, atribuyo see atribuir.

a·tri·bu·ye·ra, atribuyó see atribuir.

a·tril m. lectern.

a·trin·che·ra·mien·to m. MIL. entrenchment.

a·trin·che·rar tr. MIL. to entrench, surround with trenches —reflex. to entrench oneself, dig in.

a·trio m. ARCHIT. *(patio)* atrium; *(andén)* portico, porch; *(entrada)* entrance, vestibule; MIN. upper end of washing trough.

a·tri·to, -ta adj. THEOL. repentant.

a·tro·ci·dad f. *(barbarie)* atrocity, outrage; COLL. *(exceso)* excess, enormity; *(necedad)* stupidity, foolish action or remark.

a·tro·char intr. to take a shortcut.

a·tro·fia f. atrophy.

a·tro·fia·do, -da I. past part. see atrofiar II. adj. atrophied, atrophic.

a·tro·fiar tr. & intr. to atrophy, diminish —reflex. ANAT., MED. to suffer atrophy.

a·tro·jar tr. *(las mieses)* to store (grain) in bins; CUBA to wear out; MEX. to worry, vex —reflex. to be stumped (by a problem).

a·tro·na·do, -da I. past part. see atronar II. adj. hasty, reckless.

a·tro·na·dor, -do·ra adj. thundering, deafening.

a·tro·nar §19 tr. *(asordar)* to thunder, deafen; *(aturdir)* to stun, stupefy —reflex. ZOOL. to be frightened by thunder.

a·tro·par tr. *(tropas)* to assemble (troops); AGR. *(las mieses)* to sheaf (grain).

a·tro·pe·lla·da·men·te adv. *(con prisa)* hastily, hurriedly; *(en desorden)* helter-skelter, pell-mell.

a·tro·pe·lla·do, -da I. past part. see atropellar II. hasty, hurried.

a·tro·pe·lla·dor, -do·ra I. adj. trampling II. m.f. trampler.

a·tro·pe·lla·mien·to m. var. of atropello.

a·tro·pe·llar tr. *(pisotear)* to trample, stomp on; *(derribar)* to knock down, run over; FIG. *(agraviar)* to bully, abuse; *(hacer precipitadamente)* to do hurriedly, rush through; *(agobiar)* to overwhelm, oppress —intr. ♦ **a. por** to push violently through <*a. por la concurrencia* to push violently

through the crowd> —reflex. to rush, act hastily or recklessly.

a·tro·pe·llo m. *(ataque)* attack, assault; FIG. *(abuso)* violation, abuse.

a·troz adj. [pl. **-tro·ces**] *(cruel)* atrocious, cruel; COLL. *(grave)* serious; *(enorme)* enormous, huge; *(desagradable)* atrocious, awful.

a·troz·men·te adv. atrociously.

a·true·ne see atronar.

a·tuen·do m. *(vestido)* attire, dress; *(pompa)* pomp, ostentation.

a·tu·fa·mien·to m. anger, annoyance.

a·tu·far tr. FIG. *(enfadar)* to anger, annoy —reflex. *(oler mal)* to smell bad; *(enfadarse)* to get angry; *(marearse)* to become nauseated; ECUAD. to become dazed or confused.

a·tún m. ICHTH. tuna (fish), tunny (G.B.).

a·tur·di·do, -da I. past part. see aturdir II. adj. *(estupefacto)* stunned, shocked; FIG. *(turbado)* confused, bewildered; MED. dizzy, light-headed.

a·tur·di·mien·to m. *(choque)* shock; FIG. *(turbación)* confusion, bewilderment; MED. dizziness, vertigo.

a·tur·dir tr. *(dejar sin sentido)* to stun, shock; FIG. *(turbar)* to confuse, bewilder; MED. to cause dizziness or vertigo.

a·tur·que·sa·do, -da adj. *(azul)* turquoise (blue); *(parecido a la turquesa)* turquoise-like.

a·tu·rru·llar tr. COLL. to baffle, bewilder —reflex. to become flustered or bewildered.

a·tu·sar tr. *(recortar)* to trim, cut; *(alisar)* to smooth, slick back (hair); ARG. to shear, trim —reflex. FIG. to deck out, spruce up; ARG. to get angry.

a·tu·vie·ra, atuvo see atenerse

au·da·cia f. audacity, boldness.

au·daz [pl. **-da·ces**] I. adj. audacious, bold II. m.f. daredevil, audacious or bold person.

au·daz·men·te adv. audaciously, boldly.

au·di·ble adj. audible.

au·di·ción f. *(facultad de oír)* hearing, audition; *(programa)* broadcast, program; THEAT. *(prueba)* audition, tryout.

au·dien·cia f. *(entrevista)* audience, hearing; LAW *(tribunal)* district or high court; *(edificio)* courthouse, hall of justice; AMER. *(auditorio)* audience, public ♦ **conceder** or **dar a.** to give or grant an audience.

au·dí·fo·no m. *(aparato)* hearing aid; *(auricular)* earphone, headphone.

au·dió·me·tro m. audiometer.

au·dio·vi·sual adj. audio-visual.

au·di·ti·vo, -va adj. auditive, auditory.

au·di·tor, -to·ra m.f. *(oyente)* adviser, counselor; COM. *(interventor)* auditor.

au·di·to·rí·a f. ACC. *(cargo)* auditorship; *(oficio)* auditing; LAW *(cargo)* office of judge advocate; *(tribunal)* judge advocate's court.

au·di·to·rio, -ria I. m. *(público)* audience, listeners; *(sala)* auditorium, hall II. adj. auditive, auditory.

au·ge m. *(punto máximo)* peak, climax; *(prosperidad)* prosperity; COM. boom; ASTRON. apogee, zenith ♦ **a. económico** economic boom or expansion.

au·gu·ra·dor, -do·ra adj. auguring.

au·gu·ral adj. augural.

au·gu·rar tr. to augur, predict, foretell.

au·gu·rio m. augury, omen.

au·gus·to, -ta I. adj. august, illustrious II. m. clown.

au·la f. *(clase)* classroom, lecture hall; POET. palace ♦ **a. magna** main hall.

áu·li·co, -ca I. adj. aulic, courtly II. m.f. courtier.

au·lla·dor, -do·ra I. adj. howling II. m. ZOOL. howler monkey.

au·llar §82 intr. to howl, wail.

au·lli·do or **a·ú·llo** m. howl, wail ♦ **dar aullidos** to howl, wail.

au·men·ta·ción f. augmentation, increase.

au·men·ta·dor, -do·ra adj. augmenting, increasing.

au·men·tar tr. *(acrecentar)* to increase, augment; OPT. to magnify; PHOTOG. to enlarge; RAD. to amplify; *(mejorar)* to raise <*a. un sueldo* to raise a salary> —intr. to increase, augment.

au·men·ta·ti·vo, -va adj. & m. GRAM. augmentative.

au·men·to m. *(acrecentamiento)* increase, rise; OPT. magnification; PHOTOG. enlargement; RAD. amplification; *(de sueldo)* raise; AMER. postscript ♦ **ir en a.** to increase, be on the increase.

aun adv. even <*a. los ricos quieren más dinero* even the rich want more money> ♦ **a. así** even so • **a. cuando** although, even though.

a·ún adv. still, yet <*a. están enfermos* they are still sick> ♦ **a. no** not yet <*a. no han llegado* they have not yet arrived> • **más a.** furthermore.

au·nar §82 tr. *(unir)* to join, unite; *(combinar)* to combine —reflex. to join together, unite.

aun·que conj. *(si bien)* although, even though <*a. es severo, es justo* although he is severe, he is fair>; even if <*iré a. llueva* I'll go even if it rains> ♦ **a. más** however much, no matter how much <*a. más traté, no logré convencerla* no matter how much I tried, I couldn't convince her>.

¡a·ú·pa! interj. up!, get up! ♦ **de a.** COLL. terrific, tremendous.

au·par §82 tr. COLL. *(ayudar a levantarse)* to help up, lift up; FIG. *(enaltecer)* to praise, exalt.

au·ra f. *(atmósfera)* aura; *(brisa)* gentle breeze; FIG. *(favor)* popularity, acceptance; AMER., ORNITH. turkey buzzard.

á·u·re·o, -a I. adj. *(de oro)* gold; *(de color dorado)* golden **II.** m. NUMIS. aureus.

au·re·o·la f. RELIG. halo; *(mancha)* aureole, circular stain; FIG. *(fama)* aureole; ASTRON. aureole.

au·re·o·la·do, -da I. past part. see **aureolar II.** adj. haloed, adorned with a halo *or* aureole.

au·re·o·lar tr. *(ceñir)* to halo; FIG. *(glorificar)* to glorify, exalt.

au·rí·cu·la f. ANAT., BOT. auricle.

au·ri·cu·lar I. adj. auricular, aural **II.** m. ANAT. little finger; TELEC. receiver, earpiece ♦ **auriculares** headphones, earphones.

au·rí·fe·ro, -ra adj. GEOL., MIN. auriferous, gold-bearing.

au·ro·ra f. *(alba)* dawn; FIG. *(principio)* beginning, dawn; BOT. sagebrush; C. AMER., ORNITH. small owl ♦ **a. austral** ASTRON. aurora australis, southern lights • **a. boreal** ASTRON. aurora borealis, northern lights.

aus·cul·ta·ción f. MED. auscultation (diagnostic monitoring by sound).

aus·cul·tar tr. MED. to auscultate, diagnose by sound.

au·sen·cia f. absence ♦ **en a. de** in the absence of • **brillar uno por su a.** to be conspicuous by one's absence.

au·sen·tar tr. to send *or* keep away —reflex. *(alejarse)* to leave, absent oneself; *(no volver)* to stay away from.

au·sen·te I. adj. *(separado)* absent; FIG. *(distraído)* distracted, absent-minded **II.** m.f. absentee; LAW missing person.

au·sen·tis·mo m. absenteeism.

aus·pi·ciar tr. AMER. to sponsor, support, foster.

aus·pi·cio m. auspice, omen ♦ **auspicios** auspices, sponsorship • **bajo los auspicios de** under the auspices of, sponsored by.

aus·pi·cio·so, -sa adj. AMER. auspicious, favorable.

aus·te·ri·dad f. austerity, severity.

aus·te·ro, -ra adj. *(sin adorno)* austere; *(severo)* severe, stern.

aus·tral adj. GEOG. austral, southern.

Aus·tra·lia f. Australia.

aus·tra·lia·no, -na adj. & m.f. Australian.

Aus·tria f. Austria.

aus·trí·a·co, -ca adj. & m.f. Austrian.

aus·tro m. south wind.

au·tar·quí·a f. POL., ECON. autarchy, autarky.

au·tár·qui·co, -ca adj. POL., ECON. autarchic, autarkic.

au·tén·ti·ca I. f. certificate, attestation **II.** adj. see **auténtico, -ca.**

au·ten·ti·ca·ción f. authentication.

au·tén·ti·ca·men·te adv. authentically.

au·ten·ti·car §70 tr. to authenticate.

au·ten·ti·ci·dad f. authenticity, genuineness.

au·tén·ti·co, -ca I. adj. authentic, genuine **II.** f. see **auténtica.**

au·ten·ti·fi·car §70 tr. var. of **autenticar.**

au·tis·mo m. PSYCH. autism.

au·tis·ta adj. PSYCH. autistic.

au·to¹ m. LAW *(resolución judicial)* judicial decree *or* ruling;

(composición dramática) short play ♦ **autos** LAW case file • **poner a alguien en autos** to brief someone, fill someone in.

au·to² m. COLL. car, auto.

au·to·ad·he·si·vo, -va adj. self-adhesive.

au·to·bio·gra·fí·a f. autobiography.

au·to·bio·grá·fi·co, -ca adj. autobiographic, autobiographical.

au·to·bom·bo m. self-praise.

au·to·bús m. bus ♦ **a. de dos pisos** double-decker bus.

au·to·ca·mión m. truck.

au·to·car m. bus, motorcoach.

au·to·cla·ve f. autoclave.

au·to·cra·cia f. POL. autocracy, despotism, tyranny.

au·tó·cra·ta m.f. autocrat.

au·to·crá·ti·ca·men·te adv. autocratically.

au·to·crá·ti·co, -ca adj. autocratic, autocratical.

au·to·crí·ti·ca f. self-criticism.

au·tóc·to·no, -na I. adj. native, indigenous **II.** m.f. native.

au·to·des·truc·ción f. self-destruction.

au·to·de·ter·mi·na·ción f. self-determination.

au·to·di·dac·to, -ta I. adj. autodidactic, self-taught **II.** m.f. autodidact, self-taught person.

au·tó·dro·mo m. racetrack, racecourse.

au·to·en·cen·di·do m. self-ignition.

au·to·fe·cun·da·ción f. BOT. self-fertilization, self-pollination.

au·to·fi·nan·cia·ción f. *or* **au·to·fi·nan·cia·mien·to** m. self-financing.

au·to·fi·nan·ciar tr. to self-finance —reflex. to be self-financed.

au·tó·ge·no, -na adj. autogenous (soldering).

au·to·gi·ro m. AVIA. autogiro, autogyro.

au·tó·gra·fo, -fa I. adj. autographic. **II.** m. autograph.

au·to·in·duc·ción f. ELEC. self-induction.

au·to·ma·ción f. automation.

au·to·mar·gi·na·ción f. self-margination.

au·tó·ma·ta m. *(maquina)* automaton, robot; FIG. *(persona)* robot, puppet.

au·to·má·ti·ca·men·te adv. automatically.

au·to·ma·ti·cé, automatice see **automatizar.**

au·to·má·ti·co, -ca I. adj. MECH. automatic; FIG. *(instintivo)* automatic, instinctive **II.** m. *(corchete)* clasp, snap —f. *(ciencia)* automation; ARG. self-service restaurant.

au·to·ma·tis·mo m. automatism.

au·to·ma·ti·za·ción f. automatization.

au·to·ma·ti·zar §04 tr. to automate, automatize.

au·to·me·di·car·se §70 REFLEX. to self-medicate.

au·to·mo·tor, -triz I. adj. [f.pl. **-tri·ces**] self-propelled, automotive; AMER. automotive, automobile **II.** m. *(vehiculo ferroviario)* electric *or* diesel railcar; S. AMER. self-propelled vehicle.

au·to·mó·vil I. adj. self-propelled, automotive **II.** m. automobile, car ♦ **a. de carreras** racing car.

au·to·mo·vi·lis·mo m. motoring; *(industria)* automobile industry ♦ **a. deportivo** car racing.

au·to·mo·vi·lis·ta I. m.f. driver, motorist **II.** adj. automobile.

au·to·mo·vi·lís·ti·co, -ca adj. automobile <*industria a.* automobile industry>.

au·to·no·mí·a f. *(libertad)* autonomy, self-government; AVIA., MARIT. cruising range.

au·tó·no·mo, -ma adj. *(libre)* autonomous; PHYSIOL. autonomic.

au·to·pis·ta f. expressway, superhighway ♦ **a. de peaje** toll road, turnpike • **a. perimetral** bypass.

au·to·pro·pul·sa·do, -da adj. self-propelled.

au·to·pro·pul·sión f. self-propulsion.

au·top·sia f. autopsy, postmortem.

au·tor, -to·ra m.f. *(escritor)* author, writer; *(originador)* creator; *(responsable)* person responsible *or* concerned; *(perpetrador)* perpetrator —f. authoress.

au·to·ri·cé, autorice see **autorizar.**

au·to·ri·dad f. *(poder)* authority; *(oficial)* official; *(experto)* expert, authority; *(ostentación)* show, ostentation ♦ **con a.** authoritatively • **presentarse a la a.** to give oneself up (to the police).

au·to·ri·ta·ria·men·te adv. in an authoritarian way, dictatorially.

au·to·ri·ta·rio, –ria I. adj. *(dictatorial)* authoritarian; *(imperioso)* imperious II. m.f. authoritarian, despot.

au·to·ri·ta·ris·mo m. authoritarianism.

au·to·ri·za·ble adj. authorizable.

au·to·ri·za·ción f. authorization, permission.

au·to·ri·za·do, –da adj. *(digno de respeto)* authoritative, reliable; *(oficial)* authorized, official.

au·to·ri·zan·te adj. authorizing.

au·to·ri·zar §04 tr. *(dar autoridad)* to authorize, empower; *(dar permiso)* to approve, permit; *(legalizar)* to authorize, legalize; *(justificar)* to justify <*la necesidad autoriza tales medidas* necessity justifies such measures>.

au·to·rre·gu·la·ción f. self-regulation.

au·to·rre·tra·to m. self-portrait.

au·to·ser·vi·cio m. self-service.

au·to·stop m. hitchhiking ♦ **hacer a.** to hitchhike.

au·to·su·fi·cien·cia f. self-sufficiency.

au·to·su·ges·tión f. autosuggestion, self-suggestion.

au·to·su·ges·tio·nar·se reflex. to induce in one's own thought.

au·tum·nal adj. autumnal.

au·xi·lia·dor, –do·ra I. adj. helping, assisting II. m.f. helper, assistant.

au·xi·liar¹ I. adj. auxiliary, assistant; GRAM. auxiliary II. m.f. *(subalterno)* assistant, helper; *(maestro)* assistant teacher —m. GRAM. auxiliary.

au·xi·liar² tr. *(ayudar)* to assist, aid; *(consolar)* to attend (a dying person).

au·xi·lio m. assistance, aid ♦ **a. social** social work • **primeros auxilios** first aid • **auxilios espirituales** last rites.

a·val m. COM. endorsement; *(garantía)* guarantee ♦ **por a.** as a guarantee.

a·va·lan·cha f. avalanche.

a·va·lar tr. COM. to endorse, guarantee with an endorsement; *(garantizar)* to answer for (a person), be the guarantor of.

a·va·len·to·nar·se reflex. to brag, boast.

a·va·lis·ta m.f. COM. guarantor.

a·va·lo·rar tr. *(una cosa)* to value, appraise; FIG. *(una persona)* to encourage, inspire.

a·va·luar §67 tr. to appraise, calculate the value of.

a·va·lú·o m. appraisal, valuation.

a·van·ce¹ m. *(adelanto)* advance; COM. *(avanzo)* balance sheet, estimate; MECH. feed, lead; CUBA vomit; ARG. lucrative offer; MEX. *(saqueo)* looting, sacking; *(gesto)* friendly gesture.

a·van·ce² m. CINEM. preview.

a·van·za·do, –da I. past part. see **avanzar** II. adj. advanced III. f. MIL. advance guard, outpost.

a·van·zar §04 tr. *(adelantar)* to advance; CUBA to vomit; MEX. *(saquear)* to loot; *(robar)* to steal —intr. & reflex. to advance.

a·van·zo m. COM. balance sheet, balance; *(presupuesto)* estimate.

a·va·ra·men·te adv. avariciously, greedily.

a·va·ri·cia f. avarice, greed.

a·va·ri·cio·so, –sa *or* **a·va·rien·to, –ta** I. adj. *(tacaño)* avaricious, miserly; *(codicioso)* greedy II. m.f. *(tacaño)* miser; *(codicioso)* greedy person.

a·va·ri·cio·sa·men·te adv. *(codiciosamente)* avariciously, greedily; *(tacañamente)* stingily.

a·va·ro, –ra I. adj. *(tacaño)* avaricious, miserly; *(codicioso)* greedy II. m.f. *(tacaño)* miser; *(codicioso)* greedy person ♦ **ser a. de alabanzas** to be sparing in one's praise.

a·va·sa·lla·dor, –do·ra I. adj. subjugating, subduing II. m.f. subjugator, subduer.

a·va·sa·lla·mien·to m. subjection, subjugation.

a·va·sa·llar tr. to subjugate, subdue —reflex. *(hacerse vasallo)* to become a subject *or* vassal; *(someterse)* to submit, yield.

a·ve f. bird ♦ **a. cantora** songbird • **a. de corral** barnyard fowl • **a. del Paraíso** bird of Paradise • **a. de paso** FIG. wanderer, rover • **a. de rapiña** bird of prey • **a. negra** ARG., FIG. shyster.

a·ve·cé, avece see **avezar.**

a·ve·cin·dar tr. to domicile —reflex. to settle, take up residence.

a·ve·chu·cho m. ugly bird.

a·ve·jen·tar tr. & reflex. to age prematurely.

a·ve·ji·gar §47 tr. to blister.

a·ve·lla·nar tr. MECH. to countersink —reflex. FIG. to shrivel, wither.

a·ve·lla·no, –na I. adj. *(color)* hazel, hazel-colored; *(arrugado)* wizened, shriveled II. m. BOT. hazel (tree and wood) —f. hazelnut.

a·ve·ma·rí·a f. RELIG. *(oración)* Ave Maria, Hail Mary; *(del rosario)* small rosary bead ♦ **al a.** at dusk *or* nightfall • **en un a.** FIG., COLL. in a flash *or* twinkling.

¡a·ve ma·rí·a! interj. good heavens!

a·ve·na f. oat, oats.

a·ve·na·do, –da I. past part. see **avenar** II. adj. touched, deranged.

a·ve·na·mien·to m. drainage.

a·ve·nar tr. to drain.

a·ve·na·te m. CUL. oat gruel.

a·ven·drá, avendría see **avenir.**

a·ve·nen·cia f. *(acuerdo)* agreement; *(arreglo)* compromise; COM. *(transacción)* deal.

a·ven·ga, avengo see **avenir.**

a·ve·ni·ble adj. *(conciliable)* reconciliable, conciliable; *(adaptable)* agreeable, adaptable.

a·ve·ni·da I. f. *(calle)* avenue; *(desbordamiento)* flood; FIG. *(afluencia)* gathering II. adj. see **avenido, –da.**

a·ve·ni·do, –da I. past part. see **avenir** II. adj. ♦ **bien a.** in agreement • **mal a.** in disagreement III. f. see **avenida.**

a·ve·ni·mien·to m. *(reconciliación)* reconciliation, conciliation; *(acuerdo)* agreement, accord.

a·ve·nir §76 tr. to reconcile, conciliate —intr. to happen, occur —reflex. *(entenderse)* to agree, come to an agreement; *(armonizar)* to harmonize, go together.

a·ven·ta·ja·do, –da I. past part. see **aventajar** II. adj. *(notable)* outstanding, superior; *(ventajoso)* advantageous, favorable.

a·ven·ta·jar tr. *(superar)* to excel, surpass; *(ganar)* to beat; *(llevar ventaja)* to lead, be ahead of; *(mejorar)* to improve, give an advantage to; *(preferir)* to prefer, put before —reflex. to excel, surpass; *(avanzar)* to advance, get ahead.

a·ven·ta·mien·to m. AGR. winnowing.

a·ven·tar §49 tr. *(abanicar)* to fan; *(echar al aire)* to cast to the winds; *(empujar)* to blow away; FIG., COLL. *(arrojar)* to throw out, drive out; AGR. to winnow (grain); CUBA, MEX., AGR. to dry in the sun; MEX. *(tirar)* to throw, hurl —reflex. *(llenarse)* to swell up *or* be filled with air; FIG., COLL. *(huirse)* to beat it, scram.

a·ven·tu·ra f. *(andanza)* adventure, escapade; *(riesgo)* risk, vicissitude <*las aventuras de la vida* the vicissitudes of life>.

a·ven·tu·ra·do, –da I. past part. see **aventurar** II. adj. daring, adventurous.

a·ven·tu·rar tr. *(arriesgar)* to risk, venture (money, capital); to venture, hazard <*a. una opinión* to venture an opinion> —reflex. to take a risk, dare.

a·ven·tu·re·ro, –ra I. adj. adventurous II. m. adventurer —f. adventuress.

a·ver·gon·zar §09 tr. to shame, embarrass —reflex. to be ashamed *or* embarrassed ♦ **avergonzarse de** to be ashamed to <*me avergüenzo de tener que decírtelo* I am ashamed to have to tell you> • **avergonzarse por** to be ashamed of <*no te avergüences por tu pasado* don't be ashamed of your past>.

a·ve·rí·a f. *(daño)* damage, spoilage; *(rotura)* breakdown, failure (of machinery).

a·ve·ria·do, –da I. past part. see **averiar** II. adj. *(estropeado)* damaged; *(echado a perder)* spoiled; *(roto)* broken (down), faulty.

a·ve·riar §30 tr. *(estropear)* to damage; *(echar a perder)* to spoil; *(romper)* to break —reflex. *(estropearse)* to become damaged; *(arruinarse)* to spoil, become spoiled; *(descomponerse)* to break (down), become faulty.

a·ve·ri·gua·ble adj. verifiable, ascertainable.

a·ve·ri·gua·ción f. *(comprobación)* ascertainment; *(investigación)* inquiry, investigation; *(verificación)* verification; C. AMER., MEX. argument, dispute.

a·ve·ri·guar §10 tr. *(comprobar)* to ascertain; *(investigar)* to inquire into, investigate; *(verificar)* to verify, check; *(adivinar)* to guess —intr. C. AMER., MEX. to argue, dispute.

a·ve·rru·ga·do, –da I. past part. see **averrugarse** II. adj. warty.

a·ve·rru·gar·se §47 reflex. to become warty.

a·ver·sión f. aversion, dislike ♦ **cobrar** or **coger una a.** to develop an aversion to.

a·ves·truz m. [pl. **-tru·ces**] ORNITH. ostrich; S. AMER., FIG., COLL. dimwit, dummy.

a·ve·ta·do, –da adj. veined.

a·ve·zar §04 tr. to accustom.

a·via·ción f. *(navegación aérea)* aviation; *(cuerpo militar)* air force.

a·via·dor, –do·ra I. adj. flying II. m. *(piloto)* pilot, aviator, flier; *(barrena)* caulking auger —f. pilot, aviatrix, flier.

a·via·mien·to m. var. of **avío**.

a·viar §30 tr. *(prevenir)* to prepare, get ready; COLL. *(una persona)* to dress or spruce up; *(despachar)* to hurry up; *(proporcionar)* to provide, supply; AMER. to outfit, equip.

a·ví·co·la adj. poultry-breeding.

a·vi·cul·tor, –to·ra m.f. poultry breeder, chicken farmer.

a·vi·cul·tu·ra f. poultry breeding, aviculture.

á·vi·da·men·te adv. *(ansiosamente)* avidly, eagerly; *(avariciosamente)* greedily, avariciously.

a·vi·dez f. *(ansia)* avidity, eagerness; *(codicia)* greed ♦ **con a.** *(ansiosamente)* eagerly; *(avariciosamente)* greedily.

á·vi·do, –da adj. *(ansioso)* avid, eager; *(codicioso)* greedy ♦ **a. de sangre** bloodthirsty.

a·vien·te, aviento see **aventar**.

a·vie·sa·men·te adv. perversely, twistedly.

a·vie·so, –sa I. adj. *(torcido)* twisted, distorted; FIG. *(malicioso)* malicious, perverse II. m. COL. abortion.

Á·vi·la Avila.

a·vi·lés, –le·sa I. adj. of Avila II. m.f. native of Avila.

a·vi·lla·na·do, –da adj. rude, boorish.

a·vi·na·gra·do, –da I. past part. see **avinagrar** II. adj. *(ácido)* sour, acid; FIG. *(agrio)* sour, bitter.

a·vi·na·grar tr. to sour, make sour —reflex. *(ponerse ácido)* to turn sour; FIG. *(agriarse)* to become sour or embittered.

a·vi·nie·ra, avino see **avenir**.

A·vi·ñón Avignon.

a·ví·o m. *(prevención)* prevention, foresight; *(provisiones)* provisions (food carried by shepherds); AMER. loan (to a farmer or miner) ♦ **avíos** equipment, materials • **avíos de pesca** fishing tackle.

a·vión m. *(vehículo)* airplane, plane, aircraft ♦ **a. de caza** fighter plane • **a. de bombardeo** bomber • **a. a chorro** or **de reacción** jet plane • **por a.** by air mail.

a·vio·ne·ta f. light airplane.

a·vi·sa·do, –da I. past part. see **avisar** II. adj. prudent, discreet ♦ **mal a.** rash, ill-advised.

a·vi·sar tr. *(dar noticias)* to inform, notify; *(advertir)* to advise, warn.

a·vi·so m. *(noticia)* notice, notification; *(advertencia)* warning, admonition; *(anuncio)* advertisement; *(prudencia)* prudence, discretion; MARIT. dispatch boat ♦ **avisos de ocasión** classified advertisements • **estar sobre a.** to be on the alert.

a·vis·pa f. ENTOM. wasp; COLL. *(astuto)* shrewd or sly person; MEX. thief.

a·vis·pa·do, –da I. past part. see **avispar** II. adj. FIG., COLL. *(despabilado)* clever, quick-witted; COLL. *(astuto)* shrewd, sly.

a·vis·par tr. *(avivar)* to whip, spur (a horse); FIG., COLL. *(despabilar)* to make alert or quick-witted; CHILE to frighten, scare —reflex. *(inquietarse)* to worry, fret; FIG., COLL. *(despabilarse)* to become alert or quick-witted; MEX. to become alarmed.

a·vis·pe·ro m. *(panal)* honeycomb; *(nido)* wasps' nest; MED. hives, carbuncle ♦ **meterse en un a.** to get into a big mess.

a·vis·pón m. ENTOM. hornet.

a·vis·tar tr. to sight, make out —reflex. to meet (to discuss business).

a·vi·ta·mi·no·sis f. [pl. **-sis**] MED. avitaminosis.

a·vi·tua·lla·mien·to m. provisioning.

a·vi·tua·llar tr. to provision, supply with food.

a·vi·va·dor, –do·ra I. adj. livening, reviving II. m. ARCHIT. quirk; CARP. rabbet plane.

a·vi·va·mien·to m. *(animación)* enlivening, animation; *(de colores)* brightening, heightening; *(renacimiento)* revival, reviving; FIG. *(encendimiento)* rousing, exciting; *(de un fuego)* stoking, stirring.

a·vi·var tr. *(animar)* to spur on, animate; *(colores)* to brighten, heighten; FIG. *(un fuego)* to stoke; *(encender)* to inflame, arouse —intr. & reflex. to revive, liven up.

a·vi·zor, –zo·ra I. adj. watching, watchful ♦ **estar ojo a.** to keep one's eyes open, be on the lookout II. m.f. watcher, observer, spy.

a·vi·zo·rar tr. to watch, spy on.

a·xial or **a·xil** adj. axial, axal.

a·xi·la f. BOT. axil; ANAT. axilla, armpit.

a·xio·ló·gi·co, –ca adj. axiological.

a·xio·ma m. axiom.

a·xio·má·ti·co, –ca adj. axiomatic.

¡ay! I. interj. *(para expresar dolor)* ow!, ouch!; *(para expresar aflicción)* oh dear!, alas!; *(para expresar admiración)* oh!, wow! ♦ **¡a. de mí!** woe is me! II. m. sigh, moan ♦ **dar ayes** to sigh, moan • **estar en un a.** FIG. to be in pain.

a·yer I. adv. yesterday; FIG. *(en el pasado)* formerly, in the past ♦ **a. no más** only yesterday • **de a. a hoy** FIG. recently II. m. yesterday, past.

ay·ma·rá var. of **aimará**.

a·yo, –ya m.f. tutor.

a·yu·da f. *(auxilio)* help, assistance, aid; *(golpe)* prod, spur; *(dinero)* financial aid; MED. *(jeringa)* syringe; *(lavativa)* enema; MARIT. rope; EDUC. grant, partial scholarship ♦ **a. de cámara** valet.

a·yu·dan·te, –ta I. adj. helping II. m.f. *(auxiliar)* assistant, aide; MIL. adjutant ♦ **a. de campo** MIL. aide-de-camp.

a·yu·dan·tí·a f. assistantship; *(oficina)* assistant's office; MIL. *(cargo)* adjutancy; *(oficina)* adjutant's office.

a·yu·dar tr. to help, assist, aid ♦ **a. a** to help to <*le ayudé a bajar* I helped her to get down>.

a·yu·na·dor, –do·ra I. adj. fasting II. m.f. person who fasts.

a·yu·nar intr. *(abstenerse)* to fast; *(privarse)* to do or go without.

a·yu·no, –na I. adj. *(que no ha comido)* unfed, fasting; FIG. *(sin saber)* uninformed, ignorant <*estar a. de un asunto* to be uninformed about a matter> ♦ **en a.** or **ayunas** *(en abstinencia)* fasting; *(sin desayunar)* unfed, before breakfast; FIG. *(sin saber)* in the dark, all at sea • **quedarse en ayunas** FIG. to not understand a thing, be completely in the dark II. m. fast, fasting.

a·yun·ta·mien·to m. *(acción de ayuntar)* joining, uniting; *(reunión)* meeting; *(corporación)* city council; *(edificio)* city hall; *(coito)* sexual intercourse.

a·yun·tar tr. to join, unite —reflex. to have sexual intercourse.

a·za·ba·che m. MIN. jet; *(color)* jet; ORNITH. titmouse.

a·za·cán, –ca·na I. adj. menial II. m.f. *(trabajador servil)* menial, drudge —m. *(aguador)* water carrier.

a·za·ca·ne·ar intr. to toil, slave.

a·za·che adj. TEX. coarse, rough (silk).

a·za·da f. hoe.

a·za·dón m. large hoe ♦ **a. de peto** or **pico** pickax, mattock • **a. mecánico** backdigger, trench hoe.

a·za·do·nar tr. to hoe, dig with a hoe.

a·za·fai·fa f. BOT. jujube.

a·za·fa·ta f. AVIA. airline stewardess, hostess; *(criada)* lady-in-waiting, handmaiden.

a·za·fa·te m. *(cesta)* flat wicker basket; AMER. wicker tray.

a·za·frán m. BOT. saffron; MARIT. rudderstock; *(color)* saffron.

a·za·ga·ya f. assagai, javelin.

a·za·har f. BOT. orange, lemon, or citron blossom.

a·za·lá m. Moslem prayer.

a·za·le·a f. BOT. azalea.

a·zar m. *(casualidad)* chance, hazard; *(desgracia)* misfortune, accident; *(en la pelota)* hazard, obstacle ♦ **al a.** at random • **por a.** by chance, accidentally.

a·za·ran·dar tr. to strain, sieve.

a·za·rar tr. to embarrass, fluster —reflex. *(malograrse)* to go wrong, turn out badly; *(sobresaltarse)* to become flustered.

a·za·ro·sa·men·te adv. *(con azar)* hazardously; *(desgraciadamente)* unfortunately.

a·za·ro·so, –sa adj. *(arriesgado)* hazardous, risky; *(desgraciado)* unlucky, troubled.

á·zi·mo adj. unleavened (bread).

a·zo·car §70 tr. to press, pack.

a·zó·far m. brass.

a·zo·ga·do, –da I. past part. see **azogar** II. adj. quicksilvered, silvered (mirror); FIG. *(inquieto)* restless, fidgety; MED. suffering from mercurialism III. m.f. MED. person with mercurialism; *(inquieto)* restless *or* fidgety person —m. *(azogamiento)* quicksilvering, silvering ♦ **temblar como un a.** to shake like a leaf.

a·zo·gar §47 tr. METAL. to quicksilver, silver; MIN. to slake —reflex MED. to get mercury poisoning; FIG. *(inquietarse)* to be restless *or* fidgety.

a·zo·gue m. MIN. mercury, quicksilver; *(plaza)* marketplace ♦ **ser un a.** FIG. to be restless.

a·zol·var·se reflex. to become blocked *or* clogged (a drain).

a·zo·qué, azoque see azocar.

a·zo·ra·mien·to m. *(sobresalto)* sudden fright *or* upset, alarm; *(turbación)* confusion, fluster, embarrassment.

a·zo·ran·te adj. *(sobresaltante)* alarming, startling; *(desconcertante)* confusing, bewildering; *(irritante)* exciting, rousing.

a·zo·rar tr. *(sobresaltar)* to alarm, startle; *(confundir)* to confuse, bewilder; *(irritar)* to excite, rouse —reflex. *(sobresaltarse)* to be alarmed *or* startled; *(confundirse)* to become confused *or* bewildered; *(irritarse)* to become excited *or* roused.

A·zo·res f.pl. Azores.

a·zo·rra·do, –da adj. *(parecido a la zorra)* foxy; FIG. *(adormilado)* sleepy, drowsy.

a·zo·rra·mien·to m. sleepiness, drowsiness.

a·zo·rrar·se reflex. to become drowsy.

a·zo·ta·ca·lles m.f. FIG., COLL. loafer, bum.

a·zo·ta·do, –da I. past part. see *azotar* II. adj. *(abigarrado)* multicolored, motley; CHILE striped III. m. *(reo)* criminal sentenced to be whipped; RELIG. *(disciplinante)* penitent, flagellant.

a·zo·tai·na f. COLL. flogging, whipping, lashing.

a·zo·ta·mien·to m. whipping, flogging.

a·zo·tar tr. *(golpear)* to flog, whip; FIG. to lash, beat upon <las olas azotan la playa the waves lash the beach> —reflex. to flog *or* whip oneself; AMER. to throw oneself, plunge; MEX. to roam, wander.

a·zo·ta·zo m. *(azote)* lash, lashing; COLL. *(manotazo)* smack, spank.

a·zo·te m. *(látigo)* whip; *(golpe)* lash; *(zurra)* spanking, licking; FIG. *(embate)* beating, pounding; *(calamidad)* calamity, catastrophe; *(persona)* scourge.

a·zo·te·a f. *(tejado)* terraced roof; COLL. *(cabeza)* head; AMER. flat-roofed house.

a·zo·ti·na f. COLL. drubbing, thrashing.

az·te·ca adj. & m.f. Aztec.

a·zú·car m. *or* f. sugar ♦ **a. candi** rock candy • **a. de caña** cane sugar • **a. en terrones** lump sugar • **a. en polvo** powdered sugar • **a. moreno** *or* **negro** brown sugar.

a·zu·ca·ra·do, –da I. past part. see *azucarar* II. adj. *(dulce)* sweet, sugary; FIG., COLL. *(afable)* nice.

a·zu·ca·rar tr. *(endulzar)* to sugar-coat, sugar; FIG., COLL. *(suavizar)* to sweeten, temper —reflex. *(almibarar)* to become sugary; AMER. *(cristalizar)* to become crystallized (sugar).

a·zu·ca·re·ro, –ra I. adj. sugar II. f. *(vaso)* sugar bowl; *(fábrica)* sugar factory.

a·zu·cé, azuce see azuzar.

a·zu·ce·na f. BOT. white *or* Madonna lily; CUBA, BOT. nard; FIG. pure *or* delicate person ♦ **a. anteada** day *or* fire lily • **a. atigrada** tiger lily • **a. de agua** water lily.

a·zud m. *or* **a·zu·da** f. *(rueda)* water wheel; *(presa)* dam.

a·zu·fai·fa f. jujube (fruit).

a·zu·fra·do, –da I. past part. see *azufrar* II. adj. CHEM. sulfurous, sulfureous; *(color)* sulfur-colored III. m. CHEM. sulfuring, sulfurization, sulfuration.

a·zu·frar tr. *(impregnar de azufre)* to sulfur; *(sahumar)* to fumigate with sulfur.

a·zu·fre m. CHEM. sulfur, sulphur ♦ **a. vegetal** BOT. lycopodium (powder).

a·zu·fro·so, –sa adj. sulfurous.

a·zul I. adj. blue II. m. *(color)* blue; AMER. bluing, blue dye ♦ **a. celeste** sky blue • **a. marino** navy blue • **a. turquí** indigo.

a·zu·la·do, –da adj. bluish, colored blue.

a·zu·le·jo m. *(teja)* glazed tile; ORNITH. bee eater; BOT. bluebell; SALV., ORNITH. thrush; CHILE, ICHTH. blue shark; CUBA, MEX., SL. copper.

a·zu·li·no, –na adj. bluish.

a·zum·bre f. Spanish liquid measurement (approx. half gallon).

a·zu·zar §04 tr. *(incitar)* to sic, set the dogs on; FIG. *(estimular)* to excite, stir.

a·zu·zón, –zo·na I. adj. inciting II. m.f. inciter, troublemaker.

B

b, B f. second letter of the Spanish alphabet.

ba·ba f. *(saliva)* spittle, saliva; BOT. sap; ZOOL. slime, mucous secretion; COL., VEN., ZOOL. caiman, alligator; P. RICO, FIG. drivel, nonsense ♦ **caérsele a uno la b.** FIG., COLL. to drool (over something or someone), dote (on someone) • **echar b.** to drool, slobber.

ba·ba·da f. ZOOL. *(babilla)* stifle, knee; P. RICO foolish *or* silly remark.

ba·ba·de·ro *or* **ba·ba·dor** m. bib.

ba·bar·se tr. to dribble, salivate.

ba·ba·za f. *(baba)* slime, mucus; ZOOL. slug.

ba·be·ar intr. *(echar la baba)* to drool, dribble; FIG., COLL. *(babosear)* to drool, dote —reflex. AMER. to feel flattered ♦ **babearse por** MEX. to yearn for.

ba·bel m.f. FIG., COLL. babel, confusion, bedlam ♦ **Babel** BIBL. Babel.

ba·bé·li·co, –ca adj. *(confuso)* confused, chaotic; *(ininteligible)* unintelligible.

ba·be·o m. dribbling, salivating.

ba·be·ra f. *(pieza de armadura)* beaver (of a helmet); *(babero)* bib.

ba·be·ro m. bib; *(guardapolvos)* dust cover, dust sheet.

Ba·bia f. ♦ **estar en B.** FIG., COLL. to be woolgathering.

ba·bie·ca COLL. I. adj. simple, stupid II. m.f. simpleton, fool.

Ba·bi·lo·nia f. Babylon.

ba·bi·lo·nio, –nia adj. & m.f. Babylonian.

ba·bi·lla f. *(rótula)* kneecap; VET. muscles and tendons around the knee *or* stifle; MEX. swelling of a fractured bone.

ba·bor m. MARIT. port, portside.

ba·bo·sa I. f. ZOOL. slug; CUBA cattle tick; VEN. kind of snake II. adj. see **baboso, –sa**.

ba·bo·se·ar tr. to drool *or* dribble over —intr. to dote, drool.

ba·bo·se·o m. *(acción de babosear)* dribbling, salivating; FIG., COLL. *(enamoramiento tonto)* youthful infatuation.

ba·bo·so, –sa I. adj. *(salivoso)* dribbling, drooling; FIG., COLL. *(sentimental)* mushy, maudlin; C. AMER. foolish, simple II. m.f. *(que saliva mucho)* dribbler, drooler; FIG., COLL. *(persona infantil)* immature person; AMER. fool, simpleton —f. see **babosa**.

ba·bu·cha f. slipper; DOM. REP. blouse ♦ **a b.** ARG., COLL. on one's shoulders, piggyback.

ba·ca f. luggage rack, carrier.

ba·ca·la·o m. ICHTH. codfish; CHILE miser ♦ **cortar el b.** COLL. to be in charge.

ba·cán m. CUBA tamale; ARG., URUG. *(holgazán)* idler, loafer; *(amante)* lover, sugar daddy.

ba·ca·nal f. *(orgía)* bacchanal, orgy ♦ **bacanales** HIST. Bacchanalia, bacchanals.

ba·can·te f. HIST. bacchante; FIG. *(mujer ebria)* loud drunken woman.

ba·ca·rá or **ba·ca·rrá** m. baccarat, blackjack, twenty-one.
ba·ce·ta f. stock, widow (cards left over after dealing a hand).
ba·ci·lo m. BIOL. bacillus.
ba·cín m. *(orinal grande)* large chamber pot; *(bacineta de mendigo)* beggar's bowl; FIG., COLL. *(hombre despreciable)* contemptible man.
ba·ci·ne·te m. *(pieza de armadura)* basinet (helmet); *(soldado)* cuirassier; ANAT. pelvis.
ba·ci·ni·ca or **ba·ci·ni·lla** f. *(bacín de mendigo)* beggar's bowl; *(orinal)* small chamber pot.
Ba·co m. MYTH. Bacchus.
bac·te·ria f. [pl. **-ria**] bacterium.
bac·te·rio·lo·gí·a f. bacteriology.
bac·te·rio·ló·gi·co, –ca adj. BACT. bacteriological.
bac·te·rió·lo·go, –ga m.f. bacteriologist.
bá·cu·lo m. *(cayado)* staff, walking stick; FIG. *(apoyo)* support; *(consuelo)* comfort, support <*b. de la vejez* comfort in one's old age>; *(alivio)* relief, alleviation ✦ **b. pastoral** RELIG. bishop's crozier.
ba·che m. *(hoyo)* pothole, hole; AER. air pocket; FIG., COLL. *(aprieto)* bad moment, rough spot.
ba·chi·ller m.f. student who has completed the studies necessary for admission into an advanced university program.
ba·chi·ller, –lle·ra FIG., COLL. **I.** m.f. chatterbox, prattler **II.** adj. talkative, chatty.
ba·chi·lle·rar tr. to confer a bachelor's degree on —reflex. to be graduated as a bachelor.
ba·chi·lle·ra·to m. course of studies which enables a student to enter an advanced university program.
ba·chi·lle·re·ar intr. FIG., COLL. to babble, chatter.
ba·chi·lle·rí·a f. COLL. *(locuacidad impertinente)* babble, chatter; *(tontería)* nonsense.
ba·da·ja·da f. or **ba·da·ja·zo** m. *(golpe)* stroke (of the clapper against the bell), chime; FIG., COLL. *(necedad)* piece of gossip, idle talk.
ba·da·je·ar intr. FIG., COLL. to talk nonsense.
ba·da·jo m. clapper (of a bell); FIG., COLL. *(charlatán)* chatterbox.
ba·da·na f. *(piel)* sheepskin ✦ **zurrarle a alguien la b.** FIG., COLL. *(golpear)* to tan someone's hide; *(con palabras)* to give someone a tongue-lashing.
ba·de·a f. *(cosa sin substancia)* something tasteless; *(fruta)* insipid muskmelon, watermelon, or cucumber; FIG., COLL. *(persona floja)* lazy, dull person.
ba·dén m. *(zanja)* gully, channel (made by rainfall); *(cauce empedrado)* catchwater conduit (built across a road); *(bache)* pothole, hole (in a road).
ba·dil m. or **ba·di·la** f. fire shovel.
ba·di·le·jo m. mason's trowel.
ba·du·la·que **I.** adj. COLL. foolish, stupid **II.** m. COLL. *(tonto)* nincompoop, fool; AMER. rogue.
ba·du·la·que·ar intr. ARG., CHILE, COL. *(hacer bellaquerías)* to cheat, swindle; ARG. *(encabritarse un caballo)* to buck, rear (horses); *(ser terco)* to be stubborn.
ba·ga·je m. MIL. baggage, equipment; *(acémila)* mule, beast of burden; FIG. *(caudal)* baggage, stock of knowledge; S. AMER. baggage, luggage.
ba·gar §47 intr. to pod, go to seed.
ba·ga·te·la f. trifle, bagatelle.
ba·ga·yo m. ARG., COLL. *(atado)* bundle of clothing; *(tarasca)* hag.
ba·ga·zo m. *(caña de azúcar)* bagasse (sugar cane pulp); *(linaza)* linseed pulp or husks; *(frutas)* marc (waste pulp); C. AMER., COLL. cur, contemptible person.
Bag·dad Baghdad.
ba·gre m. ICHTH. catfish; S. AMER., DEROG. hag, ugly woman; C. RICA prostitute; C. AMER. astute person; BOL., COL. oaf, lout; MEX. fool, dolt.
ba·gual **I.** adj. AMER. *(feroz)* wild, untamed; *(descortés)* rough, ill-mannered **II.** m. *(caballo)* wild horse; S. AMER., FIG. lout, oaf.
ba·gue see **bagar**.
¡bah! interj. bah!
Ba·ha·mas f. Bahamas.
ba·ha·més, –me·sa adj. & m.f. Bahamian.
ba·hí·a f. GEOG. bay.

ba·ho·rri·na f. COLL. *(conjunto de cosas asquerosas)* slops, filth; FIG., COLL. *(conjunto de gente soez)* mob, rabble.
Bah·rein Bahrein, Bahrain.
bai·la·dor, –do·ra **I.** adj. dancing **II.** m.f. dancer.
bai·lar intr. *(danzar)* to dance; *(girar)* to spin (tops); *(retozar)* to romp (around), frolic; EQUIT. to prance ✦ **b. al son que tocan** FIG. to adapt to the circumstances ✦ **b. el agua** FIG., COLL. to flatter • **ese es otro que bien baila** FIG. there's another one of the same ilk —tr. to dance <*b. una polca* to dance a polka>; *(hacer girar)* to spin (a top).
bai·la·rín, –ri·na **I.** adj. dancing **II.** m.f. dancer —f. ballerina.
bai·le¹ m. *(acción)* dancing; dance <*b. de figuras* square dance>; *(fiesta)* dance, ball; THEAT. ballet ✦ **b. de etiqueta** formal dance, ball • **b. de máscaras** or **disfraces** costume ball, masked ball • **b. de San Vito** MED. St. Vitus' dance • **b. de trajes** fancy dress ball.
bai·le² m. ARCH. alderman, bailiff.
bai·le·te m. short ballet.
bai·lí·a f. bailiwick.
bai·lon·go m. AMER. public or village dance.
bai·lo·te·ar intr. *(bailar mucho)* to dance a lot, dance frequently; *(bailar sin esmero)* to dance clumsily.
bai·lo·te·o m. dancing about.
bai·vel m. bevel square, miter square.
ba·ja f. **I.** f. *(disminución)* drop, fall <*una b. de la temperatura* a drop in temperature>; MIL. casualty, loss; COM. rebate, reduction; CUBA weak spot ✦ **dar de b.** *(eliminar)* to expel, drop; MIL. to discharge (a soldier) • **darse de b.** to drop out, withdraw • **estar en b.** or **ir de b.** to decline, lose value **II.** adj. see **bajo, –ja**.
ba·já m. pasha, bashaw.
ba·ja·da f. *(disminución)* descent, drop; *(camino)* sloped path ✦ **b. de aguas** downspout.
ba·ja·mar f. low tide.
ba·ja·men·te adv. basely, meanly.
ba·jan·te f. AMER. low tide.
ba·jar intr. *(descender)* to descend, go or come down; *(apearse)* to alight, get off; *(disminuir)* to drop, fall <*los precios bajaron* the prices dropped> —tr. to lower, let down <*b. la persiana* to lower the shade>; to bring or take down <*b. las maletas al primer piso* to take the suitcases down to the first floor>; *(ir abajo)* to go down, descend <*bajó la escalera* she went down the stairs>; *(disminuir)* to lower, reduce <*bajaron los precios* they reduced the prices>; *(inclinar)* to bow, lower <*bajó la cabeza* he bowed his head>; *(apear)* to help down; FIG. *(humillar)* to humble, humiliate; CUBA, DOM. REP. to pay, cough up —reflex. *(descender)* to descend, go down; *(apearse)* to alight, get down or off; *(agacharse)* to bend down, stoop; FIG. *(humillarse)* to humble oneself; ARG., PAR. to lodge, stay ✦ **bajarse de las nubes** FIG. to come back to earth.
ba·jel m. vessel, ship.
ba·je·ro, –ra **I.** adj. under, lower **II.** f. AMER. saddle blanket; C. AMER. bad tobacco.
ba·je·za f. *(calidad de bajo)* lowliness, lowness; *(villanía)* baseness, vileness; *(hecho vil)* vile action or deed ✦ **b. de ánimo** timidity.
ba·jial m. PERU marsh.
ba·jí·o m. *(banco de arena)* sandbank, shallows; *(terreno bajo)* low-lying ground.
ba·jis·ta m.f. FIN. bear (in stock market).
ba·jo **I.** m. *(tierra baja)* lowland, hollow; *(bajío)* shoal, sandbank; MUS. *(voz)* bass; *(violoncelo)* cello ✦ **bajos** *(piso)* ground floor; *(enaguas)* underskirt; *(barrio)* slums **II.** adv. *(abajo)* down, below; *(en voz baja)* low, softly <*ella habla más b. que él* she speaks more softly than he> ✦ **por lo b.** *(secretamente)* secretly; in an undertone <*lo dijo por lo b.* he said it in an undertone> **III.** prep. under, beneath, underneath ✦ **b. contrato** under contract • **b. juramento** under oath • **b. llave** under lock and key • **b. palabra** on parole • **b. pena de** under penalty of • **b. protesta** under protest **IV.** adj. see **bajo, –ja**.
ba·jo, –ja **I.** adj. *(poco elevado)* low; *(de estatura)* short; *(en posición inferior)* lower; *(inclinado hacia abajo)* lowered, downcast; *(poco vivo)* dull, pale <*azul b.* pale blue>; soft, low <*en voz b.* in a soft voice>; deep <*un sonido b.* a deep sound>; FIG. *(vulgar)* coarse, vulgar; *(abyecto)* abject;

(humilde) common, humble; cheap, low *<un precio b. a cheap price>* ♦ **b. de ley** METAL. base • **b. octanaje** AUTO. low octane • **b. relieve** ARTS bas-relief **II.** f. see **baja** —m. see **bajo III.** adv. & prep. see **bajo.**

ba·jón¹ m. MUS. bassoon.

ba·jón² m. drop, slump ♦ **dar un b.** to take a turn for the worse.

ba·jon·ci·llo m. MUS. instrument resembling a tenor *or* alto bassoon, treble bassoon.

ba·jo·nis·ta m.f. bassoonist, bassoon player.

ba·jo·rre·lie·ve *or* **ba·jo re·lie·ve** m. bas-relief.

ba·ju·no, –na adj. low, vile, contemptible.

ba·ju·ra f. lowness; *(estatura)* shortness.

ba·la f. *(proyectil)* bullet; *(de cañón)* cannonball; *(de carabina)* shot; *(fardo)* bale; PRINT. *(almohadilla)* inking ball ♦ **b. fría** spent bullet • **b. perdida** stray bullet • **b. rasa** FIG. joker, clown • **como una b.** FIG., COLL. like a shot • **lanzar la b.** SPORT. to put the shot • **ni a b.** S. AMER. by no means, no way • **no entrarle a uno b.** CHILE *(ser fuerte)* to have a strong constitution; *(ser inflexible)* to be unyielding.

ba·la·da f. MUS., POET. ballad, ballade.

ba·la·dí adj. [pl. **-dí·es**] insignificant, trivial.

ba·la·drar intr. to yell, shout.

ba·la·dro m. *(grito)* shout; *(chillido)* shriek, scream.

ba·la·drón, –dro·na I. adj. boasting, blustering **II.** m.f. braggart, swaggerer.

ba·la·dro·na·da f. boast, brag.

ba·la·dro·ne·ar intr. to boast, brag.

bá·la·go m. *(paja larga de los cereales)* grain stalk, straw; *(espuma de jabón)* soapsuds.

ba·la·gue·ro m. haystack, mow.

ba·la·lai·ca f. MUS. balalaika.

ba·lan·ce m. *(movimiento)* rocking, swaying; COM. balance, balance sheet; MARIT. rocking, roll; FIG. *(vacilación)* vacillation, wavering; *(resultado)* result, balance; COL. deal, transaction; CUBA rocking chair ♦ **b. comercial** ECON. balance of trade • **b. pendiente** balance due, outstanding balance.

ba·lan·ce·ar intr. *(oscilar)* to rock, sway; MARIT. to roll; FIG. *(fluctuar)* to vacillate, waver —tr. to balance —reflex. to rock, sway.

ba·lan·ce·o m. *(oscilación)* rocking, swaying; FIG. *(vacilación)* vacillation, wavering.

ba·lan·cín m. AUTO. whiffletree; MECH. rocker arm; MARIT. outrigger; *(contrapeso)* acrobat's balancing pole; *(volante)* minting mill; *(juguete)* seesaw; *(mecedora)* rocker, rocking chair; PERU jalopy ♦ **balancines** MARIT. sheets, yard lifts.

ba·lan·dra f. MARIT. sloop.

ba·lan·drán m. cassock (worn by monks).

ba·lan·dro m. *(balandra pequeña)* small sloop; CUBA fishing boat.

bá·la·no *or* **ba·la·no** m. ANAT. glans penis; ZOOL. acorn barnacle.

ba·lan·za f. *(instrumento)* scales, balance; FIG. *(comparación)* comparison, judgment; AMER. acrobat's balancing pole ♦ **Balanza** ASTROL. the Scales (Libra) • **b. comercial** *or* **mercantil** ECON. balance of trade • **b. de pagos** ECON. balance of payments • **en la b.** FIG. in the balance, undecided.

ba·lan·zón m. *(vasija de platero)* cleaning pan; *(platillo de balanza)* pan (of scales); MEX. grain-sorting sieve.

ba·lar intr. to bleat, baa.

ba·las·tar tr. to ballast.

ba·las·te·ra f. ballast pit.

ba·las·to m. ballast; COL. gravel bed (spread on roads before the final paving).

ba·laus·tra·da f. **I.** balustrade, balusters **II.** adj. see **balaustrado, –da.**

ba·laus·tra·do, –da I. adj. *(provisto de balaustres)* balustered; *(de figura de balaustre)* baluster-shaped **II.** f. see **balaustrada.**

ba·laus·trar tr. to build a balustrade on.

ba·laus·tre *or* **ba·la·ús·tre** m. baluster, banister; AMER., MAS. trowel.

ba·lay m. AMER. wicker basket; CUBA wooden bowl used to wash rice; COL. fishing net made of reed.

ba·la·zo m. *(golpe)* shot; *(herida)* bullet wound ♦ **ser b.** CHILE to be a whiz, be adept.

bal·bo·a m. FIN. balboa (currency of Panama).

bal·bu·ce·ar intr. var. of **balbucir.**

bal·bu·ce·o m. *(articulación dificultosa)* stammering, stuttering; *(niños)* babbling.

bal·bu·cien·te adj. *(que balbuce)* stammering, stuttering; *(niños)* babbling.

bal·bu·cir §38 intr. *(articular dificultosamente)* to stammer, stutter; *(niños)* to babble.

Bal·ca·nes m.pl. Balkans, Balkan States.

bal·cón m. *(balaustrada)* balcony; FIG. *(mirador)* vantage *or* observation point ♦ **es cosa de alquilar balcones** FIG. it is something that is worth seeing *or* should not be missed.

bal·da f. cupboard, shelf.

bal·da·da f. ARG. bucketful.

bal·da·du·ra f. *or* **bal·da·mien·to** m. disability, handicap.

bal·da·quín *or* **bal·da·qui·no** m. *(palio)* pallium; *(pabellón)* canopy, baldachin.

bal·dar tr. *(lisiar)* to cripple, disable; *(en los naipes)* to trump; FIG. *(molestar)* to inconvenience, put out —reflex. *(lisiarse)* to become crippled *or* disabled; COLL. *(cansarse)* to tire, become exhausted.

bal·de¹ m. *(cubo)* pail, bucket; ARG. well ♦ **caerle a uno como un b. de agua fría** FIG. to be hit like a ton of bricks.

bal·de² adv. ♦ **de b.** *(gratuitamente)* free, for nothing; *(sin motivo)* without reason • **en b.** in vain • **estar de b.** to be in excess.

bal·de·ar tr. *(regar)* to wash down (a floor); *(achicar)* to bail out (a boat).

bal·dí·o, –a I. adj. AGR. uncultivated, untilled; *(vano)* useless, vain; *(vagabundo)* vagrant **II.** m. uncultivated land.

bal·dón m. *(afrenta)* insult, affront; *(mancha en la honra)* blot, blemish.

bal·do·sa f. floor tile.

ba·le·ar tr. AMER. *(fusilar)* to shoot (someone); *(tirotear)* to shoot at; C. AMER. *(estafar)* to swindle, cheat —reflex. to exchange fire, shoot at one another.

ba·le·á·ri·co, –ca I. adj. Balearic **II.** m.f. native of the Balearic Islands.

ba·le·ro m. *(molde de balas)* bullet mold; AMER. cup and ball (children's game).

ba·li·cé, balice see **balizar.**

ba·li·do m. bleat, bleating.

ba·lín m. pellet, small bullet ♦ **balines** shot, buckshot.

ba·lís·ti·co, –ca I. adj. ballistic **II.** f. ballistics.

ba·li·ta·de·ra f. HUNT. reed pipe used for calling deer.

ba·li·tar intr. to bleat repeatedly.

ba·li·za f. MARIT. buoy; AVIA. beacon.

ba·li·zar §04 tr. MARIT. to mark with buoys.

bal·ne·a·rio, –ria I. adj. bathing **II.** m. bathing resort; *(medicinal)* health resort, spa.

ba·lom·pié m. soccer.

ba·lón m. *(pelota)* ball, football; *(fardo)* large bundle, bale; *(recipiente)* glass flask; *(globo)* balloon.

ba·lon·ces·to m. basketball.

ba·lon·ma·no m. handball.

ba·lon·vo·le·a m. volleyball.

ba·lo·ta f. ballot.

ba·lo·ta·da f. EQUIT. ballotade.

ba·lo·ta·je m. AMER. *(votación)* balloting, voting; MEX. recount (of votes).

ba·lo·tar intr. to vote by ballot.

bal·sa f. *(charca)* pool, pond; *(embarcación)* raft, float; BOT. balsa (tree); MEX. marsh, swamp; ECUAD. floating hut ♦ **b. de aceite** FIG. tranquil place.

bal·sá·mi·co, –ca adj. balsamic, balsamy.

bál·sa·mo m. *(linimento)* balm; BOT. balsam; FIG. *(consuelo)* balm, solace.

bal·se·ro m. ferryman.

bál·ti·co, –ca adj. Baltic.

ba·luar·te m. *(fortificación)* bastion, bulwark; FIG. *(defensa)* defense, bulwark.

ba·lum·bo m. bulky *or* cumbersome thing.

ba·lle·na f. ZOOL. whale; *(de un corsé)* stay, bone.

ba·lle·na·to m. whale calf.

ba·lle·ne·ro, –ra I. adj. whaling **II.** m. whaler.

ba·lles·ta f. *(arma)* crossbow; MECH. *(de un coche)* spring (of a car).

ba·lles·te·ar tr. to shoot (with a crossbow).

ba·lles·te·ra f. loophole for crossbows.

ba·lles·te·rí·a f. *(deporte)* archery; *(ballesteros)* crossbowmen.

ba·lles·te·ro m. crossbowman.

ba·lles·ti·lla f. *(balancín del carro)* small whiffletree; ASTRON. cross-staff; VET. fleam (for letting blood).

ba·llet m. [pl. **-llets**] ballet.

bam·ba·le·ar intr. *(bambolear)* to sway, swing; FIG. *(tambalearse)* to totter, reel.

bam·ba·li·na f. THEAT. top curtain (hanging from flies) ♦ **tras** *(or* **detrás de las***) bambalinas* FIG. behind the scenes, in the wings.

bam·ba·rria m.f. *(tonto)* idiot, fool —f. fluke, scratch (in billiards).

bam·bo·che m. COLL. chubby, red-faced person.

bam·bo·le·ar intr. & reflex. to totter, wobble, be unsteady.

bam·bo·le·o m. tottering, wobble, unsteadiness.

bam·bo·lla f. COLL. *(boato)* show, ostentation; AMER. *(charla)* chatter; *(fanfarronería)* bragging, boasting.

bam·bo·lle·ro, -ra adj. COLL. showy, ostentatious.

bam·bo·ne·ar intr. var. of **bambolear**.

bam·bo·ne·o m. swaying, swinging.

bam·bú m. [pl. **-bú·es**] BOT. bamboo.

ba·nal adj. banal, trivial.

ba·na·na f. *or* **ba·na·no** m. BOT. banana (tree and fruit).

ba·na·nal *or* **ba·na·nar** m. *(plantío)* banana grove; *(plantación)* banana plantation.

ba·na·ne·ro, -ra I. adj. banana II. m. banana tree.

ba·nas·ta f. large wicker basket, hamper.

ba·nas·te·ro m. basket maker.

ba·nas·to m. round basket.

ban·ca f. *(asiento)* bench; *(puesto)* stand, stall; COM. banking; *(embarcación)* banca (Philippine canoe); *(juego)* baccarat; *(en el juego)* bank (in a game) ♦ **b. inversionista** COM. investment banking • **hacer saltar la b.** to break the bank • ARG., URUG. to have influence *or* pull.

ban·ca·da f. *(asiento)* stone bench; *(mesa)* large table; MARIT. *(banco de remeros)* rower's bench, thwart; MIN. *(escalón)* stope; MECH. *(soporte)* bedplate, bed; ARCHIT. *(trozo de obra)* piece of masonry.

ban·cal m. *(pedazo de tierra)* oblong garden plot, bed; *(parte de huerta que forma escalón)* terrace; *(tapete)* bench cover; *(arena montada en la orilla del mar)* sandbank, sandbar.

ban·ca·rio, -ria adj. banking, bank; *(financiero)* financial.

ban·ca·rro·ta f. COM. bankruptcy; FIG. *(desastre)* disaster, failure.

ban·co m. *(asiento)* bench, seat; *(caballete)* workbench; COM. bank; MAS. row of bricks; MARIT. bank, bar; *(cardumen)* shoal, school (of fish); GEOL. stratum, layer; ARCHIT. impost; CUBA bank (in a game); ECUAD. fertile alluvial land; COL. plain; VEN. plateau ♦ **b. de ahorros** savings bank • **b. de arena** sandbar • **b. de datos** data bank • **b. de esperma** sperm bank • **b. de liquidación** clearing house • **b. de nieve** snowbank • **b. de ojos** eye bank • **b. de órganos** organ bank • **b. de préstamo** loan bank • **b. de pruebas** TECH. testing bench • **b. de sangre** blood bank • **b. hipotecario** mortgage bank • **Banco Mundial** World Bank.

ban·da[1] f. *(faja)* band, strip; *(cinta)* sash, ribbon; *(lado)* side <*de la b. de acá del valle* on this side of the valley>; *(baranda de billar)* cushion (of a billiard table); MARIT. side (of a ship) ♦ **b. sonora** *or* **de sonido** CINEM. soundtrack • **b. transportadora** conveyor belt • **cerrarse en b.** FIG., COLL. to stick to one's guns • **irse a la b.** MARIT. to list.

ban·da[2] f. MIL. troop, band; *(pandilla)* band, gang; *(partido)* party, faction; *(bandada)* flock, covey; MUS. band ♦ **llevarse en b.** COL. to gang up.

ban·da·da f. *(grupo)* band, group; *(de aves)* flock, covey; *(de peces)* shoal, school.

Banda Oriental f. former name for Uruguay.

ban·da·zo m. MARIT. violent roll of a boat to one side; COLL. *(paseo)* stroll; *(tumbo)* fall.

ban·de·a·do, -da I. past part. see **bandear** II. adj. *(listado)* striped; C. AMER. wounded severely.

ban·de·ar tr. ARG., CHILE to cross, go right across; C. AMER. *(perseguir a uno)* to pursue, chase; *(herir gravemente)* to wound severely; GUAT. to court —reflex. to look after oneself, manage.

ban·de·ja f. *(platillo)* tray; AMER. *(plato)* serving dish, platter ♦ **pasar la b.** FIG. to pass the plate • **servir en b. de plata** FIG., COLL. to hand over on a silver platter.

ban·de·ra f. *(pabellón)* flag, pennant; *(estandarte)* banner, standard ♦ **a banderas desplegadas** FIG. openly, freely • **arriar b.** MARIT. to surrender • **b. negra** pirate's flag • **b. de parlamento** *or* **de paz** white flag, flag of truce • **dar la b. a** FIG. to cede the place of honor to • **de b.** FIG., COLL. great, terrific • **jurar la b.** to pledge allegiance (to the flag) • **salir con banderas desplegadas** to come out with flying colors.

ban·de·rí·a f. band, faction, party.

ban·de·ri·cé, banderice see **banderizar**.

ban·de·ri·lla f. TAUR. banderilla, barbed dart; PRINT. correction note *or* sticker pasted on a proof; AMER. swindle, trick; FIG. *(tapa)* hors d'oeuvre on a toothpick ♦ **b. de fuego** *or* **banderillas negras** banderilla with fireworks attached • **poner banderillas a uno** FIG., COLL. to taunt *or* tease someone.

ban·de·rín m. *(bandera pequeña)* small flag, pennant; *(soldado de guía)* infantry guide; *(depósito para enganchar reclutas)* recruiting post.

ban·de·ri·zar §04 tr. to divide into bands *or* factions.

ban·de·ri·zo, -za adj. *(que sigue un bando)* partisan; FIG. *(sedicioso)* seditious; *(alborotado)* headstrong, rash.

ban·de·ro·la f. *(bandera)* banderole; MIL. *(pendón)* pennant, streamer; ARG. *(de una puerta)* transom.

ban·di·da·je m. banditry.

ban·di·do m. *(ladrón)* bandit, outlaw; COLL. *(pícaro)* rogue, rascal.

ban·dín m. MARIT. rowing bench in the galleys, seat in a row galley.

ban·do m. *(edicto)* edict, proclamation; *(facción)* faction, party; *(de peces)* school (of fish); *(de aves)* flock, covey ♦ **bandos** marriage banns • **echar b.** to issue an edict *or* proclamation.

ban·do·la f. MUS. mandolin; MARIT. jury mast.

ban·do·le·ra f. bandoleer.

ban·do·le·ris·mo m. banditry, brigandage.

ban·do·le·ro m. bandit.

ban·do·lín *or* **ban·do·li·no** m. MUS. mandolin, bandore.

ban·do·li·na f. *(cosmético)* bandoline, hair pomade; MUS. mandolin, bandore.

ban·do·li·nis·ta m.f. mandolin player.

ban·do·lón m. large mandolin.

ban·do·ne·ón m. MUS. concertina.

ban·du·rria f. MUS. lute-like Spanish instrument.

Ban·gla·desh Bangladesh.

ban·jo m. MUS. banjo.

ban·que·ro m. banker.

ban·que·ta f. *(asiento)* stool; *(para los pies)* footstool; MIL. *(fortificación)* banquette; GUAT., MEX. *(acera)* sidewalk; P. RICO, DOM. REP. crowbar.

ban·que·te m. banquet, feast.

ban·qui·llo m. *(asiento)* stool; *(para los pies)* footstool; *(asiento del acusado)* dock, defendant's seat; SPORT. *(banco)* bench; AMER. *(patíbulo)* gallows.

ban·zo m. SEW. *(bastidor)* cheek (of an embroidery frame); *(de una escalera)* cheek, side piece; *(de una silla)* upright; *(quijero)* sloping side (of an irrigation ditch).

ba·ña·de·ra f. AMER. bath, bathtub.

ba·ña·de·ro m. water hole, bathing place (for animals).

ba·ña·do, -da I. past part. see **bañar** II. m. AMER. swamp, marsh.

ba·ña·dor, -do·ra I. adj. bathing II. m.f. *(persona)* bather, swimmer; *(recipiente)* dipping tub; *(traje de baño)* bathing suit, swimsuit.

ba·ñar tr. *(mojar)* to bathe, wet; *(lavar)* to bathe, wash; *(sumergir)* to immerse, dip; *(cubrir)* to cover, coat; *(tocar)* to lap, wash <*las olas bañan el rompeolas* the waves wash the sea wall>; FIG. *(llenar)* to cover, fill <*b. en lágrimas* to

fill with tears>; to bathe, flood <*la luz baña la sala* light
floods the room> —reflex. to bathe, take a bath.
ba·ñe·ra f. bath, bathtub.
ba·ñe·ro m. bathhouse owner *or* keeper.
ba·ñis·ta m.f. bather, swimmer.
ba·ño m. *(ducha)* bath; *(bañera)* bathtub; *(cuarto de baño)*
bathroom, lavatory; *(capa)* coat, coating; *(cárcel)* bagnio
(Moorish prison); FIG. *(tintura)* dye; *(apariencia)* veneer
<*un b. de cultura* a veneer of culture>; CHEM. bath ♦ **b. de
María** CUL. double boiler, bain-marie • **b. de sangre** FIG.
blood bath • **b. de sol** sunbath • **b. turco** Turkish bath,
steam bath • **baños** baths, spa • **dar un b.** FIG. to teach
a lesson to.
ba·o m. MARIT. beam.
bap·tis·te·rio m. baptistry, baptistery.
ba·que m. thump, thud (of falling object).
ba·que·li·ta f. CHEM. bakelite.
ba·que·ta f. MIL. *(varilla)* ramrod; *(castigo)* gauntlet;
ARCHIT. *(moldura)* beading ♦ **mandar a la b.** to rule with
an iron fist, rule despotically • **tratar a la b.** to treat
harshly • **baquetas** MUS. drumsticks.
ba·que·ta·zo m. *(golpe con baqueta)* blow with a ramrod;
COLL. *(caída)* fall.
ba·que·te·a·do, –da I. past part. see **baquetear** I. adj. FIG.
(endurecido) hardened; *(experimentado)* experienced.
ba·que·te·ar tr. *(ejercitar)* to exercise, practice; *(tratar mal)*
to mistreat; *(castigar con baquetas)* to force someone to
run the gauntlet; FIG. *(incomodar mucho)* to harass, vex.
ba·que·te·o m. *(molestia)* burden, imposition; *(cansancio)*
fatigue, exhaustion; *(traqueteo)* jolting, shaking.
ba·quia·no, –na I. adj. S. AMER. familiar with a region;
ARG., COL. *(experto)* expert, skillful II. m.f. S. AMER.
guide; ARG., COL. expert.
bá·qui·co, –ca adj. bacchic, bacchanalian.
bar¹ m. bar, barroom.
bar² m. PHYS. bar.
ba·ra·hún·da f. uproar, tumult.
ba·ra·ja f. *(naipes)* deck (of cards); AMER. playing card ♦
entrarse en b. *(en el juego)* to throw in one's hand; FIG.
(desistir) to give up • **jugar con dos barajas** FIG., COLL. to
double-deal.
ba·ra·ja·du·ra f. *(mezcla de cartas)* shuffling (of cards);
(confusión) confusion, mix-up; *(disputa)* dispute, quarrel.
ba·ra·jar tr. *(los naipes)* to shuffle; FIG. *(mezclar)* to jumble,
mix up; *(cifras)* to juggle, manipulate (figures); ARG.,
CHILE, MEX., COLL. *(estorbar)* to hinder, delay; ARG.,
PAR., URUG. *(agarrar)* to grab, snatch ♦ **b. en el aire**
ARG., URUG., FIG. to grasp quickly (intentions, ideas) • **b.
ideas** to toy with ideas —intr. to fight, quarrel —reflex.
(mezclarse) to get jumbled *or* mixed up; PAR. to brawl,
mix it up.
ba·ran·da f. *(de escalera)* banister, handrail; *(de billar)*
cushion.
ba·ran·da·do *or* **ba·ran·da·je** m. railing, banister.
ba·ran·di·lla f. *(de escalera)* banister, handrail; *(balaustrada)* balustrade, railing; AMER. siderail (of a car); CHILE
altar rail; MEX. plank bridge.
ba·ra·ta I. f. *(trueque)* barter, exchange; COL., MEX. bargain sale; CHILE, PERU cockroach ♦ **a la b.** ECUAD. in
disorder, in a mess II. adj. see **barato, –ta**.
ba·ra·te·ar tr. to sell at a discount, sell cheap.
ba·ra·te·rí·a f. LAW fraudulent sale; MARIT. barratry.
ba·ra·te·ro I. m. person who collects money from gamblers
II. adj. who sells cheap; AMER. cheap.
ba·ra·ti·ja f. trinket, bauble ♦ **baratijas** junk.
ba·ra·ti·lle·ro, –ra m.f. peddler.
ba·ra·ti·llo m. *(mercancías)* secondhand goods; *(tienda)*
secondhand store, junk shop; *(venta)* bargain sale.
ba·ra·to, –ta I. adj. cheap, inexpensive II. m. bargain sale
—f. see **barata** III. adv. cheaply, inexpensively ♦ **de b.** for
free, gratis • **echar** *or* **meter a b.** to heckle.
bá·ra·tro m. POET. hell.
ba·ra·ún·da f. var. of **barahúnda**.
bar·ba f. *(barbilla)* chin; *(pelo)* beard; ORNITH. wattle, gill;
BOT. beard ♦ **a b. regalada** abundantly, in abundance •
Barba Azul Bluebeard • **b. cerrada** heavy beard • **b. corrida** full beard • **b. de ballena** whalebone • **b. honrada**
distinguished person • **barbas** *(pelo)* whiskers; BOT. root

hairs; *(bordes del papel)* deckle *or* rough edges; *(filamen-
tos)* barbs • **barbas de chivo** goatee • **en las barbas de
uno** under one's nose; *(en presencia de)* in one's face •
hacer la b. *(afeitar)* to shave, give a shave to; FIG. *(adular)* to flatter, fawn over; *(fastidiar)* to annoy, pester •
mentir por la b. to tell a bare-faced lie • **por b.** COLL.
apiece, each • **subirse a las barbas de** FIG., COLL. to be
insolent to —m. character actor.
bar·ba·ca·na f. *(obra de defensa)* barbican; *(muro bajo de
iglesia)* churchyard wall; *(saetera)* loophole, embrasure.
bar·ba·co·a f. C. AMER., MEX., VEN. *(carne)* barbecued
meat; MEX. *(parrilla)* barbecue grill; AMER. *(catre)* makeshift cot; C. RICA, ECUAD. *(emparrado)* trellis; PERU *(desván)* loft, garret; BOL. *(baile)* tap dance.
bar·ba·da I. f. *(caballo)* lower jaw (of a horse); *(cadenilla de
freno)* curb strap; ICHTH. flounder, dab; PERU chin strap
II. adj. see **barbado, –da**.
bar·ba·den·se adj. & m.f. Barbadian.
bar·ba·do, –da I. past part. see **barbar** II. adj. bearded
III. m. *(hombre con barbas)* bearded man; *(sarmiento)*
seedling, shoot; *(hijuelo del árbol)* transplanted vine *or*
tree ♦ **plantar de b.** to plant as a seedling, transplant —f.
see **barbada**.
Bar·ba·dos Barbados.
bar·ba·ja f. BOT. cut-leaved viper's grass ♦ **barbajas** AGR.
first roots.
bar·bar intr. *(echar barbas)* to grow a beard; *(criar abejas)*
to breed bees; AGR. to take root.
bár·ba·ra·men·te adv. *(de manera bárbara)* barbarously,
savagely; COLL. *(muy bien)* terribly well, very well.
bar·ba·ri·cé, barbarice see **barbarizar**.
bar·bá·ri·co, –ca adj. barbaric, barbarian.
bar·ba·ri·dad f. *(calidad de bárbaro)* barbarity; *(necedad)*
foolish act, nonsense; COLL. *(gran cantidad)* an enormous
amount <*una b. de comida* an enormous amount of food>
♦ **decir barbaridades** to say outrageous things • **¡qué barbaridad!** how awful!
bar·ba·rie f. *(falta de cultura)* barbarousness, barbarism;
(fiereza) barbarity, savagery.
bar·ba·ris·mo m. GRAM. barbarism; *(fiereza)* barbarism,
savagery.
bar·ba·ri·zar §04 tr. *(hacer bárbara una cosa)* to make barbarous; *(adulterar con barbarismos)* to fill with barbarisms
(a language) —intr. to talk nonsense.
bár·ba·ro, –ra I. adj. HIST. barbarian; FIG. *(cruel)* barbaric,
barbarous; *(temerario)* bold, reckless; *(inculto)* uncivilized, barbarian; COLL. *(espléndido)* tremendous, terrific;
(grande) huge, enormous II. m.f. barbarian.
bar·be·ar tr. *(tocar con la barba)* to reach with the chin;
FIG., MEX. to butter up, flatter; COL., MEX. to bulldog,
throw to the ground —intr. *(llegar casi a la altura de otras
cosas)* to be almost the same height; *(hacer la barba)* to
shave; *(trabajar de barbero)* to (work as a) barber —reflex. to stand firm, be adamant.
bar·be·char tr. AGR. *(dejar descansar)* to leave fallow;
(arar) to plow for sowing.
bar·be·cho m. AGR. *(tierra)* fallow; *(acción)* following ♦
estar *or* **quedar en b.** AGR. to be left fallow, be in fallow •
firmar en b. *or* **firmar como en un b.** FIG., COLL. to sign
something without examining it carefully.
bar·be·rí·a f. *(tienda)* barbershop; *(oficio)* barbering, barber's trade.
bar·be·ro, –ra I. m. barber II. adj. MEX. flattering, wheedling.
bar·bi·blan·co, –ca adj. white-bearded.
bar·bi·ca·no, –na adj. *(cana)* gray-bearded; *(blanca)*
white-bearded.
bar·bies·pe·so, –sa adj. with a bushy *or* thick beard, thick-
bearded.
bar·bi·he·cho, –cha adj. fresh-shaved, newly shaved.
bar·bi·lam·pi·ño, –ña adj. smooth-faced, beardless.
bar·bi·lin·do *or* **bar·bi·lu·cio** adj. dandy, foppish.
bar·bi·lla f. ANAT. (tip of the) chin; ICHTH. barb, barbel;
CARP. *(empalme)* tenon, rabbet ♦ **barbillas** COL., COLL.
scantily bearded man.
bar·bi·que·jo m. *(barboquejo)* chin strap, bonnet ribbon;
MARIT. bobstay; AMER. *(cabestro)* halter; *(pañuelo)* handkerchief *or* scarf.

bar·bi·rru·bio, –bia adj. blond-bearded.
bar·bi·tú·ri·co, –ca PHARM. I. adj. barbituric II. m. barbiturate, barbituric acid.
bar·bón m. *(hombre barbado)* bearded man; ZOOL. goat, billy goat; RELIG. Carthusian lay brother; FIG., COLL. *(persona anciana)* serious and stern-looking old person.
bar·bo·que·jo m. chin strap, bonnet ribbon.
bar·bo·tar *or* **bar·bo·te·ar** tr. & intr. to mutter, mumble.
bar·bo·te m. *(babera)* beaver (of a helmet); ARG. ornamental plug imbedded in the bottom lip of some Indians.
bar·bo·te·o m. murmuring.
bar·bu·do, –da I. adj. heavily bearded II. m. BOT. offshoot, seedling.
bar·bu·lla f. COLL. jabbering, chatter.
bar·bu·llar intr. COLL. to jabber, chatter.
bar·bu·llón, –llo·na I. adj. jabbering, chattering II. m.f. babbler, chatterer.
bar·ca f. small boat ◊ **b. de pasaje** ferryboat.
bar·ca·da f. MARIT. *(carga)* boatload; *(viaje)* crossing, boat trip.
bar·ca·za f. MARIT. launch, lighter ◊ **b. de desembarco** MARIT., MIL. landing craft.
Bar·ce·lo·na Barcelona.
bar·ce·lo·nés, –ne·sa I. adj. of Barcelona II. m.f. native of Barcelona.
bar·ce·no, –na adj. roan, brindled.
bar·cia f. chaff.
bar·ci·na I. f. *(saco)* esparto net sack; *(paja)* bundle of straw II. adj. see **barcino, –na**.
bar·ci·no, –na adj. ZOOL. roan, brindled; ARG., FIG. opportunistic II. f. see **barcina**.
bar·co m. *(buque)* boat, ship; *(barranco)* shallow ravine ◊ **b. de carga** freighter • **b. de guerra** warship. • **b. de vela** sailboat • **como b. sin timón** FIG. aimlessly • **ir en b.** to go by boat.
bar·chi·lón, –lo·na m.f. ECUAD., PERU hospital nurse; BOL. quack.
bar·da f. *(armadura)* bard, armor for a horse; *(cubierta de ramaje)* protective fence *or* border of brambles and thorns; METEOROL. thundercloud.
bar·da·gue·ra f. BOT. willow.
bar·dal m. fence of brambles and thorns.
bar·dar tr. to cover with brambles and thorns.
ba·rio m. CHEM. barium.
ba·rí·to·no m. MUS. baritone; *(bombardón)* bombardon, bass tuba.
bar·lo·a f. MARIT. mooring cable *or* rope.
bar·lo·ar tr. MARIT. to moor.
bar·lo·ven·te·ar intr. MARIT. *(navegar de bolina)* to tack *or* ply to windward; FIG., COLL. *(vagabundear)* to wander about, meander.
bar·lo·ven·to m. MARIT. windward.
bar·ni·cé, barnice see **barnizar**.
bar·niz m. [pl. **-ni·ces**] *(laca)* varnish, lacquer; CERAM. glaze; *(maquillaje)* make-up, cosmetics; FIG. *(capa)* veneer, thin coat.
bar·ni·za·do I. past part. see **barnizar** II. m. *(capa)* varnish *or* lacquer coat; *(acción)* varnishing, lacquering.
bar·ni·zar §04 tr. *(dar barniz)* to varnish, lacquer; CERAM. *(vidriar)* to glaze.
ba·ro·mé·tri·co, –ca adj. METEOROL. barometric.
ba·ró·me·tro m. METEOROL. barometer ◊ **b. altimétrico** PHYS. altitude barometer.
ba·rón m. baron.
ba·ro·ne·sa f. baroness.
bar·que·ar tr. to cross in a boat —intr. to go about in a boat.
bar·que·ro, –ra m. MARIT. boatman; ENTOM. water bug —f. MARIT. boatwoman.
bar·qui·lla f. *(barca)* small boat; MARIT. log (device to measure ship's speed); AVIA. car, basket, nacelle; DOM. REP., P. RICO (ice cream) cone.
bar·qui·llo m. CUL. *(de forma cónica)* cone; *(de canuto)* rolled wafer.
bar·quín m. large bellows.
bar·qui·na·zo m. COLL. *(porrazo)* bump, jolt; *(vuelco)* rollover, roll ◊ **dar barquinazos** to jolt, roll.
ba·rra f. bar <**b. de acero** steel bar>; *(barandilla)* railing;

(mostrador) counter, bar; *(banco de arena)* sandbar, sandbank; MECH. rod, lever; AMER. *(público)* public, spectators; MIN. stake *or* share in a mine; *(desembocadura)* mouth of a river; ARG., URUG., COLL. gang, group of friends ◊ **b. de labios** lipstick • **b. espaciadora** space bar (on a typewriter) • **b. fija** SPORT. horizontal bar • **barras paralelas** SPORT. parallel bars • **sin pararse en barras** FIG. to stop at nothing • **tirar la b.** FIG. to sell at the highest price.
ba·rra·bás m. [pl. **-ba·ses**] FIG. scoundrel, rascal.
ba·rra·ba·sa·da f. COLL. dirty *or* mean trick.
ba·rra·ca f. *(chabola)* hut, cabin; AMER. warehouse; ECUAD. stall, booth.
ba·rra·cón m. stall, booth (at a market or fair) ◊ **b. de tiro al blanco** shooting gallery.
ba·rra·cu·da f. ICHTH. barracuda.
ba·rra·do, –da I. past part. see **barrar** II. adj. TEX. *(con listas)* striped *or* streaked with different colors; HER. *(que tiene barras)* barred.
ba·rra·gán m. TEX. *(tela de lana)* waterproof woolen material; *(abrigo)* waterproof woolen overcoat; MEX. woolen underskirt *or* petticoat.
ba·rra·ga·na f. concubine.
ba·rran·ca f. var. of **barranco**.
ba·rran·co m. GEOG. *(abismo)* ravine, gorge; *(precipicio)* precipice, cliff; FIG. *(obstáculo)* obstacle, difficulty.
ba·rran·cón m. gully, ravine.
ba·rran·co·so, –sa adj. full of ravines and gorges.
ba·rran·que·ra f. var. of **barranco**.
ba·rra·que·ro, –ra m.f. *(constructor de chabola)* builder of a cottage *or* hut; AMER. warehouse owner.
ba·rrar tr. to smear *or* cover with mud.
ba·rre·ar tr. *(fortificar)* to barricade, close (up); *(barretear)* to bar, fasten with bars; VEN. to handcuff, tie (someone's) hands together —reflex. to wallow in mud (a hog).
ba·rre·de·ra f. street sweeper (machine).
ba·rre·de·ro, –ra I. adj. FIG. dragging, sweeping II. m. CUL. *(vara con trapos)* baker's mop for cleaning bread ovens —f. *(máquina que barre la calle)* street sweeper.
ba·rre·dor, –do·ra I. adj. sweeping II. m.f. sweeper ◊ **b. eléctrica** vacuum cleaner.
ba·rre·du·ra f. sweeping ◊ **barreduras** *(inmundicia)* sweepings, refuse; *(residuos)* residue.
ba·rre·na f. MECH. *(instrumento)* drill, gimlet; *(barra)* (drill) bit; AVIA. spin <*el avión entró en b.* the airplane went into a spin> ◊ **b. picada** AVIA. tailspin.
ba·rre·na·do, –da I. past part. see **barrenar** II. adj. COLL. with holes in one's head, screwy, nuts.
ba·rre·nar tr. MECH. to drill, bore; MARIT. to scuttle; FIG. *(desbaratar)* to foil, undermine; LAW *(violar)* to violate, infringe; TAUR. to twist (the pike into the bull).
ba·rren·de·ro, –ra m.f. sweeper, street sweeper (person).
ba·rre·ne·ro m. MIN. driller, borer.
ba·rre·ni·llo m. ENTOM. boring insect, borer; BOT. *(enfermedad)* disease caused by a boring insect; CUBA mania, craze.
ba·rre·no m. MECH. *(instrumento)* large drill, auger; *(agujero)* bore, drill hole; MECH., MIN. *(agujero relleno)* blasting hole; CHILE, MEX. mania, obsession ◊ **dar b.** MARIT. to scuttle • **llevarle el b. a uno** MEX. to humor *or* indulge someone.
ba·rre·ño m. *(vasija)* small tub *or* bucket; GUAT. type of dance.
ba·rrer tr. *(limpiar)* to sweep; FIG. *(quitar todo)* to sweep clean, sweep away; *(arrastrar)* to sweep, trail along (the floor); *(rozar)* to graze, touch lightly; COL. to overwhelm, sweep aside —intr. to sweep ◊ **b. con todo** FIG., COLL. to make a clean sweep • **b. hacia adentro** FIG. to look out for number one • **comprar al b.** AMER. to buy without careful selection —reflex. MEX. to shy (horses).
ba·rre·ra¹ f. *(valla)* barrier; FIG. *(obstáculo)* obstacle, hindrance; TAUR. wooden fence surrounding the bullring ◊ **b. del sonido** sound barrier • **b. de peaje** tollgate.
ba·rre·ra² f. *(sitio donde se saca el barro)* clay pit; *(alacena)* crockery cupboard.
ba·rre·ro m. *(alfarero)* potter; *(barrera)* clay pit; *(barrizal)* mud hole, mire; AMER. salt marsh.
ba·rre·ta f. *(barra pequeña)* small bar; *(tira de cuero)*

leather reinforcement (on a seam of a shoe); AMER. pick, pickax.

ba·rre·te·ar tr. *(afianzar)* to bar, fasten with bars; AMER. *(abrir hoyos)* to drill, bore; COL. to cover in mud *or* clay.

ba·rria·da f. neighborhood, quarter, district.

ba·rrial m. *(gredal)* clay pit; *(barrizal)* bog, mire.

ba·rri·ca f. medium-sized barrel *or* cask.

ba·rri·ca·da f. barricade, barrier.

ba·rri·da f. S. AMER. sweep, sweeping; *(acción policial)* sweep, police raid.

ba·rri·do, –da I. past part. see **barrer** II. m. sweep, sweeping ♦ **barridos** sweepings —f. see **barrida.**

ba·rri·ga f. ANAT. *(abdomen)* abdomen, stomach; COLL. *(panza)* paunch, belly; FIG. *(de una vasija)* belly, bulge (of a container); *(de una pared)* bulge ♦ **b. llena, corazón contento** a full stomach, a happy heart • **echar b.** to get a paunch *or* belly • **llenarse la b.** COLL. to fill one's belly, eat heartily • **rascarse la b.** FIG., COLL. to lounge about, twiddle one's thumbs.

ba·rri·gón, –go·na *or* **ba·rri·gu·do, –da** I. adj. COLL. big-bellied, potbellied II. m.f. CUBA, P. RICO tot, small fry.

ba·rri·gue·ra f. EQUIT. cinch, bellyband.

ba·rril m. *(tonel)* barrel, cask, keg; *(jarro)* water jug ♦ **comer del b.** COL., COLL. to eat slop *or* swill • **irse al b.** CUBA, COM. to go into bankruptcy.

ba·rri·le·rí·a f. *(conjunto de barriles)* stock *or* quantity of barrels; *(fábrica)* barrel factory; *(tienda)* barrel store.

ba·rri·le·te m. CARP. clamp, dog; ARTIL. cylinder; ZOOL. fiddler crab; AMER. *(cometa)* kite; ARG. ugly woman; BOL. flirt; MEX. junior lawyer.

ba·rri·llo m. blackhead, pimple.

ba·rrio n. *(distrito)* district, neighborhood; *(arrabal)* suburb ♦ **barrios bajos** slums • **el otro b.** COLL. the other world.

ba·rris·ta m.f. SPORT. gymnast who works on the horizontal bars.

ba·rri·zal m. mud hole, mire.

ba·rro m. *(lodo)* mud; *(arcilla)* clay; *(vaso)* earthenware vessel; *(granillo)* blackhead; ARG., URUG., FIG. blunder, error.

ba·rro·co, –ca I. adj. baroque; FIG. *(extravagante)* ornate, elaborate II. m. baroque period *or* style.

ba·rro·so, –sa adj. *(lleno de barro)* muddy; *(color)* mud-colored; *(granoso)* pimply; ARG., PERU grayish, dun (said of horses).

ba·rro·te m. *(barra)* heavy bar, rail; *(sostén)* rung; CARP. *(puntal)* crosspiece.

ba·rrue·co m. JEWEL. *(perla)* irregularly shaped pearl; GEOL. nodule (found on certain rocks).

ba·rrun·ta·dor, –do·ra adj. surmising, conjecturing.

ba·rrun·tar tr. to suspect, guess.

ba·rrun·te *or* **ba·rrun·to** m. *(sospecha)* feeling, suspicion; *(indicio)* sign, clue.

bar·to·la ♦ **a la b.** without a care in the world, nonchalantly • **echarse a la b.** to let oneself go.

bar·to·le·ar intr. CHILE to idle, loaf.

bar·tu·le·ar *or* **bar·tu·lar** intr. CHILE to ponder, muse.

bár·tu·los m.pl. FIG. *(enseres domésticos)* household goods, belongings; MECH. *(herramientas)* equipment, gear ♦ **liar los b.** FIG., COLL. to pack up, get ready for a trip.

ba·ru·lle·ro, –ra COLL. I. adj. rowdy, noisy II. m.f. *(gritón)* loudmouth; *(entremetido)* busybody, gossip.

ba·ru·llo m. COLL. racket, rowdiness.

bar·zón m. *(paseo)* stroll, leisurely walk; AGR. *(anillo)* yoke ring to which the plow is attached; *(arzón)* bow of a saddle; C. RICA strap for yoking oxen ♦ **dar** *or* **hacer barzones** to take a stroll.

bar·zo·ne·ar intr. to stroll, ramble.

ba·sa f. ARCHIT. *(asiento de columna)* base; FIG. *(principio)* basis, foundation.

ba·sál·ti·co, –ca adj. GEOL. basaltic.

ba·sal·to m. GEOL. basalt.

ba·sa·men·to m. ARCHIT. base and pedestal of a column.

ba·sar tr. ARCHIT. *(asentar)* to build on a base; FIG. *(apoyar)* to base, support —reflex. to be based <*sus ideas se basan en la experiencia* his ideas are based on experience>.

bas·ca f. MED. nausea, queasiness ♦ **dar bascas** to make nauseous *or* queasy.

bas·co·si·dad f. *(suciedad)* filth, dirt; MED. *(náuseas)* nausea, queasiness; FIG. *(asco)* repugnance, revulsion; ECUAD. obscenity, dirty word.

bas·co·so, –sa adj. *(sucio)* dirty, filthy; MED. nauseated, queasy; FIG. *(asqueroso)* repugnant, revolting; ECUAD. vulgar, obscene.

bás·cu·la f. TECH. bascule; *(balanza)* platform scale, balance.

bas·cu·la·dor m. tipcart.

ba·se f. *(cimiento)* base; FIG. *(fundamento)* basis, foundation; MIL. base, station; CHEM., MATH. base ♦ **a b. de** with <*este flan está hecho a b. de huevos* this flan is made with eggs> • **b. aérea** MIL. air base • **b. de operaciones** MIL. base of operations • **b. imponible** tax base • **b. naval** MIL. naval base • **en b. a** on the basis of <*el plan se efectuará en b. a lo convenido* the plan will be carried out on the basis of the terms agreed upon>.

BA·SIC m. COMPUT. BASIC (language).

bá·si·co, –ca adj. *(fundamental)* basic; CHEM. basic, basal.

ba·sí·li·co, –ca I. f. ARCHIT. basilica; ANAT. basilic vein II. adj. ANAT. basilic.

ba·si·lis·co m. MYTH., ZOOL. basilisk ♦ **estar hecho un b.** COLL. to be furious *or* enraged.

bas·que·ar intr. MED. to feel nauseated *or* queasy —tr. to nauseate, make queasy.

bas·qui·ña f. (outer) skirt.

bas·ta I. f. SEW. *(hilván)* basting, tacking; *(puntada de colchón)* mattress tufting II. interj. (that's) enough!, stop! III. adj. see **basto, –ta.**

bas·tan·te I. adj. enough, sufficient II. adv. enough, sufficiently <*no he comido b.* I have not eaten enough>; *(muy)* rather, quite <*llegaron b. tarde* they arrived rather late>.

bas·tar intr. to be enough, suffice <*eso nos bastará* that will be enough for us> <*basta saber que llegaste bien* it is enough to know that you arrived safely> ♦ **¡basta!** that's enough of that! • **bastar a** *or* **para** to be enough to *or* for —reflex. to be self-sufficient.

bas·tar·da I. f. *(lima)* locksmith's file; ARTIL. small culverin II. adj. see **bastardo, –da.**

bas·tar·de·ar intr. to degenerate, decline —tr. to bastardize, adulterate.

bas·tar·de·o m. *(degeneración)* degeneration, decline; FIG. *(adulteración)* bastardization, adulteration.

bas·tar·dí·a f. *(calidad de bastardo)* bastardy, illegitimacy; FIG. *(dicho)* nasty *or* unkind remark; *(hecho)* mean *or* dirty trick.

bas·tar·di·llo, –lla I. adj. PRINT. italic II. f. PRINT. italic, italics; MUS. type of flute.

bas·tar·do, –da I. m.f. *(ilegítimo)* bastard; BOT., ZOOL. crossbreed, hybrid —m. ZOOL. *(serpiente)* boa; MARIT. *(racamento)* parrel, parral —f. see **bastarda** II. adj. *(ilegítimo)* bastard, illegitimate; BOT., ZOOL. hybrid, crossbred; FIG. *(mezclado)* hybrid, mixed.

bas·te m. SEW. *(hilván)* basting, tacking; EQUIT. *(almohadillado)* saddle pack.

bas·te·ar tr. SEW. to baste, tack.

bas·ti·dor m. *(armazón)* frame, framework; THEAT. *(decorado)* flat, wing; AUTO. chassis; CHILE, COL. lattice window; CUBA, DOM. REP. bedstead ♦ **entre bastidores** FIG. behind the scenes; THEAT. off-stage.

bas·ti·lla f. SEW. hem.

bas·ti·men·tar tr. to provision, supply with provisions.

bas·ti·men·to m. supplies, provisions.

bas·tión m. ARCHIT. bastion.

bas·to I. m. *(albarda)* packsaddle; AMER., EQUIT. saddle pad; *(as de bastos)* ace of clubs ♦ **bastos** clubs (in cards). II. adj. see **basto, –ta.**

bas·to, –ta I. adj. *(tosco)* coarse, rough; FIG. *(rústico)* rude, coarse II. m. see **basto** —f. see **basta.**

bas·tón m. *(apoyo)* cane, walking stick; *(vara)* truncheon, staff; FIG. *(mando)* authority, command <*empuñar el b.* to take command> ♦ **b. de esquiar** SPORT. ski pole.

bas·to·na·da f. *or* **bas·to·na·zo** m. blow *or* hit with a cane.

bas·to·ne·ar tr. to cane, beat with a stick.

bas·to·ne·o m. caning, cudgeling, beating with a cane.

bas·to·ne·ra f. umbrella stand.

bas·to·ne·ro m. *(que hace o vende bastones)* cane maker *or* seller; *(director de baile)* marshal, leader (who calls figures at a dance); *(carcelero)* assistant warden *or* jailer; VEN. hoodlum, tough.

ba·su·ra f. *(desperdicio)* garbage, trash, rubbish; *(estiércol)* dung, horse manure ♦ **estar para la b.** FIG. to be a wreck *or* worn out.

ba·su·ral m. AMER. (garbage) dump.

ba·su·re·ar tr. ARG., COLL. to slander, sling mud on.

ba·su·re·ro, –ra m. *(recogedor)* garbage *or* trash collector, garbage man; *(cubo)* garbage pail, trash can; *(basural)* (garbage) dump.

ba·ta f. *(de casa)* housecoat, robe; *(de trabajo)* frock, smock; CHILE, SPORT. bat, paddle.

ba·ta·ca·zo m. *(ruido)* bump, thud; *(caída)* fall.

ba·ta·ho·la f. COLL. rumpus, ruckus.

ba·ta·lla f. *(combate)* battle, combat; FIG. *(lucha)* battle, struggle; *(de la ballesta)* groove, notch (of a crossbow); MECH. wheel base ♦ **b. campal** pitched battle • **dar** *or* **librar b.** to do battle • **de b.** ordinary, everyday <*ropa de b.* everyday clothes>.

ba·ta·lla·dor, –do·ra I. adj. *(que batalla)* battling, fighting; FIG. *(agresivo)* aggressive, assertive II. m. *(luchador)* battler, fighter; SPORT. *(esgrimidor)* fencer.

ba·ta·llar intr. *(luchar)* to battle, fight; FIG. *(disputar)* to dispute, argue <*b. por detalles* to argue over details>; *(vacilar)* to vacillate, waver; SPORT. *(practicar esgrima)* to fence.

ba·ta·llón m. MIL. battalion.

ba·tán m. TEX. *(máquina)* fulling mill; *(zurra)* beating, drubbing; COL. agitation, excitement; ECUAD., PERU grinding stone (for corn).

ba·ta·ne·ar tr. FIG. to shake *or* beat up.

ba·ta·ne·ro m. TEX. fuller.

ba·tan·ga f. PHILIP., MARIT. bamboo outrigger.

ba·ta·ta f. BOT. sweet potato, yam; ARG., COLL. shyness, bashfulness; P. RICO, URUG., COLL. fool, dolt.

ba·ta·ta·zo m. AMER. lucky shot, fluke ♦ **dar b.** *(ganar los caballos)* to win by an upset; *(tener chiripa)* to make a lucky shot *or* fluke (in billiards).

ba·te m. SPORT. bat; CUBA, FIG. busybody.

ba·te·a f. *(bandeja)* painted *or* wicker tray; *(artesilla)* deep trough; MARIT. scow, punt; RAIL. *(plataforma)* flatcar, platform car; AMER. *(herrada)* pail, bucket; *(tina de lavar)* washing trough, washtub.

ba·te·a·dor, –do·ra m.f. SPORT. batter, hitter.

ba·te·ar tr. SPORT. to bat, hit.

ba·tel m. MARIT. boat, vessel.

ba·te·le·ro, –ra m. boatman —f. boatwoman.

ba·te·rí·a f. ELEC., MIL. battery; *(bombardeo)* battering; THEAT. *(luces)* footlights; MUS. *(percusión)* drums, percussion; *(músico)* drummer, percussionist ♦ **b. de cocina** kitchen utensils • **dar b. a** MEX. to make trouble for.

ba·tey m. AMER., AGR. *(comunidad)* sugar-mill town; CUBA machinery in a sugar mill *or* refinery.

ba·ti·bo·rri·llo *or* **ba·ti·bu·rri·llo** m. hodgepodge.

ba·ti·co·la f. *(correa)* crupper; *(taparrabo)* loin cloth.

ba·ti·da I. f. *(cacería)* beat, beating (in a hunt); *(registro)* search; ARG., PERU police raid II. adj. see **batido, –da.**

ba·ti·de·ra f. *(pala)* beater, paddle (for mixing concrete); *(cuchilla)* honeycomb cutter.

ba·ti·de·ro m. *(golpeo continuo)* banging, continual beating *or* striking; *(lugar)* beating *or* banging place; *(terreno)* uneven *or* rutty ground ♦ **batideros** MARIT. washboard.

ba·ti·do, –da I. past part. see **batir** II. adj. TEX. shot, chatoyant; *(andado)* beaten, well-trodden III. m. *(acción)* beating; CUL. batter; *(bebida)* shake ♦ **b. de leche** milkshake —f. see **batida.**

ba·ti·dor, –do·ra I. adj. beating II. m. CUL. beater, whisk; *(peine)* large-toothed comb; MIL. scout, reconnoiterer; HUNT. *(el que levanta la caza)* beater; GUAT. pot (for grinding chocolate) —f. AMER., CUL. mixing bowl ♦ **b. de oro** gold beater.

ba·tien·te I. adj. beating II. m. CONSTR. *(marco)* jamb; *(hoja de puerta)* leaf (of a door); *(lugar de costa)* surf-beaten spot, place where waves break; MUS. damper; MARIT. vertical frame of a gun port.

ba·ti·fon·do m. ARG., COLL. rumpus, uproar.

ba·ti·ho·ja m. gold *or* silver beater.

ba·ti·me·trí·a f. MARIT. bathymetry.

ba·tin·tín m. MUS. gong.

ba·tir tr. *(golpear)* to beat, hit; *(derribar)* to demolish, knock down; *(martillar)* to beat, hammer; *(revolver)* to beat, mix; *(agitar)* to beat, flap; to beat on <*el sol bate la pared* the sun beats on the wall>; *(peinar)* to comb, tease; *(registrar)* to scour, search <*los hombres batían el campo* the men searched the countryside>; *(vencer)* to beat, defeat; *(superar)* to beat, outdo <*el chico batió el récord* the boy beat the record>; NUMIS. to mint; CHILE, GUAT., PERU to rinse (clothes); ARG., COLL. to denounce, turn in ♦ **b. el vuelo** FIG. to scram, beat it • **b. palmas** to clap hands • **b. tiendas** MIL. to break camp —intr. *(el corazón)* to beat violently, pound —reflex. to fight ♦ **batirse a duelo** to fight a duel • **batirse en retirada** to beat a retreat.

ba·tis·ca·fo m. MARIT. bathyscaph.

ba·tis·ta f. TEX. batiste, fine cambric.

ba·to m. COLL. *(rústico)* yokel, bumpkin; *(tonto)* simpleton, dimwit; *(padre)* old man, pop; ORNITH. jabiru.

ba·to·lo·gí·a f. RHET. needless repetition.

ba·tra·cio, –cia ZOOL. I. adj. batrachian, amphibian II. m. batrachian.

ba·tu·da f. SPORT. series of jumps on a springboard *or* trampoline.

ba·tu·que m. ARG. uproar, din <*meter b.* to cause an uproar>.

ba·tu·que·ar tr. AMER. *(batir)* to shake, shake up; GUAT. to scold, reprimand.

ba·tu·rri·llo m. hodgepodge, mishmash.

ba·tu·ta f. MUS. baton ♦ **llevar la b.** FIG., COLL. to be the boss.

ba·úl m. *(cofre)* coffer, chest; *(maleta)* trunk, case; AUTO. trunk; FIG., COLL. *(barriga)* paunch, belly <*llenar el b.* to fill one's belly>.

bau·prés m. MARIT. bowsprit.

bau·sa f. PERU, COLL. laziness, idleness.

bau·sán, –sa·na I. m.f. *(maniquí)* mannequin, dummy; FIG. *(necio)* dummy, blockhead II. adj. lazy, idle.

bau·ti·cé, bautice see **bautizar.**

bau·tis·mal adj. baptismal.

bau·tis·mo m. RELIG. baptism, christening; FIG. *(iniciación)* baptism, initiation ♦ **b. de aire** AVIA. first flight • **b. de fuego** MIL. first combat • **romperle el b. a uno** FIG., COLL. to beat someone up, smash someone's head in.

bau·tis·ta m.f. *(persona que bautiza)* baptizer; RELIG. Baptist ♦ **El Bautista** Saint John the Baptist.

bau·tis·te·rio m. RELIG. baptistry, baptistery.

bau·ti·zar §04 tr. RELIG. to baptize, christen; FIG., COLL. *(nombrar)* to name, call <*b. una calle* to name a street>; *(apodar)* to nickname; *(mezclar con agua)* to water (down), dilute <*vino bautizado* watered-down wine>; *(mojar)* to drench, soak (as a prank).

bau·ti·zo m. RELIG. *(bautismo)* baptism, christening; *(fiesta)* christening party.

bau·xi·ta f. MIN. bauxite.

bá·va·ro, –ra adj. & m.f. Bavarian.

Ba·vie·ra f. Bavaria.

ba·ya·de·ra f. female dancer and singer of India.

ba·yal¹ adj. TEX. cambric-like; BOT. long-stem (flax).

ba·yal² m. lever used to lift millstones.

ba·ye·ta f. TEX. baize, flannel; *(para fregar)* floor cloth; COL. weakling.

ba·yo, –ya I. adj. bay II. m. *(caballo)* bay (horse) ENTOM. silkworm butterfly; CHILE bier —f. BOT. berry; CUBA mussel; CHILE chicha (liquor).

ba·yo·ne·ta f. ARM. bayonet; AMER., BOT. yucca.

ba·yo·ne·ta·zo m. ARM. *(golpe)* bayonet thrust; *(herida)* bayonet wound.

ba·za I. f. *(en los naipes)* trick (in cards) FIG. *(oportunidad)* opportunity, stroke of luck ♦ **hacer b.** to succeed • **meter b.** FIG., COLL. to butt in • **no dejar meter b. a nadie** not to let anyone get a word in edgewise II. adj. see **bazo, –za.**

ba·zar m. bazaar, marketplace.

ba·zo, –za I. adj. yellowish-brown II. m. ANAT. spleen —f. see **baza.**

ba·zo·fia f. *(sobras)* leftovers, table scraps; FIG. *(mala comida)* slop, swill; *(suciedad)* filth, rubbish.

ba·zu·ca m. ARM. bazooka.

ba·zu·car §70 *or* **ba·zu·que·ar** tr. to shake (a liquid).

be f. bee (the letter b) ♦ **b. por b.** down to the last detail • **tener las tres bes** to have everything, be perfect.

be·a·gle m. ZOOL. beagle.

be·a·ta I. f. *(religiosa)* lay sister; *(piadosa)* devout woman; COLL. *(santurrona)* sanctimonious woman, prude II. adj. see **beato, –ta.**

be·a·te·rí·a f. sanctimoniousness, false piety.

be·a·ti·fi·ca·ción f. beatification.

be·a·ti·fi·car §70 tr. *(venerar)* to beatify, bless; C. AMER. to give extreme unction *or* last rites to.

be·a·tí·fi·co, –ca adj. beatific, beatifical.

be·a·ti·tud f. *(bienaventuranza)* beatitude, blessedness; COLL. *(alegría)* happiness, bliss.

be·a·to, –ta I. adj. *(feliz)* blissful, joyful; *(beatificado)* beatified, blessed; *(piadoso)* devout, pious; COLL. *(santurrón)* sanctimonious, prudish II. m. *(religioso)* lay brother; *(piadoso)* devout man; COLL. *(santurrón)* sanctimonious man, prude —f. see **beata.**

be·bé m. *(nene)* baby; SL. *(muñeca)* babe, doll.

be·be·de·ro, –ra I. adj. drinkable, potable II. m. *(abrevadero)* watering place, water trough; *(de aves)* birdbath; *(pico de vasija)* lip, spout; PERU refreshment stand —f. MEX. drinking bout, bender.

be·be·di·zo, –za I. adj. drinkable II. m. *(poción medicinal)* medicinal potion; *(filtro mágico)* magic philter; *(veneno)* poison.

be·be·dor, –do·ra I. adj. drinking II. m.f. *(que bebe)* drinker; *(borracho)* heavy drinker, boozer.

be·ber tr. *(libar)* to drink; FIG. *(absorber)* to drink in, imbibe ♦ **b. a sorbos** to sip • **b. a tragos** to gulp (down) • **b. los vientos por (alguien)** FIG. to long *or* yearn for (someone) —intr. to drink (too much), booze ♦ **b. a la salud de** to toast, drink to • **b. como una cuba** *or* **esponja** FIG., COLL. to drink like a fish.

be·bi·ble adj. COLL. drinkable.

be·bi·da I. f. *(líquido)* drink, beverage; *(vicio)* drink, drinking; MEX. potion, concoction ♦ **b. blanca** ARG. liquor, spirits • **tener mala b.** to get mean when drinking • **darse a la b.** to take to drink II. adj. see **bebido, –da.**

be·bi·do, –da I. past part. see **beber** II. adj. tipsy, drunk III. f. see **bebida.**

be·bis·tra·jo m. COLL. concoction, brew.

be·bo·rro·te·ar intr. COLL. to sip, tipple.

be·ca f. EDUC. *(embozo)* sash, hood; *(colegiatura)* grant, scholarship, fellowship; *(pensión)* living allowance, room and board; RELIG. tippet, hood (of a gown).

be·ca·rio, –ria m.f. scholarship student, fellow.

be·ce·rro, –ra m. ZOOL. yearling bull, bull calf; *(piel)* calfskin; RELIG. register, cartulary —f. ZOOL. heifer, yearling calf; BOT. snapdragon ♦ **b. marino** ZOOL. seal, sea calf • **b. de oro** FIG. wealth, golden calf.

be·cua·dro m. MUS. natural sign.

be·cha·mel f. CUL. white *or* béchamel sauce.

be·del m. EDUC. proctor.

be·dui·no, –na adj. & m.f. Bedouin, Beduin.

be·fa I. f. mockery, jeering II. adj. see **befo, –fa.**

be·fo, –fa I. adj. *(de labio grueso)* thick-lipped; *(zambo)* knock-kneed II. m. thick lower lip, chops (of an animal) —f. see **befa.**

be·go·nia f. BOT. begonia.

be·he·trí·a f. HIST. free town whose inhabitants could choose their own master; FIG. *(confusión)* confusion, bedlam.

Bei·rut Beirut.

béis·bol m. SPORT. baseball.

be·ju·co m. BOT. rattan.

bel m. bel (measure of sound intensity).

Bel·ce·bú m. RELIG. Beelzebub.

bel·dad f. *(belleza)* beauty; *(mujer)* beauty, belle.

be·lén m. FIG. *(nacimiento)* crèche, nativity scene; COLL. *(confusión)* confusion, bedlam ♦ **Belén** Bethlehem • **estar en b.** FIG. to daydream • **meterse en belenes** FIG., COLL. to get mixed up in trouble.

bel·fo, –fa I. adj. *(de labio grueso)* thick-lipped II. m. thick lower lip, chops (of a horse).

bel·ga adj. & m.f. Belgian.

Bél·gi·ca f. Belgium.

Bel·gra·do Belgrade.

Be·li·ce Belize.

be·li·cis·mo m. warmongering, militarism.

be·li·cis·ta I. adj. warmongering, militaristic II. m.f. warmonger, militarist.

bé·li·co, –ca adj. MIL. bellicose, warlike, martial.

be·li·co·si·dad f. MIL. bellicosity.

be·li·co·so, –sa adj. MIL. bellicose, warlike; FIG. *(agresivo)* aggressive, quarrelsome.

be·li·ge·ran·cia f. belligerency.

be·li·ge·ran·te adj. & m. belligerent.

be·lio m. PHYS. bel.

be·li·tre COLL. I. adj. sly, roguish II. m.f. rascal, rogue.

be·lla·men·te adv. knavishly, roguishly.

be·lla·co, –ca I. adj. *(astuto)* sly, cunning; *(pícaro)* knavish, roguish; ARG., MEX., URUG. balky (said of horses); ECUAD., PAN. brave II. m.f. rascal, rogue.

be·lla·men·te adv. beautifully, gracefully.

be·lla·que·ar intr. *(trampear)* to cheat, trick; ARG., BOL., URUG. *(un caballo)* to buck, rear; ARG., URUG., FIG. *(resistir)* to balk, resist.

be·lla·que·rí·a f. *(astucia)* slyness, cunning; *(maldad)* knavishness, roguishness; *(trampa)* sly trick.

be·lle·za f. *(hermosura)* beauty; *(mujer)* beauty, beautiful woman ♦ **decir bellezas** FIG. to speak eloquently *or* beautifully.

be·llo, –lla adj. *(hermoso)* beautiful, lovely; FIG. *(bueno)* fine, noble ♦ **bellas artes** fine arts.

be·llo·ta f. BOT. acorn; *(capullo del clavel)* carnation bud; *(borla)* tassel, pompom.

be·llo·te·ar intr. to feed on acorns.

be·llo·te·ro, –ra m.f. *(cogedor)* acorn gatherer; *(vendedor)* acorn seller; *(cosecha)* acorn harvest time —f. *(cosecha de bellotas)* acorn harvest.

bem·ba f. *or* **bem·bo** m. AMER. *(hocico)* muzzle, snout; DEROG. thick lips; VEN. fool, simpleton.

bem·bón, –bo·na *or* **bem·bu·do, –da** adj. AMER., DEROG. thick-lipped.

be·mol MUS. m. & adj. flat ♦ **doble b.** double flat • **tener muchos bemoles** COLL. to be a tough job.

be·mo·la·do, –da adj. MUS. flatted.

ben·ci·na f. CHEM. benzine, benzin.

ben·de·cir §11 tr. RELIG. to bless; *(consagrar)* to consecrate; *(alabar)* to praise, extol; FIG. *(agradecer)* to bless, thank ♦ **b. la comida** *or* **la mesa** to say grace.

ben·di·ción f. blessing; RELIG. benediction ♦ **b. de la mesa** grace • **bendiciones nupciales** wedding ceremony • **echar la b. a** *(bendecir)* to give one's blessing to; FIG., COLL. *(renunciar)* to give up on, renounce • **ser una b.** FIG., COLL. to be marvelous, be a blessing.

ben·di·ga, bendigo see **bendecir.**

ben·di·je·ra, bendijo see **bendecir.**

ben·di·to, –ta I. past part. see **bendecir** II. adj. *(santo)* holy, blessed; *(dichoso)* fortunate, lucky; COLL. *(tonto)* simple, simple-minded ♦ **como el pan b.** FIG. like hot cakes III. m.f. *(santo)* saint; *(bonachón)* good soul; COLL. *(tonto)* simpleton, fool —m. *(oración)* prayer; AMER. *(nicho)* niche; *(toldo)* canopy; VEN. *(cura)* local priest.

be·ne·dic·ti·no, –na I. adj. Benedictine II. m.f. RELIG. Benedictine —m. *(licor)* Benedictine (liqueur).

be·ne·fac·tor, –to·ra I. adj. beneficent II. m. benefactor —f. benefactress.

be·ne·fi·cen·cia f. *(benevolencia)* beneficence, benevolence (a charitable act); *(asistencia social)* welfare, public assistance.

be·ne·fi·cia·do, –da I. past part. see **beneficiar** II. m.f. beneficiary.

be·ne·fi·cia·dor, –do·ra I. adj. benefiting II. m.f. benefactor.

be·ne·fi·ciar tr. *(mejorar)* to benefit; AGR. to cultivate <**b. la tierra** to cultivate the land>; MIN. *(extraer)* to develop *or* work (a mine); *(tratar)* to smelt, treat; COM. to sell at a discount; AMER. to slaughter (cattle for public sale); C. AMER., AGR. to process agricultural products; GUAT., FIG. to execute, shoot II. intr. to be of benefit III. reflex. to profit ♦ **beneficiarse de** to take advantage of, profit by *or* from.

be·ne·fi·cia·rio, –ria I. adj. benefiting, benefited II. m.f.

beneficiary ♦ **b. de cheque** COM. payee ♦ **b. de patente** COM. patentee.

be·ne·fi·cio m. *(favor)* benefit, advantage; *(ganancia)* profit, gain; AGR. *(cultivo)* cultivation; MIN. *(desarrollo)* working, development (of a mine); *(tratamiento)* smelting, treatment; THEAT. benefit (performance); RELIG. benefice; AMER. slaughter (of cattle for public sale); C. AMER., AGR. processing plant, refinery <*b. de azúcar* sugar refinery>; CHILE fertilizer ♦ **a b. de** for the benefit of • **a b. de inventario** LAW with reservations • **en b. propio** in one's own interest, for one's own benefit • **no tener oficio ni b.** to be without means.

be·ne·fi·cio·so, –sa adj. beneficial, advantageous.

be·né·fi·co, –ca adj. *(caritativo)* beneficent, charitable; *(provechoso)* beneficial.

be·ne·mé·ri·to, –ta adj. meritorious, worthy ♦ **La Benemérita** SP. the Spanish Civil Guard.

be·ne·plá·ci·to m. approval, consent.

be·ne·vo·len·cia f. benevolence, kindness.

be·né·vo·lo, –la adj. benevolent, kind.

ben·ga·la f. *(caña)* cane.

Ben·ga·la f. Bengal ♦ **luz de B.** sparkler, flare.

ben·ga·lí adj. & m.f. Bengalese —m. *(idioma)* Bengali (language of Bengal).

be·nig·ni·dad f. benignity.

be·nig·no, –na adj. benign.

Be·nin Benin.

be·ni·nés, –ne·sa adj. & m.f. Beninese.

ben·ja·mín m. youngest son, baby of the family.

ben·juí m. benzoin, benjamin (aromatic resin).

ben·zo·a·to m. CHEM. benzoate.

be·o·dez f. [pl. **-de·ces**] drunkenness, inebriation.

be·o·do, –da I. adj. drunk, inebriated II. m.f. drunk, drunkard.

be·que m. MARIT. *(de proa)* figurehead; *(retrete)* crew's latrines; AMER. toilet, head.

ber·be·re·cho m. ICHTH. cockle.

Ber·be·rí·a f. Barbary.

be·ré·ber adj. & m.f. Berber.

be·ren·je·na f. BOT. eggplant.

ber·ga·mo·ta f. BOT. bergamot.

ber·gan·te m. COLL. scoundrel, rascal.

ber·gan·tín m. MARIT. brig; DOM. REP., P. RICO black eye.

be·ri·lio m. CHEM. beryllium.

ber·ke·lio m. CHEM. berkelium.

Ber·lín m. Berlin.

ber·li·na f. *(coche)* berlin; *(departamento)* closed compartment (of train or stagecoach) ♦ **ponerle a alguien en b.** FIG. to put someone in a ridiculous position.

ber·li·nés, –ne·sa I. adj. of Berlin II. m.f. Berliner.

ber·lin·ga f. SP. clothesline pole; MARIT. round timber.

ber·ma f. MIL. berm.

ber·me·je·ar intr. *(ser bermejo)* to be reddish; *(tirar a bermejo)* to turn reddish.

ber·me·jo, –ja adj. bright red.

ber·me·llón m. vermilion.

ber·mu·da f. BOT. Bermuda grass ♦ **bermudas** Bermuda shorts.

Ber·mu·das f. Bermuda.

ber·nar·do, –da adj. & m.f. RELIG. Bernardine.

ber·ne·gal m. *(taza)* cup with scalloped edge; VEN. clay jug.

ber·nia f. *(tejido)* rough woolen cloth; *(capa)* rough woolen cape —m.f. HOND. loafer, idler.

be·rra f. BOT. watercress.

be·rre·ar intr. *(balar)* to bleat; *(gritar)* to howl, scream <*el nene berreaba por horas* the baby screamed for hours>; COLL. *(cantar)* to sing off-key.

be·rre·o m. temper tantrum, rage.

be·rri·do m. *(balido)* bleat; FIG. *(chillido)* shriek.

be·rrín m. COLL. hothead.

be·rrin·che m. COLL. rage, tantrum; ECUAD. argument, dispute.

be·rri·zal m. watercress bed.

be·rro m. BOT. watercress.

be·rro·cal m. craggy *or* rocky place.

be·rrue·co m. *(roca)* granite rock; *(perla)* baroque pearl; MED. tumor of the eye.

ber·za f. BOT. cabbage ♦ **mezclar berzas con capachos** FIG., COLL. to bring in irrelevant details.

be·sa·na f. AGR. *(espacio entre surcos)* space between furrows; *(primer surco)* first furrow; *(medida)* Catalonian agrarian measurement.

be·sar tr. to kiss; FIG., COLL. *(rozar)* to graze, touch —reflex. to kiss one another.

be·so m. *(acción de besar)* kiss; FIG. *(roce)* brush, glance ♦ **b. de Judas** FIG. kiss of Judas, deceitful kiss • **tirar un b.** to blow a kiss.

bes·tia I. f. ZOOL. animal, beast —m.f. FIG., COLL. *(bruto)* beast, brute; *(imbécil)* idiot, blockhead ♦ **b. de carga** pack animal • **b. de carga** beast of burden • **gran b.** ZOOL. tapir II. adj. FIG., COLL. stupid, ignorant.

bes·tia·je m. beasts of burden.

bes·tial adj. *(brutal)* bestial, beastly; COLL. *(magnífico)* terrific, fabulous; *(enorme)* huge, gigantic.

bes·tia·li·dad f. *(brutalidad)* beastliness, bestiality; COLL. *(estupidez)* stupidity, foolishness; *(gran cantidad)* a lot <*pagué una b. por este coche* I paid a lot for this car> ♦ **¡qué b.!** how awful!

bes·tia·li·zar §04 tr. to bestialize, brutalize —reflex. to become bestialized.

be·su·ca·dor, –do·ra COLL. I. adj. fond of kissing II. m.f. kisser.

be·su·car §70 tr. var. of **besuquear**.

be·su·cón, –co·na adj. & m.f. COLL. var. of **besucador, –dora**.

be·su·go m. ICHTH. sea bream; FIG., COLL. *(idiota)* idiot, twerp.

be·su·que·ar tr. COLL. smooch, lavish kisses on.

be·su·que·o m. COLL. smooching, repeated kissing.

be·ta·rra·ga *or* **be·ta·rra·ta** f. BOT. beet.

bet·le·mi·ta adj. & m.f. Bethlehemite.

be·tún m. *(brea)* bitumen, tar, pitch; *(bola)* shoe polish; CONSTR. *(zulaque)* lute, mastic; CHILE, CUL. icing ♦ **b. de Judea** asphalt.

be·tu·nar *or* **be·tu·ne·ar** tr. CUBA, ECUAD. *(pulir)* to shine, polish; *(asfaltar)* to tar, asphalt.

be·za·ar *or* **be·zar** m. MED. bezoar.

be·zo m. *(belfo)* thick lip; *(de una herida)* proud flesh.

be·zo·á·ri·co m. antidote.

be·zu·do, –da adj. thick-lipped.

Bhu·tán Bhutan.

bhu·ta·nés, –ne·sa adj. & m.f. Bhutanese.

bian·gu·lar adj. biangular.

bia·tó·mi·co, –ca adj. CHEM. diatomic.

bia·za f. leather saddlebag.

bi·bá·si·co, –ca adj. CHEM. bibasic, dibasic.

bi·be·rón m. baby bottle.

Bi·blia f. Bible ♦ **la b. en pasta** COLL. too much, a lot.

bí·bli·co, –ca adj. Biblical, biblical.

bi·blió·fi·lo, –la m.f. bibliophile, booklover.

bi·blio·gra·fí·a f. bibliography.

bi·blio·grá·fi·co, –ca adj. bibliographic, bibliographical.

bi·blió·gra·fo, –fa m.f. bibliographer.

bi·blio·lo·gí·a f. bibliology (historical and technical study of the book).

bi·blio·ma·ní·a f. bibliomania.

bi·blió·ma·no, –na m.f. bibliomaniac, bibliomane.

bi·blio·te·ca f. library; AMER. *(estantes)* bookcase, bookshelves ♦ **b. circulante** mobile library. • **b. de consulta** reference library • **b. de préstamo** lending library

bi·blio·te·ca·rio, –ria m.f. librarian.

bi·car·bo·na·ta·do, –da adj. containing bicarbonate.

bi·car·bo·na·to m. CHEM. bicarbonate ♦ **b. de sodio** *or* **de sosa** sodium bicarbonate, bicarbonate of soda; CUL. baking soda.

bi·cé·fa·lo, –la adj. bicephalic, bicephalous.

bi·cen·te·na·rio m. bicentennial, bicentenary.

bí·ceps m. [pl. **-ceps**] ANAT. biceps.

bi·ci f. COLL. bike.

bi·ci·cle·ta f. bicycle ♦ **andar** *or* **ir en b.** to go by bicycle • **montar en b.** to bicycle, ride a bicycle.

bi·ci·clo m. velocipede.

bi·cí·pi·te adj. bicipital.

bi·co·ca f. COLL. trifle, trinket; *(ganga)* bargain; ARG.,

CHILE skullcap; CHILE slap (on the head) ♦ **por una b.** for a song.

bi·co·lor adj. bicolor, two-tone.

bi·cón·ca·vo, –va adj. OPT. biconcave.

bi·con·ve·xo, –xa adj. OPT. biconvex.

bi·cor·ne adj. bicorn.

bi·cor·nio m. two-cornered hat.

bi·cos m.pl. gold trimmings (on caps).

bi·cro·má·ti·co, –ca adj. dichromatic, two-color.

bi·cro·mí·a f. two-color print.

bi·cús·pi·de adj. bicuspid.

bi·che·ro m. MARIT. boat hook.

bi·cho m. ENTOM. bug, insect; *(animal)* beast, animal; *(toro)* bull; FIG. *(fenómeno)* freak, odd person; PERU spite, envy; C. AMER. brat, imp ♦ **de puro b.** S. AMER. out of pure spite • **mal b.** FIG. villain, bad character • **todo b. viviente** COLL. every living creature, everyone.

bi·cho·co, –ca adj. S. AMER. old, decrepit (horse).

bi·dé m. bidet.

bi·den·te I. adj. bidentate II. m. two-pronged spade.

bi·dón m. large can, drum.

bie·la f. MECH. connecting rod, pitman.

biel·dar tr. AGR. to winnow.

biel·do m. AGR. winnowing fork.

Bie·lo·rru·sia f. Byelorussia.

bie·lo·rru·so, –sa adj. & m.f. Byelorussian.

bien §G29 I. m. good, goodness <*el b. y el mal* good and evil>; *(provecho)* good, benefit <*el b. común* the public good> ♦ **bienes** wealth, property, goods • **bienes de consumo** consumer goods • **bienes de dominio público** public property • **bienes dotales** dowry • **bienes gananciales** community property (in a marriage) • **bienes inmuebles** *or* **raíces** real estate • **bienes muebles** chattels, personal property • **bienes patrimoniales** capital assets • **bienes relictos** estate, inheritance • **bienes semovientes** livestock • **en b. de** for the good *or* benefit of • **hacer (el) b.** to do good II. adv. well <*las cosas van b.* things are going well>; *(apropiadamente)* well <*b. hablado* well-spoken>; *(sano)* well <*no me siento b.* I don't feel well>; *(justamente)* right, correctly <*ella contestó b.* she answered correctly>; *(con éxito)* successfully <*lo terminaron b.* they completed it successfully>; *(de buena gana)* willingly, readily <*b. lo haríamos* we would do it willingly>; *(sin dificultad)* easily <*b. se puede ver la diferencia* one can easily see the difference>; *(bastante)* quite, very <*el discurso era b. interesante* the speech was quite interesting>; *(sí)* okay <*¿vienes conmigo? b., iré contigo* are you coming with me? okay, I will go with you> ♦ **ahora b.** (well) now • **bien . . . bien** either <*te lo enviaré b. por correo o b. por mensajero* I will send it to you either by mail or by messenger> • **b. que** *or* **si b.** although <*él pagó la cuenta, si b. acordamos que nos repartiríamos los gastos* he paid the bill although we had agreed that we would share the expenses> • **de b. en mejor** better and better • **hacer b. en** to do well to, to be right in • **más b.** rather <*no voy a escribirlo ahora; más b. lo haré mañana* I am not going to write it now; rather I will do it tomorrow> • **no b.** just as, as soon as <*no b. llegaron, comenzó a llover* just as they arrived it began to rain> • **o b.** or else, otherwise <*lo pago en efectivo o b. lo cargas a mi cuenta* I will pay in cash or else you will charge it to my account> • **por b.** willingly • **pues b.** then, well now • **tener a b.** to be good enough to, see fit to • **y b.** well then III. adj. well-to-do <*gente b.* well-to-do people>.

bie·nal adj. & f. biennial.

bie·nan·dan·te adj. happy, fortunate.

bie·nan·dan·za f. good fortune, prosperity.

bie·na·ven·tu·ra·do, –da I. adj. *(afortunado)* fortunate, lucky; *(inocente)* simple, naive; RELIG. blessed II. m.f. *(afortunado)* fortunate *or* lucky person; *(inocente)* simpleton, naive person; RELIG. blessed person.

bie·na·ven·tu·ran·za f. RELIG. beatific vision; *(felicidad)* happiness, well-being ♦ **bienaventuranzas** RELIG. Beatitudes.

bie·nes·tar m. *(vida holgada)* well-being, welfare; *(comodidad)* comfort.

bien·ha·bla·do, –da adj. well-spoken, courteous.

bien·ha·da·do, –da adj. lucky, fortunate.

bien·he·chor, –cho·ra I. adj. beneficent, beneficial II. m. benefactor —f. benefactress.

bien·in·ten·cio·na·do, –da I. adj. well-meaning II. m.f. well-meaning person.

bie·nio m. biennium.

bien·man·da·do, –da adj. obedient, well-behaved.

bien·que·ren·cia f. *or* **bien·que·rer** m. good will, esteem.

bien·que·rer §55 tr. to like, to be fond of.

bien·quis·tar tr. to reconcile, conciliate —reflex. to become reconciled, to make up (with someone).

bien·ve·ni·da f. safe arrival; *(salutación)* welcome, greeting ♦ **dar la b.** to welcome.

bien·vi·vir intr. *(vivir con holgura)* to live in ease; *(vivir honestamente)* to live an honest life.

biés m. SEW. bias; *(tira de tela)* bias, binding ♦ **al b.** SEW. on the bias.

bi·fá·si·co, –ca adj. ELEC. diphase, diphasic.

bi·fe m. AMER. steak, beefsteak; ARG., URUG., COLL. slap.

bí·fe·ro, –ra adj. BOT. bearing fruit twice a year.

bí·fi·do, –da adj. BOT. bifid.

bi·fo·cal adj. OPT. bifocal.

bi·for·me adj. biform.

bí·fo·ro, –ra adj. having two doors *or* entrances.

bi·fron·te adj. having two faces.

bif·tec m. [pl. **-tecs**] steak, beefsteak.

bi·fur·ca·ción f. *(desvío)* bifurcation, branch; *(de un camino)* fork; *(en ferrocarriles)* junction.

bi·fur·ca·do, –da. I. past part. see **bifurcarse** II. adj. forked, bifurcate.

bi·fur·car·se §70 reflex. *(desviarse)* to bifurcate, branch (off); *(dividirse un camino)* to fork.

bi·ga·mia f. bigamy.

bí·ga·mo, –ma I. adj. bigamous II. m.f. bigamist.

bi·gar·de·ar intr. COLL. to wander, roam.

bi·gar·do, –da *or* **bi·gar·dón, –do·na** FIG. I. adj. *(vago)* idle, vagrant; *(libertino)* libertine, licentious II. m.f. *(vago)* idler, loafer; *(libertino)* libertine.

bi·ga·rra·do, –da adj. multicolored, motley.

bi·gor·nia f. two-beaked anvil.

bi·go·te m. mustache; PRINT. tapered dash; MIN. slag tap; MEX. croquette ♦ **b. retorcido** handlebar mustache • **bigotes** whiskers • **bigotes de foca** walrus mustache • **tener bigotes** *or* **ser hombre de bigotes** FIG., COLL. to be firm *or* stern • **ser** *or* **estar de bigotes** to be terrific.

bi·go·te·ra f. *(que cubre los bigotes)* mustache cover; FIG. *(bocera en el labio)* mustache (after drinking); *(cintas)* ribbon ornament; *(en los coches)* folding seat; *(del calzado)* shoe tap; *(compás)* bow compass.

bi·go·tu·do, –da adj. mustached, mustachioed.

bi·gu·dí m. hair curler.

bi·ja f. BOT. annatto (tree and fruit); *(tintura)* dye.

bi·ki·ni m. bikini.

bi·la·bia·do, –da adj. BOT. bilabiate.

bi·la·bial PHONET. adj. & f. bilabial.

bi·la·te·ral adj. bilateral.

bil·ba·í·no, –na I. adj. of Bilbao II. m.f. native of Bilbao.

Bil·ba·o Bilbao.

bi·liar *or* **bi·lia·rio, –ria** adj. biliary.

bi·lin·güe adj. bilingual.

bi·lin·güis·mo m. bilingualism.

bi·lio·so, –sa adj. MED. bilious; FIG. *(desabrido)* ill-tempered, bilious.

bi·lis f. [pl. **-lis**] MED. bile ♦ **descargar la b.** FIG. to vent one's spleen • **exaltársele a uno la b.** FIG. to get annoyed *or* angry.

bi·lo·bu·la·do, –da adj. bilobate.

bi·lo·ca·ción f. THEOL. bilocation.

bi·lo·car·se §70 reflex. THEOL. to be in two places at once; ARG., COLL. to go crazy.

bi·llar m. *(juego)* billiards; *(mesa)* billiard table; *(lugar)* billiard room ♦ **b. automático** *or* **romano** pinball • **b. ruso** snooker.

bi·lle·te m. *(boleto)* ticket <*b. de tren* train ticket>; *(de lotería)* lottery ticket; *(papel moneda)* bill <*un b. de cinco dólares* a five-dollar bill>; *(carta)* note, short letter ♦ **b. de ida** one-way ticket • **b. de ida y vuelta** round-trip ticket • **b. kilométrico** mileage ticket • **b. de vuelta** return ticket • **medio b.** half fare.

bi·lle·te·ra f. *or* **bi·lle·te·ro** m. *(cartera)* wallet, billfold; MEX., CARIB. lottery ticket vendor.
bi·llón m. trillion (U.S.), billion (G.B.).
bi·llo·né·si·mo, –ma adj. & m. trillionth (U.S.), billionth (G.B.).
bi·men·sual adj. bimonthly, twice a month.
bi·mes·tral adj. bimonthly, bimestrial.
bi·mes·tre I. adj. bimonthly, bimestrial II. m. two-month period; *(pago)* bimonthly payment.
bi·me·ta·lis·mo m. ECON. bimetallism.
bi·mo·tor I. adj. twin-engine II. m. twin-engine plane.
bi·na f. AGR. second plowing *or* hoeing.
bi·na·dor, –do·ra m.f. AGR. *(persona que bina)* digger, plower; *(herramienta)* hoe.
bi·nar tr. AGR. to plow *or* hoe a second time —intr. RELIG. to celebrate two masses on the same day (said of a priest).
bi·na·rio, –ria adj. binary.
bin·cha f. var. of **vincha**.
bin·gue·ro, –ra I. adj. fond of bingo II. m.f. bingo caller.
bi·no·cu·lar adj. binocular.
bi·nó·cu·lo m. pince-nez.
bi·no·mio m. MATH. binomial ♦ **b. de Newton** MATH. binomial theorem.
bio·di·ná·mi·ca f. biodynamics.
bio·fí·si·ca f. biophysics.
bio·gra·fí·a f. biography.
bio·gra·fiar §30 tr. to write a biography of.
bio·grá·fi·co, –ca adj. biographic, biographical.
bió·gra·fo, –fa m.f. biographer.
bio·lo·gí·a f. biology.
bio·ló·gi·co, –ca adj. biologic, biological.
bió·lo·go, –ga m.f. biologist.
bio·ma·sa f. BIOL. biomass.
biom·bo m. folding screen.
bio·me·cá·ni·ca f. biomechanics.
biop·sia f. MED. biopsy.
bio·quí·mi·co, –ca I. adj. biochemical II. m.f. biochemist —f. biochemistry.
bios·fe·ra f. biosphere.
bio·sín·te·sis f. BIOCHEM. biosynthesis.
bió·xi·do m. CHEM. dioxide ♦ **b. de carbono** CHEM. carbon dioxide.
bi·par·ti·dis·mo m. POL. two-party system.
bi·par·ti·dis·ta adj. POL. bipartisan, two-party <*sistema b.* two-party system>.
bi·par·ti·to, –ta *or* **bi·par·ti·do, –da** adj. bipartite <*un tratado b.* a bipartite treaty>.
bí·pe·de *or* **bí·pe·do, –da** ZOOL. I. adj. biped, bipedal II. m. biped.
bi·pla·no m. AVIA. biplane.
bi·po·lar adj. bipolar.
bi·rim·ba·o m. MUS. jew's-harp.
bir·lar tr. FIG., COLL. *(derribar)* to kill *or* knock down with one blow; *(robar)* to steal, swipe.
bir·lo·cha f. kite (toy).
bir·lo·cho m. four-wheeled carriage.
Bir·ma·nia f. Burma.
bir·ma·no, –na adj. & m.f. Burmese, Burman —m. *(idioma)* Burmese.
bi·rre·frin·gen·te adj. PHYS. birefringent.
bi·rre·ta f. biretta.
bi·rre·te m. RELIG. biretta; *(de un magistrado)* cap; *(bonete)* cap, bonnet.
bi·rria f. COLL. *(adefesio)* grotesque *or* ridiculous thing; COL. grudge, aversion ♦ **jugar de b.** COL. to play half-heartedly.
bis adv. MUS., PRINT. bis, again; *(dirección)* (number) A <*calle Madero, 31 bis* Madero St., number 31A>.
bi·sa·bue·lo, –la m.f. great-grandparent —m. great-grandfather —f. great-grandmother.
bi·sa·gra f. hinge.
bi·sa·nuo, –nua adj. BOT. biennial.
bis·bi·sar tr. COLL. to mutter, mumble.
bis·bi·se·o m. muttering, mumbling.
bi·se·car §70 tr. GEOM. to bisect.
bi·sec·tor, –triz [f.pl. **-tri·ces**] GEOM. I. adj. bisecting II. f. bisector.
bi·sel m. bevel, beveled edge.

bi·se·la·do I. past part. see **biselar** II. m. beveling.
bi·se·lar tr. to bevel.
bi·se·ma·nal adj. biweekly, semiweekly.
bi·se·qué, biseque see **bisecar**.
bi·se·xual adj. & m.f. bisexual.
bi·sies·to I. adj. bissextile, leap <*año b.* leap year> II. m. leap year.
bi·si·lá·bi·co, –ca adj. var. of **bisílabo, –ba**.
bi·sí·la·bo, –ba adj. bisyllabic, disyllabic.
bis·mu·ti·ta f. bismutite.
bis·mu·to m. CHEM. bismuth.
bis·nie·to, –ta m.f. great-grandchild —m. great-grandson —f. great-granddaughter ♦ **bisnietos** great-grandchildren.
bi·so·jo, –ja I. adj. cross-eyed, squinting II. m.f. cross-eyed person.
bi·son·te m. ZOOL. bison.
bi·so·ña·da *or* **bi·so·ñe·rí·a** f. FIG., COLL. blunder *or* mistake due to inexperience.
bi·so·ñé m. toupee, hairpiece.
bi·so·ño, –ña I. adj. inexperienced, green II. m.f. novice, greenhorn; MIL. recruit.
bis·pón m. roll of oilcloth.
bis·té *or* **bis·tec** m. beefsteak.
bis·tre m. bister.
bis·tu·rí m. [pl. **-rí·es**] SURG. scalpel, bistoury.
bi·su·te·rí·a f. costume jewelry, paste.
bi·ta f. MARIT. bitt.
bi·tá·co·ra f. MARIT. binnacle ♦ **cuaderno de b.** logbook.
bi·tio m. COMPUT. bit.
bi·ton·go, –ga adj. ♦ **niño b.** COLL. big baby, child who acts young for his age.
bi·to·que m. *(de tonel)* bung, plug; MEX. faucet, tap; AMER. cannula (of syringe); C. AMER. sewer.
bi·tu·mi·no·so, –sa adj. MIN. bituminous.
bi·va·len·te adj. CHEM. bivalent.
Bi·zan·cio m. Byzantium.
bi·zan·ti·no, –na I. adj. *(de Bizancio)* Byzantine; FIG. *(demasiado sutil)* intricate, labyrinthine <*una discusión b.* a labyrinthine discussion>; *(decadente)* decadent II. m.f. Byzantine.
bi·za·rre·ar intr. *(mostrar valor)* to act bravely; *(mostrar generosidad)* to act generously.
bi·za·rrí·a f. *(valor)* bravery, courage; *(generosidad)* generosity, magnanimity.
bi·za·rro, –rra adj. *(valiente)* brave, gallant; *(generoso)* generous, magnanimous.
bi·za·za f. saddlebag.
biz·car §70 intr. to squint, be cross-eyed —tr. to wink at.
biz·co, –ca I. adj. squinting, cross-eyed II. m.f. squinter, cross-eyed person ♦ **dejar a uno b.** to dumbfound, flabbergast • **quedarse b.** to be dumbfounded *or* flabbergasted.
biz·co·cho I. m. sponge cake; MARIT. hardtack; CERAM. bisque, biscuit ♦ **b. borracho** rum cake • **embarcarse con poco b.** FIG. to set out unprepared II. adj. MEX. *(de mala calidad)* poor-quality; MEX. *(cobarde)* cowardly.
biz·co·te·la f. CUL. sponge cake with icing.
biz·ma f. MED. poultice.
biz·nie·to, –ta m. var. of **bisnieto, –ta**.
biz·qué, bizque see **bizcar**.
biz·que·ar intr. COLL. to squint.
biz·que·ra f. OPHTHAL. strabismus.
blan·ca I. f. MUS. half note; NUMIS. ancient Spanish coin ♦ **estar sin b.** COLL. to be broke *or* penniless II. adj. see **blanco, –ca**.
blan·co, –ca I. adj. *(albo)* white; *(de color claro)* fair, light; FIG., COLL. *(cobarde)* yellow, chicken ♦ **b. como la nieve** FIG. white as snow, innocent • **más b. que el papel** FIG. as white as a sheet II. m.f. *(caucásico)* white (person); FIG., COLL. *(cobarde)* coward, chicken —m. white (color); *(tiro)* target; *(centro)* center <*ser el b. de todas las miradas* to be the center of attention>; *(espacio)* blank space, blank; *(intermedio)* interval, gap; FIG. *(fin)* goal, aim; P. RICO blank form ♦ **b. de España** CHEM. whiting • **b. del ojo** white of the eye • **calentar al b.** to make white-hot • **dar en el b.** *or* **hacer b.** FIG. to hit the target, hit the nail on the head • **pasar una noche en b.** to spend a sleepless

night • **quedarse en b.** FIG., COLL. to draw a blank • **tiro al b.** target practice —f. see **blanca.**

blan·cu·ra f. *or* **blan·cor** m. whiteness.

blan·cuz·co, –ca adj. whitish.

blan·de·ar intr. & reflex. to soften, yield —tr. to coax, blandish.

blan·di·cia f. *(molicie)* softness; *(halago)* flattery.

blan·dien·te adj. brandishing, waving.

blan·dir tr. *(un arma)* to brandish, wave —intr. to quiver, shake.

blan·do, –da adj. *(suave)* soft; *(tierno)* tender; *(fláccido)* flabby, pliant; *(amable)* gentle, kind; *(indulgente)* indulgent, soft; *(cobarde)* cowardly, weak ♦ **b. de carácter** weak-willed • **b. de carnes** flabby • **b. de corazón** sentimental, soft-hearted.

blan·dón m. *(hachón)* large wax candle; *(candelero)* candlestick.

blan·du·ra f. *(suavidad)* softness; *(ternura)* tenderness; *(flaccidez)* flabbiness; *(amabilidad)* gentleness, kindness; *(indulgencia)* indulgence, softness; *(cobardía)* cowardice, weakness; *(lisonja)* blandishment, flattery; *(emplasto)* poultice, plaster; GEOL. soft layer (in limestone).

blan·duz·co, –ca adj. COLL. softish.

blan·que·a·do I. past part. see **blanquear II.** m. *(acción)* whitening; *(encalado)* whitewashing; *(decoloración)* bleaching; *(encerado)* waxing (a honeycomb); METAL. blanching.

blan·que·a·dor, –do·ra I. adj. whitening; *(que encala)* whitewashing; *(que decolora)* bleaching **II.** m.f. whitener; *(cal)* whitewasher; *(líquido)* bleach.

blan·que·a·du·ra f. *or* **blan·que·a·mien·to** m. var. of **blanqueo.**

blan·que·ar tr. *(poner blanco)* to whiten; *(dar cal)* to whitewash; *(lavar)* to bleach (clothes); *(encerar)* to wax (a honeycomb); METAL. to blanch —intr. *(volverse blanco)* to turn white, bleach; *(tirar a blanco)* to turn whitish, fade.

blan·que·cer §17 tr. *(un metal)* to blanch (metals); *(blanquear)* to whiten.

blan·que·ci·no, –na adj. whitish.

blan·que·o m. *(acción)* whitening; *(encalado)* whitewashing; *(decoloración)* bleaching; *(encerado)* waxing (a honeycomb); METAL. blanching.

blan·qui·llo, –lla I. adj. white (bread) **II.** m. MEX. egg; CHILE, PERU white peach.

blan·qui·men·to *or* **blan·qui·mien·to** m. *(para la ropa)* bleaching solution; *(para metales)* blanching solution.

blan·qui·zal *or* **blan·qui·zar** m. clay pit.

blas·fe·mar intr. to blaspheme; FIG. *(maldecir)* to curse, swear.

blas·fe·ma·to·rio, –ria adj. blasphemous.

blas·fe·mia f. blasphemy; FIG. *(palabrota)* curse, swearword.

blas·fe·mo, –ma I. adj. blasphemous **II.** m.f. blasphemer.

bla·són m. *(ciencia heráldica)* heraldry; *(escudo)* coat of arms, escutcheon; FIG. *(honor)* honor, glory.

bla·so·na·do, –da I. past part. see **blasonar II.** adj. noble, blue-blooded.

bla·so·na·dor, –do·ra adj. boastful, bragging.

bla·so·nar tr. HER. to emblazon —intr. to boast, brag.

bla·so·ne·rí·a f. braggadocio, boasting.

bla·so·nis·ta m.f. heraldry expert.

ble·do m. ♦ **no importarle un b.** FIG. not to give a darn *or* hoot about • **no valer un b.** FIG. not to be worth two cents, not to matter in the least.

blen·da f. MIN. blende.

blin·da f. MIL. blind.

blin·da·do, –da I. past part. see **blindar II.** adj. armored, armor-plated.

blin·da·je m. *(revistamiento)* armor, armor plate; *(chapas)* armor plating.

blin·dar tr. to armor, cover with armor plate.

bloc m. writing pad *or* tablet.

blo·ca·o m. MIL. portable blockhouse.

blon·do, –da I. adj. blond, fair **II.** f. silk lace.

blo·que m. *(masa)* block *<un b. de mármol* a block of marble>; *(grupo)* bloc, coalition; *(papel)* pad, notepad ♦ **b. del motor** AUTO. engine block• **en b.** en bloc, all together.

blo·que·a·dor, –do·ra I. adj. MIL. blockading; *(que obstruye)* blocking, obstructing **II.** m.f. blockader.

blo·que·ar tr. MIL. *(asediar)* to blockade, cut off; FIG. *(impedir)* to block, obstruct; MECH. *(frenar)* to brake; *(obstruir)* to jam, block *<los escombros bloquearon la bomba* debris blocked the pump>; COM. to freeze (assets).

blo·que·o m. MIL. *(asedio)* blockade; FIG. *(obstáculo)* block, obstacle; COM. freeze (of accounts) ♦ **violar el b.** to run the blockade.

blu·sa f. blouse.

blu·són m. long blouse, smock.

bo·a f. ZOOL. boa —m. *(adorno)* boa.

bo·ar·di·lla f. attic, garret.

bo·a·to m. show, ostentation.

bo·ba·da f. foolish act *or* remark ♦ **decir bobadas** to talk nonsense.

bo·ba·lí·as m.f. COLL. fool, idiot.

bo·ba·li·cón, –co·na I. adj. silly, stupid **II.** m.f. fool, nitwit.

bo·ba·tel m. COLL. fool, idiot.

bo·bá·ti·co, –ca adj. silly, foolish.

bo·be·ar intr. *(hacer tonterías)* to fool around, do silly things; *(decir boberías)* to talk nonsense.

bo·be·ra *or* **bo·be·rí·a** f. foolish act *or* remark.

bó·bi·lis, bó·bi·lis adv. ♦ **de b.** COLL. *(de balde)* for nothing; *(sin trabajo)* without lifting a finger.

bo·bi·llo m. *(jarro)* big-bellied jug; *(encaje)* lace fichu.

bo·bi·na f. *(carrete)* spool, reel; SEW. bobbin; ELEC. coil ♦ **b. de campo** *or* **de excitación** ELEC. field coil • **b. de encendido** AUTO. ignition coil.

bo·bo, –ba I. adj. *(tonto)* silly, foolish; *(cándido)* gullible, naive **II.** m.f. *(tonto)* idiot, fool —m. *(gracioso)* clown, jester; *(adorno)* ruff, flounce; C. AMER. fresh-water fish ♦ **b. de Coria** village idiot.

bo·bón, –bo·na adj. COLL. dumb, stupid.

bo·bo·te, –ta COLL. **I.** adj. dumb, stupid **II.** m.f. dummy, idiot.

bo·ca f. ANAT., ZOOL. mouth; ZOOL. *(pinza)* pincer; GEOG. mouth; ARTIL. muzzle; FIG. *(entrada)* entrance, opening; mouth, person *<una b. más para alimentar* one more mouth to feed>; *(filo)* cutting edge; *(sabor)* flavor, bouquet (wine); GUAT. snack, appetizer ♦ **a b. de costal** freely, abundantly • **a b. de jarro** FIG. pointblank, at close range • **abrir** *or* **hacer b.** COLL. to whet the appetite • **abrir tanta b.** MEX., PERU, P. RICO to be amazed • **andar de b. en b.** FIG. to be the subject of gossip • **a pedir de b.** exactly as one pleases, perfectly • **b. abajo** face down • **b. abierta** COLL. bigmouth, blabbermouth • **b. a b.** mouth-to-mouth resuscitation • **b. arriba** face up • **b. de agua** *or* **de riego** hydrant • **b. de dragón** BOT. snapdragon • **b. de escorpión** FIG. evil tongue • **b. de fuego** firearm • **b. del estómago** pit of the stomach • **b. de oro** FIG. silver tongue • **buscar a uno la b.** FIG. to draw someone out, pump someone • **¡cállate la b.!** COLL. be quiet! shut up! • **cerrar la b. a** FIG. to leave speechless • **decir lo que se le viene a la b.** FIG. to talk off the top of one's head • **estar (algo) en b. de todos** FIG. to be common knowledge • **hablar por b. de ganso** FIG., COLL. to repeat what one has heard • **hacerse agua la b.** COLL. to make one's mouth water • **meterse en la b. del lobo** FIG. to step into the lion's den • **no decir esta b. es mía** COLL. not to open one's mouth • **oscuro como b. de lobo** pitch-dark, pitch-black • **quedarse con la b. abierta** FIG., COLL. to be astonished *or* amazed.

bo·ca·ca·lle f. intersection.

bo·ca·caz m. [pl. **-ca·ces**] HYDRAUL. spillway.

bo·ca·cí m. TEX. fine glazed buckram.

bo·ca·cha f. COLL. *(boca grande)* bigmouth, blabbermouth; *(trabuco)* blunderbuss.

bo·ca·di·llo m. *(comida ligera)* snack, tidbit; *(emparedado)* sandwich; *(lienzo)* thin linen; *(cinta)* narrow ribbon.

bo·ca·do m. mouthful *<un b. de pan* a mouthful of bread>; *(trozo)* morsel, bite; EQUIT. *(freno)* bridle, bit ♦ **b. de Adán** ANAT. Adam's apple • **b. de cardenal** choice morsel • **b. sin hueso** COLL. cushy job • **bocados** dried preserves • **con el b. en la boca** while swallowing the last bite • **no tener para un b.** COLL. to be broke *or* penniless.

bo·ca·ja·rro adv. ♦ **a b.** *(a quemarropa)* pointblank; *(de improviso)* unexpectedly.
bo·cal m. jar, jug.
bo·ca·lla·ve f. keyhole.
bo·ca·man·ga f. cuff, wristband.
bo·ca·mi·na f. pithead, mine entrance.
bo·ca·na f. AMER. estuary, inlet.
bo·ca·na·da f. *(de líquido)* swallow, swig; *(de humo)* puff; *(ráfaga)* gust, rush (of air); *(de gente)* throng, stream (of people).
bo·ca·te·ja f. front tile (of a roof).
bo·ca·ti·je·ra f. socket for a carriage pole.
bo·ca·to·ma f. AMER. sluice (in an irrigation ditch).
bo·ca·za f. *(boca grande)* big mouth —m.f. COLL. bigmouth, blabbermouth.
bo·ce·ar intr. to move the lips from side to side (said of horses).
bo·ce·cé, bocece see **bocezar.**
bo·cel m. ARCHIT. *(moldura)* torus, convex molding; *(instrumento)* molding plane ♦ **cuarto b.** quarter round • **medio b.** half round.
bo·ce·lar tr. ARCHIT. to make moldings on, emboss.
bo·ce·ra f. mustache (smear on lips) ♦ **boceras** chatterbox.
bo·ce·tar tr. to sketch, draft.
bo·ce·to m. sketch, draft.
bo·ce·zar §04 intr. to move the lips (said of animals).
bo·ci·na f. AUTO. horn; MARIT. foghorn; MUS. trumpet, horn; *(megáfono)* megaphone; *(de un fonógrafo)* horn; *(caracol)* conch shell; AMER., TELEC. mouthpiece; CHILE, COL. ear trumpet; MEX. loudspeaker.
bo·ci·nar intr. to play or sound a horn.
bo·ci·na·zo m. COLL. honk, toot.
bo·cio m. MED. goiter.
bo·cón, –co·na I. adj. COLL. *(de boca grande)* bigmouthed; *(fanfarrón)* boastful, bragging II. m.f. COLL. *(chismoso)* bigmouth, blabbermouth; *(fanfarrón)* braggart —m. ZOOL. Antillian sardine.
bo·coy m. barrel, cask.
bo·cha f. *(pelota)* wooden ball; ARG., PAR., URUG., SL. *(cabeza)* nut, noggin ♦ **bochas** SPORT. bowls.
bo·char tr. *(en el juego)* to displace (a bowl); AMER., FIG., COLL. to reject, rebuff; ARG. to fail, flunk.
bo·cha·zo m. blow of one bowl against another.
bo·che m. *(hoyo)* hole in the ground (in game of marbles); VEN. *(bochazo)* shock of one bowl hitting another (in game of bowls); FIG., COLL. *(repulsa)* rebuff, slight; CHILE, PERU *(pendencia)* fight, quarrel; CHILE, FIG. *(bochinche)* uproar, tumult ♦ **dar b. a uno** VEN. to give someone the cold shoulder.
bo·chin·che m. COLL. *(tumulto)* uproar, commotion; *(taberna)* dive, low-class bar; COL., P. RICO gossip; MEX. dance, party; C. RICA fight.
bo·chin·che·ar intr. AMER. to cause an uproar or commotion.
bo·chin·che·ro, –ra COLL. I. adj. *(alborotador)* rowdy, brawling; COL., P. RICO gossipy II. m.f. *(alborotador)* rowdy, brawler; COL., P. RICO gossip.
bo·chor·no m. FIG. *(vergüenza)* embarrassment, shame; *(sonrojo)* flush, blush; *(calor)* suffocating heat; METEOROL. sultry weather.
bo·chor·no·so, –sa adj. FIG. *(vergonzoso)* disgraceful, shameful; *(desconcertante)* embarrassing; *(sofocante)* suffocating, stifling; METEOROL. sultry.
bo·da f. wedding, marriage ♦ **b. de negros** FIG. bawdy party • **bodas de Camacho** feast, banquet • **bodas de diamante** diamond jubilee • **bodas de oro** golden anniversary • **bodas de plata** silver anniversary.
bo·de·ga f. *(para vino)* wine cellar; *(despensa)* pantry; MARIT. hold; *(granero)* granary, barn; *(taberna)* tavern, bar; *(depósito)* warehouse, storeroom; AMER. grocery store.
bo·de·ga·je m. *(almacenaje)* storage; CHILE storage fee.
bo·de·gón m. COLL. *(tabernucha)* cheap restaurant, dive; *(taberna)* tavern, bar; ARTS *(pintura)* still life.
bo·de·go·ne·ar intr. COLL. to go barhopping.
bo·de·gue·ro, –ra I. m.f. owner or keeper of a wine cellar; AMER. *(abacero)* grocer II. adj. CUBA coarse, common.
bo·di·jo m. COLL. *(boda desigual)* unequal match, misalliance; *(sin pompa)* quiet wedding, small wedding.

bo·do·cal m. black grape.
bo·do·que m. *(de ballesta)* clay pellet (shot from a crossbow); *(del colchón)* tuft (of a mattress); FIG., COLL. *(persona torpe)* blockhead, dunce; *(burujo)* lump; MEX. lump, swelling.
bo·do·que·ra f. *(molde)* pellet mold; *(de ballesta)* cradle (of a crossbow); *(cerbatana)* blowpipe.
bo·drio m. COLL. *(comida)* poorly made soup or stew; FIG. *(confusión)* muddle, confusion.
bo·fe I. adj. C. AMER. disagreeable, unpleasant II. m. *(pulmón)* lung; P. RICO easy work, child's play ♦ **echar los bofes** FIG., COLL. to break one's back • **ser un b.** FIG., COLL. to be a bore.
bo·fe·ta·da f. or **bo·fe·tón** m. *(golpe)* slap; COLL. *(afrenta)* insult; CHILE punch.
bo·ga f. *(acción de bogar)* rowing; FIG., COLL. *(moda)* fashion, vogue —m.f. *(bogador)* rower; COL. ill-bred person ♦ **estar en b.** to be in fashion or in vogue.
bo·ga·da f. distance covered in one oarstroke.
bo·ga·dor, –do·ra m.f. rower.
bo·gar §47 tr. & intr. *(remar)* to row; *(navegar)* to sail.
bo·ga·van·te m. *(remero)* stroke *(oarsman)*; ZOOL. lobster.
bo·he·mio, –mia FIG. adj. & m.f. bohemian.
bo·hí·o m. AMER. hut, shack.
bo·hor·do m. *(lanza)* javelin, dart; BOT. scape, stalk.
boi·co·te·ar tr. to boycott.
boi·co·te·o m. *(cesación)* boycott; *(acción)* boycotting.
bo·íl m. ox stall.
boi·na f. beret, cap.
boi·te f. nightclub.
boj or **bo·je** m. BOT. box tree, boxwood.
bo·je·dal m. boxwood grove.
bo·jo m. MARIT. measuring of the perimeter (of an island).
bo·la f. *(masa)* ball <*una b. de cera* a ball of wax; *(canica)* marble; *(betún)* shoe polish; FIG., COLL. *(mentira)* lie, fib; CHILE kite; VEN. tamale; CUBA rumor, gossip; MEX. *(tumulto)* tumult, uproar; *(motín)* uprising ♦ **andar como b. sin manija** S. AMER. to wander around • **b. de alcanfor** or **de naftalina** mothball • **b. del mundo** globe • **b. de nieve** snowball; COL. paddy wagon • **b. negra** blackball • **bolas** CHILE, CUBA croquet; ARG. bolas • **¡dale b.!** come off it! • **dejar rodar la b.** FIG. to let (something) ride, let things take their course • **estar** or **meterse en b.** CUBA to participate • **no dar pie con b.** FIG., COLL. to miss the mark.
bo·la·da f. *(en el billar)* stroke, billiard shot; AMER. *(oportunidad)* opportunity, lucky break; *(mentira)* lie, fib; COL. dirty trick; CHILE sweet, candy ♦ **b. de aficionado** ARG., URUG. mediation, arbitration • **no hay b. con él** P. RICO, COLL. there is no one else like him.
bo·la·do m. CUL. fondant made of syrup, egg white and lemon.
bo·la·zo m. *(golpe)* blow with a ball; ARG. *(disparate)* silly or foolish remark; *(mentira)* lie, fib ♦ **de b.** hurriedly, carelessly.
bol·che·vi·que adj. & m.f. POL. Bolshevik.
bol·che·vis·mo m. POL. Bolshevism.
bo·le·a·da f. ARG. hunting with bolas.
bo·le·a·do·ras f.pl. ARG., CHILE, URUG. bolas.
bo·le·ar tr. ARG. *(cazar)* to catch or hunt (with bolas); FIG. *(engañar)* to entangle, entrap; COL. to blackball; MEX. to polish or shine (shoes) —intr. *(jugar)* to play (billiards) for fun; COLL. *(mentir)* to fib, lie —reflex. AMER. to rear and fall, roll over (horses); ARG., URUG., FIG. *(tropezar)* to stumble, falter; *(ruborizarse)* to get flustered or embarrassed; *(un coche)* to overturn.
bo·le·o m. *(acción de jugar a bolos)* bowling; *(sitio)* bowling green or alley.
bo·le·ra I. f. bowling alley II. adj. see **bolero, –ra.**
bo·le·ro, –ra I. adj. *(truhán)* truant; FIG., COLL. *(mentiroso)* lying, fibbing II. m.f. *(novillero)* truant; *(mentiroso)* liar, fibber —m. MUS. bolero; *(chaqueta)* bolero (jacket); AMER. *(juguete)* cup and ball (toy); GUAT., HOND. top hat; MEX. bootblack, shoeshine boy —f. see **bolera.**
bo·le·ta f. *(de entrada)* admission ticket; MIL. billet; *(vale)* voucher; AMER. *(de votación)* ballot, voting slip; *(certificación)* certificate.
bo·le·ta·je m. AMER. tickets, ticket sales.

bo·le·te·rí·a f. AMER. ticket office, box office.

bo·le·te·ro, –ra m.f. ticket seller.

bo·le·tín m. bulletin; *(periódico)* bulletin, gazette; *(billete)* ticket; CUBA train ticket.

bo·le·to m. AMER. ticket; *(de lotería)* lottery ticket.

bo·li·che m. *(bolín)* jack (in bowls); *(juego)* bowling, ninepins; *(juguete)* cup and ball (toy); *(horno)* smelting furnace; *(jábega)* small dragnet; P. RICO inferior tobacco; AMER., COLL. *(almacén)* small store; *(taberna)* dive, cheap restaurant; CHILE gambling casino ♦ **caerse en b.** VEN. to fall on one's face.

bo·li·che·ro, –ra m.f. *(de un juego de bochas)* owner of a bowling set; *(de un pescado)* fishmonger; AMER. owner of a small store.

bó·li·do m. ASTRON. fireball, meteorite; FIG. *(vehículo rápido)* bullet *‹el tren pasó como un b.* the train went by like a bullet›.

bo·lí·gra·fo m. ballpoint pen.

bo·li·llo m. bobbin; *(de un caballo)* fetlock; MEX. roll, bun ♦ **bolillos** S. AMER., MUS. drumsticks; *(dulces)* candy bars.

bo·lín m. jack (in bowling) ♦ **de b., de bolán** COLL. carelessly, at random.

bo·li·na f. MARIT. *(cuerda)* bowline; *(castigo)* flogging; *(sonda)* sounding line; FIG., COLL. *(ruido)* din, uproar ♦ **ir** or **navegar de b.** MARIT. to sail close-hauled, sail close to the wind.

bo·li·ne·ar intr. MARIT. to sail close-hauled or close to the wind.

bo·lí·var m. FIN. bolivar (currency of Venezuela).

bo·li·va·ria·no, –na adj. Bolivarian, relating to Simón Bolívar.

Bo·li·via f. Bolivia.

bo·li·via·no, –na adj. & m.f. Bolivian.

bo·lo m. *(palo)* pin, ninepin; FIG., COLL. *(tonto)* dunce, dummy; ARCHIT. *(nabo)* newel post; PHARM., COLL. large pill; PHILIP. machete ♦ **andar a b.** COL. to be naked • **b. alimenticio** PHYSIOL. bolus • **bolos** bowling, ninepins • **echar a rodar los bolos** COLL. to stir up trouble • **ir en b.** CUBA to run, go running along • **jugar a los bolos** to bowl • **tumbar b.** COL. to succeed.

Bo·lo·nia f. Bologna.

bo·lo·nio, –nia FIG., COLL. **I.** adj. dumb, ignorant **II.** m.f. dunce, ignoramus.

bo·lo·ñés, –ñe·sa adj. & m.f. Bolognan, Bolognese.

bol·sa f. *(saco)* sack, bag; *(bolso)* purse, pocketbook; ANAT. pocket, sac; MIN. pocket, lode; FIN. stock exchange or market; FIG. *(caudal)* wealth, money; SPORT. *(premio)* purse, prize money; C. AMER., MEX., PERU pocket (in clothing); ♦ **aflojar la b.** COLL. to loosen the pursestrings • **b. alcista** FIN. bull market • **b. bajista** FIN. bear market • **b. de agua caliente** hot-water bottle • **b. de comercio** commodity exchange • **b. de hielo** ice pack • **b. de valores** stock exchange • **b. negra** black market • **hacer b.** ARG., CHILE to abuse • **hacer bolsas** to bag, sag • **de b.** CHILE at someone else's expense • **jugar a la b.** to play the (stock) market • **¡la bolsa o la vida!** your money or your life!

bol·se·ar intr. ARG. to bag, sag —tr. C. AMER., MEX. *(robar)* to pickpocket; AMER. *(dar calabazas)* to jilt, throw over; CHILE *(sacar de gorra)* to sponge on, cadge from.

bol·se·ra f. hairnet, snood.

bol·si·llo m. pocket; FIG. *(dinero)* purse, money ♦ **de b.** pocket *‹edición de b.* pocket edition› • **meterse a uno en el b.** COLL. to win someone over.

bol·sín m. *(reunión)* meeting of stockbrokers after exchange hours; *(sitio)* stockbrokers' meeting place.

bol·sis·ta m.f. COM. stockbroker; AMER. pickpocket.

bol·so m. purse, pocketbook.

bol·són m. *(bolsa grande)* large purse or handbag; AMER. school bag; COL. dunce, ignoramus; BOL., MIN. pocket (of ore); MEX. *(laguna)* lagoon; *(depresión en la tierra)* hollow (in the land).

bo·lla·du·ra f. *(abolladura)* dent; *(protuberancia)* bump; *(decoración)* embossing.

bo·llar f. *(sellar)* to stamp; *(abollonar)* to emboss.

bo·lle·ro, –ra m.f. baker.

bo·llo m. *(pan)* bun, roll; *(hueco)* dent; *(plegado)* fold, crease; FIG. *(chichón)* lump, bump; COLL. *(lío)* fuss, to-do; ARG., HOND. punch; COL. tamale ♦ **armar un b.** to

kick up a fuss • **bollos** COL. troubles, difficulties • **no pelar b.** VEN. never to be wrong.

bo·llón m. *(clavo)* boss, stud; *(pendiente)* button earring, stud; BOT. bud (of grapevine).

bo·llo·na·do, –da adj. studded, embossed.

bom·ba I. f. MIL. bomb, shell; TECH. pump; *(globo)* globe, glass (for lamps); FIG. *(sorpresa)* bombshell, stunning news; COL. *(burbuja)* bubble; COL., GUAT., PERU *(mentira)* lie, fib; CHILE, GUAT., HOND., PERU *(borrachera)* drinking bout; CUBA, MEX. *(sombrero)* top hat; ECUAD., VEN. hot-air balloon; ARG., CUBA, PAR., URUG. *(cometa)* circular kite ♦ **a prueba de bombas** bombproof • **b. alimenticia** feed pump • **b. aspirante** suction pump • **b. atómica** atomic bomb • **b. centrífuga** centrifugal pump • **b. de cobalto** cobalt bomb • **b. de hidrógeno** hydrogen bomb • **b. de mano** TECH. hand pump; MIL. grenade • **b. gástrica** MED. stomach pump • **b. impelente** force pump • **b. lacrimógena** tear-gas bomb • **b. neumática** pneumatic pump • **b. termonuclear** thermonuclear bomb • **caer como una b.** FIG., COLL. to hit like a bombshell • **estar echando bombas** FIG., COLL. to be boiling hot • **estar en b.** AMER. to be drunk • **éxito b.** smashing success • **pasarlo b.** to have a ball **II.** adj. see **bombo, –ba**.

bom·ba·chas f.pl. or **bom·ba·cha** f. ARG., PAR., URUG. baggy trousers (worn by peasants).

bom·ba·cho I. adj. baggy, loose-fitting **II.** m. baggy trousers.

bom·bar·da f. MARIT., MIL. bombard (warship and artillery); MUS. bombardon (instrument and organ stop).

bom·bar·de·ar tr. MIL. to bombard, shell, bomb.

bom·bar·de·o m. MIL. bombardment, shelling, bombing ♦ **b. en picado** dive bombing.

bom·bar·de·ro, –ra I. m. *(avión)* bomber; *(soldado)* bombardier, gunner, bomber **II.** adj. bombing.

bom·bar·di·no m. MUS. saxhorn.

bom·bar·dón m. MUS. bombardon.

bom·ba·sí m. bombazine, fustian (fabric).

bom·bás·ti·co, –ca adj. bombastic.

bom·ba·zo m. *(explosión)* explosion (of a bomb); *(daño)* damage (caused by exploding bomb); ARG. barbarity.

bom·bé m. gig (two-seat carriage).

bom·be·ar tr. MIL. to bomb, shell; *(sacar)* to pump *‹b. agua* to pump water›; *(abombar)* to make convex; FIG. COLL. *(dar bombo a)* to give a buildup to, make a fuss over; ARG., URUG. to scout, reconnoiter; COL. to dismiss, fire; GUAT. to steal.

bom·be·o m. *(convexidad)* bulge, convexity; *(de un líquido)* pumping (of a liquid); *(de una carretera)* crown (of a road).

bom·be·ro, –ra I. m. fireman, firefighter; ARG. *(explorador)* scout, explorer; ARG. *(espía)* spy **II.** adj. CUBA inane, foolish.

bom·bi·lla f. light bulb; MARIT. *(farol)* lantern; *(tubo)* tube (for removing liquids); MEX. ladle; AMER. *(caña)* metal straw (for drinking maté) ♦ **b. de destello** ELEC., PHOTOG. flash bulb.

bom·bi·llo m. trap (in a drain); MARIT. *(bomba de mano)* hand pump; AMER. light bulb.

bom·bín m. COLL. bowler, derby; *(inflador)* bicycle pump.

bom·bo, –ba I. adj. COLL. *(atónito)* dazed, dumbfounded; CUBA *(tibio)* lukewarm; *(tonto)* foolish; *(sin sabor)* tasteless, flat; MEX. tainted, spoiled (food) ♦ **noticia b.** sensational news **II.** m. *(tambor)* bass drum; *(músico)* bass drummer; *(barco)* barge; *(caja)* revolving drum (for raffles); FIG. *(publicidad)* fanfare, buildup; P. RICO, DOM. REP. bowler hat ♦ **a** or **con b. y platillos** FIG., COLL. with a fanfare, with a great to-do • **dar b. a** COLL. to give a buildup to, make a fuss over • **irse al b.** ARG., URUG. to fail, come to no good • **mandar a uno al b.** ARG., SL. to knock someone off, kill someone • **poner a uno b.** MEX. *(insultar)* to insult someone; *(golpear)* to hit someone —f. see **bomba**.

bom·bón m. bonbon, chocolate; COLL. *(persona)* gem, peach; *(vasija)* bamboo bowl; CUBA ladle.

bom·bo·na f. *(damajuana)* demijohn (bottle used for storing wine); *(vasija metálica)* carboy (container for volatile or corrosive liquids) ♦ **b. de gas** gas tank (for bottled gas).

bom·bo·ne·ra f. *(caja)* candy *or* chocolate box; COLL. *(sitio)* cute little place, cozy cottage.
bo·na·chón, –cho·na I. adj. COLL. *(bueno)* good-natured, genial; FIG., COLL. *(crédulo)* gullible, naive II. m.f. COLL. *(persona buena)* good-natured person; FIG., COLL. *(sencillote)* gullible person.
bo·nan·ci·ble adj. calm, tranquil.
bo·nan·za f. MARIT. fair *or* calm weather; FIG. *(prosperidad)* bonanza, prosperity; MIN. bonanza, rich lode ♦ **ir en b.** to be fortunate.
bo·na·par·tis·mo m. HIST., POL. Bonapartism.
bon·dad f. goodness, kindness ♦ **tener la b. de** to be so kind as to <*tenga la b. de explicar* would you be so kind as to explain>.
bon·da·do·so, –sa adj. good, kind.
bo·ne·ta f. MARIT. bonnet (strip of canvas used to increase sail area).
bo·ne·te m. *(gorro)* bonnet, cap; RELIG. biretta; *(dulcera)* candy dish; *(fortificación)* bonnet; ZOOL. reticulum; FIG. *(clérigo secular)* secular priest ♦ **a tente b.** doggedly, insistently.
bo·ne·te·rí·a f. AMER. notions shop.
bon·go m. C. AMER. canoe; CUBA raft.
bon·gó m. CUBA bongo drum.
bo·nia·to m. BOT. sweet potato.
bo·ni·fi·ca·ción f. *(mejora)* improvement, amelioration; *(rebaja)* discount, reduction.
bo·ni·fi·car §70 tr. *(mejorar)* to improve, ameliorate; *(rebajar)* to discount, reduce the price of.
bo·ni·to I. m. ICHTH. tuna, bonito II. adj. see **bonito, –ta**.
bo·ni·to, –ta I. adj. *(lindo)* pretty, nice-looking; *(bueno)* good, satisfactory ♦ **¡muy bonito!** IRON. oh great!, that's nice! II. m. see **bonito**.
Bonn m. Bonn.
bo·no m. *(vale)* voucher, certificate; COM. *(fianza)* bond.
bo·no·te m. AGR. coconut fiber.
bo·ñi·ga f. cattle dung *or* manure.
bo·que·a·da f. gasp ♦ **dar la última b.** to give one's last gasp.
bo·que·ar intr. *(jadear)* to gasp; FIG., COLL. *(estar a punto de morirse)* to be about to die, be at death's door —tr. to mouth, utter.
bo·que·ra f. AGR. sluice; MED. *(llaga)* lip sore, mouth ulcer; *(ventana)* window (in a hayloft).
bo·que·rón m. *(abertura)* large aperture *or* hole; *(bocaza)* big mouth; ICHTH. small sardine.
bo·que·te m. *(entrada)* gap, narrow entrance *or* opening; *(agujero)* hole, breach.
bo·quia·bier·to, –ta adj. *(con la boca abierta)* open-mouthed, gaping; FIG. *(atónito)* amazed, astonished.
bo·quian·cho, –cha adj. large-mouthed, wide-mouthed.
bo·quian·gos·to, –ta adj. narrow-mouthed.
bo·quifres·co, –ca adj. *(boquiblando)* tender-mouthed (said of horses); FIG., COLL. *(descarado)* fresh, impudent.
bo·qui·lla f. MUS. mouthpiece; *(del cigarrillo)* cigarette holder; *(filtro)* filter tip; *(de la pipa)* mouthpiece; *(mechero)* nozzle; *(de pantalones)* pant leg opening; AGR. irrigation outlet; CARP. mortise; ARTIL. fuse hole; ECUAD. rumor, gossip ♦ **de b.** idle, empty (words).
bo·qui·mue·lle adj. *(boquiblando)* tender-mouthed; FIG. *(manejable)* docile, tractable; *(crédulo)* gullible, dupable.
bo·qui·rro·to, –ta adj. FIG., COLL. gabby, talkative.
bo·qui·rru·bio, –bia I. adj. FIG. *(boquirroto)* blabbing, loose-tongued; *(inexperto)* inexperienced, naive II. m. dandy.
bo·qui·tuer·to, –ta adj. wry-mouthed.
bo·ra·ci·ta f. MIN. boracite.
bo·ra·to m. CHEM. borate.
bó·rax m. CHEM. borax.
bor·bo·llar *or* **bor·bo·lle·ar** intr. *(hacer borbollones)* to bubble (boiling water), boil; FIG. *(tartamudear)* to stutter, stammer.
bor·bo·lle·o m. bubbling (water), boiling.
bor·bo·llón m. bubbling ♦ **a borbollones** furiously, gushing ♦ **hablar a borbollones** to talk furiously.
bor·bo·llo·ne·ar intr. var. of **borbollar**.
bor·bó·ni·co, –ca adj. Bourbon, Bourbonic.
bor·bo·tar *or* **bor·bo·te·ar** intr. to boil, bubble.

bor·bo·te·o m. boiling, bubbling.
bor·bo·tón m. boiling, bubbling ♦ **a borbotones** FIG., COLL. gushing, in torrents.
bor·da f. MARIT. *(costado)* gunwale; *(vela)* mainsail; *(choza)* hut, cabin ♦ **echar** *or* **tirar por la b.** to throw overboard.
bor·da·da f. MARIT. tack, board; FIG., COLL. well-trodden path ♦ **dar una b.** MARIT. to tack, make a board.
bor·da·do I. past part. see **bordar** II. m. embroidery, embroidering.
bor·da·dor, –do·ra m.f. embroiderer.
bor·da·du·ra f. embroidery.
bor·dar tr. to embroider; FIG. *(embellecer)* to embellish.
bor·de¹ m. *(orilla)* border, edge; *(canto)* brim, rim; MARIT. board, side ♦ **al b. de** on the edge *or* border of; FIG. *(al punto de)* on the verge *or* brink of.
bor·de² I. adj. *(planta)* wild (plant); *(persona)* bastard, illegitimate (person); *(mal intencionado)* mean, bastardly (person) II. m.f. *(bastardo)* bastard.
bor·de·ar tr. to border <*las flores bordean el camino* flowers border the road>; *(ir por el borde)* to skirt, go around; FIG. *(aproximarse)* to approach, come near to —intr. MARIT. to tack.
bor·di·llo m. *(de la acera)* curb (of a sidewalk).
bor·do m. MARIT. board, shipboard; *(bordada)* tack; GUAT., MEX. dam, dike ♦ **a b.** on board, aboard • **al b.** MARIT. alongside • **de alto b.** large, sea-going (vessel).
bor·do·lés, –le·sa I. adj. of Bordeaux II. m.f. native of Bordeaux.
bor·dón m. *(bastón)* staff; *(estribillo)* refrain (verse); FIG. *(frase repetida)* pet phrase; *(guía)* helping hand, guide; MUS. bass string; COL., PAN. *(benjamín)* youngest-born male.
bor·don·ci·llo m. refrain.
bor·do·ne·ar intr. *(zumbar)* to buzz, hum; MUS. to strum; FIG. *(vagar)* to loaf, idle.
bor·do·ne·o m. buzz, buzzing, humming.
bor·do·ne·rí·a f. *(vagueo)* loafing; *(vagabundeo)* idle wandering.
bor·do·ne·ro, –ra adj. & m.f. vagrant.
bo·re·al adj. boreal, northern.
bó·re·as m. Boreas, north wind.
bor·go·ña m. Burgundy (wine).
Bor·go·ña f. Burgundy.
bor·go·ñón, –ño·na adj. & m.f. Burgundian.
bó·ri·co adj. CHEM. boric.
Bo·rin·quén m. Puerto Rico.
bo·rin·que·ño, –ña adj. & m.f. Puerto Rican.
bor·la f. *(hebras)* tassel; *(de polvera)* powder puff ♦ **borlas** BOT. amaranth • **tomar la b.** to get one's doctorate.
bor·lar·se reflex. AMER. to get one's doctorate.
bor·ne m. *(extremo)* point, tip (of a lance); ELEC. terminal.
bor·ne·a·di·zo, –za adj. pliable, flexible.
bor·ne·ar tr. *(torcer)* to twist, bend; ARCHIT. *(colocar)* to set *or* put into place (building stones); *(guiñar)* to squint one's eyes (to check the alignment of something) —intr. MARIT. to swing *or* turn on its moorings (a ship) —reflex. to warp, become warped.
bor·ne·o m. *(torcimiento)* twisting, bending; *(del cuerpo)* swinging, twisting (of the body); MARIT. swinging at anchor (ship).
bo·ro m. CHEM. boron.
bo·ro·na f. *(mijo)* millet; *(maíz)* corn, maize; *(pan de maíz)* cornbread; AMER. *(migaja)* breadcrumb.
bo·rra f. *(del café)* coffee grounds; *(sedimento)* dregs; *(relleno)* flock, stuffing; *(seda)* floss; ZOOL. goat's hair; COLL. *(palabras inútiles)* empty words, padding.
bo·rra·cha f. COLL. wineskin.
bo·rra·che·ar intr. COLL. to booze, drink in excess.
bo·rra·che·ra f. *(ebriedad)* drunkenness, inebriation; *(parranda)* binge, drinking spree; FIG., COLL. *(exaltación)* ecstasy, exultation; *(disparate)* nonsense.
bo·rra·chez f. *(embriaguez)* drunkenness; FIG. *(turbación)* delirium.
bo·rra·chín m. COLL. drunkard, sot.
bo·rra·cho, –cha I. adj. *(ebrio)* drunk, inebriated; *(alcoholizado)* drunken, alcoholic; *(morado)* violet, purple; *(de ron)* rum-soaked; FIG., COLL. *(dominado)* blind, wild <*b.*

de celos wild with jealousy>; CHILE overripe ♦ **b. como una cuba** COLL. drunk as a skunk **II.** m.f. drunken person; *(alcohólico)* drunkard, alcoholic —m. rum baba ♦ **b. perdido** COLL. hopeless drunk. —f. see **borracha.**

bo·rra·dor m. *(escrito)* rough draft, first draft; *(papel)* scratch paper *or* pad; COM. daybook; *(goma de borrar)* eraser.

bo·rra·du·ra f. erasure, deletion.

bo·rra·je·ar tr. COLL. to doodle, scribble.

bo·rra·jo m. ember, cinder.

bo·rrar tr. *(obliterar)* to erase, rub out; FIG. *(desvanecer)* to erase, wipe away.

bo·rras·ca f. *(tempestad)* storm, tempest; FIG. *(riesgo)* hazard, danger; ARG., MEX., MIN. absence of ore in a vein.

bo·rras·co·so, -sa adj. *(tempestuoso)* stormy, tempestuous; *(desordenado)* rowdy.

bo·rras·que·ro, -ra adj. COLL. *(escandaloso)* rowdy; *(licencioso)* licentious.

bo·rre·ga·da f. flock (of lambs); ECUAD., COLL. nap, siesta.

bo·rre·go, -ga m.f. *(cordero)* young sheep *or* lamb; FIG. *(tonto)* simpleton, fool; CUBA, MEX. rumor, hoax.

bo·rre·guil adj. *(corderino)* sheep-like; FIG. *(conformista)* sheep-like.

bo·rri·ca f. *(asna)* she-ass; FIG. *(mujer ignorante)* dull *or* stupid woman; dimwit.

bo·rri·ca·da f. *(rebaño)* herd of donkeys; *(cabalgata)* donkey ride; FIG., COLL. *(necedad)* foolish remark *or* act.

bo·rri·co m. *(asno)* ass, donkey; *(de carpintero)* sawhorse; FIG. COLL. *(idiota)* ass, dimwit.

bo·rri·cón *or* **bo·rri·co·te** m. COLL. *(tonto)* nitwit, idiot; *(persona laboriosa)* plodder; *(caballete)* sawhorse.

bo·rri·que·ro I. adj. ♦ **cardo b.** BOT. cotton thistle **II.** m. donkey driver.

bo·rri·que·te m. sawhorse.

bo·rro m. *(cordero)* yearling lamb; *(impuesto)* sheep tax.

bo·rrón m. *(mancha)* ink blot, smudge; *(borrador)* rough draft, first draft; PAINT. *(de una pintura)* preliminary sketch; FIG. *(defecto)* blemish; *(acción indigna)* stigma, blemish ♦ **b. y cuenta nueva** FIG., COLL. clean slate • **borrones** FIG. jottings, scribbling.

bo·rro·ne·ar tr. *(escribir)* to scribble, scrawl; *(esbozar)* to outline.

bo·rro·si·dad f. blurriness; fuzziness.

bo·rro·so, -sa adj. *(indistinto)* blurred, fuzzy; *(confuso)* confused, unclear.

bo·ru·ca f. COLL. din, uproar, noise ♦ **armar b.** to raise hell.

bo·ru·jo m. *(bulto)* lump, bulky object; *(aceitunas)* oil cake (from pressed olives).

bo·rus·ca f. *(hojas)* fallen leaves; *(ramaje)* brushwood.

bos·ca·je m. *(conjunto de árboles)* thicket, copse; *(pintura)* landscape.

bos·co·so, -sa adj. wooded, woody.

bós·fo·ro m. GEOG. strait.

Bós·fo·ro m. Bosphorous.

bos·que m. *(árboles)* woods, forest; FIG. *(confusión)* confusion, woods ♦ **b. maderable** timber forest.

bos·que·jar tr. *(trazar)* to sketch, outline, draft; *(una escultura)* rough-hew.

bos·que·jo m. sketch, outline, draft.

bos·que·te m. small woods, thicket.

bos·ta f. manure.

bos·te·zar §04 intr. to yawn.

bos·te·zo m. yawn.

bo·ta I. f. *(calzado)* boot; *(odre)* wineskin, leather wine container; *(tonel)* wooden cask; *(medida)* liquid measure (516 liters) ♦ **estar con las botas puestas** FIG., COLL. to be ready to go • **ponerse las botas** FIG., COLL. to strike it rich **II.** adj. see **boto, -ta.**

bo·ta·do, -da I. past part. see **botar II.** adj. AMER., COLL. *(expulsado)* fired, kicked out; *(barato)* cheap **III.** m.f. *(expósito)* foundling; MEX., COLL. *(borracho)* drunkard.

bo·ta·dor, -do·ra I. adj. bucking (said of a horse) **II.** m. *(sacaclavos)* nail puller; *(instrumento dental)* forceps (dentist's); *(palo de barquero)* pole (to push a boat) —m.f. AMER., COLL. spendthrift.

bo·ta·fue·go m. ARTIL. linstock; COLL. *(persona)* spitfire, person with a short temper.

bo·ta·lón m. MARIT. boom; COL., VEN. post, stake.

bo·ta·men m. *(farmacia)* collection of pots and jars (in a drugstore); MARIT. *(botas en un buque)* water and wine casks (on board a ship).

bo·ta·na f. *(remiendo)* patch (on a wineskin); *(tapón)* stopper (on wine barrel); COLL. *(parche en una llaga)* patch, plaster (on a wound); *(cicatriz)* scar; COL., CUBA *(vainita de espolones)* leather scabbard on the spurs of fighting cocks; GUAT., MEX. *(tapas)* cocktail snacks.

bo·tá·ni·co, -ca I. adj. botanical **II.** m.f. botanist —f. botany.

bo·ta·nis·ta m.f. botanist.

bo·tar tr. *(arrojar)* to fling, hurl; COLL. *(despedir)* to dismiss, fire; MARIT. to turn <**b. a babor** to turn to port>; *(lanzar al agua)* to launch; AMER. *(tirar)* to throw away; *(malgastar)* to waste, squander —intr. to bounce <*la pelota botó en el suelo* the ball bounced on the floor>; *(el caballo)* to buck, kick up the heels —reflex *(volverse)* to become; CHILE to change jobs.

bo·ta·ra·ta·da f. COLL. stupidity, foolish act.

bo·ta·ra·te m. COLL. *(tonto)* fool, idiot; AMER. spendthrift, squanderer.

bo·tar·ga f. ARCH. loose breeches, galligaskins; *(disfraz)* ridiculous costume; COLL. *(mamarracho)* clown, ridiculous *or* outlandish person.

bo·ta·si·lla f. MIL. boots and saddles (bugle call).

bo·ta·van·te m. MARIT. boarding pike.

bo·ta·va·ra f. MARIT. gaffsail.

bo·te m. *(golpe)* thrust, blow; *(brinco)* prance, caper; *(rebote)* bounce; *(pote)* pot, jar; *(lata)* tin can; *(barco)* rowboat; COLL. *(caja)* tip jar; MEX., SL. jug, slammer ♦ **b. de carnero** bucking (of a horse) • **b. de salvamento** lifeboat • **chupar del b.** FIG. to take advantage • **dar el b. a** COLL. to give the boot, fire • **dar un b.** to jump • **darse el b.** to go away • **de b. y voleo** immediately, instantly • **de b. en b.** full, jammed • **tener a alguien metido en el b.** FIG. to have someone in one's pocket.

bo·te·lla f. bottle (container and contents); CARIB. sinecure, political patronage job ♦ **b. de Leiden** ELEC. Leyden jar • **b. termo** thermos (bottle) • **en b.** bottled.

bo·te·lla·zo m. blow struck with a bottle.

bo·te·rí·a f. MARIT. water casks on board a ship; *(tienda)* wineskin shop; ARG., CHILE *(zapatería)* boot store.

bo·te·ro m. *(el que hace botas)* bootmaker; *(el que vende botas)* boot seller; MARIT. skipper ♦ **Pedro B.** COLL. the devil.

bo·ti·ca f. *(farmacia)* pharmacy, drugstore; FIG. *(medicamentos)* medicines; *(tienda)* shop, store.

bo·ti·ca·rio, -ria m.f. pharmacist, druggist ♦ **como pedrada en ojo de b.** in the nick of time.

bo·ti·ja f. *(vasija)* earthenware jar; C. AMER. buried treasure; URUG., COLL. child, baby ♦ **b. verde** COLL. insult • **estar hecho una b.** FIG., COLL. *(ser gordo)* to be very fat; *(enojarse)* to be cranky.

bo·ti·je·ro, -ra m.f. *(persona que hace botijos)* potter; *(persona que vende botijos)* pottery seller.

bo·ti·jo m. *(vasija)* earthenware jug; COLL. *(persona gorda)* chubby person.

bo·ti·lle·rí·a f. *(de bebidas)* refreshment stand; *(de helados)* ice cream stand; CHILE liquor store.

bo·ti·lle·ro m. *(vendedor)* attendant (of a refreshment stand); *(el que hace helados)* ice cream maker; *(vendedor de helados)* ice cream vendor.

bo·tín¹ m. *(calzado)* ankle boot, half boot; *(polaina)* spat, gaiter; CHILE *(calcetín)* sock.

bo·tín² m. booty, spoils.

bo·ti·na f. ankle boot, high-cut shoe.

bo·ti·ne·rí·a f. *(de botas)* boot store; *(de zapatos)* shoe store.

bo·ti·ne·ro, -ra I. adj. black-footed (cattle) **II.** m.f. *(persona que hace botines)* bootmaker, cobbler; *(vendedor de botines)* boot seller.

bo·ti·quín m. medicine chest *or* cabinet; *(estuche)* first-aid kit; VEN. wine shop.

bo·ti·vo·le·o m. returning *or* striking a ball on the bounce; *(baloncesto)* dribble (basketball).

bo·to, -ta I. adj *(romo)* blunt, dull; FIG. *(torpe)* dense, obtuse (person) **II.** m. riding boot —f. see **bota.**

bo·tón m. *(disco)* button; *(llamador)* doorbell, buzzer; BOT.

bud, gemma; MUS. key (of a wind instrument); ARG., CHILE, URUG. cop; CUBA reproach ♦ **al b.** AMER. in vain • **b. de arranque** AUTO. starter • **b. de florete** FENC. protective tip • **b. de fuego** cautery • **b. de muestra** sample • **b. de oro** BOT. buttercup • **botones** bellhop.

bo·to·na·du·ra f. buttons, set of buttons.

bo·to·ne·rí·a f. *(fábrica)* button factory; *(tienda)* button store, notions store.

bo·to·ne·ro, –ra m.f. *(fabricante)* button maker; *(vendedor)* button seller.

bo·to·nes m.pl. COLL. bellboy, bellhop.

Bot·swa·na m. Botswana.

bot·swa·nés, –ne·sa adj. & m.f. Botswanan, Botswanese.

bo·tu·lis·mo m. MED. botulism.

bou m. *(pesca)* seine fishing; *(barco)* seiner.

bó·ve·da f. ARCHIT. vault; *(techo)* dome, cupola; *(cripta)* crypt; *(caverna)* cave, cavern ♦ **b. celeste** firmament, heavens • **b. craneal** ANAT. cranial cavity • **b. palatina** ANAT. palate, roof of the mouth.

bo·vi·no, –na adj. ZOOL. bovine.

bo·xe·a·dor m. SPORT. boxer.

bo·xe·ar intr. SPORT. to box.

bo·xe·o m. SPORT. boxing.

bo·ya f. MARIT. buoy; *(corcho)* float, floating cork (for fishing nets) ♦ **b. de salvamento** or **salvavidas** life buoy.

bo·ya·da f. drove of oxen.

bo·yan·te adj. *(que flota)* buoyant, floating; *(próspero)* prosperous, thriving; TAUR. easy to fight (bull).

bo·yar intr. to float, to buoy.

bo·zal **I.** m. *(frenillo)* muzzle; AMER. halter, headstall —m.f. COLL. *(idiota)* simpleton, fool; FIG. *(novato)* novice, greenhorn **II.** adj. COLL. *(tonto)* stupid, ignorant; FIG. *(novato)* raw, green; *(salvaje)* wild, untamed.

bo·zo m. *(vello)* down, fuzz (on upper lip); *(boca)* mouth (external part only); *(cabestro)* halter (for horses).

bra·ban·te m. TEX. brabant (linen cloth).

bra·ce·a·da f. swing of the arms; *(natación)* stroke (in swimming).

bra·ce·a·je m. *(de monedas)* minting, coining; MARIT. fathomage, depth in fathoms.

bra·ce·ar intr. to flail or wave one's arms; *(nadar)* to swim; EQUIT. *(un caballo)* to step high; FIG. *(esforzarse)* to struggle, strive.

bra·ce·o m. flailing, waving of the arms; *(natación)* stroke (in swimming).

bra·ce·ro, –ra **I.** adj. throwing <*lanza b.* throwing spear> **II.** m. laborer, worker ♦ **de b.** arm in arm.

brac·mán m. RELIG. Brahman.

bra·co, –ca **I.** adj. pug-nosed, snub-nosed **II.** m.f. *(perro de caza)* pointer, setter (dog); COLL. pug nose (person).

bra·ga f. *(cuerda)* sling, rope (for hoisting); *(pañal)* diapers; *(calzón femenino)* panties, knickers; *(calzones anchos de hombre)* wide breeches.

bra·ga·da **I.** f. gaskin, inner part of the hind-leg thigh of a horse or related animal **II.** adj. see **bragado, –da.**

bra·ga·do, –da **I.** adj. *(firme)* resolute; *(enérgico)* energetic; *(valiente)* gutsy; *(animal)* having the gaskin of a different color from the rest of the body (horse or related animal); *(persona)* trouble-making **II.** f. see **bragada.**

bra·ga·du·ra f. crotch.

bra·ga·zas m. [pl. **-zas**] COLL. henpecked husband.

bra·gue·ro m. MED. truss; EQUIT. *(de un caballo)* martingale.

bra·gue·ta f. fly (of pants).

Brah·ma m. RELIG. Brahma (Hindu god).

brah·man m. RELIG. Brahman, Brahmin.

brah·ma·nis·mo m. RELIG. Brahmanism.

bra·ma f. rut, rutting season.

bra·ma·de·ra f. *(tablita que se voltea en el aire)* bull-roarer; *(instrumento musical)* reed pipes; CUBA vent (of an oven).

bra·ma·de·ro m. *(sitio de brama)* rutting place; AMER. *(poste)* tethering post.

bra·ma·dor, –do·ra adj. *(vacas)* lowing (cows); *(toros)* bellowing, roaring (bulls).

bra·man·te **I.** adj. bellowing, roaring **II.** m. twine (of reed fiber).

bra·mar intr. *(dar bramidos)* to roar, bellow; FIG. to howl

<*el viento brama* the wind is howling>; to bellow, roar <*su padre bramó de ira* his father roared in anger>.

bra·mi·do m. *(mugido)* roar, bellow; FIG. *(gran ruido)* roaring, howl.

bran·ca·da f. trammel net.

bran·dal m. MARIT. backstay.

Bran·de·bur·go or **Bran·den·bur·go** Brandenburg.

bran·quia f. ICHTH. branchia, gill.

bran·quial adj. branchial.

bran·quí·fe·ro, –ra adj. branchial, having gills.

bra·quial adj. ANAT. brachial, of the arm.

bra·qui·gra·fí·a f. shorthand, stenography.

bra·sa f. live or hot coal.

bras·ca f. METAL. fettling.

bra·se·ro m. *(fuego)* brazier; MEX. fireplace, hearth; COL. bonfire.

bra·sil m. BOT. brazilwood; ARCH. *(afeite)* rouge (cosmetic).

Bra·sil m. Brazil.

bra·si·le·ño, –ña adj. & m.f. Brazilian.

Bra·sí·lia f. Brasília.

bra·va·ta f. *(reto)* dare, threat; *(jactancia)* boast, brag.

bra·ve·a·dor, –do·ra **I.** adj. bullying, blustering **II.** m.f. bully.

bra·ve·ar intr. COLL. *(jactarse)* to boast, bluster; *(aplaudir)* to cheer, shout (bravo!).

bra·ve·ra f. vent (of furnace).

bra·ve·za f. *(valentía)* bravery, courage; *(fiereza)* fury, roughness (of sea, elements).

bra·ví·o, –a **I.** adj. *(feroz)* wild, untamed; FIG. *(silvestre)* wild, uncultivated; *(rústico)* uncouth, coarse **II.** m. fierceness, ferocity.

bra·vo, –va adj. *(valiente)* brave, valiant; *(excelente)* excellent, great; ZOOL. *(feroz)* ferocious, wild; rough, stormy <*un mar b.* a stormy sea>; *(áspero)* craggy, rugged; COLL. *(valentón)* boastful, swaggering; *(enojado)* angry, furious; FIG., COLL. *(de mal genio)* rude, ill-tempered; CUBA ambitious ♦ **¡bravo!** bravo!, well done!

bra·vu·cón, –co·na COLL. **I.** adj. boastful, swaggering **II.** m.f. boaster, swaggerer.

bra·vu·co·ne·ar intr. to boast, swagger.

bra·vu·ra f. *(fiereza)* fierceness, ferocity (of wild beasts); *(valentía)* bravery, courage; *(bravata)* bluster, bravado; MUS. bravura.

bra·za f. MARIT. *(medida)* fathom; *(cabo)* brace; *(modo de nadar)* breaststroke ♦ **nadar a la b.** to swim breaststroke.

bra·za·da f. *(gesto)* uplifting or extension of the arms; SPORT. *(natación)* stroke; *(brazado)* armful; AMER. fathom ♦ **b. de espaldas** SPORT. backstroke • **b. de pecho** breaststroke • **b. de piedra** MEX. cubic measure.

bra·za·do m. armful.

bra·zal m. *(pieza de armadura)* brassard; *(embrazadura)* handle (of shield); *(acequia)* irrigation ditch; *(insignia)* armband.

bra·za·le·te m. *(pulsera)* bracelet; MIL. armlet, armband.

bra·zo m. ANAT. arm; *(parte superior)* upper arm; ZOOL. foreleg; arm <*los brazos de una silla* the arms of a chair>; *(de una balanza)* arm, crosspiece; FIG. power, strength ♦ **a b. partido** *(sin armas)* bare-fisted; FIG. hard, fast and furiously <*trabajamos a b. partido* we worked fast and furiously> • **asidos** or **cogidos del b.** arm in arm • **b. de árbol** BOT. branch • **b. (de) gitano** CUL. jellyroll • **b. de grúa** MARIT. jib, arm • **b. de mar** inlet • **b. derecho** FIG. right-hand man, right arm • **brazos** FIG. *(jornaleros)* hands, laborers; *(valedores)* backers, supporters • **con los brazos abiertos** with open arms • **cruzarse de brazos** FIG. to cross one's arms and do nothing • **dar el b. a** FIG. to lend a hand to • **dar el b. a torcer** FIG. to give in, let one's arm be twisted • **dar un b. por** FIG. to give one's right arm for.

bre·a f. *(alquitrán)* tar, pitch; MARIT. caulking pitch; *(lienzo)* tarpaulin, waterproof canvas; MEX., FIG. excrement ♦ **b. mineral** mineral pitch, asphalt • **b. seca** rosin, coalophony.

bre·ar tr. FIG., COLL. *(maltratar)* to abuse, ill-treat; *(chasquear)* to make fun of, tease ♦ **b. de golpes** to beat up • **b. de preguntas** to shower with questions —reflex. ♦ **brearse de trabajo** to work one's fingers to the bone.

bre·ba·je m. unpalatable concoction or brew.

bré·col m. *or* **bré·co·les** m.pl. BOT. broccoli.
bre·cha f. MIL. breach; *(aberturc)* gap, opening; FIG. *(impresión)* impression <*nada hace b. en él* nothing makes an impression on him> ♦ **abrir b.** MIL. to breach, make a breach; FIG. to make an impression • **batir en b.** MIL. to batter • **estar siempre en la b.** FIG. to be on the alert, be on one's toes.
bre·ga f. *(pelea)* fight, scrap; *(trabajo)* hard work, task; *(burla)* practical joke, trick ♦ **andar a la b.** to toil, work hard • **dar b. a** to tease, play a trick on.
bre·gar §47 intr. *(pelear)* to fight, scrap; *(trabajar)* to toil, slave away; FIG. *(esforzarse)* to struggle, fight —tr. CUL. to knead with a rolling pin.
Bre·ma Bremen.
bren·ca f. sluice post.
bre·ña f. scrub, rough ground.
bre·ñal m. brambly, rugged ground.
bre·ño·so, –sa adj. rough, craggy (ground).
bre·que m. ICHTH. bleak, blay; AMER. *(brete)* fetter, shackle; *(freno)* hand brake; *(vagón)* luggage van.
bre·que·ro m. AMER. brakeman.
bre·ta·ña f. *(tela)* Brittany cloth; BOT. *(jacinto)* hyacinth.
Bre·ta·ña f. Brittany.
bre·te m. *(grillete)* shackle, fetter; FIG. *(aprieto)* jam, tight spot; BOT. betel; ARG., AGR. branding *or* butchering chute; P. RICO, FIG. love affair.
bre·tón, –to·na I. adj. Breton II. m.f. *(persona)* Breton —m. *(idioma)* Breton; BOT. Brussels sprout ♦ **bretones** Brussels sprouts.
bre·va f. BOT. *(higo)* early fig; *(bellota)* early acorn; *(puro)* flat cigar; FIG. *(ventaja)* windfall, piece of luck <*me cayó una buena b.* I had a real piece of luck>; AMER. chewing tobacco ♦ **estar** *or* **ponerse más blando que una b.** to be as gentle as a lamb. • **¡no caerá esa b.!** no such luck!
bre·ve I. adj. *(corto)* brief, short; PHONET. short ♦ **en b.** *(pronto)* shortly, soon; *(con brevedad)* in short, in brief II. m. RELIG. papal brief —f. MUS., PHONET. breve.
bre·ve·dad f. briefness, brevity ♦ **a la mayor b. posible** COM. as soon as possible.
bre·ve·men·te adv. briefly, in brief.
bre·via·rio m. RELIG. breviary; *(compendio)* compendium, abstract; FIG. *(lectura habitual)* favorite author *or* reading; PRINT. *(letra)* brevier (type size).
bria·ga f. *(cuerda)* esparto rope; MEX. drinking binge, drunk.
bri·ba f. idle life, vagabond's life ♦ **andar** *or* **vivir a la b.** to loaf around, bum around.
bri·bón, –bo·na I. adj. *(perezoso)* lazy, loafing; *(pícaro)* rascally, roguish II. m.f. *(holgazán)* loafer, bum; *(pícaro)* rascal, rogue.
bri·bo·na·da f. *(cualidad)* roguishness; *(acción)* trickery, knavery.
bri·bo·ne·ar intr. *(holgazanear)* to loaf about, bum around; *(hacer bribonadas)* to play mischievous tricks.
bri·bo·ne·rí·a f. *(vida)* life of loafing, bum's life; *(picardía)* dirty *or* roguish trick.
bri·cho m. gold *or* silver spangle (used in embroidery).
bri·da f. EQUIT. bridle; MED. *(adhesión)* adhesion *or* abcess fiber; MECH. *(collarín)* flange; *(grapa)* splice bar, clamp ♦ **a toda b.** EQUIT. at full gallop; FIG. *(a velocidad máxima)* at full speed.
bridge m. *(naipes)* bridge; DENT. *(prótesis)* bridge, bridge-work ♦ **b. contrato** contract bridge.
bri·ga·da f. MIL. *(regimiento)* brigade; *(división)* squad, unit; *(de bestias)* team, train; *(de máquinas)* fleet; *(grado)* sergeant first class, sergeant major; FIG. *(equipo)* gang, team.
bri·ga·dier m. MIL. brigade leader, brigadier general.
bri·llan·te I. adj. brilliant, shining II. m. JEWEL. brilliant.
bri·llan·tez f. brilliance, brightness.
bri·llan·ti·na f. *(cosmético)* brilliantine, hair cream; *(tela)* brilliantine, shiny percaline.
bri·llar intr. *(resplandecer)* to shine, to sparkle; FIG. *(sobresalir)* to shine, stand out.
bri·llo m. *(lustre)* brilliance, shine; FIG. *(gloria)* distinction, glory ♦ **dar** *or* **sacar b. a** to shine, polish.
brin m. *(tela)* fine canvas, duck; *(brizna)* thread of saffron.
brin·car §70 intr. *(saltar)* to jump (up and down), leap

about; *(retozar)* to frolic, gambol; FIG., COLL. *(enfadarse)* to get angry, flare up ♦ **está que brinca** she's hopping mad —tr. to bounce, dandle (a child).
brin·co m. jump, hop, skip ♦ **en** *or* **de un b.** AMER., FIG., COLL. in a jiffy • **quitar los brincos a** COL., VEN. to bring down a peg.
brin·dar intr. to toast, drink a toast ♦ **b. a** *or* **por** to toast, drink to —tr. *(ofrecer)* to offer <*los techos brindaban protección durante la tormenta* the roofs offered protection during the storm>; *(convidar)* to invite <*la buena voluntad brinda a grandes obras* good will invites great works> —reflx. to offer, volunteer <*ella se brindó a ir conmigo* she volunteered to go with me>.
brin·dis m. toast (drink or speech) ♦ **echar** *or* **anunciar un b.** to toast, drink to one's health.
brin·qué, brinque see **brincar.**
brí·o m. *(vigor)* strength, vigor; FIG. *(espíritu)* mettle, pluck; *(garbo)* grace, charm ♦ **cortar** *or* **bajar los bríos** to humble, dash (one's) hopes.
briol m. MARIT. buntline.
¡brios! interj. COLL. damn!
brio·so, –sa adj. *(enérgico)* energetic, vigorous; *(determinado)* determined, resolute; FIG. *(animoso)* fiery, spirited; *(garboso)* graceful, charming.
bri·que·ta f. charcoal briquette.
bri·sa f. breeze, light wind; AGR. bagasse.
bris·ca·do, –da I. past part. see **briscar** II. adj. brocaded, woven with silk and metallic threads.
bris·car §70 tr. to brocade.
bris·tol m. Bristol board.
bri·tá·ni·co, –ca adj. British, English.
bri·ta·no, –na I. adj. British, English II. m.f. Briton —m. Englishman —f. Englishwoman ♦ **los britanos** the British.
briz·na f. BOT. string, fiber, blade; FIG. *(trozo)* bit, piece; VEN. drizzle.
briz·no·so, –sa adj. stringy, fibrous.
bro·ca f. SEW. *(rodajuela)* bobbin, reel; MECH. *(taladro)* drill, bit; *(clavo)* shoemaker's tack.
bro·ca·do, –da I. adj. brocaded II. m. brocade.
bro·cal m. *(de un pozo)* curb (of a well); *(de una bota)* mouthpiece (of a wineskin); *(de un escudo)* ornamental steel rim (on a shield); MIL. *(de un cañón)* bushing, flange (on the mouth of a cannon); MIN. shaft mouth *or* opening; ARM. metal ring *or* mouth (of a scabbard).
bro·cé, broce see **brozar.**
bro·ce·ar·se reflx. AMER., MIN. to become mined out (vein, deposit); *(estropearse)* to fail, fold up (business).
bro·ce·o m. AMER., MIN. exhaustion, depletion (of a mine).
bró·cu·li m. BOT. broccoli.
bro·cha f. PAINT. *(pincel)* paintbrush; *(de afeitar)* shaving brush; *(dado)* loaded die; CUBA, SPORT. quoits; C. AMER. meddler, flatterer ♦ **de b. gorda** ARTS, FIG., COLL. second-rate, heavy-handed • **hacerse b.** GUAT. to play the fool.
bro·cha·da f. brush stroke II. adj. see **brochado, –da.**
bro·cha·do, –da I. adj. brocade II. f. see **brochada.**
bro·cha·zo m. brush stroke.
bro·che m. *(enganche)* clasp, hook and eye, metal snap; *(prendedor)* brooch; AMER. paper clip ♦ **b. de oro** FIG. crowning glory • **broches** AMER. cuff links.
bro·che·ta f. CUL. brochette, skewer.
bro·ma f. *(chanza)* joke, prank; *(diversión)* fun, jest; ZOOL. shipworm ♦ **b. pesada** practical joke, prank • **¡déjate de bromas!** COLL. stop kidding around! • **en b.** in jest, jokingly • **entre bromas y veras** half joking • **estar de b.** to be joking • **gastar** *or* **hacer una b. a** to play a joke on • **ni en b.** not for a second, not on your life • **no estar para bromas** not to be in the mood for jokes • **tomar en b.** to take as a joke.
bro·mar tr. to gnaw, bore (shipworm).
bro·ma·to m. CHEM. bromate.
bro·ma·zo m. stupid *or* tasteless joke.
bro·me·ar intr. to joke, jest.
bro·mis·ta I. adj. joking II. m.f. joker, jokester.
bro·mo m. CHEM. bromine; BOT. brome grass.
bro·mu·ro m. CHEM. bromide.
bron·ca I. f. *(riña)* row, quarrel; *(reprensión)* telling off, scolding; *(desagrado)* jeering, booing; ARG. rage, anger ♦

armar b. to kick up a rumpus, start a row • **echar una b. a** to tell off, give a piece of one's mind to **II.** adj. see **bronco, –ca.**

bron·ce m. MIN. bronze; NUMIS. copper coin; POET. cannon, bell, trumpet ♦ **b. amarillo** METAL. brass • **ser un b. or de b.** COLL. *(ser insensible)* to be hard-hearted, have a heart of stone; *(ser enérgetico)* to be robust and tireless.

bron·ce·a·do, –da I. past part. see **broncear II.** adj. *(color)* bronze, bronze-colored; *(tostado)* tanned, bronzed **III.** m. ARTS, METAL. bronzing; *(piel tostada)* suntan.

bron·ce·ar tr. ARTS, METAL. to bronze; *(piel)* to tan, suntan —reflex. to get a tan, suntan.

bron·cis·ta m. bronzesmith.

bron·co, –ca I. adj. *(tosco)* rough, coarse; METAL. *(quebradizo)* brittle; *(desapacible)* harsh, gruff; FIG. *(desabrido)* surly, gruff **II.** f. see **bronca.**

bron·co·neu·mo·ní·a f. MED. bronchopneumonia.

bron·que·dad or **bron·que·ra** f. *(tosquedad)* coarseness, roughness; *(aspereza)* harshness, gruffness (of voice, character); *(calidad de quebradizo)* brittleness (metals).

bron·quial adj. ANAT. bronchial.

bron·quiec·ta·sia f. MED. bronchiectasis.

bron·qui·na f. COLL. quarrel, row.

bron·quio m. ANAT. bronchus, bronchial tube.

bron·quio·lo m. ANAT. bronchiole.

bron·qui·tis f. MED. bronchitis.

bro·quel m. *(escudo)* buckler, small shield; FIG. *(amparo)* shield, protection.

bro·que·lar·se reflex. to shield oneself, protect oneself.

bro·que·ta f. CUL. brochette, skewer.

bro·ta·du·ra f. sprouting, budding.

bro·tar intr. BOT. *(germinar)* to bud, sprout; to spring, flow <*el agua brota de la fuente* water flows from the fountain>; FIG. to flow, stream <*las lágrimas brotaban de sus ojos* tears streamed from his eyes>; to break out, spring up <*el descontento brotó por todas partes de la ciudad* discontent sprang up all over the city>; MED. to break out, appear (pimples) —tr. BOT. to sprout <*mi jardín brotó flores en dos semanas* my garden sprouted flowers in two weeks>.

bro·te m. BOT. bud, sprout; FIG. outbreak, rash <*un b. de violencia* an outbreak of violence>; *(comienzo)* origin, germ.

bro·za f. *(hojas muertas)* dead leaves; *(ramas)* brushwood, dead wood; *(deshechos)* rubbish, refuse; *(maleza)* undergrowth, underbrush; FIG. *(paja)* rubbish, trash <*hay mucha b. en esa novela* there is a lot of trash in that novel>; PRINT. *(bruza)* printer's brush.

bro·zar §04 tr. PRINT. to brush, clean with a brush (typeface).

bro·zo·so, –sa adj. *(cubierto de broza)* brushy; *(lleno de broza)* full of rubbish.

bru·cé, bruce see **bruzar.**

bru·ces ♦ **a** or **de b.** adv. face down, on one's face • **caer de b.** to fall flat on one's face.

bru·ja f. *(mujer)* witch, sorceress; FIG., COLL. *(tarasca)* old witch, hag; ORNITH. barn owl ♦ **estar b.** CUBA, MEX., P. RICO, COLL. to be penniless or broke.

bru·je·ar intr. to practice witchcraft.

bru·je·rí·a f. witchcraft, sorcery, magic.

bru·jo m. *(adivino)* sorcerer, wizard; *(de una tribu)* witch doctor, medicine man.

brú·ju·la f. compass; ARM. *(mira)* sight; FIG. *(norma)* standard, norm ♦ **perder la b.** FIG. to lose one's bearings.

bru·lo·te m. MARIT., MIL. fire ship; AMER. *(palabrota)* offensive word, swear word; *(escrito satírico)* satiric article, incendiary article.

bru·ma f. fog, mist.

bru·mal adj. misty, foggy.

bru·ma·zón m. heavy or thick fog.

bru·mo m. refined wax, pure wax (for dipping church tapers).

bru·mo·so, –sa adj. foggy, misty.

bru·no, –na adj. dark-colored, black <*cabello b.* dark-colored hair>.

bru·ñi·do, –da I. past part. see **bruñir II.** m. *(acción)* burnishing, polishing; *(brillo)* shine, gloss **III.** adj. burnished, polished.

bru·ñi·dor, –do·ra I. adj. polishing, burnishing **II.** m.f. polisher, burnisher —m. polishing tool.

bru·ñi·du·ra f. or **bru·ñi·mien·to** m. *(acción)* polishing, burnishing; *(brillo)* shine, polish.

bru·ñir §12 tr. *(pulir)* to burnish, polish; AMER., COLL. to annoy, pester —reflex. FIG., COLL. to put on make-up.

brus·co, –ca I. adj. *(áspero)* curt, brusque; *(súbito)* sudden, abrupt **II.** m. BOT. butcherbroom, butcher's broom.

Bru·se·las f. Brussels.

bru·se·len·se I. adj. of Brussels **II.** m.f. native of Brussels.

brus·que·dad f. *(aspereza)* curtness, brusqueness; *(lo repentino)* suddenness, abruptness.

bru·tal I. adj. *(cruel)* brutal; FIG. *(formidable)* terrific, tremendous <*un ruido b.* a tremendous noise> **II.** m. brute, beast.

bru·ta·li·dad f. *(crueldad)* brutality; FIG. *(incapacidad)* stupidity, foolishness; *(gran cantidad)* loads, slew <*compraron una b. de comida* they bought a slew of food>.

bru·ta·li·zar §04 tr. to brutalize, maltreat —reflex. to be brutalized.

bru·te·za f. *(grosería)* brutishness, boorishness; *(tosquedad)* roughness, crudeness.

bru·to, –ta I. adj. *(necio)* stupid, ignorant; *(grosero)* brutish, boorish; *(rough, uncut)* <*un diamante b.* an uncut diamond>; COLL. *(enorme)* huge, enormous; COM. gross <*peso b.* gross weight>; CHILE inferior ♦ **a la b.** or **a lo b.** S. AMER. roughly, crudely • **en b.** in the rough, in a rough state; DOM. REP., P. RICO to excess, excessively • **noble b.** POET. horse **II.** m. *(persona)* brute; *(animal)* beast, animal.

bru·za f. *(cepillo fuerte)* coarse brush, scrubbing brush; *(cepillo de caballería)* horse brush; *(cepillo de imprenta)* printer's brush.

bru·zar §04 tr. to brush, clean with a coarse brush.

bu m. bogeyman ♦ **hacer el b. a uno** to scare someone.

bú·a f. MED. bubo, pustule.

bu·ba f. *(tumor)* pustule, small tumor; *(ganglio linfático)* yaws, pian.

bu·bón m. MED. large tumor or swelling.

bu·bó·ni·co, –ca adj. MED. bubonic.

bu·cal adj. ANAT. buccal, oral.

bu·ca·ne·ro m. HIST. buccaneer, pirate.

Bu·ca·rest m. Bucharest.

bú·ca·ro m. *(arcilla)* fragrant clay; *(botijo)* clay water jug; *(florero)* ceramic flower vase; HOND., BOT. kind of lily.

bu·ce see **buzar.**

bu·ce·ar intr. *(nadar)* to swim under water; *(oficio)* to dive, work as a diver; FIG. *(explorar)* to delve into, explore.

bu·ce·o m. *(natación)* underwater swimming; FIG. *(exploración)* exploration, searching.

bu·cle m. *(cabellos)* ringlet, curl; AVIA. spin, loop.

bu·có·li·co, –ca I. adj. bucolic, pastoral **II.** f. *(poema)* bucolic, pastoral poem; COLL. *(comida)* meal; *(hambre)* hunger.

bu·co·lis·mo m. liking for bucolic poetry.

bu·cha·da f. mouthful.

bu·che m. ORNITH. crop, craw; ZOOL. maw; *(porción)* mouthful, swallow <*un b. de café* a swallow of coffee>; *(pliegue)* sag, pucker; COLL. *(estómago)* belly, gut; FIG., COLL. *(pecho)* chest, bosom; ECUAD. top hat; MEX. goiter; CUBA bum.

bu·che·te m. puffed-up cheek.

bu·chón, –cho·na adj. *(paloma)* pouter, pouting (pigeon); CUBA *(bonachón)* nice, good-natured; VEN. *(trampista)* dishonest (public official).

Bu·da m. RELIG. Buddha.

bu·dín m. CUL. pudding.

bu·dis·mo m. RELIG. Buddhism.

bu·dis·ta adj. & m.f. RELIG. Buddhist.

buen adj. [contr. of **bueno** used before m. sing. nouns] good fine <*hace b. tiempo* the weather is fine> —see **bueno, –na.**

bue·nan·dan·za f. var. of **bienandanza.**

bue·na·ven·tu·ra f. *(suerte)* good fortune, luck; *(adivinación)* fortune <*decirle a uno la b.* to tell someone's fortune>.

bue·no, –na §G21, 24 **I.** adj. good; *(bondadoso)* kind, benevolent; *(útil)* fit, appropriate; *(sano)* well, healthy;

(agradable) nice, polite; *(grande)* considerable, goodly <*una b. cantidad de comida* a goodly amount of food>; *(no deteriorado)* in good condition; *(bonachón)* innocent, naive ♦ *a or por las buenas* FIG. willingly • **a la b. de Dios** carelessly, any old way • **¡buenas!** greetings! • **buenas noches** good night, good evening • **buenas tardes** good afternoon • **¡b. está!** that's enough! • **buenos días** good morning • **dar por b.** to approve • **de buenas a primeras** all of a sudden • **estar de buenas** to be in a good mood • **estar en la b.** S. AMER., COLL. to be on a roll • **librarse de una b.** COLL. to escape just in time II. adv. very well, all right, okay <*¿Te acompaño hasta la esquina? Bueno.* May I accompany you to the corner? Okay.> III. m. good <*separar lo b. de lo malo* to separate good from evil> ♦ **lo b. es que** the best part *or* funny thing is • **los buenos** good *or* decent people.

buey m. ZOOL. ox, bullock; MEX., FIG. cuckold; ARG., URUG. meddler, busybody; P. RICO fortune ♦ **b. corneta** AMER., FIG. troublemaker • **b. de agua** hydraulic measure • **b. de cabestrillo** hunting blind • **b. de Tibet** ZOOL. yak • **b. marino** ZOOL. sea cow • **b. muerto** P. RICO bargain • **b. suelto** free agent; COLL. *(soltero)* bachelor • **conversar** *or* **hablar de bueyes perdidos** COLL. to prattle, chatter • **pegar bueyes** C. AMER. to go to sleep • **saber los bueyes con que ara** COLL. to know who can (and cannot) be trusted • **trabajar como un b.** COLL. to work like a dog.

bue·ya·da f. AMER. var. of **boyada**.

bú·fa·lo, -la m.f. ZOOL. *(buey salvaje)* buffalo; *(bisonte)* bison.

bu·fan·da f. scarf, muffler.

bu·far intr. *(resoplar)* to snort; FIG., COLL. *(enojarse)* to snort, puff *(with anger)* —reflex. MEX. to bulge, blister.

bu·fe·te m. *(escritorio)* writing desk *or* table; FIG. *(despacho)* lawyer's office; *(clientela)* lawyer's clientele, practice ♦ **abrir b.** LAW to set up practice, open a law office.

bu·fi·do m. bellow, snort.

bu·fo, -fa I. adj. comic, farcical II. m. clown, buffoon.

bu·fón, -fo·na I. adj. buffoonish, clownish II. m.f. buffoon, clown, jester.

bu·fo·na·da *or* **bu·fo·ne·rí·a** f. *(broma)* buffoonery, jest; *(sarcasmo)* sarcastic joke *or* remark.

bu·fo·ne·ar·se reflex. *(hacer bufonadas)* to play the fool; *(burlarse)* to make fun.

bu·fo·nes·co, -ca adj. comical, clownish.

bu·fo·ni·zar §04 intr. to joke, jest.

bu·har·da *or* **bu·har·di·lla** f. ARCHIT. *(ventana)* dormer; *(desván)* attic, garret.

bú·ho m. ORNITH. eagle owl, horned owl; FIG., COLL. *(recluso)* recluse, hermit.

bu·ho·ne·rí·a f. peddler's wares, trinkets.

bu·ho·ne·ro m. peddler, hawker.

bui·do, -da adj. *(afilado)* sharp; *(acanalado)* grooved.

bui·tre m. ORNITH. vulture.

bui·tre·ra I. f. vulture trap ♦ **estar ya para b.** to be ready for the vultures, be about to die (animal) II. adj. see **buitrero, -ra**.

bui·tre·ro, -ra I. adj. vulturine II. m. vulture hunter —f. see **buitrera**.

bui·trón m. *(nasa)* fish trap, weir; *(red)* game hunting net; *(trampa)* snare, trap; MIN. *(cenicero)* ashpit (of furnace); AMER., MIN. *(horno)* silver-smelting furnace; *(era)* working yard for silver ore.

bu·je m. MECH. axle box, bushing.

bu·je·rí·a f. knickknack, trinket.

bu·je·ta f. *(caja)* wooden box; *(estuche)* perfume box; *(pomo)* perfume bottle.

bu·jí·a f. *(vela)* candle; *(candelero)* candlestick; PHYS. *(medida luminosa)* candle, candlepower; ELEC. spark plug; MED. bougie, suppository.

bu·la f. *(sello)* metal seal, bulla; RELIG. papal bull ♦ **hay bulas para difuntos** COLL. where there's a will, there's a way.

bul·bo m. ANAT., BOT. bulb.

bul·dog *or* **bull·dog** m. ZOOL. bulldog.

bu·le·var m. boulevard.

Bul·ga·ria f. Bulgaria.

búl·ga·ro, -ra adj. & m.f. Bulgarian, Bulgar —m. *(idioma)* Bulgarian.

bu·li·mia f. MED. bulimia.

bu·lo m. COLL. false report, hoax.

bul·to m. *(tamaño)* bulk, size; *(forma)* form, shape <*no puede ver más que bultos en la neblina* he can see only shapes in the fog>; *(fardo)* package, bundle; MED. swelling, lump; ARTS bust, statue; AMER. briefcase, satchel ♦ **a b.** broadly; COM. wholesale • **buscar el b. a alguien** FIG., COLL. to try to get someone's goat • **coger en el b. a** FIG., COLL. to grab, catch • **de b.** important • **de gran b.** bulky • **escurrir el b.** to duck, dodge • **hacer b.** to take up space, provide filler.

bu·lu·lú m. *(farsante)* strolling player (performing alone); AMER. *(alboroto)* racket, commotion.

bu·lla f. *(ruido)* noise, racket; *(muchedumbre)* crowd, mob; FIG. *(prisa)* bustling, rush; AMER. argument, row ♦ **armar b.** to make a racket, create a stir • **tener b.** to be in a hurry.

bu·llan·gue·ro, -ra I. adj. noisy, rowdy II. m.f. noisy *or* boisterous person.

bu·lle·bu·lle m. COLL. busybody, nosy person.

bu·lli·cio m. bustle, hubbub.

bu·lli·cio·so, -sa adj. *(animado)* bustling; *(alborotador)* riotous, tumultuous.

bu·lli·dor, -do·ra adj. bustling, lively.

bu·llir §13 intr. *(hervir)* to boil; *(agitarse)* to bubble (up); FIG. *(moverse)* to bustle about; ZOOL. *(pulular)* to swarm; to bustle <*la conferencia bullía con nuevas ideas* the conference bustled with new ideas> —tr. to bulge, move —reflex. to budge, stir <*no quería bullirse* he didn't want to budge>.

bu·llón m. *(clavo)* ornamental stud (on book binding); *(bollo)* puff (on a dress).

bu·me·rán m. boomerang.

bu·nia·to m. var. of **boniato**.

bu·ño·le·rí·a f. stand *or* shop selling fried dough.

bu·ño·le·ro, -ra m.f. fried dough seller.

bu·ñue·lo m. *(churro)* fried dough, fritter; COLL. *(algo mal hecho)* mess, bungle.

bu·que m. *(barco)* ship, vessel; *(casco)* hull ♦ **b. almirante** flagship • **b. carguero** *or* **de carga** freighter, cargo ship • **b. de cabotaje** coaster • **b. de cruz** square-rigger • **b. de guerra** warship • **b. de vapor** steamer, steamship • **b. mercante** merchant ship • **b. petrolero** oil tanker • **b. tanque** tanker • **b. velero** *or* **de vela** sailboat, sailing ship.

bu·qué m. bouquet.

bu·ra·to m. *(tejido)* Canton crepe; *(manto)* transparent veil of light silk.

bur·bu·ja f. bubble.

bur·bu·je·ar intr. to bubble.

bur·del I. adj. lustful, licentious II. m. brothel, whorehouse.

bur·de·os I. adj. maroon, deep red II. m. Bordeaux (wine).

Bur·de·os m. Bordeaux.

bur·do, -da adj. coarse, rough.

bu·re·o m. entertainment, amusement ♦ **darse un b.** COLL. to take a walk • **ir de b.** to go off and have a good time.

bur·ga f. hot springs, spa.

bur·ga·lés, -le·sa I. adj. of Burgos II. m.f. native of Burgos.

bur·go·ma·es·tre m. burgomaster, mayor.

Bur·gos Burgos.

bur·gués, -gue·sa I. adj. bourgeois, middle-class II. m.f. bourgeois, middle-class person; HIST. burgher.

bur·gue·sí·a f. bourgeoisie, middle class.

bu·ril m. burin, graver.

bu·ri·la·du·ra f. engraving.

bu·ri·lar tr. to engrave.

bur·ja·ca f. large leather bag (used by beggars, pilgrims).

bur·la f. *(mofa)* jeer, taunt; *(chanza)* joke, jest; *(engaño)* trick, hoax ♦ **b. burlando** COLL. *(sin advertirlo)* unawares; *(disimuladamente)* on the sly; *(en broma)* jokingly • **burlas aparte** joking aside • **de burlas** in fun, for fun • **hacer b. de** to make fun of, mock.

bur·la·de·ro m. TAUR. covert, refuge in bull ring (allowing bullfighter to escape animal).

bur·la·dor, -do·ra I. adj. mocking, jesting II. m.f. mocker —m. *(libertino)* seducer, Don Juan.

bur·lar tr. to make fun of, mock; *(frustrar)* to frustrate, thwart <*el veredicto burló sus esperanzas de libertad* the verdict thwarted his hopes for liberty> —reflex. to make fun, joke ♦ **burlarse de** to make fun of, ridicule.

bur·le·rí·a f. *(engaño)* deception, trick; *(mofa)* mockery, scoffing; *(cuento)* tall tale.

bur·les·co, -ca adj. burlesque; COLL. *(jocoso)* funny, comical.

bur·le·te m. weather stripping.

bur·lón, -lo·na I. adj. *(que se mofa)* jeering, mocking; *(bromista)* joking II. m.f. *(mofador)* jeerer, mocker; *(bromista)* joker, jokester.

bu·ro·cra·cia f. bureaucracy.

bu·ró·cra·ta m.f. bureaucrat.

bu·ro·crá·ti·co, -ca adj. bureaucratic.

bu·rra f. ZOOL. she-ass, jenny; FIG., COLL. *(ignorante)* stupid woman, dunce; *(trabajadora)* hard worker, slave, C. AMER. *(caballete)* sawhorse ♦ **caer uno de su b.** COLL. to acknowledge one's errors • **írsele a uno la b.** COLL. to let the cat out of the bag, spit something out.

bu·rra·da f. ZOOL. drove of asses *or* donkeys; FIG., COLL. *(necedad)* asinine action *or* remark; *(atrocidad)* vulgar *or* obscene action ♦ **una b.** a lot, tons • **decir burradas** to talk nonsense.

bu·rra·jo, -ja I. m. dry stable dung II. adj. coarse, rude.

bu·rre·ro m. donkey driver.

bu·rro m. ZOOL. donkey, jackass; *(caballete)* sawhorse, sawbuck; *(rueda)* cogwheel; FIG. *(borrico)* ass, dunce; SPORT. *(instrumento de gimnasia)* horse (in gymnastics); MARIT. feed pump; MEX. *(escalera)* stepladder; *(pelo)* bangs; *(mesa para planchar)* ironing board ♦ **b. cargado de letras** FIG., COLL. pompous ass • **b. de carga** FIG., COLL. hard worker, drudge • **apearse** *or* **caerse del b.** to acknowledge a mistake, back down • **ver burros negros** VEN. to see stars.

bur·sá·til adj. COM. stock, stock market.

bu·ru·jo m. *(bulto)* lump (in paste, dough); *(nudo)* tangle, knot (in ball of wool); *(pasto)* cattle cake (made of ground olives).

Bu·run·di Burundi.

bu·run·dia·no, -na I. adj. of Burundi II. m.f. native of Burundi.

bus·ca I. f. *(búsqueda)* search; HUNT. *(cacería)* party of hunters II. f.pl. AMER., COLL. perks, extra benefits (of a job) ♦ **ir en** *or* **a la b. de** to go in search of.

bus·ca·da f. search, pursuit.

bus·ca·dor, -do·ra I. adj. searching II. m.f. searcher, seeker —m. TECH. finder (in optical instruments).

bus·ca·pié m. FIG. feeler, insinuation (in conversation).

bus·ca·piés m. [pl. **-piés**] firecracker, squib.

bus·car §70 tr. *(inquirir)* to search *or* look for, seek; COLL. to provoke <*no me busques, que me encontrarás* don't provoke me, or you'll get it>; AMER. to ask *or* look for <*estoy buscando a Juan Pérez* I am looking for Juan Pérez> —reflex. ♦ **buscársela** *(ingeniarse)* to get by, manage; *(provocar)* to look for trouble.

bus·ca·rrui·dos m.f. [pl. **-dos**] COLL., FIG. troublemaker.

bus·ca·vi·das m.f. [pl. **-das**] FIG., COLL. *(entremetido)* snoop, busybody; *(ambicioso)* hustler, go-getter; MEX. gossip, tattletale.

bus·co m. base of a sluice gate.

bus·cón, -co·na I. adj. searching, seeking II. m.f. *(ratero)* pickpocket; *(ladrón)* pretty thief; *(estafador)* swindler, chiseler —f. COLL. streetwalker, prostitute.

bus·co·ne·ar intr. to pry, snoop.

bu·si·lis m. [pl. **-lis**] COLL. *(clave)* crux of a matter; *(dificultad)* hitch, snag ♦ **ahí esta el b.** there's the rub, there's the catch.

bus·qué, busque see **buscar.**

bús·que·da f. *(busca)* search, quest; *(investigación)* investigation, research.

bus·to m. ANAT. chest, bust; SCULP. bust.

bus·tró·fe·don m. LIT. boustrophedon (writing lines alternately from left to right and right to left).

bu·ta·ca f. *(sillón)* armchair, easy chair; THEAT. orchestra *or* box seat.

bu·ta·no m. CHEM. butane.

bu·ti·fa·rra f. *(longaniza)* pork sausage; PERU *(bocadillo)*

---

ham, lettuce and onion sandwich; COLL. *(media)* baggy, loose stocking; ARG., COLL. *(farra)* spree, wild party.

bu·ti·le·no m. CHEM. butylene.

buz m. formal kiss, kiss of respect ♦ **hacer el b.** to bow and scrape.

bu·zar §04 intr. GEOL. to dip.

bu·zo m. (deep-sea) diver.

bu·zón m. *(correo)* mailbox, letter box; *(conducto)* sluice, canal; *(tapón)* stopper, plug.

C

c, C f. third letter of the Spanish alphabet.

ca·bal I. adj. *(exacto)* exact, precise; FIG. *(recto)* just, fair <*un hombre recto* a fair man>; *(completo)* complete, total II. adv. exactly, precisely ♦ **en sus cabales** FIG. in one's right mind • **por sus cabales** exactly, precisely.

cá·ba·la f. RELIG. *(doctrina)* cabala, kabbala; *(adivinación)* superstitious divination; FIG. *(cálculo)* esoteric calculation; FIG., COLL. *(intriga)* intrigue, cabal ♦ **hacer cábalas sobre algo** to conjecture, speculate about something.

ca·bal·ga·da f. *(tropa de jinetes)* cavalry troop; *(correría)* cavalry raid, foray.

ca·bal·ga·dor, -do·ra m.f. rider —m. horseman —f. horsewoman.

ca·bal·gar §47 intr. EQUIT. *(pasear)* to ride horseback, to go riding <*c. sobre un caballo blanco* to go riding on a white horse> ♦ **c. a mujeriegas** EQUIT. to ride sidesaddle —tr. to ride, mount; ZOOL. to cover, copulate with.

ca·bal·ga·ta f. procession, parade, cavalcade.

ca·ba·lis·ta m. *(estudioso)* cabalist; *(intrigante)* intriguer.

ca·ba·lís·ti·co, -ca adj. *(de la cábala)* cabalistic; FIG. *(misterioso)* mysterious, occult.

ca·bal·men·te adv. *(totalmente)* totally, fully; *(precisamente)* exactly, precisely; *(justamente)* justly, fairly.

ca·ba·lla f. ICHTH. mackerel.

ca·ba·lla·da f. *(manada)* herd of horses; AMER. asinine remark *or* action ♦ **hacer caballadas** to make a fool of oneself.

ca·ba·llar adj. equine, pertaining to *or* resembling horses.

ca·ba·lla·za f. AMER. trampling, collision (on horseback).

ca·ba·lle·ar intr. COLL. to go horseback riding frequently.

ca·ba·lle·res·ca·men·te adv. gallantly, chivalrously.

ca·ba·lle·res·co, -ca adj. *(de un caballero andante)* chivalric, knightly; *(cortés)* chivalrous, gentlemanly; FIG. *(elevado)* noble, refined.

ca·ba·lle·rí·a f. *(animal)* mount, steed; *(orden militar)* order of knights; *(hidalguía)* chivalry; MIL. cavalry ♦ **andarse en caballerías** FIG., COLL. to bow and scrape, be overly courteous • **c. andante** knight-errantry • **c. ligera** MIL. light cavalry • **c. mayor** mule, horse • **c. menor** donkey, ass.

ca·ba·lle·ri·za f. *(cuadra)* stable, barn; *(caballos)* stud, stable; *(criados)* stablehands, staff of grooms.

ca·ba·lle·ri·zo m. groom, stableman ♦ **c. mayor del rey** Master of the Horse.

ca·ba·lle·ro, -ra I. m. *(noble)* noble, nobleman; *(persona condecorada)* knight; *(señor)* gentleman <*ser todo un c.* to be a real gentleman>; sir <*perdone usted, c.* excuse me, sir> ♦ **armar c. a** to knight, dub • **c. andante** knight-errant • **c. cubierto** SP. grandee • **c. de (la) industria** FIG. swindler, con man • **c. solitario** FIG. lone wolf II. adj. riding, mounted <*c. sobre un borrico* mounted on a donkey>; FIG. obstinate, stubborn <*c. en sus intenciones* stubborn in his intentions>.

ca·ba·lle·ro·si·dad f. chivalry, gentlemanliness.

ca·ba·lle·ro·so, -sa adj. *(noble)* noble, chivalrous; *(cortés)* gallant, gentlemanly.

ca·ba·lle·te m. ARCHIT. *(borde)* ridge (of a roof); *(soporte)* sawhorse; PAINT. *(trípode)* easel; AGR. ridge; ANAT. bridge (of the nose); rack <*lo torturaron en el c.* they tortured him on the rack>.

ca·ba·llis·ta m. *(experto)* expert on horses *or* horsemanship; *(jinete)* expert rider, horseman —f. horsewoman.

ca·ba·lli·to m. *(caballo pequeño)* pony; *(juguete)* hobbyhorse ♦ **c. del diablo** AMER., ENTOM. dragonfly, devil's darning needle • **c. de mar** sea horse • **caballitos** merry-go-round.

ca·ba·llo m. ZOOL. horse; *(jinete)* rider, horseman *<una tropa de quinientos caballos* a troop of five hundred horsemen>; *(pieza de ajedrez)* knight (in chess); *(en los naipes)* Spanish playing card; FIG., COLL. *(bestia)* brute, beast; *(bruto)* oaf, dolt; CARP. sawhorse; MIN. vein of barren rock ♦ **a c.** mounted, on horseback • **a c. de** astride • **a mata c.** at breakneck speed • **c. blanco** FIG., COLL. financial backer, sponsor • **c. de agua o de mar** ZOOL. hippopotamus; ICHTH. sea horse • **c. de batalla** charger, steed; FIG. forte, specialty *<la química es su c. de batalla* chemistry is his forte>; central issue, focal point *<el c. de batalla de la controversia es el dinero* the focal point of the controversy is money> • **c. de buena boca** FIG., COLL. easygoing person • **c. de carga** packhorse • **c. de carrera** ZOOL. racehorse • **c. de Frisa** or **Frisia** MIL. cheval-de-frise • **c. de fuerza** or **de vapor** MECH. horsepower • **c. del diablo** ENTOM. dragonfly • **c. de montar** or **de silla** saddle horse • **c. de posta** post horse • **c. de tiro** draft horse • **c. de Troya** FIG. Trojan horse • **c. hora** MECH. horsepower-hour • **c. marino** ZOOL. hippopotamus; ICHTH. sea horse • **c. mecedor** rocking horse • **c. negro** POL. dark horse • **c. padre** stallion • **c. blanco** MIL. cavalry, cavalrymen; MECH. horsepower *<un motor de ocho caballos* an eight-horsepower engine> • **c. semental** studhorse • **como c. desbocado** FIG. hastily, rashly • **montar a c.** to ride, go horseback riding.

ca·ba·ña f. *(choza)* hut, cabin; ZOOL. herd, drove; ARG., URUG. cattle ranch.

ca·ba·ñe·ro, –ra I. adj. of livestock or herds II. m. *(pastor)* shepherd; *(caballerizo)* stableman.

ca·ba·ret m. night club, cabaret.

ca·be·ce·ar intr. to toss the head (a horse); *(negar)* to shake one's head (in refusal, disagreement); to nod (sleepily); AVIA., MARIT. to pitch; AUTO. to lurch —tr. SEW. *(poner ribete a)* to bind; SPORT. *(en fútbol)* to head (a ball); CUBA to bind (tobacco).

ca·be·ce·o m. shaking, toss (of the head); AVIA., MARIT. pitch; AUTO. lurch.

ca·be·ce·ra f. *(lugar principal)* head *<la c. de la mesa* the head of the table>; *(principio)* source, beginning *<la c. de un río* the source of a river>; *(parte de una cama)* headboard; *(almohada)* pillow, bolster; *(título)* heading, title; POL. capital, seat; BKB. *(de un libro)* headband ♦ **c. de puente** MIL. bridgehead • **c. de río** headwaters • **cabeceras** PRINT. quoins • **de c.** bedside *<libro de c.* bedside book> • **médico de c.** attending physician.

ca·be·ci·lla m.f. *(extremista)* hothead —m. *(jefe)* ringleader, rabble-rouser —f. small head.

ca·be·lle·ra f. *(pelo)* hair, head of hair; *(peluca)* wig, toupee; ASTRON. tail (of a comet).

ca·be·llo m. hair, head of hair ♦ **asirse de un c.** FIG., COLL. to grasp at straws • **cabellos** hair *<cabellos rubios* blond hair>; BOT. corn silk • **cortar un c. en el aire** FIG., COLL. to be keen-sighted • **en c.** with one's hair down or loose • **en cabellos** bareheaded • **estar pendiente de un c.** FIG., COLL. to be hanging by a thread • **ponérsele a uno los cabellos de punta** FIG., COLL. (said of hair) to stand on end *<se me pusieron los cabellos de punta* my hair stood on end> • **traer (una cosa) por los cabellos** FIG., COLL. to be irrelevant, be out in left field *<para mí esa conclusión está traída por los cabellos* in my opinion that conclusion is out in left field>.

ca·be·llu·do, –da adj. *(peludo)* hairy, shaggy; BOT. fibrous, filamentous ♦ **cuero c.** scalp.

ca·ber §14 intr. to fit *<no cabe en el estante* it doesn't fit on the shelf>; to be one's duty or honor, fall to *<me cupo a mí darle las noticias* it fell to me to give him the news>; to be possible *<todo cabe ahora* anything is possible now> ♦ **cabe decir** it is possible to say • **no cabe duda** there is no doubt • **no cabe más** FIG. that's the limit • **no c. en sí** FIG. to be bursting or beside oneself *<ella no cabía en sí de alegría* she was beside herself with joy>; *(jactarse)* to be arrogant or boastful • **no c. un alfiler** FIG. to be full • **no me cabe en la cabeza** it's beyond me.

ca·bes·trar tr. to halter; AMER. to lead by the halter.

ca·bes·tri·llo m. MED. sling; *(cadena)* chain, necklace; MECH. *(abrazadera)* bracket, brace.

ca·bes·tro m. *(rienda)* halter, lead; *(buey guía)* lead or leading ox; FIG., COLL. *(necio)* sucker, dupe ♦ **llevar del c.** FIG. to lead by the nose.

ca·be·za f. ANAT. head; *(cráneo)* skull; *(parte superior)* head, top *<la c. de un alfiler* the head of a pin>; *(jefe)* chief, head; FIG. *(talento)* head, mind *<ella tiene buena c. para los números* she has a good head for numbers>; *(juicio)* judgment *<él no tiene c. para nada* he has no judgment at all>; *(persona)* head, person *<costará cinco pesos por c.* it will cost five pesos a head>; *(res)* head, cattle; *(fuente)* headwaters, source (of a river); *(capital)* capital, seat; *(vida)* life, head *<se jugó la c.* he risked his life> ♦ **a la c. de** *(delante de)* at the head of *<ir a la c. del ejército* to march at the head of the army>; in charge of, directing *<estar a la c. de la empresa* to be in charge of the enterprise> • **alzar c.** COLL. to get back on one's feet • **andársele** or **írsele la c.** COLL. to feel dizzy • **bajar** or **doblar la c.** COLL. to give in, submit • **c. de ajo** garlic bulb • **c. de combate** or **de guerra** MIL. warhead • **c. de chorlito** COLL. featherbrain, empty-headed person • **c. de dragón** BOT. snapdragon • **c. de grabación** TELEC. recording head • **c. de hierro** FIG., COLL. stubborn mule, ox • **c. de lectura** TELEC. playback head • **c. de partido** POL. county or district seat • **c. de playa** MIL. beachhead • **c. de proceso** LAW court order • **c. de puente** MIL. bridgehead • **c. de turco** FIG., COLL. scapegoat • **c. mayor** cattle • **c. menor** *(ovejas)* sheep; *(cabras)* goats • **c. redonda** COLL. blockhead • **calentarse la c.** FIG., COLL. to tire oneself out (mentally) • **dar de c.** FIG., COLL. to fall on hard times • **dar en la c.** to thwart, frustrate • **de c.** by heart *<lo aprendieron de c.* they learned it by heart>; pressed, in a hurry *<siempre anda de c.* she is always in a hurry> • **de la c. de uno** of one's own invention *<este plan es de mi c.* this plan is of my own invention> • **en c.** ARG. bareheaded • **escarmentar en c. ajena** FIG. to learn from another's mistakes • **estar metido de c. con** to be head over heels in love with • **hacer c.** to lead, be ahead • **ir. c. abajo** FIG., COLL. to go to the dogs • **ir de c.** COLL. to be snowed under • **írsele de la c.** to go out of one's mind • **levantar c.** FIG., COLL. to get back on one's feet • **meter la c.** FIG., COLL. to get one's foot in the door • **meterse de c. en** FIG., COLL. to plunge into • **metérsele en la c.** to take it into one's head *<se le metió en la c. la idea de ir* he took it into his head to go> • **no tener dónde volver la c.** FIG. to have nowhere to turn • **otorgar de c.** to nod assent • **pasarle a uno por la c.** FIG., COLL. to come into one's head, occur to one • **perder la c.** FIG. to lose one's head • **quebrarle** or **romperle la c.** FIG., COLL. to tire, bore • **quebrarse** or **romperse la c.** FIG., COLL. to rack one's brains • **sacar la c.** FIG., COLL. *(aparecer)* to show one's face; *(atreverse)* to speak up • **sentar la c.** FIG., COLL. to settle down • **subirse a la c.** to go to one's head • **tener la c. a las once** or **a pájaros** FIG., COLL. to be distracted • **tener la c. como una olla de grillos** FIG., COLL. to be confused • **tener mala c.** FIG., COLL. to act foolishly • **tocado de la c.** FIG., COLL. touched in the head.

ca·be·za·da f. *(con la cabeza)* butt; *(en la cabeza)* blow to the head; *(inclinación de cabeza)* nod; *(arreo)* headstall; MARIT. pitch; ARG., ECUAD., PAR. saddlebow ♦ **dar cabezadas** FIG., COLL. to rack one's brains • **tirarse de c.** to dive.

ca·be·zal m. *(almohada)* pillow, bolster; *(colchoncillo)* small mattress; *(de sillones)* headrest; MED. compress; MECH. headstock; MEX., CHILE doorpost, doorjamb.

ca·be·za·zo m. *(golpe con la cabeza)* butt, blow with the head; SPORT. *(fútbol)* header.

ca·be·zo m. *(cumbre)* summit, peak (of mountain); *(cerro alto)* high hill; *(montecillo)* small hill, hillock; *(cabezón)* collar (of shirt); MARIT. *(escollo)* reef.

ca·be·zón, –zo·na I. adj. COLL. *(terco)* pigheaded, stubborn; *(cabezudo)* bigheaded, largeheaded; CHILE strong, heady (said of liquor) II. m. SEW. *(cuello)* collarband; *(abertura)* neck; EQUIT. *(cabezada)* headstall; *(lista)* tax roll; COL. eddy, whirlpool.

ca·be·zo·na·da f. COLL. stubborn act, pigheaded action.

ca·be·zo·ta I. m.f. FIG., COLL. *(terco)* pigheaded person, mule; COLL. *(persona de cabeza grande)* largeheaded *or* bigheaded person —f. large *or* big head **II.** adj. pigheaded, stubborn.

ca·be·zu·do, –da I. adj. bigheaded, largeheaded; FIG., COLL. *(terco)* stubborn, pigheaded; *(espiritoso)* heady, intoxicating **II.** m. ICHTH. mullet.

ca·bi·da f. *(capacidad)* space, room, capacity; *(alcance)* extent, range ♦ **dar c. a** to make room for • **tener c. en** FIG. to be suitable for, have a place in.

ca·bil·da·da f. COLL. rash, imprudent proceeding (of town council).

ca·bil·dan·te m. councilman.

ca·bil·de·ar intr. *(influir)* to lobby; *(intrigar)* to scheme, maneuver (for votes).

ca·bil·de·o m. *(propaganda)* lobbying; *(intriga)* scheming, political maneuvering.

ca·bil·de·ro m. *(intrigante)* schemer; *(propagandista)* lobbyist.

ca·bil·do m. RELIG. *(capítulo)* chapter; *(reunión)* chapter meeting; *(sala)* chapter house; POL. *(ayuntamiento)* town council; *(junta)* town council meeting; *(sala)* town hall, city hall; *(corporación)* organization in the Canary Islands formed of representatives from all the towns.

ca·bi·na f. booth; MARIT. cabin, berth; AVIA. cockpit, cabin; AUTO. cab, cabin; CINEM. projection booth ♦ **c. anticlimática** *or* **presurizada** AVIA. pressurized cabin • **c. de cambio de agujas** RAIL. signal tower, signal box (G.B.) • **c. electora** voting booth • **c. insonorizada** RAD., TELEV. soundproof *or* isolation booth • **c. telefónica** telephone booth.

ca·biz·ba·jo, –ja adj. crestfallen, downhearted.

ca·ble m. cable; MARIT. cable's length; TELEC. cable, cablegram ♦ **c. aéreo** overhead cable • **c. de remolque** towline • **c. eléctrico** electric cable • **echar un cable** FIG., COLL. to throw a line to, help out.

ca·ble·gra·fiar §30 tr. & intr. TELEC. to cable.

ca·ble·grá·fi·co, –ca adj. TELEC. pertaining to cablegrams.

ca·ble·gra·ma m. TELEC. cable, cablegram.

ca·ble·ro m. MARIT. cable ship.

ca·ble·vi·sión f. TELEV. cable television.

ca·bo m. *(extremo)* end, extremity <*el c. de la soga* the end of the rope>; *(fin)* end, conclusion <*llegar al c. de una tarea* to arrive at the end of a task>; *(pedazo)* stub, bit; handle <*c. de hacha* ax handle>; *(hilo)* thread, strand; *(bulto)* package, bundle; GEOG. cape, point; MARIT. rope, cable; MIL. corporal ♦ **al c. de** at the end of • **al fin y al c.** FIG. after all, in the end • **atar cabos** FIG. to put two and two together • **c. de año** RELIG. anniversary mass • **c. de cañón** MIL. gunner • **c. de desgarre** ripcord • **c. de escuadra** MIL. squadron commander • **c. de maestranza** foreman • **c. de mar** MARIT. petty officer • **c. de ronda** MIL. patrol leader • **cabos** *(accesorios)* accessories; MIL. braid; EQUIT. mane and tail • **c. suelto** FIG., COLL. loose end • **dar c. a** to put the finishing touches on • **dar c. de** to put an end to, finish off • **de c. a rabo** COLL. from start to finish • **estar al c. de** to be on the verge of • **estar al c. de la calle** FIG., COLL. to know what's what • **llevar a c.** to carry out, see through <*llevó a c. el plan* she carried out the plan> • **no dejar c. suelto** FIG., COLL. to leave no loose ends • **ponerse al c. de** to get to the heart of.

Cabo de Buena Esperanza m. Cape of Good Hope.

ca·bo·ta·je m. MARIT. cabotage, coastal sailing; COM. coastal trading.

Cabo Verde m. Cape Verde.

ca·bo·ver·dia·no, –na adj. & m.f. Cape Verdean.

ca·bra f. ZOOL. goat, nanny goat; ARM. *(catapulta)* catapult; CHILE *(carruaje)* gig, cabriolet; *(cabrilla)* sawhorse; COL., CUBA, VEN. loaded die ♦ **c. de almizcle** ZOOL. musk deer • **c. montés** ZOOL. mountain goat • **estar loco como una c.** FIG., COLL. to be crazy as a loon • **la c. siempre tira la monte** FIG. a leopard never changes its spots.

ca·bre·ro, –ra I. m.f. goatherd **II.** adj. ARG. hotheaded, hot-tempered.

ca·bres·tan·te m. MARIT. capstan, winch.

ca·bria f. derrick, crane.

ca·bri·lla f. ICHTH. cabrilla; CARP. *(trípode)* sawhorse ♦ **cabrillas** ASTRON. the Pleiades; *(manchas)* burn marks

(from coming too close to the fire); *(olas)* whitecaps; *(juego)* ducks and drakes.

ca·bri·lle·ar intr. *(formarse olas blancas)* to form whitecaps, break into foam; *(rielar)* to glimmer, sparkle.

ca·brí·o, –a I. adj. caprine, hircine **II.** m. herd of goats.

ca·brio·la f. *(salto)* jump, leap; *(voltereta)* somersault, tumble; EQUIT. capriole ♦ **dar cabriolas** *(saltar)* to jump, leap; *(voltear)* to caper (about), tumble.

ca·brio·lar intr. *(saltar)* to jump, leap; *(voltear)* to caper (about), tumble; EQUIT. to capriole.

ca·brio·lé m. *(birlocho)* cabriolet; *(coche descapotable)* convertible automobile; *(capote)* short sleeveless cape.

ca·bri·ti·lla f. lambskin, kid.

ca·bri·to m. ZOOL. kid, young goat ♦ **cabritos** CHILE popcorn.

ca·brón m. ZOOL. goat; VULG. *(cornudo)* cuckold; *(cretino)* bastard; CHILE pimp.

ca·bro·na·da f. COLL. dirty *or* nasty trick.

ca·bro·na·zo, –za m.f. COLL. prankster, trickster.

ca·bru·no, –na adj. of goats, goatlike.

ca·bu·jón *or* **ca·bu·chón** m. *(piedra)* cabochon (uncut stone); *(cabeza de clavo)* ornamental head of nail.

ca·bu·ya f. BOT. agave; *(fibra de pita)* pita fiber, hemp; *(cuerda)* cord, string; MARIT. *(cabos)* cordage ♦ **dar c.** AMER. to tie up, moor • **ponerse en la c.** AMER., COLL. to catch on, catch the drift.

ca·bu·ye·rí·a f. MARIT. cordage.

ca·ca f. VULG. shit.

ca·ca·hua·te *or* **ca·ca·hué** m. var. of cacahuete.

ca·ca·hue·te m. BOT. peanut (plant and seed).

ca·ca·huey m. var. of cacahuete.

ca·ca·o m. BOT. cacao (tree and bean); CUL. cocoa, chocolate; COLL. *(lío)* commotion, mess ♦ **no valer un c.** COLL. to be worthless *or* of little importance • **pedir c.** AMER. to beg for mercy • **tener mucho c.** GUAT. to be strong and brave.

ca·ca·ra·ña f. pockmark.

ca·ca·re·a·dor, –do·ra adj. clucking, cackling; FIG., COLL. *(jactancioso)* boasting, crowing.

ca·ca·re·ar intr. to cluck, cackle —tr. FIG., COLL. to boast *or* crow about.

ca·ca·re·o m. *(cloqueo)* clucking, cackling; FIG., COLL. *(jactancia)* boasting, crowing.

ca·ca·tú·a f. ORNITH. cockatoo.

ca·cé, cace see cazar.

ca·ce·ar tr. to stir with a ladle.

ca·ce·ra f. irrigation ditch.

ca·ce·rí·a f. SPORT. *(caza)* hunting; *(partida)* hunt, hunting party; *(animales muertos)* bag, game bagged; PAINT. *(escena)* hunting scene ♦ **ir de c.** to go hunting.

ca·ce·ri·na f. cartridge pouch.

ca·ce·ro·la f. casserole, pot.

ca·ci·ca·to m. *or* **ca·ci·ca·tu·ra** f. var. of cacicazgo.

ca·ci·caz·go m. *(dignidad)* chieftainship; *(territorio)* territory, jurisdiction (of the chief); *(autoridad)* authority, power (of the chief).

ca·cim·ba f. *(hoyo)* hole, shallow well (used to find drinking water); *(balde)* pail, bucket.

ca·ci·que m. *(indio)* Indian chief, cacique; FIG., COLL. *(jefe político)* political leader *or* boss; *(déspota)* tyrant; CHILE, FIG. *(rico)* king, rich man; COL., ORNITH. cacique, tropical oriole.

ca·ci·que·ar intr. COLL. *(mandar)* to boss people around; *(mangonear)* to run things, organize affairs.

ca·ci·quis·mo m. domination of local political bosses.

ca·co m. FIG. *(ladrón)* thief, burglar; COLL. *(cobarde)* coward, chicken.

ca·co·fo·ní·a f. MUS., PHONET. cacophony.

ca·co·grá·fi·a f. cacography, poor penmanship.

ca·co·lo·gí·a f. GRAM., RHET. solecism.

ca·co·qui·mi·co, –ca adj. FIG. *(achacoso)* ailing.

ca·co·qui·mio, –mia m.f. melancholy person.

cac·to *or* **cac·tus** m. BOT. cactus.

ca·cu·men m. FIG., COLL. acumen, astuteness.

ca·cha I. f. *(pieza de mango)* handle plate; *(mango)* handle, grip; ANAT., ZOOL. buttock; *(engaño)* trick, deceit; COL., ZOOL. horn; BOL. wooden chest ♦ **hacer cachas** GUAT. to run errands; CHILE to make fun of someone •

hasta las cachas FIG., COLL. up to one's neck, up to here **II.** adj. see **cacho, –cha.**

ca·cha·co, –ca I. adj. COL., ECUAD., VEN. foppish, dandy **II.** m. PERU cop, policeman.

ca·cha·da f. AMER., TAUR. goring, ramming; ARG., URUG. (broma) mockery, joke.

ca·cha·lo·te m. ZOOL. sperm whale.

ca·char tr. (astillar) to chip; (aserrar) to split (wood); AMER. (burlar) to tease; (engañar) to trick, deceive; (acornear) to gore; (agarrar) to nab, grab; (sorprender) to catch; (robar) to rob, steal; CHILE to get, understand.

ca·char·pas f.pl. AMER. junk, useless objects.

ca·cha·rra·zo m. COLL. (golpe) blow, bump; AMER., COLL. (trago) drink, swig.

ca·cha·rre·ro, –ra m.f. pottery vendor.

ca·cha·rro m. (vasija) earthenware vessel, crock; (pedazo) shard, COLL. (trasto) piece of junk or rubbish; (máquina vieja) wreck; (coche) jalopy; C. AMER. jail, prison ♦ **cacharros** (utensilios) utensils, tools.

ca·cha·za f. (lentitud) slowness, sluggishness; (flema) phlegm, coolness; (aguardiente) cheap rum.

ca·cha·zu·do, –da I. adj. (lento) slow, sluggish; (flemático) calm, placid **II.** m.f. (flemático) phlegmatic person; (lento) slowpoke, sluggish person —m. CUBA, ENTOM. tobacco worm.

ca·che adj. ARG. sloppy, slovenly.

ca·che·ar tr. (registrar) to search, frisk; CHILE, MEX. (acornear) to gore.

ca·che·mi·ra f. or **ca·che·mir** m. cashmere.

ca·che·o m. searching, frisking.

ca·che·ta·da f. AMER. slap.

ca·che·te m. (carrillo) puffy or plump cheek; (cachetada) slap; ARM. (puñal) dagger, stiletto.

ca·che·te·ar tr. to slap.

ca·che·te·ro m. (puñal) dagger; TAUR. (matador) bullfighter who finishes off the bull with a dagger; FIG., COLL. (el que remata) hatchet man; COL. (peso) heavy weight.

ca·che·ti·na f. fist fight.

ca·che·tu·do, –da adj. chubby-cheeked, plump-cheeked.

ca·chi·cán I. m. (mayoral) farm overseer, foreman; FIG., COLL. (hombre astuto) shrewd fellow, sly sort **II.** adj. COLL. crafty, sly.

ca·chi·fo·llar tr. COLL. (humillar) to humiliate, discomfit; (apabullar) to crush, flatten.

ca·chim·ba f. AMER. (pipa) pipe (for smoking); ARG. (pozo) shallow well; HOND., ARM. empty cartridge shell; CUBA loose woman; CHILE revolver, pistol.

ca·chim·bo m. AMER. (pipa) pipe (for smoking); CUBA small sugar mill; PERU second-rate musician ♦ **chupar c.** VEN. (fumar) to smoke a pipe; COLL. (chuparse el dedo) to suck one's thumb.

ca·chi·po·rra f. ARM. club, bludgeon; CUBA, ORNITH. black-necked stilt —m. CHILE charlatan.

ca·chi·po·rra·zo m. (golpe) blow with a club; (acción) clubbing, bludgeoning.

ca·chi·ru·lo m. (vasija) flask (for liquor); (barco) small three-masted ship; (adorno) hair ornament formerly used by women; COLL. (novio) beau, sweetie; (sombrero) hat; MEX. (forro) chamois reinforcement on riding breeches ♦ **cachirulos** junk.

ca·chi·va·che m. (trasto) piece of junk, bauble; FIG., COLL. (miserable) good-for-nothing ♦ **cachivaches** COLL. (utensilios) pots and pans; (cacharro) junk, trash.

ca·cho, –cha I. adj. bent, crooked **II.** m. (pedazo) piece, morsel; AMER., ZOOL. (cuerno) horn; (cubilete) dice box; (cuento) story; (embuste) trick, hoax; ARG., URUG. (plátanos) bunch of bananas; VEN. (burla) joke, mockery; CHILE (clavo) white elephant (unwanted merchandise) ♦ **estar c.** COL. to excel • **estar fuera de c.** COLL. to be out of harm's way • **un c.** SL. a little, a bit <voy a dormir un c. I am going to sleep a bit> —f. see **cacha.**

ca·chón I. m. cresting wave, breaker **II.** adj. C. AMER., COL. having large horns (animal).

ca·chon·de·ar·se reflex. COLL. (bromear) to kid, joke around ♦ **c. de** to tease, make fun of.

ca·chon·de·o m. COLL. (guasa) leg-pulling, teasing; (burla) joking; (jarana) horseplay, fooling around; (farsa) farce.

ca·chon·dez f. (celo) heat, rut; (lujuria) lust.

ca·chon·do, –da adj. (en celo) in heat, in rut; FIG. (libidinoso) libidinous, lustful; FIG., COLL. (gracioso) funny, amusing <una película muy c. a very amusing movie>.

ca·cho·pín, –pi·na m.f. var. of **cachupín, –pina.**

ca·cho·rro, –rra I. m.f. ZOOL. (perro) puppy, pup; (cría de otros mamíferos) cub, whelp —m. ARM. (pistola) handgun, pistol **II.** adj. AMER. (lleno de desprecio) spiteful, hateful; (malcriado) ill-mannered, rude.

ca·chu·cha f. (gorra) cap; (baile) cachucha (Andalusian dance); MARIT. (bote) small boat; BOL. (cachaza) cheap rum; CHILE (bofetada) slap.

ca·chu·che·ar tr. (mimar) to indulge, spoil; (adular) to flatter.

ca·chu·cho m. (medida) oil measure; (alfiletero) pin box; MARIT. (cachucha) small boat; (cachirulo) small jar; CUBA (pez) type of snapper.

ca·chue·la f. (guisado) stew; (molleja) gizzard, sweetbread; BOL., PERU (rápido) rapids.

ca·chue·lo m. PERU (propina) tip.

ca·chum·bo m. (cáscara) husk, shell; COL. (rizo) curl.

ca·chun·de f. cachou (breath lozenge).

ca·chu·pín, –pi·na or **ga·chu·pín, –pi·na** m.f. AMER., DEROG. Spanish settler (in South America).

ca·da adj. each <c. empleado tiene un escritorio each employee has a desk>; every <c. tres días every three days> ♦ **c. cual** or **c. uno** each one, everyone • **¿c. cuánto?** how often? • **c. quisque** COLL. each one, everyone • **c. vez más** more and more • **c. vez menos** less and less • **c. vez peor** worse and worse • **c. vez que** every time that, whenever.

ca·dal·so m. (tablado) platform, stage (erected for a solemn function); (horca) scaffold, gallows.

ca·dá·ver m. corpse, cadaver.

ca·da·vé·ri·co, –ca adj. (muerto) cadaverous; FIG. (pálido) deathly pale.

ca·de·jo m. (enredo) tangle, snarl (in hair); (hilos) cluster of threads (for making tassels); (madeja) small skein; MEX. (guedeja) long hair, mane; C. AMER., COLL. (animal fantástico) imaginary animal that lurks at night.

ca·de·na f. chain; (fila de presidiarios) chain gang; (castigo) imprisonment; (joya) chain; FIG. (ligadura) bond, link; (serie) chain, series <c. de acontecimientos chain of events>; (grupo de empresas) chain <una c. de hoteles a chain of hotels>; ARCHIT. frame; CHEM. chain; CHILE crochet ♦ **c. de agrimensor** surveyor's chain • **c. de emisoras** TELEC. network • **c. de fabricación** or **de montaje** production line, assembly line • **c. de montañas** mountain range • **c. perpetua** life imprisonment • **reacción en c.** chain reaction.

ca·den·cia f. (ritmo) cadence, rhythm, beat; MUS. cadenza, cadence.

ca·den·cio·so, –sa adj. (rítmico) cadenced, rhythmical; (melodioso) lilting, melodious.

ca·de·ne·ro m. SURV. (agrimensor) chainman; AMER. (caballo) workhorse.

ca·de·ne·ta f. SEW. chain stitch; (encuadernación) headband; (adorno de papel) paper chain.

ca·de·ni·lla f. small ornamental chain.

ca·den·te adj. lilting, rhythmical.

ca·de·ra f. ANAT. hip, hip joint ♦ **caderas** bustle (of a dress).

ca·de·ta·da f. COLL. frivolous act, youthful indiscretion.

ca·de·te m.f. MIL. cadet; ARG., BOL. apprentice, trainee ♦ **hacer el c.** COLL. to play pranks.

Cá·diz Cádiz.

cad·mio m. CHEM. cadmium.

ca·du·car §70 intr. (chochear) to dote, become senile; to lapse, expire <el abono ha caducado the subscription has expired>; LAW (anularse) to become null and void, be invalid; BIOL. (extinguirse) to become extinct; FIG. (gastarse) to wear out, deteriorate.

ca·du·ce·o m. MED., MYTH. caduceus, Mercury's staff.

ca·du·ci·dad f. (senilidad) senility, decrepitude; LAW (anulación) caducity, voidance ♦ **c. de la fianza** COM. forfeiture of a bond • **c. de la instancia** LAW discontinuance of suit.

ca·du·co, –ca adj. (senil) senile, decrepit; (extinguido) lapsed, expired; LAW (anulado) null and void, canceled;

BOT. withering, deciduous; *(perecedero)* fleeting, imperma-
nent.

ca·du·qué, caduque see caducar.

ca·e·di·zo, –za adj. BOT. *(caduco)* deciduous; *(precípite)*
about to fall, in danger of falling; AMER. *(saledizo)* projecting (ledge, overhang).

ca·er §15 intr. to fall <*las hojas caen en el otoño* the leaves
fall in autumn>; to drop <*c. de rodillas* to drop to one's
knees>; *(derrumbarse)* to fall down, collapse; *(colgar)* to
hang down <*el cabello le caía sobre los hombros* her hair
hung down to her shoulders>; FIG. to befall <*nos cayó la
mala suerte* bad luck befell us>; to get, receive <*me cayó el
premio* I got the prize>; to lapse, subside <*la conversación
cayó en cuanto entró el profesor* the conversation subsided
as soon as the professor entered>; to fade, become faint
<*su voz empezó de c.* her voice began to fade>; to be, be
situated <*el museo cae a la izquierda* the museum is on the
left>; to be included, fall <*eso no cae en este capítulo* that
does not fall in this chapter>; to occur, fall <*su cumpleaños
cae en agosto* her birthday falls in August>; to drop, decrease <*los precios cayeron súbitamente* the prices dropped
suddenly>; to fall <*el imperio romano cayó en el siglo V*
the Roman empire fell in the fifth century>; to set <*el sol
caía lentamente* the sun was slowly setting>; FIG., COLL. to
die, fall <*miles de soldados cayeron en esa batalla* thousands of soldiers fell in that battle>; to understand, see
<*ahora caigo en lo que dices* now I see what you are say-
ing>; COM. to fall due ♦ **al c. la noche** at nightfall • **c. a**
to overlook, look out on <*la ventana caía a la plaza* the
window looked out on the square> • **c. bien** FIG., COLL. to
suit <*ese vestido le cae bien* that dress suits her>; to make
a good impression on <*el nuevo alumno me cayó bien* the
new student made a good impression on me>; to agree
with <*los pimientos no me caen bien* peppers do not agree
with me> • **c. de cabeza** to fall on one's head • **c. de
espaldas** to fall on one's back; FIG. *(pasmarse)* to be
stunned or taken aback • **c. del burro** FIG. to recognize
one's mistake • **c. de pie** FIG. to land on one's feet • **c. de
plano** to fall flat • **c. en** to fall on or into <*el niño cayó en
el pozo* the boy fell into the well>; FIG. to fall into <*c. en
la trampa* to fall into the trap> • **c. enfermo** or **en cama**
to fall ill • **c. en gracia** FIG. to make a good impression on
• **c. en la cuenta** FIG. to realize • **c. en mora** COM. to
become delinquent • **c. ligero** CUBA, P. RICO to please • **c.
mal** FIG., COLL. to fit poorly <*la camisa le cae mal* the
shirt fits him poorly>; *(no gustar)* to displease, make a
bad impression on; *(indigestar)* to disagree with, upset
one's stomach • **c. parado** AMER., FIG. to land on one's
feet • **c. pesado** FIG., COLL. to be a nuisance • **c. por su
propio peso** FIG. to be self-evident • **c. sobre** to descend
upon • **estar al c.** FIG. to be about to arrive —reflex. to
fall <*el niño se cayó en la vereda* the boy fell on the side-
walk>; to drop <*se me cayó el libro* I dropped the book>;
to fall out <*se le cayó todo el pelo* his hair fell out> ♦
caerse de risa FIG. to die laughing • **caerse de suyo** or **de
sí mismo** FIG. to be evident or obvious • **caerse de tonto**
to be very foolish • **caérsele el alma a las pies** FIG., COLL.
to become disheartened • **caerse muerto** to drop dead •
caerse redondo FIG. to fall in a heap, collapse • **no tener
dónde caerse muerto** FIG. to be destitute —tr. ♦ **hacer c.**
to knock down, make fall <*el fuerte viento hizo c. los frutos
del árbol* the strong wind knocked the fruit down from the
tree>.

ca·fé I. m. coffee (drink, bean, and plant); *(establecimiento)*
café, coffee shop; S. AMER., COLL. reprimand, scolding;
MEX. annoyance ♦ **c. cantante** or **c. concierto** coffee
house • **c. con leche** coffee with milk • **c. de recuelo** drip
coffee • **c. instantáneo** instant coffee • **c. molido** ground
coffee • **c. negro** or **solo** black coffee • **c. tostado** roasted
coffee • **de mal c.** COLL. out of sorts, in a bad mood
II. adj. coffee, coffee-colored.

ca·fe·í·na f. CHEM. caffeine.

ca·fe·tal m. AGR. coffee plantation.

ca·fe·ta·le·ro, –ra I. adj. coffee <*la industria c.* the coffee
industry> II. m. coffee grower, owner of a coffee plantation.

ca·fe·te·ra I. f. CUL. coffeepot, coffeemaker; *(hervidor)* kettle; AUTO. jalopy, wreck; COLL. *(trasto)* piece of junk,

wreck ♦ **c. de filtro** CUL. percolator, drip coffeemaker •
estar como una c. COLL. to be nuts or batty II. adj. see
cafetero, –ra.

ca·fe·te·rí·a f. coffee shop, café, snack bar.

ca·fe·te·ro, –ra I. adj. *(del café)* coffee <*la industria c.* the
coffee industry>; COLL. *(aficionado)* coffee-loving, fond of
coffee II. m.f. *(obrero)* coffee worker; *(comerciante)* coffee merchant; *(dueño de un café)* café owner, proprietor of
a coffee shop —f. see **cafetera.**

ca·fe·tín m. small café or coffee shop.

ca·fe·to m. BOT. coffee tree.

cá·fi·la f. COLL. *(muchedumbre)* crowd, mob; *(multitud)*
flock (of animals); *(conjunto)* large number (things); *(serie)* series, string <*una c. de disparates* a string of inani-
ties>.

ca·ga·da I. f. VULG. *(excremento)* crap, shit; *(desacierto)*
blunder, stupid thing (to do) II. adj. see **cagado, –da.**

ca·ga·de·ro m. COLL. john, latrine.

ca·ga·do, –da I. past part. see **cagar** II. adj. COLL. yellow,
cowardly III. f. see **cagada.**

ca·ga·le·ra or **ca·ga·le·ta** f. COLL. *(diarrea)* diarrhea, the
runs; *(miedo)* fear ♦ **tener c.** to be scared stiff.

ca·gar §47 intr. COLL. to shit —tr. COLL. to mess up, bungle —reflex. COLL. *(acobardarse)* to become frightened,
lose one's nerve ♦ **cagarla** COLL. to put one's foot in it.

ca·ga·rru·ta f. *(excremento)* droppings (of sheep, mice,
goats); FIG. *(hombre insignificante)* nobody, insignificant
fellow.

ca·ga·tin·ta or **ca·ga·tin·tas** m. [pl. -tas] COLL., DEROG. office worker, pencil-pusher.

ca·gón, –go·na adj. COLL. *(que tiene diarrea)* diarrheic,
suffering from diarrhea; *(cobarde)* cowardly, yellow.

ca·gué, cague see **cagar.**

ca·gue·ta f. diarrhea —m.f. COLL. coward, chicken.

ca·híz m. AGR. dry measure (twelve bushels).

ca·í·da I. f. fall, falling; *(tumbo)* tumble, spill; *(declive)*
slope, grade; *(de tela)* hang; drop, decrease <*c. de la temperatura* a drop in temperature>; FIG. *(ruina)* downfall,
collapse; GEOL. dip; MARIT. *(calma)* calm; *(altura de las
velas)* drop, hoist ♦ **a la c. de la tarde** at dusk • **a la c. del
sol** at sunset • **c. de agua** waterfall • **caídas** *(lana)*
coarse wool; COLL. *(dichos)* witticisms • **c. pluvial** METE-
OROL. rainfall • **c. radioactiva** (radioactive) fallout • **La
Caída** RELIG. the Fall (of Adam and Eve) II. adj. see
caído, –da.

ca·í·do, –da I. past part. see **caer** II. adj. *(alicaído)* weak,
tired; FIG. *(amilanado)* crestfallen, downhearted; COM.
due, matured ♦ **andar de capa c.** FIG., COLL. to suffer a
setback • **c. del cielo** out of the blue • **c. de un nido** FIG.,
COLL. naive, innocent • **c. en desuso** fallen into disuse
III. m.pl. **caídos** COM. *(atrasos)* arrears; C. AMER. perquisites ♦ **los caídos** MIL. the fallen, the dead.

cai·ga, caigo see **caer.**

cai·mán m. ZOOL. cayman, alligator; FIG. *(zorro)* cunning
person, sly fox.

Ca·ín BIBL. Cain ♦ **con las de C.** with evil intentions •
pasar or **sufrir las de C.** to have a terrible time, go
through a rough time.

cai·rel m. *(peluca)* wig, hairpiece; *(pasamanería)* fringe
trimming.

Cai·ro, El m. Cairo.

cai·ro·ta or **cai·ri·ño, –ña** adj. & m.f. Cairene.

ca·ja f. *(recipiente)* box (container and contents); *(de madera)* chest, case; *(de hierro)* safe, strongbox; *(ataúd)* coffin, casket; COM. *(sitio)* cashier's window; *(dinero)* cash,
cash on hand; MECH. casing, box; MUS. *(tambor)* drum;
(armazón) cabinet, box; ARM. gun stock; ARCHIT. well,
shaft <*c. de ascensor* elevator shaft>; CARP. socket, mortise; THEAT. wings; BOT. seed capsule; PRINT. type case;
PERU water tank; CHILE dry riverbed ♦ **c. chica** or **de
menores** COM. petty cash • **c. de ahorros** COM. savings
bank • **c. de amortización** COM. sinking fund • **c. de cambios** or **de engranajes** AUTO. transmission • **c. de caudales** safe, strongbox • **c. de colores** paint box • **c. de
conexiones** ELEC. junction box • **c. de dientes** COL. false
teeth • **c. de embalaje** packing case • **c. de enchufe** ELEC.
outlet • **c. de fuego** MECH. firebox • **c. de fusibles** ELEC.
fuse box • **c. de herramientas** toolbox • **c. de hierro**

AMER. safe, strongbox • **c. de jubilaciones** pension fund • **c. de las muelas** ANAT., COLL. gums • **c. del tambor** *or* **del tímpano** ANAT. middle ear • **c. de música** music box • **c. de reclutamiento** MIL. recruiting office • **c. de registro** manhole • **c. de resistencia** ELEC. resistance box; POL. strike fund • **c. de resonancia** MUS. sound box • **c. de seguridad** safe-deposit box, safety-deposit box • **c. de sorpresa** jack-in-the-box • **c. de velocidades** AUTO. transmission • **c. efectivo** COM. cash on hand • **c. fuerte** safe, strongbox • **c. negra** AVIA. black box • **c. recaudadora** tax bureau • **c. registradora** COM. cash register, till • **c. toráxica** ANAT. chest • **c. y espina** CARP. mortise and tenon • **echar a alguien con cajas destempladas** FIG., COLL. to send someone packing.

ca·je·ro m. COM. teller, cashier; *(fabricante)* box *or* case maker.

ca·je·ta f. MARIT. *(filástica)* sennit, braided rope; AMER. *(caja pequeña)* little box; *(tabaquera)* tobacco box; *(caja para dulces)* small round box (for sweets, jelly); *(dulce)* jelly candy *or* nougat; MEX. coward, chicken ♦ **de c.** first-rate, excellent.

ca·je·ti·lla f. *(paquete)* pack, box <*una c. de cigarrillos* a pack of cigarettes> —m. ARG., COLL. dandy, dude.

ca·je·tín m. PRINT. *(compartimiento)* individual compartment in type case, letter case; ELEC. *(aislador)* cleat insulator.

ca·jis·ta m.f. PRINT. typesetter, compositor.

ca·jón m. *(caja grande)* large box *or* case; *(gaveta)* drawer; *(caseta)* stall, booth; MIL. caisson; S. AMER. *(ataúd)* coffin, casket; CHILE ravine; MEX., PERU grocery store ♦ **c. de sastre** FIG., COLL. *(cosas sueltas)* hodgepodge; *(bobo)* featherbrain • **de c.** customary.

ca·jo·ne·ra f. *(armario)* chest of drawers in a vestry; ECUAD. *(vendedora)* itinerant saleswoman.

ca·jo·ne·rí·a f. set of drawers (in piece of furniture).

cal f. MIN. lime ♦ **c. apagada** *or* **muerta** slaked *or* hydrated lime • **c. blanca** high-calcium lime • **c. hidráulica** hydraulic lime • **c. viva** quicklime • **c. y canto** stone masonry • **de c. y canto** FIG. firmly, solidly • **una de c. y otra de arena** FIG. six of one and a half dozen of the other.

ca·la f. GEOG. *(bahía)* cove, small bay; *(trozo)* slice, sample, taste; MED. *(supositorio)* suppository; MARIT. *(bodega)* hold, draft; *(pescar)* fishing ground; BOT. calla, calla lily; *(muro)* test boring; FIG. *(sondeo de opinión)* opinion poll; Sp., COLL. peseta ♦ **vender c. y cata** COM. to offer samples of merchandise.

ca·la·ba·ce·ar tr. COLL. *(suspender)* to fail, flunk (an exam); *(dejar plantado)* to jilt.

ca·la·ba·cín m. *(calabaza pequeña)* squash; *(tonto)* dope, pumpkin head.

ca·la·ba·ci·no m. calabash (used as a container).

ca·la·ba·za f. BOT. calabash, gourd, squash (plant and fruit); FIG., COLL. *(tonto)* blockhead, fathead; MARIT., COLL. tub, unseaworthy vessel ♦ **c. confitera** *or* **totanera** BOT. pumpkin • **c. vinatera** BOT. bottle gourd • **dar calabazas a** COLL. *(suspender a)* to fail *or* flunk (someone) on an examination; *(rechazar)* to jilt, reject • **recibir** *or* **llevarse calabazas** COLL. *(ser suspendido)* to flunk *or* fail an exam; *(ser rechazado)* to be jilted *or* given the brush-off.

ca·la·ba·za·da f. *(golpe con la cabeza)* butt, blow (with the head); *(golpe en la cabeza)* blow, bump on the head.

ca·la·ba·zo m. var. of **calabaza.**

ca·la·bo·bos m. light rain, drizzle.

ca·la·bo·ce·ro m. jailer.

ca·la·bo·zo m. *(cárcel)* dungeon, underground prison; *(celda)* jail cell; HORT. pruning knife *or* hook.

ca·la·bria·da f. *(vino)* mixture of red and white wine; FIG. *(mezcolanza)* jumble, hodgepodge.

ca·la·bro·te m. MARIT. *(cabo)* cable, hawser; VEN. *(calavera)* madcap, rake.

ca·la·da f. *(mojada)* soaking, drenching; ORNITH. *(ascenso)* soaring; *(descenso)* swoop, dive; COLL. *(chupada)* puff, drag (of cigarette).

ca·la·do I. past part. see **calar²** II. m. SEW. *(bordado)* drawnwork, hemstitching; ARCHIT. *(grecas)* openwork, fretwork; MARIT. *(profundidad)* depth; *(bodega)* hold, draft; MECH. stalling.

ca·la·dor m. MECH. *(taladrador)* driller, borer; MARIT. *(he-*

rramienta) caulking iron; MED. *(instrumento)* probe; AMER. *(sonda)* sampler, probe (for taking samples from packaged goods).

ca·la·fa·te·ar tr. to caulk, plug *or* seal (up).

ca·la·í·ta f. MIN. turquoise.

ca·la·mar tr. ICHTH. squid.

ca·lam·bre m. PHYSIOL. *(espasmo)* spasm; *(rampa)* cramp; ELEC. shock ♦ **c. del escribiente** writer's cramp • **c. de estómago** stomach cramp.

ca·lam·bu·co m. BOT. calaba tree; CUBA, COLL. *(beato)* pious fellow, ultra-religious man.

ca·la·mi·dad f. *(desastre)* calamity, disaster, misfortune; FIG., COLL. *(descuidado)* mess, disgrace <*ese hombre es una c.* that man is a disgrace>.

ca·la·mi·ta f. *(brújula)* compass; *(piedra imán)* lodestone.

ca·la·mi·to·so, –sa adj. *(desastroso)* calamitous, disastrous; FIG., COLL. *(desgraciado)* disgraceful, wretched.

cá·la·mo m. BOT. *(planta aromática)* calamus; *(flauta)* ancient reed flute; POET. *(caña)* reed, stalk; *(pluma)* pen <*empuñar el c.* to take up one's pen>.

ca·la·mo·co m. icicle.

ca·la·mo·cha f. yellow ochre.

ca·lan·dra f. ornamental radiator grille.

ca·lan·dra·jo m. COLL. *(jirón)* tatter, rag (hanging from garment); *(trapo)* rag; FIG., COLL. *(persona despreciable)* dope, fool.

ca·lan·drar tr. to calender (paper, cloth).

ca·lan·dria f. ORNITH. type of lark; MECH., TEX. calender, mangle; MECH. *(torno)* hoisting treadmill —m.f. COLL. *(enfermo fingido)* malingerer, faker.

ca·la·ña f. *(modelo)* pattern, model; *(abanico)* reed hand fan; FIG. *(índole)* nature, character.

ca·lar¹ I. adj. calcareous, limy II. m. limestone deposit.

ca·lar² tr. *(mojar)* to soak, drench; *(penetrar)* to penetrate, pierce; *(vestir)* to pull *or* jam on (apparel); COLL. *(descubrir)* to see through, understand <*traté de c. sus intenciones* I tried to understand his intentions>; SEW. *(bordar)* to hemstitch; ARCHIT. to do openwork on; *(cortar)* to cut a sample of (fruit); MARIT. *(bajar)* to lower, let down (sails, nets); to draw <*el buque cala quince metros* the boat draws fifteen meters>; MIL. to fix, aim (weapons); COL. to flatten, humiliate; MEX. to sample; ARG., URUG. to stare at —intr. ORNITH. to swoop, dive —reflex. *(mojarse)* to get soaked *or* drenched; *(entrar)* to slip *or* sneak in; *(ponerse)* to pull *or* put on <*calarse las gafas* to put on one's glasses>; ORNITH. to swoop, dive; MECH. to stop, stall ♦ **calarse hasta los huesos** FIG. to get soaked to the skin.

ca·la·ve·ra f. *(cráneo)* skull, death's-head; ENTOM. death's-head moth —m. *(juerguista)* reveler; *(alocado)* madcap; *(vicioso)* devil, scum.

ca·la·ve·ra·da f. reckless escapade, tomfoolery.

ca·la·ve·re·ar intr. *(andar de juerga)* to live it up, have a wild time; *(comportarse temerariamente)* to act recklessly, lead a dissolute life.

cal·ca·do m. tracing.

cal·ca·dor, –do·ra m.f. *(persona)* tracer, copier —m. *(instrumento)* tracer.

cal·ca·ñal *or* **cal·ca·ñar** m. ANAT. heel, heel bone.

cal·car §70 tr. to trace, transfer, copy; FIG. *(imitar)* to copy, imitate.

cal·cá·re·o, –a adj. calcareous, limy.

cal·ce m. *(llanta)* steel rim *or* tire; MECH. *(corte)* steel blade reinforcement; *(cuña)* wedge, shim; C. AMER., MEX. foot, bottom (of a document).

cal·cé, calce see **calzar.**

cal·ce·do·nia f. MIN. chalcedony.

cal·ce·ta f. knee-high sock *or* stocking ♦ **hacer c.** to knit (socks).

cal·ce·te·rí·a f. *(producto)* hosiery; *(tienda)* hosiery shop.

cal·ce·tín m. sock.

cal·ci·fi·ca·ción f. CHEM., MED. calcification.

cal·ci·fi·car §70 tr. CHEM., MED. to calcify.

cal·ci·na f. concrete.

cal·ci·na·ción f. CHEM. calcination.

cal·ci·nar tr. to calcine; FIG. *(quemar)* to roast, burn; COLL. *(fastidiar)* to burn (someone) up, aggravate.

cal·cio m. CHEM. calcium.

cal·co m. (*dibujo*) tracing, traced copy; FIG. (*copia*) copy, imitation ♦ **c. heliográfico** blueprint.

cal·co·gra·fí·a f. PRINT. chalcography (engraving on metal).

cal·co·gra·fiar §30 tr. PRINT. (*grabar*) to engrave on metal; (*reproducir*) to print by means of metal engravings.

cal·co·ma·ní·a f. PRINT. decal, transfer.

cal·cu·la·ble adj. calculable.

cal·cu·la·dor, –do·ra I. f. (*máquina de calcular*) calculator; (*electrónica*) computer —m.f. (*persona*) calculator ♦ **c. electrónica** computer II. adj. calculating; FIG. (*astuto*) shrewd, calculating.

cal·cu·lar tr. (*computar*) to calculate, compute; FIG. (*proyectar*) to estimate, reckon <*calculo que no llegarán hasta el lunes* I estimate that they will not arrive until Monday>.

cal·cu·lis·ta I. adj. calculating II. m.f. COM. calculator, planner.

cál·cu·lo m. (*proceso*) calculation, computation; (*suposición*) estimate, calculation; (*prudencia*) caution, forethought; MATH. stone, calculus; MATH. calculus ♦ **c. biliar** MED. gallstone • **c. diferencial** MATH. differential calculus • **c. integral** MATH. integral calculus • **c. mental** mental arithmetic • **c. prudencial** estimate, approximation • **c. renal** MED. kidney stone • **obrar con mucho c.** to act shrewdly.

cal·de·a·mien·to m. warming, heating.

cal·de·ar tr. (*calentar*) to heat *or* warm (up); METAL. to fire, make red-hot; FIG. to enliven, liven up <*su música caldeaba la fiesta* his music livened up the party>.

cal·de·o m. warming, heating.

cal·de·ra f. caldron, vat (container and contents); MECH. boiler; MIN. sump; MUS. kettledrum case *or* shell; ARG. teakettle; ECUAD. volcanic crater ♦ **c. de vapor** MECH. steam boiler • **las calderas de Pedro Botero** COLL. hell.

cal·de·re·rí·a f. (*oficio*) boilermaking, caldronmaking; (*tienda*) boilermaker's *or* caldronmaker's shop; METAL. (*herrería*) ironworks, smithery.

cal·de·re·ro m. boilermaker.

cal·de·ro m. pot, small caldron (container and contents).

cal·de·rón m. large caldron *or* vat; MATH. (*mil*) symbol designating a thousand; GRAM., PRINT. (*párrafo*) paragraph mark; MUS. pause sign.

cal·do m. CUL. (*consomé*) stock, broth, bouillon; (*aderezo*) dressing, sauce; (*jugo*) juice; AMER. sugarcane juice ♦ **c. de cultivo** BIOL. culture medium • **caldos** CUL. liquid foodstuffs *or* condiments • **hacer a uno el c. gordo** FIG. to make something easy for someone, play into someone's hands.

cal·du·cho m. DEROG. (*caldo*) thin *or* poorly seasoned broth; CHILE (*asueto*) day off, brief vacation.

ca·le·cer §17 intr. to heat up, become heated.

ca·le·fac·ción f. heat, heating <*c. central* central heat>.

ca·le·fac·tor m. (*técnico*) heating engineer; (*calentador*) heater.

ca·len·da·rio m. calendar; (*programa*) schedule ♦ **c. exfoliador** *or* **americano** *or* **de taco** desk calendar • **c. gregoriano** *or* **nuevo** *or* **reformado** Gregorian calendar • **c. judicial** court calendar • **c. juliano** Julian calendar • **hacer calendarios** FIG. (*pensar*) to ponder, muse; (*conjeturar*) to conjecture.

ca·len·das f.pl. HIST. (*primer día*) calends; COLL. (*época*) time, epoch.

ca·lén·du·la f. BOT. calendula, pot marigold.

ca·len·ta·dor, –do·ra I. adj. heating, warming II. m. heater; (*para agua*) water heater; (*de cama*) warming pan, bed warmer; COLL. (*reloj*) cumbersome pocketwatch.

ca·len·ta·mien·to m. heating *or* warming (up); VET. inflammation.

ca·len·tar §49 tr. to warm *or* heat (up) <*c. el agua* to heat up water>; COLL. (*avivar*) to liven up; (*azotar*) to beat, thrash; CHILE to annoy, irritate ♦ **c. al blanco** to make white-hot • **c. al rojo** to make red-hot • **c. las orejas a** FIG., COLL. (*reprender*) to scold, chide; (*fastidiar*) to pester, talk (someone's) ears off; (*chismear*) to gossip; (*pegar*) to box (someone's) ears • **c. la sangre a** FIG. to anger, make (someone's) blood boil • **c. la silla** FIG. to stay too long, overstay one's welcome —reflex. to warm oneself up, get hot *or* warm; ZOOL. to be in heat; COLL. (*excitarse*) to become aroused *or* horny; (*alterarse*) to get worked up

or excited; AMER. to get angry *or* annoyed ♦ **calentarse a la lumbre** to warm oneself by the fire.

ca·len·tón, –to·na I. adj. COLL. (*sexualmente*) horny, hot II. m. (*calor excesivo*) overheating; PERU, FIG. fit of anger, rage.

ca·len·tu·ra f. MED. fever, temperature; CHILE tuberculosis, consumption; CUBA, BOT. type of milkweed; CUBA, AGR. fermentation of tobacco; COL. fit of anger, rage ♦ **c. de pollo** FIG., COLL. feigned illness, malingering.

ca·len·tu·rien·to, –ta adj. MED. feverish; FIG. (*exaltado*) feverish, restless; CHILE tubercular, consumptive.

ca·le·ro, –ra I. adj. calcareous, of lime *or* limestone II. m. (*obrero*) lime burner; (*dueño*) lime maker *or* seller —f. (*cantera*) limestone quarry; (*horno*) limekiln.

ca·le·sa f. calash, calèche (light carriage).

ca·le·se·ra f. (*chaqueta*) short jacket (worn by carriage driver); (*cante*) Andalusian folk song.

ca·le·ta f. MARIT. (*ensenada*) cove, inlet; (*descargadores*) unit of docking and unloading vessels (in a seaport); AMER. (*puerto*) small port; (*barco*) small coaster; VEN. (*asociación*) port workers' association.

ca·le·te·ar intr. CHILE, PERU, MARIT. to dock at all ports.

ca·le·te·ro m. VEN., MARIT. (*descargador*) stevedore, dockworker; AMER. (*vapor*) coaster.

ca·lez·ca see **calecer.**

ca·li·bra·ción f. TECH. calibration.

ca·li·bra·dor m. TECH. calibrator, calipers ♦ **c. a cursor** slide caliper • **c. de alambres** wire gauge • **c. de brocas** drill gauge • **c. de cubo** socket gauge • **c. micrométrico** vernier calipers.

ca·li·brar tr. TECH. (*medir*) to calibrate, gauge, measure; (*graduar*) to calibrate, graduate; (*mandrilar*) to bore.

ca·li·bre m. ARM. caliber, bore, gauge; TECH. (*tubo*) bore, diameter; (*alambre*) gauge, thickness; FIG. (*tamaño*) size, importance; (*calidad*) caliber, quality ♦ **c. de nonio** TECH. vernier calipers.

ca·li·can·to m. stone masonry ♦ **de c.** firm, solid.

ca·li·có m. TEX. calico.

ca·li·che m. (*piedrecilla*) pebble (in a brick); (*costrilla*) flake of whitewash (that peels off a wall); (*maca*) bruise (of fruit); AMER., MIN. (*salitre*) saltpeter; (*calichera*) ground rich in nitrate.

ca·li·che·ra f. BOL., CHILE, PERU, MIN. ground rich in nitrate.

ca·li·dad f. (*clase*) quality, class <*cuero de primera c.* first-quality leather>; (*nobleza*) quality <*él es un hombre de c.* he is a man of quality>; (*capacidad*) position, capacity <*en c. de alcalde* in the capacity of mayor>; (*índole*) nature, character; FIG. (*importancia*) importance, seriousness <*un asunto de c.* a matter of importance>; COM. stipulation, term ♦ **a c. de que** providing that, on the condition that • **en c. de** as <*vino en c. de emisario* he came as an envoy>.

cá·li·do, –da adj. METEOROL. warm, hot; CUL. (*picante*) hot, spicy; PAINT. (*color*) warm (tone).

ca·li·dos·co·pio *or* **ca·lei·dos·co·pio** m. kaleidoscope.

ca·lien·ta·ca·mas m. electric blanket.

ca·lien·ta·piés m. foot warmer.

ca·lien·ta·pla·tos m. plate warmer, hot plate.

ca·lien·te adj. (*que tiene calor*) warm, hot; FIG. (*acalorado*) heated, spirited; PAINT. (*color*) warm (tone); ZOOL. in heat; COLL. (*excitado*) horny, aroused; COL., FIG. daring, bold ♦ **c. de cascos** FIG. hotheaded, hot-tempered • **en c.** FIG. at once, right away • **estar c.** ZOOL. to be in heat; COLL. (*estar excitado*) to be aroused *or* horny.

ca·lien·te, caliento see **calentar.**

ca·li·fa m. caliph.

ca·li·fa·to m. caliphate.

ca·li·fi·ca·ble adj. qualifiable.

ca·li·fi·ca·ción f. (*evaluación*) assessment; (*clasificación*) classification, qualification; (*nota*) grade, mark.

ca·li·fi·ca·do, –da I. past part. see **calificar** II. adj. (*capaz*) competent, qualified; (*eminente*) eminent; (*probado*) proven.

ca·li·fi·ca·dor, –do·ra I. adj. assessing; (*clasificador*) classifying, qualifying; (*examinador*) examining II. m.f. assessor; (*clasificador*) classifier, qualifier ♦ **c. del Santo Oficio** censor of the Inquisition.

ca·li·fi·car §70 tr. (*evaluar*) to assess; (*clasificar*) to classify, qualify; *(dar una nota a)* to grade, mark; FIG. *(ennoblecer)* to ennoble, exalt; *(tratar)* to call *<me calificó de estafador* she called me a swindler>; GRAM. to qualify —reflex. to prove one's noble birth.

ca·li·fi·ca·ti·vo, –va GRAM. **I.** adj. qualifying **II.** m. qualifier.

Ca·li·for·nia f. California.

ca·li·for·nia·no, –na adj. & m.f. Californian.

ca·li·for·nio m. CHEM. californium.

ca·lí·gi·ne f. POET. *(niebla)* mist, fog; *(tinieblas)* darkness, gloom; *(bochorno)* sultriness.

ca·li·gra·fí·a f. calligraphy.

ca·lí·gra·fo, –fa m.f. calligrapher ♦ **c. perito** handwriting expert.

ca·li·na f. *(niebla)* mist, haze; *(calor)* heat.

ca·li·no·so, –sa adj. *(brumoso)* misty, hazy; *(caluroso)* hot, warm.

ca·lis·te·nia f. calisthenics.

cá·liz m. [pl. **–li·ces**] RELIG. chalice; POET. goblet, cup; BOT. calyx ♦ **c. de amarguras** *or* **de dolor** FIG. cup of bitterness *or* sorrows.

ca·li·zo, –za **I.** adj. calcareous, limy **II.** f. limestone.

cal·ma **I.** f. *(tranquilidad)* calm, tranquility; *(cesación)* lull, abatement; FIG. *(serenidad)* calmness, composure; COLL. *(pachorra)* sluggishness, sloth ♦ **c. chicha** MARIT. dead calm • **con c.** calmly • **en c.** calm; COM. in a slack period • **perder la c.** to lose one's composure **II.** adj. see **calmo, –ma.**

cal·man·te **I.** adj. soothing, calming; MED. sedative, tranquilizing **II.** m. MED. sedative, tranquilizer.

cal·mar tr. to soothe, calm (down) —intr. to calm (down), abate —reflex. to become calm, calm down.

cal·mo, –ma **I.** adj. *(sin árboles)* barren, treeless; *(tranquilo)* calm **II.** f. see **calma.**

cal·mo·so, –sa adj. *(tranquilo)* calm, quiet; COLL., FIG. *(indolente)* lazy, sluggish; *(lento)* slow, phlegmatic.

ca·ló m. *(lenguaje gitano)* gypsy dialect; *(jerga)* slang, argot.

ca·lo·friar·se §30 reflex. to have a chill.

ca·lo·frí·o m. chill, shiver.

ca·lor m. PHYS. heat; warmth, heat *<el c. del sol* the warmth of the sun>; *(pasión)* ardor, passion; FIG. warmth *<se impresionaron con el c. de la acogida* they were impressed by the warmth of the reception>; heat, thick *<en el c. de la batalla* in the thick of battle> ♦ **c. animal** PHYSIOL. animal heat • **c. blanco** white heat • **c. canicular** stifling heat • **c. específico** PHYS. specific heat • **c. latente** PHYS. latent heat • **c. natural** PHYSIOL. natural body heat • **c. rojo** red heat • **dar c. a** FIG. to encourage • **entrar en c.** to get warm, warm up • **hacer c.** to be hot *or* warm *<hacía c. ayer* it was hot yesterday> • **tener c.** to be hot *or* warm *<tengo c.* I'm hot>.

ca·lo·rí·a f. PHYS. calorie.

ca·ló·ri·co, –ca PHYS. **I.** m. caloric, heat **II.** adj. caloric.

ca·lo·rí·fe·ro, –ra **I.** adj. heat-producing **II.** m. heater, heating system ♦ **c. de aire** air heater • **c. de vapor** radiator, steam heater • **c. mural** wall radiator.

ca·lo·rí·fu·go, –ga adj. heat-resistant; *(incombustible)* fireproof, incombustible.

ca·lo·rí·me·tro m. PHYS. calorimeter.

ca·lo·ro·so, –sa adj. var. of **caluroso, –sa.**

ca·los·tro m. PHYSIOL. colostrum.

cal·qué, calque see **calcar.**

ca·lum·nia f. calumny, slander.

ca·lum·nia·dor, –do·ra **I.** adj. calumniatory, slanderous **II.** m.f. calumniator, slanderer.

ca·lum·niar tr. to calumniate, slander.

ca·lum·nio·so, –sa adj. calumnious, slanderous.

ca·lu·ro·so, –sa adj. *(caliente)* warm, hot; FIG. *(ardiente)* warm, enthusiastic.

cal·va **I.** f. bald spot; *(de una bosque)* clearing; *(en una tela)* bare *or* threadbare spot **II.** adj. see **calvo, –va.**

cal·va·rio m. RELIG. Calvary; *(vía crucis)* Stations of the Cross; *(cruz)* calvary; FIG. *(sufrimiento)* tribulations, burden; FIG., COLL. *(deudas)* string of debts.

cal·ve·ro m. *(claro)* clearing, glade; *(gredal)* clay pit, marl pit.

cal·vez *or* **cal·vi·cie** f. baldness.

cal·vi·nis·mo m. RELIG. Calvinism.

cal·vi·nis·ta adj. & m.f. Calvinist.

cal·vo, –va **I.** adj. bald; *(yerma)* bare, barren; *(raído)* threadbare, worn ♦ **quedarse c.** to go bald **II.** m.f. bald person —f. see **calva.**

cal·za f. *(cuña)* wedge, chock; *(liga)* identification tag *or* band (for animals); COLL. *(media)* stocking, hose; HER. *(blasón)* pile; COL., DENT. filling ♦ **calzas** breeches • **en calzas prietas** FIG., COLL. in a tight spot, in a jam.

cal·za·da **I.** f. highway, road **II.** adj. see **calzado, –da.**

cal·za·de·ra f. *(cuerda)* hemp cord (for tying sandals); *(calce)* chock, wedge.

cal·za·do, –da **I.** past part. see **calzar** **II.** m. *(zapatos)* footwear; *(medias)* hosiery ♦ **tienda de c.** shoe store —f. see **calzada** **III.** adj. *(que lleva zapatos)* shod; ORNITH. feathered to the claws; ZOOL. with feet of a different color; RELIG. calced.

cal·za·dor m. shoehorn; ARG., BOL. *(portaplumas)* penholder; *(para lápices)* pencil holder.

cal·zar §04 tr. *(poner zapatos)* to shoe, put shoes on; *(llevar)* to wear, take *<qué número calza usted?* what size do you take?>; *(poner calces)* to wedge, chock; COLL. *(comprender)* to grasp, understand; ARM. to carry, take (a certain caliber); AUTO. to put tires on; PRINT. *(grabar en relieve)* to raise; COL., DENT. to fill; GUAT., AGR. to bank, hill —reflex. *(ponerse los zapatos)* to put on shoes; *(ponerse)* to put on *<calzarse las botas* to put on boots>; AMER. to get, obtain.

cal·zo m. *(calce)* wedge, chock; *(fulcro)* fulcrum; MARIT. *(madero)* stowing chock, skid ♦ **calzos** legs (of horse).

cal·zón m. *(pantalones)* pants, trousers; AMER. underpants, panties; CHILE boxer shorts; BOL. pork stew; MEX. chaps ♦ **a c. quitado** COLL. boldly, fearlessly • **amarrarse los calzones** AMER., COLL. to stand firm • **calzones cortos** shorts • **tener bien puestos los calzones** FIG., COLL. to be quite a man • **tener muchos calzones** FIG., COLL. to be daring, have guts.

cal·zo·na·zos m. [pl. **-zos**] FIG., COLL. *(hombre débil)* weakling, milquetoast; *(bragazas)* henpecked husband.

cal·zon·ci·llos m.pl. underwear, (boxer) shorts.

cal·zo·rras m. [pl. **-rras**] FIG., COLL. weakling, drip.

ca·lla·da **I.** f. *(silencio)* silence; MARIT. *(recalmón)* lull, calm (in wind, waves); *(comida)* tripe dinner ♦ **a la. c.** *or* **de c.** on the quiet, secretly • **dar la c. por respuesta** to say nothing in reply, keep silent **II.** adj. see **callado, –da.**

ca·lla·do, –da **I.** past part. see **callar** **II.** adj. *(silencioso)* quiet, silent; *(reservado)* reticent, reserved; *(tácito)* tacit, unspoken **III.** f. see **callada.**

ca·lla·na f. S. AMER. *(cazuela)* earthenware dish (for roasting corn); PERU, MIN. *(escoria)* dross which still can be refined; *(vasija rota)* shard, crock; CHILE *(reloj)* large pocket watch.

ca·llan·di·co *or* **ca·llan·di·to** adv. COLL. *(con disimulo)* on the sly, secretly; *(en silencio)* softly, quietly.

ca·lla·o m. *(guijarro)* pebble; *(terreno)* stretch of land paved with pebbles.

ca·llar intr. *(silenciarse)* to be quiet *or* silent; *(dejar de hacer ruido)* to become quiet, quiet down ♦ **¡calla!** *or* **¡calle!** COLL. you don't say! • **calla callando** COLL. quietly • **calla y cuez** FIG. *(ocuparse de sus propios asuntos)* mind your own business; *(atender al trabajo útil)* stick to the business at hand —tr. *(silenciar)* to quiet, silence; *(guardar secreto)* to keep secret, hush up; *(no mencionar)* not to mention *<callaba lo que sabía* he did not mention what he knew> —reflex. *(silenciarse)* to be quiet *or* silent; to keep quiet *<callarse de miedo* to keep quiet out of fear> ♦ **¡cállate!** be quiet! • **¡cállate la boca!** COLL. shut up!

ca·lle f. *(vía)* street; *(paso)* room, way *<abrir c.* to make way>; SPORT. lane; COLL. neighborhood *<toda la. c. te puede oír* the whole neighborhood can hear you> ♦ **azotar calles** FIG., COLL. to wander *or* roam the streets • **c. de doble sentido** two-way street • **c. de la amargura** FIG. long, hard road • **c. de dirección única** one-way street • **c. mayor** main street • **dejar a uno en la. c.** FIG., COLL. to leave someone out in the cold • **echar a la. c.** FIG., COLL. to throw out of the house • **echarse a la c.** FIG., COLL. to take to the streets • **echar por la c. de en medio** FIG. to

forge ahead • **poner en la c.** FIG. to put out on the street
• **quedarse en la c.** FIG., COLL. to be out in the cold.

ca·lle·je·ar intr. to wander *or* walk the streets.

ca·lle·je·o m. *(paseo)* roaming *or* strolling about; *(vagabundeo)* loitering.

ca·lle·je·ro, –ra I. adj. fond of wandering the streets ♦ **perro c.** stray dog II. m. street guide, city map.

ca·lle·jón m. alley, narrow street; TAUR. passage between barriers of a bullring ♦ **c. sin salida** blind alley; FIG., COLL. *(dificultad)* deadlock, impasse.

ca·lle·jue·la f. back street, alley.

ca·llis·ta m.f. chiropodist.

ca·llo m. MED. callus, corn; SURG. *(cicatriz)* callus; EQUIT. calk (on a horseshoe); COLL. *(mujer)* unattractive woman ♦ **callos** CUL. tripe.

ca·llo·si·dad f. callosity, callus.

ca·llo·so, –sa adj. calloused, callous.

ca·ma f. *(lecho)* bed; *(armazón)* bedstead; bed <*un hospital de cincuenta camas* a hospital with fifty beds>; *(suelo)* floor, bed (of a truck); ZOOL. *(guarida)* lair, burrow; *(mullido de paja)* litter, straw bed; *(camada)* litter (of young); CUL. layer ♦ **c. de roca** GEOL. bedrock • **c. de tijera** folding cot • **caer en c.** to fall ill • **c. gemela** twin bed • **c. individual** single bed • **c. matrimonial** double bed • **c. turca** day bed, divan • **guardar c.** *or* **estar en c.** to stay in bed • **hacer la c.** to make the bed • **hacerle la c. a uno** FIG., COLL. to fix someone's wagon • **irse a la c.** to go to bed.

ca·ma·da f. ZOOL. litter; ORNITH. brood; *(capa)* layer; FIG. *(cuadrilla)* gang *or* band (of thieves).

ca·ma·fe·o m. cameo.

ca·mal m. *(cabestro)* halter; *(palo)* gambrel, meathook; BOL., PERU *(matadero)* slaughterhouse.

ca·ma·le·ón I. m. ZOOL. chameleon; FIG. *(persona inconstante)* chameleon, changeable person; BOL., ZOOL. iguana; C. RICA, ORNITH. falcon II. adj. *(inconstante)* chameleon-like, changeable.

ca·ma·le·ro m. PERU slaughterer, butcher.

ca·ma·lo·tal m. ARG., BOT. water hyacinth bed.

ca·ma·lo·te m. ARG., BOT. water hyacinth.

ca·ma·ma f. SL. swindle, hoax.

ca·mán·du·la f. RELIG. *(camáldula)* Order of the Camaldolites; *(rosario)* rosary; COLL. *(astucia)* cunning, slyness; *(hipocresía)* hypocrisy ♦ **tener muchas camándulas** COLL. to be a sly one, be full of tricks *or* hypocrisy.

ca·man·du·le·ar intr. COLL. *(ostentar devoción)* to be falsely devout, be hypocritical; AMER. to intrigue.

ca·man·du·len·se adj. & m.f. Camaldolite.

ca·man·du·le·ro, –ra COLL. I. adj. hypocritical; AMER. sly, cunning II. m.f. hypocrite; AMER. intriguer.

cá·ma·ra f. *(sala)* hall, parlor; *(departamento)* chamber <*c. de compresión* compression chamber>; *(junta)* chamber, board <*c. de comercio* chamber of commerce>; AGR. *(granero)* granary; AUTO. *(neumático)* inner tube; POL. house, chamber; MARIT. stateroom, cabin; ANAT. cavity, chamber; ARM. chamber, breech; PHOTOG., FILM. camera ♦ **c. clara** *or* **lúcida** OPT. camera lucida • **c. de aire** air chamber • **c. cinematográfica** movie camera • **c. de combustión** combustion chamber • **c. de compensación** COM. clearing house • **c. de gas** gas chamber • **c. de juez** judge's chambers • **c. de los Comunes** POL. House of Commons • **c. de los Lores** POL. House of Lords • **c. de niebla** PHYS. cloud chamber • **c. de oxígeno** oxygen tent • **c. de Representantes** POL. House of Representatives • **c. de televisión** television *or* video camera • **c. de tortura** torture chamber • **c. de vacío** vacuum chamber • **c. fotográfica** camera • **c. frigorífica** cold storage chamber • **c. lenta** PHOTOG. slow motion • **c. mortuoria** funeral chamber • **c. obscura** PHOTOG., OPT. camera obscura • **cámaras** MED. diarrhea • **de c.** court, royal <*pintor de c.* court painter> • **música de c.** chamber music.

ca·ma·ra·da m.f. companion, comrade ♦ **c. de colegio** classmate • **c. de trabajo** workmate, colleague.

ca·ma·ra·de·rí·a f. camaraderie, comradeship.

ca·ma·re·ra f. *(de restaurante)* waitress; *(criada)* maid; MARIT. stewardess ♦ **c. mayor** chief lady in waiting.

ca·ma·re·ro m. *(de restaurante)* waiter; MARIT. steward; *(oficial)* chamberlain, steward ♦ **c. mayor** royal chamberlain • **c. principal** headwaiter.

ca·ma·re·ta f. MARIT. *(cámara)* small cabin, deck cabin; AMER. *(morterete)* small cannon (for shooting fireworks).

ca·ma·ri·lla f. *(grupo)* clique, coterie; POL. lobby.

ca·ma·rín m. RELIG. niche, alcove; THEAT. dressing room; *(tocador)* boudoir; *(despacho)* study, private office.

ca·ma·rón m. ZOOL. shrimp, prawn; C. AMER. tip, gratuity; COL., PAN. bargain; PERU turncoat.

ca·ma·ro·te m. MARIT. cabin, berth.

ca·ma·ro·te·ro m. AMER., MARIT. steward.

ca·mas·quin·ce m.f. COLL. busybody, meddler.

ca·mas·tro m. COLL. makeshift bed; MIL. cot.

ca·mas·trón, –tro·na I. adj. cunning, sly II. m.f. cunning person.

cam·ba I. f. EQUIT. *(cama)* cheek piece (of bit); *(calzadura)* felly, segment of wheel rim —m.f. BOL. Indian of the Chaco region ♦ **cambas** gores of circular garment II. adj. BOL. Indian, native.

cam·ba·do, –da adj. S. AMER. bowlegged.

cam·ba·la·che m. COLL. *(trueque)* swap, trade; AMER. second-hand store.

cam·ba·la·che·ar tr. COLL. to swap, trade.

cam·ba·la·che·ro, –ra I. adj. swapping, trading II. m.f. swapper, trader; AMER. owner of a second-hand store.

cám·ba·ro m. ZOOL. crayfish, crawfish.

cam·bia·ble adj. *(que se puede alterar)* changeable; *(que se puede cambiar por otra cosa)* exchangeable.

cam·bia·di·zo, –za adj. changeable, variable.

cam·bia·dor, –do·ra I. adj. changing II. m.f. moneychanger —m. CHILE, MEX., RAIL. *(guardagujas)* switchman; *(mando)* control switch ♦ **cambiador automático** *or* **de discos** record changer.

cam·bian·te I. adj. *(variable)* changing, variable; *(caprichoso)* changeable, fickle II. m. moneychanger ♦ **cambiantes** iridescence, luster.

cam·biar tr. *(alterar)* to change, alter <*c. el horario* to change the schedule>; *(reemplazar)* to change, replace <*c. la bombilla eléctrica* to change the light bulb>; *(trocar)* to exchange <*cambiaron estos libros por los otros* they exchanged these books for the others>; COM. to exchange, change <*c. pesos por francos* to exchange pesos for francs> —intr. to change <*c. de asiento* to change seats>; METEOROL. to change <*el viento cambió* the wind shifted>; AUTO. to shift gears ♦ **c. de casa** to move • **c. de color** to change color • **c. de dueño** to change hands • **c. de parecer** to change one's mind • **c. de ropa** to change clothes —reflex. to change; METEOROL. to change, shift.

cam·bia·ví·a m. RAIL. *(cambio)* switch; CUBA, MEX., P. RICO *(guardagujas)* switchman.

cam·bia·zo m. COLL. change, switch ♦ **dar un c.** *(cambiar mucho)* do a complete change *or* switch; *(substituir fraudulentamente)* to pull a switch.

cam·bio m. *(alteración)* change, alteration; *(trueque)* exchange, barter; *(monedas)* change <*¿tienes c.?* do you have change?>; COM. *(tipo de cambio)* rate of exchange; *(prima)* premium (paid on a bill of exchange); *(cotización)* quotation price; RAIL. switch; AUTO. transmission ♦ **a c. de** in exchange for • **a las primeras de c.** from the start • **c. automático** AUTO. automatic transmission • **c. de domicilio** change of address • **c. de marchas** *or* **velocidades** AUTO. gearshift • **c. de tiempo** change in the weather • **c. de tribunal** LAW change of venue • **c. extranjero** FIN. foreign exchange • **casa de c.** foreign exchange office • **en c.** *(en vez de)* instead; *(por otra parte)* on the other hand • **libre c.** COM. free trade.

cam·bis·ta m.f. moneychanger, broker; *(banquero)* banker —m. ARG., RAIL. switchman.

Cam·bo·ya f. Cambodia.

cam·bo·ya·no, –na adj. & m.f. Cambodian.

cam·bray m. TEX. chambray.

cam·bria·no, –na *or* **cám·bri·co, –ca** adj. & m. GEOL. Cambrian.

cam·bu·jo, –ja I. adj. C. AMER., MEX. *(morcillo)* reddish black (donkey); *(moreno)* dark, swarthy II. m.f. C. AMER., MEX. Indian, mestizo.

ca·me·la·dor, –do·ra I. adj. flattering II. m.f. flatterer.

ca·me·lar tr. COLL. *(halagar)* to flatter; *(enamorar)* to court, woo; *(engañar)* to deceive, cajole; *(convencer)* to convince; MEX. to watch, observe.

ca·me·le·ar tr. COLL. to deceive.

ca·me·le·o m. COLL. flattery, wheedling.

ca·me·lia f. BOT. camellia.

ca·me·lis·ta I. adj. wheedling, cajoling II. m.f. humbug, wheedler.

ca·me·lo m. COLL. *(galanteo)* courting, flirting; *(chasco)* teasing, joking; *(mentira)* lie, hoax ♦ **dar c. a** to make fun of, tease.

ca·me·llo m. ZOOL. camel; MARIT. camel, watertight drum; COLL. *(traficante)* drug dealer.

ca·me·llón m. *(caballón)* ridge (of furrow); *(camelote)* camlet (cloth); *(artesa)* drinking trough; MEX. *(tierra)* cultivated land on islets in the Valley of Mexico.

ca·me·ri·no m. THEAT. dressing room.

ca·me·ro, –ra adj. double <*cama c.* double bed>.

Ca·me·rún, República Unida de f. United Republic of Cameroon.

ca·me·ru·nés, –ne·sa adj. & m.f. Cameroonian.

ca·mi·lla f. *(cama)* small bed; MED. stretcher; *(mesa)* table with a heater underneath.

ca·mi·lle·ro m. stretcher-bearer.

ca·mi·na·dor, –do·ra adj. fond of walking.

ca·mi·nan·te I. adj. walking, traveling II. m.f. walker, traveler —m. footman, groom.

ca·mi·nar intr. *(andar)* to walk; *(viajar)* to travel, go; FIG. to move along, make its way <*la carreta camina lentamente por la calle* the wagon makes its way slowly down the street> ♦ **c. derecho** to act properly —tr. to walk, go <*han caminado cinco kilómetros* they have gone five kilometers>.

ca·mi·na·ta f. *(paseo)* stroll, walk; COLL. *(recorrido largo)* hike, trek.

ca·mi·no m. *(senda)* road, path, trail; *(vía)* route <*el c. más corto* the shortest route>; *(viaje)* journey, trip; FIG. *(modo)* way, means; AMER. runner, narrow strip of carpet ♦ **abrir c.** to make way; FIG. to find a way • **allanar el c.** COLL. to smooth the way • **a medio c.** halfway • **c. carretero** or **carretil** carriage road • **c. de** on the way to, towards • **c. de acceso** access road • **c. de herradura** bridle path • **c. de hierro** railway • **c. de mesa** AMER. table runner • **C. de Santiago** ASTRON. Milky Way • **c. de sirga** towpath • **c. real** king's highway • **c. trillado** frequented road; FIG. beaten path • **c. vecinal** municipal road • **de c.** *(de paso)* on the way; FIG. *(casualmente)* in passing <*lo mencionó de c.* he mentioned it in passing> • **en c.** on the way • **en c. de** FIG. on the way to <*está en c. de extinguirse* it is on the way to becoming extinct> • **ir fuera de c.** FIG. to go astray • **ponerse en c.** to set out, get started • **por buen c.** FIG. on the right track • **traer a buen c.** FIG. to put on the right track.

ca·mión m. *(vehículo)* truck, lorry (G.B.); MEX. bus ♦ **c. blindado** armored truck • **c. cisterna** tank truck • **c. de bomberos** fire engine • **c. de la basura** garbage truck • **c. de mudanzas** moving van • **c. remolcador** tow truck • **c. de volteo** dump truck.

ca·mio·na·je m. truckage, haulage.

ca·mio·ne·ro, –ra m.f. truck driver.

ca·mio·ne·ta f. van, light truck.

ca·mi·sa f. shirt <*él llevó una c. de algodón* he wore a cotton shirt>; *(envoltura)* cover, jacket; BOT. skin, husk; ZOOL. slough; MECH. casing, jacket ♦ **c. de agua** MECH. water jacket • **c. de dormir** nightshirt • **c. de fuerza** straitjacket • **dejar sin c. a** FIG., COLL. to leave penniless • **en c.** without a dowry • **en mangas de c.** in shirtsleeves • **meterse en c. de once varas** COLL. to bite off more than one can chew • **perder hasta la c.** FIG., COLL. to lose the shirt off one's back.

ca·mi·se·ta f. *(polera)* T-shirt; *(ropa interior)* undershirt; SPORT. shirt, jersey.

ca·mi·so·la f. *(de mujer)* camisole; *(camiseta)* shirt; *(camisa de hombre)* man's dress shirt; CHILE woman's blouse.

ca·mi·so·lín m. dickey, shirt front.

ca·mi·són m. *(camisa grande)* long or wide shirt; *(camisa de dormir)* nightgown, nightdress; AMER. chemise, shift.

ca·mo·mi·la f. BOT. camomile, chamomile.

ca·món m. *(trono)* portable throne; *(mirador)* oriel, en-

closed balcony; *(cama)* large bed; ARCHIT. *(armazón)* arched rafter; CUBA *(pina)* felly, rim (of wheel) ♦ **camones** oak tires of cart wheels • **c. de vidrios** glass partition.

ca·mo·rra f. COLL. squabble, quarrel ♦ **armar c.** to pick or start a fight • **buscar c.** to go looking for trouble.

ca·mo·rre·ar intr. COLL. to squabble, quarrel.

ca·mo·rre·ro, –ra adj. & m.f. var. of **camorrista**.

ca·mo·rris·ta I. adj. quarrelsome, rowdy II. m.f. quarrelsome person, rowdy.

ca·mo·te m. AMER., BOT. *(batata)* sweet potato; *(bulbo)* tuber, bulb; AMER., COLL. *(enamoramiento)* infatuation; *(amante)* lover, sweetheart; *(embuste)* lie, fib; C. AMER. bruise, bump; ECUAD., MEX. fool; MEX. scoundrel, rascal ♦ **tener un c.** AMER. to be infatuated • **tragar c.** MEX. to stammer.

ca·mo·ti·llo m. CHILE, PERU *(dulce)* sweet made of mashed sweet potatoes; MEX. *(madera)* violet-colored wood streaked with black; C. AMER., BOT. turmeric.

cam·pal adj. ♦ **batalla c.** pitched battle.

cam·pa·men·to m. *(acción)* camping, encamping; *(lugar)* camp, encampment ♦ **c. de verano** summer camp.

cam·pa·na f. *(cascabel)* bell; *(objeto acampanado)* bell-shaped object; *(queda)* curfew; *(parroquia)* parish; CUBA, BOT. floripondio; ARG. lookout (in a crime) ♦ **c. de aire** ENGIN. air chamber • **c. de bucear** or **de buzo** diving bell • **c. de vidrio** or **de cristal** bell jar • **a c. herida** or **tañida** at the sound of the bell • **echar las campanas a vuelo** to rejoice • **oír campanas y no saber dónde** FIG., COLL. to misunderstand • **tañer** or **tocar las campanas** to ring the bells.

cam·pa·na·da f. *(toque)* stroke, ring (of a bell); *(sonido)* ringing; FIG. *(escándalo)* scandal, sensation ♦ **dar una c.** to cause a sensation.

cam·pa·na·rio m. bell tower, belfry ♦ **de c.** mean, despicable.

cam·pa·ne·ar intr. to ring the bells; ARG. to be the lookout (in a crime).

cam·pa·ne·o m. ringing or pealing of bells.

cam·pa·ne·ro m. *(fundidor)* bell founder or maker; *(tocador)* bell ringer; COL., VEN., ORNITH. campanero, bellbird.

cam·pa·nil I. adj. bell <*bronce c.* bell bronze> II. m. belfry, bell tower.

cam·pa·ni·lla f. *(campana)* hand bell; *(timbre)* doorbell; *(burbuja)* bubble; ANAT. uvula; BOT. campanula, bellflower; SEW. tassel; BOT. liana ♦ **c. de invierno** BOT. snowdrop • **de muchas campanillas** of great importance.

cam·pan·te adj. *(sobresaliente)* outstanding; COLL. *(tranquilo)* unruffled, relaxed; *(satisfecho)* self-satisfied, smug.

cam·pa·nu·do, –da adj. *(campaniforme)* bell-shaped; FIG. *(retumbante)* grandiloquent, high-flown <*retórica c.* grandiloquent rhetoric>.

cam·pa·ña f. *(llanura)* plain, open country; FIG. campaign, drive <*una c. publicitaria* a publicity campaign>; MIL., POL. campaign; MARIT. cruise, expedition; *(período)* season <*c. teatral* theater season>; AMER. countryside ♦ **batir** or **correr la c.** to reconnoiter • **hacer c.** to campaign • **tienda de c.** tent.

cam·pa·ñol m. ZOOL. vole, field mouse.

cam·par intr. *(acampar)* to camp; *(sobresalir)* to stand out, excel ♦ **c. por sus respetos** to do as one pleases.

cam·pe·a·dor adj. mighty or heroic in battle.

cam·pe·ar intr. *(pacer)* to graze, go out to pasture (animals); *(verdear)* to green, turn green; FIG. *(sobresalir)* to stand out, excel; *(abundar)* to abound; MIL. to reconnoiter; AMER. to search or scour the countryside; COL. to bluster.

cam·pe·cha·ní·a or **cam·pe·cha·ne·rí·a** f. *(buen humor)* good humor, geniality; *(generosidad)* generosity, bigheartedness; *(franqueza)* openness, straightforwardness.

cam·pe·cha·no, –na COLL. adj. *(amistoso)* genial, good-natured; *(generoso)* generous.

cam·pe·che m. BOT. campeachy wood, logwood.

cam·pe·ón, –o·na m.f. champion; FIG. *(defensor)* champion, defender.

cam·pe·o·na·to m. championship ♦ **de c.** COLL. terrific, great.

cam·pe·ro, –ra I. adj. *(al aire libre)* open-air, in the open;

ARG., URUG. expert at ranching *or* farming **II.** m. *(jeep)* jeep, land rover; *(religioso)* friar who farms.

cam·pe·si·na·do m. peasantry.

cam·pe·si·no, –na **I.** adj. country, field <*ratón c.* field mouse>; *(aldeano)* rural, rustic **II.** m.f. peasant, farmer.

cam·pes·tre adj. *(campesino)* rural, country; BOT. wild.

cam·pi·ña f. large field <*una c. de trigo* a large field of wheat>; *(campo)* country, countryside ♦ **cerrarse uno de c.** COLL. to stand firm.

cam·po m. *(campaña)* country, countryside; field <*un c. de maíz* a field of corn>; *(campamento)* camp, encampment; FIG. *(área)* sphere, field <*un c. de interés* a field of interest>; *(partido)* faction, camp, side; ARTS background; SPORT., MIL., PHYS., MATH., HER. field; COL. farm, ranch; CHILE, PERU mining concession ♦ **a c. raso** out in the open • **a c. traviesa** cross-country • **casa de c.** country house • **c. de Agramante** FIG. pandemonium, bedlam • **c. de aterrizaje** AVIA. landing field • **c. de aviación** airfield • **c. de batalla** battlefield • **c. de concentración** concentration camp • **c. de deportes** athletic field • **c. de fútbol** soccer field • **c. de instrucción** training camp • **c. de juego** playground • **c. del honor** FIG. field of honor, battlefield • **c. de minas** MIL. minefield • **c. de tiro** firing range • **c. eléctrico** electric field • **c. gravitatorio** PHYS. gravitational field • **c. magnético** PHYS. magnetic field • **c. operatorio** MED. surgical area • **c. petrolífero** oil field • **c. raso** open country • **c. santo** cemetery • **c. visual** field of vision • **dar c. a** FIG. to give ground to • **dejar el c. abierto** *or* **libre** FIG. to leave the field open • **hacérsele a uno el c. orégano** ARG., COLL. to succeed with ease • **levantar el c.** MIL. to strike camp; FIG. *(ceder)* to give up • **quedar en el c. de batalla** FIG. to die in battle • **reconocer el c.** MIL. to reconnoiter; COM. to scout out the difficulties • **trabajo de c.** field work.

cam·po·san·to m. cemetery, graveyard.

ca·mu·fla·je m. camouflage.

ca·mu·flar tr. to camouflage.

can m. *(perro)* dog; ARM. *(gatillo)* trigger; ARCHIT. *(modillón)* modillion; *(de una viga)* corbel ♦ **C. Mayor** ASTRON. Canis Major • **C. Menor** ASTRON. Canis Minor.

ca·na **I.** f. *(cabello)* white *or* gray hair; CUBA, BOT. palm tree; AMER., COLL. jail ♦ **echar una c. al aire** to let one's hair down, have fun **II.** adj. see **cano, –na.**

Ca·na·dá m. Canada.

ca·na·dien·se adj. & m.f. Canadian.

ca·nal m. canal <*el c. de Panamá* the Panama Canal>; *(estrecho)* strait, channel; *(de puerto)* navigation channel; *(tubo)* pipe, conduit, tube; ANAT. canal, duct, tract <*c. digestivo* digestive tract>; ARCHIT. *(gotera)* gutter, downspout; RAD., TELEV. channel —f. *(delantera de un libro)* front edge of a book; *(res muerto)* dressed carcass; ARCHIT. *(estría)* groove, fluting ♦ **abrir en c.** to split from top to bottom.

ca·na·le·ta f. *(canal)* chute, conduit; ARG. gutter.

ca·na·le·te m. paddle.

ca·na·li·za·ble adj. capable of being channeled.

ca·na·li·za·ción f. *(acción)* canalization, channeling; TECH. piping, tubing; ELEC. wiring; AMER. sewers, sewage system.

ca·na·li·zar §04 tr. *(abrir canales)* to canalize; *(controlar aguas)* to channel; *(por tuberías)* to pipe; FIG. *(orientar)* to channel, direct.

ca·na·lón m. *(cañería)* gutter, drainpipe (on roof of house); *(sombrero)* shovel hat.

ca·na·lla COLL. m. *(hombre ruin)* scoundrel, dirty rascal —f. *(populacho)* rabble, riffraff.

ca·na·lla·da f. dirty trick.

ca·na·lles·co, –ca adj. *(vil)* low, despicable; *(pícaro)* rascally, roguish <*risa c.* roguish laughter>.

ca·na·na f. *(cinto)* cartridge belt; AMER. *(bocio)* goiter; COL. *(camisa de fuerza)* straitjacket ♦ **cananas** COL. handcuffs.

ca·na·pé m. *(sofá)* sofa, couch; CUL. canapé, hors d'oeuvre.

Ca·na·rias f.pl. Canary Islands, Canaries.

ca·na·rio, –ria **I.** adj. Canarian, of the Canary Islands **II.** m.f. Canarian —m. ORNITH. canary; *(embarcación)* small boat; CHILE *(persona generosa)* big tipper; *(pito)* toy whistle.

ca·nas·ta f. *(cesta)* basket; *(cesto grande)* hamper; *(naipes)* canasta; SPORT. *(en baloncesto)* basket; MARIT. bowknot.

ca·nas·te·ro, –ra m.f. basket maker; AMER. street vendor.

ca·nas·ti·lla f. *(canasta pequeña)* small basket; *(de bebé)* layette; AMER. trousseau.

ca·nas·to m. narrow-mouthed basket ♦ **¡canastos!** good heavens!

cán·ca·mo m. MARIT. *(armella)* eyebolt; *(cabilla)* treenail ♦ **c. de mar** slap *or* crash of a large wave.

can·ca·mu·sa f. trick, deception ♦ **armar una c. a uno** to pull the wool over someone's eyes.

cán·ca·na f. *(banquilla)* dunce's bench; ENTOM. large brown spider; ARG., CHILE, PERU *(asador)* spit; COL. *(persona flaca)* thin person.

can·ca·ne·ar intr. COLL. *(vagar)* to wander *or* roam around; AMER. *(tartamudear)* to stutter, stammer; *(explicarse con dificultad)* to express oneself with difficulty; ARG., URUG. *(bailar)* to dance the cancan; *(proceder de modo inmoral en política)* to engage in dirty politics.

can·ca·ne·o m. AMER., COLL. *(vagabundeo)* loitering, loafing; *(tartamudeo)* stuttering, stammering; *(detonación)* sputter of a stalling motor.

cán·ca·no m. COLL. louse.

can·cel m. *(puerta)* storm door; *(mámpara)* partition; AMER. folding screen.

can·ce·la f. iron gate.

can·ce·la·ción f. cancellation.

can·ce·lar tr. *(anular)* to cancel; *(saldar)* to pay off, settle (a debt); FIG. *(borrar)* to dispel, wipe out.

cán·cer m. cancer ♦ **Cáncer** ASTROL. Cancer.

can·ce·rar·se reflex. *(un tumor)* to become cancerous; *(una persona)* to get cancer; FIG. *(corromperse)* to become corrupt.

can·cer·be·ro m. *(portero)* severe guard *or* doorman; SPORT. *(guardameta)* goaltender, goalkeeper.

can·ce·rí·ge·no, –na adj. MED. carcinogenic, cancerogenic.

can·ce·ró·lo·go, –ga m.f. MED. cancer specialist.

can·ce·ro·so, –sa adj. MED. cancerous.

can·ci·ller m. chancellor; AMER. Minister of Foreign Affairs.

can·ci·lle·rí·a f. *(oficio y lugar)* chancellery; *(oficio)* chancellorship; AMER. Ministry of Foreign Affairs.

can·ción f. *(canto)* song; POET. song, ballad ♦ **c. de cuna** lullaby, cradle song • **c. de gesta** epic poem • **c. infantil** nursery rhyme • **volver a la misma c.** FIG., COLL. to harp on the same old subject.

can·cio·ne·ro m. MUS. songbook; LIT. anthology, collection.

can·cio·nis·ta m.f. *(compositor)* songwriter, composer; *(cantante)* singer, vocalist.

can·cro m. MED. cancer; BOT. canker.

can·cha f. *(campo)* field, ground <*c. de fútbol* soccer field>; *(de tenis)* court; *(de pelea de gallos)* cockpit; AMER. *(terreno abierto)* open space *or* ground; *(corral)* fenced yard; COL. *(pago)* gaming fee; URUG. *(senda)* path, lane; COL., PERU *(maíz)* toasted corn, popcorn ♦ **abrir** *or* **dar c. a** ARG., CHILE, C. RICA to give the advantage to • **¡cancha!** ARG., URUG. make way! • **c. de carreras** S. AMER. racetrack • **estar uno en su c.** ARG., CHILE, URUG. to be in one's element • **tener c.** ARG. to be experienced.

can·che·ro, –ra **I.** m.f. AMER. expert, experienced person; AMER. groundskeeper; CHILE loafer, lazy person; CHILE, SPORT. scorekeeper **II.** adj. AMER. expert, skilled.

can·cho m. *(peñasco)* boulder, large rock; CHILE *(propina)* tip; CHILE, PERU, COLL. *(salario)* pay, wage.

can·da·do m. padlock ♦ **c. de combinación** combination padlock • **estar con c.** to be padlocked • **poner bajo c.** to lock safely away.

can·de adj. candied, crystallized.

can·de·al **I.** adj. white <*pan c.* white bread> **II.** m. ARG., CHILE, PERU hot beverage made with cognac, milk and eggs.

can·de·la f. *(vela)* candle; *(candelero)* candlestick; COLL. *(lumbre)* fire, heat; light <*necesito c. para encender el cigarillo* I need a light for my cigarette>; PHYS. candle; BOT. chestnut blossom ♦ **arrimar c. a** COLL. to thrash, beat • **candelas** COL. love affairs • **dar c. a** AMER. to pester, annoy • **en c.** MARIT. vertical • **estar con la c. en la mano** FIG., COLL. to be at death's door.

can·de·la·bro m. candelabrum, ARG., BOT. cactus.

can·de·la·da f. bonfire.

can·de·la·ria f. RELIG. Candlemas; BOT. great mullein.

can·de·le·ro m. *(candelabro)* candlestick; *(velón)* oil lamp; MARIT. stanchion; MEX., BOT. cactus; VEN., BOT. ivy; COL. stoker, fireman • **estar en el c.** to be high up, be at the top; *(ser popular)* to be very popular • **poner en el c.** to put at the top; *(hacer popular)* to make very popular.

can·de·li·lla f. *(candela pequeña)* small candle; MED. *(instrumento)* bougie, catheter; BOT. *(amento)* catkin, ament; *(planta)* euphorbia; AMER. *(fuego fatuo)* will-o'-the-wisp; *(luciérnaga)* firefly, glowworm; ARG., CUBA *(bastilla)* hemstitch, overstitch; CUBA, ENTOM. insect which attacks leaves of tobacco plant • **se le hacen candelillas los ojos** he's tipsy or merry (from drinking).

can·den·te adj. *(incandescente)* candescent, white-hot; *(ardiente)* glowing, burning; FIG. charged <*una atmósfera c.* a charged atmosphere>; *(grave)* burning, important <*cuestión c.* burning question>.

can·di adj. candied, crystallized.

can·di·da·to, -ta m.f. candidate.

can·di·da·tu·ra f. candidacy; *(lista)* list of candidates.

can·di·dez f. *(franqueza)* frankness, candor; FIG. *(ingenuidad)* naiveté, ingenuousness.

cán·di·do, -da adj. *(franco)* frank, candid; FIG. *(ingenuo)* naive, ingenuous; POET. *(blanco)* white, snowy.

can·dil m. *(luz)* oil lamp; COLL. *(pico del sombrero)* peak, cock (of a hat); ZOOL. crown, tine (of an antler); BOT. wake-robin; MEX. chandelier.

can·di·le·ja f. oil reservoir (of a lamp); *(candil)* small oil lamp; BOT. nigella • **candilejas** THEAT. footlights.

can·dom·be m. AMER. *(baile)* dance of South American blacks; *(sitio)* dance hall; *(tambor)* small drum; ARG. *(desgobierno)* corrupt government.

can·don·ga I. f. *(zalamería)* flattery, blarney; COLL. *(chasco)* trick; *(broma)* practical joke; *(burla)* teasing, kidding; *(mula)* draft mule; MARIT. *(vela)* storm sail on mizzen mast; C. AMER., P. RICO *(lienzo)* stomach band (to bind newborn's navel) • **candongas** CUBA, ECUAD. earrings • **dar c.** to tease, kid II. adj. see **candongo, -ga.**

can·don·go, -ga COLL. I. adj. *(zalamero)* flattering, ingratiating; *(astuto)* sly, cunning; *(holgazán)* lazy, malingering II. m.f. *(zalamero)* flatterer, wheedler; *(astuto)* sly one, crafty fellow; *(holgazán)* layabout, malingerer —f. see **candonga.**

can·don·gue·ar COLL. tr. to kid, tease —intr. to malinger, shirk.

can·don·gue·ro, -ra adj. COLL. *(bromista)* joking, kidding; *(holgazán)* lazy, malingering.

can·dor m. *(candidez)* frankness, candor; *(ingenuidad)* naiveté, ingenuousness; POET. *(blancura)* whiteness.

can·do·ro·so, -sa adj. *(franco)* frank, candid; *(ingenuo)* naive, ingenuous.

ca·ne·ar intr. to grow gray-haired.

ca·ne·ca f. MEX. *(frasco de barro)* glazed earthenware bottle (for liquors); ARG. *(balde)* wooden bucket; CUBA *(medida)* liquid measure; *(botella)* hot-water bottle; *(porrón)* wine bottle (with spout).

ca·ne·la f. BOT., CUL. cinnamon; FIG. *(joya)* exquisite object, gem; CARIB. mulatto girl • **¡canela!** good gracious!

ca·ne·lón m. *(cañería)* roof gutter; *(carámbano)* icicle; *(labor)* tubular braid; *(confite)* cinnamon candy; COLL. *(punta)* pointed tip of scourge or lash; GUAT., VEN. *(rizo)* corkscrew curl.

ca·ne·lo·nes m.pl. CUL. cannelloni (pasta).

ca·ne·sú m. *(de una camisa)* yoke; *(de un vestido)* bodice.

can·gi·lón m. *(cántaro)* large jug or pitcher; *(cubo)* bucket, scoop (of waterwheel); *(pliegue)* curved pleat (of a ruff); *(tambor)* drum; AMER. *(carril)* rut; *(bache)* pothole.

can·gre·jo m. *(de río)* crayfish; *(de mar)* crab; TECH. caulking bit; MARIT. gaff; RAIL. *(vagón)* trolley; ECUAD. idiot, fool; PERU rogue, rascal • **C.** ASTRON. the Crab (Cancer) • **c. de mar** crab • **c. de río** crayfish • **c. hermitaño** hermit crab.

can·gre·na f. var. of **gangrena.**

can·gue·lo m. COLL. fear.

can·gu·ro m. ZOOL. kangaroo.

ca·ní·bal I. adj. cannibalistic; FIG. *(feroz)* fierce, savage II. m.f. cannibal.

ca·ni·ba·lis·mo m. cannibalism; FIG. *(ferocidad)* fierceness, savageness.

ca·ni·ca f. *(bolita)* marble; CUBA, BOT. wild cinnamon • **canicas** (game of) marbles.

ca·ni·cie f. whiteness, grayness (of person's hair).

ca·ní·cu·la f. ASTRON. Sirius, Dog Star; *(período)* dog days, midsummer heat.

cá·ni·do, -da ZOOL. I. adj. canine II. m. canine • **cánidos** Canidae.

ca·ni·jo, -ja adj. COLL. weak, feeble.

ca·ni·lla f. ANAT. long bone; *(carretillo)* bobbin, spool; *(caño)* tap, spout; TEX. *(raya)* stripe, rib; AMER., ANAT. shin, shinbone; PERU dice game; MEX., FIG. *(fuerza)* strength; COLL. *(pierna)* skinny leg • **a c.** MEX. by force.

ca·ni·lle·ra f. *(espinillera de armadura)* greave; *(almohadilla)* shin pad; AMER. *(cobardía)* cowardice; *(temblor)* shaking, trembling (with fear); COL. *(pánico)* panic, terror.

ca·ni·lli·ta m. S. AMER. newspaper boy.

ca·ni·no, -na I. adj. canine; *(hambre)* ravenous <*hambre c.* ravenous hunger> II. m. DENT. canine, cuspid —f. dog droppings.

can·je m. exchange, trade.

can·je·a·ble adj. exchangeable.

can·je·ar tr. to exchange, trade.

ca·no, -na I. adj. white-haired, gray-haired; FIG *(viejo)* old; *(blanco)* white, snowy II. f. see **cana.**

ca·no·a f. canoe; *(bote de remos)* rowboat; AMER. *(acueducto)* aqueduct, conduit; *(artesa)* trough; AMER. gutter, drainpipe.

ca·nó·dro·mo m. dog or greyhound track.

ca·non m. *(precepto)* canon, tenet; RELIG., MUS., ARTS canon; *(de la misa)* Canon (part of the Mass); *(lista)* authorized list or catalogue; *(impuesto)* tax, levy; *(alquiler)* rent • **c. de arrendamiento** rental rate • **cánones** RELIG. canon law.

ca·no·ni·cé, canonice see **canonizar.**

ca·nó·ni·co, -ca I. adj. canonical, canonic II. f. canonical life.

ca·nó·ni·go I. m. canon, prebendary II. adj. COL. irascible, irritable • **llevar una vida de c.** or **vivir como un c.** to live like a lord.

ca·no·ni·za·ble adj. worthy of canonization.

ca·no·ni·za·ción f. canonization.

ca·no·ni·zar §04 tr. RELIG. to canonize; FIG. *(alabar)* to applaud, praise; *(aprobar)* to approve.

ca·no·ro, -ra adj. *(melodioso)* melodious, musical; FIG. *(lírico)* lyrical, graceful • **ave c.** songbird.

ca·no·so, -sa adj. white-haired, gray-haired.

can·sa·do, -da I. past part. see **cansar** II. *(fatigado)* tired, weary; *(agotado)* worn, used-up; *(fastidioso)* bothersome, tiresome • **a las cansadas** ARG., P. RICO, URUG. after much delay, finally.

can·san·cio m. *(fatiga)* tiredness, weariness; MED. exhaustion, fatigue • **muerto de c.** FIG. dog-tired.

can·sar tr. *(fatigar)* to tire, make tired; MED. to exhaust, fatigue; *(aburrir)* to bore; *(fastidiar)* to bother, annoy; AGR. to exhaust, deplete • **c. la vista** to strain one's eyes —reflex. to become or get tired —intr. to be tiring <*este trabajo cansa mucho* this work is very tiring>; to be boring <*la lectura de los clásicos puede c.* reading the classics can be boring>.

can·si·no, -na adj. *(lento)* slow, weary <*paso c.* slow pace>; *(molesto)* bothersome, annoying; *(enervado)* worn-out, exhausted.

can·ta·ble MUS. I. adj. singable <*un trozo c.* a singable piece>; *(despacio)* to be sung slowly II. m. *(melodía)* cantabile; *(letra)* lyrics.

Cán·ta·bros m.pl. GEOG. Cantabrian Mountains.

can·ta·dor, -do·ra m.f. singer (of traditional or folk songs).

can·tal m. *(canto)* boulder, stone block; *(cantizal)* stony ground.

can·ta·le·ta f. *(algazara)* noisy mock serenade; *(chasco)* scoffing, banter • **dar c.** to make fun of, deride • **estar con la misma c.** to harp on the same subject.

can·tan·te I. adj. singing ♦ **llevar la voz c.** FIG. to be in charge. **II.** m.f. singer, vocalist.
can·tar¹ m. song, folk song; CHILE gossip ♦ **c. de gesta** epic poem • **C. de los Cantares** BIBL. Song of Songs • **eso es otro c.** FIG., COLL. that is another story.
can·tar² tr. to sing <*cantaban una canción gallega* they sang a Galician song>; (*canturrear*) to chant; (*recitar*) to recite; FIG. (*alabar*) to sing the praises of, praise <*c. la belleza de una mujer* to praise the beauty of a woman> ♦ **cantarlas claras** to tell it straight —intr. to sing <*c. en voz alta* to sing out loud>; (*chirriar*) to chirp, cheep <*los grillos cantan por la noche* the crickets chirp at night>; (*rechinar*) to creak, squeak; FIG. (*confesar*) to confess, sing; MARIT. to blow a whistle ♦ **c. de plano** FIG. to confess to everything, make a full confession • **en menos de lo que canta un gallo** in a jiffy.
cán·ta·ra f. (*cántaro*) pitcher; (*medida*) liquid measure.
can·ta·re·la f. MUS. (*cuerda*) first or highest string (of violin or guitar); BOT. (*hongo*) chanterelle.
can·ta·rín, –ri·na I. adj. COLL. fond of singing, always singing **II.** m.f. singer.
cán·ta·ro m. (*jarro*) pitcher, jug (container and contents); MEX., MUS. bassoon ♦ **a cántaros** COLL. in abundance • **llover a cántaros** COLL. to rain cats and dogs.
can·ta·ta f. MUS. cantata.
can·ta·triz f. [pl. **-tri·ces**] woman singer, chanteuse.
can·te·ar tr. to place bricks on edge; CHILE to cut stone.
can·te·ra f. (*pedrera*) quarry, pit; FIG. (*talento*) talent, ability; MEX., MAS. freestone, ashlar.
Can·ter·be·ry Canterbury.
can·te·rí·a f. (*arte*) art of hewing stone, stonecutting; (*obra*) stonework, something made of hewn stone.
can·te·ro m. (*pedrero*) quarry worker, stonemason; crust <*un c. de pan* a crust of bread>; (*de tierra*) plot, strip of land; ARG., URUG. flowerbed.
cán·ti·co m. RELIG. canticle, hymn; FIG. (*canción*) song.
can·ti·dad f. (*cuantía*) quantity; (*suma*) amount, sum ♦ **c. alzada** lump sum • **c. de movimiento** PHYS. momentum • **c. variable** MATH. variable.
can·til m. (*acantilado*) cliff; AMER. cliff edge; GUAT. large snake.
can·ti·le·na f. MUS. cantilena, ballad; FIG., COLL. (*repetición*) same old song or story.
can·tim·plo·ra f. (*vasija*) water bottle, canteen; (*sifón*) syphon; GUAT., MED. mumps.
can·ti·na f. cafeteria, canteen; (*sótano de vinos*) wine cellar; (*portacomidas*) lunch or picnic basket; AMER. tavern, saloon ♦ **cantinas** saddlebags.
can·ti·ne·la f. var. of **cantilena.**
can·ti·ne·ro, –ra m.f. bartender, saloonkeeper.
can·ti·zal m. stony ground.
can·to¹ m. (*canción*) song; chant <*c. gregoriano* Gregorian chant>; (*arte de cantar*) singing; (*melodía*) melody, tune; (*letra de una canción*) lyrics; (*poema*) short heroic poem; (*estrofa*) canto, stanza ♦ **al c. del gallo** COLL. at cockcrow or daybreak • **c. del cisne** FIG. swan song • **con un c. en el pecho** COLL. gladly, with a song in one's heart • **en c. llano** COLL. in plain language.
can·to² m. (*extremo*) end, edge; (*borde*) rim, border <*el c. del vestido* the border of the dress>; (*esquina*) corner; (*cantero*) crust <*un c. de pan* a crust of bread>; blunt edge <*el c. de un sable* the blunt edge of a saber>; (*de un libro*) front edge (of a book); (*guijarro*) pebble, stone; COL. lap; P. RICO piece, bit ♦ **c. pelado** or **rodado** boulder • **de c.** (*de lado*) on end, on edge; (*grueso*) thick <*el libro tiene dos pulgadas de c.* the book is two inches thick>.
can·tón m. (*esquina*) corner; (*región*) region, district; (*división administrativa*) canton; ARG., CHILE, MEX. fine crepe.
can·to·na·da f. ♦ **dar c.** to give (someone) the slip.
can·to·nal I. adj. cantonal, pertaining to a canton or district **II.** m.f. supporter of cantonalism.
can·to·na·lis·mo m. (*sistema político*) cantonalism; FIG. (*desconcierto político*) anarchic subdivision of authority in a country.
can·to·nar tr. MIL. to canton, quarter (troops).
can·to·ne·ar intr. to idle, roam aimlessly —reflex. to strut, walk in an affected way.

can·to·ne·ra I. f. (*pieza de refuerzo*) cornerpiece, corner band; (*estante*) corner table; (*prostituta*) prostitute, streetwalker **II.** adj. see **cantonero, –ra.**
can·to·ne·ro, –ra I. adj. idling, loafing **II.** m.f. idler, loafer —m. BKB. instrument for gilding book corners —f. see **cantonera.**
can·to·nés, –ne·sa adj. & m.f. Cantonese ♦ **los cantoneses** the Cantonese.
can·tor, –to·ra I. adj. singing **II.** m.f. singer; (*poeta*) poet, bard —m. ORNITH. songbird —f. CHILE bedpan, urinal.
can·to·ral m. choir book.
can·tu·rí·a f. (*ejercicio de cantar*) singing exercise; (*canto de música*) vocal music; (*canto monótono*) monotonous singing; (*modo de cantar*) musical quality.
can·tu·rre·ar or **can·tu·rriar** intr. COLL. to sing softly, croon.
cá·nu·la f. (*caña*) small reed; MED. cannula, tube.
ca·nu·te·ro m. pincushion; AMER. stem, penholder.
ca·nu·to m. BOT. internode; (*tubo*) tube; (*canutero*) pincushion; C. AMER. stem, penholder ♦ **dar el c. a** MIL. to discharge, give a discharge to.
ca·ña f. BOT. cane, reed <*c. de azúcar* sugar cane>; (*tallo*) stem, stalk; ANAT. (*hueso*) long bone; (*tuétano*) marrow; ARM. (*grieta*) groove, notch (of a sword); (*del fusil*) tipstock (front end of a gunstock); ZOOL. shank; ARCHIT. (*fuste*) shaft of a column; (*de una bota*) leg (of a boot); (*vaso*) wine glass; MIN. gallery; AMER. (*caña de azúcar*) sugar cane; (*ron*) tafia, crude rum; COL., COLL. (*bravata*) boast, brag; COL., ECUAD., VEN. (*noticia falsa*) hoax, false rumor; VEN. (*trago*) drink, swig; MEX. (*vaso*) shot glass ♦ **c. brava** BOT. ditch reed • **c. de Batavia** or **c. espina** BOT. kind of bamboo • **c. de Bengala** or **de Indias** BOT. rattan • **c. de Castilla** COL., MEX. sugar cane • **c. de cuentas** or **de la India** BOT. canna, Indian reed • **c. del pulmón** ANAT. trachea • **c. del timón** MARIT. tiller • **c. de pescar** fishing rod • **c. dulce** or **melar** BOT. sugar cane • **correr cañas** to joust (with sharp canes) • **echar cañas** COL., COLL. to boast, brag.
ca·ña·da f. (*barranca*) gorge, ravine; (*para rebaños*) drover's road, cattle trail; AMER. stream.
ca·ña·dón m. AMER. gorge, ravine; (*arroyo profundo*) deep stream.
ca·ña·dul·za or **ca·ña·du·zal** m. AMER. sugar-cane plantation.
ca·ñal m. (*cañaveral*) cane thicket; (*cañadulza*) sugar-cane plantation; (*cerco de cañas*) cane fence for trapping fish; (*canal pequeño*) small channel for trapping river fish.
ca·ña·ma·zo m. (*tela*) burlap; (*para bordar*) canvas; FIG. (*boceto*) sketch, draft.
ca·ña·me·lar m. sugar-cane plantation.
ca·ña·me·ro, –ra adj. hemp.
ca·ña·miel f. BOT. sugar cane.
ca·ña·mo m. BOT. hemp; (*lienzo*) hempen cloth; AMER. (*bramante*) hemp rope ♦ **c. de Manila** BOT. Manila hemp, abaca.
ca·ña·ve·ra f. BOT. reed-grass.
ca·ña·ve·ral m. cane thicket, canebrake; (*plantación*) sugar-cane plantation.
ca·ña·zo m. (*golpe*) blow given with a reed or cane; AMER. (*aguardiente*) sugar-cane brandy; AMER. swig, drink ♦ **dar c. a** FIG., COLL. to disappoint, sadden • **darse c.** CUBA to be disappointed.
ca·ñe·rí·a f. (*tubo*) pipe, conduit; (*tubería*) pipeline.
ca·ñe·ro m. (*persona*) pipe fitter, pipe layer; MEX. storeroom in a sugar mill; CUBA sugar-cane vendor.
ca·ñi·zo m. wattle screen.
ca·ño m. (*tubo*) pipe, tube; (*albañal*) drain, sewer; (*chorro*) spurt, jet (of water); (*grifo*) tap, faucet; (*bodega*) cellar (for cooling water); MARIT. narrow channel; MUS. organ pipe; MIN. gallery; COL., VEN., MARIT. navigable river ♦ **c. de bridas** flanged pipe • **c. de drenaje** drainpipe.
ca·ñón m. (*tubo*) pipe, tube; MUS. organ pipe; MIL. cannon, gun; ARM. barrel; GEOG. canyon, gorge; (*hueco de la pluma*) quill, shaft; ORNITH. (*pluma naciente*) pinfeather; (*humero*) chimney flue; (*de la escalera*) stairwell; (*de la barba*) stubble; COLL. (*vago*) tramp, vagrant; SEW. (*pliegue*) flute, fold; EQUIT. bridle bit; MIN. gallery; MECH. socket; COL., BOT. tree trunk; MEX., PERU mountain path

♦ **c. antiaéreo** antiaircraft gun • **c. antitanque** or **anticarro** antitank gun • **c. de avancarga** muzzle-loader • **c. de campaña** field gun • **c. de escobén** MARIT. hawse pipe • **c. de gran** or **largo alcance** long-range gun • **c. de plaza** or **sitio** siege or heavy field gun • **c. de torre** turret gun • **c. lanzacabos** linethrowing gun • **c. lanzacemento** cement gun • **c. obús** howitzer • **c. rayado** rifled barrel • **ni a c. rayado** AMER. by no means, no way.

ca·ño·na·zo m. (tiro) cannon shot; (ruido) cannonry; COLL. (noticia inesperada) bombshell, bolt from the blue; SPORT. (fútbol) shot (on goal).

ca·ño·ne·ar tr. to cannonade, shell.

ca·ño·ne·o m. cannonade, shelling.

ca·ño·ne·ra I. f. MIL. (tronera) embrasure (for cannons); MARIT. gunport; AMER. holster II. adj. see cañonero, –ra.

ca·ño·ne·ro, –ra I. adj. armed with cannons II. m. gunboat —f. see cañonera.

ca·ñu·te·ro m. pin or needle case.

ca·ñu·ti·llo m. (abalorio) bead; (bordado) gold or silver embroidery twist.

ca·ñu·to m. (canuto) small tube or pipe; FIG., COLL. (soplón) tattletale.

ca·o·ba f. BOT. mahogany (tree and wood).

ca·o·lín m. kaolin, china clay.

ca·os m. chaos; FIG. (desorden) chaos, disorder.

ca·ó·ti·co, –ca adj. chaotic, disordered.

ca·pa f. (manto) cape, cloak; coat, coating <una c. de pintura a coat of paint>; (estrato) layer; (cubierta) cover, covering; ply <madera de tres capas three-ply wood>; FIG. (pretexto) cover, pretext; COLL. (encubridor) harborer, concealer; MAS. course, bed; GEOL. stratum, layer; ZOOL. (pelo) coat; (mamífero) paca (South American rodent); COM. primage (paid to a ship's captain); HOND. beating, thrashing ♦ **a c. y espada** FIG. through thick and thin • **andar** or **ir de c. caída** COLL. (decaer) to be in rough shape; (estar triste) to be depressed • **c. aguadera** or **gascona** waterproof cape • **c. del cielo** FIG. canopy of heaven, firmament • **c. pluvial** RELIG. cope • **c. torera** bullfighter's cape • **de c. y espada** cloak-and-dagger • **estar** or **ponerse a la c.** MARIT. to lie to; FIG. to be on the lookout • **hacer de su c. un sayo** COLL. to do as one pleases • **so c. de** under the pretext of.

cap·a·ce·te m. (bacinete) helmet, casque; AMER. hood (of a car).

ca·pa·ci·dad f. capacity <la c. de un barco the capacity of a boat>; (espacio) space, room <c. para trescientas personas room for three hundred people>; FIG. (talento) ability, talent <yo no tengo c. para matemáticas I have no talent for mathematics>; LAW capacity <c. procesal capacity to sue> ♦ **c. adquisitiva** purchasing power • **c. de arrastre** drawing power • **c. de ganancia** earning power • **c. eléctrica** capacitance.

ca·pa·ci·ta·ción f. training, drilling.

ca·pa·ci·tar tr. (instruir) to train, drill; (calificar) to qualify, entitle; (autorizar) to empower, authorize —reflex. to train oneself; (ser competente) to be competent or qualified.

ca·pa·cha f. (capacho) two-handled basket; (esportilla de palma) wicker fruit basket; FIG., COLL. (orden de San Juan de Dios) Order of St. John of God; AMER. jail, prison.

ca·pa·che·ro m. porter, one who carries things in a basket.

ca·pa·cho m. (espuerta) two-handled basket; (sera de esparto) large basket (usually without handles); ORNITH. night heron; CONSTR. leather hod (for carrying mortar); AMER. (bolsillo) pocket; (alforja) knapsack; (sombrero viejo) old hat; VEN., BOT. edible canna; FIG., COLL. (cura) monk of the Order of St. John of God.

ca·pa·dor m. (persona que capa animales) gelder, castrator; (pito) gelder's whistle.

ca·pa·du·ra f. (castración) castration; (cicatriz) castration scar; (hoja de tabaco) tobacco leaf (used for filler in cigars).

ca·par tr. (castrar) to castrate, geld; FIG., COLL. (disminuir) to reduce, diminish; MEX. to prune, cut back; BOL., VEN. to begin to eat.

ca·pa·ra·zón m. caparison; (cubierta) cover, tarpaulin; ZOOL. shell, carapace; (morral) feed bag.

ca·pa·rrón m. BOT. bud (of a tree).

ca·pa·rro·sa f. CHEM. copperas ♦ **c. azul** blue vitriol • **c. blanca** white vitriol • **c. roja** red vitriol • **c. verde** green vitriol.

ca·pa·taz m. [pl. **-ta·ces**] foreman, overseer.

ca·paz adj. [pl. **-pa·ces**] (grande) spacious, roomy; FIG. (apto) able, capable ♦ **c. de** or **para** big enough for, with room for <una caja c. de doce botellas a case with room for twelve bottles>; capable of <él es c. de hacerlo he is capable of doing it>.

ca·pa·zo m. (espuerta grande) large basket; (golpe) blow given with a cape or cloak.

cap·cio·so, –sa adj. captious, deceitful ♦ **pregunta c.** tricky question.

ca·pe·ar tr. FIG., COLL. (engañar) to take in, fool; (eludir) to dodge, avoid; MARIT. to ride out, weather (a storm); TAUR. to make cape passes at —intr. GUAT. to play hooky; MARIT. to lie to.

ca·pe·lo m. RELIG. (sombrero) cardinal's hat; (dignidad de cardenal) cardinalship, cardinalate; AMER. bell glass.

ca·pe·llán m. chaplain; (sacerdote) clergyman, priest.

ca·pe·lla·ní·a f. ECC. chaplaincy; COL., COLL. animosity, ill will.

ca·pe·ro m. (cuelgacapas) hat and coat stand; RELIG. priest who carries the cope.

ca·pe·ru·za f. (gorro) pointed hood or cap; (de una chiminea) cowl, hood (of a chimney); cap <la c. de una pluma the cap of a pen> ♦ **Caperucita Roja** Little Red Riding Hood.

ca·pe·ta f. short cape or cloak.

ca·pi·cú·a f. palindrome.

ca·pi·cho·la f. TEX. ribbed silk fabric.

ca·pi·go·rris·ta f. or **ca·pi·go·rrón** m. COLL. (holgazán) bum, loafer; (clérigo) minor cleric (who is not qualified for major orders).

ca·pi·lar I. adj. capillary II. m. ANAT. capillary.

ca·pi·la·ri·dad f. capillarity.

ca·pi·lla f. (capucha) hood, cowl; RELIG. (iglesia) chapel; (oratorio) oratory; (junta) body of chaplains or priests; MUS. choir; FIG., COLL. (fraile) clergyman, friar; (camarilla) clan; PRINT. (pliego) proof or advance sheet; TECH. hood, cowl ♦ **c. ardiente** funeral chapel • **c. mayor** main chapel • **estar en (la) c.** CRIMIN. to be awaiting execution; FIG. (esperar) to be in suspense or on tenterhooks • **estar en c. ardiente** to lie in state • **estar en capillas** PRINT. to be in proofs.

ca·pi·lle·ro m. sexton, churchwarden.

ca·pi·llo m. (de niño) baby bonnet or cap; (de bautizo) baptismal cape; (del calzado) toe lining (of shoe); (red) rabbit net; (colador) filter, strainer; BOT. (capullo) silk cocoon; MARIT. binnacle or shroud-end cover; PHARM. seal (on a bottle); TEX. head of a distaff; AMER. clay pot for melting tin or lead • **c. de hierro** helmet.

ca·pi·ro·ta·zo m. fillip, flick (with a finger).

ca·pi·ro·te I. m. (gorro puntiagudo) hood; (muceta) hood (worn by certain academics); (cucurucho de cartón) paper cone or hood (worn in certain processions); (cubierta de cuero de las aves) leather hood or mask; (capirotazo) flip (with a finger) ♦ **tonto de c.** fool, sucker II. adj. with a different color head than the rest of the body (in cattle).

ca·pi·ru·cho m. COLL. hood, cap.

ca·pi·sa·yo m. (vestidura corta) mantelet; (vestidura de los obispos) bishop's mantelleta; COL. undershirt.

ca·pi·ta·ción f. capitation, head tax.

ca·pi·tal I. adj. capital <ciudad c. capital city>; (esencial) essential, vital <de importancia c. of vital importance>; capital <pena c. capital punishment>; AMER. capital, upper-case <letra c. capital letter> ♦ **lo c.** the most important thing II. m. FIN. (caudal) capital; (principal) principal (as opposed to interest) ♦ **c. activo** working capital • **c. aventurado** venture capital • **c. circulante** working capital • **c. de inversión** investment capital • **c. disponible** available funds • **c. en giro** operating capital • **c. fijo** fixed capital • **c. físico** CHILE, COM. capital assets • **c. líquido** net worth • **c. lucrativo** productive capital • **c. propio** equity capital • **c. social** capital stock —f. capital, capital city <Caracas es la c. de Venezuela Caracas is the capital of Venezuela>.

ca·pi·ta·li·cé, capitalice see capitalizar.

ca·pi·ta·li·no, –na I. adj. of the capital II. m.f native *or* inhabitant of the capital.

ca·pi·ta·lis·mo m. capitalism.

ca·pi·ta·lis·ta I. adj. capitalist, capitalistic II. m.f. capitalist.

ca·pi·ta·li·za·ble adj. capitalizable.

ca·pi·ta·li·za·ción f. capitalization.

ca·pi·ta·li·zar §04 tr. to capitalize; *(interés)* to compound.

ca·pi·tán, –ta·na m. MIL., MARIT. captain; *(líder)* leader, chief ♦ **c. de corbeta** MARIT. lieutenant commander • **c. de fragata** MARIT. commander • **c. de industria** FIG. captain of industry • **c. del puerto** harbormaster • **c. general** MIL. commander in chief —m.f. SPORT. *(de un equipo)* team captain.

ca·pi·ta·ne·ar tr. *(gobernar)* to captain; FIG. *(ordenar)* to command, lead.

ca·pi·ta·ní·a f. *(cargo de capitán)* captainship, captaincy; MIL. *(compañía)* company (of troops); *(derecho)* port or harbor charges *or* taxes; *(oficina del capitán)* harbormaster's office ♦ **c. general** MIL. captaincy general; AMER., HIST. territory governed by a captain general (during colonial times).

ca·pi·tel m. ARCHIT. capital (of a column).

ca·pi·to·lio m. capitol; FIG. *(edificio majestuoso)* majestic building; *(acrópolis)* acropolis ♦ **Capitolio** Capitol.

ca·pí·tu·la f. RELIG. passage of scripture (read at divine service).

ca·pi·tu·la·ción f. *(entrega)* capitulation, surrender; *(convenio)* agreement, pact ♦ **capitulaciones** marriage settlement *or* contract.

ca·pi·tu·lar¹ adj. capitular, capitulary.

ca·pi·tu·lar² intr. *(rendir)* to capitulate, surrender; *(pactar)* to reach an agreement *or* pact; RELIG. *(cantar)* to sing prayers —tr. to charge, impeach.

ca·pi·tu·la·rio m. RELIG. book containing passages of scriptures read at divine service.

ca·pí·tu·lo m. chapter <*el segundo c. del libro* the second chapter of the book>; *(reunión)* meeting, assembly; *(lugar)* chapter house; RELIG. *(reprensión)* public reprimand; *(determinación)* determination, resolution; FIG. *(tema)* subject, matter; ANAT., BOT. capitulum ♦ **c. de culpas** accusation • **capítulos matrimoniales** marriage contract • **dar un c.** FIG. to reprimand severely • **ganar c.** FIG. to make one's point, attain one's objective • **llamar** *or* **traer a c.** FIG. to take to task, call to account.

ca·pó m. AUTO. hood.

ca·pón I. adj. castrated, gelded II. m. *(pollo)* capon; COLL. *(golpe)* rap on the head (with the knuckles); MARIT. anchor stopper; ARG., URUG. *(carnero)* castrated sheep.

ca·po·ne·ar·se reflex. COL. to pop (corn).

ca·po·ne·ra f. *(jaula)* coop (to fatten poultry); FIG., COLL. *(lugar donde se recibe comida gratis)* place where one gets free food and/or handouts; *(cárcel)* jail; MIL. caponiere.

ca·po·ral m. *(capataz)* foreman, overseer; MIL. corporal; FIG. leader, boss.

ca·po·ta f. *(sombrero de mujer)* bonnet; *(cubierta de coche)* hood, bonnet (G.B.); *(capa corta)* short cape (without a hood); AUTO. folding top of a convertible; ARG. long cloak.

ca·po·ta·je m. somersault, rollover (of a car, plane).

ca·po·tar intr. AUTO. to turn over, roll over; AVIA. to nosedive.

ca·po·te m. *(capa)* capote, cloak; TAUR. cape; MIL. greatcoat; *(en naipes)* slam (in cards); FIG. *(ceño)* frown, scowl; METEOROL. blanket of clouds; CHILE, MEX. beating, thrashing ♦ **a** *or* **para mi c.** FIG. in my opinion, to my way of thinking • **c. de brega** TAUR. working cape • **c. de montar** riding cape • **c. de monte** poncho • **c. de paseo** TAUR. show cape • **dar c.** to make every trick (in cards); CHILE, MEX. to trick, deceive • **darse c.** MEX. to give up, quit • **de c.** MEX. secretly, on the sly • **decir para su c.** to say to oneself • **echar un c.** FIG. *(desviar una conversación)* to change the subject; *(ayudar)* to lend a hand • **llevar** *or* **quedar c.** to be left without a trick (in cards) • **poner c.** FIG. to frown, scowl.

ca·po·te·ar tr. TAUR. to distract (the bull) with a cape; FIG., COLL. *(atascar)* to stall, put off; *(eludir)* to duck, dodge.

Ca·pri·cor·nio m. ASTROL. Capricorn.

ca·pri·cho m. caprice, whim <*los caprichos de un niño* the whims of a child>; *(antojo)* fancy, desire; MUS. *(composición)* caprice, capriccio; ARTS caprice ♦ **tener c. por** to fancy, take a liking to.

ca·pri·cho·so, –sa adj. capricious, whimsical; *(inconstante)* fickle.

cáp·su·la f. BOT., PHARM. capsule; *(tapa)* metal cap *or* seal (on bottles); ARM. cartridge shell; CHEM. laboratory dish ♦ **c. atrabiliaria** *or* **renal** ANAT. atrabiliary gland, renal capsule *or* gland • **c. detonante** *or* **fulminante** ARM. blasting *or* percussion cap • **c. espacial** space capsule • **c. sinovial** ANAT. synovial capsule • **c. suprarrenal** ANAT. suprarenal capsule *or* gland.

cap·su·lar adj. capsular ♦ **en forma c.** in capsule form.

cap·tar tr. *(atraer)* to attract, win <*c. el respeto del público* to win the public's respect>; *(recoger aguas)* to harness (waters); *(aprehender)* to grasp, understand; RAD. to receive, pick up —reflex. to attract, win.

cap·tu·ra f. capture, apprehension.

cap·tu·rar tr. to capture, apprehend.

ca·pu·cha f. *(sombrero)* hood, cowl; *(acento)* circumflex accent.

ca·pu·chi·no, –na I. adj. RELIG. Capuchin; CHILE small (fruit) II. m.f. RELIG. Capuchin —m. ZOOL., ORNITH. capuchin; P. RICO small paper kite.

ca·pu·llo m. ENTOM. cocoon; *(tela de seda)* coarse silk; BOT. *(brote)* bud; *(de la bellota)* cup (of an acorn); COLL. *(prepucio)* foreskin, prepuce; *(idiota)* idiot, fool; *(novato)* novice, beginner ♦ **c. de rosa** rosebud.

ca·qui m. BOT. kaki (tree and fruit); *(tela y color)* khaki (cloth and color).

ca·ra I. f. ANAT. face; *(semblante)* look, expression; *(superficie)* surface, face; *(frente)* façade, front; FIG. *(aspecto)* appearance, look; COLL. *(descaro)* nerve, cheek; GEOM. plane, face; NUMIS. *(anverso)* heads, obverse (of coins) ♦ **a c. descubierta** openly • **asomar la c.** to show one's face • **caérsele la c. de vergüenza** FIG., COLL. to blush with shame • **c. a c.** face to face • **c. de acelga** FIG., COLL. sad face • **c. de hereje** FIG., COLL. mug, ugly face • **c. de juez** FIG., COLL. stern look • **c. de pascua** FIG., COLL. happy face • **c. de pocos amigos** FIG., COLL. unfriendly face • **c. de rallo** FIG. pockmarked face • **c. de risa** FIG., COLL. *(sonriendo)* smiling face; *(cómico)* funny face • **c. de viernes** FIG., COLL. long face • **c. de vinagre** FIG., COLL. sour expression • **c. dura** FIG. nerve, cheek • **c. larga** FIG., COLL. long face • **c. o cruz** heads or tails • **c. sin expresión** deadpan look • **cruzar la c. a** to slap • **dar c. a** FIG. to face, confront • **dar la c.** FIG. to face the consequences, face the music • **dar la c. por** FIG., COLL. to defend, stick up for • **de dos caras** FIG. two-faced • **echar c. o cruz** to toss a coin • **echar en c.** FIG. to reproach • **hacer c. a** FIG. to face, confront • **lavar la c. a** FIG., COLL. to fawn over, flatter • **por su linda c.** FIG.., COLL. without any right *or* justification • **sacar la c. por** FIG., COLL. to stick up for • **saltar a la c.** FIG. to hit the eye immediately, be evident • **sin c.** FIG. faceless • **tener c. de** COLL. to look like <*ella tiene c. de ángel* she looks like an angel> • **tener c. para** COLL. to have the nerve to <*no teníamos c. para hacerlo* we didn't have the nerve to do it> • **verse las caras** FIG., COLL. to have it out II. adv. facing <*c. al sol* facing the sun> ♦ **c. adelante** facing forward • **c. atrás** looking backwards • **de c.** facing <*de c. al sur* facing south> III. adj. see **caro, –ra.**

ca·ra·be·la f. MARIT. caravel.

ca·ra·bi·na f. carbine; FIG., COLL. *(señora de acompaña)* chaperon; CUBA small wager ♦ **ser la c. de Ambrosio** FIG., COLL. to be good for nothing.

ca·ra·bi·ne·ro m. *(soldado)* carbineer; *(guardia)* soldier who pursues smugglers; *(crustáceo)* large prawn; COLL. *(persona severa y adusta)* severe and austere person.

Ca·ra·cas f. Caracas.

ca·ra·col m. ZOOL. snail; *(concha)* conch, sea shell; *(espiral)* spiral; *(rizo)* curl; EQUIT. caracole, caracol; ANAT. cochlea; *(del reloj)* fusee (of a watch); MEX. *(camisón de mujer)* nightgown; *(blusa)* blouse ♦ **¡caracoles!** my goodness! • **de c.** spiral <*escalera de c.* spiral staircase> • **hacer caracoles** to zigzag, weave • **subir en c.** to spiral upwards.

ca·ra·co·la f. conch.

ca·ra·co·le·ar intr. EQUIT. to caracole, turn.

ca·ra·co·li·llo m. BOT. Australian pea; *(café)* pea-bean coffee; *(caoba)* veined mahogany; ARG., URUG. shell-shaped noodle.

ca·rác·ter m. *(índole)* character, nature <*ella tiene un c. amable* she has an agreeable nature>; *(individualidad moral)* strong character <*es un hombre de c.* he is a man of strong character>; *(rasgo)* characteristic, trait; *(dignidad)* status, capacity <*en c. de juez* in the capacity of judge>; *(signo)* character, letter; *(forma de letra)* handwriting <*c. legible* legible handwriting>; *(estilo)* style; AGR. *(marca)* brand; AMER. *(virtud)* virtue, moral character; *(personaje)* fictional character ♦ **c. adquirido** BIOL. acquired trait • **c. de imprenta** PRINT. type style, typeface • **c. dominante** BIOL. dominant trait • **c. heredado** BIOL. inherited trait • **c. recesivo** BIOL. recessive trait • **de medio c.** indeterminate, neither one thing nor the other.

ca·rac·te·ri·cé, caracterice see **caracterizar.**

ca·rac·te·rís·ti·co, –ca I. adj. characteristic, typical II. m. THEAT. character actor —f. *(rasgo)* characteristic, feature; THEAT. character actress; MATH., MECH. characteristic; ARG., TELEC. telephone exchange ♦ **c. anódica** plate characteristic • **c. de traspaso** RAD. transfer characteristic.

ca·rac·te·ri·za·do, –da I. past part. see **caracterizar** II. adj. distinguished, outstanding.

ca·rac·te·ri·za·dor, –do·ra I. adj. distinguishing, characterizing II. m.f. THEAT. make-up assistant.

ca·rac·te·ri·zar §04 tr. *(distinguir)* to distinguish, confer an honor upon; THEAT. to portray (a role) expressively —reflex. to be characterized; THEAT. *(maquillarse)* to make up or dress (for a role).

ca·ra·cú m. AMER. bone marrow.

ca·ra·cul m. ZOOL. karakul (sheep and pelt).

ca·ra·cha f. or **ca·ra·che** m. mange, itch.

ca·ra·du·ra I. adj. shameless II. m.f. shameless person.

ca·ra·jo m. VULG. prick, cock ♦ **¡carajo!** VULG. shit!, damn! • **de c.** fantastic • **ni c.** nothing at all • **no me importa un c.** I don't give a damn • **¡vete al c.!** go to hell!

¡ca·ram·ba! interj. *(asombro)* good heavens!, goodness!, my God!; *(enfado)* damn it!

ca·rám·ba·no m. icicle.

ca·ram·bo·la f. carom (in billiards); FIG., COLL. *(doble resultado)* killing two birds with one stone; *(casualidad)* chance, accident; *(embuste)* trick, ruse ♦ **por c.** *(indirectamente)* indirectly, in a roundabout way; *(por casualidad)* by chance, by accident.

ca·ram·bo·le·ar intr. to carom (in billiards).

ca·ra·me·li·zar §04 tr. *(bañar)* to cover with caramel; *(convertir)* to caramelize.

ca·ra·me·lo m. caramel; *(dulce)* candy, sweet ♦ **de c.** COLL. excellent, fine.

ca·ra·mi·llo m. *(flautilla de caña)* small flute; *(montón de cosas)* untidy heap or pile; BOT. saltwort; FIG. *(chisme)* gossip; *(enredo)* fuss.

ca·ran·cho m. AMER., ORNITH. carrion hawk; PERU owl.

ca·ran·to·ña f. COLL. *(máscara fea)* frightening mask; *(mujer vieja)* painted-up old hag ♦ **carantoñas** COLL. cajolery, flattery.

ca·ran·to·ñe·ro, –ra I. adj. fawning, flattering II. m.f. *(persona que hace máscaras)* person who makes frightening masks; *(persona que hace halagos)* cajoler, flatterer.

ca·ra·pa·cho m. ZOOL. shell, carapace.

ca·ra·que·ño, –ña I. adj. Caracan, of Caracas II. m.f. native of Caracas.

ca·ra·te m. AMER. brown spots (on the skin).

ca·rá·tu·la f. *(careta)* mask; FIG. *(profesión de comediante)* theatrical profession, stage; AMER. title page; AMER. dial, face (of a watch).

ca·ra·va·na f. caravan; FIG., COLL. *(grupo de viajeros)* caravan, group of travelers; *(línea de carros)* long line of cars (on highway); COL., ORNITH. *(alcaraván)* stone curlew ♦ **caravanas** MEX., COLL. courtesies; AMER. *(pendientes)* earrings, hoops.

¡ca·ray! interj. damn!

cár·ba·so m. fine linen.

car·bo·hi·dra·to m. carbohydrate.

car·bol m. CHEM. phenol.

car·bón m. coal; *(de leña)* charcoal; *(brasa)* dead ember or cinder; *(lápiz)* charcoal, carbon pencil; *(papel)* carbon (paper); AGR. smut, charcoal rot; ELEC. carbon ♦ **c. activado** activated carbon • **c. animal** boneblack • **c. bituminoso** bituminous coal • **c. de gas** or **retorta** gas carbon • **c. de leña** charcoal • **c. de piedra** or **mineral** coal • **c. menudo** slack, small coal • **c. vegetal** or **de palo** charcoal • **negro como el c.** black as the ace of spades.

car·bo·na·do m. MIN. black diamond, carbonado.

car·bo·nar tr. to char, make into charcoal —reflex. to become carbonized or charred.

car·bo·na·ta·do, –da adj. CHEM. carbonated.

car·bo·na·to m. CHEM. carbonate.

car·bon·ci·llo m. ARTS charcoal pencil; MIN. *(carbonilla)* small coal, slack.

car·bo·ne·ra I. f. *(pila de leña)* charcoal pile; *(lugar donde se guarda el carbón)* coal bunker, coal bin; *(vendedora de carbón)* woman who sells charcoal or coal; *(mina de hulla)* coal mine; RAIL. coal tender II. adj. see **carbonero, –ra.**

car·bo·ne·rí·a f. coal shop.

car·bo·ne·ro, –ra I. adj. coal, charcoal II. m. coaler, coal supplier; MARIT. coal ship —f. see **carbonera.**

car·bo·ní·fe·ro, –ra adj. & m. carboniferous.

car·bo·ni·lla f. coal dust; *(de la locomotora)* soot; ARG. charcoal pencil.

car·bo·ni·za·ción f. carbonization.

car·bo·ni·zar §04 tr. to carbonize, char.

car·bo·no m. CHEM. carbon.

car·bo·run·do m. CHEM. carborundum.

car·bun·clo m. MIN. *(carbúnculo)* carbuncle; MED. *(carbunco)* anthrax, carbuncle.

car·bún·cu·lo m. carbuncle, ruby.

car·bu·ra·ción f. carburization, carburetion.

car·bu·ra·dor m. MECH. carburetor, carburettor (G.B.).

car·bu·ran·te I. m. fuel II. adj. containing a hydrocarbon.

car·bu·rar tr. to carburize —intr. COLL. *(funcionar)* to function, run.

car·bu·ro m. CHEM. carbide ♦ **c. de calcio** calcium carbide • **c. de hidrógeno** hydrogen carbide.

car·ca·ja·da f. guffaw, loud laughter ♦ **reír a carcajadas** to split one's sides laughing.

car·ca·mal m. COLL. old fogy, old decrepit person.

car·ca·mán m. MARIT. tub, old ship; CUBA low-class foreigner; AMER. pretentious person; PERU old person, wreck.

cár·ca·va f. *(zanja)* ditch, gully; *(foso)* pit, hole; *(sepultura)* grave.

car·ca·za f. *(aljaba)* quiver (for arrows); *(cuja)* holder (for a flag); MEX. holster; AMER. leather rifle case (on a saddle).

cár·cel f. *(prisión)* jail, prison; TECH. *(herramienta)* clamp, vise; *(ranura)* groove.

car·ce·le·rí·a f. *(detención forzada)* imprisonment; *(fianza carcelera)* bail.

car·ce·le·ro, –ra I. m.f. jailer, warden. II. adj. prison, jail.

car·ci·no·ma f. MED. carcinoma, cancer.

car·ci·no·ma·to·so, –sa adj. MED. carcinomatous.

car·co·ma f. *(insecto)* woodborer; *(polvo de la madera)* wood dust; *(persona gastosa)* spendthrift; FIG. *(preocupación)* anxiety, grief, preoccupation.

car·co·mer tr. *(roer)* to eat away, gnaw; FIG. to consume, eat away at <*la duda me carcome las entrañas* doubt eats away at my insides> —reflex. to rot, decay.

car·da f. TEX. *(acción)* carding; *(instrumento)* teasel, card; BOT. teasel; FIG., COLL. *(reprensión)* reprimand, scolding ♦ **dar una c. a** to reprimand, scold.

car·da·dor, –do·ra m.f. TEX. *(persona)* carder —f. *(máquina)* carder, carding machine —m. ENTOM. millipede.

car·dal m. PAR., BOT. agave; BOT. thistle patch.

car·dán m. MECH. cardan or universal joint.

car·dar tr. TEX. to card, comb; *(sacar el pelo)* to teasel; FIG., COLL. *(reprender)* to reprimand, scold.

car·de·nal m. RELIG. cardinal; AMER., ORNITH. cardinal; CHILE, BOT. geranium; MED., COLL. bruise, welt.

car·de·na·li·cio, –cia adj. RELIG. pertaining to a cardinal.

car·de·ni·llo m. CHEM. verdigris; *(color)* verdigris, Paris green.

cár·de·no, –na adj. *(morado)* purple, violet; opaline, opalescent <*agua c.* opalescent water>; ZOOL. grayish.

car·dia·co, –ca or **car·dí·a·co, –ca** I. adj. MED. cardiac, heart II. m.f. cardiac or heart patient ♦ **ataque c.** heart attack.

car·dial·gia m. MED. cardialgia.

car·dias m. ANAT. cardia, cardiac orifice of the stomach.

car·di·nal adj. cardinal ♦ **puntos cardinales** cardinal points • **virtudes cardinales** cardinal virtues • **números cardinales** cardinal numbers.

car·dio·gra·fí·a f. MED. *(estudio)* cardiography, electrocardiography; *(aparato)* cardiograph, electrocardiograph.

car·dió·gra·fo, –fa MED. m.f. *(médico)* cardiologist —m. *(aparato)* cardiograph, electrocardiograph.

car·dio·gra·ma m. MED. cardiogram, electrocardiogram.

car·dio·lo·gí·a f. MED. cardiology.

car·dió·lo·go, –ga m.f. MED. cardiologist.

car·do m. BOT. thistle; COLL. *(mujer fea)* ugly woman; *(arisco)* unruly person.

car·du·me or **car·du·men** m. ICHTH. school, shoal (of fish); CHILE abundance, great quantity.

car·du·zar §04 tr. TEX. to card or comb (wool or cotton).

ca·re·ar tr. *(confrontar)* to confront, bring face to face; FIG. *(cotejar)* to check, compare <*él careaba la copia con el original* he was comparing the copy with the original> —intr. to face, look towards <*la casa carea al mar* the house faces the sea> —reflex. *(confrontarse)* to meet face to face.

ca·re·cer §17 intr. to lack, be without <*carecían de fondos* they lacked funds>; URUG. to require, be necessary.

ca·rel m. border, rim (of a plate or other vessel).

ca·re·na f. MARIT. *(reparación)* careen (repairing of a ship); FIG., COLL. *(burla)* mocking.

ca·ren·cia f. *(falta)* lack, shortage; MED. deficiency.

ca·ren·te adj. lacking (in), devoid of <*c. de conocimiento* lacking (in) knowledge>.

ca·re·o m. *(confrontación)* confrontation; *(cotejo)* checking, comparison; *(reunión)* meeting; AMER. pause in a cockfight.

ca·re·ro, –ra adj. expensive, high-priced (said of a person, shopkeeper).

ca·res·tí·a f. *(escasez)* shortage, scarcity; *(hambre)* famine; COM. high price or cost ♦ **c. de la vida** high cost of living.

ca·re·ta I. f. mask ♦ **c. antigás** gas mask • **c. de esgrima** fencing mask • **quitarle a uno la c.** FIG. to unmask someone II. adj. see **careto, –ta.**

ca·re·to, –ta I. adj. white-faced (cattle and horses) II. f. see **careta.**

ca·rey m. ZOOL. sea turtle; *(caparazón)* tortoiseshell; CUBA, BOT. rough-leaved liana.

ca·rez·ca, carezco see **carecer.**

car·ga f. *(acción)* loading; load <*con plena c.* with a full load>; *(flete)* cargo, freight; FIG. *(peso)* burden, load <*la c. fiscal* the tax burden>; *(obligación)* obligation, duty; *(responsabilidad)* onus, responsibility; *(impuesto)* tax, duty; MIL. *(ataque)* attack, charge; *(pólvora y plomo)* charge (of a weapon); HYDRAUL. head; ELEC. charge; *(capacidad)* load <*c. máxima* maximum load>; VET. poultice ♦ **a cargas** in great abundance • **bestia de c.** beast of burden • **c. aérea** air freight • **c. bruta** gross tonnage • **c. de caballería** MIL. cavalry charge • **c. de pago** COM. payload • **c. de pólvora** MIN. blasting charge • **c. de profundidad** depth charge • **c. de la prueba** LAW burden of proof • **c. de rotura** MECH. breaking load • **c. fija** or **muerta** MECH. dead load • **c. personal** personal obligation • **c. real** property tax • **c. útil** payload • **echar las cargas a** FIG., COLL. to put the blame on • **llevar la c. de** FIG. to be responsible for • **tomar c.** to load, take on cargo • **volver a la c.** FIG. to persist, insist.

car·ga·da I. f. MEX. loading; ARG. practical joke II. adj. see **cargado, –da.**

car·ga·de·ro m. *(sitio de carga y descarga)* loading platform, freight station; ARCHIT. lintel; TECH. throat.

car·ga·do, –da I. past part. see **cargar** II. adj. strong, dark <*café muy c.* very strong coffee>; *(bochornoso)* sultry, heavy; loaded, laden <*c. de fruto* laden with fruit>; ELEC. charged ♦ **c. de años** old, ancient • **c. de espaldas** round-shouldered, stoop-shouldered • **c. de vino** drunk III. f. see **cargada.**

car·ga·dor m. *(portador)* loader, porter; *(bieldo)* pitchfork;

ARTIL. rammer, ramrod ♦ **c. de acumuladores** ELEC. battery charger • **cargadores** COL. suspenders.

car·ga·men·to m. load, cargo.

car·gan·te adj. FIG., COLL. tiresome, burdensome.

car·gar §47 tr. to load <*c. un barco* to load a boat>; *(llenar)* to load, fill <*c. una cámara* to load a camera>; FIG. *(imputar)* to attribute, ascribe <*le cargaron la culpa a ella* they ascribed the blame to her>; *(gravar)* to burden, impose <*nos cargó con la responsabilidad del proyecto* he burdened us with the responsibility for the project>; *(imponer)* to impose (taxes, duties); FIG., COLL. *(importunar)* to pester, annoy; *(aburrir)* to weary, tire; *(comer demasiado)* to overeat; *(beber demasiado)* to drink too much; ARM. to load, charge; ELEC. to charge; MIL. to charge, attack; COM. to charge, debit; MARIT. to furl, take in (sails); AMER. to carry, wear <*c. anteojos* to wear glasses>; CHILE, PERU to attack ♦ **c. de menos** COM. to undercharge • **c. la mano a** FIG. *(exigir mucho)* to be exacting; *(apremiar)* to press • **cargarle a uno en la cuenta** COM. to charge to one's account —intr. to load, take on a load; ARCHIT. to lean, rest; AGR. to produce a good crop; GRAM. to fall <*el acento carga en la i* the accent falls on the i>; METEOROL. to turn, veer (a storm) ♦ **c. con** *(llevarse)* to carry or take away; to take on, shoulder <*cargaré con toda la responsabilidad* I will shoulder all of the responsibility> —reflex. COLL. *(molestarse)* to become annoyed; *(aburrirse)* to get bored; FIG., COLL. *(matar)* to kill, bump off; *(eliminar)* to get rid of; *(derribar)* to defeat, break; ARCHIT. to rest, lean; METEOROL. *(nublarse)* to become cloudy; to turn, veer <*el viento se cargaba* the wind veered>; COM., ELEC. to be charged ♦ **cargarse de** to abound in, have a lot of <*cargarse de hijos* to have a lot of children>; to fill with, be full of <*se le cargaban de lágrimas los ojos* his eyes filled with tears> • **cargarse de años** to be advanced in age • **cargársela** to take the blame.

car·ga·zón f. *(carga)* load; *(pesadez)* heaviness (of the head or stomach); *(cúmulo de nubes)* overcast sky; ARG. contraption; CHILE heavy load of fruit.

car·go m. *(peso)* weight, load; FIG. *(dignidad)* post, position; *(dirección)* charge, direction <*el plan está a mi c.* the plan is under my direction>; *(obligación)* duty, obligation; *(acusación)* charge, accusation; COM. charge, debit; MARIT. freighter; AGR. load, batch (of grapes or olives) ♦ **a c. de** *(al cuidado de)* in the charge or care of; COM. charged to the account of • **c. de conciencia** remorse • **hacer c. a uno de** FIG. to hold someone responsible for • **hacerse c. de** to take charge of.

car·go·se·ar tr. ARG., CHILE, PERU to pester, bother.

car·go·so, –sa adj. AMER. bothersome, tiresome.

car·gué, cargue see **cargar.**

car·gue·ro, –ra I. adj. freight, cargo <*tren c.* freight train>; AMER. work, of burden <*bestia c.* beast of burden> II. m. MARIT. freighter, cargo boat; AVIA. cargo or transport plane; AMER. beast of burden.

ca·ria·con·te·ci·do, –da adj. COLL. crestfallen, glum.

ca·ria·do, –da adj. MED. decayed, carious.

ca·riar MED. tr. to cause to decay, cause decay in —reflex. to decay, become decayed.

ca·ri·be I. adj. Caribbean <*Mar Caribe* Caribbean Sea> II. m.f. *(persona)* Carib —m. *(lengua)* Carib; FIG. *(hombre cruel)* cruel person; ICHTH. caribe, piranha.

ca·ri·be·ño, –ña I. adj. Caribbean II. m.f. Caribbean person.

ca·ri·ca·to m. *(actor)* comedian; *(bufo)* basso buffo; AMER. caricature.

ca·ri·ca·tu·ra f. caricature.

ca·ri·ca·tu·rar tr. to caricature.

ca·ri·ca·tu·res·co, –ca adj. caricatural.

ca·ri·ca·tu·ris·ta m.f. caricaturist.

ca·ri·ca·tu·ri·zar §04 tr. to caricature.

ca·ri·cia f. caress ♦ **hacer caricias a** to caress, fondle.

ca·ri·dad f. *(virtud)* charity; *(limosna)* alms, charity; MARIT. spare anchor; MEX. prison food ♦ **¡por c.!** for pity's sake! • **la c. bien entendida empieza por uno mismo** charity begins at home.

ca·ri·do·lien·te adj. mournful, glum.

ca·ries f. [pl. **ca·ries**] MED. caries, decay <*la c. dentaria* tooth decay>; AGR. blight.

ca·ri·lla f. *(página)* page, side (of a sheet of paper); *(de colmenero)* beekeeper's mask.

ca·ri·llón m. MUS. carillon.

ca·ri·ño m. *(afecto)* affection, fondness; *(amor)* love; FIG. *(caricia)* caress; *(esmero)* care, attention; CHILE, NIC. gift ♦ **cariños** endearments; love (in a letter) • **sentir c. por** or **tener c. a** to like, be fond of • **tomar c. a** to take a liking to.

ca·ri·ño·so, -sa adj. affectionate, loving.

ca·ris·ma m. charisma.

ca·ris·má·ti·co, -ca adj. charismatic.

ca·ri·ta·ti·vo, -va adj. charitable.

ca·riz m. [pl. **-ri·ces**] METEOROL. look, aspect; FIG., COLL. prospects, outlook <*esto toma mal c.* the prospects look grim>.

car·lan·ca f. *(collar)* mastiff's spiked collar; COLL. *(picardía)* trick; CHILE, HOND. annoyance, bother; HOND. nuisance, pest; C. AMER., COL., PAN. shackle.

car·lan·cón, -co·na I. adj. cunning, crafty II. m.f. cunning person.

car·le·ar intr. to gasp, pant.

car·lin·ga f. MARIT. mast step; AVIA. cabin, compartment.

car·me·li·ta I. adj. RELIG. Carmelite; AMER. brown II. m.f. RELIG. Carmelite —f. BOT. nasturtium flower.

car·me·nar tr. *(desenredar)* to disentangle, comb; FIG., COLL. *(tirar del pelo)* to pull the hair of; *(robar)* to rob, swindle.

car·me·sí [pl. **-sí·es**] I. adj. crimson II. m. *(color)* crimson; *(polvo)* cochineal or kermes powder; *(seda)* crimson-colored silk.

car·mín I. adj. carmine, crimson II. m. *(color)* carmine, crimson; *(tinta)* carmine; BOT. *(rosal)* wild or mallow rose ♦ **c. de labios** lipstick.

car·mí·ne·o, -a adj. carmine.

car·na·da f. *(cebo)* bait; FIG. *(trampa)* trap, snare ♦ **c. viva** live bait.

car·nal adj. carnal; *(sensual)* sensual, lustful; full, blood <*hermano c.* full brother>; FIG. *(terrenal)* worldly, material.

car·na·li·dad f. carnality, lust.

car·na·val m. carnival; RELIG. Shrovetide ♦ **carnavales** Mardi gras.

car·na·za f. *(cara interior de la piel)* fleshy side of the skin; *(abundancia de carne)* abundance of meat; *(cebo)* bait; COLL. *(abundancia de carnes)* corpulence.

car·ne f. ANAT. flesh; CUL. meat; BOT. pulp; FIG. flesh <*la c. es débil* the flesh is weak>; *(vicio)* carnality; AMER. heart (of wood) ♦ **c. asada al horno** roast (of meat) • **c. asada a la parrilla** broiled meat ♦ **c. de cañón** FIG. cannon fodder • **c. de carnero** mutton • **c. de cerdo** or **de puerco** pork • **c. de cordero** or **oveja** lamb • **c. de gallina** FIG., COLL. goose bumps • **c. de membrillo** quince jelly • **c. de res** AMER. beef • **c. de ternera** veal • **c. de vaca** beef • **c. de venado** venison • **c. magra** lean meat • **c. picada** chopped meat • **c. sin hueso** CUL. boneless meat; FIG. cushy job • **c. viva** MED. raw flesh, quick • **carnes frías** cold cuts • **cobrar** or **echar carnes** to put on weight • **de c. y hueso** FIG. of flesh and blood • **en carnes** naked • **en c. viva** raw, sore • **metido en carnes** pudgy, plump • **ni c. ni pescado** FIG. neither fish nor fowl • **perder carnes** to lose weight • **poner toda la c. en el asador** FIG. to put all one's eggs in one basket • **ser uña y c.** FIG. to be very close or intimate • **temblarle las carnes a uno** FIG., COLL. to be very frightened.

car·ne·a·da ARG. f. *(acción)* slaughtering, butchering; *(lugar)* slaughterhouse.

car·ne·ar tr. AMER. to slaughter and dress (animals); ARG., CHILE *(engañar)* to deceive, take in; ARG., URUG. *(asesinar)* to murder, butcher; MEX. to knife to death.

car·ne·ro¹ m. ZOOL. sheep; *(macho)* ram; CUL. mutton; AMER., FIG. sheep, weak-willed person; ARG., CHILE, PAR. *(trabajador)* scab, strikebreaker ♦ **c. de la sierra** or **de la tierra** S. AMER. llama, alpaca • **c. del cabo** ORNITH. albatross • **c. marino** ZOOL. seal • **c. verde** mutton stew • **no hay tales carneros** COLL. there's no such thing.

car·ne·ro² m. *(cementerio)* cemetery, burial ground; *(osario)* vault, charnel house ♦ **cantar para el c.** ARG. to kick the bucket • **mandar al c.** FIG. to kill, bump off.

car·net or **car·né** m. [pl. **car·nés**] card <*c. de identidad* identification card>.

car·ni·ce·rí·a f. butcher shop; FIG. *(matanza)* butchery, carnage; ECUAD. slaughterhouse.

car·ni·ce·ro, -ra I. adj. *(carnívoro)* carnivorous, meat-eating; COLL. *(cruel)* cruel, savage II. m.f. butcher —m. ZOOL. carnivore; ECUAD. slaughter.

car·ni·se·co, -ca adj. lean, scrawny.

car·ní·vo·ro, -ra I. adj. carnivorous, meat-eating II. m. ZOOL. carnivore ♦ **carnívoros** Carnivora.

car·no·si·dad f. MED. growth; *(gordura)* obesity, corpulence.

car·no·so, -sa or **car·nu·do, -da** adj. fleshy, meaty.

ca·ro, -ra I. adj. *(costoso)* expensive, costly; *(amado)* dear, beloved II. adv. expensively, at a high price <*este coche se vende muy c.* this car sells at a very high price> III. f. see **cara.**

ca·rón, -ro·na I. adj. AMER. fat-faced; COL. brazen II. f. see **carona.**

ca·ro·na I. f. *(tela)* saddle padding; *(parte de la albarda)* interior part of a packsaddle; *(parte del lomo)* part of animal's back which the saddle lies on II. adj. see **carón, -rona.**

ca·ro·ti·na f. CHEM. carotene.

ca·ro·zo m. *(del maíz)* corncob; *(de una fruta)* stone, pit.

car·pa¹ f. ICHTH. carp ♦ **c. dorada** goldfish.

car·pa² f. AMER. *(tienda)* tent; *(toldo)* awning.

car·pe·ta f. *(cubierta)* folder; *(cartapacio)* portfolio, briefcase; *(tapete)* table cover; AMER., COLL. desk.

car·pe·ta·zo m. ♦ **dar c.** FIG. *(suspender una tramitación)* to lay aside, shelve; *(dar por terminado)* to consider (a matter) closed.

car·pe·te·ar tr. VEN. *(esconder)* to hide; *(estafar)* to trick.

car·pin·cho m. AMER., ZOOL. capybara.

car·pin·te·rí·a f. *(oficio)* carpentry, woodworking; *(taller)* carpenter shop.

car·pin·te·ro m. carpenter, woodworker; S. AMER. annoying person; ENTOM. carpenter bee; ORNITH. woodpecker ♦ **c. de blanco** cabinetmaker • **c. de carretas** or **de prieto** cartwright • **c. de navío** or **de ribera** shipwright.

car·pir tr. to stun; AMER. to weed, hoe —reflex. to be stunned.

ca·rra·ca f. *(nave antigua)* carrack, galleon; *(barco grande)* old hulk; *(instrumento)* rattle; COL. jaw.

ca·rra·da f. cartload.

ca·rras·pe·ar intr. *(estar ronco)* to be hoarse; *(aclararse la voz)* to clear one's throat.

ca·rras·pe·o m. *(ronquera)* hoarseness; *(aclaramiento de la voz)* act of clearing one's throat.

ca·rras·pe·ra f. COLL. var. of **carraspeo.**

ca·rras·po·so, -sa I. adj. *(que padece carraspera)* chronically hoarse; AMER. rough (to the touch) II. f. COL. plant with rough leaves.

ca·rre·ra f. *(espacio recorrido)* run <*una c. de dos cuadras* a two-block run>; *(competencia)* race <*la c. de los cien metros* the hundred-meter race>; *(pista)* racetrack, racecourse; *(camino)* king's highway; *(en las medias)* run (in stockings); FIG. *(profesión)* career, profession; *(estudios)* professional studies; SPORT. run (baseball); *(vida)* life, life span; *(raya del pelo)* part (in the hair); *(hilera)* row, line <*c. de dientes* row of teeth>; *(viaje)* ride (taxi); ASTRON. course, path; MARIT. route; MAS. course (of bricks); ARCHIT. girder, beam; MECH. stroke (of a piston); MUS. run, rapid passage ♦ **a c. abierta** or **tendida** at full speed • **a la c.** at a run, running • **c. a campo traviesa** cross-country race • **c. a pie** footrace • **c. armamentista** or **de armamentos** MIL. arms race • **c. ascendente** MECH. upstroke • **c. ciclista** bicycle race • **c. de baquetas** running of the gauntlet • **c. de caballos** horse race • **c. descendente** MECH. downstroke • **c. de fondo** long-distance race • **c. de obstáculos** obstacle race, steeplechase • **c. de relevos** relay race • **carreras** races, racing • **darle c. a alguien** FIG. to pay for someone's professional studies • **de c.** career <*un diplomático de c.* a career diplomat>; race, racing <*un coche de c.* a race car>; FIG. *(sin reflexión)* hastily, rashly • **hacer c.** to enter a profession; EDUC. to major • **no poder hacer c. con** FIG. to be unable to reason with, make no headway with • **tomar c.** to get a running start.

ca·rre·ris·ta m.f. *(aficionado)* racing fan; *(participante)* racer; f. COLL. *(prostituta)* prostitute, whore.

ca·rre·ta f. *(carro)* cart, wagon; COL. wheel; ECUAD. spool, bobbin; VEN. wheelbarrow ♦ **c. de bueyes** oxcart • **c. de mano** wheelbarrow • **andar como una c.** to go at a snail's pace.

ca·rre·ta·da f. *(carga)* cartload; COLL. *(gran cantidad)* load, great amount; MEX. weight measure.

ca·rre·te m. *(bobina)* reel, bobbin; *(de la caña de pescar)* reel, fishing reel; ELEC. coil; PHOTOG. roll, reel ♦ **c. de encendido** AUTO. ignition coil • **c. de inducción** ELEC. induction coil • **dar c.** to play out (fishing line) • **darle c. a uno** FIG. to keep someone dangling • **revelar un c.** PHOTOG. to develop a roll of film.

ca·rre·te·ar tr. *(conducir en carro)* to cart, haul (a load); *(gobernar el carro)* to drive (a wagon *or* cart); AER. to taxi (an airplane) —intr. AER. to taxi.

ca·rre·tel m. *(para la pesca)* spool, fishing reel; MARIT. log reel, winch.

ca·rre·te·ra f. highway, road ♦ **c. de circunvalación** bypass • **c. de cuatro vías** four-lane highway • **c. de vía libre** expressway.

ca·rre·te·ro m. *(persona que hace carros)* cartwright, cart maker; *(persona que guía carros)* teamster, driver (of carts and wagons) ♦ **jurar como un c.** to swear like a trooper.

ca·rre·ti·lla f. *(carro pequeño)* cart, handcart; *(de una rueda)* wheelbarrow; *(del niño)* baby walker; *(de compras)* shopping cart; *(buscapiés)* squib, firecracker; CUL. cake *or* bread decorator; ARG., BOT. burr; ARG., CHILE jawbone; GUAT. nonsense; COL. series, string ♦ **c. elevadora** *or* **de horquilla** fork lift • **c. de equipaje** baggage truck • **de c.** mechanically, automatically.

ca·rre·ti·lla·da f. cartload.

ca·rre·tón m. *(carro pequeño)* small cart; *(coche pequeño)* go-cart; *(carretilla)* baby walker; GUAT., HOND., P. RICO spool (of thread).

ca·rri·co·che m. COLL. *(carro cubierto)* covered cart *or* wagon; DEROG. *(coche viejo)* decrepit carriage.

ca·rril m. *(surco)* rut, groove; AGR. furrow; *(camino)* lane, narrow road; *(de tránsito)* lane; RAIL. rail; CHILE, P. RICO, COLL. train ♦ **c. americano** contact rail • **c. conductor** contact rail • **c. de cambio** *or* **de aguja** switch rail • **c. de toma** third rail • **c. maestro** running rail • **c. único** monorail • **entrar en el c.** FIG. to get on the right track.

ca·rri·le·ra f. *(carril)* track *or* rut (of a wheel); CUBA siding; COL. grillage.

ca·rri·lle·ra f. *(quijada)* jaw (of an animal); *(correa)* chin strap (on helmets).

ca·rri·llo m. ANAT. jowl; TECH. *(garrucha)* pulley ♦ **comer a dos carrillos** COLL. *(comer)* to gobble, stuff oneself; FIG., COLL. *(sacar provecho)* to have the best of both worlds.

ca·rri·llu·do, –da adj. plump-cheeked.

ca·rri·zo I. m. BOT. ditch reed II. interj. C. AMER., COL., VEN. boy!, wow!

ca·rro m. *(vehículo)* cart, wagon; AMER. *(automóvil)* car, automobile; *(contenido)* cartload, wagonload <*un c. de trigo* a cartload of wheat>; MECH. carriage <*el c. de una máquina de escribir* the carriage of a typewriter>; MIL. tank; AMER. *(tranvía)* trolley, streetcar; RAIL. *(de ferrocarril)* car, wagon; CUBA, SL. doll, beauty; P. RICO, FIG. bum, loafer ♦ **c. alegórico** parade float • **c. blindado** MIL. armored car • **c. de asalto** MIL. heavy tank • **c. de combate** MIL. tank • **c. fuerte** dray • **C. Mayor** ASTRON. Big Dipper • **C. Menor** ASTRON. Little Dipper • **c. urbano** AMER. streetcar • **carros y carretas** FIG., COLL. trials and tribulations • **pare usted el c.** FIG., COLL. hold your horses • **untar el c.** FIG., COLL. to grease the palm, bribe.

ca·rro·ce·rí·a AUTO. body, body work; *(taller)* body shop, auto repair shop.

ca·rro·ma·to m. covered wagon.

ca·rro·ño, –ña I. adj. *(podrido)* rotten, decayed; COL., COLL. cowardly II. f. carrion; FIG. *(gente vil)* trash.

ca·rro·za f. *(coche)* large coach *or* carriage; *(de desfile)* float; MARIT. awning; AMER. hearse.

ca·rrua·je m. *(vehículo)* coach, carriage; *(caravana)* caravan.

ca·rru·cha f. pulley.

ca·rru·ja·do, –da I. adj. crinkled, wrinkled II. m.f. gathering.

ca·rru·sel m. carousel, merry-go-round.

car·ta f. letter <*c. familiar* personal letter>; *(naipe)* playing card; *(constitución)* constitution, charter; *(documento)* document; *(lista de platos)* menu; *(mapa)* map, chart ♦ **a c. cabal** in every respect, thoroughly • **a la c.** a la carte • **c. abierta** open letter • **c. aérea** airmail letter • **c. amorosa** *or* **de amor** love letter • **c. blanca** FIG. carte blanche, unconditional authority • **c. certificada** certified letter • **c. credencial** DIPL. credentials • **c. de ajuste** TELEV. test pattern • **c. de contramarca** MARIT. letter of reprisal • **c. de crédito** COM. letter of credit • **c. de fletamento** MARIT. charter party • **c. de hidalguía** letters patent of nobility, pedigree • **c. de marca** MARIT. letters of marque • **c. de marear** sea chart • **c. de naturaleza** naturalization papers • **c. de pedido** COM. order • **c. de pésame** letter of condolence • **c. de porte** COM. bill of lading • **c. de presentación** letter of introduction • **c. de venta** COM. bill of sale • **c. de vinos** wine list • **c. falsa** low card • **c. general** COM. form letter • **C. Magna** Magna Charta • **c. meteorológica** weather map • **c. pastoral** RELIG. pastoral letter • **c. postal** AMER. post card • **echar una c. al correo** to mail a letter • **jugar a cartas vistas** COLL. to act with certainty • **jugar la última c.** FIG. to play one's last card • **poner las cartas sobre la mesa** FIG. to put one's cards on the table • **tomar cartas** COLL. to intervene.

car·ta·bón m. *(instrumento de dibujo)* drawing triangle, set square; *(regla de zapatero)* foot gauge, shoemaker's size stick; ARCHIT. angle formed by two slopes of a roof; TOP. octagonal prism (used as surveyor's cross); AMER. measuring stick.

car·ta·gi·nés, –ne·sa *or* **car·ta·gi·nen·se** adj. & m.f. Carthaginian.

Car·ta·go f. Carthage.

car·ta·pa·cio m. *(bolsa)* bookbag, satchel; *(cuaderno)* notebook, exercise book; AMER. portfolio.

car·te·ar intr. to play low (in cards) —reflex. *(escribir cartas)* to correspond, write letters; *(escribirse)* to write to each other <*se cartearon por cinco años* they wrote letters to each other for five years>.

car·tel m. *(anuncio)* poster, bill; *(en la escuela)* wall chart; *(pasquín)* pasquinade, lampoon; *(documento)* cartel; *(desafío)* dare, challenge; COM., FIN. cartel, trust ♦ **tener c.** COLL. to be a hit, be a star.

cár·tel m. cartel, trust.

car·te·la f. *(tarjeta)* writing tablet, card; ARCHIT. *(ménsula)* modillion, bracket; *(hierro que sostiene un balcón)* iron stay for supporting a balcony; HER. billet, rectangular emblem.

car·te·le·ra f. billboard; *(de un periódico)* entertainment section.

car·te·o m. correspondence, exchange of letters.

cár·ter m. MECH. housing, casing ♦ **c. del cigüeñal** AUTO. crankcase • **c. de engranajes** AUTO. gearbox.

car·te·ra f. *(de hombre)* wallet, billfold; *(de mujer)* pocketbook, handbag; *(portadocumentos)* portfolio, briefcase; *(tira de tela)* pocket flap; FIG. *(clientela)* clientele, portfolio; *(ministerio)* cabinet post; COM., FIN. holdings, portfolio ♦ **tener en c.** to be planning.

car·te·ris·ta m. pickpocket, thief.

car·te·ro m. mailman, postman.

car·te·sia·no, –na adj. & m.f. PHILOS. Cartesian.

car·ti·la·gi·no·so, –sa adj. ANAT. cartilaginous.

car·tí·la·go m. ANAT. cartilage.

car·ti·lla f. *(abecedario)* primer; book, card <*c. de racionamiento* ration book>; *(folleto)* booklet, leaflet; RELIG. *(añalejo)* ordo, liturgical calendar; *(certificado)* certificate of ordination ♦ **cantarle** *or* **leerle la c. a** FIG., COLL. to read the riot act to • **c. de ahorros** bankbook, passbook • **no estar en la c.** FIG. to be out of the ordinary • **no saber la c.** COLL. to be ignorant, know absolutely nothing.

car·to·gra·fí·a f. cartography, mapmaking.

car·tó·gra·fo, –fa m.f. cartographer, mapmaker.

car·to·man·cia f. cartomancy, fortunetelling (with cards).

car·to·mán·ti·co, –ca I. adj. card reading, fortunetelling II. m.f. card reader, fortuneteller.

car·tón m. *(papel endurecido)* cardboard, pasteboard; *(caja)* carton, cardboard box; *(de cigarillos)* carton (of cigarettes); *(dibujo)* cartoon, sketch; BKB. *(de un libro)* board; *(adorno)* leaf-shaped ornament; ARCHIT. bracket, corbel ♦ **c. alquitranado** tarpaper • **c. de encuadernar** millboard • **c. de paja** strawboard • **c. ondulado** corrugated cardboard • **c. piedra** papier-mâché • **c. yeso** plasterboard.

car·to·ne·rí·a f. *(fábrica)* cardboard factory; *(industria)* cardboard industry.

car·tu·che·ra MIL. f. *(caja)* cartridge box *or* case; *(cinturón)* cartridge belt.

car·tu·che·rí·a f. MIL. *(fábrica)* munition plant; *(armas)* munitions.

car·tu·cho m. MIL. cartridge; *(de monedas)* roll of coins; *(cono)* paper cone, cornucopia; *(bolsa)* paper bag ♦ **c. de dinamita** dynamite stick • **c. sin bala** *or* **en blanco** blank cartridge • **quemar uno el último c.** FIG. to use up one's last resource, play one's last card.

car·tu·li·na f. pasteboard, fine cardboard.

car·va·llo m. BOT. oak tree.

car·vi m. caraway seed.

ca·sa f. *(edificio)* house; *(residencia)* home, dwelling; *(familia)* household, family; house, line *<la c. de Borbón* the house of Bourbon>; *(establecimiento)* business establishment, firm; *(escaque)* square (of a board game) ♦ **caérsele la c. encima** FIG., COLL. to be overwhelmed • **C. Blanca** White House • **c. celeste** ASTROL. house • **c. central** central office • **c. consistorial** town hall • **c. de altos** ARG., CHILE, PAR. multistory building • **c. de asistencia** AMER. boarding house • **c. de banca** COM. banking house • **c. de beneficencia** settlement house, poorhouse • **c. de campo** country house • **c. de caridad** poorhouse • **c. de citas** house of assignation • **c. de comercio** business firm • **c. de corrección** house of correction, reformatory • **c. de correos** post office • **c. de cuna** *(orfanatorio)* foundling home; *(guardería)* nursery • **c. de departamentos** S. AMER. apartment house • **c. de Dios** *or* **del Señor** RELIG. house of God, church • **c. de empeños** pawnshop • **c. de expósitos** foundling home, orphanage • **c. de fieras** menagerie, zoo • **c. de juego** gambling house, casino • **c. de labor** *or* **de labranza** farmhouse • **c. de locos** *or* **de orates** insane asylum, madhouse • **C. de la Moneda** mint • **c. de oración** RELIG. house of prayer • **c. de postas** post house, inn • **c. de socorro** first aid station • **c. de tócame Roque** COLL. messy house • **c. de vecindad** tenement house • **c. editorial** publishing house • **c. exportadora** exporter • **c. importadora** importer • **c. matriz** RELIG. motherhouse • **c. mortuoria** house of mourning • **c. paterna** paternal home • **c. pública** brothel • **c. real** *(palacio)* royal palace; *(familia)* royal family • **c. rectoral** rectory • **c. religiosa** convent • **C. Rosada** Pink House (official residence of the Argentinian president) • **c. solariega** ancestral home, family seat • **c. y comida** room and board • **como Pedro por su c.** right at home • **de c. en c.** from house to house • **echar la c. por la ventana** FIG., COLL. to roll out the red carpet, go all out • **empezar la c. por el tejado** FIG. to put the cart before the horse • **en c.** at home, in • **en c. de** at the home of • **estar de c.** to be casually dressed • **estar fuera de c.** to be out • **franquear la c. a** to open one's home to • **hacer c.** to get rich • **ir a c.** to go home • **llevar la c.** COLL. to run the house, wear the pants in the family • **no tener c. ni hogar** to be homeless • **poner c.** to set up housekeeping • **sentirse como en la c. de uno** to feel at home • **ser de c.** COLL. to be a close friend of the family; *(ser hogareño)* to be a homebody.

ca·sa·be m. BOT. cassava; ICHTH. amberfish; AMER. round, thin cake made of cassava meal.

ca·sa·ca f. *(vestido)* dress coat; COLL. *(boda)* wedding, marriage; HOND. whispered conversation ♦ **cambiar** *or* **volver c.** FIG. to be a turncoat, change sides.

ca·sa·ción f. LAW cassation, annulment.

ca·sa·de·ro, –ra adj. marriageable, of marrying age.

ca·sa·do, –da I. past part. see **casar¹** II. adj. married *<mal c.* unhappily married> ♦ **estar c.** to be married • **c. y arrepentido** marry in haste, repent in leisure III. m.f. married person —m. PRINT. imposition; S. AMER., CUL. two different foods eaten together ♦ **recién casados** newlyweds.

ca·sa·ma·ta f. MIL. casemate.

ca·sa·men·te·ro, –ra I. adj. matchmaking II. m.f. matchmaker, marriage broker.

ca·sa·mien·to m. marriage, wedding ♦ **c. a la fuerza** shotgun wedding • **c. de braguéta** marriage of convenience.

ca·sar¹ intr. to marry *<c. con una joven* to marry a young girl>; *(cuadrar)* to balance, tally *<las cuentas no casan* the accounts do not tally>; *(armonizarse)* to match, harmonize *<estos colores no casan* these colors do not match> —tr. to marry, wed; to marry off *<c. a la hija* to marry off one's daughter>; FIG. *(juntar)* to match, pair; PRINT. to impose —reflex. *(matrimoniarse)* to marry, get married; FIG. *(armonizar)* to match, harmonize ♦ **antes que te cases mira lo que haces** FIG., COLL. look before you leap • **casarse con** to get married to • **casarse en segundas nupcias** to remarry • **casarse por interés** to marry for money • **casarse por detrás de la iglesia** FIG. to live together, cohabit • **casarse por poderes** to marry by proxy • **no casarse con nadie** FIG. to maintain one's independence.

ca·sar² m. hamlet.

ca·sa·tien·da f. store and home combined.

cas·ca f. *(hollejo)* bagasse of pressed grapes; *(corteza)* tanning bark; *(rosca)* fruitcake made of marzipan and cider *or* sweet potato covered with sugar; *(cáscara)* shell, peel, rind.

cas·ca·bel m. small bell ♦ **de c. gordo** FIG., COLL. trashy, inartistic • **echar el c.** FIG. to drop a hint • **poner el c. al gato** FIG. to bell the cat, stick one's neck out • **ser alegre como un c.** FIG. to be as happy as a lark • **ser un c.** COLL. to be a scatterbrain • **serpiente de c.** rattlesnake • **tener un c.** FIG. to be worried *or* anxious.

cas·ca·be·la f. C. RICA, ZOOL. rattlesnake.

cas·ca·be·la·da f. *(fiesta)* noisy party; FIG., COLL. *(tontería)* scatterbrained remark *or* action.

cas·ca·be·le·ar tr. COLL. to take in, entice —intr. *(sonar)* to jingle, tinkle; FIG., COLL. *(portarse con ligereza)* to act in a scatterbrained manner; CHILE to grumble, growl.

cas·ca·be·le·ro, –ra I. adj. FIG., COLL. scatterbrained II. m.f. FIG., COLL. scatterbrain —m. *(sonajero)* baby's rattle.

cas·ca·bi·llo m. *(cascabel)* small bell; *(cascarillo)* husk (of wheat *or* corn); *(cúpula de la bellota)* acorn cup.

cas·ca·ci·rue·las m.f. FIG., COLL. good-for-nothing person.

cas·ca·da I. f. cascade, waterfall ♦ **en c.** ELEC. cascade II. adj. see **cascado, –da**.

cas·ca·do, –da I. past part. see **cascar** II. adj. *(roto)* broken, cracked; COLL. *(decrépito)* decrepit, worn-out; *(sin sonoridad)* flat, cracked III. f. see **cascada**.

cas·ca·du·ra f. break, crack.

cas·ca·jo m. *(guijo)* gravel; *(nuez)* nut; COLL. *(trasto)* rubbish, scrap; *(fragmento)* piece, shard (of pottery); FIG., COLL. *(moneda)* copper coin; DOM. REP., P. RICO money ♦ **estar hecho un c.** FIG., COLL. to be a wreck.

cas·ca·jo·so, –sa adj. gravelly.

cas·ca·ma·jar tr. to break, crush.

cas·ca·mien·to m. breaking, crushing, cracking.

cas·ca·nue·ces m. [pl. **-nue·ces**] nutcracker; ORNITH. nutcracker.

cas·ca·pi·ño·nes m. nutcracker.

cas·car §70 tr. *(quebrantar)* to break, crack *<c. un huevo* to break an egg>; COLL. *(pegar)* to hit, beat; COLL. *(arruinar la salud)* to ruin, undermine (one's health) —intr. COLL. *(morir)* to kick the bucket; *(charlar)* to chatter, prattle —reflex. *(romperse)* to break, crack; *(enfermarse)* to fall ill, become sick.

cás·ca·ra f. *(de huevo, de nuez)* shell; *(de fruta)* skin, peel; *(de queso, de fruta)* rind; *(de cereal)* husk, hull; AMER. bark (of a tree); ♦ **¡cáscaras!** good heavens! • **c. sagrada** PHARM. cascara • **ser de la c. amarga** COLL. *(ser travieso)* to be a troublemaker; *(tener ideas avanzadas)* to have advanced ideas.

cas·ca·ri·lla I. f. cascarilla (bark); *(quina)* quinine, Peruvian bark; *(de cacao)* cacao-leaf tea; *(de metal)* lamina, foil; *(afeite)* powdered eggshell cosmetic; AMER. quick-tempered person II. adj. AMER. quick-tempered, touchy.

cas·ca·rón m. *(cáscara)* thick peel *or* rind; *(de huevo)* eggshell (esp. broken); ARCHIT. vault, dome; AMER. confetti-filled eggshell; URUG., BOT. cork oak tree ♦ **aún no haber salido del c.** FIG. to be inexperienced • **c. de nuez** MARIT. very small boat.

cas·ca·rra·bias m.f. [pl. **-bias**] COLL. grouch, ill-tempered person.

cas·ca·rrón, –rro·na adj. COLL. rough, harsh.

cas·co m. MIL. helmet; *(tonel)* cask, barrel, keg; *(botella)* bottle; MARIT. hull; ZOOL. hoof; MECH. casing; BOT. fleshy part, pulp (of an onion); ANAT. skull, cranium; *(copa de sombrero)* crown (of a hat); *(fragmento)* shard, potsherd; *(recinto)* limits, confines <*dentro del c. de la ciudad* within city limits>; AMER. segment, slice (of fruit); PHILIP. boat; PERU chest, breast; MEX. compound, complex; ARG. area, section (of an estate) ♦ **c. de buzo** diver's helmet • **c. de casa** framework of a house • **cascos** ZOOL. nut, noggin • **c. sideral** space helmet • **lavar el c. a** COLL. to flatter, soft-soap • **levantar de cascos a** COLL. to egg on with false hopes • **ligero de cascos** COLL. scatterbrained • **romperle los cascos a** FIG., COLL. to bore, weary • **romperse los cascos** FIG., COLL. to rack one's brains • **sentar los cascos** FIG., COLL. to settle down.

cas·co·te m. rubble, debris.

cas·co·te·ar tr. AMER. to throw out rubbish.

ca·se·a·ción f. caseation, curdling (of milk).

ca·se·o·so, –sa adj. *(relativo al queso)* caseous; *(parecido al queso)* cheese-like, cheesy.

ca·se·rí·a f. *(casa)* country house; *(gobierno de la casa)* housekeeping; AMER. customers (of a store).

ca·se·rí·o m. *(pueblo)* hamlet; *(cortijo)* country house or estate; P. RICO housing project.

ca·ser·na f. MIL. casern, bombproof bunker.

ca·se·ro, –ra I. adj. household, domestic <*animal c.* domestic animal>; family <*una reunión c.* a family gathering>; *(hecho en casa)* homemade; *(hogareño)* home-loving ♦ **cocina c.** home cooking II. m.f. *(dueño)* owner, landlord; *(administrador)* caretaker; *(inquilino)* tenant; *(persona hogareña)* homebody, stay-at-home; Amer. *(cliente)* customer; *(tendero)* shopkeeper; CHILE, CUBA door-to-door salesman —f. landlady.

ca·se·rón m. *(casa grande)* large house, mansion; *(casa destartalada)* large ramshackle or dilapidated house.

ca·se·ta f. *(casilla)* small house, cottage; *(barraca)* stand, booth, stall; SPORT. *(vestuario)* dressing room or hut ♦ **c. de cambios de agujas** RAIL. signal tower or box • **c. de derrota** or **del timón** MARIT. wheel house, pilothouse • **c. de peaje** tollbooth • **c. telefónica** TELEC. telephone booth.

ca·se·te m.f. cassette, tape cartridge.

ca·si adv. almost, nearly <*tengo c. veinte años* I am almost twenty years old> ♦ **c. c.** COLL. very nearly • **c. nada** almost nothing, next to nothing • **c. nunca** hardly ever, almost never.

ca·si·con·tra·to m. LAW quasi-contract.

ca·si·lla f. *(casa pequeña)* cabin, cottage; *(caseta)* watchman's hut; *(del mercado)* booth, stall; THEAT. *(taquilla)* box office; *(de un papel)* box, square (on ruled paper); *(de un casillero)* pigeonhole, compartment; *(escaque)* square (on chessboard); COLL. *(prisión)* clink, slammer; AUTO., RAIL. cab, compartment; AMER. post-office box; CUBA bird snare; ECUAD. toilet, lavatory ♦ **c. telefónica** telephone booth • **sacar a uno de sus casillas** FIG. *(alterar)* to change a person's habits; FIG., COLL. *(enfurecer)* to infuriate • **salir uno de sus casillas** FIG., COLL. to lose one's temper, fly off the handle.

ca·si·lle·ro m. *(escritorio)* desk with pigeonholes; *(archivador)* filing cabinet; SPORT. *(marcador)* scoreboard.

ca·si·no m. *(casa)* country house; *(recreo)* casino; *(asociación)* club, association; *(salón de asamblea)* meeting hall, clubhouse.

ca·so m. *(acontecimiento)* event, occasion; *(circunstancia)* circumstance, case <*en tal c.* in such a case>; *(asunto)* case, affair, question; GRAM., LAW, MED. case ♦ **c. de honra** question of honor • **c. de prueba** LAW test case • **c. fortuito** unexpected event; LAW act of God • **c. perdido** FIG. lost cause, hopeless case • **el c. es que** that fact is that • **en c. de** in the event of • **en c. de que** or **dado c. que** in case <*en c. de que lleguen temprano* in case they arrive early> • **en el mejor de los casos** at best • **en el peor de los casos** at worst • **en todo c.** in any case • **en último c.** as a last resort • **hablar al c.** to speak to the question • **hacer or venir al c.** COLL. to be relevant • **hacer c. a** to notice, heed • **hacer c. de** to pay attention to • **hacer c. omiso de** to ignore • **no hacer or venir al c.** COLL. to be beside the point • **poner por c.** to take as an example <*pongamos por c. a Juan* let's take John as an example> • **vamos al c.** let's get to the point • **verse en el c. de** to be obliged or compelled to.

ca·són m. or **ca·so·na** f. large house, mansion.

ca·so·rio m. COLL. mismatch, unwise marriage.

cas·pa f. MED. dandruff, scurf (of the scalp); *(costra)* scab, crust; METAL. patina (of copper).

¡cás·pi·ta! interj. COLL. holy cow!, wow!, gee!

cas·po·so, –sa f. full of dandruff.

cas·qué, casquear see cascar.

cas·que·te m. MIL. helmet, casque; RELIG. *(gorro)* skullcap; *(gorro de mujer)* toque; *(peluca de hombre)* toupee; *(peluca de mujer)* wiglet; MED. ringworm cap; MECH. cap, bonnet ♦ **c. esférico** GEOM. one-base spherical segment • **c. glaciar** GEOL. ice cap.

cas·qui·jo m. gravel, broken stone.

cas·qui·lla f. ZOOL. covering of queen bee cells; JEWEL. silver weights used by jewelers.

cas·qui·llo m. MECH. collar, sleeve (on a tool); cap <*c. de bayoneta* bayonet cap>; *(de la saeta)* iron arrowhead; ARM. *(cartucho vacío)* case, empty cartridge; ELEC. base (of light bulb); AMER. horseshoe; GUAT., HOND. hat lining; C. RICA penholder ♦ **c. escariador** reaming shell • **c. partido** MECH. split bushing.

cas·qui·va·no, –na adj. COLL. featherbrained.

cas·set·te m.f. cassette.

cas·ta I. f. ZOOL. breed, line, stock; *(de personas)* lineage, stock, descent; *(de la sociedad)* caste; FIG. *(calidad)* quality, class; MEX., PRINT. font ♦ **cruzar las castas** to crossbreed • **de c.** *(de animales)* thoroughbred, purebred; *(de personas)* of breeding; *(auténtico)* real, genuine • **de c. le viene al galgo** like father, like son • **cruzar las castas** to crossbreed • **le viene de c.** it runs in the family II. adj. see **casto, –ta.**

cas·ta·ña I. f. BOT. chestnut (fruit); *(damajuana)* demijohn; *(moño)* bun, chignon; FIG., COLL. *(borrachera)* spree, bender; *(puñetazo)* punch <*arrear una c.* to land a punch>; MEX. keg; CUBA, TECH. journal bearing in roller of sugar mill ♦ **c. apilada** or **pilonga** dried chestnut • **c. del Brasil** or **de Pará** Brazil nut • **c. regoldana** or **de Indias** horse chestnut • **dar a uno la c.** FIG., COLL. to play a trick on someone • **dar a uno para castañas** to threaten to punish someone • **sacar las castañas del fuego** to expose oneself to danger for another's advantage II. adj. see **castaño, –ña.**

cas·ta·ña·zo m. COLL. *(puñetazo)* punch, sock; *(trompetazo)* bump, blow.

cas·ta·ñe·da f. chestnut grove.

cas·ta·ñe·ta f. *(chasquido)* snap of the fingers; *(instrumento)* castanet.

cas·ta·ñe·ta·zo m. *(de las castañas)* cracking or crackling (roasting) of chestnuts; MUS. *(de las castañuelas)* clack of a castanet; *(de los dedos)* snap or click (of fingers); *(de los huesos)* crack (of joints); COLL. *(golpe)* punch, blow.

cas·ta·ñe·te·ar tr. MUS. to play on the castanets; *(los dedos)* to snap, click (one's fingers) — intr. *(los dientes)* to chatter; *(los huesos)* to crack; *(perdiz)* to cry, squawk.

cas·ta·ñe·te·o m. MUS. *(de las castañuelas)* clacking, clapping; *(de los dedos)* snapping, clicking; *(de los huesos)* cracking; *(de los dientes)* chattering; ORNITH. squawking.

cas·ta·ño, –ña I. adj. chestnut, brown II. m. chestnut (tree and wood) ♦ **c. de Indias** horse chestnut • **pasar algo de c. obscuro** FIG., COLL. to go too far, become really serious —f. see **castaña.**

cas·ta·ñue·la f. MUS. castanet; BOT. type of sedge ♦ **estar como unas castañuelas** FIG., COLL. to be in a jolly or festive mood.

cas·te·lla·ni·zar §04 tr. to Hispanicize, make Spanish.

cas·te·lla·no, –na I. adj. Castilian II. m.f *(habitante de Castilla)* Castilian —m. *(idioma)* Spanish; *(dialecto)* Castilian; *(dueño de un castillo)* castellan, lord of a castle.

cas·ti·ci·dad f. *or* **cas·ti·cis·mo** m. purity, correctness (of language); genuineness, authenticity (persons).
cas·ti·dad f. *(pudor)* chastity, continence; *(soltería)* celibacy, chastity.
cas·ti·ga·dor, –do·ra I. adj. *(que castiga)* punitive, chastising; COLL. *(coquetón)* flirtatious II. m.f *(que castiga)* punisher, chastiser —m. COLL. *(tenorio)* lady-killer, Don Juan.
cas·ti·gar §47 tr. *(penar)* to punish, chastise, castigate; *(mortificar)* to mortify, discipline <*c. el cuerpo* to discipline one's body>; SPORT. *(en los deportes)* to penalize; FIG. *(enmendar)* to correct, emend; *(reducir)* to reduce, cut <*c. los gastos* to cut expenses>; *(afligir)* to afflict, cause damage to; *(coquetear)* to seduce, lead on; TAUR. to wound; MEX. to squeeze, tighten ♦ **c. el estómago** to starve, fast • **c. la vista** to strain one's eyes.
cas·ti·go m. *(pena)* punishment, chastisement, castigation; *(mortificación)* mortification, self-denial; *(aflicción)* affliction, damage; *(pena)* penalty; SPORT. *(sanción)* penalty; FIG. *(corrección)* correction, emendation; TAUR. wound ♦ **c. corporal** LAW corporal punishment • **levantar el c.** to withdraw the sentence *or* penalty • **ser de c. una cosa** to be hard *or* grueling.
cas·ti·gué, castigue see castigar.
Cas·ti·lla la Nueva f. New Castile.
Cas·ti·lla la Vieja f. Old Castile.
cas·ti·llo m. castle; MARIT. forecastle; *(pollera)* baby walker; *(cabida)* load, capacity of a cart; MIL. howdah; ENTOM. queen cell ♦ **c. de fuego** fireworks • **c. de naipes** FIG. house of cards • **c. de popa** MARIT. poop deck • **c. de proa** MARIT. foredeck • **castillos en el aire** FIG. castles in the air.
casti·zo, –za I. adj. *(de casta)* purebred, pureblooded; FIG. *(verdadero)* genuine, authentic; *(típico)* typical, traditional <*ella es una española c.* she is a typical Spaniard>; LIT. *(puro)* pure, unbastardized II. m.f. AMER. quadroon (offspring of a mestizo and a Spaniard); LIT. *(autor)* author whose style is pure —m. COL. very fertile animal.
cas·to, –ta I. adj. *(virgen)* chaste, virginal; *(puro)* pure, clean II. f. see casta.
cas·tor m. ZOOL. beaver (animal and fur); *(sombrero)* beaver-skin cap *or* hat, castor.
cas·tra *or* **cas·tra·ción** f. ZOOL. castration; FIG. *(apocamiento)* emasculation; HORT. pruning.
cas·tra·do, –da I. past part. see castrar II. adj. ZOOL. castrated; FIG. *(apocado)* emasculated III. m. *(hombre)* eunuch; *(caballo)* gelding.
cas·trar tr. ZOOL. to castrate, geld, fix; FIG. *(apocar)* to emasculate; HORT. to prune; MED. to dry up (sores *or* wounds).
cas·tra·zón f. extraction of honeycombs from the beehive.
cas·tren·se adj. military <*tradición c.* military tradition>.
ca·sual adj. chance, accidental, coincidental.
ca·sua·li·dad f. chance ♦ **dar la c.** to just so happen that <*dio la c. que los vi cuando llegaron* it just so happened that I saw them when they arrived> • **de c.** by chance *or* accident • **por c.** by any chance.
ca·sual·men·te adv. by chance *or* accident, accidentally; AMER. precisely, exactly.
ca·su·lla f. RELIG. chasuble; HOND. rice grain with husk.
ca·ta f. *(acción de probar)* tasting, sampling; *(porción)* taste, sample; COL., MEX., MIN. prospecting pit; COL. hidden *or* secret thing; CHILE, ARG., ORNITH. parakeet.
ca·ta·cal·dos m.f. [pl. **-dos**] FIG., COLL. dabbler, dilettante.
ca·ta·clis·mo m. *(catástrofe)* cataclysm, natural disaster; FIG. *(trastorno)* disruption, upheaval.
ca·ta·cum·bas f.pl. HIST. catacombs.
ca·ta·dor, –do·ra m.f. CUL. taster, sampler.
ca·ta·du·ra f. CUL. tasting, sampling; FIG., COLL. *(semblante)* appearance, aspect.
ca·ta·fal·co m. catafalque.
ca·ta·lán, –la·na adj. & m.f. Catalonian, Catalan.
ca·ta·le·jo m. spyglass, small telescope.
ca·ta·lep·sia f. MED. catalepsy.
ca·ta·lép·ti·co, –ca adj. & m.f. MED. cataleptic.
ca·ta·li·na f. ♦ **rueda c.** escape wheel (of a watch).
ca·tá·li·sis f. [pl. **-sis**] CHEM. catalysis.
ca·ta·lí·ti·co, –ca adj. CHEM. catalytic.

ca·ta·li·za·dor m. CHEM. catalyst, catalyzer.
ca·ta·lo·ga·ción f. cataloguing.
ca·ta·lo·ga·dor, –do·ra I. adj. cataloguing II. m.f. cataloguer.
ca·ta·lo·gar §47 tr. to catalogue, list.
ca·tá·lo·go m. catalogue.
Ca·ta·lu·ña f. GEOG. Catalonia.
ca·ta·plas·ma f. MED. cataplasm, poultice; FIG., COLL. *(persona pesada)* bore, boring person.
¡ca·ta·plum! *or* **¡ca·ta·plún!** interj. crash!, bang!
ca·ta·pul·ta f. ARM., AVIA. catapult.
ca·ta·pul·tar tr. to catapult.
ca·tar tr. *(saborear)* to sample, taste; *(examinar)* to examine, inspect; *(colmena)* to remove, extract (honeycombs from the hive).
ca·ta·ra·ta f. *(cascada)* waterfall, cataract; MED. cataract ♦ **cataratas** rainclouds • **la c. del Niágara** Niagara Falls • **tener c.** FIG., COLL. to be blind (with ignorance or passion).
ca·ta·rro m. MED. cold, catarrh ♦ **coger un c.** to catch a cold.
ca·ta·rro·so, –sa MED. I. adj. *(acatarrado)* catarrhal; *(propenso a acatarrarse)* subject to colds II. m.f. person suffering from a cold.
ca·tar·sis f. [pl. **-sis**] *(purificación)* catharsis, purification; MED. *(purgación)* catharsis, purgation; PSYCH. catharsis.
ca·tár·ti·co, –ca adj. MED., PHARM. cathartic, laxative.
ca·tás·ta·sis f. THEAT. catastasis, climax of a play.
ca·tas·tral adj. cadastral.
ca·tas·tro m. cadaster, official land register.
ca·tás·tro·fe f. *(desastre)* catastrophe, disaster; LIT., THEAT. *(desenlace)* denouement, conclusion (of a play).
ca·tas·tró·fi·co, –ca adj. catastrophic, disastrous.
ca·ta·vi·nos m. [pl. **-nos**] *(enólogo)* wine taster, connoisseur; FIG., COLL. *(borracho)* boozer, drunk.
ca·te·ar tr. AMER. *(minas)* to prospect (for minerals); *(una casa)* to watch, spy on (a house); *(buscar)* to seek, search for; COLL. *(un alumno)* to flunk, fail (a student).
ca·te·cis·mo m. EDUC., RELIG. catechism (book).
cá·te·dra I. f. *(rango)* professorial chair, professorship; *(asiento)* professor's chair; *(aula)* classroom, lecture hall; *(asignatura)* subject; RELIG. cathedra, see; CUBA, VEN. wonder, marvel ♦ **c. de San Pedro** the Holy See • **c. del Espíritu Santo** pulpit • **explicar una c.** to hold a chair • **opositar a una c.** to compete for a chair • **poner c.** FIG., COLL. to pontificate, speak pedantically • **ser la c.** CUBA, COLL. to be very knowledgeable II. adj. CUBA, VEN. wonderful, marvelous.
ca·te·dral f. cathedral ♦ **como una c.** FIG., COLL. huge, enormous.
ca·te·drá·ti·co m. EDUC. university professor.
ca·te·go·rí·a f. *(clase)* category, class, type; FIG. *(rango)* position, standing ♦ **de c.** FIG. prominent, important • **de primera c.** first-rate • **de segunda c.** second-rate.
ca·te·gó·ri·ca·men·te adv. categorically, absolutely.
ca·te·gó·ri·co, –ca adj. categorical, absolute, unqualified.
ca·te·na·ria GEOM. adj. & f. catenary.
ca·te·que·sis f. *or* **ca·te·quis·mo** m. EDUC., RELIG. catechism, catechization.
ca·te·quis·ta m.f. RELIG. catechist.
ca·te·qui·zar §04 tr. EDUC., RELIG. to catechize, teach religious principles to; FIG. *(persuadir)* to convince, convert.
ca·ter·va f. *(multitud)* crowd, throng; *(pandilla)* band, gang <*c. de pillos* band of rascals>.
ca·té·ter m. SURG. catheter.
ca·te·to m. GEOM. leg of a right triangle.
ca·ti·li·na·ria I. adj. violently satirical II. f. diatribe, outburst.
ca·tin·ga f. AMER. foul smell, body odor; BOT. stunted forest.
ca·ti·te m. *(de azúcar)* loaf of high-quality refined sugar; MEX. silk fabric; *(sombrero)* conical hat; *(golpe)* slap, cuff ♦ **dar c.** COLL. to hit, beat.
ca·to m. *(de acacia)* catechu; BOL. agrarian measure.
ca·tó·di·co, –ca adj. PHYS. cathodic, cathode.
ca·to·li·cé, catolice see catolizar.
ca·to·li·ci·dad f. RELIG. *(catolicismo)* Catholicism; *(mundo*

católico) Catholics; *(universalidad)* universality, catholicity.

ca·to·li·cis·mo m. RELIG. Catholicism.

ca·tó·li·co, –ca I. adj. RELIG. Catholic; FIG., COLL. *(sano)* healthy, chipper ♦ **no ser muy c.** to be *or* look suspicious II. m.f. RELIG. Catholic.

ca·to·li·zar §04 tr. to catholicize.

ca·tor·ce I. adj. fourteen *<c. libros* fourteen books>; *(decimocuarto)* fourteenth II. m. fourteen.

ca·tre m. cot ♦ **c. de tijera** *or* **de viento** folding canvas cot • **c. de balsa** ARG. raft, float.

ca·tri·co·fre m. box containing a folding bed.

ca·trín, –tri·na MEX. m. dandy —f. clotheshorse.

cau·cá·se·o, –a *or* **cau·cá·si·co, –ca** adj. & m.f. Caucasian.

cau·ce m. *(lecho de río)* riverbed; *(acequia)* ditch, trench.

cau·ción f. *(precaución)* caution, precaution; *(advertencia)* caveat, warning; *(depósito)* security, pledge; LAW *(fianza)* bail, bond; FIN. *(bolsa)* cover, margin ♦ **bajo c.** LAW on bail • **c. de indemnidad** LAW bond of indemnity.

cau·cio·nar tr. LAW to put up *or* post bail; *(precaver)* to caution *or* warn against.

cau·che·ro, –ra I. adj. rubber II. m.f. rubber gatherer *or* worker —f. BOT. rubber plant.

cau·cho m. BOT. *(goma)* rubber; *(planta)* rubber plant *or* tree; COL. slicker, rain poncho ♦ **c. esponjoso** foam rubber • **c. vulcanizado** vulcanized rubber.

cau·dal I. adj. ZOOL. caudal; *(caudaloso)* carrying *or* holding a lot of water II. m. *(riqueza)* wealth, fortune; *(volumen de agua)* volume; *(flujo de agua)* flow; FIG. *(copia)* abundance, plenty ♦ **c. relicto** LAW estate of the deceased • **hacer c. de** to esteem, hold in high regard.

cau·da·lo·so, –sa adj. deep, swift (river, lake); *(rico)* wealthy, rich.

cau·di·lla·je *or* **cau·di·llis·mo** m. POL. *(mando)* leadership, rule by a leader *or* chief; ARG., CHILE succession of power; AMER. *(caciquismo)* bossism, tyranny.

cau·di·llo m. MIL., POL. leader, chief, commander; AMER. political boss.

cau·ro m. northwest wind.

cau·sa f. *(principio)* cause, reason *<su avaricia era la c. de toda su miseria* his avarice was the cause of all of his unhappiness>; *(motivo)* cause, motive; *(partido)* cause *<luchaban por la c. de la justicia* they fought for the cause of justice>; LAW *(pleito)* lawsuit, trial; PERU potato salad; CHILE light meal, snack *<echar una c.* to have a snack> ♦ **a c. de** because of • **c. común** common cause • **c. eficiente** PHILOS. efficient cause • **c. final** PHILOS. final cause • **c. primera** PHILOS. prime mover • **formar** *or* **instruir c.** LAW to prosecute, bring legal action • **sin c.** without good reason.

cau·sa·dor, –do·ra I. adj. causing, causative II. m.f. agent, cause.

cau·sa·ha·bien·te m. LAW assignee.

cau·sal I. adj. GRAM., LOG. causal, causative II. f. reason, cause, motive.

cau·sa·li·dad f. LOG. causality, causation; *(origen)* origin, cause.

cau·san·te I. adj. causing, causative II. m.f. causer, originator; LAW person from whom a right is derived.

cau·sar tr. to cause, occasion; to provoke (anger).

cau·sa·ti·vo, –va adj. causative.

caus·ti·ci·dad f. causticity; FIG. *(mordacidad)* mordacity, sarcasm.

cáus·ti·co, –ca I. adj. *(corrosivo)* caustic; FIG. *(mordaz)* caustic, scathing II. m. MED. blistering plaster, vesicatory.

cau·ta·men·te adv. cautiously, warily.

cau·te·la f. *(prudencia)* caution, wariness; *(astucia)* astuteness, cunning ♦ **tener c.** to take precautions.

cau·te·lo·so, –sa adj. cautious, wary.

cau·te·rio m. SURG. *(cauterización)* cauterization; *(lo que cauteriza)* cautery; FIG. *(remedio)* remedy, cure.

cau·te·ri·za·dor, –do·ra I. adj. cauterizing II. m.f. cauterizer.

cau·te·ri·zar §04 tr. MED. to cauterize; FIG. *(corregir)* to correct *or* reproach with severity; *(extirpar)* to eradicate, do away with *<c. un vicio* to eradicate a vice>.

cau·ti·van·te adj. captivating, charming.

cau·ti·var tr. *(aprisionar)* to capture, take prisoner; FIG. *(ganar)* to capture, hold (captive) *<c. el interés del público* to capture the public interest>; *(fascinar)* to charm, captivate.

cau·ti·ve·rio m. *or* **cau·ti·vi·dad** f. captivity, confinement.

cau·ti·vo, –va adj. & m.f. captive.

cau·to, –ta adj. cautious, wary, prudent.

ca·va f. AGR. digging, cultivation; MIL. *(foso)* moat; *(bodega)* (royal) wine cellar.

ca·va·co·te m. mound of earth.

ca·va·do, –da I. past part. see **cavar** II. adj. concave.

ca·va·dor, –do·ra m.f. digger.

ca·var tr. to dig, excavate —intr. FIG. to delve into, probe.

ca·ver·na f. cavern, cave; MED. cavity (in the lung).

ca·ver·na·rio, –ria adj. *(relativo a las cavernas)* cave, of a cave; *(cavernícola)* cave-dwelling.

ca·ver·ní·co·la I. adj. cave-dwelling; POL., FIG. *(retrógrado)* reactionary II. m.f. cave dweller *or* cave man *or* woman; POL., FIG. reactionary.

ca·ver·no·so, –sa adj. cavernous; FIG. deep, low *<una voz c.* a deep voice>.

ca·vial *or* **ca·viar** m. caviar.

ca·vi·dad f. cavity.

ca·vi·la·ción f. pondering, meditation, rumination.

ca·vi·lar intr. to ponder, meditate, ruminate.

ca·vi·lo·se·ar intr. *(ponderar)* to ponder, meditate; C. AMER. to gossip.

ca·vi·lo·so, –sa adj. COLL. *(pensativo)* pensive; C. AMER. gossipy, talebearing; COL. *(sensible)* touchy, irritable; *(puntilloso)* fussy, finicky.

Ca·ye·na f. Cayenne.

ca·ye·ra, cayó see **caer.**

ca·yo m. MARÍT. key, islet ♦ **C. Hueso** Key West.

ca·yu·co m. AMER. Indian canoe.

caz m. ditch, canal.

ca·za f. *(cacería)* hunting, hunt; *(animales)* game ♦ **andar** *or* **ir a c. de** FIG., COLL. to be on the lookout for • **dar c.** to give chase, pursue • **dar c. a** FIG. to hunt down, sniff out • **ir de c.** to go hunting —m. AVIA. fighter plane, fighter.

ca·za·be m. AMER., CUL. cassava bread.

ca·za·cla·vos m. nail lifter, claw.

ca·za·dor, –do·ra I. adj. hunting; ZOOL. predatory II. m. hunter, huntsman; MIL. chasseur ♦ **c. de alforja** *or* **de pieles** trapper • **c. de cabezas** head-hunter • **c. furtivo** poacher • **c. mayor** royal huntsman —f. see **cazadora.**

ca·za·do·ra I. f. hunter, huntress; hunting jacket; C. AMER. light truck; C. RICA, ORNITH. yellow warbler II. adj. see **cazador, –dora.**

ca·zar §04 tr. to hunt *<c. conejos* to hunt rabbits>; *(coger)* to catch, bag; FIG. *(a una persona)* to track down; *(conseguir)* to land *<cazó un buen trabajo* he landed a good job>; *(prender la voluntad)* to take in, win over; *(sorprender)* to catch, surprise; MARIT. to haul in (a sail) ♦ **c. al vuelo** to catch on quickly • **c. furtivamente** *or* **en vedado** to poach.

caz·ca·le·ar intr. COLL. to scurry, bustle.

caz·ca·rria f. *(lodo)* mud; ARG. dung, excrement.

caz·ca·rrien·to, –ta adj. COLL. splattered with mud.

ca·zo m. CUL. *(cucharón)* dipper, ladle; *(cacerola)* small pot, saucepan; CARP. gluepot; *(recazo del cuchillo)* blunt edge of a knife ♦ **c. de fundidor** *or* **de colada** METAL. casting ladle, founder's scoop.

ca·zo·le·ro I. adj. fussy II. m. fussbudget, sissy.

ca·zo·le·ta f. ARTIL. pan (of a musket); *(de espada)* hand guard (of a sword); *(perfume)* kind of perfume; *(pebetero)* incense burner; *(de pipa)* bowl (of a pipe).

ca·zón m. ICHTH. dogfish, small shark.

ca·zo·nal m. *(arreos de pescar)* fishing tackle; *(red)* large fishing net; FIG., COLL. *(enredo)* tight spot, mess.

ca·zue·la f. CUL. *(de arcilla o vidrio)* casserole; *(metálico)* saucepan; *(guisado)* stew, casserole; THEAT. *(gallinero)* rear balcony, gallery; PRINT. *(componedor)* wide composing stick.

ca·zum·brar tr. to caulk.

ca·zum·bre m. caulking (for wine casks).

ca·zu·rro, –rra I. adj. taciturn, reserved II. m.f. taciturn person.

ce f. *(letra)* cee ♦ **ce por be** in great detail • **por ce o por be** one way or the other.

¡ce! interj. psst!

ce·ba f. *(alimento)* special feed (to fatten animals); FIG. *(alimentación)* fattening (of animals); AMER., ARM. *(cebo de escopeta)* primer (of a gun); *(acción)* priming.

ce·ba·da I. f. BOT. barley ♦ **c. perlada** pearl barley II. adj. see **cebado, -da.**

ce·ba·dar tr. to feed barley to.

ce·ba·de·ra f. *(manta)* nose bag, feed bag; *(arca)* barley hopper *or* bin; MARIT. spritsail; MIN. furnace charger.

ce·ba·de·ro m. *(vendedor)* barley dealer; *(mozo de posada)* stable boy; *(caballería)* lead mule (of a mule train); *(lugar)* feeding place (for animals); *(adiestrador de aves)* hawk trainer; MIN. mouth (for feeding a furnace).

ce·ba·do, -da I. past part. see **cebar** II. adj. AMER., ZOOL. man-eating; fattened (animal); *(gordo)* very fat III. f. see **cebada.**

ce·ba·dor, -do·ra I. adj. feeding, fattening II. m. ARM. powder horn *or* flask.

ce·ba·du·ra f. AGR. fattening (of animals); ARG. preparation of maté.

ce·bar tr. *(nutrir)* to feed, fatten; *(con un imán)* to remagnetize; *(un fuego)* to fire, stoke; *(un anzuelo)* to bait (a hook); FIG. *(fomentar)* to excite, fuel; ARM. to prime; MECH. to start up; ARG., BOL. to prepare, brew (maté) —intr. *(penetrar)* to penetrate, go in; *(agarrar)* to grip, hold fast —reflex. FIG. *(excitarse)* to become excited; *(entregarse)* to devote oneself; C. RICA, MEX. to fail ♦ **c. en** to set upon, vent one's fury on; to rage <*la plaga se cebó en todo el pueblo* the plague raged throughout the town>.

ce·bi·che m. AMER., CUL. raw fish marinated in lemon and garlic.

ce·bo m. *(alimento)* feed, fodder; *(detonador)* fuel, charge; *(del anzuelo)* bait, fish bait; FIG. *(aliciente)* bait, enticement; *(fomento)* food, fuel; ARM. primer ♦ **c. de gelatina** ARM. gelatin primer • **c. fulminante** ARM. blasting *or* percussion cap • **c. vivo** live bait.

ce·bo·lla f. BOT. onion; bulb <*c. de tulipán* tulip bulb>; *(del madero)* core *or* heart of a tree; *(del velón)* oil receptacle (of a lamp); *(filtro)* filter, strainer; C. AMER., COLL. power, command <*agarrar la c.* to seize power> ♦ **c. albarrana** *or* **escila** BOT. squill • **c. escalonia** BOT. shallot.

ce·bo·lli·no m. *(sementero)* onion seed; *(cebollana)* chives ♦ **escardar cebollinos** FIG., COLL. to waste time on trifles • **enviar a uno a escardar cebollinos** FIG., COLL. to tell someone to go jump in a lake.

ce·bón, -bo·na I. adj. fattened II. m.f. fattened animal —m. *(puerco)* fattened hog *or* pig.

ce·bra f. ZOOL. zebra.

ce·bru·no, -na adj. bay, reddish-brown.

ce·bú m. [pl. **-bú·es**] ZOOL. zebu, Asiatic ox.

ce·ca f. royal mint ♦ **ir de la C. a la Meca** FIG., COLL. to go from place to place.

ce·ce·ar intr. to lisp; SP. to pronounce "s" as "th".

ce·ce·o m. *(defecto)* lisp; SP. pronunciation of "s" as "th".

ce·cial m. dried and cured fish.

ce·ci·na f. CUL. cured meat; ARG. jerky, charqui.

ce·ci·nar tr. CUL. to cure (meat).

ce·da f. *(letra)* zee.

ce·da·zo m. CUL. sieve, sifter; *(red)* large fishing net; CUBA a type of waltz ♦ **pasar por c.** to sift.

ce·der tr. *(entregar)* to cede, hand over; *(transferir)* to transfer; *(abandonar)* to abandon, relinquish; SPORT. to pass —intr. to cede; *(rendirse)* to yield, give in *or* up; *(disminuirse)* to diminish, abate <*la fiebre cedía* the fever abated>; *(resultar)* to result, turn out; to be inferior <*no cede a nadie en conocimiento* she is inferior to no one in knowledge> ♦ **c. de** de renounce, give up.

ce·di·lla f. GRAM. cedilla.

ce·di·zo, -za adj. spoiled (food).

ce·dro m. BOT. cedar (tree and wood) ♦ **c. amargo** *or* **blanco** C. RICA white cedar • **c. colorado** red cedar • **c. deodara** *or* **de la India** deodar • **c. de España** savin, Spanish juniper • **c. de Singapur** toon • **c. de las Antillas** Spanish cedar • **c. del Líbano** cedar of Lebanon.

cé·du·la f. *(papeleta)* slip of paper; *(pedazo de pergamino)*

piece of parchment; *(escrito)* certificate, document; *(pagaré)* promissory note ♦ **c. ante diem** summons (to a meeting) • **c. de cambio** COM. bill of exchange, draft • **c. de identidad** identification card *or* papers • **c. en blanco** blank form • **c. real** royal issue • **c. testamentaria** LAW codicil (of a will).

cé·fi·ro m. zephyr.

ce·ga·dor, -do·ra adj. dazzling, blinding.

ce·gar §52 intr. to go blind, lose one's sight —tr. *(quitar la vista)* to blind; FIG. to blind <*el amor le ha cegado el juicio* love has blinded his judgment>; *(tapar)* to obstruct, clog, block —reflex. FIG. to be blinded <*cegarse de ira* to be blinded by anger>.

ce·ga·to, -ta COLL. I. adj. shortsighted, nearsighted II. m.f. shortsighted *or* nearsighted person.

ce·ga·to·so, -sa I. adj. bleary-eyed II. m.f. bleary-eyed person.

ce·gué see **cegar.**

ce·gue·dad f. *(ceguera)* blindness; FIG. *(alucinación)* hallucination.

ce·gue·ra f. *(ceguedad)* blindness; *(inflamación)* type of ophthalmia; FIG. *(turbación)* blindness, obfuscation.

cei·ba f. BOT. ceiba, silk-cotton tree; MARIT. *(alga)* sea moss, alga.

Cei·lán m. Ceylon.

ce·ja f. ANAT. brow, eyebrow; *(saliente)* projection; *(borde)* border, edge; FIG. *(cima)* summit, peak; METEOROL. cloud cover; MUS. *(listón)* bridge; *(cajuela)* capo; BOL., CUBA path, lane ♦ **arquear las cejas** to arch one's eyebrows • **c. de monte** AMER. copse, wooded area • **fruncir las cejas** to knot one's brow, frown • **hasta las cejas** FIG. up to one's neck • **meterse algo entre c. y c.** FIG., COLL. to get something into one's head • **quemarse las cejas** FIG., COLL. to burn the midnight oil • **tener entre c. y c.** FIG., COLL. to look upon with disfavor, hold a grudge against.

ce·jar intr. *(retroceder)* to back up, move backwards; FIG. *(aflojar)* to slacken, relax.

ce·ji·jun·to, -ta adj. *(de cejas juntas)* thick-browed, having eyebrows that meet; *(ceñudo)* frowning, scowling.

ce·jo m. *(niebla)* fog *or* mist (rising from rivers); *(ceño)* ring, hoop; *(atadero de esparto)* cord of esparto grass.

ce·ju·do, -da adj. bushy-browed, thick-browed.

ce·la·da f. *(pieza de armadura)* sallet; *(soldado)* horse soldier with sallet; *(emboscada)* ambush, ambuscade; FIG. *(trampa)* trap, trick; *(asechanza)* snare.

ce·la·dor, -do·ra I. adj. watchful, vigilant II. m.f. *(observador)* watcher; *(en la escuela)* monitor; *(supervisor de prisión)* guard, warden; *(policía)* police officer; *(guardia)* guard, watchman; *(director de museo)* curator; *(conserje)* janitor, maintenance man.

ce·la·je m. *(claraboya)* skylight; FIG. *(presagio)* presage, sign; DOM. REP., PERU, P. RICO ghost ♦ **celajes** *(nubecillas)* swift-moving clouds; MARIT. clouds.

ce·lar[1] tr. *(cumplir)* to comply with, fulfill (laws, duty); *(vigilar)* to watch over, keep an eye on ♦ **c. por** *or* **sobre** to watch out for, take care of.

ce·lar[2] tr. *(ocultar)* to hide, conceal; *(esculpir)* to engrave, carve, sculpt.

cel·da f. cell (of a jail, monastery) ♦ **c. galvánica** galvanic cell.

cel·di·lla f. *(celda pequeña)* cellule; FIG. *(hornacina)* niche, recess (in a wall); BOT., ENTOM. cell.

ce·le·bra·ción f. celebration; *(aclamación)* praise.

ce·le·bran·te adj. I. celebrating II. m.f. participant in a celebration —m. RELIG. celebrant (priest).

ce·le·brar tr. *(conmemorar)* to celebrate; *(alabar)* to extol, praise; *(venerar)* to venerate, respect; to hold, have <*c. una reunión* to hold a meeting>; to reach, conclude <*c. un acuerdo* to reach an agreement>; RELIG. to celebrate *or* say (Mass); CUBA to fall in love with —intr. RELIG. to celebrate *or* say Mass —reflex. to be celebrated *or* fall on <*mi cumpleaños se celebra el dos de octubre* my birthday falls on October 2>; to take place <*la reunión se celebrará el viernes* the meeting will take place on Friday>; CUBA to fall in love.

cé·le·bre adj. *(famoso)* celebrated, famous; COLL. *(gracioso)* funny, witty; AMER. attractive, good-looking.

ce·le·bri·dad f. *(fama)* celebrity, fame, renown; *(persona)* celebrity; *(festival)* festival, celebration.

ce·le·mín m. dry measure equivalent to 4.625 liters.

cé·le·re **I.** adj. prompt, rapid **II.** m.pl. **Céleres** *(cuerpo de caballería)* one of the select three hundred knights of ancient Roman nobility —f.pl. MYTH. the hours.

ce·le·ri·dad f. *(rapidez)* rapidity, swiftness, celerity; *(prontitud)* promptness, dispatch ♦ **con toda c.** as quickly as possible.

ce·les·te **I.** adj. *(del cielo)* celestial, heavenly; *(azul)* sky-blue, azure; HIST. Chinese <*el c. imperio* the Chinese Empire>; MUS. muting or soft (organ pedal) ♦ **cuerpo c.** heavenly body **II.** m. *(color)* sky blue, azure; MUS. celeste, organ stop.

ce·les·tial adj. *(del cielo)* celestial, heavenly; FIG. *(delicioso)* delightful, heavenly; COLL. *(bobo)* silly, stupid.

ce·les·ti·na¹ f. FIG. procuress, madam.

ce·les·ti·na² f. MIN. celestite.

ce·li·ba·to m. *(soltería)* celibacy; COLL. *(soltero)* bachelor, single man.

cé·li·be **I.** adj. celibate, single, unmarried **II.** m.f. celibate, unmarried person.

ce·lo m. *(cuidado)* fervor, diligence; *(entusiasmo)* zeal, ardor; *(envidia)* jealousy, envy; ZOOL. heat ♦ **celos** jealousy • **dar celos** to make jealous or envious • **estar en celo** ZOOL. to be in heat; • **tener celos** to be jealous.

ce·lo·fán m. cellophane.

ce·lo·sí·a f. *(ventana)* lattice window; *(enrejado)* grating, lattice, latticework; *(celos)* jealousy, envy ♦ **c. de ventilación** louver.

ce·lo·so, –sa adj. *(que tiene celos)* jealous, envious; *(suspicaz)* suspicious, mistrustful; *(inspirado)* zealous, enthusiastic; AMER., MARIT. unstable, easily capsized; AMER., ARM. liable to go off, hair-trigger.

ce·lo·ti·pia f. jealousy.

cel·si·tud f. *(elevación)* grandeur, loftiness; *(excelencia)* excellence; *(alteza)* highness.

cel·ta HIST. **I.** adj. Celtic **II.** m.f. *(persona)* Celt —m. *(idioma)* Celtic.

cel·ti·bé·ri·co, –ca or **cel·tí·be·ro, –ra** or **cel·tí·be·ro, –ra** HIST. adj. & m.f. Celtiberian.

cél·ti·co, –ca adj. Celtic.

cel·tis·mo m. Celticism.

cel·tis·ta m.f. Celticist.

cel·to·his·pa·no, –na or **cel·to·his·pá·ni·co, –ca** adj. Celtic-Spanish, Celto-Spanish.

cé·lu·la f. *(celda)* cell; BIOL., ELEC., ZOOL. cell; AER. *(armazón)* airframe; POL. cell <*c. comunista* Communist cell> ♦ **c. embrionaria** or **germen** BACT. germ cell • **c. fotoeléctrica** or **fotoemisora** ELEC., PHOTOG. photoelectric cell, electric eye.

ce·lu·la·do, –da adj. cellular, cell-like.

ce·lu·lar adj. ANAT., BIOL. cellular, cellulous; CRIMIN. celled, having individual cells.

ce·lu·li·tis f. MED. cellulitis.

ce·lu·loi·de m. CHEM. celluloid; CINEM., PHOTOG. *(película)* celluloid, film.

ce·lu·lo·so, –sa **I.** adj. cellulous, cellular **II.** f. BOT. cellulose.

ce·llis·ca f. METEOROL. sleet (storm).

ce·llis·que·ar intr. METEOROL. to sleet.

ce·men·ta·ción f. cementation.

ce·men·tar tr. METAL. to face-harden.

ce·men·te·rio m. cemetery, graveyard, burial ground.

ce·men·to m. CONST. cement; *(hormigón)* concrete; DENT. *(de los dientes)* cementum ♦ **c. armado** CONST. reinforced concrete • **c. de goma** rubber cement • **c. romano** quick-drying cement.

ce·na f. dinner, supper, evening meal ♦ **santa** or **última c.** RELIG. the Last Supper.

ce·na·a·os·cu·ras m.f. FIG., COLL. *(ermitaño)* recluse; *(avaro)* miser, skinflint.

ce·ná·cu·lo m. RELIG. cenacle (room where Christ and his apostles had the Last Supper); *(círculo)* cenacle, coterie.

ce·na·cho m. wicker basket (for fruit or vegetables).

ce·na·dor, –do·ra **I.** adj. pertaining to dinner **II.** m.f. diner —m. *(pabellón)* arbor, bower; *(galería)* loggia or gallery around a courtyard (of houses in Granada).

ce·na·gal m. *(cloaca)* bog, swamp; FIG. *(lío)* jam, mess, fix ♦ **estar metido en un c.** to be in a fix or tight spot.

ce·nar intr. to have dinner or supper, dine, sup —tr. to have (something) for dinner or supper <*cenamos una tortilla* we had an omelet for dinner>.

cen·ce·ño, –ña adj. thin, slender, lean.

cen·ce·rre·ar intr. *(sonar)* to clang or ring bells; MUS., FIG., COLL. *(tocar mal)* to play poorly or out of tune; MECH. *(chirriar)* to rattle, squeak, creak; *(mover un diente)* to play or fidget with a loose tooth.

cen·ce·rre·o m. *(campanilla)* clanging, ringing; *(clamoreo)* row, din; MECH. *(chirrido)* rattling, squeaking, creaking.

cen·ce·rro m. cowbell, bell ♦ **a cencerros tapados** FIG. stealthily, on the sly.

cen·dal m. *(tela)* sendal, sheer silk or linen fabric; *(vestidura sacerdotal)* humeral veil; *(barbas de la pluma)* barbs (of a feather).

ce·ne·fa f. *(borde)* border, edging, trim; *(doselera)* valance; *(volante)* flounce; MARIT. *(madero grueso)* top rim; *(vapor)* paddle-box rim; *(tira de lona)* awning.

ce·ni·ce·ro m. *(platillo)* ashtray; *(cenizal)* ashpit, ashpan.

ce·ni·cien·to, –ta adj. ashen, ashy, ash-gray ♦ **Cenicienta** Cinderella.

ce·nit m. ASTRON. zenith.

ce·ni·za **I.** f. *(polvo)* ash, ashes; *(restos)* ashes, remains; BOT. oidium; PAINT. *(cernada)* priming, sizing; *(pintura)* copper-based paint ♦ **reducir a cenizas** FIG. to reduce to ashes, destroy • **tomar la c.** RELIG. to receive ashes on Ash Wednesday **II.** adj. see **cenizo, –za.**

ce·ni·zo, –za **I.** adj. ashen, ash-colored **II.** m. BOT. goosefoot; *(oídio)* oidium; COLL. *(aguafiestas)* party pooper, killjoy; *(gafe)* jinx ♦ **tener el c.** COLL. to have bad luck, be jinxed —f. see **ceniza.**

ce·no·bi·ta m.f. RELIG. cenobite —m. *(monje)* monk.

ce·no·bí·ti·co, –ca adj. cenobitic, monastic.

ce·no·jil m. garter.

ce·no·ta·fio m. cenotaph (monument honoring a dead person).

ce·no·te m. MEX. natural water well.

cen·sa·ta·rio, –ria m.f. person who pays an annuity out of his estate.

cen·so m. census <*el c. de 1980* the 1980 census>; *(lista)* roll <*c. electoral* electoral roll>; *(renta)* annuity, pension; *(impuesto)* tax; *(arrendamiento)* rental, lease; RELIG. stipend ♦ **levantar el c.** to take a census • **ser un c.** FIG. to be a financial burden, be a drain.

cen·sor m. *(examinador)* censor; *(crítico)* critic, censor; *(en los colegios)* proctor.

cen·so·rio, –ria adj. censorial.

cen·sua·lis·ta m.f. *(rentista)* annuitant; *(alquilador)* lessor.

cen·su·ra f. *(reprobación)* censure; *(examinación de textos)* censorship; *(crítica)* criticism, censure.

cen·su·ra·ble adj. censurable, reprehensible.

cen·su·ra·dor, –do·ra **I.** adj. censorious **II.** m.f. censurer, critic.

cen·su·rar tr. to censor <*c. un texto* to censor a text>; *(reprobar)* to censure, reproach; *(criticar)* to disapprove of, criticize.

cen·tau·ro m. centaur.

cen·ta·vo, –va **I.** adj. hundredth **II.** m. *(centésimo)* hundredth (part); AMER., FIN. cent.

cen·te·lla f. *(rayo)* flash or streak of lightning; *(chispa)* spark; FIG. spark <*una c. de amor* a spark of love>; CHILE, BOT. crowfoot, ranunculus.

cen·te·lle·an·te adj. *(que centellea)* sparkling; *(que destella)* twinkling; *(que chispea)* flickering.

cen·te·lle·ar or **cen·te·llar** intr. *(fulgurar)* to sparkle, glitter; *(destellar)* to twinkle (stars); *(chispear)* to flicker.

cen·te·lle·o m. *(fulgor)* sparkling, glittering; *(destello)* twinkling; *(chispazo)* flickering.

cen·te·na f. (one) hundred.

cen·te·nar m. *(centena)* (one) hundred; *(centenario)* centenary ♦ **a centenares** in hundreds, by the hundreds.

cen·te·na·rio, –ria **I.** adj. centenarian; *(aniversario)* centennial, centenary **II.** m.f. *(viejo)* centenarian —m. *(aniversario)* centennial, centenary.

cen·te·no m. BOT. rye.

cen·te·si·mal adj. centesimal, of or divided into hundredths.

cen·té·si·mo, –ma I. adj. hundredth II. m. hundredth; CHILE, PAR., URUG. centesimo (coin).

cen·tí·gra·do, –da adj. centigrade.

cen·ti·gra·mo m. centigram.

cen·ti·li·tro m. centiliter.

cen·tí·me·tro m. centimeter ♦ **c. cuadrado** square centimeter • **c. cúbico** cubic centimeter.

cén·ti·mo, –ma I. adj. hundredth II. m. FIN. cent.

cen·ti·ne·la m.f. MIL. sentinel, sentry; FIG. (persona que vigila) lookout, sentinel ♦ **estar de c.** MIL. to be on guard, stand sentry • **hacer c.** FIG. to be on the lookout.

cen·to·lla f. ZOOL. spider crab.

cen·tón m. (manta) patchwork quilt; FIG. (obra literaria) cento.

cen·tra·do, –da I. past part. see **centrar** II. adj. centered; FIG. (mesurado) balanced.

cen·tral I. adj. central <oficina c. central office>; (en el centro) centered II. f. (oficina) main office, headquarters; ELEC. power plant; CUBA, PERU sugar mill ♦ **c. de correos** main post office • **c. hidroeléctrica** ELEC. hydroelectric power plant • **c. nuclear** ELEC. nuclear power plant • **c. telefónica** central telephone exchange.

cen·tra·lis·mo m. centralism.

cen·tra·lis·ta adj. & m.f. centralist.

cen·tra·li·ta f. telephone exchange.

cen·tra·li·za·ción f. centralization.

cen·tra·li·zar §04 tr. to centralize —reflex. to be or become centralized.

cen·trar tr. (colocar en el centro) to center; (determinar el centro) to find the center of; (enfocar) to center, focus; (apuntar) to aim, point; CARP. to true; SPORT. to center.

cén·tri·co, –ca adj. central, centric.

cen·tri·fu·ga·do·ra f. centrifuge.

cen·tri·fu·gar §47 tr. to centrifuge.

cen·trí·fu·go, –ga adj. centrifugal.

cen·trí·pe·to, –ta adj. centripetal.

cen·tris·mo m. POL. centrism.

cen·tris·ta POL. adj. & m.f. centrist.

cen·tro m. (punto) center; (medio) middle, midst <en el c. de la muchedumbre in the middle of the crowd>; headquarters <c. administrativo administrative headquarters>; club, center <c. social community center>; FIG. (núcleo) core, heart; (fin) objective, goal; (ciudad) downtown, center city; SPORT. center; CUBA center; ECUAD. short flannel skirt; BOL., COL. underskirt; GUAT., PAN. vest ♦ **c. comercial** shopping center • **c. de atracción** or **gravitación** ASTRON. center of attraction • **c. de gravedad** PHYS. center of gravity • **c. de masa** PHYS. center of mass • **c. de mesa** centerpiece • **c. demográfico** center of population • **c. nervioso** ANAT. nerve center • **c. turístico** tourist center • **estar en su c.** FIG., COLL. to be in one's element.

Centro América or **Cen·tro·a·mé·ri·ca** f. Central America.

cen·tro·a·me·ri·ca·no, –na adj. & m.f. Central American.

cen·tu·pli·car §70 tr. (hace cien veces mayor) centuple, to multiply a hundredfold; (multiplicar por ciento) to centuplicate, multiply by one hundred.

cén·tu·plo, –pla I. adj. centuple, hundredfold II. m.f. hundredfold.

cen·tu·rión m. HIST. centurion (commanding officer in Roman times).

ce·ñi·dor m. sash, waistband.

ce·ñir §59 tr. (rodear) to encircle, put around; (atar) to bind, restrain <le ciñeron con cadenas they bound him with chains>; to fit tightly, be tight on <el cinturón le ciñe the belt is tight on him>; FIG. (abreviar) to condense, shorten ♦ **c. el viento** MARIT. to sail close to the wind —reflex. (moderarse) to hold oneself in check, limit oneself; FIG. to adjust, conform <ceñirse a un trabajo to adjust to a job> ♦ **ceñirse al tema** to stick to the subject • **ceñirse la espada** to buckle or gird one's sword.

ce·ño m. (gesto) frown, scowl; FIG. (aspecto amenazador) threatening appearance <el c. del cielo the threatening appearance of the sky> ♦ **arrugar** or **fruncir el c.** to frown, knit one's brow.

ce·ño·so, –sa or **ce·ñu·do, –da** adj. (desabrido) frowning, scowling; FIG. (amenazador) threatening.

ce·pa f. BOT. stump (of a tree); (tronco de la vid) rootstalk; (vid) vine, stock; FIG. (linaje) stock, origin; ARCHIT. pier, pillar; METEOROL. nucleus of a cloud formation; GUAT., HOND., P. RICO group of trees or plants having a common root; MEX. pit, hole ♦ **c. caballo** BOT. carline thistle • **c. virgen** BOT. vine-like plant • **de buena c.** FIG. of good stock • **de pura c.** FIG. genuine, authentic.

ce·pi·lla·do m. or **ce·pi·lla·du·ra** f. CARP. planing.

ce·pi·llar tr. (limpiar) to brush; CARP. to plane; COLL. (robar) to rob, clean out; FIG. (adular) to flatter, butter up —reflex. COLL. (suspender) to fail; (matar) to kill, rub out; (acabar) to polish off, finish.

ce·pi·llo m. (limpiadera) brush; (arquilla) alms or poor box; CARP. plane; C. RICA, COLL. flatterer ♦ **c. biselador** CARP. chamfer plane • **c. bocel** CARP. fluting plane • **c. de achaflanar** CARP. bevel plane • **c. de dientes** toothbrush • **c. mecánico** CARP. planer, jointer • **c. para el pelo** hairbrush • **c. para el suelo** scrub brush • **c. para la ropa** clothes brush • **c. para las uñas** nailbrush • **c. universal** CARP. jointing plane.

ce·po m. BOT. branch, bough; (del yunque) base of an anvil; (del reo) pillory, stocks; (para la seda) reel (for winding silk); (armadijo) trap, snare; (de limosnas) alms or collection box; TECH. (para sujetar) clamp, clasp; ARCHIT. pile; ARM. stock (of a gun); MARIT. anchor stock ♦ **caer en el c.** FIG. to fall into the trap.

ce·ra f. wax <c. blanca bleached wax>; (de los oídos) earwax, cerumen; (de lustrar) polish; AMER. candle; CUBA, BOT. liana ♦ **c. aleda** ENTOM. bee glue, propolis • **c. amarilla** ENTOM. yellow wax • **c. toral** unbleached wax • **c. vana** or **virgen** virgin wax • **ceras** ENTOM. honeycomb • **sacar c.** VEN. (alejarse) to stay away from; (obtener una ganga) to get a bargain • **ser una c.** FIG., COLL. to be pliable or docile.

ce·rá·mi·co, –ca I. adj. ceramic II. f. ceramics, pottery.

cer·ba·ta·na f. (bodoquera) blowpipe, blowgun; (trompetilla para los sordos) ear trumpet.

cer·ca¹ f. (barrera) fence, wall; MIL. square (formation) ♦ **c. alambrada** wire fence • **c. viva** hedge.

cer·ca² I. adv. nearby, close by <el museo está c. the museum is nearby> ♦ **c. de** near, close to <vivían c. del mar they lived near the sea>; about <hay c. de cien hombres aquí there are about one hundred men here>; POL. to <el embajador c. de las Naciones Unidas the ambassador to the United Nations> • **de c.** from a short distance, closely <le perseguían de c. they pursued him closely> II. m.pl. **cercas** PAINT. objects in the foreground —f. see **cerca¹**.

cer·ca·do I. past part. see **cercar** II. m. (huerto) enclosed or fenced-in garden; (valla) fence, wall; PERU (distrito) district, territorial division.

cer·ca·ní·a f. nearness, proximity ♦ **cercanías** outskirts, suburbs.

cer·ca·no, –na adj. (próximo) near, close; (vecino) neighboring, nearby; FIG. (inminente) impending ♦ **Cercano Oriente** Near East.

cer·car §70 tr. (rodear con cerco) to fence or wall in, enclose; MIL. (asediar) to besiege, lay siege to; (rodear) to surround, encircle.

cer·cén or **cer·cen** adv. ♦ **a c.** completely, all around.

cer·ce·na·du·ra f. or **cer·ce·na·mien·to** m. (cortadura) cutting, trimming; (mondadura) paring; (reducción) curtailment, reduction.

cer·ce·nar tr. (cortar) to cut, trim; (disminuir) to cut down, reduce; (abreviar) to shorten, abridge; (amputar) to amputate, cut off.

cer·cio·rar tr. to assure —reflex. to ascertain, make sure ♦ **cerciorarse de** to make sure of, find out about.

cer·co m. (círculo) circle, ring; (de un tonel) hoop, ring (of a barrel); TECH. rim; MIL. siege; (borde) edge, border; (corrillo) circle, social group; (giro) gyration; RELIG. halo; ASTRON., METEOROL. corona, halo; ARCHIT. frame; AMER. (seto) hedge; (cercado) enclosure; PERU small walled property ♦ **c. policíaco** police cordon or line • **en c.** round about • **levantar** or **alzar un c.** MIL. to raise or end a siege • **poner c. a** to besiege, lay siege to • **saltar el c.** ARG., POL. to change sides.

cer·cha f. (patrón) curved template; ARCHIT. (aro de hierro) truss; (regla plana) flexible rule for measuring curved surfaces; CARP. *(segmento)* segment of a rim; MARIT. *(rueda del timón)* outer rim (of a steering wheel); CUBA rod, rib.

cer·da f. horsehair, bristle; ZOOL. sow; *(lazo)* snare, noose; VEN. bargain; COL. track, path.

cer·da·da f. COLL. dirty *or* lousy trick.

cer·de·ar intr. *(flaquear un animal)* to become weak in the forelegs (animals); *(sonar desagradablemente)* to screech (a stringed instrument); FIG., COLL. *(hacer algo sucio)* to do something filthy; *(resistirse a hacer algo)* to refuse *or* decline to do something; ARG., URUG. to cut a horse's mane.

Cer·de·ña f. Sardinia.

cer·do m. ZOOL. pig; FIG., COLL. *(hombre sucio)* pig, slob ♦ **carne de c.** pork • **c. marino** ZOOL. porpoise.

ce·re·al adj. & m. cereal ♦ **cereales** cereals, grain.

ce·re·be·lo m. ANAT. cerebellum.

ce·re·bral adj. cerebral.

ce·re·bro m. ANAT. brain, cerebrum; FIG. *(inteligencia)* brains, intelligence ♦ **c. electrónico** electronic brain.

ce·re·mo·nia f. *(rito)* ceremony; RELIG. ceremony, service; *(aparato)* ceremony, pomp; *(cumplido)* affected gesture *or* compliment ♦ **con c.** ceremoniously • **de c.** formal, ceremonious • **guardar c.** to observe formalities • **hacer ceremonias** to stand on ceremony • **por c.** as a matter of form.

ce·re·mo·nial I. adj. ceremonial II. m. ceremonial; RELIG. *(libro)* book of ceremonies.

ce·re·mo·niá·ti·co, -ca adj. very ceremonious.

ce·re·mo·nio·so, -sa adj. *(afectado)* ceremonious; formal *<una recepción c.* a formal reception>.

ce·re·rí·a f. *(negocio)* candlemaker's shop; *(oficio)* candle-maker's trade.

ce·re·za f. BOT. cherry; *(color)* cerise, cherry; AMER., BOT. husk of coffee bean ♦ **c. gordal** *or* **garrafal** BOT. white heart cherry • **c. pasa** dried cherry • **c. póntica** BOT. sour cherry • **c. silvestre** BOT. wild cherry.

ce·re·zo m. BOT. cherry (tree and wood).

ce·ri·lla f. *(vela)* wax taper; *(fósforo)* match; ANAT. *(de los oídos)* earwax.

ce·ri·lle·ra f. *or* **ce·ri·lle·ro** m. *(caja)* matchbox; *(vendedor)* match vendor.

ce·ri·llo m. BOT. soapberry tree; AMER. *(fósforo)* match.

ce·ri·na f. *(cera del alcornoque)* cerin (from the cork tree); MIN. cirium silicate; CHEM. substance obtained from white wax.

ce·rio m. CHEM. cerium.

cer·na·da f. *(escabrillo)* cinder; *(aparejo)* priming, sizing; VET. poultice; BOL. vomitive, emetic.

cer·na·de·ro m. *(lienzo grueso)* leach of coarse cloth; *(lienzo fino)* linen *or* silk fabric.

cer·ne·dor, –do·ra m.f. *(persona)* sifter —m. *(cedazo)* sifter, sieve.

cer·ner §50 tr. *(tamizar)* to sift, sieve; FIG. *(observar)* to scan, keep an eye on; *(depurar)* to clarify, distill *<c. las ideas* to distill one's ideas> —intr. BOT. to bud, blossom; METEOROL. to drizzle —reflex. *(caminar)* to sway one's hips, waddle; ORNITH. to hover, soar; FIG. to hang, loom *<la posibilidad de derroto se cernía sobre la tropa* the possibility of defeat hung over the troops>.

cer·ní·ca·lo m. ORNITH. kestrel, sparrow hawk; FIG., COLL. *(hombre ignorante)* lout, brute; SL. *(borrachera)* drunken spree.

cer·ni·do m. *(acción de cerner)* sifting; *(harina)* sifted flour.

cer·ni·dor m. sieve.

cer·ni·du·ra f. *(cernido)* sifting ♦ **cerniduras** *(cribaduras)* dregs of flour (after sifting).

cer·nir §25 tr. to sift, sieve.

ce·ro m. zero ♦ **c. absoluto** PHYS. absolute zero • **ser un c. a la izquierda** FIG., COLL. to be totally useless.

ce·ro·llo, –lla adj. AGR. reaped while still green.

ce·ro·so, –sa adj. *(parecido a la cera)* waxy; MEX. soft *<huevo c.* soft-boiled egg>.

ce·ro·te m. *(de zapatero)* cobbler's wax; FIG., COLL. *(miedo)* fear; BOL. wax taper.

cer·qué, cerque see **cercar**.

cer·qui·llo m. *(de un monje)* tonsure; ARG., MEX. bangs (hair).

ce·rra·de·ro, –ra I. adj. closing, shutting II. m. *(de cerra-*

dura) catch, staple (of a bolt); *(de bolsa)* drawstrings, purse strings.

ce·rra·do, –da I. past part. see **cerrar** II. adj. closed *<boca c.* closed mouth>; FIG. *(obscuro)* obscure, incomprehensible; *(nublado)* overcast, cloudy; COLL. *(callado)* quiet, reserved; *(torpe)* dense, stupid; *(con acento regional)* heavily accented; thick, full *<barba c.* full beard>; PHONET. closed; ARG., PERU obstinate, stubborn ♦ **a puerta c.** behind closed doors • **c. de mollera** COLL. stupid, dense III. m. fenced-in garden.

ce·rra·dor, –do·ra I. adj. closing II. m. *(pestillo)* bolt, latch; *(cerradura)* lock.

ce·rra·du·ra f. *(acción)* closing, shutting; *(aparato)* lock ♦ **c. de cilindros** cylinder lock • **c. de combinación** combination lock • **c. de golpe** *or* **de muelle** spring lock • **c. de seguridad** safety lock • **c. embutida** mortise lock.

ce·rra·ja f. *(mecanismo)* lock; BOT. sow thistle.

ce·rra·je·rí·a f. *(oficio)* locksmith's trade; *(taller)* locksmith shop.

ce·rra·je·ro m. locksmith.

ce·rra·jón m. steep cliff.

ce·rrar §49 tr. to close, shut *<¡cierre la puerta!* close the door!>; *(echar el cerrojo a)* to bolt; *(doblar)* to close up *<cerró el paraguas* he closed up his umbrella>; *(cercar)* to enclose, close in; *(tapar)* to fill in *<c. un agujero* to fill in a hole>; to seal (up) *<c. un paquete* to seal a package>; to close down *<van a c. la fábrica* they are going to close down the factory>; to turn off *<cerró la llave del agua* I turned off the faucet>; to bring up the rear of *<los niños cerraban la procesión* the children brought up the rear of the procession>; FIG. to block off, close off *<el ejército cerró el camino* the army closed off the road>; *(concluir)* to close, conclude *<c. un debate* to conclude a debate>; to close out *<c. una cuenta* to close out an account>; MIL. to close *<c. filas* to close ranks> ♦ **c. con llave** to lock • **c. la boca** to be quiet • **c. los oídos a** FIG. to turn a deaf ear to • **c. los ojos** FIG. to die • **c. los puños** to clench one's fists —intr. to close, shut *<esta puerta no cierra bien* this door does not shut properly>; to set in, close in *<cierra la noche* night is setting in>; MED. to close up, heal *<está cerrando la llaga* the wound is healing> —reflex. to close, shut; FIG. *(insistir)* to persist, insist *<se cierran en hablar de sí mismos* they persist in talking about themselves>; MED. to close up, heal; MIL. to close ranks; METEOROL. to cloud over ♦ **cerrársele todas las puertas** FIG. to find all avenues blocked.

ce·rra·zón f. *(cielo)* dark *or* overcast sky; FIG. *(torpeza)* denseness, slowness; COL. spur (of a mountain range).

ce·rre·ro, –ra adj. *(que anda libre)* wandering, roaming; *(cerril)* wild, untamed; AMER., FIG. *(bruto)* rough, coarse; VEN. bitter *<café c.* bitter coffee>.

ce·rril adj. *(áspero)* rough, uneven (ground); *(salvaje)* wild, untamed (animal); FIG. *(obstinado)* stubborn, obstinate; COLL. *(bruto)* rough, uncouth.

ce·rro[1] m. *(colina)* hill; ZOOL. *(cuello)* neck; *(espinazo)* backbone ♦ **andar por los cerros de Úbeda** FIG., COLL. to go off on a tangent, stray from the point • **en c.** EQUIT. bareback.

ce·rro[2] m. bundle of dressed hemp *or* flax.

ce·rro·jo m. *(pestillo)* bolt, latch; ARM. bolt (of a gun); SPORT. stonewalling, blanket defense.

cer·te·ro, –ra adj. *(diestro)* accurate, skillful; *(sabedor)* well-informed, knowledgeable; accurate, good *<él es un tirador c.* he is a good shot>.

cer·te·za *or* **cer·ti·dum·bre** f. certainty, certitude.

cer·ti·fi·ca·ción f. *(acción)* certification; *(certificado)* certificate; *(de cartas)* registration (of mail).

cer·ti·fi·ca·do, –da I. past part. see **certificar** II. adj. certified; *(cartas)* registered (mail) III. m. certificate ♦ **c. de acciones** COM. stock certificate • **c. de defunción** death certificate • **c. de penales** police record • **c. de vacuna** vaccination certificate • **c. médico** medical certificate.

cer·ti·fi·ca·dor, –do·ra I. adj. certifying II. m.f. certifier.

cer·ti·fi·car §70 tr. *(verificar)* to certify, attest; *(cartas)* to register (mail).

cer·ti·fi·ca·ti·vo, -va *or* **cer·ti·fi·ca·to·rio, -ria** adj. certifying.

cer·ti·tud f. certainty, certitude.
ce·rú·le·o, –a adj. cerulean, sky-blue.
ce·ru·men m. ANAT. earwax.
ce·ru·mi·no·so, –sa adj. *(del cerumen)* ceruminous; *(parecido a la cera)* waxy.
cer·val adj. deer-like, cervine ◆ **tener un miedo c.** to be scared stiff.
cer·van·tes·co, –ca adj. Cervantine, of Cervantes <*la crítica c.* Cervantine criticism>.
cer·van·tis·ta m.f. Cervantes scholar, specialist in Cervantes.
cer·ve·ce·rí·a f. *(fábrica)* brewery; *(taverna)* bar, pub.
cer·ve·za f. beer, ale ◆ **c. de barril** *or* **al grifo** draft beer • **c. negra** dark beer.
cer·vi·cal adj. ANAT. cervical.
cer·viz f. [pl. -**vi·ces**] ANAT. cervix, nape ◆ **de dura c.** stubborn, headstrong • **doblar** *or* **bajar la c.** FIG. to submit, humble oneself • **levantar la c.** FIG. to lift up one's head, become proud.
ce·sa·ción f. cessation, discontinuance.
ce·sa·mien·to m. cessation, suspension.
ce·san·te I. adj. jobless, unemployed ◆ **dejar c. (a alguien)** to dismiss (someone) II. m.f. unemployed *or* jobless person.
ce·san·tí·a f. suspension; *(desempleo)* unemployment.
ce·sar intr. *(terminar)* to end, stop <*cesó toda conversación* all conversation stopped>; *(dejar de)* to cease, stop <*cesaron de llorar* they stopped crying>; *(dimitir)* to leave, quit —tr. to fire, dismiss ◆ **sin c.** unceasingly, without stopping.
ce·sá·re·a adj. & f. MED. Caesarean section.
ce·sá·re·o, –a adj. Caesarean, imperial.
ce·se m. COM. order for suspension (of payments); *(suspensión)* cessation, suspension; *(revocación de un funcionario)* dismissal; *(de un empleado)* firing, dismissal ◆ **c. de fuego** *or* **hostilidades** cease-fire.
ce·si·ble adj. LAW transferable, assignable.
ce·sio m. CHEM. cesium.
ce·sión f. cession, surrender <*c. de territorios* surrender of territories; LAW *(transmisión)* transfer, cession ◆ **c. de bienes** LAW surrender of property.
ce·sio·na·rio, –ria m.f. LAW cessionary, transferee.
ce·sio·nis·ta m.f. COM., LAW transferor, assignor.
cés·ped m. *(prado)* lawn, grass; *(gallón)* sod, turf; SPORT. *(campo de deportes)* field.
ces·pi·tar intr. to hesitate, vacillate.
ces·ta f. basket; *(cestada)* basketful; *(cochecillo)* wicker cart; SPORT. *(pala)* jai alai racket; SPORT. *(baloncesto)* basket ◆ **c. de costura** sewing basket • **c. de la compra** shopping basket • **c. para papeles** wastepaper basket • **llevar la c.** COLL. *(acompañar)* to chaperon; VULG. *(procurar)* to pimp, procure.
ces·to m. *(cesta)* hamper, large basket; *(guante romano)* cestus ◆ **c. de** *or* **para papeles** wastepaper basket.
ces·tón m. *(cesto grande)* large basket *or* pannier; MIL. *(gavión)* gabion.
ce·tá·ce·o m. ZOOL. cetacean ◆ **cetáceos** Cetacea.
ce·ti·na f. cetene, spermaceti.
ce·tre·rí·a f. falconry, hawking.
ce·tre·ro, –ra I. adj. of falconry II. m. RELIG. *(sacerdote)* verger; *(cazador)* falconer.
ce·tri·no, –na adj. *(verdoso amarillento)* sallow, olive (complexion); *(color)* citron, greenish-yellow; FIG. *(melancólico)* melancholy, dispirited.
ce·tro m. *(bastón de mando)* scepter; RELIG. rod, staff; *(para pájaros)* perch; FIG. *(reinado)* dominion, rule; *(superioridad)* power, sovereignty ◆ **c. de bufón** fool's scepter • **empuñar el c.** to ascend to the throne; FIG. to take command of things.
cia·na·to m. CHEM. cyanate.
cia·no·sis f. MED. cyanosis.
cia·nu·ra·ción f. METAL. cyanidation, cyaniding.
cia·nu·ro m. CHEM. cyanide ◆ **c. de potasio** CHEM. potassium cyanide.
ciar §30 intr. *(retroceder)* to back up, go backwards; MARIT. *(remar)* to back water, back the oars; FIG. *(ceder)* to back down, back out ◆ **c. en sus pretensiones** to give up *or* drop one's claims.

ciá·ti·co, –ca I. adj. MED., ANAT. sciatic II. f. MED. sciatica, lumbago.
ci·be·li·na f. ZOOL. sable.
ci·be·ra I. adj. feeding II. f. *(de un molino)* load, primer (of a mill); *(grano alimenticio)* feed, fodder; *(residuos)* marc, residue (of pressed fruit, grain).
ci·ber·né·ti·ca f. cybernetics.
ci·bi·ca f. *(barreta de hierro)* clout, iron plate (nailed to wooden axle tree); MARIT. staple, clamp.
ci·bo·lo m. ZOOL. bison.
ci·bo·rio m. RELIG. *(baldaquino)* ciborium (altar canopy); *(copa)* ciborium (goblet).
ci·ca·te·ar intr. COLL. to be stingy, miserly, *or* mean.
ci·ca·te·rí·a f. stinginess, miserliness.
ci·ca·te·ro, –ra I. adj. stingy, miserly II. m.f. miser, skinflint.
ci·ca·tri·cé, cicatrice see cicatrizar.
ci·ca·triz f. [pl. -**tri·ces**] MED. scar, cicatrix; FIG. scar <*la experiencia le dejó con cicatrices emocionales* the experience left him with emotional scars>.
ci·ca·tri·za·ción f. MED. healing, cicatrization.
ci·ca·tri·zan·te MED. I. adj. healing, cicatricial II. m. healing agent, cicatrizant.
ci·ca·tri·zar §04 tr. & intr. MED. to heal, cicatrize.
ci·ce·ro·ne m. guide, cicerone.
cí·cli·co, –ca adj. cyclical, cyclic.
ci·clis·mo m. SPORT. cycling; *(carrera)* cycle racing.
ci·clis·ta I. adj. cycling, cycle II. m.f. cyclist.
ci·clo m. *(serie)* cycle, series ◆ **c. de conferencias** a series of lectures>; LIT. cycle <*c. troyano* Trojan cycle>; AMER. studies, course <*un c. universitario* a university course> ◆ **c. lunar** lunar cycle • **c. solar** solar cycle.
ci·cloi·de f. GEOM. cycloid.
ci·clo·mo·tor m. moped, motorbike.
ci·clón m. cyclone ◆ **entrar como un c.** to burst in.
ci·clo·pe m. MYTH. Cyclops.
ci·cló·pe·o, –a adj. cyclopean, huge.
ci·clo·sti·lo m. cyclostyle (duplicating machine).
ci·clo·ti·mia f. MED. cyclothymia.
ci·clo·trón m. PHYS. cyclotron.
ci·cu·ta f. BOT. hemlock.
cid m. FIG. brave man, valiant man.
ci·dra f. BOT. citron (fruit).
cie·go, –ga I. adj. *(privado de la vista)* blind; FIG. *(enloquecido)* blind <*c. de rabia* blind with rage>; *(atascado)* blocked, stopped-up <*una cañería c.* a stopped-up pipe>; CUL. without holes (bread, cheese) ◆ **c. como un topo** blind as a bat II. m.f. blind person —m. ANAT. caecum, blind gut; CUL. *(morcilla)* blood pudding *or* sausage; FIG. *(hacienda)* country house; ARG., PERU, URUG. loser (at cards); CUBA hilly plot of land; ECUAD., ICHTH. river fish ◆ **a ciegas** blindly; FIG. *(sin reflexión)* thoughtlessly, carelessly • **andar a ciegas** to grope one's way • **los ciegos** the blind, blind people • **quedar c.** to go blind.
cie·go, ciegue see cegar.
cie·lo m. sky; *(atmósfera)* atmosphere; *(paraíso)* heaven; FIG. *(la Providencia)* Heaven; *(parte superior)* top; COLL. *(querido)* dear, darling ◆ **a c. abierto** *or* **a c. raso** out in the open, in the open air • **bajado del c.** FIG., COLL. wonderful, excellent • **caído** *or* **llovido del c.** FIG., COLL. heaven-sent • **cerrarse el c.** to cloud up • **cerrársele el cielo a uno** FIG., COLL. to have no way out • **c. de la boca** ANAT. palate, roof of the mouth • **c. de la cama** canopy (of a bed) • **c. máximo** AVIA. ceiling • **c. raso** ARCHIT. ceiling • **¡cielos!** good heavens! • **escupir al c.** FIG. to spit into the wind • **ganarse el c.** FIG. to go to heaven • **juntarse el c. con la tierra** COLL. to be in big trouble • **medio c.** ASTRON. meridian • **mover c. y tierra** FIG., COLL. to move heaven and earth • **poner por los cielos** FIG. to praise to the skies • **tomar el c. con las manos** FIG., COLL. to hit the roof • **venirse el c. abajo** FIG., COLL. *(llover)* to rain cats and dogs; *(arruinarse)* to have no way out • **ver el c. abierto** FIG., COLL. to see a way out.
ciem·piés m. [pl. -**piés**] ENTOM. centipede; FIG., COLL. *(necedad)* incoherent *or* nonsensical act.
cien §G21 adj. [contr. of **ciento** used before nouns and numerals] a hundred, one hundred <*c. casas* a hundred houses> ◆ **c. mil** one hundred thousand.

cié·na·ga f. swamp, marsh.

cien·cia f. science; FIG. *(erudición)* erudition, knowledge; *(habilidad)* skill, art ♦ **a** or **de c. cierta** for certain, with complete certainty • **a c. y paciencia** with sufferance, with someone's knowledge and permission • **c. del hogar** home economics • **c. ficción** science fiction • **c. infusa** RELIG. intuition • **ciencias exactas** exact sciences • **ciencias naturales** natural sciences • **ciencias ocultas** occult sciences • **gaya c.** the art of poetry.

cie·no m. mire, muck.

cien·tí·fi·co, –ca I. adj. scientific II. m.f. scientist.

cien·to §G17, 21 I. adj. a hundred, one hundred <*c. coches* a hundred cars>; *(centésimo)* hundredth II. m. one hundred, a hundred <*naranjas se venden por veinte pesos el c.* oranges sell at twenty pesos the hundred> ♦ **c. por c.** FIG. completely, one hundred per cent • **el c. y la madre** FIG., COLL. too many people • **por c.** per cent <*treinta por c.* thirty per cent>.

cier·na, cierno see **cerner** or **cernir**.

cier·ne m. BOT. budding, blossoming ♦ **en c.** BOT. in bud or blossom; FIG. *(principiante)* just beginning, in infancy.

cie·rre m. *(acción)* closing, shutting; *(cerradura)* lock, seal; COM. *(clausura)* shutdown; JOURN. deadline; MEX. zipper ♦ **c. de cremallera** zipper • **c. hermético** hermetic seal • **c. metálico** iron grating (used to close stores) • **c. patronal** COM. lockout • **c. relámpago** ARG., PAR., URUG. zipper.

cie·rre, cie·rro see **cerrar**.

cier·to, –ta §G17 I. adj. *(seguro)* certain, sure <*estamos ciertos de la fecha* we are sure of the date>; *(determinado)* certain, definite <*nos reuniremos a c. hora* we will meet at a definite hour>; *(verdadero)* true <*eso no es c.* that is not true>; *(alguno)* certain, some <*ciertos pintores* some painters>; *(asegurado)* certain, assured <*nuestra victoria es c.* our victory is assured> II. adv. certainly, of course ♦ **de c.** certainly, for certain • **estar en lo c.** to be right • **lo c. es que** the fact is that • **por c.** *(a propósito)* by the way, incidentally; *(ciertamente)* certainly • **por c. que** of course.

cier·vo m. ZOOL. deer; *(macho)* stag, hart ♦ **c. común** red deer • **c. volante** ENTOM. stag beetle.

cier·zo m. north wind.

ci·fra f. *(número)* numeral <*c. romana* Roman numeral>; figure, digit <*número de cuatro cifras* a four-digit number>; *(cantidad)* quantity, amount; *(total)* sum (total); *(clave)* code, cipher; *(monograma)* monogram, initials; *(abreviatura)* abbreviation; FIG. *(compendio)* compendium, summary ♦ **en c.** *(secretamente)* in code; *(en compendio)* in brief, concisely.

ci·frar tr. *(escribir en cifra)* to encode, encipher; FIG. *(compendiar)* to summarize, condense ♦ **c. en** FIG. to place in <*cifra la felicidad en el dinero* he places happiness in money> —reflex. to be summarized or condensed ♦ **cifrarse en** to amount or come to.

ci·ga·rra f. ENTOM. cicada.

ci·ga·rre·ra f. *(caja)* cigar box or case; *(petaca)* tobacco pouch.

ci·ga·rre·rí·a f. AMER. tobacco or smoke shop.

ci·ga·rri·llo m. cigarette.

ci·ga·rro m. cigar <*c. habano* Cuban cigar>; *(pitillo)* cigarette; ECUAD., ENTOM. dragonfly ♦ **c. puro** cigar • **c. de papel** cigarette.

ci·go·ñi·no m. ORINTH. young stork.

ci·go·to m. BIOL. zygote, fertilized egg.

ci·gua·to, –ta I. adj. jaundiced, suffering from food poisoning II. m.f. *(el que padece ciguatera)* one suffering from food poisoning; *(simple)* simpleton, fool; MEX., VEN. *(pálido)* anemic person.

ci·güe·ña f. ORNITH. stork; *(de una campana)* yoke (of a bell); *(manubrio)* winch, crank; HOND. barrel organ.

ci·güe·ñal m. MECH. crank, winch; *(de un motor)* crankshaft.

ci·lan·tro m. BOT. coriander.

ci·lia·do, –da I. adj. BIOL. ciliated II. m.pl. **ciliados** ZOOL. ciliates.

ci·liar adj. ANAT. ciliary.

ci·lin·dra·da f. MECH. cylinder capacity.

ci·lin·drar tr. *(comprimir)* to calender, press; *(carreteras)* to roll, steamroller.

ci·lín·dri·co, –ca adj. cylindrical, cylindric.

ci·lin·dro m. GEOM. cylinder; *(rodillo)* roller; COLL. *(sombrero)* top hat; MEX. barrel organ ♦ **c. compresor** or **de caminos** steamroller • **c. maestro** AUTO. master cylinder.

ci·lio m. BIOL. cilium.

ci·lla f. AGR. *(granero)* granary; *(renta)* tithe.

ci·lle·ri·zo m. granary keeper.

ci·lle·ro m. *(cillerizo)* granary keeper; *(despensa)* storeroom, cellar; *(granero)* granary.

ci·ma f. *(cumbre)* summit, peak, top; FIG. *(colmo)* height, pinnacle; *(remate)* end; BOT. *(tallo)* stalk, stem; *(inflorescencia)* cyme ♦ **dar c. a** to finish off or up, complete • **por c.** on top; *(superficialmente)* superficially, cursorily.

ci·ma·rrón, –rro·na I. adj. AMER. *(fugitivo)* runaway, fugitive; BOT., ZOOL. wild; CHILE lazy II. m.f. *(fugitivo)* runaway or fugitive slave; *(marinero)* lazy sailor.

ci·ma·rro·ne·ar intr. AMER. *(huir)* to run away, escape; ARG. *(tomar mate)* to drink unsweetened maté.

cim·ba·le·ro or **cim·ba·lis·ta** m. MUS. cymbalist.

cím·ba·los m.pl. MUS. cymbals.

cim·bel m. *(cordel)* rope used to tie decoys; *(señuelo)* decoy bird; FIG. *(aliciente)* lure, enticement; FIG., COLL. *(soplón)* tattletale, telltale; *(informador)* informer, squealer.

cim·bra f. ARCHIT. *(armazón)* form, centering (of arch or vault); MARIT. *(curvatura)* curvature (of boards); ARG., PAR. *(trampa)* trap (for birds).

cim·brar tr. *(vibrar)* to vibrate, shake; FIG., COLL. *(golpear)* to bash, beat; ARCHIT. *(colocar)* to put or erect the centering for (an arch) —reflex. to sway, swing.

cim·bre·ar tr. & reflex. var. of **cimbrar**.

cim·bre·ño, –ña adj. *(flexible)* flexible, pliable; COLL., FIG. *(juncal)* willowy, supple <*talle c.* willowy figure>.

cim·bre·o m. *(doblamiento)* bending; *(temblor)* shaking, quivering; *(oscilación)* swaying, swinging.

cim·bro·na·zo m. *(cintarazo)* blow with the flat of a sword; AMER. *(estremecimiento nervioso)* strong nervous convulsion; VEN. *(temblor de tierra)* earthquake.

ci·men·ta·ción f. *(acción)* laying of foundations; *(cimiento)* foundation.

ci·men·tar §49 tr. CONSTR. to lay the foundation of; FIG. *(fundar)* to establish, found <*c. una civilización* to establish a civilization>; *(afirmar)* to strengthen, consolidate <*c. el movimiento feminista* to consolidate the feminist movement>; METAL. to refine (gold); METAL. to face-harden.

ci·men·to m. var. of **cimiento**.

ci·me·ra I. f. *(del casco)* crest (of helmet); HER. *(del escudo)* crest (of coat of arms) II. adj. see **cimero, –ra**.

ci·me·ro, –ra I. adj. *(en alto)* uppermost, top; FIG. *(eximio)* renowned, eminent II. f. see **cimera**.

ci·mien·te, cimiento see **cimentar**.

ci·mien·to m. CONSTR. foundation; FIG. *(origen)* source, origin ♦ **abrir los cimientos** to dig the foundation • **c. real** METAL. compound for purifying gold • **c. romano** AMER. hydraulic lime • **cimientos** CONSTR. foundations; FIG. *(fundamentos)* fundamentals • **desde los cimientos** FIG. from the very start • **echar los cimientos** to lay the foundation.

ci·mi·ta·rra f. scimitar.

cinc m. CHEM. zinc.

cin·cel m. chisel.

cin·ce·lar tr. to chisel, carve (with a chisel).

cin·co I. adj. five <*tengo c. hermanos* I have five brothers>; *(quinto)* fifth ♦ **las c.** five o'clock II. m. *(número)* five; AMER. guitarra five-string guitar; *(moneda)* five-cent piece; MEX., COLL. bottom, backside ♦ **decir cuántos son c.** COLL. to tell off • **estar sin un c.** to be broke • **saber cuántos son c.** COLL. to know what's what.

cin·cuen·ta I. adj. fifty <*hay c. estados en los Estados Unidos* there are fifty states in the United States>; *(quincuagésimo)* fiftieth II. m. fifty.

cin·cuen·ta·vo, –va adj. & m.f. fiftieth.

cin·cuen·te·na I. f. fifty, group of fifty <*una c. de niños* a group of fifty children> II. adj. see **cincuenteno, –na**.

cin·cuen·te·na·rio m. fiftieth anniversary, golden anniversary.

cin·cuen·te·no, –na I. adj. fiftieth II. f. see **cincuentena**.

cin·cuen·tón, –to·na I. adj. fifty-year-old II. m.f. fifty-year-old person.

cin·cha f. girth, cinch ♦ **a revienta cinchas** *(de mala gana)* unwillingly, reluctantly; *(rápido)* at breakneck speed.

cin·char tr. EQUIT. *(ceñir)* to girth, cinch; *(enarcar)* to hoop, band.

cin·che·ra f. *(vientre)* belly (of horse); VET. *(desolladura)* girth gall.

cin·cho m. *(faja)* belt, girdle; *(zuncho)* metal hoop *or* band (of a barrel); *(de una rueda)* iron rim (of a wheel); ARCHIT. projecting rib of an arch; VET. ring on top of horse's hoof; AMER. girth, cinch (of a horse).

ci·ne m. *(arte)* cinema; INDUS. motion pictures, films, movies; PHOTOG., TECH. cinematography; COLL. *(espectáculo)* movies, pictures, flicks; *(teatro)* movie house *or* theater ♦ **c. de estreno** first-run movie theater • **c. de sesión continua** continuous-showing movie theater • **c. en colores** color films • **hacer c.** to make films *or* (motion) pictures • **c. mudo** silent films *or* movies • **c. parlante** *or* **sonoro** talking pictures, talkies.

ci·ne·as·ta m. CINEM. *(actor)* movie actor —f. *(actriz)* movie actress —m.f. *(general)* person who works in the film industry; *(director)* movie director, filmmaker; *(productor)* film *or* movie producer.

ci·ne·ma·sco·pe m. CINEM. cinemascope.

ci·ne·ma·te·ca f. CINEM. film library *or* archive.

ci·ne·má·ti·ca f. PHYS. kinematics.

ci·ne·ma·to·gra·fí·a f. cinematography.

ci·ne·ma·to·gra·fiar §30 tr. to film, shoot (a scene).

ci·ne·ma·to·grá·fi·co, –ca adj. cinematographic, film, cinematic.

ci·ne·ma·tó·gra·fo m. CINEM. *(cámara)* cinematograph, motion-picture camera; *(proyector)* (film) projector; *(teatro)* cinema, movie house *or* theater.

ci·ne·ra·rio, –ria adj. cinerary <*urna c.* cinerary urn>; *(ceniciento)* cinereous, ashen.

ci·ne·sia *or* **ci·ne·sis** f. MED. kinesitherapy, kinesiatrics.

ci·ne·sio·lo·gí·a f. kinesiology.

ci·ne·si·te·ra·pia f. MED. kinesitherapy.

ci·né·ti·co, –ca PHYS. I. adj. kinetic II. f. kinetics.

cin·ga·lés, –le·sa adj. & m.f. Ceylonese.

cín·ga·ro, –ra adj. & m.f. gypsy.

cin·glar tr. METAL. to shingle, puddle (iron); MARIT. to scull.

cí·ni·co, –ca I. adj. PHILOS. cynical; *(impudente)* shameless, impudent II. m.f. cynic.

ci·nis·mo m. PHILOS. cynicism; *(descaro)* impudence, shamelessness.

ci·nó·dro·mo m. greyhound track.

cin·ta f. *(listón)* ribbon, sash; tape, strip <*c. magnética* magnetic tape>; *(película)* film; *(flanco de la acera)* curb (of a sidewalk); ARCHIT. listel, scroll; MAS. first row of tiles; VET. coronet; BOT. ribbon grass; S. AMER. tin can ♦ **c. adhesiva** *or* **adherente** adhesive tape • **c. cinematográfica** movie film • **c. de freno** MECH. brake lining • **c. de medir** measuring tape • **c. de teletipo** ticker tape • **c. transportadora** conveyor belt • **c. magnetofónica** recording tape • **c. métrica** tape measure • **cintas** MARIT. wales.

cin·ta·ra·zo m. blow with the flat of a sword.

cin·te·rí·a f. *(cintas)* ribbons; *(industria)* ribbon trade; *(tienda)* notions shop, ribbon shop.

cin·ti·lar tr. to sparkle, twinkle.

cin·to m. *(ceñidor)* belt, girdle, waistband; ANAT. *(cintura)* waist, waistline ♦ **c. de oro** money belt.

cin·tu·ra f. ANAT. waist, waistline; *(ceñidor)* belt, girdle; ARCHIT. chimney throat; MARIT. rigging knot ♦ **c. pelviana** ANAT. pelvic girdle *or* arch • **doblarse por la c.** FIG., COLL. to be in stitches, be bent over in laughter • **meter en c.** FIG., COLL. to discipline, straighten out.

cin·tu·rón m. *(vestidura)* belt, sash; FIG. *(cadena)* series, chain <*un c. de fortalezas* a chain of forts>; MIL. *(bloqueo)* cordon, blockade, line; *(zona)* belt, zone; SPORT. belt <*c. negro* black belt> ♦ **apretarse el c.** FIG. to tighten one's belt, budget oneself • **c. de castidad** HIST. chastity belt • **c. de seguridad** AUTO., AVIA. seat *or* safety belt • **c. salvavidas** *or* **salvamento** MARIT. life belt, life preserver.

cin·zo·lín m. reddish-violet, fuchsia.

ci·ña, ciño see ceñir.

ci·ñe·ra, ciñó see ceñir.

ci·pa·yo m. HIST. *(soldado indio)* sepoy; ARG., DEROG. *(político)* politician in the service of foreign business interests; CUBA, P. RICO *(nativo)* name given to natives who joined the Spanish army.

ci·po m. *(lápida)* cippus, gravestone; *(hito)* milepost, milestone; COL. *(trozo grande)* chunk, large piece.

ci·po·li·no, –na I. adj. cipolin II. m. cipolin marble.

ci·prés m. BOT. cypress; MEX., RELIG. main altar.

cir·cen·se adj. *(del circo romano)* circensian; *(del circo actual)* circus.

cir·co m. *(espectáculo)* circus; HIST. *(anfiteatro)* circus, amphitheater; GEOL. cirque; MEX. acrobatic troupe.

cir·cón m. JEWEL., MIN. zircon.

cir·co·nio m. CHEM. zirconium.

cir·cuir §18 tr. to surround, encircle.

cir·cui·to m. *(movimiento circular)* circuit; *(circunferencia)* circumference; network <*un c. de carreteras* a network of highways>; *(viaje)* trip, tour; ELEC. circuit ♦ **c. abierto** ELEC. open circuit • **c. cerrado** ELEC. closed circuit • **c. impreso** ELEC. printed circuit • **c. magnético** ELEC. magnetic circuit • **corto c.** ELEC. short circuit.

cir·cu·la·ción f. *(movimiento)* circulation, movement; FIG. *(transmisión)* propagation, dissemination; ANAT. circulation; COM., FIN. circulating notes *or* bills, currency; AUTO. *(tráfico)* traffic ♦ **fuera de c.** out of circulation • **poner en c.** to put into circulation.

cir·cu·lan·te adj. circulating <*capital c.* circulating capital>.

cir·cu·lar¹ I. adj. circular II. f. circular, flier.

cir·cu·lar² intr. to circulate <*el aire circula por el cuarto* air circulates about the room>; to move <*la gente circulaba por el museo* people were moving about the museum>; to circulate, pass from hand to hand <*el decreto circulaba por el pueblo* the decree passed from hand to hand throughout the town>; FIG. to circulate, spread <*circulan noticias de la guerra* news of the war is spreading>; COM., FIN. to circulate, flow —tr. to circulate, pass around <*circularon el memorándum* they passed around the memorandum>.

cir·cu·lar·men·te adv. circularly.

cir·cu·la·to·rio, –ria adj. ANAT. circulatory; AUTO. traffic <*problemas circulatorios* traffic problems>.

cír·cu·lo m. GEOM. circle; *(circunferencia)* circumference, ring; *(grupo)* circle, group <*c. social* social circle>; FIG. *(extensión)* scope, range ♦ **c. horario** ASTRON. hour circle • **c. máximo** GEOM. great circle • **c. polar antártico** Antarctic Circle • **c. polar ártico** Arctic Circle • **c. vicioso** vicious circle, circular argument.

cir·cum·po·lar adj. circumpolar.

cir·cun·ci·dar tr. RELIG., SURG. to circumcise; FIG. *(cortar)* to clip, curtail, diminish.

cir·cun·ci·sión f. RELIG., SURG. circumcision.

cir·cun·ci·so, –sa I. past part. see **circuncidar** II. adj. RELIG., SURG. circumcised; FIG. *(disminuido)* clipped, curtailed, diminished III. m. circumcised man.

cir·cun·dan·te adj. surrounding.

cir·cun·dar tr. to surround, encircle, encompass.

cir·cun·fe·ren·cia f. circumference.

cir·cun·fe·rir §65 tr. to circumscribe, limit.

cir·cun·fle·jo, –ja adj. & m. PHONET. circumflex.

cir·cun·lo·cu·ción f. *or* **cir·cun·lo·quio** m. circumlocution, periphrasis.

cir·cun·na·ve·ga·ción f. MARIT. circumnavigation.

cir·cuns·cri·bir §85 tr. GEOM. to circumscribe, encircle; FIG. *(limitar)* to circumscribe, limit, confine —reflex. to restrict *or* limit oneself.

cir·cuns·crip·ción f. GEOM. circumscription, circumscribing; *(limitación)* limitation, restriction; *(territorio)* district, territory.

cir·cuns·cri·to, –ta *or* **cir·cuns·crip·to, –ta** I. past part. see **circunscribir** II. adj. circumscriptive.

cir·cuns·pec·ción f. *(atención)* circumspection; *(prudencia)* caution, prudence.

cir·cuns·pec·to, –ta adj. circumspect; *(prudente)* cautious, prudent.

cir·cuns·tan·cia f. *(momento)* circumstance, situation <*una c. grave* a serious situation>; *(particularidad)* circumstance, condition <*hay circunstancias atenuantes* there are extenuating circumstances> ♦ **bajo las circunstancias** under the circumstances • **circunstancias agravantes** LAW aggravating circumstances • **circunstancias eximentes** LAW exculpatory circumstances • **de circunstancias** circumstantial • **en las circunstancias actuales** under the present circumstances.

cir·cuns·tan·cia·do, –da adj. detailed, minute.

cir·cuns·tan·cial adj. circumstantial; GRAM. adverbial <*complemento c.* adverbial complement>.

cir·cuns·tan·ciar tr. to circumstantiate, verify in detail.

cir·cuns·tan·te I. adj. *(alrededor)* surrounding; *(presente)* present, attending II. m.f. spectator, onlooker ♦ **los circunstantes** those present.

cir·cun·va·la·ción f. MIL. circumvallation ♦ **línea de c.** AUTO., RAIL. loop, circular route.

cir·cun·va·lar tr. *(cercar)* to surround, encircle; MIL. circumvallate, surround.

cir·cun·ve·ci·no, –na adj. adjacent, neighboring.

cir·cun·vo·lu·ción f. circumvolution; ANAT. convolution, fold ♦ **c. cerebral** ANAT. cerebral convolution.

cir·cu·ya, circuyo see **circuir.**

ci·ri·ne·o m. COLL., FIG. helper, assistant.

ci·rio m. RELIG. church candle; CUBA, BOT. pine-like ornamental tree; AMER. *(cacto)* cereus, saguaro cactus.

ci·rro m. BOT., METEOROL., ZOOL. cirrus; MED. scirrhus (tumor).

ci·rro·sis f. MED. cirrhosis.

ci·rue·la f. BOT. plum; *(pasa)* prune ♦ **c. amarilla** mirabelle plum • **c. claudia** *or* **verdal** greengage • **c. damascena** damson (plum) • **c. de yema** yellow plum • **c. pasa** dried plum, prune.

ci·rue·lo m. BOT. plum tree; COLL. *(tonto)* fool, sap; AMER., PHILIP. hog plum *or* yellow mombin tree.

ci·ru·gí·a f. surgery ♦ **c. plástica** *or* **estética** plastic *or* cosmetic surgery ♦ **c. mayor** major surgery • **c. menor** *or* **ministrante** minor surgery.

ci·ru·ja·no, –na m.f. surgeon ♦ **c. dentista** dental *or* oral surgeon.

ci·san·di·no, –na adj. cisandine (on this side of the Andes).

cis·car §70 tr. COLL. *(ensuciar)* to dirty, soil; CUBA, MEX. *(avergonzar)* to embarrass; *(molestar)* to bother, annoy —reflex. COLL. to soil oneself.

cis·co m. *(carbón)* slack (coal); COLL. *(alboroto)* rumpus, uproar; *(reyerta)* wrangle, squabble ♦ **hacer c.** to smash to smithereens • **meter c.** *or* **armar un c.** to raise a rumpus, kick up a row.

ci·sión f. incision.

cis·ma m. *(separación)* schism, split, division; *(discordia)* discord, dissension; COL. affectedness, affectation.

cis·má·ti·co, –ca I. adj. *(disidente)* schismatic, dissident; COL. *(chismoso)* gossipy; *(melindroso)* finicky, prudish II. m.f. schismatic, dissident.

cis·mon·ta·no, –na adj. cismontane.

cis·ne m. ORNITH. swan; FIG. *(poeta)* bard, great poet *or* singer; ARG. powder puff ♦ **C.** ASTRON. Swan, Cygnus.

cis·qué, cisque see **ciscar.**

cis·que·ro m. *(comerciante)* slack maker *or* seller; *(muñequilla)* pounce bag.

cis·ter·na f. cistern, tank, reservoir.

cis·ti·tis f. MED. cystitis.

ci·su·ra f. scission, fissure.

ci·ta f. *(entrevista)* appointment, engagement, meeting; date <*tengo una c. con mi novio a las nueve* I have a date with my boyfriend at nine o'clock>; *(referencia)* quotation, quote ♦ **c. espacial** ASTRONAUT. space linkup *or* docking • **darse** to set up a meeting *or* date with someone.

ci·ta·ción f. LAW *(emplazamiento)* writ of summons, citation, subpoena; *(referencia)* citation, quotation ♦ **c. de evicción** LAW eviction notice • **c. de remate** LAW notice of public sale.

ci·ta·dor, –do·ra I. adj. quoting, citing II. m.f. quoter, citer.

ci·tar tr. *(convocar)* to arrange to meet, make an appointment *or* date with; *(referirse)* to cite, quote, refer to; LAW *(emplazar)* to cite, summon; TAUR. to incite *or* attack (the bull) ♦ **para no c. otros** to mention but a few, name only a few.

cí·ta·ra f. MUS. zither, zithern.

ci·ta·to·rio, –ria I. adj. LAW citatory, summoning II. f. LAW citation, summons.

ci·té·re·o, –a adj. POET. Cytherean.

ci·te·rior adj. hithermost, near.

cí·to·la f. mill clapper.

ci·to·lo·gí·a f. BIOL. cytology.

ci·to·plas·ma m. BIOL. cytoplasm.

cí·tri·co, –ca I. adj. CHEM. citric; BOT. citrus II. m. ♦ **cítricos** citrus fruits.

ci·tri·na f. lemon oil.

ciu·dad f. city ♦ **C. de Guatemala** Guatemala City • **C. del Vaticano** Vatican City • **C. de México** Mexico City • **c. hermana** sister city • **c. hongo** boom town • **c. universitaria** university campus.

ciu·da·da·ní·a f. *(derecho)* citizenship; *(población)* townspeople, citizens, citizenry.

ciu·da·da·no, –na I. adj. civic, city II. m.f. *(habitante)* citizen, city dweller; *(con derechos)* citizen.

ciu·da·de·la f. *(fortaleza)* citadel, fortress; AMER. *(casa de vecindad)* tenement.

cí·vi·co, –ca I. adj. civic <*responsabilidad c.* civic responsibility>; *(civil)* civil, civilian; FIG. *(patriótico)* patriotic, civic-minded II. m. AMER. policeman.

ci·vil I. adj. *(ciudadano)* civic, civil <*derechos civiles* civil rights>; *(no militar)* civil, civilian; *(no religioso)* lay, secular; *(gentil)* civil, polite, courteous; LAW civil <*código c.* civil code> II. m.f. civilian —m. SP., COLL. civil guard.

ci·vi·li·cé, civilice see **civilizar.**

ci·vi·li·dad f. civility, courtesy, urbanity.

ci·vi·lis·ta m. *(jurisconsulto)* professor *or* person versed in civil law; AMER. opponent of military and church influence in politics.

ci·vi·li·za·ción f. civilization.

ci·vi·li·za·do, –da I. past part. see **civilizar** II. adj. civilized, educated, refined.

ci·vi·li·za·dor, –do·ra I. adj. civilizing II. m.f. civilizer.

ci·vi·li·zar §04 tr. to civilize —reflex. to become civilized.

ci·vil·men·te adv. civilly.

ci·vis·mo m. good citizenship, civic-mindedness.

ci·za·lla f. *(tijeras)* shears, clippers (for cutting metal); *(cortadura)* metal clippings *or* shavings ♦ **c. de guillotina** guillotine shears (for cutting paper).

ci·za·llar tr. to shear.

ci·za·ña f. BOT. (bearded) darnel; BIBL. tare; FIG. *(vicio)* vice, evil; *(influencia mala)* bad *or* corrupting influence; *(disensión)* discord, dissension ♦ **meter** *or* **sembrar c.** FIG. to sow discord, cause trouble • **separar la c. del buen grano** FIG. to separate the chaff from the wheat.

ci·za·ñar tr. FIG. to sow discord in, cause *or* make trouble for.

ci·za·ñe·ro, –ra FIG. I. adj. troublemaking, mischief-making II. m.f. troublemaker, mischief-maker.

clac m. [pl. **cla·ques**] *(sombrero plegable)* opera hat; *(sombrero de tres picos)* cocked hat; THEAT. claque.

cla·mar intr. to clamor, cry out <*todos clamaban por la paz* everyone was clamoring for peace>; FIG. to require, demand <*la planta clama por agua* the plant requires water> —tr. to clamor for, cry out for <*c. venganza* to cry out for vengeance>.

cla·mor m. clamor, outcry; *(queja)* plaint, moan; *(toque de campanas)* knell, toll.

cla·mo·re·ar tr. to cry out for, beg for <*clamoreaban noticias de la guerra* they begged for news of the war> —intr. to clamor, cry out <*c. por una reforma* to clamor for reform>; *(doblar)* to toll, knell.

cla·mo·re·o m. *(ruido)* clamor, clamoring; *(ruego)* pleading, imploring.

cla·mo·ro·so, –sa adj. *(ruidoso)* loud, clamorous; *(quejoso)* complaining, moaning ♦ **éxito c.** resounding success.

clan m. *(familia)* clan; FIG. *(partido)* faction, cause.

clan·des·ti·na·men·te adv. clandestinely, secretly.

clan·des·ti·ni·dad f. clandestinity, secrecy.

clan·des·ti·no, –na adj. *(secreto)* clandestine, secret; POL. underground.

clan·gor m. POET. clarion (trumpet sound).

cla·que·tas f.pl. MUS. clappers.

cla·ra I. f. white <*la c. del huevo* egg white>; *(de la cabeza)* bald spot *or* patch; TEX. threadbare *or* badly woven patch of cloth; COLL. *(escampada)* break, clearing (in a rain); *(claridad)* clearness; AMER. *(monja)* nun (of the order of Saint Clare) **II.** adj. & adv. see **claro, -ra.**

cla·ra·bo·ya f. ARCHIT. skylight ♦ **c. de bóveda** vault light.

cla·ra·men·te adv. clearly.

cla·re·ar tr. *(aclarar)* to lighten, make lighter; FIG. *(explicar)* to clarify; MEX. to go *or* pass through (a bullet) —intr. *(amanecer)* to dawn; METEOROL. to clear *or* brighten up ♦ **al c. el día** at the break of dawn —reflex. *(quedarse raído)* to wear thin, become threadbare; *(transparentarse)* to be transparent, let the light through; FIG., COLL. to give oneself away.

cla·re·cer §17 intr. to dawn.

cla·re·te adj. & m. claret (wine).

cla·re·za f. var. of **claridad.**

cla·ri·dad f. *(luz)* brightness, light; *(nitidez)* clarity, clearness; *(dote)* splendor, radiance; FIG. *(fama)* fame ♦ **c. de la vista** *or* **de los ojos** clear-sightedness, perspicacity • **claridades** FIG. plain language, blunt remarks • **con c.** clearly.

cla·ri·fi·ca·ción f. *(purificación)* clarification, refining; *(iluminación)* illumination, lighting up; FIG. *(aclaración)* clarification, explanation.

cla·ri·fi·car §70 tr. *(poner claro)* to clarify, refine; *(iluminar)* to illuminate, light up; FIG. *(aclarar)* to clarify, explain.

cla·ri·fi·ca·ti·vo, -va adj. clarifying.

cla·rín m. MUS. *(instrumento)* bugle, clarion; *(músico)* bugler, trumpet player; TEX. *(batista)* fine batiste *or* cambric; CHILE. BOT. sweet pea ♦ **c. de la selva** ORNITH. American thrush.

cla·ri·ne·te m. MUS. *(instrumento)* clarinet; *(músico)* clarinet player, clarinetist.

cla·ri·ne·tis·ta m.f. MUS. clarinetist.

cla·rión m. white crayon, chalk.

cla·ri·vi·den·cia f. clairvoyance; *(perspicacia)* perspicacity, insight.

cla·ri·vi·den·te adj. clairvoyant; *(perspicaz)* perspicacious, insightful.

cla·ro, -ra **I.** adj. clear; *(luminoso)* bright, well-lit; *(despejado)* clear, cloudless; *(cristalino)* limpid, transparent; clear, distinct *<ella habla con voz c.* she speaks in a distinct voice>; light *<verde c.* light green>; thin, weak *<sopa c.* thin soup>; *(manifiesto)* evident, obvious, plain: *(inteligible)* intelligible, lucid; straightforward *<lenguaje c.* straightforward language>; FIG. *(perspicaz)* sharp, keen *<tiene una inteligencia c.* she has a sharp mind>; *(célebre)* famous, illustrious ♦ **a las claras** openly, publicly • **c. como el agua** FIG. as plain as the nose on your face **II.** adv. clearly, plainly *<hablemos c.* let's speak plainly> ♦ **¡claro!** *or* **¡c. que sí!** of course!, sure! • **¡c. que no!** of course not! • **por lo c.** clearly, plainly **III.** m. *(abertura)* gap, space *<una c. en la fila* a gap in the row>; clearing, opening *<lo vi en un c. del bosque* I saw it in a clearing in the woods>; METEOROL. clearing, break (in clouds); PAINT. highlight; ARCHIT. skylight ♦ **c. de luna** brief period of moonlight • **pasar la noche en c.** FIG. to pass a sleepless night • **poner** *or* **sacar en c.** to clarify, explain —f. see **clara.**

cla·ros·cu·ro m. PAINT. chiaroscuro, contrast of light and shadows.

cla·se f. *(tipo)* class, kind, sort; *(categoría social)* class *<la c. obrera* the working class>; *(cualidad)* class *<primera c.* first class>; EDUC. lesson, class *<una c. de historia* a history class>; class, grade *<las clases elementales* the elementary grades>; *(aula)* classrom; BOT., ZOOL. class ♦ **c. alta** upper class • **c. baja** lower class • **c. media** middle class • **clases** MIL. noncommissioned officers • **c. turista** *or* **turística** tourist class, coach • **de c.** distinguished, of distinction • **toda c. de** all kinds of.

cla·si·cis·mo m. ARTS classicism.

cla·si·cis·ta adj. & m.f. classicist.

clá·si·co, -ca **I.** adj. ARTS classic, classical; *(notable)* remarkable, outstanding; FIG. classic *<un vestido c.* a classic dress> **II.** m.f. *(autor)* classic author; *(partidario del clasicismo)* classicist —m. *(obra)* classic.

cla·si·fi·ca·ción f. classification.

cla·si·fi·ca·dor, -do·ra **I.** adj. classifying **II.** m.f. *(persona)* classifier —m. *(mueble)* filing cabinet —f. MECH. sorter.

cla·si·fi·car §70 tr. *(ordenar)* to classify, class; *(archivar)* to sort, file —reflex. SPORT. to qualify.

clau·di·ca·ción f. FIG. *(evasión)* shirking; *(abandono)* backing down; *(cojera)* limp, lameness.

clau·di·car §70 intr. FIG. *(evadir)* to shirk; *(ceder)* to give up, back down; *(cojear)* to limp, hobble.

claus·tro m. RELIG. *(galería)* cloister; *(estado)* monastic state *or* life; EDUC. *(conjunto)* academic staff, faculty ♦ **c. materno** ANAT. womb.

claus·tro·fo·bia f. MED. claustrophobia.

cláu·su·la f. LAW clause, article, proviso; GRAM. *(período)* sentence; *(frase)* clause ♦ **c. absoluta** GRAM. *(latín)* ablative absolute; *(inglés)* absolute construction • **c. compuesta** GRAM. complex sentence • **c. de escape** LAW escape clause • **c. penal** LAW penalty *or* forfeit clause • **c. resolutoria** LAW defeasance clause • **c. simple** GRAM. simple sentence.

clau·su·ra f. RELIG. *(abadía)* cloister, monastery, convent; *(estado)* monastic reclusion *or* life; *(conclusión)* closing ceremony; AMER. *(cierre)* closing, closure; EDUC. commencement, graduation ceremony.

clau·su·rar tr. *(terminar)* to conclude, (bring to a) close, adjourn; *(cerrar)* to close, shut.

cla·va f. *(porra)* club, cudgel; MARIT. scupper.

cla·va·do, -da **I.** past part. see **clavar** **II.** adj. *(con claves)* nail-studded; *(fijo)* fixed, stuck; *(en punto)* sharp, on the dot *<llamó a las cuatro clavadas* she called at four o'clock on the dot>; FIG. perfect *<esa camisa te está c.* that shirt fits you perfectly>; just like, identical *<el chico es c. a su abuelo* the child looks just like his grandfather> ♦ **c. para** perfect *or* ideal for • **dejar a uno c.** to leave someone speechless • **quedar c.** to be dumbfounded.

cla·va·du·ra f. piercing of a horse's hoof (in shoeing).

cla·var tr. *(introducir clavos)* to nail; *(hincar)* to thrust, drive *<clavó la bayoneta en el pecho de su enemigo* he thrust the bayonet into his enemy's chest>; *(enclavar)* to fasten, fix; FIG. *(fijar)* to fix *or* rivet on *<c. los ojos en una persona* to rivet one's eyes on someone>; FIG., COLL. *(engañar)* to cheat, swindle; JEWEL. to set, mount; MIL. to spike; VET. to prick, pierce ♦ **c. un clavo con la cabeza** FIG. to be very stubborn • **clavarle el diente** to try, taste —reflex. to prick oneself, get a splinter; MEX. *(embolsarse algo)* to pocket, steal; *(ser engañado)* to be cheated *or* swindled; PERU to crash, come uninvited ♦ **clavársela** C. AMER. to get drunk.

cla·va·zón f. set of nails.

cla·ve **I.** f. *(cifra)* code; *(esencia)* key *<la c. del problema* the key to the problem>; ARCHIT. keystone; MUS. clef ♦ **c. de cifra** cipher key • **c. de do** MUS. tenor *or* alto clef • **c. de fa** MUS. base clef • **c. de sol** MUS. treble clef • **echar la c.** FIG. to close a matter • **escribir en c.** to write in code; m. MUS. clavichord **II.** adj. key *<cuestión c.* key question>.

cla·ve·cín m. MUS. *(macillo)* clavichord; *(plectro)* cembalo, harpsichord.

cla·vel m. BOT. carnation, pink ♦ **c. coronado** BOT. grass pink, common garden pink • **c. de las Indias** BOT. French marigold • **c. del Japón** BOT. sweet William • **c. doble** *or* **reventón** BOT. double carnation, clove pink.

cla·ve·li·to m. BOT. sweet William, small pink.

cla·ve·que m. rock crystal.

cla·ve·ra f. *(molde)* nail mold; *(agujero)* nail hole.

cla·ve·rí·a f. *(oficio)* office of the keybearer (in knightly orders); MEX. treasury of a cathedral.

cla·ve·ro m.f. *(llavero)* keeper of the keys; BOT. clove tree; MEX. peg, hook —m. MIL., RELIG. keeper of the keys; BOT. clove tree; MEX. peg, hook.

cla·ve·te m. *(clavo pequeño)* small nail, tack; MUS. plectrum.

cla·ve·te·ar tr. *(adornar con clavos)* to stud; *(herretear)* to tip, tag; FIG. *(terminar)* to wind up, clinch *<c. un negocio* to clinch a deal>.

cla·ve·te·o m. *(con clavos)* studding; FIG. *(término)* windup, clinching.

cla·vi·cém·ba·lo m. MUS. harpsichord, cembalo.

cla·vi·cor·dio m. MUS. clavichord.

cla·ví·cu·la f. ANAT. clavicle, collarbone.

cla·vi·ja f. *(clavo)* peg, pin; CARP. peg, dowel; ELEC. plug; MUS. peg ♦ **adjustarle** *or* **apretarle a uno las clavijas** COLL. to put the screws on *or* to someone • **c. de dos contactos**

or **de enchufe** ELEC. two-pin plug • **c. hendida** *or* **de dos patas** cotter pin • **c. maestra** MECH. kingpin.

cla·vi·je·ro m. MUS. pegbox; *(percha)* clothes hook; AGR. clevis (of a plow); ELEC. plug.

cla·vo m. TECH. nail; BOT. clove; MED. corn; ARG., CHILE *(mercadería)* white elephant; ARG. *(situación desagradable)* bad spot, nasty business; HOND., MEX., MIN. rich vein ♦ **agarrarse a** *or* **de un c. ardiendo** FIG. to do anything to achieve one's purpose • **c. de chilla** roofing nail • **c. de rosca** round-headed screw • **c. de roseta** ornamental nail • **c. romano** brass-headed nail • **c. tachuela** tack • **como un c.** FIG. punctually • **dar en el c.** FIG., COLL. to hit the nail on the head • **de c. pasado** COLL. *(evidente)* obvious, self-evident; *(fácil)* easy • **remachar el c.** FIG., COLL. *(empeorar una situación)* to make matters worse, compound one's error; *(establecer el punto en una discusión)* to drive home the point.

cla·xon m. AUTO. horn ♦ **tocar el c.** AUTO. to honk *or* toot the horn.

cle·men·cia f. clemency, mercy.

cle·men·te adj. clement, merciful.

clep·si·dra f. clepsydra (water clock).

clep·to·ma·ní·a f. PSYCH. kleptomania.

clep·tó·ma·no, –na adj. & m.f. PSYCH. kleptomaniac.

cle·re·cí·a f. RELIG. *(clero)* clergy; *(oficio)* priesthood.

cle·ri·cal I. adj. RELIG. clerical II. m.f. POL., RELIG. clericalist; C. AMER. clergyman.

cle·ri·ca·lis·mo m. clericalism.

cle·ri·ca·to m. *or* **cle·ri·ca·tu·ra** f. RELIG. priesthood.

clé·ri·go m. RELIG. clergyman, cleric; EDUC., HIST. *(escolar)* clerk, scholar.

cle·ro m. RELIG. clergy ♦ **c. regular** regular clergy • **c. secular** secular clergy.

cle·ro·fo·bia f. anticlericalism.

cli·ché m. PRINT. *(plancha)* cliché, (stereotype) plate; PHOTOG. negative; FIG. *(frase hecha)* cliché, trite *or* hackneyed expression.

clien·te m.f. COM. client, customer; DENT., MED. patient; law client.

clien·te·la f. COM. customers, clientele; DENT., MED. practice, patients; LAW clients.

cli·ma m. METEOROL. climate; GEOG. *(zona)* climatic zone *or* region; FIG. *(ambiente)* climate, atmosphere *<el c. político* the political climate>.

cli·ma·té·ri·co, –ca adj. *(crítico)* critical, climacteric *<año c.* critical year>; COLL. *(peligroso)* dangerous; FIG. *(de mal talante)* ill-humored.

cli·má·ti·co, –ca adj. climatic.

cli·ma·ti·za·ción f. air conditioning.

cli·ma·ti·zar §04 tr. to air-condition.

cli·ma·to·lo·gí·a f. climatology.

cli·ma·to·ló·gi·co, –ca adj. climatological.

clí·max m. [pl. **-max**] climax.

clí·ni·ca I. f. *(hospital privado)* private hospital; *(hospital de práctica)* teaching hospital; *(enseñanza)* clinical medicine instruction II. adj. see **clínico, –ca.**

clí·ni·co, –ca I. adj. clinical II. m. clinician —f. see **clínica.**

clip m. [pl. **clips**] *(sujetapapeles)* paper clip; *(aro)* earring.

clí·per m. AVIA., MARIT. clipper.

cli·sé m. PRINT. stereotype plate; PHOTOG. negative; FIG. *(frase hecha)* cliché.

clí·to·ris m. ANAT. clitoris.

clo·a·ca f. *(alcantarilla)* drain, sewer; FIG. *(cenagal)* sewer, cesspool; ZOOL. cloaca ♦ **c. pluvial** storm sewer, storm drain.

clo·car §73 intr. ORNITH. to cluck, cackle.

clon m. BIOL. clone.

clo·que m. MARIT. *(bichero)* boathook; *(garfio)* gaff.

clo·que·ar intr. ORNITH. to cluck, cackle.

clo·que·ra f. ORNITH. brooding, broodiness.

clo·ral m. CHEM. chloral.

clo·ra·to m. CHEM. chlorate ♦ **c. de potasio** CHEM. potassium chlorate • **c. de sodio** CHEM. sodium chlorate.

clor·hi·dra·to m. CHEM. hydrochloride.

clor·hí·dri·co, –ca adj. CHEM. hydrochloric.

cló·ri·co, –ca adj. CHEM. chloric.

clo·ro m. CHEM. chlorine.

clo·ro·fi·la f. BOT. chlorophyll.

clo·ro·for·mi·zar §04 tr. MED. to chloroform.

clo·ro·for·mo m. CHEM., MED. chloroform.

clo·ro·mi·ce·ti·na f. CHEM. Chloromycetin (trademark).

clo·ru·ro m. CHEM. chloride • **c. cálcico** *or* **de calcio** calcium chloride • **c. de cal** chloride of lime **c. de potasio** potassium chloride • **c. mercúrico** mercury *or* mercuric chloride • **c. sódico** *or* **de sodio** sodium chloride, salt.

club m. [pl. **clubs** *or* **clu·bes**] club *<c. literario* literary club>.

clu·bis·ta m.f. club member.

clue·co, –ca I. adj. ORNITH. broody; COLL. *(decrépito)* decrepit, feeble II. f. ORNITH. brooder, broody hen.

clue·que see **clocar.**

co·a f. CUBA, AGR. wooden rod used by Indians to till the soil; MEX. hoe; CHILE prison slang.

co·ac·ción f. coercion, compulsion, coaction; LAW duress *<bajo c.* under duress>.

co·ac·cio·nar tr. to coerce, compel, force.

co·a·cer·var tr. to pile *or* heap up.

co·a·cre·e·dor, –do·ra m.f. joint creditor.

co·ac·ti·vo, –va adj. coercive, compelling, coactive.

co·a·cu·sa·do, –da LAW I. m.f. codefendant II. adj. jointly accused.

co·ad·ju·tor, –to·ra m.f. coadjutor.

co·ad·ju·to·rí·a f. coadjutorship.

co·ad·qui·ri·dor, –do·ra m.f. LAW joint purchaser *or* acquirer.

co·ad·qui·si·ción f. joint acquisition.

co·a·du·nar tr. to join, combine.

co·ad·yu·tor m. coadjutor.

co·ad·yu·to·rio, –ria adj. helping, assisting.

co·ad·yu·van·te adj. coadjuvant, helping, assisting.

co·ad·yu·var tr. to help, assist —intr. to collaborate, contribute *<c. al bien público* to contribute to the common good>.

co·a·gen·te m.f. coagent.

co·a·gu·la·ble adj. coagulable.

co·a·gu·la·ción f. *(cuajamiento)* congealing, coagulation; MED. coagulation, clotting; *(leche)* curdling.

co·a·gu·la·dor, –do·ra adj. coagulant, coagulative.

co·a·gu·lan·te adj. coagulating, coagulative.

co·a·gu·lar tr. & reflex. *(cuajar)* to coagulate, congeal, thicken; MED. to coagulate, clot; *(leche)* to curdle.

co·á·gu·lo m. coagulation, coagulum; MED. clot; *(leche)* curd.

co·a·li·ción f. coalition, league, alliance.

co·ar·ta·ción f. *(restricción)* restriction, limitation; RELIG. obligation to become an ordained priest within a specific period of time.

co·ar·ta·da f. LAW alibi ♦ **probar** *or* **presentar** *or* **alegar una c.** LAW to establish *or* provide an alibi.

co·ar·tar tr. to hinder, restrict, limit.

co·a·tí m. ZOOL. coati.

co·au·tor, –to·ra m.f. co-author, joint author.

co·a·xial adj. ENGIN., MATH. coaxial.

co·ba f. COLL. *(embuste)* tall tale, amusing fib; *(halago)* soft soap, flattery; *(tienda de campaña)* sultan's tent; ARCHIT. *(cúpula)* dome, domed structure; CHILE, CHEM. type of layer found on sodium nitrate ♦ **dar c.** *or* **la c.** COLL. to soft-soap, flatter.

co·bal·to m. CHEM. cobalt.

co·bar·de I. adj. cowardly, faint-hearted II. m.f. coward.

co·bar·de·ar intr. to be a coward, show cowardice.

co·bar·dí·a f. cowardice, cowardliness.

co·bar·dón, –do·na I. adj. very cowardly II. m.f. big chicken *or* coward.

co·ba·yo m. *or* **co·ba·ya** f. ZOOL. guinea pig.

co·be·ar intr. COLL. to soft-soap, flatter.

co·ber·te·ra f. *(cubierta)* lid, cover, top; COLL. *(alcahueta)* madam, procuress; BOT. white water lily; ORNITH. tail covert.

co·ber·ti·zo m. *(protección)* lean-to, shelter; *(barraca)* shed, hut; AUTO. *(cochera)* garage, carport ♦ **c. de fletes** RAIL. freight shed.

co·ber·tor m. *(colcha)* bedspread, coverlet; *(colcha de plumas)* quilt, comforter; *(manta)* blanket.

co·ber·tu·ra f. *(cubierta)* cover, covering; SP. *(cobertor)* bedspread, coverlet.

co·bi·ja f. *(teja)* ridge tile; *(cubierta)* cover, covering; ORNITH. covert; AMER. blanket; MEX. *(chal)* short shawl, wrap; CUBA thatched roof; VEN., BOT. type of palm ♦ **cobijas** AMER. bedclothes.

co·bi·ja·dor, –do·ra I. adj. covering, protective II. m.f. coverer, protector.

co·bi·ja·mien·to m. *(cubrimiento)* covering; *(protección)* protection, shelter; *(albergue)* lodging, lodgings.

co·bi·jar tr. *(cubrir)* to cover (up), enclose, wrap; FIG. *(albergar)* to harbor, shelter, lodge; CUBA to thatch (a roof).

co·bi·jo m. *(cubrimiento)* covering; *(protección)* protection, shelter; *(albergue)* lodging, lodgings; ECUAD. *(ropa)* bedclothes; *(manta)* blanket.

co·bis·ta I. adj. soft-soaping, flattering II. m.f. soft-soaper, flatterer.

co·bra f. ZOOL. cobra; *(coyunda)* rope for yoking oxen; HUNT. *(en la caza)* retrieval ♦ **c. de capuchón** ZOOL. hooded cobra.

co·bra·ble adj. collectible, cashable.

co·bra·de·ro, –ra adj. *(cobrable)* collectible; *(recuperable)* retrievable, recoverable.

co·bra·dor, –do·ra I. adj. HUNT. retrieving II. m.f. *(recaudador)* bill or tax collector; HUNT. *(perro)* retriever; *(de tranvía)* conductor.

co·bran·za f. *(cobro)* collection, collecting; *(recuperación)* retrieval, recovery; *(de un cheque)* cashing; *(pago)* payment; HUNT. retrieval.

co·brar tr. *(recibir)* to collect <*c. un sueldo* to collect a salary>; *(recuperar)* to retrieve, recover; to charge <*me cobraron treinta dólares* they charged me thirty dollars>; to cash <*c. un cheque* to cash a check>; *(tirar)* to haul or pull in (rope); FIG. to summon, muster <*c. valor* to muster courage>; HUNT. to retrieve, fetch; S. AMER. to dun, press for payment ♦ **c. afecto** or **cariño a** to take a liking to • **c. ánimo** to take heart • **c. conciencia** to regain consciousness • **c. fama de** to get a reputation for • **c. fuerza** to gather strength —reflex. *(recuperarse)* to recover, recuperate; *(pagarse)* to recoup one's losses.

co·bre m. CHEM., METAL. copper; MUS. brass instrument; AMER. cent ♦ **batir el c.** to go all out (for something) • **c. quemado** copper sulfate • **c. verde** malachite • **mostrar el c.** AMER. to show one's bad side • **quedarse sin un c.** PERU to be broke.

co·bri·zo, –za adj. MIN. cupreous, cupriferous; *(color)* copper, copper-colored.

co·bro m. *(cobranza)* collection, collecting; *(recuperación)* retrieval, recuperation; *(de un cheque)* cashing; *(pago)* payment; HUNT. retrieval ♦ **c. a la entrega** collect on delivery • **poner al** or **en c.** to make payable; *(enviar)* to send (out) • **poner algo en c.** to put or store something in a safe place • **poner c. en una cosa** to try hard to get or collect something • **ponerse uno en c.** to take refuge • **presentar al c.** to cash, present for cashing.

co·ca¹ f. BOT. coca (shrub and leaf); PHARM. cocaine ♦ **c. de Levante** BOT. Indian berry tree.

co·ca² f. *(división del pelo)* hair on either side of the part; *(moño)* bun (of hair); *(de un cabo)* bend, kink; COLL. *(cabeza)* head; *(golpe)* rap on the head ♦ **de c.** MEX., COLL. *(gratis)* free, gratis; *(en vano)* vainly.

co·ca·cho I. adj. PERU, CUL. said of hard and improperly cooked beans II. m. AMER. rap or blow on the head.

co·ca·da f. CUL. *(dulce)* macaroon, sweet made with shredded coconut; *(amasijo para mascar)* lump of coca for chewing; PERU supply of coca leaves.

co·ca·í·na f. PHARM. cocaine.

co·ca·ís·mo or **co·cai·nis·mo** m. cocainism, cocaine addiction.

co·cal m. AMER., AGR. *(cocotal)* coconut grove; *(árboles de coca)* coca plantation.

co·car §70 tr. COLL. *(adular)* to flatter, wheedle; *(hacer muecas)* to make eyes at, flirt with.

coc·ción f. *(acción de cocer)* cooking; *(hervor)* boiling; *(en un horno)* baking; TECH. firing, baking.

cóc·cix m. [pl. **-cix**] ANAT. coccyx.

co·ce·ar intr. ZOOL. to kick; FIG., COLL. *(resistir)* to resist, kick.

co·cer §71 tr. to cook <*c. la carne* to cook the meat>; *(hervir)* to boil; *(en un horno)* to bake; TECH. to fire, bake; SURG. to maturate, suppurate —intr. to cook <*la carne cuece* the meat is cooking>; *(hervir)* to boil; *(fermentar)* to ferment, brew; TEX. to ret —reflex. *(guisar)* to cook; FIG. *(sufrir)* to suffer intensely, be in great pain ♦ **no cocérsele a uno el pan** COLL. to be very impatient.

co·ci·do, –da I. past part. see **cocer** II. adj. boiled, cooked III. m. boiled dinner.

co·cien·te m. MATH. quotient ♦ **c. intelectual** intelligence quotient.

co·ci·mien·to m. *(acción de hervir)* boiling, cooking; *(acción de poner al horno)* baking; *(líquido)* medicinal decoction or extraction; TEX. *(baño)* solution for preparing wool for dyeing.

co·ci·na f. *(cuarto)* kitchen; *(aparato)* stove, range; cooking, cuisine <*c. francesa* French cuisine>; *(caldo)* broth, soup ♦ **de c.** kitchen, culinary • **hacer la c.** to cook, do the cooking • **libro de c.** cookbook.

co·ci·nar tr. *(guisar)* to cook; COL. to bake <*c. el pan* to bake bread> —intr. *(guisar)* to cook; FIG. *(entremeterse)* to meddle.

co·ci·ne·ro, –ra m.f. cook, chef ♦ **haber sido c. antes que fraile** FIG. to know what one is talking about.

co·ci·ni·lla f. *(infiernillo)* portable or camp stove; *(cuarto)* small kitchen, kitchenette.

co·co m. BOT. coconut (tree, shell and fruit); BACT. coccus; ENTOM. mealy bug, maggot; COLL. *(cabeza)* head, noggin; *(espantajo)* boogieman, hobgoblin; *(mueca)* grimace, face; COL., ECUAD. derby hat; PERU, URUG. percale; CUBA, ORNITH. white ibis ♦ **c. de Levante** Indian berry tree • **hacer cocos** *(lisonjear)* to coax, cajole; *(hacer carantoñas)* to flirt, make eyes • **parecer** or **ser un c.** COLL. to be a sight, be very ugly.

co·co·dri·lo m. ZOOL. crocodile.

co·co·li·che m. ARG., URUG. pidgin Spanish of Italian immigrants; COLL. *(el italiano)* Italian (language).

có·co·ra I. adj. COLL. annoying, bothersome II. m.f. COLL. *(persona molesta)* nuisance, pest; COL., CUBA, P. RICO *(cólera)* anger, rage; CUBA, P. RICO *(escozor)* irritation; PERU animosity, ill will; DOM. REP. fear, aversion.

co·co·ro·có m. cock-a-doodle-doo.

co·co·tal m. AGR. coconut grove.

co·co·te·ro m. BOT. coconut palm.

cóc·tel m. *(bebida)* cocktail; *(reunión)* cocktail party ♦ **c. Molotov** Molotov cocktail.

coc·te·le·ra f. *(recipiente)* cocktail shaker; FIG. *(mezcla)* mixture.

co·cu·yo m. ENTOM. *(insecto)* glowworm, firefly; CUBA, BOT. type of tree.

co·cha f. METAL. *(estanque)* water tank (adjacent to a washing tank); PERU pampa, plain; CHILE, ECUAD. pool, puddle.

co·cham·bre m.f. COLL. *(objeto)* filthy and smelly object; *(suciedad)* filth, dirt.

co·cham·bre·rí·a f. COLL. rubbish, filth.

co·cham·bro·so, –sa I. adj. filthy, dirty II. m.f. filthy or dirty person.

co·cha·rro m. wooden or stone cup.

co·che m. *(carruaje)* coach, carriage; *(automóvil)* automobile, car; RAIL. *(vagón)* coach, car ♦ **c. blindado** armored car • **c. cama** RAIL. sleeper, sleeping car • **c. comedor** RAIL. dining car • **c. de alquiler** *(taxi)* taxi, cab; *(alquilado)* rental car • **c. de carreras** race car • **c. de plaza** or **de punto** taxi, cab • **c. de sitio** MEX. dispatched cab • **c. fúnebre** hearse • **ir en el c. de San Fernando** or **de San Francisco** COLL. to go on foot, walk.

co·che·ra I. adj. carriage, coach <*puerta c.* carriage door> II. f. carriage or coach house; AUTO. garage.

co·che·ril adj. COLL. pertaining to a coachman.

co·che·ro m. coachman ♦ **de c.** COLL. *(lenguaje)* foul.

co·chi·fri·to m. CUL. *(guisado de cabrito)* kid or goat stew; *(guisado de cordero)* lamb stew.

co·chi·na·da or **co·chi·ne·rí·a** f. FIG., COLL. *(suciedad)* dirt, filth; *(cosa dicha)* obscenity, dirty word; *(acto)* dirty trick ♦ **decir cochinadas** to use foul language.

co·chi·ne·ar intr. COLL. to act or behave like a pig.

co·chi·ne·ro, –ra adj. *(de pobre calidad)* fit for hogs or pigs;

COLL. slow and gentle *<trote c.* slow and gentle trot>; *(habitual)* routine, habitual.

co·chi·ni·lla f. ENTOM. cochineal insect; *(materia colorante)* cochineal; ZOOL. wood louse, sow bug ♦ **c. de humedad** pill bug • **c. de San Antón** ladybug.

co·chi·ni·llo m. piglet, suckling pig.

co·chi·no, –na I. m.f. ZOOL. pig, hog; FIG., COLL. *(persona)* pig, swine; *(tacaño)* miser, tightwad —m. CUBA, ICHTH. triggerfish ♦ **c. montés** *or* **de monte** wild pig II. adj. *(sucio)* filthy, dirty; COLL. *(ruin)* rotten, miserable *<suerte c.* rotten luck>.

co·chi·que·ra f. COLL. pigsty.

co·chi·te her·vi·te COLL. I. adv. helter-skelter, pell-mell II. m. madcap, frenzied person.

co·chi·tril m. COLL. *(pocilga)* pigsty; FIG. *(barraca)* dirty hovel, pigsty.

co·chi·zo m. MIN. richest part of a mine.

co·cho, –cha I. past part. see **cocer** II. adj. CUL. *(cocido)* cooked; *(sucio)* dirty, filthy; COL. coarse, raw II. m. ZOOL. pig; CHILE, CUL. gruel *or* porridge made with corn meal; ARG. mixture of corn meal and carob —f. ZOOL. sow.

co·chu·ra f. *(acción de hervir)* cooking, boiling; *(acción de poner al horno)* baking; *(masa de pan)* batch of fresh bread dough.

co·da¹ f. MUS. coda.

co·da² f. CARP. wedge.

co·dal I. adj. elbow, elbow-shaped II. m. *(pieza de armadura)* armor piece for elbow; CARP., CONSTR. frame; ARCHIT. shore, prop; BOT. layer (of a grapevine); MIN. brick arch (in a mine gallery); MEX. large candle.

co·das·te m. MARIT. sternpost.

co·da·zo m. jab, poke (with one's elbow) ♦ **abrirse paso a codazos** to elbow one's way through • **dar un c.** to jab, elbow • **dar codazos** to nudge.

co·de·a·dor, –do·ra AMER. I. adj. mooching, sponging II. m.f. moocher, sponger.

co·de·ar intr. *(abrirse paso)* to elbow, jostle; CHILE, ECUAD., PERU to wheedle, cajole —reflex. COLL. to rub elbows with, hobnob with.

co·de·í·na f. PHARM. codeine.

co·de·lin·cuen·te LAW I. adj. codelinquent II. m.f. accomplice, accessory.

co·de·o m. elbowing, jostling; CHILE, ECUAD., PERU wheedling, cajoling.

co·de·ra f. *(remiendo)* elbow patch; MARIT. mooring cable.

co·deu·dor, –do·ra m.f. codebtor, joint debtor.

có·di·ce m. codex, manuscript.

co·di·cia f. *(avaricia)* greed, avarice; *(envidia)* envy, covetousness; FIG. *(ambición)* desire, thirst *<c. de saber* thirst for knowledge>; TAUR. fighting spirit.

co·di·cia·dor, –do·ra I. adj. covetous, coveting II. m.f. coveter.

co·di·ciar tr. to covet, desire.

co·di·ci·lar adj. LAW codicillary.

co·di·ci·lo m. LAW codicil.

co·di·cio·so, –sa I. adj. greedy, avaricious; FIG., COLL. *(trabajador)* hard-working, industrious ♦ **ser c. de** to be greedy for, covet II. m.f. greedy *or* avaricious person; FIG., COLL. *(trabajador)* hard worker, industrious person.

co·di·fi·ca·ción f. LAW codification; *(de mensajes)* encoding.

co·di·fi·ca·dor, –do·ra I. adj. codifying II. m.f. codifier.

co·di·fi·car §70 tr. LAW to codify *<c. leyes* to codify laws>; to encode *<c. un mensaje* to encode a message>.

có·di·go m. LAW code *<c. civil* civil code>; *(cifra)* code, cipher; *(reglamento)* set of rules, code *<c. de la circulación* traffic code> ♦ **c. de comercio** commercial code • **c. de edificación** building code • **c. de leyes** legal code • **c. del honor** honor code • **c. fiscal** tax code • **c. militar** articles of war • **c. penal** penal code • **c. postal** zip code.

co·di·llo m. ZOOL. elbow, forearm; *(tubo)* elbow pipe; BOT. stump of a cut branch; CUL. shoulder; EQUIT. *(estribo)* stirrup; MARIT. either end of the keel ♦ **dar c.** to trick, outwit • **tirar a uno al c.** COLL. to try to ruin someone • **jugársela uno de c. a otro** COLL. to trick, outwit.

co·di·rec·tor, –to·ra I. adj. *(de una empresa)* co-managing;

CINEM. co-directing II. m.f. *(uno de varios jefes)* co-manager; CINEM. co-director.

co·do m. ANAT. elbow; ZOOL. elbow, knee; *(medida antigua)* cubit; TECH. elbow (pipe, joint); FIG. *(en un río, camino)* bend, turn ♦ **a base de codos** by sheer hard work • **alzar el c.** to drink, booze it up • **c. con c.** neck and neck • **dar con el c.** to nudge • **hablar por los codos** to blabber, be a chatterbox • **mentir por los codos** to lie like a trooper • **romperse los codos** to grind, study hard.

co·e·fi·cien·te I. adj. coefficient, cooperating II. m. MATH. coefficient; *(valor relativo)* correlation coefficient ♦ **c. de dilatación** PHYS. coefficient of expansion • **c. de inteligencia** intelligence quotient.

co·er·ci·ble adj. coercible, restrainable.

co·er·ción f. coercion.

co·er·ci·ti·vo, –va adj. coercive, restrictive.

co·e·tá·ne·o, –a I. adj. contemporary, coetaneous II. m.f. contemporary.

co·e·ter·ni·dad f. THEOL. coeternity.

co·e·xis·ten·cia f. coexistence.

co·e·xis·ten·te adj. coexistent.

co·e·xis·tir intr. to coexist.

co·ex·ten·der·se §50 reflex. to coextend.

co·fa f. MARIT. top (of the lower mast) ♦ **c. para el vigía** crow's-nest • **c. mayor** maintop.

co·fia f. *(red)* hair net; *(gorro)* cap, bonnet; BOT. calyptra.

co·fra·de m.f. *(miembro)* member (of a society) —m. RELIG. brother —f. RELIG. sister.

co·fra·dí·a f. *(de hombres)* brotherhood, confraternity; *(de mujeres)* sisterhood, society; *(gremio)* guild, association; *(pandilla)* gang, band *<una c. de ladrones* a band of thieves>.

co·fre m. *(arca)* chest, trunk; *(caja pequeña)* case, box; ICHTH. boxfish, trunkfish.

co·ge·de·ro, –ra I. adj. ripe, ready for picking II. m. *(asidero)* handle —f. *(palo para frutas)* pole for picking fruit; COL. rope headstall.

co·ge·dor, –do·ra I. adj. picking, gathering II. m.f. *(persona)* picker, gatherer —m. *(cajón para recoger la basura)* dustpan; *(cucharón)* ash *or* coal shovel; ECUAD. *(trago)* shot (of liquor); *(agente)* government conscription agent.

co·ger §34 tr. *(agarrar)* to take hold of, seize, grasp *<le cogí de la mano* I took hold of his hand>; *(recoger)* to collect, gather up *<cogimos aceitunas* we gathered olives>; *(apresar)* to catch, capture *<cogieron al asesino* they captured the assassin>; *(contener)* to contain, hold *<esta caja no coge mucho* this box does not hold much>; *(ocupar)* to occupy, take up *<la cama coge mucho espacio* the bed takes up a lot of space>; *(absorber)* to absorb, soak up *<este tipo de esponja coge mucha agua* this type of sponge absorbs a lot of water>; *(alcanzar)* to catch up with, overtake *<le cogí a pocos pasos de la puerta* I caught up with him a few steps from the door>; *(encontrar)* to find *<esperan cogerle de buen humor* they hope to find him in a good mood>; *(sorprender)* to surprise, catch by surprise *<la noche me cogió en camino a casa* nightfall caught me by surprise on the way home>; *(atropellar)* to run over *or* down *<el coche le cogió* the car ran him over>; MED. to catch, contract *<cogí un resfriado* I caught a cold>; TAUR. to gore; FIG. *(entender)* to understand, get *<no podían c. lo que dijo* they could not understand what he said>; AMER., VULG. to screw, fuck ♦ **cogerle las vueltas** FIG. to know someone's game, have someone's number —intr. *(hallarse)* to be, be located; to fit in *<la silla no coge allí* the chair does not fit in there>; COLL. *(decidir)* to decide *<cogió y se fue* he decided to go> —reflex. to grab, seize *<se cogió un pedazo de pan* he grabbed a piece of bread>; *(robar)* to steal, make off with; DOM. REP., P. RICO *(incurrir)* to fall into a life of crime; *(acostumbrarse)* to get used to; *(llevarse bien)* to get along *<no nos cogemos* we do not get along> ♦ **cogerse los dedos** FIG. to get burned, be had.

▲ In many Latin-American countries (esp. ARG., BOL., CUBA, MEX., PAR., URUG.) *coger* is commonly used in its vulgar meaning "to screw, fuck." In those countries it is almost invariably replaced by a synonym such as *tomar* or *agarrar.*

co·ges·tión f. *(administración por varios)* comanagement;

(gestión por jefes y trabajadores) labor and management copartnership.

co·ges·tio·na·rio, –ria adj. comanaging.

co·gi·da f. AGR. *(cosecha)* harvest, crop; *(acto de esquilmar)* harvesting, reaping; TAUR. goring, horning.

co·gi·do I. past part. see **coger II.** m. SEW. pleat, fold.

co·gi·ta·bun·do, –da adj. pensive, meditative.

cog·na·ción f. *(parentesco por la línea femenina)* cognation, blood relationship (on the female side); *(parentesco)* relationship.

cog·na·do, –da m.f. cognate.

cog·ni·ción f. cognition.

cog·no·men·to m. cognomen.

cog·nos·ci·ble adj. cognoscible, knowable.

cog·nos·ci·ti·vo, –va adj. cognitive.

co·go·llo m. *(parte interior)* heart (of lettuce); BOT. *(renuevo)* shoot, bud; *(del pino)* top of a pine tree; FIG. *(lo sustancioso)* heart, core <el c. de un asunto the heart of a matter>; *(lo mejor)* cream <el c. de la sociedad the cream of society>; AMER. sugarcane top; CHILE flattery, praise; ARG., ENTOM. large cricket; COL., MIN. outcrop.

co·go·te m. ANAT. nape of the neck ♦ **ponérselas en el c.** C. AMER., COLL. to scram, beat it • **tieso de c.** arrogant.

co·go·te·ra f. *(cubrenuca)* neck cover, havelock; *(sombrero para bestias)* sunshade for beasts of burden; ARG. cow's dewlap.

co·go·tu·do, –da AMER., COLL. **I.** m.f. *(rico)* wealthy or influential person; *(orgulloso)* arrogant person **II.** adj. *(rico)* wealthy, influential; *(orgulloso)* arrogant.

co·gu·jón m. corner or point (of a mattress, sack).

co·ha·bi·ta·ción f. cohabitation.

co·ha·bi·tar intr. to live together, cohabit.

co·he·cha·dor, –do·ra I. adj. bribing **II.** m.f. briber.

co·he·char tr. *(sobornar)* to bribe; AGR. to till fallow land.

co·he·cho m. *(soborno)* bribe, bribery; AGR. tilling of fallow land.

co·hen m.f. *(hechicero)* soothsayer, seer —m. *(alcahuete)* procurer —f. *(tercera)* procuress.

co·he·re·de·ro, –ra m. coheir, joint heir —f. coheiress, joint heiress.

co·he·ren·cia f. coherence <la c. de un discurso the coherence of a speech>; PHYS. cohesion.

co·he·ren·te adj. coherent.

co·he·sión f. PHYS. cohesion; FIG. *(unión)* cohesion, unity <la c. de un equipo the unity of a team>.

co·he·si·vo, –va adj. cohesive.

co·he·sor m. RAD. coherer.

co·he·te m. *(petardo)* rocket, skyrocket; MIL. rocket, missile; C. AMER., MEX. *(pistola)* pistol; MEX. *(agujero)* blasting hole ♦ **al c.** ARG., BOL., COLL. in vain • **c. balístico** ballistic missile • **c. chispero** shower rocket • **c. de señales** flare, signal rocket • **c. de tres cuerpos** three-stage rocket • **c. sonda** sounding rocket • **c. tronador** detonating rocket • **cohetes** fireworks • **escapar** or **salir como un c.** to be off like a shot.

co·he·te·rí·a f. rocketry.

co·hi·bi·ción f. restraint, restriction.

co·hi·bir tr. *(inhibir)* to restrain, inhibit; *(desasosegar)* to make uneasy —reflex. *(inhibirse)* to be or feel inhibited; *(desasosegar)* to be or feel uneasy.

co·ho·nes·tar tr. to give an honest appearance to (an action).

co·hor·te f. cohort.

coi·ma f. *(del garitero)* rake-off (in a gambling house); *(concubina)* concubine; AMER. bribe, payola.

co·in·ci·den·cia f. *(ocurrencia casual)* coincidence; agreement <en c. con in agreement with>.

co·in·ci·den·te adj. coincidental, coincident.

co·in·ci·dir intr. to coincide <su cumpleaños coincide con la Navidad her birthday coincides with Christmas>; *(acordar)* to agree, coincide <tus ideas coinciden con las mías your ideas agree with mine>; *(encontrarse)* to meet <coincidieron en el mercado they met in the market place>.

co·in·qui·li·no, –na I. adj. pertaining to cotenancy or joint tenancy **II.** m.f. cotenant, joint tenant.

co·in·te·re·sa·do, –da I. adj. jointly interested **II.** m.f. partner, jointly interested party.

coi·to m. coitus, sexual intercourse.

co·ja, cojo see **coger.**

co·je·ar intr. *(renquear)* to limp, hobble; to wobble <una mesa que cojea a table that wobbles>; COLL. *(obrar mal)* to slip up, be at fault ♦ **saber de qué pie cojea** COLL. to know someone's faults.

co·je·ra f. limp, lameness.

co·ji·jo m. *(desazón)* discontent, peevishness; *(sabandija)* bug, insect.

co·jín m. *(almohadón)* cushion, hassock; MARIT. bolster, fender ♦ **c. de aire** air cushion.

co·ji·ne·te m. *(almohadilla)* small cushion; RAIL. chair, socket; MECH. *(de un eje)* bearing, bolster; PRINT. roller clamp ♦ **c. de agujas** needle bearing • **c. de bolas** or de **bolillas** ball bearing • **c. de collares** collar bearing • **c. de rodillos** roller bearing • **c. de roscar** screw plate • **cojinetes** COL., MEX., VEN. saddlebags.

co·jo, –ja I. adj. *(tullido)* lame, crippled; *(un mueble)* wobbly; FIG. feeble, faulty <razonamiento c. faulty reasoning> ♦ **no ser c. ni manco** FIG., COLL. to be all there **II.** m.f. lame person, cripple.

co·jón m. VULG. testicle, ball.

co·jo·nu·do, –da adj. VULG. *(estupendo)* great, fantastic; *(valiente)* gutsy, ballsy.

co·ju·do, –da adj. *(no castrado)* entire, not gelded or castrated; *(bobo)* dimwitted, retarded.

col f. cabbage ♦ **c. de Bruselas** Brussels sprouts • **c. morada** or **roja** red cabbage • **c. rizada** kale • **entre c. y c., lechuga** variety is the spice of life.

co·la¹ f. ASTRON., ORNITH., ZOOL. tail; train <la c. de un vestido the train of a dress>; *(fila)* line, queue; *(parte final)* end, rear; MUS. prolonged final note; ARCHIT. tailing, inside joint; GUAT. bodyguard; VEN. sinecure ♦ **a la c.** at the end, last • **c. de caballo** BOT. horsetail; *(pelo)* ponytail • **c. de milano** or **de pato** ARCHIT. dovetail tenon • **c. de zorra** BOT. foxtail • **comer c.** ARG., URUG. to suffer a setback • **hacer c.** to line up, form a line • **piano de c.** grand piano • **ser arrimado a la c.** FIG., COLL. to be short on brains • **tener** or **traer c.** FIG. to have serious consequences • **te va a salir c.** MEX., COLL. you will have to face the consequences.

co·la² f. glue, gum ♦ **c. de boca** solid glue pastille (for stamps, envelopes) • **c. de pescado** fish glue, isinglass • **c. de retal** PAINT. size (for preparing canvas) • **eso no pega ni con c.** COLL. that's nonsense.

co·la·bo·ra·ción f. *(cooperación)* collaboration, cooperation; LIT. contribution.

co·la·bo·ra·cio·nis·mo m. POL. collaboration (with an enemy).

co·la·bo·ra·cio·nis·ta POL. **I.** adj. pertaining to collaborationism **II.** m.f. collaborationist.

co·la·bo·ra·dor, –do·ra I. adj. *(cooperador)* collaborating; LIT. contributing **II.** m.f. *(cooperador)* associate, collaborator, co-worker; LIT. contributor.

co·la·bo·rar intr. *(cooperar)* to collaborate, cooperate; LIT. to contribute.

co·la·ción f. conferral, granting <la c. de un grado universitario the conferral of a university degree>; *(comparación)* comparison, collation; *(merienda)* light meal, snack; RELIG. collation (appointment to a benefice); AMER. sweet, candy ♦ **sacar** or **traer a c.** FIG. to make mention of, bring up.

co·la·cio·nar tr. to collate, compare.

co·lac·tá·ne·o, –a m. foster brother —f. foster sister (nursed by the same female).

co·la·da f. *(acción de blanquear)* bleaching, whitening; *(lejía)* bleach, whitener; *(ropa blanca)* bleached clothes; *(cañada)* cattle trail; *(cañón)* gorge, gulch; COLL. *(enredo)* mess, jam; METAL. tap (in a furnace) ♦ **salir en la c.** FIG., COLL. to come out in the wash, be exposed.

co·la·de·ra f. *(colador)* colander, strainer; AMER. sewer drain.

co·la·de·ro m. *(cedazo)* colander, strainer; *(camino)* narrow path or trail; COLL. *(sitio)* passage, opening; *(tribunal)* lenient examination committee; MIN. winze (hole for dumping ore).

co·la·do, –da I. past part. see **colar II.** adj. METAL. cast <hierro c. cast iron>; cold, drafty <aire c. cold air> ♦ **estar c. por** COLL. to be in love ♦ **hierro c.** cast iron.

co·la·dor m. *(cedazo)* colander, strainer; PRINT. leach tub; RELIG. collator.

co·la·do·ra f. *(lavandera)* laundress, washerwoman; *(máquina)* bleaching machine.

co·la·du·ra f. *(acción de colar)* straining, filtering; *(residuos)* residue (from straining or filtering); FIG. *(error)* blunder, faux pas.

co·lai·na f. split or crack in lumber.

co·lam·bre f. group of hides or skins (of animals).

co·la·ni·lla f. small sliding bolt (for securing doors and windows).

co·la·ña f. low partition or room divider.

co·lap·so m. MED. collapse, breakdown; FIG. *(ruina)* collapse ♦ **c. nervioso** nervous breakdown.

co·lar §19 tr. *(tamizar)* to strain, filter; *(blanquear)* to bleach, whiten (clothes); COLL. to pass or pass off, foist off <*c. un billete falso* to pass off a counterfeit bill>; RELIG. to collate, grant (a benefice); METAL. to cast, pour —intr. *(introducirse)* to squeeze or pass through <*el aire cuela por esta rendija* air passes through this crack>; *(rezumar)* to ooze, seep; COLL. *(beber)* to booze, tipple ♦ **no c. una cosa** COLL. to be unbelievable or unconvincing —reflex. *(infiltrarse)* to sneak in, slip in; *(equivocarse)* to blunder, slip up; COLL. *(mentir)* to lie, fib.

co·la·te·ral I. adj. collateral, side <*altar c.* side altar>; *(transversal)* collateral <*pariente c.* collateral relative> II. m.f. collateral (relative).

co·la·ti·tud f. ASTRON. colatitude.

co·la·ti·vo, –va adj. collative.

col·cha f. bedspread.

col·cha·do, –da I. past part. see **colchar** II. adj. quilted III. m. quilting.

col·cha·du·ra f. quilting.

col·char tr. to quilt ♦ **c. cabos** MARIT. to lay or twist ropes.

col·chón m. mattress ♦ **c. de aire** MECH. air cushion • **c. de muelles** or **de tela metálica** spring mattress • **c. de plumas** feather bed • **c. neumático** air mattress.

col·cho·ne·ro, –ra I. adj. SEW. tufting <*aguja c.* tufting needle> II. m.f. *(fabricante)* mattress maker or manufacturer; *(vendedor)* mattress seller.

col·cho·ne·ta f. *(cojín)* cushion; *(colchón)* light mattress.

co·le·a·da f. switch, flick (of the tail); *(de un perro)* wag (of the tail); AMER. throwing down a bull by its tail.

co·le·ar tr. TAUR. to hold (a bull) by its tail; AMER. to throw down (a bull) by its tail; C. AMER., P. RICO to border on, be close to <*colea en los cincuenta* he's close to fifty>; CHILE to fail (an examination); COL., VEN., COLL. to bother, annoy; GUAT. to follow, tail; PERU, P. RICO to prepare (cocks) for a fight; DOM. REP. to court, woo —intr. *(mover la cola)* to switch, flick its tail; *(un perro)* to wag its tail ♦ **c. todavía** FIG. to be unfinished, pend <*este asunto colea todavía* this affair is still pending> • **vivito y coleando** COLL. alive and kicking —reflex. VEN. to skid (said of a carriage).

co·lec·ción f. collection <*una c. numismática* a coin collection>; LIT. anthology.

co·lec·cio·na·dor, –do·ra m.f. collector.

co·lec·cio·nar tr. to collect, form a collection of.

co·lec·cio·nis·ta m.f. collector.

co·lec·ta f. *(recaudación)* collection (of money); RELIG. *(oración)* collect.

co·lec·ta·ción f. collection.

co·lec·tar tr. to collect <*c. un impuesto* to collect a tax>.

co·lec·ti·cio, –cia adj. MIL. *(sin experiencia)* inexperienced, novice (said of troops); *(reunido)* collected.

co·lec·ti·vi·cé, colectivice see **colectivizar**.

co·lec·ti·vi·dad f. *(agrupación)* collectivity, whole; *(propiedad)* collective ownership ♦ **la c. social** society, whole community.

co·lec·ti·vis·mo m. POL. collectivism.

co·lec·ti·vis·ta POL. I. adj. collectivistic II. m.f. collectivist.

co·lec·ti·vi·za·ción f. collectivization.

co·lec·ti·vi·zar §04 tr. to collectivize —reflex. to unionize.

co·lec·ti·vo, –va I. adj. *(agrupado)* collective; communal, joint <*esfuerzo c.* joint effort> ♦ **contrato c.** collective bargaining • **granja c.** collective farm II. m. GRAM. collec-

tive (noun); ARG., BOL., PERU small bus, minibus; PERU collection of money.

co·lec·tor I. adj. collecting II. m. collector <*c. de impuestos* tax collector>; ELEC. collector; *(sumidero)* main sewer ♦ **c. centrífugo** centrifugal collector • **c. de aceite** AUTO. drip pan • **c. de basuras** garbage chute.

co·lec·tu·rí·a f. *(recaudación)* collecting, collection; *(oficio)* collectorship; *(despacho)* tax collector's office.

co·le·ga m. colleague, associate.

co·le·ga·ta·rio, –ria m.f. LAW colegatee, joint legatee.

co·le·gia·do, –da I. past part. see **colegiarse** II. adj. collegiate III. m.f. *(miembro de un colegio)* collegian —m. SPORT. *(árbitro)* umpire, referee.

co·le·gial I. adj. *(de un colegio)* school, collegiate; MEX., COLL. inexperienced, raw II. m. *(estudiante)* schoolboy; MEX., COLL. inexperienced person ♦ **c. capellán** student monitor.

co·le·gia·la f. schoolgirl.

co·le·giar·se reflex. to enroll in a college.

co·le·gia·tu·ra f. educational grant, scholarship.

co·le·gio m. *(de enseñanza primaria)* primary or elementary school; *(de enseñanza secundaria)* secondary or high school; *(asociación)* college, association <*c. de abogados* bar association>; *(comunidad)* college <*C. de Cardenales* College of Cardinals> ♦ **c. de internos** boarding school • **c. de párvulos** nursery school • **c. electoral** POL. electoral college • **c. mayor** residence hall, dormitory.

co·le·gir §57 tr. *(reunir)* to collect, gather; *(inferir)* to infer, gather <*colijo de lo dicho que ellos no vienen* I gather from what has been said that they are not coming>.

co·le·gis·la·dor, –do·ra adj. POL. colegislative.

co·le·o m. tail wagging, tail switching.

co·le·óp·te·ro ENTOM. I. adj. coleopteral II. m. coleopteran ♦ **coleópteros** Coleoptera.

có·le·ra f. PHYSIOL. bile, choler; FIG. *(ira)* anger, fury —m. MED. cholera ♦ **c. asiático** MED. Asiatic cholera • **c. de gallinas** MED. chicken cholera • **c. esporádico** MED. sporadic or summer cholera • **c. morbo** MED. cholera morbus, gastroenteritis • **cortar la c.** COLL. to snack, have a snack • **cortar la c. a** FIG., COLL. to calm down, soothe • **dar c.** FIG. to anger, infuriate • **descargar la c. en** FIG. to vent one's anger on • **montar uno en c.** FIG. to get angry • **tomarse uno de la c.** FIG. to lose one's temper.

co·lé·ri·co, –ca I. adj. MED. choleroid, choleraic; MED. *(que padece cólera)* suffering from cholera; FIG. *(irascible)* choleric, irascible II. m.f. MED. cholera patient, person suffering from cholera; FIG. *(cascarrabias)* irascible or ill-tempered person.

co·les·te·rol m. or **co·les·te·ri·na** f. BIOL. cholesterol, cholesterin.

co·le·ta f. *(pelo)* pigtail, queue; FIG., COLL. *(adición escrita)* postscript; TEX. *(lona)* coarse material; COL., CUBA coarse canvas; ECUAD. percaline; MEX. nankeen ♦ **cortarse la c.** TAUR. to give up bullfighting; COLL. *(dejar una actividad)* to quit, give up • **tener** or **traer c.** FIG. to have serious consequences.

co·le·ta·zo m. *(golpe)* lash or blow with the tail; AUTO. sway.

co·le·to m. *(vestidura)* jerkin; FIG., COLL. oneself <*decir para su c.* to say to oneself> ♦ **echarse algo al c.** FIG., COLL. to eat or drink something right up • **echarse un libro al c.** FIG., COLL. to read a book straight through.

col·ga·de·ro, –ra I. adj. hangable II. hook, peg.

col·ga·di·zo, –za I. adj. hanging, suspended II. m. CONSTR. *(tejadillo)* lean-to; CUBA porch roof.

col·ga·do, –da I. past part. see **colgar** II. adj. *(incierto)* uncertain, pending; FIG. *(burlado)* let down, disappointed ♦ **dejar c. a** FIG. to disappoint, let down.

col·ga·dor m. *(percha)* clothes hanger; PRINT. *(tabla)* peel.

col·ga·jo m. *(jirón)* rag, tatter; *(racimo)* bunch (of fruit); DEROG. hanging, drapery; SURG. flap (of skin).

col·ga·mien·to m. hanging, suspension.

col·gan·te I. adj. hanging ♦ **puente c.** suspension bridge II. m. *(adorno)* pendant; ARCHIT. festoon; ARG., PAR., P. RICO watch chain.

col·gar §16 tr. *(suspender)* to hang, hang up; *(adornar)* to drape with hangings; *(ahorcar)* to hang, execute by hanging; COLL. *(achacar)* to hang, pin <*le colgaron la culpa a él* they pinned the blame on him>; EDUC. *(reprobar)* to fail, flunk ♦ **c. los hábitos** to give up the cloth; FIG. to give up an action or profession —intr. *(estar colgado)* to hang, be suspended; *(caer)* to hang down, dangle <*la falda cuelga de un lado* the skirt hangs down on one side>.

co·li·ba·ci·lo m. BACT. colon bacillus.

co·li·brí m. [pl. **-brí·es**] ORNITH. hummingbird.

có·li·co, –ca MED. **I.** adj. colonic **II.** m. colic ♦ **c. hepático** hepatic spasm *or* colic • **c. miserere** ileus, intestinal occlusion • **c. nefrítico** *or* **renal** nephritic spasm *or* colic • **saturnino** *or* **c. de plomo** lead *or* painter's colic —f. mild colic.

co·li·cua·ción f. *(disolución)* melting, dissolving; MED. rapid weight loss (through excessive liquid discharge).

co·li·cuar §78 tr. to dissolve or melt together.

co·li·cua·ti·vo, –va adj. MED. causing rapid weight loss (through elimination of liquid waste).

co·li·cue·cer §17 tr. var. of **colicuar.**

co·li·flor f. BOT. cauliflower.

co·li·ga·ción f. *(unión)* colligation, union; *(ligazón)* connection, link.

co·li·ga·do, –da **I.** past part. see **coligarse** **II.** adj. allied, united **III.** m.f. ally, confederate.

co·li·gar·se §47 reflex. to ally, unite, confederate.

co·li·ge see **colegir.**

co·li·ja, colijo see **colegir.**

co·li·lla f. cigarette butt.

co·li·lle·ro, –ra m.f. person who picks up cigarette butts.

co·lín **I.** adj *(de poca cola)* short-tailed, bobtailed (said of a horse); MUS. *(de tamaño pequeño)* smallish (grand piano) **II.** m. MEX., ORNITH. colin, American quail *or* bobwhite.

co·li·na f. *(cerro)* hill; BOT. cabbage seed; *(plantío)* cabbage patch.

co·lin·dan·te adj. adjacent, adjoining.

co·lin·dar intr. to be adjacent, adjoin.

co·li·ne·al adj. collinear.

co·li·ne·ta f. *(ramillete)* bouquet of flowers; VEN., CUL. egg and almond confection.

co·li·no m. AGR. *(plantío)* cabbage nursery (for seedlings); *(simiente)* cabbage seed.

co·li·rio m. MED. collyrium, eyewash.

co·li·sa f. ARTIL., MARIT. *(plataforma)* swivel gun platform; *(cañón)* swivel gun; CHILE straw hat.

co·li·se·o m. coliseum, colosseum.

co·li·sión f. *(choque)* collision; FIG. *(conflicto)* clash, conflict <*una c. de intereses* a conflict of interests> ♦ **c. de frente** head-on collision.

co·li·ti·gan·te m.f. colitigant, joint litigant.

co·li·tis f. MED. colitis, colonitis.

col·ma·do, –da **I.** past part. see **colmar** **II.** adj. *(lleno)* full, filled; *(abundante)* abundant, copious; heaping <*una cucharada c.* a heaping spoonful> **III.** m. *(café)* restaurant, café; *(almacén)* grocery store.

col·mar tr. *(llenar)* to fill (up), fill to the brim; FIG. to heap, shower <*c. a uno de alabanzas* to heap praise on someone>; FIG. *(satisfacer)* to fulfill, satisfy ♦ **eso colma la medida** FIG. that's the last straw!

col·me·na f. ENTOM. beehive, hive; FIG. hive, hub of activity <*una c. humana* a human hive>; MEX. bee.

col·me·nar m. apiary.

col·me·ne·ro, –ra m.f. beekeeper, apiarist —m. MEX., ZOOL. honey bear.

col·mi·lla·zo m. bite *or* blow with a fang *or* tusk.

col·mi·llo m. ANAT. canine tooth, eyetooth; ZOOL. *(del elefante)* tusk; *(del perro)* fang ♦ **enseñar los colmillos** COLL. to show one's teeth • **escupir por el c.** COLL. to talk big • **tener el c. retorcido** COLL. to be sly *or* crafty.

col·mi·llu·do, –da adj. ZOOL. having long fangs *or* tusks; FIG. *(astuto)* shrewd, crafty.

col·mo **I.** m. *(exceso)* overflow; FIG. height, ultimate <*el c. de la elegancia* the height of elegance>; COLL. limit, last straw <*eso es el c.* that is the last straw> ♦ **para c. de desgracias** to make matters worse, to top it all off **II.** adj. see **colmo, –ma.**

col·mo, –ma **I.** adj. filled to the brim **II.** m. see **colmo.**

co·lo·ca·ción f. *(acción)* placing, positioning; *(lugar)* place, position; *(empleo)* position, employment; COM. investment.

co·lo·car §70 tr. *(poner)* to place, position <*c. un cuadro en la pared* to place a painting on the wall>; MIL. to position, station; COM. to place, invest <*c. dinero en una hipoteca* to invest money in a mortgage>; to place, settle <*coloqué a mi hermano en un empleo* I placed my brother in a job> ♦ **c. una historia a alguien** to give someone the same old story —reflex. *(situarse)* to place *or* station oneself; to get a job <*me coloqué en una compañía minera* I got a job in a mining company>; SPORT. to place <*el equipo se colocó en segundo lugar* the team came in second>.

co·lo·dra f. *(para leche)* milk pail; *(para vino)* wine pail (used for measuring); *(cuerna)* drinking horn.

co·lo·fón m. PRINT. colophon.

co·lo·fo·nia f. rosin.

co·loi·dal *or* **co·loi·de·o, –a** adj. CHEM. colloidal.

co·loi·de m. CHEM. colloid.

Co·lom·bia f. Colombia.

co·lom·bia·no, –na adj. & m.f. Colombian.

co·lom·bi·no, –na adj. of Christopher Columbus.

co·lom·bó·fi·lo, –la **I.** adj. pigeon-breeding **II.** m.f. pigeon breeder.

co·lon m. ANAT. colon; GRAM. *(oración)* main clause; *(dos puntos)* colon; *(punto y coma)* semicolon ♦ **c. imperfecto** GRAM. subordinate *or* dependent clause • **c. perfecto** GRAM. simple sentence, main clause • **c. transverso** ANAT. transverse colon.

co·lón m. FIN. colon (currency of Costa Rica and El Salvador).

Co·lón Columbus ♦ **Cristóbal C.** Christopher Columbus.

co·lo·na·to m. AGR. tenant farming.

co·lo·nia f. *(conjunto de personas)* colony; POL. colony (dependent country or territory); *(perfume)* cologne, eau de cologne; *(cinta)* silk ribbon; CARIB. sugar-cane plantation; MEX. suburb, new district; CUBA, BOT. alpinia ♦ **c. penal** penal colony • **c. penitenciaria** labor *or* prison camp • **c. veraniega** *or* **de verano** summer camp.

Co·lo·nia Cologne.

co·lo·nia·je m. AMER. *(época)* colonial period; *(gobierno)* colonial government.

co·lo·nial **I.** adj. colonial <*el gobierno c.* the colonial government>; COM. *(ultramarino)* imported, overseas **II.** m. [pl. **-nial·es**] COM. imported goods.

co·lo·nia·lis·mo m. POL. colonialism.

co·lo·nia·lis·ta adj. & m.f. POL. colonialist.

co·lo·ni·za·ción f. colonization.

co·lo·ni·za·dor, –do·ra **I.** adj. colonizing, settling **II.** m.f. colonizer, settler.

co·lo·ni·zar §04 tr. to colonize, settle.

co·lo·no m. *(colonizador)* colonist, settler; AGR. *(arrendatario)* tenant farmer; CARIB. sugar planter.

co·lo·qué, coloque see **colocar.**

co·lo·quial adj. colloquial.

co·lo·quio m. *(conversación)* conversation, talk; *(conferencia)* colloquium, seminar; LIT. *(diálogo)* dialogue, colloquy.

co·lor m. color; *(colorante)* coloring, tint; *(afeite)* rouge; FIG. *(pretexto)* pretext, pretense <*so c. de* under the pretext of>; *(aspecto)* aspect, coloring ♦ **a c.** in color • **c. complementario** complementary color • **c. elemental** primary color • **colores** MIL. colors, flag • **c. firme** fast color • **c. local** local color • **c. vivo** bright color • **dar c.** *or* **colores** to color • **de c.** colored <*una falda de c. de rosa* a rose-colored skirt>; *(no caucásico)* colored, of color • **mudar de c.** FIG., COLL. *(sonrojarse)* to blush; *(palidecer)* to blanch, turn pale • **pintar con colores trágicos** FIG. to take a dim view of things • **ponerse de mil colores** FIG., COLL. to flush • **sacarle los colores a la cara** FIG. to embarrass, make blush • **salirle los colores a la cara** FIG. to get embarrassed • **subido de c.** off-color (joke, story) • **ver las cosas de c. de rosa** FIG., COLL. to be optimistic, see things through rose-colored glasses.

co·lo·ra·ción f. *(acción)* coloring; *(color)* coloration, coloring; BIOL. markings ♦ **c. defensiva** BIOL. protective markings.

co·lo·ra·do, –da **I.** past part. see **colorar** **II.** adj. *(que tiene color)* colored; *(rojizo)* red, reddish; FIG. off-color, risqué <*un chiste c.* a risqué joke> ♦ **ponerse c.** to blush **III.** m. *(color)* red; CUBA, MED. scarlet fever.

co·lo·ra·do·te, –ta adj. COLL. ruddy, red-faced.
co·lo·ran·te I. adj. coloring II. m. colorant.
co·lo·rar tr. *(dar de color)* to color, give color to; *(teñir)* to dye, tint; *(pintar)* to paint.
co·lo·re·ar tr. *(dar de color)* to color, give color to; FIG. *(encubrir)* to whitewash, gloss over; *(excusar)* to justify, make excuses for —intr. *(enrojecerse)* to redden, turn red; BOT. *(madurar)* to ripen.
co·lo·re·te m. rouge.
co·lo·ri·do m. *(acción)* coloring; *(mezcla de colores)* coloration; *(brillo)* verve, style <*el ensayo tiene poco c.* the essay has little style>; *(color)* color <*el c. de sus labios* the color of her lips>.
co·lo·rin·che m. ARG. combination of gaudy colors.
co·lo·rir §38 tr. *(dar de color)* to color; FIG. *(teñir)* to dye; *(pretextar)* to gloss over, rationalize —intr. to be colored.
co·lo·ris·mo m. PAINT. emphasizing color rather than line; LIT. floridity (of style).
co·lo·ris·ta PAINT. I. adj. coloristic II. m.f. colorist.
co·lo·sal adj. *(grande)* colossal, gigantic; FIG. *(extraordinario)* colossal, extraordinary.
co·lo·so m. *(estatua)* colossus; *(gigante)* giant; FIG. *(fenómeno)* colossus, phenomenon.
co·lu·dir intr. LAW to collude.
co·lum·brar tr. *(ver de lejos)* to discern, see at a distance; FIG. *(adivinar)* to guess, surmise.
co·lu·me·lar adj. DENT. canine <*diente c.* canine tooth>.
co·lum·na f. ARCHIT. column <*c. dórica* Doric column>; MIL., PHYS., PRINT. column; FIG. *(sostén)* supporter, pillar <*una c. de la iglesia* a pillar of the church> ♦ **c. de dirección** AUTO. steering column • **c. vertebral** ANAT. spine, spinal column • **quinta c.** MIL. fifth column.
co·lum·na·ta f. ARCHIT. colonnade.
co·lum·nis·ta m.f. JOURN. columnist.
co·lum·piar tr. *(mecer)* to swing, push in a swing; AMER. to understand —reflex. *(mecerse)* to swing; FIG., COLL. *(contonearse)* to swagger, sway; *(equivocarse)* to make a mistake.
co·lum·pio m. *(hamaca)* swing; CUBA rocking chair ♦ **c. basculante** or **de tabla** seesaw.
co·lu·sión f. collusion.
co·lu·to·rio m. MED. mouthwash, gargle.
co·lu·vie f. gang of rascals.
col·za f. BOT. colza, rape.
co·lla¹ f. MIL. gorget (piece of armor); *(de pesca)* fish trap.
co·lla² f. PHILIP. storm preceding the monsoons.
co·lla³ I. adj. BOL. Andean; ARG. Bolivian. II. m.f. BOL. inhabitant of the Andean plateau; ARG. Bolivian.
co·lla⁴ f. team of dockworkers.
co·lla·do m. *(cerro)* hill; *(entre dos montañas)* mountain pass.
co·llar m. *(adorno)* necklace; *(cadena)* chain; *(de animal)* collar; *(aro de hierro)* iron collar; MECH. ring, collar; ORNITH., ZOOL. collar, ruff; CUBA, MEX. harness, collar.
co·lla·rín m. *(collar pequeño)* small collar; RELIG. collar; *(de una botella)* label (on the neck of a bottle); MECH. sleeve, tube.
co·lla·zo m. *(hermano de leche)* foster brother; *(compañero de trabajo)* fellow worker; AGR. *(labrador)* farmhand, laborer; *(siervo)* serf; *(palo)* rake —f. *(hermana de leche)* foster sister; *(compañera de trabajo)* fellow worker.
co·lle·ra f. *(de un caballo)* horse collar; FIG. *(de presidiarios)* chain gang; AMER. *(yunta)* brace, yoke (of animals); *(pareja)* team, pair (of people) ♦ **colleras** ARG., CHILE cufflinks.
co·ma¹ f. GRAM. comma; MUS. comma, caesura; *(ménsula)* miserere, misericord; BOT., OPT. coma ♦ **sin faltar una c.** in the minutest detail.
co·ma² m. MED. coma.
co·ma·dre f. godmother (of a child); *(relación)* mother of the child (in relation to the godmother); *(partera)* midwife; COLL. *(alcahueta)* go-between, procuress.
co·ma·dre·ar intr. COLL. to gossip.
co·ma·dre·ja f. ZOOL. weasel; ARG. opossum.
co·ma·dre·o m. COLL. gossip, tattling.
co·ma·drón m. COLL. male midwife.
co·ma·dro·na f. midwife.

co·mal m. C. AMER., MEX. clay dish used for baking tortillas.
co·ma·lia f. VET. sheep dropsy.
co·man·dan·cia f. MIL. *(grado)* command (post of commander); *(distrito)* district (under a commander); *(edificio)* headquarters.
co·man·dan·te MIL. m. commander, commanding officer; *(grado)* major ♦ **c. de armas** commandant • **c. de barco** captain, commander • **c. en jefe** or **general** commander-in-chief.
co·man·dar tr. MIL. to command, lead.
co·man·di·ta f. ♦ **sociedad en c.** COM. silent partnership.
co·man·di·tar tr. COM. to finance (an enterprise) as a silent partner.
co·man·di·ta·rio, –ria COM. I. adj. silent <*sociedad c.* silent partnership> II. m.f. silent partner.
co·man·do m. MIL. commando, assault unit; MIL. *(mando)* command; TECH. control ♦ **c. a distancia** TECH. remote control • **c. aéreo** MIL. air command.
co·mar·ca f. region, district.
co·mar·ca·no, –na adj. nearby, neighboring.
co·mar·car §70 intr. to border on, adjoin —tr. to plant trees in straight lines.
co·ma·to·so, –sa adj. MED. comatose.
com·ba I. f. *(convexidad)* bend, curve; *(alabeo)* warp; *(juego y cuerda)* skipping rope, jump rope (game and rope); PERU large hammer • **hacer combas** COLL. to swing one's hips • **no perder c.** COLL. to not miss a chance • **saltar a la comba** to skip rope, jump rope II. adj. see **combo, –ba.**
com·ba·du·ra f. bending, curving.
com·bar tr. *(encorvar)* to bend, curve; *(alabear)* to warp —reflex. *(encorvarse)* to bend, curve; *(alabearse)* to warp.
com·ba·te m. *(lucha)* combat; FIG. *(desasosiego)* struggle, conflict; SPORT. *(concurso)* fight, contest ♦ **c. naval** naval or sea battle • **c. nulo** draw • **fuera de c.** out of action • **ganar por fuera de c.** SPORT. to win by a knockout.
com·ba·ti·ble adj. combatable.
com·ba·tien·te I. adj. combatant, fighting II. m. *(luchador)* combatant, fighter; MIL. soldier.
com·ba·tir intr. *(pelear)* to fight, battle —tr. to fight, combat <*el bombero combatió el fuego* the fireman fought the fire>; *(acometer)* to attack, rush; FIG. to beat upon, lash <*las olas combatían el malecón* the waves beat upon the sea wall>; *(agitar)* to agitate, convulse; *(impugnar)* to oppose —reflex. to fight, struggle; FIG. *(agitarse)* to become agitated.
com·ba·ti·vi·dad f. combativeness.
com·ba·ti·vo, –va adj. combative.
com·bi·na·ción f. combination <*c. de colores* color combination>; *(bebida)* cocktail; *(prenda)* slip, petticoat; FIG. *(plan)* plan, scheme; CHEM. compound; RAIL. connection; MATH. permutation ♦ **c. métrica** POET. rhyme scheme.
com·bi·na·do I. past part. see **combinar** II. m. *(bebida)* cocktail; *(complejo industrial)* industrial complex; CHEM. compound.
com·bi·nar tr. *(unir)* to combine <*c. lo dulce con lo amargo* to combine the bitter with the sweet>; *(arreglar)* to arrange, work out <*c. ideas* to work out ideas>; CHEM. to compound, combine —reflex. CHEM. to coalesce, combine.
com·bi·na·to·rio, –ria MATH. I. adj. combinatorial II. f. combinatorics.
com·bo, –ba I. adj. bent, curved II. m. *(asiento)* stand on which wine casks are placed; ARG., CHILE *(martilla)* sledge hammer; CHILE *(puñetazo)* punch, blow —f. see **comba.**
com·bu·ren·te PHYS. I. adj. causing combustion II. m. combustive agent.
com·bus·ti·bi·li·dad f. combustibility.
com·bus·ti·ble I. adj. combustible II. m. fuel ♦ **c. fósil** CHEM., GEOL. fossil fuel.
com·bus·tión f. combustion ♦ **c. espontánea** spontaneous combustion.
co·me·de·ro, –ra I. adj. edible II. m. *(para animales)* feeding trough; *(comedor)* dining room.
co·me·dia f. *(género cómico)* comedy; *(obra)* play, drama; *(edificio)* theater; FIG. *(fingimiento)* pretense, farce ♦ **c.**

alta high comedy • **c. de capa y espada** cloak-and-dagger play • **c. de costumbres** comedy of manners • **c. de enredo** comedy of intrigue • **c. en un acto** one-act play • **c. ligera** light comedy • **hacer la c.** COLL. to pretend, make believe.

co·me·dian·te, –ta m. (comic) actor —f. (comic) actress —m.f. COLL., FIG. (hipócrita) hypocrite.

co·me·di·do, –da I. past part. see **comedirse** II. adj. (cortés) courteous, polite; (reservado) reserved; S. AMER. (servicial) obliging; ECUAD. meddling.

co·me·di·mien·to m. (moderación) moderation, restraint; (cortesía) courtesy, politeness.

co·me·dio m. (de lugar) center, middle (of a territory); (de tiempo) interval (of time).

co·me·dir·se §48 reflex. (moderarse) to control oneself, restrain oneself; ARG., ECUAD. to meddle, interfere.

co·me·dor, –do·ra I. adj. gluttonous II. m.f. glutton, big eater ♦ **coche c.** dining car —m. (pieza) dining room; (restaurante) restaurant; (muebles) dining room suite.

co·men·cé see **comenzar.**

co·men·da·dor m. MIL. (caballero) knight commander (of a military order); (dignatario) middle-ranking commander; RELIG. prelate.

co·men·da·do·ra f. RELIG. mother superior.

co·men·sal m.f. (convidado) commensal, mealtime companion; (persona a cargo) dependent.

co·men·ta·dor, –do·ra m.f. (persona que comenta) commentator; (chismoso) malicious gossip.

co·men·tar tr. (discutir) to comment on, talk about; (explicar) to make comments on, annotate.

co·men·ta·rio m. (observación) commentary, observation ♦ **comentarios** (memorias históricas) commentaries, historical memoirs; (chisme) gossip, malicious remarks • **sin c.** no comment.

co·men·ta·ris·ta m.f. commentator.

co·men·to m. (de una obra) commentary, annotation; (observación) observation, comment.

co·men·zar §29 tr. & intr. to begin, start ♦ **c. a** to begin <comenzaron a llorar they began to cry> • **c. con** to begin with • **c. por** to begin with <comenzó por el segundo he began with the second one>; to begin by <comenzó por explicar las reglas she began by explaining the rules>.

co·mer tr. to eat <comimos mucho pan we ate a lot of bread>; (roer) to corrode, erode; to consume <la estufa come mucha leña the stove consumes a lot of wood>; FIG. (descolorar) to fade (colors); (en los juegos) to take (a piece in chess or checkers) ♦ **sin comerlo ni beberlo** FIG., COLL. without having had anything to do with it —intr. to eat <comieron en casa they ate at home>; (cenar) to dine, eat a meal • **c. y callar** COLL. beggars can't be choosers • **dar de c.** to feed • **ser de buen c.** COLL. to have a healthy appetite • **tener qué c.** to have enough to live on —reflex. to eat up <me lo comí todo I ate it all up>; FIG. (disipar) to eat up, squander; (pasar) to skip, skip over <el orador se comía palabras the speaker skipped over words>; (pelear) to have it in for one another; (ser mejor) to beat, beat out <mi trabajo se come al tuyo my job beats yours>.

co·mer·cia·ble adj. (con que se puede comerciar) marketable; FIG. (sociable) sociable, affable.

co·mer·cial I. adj. commercial, business <distrito c. business district> ♦ **centro c.** shopping center II. m. AMER. commercial, advertisement.

co·mer·cia·lis·mo m. commercialism.

co·mer·cia·li·za·ción f. commercialization.

co·mer·cia·li·zar §04 tr. to commercialize.

co·mer·cian·te I. adj. trading II. m.f. merchant —m. businessman, shopkeeper —f. businesswoman ♦ **c. al por mayor** wholesaler • **c. al por menor** retailer.

co·mer·ciar intr. to trade, traffic <c. en algodón to trade in cotton>; to have dealings, do business <no comercio con esa compañía I don't do business with that company>.

co·mer·cio m. (negocio) commerce, business, trade; (conjunto de comerciantes) business world; (tienda) store, business ♦ **c. exterior** foreign trade • **c. interior** domestic trade.

co·mes·ti·ble I. adj. edible, eatable II. m. food, foodstuff ♦ **comestibles** groceries, provisions.

co·me·ta m. ASTRON. comet —f. (juguete) kite.

co·me·ter tr. (encargar) to entrust, charge with <me cometieron la realización del plan they charged me with carrying out the plan>; (un crimen) to commit, perpetrate; (un error) to make, commit <cometió cinco errores he made five mistakes>.

co·me·ti·do I. past part. see **cometer** II. m. assignment, charge.

co·me·zón f. (picazón) itch, itching; FIG. (deseo) itch, longing.

co·mi·ble adj. COLL. edible, fit to eat.

co·mi·cas·tro m. second-rate actor.

co·mi·ci·dad f. comedy, humor.

co·mi·cio m. POL. (elecciones) elections, voting; HIST. (asamblea) comitia (of Romans).

có·mi·co, –ca I. adj. comical, funny II. m. (actor) comic actor; (gracioso) comic, comedian —f. (actriz) comic actress; (graciosa) comic, comedienne ♦ **c. de la legua** strolling player.

co·mi·da, comido see **comedirse.**

co·mi·da I. f. (alimento) food, nourishment; meal <hacemos tres comidas al día we have three meals a day>; (almuerzo) lunch; (acción) eating; COL., BOT. medulla, pith ♦ **cambiar la c.** to vomit, throw up • **c. campestre** picnic • **c. corrida** AMER. table d'hote II. adj. see **comido, –da.**

co·mi·die·ra, comidió see **comedirse.**

co·mi·di·lla f. FIG., COLL. favorite pastime <el tenis es su c. tennis is her favorite pastime>; COLL. (objeto de conversación) talk, topic of conversation <ser la c. del pueblo to be the talk of the town>.

co·mi·do, –da I. past part. see **comer** II. adj. fed, having eaten ♦ **c. de gusanos** eaten by worms, worm-eaten • **c. y bebido** COLL. supported, kept • **estar c.** to have eaten • **ser c. por servido** FIG., COLL. to be unprofitable • **sin haberlo c. ni bebido** through no fault of one's own, for no apparent reason III. f. see **comida.**

co·mien·ce, comienzo see **comenzar.**

co·mien·zo m. (empiezo) beginning, start; MED. onset ♦ **al c.** at first • **dar c.** to begin, start.

co·mi·lón, –lo·na I. adj. gluttonous II. m.f. glutton, big eater —f. COLL. feast, spread ♦ **darse una c.** to have a feast.

co·mi·llas f.pl. quotation marks ♦ **abrir c.** to open quotation marks • **cerrar c.** to close quotation marks • **entre c.** in quotes.

co·mi·no m. BOT. cumin (plant and seed) ♦ **no importarle a uno un c.** FIG., COLL. to not give a damn about • **no valer un c.** FIG., COLL. to be worthless.

co·mi·sar tr. to seize, confiscate.

co·mi·sa·rí·a f. or **co·mi·sa·ria·to** m. (cargo) commissariat; (oficina) office of a commissioner; AMER. police station ♦ **c. de policía** police station.

co·mi·sa·rio m. commissioner, commissary <c. de policía police commissioner>; POL. commissar; AMER. chief of police; P. RICO deputy mayor.

co·mis·car §70 tr. to nibble, pick at (food).

co·mi·sión f. committing, commission <la c. de un delito the commission of a crime>; (encargo) task, assignment; (delegación) commission, committee; COM. commission, percentage; MEX. type of policeman ♦ **a c.** COM. on a commission basis • **c. mercantil** COM. agency contract; (porcentaje) commission, percentage • **c. mixta** joint committee • **c. permanente** standing committee • **c. planificadora** planning board.

co·mi·sio·na·do, –da I. past part. see **comisionar** II. adj. commissioned, authorized III. m.f. (comisario) commissioner; FIN., POL. committee or board member; CUBA sheriff ♦ **c. de apremio** tax collector.

co·mi·sio·nar tr. to commission, authorize.

co·mi·sio·nis·ta m.f. COM. commission merchant.

co·mi·so m. LAW. (confiscación) confiscation, seizure; (objeto) confiscated goods.

co·mi·so·rio, –ria adj. LAW valid for a specified period.

co·mis·qué, comisque see **comiscar.**

co·mis·tra·jo m. COLL. hodgepodge, mess (food).

co·mi·su·ra f. ANAT. commissure, corner <la c. de los párpados the corner of the eyelids>.

co·mi·té m. committee.

co·mi·ten·te I. adj. commissioning, entrusting II. m.f. client.

co·mi·ti·va f. retinue, party ♦ **c. fúnebre** cortege, funeral procession.

co·mo §G17, 46 I. adv. *(lo mismo que)* as <*ella no es tan alta c. yo* she is not as tall as I>; *(de tal modo)* like <*nadan c. peces* they swim like fish>; *(en calidad de)* as, in the capacity of <*c. presidente que es, tiene que asistir* as president he must attend>; *(casi)* about, approximately <*había c. cien personas en la reunión* there were about one hundred people at the meeting>; *(según)* as <*c. dice la Biblia* as the Bible says> ♦ **c. quiera que** however, no matter how • **c. sea** one way or the other, however II. conj. *(puesto que)* as, since <*c. no teníamos tiempo, no pudimos terminar el proyecto* since we did not have time, we were not able to finish the project>; *(si)* if <*c. no me digas la verdad, no te voy a ayudar* if you do not tell me the truth, I am not going to help you>; *(así que)* as <*c. llegó, la orquesta empezó a tocar* as he arrived, the orchestra began to play>; *(por ejemplo)* such as, like <*me gustan los deportes c. el tenis y el golf* I like sports such as tennis and golf> ♦ **así c.** as soon as • **c. que** as if • **c. quien dice** so to speak • **c. no sea para** unless to • **c. si** as if • **hacer como si** to pretend.

có·mo I. adv. *(en qué condiciones)* how <*¿c. está usted?* how are you?>; *(por qué)* why, how come <*¿c. no viniste ayer?* why didn't you come yesterday?> ♦ **¿a c.?** how much, at what price? <*¿a c. están las fresas hoy?* how much are strawberries today?> • **¿c. así?** how is that possible? • **¿c. no?** why not? II. interj. *(que expresa sorpresa)* what, what did you say; how <*¡c. nieva!* how it is snowing!> ♦ **¡c. no!** AMER. sure, of course III. m. how <*el c. y el cuándo* the how and the when>.

có·mo·da f. I. f. chest of drawers, bureau II. adj. see **cómodo, –da.**

có·mo·da·men·te adv. *(confortablemente)* comfortably; *(convenientemente)* conveniently.

co·mo·di·dad f. *(confort)* comfort, comfortableness; *(conveniencia)* convenience; *(ventaja)* advantage, interest ♦ **comodidades** comforts, amenities.

co·mo·dín I. adj. AMER. comfort-loving II. m. AMER. comfort lover; *(naipes)* joker, wild card; FIG. *(aparato)* all-purpose gadget; *(pretexto)* weak excuse.

có·mo·do, –da I. adj. *(confortable)* comfortable <*un sofá c. a comfortable sofa*>; *(útil)* handy, convenient; comfortable, relaxed <*ella se siente muy c. con ustedes* she feels very comfortable with you> II. f. see **cómoda.**

co·mo·dón, –do·na adj. comfort-loving.

co·mo·do·ro m. MARIT. commodore.

co·mo·quie·ra adv. anyway, anyhow.

Co·mo·ras f. Comoros.

com·pac·tar tr. to compact, compress.

com·pac·to, –ta adj. *(apretado)* compact; *(denso)* dense, tight; PRINT. close, compact; AUTO. compact.

com·pa·de·cer §17 tr. to sympathize with, commiserate with <*compadezco los problemas del director* I sympathize with the problems of the director>; *(tener lástima)* to pity, feel sorry for —reflex. *(tener compasión)* to sympathize, commiserate <*él se compadece del dolor ajeno* he sympathizes with the pain of others>; *(tener lástima)* to pity <*se compadecían a los pobres* they pitied the poor>; *(armonizar)* to harmonize <*sus ideas no se compadecen con las mías* their ideas don't harmonize with mine>; *(acordarse)* to agree <*no me compadezco con ustedes* I don't agree with you>.

com·pa·dra·je m. *(entre compadres)* relationship between parents and godparents; *(conspiración)* conspiracy, cabal.

com·pa·drar intr. *(contraer compadrazgo)* to become a godfather *or* godmother; *(hacerse amigo)* to become friends.

com·pa·draz·go m. *(parentesco)* godfatherhood *or* godmotherhood; *(compadraje)* relationship between parents and godparents; MEX. ring, cabal.

com·pa·dre m. godfather (of the child); *(relación)* father of the child (in relation to the godfather); COLL. friend, pal; ARG., COLL. braggart, show-off.

com·pa·dre·ar intr. *(ser amigos)* to be friends; ARG., COLL. *(jactarse)* to brag, show off.

com·pa·gi·na·ción f. *(ordenamiento)* arranging, putting in order; PRINT. page make-up.

com·pa·gi·na·dor, –do·ra m.f. PRINT. pager; *(ordenador)* arranger.

com·pa·gi·nar tr. *(arreglar)* to arrange, put in order; FIG. *(reconciliar)* to reconcile; *(acordar)* to be in keeping, to agree; PRINT. to make up —reflex. to go together, be compatible.

com·pa·ñe·ris·mo m. camaraderie, comradeship.

com·pa·ñe·ro, –ra m.f. *(amigo)* companion, comrade; *(colega)* colleague, associate; FIG. *(de una pareja)* mate, counterpart ♦ **c. de armas** comrade in arms • **c. de clase** classmate • **c. de colegio** schoolmate • **c. de cuarto** roommate • **c. de las fatigas** fellow sufferer • **c. de trabajo** fellow worker, workmate • **c. de viaje** traveling companion.

com·pa·ñí·a f. COM., MIL., THEAT. company; *(acompañamiento)* company, companionship ♦ **c. anónima** COM. stock company • **c. comanditaria** COM. silent partnership • **C. de Jesús** Society of Jesus, the Jesuits • **c. de seguros** COM. insurance company • **c. tenedora** COM. holding company • **hacer c. a alguien** to keep someone company • **señora de c.** attendant, lady companion • **y C.** COM. and Company.

com·pa·ra·ble adj. comparable.

com·pa·ra·ción f. *(similitud)* comparison; GRAM. comparison; LIT. simile ♦ **en c. con** in comparison with *or* to, compared with *or* to • **sin c.** beyond comparison.

com·pa·rar tr. *(relacionar)* to compare; *(cotejar)* to collate, check.

com·pa·ra·ti·va·men·te adv. comparatively.

com·pa·ra·ti·vo, –va adj. & m. comparative.

com·pa·re·cen·cia f. LAW appearance ♦ **orden de c.** summons.

com·pa·re·cer §17 intr. LAW to appear <*compareció ante el juez* he appeared before the judge>.

com·pa·re·cien·te LAW I. adj. appearing II. m.f. person appearing.

com·pa·ren·cia f. ARG., CHILE, LAW appearance.

com·pa·ren·do m. LAW summons, subpoena.

com·pa·ri·ción f. LAW. *(comparecencia)* appearance; *(orden)* summons.

com·par·sa m.f. THEAT. *(actor)* extra, supernumerary —f. THEAT. *(séquito)* chorus, extras; *(banda de máscaras)* masquerade, costumed group.

com·par·ti·men·to *or* **com·par·ti·mien·to** m. *(división)* division; *(participación)* sharing; *(departamento)* compartment ♦ **c. estanco** MARIT. watertight compartment.

com·par·tir tr. *(repartir)* to divide (up); to share <*c. la responsabilidad* to share the responsibility>.

com·pás m. MATH. compass, compasses; MARIT. compass; MUS. *(ritmo)* time; bar, measure <*c. de espera* rest measure>; RELIG. monasterial territory; FIG. *(regla)* rule, norm ♦ **al c. de** in step with, in time with • **c. binario** MUS. double time • **c. de calibres** calipers • **c. de división** dividers • **c. de espesores** thickness gauge • **c. de proporción** proportional dividers • **c. ternario** MUS. triple time • **fuera de c.** out of step, off beat • **llevar el c.** MUS. to beat time, keep time • **perder el c.** MUS. to lose the beat.

com·pa·sa·do, –da I. past part. see **compasar** II. adj. moderate, prudent.

com·pa·sar tr. *(medir)* to measure with a compass; FIG. *(disponer)* to apportion, proportion; MUS. to divide into bars.

com·pa·si·llo m. MUS. common *or* four-four time.

com·pa·sión f. compassion, pity ♦ **llamar** *or* **mover a la compasión** to move to pity • **¡por c.!** for pity's sake! • **sin c.** merciless • **tener c. de** to feel sorry for.

com·pa·si·vo, –va adj. *(caritativo)* compassionate; *(clemente)* sympathetic, merciful.

com·pa·ti·bi·li·dad f. compatibility.

com·pa·ti·ble adj. compatible.

com·pa·trio·ta m.f. compatriot.

com·pe·ler tr. to compel, force.

com·pen·dia·dor, –do·ra I. adj. summarizing, abridging II. m.f. summarizer, abridger.

com·pen·diar tr. to summarize, abridge.

com·pen·dio m. summary, abridgment ♦ **en c.** in short, in brief.

com·pen·dio·so, –sa adj. concise.

com·pen·di·zar §04 tr. to summarize, abridge.

com·pe·ne·tra·ción f. *(interpenetración)* interpenetration; FIG. *(afinidad)* mutual understanding.

com·pe·ne·trar·se reflex. to interpenetrate; FIG. *(tener afinidad)* to understand each other, share each other's feelings.

com·pen·sa·ción f. *(equilibrio)* compensation; LAW recompense, redress ♦ **en c.** in exchange *or* return.

com·pen·sa·dor, –do·ra I. adj. compensating II. m. compensator (pendulum).

com·pen·sar tr. *(equilibrar)* to compensate, make up for *<c. una pérdida* to make up for a loss>; *(recompensar)* to indemnify, reimburse.

com·pen·sa·to·rio, –ria adj. compensatory.

com·pe·ten·cia f. *(competición)* competition; *(rivalidad)* rivalry; *(incumbencia)* responsibility, obligation; *(aptitud)* competence, capability; *(rama)* scope, field *<no es de mi c.* it's outside my field>; LAW *(jurisdicción)* competence, jurisdiction; AMER., SPORT. competition ♦ **a c.** competitively • **de c.** competitive • **hacer la c. a** to compete with *or* against.

com·pe·ten·te adj. *(adecuado)* appropriate, suitable; *(apto)* competent, capable; LAW competent, legally qualified *<una autoridad c.* a legally qualified authority>.

com·pe·ter intr. *(pertenecer)* to be one's business *or* concern, have to do with someone *<este asunto compete al ministerio* this matter is the concern of the ministry>; *(incumbir)* to be up to someone, be incumbent on something *<a ellos les competió encontrar una solución* it was up to them to find a solution>.

com·pe·ti·ción f. *(rivalidad)* competition, rivalry; SPORT. *(certamen)* competition, tournament.

com·pe·ti·dor, –do·ra I. adj. competing, rival II. m.f. competitor.

com·pe·tir §48 intr. *(contender)* to compete, vie; *(igualar)* to match, be on a par *<este coche compite con aquél* this car is on a par with that one>.

com·pe·ti·ti·vo, –va adj. competitive.

com·pi·la·ción f. compilation.

com·pi·la·dor, –do·ra I. adj. compiling II. m.f. compiler.

com·pi·lar tr. to compile.

com·pin·che m.f. COLL. pal, chum; *(cómplice)* accomplice.

com·pi·ta, compito see **competir**.

com·pi·tie·ra, compitió see **competir**.

com·pla·cen·cia f. contentment, complacency; *(gusto)* pleasure, satisfaction.

com·pla·cer §51 tr. to please, gratify —reflex. ♦ **complacerse en** *or* **de** to delight in, take pleasure in.

com·pla·ci·do, –da I. past part. see **complacer** II. adj. satisfied, content ♦ **c. de sí** self-satisfied, smug.

com·pla·cien·te adj. *(satisfecho)* satisfied, content; *(obsequioso)* complaisant, obliging.

com·ple·ji·dad f. complexity.

com·ple·jo, –ja I. adj. *(complicado)* complex, complicated; GRAM. complex; MATH. compound II. m. INDUS., PSYCH. complex ♦ **c. de Edipo** Oedipus complex • **c. de Electra** Electra complex • **c. de inferioridad** inferiority complex • **c. fundamental** GEOL. basal complex.

com·ple·men·tar tr. to complement, complete —reflex. to be complementary, to complement each other.

com·ple·men·ta·rio, –ria adj. complementary.

com·ple·men·to m. *(suplemento)* complement; *(perfección)* completion, culmination; GRAM. object, complement *<c. directo* direct object>.

com·ple·ta·men·te adv. completely, entirely.

com·ple·tar tr. *(integrar)* to complete, make whole; *(acabar)* to finish; *(perfeccionar)* to perfect.

com·ple·to, –ta adj. *(entero)* complete, whole; *(acabado)* completed, finished; *(íntegro)* complete, perfect; *(lleno)* full ♦ **por c.** completely.

com·ple·xi·dad f. var. of **complejidad**.

com·ple·xión f. PHYSIOL. *(físico)* build, physique; *(constitución)* constitution, make-up; FIG. *(naturaleza)* disposition, nature; RHET. anadiplosis.

com·pli·ca·ción f. complication.

com·pli·ca·do, –da I. past part. see **complicar** II. adj. *(complejo)* complicated; *(intricado)* intricate, complex; FIG. *(difícil)* difficult, sticky.

com·pli·car §70 tr. *(dificultar)* to complicate, make complicated; *(embrollar)* to embroil, entangle —reflex. *(ponerse difícil)* to become complicated; *(embrollarse)* to become involved.

cóm·pli·ce CRIMIN. I. adj. accessory, abetting II. m.f. accomplice, abettor ♦ **c. encubridor** LAW accessory after the fact • **c. instigador** LAW accessory before the fact.

com·pli·ci·dad f. complicity, abetment.

com·plot m. [pl. **-plots**] *(conspiración)* plot, conspiracy; *(intriga)* intrigue, scheme.

com·plo·tar intr. to plot, conspire.

com·pon see **componer**.

com·pon·drá, compondría see **componer**.

com·po·ne·dor, –do·ra m.f. *(árbitro)* arbitrator; PRINT. *(de textos)* compositor; S. AMER. bonesetter —m. PRINT. composing stick ♦ **amigable c.** LAW arbitrator.

com·po·nen·da f. compromise, settlement.

com·po·nen·te adj. & m. component.

com·po·ner §54 tr. *(formar)* to compose, put together, form; LIT., MUS. to compose, create; CUL. *(aderezar)* to season, dress; *(reparar)* to repair, fix; *(adornar)* to decorate, arrange *<c. una sala* to decorate a room>; *(reconciliar)* to reconcile *<c. a dos enemigos* to reconcile two enemies>; *(arreglar)* to arrange, fix *<con dinero se puede c. el negocio* with money one can fix the deal>; *(moderar)* to soothe, calm; MED., COLL. to settle *<la leche te compondrá el estómago* milk will settle your stomach>; PRINT. *(un texto)* to compose, make up; MATH. to compound; S. AMER., MED. to set (bones); ARG. to prime (fighting cocks, racehorses); CHILE, MEX. to castrate, fix —intr. LIT., MUS. to compose —reflex. to be composed *or* made up *<el grupo se compone de artistas y músicos* the group is made up of artists and musicians>; *(ataviarse)* to dress up, primp; *(reconciliarse)* to reconcile, make up; *(calmarse)* to compose oneself ♦ **componérselas** FIG., COLL. to fend for oneself, shift for oneself.

com·pon·ga, compongo see **componer**.

com·po·ni·ble adj. reconcilable.

com·por·ta·ble adj. bearable, tolerable.

com·por·ta·mien·to m. behavior, conduct.

com·por·tar tr. FIG. *(aguantar)* to bear, tolerate; *(llevar)* to involve, entail —reflex. to behave, conduct oneself ♦ **comportarse mal** to misbehave.

com·po·si·ción f. *(estructura)* composition, make-up; LIT., MUS. composition; *(redacción)* composition *<el alumno escribió una c.* the student wrote a composition>; PRINT. composition, typesetting; GRAM. composition (of words); FIG. *(mesura)* composure ♦ **hacer c. de lugar** to size up the situation.

com·po·si·tor, –to·ra I. adj. composing II. m.f. MUS. composer; PRINT. compositor, typesetter; ARG., SPORT. horse trainer; CHILE, MED. bonesetter.

com·pos·te·la·no, –na I. adj. of Santiago de Compostela II. m.f. native of Santiago de Compostela.

com·pos·tu·ra f. *(estructura)* composition, make-up; *(reparación)* repair, fixing; *(aseo)* neatness, smartness; *(mezcla)* compound, mixture; *(ajuste)* agreement, arrangement; *(circunspección)* decorum, circumspection; *(calma)* composure, calm; ARG. priming ♦ **en c.** under repair.

com·po·ta f. CUL. compote, stewed fruit.

com·po·te·ra f. CUL. compote bowl *or* dish.

com·pra f. *(acción)* buying, purchasing; *(adquisición)* purchase, buy; *(diario)* daily marketing *or* shopping ♦ **c. al contado** cash purchase • **c. a plazos** installment plan, credit purchase • **hacer compras** to shop • **hacer la c.** to do the daily marketing *or* shopping • **ir de compras** to go shopping.

com·pra·ble *or* **com·pra·de·ro, –ra** adj. purchasable.

com·pra·dor, –do·ra I. adj. purchasing, buying II. m.f. *(adquiridor)* purchaser, buyer; *(cliente)* customer, shopper.

com·prar tr. *(adquirir)* to buy, purchase; FIG. *(sobornar)* to buy, bribe ♦ **c. al contado** to pay cash for • **c. al por mayor** to buy wholesale • **c. al por menor** to purchase at retail • **c. a plazos** *or* **fiado** to buy on the installment plan *or* on credit • **c. de comer** to market, grocery shop • **c. las cosas sueltas** *or* **a bulto** to buy in lots *or* wholesale.

com·pra·ven·ta f. buying and selling; COM., LAW purchase and sale agreement.

com·pre·hen·si·vo, –va adj. var. of **comprensivo.**

com·pren·de·dor, –do·ra adj. *(que contiene)* encompassing; *(que entiende)* understanding.

com·pren·der tr. *(entender)* to understand, comprehend; *(contener)* to include, comprehend <*España comprende muchas provincias* Spain includes many provinces>.

com·pren·si·ble adj. comprehensible, understandable.

com·pren·sión f. *(entendimiento)* comprehension, understanding; LOG. intension.

com·pren·si·vo, –va adj. comprehensive.

com·pre·sa f. MED. compress ♦ **c. fría** MED. cold pack.

com·pre·si·ble adj. compressible.

com·pre·sión f. compression; GRAM. syneresis.

com·pre·si·vo, –va adj. compressive, compressing.

compre·so, –sa past part. see **comprimir.**

com·pre·sor, –so·ra I. adj. compressing, compressive II. m. MECH. compressor.

com·pri·mi·do, –da I. past part. see **comprimir** II. adj. *(apretado)* compressed; FIG. *(reprimido)* restricted, repressed III. m. PHARM. tablet, pill.

com·pri·mir tr. *(apretar)* to compress; FIG. *(reprimir)* to contain, repress.

com·pro·ba·ción f. *(verificación)* confirmation, verification; *(prueba)* proof, evidence.

com·pro·ban·te I. adj. confirming, verifying ♦ II. m. *(prueba)* proof, evidence; COM. voucher, check ♦ **c. de venta** COM. sales slip, receipt.

com·pro·bar §19 tr. *(cotejar)* to compare, check; *(verificar)* to confirm, verify.

com·pro·ba·to·rio, –ria adj. confirming, verifying.

com·pro·me·te·dor, –do·ra adj. compromising, endangering.

com·pro·me·ter tr. *(poner en peligro)* to compromise, endanger <*el traidor comprometió los intereses de la nación* the traitor endangered the interests of the nation>; to compromise, put in a compromising situation <*tu falta de sentido común le comprometió* your lack of common sense put him in a compromising situation>; to impair (health); to submit to the arbitration of <*comprometerán el acuerdo en un juez* they will submit the agreement to the arbitration of a judge>; *(obligar)* to oblige, bind —reflex. *(obligarse)* to commit *or* bind oneself; *(ponerse en peligro)* to compromise oneself <*la nación no quiere comprometerse en estas negociaciones* the nation does not want to compromise itself in these negotiations>; AMER. to get engaged ♦ **comprometerse a** to undertake to.

com·pro·me·ti·do, –da I. past part. see **comprometer** II. adj. *(envuelto)* involved, implicated; *(embarazoso)* embarrassing, compromising; *(escritor)* committed ♦ **estar c.** *(novios)* to be engaged; *(ocupado)* to be tied up *or* involved.

com·pro·me·ti·mien·to m. *(envolvimiento)* involvement, implication; *(promesa)* pledge, promise.

com·pro·mi·sa·rio I. adj. arbitrating, mediating II. m.f. *(árbitro)* arbitrator, mediator; *(delegado)* delegate, representative.

com·pro·mi·so m. *(obligación)* obligation, commitment; *(lío)* compromising situation, jam; *(convenio)* agreement, compromise; *(desposorios)* engagement, betrothal; LAW *(arbitraje)* arbitration; AMER. commercial transaction ♦ **compromisos** MEX. curls, waves • **estar en c.** to be in question • **poner en c.** to call into question • **sin c.** without obligation.

com·prue·be, compruebo see **comprobar.**

com·puer·ta f. *(esclusa)* sluice, floodgate; *(puerta)* hatch, Dutch door ♦ **c. de esclusa** sluice *or* lock gate • **c. de marea** floodgate, tide gate.

com·pues·to, –ta I. past part. see **componer** II. adj. compound *(número c.* compound number>; *(arreglado)* dressed up, decked out; ARCHIT., BOT. composite; GRAM. compound; FIG. *(mesurado)* composed, calm III. m. compound —f. BOT. composite.

com·pul·sa f. *(acción de compulsar)* collation, comparison; LAW certified *or* true copy.

com·pul·sa·ción f. comparison, collation (of documents).

com·pul·sar tr. LAW *(comparar)* to compare, collate; *(copiar)* to make an official copy *or* transcript of; AMER. *(compeler)* to oblige, compel.

com·pul·sión f. LAW compulsion, duress.

com·pun·ción f. *(remordimiento)* compunction, remorse; FIG. *(tristeza)* sorrow, sadness.

com·pun·gir §32 tr. *(mover a compunción)* to move to compunction *or* remorse; *(entristecer)* to move to tears *or* sadness —reflex. *(arrepentirse)* to feel compunction *or* remorse; *(entristecerse)* to feel sad *or* sorrowful, grieve ♦ **compungirse por** to grieve at, be distressed by.

com·pur·ga·ción f. LAW compurgation.

com·pur·gar §47 tr. AMER., LAW to try by compurgation; MEX. to finish serving a prison sentence.

com·pu·sie·ra, compuso see **componer.**

com·pu·ta·ción f. computation, calculation.

com·pu·ta·do·ra f. TECH. computer.

com·pu·ta·do·ri·zar §04 tr. var. of **computarizar.**

com·pu·tar tr. to compute, calculate.

com·pu·ta·ri·zar §04 *or* **com·pu·te·ri·zar** §04 tr. TECH. to computerize.

cóm·pu·to m. computation, calculation.

co·mul·gan·te RELIG. I. adj. communicating II. m.f. communicant.

co·mul·gar §47 tr. RELIG. to administer communion to —intr. RELIG. to take *or* receive communion; FIG. *(compartir)* to share ideas, commune ♦ **c. con ruedas de molino** COLL. to be very gullible.

co·mul·ga·to·rio m. RELIG. communion rail.

co·mún I. adj. common, general <*la opinión c.* the general opinion>; common, commonplace, customary <*esa actitud es c. entre los obreros* that attitude is commonplace among the workers>; ordinary, usual <*es una especie c. de violeta* this is an ordinary variety of violet>; shared, joint <*el proyecto representaba un esfuerzo c.* the project was a joint effort>; *(vulgar)* common, vulgar; FIN. common, public <*acciones comunes* common stocks>; GRAM. common <*nombre c.* common noun> ♦ **en c.** in common • **por lo c.** commonly, generally II. m. general public *or* population; MEX., COLL. behind, backside ♦ **comunes** EDUC. general subjects • **el c. de las gentes** the majority, most people.

co·mu·na f. commune, collective living arrangement; AMER. commune, municipality.

co·mu·nal I. adj. communal II. m. the public *or* community.

co·mu·ne·ro, –ra I. adj. *(popular)* popular, common; SP., HIST. supporting the *comunidades* of Castile; COL., PAR. supporting independence II. m.f. *(copropietario)* joint owner; SP., HIST. supporter of the *comunidades* of Castile; COL., PAR. early supporter of independence ♦ **comuneros** PERU towns with joint pasture land.

co·mu·ni·ca·bi·li·dad f. communicability.

co·mu·ni·ca·ble adj. *(transmisible)* communicable, transmittable; *(sociable)* sociable, communicative.

co·mu·ni·ca·ción f. *(trato)* communication; *(enlace)* connection <*una c. telefónica* a telephone connection>; *(escrito)* communiqué ♦ **comunicaciones** communications (postal, telegraph, telephone) • **estar en c.** to be in touch with.

co·mu·ni·ca·do I. past part. see **comunicar** II. m. communiqué ♦ **c. de prensa** *or* **c. a la prensa** JOURN. press release.

co·mu·ni·can·te I. adj. communicating II. m.f. communicator.

co·mu·ni·car §70 tr. *(informar)* to communicate, convey <*c. las noticias* to convey the news>; *(transmitir)* to communicate, transmit; *(propagar)* to spread —intr. *(tener paso)* to connect, adjoin; *(tratar)* to communicate, correspond <*comunico con mi primo* I correspond with my cousin> —reflex. *(mantener correspondencia)* to communicate, correspond; *(tener paso)* to be connected <*los dos lagos se comunican* the two lakes are connected>.

co·mu·ni·ca·ti·vo, –va adj. *(sociable)* communicative, affable; *(contagioso)* infectious, contagious <*risa c.* infectious laughter>.

co·mu·ni·dad f. *(similitud)* community, similarity <*c. de ideas* community of ideas>; *(pueblo)* community ♦ **comu-**

nidades SP., HIST. popular uprisings during reign of Charles I • **de c.** jointly, in common • **en c.** together.

co·mu·nión f. *(participación)* communion, sharing <*la c. de ideas* the sharing of ideas>; *(comunicación)* union, fellowship; RELIG. *(sacramento)* (Holy) Communion; *(congregación)* congregation.

co·mu·ni·qué, comunique see **comunicar.**

co·mu·nis·mo m. POL. communism, Communism.

co·mu·nis·ta POL. **I.** adj. communist, communistic **II.** m.f. Communist, communist.

co·mún·men·te adv. *(generalmente)* commonly, generally; *(usualmente)* usually, ordinarily.

con §G34 prep. with <*iré c. mi padre* I will go with my father>; *(a pesar de)* in spite of, despite <*c. todas nuestras diferencias, todavía nos amamos* in spite of all of our differences, we still love one another>; to, towards <*ella es amable c. todos* she is friendly towards everyone>; in, with <*c. ira* in anger> ♦ **c. que** so, so then <*c. que se fueron sin decirme* so then, you left without telling me> • **c. tal (de) que** provided that • **c. todo** nevertheless, in spite of everything.

co·na·to m. *(empeño)* conatus, effort; *(intento)* attempt <*c. de robo* robbery attempt>; *(fracaso)* failed attempt, bungle.

con·ca·de·nar tr. to link (up), concatenate.

con·ca·te·na·ción f. *(encadenación)* concatenation, linking; RHET. anadiplosis.

con·ca·vi·dad f. *(calidad de concavo)* concavity, hollowness; *(hueco)* hollow, cavity.

cón·ca·vo, -va **I.** adj. concave, hollow **II.** m. cavity, hollow.

con·ce·bi·ble adj. conceivable, imaginable.

con·ce·bir §48 tr. *(imaginar)* to conceive of, imagine; *(comprender)* to understand, comprehend; PHYSIOL. *(engendrar)* to conceive, become pregnant with; *(sentir)* to begin to feel (something) for, take a (feeling) to <*c. una antipatía por* to take a dislike to> —intr. PHYSIOL. to conceive, become pregnant; *(imaginar)* to conceive, imagine.

con·ce·den·te adj. granting, conceding.

con·ce·der tr. *(otorgar)* to grant, bestow; *(admitir)* to concede, admit.

con·ce·jal, -ja·la m.f. (town) councilor —m. alderman, councilman —f. councilwoman; *(esposa)* town councilor's wife.

con·cen·tra·ción f. concentration ♦ **c. parcelaria** AGR. land consolidation.

con·cen·tra·do, -da **I.** past part. see **concentrar** **II.** adj. *(centrado)* centered; *(condensado)* concentrated; FIG. *(reconcentrado)* uncommunicative, withdrawn.

con·cen·trar tr. *(centralizar)* to center, focus <*c. la luz sobre la página* to focus the light on the page>; *(reunir)* to concentrate, centralize; CHEM. to concentrate —reflex. *(centrarse)* to be concentrated; FIG. *(reconcentrarse)* to withdraw into oneself.

con·cén·tri·co, -ca adj. GEOM. concentric.

con·cep·ción f. PHYSIOL. conception, act of conceiving; FIG. *(idea)* conception, idea ♦ **la Inmaculada** or **Purísima C.** RELIG. the Immaculate Conception.

con·cep·tis·mo m. SP., LIT. conceptism (17th-century literary style).

con·cep·to m. *(pensamiento)* concept; *(idea)* idea, notion; *(agudeza)* pun, witticism; *(juicio)* opinion, judgment <*en mi c.* in my opinion>; *(título)* heading, section ♦ **en ningún c.** under no circumstances • **en todo c.** in every respect • **en** or **por c. de** as, by way of • **por ningún c.** by no means, in no way • **por** or **bajo todos los conceptos** in every respect, from every point of view • **tener buen c. de** or **tener en buen c. a** to think highly of, esteem.

con·cep·tual adj. conceptual.

con·cep·tua·lis·mo m. PHILOS. conceptualism.

con·cep·tuar §67 tr. to consider, judge.

con·cep·tuo·so, -sa adj. *(afectado)* affected, labored (style); *(agudo)* witty, epigrammatic.

con·cer·nien·te adj. concerning, regarding ♦ **en lo c. a** as for, with regard to.

con·cer·nir §25 tr. to concern, be pertinent to —intr. to be pertinent or related.

con·cer·ta·do, -da **I.** past part. see **concertar** **II.** adj. arranged, concerted **III.** m.f. C. RICA servant.

con·cer·ta·dor, -do·ra **I.** adj. arranging **II.** m.f. arranger.

con·cer·tar §49 tr. to arrange, concert <*c. un casamiento* to arrange a marriage>; *(conciliar)* to coordinate, bring together <*c. los esfuerzos* to coordinate efforts>; MUS. to harmonize, tune; *(concluir)* to settle, conclude (a deal) —intr. *(concordar)* to agree, go together; GRAM. to agree <*el adjetivo tiene que c. en género y número con el sustantivo* the adjective has to agree in gender and number with the noun> —reflex. *(ponerse de acuerdo)* to reach an agreement, come to terms; *(ajustarse)* to go together, harmonize; MUS. to be in tune; AMER. to hire oneself out.

con·cer·tis·ta m.f. MUS. concert performer, soloist.

con·ce·si·ble adj. grantable.

con·ce·sión f. *(derecho)* concession, grant; *(reconocimiento)* concession, admission.

con·ce·sio·na·rio, -ria **I.** adj. concessionary **II.** m.f. concessionaire, licensee.

con·ci·ba, concibo see **concebir.**

con·ci·bie·ra, concibió see **concebir.**

con·cien·cia f. *(juicio)* conscience <*c. limpia* clear conscience>; *(integridad)* conscientiousness, scruples; *(conocimiento)* consciousness, awareness ♦ **a c.** conscientiously • **ancho de c.** unscrupulous • **en c.** in good conscience or faith • **libertad de c.** freedom of worship • **remorderle a uno la c.** to have a guilty conscience • **sin c.** unscrupulous • **tener** or **tomar c.** to be or become aware of.

con·cien·zu·da·men·te adv. conscientiously, scrupulously.

con·cien·zu·do, -da adj. conscientious, scrupulous.

con·cier·na, concierne see **concernir.**

con·cier·te, concierto see **concertar.**

con·cier·to m. *(buen orden)* concert, harmony; *(ajuste)* agreement, arrangement; MUS. *(armonía)* harmony; *(función)* concert; *(obra)* concerto ♦ **de c.** in concert, together.

con·ci·lia·ble adj. conciliable, reconcilable.

con·ci·liá·bu·lo m. secret meeting.

con·ci·lia·ción f. conciliation, reconciliation.

con·ci·lia·dor, -do·ra adj. conciliatory.

con·ci·liar¹ tr. to conciliate, reconcile ♦ **c. el sueño** to get to sleep —reflex. to win, gain <*conciliarse el respeto de todos* to gain everyone's respect>.

con·ci·liar² **I.** adj. conciliar, pertaining to councils **II.** m.f. council member.

con·ci·lia·ti·vo, -va or **con·ci·lia·to·rio, -ria** adj. conciliatory, reconciliatory.

con·ci·lio m. *(reunión)* council; *(decretos)* council decrees ♦ **c. ecuménico** RELIG. ecumenical council.

con·ci·sión f. conciseness, concision.

con·ci·so, -sa adj. concise, succinct.

con·ci·tar tr. to stir up, incite.

con·ciu·da·da·no, -na m.f. fellow citizen.

cón·cla·ve or **con·cla·ve** m. RELIG. conclave; FIG. *(asamblea secreta)* conclave, closed or secret meeting.

con·cluir §18 tr. *(terminar)* to conclude, finish; *(deducir)* to conclude, deduce; LAW to sum up; SPORT. to disarm (in fencing) —intr. to finish, end • **c. con** or **en** to end with or in ♦ **c. por** to end up <*concluyeron por esperar* they ended up waiting> —reflex. to finish, end.

con·clu·sión f. *(fin)* conclusion, end; *(deducción)* conclusion, deduction; *(decision)* decision, judgment; LAW *(afirmación final)* summary, summing up ♦ **en c.** in conclusion, finally ♦ **llegar a una c.** to come to a conclusion.

con·clu·si·vo, -va adj. conclusive, final.

con·clu·so, -sa **I.** past part. see **concluir** **II.** adj. LAW closed pending sentence.

con·clu·ya, concluyo see **concluir.**

con·clu·yen·te adj. conclusive, decisive.

con·clu·yen·te·men·te adv. conclusively.

con·clu·ye·ra, concluyó see **concluir.**

con·co·mer·se reflex. COLL. to shrug one's shoulders; FIG. *(sentir comezón)* to squirm.

con·co·mi·tan·cia f. concomitance, coexistence.

con·co·mi·tan·te adj. concomitant, accompanying.

con·co·mi·tar tr. to coexist with, accompany.

con·cor·da·ción f. *(coordinación)* coordination; *(conciliación)* conciliation.

con·cor·da·dor, –do·ra I. adj. *(que coordina)* coordinating; *(que concilia)* conciliating **II.** m.f. *(coordinador)* coordinator; *(conciliador)* conciliator.

con·cor·dan·cia f. *(correspondencia)* agreement, concordance; GRAM. agreement; MUS. harmony ♦ **concordancias** LIT. concordance.

con·cor·dar §19 tr. *(conciliar)* to reconcile, bring into agreement; GRAM. to make agree —intr. *(estar de acuerdo)* to agree; *(corresponder)* to agree, tally; GRAM. to agree.

con·cor·de adj. in accord, in agreement.

con·cor·dia f. *(armonía)* concord, concordance; *(ajuste)* agreement, settlement; *(sortija)* double ring ♦ **de c.** jointly, of a common accord.

con·cre·ción f. GEOL. concretion; MED. stone, calculus <*c. biliar* gallstone>.

con·cre·ta·men·te adv. concretely.

con·cre·tar tr. *(combinar)* to combine, unite; *(resumir)* to summarize, condense; *(precisar)* to specify, state explicitly —reflex. to limit *or* confine oneself; *(tomar forma)* to take shape (a plan).

con·cre·ti·zar §04 tr. to materialize.

con·cre·to, –ta I. adj. *(real)* concrete, real; *(definido)* specific, definite; GRAM., MATH. concrete ♦ **en c.** to sum up, in conclusion *or* short **II.** m. *(concreción)* concretion; AMER. concrete.

con·cu·bi·na f. *(amante)* concubine, mistress; LAW *(esposa)* common-law wife.

con·cu·bi·na·to m. concubinage; LAW *(matrimonio consensual)* common-law marriage.

con·cuer·de, concuerdo see **concordar**.

con·cul·car §70 tr. *(pisotear)* to trample underfoot; FIG. *(una ley)* to break, violate (a law).

con·cu·ña·do, –da m. husband of one's sister-in-law —f. wife of one's brother-in-law.

con·cu·pis·cen·cia f. *(lascivia)* concupiscence, lust; *(codicia)* avarice, greed.

con·cu·pis·cen·te adj. *(lascivo)* concupiscent, lustful; *(avaro)* greedy, avaricious.

con·cu·pis·ci·ble adj. *(deseable)* desirable; *(que hace desear)* sensual <*apetito c.* sensual appetite>.

con·cu·rren·cia f. *(asamblea)* audience, crowd, gathering; *(simultaneidad)* concurrence, coincidence; *(competición)* competition, rivalry; *(auxilio)* assistance, help.

con·cu·rren·te I. adj. *(coincidente)* concurrent, coinciding; *(contendiente)* competing, contending; *(presente)* attending, in attendance **II.** m.f. *(asistente)* person in attendance; *(competidor)* competitor, contender.

con·cu·rri·do, –da I. past part. see **concurrir II.** adj. *(animado)* busy, crowded; *(popular)* well-attended, popular; *(frecuentado)* frequented.

con·cu·rrir intr. *(convenir)* to concur, agree; *(converger)* to converge, meet; *(presenciar)* to be present, attend; *(coincidir)* to coincide; *(contribuir)* to contribute; *(competir)* to compete, contend ♦ **c. en** to agree *or* concur with.

con·cur·san·te m.f. competitor, contestant.

con·cur·sar tr. LAW to declare (a person) bankrupt —intr. to compete.

con·cur·so m. *(certamen)* competition, contest; *(reunión)* concourse, crowd, gathering; concurrence <*c. de circunstancias* concurrence of circumstances>; *(ayuda)* assistance, cooperation; LAW bankruptcy proceedings ♦ **c. de acreedores** COM. meeting of creditors • **c. hípico** horse show • **fuera de c.** out of the running.

con·cu·sión f. LAW *(extorsión)* extortion, graft; *(sacudimiento)* concussion, shock.

con·cu·sio·na·rio, –ria I. adj. extortionary **II.** m.f. extortionist.

con·cha I. f. ZOOL. shell <*c. de tortuga* turtle shell>; *(molusco)* shellfish, mollusk; *(carey)* tortoise shell; MARIT. cove, inlet; THEAT. prompter's box; FIG. *(caparazón)* shell; AMER. *(descaro)* nerve, cheek; VULG. cunt; GUAT. eggshell; PERU hearth; COL., CUBA sluggishness, sloth ♦ **c. auditiva** ANAT. concha, outer ear • **meterse uno en su c.** FIG. to withdraw, crawl into one's shell • **tener muchas conchas** FIG., COLL. to be very astute; PERU, P. RICO to be sassy **II.** adj. see **concho, –cha**.

con·cha·ban·za f. *(acomodo)* comfort; COLL. *(complot)* plot, conspiracy.

con·cha·bar tr. *(unir)* to join, unite; *(mezclar)* to mix, blend; AMER. to hire, take on —reflex. COLL. to band together, gang up.

con·cha·bo m. AMER. domestic service.

con·cho, –cha I. adj. ECUAD. amber, tawny; PERU dark red **II.** m. AMER. sediment, dregs; ECUAD., BOT. corn husk; CHILE end, finish ♦ **conchos** AMER. leftovers —f. see **concha**.

con·chu·do, –da adj. ZOOL. shell-bearing; FIG., COLL. *(astuto)* shrewd, wily; *(cauteloso)* cautious, reserved; ECUAD., MEX., PERU brash, brazen.

con·da·do m. *(dignidad)* earldom, countship; *(territorio)* county, shire.

con·de m. *(título)* count, earl; *(gitano)* gypsy chief; SP., AGR. overseer.

con·de·cir §11 intr. var. of **convenir**.

con·de·co·ra·ción f. *(insignia)* decoration, medal; *(ceremonia)* decoration *or* award ceremony.

con·de·co·rar tr. to decorate, award.

con·de·na f. LAW *(juicio)* sentence; *(declaración)* conviction; *(extensión)* term, sentence ♦ **c. a perpetuidad** life sentence • **c. condicional** suspended sentence • **cumplir una c.** to serve a sentence.

con·de·na·ble adj. condemnable.

con·de·na·ción f. *(desaprobación)* condemnation; RELIG. damnation; LAW *(juicio)* sentence; *(declaración)* conviction.

con·de·na·do, –da I. past part. see **condenar II.** adj. condemned; *(culpable)* convicted, found guilty; *(réprobo)* reprobate; RELIG. damned; COLL. *(desgraciado)* damned, wretched; CHILE shrewd, astute **III.** m.f. *(prisionero)* convict; *(réprobo)* reprobate; RELIG. damned person; COLL. *(desgraciado)* wretch; CHILE sly fox.

con·de·na·dor, –do·ra I. adj. condemning **II.** m.f. condemner.

con·de·nar tr. *(castigar)* to condemn, sentence <*c. a la muerte* to sentence to death>; *(declarar culpable)* to convict, find guilty; *(reprobar)* to condemn, censure; *(desaprobar)* to disapprove of; RELIG. to damn, condemn; *(echar a perder)* to give up; *(cerrar)* to seal *or* board up; COLL. *(molestar)* to annoy, bother —reflex. *(culparse)* to condemn *or* blame oneself; RELIG. to be damned; COLL. *(molestarse)* to become annoyed ♦ **c. a alguien a presidio** to sentence someone to hard labor • **c. a alguien a una multa** to fine someone • **c. en costas** LAW to order to pay costs • **c. en rebeldía** LAW to judge by default.

con·de·na·to·rio, –ria adj. LAW condemnatory.

con·den·sa·ble adj. condensable.

con·den·sa·ción f. *(acción)* condensation, condensing; *(resultado)* condensation.

con·den·sa·dor, –do·ra I. adj. condensing **II.** m. PHYS. condenser ♦ **c. de fuerzas** MECH. accumulator • **c. eléctrico** capacitor.

con·den·sar tr. *(reducir)* to condense, compress; FIG. *(abreviar)* to shorten, abridge.

con·de·sa f. countess.

con·des·cen·cia f. compliance, acquiescence.

con·des·cen·der §50 intr. to comply, acquiesce ♦ **c. a** *or* **en** to be kind *or* gracious enough to.

con·des·cen·dien·te adj. agreeable, obliging.

con·di·ce see **condecir**.

con·di·ción f. condition, state <*estar en mala c.* to be in bad condition>; *(carácter)* nature, character <*la niña tiene c. apacible* the child has a gentle nature>; *(clase)* status, standing <*tenía las ventajas de su c. noble* he had the advantage of his noble status>; LAW *(cláusula)* stipulation, term, condition; *(calidad)* capacity <*en su c. de abogado* in his capacity as a lawyer> ♦ **a c. de que** provided that, on the condition that • **c. callada** *or* **tácita** LAW implied condition • **c. casual** LAW casual condition • **c. de hecho** LAW express condition • **c. única** LAW single condition • **condiciones** *(aptitud)* aptitude, talent; circumstances, conditions <*no puedo trabajar en estas condiciones* I cannot work under these conditions> • **condiciones acostumbradas** COM. usual terms • **condiciones convenidas** COM. terms agreed upon • **condiciones de pago** COM. terms of payment • **condiciones de venta** COM. conditions of sale • **condiciones de vida** living conditions • **estar en condi-**

ciones de to be fit for • **poner en condiciones** to prepare, get ready • **sin condiciones** unconditionally.

con·di·cio·na·do, –da I. past part. see **condicionar** II. adj. *(acondicionado)* conditioned; *(condicional)* conditional ♦ **c. a** subject to, dependent upon.

con·di·cio·nal adj. conditional.

con·di·cio·nal·men·te adv. conditionally.

con·di·cio·nar intr. to fit, agree —tr. *(hacer convenir)* to suit, adapt; *(poner condiciones)* to condition, place conditions on; *(temperature)* to condition.

con·di·ga, condigo see **condecir**.

con·dig·no, –na adj. commensurate <*c. de* commensurate with>.

con·di·je·ra, condijo see **condecir**.

con·di·men·ta·ción f. CUL. seasoning.

con·di·men·tar tr. CUL. to season, flavor.

con·di·men·to m. CUL. condiment, seasoning.

con·dis·cí·pu·lo, –la m.f. fellow student, classmate.

con·do·len·cia f. condolence, sympathy.

con·do·ler·se §78 reflex. to condole, sympathize ♦ **c. de** or **por** to sympathize with, feel sorry for.

con·do·mi·nio m. *(soberanía)* condominium, joint sovereignty *or* rule; *(propiedad)* condominium, cooperative apartment.

con·dón m. condom.

con·do·na·ción f. *(acción)* condoning, pardoning; *(resultado)* pardon, forgiveness.

con·do·nar tr. *(perdonar)* to condone, pardon; *(remitir)* to cancel, release from (a debt).

cón·dor m. ORNITH. condor; CHILE, COL., ECUAD., NUMIS. condor, gold coin.

con·drín m. PHILIP. unit of weight for precious metals.

con·duc·ción f. *(transporte)* transport, transportation; *(cañería)* piping, pipeline; AUTO. driving; PHYS. conduction; COM. *(ajuste)* wage *or* price agreement; *(porteo)* portage, cartage ♦ **permiso de c.** driver's license.

con·du·cen·te adj. conducive.

con·du·cir §22 tr. *(guiar)* to guide, lead <*me condujeron a sus habitaciones* they led me to their rooms>; *(dirigir)* to direct, manage <*c. una empresa* to manage an enterprise>; *(llevar)* to transport, carry <*conducen la carga por mar* they transport the cargo by sea>; AUTO. to drive —intr. to lead, conduce <*la avaricia conduce a la desgracia* avarice leads to unhappiness>; AUTO. to drive —reflex. to conduct oneself, behave.

con·duc·ta f. *(proceder)* conduct, behavior; *(dirección)* management, direction; POL. government, governing; *(convoy)* convoy ♦ **cambiar de c.** to change one's ways • **mala c.** misconduct.

con·duc·ti·vi·dad f. PHYS. conductivity.

con·duc·ti·vo, –va adj. PHYS. conductive.

con·duc·to m. *(canal)* conduit, pipe; ANAT. canal, duct <*c. lacrimal* tear duct>; FIG. *(agente)* means, agency <*hay que conseguir permiso por c. del gerente* it is necessary to get permission through the agency of the manager> ♦ **por c. de** by means of, through • **por c. regular** through regular channels.

con·duc·tor, –to·ra I. adj. conducting; PHYS. conductive II. m.f. AUTO. driver; PHYS. conductor; AMER. *(cobrador)* conductor (on a public vehicle).

con·due·la, conduelo see **condolerse**.

con·due·ño, –ña m.f. joint owner, co-owner.

con·du·je·ra, conduje see **conducir**.

con·duz·ca, conduzco see **conducir**.

co·nec·ta·dor m. TECH. connector.

co·nec·tar tr. MECH. *(engranar)* to connect, gear; *(acoplar)* to hook up, couple; *(enchufar)* to plug in; AMER. *relacionar)* to put in touch with —intr. AMER. to link up, be connected <*este discurso conecta con el de ayer* this discussion is connected with yesterday's>.

co·ne·ja f. ZOOL. doe rabbit ♦ **ser una c.** COLL., FIG. to be very fertile, have a lot of children.

co·ne·je·ra I. f. *(madriguera)* rabbit warren *or* burrow; *(conejal)* rabbit hutch; FIG. *(cueva)* deep and narrow cave; FIG., COLL. *(guarida)* den, haunt; *(lugar superpoblado)* warren, over-crowded living environment II. adj. see **conejero, –ra**.

co·ne·je·ro, –ra I. adj. rabbit-hunting <*perro c.* rabbit-hunting dog> II. m.f. *(criador)* rabbit breeder; *(vendedor)* rabbit seller —f. see **conejera**.

co·ne·ji·llo m. ZOOL. young rabbit, bunny ♦ **c. de Indias** ZOOL. guinea pig.

co·ne·jo m. ZOOL. rabbit; AMER., ZOOL. *(cobayo)* guinea pig; *(agutí)* agouti; CUBA, ICHTH. a salmonoid fish.

co·ne·xión f. connection ♦ **conexiones** connections, relationships.

co·ne·xio·nar·se reflex. *(contraer conexiones)* to establish contacts, make connections (social, commercial); *(ponerse en contacto)* to get in touch, get in contact.

co·ne·xo, –xa connected, related.

con·fa·bu·la·ción f. *(discusión)* conference, discussion; *(complot)* plot, conspiracy.

con·fa·bu·la·dor, –do·ra m.f. *(intrigante)* schemer, plotter; *(conferenciante)* participant in a conference *or* discussion.

con·fa·bu·lar tr. to converse, discuss —reflex. to plot, conspire.

con·fec·ción f. *(fabricación)* making, manufacture; PHARM. *(medicamento blando)* confection, concoction; TEX. *(ropa hecha)* ready-to-wear clothing.

con·fec·cio·nar tr. *(fabricar)* to make, manufacture; PHARM. *(preparar)* to compound, confect.

con·fe·de·ra·ción f. *(conjunto)* confederation, confederacy; *(liga)* league, alliance.

con·fe·de·ra·do, –da I. past part. see **confederar** II. adj. confederated, allied III. m.f. confederate, ally.

con·fe·de·rar tr. & reflex. to confederate.

con·fe·de·ra·ti·vo, –va adj. confederative.

con·fe·ren·cia f. *(discusión)* discussion; *(discurso)* lecture, talk; *(reunión)* meeting, conference; TELEC. long-distance (telephone) call ♦ **c. a cobro revertido** TELEC. collect call ♦ **c. de prensa** JOURN. press conference • **c. en la cumbre** or **de alto nivel** POL. summit conference • **poner una c.** TELEC. to make a long-distance call.

con·fe·ren·cian·te m.f. lecturer, speaker.

con·fe·ren·ciar intr. to confer, hold a conference.

con·fe·ren·cis·ta m.f. AMER. lecturer, speaker.

con·fe·rir §65 tr. *(conceder)* to confer, bestow; *(comparar)* to compare —intr. to confer, consult.

con·fe·san·te I. adj. confessing II. m.f. LAW one who makes a declaration in court.

con·fe·sar §49 tr. *(admitir)* to confess, admit <*confesó su delito* he confessed his crime>; *(proclamar)* to confess, proclaim <*c. la fe* to proclaim the faith>; RELIG. *(declarar los pecados)* to confess; *(oír en confesión)* to confess (a penitent), hear the confession of ♦ **c. de plano** to make a clean breast of —reflex. to confess.

con·fe·sión f. *(admisión)* confession, admission; LAW *(declaración del reo)* testimony; RELIG. *(credo)* confession, faith; *(acto)* confession ♦ **oír en c.** to confess, hear in confession.

con·fe·sio·na·rio m. RELIG. *(lugar)* confessional; *(tratado)* confessional procedure.

con·fe·so, –sa I. past part. see **confesar** II. adj. confessed, self-confessed <*un asesino c.* a confessed assassin>; *(converso)* converted Jew III. m.f. converted Jew —m. RELIG. lay brother.

con·fe·sor m. RELIG. *(sacerdote)* confessor; HIST., RELIG. confessor, believer.

con·fe·ti m.pl. confetti.

con·fia·ble adj. reliable, trustworthy.

con·fia·do, –da I. past part. see **confiar** II. adj. *(presumido)* confident, assured; *(crédulo)* gullible, unsuspecting; *(que se fía)* trusting.

con·fian·za f. *(fe)* confidence, trust, faith; *(seguridad)* self-confidence, self-assurance; *(presunción)* conceit, vanity; *(familiaridad)* familiarity, closeness; *(pacto)* private agreement ♦ **con toda c.** in all confidence • **de c.** *(confiable)* trustworthy, reliable; *(íntimo)* intimate, close • **defraudar la c. de alguien** to let someone down • **en c.** in confidence, confidentially • **tender c. con alguien** to be on close terms with someone • **tratar a alguien con c.** to treat someone informally.

con·fian·zu·do, –da adj. COLL. bold, fresh.

con·fiar §30 intr. *(fiar)* to trust, feel confident <*confiamos en que el plan tendrá éxito* we feel confident that the plan will succeed>; *(contar con)* to count, rely <*confió en mis* *amigos* I count on my friends>; to commit <*c. a la memoria* to commit to memory> —tr. *(encargar)* to entrust <*confiaron la tarea a un amigo íntimo* they entrusted the task to a close friend>; to confide <*c. un secreto* to confide a secret> —reflex. to trust, have faith <*me confío en usted* I have faith in you>.

con·fi·den·cia f. *(confianza)* confidence; *(revelación secreta)* secret ♦ **hacer confidencias a** to confide in.

con·fi·den·cial adj. confidential.

con·fi·den·cial·men·te adv. confidentially.

con·fi·den·te I. adj. faithful, trusty II. m.f. *(consejero)* confidant; *(informante)* informer, informant —m. *(canapé)* love seat, settee.

con·fie·ra, confiero see **conferir.**

con·fie·se, confieso see **confesar.**

con·fi·gu·rar tr. to shape, form.

con·fín I. adj. bordering, adjoining II. m. *(límite)* boundary, border; *(horizonte)* horizon ♦ **confines** confines, limits.

con·fi·na·ción f. *(destierro)* exile, deportation; *(encierro)* confinement, LAW *(limitación)* confinement (to limited area while on parole).

con·fi·na·do, –da I. past part. see **confinar** II. adj. *(limitado)* confined; *(desterrado)* exiled, deported III. m.f. *(preso)* prisoner; *(desterrado)* exile.

con·fi·na·mien·to m. *(encarcelamiento)* confinement, imprisonment; *(destierro)* exile, deportation.

con·fi·nar intr. to border, be contiguous <*Colombia confina con Venezuela* Colombia borders on Venezuela> —tr. *(encarcelar)* to confine, imprison; *(desterrar)* to exile, deport —reflex. to shut oneself away, confine oneself.

con·fi·rie·ra, confirió see **conferir.**

con·fir·ma·ción f. *(verificación)* confirmation, verification; RELIG. confirmation.

con·fir·ma·do, –da I. past part. see **confirmar** II. adj. confirmed III. m.f. RELIG. confirmed person.

con·fir·ma·dor, –do·ra I. adj. confirmatory, confirmative II. m.f. confirmer, corroborator.

con·fir·man·te I. adj. confirming II. m.f. confirmer, corroborator.

con·fir·mar tr. *(verificar)* to confirm, verify; *(corroborar)* to support, endorse; RELIG. to confirm.

con·fir·ma·to·rio, –ria adj. confirmatory, confirmative.

con·fis·ca·ble adj. confiscable.

con·fis·ca·ción f. confiscation, appropriation.

con·fis·car §70 tr. to confiscate, appropriate.

con·fi·ta·do, –da I. past part. see **confitar** II. adj. candied, sugar-coated.

con·fi·tar tr. *(azucarar)* to candy, coat with sugar; *(conservar)* to preserve (in syrup); FIG. *(endulzar)* to sweeten, soften.

con·fi·te m. candy, sweet.

con·fi·te·rí·a f. *(dulcería)* candy shop, confectionery; AMER. tearoom, café.

con·fi·te·ro, –ra m.f. confectioner —f. *(caja)* candy box; *(vasija)* candy dish.

con·fi·tu·ra f. CUL. confiture; preserve.

con·fla·gra·ción f. *(incendio)* conflagration, blaze; FIG. *(perturbación violenta)* flare-up, outbreak.

con·flic·ti·vo, –va adj. *(que implica conflicto)* of conflict <*la edad c.* the age of conflict>; *(en conflicto)* conflicting.

con·flic·to m. *(lucha)* conflict, struggle; *(choque)* conflict, clash; FIG. *(apuro)* quandary, dilemma; *(angustia)* anguish, agony.

con·fluen·cia f. confluence.

con·fluen·te I. adj. confluent, convergent II. m. confluence.

con·fluir §18 intr. *(converger)* to converge, join; FIG. *(reunirse)* to converge, assemble.

con·for·ma·ción f. conformation, shape.

con·for·mar tr. *(adaptar)* to conform, adapt <*hay que c. la conducta a las reglas* it is necessary to adapt one's behavior to the rules>; *(dar forma)* to shape, fashion —intr. *(ajustarse)* to conform; to agree, be in agreement <*estas cifras no conforman* these figures are not in agreement> —reflex. to conform, comply <*ella no quiere conformarse a las normas establecidas* she does not want to comply with the established norms>; *(resignarse)* to resign oneself <*él*

se conformaba con el sueldo que le ofrecían he resigned himself to the salary that they offered to him>; *(convenir)* to agree.

con·for·me I. adj. *(semejante)* similar, alike; in accordance, consistent <*es una decisión c. a sus principios* it is a decision consistent with his principles>; *(de acuerdo)* agreed, in agreement <*estamos conformes en este asunto* we are in agreement on this matter>; FIG. *(resignado)* resigned <*él está c. con su destino* he is resigned to his fate> II. adv. *(consistente)* in accordance, in keeping <*c. a lo dicho* in accordance with what was said>; *(tan pronto como)* as soon as <*c. anochece, se acuestan* as soon as night falls, they go to bed> III. m. approval, OK <*el jefe puso el c. al pie de la página* the boss put his OK at the bottom of the page>.

con·for·me·men·te adv. according (to), in accordance (with).

con·for·mi·dad f. *(tolerancia)* resignation, acquiescence; *(concordancia)* conformity, agreement <*la c. era normal entre los críticos* agreement was usual among the critics>; *(semejanza)* similarity, likeness ♦ **de c.** in agreement.

con·for·mis·mo m. conformism.

con·for·mis·ta adj. & m.f. conformist.

con·fort m. comfort.

con·for·ta·ble adj. *(cómodo)* comfortable; *(consolador)* comforting, consoling.

con·for·ta·ble·men·te adv. comfortably.

con·for·ta·ción f. *(consuelo)* consolation, comfort; *(fortalecimiento)* invigoration.

con·for·ta·dor, –do·ra I. adj. *(animador)* comforting, consoling; *(fortalecedor)* invigorating II. m.f. comforter, consoler.

con·for·tan·te adj. comforting, consoling.

con·for·tar tr. *(consolar)* to comfort, console; *(dar vigor)* to strengthen, invigorate; *(animar)* to cheer, encourage.

con·for·ta·ti·vo, –va I. adj. comforting, consoling II. m. *(consuelo)* comfort, consolation; *(ánimo)* encouragement; *(tónico)* tonic, restorative.

con·fra·ter·ni·dad f. fraternity, fellowship.

con·fra·ter·ni·zar §04 intr. to fraternize, consort.

con·fron·ta·ción f. *(careo)* confrontation; *(comparación)* comparison, collation; *(simpatía)* affinity, congeniality.

con·fron·tar tr. *(carear)* to confront, face; *(comparar)* to compare, collate —intr. to border, be contiguous —reflex. to be faced *or* confronted.

con·fu·cia·nis·mo m. Confucianism.

con·fu·cia·no, –na adj. & m.f. Confucianist.

con·fun·di·do, –da adj. *(avergonzado)* embarrassed; *(equivocado)* mistaken, confused.

con·fun·dir tr. *(no distinguir)* to confuse, mistake <*confundió a Elena con su hermana* he confused Elena with her sister>; *(desordenar)* to mix up, jumble <*como no sabían el orden, lo confundieron todo* since they did not know the order, they mixed everything up>; FIG. *(perturbar)* to confuse, perplex <*las muchas soluciones posibles me confundieron* the many possible solutions perplexed me>; *(avergonzar)* to embarrass, abash <*los elogios me confunden* praise embarrasses me> —reflex. *(mezclarse)* to be mixed up *or* jumbled; to blend, mingle <*confundirse con la muchedumbre* to mingle with the crowd>; *(equivocarse)* to make a mistake, get mixed up; FIG. *(turbarse)* to be confused *or* perplexed; *(avergonzarse)* to be embarrassed.

con·fu·sa·men·te adv. *(con turbación)* confusedly; *(en desorden)* in confusion *or* disorder.

con·fu·sión f. confusion, jumble <*esta composición es una c. de ideas inconexas* this composition is a jumble of unconnected ideas>; *(oscuridad)* haziness, confusion <*hay gran c. en cuanto a los datos* there is great confusion about the facts>; FIG. *(perplejidad)* confusion, perplexity; *(vergüenza)* embarrassment, abashment.

con·fu·sio·nis·mo m. mystification, confusion of ideas.

con·fu·so, –sa I. past part. see **confundir** II. adj. *(mezclado)* mixed up, jumbled; *(oscuro)* hazy, unclear; FIG. *(turbado)* confused, perplexed; *(avergonzado)* embarrassed, abashed.

con·fu·ta·ción f. confutation, disproof.

con·fu·tar tr. to confute, disprove.

con·ga f. AMER., MUS. conga; COL., ENTOM. large poisonous ant; CUBA, ZOOL. grey or reddish rodent; VEN. toupee.
con·ge·la·ble adj. *(que se puede congelar)* freezable; *(que se puede cuajar)* congealable.
con·ge·la·ción f. *(acción)* freezing, congealing; *(resultado)* congealment; MED. frostbite.
con·ge·la·dor m. freezer, freezing compartment.
con·ge·la·dos m.pl. frozen foods.
con·ge·la·mien·to m. var. of **congelación**.
con·ge·lan·te adj. freezing, congealing.
con·ge·lar tr. *(helar)* to freeze; *(coagular)* to congeal, coagulate; COM. to freeze, fix <c. sueldos to freeze wages>; MED. to affect with frostbite —reflex. *(helarse)* to become or be frozen; *(coagularse)* to become congealed or coagulated; MED. to become frostbitten.
con·gé·ne·re I. adj. congeneric, congenerous II. m. fellow, kind.
con·ge·nial adj. congenial.
con·ge·niar intr. to be compatible, get along.
con·gé·ni·to, –ta adj. congenital.
con·ges·tión f. MED. congestion; FIG. *(acumulación)* congestion ♦ **c. cerebral** stroke • **c. pulmonar** pneumonia.
con·ges·tio·nar tr. to congest, make congested —reflex. to become or be congested.
con·ges·ti·vo, –va adj. MED. congestive.
con·glo·ba·ción f. *(montón)* conglobation, heaping up; FIG. *(mezcla)* conglomeration (of words, ideas); RHET. *(acumulación)* accumulation of arguments (to prove a point).
con·glo·me·ra·ción f. conglomeration.
con·glo·me·ra·do, –da I. past part. see **conglomerar** II. adj. conglomerate III. m. COM., GEOL. conglomerate; FIG. *(colección)* conglomeration, collection.
con·glo·me·ran·te I. adj. agglutinative II. m. agglutinant, bonding or adhesive material.
con·glo·me·rar tr. & reflex. to conglomerate.
con·glu·ti·na·ción f. conglutination.
con·glu·ti·nar tr. & reflex. to conglutinate; cement.
con·glu·ti·no·so, –sa adj. conglutinative, adhesive.
con·go m. AMER. second crop tobacco leaf; C. RICA, SALV., ZOOL. howling monkey; CUBA congo (dance); HOND., ICHTH. black-striped fish; MEX., COLL. femur of a pig.
Con·go m. Congo.
con·go·ja f. *(angustia)* anguish, distress; *(pena)* sorrow, grief; *(desmayo)* dejection, depression.
con·go·jar tr. to distress, cause anguish.
con·go·jo·sa·men·te adv. distressfully, painfully.
con·go·jo·so, –sa adj. *(afligido)* distressed, anguished; *(apenado)* sad, sorrowful; *(que causa congoja)* distressing, painful.
con·go·le·ño, –ña adj. & m.f. *(habitante)* Congolese.
con·gra·cia·dor, –do·ra adj. ingratiating.
con·gra·cia·mien·to m. *(insinuación)* ingratiation; *(acto de captar simpatías)* winning over.
con·gra·ciar tr. to win over —reflex. to ingratiate oneself.
con·gra·tu·la·ción f. congratulation.
con·gra·tu·lar tr. to congratulate —reflex. to congratulate oneself, be pleased.
con·gra·tu·la·to·rio, –ria adj. congratulatory.
con·gre·ga·ción f. *(reunión)* congregation, gathering; *(cofradía)* brotherhood, fraternity; RELIG. congregation ♦ **la c. de los fieles** RELIG. the Catholic Church, Christendom.
con·gre·gar §47 tr. & reflex. to congregate, assemble.
con·gre·sal AMER. or **con·gre·sis·ta** m.f. congressman or congresswoman, delegate.
con·gre·so m. *(reunión)* congress, meeting; POL. Congress (of the United States).
con·grio m. ICHTH. conger eel.
con·grua f. RELIG. *(renta)* adequate income (required of a person to be ordained); *(cantidad supletoria)* additional emolument (given to some state functionaries).
con·gruen·cia f. *(conveniencia)* congruity; *(oportunidad)* aptness, appropriateness; MATH. *(relación)* congruence; LAW *(conformidad)* coherence, cohesion.
con·gruen·te f. *(apropiado)* suitable, fitting; MATH. congruent.
có·ni·co, –ca adj. conic, conical.
co·ní·fe·ro, –ra BOT. I. adj. coniferous II. f. conifer.
co·ni·for·me adj. coniform, cone-shaped.

con·je·tu·ra f. conjecture, guess.
con·je·tu·ra·ble adj. conjecturable, presumable.
con·je·tu·rar tr. to conjecture, guess.
con·juez m. [pl. **–jue·ces**] LAW cojudge, joint judge.
con·ju·ga·ble adj. GRAM. conjugable.
con·ju·ga·ción f. BIOL., GRAM. conjugation.
con·ju·ga·do, –da I. past part. see **conjugar** II. adj. ANAT., MATH., MECH. conjugate; *(combinado)* combined, joined.
con·ju·gar §47 tr. to join, combine <no podía c. los intereses de los dos partidos he was not able to join the interests of the two parties>; GRAM. to conjugate; ECUAD. to quarrel with —reflex. *(mezclarse)* to blend or fit together; GRAM. to be conjugated.
con·jun·ción f. *(unión)* conjunction, junction; ASTRON., GRAM. conjunction.
con·jun·ta·men·te adv. jointly, together.
con·jun·tar tr. to coordinate.
con·jun·ti·va I. f. ANAT. conjunctiva II. adj. see **conjuntivo, –va**.
con·jun·ti·vi·tis f. MED. conjunctivitis.
con·jun·ti·vo, –va I. adj. *(que une)* conjunctive, joining; GRAM., MED. conjunctive II. f. see **conjuntiva**.
con·jun·to, –ta I. adj. *(unido)* joined, combined; *(mezclado)* joint; *(aliado)* related, allied II. m. *(totalidad)* whole; *(agregado)* group, collection; *(vestido)* outfit, set (of clothes); *(de muebles)* suite (of furniture); MECH. assembly, unit; MUS. band, ensemble; THEAT. chorus ♦ **c. motriz** ARG., ENGIN. power plant • **de c.** general, overall • **en c.** altogether • **en su c.** in its entirety, as a whole.
con·ju·ra or **con·ju·ra·ción** f. conspiracy, plot.
con·ju·ra·do, –da I. past part. see **conjurar** II. adj. *(intrigante)* plotting, conspiring; *(impedido)* averted, prevented III. m.f. plotter, conspirator.
con·ju·ra·dor m. *(intrigante)* plotter, conspirator; *(exorcista)* conjurer, exorcist.
con·ju·ra·men·tar tr. to swear in, administer an oath —reflex. to take the oath.
con·ju·ran·te I. adj. *(que intriga)* plotting, conspiring; *(que suplica)* conjuring II. m.f. *(intrigante)* plotter, conspirator; *(exorcista)* conjurer, exorcist.
con·ju·rar tr. *(suplicar)* to entreat, beseech; RELIG. *(exorcizar)* to exorcise; FIG. *(alejar)* to avert, ward off <c. un peligro to ward off danger> —intr. & reflex. to conspire, plot.
con·ju·ro m. RELIG. exorcism; *(sortilegio)* incantation, spell; *(ruego)* entreaty, supplication.
con·lle·var tr. *(ayudar)* to aid, help (someone bear his troubles); *(soportar a alguien)* to put up with, tolerate (someone); *(aguantar)* to bear patiently, endure <c. una enfermedad to endure an illness>.
con·me·mo·ra·ción f. commemoration ♦ **c. de los difuntos** RELIG. All Souls' Day.
con·me·mo·rar tr. to commemorate, celebrate.
con·me·mo·ra·ti·vo, –va adj. commemorative, memorial.
con·men·su·ra·ble adj. commensurable.
con·men·su·rar tr. to make commensurate.
con·mi·go §G34 pron. with me <¿quieres ir c.? do you want to go with me?> ♦ **c. mismo** with myself.
con·mi·na·ción f. threat, menace.
con·mi·nar tr. to threaten, menace.
con·mi·na·ti·vo, –va or **con·mi·na·to·rio, –ria** adj. threatening, menacing.
con·mi·se·ra·ción f. commiseration, compassion.
con·mi·se·rar·se reflex. PERU to commiserate.
con·mi·se·ra·ti·vo, –va adj. commiserative, compassionate.
con·mis·tión or **con·mix·tión** f. commixture.
con·mo·ción f. *(sacudimiento)* shock; FIG. *(perturbación)* shock, blow <la noticia de su muerte me produjo una c. desagradable the news of her death was a nasty shock for me>; *(tumulto)* commotion, upheaval <una c. política political upheaval>; GEOL. tremor ♦ **c. cerebral** MED. concussion.
con·mo·ni·to·rio m. *(relación)* record, report; LAW *(carta acordada)* reminder from a superior judge to a lower one.
con·mo·ve·dor, –do·ra adj. moving, touching.
con·mo·ver §78 tr. *(emocionar)* to move, touch <su pobreza me conmovió mucho his poverty touched me deeply>; *(perturbar)* to disturb, shake; *(sacudir)* to shake —reflex.

(emocionarse) to be moved *or* touched; *(perturbarse)* to be disturbed *or* troubled.

con·mu·ta·bi·li·dad f. commutability.

con·mu·ta·ble adj. commutable.

con·mu·ta·ción f. *(reemplazo)* commutation, exchange; *(retruécano)* pun, play on words; LAW commutation, reduction <*la c. de una pena* the commutation of a sentence>.

con·mu·tar tr. *(cambiar)* to exchange, trade; LAW to commute (a sentence).

con·mu·ta·ti·vo, –va adj. commutative.

con·mu·ta·triz f. [pl. **-tri·ces**] ELEC. converter.

con·na·tu·ral adj. connatural, innate.

con·na·tu·ra·li·za·ción f. acclimatization, adaptation.

con·na·tu·ra·li·zar §04 tr. to acclimatize —reflex. to adapt *or* accustom oneself.

con·ni·ven·cia f. *(confabulación)* connivance; *(disimulo)* complicity.

con·no·ta·ción f. connotation; *(parentesco remoto)* distant relationship.

con·no·ta·do, –da I. adj. AMER. noted, famous <*el c. autor* the noted author> II. m. distant relationship.

con·no·tar tr. to connote, imply.

con·no·ta·ti·vo, –va adj. GRAM. connotative.

con·nu·bio m. matrimony, marriage.

con·nu·me·rar tr. to enumerate, cite.

co·no m. ANAT., BOT., GEOM. cone ♦ **c. circular** GEOM. circular cone • **c. de helado** COLL. ice-cream cone • **c. de sombra** ASTRON. umbra • **c. oblicuo** GEOM. oblique cone • **c. recto** GEOM. right cone • **c. truncado** GEOM. truncated cone.

co·no·ce·dor, –do·ra I. adj. knowledgeable, expert II. m.f. connoisseur <*ella es c. de caballos* she is a connoisseur of horses>.

co·no·cer §17 tr. to know, be acquainted with <*conozco a esa chica* I know that girl>; to meet, become acquainted with <*conocí a esa chica en Portugal* I met that girl in Portugal>; to know about <*conocemos el arte griego* we know about Greek art>; *(reconocer)* to know, recognize <*no conocen los riesgos* they do not recognize the risks>; *(conjeturar)* to presume, know <*conozco que va a nevar dado el aspecto del cielo* I presume that it is going to snow given the way that the sky looks>; FIG. *(tener trato carnal con)* to know carnally ♦ **c. de nombre** to know by name • **c. de vista** to know by sight —intr. ♦ **c. de** to know about; LAW to try <*c. de una causa* to try a case> —reflex. *(juzgarse)* to know oneself; to know one another, be acquainted <*se conocen desde hace muchos años* they have known one another for many years>.

co·no·ci·ble adj. knowable, cognizable.

co·no·ci·da·men·te adv. clearly, evidently.

co·no·ci·do, –da I. past part. see **conocer** II. adj. well-known, famous III. m.f. acquaintance.

co·no·ci·mien·to m. *(cognición)* knowledge, cognition; *(entendimiento)* understanding, intelligence; *(conocido)* acquaintance; MED. consciousness; COM. *(de embarque)* bill of lading; *(documento)* voucher, identification ♦ **con c. de causa** with full knowledge of the facts • **c. de embarque** COM. bill of lading • **conocimientos** learning, erudition • **perder el c.** MED. to lose consciousness • **poner en c. de** to inform, notify • **recobrar el c.** MED. to regain consciousness • **venir en c. de** COLL. to hear about, learn of.

co·noi·dal adj. GEOM. conoidal, conoid.

co·noz·ca, conozco see **conocer.**

con·que I. conj. and so, so <*el libro está en la biblioteca, c. no tienes que comprarlo* the book is in the library, so you don't have to buy it>; so then, well then <*c. ¿comemos aquí o en otro restaurante?* well then, shall we eat here or in a different restaurant?> II. m. COLL. *(condición)* condition, term <*es un c. esencial del acuerdo* it is an essential term of the agreement>.

con·quis·ta f. conquest.

con·quis·ta·ble adj. *(que se puede conquistar)* conquerable; FIG. *(fácil de conseguir)* attainable, achievable.

con·quis·ta·dor, –do·ra I. adj. conquering II. m.f. *(vencedor)* conqueror; FIG., COLL. *(tenorio)* ladykiller, Don Juan.

con·quis·tar tr. *(tomar)* to conquer; *(adquirir)* to win <*con-*

quisté el puesto I won the position>; FIG., COLL. *(cautivar)* to win over, win <*conquistó a todos con su sinceridad* he won everyone over with his sincerity>; *(seducir)* to conquer, win the heart of.

con·sa·bi·do, –da adj. *(tradicional)* usual, traditional <*el c. discurso inaugural* the usual opening address>; *(muy conocido)* well-known; *(anteriormente citado)* above-mentioned.

con·sa·gra·ción f. consecration.

con·sa·gra·do, –da I. past part. see **consagrar** II. adj. *(sagrado)* consecrated, sacred; *(destinado)* devoted, dedicated; *(confirmado)* recognized, time-honored <*una tradición c.* a time-honored tradition>; COLL. *(renombrado)* famous, renowned.

con·sa·gran·te I. adj. consecrating II. m. *(sacerdote)* consecrating priest; *(el que consagra)* consecrator.

con·sa·grar tr. RELIG. to consecrate; *(deificar)* to deify, apotheosize; *(destinar)* to devote, dedicate <*consagró su vida a la extirpación de la enfermedad* he dedicated his life to the eradication of disease>; *(hacer homenaje)* to commemorate, honor; *(confirmar)* to confirm, establish <*la victoria lo consagró como comandante excepcional* the victory established him as an exceptional commander>; *(autorizar)* to authorize, recognize <*c. nuevas palabras* to recognize new words> —reflex. *(dedicarse)* to devote *or* dedicate oneself; *(adquirir fama)* to become renowned, establish oneself.

con·sa·gra·to·rio, –ria adj. consecratory, consecrative.

con·san·guí·ne·o, –a I. adj. consanguineous; *(del mismo padre)* agnate (having the same father) II. m.f. *(pariente)* blood relation.

con·san·gui·ni·dad f. consanguinity, blood relationship.

cons·cien·cia f. var. of **conciencia.**

cons·cien·te adj. *(enterado)* conscious, aware; MED. conscious; *(responsable)* conscientious, responsible.

cons·cien·te·men·te adv. consciously, knowingly.

cons·crip·ción f. AMER. conscription, military draft.

cons·crip·to m. AMER. conscript, draftee.

con·se·cu·ción f. acquisition, attainment.

con·se·cuen·cia f. *(deducción)* consequence, deduction; *(resultado)* result, outcome; *(firmeza)* consistency <*obrar con c.* to act with consistency>; LOG. illation ♦ **a** *or* **como c. de** as a result *or* consequence of • **de c.** of consequence *or* importance • **en c.** accordingly, therefore • **por c.** consequently, therefore • **sacar en c.** to conclude, come to the conclusion • **tener c.** to have consequences • **traer como c.** to result in.

con·se·cuen·te I. adj. *(resultante)* resulting, consequent; *(firme)* consistent II. m. LOG., MATH. consequent.

con·se·cuen·te·men·te adv. *(por consiguiente)* consequently, therefore; *(firmemente)* consistently.

con·se·cu·ti·va·men·te adv. consecutively.

con·se·cu·ti·vo, –va adj. consecutive.

con·se·gui·mien·to m. var. of **consecución.**

con·se·guir §64 tr. *(obtener)* to obtain, get <*conseguimos los documentos* we obtained the documents>; *(lograr)* to attain, achieve <*consiguió su objetivo* he achieved his objective>; *(lograr)* to manage <*conseguí convencer a las autoridades* I managed to convince the authorities>.

con·se·ja f. tale, fable.

con·se·je·ro, –ra I. adj. advisory II. m.f. *(guía)* counselor, adviser; *(miembro de un consejo)* councilor.

con·se·jo m. counsel, advice <*siguió el c. de su padre* he followed his father's advice>; POL. council, board; LAW *(tribunal)* tribunal, court ♦ **c. de guerra** court-martial • **c. de ministros** POL. cabinet • **C. de Seguridad** POL. Security Council.

con·sen·so m. consensus.

con·sen·sual adj. LAW consensual.

con·sen·ti·do, –da I. past part. see **consentir** II. adj. *(mimado)* spoiled, pampered; *(cornudo)* cuckolded.

con·sen·ti·dor, –do·ra I. adj. *(acomodadizo)* acquiescent; COLL. *(mimoso)* pampering, spoiling II. m.f. *(persona acomodadiza)* acquiescent person; COLL. *(persona mimosa)* pamperer.

con·sen·ti·mien·to m. consent, agreement.

con·sen·tir §65 tr. *(autorizar)* to consent *or* agree to <*c. la venta* to agree to the sale>; *(creer)* to believe, think; *(per-*

mitir) to permit, allow; *(mimar)* to spoil, pamper; *(soportar)* to bear, accomodate —intr. *(acceler)* to consent, assent *<consentí en escribirlo* I consented to write it>; *(romperse)* to come loose, give (way) ♦ **c. a** *or* **con** to be indulgent with, indulge —reflex. to come loose, give (way).

con·ser·je m. *(custodio)* concierge, janitor; *(portero)* porter.

con·ser·je·rí·a f. concierge's *or* janitor's office; *(de un hotel)* reception desk.

con·ser·va f. *(confitura)* preserve, jam; *(alimentos)* preserved food; MARIT. convoy *<navegar en c.* to sail in convoy> ♦ **conservas alimenticias** canned goods • **en c.** preserved, canned.

con·ser·va·ción f. *(preservación)* conservation, preservation; *(de recursos, de energías)* conservation; *(cuidado)* maintenance, upkeep ♦ **c. de la energía** PHYS. conservation of energy • **c. de la masa** PHYS. conservation of mass • **c. de sí mismo** *or* **propia** self-preservation • **c. de suelos** soil conservation • **c. refrigerada** cold storage.

con·ser·va·dor, –do·ra I. adj. *(preservativo)* conserving, preservative; POL. conservative; *(prudente)* prudent, cautious II. m.f. POL. conservative; *(oficio)* conservator; *(curador)* curator.

con·ser·va·du·rí·a f. *(cargo)* curatorship; *(oficina)* curator's office.

con·ser·va·du·ris·mo m. conservatism.

con·ser·var tr. *(preservar)* to conserve, preserve; *(guardar)* to keep *<c. un secreto* to keep a secret>; *(cuidar)* to keep up, maintain *<c. la casa* to maintain the house>; *(mantener)* to retain, keep *<c. amigos* to retain friends>; CUL. to can, preserve —reflex. *(permanecer)* to survive, remain; *(cuidarse)* to take care of oneself; *(guardar para sí)* to reserve, keep for oneself; CUL. *(mantenerse)* to keep, stay fresh; to conserve, save *<conservarse la fuerza* to conserve one's strength> ♦ **conservarse en** *or* **con salud** to keep *or* stay well.

con·ser·va·tis·mo m. AMER. conservatism.

con·ser·va·ti·vo, –va adj. preservative.

con·ser·va·to·rio, –ria I. adj. conservatory, preservative II. m. *(escuela)* conservatory; ARG. private school; CHILE greenhouse.

con·ser·ve·rí·a f. preserving, canning; *(industria)* cannery, canning industry.

con·si·de·ra·ble adj. *(grande)* considerable, substantial *<una suma c.* a substantial sum>; *(poderoso)* powerful; *(importante)* considerable, important *<un asunto c.* an important issue>.

con·si·de·ra·ble·men·te adv. considerably, substantially.

con·si·de·ra·ción f. *(atención)* consideration, attention *<digno de c.* worthy of attention>; FIG. *(razón)* reason, motive; *(importancia)* consideration, importance; *(respeto)* respect, regard ♦ **bajo** *or* **en c.** under consideration • **de c.** considerable • **en c. a** considering, in consideration of • **por c.** out of consideration • **tomar en c.** to take into consideration *or* account.

con·si·de·ra·do, –da I. past part. see **considerar** II. adj. *(respetuoso)* considerate, thoughtful; *(respetado)* respected, esteemed; *(prudente)* prudent.

con·si·de·ran·do I. pres. part. see **considerar** II. m. LAW whereas, legal reason.

con·si·de·rar tr. *(examinar)* to consider, think about *<hay que c. las consecuencias* one must consider the consequences>; *(estimar)* to consider, regard *<le considero como loco* I regard him as a crazy person>; *(tomar en consideración)* to take into consideration —reflex. to be considered; *(a sí mismo)* to consider oneself *<me considero feliz* I consider myself blessed>.

con·sien·ta, consiento see **consentir**.

con·si·ga, consigo see **conseguir**.

con·sig·na f. *(órdenes)* orders, instructions; *(slogan)* watchword, slogan, motto; *(depósito)* checkroom, cloakroom.

con·sig·na·ción f. COM. consignment, shipment; FIN. *(depósito)* deposit; *(asignación)* appropriation, allocation.

con·sig·na·dor m.f. COM. consignor, depositor.

con·sig·nar tr. *(enviar)* to consign, send; *(depositar)* to deposit, consign; *(citar)* to note, write down; *(asignar)* to assign, allocate.

con·sig·na·to·rio m. COM. consignee; LAW *(depositario)* trustee, assignee.

con·si·go §G34 pron. with him, with her, with them, with you ♦ **c. mismo** with himself, with herself, with oneself, with themselves, with yourself, with yourselves.

con·si·guien·te I. adj. consequent, resulting ♦ **por c.** consequently, therefore II. m. RHET. consequent.

con·si·guien·te·men·te adv. consequently, therefore.

con·si·guie·ra, consiguió see **conseguir**.

con·sin·tien·te adj. consenting, agreeing.

con·sin·tie·ra, consintió see **consentir**.

con·sis·ten·cia f. *(fijeza)* consistency; *(estabilidad)* stability; *(durabilidad)* durability; *(coherencia)* consistency, coherence ♦ **sin c.** insubstantial; CUL. *(aguado)* thin, without body.

con·sis·ten·te adj. *(válido)* consistent; *(espeso)* thick *<crema c.* thick cream>; *(firme)* solid, consistent; AMER. consequent, corresponding.

con·sis·tir intr. to consist ♦ **c. en** to consist of, be composed of *<la ciudad consiste en cinco distritos* the city is composed of five districts>; *(residir)* to consist in *<la felicidad consiste en la moderación* his happiness consists in moderation>.

con·sis·to·rio m. RELIG. *(asamblea)* consistory; *(concejo)* town council; *(sala)* town hall.

con·so·cio, –cia m.f. *(colega)* fellow member (of a club); COM. *(asociado)* joint partner, copartner.

con·so·la f. *(mesa)* console table; ARCHIT. *(ménsula)* console, bracket.

con·so·la·ción f. *(consuelo)* consolation, comfort; *(en los juegos de cartas)* forfeit, penalty (in cards).

con·so·la·dor, –do·ra I. adj. consoling, comforting II. m.f. consoler, comforter.

con·so·lar §19 tr. to console, comfort —reflex. to console *or* comfort oneself.

con·so·li·da·ción f. consolidation, strengthening.

con·so·li·da·do, –da I. past part. see **consolidar** II. adj. FIN. consolidated III. m. FIN. consol, consolidated annuity.

con·so·li·dar tr. *(solidar)* to consolidate, strengthen; FIG. *(asegurar)* to consolidate, strengthen *<c. una alianza* to strengthen an alliance>; COM. to consolidate, fund (a debt) —reflex. to consolidate, become consolidated.

con·so·mé m. consommé, clear broth.

con·so·nan·cia f. *(rima)* consonace; MUS. consonance, harmony; FIG. *(conformidad)* agreement, harmony.

con·so·nan·te I. adj. *(armonioso)* consonant, harmonious; GRAM. consonantal; *(rimado)* rhyming II. f. GRAM. consonant.

con·so·nar §19 intr. MUS. to be harmonious, be in harmony; *(rimar)* to rhyme; FIG. *(concordar)* to agree, harmonize.

con·sor·cio m. *(asociación)* association, consortium *<c. bancario* banking consortium>; *(de circunstancias)* conjunction; *(unión)* fellowship.

con·sor·te m.f. *(esposo)* spouse, consort; *(compañero)* companion, partner ♦ **consortes** LAW *(litigantes)* colitigants, joint litigants; *(cómplices)* accomplices.

cons·pi·cuo, –cua adj. famous, eminent.

cons·pi·ra·ción f. conspiracy, plot.

cons·pi·ra·dor, –do·ra m.f. conspirator, plotter.

cons·pi·rar intr. *(conjurarse)* to conspire, plot; *(concurrir)* to conspire *<todo conspira a vencerle* everything conspires to defeat him>.

cons·tan·cia f. *(fidelidad)* constancy; *(perseverancia)* perseverance, steadfastness; *(certeza)* certainty; evidence, record *<dejar c. de algo* to leave a record of something>; AMER. proof, documentation.

cons·tan·te I. adj. *(continuo)* constant, unchanging; *(perseverante)* persevering, steadfast; *(duradero)* durable, lasting; *(verificador)* verifying; MATH. constant II. f. MATH. constant.

cons·tan·te·men·te adv. *(a menudo)* constantly; *(ciertamente)* certainly, undoubtedly; *(con firmeza)* steadfastly.

Cons·tan·ti·no·pla f. Constantinople.

cons·tar intr. *(ser cierto)* to be clear *or* evident *<me consta que no han llegado* it is clear to me that they have not arrived>; to be on record *<su pedido consta en el registro de*

la compañía his order is on record in the company's register>; *(consistir)* to consist *or* be composed <*el estudio consta de tres secciones* the study consists of three sections>; to appear, to figure in; POET. to have correct meter and accentuation ♦ **hacer c.** to point out • **hacer c. por escrito** to put on record • **que conste que** let it be clearly known that • **para que así conste** for the record.

cons·ta·tar tr. to verify, confirm.

cons·te·la·ción f. ASTRON. constellation.

cons·ter·na·ción f. consternation, dismay.

cons·ter·nar tr. to consternate, dismay —reflex. to be dismayed.

cons·ti·pa·do, –da I. past part. see **constipar** II. m. cold, head cold.

cons·ti·par tr. to give a cold to —reflex. to catch a cold.

cons·ti·tu·ción f. *(fundación)* constitution, establishment <*la c. de una sociedad* the establishment of a society>; *(composición)* composition <*la c. del agua* the composition of water>; LAW, POL. constitution; ANAT. constitution <*él es de c. robusta* he has a robust constitution> ♦ **c. apostólica** RELIG. papal decree • **c. atmosférica** atmospheric condition • **c. pontificia** RELIG. bull, papal letter.

cons·ti·tu·cio·nal I. adj. LAW, POL. constitutional II. m.f. POL. constitutionalist.

cons·ti·tu·cio·na·li·dad f. constitutionality.

cons·ti·tu·cio·nal·men·te adv. constitutionally.

cons·ti·tuir §18 tr. *(componer)* to constitute, form; to make (into) <*c. una ciudad en capital* to make a city the capital>; to be <*eso no constituye problema* that is not a problem>; *(poner)* to place <*c. en una obligación* to place under an obligation>; *(establecer)* to establish, found <*c. un colegio* to found a school> ♦ **c. en apuro** to put in a difficult situation —reflex. to be established *or* formed ♦ **constituirse en** *or* **por** to assume the position of • **constituirse en un lugar** to present oneself at a place, show up • **constituirse parte civil** LAW to bring a civil action • **constituirse por** *or* **en fiador de** to answer for • **constituirse prisionero** to give oneself up.

cons·ti·tu·ti·vo, –va *or* **cons·ti·tu·yen·te** I. adj. constituent, component II. m. constituent, component.

cons·tre·ñi·mien·to m. constraint, compulsion.

cons·tre·ñir §59 tr. *(compeler)* to constrain, compel; MED. *(apretar)* to constrict; *(estreñir)* to constipate.

cons·tric·ción f. constriction, contraction.

cons·tric·ti·vo, –va adj. constrictive, constraining.

cons·tric·tor, –to·ra I. adj. constrictive, constricting; MED. astringent II. m. MED. astringent.

cons·trin·gen·te adj. constringent, binding.

cons·tri·ña, constriño see **constreñir**.

cons·tri·ñe·ra, constriñó see **constreñir**.

cons·truc·ción f. *(acto)* construction, building <*la c. de un catedral* the construction of a cathedral>; *(edificio)* building, structure; GRAM. construction ♦ **c. de naval** *or* **de buques** shipbuilding • **en** *or* **en vías de c.** under construction.

cons·truc·ti·vo, –va adj. constructive <*crítica c.* constructive criticism>.

cons·truc·tor, –to·ra I. adj. construction, building <*la industria c.* the construction industry> II. m.f. constructor, builder ♦ **c. naval** *or* **de buques** shipbuilder.

cons·truir §18 tr. to construct, build; *(fabricar)* to manufacture; GRAM. to construct.

con·subs·tan·cial adj. THEOL. consubstantial.

con·sue·gro, –gra m. father-in-law of one's child (in relation to oneself) —f. mother-in-law of one's child (in relation to oneself).

con·sue·le, consuelo see **consolar**.

con·sue·lo m. *(alivio)* consolation, solace; *(alegría)* joy, delight ♦ **sin c.** inconsolable.

con·sue·ne, consueno see **consonar**.

con·sue·tu·di·na·rio, –ria adj. *(habitual)* customary, usual; *(empedernido)* hardened, confirmed ♦ **derecho c.** *(en Inglaterra)* Common Law; *(en otros países)* consuetudinary law.

cón·sul m. consul ♦ **c. general** consul general.

con·su·la·do m. *(residencia)* consulate; *(oficio)* consulship.

con·su·lar adj. consular.

con·sul·ta f. *(conferencia)* consultation; *(opinión)* opinion, advice ♦ **c. a domicilio** house call, home visit.

con·sul·ta·ción f. conference, consultation.

con·sul·tan·te I. adj. consulting, consultant II. m.f. consultant.

con·sul·tar intr. to consult (with), get advice (from) <*c. con el abogado* to consult with a lawyer> ♦ **c. con la almohada** to sleep on it —tr. *(aconsejarse)* to consult; *(buscar en)* to consult <*c. el diccionario* to consult the dictionary>; *(verificar)* to look up, check (a word, fact); *(discutir)* to discuss, talk over.

con·sul·ti·vo, –va adj. consultative, advisory.

con·sul·tor, –to·ra I. adj. consultory, advisory II. m. consultant, advisor.

con·sul·to·rio m. *(para consejos técnicos)* information bureau; MED. consulting room, doctor's office; JOURN. advice column.

con·su·ma·ción f. *(acabamiento)* consummation, completion; *(fin)* end, extinction.

con·su·ma·da·men·te adv. consummately, completely.

con·su·ma·do, –da I. past part. see **consumar** II. adj. consummate, perfect ♦ **hecho c.** accomplished fact.

con·su·mar tr. *(acabar)* to consummate, complete.

con·su·mi·ble adj. consumable.

con·su·mi·ción f. *(consumo)* consumption; *(bebida)* drink ♦ **c. mínima** cover charge.

con·su·mi·do, –da I. past part. see **consumir** II. adj. *(inquieto)* fretful, easily upset; FIG., COLL. *(flaco)* thin, emaciated.

con·su·mi·dor, –do·ra I. adj. consuming II. m.f. consumer.

con·su·mir tr. *(gastar)* to consume, use up <*consumieron toda la leña* they used up all of the firewood>; *(destruir)* to consume, destroy <*el fuego consumió la fábrica* the fire destroyed the factory>; *(malgastar)* to waste <*consumió su fortuna* he wasted his fortune>; *(evaporar)* to evaporate, dry up; FIG., COLL. *(afligir)* to consume, afflict <*le consume la pena* grief consumes him>; RELIG. to take Communion (a priest); C. AMER., COL. to submerge —reflex. to be consumed *or* used (up); *(destruirse)* to be consumed *or* destroyed; *(malgastarse)* to waste away; *(evaporarse)* to evaporate, dry up; FIG., COLL. to be consumed *or* afflicted <*consumirse de celos* to be consumed with jealousy>; CUL. to boil away.

con·su·mo m. consumption ♦ **consumos** excise tax • **de c.** consumer <*bienes de c.* consumer goods>.

con·sun·ción f. *(consumimiento)* consumption; MED. consumption.

con·su·no adv. ♦ **de c.** by mutual agreement *or* consent.

con·sun·ti·vo, –va adj. consuming.

con·sus·tan·cial adj. var. of **consubstancial.**

con·ta·bi·li·dad f. *(teneduría de libros)* accounting, bookkeeping; *(profesión)* accountancy; *(calidad de contable)* countability, computability.

con·ta·bi·li·zar §04 tr. COM. to enter, record (in the accounts).

con·ta·ble I. adj. countable, computable; *(relatable)* relatable (story) II. m. accountant, bookkeeper.

con·tac·to m. *(tacto)* contact; FIG. *(relación)* contact, touch <*me puse en c. con el ministro* I got in touch with the minister>; ELEC. contact ♦ **lentes de c.** contact lenses.

con·ta·do, –da I. past part. see **contar** II. adj. *(raro)* scarce, rare <*en contadas ocasiones* on rare occasions>; *(determinado)* specified, set ♦ **al c.** for cash, in cash • **de c.** at once, immediately • **por de c.** of course III. m. COL. installment.

con·ta·dor, –do·ra I. adj. counting II. m.f. *(tenedor de libros)* accountant, bookkeeper; LAW *(administrador judicial)* auditor, receiver; ECUAD. pawnbroker —m. *(aparato)* counter, counting device; AUTO. parking meter; TECH. meter <*c. de gas* gas meter> ♦ **c. de costos** COM. cost accountant • **c. Geiger** Geiger counter • **c. kilométrico** odometer • **c. público titulado** COM. certified public accountant.

con·ta·du·rí·a f. *(estudio)* accounting; *(oficio)* accountancy; *(oficina)* accounting office; THEAT. box office; ECUAD. pawnshop ♦ **c. general** audit office.

con·ta·giar tr. MED. to contaminate, infect; FIG. *(inficionar)* to contaminate, infect; *(pervertir)* to corrupt —reflex. MED. to become infected; FIG. *(inficionarse)* to become corrupt.

con·ta·gio m. MED. contagion; FIG. *(contaminación)* contamination, corruption.

con·ta·gio·so, –sa adj. MED. contagious, infectious; FIG. *(vicioso)* corrupting, catching.

con·ta·mi·na·ción f. *(contagio)* contamination; *(corrupción)* corruption; *(del aire, agua)* pollution.

con·ta·mi·na·dor, –do·ra adj. *(infeccioso)* contaminating, infecting; *(ensuciador)* polluting; *(profanador)* corrupting (morally).

con·ta·mi·nar tr. *(contagiar)* to contaminate, infect; *(ensuciar)* to soil, stain; to pollute <*c. el aire* to pollute the air>; FIG. *(corromper)* to corrupt, pervert; *(alterar)* to corrupt, alter <*c. un texto* to alter a text>; RELIG. to profane —reflex. *(contagiarse)* to be contaminated; *(corromperse)* to be corrupted.

con·tan·te adj. ♦ **dinero c. y sonante** cash, ready money.

con·tar §19 tr. to count, count up <*contó los libros* he counted the books>; *(incluir)* to count, include <*te cuento entre mis amigos* I count you among my friends>; *(referir)* to tell, recount —intr. <*el niño cuenta con los dedos* the child counts on his fingers> ♦ **c. con** *(confiar)* to count *or* rely on <*los niños cuentan con la ayuda de sus padres* children rely on their parents' help>; *(tener en cuenta)* to figure on, take into account <*no contaron con que nevaría* they did not figure on it snowing> • **¿que (te) cuentas?** what's up?

con·tem·pe·rar tr. to temper, moderate.

con·tem·pla·ción f. contemplation, meditation ♦ **contemplaciones** *(indulgencia)* indulgence, pampering; *(ceremonia)* ceremony <*andarse con contemplaciones* to stand on ceremony> • **sin contemplaciones** without ceremony.

con·tem·pla·dor, –do·ra I. adj. *(contemplativo)* contemplative, meditative; *(amable)* obliging II. m.f. *(persona)* contemplative person; *(religioso)* contemplative.

con·tem·plar tr. *(examinar)* to contemplate, ponder; *(mimar)* to indulge, pamper —intr. to contemplate, meditate.

con·tem·pla·ti·vo, –va I. adj. *(meditativo)* contemplative, meditative; *(indulgente)* obliging, indulgent II. m.f. contemplative person.

con·tem·po·ra·nei·dad f. contemporaneity, contemporaneousness.

con·tem·po·rá·ne·o, –a I. adj. contemporary, contemporaneous II. m.f. contemporary.

con·tem·po·ri·za·ción f. temporization, compromise.

con·tem·po·ri·za·dor, –do·ra I. adj. temporizing II. m.f. temporizer.

con·tem·po·ri·zar §04 intr. to temporize, compromise.

con·tén see **contener**.

con·ten·ción f. *(contienda)* competition, contest; *(retención)* retention, containment; LAW lawsuit, suit.

con·ten·cio·so, –sa I. adj. *(argumentador)* contentious, argumentative; LAW *(litigioso)* litigious, contentious II. m. collection of lawsuits.

con·ten·der §50 intr. to contend, fight; FIG. *(competir)* to compete; *(disputar)* to argue, dispute.

con·ten·dien·te I. adj. contending, opposing II. m.f. contender, competitor.

con·te·ne·dor, –do·ra I. adj. containing II. m. container (for shipping cargo).

con·te·ner §69 tr. *(abarcar)* to contain, hold; *(impedir)* to restrain, hold back <*c. a la muchedumbre* to hold back the crowd>; FIG. *(suprimir)* to suppress, contain <*c. la cólera* to contain one's anger>; CHILE to mean, signify —reflex. to contain *or* control oneself.

con·te·ni·do, –da I. past part. see **contener** II. adj. contained, controlled III. m. contents, content.

con·ten·ta I. f. *(agasajo)* treat, present; COM. *(endoso)* endorsement; AMER., LAW *(declaración)* acknowledgment of payment; MARIT. *(certificado)* good conduct and capability certificate II. adj. see **contento, –ta**.

con·ten·ta·di·zo, –za adj. easily pleased *or* satisfied.

con·ten·tar tr. *(satisfacer)* to content, satisfy; AMER. *(reconciliar)* to reconcile ♦ **ser de buen c.** to be easily pleased • **ser de mal c.** to be hard to please • **no caber de c.** to be

beside oneself with joy —reflex. *(estar satisfecho)* to be satisfied *or* content; AMER. to make up, reconcile.

con·ten·ti·ble adj. despicable, contemptible.

con·ten·to, –ta I. adj. *(alegre)* happy, pleased; *(satisfecho)* satisfied, content II. m. *(alegría)* happiness, gladness; *(satisfacción)* contentment, satisfaction —f. see **contenta**.

con·te·ra f. *(regatón)* tip, ferrule (on cane, umbrella); *(remate de metal)* chape (on scabbard); MIL. *(cascabel)* cascabel (on a cannon); POET. *(estribillo)* refrain; *(terceto)* last three lines of a sextain; FIG. *(remate)* end, finishing touch ♦ **por c.** to end with, finally.

con·te·rrá·ne·o, –a adj. var. of **coterráneo**.

con·tes·ta·ble adj. *(discutible)* contestable, questionable; *(que se puede contestar)* answerable.

con·tes·ta·ción f. *(respuesta)* answer, reply; *(disputa)* dispute, argument ♦ **c. a la demanda** LAW defense *or* defendant's plea.

con·tes·ta·dor m. answering machine.

con·tes·tar tr. *(responder)* to answer, reply; *(confirmar)* to confirm, corroborate; *(inpugnar)* to contest, impugn; *(corresponder)* to return (a greeting) —intr. *(responder)* to answer; *(convenir)* to agree; MEX. *(conversar)* to chat, talk; *(discutir)* to argue.

con·tex·to m. *(hilo de una narración)* context; *(contextura)* contexture.

con·tex·tu·ra f. *(enlazo)* contexture; PHYSIOL. build, frame.

con·tien·da f. *(pelea)* fight, battle; *(disputa)* dispute, argument; *(competencia)* contest.

con·tien·da, contiendo see **contender**.

con·tie·ne see **contener**.

con·ti·go §G34 pron. with you <*no queremos comer c.* we do not want to eat with you> ♦ **c. mismo** with yourself.

con·ti·guo, –gua adj. contiguous, adjacent.

con·ti·nen·cia f. continence, abstinence ♦ **c. de la causa** LAW consistency in proceedings.

con·ti·nen·tal adj. continental.

con·ti·nen·te I. adj. *(moderado)* continent; *(que contiene)* containing II. m. GEOG. continent; *(actitud)* countenance, bearing; *(recipiente)* container.

con·tin·gen·cia f. contingency, possibility.

con·tin·gen·te I. adj. contingent II. m. *(posibilidad)* contingency; *(cupo)* quota, share; MIL. contingent.

con·ti·nua·ción f. *(prolongación)* prolongation, continuance ♦ **a c.** next, following.

con·ti·nua·dor, –do·ra I. adj. continuing II. m.f. continuator.

con·ti·nua·men·te adv. continuously, continually.

con·ti·nuar §67 tr. to continue, go *or* keep on <*c. leyendo* to continue reading>; to go *or* continue on <*continuó su camino* she continued on her way> —intr. to continue, go *or* carry on <*continuó con su trabajo* he went on with his work> ♦ **continuará** to be continued.

con·ti·nua·ti·vo, –va adj. continuative.

con·ti·nui·dad f. continuity.

con·ti·nuo, –nua I. adj. *(incesante)* continuous, uninterrupted; *(constante)* continual, constant ♦ **de c.** *or* **a la continua** continually • **corriente c.** direct current II. m. continuum III. adv. continually.

con·to·ne·ar·se reflex. to sway one's hips, wiggle.

con·to·ne·o m. swaying of the hips, wiggle.

con·tor·cer·se §71 reflex. to contort oneself.

con·tor·ción f. contortion.

con·tor·na·do, –da I. past part. see **contornar** II. adj. HER. turned toward the left of the shield (animals).

con·tor·nar *or* **con·tor·ne·ar** tr. *(dar vueltas alrededor)* to skirt, go around <*c. una montaña* to skirt a mountain>; *(perfilar)* to outline.

con·tor·no m. *(perfil)* contour, outline; *(perímetro)* perimeter, periphery; *(canto de la moneda)* edge, rim (of a coin) ♦ **contornos** environs, surroundings • **en c.** around.

con·tor·sión f. *(torsión)* contortion; *(mueca)* grimace.

con·tor·sio·nis·ta m.f. contortionist.

con·tra I. prep. against <*apoyó la escala c. la pared* he leaned the ladder against the wall>; opposite, facing <*la iglesia está c. el museo* the church is opposite the museum> ♦ **c. viento y marea** against all odds • **en c. de** against <*votar en c. de la propuesta* to vote against the proposition> II. m. cons <*el pro y el c.* the pros and

cons>; MUS. organ pedal ♦ **hacerle** *or* **llevarle la c. (a al-guien)** to contradict (someone) —f. COLL. *(obstáculo)* snag, hitch; FENC. *(parada)* parry; CUBA, P. RICO bonus, extra; S. AMER. antidote ♦ **llevar la c.** to oppose, counter.
con·tra·a·cu·sa·ción f. countercharge.
con·tra·al·mi·ran·te m. MARIT. rear admiral.
con·tra·a·ta·car §70 tr. MIL. to counterattack.
con·tra·a·ta·que m. MIL. counterattack.
con·tra·ban·de·ar intr. to smuggle.
con·tra·ban·dis·ta m.f. smuggler, contrabandist.
con·tra·ban·do m. *(mercancía)* contraband; *(acción)* smuggling.
con·trac·ción f. *(encogimiento)* contraction; GRAM. contraction.
con·tra·cep·ción f. MED. contraception.
con·tra·cep·ti·vo, –va adj. & m. contraceptive.
con·tra·co·rrien·te f. countercurrent.
con·trac·ta·ble adj. contractible.
con·trac·to, –ta I. past part. see **contraer** II. adj. GRAM. contracted.
con·trac·tual adj. contractual.
con·tra·cul·tu·ra f. counterculture.
con·tra·cha·pa·do, –da *or* **con·tra·cha·pe·a·do, –da** adj. & m. plywood.
con·tra·de·cir §11 tr. to contradict —reflex. to contradict oneself.
con·tra·dic·ción f. *(objeción)* contradiction; FIG. *(incompatibilidad)* incompatibility, inconsistency.
con·tra·dic·tor, –to·ra I. adj. contradictory II. m.f. contradicter.
con·tra·dic·to·rio, –ria adj. contradictory.
con·tra·di·ga, contradigo see **contradecir**.
con·tra·di·je·ra, contradijo see **contradecir**.
con·tra·em·bos·ca·da f. counterambush.
con·tra·er §72 tr. to contract, shrink <*el frío contrae el hierro* cold contracts iron>; *(reducir)* to shorten, condense; GRAM. to contract, shorten; to contract, incur <*c. deudas* to incur debts>; MED. to contract, catch <*contrajo un resfriado* he caught a cold>; *(adquirir)* to acquire, pick up <*no quiero c. el vicio de fumar* I do not want to pick up the bad habit of smoking> ♦ **c. la frente** to wrinkle one's brow • **c. matrimonio** to marry, get married —reflex. to contract <*sus músculos se contraían* his muscles contracted>; *(reducirse)* to be limited *or* restricted; AMER. to apply oneself, work hard.
con·tra·es·cri·tu·ra f. LAW counterdeed.
con·tra·es·pio·na·je m. counterespionage.
con·tra·faz f. [pl. **-fa·ces**] reverse, other side (of a coin or medal).
con·tra·fi·lo m. sharpened back (of a sword).
con·tra·fue·go m. backfire.
con·tra·fue·ro m. violation, infringement (of a privilege).
con·tra·fuer·te m. ARCHIT. buttress; ARM. outwork; GEOG. spur (of a mountain range); *(del zapato)* heel reinforcement.
con·tra·gol·pe m. MED. contrecoup; SPORT. counter, counterblow; AUTO. kickback.
con·tra·gue·rri·lla f. antiguerrilla troops.
con·tra·ha·cer §40 tr. *(imitar)* to imitate, mimic; FIG. *(un libro)* to plagiarize; *(la moneda)* to counterfeit; *(un documento)* to forge; *(una enfermedad)* to fake, feign (illness) —reflex. to feign, pretend.
con·tra·haz f. [pl. **-ha·ces**] wrong side (of cloth).
con·tra·he·cho, –cha I. past part. see **contrahacer** II. adj. *(deforme)* deformed, hunchbacked; *(falso)* counterfeit, fake III. m.f. deformed person, hunchback.
con·tra·he·chu·ra f. *(imitación)* imitation, mimicry; *(falsificación)* falsification, fakery; *(la moneda)* counterfeiting; *(documentos)* forgery.
con·tra·hi·cie·ra, contrahizo see **contrahacer**.
con·tra·i·ga, contraigo see **contraer**.
con·tra·in·di·ca·ción f. MED. contraindication.
con·tra·in·di·car §70 tr. MED. to contraindicate.
con·tra·je·ra, contrajo see **contraer**.
con·tra·al·mi·ran·te m. var. of contraalmirante.
con·tra·lor m. comptroller, inspector.
con·tral·to m.f. MUS. contralto.
con·tra·luz m. backlighting.

con·tra·ma·es·tre m. *(en un taller)* foreman; MARIT. boatswain ♦ **c. de segunda** MARIT. chief petty officer.
con·tra·ma·nio·bra f. countermaneuver.
con·tra·ma·no adv. ♦ **a c.** in the wrong direction, the wrong way <*circulación a c.* traffic going the wrong way>.
con·tra·mar·ca f. *(segunda marca)* countermark; *(impuesto)* customs duty.
con·tra·mar·car §70 tr. to countermark.
con·tra·mar·cha f. countermarch; AUTO. reverse.
con·tra·ma·tar tr. AMER. to slam a person against something —reflex. MEX. to repent.
con·tra·mi·nar tr. MIL. to countermine; FIG. to countermine, counterplot.
con·tra·na·tu·ral I. adj. contrary to nature, unnatural II. f. unnatural thing.
con·tra·o·fen·si·va f. MIL. counteroffensive.
con·tra·o·pe·ra·ción f. counteroperation.
con·tra·or·den f. countermand.
con·tra·par·ti·da f. COM. *(corrección)* cross entry; *(compensación)* compensation.
con·tra·pa·sar intr. to cross over, change sides.
con·tra·pe·lo adv. ♦ **a c.** against the grain, the wrong way; FIG. *(contra lo normal)* contrary to normal practice; *(con desgana)* unwillingly, against one's will • **a c. de** against, counter to.
con·tra·pe·sar tr. *(contrabalancear)* to counterbalance, counterpoise; FIG. *(equilibrar)* to offset, counterbalance.
con·tra·pe·so m. *(peso)* counterweight, counterbalance; *(añadidura)* makeweight; FIG. *(compensación)* counterbalance, compensation; *(balancín)* balancing pole (used by tightrope walkers); CHILE restlessness.
con·tra·po·ner §54 tr. *(oponer)* to oppose, set against; *(comparar)* to compare, contrast —reflex. to oppose, set oneself against.
con·tra·po·si·ción f. *(oposición)* opposition; *(comparación)* comparison; *(contraste)* contrast.
con·tra·pro·du·cen·te adj. counterproductive, self-defeating.
con·tra·pro·po·si·ción f. counterproposal.
con·tra·prue·ba f. PRINT. second proof.
con·tra·puer·ta f. *(cancel)* storm door; FORT. second *or* inner door.
con·tra·pues·to, –ta past part. see **contraponer**.
con·tra·pun·te·ar tr. MUS. to sing in counterpoint; FIG. *(provocar)* to pique, taunt —intr. AMER. *(cantar)* to sing improvised verses; *(rivalizar)* to compete, rival —reflex. *(molestarse)* to be annoyed *or* piqued; *(resentirse)* to quarrel, argue.
con·tra·pun·te·o m. MUS. counterpoint; FIG. *(rivalidad)* rivalry, competition; *(provocación)* provocation; AMER. quarrel, argument.
con·tra·pun·to m. MUS. counterpoint; FIG. *(desenlace)* ending; AMER. poetry contest, poetic competition.
con·tra·pu·sie·ra, contrapuso see **contraponer**.
con·tra·riar §30 tr. *(oponer)* to oppose; *(contradecir)* to contradict; *(enfadar)* to annoy, vex; *(obstaculizar)* to obstruct, hinder.
con·tra·rie·dad f. *(oposición)* opposition; *(obstáculo)* obstacle, hindrance; *(desazón)* annoyance, vexation; *(contratiempo)* setback; *(percance)* mishap.
con·tra·rio, –ria I. adj. opposite <*en sentido c.* in the opposite direction>; *(adverso)* unfavorable, adverse <*condiciones contrarias* adverse conditions>; FIG. *(nocivo)* harmful, bad <*c. a la salud* harmful to one's health> ♦ **al c.** to the contrary • **al c. de** contrary to <*al c. de lo que dijo a usted* contrary to what he told you> • **por el** *or* **lo c.** on the contrary • **todo lo c.** quite the opposite II. m.f. opponent, adversary —m. *(obstáculo)* obstacle, snag —f. contrary, opposite ♦ **llevar la c.** COLL. to contradict, disagree.
con·tra·rres·tar tr. *(contrabalancear)* to counteract, offset; *(resistir)* to resist, oppose; SPORT. to return (the ball).
con·tra·rre·vo·lu·ción f. counterrevolution.
con·tra·rriel m. RAIL. guardrail, wing rail.
con·tra·se·llo m. counterseal.
con·tra·sen·ti·do m. *(contradicción)* contradiction, incongruity; *(interpretación incorrecta)* misinterpretation; *(disparate)* nonsense, absurdity.

con·tra·se·ña f. *(firma)* countersign, secret sign; *(contramarca)* countermark (customs mark); MIL. watchword, password; ARG. countersignature ♦ **c. de salida** readmission ticket *or* pass.

con·tras·ta·ble adj. contrastable.

con·tras·ta·dor, –do·ra I. adj. contrasting II. m.f. contraster.

con·tras·tar intr. to contrast, differ —tr. *(resistir)* to resist, stand up to; *(averiguar)* to check, verify; METAL. to assay and hallmark; NUMIS. to assay.

con·tras·te m. *(desigualdad)* contrast; *(oposición)* opposition, resistance; MARIT. sudden change in wind; METAL. *(control)* assay; *(marcador)* assayer, assay officer; *(almotacén)* public assaying office; *(marca)* hallmark; TEX. *(de la seda)* weighing of raw silk ♦ **en c. con** in contrast to • **hacer c. con** to contrast to *or* with • **por c.** in contrast.

con·tra·ta f. *(escritura)* contract, deed <*firmaron la c.* they signed the contract>; *(por precio determinado)* contract, engagement.

con·tra·ta·ción f. *(empleo)* contracting, hiring; *(negocio)* trade, commerce.

con·tra·tar tr. *(hacer un contrato)* to contract for; *(firmar un contrato)* to sign a contract for; *(emplear)* to hire, engage.

con·tra·te·rro·ris·ta adj. & m.f. counterterrorist.

con·tra·tiem·po m. *(desgracia)* contretemps, mishap; MUS. syncopation ♦ **a c.** MUS. in syncopated time, offbeat.

con·tra·tis·ta m.f. contractor ♦ **c. de edificación** *or* **obras** building contractor.

con·tra·to m. LAW contract ♦ **c. a la gruesa** *or* **a riesgo marítimo** MARIT. bottomry • **c. aleatorio** aleatory contract • **c. bilateral** bilateral contract • **c. colectivo de trabajo** labor contract • **c. de aceptación** COM. acceptance agreement • **c. de administración** management contract • **c. de ajuste** *or* **de conchabo** ARG. employment contract • **c. de arrendamiento** *or* **de locación** lease • **c. de asociación** *or* **de sociedad** partnership contract • **c. de cambio** exchange agreement • **c. de compraventa** COM. purchase agreement • **c. de fideicomiso** deed of trust • **c. de fletamento** charter party • **c. de palabra** *or* **verbal** verbal *or* parol contract • **c. de prenda** collateral contract • **c. de trabajo** *or* **de empleo** employment contract • **c. matrimonial** marriage contract • **c. pignoraticio** contract of pledge • **c. unilateral** unilateral contract.

con·tra·tor·pe·de·ro m. MIL. destroyer.

con·tra·tuer·ca f. MECH. locknut.

con·tra·ven·ción f. contravention, violation.

con·tra·ve·nir §76 intr. LAW to contravene, violate.

con·tra·ven·ta·na f. *(puertaventana)* storm window; *(postigo)* shutter.

con·tra·ven·tor, –to·ra I. adj. LAW contravening, violating II. m.f. LAW contravener, violator.

con·tra·yen·te I. adj. contracting (party) II. m.f. contracting party.

con·tre·cho, –cha adj. crippled, maimed.

con·tri·bu·ción f. *(cantidad contribuida)* contribution; *(impuesto)* tax ♦ **c. de guerra** MIL. tribute • **c. de sangre** FIG. military service • **c. directa** direct tax • **c. indirecta** indirect tax • **c. territorial** land tax • **c. urbana** property *or* real estate tax • **contribuciones** taxes, taxation • **exento de contribuciones** tax-exempt • **poner a c.** to make use of, put to use.

con·tri·bui·dor, –do·ra I. adj. contributory II. m.f. contributor.

con·tri·buir §18 tr. *(pagar)* to contribute, pay; FIG. to contribute <*c. ideas* to contribute ideas> —intr. to contribute <*el rey contribuyó con una gran cantidad de dinero* the king contributed a great deal of the money>; FIG. *(ayudar)* to contribute.

con·tri·bu·yen·te I. adj. *(que contribuye)* contributing, contributory; *(que paga impuestos)* taxpaying II. m.f. *(uno que contribuye)* contributor; *(que paga impuestos)* taxpayer.

con·tri·ción f. contrition, repentance.

con·trin·can·te m. rival, opponent.

con·tris·tar tr. to sadden, grieve —reflex. to become sad *or* downcast.

con·tri·to, –ta adj. contrite, repentant.

con·trol m. *(dominio)* control; *(inspección)* inspection;

(comprobación) check, checking; *(lugar)* control point, checkpoint; FIG. *(examen)* examination; COM. audit ♦ **bajo c.** under control • **c. de frontera** border checkpoint • **c. de la circulación** traffic control • **c. de la natalidad** birth control • **c. de precios** price control • **c. de vuelo** flight control • **c. remoto** *or* **a distancia** remote control • **c. sobre sí mismo** self-control • **fuera de c.** out of control.

con·tro·lar tr. *(dirigir)* to control, direct; *(dominar)* to control <*c. los nervios* to control one's nerves>; *(inspeccionar)* to inspect, examine; *(comprobar)* to check, verify; COM. to audit.

con·tro·ver·sia f. controversy, dispute.

con·tro·ver·ti·ble adj. controvertible, debatable.

con·tro·ver·tir §65 tr. to controvert, dispute —intr. to argue, discuss.

con·tu·ber·nio m. *(cohabitación)* cohabitation; FIG. *(confabulación)* collusion.

con·tuer·za, contuerzo see **contorcerse.**

con·tu·ma·cia f. *(obstinación)* stubbornness, obstinacy; LAW nonappearance, default.

con·tu·maz adj. *(porfiado)* stubborn, obstinate; LAW in default ♦ **condenar por c.** to convict by default.

con·tu·me·lio·so, –sa adj. insulting, offensive.

con·tun·den·cia f. *(de un arma)* bluntness (of a weapon); FIG. *(de un argumento)* weight (of an argument).

con·tun·den·te adj. *(tundente)* bruising; FIG. *(convencedor)* convincing, overwhelming <*evidencia c.* overwhelming evidence>.

con·tun·dir tr. to bruise, contuse.

con·tur·ba·ción f. uneasiness, anxiety.

con·tur·ba·do, –da I. past part. see **conturbar** II. adj. anxious, perturbed.

con·tur·ba·dor, –do·ra adj. troubling, perturbing.

con·tur·bar tr. to trouble, perturb —reflex. to become uneasy *or* perturbed.

con·tu·sión f. bruise, contusion.

con·tu·so, –sa I. adj. bruised, contused II. m.f. bruised person.

con·tu·vie·ra, contuvo see **contener.**

con·va·le·cen·cia f. *(recobramiento)* convalescence; *(lugar)* rest home, sanatorium.

con·va·le·cer §17 intr. MED. to convalesce; FIG. *(salir del peligro)* to recover, recuperate.

con·va·le·cien·te I. adj. convalescent II. m.f. convalescent patient.

con·va·li·da·ción f. confirmation, ratification.

con·va·li·dar tr. to confirm, ratify.

con·vec·ción f. PHYS. convection.

con·ve·ci·no, –na I. adj. neighboring, adjacent II. m.f. neighbor.

con·ve·ler·se reflex. MED. to contract (said of muscles).

con·ven·cer §75 tr. to convince —reflex. to be *or* become convinced.

con·ven·ci·ble adj. convincible.

con·ven·ci·do, –da I. past part. see **convencer** II. adj. *(persuadido)* convinced; *(culpable)* convicted, found guilty.

con·ven·ci·mien·to m. *(acción)* convincing; *(convicción)* conviction, certainty.

con·ven·ción f. *(pacto)* convention, pact; *(conformidad)* conformity, harmony; *(asamblea)* convention ♦ **de c.** by convention.

con·ven·cio·nal I. adj. conventional II. m. delegate, conventioneer.

con·ven·cio·na·lis·mo m. conventionality.

con·ven·cio·nal·men·te adv. conventionally.

con·ven·drá, convendría see **convenir.**

con·ven·ga, convengo see **convenir.**

con·ve·ni·ble adj. *(dócil)* easy-going, accommodating; *(precio)* fair, reasonable (price).

con·ve·ni·do I. past part. see **convenir** II. adv. agreed.

con·ve·nien·cia f. *(conformidad)* agreement, harmony; *(oportunidad)* suitability, fitness; *(lo aconsejable)* advisability, desirability; *(provecho)* advantage, profit; *(comodidad)* convenience, comfort; *(puesto)* position (as a domestic); *(acuerdo)* arrangement, agreement; *(decoro)* convention, decorum ♦ **a la primera c.** at the first *or* earliest opportunity • **conveniencias** *(renta)* income; *(propiedad)* property; *(de un trabajo)* perquisites • **ser de la c. de uno** • to be convenient for someone, suit someone.

con·ve·nien·te adj. *(util)* convenient; *(oportuno)* suitable, fit; *(aconsejable)* advisable, desirable; *(provechoso)* advantageous, profitable; *(proporcionado)* correct, proper ♦ **creer** *or* **juzgar c.** to think *or* see fit.

con·ve·nio m. *(pacto)* agreement, pact; COM. settlement ♦ **c. comercial** trade agreement • **c. de préstamos y arriendos** lend-lease agreement • **llegar a un c.** to reach an agreement.

con·ve·nir §76 intr. *(acordar)* to agree, concur <*hemos convenido en reunirnos mañana* we have agreed to meet tomorrow>; *(corresponder)* to correspond, be fitting <*al rey conviene la sabiduría* wisdom is fitting for a king>; to suit, be suitable for <*este tipo de trabajo me conviene mucho* this type of work suits me very well>; to be advisable <*no les conviene pedirle otro favor de él* it's not advisable for you to ask another favor of him>; *(juntarse)* to meet ♦ **conviene a saber** namely, that is —reflex. to agree, come to an agreement ♦ **convenirse a** *or* **en** to agree to.

con·ven·tí·cu·lo m. conventicle, secret meeting.

con·ven·ti·lle·ro, -ra m.f. ARG. gossip, meddler.

con·ven·ti·llo m. AMER. tenement house.

con·ven·to m. *(de monjas)* convent, nunnery; *(monasterio)* monastery; ECUAD., PERU rectory.

con·ven·za, convenzo see **convencer**.

con·ver·gen·cia f. convergence.

con·ver·gen·te adj. convergent, converging.

con·ver·ger §34 *or* **con·ver·gir** §32 intr. *(dirigirse al mismo punto)* to converge; FIG. *(concurrir)* to concur, agree.

con·ver·sa f. COLL. talk, chat.

con·ver·sa·ción f. conversation, talk ♦ **cambiar de c.** to change the subject • **dar c.** to make conversation • **dirigir la c. a uno** to address someone • **trabar c.** to strike up a conversation.

con·ver·sa·dor, -do·ra I. talkative, garrulous II. m.f. talker, conversationalist; S. AMER. gossip.

con·ver·sar intr. *(charlar)* to converse, talk; MIL. to wheel, change fronts — tr. CHILE, ECUAD. to relate, tell.

con·ver·sión f. *(cambio)* conversion; MIL. wheel; RHET. epistrophe.

con·ver·so, -sa I. past part. see **convertir** II. adj. converted III. m.f. convert; RELIG. lay brother —f. lay sister.

con·ver·ti·bi·li·dad f. convertibility.

con·ver·ti·ble I. adj. convertible, changeable II. m. AMER., AUTO. convertible.

con·ver·ti·dor m. ELEC., METAL. converter ♦ **c. de frecuencia** ELEC. frequency changer.

con·ver·tir §65 tr. *(cambiar)* to change, turn <*c. el agua en vino* to turn water into wine>; *(persuadir)* to convert; to turn <*c. los pensamientos hacia Dios* to turn one's thoughts to God>; COM., FIN. to convert, exchange —reflex. to convert, be converted; to change, turn <*el vino se convirtió en vinagre* the wine turned into vinegar>.

con·ve·xo, -xa adj. convex.

con·vic·ción f. conviction.

con·vic·to, -ta I. past part. see **convencer** II. adj. convicted, found guilty III. m.f. convict.

con·vi·da·do, -da I. past part. see **convidar** II. m.f. guest ♦ **como el c. de piedra** quiet, mute.

con·vi·dar tr. *(invitar)* to invite; *(incitar)* to invite, be conducive to <*el silencio convida a la meditación* silence is conducive to meditation> ♦ **c. a uno con** to treat someone to —reflex. to offer one's services, volunteer.

con·vie·ne see **convenir**.

con·vier·ta, convierto see **convertir**.

con·vin·cen·te adj. convincing.

con·vi·nie·ra, convino see **convenir**.

con·vir·ja, convirjo see **convergir**.

con·vir·tie·ra, convirtió see **convertir**.

con·vi·te m. *(invitación)* invitation; *(banquete)* banquet, feast; C. AMER., MEX. street costume party ♦ **c. a escote** Dutch treat.

con·vi·ven·cia f. living together; *(coexistencia)* coexistence (countries, factions).

con·vi·vir intr. to live together.

con·vo·ca·ción f. convocation.

con·vo·ca·dor, -do·ra I. adj. convoking, summoning II. m.f. convener.

con·vo·car §70 tr. *(llamar)* to convoke, summon; *(aclamar)* to acclaim, hail.

con·vo·ca·to·rio, -ria I. adj. convoking, summoning II. f. *(anuncio)* summons, notice; EDUC. *(época de exámenes)* examination period.

con·voy m. *(conjunto)* convoy; *(escolta)* escort, guard; *(vinagreras)* cruet; *(tren)* train; FIG., COLL. *(séquito)* procession, retinue.

con·vo·yar tr. *(escoltar)* to escort, convoy; CHILE to help, assist —reflex. P. RICO, VEN. to conspire, connive.

con·vul·sión f. MED. convulsion, spasm; FIG. *(trastorno)* upheaval, agitation <*c. política* political upheaval>; GEOL. *(temblor)* tremor, seismic movement.

con·vul·sio·nar tr. *(contraer)* to convulse; FIG. *(agitar)* to agitate, disturb.

con·vul·sio·na·rio, -ria adj. & m.f. convulsionary.

con·vul·si·va·men·te adv. convulsively.

con·vul·si·vo, -va adj. MED. *(espasmódico)* convulsive; whooping <*tos c.* whooping cough>.

con·vul·so, -sa adj. MED. convulsed; FIG. *(excitado)* agitated, excited.

con·yu·gal adj. conjugal, connubial.

cón·yu·ge m.f. spouse ♦ **cónyuges** married couple, husband and wife.

co·ñac m. [pl. **-ñacs**] cognac, brandy.

co·ño m. VULG. cunt ♦ **¡coño!** damn it!, shit!

co·o·pe·ra·ción f. cooperation.

co·o·pe·ra·dor, -do·ra *or* **co·o·pe·ran·te** I. adj. cooperating II. m.f. cooperator.

co·o·pe·rar intr. to cooperate ♦ **c. a un mismo fin** to work for a common cause.

co·o·pe·ra·ti·va I. f. cooperative II. adj. see **cooperativo, -va**.

co·o·pe·ra·ti·vis·mo m. cooperative movement.

co·o·pe·ra·ti·vis·ta adj. & m.f. cooperativist.

co·o·pe·ra·ti·vo, -va I. adj. cooperative II. f. see **cooperativa**.

co·o·po·si·tor, -to·ra m.f. rival candidate (for a position).

co·op·ta·ción f. co-option (election of a fellow member).

co·or·de·na·da f. MATH. coordinate.

co·or·di·na·ción f. coordination.

co·or·di·na·dor, -do·ra I. adj. coordinating II. m.f. coordinator.

co·or·di·nar tr. *(concertar)* to coordinate; *(ordenar)* to classify.

co·pa f. stemmed glass, goblet <*una c. de cristal* a crystal goblet>; *(contenido)* glassful, goblet <*bebió tres copas de vino* he drank three glasses of wine>; *(trago)* drink, cocktail; *(follaje)* treetop; *(de un sombrero)* crown (of a hat); *(brasero)* brazier; SPORT. *(premio)* cup, trophy ♦ **copas** suit in a Spanish deck of cards; *(del freno)* bosses (of a bridle) • **echar por copas** AMER. to exaggerate • **tomarse una c.** FIG. to have a drink *or* cocktail.

co·pai·ba f. BOT. copaiba, copaiba balsam.

co·pal m. copal (resin).

co·par tr. *(en un juego)* to cover *or* wager (the bank); POL. to win, sweep (an election); MIL. to surround, cut off.

co·par·ti·ci·pa·ción f. copartnership.

co·par·ti·ci·pe m.f. copartner.

co·pe·ar intr. *(vender)* to sell by the glassful; *(beber)* to have a few drinks.

co·pe·la f. METAL. cupel.

Co·pen·ha·gue Copenhagen.

co·pe·ro m. *(persona)* cupbearer; *(mueble)* cupboard.

co·pe·te m. *(mechón)* tuft (of hair); *(tupé)* toupee, hairpiece; ZOOL. forelock (of a horse); ORNITH. crest, crown; *(cima)* summit, top; *(del mueble)* crownwork, headpiece (on furniture); *(del zapato)* tongue (of a shoe); FIG., COLL. *(altanería)* arrogance, haughtiness; CUL. topping ♦ **de alto c.** high-class; *(importante)* important, prominent • **estar hasta el c.** AMER. to be completely fed up • **tener mucho c.** to be arrogant *or* haughty.

co·pe·tín m. AMER., COLL. drink, cocktail.

co·pe·tón, -to·na I. adj. AMER., ORNITH. tufted, crested; *(arrogante)* arrogant, haughty; COL. *(achispado)* slightly

drunk, tipsy; VEN. *(cobarde)* cowardly **II.** m. COL., OR-
NITH. crested sparrow —f. MEX. elegant woman.
co·pe·tu·do, –da **I.** adj. ORNITH. tufted, crested; *(arrogante)*
arrogant, haughty **II.** f. ORNITH. skylark; CUBA, BOT.
marigold.
co·pia f. *(reproducción)* copy, duplicate; exact likeness,
image *<él es una c. de su hermano mayor* he is the image of
his older brother>; *(gran cantidad)* abundance, profusion;
FIG. *(imitación)* imitation; ARTS copy, reproduction; CI-
NEM., PHOTOG. copy, print; *(fotocopia)* photocopy ♦ **c. al
carbón** carbon copy • **c. en limpio** fair copy • **c. fotostática** photostat • **c. heliográfica** blueprint • **c. por contacto** PHOTOG. contact print • **sacar una c.** to make a
copy.
co·pia·dor, –do·ra **I.** adj. copying **II.** m.f. *(copista)* copyist, transcriber —m. COM. *(libro)* letter book —f. *(foto-
copiador)* photocopier, copying machine.
co·piar tr. *(hacer una copia)* to copy, make a copy of; *(apuntar)* to copy down, take down; *(imitar)* to imitate, copy.
co·pi·lo·to m. AVIA. copilot.
co·pio·sa·men·te adv. copiously, abundantly.
co·pio·si·dad f. copiousness, abundance.
co·pio·so, –sa adj. copious, abundant; *(fuerte)* heavy
(rain).
co·pis·ta m.f. copyist.
co·pla f. *(canción)* popular song, ballad; *(estrofa)* verse,
stanza ♦ **coplas** COLL. verses, poetry • **coplas de ciego**
doggerel, jingles.
co·ple·ar intr. *(escribir cantos)* to write songs; *(escribir versos)* to write poetry; *(cantar)* to sing ballads.
co·ple·ro, –ra *or* **co·plis·ta** m.f. *(persona que hace coplas)*
balladist; FIG. *(mal poeta)* poetaster, bad poet.
co·po m. *(de nieve)* flake, snowflake; TEX. *(mechón)* bundle,
tuft (of flax); *(coágulo)* clot, curd; *(de una red)* bottom of
a seine; ARG., URUG. rain cloud; COL., VEN. treetop ♦ **c.
de algodón** cotton ball • **copos de avena** oatmeal, rolled
oats.
co·po·se·sión f. co-ownership.
co·po·se·sor, –so·ra m.f. co-owner.
co·po·so, –sa adj. bushy, thick-topped (tree).
co·pra f. copra.
co·pro·duc·ción f. CINEM. coproduction.
co·pro·pie·dad f. joint ownership.
co·pro·pie·ta·rio, –ria m.f. co-owner, coproprietor.
có·pu·la f. *(unión)* union, coupling; *(atadura)* link; *(coito)*
copulation, sexual intercourse; GRAM., LOG. copula.
co·pu·lar·se reflex. to copulate, have sexual intercourse.
co·pu·la·ti·vo, –va adj. copulative.
co·que m. MIN. coke.
co·qué, coque see **cocar.**
co·que·ar intr. AMER. to chew coca leaves.
co·que·ro, –ra **I.** adj. addicted to coca **II.** m.f. *(aficionado)*
coca addict; *(vendedor)* coca seller —f. *(en una piedra)*
hollow (in a stone); *(para el coque)* coke bin; BOL. place
for storing coca.
co·que·ta **I.** f. *(mujer)* coquette, flirt; *(tocador)* dressing
table **II.** adj. see **coqueto, –ta.**
co·que·te·ar intr. to flirt.
co·que·te·o m. flirtation.
co·que·te·rí·a f. *(encanto)* coquettishness, flirtatiousness;
(afectación) affectation.
co·que·to, –ta **I.** adj. COLL. *(agradable)* attractive, charming *<una casa c.* a charming house>; flirtatious *<una mujer c.* a flirtatious woman> **II.** f. see **coqueta.**
co·que·tón, –to·na COLL. **I.** adj. *(agradable)* attractive,
charming; flirtatious **II.** m.f. flirt.
co·qui·to m. *(gesto)* funny face (to amuse a child); ORNITH.
turtledove; AMER., BOT. coquito palm ♦ **hacer coquitos** to
make faces.
co·qui·za·ción f. MIN. coking.
co·ra·ce·ro m. *(soldado)* cuirassier; COLL. strong black cigar.
co·ra·cha f. leather bag.
co·ra·je m. *(ira)* anger, rage; *(valor)* courage, bravery ♦ **dar
c. a** to make angry.
co·ra·ji·na f. COLL. fit of anger.
co·ra·ju·do, –da adj. COLL. angry, ill-tempered.
co·ral[1] m. JEWEL., ZOOL. coral; CUBA, BOT. coral tree —f.

(serpiente) coral snake ♦ **corales** *(cuentas)* coral beads;
ORNITH. *(carúnculas)* caruncle, wattle and comb • **más
fino que un c.** FIG. astute, as sharp as a tack.
co·ral[2] MUS. **I.** adj. choral **II.** m. chorale.
co·ra·li·no, –na **I.** adj. coralline (animal, color) **II.** f. BOT.,
ZOOL. coralline.
co·ram·bre f. *(conjunto de cueros)* hides, skins; *(cuero)* hide
<c. de vaca cowhide>.
Co·rán m. RELIG. Koran.
co·ra·za f. *(armadura)* cuirass; FIG. *(protección)* protection,
armor; MARIT. armor plate; ZOOL. shell.
co·ra·zón m. ANAT. heart; FIG. *(figura)* heart, heart-shaped
design; *(valor)* spirit, courage; *(amor)* heart, love; *(centro)*
core, heart *<el c. de la ciudad* the heart of the city> ♦
atravesar el c. FIG. to move with pity • **blando de c.** FIG.
softhearted • **clavársele a uno en el c.** FIG. to pierce one's
heart • **con el c. en la mano** FIG. frankly, openly • **de c.**
sincerely, from the heart *<te lo digo de c.* I'm telling you
sincerely> • **duro de c.** FIG. hardhearted • **encogérsele a
uno el c.** FIG. to move with pity • **helársele a uno el c.**
FIG. to be stunned • **no caberle el c. en el pecho** FIG. to
be bursting (with joy) • **no tener c.** to be heartless • **no
tener c. para** not to have the heart to *<no tengo c. para
decirle la verdad* I do not have the heart to tell her the
truth> • **ojos que no ven, c. que no siente** out of sight,
out of mind • **tener c. de bronce** FIG. to be hardhearted •
tener c. de oro FIG. to have a heart of gold, be good-
hearted.
co·ra·zo·na·da f. *(impulso)* impulse; *(presentimiento)* premonition, presentiment; COLL. *(entrañas)* entrails.
cor·ba·ta f. tie, necktie; *(banda)* cravat; *(en una bandera)*
streamer, sash; *(insignia)* ribbon, insignia; *(en carambolas)*
two-cushion shot; THEAT. apron; ARG. neckerchief; COL.
back of a rooster's neck —m. LAW, RELIG. layman ♦ **con
c.** wearing a tie, with a tie on • **c. de lazo** *or* **mariposa**
bow tie.
cor·be·ta f. MARIT. corvette.
Cór·ce·ga f. Corsica.
cor·cel m. steed, charger.
cor·co·va·do, –da **I.** past part. see **corcovar II.** adj. hunchbacked, humpbacked **III.** m.f. hunchback, humpback.
cor·co·var tr. to curve, bend.
cor·co·ve·ar intr. *(dar corcovos)* to buck; AMER. *(refunfuñar)* to grumble, grouse; MEX. to be scared.
cor·cu·sir tr. to sew poorly.
cor·char tr. *(tapar con corcho)* to cork (a bottle); MARIT. to
lay (strands of rope); COL. to discredit.
cor·che·a f. MUS. eighth note, quaver (G.B.) ♦ **doble c.**
MUS. sixteenth note, semiquaver (G.B.).
cor·che·te m. *(broche)* hook and eye, clasp; *(macho del
broche)* hook (of clasp); FIG. *(alguacil)* constable; CARP.
bench stop *or* hook; PRINT. *(llave)* bracket, brace; *(renglón)* overrun.
cor·cho m. BOT. cork, cork bark; *(tapón)* cork, bottle stopper; *(corchera)* wine cooler; *(caja)* cork box; *(de mesa)*
cork mat; *(guardafuego)* cork fireguard; *(chanclo)* cork-
soled sandal; *(de la pesca)* float (in fishing); *(colmena)*
beehive; ARG., BOT. climbing plant ♦ **c. bornizo** *or* **virgen**
virgin cork • **c. segundero** cork from second cutting of
tree • **estar c.** COL., FIG. to be ignorant of something •
hacer el c. CHILE, FIG. to vanish, disappear rapidly • **sacar el c.** to uncork, take out the cork.
¡cór·cho·lis! interj. good heavens!, gracious!
cor·da·je m. MARIT. rigging, cordage; MUS. set of strings
(for an instrument).
cor·dal[1] adj. ♦ **muela c.** wisdom tooth.
cor·dal[2] m. MUS. tailpiece (on stringed instruments).
cor·del m. *(cuerda)* cord, thin rope; *(distancia)* length of
five paces; *(cañada)* cattle path; CHILE rope-skipping,
jump rope; CUBA agrarian measure ♦ **a c.** in a straight line
• **a hurta c.** stealthily, on the sly.
cor·de·la·do, –da adj. corded *<cinta c.* corded ribbon>.
cor·de·le·rí·a f. *(oficio)* ropemaking; *(taller)* ropemaker's
shop; *(cordería)* rope, cordage.
cor·de·le·ro, –ra m.f. rope maker; *(vendedor)* rope dealer.
cor·de·ro m. *(carnero)* lamb; *(piel)* lambskin; FIG. *(persona
mansa)* lamb ♦ **c. lechal** *or* **recental** suckling lamb ♦ **c.**

pascual RELIG. paschal lamb • **el C. de Dios** *or* **el Divino C.** RELIG. the Lamb of God.

cor·dial I. adj. *(afectuoso)* cordial, warm; PHARM. *(reconfortante)* stimulating, tonic ♦ **saludos cordiales** cordially yours (in a letter) **II.** m. tonic, cordial.

cor·dia·li·dad f. *(afectuosidad)* cordiality, warmth; *(franqueza)* frankness, sincerity.

cor·dial·men·te adv. *(afectuosamente)* cordially, warmly; *(al final de una carta)* sincerely.

cor·di·lle·ra f. chain of mountains, cordillera.

cor·di·lle·ra·no, –na adj. & m.f. Andean.

cór·do·ba m. FIN. cordoba (currency of Nicaragua).

Cór·do·ba f. Córdoba.

cor·do·bán m. cordovan leather.

cor·do·bés –be·sa adj. & m.f. Cordovan.

cor·dón m. *(cuerda)* cord, string; *(cinta)* cordon, braid; cordon, ring <*c. de policía* police cordon>; ANAT. cord <*c. umbilical* umbilical cord>; ELEC. cord, flex; ARCHIT. cordon, stringcourse; MARIT. strand (of rope); ARG. curb; CUBA, PERU liquor ♦ **cordones** MIL. aiguillettes.

cor·don·ci·llo m. *(de tela)* rib, cord (of fabrics); *(de una moneda)* milling (of coins).

cor·do·ne·rí·a f. *(conjunto)* cords, cording; *(oficio)* cordmaking; *(tienda)* cordmaker's shop.

cor·do·ne·ro, –ra m.f. *(cordelero)* rope maker *or* cord maker —m. MARIT. rigging maker.

cor·du·ra f. good sense, prudence, wisdom; *(lucidez)* sanity.

Co·re·a, República de f. Republic of Korea.

Co·re·a, República Popular Democrática de f. Democratic People's Republic of Korea.

co·re·a·no, –na adj. & m.f. Korean —m. *(idioma)* Korean.

co·re·ar tr. MUS. *(componer música)* to compose choral music; *(acompañar)* to accompany (with a chorus); FIG. *(asentir)* to agree to, approve of.

co·re·o·gra·fí·a f. choreography.

co·re·ó·gra·fo m. choreographer.

co·re·zue·lo m. *(cochinillo)* suckling pig; *(pellejo)* skin of roast suckling pig.

co·rin·tio, –tia adj. & m.f. Corinthian.

Co·rin·to m. Corinth.

co·ris·ta m.f. MUS. chorus singer; RELIG. chorister; THEAT. member of the chorus.

co·ri·to, –ta adj. *(desnudo)* naked; FIG. *(pusilánime)* pusillanimous, timid.

cor·lar *or* **cor·le·ar** tr. TECH. to varnish.

cor·ma f. *(cepo)* pillory, stocks; FIG. *(embarazo)* hindrance, obstacle.

cor·na·da f. *(golpe)* butt (with a horn); *(herida)* goring ♦ **dar una c.** to gore.

cor·na·men·ta f. ZOOL. horns; *(de un ciervo)* antlers.

cor·na·mu·sa f. MUS. bagpipe.

cór·ne·a f. ANAT. cornea ♦ **c. opaca** sclera • **c. transparente** cornea.

cor·ne·a·do, –da I. past part. see **cornear II.** adj. gored (by an animal).

cor·ne·ar tr. *(dar un golpe)* to butt; TAUR. to gore.

cor·ne·ta f. MUS. bugle; *(trompa de caza)* hunting horn; *(del porquero)* shepherd's horn; MIL. *(banderita)* cornet, calvary standard *or* pennant ♦ **c. acústica** ear trumpet • **c. de llaves** MUS. cornet • **c. de monte** hunting horn —m. MUS. bugler; MEX. car horn.

cor·ne·tín m. MUS. *(instrumento)* cornet; *(persona)* cornetist; MIL. bugle.

cor·ne·zue·lo m. *(aceituna)* kind of olive; BOT. ergot (of rye).

cor·ni·sa f. ARCHIT. cornice.

cor·ni·sa·men·to m. ARCHIT. entablature.

cor·no m. BOT. dogwood tree ♦ **c. inglés** MUS. English horn.

cor·nu·co·pia f. *(cuerno de la abundancia)* cornucopia, horn of plenty; *(espejo)* mirror with candelabra.

cor·nu·do, –da I. adj. ZOOL. horned; *(de ciervo)* antlered; COLL. *(engañado)* cuckolded, deceived ♦ **tras c.,** apaleado adding insult to injury **II.** m. COLL. cuckold.

co·ro m. MUS. *(grupo)* chorus, choir; *(obra)* chorus, chorale; THEAT. chorus; RELIG. *(de ángeles)* choir; ARCHIT.

choir, chancel ♦ **a c.** in unison • **de c.** by memory *or* rote • **hacer c. a** to back up, support.

co·ro·la f. BOT. corolla.

co·ro·la·rio m. *(consecuencia)* corollary; *(inferencia)* deduction, inference.

co·ro·na f. *(guirnalda)* crown, wreath <*c. de flores* crown of flowers>; *(diadema)* crown, coronet; ANAT. *(coronilla)* crown, top of the head; *(aureola)* halo; RELIG. tonsure; ASTRON., ARCHIT. corona; MECH. *(arandela)* washer; AUTO. *(llanta)* rim (of a wheel); DENT. *(de una muela)* crown; GEOM. annulus; FORT. crownwork; NUMIS. crown; FIG. *(dignidad real)* crown, throne; *(reino)* crown, kingdom; winder (of a watch) ♦ **ceñirse la c.** FIG. to assume the crown *or* throne • **c. de espinas** crown of thorns • **c. del casco** VET. coronet (of a horse's hoof) • **triple c.** RELIG. triple crown, papal tiara.

co·ro·na·ción f. *(ceremonia)* crowning, coronation; FIG. *(remate)* crowning, culmination; ARCHIT. corona.

co·ro·na·men·to *or* **co·ro·na·mien·to** m. *(fin)* crowning, culmination; ARCHIT. capstone; MARIT. taffrail.

co·ro·nar I. tr. *(poner corona)* to crown; *(en las damas)* to crown (in checkers); *(en ajedrez)* to queen, promote (in chess); FIG. *(premiar)* to crown, honor; *(completar)* to crown, finish <*c. una obra de arte* to crown a work of art>; to crown, top <*la nieve coronaba las montañas* snow topped the mountains>; ARG., CARIB., PERU to cuckold —reflex. to crown oneself; *(cubrirse)* to become covered (with flowers) —intr. MED. to appear, crown (the head of a fetus).

co·ro·na·rio, –ria I. adj. ANAT., BOT. coronary **II.** f. TECH. crown wheel (of a watch).

co·ro·nel m. MIL. colonel.

co·ro·ni·lla f. ANAT. crown ♦ **andar** *or* **bailar de c.** FIG. to bend over backwards, make great efforts • **dar de c.** to fall headfirst, bump one's head • **estar hasta la c.** FIG., COLL. to be at wit's end, be fed up.

co·ro·za f. *(castigo)* dunce cap (worn by convicts); *(capa)* straw cape (worn by farmers).

cor·pa·chón *or* **cor·pan·chón** m. COLL. *(cuerpo)* big *or* bulky body; ORNITH. carcass, frame.

cor·pi·ño m. *(cuerpo)* little body; *(jubón)* sleeveless bodice; ARG. bra, brassiere.

cor·po·ra·ción f. *(asociación)* group, association <*una c. literaria* a literary group>; COM. corporation, company.

cor·po·ral I. adj. corporal, bodily **II.** m. RELIG. corporal (cloth).

cor·po·ra·li·dad f. corporality.

cor·po·ra·ti·vo, –va I. adj. corporate, corporative **II.** m.f. corporate part *or* constituent.

cor·po·rei·dad f. corporeity, corporeality.

cor·po·rei·zar §04 tr. to materialize, make material *or* tangible.

cor·pó·re·o, –a adj. *(material)* corporeal, material; *(corporal)* corporal, bodily.

cor·pu·len·cia f. corpulence, obesity.

cor·pús·cu·lo m. BIOL. corpuscle.

co·rral m. *(cercado)* corral, yard; *(redil)* stockyard, pen; *(teatro)* open-air theater; GEOL. perpetually snow-covered cirque; ICHTH. fish weir; CUBA small plantation ♦ **c. de madera** lumberyard, timber yard • **c. de vacas** FIG., COLL. pigsty, dump • **hacer corrales** FIG. to play hooky.

co·rra·li·za f. corral, yard.

co·rra·lón m. *(cercado)* large corral *or* yard; *(de madera)* lumberyard, timber yard; PERU fenced-in yard *or* enclosure ♦ **c. de tránsito** MEX. car pound.

co·rre·a f. *(tira de cuero)* strap, thong; *(cinturón)* belt; *(flexibilidad)* flexibility, stretch <*el caucho tiene c.* rubber has stretch>; TECH. belt <*c. de transmisión* transmission belt>; ARCHIT. purlin ♦ **c. de ventilador** AUTO. fan belt • **tener c.** FIG., COLL. *(resignarse)* to be long-suffering; *(tener resistencia)* to be tough *or* strong.

co·rre·a·je m. straps, belts.

co·rre·a·zo m. blow with a leather strap.

co·rrec·ción f. *(acción)* correction, correcting; *(efecto)* correction, adjustment; *(reprensión)* rebuke, reprimand; *(castigo)* punishment, correction; *(urbanidad)* propriety, correctitude ♦ **c. de pruebas** *or* **de galeradas** PRINT. proofreading.

co·rrec·cio·nal I. adj. correctional, corrective II. m. *(reformatorio)* reformatory, prison.

co·rrec·ta·men·te adv. correctly, properly.

co·rrec·ti·vo, –va adj. & m. corrective.

co·rrec·to, –ta I. past part. see **corregir** II. adj. *(cabal)* correct, proper; *(cortés)* courteous, correct.

co·rrec·tor, –to·ra I. adj. correcting, corrective II. m.f. corrector; PRINT. proofreader.

co·rre·de·ra f. *(carril)* runner, slide, track; *(muela de molino)* upper millstone; *(calle)* street, road; MECH. slide valve; MARIT. log, log line; ENTOM. cockroach; ARG. river rapid; COL. diarrhea, the runs; DOM. REP. stampede (of people).

co·rre·di·zo, –za adj. *(puerta)* sliding (door); *(nudo)* running, slip (knot).

co·rre·dor, –do·ra I. adj. running, racing; ORNITH. ratite II. m.f. SPORT. runner, racer <*c. de fondo* long-distance runner> —m. *(pasillo)* corridor, hallway; *(galería)* gallery, porch; COM. broker, agent; MIL. scout; FORT. covert way —f. ORNITH. ratite ♦ **c. de apuestas** bookmaker • **c. de bolsa** or **de cambios** COM. stockbroker • **c. de lonja** or **de mercaderías** COM. sales agent • **c. de seguros** COM. insurance agent.

co·rre·du·rí·a f. FIN. brokerage.

co·rre·gi·dor, –do·ra I. adj. correcting II. m. SP., HIST. *(magistrado)* corregidor (former magistrate); *(alcalde)* mayor.

co·rre·gi·mien·to m. SP., HIST. *(empleo)* post of corregidor; *(territorio)* district of corregidor; *(oficina)* office of corregidor.

co·rre·gir §57 tr. *(enmendar)* to correct, amend; *(templar)* to temper, mitigate; *(castigar)* to punish, chastise; PRINT. to proofread; CARIB. to evacuate (one's bowels) —reflex. to reform, mend one's ways.

co·rre·la·ción f. correlation.

co·rre·la·cio·nar tr. to correlate, relate.

co·rre·la·ti·va·men·te adj. correlatively.

co·rre·la·ti·vo, –va I. adj. *(relacionado)* correlative, correlate; GRAM. correlative II. m. GRAM. correlative; CHILE laxative.

co·rre·li·gio·na·rio, –ria I. adj. RELIG. of the same religion; *(de la misma opinión)* of the same doctrine or opinion II. m.f. RELIG. coreligionist; FIG. colleague, associate.

co·rren·cia or **co·rren·tí·a** f. COLL. diarrhea, runs.

co·rren·ta·da f. AMER. strong current, roaring rapids (of a river).

co·rren·tí·o adj. *(un líquido)* running, flowing; FIG., COLL. *(suelto)* nimble, agile.

co·rren·tón, –to·na I. adj. *(trotacalles)* roving, gadding; *(bromista)* jesting, playful II. m. COL., P. RICO strong current of water.

co·rren·to·so, –sa adj. AMER. swift, rapid (river).

co·rre·o m. *(correspondencia)* mail; *(mensajero)* courier, messenger; *(cartero)* mailman, letter carrier; *(tren)* mail train; *(buzón)* mailbox; *(oficina)* post office; LAW accomplice ♦ **a vuelta de c.** by return mail • **c. aéreo** air mail • **c. certificado** registered mail • **correos** *(servicio postal)* postal service, mail service; *(oficina)* post office • **echar al c.** to mail • **por c.** by mail.

co·rre·o·so, –sa adj. *(flexible)* flexible; *(elástico)* elastic; FIG. *(que se mastica con dificultad)* tough, rubbery.

co·rrer intr. to run <*echarse a c.* to start running>; *(en una carrera)* to race, run a race; *(fluir)* to flow, run; *(soplar)* to blow <*el viento corre suavemente* the wind is blowing gently>; *(extender)* to run, extend <*el camino corre de este a oeste* the road runs from east to west>; *(pasar)* to pass, elapse <*las horas corren como minutos* the hours pass like minutes>; *(un sueldo)* to be payable; to pass, be valid <*esta moneda no corre* this coin is not valid>; *(circular)* to circulate, go around (rumor, gossip); *(venderse)* to sell <*la carne corre a seis pesos la libra* meat is selling at six pesos a pound> ♦ **a todo c.** at full speed • **c. a** to run to, hurry to <*corrió a ayudar al niño* he hurried to help the child> • **c. con** to be responsible for • **c. la voz** to be said • **c. por cuenta de** or **a cargo de** to be the responsibility of • **que corre** current <*el mes que corre* the current month> —tr. to race, run <*c. un caballo* to race a horse>; *(atravesar)* to travel, cover <*he corrido mucho mundo* I have covered a lot

of miles>; *(perseguir)* to pursue, chase; to slide over, move <*c. la mesa* to move the table>; to tip <*c. la balanza* to tip the scale>; to draw <*corra las cortinas* draw the curtains>; to shoot, slide <*c. el cerrojo* to slide the bolt>; to turn <*c. la llave* to turn the key>; to slip, unfasten <*c. un nudo* to slip a knot>; FIG. to run <*corre el riesgo de fracasar* he runs the risk of failing>; to experience, meet with <*corrió aventuras adondequiera que fue* he met with adventures wherever he went>; COLL. *(avergonzar)* to embarrass; *(confundir)* to disconcert, confuse; *(robar)* to make off with; MIL. to overrun; COM. to auction, sell at auction; AMER. to throw (someone) out ♦ **correrla** COLL. to carouse, live it up • **c. baquetas** to run the gauntlet —reflex. *(deslizarse)* to slide, slip; to slide over <*córrete a la izquierda* slide over to the left>; to run, melt <*la vela corría poco a poco* the wax melted slowly>; COLL. *(avergonzarse)* to be embarrassed; *(confundirse)* to become confused; *(excederse)* to go too far; *(ofrecer demasiado)* to offer too much (money); AMER. to run away, escape.

co·rre·rí·a f. MIL. incursion, foray; *(viaje)* short trip, excursion.

co·rres·pon·den·cia f. *(relación)* correspondence, relationship; *(conformidad)* conformity, agreement; *(comunicación)* communication, contact; *(transporte)* connection; *(cartas)* correspondence, mail; *(sinonimia)* synonymy, synonymity; *(significado)* equivalent ♦ **c. entrante** incoming mail.

co·rres·pon·der intr. *(ser igual a)* to correspond, match <*el resultado no corresponde a mis esperanzas* the result does not match my expectations>; *(tener proporción con)* to fit or go with, match; *(responder)* to respond, reply <*c. dignamente a* to respond appropriately to>; *(recompensar)* to repay, return <*él correspondió un favor con otro* he repaid one favor with another>; *(incumbir)* to be the responsibility or concern of, fall to <*me correspondió decirle la verdad* it fell to me to tell her the truth>; *(tocar)* to be one's turn to, be up to <*te corresponde a ti pagar la cuenta* it's your turn to pay the bill>; *(ser propio de)* to befit, become; to belong <*ese libro no corresponde aquí* that book doesn't belong here>; to be the share of, belong to <*a José le corresponden diez pesos* José's share is ten pesos>; ARCHIT. to connect, communicate <*estas dos habitaciones corresponden* these two rooms connect> —reflex. *(escribir)* to correspond, write; *(amarse)* to love each other; *(hacer juego)* to match, go together; ARCHIT. to connect, communicate.

co·rres·pon·dien·te I. adj. corresponding; GEOM. corresponding II. m.f. correspondent.

co·rres·pon·sal I. adj. correspondent, corresponding II. m.f. JOURN. news correspondent; COM. correspondent, agent.

co·rres·pon·sa·lí·a f. JOURN. correspondent's assignment or post.

co·rre·ta·je m. COM. *(oficio)* brokerage, brokering; *(comisión)* broker's fee or commission; HOND., AGR. sharecropper's consignment or quota.

co·rre·te·ar intr. *(vagar)* to wander or roam the streets; *(retozar)* to run about, frolic —tr. AMER. *(perseguir)* to chase, pursue; C. AMER. *(despedir)* to dismiss, drive away; CHILE to send an urgent dispatch to.

co·rre·te·o m. *(vagabundeo)* wandering or roaming the streets; *(retozo)* frolic, romp.

co·rre·ve·di·le or **co·rre·vei·di·le** m.f. FIG., COLL. *(chismoso)* gossip, gossipmonger; *(alcahuete)* pimp, go-between.

co·rri·da I. f. *(carrera)* race, run; *(canto)* Andalusian song; AMER., MIN. outcrop; CARIB., CHILE celebration, spree; CHILE row, line ♦ **c. de toros** bullfight • **dar una c.** to make a dash • **de c.** quickly • **en una c.** in an instant or a flash II. adj. see **corrido, –da**.

co·rri·do, –da I. past part. see **correr** II. adj. full, good <*un kilo c.* a full kilo>; *(cursiva)* cursive; running, straight <*tres meses corridos* three months running>; FIG. *(avergonzado)* embarrassed; *(experimentado)* experienced, worldly; ARCHIT. continuous, unbroken <*un balcón c.* a continuous balcony>; AMER. whole, completed ♦ **de c.** fluently <*leer de c.* to read fluently>; *(rápido)* quickly III. m. *(cobertizo)* projecting roof, lean-to; *(romance)* ballad; PERU fugitive ♦ **corridos** COM. accrued interest —f. see **corrida.**

co·rrien·te I. adj. running <*agua c.* running water>; current, present <*la situación c.* the current situation>; *(sabido)* well-known; common, usual <*es c. llamar antes de hacer una visita* it is usual to call before visiting>; *(ordinario)* common, ordinary; *(moderno)* current, up-to-date; *(fluido)* smooth, flowing ♦ **al c.** *(sin atraso)* on time, punctually; informed, up-to-date <*el jefe está al c. del progreso del proyecto* the boss is up-to-date on the progress of the project> • **c. y moliente** COLL. ordinary, run-of-the-mill • **poner al c.** to bring up-to-date • **tener al c.** to keep informed **II.** f. current <*la c. de un río* the current of a river>; ELEC. current; FIG. course, trend <*una nueva c.* a new trend> ♦ **c. alterna** ELEC. alternating current • **c. continua** *or* **directa** ELEC. direct current • **c. de aire** air current, draft • **C. del Golfo** GEOG. Gulf Stream • **dejarse llevar por la c.** *or* **ir con la c.** FIG. to go along with the crowd • **ir** *or* **navegar contra la c.** FIG. to go against the current • **llevarle** *or* **seguirle la c. (a alguien)** to humor (someone).

co·rrien·te·men·te adv. *(fácilmente)* fluently <*conversan c. en alemán* they converse fluently in German>; *(actualmente)* currently; *(comúnmente)* commonly, usually.

co·rri·ja, corrijo see **corregir.**

co·rri·llo m. small circle *or* group, clique.

co·rri·mien·to m. *(acción)* running; *(deslizamiento)* landslide; *(fluxión)* discharge, secretion; FIG. *(vergüenza)* embarrassment; *(empacho)* shyness; AMER. rheumatism.

co·rro m. *(cerco de personas)* group *or* circle of talkers; *(espacio redondo)* circle, ring ♦ **hacer c. aparte** FIG., COLL. *(seguir otro partido)* to follow another party; *(formar otro partido)* to create another party.

co·rro·bo·ra·ción f. *(confirmación)* corroboration, confirmation; *(fortificación)* strengthening, fortifying.

co·rro·bo·rar tr. *(confirmar)* to corroborate, confirm; *(fortificar)* to strengthen, fortify.

co·rro·bo·ra·ti·vo, –va adj. corroborative, confirmatory.

co·rro·er §61 tr. *(carcomer)* to corrode, eat *or* wear away; GEOL. *(desgastar)* to erode; FIG. *(consumir)* to eat away at, consume <*le corroe la envidia* envy is eating away at him>.

co·rrom·per tr. *(pervertir)* to corrupt, pervert; *(seducir)* to seduce; *(sobornar)* to bribe; *(pudrir)* to rot, decay; FIG. *(viciar)* to corrupt, taint <*c. el habla* to corrupt the language>; COLL. *(fastidiar)* to bother, annoy —intr. to smell, stink —reflex. *(pervertirse)* to become corrupt; *(degenerar)* to degenerate, deteriorate; *(pudrirse)* to rot, go bad.

co·rro·sión f. corrosion.

co·rro·si·vo, –va adj. corrosive.

co·rro·ya see **corroer.**

co·rro·ye·ra, corroyó see **corroer.**

co·rru·ga·ción f. corrugation.

co·rrup·ción f. *(perversión)* perversion, depravity; *(seducción)* seduction; *(soborno)* bribery, bribing; *(putrefacción)* decay, putrefaction; FIG. *(vicio)* corruption, vitiation; *(mal olor)* stink, stench.

co·rrup·ti·bi·li·dad f. corruptibility.

co·rrup·ti·ble adj. *(de personas)* corruptible, pervertible; *(de productos)* perishable.

co·rrup·ti·vo, –va adj. *(de personas)* corruptive, corrupting; *(de productos)* putrefactive, causing to rot.

co·rrup·to, –ta I. past part. see **corromper II.** adj. corrupt, corrupted.

co·rrup·tor, –to·ra I. adj. corruptive, corrupting **II.** m.f. corrupter.

cor·sa·rio, –ria I. adj. privateer **II.** m.f. corsair, privateer •

cor·sé m. corset, corselet.

cor·so, –sa adj. & m.f. Corsican —m. MARIT. privateering.

cor·ta·ca·llos m. [pl. **–llos**] MED. corn cutter *or* parer.

cor·ta·cés·ped m. lawnmower.

cor·ta·ci·ga·rros m. [pl. **–rros**] cigar cutter.

cor·ta·cir·cui·tos m. [pl. **–tos**] ELEC. circuit breaker.

cor·ta·co·rrien·te m. ELEC. current breaker, switch.

cor·ta·da I. f. AMER. cut, gash **II.** adj. see **cortado, –da.**

cor·ta·de·ro, –ra I. adj. easily cut **II.** f. *(cincel de acero)*

blacksmith's chisel; *(cuchilla de colmenero)* beekeeper's knife; AMER. bulrush with sharp leaves.

cor·ta·do, –da I. past part. see **cortar II.** adj. *(ajustado)* proportioned, fit; choppy, disjointed <*escribe en un estilo c.* he writes in a disjointed style>; ARG., CHILE, URUG., COLL. broke, penniless **III.** m. *(café)* coffee with milk; *(cabriola)* capriole, leap —f. see **cortada.**

cor·ta·dor, –do·ra I. adj. cutting **II.** m. *(el que corta)* cutter; *(carnicero)* butcher; DENT. *(diente)* cutter, incisor —f. *(máquina)* cutter, cutting machine.

cor·ta·du·ra f. *(acción)* cutting; *(incisión)* cut, gash; *(recortado)* cutting, clipping; GEOG. mountain pass, defile; FORT. parapet ♦ **cortaduras** cuttings, scraps.

cor·ta·lá·pi·ces m. [pl. **–ces**] pencil sharpener.

cor·tan·te I. adj. cutting, sharp **II.** m. *(carnicero)* butcher; *(cuchilla)* butcher's knife *or* cleaver.

cor·ta·pa·pel *or* **cor·ta·pa·pe·les** m. paperknife, letter opener.

cor·ta·pi·sa f. SEW. *(guarnición)* trimming (on a skirt); FIG. *(gracia)* elegance, grace; *(limitación)* restriction, condition.

cor·ta·plu·mas m. [pl. **–mas**] penknife, pocketknife.

cor·tar tr. to cut <*cortó el papel con las tijeras* he cut the paper with scissors>; *(recortar)* to clip, trim; to cut, carve <*c. la carne* to carve the meat>; to cut up <*cortaron el pastel y lo repartieron* they cut up the cake and distributed it>; *(separar)* to cut off, sever; *(un árbol)* to cut down, fell; SEW. to cut out (an article of clothing); *(naipes)* to cut (the deck); to cut through <*el buque cortaba las tranquilas aguas* the ship cut through the calm waters>; *(dividir)* to cut <*la cordillera corta la provincia en dos* the mountain range cuts the province in two>; MIL. to cut off; *(diluir)* to cut, dilute <*c. el aguardiente* to dilute liquor>; *(omitir)* to cut out, leave out <*cortó unas frases del ultimo párrafo* he cut out a few sentences from the last paragraph>; *(suspender)* to cut off, discontinue <*c. la conversación* to discontinue the conversation>; *(interrumpir)* to cut off, interrupt <*c. la electricidad* to cut off the electricity>; *(acortar)* to cut short, curtail <*la enfermedad de mi padre cortó mis vacaciones* my father's illness cut short my vacation>; COLL. *(criticar)* to cut up, criticize; ARG., P. RICO, URUG. to cut (through *or* across) <*c. por el campo* to cut through the field> ♦ **c. por la mitad** to cut in half —intr. to cut <*este cuchillo no corta bien* this knife does not cut well>; to be cutting <*hace un frío que corta* the cold is cutting> ♦ **c. por lo sano** to take drastic measures —reflex. *(turbarse)* to become flustered; to chap, crack <*la piel se le corta fácilmente* his skin chaps easily>; *(cuajar)* to curdle (milk); to split, fray (cloth); ARG. to be left out, be left behind; URUG. to die; MEX., PERU. P. RICO, VET. to catch a chill (said of horses).

cor·ta·ú·ñas m. [pl. **–ñas**] nail clipper, nail scissors.

cor·te[1] m. *(filo)* (cutting) edge <*el c. de un puñal* the cutting edge of a dagger>; *(acción de cortar)* cutting; *(cortadura)* cut <*c. de pelo* haircut>; *(corta)* felling (of trees); SEW. cutting (out) <*este sastre es un maestro del c.* this tailor is a master at cutting>; piece, length <*c. de tela* length of cloth>; cut, style <*no me gusta el c. de este vestido* I don't like the cut of this dress>; BKB. edge <*el libro tiene cortes dorados* the book has gilt edges>; TECH. section <*c. transversal* cross section> ♦ **c. y confección** dressmaking • **darse c.** FIG., COLL. to put on airs.

cor·te[2] f. *(residencia)* (royal) court; *(comitiva)* entourage, retinue; *(corral)* courtyard, yard; AMER. court of law ♦ **c. celestial** heaven • **C. Suprema** Supreme Court • **Cortes** SP. Cortes (legislative body) • **hacer la c. a** to court, woo.

cor·te·dad f. *(pequeñez)* shortness; *(brevedad)* briefness, brevity; FIG. *(timidez)* timidity, shyness; *(falta)* lack, dearth.

cor·te·ja·dor, –do·ra I. adj. wooing, courting **II.** m.f. wooer, courter.

cor·te·jar tr. *(galantear)* to woo, court; *(asistir)* to attend, wait upon *or* on; *(halagar)* to court, curry favor with.

cor·te·jo m. *(galanteo)* courting, courtship; *(agasajo)* gift, present; *(séquito)* entourage, cortege <*c. fúnebre* funeral cortege>; COLL. *(amante)* lover, beau.

cor·tés adj. *(atento)* courteous, polite; *(galante)* gallant, gracious.

cor·te·sa·ní·a f. *(cortesía)* courtesy; *(atención)* attentiveness; *(gallardía)* gallantry.

cor·te·sa·no, –na I. adj. *(de la corte)* of the court, courtly; *(urbano)* courteous, polite II. m. *(palaciego)* courtier —f. *(prostituta)* courtesan.

cor·te·sí·a f. *(atención)* courtesy, courteousness, politeness; *(regalo)* gift, present; *(galantería)* gallantry, charm; *(gracia)* grace, mercy; *(reverencia)* bow (of men), curtsy (of women); *(tratamiento)* title; COM. days of grace, grace period; *(en una carta)* formal close or ending (of a letter); PRINT. *(hoja en blanco)* blank page or space.

cor·tés·men·te adv. courteously, politely.

cor·te·za f. BOT. *(de un arbol)* bark; *(de una fruta)* peel, rind; ANAT., BOT. cortex; CUL. *(del pan)* crust; *(de queso, tocino)* rind; FIG. *(exterior)* outward appearance, surface; COLL. *(rusticidad)* crudeness, roughness; ORNITH. sand grouse.

cor·ti·jo m. farm, grange.

cor·ti·na f. *(paño)* curtain; *(muro de sostenimiento)* retaining wall (of a dike); FIG. screen, cover <*c. de humo* smoke screen>; FORT. curtain ♦ **c. de fuego** MIL. barrage of fire • **c. de hierro** POL. Iron Curtain • **correr la c.** to unveil, uncover.

cor·ti·na·je m. curtains, draperies.

cor·ti·so·na f. MED., PHARM. cortisone.

cor·to, –ta adj. short <*ella tiene el pelo c.* she has short hair>; *(breve)* brief, short <*escribió un ensayo c.* he wrote a short essay>; *(un tiro)* short (of the mark); *(escaso)* short <*estamos cortos de dinero* we are short of money>; FIG. *(tímido)* timid, shy ♦ **a la corta o a la larga** sooner or later • **c. circuito** ELEC. short circuit • **c. de alcances** FIG. dull, stupid • **c. de oído** hard of hearing • **c. de vista** shortsighted • **de cortas luces** FIG. not very bright • **ni c. ni perezoso** without thinking twice • **quedarse c.** to fall short.

cor·to·cir·cui·to m. ELEC. short circuit.

co·rus·car §70 intr. POET. to gleam, shine.

cor·va·du·ra f. *(curvatura)* curvature, bend; ARCHIT. curve, arch (of a vault).

cor·var tr. to curve, bend.

cor·va·to m. young crow or rook.

cor·ve·jón m. *(cuervo marino)* cormorant; ZOOL. back joint of a quadruped; *(espolón)* spur.

cor·ve·te·ar intr. EQUIT. to curvet.

cor·vi·no, –na I. adj. corvine, crowlike II. f. ICHTH. corvina, corbina.

cor·vo, –va I. adj. curved, bent II. m. *(gancho)* hook, drag; ICHTH. corvina, corbina; CHILE double-bladed knife.

cor·zue·lo m. unhusked wheat left over after threshing.

co·sa f. thing <*comprar unas cosas en el mercado* to buy some things at the market>; *(algo)* something <*¿quiere usted otra c.?* do you want something else?>; [in negative sentences] anything, nothing <*no vale c.* it is not worth anything>; FIG. affair, business <*eso es c. suya* that is his business> ♦ **a cosa hecha** *(con éxito)* successfully; *(con intención)* purposely, intentionally • **como c. tuya** as if it came from you • **como quien no quiere la c.** COLL. diffidently • **como si tal c.** COLL. as if such a thing had never happened • **c. de** COLL. about, approximately <*es c. de tres semanas* it takes about three weeks> • **c. del otro jueves** or **del otro mundo** FIG., COLL. extraordinary thing, marvel • **c. de oír** something worth hearing • **c. de ver** something worth seeing • **c. hecha** fait accompli • **c. nunca vista** FIG., COLL. something unheard of • **c. para reír** or **de risa** laughing matter • **c. perdida** FIG., COLL. lost cause, hopeless case • **c. que** AMER. so that, in order that • **c. rara** strange thing • **cosas** COLL. wild ideas or notions • **cosas de la vida** FIG. ups and downs • **c. seria** serious matter • **ni c. parecida** or **ni c. que lo parezca** nor anything of the kind • **no es gran c.** it's nothing great • **no hay tal c.** there's no such thing • **no sea c. que** lest, in case • **poquita c.** COLL. pip-squeak, squirt • **no ser c. del otro jueves** or **del otro mundo** FIG., COLL. to be nothing special • **¿qué c.?** what did you say?

co·sa·co, –ca I. adj. Cossack II. m.f. Cossack —m. FIG. *(feroz)* warrior, soldier ♦ **beber como un c.** FIG., COLL. to drink like a fish.

co·sa·rio I. adj. *(relativo al trajinero)* pertaining to carriers; *(frecuentado)* frequented; COL. tame (horse) II. m. *(ordinario)* carrier, expressman; *(cazador)* huntsman.

cos·car·se §70 reflex. to shrug (one's shoulders).

cos·cón, –co·na COLL. I. adj. cunning, crafty II. m.f. smart aleck.

cos·co·rrón m. bump or knock on the head.

co·se·can·te f. MATH. cosecant.

co·se·cha f. AGR. *(recolección)* harvest, harvesting, reaping; *(temporada)* harvest, harvest time; *(producción)* crop, harvest; FIG. *(acopio)* crop, bunch <*una c. de ideas nuevas* a crop of new ideas> ♦ **c. de vino** vintage • **de su propia c.** FIG. of one's own invention or creation • **hacer la c.** AGR. to harvest, reap.

co·se·cha·do·ra f. AGR., MECH. reaping machine, combine.

co·se·char tr. *(cultivos)* to harvest, reap; *(frutas, flores)* to pick ♦ **c. laureles** to reap the laurels —intr. to harvest, reap.

co·se·che·ro, –ra m.f. reaper, harvester.

co·se·le·te m. *(coraza ligera)* corslet, corselet; *(soldado)* pikeman; ENTOM. thorax (of insects).

co·se·no m. MATH. cosine.

co·ser tr. SEW. to sew, stitch; FIG. *(unir)* to join, unite ♦ **c. a balazos** FIG. to riddle with bullets • **c. a puñaladas** FIG. to stab full of holes, stab repeatedly • **c. y cantar** FIG., COLL. child's play, easy as pie, a snap —intr. to sew —reflex. ♦ **coserse con** to stick close to.

co·si·do I. past part. of **coser** II. m. sewing, needlework.

cos·mé·ti·co, –ca I. adj. cosmetic II. m. *(substancia)* cosmetic —f. *(arte)* cosmetology.

cós·mi·co, –ca adj. cosmic.

cos·mo·gó·ni·co, –ca adj. ASTRON., PHYS. cosmogonic.

cos·mo·gra·fí·a f. cosmography.

cos·mo·ló·gi·a f. cosmology.

cos·mo·ló·gi·co, –ca adj. cosmological.

cos·mó·lo·go m. cosmologist.

cos·mo·nau·ta m.f. ASTRONAUT. cosmonaut, astronaut.

cos·mo·po·li·ta I. adj. cosmopolitan II. m.f. cosmopolitan, cosmopolite.

cos·mo·po·li·tis·mo m. cosmopolitism, cosmopolitanism.

cos·mos m. [pl. –mos] cosmos, universe.

co·so m. *(plaza de toros)* arena (for bullfighting); *(calle principal)* main street.

cos·pe m. CARP. groove.

cos·qué, cosque see **coscarse.**

cos·qui·llas f.pl. tickling, ticklishness ♦ **buscarle a uno las c.** FIG., COLL. to annoy or tease someone • **hacer c.** *(físicamente)* to tickle; FIG. *(excitar)* to tickle one's fancy, titillate • **tener c.** to be ticklish • **tener malas c.** to be touchy or on edge.

cos·qui·lle·ar tr. to tickle.

cos·ta f. *(precio)* cost, price; *(orilla)* coast, shore; *(alisador)* cobbler's polishing tool; *(de un trabajador)* labor cost ♦ **a c.** COM. at cost • **a c. ajena** at someone else's expense • **a c. de** at the expense of; *(a fuerza de)* by dint, by means of • **a toda c.** at all costs • **barajar la c.** MARIT. to sail close to the shore • **condenar a uno en costas** LAW to order someone to pay costs • **costas** LAW fees, costs.

▲ *costa* generally refers to what is paid in time and effort, not in money <*pagó la costa de su negligencia en disgustos* he paid the price of his negligence in problems>; *coste* is used to refer to the monetary cost <*el coste de un automóvil* the price of a car>; *costo* refers to the cost of large-scale projects <*el costo de un puente* the cost of a bridge>.

Costa de Marfil f. Ivory Coast.

cos·ta·do m. ANAT., MARIT. side; MIL. flank; MEX., RAIL. platform ♦ **costados** lineage, lines (of parentage) • **dar el c.** MARIT. to turn broadside on • **de c.** sideways • **por los cuatro costados** through and through • **tenderse de c.** to lie on one's side.

cos·tal I. adj. ANAT. costal, of the ribs II. m. *(saco)* sack, bag; *(listón)* brace; *(pisón)* tamper, mallet ♦ **c. de huesos** COLL. bag of bones • **c. de los pecados** FIG. the human body • **no parecer c. de paja** COLL. to look attractive • **vaciar el c.** COLL. to tell everything, unburden oneself.

cos·ta·le·ro m. *(mozo de cuerda)* porter; RELIG. bearer (in Holy Week processions).

cos·ta·ne·ro, –ra I. adj. GEOG. coastal <*navegación c.* coastal navigation>; *(inclinado)* steep, sloping <*calle c.*

steep street> **II.** f. *(cuesta)* slope ♦ **costaneras** ARCHIT., CARP. rafters.
cos·tar §19 intr. *(valer)* to cost *<¿cuánto cuesta la lámpara?* how much does the lamp cost?>; FIG. to cost *<ese proyecto me costó muchos esfuerzos* that project cost me a great deal of effort>; to be difficult to, find it difficult to *<me cuesta mucho creer eso* I find that difficult to believe>; to take *<el trabajo me costó tres horas* the job took me three hours> ♦ **c. barato** to be cheap *or* inexpensive • **c. caro** to be expensive • **costar trabajo** to take a lot to, be difficult to • **c. un ojo de la cara** COLL. to cost a fortune • **cueste lo que cueste** at all costs, at any cost.
Costa Rica f. Costa Rica.
cos·ta·rri·cen·se adj. & m.f. Costa Rican.
cos·te m. cost *<el c. de un mueble* the cost of a piece of furniture> —see **costa.**
cos·te·ar tr. *(pagar)* to pay for, finance; MARIT. to coast, sail close to (the shore); ARG. to graze, pasture —reflex. *(mantenerse)* to pay for itself; *(pagar lo suyo)* to pay one's own way; PERU to make fun of, tease; ARG., CHILE to arrive with difficulty.
cos·te·ño, –ña I. adj. pertaining to the coast, coastal **II.** m.f. inhabitant of the coast, coastal resident.
cos·te·ro, –ra I. adj. coastal **II.** m.f. *(habitante)* coastal inhabitant *or* dweller —m. CARP. first plank of timber, wood nearest to the bark; TECH. side wall of a high furnace; MIN. side wall of an excavation —f. *(cuesta)* slope, incline; *(costa)* coast, shore; MARIT. fishing season; *(paquete)* side of a package *or* bale.
cos·ti·lla f. ANAT. rib; *(chuleta)* cutlet, chop; *(de una silla)* rung; *(de una rueda)* spoke; *(de un barril)* stave; FIG., COLL. *(esposa)* wife ♦ **a las costillas de** at the expense of • **c. falsa** ANAT. false rib • **c. flotante** ANAT. false *or* floating rib • **c. verdadera** ANAT. true rib • **costillas** COLL. back • **medirle a uno las costillas** FIG. to give someone a beating • **pasearle a uno las costillas** FIG. to trample someone.
cos·ti·llar m. ribs.
cos·ti·llu·do, –da adj. COLL. well-built, broad-shouldered.
cos·to m. cost *<el c. de la fabricación* the cost of manufacturing>; ARG., P. RICO effort ♦ **al c.** at cost • **c. de la vida** cost of living • **c. efectivo** actual cost • **c. hortense** BOT. costmary • **c., seguro y flete** cost, insurance and freight. —see **costa.**
cos·to·so, –sa adj. *(caro)* expensive, costly; FIG. *(grave)* costly, grievous.
cos·tra f. *(corteza)* crust; MED. scab, scale; *(bizcocho)* biscuit given to galley slaves ♦ **c. láctea** MED. infantile eczema.
cos·tro·so, –sa adj. crusty, having crusts; MED. scabby, scaly.
cos·tum·bre f. *(hábito)* custom, habit; *(práctica)* practice ♦ **costumbres** mores, customs • **de c.** *(usual)* usual, customary; *(usualmente)* usually, customarily • **novela de costumbres** novel of manners • **por c.** through force of habit, out of habit • **tener por c.** to be in the habit of.
cos·tum·bris·mo m. literary style that deals with typical regional *or* national customs.
cos·tum·bris·ta I. adj. folkloric **II.** m.f. folklorist.
cos·tu·ra f. SEW. *(acción y labor)* sewing, needlework; *(unión)* seam *<sentar las costuras* to iron the seams>; MARIT. seam, splice; MED. *(cicatriz)* scar ♦ **alta c.** haute couture, high fashion • **c. de soldadura** welded seam • **meter a uno en c.** COLL. to calm down *or* restrain someone • **saber de toda c.** COLL. to be worldly-wise *or* cosmopolitan • **sentar a uno las costuras** COLL. to take to task, punish • **sin c.** seamless.
cos·tu·re·ra f. SEW. seamstress, dressmaker.
cos·tu·re·ro m. SEW. *(estuche)* sewing case *or* basket; *(cuarto)* sewing room.
co·ta¹ f. HER. *(jubón)* doublet; *(armadura)* tabard, coat of arms ♦ **c. de malla** coat of mail.
co·ta² f. TOP. contour elevation reading, elevation; FIG. *(nivel)* level.
co·ta·na f. mortise hole.
co·tan·gen·te f. MATH. cotangent.
co·ta·rro m. *(recinto)* shelter (for vagrants); *(barranco)*

bank (of a ravine) ♦ **alborotar el c.** FIG., COLL. to stir up trouble, cause a disturbance.
co·te·ja·ble adj. comparable.
co·te·jar tr. to compare, collate.
co·te·jo m. *(comparación)* comparison, collation; VEN., ZOOL. type of small lizard.
co·te·rrá·ne·o, –a adj. of the same country *or* region.
co·ti·cé, cotice see **cotizar.**
co·ti·dia·na·men·te adv. daily, everyday.
co·ti·dia·no, –na adj. daily, everyday.
co·ti·le·dón m. BOT. cotyledon, seed leaf.
co·ti·lla f. *(apretador)* corset —m.f. COLL. *(chismoso)* gossip.
co·ti·lle·ar intr. COLL. to gossip.
co·ti·lle·o m. COLL. gossip, gossiping.
co·ti·lle·ro, –ra m.f. gossip.
co·ti·llo m. head (of a hammer).
co·ti·llón m. cotillion (dance).
co·ti·za f. VEN. Indian's sandal ♦ **ponerse uno las cotizas** to hide oneself, take shelter.
co·ti·za·ble adj. quotable, priceable.
co·ti·za·ción f. COM. *(acción)* quotation, quoting; *(precio)* quotation, current price; *(cuota)* share, fee.
co·ti·zar §04 tr. COM. *(anunciar)* to quote (prices); *(valorar)* to price, value; *(fijar)* to fix (fees *or* shares); PERU, P. RICO to sell —intr. *(pagar)* to pay a fee *or* dues; *(recaudar)* to collect a fee *or* dues.
co·to m. *(terreno acotado)* preserve, reserved area; *(mojón)* landmark, boundary marker; *(límite)* end, limit, boundary; *(población)* small village *or* hamlet in an estate; *(medida)* linear measurement equal to length of fist and thumb; COM. price-fixing agreement; ZOOL. howling monkey; ICHTH. miller's thumb; HUNT. *(campo de caza)* shooting *or* game preserve; AMER., MED. goiter ♦ **c. de caza** game preserve • **poner c. a** to put a stop to.
co·tón m. TEX. cotton fabric; AMER. work shirt.
co·to·na f. MEX. chamois jacket; AMER. coarse cotton undershirt.
co·to·rra f. ORNITH. *(loro)* parakeet, small parrot; *(urraca)* magpie; FIG., COLL. *(charlatán)* chatterbox, magpie.
co·to·rre·ar intr. FIG., COLL. to chatter, babble.
co·to·rre·o m. FIG., COLL. chatter, babbling.
co·to·rrón, –rro·na m.f. old person affecting youthfulness.
co·to·so, –sa *or* **co·tu·do, –da** adj. AMER. goitrous.
co·tu·fa f. BOT. Jerusalem artichoke; *(golosina)* delicacy, tidbit; *(dulce)* sweet; *(chufa)* chufa ♦ **pedir cotufas en el golfo** COLL. to ask for the moon, expect the impossible.
co·tur·no m. cothurnus, buskin ♦ **calzar el c.** to put on the buskin, use high-flown language.
co·tu·tor m. co-guardian, joint guardian.
co·va·cha f. *(cueva)* small cave, grotto; CARIB., GUAT. hut, shack; ECUAD. produce *or* greengrocer's shop; BOL. adobe bench; ARG., PERU cubbyhole *or* storage area beneath a flight of stairs; P. RICO kennel.
co·xis m. [pl. **–xis**] ANAT. coccyx.
co·ya f. HIST. *(esposa del Inca)* wife of the Inca; *(princesa)* princess.
co·yo·ta·je m. MEX. *(acción)* act of operating as a stockbroker; *(remuneración)* remuneration of the stockbroker.
co·yo·te m. ZOOL. coyote, prairie wolf; MEX., COM. *(de la bolsa)* stockbroker; *(agente)* agent, broker.
co·yo·te·ar intr. MEX. to operate as a stockbroker.
co·yo·te·o m. MEX. act of operating as a stockbroker.
co·yo·te·ro, –ra I. adj. AMER. coyote-hunting (dog) **II.** f. *(manada)* pack of coyotes; *(trampa)* coyote trap.
co·yun·da f. *(soga)* strap for yoking oxen; *(cordón)* lace (for sandals); FIG. *(unión conyugal)* marriage tie; *(dominio)* dominion, yoke; C. AMER. whip.
co·yun·tu·ra f. ANAT. joint, articulation; FIG. *(oportunidad)* opportunity, chance; *(ocasión)* occasion, juncture; *(circunstancias)* circumstance, situation.
coz f. [pl. **co·ces**] *(patada)* backward kick; COLL. *(insulto)* insult; ARM. *(retroceso)* kick, recoil; *(culata)* butt; MARIT. base of a topmast ♦ **dar** *or* **pegar** *or* **tirar coces** to kick • **dar** *or* **tirar coces contra el aguijón** FIG. to resist authority • **mandar uno a coces** COLL. to order someone about roughly • **tratar a la gente a coces** FIG., COLL. to kick people around.

crac m. FIN. *(quiebra)* crash, bankruptcy, failure; *(onomatopeya)* crack.

Cra·co·via Cracow.

cra·ne·al *or* **cra·ne·a·no, -na** adj. ANAT. cranial.

crá·ne·o m. ANAT. cranium, skull ◆ **secársele a uno el c.** COLL. to go mad.

crá·pu·la I. f. *(embriaguez)* drunkenness; *(crapuloso)* drunkard, drunk; FIG. *(disipación)* degeneracy, dissipation II. adj. *(borracho)* drunken; FIG. *(libertino)* debauched, degenerate.

cra·pu·lo·so, -sa I. adj. *(libertino)* debauched, degenerate; *(borracho)* drunken, besotted II. m.f. *(libertino)* debauched person, degenerate; *(borracho)* drunkard, drunk.

cra·sa·men·te adv. FIG. crassly, grossly.

cra·sien·to, -ta adj. greasy.

cra·so, -sa I. adj. *(grasiento)* greasy, fatty; *(grueso)* thick, fat; FIG. *(grave)* crass, gross <*un error c.* a gross error>; ARG., ECUAD. crass, coarse II. m. fat, fatness.

crá·ter m. GEOL. crater.

cre·a·ción f. *(acto de crear)* creation; *(universo)* universe, world, creation ◆ **la C.** BIBL. the Creation.

cre·a·cio·nis·mo m. POET. doctrine that proclaims the complete autonomy of the poem.

cre·a·dor, -do·ra I. adj. creative II. m.f. creator ◆ **el C.** BIBL. the Creator.

cre·ar tr. *(producir)* to create, make; *(fundar)* to found <*c. una escuela* to found a school>; *(establecer)* to establish, institute; *(nombrar)* to appoint, name; FIG. *(inventar)* to invent <*c. una nueva palabra* to invent a new word>.

cre·ce·de·ro, -ra adj. *(que puede crecer)* growing; *(rel. a la ropa de niños)* with room to grow (said of children's clothing).

cre·cer §17 intr. to grow <*los niños crecen rápidamente* children grow rapidly>; *(aumentar)* to increase, augment; *(los días)* to get longer (the days); *(la luna)* to wax (the moon); *(un río)* to rise, swell (a river); FIN. to increase in value (currency) ◆ **c. como la cizaña** FIG. to grow like weeds • **dejarse c. la barba** to grow a beard —reflex. *(tomar mayor importancia)* to become important; *(engreírse)* to become conceited *or* vain; *(alentarse)* to be encouraged.

cre·ces f.pl. increase, growth ◆ **con c.** *(ampliamente)* amply; COM. *(con interés)* with interest.

cre·ci·do, -da I. past part. see **crecer** II. adj. *(grande)* large; *(adulto)* full-grown, grown; *(engreído)* conceited, vain ◆ **crecidos** SEW. added stitches • **estar c.** *(un río)* to be in flood *or* in spate (a river) III. f. spate, freshet.

cre·cien·te I. adj. *(que crece)* growing; *(que aumenta)* increasing; *(de la luna)* crescent, waxing (moon) II. m. HER. crescent —f. *(luna)* crescent *or* waxing moon; *(marea)* rising *or* flood tide.

cre·ci·mien·to m. *(acción de crecer)* growth, growing; *(aumento)* increase; *(de la luna)* waxing (of the moon); *(de un río)* rising, swelling (of a river); FIN. increase in value (of currency).

cre·den·cial I. adj. accrediting II. f. *(documento)* credential; AMER. pass, authorization ◆ **credenciales** credentials.

cre·di·bi·li·dad f. credibility.

cré·di·to m. *(reputación)* name, reputation; *(autoridad)* authority, standing; *(asenso)* credence <*no daban c. a los rumores* they did not give credence to the rumors>; COM. credit <*c. rotativo* revolving credit>; *(carta)* letter of credit ◆ **abrir** *or* **dar c. a** COM. to give *or* extend credit to • **a c.** COM. on credit • **c. abierto** COM. open credit • **créditos activos** COM. assets • **créditos pasivos** COM. liabilities.

cre·do m. RELIG. creed, articles of faith; *(doctrina)* creed, credo, beliefs ◆ **en un c.** COLL. in a jiffy *or* flash.

cre·du·li·dad f. credulity.

cré·du·lo, -la adj. credulous, gullible.

cre·e·de·ras f.pl. COLL. gullibility.

cre·e·dor, -do·ra adj. credulous.

cre·en·cia f. *(convicción)* belief, conviction; *(fe)* belief, faith.

cre·er §43 tr. to believe <*no creo lo que dicen* I do not believe what they say>; *(imaginar)* think, imagine <*creemos que vendrán a las seis* we think that they will come at

six o'clock>; *(estimar)* to consider, regard <*lo creo capaz* I consider him competent> ◆ **c. a ciencia cierta** to be convinced of • **c. a pie juntillas** to believe blindly • **c. que no** to think not • **c. que sí** to think so • **según creo** to the best of my knowledge • **¡ya lo creo!** COLL. of course, naturally, I should say so —intr. to believe <*creo en la astrología* I believe in astrology> ◆ **ver es c.** seeing is believing —reflex. *(pensar)* to believe, think; *(estimarse)* to consider *or* regard oneself <*me creo poeta* I consider myself a poet> ◆ **creérselas** to be self-satisfied • **¿qué se cree?** who does he think he is?

cre·í·ble adj. credible, believable.

cre·í·do, -da I. past part. see **creer** II. adj. *(confiado)* trusting, credulous; *(vanidoso)* conceited, vain.

cre·ma[1] f. *(nata)* cream; *(natillas)* custard; *(cosmética)* cold cream; *(betún)* shoe polish; FIG. *(lo mejor)* cream of the crop, elite ◆ **c. batida** whipped cream • **c. de afeitar** shaving cream • **c. dental** toothpaste • **c. hidrante** moisturizer.

cre·ma[2] f. GRAM. diaresis.

cre·ma·ción f. cremation.

cre·ma·lle·ra f. MECH. rack, toothed bar, ratch; *(cierre)* zipper; RAIL. cogway, rack railway.

cre·ma·tís·ti·ca f. political economy.

cre·ma·to·rio, -ria I. adj. crematory II. m. crematory, crematorium.

cre·mo·so, -sa adj. creamy.

cren·cha f. *(raya)* parting (of hair); *(parte)* each side of parted hair.

cre·o·so·ta f. CHEM. creosote.

cre·pé m. TEX. *(tela fina)* crepe, crêpe; *(caucho)* crepe rubber.

cre·pi·ta·ción f. *(ruido)* crackling, crepitation; MED. crepitation.

cre·pi·tan·te adj. crepitating, cracking.

cre·pi·tar intr. to crackle, crepitate.

cre·pus·cu·lar *or* **cre·pus·cu·li·no, -na** adj. twilight, crepuscular.

cre·pús·cu·lo m. *(al atardecer)* twilight, dusk; *(aurora)* twilight, dawn; FIG. *(decadencia)* twilight, decline <*en el c. de su vida* in the twilight of his life>.

cre·sa f. *(larva)* larva, maggot; *(semilla)* egg of the queen bee.

cre·so m. FIG. wealthy person.

cres·po, -pa I. adj. *(ensortijado)* curly, kinky; BOT. *(hoja)* crinkled, curly; FIG. *(obscuro)* obscure, complicated <*un estilo c.* a complicated style>; *(irritado)* huffy, testy, wound-up II. f. curl, ringlet.

cres·pón m. TEX. crepe, crepon.

cres·ta f. ORNITH. *(carnosidad)* crest, comb; *(copete)* tuft, crown (of feathers); *(cima)* summit, peak; MARIT. crest (of a wave) ◆ **c. de gallo** BOT. cockscomb • **alzar** *or* **levantar la c.** COLL. to stick one's nose in the air, show arrogance • **dar en la c. a uno** COLL. to cut someone down to size, bring someone down a peg.

cres·tón m. *(cresta grande)* large crest; *(cresta de morrión)* crest (of a helmet); MIN. outcrop; COL., COLL. very infatuated young man.

cre·ta f. MIN. chalk.

Cre·ta f. Crete.

cre·tá·ceo, -cea I. adj. cretaceous II. m. GEOL. the Cretaceous period.

cre·ti·nis·mo m. MED. cretinism, myxedema; FIG., COLL. *(necedad)* stupidity, idiocy.

cre·ti·no, -na I. adj. MED. cretinous; FIG. *(necio)* idiotic, stupid II. m.f. MED. cretin; FIG. *(necio)* cretin, imbecile.

cre·to·na f. TEX. cretonne.

cre·yen·te I. adj. believing II. m.f. believer.

cre·ye·ra, creyó see **creer.**

crez·ca, crezco see **crecer.**

crí·a f. rearing, raising <*la c. de niños es un trabajo difícil* raising children is a difficult job>; *(bebé)* infant, nursling; ZOOL. *(crianza)* breeding, raising; *(animal)* young, offspring; *(camada)* brood, litter.

cria·da I. f. maid, maidservant II. adj. see **criado, -da.**

cria·de·ro, -ra m. BOT. nursery; ZOOL. breeding place; MIN. vein, bed ◆ **c. de ostras** oyster bed.

cria·di·lla f. FIG. *(panecillo redondo)* round roll of bread;

(testículo) testicle (of an animal) ♦ **c. de mar** ZOOL. polyp • **c. de tierra** BOT. truffle.

cria·do, –da I. past part. see **criar** II. adj. bred, brought up *<una persona mal c.* an ill-bred person> III. m. servant, manservant —f. see **criada.**

cria·dor, –do·ra m.f. breeder; *(vinicultor)* viniculturist.

cria·mien·to m. *(acción de criar)* breeding; *(renovación)* renovation; *(conservación)* conservation.

crian·de·ra f. AMER. wet nurse.

crian·za f. *(acción de criar)* nursing, nurturing; ZOOL. breeding, raising; *(lactancia)* lactation; FIG. *(cortesía)* breeding, manners; CHILE, ZOOL. litter ♦ **dar c.** to rear, bring up.

criar §30 tr. *(nutrir)* to nurse, suckle *<la madre misma criaba al bebé* the mother nursed the baby herself>; to raise, breed *<c. vacas* to raise cows>; *(educar)* to rear, bring up (children); *(producir)* to produce, bring forth (said of land); *(establecer)* to establish, set up; *(fomentar)* to foster, nurture ♦ **c. carnes** to put on weight —intr. to reproduce, have young —reflex. to be brought up, grow up *<me crié en una buena familia* I was brought up in a good family>; *(crecer)* to grow.

cria·tu·ra f. *(cosa creada)* creature; *(niño)* baby, infant.

cri·ba f. screen, sieve ♦ **estar como una c.** *or* **estar hecho una c.** FIG. to be riddled with holes • **c. hidráulica** MIN. jig.

cri·ba·do I. past part. see **cribar** II. m. *(acción de cribar)* sieving, sifting; ARG. *(bordado)* embroidery; *(prenda)* decorative lace garment worn under *chiripá* trousers.

cri·bar tr. to sift, screen.

cri·bo·so, –sa adj. riddled, full of holes.

cric m. MECH. jack ♦ **c. de tornillo** MECH. screw jack, jackscrew.

cri·men m. crime, criminal offense; FIG., COLL. *(lástima)* shame, pity.

cri·mi·nal adj. & m.f. criminal.

cri·mi·na·li·dad f. *(calidad)* criminality; *(índice)* crime rate.

cri·mi·na·lis·ta m.f. CRIMIN. criminologist; LAW *(abogado)* criminal lawyer.

cri·mi·nal·men·te adv. criminally.

cri·mi·no·lo·gí·a f. criminology.

cri·mi·nó·lo·go m. criminologist.

cri·mi·no·so, –sa adj. & m.f. var. of **criminal.**

crin f. ZOOL. mane; *(pelo)* horsehair ♦ **c. vegetal** vegetable fiber.

crí·o m. COLL. *(de pecho)* nursing baby, sucking infant; *(niño)* kid.

crio·llis·mo m. expression denoting what is indigenous to the New World.

crio·llo, –lla I. adj. Creole; AMER. native, American *<costumbres criollas* native customs>; COL. cowardly II. m.f. Creole (esp. person of European descent born in America); AMER. native American; COL. coward.

crip·ta f. crypt, underground vault.

crip·tón m. CHEM. krypton.

cri·quet m. SPORT. cricket.

cri·sá·li·da f. ENTOM. chrysalis, pupa.

cri·san·te·mo m. *or* **cri·san·te·ma** f. BOT. chrysanthemum.

cri·sis f. [pl. **–sis**] crisis *<c. financiera* financial crisis>; fit, attack *<c. de furia* fit of rage>; *(juicio)* judgment, conclusion; shortage *<c. de vivienda* housing shortage> MED. crisis, sudden change ♦ **c. ministerial** cabinet crisis • **c. nerviosa** nervous breakdown • **llegar a la** *or* **hacer c.** to reach crisis point, come to a head.

cris·ma m.f. RELIG. *(aceite)* chrism (consecrated oil) —f. FIG., COLL. *(cabeza)* head ♦ **romperle la c. a alguien** COLL. to bash in someone's head.

cri·sol m. TECH. crucible, melting pot; METAL. metal crucible, hearth; FIG. *(prueba)* crucible, trial.

cri·só·li·to m. MIN. chrysolite ♦ **c. de los volcanes** chrysolite, olivine • **c. oriental** yellow topaz.

cri·so·pe·ya f. alchemy.

cris·pa·du·ra f. *or* **cris·pa·mien·to** m. var. of **crispatura.**

cris·par tr. ANAT. to contract, tense; FIG., COLL. *(irritar)* to irritate, put on edge —reflex. ANAT. to twitch; FIG., COLL. *(irritarse)* to become irritated.

cris·pa·tu·ra f. *(estirón repentino)* twitching (of a muscle); *(contracción)* contraction; FIG. *(irritación)* annoyance.

cris·tal m. MIN. crystal; *(vidrio)* crystal, crystal glass; *(objeto)* glass *or* crystal ornament; *(hoja de vidrio)* pane of glass; FIG. *(espejo)* looking glass, mirror; POET. *(agua)* water; AMER. *(vaso)* drinking glass; CARIB. jelly; CUBA vegetable mucilage ♦ **c. ahumado** smoked glass • **c. armado** wire glass • **c. cilindrado** plate glass • **c. de aumento** magnifying glass, lens • **c. de patente** MARIT. bull's-eye • **c. de roca** rock crystal; MIN. flint glass • **c. de seguridad** safety glass • **c. esmerilado** ground glass • **c. estriado** ribbed glass • **c. hilado** spun glass, fiber glass • **c. inastillable** splinterproof glass • **c. irrompible** safety *or* shatterproof glass • **c. tallado** cut glass • **cristales** windows • **de c.** glass.

cris·ta·le·ra f. *(armario)* glass cabinet, sideboard; *(vidriera)* glass window *or* door.

cris·ta·le·rí·a f. *(arte)* glasswork, glassmaking; *(fábrica)* glassworks; *(tienda)* glass *or* crystal shop; *(juego)* glass *or* crystal service; *(objetos)* glassware.

cris·ta·li·no, –na I. adj. *(de cristal)* crystalline; FIG. *(diáfano)* crystal clear, transparent II. m. ANAT. crystalline lens.

cris·ta·li·za·ción f. crystallization.

cris·ta·li·za·dor m. CHEM. crystallizer.

cris·ta·li·zar §04 tr. & intr. & reflex. to crystallize.

cris·ta·loi·de m. CHEM. crystalloid.

cris·tia·nar tr. COLL. to baptize, christen.

cris·tian·dad f. RELIG. Christendom.

cris·tia·nis·mo m. RELIG. Christianity.

cris·tia·ni·za·ción f. Christianization.

cris·tia·ni·zar §04 tr. to christianize, convert to Christianity.

cris·tia·no, –na I. adj. RELIG. Christian II. m.f. RELIG. Christian; COLL. plain Spanish *<hable usted en c.* speak in plain Spanish>; living soul *<no había ni un c. en el teatro* there was not a living soul in the theater>; C. AMER. good soul, naive person.

Cris·to m. RELIG. Christ; *(crucifijo)* crucifix ♦ **estar hecho un C.** to be a pitiful sight.

cris·tus m. [pl. **–tus**] *(cruz)* christcross, crisscross; *(abecedario)* alphabet ♦ **no saber el c.** FIG., COLL. to be ignorant.

cri·sue·la f. drip pan (of an oil lamp).

cri·te·rio m. *(regla)* criterion, standard; *(juicio)* judgment, discernment; *(opinión)* view, opinion *<en mi c.* in my opinion>; SPORT. *(campeonato)* championship.

crí·ti·ca I. f. *(valoración)* criticism *<c. literaria* literary criticism>; *(reseña)* review, critique; *(censura)* censure, criticism; *(murmuración)* gossip II. adj. see **crítico, –ca.**

cri·ti·ca·ble adj. criticizable

cri·ti·ca·dor, –do·ra I. adj. critical, criticizing II. m.f. criticizer, critic.

cri·ti·car §70 tr. *(valorar)* to criticize, judge; *(censurar)* to criticize, disapprove of; *(murmurar)* to gossip about.

cri·ti·cis·mo m. PHILOS. Kantianism, critical philosophy.

crí·ti·co, –ca I. adj. critical *<un examen c.* a critical examination>; *(crucial)* crucial, critical *<el momento c.* the crucial moment> II. m.f. critic, reviewer —f. see **crítica.**

cri·ti·cón, –co·na I. adj. faultfinding, carping II. m.f. faultfinder, carper.

cri·ti·qué, critique see **criticar.**

Cro·a·cia f. Croatia.

cro·ar intr. to croak, make a croaking sound.

cro·a·ta adj. & m.f. Croatian.

cro·can·te m. almond *or* peanut brittle.

cro·ci·tar intr. to caw, croak.

cro·chet m. SEW. crochet; SPORT. *(en el boxeo)* hook.

cro·ma·do I. past part. of **cromar** II. m. chromium-plating, chroming.

cro·mar tr. TECH. to chrome, plate with chromium.

cro·má·ti·co, –ca adj. chromatic.

cro·ma·ti·na f. BIOL. chromatin.

cro·ma·tis·mo m. PHYS. chromatism.

cro·mo m. CHEM. chromium, chrome; *(estampa)* chromo, chromolithography.

cro·mo·li·to·gra·fí·a f. PRINT. chromolithography.

cro·mos·fe·ra f. ASTRON. chromosphere.

cro·mo·so·ma m. BIOL. chromosome.

cró·ni·ca I. f. *(historia)* chronicle, history; JOURN. *(artículo)* feature, article II. adj. see **crónico, –ca.**

cro·ni·ci·dad f. quality of being chronic, chronicity.

cró·ni·co, –ca I. adj. MED. chronic; *(inveterado)* chronic, inveterate **II.** f. see **crónica.**

cro·nis·ta m.f. *(historiador)* chronicler, historian; JOURN. *(periodista)* columnist, reporter.

cro·nó·gra·fo m. *(persona)* chronologer, chronologist; *(aparato)* chronograph.

cro·no·lo·gí·a f. chronology.

cro·no·ló·gi·co, –ca adj. chronologic, chronological.

cro·no·me·trar tr. to time with a chronometer.

cro·no·me·tris·ta m.f. person who makes chronometers.

cro·nó·me·tro m. chronometer, stopwatch.

cro·que·ta f. CUL. croquette, fritter.

cro·quis m. [pl. **–quis**] sketch, rough draft.

cro·sci·tar intr. to caw, croak.

cró·ta·lo m. *(castañuela antigua)* crotalum; ZOOL. rattlesnake; MUS. castanets.

crou·pier m.f. croupier.

cru·ce m. *(acción)* crossing; *(crucero)* intersection, junction; RAIL. crossing; BIOL. *(acción)* crossing, crossbreeding; *(ser híbrido)* cross, crossbreed; ELEC. short circuit; GEOM. intersection; LING. cross; RAD. interference, crossing of signals; TELEC. crossing of lines ♦ **c. a nivel** *or* **de vía** grade *or* level crossing ♦ **c. de peatones** pedestrian crossing • **c. en trébol** cloverleaf intersection • **c. giratorio** traffic circle, rotary • **c. inferior** underpass • **c. superior** overpass.

cru·cé, cruce see **cruzar.**

cru·ce·ro 1. adj. ARCHIT. cross <*arco c.* cross vault> **II.** m. *(encrucijada)* intersection, junction; RAIL. crossing; cruise <*c. de recreo* pleasure cruise>; ARCHIT. transept; CARP. batten, crossbeam; MIL. cruiser; MIN. cleavage; PRINT. *(doblez)* fold; *(listón)* crossbar (of a chase); RELIG. crossbearer, crucifer ♦ **c. de batalla** MIL. battle cruiser • **c. de bolsillo** MIL. pocket battleship • **C. del Sur** ASTRON. Southern Cross • **c. pesado** MIL. heavy cruiser.

cru·ce·ta f. *(intersección)* intersection, crosspiece; MARIT. crosstree; MECH. crosshead; PERU small mill.

cru·cial adj. *(decisivo)* crucial, decisive <*la fase c.* the crucial phase>; *(esencial)* essential, crucial; *(en forma de cruz)* cruciform, crucial.

cru·ci·fe·ra·rio m. RELIG. crucifer, crossbearer.

cru·ci·fe·ro, –ra I. adj. POET. cruciferous **II.** m. RELIG. crucifer, crossbearer.

cru·ci·fi·ca·do, –da I. past part. see **crucificar II.** adj. crucified **III.** m. ♦ **El C.** Jesus Christ, the Crucified.

cru·ci·fi·car §70 tr. *(matar)* to crucify; FIG. *(mortificar)* to torment, torture.

cru·ci·fi·jo m. crucifix.

cru·ci·fi·xión f. crucifixion.

cru·ci·for·me adj. cross-shaped, cruciform.

cru·ci·gra·ma m. crossword puzzle.

cru·de·za f. *(estado)* rawness; *(severidad)* rawness, harshness <*la c. del invierno* the harshness of winter>; FIG. *(rigor)* harshness, cruelty <*la c. de una observación* the cruelty of a remark> ♦ **con c.** harshly, cruelly.

cru·di·llo m. TEX. unbleached linen.

cru·do, –da I. adj. raw <*carne c.* raw meat>; *(verde)* unripe, green; *(difícil de digerir)* indigestible, hard to digest; *(amarillento)* yellowish; raw, untreated <*seda c.* raw silk>; crude <*petróleo c.* crude oil>; raw, harsh <*un invierno c.* a harsh winter>; FIG. harsh, cruel <*la verdad c.* the cruel truth>; MEX. hung over ♦ **medio c.** rare (meat) **II.** m. *(petróleo)* crude oil; S. AMER. burlap, sackcloth.

cruel adj. *(despiadado)* cruel, merciless; *(fiero)* savage, bloodthirsty; *(severo)* severe, cruel.

cruel·dad f. *(inhumanidad)* cruelty, inhumanity; *(ferocidad)* savagery, ferocity; *(severidad)* severity, cruelness.

cruel·men·te adv. cruelly.

cruen·to, –ta adj. bloody.

cru·jí·a f. *(pasillo)* passage; *(corredor)* corridor; *(sala de hospital)* hospital ward; *(fila de habitaciones)* large hall with rooms on either side; ARCHIT. space between two windows; MARIT. midship gangway ♦ **pasar una c.** FIG., COLL. to go through a bad time.

cru·ji·de·ro, –ra adj. cracking, creaking.

cru·ji·do I. past part. see **crujir II.** m. *(de hoja, tela)* rustle, rustling; *(de puerta)* creak, creaking; *(de dientes)* rattling,

chatter; *(de huesos)* crack, cracking; *(de quema)* crackle, crackling; ARM. *(de espada)* flaw in a sword blade.

cru·ji·dor, –do·ra adj. cracking, creaking.

cru·jien·te adj. *(de hoja, tela)* rustling; *(de puerta)* creaking; *(de dientes)* rattling, chattering; *(de huesos)* cracking; *(de quema)* crackling; CUL. *(de pan)* crusty, crisp; *(de galleta)* crispy, crunchy; *(de nuez)* crunchy; *(de otros vegetales)* crisp.

cru·jir intr. *(hoja, tela)* to rustle; *(puerta, madera)* to creak; *(dientes)* to rattle, chatter; *(huesos)* to crack; *(quema)* to crackle; *(grava)* to crunch.

cru·pal adj. MED. croupy, croupal.

crus·tá·ce·o, –a adj. & m. crustacean.

cruz f. [pl. **cru·ces**] cross; tails <*cara o c.* heads or tails>; FIG. cross, burden <*esta enfermedad es mi c.* this illness is my cross>; ZOOL. withers; BOT. crotch (of a tree); PRINT. *(signo)* dagger, obelisk; MARIT. crown (of an anchor); HER. cross, crosslet ♦ **c. de Jerusalén** BOT. scarlet lychnis • **C. de Malta** Maltese Cross • **C. de San Andrés** Saint Andrew's Cross • **C. de San Antonio** Saint Anthony's Cross, tau cross • **c. gamada** swastika • **C. Roja** Red Cross • **¡c. y raya!** COLL. that's it!, enough! • **de la c. a la fecha** from beginning to end • **en c.** cross-shaped • **hacerse cruces** to cross oneself; FIG. to show one's astonishment • **por éstas que son cruces** COLL. by all that is holy.

cru·za·da I. f. HIST., RELIG. Crusade; *(encrucijada)* crossroads, intersection; FIG. crusade, campaign <*la c. contra las armas nucleares* the campaign against nuclear arms> —m. see **cruzado, –da II.** adj. see **cruzado, –da.**

cru·za·do, –da I. past part. see **cruzar II.** adj. crossed <*espadas cruzadas* crossed swords>; BIOL., ZOOL. crossbred, hybrid; TEX. twilled; HER. crossed **III.** m. crusader —f. see **cruzada.**

cru·za·men m. MARIT. square *or* width (of a sail).

cru·za·mien·to m. *(acción de cruzar)* crossing; *(animales)* crossbreeding, interbreeding (animals).

cru·zar §04 tr. to cross, place crosswise <*c. las piernas* to cross one's legs>; to cross, intersect <*ese camino cruza el campo* that road crosses the field>; to cut across, cross <*el niño no puede c. la calle sólo* the child cannot cross the street alone>; AGR. to replow; CHILE, ECUAD., PERU to attack ♦ **cruzarle a uno la cara** FIG. to slap someone across the face —intr. MARIT. to cruise —reflx. to cross one another, intersect <*las líneas se cruzan* the lines cross one another>; to pass, cross paths <*los dos carros se cruzaron en el camino* the two cars passed each other in the road>; CHILE, ECUAD., PERU to fight ♦ **cruzarse de brazos** FIG. to remain idle, do nothing.

cru·zei·ro m. FIN. cruzeiro (currency of Brazil).

cua·der·na f. *(moneda antigua)* old Spanish coin; *(juego de tablas)* double fours; MARIT. *(costillas)* frame (of a hull), rib (of a frame) ♦ **c. vía** POET. verse form with four alexandrines.

cua·der·ni·llo m. *(papel)* quinternion; RELIG. ecclesiastical calendar, clerical directory.

cua·der·no m. *(libreta)* notebook; PRINT. *(hoja doblada)* quarto ♦ **c. de bitácora** MARIT. logbook.

cua·dra f. *(establo)* stable; *(grupo de caballos)* stable; *(grupa)* croup, rump; *(sala)* large hall *or* room; *(de hospital)* ward; *(de cuartel)* hut; MARIT. quarter; AMER. *(manzana de casas)* block, city block; *(medida)* quarter of a Roman mile; ECUAD., VEN. small rural property; PERU reception room ♦ **navegar a la c.** MARIT. to sail with the wind on the quarter.

cua·dra·di·llo m. *(regla)* ruler, straightedge; *(barra)* square-sectioned iron bar; SEW. *(de camisa)* gusset; *(azúcar)* lump *or* cube of sugar.

cua·dra·do, –da I. past part. see **cuadrar II.** adj. square; FIG. *(perfecto)* complete, consummate; COL. graceful, elegant **III.** m. GEOM. *(figura)* square; MATH. *(segunda potencia)* square <*nueve es el c. de tres* nine is the square of three>; *(regla)* square ruler; TECH. die; SEW. gusset; PRINT. quadrat, quad ♦ **c. mágico** magic square.

cua·dra·ge·na·rio, –ria adj. & m.f. quadragenarian.

cua·dra·gé·si·mo, –ma adj. & m. fortieth —f. RELIG. Quadragesima, Lent.

cua·dran·gu·lar adj. GEOM. quadrangular.

cua·drán·gu·lo, –la GEOM. I. adj. quadrangular II. m. quadrangle.
cua·dran·te m. MATH., MARIT. quadrant; *(reloj)* sundial; *(cristal)* face (of a watch); MEX. sacristy.
cua·drar I. tr. *(dar figura cuadrada)* to square, make square; CARP., GEOM., MATH. to square; *(cuadricular)* to divide into squares —intr. *(conformar)* to square, agree <*tus ideas no cuadran con las mías* your ideas do not agree with mine>; COM. to tally, balance <*las cifras no cuadran* the figures do not balance>; *(agradar)* to suit, please <*vendremos a las once si le cuadra a usted* we will come at eleven if that suits you>; CHILE to be ready —reflex. to square off <*los soldados se cuadraron frente a las tropas enemigas* the soldiers squared off facing the enemy troops>; FIG. *(resistir)* to stand firm, dig in one's heels; VEN. to shine, succeed; DOM. REP., P. RICO to strike it rich.
cua·dra·tu·ra f. *(acción y efecto de cuadrar)* squaring; ASTRON. quadrature ♦ **c. del círculo** squaring the circle.
cua·dri·ce·nal adj. done every forty years.
cua·drí·cu·la f. grid.
cua·dri·cu·la·do, –da I. past part. see **cuadricular²** II. adj. cross-sectioned, squared.
cua·dri·cu·lar¹ adj. squared, quadrille.
cua·dri·cu·lar² tr. to divide into squares, square (paper).
cua·drie·nal adj. quadrennial.
cua·drie·nio m. quadrennium, four-year period.
cua·dri·for·me adj. quadriform, four-faced.
cua·dril m. ANAT. *(hueso)* innominate bone, hipbone; *(anca)* hip; ZOOL. hindquarter, rump.
cua·dri·la·te·ral adj. quadrilateral.
cua·dri·lá·te·ro, –ra GEOM. I. adj. quadrilateral, four-sided II. m. quadrilateral.
cua·dri·lla f. *(de obreros)* team, crew; *(de malhechores)* gang, band; *(patrulla)* armed band *or* patrol; *(baile)* quadrille; TAUR. team assisting a bullfighter.
cua·dri·lle·ro m. *(cabo)* foreman; PHILIP. rural policeman; CHILE gang member.
cua·drin·gen·té·si·mo, –ma I. adj. four hundredth II. m. one four hundredth.
cua·dri·no·mio m. MATH. quadrinomial.
cua·dri·pli·car §70 tr. to quadruplicate.
cua·dri·sí·la·bo, –ba I. adj. quadrisyllabic II. m. quadrisyllable.
cua·dri·vio m. *(encrucijada)* crossroads; HIST. *(artes liberales)* quadrivium, liberal arts (in the Middle Ages).
cua·dro m. *(rectángulo)* square; ARTS painting, picture <*un c. de Goya* a painting by Goya>; LIT. picture, description <*el autor nos ofrece un c. animado de la sociedad francesa* the author offers us an animated description of French society>; ARCHIT., ARTS, TECH. *(armazón)* framework; HORT. bed, patch; THEAT. scene <*el acto tiene cinco cuadros* the act has five scenes>; MIL. *(formación)* square formation; *(conjunto de oficiales)* cadre; SPORT. *(equipo)* team; FIG. *(espectáculo)* spectacle, sight <*las montañas presentan un c. conmovedor* the mountains present a moving spectacle>; CHILE slaughterhouse ♦ **a cuadros** checked, checkered • **c. al óleo** oil painting • **c. conmutador** *or* **de distribución** ELEC., TELEC. switchboard • **c. de costumbres** LIT. sketch of regional types and customs • **c. de mandos** TECH. control panel • **c. sinóptico** table, statistical chart • **c. vivo** THEAT. tableau vivant • **en c.** square • **estar** *or* **quedarse en c.** FIG. to be all alone in the world.
cua·drú·ma·no, –na ZOOL. I. adj. quadrumanous II. m.f. quadrumane.
cua·drú·pe·do, –da ZOOL. I. adj. quadrupedal II. m.f. quadruped.
cuá·dru·ple adj. MATH. quadruple, fourfold.
cua·dru·pli·ca·ción f. quadruplication.
cua·dru·pli·car §70 MATH. tr. & intr. to quadruple, quadruplicate.
cuá·drup·lo, –la adj. & m. quadruple.
cua·ja·da I. f. curd (of milk); *(requesón)* cottage cheese II. adj. see **cuajado, –da.**
cua·ja·di·llo m. fine embroidery work (done on silk).
cua·ja·do, –da I. past part. see **cuajar²** II. adj. FIG., COLL. *(pasmado)* stunned, dumbfounded; *(dormido)* fast asleep; DOM. REP. lazy, indolent ♦ **c. de** full of <*la ciudad está c.*

de turistas the city is full of tourists> III. m. CUL. mincemeat dish —f. see **cuajada.**
cua·ja·mien·to m. *(coagulación)* coagulation; *(la leche)* curdling (of milk); *(la gelatina)* setting, jelling (of gelatine); *(solidificación)* solidification.
cua·jar¹ m. ZOOL. abomasum, fourth stomach (of a ruminant).
cua·jar² tr. *(coagular)* coagulate, congeal; *(leche)* to curdle; FIG. *(adornar)* to adorn excessively, cover <*la niña cuajó la mesa de flores* the girl covered the table with flowers> —intr. FIG., COLL. *(tener éxito)* to turn *or* work out well, succeed <*cuajó su negocio* his business succeeded>; *(gustar)* to like, please <*no me cuaja esa idea* I don't like that idea>; MEX. *(mentir)* to lie; *(charlar)* to chatter, prattle —reflex. *(coagular)* to coagulate, congeal; *(leche)* to curdle; *(dormirse)* to fall fast asleep; FIG. *(lograrse)* to turn *or* work out well, succeed; *(llenarse)* to get filled, fill up; GUAT., MEX. to get drunk.
cua·jo m. *(materia)* rennet (extract from calf's stomach); *(cuajada)* curd; ZOOL. abomasum; FIG., COLL. *(calma)* calmness, patience; *(lentitud)* slowness; CUBA solidifying of cane juice; MEX., COLL. *(charla)* chatter; *(receso)* recess, break; *(embuste)* hoax, trick ♦ **de c.** by the roots <*arrancar de c.* to pull up by the roots> • **ensanchar el c.** to have patience, be patient • **tener buen** *or* **mucho c.** *(ser paciente)* to be patient; *(ser lento)* to be slow.
cual §G42 I. rel. pron. which <*el paquete del c. te hablé* the package of which I spoke to you>; who <*yo hablaba a los estudiantes los cuales no me escuchaban* I was talking to the students, who were not listening to me>; whom <*la amiga a la c. escribí vivía en Francia* the friend to whom I wrote was living in France> ♦ **cada c.** each one, every one • **con lo c.** whereupon, upon which • **por lo c.** whereby, because of which II. adv. like, as <*la situación, c. él la describe, parece bastante difícil* the situation, as he describes it, looks quite difficult>; just as, just like <*nos ofrecieron ayuda c. requería nuestra necesidad* they offered us help just like we needed> ♦ **c. . . . tal** like. . . like • **c. si** as if • **tal c.** some, a few <*vino tal c. persona* a few people came>; okay, fair <*el enfermo se encuentra tal c.* the sick man is okay>.
cuál §G43 I. adj. which <*¿c. libro quiere usted?* which book do you want?> II. rel. pron. which (one) <*¿c. de las faldas compraste?* which one of the skirts did you buy?> III. indef. pron. some <*todos llegaron, cuáles temprano, cuáles tarde* everyone arrived, some early, some late> IV. adv. how <*¡c. sorprendido se sentirá!* how surprised he will be!>.
cua·les·quier adj. see **cualquier.**
cua·les·quie·ra adj. & indef. pron. see **cualquiera.**
cua·li·dad f. quality, characteristic.
cua·li·fi·car §70 tr. to qualify, characterize.
cua·li·ta·ti·vo, –va adj. qualitative.
cual·quier adj. [pl. **cua·les·quier**] [contr. of **cualquiera** used before nouns] any <*cualquier libro* any book>.
cual·quie·ra [pl. **cua·les·quie·ra**] I. adj. any <*en cualquier momento* at any time>; just any, any ordinary <*ella no es una chica c.* she is not just any girl> II. indef. pron. anyone, anybody <*c. lo puede hacer* anybody can do it>; any one <*c. de los chicos* any one of the boys> ♦ **un (hombre) cualquiera** a nobody III. rel. pron. whoever <*no lo creas, c. que te lo diga* don't believe it, whoever tells it to you>; whatever <*c. que sea el pretexto* whatever the pretext>; nobody <*ser un c.* to be a nobody>.
cuan adv. as <*era tan contra su gusto c. contra el buen acierto* it was as much contrary to his taste as it was against his better judgment>.
cuán adv. how <*¡c. fugaces los años!* how time flies!>.
cuan·do §G46 I. adv. when, since <*será ya de noche cuando lleguemos a casa* it will be night when we get home> ♦ **c. más** *or* **c. mucho** at the most • **c. menos** at least • **de c. en c.** from time to time II. conj. when <*comeremos c. lleguen los invitados* we will eat when the guests arrive>; *(aunque)* although, even if <*ella no mentiría c. le fuera en ello la vida* she would not tell a lie even if her life depended on it>; *(puesto que)* since <*c. él lo dice, será verdad* since he says it, it must be true>; if <*c. fuese verdad* if it were true> ♦ **aun c.** even though, although • **c. no** if not,

otherwise • **c. quiera** whenever **III.** prep. at the time of <*c. la muerte de Napoleón* at the time of Napoleon's death>; as <*c. niño* as a child>.

cuán·do I. adv. when <*¿c. llegó el tren?* when did the train arrive?> ♦ **¿de c. acá?** since when?, how come? **II.** conj. sometimes, at times <*siempre me están castigando, c. con razón, c. sin ella* they are always punishing me, sometimes with reason, sometimes without> **III.** m. when <*el cómo y el c.* the how and the when>.

cuan·ta m. PHYS. quanta.

cuan·tí·a f. *(cantidad)* quantity, amount; *(importancia)* importance, distinction; LAW *(valor)* assessed value.

cuán·ti·co, –ca adj. PHYS. quantum <*mecánica c.* quantum mechanics>.

cuan·ti·más adv. [contr. of **cuanto** and **más**] COLL. all the more.

cuan·tio·so, –sa adj. *(grande)* large, substantial; *(abundante)* abundant, copious; *(numeroso)* numerous.

cuan·ti·ta·ti·vo, –va adj. quantitative.

cuan·to¹ m. PHYS. quantum.

cuan·to² I. adv. as much as <*le voy a ayudar c. puedo* I am going to help him as much as I can>; as long as <*nos quedaremos aquí c. podamos* we will remain here as long as we can> ♦ **c. a** as to, as for • **c. antes** as soon as possible • **c. más** all the more, even more so <*se rompen las amistades recientes, c. más las antiguas* recent friendships break up, even more so the old ones>; the more <*c. más tiene, más desea* the more one has, the more one wants> • **c. más que** even more so because <*ella tendrá mucho éxito, c. más que es tan trabajadora* she will be very successful, even more so because she's so hard-working> • **en c.** as soon as <*en c. llegó, lo detuvieron* as soon as he arrived, they detained him>; *(mientras)* while • **en c. a** as to, as for • **por c.** insofar as, inasmuch as **II.** adj. & pron. see **cuanto, -ta.**

cuán·to I. adv. how <*¡c. me alegro!* how happy I am!>; how much <*¡c. cuestan las joyas!* how much jewels cost!>; how long <*¡c. ha durado esta conversación!* how long this conversation has lasted!> **II.** adj. & pron. see **cuánto, -ta.**

cuan·to, -ta §G42 I. adj. as much as <*ella les dio tanto dinero c. quisieron* she gave them as much money as they wanted> ♦ **c. más** the more <*c. más dinero te doy, más me pides* the more money I give to you, the more you ask me for> • **c. menos** the less • **cuantos** as many • **unos cuantos** a few, some **II.** pron. all that, everything <*le ofrecí c. tenía* I offered her everything I had>; as much as <*coma c. quiera* eat as much as you want> ♦ **cuantos** as many as, everyone <*reían cuantos entraban* everyone who came in laughed> • **unos cuantos** some, a few.

cuán·to, -ta §G43 I. adj. how much <*¿c. dinero necesitas?* how much money do you need?>; what a lot of <*¡cuántos problemas tiene ese chico!* what a lot of problems that boy has!> ♦ **cuántos** *or* **cuántas** how many <*¿cuántas clases tomas este semestre?* how many classes are you taking this semester?> **II.** pron. how much <*¿c. vale?* how much is it worth?> ♦ **¿a cuántos estamos hoy?** what is today's date? • **cuántos** how many <*¿cuántos tiene usted?* how many do you have?>.

cua·que·ris·mo m. Quakerism.

cuá·que·ro, -ra m.f. Quaker.

cua·ren·ta I. adj. forty <*c. páginas* forty pages>; *(cuadragésimo)* fortieth **II.** m. forty ♦ **cantarle las c. a** FIG., COLL. to give (someone) a piece of one's mind • **ésas son otras c.** ARG., PERU, URUG., COLL. that's a horse of a different color.

cua·ren·ta·vo, -va adj. fortieth.

cua·ren·te·na f. *(conjunto de cuarenta)* group of forty; MED. quarantine; RELIG. Lent; FIG., COLL. *(aislamiento)* isolation; *(suspensión)* suspension of judgement.

cua·ren·tón, -to·na adj. & m.f. forty-year-old.

cua·res·ma f. RELIG. Lent.

cuar·ta I. f. *(medida)* span (of the hand); *(naipes)* four of a kind (in cards); ASTRON. quadrant; MARIT. rhumb (compass point); MUS. fourth; AMER. quirt, riding crop ♦ **andar de la c. al pértigo** ARG., URUG., COLL. to live from hand to mouth **II.** adj. see **cuarto, -ta.**

cuar·ta·go m. ZOOL. small horse, pony.

cuar·ta·na·rio, –ria adj. MED. suffering from quartan (fever).

cuar·te·ar tr. *(dividir en cuartos)* to quarter, divide into four pieces; *(descuartizar)* to divide into pieces, cut up; *(fragmentar)* to crack; *(pujar)* to bid a fourth more for (at an auction); *(en un juego)* to make a fourth (player); *(hacer eses)* to zigzag (up a slope); MARIT. to box (a compass); MEX., P. RICO to whip —intr. TAUR. to dodge; VEN. to hedge —reflex. *(henderse)* to crack, split (a wall); FIG. *(fragmentar)* to crack, weaken; TAUR. to dodge; CUBA to challenge; ECUAD. to wait (for someone urgently needed); MEX. to go back on one's word.

cuar·tel m. *(cuarta parte)* quarter, fourth; *(barrio)* quarter, district; *(de terreno)* lot, plot; *(de jardín)* flowerbed; FIG., COLL. *(casa)* house; MIL. *(alojamiento)* barracks; quarter <*dar c. al enemigo* to give quarter to the enemy>; HER. quarter; MARIT. hatch door *or* cover; POET. quatrain ♦ **c. de bomberos** fire station, firehouse • **c. general** MIL. general headquarters • **cuarteles** MIL. quarters <*cuarteles de invierno* winter quarters> • **estar de c.** MIL. to be unassigned and on half pay (an officer) • **no dar c. a** to show no mercy to • **sin c.** merciless.

cuar·te·la·da f. *or* **cuar·te·la·zo** m. AMER. military uprising.

cuar·te·le·ro, -ra I. adj. pertaining to military barracks **II.** m. MIL. orderly *or* soldier in charge of keeping the barracks clean; ECUAD., PERU waiter.

cuar·te·o m. *(división en cuartos)* quartering; *(descuartizamiento)* dividing into pieces, cutting up; *(grieta)* crack, split; TAUR. dodge; COL. break in winter rains; VEN. hedging ♦ **al c.** TAUR. dodging.

cuar·te·ro·la f. *(barril)* quarter cask; *(medida)* unit of measure equivalent to 129 liters; CHILE water vendor's bucket; AMER. short carbine.

cuar·te·rón, -ro·na I. adj. of mulatto and Spanish parentage **II.** m.f. *(mulato)* mulatto, quadroon —m. *(cuarta parte)* quarter, fourth; *(cuarta parte de una libra)* quarter of a pound; *(postigo)* window shutter; CARP. door panel.

cuar·te·to m. POET. quatrain; MUS. quartet.

cuar·ti·lla f. *(medida de capacidad)* measure of capacity of 13.87 liters; *(medida de líquido)* liquid measure of 4.033 liters; *(cuarta parte de la arroba)* one fourth of an arroba (2.8125 kilos); *(papel)* fourth part of a large sheet of paper; *(moneda)* old silver coin from Mexico.

cuar·ti·llo m. *(nombre de medidas)* pint in liquid *or* dry measure; *(moneda)* quarter of a *real*.

cuar·to, -ta I. adj. fourth ♦ **c. dimensión** PHYS. fourth dimension **II.** m. fourth, quarter <*un c. de las chicas no saben coser* a quarter of the girls do not know how to sew>; ASTRON., ZOOL. quarter; quarter-hour, quarter <*son las ocho menos c.* it is quarter to eight>; *(vivienda)* living quarters; *(habitación)* room <*c. de costura* sewing room>; MIL. watch; NUMIS. old Spanish coin ♦ **c. creciente** ASTRON. first quarter (of the moon) • **c. de aseo** powder room • **c. de baño** bathroom • **c. de dormir** bedroom • **c. de estar** living room • **c. de final** SPORT. quarterfinal • **c. delantero** ZOOL. forequarter • **c. menguante** ASTRON. third quarter (of the moon) • **c. oscuro** PHOTOG. darkroom • **c. trasero** ZOOL. hindquarter • **c. y comida** room and board • **de tres al c.** FIG., COLL. unimportant, insignificant • **en c.** PRINT. quarto —f. see **cuarta.**

cuar·tón m. *(madera)* length *or* plank of wood; *(medida)* liquid measure; *(pieza de tierra)* oblong field of farmland.

cuar·tu·co *or* **cuar·tu·cho** m. dingy room, hovel.

cuar·zo m. MIN. quartz ♦ **c. ahumado** MIN. smoky quartz, cairngorm • **c. hialino** MIN. rock crystal.

cua·si adv. almost, quasi.

cua·si·con·tra·to m. LAW quasi contract.

cua·si·de·li·to m. LAW quasi delict.

cua·si·mo·do m. RELIG. Quasimodo Sunday, Low Sunday.

cua·te, -ta AMER. **I.** adj. *(gemelo)* twin; *(semejante)* similar, alike **II.** m.f. *(gemelo)* twin; *(amigo)* buddy, pal.

cua·ter·na f. quartern (lottery).

cua·ter·na·rio, –ria I. adj. quaternary, having four parts; GEOL. *(período)* Quaternary **II.** m. quaternary; GEOL. Quaternary (period or system).

cua·tre·re·ar tr. ARG. to steal, rustle (cattle).

cua·tre·ro, -ra I. adj. *(de caballos)* pertaining to a horse thief *or* horse thievery; *(de vacas)* cattle-rustling; PERU rascally, roguish; MEX., COLL. joking, prankish; C. AMER. traitorous, perfidious **II.** m.f. *(de caballos)* horse thief; *(de* *vacas)* cattle thief, cattle rustler; PERU *(pícaro)* rascal, rogue; MEX., COLL. joker, prankster; C. AMER. *(traidor)* traitor, betrayer.

cua·trie·nio m. var. of **cuadrienio.**

cua·tri·lli·zo, –za I. adj. pertaining to a quadruplet II. m.f. quadruplet.

cua·tri·mo·tor m. AVIA. four-engine plane.

cua·tri·sí·la·bo, –ba I. adj. four-syllable II. m. four-syllable word.

cua·tro I. adj. four <*c. horas* four hours>; *(cuarto)* fourth ♦ **las c.** four o'clock • **c. gatos** COLL. a mere handful of people (at an affair, in a place) II. m. *(número)* four; S. AMER. four-string guitar; MEX. *(ardid)* trick, ruse; *(error)* blunder ♦ **más de c.** FIG., COLL. quite a few.

cua·tro·cien·tos, –tas I. adj. four hundred <*c. marineros* four hundred sailors>; *(cuadrigentésimo)* four hundredth II. m. four hundred.

cu·ba f. *(tonel)* cask, barrel (container and contents); *(tina)* vat, tub (container and contents); FIG., COLL. *(gordo)* tub, pot-bellied person; *(borracho)* drunkard, boozer; METAL. stack (of blast furnace); RAIL. tank car; COL. youngest child, baby of the family ♦ **beber como una c.** FIG., COLL. to drink like a fish • **c. libre** rum and coke (drink) • **estar hecho una c.** FIG., COLL. to be plastered *or* drunk.

Cu·ba f. Cuba.

cu·ba·ción f. MATH. cubing.

cu·ba·no, –na adj. & m.f. Cuban.

cu·be·ro m. cooper.

cu·be·ta f. *(cubo)* bucket, pail (container and contents); *(tina)* small vat *or* tub (container and contents); *(cuñete)* keg, small cask; CHEM., PHOTOG. tray, dish; MUS. pedestal (of harp); PHYS. *(del barómetro)* mercury cistern; *(del termómetro)* bulb; MEX. top hat ♦ **c. de siembra** seed box • **c. del carburador** MECH. float chamber.

cu·bi·car §70 tr. MATH. to cube; GEOM. to determine the volume *or* capacity of a body.

cú·bi·co, –ca adj. GEOM. cubic; MATH. cube (root).

cu·bier·ta f. *(cobertura)* cover, covering; *(sobre)* envelope; *(envoltura)* wrapping, cover; FIG. *(pretexto)* pretext, cover; MARIT. deck; ARCHIT. roof; AUTO. tire, casing ♦ **bajo c.** COM. under separate cover ♦ **c. de aterrizaje** *or* **de vuelo** MARIT. flight deck • **c. de paseo** MARIT. promenade deck • **c. de sol** MARIT. sun deck.

cu·bier·to I. past part. see **cubrir** II. m. *(servicio de mesa)* cover, table setting; *(abrigo)* protection, shelter; *(comida)* plate, meal (at a fixed price); ARCHIT. roofing ♦ **a c.** under the protection of • **bajo c.** under cover • **poner los cubiertos** to set the table • **ponerse a c.** to take cover.

cu·bil m. lair, den.

cu·bi·le·te m. *(vaso)* copper *or* tin tumbler; *(molde)* copper *or* tin mold; *(hielo)* ice cube; *(de dados)* dicebox; BOT. water lily flower; C. AMER., COL., VEN. top hat.

cu·bi·le·te·ar intr. *(manejar los cubiletes)* to juggle; FIG. *(intrigar)* to intrigue, scheme.

cu·bi·le·te·o m. *(malabarismo)* juggling; FIG. *(intriga)* intrigue.

cu·bi·le·te·ro m. *(malabarista)* juggler; CUL. copper baking mold.

cu·bi·llo m. *(carraleja)* oil beetle; *(pieza de vajilla)* water cooler; THEAT. two small boxes on either side of the stage.

cu·bi·qué, cubique see **cubicar.**

cu·bis·mo m. ARTS cubism.

cu·bis·ta adj. & m.f. ARTS cubist.

cú·bi·to m. ANAT. ulna, cubitus.

cu·bo m. *(balde)* bucket, pail (container and contents); *(tina)* tub, vat (container and contents); *(de rueda)* hub; *(estanque)* millpond; *(torreón)* round turret; *(de molino)* socket (of a candlestick); ARM. socket (of a bayonet); ARCHIT., GEOM., MATH. cube; JEWEL., MECH. drum, barrel; DOM. REP. trick, deception ♦ **a cubos** abundantly • **elevar al c.** MATH. to cube • **llover a cubos** to rain cats and dogs.

cu·bre·ca·de·na m. bicycle chainguard.

cu·bre·ca·ma m. bedcover, bedspread.

cu·bre·pia·no m. covering for piano keyboard.

cu·bre·mien·to m. covering.

cu·brir §85 tr. to cover <*ella cubrió los muebles para que no se ensuciaran* she covered the furniture so that it would

not get dirty>; to cover, cover up <*el polvo cubría los muebles* dust covered the furniture>; *(proteger)* to protect, shield <*cubrió su pecho con el escudo* he protected his chest with the shield>; *(recorrer)* to go, cover <*hoy cubrimos tres kilómetros del camino* today we covered three kilometers of the road>; FIG. *(esconder)* to conceal, cover up; to shower <*lo cubrieron de honores* they showered him with honors>; MIL. to cover <*c. la retirada* to cover the retreat>; JOURN. to cover (a story); *(pagar)* to repay (a debt); ARCHIT. to roof, put a roof on; ZOOL. to cover, mate with; COM. to cover <*c. los gastos* to cover the expenses> —reflex. *(ponerse ropa)* to cover oneself; *(protegerse)* to protect oneself; COM. to cover a debt.

cu·ca I. f. BOT. chufa, sedge; ENTOM. caterpillar; COLL. *(mujer aficionada al juego)* woman gambler, woman given to gambling; SL. *(peseta)* peseta (coin); CHILE type of heron; VEN. kind of cake II. adj. see **cuco, –ca.**

cu·ca·mo·nas f.pl. COLL. cajolery, sweet talk.

cu·ca·ña f. SPORT. *(palo alto)* greased pole; FIG., COLL. *(ganga)* cinch, easy job.

cu·ca·ñe·ro, –ra FIG., COLL. I. adj. smart, resourceful II. m.f. smart cookie.

cu·car §70 tr. *(guiñar)* to wink; *(hacer burla)* to make fun of, mock.

cu·ca·ra·cha f. ENTOM. cockroach; ZOOL. wood louse, sow bug; *(tabaco)* snuff; MEX. *(tranvía)* trailer; *(coche)* jalopy, rattletrap.

cu·car·da f. *(escarapela)* cockade, rosette; *(pieza de adorno de una brida)* bridle ornament; MECH. *(martillo)* toothed finishing hammer.

cu·ca·rrón m. COL. beetle.

cu·cli·llas adv. ♦ **en c.** squatting, crouching • **ponerse** *or* **sentarse en c.** to squat, crouch.

cu·cli·llo m. ORNITH. cuckoo; FIG. *(marido de la adúltera)* cuckold.

cu·co, –ca I. adj. COLL. *(bonito)* pretty, cute; *(astuto)* clever, crafty II. m.f. *(astuto)* clever person —m. ENTOM. caterpillar; ORNITH. cuckoo; *(fantasma)* ghost, phantom; COLL. *(tahúr)* gambler; ARG., BOL. peach ♦ **cucos** panties • **hacer c. a uno** MEX. to poke fun at someone —f. see **cuca.**

cu·cú m. cuckoo (call of the cuckoo).

cu·cu·fa·to m. BOL., PERU bigot, sanctimonious person.

cu·cu·lí m. [pl. **-lí·es**] AMER. small gray dove (easily domesticated).

cu·cúr·bi·ta f. CHEM. retort; BOT. cucurbit (squash).

cu·cuy *or* **cu·cu·yo** m. var. of **cocuyo.**

cu·cha·ra f. spoon; *(cucharada)* spoonful; *(para servir)* ladle, dipper; ARTS, TECH. scoop, bucket; MARIT. bailing scoop; AMER. trowel; MEX. *(ladrón)* pickpocket; *(badila)* fire shovel ♦ **c. cafetera** teaspoon • **c. de albañil** trowel • **c. de fundición** casting ladle • **c. de palo** wooden spoon • **c. de postre** dessert spoon • **c. sopera** *or* **de sopa** soupspoon, tablespoon • **despacharse** *or* **servirse con la c. grande** FIG. to look out for number one; S. AMER. to give oneself a big helping • **hacer cucharas** AMER., FIG., COLL. to pout • **media c.** FIG., COLL. mediocre person • **meter uno su c.** FIG., COLL. to meddle, butt in.

cu·cha·ra·da f. spoonful ♦ **meter** *or* **echar uno su c.** FIG., COLL. to meddle, butt in, put one's two cents in.

cu·cha·re·ar tr. *(sacar con cuchara)* to spoon out —intr. *(revolver con la cuchara)* to stir; FIG. *(meterse en negocios ajenos)* to meddle, interfere.

cu·cha·re·te·ar intr. CUL., COLL. *(revolver)* to stir with a spoon; *(hacer ruido)* to slurp; FIG. *(entremeterse)* to meddle, interfere <*c. en todo* to meddle in everything>.

cu·cha·ri·lla f. *(cuchara pequeña)* small spoon, teaspoon; VET. liver disease (in pigs); MIN. scraper, fluke.

cu·cha·rón m. *(cuchara grande)* big spoon; *(cazo)* ladle, scoop, serving spoon; TECH. *(cubo)* bucket, scoop; ARG., ORNITH. type of wading bird ♦ **despacharse uno con el c.** FIG., COLL. to snatch *or* take the biggest part for oneself.

cu·che m. AMER. pig.

cu·che·ta f. ARG., BOL., MARIT. cabin, berth.

cu·chi·che·ar intr. to whisper.

cu·chi·che·o m. whisper, whispering.

cu·chi·lla f. *(cuchillo)* knife; *(hoja)* blade; *(de afeitar)* razor blade; FIG., COLL. *(espada)* sword; AMER. *(cumbre)* mountain crest or ridge; (cortaplumas) pocketknife, jack-knife ♦ c. de arado AGR. colter.

cu·chi·lla·da f. (golpe) stab, thrust; (herida) gash, stab wound ♦ cuchilladas SEW. (aperturas) ornamental slashes or slits; FIG. (riñas) wrangles, quarrels.

cu·chi·lla·zo m. (golpe) stab, thrust; (herida) gash, stab wound.

cu·chi·lle·rí·a f. (oficio) cutlery, knifemaking; (taller) cutler's shop.

cu·chi·lle·ro m. (persona) cutler; (abrazadera) iron ring or band; ARCHIT. cleat, wedge; AMER. troublemaker, wrangler.

cu·chi·llo m. knife <c. de monte hunting knife>; FIG. (autoridad) authority; ZOOL. lower tusk; SEW. gore, godet; ARCHIT. support, upright; ORNITH. feather; MARIT. triangular sail ♦ c. de cocina kitchen knife • c. de resorte switchblade • c. de trinchar carving knife • pasar a c. to kill.

cu·chi·pan·da f. COLL. festive dinner shared by several people; (comilona) feed.

cu·chi·tril m. COLL. (cochitril) pigsty; (agujero) hole (very small room).

cu·cho m. AGR. fertilizing mixture of manure and compost.

cu·chu·fle·ta f. COLL. (burla) joke, jest; GUAT. old shoe; MEX. type of biscuit.

cu·chu·fle·te·ro, –ra I. adj. joking II. m.f. joker, tease.

cue·ca f. popular dance of Bolivia, Peru and Chile.

cue·ce see cocer.

cue·le, cuelo see colar.

cuel·ga f. (frutas) bunch of fruit; COLL. (regalo) birthday present.

cuel·ga, cuelgue see colgar.

cuel·ga·ca·pas m. [pl. -pas] coatrack.

cue·lli·cor·to, –ta adj. short-necked.

cue·lli·er·gui·do, –da adj. stiff-necked.

cue·lli·lar·go, –ga adj. long-necked.

cue·llo m. ANAT. neck; neck <el c. de una botella the neck of a bottle>; (tira de tela) collar; BOT. stalk ♦ alargar el c. to stretch or crane one's neck • c. acanalado or alechugado or escarolado fluted collar, ruff • c. de pajarita or palomita wing collar • c. de pico V-neck • c. duro stiff collar • c. postizo detachable collar • c. romano dog collar • c. vuelto turtleneck • erguir el c. FIG. to be arrogant • hablar para el c. de su camisa FIG. to talk to oneself • levantar uno el c. COLL. to get back on one's feet • meter el c. FIG. to put one's nose to the grindstone.

cuen·ca f. (escudilla) wooden bowl; ANAT. eye socket; GEOG. (valle) valley, hollow; (hoya) river basin, watershed; MIN. field.

cuen·co m. earthenware bowl.

cuen·ta f. (nota) bill, check <le pedí la c. al mozo I asked the waiter for the bill>; (cálculo) count, calculation; (acción de contar) counting; (bolita) bead; COM. account; FIG. (explicación) account, explanation; (cargo) responsibility, business <esa tarea es c. mía that task is my responsibility>; consideration, account <tomar en c. to take into account> ♦ abonar en c. COM. to credit an account • abrir una c. COM. to open an account • a c. COM. on account • a fin de cuentas in the final analysis, when all is said and done • ajustar cuentas COLL. to settle up • caer en la c. COLL. to catch on, realize • cargar en c. COM. to debit an account • cerrar una c. COM. to close an account • c. abierta COM. active account • c. acreedora COM. credit account • c. bancaria or de banco bank account • c. corriente COM. checking account • c. de ahorros savings account • c. de gastos expense account • c. de la vieja COLL. counting on one's fingers • c. pendiente COM. outstanding account • c. por cobrar COM. account receivable • c. por pagar COM. account payable • dar c. de (contar) to relate, give an account of; COLL. (gastar) to use up <dar c. de la fortuna to use up one's fortune> • darse c. de to realize • echar cuentas to make a rough estimate • en resumidas cuentas in short, briefly • ir a cuentas COLL. to settle (a dispute) • llevar las cuentas to keep the books • más de la c. too much, more than necessary • pedir cuentas a to call to account • perder la c. de to lose track of • por c. de on behalf of • por su propia c. for oneself, on one's own account • por c. y riesgo de uno at one's

own risk • rendir cuentas de to give an account of • tener c. de to take care of • tener en c. to bear in mind • trabajar por su c. to be self-employed.

cuen·ta·go·tas m. [pl. -tas] dropper, eyedropper ♦ dar con c. FIG. to give little by little, to mete out.

cuen·ta·ki·ló·me·tros m. [pl. -tros] AUTO. odometer.

cuen·ta·rre·vo·lu·cio·nes m. [pl. -nes] revolution counter.

cuen·te, cuento see contar.

cuen·te·ar intr. C. AMER. to gossip.

cuen·te·ro, –ra I. adj. gossipy, talebearing II. m.f. gossip, gossipmonger.

cuen·tis·ta I. adj. LIT. short-story; COLL. (chismoso) gossipy, talebearing; (jactancioso) boastful, bragging II. m.f. LIT. short-story writer; COLL. (chismoso) gossip, gossipmonger; (jactancioso) boaster, braggart.

cuen·to[1] m. (relato) story, tale; LIT. short story; (cómputo) counting; COLL. (chisme) gossip; (embuste) hoax, ruse; (disgusto) upset, disagreement; MATH. million ♦ c. de fantasmas ghost story • c. de hadas fairy tale • c. del tío or del tocomocho confidence game, con game • c. de nunca acabar FIG. endless story • c. de viejas COLL. old wives' tale • dejarse or quitarse de cuentos COLL. to come to the point • ¡puro c.! all lies! • sin c. countless • traer a c. COLL. to bring up, mention • va de c. COLL. the story goes, it is said • venir a c. to be to the point • vivir del c. to live by one's wits.

cuen·to[2] m. (regatón) tip, point (of a weapon or tool); (puntal) support, prop.

cue·ra·zo m. AMER. lash, whiplash.

cuer·da I. f. (cordón) cord, string; MECH. watch spring; MUS. string <c. de violín violin string>; (extensión de la voz) range; GEOM. chord; ARCHIT. spring line; (conjunto de presos) chain gang ♦ aflojar la c. FIG. to ease up • andar en la c. floja FIG., COLL. to walk a tightrope • apretar la c. FIG. to tighten up on discipline • c. de tripa MUS. catgut • c. floja tightrope • c. guía AVIA. dragline, trail rope • cuerdas vocales ANAT. vocal cords • dar c. a uno FIG. to get someone started on a topic, encourage someone to speak • dar c. a un reloj to wind a watch • de la misma c. FIG. of the same opinion • por debajo de or bajo c. underhandedly • tirar de la c. FIG. to abuse • tocar la c. sensible FIG. to hit the right chord II. adj. see cuerdo, –da.

cuer·do, –da I. adj. (de juicio sano) sane; (prudente) prudent, sensible II. m.f. (persona de juicio sano) sane person; (persona prudente) sensible person —f. see cuerda.

cue·re·a·da f. C. AMER., COL., MEX. beating, thrashing; AMER. tanning season.

cue·re·ar tr. Amer. (azotar) to whip, lash; (desollar) to skin, flay; (adobar) to tan (hides); ARG., FIG. (criticar) to denigrate, slander.

cue·ri·za f. AMER., COLL. beating, thrashing.

cuer·na f. (cuerno de vaca) drinking horn; (cuerno) horns, antlers; (trompa de cuerno) hunting horn.

cuer·no m. ZOOL. horn; ENTOM. feeler, antenna; MUS. horn; MIL. flank; FIG. (extremidad) tip, horn ♦ ¡cuerno! oh my goodness! • c. de la abundancia horn of plenty, cornucopia • ¡cuernos! MEX. fat chance!, no way! • en los cuernos del toro FIG., COLL. in imminent danger • levantar hasta or poner en los cuernos de la luna COLL. to praise to the skies • poner los cuernos a to cuckold • saber or oler a c. quemado COLL. to be fishy or suspicious • ¡vete al c.! go to hell!

cue·ro m. ZOOL. skin, hide; leather <una chaqueta de c. a leather jacket>; (odre) wineskin; COLL. skunk <borracho como un c. drunk as a skunk>; S. AMER. (látigo) whip; (prostituta) prostitute; COL. old maid; CUBA old woman; ECUAD., MEX. mistress; CUBA, GUAT. impudence, nerve ♦ arrastrar en c. VEN. to brag, boast • arrimar el c. or dar c. AMER. to whip, flog • c. cabelludo scalp • c. charolado patent leather • en cueros naked.

cue·pe·ar intr. AMER. (esquivar) to swerve, dodge; FIG. (eludir) to shirk, avoid an obligation.

cuer·po m. body; (substancia) substance, matter; ANAT. (tronco) trunk, torso; figure, build <los atletas tienen buen c. athletes have good builds>; length <el caballo ganó por cuatro cuerpos the horse won by four lengths>; (cadáver) corpse, body; SEW. (corpiño) bodice; (volumen) volume, book; FIG. main part, body <el c. del libro the main part

of the book>; *(colección)* body, corpus <*c. de leyes* body of laws>; corps, staff <*c. diplomático* diplomatic corps>; MIL. corps <*c. de ejército* army corps>; *(espesor)* thickness, body; *(parte)* unit, component; PRINT. type size; GEOM. three-dimensional figure ♦ **a c. de rey** FIG. like a king <*el dictador vive a c. de rey* the dictator lives like a king> • **c. a c.** hand-to-hand (combat) • **c. celeste** ASTRON. heavenly body • **c. compuesto** CHEM. compound • **c. de baile** dance company • **c. de bomberos** fire department • **c. del delito** LAW corpus delicti • **C. de Paz** Peace Corps • **c. muerto** MARIT. mooring buoy • **c. simple** CHEM. element • **c. volante** MIL. flying column • **dar con el c. en la tierra** to fall down • **dar c. a** to thicken • **de c. entero** full-length <*un espejo de c. entero* a full-length mirror>; *(auténtico)* real, true <*es un hombre de c. entero* he is a real man> • **de medio c.** half-length • **en c. y alma** FIG., COLL. body and soul, wholeheartedly • **estar de c. presente** to lie in state • **hacer del c.** COLL. to relieve oneself • **tomar c.** to take shape.

cue·ru·do, –da adj. AMER. slow, sluggish (horse); C. AMER. shameless, brazen.

cuer·vo m. ORNITH. crow, raven; AMER. *(iribú)* urubu, black vulture ♦ **c. marino** cormorant • **c. merendero** rook, jackdaw.

cues·co m. *(hueso de la fruta)* pit, stone; COLL. *(pedo)* loud fart; CHILE man in love; MEX. large lump of mineral.

cues·ta f. slope, hill ♦ **a cuestas** on one's shoulders <*llevó el fardo a cuestas* he carried the bundle on his shoulders>; FIG. upon oneself <*me eché la responsabilidad a cuestas* I took the responsibility upon myself> • **c. abajo** downhill • **c. arriba** uphill • **hacérsele c. arriba** FIG., COLL. to find it hard to • **ir c. abajo** FIG. to decline, go downhill.

cues·ta, cueste see costar.

cues·ta·ción f. collection (for charity).

cues·tión f. question, issue <*es una c. candente* it is a burning issue>; question, matter <*es una c. de fe* it is a matter of faith>; *(duda)* dispute, controversy; MATH. problem ♦ **c. de derecho** LAW issue in law • **c. de gabinete** affair of state • **en c.** in question, at issue • **en c. de** in the matter of • **es c. de** it is a question of.

cues·tio·na·ble adj. questionable, debatable.

cues·tio·nar tr. to discuss, debate —intr. to argue.

cues·tio·na·rio m. *(encuesta)* questionnaire; *(examen)* test questions; *(interrogatorio)* interrogation.

cues·tor m. HIST. *(antiguo magistrado)* quaestor (Roman official); *(solicitador)* solicitor of alms.

cue·to m. inaccessible peak, fortified peak.

cue·va f. *(gruta)* cave, grotto; *(sótano)* basement, cellar ♦ **c. de ladrones** COLL. den of thieves.

cué·va·no m. *(cesto grande)* large basket, pannier; *(cesto)* small straw basket strapped to the back.

cue·za, cuezo see cocer.

cui·da·do m. care <*él se vistió con c.* he dressed with care>; caution <*manejé con c.* I drove with caution>; *(miedo)* concern, apprehension; care, charge <*lo voy a dejar a su c.* I am going to leave it in your care> ♦ **al c. de** in the care of • **con c.** *(con esmero)* carefully; *(con cautela)* cautiously; • **¡cuidado!** be careful!, watch out! • **c. con** look out for, beware of <*¡c. con el perro!* beware of the dog!> • **estar de c.** *(enfermo)* to be seriously ill; *(peligroso)* to be dangerous • **perder c.** not to worry • **poner c. en** to take care in • **sin c.** carelessly • **tener c.** to be careful.

cui·da·dor, –do·ra I. adj. caretaking II. m.f. caretaker, custodian —m. SPORT. *(entrenador)* trainer; ARG. male nurse.

cui·da·do·so, –sa adj. *(cauteloso)* careful, cautious; *(atento)* attentive, vigilant.

cui·dar tr. to look after, take care of —intr. ♦ **c. de** to look after, take care of —reflex. to take care of oneself ♦ **cuidarse de** to care about, worry about <*ella no se cuida de lo que digan* she does not care about what they may say>; *(protegerse)* to be careful about.

cui·ta f. *(aflicción)* grief, anxiety; C. AMER. bird dropping.

cui·ta·do, –da adj. *(afligido)* anxious, worried; *(apocado)* bashful, shy.

cu·ja f. *(bolsita de cuero)* lance bucket or holder (on a saddle); *(armadura de la cama)* bedstead; AMER. bed; PERU

coffin; MEX. wrapping (of a parcel); HOND., MEX. envelope.

cu·lan·tri·llo m. BOT. maidenhair, maidenhair fern.

cu·lan·tro m. BOT. coriander.

cu·la·ta f. ZOOL. haunch, hindquarters; *(del caballo)* croup; *(del arma)* butt (of a gun); *(del cañón)* breech (of a cannon); *(tornillo)* breech screw; FIG. *(posterior)* rear, back; MECH. cylinder head; ELEC. armature; ECUAD. gable wall ♦ **salir el tiro por la c.** FIG. to backfire.

cu·la·ta·zo m. *(golpe)* blow with a gun butt; ARM. *(coz)* kick, recoil.

cu·le·bra f. ZOOL. snake; *(de alambique)* coil (of a still); FIG., COLL. *(alboroto)* disturbance, din; *(broma)* trick, practical joke; MARIT. cable, line; COL., ECUAD., PERU debt, bill; MEX. waterspout ♦ **c. de anteojos** cobra • **c. de cascabel** rattlesnake • **hacer c.** to zigzag, slither.

cu·le·bra·zo m. practical joke, trick.

cu·le·bre·ar intr. to snake, zigzag, wind.

cu·le·bri·lla f. MED. ringworm; *(papel)* silk or tissue paper; ARM. *(grieta)* split, crack (in a gun barrel) ♦ **c. de agua** water snake.

cu·le·ro, –ra I. adj. lazy, sluggish II. m. *(pañal)* diaper; AMER. miner's leather belt —f. *(mancha)* diaper stain; *(remiendo)* patch (on seat of pants).

cu·lí m. coolie.

cu·li·na·rio, –ria adj. culinary, pertaining to cooking.

cul·mi·na·ción f. culmination.

cul·mi·nan·te adj. *(elevado)* culminating, highest; FIG. *(sobresaliente)* outstanding.

cul·mi·nar intr. to culminate.

cu·lo m. VULG. *(parte posterior)* butt, ass; FIG. *(extremidad posterior de una cosa)* bottom; FIG., COLL. *(fondo de líquido)* dregs (of liquid in a glass); ANAT. anus ♦ **c. de pajarero** bare-bottomed, bare-assed • **c. de mal asiento** COLL. restless or fidgety person • **c. de pollo** ill-mended part in clothes, bulge, pucker • **c. de vaso** imitation precious stone.

cu·lom·bio m. PHYS. coulomb.

cul·pa f. *(falta)* fault; *(responsabilidad)* blame, guilt <*no le alcanza la c.* no blame attaches to him> ♦ **por c. de** through the fault of • **echar la c. a uno** to blame someone • **tener la c.** to be to blame, be guilty.

cul·pa·bi·li·dad f. guilt.

cul·pa·bi·li·zar §04 tr. to accuse, blame.

cul·pa·ble I. adj. *(que tiene culpa)* guilty, culpable; *(acusado)* accused ♦ **confesarse c.** to plead guilty • **declarar c.** to find guilty II. m.f. *(reo)* culprit; *(acusado)* accused (party).

cul·pa·ción f. blaming, inculpation.

cul·pa·do, –da I. past part. see culpar II. adj. *(que tiene culpa)* guilty, culpable; *(acusado)* accused III. m.f. *(reo)* culprit; *(acusado)* accused (party).

cul·par tr. *(acusar)* to blame, accuse; *(censurar)* to censure, criticize —reflex. to blame oneself, take the blame.

cul·te·ra·nis·mo m. LIT. euphuism, Gongorism.

cul·ti·par·lar intr. to speak in an affected manner.

cul·tis·mo m. *(culteranismo)* euphuism, Gongorism; *(palabra)* learned or scholarly word.

cul·ti·va·ble adj. cultivatable, arable.

cul·ti·va·ción f. cultivation.

cul·ti·va·dor, –do·ra I. adj. cultivating II. m.f. cultivator.

cul·ti·var tr. *(arar)* to cultivate, farm <*c. la tierra* to farm the land>; *(plantar)* to grow <*c. cereales* to grow grain>; FIG. *(entregarse)* to dedicate oneself to; *(desarrollar)* to develop, cultivate <*c. amistades* to cultivate friendships>; BIOL. to culture; *(entrenar)* to train, develop (memory).

cul·ti·vo m. *(labor)* cultivation, growing; *(cosecha)* crop; BIOL. culture ♦ **caldo de c.** culture fluid • **c. de hortalizas** market gardening • **c. de regadío** irrigation farming • **poner en c.** to cultivate.

cul·to, –ta I. adj. *(civilizado)* cultured, refined; FIG. *(afectado)* affected; learned, scholarly <*palabra c.* learned word>; AGR. cultivated II. m. RELIG. *(secto)* cult; *(religión)* religion; *(homenaje)* worship; *(rito)* ritual; FIG. *(admiración)* admiration ♦ **c. de la personalidad** personality cult • **c. de dulía** worship of angels and saints • **c. externo** external ritual • **c. indebido** superstitious ritual • **c. interno** personal worship, faith • **c. superfluo** empty ritual • **rendir c. a** to worship; FIG. *(homenajear)* to pay homage *or* tribute to.

cul·tu·ra f. *(civilización)* culture; *(educación)* refinement, breeding; *(cultivo)* cultivation.

cul·tu·ral adj. cultural.

cum·bre m. *(cima)* summit, crest; FIG. *(culminación)* height, pinnacle.

cum·bre·ra f. *(cumbre)* summit, top; *(cima)* peak; CARP. large beam; ARCHIT. *(dintel)* lintel; *(hilera)* ridgepole.

cúm·pla·se m. *(fórmula)* official approval; CHILE writ of execution (of a judgment).

cum·ple·a·ños m. [pl. **-ños**] birthday ◆ **feliz c.** happy birthday.

cum·pli·de·ro, -ra adj. *(que ha de cumplir)* expiring; *(conveniente)* convenient, suitable.

cum·pli·do, -da I. past part. see **cumplir II.** adj. *(completo)* complete; *(abundante)* full, ample; *(perfecto)* perfect <*un caballero c.* a perfect gentleman>; *(confiable)* trustworthy, reliable; *(cortés)* courteous, polite **III.** m. *(cortesía)* courtesy, polite gesture; *(piropo)* compliment.

cum·pli·dor, -do·ra I. adj. *(confiable)* trustworthy, reliable; *(cortés)* courteous, polite **II.** m.f. *(persona confiable)* reliable person; *(persona cortés)* courteous person.

cum·pli·men·tar tr. *(felicitar)* to congratulate; *(hacer visita a)* to pay one's respects to; LAW *(ejecutar)* to execute, carry out.

cum·pli·mien·to m. fulfillment <*el c. de una promesa* the fulfillment of a promise>; *(cortesía)* courtesy, polite gesture; *(piropo)* compliment, formality <*lo llamaré por c.* I will call him as a formality>.

cum·plir tr. to carry out, realize <*c. una amenaza* to carry out a threat>; to fulfill, keep <*c. la palabra* to keep one's word>; to be, reach <*hoy cumple doce años* today he is twelve years of age>; *(obedecer)* to obey, observe (laws); CRIMIN. to serve (a sentence) —intr. to do one's duty, fulfill one's obligations; MIL. to complete one's military service; *(terminar)* to expire, end; COM. to fall due; to behoove, be proper to <*le cumple llegar a tiempo* it behooves him to arrive on time> ◆ **c. con** to fulfill <*c. con una promesa* to fulfill a promise>; to fulfill one's obligations to <*c. con Dios* to fulfill one's obligations to God> • **c. uno por otro** to pay another's respects <*cumpla usted por mí* pay my respects> • **por c.** as a formality —reflex. to be fulfilled; COM. to fall due.

cu·mu·lar tr. to accumulate.

cu·mu·la·ti·vo, -va adj. cumulative.

cú·mu·lo m. *(montón)* heap, pile; *(nube)* cumulus; FIG. *(gran cantidad)* load, great quantity.

cu·na f. *(cama)* cradle; *(inclusa)* foundling hospital; *(puente)* rope bridge; FIG. *(origen)* origin, stock <*de c. humilde* of humble stock>; *(lugar de nacimiento)* birthplace; ZOOL. space between animal's horns ◆ **canción de c.** lullaby.

cun·di·do I. past part. see **cundir II.** m. CUL. sandwich spread.

cun·dir intr. *(extenderse)* to spread <*la noticia cundió* the news spread>; *(inflar)* to swell, expand <*el arroz cunde al cocerse* rice expands when cooked>; *(adelantar)* to progress, make headway; FIG. *(rendir)* to yield, deliver ◆ **cunde la voz que** rumor hast it that.

cu·ne·ar tr. to rock (a cradle) —reflex. FIG., COLL. to rock, sway.

cu·nei·for·me adj. cuneiform, wedge-shaped; BOT. cuneate, wedge-shaped.

cú·ne·o m. HIST. cuneus (space between two vomitories in Roman amphitheaters); MIL. triangular formation of troops.

cu·ne·ro, -ra I. adj. *(expósito)* foundling; TAUR. of unknown stock; FIG. *(de autoría desconocida)* of unknown authorship; POL. alien (said of a little-known representative elected with the support of the government) **II.** m.f. foundling.

cu·ne·ta f. *(de un foso)* ditch; *(de una calle)* gutter; *(arcén)* shoulder, curb.

cu·ña f. *(calza)* wedge; *(adoquín)* wedge-shaped paving stone; FIG. *(apoyo)* help, support; *(palanca)* pull, influence; ANAT. cuneiform *or* tarsal bone; PRINT. quoin; S. AMER., COLL. big shot; CARIB., C. AMER. two-seater car;

COL., RAD. advertisement, plug ◆ **meter c.** to sow discord • **no hay peor c. que la del mismo palo** a person's worst enemies are often those of his own home • **tener cuñas** ARG., CHILE to have pull *or* influence.

cu·ña·do, -da m. brother-in-law —f. sister-in-law.

cu·ñe·te m. small barrel, keg.

cu·ño m. *(troquel)* die; *(impresión)* stamp, impression; FIG. *(huella)* stamp, mark <*el trabajo muestra el c. del artesano* the work shows the mark of the artisan> ◆ **de nuevo c.** new, modern.

cuo·cien·te m. var. of **cociente**.

cuo·ta f. *(parte)* quota, share; *(pago)* fee, dues ◆ **c. de admisión** admission fee • **c. del gremio** union dues.

cu·pé m. AUTO. coupé.

cu·pi·do m. FIG. young Casanova ◆ **C.** MYTH. Cupid, god of love.

cu·pie·ra, cupo see **caber**.

cup·lé m. popular song, variety song.

cu·po m. *(cuota)* quota, share; MIL. contingent, quota; AMER. capacity, room; MEX., COLL. jail.

cu·pón m. coupon.

cú·pri·co, -ca adj. CHEM. cupric, pertaining to copper.

cu·pri·ta f. MIN. cuprite.

cu·pro·so, -sa adj. CHEM. cuprous.

cú·pu·la f. ARCHIT. dome, cupola; BOT. shell, cupule; MARIT. turret ◆ **c. de vapor** *or* **caldera** GEOL. steam dome.

cu·qué, cuque see **cucar**.

cu·qui·llo m. ORNITH. cuckoo.

cu·ra¹ m. RELIG. vicar, parish priest; COLL. *(sacerdote)* Catholic priest; *(saliva)* spray; COL., VEN. avocado ◆ **c. de almas** *or* **de parroco** parish priest • **c. de misa y olla** COLL. ignorant priest • **c. económo** substitute parish priest • **este c.** FIG., COLL. yours truly (the speaker).

cu·ra² f. MED. *(curación)* cure, treatment; *(apósito)* dressing, bandage; CHILE drunkenness ◆ **alargar la c.** FIG. to prolong (business) for one's own profit • **c. de almas** RELIG. care of souls • **curas médicas** medical care • **encarecer la c.** FIG. to exaggerate one's efforts • **no tener c.** COLL. to be incorrigible • **ponerse en c.** MED. to begin treatment • **primera c.** first aid • **tener c.** MED. to be curable.

cu·ra·ble adj. curable.

cu·ra·ca m. ARG., CHILE, PERU Indian chief, headman.

cu·ra·ción f. cure, treatment.

cu·ra·di·llo m. ICHTH. codfish.

cu·ra·do, -da I. past part. see **curar II.** adj. FIG. *(endurecido)* hardened, inured; *(curtido)* tanned; TECH. cured; AMER., COLL. drunk, pickled ◆ **estoy c. de espanto** nothing can shock me anymore.

cu·ra·dor, -do·ra I. adj. curing, healing **II.** m.f. *(guardián)* caretaker; LAW guardian; CUL. curer; *(charlatán)* quack, healer ◆ **c. ad bona** *or* **ad hoc** LAW guardian of an invalid • **c. ad litem** LAW guardian of a minor.

cu·ra·du·rí·a f. guardianship, tutorship.

cu·ran·de·rí·a f. MED. quackery.

cu·ran·de·ris·mo m. MED. quackery.

cu·ran·de·ro, -ra m.f. MED. quack.

cu·rar intr. ◆ **c. de** MED. *(sanar)* to recover from; *(hacer caso)* to take notice of, heed —tr. MED. *(sanar)* to cure; *(tratar)* to treat; *(vendar)* to dress (a wound); FIG. *(remediar)* to remedy; to soothe, heal <*c. el alma* to soothe the soul>; *(curtir)* to tan, dress; *(madera)* to season (wood); CUL. *(conservar)* to cure; TEX. *(tela)* to bleach ◆ **c. al humo** to smoke (meat) ◆ **c. en salud** to recover from an illness before it becomes serious —reflex. *(recobrarse)* to recover, get well; *(sanarse)* to heal; CHILE, COLL. to get drunk.

cu·ra·re m. curare.

cu·ra·te·la f. guardianship, tutorship.

cu·ra·ti·vo, -va adj. & f. curative.

cu·ra·to m. RELIG. *(cargo de cura de almas)* curacy; *(parroquia)* parish.

Cu·ra·za·o *or* **Cu·ra·ça·o** m. Curaçao.

cur·cu·cho, -cha adj. AMER. hunchbacked.

cúr·cu·ma f. curcuma, turmeric.

cur·da COLL. m. *(persona)* drunk —f. *(borrachera)* drunkenness, drunk ◆ **coger una c.** to get drunk.

cu·ria f. HIST. curia; *(tribunal)* tribunal, court; LAW bar, legal profession ♦ **C. Romana** Curia Romana.
cu·rial I. adj. curial II. m. Officer of the Curia Romana.
cu·rio m. CHEM. curium.
cu·rio·se·ar COLL. intr. *(andar husmeando)* to snoop, pry; *(callejear)* to look *or* wander around —tr. *(fisgonear)* to pry *or* nose into.
cu·rio·si·dad f. curiosity, inquisitiveness <*despertar la c. de uno* to arouse one's curiosity>; *(indiscreción)* indiscretion; *(limpieza)* neatness, cleanliness; *(cuidado)* care, carefulness; *(cosa curiosa)* curio, curiosity ♦ **curiosidades** sights, attractions.
cu·rio·so, –sa I. adj. *(entremetido)* curious, inquisitive; *(indiscreto)* indiscreet; *(limpio)* neat, clean; *(cuidadoso)* careful; *(excepcional)* odd, curious II. m.f. *(entremetido)* curious person, busybody; *(espectador)* onlooker, spectator; AMER. witch doctor.
cu·rri·cu·lum vi·tae m. resumé, curriculum vitae.
cu·rru·ta·co, –ca I. adj. *(alechuguinado)* dandyish; AMER. *(regordete)* chubby, plump II. m.f. *(galán)* dandy, dude ♦ **currutacos** C. AMER. diarrhea.
cur·sa·do, –da I. past part. see **cursar** II. adj. skilled, versed.
cur·san·te I. adj. frequenting II. m. student, pupil.
cur·sar tr. *(estudiar)* to study, take (a course) <*c. teología* to study theology>; *(dar curso a)* to dispatch, attend to; *(frecuentar)* to frequent.
cur·si I. adj. *(presumido)* affected, pretentious; *(de mal gusto)* tasteless, cheap II. m.f. affected *or* pretentious person.
cur·si·le·rí·a s. pretentiousness, snobbery.
cur·si·llo m. *(curso corto)* short course; *(serie de conferencias)* series of lectures.
cur·si·vo, –va I. adj. cursive, running; PRINT. italic II. f. cursive script; PRINT. italics.
cur·so m. course, flow <*el c. del río* the course of the river>; *(dirección)* direction, course; FIG. course <*en el c. de la vida* in the course of a lifetime>; EDUC. course, subject <*tomé un c. de física* I took a physics course>; ASTRON. course, route; FIN. currency, circulation ♦ **c. acelerado** crash course • **c. por correspondencia** correspondence course • **dar libre c. a** to give free rein • **en c.** under way, in process • **tener c. legal** FIN. to be legal tender.
cur·ti·do I. past part. see **curtir** II. m. tanning ♦ **curtidos** tanned leather.
cur·ti·dor m. tanner.
cur·ti·du·rí·a f. tannery.
cur·tiem·bre m. *(proceso)* tanning; AMER. tannery.
cur·tien·te I. adj. tanning, curing II. m. tanning agent.
cur·ti·mien·to m. tanning, curing.
cur·tir tr. *(adobar)* to tan (hides); *(broncear)* to tan, bronze; *(acostumbrar)* to inure, harden —reflex. *(broncearse)* to become tanned; *(por la intemperie)* to become weather-beaten; *(acostumbrarse)* to become inured *or* hardened; AMER. to get dirty.
cur·va I. f. *(línea)* curve; *(recodo)* curve, bend (in a road); MARIT. knee ♦ **c. acampanada** bell curve • **c. cerrada** sharp curve • **c. de enlace** RAIL. connecting curve • **c. de frecuencias acumuladas** frequency curve • **c. de nivel** TOP. contour line • **c. en herradura** hairpin curve • **c. inversa** RAIL. reverse curve • **c. isóbata** TOP. depth contour • **c. isócora** PHYS. isochor, isochore • **c. sedástica** sedastic curve • **c. sinusoidal** MATH. sine curve • **c. suave** easy curve II. adj. see **curvo, -va.**
cur·va·do, –da I. past part. see **curvar** II. adj. curved, bent.
cur·var tr. to curve, bend.
cur·va·tu·ra f. *(recodo)* curvature, bend; *(acción)* curving, bending.
cur·ve·ar intr. to curve.
cur·vi·lí·ne·o, –a adj. GEOM. curvilinear.
cur·vo, –va I. adj. *(curvado)* curved, bent; COL. bow-legged; P. RICO left-handed II. f. see **curva.**
cus·cu·rro or **cus·cu·rrón** m. crust of bread.
cus·ma f. ECUAD., PERU sleeveless wool shirt worn by the Indians.
cús·pi·de f. *(cima)* summit, peak; FIG. *(culminación)* height, pinnacle; ANAT., BOT. cusp; MATH. apex.

cus·to·dia f. *(vigilia)* custody, care; *(persona)* custodian; RELIG. *(pieza)* monstrance; *(tabernáculo)* tabernacle ♦ **c. preventiva** protective custody.
cus·to·diar tr. *(cuidar)* to look after, take care of; *(vigilar)* to guard, watch over; *(proteger)* to protect, defend.
cus·to·dio I. adj. guardian <*ángel c.* guardian angel> II. m. guardian, custodian.
cu·tá·ne·o, –a adj. cutaneous, skin.
cú·ter m. MARIT. cutter.
cu·tí·cu·la f. cuticle.
cu·tis m. [pl. **-tis**] skin, complexion.
cuy m. AMER. guinea pig; ECUAD. rocket, firecracker.
cu·yo, –ya §G42 rel. pron. whose, of whom <*mi padre, cuyas costumbres bien conoces, se enojó mucho* my father, whose habits you well know, got very angry>; whose, of which <*una casa cuyos cuartos son inmensos* a house whose rooms are immense>.
▲ *cuyo, -ya* refers to both persons and things. In number and gender it agrees with the noun it identifies and not with its antecedent <*mi padre, cuyas costumbres bien conoces, se enojó mucho*>.

CH

ch, Ch f. fourth letter of the Spanish alphabet.
cha·ba·ca·ne·ar intr. to behave in a coarse *or* crude way.
cha·ba·ca·ne·rí·a f. *(falta de gusto)* tastelessness, vulgarity; *(grosería)* coarse *or* crude thing.
cha·ba·ca·no, –na I. adj. *(sin gusto)* tasteless, vulgar; *(grosero)* coarse, crude; *(mal hecho)* shoddy, sloppy II. m. MEX., BOT. species of apricot tree.
cha·bo·la f. *(caseta)* hut, shed; *(de un pobre)* shanty ♦ **las chabolas** shantytown.
cha·bo·lis·mo m. NEOL. shantytown, slum.
cha·cal m. ZOOL. jackal.
chá·ca·ra f. AMER. small farm; COL., VEN. large leather bag; C. AMER., COLL. sore.
cha·ca·re·ro, –ra I. adj. AMER. farming, peasant II. m.f. AMER. *(campesino)* farmer, peasant; COL. *(curandero)* quack —f. ARG., BOL., URUG. *(baile)* peasant dance.
cha·ci·na f. CUL. spiced pork.
cha·ci·ne·rí·a f. sausage shop.
cha·ci·ne·ro, –ra m.f. pork butcher.
cha·co m. AMER. Indian style of hunting.
cha·co·lo·te·ar intr. to clatter (said of horseshoe).
cha·co·lo·te·o m. clattering (of a horseshoe).
cha·co·ta f. *(bulla)* merriment, fun; *(burla)* ridicule, making fun ♦ **echar a ch.** *or* **hacer ch. de** to make fun of, ridicule • **estar de ch.** to be in a joking mood • **tomar a ch.** *(burlarse de)* to make fun of; *(tomar a broma)* to take as a joke.
cha·co·te·ar intr. *(burlarse)* to joke, kid; *(divertirse)* to have fun.
cha·co·te·o m. joking, kidding.
cha·co·te·ro, –ra I. adj. joking, kidding II. m.f. joker, kidder.
cha·cra f. AMER. farm.
cha·cua·co I. m. MIN. poorly made furnace; C. AMER. cigarette butt II. adj. *(chapucero)* clumsy, careless; DOM. REP., URUG. country bumpkin.
chá·cha·ra f. COLL. *(charla)* chatter, small talk; ECUAD. joke ♦ **cháchara**s trinkets, baubles • **estar de ch.** to chatter, make small talk.
cha·cha·re·ar intr. COLL. *(charlar)* to chatter, babble —tr. MEX. to sell, deal in.
cha·cha·re·ro, –ra I. adj. COLL. chattering, talkative II. m.f. COLL. *(charlatán)* chatterbox; MEX. trinket peddler.
cha·cho, –cha m. COLL. *(muchacho)* kid —f. COLL. *(muchacha)* girl, kid —m.f. MEX. servant; HOND. twin.
Chad m. Chad.
cha·dia·no —na adj. & m.f. Chadian.
cha·fal·di·ta f. COLL. joke, jest.
cha·fal·me·jas m.f. COLL. dauber, unskilled painter.

cha·fa·lo·ní·a f. scrap silver *or* gold.

cha·fa·llar tr. COLL. to botch, make a mess of (a repair).

cha·fa·llo m. COLL. botched repair job.

cha·fa·llón, –llo·na COLL. I. adj. slapdash, careless II. m.f. careless worker.

cha·far tr. *(aplastar)* to flatten, plaster down; *(la ropa)* to crease, rumple (clothes); FIG., COLL. *(deslucir)* to spoil, ruin; *(en una discusión)* to squelch; CHILE to fling, throw.

cha·fa·ro·te m. *(alfanje)* short wide cutlass; COLL. *(espada)* broadsword; GUAT. ignorant *or* uneducated military officer.

cha·fa·rri·na·da f. stain, blot.

cha·fa·rri·nar tr. to stain, spot.

cha·flán m. CARP. bevel, chamfer; *(esquina)* cant (of a building) ◆ **de ch.** VEN. obliquely.

cha·fla·nar tr. CARP. to bevel, camfer.

cha·gra I. m. ECUAD. farmer, peasant —f. CUBA shoemaker's knife; COL., ECUAD. small farm II. adj. ECUAD. boorish, uncouth.

cha·gua·lón m. COL., BOT. incense tree.

cha·guar¹ §10tr. ARG. to wring out (wet clothes).

cha·guar² m. AMER. kind of fiber rope.

cha·gua·ra·ma f. C. AMER., BOT. royal palm.

cha·huist·le m. BOT. rust, blight.

chai·na f. PERU, ORNITH. goldfinch; MUS. reed flute.

chai·ra f. *(cuchilla)* shoemaker's knife; *(afilador)* knife sharpener; BOL., CUL. meat and potato stew.

cha·já m. ARG., ORNITH. crested screamer.

chal m. shawl.

cha·la f. AMER. *(farfolla)* corn husk *or* shuck; ARG., COLL. *(dinero)* dough, money ◆ **pelarle la ch. a uno** to rob someone.

cha·lán, –la·na I. adj. horse-trading II. m.f. *(comerciante)* horse dealer *or* trader —m. AMER. horse trainer —f. see **chalana**.

cha·la·na I. f. MARIT. barge, flat-bottomed boat II. adj. see **chalán, –lana**.

cha·la·ne·ar intr. *(negociar)* to wheel and deal, make horse trades —tr. AMER., COLL. to break horses; ARG. to humiliate, jeer at; C. AMER. to play a joke on.

cha·la·ne·o m. *(en los negocios)* wheeling and dealing, horse trading; AMER., COLL. horse breaking.

cha·la·ne·rí·a f. tricks, wiles.

cha·la·nes·co, –ca adj. wily, sharp.

cha·lar tr. to drive mad *or* crazy —reflex. to fall head over heels in love.

cha·le·co m. vest ◆ **ch. antibalas** bulletproof vest • **ch. de fuerza** AMER. straitjacket • **ch. salvavidas** life jacket.

cha·let m. [pl. **-lets**] *(casa)* chalet, cottage; *(de playa)* bungalow, beach house; *(de lujo)* villa.

cha·li·na f. *(corbata)* cravat; AMER. *(chal)* narrow shawl.

cha·lón m. ARG., CHILE shawl.

cha·lo·na f. ARG., BOL., PERU jerked *or* salted mutton.

cha·lo·te m. BOT. shallot.

cha·lu·pa f. MARIT. launch, boat; AMER. small canoe; MEX. corn tortilla.

cha·ma f. SL. swap, trade.

cha·ma·co, –ca m.f. CARIB., MEX. kid, youngster.

cha·ma·da f. *(leña)* brushwood; SP. run of bad luck.

cha·mal m. ARG., BOL., CHILE blanket worn by Indians.

cha·mar tr. SL. to swap, trade.

chá·ma·ra *or* **cha·ma·ras·ca** f. *(leña)* brushwood; *(llama)* brushfire.

cha·ma·ri·le·ar intr. to swap, barter.

cha·ma·ri·le·o m. swapping, trading.

cha·ma·ri·le·ro, –ra m.f. junk dealer.

cha·ma·rra f. *(chaquetón)* coarse cloth jacket; C. AMER., VEN. blanket; C. AMER. fraud, swindle.

cha·ma·rre·ar tr. C. AMER. to swindle, cheat.

cha·ma·rre·ta f. short and loose jacket.

cham·ba f. COLL. *(chiripa)* fluke, lucky break; ARG., ECUAD. turf, sod; MEX. ditch; MEX. job, employment; BOL., MIN. natural zinc sulfate ◆ **de** *or* **por ch.** by a fluke.

cham·be·ar intr. ECUAD. to fill in land with sod; COL. to shave, trim —intr. COL., ECUAD. to go through the grasslands; MEX. to work, do a job.

cham·be·lán m. chamberlain.

cham·ber·go m. broad-brimmed soft hat.

cham·be·ro, –ra m.f. MEX. itinerant worker.

cham·bón, –bo·na COLL. I. adj. *(torpe)* awkward, clumsy; *(afortunado)* lucky II. m.f. *(chapucero)* bungler, botcher; *(jugador)* unskilled but lucky player.

cham·bo·na·da f. COLL. *(torpeza)* awkwardness, clumsiness; *(chiripa)* fluke, stroke of luck; AMER. bungle, blunder.

cham·bo·ne·ar intr. *(ganar)* to win by a fluke; AMER. to bungle, blunder.

cham·bra f. *(vestidura)* camisole; VEN. tumult, uproar.

cha·mi·co m. BOT. thorn apple, Jimson weed ◆ **dar ch. a** FIG. to bewitch, seduce.

cha·mi·za f. BOT. chamiso; *(leña)* brushwood.

cha·mi·zar §04 tr. to thatch (with chamiso).

cha·mi·zo m. *(leño quemado)* half-burnt log; *(choza)* thatched hut; FIG., COLL. *(garito)* joint, hangout.

cha·mo·rro, –rra adj. *(una persona)* shorn, clipped; AGR. beardless (wheat).

cham·pa f. CHILE, PERU sod, turf; AMER. tangle, snarl; ECUAD., BOT. agave, century plant; C. AMER. palm leaf tent; GUAT. primitive hut.

cham·pán m. *(vino)* champagne; AMER. sampan (barge).

cham·pa·ña m. champagne.

cham·par tr. COLL. to say something unpleasant to someone.

cham·pe·ar tr. CHILE, ECUAD., PERU to fill with sod.

cham·pi·ñón m. mushroom, champignon.

cham·po·la f. C. AMER., CUBA, CUL. drink made from custard apple pulp.

cham·pú m. [pl. **-pú·es** *or* **-pús**] shampoo.

cham·pu·rra·do I. past part. see **champurrar** II. m. *(coctel)* mixture of liquors, cocktail; MEX. *(bebida)* chocolate flavored drink; FIG. *(mezcolanza)* hodgepodge, mess.

cham·pu·rrar tr. COLL. to mix (drinks).

cham·pu·rro m. COLL. mixed drink.

cham·pús *or* **cham·puz** m. ECUAD., PERU, CUL. cornmeal mush flavored with orange juice and sugar.

cha·mu·chi·na f. AMER. crowd, throng; ECUAD., VEN. fight, quarrel; ARG., HOND., MEX. rabble, riffraff; BOL. trifle, nonsense.

cha·mu·llar intr. SL. to talk, speak.

cha·mus·car §70 tr. *(quemar)* to singe, scorch; MEX. to sell cheaply —reflex. *(quemarse)* to get singed *or* scorched; COL. to become furious.

cha·mus·qui·na f. *(acción de chamuscar)* burning, scorching; FIG. *(riña)* fight, quarrel ◆ **oler a ch.** to look like trouble, smell fishy.

cha·na·da f. COLL. trick, ruse.

chan·ca·do·ra f. AMER., MIN. crusher, grinder.

chan·car §70 tr. AMER. to crush, grind.

chan·ce m. AMER. *(oportunidad)* chance, opportunity; *(suerte)* good luck.

chan·ce·ar intr. & reflex. to joke, fool around ◆ **chancearse de uno** to make fun of someone.

chan·ci·ller m. var. of **canciller**.

chan·ci·lle·rí·a f. *(tribunal)* chancery; *(derechos)* chancellor's fees.

chan·cle·ta m.f. COLL. *(inepto)* good-for-nothing, nincompoop —f. *(zapatilla)* slipper; AMER., COLL. baby girl ◆ **largar la ch.** CUBA, COLL. to kick the bucket.

chan·cle·ta·zo m. blow *or* spanking with a slipper.

chan·cle·te·ar intr. to shuffle about, drag around (in slippers); CUBA to flee.

chan·cle·te·o m. noise *or* shuffle of slippers.

chan·cle·te·ro, –ra adj. CARIB., COL., MEX. of low social status.

chan·clo m. *(zueco)* clog, thick-soled overshoe; *(zapato de goma)* rubber overshoe, galosh.

chan·cro m. MED. chancre.

chan·cha I. f. AMER., ZOOL. sow; CHILE small wooden cart; COL., COLL. mouth, trap ◆ **hacer la ch.** AMER. to play hookie II. adj. see **chancho, –cha**.

chan·cha·da f. AMER., COLL. dirty trick; *(porquería)* mess.

chán·cha·rras mán·cha·rras f.pl. COLL. pretexts, excuses ◆ **andar en ch. m.** to beat around the bush.

chan·che·rí·a f. ARG., CHILE sausage shop.

chan·cho, –cha I. adj. AMER. dirty, filthy II. m. ZOOL. pig, hog; AMER. *(en el ajedrez)* blocked piece (in chess); CHILE grinder, crusher ✦ **hacer un ch.** CHILE, SL. to belch, burp • **hacerse un ch. rengo** AMER. to pretend not to notice • **quedar como ch.** AMER. to let someone down, make a bad impression • **ser como chanchos** AMER. to be close friends —f. see **chancha.**

chan·chu·lle·ro, –ra I. adj. crooked, swindling II. m.f. crook, swindler.

chan·chu·llo m. COLL. crooked deal, swindle ✦ **andar en chanchullos** COLL. to be involved in swindles.

chan·fai·na f. CUL. stew made of liver and lungs.

chan·flón, –flo·na adj. coarse, crude.

chan·ga I. f. COLL. (*arreglo*) small business deal; ARG., BOL. porterage; CUBA joke, jest; ARG., COLL. payment, tip II. adj. see **chango, –ga.**

chan·ga·dor m. ARG., BOL. porter.

chan·gar §47 intr. ARG., BOL. to work as a porter; (*picholear*) to do odd jobs.

chan·go, –ga I. adj. CARIB., MEX. (*bromista*) playful, joking; MEX. (*listo*) clever, alert; CHILE (*fastidioso*) tedious, annoying ✦ **estar ch.** CARIB., MEX. to be plentiful and cheap • **ponerse ch.** MEX. to be on one's guard, take precautions II. m.f. CARIB., MEX. (*bromista*) joker, prankster; CHILE (*fastidioso*) tedious person; MEX. (*muchacho*) youngster —m. MEX. (*mono*) small monkey; ARG., URUG. (*mozo*) houseboy, servant • **changos** VEN. rags —f. see **changa.**

chan·gué, changue see **changar.**

chan·gue·ar intr. AMER. to joke, jest.

chan·gue·ro, –ra AMER. I. adj. humorous, jocose II. m.f. joker, jester.

chan·güí m. COLL. (*engaño*) hoax, trick; CUBA country dance.

chan·qué, chanque see **chancar.**

chan·ta·je m. blackmail.

chan·ta·jis·ta m.f. blackmailer.

chan·tar tr. (*vestir*) to put on (clothes); (*clavar*) to stick or drive in; COLL. to tell to someone's face <*se la chantó* she told him to his face>; ARG., CHILE (*golpear*) to beat; ARG. (*tirar*) to throw; (*dejar plantado*) to abandon; URUG. to stand up, leave in the lurch.

chan·ti·llí m. whipped cream.

chan·tre m. RELIG. precentor.

chan·trí·a f. RELIG. precentorship.

chan·za f. joke, jest ✦ **de o en ch.** in fun • **entre chanzas y veras** half in fun and half in earnest • **estar de ch.** to be joking • **gastar chanzas** to crack jokes.

cha·pa f. (*de metal*) sheet, plate; (*de madera*) sheet, panel (of wood); (*chapeta*) flush (of the face); (*de maquillaje*) rouge, blusher; (*insignia*) insignia; FIG. (*seso*) good sense or judgment; AMER. (*cerradura*) lock; AMER., AUTO. license plate; ECUAD., COLL. policeman; SP., REG. snail • **chapas** (*juego*) coin-tossing game; PERU, COLL. rosy cheeks • **ch. de estarcir** stencil • **ch. metálica** sheet metal • **ch. ondulada** corrugated iron.

cha·pa·do, –da I. past part. see **chapar** II. adj. covered with metal sheets, plated; (*de madera*) veneered ✦ **c. a la antigua** FIG. old-fashioned.

cha·pa·le·ar intr. (*chapotear*) to splash; (*chacolotear*) to clatter.

cha·pa·le·o m. (*chapoteo*) splash; (*acción*) splashing; (*chacoloteo*) clatter; (*acción*) clattering.

cha·pa·po·te m. COL., CUBA, VEN. asphalt, mineral tar.

cha·par tr. (*cubrir con metal*) to plate, cover with plates; (*cubrir con madera*) to veneer; FIG. (*encajar*) to come out with, say (a remark); COL., ECUAD., PERU (*acechar*) to spy on; PERU (*alcanzar*) to catch up with; (*agarrar*) to seize, grasp; (*apresar*) to catch, capture.

cha·pa·rral m. thicket, chaparral.

cha·pa·rro, –rra I. adj. short and thick II. m. BOT. dwarf or scrub oak; FIG. (*persona*) short chubby person; MEX. (*niño*) child, kid.

cha·pa·rrón m. (*lluvia*) downpour, cloudburst; FIG., COLL. (*gran cantidad*) shower, rain <*un ch. de insultos* a shower of insults>.

cha·pe·ar tr. (*cubrir con metal*) to plate, cover with plates; (*cubrir con madera*) to veneer; AMER. to clear (the land) —intr. to clatter.

cha·pe·tón, –to·na I. adj. (*recién llegado*) newly arrived from Europe; AMER., FIG. green, inexperienced; ARG. boastful II. m.f. (*inmigrante*) newly arrived European immigrant; (*bisoño*) novice —m. (*aguacero*) downpour, cloudburst; MED. illness suffered by Europeans arriving in America; MEX., EQUIT. horse brass ✦ **pasar el ch.** COLL. to emerge from a danger or difficulty.

cha·pis·ta m. (*obrero*) sheet-metal worker; AUTO. body repairman.

cha·po·dar tr. (*un árbol*) to prune, cut back (a tree); FIG. (*cercenar*) to reduce, trim.

cha·po·do m. pruned branch.

cha·po·la f. COL. butterfly.

cha·pón m. ink blot.

cha·po·te·ar tr. to moisten, dampen —intr. to splash.

cha·po·te·o m. splash.

cha·pu·cé, chapuce see **chapuzar.**

cha·pu·ce·ar tr. COLL. (*chafallar*) to botch, bungle; MEX. (*engañar*) to deceive.

cha·pu·ce·rí·a f. COLL. (*obra mal hecha*) sloppy job, slipshod piece of work; (*mentira*) lie, fib.

cha·pu·ce·ro, –ra I. adj. COLL. shoddy, sloppy II. m.f. (*desmañado*) bungler, careless worker; (*mentiroso*) liar —m. (*herrero*) blacksmith.

cha·pu·rra·do, –da I. past part. see **chapurrar** II. m. CUBA drink made of water, plums, sugar and cloves boiled together.

cha·pu·rrar or **cha·pu·rre·ar** tr. to speak poorly or with difficulty (a foreign language); COLL. (*los licores*) to mix (liquor).

cha·puz m. [pl. **-pu·ces**] (*obra*) odd job; (*acción de chapuzar*) ducking; (*chapucería*) botched job.

cha·pu·za f. COLL. botched job.

cha·pu·zar §04 tr. to duck (a person) under water.

cha·pu·zón m. dip, swim <*darse un ch.* to go for a swim>; (*forzado*) duck, ducking; (*zambullida*) dive.

cha·qué or **cha·quet** m. morning coat.

cha·que·ta f. jacket ✦ **ch. de fumar** smoking jacket • **ch. salvavidas** life jacket.

cha·que·te·ar intr. (*volverse atrás*) to retreat, back down; (*mudar de opinión*) to change one's mind; (*huir*) to flee, run away.

cha·que·te·o m. escape, flight.

cha·que·ti·lla f. short jacket, bolero.

cha·que·tón m. overcoat.

cha·qui·ra f. PERU, HIST. glass bead (used as currency by Indians).

cha·ra·da f. charade.

cha·ra·mus·ca f. MEX. candy twist; AMER. (*leña*) brushwood, firewood; CUBA, P. RICO noise, din.

cha·ran·ga f. (*orquesta*) brass band; C. RICA, MEX., PERU informal dance.

cha·ran·go m. AMER., MUS. small five-stringed Andean guitar.

cha·ran·gue·ro, –ra I. adj. careless, slipshod II. m.f. (*chapucero*) bungler; (*buhonero*) hawker, peddler —m. (*barco*) small coastal trading boat.

cha·ra·pa f. ECUAD., PERU, ZOOL. type of turtle.

cha·ra·pe m. MEX. spicy fermented beverage made with pulque.

char·ca f. pond, pool.

char·cal m. marshy area.

char·co m. puddle, pool ✦ **pasar el ch.** FIG., COLL. to cross the ocean.

char·la f. (*conversación*) chat, conversation; (*conferencia simple*) talk; ORNITH. missel thrush.

char·la·dor, –do·ra I. adj. talkative, garrulous II. m.f. chatterbox, chatterer.

char·la·du·rí·a f. gossip, chatter.

char·lar intr. COLL. (*parlotear*) to chatter, prattle; (*hablar*) to chat, talk.

char·la·tán, –ta·na I. adj. (*parlanchín*) talkative, garrulous; (*chismoso*) gossipy, gossiping II. m.f. (*parlanchín*) chatterbox, chatterer; (*murmurador*) gossip; (*curandero*) charlatan, quack; (*vendedor ambulante*) peddler.

char·la·ta·ne·ar intr. (*parlotear*) to chatter, prattle; (*hablar indiscretamente*) to gossip.

char·la·ta·ne·rí·a f. (*palabreo*) talkativeness, garrulousness; (*curanderismo*) charlatanry, quackery.

char·la·ta·nis·mo m. charlatanism.
char·lis·ta m.f. lecturer.
char·lo·te·ar intr. COLL. to chatter, prattle.
char·lo·te·o m. COLL. chatter, prattle.
char·ne·ca f. BOT. mastic tree.
char·ne·la f. CARP., ZOOL. hinge.
cha·rol m. *(barniz)* varnish, lacquer; *(cuero)* patent leather; AMER. *(bandeja)* tray ♦ **darse ch.** COLL. to brag, blow one's own horn.
cha·ro·la f. AMER. tray.
cha·ro·la·do, –da I. past part. see **charolar** II. adj. *(barnizado)* varnished, polished; *(lustroso)* shiny, glossy.
cha·ro·lar tr. to varnish, lacquer.
cha·ro·lis·ta m.f. varnisher.
char·pa f. *(tahalí)* pistol belt; MED. sling.
char·que m. ARG., MEX. jerked beef, jerky.
char·que·ar tr. *(acecinar)* to dry, cure; ARG., COLL. *(herir)* to slash, cut to pieces (a person).
char·qui m. AMER. *(carne)* jerked meat, jerky; CHILE *(fruta)* dried fruit.
char·qui·cán m. BOL., CHILE, PERU, CUL. stew made from jerked meat, potatoes, beans and seasonings.
cha·rra·da f. *(torpeza)* coarseness, boorishness; *(baile)* peasant dance; FIG., COLL. *(adorno tosco)* gaudy ornament.
cha·rrán I. adj. scoundrelly, rascally II. m.f. scoundrel, rascal.
cha·rra·ne·ar intr. to behave like a scoundrel.
cha·rra·ne·rí·a f. *(acción)* dirty trick; *(comportamiento)* scoundrelly behavior.
cha·rras·ca f. COLL. *(sable)* saber, cutlass; *(navaja)* jackknife.
cha·rras·que·o m. jangle, clatter.
cha·rre·te·ra f. MIL. epaulet, epaulette.
cha·rro, –rra I. adj. FIG. *(tosco)* rustic, unsophisticated; FIG., COLL. *(de mal gusto)* gaudy, flashy; MEX. *(pintoresco)* picturesque; *(diestro)* skilled in horsemanship II. m.f. *(campesino)* Salamancan peasant; *(tosco)* yokel, bumpkin —m. CUBA game similar to marbles; MEX. *(jinete)* charro, cowboy; *(sombrero)* wide-brimmed hat.
cha·rrú·a f. small tugboat.
¡chas! m. interj. pow!, wham!
chas·ca f. *(leña)* brushwood, kindling; AMER. tangled or matted hair.
chas·car §70 intr. *(la madera)* to crack; *(la lengua)* to click (one's tongue) —tr. to crunch.
chas·co m. *(burla)* trick, joke; *(decepción)* disappointment.
chas·sis m. [pl. **-sis**] AUTO. chassis, framework; PHOTOG. plate holder.
chas·po·na·zo m. bullet mark, graze.
chas·que·ar[1] tr. *(burlarse de)* to play a joke on, trick; *(decepcionar)* to disappoint, let down; *(faltar)* to break, fail to keep (a promise) —reflex. to come to naught.
chas·que·ar[2] tr. to crack, snap <*ch. un látigo* to crack a whip>; to snap <*ch. los dedos* to snap one's fingers>; COL. to champ (a bit) —intr. to crack, crackle (wood).
chas·qui m. AMER. *(mensajero)* messenger; *(correo)* mail.
chas·qui·do m. crack, snap.
cha·ta I. f. *(embarcación)* barge, scow; *(carro)* flatcar; *(bacín)* bedpan; COLL. *(querida)* darling, honey II. adj. see **chato, -ta.**
cha·ta·rra f. scrap, scrap iron.
cha·ta·rre·rí·a f. junk yard.
cha·ta·rre·ro, –ra m.f. scrap dealer.
cha·te·ar tr. COLL. to have a few (drinks).
cha·te·dad f. flatness.
cha·to, –ta I. adj. *(de nariz aplastada)* flat-nosed, snub-nosed; flat, snub <*nariz ch.* snub nose>; *(bajo)* low <*torre ch.* low tower>; *(llano)* shallow, flat <*plato ch.* flat plate>; *(embotado)* blunt; AMER., COLL. commonplace, ordinary; DOM. REP., P. RICO cowardly ♦ **dejar ch.** AMER. to defeat, crush; MEX. to deceive, swindle • **quedarse ch.** AMER. to fail • **quedarse ch. con** MEX. to appropriate, take possession of II. m. *(querido)* darling; *(vaso)* small wine glass ♦ **tomarse unos chatos** to have a few (drinks) —f. see **chata.**
cha·tón m. large mounted gem.
cha·tu·ra f. flatness, snubness.

¡chau! interj. AMER. goodbye, ciao.
chau·cha I. f. S. AMER. *(patata)* new potato; BOL., CHILE, PERU *(dinero)* money; ARG. *(judía)* string bean; ECUAD. *(beneficio)* small profit; *(estipendio)* small stipend; PERU *(comida)* food ♦ **pelar la ch.** FIG. to brandish a knife II. adj. ARG. *(de mala clase)* poor-quality; *(insípido)* insipid, dull.
chau·vi·nis·mo m. chauvinism.
chau·vi·nis·ta I. adj. *(patriotero)* chauvinistic, fanatically patriotic II. m.f. chauvinist, fanatical nationalist.
cha·val, –va·la I. adj. young II. m. lad, youngster —f. lass, young girl.
cha·va·le·rí·a f. SP., COLL. kids, children.
cha·ve·ta f. *(clavija)* key, cotter; COLL. *(chiflado)* nut, crackpot ♦ **perder la ch.** FIG., COLL. to go off one's rocker.
cha·yo·te m. BOT. chayote (plant and fruit); C. AMER., COLL. fool, nincompoop; HOND. coward.
che f. name of the letter **ch.**
¡che! interj. AMER. hey!, listen!
che·co, –ca adj.& m.f. Czech, Czechoslovak —m. *(idioma)* Czech.
che·cos·lo·va·co, –ca adj. & m.f. Czechoslovak, Czechoslovakian.
Che·cos·lo·va·quia f. Czechoslovakia.
che·lín m. FIN. shilling.
che·lo I. m. MUS. cello II. adj. MEX. blond, white-haired.
chen·cha adj. MEX. lazy, idle.
che·pa f. COLL. hump, hunch; C. AMER. luck, chance.
che·que m. check, cheque (G.B.) ♦ **ch. abierto** or **al portador** open check • **ch. cruzado** crossed check • **ch. de viaje** or **viajero** travelers check • **ch. en blanco** blank check.
che·que·ar tr. AMER. *(inspeccionar)* to check, inspect; *(cotejar)* to compare; C. AMER. *(facturar)* to check, register (luggage); MED. to give a checkup to.
che·que·o m. AMER. *(inspección)* inspection, check; MED. checkup, examination.
che·que·ra f. or **che·que·ro** m. checkbook.
Cher·bur·go Cherbourg.
cher·na f. ICHTH. sea bass.
cher·va f. BOT. castor oil plant.
cheu·to, –ta adj. CHILE harelipped.
chí·a f. *(manto)* short black coat; *(beca)* hood, cowl; MEX., BOT. kind of sage; *(refresco)* drink from sage seeds, lemon juice and sugar.
chi·ba·le·te m. PRINT. composing stand.
chib·chas m.pl. COL., HIST. Chibchas (ancient Indian tribe).
chi·bo·lo m. AMER. swelling, bump.
chi·bu·quí m. chibouk (Turkish pipe).
chic I. adj. chic, stylish II. m. stylishness, elegance.
chi·ca I. f. *(muchacha)* girl, child; *(criada)* maid, servant; *(chicha)* corn liquor; ARG., URUG. plug of chewing tobacco or chewing gum; C. AMER. small lottery prize II. adj. see **chico, -ca.**
chi·ca·da f. childish prank.
chi·ca·na I. f. AMER. chicanery, trickery II. adj. see **chicano, –na.**
chi·ca·ne·ar intr. to engage in chicanery or trickery.
chi·ca·no, –na adj. & m.f. Chicano, Mexican-American.
chi·cle m. *(goma de mascar)* chewing gum; *(gomorresina)* chicle; MEX. *(suciedad)* filth, dirt.
chi·co, –ca I. adj. small, little II. m. *(muchacho)* boy, child; *(medida)* measure for wine (168 milliliters); AMER. game, round; GUAT., HOND., BOT. sapodilla —f. see **chica.**
chi·co·le·ar intr. COLL. to pay compliments —reflex. ARG., PERU to enjoy oneself.
chi·co·le·o m. COLL. compliment, flattering remark ♦ **decir chicoleos** to pay compliments.
chi·co·ria f. BOT. chicory.
chi·co·ta·zo m. AMER. whiplash.
chi·co·te m. AMER. whip; MARIT. end of a rope or cable; FIG., COLL. *(cigarro)* cigar stub; C. AMER. string, line.
chi·co·te·ar tr. AMER. to ship, flog; COL. to kill.
chi·cha f. *(bebida)* chicha, corn whiskey; COLL. *(carne)* meat; C. AMER., ECUAD. ill humor; ARG., COLL. blood ♦ **ch. de uva** ARG., PERU unfermented grape juice • **de ch. y**

nabo insignificant • **estar ch.** MEX. to be pleasant or amusing • **estar como ch.** COL. to be plentiful • **estar de ch.** C. AMER., ECUAD. to be ill-humored or in a bad mood • **estar hecho una ch.** ECUAD. to be very dirty • **sacar la ch.** FIG. to get blood from a stone.

chí·cha·ro m. BOT. pea; COL., COLL. bad cigar.

chi·cha·rra f. ENTOM. cicada; (juguete) kazoo; FIG., COLL. (persona) chatterbox; SP. nuisance ♦ **hablar como una ch.** to be a real chatterbox.

chi·cha·rre·ro m. FIG. hot place, oven <esta oficina es un ch. this office is an oven>.

chi·cha·rro m. ICHTH. caranx, horse mackerel; (chicharrón) fried pork rind.

chi·cha·rrón m. (cerdo) crisp pork rind; FIG. (manjar requemado) overcooked or burned food; FIG., COLL. (persona) very tanned person.

chi·che I. m. AMER. (pecho), breast, teat (of a wet nurse); (persona) skillful or elegant person; (lugar) well-decorated place; ARG. (juguete) toy; ARG., CHILE (alhaja) trinket, bauble; MEX. (nodriza) wet nurse II. adj. C. AMER. easy, comfortable III. adv. C. AMER. easily, comfortably.

chi·che·ar intr. to hiss.

chi·che·rí·a f. AMER. store where corn whiskey is sold.

chi·che·ro m.f. AMER. person who makes or sells corn whiskey.

chi·chi m. AMER., ANAT. nipple —m.f. C. AMER. baby.

chi·chi·gua C. AMER., MEX. I. adj. of a wet nurse II. f. wet nurse.

chi·chi·me·ca m.pl. MEX., HIST. Chichimecans (Indians).

chi·chis·be·o m. (galantería) wooing, courtship; (hombre) suitor.

chi·cho m. curl on the forehead.

chi·chón m. bump, lump (on the head).

chi·cho·ne·ar intr. S. AMER., COLL. to make or play jokes.

chi·cho·ne·ra f. padded cap or hood.

chi·cho·ta f. BOT. chick-pea; AMER. bump, lump (on the head) ♦ **sin faltar ch.** FIG. down to the last detail.

chi·fla f. (acción de chiflar) whistling; (silbato) whistle; (cuchillo) paring knife; MEX. bad mood.

chi·fla·do, –da I. past part. see **chiflar** II. adj. COLL. (loco) crazy, nuts; (enamorado) in love.

chi·fla·du·ra f. COLL. (locura) craziness, madness; (silbido) whistle, whistling.

chi·flar[1] intr. to whistle; MEX., ORNITH. to sing —tr. to hiss at, boo <ch. a un actor to boo an actor>; COLL. (beber rápidamente) to guzzle, gulp —reflex. (volverse loco) to go crazy or mad; (enamorarse) to fall in love; COLL. (gustar) to be crazy about (something).

chi·flar[2] tr. to pare, trim (leather).

chi·fle m. (silbato) whistle; (reclamo) bird call, decoy; (para la pólvora) powder horn.

chi·fli·do m. whistle.

chi·flón m. AMER. draft, air current; MEX. (de agua) jet, spout; MIN. cave-in; CHILE rockfall; C. AMER. waterfall.

chi·hua·hua m. ECUAD. kind of fireworks; (perro) chihuahua (dog).

chi·í·ta adj. & m.f. RELIG. Shiite.

chi·la·ca·yo·te m. BOT. bottle gourd.

chi·lar m. chili or pepper patch.

chi·la·te m. C. AMER. drink made with corn, peppers and cocoa.

chi·le m. AMER. pepper, chili; C. AMER. (patraña) story, hoax.

Chi·le m. Chile.

chi·le·no, –na adj. & m.f. Chilean.

chi·lin·dri·na f. COLL. (cosa sin importancia) trifle; (anécdota) anecdote, funny story; MEX., CUL. bread sprinkled with sugar.

chi·lin·dri·ne·ro, –ra I. adj. joking, bantering II. m.f. joker.

chi·lo·te, –ta I. adj. CHILE of or from Chiloé province II. m.f. CHILE Chiloé inhabitant —m. MEX. drink made of chili and pulque; C. AMER. ear of green corn.

chil·pe m. ECUAD. (de cabuya) dried agave leaf; (de maíz) dried corn leaf ♦ **chilpes** CHILE, ECUAD. rags, tatters.

chi·lla I. f. HUNT. decoy call; CARP. lath; ARG., BOT. down II. adj. see **chillo, –lla.**

chi·lla·do I. past part. see **chillar** II. m. CARP. roof made of laths and shingles.

chi·lla·dor, –do·ra I. adj. screaming, shrieking II. m.f. screamer.

chi·llan·te adj. screaming, shrieking.

chi·llar intr. (gritar) to scream, shriek; (chirriar) to squeak, creak; (destacarse) to clash, be loud (colors); COLL. (alborotar) to complain, protest; HUNT. to call; HONG., P. RICO to squeal, be an informer —reflex. AMER. (ofenderse) to take offense; C. AMER. (avergonzarse) to become ashamed.

chi·lle·rí·a f. (alboroto) screaming, yelling; (regaño) scolding, reprimand.

chi·lli·do m. (grito) scream, shriek; (chirrido) squeak, creak.

chi·llo, –lla I. m. CARP. lath; C. AMER. debt; ECUAD. anger, resentment —f. see **chilla** II. adj. PERU dark black.

chi·llón, –llo·na I. adj. COLL. (gritón) screaming, shrieking; (estridente) clashing, loud <colores chillones loud colors> II. m.f. screamer.

chi·ma·chi·ma or **chi·man·go** m. AMER., ORNITH. kind of vulture.

chim·ba I. f. CHILE, PERU opposite bank (of a river); CHILE noncentral part of town; PERU ford, crossing; COL., ECUAD. braid of hair II. adj. see **chimbo, –ba.**

chim·ba·dor m. PERU person expert in fording rivers.

chim·bar tr. ECUAD. to make phony deals; PERU to ford (a river) —intr. PERU to turn out well.

chim·bo, –ba I. adj. COL. worn-out, exhausted II. m. COL. piece of meat —f. see **chimba.**

chi·me·ne·a f. (conducto) chimney; (hogar) fireplace, hearth; INDUS., RAIL. chimney, smokestack; ARM. nipple, inner casing; THEAT. wooden channel (for scenery counterweights); MARIT. funnel, stack; AMER., MIN. shaft, opening ♦ **caerle a uno una cosa por la ch.** COLL. to receive a windfall, have something fall in one's lap • **ch. de aire** MIN. air shaft • **ch. de campana** canopy fireplace • **ch. de paracaídas** parachute vent • **ch. estufa** closed stove • **ch. francesa** mantelpiece • **ch. refrigeradora** cooling tower • **ch. volcánica** volcanic chimney or vent.

chim·pan·cé m. ZOOL. chimpanzee.

chi·na[1] f. (piedra pequeña) pebble, small stone; (juego) guessing game; (tejido) Chinese silk; (porcelana) porcelain, china; P. RICO orange ♦ **poner chinas** FIG., COLL. to put obstacles in someone's way • **tocarle a uno la ch.** COLL. to win the draw.

chi·na[2] I. f. (mujer de la China) Chinese woman; CHILE, COL., ECUAD. servant, maid; C. AMER. nanny, nurse; AMER. young Indian woman; COL. bellows; BOT. sarsaparilla root II. adj. see **chino, –na.**

Chi·na f. China.

chi·nam·pa f. MEX. floating garden near Mexico City.

chi·nam·pe·ro, –ra MEX. I. adj. pertaining to floating gardens II. m.f. cultivator of floating gardens.

chin·char tr. (molestar) to pester, bug; (causar molestia) to annoy, bother <me chincha tener que hacerlo it bothers me to have to do it>; (matar) to do in, kill —reflex. (molestarse) to get cross, get upset ♦ **¡chínchate!** tough luck!

chin·cha·rra·zo m. COLL. slap.

chin·cha·rre·ro m. ENTOM. bug-infested place; AMER. small fishing boat.

chin·che f. ENTOM. bug, bedbug; (clavito) thumbtack —m.f. FIG., COLL. (pesado) bore, boring person ♦ **morir como chinches** FIG., COLL. to drop like flies.

chin·che·ro m. ENTOM. bug-infested place; GUAT. sunny part of the bull ring.

chin·che·ta f. thumbtack.

chin·chi·lla f. ZOOL. chinchilla (animal and fur).

chin·chín m. COLL. (ruido de música) oom-pah-pah; (música callejera) street music; CUBA drizzle, light rain; C. AMER. baby's rattle; CHILE, BOT. evergreen shrub.

chin·cho·na f. AMER. quinine.

chin·cho·rre·rí·a f. FIG., COLL. (impertinencia) impertinence, nerve; (pesadez) nuisance, annoyance; (cuento) gossip, rumor.

chin·cho·rre·ro, –ra COLL. I. adj. gossipy II. m.f. gossip, tattler.

chin·cho·rro m. (red) small or sweep net; (bote de remos) rowboat, dinghy; COL., VEN. hammock; MEX. small herd; DOM. REP., P. RICO small store; C. RICA tenement.

chin·cho·so, –sa adj. COLL. boring, tedious.

chin·chu·do, –da adj. ARG. tiresome, boring.

chi·ne·la f. (babucha) slipper; (chanclo) clog.

chi·ne·ro m. china closet, cupboard.

chi·nes·co, –ca I. adj. Chinese II. m. MUS. Chinese pavilion (instrument).

chin·ga f. (barato) fee paid by gamblers; C. AMER., VEN. cigar butt; AMER., ZOOL. skunk; VEN. drunkenness.

chin·ga·da VULG. I. past part. see **chingar** II. f. fuck-up.

chin·ga·du·ra f. VULG. (molestia) fuck-up; AMER. flop.

chin·ga·ne·ar intr. ARG., PERU to go on a binge or spree.

chin·gar §47 tr. SL. (beber) to drink heavily, hit the bottle; VULG. to fuck, screw; C. RICA to dock, cut the tail off of (an animal); MEX. SALV. to bother, harass; GUAT. to train (fighting cocks); MEX., PHILIP. to outwit —reflex. (emborracharse) to get drunk; (endrogarse) to get high (on drugs); (enfadarse) to get annoyed; AMER. (fracasar) to be a flop.

chin·go, –ga adj. C. AMER. (mocho) stubby, blunt; (corto) short, ill-fitting (clothes); (desnudo) naked, without a stitch; (rabón) bobtailed, tailless; VEN. pug-nosed, flat-nosed ♦ **estar ch. por algo** to want something very badly II. m.pl. **chingos** C. AMER. underwear.

chin·gué, chingue see **chingar.**

chin·gue·ar intr. C. AMER. var. of **chingar.**

chi·no, –na[1] I. adj. Chinese II. m.f. (habitante) Chinese —m. (idioma) Chinese ♦ **los chinos** the Chinese • **trabajar como un ch.** COLL. to work like a slave —f. see **china.**

chi·no, –na[2] I. adj. AMER. of mixed ancestry; ZOOL., COL. yellowish; C. AMER. (pelón) bald, hairless; (airado) angry, irate; MEX. kinky, curly (hair) II. m.f. AMER. (mestizo) person of mixed ancestry; (niño) youngster, kid; (criado) servant, domestic; (calificativo cariñoso) honey, darling; (campesino) peasant —f. (niñera) nurse, nanny; (peonza) spinning top; see **china.**

chi·pi·cha·pe m. COLL. (zipizape) fight, ruckus; (golpe) blow.

chi·po·te or **chi·po·ta·zo** m. C. AMER. slap on the hand.

chi·po·te·ar tr. C. AMER. to slap.

Chi·pre m. Cyprus.

chi·prio·ta adj. & m.f. Cypriot, Cypriote.

chi·que·a·do·res m.pl. MEX. headache plasters; GUAT. long thin pastries.

chi·que·ro m. (pocilga) pigsty; TAUR. bullpen; ARG. cowshed.

chi·qui·cha·que m. sawyer.

chi·qui·li·cua·tro m. COLL. busybody, meddler.

chi·qui·lín m. COLL. small boy.

chi·qui·lla·da f. COLL. childish act or remark.

chi·qui·lle·rí·a f. COLL. flock of noisy children.

chi·qui·llo, –lla I. adj. small II. m.f. child, youngster.

chi·qui·tín, –ti·na I. adj. teeny, tiny II. m.f. baby, tot.

chi·qui·to, –ta I. adj. tiny, small II. m.f. (niño) infant, child —m. (vaso de vino) glass of wine; ARG., URUG. a minute, a bit <espere un ch. wait a minute> ♦ **andarse en** or **con chiquitas** FIG., COLL. to beat around the bush.

chi·ra·pa f. PERU sunshower (rain and sunshine); BOL. rags, tatters.

chi·ri·bi·ta f. spark ♦ **chiribitas** spots before the eyes • **echar ch.** FIG., COLL. to fume (be angry).

chi·ri·bi·til m. (desván) garret, attic; COLL. (cuarto pequeño) tiny room.

chi·ri·go·ta f. COLL. joke, quip.

chi·ri·go·te·ar intr. COLL. to joke, banter.

chi·ri·go·te·ro, –ra I. adj. joking, bantering II. m.f. joker.

chi·rim·bo·lo m. COLL. gadget, contraption ♦ **chirimbolos** COLL. utensils, gear.

chi·ri·mo·ya f. BOT. cherimoya (fruit).

chi·ri·mo·yo m. BOT. cherimoya tree.

chi·ri·pa f. fluke, stroke of luck (in billiards) ♦ **de** or **por ch.** FIG., COLL. by a fluke, by a piece of luck.

chi·ri·pá m. ARG., URUG. gaucho's trousers.

chi·ri·pa·zo m. AMER. fluke, stroke of luck.

chi·ri·pe·ro, –ra m.f. lucky person.

chir·la·dor, –do·ra COLL. I. adj. chattering, jabbering II. m.f. chatterer, jabberer.

chir·lar intr. COLL. to chatter, jabber.

chir·la·ta f. COLL. gambling joint.

chir·le I. adj. COLL. insipid, tasteless II. m. droppings, dung.

chir·lo m. (herida) slash, gash (on face); (cicatriz) scar.

chir·lo·mir·lo m. tidbit, snack.

chi·ro·la f. AMER. (moneda) coin of little value; (cárcel) slammer, jail.

chi·ro·te m. AMER., ORNITH. linnet; FIG. (tonto) fool, nincompoop.

chi·rre·ar intr. var. of **chirriar.**

chi·rria·do, –da I. past part. see **chirriar** II. adj. COL. charming, graceful.

chi·rria·dor, –do·ra or **chi·rrian·te** adj. (un gozne) creaking, squeaking; (al freírse una cosa) sizzling, hissing; (un pájaro) cheeping, chirping; COLL. (una voz) shrill.

chi·rriar §30 intr. (rechinar) to creak, squeak <las ruedas chirrían the wheels squeak>; (al freír) to sizzle <el tocino chirria en la sarten bacon sizzles in the frying pan>; ORNITH. to screech, shriek; FIG., COLL. (cantar) to sing out of tune; COL. (tiritar) to shiver; (ir de juerga) to go on a spree.

chi·rri·do m. (ruido desagradable) screeching, shrieking; FIG., COLL. (grito) yell, shriek; (al freír) sizzling, sizzle.

chi·rrión m. (carro) heavy cart; AMER. horsewhip; C. AMER. string, chain.

chi·ru·la f. MUS. Basque flute.

chi·ru·men m. COLL. common sense.

¡chis! interj. sh!, hush!

chis·ca·rra f. MIN. soft crumbly limestone.

chis·cón m. SL. garret, closet (small room).

chis·chás m. clash (of swords).

chis·ga·ra·bís m. COLL. busybody, meddler.

chis·gue·te m. COLL. (trago) swig, drink; (chorro) jet, spurt; AMER., BOT. rubber tree.

chis·mar intr. var. of **chismear.**

chis·me m. (murmuración) gossip, rumor; COLL. (baratija) trinket, knicknack.

chis·me·ar intr. to gossip, tell tales.

chis·me·rí·a f. gossip.

chis·me·ro, –ra I. adj. gossiping, tattling II. m.f. gossip, tattler.

chis·mo·gra·fí·a f. COLL. (afición a los chismes) fondness for gossip; (relación de chismes) gossiping.

chis·mo·rre·ar intr. to gossip, tell tales.

chis·mo·so, –sa I. adj. gossipy, gossiping II. m.f. gossip, gossipmonger.

chis·pa I. f. (chiribita) spark; (relámpago) flash; FIG. (pedazo) little bit, small amount <bebí una ch. de vino I drank a little bit of wine>; (de lluvia) sprinkle, drop (of rain); (viveza) wit, liveliness; COLL. (borrachera) drunkenness; JEWEL. diamond chip; COL. rumor; GUAT., MEX., COLL. success; MEX. two-wheeled horse-drawn cart ♦ **dar chispas** (lucir) to be bright; GUAT., MEX. to be successful • **echar chispas** FIG. to fume (with anger) • **ni chispas** not the least bit, nothing at all • **ser una ch.** or **tener mucha ch.** to be a live wire, be witty II. adj. MEX. amusing, funny.

chis·par tr MEX. to take out —reflex. COLL. (embriagarse) to get drunk or tipsy; GUAT., MEX. to run away.

chis·pa·zo m. (destello) spark; (chisme) gossip, rumor; FIG. (momento brillante) spark, flash <un ch. de ingenio a spark of genius>.

chis·pe·an·te adj. (que chispea) sparkling; FIG. (ingenioso) brilliant, sharp.

chis·pe·ar intr. (destellar) to spark, give off sparks; (relucir) to sparkle; (lloviznar) to drizzle; FIG. (brillar) to be brilliant —reflex. ARG., DOM. REP. to get tipsy.

chis·pe·ro, –ra I. m. (herrero) blacksmith; SP., COLL. ruffian, rogue; DOM. REP. revolver, pistol II. adj. sparkling.

chis·po, –pa COLL. I. adj. (borracho) tipsy, tight II. m. COLL. drink, swig.

chis·po·le·to, –ta adj. alert, wide awake.

chis·po·rro·te·ar intr. to spark, crackle.

chis·po·rro·te·o m. COLL. (siseo) spitting, sizzling (of oil); (de la leña) crackling.

chis·po·so, –sa adj. sparking, crackling.

chis·que·ro m. *(esquero)* leather pouch; *(encendedor)* cigarette lighter.

¡chist! interj. sh!, hush!

chis·tar intr. to speak ♦ **sin ch. ni mistar** without a word, without saying anything.

chis·te m. *(burla)* joke, jest; *(gracia)* witty remark ♦ **caer en el ch.** COLL. to get the joke, get it • **ch. colorado** *or* **verde** dirty *or* off-color joke • **dar en el ch.** COLL. to guess the trouble • **hacer ch. de** to make a joke of.

chis·te·ra f. *(cesta de pescador)* fisherman's basket; FIG., COLL. *(sombrero de copa)* top hat; *(cesta del pelotari)* jai alai basket.

chis·ti·do m. whistle.

chis·to·so, –sa adj. funny, humorous.

chi·ta f. ANAT. anklebone; *(juego)* game of throwing stones at an upright bone ♦ **a la ch. callando** on the quiet *or* sly • **dar en la ch.** to hit the nail on the head.

chi·tar intr. var. of **chistar**.

chi·ti·ca·lla m.f. COLL. discreet *or* close-mouthed person.

chi·ti·ca·llan·do adv. ♦ **a la ch.** COLL. stealthily, on the quiet.

¡chi·to! interj. hush!, sh!

¡chi·tón! interj. COLL. hush!, quiet!

chi·va f. AMER. *(barba)* goatee, beard; C. AMER. *(manta)* blanket, coverlet; ARG., HOND., URUG. *(borrachera)* drunknness; C. RICA *(berrinche)* rage, fit of anger; COL., PAN. *(omnibús)* bus; CHILE, HOND. *(marimacho)* tomboy; ARG., P. RICO *(traviesa)* naughty girl; VEN. *(red)* net bag; *(molicha)* knapsack ♦ **chivas** MEX. odds and ends.

chi·var tr. COLL. *(fastidiar)* to annoy, upset; *(delatar)* to denounce —reflex. COLL. *(fastidiarse)* to become *or* get annoyed; AMER. *(enfadarse)* to become *or* get angry.

chi·va·te·o m. COLL. *(delación)* informing; AMER. *(vocinglería)* noise, shouting.

chi·va·to, –ta m. ZOOL. kid (less than one year old); COLL. *(delator)* informer, tattletale; COL. rascal, rogue —m. BOL. apprentice; VEN. talented man; CHILE firewater, cheap liquor.

chi·vo, –va m.f. ZOOL. kid, young goat ♦ **ch. expiatorio** FIG. scapegoat —m. *(poza)* pit for oil lees; AMER. *(cólera)* rage, fit of anger; C. AMER. *(juego)* dice game; CUBA *(golpe)* punch, blow; ECUAD., GUAT. *(travieso)* naughty boy; MEX. *(salario)* day's wages; CUBA, P. RICO *(tráfico ilícito)* illegal trade; *(contrabando)* contraband, smuggled goods —f. see **chiva**.

¡cho! interj. whoa!

cho·ca·dor, –do·ra I. adj. shocking II. m.f. shocker.

cho·can·te adj. *(desagradable)* offensive, disagreeable; *(chocorrero)* vulgarly amusing; ARG. *(impropio)* inappropriate, unsuitable; MEX. annoying, bothersome.

cho·car §70 intr. *(topar)* to crash, collide; *(pelear)* to clash, fight; *(provocar)* to provoke, annoy; COLL. *(disgustar)* to displease, offend ♦ **chocarla** COLL. to shake hands • **ch. de frente** to hit head on.

cho·ca·rre·ar intr. to tell dirty jokes.

cho·ca·rre·rí·a f. dirty joke.

cho·ca·rre·ro, –ra I. adj. coarse, vulgar II. m.f. teller of dirty jokes.

cho·clo m. *(chanclo)* clog; AMER. *(maíz)* corncob, ear of corn; PERU *(conjunto)* bunch, group; ARG. *(dificultad)* difficulty, trouble; *(carga)* burden, worry ♦ **meter el ch.** MEX. to make a mistake.

cho·co I. m. ICHTH. small cuttlefish; ZOOL., CHILE, PERU spaniel; CHILE, FIG. curly-haired person; AMER. handicapped *or* disabled person; BOL. dark red; COL. *(persona morena)* dark-skinned person; *(cuyabra)* gourd; GUAT. one-eyed person; PERU, ZOOL. white wooly monkey; CHILE *(muñón)* tree stump; AUTO. brake shoe II. adj. AMER. handicapped, disabled; HOND. one-eyed.

cho·co·la·te I. adj. chocolate II. m. *(dulce)* chocolate; *(bebida)* hot chocolate, cocoa ♦ **chocolates surtidos** assorted chocolates • **sacar ch.** AMER. to make someone's nose bleed.

cho·co·la·te·ra I. f. *(vasija)* pot for making chocolate; FIG., COLL. *(barco)* old tub *or* hulk; *(automóvil)* jalopy II. adj. see **chocolatero**.

cho·co·la·te·rí·a f. *(fábrica)* chocolate factory; *(tienda)* chocolate shop.

cho·co·la·te·ro, –ra I. m.f. *(fabricante)* chocolate maker; *(vendedor)* chocolate seller; *(aficionado al chocolate)* chocolate lover —f. see **chocolatera** II. adj. fond of chocolate.

cho·cha·per·diz f. [pl. **-di·ces**] ORNITH. woodcock.

cho·char intr. AMER. var. of **chochear**.

cho·che·ar intr. *(caducar)* to be doddering, be senile; FIG., COLL. *(enamorarse locamente)* to be madly in love.

cho·che·ra *or* **cho·chez** f. *(senilidad)* dotage, senility; COLL. *(admiración excesiva)* doting, excessive fondness; *(favorito)* pet, favorite.

cho·cho I. m. BOT. lupine seed; *(confite)* cinnamon candy II. adj. see **chocho, –cha**.

cho·cho, –cha I. adj. *(caduco)* doddering, senile; COLL. *(lelo)* doting II. m. see **chocho**.

chó·fer *or* **cho·fer** m. chauffeur.

cho·fes m.pl. CUL. livers and lights.

cho·la f. COLL. bean, noggin.

cho·la·da f. DEROG. action typical of an Indian *or* mestizo.

cho·le·rí·o m. DEROG. group of Indians *or* mestizos.

cho·lo, –la I. adj. *(mestizo)* half-breed, mestizo; CHILE cowardly II. m.f. *(mestizo)* half-breed, mestizo; PAN. *(indio civilizado)* civilized Indian; CHILE *(indio puro)* pure Indian; *(cobarde)* coward; ECUAD., PERU, VEN. *(querido)* darling, dear.

cho·lo·ques m.pl. PERU, BOT. soapberries.

cho·lla f. COLL. *(cabeza)* bean, noggin; AMER., SL. *(flema)* calmness, sluggishness.

cho·llo m. COLL. *(sinecura)* cushy job; *(ganga)* bargain.

chom·ba f. CHILE jersey, sweater.

chom·pa f. AMER. jersey, sweater.

chon·go m. GUAT. curl, lock (of hair); MEX. *(moño)* bun, chignon; *(dulce)* sweet, dessert; COLL. *(broma)* joke; PERU bordello.

chon·ta f. AMER., BOT. palm tree; ZOOL. black snake.

cho·pe·ra f. BOT. poplar grove.

cho·po m. BOT. black poplar; COLL. *(fusil)* rifle, gun.

cho·que m. *(colision)* crash, collision; *(impacto)* impact; FIG. *(pelea)* clash, skirmish; *(disputa)* dispute, quarrel; ELEC., MED. shock ♦ **ch. de agua** *or* **ariete** HYDRAUL. water hammer • **ch. de frente** head-on collision • **ch. eléctrico** electric shock • **ch. nervioso** nervious shock • **entrar en ch.** to clash.

cho·qué, choque see **chocar**.

chor·cha f. ORNITH. woodcock; MEX. gang, mob.

chor·dón m. BOT. raspberry (bush and fruit).

cho·re·ar intr. CHILE, COLL. to grumble, moan; PERU to pinch, steal.

cho·re·o m. CHILE, COLL. grumbling, moaning; PERU pinching, stealing.

cho·ri·ce·rí·a f. sausage shop.

cho·ri·ce·ro, –ra m.f. *(fabricante)* sausage maker; *(vendedor)* sausage seller; SP., FIG. frontier dweller.

cho·ri·zo m. *(carne)* sausage; *(balancín)* balancing pole (for tightrope walkers); COLL. *(ladrón)* thief; COL. *(bobo)* fool, idiot; ARG., URUG. daub, plastering material; CUBA, DEROG. mulatto.

chor·li·to m. ORNITH. plover; FIG., COLL. *(tonto)* scatterbrain.

chor·lo m. MIN. schorl, tourmaline; C. AMER., COL. great-great-great-grandson.

cho·ro m. CHILE, PERU large mussel.

cho·ro·te m. COL. unglazed pot for making chocolate; CUBA any thick beverage; VEN. mixture of chocolate, water and brown sugar.

cho·rre·a·do, –da I. past part. see **chorrear** II. adj. *(un animal)* striped; AMER. spotted, stained; ECUAD. soaked, wet III. m. P. RICO folk dance.

cho·rre·a·du·ra f. *(chorrea)* dripping; *(mancha)* stain.

cho·rre·ar intr. *(fluir)* to gush, spout; *(gotear)* to drip, trickle —tr. *(derramar)* to pour; FIG., COLL. *(dar poco a poco)* to give in dribs and drabs; CUBA to tell off; ECUAD. to soak; ARG., URUG. to steal —reflex. COL. to steal.

cho·rre·o m. *(efusión)* gushing, spouting; *(goteo)* drip, trickle; FIG. *(inundación)* flood <*un ch. de turistas* a flood of tourists>.

cho·rre·ra f. *(canal)* channel, gully; *(de un río)* rapids;

(adorno) frill; AMER. *(serie)* string; CUBA scolding, reprimand.

cho·rri·llo m. FIG., COLL. *(chorro)* flow, stream ♦ **irse por el ch.** COLL. to follow the crowd, go with the flow • **sembrar a ch.** ARG. to sow in a straight line.

cho·rro m. *(hilo)* spout, jet <*un ch. de agua* a spout of water>; FIG. *(inundación)* flood, shower <*un ch. de luz* a flood of light>; C. AMER. tap, faucet; BOL. lash, thong (of a whip); CUBA, P. RICO reprimand, scolding; ARG., COLL. thief ♦ **a chorros** abundantly • **como los chorros del oro** clean as a whistle • **llover a chorros** to pour, rain cats and dogs • **salir a chorros** to gush, spurt out.

cho·rro·bo·rro m. COLL. flood.

cho·rrón m. dressed hemp.

chor·tal m. fountain, spring.

cho·ta·ca·bras m.pl. ORNITH. nightjar, goatsucker.

cho·te·ar COLL. tr. & reflex. to make fun (of), tease.

cho·te·o m. COLL. teasing, ribbing.

cho·tis f. schottische (dance).

cho·to, -ta I. m.f. ZOOL. *(cabrito)* kid, young goat; *(ternero)* calf; HOND. reddish yellow II. adj. COL. tame; ARG. swindling, cheating.

cho·tu·no, -na adj. ZOOL. of a kid *or* young goat ♦ **oler a ch.** to stink to high heaven.

cho·va f. ORNITH. chough, jackdaw.

cho·za f. hut. shack.

choz·no, -na m. great-great-grandson —f. great-great-granddaughter.

cho·zo m. var. of **choza.**

choz·po m. gambol, caper.

chu·bas·co m. *(lluvia)* squall, downpour; FIG. *(contratiempo)* setback, difficulty.

chu·bas·co·so, -sa adj. METEOROL. squally, stormy.

chu·bas·que·ro m. raincoat, slicker.

chú·ca·ro, -ra I. adj. AMER. *(salvaje)* wild, untamed; *(huraño)* shy II. m.f. ECUAD. wild *or* untamed mule.

chu·cé, chuce see **chuzar.**

chu·ce·ar tr. AMER. to wound with a pike *or* lance.

chu·cha I. f. COLL. *(perra)* bitch, female dog; *(galbana)* laziness, sloth; COL., ZOOL. opossum; *(sobaquina)* body odor; COL., VEN., MUS. maraca; BOL., CHILE, PERU, VULG. cunt II. adj. see **chucho, -cha.**

chu·che·ar intr. *(cazar)* to trap, snare (game); *(cuchichear)* to whisper; SP. to nibble sweets.

chu·che·rí·a f. *(baratija)* trinket, trifle; *(dulce)* piece of candy, sweet.

chu·che·ro m. *(cazador)* hunter, trapper; COL. peddler, hawker; CUBA, RAIL. switchtender.

chu·cho, -cha I. m. COLL. *(perro)* dog, hound; AMER. *(escalofrío)* chill, shivers; *(fiebre)* ague, fever; AMER., ICHTH. herring-like fish; ARG. *(susto)* fear, fright; CARIB., RAIL. switch; COL. *(buhonería)* peddler's wares; CUBA, ICHTH. type of stingray; CUBA, VEN. *(látigo)* whip; CHILE *(cárcel)* jail; CHILE, ORNITH. pygmy *or* gnome owl ♦ **¡chucho!** shoo! (said to dogs) II. adj. COL. *(aguanoso)* soft, watery (fruit); *(arrugado)* wrinkled (person); GUAT., HOND. stingy.

chu·chu·me·co m. COLL., DEROG. *(monigote)* boob, jerk.

chue·ca I. f. ANAT. ball (of a socket joint); *(juego)* game resembling hockey; *(tocón)* tree stump; FIG., COLL. *(burla)* joke II. adj. see **chueco, -ca.**

chue·co, -ca I. adj. *(patizambo)* bowlegged; *(torcido)* crooked, bent II. f. see **chueca.**

chu·far intr. to mock, make fun of.

chu·fla f. COLL. joke, jest.

chu·flar·se reflex. to tease, make fun of.

chu·fle·ta f. COLL. joke, jest.

chu·fle·te·ar intr. COLL. to joke, jest.

chu·fle·te·ro, -ra I. adj. joking, bantering II. m.f. joker.

chu·la·da f. *(acción indecorosa)* coarse *or* vulgar action; COLL. *(gracia)* ease, self-assurance; *(jactancia)* showing off.

chu·la·pe·ar intr. to lead a roguish life.

chu·la·po, -pa *or* **chu·la·pón, -po·na** I. adj. natty, sharp II. m.f. sharp dresser, dandy.

chu·le·ar tr. *(vivir a costa de una mujer)* to live off a woman; MEX. to court, flirt with; COLL. to play a joke on —reflex.

(burlarse) to make fun of, tease; COLL. *(presumir)* to show off.

chu·le·rí·a f. COLL. *(donaire)* wit, verve; *(desfachatez)* brazenness, insolence.

chu·les·co, -ca I. adj. *(descarado)* brazen, insolent; *(vistoso)* flashy, natty II. m.f. sharp dresser, dandy.

chu·le·ta f. *(carne)* cutlet, chop; FIG., COLL. *(bofetada)* slap; COLL. *(de estudiantes)* crib sheet, cheat sheet ♦ **chuletas** muttonchops, side whiskers.

chu·lo, -la I. adj. *(picaresco)* roguish, rascally; *(chulesco)* fresh, showy; *(descarado)* fresh, impudent; GUAT., HOND., MEX. pretty, cute II. m.f. SP. lower-class Madrilenian —m. *(rufián)* ruffian, rascal; *(del matadero)* butcher's assistant; *(alcahuete)* pimp; TAUR. bullfighter's assistant; AMER., ORNITH. turkey buzzard; BOL., PERU woolen cap.

chu·ma·ce·ra f. MECH. axle bearing, journal bearing; MARIT. rowlock.

chum·bar tr. ARG. to attack (said of dogs); BOL. to shoot; COL. to swaddle.

chum·be m. AMER. sash, belt (worn by Indians); BOL., MIN. zinc sulfide.

chum·bo, -ba I. adj. BOT. prickly <*higo ch.* prickly pear> II. m. ARG. bullet.

chun·cho m. PERU, BOT. pot marigold; CHILE, ORNITH. owl.

chun·ga f. COLL. joke, jest ♦ **tomar a** *or* **en ch.** to take as a joke.

chun·gue·ar·se reflex. COLL. to joke.

chun·gue·o m. COLL. joke, jest.

chu·ño m. AMER. potato starch.

chu·pa f. *(prenda)* waistcoat; PHILIP. unit of measurement; C. AMER., ARG. drunkenness ♦ **poner a uno como ch. de dómine** FIG., COLL. to wipe the floor with someone.

chu·pa·ci·rios m. [pl. **-rios**] COLL. sanctimonious person.

chu·pa·da I. f. sucking II. adj. see **chupado, -da.**

chu·pa·de·ro, -ra I. adj. sucking II. m. teething ring, pacifier.

chu·pa·do, -da I. past part. see **chupar** II. adj. FIG., COLL. *(flaco)* thin, emaciated; tight <*falda ch.* tight skirt>; ARG., CHILE, CUBA drunk ♦ **estar ch.** to be as easy as pie III. f. see **chupada.**

chu·pa·dor, -do·ra I. adj. sucking II. m. *(chupete)* pacifier; *(de biberón)* nipple (of a bottle) —m.f. *(bebedor)* boozer, heavy drinker.

chu·pa·du·ra f. sucking.

chu·pa·flor m. VEN., ORNITH. hummingbird.

chu·pa·mir·to m. MEX., ORNITH. hummingbird.

chu·par tr. to suck <*ch. un limón* to suck a lemon>; *(absorber)* to absorb, soak up; *(fumar)* to puff on, smoke; *(beber)* to sip; COLL. *(aguantar)* to put up with; FIG., COLL. to milk, bleed <*chuparle el dinero a uno* to bleed someone of his money> —intr. to suck —reflex. *(adelgazarse)* to become emaciated, waste away; AMER. *(beber)* to drink ♦ **chuparse el dedo** COLL. to be naive • **chuparse los dedos** COLL. to lick one's fingers • **chuparse un insulto** AMER. to swallow an insult • **¡chúpate esa!** COLL. take that!

chu·pa·tin·tas m. [pl. **-tas**] COLL. pencil-pusher (petty clerk).

chu·pa·ti·vo, -va adj. sucking.

chu·pe m. COL., PERU, CUL. stew made with potatoes, eggs, meat and fish; COLL. *(chupete)* pacifier.

chu·pe·ta f. MARIT. roundhouse; CHILE drunkenness; C. AMER. pacifier.

chu·pe·te m. *(chupador de niños)* pacifier; *(pezón)* nipple (of a bottle); *(dulce)* lollipop.

chu·pe·te·ar intr. to suck at.

chu·pe·te·o m. sucking.

chu·pe·tón m. strong sucking.

chu·po m. MED., AMER. boil; COL. pacifier.

chu·pón, -po·na I. adj. sucking II. m.f. FIG. *(parásito)* parasite, leech —m. BOT. sucker, shoot; ORNITH. live feather; COLL. *(beso)* hickey; MIN. piston, plunger; AMER. *(biberón)* baby bottle; *(chupete)* pacifier; *(pezón)* nipple (of a bottle); ARG., CHILE, MED. boil.

chur·dón m. raspberry jam.

chur·la f. *or* **chur·lo** m. burlap bag.

chu·ro m. ECUAD. *(rizo de pelo)* curl (of hair); *(escalera de caracol)* spiral staircase.

chu·rras·co m. AMER. grilled *or* broiled steak.

chu·rras·que·ar intr. AMER. to have a barbecue.

chu·rre m. *(pringue)* thick grease *or* fat; COLL. *(suciedad)* filth, grime.

chu·rre·rí·a f. place where fritters are sold.

chu·rre·ro, –ra m.f. *(fabricante)* fritter maker; *(vendedor)* fritter seller.

chu·rre·te m. spot, stain.

chu·rrien·to, –ta adj. *(sucio)* greasy, grimy; AMER. suffering from diarrhea.

chu·rri·gue·ris·mo m. ARCHIT. baroque; FIG. *(exceso de ornamentación)* ornateness, overdecoration.

chu·rro, –rra I. adj. coarse (said of wool) II. m. CUL. fritter; COLL. *(chapuza)* botch, mess.

chu·rru·lle·ro, –ra I. adj. garrulous, talkative II. m.f. talkative person.

chu·rrus·car·se §70 reflex. to start to burn (food).

chu·rrus·co m. burnt toast.

chu·rum·bel m. COLL. kid, youngster.

chu·rum·be·la f. MUS. wind instrument; COL. *(pipa)* pipe; AMER. tube for drinking maté; COL. *(cuidado)* care, worry.

chu·ru·mo m. COLL. juice.

chus·ca·da f. joke, witticism.

chus·co, –ca I. adj. *(gracioso)* witty, funny; PERU common, ordinary II. m. COLL. *(panecillo)* roll, bun; PERU mongrel.

chus·ma f. *(galeotes)* crew of galley slaves; *(gentuza)* rabble, riffraff; COLL. *(multitud)* crowd, throng; ARG. crowd of Indians.

chus·pa f. ARG., PERU knapsack.

chu·te m. SALV., GUAT. barb, spike.

chu·za f. MEX. strike (in bowling).

chu·zar §04 tr. COL. to prick, stab.

chu·za·zo m. stabbing.

chuz·nie·to m. ECUAD. great-great-grandson.

chu·zo m. *(pica)* pike; *(bastón)* stick, club; CHILE *(rocín)* nag, worn-out horse; AMER. *(látigo)* horsewhip; *(aguijada)* goad; CHILE *(de agua)* water jet; ECUAD. sharp object ◆ **llover a chuzos** COLL. to rain cats and dogs.

chu·zón, –zo·na I. adj. astute, sharp II. m.f. joker, clown —m. COL. prick, jab.

D

d, D f. fifth letter of the Spanish alphabet.

da·ble adj. possible, feasible.

da·ca interj. COLL. hand over, give me <*d. la carta* give me the letter> ◆ **en d. las pajas** in a jiffy • **toma y d.** give-and-take.

dac·ti·lar adj. digital, finger.

dac·ti·lo·gra·fí·a f. typewriting, typing.

dac·ti·ló·gra·fo m.f. typist.

dac·ti·lo·lo·gí·a f. dactylology (sign language).

dac·ti·los·co·pia f. dactyloscopy (study of fingerprints).

dá·di·va f. *(regalo)* present, gift; *(contribución)* contribution, grant.

da·di·vo·si·dad f. generosity, liberality.

da·di·vo·so, –sa adj. generous, lavish.

da·do I. m. *(en el juego)* die; ARCHIT. pedestal, dado; MECH. block ◆ **cargar los dados** to load the dice • **correr el d.** COLL. to be in luck • **dados** dice • **dados cargados** *or* **falsos** loaded dice • **dar** *or* **echar el d.** COLL. to trick II. adj. see **dado, –da.**

da·do, –da I. past part. see **dar** II. adj. given <*un caso d.* a given case>; given, inclined <*Miguel es d. a charlar* Michael is given to chattering> ◆ **d. que** since, given that III. m. see **dado.**

da·dor, –do·ra I. adj. giving II. m.f. *(persona que da)* giver, donor; *(portador)* bearer; COM. drawer (of a letter of exchange) ◆ **d. de sangre** blood donor.

da·ga f. *(puñal)* dagger; AMER. machete ◆ **llegar a las dagas** FIG. to reach the most critical point.

da·gue·rro·ti·po m. PHOTOG. daguerreotype.

dai·fa f. concubine, mistress.

da·lia f. BOT. dahlia.

dal·má·ti·ca f. dalmatic (ceremonial vestment).

dal·má·ti·co, –ca adj. & m.f. Dalmatian.

dal·to·nis·mo m. MED. colorblindness, daltonism.

da·llar tr. to scythe, mow.

da·lle m. scythe, sickle.

da·ma f. *(mujer)* lady; *(noble)* lady, gentlewoman; *(de la reina)* lady-in-waiting; *(manceba)* mistress, concubine; *(actriz)* actress; *(en damas)* king (in checkers); *(en ajedrez, naipes)* queen (in cards, chess) ◆ **d. de honor** maid of honor • **d. de noche** BOT. morning glory • **d. joven** THEAT. ingénue • **primera d.** leading lady • **segunda d.** supporting actress • **damas** checkers, draughts (G.B.)

da·ma·ju·a·na f. demijohn.

da·mas·ce·no, –na adj. & m.f. Damascene.

da·mas·co m. TEX. damask; BOT. damson plum.

Da·mas·co m. Damascus.

da·mas·qui·llo m. *(tejido)* damassin (light cloth resembling damask); BOT. *(albaricoque)* apricot.

da·mas·qui·nar tr. to damascene.

da·mas·qui·no, –na adj. Damascene, of Damascus.

da·me·ro m. checkerboard.

da·mi·se·la f. *(moza)* damsel, young lady (used ironically); *(cortesana)* courtesan.

dam·na·ción f. ARCH. damnation, condemnation.

dam·ni·fi·car §70 tr. *(cosa)* to damage, mar; *(persona)* to injure, harm.

dam·ni·fi·ca·do, –da I. past part. see **damnificar** II. adj. *(cosa)* damaged, harmed; *(persona)* injured, harmed III. m.f. victim.

dan·cé, dance see **danzar.**

dan·dis·mo m. dandyism, foppishness.

da·nés, –ne·sa I. adj. Danish II. m.f. *(habitante)* Dane —m. *(idioma)* Danish.

dan·ta f. ZOOL. *(anta)* elk; *(tapir)* tapir.

dan·te·lla·do, –da adj. HER. dentated, serrated.

dan·tes·co, –ca adj. *(de Dante)* of Dante, Dantesque; FIG. *(espantoso)* horrific, terrifying.

Da·nu·bio m. Danube.

dan·za f. *(baile)* dance; FIG., COLL. *(negocio)* shady business deal; *(riña)* quarrel, argument; CUBA habanera (dance) ◆ **andar** *or* **estar en la d.** FIG., COLL. to be mixed up in a shady deal • **baja d.** allemande • **d. de arcos** arcade • **d. de cintas** Maypole dance • **d. de espadas** *(baile)* sword dance; FIG. *(riña)* quarrel, argument • **d. de figuras** square dance • **d. macabra** *or* **de la muerte** dance of death, danse macabre.

dan·za·dor, –do·ra I. adj. dancing II. m.f. dancer.

dan·zan·te I. adj. dancing II. m.f. *(bailarín)* dancer; FIG., COLL. *(estafador)* sharp operator, hustler; *(cabeza de chorlito)* scatterbrain; *(entremetido)* meddler, busybody.

dan·zar §04 tr. to dance —intr. *(bailar)* to dance; *(temblar)* to dance, bob up and down; FIG., COLL. *(entremeterse)* to get mixed up *or* involved.

dan·za·rín, –ri·na m.f. dancer.

dan·zón m. CUBA *(baile)* Cuban dance (derived from the habanera); *(música)* music of this dance.

da·ña·ble adj. harmful, hurtful.

da·ña·do, –da I. past part. see **dañar** II. adj. *(malo)* evil, wicked; *(lastimado)* damaged, injured; *(echado a perder)* spoiled, damaged.

da·ña·dor, –do·ra I. adj. damaging, harmful II. m.f. damager.

da·ñar tr. *(causar daño)* to damage, mar; *(personas)* to injure, harm —reflex. *(lastimarse)* to become damaged *or* injured; *(echarse a perder)* to spoil, go bad.

da·ñi·no, –na adj. damaging, harmful.

da·ño m. damage, injury ◆ **hacer d.** *(doler)* to hurt <*me hace d. el brazo* my arm hurts>; *(perjudicar)* to harm, injure • **daños punitivos** LAW punitive *or* vindictive damages • **daños y perjuicios** LAW damages • **sin d. de barras** without danger for anyone.

da·ño·so, –sa adj. damaging, harmful.

dar §20 tr. *(entregar)* to give, hand <*dame la sal, por favor* hand me the salt, please>; *(regalar)* to give, donate <*dio sus bienes a los pobres* he gave his fortune to the poor>; *(proporcionar)* to give, provide <*te daré más trabajo si lo* *necesitas* I will give you more work if you need it>; *(conferir)* to confer, grant <*recientemente me dieron el título de doctor* I was recently granted the title of doctor>; *(conceder)* to concede, grant <*el Papa le dio una audiencia* the Pope granted him an audience>; *(proponer)* to propose, offer <*el profesor nos dio el tema para la discusión* the professor proposed the topic for our discussion>; *(sacrificar)* to give up <*el patriota dio la vida por su país* the patriot gave up his life for his country>; *(repartir)* to deal <*d. las cartas* to deal the cards>; *(producir)* to produce, bear <*este árbol da buen fruto* this tree bears good fruit>; FIN. to bear, yield <*el negocio dio buenas ganancias* the business yielded good profits>; *(soltar)* to give off, emit <*el horno da mucho humo* the oven gives off a lot of smoke>; *(propinar)* to deal <*el ladrón le dio un tremendo golpe* the thief dealt him a tremendous blow>; *(administrar)* to administer <*la enfermera me dio la medicina* the nurse administered the medicine to me>; *(imponer)* to impose <*d. leyes* to impose laws>; *(sonar)* to strike <*el reloj acaba de d. las dos* the clock has just struck two>; *(celebrar)* to give, have <*dieron un banquete en mi honor* they gave a banquet in my honor>; THEAT. to show <*¿qué película dan hoy?* what movie are they showing today?>; to take <*d. un paseo* to take a walk>; *(aplicar)* to apply, put on <*d. una capa de pintura* to put on a coat of paint>; *(causar)* to cause, give <*su ausencia nos da pena* her absence causes us grief>; *(comunicar)* to express, convey <*d. la enhorabuena* to express congratulations> ♦ *ahí me las den todas* COLL. I don't give a hoot • **d. a conocer** to make known • **d. a entender** *(insinuar)* to insinuate, hint (at); *(explicar)* to explain • **d. a luz** *(tener hijos)* to give birth; FIG. *(publicar)* to publish, print • **d. audiencia** LAW to give a hearing • **d. aviso** to give notice • **d. barreno** MARIT. to scuttle • **d. cabezadas** to nod, doze • **d. caza a** to give chase to, pursue • **d. celos** to make jealous • **d. coces** to kick • **d. comienzo** *or* **principio a** to start • **d. como** *(considerar)* to regard, consider <*d. como falso* to consider (something) false>; *(producir)* to produce <*d. como resultado* to produce as a result> • **d. contramarcha** *or* **marcha atrás** MECH. to go into reverse • **d. crédito a** *(creer)* to believe, credit; COM. to give credit to • **d. cuenta de** to report on, give a report of <*quiero que me des cuenta de tus acciones* I want you to give me a report on your actions>; to account for <*te daré cuenta de los gastos en cuanto lleguemos* I will account for the expenses as soon as we arrive> • **d. cuerda a** *(relojes)* to wind (clocks); FIG. *(alargar)* to prolong; *(animar)* to encourage, get (someone) started • **d. de alta** to discharge (a patient) • **d. de baja** MIL. to discharge (a soldier) • **d. de beber** to give to drink • **d. de comer** to give to eat • **d. de lado** to shun, ignore • **d. diente con diente** to shiver • **d. el pésame** to express condolences • **d. el santo y seña** MIL. to give the password • **d. el sí** *(ceder)* to assent; *(casarse)* to agree to marry • **d. en cara** to reproach, scold • **d. en prenda** *(prometer)* to pledge; *(empeñar)* to hock, pawn • **d. fe** to certify • **d. fiado** COM. to give credit • **d. fianza** to post bail, bail out • **d. fin a** to complete, finish • **d. fondo** MARIT. to anchor, drop anchor • **d. frente a** to face, be facing • **darle ganas de** to feel like, have a mind to • **d. garantía** to guarantee • **d. garrote** to garrote, strangle • **d. gemidos** to groan • **d. gritos** to shout • **d. gusto a** *(alegrar)* to please, make happy; *(sazonar)* to enhance the flavor of • **d. la bienvenida** to welcome • **d. la cara por** to stand up for (someone) • **d. la casualidad que** to just so happen that <*dio la casualidad que la vi en Roma* it just so happened that I saw her in Rome> • **d. la lata** COLL. to pester • **d. la mano a** to shake hands with • **d. la razón a** to agree with, support • **d. las espaldas** to turn one's back on • **d. las gracias** to thank • **d. lectura a** to read out loud • **d. licencia para** to give permission to <*les di licencia a mis alumnos para que me llamen Diane* I gave my students permission to call me Diane> • **d. los buenos días** to greet, say good morning • **d. margen** to afford an opportunity • **d. muerte a** to kill • **d. pábulo a** FIG. to feed, foster • **d. palmadas** *(aplaudir)* to applaud, clap hands; *(pegar)* to spank • **d. parte de** LAW to report • **d. poder a** to empower, authorize • **d. por** to consider, regard <*le doy por inocente* I consider him innocent> • **d.**

por hecho que to take for granted that • **d. por muerto** to presume dead • **d. prestado** to lend • **d. punto final** to conclude • **d. saltos de alegría** to jump for joy • **d. satisfacción** *(disculparse)* to apologize; *(satisfacer)* to please, satisfy • **d. señales de** to show signs of • **d. suspiros** to sigh • **d. un abrazo** to hug • **d. una carcajada** to guffaw • **d. una cita** to make an appointment • **d. una mano a** to help, give a hand • **d. un vistazo** to glance • **d. una vuelta** to take a stroll • **d. vista** LAW to give a hearing • **no d. un bledo** COLL. not to give a hoot —*intr. (tener vista de)* to overlook, face <*la ventana da a la plaza* the window overlooks the plaza>; *(ocurrir)* to arise, occur <*si diera el caso, lo volvería a hacer* if the situation arose, I would do it again>; *(sobrevenir)* to come over, set in <*le dio fiebre* a fever set in>; FIG. *(presagiar)* to tell <*me da el corazón que no vendrán* my heart tells me that they will not come> ♦ **¡dale!** COLL. *(¡apúrate!)* hurry up!; *(¡adelante!)* keep it up! • **d. con** to find, hit on <*d. con la solución* to hit on the solution>; to meet, run into <*di con ella en el mercado* I ran into her in the market>; to hit, bang <*dio con la cabeza contra la puerta* he hit his head on the door • **d. de** to fall on <*d. de cabeza* to fall on one's head> • **d. de narices** to fall flat on one's face • **d. de sí** TEX. *(ensancharse)* to stretch, give • **d. en** *(caer)* to fall <*d. en el suelo* to fall on the floor>; FIG. to fall into <*d. en la trampa* to fall into the trap>; *(empeñarse)* to be bent on <*d. en irse* to be bent on going>; *(acertar)* to catch on to, get <*d. en el chiste* to catch on to the joke> • **d. en el clavo** FIG. to hit the nail on the head • **d. igual** *or* **lo mismo** to be all the same <*a mí me da igual* it is all the same to me> • **darle al codo** FIG., COLL. to booze, tipple • **darle por** to take it into one's head <*esta tarde me dio por ir al cine* this afternoon I took it into my head to go to the movies> • **d. sobre** to look out on • **d. tras alguien** to chase, pursue (someone) —*reflex. (entregarse)* to give oneself up, surrender <*el ladrón se dio a las autoridades* the thief surrendered to the authorities>; *(suceder)* to arise, occur <*lo haría otra vez si se dieran las mismas circunstancias* I would do it again if the same circumstances arose>; FIG. *(dedicarse)* to devote oneself <*mi hijo se dio al estudio de lleno* my son devoted himself completely to his studies>; *(tomar el hábito de)* to take to, give in to <*darse a la bebida* to take to drink>; AGR. to grow, come up <*el maíz se da bien en esta región* corn grows well in this area> ♦ **darse a conocer** *(presentarse)* to introduce oneself; FIG. *(revelarse)* to reveal oneself, show one's true colors • **darse a entender** to make oneself understood; *(ser evidente)* to become evident *or* clear • **darse con** *or* **contra** to hit, bump against • **darse corte** AMER. to put on airs • **darse cuenta de** to realize • **dárselas de** to consider oneself, to act like <*él se las da de experto* he considers himself an expert> • **darse las manos** *or* **la mano** to shake hands • **dársele a uno** to care about <*poco se me da lo que ocurre ahora* I care little about what happens now> • **dársele bien** to be lucky • **darse maña** to manage ably • **darse por** to consider oneself • **darse por notificado** LAW to accept service, be served (with a document) • **darse por ofendido** to take offense • **darse por perdido** to give oneself up for lost • **darse por vencido** to give up, surrender • **darse prisa** to hurry • **darse tono** to put on airs • **darse una panzada** COLL. to stuff oneself, gorge • **darse vuelta** ARG., PAR., FIG. to do an about-face.
▲ Used with some nouns, the transitive verb *dar* conveys the action associated with the noun. Thus *dar un abrazo* conveys the action "to hug" and *dar saltos* conveys the action "to jump."

Dar·da·ne·los m.pl. Dardanelles.
dar·do m. *(flecha)* dart, arrow; FIG. *(sátira)* cutting remark, barb; ICHTH. dace, bleak; ZOOL. sting.
da·res y to·ma·res m.pl. COLL. *(lo que se da y se recibe)* give-and-take; *(disputas)* arguments, disputes ♦ **andar en d. y t.** to argue, quarrel.
dár·se·na f. MARIT. inner harbor, dock.
dar·wi·nis·mo m. *SCI.* Darwinism.
da·ta f. *(fecha)* date; COM. data, items; *(de agua)* outlet (for water).
da·tar tr. *(poner fecha)* to date; COM. to enter, credit (in the books) —*intr.* to date, begin ♦ **d. de** to date from.

dá·til m. BOT. date; ICHTH. date mussel *or* shell ♦ **dátiles** COLL. fingers.

da·ti·vo, –va GRAM. adj. & m. dative.

da·to m. *(hecho)* fact, datum; *(documento)* document ♦ **datos** data, information • **datos personales** personal details.

de[1] prep. §G16, 17, 25 □ POSSESSION of *<las joyas de la reina* the jewels of the queen>; -'s *<las joyas de la reina* the queen's jewels>; -s' *<los amigos de mis hermanos* my brothers' friends> □ SUBSTANCE, SUBJECT of *<un fajo de billetes* a wad of bills>; about *<ellos hablaban de la situación económica* they were talking about the economic situation>; on *<él escribió un libro de filosofía* he wrote a book on philosophy>; [not translated] *<un broche de oro* a gold pin> *<una clase de historia* a history class> □ CONTENT of *<una caja de cigarros* a box of cigars> □ ORIGIN, INFERENCE from *<soy de Venezuela* I am from Venezuela>; from, according to *<de lo que dicen se puede deducir que no comprenden la situación* from what they say, one can deduce that they do not understand the situation>; [not translated] *<sal de mar* sea salt> □ DISTANCE from *<lejos de aquí* far from here> *<de casa en casa* from house to house>; FIG. from *<de amigo a amigo* from one friend to another> □ MANNER in, with *<lo bebí de un trago* I drank it in one swallow>; on *<de rodillas* on one's knees>; as *<trabajó de abogado* he worked as a lawyer>; [not translated] *<de mala gana* unwillingly> □ DESCRIPTION of *<un hombre de empuje* a man of energy>; in, with *<la mujer del abrigo azul* the woman in the blue coat> □ VALUE, MEASURE of *<acumulé una cuenta de veinte dólares* I ran up a bill of twenty dollars>; [not translated] *<un billete de cinco dólares* a five-dollar bill> *<un viaje de cien kilómetros* a one hundred kilometer trip> □ PURPOSE [not translated] *<un tren de pasajeros* a passenger train> □ TIME in *<a las cuatro de la tarde* at four o'clock in the afternoon>; at, by *<de noche* at night>; from *<de las ocho a las diez de la mañana* from eight to ten o'clock in the morning> □ CAUSE, REASON from, with *<el niño tiritaba de frío* the child shivered with cold>; out of *<lo ayudé de lástima* I helped him out of pity>; from, of *<morir de hambre* to die of hunger> □ ENERGY SOURCE [not translated] *<un molino de viento* a windmill> □ PASSIVE AGENT by *<ella es respetada de todos los estudiantes* she is respected by all of the students> *<es una novela de García Márquez* it is a novel by García Márquez> □ PARTITIVE some *<bebió del vino* he drank some wine> □ COMPARISON than *<ella necesita más de cien dólares* she needs more than a hundred dollars>; of, in *<soy el mejor alumno de la clase* I am the best student in the class> □ APPOSITION of *<la isla de Puerto Rico* the island of Puerto Rico>; on, at *<la casa de la izquierda* the house on the left> □ EMPHASIS [not translated] *<el bueno de Jorge* good old George> □ WITH AN INFINITIVE to *<es hora de comer* it is time to eat>; if *<de seguir así nos arruinaremos* if we go on like this we will be ruined> □ MARRIED NAMES [not translated, see §G47] *<la señora Sara Sola de Fernández* Mrs. Sara Fernández (née Sola)>.

de[2] f. dee (letter)

dé see **dar**.

de·am·bu·lar intr. *(vagar)* to wander *or* roam around; *(pasear)* to stroll.

de·am·bu·la·to·rio m. ARCHIT. ambulatory.

de·án m. RELIG. dean.

de·ba·jo adv. underneath, below ♦ **d. de** underneath, below • **por d.** underneath, below.

de·ba·te m. debate, discussion.

de·ba·tir tr. *(discutir)* to debate, discuss; *(combatir)* to fight, struggle.

de·be m. COM. debit.

de·be·la·dor, –do·ra I. adj. conquering, victorious II. m.f. conqueror, victor.

de·be·lar tr. to conquer, defeat.

de·ber[1] tr. to owe *<le debo diez dólares* I owe him ten dollars>; to ought to *<debemos proteger nuestros recursos naturales* we ought to protect our natural resources> ♦ **d. de** to be probable *<debe de estar en su oficina* he's probably in his office> —reflex. to be due to *<su falta de apetito se debe a la fiebre* his lack of appetite is due to fever>.

de·ber[2] m. *(obligación)* duty, obligation; *(faena)* chore;

(deuda) debt ♦ **cumplir con un d.** to carry out an obligation • **deberes** homework.

de·bi·da·men·te adv. properly, duly.

de·bi·do, –da I. past part. see **deber** II. adj. due *<la suma d.* the sum due>; *(apropiado)* proper, fitting ♦ **d. a** owing *or* due to, because of • **en d. forma** in due form.

dé·bil I. adj. *(debilitado)* weak, frail *<el enfermo está muy d.* the patient is very weak>; FIG. *(pasivo)* weak, ineffectual *<es un hombre d. de carácter* he is a man of weak character>; *(marchito)* faint, faded *<un color d.* a faint color>; *(la voz)* faint, feeble *<una voz d.* a feeble voice> II. m.f. weakling ♦ **los débiles** the weak.

de·bi·li·dad f. *(falta de vigor)* weakness, feebleness; FIG. *(inclinación)* weakness, soft spot ♦ **d. mental** mental deficiency.

de·bi·li·ta·ción f. *(acción de debilitar)* debilitation, weakening; *(debilidad)* weakness, feebleness.

de·bi·li·ta·dor, –do·ra adj. debilitating, weakening.

de·bi·li·tan·te adj. debilitating, weakening.

de·bi·li·tar tr. to debilitate, weaken —reflex. to become debilitated *or* weakened.

dé·bi·to m. *(deuda)* debt; COM. debit.

de·but m. debut, opening.

de·bu·tan·te I. adj. beginning II. m.f. *(principiante)* beginner, newcomer —f. debutante.

de·bu·tar intr. *(principiar)* to begin; THEAT. *(una persona)* to make a debut; *(obra)* to open.

dé·ca·da f. *(años)* decade; *(días)* ten days; *(volúmenes)* ten volumes.

de·ca·den·cia f. decadence, decline *<d. del Imperio Romano* decline *or* fall of the Roman Empire>.

de·ca·den·te I. adj. decadent, declining II. m.f. decadent.

de·ca·er §15 intr. *(disminuir)* to decline, fall; *(pudrir)* to decay; MARIT. to drift off course.

de·cá·go·no m. GEOM. decagon.

de·ca·gra·mo m. decagram.

de·ca·í·do, –da I. past part. see **decaer** II. adj. *(débil)* weak, run-down; *(deprimido)* depressed, discouraged.

de·cai·mien·to m. *(decadencia)* decadence, decline; *(debilidad)* weakness, feebleness; *(desaliento)* discouragement, dejection.

de·ca·li·tro m. decaliter.

de·cá·lo·go m. RELIG. Decalogue, Ten Commandments.

de·cá·me·tro m. decameter.

de·ca·no m.f. EDUC. dean; *(miembro más viejo)* doyen, senior member.

de·can·ta·ción f. decanting, pouring off.

de·can·tar tr. *(un líquido)* to decant, pour off; *(engrandecer)* to exaggerate, aggrandize.

de·ca·pi·ta·ción f. decapitation, beheading.

de·ca·pi·tar tr. to decapitate, behead.

de·ca·sí·la·bo, –ba I. adj. decasyllabic, ten-syllable II. m. decasyllable.

de·cat·lón m. SPORT. decathlon.

de·ca·ye·ra, decayó see **decaer**.

de·ce·le·ra·ción f. PHYS. deceleration.

de·ce·na f. MATH. ten, group of ten; MUS. tenth.

de·cen·cia f. *(honradez)* decency, honesty *<portarse con d.* to act with decency>; *(modestia)* decency, modesty.

de·ce·nio m. decennium, decade.

de·cen·tar §49 tr. *(empezar)* to start, begin; *(empezar a mermar)* to begin to deteriorate *or* decline —reflex. to get bedsores.

de·cen·te adj. *(honrado)* decent, honorable *<comportamiento d.* decent behavior>; *(adecuado)* decent, adequate *<un salario d.* a decent wage>; *(limpio)* clean, decent *<ropa d.* decent clothes>; *(de buena calidad)* decent, good *<estos zapatos todavía están decentes* these shoes are still good>.

de·cen·te·men·te adv. *(decorosamente)* decently; *(pulcramente)* neatly.

de·cen·vi·ro m. HIST. decemvir.

de·cep·ción f. *(engaño)* deception, trickery; *(desengaño)* disenchantment, disappointment.

de·cep·cio·nar tr. to disenchant, disappoint.

de·ce·so m. decease, death.

de·ci·bel *or* **de·ci·be·lio** m. decibel.

de·ci·ble adj. *(que se puede decir)* utterable, mentionable; *(que se puede explicar)* expressible, communicable.

de·ci·di·do, –da I. past part. see **decidir** II. adj. determined, resolute.

de·ci·dir tr. *(resolver)* to decide, resolve (a matter); *(persuadir)* to persuade, convince <*lo decidí a quedarse* I convinced him to stay>; *(tomar decisión)* to decide, resolve <*decidimos viajar por avión* we decided to travel by plane> —intr. to decide <*el juez decidirá* the judge will decide> ♦ **d. de** to decide <*d. del suerte de un reo* to decide a prisoner's fate> • **d. en** to decide on <*d. en una cuestión* to decide on a question> —reflex. to decide, make up one's mind <*nos decidimos a visitar la capital* we made up our minds to visit the capital>.

de·cien·te, deciento see decentar.

de·ci·gra·mo m. decigram.

de·ci·li·tro m. deciliter.

dé·ci·ma I. f. tenth; RELIG. tithe; POET. ten-line stanza; *(fiebre)* tenth of a degree (on a centigrade thermometer) II. adj. see **décimo, –ma.**

de·ci·mal adj. & m. decimal.

de·cí·me·tro m. decimeter.

dé·ci·mo, –ma I. adj. tenth II. m. tenth; COL., ECUAD., MEX. ten-cent coin —f. see **décima.**

de·ci·moc·ta·vo, –va adj. eighteenth.

de·ci·mo·cuar·to, –ta adj. fourteenth.

de·ci·mo·no·no, –na or **de·ci·mo·no·ve·no, –na** nineteenth.

de·ci·mo·quin·to, –ta adj. fifteenth.

de·ci·mo·sép·ti·mo, –ma adj. seventeenth.

de·ci·mo·sex·to, –ta adj. sixteenth.

de·ci·mo·ter·ce·ro, –ra adj. thirteenth.

de·cir[1] m. *(refrán)* saying; *(ocurrencia)* witticism, witty remark; *(modo de hablar)* language; *(suposición)* figure of speech ♦ **decires de la gente** gossip, talk.

de·cir[2] §21 tr. *(expresar con palabras)* to say <*siempre digo lo que pienso* I always say what I think>; *(estar escrito)* to say <*la Biblia lo dice* the Bible says so>; *(relatar)* to tell <*dígame lo que pasó* tell me what happened>; *(hablar)* to talk, speak <*no digas tonterías* don't talk nonsense>; *(ordenar)* to tell, order <*nos dijeron que nos fuéramos* they told us to go away>; *(divulgar)* to tell, divulge <*me dijo el secreto* he told me the secret>; *(predecir)* to tell <*d. la buenaventura* to tell one's fortune>; *(asegurar)* to tell, assure <*te digo que ella no está mintiendo* I assure you that she is not lying>; *(celebrar)* to say <*d. misa* to say Mass>; FIG. *(mostrar)* to show, reveal <*su semblante dice su alegría* his face shows his happiness>; COLL. *(nombrar)* to call, name <*me dicen Paco* they call me Frank> ♦ **a d. verdad** to tell the truth • **al d. esto** with these words • **como quien dice** or **como si dijéramos** COLL. so to speak, to use that expression <*trabajé como un caballo, como quien dice* I worked like a horse, so to speak> • **d. adiós** to say goodbye • **d. entre** or **para sí** to say to oneself • **d. lo que se le viene a la boca** COLL. to say whatever comes into one's head • **d. por d.** to talk for the sake of talking • **d. que no** to say no • **d. que sí** to say yes, to say so; *(estar de acuerdo)* to agree • **¡diga!** hello! (when answering a telephone) • **el qué dirán** what people may say • **es d.** that is (to say) • **no d. esta boca es mía** COLL. not to say a word • **¡no me digas!** you don't say!, really! • **por decirlo así** so to speak • **que digamos** COLL. to speak of, worth mentioning <*él no tiene mucho dinero, que digamos* he does not have much money to speak of>; particularly, what one would call <*él no es muy inteligente, que digamos* he is not what one would call intelligent> • **querer d.** to mean • **según el d. general** by all accounts.

de·ci·sión f. *(resolución)* decision <*tomar una d.* to make a decision>; *(firmeza)* determination, resoluteness; *(sentencia)* verdict, ruling.

de·ci·si·vo, –va adj. decisive, conclusive.

de·cla·ma·ción f. *(arte)* declamation, oratory; *(perorata)* harangue, tirade; *(recitación)* recital, recitation.

de·cla·ma·dor, –do·ra I. adj. declaiming II. m.f. declaimer, orator.

de·cla·mar tr. & intr. to declaim, recite.

de·cla·ra·ción f. *(afirmación)* declaration, statement; LAW *(testimonio)* deposition, evidence; *(en los juegos de cartas)* bid, call ♦ **d. de derechos** bill of rights • **d. de no culpabilidad** verdict of not guilty • **d. jurada** sworn statement.

de·cla·ra·da·men·te adv. manifestly, openly.

de·cla·ran·te I. adj. declaring II. m.f. LAW declarant, witness.

de·cla·rar tr. *(decir)* to declare, state; *(anunciar)* to declare <*declaró sus intenciones* he declared his intentions>; *(proclamar)* to declare <*d. la guerra* to declare war>; *(en los juegos de cartas)* to bid, declare; LAW *(derecho)* to find, pronounce <*el juez lo declaró culpable* the judge found him guilty> —intr. *(manifestar)* to declare; LAW *(dar testimonio)* to testify, give evidence —reflex. *(dar a conocer los sentimientos)* to declare oneself; *(el amor)* to declare one's love ♦ **declararse culpable** LAW to plead guilty • **declararse inocente** LAW to plead not guilty.

de·cla·ra·ti·vo, –va or **de·cla·ra·to·rio, –ria** adj. declarative, declaratory.

de·cli·na·ble adj. GRAM. declinable.

de·cli·na·ción f. *(descenso)* decline, descent; FIG. *(decadencia)* decadence, decline; GRAM. declension; ASTRON. declination.

de·cli·nan·te adj. declining <*poder d.* declining power>.

de·cli·nar intr. *(inclinarse)* to decline, slope downward; FIG. *(ir hacia su fin)* to wane, draw to a close <*declina el día* the day is waning>; *(una brújula)* to vary from the true meridian (said of a compass); FIG. *(disminuir)* to decline, diminish <*su fuerza está declinando* his energy is declining> —tr. *(rechazar)* to decline, refuse; GRAM. to decline.

de·cli·ve m. *(pendiente)* slope, incline; FIG. *(decadencia)* decadence, decline.

de·co·lo·ra·ción f. *(acción de decolorar)* discoloration, fading; *(del pelo)* bleaching (hair).

de·co·lo·ran·te m. decolorant, bleaching agent.

de·co·lo·rar tr. to discolor, fade.

de·co·mi·sar tr. to confiscate, seize.

de·co·mi·so m. *(acción)* confiscation, seizure; *(objeto)* confiscated object or article.

de·co·ra·ción f. *(acción de decorar)* decoration; *(cosa que decora)* decoration; THEAT. scenery, set.

de·co·ra·do I. past part. see **decorar** II. m. THEAT. scenery, set; *(acción)* decoration.

de·co·ra·dor, –do·ra I. adj. decorative, ornamental II. m.f. decorator ♦ **d. de escaparates** window-dresser

de·co·rar tr. *(adornar)* to decorate, adorn; *(condecorar)* to decorate, bestow honors upon; *(memorizar)* to memorize, learn by heart.

de·co·ra·ti·vo, –va adj. decorative, ornamental.

de·co·ro m. *(respeto)* respect, honor <*tratar a alguien con d.* to treat somone with respect>; *(recato)* decorum, propriety; *(decencia)* decency, decorum <*comportarse con d.* to behave decently>; ARCHIT. ornamentation (of buildings).

de·co·ro·so, –sa adj. *(decente)* decorous, decent; *(digno)* respectable, honorable.

de·cre·cer §17 intr. to decrease, diminish.

de·cre·cien·te adj. decreasing, diminishing.

de·cre·ci·mien·to m. decrease, diminution.

de·cre·men·to m. *(decrecimiento)* decrease, diminution; COMPUT., MATH. decrement.

de·cré·pi·to, –ta adj. decrepit, aged.

de·cre·pi·tud f. decrepitude, old age.

de·cre·tar tr. to decree, order.

de·cre·to m. decree, order ♦ **d. ley** decree-law.

de·crez·ca, decrezco see decrecer.

de·cú·bi·to m. MED. decubitus, reclining position • **d. prono** prone position

de·cu·plar tr. to decuple, multiply by ten.

dé·cu·plo, –pla I. adj. decuple, tenfold II. m. tenfold.

de·cur·so m. passage, course <*en el d. del tiempo* in the course of time>.

de·cha·do m. *(modelo)* model, perfect example <*d. de virtudes* model of virtues>; SEW. sampler.

de·da·da f. pinch, small amount ♦ **dar una d. de miel a alguien** FIG. to keep someone's hopes up.

de·dal m. thimble.

de·de·o m. dexterity, agility of fingers (in playing an instrument).

de·di·ca·ción f. dedication.

de·di·car §70 tr. *(consagrar)* to dedicate, consecrate <*d. una* *iglesia* to consecrate a church>; *(destinar)* to dedicate, devote *<ella dedicó mucho tiempo al estudio* she devoted a lot of time to her studies>; *(dirigir como homenaje)* to dedicate *<dedicó el libro a su esposa* he dedicated the book to his wife> —reflex. to dedicate *or* devote oneself.

de·di·ca·to·ria I. f. dedication, inscription **II.** adj. see **dedicatorio, –ria.**

de·di·ca·to·rio, –ria I. adj. dedicatory, dedicative **II.** f. see **dedicatoria.**

de·di·llo m. little finger, pinky ♦ **al d.** COLL. perfectly, thoroughly • **saber al d.** to know by heart.

de·di·qué, dedique see **dedicar.**

de·do m. ANAT. *(de la mano)* finger; *(del pie)* toe; *(medida)* finger, *(porción)* bit, smidgen ♦ **a dos dedos de** FIG., COLL. within an inch of • **cogerse los dedos** FIG. to get caught • **contar con los dedos** to count on one's fingers • **chuparse los dedos** *(comer)* to eat with relish; FIG., COLL. *(gozar)* to smack one's lips • **d.** anular ring finger • **d. cordial** *or* **del corazón** middle finger • **d. índice** index finger, forefinger • **d. meñique** little finger, pinky • **d. pulgar** *or* **gordo** *(de la mano)* thumb; *(del pie)* big toe • **el d. de Dios** FIG. the hand of God • **mamarse** *or* **chuparse el d.** FIG., COLL. to be a fool • **meterle a alguien los dedos** FIG., COLL. to pump someone (for information) • **morderse los dedos** to bite one's nails; FIG., COLL. *(arrepentirse)* to regret • **no mamarse** *or* **chuparse el d.** FIG., COLL. to be shrewd • **no tener dos dedos de frente** COLL. to lack intelligence • **poner bien los dedos** MUS. to play well • **poner el d. en la llaga** FIG. to pinpoint the trouble spot • **poner los cinco dedos en la cara a alguien** FIG. to slap someone across the face • **señalar a alguien con el d.** FIG. to point the finger at someone, accuse someone.

de·duc·ción f. *(acción de deducir)* deduction; LOG. inference; MUS. diatonic scale.

de·du·cir §22 tr. *(concluir)* to deduce, conclude; *(rebajar)* to deduct, subtract.

de·duc·ti·vo, –va adj. deductive.

de·fal·car §70 tr. *(rebajar)* to deduct; *(robar)* to embezzle.

de·fe·ca·ción f. defecation.

de·fe·car §70 I. tr. to defecate (clarify a chemical solution) **II.** intr. to defecate.

de·fec·ción f. defection, desertion.

de·fec·ti·vo, –va I. adj. *(defectuoso)* defective, faulty; GRAM. defective **II.** m. GRAM. defective verb.

de·fec·to m. *(imperfección)* defect, flaw; *(falta)* absence, lack ♦ **defectos** PRINT. sheets left over *or* lacking • **en d. de** in the absence of, for want of.

de·fec·tuo·so, –sa adj. defective, faulty.

de·fen·der §50 tr. *(proteger)* to defend, protect; LAW *(derecho)* to defend —intr. & reflex. *(protegerse)* to defend *or* protect oneself; *(arreglárselas)* to manage, get by.

de·fen·di·ble adj. defensible.

de·fen·di·do, –da I. past part. see **defender II.** adj. defended **III.** m.f. LAW defendant.

de·fen·sa f. *(resistencia)* defense; *(protección)* protection, defense; LAW *(apología)* defense, speech for the defense; MIL. defense; SPORT. *(deportes)* defense, defenders; MARIT. fender (of a boat) ♦ **d. propia** *or* **legítima d.** self-defense.

de·fen·si·va I. f. defensive *<estar a la d.* to be on the defensive> **II.** adj. see **defensivo, –va.**

de·fen·si·vo, –va I. adj. defensive, protective **II.** m. *(resguardo)* defense, safeguard; MED. wet compress —f. see **defensiva.**

de·fen·sor, –so·ra I. adj. defending, protecting **II.** m.f. defender, protector —m. LAW defense counsel.

de·fe·qué, defeque see **defecar.**

de·fe·ren·cia f. deference.

de·fe·ren·te adj. *(respetuoso)* deferential; ANAT. deferent.

de·fe·rir §65 intr. to defer —tr. to refer, delegate.

de·fi·cien·cia f. deficiency, lack.

de·fi·cien·te adj. *(insuficiente)* deficient, lacking • *(defectuoso)* defective, poor.

dé·fi·cit m. [pl. **–cits**] COM. deficit; FIG. *(carencia)* shortage, lack.

de·fi·ci·ta·rio, –ria adj. showing a deficit.

de·fien·da, defiendo see **defender.**

de·fie·ra, defiero see **deferir.**

de·fi·ni·ción f. *(acción de definir)* definition; *(determinación)*

determination, decision ♦ **definiciones** MIL. rules, statutes • **por d.** by definition.

de·fi·ni·do, –da I. past part. see **definir II.** adj. *(explicado)* defined *<bien d.* well defined>; GRAM. definite *<artículo d.* definite article> **III.** m. definition.

de·fi·nir tr. *(fijar)* to define *<d. una palabra* to define a word>; *(determinar)* to determine, decide; PAINT. to complete, finish.

de·fi·ni·ti·vo, –va adj. definitive, final♦ **en definitiva** *(por fin)* once and for all, finally; *(de verdad)* really, exactly *<no sé en definitiva* I don't really know>; *(en resumen)* in short.

de·fi·rie·ra, defirió see **deferir.**

de·fla·ción f. deflation.

de·fla·gra·ción f. deflagration, intense combustion.

de·fla·gra·dor, –do·ra I. adj. deflagrating **II.** m. electric detonator (for exploding dynamite).

de·fla·grar intr. to deflagrate.

de·flec·tor m. TECH. deflector, baffle.

de·fo·lia·ción f. BOT. defoliation.

de·fo·lian·te m. CHEM. defoliant.

de·for·ma·ción f. *(acción de deformar)* deformation; RAD. distortion; MECH. strain; *(alabeo)* warp ♦ **d. lindera** *or* **de límite** GEOL. boundary deformation.

de·for·ma·dor, –do·ra I. adj. deforming **II.** m.f. deformer.

de·for·mar tr. *(alterar la forma)* to deform; RAD. to distort; MECH. to strain; *(alabear)* to warp —reflex. to be *or* become deformed.

de·for·me adj. deformed, misshapen.

de·for·mi·dad f. *(física)* deformity; FIG. *(moral)* moral shortcoming.

de·frau·da·ción f. *(fraude)* fraud, cheating; *(decepción)* disappointment ♦ **d. fiscal** *or* **de impuestos** tax evasion.

de·frau·da·dor, –do·ra I. adj. *(engañador)* deceiving, cheating; *(decepcionante)* disappointing **II.** m.f. *(evasor)* evader *<d. fiscal* tax evader>; *(estafador)* swindler, cheat.

de·frau·dar tr. *(estafar)* to defraud, cheat; *(decepcionar)* to disappoint; FIG. *(frustrar)* to dash, thwart (hopes); FIG. *(turbar)* to disturb, spoil; *(en los impuestos)* to evade; PHYS. to block, cut off (light).

de·fun·ción f. demise, death.

de·ge·ne·ra·ción f. *(acción de degenerar)* degeneration; *(de moral)* degeneracy; MED. degeneration, deterioration.

de·ge·ne·ra·do, –da I. past part. see **degenerar II.** adj. & **III.** m.f. degenerate.

de·ge·ne·rar intr. *(declinar)* to degenerate; *(perder mérito)* to decline, decay; MED. to degenerate, deteriorate.

de·glu·tir tr. & intr. to swallow.

de·go·lla·ción f. *(degüello)* throat cutting; *(decapitación)* beheading, decapitation; FIG. *(matanza)* massacre, slaughter.

de·go·lla·de·ro m. ANAT. throat, windpipe; *(del vestido)* neckline; *(matadero)* slaughterhouse; *(cadalso)* scaffold, block (for executions) ♦ **llevar al d.** COLL. to lead to the slaughterhouse, throw to the dogs.

de·go·lla·do, –da I. past part. see **degollar II.** m. décolletage, low neckline.

de·go·lla·du·ra f. *(herida)* cut (in throat); *(escote)* low neckline; ARCHIT. shaft (of balustrade); *(junta entre ladrillos)* joint (between two bricks).

de·go·lla·mien·to m. var. of **degollación.**

de·go·llar §19 tr. *(guillotinar)* to cut *or* slit the throat of; *(decapitar)* to behead, decapitate; FIG. *(masacrar)* to massacre, slaughter; *(destruir)* to destroy, ruin; SEW. *(escotar)* to cut a low neckline; MARIT. to slash (a sail); FIG., COLL. *(aburrir)* to bore to death *<Juan me degüella* John bores me to death>.

de·gra·da·ción f. degradation, debasement; MIL. demotion, lowering in rank; PAINT. gradation.

de·gra·dan·te adj. degrading, debasing.

de·gra·dar tr. *(envilecer)* to degrade, debase; MIL. to demote, lower in rank; PAINT. to gradate —reflex. to degrade *or* lower oneself.

de·güe·lle, degüello see **degollar.**

de·güe·llo m. throat cutting; *(decapitación)* beheading, decapitation; FIG. *(matanza)* massacre, slaughter; *(del arma)* shaft, narrow part (of a weapon) ♦ **entrar a d.** to massacre, put to the sword • **tirar a d.** to endeavor to harm.

de·gus·ta·ción f. tasting, sampling.

de·he·sa f. pasture, grazing land.

dei·ci·da I. adj. deicidal II. m.f. deicide (killer of a god).

dei·ci·dio m. deicide (killing of a god).

dei·dad f. deity, divinity.

dei·fi·ca·ción f. deification.

dei·fi·car §70 tr. (divinizar) to deify; (ensalzar) to glorify, exalt.

de·ja·dez f. (negligencia) carelessness, negligence; (desaliño) slovenliness, untidiness; (pereza) laziness.

de·ja·do, –da I. past part. see **dejar** II. adj. (negligente) careless, negligent; (desaliñado) slovenly, untidy; (perezoso) lazy; (deprimido) depressed, dejected ♦ **d. de la mano de Dios** FIG. godforsaken.

de·ja·dor m. (el que presta) lender; (el que cede) bequeather.

de·jar tr. (abandonar) to leave <dejé el vaso en la mesa I left the glass on the table>; (posponer) to leave <dejaron lo más difícil para más tarde they left the most difficult part for later>; (consentir) to let, allow <d. correr el agua to let the water run>; (producir) to yield, produce <este negocio me dejará buena ganancia this deal will yield me a good profit>; (desamparar) to abandon, desert <dejó a sus antiguos amigos she abandoned her old friends>; (ausentarse de) to leave, depart <dejaron la ciudad they left the city>; (encargar) to leave, entrust <me dejó al cuidado de sus asuntos he entrusted the care of his affairs to me>; (legar) to leave, bequeath <mi padre me dejó su fortuna my father left me his fortune>; (nombrar) to name, designate <el presidente de la compañía no dejó sucesor the president of the company did not name a successor>; (cesar) to stop, quit <d. la carrera to quit the race>; (no inquietar) to leave, let be <¡déjame en paz! leave me in peace!>; (prestar) to lend, loan <déjame el libro, por favor lend me the book, please> ♦ **¡deja!** or **¡déjalo!** never mind! • **d. aparte** to leave aside • **d. atrás** (abandonar) to leave behind; FIG. (superar) to surpass, outdo • **d. caer** to drop, let go of • **d. con la boca abierta** FIG. to stun, astonish • **d. dicho** or **escrito** to leave word • **d. el paso libre** to let pass • **d. en blanco** to leave blank • **d. fresco a** COLL. to baffle, perplex • **d. mal** FIG. to let down <me dejó mal he let me down> • **d. plantado** COLL. to leave in the lurch, stand up • **d. que** to leave <su trabajo deja mucho que desear his work leaves a lot to be desired> • **d. saber** AMER. to let know • **d. ver** to show —intr. ♦ **d. de** to stop, leave off <dejó de correr he stopped running> • **d. de existir** to die • **no d. de** to not neglect to, not fail to <no dejes de llamarme don't fail to call me> —reflex. (descuidarse) to let oneself go, become sloppy; (abandonarse) to give oneself up to, abandon oneself to <me dejé al arbitrio de la fortuna I abandoned myself to the winds of fortune>; (permitirse) to allow oneself to be <no te dejes manipular don't allow yourself to be manipulated> ♦ **dejarse caer** (caerse) to fall, flop <se dejó caer en el sillón he flopped into the armchair>; FIG., COLL. (insinuar) to drop a hint, insinuate; (presentarse) to drop in unexpectedly • **dejarse decir** to let slip, let out <se dejó decir que no tenía el dinero he let slip that he did not have the money> • **dejarse de rodeos** to stop beating around the bush, come to the point • **dejarse llevar de** to get carried away with • **dejarse ver** (aparecer) to show; (presentarse) to show up (at a social gathering) • **no dejarse ensillar** FIG., COLL. to stand firm.

de·jo m. (dejación) abandonment, relinquishment; (fin) end, termination; (acento) accent, lilt; (inflexión) drop (in voice); (gusto) aftertaste; (flojedad) neglect, indolence; FIG. aftertaste <me quedé con un d. de amargura después de su visita I was left with a bitter aftertaste after his visit>.

del §G16 [contr. of **de** and **el**] of the <el poder del presidente the power of the president>; from the <vengo del norte I come from the north> —see **de¹**.

de·la·ción f. denunciation, accusation.

de·lan·tal m. (sin faja) apron; (con peto) pinafore.

de·lan·te adv. (con prioridad) in front, ahead <ir d. to walk in front>; (enfrente) facing, opposite ♦ **de d.** in front, front <el caballo de d. the front horse> • **d. de** in front of,

before <confesar d. del juez to confess before a judge>; in front of, ahead <andar d. de los otros to walk ahead of the others> • **tener algo d. de las narices** to have something under one's nose • **tener algo por d.** to have something ahead of one.

de·lan·te·ra I. f. (frente) front, front part; (ventaja) advantage, lead; (de un libro) front edge (of a book); THEAT. front row; SPORT. forward line ♦ **delanteras** overalls • **coger** or **tomar la d.** to take the lead • **llevar la d.** to lead, be in the lead II. adj. see **delantero, –ra.**

de·lan·te·ro, –ra I. adj. front, fore II. m. (de un vestido) front; SPORT. forward —f. see **delantera.**

de·la·tar tr. (denunciar) to denounce, inform on; (revelar) to reveal, expose.

de·la·tor, –to·ra I. adj. denouncing, informing II. m.f. denouncer, informer.

de·le·ble adj. erasable, delible.

de·lec·ta·ción f. delight, delectation.

de·le·ga·ción f. (acción de delegar) delegation; (cargo y oficina) office; (sucursal) branch, local office.

de·le·ga·do, –da I. past part. see **delegar** II. adj. delegated III. m.f. delegate, representative.

de·le·gar §47 tr. to delegate.

de·lei·ta·ble adj. delightful, enjoyable.

de·lei·ta·ción f. or **de·lei·ta·mien·to** m. delight, pleasure.

de·lei·tar tr. to delight, please —reflex. ♦ **deleitarse con** or **en** to take pleasure in, delight in <me deleito en leer I take pleasure in reading>.

de·lei·te m. delight, pleasure.

de·lei·to·so, –sa adj. delightful, pleasing.

de·le·té·re·o, –a adj. deleterious, noxious.

de·le·tre·ar tr. (pronunciar) to spell (out); FIG. (descifrar) to decipher, interpret; CHILE to observe closely.

de·le·tre·o m. (de palabras o sílabas) spelling; (desciframiento) deciphering.

de·lez·na·ble adj. (que se rompe fácilmente) crumbly <arcilla d. crumbly clay>; (resbaladizo) slippery; (quebradizo) brittle, fragile; FIG. frail, weak <excusa d. weak excuse>.

del·fín m. ZOOL. dolphin; (príncipe) dauphin.

Del·fos Delphi.

del·ga·dez f. (esbeltez) slenderness, slimness; (flacura) thinness.

del·ga·do, –da I. adj. (esbelto) slender, slim; (flaco) thin; FIG. (tenue) tenuous, delicate; (agudo) sharp, clever; AGR. poor, exhausted (soil) ♦ **hilar d.** FIG., COLL. to split hairs • **ponerse d.** to lose weight II. m.pl. **delgados** flanks (of animals).

de·li·be·ra·ción f. deliberation.

de·li·be·ra·da·men·te adv. deliberately, on purpose.

de·li·be·ra·do, –da I. past part. see **deliberar** II. adj. deliberate, intentional.

de·li·be·rar intr. to deliberate, ponder —tr. to decide, resolve.

de·li·ca·dez f. (debilidad) weakness, frailty; (indolencia) indolence, laziness; (sensibilidad) touchiness, hypersensitivity.

de·li·ca·de·za f. delicacy <admiraron la d. del encaje they admired the delicacy of the lace>; (ligereza) fineness, daintiness; (finura) subtlety, refinement; (sensibilidad) touchiness, hypersensitivity; (discreción) tactfulness, discretion; (debilidad) weakness, frailty ♦ **con d.** gently; (con tacto) tactfully • **tener la d. de** to be thoughtful enough to.

de·li·ca·do, –da adj. delicate <un perfume d. a delicate perfume>; (exquisito) exquisite, fine; (bien parecido) fine, delicate <facciones delicadas fine features>; difficult, delicate <una operación d. a difficult operation>; (embarazoso) delicate <una situación d. a delicate situation>; (fino) refined, polite; (atento) considerate, thoughtful; (exigente) demanding, exacting; (enojadizo) touchy, hypersensitive; (quebradizo) fragile, delicate; (enfermizo) frail, delicate; FIG. (de buen juicio) refined, subtle <paladar d. subtle palate>.

de·li·cia f. delight, pleasure.

de·li·cio·sa·men·te adv. (con encanto) delightfully; (sabrosamente) deliciously.

de·li·cio·so, –sa adj. (agradable) delightful; (sabroso) delicious.

de·lic·ti·vo, –va *or* de·lic·tuo·so, –sa adj. criminal.
de·li·mi·tar tr. to delimit, mark the boundaries of.
de·lin·ca, delinco see delinquir.
de·lin·cuen·cia f. delinquency, criminality ♦ d. Juvenil *or* de menores juvenile delinquency.
de·lin·cuen·te adj. & m.f. delinquent ♦ d. primario *or* sin antecedente penal first offender • d. habitual hardened criminal • d. Juvenil juvenile delinquent.
de·li·ne·a·dor, –do·ra I. adj. delineating, outlining II. m.f. *(persona que delinea)* delineator; *(dibujante)* draftsman.
de·li·ne·a·men·to *or* de·li·ne·a·mien·to m. *(acción)* delineation, outlining; *(dibujo)* sketch, draft.
de·li·ne·an·te m. draftsman.
de·li·ne·ar tr. to delineate, outline.
de·lin·quir §23 intr. to break the law, trangress.
de·li·ran·te adj. delirious.
de·li·rar intr. *(sufrir delirio)* to be delirious, suffer from delirium; FIG. *(decir tonterías)* to rave, talk nonsense.
de·li·rio m. *(desvarío)* delirium; FIG. *(manía)* mania, frenzy; COLL. *(disparate)* raving ♦ con d. madly • d. de grandeza delusions of grandeur • tener d. por to be crazy about.
de·li·to m. offense, crime ♦ d. común common law offense • d. de incendio arson • d. de mayor cuantía felony • d. de menor cuantía misdemeanor • cogido en flagrante d. caught red-handed.
del·ta m. GEOG. delta —f. delta (Greek letter).
de·lu·si·vo, –va *or* de·lu·so·rio, –ria adj. delusive, deceptive.
de·ma·cra·do, –da adj. emaciated, wasted away.
de·ma·crar·se reflex. to become emaciated, waste away.
de·ma·go·gia f. demagogy, demagoguery.
de·ma·gó·gi·co, –ca adj. demagogic, demagogical.
de·ma·go·go, –ga I. m.f. demagogue II. adj. demagogic.
de·man·da f. *(pedida)* demand; *(petición)* appeal, request; *(limosna)* alms; *(pregunta)* question, inquiry; *(empresa)* enterprise; *(empeño)* perseverance; COM. demand *<este producto no tiene d. hoy día* this product is not in demand these days>; *(pedido)* order; ELEC. load *<d. máxima* peak load>; LAW *(escrito)* writ; *(acción)* lawsuit, action; THEAT. call ♦ d. por daños y perjuicios LAW claim for damages • demandas y respuestas haggling • entablar *or* poner una d. LAW to bring suit • estimar una d. LAW to allow a claim • ir en d. de to go in search of • salir uno a la d. LAW to oppose an action; FIG. *(defender)* to defend.
de·man·da·do, –da I. past part. see demandar II. m.f. LAW defendant.
de·man·da·dor, –do·ra m.f. LAW plaintiff; *(de limosnas)* alms-collector.
de·man·dan·te m.f. LAW plaintiff.
de·man·dar tr. *(pedir)* to request, ask for; *(preguntar)* to ask; *(desear)* to desire, long for; LAW to sue, file suit against.
de·mar·ca·ción f. demarcation.
de·mar·car §70 tr. to demarcate, delimit.
de·más I. adj. other, rest of the *<nosotros llegamos a las cuatro y la d. gente, más tarde* we arrived at four o'clock and the other people, later> ♦ lo d. the rest • por d. *(en demasía)* excessively, too much; *(inútilmente)* in vain • por lo d. otherwise, other than that *<es un coche viejo pero por lo d. anda bien* it is an old car but other than that it runs well> • todo lo d. everything else • y d. etcetera, and so on; *(y los otros)* and the others II. adv. moreover, besides.
de·ma·sí·a f. *(exceso)* excess, surplus; *(abuso)* disregard, abuse; *(insolencia)* insolence, audacity; MIN. space between two claims ♦ en d. excessively.
de·ma·sia·do, –da I. adj. too much *or* many, excessive II. adv. too *<es d. pesado* it is too heavy>; too much *<comer d.* to eat too much>.
de·men·cia f. *(locura)* madness, insanity; MED. dementia.
de·men·tar tr. to drive mad *or* insane.
de·men·te I. adj. insane, demented II. m.f. insane person, lunatic —m. madman —f. madwoman.
de·me·ri·to·rio, –ria adj. unworthy, undeserving.
de·mi·sión f. submission, humility.
de·mo·ción f. demotion.

de·mo·cra·cia f. democracy.
de·mó·cra·ta I. adj. democratic II. m.f. democrat.
de·mo·crá·ti·co, –ca adj. POL. democratic; FIG. *(popular)* popular, widespread.
de·mo·cra·ti·za·ción f. democratization.
de·mo·cra·ti·zar §04 tr. to democratize, make democratic.
de·mo·gra·fí·a f. demography.
de·mo·grá·fi·co, –ca adj. demographic.
de·mó·gra·fo, –fa m.f. demographer.
de·mo·le·dor, –do·ra I. adj. *(destructivo)* demolishing, destructive; FIG. *(arruinador)* devastating *<crítica demoledora* devastating criticism> II. m.f. demolisher, wrecker.
de·mo·ler §78 tr. to demolish, destroy.
de·mo·li·ción f. demolition, destruction.
de·mo·nia·co, –ca adj. demoniacal, demonic.
de·mo·nio m. *(diablo)* demon, devil; *(genio)* evil spirit; FIG., COLL. *(travieso)* rascal, mischievous person ♦ ¿cómo demonios . . .? how in the hell . . .? • como el d. like the devil, like hell *<ir como el d.* to go like hell> • darse a todos los demonios COLL. to fly off the handle • de mil *or* todos los demonios a hell of a *<una sorpresa de mil demonios* a hell of a surprise> • ¡demonios! hell!, damn! • ¡que me lleve el d.! I'll be damned! • tener el d. en el cuerpo FIG., COLL. to be full of the devil.
de·mo·no·la·trí·a f. demonolatry.
de·mo·ra f. *(tardanza)* delay, wait; MARIT. bearing.
de·mo·rar tr. to delay, hold up —intr. *(detenerse)* to linger, stay; MARIT. to bear —reflex. to take a long time, delay *<demorarse en contestar* to take a long time to answer>.
de·mos·tra·ción f. *(muestra)* demonstration; *(ostentación)* show, display; *(prueba)* proof; AMER. public demonstration ♦ d. de cariño show of affection • d. de cólera display of anger.
de·mos·trar §19 tr. to demonstrate, show; *(probar)* to prove.
de·mos·tra·ti·vo, –va I. adj. demonstrative ♦ adjetivo, pronombre p. GRAM. demonstrative adjective, pronoun II. m. GRAM. demonstrative.
de·mu·dar tr. to change, turn pale —reflex. *(la cara)* to change, turn pale (said of the face); *(alterarse)* to become suddenly upset *or* agitated.
de·mue·la, demuelo see demoler.
de·mues·tre, demuestro see demostrar.
de·ne·gar §52 tr. *(rechazar)* to refuse, reject; *(negar)* to deny.
den·go·so, –sa adj. hypersensitive, finicky.
den·gue m. *(melindre)* affectation, coyness; *(esclavina)* woman's cape; MED. dengue fever; CHILE, BOT. marvel of Peru; SP., SL. devil, evil spirit ♦ no me vengas con dengues don't put on airs.
de·nie·go, deniegue see denegar.
de·ni·gra·ción f. denigration, disparagement.
de·ni·gra·dor, –do·ra *or* de·ni·gran·te I. adj. denigrating, disparaging II. m.f. denigrator, disparager.
de·ni·grar tr. *(desacreditar)* to denigrate, disparage; *(injuriar)* to insult.
de·no·da·do, –da adj. bold, intrepid.
de·no·mi·na·ción f. *(acción)* denomination, naming; *(nombre)* denomination, name.
de·no·mi·na·do, –da I. past part. see denominar II. adj. ATH. denominate, compound *<número d.* compound number>.
de·no·mi·na·dor, –do·ra I. adj. denominating, denominative II. m.f. denominator —m. MATH. denominator.
de·no·mi·nar tr. to denominate, name.
de·nos·tar §19 tr. to abuse, insult.
de·no·tar tr. *(indicar)* to denote, designate; *(significar)* to denote, mean.
den·si·dad f. *(calidad de denso)* density, thickness; PHYS. density ♦ d. absoluta PHYS. true specific gravity • d. de radiación PHYS. radiation flux.
den·so, –sa adj. *(espeso)* dense, thick; *(sólido)* heavy, solid; FIG. *(oscuro)* dark, black.
den·ta·do, –da I. past part. see dentar II. adj. *(que tiene dientes)* dentate, toothed; HER. crenelated III. m. *(borde)* perforation —f. AMER. bite.

den·ta·du·ra f. DENT. (set of) teeth ♦ **d. postiza** false teeth, dentures.

den·tal I. adj. DENT., PHONET. dental II. f. PHONET. dental consonant.

den·tar §49 tr. *(formar dientes)* to tooth, put teeth in; *(endentecer)* to serrate.

den·te·lla·da I. f. *(movimiento)* snap of the jaws; *(mordisco)* bite; *(señal)* tooth mark ♦ **a dentelladas** with the teeth • **dar dentelladas** to bite II. adj. see **dentellado, –da.**

den·te·lla·do, –da I. past part. see **dentellar** II. adj. *(que tiene dientes)* dentate, toothed; HER. engrailed III. f. see **dentellada.**

den·te·llar intr. to chatter (said of the teeth).

den·te·lle·ar tr. to nibble, bite.

den·te·ra f. *(en los dientes)* setting (the teeth) on edge; FIG. *(envidia)* envy, jealousy; *(deseo intenso)* vehement desire, longing ♦ **dar a alguien d.** *(incomodar)* to set someone's teeth on edge; *(dar envidia)* to make someone jealous.

den·ti·ción f. *(acción)* teething; *(período)* teething period; ANAT. set of teeth ♦ **primera d.** first set of teeth.

den·tí·fri·co, –ca I. adj. ♦ **pasta d.** toothpaste II. m. toothpaste, dentifrice.

den·tis·ta m.f. dentist.

den·tro adv. *(en el interior)* inside, within, in; *(de un edificio)* inside, indoors ♦ **d. de** inside, within, in • **d. de poco** shortly, soon • **de** *or* **desde d.** from (the) inside • **¡d. o fuera!** COLL. yes or no!, make up your mind! • **hacia d.** toward the inside *or* interior • **por d.** inside, inwardly, on the inside.

den·tu·do, –da I. adj. large-toothed, toothy II. m. CUBA, ICHTH. type of shark.

de·nue·do m. bravery, courage.

de·nues·te, denuesto see **denostar.**

de·nues·to m. insult, affront.

de·nun·cia f. *(declaración)* declaration, report; *(acusación)* accusation, denunciation; DIPL. denouncement (of a treaty).

de·nun·cia·ble adj. punishable (offense).

de·nun·cia·ción f. denunciation.

de·nun·cia·dor, –do·ra *or* **de·nun·cian·te** I. adj. denouncing, accusing II. m.f. denouncer, accuser.

de·nun·ciar tr. *(declarar)* to declare, announce <*d. la guerra* to declare war>; *(acusar)* to accuse, denounce; *(pronosticar)* to foretell, prophesy; DIPL. *(anular)* to denounce, revoke (a treaty); FIG. *(indicar)* to indicate, reveal; *(delatar)* to denounce, censure; AMER., MIN. to register a claim.

de·nun·cio m. MIN. registration of a claim; AMER. denunciation.

de·on·to·lo·gí·a f. PHILOS. deontology.

de·pa·rar tr. to supply, provide ♦ **la primera casa que me deparó la suerte** the first house I chanced upon.

de·par·ta·men·tal adj. departmental.

de·par·ta·men·to m. *(parte)* department, section; *(distrito)* province, district; *(compartimiento)* compartment; *(piso)* apartment, flat (G.B.) ♦ **d. de bienes raíces** real estate department • **d. de máquinas** MARIT. engine room • **d. de mercería** notions counter *or* department • **d. jurídico** legal department.

de·par·tir intr. to talk, converse.

de·pau·pe·ra·ción f. *(empobrecimiento)* impoverishment; MED. weakness, exhaustion.

de·pau·pe·rar tr. *(empobrecer)* to impoverish; MED. to weaken, exhaust —reflex. *(empobrecerse)* to become needy *or* impoverished; MED. to become weak *or* exhausted.

de·pen·den·cia f. *(subordinación)* dependence, reliance; *(parentesco)* relationship, kinship; *(amistad)* friendship, relationship; COM. *(sucursal)* branch (office); *(negocio)* business, agency; *(empleados)* employees, subordinates ♦ **d. de la droga** MED., PSYCH. drug addiction • **dependencias** accessories.

de·pen·der intr. to depend ♦ **d. de** *(estar bajo de uno)* to depend *or* rely on, be dependent on; *(ser consecuencia de)* to depend on, be contingent on.

de·pen·dien·te, –ta I. adj. dependent, subordinate II. m.f. *(empleado)* employee; *(de tienda)* clerk, salesperson.

de·pi·la·ción f. depilation.

de·pi·lar tr. to depilate, remove hair from.

de·plo·ra·ble adj. deplorable, lamentable.

de·plo·rar tr. to deplore, lament.

de·po·nen·te I. adj. GRAM. deponent (verb) II. m.f. LAW deponent, witness; GRAM. deponent verb.

de·po·ner §54 tr. *(apartar)* to lay *or* put aside; *(privar)* to depose, deprive of office; LAW *(afirmar)* to testify, provide testimony for; *(bajar)* to lower, bring *or* take down; GUAT., HOND., MEX. to vomit, regurgitate —intr. *(defecar)* to defecate, move the bowels; LAW *(dar testimonio)* to testify, make a deposition.

de·por·ta·ción f. deportation.

de·por·tar tr. to deport, exile.

de·por·tis·ta I. adj. *(perteneciente a los deportes)* sporting, sporty; COLL. *(aficionado)* fond of sports II. m.f. *(aficionado)* sports fan —m. sportsman —f. sportswoman.

de·por·ti·vo, –va adj. *(relativo a los deportes)* sporting, sports <*club d.* sports club>; *(aficionado a los deportes)* sportive, fond of sports.

de·po·si·ción f. *(de un rey)* deposition, deposal; LAW deposition, tesimony; PHYSIOL. defecation, bowel movement.

de·po·si·tan·te I. adj. depositing II. m.f. depositor.

de·po·si·tar tr. to deposit <*d. dinero en el banco* to deposit money in the bank>; *(almacenar)* to deposit, store <*d. mercancía en un almacén* to deposit merchandise in a warehouse>; *(sedimentar)* to deposit, leave (sediment); FIG. *(encomendar)* to place <*deposité la confianza en mi abogado* I placed my confidence in my lawyer> —reflex. to settle.

de·po·si·ta·rio, –ria m.f. *(de un depósito)* depositary, trustee —m. *(cajero)* cashier; *(tesorero)* treasurer.

de·pó·si·to m. deposit <*d. de ahorros* savings deposit>; *(almacén)* warehouse, storehouse; *(cisterna)* cistern, tank; *(desembolso inicial)* deposit, down payment; CHEM. deposit, sediment; GEOL., MIN. deposit; MIL. depot, dump ♦ **d. a la vista** *or* **disponible** COM. demand deposit • **d. compresor** pressure tank • **d. de agua** reservoir, water tank • **d. de cadáveres** mortuary, morgue • **d. de equipaje** checkroom, baggage room • **d. de libros** book stack, stacks • **d. de locomotoras** RAIL. roundhouse • **d. de maderas** lumberyard • **d. de municiones** MIL. ammunition dump • **d. indistinto** COM. joint deposit.

de·pra·va·ción f. *(alteración)* alteration; FIG. *(corrupción)* corruption, depravity.

de·pra·va·do, –da I. past part. see **depravar** II. adj. depraved, corrupted III. m.f. depraved person, degenerate.

de·pra·va·dor, –do·ra I. adj. depraving II. m.f. depraver, corrupter.

de·pra·var tr. *(echar a perder)* to harm, damage; FIG. *(corromper)* to deprave, corrupt.

de·pre·ca·ción f. entreaty, petition.

de·pre·can·te I. adj. imploring, beseeching II. m.f. implorer, suppliant.

de·pre·car §70 tr. to beg, implore.

de·pre·ca·to·rio, –ria adj. supplicatory, imploring.

de·pre·cia·ción f. depreciation, decrease in value ♦ **d. de línea recta** *or* **simplista** ECON. straight-line depreciation.

de·pre·ciar tr. to depreciate, decrease the value of.

de·pre·da·ción f. *(saqueo)* depredation, pillaging; *(malversación)* embezzlement, misappropriation.

de·pre·da·dor m.f. plunderer, pillager.

de·pre·dar tr. to plunder, pillage.

de·pre·qué, depreque see **deprecar.**

de·pre·sión f. *(hundimiento)* depression, pressing in *or* down; GEOL. depression, hollow; MED. depression, debilitation; PSYCH. depression, dejection; METEOROL. depression, low; ECON. depression, severe and prolonged slump; FIG. *(humillación)* humiliation, embarassment ♦ **d. de horizonte** MARIT. dip (of the horizon).

de·pre·si·vo, –va adj. MED. depressive; *(deprimente)* depressing.

de·pri·men·te adj. depressing.

de·pri·mi·do, –da I. past part. see **deprimir** II. adj. depressed.

de·pri·mir tr. *(hundir)* to depress, sink; ECON., MED. *(debilitar)* to depress, weaken; PSYCH. *(abatir)* to depress, deject; METEOROL. to lower, decrease; FIG. *(humillar)* to humiliate, embarrass —reflex. PSYCH. to get depressed.

de·pu·ra·ción f. *(purificación)* depuration, purification; POL., FIG. purge, purging.

de·pu·rar tr. *(purificar)* to depurate, purify; POL., FIG. to purge.

de·pu·sie·ra, depuso see **deponer.**

de·re·cha·zo m. *(en boxeo)* right, blow with the right; TAUR. right-handed pass with the final cape.

de·re·chis·mo m. POL. rightism.

de·re·chis·ta POL. **I.** adj. right-wing, rightist **II.** m.f. right-winger, rightist.

de·re·cho I. m. *(autoridad)* right, authority <*ellos no tienen el d. de entrar aquí* they do not have the right to enter here>; *(privilegio)* right, privilege <*los derechos que da la amistad* the privileges that friendship offers>; *(conjunto de leyes)* law <*d. municipal* municipal law>; *(justicia)* justice; *(estudio)* law <*un estudiante de d.* a law student>; TEX. *(de tela)* right side ◊ **ambos derechos** both canon and civil law • **con d. a** with a right to • **de d.** LAW de jure, by right • **d. administrativo** administrative law • **d. canónico** RELIG. canon law • **d. civil** civil law • **d. consuetudinario** common law • **d. de paso** right of way • **d. de propiedad literaria** copyright • **d. de reunión** right of assembly • **d. de votar** right to vote, franchise • **d. divino** divine right • **d. escrito** *or* **positivo** statute law • **d. internacional** international law • **d. mercantil** business law • **d. natural** natural law • **d. penal** criminal law • **derechos** *(impuestos)* duties, taxes; *(honorarios)* fees, charges • **derechos arancelarios** *or* **de aduana** customs duties • **derechos civiles** civil rights • **derechos de autor** royalties • **derechos de entrada** import duties • **derechos de puerto** harbor dues • **hacer valer sus derechos** to exercise one's rights • **hecho y d.** complete, full • **tener d. a** to have a right to **II.** adv. *(por el camino más recto)* straight, right <*fue d. a su casa* he went right home>; COLL. right, honestly <*vamos a hacerlo d.* let's do it right> ◊ **todo d.** straight ahead <*siga todo d. para llegar al museo* continue straight ahead to reach the museum> **III.** adj. see **derecho, –cha.**

de·re·cho, –cha I. adj. right <*el brazo d.* the right arm>; right-hand <*el margen d.* the right-hand margin>; *(vertical)* upright, erect <*esta estaca no está d.* this post is not upright>; *(recto)* straight, even; AMER. lucky, fortunate ◊ **a derechas** right, properly • **estar derechos** ARG., PAR. to be even, owing nothing **II.** f. *(lado derecho)* right side, right-hand side; *(diestra)* right hand; POL. right, right wing ◊ **a la d.** to the right <*torcer a la d.* to turn to the right>; on the right <*la iglesia está a la d.* the church is on the right> • **¡derecha!** MIL. right face! —m. see **derecho III.** adv. see **derecho.**

de·ri·va f. AVIA., MARIT. drift, deviation ◊ **ir a la d.** AVIA., MARIT. to drift, go off course; FIG. *(carecer de rumbo)* to drift, be adrift.

de·ri·va·ción f. *(acción de derivar)* derivation, deriving; GRAM., MATH. derivation; *(de un arroyo)* drawing *or* leading off (of water); MED. removal *or* healing of an inflammation; ELEC. *(pérdida)* loss of current; *(circuito)* by-pass, shunt.

de·ri·va·do, –da I. past part. see **derivar II.** adj. CHEM., GRAM., MATH. derived, derivative **III.** m. CHEM., GRAM. derivative —f. MATH. derivative.

de·ri·var tr. CHEM., GRAM. to derive; *(dirigir)* to lead, direct, channel —intr. *(traer origen)* to derive, be derived; AVIA., MARIT. to drift, go off course —reflex. to be derived *or* come from.

der·ma·to·lo·gí·a f. MED. dermatology.

der·ma·tó·lo·go, –ga m.f. MED. dermatologist.

dér·mi·co, –ca adj. ANAT. dermic, cutaneous.

der·mis f. ANAT. derma, dermis.

de·ro·ga·ción f. LAW derogation, repeal; *(disminución)* decrease, deterioration.

de·ro·gar §47 tr. LAW to derogate, repeal; *(destruir)* to destroy, abolish.

de·ro·ga·to·rio, –ria I. adj. LAW repealing, abolishing **II.** f. AMER., LAW derogation, repeal.

de·rra·ma f. *(repartimiento)* apportionment, sharing (of a tax); *(impuesto extraordinario)* special *or* additional tax.

de·rra·ma·de·ro m. *(desaguadero)* sink, drain; *(aliviadero)* spillway, wasteway; *(sitio para la basura)* dump, dumping ground.

de·rra·ma·do, –da I. past part. see **derramar II.** adj. FIG., COLL. prodigal, extravagant.

de·rra·ma·dor, –do·ra I. adj. prodigal, extravagant **II.** m.f. prodigal *or* extravagant person.

de·rra·ma·mien·to m. *(acción de derramar)* spilling; *(rebosamiento)* overflowing; *(dispersión)* dispersion, scattering; FIG. *(despilfarro)* squandering, wasting ◊ **d. de sangre** bloodshed, spilling of blood.

de·rra·mar tr. *(verter)* to spill, pour out; *(sangre)* to spill, shed; *(lágrimas)* to shed; *(dispersar)* to scatter, spread; FIG. *(diseminar)* to spread, make known; *(impuestos)* to apportion (taxes) —reflex. to overflow, spill over.

de·rra·me m. *(derramamiento)* spilling, pouring out; *(sangre)* spilling, shedding; *(lágrimas)* shedding; *(dispersión)* scattering, spreading, dispersion; *(diseminación)* spreading, dissemination; *(pérdida)* leakage, waste; *(rebosamiento)* overflow; MED. extravasation, effusion; ARCHIT. chamfer, splay; *(declive)* slope, incline; MARIT. draft, leakage (in a sail) ◊ **d. cerebral** MED. cerebral hemorrhage • **d. sinovial** MED. water on the knee.

de·rre·dor m. periphery, circumference ◊ **al** *or* **en d.** around • **por todo el d.** all around.

de·rre·lic·to, –ta I. past part. see **derrelinquir II.** adj. derelict, abandoned **III.** m. MARIT. derelict (abandoned ship).

de·rre·lin·quir §23 tr. to abandon, relinquish.

de·rren·ga·do, –da I. past part. see **derrengar II.** adj. *(torcido)* bent, twisted; FIG. *(cansado)* exhausted, pooped.

de·rren·gar §47 tr. *(el espinazo)* to break the back of; *(cansar)* to exhaust, wear out; *(torcer)* to twist, bend.

de·rre·ti·do, –da I. past part. see **derretir II.** adj. FIG. madly in love <*él está d. por Carmen* he is madly in love with Carmen> **III.** m. concrete, cement.

de·rre·tir §48 tr. *(liquidar)* to liquefy, dissolve; *(hielo)* to melt, thaw; METAL. to fuse, found; FIG. *(consumir)* to squander, waste, exhaust —reflex. *(enamorarse)* to fall madly in love; FIG., COLL. *(inquietarse)* to worry, fret; *(impacientarse)* to be restless *or* impatient.

de·rri·bar tr. *(echar abajo)* to knock *or* tear down, demolish; *(tumbar)* to knock down, bring to the ground; *(subvertir)* to overthrow, topple <*d. la monarquía* to overthrow the monarchy>; AVIA., MIL. to shoot down (a plane); FIG. *(humillar)* to humiliate, prostrate —reflex. *(tirarse)* to throw oneself to the ground; *(caerse)* to tumble *or* fall to the ground.

de·rri·bo m. *(demolición)* demolition; *(sitio)* demolition site ◊ **derribos** rubble, debris.

de·rri·ta, derrito see **derretir.**

de·rri·tie·ra, derritió see **derretir.**

de·rro·ca·mien·to m. *(despeño)* hurling *or* throwing down; *(demolición)* demolition, knocking down; *(subversión)* overthrow, ousting.

de·rro·car §70 tr. *(despeñar)* to hurl *or* throw down; FIG. *(arruinar)* to demolish, knock down; *(subvertir)* to oust, overthrow.

de·rro·cha·dor, –do·ra I. adj. wasteful, squandering **II.** m.f. spendthrift, squanderer.

de·rro·char tr. to squander, waste.

de·rro·che m. squandering, waste.

de·rro·ta f. MIL. defeat, rout; *(camino)* route, path; MARIT. ship's course, tack; FIG. *(desorden)* disorder, shambles.

de·rro·ta·do, –da I. past part. see **derrotar II.** adj. shabby, ragged.

de·rro·tar tr. *(vencer)* to defeat, beat; MIL. to defeat, rout; *(arruinar)* to ruin, spoil; *(echar a perder)* to waste, squander; TAUR. to butt, gore —reflex. MARIT. to drift *or* be driven off course.

de·rro·te·ro m. MARIT. *(rumbo)* course, tack; *(guía)* pilot book, navigation track; FIG. *(modo de obrar)* course, plan of action; *(tesoro)* hidden *or* buried treasure.

de·rro·tis·mo m. defeatism.

de·rro·tis·ta adj. & m.f. defeatist.

de·rru·bio m. *(desgaste)* erosion, washing away; *(tierra)* alluvium, sediment deposit.

de·rruir §18 tr. to knock down, demolish.

de·rrum·ba·de·ro m. *(despeñadero)* precipice, cliff; FIG. *(peligro)* pitfall, hazard.

de·rrum·ba·mien·to m. *(caída)* plunge, headlong fall; *(demolición)* demolition; *(desplome)* collapse, falling down; FIG. *(ruina)* collapse, fall; *(derrocamiento)* overthrow; MIN. cave-in • **d. de tierra** landslide.

de·rrum·bar tr. *(despeñar)* to hurl *or* cast down; *(demolir)* to knock down, demolish —reflex. *(caerse)* to collapse, fall; *(tirarse)* to throw oneself headfirst; MIN. to cave in, collapse; AMER. to fail.

de·rrum·be *or* **de·rrum·bo** m. *(despeñadero)* precipice, cliff; MIN. *(socavón)* cave-in; *(de tierra)* landslide; *(demolición)* demolition, knocking down; *(desplome)* falling down, collapse.

de·rru·ya, derruyo see **derruir.**

de·rru·ye·ra, derruyó see **derruir.**

de·sa·bas·te·cer §17 tr. to leave without provisions *or* supplies.

de·sa·bo·no m. *(cancelación)* cancellation of a subscription; *(descrédito)* discredit, disgrace.

de·sa·bo·to·nar tr. to unbutton, undo —intr. BOT. to blossom, bloom (said of flowers) —reflex. to come undone, be unbuttoned.

de·sa·bri·do, –da I. past part. see **desabrir** II. adj. *(de poco sabor)* tasteless, insipid; *(de mal sabor)* bad-tasting, unsavory; ARTIL. kicking *or* recoiling (weapon); METEOROL. inclement, unpleasant (weather); FIG. *(áspero)* gruff, surly.

de·sa·bri·ga·do, –da I. past part. see **desabrigar** II. adj. *(descubierto)* unprotected, exposed; FIG. *(desamparado)* unprotected, defenseless.

de·sa·bri·gar §47 tr. *(descubrir)* to uncover; *(quitar la ropa)* to undress; *(desamparar)* to deprive of shelter *or* protection.

de·sa·bri·mien·to m. *(sabor desagradable)* unpleasant taste; *(falta de sazón)* tastelessness, insipidness; *(aspereza)* rudeness, harshness; *(del tiempo)* unpleasantness (of weather).

de·sa·brir tr. *(no sazonar)* to make tasteless *or* insipid; *(dar mal sabor)* to spoil the taste of; FIG. *(molestar)* to harass, annoy.

de·sa·bro·char tr. *(la ropa)* to undo, unfasten (clothing); FIG. *(abrir)* to open, uncover —reflex. *(desvestirse)* to undo *or* unfasten one's clothing, FIG., COLL. *(confiarse)* to unburden oneself, confide • **d. con** to confide in.

de·sa·ca·lo·rar·se reflex. to cool off *or* down.

de·sa·ca·tar tr. to show disrespect *or* contempt for —reflex. to behave disrespectfully *or* irreverently.

de·sa·ca·to m. *(falta de respeto)* disrespect, irreverence; LAW contempt <*d. al tribunal* contempt of court>.

de·sa·cei·ta·do, –da I. past part. see **desaceitar** II. adj. lacking oil.

de·sa·cei·tar tr. to remove oil *or* grease from.

de·sa·cer·ta·do, –da I. past part. see **desacertar** II. adj. mistaken, misguided.

de·sa·cer·tar §49 intr. to be wrong, err.

de·sa·cier·to m. error, mistake.

de·sa·co·mo·da·do, –da I. past part. see **desacomodar** II. adj. *(molesto)* inconvenient, troublesome; *(pobre)* badly off, poor; *(incómodo)* uncomfortable; *(sin empleo)* unemployed, out of work; AMER. untidy, messy.

de·sa·co·mo·dar tr. *(molestar)* to inconvenience, bother; *(despedir)* to discharge, dismiss —reflex. to lose one's job.

de·sa·co·mo·do m. *(molestia)* inconvenience, bother; *(incomodidad)* discomfort; *(desempleo)* unemployment, joblessness; *(despedida)* discharge, dismissal.

de·sa·com·pa·ñar tr. to leave (alone), take leave of.

de·sa·con·se·ja·do, –da I. past part. see **desaconsejar** II. adj. unwise III. m.f. unwise *or* imprudent person.

de·sa·con·se·jar tr. to dissuade, advise against.

de·sa·co·plar tr. to uncouple, disconnect.

de·sa·cor·dar §19 tr. MUS. to put out of tune, make discordant —reflex. *(olvidarse)* to be forgetful; MUS. to become discordant, get out of tune.

de·sa·cor·de adj. MUS. discordant, out of tune; FIG. *(sin armonía)* discordant, conflicting.

de·sa·co·rra·lar tr. to let (an animal) out of a corral *or* pen.

de·sa·cos·tum·bra·do, –da I. past part. see **desacostumbrar** II. adj. unusual, uncommon.

de·sa·cos·tum·brar tr. to break of the habit (of) —reflex. to break oneself of the habit (of).

de·sa·co·tar tr. *(levantar el coto)* to open up (reserved or restricted land); *(rechazar)* to reject, refuse; *(suspender)* to lift *or* suspend (the rules of a game) —intr. to withdraw from an agreement *or* deal.

de·sa·cre·di·ta·do, –da I. past part. see **desacreditar** II. adj. discredited, disgraced.

de·sa·cre·di·tar tr. to discredit, disgrace.

de·sac·ti·va·do, –da I. past part. see **desactivar** II. adj. deactivated III. m. deactivation.

de·sac·ti·var tr. to deactivate.

de·sa·cuer·de, desacuerdo see **desacordar.**

de·sa·cuer·do m. *(discordia)* disagreement, discord <*estar en d. con* to be in disagreement with>; *(error)* error, mistake; *(olvido)* forgetfulness, loss of memory.

de·sa·dor·me·cer §17 tr. *(despertar)* to wake, rouse; *(desentumecer)* to rid of numbness —reflex. *(despertarse)* to wake up; *(desentumecerse)* to regain feeling.

de·sad·ver·tir §65 tr. to fail to notice, be unaware of.

de·sa·fec·ción f. disaffection, dislike.

de·sa·fec·to, –ta I. adj. *(que no siente afecto)* disaffected; *(opuesto)* hostile, opposed II. m. disaffection, dislike.

de·sa·fia·dor, –do·ra I. adj. defying, challenging II. m.f. challenger.

de·sa·fiar §30 tr. *(retar)* to challenge, dare; *(competir)* to oppose, compete with.

de·sa·fi·lar tr. to blunt, dull.

de·sa·fi·nar intr. MUS. *(desacordarse)* to be out of tune; *(tocar)* to play out of tune; *(cantar)* to sing out of tune; FIG., COLL. *(decir algo importuno)* to speak out of turn *or* indiscreetly —reflex. MUS. to become discordant, go out of tune.

de·sa·fí·o m. *(reto)* challenge, defiance; *(duelo)* duel; *(competencia)* competition, rivalry.

de·sa·fo·ra·da·men·te adv. *(con exceso)* excessively; *(escandalosamente)* outrageously; *(desenfrenadamente)* lawlessly, rowdily; *(descortésmente)* rudely, insolently ♦ **gritar d.** to shout one's head off, shout at the top of one's voice.

de·sa·fo·ra·do, –da I. past part. see **desaforar** II. adj. *(gigantesco)* huge, gigantic; *(excesivo)* huge, excessive; *(sin límite)* boundless <*ambición d.* boundless ambition>; *(contra fuero)* illegal, unlawful.

de·sa·fo·rar §19 tr. *(violar los fueros)* to violate (a person's) rights; *(privar del fuero)* to deprive (a person) of rights —reflex. to lose control, fly off the handle.

de·sa·for·tu·na·do, –da adj. unlucky, unfortunate.

de·sa·fue·ro m. *(violación de las leyes)* infringement, violation; *(violación de los fueros)* infringement, encroachment; *(abuso)* outrage, excess.

de·sa·gra·cia·do, –da adj. *(desdichado)* unhappy, unfortunate; *(sin gracia)* graceless, artless; CARIB. shameless.

de·sa·gra·da·ble adj. unpleasant, disagreeable.

de·sa·gra·dar tr. to displease, offend.

de·sa·gra·de·cer §17 tr. to be ungrateful *or* unappreciative of.

de·sa·gra·de·ci·do, –da I. past part. see **desagradecer** II. adj. ungrateful III. m.f. ungrateful person, ingrate.

de·sa·gra·do m. displeasure, discontent ♦ **con d.** ungraciously, reluctantly.

de·sa·gra·viar tr. to indemnify, make amends to —reflex. to obtain satisfaction *or* compensation.

de·sa·gra·vio m. compensation, amends ♦ **desagravios** MEX., RELIG. acts of atonement (traditional rite of September) • **en d. de** in amends for.

de·sa·gre·gar §47 tr. to disintegrate, break up.

de·sa·gua·de·ro m. drain, outlet.

de·sa·gua·dor m. drain, outlet.

de·sa·guar §10 tr. *(sacar agua)* to drain, empty of water; FIG. *(malgastar)* to waste, consume —intr. MARIT. to empty *or* flow into the sea —reflex. FIG. *(vomitar)* to vomit; *(defecar)* to defecate, move one's bowels.

de·sa·güe m. *(avenamiento)* draining, drainage; *(desaguadero)* drain, outlet ♦ **d. de azotea** roof drain • **d. superficial** surface drainage.

de·sa·gui·sa·do, –da I. adj. *(contra la ley)* unlawful, illegal; *(contra razón)* outrageous, unreasonable **II.** m. *(delito)* offense, outrage; AMER. disorder, mess.

de·sa·hi·jar §81 tr. to wean, separate offspring from —reflex. ENTOM. to swarm.

de·sa·ho·ga·do, –da I. past part. see **desahogar II.** adj. *(descarado)* brazen, fresh; *(despejado)* clear, open *<un camino d.* an open road>; *(espacioso)* roomy, spacious; *(acomodado)* relaxing, easy *<una vida d.* an easy life>.

de·sa·ho·gar §47 tr. *(aliviar)* to alleviate, ease; *(dar rienda suelta)* to vent, give rein to *<d. la ira* to vent one's anger> —reflex. *(dar rienda suelta)* to let off steam; *(descargarse)* to get something off one's chest; *(confiarse)* to confide *<es mejor desahogarse con un amigo íntimo* it is better to confide in a close friend>; *(descansar)* to relax, take it easy; *(recobrarse)* to recover, feel better; *(desempeñarse)* to extricate oneself from difficulty.

de·sa·ho·go m. *(alivio)* relief, alleviation; *(descanso)* rest, respite; *(expansión)* space, room; *(libertad)* freedom; *(comodidad)* comfort, ease *<vivir con d.* to live in comfort>; *(descaro)* brazenness, impudence; *(salida)* outlet *<esta actividad le sirve de d.* this activity serves as an outlet for him>.

de·sa·ho·gué, desahogue see **desahogar.**

de·sa·hu·ciar tr. *(quitar toda esperanza)* to remove all hope from; *(desesperar)* to lose hope for; *(un inquilino)* to evict (a tenant).

de·sai·ra·do, –da I. past part. see **desairar II.** adj. *(sin garbo)* ungraceful, clumsy; FIG. *(sin éxito)* unsuccessful.

de·sai·rar §81 tr. *(rechazar)* to reject, rebuff; *(desestimar)* to value lightly, underestimate.

de·sai·re m. *(falta de gracia)* gracelessness, lack of charm; *(desprecio)* slight, snub; *(rechazo)* rebuff ♦ **dar** or **hacer un d. a uno** to slight or snub someone • **sufrir un d.** to suffer a rebuff.

de·sa·jus·tar tr. *(desconcertar)* to disturb, put out of order; *(estropear)* to spoil, upset —reflex. to go wrong, get out of order; FIG. *(romper)* to break (an agreement).

de·sa·jus·te m. *(mal ajuste)* maladjustment; *(avería)* breakdown, failure; FIG. *(ruptura)* breaking (of an agreement).

de·sa·la·bar to disparage, belittle.

de·sa·la·do, –da I. past part. see **desalar II.** adj. *(apresurado)* hurried, pressured; *(ansioso)* anxious, eager.

de·sa·lar tr. *(quitar la sal)* to remove salt from, desalinate; *(quitar las alas)* to remove or clip the wings of —intr. FIG. *(apresurarse)* to hurry, rush; *(desear)* to yearn or long ♦ **desalarse por** to yearn or long for.

de·sa·len·ta·dor, –do·ra adj. discouraging, disheartening.

de·sa·len·tar §49 tr. *(quitar el aliento)* to leave breathless, put out of breath; FIG. *(desanimar)* to discourage, dishearten —reflex. to become discouraged or disheartened.

de·sa·lien·to m. FIG. discouragement.

de·sa·li·ña·do, –da I. past part. see **desaliñar II.** adj. *(desaseado)* slovenly, untidy; FIG. *(descuidado)* careless, neglectful.

de·sa·li·ñar tr. to disarrange, make untidy; *(arrugar)* to crease —reflex. to become disarranged or untidy.

de·sa·li·ño m. *(descompostura)* slovenliness, untidiness; FIG. *(descuido)* carelessness, neglect ♦ **desaliños** long earrings.

de·sal·ma·do, –da I. past part. see **desalmar II.** adj. heartless, cruel.

de·sal·mar tr. FIG. *(debilitar)* to weaken, debilitate; *(desasosegar)* to disturb, upset —reflex. to become disturbed or upset ♦ **d. por** to crave, long for.

de·sa·lo·ja·mien·to m. dislodging, removal.

de·sa·lo·jar tr. *(sacar)* to remove, expel; *(desplazar)* to dislodge, displace; *(abandonar)* to abandon, evacuate —intr. to move out of, leave.

de·sa·lo·jo m. *(acción de sacar)* removal, expulsion; *(desplazamiento)* dislodgement, displacement; *(abandonamiento)* abandonment, evacuation.

de·sal·qui·lar tr. *(dejar de tener alquilado)* to stop renting; *(mudarse)* to move out of, vacate —reflex. to become vacant.

de·sal·te·rar tr. to calm, soothe.

de·sa·mar tr. *(dejar de amar)* to stop loving; *(aborrecer)* to hate, detest.

de·sa·ma·rrar tr. *(desatar)* to untie, unloose; MARIT. to cast off —reflex. to come untied.

de·sa·mor m. *(frialdad)* indifference, lack of affection; *(antipatía)* enmity, dislike.

de·sa·mo·rar tr. to lose love for —reflex. to cease or stop loving.

de·sa·mor·ti·zar §04 tr. LAW to disentail.

de·sam·pa·ra·dor, –do·ra I. adj. forsaking, abandoning **II.** m.f. one who forsakes or abandons another.

de·sam·pa·rar tr. to forsake, abandon.

de·sam·pa·ro m. helplessness, abandonment.

de·sa·mue·blar tr. to strip (a dwelling) of furniture.

de·san·clar or **des·an·co·rar** tr. MARIT. to weigh the anchor of (a ship).

de·san·dar §05 tr. to retrace (one's steps), go back.

de·san·gra·mien·to m. profuse bleeding.

de·san·grar tr. *(sacar la sangre)* to bleed; *(vaciar)* to drain, empty; FIG. *(empobrecer)* to impoverish, bleed dry —reflex. *(perder la sangre)* to bleed profusely; *(morir)* to bleed to death.

de·sa·ni·ma·do, –da I. past part. see **desanimar II.** adj. *(falto de valor)* downhearted, discouraged; *(poco animado)* dull, lifeless.

de·sa·ni·mar tr. to discourage, depress —reflex. to become discouraged or depressed.

de·sá·ni·mo m. discouragement, dejection.

de·sa·nu·dar or **des·a·ñu·dar** tr. *(un nudo)* to untie, unknot; FIG. *(desenmarañar)* to straighten out, clarify.

de·sa·pa·ci·ble adj. unpleasant, disagreeable.

de·sa·pa·re·cer §17 tr. to make disappear, cause to vanish —intr. & reflex. *(desvanecer)* to disappear, vanish; *(disipar)* to wear off ♦ **d. del mapa** COLL. to vanish from the face of the earth.

de·sa·pa·ri·ción f. disappearance, vanishing.

de·sa·pa·sio·na·do, –da I. past part. see **desapasionar II.** adj. dispassionate, impartial.

de·sa·pa·sio·nar tr. to take away interest (in) or enthusiasm (for) —reflex. to lose interest (in) or enthusiasm (for).

de·sa·pe·gar §47 tr. *(desprender)* to unstick; *(separar)* to separate, detach; FIG. *(desaficionar)* to estrange, alienate —reflex. *(desprenderse)* to come unstuck; *(separarse)* to become separated or detached; FIG. *(desaficionarse)* to become estranged or alienated.

de·sa·pe·go m. *(frialdad)* indifference, lack of love; *(desafición)* estrangement; *(imparcialidad)* impartiality.

de·sa·per·ci·bi·do, –da adj. *(no preparado)* unprepared, unready; *(inadvertido)* unnoticed, unseen *<pasar d.* to go or be unnoticed> ♦ **coger d.** to catch unawares, take by surprise.

de·sa·pli·ca·do, –da I. adj. lazy, idle **II.** m.f. lazybones, idler.

de·sa·po·de·rar tr. *(quitar)* to dispossess; *(privar del poder)* to remove from power.

de·sa·po·li·llar tr. to rid or clear of moths —reflex. FIG., COLL. to clear the cobwebs from one's mind.

de·sa·pre·ciar tr. to underestimate.

de·sa·pren·der tr. to unlearn, forget (something previously learned).

de·sa·pren·sar tr. *(sacar el lustre de)* to take the gloss or finish off; FIG. *(soltar)* to extricate, free.

de·sa·pren·sión f. unscrupulousness, lack of scruples.

de·sa·pren·si·vo, –va adj. unscrupulous, unconscientious.

de·sa·pre·tar §49 tr. to loosen, make loose.

de·sa·pro·ba·ción f. disapproval.

de·sa·pro·ba·dor, –do·ra adj. disapproving, unfavorable.

de·sa·pro·bar §19 tr. to disapprove (of), condemn.

de·sa·pro·ve·cha·do, –da I. past part. see **desaprovechar II.** adj. *(perezoso)* idle, lazy *<estudiante d.* lazy student>; *(desperdiciado)* wasted **III.** m.f. idle or lazy person.

de·sa·pro·ve·cha·mien·to m. *(desperdicio)* waste, ill use; *(falta de progreso)* backwardness, lack of progress.

de·sa·pro·ve·char tr. to waste, misuse —intr. to lose ground, go backwards.

de·sa·prue·be, desapruebo see **desaprobar.**

de·sar·bo·lar tr. MARIT. to dismast, strip of masts; CARIB., PERU, SL. to mess up, make a mess of.

de·sa·re·nar tr. to remove sand from, clear of sand.

de·sar·ma·do, –da I. past part. see **desarmar II.** adj. *(desprovisto)* unarmed; *(desmontado)* in pieces, dismantled.

de·sar·mar tr. *(quitar las armas)* to disarm; *(desmontar)* to take apart, dismantle; FIG. *(templar)* to calm, appease; *(encantar)* to disarm <*la sonrisa del estudiante le desarmó* the student's smile disarmed her>; MARIT. to lay up (a ship); MIL. to discharge, disband (troops) —intr. & reflex. to disarm; *(desmontar)* to come or fall apart, fall to pieces.

de·sar·me m. *(acción de desarmar)* disarmament; *(desmontaje)* taking apart, dismantling ♦ **d. nuclear** nuclear disarmament.

de·sar·mo·ní·a f. disharmony.

de·sar·mo·ni·zar §04 tr. to make inharmonious.

de·sa·rrai·ga·do, –da I. past part. see **desarraigar** II. adj. *(árbol)* uprooted; FIG. *(persona)* rootless III. m.f. rootless person.

de·sa·rrai·gar §47 tr. *(arrancar de raíz)* to uproot, dig up; FIG. *(extirpar)* to extirpate, eradicate; FIG. *(apartar de una opinión)* to make (someone) give up an opinion; FIG. *(desterrar)* to banish, expel —reflex. to become uprooted; *(extirparse)* to be extirpated or eradicated.

de·sa·rrai·go m. *(acción de desarraigar)* uprooting; FIG. *(extirpación)* extirpation, eradication; FIG. *(destierro)* banishment, expulsion.

de·sa·rra·pa·do, –da adj. ragged, tattered.

de·sa·rre·bu·jar tr. *(desarropar)* to loosen, unfasten; *(desenvolver)* to disentangle, unwind; FIG. *(explicar)* to explain, unravel (a mystery).

de·sa·rre·gla·do, –da I. past part. see **desarreglar** II. adj. *(desaliñado)* untidy, messy; FIG. *(desordenado)* disorderly; MECH. *(roto)* out of order, broken (down).

de·sa·rre·glar tr. *(descomponer)* to make untidy, mess (up); FIG. *(estropear)* to spoil, upset; MECH. *(quebrar)* to put out of order, break —reflex. *(descomponerse)* to become untidy or messy; MECH. *(quebrar)* to get out of order, break (down).

de·sa·rre·glo m. *(descompostura)* untidiness; *(confusión)* disorder, confusion; MECH. *(de un mecanismo)* breakdown, trouble.

de·sa·rren·dar §49 tr. *(dejar de arrendar)* to stop leasing; *(dejar de alquilar)* to stop renting.

de·sa·rri·mar tr. *(apartar)* to separate, remove; FIG. *(disuadir)* to dissuade, cause to change one's opinion.

de·sa·rro·lla·do, –da I. past part. see **desarrollar** II. adj. developed <*los países desarrollados* the developed countries>.

de·sa·rro·llar tr. *(deshacer)* to unroll, unfold; *(extender)* to develop, expand <*d. la industria nacional* to develop domestic industry>; *(explicar)* to expound, elaborate; CHEM. to expand; MATH. to expand, work out —reflex. *(deshacerse)* to unroll, unfold; *(extenderse)* to develop, expand; *(tener lugar)* to take place.

de·sa·rro·llo m. *(despliegue)* unrolling, unfolding; *(extensión)* development, expansion <*d. del movimiento progresista* development of the progressive movement>; *(explicación)* exposition, elaboration; *(de los sucesos)* development, course of events); MATH. expansion.

de·sa·rru·gar §47 tr. to unwrinkle, smooth the wrinkles from —reflex. to become unwrinkled.

de·sar·ti·cu·la·ción f. disarticulation, dislocation (of bones).

de·sar·ti·cu·lar tr. *(un hueso)* to dislocate, throw out of joint; MECH. to disassemble, take apart; FIG. *(quebrantar)* to take apart, break up —reflex. to become dislocated or out of joint.

de·sa·se·a·do, –da I. past part. see **desasear** II. adj. *(sucio)* dirty, unclean; *(desarreglado)* untidy, messy III. m.f. *(sucio)* dirty or unclean person; *(desarreglado)* untidy or messy person, slob.

de·sa·se·ar tr. *(ensuciar)* to dirty, soil; *(poner en desorden)* to mess up, disorder.

de·sa·se·gu·rar tr. *(una cosa)* to unbrace, make unsteady; COM. *(con contrato de seguro)* to cancel an insurance policy.

de·sa·sen·tar §49 tr. *(remover)* to move, remove; FIG. *(sentar mal)* to displease —reflex. to rise from one's seat.

de·sa·se·o m. *(suciedad)* dirtiness, uncleanliness; *(desarreglo)* untidiness, messiness.

de·sa·si·mien·to m. *(cesión)* releasing, letting go; FIG. *(desinterés)* disinterestedness, unselfishness.

de·sa·sir §08 tr. to release, let go —reflex. to yield, give up.

de·sa·so·ciar tr. to dissociate, separate.

de·sa·so·se·gar §52 I. tr. to make uneasy, disturb —reflex. to become uneasy or disturbed.

de·sa·so·sie·go m. uneasiness, restlessness.

de·sas·tar tr. to remove horns (from an animal).

de·sas·tra·do, –da I. adj. *(sucio)* dirty, slovenly; *(desgraciado)* wretched, unfortunate II. m.f. slovenly person.

de·sas·tre m. disaster, catastrophe.

de·sas·tro·so, –sa adj. disastrous, catastrophic.

de·sa·ta·car §70 tr. *(una prenda)* to unbutton, unfasten; *(una arma)* to withdraw ramrods from a (firearm) —reflex. to unbutton one's trousers.

de·sa·ta·dor, –do·ra I. adj. untying, unfastening II. m.f. someone or something that unfastens.

de·sa·ta·du·ra f. untying, unfastening.

de·sa·tan·car §70 tr. to clear out, unblock (a pipe) —reflex. to free oneself, pull oneself loose.

de·sa·ta·qué, desataque see **desatacar.**

de·sa·tar tr. *(deshacer)* to untie, undo; *(soltar)* to unleash, let go; FIG. *(aclarar)* to unravel, solve <*d. un misterio* to unravel a mystery> —reflex. to come untied or undone; *(soltarse)* to break away or loose; *(hablar con exceso)* to chatter, talk excessively; FIG. *(descomedirse)* to be rude, let oneself go; *(perder el encogimiento)* to loosen up, stop feeling self-conscious; *(descencadenarse)* to break loose; METEOROL. to break, burst ♦ **desatarse de** to get out of, rid oneself of.

de·sa·tas·car §70 tr. *(sacar de un atascadero)* to pull out of the mud; *(desatancar)* to clear, unblock; FIG. *(ayudar)* to get someone out of a jam —reflex. to get out of the mud.

de·sa·ta·ví·o m. untidiness, disarray.

de·sa·te m. *(de palabras)* flood (of speech); *(una acción)* letting loose, unleashing ♦ **d. de vientre** diarrhea.

de·sa·ten·ción f. *(falta de atención)* inattention, disregard; *(descortesía)* discourtesy, disrespect.

de·sa·ten·der §50 tr. *(no hacer caso)* to neglect; *(no prestar atención)* to ignore, disregard.

de·sa·ten·tar §49 tr. to confuse, disorient.

de·sa·ten·to, –ta I. adj. *(que no pone atención)* inattentive; *(descortés)* discourteous, impolite II. m.f. discourteous or impolite person.

de·sa·ti·na·do, –da I. past part. see **desatinar** II. adj. *(necio)* foolish, silly; *(imprudente)* rash, reckless III. m.f. fool.

de·sa·ti·nar tr. *(exasperar)* to exasperate, bewilder; *(atolondrar)* to make lose one's head; —intr. *(cometer desaciertos)* to make blunders; *(disparatar)* to rave, talk nonsense.

de·sa·ti·no m. *(falta de tino)* folly, foolishness; *(acción)* silly or foolish act ♦ **decir desatinos** to talk nonsense.

de·sa·ton·tar·se reflex. to come to one's senses.

de·sa·to·rar tr. MARIT. to break out, unload; MIN. to clear of debris.

de·sa·tor·ni·lla·dor m. AMER. screwdriver.

de·sa·tra·car §70 MARIT. —tr. to cast off (moorings) —intr. to steer away from the coast.

de·sa·tran·car §70 tr. *(la puerta)* to unbar, unbolt (a door); *(desatrampar)* to clear, unblock.

de·sa·tu·far·se reflex. *(tomar el aire fresco)* to get some fresh air; FIG. *(desenojarse)* to calm down, cool off.

de·sa·tur·dir tr. to bring to, revive.

de·sau·to·ri·za·ción f. withdrawal of authority.

de·sau·to·ri·za·do, –da I. past part. see **desautorizar** II. adj. *(falta de autoridad)* unauthorized; *(desmentido)* denied; *(prohibido)* prohibited.

de·sau·to·ri·zar §04 tr. *(quitar la autoridad)* to deprive of authority; *(desmentir)* to deny; *(prohibir)* to prohibit.

de·sa·ve·nen·cia f. discord, enmity.

de·sa·ve·ni·do, –da I. past part. see **desavenir** II. adj. *(incompatible)* incompatible; *(opuesto)* opposing.

de·sa·ve·nir §76 tr. to cause discord or enmity between —reflex. to disagree, quarrel.

de·sa·ven·ta·ja·do, –da adj. disadvantaged.

de·sa·ven·tu·ra f. misadventure, misfortune.

de·sa·vi·sa·do, –da I. past part. see **desavisar** II. adj. uninformed, unaware.

de·sa·vi·sar tr. to countermand.

de·sa·yu·na·do, –da I. past part. see **desayunar** II. adj. having breakfasted.

de·sa·yu·nar intr. to have breakfast, breakfast ♦ **d. con** to have for breakfast —reflex. to have breakfast, breakfast; FIG. *(enterarse)* to receive the first news of —tr. to breakfast on, have for breakfast.

de·sa·yu·no m. breakfast.

de·sa·zón f. *(falta de sazón)* tastelessness, insipidity; FIG. *(disgusto)* annoyance, irritation; *(desasosiego)* anxiety, uneasiness; MED. upset, discomfort; AGR. poorness (of soil).

de·sa·zo·na·do, –da I. past part. see **desazonar** II. adj. *(soso)* tasteless, insipid; MED. upset, unwell; AGR. poor (soil.).

de·sa·zo·nar tr. *(hacer insípido)* to make tasteless, take the flavor out of; FIG. *(disgustar)* to annoy, irritate —reflex. MED. to feel unwell, be out of sorts; FIG. *(disgustarse)* to become annoyed *or* irritated.

des·ban·car §70 tr. *(en el juego)* to break the bank; FIG. *(suplantar)* to supplant, replace.

des·ban·da·da f. *(acción de desbandarse)* disbandment; MIL. rout ♦ **a la d.** in confusion, helter-skelter.

des·ban·dar·se reflex. *(huir en desorden)* to flee in disorder, disband; FIG. *(dispersarse)* to disperse, scatter.

des·ba·ra·jus·tar tr. to disarrange, disorder.

des·ba·ra·jus·te m. confusion, disorder.

des·ba·ra·ta·do, –da I. past part. see **desbaratar** II. adj. *(desordenado)* wild, unruly; *(roto)* wrecked, broken down III. m.f. *(ruina)* ruin, wreck; COLL. *(libertino)* libertine, debauchee.

des·ba·ra·tar tr. *(arruinar)* to ruin, wreck; *(malgastar)* to squander, waste; FIG. *(estorbar)* to hinder, frustrate; MECH. to break, put out of order; MIL. to rout, throw into confusion —intr. to talk *or* act wildly —reflex. *(descomponerse)* to be ruined *or* wrecked; *(malgastarse)* to be squandered *or* wasted; *(disparatarse)* to talk *or* act wildly; MECH. to break down, fall apart.

des·bar·ba·do, –da I. past part. see **desbarbar** II. adj. *(que no tiene barba)* beardless; *(afeitado)* shaved.

des·bar·bar tr. AGR. to trim, prune; COLL. *(la barba)* to shave —reflex. to shave.

des·ba·rrar intr. *(deslizar)* to slip, slide; FIG. *(desatinar)* to talk nonsense; *(con una barra)* to throw an iron bar as far as possible.

des·ba·rri·gar §47 tr. COLL. to rip open the belly of —intr. CUBA to become known.

des·ba·rro m. *(desliz)* slip, skid; *(error)* blunder, mistake.

des·bas·ta·dor m. CARP. plane.

des·bas·tar tr. CARP. to plane; *(suavizar)* to smooth; *(desgastar)* to wear out, weaken; FIG. *(una persona)* to educate, polish.

des·bas·te m. CARP. planing ♦ **en d.** rough-hewn.

des·bas·te·ci·do, –da adj. without provisions.

des·ba·za·de·ro m. wet and slippery place.

des·be·ce·rrar tr. to wean (a calf).

des·blo·que·ar tr. COM. to unfreeze, unblock; MIL. to lift a blockade from (a port).

des·bo·ca·do, –da I. past part. see **desbocar** II. adj. *(roto)* chipped, having a broken rim *or* mouth; *(mellado)* nicked, damaged; FIG., COLL. *(malhablado)* foul-mouthed; ARM. wide-mouthed; EQUIT. runaway; S. AMER. overflowing III. m.f. FIG., COLL. foul mouth, foul-mouthed person.

des·bo·ca·mien·to m. *(de un caballo)* bolting (of a horse); FIG. *(injurias)* insults, abuse.

des·bo·car §70 tr. *(astillar)* to chip, break the rim *or* mouth of; *(mellar)* to nick —intr. *(dirigir a)* to lead *or* open into <*la calle desboca en la avenida* the street leads into the avenue>; *(desembocar)* to flow *or* empty into <*el río desboca en el lago* the river empties into the lake> —reflex. EQUIT. to bolt, run away; FIG. *(injuriar)* to start to swear, break into a stream of insults.

des·bor·da·ble adj. which can overflow.

des·bor·da·mien·to m. *(inundación)* overflowing, running over; FIG. *(de cólera)* outburst; MIL. outflanking.

des·bor·dan·te adj. *(que desborda)* overflowing; FIG. *(que sale de sus límites)* boundless, unrestrained.

des·bor·dar intr. *(derramarse)* to overflow, run over; FIG.

(rebosar) to burst *or* brim with —reflex. *(derramarse)* to overflow, run over; FIG. *(rebosar)* to burst *or* brim with; *(desmandarse)* to lose one's self-control —tr. to pass, go beyond <*el trabajo desborda el tema asignado* the paper goes beyond the assigned topic>.

des·bor·de m. var. of **desbordamiento**.

des·bo·rrar tr. TEX. to burl.

des·bra·ga·do I. adj. COLL. *(sin bragas)* without breeches; FIG. *(descamisado)* ragged, destitute II. m. FIG. bum, tramp.

des·bra·var tr. to tame, break in (horses) —intr. *(perder la braveza)* to become less fierce; FIG. *(disminuir)* to diminish, abate —reflex. to lose strength (liquor).

des·briz·nar tr. CUL. to chop, mince; BOT. to remove the stamens from (a crocus).

des·bro·zar §04 tr. to clear of rubbish *or* undergrowth.

des·bro·zo m. *(acción)* clearing away of rubbish *or* undergrowth; *(basura)* rubbish; *(maleza)* undergrowth.

des·ca·bal adj. incomplete.

des·ca·ba·lar tr. to leave incomplete.

des·ca·bal·gar §47 —intr. to dismount (from a horse) —tr. ARTIL. to dismount (a gun) —reflex. ARTIL. to be put out of action (a gun).

des·ca·be·cé, descabece see **descabezar**.

des·ca·be·lla·do, –da I. past part. see **descabellar** II. adj. FIG. wild, crazy.

des·ca·be·llar tr. *(el pelo)* to tousle, ruffle (hair); TAUR. to kill the bull with one thrust of the sword in the neck.

des·ca·be·za·do, –da I. past part. see **descabezar** II. adj. *(sin cabeza)* headless; FIG. *(imprudente)* rash, wild III. m.f. FIG. rash *or* wild person.

des·ca·be·za·mien·to m. *(decapitación)* decapitation, beheading; *(de un árbol)* cutting off the top (of a tree).

des·ca·be·zar §04 tr. *(decapitar)* to behead, decapitate; *(desmochar)* to top, cut the top of; FIG., COLL. *(vencer)* to get over the worst of, surmount <*hemos descabezado la dificultad* we have surmounted the difficulty>; MIL. to move front ranks to a new position ♦ **d. el sueño** to take a nap, get forty winks —intr. to abut, border on —reflex. FIG., COLL. *(descalabazarse)* to rack one's brains; AGR. to shed grain.

des·ca·bu·llir·se §13 reflex. to sneak off, steal away.

des·ca·char tr. AMER. to remove the horns from.

des·ca·e·cer §17 intr. to decline, deteriorate.

des·ca·fei·na·do, –da I. adj. decaffeinated II. m. decaffeinated coffee.

des·cai·mien·to m. decline, weakness.

des·ca·la·ba·zar·se §04 reflex. FIG., COLL. to rack one's brains.

des·ca·la·bra·do, –da I. past part. see **descalabrar** II. adj. *(herido)* injured *or* wounded in the head; FIG. *(que pierde)* losing, unsuccessful <*salir d.* to come out losing> III. m.f. loser.

des·ca·la·brar tr. *(herir)* to injure, wound; *(en la cabeza)* to injure *or* wound in the head; COLL. *(causar daño)* to damage, harm; CUBA to be thwarted *or* frustrated —reflex. to injure one's head.

des·ca·la·bro m. *(desgracia)* setback, misfortune; MIL. defeat.

des·ca·lan·dra·jar tr. to rip to shreds (a garment).

des·cal·ce m. undermining.

des·cal·ci·fi·ca·ción f. MED. decalcification.

des·ca·li·fi·ca·ción f. *(pérdida de calificación)* disqualification; *(descrédito)* discredit.

des·ca·li·fi·car §70 tr. to disqualify.

des·cal·zar §04 tr. *(quitar el calzado)* to take off *or* remove footwear; *(quitar un calzo)* to remove a wedge *or* block from; *(socavar)* to dig under, undermine —reflex. *(quitarse el calzado)* to take off *or* remove footwear; *(desherrarse)* to lose a shoe (a horse).

des·cal·zo, –za I. irr. past part. see **descalzar** II. adj. *(con los pies desnudos)* barefoot(ed), shoeless; FIG. *(pobre)* destitute, poor; RELIG. discalced III. m.f. RELIG. discalced monk *or* nun.

des·cam·biar tr. to change back again.

des·ca·mi·nar tr. *(hacer perder el camino)* to misdirect, misguide; FIG. *(desviar)* to mislead, lead astray; *(meter de contrabando)* to smuggle; S. AMER. to hold up, delay

—reflex. *(desviarse)* to lose one's way, get lost; *(salir del camino)* to run off the road; FIG. *(errar)* to go astray.

des·ca·mi·sa·do, –da I. adj. COLL. *(sin camisa)* shirtless; *(pobre)* poor, ragged II. m.f. *(pobre)* pauper, wretch; ARG. proletarian, worker.

des·cam·pa·do, –da I. adj. open, clear *(land)* II. m. open field ♦ **en d.** in the open country.

des·cam·par intr. to clear up (weather).

des·can·sa·de·ro m. resting place.

des·can·sa·do, –da I. past part. see **descansar** II. adj. *(tranquilo)* restful, tranquil; *(refrescado)* rested, relaxed.

des·can·sar intr. *(cesar el trabajo)* to rest, take a rest; *(calmarse)* to relax; *(reposar)* to repose, to rest; *(fiarse)* to rely on; *(basarse)* to be based on; *(apoyarse)* to rest or lean on; AGR. to lie fallow (land); *(yacer)* to lie, rest —tr. *(aliviar)* to rest, give rest to; *(ayudar)* to help, aid; *(apoyar)* to rest or lean (something) on —reflex. to rest, take a rest ♦ **descansarse en uno** to rely on someone, have trust in someone.

des·can·so m. *(reposo)* rest, repose; *(alivio)* relief; *(período)* break; *(licencia)* leave; SPORT. half time; THEAT. intermission; ARCHIT. landing; TECH. support, seat; CHILE toilet.

des·can·tar tr. to clear of stones.

des·can·ti·llar tr. *(una piedra)* to chip; *(rebajar)* to deduct, subtract —reflex. to get chipped.

des·can·to·nar tr. *(romper)* to chip, bevel (the edges of); FIG. *(rebajar)* to deduct.

des·ca·ño·nar tr. *(desplumar)* to pluck (the feathers of a bird); *(afeitar)* to shave close; FIG., COLL. *(en el juego)* to skin or fleece someone out of their money.

des·ca·po·ta·ble AUTO. adj. & m. convertible.

des·ca·ra·da·men·te adv. shamelessly, brazenly.

des·ca·ra·do, –da I. past part. see **descararse** II. adj. shameless, brazen III. m.f. scoundrel, shameless person.

des·ca·rar·se reflex. to be rude or insolent ♦ **d. a** to have the nerve to.

des·car·bu·rar tr. to decarbonize.

des·car·ga f. *(desembarco)* unloading; ARM. *(disparo)* discharge, firing; ARCHIT. *(aligeramiento)* reduction of weight; ELEC. discharge ♦ **d. cerrada** MIL. volley.

des·car·ga·de·ro m. pier, unloading dock.

des·car·ga·dor m. *(portador)* stevedore; MIL. wad-hook.

des·car·gar §47 tr. *(desembarcar)* to unload (boats); ARM. *(disparar)* to discharge, shoot; *(extraer la carga de)* to unload, disarm; ELEC. to discharge; *(golpear)* to deal <*le descargué un golpe* I dealt him a blow>; FIG. *(liberar)* to release, free <*este decreto le descarga de su obligación* this decree releases him from his obligation>; *(aliviar)* to ease, relieve; LAW *(absolver)* to acquit, clear —intr. *(desaguar)* to flow, empty <*el río descarga en el mar* the river empties into the sea; METEOROL. to burst, break (said of clouds, storms) —reflex. *(dimitir)* to resign, quit; *(eximirse)* to unburden oneself; LAW *(exonerarse)* to clear oneself (of charges) ♦ **descargarse de algo en alguien** FIG. to unload something on someone else.

des·car·go m. *(acción de descargar)* unloading; COM. entry; *(excusa)* excuse; *(dispensa)* release (from an obligation).

des·car·gue m. unloading.

des·ca·ri·ñar·se reflex. *(faltar cariño para)* to lose one's affection or love for; *(ser indiferente a)* to become indifferent to.

des·ca·ri·ño m. *(falta de cariño)* lack of affection; *(indiferencia)* indifference.

des·car·na·da·men·te adv. FIG. frankly, plainly.

des·car·nar tr. DENT. to scrape flesh from; *(desmoronar)* to wear or eat away; FIG. *(desapegar)* to disembody —reflex. to wear away, be eaten away.

des·ca·ro m. shamelessness, brazenness.

des·ca·ro·zar §04 tr. AMER. to pit, stone (fruit).

des·ca·rriar §30 tr. *(una persona)* to misdirect, send the wrong way; *(un animal)* to separate from the herd; FIG. *(apartar de la razón)* to lead astray —reflex. *(desviarse)* to stray, get lost; FIG. *(apartarse de la razón)* to err, go astray.

des·ca·rri·la·mien·to m. RAIL. derailment; FIG. *(descarrío)* act of going astray.

des·ca·rri·lar intr. *(un tren)* to be derailed, jump the track;

FIG. *(una persona)* to get off the track, wander from the point.

des·ca·rrí·o m. losing one's way, going astray.

des·car·tar tr. to discard, put aside —reflex. to discard (in cards) ♦ **descartarse de** to excuse oneself from.

des·car·te m. *(acción)* discard, discarding; *(naipes descartados)* discard, discarded cards; FIG. *(excusa)* excuse.

des·ca·sar tr. *(separar a los casados)* to separate; *(anular el matrimonio)* to annul the marriage of; *(turbar)* to disturb, upset; PRINT. to change the position of pages on a sheet; GUAT., PERU, P. RICO to break an agreement —reflex. *(separarse)* to separate; *(divorciarse)* to get divorced; *(turbarse)* to be disturbed.

des·cas·car §70 tr. to shell, peel —reflex. *(romperse)* to break into pieces; FIG. *(charlar mucho)* to blab, run off at the mouth.

des·cas·ca·rar tr. to shell, peel —reflex. to peel (off), lose the peel.

des·cas·ca·ri·llar tr. to peel, husk.

des·cas·ta·do, –da I. past part. see **descastar** II. adj. cold, indifferent to affection III. m.f. person who shows little love or affection for his family.

des·cas·tar tr. to exterminate (animals).

des·ca·to·li·zar §04 tr. to induce (a person or a people) to abandon Catholicism, dechristianize.

des·cen·den·cia f. *(hijos)* descendants, offspring; *(linaje)* descent, origin.

des·cen·den·te adj. *(que desciende)* descending, downward; MARIT. ebb (tide).

des·cen·der §50 intr. *(bajar)* to descend, go down; *(proceder)* to descend or be descended from; *(un líquido)* to run or flow down; *(de nivel)* to drop, fall; FIG. *(derivar)* to derive or come from —tr. *(bajar)* to descend, go down <*d. la escalera* to go down the stairs>; *(bajar una cosa)* to lower, bring down.

des·cen·dien·te I. adj. descending II. m.f. descendant, offspring.

des·cen·so m. *(descensión)* descent, going down; *(de nivel)* fall, drop; *(degradación)* demotion; FIG. *(decaimiento)* drop, decline.

des·cen·tra·ción f. putting off center.

des·cen·tra·do, –da I. past part. see **descentrar** II. adj. off-center.

des·cen·tra·li·za·ción f. decentralization.

des·cen·trar tr. to put off center, uncenter —reflex. to become off center or out of plumb.

des·ce·ñi·do, –da I. past part. see **desceñir** II. adj. loose, loose-fitting.

des·ce·ñir §59 tr. to unbelt, ungird.

des·ce·par tr. *(una planta)* to uproot, pull up by the roots; FIG. *(extirpar)* to extirpate.

des·cer·car §70 tr. *(una muralla)* to destroy, demolish (a fence or wall); *(una ciudad)* to raise or lift (a siege).

des·ce·rra·jar tr. *(una cerradura)* to force, break open (a lock); FIG., COLL. *(descargar)* to fire, discharge (a shot).

des·cien·da descendo, see **descender**.

des·ci·fra·mien·to m. *(de una escritura)* deciphering; *(con clave)* decoding.

des·ci·frar tr. *(una escritura)* to decipher; *(con clave)* to decode; FIG. *(aclarar)* to make out.

des·ci·ña, desciño see **desceñir**.

des·ci·ñe·ron, desciñó see **desceñir**.

des·cla·var tr. *(quitar los clavos)* to remove the nails from; *(desabrochar)* to unfasten.

des·co·a·gu·lan·te adj. liquefying, dissolving.

des·co·ca·do, –da I. past part. see **descocar** II. adj. brazen, forward III. m.f. brazen or forward person.

des·co·car §70 tr. to clean insects (from trees) —reflex. to be impudent or brazen.

des·co·di·fi·ca·ción f. decodification, decoding.

des·co·di·fi·car §70 tr. to decode.

des·co·ger §34 tr. to unfold, spread.

des·co·lar tr. *(cortar la cola)* to cut off or dock the tail of; MEX., COLL. to show contempt for.

des·col·gar §16 tr. *(quitar)* to take down <*d. un cuadro* to take down a painting>; *(bajar)* to lower, let down; SPORT. to lead; TELEC. to pick up (a telephone receiver) —reflex. *(caer)* to come or fall down; *(bajarse)* to climb or come down; *(por una cuerda)* to lower oneself, descend (on a rope); *(presentarse)* to show up, drop in; METEOROL. to come on suddenly ♦ **descolgarse con** to come up with *<se descolgó con una idea buenísima* she came up with a great idea>.

des·co·lo·ran·te I. adj. *(que descolora)* discoloring; *(de un color)* fading; *(del pelo)* bleaching **II.** m. bleach, bleaching agent.

des·co·lo·rar tr. *(hacer perder el color)* to discolor; *(desteñir)* to fade; *(blanquear)* to bleach —reflex. *(perder el color)* to be discolored; *(desteñirse)* to become faded; *(quedar blanco)* to be bleached; *(teñirse el pelo)* to bleach one's hair.

des·co·lo·ri·do, –da I. past part. see **descolorir II.** adj. discolored; *(pálido)* pallid, colorless; *(desteñido)* faded; *(blanqueado)* whitened, bleached.

des·co·lo·ri·mien·to m. fading, discoloration.

des·co·lo·rir §38 tr. to fade, discolor.

des·co·llar §19 intr. to stand out, be outstanding.

des·com·brar tr. to disencumber, clear (of obstacles).

des·com·bro m. disencumbering, clearing.

des·co·me·di·do, –da I. past part. see **descomedirse II.** adj. *(excesivo)* excessive; *(grosero)* rude; *(descortés)* impolite.

des·co·me·dir·se §48 reflex. to be rude, impolite.

des·com·pa·gi·nar tr. *(descomponer)* to disarrange; FIG. *(perturbar)* to disrupt, upset.

des·com·pás m. lack of proportion, excess.

des·com·pa·sar tr. to go too far —reflex. to be rude, be impolite.

des·com·po·ner §54 tr. *(desordenar)* to disarrange, mess up; *(deshacer)* to separate, break up; CHEM. to decompose, analyze; *(podrir)* to decompose, cause to rot; MECH. to break, put out of order; FIG. *(trastornar)* to upset, disturb *<su presencia la descomponía* his presence disturbed her> —reflex. *(corromperse)* to rot, decompose; CHEM. to decompose, break down; MECH. to break down; FIG. *(indisponerse)* to feel sick *<se descompuso del estómago* he felt sick to his stomach>; *(irritarse)* to become disturbed, get upset; METEOROL. to become inclement.

des·com·po·ni·ble adj. decomposable.

des·com·po·si·ción f. *(putrefacción)* decomposition, decay; CHEM. decomposition, breakdown; *(desarreglo)* disorder, disarrangement.

des·com·pos·tu·ra f. *(desarreglo)* disorder, disarrangement; *(desaseo)* slovenliness, messiness; FIG. *(descaro)* impudence, brazenness; *(falta de cortesía)* rudeness; MECH. breakdown.

des·com·pre·sión f. decompression.

des·com·pri·mir tr. to decompress.

des·com·pues·to, –ta I. past part. see **descomponer II.** adj. *(podrido)* decomposed, rotten; *(desarreglado)* slovenly, messy; MECH. out of order, broken; FIG. *(perturbado)* upset; *(descarado)* impudent, brazen; *(descortés)* rude, impolite; S. AMER. tipsy.

des·com·pu·sie·ra, descompuso see **descomponer.**

des·co·mul·gar §47 tr. to excommunicate.

des·co·mu·nal adj. *(enorme)* enormous, huge; FIG. *(extraordinario)* extraordinary.

des·co·mu·nal·men·te adv. excessively, extraordinarily *<beber d.* to drink excessively>.

des·con·cep·tuar §67 tr. to discredit. —reflex. to be discredited.

des·con·cer·ta·do, –da I. past part. see **desconcertar II.** adj. FIG. wild, unruly.

des·con·cer·tan·te adj. disconcerting, upsetting.

des·con·cer·tar §49 tr. *(aturdir)* to disconcert, upset; *(descomponer)* to put out of order; *(desordenar)* to disarrange, disrupt; MED. to dislocate —reflex. *(aturdirse)* to be disconcerted *or* upset; *(descomponer)* to get out of order; *(desavenirse)* to fall out, disagree; FIG. *(descomedirse)* to go off the deep end; MED. to become dislocated.

des·con·cor·dia f. discord, disagreement.

des·co·nec·tar tr. to disconnect; ELEC. to unplug, turn off —reflex. to become disconnected.

des·con·fia·do, –da I. past part. see **desconfiar II.** adj. distrustful, suspicious **III.** m.f. distrustful *or* suspicious person.

des·con·fian·za f. distrust, mistrust.

des·con·fiar §30 intr. to distrust, mistrust.

des·con·ge·lar tr. *(deshelar)* to thaw; *(la nevera)* to defrost; COM. to unfreeze (assets).

des·con·ges·tio·nar tr. PHYSIOL. to clear (congestion from); FIG. *(desatascar)* to clear, unblock *<d. el tráfico de la plaza* to clear traffic from the square>.

des·co·no·ce·dor, –do·ra adj. unknowing, unaware (of).

des·co·no·cer §17 tr. *(no conocer)* not to know, to be unacquainted (with); *(ignorar)* to be ignorant of; *(no recordar)* not to remember, to fail to remember; FIG. *(no reconocer)* not to recognize, to fail to recognize; *(negar)* to deny, disavow; *(desentenderse)* to pretend not to know, ignore.

des·co·no·ci·do, –da I. past part. see **desconocer II.** adj. *(ignorado)* unknown, ignored; *(desagradecido)* ungrateful, unthankful; *(muy cambiado)* greatly changed, unrecognizable; *(extraño)* strange, unfamiliar **III.** m.f. *(extraño)* stranger, unknown person; *(recién llegado)* newcomer ♦ **lo desconocido** the unknown.

des·co·no·ci·mien·to m. *(ignorancia)* ignorance; *(despreocupación)* disregard, lack of acknowledgement; *(ingratitud)* ingratitude, ungratefulness; *(olvido)* forgetfulness, lack of memory.

des·co·noz·ca, desconozco see **desconocer.**

des·con·si·de·ra·ción f. inconsiderateness, thoughtlessness.

des·con·si·de·ra·do, –da I. past part. see **desconsiderar II.** adj. inconsiderate, thoughtless **III.** m.f. inconsiderate *or* thoughtless person.

des·con·si·de·rar tr. to be inconsiderate *or* thoughtless toward.

des·con·so·la·do, –da I. past part. see **desconsolar II.** adj. *(triste)* disconsolate, sad; *(el estómago)* empty, starved.

des·con·so·la·dor, –do·ra adj. distressing, heartbreaking.

des·con·so·lar §19 tr. to distress, grieve —reflex. to lose heart, become distressed.

des·con·sue·lo m. *(pena)* grief, distress; *(del estómago)* empty feeling (in the stomach).

des·con·ta·mi·nar tr. to decontaminate, disinfect.

des·con·tar §19 tr. *(quitar)* to deduct, take away *<lo descontaron de mi sueldo* they deducted it from my salary>; FIG. *(rebajar)* to disregard, discount; *(dar por cierto)* to take for granted, assume; COM. to discount ♦ **dar por descontado** to take for granted.

des·con·ten·ta·di·zo, –da I. adj. fastidious, hard to please. **II.** m.f. person who is hard to please.

des·con·ten·tar tr. to discontent, displease —reflex. to become discontented *or* displeased.

des·con·ten·to, –ta I. past part see **descontentar II.** adj. discontented, dissatisfied **III.** m. discontent, dissatisfaction.

des·con·ve·nir §76 intr. to disagree.

des·co·qué, descoque see **descocar.**

des·co·ra·zo·na·mien·to m. FIG. discouragement, dejection.

des·co·ra·zo·nar tr. *(arrancar el corazón de)* to tear out the heart of; FIG. *(desanimar)* to discourage, dishearten —reflex. to lose heart, become discouraged.

des·cor·char tr. *(un árbol)* to remove the bark from, decorticate (a tree); *(una botella)* to uncork (a bottle); *(una colmena)* to break (a beehive).

des·cor·nar §19 tr. to dehorn, remove the horns from —reflex. FIG., COLL. to rack one's brains.

des·co·ro·nar tr. to depose, remove the crown from (a king).

des·co·rrer tr. *(volver a correr)* to run back over (ground already covered); *(cortinas)* to draw back, open (curtains) —intr. & reflex. to flow (said of liquids).

des·cor·tés I. adj. discourteous, rude **II.** m.f. rude *or* impolite person.

des·cor·te·sí·a f. discourtesy, rudeness.

des·cor·tés·men·te adv. discourteously, rudely.

des·cor·te·zar §04 tr. to strip the bark from, decorticate; *(el pan)* to remove the crust from (bread); *(la fruta)* to peel (fruit); FIG., COLL. *(desbastar)* to refine, knock the rough edges off.

des·co·ser tr. SEW. to unstitch, rip (a seam) —reflex. SEW.

to come unstitched, rip (a seam); FIG. *(revelar indiscreta-mente)* to let out, blurt out; FIG., COLL. *(peerse)* to fart ♦ **no descoser los labios** FIG. to keep silent, keep one's lips sealed.

des·co·si·do, –da I. past part. see **descoser II.** adj. SEW. unstitched, ripped; *(indiscreto)* indiscreet, talkative; FIG. *(desordenado)* disorderly, chaotic; FIG. *(excesivo)* immoderate, excessive **III.** m. SEW. open seam, rip ♦ **como un descosido** FIG., COLL. immoderately, excessively • **beber como un descosido** FIG., COLL. to drink like a fish.

des·co·tar·se reflex. to wear a low-cut neckline.

des·cote m. low-cut neckline, décolletage.

des·co·yun·ta·mien·to m. MED. *(dislocación)* dislocation, luxation; *(fatiga)* fatigue, exhaustion.

des·co·yun·tar tr. MED. to dislocate; FIG. *(molestar)* to bother, annoy —reflex. MED. to become dislocated ♦ **descoyuntarse de risa** FIG. to split one's sides with laughter.

des·cré·di·to m. discredit, disrepute.

des·cre·er §43 tr. *(no creer)* to disbelieve; *(negar el debido crédito)* to deny due recognition to; *(negar)* to disown.

des·cre·í·do, –da I. past part. see **descreer II.** adj. disbelieving, incredulous; RELIG. unbelieving **III.** m.f. *(persona que descree)* disbeliever; RELIG. nonbeliever, infidel.

des·crei·mien·to m. disbelief, incredulousness.

des·cri·bi·ble adj. describable.

des·cri·bir §85 tr. *(hacer la descripción de)* to describe; *(trazar)* to trace, describe <*d. un círculo* to describe a circle>.

des·crip·ción f. *(acción de describir)* description; LAW *(inventario)* inventory.

des·crip·ti·ble adj. describable.

des·crip·ti·vo, –va adj. descriptive.

des·cris·mar tr. RELIG. to remove the chrism from; COLL. *(dar un golpe en la cabeza)* to bash over the head —reflex. *(enfadarse)* to lose one's patience; *(devanarse los sesos)* to rack one's brains.

des·cris·tia·ni·zar §04 tr. to dechristianize, turn away from Christianity.

des·cri·to, –ta or **des·crip·to, –ta** past part. see **describir.**

des·cua·der·nar tr. *(desencuadernar)* to unbind, take the binding from; FIG. *(turbar)* to confuse, upset.

des·cua·dri·llar·se reflex. VET. to sprain the haunches (said of a horse).

des·cua·jar tr. *(liquidar)* to liquefy, dissolve; FIG., COLL. *(desanimar)* to discourage, dishearten; *(arrancar de raíz)* to uproot, pull up by the root.

des·cua·ja·rin·gar·se §47 reflex. COLL. *(agotarse)* to be exhausted or worn out; *(relajarse)* to relax, take it easy.

des·cuar·ti·zar §04 tr. to quarter, cut up.

des·cu·bier·to, –ta I. past part. see **descubrir II.** adj. *(no cubierto)* uncovered, exposed; clear <*un cielo d.* a clear sky>; *(yermo)* bare, barren; *(sin sombrero)* bareheaded, without a hat ♦ **a d.** uncovered; COM. unbacked • **al d.** COM. short; FIG. *(abiertamente)* openly, in the open • **estar en d.** COM. to be overdrawn; FIG. *(quedarse cortado)* to be at a loss for words • **girar en d.** COM. overdraw **III.** m. COM. deficit, shortage; RELIG. exposition (of the sacrament).

des·cu·bri·dor, –do·ra I. adj. MARIT. scouting, reconnaissance (ship); *(que descubre)* discovering, exploring **II.** m.f. *(explorador)* discoverer, explorer —m. MIL. scout.

des·cu·bri·mien·to m. *(acción de descubrir)* discovery <*el d. del Nuevo Mundo* the discovery of the New World>; *(revelación)* disclosure, revelation; *(inauguración)* unveiling.

des·cu·brir §85 tr. *(hallar)* to discover, find; *(inventar)* to discover, invent; *(revelar)* to reveal, uncover; *(alcanzar a ver)* to be able to see, make out; *(inaugurar)* to unveil; FIG. *(enterarse)* to find out; MIL. to reconnoiter; RELIG. to expose —reflex. *(quitarse el sombrero)* to take off or remove one's hat; *(dejarse ver)* to reveal oneself, show oneself ♦ **descubrirse a** or **con alguien** to confess to or confide in someone.

des·cuel·go, descuelgue see **descolgar.**

des·cue·lle, descuello see **descollar.**

des·cuen·te, descuento see **descontar.**

des·cuen·to m. *(rebaja)* discount, reduction; *(acción de descontar)* deduction ♦ **al** or **con d.** at a discount.

des·cue·rar tr. *(despellejar)* to skin, flay; FIG. *(criticar)* to criticize, tear apart.

des·cuer·ne, descuerno see **descornar.**

des·cui·da·do, –da I. past part. see **descuidar II.** adj. *(negligente)* careless, thoughtless; *(desaliñado)* untidy, slovenly; *(desprevenido)* unprepared, off guard; *(abandonado)* neglected, abandoned; *(despreocupado)* carefree, easygoing ♦ **coger d. a uno** to catch someone unawares or off guard **III.** m.f. *(negligente)* careless or thoughtless person; *(desaliñado)* sloppy or untidy person, slob.

des·cui·dar tr. *(libertar)* to relieve, free of an obligation; *(no cuidar)* to neglect, forget; *(distraer)* to distract, make careless —intr. to be careless or thoughtless ♦ **d. de** to neglect, forget —reflex. *(no cuidar)* to be careless or thoughtless; *(desaliñarse)* to neglect oneself, not take care of oneself ♦ **descuidarse de** to neglect, forget.

des·cui·do m. *(negligencia)* carelessness, negligence; *(olvido)* forgetfulness; *(desaliño)* untidiness, slovenliness; *(desatención)* slip, oversight; *(falta)* error, mistake ♦ **al d.** nonchalantly, casually • **con d.** carelessly, thoughtlessly • **en un d.** AMER. when least expected.

des·cui·ta·do, –da adj. carefree, untroubled.

des·cu·lar tr. to break the bottom of.

des·cha·ve·ta·do, –da I. past part. see **deschavetarse II.** adj. AMER., COLL. crazy, loony.

des·cha·ve·tar·se reflex. AMER., COLL. to go crazy, go off one's rocker.

des·de prep. from <*d. el primero hasta el último* from the first to the last>; since <*d. niño* since childhood> ♦ **d. ahora** from now on • **d. entonces** since then • **d. hace** for <*no le hemos visto d. hace un año* we have not seen him for a year> • **d. luego** of course • **d. que** since <*d. que nací* since I was born> • **d. ya** AMER. right now.

des·de·cir §11 intr. ♦ **d. de** *(no corresponder a su origen)* not to live up to, to fall short of; FIG. *(no convenir)* to differ, not to match; *(venir a menos)* to degenerate, decline —reflex. ♦ **desdecirse de** *(retractarse)* to retract, withdraw; *(contradecirse)* to contradict oneself, say the opposite.

des·dén m. disdain, scorn ♦ **al d.** carelessly, nonchalantly.

des·den·ta·do, –da I. past part. see **desdentar II.** adj. *(sin dientes)* toothless; ZOOL. edentate.

des·den·tar §49 tr. *(extraer dientes a)* to pull or extract teeth from; *(dejar sin dientes)* to leave without teeth.

des·de·ña·ble adj. despicable, contemptible.

des·de·ñar tr. to disdain, scorn —reflex. to be disdainful ♦ **desdeñarse de** not to deign to.

des·de·ño·so, –sa I. adj. disdainful, scornful **II.** m.f. disdainful person, snob.

des·di·bu·ja·do, –da I. past part. see **desdibujarse II.** adj. blurred, faded (said of a drawing).

des·di·bu·jar·se reflex. to become blurred or faded.

des·di·ce see **desdecir.**

des·di·cha f. *(desgracia)* misfortune; *(pobreza)* poverty, misery ♦ **por d.** unfortunately.

des·di·cha·do, –da I. adj. *(desgraciado)* unfortunate, pitiful; *(infeliz)* unhappy, wretched ♦ **¡d. de mí!** woe is me! **II.** m.f. *(infelizote)* poor devil or wretch; *(cuitado)* spiritless or timid person.

des·dien·te, desdiento see **desdentar.**

des·di·ga, desdigo see **desdecir.**

des·di·je·ra, desdijo see **desdecir.**

des·do·bla·mien·to m. *(extensión)* unfolding, spreading out; *(fraccionamiento)* splitting, breaking down; FIG. *(aclaración)* explanation, elucidation ♦ **d. de la personalidad** PSYCH. split personality.

des·do·blar tr. *(extender)* to unfold, spread out; *(separar)* to split, break down.

des·do·rar tr. *(quitar lo dorado)* to remove the gilt from; FIG. *(deslustrar)* to tarnish, sully (a reputation).

des·do·ro m. blemish, stain (on a reputation).

de·se·a·ble adj. desirable.

de·se·ar tr. to wish, desire.

de·se·car §70 tr. *(secar)* to dry, desiccate; FIG. *(volver insensible)* to dry up, harden <*d. el corazón* to harden the heart>.

de·se·ca·ti·vo, –va adj. desiccative, drying.

de·se·char tr. *(rechazar)* to reject, decline <*desechó mi consejo* he rejected my advice>; *(renunciar)* to refuse, turn down <*d. un empleo* to turn down a job>; *(apartar)* to put *or* cast aside, banish, get rid of; *(arrojar)* to discard, throw away *or* out; *(menospreciar)* to underrate, undervalue; *(despreciar)* to scorn, be disdainful of.

de·se·cho m. *(residuo)* residue, remainder; *(desperdicio)* waste, rubbish; *(lo peor)* scum, dregs; *(carne)* offal; *(metal)* scrap; FIG. *(desprecio)* scorn, contempt; CUBA, AGR. grade- *or* class-A tobacco ♦ **de d.** discarded, scrap • **desechos** AGR., MIN. tailings • **desechos radiactivos** ARM., INDUS. radioactive waste.

de·sem·ba·la·je m. unpacking.

de·sem·ba·lar tr. to unpack.

de·sem·ba·nas·tar tr. *(desempaquetar)* to unpack, take out of a basket; *(hablar mucho)* to chatter, babble; COLL. *(la espada)* to draw (a sword) —reflex. FIG. *(un animal)* to break out (a caged animal); COLL. *(desembarcar)* to alight (from a carriage).

de·sem·ba·ra·za·do, –da I. past part. see **desembarazar** II. adj. *(libre)* free, clear; *(desenvuelto)* free and easy.

de·sem·ba·ra·zar §04 tr. *(despejar)* to clear, rid of obstacles; AMER. to give birth to; *(evacuar)* to evacuate, leave (a house) —reflex. FIG. to free oneself, get rid (of).

de·sem·ba·ra·zo m. *(despejo)* clearing, freeing; *(desenfado)* ease, naturalness; AMER. childbirth.

de·sem·bar·ca·de·ro m. pier, wharf.

de·sem·bar·car §70 tr. to disembark, unload —intr. *(salir de un barco)* to disembark, go ashore; FIG., COLL. *(descender de un carruaje)* to alight (from a carriage); *(una escalera)* to end in a landing (stairs).

de·sem·bar·co m. *(acción)* landing, disembarkation; MIL. landing (of troops); *(escalera)* landing (of stairs).

de·sem·bar·gar §47 tr. *(desembarazar)* to clear, remove obstacles from; LAW *(quitar el embargo)* to raise *or* lift the embargo on.

de·sem·bar·que m. *(de mercancías)* debarkation, unloading; *(de pasajeros)* disembarkation, landing.

de·sem·bar·qué, desembarque see **desembarcar**.

de·sem·ba·rrar tr. to clear of mud.

de·sem·bau·lar §82 tr. *(desembalar)* to unpack; FIG., COLL. *(desahogarse)* to unbosom oneself, get something off one's chest.

de·sem·be·le·sar·se reflex. to recover from one's amazement.

de·sem·bo·ca·de·ro m. *(bocacalle)* entrance *or* end (of a street); *(de un río)* mouth, outlet (of a river).

de·sem·bo·ca·du·ra f. *(de un río)* mouth, outlet; *(de una calle)* entrance, outlet.

de·sem·bo·car §70 intr. *(río)* to flow, run; *(calle)* to lead to, run; *(abrirse paso)* to squeeze through a narrow place.

de·sem·bo·cé, desemboce see **desembozar**.

de·sem·bol·sar tr. *(sacar de la bolsa)* to take out of a purse *or* bag; FIG. *(pagar)* to disburse, pay.

de·sem·bol·so m. *(pago)* disbursement, payment; FIG. *(gasto)* expenditure, outlay ♦ **d. inicial** down payment, initial outlay.

de·sem·bo·que var. of **desembocadero**.

de·sem·bo·qué, desemboque see **desembocar**.

de·sem·bo·tar tr. FIG. *(aguzar lo embotado)* to sharpen, hone (a blunt edge); *(avivar)* to rouse, sharpen (someone's wits).

de·sem·bo·zar §04 tr. to uncover the face of, unmask —reflex. to uncover one's face, unmask oneself.

de·sem·bra·gar §47 tr. MECH. to declutch, disengage (gears).

de·sem·bra·ve·cer §17 tr. *(amansar)* to tame, domesticate; *(calmar)* to calm.

de·sem·bria·gar §47 tr. to sober up.

de·sem·bro·llar tr. COLL. *(desenredar)* to unravel, untangle; *(aclarar)* to sort out, clear up.

de·sem·bu·char tr. ORNITH. to disgorge; FIG., COLL. *(revelar)* tell, reveal.

de·se·me·jan·te adj. different, dissimilar.

de·sem·pa·car §70 tr. to unpack, unwrap.

de·sem·pa·char tr. to relieve of indigestion —reflex. FIG. to become vivacious.

de·sem·pa·cho m. FIG. ease, self-confidence.

de·sem·pa·la·gar §47 tr. *(quitar el empalago)* to settle the stomach of, restore the appetite of; *(un molino)* to clear of stagnant water (a mill).

de·sem·pa·ñar tr. *(un cristal)* to clean, polish (glass); *(un niño)* to remove diapers from, unswaddle *(a child)*.

de·sem·pa·pe·lar tr. *(quitar el papel)* to remove paper from (a wall); *(desenvolver)* to unwrap; LAW *(sobreseer un proceso)* to discontinue an action (against someone).

de·sem·pa·que m. unpacking.

de·sem·pa·qué, desempaque see **desempacar**.

de·sem·pa·que·tar tr. to unpack, unwrap.

de·sem·pa·tar tr. *(deshacer el empate)* to break a tie between; COL., CUBA, P. RICO to untie, separate.

de·sem·pe·drar §49 tr. *(remover las piedras)* to remove cobblestones from, unpave; COLL. *(ir de prisa)* to rush along (the street).

de·sem·pe·ñar tr. *(rescatar)* to recover, redeem (pawned goods); *(pagar las deudas)* to get out of debt, free from debt; *(cumplir)* to fulfill, carry out <d. un cargo to carry out a mission>; *(sacar de apuro)* to get (someone) out of trouble; THEAT. to play, perform (a part) —reflex. *(pagar las deudas)* to get oneself out of debt; *(sacarse de apuro)* to get oneself out of trouble.

de·sem·pe·ño m. *(rescate)* redemption, redeeming; *(de deudas)* freeing from debt; *(cumplimiento)* fulfillment; THEAT. performance.

de·sem·per·nar tr. to unbolt.

de·sem·pie·dre, desempiedro see **desempedrar**.

de·sem·ple·a·do, –da I. adj. unemployed, out of work II. m.f. unemployed person.

de·sem·ple·o m. unemployment.

de·sem·plu·mar tr. to pluck, take the feathers out of.

de·sem·pol·var tr. *(quitar el polvo)* to remove the dust from, dust; FIG. *(desenterrar)* to revive, brush up (something forgotten).

de·sen·a·mo·rar tr. to destroy the love *or* affection of —reflex. to lose one's love or affection for.

de·sen·ca·de·na·mien·to m. unchaining, unleashing.

de·sen·ca·de·nar tr. *(quitar la cadena)* to unchain, unfetter; *(liberar)* to free, unleash, set *or* let loose; FIG. *(incitar)* to start, spark, incite —reflex. *(soltarse)* to break loose; FIG. *(pasiones)* to become unleashed, run wild; METEOROL. *(tormenta)* to rage, break out; *(guerra)* to break out.

de·sen·ca·jar tr. MED. to dislocate (bones); *(desconectar)* to disconnect, take apart; *(sacar)* to remove, take out —reflex. *(el rostro)* to become distorted *or* contorted (said of the face); *(deshacerse)* to fall apart, become disconnected.

de·sen·ca·llar tr. MARIT. to refloat, free (a ship) from a shoal.

de·sen·ca·mi·nar tr. to lead astray, misdirect.

de·sen·can·tar tr. to disillusion, disenchant.

de·sen·can·to m. disenchantment, disillusionment.

de·sen·ca·po·tar tr. *(quitar el capote)* to uncloak, remove the cloak *or* cape from; FIG., COLL. *(hacer patente)* to uncloak, reveal; EQUIT. to make (a horse) raise its head —reflex. METEOROL. to clear up (said of the sky); FIG. *(desenojarse)* to calm down.

de·sen·ca·pri·char·se tr. to rid oneself of a caprice *or* whim.

de·sen·car·ce·lar tr. CRIMIN. to set free, release (from a prison).

de·sen·ce·rrar §49 tr. *(sacar del encierro)* to free (from confinement); *(abrir)* to open, unlock; FIG. *(descubrir)* to bring to light, reveal.

de·sen·cin·char tr. AMER. to ungirth, uncinch (a horse).

de·sen·cla·var tr. *(desclavar)* to remove the nails from; FIG. *(sacar violentamente)* to tear out.

de·sen·cla·vi·jar tr. *(quitar las clavijas)* to remove the pegs from (a musical instrument); FIG. *(desencajar)* to disconnect, loosen.

de·sen·co·ger §34 tr. *(extender)* to stretch *or* spread out; *(desdoblar)* to unfold —reflex. FIG. to come out of one's shell, lose one's shyness.

de·sen·co·gi·mien·to m. *(extensión)* stretching *or* spreading out; *(desdoblamiento)* unfolding; *(desembarazo)* ease, self-confidence.

de·sen·co·lar tr. to unglue, unstick.

de·sen·co·le·ri·zar §04 tr. to calm, pacify.

de·sen·co·nar tr. MED. to relieve the inflammation of; *(desahogar)* to soothe, pacify; *(moderar)* to control, restrain —reflex. *(suavizarse)* to become smooth; *(contenerse)* to calm down, cool off.

de·sen·co·no m. MED. relief of inflammation; *(apaciguamiento)* calming, pacification; *(contención)* restraint, control.

de·sen·cor·dar §19 tr. to unstring (a musical instrument).

de·sen·cua·der·nar tr. to unbind (a book).

de·sen·chu·far tr. ELEC. to unplug, disconnect.

de·sen·dio·sar tr. FIG. to knock off a pedestal, bring down to earth.

de·sen·fa·da·do, –da I. past part. see **desenfadar** II. adj. *(desenvuelto)* confident, self-assured; *(despreocupado)* carefree, uninhibited; *(espacioso)* spacious, ample.

de·sen·fa·dar tr. to soothe, pacify —reflex. to calm down, cool off.

de·sen·fa·do m. *(desenvoltura)* confidence, self-assurance; *(facilidad)* ease, naturalness.

de·sen·fo·que m. incorrect focus, being out of focus.

de·sen·fre·nar tr. EQUIT. to unbridle —reflex. FIG. *(entregarse al vicio)* to surrender oneself, give oneself over (to vice); *(las pasiones)* to break loose, be unleashed (passions); *(una tempestad)* to break, burst (a storm).

de·sen·fre·no m. FIG. *(vicio)* wantonness, licentiousness; *(de las pasiones)* unleashing, unbridling (of passions) ♦ **d. de vientre** MED. diarrhea.

de·sen·fun·dar tr. to unsheath, remove the covering from.

de·sen·gan·char tr. *(soltar una cosa enganchada)* to unhook, unfasten; *(caballerías)* to unhitch, unharness.

de·sen·ga·ña·do, –da I. past part. see **desengañar** II. adj. *(desilusionado)* disillusioned; *(aleccionado)* taught *or* schooled by experience; CHILE, ECUAD. ugly, hideous.

de·sen·ga·ña·dor, –do·ra I. adj. disillusioning II. m.f. disillusioner.

de·sen·ga·ñar tr. *(desilusionar)* to disillusion, open the eyes of; *(desencantar)* to disillusion, disenchant —reflex. *(desilusionarse)* to open one's eyes, not to fool oneself; *(desencantarse)* to become disillusioned *or* disenchanted.

de·sen·ga·ño m. *(comprensión)* enlightenment, realization; *(desilusión)* disillusionment ♦ **desengaños** bitter lessons of life *or* experience.

de·sen·gas·tar tr. JEWEL. to remove (a jewel) from its setting.

de·sen·go·mar tr. to unglue, unstick.

de·sen·gra·nar tr. MECH. to disengage (gears or cogged wheels).

de·sen·gra·sar tr. *(limpiar)* to remove the fat *or* grease from; CHILE to eat dessert —intr. FIG. *(enflaquecer)* to lose weight, grow slim; *(variar el trabajo)* to change jobs (to make work easier); COLL. *(quitar un sabor grasiento)* to remove a greasy taste.

de·sen·la·ce m. *(acción de desenlazar)* untying, unfastening; LIT. denouement, ending; FIG. *(resultado)* result, outcome.

de·sen·la·zar §04 tr. *(desatar)* to unfasten, untie; FIG. *(resolver)* to clear up, resolve; LIT. to unravel (a plot) —reflex. *(desatarse)* to become untied *or* loose; LIT. to reach a denouement.

de·sen·lu·tar tr. to bring (someone) out of mourning, make (someone) give up mourning.

de·sen·ma·ra·ñar tr. *(desenredar)* to untangle, unravel; FIG. *(aclarar)* to clear up, solve.

des·en·mas·ca·rar tr. *(quitar la máscara)* to unmask; FIG. *(descubrir)* to reveal, expose.

de·sen·mo·he·cer §17 tr. *(quitar el herrumbre)* to remove rust from; *(quitar el moho)* to remove mildew from.

de·sen·mu·de·cer §17 tr. *(libertar del impedimento natural)* to rid of a speech impediment; FIG. *(hacer que vuelva a hablar)* to cause to break a long silence —intr. *(libertarse del impedimento natural)* to rid oneself of a speech impediment; FIG. *(volver a hablar)* to break a long silence.

de·sen·o·jar tr. to calm, pacify —reflex. *(calmarse)* to become calm; *(distraerse)* to rest, amuse oneself.

de·sen·o·jo m. calm, calmness (after anger).

de·sen·re·dar tr. *(desenmarañar)* to disentangle, unravel; FIG. *(poner en orden)* to put in order, straighten out —reflex. FIG. to extricate *or* free oneself.

de·sen·re·do m. *(acción de desenredar)* disentangling, untangling; *(efecto de desenredar)* disentanglement; FIG.

(aclaración) putting in order, straightening out; LIT. *(desenlace)* denouement, ending; *(de peligro)* extrication, disinvolvement.

de·sen·ro·llar tr. to unroll, unwind.

de·sen·ros·car §70 tr. to unwind, uncoil.

de·sen·sam·blar tr. to take apart, disassemble.

de·sen·sa·ñar tr. to soothe, appease.

de·sen·se·bar tr. to strip of fat —intr. FIG. *(variar de ocupación)* to change one's occupation (to make work easier); *(quitar el sabor a grasa)* to remove the taste of fat (by eating something else).

de·sen·se·ñar tr. to re-educate, teach correctly.

de·sen·si·bi·li·zar §04 tr. MED., PHOTOG., PHYSIOL. to desensitize.

de·sen·si·llar tr. EQUIT. to unsaddle.

de·sen·so·ber·be·cer §17 tr. to humble, make humble.

de·sen·ta·blar tr. *(arrancar las tablas)* to rip up planks *or* boards from; FIG. *(desarreglar)* to disarrange, disturb; *(deshacer)* to break up <*d. una amistad* to break up a friendship>.

de·sen·ten·der·se §50 reflex. to feign ignorance, pretend not to know ♦ **d. de** to take no part in, have nothing to do with.

de·sen·te·rrar §49 tr. *(exhumar)* to unearth, dig up; FIG., COLL. *(traer a la memoria)* to dig up, recall.

de·sen·to·na·ción f. dissonance, tunelessness.

de·sen·to·nar tr. to humiliate, humble —intr. MUS. to be out of tune; FIG. *(discordar)* to clash, not to match —reflex. *(descomedirse)* to be rude *or* insolent; *(alzar la voz)* to raise one's voice.

de·sen·to·no m. MUS. dissonance, inharmoniousness; FIG. *(descompostura)* rude *or* insolent tone of voice.

de·sen·tor·pe·cer §17 tr. *(sacudir la torpeza)* to rid of numbness *or* stiffness (a leg or arm); *(hacer capaz)* to make alert *or* intelligent —reflex. *(sacudirse la torpeza)* to come back to life (a leg or arm); *(volverse capaz)* to become alert *or* intelligent.

de·sen·tra·ñar tr. *(arrancar las entrañas)* to eviscerate, disembowel; FIG. *(solucionar)* to get to the bottom of (a matter) —reflex. to give one's all.

de·sen·tu·me·cer §17 tr. to rid of numbness, restore feeling to.

de·sen·vai·nar tr. *(un sable)* to draw, unsheathe (a sword); FIG. *(las uñas)* to bare claws (said of an animal); FIG., COLL. *(sacar a relucir)* to uncover, expose.

de·sen·vol·tu·ra f. FIG. *(confianza)* naturalness, confidence; *(elocuencia)* eloquence, facility; *(desvergüenza)* forwardness, brazenness.

de·sen·vol·ver §78 tr. *(desarrollar)* to unroll, unwrap; *(explicar)* to develop, expand <*d. una idea* to develop an idea>; FIG. *(aclarar)* to unravel, disentangle —reflex. *(desarrollarse)* to come unrolled *or* unwrapped; *(desempacharse)* to become self-assured; FIG. *(aclararse)* to become unravelled *or* disentangled; COLL. *(desenredarse)* to get oneself out of trouble.

de·sen·vol·vi·mien·to m. *(desarrollo)* unrolling, unwrapping; *(explicación)* development, expansion; FIG. *(aclaración)* unravelling, disentanglement; COLL. *(desenredo)* way out, escape (from trouble).

de·sen·vuel·to, –ta I. past part. see **desenvolver** II. adj. *(confiado)* natural, confident; *(elocuente)* eloquent, fluent; *(desvergonzado)* forward, brazen.

de·sen·vuel·va, desenvuelvo see **desenvolver**.

de·se·o m. desire, wish ♦ **a medida de sus deseos** to one's liking • **buenos deseos** good intentions.

de·se·o·so, –sa adj. desirous, anxious.

de·se·qué, deseque see **desecar**.

de·se·qui·li·bra·do, –da I. past part. see **desequilibrar** II. adj. *(una cosa)* unbalanced, lopsided; *(una persona)* (mentally) unbalanced, unstable III. m.f. (mentally) unbalanced *or* unstable person.

de·se·qui·li·brar tr. *(una cosa)* to throw off balance; FIG. *(una persona)* to unbalance mentally —reflex. *(perder el equilibrio)* to lose one's balance; FIG. *(dementarse)* to become mentally unbalanced *or* unstable.

de·se·qui·li·brio m. *(falta de equilibrio)* lack of equilibrium, imbalance; FIG. *(de la mente)* unbalanced mental condition, derangement.

de·ser·ción f. *(abandono)* desertion, abandonment; MIL. desertion; LAW *(de una apelación)* forfeiture (of a suit).

de·ser·tar tr. to desert, abandon; LAW *(apelación)* to abandon, drop (a suit) ♦ **d. a** MIL., POL. to defect, go over to • **d. de** FIG., COLL. to stop frequenting —intr. & reflex. MIL. to desert.

de·sér·ti·co, –ca adj. *(como un desierto)* desert-like, barren; *(sin habitantes)* deserted, unpopulated.

de·ser·tor, –to·ra m.f. deserter.

de·ser·vir §48 tr. to fail to do (one's duty).

de·ses·ca·la·da f. MIL. de-escalation.

de·ses·pe·ra·ción f. *(desaliento)* despair, desperation; *(cólera)* anger, exasperation ♦ **ser una d.** COLL. to be exasperating *or* unbearable.

de·ses·pe·ra·do, –da I. past part. see **desesperar** II. adj. hopeless, despairing ♦ **a la desesperada** in desperation, as a last hope III. m.f. hopeless *or* desperate person.

de·ses·pe·ran·te adj. *(que impacienta)* exasperating, infuriating; *(descorazonador)* discouraging, causing despair.

de·ses·pe·ran·za f. despair, hopelessness.

de·ses·pe·ran·zar §04 tr. to deprive of hope, discourage —intr. & reflex. to lose hope, lose hope.

de·ses·pe·rar tr. *(desesperanzar)* to drive to despair, discourage; COLL. *(irritar)* to exasperate —intr. & reflex. to lose hope, despair.

de·ses·pe·ro m. var. of **desesperación**.

de·ses·ti·ma *or* **des·es·ti·ma·ción** f. disesteem, lack of respect.

de·ses·ti·mar tr. to think little of, hold in low esteem.

des·fa·cha·ta·do, –da adj. COLL. cheeky, insolent.

des·fa·cha·tez f. COLL. cheek, nerve.

des·fal·car §70 tr. *(quitar una parte)* to remove part of; *(robar)* to embezzle, defalcate.

des·fal·co m. *(malversación)* embezzlement, defalcation; *(eliminación)* removal, taking away.

des·fa·lle·cer §17 tr. *(debilitar)* to weaken, debilitate —intr. MED. *(perder fuerzas)* to weaken; *(desmayarse)* to faint, pass out.

des·fa·lle·ci·do, –da I. past part. see **desfallecer** II. adj. MED. faint, dizzy.

des·fa·lle·ci·mien·to m. *(debilidad)* weakness, debilitation; MED. fainting, swooning.

des·fa·sa·do, –da MECH., PHYS. out of phase ♦ **estar d.** to be out of step (with the times).

des·fa·vo·ra·ble adj. unfavorable, adverse.

des·fa·vo·re·cer §17 tr. *(dejar de favorecer)* to disfavor, hold in low esteem; *(oponer)* to oppose, contradict.

des·fi·bra·do m. TECH. removal of fibers.

des·fi·bra·do·ra f. TECH. fiber-removing machine.

des·fi·gu·ra·ción f. *(persona)* disfiguring, disfigurement; *(objeto)* distortion, misrepresentation; *(hecho)* distortion, misrepresentation; *(disfraz)* disguise, camouflage.

des·fi·gu·ra·mien·to m. var. of **desfiguración**.

des·fi·gu·rar tr. *(afear)* to disfigure, mar; *(deformar)* to deform, misshape; *(mutilar)* to deface, mar; FIG. *(disfrazar)* to disguise, camouflage *<d. las intenciones* to disguise one's intentions;*> (desvirtuar)* to distort, misrepresent *<d. los hechos* to distort the facts> —reflex. to be disfigured.

des·fi·jar tr. to pull off, remove.

des·fi·la·de·ro m. defile, narrow pass.

des·fi·lar intr. to parade, march.

des·fi·le m. *(procesión)* march, procession; MIL. parade.

des·fle·car §70 tr. *(una tela)* to fringe (cloth); CUBA, P. RICO to whip.

des·flo·ra·ción f. *or* **des·flo·ra·mien·to** m. defloration, deflowering.

des·flo·rar tr. *(quitar la flor)* to strip the flowers from; *(ajar)* to tarnish, spoil; FIG. *(tratar superficialmente)* to treat superficially, touch lightly on (a subject); *(desvirgar)* to deflower (a woman).

des·flo·re·cer §17 intr. & reflex. to wither, lose its flowers (said of a plant).

des·flo·re·ci·mien·to m. loss of flowers, withering.

des·fo·gar §47 tr. *(dar salida al fuego)* to make an opening *or* vent in (to allow fire to escape); *(apagar)* to slake (lime); FIG. *(soltar)* to vent, give vent to *<desfogó su cólera en el empleado* he vented his anger on the employee>

—intr. MARIT. to break, burst (storm) —reflex. to vent one's anger, let off steam.

des·fo·gue m. *(agujero)* vent; FIG. *(desahogo)* letting off steam, venting (anger, passion); MEX. *(desagüe)* outlet (of a pipe).

des·fo·llo·nar tr. to prune, strip off (leaves and shoots).

des·fon·da·mien·to m. *(acción de desfondarse)* breaking the bottom; SPORT. defeat, beating.

des·fon·dar tr. *(quitar el fondo)* to knock the bottom out of, break the bottom of *<d. un tonel* to knock the bottom out of a barrel>; AGR. to plough deeply; MARIT. to damage the bottom of a ship, bilge —reflex. *(perder el fondo)* to have the bottom fall out *<la silla se ha desfondado* the bottom has fallen out of the chair>; FIG. *(agotarse)* to wear oneself out, exhaust oneself.

des·fon·de m. *(rompimiento)* breaking of the bottom; MARIT. bilging; FIG. *(cansancio)* exhaustion.

des·for·mar tr. to deform, disfigure.

des·for·ta·le·cer §17 tr. to demolish, dismantle (fortifications).

des·fre·nar tr. to unbridle.

des·frun·cir §35 tr. to unfold, unfurl.

des·gai·re m. *(desaliño)* slovenliness, sloppiness; *(descuido afectado)* affected carelessness, nonchalance; *(gesto de desprecio)* scornful gesture, disdain ♦ **al d.** nonchalantly, carelessly • **vestido al d.** sloppily dressed.

des·ga·jar tr. to rip *or* tear off —reflex. to come *or* break off.

des·ga·je m. *(despedazamiento)* ripping *or* tearing apart; *(arrancamiento)* breaking *or* tearing off.

des·ga·lo·nar tr. to strip, remove (military stripes).

des·ga·na f. *(falta de apetito)* lack of appetite; *(renuencia)* reluctance, unwillingness ♦ **hacer algo a d.** to do something reluctantly.

des·ga·na·do, –da I. past part. see **desganar** II. adj. *(sin apetito)* without appetite, not hungry; *(sin entusiasmo)* indifferent, unenthusiastic.

des·ga·nar tr. to take away (a person's) desire *or* interest —reflex. *(perder el apetito)* to lose one's appetite; FIG. *(cansarse)* to get bored, lose interest.

des·gan·char tr. *(quitar los ganchos)* to lop off branches from; C. AMER. to unhook, unfasten.

des·ga·no m. var. of **desgana**.

des·ga·ñi·tar·se reflex. to scream *or* yell at the top of one's lungs.

des·gar·ba·do, –da adj. awkward, ungainly.

des·gar·bo m. ungainliness, awkwardness.

des·gar·gan·tar·se reflex. COLL. to yell at the top of one's lungs, scream one's head off.

des·ga·ri·tar intr. to lose the way —reflex. *(descarriarse)* to go astray, get lost; FIG. *(abandonar un proyecto)* to give up, abandon (an idea, plan).

des·ga·rra·do, –da I. past part. see **desgarrar** II. adj. *(roto)* torn, ripped; COLL. *(desvergonzado)* impudent, shameless.

des·ga·rra·dor, –do·ra adj. *(que desgarra)* heartbreaking, heartrending; *(que da miedo)* bloodcurdling.

des·ga·rra·mien·to m. *(rasgadura)* rip, tear; *(acción de romper)* ripping, tearing.

des·ga·rrar tr. *(rasgar)* to rip, tear; FIG. *(afligir)* to break (a person's heart); *(expectorar)* to spit, expectorate —reflex. *(romperse)* to rip, tear; *(apartarse)* to break away, go off by oneself.

des·ga·rro m. *(rompimiento)* rip, tear; FIG. *(baladronada)* boast, brag; FIG. *(arrojo)* boldness, impudence; AMER., MED. sputum.

des·gas·tar tr. *(gastar poco a poco)* to wear away, wear down; FIG. *(debilitar)* to weaken —reflex. FIG. *(perder fuerza)* to become weak *or* feeble; *(agotarse)* to wear oneself out.

des·gas·te m. *(erosión)* erosion, wearing away; *(daño)* damage, wear; FIG. *(debilitación)* weakening, debilitation ♦ **guerra de d.** MIL. war of attrition.

des·gaz·na·tar·se reflex. to yell at the top of one's lungs, scream one's head off.

des·glo·sar tr. *(quitar la glosa)* to remove footnotes *or* marginal comments from (manuscript); *(separar)* to detach, tear out (a page from bound copy); CINEM. to cut, edit (film).

des·glo·se m. *(eliminación de glosas)* removal of footnotes (from a manuscript); *(separación de hojas)* removal of pages (from a bound book); *(detalle)* breakdown <d. de los gastos breakdown of expenses>; CINEM. cutting, editing.

des·go·ber·nar §49 tr. *(un país)* to misgovern, misrule (a country); *(huesos)* to dislocate (bones); *(llevar mal)* to mismanage, handle badly; MARIT. to steer badly —reflex. to lose control, go crazy.

des·go·bier·no m. *(en un país)* misrule, misgovernment (of a country); *(desorden)* disorder, confusion; *(incompetencia)* mismanagement, bad handling.

des·go·lle·tar tr. *(una vasija)* to break the neck off (a bottle or vase); *(aflojar la ropa)* to loosen *or* remove clothing covering the neck.

des·gon·zar *or* **des·goz·nar** tr. to unhinge, remove the hinges from —reflex. *(descoyuntarse)* to be dislocated, disjointed; FIG. *(desgobernarse)* to lose control, become unhinged.

des·gra·cia f. *(adversidad)* misfortune, adversity; *(accidente)* mishap, setback; *(pérdida de favor)* disgrace, disfavor; *(desagrado)* displeasure *(falta de gracia)* gracelessness, clumsiness ♦ **caer en d.** to fall into disgrace • **por d.** unfortunately • **tener la d. de** to be unfortunate enough to.

des·gra·cia·da·men·te adv. unfortunately.

des·gra·cia·do, –da I. past part. see **desgraciar** II. adj. *(desdichado)* unfortunate, unlucky; *(infeliz)* unhappy; *(sin gracia)* graceless, clumsy; *(desagradable)* unpleasant, disagreeable; *(sinvergüenza)* wretched, despicable III. m.f. *(desdichado)* unfortunate person; *(infeliz)* unhappy person; *(sinvergüenza)* wretch, despicable person.

des·gra·ciar tr. to displease, annoy; *(estropear)* to ruin, spoil; COLL. *(seducir)* to seduce —reflex. *(perder favor)* to lose favor *or* fall out; *(estropearse)* to be ruined *or* spoiled; *(malograrse)* to fail, fall through; S. AMER. to wound *or* kill someone.

des·gra·na·dor, –do·ra I. adj. *(trigo)* threshing; *(guisantes)* shelling II. m.f. *(persona)* thresher, sheller —f. *(máquina)* threshing machine.

des·gra·nar tr. AGR. to shell; *(trigo)* to thresh, shell —reflex. *(maíz)* to lose its corn; *(uvas)* to lose its grapes; *(las cuentas)* to become unstrung (beads); ARTIL. to wear away the venthole of a cannon; ARG., CHILE to disperse, break up.

des·gra·ne m. shelling, threshing; *(las cuentas)* unstringing (beads).

des·gra·sar tr. to remove grease from.

des·gra·se m. removing grease, degreasing.

des·gra·var tr. *(rebajar)* to reduce taxes *or* duties; *(eximir)* to exempt (an item) from taxes *or* duties; *(aligerar)* to lighten, reduce the weight of.

des·gre·ña·do, –da I. past part. see **desgreñar** II. adj. disheveled, unkempt.

des·gre·ñar tr. to dishevel, tousle (the hair) —reflex. *(despeinarse)* to become disheveled *or* tousled; *(reñir)* to have a heated argument.

des·gua·ce m. *(rompimiento)* breaking up (a car or ship); *(desbaste)* rough dressing, roughhewing (lumber).

des·guar·ne·cer §17 tr. *(quitar los adornos)* to remove the trimmings, strip down; *(desarmar)* to dismantle; *(un caballo)* to unharness, remove the harness; *(quitar la fuerza de una plaza fuerte)* to remove the garrison.

des·gua·zar §04 tr. *(desbastar)* to roughhew, rough-dress (lumber); *(deshacer)* to break up (a car or ship).

des·ha·bi·ta·do, –da I. past part. see **deshabitar** II. adj. uninhabited, unoccupied.

des·ha·bi·tar tr. to vacate, leave; *(despoblar)* to depopulate, leave without inhabitants.

des·ha·bi·tuar §67 tr. to break of a habit, disaccustom —reflex. to lose *or* get out of the habit.

des·ha·ce·dor, –do·ra I. adj. undoing II. m.f. undoer ♦ **d. de agravios** *or* **de entuertos** righter of wrongs.

des·ha·cer §40 tr. to undo <ella deshizo el nudo she undid the knot>; *(destruir)* to destroy, ruin; *(desgastar)* to wear out; *(dividir)* to cut up, cut into pieces; *(desarmar)* to take apart <d. un reloj to take apart a watch>; *(disolver)* to

melt, dissolve; MIL. to vanquish, rout; FIG. *(desconcertar)* to break <d. un contrato to break a contract> ♦ **d. agravios** to right wrongs —reflex. *(descomponerse)* to fall apart, break; *(disolverse)* to melt, dissolve; *(desaparecer)* to vanish, disappear; FIG. *(inquietarse)* to go to pieces, get worked up; *(desvivirse)* to go out of one's way <se deshizo por conseguir lo que quería he went out of his way to get what he wanted>; *(extenuarse)* to weaken, become weak ♦ **deshacerse de** to get rid of • **deshacerse en** to dissolve into <el chico se deshizo en lágrimas the boy dissolved into tears>.

des·he·cha f. *(disimulo)* pretense, evasion; *(despedida)* polite farewell; *(salida)* speedy departure, swift exit; *(cancioncita)* short song at the end of a poem ♦ **hacer uno la d.** to feign, pretend.

des·he·cho, –cha I. past part. see **deshacer** II. adj. undone; *(cansado)* tired, worn out; METEOROL. strong, violent (said of storms, winds) III. m. S. AMER. short cut.

des·he·lar §49 tr. & reflex. to melt, thaw.

des·he·re·da·do, –da I. past part. see **desheredar** II. adj. *(excluido de la herencia)* disinherited; *(pobre)* poor, underprivileged III. m.f. *(persona excluida de la herencia)* disinherited person; *(pobre)* poor *or* underprivileged person.

des·he·re·dar tr. to disinherit.

des·her·ma·nar tr. to make unlike, make different —reflex. to forsake one's brother.

des·he·rrar §49 tr. *(quitar los hierros)* to unshackle, unchain (a prisoner); *(quitar las herraduras)* to remove the shoes from (a horse) —reflex. *(librarse)* to free oneself from shackles *or* chains; *(perder las herraduras)* to lose a shoe (said of a horse).

des·hi·cie·ra, deshice see **deshacer**.

des·hi·dra·ta·ción f. dehydration.

des·hi·dra·tar tr. to dehydrate —reflex. to become dehydrated.

des·hi·dro·ge·nar tr. to dehydrogenate, dehydrogenize.

des·hie·le see **deshelar**.

des·hie·lo m. *(del tiempo)* thaw; *(de un río)* thawing; *(de una nevera)* defrosting.

des·hie·rre, deshierro see **desherrar**.

des·hi·jar tr. *(apartar las crías)* to separate young animals from the mother); CUBA, HOND., MEX. to remove suckers from (plants).

des·hi·la·char tr. to ravel, remove threads from (cloth) —reflex. to fray, become frayed.

des·hi·la·do, –da I. adj. in single file II. m. openwork embroidery ♦ **a la d.** *(en fila india)* in single file; *(con disimulo)* secretly, sneakily.

des·hi·lar tr. *(deshacer)* to undo, unravel; FIG. *(reducir a hilos)* to cut to ribbons *or* pieces; *(abejas)* to lead *or* distract bees to a new hive —intr. to get *or* grow thin —reflex. to become frayed.

des·hil·va·na·do, –da I. past part. see **deshilvanar** II. adj. FIG. disjointed, disconnected.

des·hil·va·nar tr. SEW. to remove tacking or basting from.

des·hin·car §70 tr. to pull out, draw out.

des·hin·char tr. *(quitar la hinchazón)* to reduce the swelling of; *(un balón)* to deflate; *(la cólera)* to give vent to —reflex. *(la hinchazón)* to go down (swelling); FIG., COLL. *(perder la presunción)* be taken down a peg or two.

des·hi·po·te·ca f. paying off the mortgage.

des·hi·po·te·car §70 tr. to pay off the mortgage on.

des·hi·zo see **deshacer**.

des·ho·ja·du·ra f. *or* **des·ho·ja·mien·to** m. stripping of leaves, defoliation.

des·ho·jar tr. to defoliate, strip the leaves from —reflex. to lose leaves.

des·ho·je m. falling of leaves.

des·ho·lle·jar tr. to peel, pare (fruit or vegetable).

des·ho·lli·na·dor, –do·ra I. adj. chimney-sweeping; FIG. *(escudriñador)* nosy, inquisitive II. m.f. *(persona que deshollina)* chimney sweep; FIG. *(escudriñador)* busybody, snoop —m. *(aparato)* chimney-sweeping machine; *(escoba)* long-handled brush.

des·ho·lli·nar tr. *(quitar el hollín)* to sweep chimneys, clean off soot; FIG. *(escudriñar)* to scrutinize, examine closely.

des·ho·nes·ti·dad f. *(calidad de deshonesto)* dishonesty; *(indecencia)* indecency, impropriety.

des·ho·nes·to, –ta adj. *(no honesto)* dishonest; *(indecente)* indecent, improper.

des·ho·nor m. *(pérdida del honor)* dishonor, disgrace; *(afrenta)* insult, affront.

des·hon·ra f. *(pérdida de la honra)* dishonor, disgrace; *(cosa deshonrosa)* dishonorable *or* disgraceful act.

des·hon·ra·bue·nos m.f. [pl. **-nos**] COLL. *(calumniador)* slanderer; *(inútil)* good-for-nothing, black sheep.

des·hon·ra·dor, –do·ra I. adj. dishonorable, disgraceful II. m.f. dishonorer, disgracer.

des·hon·rar tr. *(quitar la honra)* to dishonor, disgrace; *(afrentar)* to insult, affront; *(a una mujer)* to disgrace, seduce.

des·hon·ro·so, –sa adj. dishonorable, disgraceful.

des·ho·ra f. inconvenient time ♦ **a d.** *or* **a deshoras** at an inconvenient moment, inopportunely.

des·hor·nar tr. to take out of the oven.

des·hue·sar tr. *(carne)* to debone, remove the bones from (meat); *(fruta)* to remove the pits from (fruit).

des·hue·se, deshueso see **desosar.**

des·hu·ma·ni·za·ción f. dehumanization.

des·hu·ma·ni·zar §04 tr. to dehumanize.

des·hu·me·de·cer §17 tr. to dehumidify, dry out —reflex. to dry out.

de·si·dia f. *(negligencia)* negligence, carelessness; *(pereza)* laziness, indolence.

de·si·dio·so, –sa I. adj. lazy, indolent II. m.f. lazy person, idler.

de·sier·to, –ta I. adj. *(despoblado)* deserted, uninhabited; *(desolado)* desolate, bleak II. m. desert, wasteland ♦ **predicar en el d.** FIG. to cry in the wilderness.

de·sig·na·ción f. *(nombramiento)* designation, appointment; *(nombre)* designation, name.

de·sig·nar tr. *(tener propósito)* to design, plan; *(nombrar)* to designate, appoint <**d. a una persona para un puesto** to appoint a person to a post>; *(señalar)* to point out; *(fijar)* to decide on, fix <**d. una hora** to decide on a time>.

de·sig·nio m. design, plan.

de·si·gual adj. *(no igual)* unequal; *(quebrado)* uneven <*terreno d.* uneven terrain>; *(diferente)* different; *(injusto)* unfair, inequitable <*tratamiento d.* inequitable treatment>; *(arduo)* arduous, difficult; *(inconstante)* changeable, inconstant <*tiempo d.* changeable weather>.

de·si·gua·lar tr. *(hacer desigual)* to make unequal (two things); *(desemejar)* to make different; *(desemparejar)* to make unequal *or* uneven <**d. una lucha** to make a fight unequal>; *(hacer fragoso)* to make uneven *or* rough (ground) —reflex. *(aventajar)* to excel; *(adelantarse)* to get ahead, advance.

de·si·gual·dad f. *(desemejanza)* inequality, disparity; *(aspereza)* roughness, ruggedness; *(diferencia)* difference, inequality; *(inconstancia)* inconstancy, changeableness.

de·si·lu·sion f. disillusionment, disappointment.

de·si·lu·sio·nar tr. to disillusion, disappoint —reflex. to become disillusioned *or* disappointed.

de·si·man·ta·ción f. demagnetization.

de·si·man·tar tr. to demagnetize.

de·sim·pre·sio·nar tr. to enlighten, open the eyes of —reflex. to become enlightened, have one's eyes opened.

de·sin·cor·po·rar tr. to dissolve, break up.

de·sin·fec·ción f. disinfection.

de·sin·fec·tan·te MED. adj. & m. disinfectant.

de·sin·fec·tar tr. to disinfect.

de·sin·fla·mar tr. MED. to reduce inflammation *or* swelling in.

de·sin·flar tr. *(un neumático)* to deflate, let air out of —reflex. *(un neumático)* to deflate, collapse; COLL. *(rajarse)* to lose one's nerve.

de·sin·te·gra·ción f. disintegration, decay ♦ **d. atómica** atomic fission • **d. nuclear** nuclear fission.

de·sin·te·grar tr. *(disociar)* to disintegrate, break up; PHYS. to split <**d. un átomo** to split an atom>.

de·sin·te·rés m. disinterestedness, unselfishness.

de·sin·te·re·sa·do, –da I. past part. see **desinteresarse** II. adj. *(imparcial)* disinterested, impartial; *(generoso)* altruistic, unselfish.

de·sin·te·re·sar·se reflex. to lose interest, take no interest in.

de·sin·to·xi·ca·ción f. MED. detoxification.

de·sin·to·xi·car §70 intr. to detoxify, detoxicate.

de·sir·va, desirvo see **deservir.**

de·sir·vie·ra, desirvió see **deservir.**

de·sis·ti·mien·to m. *(abandono)* desistance, giving up; LAW *(de un derecho)* waiving (a right).

de·sis·tir intr. *(de una empresa)* to desist, give up; LAW *(de un derecho)* to waive (a right) ♦ **d. de** to desist from, stop.

des·ja·rre·tar tr. *(un animal)* to hamstring, hock (an animal); FIG., COLL. *(debilitar)* to weaken, debilitate.

des·jui·cia·do, –da adj. injudicious, lacking sense.

des·jun·tar tr. & reflex. to separate, divide.

des·la·bo·nar tr. *(soltar)* to unlink, disconnect the links of <**d. una cadena** to unlink a chain>; FIG. *(desunir)* to disjoin, disconnect; *(desconcertar)* to upset; *(deshacer)* to ruin, destroy <**d. un proyecto** to ruin a project> —reflex. *(desunirse)* to come apart, become disconnected; *(deshacerse)* to fail, fall apart (project); *(apartarse)* to break away, withdraw (from someone's company).

des·la·cé, deslace see **deslazar.**

des·la·var tr. *(lavar)* to rinse, wash superficially; *(desteñir)* to wash out, fade (fabric); *(quitar fuerza)* to take away force *or* vigor; MEX. to wear away the riverbank.

des·la·va·zar §04 tr. *(aclarar)* to rinse through; *(desteñir)* to fade, wash out; *(volver flojo)* to make limp.

des·la·zar §04 tr. to unlace, untie.

des·le·al adj. disloyal, traitorous II. m.f. traitor.

des·le·al·men·te adv. disloyally.

des·le·al·tad f. disloyalty, treachery.

des·le·ír §58 tr. *(disolver)* to dissolve, liquefy; FIG. *(un discurso)* to dilute, weaken (a speech) —reflex. to dissolve.

des·len·gua·do, –da I. past. part. see **deslenguar** II. adj. FIG. *(grosero)* foul-mouthed, coarse; *(descarado)* rude, insolent.

des·len·guar §10 tr. to cut out *or* remove the tongue from —reflex. FIG., COLL. *(descararse)* to be insolent *or* rude; *(hablar groseramente)* to use foul language, swear.

des·lí·a, deslío see **desleir.**

des·liar §30 tr. *(desatar)* to untie, undo; *(desenvolver)* to unwrap; *(separar las lías)* to separate lees from (grape must).

des·li·cé, deslice see **deslizar.**

des·lie·ra, deslió see **desleir.**

des·li·ga·du·ra f. *(desatadura)* untying, unfastening; FIG. *(desenredo)* disentanglement, clearing up; *(dispensa)* freeing (from an obligation).

des·li·gar §47 tr. *(desatar)* to untie, unfasten; FIG. *(desenredar)* to untangle, unravel; *(dispensar)* to dispense, administer; *(absolver)* to absolve, exonerate; MUS. to pick —reflex. *(desatarse)* to become untied *or* unfastened; *(librarse)* to extricate oneself, break away.

des·lin·dar tr. to delimit, mark the boundaries of; FIG. *(aclarar)* to clarify, elucidate.

des·lin·de m. *(señalamiento de los límites)* delimitation, setting boundaries; FIG. *(aclaración)* clarification, elucidation.

des·liz m. [pl. **-li·ces**] *(acción de deslizar)* slipping, slip; FIG. *(error)* slip, mistake ♦ **d. de lengua** slip of the tongue.

des·li·za·ble adj. *(que se desliza)* slippery; *(corredizo)* sliding.

des·li·za·di·zo, –za adj. slippery.

des·li·za·mien·to m. *(desliz)* slip, slipping; *(resbalamiento)* slide, sliding ♦ **d. de tierra** landslide.

des·li·zan·te adj. slippery.

des·li·zar §04 tr. *(escurrir)* to slip, slide; *(decir por descuido)* to let slip —intr. to slide, slip —reflex. *(resbalar)* to slide; *(caerse)* to slip; *(sobre el agua)* to glide; *(escaparse)* to slip away, escape; FIG., COLL. *(caerse)* to slip <*deslizarse en un vicio* to slip into a bad habit>; FIG. *(meter la pata)* to slip up, make a mistake.

des·lo·mar tr. *(romper los lomos)* to break the back of; *(cansar)* to exhaust, wear out —reflex. COLL. to exhaust oneself, wear oneself out.

des·lu·ci·do, –da I. past. part. see **deslucir** II. adj. *(sin brillo)* tarnished, dull; *(sin vida)* lackluster, mediocre <*la* *compañía hizo una actuación d.* the company gave a lackluster performance>.

des·lu·ci·mien·to m. *(falta de vitalidad)* dullness, lifelessness; *(falta de gracia)* inelegance, gracelessness; *(falta de brillantez)* unimpressiveness, insignificance.

des·lu·cir §44 tr. *(estropear)* to spoil, ruin; *(quitar el brillo a)* to dull, tarnish; FIG. *(desacreditar)* to discredit —reflex. *(perder el brillo)* to become dull or tarnished; *(desacreditarse)* to become discredited.

des·lum·bra·dor, –do·ra adj. *(brillante)* dazzling, brilliant; FIG. *(asombrante)* overwhelming, bewildering.

des·lum·bra·mien·to m. *(ceguera)* dazzling, dazzle; *(confusión)* confusion, bewilderment.

des·lum·bran·te adj. var. of deslumbrador, –dora.

des·lum·brar tr. *(cegar)* to dazzle, blind; FIG. *(confundir)* to overwhelm, bewilder.

des·lus·trar tr. *(quitar el lustre)* to take the shine off, tarnish; *(quitar el brillo)* to remove the finish from (cloth); *(quitar la transparencia)* to frost (glass); FIG. *(deslucir)* to dull, tarnish; *(desacreditar)* to tarnish the reputation of, disgrace.

des·lus·tre m. *(falta de brillo)* dullness, lack of shine; *(el quitar el lustre)* removal of finish (from cloth); *(esmerilado)* frosting (glass); *(empañadura)* tarnishing, dulling (metal); FIG. *(deshonra)* dishonor, disgrace (reputation).

des·lus·tro·so, –sa adj. FIG. *(indecoroso)* unbecoming, unsuitable; *(feo)* disgraceful.

des·luz·ca, desluzco see deslucir.

des·ma·de·jar tr. FIG. to weaken, enervate.

des·ma·dra·do, –da I. past part. see desmadrar II. adj. abandoned by or separated from its mother (said of an animal).

des·ma·drar tr. to take (an animal) away from its mother.

des·ma·le·zar §04 tr. AMER. to weed, clear of underbrush.

des·mán m. *(ultraje)* outrage, abuse; *(desgracia)* misfortune, mishap; ZOOL. muskrat.

des·man·char tr. AMER. to clean, remove stains from —reflex. AMER. *(apartarse)* to go one's own way.

des·man·da·do, –da I. past part. see desmandar II. adj. disobedient, intractable.

des·man·dar I. tr. to countermand, rescind II. reflex. *(propasarse)* to go too far, get out of hand; *(demanarse)* to stray from the herd or flock.

des·ma·no adv. ♦ a d. out of reach.

des·ma·no·ta·do, –da adj. FIG., COLL. I. adj. clumsy, awkward II. m.f. clumsy person, fumbler.

des·man·te·car §70 tr. *(quitar la manteca)* to skim (milk); *(quitar la grasa)* to remove the fat or grease from ♦ leche desmantecada skim milk.

des·man·te·la·do, –da I. past part. see desmantelar II. adj. *(desarmado)* dismantled, disassembled; *(mal cuidado)* dilapidated, run-down.

des·man·te·la·mien·to m. *(desarmadura)* dismantling, disassembling; *(estado ruinoso)* dilapidation.

des·man·te·lar tr. *(derribar)* to knock down, dismantle; FIG. *(una casa)* to vacate, abandon (a house); MARIT. to dismast, unmast.

des·man·te·qué, desmanteque see desmantecar.

des·ma·ña f. or **des·ma·ño** m. clumsiness, awkwardness.

des·ma·ña·do, –da I. adj. clumsy, awkward II. m.f. clumsy person, bungler.

des·ma·ra·ñar tr. to disentangle, unravel.

des·ma·rri·do, –da adj. *(alicaído)* dejected, crestfallen; *(desfallecido)* weak, exhausted.

des·ma·tar or **des·ma·to·nar** tr. to clear of underbrush, weed.

des·ma·ya·do, –da I. past part. see desmayar II. adj. *(sin sentido)* unconscious; *(un color)* dull, wan; *(desanimado)* discouraged, disheartened; *(hambriento)* faint (from hunger); *(agotado)* exhausted, worn out.

des·ma·yar tr. to make faint, cause to faint —intr. FIG. to lose heart, be discouraged —reflex. to faint, swoon.

des·ma·yo m. *(síncope)* faint, swoon; *(estado)* unconsciousness; *(desánimo)* depression, downheartedness; BOT. weeping willow.

des·me·di·do, –da I. past part. see desmedirse II. adj. *(excesivo)* excessive, immoderate; *(sin límite)* boundless, limitless.

des·me·dir·se §48 reflex. to go too far, forget oneself.

des·me·drar tr. to impair, damage —intr. to decline, deteriorate.

des·me·dro m. decline, deterioration.

des·me·jo·rar tr. to impair, damage —intr. & reflex. to deteriorate, get worse.

des·mem·bra·ción f. or **des·mem·bra·mien·to** m. *(despedazamiento)* dismemberment; FIG. *(división)* division, breaking up.

des·mem·brar tr. to dismember, cut into pieces.

des·me·mo·ria·do, –da I. past part. see desmemoriarse II. adj. forgetful, absent-minded III. m.f. forgetful or absent-minded person.

des·me·mo·riar·se reflex. to become forgetful, lose one's memory.

des·men·ti·da f. *(negación)* denial; *(contradicción)* contradiction.

des·men·tir §65 tr. *(negar)* to deny; *(contradecir)* to contradict; *(refutar)* to refute, disprove; *(proceder contrariamente)* to act contrary, go against <*d. uno su carácter* to go against one's own nature> —intr. to deviate, go out of line —reflex. *(contradecirse)* to contradict oneself; *(faltar a su palabra)* to go back on one's word.

des·me·nu·za·dor, –do·ra I. adj. *(que examina)* investigating, analyzing; *(que desmigaja)* crumbling, shredding II. m.f. *(investigador)* investigator; *(despedazador)* shredder.

des·me·nu·zar §04 tr. *(deshacer)* to crumble, break into pieces; FIG. *(examinar)* to examine closely, scrutinize.

des·me·o·llar tr. to remove marrow from.

des·me·re·ce·dor, –do·ra adj. unworthy, undeserving.

des·me·re·cer §17 tr. to be unworthy or undeserving of —intr. *(decaer)* to deteriorate; *(ser inferior)* to be inferior, compare unfavorably.

des·me·re·ci·mien·to m. demerit, unworthiness.

des·me·su·ra f. excess, lack of moderation.

des·me·su·ra·da·men·te adv. *(excesivamente)* excessively, extremely; *(descomunalmente)* uncommonly, extremely.

des·me·su·ra·do, –da I. past part. see desmesurar II. adj. *(desmedido)* excessive, inordinate; *(sin límite)* boundless, limitless; *(insolente)* insolent, impudent.

des·me·su·rar tr. *(desordenar)* to put in disorder; *(descomponer)* to disturb, upset —reflex. to go too far, forget oneself.

des·mi·da, desmido see desmedirse.

des·mi·die·ra, desmidió see desmedirse.

des·mien·ta, desmiento see desmentir.

des·mi·gar §47 tr. to crumble (bread).

des·mi·li·ta·ri·zar §04 tr. to demilitarize.

des·mi·ne·ra·li·za·ción f. MED. demineralization.

des·min·tie·ra, desmintió see desmentir.

des·mo·char tr. *(un árbol)* to cut the top off, lop (a tree); *(una res)* to blunt the horns of (an animal); FIG. *(una obra)* to cut (a text).

des·mol·dar tr. to unmold.

des·mo·ne·ti·za·ción f. ECON. demonetization.

des·mon·ta·ble I. adj. *(que se puede desmontar)* capable of being disassembled; *(que se quita)* detachable II. m. tire iron.

des·mon·ta·je m. *(desarme)* dismantling, disassembly; *(demolición)* demolition; *(de pistola)* uncocking (a firearm).

des·mon·tar tr. *(desarmar)* to dismantle, disassemble; *(bajar)* to dismount; *(árboles)* to fell, cut down (trees); *(terreno)* to level (ground); *(arma de fuego)* to uncock —intr. & reflex. to dismount.

des·mon·te m. *(tala de árboles)* clearing (of trees); *(nivelación)* leveling; *(terreno sin árboles)* clearing; *(árboles talados)* felled trees; MIN. slag, refuse.

des·mo·ra·li·za·ción f. *(desaliento)* demoralization; *(corrupción)* corruption.

des·mo·ra·li·za·dor, –do·ra I. adj. demoralizing II. m.f. demoralizer.

des·mo·ra·li·zar §04 tr. *(desalentar)* to demoralize; *(corromper)* to corrupt —reflex. *(desalentarse)* to become demoralized; *(corromperse)* to become corrupt or depraved.

des·mo·ro·na·mien·to m. decay, crumbling.

des·mo·ro·nar tr. to wear away, erode —reflex. to crumble, fall to pieces.

des·mo·ta·de·ra f. TECH., TEX. burling iron; AMER. cotton gin.

des·mo·ta·dor, –do·ra m.f. burler (person who removes threads from cloth) —f. cotton gin.

des·mo·tar tr. (lana) to burl (cloth or wool); AMER. to gin (cotton).

des·mo·te m. (de lana) burling (of cloth or wool); AMER. ginning (of cotton).

des·mo·vi·li·za·ción f. demobilization.

des·mo·vi·li·zar §04 tr. MIL. to demobilize; FIG. (quitar energía) to dispel energy or enthusiasm.

des·na·cio·na·li·za·ción f. denationalization.

des·na·cio·na·li·zar §04 tr. to denationalize.

des·na·ta·do·ra f. cream separator, skimmer.

des·na·tar tr. (quitar la nata) to skim the cream off (milk); FIG. (sacar lo mejor) to take the cream or the best of ♦ **leche sin d.** whole milk.

des·na·tu·ra·li·cé, desnaturalice see desnaturalizar.

des·na·tu·ra·li·za·ción f. (de un ciudadano) denaturalization; (del carácter) perversion, corruption; (de un texto) misrepresentation, distortion.

des·na·tu·ra·li·za·do, –da I. past part. see desnaturalizar II. adj. (sin nacionalidad) denaturalized; (corrompido) perverted, corrupted; (malo) cruel, unnatural; CHEM. denatured, denaturized <alcohol d. denatured alcohol>.

des·na·tu·ra·li·zar §04 tr. (un ciudadano) to denaturalize; (corromper) to pervert, corrupt; CHEM. to denature, denaturize —reflex. to become denaturalized, give up one's nationality.

des·ni·tri·fi·car §70 tr. to denitrify.

des·ni·vel m. (falta de nivel) unevenness; (depresión) depression, drop (in level); FIG. (diferencia) difference, disparity.

des·ni·ve·lar tr. (sacar de nivel) to make uneven; FIG. (desequilibrar) to throw out of balance, unbalance; (una balanza) to tip, tilt.

des·nu·car §70 tr. to break the neck of —reflex. to break one's neck.

des·nu·dar tr. (desvestir) to strip, undress; FIG. (descubrir) to lay bare, uncover; ARM. to bare, draw; COLL. (en el juego) to fleece, clean out; MARIT. to unrig ♦ **d. un santo para vestir a otro** COLL. to rob Peter to pay Paul —reflex. to get undressed, strip ♦ **desnudarse de** to free or rid oneself of.

des·nu·dez f. nudity, nakedness.

des·nu·dis·mo m. nudism.

des·nu·dis·ta adj. & m.f. nudist.

des·nu·do, –da I. adj. (sin vestido) undressed; (en cueros) naked, nude; FIG. (despojado) stripped, bare; (pobre) dispossessed, destitute; (patente) clear, naked <la verdad d. the naked truth>; ARM. drawn, bared ♦ **d. de** devoid of, lacking II. m. PAINT., SCULP. nude (figure).

des·nu·qué, desnuque see desnucar.

des·nu·tri·ción f. MED. malnutrition, undernourishment.

de·so·be·de·cer §17 tr. to disobey.

de·so·be·dien·cia f. disobedience.

de·so·be·dien·te I. adj. disobedient II. m.f. disobedient person.

de·so·bli·gar §47 tr. (librar) to free from an obligation; FIG. (ofender) to offend, alienate.

de·so·cu·pa·ción f. (desempleo) unemployment; (ociosidad) idleness.

de·so·cu·pa·do, –da I. past part. see desocupar II. adj. (sin empleo) unemployed, out of work; (sitio) vacant, unoccupied; III. m.f. (ocioso) idler; (persona sin empleo) unemployed person.

de·so·cu·par tr. (una casa) to vacate, move out of (a house); (una vasija) to empty (a container) —reflex. (de un trabajo) to leave, quit (a job); ARG., CHILE, VEN. to give birth.

de·so·do·ran·te I. adj. deodorizing II. m. deodorant.

de·so·do·ri·zar §04 tr. to deodorize.

de·so·ír §45 tr. to ignore, pay no attention to.

de·so·jar tr. to break the eye of (a needle) —reflex. to strain one's eyes.

de·so·la·ción f. (ruina) desolation, ruin; (soledad) loneliness, solitariness; FIG. (aflicción) affliction, distress.

de·so·la·dor, –do·ra adj. (asolador) destructive, devastating; FIG. (aflictivo) desolating, distressing.

de·so·lar §19 tr. (asolar) to desolate, ravage —reflex. FIG. to be grieved, be distressed.

de·so·lla·do, –da I. adj. COLL. impudent, fresh II. m.f. impudent or cheeky person.

de·so·lla·dor, –do·ra I. adj. (que desuella) skinning; FIG., COLL. (caro) exorbitant, high-priced II. m.f. (en el matadero) skinner (in a slaughterhouse); FIG., COLL. (comerciante) cut-throat, fleecer —m. ORNITH. butcherbird.

de·so·lla·du·ra f. (de las reses) skinning, flaying; (arañazo) abrasion, graze; FIG. (robo) extortion, fleecing.

de·so·llar §19 tr. (despellejar) to skin, flay; FIG. (dañar) to harm, injure; (hacer pagar mucho) to skin, fleece; (criticar) to flay, criticize; COLL. (murmurar de) to slander ♦ **d. a alguien vivo** COLL. to skin someone alive.

de·sor·bi·tar tr. (exagerar) to exaggerate, carry to extremes; ARG. (enloquecer) to drive mad —reflex. (los ojos) to bulge (eyes); (un satélite) to leave its orbit (said of a satellite); FIG. (descomedirse) to go to extremes, lose one's sense of proportion ♦ **d. un asunto** to misinterpret a matter.

de·sor·den m. (confusión) disorder, disarray; COLL. (lío) muddle, mess; (conducta) disorderliness, unruliness; (tumulto) disturbance, disorder; MED. upset, disorder; (exceso) excess, license ♦ **poner en d.** to upset, disarrange.

de·sor·de·na·da·men·te adv. (sin orden) in a disorderly or unruly way; (confusamente) confusedly.

de·sor·de·na·do, –da I. past part. of desordenar II. adj. (sin arreglo) disorderly, disarranged; (falta de aseo) slovenly, untidy; (excesivo) excessive, inordinate; (conducta) unruly, wild.

de·sor·de·nar tr. (poner en desorden) to disorder, disarrange; (causar confusión) to throw into confusion; (desasear) to make untidy or messy —reflex. (ponerse en desorden) to become disarranged or disorderly; (salir de la regla) to get out of order or out of control.

de·so·re·ja·do, –da I. past part. see desorejar II. adj. COLL. (infame) despicable, abject; AMER. (sin asas) without handles; BOL., PERU (que tiene mal oído) tone-deaf; CUBA (pródigo) lavish; (derrochador) wasteful; GUAT. silly, foolish.

de·so·re·jar tr. to cut off or crop the ears of.

de·sor·ga·ni·za·ción f. disorganization.

de·sor·ga·ni·zar §04 tr. to disorganize, disrupt.

de·so·rien·ta·ción f. disorientation.

de·so·rien·tar tr. (hacer perder la orientación) to disorient, mislead; FIG. (confundir) to confuse —reflex. (extraviarse) to lose one's way, be disoriented; (confundirse) to become confused.

de·so·sar §24 tr. (carne) to bone (meats); (fruta) to pit, remove the stone from (fruit).

de·so·vi·llar tr. (un ovillo) to unwind, unravel (a ball of wool); FIG. (aclarar algo) to unravel, solve (a mystery or problem); (dar ánimo) to encourage.

de·so·xi·rri·bo·nu·clei·co, –ca adj. ♦ **ácido d.** BIOCHEM. DNA.

de·so·ye·ra, desoyó see desoír.

des·pa·bi·la·dor m. candle snuffer.

des·pa·bi·lar tr. (recortar) to trim (a candle wick); (apagar) to snuff (a candle); FIG. (robar) to steal, pinch; (avivar) to liven up, stimulate; FIG., COLL. (malgastar) to squander, go through rapidly; (despachar) to finish quickly; (matar) to kill, snuff out —reflex. FIG. (despertarse) to wake up; (avivarse) to liven up; AMER. to leave, disappear.

des·pa·cio I. adv. (lentamente) slowly, slow; (poco a poco) little by little, gradually; AMER. in a low voice, quietly II. interj. easy does it!, take it easy!.

des·pa·cha·de·ras f.pl. (brusquedad) curtness, sharpness; (insolencia) insolence, brazenness; (habilidad) resourcefulness, business sense ♦ **tener buenas d.** to be on the ball.

des·pa·cha·dor, –do·ra I. adj. efficient, quick II. m. (el que despacha) expediter, dispatcher; AMER. excavator.

des·pa·chan·te m. ARG. clerk, employee ♦ **d. de aduana** customs officer.

des·pa·char tr. (concluir) to complete, conclude <despachó

el negocio en una semana he concluded the business deal within a week>; *(resolver)* to resolve, settle <*quiere d. el problema lo más pronto posible* he wants to resolve the problem as soon as possible>; *(enviar)* to dispatch, send; *(despedir)* to fire, dismiss; *(vender)* to sell; *(expedir)* to expedite, hurry along; FIG., COLL. *(acabar con)* to polish or knock off <*despacharon dos botellas de ron* they knocked off two bottles of rum>; *(matar)* to kill, knock off <*despachó a su rival* he knocked off his rival> —intr. *(darse prisa)* to hurry up; *(hablar)* to speak one's mind; COM. to do business <*no despachan los domingos* they do not do business on Sundays> —reflex. *(darse prisa)* to hurry up ♦ **despacharse de** to get rid of.

des·pa·cho m. *(envío)* dispatch, sending; *(oficina)* office, bureau; *(estudio)* study <*el tiene un d. en su casa* he has a study in his home>; *(tienda)* store, shop; *(venta)* sale (of goods); *(comunicación)* dispatch, message <*d. diplomático* diplomatic dispatch>; *(resolución)* efficiency; *(cédula)* commission; CHILE general store ♦ **d. telegráfico** telegram • **tener buen d.** to be efficient.

des·pa·chu·rra·mien·to m. crushing, squashing.

des·pa·chu·rrar tr. COLL. *(aplastar)* to crush, squash; *(una cuenta)* to confuse, mix up (a story); FIG. *(una persona)* to silence, squelch.

des·pal·ma·du·ra f. MARIT. careening, caulking (a ship); VET. paring a horse's hoof ♦ **despalmaduras** parings from a horse's hooves.

des·pal·mar tr. MARIT. to careen, caulk (a ship's bottom); CARP. to bevel, chamfer; VET. to pare (a horse's hooves); *(arrancar)* to pull up (grass).

des·pam·pa·nan·te adj. COLL. astounding, stunning.

des·pam·pa·nar tr. AGR. to prune, trim young shoots from (plants); FIG., COLL. *(desconcertar)* to confuse, bewilder; *(dejar atónito)* to amaze, bowl over —intr. FIG., COLL. to speak one's mind, unburden oneself —reflex. COLL. to hurt oneself falling down, take a nasty fall or spill.

des·pan·ci·jar tr. COLL. var. of **despanzurrar.**

des·pan·zu·rrar or **des·pan·chu·rrar** tr. COLL. to rip open the belly of, disembowel.

des·pa·re·jo, –ja adj. odd, not matching.

des·par·pa·jar tr. to ruin, wreck —intr. to prattle, talk one's head off.

des·par·pa·jo m. COLL. *(desenvoltura)* ease, confidence; *(descaro)* pertness, freshness; C. AMER. disorder, confusion.

des·pa·rra·ma·do, –da I. past part. see **desparramar** II. adj. *(esparcido)* spread, scattered; *(derramado)* spilt, splashed; *(espacioso)* sprawling, wide-open.

des·pa·rra·mar tr. *(esparcir)* to scatter, spread; *(diseminar)* to spread, disperse <*d. la noticia* to spread the news>; *(derramar)* to spill, splash; FIG. *(malgastar)* to squander, lavish; ARG. to thin out, dilute —reflex. *(esparcirse)* to scatter, spread; FIG. *(divertirse)* to let oneself go, let one's hair down.

des·par·tir tr. *(dividir)* to divide, separate; *(reconciliar)* to make peace (between or among), reconcile.

des·pa·ta·rra·da f. COLL. splits (step in some dances).

des·pa·ta·rrar tr. COLL. *(abrir las piernas)* to make a person open his legs wide; *(aturdir)* to astonish, flabbergast ♦ **dejar a alguien despatarrado** to flabbergast someone —reflex. *(abrirse de piernas)* to open one's legs wide; *(caerse)* to fall with legs apart; *(aturdirse)* to be astonished or flabbergasted ♦ **despatarrarse de risa** COLL. to split one's sides laughing.

des·pa·vo·ri·do, –da I. past part. see **despavorir** II. adj. terrified, afraid.

des·pa·vo·rir §38 intr. & reflex. to be terrified or afraid.

des·pe·ar·se reflex. *(cansarse)* to be footsore, hurt one's feet (by walking); VET. to become bruised (said of a horse's hooves).

des·pec·ti·va·men·te adv. disparagingly, pejoratively.

des·pec·ti·vo, –va adj. disparaging, pejorative.

des·pe·char tr. *(enojar)* to anger, make angry or spiteful; *(causar disgusto a)* to displease, disgust; *(irritar)* to vex, peeve; COLL. *(destetar)* to wean —reflex. *(enfadarse)* to become angry or spiteful.

des·pe·cho m. *(ira)* spite, wrath; *(descontento)* displeasure, disgust; *(irritación)* vexation, peevishness; *(desesperación)* despair, dejection; *(rencor)* grudge, resentment; CHILE, SP. weaning ♦ **a d. de** in spite of, in defiance of • **por d.** out of spite.

des·pe·chu·gar §47 tr. to cut or carve the breast of (a fowl) —reflex. COLL. to bare one's breast.

des·pe·da·za·mien·to m. *(acción de hacer pedazos una cosa)* breaking or tearing to pieces; FIG. *(ruina)* ruin, destruction.

des·pe·da·zar §04 tr. to break or tear to pieces —reflex. *(caerse)* to fall or break into pieces; *(arruinarse)* to be ruined, be destroyed.

des·pe·di·da f. *(adiós)* good-bye, farewell; *(despacho)* dismissal, firing; *(copla final)* final verse.

des·pe·dir §48 tr. *(soltar)* to throw (out), eject; to say good-bye to, see off or out <*le vamos a d. mañana* we'll say good-bye to him tomorrow>; *(despachar)* to dismiss, fire <*d. a un empleado* to fire an employee>; FIG. *(deshacerse de)* to get rid of, throw out; *(emitir)* to emit, give off —reflex. to say good-bye ♦ **despedirse a la francesa** to leave without saying good-bye, take French leave • **despedirse de** to say good-bye to.

des·pe·dre·gar §47 tr. to remove rocks or stones from.

des·pe·ga·ble adj. detachable.

des·pe·ga·do, –da I. past part. see **despegar** II. adj. FIG. cold, detached.

des·pe·ga·du·ra f. *(desprendimiento)* unsticking, ungluing; FIG. *(desapego)* coldness, detachment.

des·pe·ga·mien·to m. indifference, detachment.

des·pe·gar §47 tr. *(separar cosas pegadas)* to unstick, unglue; *(separar)* to detach, separate; *(quitar)* to remove, take off; *(carta)* to open; MEX. to unhitch, unharness (horses) ♦ **no d. los labios** to keep one's lips sealed, remain silent —intr. AVIA. to take off; ASTRONAUT. to blast off —reflex. *(separarse lo pegado)* to become unstuck or unglued; *(separarse)* to become detached or separated; FIG. *(desapegarse)* to lose affection, grow indifferent.

des·pe·gue m. AVIA. takeoff; ASTRONAUT. blastoff, launching.

des·pei·nar tr. to disarrange the hair of.

des·pe·ja·do, –da I. past part. see **despejar** II. adj. *(lleno de confianza)* confident, sure of oneself; *(listo)* clever, bright; METEOROL. clear, cloudless <*un día d.* a clear day>; *(sin impedimento)* clear, open; *(espacioso)* spacious, wide.

des·pe·jar tr. *(desocupar)* to clear, free from obstruction or encumbrance; *(quitar)* to get rid of, remove; FIG. *(aclarar)* to clear up, sort out <*d. una situación* to clear up a situation>; MATH. to find the value of, solve for (an unknown) —reflex. *(adquirir soltura)* to become self-confident; *(mostrar soltura)* to display self-confidence; METEOROL. to clear up; *(divertirse)* to enjoy or amuse oneself; MED. to abate, go down (fever).

des·pe·lu·zar §04 tr. *(desmelenar)* to dishevel, muss (hair); *(erizar)* to make (someone's) hair stand on end; CUBA to fleece, rob —reflex. *(despeinarse)* to muss one's hair up, get one's hair ruffled; *(aterrarse)* to be frightened.

des·pe·luz·nan·te adj. horrifying, terrifying.

des·pe·lle·ja·du·ra f. skinning, flaying.

des·pe·lle·jar tr. *(desollar)* to skin, flay; FIG. *(criticar)* to flay, criticize.

des·pe·nar tr. *(consolar)* to console, comfort; FIG., COLL. *(matar)* to finish off, kill; CHILE to deprive of hope.

des·pen·de·dor, –do·ra I. adj. wasteful, spendthrift II. m.f. wastrel, spendthrift.

des·pen·sa f. *(lugar)* larder, pantry; *(provisiones)* provisions, supplies; *(oficio)* post of steward or butler, stewardship; MARIT. steward's room; MEX., MIN. strong room (for precious metals); ARG. store house, warehouse.

des·pen·se·ro, –ra m. steward, butler —f. housekeeper.

des·pe·ña·de·ro, –ra I. adj. steep, precipitous II. m. *(precipicio)* precipice, cliff; FIG. *(peligro)* danger, risk.

des·pe·ñar tr. *(despedir)* to hurl, throw —reflex. *(precipitarse)* to hurl or throw oneself; FIG. *(entregarse)* to throw oneself into, give oneself up to <*d. en el vicio* to give oneself up to vice>.

des·pe·ño m. *(acción de despeñar)* hurling, throwing; *(caída)* plunge or fall (from a height); MED. diarrhea; FIG.

(fracaso) failure, ruin <*d. de un negocio* failure of a business>.

des·pe·pi·tar tr. to remove pits or seeds from (fruit) —reflex. *(gritar)* to shout, rant; *(proceder descomedidamente)* to act rashly, forget oneself ♦ **despepitarse por algo** to be mad for something, dying for something.

des·per·di·cia·do, –da I. past part. see **desperdiciar** II. adj. wasted, squandered.

des·per·di·cia·dor, –do·ra I. adj. wasteful, spendthrift II. m.f. *(malgastador)* spendthrift, prodigal; ECUAD., FIG. *(sinvergüenza)* scoundrel, rogue.

des·per·di·ciar tr. *(malgastar)* to waste, squander; *(no aprovecharse de)* to fail to take advantage of, miss.

des·per·di·cio m. *(acción)* waste, squandering; *(residuo)* waste, remains ♦ **no tener d.** FIG., COLL. to be wholly good or useful, contain no waste.

des·per·di·gar §47 tr. to scatter, disperse —reflex. to become scattered or dispersed.

des·pe·re·zar·se §04 reflex. to stretch one's limbs.

des·pe·re·zo m. *(estirón)* stretching, stretch; *(despertamiento)* waking up, shaking off sleep.

des·per·fec·to m. *(falta)* flaw, blemish; *(deterioro)* wear and tear, slight deterioration.

des·per·ta·dor, –do·ra I. adj. awakening, arousing II. m.f. one who wakes people up —m. *(reloj)* alarm clock; FIG. *(aviso)* warning.

des·per·ta·mien·to m. waking up, awakening.

des·per·tar §49 tr. *(desvelar)* to wake up, awaken; *(resucitar)* to revive, resuscitate; FIG. *(suscitar)* to awaken, revive <*despertó sus antiguas sospechas* it revived his old suspicions>; *(excitar)* to whet, excite <*el olor de la comida le despertó el apetito* the smell of food whetted his appetite> —intr. *(dejar de dormir)* to wake up, awaken; *(ser más listo)* to wise up —reflex. to wake up, awaken.

des·pe·sar m. displeasure, annoyance.

des·pe·zu·ñar·se reflex. *(la pezuña)* to become useless (said of an animal's hoof); AMER., FIG. *(caminar de prisa)* to walk very quickly; *(esforzarse)* to exert oneself, put a great deal of effort into; *(desvivirse)* to be very eager (to do something).

des·pia·da·da·men·te adv. pitilessly, mercilessly.

des·pia·da·do, –da adj. pitiless, merciless.

des·pi·car §70 tr. to appease, calm down —reflex. *(satisfacerse)* to get revenge, get one's own back; *(romperse el pico)* to break its beak (said of a bird); VEN., FIG. to fall into disgrace.

des·pi·da, despido see **despedir.**

des·pi·die·ra, despidió see **despedir.**

des·pi·do m. dismissal, firing.

des·pier·ta, despierto see **despertar.**

des·pier·to, –ta I. past part. see **despertar** II. adj. *(no dormido)* awake; FIG. *(despabilado)* alert, wide-awake; *(listo)* clever, sharp.

des·pig·men·ta·ción f. depigmentation.

des·pi·la·rar tr. AMER. to remove the props from (mines).

des·pil·fa·rra·dor, –do·ra I. adj. wasteful, spendthrift; II. m.f. wastrel, spendthrift.

des·pil·fa·rrar tr. to squander, waste —reflex. to squander or misspend a fortune.

des·pil·fa·rro m. *(destrozo)* spoiling, ruining; *(gasto excesivo)* waste, extravagance.

des·pin·tar tr. *(borrar lo pintado)* to take the paint off of; FIG. *(desfigurar)* to distort, misrepresent —intr. to be no worse <*esa chica no dispinta de su familia* that girl is no worse than the rest of her family> —reflex. to fade ♦ **no despintársele a uno** not to fade from one's memory.

des·pio·jar tr. *(espulgar)* to delouse; FIG., COLL. *(sacar de miseria)* to free from poverty, rescue from the gutter.

des·pi·qué, despique see **despicar.**

des·pis·ta·do, –da I. past part. see **despistar** II. adj. absent-minded, confused III. m.f. absent-minded person, scatterbrain.

des·pis·tar tr. to lead astray, throw off the track —reflex. to be disoriented, lose one's bearings.

des·pis·te m. *(confusión)* confusion, bewilderment; *(de un coche)* leaving the road (said of a car).

des·pla·cé, desplace see **desplazar.**

des·pla·cer §17 tr. to displease, annoy.

des·plan·ta·ción f. uprooting.

des·plan·tar tr. *(desarraigar)* to uproot, pull up; *(desviar)* to deviate from the vertical —reflex. to lose one's erect posture (in fencing or dancing).

des·plan·te m. *(postura irregular)* bad posture (in dance or fencing); *(dicho arrogante)* arrogant remark; *(hecho arrogante)* arrogant action; TAUR. defiant stance (facing the bull).

des·pla·za·mien·to m. MARIT., PHYS. displacement; *(traslado)* moving, shifting.

des·pla·zar §04 tr. MARIT., PHYS. to displace; *(trasladar)* to move, shift.

des·plaz·ca, desplazco see **desplacer.**

des·ple·gar §52 tr. *(desdoblar)* to unfold, open or spread out; *(bandera)* to unfurl; MIL. to deploy, fan out; FIG. *(aclarar)* to explain, unfold; *(mostrar)* to display, show —reflex. *(desdoblarse)* to unfold, spread out; MIL. to fan out.

des·plie·gue m. *(abertura)* unfolding, spreading out; *(bandera)* unfurling; MIL. deployment, fanning; FIG. *(muestra)* display, show.

des·plo·mar tr. *(inclinar)* to put or throw out of a plumb; VEN. to scold, reprimand —reflex. *(inclinarse)* to lean, get out of plumb; *(caerse)* to fall down, collapse; FIG. *(desmayarse)* to faint, collapse; ECON. to plummet, drop <*los precios se desplomaron* prices plummeted>.

des·plo·me m. *(inclinación)* leaning, getting out of plumb; *(caída)* collapse, fall; ARCHIT. overhang; FIG. *(desmayo)* fainting, collapsing ♦ **en d.** ARCHIT. overhanging.

des·plu·mar tr. *(un ave)* to pluck, remove the feathers from (a bird); COLL. *(sacar dinero)* to fleece, skin (a person).

des·po·bla·do I. past part. see **despoblar** II. m. wilderness, deserted or uninhabited place ♦ **en d.** in the wilds.

des·po·blar §19 tr. *(disminuir la población)* to depopulate; FIG. *(despojar)* to clear, strip; *(devastar)* to lay waste, ravage —reflex. to become depopulated or deserted.

des·po·ja·dor, –do·ra I. adj. *(expoliador)* plundering, despoiling; *(privativo)* depriving II. m.f. plunderer, pillager.

des·po·jar tr. *(privar)* to deprive, dispossess <*d. a uno de sus derechos*> to deprive someone of his rights>; *(quitar)* to strip <*d. un árbol de su corteza* to strip a tree of its bark>; *(robar)* to rob —reflex. *(desnudarse)* to undress, strip; FIG. *(desposeerse)* to give up, relinquish <*despojarse de su fortuna* to give up one's fortune>.

des·po·jo m. *(desposeimiento)* depriving, dispossession; *(botín)* loot, plunder; *(desnudamiento)* undressing; ZOOL. offal; ORNITH. giblets; FIG. *(víctima)* prey, victim <*la juventud es d. del tiempo* youth is the prey of time> ♦ **despojos** CONST. scrap, usable rubble; *(restos mortales)* remains, corpse; *(sobras)* leftovers; COL., MIN low-grade minerals • **despojos de hierro** scrap iron.

des·pol·var tr. to dust, remove the dust from.

des·po·pu·la·ri·za·ción f. loss of popularity.

des·po·sa·do, –da I. past part. see **desposar** II. adj. *(recién casado)* newly wed; *(aprisionado)* handcuffed III. m.f. *(recién casado)* newlywed; *(aprisionado)* person in handcuffs.

des·po·sar tr. *(casar)* to marry, perform a marriage ceremony for —reflex. *(contraer esponsales)* to become engaged or betrothed; *(contraer matrimonio)* to marry, wed.

des·po·se·er §43 tr. *(privar)* to dispossess, divest —reflex. to renounce, give up.

des·po·se·í·mien·to m. dispossession.

dés·po·ta m.f. despot, tyrant.

des·pó·ti·co, –ca adj. despotic, tyrannical.

des·po·tis·mo m. despotism, tyranny.

des·po·tri·car §70 tr. MEX. to destroy, ruin —intr. COLL. to rant, rave.

des·pre·cia·ble adj. abject, despicable.

des·pre·ciar tr. *(desdeñar)* to disdain, look down on; *(desairar)* to slight, snub —reflex. to disdain, not to deign <*no despreciarse de recibirnos* not to deign to receive us>.

des·pre·cia·ti·vo, –va adj. scornful, contemptuous.

des·pre·cio m. *(desdeño)* disdain, scorn; *(desaire)* slight, snub.

des·pren·der tr. *(desunir)* to unfasten, detach; *(soltar)* to loosen; *(emitir)* to emit, give off —reflex. *(separarse)* to come undone, become detached; *(ser emitido)* to issue, emanate; *(proceder)* to be inferred, follow *<de lo que dijo se desprende que el plan no tendrá exito* from what he said it follows that the plan will not succeed>; MED. to be detached ♦ **desprenderse de** to give up, part with *<se desprendió de sus bienes* he gave up his fortune>.

des·pren·di·do, –da I. past part. see **desprender** II. adj. *(desunido)* detached, loose; FIG. *(generoso)* generous, unselfish; *(desinteresado)* disinterested, detached; MED. detached.

des·pren·di·mien·to m. *(separación)* detachment; *(emisión)* emission, release; *(caída de tierra)* landslide; FIG. *(generosidad)* generosity, largesse; *(desapego)* disinterest, detachment; MED. detachment ♦ **d. termiónico** RAD. Edison effect.

des·pre·o·cu·pa·ción f. *(falta de preocupación)* unconcern, nonchalance; *(imparcialidad)* impartiality, open-mindedness; *(falta de conformidad)* unconventionality; *(descuido)* carelessness, negligence.

des·pre·o·cu·pa·do, –da I. past part. see **despreocuparse** II. adj. *(calmoso)* unconcerned, nonchalant; *(imparcial)* impartial, open-minded; *(descuidado)* untidy, sloppy; *(que no conforma)* unconventional.

des·pre·o·cu·par·se reflex. *(dejar de preocuparse)* to stop worrying, forget one's cares or worries; *(descuidarse)* to become negligent or careless ♦ **d. de** *(olvidarse de)* to forget, neglect; *(no hacer caso de)* not to care about, to disregard.

des·pres·ti·giar tr. *(hacer perder el prestigio)* make (someone) lose prestige; to ruin (someone's) reputation; COLL. *(desacreditar)* to discredit, disparage —reflex. to lose one's reputation or prestige.

des·pres·ti·gio m. loss of reputation or prestige.

des·pre·ven·ción f. improvidence, lack of caution.

des·pre·ve·ni·do, –da adj. unprepared, off guard *<coger a una persona d.* to catch a person off guard>.

des·pro·por·ción f. disproportion.

des·pro·por·cio·nar tr. to disproportion, mismatch.

des·pro·pó·si·to m. absurdity, nonsense; *(metedura de pata)* blunder, faux pas.

des·pro·ve·er §43 tr. to deprive of provisions or necessities.

des·pue·ble, despueblo see **despoblar**.

des·pués adv. afterward, later *<nos veremos d.* we will see each other later>; next, then *<¿qué pasó d.?* what happened then>?; later *<un día d.* one day later> ♦ **d. de** after *<d. de comer* after eating>; next to *<d. de él, soy el mejor de la clase* next to him I am the best in the class> • **d. (de) que** after *<d. que llamó, salí de la oficina* after he called, I left the office> • **d. de todo** after all is said and done • **poco d.** soon after, shortly after.

des·pun·tar tr. *(quitar la punta)* to break off or dull the point of; *(descerar)* to remove dry combs of (a beehive); MARIT. to sail around, round *<d. el cabo* to round the cape> —intr. to begin, break *<despunta el día* day is breaking; *(manifestar agudeza)* to show wit or intelligence; FIG. *(sobresalir)* to excel, stand out; BOT. to bud, sprout —reflex. to break its point.

des·pun·te m. *(acción)* blunting, breaking a point; AMER. cuttings, twigs.

des·que·rer §55 tr. to lose affection or liking for.

des·qui·cia·dor, –do·ra I. adj. *(que desgozna)* unhinging; *(que turba)* disturbing, distressing; *(que desorganiza)* disruptive II. m.f. one who unsettles or disturbs.

des·qui·cia·mien·to m. *(desencajamiento)* unhinging; FIG. *(perturbación)* perturbation, mental unrest; *(trastorno)* disturbance, disruption.

des·qui·ciar tr. *(sacar de quicio)* to unhinge; *(desconectar)* to loosen, disconnect; FIG. *(descomponer)* to unsettle, undermine; *(trastornar)* to upset, unhinge; FIG., COLL. *(quitar la confianza)* to deprive (someone) of favor, oust —reflex. *(salir de quicio)* to become unhinged, come off its hinges; *(desconectarse)* to come loose, become disconnected; FIG. *(descomponerse)* to become unsettled; *(trastornarse)* to become upset or unhinged.

des·quie·ra, desquiero see **desquerer**.

des·qui·la·tar tr. to lessen the intrinsic value of.

des·qui·sie·ra, desquiso see **desquerer**.

des·qui·tar tr. to compensate —reflex. ♦ **desquitarse de**

(resarcirse de) to recoup, win back; *(tomar satisfacción)* to take revenge on, get even with.

des·qui·te m. *(de pérdida)* recovery, recouping (of a loss); *(compensación)* compensation, restitution; *(venganza)* revenge, retaliation; SPORT. return match or game ♦ **en d.** in return, in retaliation.

des·rai·zar tr. AMER. to uproot.

des·ra·zo·na·ble adj. COLL. unreasonable, irrational.

des·ta·ca·men·to m. MIL. *(tropa destacada)* detachment, detail; *(lugar)* post, station.

des·ta·car §70 tr. FIG. *(subrayar)* to emphasize, highlight *<d. los méritos de alguien* to highlight someone's merits>, MIL. to detail, assign; PAINT. to make stand out, highlight —intr. *(sobresalir)* to stand out, be outstanding; PAINT. to stand out, be highlighted —reflex. *(sobresalir)* to stand out, be outstanding; *(aventajarse)* to break away, draw ahead.

des·ta·co·nar tr. to wear out the heels of (shoes).

des·ta·jar tr. *(acordar)* to contract for, settle the conditions for (a job); *(naipes)* to cut (a deck of cards); AMER. to cut up, quarter (a carcass).

des·ta·je·ro, –ra m.f. pieceworker, jobber.

des·ta·jo m. *(trabajo)* piecework; *(tajo)* job, stint ♦ **a d.** by the job or piece; *(diligentemente)* diligently; COLL. *(por adivinación)* at a guess, roughly; CHILE *(a bulto)* in bulk, wholesale • **hablar a d.** to chatter, talk excessively.

des·ta·pa·du·ra f. *(acción de descorchar)* uncorking; *(acción de destaponar)* uncapping, removing the lid from; FIG. *(revelación)* revelation, discovery.

des·ta·par tr. *(abrir)* to open, uncover; *(una botella)* to uncork, uncap; *(una caja)* to take the lid off, open; FIG. *(descubrir)* to reveal, discover —intr. MEX. to bolt (a horse) —reflex. *(revelarse)* to show one's true colors; *(desahogarse)* to unburden oneself, open one's heart; COLL. *(desnudarse)* to take off one's clothes.

des·ta·pe m. *(acción)* uncovering, revealing; COLL. *(desnudo)* nude (in pornography); *(liberalización)* liberalization of any prohibitive law or custom.

des·ta·po·nar tr. *(una botella)* to uncork; *(el taponamiento)* to unplug, unstop.

des·ta·qué, destaque see **destacar**.

des·tar·ta·la·do, –da adj. *(mal dispuesto)* ramshackle, dilapidated; *(desproporcionado)* rambling, disproportionate.

des·te·char tr. to remove the roof from, unroof.

des·te·jar tr. *(quitar las tejas)* to remove the tiles from; FIG. *(dejar sin defensa)* to leave defenseless.

des·te·jer tr. *(lo tejido)* to unweave, unravel; *(descoser)* to unstitch, take stitches out of; FIG. *(desbaratar)* to upset, disrupt.

des·te·llar tr. to flash —intr. *(despedir destellos)* to flash; *(centellar)* to sparkle, glitter; *(una estrella)* to twinkle; ARCH. to distill, drip.

des·te·llo m. *(luz repentina)* flash (of light); *(centelleo)* sparkle, glitter; *(de una estrella)* twinkle; TECH. signal or flashing light ♦ **destellos** signs, indications *<destellos de genio* signs of genius>.

des·tem·pla·do, –da I. past part. see **destemplar** II. adj. *(desmesurado)* immoderate, intemperate; *(desigual)* uneven, irregular (rhythm); METAL. untempered; MUS. *(desafinado)* untuned, out of tune; *(disonante)* dissonant, inharmonious; PAINT. inharmonious, having uneven colors; MED. *(irregular)* irregular (said of pulse); *(indispuesto)* indisposed, feverish; METEROL. unsettled, variable.

des·tem·plan·za f. *(inclemencia)* inclemency, harshness (climate); *(inestabilidad)* instability, variability (weather); MED. *(irregularidad)* irregularity, unevenness (of pulse); *(desazón)* indisposition; FIG. *(inmoderación)* intemperance, lack of moderation (in speech, behavior).

des·tem·plar tr. *(alterar)* to disturb the order or harmony of; *(poner en infusión)* to steep, infuse; METAL. to untemper; MUS. to put out of tune, untune —reflex. FIG. *(descomponerse)* to get upset or worked up; METAL. to lose temper; MUS. to go or get out of tune; MED. *(sentir calentura)* to have a slight fever; *(el pulso)* to become irregular (said of pulse); AMER. to have one's teeth on edge.

des·tem·ple m. MUS. *(desafinación)* dissonance, disharmony (instrument); MED. *(indisposición)* indisposition; FIG. *(desconcierto)* confusion, disorder.

des·ten·tar §49 tr. to dissuade from temptation.
des·te·ñir §59 tr. *(quitar el tinte)* to fade, remove the color of; *(descolorar)* discolor —intr. *(perder el tinte)* to fade, lose its color; *(descolorarse)* to discolor, become discolored.
des·ter·ni·llar·se reflex. to tear a cartilage ♦ **d. de risa** to split one's sides laughing.
des·te·rrar §49 tr. *(de un país)* to exile, banish; FIG. *(alejar)* to banish, expel; AGR. to remove the soil from —reflex. to exile oneself, go into exile.
des·te·tar tr. to wean —reflex. *(dejar de mamar)* to be weaned; *(deshabituarse)* to break a habit ♦ **d. con** FIG. to have been weaned on, been brought up on.
des·te·te m. weaning.
des·tiem·po adv. ♦ **a d.** inopportunely, at the wrong moment.
des·tien·te, destiento see **destentar.**
des·tie·rre, destierro see **desterrar.**
des·tie·rro m. *(exilio)* exile, banishment; FIG. *(lugar apartado)* wilderness, remote place.
des·ti·la·ble adj. distillable.
des·ti·la·ción f. *(acción de destilar)* distillation, filtration ♦ **d. fraccionada** CHEM. fractional distillation.
des·ti·lar tr. *(evaporar)* to distill; *(filtrar)* to filter; *(exudar)* to exude, ooze —intr. *(gotear)* to drip, trickle; *(exudar)* to exude, ooze.
des·ti·le·rí·a f. distillery ♦ **d. de petróleo** oil refinery.
des·ti·na·ción f. *(asignación)* assignment; *(destino)* destination.
des·ti·nar tr. *(señalar)* to destine, intend; *(asignar)* to assign, appoint; *(mandar)* to send; COM. to allot, earmark; MIL. to post, station; MARIT. to station ships —reflex. to intend to go into *or* take up.
des·ti·na·ta·rio, –ria m.f. *(de una carta)* addressee; *(de un giro)* payee.
des·ti·no m. *(sino)* destiny, fate; *(destinación)* destination; *(empleo)* job, position; use, function <*dar d. a algo* to find a use for something>; COM. allotment, earmarking; MIL. post, station ♦ **con d.** bound for <*el vuelo con d. a Bogotá* the flight bound for Bogotá>.
des·ti·ña, destiño see **desteñir.**
des·ti·ñe·ra, destiñó see **desteñir.**
des·ti·tu·ción f. dismissal, removal from an office.
des·ti·tuir §18 tr. *(revocar)* to dismiss, remove (from an office); *(privar)* to deprive.
des·tor·cer §71 tr. *(deshacer lo retorcido)* to untwist, undo; FIG. *(enderezar)* to straighten, rectify —reflex. MARIT. to go off course, drift.
des·tor·ni·lla·do, –da I. past part. see **destornillar** II. adj. FIG. crazy, harebrained III. m.f. FIG. screwball, nut.
des·tor·ni·lla·dor m. screwdriver.
des·tor·ni·llar tr. to unscrew —reflex. *(un tornillo)* to come unscrewed; FIG. *(perder el juicio)* to go crazy.
des·to·ser·se reflex. to feign a cough, clear one's throat.
des·tra·bar tr. *(desatar)* to untie, unfetter; *(desprender)* to separate, disconnect (two things).
des·tren·zar §04 tr. to unbraid, unplait.
des·tre·za f. skill, dexterity.
des·tri·cé, destrice see **destrizar.**
des·tri·pa·cuen·tos m. [pl. -tos] COLL. interrupter, person who butts in.
des·tri·pa·dor, –do·ra I. adj. disemboweling II. m.f. disemboweler, ripper ♦ **el Destripador de Londres** *or* **Juanito el Destripador** Jack the Ripper.
des·tri·par tr. *(sacar las tripas)* to gut, disembowel; *(sacar lo interior)* to remove the stuffing from; *(despachurrar)* to crush, squash; FIG., COLL. *(socavar)* to spoil, take the punch out of (a story); AGR. to break up clods (of earth) —intr. MEX. to drop out (of school).
des·tri·zar §04 tr. *(hacer trizas)* to tear into strips; *(desmenuzar)* to crumble, shred —reflex. to be heartbroken, overcome with grief.
des·tro·cé, destroce see **destrozar.**
des·tro·na·mien·to m. *(acción de quitar el trono)* dethronement; FIG. *(derrocamiento)* overthrow.
des·tro·nar tr. *(echar del trono)* to dethrone; FIG. *(desposeer)* to overthrow, bring down.
des·tron·ca·do·ra f. pruning hook.

des·tron·ca·mien·to m. *(tala)* lopping off, pruning (branches, twigs); FIG. *(destrucción)* ruination.
des·tron·car §70 tr. *(tronchar)* to cut down, fell (a tree); FIG. *(interrumpir)* to cut off, interrupt <*d. un discurso* to interrupt a speech>; *(descoyuntar)* to dislocate; *(mutilar)* to maim, mutilate; *(cansar)* to exhaust, tire out; *(arruinar)* to ruin (someone); AMER. *(arrancar)* to uproot; *(aplastar)* to crush, tread underfoot (plants).
des·tron·que m. AMER. uprooting.
des·tro·za·dor, –do·ra I. adj. destructive II. m.f. destroyer, wrecker.
des·tro·zar §04 tr. *(despedazar)* to smash, break into pieces; FIG. *(arruinar)* to destroy, ruin; *(estropear)* to spoil, shatter; MIL. to wipe out, crush —reflex. to smash, break into pieces.
des·tro·zo m. *(daño)* damage; *(destrucción)* destruction, ruin; MIL. defeat.
des·tro·zón, –zo·na I. adj. *(destructor)* destructive; *(que rompe la ropa)* hard on one's clothes II. m.f. destructive person.
des·truc·ción f. *(destrozo)* destruction; *(ruina)* damage, havoc.
des·truc·ti·ble adj. destructible.
des·truc·ti·vo, –va adj. destructive.
des·truc·tor, –to·ra I. adj. destructive II. m.f. *(persona)* destructive person, spoiler —m. MARIT. destroyer.
des·truir §18 tr. *(arruinar)* to destroy, ruin; *(malgastar)* to squander, waste; FIG. *(deshacer)* to shatter, dash <*d. las esperanzas* to shatter the hopes> —reflex. MATH. to cancel (each other) out.
des·tru·yen·te adj. destructive
des·tuer·za, dertuerzo see **destorcer.**
de·su·dar tr. to wipe the sweat off.
de·sue·le, desuelo see **desolar.**
de·sue·lle, desuello see **desollar.**
de·sue·rar tr. to drain whey from (milk).
de·su·nión f. *(separación)* disunion, separation; FIG. *(discordia)* discord, dissension.
de·su·nir tr. *(separar)* to disunite, separate; FIG. *(enemistar)* to cause discord *or* a rift; TECH. to disconnect, disengage —reflex. to separate, break apart.
de·su·ñar tr. *(las uñas)* to tear out the nails of; *(raíces)* to pull out the roots of —reflex. *(empeñarse)* to work one's fingers to the bone; *(dedicarse al vicio)* to indulge in vice.
de·sur·dir tr. *(una tela)* to unweave, undo the warp of (fabric); FIG. *(una intriga)* to thwart, frustrate (a plot).
de·su·sa·do, –da I. past part. see **desusar** II. adj. *(fuera de uso)* obsolete, out of date; *(poco usado)* uncommon, rare; *(extraño)* strange, unusual.
de·su·sar tr. to stop using, discontinue the use of —reflex. to become obsolete *or* out of date.
de·su·so m. disuse, obsolescence ♦ **caer en d.** to fall into disuse, become obsolete.
de·sus·tan·ciar tr. *(debilitar)* to enervate, deprive of strength; *(diluir)* to weaken, dilute —reflex. to become weak *or* diluted.
des·va·í·do, –da adj. *(desgalichado)* lanky, gawky; *(apagado)* dull, faded (color); FIG. *(insignificante)* dull, lackluster (personality).
des·vá·li·do, –da I. adj. needy, destitute II. m.f. needy *or* destitute person.
des·va·li·jar tr. to rob, plunder.
des·va·lo·rar tr. *(desvalorizar)* to depreciate; *(una moneda)* to devalue, devaluate; *(despreciar)* to disdain.
des·va·lo·ri·za·ción f. *(depreciación)* depreciation; *(de una moneda)* devaluation.
des·va·lo·ri·zar §04 tr. *(disminuir el valor)* to devalue, reduce the value of; *(una moneda)* to devalue, devaluate —reflex. to depreciate, lose value.
des·va·lua·ción f. devaluation, depreciation.
des·ván m. attic, garret.
des·va·ne·cer §17 tr. *(difundir)* to make vanish *or* disappear; *(envanecer)* to make vain *or* presumptuous; *(hacer desmayar)* to make dizzy; FIG. *(disipar)* to remove, dispel <*d. las dudas* to dispel doubts>; PAINT. to tone down (colors); PHOTOG. to mask; RAD. to fade —reflex. *(desaparecer)* to vanish, disappear; *(envanecerse)* to become vain;

(evaporarse) to evaporate; *(desmayarse)* to become dizzy, faint; RAD. to fade (out).

des·va·ne·ci·mien·to m. *(desaparición)* vanishing, disappearance; *(desmayo)* dizziness, faintness; *(evaporación)* evaporation; *(altanería)* arrogance, haughtiness; PAINT. toning down (of colors); PHOTOG. masking; RAD. fade, fading.

des·va·nez·ca, desvanezco see **desvanecer**.

des·va·rar tr. *(resbalar)* to slip, slide; MARIT. to refloat (a grounded ship).

des·va·riar §30 intr. *(delirar)* to be delirious; *(disparatar)* to rave, talk nonsense.

des·va·rí·o m. *(delirio)* delirium, madness; *(disparate)* raving, nonsense; *(tontería)* foolish remark *or* act; *(capricho)* whim; FIG. *(monstruosidad)* monstrosity.

des·ve·lar tr. to keep awake, stop from sleeping —reflex. *(no poder dormir)* to stay awake, go without sleep; *(dedicarse)* to devote *or* dedicate oneself ♦ **d. por** to be watchful for, take great care over.

des·ve·lo m. *(insomnio)* sleeplessness, insomnia; *(esfuerzo)* effort; *(esmero)* watchfulness, care; *(devoción)* devotion, dedication ♦ **desvelos** trouble.

des·ven·ci·ja·do, –da I. past part. see **desvencijar II.** adj. *(de una estructura)* ramshackle, tumbledown; *(de muebles)* rickety, shaky; *(de una máquina)* broken-down, out of order.

des·ven·ci·jar tr. *(aflojar)* to loosen, weaken; *(estropear)* to ruin; *(romper)* to break; *(agotar)* to exhaust —reflex. *(romperse)* to break, come apart; COLL. *(estar agotado)* to be exhausted; *(descansar)* to relax; MED. to rupture oneself.

des·ven·dar tr. to unbandage.

des·ven·ta·ja f. disadvantage, drawback ♦ **estar en d.** to be at a disadvantage.

des·ven·ta·jo·so, –sa adj. disadvantageous, unfavorable.

des·ven·tu·ra f. misfortune, bad luck.

des·ven·tu·ra·do, –da I. adj. *(desgraciado)* unfortunate, unlucky; *(tímido)* timid, fainthearted; *(pobre)* poor **II.** m.f. *(miserable)* poor devil, loser; *(tímido)* timid person.

des·ver·gon·za·do, –da I. past part. see **desvergonzarse II.** adj. impudent, shameless **III.** m.f. shameless *or* impudent person.

des·ver·gon·zar·se §09 reflex. *(descomedirse)* to act rudely, behave shamelessly; *(insolentarse)* to speak rudely *or* impudently.

des·ver·güen·za f. *(falta de vergüenza)* shamelessness, brazenness; *(insolencia)* insolence.

des·ves·tir §48 tr. to undress; FIG. *(revelar)* to lay bare, reveal —reflex. undress.

des·via·ción f. *(rodeo)* detour, diversion; *(de un golpe)* deflection (of a blow); FIG. *(de una norma)* deviation, departure; MED. extravasation; PHYS. deviation, deflection ♦ **d. electromagnética** RAD. electromagnetic deflection ♦ **d. magnética** RAD. magnetic deviation • **d. normal** standard deviation.

des·viar §30 tr. *(extraviar)* to divert <**d. un río** to divert a river>; to deflect <**d. un golpe** to deflect a blow>; FIG. *(disuadir)* to dissuade; SPORT. to deflect (a shot); *(en la esgrima)* to parry (in fencing) ♦ **d. la mirada** to look away, avoid someone's eyes —reflex. *(salir de)* to turn off; *(perder la ruta)* to go off course; *(mudar de dirección)* to change direction *or* course; *(hacer un rodeo)* to take a detour <*nos desviamos porque había obras en la carretera* we took a detour because of the road work on the highway>; FIG. *(apartarse)* to deviate.

des·vin·cu·lar tr. *(desconectar)* to separate (someone from), break ties with; LAW *(librar)* to free, release (from mortmain); ARG., CHILE to amortize —reflex. ♦ **d. de** *or* **con** to break contact with, dissociate oneself from.

des·ví·o m. *(rodeo)* detour, diversion; FIG. *(desapego)* indifference, coolness; *(desagrado)* aversion, displeasure; PHYS. deviation, deflection; RAIL. siding ♦ **d. de atajo** RAIL. catch siding • **d. de frecuencia** RAD. frequency drift • **d. de la brújula** PHYS. compass error.

des·vi·rar tr. *(la suela)* to pare off the rough edge (of the sole of a shoe); *(un libro)* to trim (a book); MARIT. to reverse the capstan.

des·vir·gar §47 tr. to deflower.

des·vir·tuar §67 tr. *(echar a perder)* to spoil, impair; *(adulterar)* to adulterate; *(quitar valor a)* to detract from; *(viciar)* to distort —reflex. to spoil, go bad.

des·vis·ta, desvisto see **desvestir**.

des·vis·tie·ra, desvistió see **desvestir**.

des·vi·vir·se reflex. *(mostrar interés)* to be eager, show a great desire <*se desvive por ayudar a los amigos* he is eager to help his friends>; *(estar enamorado)* to be madly in love; *(esforzarse)* to strive, do one's utmost; *(dedicarse)* to dedicate *or* devote oneself.

des·ye·mar tr. to remove buds (from a tree).

des·yer·bar tr. to weed.

de·ta·lla·da·men·te adv. in detail.

de·ta·llar tr. *(contar con detalles)* to detail, relate in detail; *(especificar)* to specify, itemize; COM. to sell retail.

de·ta·lle m. *(pormenor)* detail, particular; *(gesto)* gesture, kind thought; AMER., COM. retailing ♦ **al d.** AMER., COM. retail • **con todo d.** in full detail.

de·ta·llis·ta I. adj. retail <*comercio d.* retail trade> **II.** m.f. COM. retailer; *(considerado)* thoughtful person.

de·tec·ción f. detection ♦ **d. audible** audible detection.

de·tec·tar tr. to detect.

de·tec·ti·ve m. detective.

de·tec·tor, –to·ra I. m. detector; *(de radar)* scanner, monitor ♦ **d. de mentiras** lie detector **II.** adj. detecting.

de·ten see **detener**.

de·ten·ción f. *(acción)* stopping, halting; *(estado)* stoppage, standstill; *(retraso)* delay; *(arresto)* arrest; *(prisión)* detention; *(cuidado)* care, thoroughness; MARIT. demurrage, embargo ♦ **d. de juego** SPORT. stoppage of play • **d. en masa** mass arrest.

de·te·ner §69 tr. *(parar)* to stop, halt; *(retrasar)* to delay; *(arrestar)* to arrest; *(encarcelar)* to detain; *(retener)* to keep, retain —reflex. *(pararse)* to stop; *(retardarse)* to linger, tarry; *(dilatarse)* to dwell upon.

de·te·ni·da·men·te adv. thoroughly, closely.

de·te·ni·do, –da I. past part. see **detener II.** adj. *(cuidadoso)* thorough, close; *(tímido)* timid, fainthearted; *(escaso)* sparing; *(dilatorio)* dilatory; *(arrestado)* arrested; *(preso)* detained, in custody **III.** m.f. person under arrest.

de·te·ni·mien·to m. var. of **detención**.

de·ten·ta·ción f. LAW deforcement.

de·ten·tar tr. LAW to deforce.

de·ten·tor, –to·ra m.f. SPORT. record holder.

de·ter·gen·te adj. & m. detergent.

de·te·rio·ra·ción f. *(estropeo)* deterioration, spoiling; *(daño)* damage, harm; *(con el uso)* wear, wear and tear.

de·te·rio·rar tr. *(estropear)* to damage, spoil; *(desgastar)* to wear (out), cause wear on —reflex. *(estropearse)* to deteriorate, spoil; *(dañarse)* to damage, harm; *(desgastarse)* to wear out.

de·te·rio·ro m. *(deterioración)* deterioration; *(daño)* harm, damage.

de·ter·mi·na·ción f. *(decisión)* decision; *(fijación)* specifying, fixing; *(resolución)* determination, resolve.

de·ter·mi·na·do, –da I. past part. see **determinar II.** adj. *(resoluto)* determined, resolute; *(preciso)* specific, particular; GRAM. definite.

de·ter·mi·nan·te I. adj. determining, determinant **II.** m. MATH. determinant.

de·ter·mi·nar tr. *(descubrir)* to determine; *(convencer)* to convince, decide <*la promoción me determinó a asistir* the publicity convinced me to attend>; *(fijar)* to specify, fix (a date); *(causar)* to cause, bring about; *(distinguir)* to distinguish, discern <*no pude d. quién era* I could not discern who he was>; LAW *(juzgar)* to settle, decide; *(estipular)* to stipulate, specify —reflex. to decide, make up one's mind.

de·ter·mi·na·ti·vo, –va adj. determinative.

de·ter·mi·nis·mo m. PHILOS. determinism.

de·ter·mi·nis·ta PHILOS. **I.** adj. deterministic **II.** m.f. determinist.

de·ter·sión f. cleansing.

de·ter·si·vo, –va *or* **de·ter·so·rio, –ria I.** adj. detersive, detergent **II.** m. detergent.

de·tes·ta·ble adj. detestable, hateful.

de·tes·ta·ción f. detestation, hatred.

de·tes·tar tr. to detest, hate.

de·tie·ne see **detener.**

de·to·na·ción f. *(acción de detonar)* detonation, explosion; *(ruido)* report, blast.

de·to·na·dor m. detonator.

de·to·nan·te I. adj. detonating, explosive II. m. explosive.

de·to·nar intr. to detonate, explode.

de·trac·ción f. *(denigración)* denigration, disparagement; *(retiro)* withdrawal.

de·trac·tar tr. to denigrate, disparage.

de·trac·tor, –to·ra I. adj. detracting, defamatory II. m.f. detractor, defamer.

de·tra·er §72 tr. *(denigrar)* to denigrate, defame; *(quitar)* to remove.

de·trás adv. behind <*irán d.* they will follow behind> ♦ **d. de** behind, in back of • **por d.** from behind <*me atacaron por d.* they attacked me from behind>; FIG. *(en ausencia)* behind one's back <*hablan por d. de ella* they talk behind her back>.

de·tri·men·to m. detriment, damage ♦ **en d. de** to the detriment of.

de·tri·to or **de·tri·tus** m. GEOL., MED. detritus; *(basura)* waste, debris ♦ **d. radioactivo** radioactive waste.

de·tu·vie·ra, detuvo see **detener.**

deu·da f. *(deber)* debt; RELIG. sin, trespass ♦ **contraer deudas** to get into debt • **d. a largo plazo** long-term debt • **d. exterior** foreign debt • **d. incobrable** or **morosa** bad debt • **d. pública** national debt • **deudas activas** assets • **deudas pasivas** liabilities —m.f. see **deudo, –da.**

deu·do, –da m.f. relative —m. relationship, kinship —f. see **deuda.**

deu·dor, –do·ra I. adj. debit <*saldo d.* debit balance>; FIG. *(que debe)* indebted II. m.f. debtor.

deu·tó·xi·do m. CHEM. deutoxide, dioxide.

de·va·lua·ción f. devaluation.

de·va·luar §67 tr. to devaluate.

de·va·na·de·ra f. *(bobina)* reel, spool; *(marco)* winding frame; MARIT. log-reel; THEAT. mechanism for revolving sets.

de·va·na·do m. ELEC. winding, coiling ♦ **d. inductor** or **de campo** ELEC. field winding.

de·va·na·dor, –do·ra I. adj. winding II. m.f. *(persona)* winder —m. *(del ovillo)* spool; AMER. winder, reel.

de·va·nar tr. to reel, wind —reflex. CUBA, MEX. to double up with pain or laughter ♦ **devanarse los sesos** COLL. to rack one's brain.

de·va·ne·ar intr. to rave, talk deliriously.

de·va·ne·o m. *(delirio)* delirium, madness; *(disparate)* nonsense, raving; *(pasatiempo)* idle pastime, frivolity; *(amorío)* affair, flirtation.

de·vas·ta·ción f. devastation.

de·vas·ta·dor, –do·ra I. adj. devastating, destroying II. m.f. devastator, destroyer.

de·vas·tar tr. to devastate, destroy.

de·ve·lar tr. to reveal.

de·ven·gar §47 tr. to have due, be owed; *(interés)* to earn, yield.

de·ven·go m. amount due.

de·ve·nir §76 intr. *(suceder)* to happen, come about; *(llegar a ser)* to become, evolve into.

de·vo·ción f. RELIG. devotion; *(piedad)* devoutness, piety; *(afición)* affection, attachment ♦ **estar a la d. de uno** to be at someone's disposal • **tener por d.** to be in the habit of.

de·vo·cio·na·rio m. prayer book.

de·vo·lu·ción f. *(vuelto)* return; *(restauración)* restoration; COM. refund; LAW devolution.

de·vo·lu·ti·vo, –va adj. LAW returnable, restorable.

de·vol·ver §78 tr. to return, give back <*d. un libro perdido* to return a lost book>; *(corresponder)* to return <*d. un favor* to return a favor>; *(restaurar)* to restore; *(vomitar)* to throw up, vomit; COM. to refund —reflex. AMER. to return, go or come back.

de·vo·ra·dor, –do·ra I. adj. devouring, ravenous <*hambre d.* ravenous hunger> II. m.f. devourer.

de·vo·ran·te adj. voracious, ravenous.

de·vo·rar tr. *(comer)* to devour, eat up; *(disipar)* to squander, waste; *(arruinar)* to ruin, destroy; FIG. *(consumir)* to consume.

de·vo·te·rí·a f. COLL. false piety, sanctimoniousness.

de·vo·to, –ta I. adj. RELIG. *(piadoso)* devout, pious; RELIG. devotional <*imagen d.* devotional image>; *(venerable)* venerable, revered; *(aficionado)* devoted, attached II. m.f. RELIG. devout person; *(aficionado)* devotee, enthusiast.

de·vuel·to, –ta I. past part. see **devolver** II. f. COL., DOM. REP., P. RICO change (coins).

de·vuel·va, devuelvo see **devolver.**

dex·te·ri·dad f. dexterity, skillfulness.

dex·tro·sa f. CHEM. dextrose.

de·yec·ción f. MED. dejection, defecation ♦ **deyecciones** MED. dejecta, feces; GEOL. ejecta.

de·yec·tor m. TECH. device for preventing formation of crust inside steam boilers.

di see **dar** or **decir²**.

dí·a m. day <*hay 365 días en un año* there are 365 days in a year>; *(tiempo de claridad)* daytime, daylight; *(tiempo)* weather <*hace buen d.* it is good weather> ♦ **a días** some days, once in a while • **al d.** *(al corriente)* up to date; per day, a day <*pagué treinta dólares al d. por la habitación* I paid thirty dollars a day for the room> • **al d. siguiente** or **al otro d.** on the following day, the next day • **a los pocos días** a few days later • **a tantos días fecha** or **vista** COM. to be paid on the date stated • **¡buenos días!** good morning • **cada dos días** every other day • **¡cualquier d.!** COLL. not on your life! • **dar los buenos días** to say good morning to • **de d.** by day • **de d. en d.** from day to day • **de días** old <*esa idea es ya de días* that is an old idea> • **d. a d.** AMER. from day to day • **d. astronómico** astronomical day • **d. civil** calendar day • **d. de Año Nuevo** New Year's Day • **d. de asueto** day off • **d. de ayuno** RELIG. fast day • **d. de fiesta** holiday • **d. de guardar** RELIG. holy day, day of obligation • **d. del juicio** Judgment Day, doomsday • **d. de los difuntos** RELIG. All Souls' Day • **d. de los Reyes** RELIG. Epiphany • **d. de todos los santos** RELIG. All Saints' Day • **d. de trabajo** workday, working day • **d. de vigilia** RELIG. day of abstinence • **d. entre semana** weekday • **d. feriado** or **festivo** holiday • **d. hábil** workday, business day • **d. laborable** workday, working day • **d. por d.** day by day • **días** *(cumpleaños)* saint's day, birthday; FIG. *(vida)* life <*al fin de sus días* at the end of his life> • **d. santo** saint's day, birthday • **días de gracia** COM. days of grace • **d. señalado** red-letter day • **d. tras d.** day after day • **el d. de hoy** today • **el d. de mañana** *(mañana)* tomorrow; *(pronto)* soon, in the near future • **el d. menos pensado** when one least expects it • **el mejor d.** some fine day • **en mis días** in my day or time • **en pleno d.** in broad daylight • **en su d.** in due time • **entrado en días** advanced in age • **estar al d.** to be up-to-date • **hoy (en) d.** nowadays, these days • **ocho días** a week • **poner al d.** to bring up to date • **quince días** two weeks, fortnight • **todo el santo d.** all day long, all the livelong day • **todos los días** every day, daily • **un d. de estos** one of these days • **un d. sí y otro no** every other day • **vivir al d.** to live from hand to mouth, live one day at a time.

dia·be·tes f. MED. diabetes.

dia·bé·ti·co, –ca adj. & m.f. MED. diabetic.

dia·bla f. COLL. *(diablo hembra)* she-devil; *(coche)* two-wheeled carriage; THEAT. footlights ♦ **a la d.** COLL. any old way, carelessly • **cosido a la d.** BKB. paperbound.

dia·ble·ar intr. COLL. to play pranks.

dia·ble·sa f. COLL. she-devil.

dia·bli·llo m. *(enmascarado)* person disguised as a devil; FIG., COLL. *(persona traviesa)* devil, imp ♦ **diablillos** COLL. short hairs at the back of the neck.

dia·blo m. *(demonio)* devil, demon; FIG. *(travieso)* scamp, devil; *(requetefeo)* monster, ugly person; CHILE *(vehículo)* ox-cart, dray; PERU *(en billiards)* ♦ **al d.** or **como el d.** COLL. like the devil, a hell of a lot <*me pica como el d.* it stings like the devil> • **darse al d.** FIG. to get angry • **¡diablo!** or **¡diablos!** COLL. wow! • **d. encarnado** FIG. devil incarnate, devil himself • **d. marino** ICHTH. scorpene • **diablos azules** CHILE, C. RICA, HOND. delirium tremens • **donde el d. perdió el poncho** ARG., CHILE in the middle of nowhere • **pobre d.** FIG. poor devil • **¡qué diablos!** what the hell! • **tener el d. en el cuerpo** FIG. to be full of the devil, be full of mischief.

dia·blu·ra f. deviltry, prank.

dia·bó·li·co, –ca adj. diabolical, devilish.
dia·co·na·do or **dia·co·na·to** m. RELIG. diaconate, deaconship.
dia·co·ni·sa f. RELIG. deaconess.
diá·co·no m. RELIG. deacon.
dia·crí·ti·co, –ca adj. GRAM. diacritical; MED. diagnostic.
dia·cús·ti·ca f. diacoustics.
dia·de·ma f. diadem, crown.
dia·fa·ni·dad f. diaphanousness, transparency.
diá·fa·no, –na adj. diaphanous, transparent.
dia·fo·re·sis f. MED. diaphoresis, perspiration.
dia·frag·ma m. diaphragm.
diag·no·sis f. diagnosis.
diag·nos·ti·car §70 tr. MED. to diagnose.
diag·nós·ti·co, –ca MED. I. adj. diagnostic II. m. *(de una enfermedad)* diagnosis, diagnostic; *(ciencia)* diagnostics.
dia·go·nal adj. & f. diagonal ♦ **en d.** diagonally.
dia·gra·ma m. diagram ♦ **d. de fabricación** COM., INDUS. flow chart or diagram.
dial I. adj. daily II. m. (radio) dial ♦ **diales** diary, journal.
dia·léc·ti·ca f. dialectics.
dia·léc·ti·co, –ca I. adj. dialectical II. m.f. dialectician.
dia·lec·to m. dialect.
dia·lec·to·lo·gí·a f. dialectology.
diá·li·sis f. CHEM. dialysis.
dia·li·za·dor m. CHEM. dialyzer.
dia·li·zar §04 tr. CHEM. to dialyze.
dia·lo·ga·do, –da I. past part. see **dialogar** II. adj. written in dialogue.
dia·lo·gar §47 intr. to dialogue, converse —tr. to write in dialogue form.
diá·lo·go m. dialogue.
dia·lo·guis·ta m.f. dialogist.
dia·man·ta·do, –da adj. glittering (like a diamond).
dia·man·te m. *(joya)* diamond; *(naipe)* diamond (card suit) ♦ **d. brillante** cut diamond • **d. en bruto** uncut diamond • **d. falso** paste.
dia·man·ti·no, –na adj. *(relativo al diamante)* diamantine, diamond-like; FIG., POET. *(duro)* adamantine, unbreakable.
dia·man·tis·ta m.f. diamond cutter.
dia·me·tral adj. diametric, diametrical.
dia·me·tral·men·te adv. diametrically <*d. opuesto* diametrically opposed>.
diá·me·tro m. GEOM. diameter.
dia·na f. MIL. *(toque)* reveille; *(punto central)* bull's-eye.
dia·pa·són m. MUS. diapason, tuning fork; *(escala)* scale, range (of an instrument); *(del violín)* fingerboard; *(de la voz)* tone.
dia·po·si·ti·va f. PHOTOG. slide, transparency.
dia·ria·men·te adv. daily, every day.
dia·rie·ro m. AMER. newspaper seller.
dia·rio, –ria I. adj. daily II. m. *(periódico)* daily paper, daily; *(relación)* diary, journal; *(gasto)* daily expenses; COM. journal, daybook ♦ **d. de navegación** MARIT. log (book) • **d. hablado** RAD. news, news broadcast • **d. matinal** or **de la mañana** morning newspaper • **d. vespertino** or **de la noche** evening newspaper III. adv. daily ♦ **a d.** daily, every day • **de d.** *(diariamente)* daily, every day; *(ordinario)* everyday <*un vestido d.* an everyday suit>.
dia·ris·ta m.f. *(persona que escribe un diario)* diarist; AMER. journalist.
dia·rre·a f. MED. diarrhea.
diás·po·ra f. dispersion.
diás·to·le f. PHYSIOL., POET. diastole.
dia·tri·ba f. diatribe, invective.
dia·tro·pis·mo m. BOT. diatropism.
di·bu·jan·te I. adj. drawing, sketching II. m. *(artista)* drawer, sketcher; *(de dibujos animados)* cartoonist; TECH. draftsman.
di·bu·jar tr. *(esbozar)* to draw, sketch; FIG. *(describir)* to describe, depict <*d. un carácter* to depict a character> —reflex. *(delinearse)* to be outlined, stand out <*un árbol se dibuja a lo lejos* a tree stands out in the distance>; *(aparecer)* to appear, be traced.
di·bu·jo m. *(esbozo)* drawing, sketch; FIG. *(descripción)* description, depiction; ARTS sketching, drawing ♦ **d. del natu-**

ral ARTS drawing or sketching from life or nature • **dibujos animados** cartoons.
di·caz adj. sharp, caustic.
dic·ción f. diction.
dic·cio·na·rio m. dictionary.
dic·cio·na·ris·ta m.f. lexicographer.
di·ce see **decir²**.
di·ciem·bre m. December.
di·co·to·mí·a f. dichotomy.
di·cro·má·ti·co, –ca adj. dichromatic (having two colors).
dic·ta·do I. past part. see **dictar** II. m. *(título)* title (of nobility); *(acción de dictar)* dictation ♦ **dictados** FIG. dictates.
dic·ta·dor m. dictator.
dic·ta·du·ra f. dictatorship.
dic·tá·fo·no m. dictaphone.
dic·ta·men m. *(juicio)* opinion, judgment; *(consejo)* advice; *(informe)* report ♦ **d. médico** diagnosis.
dic·ta·mi·nar intr. to express an opinion.
dic·tar tr. to dictate <*d. una carta* to dictate a letter>; *(sentencia)* to pronounce, pass; *(inspirar)* to dictate, direct <*la sabiduría dicta sus palabras* wisdom dictates his words>; AMER. *(una conferencia)* to give, deliver; *(una clase)* to give, teach.
dic·ta·to·rial or **dic·ta·to·rio, –ria** adj. POL. dictatorial; FIG. *(arbitrario)* arbitrary, domineering.
dic·te·rio m. insult.
di·cha I. f. *(felicidad)* happiness; *(suerte)* good fortune ♦ **a** or **por d.** fortunately, happily II. adj. see **dicho, –cha.**
di·cha·ra·che·ro, –ra COLL. I. adj. *(gracioso)* witty, racy; *(hablador)* talkative, loquacious II. m.f. *(gracioso)* joker, wag; *(hablador)* chatterbox.
di·che·ro, –ra I. adj. witty, amusing II. m.f. clever person, amusing conversationalist.
di·cho, –cha I. past part. see **decir** II. adj. said, aforementioned <*en d. libro* in the aforementioned book> ♦ **d. de otro modo** in other words • **d. y hecho** FIG. no sooner said than done • **¡haberlo d.!** you should have said so! • **mejor d.** rather, more accurately III. m. *(refrán)* saying, proverb; *(ocurrencia)* witticism, witty remark; COLL. *(expresión insultante)* insulting remark; LAW statement, deposition ♦ **d. de las gentes** gossip, talk • **dichos** marriage vows <*tomarse los dichos* to exchange marriage vows> —f. see **dicha.**
di·cho·so, –sa adj. *(feliz)* happy, contented; *(afortunado)* lucky, fortunate; COLL. *(enfadoso)* blessed, blasted <*d. trabajo* blessed or blasted work>.
di·dác·ti·ca I. f. didactics II. adj. see **didáctico, –ca.**
di·dác·ti·co, –ca I. adj. didactic, pedagogical II. f. see **didáctica.**
die·ci·nue·ve I. adj. nineteen <*d. testigos* nineteen witnesses>; *(decimonoveno)* nineteenth II. m. nineteen.
die·cio·cho I. adj. eighteen <*d. aviones* eighteen planes>; *(decimoctavo)* eighteenth II. m. eighteen.
die·ci·séis I. adj. sixteen <*d. plumas* sixteen pens>; *(decimosexto)* sixteenth II. m. sixteen.
die·ci·sie·te I. adj. seventeen <*d. libras* seventeen pounds>; *(decimoséptimo)* seventeenth II. m. seventeen.
dien·ta, dien·to see **dentar.**
dien·te m. ANAT. tooth; ZOOL. fang; ORNITH. temium; MECH. cog <*los dientes de una rueda* the cogs of a wheel>; tooth <*los dientes de una sierra* the teeth of a saw>; prong, tine <*los dientes de un tenedor* the prongs of a fork>; BOT. clove <*d. de ajo* garlic clove> ♦ **aguzarse** or **afilarse los dientes** FIG. to whet one's appetite • **alargársele los dientes** FIG., COLL. to have one's heart set on • **dar d. con d.** to chatter (said of teeth) • **de dientes afuera** FIG. insincerely, as lip service • **diente canino** ANAT. canine tooth, eyetooth • **d. de león** BOT. dandelion • **d. de lobo** JEWEL. burnisher; *(clavo)* spike • **d. de maíz** corn kernel • **d. de perro** TECH. chisel; ARCHIT. dogtooth; BOT. dogtooth violet • **d. incisivo** ANAT. incisor • **d. molar** ANAT. molar • **d. tierno** or **de leche** ANAT. milk tooth, baby tooth • **dientes postizos** false teeth • **enseñar** or **mostrar los dientes** FIG. to show or bare one's teeth• **estar a d.** to be famished or ravenous • **hablar entre dientes** to mumble, mutter • **hincar el d. en** to get or sink one's teeth into • **pelar el d.**

AMER. *(coquetear)* to flirt; *(adular)* to flatter • **tener buen d.** FIG. to have a good appetite.

die·ra, dieron see **dar**.

dié·re·sis f. GRAM. dieresis.

die·sel m. diesel (engine).

dies·tro, –tra I. adj. *(hábil)* deft, dexterous; *(derecho)* right; *(astuto)* shrewd, astute **II.** m. TAUR. matador, bull-fighter; *(esgrimista)* swordsman —f. *(mano derecha)* right hand ♦ **a d. y siniestra** all over, right and left.

die·ta f. diet ♦ **d. hídrica** water diet • **d. láctea** milk diet • **estar a d.** to diet, be on a diet • **poner a d.** to put on a diet • **ponerse a d.** to go *or* put oneself on a diet • **tener d.** VEN. to be patient.

die·ta·rio m. *(agenda)* diary; *(libro de cuentas)* account book; *(libro de crónicas)* book of chronicles *or* notable events.

die·té·ti·ca I. f. dietetics **II.** adj. see **dietético, –ca**.

die·té·ti·co, –ca I. adj. dietetic, dietary **II.** m.f. dietician — f. see **dietética**.

diez I. adj. ten <*este verso tiene d. sílabas* this verse has ten syllables>; *(décimo)* tenth ♦ **las d.** ten o'clock **II.** m. *(número)* ten; RELIG. decade (of a rosary); CHILE, C. RICA ten-cent piece ♦ **hacer las d. de última** FIG. to hurt one's own chances.

diez·mar tr. *(matar de cada diez uno)* to decimate; *(pagar el diezmo)* to pay the tithe (to the Church); FIG. *(causar gran mortandad)* to decimate, ravage <*la peste diezmó el ejército* the plague decimated the army>.

diez·mo m. *(impuesto)* tithe; *(décima parte)* tenth part.

diez y nueve adj. & m. var. of **diecinueve**.

diez y ocho adj. & m. var. of **dieciocho**.

diez y seis adj. & m. var. of **dieciséis**.

diez y siete adj. & m. var. of **diecisiete**.

di·fa·ma·ción f. *(hablando)* defamation, slander; LAW *(por escrito)* libel.

di·fa·ma·dor, –do·ra I. adj. *(de palabra)* defamatory, slanderous; LAW *(por escrito)* libelous **II.** m.f. *(de palabra)* defamer, slanderer; LAW *(por escrito)* libeler.

di·fa·mar tr. to defame, slander.

di·fa·ma·to·rio, –ria adj. *(de palabra)* defamatory, slanderous; LAW *(por escrito)* libelous.

di·fe·ren·cia f. *(desemejanza)* difference, dissimilarity; FIG. *(disensión)* difference, disagreement; MATH. difference ♦ **a d. de** unlike, in contrast to • **hacer d. entre** to make *or* draw a distinction between • **partir la d.** to split the difference.

di·fe·ren·cia·ción f. differentiation.

di·fe·ren·cial I. adj. differential **II.** f. MATH. differential —m. MECH. differential (gear).

di·fe·ren·ciar tr. *(distinguir)* to differentiate, distinguish; *(variar)* to vary *or* change (the use of); MATH. to differentiate —intr. to differ, disagree —reflex. *(hacerse famoso)* to distinguish oneself; *(ser diferente)* to differ, be different; BIOL. to differentiate.

di·fe·ren·te I. adj. different, dissimilar ♦ **diferentes** various, several <*eso me ha pasado diferentes veces* that's happened to me several times> **II.** adv. differently.

di·fe·ren·te·men·te adv. differently.

di·fe·rir §65 tr. to defer, postpone —intr. to differ, be different.

di·fí·cil adj. *(arduo)* difficult, hard; *(descontentado)* difficult, hard to please.

di·fí·cil·men·te adv. difficultly, with difficulty.

di·fi·cul·tad f. *(obstáculo)* difficulty, obstacle; *(objeción)* objection, doubt.

di·fi·cul·tar tr. to make difficult, complicate.

di·fi·cul·to·so, –sa adj. *(arduo)* difficult, hard; FIG., COLL. *(feo)* ugly, unpleasant; COLL. *(fastidioso)* difficult, fussy.

di·fi·den·cia f. mistrust, diffidence.

di·fie·ra, difiero see **diferir**.

di·fi·rie·ra, difirió see **diferir**.

dif·te·ria f. MED. diphtheria.

di·fun·dir tr. *(extender)* to diffuse; *(derramar)* to spread, scatter; *(divulgar)* to divulge, make known; *(diseminar)* to disseminate, propagate —reflex. to spread, be diffused.

di·fun·to, –ta I. adj. deceased, dead **II.** m.f. *(muerto)* deceased, dead person; *(cadáver)* corpse, cadaver.

di·fu·sión f. *(extensión)* diffusion, spreading; *(prolijidad)* diffusiveness, prolixity (of style); *(radio)* broadcasting.

di·fu·si·vo, –va adj. diffusive.

di·fu·so, –sa I. past part. see **difundir II.** adj. *(redundante)* diffuse, wordy; *(ancho)* wide, extended; *(vago)* vague, hazy.

di·fu·sor, –so·ra I. adj. diffusing, spreading **II.** m. diffuser (sugar manufacturing) —f. RAD. broadcasting station.

di·ga, digo see **decir²**.

di·ge·rir §65 tr. PHYSIOL. to digest; FIG. *(sufrir)* to suffer, endure <*d. una afrenta* to suffer an insult>; FIG. *(examinar con cuidado)* to digest, assimilate.

di·ges·ti·ble adj. digestible.

di·ges·tión f. PHYSIOL. digestion.

di·ges·ti·vo, –va I. adj. & **II.** m. digestive.

di·gi·ta·do, –da adj. BOT., ZOOL. digitate.

di·gi·tal adj. digital.

dí·gi·to m. MATH. digit.

dig·na·ción f. condescension, accomodation.

dig·nar·se reflex. to deign, condescend.

dig·na·ta·rio m. dignitary.

dig·ni·dad f. *(respeto de sí mismo)* dignity, self-respect; *(honor)* dignity, honor; *(cargo)* post, rank.

dig·ni·fi·can·te adj. THEOL. dignifying.

dig·ni·fi·car §70 tr. to dignify, honor.

dig·no, –na adj. *(merecedor)* worthy, deserving; *(apropiado)* proper, fitting; *(honrado)* worthy, honorable; *(mesurado)* dignified; *(decente)* decent.

di·gre·sión f. digression, deviation.

di·je m. *(adorno)* trinket, charm; FIG., COLL. *(persona)* jewel, gem <*esa criada es un d.* that maid is a jewel> ♦ **dijes** boasting, bravado.

di·je, dijo see **decir²**.

di·je·ra, dijeron see **decir²**.

di·la·ce·ra·ción f. laceration, tearing.

di·la·ce·rar tr. to lacerate, tear.

di·la·ción f. delay, delaying ♦ **sin d.** without delay, immediately.

di·la·pi·da·ción f. waste, squandering.

di·la·pi·dar tr. to waste, squander.

di·la·ta·ble adj. dilatable, expandable.

di·la·ta·ción f. *(expansión)* dilation, expansion; *(alargamiento)* prolongation, protraction; FIG. *(prolijidad)* diffuseness, long-windedness; *(desahogo)* serenity, calmness; SURG. dilatation, dilation; PHYS. expansion.

di·la·ta·dor, –do·ra I. adj. dilating, expanding **II.** m. SURG. dilator.

di·la·tar tr. *(extender)* to dilate, expand; FIG. *(retrasar)* to postpone, delay; *(propagar)* to spread; *(alargar)* to prolong, protract —reflex. *(extenderse)* to dilate, expand; FIG. *(ser muy prolijo)* to be diffuse *or* long-winded; *(propagarse)* to extend, stretch; AMER. to take a long time, be slow.

di·la·to·ria I. f. delay ♦ **andar con dilatorias** to waste time, use delaying tactics **II.** adj. see **dilatorio, –ria**.

di·la·to·rio, –ria I. adj. LAW dilatory, delaying **II.** f. see **dilatoria**.

di·lec·ción f. true love, sincere affection.

di·lec·to, –ta adj. beloved, loved.

di·le·ma m. dilemma.

di·let·tan·te or **di·le·tan·te** m.f. dilettante (lover of the arts).

di·li·gen·cia f. *(cuidado)* diligence, care; *(prisa)* speed, briskness; *(negocio)* affair, piece of business; *(empeño)* errand, task; *(coche)* stagecoach; LAW *(derecho)* proceeding ♦ **hacer una d.** to run an errand.

di·li·gen·ciar tr. *(tramitar)* to take the necessary measures *or* steps to obtain; LAW *(ejecutar)* to deal with, handle.

di·li·gen·te adj. *(cuidadoso)* diligent, careful; *(rápido)* speedy, quick.

di·li·gen·te·men·te adv. *(con cuidado)* diligently, carefully; *(con rapidez)* speedily, quickly.

di·lu·ci·da·ción f. elucidation, explanation.

di·lu·ci·dar tr. to elucidate, explain.

di·luen·te or **di·lu·yen·te** adj. diluent, diluting.

di·luir §18 tr. *(un sólido en un líquido)* to dissolve; *(líquidos)* to dilute; FIG. *(debilitar)* to water down, weaken.

di·lu·via·no, –na adj. diluvian, diluvial.

di·lu·viar intr. to pour down, teem (rain).

di·lu·vio m. *(inundación)* flood, deluge; FIG. *(gran cantidad)* flood, torrent ♦ **el Diluvio** BIBL. the Flood.

di·ma·nar intr. *(nacer)* to flow from, have its source in (water); FIG. *(originarse)* to originate in; *(proceder)* to proceed from, spring from; *(radicar)* to be due to <*su éxito dimana de su talento* his success is due to his abilities>.

di·men·sión f. *(tamaño)* dimension, size; FIG. *(importancia)* importance, dimension.

di·men·sio·nal adj. dimensional.

di·mi·nu·ción f. diminution, lessening.

di·mi·nuir §18 tr. to diminish, lessen.

di·mi·nu·ta·men·te adv. *(con escasez)* minutely, in small quantities; *(al por menor)* retail.

di·mi·nu·ti·vo, –va adj. & m. diminutive.

di·mi·nu·to, –ta adj. diminutive, little.

di·mi·sión f. resignation (from office).

di·mi·sio·na·rio, –ria adj. resigning II. m.f. resigner.

di·mi·ten·te I. adj. resigning II. m.f. resigner.

di·mi·tir intr. & tr. to resign, relinquish.

di·mos see **dar.**

din m. [contr. of **dinero**] COLL. bread, dough ♦ **el d. y el don** money and rank.

di·na f. PHYS. dyne.

Di·na·mar·ca f. Denmark.

di·na·mar·qués, –que·sa I. adj. Danish II. m.f. *(habitante)* Dane —m. *(idioma)* Danish.

di·ná·mi·ca I. f. PHYS. dynamics; FIG. *(impulso)* dynamics <*d. social* social dynamics> ♦ **d. de gases** gas dynamics II. see **dinámico, –ca.**

di·ná·mi·co, –ca I. adj. dynamic. II. f. see **dinámica.**

di·na·mis·mo m. dynamism.

di·na·mi·ta f. dynamite.

di·na·mi·tar tr. to dynamite, blast.

di·na·mi·te·ro, –ra m.f. dynamiter.

di·na·mo or **di·na·mo** f. dynamo.

di·na·mo·e·léc·tri·co, –ca adj. dynamoelectric.

di·na·mo·mé·tri·co, –ca adj. dynamometric, dynamometrical.

di·nas·tí·a f. dynasty.

di·ne·ra·da f. or **di·ne·ral** m. fortune, enormous sum of money <*gastar un d.* to spend a fortune>.

di·ne·ro m. money <*ganan mucho d.* they earn a lot of money>; *(caudal)* wealth, fortune ♦ **d. al contado** or **al contante** ready cash • **d. de curso legal** legal tender • **d. en caja** cash on hand • **d. rentado** or **prestado** loan, borrowed money • **d. suelto** loose change • **podrido en d.** AMER. filthy rich.

di·no·sau·rio m. PALEON. dinosaur.

din·tel m. ARCHIT. lintel.

dio see **dar.**

dio·ce·sa·no, –na adj. & m. diocesan.

dió·ce·sis f. RELIG. diocese.

dio·do m. ELEC. diode.

Dios m. God ♦ **a la buena de D.** COLL. haphazardly • **como D. manda** as it should be, properly • **de D.** COLL. abundantly • **¡D. bendito!** or **¡Bendito D.!** oh God! • **D. dirá** God will decide • **D. mediante** God willing • **¡D. mío!** my God!, oh my! • **D. sabe** goodness only knows, God only knows • **gracias a D.** thank heavens, thank God • **por D.** for God's sake • **por la gracia de D.** by or for the grace of God • **¡válgame D.!** goodness gracious! • **¡vaya con D.!** good-by • **¡venga D. y véalo!** as God is my witness!

dios m. god <*los dioses griegos* the Greek gods>.

dio·sa f. goddess.

di·plo·ma m. diploma, certificate.

di·plo·ma·cia f. POL. diplomacy; FIG., COLL. *(tacto)* diplomacy, tact; *(carera diplomática)* diplomatic service.

di·plo·ma·do, –da I. past part. see **diplomar** II. adj. *(educado)* qualified, trained; *(que tiene diploma)* having a diploma or academic degree III. m.f. *(persona educada)* qualified or trained person; *(graduado)* graduate.

di·plo·mar tr. to graduate, grant a diploma to —reflex. to graduate, earn a diploma.

di·plo·má·ti·ca I. f. *(paleografía)* diplomatics (study of documents); *(diplomacia)* diplomacy II. adj. see **diplomático, –ca.**

di·plo·má·ti·co, –ca I. adj. POL. diplomatic; FIG., COLL.

(astuto) diplomatic, tactful II. m.f. diplomat —f. see **diplomática.**

dip·so·ma·no, –na or **dip·so·ma·ní·a·co, –ca** adj. & m.f. MED. dipsomaniac, alcoholic.

dip·ton·go m. GRAM. diphthong.

di·pu·ta·ción f. *(delegación)* delegation, deputation; *(conjunto)* delegation, committee; *(cargo)* post (of congressman, Member of Parliament, member of Spanish Cortes); *(duración)* term (as member of a delegation); AMER. *(ayuntamiento)* town hall.

di·pu·ta·do, –da I. past part. see **diputar** II. m.f. *(representante)* delegate, representative; *(en Gran Bretaña)* member of Parliament; *(en los Estados Unidos)* Congressman ♦ **d. a Cortes** member of the Spanish Parliament or the Cortes.

di·pu·tar tr. *(elegir)* to appoint, deputize (as one's representative); *(delegar)* to delegate, empower; *(reputar)* to deem, consider.

di·que m. *(malecón)* dike, sea wall; *(para carenar)* dry dock; FIG. *(restricción)* check, restriction; GEOL. dike, outcrop ♦ **dar d.** ARG., COLL. to deceive • **d. de carena** or **seco** dry dock • **d. de contención** dam • **d. flotante** floating dock • **d. de marea** wet dock • **d. de retardo** HYDRAUL. current retard • **entrar en d.** to dock • **poner un d. a** FIG. to check, restrict.

di·rá, di·ría see **decir².**

di·rec·ción f. *(acción de dirigir)* direction, management; *(sentido)* direction, way; *(rumbo)* direction, course; *(enseñanza)* guidance, direction; *(tendencia)* tendency, trend; *(junta)* board of directors, executive board; *(cargo de director)* directorship, managership; *(oficina)* director's or manager's office; *(ministerio)* office, department <*D. de Bienestar Público* Office of Public Welfare>; *(señas)* address <*d. del remitente* return address>; AUTO., TECH. steering (mechanism); GEOL. strike ♦ **con** or **en d. a** in the direction of, towards • **d. de tiro** MARIT., MIL. fire control • **d. general** headquarters, head office • **d. prohibida** no entry • **en d. a** in the direction of, towards • **llevar la d.** to direct.

di·rec·ti·vo, –va I. adj. directing, managing II. m.f. director, board member —f. *(orden)* directive, instruction; *(junta)* board of directors.

di·rec·to, –ta I. adj. *(derecho)* straight; *(sin intermediario)* direct; direct, through <*tren d.* direct train>; GRAM. direct <*complemento d.* direct object> ♦ **en d.** TELEC. live <*transmitir en d.* to broadcast live> II. m. SPORT. straight punch —f. AUTO. high gear <*poner la d.* to go into high gear>.

di·rec·tor, –to·ra I. adj. *(que dirige)* directing, managing; master <*esquema d.* master plan>; GEOM. director; TECH. controlling, steering II. m.f. *(gerente)* director, manager; *(de escuela)* principal, headmaster; MUS. conductor —f. *(gerente)* directress; *(de escuela)* principal, headmistress ♦ **d. de cine** film or movie director • **d. de escena** or **escénico** THEAT. stage manager • **d. de funeraria** funeral director, mortician • **d. de orquesta** conductor • **d. gerente** managing director • **d. visitante** MUS. guest conductor.

di·rec·to·rio, –ria I. adj. directory, directive II. m. *(instrucción)* manual, directory; *(junta)* directorate, governing body; AMER. telephone directory.

di·rec·triz [pl. **-tri·ces**] GEOM. directrix.

di·ri·gen·te I. adj. directing, leading II. m.f. *(jefe)* leader; *(director)* manager.

di·ri·gi·ble I. adj. AER. dirigible; MARIT. navigable II. m. dirigible.

di·ri·gir §32 tr. *(enderezar)* to direct <*d. la mirada hacia la pantalla* to direct one's eye to the screen>; *(administrar)* to manage, run <*d. una empresa* to run a company>; *(una carta)* to address; *(guiar)* to guide, advise; *(dedicar)* to dedicate <*d. los estudios al descubrimiento de la verdad* to dedicate one's studies to the discovery of truth>; AUTO. to drive, steer; AVIA., MARIT. to pilot, steer; MUS. to conduct; CINEM., THEAT. to direct —reflex. *(encaminarse)* to go, make one's way; *(hablar)* to address, speak.

di·ri·mir tr. *(anular)* to annul, dissolve; *(resolver)* to resolve, settle (problem, dispute).

dis·can·tar tr. *(cantar)* to sing, chant; FIG. *(recitar)* to recite; *(componer)* to compose (verses); *(glosar)* to comment, discourse (at great length); *(echar contrapunto)* to descant, sing in counterpoint.

dis·can·te m. *(tiple)* small guitar; *(concierto)* musical concert (of string instruments); PERU folly, craziness.

dis·cer·ni·ble adj. discernible.

dis·cer·ni·mien·to m. *(percepción)* discernment, perception; *(juicio)* judgment, discernment; LAW *(designación)* appointment.

dis·cer·nir §25 tr. *(distinguir)* to discern, distinguish; LAW *(designar)* to appoint.

dis·ci·pli·na f. *(subordinación)* discipline; *(asignatura)* subject, discipline; *(doctrina)* doctrine; *(azote)* whip.

dis·ci·pli·na·do, –da I. past part. see **disciplinar** II. adj. *(ordenado)* disciplined; FIG. *(matizado)* variegated <*clavel d.* variegated carnation>.

dis·ci·pli·nar tr. *(imponer disciplina)* to discipline; *(enseñar)* to teach, instruct; *(azotar)* to whip, scourge; FIG. *(dominar)* to dominate, control <*d. la ira* to control one's anger> —reflex. to discipline oneself.

dis·ci·pli·na·rio, –ria adj. disciplinary.

dis·cí·pu·lo, –la m.f. *(adherente)* disciple, follower; *(alumno)* student, pupil.

dis·co m. *(plato)* disk, disc; *(para escuchar)* record <*poner un d.* to play a record>; *(para el tránsito)* traffic signal; FIG., COLL. *(cosa pesada)* broken record; SPORT. discus; ANAT., ASTRON., BOT. disk, disc; COMPUT. diskette; TECH. disk, plate; TELEC. telephone dial ♦ **d. cromático** OPT. color disk • **d. de señales** RAIL. semaphore, signal • **d. flexible** COMPUT. floppy disk • **d. intervertebral** ANAT. spinal disk • **d. motor** AUTO. driving disk • **d. volador** flying saucer • **saltarse un d. rojo** to run a red light • **soltar un d.** FIG., COLL. to repeat a familiar tale.

dis·co·grá·fi·co, –ca adj. pertaining to records or recordings.

dís·co·lo, –la adj. wayward, intractable.

dis·con·for·me adj. disagreeing, differing.

dis·con·for·mi·dad f. *(diferencia)* difference, divergence; *(desacuerdo)* disagreement, difference.

dis·con·ti·nuar §67 tr. to discontinue, interrupt.

dis·con·ti·nui·dad f. discontinuity.

dis·con·ti·nuo, –nua adj. discontinuous.

dis·con·ve·nien·cia f. incongruity.

dis·con·ve·nir §76 intr. *(estar en desacuerdo)* to disagree, differ (in opinion); *(no concordar)* not to match.

dis·cor·dan·cia f. discordance, disagreement.

dis·cor·dan·te adj. discordant, disagreeing.

dis·cor·dar §19 intr. *(no convenir)* to differ, disagree; MUS. to be out of tune or dissonant.

dis·cor·de adj. *(desconveniente)* disagreeing, discordant; MUS. discordant, dissonant.

dis·cor·dia f. discord, disagreement.

dis·co·te·ca f. *(colección)* record library or collection; *(salón de baile)* discotheque.

dis·cre·ción f. *(prudencia)* discretion, tact; *(astucia)* wisdom, shrewdness ♦ **a d.** at one's discretion.

dis·cre·cio·nal adj. discretionary, optional.

dis·cre·pan·cia f. *(diferencia)* discrepancy, divergence; *(desacuerdo)* disagreement, dissent.

dis·cre·pan·te adj. *(diferente)* divergent, differing; *(disidente)* dissenting.

dis·cre·par intr. to differ, disagree.

dis·cre·ta·men·te adv. discreetly, prudently.

dis·cre·te·ar intr. to act witty.

dis·cre·te·o m. witty behavior.

dis·cre·to, –ta I. adj. *(prudente)* prudent, circumspect; *(ingenioso)* witty, clever; *(poco llamativo)* discreet, subdued; FIG. *(moderado)* discreet, tactful; reasonable, average <*de inteligencia d.* of reasonable intelligence>; MATH., MED., PHYS. discrete ♦ **a lo d.** *(a la discreción de uno)* at one's discretion; *(discretamente)* discreetly II. m.f. *(persona prudente)* discreet person; RELIG. superior's advisor.

dis·cri·mi·na·ción f. discrimination.

dis·cri·mi·nan·te m. MATH. discriminant.

dis·cri·mi·nar tr. *(distinguir)* to discriminate, distinguish; *(perjudicar)* to discriminate against.

dis·cri·mi·na·to·rio, –ria adj. discriminatory.

dis·cuer·de, discuerdo see **discordar**.

dis·cul·pa f. *(por una ofensa)* apology; *(excusa)* excuse ♦

dar disculpas to make excuses • **pedir disculpas** to ask someone's pardon, apologize.

dis·cul·par tr. to excuse, pardon —reflex. to apologize ♦ **d. con alguien** to apologize to someone • **d. de** or **por algo** to apologize for something.

dis·cu·rrir intr. *(andar)* to roam, wander; *(reflexionar)* to reflect, ponder; *(hablar)* to speak, discourse; *(fluir)* to flow, run; *(el tiempo)* to pass ♦ **d. poco** to do or produce little, be inactive —tr. to invent, think up.

dis·cur·sar or **dis·cur·se·ar** intr. to discourse or lecture on <*d. sobre la política* to lecture on politics>.

dis·cur·sis·ta m.f. glib talker.

dis·cur·si·vo, –va adj. *(dado a discurrir)* discursive; *(meditativo)* meditative, reflective.

dis·cur·so m. *(conferencia)* speech, discourse; *(tratado)* discourse, treatise; *(facultad)* reasoning, ratiocination; *(transcurso)* passage, course <*en el d. del tiempo* with the passage of time>; GRAM. speech <*las partes del d.* the parts of speech> ♦ **pronunciar** or **dictar un d.** to make or deliver a speech.

dis·cu·sión f. *(debate)* discussion; *(disputa)* dispute, argument ♦ **en d.** under discussion.

dis·cu·ti·ble adj. *(contestable)* debatable, disputable; *(dudoso)* doubtful, questionable.

dis·cu·ti·dor, –do·ra I. adj. argumentative II. m.f. arguer.

dis·cu·tir tr. *(debatir)* to discuss, debate; *(disputar)* to argue about or over; *(cuestionar)* to question, contest —intr. *(debatir)* to discuss, talk about; *(disputar)* to argue.

di·se·car §70 tr. *(dividir en partes)* to dissect; *(conservar)* to stuff; FIG. *(analizar)* to dissect, analyze.

di·sec·ción f. dissection.

di·se·mi·na·ción f. dissemination, spreading.

di·se·mi·nar tr. to disseminate, spread —reflex. to become disseminated, spread.

di·sen·sión f. dissension, strife.

di·sen·te·rí·a f. MED. dysentery.

di·sen·ti·mien·to m. dissent, disagreement.

di·sen·tir §65 intr. to dissent, differ <*disentimos en eso* we differ on that>.

di·se·ñar tr. *(crear)* to design; *(dibujar)* to draw, sketch; *(bosquejar)* to outline.

di·se·ño m. *(plan)* design; *(dibujo)* drawing, sketch; *(bosquejo)* outline.

di·se·qué, diseque see **disecar**.

di·ser·ta·ción f. dissertation, discourse.

di·ser·ta·dor, –do·ra adj. fond of making speeches.

di·ser·tan·te I. adj. dissertating II. m.f. dissertator, lecturer.

di·ser·tar intr. to discourse, expound ♦ **d. sobre** or **acerca de** to discourse upon, expound on.

dis·for·me adj. *(deformado)* deformed; *(sin forma)* shapeless; *(feo)* ugly, hideous; *(enorme)* huge, enormous <*un error d.* a huge error>.

dis·fraz m. [pl. **-fra·ces**] *(estado)* disguise; *(traje)* disguise, costume; *(máscara)* mask; FIG. *(pretexto)* pretext, excuse; *(disimulo)* dissimulation, dissembling; MIL. camouflage ♦ **sin disfraz** plainly.

dis·fra·zar §04 tr. *(encubrir)* to disguise; *(enmascarar)* to mask, cloak; *(disimular)* to dissimulate, dissemble; MIL. to camouflage —reflex. to disguise oneself.

dis·fru·tar tr. to enjoy, have the benefit of <*disfruta una renta de su finca* he enjoys an income from his property>; *(aprovechar)* to make the most of <*d. una buena oportunidad* to make the most of a good opportunity> —intr. to enjoy <*he disfrutado mucho en este curso* I've enjoyed this course very much> ♦ **d. de** or **con** *(gozar de)* to enjoy; *(aprovechar)* to enjoy, have the benefit of.

dis·fru·te m. *(gozo)* enjoyment; *(provecho)* benefit; *(uso)* use; *(posesión)* possession.

dis·gre·ga·ción f. disintegration, breaking up.

dis·gre·gar §47 tr. & reflex. to disintegrate, break up.

dis·gus·ta·do, –da I. past part. see **disgustar** II. adj. *(enojado)* annoyed, displeased; *(inquieto)* worried, anxious; MEX. finicky.

dis·gus·tar tr. to annoy, displease —reflex. *(desagradarse)* to be annoyed or displeased; *(desazonarse)* to fall out <*disgustarse con alguien* to fall out with someone> ♦ **dis-**

gustarse de algo to get annoyed at *or* fed up with something.

dis·gus·to m. *(desagrado)* annoyance, displeasure; *(contienda)* quarrel, disagreement; *(inquietud)* worry, anxiety ♦ **a d.** unwillingly.

di·si·den·cia f. dissidence, disagreement.

di·si·den·te I. adj. dissenting, dissident II. m.f. dissenter, dissident.

di·si·dir intr. to dissent.

di·sien·ta, disiento see **disentir.**

di·sí·mil adj. dissimilar, unlike.

di·si·mi·lar tr. to dissimilate.

di·si·mi·li·tud f. dissimilarity, unlikeness.

di·si·mu·la·ble adj. excusable, pardonable.

di·si·mu·la·ción f. *(simulación)* dissimulation, dissembling; *(encubrimiento)* concealment, hiding; *(tolerancia)* toleration, tolerance.

di·si·mu·la·do, –da I. past. part. see **disimular** II. adj. *(simulado)* dissimulating, dissembling; *(encubierto)* concealed, hidden II. m.f. dissimulator, dissembler ♦ **hacerse el d.** to act dumb, feign ignorance.

di·si·mu·la·dor, –do·ra I. adj. dissimulating, dissembling II. m.f. dissimulator, dissembler.

di·si·mu·lar tr. *(simular)* to dissimulate, dissemble; *(encubrir)* to conceal, hide; *(fingir)* to feign, pretend <*d. ignorancia* to feign ignorance>; *(disfrazar)* to disguise, cloak; *(tolerar)* to tolerate, overlook <*d. las culpas de un amigo* to overlook the faults of a friend>; *(perdonar)* to pardon, excuse —intr. to dissimulate, dissemble.

di·si·mu·lo m. *(simulación)* dissimulation, dissembling; *(encubrimiento)* concealment, hiding; *(fingimiento)* feigning, pretending; *(tolerancia)* tolerance, toleration ♦ **con d.** furtively.

di·sin·tie·ra, disintió see **disentir.**

di·si·pa·ción f. *(evaporación)* dissipation; *(dispersión)* dispersion, scattering; *(derroche)* squandering, wasting; *(libertinaje)* dissipation, dissolution.

di·si·pa·do, –da I. past. part. see **disipar** II. adj. *(evaporado)* dissipated; *(libertino)* dissolute; *(derrochador)* squandering, wasteful II. m.f. *(libertino)* dissolute person; *(derrochador)* squanderer, wasteful person.

di·si·pa·dor, –do·ra I. adj. wasteful, extravagant II. m.f. spendthrift.

di·si·par tr. *(evaporar)* to dissipate, cause to disappear; *(dispersar)* to disperse, scatter; *(derrochar)* to squander, waste; *(una duda)* to dispel (a doubt) —reflex. *(desaparecer)* to disappear, vanish; *(dispersarse)* to disperse, scatter; *(derrocharse)* to be squandered *or* wasted.

dis·lo·ca·ción f. MED. dislocation; FIG. *(desmembramiento)* overturning, unseating; FIG. *(dispersión)* breakup, scattering; GEOL. fault, slip.

dis·lo·car §70 tr. MED. to dislocate; FIG. *(desmembrar)* to overturn, unseat; FIG. *(dispersar)* to break up —reflex. MED. to dislocate; FIG. *(dispersarse)* to break up.

dis·mi·nu·ción f. *(reducción)* diminution, decrease, reduction; ARCHIT. diminution, taper; VET. hoof disease ♦ **ir en d.** to diminish, be on the decrease.

dis·mi·nuir §18 tr., intr., & reflex. to diminish, decrease.

di·so·cia·ble adj. dissociable, separable.

di·so·cia·ción f. dissociation, separation.

di·so·ciar tr. to dissociate, separate —reflex. to dissociate *or* separate oneself.

di·so·lu·ble adj. dissoluble.

di·so·lu·ción f. *(dispersión)* dissolution; FIG. *(libertinaje)* dissoluteness, dissipation; *(ruptura)* breakup <*la d. de la familia* the breakup of the family>; AUTO. rubber solution; COM. liquidation; CHEM. solution.

di·so·lu·ti·vo, –va adj. solvent.

di·so·lu·to, –ta I. adj. dissolute, licentious II. m.f. dissolute *or* licentious person.

di·sol·ven·te I. adj. *(que disuelve)* dissolvent, solvent; FIG. *(corruptivo)* corrupting II. m. dissolvent, solvent.

di·sol·ver §78 tr. *(diluir)* to dissolve; *(dispersar)* to break up; *(anular)* to annul <*d. un matrimonio* to annul a marriage>; *(resolver)* to resolve; COM. to liquidate —reflex. *(diluirse)* to dissolve; *(dispersarse)* to break up; COM. to liquidate, go into liquidation.

di·so·nan·cia f. *or* **di·són** m. MUS. dissonance.

di·so·nan·te adj. dissonant, discordant.

di·so·nar §19 intr. MUS. to be dissonant, be out of tune; *(faltar armonía)* to lack harmony; FIG. *(no estar de acuerdo)* to disagree ♦ **d. con** to clash with, be out of keeping with.

dis·par adj. *(desigual)* uneven, unequal; *(diferente)* different, unlike.

dis·pa·ra·de·ro m. trigger ♦ **poner a uno en el d.** FIG., COLL. to push someone too far.

dis·pa·ra·dor, –do·ra m.f. *(persona)* shooter, firer —m. *(de una arma)* trigger; PHOTOG. shutter release; *(de un reloj)* escapement; MARIT. anchor tripper; MEX. spendthrift.

dis·pa·rar tr. ARM. to fire, shoot; *(echar)* to throw, hurl; SPORT. to shoot —intr. ARM. to fire, shoot; FIG. *(disparatar)* to act foolishly; AMER. to run *or* dart off, flee; MEX. to be a spendthrift —reflex. ARM. to go off; *(irse corriendo)* to rush *or* dash off; *(un caballo)* to bolt (a horse); FIG. *(enfurecerse)* to lose one's patience, become furious.

dis·pa·ra·ta·do, –da I. past part. see **disparatar** II. adj. *(absurdo)* absurd, nonsensical; COLL. *(excesivo)* excessive, enormous.

dis·pa·ra·tar intr. *(decir disparates)* to talk nonsense; *(hacer disparates)* to act foolishly *or* absurdly.

dis·pa·ra·te m. *(desatino)* absurd *or* nonsensical thing; COLL. *(cantidad)* enormous amount ♦ **disparates** nonsense.

dis·pa·ra·te·ro, –ra AMER. I. adj. absurd, foolish II. m.f. person who says absurd *or* foolish things.

dis·pa·re·jo, –ja adj. *(distinto)* different, disparate; *(desigual)* uneven, enequal.

dis·pa·ri·dad f. disparity, dissimilarity.

dis·pa·ro m. *(echada)* throwing, hurling; ARM. *(acción de disparar)* firing, shooting; *(tiro)* shot; FIG. *(disparate)* foolishness, nonsense; MECH. release, trip; SPORT. shot ♦ **d. de aviso** *or* **de advertencia** warning shot • **d. de ensayo** trial shot.

dis·pen·dio m. waste, extravagance.

dis·pen·dio·so, –sa adj. costly, extravagant.

dis·pen·sa f. *(dispensación)* dispensation, exemption; *(certificado)* certificate of dispensation.

dis·pen·sa·ble adj. pardonable, excusable.

dis·pen·sa·ción f. *(acción de dispensar)* dispensation, exemption; *(certificado)* certificate of dispensation.

dis·pen·sa·dor, –do·ra I. adj. dispensing II. m.f. dispenser.

dis·pen·sar tr. *(dar)* to dispense, give out; *(conferir)* to confer, bestow; *(eximir)* to exempt, excuse; *(perdonar)* to forgive, excuse —reflex. to excuse oneself (from doing something).

dis·pen·sa·rio m. dispensary, clinic ♦ **d. de alimentos** soup kitchen.

dis·pep·sia f. MED. dyspepsia, indigestion.

dis·per·sa·dor, –do·ra I. adj. dispersive II. m.f. disperser.

dis·per·sar tr. *(esparcir)* to disperse, scatter; FIG. *(poner en fuga)* to disperse, break up <*d. una manifestación* to break up a demonstration>; *(dividir)* to divide <*d. sus esfuerzos* to divide one's efforts>; MIL. to break up, rout —reflex. *(esparcirse)* to disperse, scatter; MIL. to deploy, spread out.

dis·per·sión f. *(separación)* dispersion, dispersal; PHYS. dispersion ♦ **d. magnético** PHYS. magnetic dispersion • **d. nuclear** PHYS. nuclear scattering • **d. retrógrada** PHYS. backscattering.

dis·per·so, –sa I. adj. dispersed, scattered II. m. MIL., ARCH. unattached soldier.

dis·per·sor, –so·ra adj. dispersive.

dis·pla·cer §17 tr. to displease.

dis·pli·cen·cia f. *(indiferencia)* indifference, coolness; *(desaliento)* lack of enthusiasm.

dis·pli·cen·te adj. *(desagradable)* disagreeable, unpleasant; *(indiferente)* indifferent, cool.

dis·po·ne·dor, –do·ra I. adj. arranging, organizing II. m.f. arranger, organizer.

dis·po·ner §54 tr. *(colocar)* to arrange, place; *(preparar)* to prepare, get ready; *(ordenar)* to order; LAW to provide, stipulate; MIL. to form *or* line up ♦ **d. la mesa** to set the table —intr. **d. de** *(poseer)* to have, have at one's disposal <*no dispongo de tiempo libre* I don't have any free time>;

(utilizar) to make use of; to dispose of *<quería d. de la empresa* she wanted to dispose of the business> —reflex. *(prepararse)* to prepare, get ready *<se dispone a marchar* he is getting ready to go>; *(prepararse a morir)* to prepare to die, make one's will; MIL. to form *or* line up.

dis·po·ni·bi·li·dad f. availability ♦ **disponibilidades** resources, means.

dis·po·ni·ble adj. *(utilizable)* available, on hand; MIL. ready for action.

dis·po·si·ción f. disposal *<a la d. de uno* at one's disposal>; *(distribución)* arrangement, disposition; FIG. *(temperamento)* disposition, temperament; *(inclinación)* disposition, inclination; *(aptitud)* aptitude, talent *<mostrar gran d. para las ciencias* to show great aptitude for sciences>; ARCHIT. layout; LAW *(precepto)* provision; *(orden)* decreee, order *<d. ministerial* ministerial decree>; MIL. formation; RHET. organization ♦ **disposiciones** preparations, measures • **estar en** *or* **hallarse en d. de** to be ready to, be in a position to • **última d.** last will and testament.

dis·po·si·ti·vo, –va I. adj. dispositive II. m. device, mechanism *<d. de arranque* starting mechanism>.

dis·pro·sio m. CHEM. dysprosium.

dis·pues·to, –ta I. past part. see **disponer** II. adj. *(apuesto)* good-looking, elegant; *(hábil)* clever, capable *<es un muchacho muy d.* he's a very capable young man> ♦ **bien d.** *(bien intencionado)* well-disposed; *(saludable)* well, not sick • **estar d. a** to be prepared *or* willing to • **estar poco d. a** to be reluctant (to) • **mal d.** *(mal intencionado)* ill-disposed; *(enfermo)* ill, indisposed.

dis·pu·sie·ra, dispuso see **disponer**.

dis·pu·ta f. *(altercado)* dispute, argument; *(discusión)* discussion, debate ♦ **sin d.** indisputably, undoubtedly.

dis·pu·ta·ble adj. disputable, debatable.

dis·pu·ta·dor, –do·ra I. adj. disputatious, argumentative II. m.f. disputant, arguer.

dis·pu·tar tr. *(contender)* to dispute, challenge; *(discutir)* to debate, discuss; *(competir)* to compete *or* contend for —intr. to argue, quarrel —reflex. *(discutirse)* to be debated *or* discussed; *(competir)* to contend *or* compete for.

dis·qui·si·ción f. disquisition ♦ **disquisiciones** side comments, digressions.

dis·tan·cia f. *(intervalo)* distance; FIG. *(diferencia)* difference *<hay gran d. entre lo que prometió y lo que hizo* there is a great difference between what he promised and what he did> ♦ **a (la) d.** at *or* from a distance • **a larga d.** long-distance • **d. focal** *or* **de enfoque** PHOTOG. focal length *or* distance • **d. del suelo** clearance, height off the ground • **acortar las distancias** to meet halfway • **mantenerse a d.** to keep one's distance.

dis·tan·ciar tr. *(separar)* to separate, space out; *(alejar)* to put *or* place at a distance; *(dejar atrás)* to outdistance —reflex. *(separarse)* to become separated; *(enajenarse)* to become estranged, drift away.

dis·tan·te adj. *(lejos)* distant, far; *(remoto)* far-off, remote.

dis·tar intr. to be a certain distance from *<dista cincuenta kilómetros de aquí* it's fifty kilometers from here>; FIG. *(diferenciarse)* to be different *or* far from *<dista mucho de ser posible* it's far from possible>.

dis·te see **dar**.

dis·ten·der §50 tr. *(torcer)* to distend, stretch; *(aflojar)* to loosen, slacken —intr. *(torcerse)* to become distended *or* stretched; *(aflojarse)* to become loose *or* slack.

dis·ten·sión f. *(torcedura)* distension, stretching; *(aflojamiento)* slackening.

dis·tin·ción f. *(diferencia)* distinction; *(honor)* honor, privilege; *(elegancia)* refinement, elegance; *(trato)* respect, deference; *(claridad)* clarity, clearness ♦ **a d. de** as distinct from, in contrast to • **sin d.** indiscriminately, without distinction.

dis·tin·gui·do, –da I. past part. see **distinguir** II. adj. *(notable)* distinguished, illustrious; *(refinado)* distinguished, refined.

dis·tin·guir §26 tr. *(diferenciar)* to distinguish, tell *or* see the difference between; *(caracterizar)* to distinguish, characterize; *(discernir)* to distinguish, discern; *(divisar)* make out, see in the distance; *(preferir)* to favor, show preference for; *(honrar)* to pay tribute to, honor —intr. to

distinguish, discriminate —reflex. *(ser distinto)* to be distinguished, differ; *(sobresalir)* to distinguish oneself, excel.

dis·tin·ta·men·te adv. distinctly, clearly.

dis·tin·ti·vo, –va I. adj. distinctive, distinguishing II. m. *(insignia)* badge, emblem; FIG. distinguishing mark *or* characteristic.

dis·tin·to, –ta adj. *(diferente)* distinct, different; *(claro)* distinct, clear.

dis·tor·sión f. *(deformación)* distortion; MED. twist, sprain.

dis·tor·sio·nar tr. *(deformar)* to distort; MED. to twist, sprain.

dis·trac·ción f. *(acción)* distraction, distracting; *(diversión)* amusement, entertainment; *(descuido)* distraction, absent-mindedness; *(libertinaje)* dissoluteness, libertinage; *(error)* slip, oversight; FIN. embezzlement, misappropriation ♦ **por d.** through an oversight.

dis·tra·er §72 tr. *(alejar)* to distract, divert (attention); *(descaminar)* to lead astray; *(entretener)* to amuse, entertain; FIN. to embezzle, misappropriate; MED. to draw away (fluids); MIL. divert —intr. *(entretener)* to be relaxing *or* entertaining *<la lectura distrae mucho* reading is very relaxing> —reflex. *(entretenerse)* to amuse *or* entertain oneself; *(descuidarse)* to be distracted, let one's mind wander.

dis·tra·í·do, –da I. past part. see **distraer** II. adj. *(divertido)* amusing, entertaining; *(desatento)* inattentive, absent-minded; *(libertino)* dissolute, libertine; CHILE, MEX. ragged, dirty III. m.f. *(persona desatenta)* inattentive *or* absent-minded person; *(libertino)* dissolute person, libertine ♦ **hacerse el d.** to pretend not to notice.

dis·trai·ga, distraigo see **distraer**.

dis·trai·mien·to m. var. of **distracción**.

dis·tra·je·ra, distrajo see **distraer**.

dis·tri·bu·ción f. *(reparto)* distribution; *(entrega)* delivery; *(red)* supply system; ARCHIT. layout, floor plan; MECH. timing gears; MEX., AUTO. distributor.

dis·tri·bui·dor, –do·ra I. adj. distributing, distributive; II. m.f. distributor; COM. dealer, agent —m. AUTO., TELEC. distributor ♦ **d. automático** vending machine.

dis·tri·buir §18 tr. *(repartir)* to distribute; *(entregar)* to deliver; *(abastecer)* to supply; ARCHIT. to lay out, plan; *(un golpe)* to deal (out) —reflex. to be distributed.

dis·tri·bu·ti·vo, –va adj. distributive.

dis·tri·to m. district, zone.

dis·tro·fí·a f. MED. dystrophy.

dis·tur·bar tr. to disturb.

dis·tur·bio m. disturbance, trouble.

di·sua·dir tr. to dissuade, discourage.

di·sua·sión f. dissuasion ♦ **fuerza** *or* **poder de d.** MIL. deterrent force.

di·sua·si·vo, –va adj. dissuasive.

di·suel·to, –ta past part. see **disolver**.

di·suel·va, disuelvo see **disolver**.

di·sue·ne, disueno see **disonar**.

dis·yun·ción f. disjunction.

dis·yun·ti·va f. disjunctive, alternative.

dis·yun·ti·vo, –va I. adj. disjunctive II. f. see **disyuntiva**.

dis·yun·tor m. ELEC. circuit breaker.

di·ta f. COM. *(garantía)* guarantee, surety; AMER. debt; SP. credit ♦ **vender a d.** to sell on credit.

diu·ré·ti·co, –ca MED. adj. & m. diuretic.

diur·no I. adj. diurnal, day II. m. RELIG. diurnal.

di·va·ga·ción f. digression, rambling ♦ **divagaciones** wanderings.

di·va·ga·dor, –do·ra I. adj. wandering II. m.f. wanderer.

di·va·gar §47 intr. *(errar)* to digress, ramble; *(vagar)* to wander, roam.

di·ván m. *(sofá)* divan, couch; *(consejo turco)* divan (Turkish council); POET. divan.

di·ver·gen·cia f. divergence.

di·ver·gen·te adj. divergent, diverging.

di·ver·gir §32 intr. to diverge, differ.

di·ver·si·dad f. *(variedad)* diversity, variety; *(abundancia)* abundance.

di·ver·si·fi·ca·ción f. diversification.

di·ver·si·fi·car §70 tr. to diversify.

di·ver·sión f. *(entretenimiento)* diversion, amusement; MIL. diversion.

di·ver·so, –sa adj. diverse, different ♦ **diversos** several, various.
di·ver·ti·do, –da I. past part. see **divertir** II. adj. *(entretenido)* amusing, entertaining; *(cómico)* funny, comical; AMER. drunk.
di·ver·tir §65 tr. *(entretener)* to amuse, entertain; *(distraer)* to divert, distract; MED. to draw away (a fluid); MIL. to divert —reflex. *(entretenerse)* to amuse *or* entertain oneself, have a good time; *(distraerse)* to be diverted *or* distracted.
di·vi·den·do m. COM., MATH. dividend.
di·vi·dir tr. MATH. to divide; *(separar)* to divide, separate; *(repartir)* to divide (up), split (up); *(desunir)* to divide, cause a split between —reflex. to divide; *(separarse)* to separate.
di·vier·ta, divierto see **divertir**.
di·vie·so m. MED. boil, furuncle.
di·vi·na·men·te adv. *(con divinidad)* divinely; FIG. *(admirablemente)* admirably, wonderfully.
di·vi·na·to·rio, –ria adj. divinatory.
di·vi·ni·dad f. *(calidad)* divinity; *(del paganismo)* divinity, deity; *(persona o cosa bella)* beautiful person *or* thing.
di·vi·ni·zar §04 tr. *(hacer divino)* to deify; FIG. *(exaltar)* to exalt, glorify.
di·vi·no, –na adj. RELIG. divine, godlike; FIG. *(excelente)* divine, marvelous.
di·vir·tie·ra, divirtió see **divertir**.
di·vi·sa f. *(insignia)* emblem, insignia; COM. currency; HER. motto ♦ **divisas** COM. foreign currency *or* exchange.
di·vi·sar tr. to discern, make out.
di·vi·si·bi·li·dad f. divisibility.
di·vi·si·ble adj. divisible.
di·vi·sión f. *(partición)* dividing, division; *(parte)* division, section; FIG. *(desunión)* division, discord; GRAM. dash, hyphen; MARIT., MATH., MIL. division; RHET. distribution of points of discussion ♦ **d. acorazada** *or* **blindada** MIL. armored division • **d. continental** GEOL. continental divide.
di·vi·sio·nal adj. divisional.
di·vi·sio·nis·mo m. PAINT. divisionism.
di·vi·sor, –so·ra I. adj. dividing; MATH. factorial II. m. divider; MATH. divisor, denominator ♦ **d. común** MATH. common denominator.
di·vi·so·rio, –ria I. adj. *(que divide)* dividing, separating; *(divisivo)* divisive II. m. PRINT. copy holder —f. dividing line; GEOL. divide ♦ **d. de aguas** watershed • **d. continental** continental divide.
di·vo, –va I. adj. POET. divine II. m.f. leading (operatic) singer —f. diva.
di·vor·cia·do, –da I. past part. see **divorciar** II. adj. divorced III. m. divorcé —f. divorcée.
di·vor·ciar tr. *(cónyuges)* to divorce; FIG. *(separar)* to separate, divide —reflex. to divorce, get divorced.
di·vor·cio m. *(de cónyuges)* divorce; FIG. *(separación)* separation, division; COL. women's jail.
di·vul·ga·ción f. *(revelación)* disclosure, revelation; *(propagación)* spreading, circulation; *(popularización)* popularization.
di·vul·ga·dor, –do·ra I. adj. divulging, revealing II. m.f. divulger, revealer.
di·vul·gar §47 tr. *(revelar)* to divulge, disclose; *(propagar)* to spread, circulate; *(popularizar)* to popularize —reflex. to be divulged *or* disclosed.
Dji·bou·ti Djibouti.
do m. MUS. do, C; FIG., COLL. *(mayor esfuerzo)* supreme effort (made to achieve something) ♦ **dar el d. de pecho** FIG., COLL. to knock oneself out • **d. de pecho** MUS. high C.
do·bla·di·llar tr. SEW. to hem, cuff.
do·bla·di·llo m. SEW. *(de vestido)* hem; *(de pantalón)* cuff; *(hilo)* strong knitting yarn.
do·bla·do, –da I. past part. see **doblar** II. adj. *(regordete)* stocky, thickset; *(desigual)* rough, uneven <*terreno d.* rough terrain>; *(plegado)* bent, doubled; FIG. *(disimulado)* false, deceitful.
do·bla·dor m. GUAT. corn husk (for rolling tobacco).
do·bla·du·ra f. fold, crease.
do·bla·je m. CINEM. dubbing.
do·bla·mien·to m. bending, folding.

do·blar tr. to double <*Enrique dobló la apuesta* Henry doubled the bet>; *(plegar)* to double, fold; *(encorvar)* to bend; to turn <*d. la esquina* to turn the corner>; MARIT. to round <*d. el cabo* to round the cape>; CINEM. to dub; CUBA to embarrass; MEX. to shoot down ♦ **d. el brazo a** FIG. to twist someone's arm —intr. *(tocar)* to toll, ring; THEAT. to double, play two roles; COM. to postpone —reflex. *(plegarse)* to fold; to bend *or* double over <*doblarse de dolor* to double over in pain>; *(ceder)* to yield, give in; CUBA to be embarrassed.
do·ble I. adj. double <*d. sentido* double meaning>; *(duplo)* double, twofold; *(grueso)* thick, heavy; FIG. *(disimulado)* insincere; CHEM. binary II. m. double; *(pliegue)* fold, crease; *(toque)* death knell; *(copia)* copy, reproduction; COM. margin —m.f. *(actor)* double, stand-in ♦ **al d.** doubly III. adv. doubly.
do·ble·ga·ble *or* **do·ble·ga·di·zo, –za** adj. pliant, flexible.
do·ble·gar §47 tr. *(doblar)* to fold, crease; *(curvar)* to bend, flex; *(blandir)* to brandish; *(hacer ceder)* to force someone to yield *or* give in —reflex. *(doblarse)* to fold, crease; *(encorvarse)* to bend, flex; *(ceder)* to yield, give in.
do·ble·men·te adv. *(dos veces)* doubly; FIG. *(maliciosamente)* falsely, deceitfully.
do·ble·te I. adj. medium thick II. m. JEWEL., PHILOL. doublet.
do·blez m.f. [pl. **–ble·ces**] *(disimulo)* duplicity, two-facedness —m. *(pliegue)* fold, crease; *(dobladillo)* hem.
do·blón m. doubloon (ancient coin) ♦ **d. de a ocho** piece of eight • **escupir doblones** COLL. to parade one's wealth.
do·ce I. adj. twelve <*hay d. huevos en una docena* there are twelve eggs in a dozen>; *(duodécimo)* twelfth ♦ **las d.** twelve o'clock II. m. twelve.
do·ce·na f. dozen ♦ **a** *or* **por docenas** by the dozens • **d. de fraile** baker's dozen.
do·cen·cia f. teaching, instruction.
do·cen·te adj. *(que enseña)* teaching <*personal d.* teaching staff>; *(relativo a la enseñanza)* of education, educational <*institución d.* educational institution>.
dó·cil adj. *(obediente)* docile, obedient; *(dúctil)* ductile.
do·ci·li·dad f. *(obediencia)* docility, obedience; *(ductilidad)* ductility.
do·ci·li·tar tr. to make docile *or* obedient.
dó·cil·men·te adv. docilely, obediently.
doc·ta·men·te adv. learnedly, eruditely.
doc·to, –ta I. adj. learned, erudite II. m.f. learned person, erudite.
doc·tor, –to·ra m.f. doctor <*d. en matemáticas* doctor of mathematics>; *(maestro)* teacher, professor; COLL. *(médico)* doctor, physician —f. COLL. *(mujer del médico)* doctor's wife; *(mujer pedante)* pedantic woman, bluestocking.
doc·to·ra·do m. doctorate.
doc·to·ral adj. *(relativo al doctor)* doctoral; COLL. *(pedantesco)* pedantic, pompous.
doc·to·rar tr. to confer a doctor's degree on —reflex. to receive a doctor's degree.
doc·tri·na f. *(enseñanza)* doctrine, teaching; *(conocimiento)* knowledge, learning; RELIG. catechism, religious instruction.
doc·tri·nal RELIG. I. adj. doctrinal II. m. catechism.
doc·tri·nar tr. to teach, instruct.
doc·tri·na·rio, –ria adj. & m.f. doctrinaire.
doc·tri·ne·ro m. RELIG. catechist; AMER. parish priest.
doc·tri·no m. orphan ♦ **parecer un d.** to be timid.
do·cu·men·ta·ción f. documentation.
do·cu·men·ta·do, –da I. past part. see **documentar** II. adj. *(acompañado de documentos)* documented, with the necessary papers; *(informado)* well-informed, well-read.
do·cu·men·tal I. adj. documentary II. m. CINEM. documentary (film).
do·cu·men·tar tr. *(probar)* to document, prove with documents; *(educar)* to educate, inform about —reflex. to research, investigate.
do·cu·men·to m. *(escrito)* document, paper; *(prueba)* proof, evidence ♦ **documentos** papers • **d. a la vista** COM., FIN. sight bill, draft • **d. comercial** COM., FIN. commercial paper, corporate note • **d. de identidad** proof of identity, identity papers • **d. justificativo** COM., FIN. voucher, certificate.

do·de·ca·e·dro m. GEOM. dodecahedron.
do·de·cá·go·no, –na GEOM. **I.** adj. dodecagonal **II.** m. dodecagon.
do·gal m. *(de caballo)* halter; *(para ahorcar)* noose, hangman's rope ♦ **estar con el d. al cuello** *or* **a la garganta** FIG., COLL. to be in a tight spot, have a noose around one's neck.
dog·ma m. dogma.
dog·má·ti·co, –ca **I.** adj. dogmatic **II.** m.f. *(persona)* dogmatist —f. dogmatics.
dog·ma·tis·mo m. dogmatism.
dog·ma·ti·za·dor, –ra **I.** adj. dogmatic **II.** m.f. dogmatist.
dog·ma·ti·zan·te adj. dogmatic.
dog·ma·ti·zar §04 tr. & intr. to dogmatize.
do·go, –ga m.f. bulldog.
do·la·dor m. *(de piedra)* stonecutter; *(de madera)* woodcutter.
do·la·du·ra f. cutting, hewing (wood or stone).
dó·lar m. FIN. dollar.
do·len·cia f. illness, ailment.
do·ler §78 intr. to hurt, ache *<me duele el estómago* my stomach hurts>; *(disgustar)* to pain, distress *<me duele decirte que lo has perdido todo* it distresses me to tell you that you have lost everything> —reflex. *(arrepentirse)* to repent *<se dolió de sus pecados* he repented his sins>; *(sentir)* to regret < *se duele de la situación en que los encuentra* he regrets the situation in which he finds them>; *(compadecerse)* to sympathize, be sorry *<me duelo de las desgracias de mis vecinos* I am sorry about the misfortunes of my neighbors>; *(quejarse)* to complain *<dolerse con los amigos* to complain to friends>.
do·lien·te **I.** adj. *(enfermo)* ill, ailing; *(adolorido)* sore, aching; *(apenado)* mournful, bereaved **II.** m.f. *(enfermo)* sick person; *(pariente del difunto)* mourner.
do·lo m. *(fraude)* fraud, deceit; LAW fraud.
do·lor m. pain, ache *<tengo d. de estómago* I have a stomachache>; *(congoja)* sorrow, distress; *(arrepentimiento)* repentance, regret ♦ **d. de cabeza** headache • **d. de corazón** FIG. repentance, regret • **d. de muela** *or* **de diente** toothache • **d. de oído** earache • **d. de partera** *or* **de viuda** FIG. sharp shooting pain • **dolores del parto** labor pains • **d. sordo** FIG. chronic dull pain • **tener d.** to be in pain.
do·lo·ri·do, –da adj. sore, aching *<tengo la pierna d.* I have a sore leg>; *(desconsolado)* pained, distressed.
do·lo·ro·so, –sa adj. *(lastimoso)* pitiful, distressing; *(sensible)* painful *<la herida es muy d.* the wound is very painful>.
do·lo·so, –sa adj. fraudulent, deceitful.
do·ma f. *(de un caballo)* taming, breaking (a horse); FIG. *(las pasiones)* taming, controlling (the passions).
do·ma·ble adj. tamable, conquerable.
do·ma·dor, –do·ra m.f. *(de fieras)* tamer, trainer; *(de caballos)* horsebreaker, broncobuster.
do·ma·du·ra f. *(de fieras)* taming, training; *(de caballos)* breaking in.
do·mar tr. *(fieras)* to tame, domesticate; *(un caballo)* to break (in) (a horse); *(adiestrar)* to train; FIG. *(vencer)* to subdue, master.
do·me·ñar tr. to subdue, bring under control.
do·mes·ti·ca·ble adj. which can be domesticated.
do·mes·ti·ca·ción f. domestication.
do·mes·ti·car §70 tr. *(fieras)* to tame, domesticate; *(un caballo)* to break (in) (a horse); *(adiestrar)* to train; FIG. *(vencer)* to subdue, conquer; *(educar)* to educate, refine.
do·mes·ti·ci·dad f. domesticity.
do·més·ti·co, –ca **I.** adj. *(relativo a la casa)* domestic, pertaining to the home; *(un animal)* domestic, domesticated **II.** m.f. *(criado)* domestic, household servant; SPORT. domestic in bicycle racing.
do·mes·ti·qué, domestique see **domesticar.**
do·mi·ci·liar tr. *(dar domicilio)* to domicile, establish in a residence; MEX. to (put an) address (on a letter) —reflex. to settle, take up residence.
do·mi·ci·lia·rio, –ria **I.** adj. domiciliary **II.** m.f. resident, inhabitant.
do·mi·ci·lio m. *(morada)* domicile, residence; LAW *(morada e intereses)* legal residence, domicile ♦ **adquirir** *or* **elegir d.** to settle, take up residence • **a d.** at home • **d. particular**

private residence • **d. social** LAW, COM. head *or* home office, corporate headquarters • **sin d. fijo** LAW with no fixed abode *or* residence.
do·mi·na·ción f. *(acción de dominar)* domination; *(señorío)* rule, dominion; MIL. commanding position, high ground ♦ **dominaciones** RELIG. dominations, dominions.
do·mi·na·dor, –do·ra **I.** adj. *(que domina)* dominating; *(avasallador)* domineering, overbearing **II.** m.f. *(soberano)* dominator; *(avasallador)* domineering *or* overbearing person.
do·mi·nan·te **I.** adj. *(prevaleciente)* dominant, prevalent; *(avasallador)* domineering, overbearing; FIG. *(característico)* dominant, characteristic; ASTROL. dominant **II.** f. BIOL., MUS. dominant.
do·mi·nar tr. *(mandar)* to dominate, rule; *(someter)* to subdue; *(sujetar)* to control, master *<d. sus deseos* to control one's desires>; *(sobresalir)* to dominate *<la torre domina el pueblo* the tower dominates the town>; FIG. *(saber a fondo)* to know well, master —intr. to dominate, stand out —reflex. to control *or* restrain oneself.
do·min·ga·da f. Sunday party *or* festival.
do·min·go m. Sunday ♦ **d. de Adviento** Advent Sunday ♦ **d. de Pentecostés** Pentecost, Whitsunday • **d. de Ramos** Palm Sunday ♦ **d. de Resurrección** Easter Sunday • **guardar el d.** to keep the Sabbath • **hacer d.** to take a day off • **salir con un** *or* **su d. siete** to make an uncalled-for remark.
do·min·gue·ro, –ra **I.** adj. pertaining to Sunday *<ropa d.* Sunday clothes> **II.** m. AUTO. Sunday driver.
Do·mi·ni·ca f. Dominica.
do·mi·ni·cal adj. dominical (pertaining to Sunday).
do·mi·ni·ca·no, –na adj. & m.f. Dominican.
do·mi·ni·co, –ca RELIG. adj. & m.f. Dominican.
do·mi·nio m. *(poder)* dominion, power; *(superioridad)* dominance, supremacy *<d. de los mares* naval supremacy>; *(maestría)* mastery, command *<tiene un buen d. del italiano* she has a good command of Italian>; *(tierra)* domain, dominion *<el D. del Canadá* the Dominion of Canada>; LAW ownership ♦ **d. de sí mismo** self-control • **d. directo** legal ownership • **d. eminente** eminent domain • **d. público** public domain • **ser del d. público** to be in the public domain; *(ser de conocimiento común)* to be common knowledge.
do·mi·nó m. *(juego)* dominoes; *(disfraz)* domino (hooded cape).
do·mo m. ARCHIT. dome, cupola.
dom·pe·dro m. BOT. morning glory; COLL. *(orinal)* urinal.
don¹ m. *(regalo)* gift, present; *(gracia)* gift, talent, knack ♦ **d. de acierto** knack for doing the right thing • **d. de errar** knack for doing the wrong thing • **d. de gentes** winning way, personal charm • **d. de hablar** *or* **de la palabra** eloquence, way with words • **d. de lenguas** gift for languages • **d. de mando** leadership ability.
don² §G47 m. Don (title of respect used before a man's first name) ♦ **d. cómodo** sybarite • **d. Diego** BOT. four-o'clock • **D. Juan** Don Juan, ladykiller.
do·na·ción f. *(a una institución)* donation, contribution; *(regalo)* gift, present; *(testamento)* bequest.
do·na·do, –da **I.** past part. see **donar II.** m. RELIG. lay brother —f. RELIG. lay sister.
do·na·dor, –do·ra m.f. donor.
do·nai·re m. *(gracia)* grace, gentility; *(porte)* graceful posture, poise; *(agudeza)* witticism, quip; *(humor en el hablar)* wit, clever humor ♦ **hacer d. de** to laugh wittily at.
do·nai·ro·so, –sa adj. graceful, elegant.
do·nan·te **I.** adj. donating **II.** m.f. donor.
do·nar tr. to donate, give.
do·na·ta·rio, –ria m.f. recipient of a donation.
do·na·ti·vo m. donation, gift.
don·cel **I.** m. *(joven noble)* young nobleman *or* squire; *(paje)* page of honor; *(virgen)* virgin male **II.** adj. mellow, mild.
don·ce·lla f. *(virgen)* virgin, maiden; *(criada)* maid, housemaid; *(chica)* girl, lass; ICHTH. blenny; COL., VEN., MED. whitlow ♦ **La D. de Orléans** HIST. Maid of Orleans, Joan of Arc.
don·ce·llez f. virginity.
don·ce·llu·ca f. COLL. old maid, spinster.

don·de adv. where <*éste es el lugar d. pasamos el verano* this is the place where we spent the summer>; which <*allí está la casa en d. nací* there is the house in which I was born> ♦ **d. no** otherwise • **por d.** whereby **II.** prep. S. AMER. to *or* at the house of <*estuve d. mi amigo* I was at the house of my friend>.

dón·de adv. where <*¿d. encontraste el libro?* where did you find the book?> ♦ **¿a d.?** where • **¿de d.?** from where, where . . . from <*¿de d. viene?* where does she come from?> • **¿por d.?** why <*¿por d. tengo que creerlo?* why should I believe it?>.

don·de·quie·ra adv. anywhere ♦ **d. que** wherever • **por d.** everywhere, all over the place.

don·die·go *or* **don·die·go de no·che** m. BOT. marvel of Peru, four-o'clock ♦ **d. de día** BOT. morning glory.

don·gón m. BOT. dungen (tree producing wood for ship-building).

do·no·si·dad f. (*gracia*) wit, humor; (*elegancia*) elegance, poise.

do·no·so, –sa adj. COLL. (*gracioso*) witty, funny; (*elegante*) elegant, poised.

do·no·su·ra f. (*gracia*) grace, gentility; (*porte*) graceful posture, poise; (*agudeza*) witticism, quip; (*humor en el hablar*) wit, clever humor.

do·ña §G47 f. (*título*) Mrs., Madame; ECUAD. Indian woman ♦ **la D.** AMER., COLL. lady of the house.

do·quier *or* **do·quie·ra** adv. var. of **dondequiera**.

do·ra·do, –da I. past part. see **dorar II.** adj. (*color*) golden; (*cubierto de oro*) gilt, gilded; FIG. (*esplendoroso*) golden <*la juventud d.* the golden years of youth>; CUL. golden-brown, lightly fried *or* toasted; ZOOL. bay **III.** m. ICHTH. dorado; (*doradura*) gilding; (*adorno*) gilt, gilding —f. see **dorada.**

do·ra·dor, –do·ra m.f. gilder.

do·ra·du·ra f. gilding.

do·rar tr. (*cubrir con oro*) to gild, cover with gold; JEWEL., METAL. to gold-plate; CUL. to fry *or* toast golden brown, brown lightly; FIG. (*paliar*) to palliate, minimize ♦ **d. la píldora** FIG., COLL. to make something easier to swallow —reflex. FIG. to take on a golden tint, become golden *or* gilded.

dó·ri·co, –ca adj. ARCHIT., HIST. Doric <*orden d.* Doric order>.

dor·mi·da f. (*de animales*) lair, den; (*de aves*) roost; COLL. (*sueño*) a night's sleep; AMER. alcove.

dor·mi·de·ra f. BOT. opium poppy; CUBA, C. AMER., BOT. sensitive plant ♦ **dormideras** COLL. sleepiness • **tener buenas dormideras** COLL. to have no trouble sleeping.

dor·mi·de·ro, –ra I. adj. soporific, sleep-inducing **II.** m. place where cattle are penned for the night —f. see **dormidera.**

dor·mi·lón, –lo·na I. adj. sleepyheaded, sleepy **II.** m.f. COLL. (*persona*) sleepyhead —m. AMER., ORNITH. goatsucker, nightjar —f. (*poltrona*) easy chair, comfortable armchair (for napping); VEN. nightgown ♦ **dormilonas** pearl *or* diamond earrings.

dor·mir §27 intr. (*reposar*) to sleep; (*pernoctar*) to spend the night <*dormimos al raso* we spent the night in the open air>; FIG. (*sosegarse*) to grow calm, subside <*sus pasiones dormían* his passions subsided> ♦ **d. como una piedra** *or* **como un lirón** FIG. to sleep like a log • **d. de un tirón** *or* **a pierna suelta** FIG. to sleep soundly • **d. sobre algo** FIG. to sleep on something, consider something seriously —reflex. (*adormecerse*) to fall asleep; FIG. (*tornarse insensible*) to fall asleep, go numb <*se me durmió el brazo* my arm fell asleep>; MARIT. to heel, list ♦ **dormirse con el dinero** COLL. to delay payment • **dormirse en los laureles** FIG. to rest on one's laurels —tr. to put to sleep <*la madre durmió al niño* the mother put the child to sleep>; C. AMER. to seduce; ARG. to knock out ♦ **d. la mona** COLL. to sleep it off • **d. la siesta** to take a nap.

dor·mi·tar intr. to doze, snooze.

dor·mi·to·rio m. (*alcoba*) bedroom; (*residencia*) dormitory.

dor·sal I. ANAT., PHONET. adj. dorsal. **II.** m. SPORT. number worn by a player *or* athlete.

dor·so m. ANAT. back; FIG. (*revés*) back, reverse side ♦ **al d. de** on the back of.

dos I. adj. two <*tengo d. hijos* I have two children>; (se-

gundo) second ♦ **las d.** two o'clock **II.** m. (*número*) two; (*naipe*) deuce ♦ **cada d. por tres** COLL. frequently • **de d. en d.** two by two, by twos • **en un d. por tres** COLL. in a jiffy • **los** (*or* **las**) **d.** both.

dos·cien·tos, –tas I. adj. two hundred <*d. kilómetros* two hundred kilometers>; (*ducentésimo*) two hundredth **II.** m. two hundred.

do·sel m. (*pabellón*) canopy; (*baldaquín*) dais; (*antepuerta*) portière.

do·se·le·ra f. valance (drapery around a canopy).

do·si·fi·ca·ción f. MED., PHARM. dosage.

do·si·fi·car §70 tr. MED., PHARM. to dose; FIG. (*repartir*) to measure out, proportion.

do·sis f. [pl. **-sis**] MED., PHARM. dose; FIG. (*cantidad*) portion, quantity ♦ **d. de recuerdo** MED., PHARM. booster • **a** *or* **en pequeñas d.** in small doses • **tener una buena d. de** to have one's share *or* fill of.

do·ta·ción f. (*fundación*) endowment, bequest; (*dote*) dowry; MARIT. (*tripulación*) crew, complement; (*personal*) staff, personnel.

do·tar tr. (*proveer*) to endow, provide; (*bodas*) to give as a dowry, give a dowry; (*viuda*) to dower; (*testamento*) to bequeath, leave; MARIT. to man (a ship), COM. to staff, man; (*subvencionar*) to endow with money, fund ♦ **d. de** (*proveer*) to furnish *or* provide with; (*talentos*) to endow with.

do·te m.f. (*bodas*) dowry, marriage portion; (*viuda*) dower —m. (*naipes*) player's score *or* number of points —f. (*talentos*) talent, gift, endowment; (*habilidad*) ability ♦ **dotes de mando** leadership ability, qualities of a leader.

do·ve·la f. ARCHIT. voussoir (wedge-shaped stone).

doy see **dar.**

do·za·vo, –va adj. & m.f. twelfth ♦ **en d.** PRINT. duodecimo, twelvemo (page size).

drac·ma m.f. FIN. drachma; (*peso*) dram (weight).

dra·co·nia·no, –na adj. draconian, harsh.

dra·ga f. MARIT. (*máquina*) dredge, dredging machine; (*barco*) dredge, dredger ♦ **d. cavadora** MARIT. dragline excavator • **d. de cucharón de mordazas** *or* **de balde** MARIT. clamshell dredge.

dra·ga·do m. (*excavación*) dredging; (*búsqueda*) dragging.

dra·gar §47 tr. MARIT. (*limpiar*) to dredge; (*buscar*) to drag (a body of water).

dra·go·man m. dragoman, interpreter.

dra·gón m. (*monstruo*) dragon; BOT. snapdragon; METAL. feed opening, mouth (of a furnace); MIL. dragoon; VET. type of leucoma (on pupil of an animal's eye); ZOOL. flying dragon.

dra·go·na f. MIL. epaulette; MEX. man's cape.

dra·go·ne·ar intr. AMER. (*impersonar*) to pass oneself off as, impersonate; (*manipular*) to manipulate; (*jactarse*) to boast.

dra·gué, drague see **dragar.**

dra·ma m. THEAT. drama, play; FIG. (*catástrofe*) catastrophe, dramatic event.

dra·má·ti·ca f. (*arte dramático*) dramatic art; (*dramaturgia*) dramaturgy, playwriting.

dra·má·ti·co, –ca I. adj. THEAT. dramatic; FIG. (*emocionante*) dramatic, moving **II.** m.f. THEAT. (*dramaturgo*) dramatist, playwright —m. actor —f. actress.

dra·ma·tis·mo m. drama, dramatism.

dra·ma·ti·zar §04 tr. to dramatize.

dra·ma·tur·gia f. THEAT. dramaturgy, dramatic art.

dra·ma·tur·go, –ga m.f. THEAT. playwright, dramaturge.

drás·ti·co, –ca adj. drastic.

dre·na·je m. drainage ♦ **tubo de d.** drain, drainpipe.

dre·nar tr. to drain.

Dres·de Dresden.

dril m. TEX. drill, linen twill; ZOOL. mandrill.

dro·ga f. MED., PHARM. drug, medicine; FIG. (*embuste*) fib, lie; (*trampa*) trick, deception; (*molestia*) nuisance, bother; AMER. bad debt ♦ **d. dura** MED., PHARM. hard drug, narcotic • **mandar a uno a la d.** COLL. to tell someone to go jump in the lake.

dro·ga·dic·ción f. MED., PHARM. drug addiction.

dro·ga·dic·to, –ta MED., PHARM. **I.** adj. pertaining to drug addiction **II.** m.f. drug addict.

dro·ga·do, –da MED., PHARM. **I.** past part. see **drogar**

II. adj. drugged, doped **III.** m.f. *(drogadicto)* drug addict —m. *(administración de drogas)* drugging, doping.
dro·gar §47 tr. MED., PHARM. to drug, dope.
dro·gue·rí·a f. *(farmacia)* drugstore, pharmacy; *(comercio)* drug trade; *(fabricación)* drug manufacturing *or* processing.
dro·gue·ro, –ra m.f. *(comerciante)* druggist, pharmacist; COLL. *(drogadicto)* drug addict; MEX., PERU *(estafador)* swindler; *(tramposo)* cheater.
dro·guis·ta m. *(comerciante)* druggist, pharmacist; MEX., PERU *(estafador)* swindler; *(tramposo)* cheater.
dro·me·da·rio m. ZOOL. dromedary.
dru·i·da m. RELIG. Druid.
dual GRAM. adj. & m. dual ♦ **número d.** dual number.
dua·li·dad f. *(calidad)* duality; MIN. dimorphism; CHILE tie, draw.
dua·lis·mo m. PHILOS., POL. dualism.
du·bi·ta·ción f. *(duda)* doubt, uncertainty; RHET. rhetorical question.
du·bi·ta·ti·vo, –va adj. *(que expresa duda)* doubtful, uncertain; GRAM. dubitative.
Du·blín Dublin.
du·ca·do m. *(territorio)* duchy, dukedom; *(dignidad)* dukedom; NUMIS. ducat, gold coin.
du·cal adj. ducal <*palacio d.* ducal palace>.
dúc·til adj. METAL. ductile; FIG. *(flexible)* pliant, docile.
duc·ti·li·dad f. ductility.
du·cha **I.** f. *(baño)* shower; MED. douche, irrigation; TEX. *(lista)* stripe (in cloth) ♦ **tomar** *or* **darse una d.** to take a shower, shower **II.** adj. see **ducho, –cha.**
du·char tr. *(dar una ducha)* to shower, give a shower to; MED. to douche —reflex. *(darse una ducha)* to shower, take a shower; MED. to douche, take a shower.
du·cho, –cha **I.** adj. skillful, expert **II.** f. see **ducha.**
du·da f. doubt, uncertainty ♦ **en d.** in question *or* doubt • **no cabe** *or* **no hay d.** (there is) no doubt • **poner en d.** to question, doubt • **sacar de dudas** to dispel *or* remove doubt from • **sin d.** *or* **sin d. alguna** doubtlessly, without (a *or* any) doubt • **sin la menor d.** without the slightest doubt • **sin sombra de d.** beyond the shadow of a doubt.
du·da·ble adj. doubtful, dubious.
du·dar tr. *(no creer)* to doubt, question —intr. *(no creer)* to doubt; *(vacilar)* to vacillate, waver, hesitate.
du·do·so, –sa adj. *(incierto)* doubtful, uncertain; *(sospechoso)* questionable, dubious; *(vacilante)* hesitant, wavering.
due·la, duelo see **doler.**
due·lis·ta m. dueler, duelist.
due·lo¹ m. duel ♦ **batirse a** *or* **en d.** to fight a duel.
due·lo² m. *(dolor)* grief, sorrow; *(luto)* mourning, bereavement; *(los afligidos)* mourners, mourning party ♦ **duelos** troubles, hardship • **estar de d.** to be in mourning • **sin d.** unrestrainedly.
duen·de m. *(fantasma)* goblin, ghost; SP., FIG. enchanting quality, magic; TEX. cloth of gold *or* silver threads.
duen·do, –da adj. domesticated, tame.
due·ña f. *(propietaria)* owner; *(ama)* lady of the house, mistress; *(señora)* lady, matron.
due·ño m. *(propietario)* owner; *(amo)* master (of a house); *(de un negocio)* owner, proprietor; *(de una casa alquilada)* owner, landlord ♦ **hacerse uno d. de una cosa** *(tomar posesión de)* to take possession of something; *(aprender)* to master something • **ser d. de** to own, be the owner of • **ser d. de sí mismo** to have self-control • **ser (muy) d. de hacer una cosa** to be free to do something.
duer·ma, duermo see **dormir.**
Due·ro m. GEOG. Douro (River).
due·tis·ta m. MUS. duettist.
due·to m. MUS. duet, duo.
du·la f. AGR. plot watered by a common ditch.
dul·ce **I.** adj. *(azucarado)* sweet; *(dúctil)* soft, ductile; fresh <*agua d.* fresh water>; FIG. *(dócil)* sweet, gentle; *(agradable)* soft, pleasant <*voz d.* pleasant voice> **II.** m. *(confite)* candy, sweet; *(golosinas)* sweets, sweet things; C. AMER. brown sugar ♦ **d. de arroz** rice pudding • **d. de fruta** candied fruit • **d. de leche** custard cream • **en d.** *(confitado)* candied; *(en almíbar)* in syrup **III.** adv. gently, softly.

dul·ce·dum·bre f. *(calidad de dulce)* sweetness; *(suavidad)* softness.
dul·ce·men·te adv. sweetly.
dul·ce·ra f. compote, candy dish.
dul·ce·rí·a f. candy store, confectioner's (shop).
dul·ce·ro, –ra **I.** adj. fond of sweets, sweet-toothed ♦ **ser dulcero** to have a sweet tooth **II.** m.f. confectioner —f. see **dulcera.**
dul·ci·fi·ca·ción f. *(acción de dulcificar)* sweetening; FIG. *(sosiego)* soothing.
dul·ci·fi·car §70 tr. *(endulzar)* to sweeten; FIG. *(mitigar)* to soften, soothe —reflex. to become softer *or* milder.
dul·ci·ne·a f. COLL. *(amada)* beloved; *(mujer ideal)* woman of one's dreams; FIG. *(quimera)* ideal, dream.
dul·cí·so·no, –na adj. POET. sweet-sounding.
dul·za·rrón, –rro·na *or* **dul·zón, –zo·na** adj. COLL. too sweet, cloying.
dul·zu·ra f. *(sabor)* sweetness; *(mansedumbre)* mildness; FIG. *(bondad)* gentleness, kindliness; *(afabilidad)* pleasantness, pleasing manner; *(caricia verbal)* endearment, sweet nothing.
du·na f. GEOL. dune.
Dun·ker·que Dunkirk.
dú·o m. MUS. duet, duo.
du·plex m. RAD. duplex telegraphy; *(piso)* duplex, split-level (apartment).
du·pli·ca·ción f. duplication, doubling.
du·pli·ca·do m. copy, duplicate ♦ **por d.** in duplicate.
du·pli·ca·dor, –do·ra **I.** adj. *(que copia)* duplicating, copying; *(que dobla)* doubling **II.** m.f. *(persona)* duplicator —m. PHOTOG. copier, copying machine ♦ **duplicador de voltaje** RAD. voltage doubler.
du·pli·car §70 tr. *(copiar)* to duplicate, copy; *(doblar)* to double, increase twofold; LAW *(contestar)* to rejoin, reply.
du·pli·ci·dad f. duplicity, falseness.
du·plo, –pla **I.** adj. MATH. double, twice **II.** m. double <*seis es el duplo de tres* six is the double of three>.
du·que m. duke ♦ **d. de alba** MARIT. clump of piles used for a mooring • **gran d.** ORNITH. grand duke (owl).
du·que·sa f. duchess.
du·ra·bi·li·dad f. durability, endurance.
du·ra·ble adj. durable, lasting.
du·ra·ción f. *(permanencia)* duration, continuance; *(período)* duration, length ♦ **de corta** *or* **poca d.** short, short-lived • **de larga d.** long, long-lasting; *(disco)* long-playing.
du·ra·de·ro, –ra adj. durable, lasting.
du·ra·men·te adv. *(con aplicación)* hard, earnestly; *(con severidad)* severely, harshly.
du·ran·te prep. during <*charlamos d. el viaje* we chatted during the trip>; for <*viajamos d. cuatro horas* we travelled for four hours>.
du·rar intr. *(continuar)* to last, endure; *(quedar)* to remain; *(ropa)* to last, wear (well).
du·raz·ne·ro m. BOT. peach tree.
du·raz·no m. BOT. peach (fruit and tree).
du·re·za f. *(solidez)* hardness; *(resistencia)* toughness; *(fuerza)* strength; *(dificultad)* difficulty; *(severidad)* severity, harshness; *(obstinación)* obstinacy, stubbornness; FIG. *(indiferencia)* indifference; MED. *(callosidad)* callosity, hard patch ♦ **d. de corazón** COLL. cold-heartedness.
dur·mien·te adj. *(que duerme)* asleep, sleeping; *(inactivo)* dormant, inactive ♦ **la Bella D.** LIT. Sleeping Beauty **II.** m.f. *(descansador)* sleeper; *(inactividad)* something *or* someone lying dormant —m. RAIL. sleeper, tie, crosstie ARCHIT., CARP. girder, rafter, crossbeam.
dur·mie·ra, –ra see **dormir.**
du·ro, –ra **I.** adj. *(sólido)* hard <*el vidrio no es tan d. como un diamante* glass is not as hard as a diamond>; *(penoso)* tough, hard <*los tiempos son duros* times are hard>; *(difícil)* hard, difficult <*es un trabajo d.* it is a difficult job>; *(de agua)* hard (said of water); FIG. *(fuerte)* tough, strong <*el campeón es muy d.* the champion is very tough>; *(resistente)* resistent, resilient <*soy d. al frío* I am resistent to the cold>; *(cruel)* callous, cruel; *(obstinado)* stubborn, obstinate; *(terco)* mean, stingy; *(áspero)* harsh <*ella tiene una voz d.* she has a harsh voice>; *(arts)* crude <*un estilo d.* a crude style>; MEX., URUG. drunk ♦ **a duras penas** with

difficulty • **d. de corazón** hardhearted • **d. de mollera** or **de cabeza** hardheaded • **d. de oído** hard of hearing • **más d. que una piedra** FIG. as hard as nails **II.** adv. hard *<trabajar d.* to work hard> **III.** m. SP. five-peseta coin.

E

e, E f. sixth letter of the Spanish alphabet.
e §G46 conj. [used instead of **y** before words beginning with *i* or *hi*] and *<madre e hija* mother and daughter>.
¡e·a! interj. come on!, come along!
e·ba·nis·ta m. CARP. cabinetmaker, woodworker.
e·ba·nis·te·rí·a f. CARP. *(arte)* cabinetmaking; *(muebles)* cabinetwork; *(taller)* cabinetmaker's workshop.
é·ba·no m. BOT. ebony (tree and wood).
e·brie·dad f. inebriation, intoxication.
e·brio, –bria I. adj. *(embriagado)* inebriated, intoxicated; FIG. *(ciego)* blind, beside oneself *<estar e. de ira* to be blind with anger> **II.** m.f. drunk, drunkard.
e·bu·lli·ción f. *(hervor)* boiling; FIG. *(efervescencia)* ebullience, effervescence; *(agitación pasajera)* outpouring, outburst ♦ **estar en e.** FIG. to be overflowing or bubbling over.
ec·ce·ho·mo or **ec·ce ho·mo** m. RELIG. Ecce Homo; FIG. *(persona)* pitiful wretch ♦ **estar hecho un e.** to be in a sorry state, cut a sorry figure.
e·cléc·ti·co, –ca adj. & m.f. eclectic.
E·cle·sias·tés m. BIBL. Ecclesiastes.
e·cle·siás·ti·co, –ca I. adj. ecclesiastical, ecclesiastic **II.** m. ecclesiastic, clergyman ♦ **Eclesiástico** BIBL. Ecclesiasticus.
e·clip·sar tr. ASTRON. to eclipse; FIG. *(oscurecer)* to overshadow, eclipse —reflex. ASTRON. to be eclipsed; FIG. *(desaparecer)* to disappear, vanish.
e·clip·se m. ASTRON. eclipse; FIG. *(desaparición)* downfall, eclipse ♦ **e. anular** annular eclipse • **e. lunar** or **de luna** lunar eclipse • **e. parcial** partial eclipse • **e. solar** or **de sol** solar eclipse • **e. total** total eclipse.
e·co m. *(sonido)* echo; MUS., POET. echo, repetition of a syllable or word; FIG. *(noticia)* news *<ecos de sociedad* society news>; echo, reflection *<el problema actual es un e. de los del pasado* the present problem is an echo of those of the past>; *(acogida)* response, reception ♦ **Eco** MYTH. Echo • **hacerse e.** to repeat, spread (a rumor, opinion) • **tener e.** to catch on, be popular.
e·co·lo·gí·a f. ecology.
e·co·ló·gi·co, –ca adj. ecological.
e·có·lo·go, –ga or **e·co·lo·gis·ta** m.f. ecologist.
e·co·no·ma·to m. LAW *(cargo administrativo)* trusteeship, guardianship; RELIG. *(oficio eclesiástico)* post of ecclesiastical administrator; COM. *(tienda)* commissary; *(tienda cooperativa)* co-op, cooperative.
e·co·no·mí·a f. economy *<la e. francesa* the French economy>; *(ciencia)* economics; *(parsimonia)* thrift, frugality; *(escacez)* scantiness, scarcity; *(miseria)* poverty, want; *(ahorro)* economy, saving; *(buena distribución)* good use ♦ **economías** savings • **e. dirigida** planned economy • **e. doméstica** home economics, household management • **e. política** political economy, economics • **hacer economías** to economize, save.
e·co·nó·mi·ca·men·te adv. *(con economía)* economically; *(sin mucho gasto)* cheaply, inexpensively.
e·co·nó·mi·co, –ca adj. *(monetario)* economic; *(ahorrador)* economical, money-saving; *(barato)* inexpensive, cheap.
e·co·no·mis·ta m.f. economist.
e·co·no·mi·zar §04 tr. *(ahorrar)* to save, economize on; *(reservar)* to reserve, hold in reserve.
e·có·no·mo I. adj. RELIG. acting, provisional **II.** m. RELIG. *(sacerdote)* acting or provisional priest; *(administrador)* ecclesiastical administrator; LAW *(guarda)* trustee, guardian.
e·co·sis·te·ma m. ECOL. ecosystem.
ec·to·plas·ma f. ectoplasm.
e·cua·ción f. equation ♦ **e. cuadrática** or **de segundo grado** MATH. quadratic equation • **e. de primer grado**

MATH. simple equation • **e. de tiempo** equation of time • **e. diferencial** MATH. differential equation • **e. lineal** MATH. linear equation • **e. personal** personal equation, personal margin of error • **e. química** chemical equation.
E·cua·dor m. Ecuador.
e·cua·dor m. ASTRON., GEOG., GEOM. equator ♦ **e. celestial** celestial equator • **e. magnético** magnetic equator, aclinic line • **pasar el e.** COLL. to cross the line, pass the halfway mark.
e·cuá·ni·me adj. *(equilibrado)* even-tempered, levelheaded; *(imparcial)* impartial, fair-minded.
e·cua·ni·mi·dad f. *(equilibrio)* equanimity, levelheadedness; *(imparcialidad)* impartiality, fair-mindedness.
e·cua·to·rial I. adj. equatorial **II.** m. equatorial telescope!
e·cua·to·ria·no, –na adj. & m.f. Ecuadorian.
e·cues·tre adj. equestrian.
e·cu·mé·ni·co, –ca adj. ecumenical, universal.
e·cu·me·nis·mo m. RELIG. ecumenism.
ec·ze·ma m. MED. eczema.
e·cha·can·tos m. [pl. **-tos**] COLL. good-for-nothing, worthless fellow.
e·cha·cuer·vos m. [pl. **-vos**] *(alcahuete)* pimp, procurer; *(embustero)* cheat, swindler.
e·cha·da f. *(lanzamiento)* throw, cast; *(espacio)* length *<ganó por dos echadas* he won by two lengths>; AMER. *(fanfarronada)* boast.
e·cha·de·ro m. place of rest, spot for lying down.
e·cha·di·zo, –za I. adj. *(atisbador)* spying, sent to spy; *(esparcido)* spread about secretly, circulated in a clandestine way; *(inútil)* useless, discarded; COLL. *(expósito)* abandoned **II.** m.f. *(espía)* spy; *(desperdicios)* refuse, waste; *(inclusero)* foundling.
e·cha·dor, –do·ra I. adj. *(que echa)* throwing; AMER. *(fanfarrón)* boastful, bragging **II.** m.f. thrower —m. *(mozo)* waiter who pours coffee and milk; AMER. *(fanfarrón)* braggart, boaster.
e·cha·mien·to m. *(lanzamiento)* throwing, casting; *(echada)* throw, pitch; *(evicción)* expulsion, ejection.
e·char tr. *(arrojar)* to throw, cast, toss *<Martín echó una piedra por la ventana* Martin threw a stone through the window>; *(expulsar)* to throw out, expel *<le echaron de la oficina* they threw him out of the office>; *(destituir)* to dismiss, fire; *(desechar)* to throw out or away; *(derramar)* to shed *<e. lágrimas* to shed tears>; *(emitir)* to emit, give off *<las flores echan un olor delicioso* the flowers give off a delightful fragrance>; *(verter)* to pour *<e. el vino* to pour the wine>; *(añadir)* to add, put in *<la cocinera echó sal a la sopa* the cook added salt to the soup>; BOT. to sprout, begin to grow *<la planta echó raíces* the plant began to grow roots>; *(salir)* begin to grow *<e. pelo* to begin to grow hair>; *(los dientes)* to cut *<la bebé echó los dientes* the baby cut her teeth>; *(tomar)* to take *<eché un trago* I took a gulp>; *(aplicar)* to put on, apply; *(imponer)* to impose, give *<me echaron una multa* they gave me a traffic ticket>; *(condenar)* to condemn, sentence *<e. a presidio* to sentence to imprisonment>; *(jugar)* to play *<eché un as* I played an ace>; *(repartir)* to deal *<eche usted las cartas* deal the cards>; *(apostar)* to wager, gamble *<mi tío echó cien dólares a la rifa* my uncle gambled a hundred dollars on the raffle>; *(cerrar)* to turn (a key), shoot (a bolt); *(hacer)* to do *<echaron cálculos* they did the calculations>; *(publicar)* to publish, issue *<la editorial echó una edición nueva* the publishing house issued a new edition>; *(representar)* to put on, present *<echan una comedia de Cervantes* they are presenting a play by Cervantes>; *(pronunciar)* to give, deliver *<e. un sermón* to deliver a sermon>; *(decir)* to utter, say *<e. la suerte* to tell one's fortune>; *(presentar)* to bring, present *<les echaré un referéndum* I will present a referendum to them>; *(conjeturar)* to attribute, guess to be *<¿qué edad le echas?* what age do you guess him to be?>; *(adquirir)* to develop, get *<su padre echó barriga* her father developed a paunch>; ZOOL. to mate, couple; ARG., P. RICO to urge on (animals) ♦ **e. abajo** or **en tierra** *(derribar)* to demolish, knock down; *(derrotar)* to overthrow • **e. al correo** or **al buzón** to mail, post • **e. al mar** to jettison • **e. al vuelo** AVIA. to take off; *(hacer público)* to make public • **e. a perder** *(arruinar)* to spoil, ruin; *(pervertir)* to corrupt;

(malograr) to waste • **e. a pique** MARIT. to scuttle, sink; FIG. *(arruinar)* to ruin, wreck • **e. a un lado** to push aside • **e. baladronadas** *or* **bravadas** to boast, brag • **e. de comer** • **e. de menos a** to miss *<echo de menos a mi ciudad natal* I miss the city of my birth>; *(descuidar)* to neglect *<me has echado de menos recientemente* you have neglected me lately> • **e. de ver** to notice, observe • **e. en cara** to flaunt, throw in one's face • **e. humo** *(fumar)* to smoke • **echarla de** to pose as, pretend to be • **echarlas** *or* **echarlos** CHILE to run away • **e. largo** to consider carefully • **e. mano a** to grab, get a hold of • **e. pareja** ZOOL. to mate • **e. por mayor** *or* **por arrobas** to exaggerate • **e. rayas** *or* **centellas** *or* **luces** FIG. to blow a fuse, blow one's stack • **e. suerte** to play the lottery • **e. suertes** to draw lots • **e. tierra a** FIG. to hush *or* cover up • **e. una mirada** to cast a glance, eye • **e. una siesta** to take a nap —intr. to grow, sprout ♦ **e. a** *(empezar)* to begin, start; *(romper)* to burst out *<echó a reír* he burst out laughing> • **e. por** *(seguir una carrera)* to choose, go into; *(ir)* to go *<e. por la derecha* to go to the right> —reflex. *(arrojarse)* to throw oneself; *(tenderse)* to lie down, stretch out; ORNITH. to brood; METEOROL. to fall, die down (wind); *(dedicarse)* to apply *or* dedicate oneself ♦ **echarse a** *(empezar)* to begin, start; *(romper)* to burst out • **echarse a cuenta** to take into account • **echarse adelante** to succeed, get ahead • **echarse a dormir** *(acostarse)* to go to bed; *(descuidar)* to let things slide • **echarse a la brava** to go berserk • **echarse a morir** FIG. to despair • **echarse a perder** *(arruinarse)* to spoil, go bad; *(decaer)* to go to the dogs, go astray • **echarse atrás** *(recostarse)* to lean back; *(desdecirse)* to retract, back out • **echarse de ver** to be obvious, be easy to see • **echárselas de** to pose as, pretend to be • **echarse sobre** *or* **encima** to rush at, fall upon.

e·char·pe m. stole, shawl.

e·dad f. *(años)* age *<la niña tiene diez años de e.* the girl is ten years of age>; *(período)* time *<la adolescencia es la e. que recuerdo con más nostalgia* adolescence is the time I remember most fondly>; *(época)* era, epoch *<la E. Moderna* the modern era> ♦ **e. avanzada** old age • **e. crítica** menopause, change of life • **E. de Oro** *or* **Dorada** Golden Age • **E. de Piedra** Stone Age • **e. del pavo** *or* AMER. **del chivateo** puberty • **E. Media** Middle Ages • **e. viril** prime of life (said of men) • **mayor de e.** of age • **menor de e.** underage • **¿qué e. tienes?** how old are you?

e·de·cán m. MIL. aide-de-camp; FIG. *(ayudante)* assistant, aide.

e·de·ma m. MED. edema.

e·dén m. BIBL. (Garden of) Eden, Paradise; FIG. paradise.

e·dé·ni·co, -ca adj. paradisiacal.

e·di·ción f. PRINT. *(publicación)* publication; *(conjunto de libros)* edition; JOURN. *(conjunto de periódicos)* edition; *(conjunto de revistas)* issue; ♦ **Ediciones** Press, Publications • **e. abreviada** abridged edition • **e. crítica** annotated *or* critical edition • **e. de bolsillo** *or* **en rústica** pocket *or* paperback edition • **e. escolar** school *or* student edition • **e. príncipe** *or* **princeps** first edition, editio princeps • **segunda e.** FIG., COLL. spitting image, carbon copy.

e·dic·to m. edict, proclamation ♦ **e. emplazatorio** LAW summons.

e·dí·cu·lo m. *(edificio)* small building; *(templete)* shrine.

e·di·fi·ca·ción f. *(construcción)* building, construction; FIG. *(mejoramiento)* edification, enlightenment.

e·di·fi·ca·dor, -do·ra I. adj. *(constructor)* construction, building; FIG. *(ejemplar)* edifying, enlightening II. m.f. *(constructor)* constructor, builder; *(ejemplar)* edifier, enlightener.

e·di·fi·can·te adj. edifying, enlightening.

e·di·fi·car §70 tr. *(construir)* to build, construct; FIG. *(establecer)* to establish, form *<e. una alianza nacional* to form a national alliance>; *(mejorar)* to edify, enlighten.

e·di·fi·cio m. *(construcción)* building, edifice; FIG. structure, fabric *<el e. social* the social structure>.

e·dil m. *(concejal)* alderman, councilor; HIST. aedile, Roman magistrate.

e·di·li·cio, -cia adj. civic, municipal.

E·dim·bur·go Edinburgh.

e·di·tar tr. to publish.

e·di·tor, -to·ra I. adj. publishing *<casa editora* publishing house> II. m.f. publisher.

e·di·to·rial I. adj. publishing II. m. *(artículo)* editorial —f. *(casa editora)* publishing house.

e·di·to·ria·lis·ta m.f. JOURN. editorial writer.

e·dre·dón m. eiderdown.

e·du·ca·ble adj. educable, teachable.

e·du·ca·ción f. *(enseñanza)* education, training; *(crianza)* upbringing, rearing; *(cortesía)* good manners *or* breeding ♦ **e. física** physical education • **e. nacional** public education • **mala e.** bad manners, impoliteness.

e·du·ca·cio·nal adj. educational.

e·du·ca·do, -da I. past part. see **educar** II. adj. *(enseñado)* educated, trained; *(cortés)* well-mannered, polite ♦ **bien e.** well-bred, well-mannered • **mal e.** ill-bred, bad-mannered.

e·du·ca·dor, -do·ra I. adj. educating, instructing II. m.f. educator, instructor.

e·du·car §70 tr. *(enseñar)* to educate, teach; *(criar)* to raise, bring up; FIG. *(desarrollar)* to develop, train *<e. el oído* to train one's ear>.

e·du·ca·ti·vo, -va adj. educational, educative.

e·dul·co·rar tr. PHARM. to edulcorate, sugar-coat.

e·fe f. ef (name of the letter f).

e·fe·bo m. youth, adolescent.

e·fec·tis·mo m. ARTS, LIT. striving for effect, sensationalism.

e·fec·ti·va·men·te adv. *(en realidad)* really, in fact; *(por supuesto)* indeed, certainly.

e·fec·ti·vi·dad f. *(adecuación)* effectiveness, effectuality; MIL. *(grado)* nominal rank.

e·fec·ti·vo, -va I. adj. *(eficaz)* effective; *(verdadero)* real, actual; *(permanente)* permanent, regular *<un empleo e.* a regular job> II. m. *(dinero)* (hard) cash; *(número total)* total number ♦ **en e.** in cash • **e. en caja** ACC. cash on hand • **hacer e.** to cash.

e·fec·to m. *(resultado)* effect, result *<el analfabetismo es un e. de la falta de escuelas* illiteracy is a result of the lack of schools>; *(fin)* end, purpose *<a este e.* to this end>; *(impresión)* impression, impact *<su aviso causó un gran e.* his announcement made a great impression>; *(rotación)* spin; COM. commercial paper ♦ **a efectos de** for the purpose of • **con** *or* **en e.** *(efectivamente)* in effect, in fact; *(en conclusión)* indeed, precisely • **dar e.** CINEM. to produce sound effects • **efectos** *(bienes)* effects, property; *(mercancía)* goods, merchandise; FIN. bills, securities • **efectos a pagar** bills payable • **efectos a recibir** bills receivable • **efectos de consumo** consumer goods • **efectos de resultado** *or* **de residuo** COMPUT. output • **efectos públicos** *or* **del estado** government securities • **efectos sonoros** *or* **de sonido** TELEC. sound effects • **e. útil** MECH. output • **hacer e.** *(dar resultado)* to have an effect; *(producir impresión)* to have an impact, make an impression • **llevar a** *or* **poner en e.** to put into effect, implement • **sentir e.** to feel the effect • **surtir e.** to have the desired effect, work • **tener e.** *(efectuarse)* to take effect; *(ocurrir)* to take place.

e·fec·tuar §67 tr. to effect, bring about, carry out —reflex. to be carried out *or* accomplished, take effect.

e·fe·mé·ri·des f.pl. ASTRON. ephemeris; *(calendario)* list *or* calendar of anniversary dates.

e·fer·ves·cen·cia f. CHEM. *(desprendimiento de gas)* effervescence, effervescency; FIG. *(vivacidad)* excitement, vivacity.

e·fer·ves·cen·te adj. CHEM. effervescent, bubbly; FIG. *(animado)* vivacious, excited.

e·fi·ca·cia f. efficacy, effectiveness.

e·fi·caz adj. [pl. **-ca·ces**] efficacious, effective.

e·fi·caz·men·te adv. efficaciously, effectively.

e·fi·cien·cia f. efficiency.

e·fi·cien·te adj. *(eficaz)* efficient, effective; *(competente)* competent, capable.

e·fi·gie f. *(imagen)* effigy, image; FIG. *(personificación)* personification, embodiment.

e·fí·me·ro, -ra adj. BOT., ZOOL. ephemeral; FIG. *(pasajero)* ephemeral, short-lived.

e·flu·vio m. PHYSIOL. effluvium, emanation; ELEC. *(emisión)* effluvium, discharge; FIG. *(vibración)* vibration, aura *<efluvios de simpatía* good vibrations>.

e·fu·gio m. evasion, subterfuge.

e·fu·sión f. *(derramamiento)* effusion; FIG. *(intensidad)* effusiveness, intensity ♦ **con e.** effusively • **e. de sangre** bloodshed, spilling of blood.

e·fu·si·vi·dad f. effusiveness.

e·fu·si·vo, –va adj. effusive.

E·ge·o m. Aegean (Sea).

é·gi·da f. FIG. aegis, protection ♦ **bajo la e. de** under the protection *or* sponsorship *or* auspices of.

e·gip·cio, –cia adj. & m.f. Egyptian.

E·gip·to m. Egypt.

e·gip·to·lo·gí·a f. Egyptology.

e·go m. PHILOS., PSYCH. ego, the self.

e·go·cén·tri·co, –ca adj. egocentric, self-centered.

e·go·cen·tris·mo m. egocentricity, self-centeredness.

e·go·ís·mo m. egoism.

e·go·ís·ta I. adj. egoistic, egoistical II. m.f. egoist, selfish person.

e·gó·la·tra adj. self-worshipping, narcissistic.

e·go·la·trí·a f. self-worship, narcissism.

e·go·tis·mo m. egotism, ego.

e·go·tis·ta I. adj. egotistic, egotistical II. m.f. egotist.

e·gre·gio, –gia adj. illustrious, distinguished.

e·gre·sa·do, –da AMER. I. past part. see **egresar** II. adj. & m.f. graduate.

e·gre·sar intr. AMER. to leave school upon graduation.

e·gre·so m. *(salida)* departure; AMER. leaving school upon graduation.

¡eh! interj. *(para llamar la atención)* hey!; *(para confirmar)* all right?, okay? *<lo traigo mañana, ¿eh?* I'll bring it tomorrow, okay?>.

eins·te·nio m. CHEM. einsteinium.

e·je m. axis *<el mundo gira sobre su e.* the world spins on its axis>; FIG. *(lo fundamental)* crux, main point; MECH., TECH. shaft, axle; BOT., GEOM. axis ♦ **e. de abscisas** MATH. y-axis • **e. de ordenadas** MATH. x-axis • **partir por el e.** COLL. to foul up.

e·je·cu·ción f. *(cumplimiento)* execution, realization *<la e. de un plan* the execution of a plan>; CRIMIN. execution *<la e. de un criminal* the execution of a criminal>; MUS. performance, rendition; LAW *(embargo)* attachment, distraint, distrainment.

e·je·cu·ta·ble adj. executable, workable; MUS. performable; LAW *(embargable)* attachable.

e·je·cu·tan·te I. m.f. MUS. executant, performer; LAW *(embargador)* distrainer II. adj. LAW distraining.

e·je·cu·tar tr. *(realizar)* to execute, carry out *<e. un plan* to execute a plan>; CRIMIN. to execute, put to death *<e. a un reo* to put a criminal to death>; MUS. to perform, play *<e. una sinfonía* to perform a symphony>; LAW *(embargar)* to attach, distrain.

e·je·cu·ti·vo, –va I. adj. *(dirigente)* executive, administrative; *(apremiante)* pressing, urgent; POL. executive *<poder e.* executive power> II. m. *(director)* executive, administrator; POL. *(poder dirigente)* the executive.

e·je·cu·tor, –to·ra I. adj. executing; MUS. performing II. m.f. executor; MUS. performer, executant ♦ **e. de la justicia** executioner • **e. testamentaria** executrix • **e. testamentario** executor (of a will).

e·je·cu·to·ria I. f. *(título)* letters patent of nobility; FIG. *(historial)* record of accomplishments; *(nobleza)* noble quality, ennobling deed; LAW *(sentencia)* final judgment; *(despacho)* writ of execution II. adj. see **ejecutorio, –ria.**

e·je·cu·to·rio, –ria I. adj. LAW executory II. f. see **ejecutoria.**

¡e·jem! interj. ahem!, humph!

e·jem·plar I. adj. *(modélico)* exemplary, model *<conducta e.* model behavior>; exemplary *<castigo e.* exemplary punishment>* II. m. *(ejemplo)* example; PRINT. copy *<un e. de la Biblia* a copy of the Bible>; *(número)* number, issue; *(precedente)* precedent; SCI. specimen ♦ **e. de regalo** complimentary copy • **¡menudo e.!** COLL. sly *or* wily bird • **sin e.** unprecedented, unique.

e·jem·pli·fi·ca·ción f. exemplification, illustration.

e·jem·pli·fi·car §70 tr. to exemplify, illustrate.

e·jem·plo m. *(caso)* example, instance; *(modelo)* example, model *<ella es un e. de modestia* she is a model of modesty>* ♦ **dar e.** to set an example • **hacer un e. de** to make

an example of • **por e.** for example, for instance • **sin e.** unprecedented.

e·jer·cer §75 tr. to exercise *<e. la autoridad* to exercise authority>; *(desempeñar)* to practice *<e. una profesión* to practice a profession>* —intr. to be in practice, practice a profession.

e·jer·ci·cio m. *(uso)* exercise, use *<el e. del poder* the exercise of power>; *(desempeño)* practice *<el e. de una profesión* the practice of a profession>; *(tarea)* exercise, drill *<ejercicios de matemáticas* math exercises>; *(movimiento)* exercise *<el e. es necesario para mantener la buena salud* exercise is necessary to maintain good health>; *(prueba)* examination (for a public post); MIL. exercise, drill; POL. tenure ♦ **e. económico** COM. fiscal year • **ejercicios espirituales** RELIG. retreat.

e·jer·ci·ta·ción f. exercise, use *<la e. de un derecho* the exercise of a right>; *(desempeño)* practice *<la e. de una profesión* the practice of a profession>.

e·jer·ci·tar tr. *(desempeñar)* to practice *<e. la medicina* to practice medicine>; *(adiestrar)* to train, drill —reflex. to train, drill.

e·jér·ci·to m. MIL. army; FIG. *(multitud)* army, flock ♦ **E. del Aire** Air Force • **E. de Salvación** Salvation Army.

e·jer·za, ejerzo see **ejercer.**

e·ji·do m. common *or* public land.

e·jo·te m. MEX., C. AMER. green bean, string bean.

el §G16 I. def. art. the *<el teléfono* the telephone> II. pron. the one *<¿no puedes encontrar el de Madrid?* can't you find the one from Madrid?> ♦ **el que** the one that *<no me gusta el que me envió Enrique* I do not like the one that Henry sent me>; he who *<el que imita buenos modelos será bueno* he who imitates good models will become good>.

él §G30 pron. [pl. **e·llos**] he *<no sé si él viene o no* I do not know if he is coming or not>; him *<iremos con él* we will go with him>; it *<compró un cuaderno y se puso a escribir en él* she bought a notebook and began to write in it> ♦ **¡a ellos!** let's get them! • **de él** his *<aquí están mis guantes y los de él* here are my gloves and his> • **de ellos** theirs • **ellos** they *<ellos no pueden venir* they are not able to come>; them *<hay que tener paciencia con ellos* one must have patience with them> • **él mero** MEX. he alone • **él mismo** he himself • **ellos mismos** they themselves.

e·la·bo·ra·ble adj. workable *<es un sistema e.* it is a workable system>.

e·la·bo·ra·ción f. *(producción)* production, manufacture; *(preparación)* preparation, working out *<la e. de un proyecto* the preparation of a project>.

e·la·bo·ra·dor, –do·ra I. adj. manufacturing, elaborating II. m.f. manufacturer, producer.

e·la·bo·rar tr. *(fabricar)* to manufacture, produce *<el carbón es indispensable para e. el acero* carbon is essential in order to produce steel>; *(crear)* to make, create *<las abejas elaboran la miel* bees make honey>; *(labrar)* to work *<e. la madera* to work wood>; *(preparar)* to prepare, work out *<e. un plan* to work out a plan>.

e·lan m. élan, zest.

e·lás·ti·ca I. f. undershirt, T-shirt II. adj. see **elástico, –ca.**

e·las·ti·ci·dad f. elasticity; FIG. *(flexibilidad)* flexibility, give; resiliency • **e.** *moral* moral resiliency>.

e·lás·ti·co, –ca I. adj. elastic; flexible *<una regla e.* a flexible rule>; resilient *<un espíritu e.* a resilient spirit> II. m. elastic, elastic band ♦ **elásticos** suspenders —f. see **elástica.**

e·le f. el (the name of the letter l).

e·lec·ción f. POL. election; *(selección)* selection, choice ♦ **e. primaria** POL. primary election • **elecciones** POL. election • **elecciones generales** POL. general election.

e·lec·cio·na·rio, –ria adj. AMER. electoral.

e·lec·ti·vo, –va adj. elective.

e·lec·to, –ta I. past part. see **elegir** II. adj. elect, chosen III. m.f. elect, chosen *or* elected person.

e·lec·tor, –to·ra I. adj. electing II. m.f. *(votante)* elector, voter —m. elector (German prince).

e·lec·to·ra·do m. electorate.

e·lec·to·ral adj. electoral.

e·lec·tri·cé, electrice see **electrizar.**

e·lec·tri·ci·dad f. electricity ♦ **e. estática** static electricity.

e·lec·tri·cis·ta I. adj. electrical <*ingeniero e.* electrical engineer> **II.** m.f. electrician.
e·léc·tri·co, –ca adj. electric, electrical; FIG. (*rápido*) lightning-fast.
e·lec·tri·fi·ca·ción f. electrification.
e·lec·tri·fi·car §70 tr. to electrify.
e·lec·tri·za·ble adj. electrifiable.
e·lec·tri·za·dor, –do·ra I. adj. electrifying **II.** m.f. electrifier.
e·lec·tri·zan·te adj. electrifying; FIG. (*apasionante*) electrifying, exciting.
e·lec·tri·zar §04 tr. to electrify; FIG. (*entusiasmar*) to electrify, excite.
e·lec·tro·car·dió·gra·fo m. MED. electrocardiograph.
e·lec·tro·car·dio·gra·ma m. MED. electrocardiogram.
e·lec·tro·cu·ción f. electrocution.
e·lec·tro·cu·tar tr. to electrocute.
e·lec·tro·do m. ELEC. electrode.
e·lec·tro·do·més·ti·co, –ca adj. electric, household <*aparato e.* household appliance>.
e·lec·tro·en·ce·fa·lo·gra·ma m. MED. electroencephalogram.
e·lec·tró·ge·no, –na I. adj. generating **II.** m. electric generator.
e·lec·tro·i·mán m. PHYS. electromagnet.
e·lec·tró·li·sis f. CHEM. electrolysis.
e·lec·tró·li·to m. CHEM. electrolyte.
e·lec·tro·mag·né·ti·co, –ca adj. electromagnetic.
e·lec·tro·mag·ne·tis·mo m. electromagnetism.
e·lec·tro·me·cá·ni·co, –ca MECH. **I.** adj. electromechanical **II.** f. electromechanics.
e·lec·tro·mo·tor, –to·ra I. adj. electromotive **II.** m. electromotor.
e·lec·tro·mo·triz adj. [pl. **-tri·ces**] electromotive.
e·lec·trón m. PHYS. electron.
e·lec·tró·ni·co, –ca I. adj. electronic **II.** f. electronics.
e·lec·tros·tá·ti·co, –ca I. adj. electrostatic **II.** f. electrostatics.
e·lec·tro·tec·nia f. TECH. electrical engineering, electrotechnology.
e·lec·tro·te·ra·pia f. MED. electrotherapy.
e·le·fan·ta f. ZOOL. female elephant, cow.
e·le·fan·te m. ZOOL. elephant ♦ **e. blanco** S. AMER., FIG. white elephant • **e. marino** ZOOL. elephant seal.
e·le·fan·tia·sis f. MED. elephantiasis.
e·le·gan·cia f. elegance, polish.
e·le·gan·te adj. (*esbelto*) elegant, stylish; well-turned <*una frase e.* a well-turned phrase>.
e·le·gan·te·men·te adv. elegantly, stylishly.
e·le·gan·tón, –to·na adj. COLL. very elegant *or* stylish.
e·le·gí·a f. POET. elegy.
e·le·gi·bi·li·dad f. eligibility.
e·le·gi·ble adj. eligible.
e·le·gi·do, –da I. past part. of **elegir II.** m.f. RELIG. chosen (one).
e·le·gir §57 tr. (*escoger*) to choose, select; POL. to elect.
e·le·men·tal adj. CHEM. elemental; (*obvio*) elementary, obvious; FIG. (*fundamental*) fundamental, essential.
e·le·men·to m. CHEM., MATH., PHYS. element; (*componente*) element, component; element, milieu <*Carlos está en su e. cuando juega en el casino* Charles is in his element when he gambles in the casino>; (*miembro*) member; element <*el e. radical grita por la justicia* the radical element cries for justice>; BIOL. natural habitat, element; ELEC. cell (of a battery); AMER. dimwit, blockhead; P. RICO person, guy <*un buen e.* a good guy> ♦ **elementos** (*rudimentos*) rudiments, basic principles; (*recursos*) resources, means; (*fuerzas atmosféricas*) elements <*los marineros tienen que luchar contra los elementos* sailors have to fight the elements> • **los cuatro elementos** the four elements (earth, air, fire, water).
e·len·co m. (*catálogo*) catalogue, list; THEAT. (*compañía*) company (of actors); (*reparto*) cast.
e·le·pé m. COLL. long-playing album, LP.
e·le·va·ción f. (*alzamiento*) elevation, raising; (*construcción*) erection, building <*la e. de un monumento* the erection of a monument>; (*altitud*) elevation, height; (*nobleza*) elevation, loftiness; FIG. promotion <*su e. al puesto de director*

era inexplicable his promotion to the position of director was inexplicable>; (*enajenamiento*) rapture, ecstasy; RELIG. Elevation (of the host); MATH. raising (to a power).
e·le·va·da·men·te adv. elevatedly, loftily.
e·le·va·do, –da I. past part. see **elevar II.** adj. (*alto*) tall, high <*precios elevados* high prices>; FIG. (*sublime*) elevated, lofty <*estilo e.* lofty style>.
e·le·va·dor, –do·ra I. adj. elevatory **II.** m. AMER. (*ascensor*) elevator; (*montacargas*) freight elevator ♦ **e. eléctrico** *or* **de voltaje** ELEC. booster.
e·le·va·mien·to m. var. of **elevación.**
e·le·var tr. (*alzar*) to raise, lift; FIG. (*ennoblecer*) to elevate, ennoble; to promote, elevate <*e. al puesto de director* to promote to the position of director>; MATH. to raise (to a power) ♦ **e. al cuadrado** to square • **e. al cubo** to cube.
e·li·dir tr. GRAM. to elide; (*debilitar*) to weaken.
e·li·gie·ra, eligió see **elegir.**
e·li·ja, elijo see **elegir.**
e·li·mi·na·ción f. elimination, disposal.
e·li·mi·nar tr. (*apartar*) to eliminate, remove; (*excluir*) to exclude, leave out; MED. to eliminate, excrete; MATH. to eliminate —reflex. MEX. to go away.
e·li·mi·na·to·rio, –ria I. adj. eliminatory **II.** f. SPORT. preliminary, preliminary round.
e·lip·se f. GEOM. ellipse.
e·lip·sis f. GRAM. ellipsis.
e·líp·ti·co, –ca adj. GEOM., GRAM. elliptical, elliptic.
e·lí·se·o, –a I. adj. Elysian, blissful ♦ **Campos Elíseos** Elysian Fields **II.** m. MYTH. Elysium, paradise.
e·li·tis·mo m. elitism.
e·li·tis·ta adj. elitist.
e·li·xir m. PHARM. elixir; FIG. (*medicamento*) elixir, panacea.
e·lo·cu·ción f. elocution.
e·lo·cuen·cia f. eloquence.
e·lo·cuen·te adj. (*persuasivo*) eloquent; (*expresivo*) telling, significant.
e·lo·cuen·te·men·te adv. eloquently, with eloquence.
e·lo·gia·ble adj. praiseworthy, laudable.
e·lo·gia·dor, –do·ra I. adj. eulogistic, laudatory **II.** m.f. eulogist, praiser.
e·lo·giar tr. to eulogize, praise.
e·lo·gio m. eulogy, praise.
e·lo·gio·so, –sa adj. eulogistic, laudatory.
e·lo·te m. C. AMER., MEX. ear of tender corn.
El Sal·va·dor m. El Salvador.
e·lu·ci·da·ción f. elucidation, explanation.
e·lu·ci·dar tr. to elucidate, explain.
e·lu·cu·bra·ción f. lucubration.
e·lu·di·ble adj. eludible, avoidable.
e·lu·dir tr. to elude, avoid.
e·lu·si·vo, –va adj. elusive, evasive.
e·lla §G30 pron. she <*e. leía mientras yo cantaba* she was reading while I was singing>; her <*hice mi declaración ante e.* I made my statement in front of her>; it <*trató de levantarse de la silla y quedó anclado en e.* he tried to get up from the chair and got stuck in it>; COLL. the trouble <*ahora es e.* now is when the trouble begins> ♦ **de e.** hers <*esta pluma no es mía; es de e.* this pen is not mine; it is hers> • **de ellas** theirs • **ellas** they <*ellas estudian la biología* they are studying biology>; them <*cuento con ellas* I am relying on them> • **e. misma** she herself • **ellas mismas** they themselves.
e·lle f. name of the Spanish letter ll.
e·llo §G30, 39 pron. it <*no te preocupes con e.* don't worry about it>; COLL. the trouble <*allí fue e.* there the trouble began>.
e·llos, e·llas pron. see **él, ella.**
e·ma·cia·do, –da adj. MED. emaciated.
e·ma·na·ción f. emanation, efflux.
e·ma·nan·te adj. emanating.
e·ma·nar intr. to emanate, flow.
e·man·ci·pa·ción f. emancipation, liberation.
e·man·ci·pa·dor, –do·ra I. adj. emancipating, liberating **II.** m.f. emancipator, liberator.
e·man·ci·par tr. to emancipate, liberate —reflex. to become emancipated *or* liberated.
e·mas·cu·lar tr. to emasculate, castrate.

em·ba·bu·car §70 tr. to deceive, trick.

em·ba·cé, embace see **embazar.**

em·ba·dur·nar tr. to smear, daub —reflex. to become smeared *or* bedaubed.

em·bai·dor, –do·ra I. adj. deceptive, misleading II. m.f. *(estafador)* cheat, swindler; *(engañador)* deceiver.

em·bai·mien·to m. deception, delusion.

em·ba·ír §83 tr. [used in infinitive or past part. only] to deceive, mislead.

em·ba·ja·da f. *(casa)* embassy; *(cargo)* ambassadorship; *(mensaje)* message, commission; COLL. *(proposición)* impertinent proposition or demand.

em·ba·ja·dor m. DIPL. ambassador; FIG., COLL. *(mensajero)* messenger, envoy.

em·ba·ja·do·ra f. DIPL. ambassador; *(esposa)* ambassador's wife; FIG., COLL. *(mensajera)* messenger, envoy.

em·ba·la·dor m. packer.

em·ba·la·du·ra f. CHILE, PERU packing, crating.

em·ba·la·je m. *(acción de embalar)* packing, crating; *(materia)* packing material; *(costa)* packaging cost or expense.

em·ba·lar tr. *(empaquetar)* to pack, crate; *(acelerar)* to rev (a motor) —intr. to chase fish into nets; SPORT. *(correr)* to race, sprint —reflex. AUTO. to rev (a motor); FIG. *(entusiasmarse)* to be carried away (by emotion).

em·bal·do·sa·do m. *(acción de embaldosar)* tiling; *(suelo)* tiled floor.

em·bal·do·sar tr. to tile.

em·bal·sa·de·ro m. bog, swamp.

em·bal·sa·ma·mien·to m. embalming.

em·bal·sa·mar tr. *(un cadáver)* to embalm; *(perfumar)* to perfume, scent —reflex. to become fragrant or perfumed.

em·bal·sar tr. *(agua)* to dam up, dam; *(izar)* to sling, hoist —reflex. to be dammed up.

em·bal·se m. *(acción de embalsar)* damming up, damming; *(lago artificial)* dam, reservoir; *(presa)* dam; MARIT. hoisting, slinging.

em·ba·lu·mar tr. to load with large, bulky objects —reflex. FIG. to overload oneself, overburden oneself (with work).

em·ba·lle·nar tr. to stiffen with whalebone stays.

em·ba·nas·tar tr. *(meter en banasta)* to put into a basket; FIG. *(apiñar)* to pack in, crowd in (people).

em·ban·car·se §70 reflex. MARIT. to run aground; CHILE, ECUAD. to silt up, become blocked by silt (a river); MEX., METAL. to stick to the walls of a furnace.

em·ban·de·rar tr. to decorate with flags.

em·ban·que·ta·do m. MEX. sidewalk, pavement.

em·ba·ra·cé, embarace see **embarazar.**

em·ba·ra·za·da I. f. pregnant woman, expectant mother II. adj. see **embarazado, –da.**

em·ba·ra·za·da·men·te adv. *(encogidamente)* embarrassedly, with embarrassment; *(con dificultad)* with difficulty, difficultly.

em·ba·ra·za·do, –da I. past part. see **embarazar** II. adj. *(preñado)* pregnant; *(molestado)* troubled, bothered III. f. see **embarazada.**

em·ba·ra·za·dor, –do·ra adj. *(penoso)* embarrassing, awkward; *(que estorba)* hindering, impeding; *(que molesta)* troubling, upsetting.

em·ba·ra·zar §04 tr. *(estorbar)* to hinder, impede; *(preñar)* to impregnate, make pregnant; FIG. *(molestar)* to bother, embarrass —reflex. *(estorbarse)* to be hindered or hampered; *(preñarse)* to become pregnant.

em·ba·ra·zo m. *(preñado)* pregnancy; *(dificultad)* difficulty, obstruction; *(timidez)* shyness, embarrassment.

em·ba·ra·zo·so, –sa adj. cumbersome, troublesome.

em·bar·bas·car·se §70 reflex. *(enredarse el arado)* to become entangled in the roots (said of a plow); FIG. *(confundirse)* to become confused or mixed up.

em·bar·be·cer §17 intr. to grow a beard.

em·bar·ca·ción f. MARIT. boat, vessel; *(embarco)* embarkation; *(viaje)* voyage ♦ **e. de desembarco** MIL. landing craft • **e. de pesca** *or* **pesquera** fishing boat • **e. de recreo** pleasure boat.

em·bar·ca·de·ro m. MARIT. landing stage, pier; *(muelle para mercancías)* wharf, dock; AMER. *(de ferrocarriles)* loading platform.

em·bar·ca·dor m. shipper, freighter.

em·bar·car §70 tr. *(dar ingreso)* to embark (passengers); *(poner a bordo)* to load, ship aboard (goods); FIG. *(incluir)* to involve <le embarcaron en una empresa dudosa they involved him in a dubious enterprise>; AMER. *(engañar)* to deceive —reflex. *(subir a bordo)* to embark, go aboard; FIG. *(lanzarse)* to embark on, launch into; *(enredarse)* to get involved in, engage in (a matter) ♦ **embarcarse para** to sail for.

em·bar·co m. embarkation.

em·bar·ga·ble adj. LAW subject to embargo.

em·bar·ga·dor m. one who applies an embargo.

em·bar·gan·te adj. impeding, restraining ♦ **no e.** notwithstanding, nevertheless.

em·bar·gar §47 tr. *(estorbar)* to impede, hamper; LAW *(derecho)* to lay an embargo on, distrain; FIG. *(una emoción)* to overcome (an emotion).

em·bar·go m. MARIT. embargo; LAW *(derecho)* seizure, distraint; MED. indigestion ♦ **sin e.** however, nevertheless.

em·bar·ni·zar §04 tr. to varnish.

em·bar·que m. loading, shipment.

em·bar·qué, embarque see **embarcar.**

em·ba·rra·da f. ARG., CHILE blunder, stupidity.

em·ba·rra·dor, –do·ra I. adj. *(que embarra)* staining; *(enredador)* mischief-making II. m.f. mischief-maker.

em·ba·rra·du·ra f. smearing, splattering (with mud).

em·ba·rran·car §70 tr. MARIT. to ground (a ship) —intr. MARIT. to run aground; FIG. *(en una dificultad)* to bog down, get stuck —reflex. to run into a ditch.

em·ba·rrar tr. *(untar de barro)* to splash with mud; *(manchar)* to smear, stain; AMER. *(fastidiar)* to annoy, irritate; C. AMER. *(en un asunto)* to implicate, involve (in a matter) —reflex. *(mancharse)* to become smeared or covered with mud; *(las perdices)* to take refuge in trees (said of partridges).

em·ba·rri·lar tr. to barrel, pack in barrels.

em·ba·ru·llar tr. COLL. *(mezclar)* to muddle, mix up; *(hacer atropelladamente)* to bungle, do clumsily.

em·bas·tar tr. *(una tela)* to put (cloth) in an embroidery frame; *(un colchón)* to quilt; *(hilvanar)* to baste, tack; *(caballos)* to put a packsaddle on, load.

em·bas·te·cer §17 intr. to get fat, grow stout —reflex. to become coarse or crude.

em·ba·te m. MARIT. *(golpe de las olas)* dashing, pounding (of the waves); *(viento)* sea breeze; *(acometida impetuosa)* sudden attack.

em·bau·ca·dor, –do·ra I. adj. deceiving, swinding II. m.f. deceiver, swindler.

em·bau·ca·mien·to m. deception, swindling.

em·bau·car §70 tr. to deceive, swindle.

em·bau·lar §82 tr. *(meter en un baúl)* to pack in a trunk; FIG., COLL. *(comer mucho)* to cram, stuff (food); FIG. *(en un lugar pequeño)* to pack, cram (in a small place).

em·ba·zamien·to m. amazement, astonishment.

em·ba·zar §04 tr. *(teñir)* to dye brown; *(embarazar)* to hinder, impede; FIG. *(dejar admirado)* to astound, amaze —intr. to be dumbfounded —reflex. *(hartarse)* to have had enough; *(meterse en bazas)* to make tricks (in cards); *(cansarse)* to get tired of, get bored with (something).

em·be·be·cer §17 tr. *(entretener)* to amuse, entertain; *(embelesar)* to fascinate, delight —reflex. to be fascinated or enchanted.

em·be·be·ci·mien·to m. fascination, captivation.

em·be·ber tr. *(absorber)* to absorb, soak up; *(empapar)* to soak, wet; *(contener)* to contain, enclose; FIG. *(incorporar)* to incorporate, add; *(estrechar)* to take in, shorten (clothes) —intr. to shrink —reflex. *(embebecerse)* to be absorbed, engrossed or enthralled; FIG. *(empaparse)* to soak or steep oneself (in a subject).

em·be·bez·ca, embebezco see **embebecer.**

em·be·le·ca·dor, –do·ra I. adj. deceptive, tricky II. m.f. *(engañador)* deceiver, trickster; *(estafador)* cheat, duper.

em·be·le·ca·mien·to m. *(engaño)* deception, trickery; *(estafa)* swindle, fraud.

em·be·le·car §70 tr. *(engañar)* to deceive, trick; *(embaucar)* to swindle, cheat.

em·be·le·co m. *(embuste)* deceit, fraud; COLL., FIG. *(persona enfadosa)* nuisance, bore.

em·be·le·sa·dor, –do·ra adj. enchanting, charming.

em·be·le·sa·mien·to m. enthrallment, fascination.

em·be·le·sar tr. to enthrall, fascinate —reflex. to be enthralled or fascinated.

em·be·le·so m. (encanto) delight, enchantment; CUBA, BOT. leadwort.

em·be·lla·que·cer·se §17 reflex. to become a rogue, become cunning.

em·be·lle·ce·dor, –do·ra I. adj. beautifying, embellishing II. m. AUTO. hubcap.

em·be·lle·cer §17 tr. to beautify, embellish.

em·be·lle·ci·mien·to m. beautification, embellishment.

em·ber·me·jar tr. (teñir) to redden, dye red; (poner colorado) to make blush; (avergonzar) to put to shame, embarrass —intr. to turn red or reddish —reflex. to blush, turn red.

em·bes·ti·da f. (ataque) attack, onslaught; (de un toro) charge (of a bull); FIG., COLL. (acción de molestar) touching, pestering (a person for money).

em·bes·ti·dor, –do·ra I. adj. attacking, charging II. m. COLL. sponger.

em·bes·tir §48 tr. (atacar) to attack, charge; COLL. (molestar) to touch or pester (for money) —intr. to attack, rush.

em·be·tu·nar tr. to polish, black (shoes); (asfaltar) to cover with pitch or tar.

em·bi·jar tr. (pintar) to paint with annatto dye or vermillion; AMER. (ensuciar) to soil, make dirty.

em·blan·de·cer §17 tr. to soften, mollify —intr. to soften.

em·blan·que·cer §17 tr. to whiten, bleach —reflex. to become whitened or bleached.

em·ble·ma m. emblem, symbol.

em·bo·ba·mien·to m. fascination, stupefaction.

em·bo·bar tr. to stupefy, fascinate —reflex. to be stupefied, be fascinated.

em·bo·be·cer §17 tr. to make foolish or silly —reflex. to become silly or foolish.

em·bo·be·ci·mien·to m. stupefaction.

em·bo·ca·de·ro m. outlet, narrow channel.

em·bo·ca·du·ra f. MUS. mouthpiece; (del caballo) bit; (desembocadura) mouth (of a river); (sabor) taste (of wine); THEAT. proscenium arch.

em·bo·car §70 tr. (meter por la boca) to put in the mouth; (entrar) to enter; FIG. (engañar) to make someone swallow, make someone believe (a story); FIG., COLL. (engullir) to gorge, gulp down (food); (comenzar) to begin, undertake —reflex. to enter, go into.

em·bo·cé, emboce see **embozar.**

em·bo·chin·char tr. AMER. to raise a ruckus, throw into confusion.

em·bo·de·gar §47 tr. to store, put in storage.

em·bo·la·do m. THEAT. bit part, minor role; (toro) bull with protective wooden balls on its horns; COLL. (artificio) deception, trick; (embrollo) troublesome situation, mess.

em·bo·lar tr. (poner bolas) to tip a bull's horns with wooden balls; (dar betún) to shine, polish (shoes); (dar bola) to size (for gilding); C. AMER., MEX. to make drunk.

em·bo·lia f. MED. embolism, clot.

em·bo·lis·ma·dor, –do·ra I. adj. detracting, disparaging II. m.f. detractor, disparager.

em·bo·lis·mar tr. COLL. (chismear) to gossip about, carry tales about; CHILE to incite, agitate.

em·bo·lis·mo m. (intercalación) insertion (of time in the calendar); FIG. (enredo) confusion, muddle; (mentira) lie, falsehood; (chisme) gossip.

ém·bo·lo m. MECH. piston.

em·bol·sar tr. to pocket, collect.

em·bol·si·car §70 tr. AMER. to pocket.

em·bol·so m. pocketing.

em·bo·nar tr. (mejorar) to improve; MARIT. to sheathe (a ship); AMER. (empalmar) to join, unite; (acomodar) to suit, look good on <le embona ese traje that suit looks good on him>; (abonar) to manure.

em·bo·que m. (paso) passage through a narrow place; COLL. (engaño) trick, hoax; CHILE cup and ball (toy).

em·bo·qué, emboque see **embocar.**

em·bo·qui·lla·do, –da adj. filter-tipped (cigarette).

em·bo·rra·char tr. (embriagar) to intoxicate, make drunk;

(adormecer) to make sleepy or drowsy —reflex. to get drunk.

em·bo·rras·car §70 tr. to irritate, annoy —reflex. (el tiempo) to become stormy (said of the weather); (irritarse) to become irritated or annoyed; (fracasar) to fail, go wrong; MIN. to become exhausted (a mine).

em·bo·rri·car·se §70 reflex. (aturdirse) to be stunned or bewildered; COLL. (enamorarse) to be madly in love.

em·bo·rro·nar tr. to cover (paper) with smudges or blots; FIG. (escribir) to scribble.

em·bos·ca·da f. ambush.

em·bos·car §70 tr. to ambush —reflex. (ocultarse) to ambush, lie in ambush; FIG. (procurarse un trabajo fácil) to find an easy way out.

em·bo·ta·du·ra f. bluntness, dullness (of weapons).

em·bo·ta·mien·to m. blunting, dulling <e. de los sentimientos dulling of the senses>.

em·bo·tar tr. (desafilar) to blunt, dull; FIG. (entorpecer) to dull, make weak; (embotellar) to put into a jar or container —reflex. (desafilarse) to become blunt; FIG. (entorpecerse) to become dull or weakened; (ponerse las botas) to put on one's boots.

em·bo·te·lla·do, –da I. past part. see **embotellar** II. adj. prepared beforehand (speech) III. m. bottling.

em·bo·te·lla·dor, –do·ra I. adj. bottling II. m.f. (persona) bottler —f. (máquina) bottling machine.

em·bo·te·lla·mien·to m. (acción de embotellar) bottling; FIG. (obstrucción de la circulación) traffic jam, bottleneck.

em·bo·te·llar tr. (poner en botellas) to bottle; FIG. (obstruir) to jam, block <e. la circulación to block traffic>; (acorralar) to corner (a person); (inmovilizar) to paralyze, block <e. un negocio to block a transaction>; FIG. (memorizar) to learn by heart, memorize.

em·bo·ti·jar tr. (meter en botijas) to put in jugs; (poner botijas debajo del suelo) to place jars under a tile floor (for drainage) —reflex. FIG., COLL. (hincharse) to swell, become swollen; (irritarse) to become angry or annoyed.

em·bo·ve·da·do m. ARCHIT. vault, arch.

em·bo·za·lar tr. to muzzle, put a muzzle on.

em·bo·zar §04 tr. (cubrir) to cover (the lower part of the face); FIG. (ocultar) to disguise, conceal <la policía embozó sus planes the police concealed their plans>; (un animal) to muzzle, put a muzzle on —reflex. to cover one's face.

em·bra·gar §47 tr. (abrazar) to connect, engage; AUTO. to engage (the clutch).

em·bra·gue m. AUTO. (mecanismo) clutch; (acción) engaging the clutch ♦ e. automático automatic clutch • e. de fricción MECH. friction clutch.

em·bra·ve·cer §17 tr. to irritate, infuriate —intr. to flourish, thrive (said of plants) —reflex. (irritarse) to become irritated; (el mar) to become choppy (said of the sea).

em·bra·ve·ci·mien·to m. fury, rage.

em·bre·ar tr. to cover with tar or pitch.

em·bre·gar·se §47 reflex. to quarrel, wrangle.

em·bria·ga·dor, –do·ra or **em·bria·gan·te** adj. intoxicating.

em·bria·gar §47 tr. (emborrachar) to intoxicate; FIG. (enajenar) to enrapture, intoxicate —reflex. to get drunk.

em·bria·guez f. (borrachera) intoxication, drunkenness; FIG. (enajenación) rapture, intoxication.

em·bri·dar tr. to put a bridle on, bridle.

em·brio·lo·gí·a f. BIOL. embryology.

em·brión m. BIOL., BOT. embryo; FIG. (principio) embryo, germ <el e. de una idea the embryo of an idea> ♦ en e. in embryo.

em·brio·na·rio, –ria adj. BIOL., BOT. embryonic; FIG. (no acabado) embryonic.

em·bro·ca·ción f. (embroca) poultice, cataplasm; MED. (loción) embrocation; (líquido) embrocation, liniment.

em·bro·car §70 tr. (vaciar) to empty, pour (from one container into another); (devanar) to wind (thread onto a bobbin); (clavar) to tack, nail (sole of shoe); (poner boca abajo) to turn upside down; TAUR. (arrebatar) to catch between the horns —reflex. MEX. (vestirse) to put a garment on over one's head; GUAT. (salir mal) to come out poorly (on a deal).

em·bro·lla f. COLL. (embrollo) muddle, mess; (enredo) tangle, confusion.

em·bro·lla·dor, –do·ra I. adj. confusing, embroiling II. m.f. troublemaker.

em·bro·llar tr. to confuse, embroil.

em·bro·llo m. *(enredo)* confusion, tangle; *(embuste)* trick, fraud; FIG. *(lío)* entanglement, jam <salir del e. to get out of a jam>.

em·bro·llón, –llo·na COLL. I. adj. confusing, embroiling II. m.f. troublemaker.

em·bro·llo·so, –sa adj. COLL. muddling, confusing.

em·bro·ma·dor, –do·ra I. adj. *(bromista)* joking, teasing; *(engañador)* tricking, cheating II. m.f. *(bromista)* jokester, tease; *(engañador)* trickster, cheat.

em·bro·mar tr. *(burlarse de)* to make fun of, tease; *(engañar)* to cheat, hoodwink; AMER. *(fastidiar)* to annoy; ARG., CHILE *(hacer daño a)* to harm, damage; CHILE, MEX. *(detener)* to detain, delay —reflex. AMER. to get annoyed *or* cross.

em·bro·qué, embroque see **embrocar.**

em·bro·que·lar·se reflex. to shield oneself.

em·bru·ja·mien·to m. bewitchment.

em·bru·jar tr. to bewitch, cast a spell on.

em·bru·jo m. spell, charm.

em·bru·te·ce·dor, –do·ra adj. brutalizing, stupefying.

em·bru·te·cer §04 tr. *(degradar)* to brutalize; *(entorpecer)* stupefy, benumb.

em·bru·te·ci·mien·to m. *(degradación)* brutalization; *(entorpecimiento)* stupefying, stupefaction.

em·bu·cha·do I. past part. see **embuchar** II. m. CUL. pork sausage; FIG. *(enojo)* feigned anger; *(engaño)* fraud, deception; *(improvisación)* ad-libbing; *(de votos)* fraudulent voting.

em·bu·char tr. *(en el buche de un animal)* to cram the maw of (an animal); CUL. *(embutir)* to stuff (an animal) with mincemeat; COLL. *(tragar)* to gulp down, wolf down; FIG., COLL. *(hacer creer)* to try to make (someone) swallow (something), put (something) over on (someone) —reflex. CUBA to pretend to be angry.

em·bu·dar tr. *(poner el embudo)* to put a funnel into; FIG. *(hacer trampas)* to trick; HUNT. *(acorralar)* to surround, enclose (game).

em·bu·do m. *(instrumento)* funnel; MIL. *(oquedad)* shell hole; FIG. *(trampa)* trick, fraud.

em·bu·llar tr. *(animar)* to liven up, excite; *(hacer participar)* to get (someone) to join the crowd.

em·bu·ru·jar tr. COLL. *(amontonar)* to heap together, jumble together; *(aborujar)* to make lumpy; CUBA, P. RICO *(confundir)* to bewilder, confuse —reflex. AMER. to wrap oneself up.

em·bus·te m. *(engaño)* hoax, fraud; *(mentira)* lie, fib ♦ **embustes** trinkets.

em·bus·te·ar intr. to lie, fib.

em·bus·te·rí·a f. COLL. *(mentira)* lying; *(engaño)* deceit.

em·bus·te·ro, –ra I. adj. *(engañador)* lying, deceitful; GUAT. *(orgulloso)* haughty; *(melindroso)* finicky II. m.f. liar, cheat; CHILE bad speller.

em·bu·ti·do I. past part. see **embutir** II. m. *(acción de llenar)* stuffing, cramming; *(marquetería)* inlay, marquetry; CUL. *(embuchado)* sausage; AMER. *(entredós)* strip of lace.

em·bu·tir tr. *(taracear)* to inlay; *(llenar)* to stuff, cram; COLL. *(tragar)* to swallow —reflex. COLL. to stuff oneself, gorge.

e·me f. em (name of the letter m).

e·mer·gen·cia f. *(surgimiento)* emergence; *(accidente)* emergency.

e·mer·gen·te adj. emergent.

e·mer·ger §34 intr. *(surgir)* to emerge, surface; FIG. *(asomar)* to appear, show.

e·mé·ri·to, –ta adj. emeritus, retired.

e·mi·gra·ción f. emigration, migration.

e·mi·gra·do, –da I. past part. see **emigrar** II. m.f. emigrant, émigré.

e·mi·gran·te I. adj. emigrating, migrating II. m.f. emigrant, émigré.

e·mi·grar intr. *(salir de su país)* to emigrate; ZOOL. to migrate.

e·mi·nen·cia f. GEOG. eminence, hill; FIG. *(grandeza)* eminence, distinction; *(persona)* eminent person ♦ **Eminencia** RELIG. Eminence • **e. gris** FIG. gray eminence.

e·mi·nen·te adj. *(elevado)* high, lofty; FIG. *(distinguido)* eminent, distinguished.

e·mir m. emir (Moslem prince or leader).

E·mi·ra·tos Á·ra·bes U·ni·dos m. United Arab Emirates.

e·mi·sa·rio, –ria m.f. *(mensajero)* emissary, secret agent —m. *(desaguadero)* outlet of a pond or lake.

e·mi·sión f. *(acción de emitir)* emission; TELEC. transmission, broadcast; COM. *(puesta en circulación)* issuance; *(conjunto de efectos diseminados)* issue ♦ **e. espectral** OPT. spectral emission • **e. secundaria** RAD. secondary emission • **neuva e.** COM. new issue.

e·mi·sor, –so·ra I. adj. *(que emite)* emitting; TELEC. broadcasting <estación e. broadcasting station>; COM. issuing <banco e. issuing bank> II. m.f. *(que emite)* issuer; TELEC. *(aparato)* transmitter; RAD., TELEV. *(estación)* broadcasting station.

e·mi·tir tr. *(arrojar)* to emit, throw off; COM. *(poner en circulación)* to issue; FIG. *(expresar)* to utter, express —intr. TELEC. to broadcast, transmit.

e·mo·ción f. *(sentimiento)* emotion, feeling; *(agitación)* excitement, thrill.

e·mo·cio·nal adj. emotional.

e·mo·cio·nan·te adj. *(conmovedor)* touching, moving; *(excitante)* thrilling, exciting.

e·mo·cio·na·do, –da I. past part. see **emocionar** II. adj. *(conmovido)* moved, touched; *(perturbado)* upset, distressed.

e·mo·cio·nar tr. to move, affect —reflex. to be moved *or* affected.

e·mo·lien·te adj. & m. MED. emollient.

e·mo·lu·men·to m. emolument, wage.

e·mo·ti·vi·dad f. emotionality, emotiveness.

e·mo·ti·vo, –va adj. emotive, emotional.

em·pa·ca·dor, –do·ra I. adj. packing, baling II. m.f. *(persona)* packer, baler —f. *(máquina)* packing *or* baling machine.

em·pa·ca·mien·to m. *(obstinación)* stubbornness, obstinacy; AMER. *(de un caballo)* balking (of a horse).

em·pa·car §70 tr. *(empaquetar)* to pack, bale; AMER. to annoy, anger —intr. MEX. to pack (one's bags). —reflex. *(obstinarse)* to be stubborn, be obstinate; *(turbarse)* to be flustered, be embarrassed; AMER. *(un caballo)* to balk (said of a horse).

em·pa·cha·do, –da I. past part. see **empachar** II. adj. awkward, clumsy ♦ **estar e.** *(ahitarse)* to have indigestion; *(estar harto)* to be fed up, be sick and tired.

em·pa·char tr. *(ahitar)* to give indigestion to; *(estorbar)* to obstruct, hinder; *(disfrazar)* to disguise, cloak; *(hacer pasar un apuro)* to embarrass —reflex. *(ahitarse)* to have indigestion; *(embarazarse)* to become embarassed *or* flustered; MEX. to become clogged *or* filled with wax (a candlestick holder).

em·pa·cho m. *(ahíto)* indigestion; *(apuro)* embarrassment, shame; *(timidez)* shyness, bashfulness; *(estorbo)* hindrance, obstacle; *(turbación)* confusion, perplexity ♦ **sin e.** without overindulgence *or* ceremony.

em·pa·cho·so, –sa adj. *(que causa indigestión)* indigestible, causing indigestion; *(vergonzoso)* shameful, embarrassing; *(tímido)* shy, bashful; *(que turba)* confusing, perplexing; *(que estorba)* annoying, bothersome.

em·pa·dro·na·dor m. census taker.

em·pa·dro·na·mien·to m. *(censo)* census; *(acción de empadronar)* census-taking.

em·pa·dro·nar tr. to take a census of.

em·pa·jar tr. *(cubrir con paja)* to cover with straw; AMER. to thatch; CHILE to mix straw into (clay) —reflex. AMER., BOT. to bear much stalk and little grain; *(hartarse)* to stuff oneself with snacks; MEX. to make a good profit.

em·pa·la·ga·mien·to m. var. of **empalago.**

em·pa·la·gar §47 tr. *(causar hastío)* to cloy, surfeit; *(fastidiar)* to annoy, tire —intr. *(causar hastío)* to be boring, be tiresome —reflex. *(fastidiarse)* to be annoyed (with), be tired (of).

em·pa·la·go m. *(exceso)* surfeit, excess; *(repugnancia)* disgust, repugnance; FIG. *(molestia)* annoyance, irritation; *(cansancio)* boredom.

em·pa·la·go·so, –sa I. adj. *(excesivamente dulce)* cloying, sickening; *(fastidioso)* annoying, tiresome. **II.** m.f. pest, nuisance.

em·pa·la·gué, empalague see **empalagar.**

em·pa·la·mien·to m. impalement, impaling.

em·pa·lar tr. to impale —reflex. *(obstinarse)* to be persistent *or* obstinate; CHILE *(entumecerse)* to become numb *or* stiff; CHILE, PERU *(quedar seco el pan)* to turn out hard (said of bread).

em·pa·li·za·da I. past part. see **empalizar II.** f. MIL. palisade, stockade; *(valla)* (picket) fence.

em·pa·li·zar §04 tr. MIL. to palisade, stockade; *(vallar)* to fence (in).

em·pal·mar tr. *(unir)* to connect, join; CARP. to join; PHOTOG. to splice; FIG. *(combinar)* to link (up), combine —intr. *(juntarse)* to meet, join; RAIL. *(combinarse)* to connect, join ♦ **e. con** to follow —reflex. *(juntarse)* to meet, join; RAIL. *(combinarse)* to connect, join; *(ocultar una navaja)* to conceal a knife in one's palm and sleeve.

em·pal·me f. *(conexión)* join, joint; *(combinación)* combination, combining; *(acción de conectar)* connecting, joining; CARP. joint; RAIL. *(cruce de vías)* junction, crossing; *(conexión entre trenes)* connection; AUTO. junction, intersection; PHOTOG. *(conexión de películas)* splice; *(acción de conectar películas)* splicing.

em·pa·na·da f. CUL. turnover; FIG. *(fraude)* fraud, deception ♦ **e. mental** COLL. confusion, bewilderment.

em·pa·na·do, –da I. past part. see **empanar II.** adj. CUL. breaded; *(sin ventilación directa)* dark and stuffy (room) **III.** m. room without direct sunlight *or* ventilation —f. see **empanada.**

em·pa·nar tr. to coat with breadcrumbs; AGR. *(sembrar)* to sow (wheat) —reflex. AGR. to be choked (land too closely sown).

em·pan·ta·nar tr. *(inundar)* to swamp, flood; FIG. *(detener)* to hold up, bog down.

em·pan·zar·se §04 reflex. CHILE, HOND. to be full, be surfeited (with food and drink).

em·pa·ña·mien·to m. *(con pañales)* diapering, swaddling; *(obscurecimiento)* blurring, clouding; FIG. *(de la reputación)* tarnishing, blemishing (the reputation).

em·pa·ñar tr. *(con pañales)* to diaper, swaddle; *(obscurecer)* to blur, mist; FIG. *(manchar la reputación)* to tarnish, blemish (the reputation).

em·pa·ñe·tar tr. AMER. *(enlucir)* to plaster; *(encalar)* to whitewash.

em·pa·par tr. *(humedecer)* to soak; *(mojar completamente)* to saturate, drench; *(absorber)* to absorb, soak up —reflex. *(mojarse)* to get soaked; *(imbuirse)* to become imbued *or* inspired <empaparse de ideas revolucionarias to become imbued with revolutionary ideas>; COLL. *(ahitarse)* to stuff oneself, gorge oneself.

em·pa·pe·la·do I. past part. see **empapelar II.** m. *(acción de empapelar)* papering, lining; *(papel)* paper (for wrapping or lining).

em·pa·pe·la·dor, –do·ra m.f. paperhanger, paperer.

em·pa·pe·lar tr. *(forrar en papel)* to wrap in paper; *(forrar de papel)* to paper, line with paper <e. un cuarto to paper a room>; FIG., COLL. *(formar causa criminal)* to serve papers on (a person).

em·pa·pi·ro·tar tr. & reflex. COLL. to dress up, put on one's Sunday best.

em·pa·que m. *(acción de empacar)* packing, wrapping; *(materiales empleados)* packing, packing material; COLL. *(aspecto)* appearance, air; *(seriedad)* affected gravity *or* seriousness; AMER. *(descaro)* brazenness, nerve; MEX. package, container.

em·pa·qué, empaque see **empacar.**

em·pa·que·ta·dor, –do·ra m.f. packer, wrapper.

em·pa·que·tar tr. *(embalar)* to pack, wrap; FIG. *(muchas personas en un lugar)* to stuff, pack; *(emperejilar)* to dress up.

em·pa·ra·mar·se reflex. S. AMER. to freeze to death.

em·pa·re·da·do, –da I. past part. see **emparedar II.** adj. *(encarcelado)* imprisoned, confined; *(retirado)* reclusive **III.** m.f. *(prisionero)* prisoner, captive; *(hermitaño)* recluse, hermit —m. CUL. *(bocadillo)* sandwich.

em·pa·re·dar tr. *(encerrar entre paredes)* to immure, wall in;

(encarcelar) to imprison, confine; *(esconder entre paredes)* to hide *or* conceal (something) between walls.

em·pa·re·ja·du·ra f. *or* **em·pa·re·ja·mien·to** m. *(acción de alisar)* smoothing, leveling; *(acción de poner en parejas)* matching, pairing.

em·pa·re·jar tr. *(poner parejas)* to match, pair (off); *(poner a nivel)* to (make) level; *(alisar)* to smooth, even *or* level off; *(encerrar)* to close flush *or* without locking —intr. *(alcanzar)* to catch up, draw abreast; *(ser pareja)* to match; FIG. *(igualar)* to be considered an equal *or* rival (of someone) —reflex. *(ponerse en parejas)* to form pairs, pair off; MEX. to find the necessary steps *or* measures for success.

em·pa·ren·tar §49 intr. to become related by marriage ♦ **e. con** to marry into (a family).

em·pa·rrar tr. HORT. to make into a vine arbor *or* bower.

em·pa·rri·llar tr. CUL. to grill, broil on a grill.

em·par·var tr. AGR. to lay (grain) for threshing.

em·pas·tar tr. *(cubrir de pasta)* to cover with paste; BKB. to bind (a book); DENT. to fill (a tooth); PAINT. to apply paint thickly to (a canvas); AMER., AGR. to turn (land) into pasture —reflex. CHILE to become overgrown with weeds.

em·pas·te m. DENT. (tooth) filling; BKB. bookbinding; PAINT. impasting.

em·pa·tar tr. *(igualar)* to tie, equal; *(estorbar)* to impede, hold up; AMER. to couple, join; SALV. to fix, fasten; VEN. to pester, bother —intr. to tie, be equal —reflex. to result in a tie *or* draw ♦ **empatársela a uno** *(igualarle)* to equal someone's performance, be a match for someone; HOND. to fool *or* deceive someone.

em·pa·te m. *(equivalencia)* tie, draw; *(acción de igualar)* tying, equaling; *(estorbo)* obstacle, impediment; *(acción de estorbar)* obstructing, impeding; AMER. *(unión)* joint, connection; COL. penholder; VEN. waste of time, cause for procrastination.

em·pa·var tr. PERU, COLL. to tease, kid; ECUAD. to annoy, irritate —reflex. PERU, VEN. to become embarrassed.

em·pa·ve·sa·do, –da I. past part. see **empavesar II.** adj. armed with a shield **III.** m. *(soldado)* soldier armed with a shield; MARIT. bunting, dressing (of ship).

em·pa·ve·sar tr. MARIT. to dress, decorate with bunting (a ship); *(decorar)* to deck, decorate (streets for festivities); *(echar velo sobre)* to veil (a statue or monument before inauguration).

em·pa·vo·nar tr. *(pavonar)* to blue (metals); AMER. to grease —reflex. C. AMER. to dress up.

em·pe·ca·ta·do, –da adj. *(incorregible)* incorrigible; *(desgraciado)* ill-fated, unfortunate.

em·pe·cé see **empezar.**

em·pe·cer §17 tr. to harm, damage —intr. to impede, obstruct ♦ **lo que no empece** which does not prevent.

em·pe·ci·na·do, –da I. past part. see **empecinar II.** adj. *(terco)* stubborn, obstinate; *(empeñado)* persistent, determined **III.** m. maker *or* seller of pitch.

em·pe·ci·na·mien·to m. *(terquedad)* stubbornness, obstinacy; *(aferramiento)* insistence, determination.

em·pe·ci·nar tr. to cover *or* smear with pitch —reflex. to be stubborn *or* obstinate.

em·pe·dar·se reflex. ARG., MEX., COLL. to get drunk.

em·pe·der·ni·do, –da I. past part. see **empedernir II.** adj. FIG. *(duro de corazón)* hardhearted, insensitive; *(inveterado)* hardened, inveterate <un criminal e. a hardened criminal>.

em·pe·der·nir §38 tr. to harden, toughen —reflex. FIG. *(endurecerse)* to harden, toughen; *(hacerse insensible)* to harden, become callous.

em·pe·dra·do, –da I. past part. see **empedrar II.** adj. *(un caballo)* dappled, spotted (said of a horse) **III.** m. cobblestones, cobblestone pavement.

em·pe·drar §49 tr. *(cubrir con piedras)* to pave (with stones); FIG. *(cubrir)* to strew, scatter <e. de citas to strew with quotations>.

em·pe·gar §47 tr. *(bañar)* to coat with pitch; *(señalar)* to mark with pitch (sheep, cattle).

em·pei·ne m. ANAT. *(del vientre)* groin; *(del pie)* instep; *(de la bota)* instep, vamp (of a boot); MED. impetigo; BOT. liverwort, hepatica.

em·pe·lo·tar tr. COLL. to wrap up —reflex. COLL. *(reñir)* to get into a row, quarrel; AMER. *(desnudarse)* to strip naked *or* to the skin ♦ **empelotarse con** *or* **por** to fall madly in love with, go crazy over.

em·pe·llar *or* **em·pe·ller** §28 tr. to push, shove.

em·pe·llón m. push, shove ♦ **a empellones** FIG. roughly, violently.

em·pe·ñar tr. *(dar en prenda)* to pawn, pledge as security; *(obligar)* to oblige, compel; *(poner por medianero)* to have (someone) mediate *or* intercede <*empeñaron a Miguel en la disputa* they had Michael mediate the dispute>; MIL. *(comenzar)* to engage in, begin; *(enredar)* to embroil, involve ♦ **e. hasta la camisa** COLL. to stake *or* risk losing one's shirt —reflex. *(entramparse)* to fall *or* go into debt; *(insistir)* to insist, persist; MIL. *(trabarse)* to begin, start ♦ **empeñarse en** to be bent on *or* determined to • **empeñarse por** *or* **con** to intercede *or* mediate on behalf of.

em·pe·ño m. *(acción de dar en prenda)* pawning, pledging; *(prenda)* pawn, pledge; *(deudor)* debtor; *(obligación)* obligation, pledge; *(constancia)* insistence, tenacity; *(deseo)* desire, longing; *(protector)* patron, supporter; *(afán)* ambition, zeal; *(participación)* involvement, embroilment; *(recomendación)* recommendation, endorsement; MEX. pawnshop, hock shop ♦ **con e.** persistently, tenaciously • **poner** *or* **tomar e. en** to take great pains in • **tener e.** *(desear)* to want, desire; *(afanarse)* to be eager *or* persistent.

em·pe·ño·so, –sa adj. AMER. persevering, tenacious.

em·pe·o·ra·mien·to m. deterioration, worsening.

em·pe·o·rar tr. to make worse —intr. & reflex. to worsen, deteriorate.

em·pe·que·ñe·cer §17 tr. *(disminuir)* to diminish, make small; FIG. *(desprestigiar)* to belittle, disparage.

em·pe·que·ñe·ci·mien·to m. *(disminución)* diminishing, making smaller; FIG. *(desprestigio)* belittling, disparagement.

em·pe·ra·dor m. *(soberano)* emperor; CUBA, ICHTH. swordfish.

em·pe·ra·triz f. [pl. **-tri·ces**] empress.

em·per·char tr. to put on a hanger, hang up —reflex. HUNT. to become caught in a snare.

em·pe·re·ji·lar tr. COLL. to dress up, doll up —reflex. to get dressed up, doll (oneself) up.

em·per·ga·mi·nar tr. BKB. to bind in parchment.

em·pe·ri·fo·llar tr. & reflex. COLL. var. of **emperejilar.**

em·per·nar tr. TECH. to bolt, fasten down with bolts.

em·pe·ro conj. but, however.

em·pe·rra·mien·to m. COLL. *(rabia)* rage, anger; *(obstinación)* obstinacy, stubbornness.

em·pe·rrar·se reflex. COLL. *(encolerizarse)* to flare up, lose one's temper; *(obstinarse)* to be dead set, be determined.

em·per·ti·gar §47 tr. CHILE to yoke (oxen).

em·pe·zar §29 tr. & intr. *(comenzar)* to begin, commence ♦ **al e.** at the beginning *or* start • **e. a** to begin *or* start, to begin to <*e. a leer* to start reading> • **e. por** to begin by • **e. la casa por el tejado** to put the cart before the horse • **para e.** to begin with, first.

em·pez·ca, empezco see **empecer.**

em·pi·car·se §70 reflex. to become infatuated, become overly fond.

em·pi·co·tar tr. to pillory, put in the stocks.

em·pie·ce see **empezar.**

em·pie·dre, empiedro see **empedrar.**

em·pie·zo see **empezar.**

em·pi·na·do, –da I. past part. see **empinar** II. adj. *(muy alto)* very high, lofty; FIG. *(orgulloso)* proud, haughty.

em·pi·na·du·ra f. *or* **em·pi·na·mien·to** m. elevation, raising.

em·pi·nar tr. *(poner derecho)* to stand (up), set straight; *(elevar)* to raise, lift ♦ **e. el codo** FIG., COLL. to drink heavily, lift one's elbow (G.B.) —reflex. *(un caballo)* to rear; *(una persona)* to stand on tiptoe; *(una estructura)* to tower, rise up.

em·pin·go·ro·ta·do, –da I. past part. see **empingorotar** II. adj. haughty, stuck-up.

em·pin·go·ro·tar tr. COLL. to place an object above something else —reflex. *(subirse)* to climb on top of something; COLL. *(engreírse)* to become haughty *or* stuck-up.

em·pi·pa·da f. AMER., COLL. *(atracón)* big feed, bellyful; *(hartazgo)* satiety, surfeit.

em·pi·qué, empique see **empicarse.**

em·pí·re·o, –a I. adj. empyreal, celestial II. m. MYTH. *(esfera)* empyrean; *(cielo)* sky, firmament.

em·pí·ri·co, –ca I. adj. empirical II. m.f. empiricist.

em·pi·za·rra·do, –da I. past part. see **empizarrar** II. m. slate roof.

em·pi·za·rrar tr. to cover *or* roof with slate.

em·pla·cé, emplace see **emplazar.**

em·plas·tar tr. PHARM. *(poner parches)* to plaster, apply a plaster to; FIG. *(maquillar)* to make up, apply cosmetics to; FIG., COLL. *(detener)* to hamper, hold up —reflex. *(ensuciarse)* to become smeared *or* covered; *(maquillarse)* to make up (one's face); HOND. to leave a mark on the skin.

em·plas·te·cer §17 tr. to smooth (a surface).

em·plas·to m. *(medicamento)* plaster, poultice; FIG., COLL. *(enfermizo)* weakling, sickly person; *(componenda)* doubtful *or* unsatisfactory agreement; AMER. *(parche)* patch; *(aburrido)* boring *or* annoying person ♦ **e. de ranas** COLL. money.

em·pla·za·mien·to m. LAW *(acción de citar)* summoning, summons; *(escrito)* (writ of) summons; *(situación)* situation, positioning; *(sitio)* location, site ♦ **e. arqueológico** ARCHEOL. archaeological site.

em·pla·zar §04 tr. *(convocar)* to call together, convene; LAW *(citar ante un juez)* to summon to appear in court; *(situar)* to place, situate; HUNT. to reconnoiter —reflex. TAUR. to go into the center of the bullring.

em·ple·a·do, –da I. past part. see **emplear** II. m.f. employee ♦ **e. del estado** civil servant.

em·ple·a·dor, –do·ra I. adj. employing II. m.f. employer.

em·ple·ar tr. *(usar)* to use, employ; *(ocupar)* to employ, hire; *(nombrar)* to appoint to a position; *(gastar)* to spend (time or money); *(invertir)* to invest —reflex. to get a job, become employed ♦ **empleársele bien a uno** to get what one deserves, get one's just deserts.

em·ple·o m. *(ocupación)* job, occupation; *(uso)* use, utilization; MIL. rank, position; *(gasto de dinero)* expense; *(gasto de tiempo)* spending, use; *(inversión)* investment ♦ **sin e.** unemployed.

em·plo·mar tr. *(revestir de plomo)* to cover *or* line with lead; *(techar)* to roof with lead; *(poner sellos)* to seal with lead; AMER., DENT. to fill (a tooth); COL., GUAT. to fool, dupe.

em·plu·mar tr. *(poner plumas a)* to feather, adorn with feathers; *(castigar)* to tar and feather; CARIB., C. AMER. *(engañar)* to fool, dupe; GUAT., HOND. *(zurrar)* to give a beating to; CUBA *(despedir)* to dismiss, fire; ECUAD., VEN. exile, banish ♦ **emplumarlas** CHILE, COLL. to beat it, split —intr. ORNITH. *(enplumecer)* to fledge, grow feathers; AMER. to flee, take flight.

em·po·bre·cer §17 tr. to impoverish —intr. & reflex. *(venir a menos)* to become poor *or* impoverished.

em·po·bre·ci·do, –da I. past part. see **empobrecer** II. adj. impoverished.

em·po·bre·ci·mien·to m. impoverishment.

em·po·cé, empoce see **empozar.**

em·pol·var tr. *(echar polvo)* to powder, sprinkle with powder; *(ensuciar)* to cover with dust —reflex. *(ponerse polvos)* to dust oneself with powder, powder (oneself); *(ensuciarse)* to get dusty; MEX., FIG. to be rusty, be out of practice; DOM. REP. to run away, flee.

em·po·llar tr. ORNITH. to hatch, brood; FIG. *(estudiar mucho)* to bone up on <*e. la química* to bone up on chemistry>; *(meditar)* to brood *or* dwell on —intr. ENTOM. to breed, brood; *(estudiar mucho)* to grind, cram; AMER. to develop blisters.

em·po·llón, –llo·na adj. & m.f. DEROG. grind (student who studies a lot).

em·pon·cha·do, –da I. past part. see **emponcharse** II. adj. AMER. wearing a poncho; ARG., PERU, FIG. suspicious.

em·pon·char·se reflex. AMER. to wrap oneself in a poncho.

em·pon·zo·ñar tr. to poison.

em·por·car §73 tr. to soil, dirty —reflex. to become soiled *or* dirty.

em·po·rio m. *(centro comercial)* emporium, market; *(lugar* *famoso*) capital, center <*e. artístico* art capital>; AMER. department store.

em·po·trar tr. (*fijar con cemento*) to embed; ENTOM. to put (beehives) into a pit.

em·po·zar §04 tr. (*echar en un pozo*) to throw in a well; TEX. to ret, soak (flax) —intr. to form puddles, stagnate —reflex. FIG. to be shelved *or* forgotten.

em·pren·de·dor, –do·ra adj. enterprising, plucky.

em·pren·der tr. to begin, set about ♦ **e. a** *or* **con** to address, accost • **emprenderla a bofetadas con** to punch, begin hitting • **emprenderla con** to quarrel *or* wrangle with • **emprenderla para** to set out for.

em·pre·ñar tr. to impregnate, make pregnant.

em·pre·sa f. (*proyecto*) enterprise, undertaking; (*sociedad*) company, firm; (*dirección*) management; (*lema*) emblem, legend; (*designio*) design, intention ♦ **e. funeraria** undertaker's • **e. privada** private enterprise.

em·pre·sa·ria·do m. group of employers.

em·pre·sa·rial adj. managerial, management ♦ **empresariales** management studies.

em·pre·sa·rio, –ria m.f. (*gerente*) manager, director; THEAT. impresario, theater producer ♦ **e. de pompas fúnebres** undertaker, funeral director.

em·prés·ti·to m. loan ♦ **e. público** government *or* public loan • **lanzar** *or* **hacer un e.** FIN. to float a loan.

em·pri·mar tr. (*cardar*) to give a second carding to (wool); COLL. (*engañar*) to dupe, deceive (an inexperienced person); PAINT. to prime (canvas).

em·puer·que, empuerco see **emporcar**.

em·pu·jar tr. (*impeler*) to push, shove; (*apretar*) to press <*e. el botón* to press the button>; FIG. (*despedir*) to oust, push (someone) out of a job *or* position; (*hacer presión*) to press, put pressure on.

em·pu·je m. (*efecto de empujar*) push, shove; (*presión*) pressure; (*impulso*) thrust <*el e. del motor* the thrust of the motor>; FIG. (*energía*) energy, drive.

em·pu·jón m. push, shove ♦ **a empujones** (*bruscamente*) roughly, brusquely; (*con interrupciones*) intermittently, in fits and starts.

em·pul·gar §47 tr. (*armar*) to tighten the string of (a crossbow); (*llenar de pulgas*) to fill with fleas.

em·pun·tar tr. (*sacar punta*) to put a point on; COL. (*dirigir*) to direct towards ♦ **empuntarlas** COL. to run away, scram —reflex. VEN. to be obstinate, dig one's heels in.

em·pu·ña·du·ra f. (*de espada*) hilt (of a sword); (*de paraguas*) handle (of an umbrella); FIG., COLL. (*principio de un cuento*) beginning of a story.

em·pu·ñar tr. (*asir*) to seize, grasp; (*levantar*) to take up <*e. la espada* to take up the sword>; FIG. (*obtener un trabajo*) to land (a job); CHILE (*hacer un puño*) to make a fist.

em·pur·pu·ra·do, –da dressed in purple.

em·pu·te·cer §17 tr. to prostitute, corrupt.

e·mu·la·ción f. emulation.

e·mu·la·dor, –do·ra I. adj. emulating, rivaling II. m.f. emulator, rival.

e·mu·lar tr. to emulate, rival.

é·mu·lo, –la I. adj. emulating, rivaling II. m.f. emulator, rival.

e·mul·sión f. emulsion.

en prep. □ LOCATION in <*ellos están en la Argentina* they are in Argentina>; in, into <*lo puse en el banco* I put it into the bank>; at <*¿está en casa su padre?* is your father at home?>; on, upon <*las llaves están en la mesa* the keys are on the table> □ TIME in <*llegaremos en junio* we will arrive in June>; at <*en aquel momento* at that time>; as soon as <*en entrando el profesor, los estudiantes empezaron a leer* as soon as the professor entered, the students began to read> □ MANNER in <*lo dijo en broma* he said it in jest>; by <*hicieron el viaje en avión* they made the trip by plane>; at, for <*los vendimos en cien pesos* we sold them for one hundred pesos>; if <*en tomando el tren, llegarás a tiempo* if you take the train, you will arrive on time>; in, into <*el vino se convirtió en vinagre* the wine turned into vinegar>.

en·a·guar tr. to soak, drench.

e·na·guas f.pl. petticoat, underskirt.

en·a·je·na·ble adj. alienable.

en·a·je·na·ción f. alienation; FIG. (*distracción*) distraction,

absent-mindedness; (*éxtasis*) rapture, ecstasy ♦ **e. mental** mental derangement, madness.

en·a·je·nar tr. (*alienar*) to alienate; FIG. (*turbar*) to drive crazy, drive to distraction —reflex. (*apartarse*) to become alienated *or* estranged; (*extasiarse*) to become enraptured.

en·al·bar·dar tr. (*poner la albarda*) to saddle; FIG. (*rebozar con harina*) to coat with flour, bread; (*emborazar*) to lard, cover with bacon strips.

en·al·te·ce·dor, –do·ra adj. extolling, praising.

en·al·te·cer §17 tr. to extol, praise.

en·al·te·ci·mien·to m. extolling, praising.

en·a·mo·ra·da·men·te adv. lovingly, affectionately; (*con pasión*) passionately.

en·a·mo·ra·di·zo, –za adj. easily infatuated, always falling in love.

en·a·mo·ra·do, –da I. past part. see **enamorar** II. adj. (*que tiene amor*) enamored, in love; (*enamoradizo*) easily infatuated, always falling in love ♦ **e. de** in love with, enamored of III. m.f. (*novio*) sweetheart, lover; FIG. (*aficionado*) lover <*e. de las artes* lover of the arts>.

en·a·mo·ra·mien·to m. falling *or* being in love; (*amor*) love.

en·a·mo·rar tr. (*inspirar amor*) to enamor, inspire love; (*cortejar*) to court, woo —reflex. (*sentir amor*) to fall in love <*enamorarse de alguien* to fall in love with someone>; (*aficionarse*) to become enamored <*enamorarse de una teoría* to become enamored with a theory>.

en·a·mo·ri·car·se §70 *or* **e·na·mo·ris·car·se** §70 reflex. to be infatuated ♦ **e. de** to be infatuated with, take a fancy to.

en·an·car·se §70 reflex. AMER. to ride on a horse's haunches; MEX. to rear up (said of a horse).

e·na·no, –na I. adj. FIG. small, minute II. m.f. dwarf.

en·ar·bo·lar tr. to raise, hoist —reflex. (*encabritarse*) to rear up (said of a horse); (*enfadarse*) to be angry.

en·ar·car §70 tr. (*arquear*) to bend, arch; (*echar arcos a*) to hoop (barrels) —reflex. (*encogerse*) to bend, arch ♦ **e. las cejas** to raise one's eyebrows.

en·ar·de·ce·dor, –do·ra adj. fiery, inflammatory.

en·ar·de·cer §17 tr. FIG. to ignite, set aflame —reflex. to be ignited.

en·a·re·nar tr. (*cubrir de arena*) to cover with sand, sand; MIN. to mix (ore) with sand —reflex. MARIT. to run aground.

en·ar·qué, enarque see **enarcar**.

en·as·tar tr. to put a handle *or* shaft on.

en·ca·bal·gar §47 intr. to rest upon, lean on —tr. (*montar*) to mount a horse; (*proveer*) to provide with horses.

en·ca·ba·llar tr. (*traslapar*) to overlap, imbricate PRINT. to pie, mix up —reflex. PRINT. to become pied, get mixed up.

en·ca·be·cé, encabece see **encabezar**.

en·ca·bes·trar tr. (*poner el cabestro*) to put a halter on; FIG. (*atraer*) to attract, seduce —reflex. to become tangled up in the halter (said of a horse).

en·ca·be·za·mien·to m. (*titular*) caption, headline; (*de una carta*) heading; (*registro*) census list *or* register; (*impuestos*) tax roll.

en·ca·be·zar §04 tr. FIG. (*estar a la cabeza*) to head, lead; (*un periódico*) to title, head; (*una carta*) to head; (*registrar*) to register, enroll; (*vino*) to fortify (wine); CARP. to join —reflex. to agree, come to terms.

en·ca·bri·tar·se reflex. (*un caballo*) to rear up (said of a horse); (*un vehículo*) to pitch upwards (said of a vehicle); COLL. (*enfadarse*) to get angry.

en·ca·bro·nar tr. CUBA to infuriate —reflex. to become furious.

en·ca·de·na·ción f. *or* **en·ca·de·na·du·ra** f. *or* **en·ca·de·na·mien·to** m. (*acción de encadenar*) enchainment, chaining; (*conexión*) connection, linking.

en·ca·de·na·do, –da I. past part. see **encadenar** II. adj. POET. linked III. m. ARCHIT. buttress, reinforcement; CINEM. dissolve.

en·ca·de·nar tr. (*atar con cadena*) to enchain, chain; (*inmovilizar*) to chain up; FIG. (*sujetar*) to chain down; (*conectar*) to connect, link.

en·ca·jar tr. (*introducir*) to fit, insert <*e. el anillo al dedo* to fit the ring on the finger>; (*ajustar*) to force; (*dar a enten-*

der) to slip in, drop; FIG., COLL. *(engañar)* to pass off <*le encajaron un billete falso* they passed off a counterfeit bill on him>; COLL. *(dar)* to deal, land <*le encajó un palo* he dealt him a blow>; *(hacer oír)* to give <*el maestro nos encajó un discurso con respeto a nuestra disciplina* the teacher gave us a speech about our discipline> —intr. *(juntarse bien)* to fit (well); FIG., COLL. to square <*estos hechos no encajan* these facts don't square> —reflex. *(meterse)* to squeeze in; FIG. *(ponerse)* to put on (clothes); ARG., AUTO. to get stuck.

en·ca·je m. TEX. lace; *(inserción)* insertion, inserting; *(unión)* joining, fitting; TECH. *(marquetería)* inlay; *(hueco)* socket ♦ **encajes** COM. cash reserve.

en·ca·je·tar tr. to insert, put in.

en·ca·jo·na·do I. past part. see **encajonar** II. m. ARCHIT. *(tapia)* boxing work, packed work; CONSTR. *(ataguía)* cofferdam.

en·ca·jo·na·mien·to m. *(acción de meter en cajón)* boxing, crating; *(de un río, camino)* narrowness, narrowing.

en·ca·jo·nar tr. *(meter en cajón)* to box, crate; *(estrechar)* to squeeze in; ARCHIT. *(reforzar)* to reinforce, buttress —reflex. to run through a narrow place.

en·ca·la·bo·zar §04 tr. COLL. to lock up in a cell *or* dungeon.

en·ca·la·bri·nar tr. *(inebriar)* to go to the head of, intoxicate <*el vino me encalabrinó* the wine went to my head>; *(irritar)* to irritate, exasperate —reflex. *(encapricharse)* to become obsessed with, become infatuated with; *(obstinarse)* to get dead set on, be stubborn.

en·ca·la·do m. *or* **en·ca·la·du·ra** f. whitewashing.

en·ca·lar tr. *(blanquear)* to whitewash; AGR. *(dar de cal)* to lime, sprinkle with lime.

en·cal·ve·cer §17 intr. to lose one's hair, go bald.

en·ca·lla·de·ro m. MARIT. shoal, sandbank; FIG. *(atascadero)* obstruction, stumbling block.

en·ca·llar intr. MARIT. to run aground; FIG. *(enredarse)* to founder, bog down —reflex. to harden (food while cooking).

en·ca·lle·cer §17 intr. & reflex. to develop corns, become callused; FIG. *(endurecerse)* to harden, become callous.

en·ca·lle·ci·do, –da I. past part. see **encallecer** II. adj. hardened, calloused.

en·ca·lle·jo·nar tr. to lead through a narrow passage *or* alley.

en·ca·ma·rar tr. to store in a granary.

en·ca·mar·se reflex. COLL. to stay in bed (due to illness); AGR. to be beaten down, droop (said of crops).

en·cam·bro·nar tr. *(cercar)* to hedge with brambles; *(fortificar)* to strengthen with iron.

en·ca·mi·na·mien·to m. *or* **en·ca·mi·na·du·ra** f. *(dirección)* guiding, directing; FIG. *(orientación)* guidance.

en·ca·mi·nar tr. to direct, guide —reflex. to make for, set out for.

en·ca·mi·sa·do m. *(máscaras)* masquerade; MECH. putting new linings on (piece of machinery).

en·ca·mi·sar tr. *(vestir)* to put a shirt on; *(enfundar)* to put a cover on, cover up; *(envolver)* to wrap; MECH. to put new linings on (piece of machinery); FIG. *(disfrazar)* to disguise —reflex. MIL. to disguise for a night attack.

en·ca·mo·ta·do, –da I. past part. see **encamotarse** II. adj. AMER., COLL. in love.

en·ca·mo·tar·se reflex. AMER., COLL. to fall in love.

en·cam·pa·nar tr. P. RICO, VEN. to raise, lift; MEX. *(dejar a uno colgado)* to leave (a person) in the lurch —reflex. *(ensancharse)* to put on airs; PERU to become complicated *or* involved (a situation); TAUR. to raise the head defiantly (said of a bull).

en·ca·na·lar tr. to channel through pipes *or* conduits.

en·ca·na·li·zar §04 tr. var. of **encanalar.**

en·ca·na·llar·se reflex. *(corromperse)* to become degenerate, become depraved; *(alternar)* to associate with corrupt people, keep bad company.

en·ca·nar tr. ARG. to jail, incarcerate.

en·ca·nas·tar tr. to put in a basket.

en·can·de·cer §17 tr. to make incandescent.

en·can·de·lar intr. to blossom (said of trees) —tr. CUBA to bother, annoy.

en·can·de·li·llar tr. AMER., SEW. to overstitch; *(deslumbrar)* to dazzle.

en·can·di·la·do, –da I. past part. see **encandilar** II. adj. COLL. erect, tall.

en·can·di·lar tr. *(deslumbrar)* to dazzle, blind; FIG. *(engañar)* to dazzle, delude; *(avivar la lumbre)* to stir, rake (coals); FIG. *(excitar el sentimiento)* to kindle, excite (feelings) —reflex. to light up (eyes, face).

en·ca·ne·cer §17 intr. & reflex. *(ponerse cano)* to go gray; FIG. *(envejecerse)* to age, grow old; *(ponerse mohoso)* to become moldy —tr. to age.

en·ca·ni·jar·se reflex. to grow weak, become emaciated.

en·ca·ni·llar tr. to wind on a spool or bobbin (thread).

en·can·ta·ción f. var. of **encantamiento.**

en·can·ta·do, –da I. past part. see **encantar** II. adj. *(muy satisfecho)* delighted, charmed; *(distraído)* absentminded, distracted; haunted <*una casa e.* a haunted house>.

en·can·ta·dor, –do·ra I. adj. enchanting, charming II. m.f. *(seductor)* charmer —m. *(mago)* magician, sorcerer —f. *(hechicera)* sorceress; *(seductora)* seductress ♦ **e. de serpientes** snake charmer.

en·can·ta·mien·to m. *(encanto)* enchantment; *(hechizo)* bewitchment, spell.

en·can·tar tr. *(hechizar)* to bewitch, cast a spell on; FIG. *(embelesar)* to captivate, enchant; *(causar placer)* to delight, charm.

en·can·te m. *(subasta)* auction, public sale; *(lugar)* auction room.

en·can·to m. *(hechizo)* enchantment, bewitchment; FIG. *(fascinación)* delight, fascination; *(magia)* magic ♦ **encantos** charms.

en·ca·ñar[1] tr. *(conducir agua)* to channel, pipe (water); *(sacar humedad)* to drain (land).

en·ca·ñar[2] tr. *(poner caña)* to stake, prop up (plants) —intr. to form stalks (said of cereal plants).

en·ca·ño·nar tr. *(encañar)* to channel, pipe; *(apuntar con arma)* to take aim at; *(encanillar)* to wind on a spool or bobbin; *(planchar)* to goffer, crimp —intr. to grow feathers, fledge.

en·ca·pi·llar tr. MARIT. to rig; MIN. to open a new gallery (in a mine); *(poner en capilla)* to put (a condemned prisoner) in a chapel —reflex. to put clothes on (over the head).

en·ca·po·ta·do, –da I. past part. see **encapotar** II. adj. *(nublado)* overcast, cloudy; *(encapuchado)* cloaked; CUBA, MEX. *(alicaído)* downcast, dejected.

en·ca·po·tar tr. to cover with a cloak —reflex. FIG. *(poner rostro ceñudo)* frown; *(nublarse)* to become cloudy or overcast; *(bajar la cabeza)* to lower the head (said of a horse); CUBA, MEX., P. RICO to become sick or listless (said of a bird).

en·ca·pri·cha·mien·to m. whim, fancy.

en·ca·pri·char·se reflex. to take it into one's head, take a fancy ♦ **e. por** *or* **con** to become infatuated with, take a fancy to.

en·ca·pu·char tr. to hood, cover with a hood.

en·ca·ra·do, –da adj. ♦ **bien e.** good-looking • **mal e.** ugly-looking.

en·ca·ra·mar tr. *(levantar)* to lift, raise; FIG. *(a un puesto elevado)* to elevate, promote; *(elogiar)* to extol, praise; COL. *(abochornar)* to embarrass, make blush —reflex. *(subir)* to climb up; *(alcanzar un puesto elevado)* to reach a high position; *(abochornarse)* to blush.

en·ca·ra·mien·to m. encounter, confrontation.

en·ca·rar intr. & reflex. to face, confront —tr. *(apuntar con arma)* to take aim at; FIG. *(confrontar)* to confront, face.

en·car·ce·la·mien·to m. incarceration, imprisonment.

en·car·ce·lar tr. *(poner en la cárcel)* to incarcerate, imprison; *(empotrar)* to imbed, embed; CARP. to clamp.

en·ca·re·ce·dor, –do·ra I. adj. praising, extolling II. m.f. praiser, extoller.

en·ca·re·cer §17 tr. *(hacer más caro)* to raise the price of; FIG. *(elogiar)* to extol, praise; *(recomendar)* to recommend, urge —intr. & reflex. to become more expensive.

en·ca·re·ci·da·men·te adv. earnestly, insistently.

en·ca·re·ci·mien·to m. *(aumento de precio)* rise in price;

(alabanza) praise; *(recomendación)* recommendation, urging ♦ **con e.** earnestly, insistently.

en·car·ga·do, –da I. past part. see **encargar** II. adj. in charge <*debe usted hablar con la persona encargada de eso* you should speak with the person in charge of that> III. m.f. person in charge ♦ **e. de negocios** DIPL. chargé d'affaires.

en·car·gar §47 tr. *(encomendar)* to entrust, put in charge; *(pedir)* to advise, recommend <*cuando salí de casa mamá me encargó que volviera temprano* when I left the house, Mother advised me to be back early>; *(ordenar)* to order, request —reflex. to take charge *or* responsibility <*me encargué de los niños* I took charge of the children>.

en·car·go m. *(recado)* errand, task; *(cosa encargada)* charge; *(trabajo)* assignment, job; *(empleo)* post ♦ **como hecho de e.** as if made to order.

en·car·gue m. ARG. var. of **encargo**.

en·ca·ri·ñar tr. to make fond of, endear —reflex. to become fond ♦ **encariñarse con** to become fond of.

en·car·na·ción f. RELIG. Incarnation; FIG. *(personificación)* incarnation; *(color)* flesh color.

en·car·na·do, –da I. past part. see **encarnar** II. adj. *(de color de carne)* flesh-colored; *(colorado)* red; *(personificado)* incarnate; *(complexión)* ruddy III. m. *(color de carne)* flesh color; *(rojo)* red.

en·car·nar intr. *(tomar forma carnal)* to become incarnate; *(cicatrizar)* to heal, close up (a wound); *(herir)* to penetrate the flesh *or* skin; FIG. *(impresionar)* to make a great impression —tr. *(personificar)* to personify, embody; *(cebar)* to blood (hounds); THEAT. to play (a role); ARTS *(colorar)* to give flesh color (to a sculpture) —reflex. to mix, join.

en·car·ni·cé, encarnice see **encarnizar**.

en·car·ni·za·do, –da I. past part. see **encarnizar** II. adj. *(ensangrentado)* bloodshot; *(sangriento)* bloody; *(intenso)* fierce, bitter.

en·car·ni·za·mien·to m. HUNT. eating *or* gorging on meat; FIG. *(crueldad)* bloodthirstiness, extreme cruelty.

en·car·ni·zar §04 tr. HUNT. to blood (hounds); FIG. *(enfurecer)* to make cruel, brutalize <*la guerra encarniza a los hombres* war brutalizes men> —reflex. HUNT. to gorge on meat; FIG. *(encrudecerse)* to become cruel *or* brutal; *(pelear)* to fight bitterly *or* fiercely.

en·ca·ro m. facing, confronting; *(puntería)* aiming (at); *(trabuco)* blunderbuss; *(parte de la culata)* cheek rest (on a rifle).

en·car·pe·tar tr. *(guardar en carpeta)* to file (away), put in a file; *(dar carpetazo)* to shelve, pigeonhole.

en·ca·rri·lar *or* **en·ca·rri·llar** tr. *(encaminar)* to direct, guide; *(colocar sobre rieles)* to put on tracks; FIG. *(dar una buena orientación)* to put on the right track —reflex. MARIT. to get fouled up (a rope on a pulley).

en·ca·rru·jar tr. *(encarrilar)* to direct, guide; AMER. to gather, shirr —reflex. to become twisted, curl up.

en·car·tar tr. *(condenar)* to proscribe, outlaw (a criminal); *(emplazar)* to summon; *(incluir en los padrones)* to register, enroll (for taxes); *(introducir)* to insert, include <*e. un prospecto en una revista* to insert a brochure in a magazine>; *(implicar)* to implicate, involve <*las personas encartadas en este asunto* the people involved in this affair>; *(jugar)* to lead (in cards) —intr. FIG., COLL. *(ser conveniente)* to be suitable *or* opportune; *(encajar)* to go, fit in <*eso no encarta con mis proyectos* that doesn't fit in with my plans> —reflex. to have to follow suit (in card games).

en·car·to·nar tr. to bind *or* cover with cardboard.

en·cas·ca·be·lar tr. to decorate with jingle bells.

en·cas·co·tar tr. to fill with debris *or* rubble.

en·ca·si·lla·do, –da I. past part. see **encasillar** II. adj. CHILE, PERU checkered III. m. (set of) pigeonholes.

en·ca·si·llar tr. *(poner en casillas)* to pigeonhole; *(clasificar)* to classify, class; *(designar a un candidato)* to designate as a government candidate.

en·cas·que·tar tr. *(vestir)* to pull on, put on (a hat); FIG. *(meter en la cabeza)* to put into someone's head (an idea); *(hacer oír)* to make listen, make sit through <*nos encasquetó un discurso aburrido* he made us sit through a boring speech> —reflex. *(vestirse)* to pull on (a hat); FIG. *(obsti-*

narse) to take it into one's head <*se le encasquetó la idea de viajar por barco* he took it into his head to travel by boat>.

en·cas·qui·lla·dor m. AMER. blacksmith, farrier.

en·cas·qui·llar tr. AMER. to shoe (a horse) —reflex. *(atascarse)* to jam, get stuck (pistol); CUBA to get frightened.

en·cas·ti·llar tr. *(fortificar)* to fortify with castles; *(apilar)* to pile, pile up; *(armar un andamio)* to build a scaffold, erect scaffolding —reflex. *(defenderse)* to defend oneself (in a castle); *(acogerse)* to take refuge <*e. en un risco* to take refuge in a cliff>; FIG. *(empeñarse)* to persist in, stick to one's guns.

en·cas·trar tr. MECH. to mesh, engage; *(empotrar)* to insert, fit in.

en·cau·char tr. to rubberize (fabric).

en·cau·sar tr. LAW to prosecute, sue.

en·cau·zar §04 tr. to channel, direct.

en·ce·ba·dar VET. tr. to feed too much (to horses) —reflex. to become bloated *or* flatulent (said of horses).

en·ce·bo·llar tr. to season with onions.

en·ce·fá·li·co, –ca adj. MED. encephalic.

en·ce·fa·li·tis f. MED. encephalitis.

en·cé·fa·lo m. ANAT. encephalon, brain.

en·ce·fa·lo·gra·ma m. MED. encephalogram.

en·ce·lar tr. to make jealous —reflex. *(concebir celos)* to become jealous; *(estar en celo)* to be in heat (animals).

en·cel·dar tr. to put in a cell, incarcerate.

en·ce·lla f. cheese mold.

en·ce·na·ga·do, –da I. past part. see **encenagarse** II. adj. *(manchado con cieno)* muddy, stained with mud; FIG. *(enviciado)* vice-ridden, depraved.

en·ce·na·gar·se §47 reflex. to wallow.

en·cen·de·dor m. *(chisquero)* lighter; *(hombre)* lamplighter.

en·cen·der §50 tr. to light <*e. un cigarrillo* to light a cigarette>; *(pegar fuego)* to ignite; *(incendiar)* to set on fire; to turn on <*e. la luz* to turn on the light>; FIG. *(excitar)* to arouse, excite; *(causar)* to spark, start <*el incidente diplomático encendió la guerra* the diplomatic incident sparked the war>; *(provocar)* to provoke —reflex. to light <*esta cerilla no se enciende* this match won't light>; *(incendiarse)* to catch on fire; FIG. *(excitarse)* to get excited; *(estallar)* to break out <*la guerra se encendió* war broke out>; *(ruborizarse)* to blush.

en·cen·di·do, –da I. past part. see **encender** II. adj. lit, switched on <*la lámpara está e.* the lamp is lit>; *(hecho ascua)* red, red-hot; *(inflamado)* inflamed, red III. m. AUTO. ignition; *(acción de inflamar)* firing.

en·ce·ni·zar §04 tr. to cover with ashes.

en·cen·tar §49 tr. *(empezar)* to begin; *(decentar)* to cut the first slice from.

en·ce·par tr. *(a un prisionero)* to put in the stocks, pillory; CARP. to join (using clamps); ARTIL., MARIT. to stock (a gun or anchor) —intr. BOT. to take deep root.

en·ce·ra·do, –da I. past part. see **encerar** II. adj. *(de color de cera)* wax-colored; *(pulido con cera)* waxed, polished III. m. *(acción de pulir)* waxing, polishing; *(cera)* wax; *(pizarra)* blackboard; *(tela)* oilcloth, oilskin; MARIT. tarpaulin.

en·ce·ra·dor, –do·ra m.f. *(persona)* floor polisher *or* waxer —f. *(aparato)* floor polisher *or* waxer.

en·ce·rar tr. *(dar cera)* to wax, polish; *(manchar)* to stain *or* soil with wax; *(espesar)* to thicken (lime or mortar); MEX., RELIG. to furnish *or* provide with candles —intr. & reflex. ARG. to turn yellow, ripen.

en·ce·rra·du·ra f. *or* **en·ce·rra·mien·to** m. *(acción de meter sin salida)* confining; *(confinamiento)* confinement; *(recinto)* enclosure; *(retiro)* seclusion, retreat; *(cárcel)* jail, cell.

en·ce·rrar §49 tr. *(meter sin salida)* to enclose, confine; AGR. *(poner en un corral)* to pen, corral; FIG. *(incluir)* to hold, contain; *(implicar)* to involve, entail; *(en el ajedrez)* to mate, checkmate —reflex. to go into seclusion.

en·ces·pe·dar tr. to (cover with) turf.

en·ces·tar tr. *(meter en una cesta)* to put in a basket; SPORT. to score in basketball.

en·cí·a f. ANAT., DENT. gum, gingiva.

en·cí·cli·ca f. RELIG. encyclical (letter).

en·ci·clo·pe·dia f. encyclopedia, encyclopaedia.

en·ci·clo·pé·di·co, –ca adj. encyclopedic, encyclopaedic.

en·ci·clo·pe·dis·mo m. encyclopedism, encyclopaedism.

en·ci·clo·pe·dis·ta I. adj. encyclopedic, encyclopaedic **II.** m.f. encyclopedist, encyclopaedist.

en·cien·da, enciendo see **encender.**

en·cien·te, enciento see **encentar.**

en·cie·rre, encierro see **encerrar.**

en·cie·rro m. *(acción de encerrar)* shutting, closing; *(recinto)* enclosure; *(clausura)* seclusion; *(retiro)* retirement; *(prisión)* narrow prison; TAUR. penning (of bulls).

en·ci·ma adv. *(sobre)* on top <*ponga los libros e. de la mesa* put the books on top of the table>; *(además)* in addition, besides <*yo pagué los tragos e. la comida* I paid for the drinks in addition to the food> ♦ **de e.** CHILE in addition, besides ♦ **echarse e.** to throw oneself onto *or* at ♦ **echarse e. una responsabilidad** to take upon oneself, undertake ♦ **e. de** above ♦ **estar e. de** FIG., COLL. to be on top of ♦ **llevar** *or* **tener e.** to have (money) on oneself ♦ **por e.** superficially ♦ **por e. de** in spite of.

en·ci·mar tr. *(poner encima)* to place *or* put on top; *(poner en alto)* to raise *or* hold high; *(dar de más)* to give an extra measure; *(apostar)* to raise (in card games), CHILE to cap, top —intr. CHILE to reach the top *or* summit —reflex. to rise above, tower.

en·ci·na f. *or* **en·ci·no** m. BOT. evergreen *or* holm oak.

en·cin·ta adj. pregnant, with child.

en·cin·tar tr. *(adornar)* to beribbon, adorn with ribbon; *(poner el cintero)* to bridle, put a bridle on (a young bull); *(pasar las cintas)* to rim with a curbstone; MARIT. to put wales on (a ship).

en·clan·char·se reflex. HOND. to put on a garment.

en·claus·trar tr. *(meter en un claustro)* to put in a cloister; FIG. *(esconder)* to hide, conceal.

en·cla·va·do, –da I. past part. see **enclavar II.** adj. *(juntado con)* joined (to); *(encajado)* embedded (in); GEOG., POL. *(encerrado)* enclaved **III.** m. GEOG., POL. enclave.

en·cla·var tr. CARP. to nail (down); VET. to wound (a horse while shoeing); FIG. *(traspasar)* to pierce, transfix; *(ubicar)* to locate, situate; COLL. *(engañar)* to trick, dupe.

en·cla·ve m. GEOG., POL. enclave.

en·cla·vi·jar tr. CARP. to peg, join with pegs; MUS. to peg, put pegs on (a stringed instrument).

en·clen·que I. adj. *(enfermizo)* weak, sickly; *(muy flaco)* skinny, thin **II.** m.f. weak *or* sickly person.

en·clo·car §73 intr. & reflex. ORNITH. to go broody (a hen).

en·co·bra·do, –da I. past part. see **encobrar II.** adj. MIN. coppery, containing copper **III.** m. coppering, coating with copper.

en·co·brar tr. to cover *or* coat with copper.

en·co·co·rar tr. COLL. to annoy, vex —reflex. to be annoyed *or* vexed.

en·co·fra·do I. past part. see **encofrar II.** m. ARCHIT. plank molding, formwork; MIN. plank lining, timbering.

en·co·frar tr. MIN. to plank, timber.

en·co·ger §34 tr. *(contraer)* to contract, draw in; *(reducir)* to shrink, make smaller; FIG. *(apocar el ánimo de)* to intimidate, cow —intr. & reflex. *(contraerse)* to contract; *(reducirse)* to shrink, become smaller; FIG. *(achicarse)* to lose courage, feel timid ♦ **encogerse de hombros** to shrug one's shoulders.

en·co·gi·do, –da I. past part. see **encoger II.** adj. FIG. *(tímido)* shy, bashful; *(pusilánime)* faint-hearted, cowardly **III.** m.f. *(persona tímida)* shy *or* bashful person; *(persona pusilánime)* coward, faint-hearted person.

en·co·gi·mien·to m. *(constricción)* contraction, constriction; *(reducción)* shrinkage, dimunition; FIG. *(timidez)* shyness, bashfulness; *(cobardía)* cowardice, faint-heartedness ♦ **e. de hombros** *(acción)* shrugging (of the shoulders); *(efecto)* shrug.

en·co·ja, encojo see **encoger.**

en·co·jar tr. to lame, cripple —reflex. *(ponerse cojo)* to become lame *or* crippled; FIG., COLL. *(caer enfermo)* to become sick, fall ill; *(fingir enfermedad)* to malinger, feign illness.

en·co·la·do, –da I. past part. see **encolar II.** adj. CHILE, MEX., FIG. *(gomoso)* dandified, foppish **III.** m. clarification (of wine).

en·co·la·du·ra f. *(pegadura)* sticking, gluing; *(clarificación)* clarification, clarifying (of wine); PAINT., TEX. priming, sizing.

en·co·lar tr. *(pegar)* to glue, stick; *(clarificar)* to clarify (wine); PAINT., TEX. to prime, size; *(arrojar)* to throw out of reach.

en·co·le·ri·zar §04 tr. to anger, enrage —reflex. to become angry *or* enraged.

en·co·men·dar §49 tr. *(confiar)* to entrust, commend; HIST. *(hacer comendador)* to bestow the rank of knight commander on —intr. HIST. to become a knight commander —reflex. *(confiarse)* to entrust *or* commend oneself; *(enviar recuerdos)* to send one's regards.

en·co·men·de·ro m. *(comisionista)* commissioner, agent; HIST. *(gobernador)* Spanish colonist in charge of Indian laborers; CUBA *(suministrador)* wholesale meat supplier; PERU *(abacero)* grocer.

en·co·mia·dor, –do·ra I. adj. laudatory, encomiastic **II.** m.f. praiser, encomiast.

en·co·miar tr. to praise, extol.

en·co·miás·ti·co, –ca adj. laudatory, complimentary.

en·co·mien·da f. *(encargo)* commission, task; *(dignidad)* commandery, commandry (of a military order); *(cruz)* knight commander's cross; *(recomendación)* praise, commendation; *(amparo)* care, protection; AMER. postal parcel *or* package ♦ **encomiendas** regards, compliments.

en·co·mien·de, encomiendo see **encomendar.**

en·co·mio m. encomium, praise.

en·com·pa·drar intr. COLL. *(contraer compadrazgo)* to become a godparent (to someone's child); *(hacerse compadres)* to become pals.

en·co·na·mien·to m. MED. inflammation (of a wound); FIG. *(rencor)* rancor, ill will; CHILE, COL. wound, sore.

en·co·nar tr. MED. to inflame, irritate (a wound) FIG. *(enfadar)* to anger, irritate; *(cargar la conciencia de mala acción)* to burden (the conscience) with feelings of guilt —reflex. MED. to become inflamed *or* irritated; FIG. *(enfadarse)* to become angry *or* irritated.

en·con·cha·do m. PERU mother-of-pearl inlay.

en·con·gar·se §47 reflex. MEX. to become annoyed *or* irritated.

en·co·no m. *(rencor)* rancor, ill will; MED. inflammation (of a wound); CHILE, COL. *(llaga)* wound, sore.

en·co·no·so, –sa adj. FIG. *(rencoroso)* crabby, irascible; *(una llaga)* sore, inflamed.

en·con·tra·do, –da I. past part. see **encontrar II.** adj. *(puesto enfrente)* facing *or* opposite one another; *(antitético)* contrary, opposing.

en·con·trar §19 tr. *(hallar)* to find <*encontré la clave del enigma* I found the key to the enigma>; *(topar)* to meet, encounter <*mi padre encontró a un amigo en el parque* my father met a friend in the park> —intr. to meet —reflex. *(tropezar)* to meet, encounter <*nos encontramos con un obstáculo insuperable* we met with an insurmountable obstacle>; *(concurrir)* to meet <*se encontraron en el museo* they met in the museum>; *(chocar)* to clash, differ <*las ideas de ambos se encuentran* the two ideas clash>; *(enemistarse)* to have a falling out, become enemies; *(estar)* to be, be located <*¿dónde se encuentra el teatro?* where is the theater?>; *(sentirse)* to find oneself <*ella se encuentra sola* she finds herself alone> ♦ **encontrarse con** *(hallar)* to find, run across; *(topar)* to meet, run into.

en·con·trón *or* **en·con·tro·na·zo** m. *(golpe)* crash, collision; *(riña)* quarrel, dispute.

en·co·pe·ta·do, –da I. past part. see **encopetar II.** adj. FIG. *(presumido)* arrogant, haughty; *(de alto copete)* of noble birth *or* descent.

en·co·pe·tar tr. to raise high —reflex. FIG. to put on airs, be conceited.

en·co·ra·jar tr. to encourage, hearten —reflex. to become incensed *or* angry.

en·co·ra·ji·nar·se reflex. COLL. *(encolerizarse)* to get angry, lose one's temper; CHILE to fail, fall through (a deal).

en·co·rar §19 tr. *(cubrir)* to cover with leather; *(encerrar)* to wrap up in leather; *(curar)* to help the formation of new skin, make wounds heal —intr. to heal, grow new skin (wounds).

en·cor·cha·dor, –do·ra I. adj. corking **II.** m.f. *(persona)* person who corks bottles —f. *(máquina)* corking machine.

en·cor·char tr. ENTOM. to put (bees) into a hive; *(poner tapones)* to cork (bottles).

en·cor·che·tar tr. SEW. *(poner corchetes)* to fit with a clasp *or* hook and eye; *(sujetar)* to fasten with a clasp *or* hook and eye.

en·cor·dar §19 tr. MUS. to string (an instrument); *(apretar con una cuerda)* to bind with a cord.

en·cor·de·lar tr. *(atar con cordeles)* to tie *or* bind with cord; *(adornar)* to decorate with braid *or* gimp.

en·cor·do·na·do, –da I. past part. see **encordonar** II. adj. decorated with braid *or* gimp.

en·cor·do·nar tr. to bind with cord.

en·co·ria·ción f. healing (of a wound).

en·cor·na·do, –da adj. ZOOL. horned.

en·co·rra·lar tr. to corral, pen (cattle).

en·cor·ti·nar tr. to provide with curtains.

en·cor·va·du·ra f. *or* **en·cor·va·mien·to** m. *(doblamiento)* bending, curving; *(curva)* bend, curve.

en·cor·var tr. to bend, curve —reflex. *(ladearse)* to stoop, bend down; EQUIT. to buck (said of a horse); FIG. *(inclinarse)* to lean toward, be partial to.

en·cos·trar tr. to cover with a crust —intr. & reflex. to form a crust.

en·cres·par tr. *(ensortijar)* to curl; *(erizar)* to make (one's hair) stand on end —reflex. *(ensortijarse)* to curl; *(erizarse)* to stand on end (hair); MARIT. to become choppy (said of waves); FIG. *(enredarse)* to become complicated; *(enardecerse)* to become agitated *or* excited.

en·cru·ci·ja·da f. *(cruce de vías)* crossroads, intersection; FIG. *(emboscada)* ambush, snare; *(dilema)* dilemma.

en·cru·de·cer §17 tr. *(hacer parecer crudo)* to make rough *or* raw; FIG. *(irritar)* to irritate, exasperate —intr. & reflex. METEOROL. to become harsh *or* rough.

en·cua·der·na·ción f. BKB. *(acción de encuadernar)* bookbinding; *(taller)* bindery ♦ **e. en cuero** leather binding • **e. en tela** cloth binding.

en·cua·der·na·dor, –do·ra m.f. BKB. bookbinder —m. *(sujetador)* paper clip.

en·cua·der·nar tr. BKB. to bind.

en·cua·drar tr. *(poner en un marco)* to frame; FIG. *(encajar)* to fit in, insert; *(rodear)* to surround, enclose; *(incorporar)* to put in, incorporate.

en·cuar·te·lar tr. AMER. var. of **acuartelar**.

en·cu·bar tr. *(echar en cubas)* to pour into a vat *or* cask; MIN. to shore up.

en·cu·bier·to, –ta I. past part. see **encubrir** II. adj. hidden, concealed.

en·cu·bri·dor, –do·ra I. adj. concealing, harboring II. m.f. *(persona que encubre)* concealer; *(amparador de un criminal)* harborer (of a criminal); LAW *(en un delito)* accessory after the fact.

en·cu·bri·mien·to m. *(ocultación)* hiding, concealment; LAW *(amparo de un criminal)* harboring a criminal.

en·cu·brir §85 tr. *(ocultar)* to hide, conceal; *(amparar un criminal)* to harbor (a criminal).

en·cu·cli·llar·se reflex. MEX. to squat, crouch.

en·cuen·tre, encuentro see **encontrar**.

en·cuen·tro m. *(reunión)* meeting, encounter <*un e. entre amigos* a meeting among friends>; *(choque)* crash, collision; *(oposición)* clash, conflict; *(hallazgo)* find, discovery; MIL. clash, skirmish; SPORT. *(competición)* match, game; ARCHIT. *(juntura)* joint; ZOOL. *(tope)* ramming, butting; *(axila)* shoulder joint ♦ **encuentros** ORNITH. wing joints • **salir al e.** *(recibir)* to go out to meet; FIG. *(oponer)* to oppose, confront; *(prevenir)* to anticipate.

en·cue·ra·do, –da I. past part. see **encuerar** II. adj. AMER. naked, nude.

en·cue·rar tr. CUBA, MEX. to strip, undress; ARG. to put in a straitjacket —reflex. VEN. to cohabit.

en·cuer·de, encuerdo see **encordar**.

en·cue·re, encuero see **encorar**.

en·cues·ta f. *(investigación)* investigation, inquiry; *(sondeo)* survey, poll.

en·cues·ta·dor, –do·ra m.f. *(investigador)* investigator; *(persona que hace sondeos)* pollster, survey taker.

en·cui·tar·se reflex. to grieve.

en·cum·bra·do, –da I. past part. see **encumbrar** II. adj. high, lofty.

en·cum·bra·mien·to m. *(levantamiento)* raising, lifting; *(altura)* height, elevation; FIG. *(exaltación)* exaltation, elevation.

en·cum·brar tr. *(levantar en alto)* to raise, lift; FIG. *(elevar)* to exalt, honor —intr. to reach *or* scale the summit —reflex. *(envanecerse)* to put on airs, become haughty; *(elevarse mucho)* to tower, rise.

en·cu·nar tr. *(poner en la cuna)* to put in the cradle; TAUR. to catch between the horns (said of a bull).

en·cur·de·lar·se reflex. COLL. to get drunk.

en·cur·ti·do m. CUL. pickled fruit *or* vegetable.

en·cur·tir tr. CUL. to pickle, preserve in vinegar; ECUAD. to tan (leather).

en·chan·cle·tar tr. *(poner las chancletas)* to put on slippers; *(llevar los zapatos como chancletas)* to scuff *or* drag (one's shoes) like slippers —reflex. to put on slippers.

en·cha·pa·do, –da I. past part. see **enchapar** II. m. TECH. *(chapa de madera)* veneer, overlay; *(acción)* veneering, plating.

en·cha·par tr. CARP. to veneer, overlay; METAL. to plate.

en·char·car §70 tr. to flood (land) —reflex. *(enaguacharse)* to become flooded, become swamped; FIG. *(encenagarse)* to wallow (in vice).

en·chi·char·se reflex. AMER. *(embriagarse)* to get drunk on chicha (fermented liquor); *(irritarse)* to get angry, get riled.

en·chi·la·da I. past part. see **enchilar** II. f. C. AMER., MEX. enchilada (rolled tortilla filled with meat or cheese and served with a chili sauce).

en·chi·la·do, –da I. past part. see **enchilar** II. adj. CUL. seasoned with chili; *(rojo)* (bright) red, vermillion; MEX., FIG. irascible, bad-tempered III. m. CUBA, MEX., CUL. shellfish stew with chili and tomatoes and onions.

en·chi·lar tr. AMER., CUL. to season with chili; MEX., FIG. *(irritar)* to irritate, annoy; C. RICA to play a joke on —intr. CUL. to burn the mouth (red pepper).

en·chin·char tr. GUAT. to annoy, bother; MEX. to waste (a person's) time —reflex. AMER. to become infested with bedbugs.

en·chi·que·rar tr. TAUR. to shut in the bullpen; FIG., COLL. *(encarcelar)* to imprison, jail.

en·chi·var·se reflex. AMER. to fly into a rage.

en·chue·car §70 tr. CHILE, MEX. to twist, bend.

en·chu·fa·do, –da I. past part. see **enchufar** II. adj. COLL. well-connected III. m. f. well-connected person.

en·chu·far tr. ELEC. to connect, plug in; *(acoplar tubos)* to fit together, couple (pipes); COM. to combine, merge (businesses); FIG., COLL. *(ejercer influencia)* to pull strings for —reflex. *(obtener un puesto por influencia)* to land *or* get a job through connections; P. RICO *(enojarse)* to get angry *or* mad; *(ponerse serio)* to become serious *or* sober.

en·chu·fe m. ELEC. *(acción de conectar)* plugging in, connecting; *(conexión)* connection; *(hembra)* socket; *(macho)* plug; TECH. *(acoplamiento de tubos)* pipe coupling; *(conexión de tubos)* joint, connection; COLL. *(puesto)* cushy job, sinecure; *(relaciones)* contacts, pull ♦ **e. fusible** ELEC. fuse plug, adapter • **tener e.** FIG., COLL. to have connections *or* pull.

en·chu·fis·ta m.f. COLL., DEROG. person who holds sinecures.

en·de adv. ♦ **por e.** therefore, consequently.

en·de·ble adj. weak, flimsy.

en·de·blez f. weakness, flimsiness.

en·de·ca·sí·la·bo, –ba POET. I. adj. hendecasyllabic II. m. hendecasyllabic verse.

en·de·cha·de·ra f. professional mourner, hired mourner.

en·de·char tr. to sing (dirges *or* laments) —reflex. to grieve, lament.

en·dé·mi·co, –ca adj. MED. endemic; FIG. *(frecuente)* persistent, frequent.

en·de·mo·nia·do, –da I. past part. see **endemoniar** II. adj. *(poseído)* possessed (by the devil); FIG. *(perverso)* devilish, fiendish III. m.f. person possessed (by the devil).

en·de·mo·niar tr. *(introducir los demonios)* to bedevil, possess with the devil; FIG. *(encolerizar)* to enrage, infuriate —reflex. FIG. to get furious, fly into a rage.

en·den·tar §49 tr. *(encajar)* to engage, mesh; *(poner dientes)* to tooth, serrate.

en·den·te·cer §17 intr. to teethe, cut teeth.

en·de·re·za·mien·to m. straightening <*el e. de un clavo torcido* the straightening of a twisted nail>; FIG. *(enmienda)* correction, redress.

en·de·re·zar §04 tr. *(poner derecho)* to straighten; *(poner vertical)* to set or stand up straight; *(encaminar)* to direct, guide; FIG. *(enmendar)* to correct, rectify; *(castigar)* to punish, discipline; MARIT. to right —intr. *(dirigirse)* to go straight to —reflex. *(ponerse derecho)* to become straight; *(ponerse vertical)* to stand up straight.

en·deu·dar·se reflex. *(llenarse de deudas)* to fall into debt; *(reconocerse obligado)* to become indebted or obligated.

en·dia·bla·do, –da I. past part. see endiablar II. adj. *(propio del diablo)* devilish, diabolical; FIG. *(feísimo)* hideous, repulsive; *(colérico)* irascible, ill-tempered; *(muy animado)* wild, frenzied; *(perverso)* perverse, wicked.

en·dia·blar tr. *(endemoniar)* to bedevil, possess with the devil; *(corromper)* to pervert, corrupt —reflex. to become enraged, fly off the handle.

en·di·bia f. BOT. endive.

en·dien·te, endiento see endentar.

en·dil·ga·dor, –do·ra I. adj. COLL. directing, guiding II. m.f. *(guía)* director, guide; *(alcahuete)* pimp.

en·dil·gar §47 tr. COLL. *(encaminar)* to send off, dispatch; COLL. *(encajar)* to foist or palm off.

en·dio·sa·mien·to m. FIG. *(orgullo)* pride, vanity; *(enajenamiento)* preoccupation, absorption.

en·dio·sar tr. to deify —reflex. FIG. *(envanecerse)* to become vain or conceited; *(enajenarse)* to become absorbed or preoccupied.

en·do·cri·no, –na adj. PHYSIOL. endocrine.

en·do·min·gar·se §47 reflex. to dress up (in one's Sunday best).

en·do·sa·ble adj. endorsable.

en·do·san·te I. adj. endorsing II. m.f. endorser.

en·do·sar tr. *(ceder un cheque)* to endorse; FIG. *(encajar)* to foist or palm off.

en·do·sa·ta·rio m. endorsee.

en·dos·co·pio m. MED. endoscope.

en·do·so m. COM. endorsement.

en·do·ve·no·so, –sa adj. MED. intravenous.

en·dro·gar·se §47 reflex. AMER. *(tomar drogas)* to take drugs, use drugs; *(entramparse)* to get into debt.

en·dul·zar §04 tr. *(poner dulce)* to sweeten; FIG. *(suavizar)* to soften, ease.

en·du·re·cer §17 tr. *(poner duro)* to harden, make hard; FIG. *(robustecer)* to toughen (up), make hardy; *(encruelecer)* to harden, inure <*el sufrimiento endureció su corazón* suffering hardened his heart> —reflex. *(ponerse duro)* to harden, become hard; *(robustecerse)* to become tough or hardy; *(encruelecerse)* to become hardhearted or cruel.

en·du·re·ci·mien·to m. *(dureza)* hardness; *(acción)* hardening; FIG. *(obstinación)* stubbornness, obstinacy; FIG. *(insensibilidad)* hardheartedness, insensibility.

e·ne f. *(letra)* en (name of the letter n); *(número)* x, so many (indeterminate number) <*después de ene* (or *n*) *días* after so many days>.

e·ne·bro m. BOT. juniper (tree and wood).

e·nel·do m. BOT. dill.

e·ne·ma f. MED. enema.

e·ne·mi·go, –ga I. adj. enemy, opposing II. m.f. enemy, adversary ♦ **el e. (malo)** COLL. the devil —f. enmity.

e·ne·mis·tad f. animosity, enmity.

e·ne·mis·tar tr. to make enemies of, antagonize —reflex. to become enemies ♦ **enemistarse con** to fall out with.

e·ner·gé·ti·co, –ca I. adj. PHYS. energy, pertaining to energy II. f. PHYS. energetics.

e·ner·gí·a f. PHYS. energy; *(poder)* power, energy; FIG. *(vigor)* vitality, vigor; *(eficacia)* efficacy, effectiveness; *(ánimo)* spirit ♦ **e. atómica** atomic energy • **e. calórica** heat energy • **e. cinética** kinetic energy • **e. eléctrica** electric power • **e. hidráulica** water power • **e. libre** CHEM., PHYS. free energy • **e. nuclear** nuclear power or energy • **e. potencial** potential energy.

e·nér·gi·ca·men·te adv. energetically, vigorously.

e·nér·gi·co, –ca adj. *(vigoroso)* energetic, vigorous; strenuous <*ejercicios enérgicos* strenuous exercises>; *(enfático)* emphatic; *(eficaz)* strong, vigorous <*un ataque e.* a strong attack>.

e·ner·gú·me·no, –na m.f. *(persona poseída del demonio)* person possessed by the devil, energumen; FIG. *(loco)* insane or crazy person.

e·ne·ro m. January.

e·ner·va·ción f. or **e·ner·va·mien·to** m. *(debilitación)* enervation, weakening; *(afeminación)* effeminacy.

e·ner·va·dor, –do·ra or **e·ner·van·te** adj. enervating, weakening.

e·ner·var tr. to enervate, weaken.

e·né·si·mo, –ma adj. nth, umpteenth <*por la enésima vez* for the umpteenth time>.

en·fa·da·di·zo, –za adj. touchy, irritable.

en·fa·dar tr. to anger, annoy —reflex. to get angry or annoyed.

en·fa·do m. *(molestia)* annoyance, irritation; *(enojo)* anger.

en·fa·do·so, –sa adj. *(molesto)* annoying, irritating; *(desagradable)* disagreeable, unpleasant.

en·fa·jar tr. to girdle.

en·fal·da·do, –da adj. fond of women's company (said of a man).

en·fal·dar tr. *(recoger las faldas)* to draw up the skirts of; *(cortar las ramas)* to prune or trim the lower branches of (a tree) —reflex. to draw up one's skirts.

en·fan·gar §47 tr. to cover with mud —reflex. FIG., COLL. *(meterse en negocios sucios)* to get involved in dirty business; FIG. *(entregarse a los placeres)* to wallow in vice; *(ensuciarse)* to become muddy.

en·far·dar tr. to pack, bale.

en·far·de·lar tr. to bundle, bale.

én·fa·sis m. *(insistencia)* emphasis, stress; *(afectación)* affectation, exaggeration.

en·fá·ti·co, –ca adj. emphatic.

en·fer·mar intr. to get sick, become sick —tr. *(causar enfermedad)* to make ill; FIG. *(irritar)* to make sick or ill <*la idea del trabajo me enferma* the idea of work makes me sick>; *(debilitar)* to weaken.

en·fer·me·dad f. *(indisposición)* illness, sickness; FIG. *(anormalidad)* malady, illness ♦ **e. contagiosa** contagious disease • **e. del sueño** sleeping sickness • **e. mental** mental illness • **e. profesional** occupational disease • **e. venérea** venereal disease.

en·fer·me·rí·a f. infirmary, hospital; MARIT. sick bay <*e. del submarino* the sick bay of the submarine>; *(pacientes)* patients (of a hospital).

en·fer·me·ro, –ra m.f. nurse ♦ **e. graduado** registered nurse • **e. auxiliar** nurse's aide.

en·fer·mi·zo, –za adj. sickly, unhealthy, morbid <*una curiosidad e.* a morbid curiosity>.

en·fer·mo, –ma I. adj. sick, ill ♦ **e. de amor** lovesick • **e. de aprensión** hypochondriac • **e. de gravedad** seriously ill II. m.f. sick person; *(inválido)* invalid; *(paciente)* patient.

en·fer·mu·cho, –cha adj. COLL. sickly, ailing.

en·fer·vo·ri·zar §04 tr. *(infundir fervor)* to enliven, enthuse; *(animar)* to encourage.

en·feu·dar tr. to enfeoff, give in vassalage.

en·fie·lar tr. to balance (scales).

en·fie·re·cer·se §17 reflex. to become furious, get raving mad.

en·fies·tar·se reflex. AMER. to live it up, make merry.

en·fi·lar tr. *(poner en fila)* to line up, put in line; *(enhebrar)* to thread, string <*e. los abalorios* to thread beads>; *(apuntar)* to direct, point; *(seguir)* to go down or along <*el chico enfiló la avenida* the boy went down the avenue>; MIL. to enfilade, rake (with gunfire).

en·fi·se·ma m. MED. emphysema.

en·fla·que·cer §17 tr. *(adelgazar)* to make thin; FIG. *(debilitar)* to weaken, debilitate —intr. *(adelgazarse)* to grow thin, lose weight; FIG. *(desanimarse)* to weaken, lose heart.

en·fla·que·ci·mien·to m. *(adelgazamiento)* thinning, slimming; FIG. *(debilitación)* weakening, debilitacion; *(desanimación)* weakening, losing heart.

en·flau·ta·do, –da I. past part. see enflautar II. adj. COLL. pompous, high-flown III. f. GUAT., HOND., PERU blunder.

en·flau·ta·dor, –do·ra COLL. I. adj. cheating, swindling

II. m.f. *(estafador)* cheat, swindler; *(alcahuete)* pimp, pander.

en·flau·tar tr. *(hinchar)* to inflate, blow up; COLL. *(engañar)* to cheat, deceive; *(alcahuetear)* to pimp, procure; AMER. to force (something) on, unload (something) on (someone).

en·flo·rar tr. to adorn with flowers.

en·flo·re·cer §17 intr. to flower, bloom.

en·fo·car §70 tr. OPT. to focus; FIG. *(considerar)* to consider, approach <*e. un asunto de todo punto de vista* to consider a subject from all points of view>.

en·fo·que m. *(acción de enfocar)* focusing, putting into focus; *(foco)* focus.

en·fos·car §70 tr. ARCHIT. *(tapar)* to fill with mortar (holes); *(enyesar)* to plaster (a wall) —reflex. *(ponerse hosco)* to be sullen *or* ill-tempered; *(engolfarse)* to plunge into, become deeply involved in (a business); *(encapotarse)* to cloud over (the sky).

en·fras·ca·mien·to m. entanglement, involvement.

en·fras·car §70 tr. to bottle, put in bottles —reflex. *(meterse en una maleza)* to enter a thicket; FIG. *(enredarse)* to become entangled *or* involved; *(absorberse)* to become absorbed *or* engrossed.

en·fre·nar tr. EQUIT. to bridle, rein in; *(aplicar el freno)* to brake, apply the brake; FIG. *(refrenar)* to curb, check.

en·fren·tar tr. *(poner frente a frente)* to bring *or* put face to face —intr. to face —reflex. to confront, face <*el soldado se enfrentó con el peligro sin miedo* the soldier confronted the danger without fear>.

en·fren·te adv. facing, opposite <*mi casa está e. del teatro* my house is facing the theater>; *(delante)* in front; *(en contra)* against, in opposition to <*su familia se le puso e.* his family was against him>.

en·fria·dor, –do·ra **I.** adj. cooling **II.** m. cooling place.

en·fria·mien·to m. *(acción de enfriar)* cooling; MED. chill, cold.

en·friar §30 tr. *(poner frío)* to cool, chill; FIG. *(templar las pasiones)* to cool down, dampen (passions); FIG., COLL. *(matar)* to kill —intr. to cool, become cold —reflex. *(tener frío)* to be cold; *(contraer un catarro)* to catch a cold.

en·fron·tar tr. to confront, face.

en·fu·llar tr. COLL. to cheat (in cards).

en·fun·dar tr. to put in a case, to sheathe.

en·fu·re·cer §17 tr. to madden, infuriate —reflex. *(irritarse)* to become furious, lose one's temper; FIG. *(alborotarse)* to become rough *or* stormy (said of the sea).

en·fu·re·ci·mien·to m. rage, fury.

en·fu·rru·ña·mien·to m. anger, wrath.

en·fu·rru·ñar·se *or* **en·fu·rrus·car·se** §70 reflex. to become angry.

en·fur·tir tr. TEX. *(abatanar los paños)* to full (cloth); *(abatanar el fieltro)* to felt, press together.

en·gai·tar tr. COLL. to trick, bamboozle.

en·ga·la·nar tr. *(adornar)* to adorn, decorate; *(vestir)* to dress up, deck out —reflex. *(adornarse)* to adorn oneself; *(vestirse)* to dress up, deck oneself out.

en·ga·llar·se reflex. FIG. to put on airs, be arrogant.

en·gan·char tr. *(agarrar)* to hook, catch on a hook; *(colgar)* to hang, hook (up); EQUIT. to hitch (up) <*e. el caballo* to hitch the horse>; FIG. *(comprometer)* to wheedle, persuade; MIL. *(reclutar)* to enlist, recruit; TAUR. *(empitonar)* to gore, catch with the horns —reflex. *(agarrarse)* to get caught *or* hooked up; MIL. *(alistarse)* to enlist.

en·gan·che m. *(acción)* hooking (up); *(gancho)* hook; *(acoplamiento)* coupling; MIL. *(reclutamiento)* enlistment, recruitment.

en·gan·gre·nar·se reflex. ECUAD., MED. to become gangrenous.

en·ga·ña·bo·bos m.f. [pl. **-bos**] COLL. cheat, swindler —m. *(engaño)* fraud, swindle.

en·ga·ña·di·zo, –za adj. gullible, credulous.

en·ga·ña·dor, –do·ra **I.** adj. deceiving, deceptive **II.** m.f. deceiver, trickster.

en·ga·ña·pi·chan·ga f. ARG., CHILE trick, fraud.

en·ga·ñar tr. *(burlar)* to deceive, trick; *(encornudar)* to cuckold, be unfaithful; *(distraer)* to ward *or* stave off <*e. la hambre* to stave off hunger>; *(pasar)* to kill, while away <*e. las horas* to while away the hours> —intr. to be

deceptive *or* misleading —reflex. *(cerrar los ojos)* to deceive oneself; *(equivocarse)* to be mistaken *or* wrong.

en·ga·ñi·fa *or* **en·ga·ñi·fla** f. COLL. trick, swindle.

en·ga·ño m. *(equivocación)* error, mistake; *(trampa)* deception, trick; *(estafa)* swindle, fraud; TAUR. *(muleta)* muleta, cape; *(armadijo para pescar)* tackle, lure.

en·ga·ño·so, –sa adj. *(burlador)* deceiving, tricking; *(deshonesto)* dishonest, deceitful; *(mentiroso)* misleading, wrong <*consejos engañosos* misleading advice>.

en·ga·ra·ba·tar tr. to hook, grapple —reflex. to become hooked *or* crooked.

en·ga·ra·bi·tar·se reflex. COLL. *(subir)* to climb, go up; *(entumecerse)* to become numb (from cold).

en·gar·bu·llar tr. COLL. to confuse, entangle.

en·gar·ce m. *(acción de engarzar)* stringing, threading; *(encadenamiento)* linking, joining; JEWEL. *(engaste)* setting, mounting.

en·gar·cé, engarce see **engarzar**.

en·gar·go·lar tr. to fit together, join.

en·ga·ri·tar tr. COLL. *(engañar)* to trick, deceive; *(fortificar con garitas)* to furnish with turrets *or* sentry boxes.

en·gar·nio m. COLL. good-for-nothing.

en·ga·rra·far tr. COLL. to seize, grab tightly.

en·ga·rriar intr. to climb.

en·ga·rro·tar tr. ARG., SALV. *(entumecer)* to make numb (from cold); *(agarrotar)* to garrote, strangle.

en·gar·za·dor, –do·ra **I.** adj. stringing, threading; JEWEL. setting, mounting **II.** m.f. JEWEL. setter, mounter.

en·gar·zar §04 tr. *(reunir con un hilo)* to string, thread; *(engastar)* to set, mount; *(rizar)* to curl; *(encadenar)* to link, join —reflex. COL. to fight, quarrel.

en·ga·sar tr. to cover with gauze.

en·gas·ta·dor, –do·ra JEWEL. **I.** adj. setting **II.** m.f. setter, mounter.

en·gas·tar tr. JEWEL. to set, mount.

en·gas·te m. JEWEL. setting, mounting; *(perla)* imperfect pearl.

en·ga·tar tr. COLL. to wheedle, deceive (by flattery *or* guile).

en·ga·tu·sa·dor, –do·ra COLL. **I.** adj. coaxing, cajoling **II.** m.f. wheedler, soft-soap artist.

en·ga·tu·sa·mien·to m. COLL. coaxing, cajoling.

en·ga·tu·sar tr. COLL. to cajole, coax, soft-soap.

en·gen·dra·dor, –do·ra **I.** adj. begetting, engendering **II.** m.f. begetter, engenderer.

en·gen·dra·mien·to m. begetting, engendering.

en·gen·drar tr. *(procrear)* to beget, engender; *(producir)* to engender, produce; *(causar)* to cause; MATH. to generate.

en·gen·dro m. *(embrión)* fetus; *(niño informe)* deformed *or* stunted child; *(monstruo)* monster, freak; *(chambonada)* botch, abortion ♦ **mal e.** little monster, bad boy.

en·glo·bar tr. to include, comprise.

en·go·la·do, –da adj. *(que tiene gola)* having a gorget *or* neck piece; FIG. *(presuntuoso)* presumptuous, arrogant; FIG. *(pomposo)* pompous, bombastic.

en·gol·far intr. MARIT. to sail far out to sea, lose sight of land —reflex. MARIT. to sail out to sea; FIG. *(absorberse en alguna cosa)* to become absorbed *or* engrossed (in something).

en·go·li·lla·do, –da adj. COLL. *(con la golilla puesta)* wearing a gorget *or* ruff; FIG., COLL. *(chapado a la antigua)* old-fashioned, clinging to old customs.

en·go·lon·dri·nar·se reflex. COLL. *(engreírse)* to become conceited; *(envanecerse)* to become vain; FIG. *(enamoricarse)* to become infatuated (with), have a crush (on).

en·go·lo·si·nar tr. to entice, tempt —reflex. *(aficionarse)* to develop a taste (for), take a liking (to); *(habituarse)* to become accustomed (to) ♦ **engolosinarse con** to develop a taste for, take a liking to.

en·go·lle·ta·do, –da **I.** past part. see **engolletarse** **II.** adj. COLL. *(engreído)* conceited; *(altivo)* proud, haughty.

en·go·lle·tar·se reflex. COLL. *(engreírse)* to become conceited; *(altivarse)* to become proud.

en·go·ma·do, –da **I.** past part. see **engomar** **II.** adj. gummy, gluey **III.** m. TEX. gumming, sizing.

en·go·mar tr. *(untar con goma)* to glue, gum; TEX. to size.

en·go·mi·nar tr. to put on hairdressing *or* hair cream.

en·gor·da f. CHILE, MEX. *(ceba)* fattening; *(ganado)* cattle fattened for slaughter.

en·gor·da·de·ro m. *(sitio)* feedlot; *(tiempo de engorde)* fattening period *or* season; *(alimento)* fattening fodder.

en·gor·dar tr. to fatten (livestock) —intr. *(ponerse gordo)* to get fat; COLL. *(hacerse rico)* to get rich.

en·gor·de m. fattening (of livestock).

en·go·rro m. obstacle, impediment.

en·go·rro·so, –sa adj. annoying, troublesome.

en·goz·nar tr. to hinge.

en·gra·na·je m. MECH. gear; *(acción)* engaging, meshing; *(conjunto de dientes)* teeth, gear teeth; COLL. *(conexión)* connection, link.

en·gra·nar intr. MECH. to mesh, engage; *(enlazar)* to connect, link.

en·gran·de·cer §17 tr. *(aumentar)* to augment, increase; *(alabar)* to laud, praise; *(elevar)* to enhance, heighten <*e. la emocion* to heighten the emotion>; *(exagerar)* to exaggerate —reflex. FIG. *(exaltarse)* to become exalted; *(elevarse)* to rise, be promoted.

en·gran·de·ci·mien·to m. *(exaltación)* exaltation, elevation; *(aumento)* increase, enlargement; *(exageración)* exaggeration.

en·gra·ne·rar tr. to store in a granary.

en·gra·nu·jar·se reflex. *(llenarse de granos)* to become covered with pimples, become pimply; *(hacerse granuja)* to become a rascal, become a rogue.

en·gra·pa·do·ra f. stapler.

en·gra·par tr. TECH. to clamp, cramp; *(presillar)* to staple.

en·gra·sa·do I. past part. see **engrasar** II. m. *(acción de engrasar)* greasing, lubrication; *(substancia lubricante)* grease, lubricant.

en·gra·sa·dor, –do·ra I. adj. greasing, lubricating II. m. grease gun.

en·gra·sar tr. *(untar)* to grease; *(aceitar)* to oil; *(fertilizar)* to spread with manure —reflex. MEX. to become ill with lead poisoning.

en·gra·se *or* **en·gra·sa·mien·to** m. *(engrasación)* greasing, lubrication; *(substancia lubricante)* lubricant.

en·gre·í·do, –da I. past part. see **engreír** II. adj. *(presumido)* conceited, arrogant; AMER. spoiled ♦ **e. de sí mismo** stuck-up, full of oneself.

en·grei·mien·to m. pride, haughtiness.

en·gre·ír §58 tr. *(envanecer)* to make vain *or* conceited; AMER. *(mimar)* to spoil, pamper —reflex. *(envanecerse)* to become vain *or* conceited; AMER. *(mimarse)* to become spoiled *or* pampered; *(encariñarse)* to grow fond.

en·gres·car §70 tr. *(incitar a disputa)* to incite *or* goad into fighting; FIG. *(alegrar)* to make merry; *(excitar)* to incite, urge on.

en·gri·far tr. to curl, crimp —reflex. *(un caballo)* to rear up; COLL. *(drogarse)* to take drugs.

en·gri·llar tr. *(meter en grillos)* to put in irons, shackle; FIG. *(sujetar)* to bring under control, subdue —reflex. AMER. *(encapotarse)* to lower the head (a horse); COL., PAN. to get *or* go into debt; P. RICO, VEN. to become fond of.

en·grin·gar·se §47 reflex. AMER., COLL. to adopt the ways of foreigners (esp. Americans and English).

en·gro·sa·mien·to m. *(de una persona)* fattening; *(espesamiento)* thickening; *(aumento)* increase, enlargement.

en·gro·sar §19 tr. *(hacer gruesa)* to make thick, thicken; FIG. *(aumentar)* to increase, swell (enrollment) —intr. *(engordar)* to get fat, put on weight; *(crecer)* to grow.

en·gru·dar tr. to paste —reflex. to take the consistency of a paste.

en·gru·do m. paste.

en·gua·tar tr. to wad, pad.

en·gue·de·ja·do, –da I. past part. see **enguedejar** II. adj. *(que está hecho guedejas)* in long tresses (hair); *(que trae así la cabellera)* long-haired (person).

en·gue·de·jar tr. to comb (hair) in long tresses.

en·gui·ja·rrar tr. to pave with cobblestones.

en·gui·llo·tar·se tr. to be absorbed (in).

en·guir·nal·dar tr. to decorate with garlands.

en·gu·lli·dor, –do·ra I. adj. gulping, gobbling II. m.f. gulper, gobbler.

en·gu·llir §13 tr. to gulp down, gobble.

en·gu·rru·ñar tr. to wrinkle, crease —reflex. *(encogerse)* to become wrinkled; COLL. *(enmantarse)* to get sad, be melancholy.

en·ha·ci·nar tr. to pile, heap.

en·ha·ri·nar tr. to flour, coat with flour.

en·has·tiar §30 tr. to bore, annoy.

en·he·bi·llar tr. to put a buckle on.

en·he·brar tr. SEW. to thread (a needle); *(ensartar)* to string <*e. cuentas* to string beads>; FIG. *(conectar ideas)* to link, connect (ideas) ♦ **e. una mentira tras otra** to tell a string *or* pack of lies.

en·hes·tar §49 tr. *(levantar)* to raise, lift; *(poner derecho)* to erect, set upright —reflex. *(levantarse)* to be raised *or* lifted; *(ponerse derecho)* to stand erect *or* upright.

en·hie·lar tr. *(mezclar con hiel)* to mix with bile; *(volver amargo)* to make bitter.

en·hies·to, –ta I. past part. see **enhestar** II. adj. upright, erect.

en·hi·lar tr. SEW. *(una aguja)* to thread (a needle); *(enfilar)* to string, thread (beads); FIG. *(ordenar)* to order, arrange; *(dirigir)* to direct, guide —intr. to set out for, make for.

en·ho·ra·bue·na I. f. congratulations ♦ **dar la e. a** to congratulate II. adv. *(felizmente)* luckily, fortunately; *(con mucho gusto)* welcome, with pleasure <*venga usted e.* you're welcome to come>.

en·ho·ra·ma·la adv. *(desgraciadamente)* unfortunately; *(inoportunamente)* inopportunely, at the wrong time <*e. llegó* he arrived at the wrong time> ♦ **¡irse e.!** COLL. go to blazes!, good riddance!.

en·hor·car §70 tr. to string (onions or garlic).

en·hor·nar tr. to put in an oven.

en·hue·car §70 tr. var. of **ahuecar**.

en·hue·rar tr. to addle, make addled —intr. to become addled.

e·nig·ma m. enigma, riddle.

e·nig·má·ti·ca·men·te adv. enigmatically.

e·nig·má·ti·co, –ca adj. enigmatic, enigmatical.

en·ja·bo·na·do I. past part. see **enjabonar** II. adj. CUBA, PERU mottled, piebald (a horse) III. m. soaping, lathering.

en·ja·bo·nar tr. *(jabonar)* to soap, wash with soap; FIG., COLL. *(adular)* to soft-soap, flatter; *(reprender)* to scold, reprimand.

en·ja·e·zar §04 tr. *(poner los jaeces)* to put trappings on, harness (a horse); AMER. to saddle (a horse).

en·ja·güe m. MARIT. adjudication made in favor of a ship's creditors; *(enjuague)* rinse, rinsing.

en·jal·be·gar §47 tr. *(blanquear)* to whitewash; FIG. *(maquillar)* to make up, apply cosmetics.

en·jal·ma f. packsaddle.

en·jal·mar tr. to put a packsaddle on —intr. to make packsaddles.

en·jam·brar tr. ENTOM. tr. *(encerrar en una colmena)* to (collect into a) hive; *(sacar un enjambre)* to swarm, extract a swarm from —intr. *(irse de una colonia)* to (leave as a) swarm; FIG. *(multiplicar)* to multiply, abound.

en·jam·bra·zón f. swarming (of bees).

en·jam·bre m. ENTOM. swarm; FIG. *(multitud)* crowd, throng; ASTRON. cluster; CUBA, ICHTH. cabrilla-like fish.

en·jau·lar tr. to put a halter on.

en·jar·di·nar tr. to trim (trees and flowers).

en·ja·re·tar tr. *(pasar por una jareta)* to thread through, run a string through (e.g., a hem); FIG., COLL. *(hacer de prisa)* to rush through, do in a rush; *(decir sin cuidado)* to reel *or* rattle off; *(endilgar)* to palm off, foist off (something unpleasant); COLL. *(intercalar)* to insert.

en·jau·lar tr. *(poner dentro de una jaula)* to cage, put in a cage; *(encarcelar)* to jail.

en·je·bar tr. *(meter en alumbre)* to bleach, steep in lye (before dying); *(blanquear)* to whitewash.

en·jer·gar §47 tr. COLL. to start and conduct (a business).

en·jer·ta·ción f. grafting.

en·jer·tar tr. var. of **injertar.**

en·jo·yar tr. *(adornar con joyas)* to adorn with jewels; *(engastar)* to set with precious stones *or* jewels; FIG. *(embellecer)* to embellish, beautify.

en·jo·ye·la·do, –da adj. *(convertida en joya)* wrought into jewelry (gold or silver); *(adornado con joyeles)* bejeweled.

en·jua·ga·dien·tes m. COLL. mouthwash.

en·jua·gar §47 tr. & reflex. to rinse.

en·jua·gue *or* **en·jua·ga·to·rio** m. *(acción de enjuagar)* rinsing; *(líquido)* rinse, rinsing water; *(recipiente)* washbowl, rinsing cup; FIG. *(estratagema)* scheme, plot.

en·ju·ga·dor, –do·ra I. adj. drying **II.** m. *(sahumador)* clothes dryer or rack; MECH. clothes dryer; PHOTOG. photographic plate dryer.

en·ju·ga·ma·nos m. [pl. **-nos**] towel.

en·ju·gar §47 tr. *(secar)* to dry; *(quitar la humedad)* to wipe (dry), mop up; FIG. *(cancelar)* to wipe out, settle (a debt) —reflex. *(adelgazarse)* to grow thin or lean; *(quitarse la humedad)* to wipe, dry <enjugarse las manos to wipe one's hands> ♦ **enjugarse las lágrimas** to wipe away or dry one's tears.

en·jui·cia·ble adj. indictable, deserving of prosecution.

en·jui·cia·mien·to m. LAW *(acción de juzgar)* judgment, judging; *(proceso)* trial, prosecution; *(pleito)* lawsuit; *(procedimiento)* procedure.

en·jui·ciar tr. LAW *(juzgar)* to judge, examine; *(instruir una causa)* to institute (legal proceedings); *(sujetar a juicio)* to indict, prosecute.

en·jun·car §70 tr. *(cubrir de juncos)* to cover with rushes; MARIT. *(atar)* to lash with rush ropes (a sail); *(substituir los tomadores)* to unlash the gaskets and lash with rope-yarn (sails).

en·jun·dia f. ORNITH. fat (in the ovary of a fowl); ZOOL. grease, fat (of an animal); FIG. *(substancia)* essence, substance; *(vigor)* strength, vitality; *(carácter)* character, personality.

en·jun·dio·so, –sa adj. *(grasiento)* fatty; FIG. *(sustancioso)* substantial; *(vigoroso)* vigorous, forceful; *(de mucho carácter)* having a strong character or personality.

en·jun·qué, enjunque see **enjuncar.**

en·ju·ta f. ARCHIT. spandrel.

en·ju·tar tr. *(secar)* to dry (plaster); ARCHIT. to fill up (spandrels).

en·ju·tez f. dryness.

en·ju·to, –ta I. past part. see **enjugar II.** adj. *(seco)* dry; FIG. *(delgado)* skinny, lean **III.** m.pl. *(tascos)* brushwood, kindling; *(tapas)* snacks, tidbits.

en·la·biar tr. *(aplicar los labios a)* to bring or press one's lips to; *(seducir)* to sweet talk, bamboozle.

en·la·bio m. deception, bamboozling.

en·la·ce m. *(acción de enlazar)* connecting, linking; *(conexión)* connection, link, relationship; FIG. *(casamiento)* marriage, matrimony; *(parentesco)* tie, bond; *(intermediario)* intermediary, liaison; RAIL. *(empalme de vías)* junction, crossing; *(empalme de trenes)* connection; CHEM. bond ♦ **e. covalente** CHEM. covalent bond.

en·la·cé, enlace see **enlazar.**

en·la·ciar tr. to make flaccid or limp —reflex. to become flaccid or limp.

en·la·dri·lla·do I. past part. see **enladrillar II.** m. brick pavement.

en·la·dri·lla·dor m. bricklayer.

en·la·dri·llar tr. to pave with bricks.

en·la·jar tr. VEN. to pave with flagstones or tiles.

en·la·na·do, –da adj. covered with wool.

en·lar·dar tr. CUL. to lard, baste.

en·la·tar tr. *(meter en latas)* to can, put in cans; AMER. to roof with tin.

en·la·za·dor, –do·ra I. adj. linking, connective **II.** m.f. binder, connector.

en·la·zar §04 tr. *(coger con lazos)* to lace, interlace; *(trabar)* to link, connect; *(agarrar)* to lasso, rope —intr. RAIL. to connect —reflex. *(unirse)* to become linked or connected; FIG. *(casarse)* to marry, get married; *(contraer parentesco)* to become related by marriage.

en·le·ga·jar tr. to file, docket (papers).

en·le·jiar §30 tr. *(meter en lejía)* to bleach, steep in lye; CHEM. to dissolve (an alkali) in water.

en·lo·cé, enloce see **enlozar.**

en·lo·da·du·ra f. or **en·lo·da·mien·to** m. muddying, filling with mud.

en·lo·dar tr. *(cubrir de lodo)* to muddy, cover with mud; *(manchar de lodo)* to splash or stain with mud; FIG. *(infamar)* to besmirch, stain (a reputation); MIN. to lute, seal up (sides of a mine) —reflex. to become muddy.

en·lo·que·ce·dor, –do·ra adj. *(que vuelve loco)* maddening; *(que trastorna)* moving, enthralling.

en·lo·que·cer §17 tr. *(hacer perder el juicio)* to drive mad or insane, madden; FIG. *(excitar)* to excite, drive crazy <la danza moderna me enloquece modern dance excites me> —intr. *(perderse el juicio)* to go insane or crazy; AGR. *(dejar de dar fruto)* to become barren; *(dar fruto con irregularidad)* to bear fruit irregularly; FIG. *(trastornar)* to get excited, go crazy —reflex. *(perderse el juicio)* to go insane or crazy; *(trastornarse)* to get excited, go crazy.

en·lo·que·ci·mien·to m. *(locura)* madness, insanity; *(proceso)* process of going insane.

en·lo·sa·do I. past part. see **enlosar II.** m. tiled floor.

en·lo·sa·dor m. tiler, tile layer.

en·lo·sar tr. to tile, pave with tiles.

en·lo·zar §04 tr. AMER. to cover or coat with enamel.

en·lu·ci·do, –da I. past part. see **enlucir II.** adj. *(una pared)* plastered; *(blanqueado)* whitewashed **III.** m. plaster, coat of plaster.

en·lu·ci·dor m. *(de paredes)* plasterer; *(de metales)* polisher (of metals).

en·lu·cir §44 tr. *(poner yeso)* to plaster; *(blanquear)* to whitewash; *(limpiar metales)* to polish (metals).

en·lu·ta·do, –da I. past part. see **enlutar II.** adj. in mourning.

en·lu·tar tr. *(vestir de luto)* to dress in mourning; *(poner de luto)* to cast into mourning, bereave; FIG. *(obscurecer)* to darken, make gloomy; *(entristecer)* to sadden —reflex. *(ponerse de luto)* to go into mourning; *(obscurecerse)* to get dark or gloomy.

en·luz·ca, enluzco see **enlucir.**

en·llan·tar tr. to rim or shoe (a wheel).

en·llen·te·cer §17 tr. to blandish, soften.

en·ma·de·ra·do or **en·ma·de·ra·mien·to** m. CARP. timbering, woodwork.

en·ma·de·rar tr. CARP. to plank, timber.

en·ma·le·cer·se §17 reflex. AMER. to become covered with undergrowth or weeds, get overgrown with weeds.

en·ma·le·zar·se §04 reflex. var. of **enmalecerse.**

en·ma·llar·se reflex. to get caught in the meshes of a net (a fish).

en·man·gar §47 tr. to put a handle or haft on.

en·man·tar tr. to cover with a blanket —reflex. FIG. to become melancholy or sad.

en·ma·ra·ña·mien·to m. *(de cosas)* tangle, snarl; FIG. *(de un asunto)* embroilment, confusion.

en·ma·ra·ñar tr. *(enredar)* to entangle, snarl; FIG. *(confundir)* to muddle, confuse —reflex. *(enredarse)* to become tangled or snarled; FIG. *(confundirse)* to become muddled or confused; METEOROL. to become cloudy or overcast (the sky).

en·ma·rar·se reflex. MARIT. to sail out into the high seas.

en·mar·car §70 tr. *(en un marco)* to frame; FIG. *(rodear)* to surround.

en·ma·ri·dar intr. & reflex. to marry (said of a woman), take a husband.

en·ma·ri·lle·cer·se §17 reflex. to turn yellow or yellowish.

en·ma·ro·mar tr. to tie with a rope, rope.

en·mas·ca·ra·do, –da I. past part. see **enmascarar II.** m.f. masked person.

en·mas·ca·rar tr. *(cubrir con máscara)* to mask, cover with a mask, FIG. *(disfrazar)* to conceal, disguise —reflex. to put on a mask.

en·ma·si·llar tr. to putty, caulk.

en·me·lar §49 tr. *(untar con miel)* to smear with honey; *(agregar miel)* to add honey to; FIG. *(endulzar)* to sweeten; *(hacer agradable)* to make pleasant; *(suavizar)* to make soft —intr. to make honey (bees).

en·men·da·ble adj. amendable, rectifiable.

en·men·da·ción f. correction, amendment.

en·men·da·dor, –do·ra I. adj. corrective, amending **II.** m.f. corrector, amender.

en·men·dar §49 tr. *(corregir)* to correct, amend; *(resarcir)* to make amends for, compensate; LAW *(reformar)* to revise, amend; MARIT. to alter or change (course) —reflex. to mend one's ways.

en·mie·le, enmielo see **enmelar.**

en·mien·da f. *(corrección)* correction, amendment; *(reparo)* reparation, compensation; *(premio)* award, prize; *(pro-

puesta de variante) amendment, revision; AGR. mineral fertilizer.

en·mien·de, enmiendo see **enmendar.**

en·mo·he·cer §17 tr. *(materia orgánica)* to make moldy or mildewy; *(metales)* to rust; FIG. *(la memoria)* to make rusty (memory) —reflex. *(materia orgánica)* to become moldy or mildewy; *(metales)* to get rusty.

en·mo·he·ci·mien·to m. *(de materias orgánicas)* molding, mildewing; *(de metales)* rusting; FIG. *(embotamiento)* rustiness.

en·mo·lle·cer §17 tr. to soften, mollify.

en·mon·tar·se reflex. C. AMER., COL. to turn into a wilderness.

en·mor·da·zar §04 tr. to gag, muzzle.

en·mu·de·cer §17 tr. to silence, hush —intr. *(callarse)* to be silent, keep quiet; *(quedar mudo)* to become speechless or dumb.

en·mu·grar tr. & reflex. AMER. var. of **enmugrecer.**

en·mu·gre·cer §17 tr. to soil, dirty —reflex. to become soiled or dirty.

en·ne·gre·cer §17 tr. *(poner negro)* to blacken; FIG. *(obscurecer)* to darken —reflex. *(ponerse negro)* to turn black; FIG. *(obscurecerse)* to darken.

en·ne·gre·ci·mien·to m. *(acción de ennegrecer)* blackening, turning black; FIG. *(obscurecimiento)* darkening.

en·no·ble·cer §17 tr. *(hacer noble)* to ennoble, make noble; FIG. *(dar lustre)* to adorn, embellish.

en·no·ble·ci·mien·to m. ennobling, ennoblement.

e·no·ja·di·zo, –za adj. quick-tempered, touchy.

e·no·jar tr. *(enfadar)* to anger, make angy; *(disgustar)* to displease, offend —reflex. *(enfadarse)* to become angry or angered; *(disgustarse)* to be displeased or offended; METEOROL. to become rough or stormy.

e·no·jo m. *(ira)* anger; *(disgusto)* displeasure, offense; *(molestia)* bother, annoyance; *(trabajo)* trouble, work.

e·no·jo·sa·men·te adv. *(con ira)* angrily, crossly; *(con disgusto)* offensively, displeasingly; *(con molestia)* annoyingly, troublesomely.

e·no·jo·so, –sa adj. *(que causa enojo)* irritating, vexatious; *(desagradable)* displeasing, offensive; *(molestoso)* bothersome, annoying; *(que causa trabajo)* troublesome.

e·no·lo·gí·a f. oenology (study of wine).

e·nó·lo·go, –ga I. adj. oenological II. m.f. oenologist.

e·nor·gu·lle·cer §17 tr. to make proud, fill with pride —reflex. to be proud, pride oneself ♦ **enorgullecerse de** to take pride in, pride oneself on.

e·nor·me adj. *(muy grande)* enormous, huge *<un disparate e. a huge blunder>;* FIG. *(perverso)* perverse, wicked.

e·nor·me·men·te adv. enormously, extremely.

e·nor·mi·dad f. *(grandeza)* enormity, hugeness; FIG. *(monstruosidad)* wickedness, monstrousness; *(desatino)* stupidity, folly; *(gravedad)* graveness, seriousness.

e·no·tec·nia f. art of wine-making.

en·qui·ciar tr. *(una puerta)* to put (a door) on its hinges; *(una ventana)* to put (a window) in a frame; FIG. *(poner en orden)* to set right, put in order.

en·qui·llo·trar·se reflex. *(engreírse)* to become conceited; COLL. *(enamorarse)* to fall in love.

en·quis·ta·do, –da adj. MED. cystic, cyst-like; FIG. *(embutido)* embedded, inlaid.

en·ra·biar tr. to enrage, infuriate —reflex. to become enraged or furious.

en·rai·zar §06 intr. BOT. to take root.

en·ra·le·cer §17 intr. to get thin (hair).

en·ra·ma·da f. *(ramaje)* branches; *(cobertizo)* bower, arbor; *(adorno)* decoration or garland made of branches.

en·ra·mar tr. *(entretejer ramos)* to embower, interweave (branches); *(adornar)* to decorate with branches; MARIT. to fit the ribs to (a ship) —intr. to put out branches —reflex. to hide between the branches.

en·ran·ciar tr. to make rancid, spoil —reflex. to become rancid, spoil.

en·ra·re·cer §17 tr. *(el aire)* to thin; rarefy; FIG. *(hacer escaso)* to make rare or scarce —intr. FIG. to become rare or scarce —reflex. *(el aire)* to thin, rarefy; FIG. *(hacerse escaso)* to become rare or scarce.

en·ra·re·ci·mien·to m. *(rarefacción)* thinning, rarefying; *(escasez)* scarcity.

en·ra·sar tr. CONSTR. *(igualar)* to level, make flush *<e. una pared* to make a wall flush>; *(allanar)* to smooth, plane; PHYS. to level up (liquids) —intr. to be at the same level.

en·ra·yar tr. to spoke, put spokes in (a wheel).

en·re·da·de·ra BOT. I. adj. climbing, trailing *<planta e.* climbing plant> II. f. *(planta trepadora)* climbing plant, creeper; *(planta convolvulácea)* bindweed.

en·re·da·dor, –do·ra I. adj. *(que enmaraña)* entangling; COLL. *(chismoso)* gossipy; *(dañoso)* mischievous II. m.f. *(chismoso)* gossip, busybody; *(buscapleitos)* mischief-maker.

en·re·dar tr. *(atrapar)* to net; *(tender)* to lay, set *<e. una trampa* to lay a trap>; *(enmarañar)* to tangle up, snarl *<e. un ovillo de hilo* to tangle up a ball of yarn>; *(enemistar)* to cause trouble between; FIG. *(embrollar)* to complicate, confuse *<e. una situación* to complicate a situation>; *(comprometer)* to involve, embroil *<él enredó a su hermano en un negocio sucio* he involved his brother in a shady deal>* —intr. to get into mischief, cause trouble —reflex. *(enzarzarse)* to get tangled up, become snarled; *(complicarse)* to become complicated or confused; FIG. *(comprometerse)* to become involved *<me enredé en el asunto sin darme cuenta de los peligros* I became involved in the matter without realizing the dangers>; COLL. *(amancebarse)* to get involved, have an affair.

en·re·do m. *(maraña)* tangle, snarl; FIG. *(travesura)* mischief, mischievousness; *(engaño)* deceit; *(lío)* mess, muddle; *(trama)* plot (of a novel) ♦ **enredos** COLL. things, stuff.

en·re·do·so, –sa adj. *(complicado)* complicated, tricky; CHILE, MEX. *(intrigante)* troublemaking, mischievous; *(chismoso)* gossipy.

en·re·ja·do I. past part. see **enrejar** II. m. *(conjunto de rejas)* railings; *(celosía)* latticework, trellis; *(emparrillado)* grillage; SEW. openwork embroidery.

en·re·jar tr. *(cercar con rejas)* to surround with railings; *(poner rejas a una ventana)* to put latticework on (a window); *(apilar tablas)* to lay (planks of wood) crosswise; *(fijar la reja al arado)* to fit the plowshare to (a plow); VET. *(herir con la reja del arado)* to wound (the feet of an animal) with a plowshare; HOND. to tie (a nursing calf) to the leg of a cow.

en·re·ve·sa·do, –da adj. *(revesado)* intricate, complicated; FIG. *(travieso)* mischievous, unruly.

en·ri·ar §30 tr. to ret, soak.

en·rie·lar tr. METAL. *(hacer rieles)* to make into ingots or bars; *(echar en la rielera)* to pour or cast into ingot molds; AMER. *(poner rieles)* to lay or put rails on; *(encarrilar)* to set or put on rails.

en·ri·pia·do I. past part. of **enripiar** II. m. filling with rubble or gravel.

en·ri·piar tr. CONSTR. to fill with rubble or gravel.

en·ri·que·ce·dor, –do·ra adj. enriching.

en·ri·que·cer §17 tr. *(hacer rico)* to enrich, make wealthy; FIG. *(adornar)* to adorn, embellish —intr. & reflex. *(hacerse rico)* to get rich, become wealthy *<enriquecerse a costa ajena* to get rich at another's expense>; *(prosperar)* to prosper, flourish.

en·ris·ca·do, –da I. past part. see **enriscar** II. adj. craggy, rugged.

en·ris·car §70 tr. FIG. to raise, lift —reflex. to take refuge, hide (among cliffs or rocks).

en·ris·trar[1] tr. to string (garlic or onions).

en·ris·trar[2] tr. *(la lanza en el ristre)* to couch (a lance); FIG. *(ir derecho hacia)* to go straight toward; *(acertar una cosa difícil)* to overcome (a difficulty), get (something difficult) right.

en·ro·car[1] tr. & intr. to castle (in chess).

en·ro·car[2] §73 tr. TEX. to put (wool or linen) on the distaff —reflex. MARIT. to get caught in the rocks (an anchor).

en·ro·je·cer §17 tr. *(poner rojo con fuego)* to make red-hot; *(dar color rojo)* to redden, make red —intr. to blush, turn red —reflex. *(ponerse rojo por fuego)* to turn red-hot; *(ponerse rojo)* to redden, turn red; *(ruborizarse)* to blush, turn red.

en·ro·je·ci·mien·to m. reddening; *(rubor)* blush.

en·ro·lar tr. MARIT., MIL. to sign up, recruit.

en·ro·llar tr. *(arrollar)* to roll or wind up; *(empedrar)* to cobble, pave with cobblestones; COLL. (*enredar*) to entangle, involve —reflex. (*arrollarse*) to be rolled *or* wound up; COLL. to get involved (in something *or* with someone).

en·ro·mar tr. to dull, blunt (an edge or point).

en·ron·que·cer §17 tr. make hoarse —reflex. to become hoarse.

en·ron·que·ci·mien·to m. hoarseness.

en·ro·ñar tr. (*llenar de roña*) to cover with scabs; METAL. to rust, make rusty —reflex. METAL. to rust, corrode.

en·ro·qué see enrocar².

en·ros·ca·du·ra f. (*acción de enroscar*) coiling, twisting; (*rosca*) coil, twist.

en·ros·car §70 tr. (*arrollar*) to coil, twist; (*atornillar*) to screw in.

en·ru·bio m. (*acción de enrubiar*) bleaching (of hair); (*ingrediente*) hair bleach.

en·ru·de·cer §17 tr. (*hacer rudo*) to roughen, make coarse; (*entorpecer*) to dull, stupefy.

en·rue·co, enrueque see enrocar².

en·ru·lar tr. AMER. to curl.

en·sa·ba·nar tr. (*envolver con sábanas*) to cover with a sheet; CONSTR. to give (a wall) a coat of plaster —reflex. VEN. to rise up, rebel.

en·sa·car §70 tr. to bag, put into sacks.

en·sa·la·da f. CUL. salad; FIG. (*mezcla confusa*) hodgepodge, jumble; MUS. composition featuring a variety of tempos; POET. poem consisting of verses from other poems; CUBA, CUL. mint-flavored citrus drink ♦ **e. de frutas** CUL. fruit salad • **e. rusa** CUL. type of potato salad garnished with peas and carrots and ham.

en·sa·la·de·ra f. salad bowl.

en·sa·la·di·lla f. CUL. (*ensalada rusa*) diced vegetable salad; (*bocados de dulces*) assortment of sweets; JEWEL. jewel set with stones of different colors.

en·sal·cé, ensalce see ensalzar.

en·sa·li·var tr. to wet with saliva.

en·sal·ma·dor, –do·ra m.f. (*algebrista de huesos*) bone-setter; (*curandero*) quack, charlatan.

en·sal·mar tr. (*componer huesos*) to set (bones); (*curar*) to heal, cure (said of a quack).

en·sal·mis·ta m.f. quack, charlatan.

en·sal·mo m. curing by quack remedy *or* incantation ♦ **como por e.** as if by magic.

en·sa·lo·brar·se reflex. to become salty.

en·sal·za·dor, –do·ra adj. praising, exalting.

en·sal·za·mien·to m. praise, exaltation.

en·sal·zar §04 tr. (*enaltecer*) to exalt, glorify; (*alabar*) to praise, extol.

en·sam·bla·dor m. CARP. joiner.

en·sam·bla·du·ra f. *or* **en·sam·bla·je** m. CARP. (*acción de ensamblar*) joining, connecting; (*unión*) joint, connection.

en·sam·blar tr. CARP. to join, connect.

en·sam·ble m. var. of ensambladura.

en·san·cha f. widening, expanding.

en·san·cha·dor, –do·ra I. adj. widening, expanding II. m.f. widener, expander (instrument).

en·san·cha·mien·to m. (*expansión*) widening, expansion; (*extensión*) stretching, extension.

en·san·char tr. (*hacer más ancho*) to widen, expand; (*extender*) to stretch, extend —intr. & reflex. FIG. (*envanecerse*) to get puffed up *or* conceited; (*engrandecerse*) to expand, broaden.

en·san·che m. (*extensión*) extension, stretching; (*expansión*) widening, expansion; SEW. (*tela adicional*) allowance in seams for future alteration; (*barrio nuevo*) suburban development.

en·san·de·cer §17 intr. to become simple-minded.

en·san·gren·tar §49 tr. (*manchar con sangre*) to stain with blood; (*derramar sangre*) to shed blood —reflex. (*mancharse con sangre*) to become blood-stained; FIG. (*encolerizarse*) to fly into a rage, become furious ♦ **ensangrentarse con** *or* **contra** to be cruel *or* merciless toward.

en·sa·ña·mien·to m. cruelty, brutality.

en·sa·ñar tr. to enrage, infuriate —reflex. (*mostrar crueldad*) to be cruel *or* merciless.

en·sa·qué, ensaque see ensacar.

en·sar·ne·cer §17 intr. to itch all over.

en·sar·te m. SP. thread, string.

en·sar·tar tr. (*pasar por un hilo*) to string, thread; (*enhebrar*) to thread (a needle); (*atravesar*) to run through, pierce; FIG. (*decir cosas sin conexión*) to reel *or* rattle off <*e. mentiras* to rattle off lies>; CHILE, MEX., NIC. to snare, trap (a person) —reflex. FIG. to get stuck with.

en·sa·ya·dor, –do·ra m.f. METAL. assayer.

en·sa·yar tr. (*probar*) to test, try out; THEAT. to rehearse, practice; MIN. to assay, test; (*adiestrar*) to train, teach; (*intentar*) to try *or* attempt —reflex. to practice, rehearse.

en·sa·yis·ta m.f. essayist.

en·sa·yo m. (*prueba*) test, trial; (*ejercicio*) exercise, practice; FIG. (*intento*) attempt; LIT. essay; METAL. assay, assaying; (*rugby*) try; THEAT. rehearsal ♦ **de d.** test, trial <*viaje de e.* trial run> • **e. biológico** bioassay • **e. general** THEAT. dress rehearsal • **hacer ensayos** to practice (on).

en·se·bar tr. to grease.

en·se·gui·da *or* **en seguida** adv. immediately, at once.

en·se·na·da f. (*golfo*) cove, inlet; ARG. small fenced pasture.

en·se·ña f. badge, emblem.

en·se·ña·do, –da I. past part. see enseñar II. adj. (*educado*) educated; housebroken <*perro e.* housebroken dog>.

en·se·ña·dor, –do·ra I. adj. teaching II. m.f. teacher.

en·se·ñan·za f. (*arte de enseñar*) teaching; (*instrucción*) instruction, training; (*educación*) education <*e. técnica* technical education>; (*lección*) lesson; RELIG. doctrine, teaching ♦ **e. primaria** *or* **primera e.** elementary *or* primary education • **e. secundaria** *or* **segunda e.** secondary education • **e. superior** higher education • **e. universitaria** university education, college education.

en·se·ñar tr. (*instruir*) to teach, instruct; (*indicar*) to indicate, point out; (*mostrar*) to show ♦ **e. a alguien a hacer algo** to teach *or* show someone (how) to do something —reflex. (*acostumbrarse*) to accustom oneself to, get used to; S. AMER. to learn.

en·se·ño·re·ar·se reflex. to take over, take possession ♦ **e. de** to take possession of, take over.

en·se·res m.pl. equipment, accouterments ♦ **e. de pescar** fishing tackle • **e. domésticos** household goods.

en·se·riar·se reflex. AMER. to become serious.

en·si·la·je m. AGR. ensilage.

en·si·lar tr. to store in a silo, ensile.

en·si·lla·do, –da I. past part. see ensillar II. adj. saddlebacked.

en·si·llar tr. to saddle, put a saddle on.

en·si·mis·ma·do, –da I. past part. see ensimismarse II. adj. (*absorto*) pensive, absorbed in thought; (*engreído*) conceited, vain.

en·si·mis·ma·mien·to m. (*acción de ensimismarse*) pensiveness, absorption; (*engreimiento*) conceit, vanity.

en·si·mis·mar·se reflex. (*quedar pensativo*) to be *or* become absorbed in thought; (*engreírse*) to become conceited *or* vain.

en·so·ber·be·cer §17 tr. to make proud *or* arrogant —reflex. (*enorgullecerse*) to become proud *or* arrogant; MARIT. to become rough (the sea).

en·so·gar §47 tr. (*atar con soga*) to rope, tie with a rope; (*forrar con soga*) to cover *or* bind with rope.

en·sol·ver §78 tr. (*incluir*) to include; (*contraer*) to reduce, condense; MED. to resolve, dissipate (a tumor).

en·som·bre·cer §17 tr. (*obscurecer*) to darken; FIG. (*eclipsar*) to overshadow, eclipse —reflex. (*obscurecerse*) to darken, get dark; FIG. (*entristecerse*) to become sad *or* gloomy.

en·so·ña·dor, –do·ra I. adj. dreamy II. m.f. dreamer.

en·so·par tr. (*empapar*) to soak, drench; (*sopetear*) to dip, dunk —reflex. to get soaked *or* drenched.

en·sor·de·ce·dor, –do·ra adj. deafening.

en·sor·de·cer §17 tr. (*causar sordera*) to make deaf, deafen; (*amortiguar*) to muffle, deaden —intr. (*contraer sordera*) to go *or* become deaf; (*enmudecer*) to pretend not to hear.

en·sor·de·ci·mien·to m. (*acción de ensordecer*) deafening; (*sordera*) deafness; (*amortiguamiento*) muffling, deadening.

en·sor·ti·ja·mien·to m. *(acción de ensortijar)* crimping, curling; *(sortijas en el cabello)* curls, ringlets.

en·sor·ti·jar tr. *(rizar)* to curl, put curls into; *(enrollar)* to coil, wind; *(la nariz)* to ring, put a ring into (an animal's nose) —reflex. to curl, become curly.

en·so·tar·se reflex. to enter a thicket.

en·su·cia·dor, –do·ra adj. dirtying.

en·su·ciar tr. *(manchar)* to dirty, soil; *(estropear)* to make a mess of, mess up; FIG. *(desacreditar)* to stain, besmirch (one's name) —intr. COLL. to soil *or* mess (one's bedding or clothing) —reflex. *(mancharse)* to become dirty *or* soiled; COLL. *(evacuarse)* to soil *or* mess (one's bedding or clothing); FIG. *(desacreditar)* to discredit oneself ♦ **ensuciarse por dinero** to accept *or* take bribes.

en·suel·va, ensuelvo see **ensolver**.

en·sue·ño m. *(sueño)* dream; FIG. *(fantasía)* fantasy, illusion ♦ **de e.** dream <*casa de e.* dream house>.

en·ta·bla·ción f. *(acción de cubrir con tablas)* boarding up; *(tablas)* boards, planks; *(comienzo)* beginning, starting (negotiations, conversation, etc.); LAW *(preparación)* bringing, filing (legal action); *(notación en las tablas de las iglesias)* registering on tablets (of church annals).

en·ta·bla·do I. past part. see **entablar** II. m. *(suelo)* floor, flooring; *(tablas)* floorboards, planks.

en·ta·bla·men·to m. ARCHIT. entablature.

en·ta·blar tr. *(cubrir con tablas)* to board (up), cover with boards; *(arreglar un tablero)* to set up the board (for chess or checkers); *(empezar)* to begin, start; MED. to splint, put in a splint; RELIG. to write on tablets; AMER., LAW to bring, file <*e. juicio a* to file suit against>; ARG. to train (livestock) to stay in a herd; PERU to boast, brag ♦ **e. amistad** to become friends —intr. AMER. to tie, draw —reflex. *(empezar)* to begin, start; *(fijarse el viento)* to settle, fix direction (the wind); EQUIT. to resist turning its head (a horse); ARG. to graze in a herd (livestock).

en·ta·ble m. *(entabladura)* boarding, planking; *(en damas, en ajedrez)* position of pieces (in chess *or* checkers); S. AMER. order, arrangement; COL. business, enterprise.

en·ta·bli·llar tr. MED. to splint, put in a splint.

en·ta·le·gar §47 tr. *(meter en talegos)* to put into pouches; *(atesorar)* to hoard, save (money).

en·ta·lin·gar §47 tr. MARIT. to clinch (a cable).

en·ta·lla·du·ra f. *or* **en·ta·lla·mien·to** m. *(escultura)* carving, sculpture; *(grabado)* engraving; *(para resinar)* incision (to extract resin); CARP. notch, groove.

en·ta·llar tr. *(esculpir)* to carve, sculpture; *(grabar)* to engrave; *(resinar)* to tap, make an incision in (to extract resin); CARP. to notch, groove; SEW. to tailor, adjust —intr. SEW. to fit well.

en·ta·lle·cer §17 intr. & reflex. BOT. to shoot, sprout.

en·ta·par tr. CHILE, BKB. to bind.

en·ta·pi·zar §04 tr. *(paredes)* to tapestry, hang with tapestries; *(muebles)* to upholster (furniture); FIG. *(cubrir)* to grow over, cover; ARG. to carpet.

en·ta·pu·jar tr. COLL. *(cubrir)* to cover; FIG. *(encubrir)* to cover up, conceal —reflex. to become covered.

en·ta·ri·ma·do I. past part. see **entarimar** II. m. parquet, parquetry.

en·ta·ri·mar tr. to parquet.

en·ta·ru·ga·do I. past part. see **entarugar** II. m. wooden paving.

en·ta·ru·gar §47 tr. to pave in wood —reflex. VEN. to pull (a hat) down over one's head.

en·te m. *(ser)* entity, being; COLL. *(persona rara)* odd character, specimen; COM. firm, company ♦ **e. de razón** imaginary being • **e. de ficción** fictional character.

en·te·co, –ca adj. sickly, puny.

en·te·char tr. AMER. to roof.

en·te·jar tr. AMER. to tile, roof with tiles.

en·te·le·ri·do, –da m.f. *(sobrecogido de frío o de pavor)* numb from cold *or* fear; AMER. weakly, sickly.

en·te·na·do, –da m. stepson —f. stepdaughter —m.f. stepchild ♦ **entenados** stepchildren.

en·ten·de·de·ras f.pl. COLL. brains, intelligence ♦ **ser corto de e.** *or* **tener malas e.** COLL. to be dim, be slow on the uptake ♦ **tener buenas e.** COLL. to be bright.

en·ten·de·dor, –do·ra I. adj. *(que entiende)* understanding; *(experto)* expert; *(listo)* clever, sharp II. m.f. *(que entiende)* one who understands; *(experto)* expert ♦ **al buen e., pocas palabras bastan** a word to the wise is sufficient.

en·ten·der §50 I. tr. *(comprender)* to understand, comprehend; *(creer)* to believe, think <*entiendo que sería mejor no decir nada* I think it would be better not to say anything>; *(querer)* mean, intend <*entiendo que me llames en seguida* I mean for you to call me immediately>; *(inferir)* to infer, take it —intr. ♦ **e. en** *or* **de** *(tener aptitud)* to be good at; *(ocuparse)* to deal with; *(tener autoridad)* to be in charge of • **dar a e.** *(manifestar)* to give to understand; *(insinuar)* to insinuate, hint at • **e. mal** to misunderstand —reflex. to be understood <*esta frase puede entenderse de dos modos* this sentence can be understood in two ways>; *(interpretarse)* to be meant <*¿qué se entiende por esta cláusula?* what is meant by this clause?>; *(comprenderse a sí mismo)* to understand oneself; *(tener motivo)* to have one's reasons <*yo me entiendo* I have my reasons>; *(ponerse de acuerdo)* to come to an agreement; *(llevarse bien)* to get along; *(tener relaciones amorosas)* to have an affair ♦ **entenderse con** to refer to, concern <*esa decisión no se entiende con nosotros* that decision does not concern us> II. m. opinion <*a mi e.* in my opinion>.

en·ten·di·do, –da I. past part. see **entender** II. adj. *(perito)* expert, informed; *(intelligente)* intelligent, smart ♦ **no darse por e.** to pretend not to understand *or* hear III. m.f. expert, connoisseur.

en·ten·di·mien·to m. *(comprensión)* understanding, comprehension; *(juicio)* judgment, sense; *(inteligencia)* intelligence, understanding.

en·te·ne·bre·cer §17 tr. to darken —reflex. to darken, become dark.

en·te·ra·do, –da I. past part. see **enterar** II. adj. *(informado)* informed, aware; *(bien informado)* well-informed; CHILE conceited, haughty ♦ **darse por e. de** to be well aware of • **estar e.** to be informed, know • **estar e. de** to know about, be aware of III. m. expert, authority; COLL. *(sabelotodo)* know-it-all.

en·te·ra·men·te adv. completely, entirely.

en·te·rar tr. *(informar)* to inform, make aware; AMER. to pay; S. AMER. to complete, make up (a quantity) —intr. CHILE to let (the days) go by —reflex. to find out, become aware ♦ **enterarse de** to find out about, learn of.

en·ter·car·se §70 reflex. to become stubborn, insist.

en·te·re·za f. *(integridad)* entirety, completeness; FIG. *(constancia)* integrity, uprightness; *(fortaleza)* fortitude, strength; *(severidad)* strictness, severity (in discipline).

en·te·ri·tis f. MED. enteritis.

en·te·ri·zo, –za adj. *(entero)* entire, whole; *(de una pieza)* in one-piece, one-piece.

en·ter·ne·ce·dor, –do·ra adj. touching, moving.

en·ter·ne·cer §17 tr. *(ablandar)* to soften, make tender; *(conmover)* to touch, move —reflex. *(conmoverse)* to be touched *or* moved; *(ceder)* to relent.

en·ter·ne·ci·mien·to m. softening; *(ternura)* tenderness; *(compasión)* compassion.

en·te·ro, –ra I. adj. *(completo)* entire, complete; *(robusto)* robust, healthy; FIG. *(justo)* just, fair; *(virtuoso)* honest, upright; *(firme)* steadfast, resolute; COLL. *(de la tela)* thick, strong (said of cloth); ZOOL. uncastrated; MATH. whole, integral; AMER., COLL. identical ♦ **por e.** entirely, completely II. m. MATH. integer, whole number; FIN. point <*la acción perdió muchos enteros* the stock lost a lot of points>; AMER. payment; CHILE balance.

en·ter·qué, enterque see **entercarse.**

en·te·rra·mien·to m. *(entierro)* burial, interment; *(sepulcro)* tomb, grave; *(sepultura)* burial place.

en·te·rrar §49 tr. *(sepultar)* to bury; *(inhumar)* to bury, inter; *(esconder)* to hide, bury; *(clavar)* to sink *or* drive in; FIG. *(olvidar)* to bury, forget; *(sobrevivir)* to outlive, survive —reflex. FIG. *(retirarse)* to withdraw, bury oneself.

en·te·sar §49 tr. *(poner tieso)* to tighten, stretch; *(dar fuerza)* to strengthen.

en·tes·ta·do, –da adj. obstinate, stubborn.

en·ti·bar intr. to rest on —tr. MIN. to shore.

en·ti·biar tr. *(poner tibio)* to make lukewarm *or* tepid; FIG. *(templar)* to temper, moderate —reflex. *(ponerse tibio)* to become lukewarm; FIG. *(moderar)* to relax, cool down.

en·ti·cé, entice see **entizar**.
en·ti·dad f. *(ser)* entity; *(esencia)* essence; *(importancia)* importance, significance; *(organización)* body, organization; COM. company, concern.
en·tien·da, entiendo see **entender**.
en·tie·rra, entierro see **enterrar**.
en·tie·rro m. *(sepelio)* burial, interment; *(funerales)* funeral; *(sepulcro)* tomb, grave; *(convoy)* funeral procession; COLL. *(tesoro)* buried treasure ♦ **Santo E.** RELIG. Good Friday procession.
en·tie·sar tr. AMER. to stiffen, make stiff.
en·tie·se, entieso see **entesar**.
en·ti·gre·cer·se §17 reflex. FIG. to get angry, become furious.
en·ti·nar tr. to place in a tub *or* vat.
en·tin·ta·do, –da PRINT. I. past part. see **entintar** II. m. inking.
en·tin·tar tr. PRINT. to ink; FIG. *(teñir)* to dye, tint.
en·ti·zar §04 tr. AMER. to chalk (a billiard cue).
en·tiz·nar tr. to soil, stain.
en·tol·dar tr. *(cubrir con toldos)* to cover with an awning, put an awning over; *(tapizar)* to tapestry, cover with a tapestry —reflex. FIG. *(engreírse)* to put on airs; METEOROL. to become overcast, cloud over.
en·to·mo·lo·gí·a f. entomology.
en·to·mo·ló·gi·co, –ca adj. entomological, entomologic.
en·to·mó·lo·go m. f. entomologist.
en·to·na·ción f. *(modulación)* intoning, modulation; *(tono)* intonation; FIG. *(arrogancia)* arrogance, conceit.
en·to·na·dor, -do·ra I. adj. *(que se ajusta al tono)* in tune (singing) II. m.f. organ blower (person).
en·to·nar tr. *(cantar)* to sing in tune; *(dar cierto tono)* to modulate; *(empezar a cantar)* to intone; *(dar viento)* to work the bellows of (an organ); FIG. *(alabar)* to sing *or* sound (praises); MED. to tone up, invigorate; PAINT. to harmonize, tone (colors) —intr. *(cantar)* to sing in tune; *(empezar a cantar)* to intone; *(armonizar)* to harmonize; PAINT. to match (colors) —reflex. *(envanecerse)* to be arrogant, put on airs; MED. to tone oneself up.
en·to·na·to·rio m. chant book (for a church choir).
en·ton·ces adv. *(en aquel momento)* then, at that time *<me di cuenta e. de lo que estaba ocurriendo* I realized then what was happening>; *(en tal caso)* then, in that case *<si estás enojado, vete e.* if you're angry, then go> ♦ **desde e.** since then, from then on • **en aquel e.** *or* **por e.** around that time, at that time • **hasta e.** till then.
en·to·ne·lar tr. to put in barrels *or* casks.
en·to·no m. environment.
en·ton·te·cer §17 tr. to make silly *or* foolish —intr. & reflex. to become silly *or* foolish.
en·ton·te·ci·mien·to m. silliness, foolishness.
en·tor·cha·do I. past part. see **entorchar** II. m. *(bordado)* gold *or* silver braid; MUS. bass string.
en·tor·char tr. *(retorcer velas)* to join (candles) to form a torch; *(entrelazar)* to braid; *(retorcer)* to twist.
en·to·ri·lar tr. TAUR. to put (a bull) in the stall.
en·tor·nar tr. *(medio cerrar)* to half-close, leave ajar *<e. una puerta* to leave a door ajar>; *(inclinar)* to tilt; *(volcar)* to upset, tip over.
en·tor·no m. environment.
en·tor·pe·ce·dor, -do·ra adj. numbing, dulling.
en·tor·pe·cer §17 tr. *(poner torpe)* to make torpid *or* slow; FIG. *(embrutecer)* to dull, deaden; *(obstaculizar)* to hamper, obstruct; MECH. to make stick.
en·tor·pe·ci·mien·to m. *(torpeza)* torpor, slowness; *(embotamiento)* dulling, deadening; FIG. *(obstrucción)* hampering, obstruction; MECH. sticking.
en·tor·tar §19 tr. *(poner tuerto)* to make crooked; *(cegar)* to make blind in one eye —reflex. to become crooked.
en·to·si·gar §47 tr. to poison.
en·to·zo·a·rio m. ZOOL. entozoan.
en·tra·da f. *(acción)* entry, entrance *<el rey hizo una e. solemne* the king made a solemn entrance>; *(acceso)* entry, entrance; *(vestíbulo)* vestibule, entrance hall; *(ingreso)* admission *<celebraron su e. a la sociedad* they celebrated her admission into the society>; *(privilegio)* admittance, entrée; *(intimidad)* familiar access; *(billete)* admission

ticket; *(taquilla)* gate, receipts; *(desembolso)* deposit, down payment; *(principio)* beginning *<la e. del año* the beginning of the year>; COM. entry; CUL. entrée; *(palabra)* entry (in a dictionary); *(pelo)* receding hairline; *(naipes)* hand (of cards); MECH. intake *<e. de aire* air intake>; COMPUT., ELEC., input; MIN. adit; MIL. invasion, encroachment; MUS., THEAT. entrance; ARG., CUBA, MEX. *(embestida)* sudden attack, onslaught; *(paliza)* beating; MEX. false start ♦ **dar e. a** to let in, admit; AUTO. to yield the right of way to • **de e.** right away, from the start • **de primera e.** at first sight • **e. a viva fuerza** forced entry • **e. de datos** COMPUT. data input • **e. de favor** complimentary ticket • **e. general** THEAT. standing room • **e. gratuita** free admission • **e. llena** THEAT. full house • **entradas** FIN. income, receipts • **tener e.** to be welcome.
en·tra·dor, -do·ra adj. *(animoso)* spirited, energetic; *(enamoradizo)* amorously inclined; *(agradable)* likeable, charming; CHILE meddling.
en·tra·ma·do I. past part see **entramar** II. m. ARCHIT. framework; FIG. *(estructura)* framework, structure.
en·tra·mar tr. ARCHIT. to build a framework for.
en·tram·bos, –bas adj. LIT. both.
en·tram·par tr. *(hacer caer en una trampa)* to trap, snare; FIG. *(engañar)* to deceive, trick; *(enredar)* to entangle, make a mess of; *(gravar con deudas)* to burden with debts —reflex. FIG., COLL. to get *or* go into debt.
en·tran·te I. adj. *(próximo)* next, coming *<la semana e.* next week>; *(nuevo)* new, incoming *<el presidente e.* the incoming president>; ARCHIT. recessed; GEOM. re-entering, re-entrant (angle); MARIT. rising, incoming (tide); MIL. relief (guard) II. m.f. person entering ♦ **entrantes y salientes** COLL. frequent visitors —m. ARCHIT. recess, niche; GEOG. inlet.
en·tra·ña f. ANAT. entrails, innards; *(esencia)* core, essence; *(centro)* center, middle; *(voluntad)* will; FIG. *(genio)* disposition, nature ♦ **arrancar las entrañas a alguien** FIG. to break someone's heart • **dar hasta las entrañas** to give one's all • **de buenas entrañas** good-natured • **de malas entrañas** heartless, callous • **echar las entrañas** COLL. to vomit, throw up • **entrañas** FIG. bowels, innermost part *<las entrañas de la tierra* the bowels of the earth> • **sin entrañas** heartless, pitiless.
en·tra·ña·ble adj. *(íntimo)* intimate, close; *(querido)* beloved, dear; deep *<afecto e.* deep affection>.
en·tra·ñar tr. *(enterrar)* to bury deep; *(llevar en sí)* to carry within *<e. un odio profundo* to carry a deep hatred within oneself>; *(acarrear)* to entail —reflex. to become deeply attached (to someone) ♦ **entrañarse en** to reach the bottom *or* very heart of.
en·tra·par tr. *(empolvar la cabeza)* to powder (one's head); AGR. to fertilize by burying rags under each plant —reflex. to get full of dirt (cloth or hair); *(embotarse el filo)* to become blunt (a knife or tool).
en·trar intr. *(pasar adentro)* to enter, go in, come in *<el ladrón entró por la ventana* the thief came in through the window>; *(ser admitido)* to be admitted *<entró en la universidad* he was admitted to the university>; *(penetrar)* to enter, go *<el clavo entró en la pared sin dificultad* the nail went into the wall without difficulty>; *(ingresar)* to join *<entraré al ejército en noviembre* I will join the army in November>; *(encajar)* to go, fit *<este libro no entra en el estante* this book does not fit on the shelf>; *(desaguar)* to flow *<el arroyo entra en el río* the creek flows into the river>; *(formar parte de)* to enter, be part *<eso no entra en sus planes* that does not enter into his plans>; *(ser contado)* to be included *or* counted *<ella entra en la lista de sus admiradores* she is included in the list of his admirers>; *(emplearse)* to go, be used *<entra mucho azúcar en esa receta* a lot of sugar is used in that recipe>; *(empezar)* to begin, come in *<el invierno entra el 21 de diciembre* winter begins on December 21>; *(atacar)* to attack, charge; MUS. to come in ♦ **e. a** *(dar principio)* to begin to *<entramos a remar* we began to row> • **e. bien** to be fitting *or* appropriate • **e. en** to enter, go in; *(abrazar)* to take up, adopt *<e. en una profesión* to take up a profession> • **e. en detalles** to go into detail • **e. en función** to go into operation • **e. en huelga** to go on strike • **e. en recelo** *(ser desconfiado)* to begin to be suspicious; *(sentir celos)* to

become jealous • **e. en vigor** to go into effect • **entrarle deseos de** to get the urge to • **no entrarle a uno** *(desagradar)* to dislike *<no me entra ese chico* I dislike that boy>; *(no comprender)* to be unable to get *<no me entran las matemáticas* I can't get mathematics> • **no e. ni salir** COLL. to be unconcerned —tr. *(meter)* to bring *or* put inside *<la criada entró los vasos* the maid brought in the glasses>; *(introducir)* to introduce, bring in *<ella entró a los huéspedes* she brought in the guests>; *(invadir)* to invade, attack; *(influir)* to influence, get at *<no hay por donde entrarle* there is no way to get at him>; MARIT. to overtake —reflex. to get in, sneak in.

en·tre prep. *(en medio de)* between *<viven e. Bogotá y Medellín* they live between Bogotá and Medellín>; *(en el intervalo)* between *<e. las dos y las cuatro de la tarde* between two and four o'clock in the afternoon>; *(en el número de)* among, amongst *<e. mis amigos* among my friends>; *(en cooperación)* between *<e. todos lo matamos* between all of us we killed him>; *(en)* in *<e. paréntesis* in parentheses>; to *<pensé e. mí* I thought to myself> ♦ **de e.** out of, from among • **e. la espada y la pared** FIG. between a rock and a hard place, between the devil and the deep blue sea • **e. tanto** meanwhile • **e. tú y yo** between you and me, confidentially • **por e.** through.

en·tre·a·bier·to, –ta I. past part. see **entreabrir** II. adj. *(medio abierto)* half-open; ajar *<dejar una puerta e.* to leave a door ajar>.

en·tre·a·brir §85 tr. to open halfway, set ajar *<e. una puerta* to set a door ajar> —reflex. to be open halfway, be ajar.

en·tre·ac·to m. THEAT. intermission, entr'acte; *(cigarro)* small cigar.

en·tre·an·cho, –cha adj. of medium width.

en·tre·ca·lle f. ARCHIT. quirk, space between two moldings.

en·tre·ca·nal m. ARCHIT. filet (between two flutings).

en·tre·ca·no, –na adj. *(cabello)* graying (hair); *(persona)* going gray.

en·tre·ca·va f. shallow digging.

en·tre·ca·var tr. to dig shallowly.

en·tre·ce·jo m. ANAT. space between the eyebrows; *(ceño)* frown ♦ **arrugar** *or* **fruncir el e.** to frown.

en·tre·ce·rrar §49 tr. to half-close, leave ajar *<e. una puerta* to leave a door ajar>.

en·tre·cla·ro, –ra adj. fairly clear, lightish.

en·tre·co·ger §34 tr. *(agarrar)* to catch, seize; FIG. *(apremiar)* to compel, force (with arguments *or* threats).

en·tre·co·mi·llar tr. to put in quotation marks.

en·tre·co·ro m. chancel.

en·tre·cor·tar tr. to cut into, cut partially; *(interrumpir)* to interrupt, cut off.

en·tre·cor·te m. incomplete *or* partial cut.

en·tre·cor·te·za f. ingrown bark (in wood).

en·tre·cru·za·do, -da I. past part. see **entrecruzar** II. adj. interwoven, intertwined.

en·tre·cru·zar §04 tr. to intercross, interweave —reflex. to be intercrossed, be interwoven.

en·tre·cu·bier·tas f.pl. MARIT. between-decks.

en·tre·cho·car·se §70 reflex. to collide.

en·tre·de·cir §11 tr. *(prohibir)* to prohibit, interdict; RELIG. to prohibit the use of the sacraments.

en·tre·di·cho, –cha I. past part. see **entredecir** II. m. *(prohibición)* prohibition, interdiction; RELIG. interdict; ARG. disagreement, split; BOL. alarm bell ♦ **estar en e.** FIG. to be in question • **poner algo en e.** FIG. to question something.

en·tre·di·ga, entredigo see **entredecir**.

en·tre·di·je·ra, entredijo see **entredecir**.

en·tre·do·ble adj. of medium thickness (cloth).

en·tre·dós m. SEW. insert, panel; *(mueble)* dresser, low cupboard; PRINT. long primer.

en·tre·fi·no, –na adj. of medium quality.

en·tre·fo·rro m. SEW. interlining.

en·tre·ga f. *(transferencia)* delivery; *(rendición)* handing over *<la e. de las joyas robadas* the handing over of the stolen jewels>; *(cuaderno)* installment, part (of a serial); ARCHIT. part of a beam embedded in wall; SPORT. pass ♦ **e. contra pago** *or* **reembolso** cash on delivery, C.O.D. • **e. inmediata** special delivery • **hacer e. de** to present, hand over.

en·tre·ga·do, –da I. past part. see **entregar** II. adj. ARCHIT. embedded.

en·tre·ga·dor, –do·ra I. adj. delivering II. m.f. deliverer.

en·tre·ga·mien·to m. *(acción de dar)* delivery, handing over; *(rendición)* surrender.

en·tre·gar §47 tr. *(dar)* to deliver; *(poner en manos)* to hand over *<e. las joyas robadas a la policía* to hand over the stolen jewels to the police>; *(hacer)* to hand *or* turn in *<e. un ensayo* to turn in an essay>; *(traicionar)* to betray; ARCHIT. to embed ♦ **e. a la voluntad de** to leave at the mercy of • **entregarla** COLL. to kick the bucket, die —reflex. *(rendirse)* to surrender, submit; *(dedicarse)* to dedicate *or* devote oneself to; *(abandonarse)* to abandon oneself to ♦ **entregarse de** to take possession of.

en·tre·jun·tar tr. CARP. to assemble, join.

en·tre·la·zar §04 tr. to interlace, interweave.

en·tre·li·ne·ar tr. to interline, write between two lines.

en·tre·li·ño m. AGR. space between rows of trees *or* vines.

en·tre·lis·ta·do, –da adj. striped, multicolored.

en·tre·lu·cir §44 intr. to show through, shine through.

en·tre·me·dias adv. *(entre dos cosas)* in between, halfway; *(mientras tanto)* in the meantime, meanwhile ♦ **e. de** between, among.

en·tre·me·dio m. AMER. *(intervalo)* interim; *(entreacto)* intermission.

en·tre·més[1] m. THEAT. interlude, entr'acte (short play).

en·tre·més[2] m. CUL. *(encurtido)* pickled fruit *or* vegetable; *(tapa)* appetizer, hors d'oeuvre.

en·tre·me·ter tr. to insert, put *or* place in between —reflex. *injerirse* to meddle, interfere *<no quiero entremeterme en tus asuntos* I don't want to meddle in your affairs>; *(una conversación)* to interrupt, butt in.

en·tre·me·ti·do, –da I. past part. see **entremeter** II. adj. meddlesome, interfering III. m.f. meddler, busybody.

en·tre·me·ti·mien·to m. *(inserción)* insertion, interposition; *(estorbo)* meddling, interfering.

en·tre·mez·clar tr. to intermingle, mix together.

en·tre·mo·rir §27 intr. to flicker, burn out (a candle).

en·tre·na·dor, –do·ra SPORT. I. adj. training, coaching II. m.f. trainer, coach ♦ **e. de pilotaje** AVIA. flight simulator.

en·tre·na·mien·to m. SPORT. training, coaching.

en·tre·nar tr. SPORT. to train, coach —reflex. to train, be in training.

en·tren·zar §04 tr. to braid, entwine.

en·tre·o·ír §45 tr. to half-hear, hear partially.

en·tre·pa·nes m.pl. fallow land.

en·tre·pa·ño m. ARCHIT. panel, bay; CARP. *(entante)* shelf; *(cuarterón)* panel.

en·tre·pa·re·cer·se §17 reflex. to show through.

en·tre·pier·na f. *or* **en·tre·pier·nas** f.pl. ANAT. crotch, inner surface of the thighs; SEW. *(refuerzo)* crotch reinforcement; CHILE swimming suit, bathing trunks.

en·tre·pi·so m. ARCHIT. mezzanine; MIN. space between galleries.

en·tre·pun·zar §04 tr. to cause intermittent shooting pains.

en·tre·rren·glo·nar tr. to interlineate, write between the lines.

en·tre·sa·ca *or* **en·tre·sa·ca·du·ra** f. thinning *or* culling out.

en·tre·sa·car §70 tr. *(elegir)* to pick out, select; *(aclarar)* to thin (out).

en·tre·si·jo m. ANAT. mesentery; FIG. *(cosa escondida)* secret, mystery ♦ **tener muchos entresijos** FIG., COLL. *(tener dificultades)* to have many ins and outs; *(una persona)* to be a mystery *or* puzzle (to others).

en·tre·sue·lo m. mezzanine.

en·tre·sur·co m. AGR. space between furrows.

en·tre·ta·lla *or* **en·tre·ta·lla·du·ra** f. bas-relief.

en·tre·ta·llar tr. *(labrar)* to engrave, carve; *(recortar)* to do openwork on (cloth); *(detener)* to hinder, impede —reflex. to fit together.

en·tre·tan·to I. adv. meanwhile, in the meantime II. m. meantime, meanwhile.

en·tre·te·cho m. AMER. attic, loft.

en·tre·te·jer tr. TEX. to interweave; *(enlazar)* to interlace, braid; FIG. *(incluir)* to insert, include <*e. citas con el texto* to insert quotations throughout the text>.

en·tre·te·la f. SEW. interlining; PRINT. *(acción de satinar)* surfacing, smoothing ♦ **entretelas** FIG., COLL. innermost soul, heart of hearts <*lo creo en mis entretelas* I believe it in my heart of hearts>.

en·tre·te·lar tr. SEW. *(reforzar)* to interline; PRINT. *(satinar)* to surface, smooth.

en·tre·ten·ción f. AMER. var. of **entretenimiento**.

en·tre·te·ne·dor, –do·ra I. adj. entertaining II. m.f. entertainer.

en·tre·te·ner §69 tr. *(divertir)* to entertain, amuse; *(mitigar)* to alleviate, make more bearable; *(ocupar)* to occupy, keep busy <*el libro me entretenía toda la mañana* the book kept me busy all morning>; *(mantener)* to maintain, keep; *(detener)* to detain, delay; *(demorar)* to stall, hold up —reflex. *(detenerse)* to dally, dawdle; *(divertirse)* to be entertained *or* amused; *(perder tiempo)* to pass the time, while away the hours.

en·tre·te·ni·do, –da I. past part. see **entretener** II. adj. *(divertido)* amusing, entertaining; HER. *(enlazado)* interlaced, interwoven III. m. trainee —f. *(amante)* lover, mistress.

en·tre·te·ni·mien·to m. *(diversión)* amusement, entertainment; *(alivio)* alleviation, easing; *(conservación de una cosa)* maintenance, upkeep; *(detenimiento)* detainment, delay.

en·tre·tiem·po m. between-season, transitional <*traje de e.* transitional suit (suitable for wear in spring or fall).

en·tre·tie·ne see **entretener**.

en·tre·tu·vie·ra, entretuvo see **entretener**.

en·tre·ve·nar·se reflex. to enter through the veins (a liquid).

en·tre·ven·ta·na f. ARCHIT. pier, space between windows.

en·tre·ver §77 tr. *(ver confusamente)* to half-see, see partially; *(adivinar)* to guess, surmise.

en·tre·ve·ra·do, –da I. past part. see **entreverar** II. adj. mixed (fat and lean) III. m. VEN., CUL. type of roasted lamb.

en·tre·ve·rar tr. to intermingle, mix —reflex. ARG. *(mezclarse)* to be mixed up *or* intermingled; MIL. to fight, skirmish.

en·tre·ve·ro m. AMER. *(mezcla)* intermingling, mixture; *(confusión)* confusion, jumble; ARG. *(pelea)* brawl.

en·tre·ví, entrevimos see **entrever**.

en·tre·ví·a f. RAIL. gauge, space between rails.

en·tre·vis·ta f. *(cita)* meeting, conference; JOURN. *(interrogación)* interview.

en·tre·vis·ta·dor, –do·ra m.f. interviewer.

en·tre·vis·tar tr. to interview <*e. a la actriz* to interview the actress> —reflex. *(celebrar una interrogación)* to hold *or* have an interview; *(celebrar una conferencia)* to hold *or* have a meeting ♦ **e. con** to interview, hold *or* have an interview with.

en·tri·pa·do, –da I. adj. ANAT. intestinal; ZOOL. *(no destripado)* with the intestines intact, not eviscerated II. m. FIG., COLL. *(enojo disimulado)* concealed anger, gnawing resentment —f. CARIB., MEX. soaking, drenching.

en·tris·te·cer §17 tr. to sadden, grieve —reflex. to become sad *or* grieved.

en·tris·te·ci·mien·to m. *(acción)* saddening; *(tristeza)* sadness.

en·tro·jar tr. to store (grain) in a granary, garner.

en·tro·me·ter tr. & reflex. var. of **entremeter**.

en·trom·par·se reflex. FIG., COLL. *(emborracharse)* to get drunk *or* intoxicated; AMER. to get angry.

en·tron·car §70 tr. *(probar el parentesco entre)* to show *or* establish the relationship between (two persons); MEX. *(reunir dos caballos)* to mate horses of the same color —intr. *(contraer parentesco)* to become related (by marriage); AMER. *(reunirse)* to connect, form a junction (railway lines).

en·tro·ne·rar tr. to pocket (a billiard ball) —reflex. to fall into a pocket (a billiard ball).

en·tro·ni·za·ción f. *or* **en·tro·ni·za·mien·to** m. *(acción de colocar en el trono)* throning, enthronement; *(ensalzamiento)* exaltation.

en·tro·ni·zar §04 tr. *(colocar en el trono)* to enthrone, put on

the throne; FIG. *(ensalzar)* to revere, praise; *(colocar en alto estado)* to raise to a lofty *or* high position —reflex. FIG. to put on airs, become puffed up.

en·tron·que m. *(relación de parentesco)* cognation, blood relationship; AUTO., RAIL. *(empalme)* junction.

en·tron·qué, entronque see **entroncar**.

en·tru·cha·da f. *or* **en·tru·cha·do** m. COLL. trick, plot.

en·tru·char tr. COLL. to trick, lure (into doing something) —reflex. MEX. to meddle (in someone else's business).

en·tru·chón, –cho·na COLL. I. adj. plotting, scheming II. m.f. plotter, schemer.

en·tru·jar tr. *(guardar en trujas)* to store in bins (olives); *(entrojar)* to store in a granary (grain); COLL. *(embolsar)* to pocket, put away.

en·tu·ba·ción f. *or* **en·tu·ba·mien·to** m. tubing.

en·tu·bar tr. to tube, insert a tube in.

en·tuer·te, entuerto see **entortar**.

en·tuer·to m. wrong, injustice ♦ **entuertos** MED. afterpains.

en·tu·lle·cer §17 tr. FIG. to check, stop —intr. & reflex. to become paralyzed *or* crippled.

en·tu·me·cer §17 tr. to (make) numb —reflex. *(entorpecerse)* to go *or* become numb; *(hincharse)* to swell, rise <*se entumece el río* the river is rising>.

en·tu·me·ci·mien·to m. *(adormecimiento)* numbness, torpor; *(crecida)* swelling, rise (of water).

en·tu·mir·se reflex. to go *or* become numb, fall asleep (part of the body).

en·tu·ni·car §70 tr. PAINT. to plaster (for fresco painting); *(poner una túnica)* to put a tunic on.

en·tu·pir tr. *(obstruir)* to clog, block (a pipe); *(comprimir)* to compress, squeeze.

en·tur·biar tr. *(poner turbio)* to cloud <*el lodo enturbió el agua* the mud clouded the water>; FIG. *(confundir)* to cloud, confuse —reflex. to become clouded *or* cloudy.

en·tu·sias·mar tr. to enthuse —reflex. to become enthusiastic.

en·tu·sias·mo m. *(exaltación)* enthusiasm; *(inspiración)* inspiration, creative impulse; FIG. *(pasión)* enthusiasm, zeal; RELIG. ardor, fervor.

en·tu·sias·ta I. adj. *(admirador)* enthusiastic; RELIG. fervorous II. m.f. enthusiast, fan <*un e. de fútbol* a soccer fan>.

en·tu·siás·ti·co, -ca adj. enthusiastic.

e·nu·me·ra·ción f. *(catálogo)* enumeration, listing; *(cómputo)* count.

e·nu·me·ra·dor, –do·ra I. adj. enumerating, enumerative II. m.f. enumerator.

e·nu·me·rar tr. *(catalogar)* to enumerate, list; *(contar)* to count.

e·nun·cia·ción f. enunciation, declaration.

e·nun·cia·do I. past part. see **enunciar** II. m. enunciation, statement.

e·nun·ciar tr. to enunciate, express clearly <*e. una doctrina* to enunciate a doctrine>.

e·nun·cia·ti·vo, –va adj. *(que expresa claramente)* enunciative, enunciatory; GRAM. declarative <*una oración e.* a declarative sentence>.

en·vai·nar tr. *(meter en la vaina)* to sheathe (a sword); *(envolver)* to enclose.

en·va·len·to·na·mien·to m. *(acción)* emboldening, encouragement; *(valentía)* boldness, courage.

en·va·len·to·nar tr. to encourage, embolden —reflex. to become bold *or* emboldened.

en·va·ne·ce·dor, –do·ra adj. ego-boosting.

en·va·ne·cer §17 tr. *(poner vanidoso)* make vain *or* conceited —reflex. *(ponerse vanidoso)* to become vain *or* conceited; CHILE, AGR. to wither, dry (fruit).

en·va·ne·ci·mien·to m. *(acción)* ego-boosting; *(vanidad)* vanity, conceit.

en·va·ra·mien·to m. stiffness, numbness.

en·va·rar·se reflex. to become numb.

en·va·sa·dor, –do·ra I. adj. *(relativo al empaque)* packing, packaging; *(relativo a botellas)* bottling II. m.f. *(empacador)* packer; *(embotellador)* bottler —m *(embudo)* large funnel.

en·va·sar tr. *(empaquetar)* to pack, package; *(embotellar)* to bottle; FIG. *(beber con exceso)* to drink to excess; *(apuñalar)* to stab.

en·va·se m. *(empaque)* packing, packaging; *(embotellamiento)* bottling; *(envío)* shipping, transport; *(paquete)* package; *(botella)* bottle; FIG. *(acción de beber con exceso)* drinking to excess; *(salto de un arma)* stab, plunge.

en·ve·di·jar·se reflex. *(enmarañarse)* to become entangled; COLL. *(enzarzarse)* to wrangle, get into a fight.

en·ve·je·cer §17 tr. *(hacer viejo)* to age, make old —intr. & reflex. to grow old, age.

en·ve·je·ci·do, –da I. past part. see **envejecer** II. adj. *(viejo)* old, aged; FIG. *(acostumbrado)* accustomed (to), experienced (in).

en·ve·je·ci·mien·to m. *(acción)* aging; *(vejez)* age.

en·ve·ne·na·dor, –do·ra I. adj. *(venenoso)* poisonous, venomous II. m.f. poisoner.

en·ve·na·mien·to m. *(emponzoñamiento)* poisoning.

en·ve·ne·nar tr. *(emponzoñar)* to poison; FIG. *(interpretar mal)* to misconstrue, interpret maliciously; *(agriar)* to embitter, poison.

en·ve·rar intr. to begin to ripen (fruits).

en·ver·de·cer §17 intr. BOT. to turn or become green.

en·ver·ga·du·ra f. MARIT. breadth, span; AVIA., ORNITH. wingspan, wingspread; FIG. *(importancia)* importance, significance <*un tema de gran e.* a subject of great importance>.

en·ver·gar §47 tr. MARIT. to fasten (sails).

en·ve·ro m. *(color)* golden red (of ripening fruit); *(uva)* type of golden red grape.

en·vés m. other side, back.

en·ve·sa·do, –da adj. showing the other or opposite side.

en·ves·tir §48 tr. var. of **investir**.

en·via·da f. var. of **envío**.

en·via·do I. past part. see **enviar** II. m. *(delegado)* representative, delegate; *(mensajero)* envoy, messenger ♦ **e. especial** or **de prensa** JOURN. special correspondent • **e. extraordinario** DIPL. envoy extraordinary, special envoy.

en·viar §30 tr. *(mandar)* to send, dispatch; *(transmitir)* to convey, transmit ♦ **e. a uno al diablo** or **noramala** FIG., COLL. to send someone to the devil • **e. a uno a pasear** or **a paseo** FIG., COLL. to send someone packing, send someone about his business • **e.** to send as <*le enviaron de embajador* they sent him as ambassador> • **e. por** to send for <*le enviaron por agua* they sent him for water> • **e. un parte** JOURN. to file a dispatch.

en·vi·ciar tr. to corrupt, pervert —intr. BOT. to bear much foliage and little fruit —reflex. *(aficionarse)* to become addicted; *(corromperse)* to become corrupt or perverted ♦ **enviciarse con** or **en** to become addicted to <*enviciarse con la televisión* to become addicted to television>.

en·vi·dia f. *(resentimiento)* envy, jealousy; *(emulación)* emulation, desire to emulate ♦ **comerse de e.** to be eaten up with jealousy or envy • **dar e.** to make jealous or envious • **muerto de e.** green with envy • **tener e. a** to envy, be envious of.

en·vi·dia·ble adj. enviable, desirable.

en·vi·diar tr. *(tener envidia)* to envy, be envious of; FIG. *(desear)* to covet, desire.

en·vi·dio·so, –sa I. adj. envious, jealous II. m.f. envier, envious or jealous person.

en·vi·gar §47 tr. to put rafters or beams in.

en·vi·le·ce·dor, –do·ra adj. debasing, degrading.

en·vi·le·cer §17 tr. to debase, degrade —reflex. to debase or degrade oneself.

en·vi·le·ci·mien·to m. debasement, degradation.

en·vi·na·grar tr. to add vinegar to, put vinegar on.

en·vi·nar tr. to mix up with wine, add wine to.

en·ví·o m. *(expedición)* sending, dispatch; *(transmisión)* conveyance, transmission; *(paquete)* package, parcel; *(remesa de dinero)* remittance; *(remesa de mercancías)* shipment, consignment; LIT. *(dedicatoria)* dedication, inscription ♦ **e. contra reembolso** COM. cash on delivery.

en·vión m. push, shove.

en·vis·car¹ §70 tr. HUNT. *(untar con liga)* to smear with birdlime —reflex. to get stuck in birdlime.

en·vis·car² §70 tr. *(azuzar)* to tease (dogs); FIG. *(enconar los ánimos)* to provoke, incite.

en·vis·ta, envisto see **envestir**.

en·vis·tie·ra, envistió see **envestir**.

en·vi·te m. *(apuesta extraordinaria)* side bet; *(apuesta aumentadora)* raise; *(empujón)* push, shove; FIG. *(ofrecimiento)* offering ♦ **acortar** or **ahorrar envites** to shorten discussion • **al primer e.** right off (the bat), from the outset or start.

en·viu·dar intr. to be widowed, become a widow or widower.

en·vol·ti·jo m. ECUAD. var. of **envoltorio**.

en·vol·to·rio m. *(lío)* bundle; *(cubierta)* wrapping, wrapper; TEX. *(defecto)* flaw in woven fabric, defective woof.

en·vol·tu·ra f. *(pañales)* swaddling clothes; *(cubierta)* cover, covering.

en·vol·ve·de·ro or **en·vol·ve·dor** m. *(cubierta)* wrapping, wrapper; *(mesa)* baby's changing table.

en·vol·ve·dor, –do·ra m.f. *(persona que cubre con papel)* wrapper; *(persona que cubre)* coverer.

en·vol·ven·te adj. *(que cubre)* enveloping, covering; MIL. *(que rodea)* surrounding, encircling; GEOM. enveloping <*un círculo e.* an enveloping circle>.

en·vol·ver §78 tr. *(cubrir)* to envelop, cover; *(empaquetar)* to pack, make into a package or bundle; *(vestir con pañales)* to swaddle, swathe; *(arrollar)* to wind <*e. hilo en un carrete* to wind thread on a spool>; MIL. *(sitiar)* to encircle, surround; FIG. to involve, mix up <*no quise envolverle en el asunto* I didn't want to involve him in the affair>; *(dejar perplejo)* to floor, stump (an opponent); *(ocultar)* to enshroud, envelop —reflex. *(cubrirse una cosa)* to be wrapped or covered; *(cubrirse una persona)* to wrap or cover oneself; FIG. *(complicarse)* to become involved or mixed up (in a matter); *(amancebarse)* to have an affair or lover; *(luchar)* to fight, mix it up with.

en·vol·vi·mien·to m. *(cubrimiento)* envelopment, covering; *(enrollamiento)* winding; MIL. *(rodeamiento)* encirclement; FIG. *(complicación)* involvement, entanglement; ZOOL. *(revolcadero)* wallow, mudhole.

en·vuel·to, –ta I. past part. see **envolver** II. m. COL., CUL. roll (made with corn or plantain); MEX. corn tortilla with filling; ECUAD. rompers, one-piece playsuit or pajamas. —f. ♦ **envueltas** swaddling clothes.

en·vuel·va, envuelvo see **envolver**.

en·ye·sar tr. *(tapar con yeso)* to plaster <*e. una pared* to plaster a wall>; *(agregar yeso a)* to add gypsum to; MED. to set in plaster or in a plaster cast <*e. un brazo roto* to set a broken arm in a plaster cast>.

en·ye·tar tr. ARG., PAR. to jinx, to give bad luck to.

en·yu·gar §47 or **en·yun·tar** tr. to yoke.

en·zar·zar §04 tr. *(poner zarzas)* to cover with brambles; FIG. *(malquistar)* to entangle, embroil —reflex. *(enredarse en zarzas)* to get caught or entangled in brambles; FIG. *(meterse en negocios arduos)* to become involved in difficult affairs; *(pelearse)* to wrangle, bicker.

en·zi·ma f. CHEM. enzyme.

en·zun·char tr. to bind with iron hoops or bands.

en·zu·ri·zar §04 tr. to incite, provoke trouble between.

en·zu·rro·nar tr. *(meter en un zurrón)* to bag, put in a bag; FIG., COLL. *(encerrar)* to enclose, put in.

e·ñe f. name of the Spanish letter "ñ".

e·ó·li·co, –ca I. adj. Aeolian, Aeolic II. m. Aeolic (dialect).

e·ón m. eon.

¡e·pa! interj. AMER. *(¡hola!)* hey!, hello!; *(¡ea!)* come on!; *(¡cuidado!)* whoa!

e·per·la·no m. ICHTH. smelt, sparling.

é·pi·ca I. f. POET. epic poetry II. adj. see **épico, –ca**.

e·pi·cen·tro m. GEOL. epicenter.

é·pi·co, –ca I. adj. POET. epic; FIG. *(heroico)* heroic, epic II. m. *(poeta)* epic poet —f. see **épica**.

e·pi·cu·re·is·mo m. PHILOS. Epicureanism; FIG. *(sensualismo)* sensualism.

e·pi·cú·re·o, –a I. adj. PHILOS. Epicurean; FIG. *(sensual)* sensual II. m.f. PHILOS. Epicurean; FIG. *(sensualista)* sensualist.

e·pi·de·mia f. MED. epidemic.

e·pi·dé·mi·co, –ca adj. MED. epidemic.

e·pi·de·mio·lo·gí·a f. MED. epidemiology.

e·pi·dér·mi·co, –ca adj. epidermal, epidermic.

e·pi·der·mis f. [pl. **-mis**] ANAT., BOT. epidermis, outer skin.

E·pi·fa·ní·a f. RELIG. Epiphany.

e·pi·gas·trio m. ANAT. epigastrium.

e·pi·glo·tis f. [pl. **-tis**] ANAT., ZOOL. epiglottis.

e·pí·go·no m. epigone, follower.

e·pí·gra·fe m. *(inscripción)* epigraph, inscription; *(cita)* quotation.

e·pi·gra·fí·a f. epigraphy.

e·pi·gra·ma m. epigram.

e·pi·lep·sia f. MED. epilepsy.

e·pi·lép·ti·co, –ca adj. & m.f. MED. epileptic.

e·pi·lo·gar §47 tr. *(resumir)* to summarize, sum up; *(terminar)* to round off *or* out; LIT. to add an epilogue to.

e·pí·lo·go m. *(conclusión)* epilogue; *(resumen)* summary, compendium; RHET. *(peroración)* peroration.

e·pis·co·pa·do m. RELIG. episcopate.

e·pis·co·pal adj. RELIG. *(obispal)* episcopal; Episcopal <*la iglesia e.* the Episcopal Church>.

e·pi·só·di·co, –ca adj. episodic, episodical.

e·pi·so·dio m. *(digresión)* episode, digression; *(suceso)* episode, incident; *(entrega)* episode, installment (of a serial).

e·pis·te·mo·lo·gí·a f. PHILOS. epistemology.

e·pís·to·la f. *(carta)* epistle, letter; BIBL. Epistle.

e·pis·to·lar adj. epistolary.

e·pis·to·la·rio m. *(colección)* epistolary, collection of letters; RELIG. Epistolary.

e·pi·ta·fio m. epitaph.

e·pi·ta·la·mio m. epithalamium (nuptial song).

e·pi·te·lio m. ANAT. epithelium.

e·pí·te·to m. epithet.

e·pi·to·mar tr. to epitomize, abridge.

e·pí·to·me m. epitome, summary.

é·po·ca f. *(era)* epoch, era <*la é. victoriana* the Victorian era>; *(período)* time, period <*en esta é.* at this time>; GEOL. age <*la é. cenozóica* the Cenozoic age> ♦ **en aquella é.** at that time • **formar** *or* **hacer é.** to make history.

e·pó·ni·mo, –ma I. adj. eponymous, eponymic II. m. eponym.

e·po·pe·ya f. POET. epic poem, epopee; FIG. *(sucesos épicos)* epic.

ép·si·lon f. epsilon (Greek letter).

ep·tá·go·no, –na GEOM. I. adj. heptagonal II. m. heptagon.

e·pu·lón m. gourmand.

e·qui·dad f. *(justicia)* equity, fairness; LAW *(justicia natural)* equity, natural law; *(moderación)* moderateness, reasonableness.

e·qui·dis·tan·cia f. equidistance.

e·qui·dis·tan·te adj. equidistant.

e·qui·lá·te·ro, –ra adj. GEOM. equilateral.

e·qui·li·bra·do, –da I. past part. see **equilibrar** II. adj. *(ecuánime)* stable, well-balanced; *(sensato)* sensible, reasonable.

e·qui·li·brar tr. *(poner en equilibrio)* to balance, equilibrate; FIG. *(armonizar)* to balance, harmonize —reflex. to balance, equilibrate.

e·qui·li·brio m. *(igualdad)* equilibrium, balance; *(contrapeso)* counterbalance, counterpoise; FIG. *(aplomo)* aplomb, poise ♦ **e. de poder** *or* **político** balance of power • **perder el e.** to lose one's balance.

e·qui·li·bris·mo m. *(acrobatismo)* acrobatics; *(del funámbulo)* tightrope walking.

e·qui·li·bris·ta m.f. *(acróbata)* acrobat; *(funámbulo)* tightrope walker, funambulist.

e·qui·no, –na I. adj. equine, horse II. m. ARG. horse.

e·qui·noc·cial ASTRON. I. adj. equinoctial II. f. equinoctial line.

e·qui·noc·cio m. ASTRON. equinox.

e·qui·pa·je m. *(bagaje)* luggage, baggage; MARIT. crew ♦ **e. de mano** hand luggage • **exceso de e.** excess luggage *or* baggage.

e·qui·pa·mien·to m. equipment, gear.

e·qui·par tr. *(proveer)* to equip, outfit; MARIT. to provision, fit out.

e·qui·pa·ra·ble adj. comparable ♦ **e. con** comparable to *or* with.

e·qui·pa·ra·ción f. comparison, comparing.

e·qui·pa·rar tr. to compare, put on the same level.

e·qui·po m. *(acción de equipar)* equipping, outfitting; *(equipamiento)* equipment, gear; *(instrumentos)* instruments, gear; SPORT. team <*e. de béisbol* baseball team>; *(de traba-*

jadores) shift, crew ♦ **e. de novia** trousseau • **e. de primeros auxilios** MED. first-aid kit • **e. quirúrgico** MED. surgical instruments.

e·quis f. *(letra)* ex (name of the letter "x"); MATH. *(número desconocido)* x (unknown number) ♦ **estar en la e.** C. AMER., COL., ECUAD. to be very skinny.

e·qui·ta·ción f. EQUIT. riding, equitation.

e·qui·ta·ti·va·men·te adv. equitably, fairly.

e·qui·ta·ti·vo, –va adj. equitable, fair.

e·qui·va·len·cia f. equivalence, equivalency.

e·qui·va·len·te adj. & m. CHEM. equivalent.

e·qui·va·ler §74 intr. *(igualar)* to be equivalent *or* equal, equal; *(significar)* to mean, amount to.

e·qui·vo·ca·ción f. *(error)* error, mistake; *(malentendido)* misunderstanding ♦ **por e.** by mistake, in error.

e·qui·vo·ca·da·men·te adv. mistakenly, by mistake.

e·qui·vo·ca·do, –da I. past part. see **equivocar** II. adj. wrong, mistaken <*Ud. está e.* you are mistaken>.

e·quí·vo·ca·men·te adv. equivocally, ambiguously.

e·qui·vo·car §70 tr. to mistake —intr. to equivocate, lie —reflex. to be mistaken *or* wrong.

e·quí·vo·co, –ca adj. *(ambiguo)* equivocal, ambiguous; FIG. *(sospechoso)* suspicious, strange II. m. *(ambigüedad)* ambiguity, ambiguous *or* equivocal expression; *(malentendido)* misunderstanding.

e·ra¹ f. *(época)* era, age; FIG. *(período)* period, time ♦ **e. atómica** atomic age • **e. común** *or* **cristiana** *or* **de Cristo** Christian era • **e. espacial** *or* **de exploración espacial** space age • **e. glacial** ice age.

e·ra² f. AGR. threshing floor; CONSTR., MIN. working yard; HORT. bed, patch; BOL. vessel where chicha is fermented.

e·ra³ see **ser²**.

e·ra·rio m. *(fondos)* treasury, public funds; *(lugar)* treasury.

er·bio m. CHEM. erbium.

e·re f. r (name of the letter "r").

e·rec·ción f. *(construcción)* erection, raising; *(fundación)* founding, establishment; PHYSIOL. erection.

e·réc·til adj. erectile.

e·rec·to, –ta adj. erect.

e·rec·tor, –to·ra I. adj. erecting II. m.f. erector, builder.

e·re·mi·ta m. hermit, eremite.

e·re·mí·ti·co, –ca adj. hermitical, eremitic.

e·res see **ser²**.

er·gio *or* **erg** m. PHYS. erg, ergon.

er·go conj. ergo, therefore.

er·go·tis·mo m. PHILOS. sophistry; MED. ergotism.

er·go·tis·ta PHILOS. I. adj. sophistic II. m.f. sophist.

er·gui·mien·to m. erection, raising up.

er·guir §31 tr. to raise, lift up —reflex. *(enderezarse)* to straighten up; FIG. *(envanecerse)* to become vain *or* conceited.

e·rial AGR. I. adj. untilled, uncultivated II. m. untilled *or* uncultivated land.

e·ri·cé, erice see **erizar.**

e·ri·gir §32 tr. *(construir)* to erect, build; *(fundar)* to found, establish —reflex. to set oneself up, establish oneself.

e·ri·na f. MED. forceps.

e·rís·ti·co, –ca adj. PHILOS. eristic, eristical.

e·ri·za·do, –da I. past part. see **erizar** II. adj. *(espinoso)* bristly, spiky; *(tieso)* rigid, stiff; FIG. *(difícil)* thorny, difficult.

e·ri·za·mien·to m. bristling, standing *or* setting on end (hair).

e·ri·zar §04 tr. *(levantar)* to make stand on end, set on end; *(un animal)* to bristle —reflex. *(levantarse)* to stand on end (hair); *(un animal)* to bristle.

e·ri·zo m. ZOOL. hedgehog; BOT. *(planta)* tibourbou; *(de la castaña)* burr; ICHTH. globefish; FIG., COLL. *(persona ruda)* surly *or* bad-tempered person ♦ **e. de mar** sea urchin.

er·mi·ta f. hermitage.

er·mi·ta·ño, –ña m.f. hermit —m. ZOOL. hermit crab.

e·ro·ga·ción f. *(distribución)* distribution; AMER. donation, contribution.

e·ro·gan·te AMER. I. adj. donating, contributing II. m.f. donor, contributor.

e·ro·gar §47 tr. to distribute (wealth); AMER. to donate, contribute.

e·ró·ge·no, –na adj. erogenous.

e·ro·sión f. *(desgaste)* erosion; MED. graze.

e·ro·si·vo, –va adj. erosive.

e·ró·ti·co, –ca I. adj. erotic, amorous II. f. POET. erotic poetry.

e·ro·tis·mo m. eroticism, erotism.

e·rra·bun·do, –da adj. wandering, roving.

e·rra·da·men·te adv. erroneously, mistakenly.

e·rra·di·ca·ción f. FIG. *(eliminación)* eradication; *(descuaje)* uprooting.

e·rra·di·car §70 tr. *(descuajar)* to uproot, tear up by the roots; FIG. *(eliminar)* to eradicate, root out.

e·rra·di·zo, –za adj. errant, wandering.

e·rra·do, –da I. past part. see **errar** II. adj. wrong, mistaken.

e·rran·te adj. errant, wandering.

e·rrar §33 tr. *(no acertar)* to miss <e. el blanco to miss the target>; *(faltar)* to fail (someone) —intr. *(vagar)* to wander, roam; *(equivocarse)* to be mistaken, make a mistake —reflex. to be mistaken, make a mistake.

e·rra·ta f. erratum.

e·rrá·ti·co, –ca adj. GEOL., MED. erratic; *(errante)* wandering, roving.

e·rrá·til adj. erratic, inconsistent.

e·rre f. name of the Spanish double "r" ♦ **e. que e.** COLL. persistently, stubbornly.

e·rró·ne·a·men·te adv. erroneously, mistakenly.

e·rró·ne·o, –a adj. erroneous, mistaken.

e·rror m. *(equivocación)* error, mistake; *(idea falsa)* misconception, fallacy ♦ **e. de copia** *or* **de pluma** clerical error • **e. de imprenta** misprint • **e. de máquina** *or* **de tecla** typing mistake *or* error • **e. judicial** LAW miscarriage of justice • **estar en un e.** to be mistaken • **por e.** by mistake.

e·ru·bes·cen·cia f. *(rubor)* blush; MED. erubescence.

e·ru·bes·cen·te adj. *(ruborizante)* blushing; MED. erubescent.

e·ruc·tar intr. to burp, belch.

e·ruc·to m. burp, belch.

e·ru·di·ción f. *(instrucción)* erudition, learning; *(conocimientos)* knowledge.

e·ru·di·ta·men·te adv. eruditely, learnedly.

e·ru·di·to, –ta I. adj. erudite, learned II. m.f. scholar, erudite ♦ **e. a la violeta** dilettante, pseudo-intellectual.

e·ru·gi·no·so, –sa adj. rusty, rusted.

e·rup·ción f. GEOL. eruption; MED. eruption, rash; FIG. *(brote)* eruption, outbreak ♦ **e. solar** solar flare.

e·rup·ti·vo, –va adj. eruptive.

es see **ser²**.

e·sa adj. see **ese, esa**.

é·sa pron. see **ése, ésa**.

es·ba·ti·men·to m. PAINT. shadow, shade.

es·bel·tez f. slenderness, svelteness.

es·bel·to, –ta adj. slender, svelte.

es·bi·rro m. *(alguacil)* sheriff, constable; FIG. *(ayudante)* henchman.

es·bo·zar §04 tr. to sketch, outline.

es·bo·zo m. sketch, outline.

es·ca·be·char tr. CUL. to pickle, marinate; FIG. *(teñir)* to dye (gray hair); FIG., COLL. *(matar)* to kill, bump off; *(suspender)* to fail, flunk <el profesor me escabechó en el examen final the professor flunked me on the final exam>.

es·ca·be·che m. *(adobo)* marinade; *(pescado)* marinated fish salad; FIG. *(tinte)* dye (for gray hair).

es·ca·bel m. *(asiento)* stool, small seat; *(para los pies)* footstool; FIG. *(trampolín)* steppingstone (to one's ambitions).

es·ca·bro m. VET. mange, scab (of sheep); BOT. scaly bark.

es·ca·bro·sa·men·te adv. FIG. *(ásperamente)* harshly, cruelly; *(atrevidamente)* scabrously, dirtily.

es·ca·bro·si·dad f. *(desigualdad)* roughness, ruggedness; FIG. *(aspereza)* harshness, asperity; *(salacidad)* scabrousness, dirtiness.

es·ca·bro·so, –sa adj. *(desigual)* rough, rugged; FIG. *(áspero)* harsh, cruel; *(atrevido)* dirty, smutty.

es·ca·bu·llir·se §13 reflex. to escape, slip away.

es·ca·fan·dra f. *or* **es·ca·fan·dro** m. diver's *or* diving suit ♦ **e. autónoma** scuba • **e. espacial** space suit.

es·ca·la f. scale <la e. barométrica the barometric scale>; *(proporción)* scale; *(escalera de mano)* ladder, stepladder; *(gama)* range <la e. de colores the range of colors>; MA-RIT. port of call; MIL. register, list <e. de reservas list of reserves>; MUS. scale ♦ **a grande e.** large-scale • **a pequeña e.** small-scale • **en grande e.** on a large scale • **en pequeña e.** on a small scale • **e. cromática** MUS. chromatic scale • **e. de popa** *or* **portalón** MARIT. accommodation ladder • **e. de viento** *or* **cuerda** MARIT. rope ladder • **e. diatónica** MUS. diatonic scale • **e. móvil** sliding scale • **hacer e.** MARIT. to put in, call.

es·ca·la·da f. *(acción de escalar)* scaling, climbing; MIL. escalation; *(intensificación)* escalation.

es·ca·la·dor, –do·ra I. adj. scaling, climbing II. m.f. *(persona que escala)* scaler, climber; *(ladrón)* housebreaker, burglar.

es·ca·la·fón m. *(registro)* list, roll (of employees); FIG. *(cuadro)* table, list.

es·ca·la·mien·to m. scaling, climbing.

es·ca·lar tr. *(trepar)* to scale, climb; MIL. to escalade <e. una plaza fuerte to escalade a fort>; *(robar)* to break in *or* into, burgle <e. un apartamento to burgle an apartment> —intr. FIG. to rise, climb (by dubious means); MIL., POL. *(aumentar)* to escalate.

es·cal·da·do, –da I. past part. of **escaldar** II. adj. FIG., COLL. *(receloso)* wary, cautious; *(deshonesta)* loose (woman).

es·cal·da·du·ra f. *(quemadura)* scald; *(acción)* scalding.

es·cal·dar tr. *(con un líquido)* to scald, burn (with hot liquid); *(abrasar)* to make red hot —reflex. chafe, to become chafed.

es·ca·le·ra f. *(peldaño)* stairs, staircase; *(escalerilla)* ladder; *(en los juegos de naipes)* straight (in cards) ♦ **de e. abajo** menial, downstairs (servants) • **e. abajo** downstairs, down the stairs • **e. de caracol** *or* **husillo** winding staircase • **e. de color** *or* **real** royal flush • **e. de incendios** fire escape • **e. de mano** *or* **de tijera** stepladder • **e. de servicio** service stairs • **e. mecánica** *or* **automática** escalator.

es·ca·le·ri·lla f. *(escalera de tijera)* stepladder; *(en los juegos de naipes)* series of three cards (in some card games); VET. speculum (instrument for keeping a horse's mouth open); MARIT. gangway.

es·cal·fa·do, –da I. past part. of **escalfar** II. adj. *(mal encalado)* blistered (wall); CUL. poached (egg).

es·cal·fa·dor m. *(jarro)* barber's pitcher; *(braserillo)* chafing dish; *(para huevos)* egg poacher.

es·cal·far tr. CUL. *(en agua)* to poach; *(quemar)* to burn (bread).

es·ca·li·na·ta f. flight of steps.

es·ca·lo·frí·o m. *(de miedo)* shiver, shudder; *(de fiebre)* chill, shiver ♦ **tener escalofríos** to shiver.

es·ca·lón m. *(peldaño)* step, stair; FIG. *(fase)* step, rung (in a career) ♦ **en escalones** unevenly.

es·ca·lo·na f. BOT. shallot.

es·ca·lo·nar tr. *(colocar)* to place *or* spread out at regular intervals; to stagger <e. la producción to stagger production>; AGR. to terrace (land); MIL. to echelon (troops).

es·ca·lo·pe m. CUL. cutlet, scaloppini.

es·cal·par tr. to scalp.

es·cal·po *or* **es·cal·po** m. scalp.

es·cal·pe·lo m. SURG. scalpel.

es·ca·ma f. ICHTH. scale; FIG. *(resentimiento)* resentment, indignation; *(recelo)* suspicion, mistrust.

es·ca·ma·do, –da I. past part. see **escamar** II. adj. COLL. suspicious, wary.

es·ca·ma·du·ra f. scaling (of a fish).

es·ca·mar tr. *(quitar las escamas)* to scale (fish); FIG., COLL. *(desconfiar)* to make suspicious *or* wary —reflex. FIG., COLL. to become suspicious *or* wary.

es·ca·mon·da f. pruning (of trees).

es·ca·mon·dar tr. *(podar)* to prune (trees); FIG. *(sacar lo inútil)* to prune, trim; *(limpiar)* to clean; *(lavar)* to wash.

es·ca·mo·ne·ar·se reflex. COLL. to become suspicious.

es·ca·mo·so, –sa adj. *(con escamas)* scaly, flaky, scaly <piel e. flaky skin>; FIG. *(receloso)* suspicious, wary.

es·ca·mo·te·a·dor, –do·ra I. adj. conjuring II. m.f. *(prestidigitador)* conjurer, magician; COLL. *(ladrón)* filcher, thief.

es·ca·mo·te·ar tr. *(hacer desaparecer)* to make disappear *or* vanish (by sleight of hand); FIG., COLL. *(robar)* to filch, steal; *(evitar)* to avoid, evade.

es·ca·mo·te·o m. *(magia)* sleight of hand; COLL. *(robo)* filching, thievery.

es·cam·pa·da f. clear spell (during a storm).

es·cam·pa·do, -da I. past part. of **escampar** II. adj. clear, open.

es·cam·par tr. to clear, open (a space) —intr. *(dejar de llover)* to stop raining, clear (up); FIG. *(aflojar)* to give up, stop making an effort; C. AMER., COL. to take shelter (from the rain).

es·ca·mu·do, -da adj. scaly.

es·can·ciar tr. to serve, pour (wine) —intr. to drink wine.

es·can·da f. BOT. spelt (wheat).

es·can·da·li·zar §04 tr. to scandalize, shock —intr. to make a fuss —reflex. to become scandalized or shocked.

es·cán·da·lo m. *(ofensa)* scandal; *(alboroto)* uproar, ruckus ♦ **armar un e.** to make a scene, cause an uproar.

es·can·da·lo·sa f. MARIT. topsail, gaff ♦ **echar la e. a uno** FIG., COLL. to give someone a piece of one's mind.

es·can·da·lo·sa·men·te adv. scandalously, shockingly.

es·can·da·lo·so, -sa adj. *(ofensivo)* scandalous, shocking; *(alborotoso)* rowdy, noisy; uproarious, hearty <*risa e.* uproarious laughter>.

es·can·da·llar tr. MARIT. to sound; COM. to price, calculate the price of.

es·can·da·llo m. MARIT. sounding lead; COM. pricing; FIG. *(ensayo)* sampling, trial.

Es·can·di·na·via f. Scandinavia.

es·can·dio m. CHEM. scandium.

es·can·sión f. POET. scansion.

es·ca·ña f. BOT. spelt (wheat).

es·ca·ño m. *(banco)* bench (with a back); POL. seat (in congress); AMER. park bench.

es·ca·ñue·lo m. footstool.

es·ca·pa·da f. *(huida)* escape, flight; *(aventura)* escapade; *(viaje corto)* quick trip ♦ **darse una e.** COLL. to slip out or away.

es·ca·par intr. *(evitar)* to escape, get away <*e. de un peligro* to escape from danger>; *(huir)* to flee, escape —reflex. *(fugarse)* to escape, get away <*se ha escapado un fugitivo de la cárcel* a fugitive has escaped from prison>; *(líquido, gas)* to escape, leak; *(pasar por alto)* to miss, overlook <*se me escapó ese detalle* I missed that detail> ♦ **escaparse la lengua** FIG., COLL. to make a slip of the tongue • **escaparse por un pelo** FIG., COLL. to have a close call —tr. EQUIT. *(hacer galopar)* to make gallop (a horse); *(librar)* to save, free.

es·ca·pa·ra·te m. *(ventana)* shop or display window; AMER. *(ropero)* wardrobe, closet.

es·ca·pa·to·ria f. *(escape)* escape, flight; COLL. *(pretexto)* excuse, pretext.

es·ca·pe m. *(fuga)* escape, flight; *(de un reloj)* escapement; AUTO. exhaust (pipe) ♦ **a e.** at full or breakneck speed.

es·ca·pu·la·rio m. RELIG. scapular, scapulary.

es·ca·que m. square (on a chessboard) ♦ **escaques** chess.

es·ca·que·a·do, -da adj. checkered.

es·ca·ra f. MED. eschar, scab.

es·ca·ra·ba·je·ar intr. *(moverse)* to mill or move about; FIG. *(garabatear)* to scribble, scrawl —tr. FIG., COLL. *(molestar)* to worry, bother.

es·ca·ra·ba·je·o m. FIG., COLL. worry, bother.

es·ca·ra·ba·jo m. ENTOM. scarab, black beetle; *(defecto)* flaw (in material); FIG., COLL. *(persona)* runt ♦ **escarabajos** COLL. scribbles, scrawls.

es·ca·ra·mu·cé, escaramuce see **escaramuzar**.

es·ca·ra·mu·ce·ar intr. var. of **escaramuzar**.

es·ca·ra·mu·jo m. BOT. wild rose; ZOOL. goose barnacle; CUBA evil eye.

es·ca·ra·mu·za f. *(combate)* skirmish; *(argumento)* quarrel, dispute.

es·ca·ra·mu·zar §04 intr. to skirmish, engage in a skirmish.

es·ca·ra·pe·la f. *(divisa)* emblem, insignia; *(riña)* dispute, free-for-all.

es·ca·ra·pe·lar intr. to quarrel, fight —tr. COL. to rumple, muss; C. AMER. to peel, flake —reflex. MEX., PERU to get goose flesh or goose pimples.

es·car·ba·dien·tes m. [pl. **-tes**] toothpick.

es·car·ba·dor, -do·ra I. adj. scratching, scraping II. m. scraper.

es·car·bar tr. *(rascar)* to scrape, scratch; to pick <*e. los dientes* to pick one's teeth>; to rake, poke <*e. el fuego* to rake the fire>; FIG. *(averiguar)* to poke around, investigate.

es·car·cé, escarce see **escarzar**.

es·car·ce·la f. *(bolsa)* belt pouch; HUNT. game bag; *(cofia)* hairnet; ARM. cuisse (piece of armor).

es·car·ce·os m.pl. *(rodeos)* wanderings, ramblings; *(cabrilleo)* small waves; EQUIT. caracoles ♦ **e. amorosos** flirtation.

es·car·ci·na f. cutlass.

es·car·cha f. frost.

es·car·cha·do, -da I. past part. see **escarchar** II. adj. *(cubierto de escarcha)* frosted, frosty; *(fruta)* candied III. m. silver or gold embroidery.

es·car·char intr. to become frosted or covered with frost —tr. *(azucarar)* to candy; to frost, ice <*e. los pasteles* to frost the pastries>.

es·car·che m. frostwork.

es·car·chi·lla f. AMER. small ice particles.

es·car·da f. AGR. *(instrumento)* weeding hoe; *(acción)* weeding.

es·car·dar tr. AGR. to weed (out); FIG. *(separar lo malo)* to weed out.

es·car·di·llo m. AGR. weeding hoe; *(luz)* reflection.

es·ca·riar tr. MECH. to ream.

es·ca·ri·fi·ca·ción f. SURG. scarification.

es·ca·ri·fi·ca·dor m. AGR. harrow; SURG. scarificator.

es·ca·ri·fi·car §70 tr. AGR., SURG. to scarify.

es·car·la·ta I. f. *(color)* scarlet; *(tela)* scarlet cloth; MED. scarlet fever II. adj. scarlet (color).

es·car·la·ti·na f. MED. scarlet fever.

es·car·me·nar tr. *(peinar)* to comb; FIG. *(castigar)* to punish, castigate; *(estafar)* to swindle little by little.

es·car·men·ta·do, -da I. past part. see **escarmentar** II. adj. taught by experience III. m.f. person who has learned from experience.

es·car·men·tar §49 tr. to chastise, teach a lesson to —intr. to learn one's lesson ♦ **e. en cabeza ajena** to learn from another's mistakes.

es·car·mien·to m. *(aviso)* warning, lesson; *(castigo)* punishment.

es·car·ne·ce·dor, -do·ra I. adj. ridiculing, mocking II. m.f. ridiculer, mocker.

es·car·ne·cer §17 tr. to ridicule, mock.

es·car·nio m. ridicule, mocking.

es·ca·ro, -ra I. adj. having crooked feet II. m.f. person with crooked feet.

es·ca·ro·la f. BOT. endive; *(collar)* ruff, ruffled collar.

es·ca·ro·la·do, -da I. past part. see **escarolar** II. adj. curled, ruffled.

es·ca·ro·lar tr. to curl, ruffle.

es·car·pa f. *(declive)* slope, scarp; MIL. escarpment.

es·car·pa·do, -da I. past part. of **escarpar** II. adj. *(pendiente)* steep, sheer; *(escabroso)* craggy, rugged.

es·car·pa·du·ra f. scarp, escarpment.

es·car·par tr. CARP., SCULP. to rasp, scrape; *(inclinar)* to scarp, slope (land).

es·car·pe m. scarp, escarpment.

es·car·pe·lo m. CARP., SCULP. rasp; MED. scalpel.

es·car·pia f. hook.

es·car·pi·dor m. large-toothed comb.

es·car·pín m. *(zapato)* pump; *(calcetín)* outer sock, woolen slipper.

es·car·zar §04 tr. to remove honeycombs from a beehive.

es·car·zo m. *(panal)* honeycomb without honey; *(acción de escarzar)* removal of honeycombs from a beehive.

es·ca·sa·men·te adv. *(con escasez)* scarcely, just <*me tomé e. una semana de vacaciones* I took scarcely one week of vacation>; *(con dificultad)* with difficulty.

es·ca·se·ar tr. to skimp, give sparingly; CARP. to bevel —intr. to become or be scarce.

es·ca·sez f. [pl. **-se·ces**] *(poquedad)* scarcity, lack; *(mezquindad)* miserliness, stinginess; *(pobreza)* poverty, need <*vivir con e.* to live in poverty>. .

es·ca·so, -sa adj. *(poco abundante)* scarce, limited; *(mezquino)* miserly, stingy; *(falto)* scanty, insufficient; *(muy económico)* skimpy, sparing.

es·ca·ti·mar tr. to skimp on, be sparing with <*e. la comida* to skimp on food>; to spare <*no e. esfuerzos* to spare no effort>.

es·ca·ti·mo·so, –sa adj. stingy, mean.

es·ca·to·lo·gí·a f. PHILOS. eschatology; (*de excrementos*) scatology.

es·ca·to·ló·gi·co, –ca adj. PHILOS. eschatological; (*excrementicio*) scatological.

es·ca·va·nar tr. AGR. to loosen (soil).

es·ca·yo·la f. (*yeso*) plaster of Paris; (*estuco*) stucco; MED. plaster cast.

es·ce·na f. THEAT. (*escenario*) stage; (*decoración*) scenery, scene <*en las operas de Wagner, la e. es muy importante* in Wagner's operas, the scenery is very important>; (*arte dramática*) theater, dramatic art; (*subdivisión del acto*) scene; (*literatura*) drama, theater; FIG. (*episodio*) scene, episode; (*lugar*) scene <*la e. del crimen* the scene of the crime> ♦ **e. retrospectiva** CINEM. flashback ♦ **hacer una e.** COLL. to make a scene • **poner en e.** THEAT. to stage, present (a play).

es·ce·na·rio m. THEAT., CINEM. stage, scenery; FIG. (*ambiente*) setting, scene.

es·cé·ni·co, –ca adj. scenic.

es·ce·ni·fi·ca·ción f. CINEM., THEAT. staging, dramatization.

es·ce·ni·fi·car §70 tr. CINEM., THEAT. to stage, dramatize.

es·ce·no·gra·fí·a f. CINEM., THEAT. scenography.

es·ce·nó·gra·fo, –fa m. CINEM., THEAT. set designer, scenographer.

es·cep·ti·cis·mo m. PHILOS. skepticism.

es·cép·ti·co, –ca I. adj. skeptical II. m.f. skeptic.

es·cin·dir tr. to divide, split —reflex. to split.

es·ci·rro m MED. scirrhus, tumor.

es·ci·sión f. (*división*) division, split; MED. excision; PHYS. fission.

es·cla·re·cer §17 tr. (*iluminar*) to illuminate, light up; FIG. (*elucidar*) to clarify, elucidate; (*ennoblecer*) to ennoble, make illustrious —intr. to get light, dawn.

es·cla·re·ci·da·men·te adv. nobly, illustriously.

es·cla·re·ci·do, –da I. past part. of **esclarecer** II. adj. illustrious, eminent.

es·cla·re·ci·mien·to m. (*iluminación*) illumination; (*explicación*) clarification, elucidation; (*ennoblecimiento*) ennoblement.

es·cla·rez·ca, esclarezco see **esclarecer.**

es·cla·vis·ta adj. pro-slavery.

es·cla·vi·tud f. (*servidumbre*) slavery, servitude; FIG. (*dominación*) slavery, domination.

es·cla·vi·zar §04 tr. (*reducir a esclavitud*) to enslave, FIG. (*dominar*) to dominate, subjugate.

es·cla·vo, –va I. adj. (*siervo*) enslaved; FIG. (*dominado*) dominated, subjugated; addicted <*es e. de las drogas* he is addicted to drugs> II. m.f. (*siervo*) slave; FIG. slave <*ser e. de sus pasiones* he is a slave to his passions> —f. (*pulsera*) bracelet, bangle.

es·cle·ro·sar tr. MED. to cause sclerosis.

es·cle·ro·sis f. [pl. **-sis**] MED. sclerosis ♦ **e. multiple** *or* **en placas** multiple sclerosis.

es·clu·sa f. (*recinto*) lock, sluice; (*compuerta*) floodgate.

es·co·ba f. broom ♦ **pasar la e.** to sweep (up).

es·co·ba·da f. sweep, stroke (with a broom).

es·co·ba·jo m. (*escoba*) old broom; (*vástago*) stalk (of a bunch of grapes).

es·co·bar tr. (*barrer*) to sweep; AGR. to separate grain (from chaff).

es·co·ba·zo m. (*golpe*) blow with a broom; (*barrido*) sweep, sweeping ♦ **echar a uno a escobazos** to kick someone out.

es·co·be·ro, –ra m.f. broom maker *or* seller.

es·co·bi·lla f. (*cepillo*) brush; (*escoba pequeña*) small broom; TECH. brush; BOT. (*cardencha*) teasel; (*brezo*) heather.

es·co·bi·llar tr. AMER. (*cepillar*) to brush; (*bailar*) to dance with quick steps.

es·co·bi·na f. (*serrín*) sawdust; (*de metal*) filings.

es·co·bón m. (*escoba*) large broom; (*deshollinador*) chimney sweep's brush; (*de mango corto*) short-handled broom.

es·co·ce·du·ra f. irritation, burning sensation.

es·co·cer §71 intr. (*picar*) to sting, smart; FIG. (*sentir desazón*) to hurt (one's feelings) —reflex. (*sahornarse*) become chafed *or* irritated; FIG. (*sentirse*) to be hurt.

es·co·cés, –ce·sa I. adj. Scottish, Scots, Scotch II. m.f. (*habitante*) Scot, Scots —m. (*habitante*) Scotsman, Scotchman; (*idioma*) Scottish, Scots —f. Scotswoman, Scotchwoman ♦ **los escoceses** the Scottish, the Scots, the Scotch.

Es·co·cia f. Scotland.

es·co·ci·mien·to m. stinging, smarting.

es·co·da f. stonecutter's hammer.

es·co·dar tr. (*labrar*) to cut, hew (stone); ZOOL. to rub (antlers).

es·co·fi·na f. coarse file, rasp.

es·co·ge·dor, –do·ra I. adj. choosing, selecting II. m.f. chooser, selector.

es·co·ger §34 tr. to choose, select.

es·co·gi·do, –da I. past part. see **escoger** II. adj. (*superior*) select, choice; (*elegido*) chosen, selected <*obras escogidas de Galdós* selected works of Galdós>.

es·co·gi·mien·to m. choosing, selection.

es·co·lar I. adj. scholastic, school II. m.f. pupil, student.

es·co·la·ri·dad f. education, schooling.

es·co·las·ti·cis·mo m. *or* **es·co·lás·ti·ca** f. (*enseñanza*) scholasticism; PHILOS., RELIG. Scholasticism.

es·co·lás·ti·co, –ca I. adj. scholastic, academic; PHILOS., RELIG. Scholastic II. m.f. Scholastic.

es·co·liar tr. LIT. to annotate.

es·co·lias·ta m.f. LIT. annotator.

es·co·li·ma·do, –da adj. COLL. weak, delicate.

es·co·li·mo·so, –sa adj. COLL. fussy, disagreeable.

es·col·ta f. escort. ♦ **dar e. a.** to escort, accompany.

es·col·tar tr. to escort.

es·co·llar intr. MARIT. to run aground, hit a reef; ARG., CHILE, FIG. to fail, run aground.

es·co·lle·ra f. MARIT. jetty, breakwater.

es·co·llo m. MARIT. reef, rock; FIG. (*peligro*) danger, pitfall; (*dificultad*) difficulty, stumbling block.

es·com·bra f. clearing, removal (of rubble).

es·com·brar tr. (*limpiar*) to sweep, clear; FIG. (*desembarazar*) to clear.

es·com·bre·ra f. dump, tip.

es·com·bro m. (*desecho*) rubble, debris; MIN. slag; (*pasa menuda*) bad raisin.

es·co·mer·se reflex. to erode, wear away.

es·con·ce m. corner, angle.

es·con·der¹ m. hide-and-seek.

es·con·der² tr. (*encubrir*) to hide, conceal; FIG. (*ocultar*) to hide <*e. sus verdaderas intenciones* to hide one's true intentions> —reflex. to hide *or* conceal oneself.

es·con·di·da·men·te adv. secretly, covertly.

es·con·di·das f.pl. AMER. hide-and-seek ♦ **a e.** secretly, covertly.

es·con·di·jo m. var. of **escondrijo.**

es·con·di·mien·to m. concealment.

es·con·di·te m. (*escondrijo*) hiding place; (*juego*) hide-and-seek.

es·con·dri·jo m. hiding place.

es·con·za·do, –da adj. angular, cornered.

es·co·ñar tr. COLL. to spoil, ruin; (*romper*) to break —reflex. to be spoiled *or* ruined; (*romperse*) to be broken; (*hacerse daño*) to hurt oneself.

es·co·pe·ta f. shotgun, rifle ♦ **como una e.** FIG. like a shot, quickly • **e. de aire** *or* **de viento** air rifle *or* gun • **e. de caza** hunting rifle • **e. de dos cañones** double-barreled rifle *or* shotgun • **e. negra** professional hunter.

es·co·pe·ta·zo m. (*tiro*) rifle shot, gunshot; (*herida*) gunshot wound; FIG. (*noticia*) bad news, blow.

es·co·pe·te·ar tr. to shoot at (with a shotgun) —reflex. FIG., COLL. to shower, barrage <*escopetearse con insultos* to shower (each other) with insults>.

es·co·pe·te·rí·a f. (*tropa*) riflemen, troops armed with rifles; (*multitud de escopetazos*) volley of gunshots.

es·co·pe·te·ro m. MIL. rifleman, soldier armed with a rifle; (*escopeta negra*) professional hunter; (*fabricante*) gunsmith, gun maker; ENTOM. bombardier beetle.

es·co·plo m. CARP. chisel ♦ **e. de cantería** TECH. stonecutter's chisel.

es·co·rar tr. MARIT. *(hacer que inclina)* to list, heel; CONSTR. *(apuntalar)* to shore or prop up —intr. MARIT. *(inclinarse)* to list, heel; *(llegar la marea al nivel bajo)* to reach low tide, ebb —reflex. MARIT. *(inclinarse)* to list, heel; *(llegar la marea al nivel bajo)* to reach low tide, ebb; CUBA, HOND. to hide oneself from view, take cover; ECUAD. *(desquitarse)* to get even; *(echar culpa)* to accuse wrongly.

es·cor·bu·to m. MED. scurvy.

es·cor·char tr. *(desollar)* to skin, flay; ARG., COLL. to annoy.

es·co·ria f. METAL. scoria, slag; GEOL. scoria, lava; FIG. *(desecho)* scum, dregs ♦ **e. de cemento** cement clinker or brick • **e. de fundición** METAL. slag.

es·co·rial m. METAL. *(vertedero)* slag dump; *(montón)* pile of slag; BOL., GEOL. gorge.

es·co·ri·fi·ca·ción f. slagging, scorification.

es·co·ri·fi·car §70 tr. to slag, scorify.

Es·cor·pio m. ASTROL., ASTRON. Scorpio.

es·cor·pión m. ENTOM. scorpion; ICHTH. scorpion fish; ARM. catapult, ancient ballister; *(azote)* scorpion, scourge ♦ **Escorpión** ASTROL., ASTRON. Scorpio.

es·cor·zo m. PAINT. *(efecto)* foreshortening; *(figura)* foreshortened figure.

es·co·tar tr. *(cortar para ajustar)* to cut or trim (to fit); *(sacar agua)* to drain or draw water from; *(partir un gasto)* to contribute, pay (one's share of an expense).

es·co·te m. SEW. *(corte del cuello)* neck, neckline; *(encaje del cuello)* lace collar or frill; *(cuota)* share, contribution ♦ **ir** or **pagar a e.** *(compartir gastos una pareja)* to go Dutch; *(compartir gastos más de dos personas)* to go in on an expense, contribute one's share (of an expense).

es·co·ti·lla f. AVIA., MARIT. hatch, hatchway.

es·co·ti·llón m. *(trampa)* trap door; MARIT. scuttle.

es·co·zor m. *(escocimiento)* smarting; FIG. *(pena)* grief, heartache.

es·cri·ba m. RELIG. scribe; COLL. *(escribano)* clerk, secretary.

es·cri·ba·na f. *(mujer que ejerce la escribanía)* female notary public; *(mujer de escribano)* wife of a notary public.

es·cri·ba·ní·a f. *(oficio de notario)* notary public's position and duties; *(oficina de notario)* notary public's office; *(oficio de secretario)* secretary's duties and position, clerkship; *(oficina de secretario)* secretary's or clerk's office; *(escritorio)* writing desk; *(recado de escribir)* writing materials; *(caja portátil)* portable writing case.

es·cri·ba·no m. *(notario público)* notary public; *(secretario)* clerk, secretary; *(pendolista)* penman, calligrapher; RARE *(maestro)* schoolteacher, schoolmaster; CUBA, ORNITH. type of wading bird ♦ **e. de agua** ENTOM. whirligig beetle • **e. de cámara** LAW clerk of a high court of justice • **e. de número** licensed notary public.

es·cri·bi·dor, –do·ra m.f. scribbler, third-rate writer.

es·cri·bien·te m.f. amanuensis, clerk (who copies or takes dictation).

es·cri·bir §85 tr. to write <*le escribió una carta a su hermana* he wrote a letter to his sister>; *(ortografiar)* to spell ♦ **e. a mano** to write by hand, write in longhand • **e. a máquina** to type —intr. to write <*le escribí desde Londres* I wrote to him from London> —reflex. *(corresponderse)* to write to each other, correspond; *(ortografiarse)* to be spelled <*¿cómo se escribe su nombre?* how is his name spelled?>; *(inscribirse)* to enroll, enlist.

es·cri·ño m. *(cesta)* straw basket; *(cofrecito)* coffer.

es·cri·to, –ta I. past part. see **escribir** II. adj. written <*un examen e.* a written test>; FIG. *(señalado)* written <*tiene la culpa e. en la cara* his guilt is written all over his face>; *(dicho)* said, stated ♦ **e. a mano** handwritten • **e. a máquina** typed, typewritten III. m. *(documento)* document, writing; *(manuscrito)* manuscript; *(obra)* literary text; *(solicitación)* petition, plea; *(examen)* written examination; LAW *(decreto judicial)* writ; *(alegato)* brief ♦ **por e.** in writing.

es·cri·tor, –to·ra m.f. writer.

es·cri·to·rio m. *(escribanía)* desk; *(despacho)* office, study; *(mueble)* jewelry cabinet.

es·cri·tor·zue·lo, –la m.f. third-rate or hack writer.

es·cri·tu·ra f. writing <*la e. del guión le tomó mucho tiempo* the writing of the script took him a lot of time>; *(caligrafía)* handwriting, penmanship; *(obra literaria)* literary work; *(sistema de signos)* script <*e. fonética* phonetic script>; LAW *(documento)* document, instrument; *(contrato)* contract, indenture <*e. de emisión de bonos* bond indenture>; deed <*e. de propiedad* title deed>; *(póliza)* policy <*e. de seguro* insurance policy>; COM. bill <*e. de venta* bill of sale> ♦ **e. aérea** skywriting • **e. corrida** longhand • **Sagradas Escrituras** RELIG. Holy Scriptures.

es·cri·tu·ra·ción f. P. RICO, S. AMER., LAW notarizing, notarization; THEAT. booking, signing (for an engagement).

es·cri·tu·rar tr. LAW to notarize, execute by deed; THEAT. to book, sign (for an engagement).

es·cro·to m. ANAT. scrotum.

es·cru·pu·li·zar §04 intr. to have scruples, hesitate.

es·crú·pu·lo m. *(duda)* scruple, hesitation; *(escrupulosidad)* scrupulousness, extreme care; *(china)* stone or pebble (lodged in one's shoe); ASTRON. minute; PHARM. scruple (weight) ♦ **con e.** scrupulously • **e. de monja** COLL. childish scruple • **no tener escrúpulos** to have no scruples, be unscrupulous • **sin escrúpulos** unscrupulous.

es·cru·pu·lo·sa·men·te adv. scrupulously.

es·cru·pu·lo·si·dad f. scrupulousness, extreme care.

es·cru·pu·lo·so, –sa I. adj. *(que tiene o causa escrúpulos)* scrupulous; FIG. *(exacto)* exact, precise II. m.f. scrupulous person.

es·cru·ta·dor, –do·ra I. adj. *(escudriñador)* scrutinizing, examining; searching <*una mirada e.* a searching look> II. m.f. electoral inspector.

es·cru·tar tr. *(indagar)* to scrutinize, examine; *(comprobar votos)* to count (votes).

es·cru·ti·nio m. *(examinación)* scrutiny, examination; *(recuento)* counting of votes, scrutiny.

es·cru·ti·ña·dor, –do·ra m.f. scrutinizer, examiner.

es·cua·dra f. *(para dibujar)* triangle; CARP. carpenter's square; *(grapa)* angle iron; MIL. *(grupo de soldados)* squad; *(cabo)* corporal; MARIT. squadron, fleet; COL. automatic pistol ♦ **a** or **de e.** at right angles • **e. de agrimensor** cross staff, surveyor's cross • **e. falsa** or **falsa e.** bevel square.

es·cua·drar tr. CARP., CONSTR. to square.

es·cua·dri·lla f. AVIA., MARIT., MIL. squadron.

es·cua·drón m. MIL. *(de caballería)* cavalry squadron; *(unidad aérea)* air squadron.

es·cua·li·dez f. *(suciedad)* squalor, filth; *(delgadez)* skinniness, emaciation.

es·cuá·li·do, –da I. adj. *(sucio)* squalid, filthy; *(delgado)* skinny, emaciated; ICHTH. squaloid II. m. ICHTH. shark, dogfish.

es·cu·cha f. *(acción de escuchar)* listening; RELIG. locutory nun, chaperone; *(criada)* maid assigned to royal sleeping chambers; *(ventana)* king's listening-in window —m. MIL. *(centinela)* night scout ♦ **escuchas** ARCHIT., MIL. small radial galleries running along the glacis • **estar a la e.** or **estar en e.** to be listening.

es·cu·cha·dor, –do·ra adj. listening.

es·cu·char tr. *(prestar atención)* to listen to <*e. un concierto* to listen to a concert>; *(atender)* to mind, heed <*e. sus consejos* to heed their advice> —reflex. to like to hear oneself talk, enjoy hearing oneself talk.

es·cu·chón, –cho·na I. adj. eavesdropping II. m.f. eavesdropper.

es·cu·dar tr. *(amparar con el escudo)* to shield, protect with a shield; FIG. *(proteger)* to protect —reflex. FIG. to shield or protect oneself.

es·cu·de·rí·a f. *(servicio)* position of a page or squire; AUTO. fleet.

es·cu·de·ro, –ra I. adj. pertaining to a page or squire II. m. *(paje)* squire, shield bearer; *(hidalgo)* nobleman; *(criado de señora)* lady's page or attendant; *(fabricante)* shield maker; HUNT. young boar accompanying an older one ♦ **e. de (a) pie** royal messenger or attendant.

es·cu·di·lla f. *(vasija ancha)* wide bowl; CUBA large cup.

es·cu·di·llar tr. CUL. *(servir)* to serve into wide bowls; *(remojar)* to soak (in broth); FIG. *(dominar)* to control, manage.

es·cu·do m. ARM. *(broquel)* shield, buckler; ARTIL. *(plancha)* sideplate, shield; HER. *(insignia)* coat of arms; *(plan-*

chuela de una cerradura) keyhole plate, escutcheon; MARIT. *(respaldo de asiento)* backboard of a boat seat; *(espejo de popa)* stern escutcheon; FIN. escudo; ZOOL. *(espaldilla de jabalí)* back *or* shoulder of a wild boar; *(escama)* scale, scute; FIG. *(egida)* shield, protection.

es·cu·dri·ña·dor, –do·ra I. adj. *(examinante)* scrutinizing, examining; *(curioso)* nosy, inquisitive **II.** m.f. *(examinador)* scrutinizer, examiner; *(curioso)* nosy *or* inquisitive person.

es·cu·dri·ña·mien·to m. scrutiny, examination.

es·cu·dri·ñar tr. to scrutinize, examine.

es·cue·la f. *(edificio)* school; *(doctrina)* school, doctrine *<la e. platónica* the Platonic school>; *(estilo)* school, style *<la e. romántica de pintura* the Romantic school of painting>; FIG. *(experiencia)* school *<la e. de la vida* the school of life> **e. de artes y oficios** trade *or* technical school • **e. de bellas artes** school of fine arts • **e. de párvulos** kindergarten • **e. nocturna** night school • **e. normal o del magisterio** normal school • **e. parroquial** parochial school • **e. primaria** elementary *or* grammar school • **e. privada** *or* **particular** private school • **e. pública** public school • **e. secundaria** high school • **tener buena e.** to be well trained *or* schooled.

es·cuer·zo m. ZOOL. toad; COLL. *(flaco)* skinny person, beanpole.

es·cue·to, –ta adj. *(conciso)* concise, direct; *(sin adorno)* unadorned, simple; *(libre)* free, unencumbered.

es·cue·za, escuezo see **escocer.**

es·cu·la·pio m. FIG., COLL. doctor, physician **Esculapio** MYTH. Aesculapius (Roman god of medicine).

es·cul·car §70 tr. *(escudriñar)* to watch, spy on; AMER. to search —reflex. AMER. to have one's pockets searched.

es·cul·pir tr. *(labrar en piedra)* to sculpt, sculpture; *(labrar en madera)* to carve; *(grabar)* to engrave **e. a cincel** to chisel.

es·cul·tor, –to·ra m.f. sculptor —f. sculptress.

es·cul·tu·ra f. *(arte y obra)* sculpture, carving; *(grabado)* engraving.

es·cul·tu·ral adj. *(escultórico)* sculptural; FIG. *(como estatua)* statuesque.

es·cu·pi·de·ra f. *(vasija para escupir)* spittoon, cuspidor; *(orinal)* chamber pot, urinal.

es·cu·pi·de·ro m. *(lugar)* spitting place; FIG. *(situación despreciable)* vulnerability to scorn *or* humiliation.

es·cu·pi·do, –da I. past part. see **escupir II.** adj. *(parecido)* being the spitting image of *<es su padre e.* he's the spitting image of his father> **III.** m. spit, spittle —f. ARG. spit, spittle.

es·cu·pi·dor, –do·ra I. adj. frequently spitting **II.** m.f. *(persona que escupe mucho)* frequent spitter —m. AMER. *(escupidera)* spittoon, cuspidor.

es·cu·pi·du·ra f. *(esputo)* spit, spittle; MED. fever blister.

es·cu·pir tr. *(arrojar escupo)* to spit; MED. to break out in, come out in (a rash); FIG. *(desdeñar)* to spit at, disdain; *(soltar)* to spit *or* spew (something) out; *(arrojar)* to throw out, cast off; *(revenir)* to exude; COLL. *(pagar)* to cough up, fork over *or* out; *(confesar)* to spill, give (information) **e. a** *or* **e. a alguien en la cara** FIG., COLL. to spit in someone's face, insult • **e. al cielo** FIG., COLL. to spit in the wind, act rashly and without consequence • **e. doblones** FIG., COLL. to boast of one's wealth • **e. sangre** to boast of one's ancestors *or* nobility —intr. to spit.

es·cu·pi·ta·jo m. var. of **escupidura.**

es·cu·rre·pla·tos m. [pl. **-tos**] dish rack (for drying).

es·cu·rri·de·ra f. spoon rack **escurrideras** GUAT., MEX., AGR. excess irrigation water, irrigation run-off.

es·cu·rri·de·ro m. *(lugar)* draining place; *(superficie)* drainboard; *(escurreplatos)* plate *or* dish rack; MIN. drainpipe; PHOTOG. drying rack.

es·cu·rri·di·zo, –za adj. slippery **hacerse uno e.** to slip *or* steal away.

es·cu·rri·dor m. *(colador)* colander; *(escurreplatos)* plate *or* dish rack; PHOTOG. drying rack (for negatives).

es·cu·rrir tr. *(apurar)* to drain; *(hacer que chorrea)* to wring (out) *<e. la ropa* to wring out the clothes> **e. la bola** *or* **el bullo** to take French leave, abscond —intr. *(caer gota a gota)* to drip, trickle; *(deslizar)* to slip, slide; *(ser resbaladizo)* to be slippery —reflex. *(quitarse de humedad)* to

drain; *(caer gota a gota)* to drip, trickle; *(deslizar)* to slip, slide *<escurrirse en el hielo* to slip on the ice>; *(escapar)* to slip out, escape; COLL. *(equivocarse)* to slip up, go too far; *(decir más de lo suficiente)* to say too much, let (something) slip; *(huirse)* to give the slip **escurrirse de** *or* **entre las manos** to slip between one's fingers.

es·cu·sa·do, –da adj. **I.** reserved, private **II.** m. bathroom, toilet.

es·drú·ju·lo, –la GRAM. **I.** adj. proparoxytonic (accented on the antepenultimate syllable) **II.** m.f. proparoxytone.

e·se f. *(letra)* ess; *(eslabón)* S-shaped link; MUS. sound hole (in the violin, viola).

e·se, e·sa §G26 adj. [pl. **e·sos, e·sas**] that *<e. chico* that boy> **esas** *or* **esos** those *<esos edificios* those buildings>.

é·se, é·sa §G41 pron. [pl. **é·sos, é·sas**] that one *<ya tengo muchos libros; no quiero é.* I already have many books; I do not want that one>; *(el primero)* the former; *(allí)* there, your town *<mañana llegaré a é.* tomorrow I will arrive in your town>; MEX., PERU, COLL. dude, guy **choque usted ésa** let's shake on it • **ésas** *or* **ésos** those *<necesito unos lápices; deme ésos, por favor* I need some pencils; give me those, please> • **ni por ésas** by no means, under no circumstances.

e·sen·cia f. *(naturaleza fundamental)* essence, pith; *(ser)* being, entity; *(extracto)* essence *<e. de café* essence of coffee>; *(perfume)* perfume, fragrance; CHEM. *(substancia volátil)* essential oil **en e.** in essence, essentially • **e. mineral** mineral oil *or* spirits • **quinta e.** quintessence.

e·sen·cial adj. essential **no e.** non-essential, inessential • **lo e.** the essential *or* main thing.

e·sen·cial·men·te adv. essentially, in essence.

e·sen·cie·ro m. essence bottle.

es·fa·ce·lo m. MED. gangrenous tissue.

es·fe·ra f. ASTRON., GEOM. sphere; *(del reloj)* dial, face (of a watch); FIG. *(medio)* sphere, circle **e. armilar** ASTRON. armillary sphere • **e. celeste** ASTRON. celestial sphere • **e. de influencia** FIG. sphere of influence • **e. terrestre** *or* **terráquea** ASTRON. earth.

es·fe·ri·ci·dad f. GEOM. sphericity.

es·fé·ri·co, –ca I. adj. GEOM. spherical **II.** m. SPORT. ball.

es·fe·ro·grá·fi·ca f. ARG. ball-point pen.

es·fe·roi·dal adj. GEOM. spheroidal.

es·fe·roi·de m. GEOM. spheroid.

es·fin·ge f. MYTH. sphinx; FIG. *(persona enigmática)* sphinx, enigmatic person; ENTOM. hawk moth **ser** *or* **parecer una e.** to be sphinxlike *or* enigmatic.

es·fín·ter m. ANAT. sphincter.

es·for·za·da·men·te adv. *(con valentía)* bravely, courageously; *(con ánimo)* spiritedly, confidently.

es·for·za·do, –da I. past part. see **esforzar II.** adj. *(valiente)* brave, courageous; *(animoso)* spirited, confident.

es·for·zar §37 tr. *(dar fuerza)* to strengthen, make strong; *(dar ánimo)* to encourage, hearten —reflex. to strive, exert much effort *<esforzarse en conquistar* to strive to conquer>.

es·fuer·zo m. *(empleo enérgico)* effort, exertion; *(valor)* courage, bravery; *(ánimo)* spirit, heart; *(intento)* attempt, endeavor **hacer esfuerzos** *or* **un e.** to make a concerted effort, try hard • **sin e.** effortlessly.

es·fu·mar tr. PAINT. *(esfuminar)* to shade, stump; *(suavizar el color)* to tone down, soften —reflex. FIG. to disappear, vanish.

es·fu·mi·no m. *(lápiz)* stump.

es·ga·rro m. spit, spittle.

es·gri·ma f. SPORT. fencing.

es·gri·mi·dor m. SPORT. fencer, swordsman.

es·gri·mir tr. *(manejar)* to wield, brandish; FIG. *(servirse de)* to use, make use of *<e. la razón* to make use of reason> —intr. SPORT. to fence, engage in fencing.

es·gri·mis·ta m.f. AMER., SPORT. fencer.

es·gua·zar §04 tr. to ford (a body of water).

es·guin·ce m. *(regate)* dodge, swerve; *(gesto de desdén)* frown, grimace; MED. sprain, twist (of a joint).

es·gun·fio m. ARG. bother, annoyance.

es·la·bón m. *(hierro enlazado)* link; *(hierro para sacar chispas)* steel (for striking sparks); *(chaira)* steel knife-sharpener; ENTOM. black scorpion; VET. (bone) spavin **e.**

giratorio *or* **de guimbalete** MARIT. swivel • **e. interruptor** ELEC. disconnecting link • **e. perdido** missing link.

es·la·bo·na·mien·to m. *(encadenación)* linking, interlinking; FIG. *(unión)* connection, union.

es·la·bo·nar tr. *(encadenar)* to link, interlink; FIG. *(unir)* to connect, unite —reflex. to be connected *or* united.

es·lo·ra f. MARIT. length (of a ship) ♦ **e. de flotación** MARIT. water-line length • **esloras** MARIT. binding strakes.

es·mal·tar tr. *(cubrir con esmalte)* to enamel; FIG. *(adornar con varios colores)* to variegate, adorn with a variety of colors; *(hermosear)* to embellish, adorn.

es·mal·te m. *(barniz vítreo)* enamel, vitreous varnish; *(objeto esmaltado)* enameled object; *(labor)* enameling, enamel work; DENT. *(superficie)* enamel; PAINT. *(color azul)* smalt, cobalt blue; HER. color, tincture; FIG. *(lustre)* luster, splendor ♦ **e. de** *or* **para uñas** nail polish *or* enamel.

es·me·ra·da·men·te adv. very carefully, with extreme care.

es·me·ra·do, –da I. past part. see **esmerar II.** adj. *(hecho con esmero)* done with extreme care; *(que se esmera)* careful, meticulous.

es·me·ral·da f. emerald.

es·me·ral·di·no, –na adj. emerald, emerald-colored.

es·me·rar tr. to polish, brighten —reflex. *(esforzarse)* to be painstaking, take great care (in doing something); *(obrar con acierto)* to do well.

es·me·ril m. MIN. emery.

es·me·ri·la·do I. past part. see **esmerilar II.** m. *(pulimento)* polishing with emery; TECH. grinding.

es·me·ri·la·dor, –do·ra m.f. polisher.

es·me·ri·lar tr. *(pulir)* to polish with emery; TECH. to grind *<e. una válvula* to grind a valve>.

es·me·ro m. extreme care, meticulousness ♦ **poner e. en** to take great care over.

es·mi·rria·do, –da adj. COLL. *(delgado)* skinny, thin; *(consumido)* run-down, spent.

es·mo·quin m. dinner jacket, tuxedo.

es·nob I. m.f. [pl. **-nobs**] snob **II.** adj. snobbish, snobby.

es·no·bis·mo m. snobbery, snobbishness.

e·so §G41 pron. that *<no quiero pensar en e.* I do not want to think about that>; *(asunto)* that business *or* matter *<e. de su linaje* that business about his parentage> ♦ **a e. de** about, around *<nos reuniremos a e. de las tres* we will meet at around three o'clock> • **e. es** that's it • **e. mismo** exactly, the same • **nada de e.** none of that • **por e.** therefore, that's why.

e·só·fa·go m. ANAT. esophagus.

e·sos, e·sas adj. see **ese, esa.**

é·sos, é·sas pron. see **ése, ésa.**

e·so·té·ri·co, –ca adj. esoteric.

e·so·te·ris·mo m. PHILOS. esotericism, esoterism.

e·so·tro, –tra I. pron. that other one *<no me gusta e.* I don't like that other one> **II.** adj. that other *<se lo di a e. chico* I gave it to that other boy>.

es·pa·cia·dor m. space bar, spacer (on a typewriter).

es·pa·cial adj. MATH. spatial; *(del espacio)* space *<nave e.* spaceship>.

es·pa·ciar tr. *(poner espacio)* to space, space *or* spread out; *(divulgar)* to spread, divulge; PRINT. *(imprenta)* to space —reflex. *(dilatarse)* to expatiate, go on at length; *(solazarse)* to enjoy *or* amuse oneself, relax.

es·pa·cio I. m. *(extensión)* space; *(período de tiempo)* space, period *<terminó el examen en el e. de dos horas* he finished the examination in the space of two hours>; FIG. *(lentitud)* slowness; MUS., PRINT. space ♦ **a doble e.** double-spaced • **e. extraterrestre** *or* **ultraterrestre** ASTRON. outer space • **e. tiempo** PHYS. space-time (continuum) • **e. vital** POL. lebensraum (additional territory for economic growth) • **geometría del e.** GEOM. solid geometry **II.** adv. MEX. slowly.

es·pa·cio·sa·men·te adv. slowly, deliberately.

es·pa·cio·so, –sa adj. *(amplio)* spacious, roomy; *(lento)* slow, deliberate.

es·pa·da f. *(arma blanca)* sword; *(espadachín)* swordsman; *(naipe)* spade (playing card); ICHTH. swordfish ♦ **colgar la e.** COLL. to retire, hang up one's spurs • **de capa y e.** cloak and dagger • **desnudar la e.** to draw one's sword • **entre la e. y la pared** FIG. between a rock and a hard

place, between the devil and the deep blue sea • **E. de Damocles** FIG. Sword of Damocles, constant threat • **e. de dos filos** FIG. double-edged sword • **E. Dorada** FIG. magic sword • **le salió la e.** FIG. he was given the ax • **salir con su media e.** FIG. to butt into a conversation —m. *(torero)* bullfighter; FIG. *(autoridad)* ace, expert.

es·pa·da·chín m. *(buen esgrimidor)* skilled swordsman; *(bravucón)* swashbuckler.

es·pa·da·ña f. BOT. cattail, bulrush; *(campanario)* belfry, bell gable; *(en un pozo)* pail hook (in a well).

es·pa·di·lla f. *(insignia)* insignia, emblem (of the order of Santiago); *(para espadar)* hemp brake; *(remo)* scull, oar; *(en naipes)* ace of spades; *(en el pelo)* hair ornament.

es·pa·di·llar tr. to brake, crush (hemp or flax).

es·pa·dín m. dress *or* ceremonial sword.

es·pa·gue·ti m. CUL. spaghetti.

es·pal·da f. *(dorso)* back; SPORT. *(natación)* backstroke; ECUAD. destiny, fate ♦ **a espaldas de alguien** behind someone's back • **caer** *or* **dar de espaldas** to fall flat on one's back • **cargado de espaldas** round-shouldered • **dar** *or* **volver la e.** to turn one's back • **de espaldas** from behind *<le vi de espaldas* I saw him from behind • **echarse a las espaldas** FIG. to put (something) behind, forget about • **echarse sobre las espaldas** FIG. to take on one's shoulders (a responsibility) • **espaldas** *(dorso)* back; MIL. rear guard • **tener buenas espaldas** FIG. to be very patient.

es·pal·dar m. back plate (of armor); *(respaldo)* back (of a chair); *(enrejado)* trellis, espalier; ZOOL. shell (back of a tortoise) ♦ **espaldares** wall hangings, tapestries (hung like a frieze).

es·pal·da·ra·zo m. *(golpe)* blow *or* slap on the back; FIG. *(apoyo)* support, backing; accolade *<dar el e. a* to give the accolade to (a knight)>.

es·pal·de·ar tr. MARIT. to poop, break over the stern of; CHILE to guard the back of (someone).

es·pal·dón, –do·na I. m. CARP. tenon; MIL. barricade **II.** adj. COL. broad-shouldered.

es·pal·du·do, –da adj. broad-shouldered, broad-backed.

es·pa·le·ra f. espalier, trellis.

es·pan·ta·di·zo, –za adj. jumpy, easily frightened.

es·pan·ta·dor, –do·ra adj. *(espantoso)* frightening, terrifying; AMER. shy, jumpy (horse).

es·pan·ta·jo m. *(espantapájaros)* scarecrow; *(coco)* bogeyman; FIG. *(persona fea)* sight, fright.

es·pan·ta·pá·ja·ros m. [pl. **-ros**] scarecrow.

es·pan·tar tr. *(asustar)* to frighten, scare; *(echar)* to frighten *or* scare away, shoo —reflex. *(asustarse)* to be frightened *or* scared; *(maravillarse)* to be astonished *or* amazed.

es·pan·to m. *(terror)* fright, scare; *(amenaza)* threat, menace; *(asombro)* astonishment, amazement; *(fantasma)* ghost, phantom ♦ **estar curado de e.** to have been through the mill, be experienced.

es·pan·to·sa·men·te adv. *(terroríficamente)* frighteningly, terrifyingly; *(asombrosamente)* astonishingly, amazingly.

es·pan·to·so, –sa adj. *(terrorífico)* frightening, terrifying; *(horrible)* horrible, dreadful; FIG. *(asombroso)* astounding, amazing.

Es·pa·ña f. Spain.

es·pa·ñol, –ño·la I. adj. Spanish **II.** m.f. *(habitante)* Spaniard —m. *(idioma)* Spanish ♦ **los españoles** the Spanish, the Spaniards.

es·pa·ño·la·do, –da I. adj. Spanish-like **II.** f. *(dicho, hecho)* typically Spanish action *or* expression; DEROG. *(exageración)* exaggerated portrait of Spain.

es·pa·ño·li·dad f. Spanishness, Spanish character.

es·pa·ño·lis·mo m. *(afán)* love of Spain; *(hispanismo)* Hispanicism; *(carácter español)* Spanishness, Spanish character.

es·pa·ño·li·zar §04 tr. to Hispanicize, make Spanish —reflex. to adopt Spanish ways.

es·pa·ra·dra·po m. MED. adhesive tape.

es·par·ci·do, –da I. past part. see **esparcir II.** adj. *(derra-*

mado) scattered, strewn; (*diseminado*) widespread; FIG. (*alegre*) merry, cheerful.

es·par·ci·mien·to m. (*dispersión*) scattering, dispersion; FIG. (*divulgación*) spreading, disseminating (of ideas); (*diversión*) amusement, entertainment; (*descanso*) relaxation; (*alegría*) merriness, gaiety.

es·par·cir §35 tr. (*dispersar*) to scatter, spread; (*divulgar*) to spread, disseminate —reflex. (*dispersarse*) to scatter, be scattered; (*descansarse*) to relax, take it easy; (*divertirse*) to amuse *or* entertain oneself.

es·pá·rra·go m. BOT. asparagus (plant and stem); (*palo*) pole, post; (*escalerilla*) peg ladder.

es·pa·rran·car·se §70 reflex. COLL. to open *or* spread one's legs, straddle.

Es·par·ta f. Sparta.

es·par·ta·no, –na adj. & m.f Spartan.

es·par·te·ña f. espadrille.

es·par·ti·zal m. AGR. esparto field.

es·par·to m. BOT. esparto.

es·par·za, esparzo see **esparcir.**

es·pas·mo m. MED. spasm.

es·pas·mó·di·co, –ca adj. MED. spasmodic.

es·pá·tu·la f. CUL. spatula; ORNITH. spoonbill.

es·pe·cia f. spice.

es·pe·cial adj. special ♦ **en e.** especially.

es·pe·cia·li·cé, especialice see **especializar.**

es·pe·cia·li·dad f. (*particularidad*) specialty; (*estudios*) major (field of studies).

es·pe·cia·lis·ta adj. & m.f. specialist.

es·pe·cia·li·za·ción f. specialization.

es·pe·cia·li·za·do, –da adj. specialized.

es·pe·cia·li·zar §04 tr., intr. & reflex. to specialize.

es·pe·cial·men·te adv. especially, specially.

es·pe·cie f. BIOL. species; (*tipo*) type, kind; FIG. (*asunto*) matter, affair <*nunca hablábamos de aquella e.* we never spoke about that affair>; (*noticia*) bit of news; (*pretexto*) pretext, appearance ♦ **especies sacramentales** RELIG. species.

es·pe·cie·rí·a f. (*tienda*) spice shop; AMER. (*especias*) spices; (*tienda de comestibles*) grocery store.

es·pe·ci·fi·ca·ción f. specification.

es·pe·ci·fi·car §70 tr. to specify.

es·pe·ci·fi·ca·ti·vo, –va adj. specific, specifying.

es·pe·ci·fi·ci·dad f. specificity.

es·pe·cí·fi·co, –ca I. adj. specific **II.** m. MED. (*medicamento*) specific; (*medicamento producido industrialmente*) patent medicine.

es·pe·ci·fi·qué, especifique see **especificar.**

es·pé·ci·men m. [pl. **-cí·me·nes**] specimen.

es·pe·cio·so, –sa adj. (*hermoso*) beautiful, perfect; FIG. (*engañoso*) specious.

es·pe·cio·ta f. COLL. hoax.

es·pec·ta·cu·lar adj. spectacular.

es·pec·tá·cu·lo, m. (*visión*) spectacle, sight; (*función*) show, spectacle; (*escándalo*) scandal, exhibition ♦ **dar un e.** to cause a scandal.

es·pec·ta·dor, –do·ra I. adj. observing, watching **II.** m.f. spectator, onlooker ♦ **espectadores** audience, public.

es·pec·tral adj. PHYS. spectral; (*fantasmal*) ghostly, spooky.

es·pec·tro m. PHYS. spectrum; (*fantasma*) ghost, spook; (*horror*) specter, horror; FIG., COLL. (*hombre cadavérico*) ghost, specter.

es·pec·tró·gra·fo m. PHYS. spectrograph.

es·pec·tros·co·pia f. PHYS. spectroscopy.

es·pec·tros·co·pio m. PHYS. spectroscope.

es·pe·cu·la·ción f. COM. speculation; (*meditación*) meditation, speculation.

es·pe·cu·la·dor, –do·ra I. adj. speculating, speculatory **II.** m.f. speculator.

es·pe·cu·lar[1] tr. (*examinar*) to examine, inspect; (*conjeturar*) to conjecture, speculate; (*meditar*) to meditate, speculate —intr. COM. to speculate in *or* on <*e. en metales preciosos* to speculate in precious metals>.

es·pe·cu·lar[2] adj. specular, mirror-like.

es·pe·cu·la·ti·va f. intellect, understanding.

es·pe·cu·la·ti·vo, –va adj. (*especulador*) speculative; (*pensativo*) thoughtful, meditative.

es·pe·ja·do, –da adj. (*claro*) clear, limpid; (*que refleja*) reflecting.

es·pe·je·ar intr. to shine, gleam.

es·pe·jis·mo *or* **es·pe·je·o** m. (*visión*) mirage; FIG. (*ilusión*) illusion, mirage.

es·pe·jo m. (*luna*) mirror; FIG. (*reflejo*) mirror, reflection <*los ojos son el e. del alma* the eyes are the mirror of the soul>; (*modelo*) model, example ♦ **e. de cuerpo entero** full-length mirror • **e. de los Incas** MIN. obsidian • **e. retrovisor** AUTO. rearview mirror.

es·pe·jue·lo m. MIN. selenite; (*hoja de talco*) flake of talc; (*conserva*) citron; HUNT. lark mirror; VET. chestnut, callosity ♦ **espejuelos** glasses, spectacles.

es·pe·le·o·lo·gí·a f. speleology (study of caves).

es·pe·luz·nan·te adj. COLL. hair-raising, horrifying.

es·pe·luz·nar tr. to ruffle, muss (hair); (*erizar*) to make stand on end (someone's hair) —reflex. to become ruffled *or* mussed; (*erizarse*) to stand on end (hair).

es·pe·luz·no m. COLL. chill, shudder.

es·pe·que m. handspike.

es·pe·ra f. (*acción de esperar*) wait, waiting <*sala de e.* waiting room>; (*calma*) restraint; LAW (*plazo*) respite; CARP. notch ♦ **en e. de** awaiting • **estar en e.** to be waiting.

Es·pe·ran·to m. Esperanto.

es·pe·ran·za f. (*confianza*) hope; (*deseo*) wish, desire; (*virtud*) hope; (*fe*) faith ♦ **dar esperanzas** to encourage, give hope • **esperanzas** prospects, hopes.

es·pe·ran·zar §04 tr. to make hopeful, give hope.

es·pe·rar tr. (*tener esperanza*) to hope <*esperamos que vendrás* we hope that you will come>; to hope for <*espero la victoria* I hope for victory>; (*aguardar*) to wait for, await <*e. a unos amigos* to wait for some friends>; (*confiar en*) to expect <*espero que llegarán a tiempo* I expect them to arrive on time>; (*detenerse*) to wait <*esperé a que sonara la hora* I waited for the hour to ring>; (*ser inminente*) to be in store, await <*el invierno cruel nos espera* the cruel winter awaits us> ♦ **e. en alguien** to trust *or* put one's faith in someone —intr. wait ♦ **e. sentado** to have a long wait.

es·per·ma f. MED. sperm, semen; AMER. candle ♦ **e. de ballena** sperm oil, spermaceti.

es·per·ma·to·zoi·de m. BOT. spermatozoid; ZOOL. spermatozoon.

es·pe·rón m. MARIT. ram; CUBA long wait.

es·per·pen·to m. COLL. (*espanto*) fright, sight; (*desatino*) absurdity, nonsense.

es·pe·sa·mien·to m. thickening.

es·pe·sar tr. (*condensar*) to thicken, make thick; (*tejer*) to weave tighter, knit closer —reflex. to grow *or* become thicker.

es·pe·so, –sa adj. (*condensado*) thick, dense; (*compacto*) compact, thick; (*grueso*) thick <*muros espesos* thick walls>; FIG. (*sucio*) dirty, unkempt.

es·pe·sor m. (*grosor*) thickness; (*densidad*) density.

es·pe·su·ra f. (*espesor*) thickness; (*densidad*) density; (*matorral*) thicket; FIG. (*suciedad*) dirtiness.

es·pe·ta·pe·rro adv. ♦ **a e.** at breakneck speed.

es·pe·tar tr. CUL. to skewer, spit; (*atravesar*) to pierce, run through; FIG., COLL. to recite, make sit through <*nos espetó una lección aburrida* he made us sit through a boring lesson> —reflex. (*ponerse tenso*) to become serious *or* solemn; FIG., COLL. (*asegurarse*) to establish oneself (in a position of authority).

es·pe·te·ra f. (*tabla*) kitchen rack; FIG., COLL. (*pecho*) breasts, woman's chest; GUAT., HOND. excuse, pretext.

es·pe·tón m. CUL. skewer, spit; ICHTH. needlefish, pipefish.

es·pí·a m.f. spy —f. MARIT. (*acción*) warping; (*cabo*) warp ♦ **e. doble** double agent.

es·piar §30 tr. to spy on, observe; —intr. (*vigilar*) to spy; MARIT. to warp.

es·pi·char tr. (*pinchar*) to prick; CHILE, PERU (*espitar*) to put a faucet *or* tap on —intr. COLL. to kick the bucket, die —reflex. MEX. to be ashamed; GUAT. to become frightened *or* cowardly; COL. to become empty *or* drained.

es·pi·che m. (*estaquilla*) spike; (*arma*) sharp weapon.

es·pi·chón m. stab wound.

es·pi·ga f. BOT. spike, ear; (*de una espada*) tang (of a sword); CARP. tenon; (*clavija*) peg, pin; MARIT. masthead.

es·pi·ga·de·ra f. gleaner.

es·pi·ga·do, –da I. past part. see **espigar** II. adj. BOT. spiky; FIG. *(alto)* slender, tall and graceful.

es·pi·ga·dor, –do·ra m.f. gleaner.

es·pi·gar §47 tr. AGR. to glean; *(rebuscar)* to cull, glean *<e. de un libro* to cull from a book>; CARP. to tenon, dovetail —intr. AGR. to tassel, grow ears *or* spikes (cereals) —reflex. to grow *or* shoot up.

es·pi·gón m. *(aguijón)* point; *(mazorca)* ear (of corn); *(cerro)* peak, butte; MARIT. breakwater, jetty.

es·pi·gue·ar intr. MEX. to move its tail up and down (a horse).

es·pi·gue·o m. *(acción)* gleaning; *(tiempo)* gleaning season.

es·pi·gui·lla f. BOT. spikelet; *(diseño)* herringbone.

es·pín m. ZOOL. porcupine; MIL. square.

es·pi·na f. BOT. thorn; *(astilla)* splinter; *(de pez)* fishbone; ANAT. spine, backbone; FIG. *(pesar)* grief, sorrow ♦ **dar mala e.** FIG. to cause suspicion • **e. blanca** BOT. cotton thistle • **e. santa** BOT. Jerusalem thorn • **estar en espinas** FIG. to be on pins and needles • **sacarse la e.** FIG., COLL. to get even.

es·pi·na·ca f. BOT. spinach.

es·pi·nal I. adj. ANAT. spinal II. m. COL., CUBA thicket.

es·pi·na·pez m. [pl. **-ces**] herringbone work.

es·pi·nar tr. *(herir)* to prick; AGR. to protect, surround (new trees with thorn branches); FIG. *(zaherir)* to hurt, offend (with words).

es·pi·na·zo m. ANAT. spine, backbone; ARCHIT. keystone ♦ **doblar el e.** FIG., COLL. to grovel.

es·pi·nel m. MARIT. boulter, trotline.

es·pi·ne·ta f. MUS. spinet.

es·pi·ni·lla f. ANAT. shinbone; *(granillo)* blackhead.

es·pi·ni·llo m. ARG., BOT. nandubay (tree and wood); CUBA, P. RICO variety of mimosa.

es·pi·no m. BOT. *(arbusto)* hawthorn, thornbush; ECUAD. thorn, thistle ♦ **e. albar** *or* **blanco** BOT. hawthorn • **e. amarillo** *or* **falso** BOT. common sea-buckthorn • **e. artificial** barbed wire • **e. cerval** *or* **hediondo** BOT. purging buckthorn • **e. de escobas** BOT. euphorbia • **e. negro** BOT. blackthorn, blackthorn.

es·pi·no·so, –sa adj. BOT., ZOOL. thorny, spiny; FIG. *(arduo)* difficult, sticky *<es una situación e.* it is a sticky situation>.

es·pio·na·je m. espionage, spying.

es·pi·ra f. GEOM. *(espiral)* spiral, helix; *(vuelta)* spire, whorl; ZOOL. spire; ARCHIT. surbase, torus.

es·pi·ra·ción f. PHYSIOL. exhalation, expiration.

es·pi·ra·dor, –do·ra adj. *(que espira)* exhaling, breathing out; ANAT. expiratory *<músculo e.* expiratory muscle>.

es·pi·ral I. adj. spiral, winding *<escalera e.* spiral staircase> II. m. *(muelle de reloj)* balance spring, hairspring; MED. *(contraceptivo)* coil —f. spiral.

es·pi·ran·te adj. *(que expele aire)* exhaling, breathing out; PHONET. aspirate.

es·pi·rar tr. *(exhalar)* to exhale, breathe out; *(exudar)* to give off, exude; THEOL. to inspire —intr. PHYSIOL. to exhale, breathe out; POET. to blow gently (wind).

es·pi·ri·ta·do, –da I. past part. see **espiritar** II. adj. COLL. skinny, thin.

es·pi·ri·tar tr. to possess with a devil —reflex. to become agitated.

es·pi·ri·tis·mo m. spiritualism, spiritism.

es·pi·ri·tis·ta I. adj. spiritualistic, spiritistic II. m.f. spiritualist, spiritist.

es·pi·ri·to·so, –sa adj. *(vivo)* spirited, lively; *(alcohólico)* spirituous, alcoholic.

es·pí·ri·tu m. *(ánima)* spirit *<los ángeles son espíritus protectores* the angels are protective spirits>; *(alma)* soul *<el e. y la carne* body and soul>; *(fantasma)* spirit, ghost; *(esencia)* spirit *<el e. humano* the human spirit>; *(tono)* spirit, tone, mood *<el e. de la época* the mood of the era>; *(tendencia)* disposition, inclination; *(demonio)* evil spirit; *(vigor)* esprit, vitality; *(mente)* intelligence, wit; FIG. *(sentido)* spirit, real sense *<el e. de la ley* the spirit of the law>; RELIG. *(don)* gift *<e. de profecía* gift of prophecy>; CHEM. spirit, essence; GRAM. spiritus, breathing (mark in Greek) ♦ **despedir** *or* **exhalar el e.** to die, give up the ghost • **e. de cuerpo** esprit de corps • **e. de sal** CHEM.

spirits of salt • **e. de vino** spirits of wine, ethyl alcohol • **E. Santo** RELIG. Holy Spirit, Holy Ghost • **levantar el e.** to cheer up • **tener e. de contradicción** to be contrary.

es·pi·ri·tual I. adj. spiritual II. m. MUS. spiritual.

es·pi·ri·tua·li·dad f. spirituality.

es·pi·ri·tua·lis·mo m. spiritualism.

es·pi·ri·tua·lis·ta I. adj. spiritualistic II. m.f. spiritualist.

es·pi·ri·tua·li·za·ción f. spiritualization.

es·pi·ri·tua·li·zar §04 tr. to spiritualize.

es·pi·ri·tual·men·te adv. spiritually.

es·pi·roi·dal adj. spiral, spiroid.

es·pi·ró·me·tro m. MED. spirometer.

es·pi·ta f. *(cañuto)* tap, spigot; FIG. *(bebedor)* drunkard, boozer.

es·pi·tar tr. to tap, put a spigot on.

es·plen·den·te adj. shining, resplendent.

es·plén·di·da·men·te adv. *(con magnificencia)* magnificently, splendorously; *(generosamente)* generously, abundantly.

es·plen·di·dez f. [pl. **-de·ces**] *(magnificencia)* splendor, magnificence *(generosidad)* generosity, abundance.

es·plén·di·do, –da adj. *(magnificente)* splendorous, magnificent; *(generoso)* generous, abundant; *(resplandeciente)* resplendent, shining.

es·plen·dor m. *(resplandor)* splendor, magnificence; *(refulgencia)* radiance, fulgency; FIG. *(gloria)* splendor, glory.

es·plen·do·ro·so, –sa adj. resplendent, shining.

es·plie·go m. BOT. lavender.

es·plín m. melancholy, depression.

es·po·le·ar tr. EQUIT. to spur, prod with a spur; FIG. *(estimular)* to incite, urge; P. RICO, SPORT. to attack with the spur (in cockfighting).

es·po·le·o m. spurring.

es·po·le·ta f. ARM. *(espiga)* fuse; ORNITH. *(horquilla)* wishbone, furcula ♦ **e. de percusión** percussion fuse • **e. de proximidad** *or* **radioproximidad** proximity fuse • **e. de retardo** delay fuse • **e. de tiempo** time fuse • **quitar la e. de** to defuse, disarm.

es·po·liar tr. to despoil, deprive.

es·po·lín m. TEX. *(lanzadera)* shuttle (for weaving patterns into cloth); *(tela)* flowered silk brocade.

es·po·lón m. ORNITH. spur; ZOOL. fetlock; MARIT. *(remate para embestir)* ram; *(tajamar)* cutwater; ARCHIT. buttress; *(malecón de mar)* sea wall, dike; *(malecón de río)* levee, embankment; *(andén)* promenade, esplanade; GEOL. spur, ridge; MED., COLL. *(sabañón)* chilblain; BOT. spur; MARIT., MIL. gun-carriage grille ♦ **embestir con el e.** MARIT., MIL. to ram • **tener más espolones que un gallo** FIG. to be very old.

es·po·lo·na·da f. sudden attack by horsemen.

es·po·lo·na·zo m. ORNITH. blow with a cock's spur; MARIT. ramming.

es·pol·vo·re·ar tr. *(despolvorear)* to dust (off), remove the dust from; *(esparcir)* to sprinkle, dust *<e. azúcar sobre las galletas* to sprinkle sugar on the cookies>.

es·pol·vo·ri·zar §04 tr. to sprinkle, dust (with powder).

es·pon·de·o m. POET. spondee.

es·pon·ja f. sponge; FIG. COLL. *(gorrón)* sponge, leech ♦ **beber como una e.** FIG., COLL. to drink like a fish • **pasar la e. por eso** FIG. to let bygones be bygones, wipe the slate clean • **tirar** *or* **arrojar la e.** FIG. to throw in the towel, give up.

es·pon·ja·du·ra f. *(acción de esponjar)* fluffing up; *(de la lana)* fluffiness; *(esponjosidad)* sponginess.

es·pon·jar tr. to make spongy *or* fluffy —reflex. *(ponerse fofo)* to become spongy; FIG. *(envanecerse)* to become puffed up, put on airs; COLL. *(rebozar de salud)* to glow with health.

es·pon·je·ar intr. *(curiosear)* to snoop, pry; CUBA to sponge dry.

es·pon·jo·so, –sa adj. spongy.

es·pon·sa·les m.pl. betrothal, engagement, espousal ♦ **contraer e.** to get engaged.

es·pon·sa·li·cio, –cia adj. pertaining to betrothal *or* engagement.

es·pon·tá·ne·a·men·te adv. spontaneously.

es·pon·ta·ne·ar·se reflex. to open up, let out one's innermost feelings.

es·pon·ta·nei·dad f. spontaneity, spontaneousness.

es·pon·tá·ne·o, –a adj. *(voluntario)* spontaneous, voluntary <*aplauso e.* spontaneous applause>; *(automático)* spontaneous <*la generación e.* spontaneous generation>; BOT. wild.

es·po·ra f. BACT., BIOL. spore.

es·po·rá·di·co, –ca adj. MED. sporadic; FIG. *(ocasional)* sporadic, intermittent.

es·por·ta·da f. basketful.

es·por·te·ar tr. to carry in baskets.

es·por·ti·lle·ro m. carrier, porter.

es·po·sa f. *(casada)* wife, spouse; AMER. episcopal ring ♦ **esposas** handcuffs, manacles.

es·po·sa·do, –da I. past part. see **esposar** II. adj. var. of **desposado, –da**.

es·po·sar tr. to handcuff, put handcuffs on.

es·po·so m. *(casado)* husband, spouse.

es·pue·la f. EQUIT. *(espolón)* spur; FIG. *(estímulo)* incitement, stimulus; AMER., ORNITH. *(espolón)* spur; *(espoleta)* wishbone, furcula ♦ **calzar** or **calzarse la e.** to be dubbed a knight, be knighted • **dar de e.** or **dar espuelas** to spur • **e. de caballero** BOT. larkspur • **estar con** or **tener las espuelas calzadas** FIG., COLL. to be ready to undertake something (a journey, business deal).

es·pue·le·ar tr. AMER. var. of **espolear**.

es·puer·ta f. two-handled basket ♦ **a espuertas** by the basketful.

es·pul·gar §47 tr. *(quitar las pulgas)* to delouse, rid of fleas or lice; FIG. *(examinar)* to scrutinize, examine closely.

es·pul·go m. *(limpieza de pulgas)* delousing, removal of lice or fleas; FIG. *(examinación)* scrutiny, close examination.

es·pu·ma f. *(burbujas)* foam; *(capa de un líquido)* froth, spume; *(capa de una cerveza)* head; *(burbujas de jabón)* lather, soap bubbles; *(desechos)* scum; TEX. *(espumilla)* voile, sheer fabric; COLL. *(lo mejor)* cream, pick ♦ **crecer como e.** or **la e.** COLL. to shoot up, spread like wildfire • **e. de caucho** foam rubber • **e. de mar** MIN. meerschaum, sepiolite • **e. de nitro** MIN. saltpeter • **e. de la sal** MARIT. sea froth • **e. de plata** CHEM. litharge of silver • **hacer e.** to foam.

es·pu·ma·de·ra f. skimmer (utensil).

es·pu·ma·je m. foaminess, frothiness.

es·pu·ma·je·ar intr. to foam or froth at the mouth.

es·pu·ma·jo·so, –sa adj. foamy, frothy.

es·pu·man·te adj. *(que hace espuma)* foaming, frothing; sparkling <*vino e.* sparkling wine>.

es·pu·mar tr. to skim, remove foam or scum from —intr. *(hacer espuma)* to foam, froth; FIG. *(crecer)* to shoot up, spread like wildfire.

es·pu·ma·ra·jo m. foam or froth (from the mouth).

es·pu·mi·lla f. TEX. voile, sheer crepe; AMER., CUL. meringue.

es·pu·mi·llón m. TEX. heavy silk cloth.

es·pu·mo·so, –sa adj. *(espumajoso)* frothy, foamy; lathery <*jabón e.* lathery soap>.

es·pun·dia f. VET. skin ulcer (in horses); AMER., MED. elephantiasis; P. RICO barb, spike.

es·pu·rio, –ria adj. *(bastardo)* illegitimate, bastard; FIG. *(falso)* spurious, counterfeit; *(adulterado)* adulterated, impure.

es·pu·ta·ción f. spitting, expectoration.

es·pu·tar tr. to spit, expectorate.

es·pu·to m. spit, spittle.

es·que·la f. *(carta breve)* note, short letter; *(invitación)* invitation; *(aviso)* notice, announcement ♦ **e. amatoria** or **amorosa** love letter • **e. mortuoria** or **de defunción** obituary notice or announcement.

es·que·lé·ti·co, –ca adj. ANAT. skeletal; FIG., COLL. *(muy flaco)* bony, emaciated.

es·que·le·to m. ANAT. skeleton, frame; FIG. *(tipo delgado)* skeleton, emaciated person; FIG. *(armadura)* skeleton, framework; AMER. form, blank ♦ **en e.** unfinished, in outline form • **estar hecho un e.** FIG., COLL. to be like a skeleton, be skin and bones.

es·que·ma m. *(plan)* scheme, plan; *(bosquejo)* outline, sketch; *(diagrama)* diagram, chart; PHILOS., RELIG. *(resumen)* schema.

es·que·má·ti·ca·men·te adv. schematically.

es·que·má·ti·co, –ca adj. schematic.

es·que·ma·tis·mo m. schematism.

es·que·ma·ti·zar §04 tr. *(poner en esquema)* to schematize; *(bosquejar)* to outline, sketch; *(poner en diagrama)* to diagram, chart.

es·quí m. [pl. **-quís**] SPORT. *(plancha)* ski; *(deporte)* skiing ♦ **e. acuático** or **náutico** *(plancha)* water ski; *(deporte)* water-skiing.

es·quia·dor, –do·ra m.f. SPORT. skier.

es·quiar §30 intr. SPORT. to ski.

es·qui·cio m. PAINT. sketch, outline.

es·qui·la¹ f. *(cencerro)* cowbell; *(campana pequeña)* small bell.

es·qui·la² f. *(esquileo)* shearing, fleecing.

es·qui·la³ f. ZOOL. prawn; ENTOM. whirligig beetle; BOT. squill.

es·qui·la·dor, –do·ra I. adj. shearing, fleecing II. m.f. *(persona)* shearer, fleecer —f. *(máquina)* shearing machine.

es·qui·lar tr. to shear, fleece.

es·qui·le·o m. *(acción)* shearing, fleecing; *(casa)* shearing or fleecing shed; *(tiempo)* shearing or fleecing season.

es·quil·mar tr. AGR. *(cosechar)* to harvest, gather (crops); *(empobrecer)* to impoverish, exhaust (the soil); FIG. *(agotar)* to exhaust; FIG., COLL. *(engañar)* to fleece.

es·quil·mo m. AGR. *(cosecha)* harvest, farm produce; MEX. farm by-products.

es·qui·mal I. adj. Eskimoan II. m.f. Eskimo.

es·qui·na f. *(ángulo)* corner; AMER. corner store ♦ **a la vuelta de la e.** just around the corner • **doblar la e.** *(dar una vuelta)* to turn the corner; AMER., FIG. to die, kick the bucket • **hacer e.** *(estar al final de la calle)* to be on the corner; *(cruzar)* to meet or intersect (to form a corner).

es·qui·na·do, –da I. past part. see **esquinar** II. adj. *(angular)* cornered, angular; FIG. *(de trato difícil)* difficult, unsociable.

es·qui·nar tr. *(formar esquina)* to form a corner with; *(poner en esquina)* to put in a corner; *(escuadrar)* to square; FIG. *(poner a mal)* to set against, estrange —intr. to form a corner (with) —reflex. ♦ **esquinarse con** FIG. to fall out or quarrel with.

es·qui·na·zo m. COLL. *(esquina)* corner; ARG., CHILE serenade ♦ **dar e. a alguien** COLL. *(dejar plantado)* to stand someone up; *(evadir)* to give someone the slip, shake someone (by turning a corner).

es·qui·ne·ra f. or **es·qui·ne·ro** m. AMER. corner piece (of furniture).

es·quir·la f. splinter.

es·qui·rol m. COLL., DEROG. *(obrero)* scab, strikebreaker.

es·quis·to m. MIN. schist ♦ **e. bituminoso** bituminous shale • **e. petrolífero** oil shale.

es·qui·te m. C. AMER., MEX., CUL. popcorn, popping corn.

es·qui·var tr. *(evitar)* to avoid, evade <*e. un encuentro* to avoid an encounter>; to dodge, avoid <*e. un golpe* to dodge a blow>; *(rehusar)* to shun, refuse <*e. una invitación* to refuse an invitation> —reflex. to withdraw, shy away.

es·qui·vez f. coldness, disdain.

es·qui·vo, –va adj. cold, disdainful.

es·qui·za·do, –da adj. mottled, flecked (marble).

es·qui·zo·fre·nia f. PSYCH. schizophrenia.

es·qui·zo·fré·ni·co, –ca adj. & m.f. schizophrenic.

es·ta adj. see **este, –ta**.

és·ta pron. see **éste, –ta**.

es·ta·ba see **estar**.

es·ta·bi·li·cé, estabilice see **estabilizar**.

es·ta·bi·li·dad f. *(firmeza)* stability, steadiness; CHEM. stableness.

es·ta·bi·li·za·ción f. stabilization.

es·ta·bi·li·za·dor, –do·ra I. adj. stabilizing II. m.f. *(persona)* stabilizer —m. AER., CHEM., MARIT. stabilizer ♦ **e. giroscópico** AER. gyrostabilizer • **e. vertical** AER. vertical stabilizer.

es·ta·bi·li·zar §04 tr. to stabilize, make stable.

es·ta·ble adj. stable.

es·ta·ble·ce·dor, –do·ra I. adj. *(que funda)* establishing, founding; *(que decreta)* decreeing, ordaining II. m.f. establisher, founder.

es·ta·ble·cer §17 tr. *(fundar)* to establish, found; *(decretar)* to decree, ordain; *(fijar)* to establish, fix firmly —reflex.

(avecindarse) to take up residence, settle down; COM. to set oneself up in business.

es·ta·ble·ci·mien·to m. *(creación)* establishment, foundation; LAW *(estatuto)* decree, edict; COM. establishment, place of business.

es·ta·blo m. AGR. *(caballeriza)* stable; CUBA carriage house.

es·ta·bu·la·ción f. stabling.

es·ta·ca f. *(palo)* stake, post; *(garrote)* club, cudgel; BOT. cutting; CARP. spike, nail; AMER., MIN. mining concession; CHILE, ORNITH. spur (of fowl).

es·ta·ca·da f. *(valla)* picket fence; MIL. stockade, palisade; HIST. *(lugar de desafío)* battlefield, dueling ground; AGR. field of cuttings; C. AMER. puncture or stab wound ♦ **dejar a alguien en la e.** COLL. to leave someone in the lurch • **quedar en la e.** COLL. *(ser vencido)* to be defeated or beaten.

es·ta·car §70 tr. *(atar)* to tie to a stake or post; *(señalar)* to stake out (land); MIL. to stockade; AMER. *(sujetar con estacas)* to fasten down with stakes; COL., VEN. *(engañar)* to fool, dupe; VEN. *(herir)* to stab, wound —reflex. FIG. *(quedarse tieso)* to freeze, stand stock-still; COL., VEN. *(engañarse)* to be fooled or duped; AMER. *(clavarse una astilla)* to get a splinter; *(pincharse)* to prick oneself; ECUAD. *(plantarse)* to balk (a horse).

es·ta·ca·zo m. *(garrotazo)* blow with a stake or club; FIG. *(varapalo)* blow, setback.

es·ta·ción f. *(estado)* position <e. horizontal horizontal position>; *(tiempo)* season <las cuatro estaciones the four seasons>; *(temporada)* season, time <la e. de las lluvias ha comenzado the rainy season has begun>; RAIL., TELEC. *(edificio)* station; ASTRON. stationary or synchronous orbit.

es·ta·cio·nal adj. seasonal; ASTRON. stationary.

es·ta·cio·na·mien·to m. *(situación)* stationing, positioning; AUTO. *(acción de aparcar)* parking; *(aparcamiento)* parking place or space.

es·ta·cio·nar tr. *(colocar)* to station, place; AUTO. *(aparcar)* to park —reflex. *(parar)* to remain stationary; *(colocarse)* to station oneself; ARG. to mate (sheep).

es·ta·cio·na·rio, –ria adj. *(parado)* stationary; ASTRON. stationary.

es·ta·da f. stay, stop (in a place).

es·ta·dí·a f. *(estancia)* stay, stop <planeó una e. de tres días en Lima he planned a three-day stop in Lima>; COM. lay day.

es·ta·dio m. SPORT. stadium <e. olímpico olympic stadium>; *(fase)* phase, stage.

es·ta·dis·ta m. POL. statesman; *(estadístico)* statistician.

es·ta·dís·ti·ca I. f. *(ciencia)* statistics; *(dato)* statistic II. adj. see **estadístico, –ca.**

es·ta·dís·ti·co, –ca I. adj. statistical II. m. statistician —f. see **estadística.**

es·ta·do m. *(modo de ser)* state <e. gaseoso gaseous state>; *(condición)* condition <en buen e. in good condition>; *(calidad)* status <e. civil marital status>; *(jerarquía)* rank, grade <e. militar military rank>; estate <el cuarto e. the fourth estate>; *(gobierno)* state, government; *(nación)* nation, state; *(división política)* state <los Estados Unidos the United States>; *(lista)* list <e. de personal personnel list>; *(resumen)* statement, report; MIL. post, garrison ♦ **e. civil** marital status • **e. de alma** or **de ánimo** state of mind • **e. de cosas** state of affairs • **e. de cuenta** COM. statement of account • **e. de emergencia** state of emergency • **e. de gracia** RELIG. state of grace • **e. de guerra** state of war • **e. de sitio** state of siege • **e. interesante** pregnancy • **e. libre asociado** POL. commonwealth • **e. llano** or **general** third estate, common people • **e. mayor** MIL. general staff • **estar en e. de merecer** to be marriageable • **tomar e.** to marry.

Estados Unidos de América m. United States of America.

es·ta·dou·ni·den·se adj. of the United States of America.

es·ta·fa f. *(trampa)* swindle, hoax; *(fraude organizado)* racket.

es·ta·fa·dor, –do·ra m.f. swindler, crook.

es·ta·far tr. to swindle, cheat.

es·ta·fe·ta f. *(correo)* mail, post; *(casa de correo)* post office; DIPL. diplomatic bag or pouch.

es·ta·fi·lo·co·co m. MED. staphylococcus.

es·ta·la f. MARIT. port of call; *(establo)* stable.

es·ta·lac·ti·ta f. GEOL. stalactite.

es·ta·lag·mi·ta f. GEOL. stalagmite.

es·ta·llan·te adj. bursting, exploding.

es·ta·llar intr. *(explotar)* to burst, explode; *(restallar)* to crack (said of a whip); FIG. *(sobrevenir)* to break out <la revolución estalló en 1868 the revolution broke out in 1868>; *(reventar)* to break loose, explode <de repente su ira estalló suddenly his anger broke loose>; to blow up, lose one's temper.

es·ta·lli·do or **es·ta·llo** m. *(explosión)* explosion; *(de un látigo)* crack (of a whip); ARM. report; FIG. outbreak <un e. de manifestaciones an outbreak of riots>; outburst <un e. de ira an outburst of anger> ♦ **dar un e.** to explode.

es·tam·bre m. TEX. *(hilo)* worsted yarn; *(tela)* worsted; *(urdimbre)* warp; BOT. stamen.

es·tam·pa f. *(imagen)* print, mark; FIG. *(aspecto)* aspect, appearance ♦ **dar a la e.** FIG. to print • **tener mala e.** COLL. *(ser feo)* to be ugly; *(lucir mal)* to be disheveled.

es·tam·pa·do, –da I. past part. see **estampar** II. adj. TEX. stamped III. m. printing, engraving.

es·tam·pa·dor m. printer, engraver.

es·tam·par tr. *(imprimir)* to print, stamp; *(grabar)* to emboss, engrave; *(dejar huella)* to leave a mark <e. el pie en la arena to leave a mark of one's foot in the sand>; COLL. *(arrojar)* to throw, hurl; FIG. to engrave, stamp <e. la fecha en la mente to stamp the date in one's mind>; *(dar un beso)* to plant (a kiss).

es·tam·pe·rí·a f. print shop.

es·tam·pí·a ♦ **de e.** suddenly, all at once.

es·tam·pi·da f. *(estallido)* explosion, bang; AMER. stampede.

es·tam·pi·do m. explosion, bang.

es·tam·pi·lla f. *(firma)* signet, seal; *(sello)* rubber stamp; AMER. *(sello de correos)* postage stamp.

es·tam·pi·llar tr. to stamp, mark with a stamp.

es·tam·pi·ta f. print.

es·tan·ca·ción f. *(de aguas)* stagnation; COM. state monopoly; FIG. *(detención)* standstill, deadlock.

es·tan·ca·mien·to m. var. of **estancación.**

es·tan·car §70 tr. *(embalsar)* to dam up, stem (waters); COM. to monopolize, convert into a monopoly; FIG. *(detener)* to delay, bring to a standstill —reflex. *(encenegarse)* to stagnate, become stagnant; COM. to be converted into a monopoly; FIG. *(detenerse)* to come to a standstill, be deadlocked.

es·tan·cia f. *(mansión)* country house, estate; *(sala)* room; *(estadía)* stay <una e. en el hospital a hospital stay>; POET. stanza; AMER. *(hacienda)* ranch, farm; *(ganadería)* cattle ranch.

es·tan·cie·ro m. AMER. rancher, farmer.

es·tan·co, –ca I. adj. watertight II. m. COM. state monopoly; *(tienda)* government or state store; FIG. *(archivos)* repository, archives; SP. tobacco shop; ECUAD. liquor store.

es·tan·dar·te m. standard, banner.

es·tan·que m. *(charca)* pond, pool; *(depósito)* tank, reservoir.

es·tan·qué, estanque see **estancar.**

es·tan·que·ro, –ra m.f. tobacconist.

es·tan·te I. adj. *(existente)* extant; *(permanente)* permanent, fixed II. m. *(armario)* shelving, shelves <e. de libros bookshelves>; *(apoyo)* leg, support; AMER. post, pillar.

es·tan·te·rí·a f. shelving, shelves.

es·tan·ti·gua f. *(fantasma)* phantom, specter; FIG., COLL. *(espantajo)* scarecrow, fright.

es·ta·ña·du·ra f. tinning, tin plating.

es·ta·ñar tr. *(bañar)* to tin, plate with tin; *(soldar)* to solder (with tin).

es·ta·ño m. CHEM. tin; ARG., COLL. counter (of a bar).

es·ta·qué, estaque see **estacar.**

es·ta·que·a·da f. AMER., COLL. beating, thrashing.

es·ta·que·ar tr. AMER. to stretch with stakes (hides).

es·ta·qui·lla f. *(espiga)* wooden peg; *(estaca)* spike, nail.

es·ta·qui·llar tr. to peg, fasten with pegs.

es·tar §36 §G9, 11, 13 intr. to be <*el lápiz está en el escritorio* the pencil is on the desk>; to be in, be at home <*¿está la señora?* is the lady of the house in?>; to be ready <*en seguida está* it will be ready in a few minutes>; COLL. *(entender)* to understand <*¿está usted?* do you understand> • **¿a cuántos estamos?** *or* **¿a qué estamos?** what is the date? • **¿cómo estás?** how are you? • **¿dónde estamos?** FIG. what have we come to? • **está bien** *or* **bien está** okay, all right • **e. a** to sell at, cost <*las manzanas están a veinte centavos* apples cost twenty cents> • **e. a dos velas** COLL. to be hard up, be down and out • **e. a extremos** to be on opposite sides • **e. a la que salta** to be ready for whatever comes up • **e. al caer** to be about to strike <*están al caer las tres* it is about to strike three>; FIG. *(a punto de ocurrir)* to be imminent, be about to happen • **e. a matar** to be bitter enemies • **e. a oscuras** FIG., COLL. to be in the dark, be ignorant • **e. bien** *(convenir)* to be suitable *or* fitting; *(gozar de buena salud)* to be well *or* healthy • **e. idle** • **e. bien con** to be on good terms with • **e. con** to have <*el niño está con fiebre* the child has a fever>; *(avistarse)* to be in agreement with • **e. de** to be <*estamos de mudanza* we are moving>; *(trabajar)* to work as, serve as <*estoy de chófer* I am working as a chauffeur> • **e. de acuerdo** to be in agreement • **e. de malas pulgas** FIG. to be jumpy or on edge • **e. de mal humor** to be in a bad mood • **e. de más** to be superfluous • **e. de ocio** ARG., MEX., PAR. to be idle • **e. de prisa** to be in a hurry • **e. de puntas** to be on pins and needles • **e. de vacaciones** to be on vacation • **e. en** *(entender)* to understand; *(consistir en)* to depend on, lie in <*está en el asunto del dinero* it depends on the question of money> • **e. en grande** to live in luxury • **e. en lo cierto** to be on firm ground • **e. en paz** to be at peace • **e. en sí** to know what one is doing • **e. en todo** to be involved in everything • **e. mal** *(no convenir)* to be unsuitable *or* inappropriate; *(padecer de mala salud)* to be ill • **e. mal con** to be on bad terms with • **e. para** *(gustar)* to be in the mood for <*no estoy para bromas* I am not in the mood for jokes>; to be about to <*estamos para salir* we are about to leave> • **e. por** *(favorecer)* to be for, be in favor of <*estoy por decirle la verdad* I am in favor of telling him the truth>; to be about to <*e. por terminarlo* to be about to finish it>; *(quedar)* to remain to be <*el resto de la carta está por escribir* the rest of the letter remains to be written>; *(tener ganas)* to have a mind to, be inclined to • **e. que bota** *or* **que hincha** COLL. to be furious • **e. sobre sí** to be on guard.
es·tar·cir §35 tr. to stencil.
és·ta·sis f. [pl. **-sis**] MED. stasis.
es·ta·tal adj. state, of the state.
es·tá·ti·ca **I.** f. MECH. statics **II.** adj. see **estático, -ca.**
es·tá·ti·co, -ca **I.** adj. *(inmóvil)* static; FIG. *(pasmado)* stunned, dumbfounded **II.** f. see **estática.**
es·ta·ti·fi·car §70 tr. to nationalize.
es·ta·tis·mo m. *(inmovilidad)* static state, immobility; POL. statism.
es·ta·tua f. *(escultura)* statue; FIG., COLL. *(persona fría)* cold fish.
es·ta·tua·rio, -ria **I.** adj. statuary **II.** m. sculptor, statuary —f. statuary, sculptures.
es·ta·tuir §18 tr. *(establecer)* to establish, enact; *(demostrar)* to demonstrate, prove <*e. una teoría* to demonstrate a theory>.
es·ta·tu·ra f. stature, height (of a person).
es·ta·tu·ta·rio, -ria adj. statutory.
es·ta·tu·to m. *(ley)* statute, law; *(regla)* rule.
es·tay m. [pl. **-ta·yes**] MARIT. stay • **e. mayor** mainstay.
es·te **I.** adj. eastern, easterly **II.** m. east; *(viento)* east wind.
es·te, -ta §G26 adj. [pl. **es·tos, -tas**] this <*e. situación* this situation> • **estas** *or* **estos** these <*estos sombreros* these hats>.
és·te, -ta §G41 pron. [pl. **és·tos, -tas**] this one <*si compro un nuevo coche, te daré é.* if I buy a new car, I will give you this one>; the latter <*ni Juan ni María viene; aquél está ocupado; ésta no quiere* neither John nor Mary is coming; the former is busy; the latter does not want to>; *(aquí)* here, this town <*me quedaré en ésta cinco días* I will remain here for five days> • **ésta y no más** COLL. nevermore, never again • **éstas** *or* **éstos** these.

es·té see estar.
es·te·a·ti·ta f. MIN. steatite, soapstone.
es·te·la¹ f. ASTRON., AVIA. trail; MARIT. wake; BOT. lady's mantle.
es·te·la² f. ARCHIT. stele.
es·te·lar adj. ASTRON. stellar, sidereal; FIG. stellar, leading <*la figura e. del movimiento* the leading figure of the movement>.
es·te·lí·fe·ro, -ra adj. POET. starry.
es·te·no·gra·fí·a f. stenography, shorthand.
es·te·nó·gra·fo, -fa m.f. stenographer.
es·te·no·ti·pia f. ARTS stenotypy; *(máquina)* stenotype.
es·ten·tó·re·o, -a adj. stentorian, loud.
es·te·pa f. steppe.
és·ter m. CHEM. ester.
es·te·ra f. matting.
es·te·rar tr. to cover with mats —intr. to bundle up, dress warmly (out of season).
es·ter·co·la·du·ra f. *or* **es·ter·co·la·mien·to** m. AGR. manuring, fertilizing.
es·ter·co·lar¹ m. dung heap, manure pile.
es·ter·co·lar² tr. to manure, fertilize —intr. to defecate (animals).
es·té·re·o **I.** adj. stereo, stereophonic **II.** f. stereo, stereophony.
es·te·re·o·fo·ní·a f. stereophony, stereo.
es·te·re·o·fó·ni·co, -ca adj. stereophonic, stereo.
es·te·re·o·gra·fí·a f. stereography.
es·te·re·os·co·pia f. PHOTOG. stereoscopy.
es·te·re·os·co·pio m. PHOTOG. stereoscope.
es·te·re·o·ti·par tr. PRINT. to stereotype; FIG. *(fijar)* to stereotype, fix.
es·te·re·o·ti·pia f. PRINT. *(arte)* stereotypy; *(oficina)* stereotyper's shop; *(máquina)* stereotype; MED. stereotypy.
es·te·re·o·tí·pi·co, -ca adj. PRINT., FIG. stereotypical, stereotypic.
es·te·re·o·ti·po m. PRINT. stereotype; FIG. *(concepción)* stereotype, conventional belief.
es·te·re·rí·a f. *(fábrica)* mat factory; *(tienda)* mat shop.
es·te·re·ro, -ra m.f. *(colocador)* mat layer; *(fabricante)* mat maker; *(vendedor)* mat seller.
es·té·ril adj. *(infecundo)* sterile, infertile; AGR. *(árido)* barren; FIG. *(fútil)* futile, fruitless.
es·te·ri·li·dad f. *(improductividad)* sterility; MED. sterility, infertility; AGR. barrenness; FIG. futility.
es·te·ri·li·za·ción f. sterilization.
es·te·ri·li·za·dor, -do·ra adj. sterilizing.
es·te·ri·li·zar §04 tr. to sterilize.
es·té·ril·men·te adv. sterilely.
es·te·ri·lla f. *(alfombrilla)* small mat; *(galón)* gold or silver braid; *(pleita)* straw braid; *(rejilla)* canework.
es·ter·li·na adj. sterling <*libra e.* pound sterling>.
es·ter·nón m. ANAT. sternum, breastbone.
es·te·ro m. *(estuario)* estuary; AMER. *(pantano)* marsh, swamp; *(charca)* puddle, pool; CHILE, ECUAD. brook, stream.
es·ter·tor m. *(sarrillo)* death rattle; MED. stertor.
es·te·ta m. aesthete.
es·té·ti·ca **I.** f. ARTS, PHILOS. aesthetics • **e. trascendental** transcendental aesthetics **II.** adj. see **estético, -ca.**
es·té·ti·ca·men·te adv. aesthetically.
es·te·ti·cis·mo m. aestheticism.
es·té·ti·co, -ca **I.** adj. aesthetic **II.** m. aesthetic, aesthete —f. see **estética.**
es·te·tis·mo m. PHILOS. aestheticism.
es·te·tos·co·pio m. MED. stethoscope.
es·te·va·do, -da **I.** adj. bowlegged **II.** m.f. bowlegged person.
es·tia·je m. *(nivel)* low water (of a river); *(período)* period of low water.
es·ti·ba·dor m. MARIT. stevedore.
es·ti·bar tr. TEX. *(apretar)* to pack tightly, compress (wool); MARIT. to stow.
es·tiér·col m. dung, manure.
es·ti·gio, -gia adj. & m.f. Stygian.
es·tig·ma m. MED., BOT., ENTOM. stigma; *(marca)* stigma, brand; FIG. *(mancha)* stigma, stain <*el e. del vicio* the stigma of vice> • **estigmas** RELIG. stigmata.

es·tig·má·ti·co, –ca adj. stigmatic.
es·tig·ma·ti·zar §04 tr. *(marrar)* to stigmatize, brand; FIG. *(infamar)* to censure, reproach; RELIG. to mark with stigmata.
es·ti·lar intr. & reflex. *(usar)* to be customary, be the custom <*no se estila llevar ropa de lana en el verano* it is not customary to wear woolen clothing in the summer>; *(estar de moda)* to be in fashion —tr. to draw up (a document); AMER. to distill.
es·ti·le·te m. *(estilo)* stylus, style; *(puñal)* stiletto; MED. probe, stylet.
es·ti·lis·mo m. LIT. stylism.
es·ti·lis·ta m.f. LIT. stylist.
es·ti·lís·ti·co, –ca I. adj. stylistic II. f. LIT. stylistics.
es·ti·li·zar §04 tr. to stylize.
es·ti·lo m. *(modo)* style; *(moda)* style, vogue; *(punzón)* style, stylus; *(indicador)* gnomon, style; BOT. style ♦ **al e. de** in the style of • **por el e.** of that sort, like that <*busco algo por el e.* I am looking for something like that>.
es·ti·lo·grá·fi·co, –ca I. adj. stylographic II. f. fountain pen, stylograph.
es·ti·ma f. *(respeto)* esteem, respect; MARIT. dead reckoning.
es·ti·ma·ble adj. estimable <*una cantidad e.* an estimable quantity>; *(valioso)* worthy of esteem, admirable.
es·ti·ma·ción f. *(respeto)* esteem, respect <*este cuadro mereció la e. del público* this painting merited the public's respect>; COM. appraisal, valuation.
es·ti·ma·dor, –do·ra I. adj. appreciative II. m. COM. appraiser.
es·ti·mar tr. *(apreciar)* to esteem, hold in esteem; COM. to estimate, appraise; *(juzgar)* to consider, deem; *(creer)* to believe —reflex. to be esteemed *or* respected.
es·ti·ma·ti·va f. *(juicio)* judgment; *(instinto)* instinct.
es·ti·mu·lan·te I. adj. stimulating II. m. stimulant.
es·ti·mu·lar tr. *(aguijonear)* to prod, push; FIG. *(incitar)* to incite, urge on <*la muchedumbre le estimuló con gritos* the crowd urged him on with their shouts>; *(excitar)* to excite, stimulate <*los aperitivos estimularon su apetito* the appetizers stimulated his appetite>; *(animar)* to encourage.
es·tí·mu·lo m. FIG. stimulus.
es·tí·o m. POET. summer.
es·ti·pen·diar tr. to give a stipend to, remunerate.
es·ti·pen·dio m. stipend, remuneration.
es·típ·ti·co, –ca adj. *(metálico)* astringent; MED. *(astringente)* styptic; *(estreñido)* constipated; FIG. *(avaro)* stingy, miserly.
es·tip·ti·quez f. ARG., COL. constipation.
es·tí·pu·la f. BOT. stipule.
es·ti·pu·la·ción f. stipulation.
es·ti·pu·lan·te adj. stipulating.
es·ti·pu·lar tr. to stipulate.
es·ti·ra f. currier's knife.
es·ti·ra·da·men·te adv. *(escasamente)* hardly, scarcely; FIG. *(forzadamente)* forcibly, violently.
es·ti·ra·do, –da I. past part. see **estirar** II. adj. *(alargado)* stretched; FIG. *(vanidoso)* pompous, haughty; *(tacaño)* stingy, tight III. f. SPORT. *(en fútbol)* dive (in soccer).
es·ti·ra·jar tr. COLL. var. of **estirar**.
es·ti·ra·mien·to m. stretching.
es·ti·rar tr. *(alargar)* to stretch; FIG. *(extender)* to extend <*el alcalde estiraba sus poderes* the mayor extended his powers>; AMER. *(matar)* to kill; BOL. to flog; PERU to swindle ♦ **e. la pata** FIG., COLL. to die, kick the bucket —reflex. to stretch oneself.
es·ti·rón m. *(tirón)* yank, tug; *(crecimiento)* rapid growth ♦ **dar un e.** to shoot up, grow quickly.
es·tir·pe f. *(linaje)* stock, lineage; LAW heirs <*la e. del difunto* the heirs of the deceased>.
es·ti·va·ción f. ZOOL. acclimation.
es·ti·val adj. summer, estival.
es·to §G41 pron. this <*e. no tiene ningún sentido* this does not make any sense>; *(asunto)* this business *or* matter <*e. de la casa no se resolverá fácilmente* this matter of the house will not be resolved easily> ♦ **con e.** herewith • **en e.** on this point • **por e.** for this reason.
es·to·ca·da f. *(golpe)* thrust (of a sword); *(herida)* stab wound.
Es·to·col·mo Stockholm.

es·to·fa f. TEX. brocade; FIG. *(calidad)* class, quality ♦ **de baja e.** low-class.
es·to·fa·do, –da I. past part. see **estofar¹, estofar²** II. adj. CUL. stewed; *(alcochado)* quilted III. m. CUL. stew; *(alcochadura)* quilting.
es·to·far¹ tr. CUL. to stew.
es·to·far² tr. *(alcochar)* to quilt; TECH. *(adornar)* to decorate with agraffe; *(preparar)* to size, prepare (wood for gilding).
es·toi·ca·men·te adv. stoically.
es·toi·cis·mo m. PHILOS. Stoicism; FIG. *(austeridad)* stoicism, impassiveness.
es·toi·co, –ca I. adj. PHILOS. Stoic; *(impasivo)* stoic, impassive II. m.f. PHILOS. Stoic; FIG. *(persona impasiva)* stoic.
es·to·la f. stole.
es·to·li·dez f. dullness, stupidity.
es·tó·li·do, –da adj. dull, stupid.
es·to·lón m. BOT. stolon.
es·to·ma m. BOT. stoma.
es·to·ma·cal I. adj. *(del estómago)* stomach; *(digestivo)* digestive, stomachic II. m. MED. stomachic.
es·to·ma·gar §47 tr. *(empachar)* to give indigestion to; COLL. *(aburrir)* to annoy, irritate.
es·tó·ma·go m. ANAT. stomach ♦ **dolor de e.** MED. stomachache • **revolver el e. a uno** to turn *or* upset one's stomach • **tener buen e.** *or* **mucho e.** FIG. to be tough, be able to stand a lot • **tener un e. de piedra** FIG. to have a cast-iron stomach.
es·to·ma·gué, estomagne see **estomagar**.
es·to·ma·gue·ro m. infant's bellyband.
es·to·pa f. *(fibra)* tow; *(tela)* burlap; MARIT. oakum ♦ **e. de acero** steel wool.
es·to·pe·rol m. MARIT. *(clavo)* tack, thumbtack; *(torcida)* tow wick; COL. pot, cauldron; AMER. stud, tack.
es·to·pi·lla f. *(estopa fina)* fine tow; *(tela)* cheesecloth.
es·to·pón m. *(estopa gruesa)* coarse tow; *(tela)* burlap, sackcloth.
es·to·que m. *(espada)* rapier, sword; *(bastón)* sword cane; TAUR. bullfighter's sword; BOT. gladiolus.
es·to·que·ar tr. to kill *or* wound with a sword.
es·to·que·o m. stabbing.
es·tor m. window shade *or* blind.
es·tor·ba·dor, –do·ra adj. *(que obstruye)* obstructing, blocking; *(que dificulta)* hindering, hampering.
es·tor·bar tr. *(obstruir)* to obstruct, block <*e. el paso* to block the way>; *(dificultar)* to hinder, hamper; *(frustrar)* to frustrate; FIG. *(molestar)* to bother, annoy.
es·tor·bo m. *(obstrucción)* obstruction, obstacle; *(dificultad)* hindrance; FIG. *(molestia)* bother, annoyance.
es·tor·bo·so, –sa adj. *(que obstruye)* obstructing, blocking; *(que dificulta)* hampering, hindering.
es·tor·nu·dar intr. to sneeze.
es·tor·nu·do m. sneeze.
es·tor·nu·ta·to·rio, –ria adj. sternutatory, sneezing <*polvo e.* sneezing powder>.
es·tos, –tas adj. see **este, –ta**.
és·tos, –tas pron. see **éste, –ta**.
es·to·tro, –tra pron. [contr. of **este** and **otro**] this other.
es·toy see **estar**.
es·tra·ci·lla f. rag, shred.
es·tra·da f. road, highway ♦ **batir la e.** MIL. to scout.
es·tra·do m. *(plataforma)* dais; *(sala)* drawing room; *(mobiliario)* drawing room furniture ♦ **estrados** LAW court-rooms.
es·tra·fa·la·ria·men·te adv. COLL. *(con extravagancia)* outlandishly, bizarrely; *(desaliñadamente)* slovenly, sloppily.
es·tra·fa·la·rio, –ria COLL. I. adj. *(extravagante)* outlandish, bizarre; *(desaliñado)* slovenly, sloppy II. m.f. eccentric.
es·tra·ga·dor, –do·ra adj. *(corruptor)* corrupting, perverting; *(destructor)* destroying, devastating.
es·tra·ga·mien·to m. destruction, devastation.
es·tra·gar §47 tr. *(corromper)* to corrupt, pervert; *(destruir)* to destroy, devastate.
es·tra·go m. destruction, devastation.
es·tra·gón m. BOT. tarragon.
es·tram·bo·te m. POET. envoi (final stanza of a poem).

es·tram·bó·ti·ca·men·te adv. COLL. outlandishly, bizarrely.
es·tram·bó·ti·co, –ca adj. COLL. outlandish, bizarre.
es·tran·gu·la·ción f. strangulation.
es·tran·gu·la·do, –da I. past part. see **estrangular** II. adj. *(ahogado)* strangled; MED. strangulated.
es·tran·gu·la·dor, –do·ra I. adj. strangulating II. m.f. *(persona)* strangler —m. AUTO. choke.
es·tran·gu·lar tr. *(ahogar)* to strangle, choke; MED. to strangulate; MECH. to choke.
es·tra·per·lis·ta COLL. I. adj. black market II. m.f. black marketeer.
es·tra·per·lo m. COLL. black market.
Es·tras·bur·go Strasbourg.
es·tra·ta·ge·ma f. MIL. stratagem; *(engaño)* trick, ruse; FIG. *(astucia)* cleverness, craftiness.
es·tra·te·ga m.f. strategist.
es·tra·te·gia f. *(plan)* strategy; *(astucia)* cleverness, craftiness; AMER. stratagem.
es·tra·té·gi·ca·men·te adv. strategically.
es·tra·té·gi·co, –ca I. adj. strategic II. m.f. strategist.
es·tra·ti·fi·ca·ción f. stratification.
es·tra·ti·fi·car §70 tr. & reflex. to stratify.
es·tra·to m. ANAT., BIOL., GEOL. stratum; METEOROL. stratus; FIG. *(nivel)* stratum, layer *<los estratos sociales* the social strata>.
es·tra·tos·fe·ra f. METEOROL. stratosphere.
es·tra·za f. rag (cloth) ♦ **papel de e.** brown wrapping paper.
es·tre·cha·men·te adv. *(angostamente)* narrowly; *(apretadamente)* tightly; FIG. *(con rigor)* rigidly, severely; *(con intimidad)* closely, intimately; *(con frugalidad)* frugally, austerely; *(con limitación)* narrow-mindedly; *(puntualmente)* punctually.
es·tre·cha·mien·to m. narrowing *<el e. de una carretera* the narrowing of a highway>; tightening *<el e. de los lazos de la amistad* the tightening of the bonds of friendship>.
es·tre·char tr. *(reducir)* to narrow, make narrower *<van a e. el camino* they are going to narrow the road>; *(apretar)* to tighten *<e. la faja* to tighten the sash>; *(sisar)* to take in *<e. un vestido* to take in a dress>; FIG. *(abrazar)* to hug, squeeze; *(oprimir)* to press, harass; *(obligar)* to compel, oblige ♦ **e. la brecha** to close the gap • **e. la mano a** to shake hands with —reflex. *(reducirse)* to narrow; *(apretarse)* to tighten, become tight; *(ceñirse)* to squeeze together *<me estreché en el banco con mi hermana* I squeezed together on the bench with my sister>; *(reducir los gastos)* to economize; FIG. *(amistarse)* to become close *or* intimate.
es·tre·chez f. *(pequeñez)* narrowness; FIG. *(aprieto)* bind, jam *<hallarse en gran e.* to be in a bind>; *(amistad)* closeness, intimacy; *(pobreza)* poverty, need; *(escasez)* shortage; *(austeridad)* austerity; MED. stricture.
es·tre·cho, –cha I. adj. *(angosto)* narrow; *(apretado)* tight *<zapatos estrechos* tight shoes>; FIG. *(tacaño)* stingy, mean; *(íntimo)* close, intimate; *(rígido)* rigid, severe; *(limitado)* narrow-minded II. m. *(paso)* strait, channel *<el E. de Gibraltar* the Strait of Gibraltar>; FIG. *(aprieto)* jam, tight spot.
es·tre·ga·de·ra f. *(cepillo)* scrubbing brush; *(para los zapatos)* footscraper.
es·tre·ga·du·ra f. *or* **es·tre·ga·mien·to** m. rubbing, scrubbing.
es·tre·gar §52 tr. *(frotar)* to rub; *(fregar)* to scrub, scour.
es·tre·lla f. ASTRON. star; *(asterisco)* asterisk; FIG. *(destino)* star, destiny *<nací con buena e.* I was born under a lucky star>; *(actor)* star *<e. del cine* movie star>; ZOOL. star, blaze (white spot on a horse's forehead) ♦ **e. de cometa** ASTRON. comet • **e. de mar** ICHTH. starfish • **e. de rabo** kite • **e. errante** ASTRON. meteorite • **e. fugaz** ASTRON. shooting star • **e. polar** ASTRON. polestar, polar star • **estrellas** star-shaped pasta • **poner sobre las estrellas** FIG. to praise to the skies • **ver las estrellas** FIG. to see stars.
es·tre·lla·do CUL. slotted spatula.
es·tre·lla·do, –da I. past part. see **estrellar** II. adj. *(de forma de estrella)* stellate, star-shaped; *(con estrellas)* starry *<un cielo e.* a starry sky> ♦ **huevos estrellados** CUL. fried eggs.
es·tre·llar tr. *(llenar de estrellas)* to cover with stars; COLL.

(romper) to smash, shatter *< el niño estrelló el vaso contra el piso* the child smashed the glass against the floor>; CUL. *(freír)* to fry (eggs) —reflex. *(llenarse de estrellas)* to become starry; COLL. *(romperse)* to smash, crash *<el coche se estrelló contra el poste de alumbrado* the car smashed into the lamppost>; *(oponerse)* to clash, disagree strongly *<me estrello a menudo con el profesor durante la clase* I often clash with the professor during class>; FIG. *(fracasar)* to fail.
es·tre·lla·to m. stardom.
es·tre·llón m. *(fuego artificial)* star-shaped firework; AMER. crash, collision.
es·tre·me·ce·dor, –do·ra adj. *(que espanta)* terrifying, frightening; *(que asusta)* startling, shocking.
es·tre·me·cer §17 tr. *(hacer temblar)* to shake, make shake *or* tremble; *(asustar)* to startle, shock; FIG. *(turbar)* to shake, disturb —reflex. to shake, tremble.
es·tre·me·ci·mien·to m. *(acción)* shaking, shuddering; *(sacudida)* shake, shudder; *(de frío)* shiver, shivering.
es·tre·na f. *(regalo)* gift, reward; *(primer uso)* first use; *(de la ropa)* first wearing.
es·tre·nar tr. *(inaugurar)* to use for the first time; *(llevar)* to wear for the first time *<estrené una nueva falda hoy* I wore a new skirt for the first time today>; CINEM., THEAT. *(representar)* to première, open (a film, play) —reflex. CINEM., THEAT. *(representarse)* to première, open *<esta película se estrenará el mes que viene* this film will première next month>; *(debutar)* to debut.
es·tre·no m. *(inauguración)* opening (house, gallery); *(debut)* debut; CINEM., THEAT. *(representación)* première.
es·tre·nui·dad f. *(vigor)* strength, vigor; *(carácter emprendedor)* enterprise.
es·tre·nuo, –nua adj. *(vigoroso)* strenuous, vigorous; *(emprendedor)* enterprising.
es·tre·ñi·do, –da I. past part. of **estreñir** II. adj. MED. constipated; FIG. *(avaro)* greedy, stingy.
es·tre·ñi·mien·to m. MED. constipation.
es·tre·ñir §59 tr. MED. to constipate —reflex. to be *or* get constipated.
es·tré·pi·to m. *(alboroto)* uproar, din; *(ostentación)* ostentation, show.
es·tre·pi·to·sa·men·te adv. *(alborotosamente)* noisily, deafeningly; *(con ostentación)* ostentatiously, showily.
es·tre·pi·to·so, –sa adj. *(alborotoso)* noisy, deafening; *(ostentoso)* ostentatious, showy.
es·trep·to·co·co m. BACT., BIOL. streptococcus.
es·trep·to·mi·ci·na f. PHARM. streptomycin.
es·trí·a f. ARCHIT. fluting, stria; *(ranura)* groove; GEOL. striation.
es·tria·do, –da I. past part. see **estriar** II. adj. striated, fluted.
es·triar §30 tr. ARCHIT. to striate, flute; *(hacer ranuras)* to groove; GEOL. to striate —reflex. to be striated *or* grooved.
es·tri·ba·de·ro m. support, prop.
es·tri·bar intr. *(apoyarse)* to rest, lie on; *(fundarse)* to be based, rest.
es·tri·be·ra f. *(estribo)* stirrup; ARG. stirrup strap.
es·tri·be·rón m. steppingstone.
es·tri·bi·llo m. POET. refrain; MUS. chorus; FIG., COLL. *(muletilla)* pet word *or* phrase.
es·tri·bo m. EQUIT. stirrup; *(de carruaje)* footboard, step; AUTO. running board; FIG. *(apoyo)* base, foundation (of an argument); TECH. bracket, brace; ANAT. stapes; ARCHIT. buttress; GEOG. spur ♦ **estar con un pie en el e.** FIG. to be ready to leave • **perder los estribos** FIG. to lose one's head, lose control.
es·tri·bor m. MARIT. starboard.
es·tric·ni·na f. CHEM. strychnine.
es·tric·ta·men·te adv. strictly.
es·tric·tez f. AMER. strictness.
es·tric·to, –ta adj. *(estrecho)* strict; *(severo)* severe.
es·tri·den·cia f. stridence, shrillness.
es·tri·den·te adj. *(agudo)* strident, shrill; *(ruidoso)* clamorous, noisy.
es·tri·dor m. stridor (shrill sound).
es·trie·go, estriegue see **estregar.**
es·tri·ña, estriño see **estreñir.**

es·tri·ñe·ra, estriñó see **estreñir.**
es·tro m. POET. inspiration; ENTOM. botfly; BIOL., ZOOL. oestrus, heat.
es·tro·bos·co·pio m. OPT., PHYS. stroboscope.
es·tro·fa f. POET. strophe, stanza.
es·tron·cio m. CHEM. strontium.
es·tro·pa·je·ar tr. to scrub, clean (a wall).
es·tro·pa·jo m. (para fregar) scourer, scrubber; (trapo) dishcloth, rag; FIG. (persona) good-for-nothing; AMER., BOT. luffa, loofah.
es·tro·pa·jo·so, –sa adj. FIG., COLL. (que pronuncia mal) stammering, stuttering; (desaseado) slovenly, unkempt; (carne) tough, leathery (meat).
es·tro·pe·ar tr. (ruinar) to damage, ruin; (romper) to break; (dañar) to hurt, injure; (malograr) to ruin, spoil <su intromisión estropeó el proyecto his interference ruined the project>; (maltratar) to mistreat, mishandle; CONSTR. to remix (mortar).
es·tro·pi·cio m. COLL. (destrozo) crash, clatter; (alboroto) row, uproar.
es·truc·tu·ra f. (orden) structure, order; (armazón) frame, framework; FIG. (forma) structure, form.
es·truc·tu·ra·ción f. construction, organization.
es·truc·tu·ral adj. structural.
es·truc·tu·ra·lis·mo m. Structuralism.
es·truc·tu·rar tr. to structure, construct.
es·truen·do m. (ruido) clamor, noise; FIG. (confusión) tumult, uproar; (pompa) pomp, show.
es·truen·do·so, –sa adj. clamorous, noisy.
es·tru·ja·dor, –do·ra I. adj. squeezing, crushing II. m. squeezer, crusher.
es·tru·jar tr. (apretar) to squeeze, crush; to press <e. uvas to press grapes>; to squeeze <e. una naranja to squeeze an orange>; (retorcer) to wring (out) <e. una camisa mojada to wring out a wet shirt>; FIG. (agotar) to squeeze dry, drain.
es·tru·jón m. (de uvas) last pressing (of grapes); COLL. (estrujadura) squeezing, pressing.
es·tua·rio m. estuary.
es·tu·ca·do I. past part. see **estucar** II. m. stucco, stuccowork.
es·tu·ca·dor m. stucco plasterer or worker.
es·tu·car §70 tr. to stucco.
es·tu·co m. stucco.
es·tu·che m. (caja) case, box; (vaina) sheath; (conjunto) set of instruments ♦ **e. de joyas** jewel box • **ser un e.** to be a jack-of-all-trades.
es·tu·dia·do, –da I. past part. see **estudiar** II. adj. studied, mannered.
es·tu·dian·ta·do m. student body, pupils.
es·tu·dian·te m.f. student, pupil.
es·tu·dian·til adj. student, pertaining to students.
es·tu·diar tr. to study <estudio mis lecciones en casa I study my lessons at home>; (cursar) to study, take (a course); (memorizar) to memorize; (examinar) to study, examine; PERU to pawn —intr. to study.
es·tu·dio m. study <el e. de las matemáticas es muy difícil the study of mathematics is very difficult>; (cuarto) study, studio; (investigación) study, investigation; (obra) study <acaba de publicar un e. sobre la obra de Cervantes he has just published a study on Cervantes' work>; FIG. (diligencia) diligence, application; ARTS (boceto) study; MUS. etude, study ♦ **dar estudios a alguien** to pay for or finance someone's education • **e. del mercado** COM. marketing, market study • **estudios** CINEM., RAD., TELEV. studio • **tener estudios** to be well educated.
es·tu·dio·si·dad f. studiousness.
es·tu·dio·so, –sa I. adj. studious II. m.f. student, studious person.
es·tu·fa f. (calentador) stove, heater; (invernáculo) hothouse, greenhouse; (sauna) steam room; (estufilla) foot stove, foot warmer; (cuarto para secar) drying chamber.
es·tu·fi·lla f. (estufa pequeña) foot stove, foot warmer; (manguito) hand muff.
es·tul·ti·cia f. stupidity, foolishness.
es·tul·to, –ta adj. foolish, stupid.
es·tu·pe·fac·ción f. stupefaction, astonishment.
es·tu·pe·fa·cien·te I. adj. (asombroso) stupefying, aston-

ishing; PHARM. narcotic, stupefacient II. m. PHARM. narcotic, stupefacient.
es·tu·pe·fac·ti·vo, –va adj. stupefying, amazing.
es·tu·pe·fac·to, –ta adj. stupefied, astonished.
es·tu·pen·da·men·te adv. stupendously, tremendously.
es·tu·pen·do, –da adj. stupendous, tremendous ♦ **¡estupendo!** great!, terrific!
es·tú·pi·da·men·te adv. stupidly, dumbly.
es·tu·pi·dez f. [pl. **-de·ces**] stupidity, idiocy ♦ **cometer una e.** to do something stupid or foolish.
es·tú·pi·do, –da I. adj. stupid, dumb II. m.f. idiot, dumbbell.
es·tu·por m. MED. stupor, torpor; FIG. (asombro) stupefaction, astonishment.
es·tu·pro m. LAW rape.
es·tu·qué, estuque see **estucar.**
es·tur·gar §47 tr. to fettle, trim (pottery).
es·tu·rión m. ICHTH. sturgeon.
es·tu·vie·ra, estuvo see **estar.**
es·vás·ti·ca f. swastika.
e·ta·no m. CHEM. ethane.
e·ta·pa f. (fase) phase, stage; (alto) leg, stage <la primera e. de la carrera the first leg of the race>; MIL. (ración) field ration; (parada) stop, halt (in a march) ♦ **de una e.** AER. single-stage (rocket) • **por etapas** in stages.
et·cé·te·ra f. et cetera.
é·ter m. CHEM., PHYS. ether; POET. ether, the heavens ♦ **e. etílico** CHEM. ethyl ether.
e·té·re·o, –a adj. CHEM., PHYS. ethereal, pertaining to ether; POET. ethereal, heavenly.
e·te·ri·za·ción f. MED. etherization; CHEM. etherification.
e·ter·nal adj. eternal, everlasting.
e·ter·na·men·te adv. eternally, everlastingly.
e·ter·ni·dad f. (tiempo sin fin) eternity, endless time; FIG. (rato largo) eternity, long time ♦ **para** or **por toda la e.** for all eternity.
e·ter·ni·zar §04 tr. (perpetuar) to eternize, perpetuate; (hacer durar) to prolong indefinitely or interminably; (inmortalizar) to immortalize, eternalize —reflex. (durar por siempre) to be everlasting or eternal; FIG. to drag on, be exceedingly slow <se eterniza la película the film is dragging on>.
e·ter·no, –na I. adj. (sin principio ni fin) eternal, everlasting; (sin fin) endless, immortal II. m. ♦ **El Eterno** RELIG. the Eternal One.
é·ti·co, –ca[1] I. adj. ethical, moral II. m.f. moralist —f. ethics.
é·ti·co, –ca[2] adj. MED. consumptive, phthisical.
e·tí·li·co, –ca adj. CHEM. ethylic; FIG. (borracho) intoxicated, drunk.
e·ti·lis·mo m. MED. alcoholism.
e·ti·lo m. CHEM. ethyl.
e·ti·mo·lo·gí·a f. etymology.
e·ti·mo·ló·gi·co, –ca adj. etymological.
e·ti·mo·lo·gi·zar §04 tr. & intr. to etymologize.
e·ti·mó·lo·go, –ga m.f. etymologist.
e·tio·lo·gí·a f. etiology.
e·ti·o·pe adj. & m.f. Ethiopian.
E·tio·pí·a f. Ethiopia.
e·ti·que·ta f. (protocolo) etiquette, ceremony; (rótulo) tag, label; FIG. (calificativo) qualifier, modifier ♦ **de e.** formal, ceremonial • **estar de e.** to be distant, stand on ceremony • **vestirse de e.** to wear formal dress.
e·ti·que·tar tr. FIG. to label, pigeonhole.
e·ti·que·te·ro, –ra adj. ceremonious, formal.
et·nia f. ethnic group.
ét·ni·co, –ca adj. ANTHR. ethnic.
et·no·cen·tris·mo m. ethnocentrism.
et·no·ci·dio m. genocide.
et·no·gra·fí·a f. ethnography.
et·no·grá·fi·co, –ca adj. ethnographic.
et·nó·gra·fo m.f. ethnographer.
et·no·lin·güís·ti·ca f. study of unwritten languages.
et·no·lo·gí·a f. ethnology.
et·no·ló·gi·co, –ca adj. ethnologic, ethnological.
et·nó·lo·go m.f. ethnologist.
e·trus·co, –ca adj. & m.f. Etruscan —m. (idioma) Etruscan.

eu·ca·lip·to m. BOT. eucalyptus.
eu·ca·ris·tí·a f. RELIG. Eucharist.
eu·ca·rís·ti·co, –ca adj. RELIG. Eucharistic.
eu·cli·dia·no, –na adj. GEOM. Euclidean.
eu·co·lo·gio m. RELIG. prayer book.
eu·cra·sia f. MED. good health.
eu·fe·mis·mo m. euphemism.
eu·fo·ní·a f. euphony.
eu·fó·ni·co, –ca adj. euphonic, euphonious.
eu·fo·ria f. euphoria.
eu·fó·ri·co, –ca adj. euphoric, jubilant.
eu·ge·ne·sia f. or **eu·ge·nis·mo** m. eugenics.
eu·ge·né·si·co, –ca adj. eugenic.
eu·nu·co m. eunuch.
eu·pep·sia f. MED. eupepsia, good digestion.
eu·ra·siá·ti·co, –ca adj. Eurasian.
eu·rit·mia f. ARTS eurythmy; FIG. *(equilibrio de las facultades)* eurythmics.
eu·rít·mi·co, –ca adj. eurythmic.
eu·ro m. POET. east wind.
eu·ro·a·fri·ca·no, –na adj. pertaining to both Europe and Africa.
eu·ro·co·mu·nis·mo m. POL. Eurocommunism.
eu·ro·co·mu·nis·ta adj. & m.f. POL. Eurocommunist.
eu·ro·dó·lar m. ECON. Eurodollar.
Eu·ro·pa f. Europe.
eu·ro·pei·za·ción f. Europeanization.
eu·ro·pei·zar §06 tr. to Europeanize.
eu·ro·pe·o, –a adj. & m.f. European.
eu·ro·pio m. CHEM. europium.
éus·ca·ro, –ra or **eus·que·ro, –ra** adj. & m. Basque.
eu·ta·na·sia f. euthanasia.
eu·tra·pe·lia f. *(moderación)* moderation, restraint; *(broma inofensiva)* harmless joke; *(recreo inocente)* innocent pastime.
E·va f. BIBL. Eve ◆ **las hijas de E.** FIG. women, womankind • **traje de E.** FIG. nudity, nakedness.
e·va·cua·ción f. evacuation.
e·va·cuan·te adj. & m. var. of **evacuativo**.
e·va·cuar tr. *(desocupar)* to evacuate, empty; PHYSIOL. *(expeler)* to discharge, evacuate; *(salir)* to quit, take leave of; LAW *(cumplir)* to carry out, transact.
e·va·cua·ti·vo, –va I. adj. *(que desocupa)* evacuating; *(purgativo)* evacuant, purgative II. m. MED. evacuant, purgative.
e·va·cua·to·rio, –ria I. adj. *(que desocupa)* evacuating; *(purgativo)* evacuant, purgative II. m. *(lugar)* evacuation site; *(retrete)* public lavatory, rest room.
e·va·dir tr. to evade, avoid —reflex. to escape, sneak away.
e·va·lua·ción f. evaluation, assessment.
e·va·luar §67 tr. to evaluate, assess.
e·va·nes·cen·te adj. evanescent, vanishing.
e·van·gé·li·ca·men·te adv. RELIG. evangelically, according to the gospel.
e·van·ge·li·cé, evangelice see **evangelizar**.
e·van·gé·li·co, –ca adj. RELIG. *(perteneciente al Evangelio)* evangelical, pertaining to the gospel; *(protestante)* Protestant.
e·van·ge·lio m. RELIG. *(doctrina cristiana)* gospel, evangel; FIG. *(religión cristiana)* Christianity; FIG., COLL. *(verdad)* gospel, undisputed truth.
e·van·ge·lis·mo m. RELIG. evangelism.
e·van·ge·lis·ta m. RELIG. evangelist (author of the Gospel); MEX. amanuensis, public clerk.
e·van·ge·li·za·ción f. evangelization, evangelizing.
e·van·ge·li·za·dor, –do·ra I. adj. evangelizing II. m.f. evangelist, evangelizer.
e·van·ge·li·zar §04 tr. to evangelize, preach the gospel to.
e·va·po·ra·ble adj. evaporable.
e·va·po·ra·ción f. evaporation.
e·va·po·rar tr. to evaporate —reflex. *(convertirse en vapor)* to evaporate; FIG. *(desvanecerse)* to vanish, disappear.
e·va·po·ri·zar §04 tr. to vaporize, evaporate.
e·va·sión f. *(fuga)* escape, flight; *(evasiva)* excuse, evasion.
e·va·si·va f. I. evasion, subterfuge II. adj. see **evasivo, –va**.
e·va·si·va·men·te adv. evasively.
e·va·si·vo, –va I. adj. evasive, elusive II. f. see **evasiva**.

e·va·sor, –so·ra adj. evading, eluding.
e·ven·to m. chance event, contingency ◆ **en cualquier e.** in any event, in any case.
e·ven·tual adj. *(casual)* fortuitous, unexpected; *(para gastos imprevistos)* contingency or incidental (funds).
e·ven·tua·li·dad f. eventuality, contingency.
e·ven·tual·men·te adv. *(por casualidad)* by chance, unexpectedly; *(posiblemente)* possibly, perhaps.
e·ver·sión f. destruction, ruin.
e·vic·ción f. eviction, dispossession.
e·vi·den·cia f. *(certeza)* certainty, obviousness; AMER. proof, evidence ◆ **en e.** FIG. *(desairado)* out in the open, in the light; *(en ridículo)* in ridicule.
e·vi·den·ciar tr. *(probar)* to prove, demonstrate; *(hacer patente)* to make evident or clear.
e·vi·den·te adj. evident, clear, obvious ◆ **¡evidente!** obviously!, of course!
e·vi·den·te·men·te adv. evidently, clearly, obviously.
e·vi·ta·ble adj. evitable, avoidable.
e·vi·tar tr. *(precaver)* to avoid, prevent; *(eludir)* to elude, escape.
e·vi·ter·no, –na adj. everlasting, eternal.
e·vo m. THEOL. eternity; POET. eon, age ◆ **el medioevo** the Middle Ages.
e·vo·ca·ble adj. evocable.
e·vo·ca·ción f. evocation, evoking.
e·vo·ca·dor, –do·ra adj. evocative.
e·vo·car §70 tr. *(recordar)* to evoke, recall; FIG. *(invocar)* to invoke, call up (spirits).
e·vo·ca·ti·vo, –va adj. evocative.
e·vo·lu·ción f. evolution <*la e. de las especies* the evolution of the species>; *(desarrollo)* evolution <*la e. de una idea* the evolution of an idea>; *(transformación)* gradual change, transformation; MIL. *(maniobra)* evolution, maneuver.
e·vo·lu·cio·nar intr. *(desarrollar)* to evolve, develop; *(transformar)* to change, transform; MIL. *(maniobrar)* to perform military maneuvers.
e·vo·lu·cio·nis·mo m. evolutionism.
e·vo·lu·cio·nis·ta I. adj. evolutionary II. m.f. evolutionist.
e·vo·lu·ti·vo, –va adj. evolutionary, evolutional.
e·vo·qué, evoque see **evocar**.
ex·a·brup·to m. abrupt or sharp remark.
ex a·brup·to adv. *(inesperadamente)* abruptly, sharply; *(arrebatadamente)* violently, recklessly.
e·xac·ción f. *(exigencia de impuestos)* exaction, levying (of taxes); *(abuso)* extortion, exaction.
e·xa·cer·ba·ción f. exacerbation, aggravation.
e·xa·cer·bar tr. to exacerbate, aggravate.
e·xac·ta·men·te adv. exactly.
e·xac·ti·tud f. *(precisión)* exactitude, exactness; *(regularidad)* correctness, accuracy; *(puntualidad)* punctuality; *(rigor)* assiduousness, rigorousness.
e·xac·to, –ta adj. *(preciso)* exact, precise; *(correcto)* correct, accurate; *(puntual)* punctual; *(riguroso)* assiduous, rigorous ◆ **¡exacto!** exactly!, quite so!
e·xac·tor m. tax collector.
e·xa·ge·ra·ción f. exaggeration.
e·xa·ge·ra·do, –da I. past part. see **exagerar** II. adj. *(inflado)* exaggerated; *(que exagera)* exaggerating, exaggerative.
e·xa·ge·ra·dor, –do·ra I. adj. exaggerating, exaggerative II. m.f. exaggerator.
e·xa·ge·ran·te adj. exaggerating, exaggerative.
e·xa·ge·rar tr. to exaggerate, overstate.
e·xá·go·no m. hexagon.
e·xal·ta·ción f. *(glorificación)* exaltation, glorification; *(aumento de los sentidos)* heightening, stimulation; *(aumento del espíritu)* exhilaration, elation; *(sobrexitación)* over-excitement, hotheadedness; RELIG. ascent or advancement to the pontificate.
e·xal·ta·do, –da I. past part. see **exaltar** II. adj. *(glorificado)* exalted, glorified; *(sobrexcitado)* over-excited, hotheaded II. m.f. hothead.
e·xal·ta·dor, –do·ra I. adj. exalting II. m.f. exalter.
e·xal·tar tr. *(glorificar)* to exalt, glorify; *(elevar)* to elevate, raise —reflex. to become worked up or hotheaded ◆ **exaltarse la bilis** or **la cólera** to become irritated or angered.

e·xa·men m. *(investigación)* investigation, inspection; *(indagación)* survey; *(prueba)* examination, exam, test; *(interrogación)* interrogation ♦ **presentarse a un e.** *or* **sufrir un e.** EDUC. to take *or* sit for an examination *or* test • **e. de conciencia** self-examination • **e. de ingreso** entrance exam • **e. de Rorschach** PSYCH. Rorschach test • **e. de testigos** LAW interrogation *or* examination of witnesses • **e. final** EDUC. final exam • **someter a. e.** to examine.

e·xa·mi·na·dor, -do·ra m.f. examiner.

e·xa·mi·nan·do, -da I. pres. part. see **examinar** II. m.f. examinee.

e·xa·mi·nan·te adj. examining.

e·xa·mi·nar tr. *(probar)* to examine, test; *(inspeccionar)* to inspect, scrutinize; *(interrogar)* to interrogate, question —reflex. to take an exam <*se examinó de biología* he took an exam in biology>.

e·xan·güe adj. *(desangrado)* exsanguine, bloodless; FIG. *(aniquilado)* weak, exhausted; *(muerto)* dead.

e·xá·ni·me adj. *(sin vida)* inanimate, lifeless; FIG. *(debilitado)* weak, faint <*se quedó e. al oír de su muerte* he felt faint upon hearing of her death>.

e·xas·pe·ra·ción f. *(enojo)* exasperation, anger; *(intensificación)* exasperation, intensification <*la e. del dolor* the intensification of pain>.

e·xas·pe·ra·dor, -do·ra adj. exasperating.

e·xas·pe·rar tr. *(intensificar)* to exasperate, exacerbate; *(irritar)* to irritate, aggravate <*la sal exaspera la herida* salt irritates the wound>; FIG. *(enojar)* to exasperate, anger <*el discurso me exasperó* the speech angered me> —reflex. FIG. *(enojarse)* to become exasperated.

ex·car·ce·la·ción f. freeing, release (of a prisoner).

ex·car·ce·lar tr. to free, release (from prison).

ex·ca·va·ción f. excavation.

ex·ca·va·dor, -do·ra I. adj. excavating, digging II. f. excavator.

ex·ca·var tr. to excavate, dig.

ex·ce·den·te I. adj. *(excesivo)* excessive; *(sobrante)* excess, surplus; *(que está de permiso)* on leave II. m. excess, surplus.

ex·ce·der tr. to exceed, surpass —reflex. *(propasarse)* to exceed oneself, go beyond oneself <*excederse uno a sí mismo* to exceed oneself>; *(sobrepasar)* to go too far, overdo.

ex·ce·len·cia f. excellence ♦ **Excelencia** Excellency • **por e.** par excellence, pre-eminently.

ex·ce·len·te I. adj. excellent II. m. *(moneda)* old Spanish gold coin.

ex·ce·len·te·men·te adv. excellently.

ex·cél·sior adv. highest, most high.

ex·cel·so, -sa adj. sublime, lofty ♦ **El Excelso** the Almighty (God).

ex·cén·tri·ca·men·te adv. eccentrically.

ex·cen·tri·ci·dad f. *(extravagancia de carácter)* eccentricity, oddness; ASTRON., GEOM. eccentricity.

ex·cen·tri·cis·mo m. eccentricity.

ex·cén·tri·co, -ca I. adj. *(extravagante)* eccentric, odd; MATH. eccentric, abaxial II. f. MECH. eccentric (wheel).

ex·cep·ción f. exception; LAW demurrer, exception ♦ **a** *or* **con e. de** except for.

ex·cep·cio·nal adj. exceptional, exceptive <*circunstancias excepcionales* exceptional circumstances>; *(extraordinario)* unusual, outstanding.

ex·cep·cio·nal·men·te adv. exceptionally.

ex·cep·ti·vo, -va adj. exceptive.

ex·cep·to prep. except, excepting.

ex·cep·tua·ción f. exclusion, exemption.

ex·cep·tuar §67 tr. to exclude, exempt —reflex. to be excluded *or* exempted.

ex·ce·si·va·men·te adv. excessively.

ex·ce·si·vo, -va adj. excessive.

ex·ce·so m. *(sobra)* excess; FIG. *(abuso)* excess, abuse <*los excesos del poder* the excesses of power>; COM. surplus ♦ **en e.** to excess, too much • **e. de equipaje** excess baggage • **e. de peso** excess weight • **e. de velocidad** speeding.

ex·ci·pien·te m. PHARM. excipient.

ex·ci·sión f. SURG. excision.

ex·ci·ta·bi·li·dad f. excitability.

ex·ci·ta·ble adj. excitable.

ex·ci·ta·ción f. *(frenesí)* excitement; BIOL. excitation, stimulation.

ex·ci·ta·dor, -do·ra I. adj. exciting, stimulating II. m. ELEC. discharging rod, exciter.

ex·ci·tan·te I. adj. stimulating II. m. stimulant.

ex·ci·tar tr. *(estimular)* to excite, arouse <*e. las pasiones* to arouse passions>; *(incitar)* to incite, provoke <*e. las masas a rebelarse* to incite the masses to revolt>; BIOL. to excite, stimulate —reflex. to become excited, get worked up.

ex·ci·ta·ti·vo, -va I. adj. excitant, stimulating II. m. excitant, stimulant.

ex·cla·ma·ción f. *(grito)* exclamation; *(signo ortográfico)* exclamation point.

ex·cla·mar intr. to exclaim.

ex·cla·ma·ti·vo, -va *or* **ex·cla·ma·to·rio, -ria** adj. exclamatory.

ex·claus·tra·do, -da m.f. secularized monk *or* nun.

ex·cluir §18 tr. *(no admitir)* to exclude, bar <*le excluí de la lista* I excluded him from the list>; *(expulsar)* to throw out, expel <*le excluyeron de la reunión* they threw him out of the meeting>; *(descartar)* to exclude, rule out <*su actitud excluye una solución amistosa* his attitude rules out a friendly solution>.

ex·clu·sión f. exclusion.

ex·clu·si·va I. f. *(repulsa)* rejection; *(privilegio)* exclusive *or* sole right II. adj. see **exclusivo, -va.**

ex·clu·si·va·men·te adv. exclusively.

ex·clu·si·ve adv. *(exclusivamente)* exclusively; *(no incluyendo)* exclusive of, not including <*hasta el cinco de mayo e.* not including the fifth of May>.

ex·clu·si·vis·mo m. exclusivism.

ex·clu·si·vis·ta adj. & m.f. exclusivist.

ex·clu·si·vo, -va I. adj. exclusive II. f. see **exclusiva.**

ex·clu·ya, excluyo see **excluir.**

ex·clu·ye·ra, excluyó see **excluir.**

ex·co·gi·tar tr. to excogitate, think out.

ex·com·ba·tien·te adj. & m.f. MIL. veteran.

ex·co·mul·ga·do, -da I. past part. see **excomulgar** II. m.f. RELIG. excommunicant, excommunicated person.

ex·co·mul·gar §47 tr. RELIG. to excommunicate.

ex·co·mu·nión f. RELIG. excommunication.

ex·co·ria·ción f. excoriation, abrasion.

ex·co·riar tr. to excoriate, chafe <*se le excorió la pierna* he chafed his leg> —reflex. to be chafed.

ex·cre·cen·cia f. excrescence.

ex·cre·ción f. excretion.

ex·cre·men·tar intr. to defecate, evacuate (the bowels).

ex·cre·men·ti·cio, -cia adj. excremental.

ex·cre·men·to m. excrement.

ex·cre·tar intr. to excrete.

ex·cre·to, -ta adj. excretory.

ex·cul·pa·ción f. exculpation, exoneration.

ex·cul·par tr. to exculpate, exonerate.

ex·cur·sión f. *(paseo)* excursion, trip <*ir de e.* to go on an excursion>; MIL. incursion, raid ♦ **e. a pie** hike • **e. campestre** picnic • **e. de caza** hunting trip.

ex·cur·sio·nis·mo m. excursions, sightseeing ♦ **e. a pie** hiking, walking.

ex·cur·sio·nis·ta I. adj. excursionary II. m.f. excursionist, sightseer ♦ **e. a pie** hiker.

ex·cu·sa f. excuse ♦ **a e.** secretly • **buscar e.** to look for an excuse • **dar excusas** to make excuses • **¡nada de excusas!** no excuses! • **presentar sus excusas a** to apologize to.

ex·cu·sa·ble adj. *(perdonable)* excusable, pardonable; *(evitable)* avoidable.

ex·cu·sa·do, -da I. past part. see **excusar** II. adj. *(reservado)* reserved, private; *(inútil)* unnecessary, superfluous; exempt <*estar e. de* to be exempt from>; *(escondido)* hidden, secret <*una puerta e.* a secret door> ♦ **e. (es) decir que** needless to say that III. m. toilet.

ex·cu·sa·dor, -do·ra I. adj. excusing, exonerating II. m. deputy, stand-in.

ex·cu·sar tr. *(disculpar)* to excuse, pardon; *(evitar)* to avoid, prevent; to have no need <*excusas venir* you have no need to come>; to exempt <*e. del pago de impuestos* to exempt from the payment of taxes> ♦ **excusarle a alguien**

de algo to excuse someone for something —reflex. to excuse oneself ♦ **excusarse de** to refuse.

ex·cu·so m. *(disculpa)* excusing; *(evitación)* avoidance, avoiding.

e·xe·cra·ble adj. execrable, abominable.

e·xe·cra·ción f. execration ♦ **proferir execraciones** to utter curses.

e·xe·cra·dor, –do·ra I. adj. execrating II. m.f. execrator.

e·xe·crar tr. *(odiar)* to loathe, execrate; *(maldecir)* to curse, execrate.

e·xe·cra·to·rio, –ria adj. execratory.

e·xé·ge·sis f. exegesis.

e·xe·ge·ta m.f. exegete.

e·xen·ción f. exemption.

e·xen·tar tr. to exempt, excuse —reflex. to exempt oneself.

e·xen·to, –ta I. past part. see **eximir** and **exentar** II. adj. *(libre)* exempt, free <*estar e. de inquietud* to be free from worry>; *(descubierto)* clear, unobstructed; ARCHIT. freestanding ♦ **e. de aduanas** duty-free • **e. de alquileres** rent-free • **e. de impuestos** tax-exempt • **no e. de riesgos** not without danger.

e·xe·quias f.pl. funeral rites, obsequies.

e·xe·qui·ble adj. attainable.

ex·fo·lia·ción f. exfoliation.

ex·fo·lia·dor, –do·ra I. adj. tear-off II. m. *(calendario)* tear-off calendar; CHILE, MEX. loose-leaf notebook.

ex·fo·liar tr. & reflex. to exfoliate.

ex·ha·la·ción f. *(respiración)* exhalation; *(vapor)* fumes, vapor; *(estrella)* shooting star; *(centella)* flash of lightning ♦ **como una e.** in a flash, like a flash.

ex·ha·la·dor, –do·ra adj. exhaling, emitting.

ex·ha·lar tr. *(despedir)* to exhale, give off (gases, odors); *(suspiros)* to breathe (a sigh) —reflex. *(respirar)* to breathe hard; *(correr)* to hurry, run.

ex·haus·ti·vo, –va adj. exhaustive.

ex·haus·to, –ta adj. exhausted.

ex·he·re·dar tr. to disinherit.

ex·hi·bi·ción f. *(exposición)* exhibition, show; *(de alta costura)* presentation (of new fashions); *(de escaparate* window display>; showing <*la pobre e. del equipo* the team's poor showing>; CINEM. showing (of a movie); LAW exhibit (in a court of law).

ex·hi·bi·cio·nis·mo m. exhibitionism.

ex·hi·bi·cio·nis·ta m.f. exhibitionist.

ex·hi·bir tr. *(mostrar)* to exhibit, display; *(manifestar)* to show <*e. un pasaporte* to show a passport>; *(modelos de alta costura)* to present (a collection of fashions); *(una película)* to show (a movie); LAW to exhibit (a document); MEX. to pay <*e. mil pesos al contado* to pay a thousand pesos in cash> —reflex. to show up, to show oneself.

ex·hor·ta·ción f. exhortation.

ex·hor·ta·dor, –do·ra I. adj. exhorting II. m.f. exhorter.

ex·hor·tar tr. to exhort.

ex·hor·ta·to·rio, –ria adj. exhortatory.

ex·hu·ma·ción f. exhumation, disinterment.

ex·hu·mar tr. to exhume, disinter.

e·xi·gen·cia f. exigency, requirement, demand ♦ **según las exigencias de la situación** as the situation demands • **tener muchas exigencias** to be very demanding.

e·xi·gen·te I. adj. demanding, exacting II. m.f. demanding person.

e·xi·gi·bi·li·dad f. liability.

e·xi·gi·ble adj. payable on demand.

e·xi·gir §32 tr. *(cobrar)* to exact <*e. una contribución a* to exact a contribution from>; *(pedir)* to demand <*e. el pago a* to demand payment from>; *(requerir)* to call for, require <*no e. comentario* not to call for any comment>.

e·xi·güi·dad f. meagerness, scantiness.

e·xi·guo, –gua adj. small, scanty.

e·xi·la·do, –da or **e·xi·lia·do, –da** I. past part. see **exilar** or **exiliar** II. adj. exiled, in exile III. m.f. exile.

e·xi·lar or **e·xi·liar** tr. to exile, banish —reflex. to be exiled or banished.

e·xi·lio m. exile, banishment ♦ **en el e.** in exile.

e·xi·men·te adj. LAW exonerating, absolving <*circunstancia e.* exonerating circumstance>.

e·xi·mio, –mia adj. *(distinguido)* distinguished, eminent; *(excelente)* select, choice.

e·xi·mir tr. to free <*e. de cualquier obligación con él* to free from any obligation to him> ♦ **e. a alguien de** to exempt someone from <*eximen al hombre de pagar los impuestos* they are exempting the man from paying taxes> —reflex. to excuse oneself.

e·xis·ten·cia f. existence ♦ **existencias** COM. stock, goods.

e·xis·ten·cial adj. existential.

e·xis·ten·cia·lis·mo m. PHILOS. existentialism.

e·xis·ten·cia·lis·ta adj. & m.f. PHILOS. existentialist.

e·xis·ten·te adj. *(que existe)* existing, existent; COM. in stock.

e·xis·tir intr. to exist, be in existence.

é·xi·to m. *(resultado)* result, outcome; *(triunfo)* success; CINEM., MUS., THEAT. hit ♦ **con é.** successfully • **é. de librería** best seller • **é. de taquilla** box-office hit *or* smash • **é. rotundo** huge *or* overwhelming success • **tener é.** to be successful.

e·xi·to·so, –sa adj. AMER. successful.

é·xo·do m. exodus ♦ **Éxodo** BIBL. Exodus.

e·xó·ge·no, –na adj. ANAT. exogenous.

e·xo·ne·ra·ción f. *(acción de exonerar)* exoneration; *(de una tarea)* freeing, relief; *(de un empleo)* dismissal.

e·xo·ne·rar tr. *(libertar)* to free, exonerate; *(despedir)* to dismiss ♦ **e. el vientre** to have a bowel movement.

e·xo·ra·ble adj. exorable, easily persuaded.

e·xo·rar tr. to implore, beseech.

e·xor·bi·tan·cia f. exorbitance, excess.

e·xor·bi·tan·te adj. exorbitant, excessive.

e·xor·cis·mo m. exorcism.

e·xor·cis·ta m. exorcist.

e·xor·ci·zar §04 tr. to exorcise.

e·xor·dio m. preamble, introduction.

e·xor·nar tr. to beautify, embellish.

e·xo·té·ri·co, –ca adj. *(común)* common, popular; PHILOS. exoteric.

e·xo·tér·mi·co, –ca adj. CHEM. exothermic.

e·xo·ti·ci·dad or **e·xo·ti·quez** f. exoticism.

e·xó·ti·co, –ca adj. exotic.

e·xo·tis·mo m. exoticism.

ex·pan·dir tr. & reflex. to expand, spread.

ex·pan·si·ble adj. expansible.

ex·pan·sión f. *(dilatación)* expansion, dilation; *(propagación)* expansion, spread; *(recreo)* relaxation, recreation; FIG. *(franqueza)* expansiveness.

ex·pan·sio·nar tr. to expand —reflex. *(dilatarse)* to expand; *(recrearse)* to relax, rest ♦ **e. con uno** to open one's heart to someone.

ex·pan·sio·nis·mo m. POL. expansionism.

ex·pan·sio·nis·ta adj. & m.f. POL. expansionist.

ex·pan·si·vo, –va adj. *(expansible)* expandable, expansible; FIG. *(franco)* open, expansive.

ex·pa·tria·ción f. expatriation.

ex·pa·triar §30 tr. to expatriate, banish —reflex. *(exiliarse)* to go into exile; *(emigrar)* to emigrate.

ex·pec·ta·ble adj. eminent, notable.

ex·pec·ta·ción f. *(anticipación)* expectation, anticipation; MED. expectation ♦ **e. de vida** life expectancy.

ex·pec·tan·te adj. expectant.

ex·pec·ta·ti·va I. f. *(anticipación)* expectation, anticipation; *(esperanza)* hope; *(perspectiva)* prospect ♦ **estar en la e. de** to be on the lookout for, to be expecting II. adj. see **expectativo, –va.**

ex·pec·ta·ti·vo, –va I. adj. expectant, hopeful II. f. see **expectativa.**

ex·pec·to·ra·ción f. expectoration.

ex·pec·to·ran·te adj. & m. expectorant.

ex·pec·to·rar tr. & intr. to expectorate.

ex·pe·di·ción f. *(excursión)* expedition; *(prontitud)* speed, dispatch; COM. shipping, shipment ♦ **e. de salvamento** rescue mission • **e. militar** military expedition.

ex·pe·di·cio·na·rio, –ria I. adj. expeditionary II. m.f. *(que participa en una expedición)* member of an expedition; *(expedidor)* sender.

ex·pe·di·dor, –do·ra m.f. sender, shipper —m. *(aparato)* dispenser.

ex·pe·dien·te I. adj. expedient II. m. *(medios)* expedient;

(facilidad) expedient, resource, device; *(título)* reason, motive; file, dossier, record <*e. policíaco* police file>; LAW proceedings <*instruir un e.* to start proceedings> ♦ **cubrir el e.** to do just enough to fulfill one's obligations • **dar e. a** to dispose of, to expedite • **e. académico** transcript • **formar** *or* **instruir e. a un funcionario** to impeach a public official • **tener recurso al e. de** to resort to.

ex·pe·dir §48 tr. *(enviar)* to send, ship; *(despachar)* to expedite, dispatch <*e. un negocio* to expedite a business deal>; *(extender)* to draw up <*e. un contrato* to draw up a contract>; *(dictar)* to issue <*e. un decreto* to issue a decree>; *(encargarse de)* to deal with.

ex·pe·di·tar tr. S. AMER. to expedite, dispatch.

ex·pe·di·ti·vo, –va adj. *(que permite obrar rápidamente)* expeditious <*un procedimiento e.* an expeditious method>; *(que obra rápidamente)* fast, efficient <*un obrero e.* a fast worker>.

ex·pe·di·to, –ta adj. *(libre de estorbos)* ready, free <*e. para obrar* free to act>; *(una vía)* clear, open.

ex·pe·len·te adj. expelling ♦ **bomba e.** force pump.

ex·pe·ler tr. to expel, eject.

ex·pen·de·dor, –do·ra I. adj. spending II. m.f. *(vendedor al detalle)* dealer, retailer; THEAT. ticket agent; *(de moneda falsa)* distributor of counterfeit money ♦ **e. automático** vending machine.

ex·pen·de·du·rí·a f. *(de tabaco)* tobacco shop; *(de billetes de teatro)* ticket office; *(de bebidas espirituosas)* liquor store.

ex·pen·der tr. *(gastar)* to expend, spend; *(hacer circular moneda falsa)* to circulate, pass (counterfeit money); *(vender al por menor)* to retail, sell.

ex·pen·dio m. *(gasto)* expense, outlay; AMER. *(tienda)* store, shop; *(venta al por menor)* retailing.

ex·pen·sar tr. GUAT., MEX. to defray the costs of.

ex·pen·sas f.pl. expenses, costs ♦ **a e. de** at the expense of • **a mis e.** at my expense.

ex·pe·rien·cia f. *(pericia)* experience; CHEM., PHYS. experiment ♦ **por e.** from experience.

ex·pe·ri·men·ta·ción f. experimentation.

ex·pe·ri·men·ta·do, –da I. past part. see **experimentar** II. adj. experienced.

ex·pe·ri·men·ta·dor, –do·ra I. adj. experimenting II. m.f. experimenter.

ex·pe·ri·men·tal adj. experimental.

ex·pe·ri·men·ta·lis·mo m. experimentalism.

ex·pe·ri·men·tal·men·te adv. experimentally.

ex·pe·ri·men·tar tr. *(probar)* to try out, test; *(sentir en sí)* to experience, undergo; *(sufrir)* to suffer (a loss); *(mostrar)* to show (a gain) ♦ **e. con** to experiment with • **e. en** to experiment on.

ex·pe·ri·men·to m. *(experiencia)* experiment <*un e. de química* a chemistry experiment>; *(acción)* experimentation.

ex·per·ti·cia f. VEN. expertise, skill.

ex·per·to adj. & m. expert.

ex·pia·ble adj. expiable.

ex·pia·ción f. expiation, atonement ♦ **Día de Expiación** RELIG. Day of Atonement.

ex·piar §30 tr. to atone for, expiate.

ex·pia·ti·vo, –va adj. expiative, expiatory.

ex·pia·to·rio, –ria adj. expiatory.

ex·pi·da, expido see **expedir**.

ex·pi·die·ra, expidió see **expedir**.

ex·pi·ra·ción f. expiration.

ex·pi·rar intr. *(morir)* to expire, die; FIG. *(acabarse)* to expire, end.

ex·pla·na·ción f. *(nivelación)* leveling, grading; FIG. *(aclaración)* explanation, elucidation.

ex·pla·na·da f. esplanade, walkway; *(fortificación)* esplanade, glacis.

ex·pla·nar tr. *(nivelar)* to level, grade; FIG. *(aclarar)* to explain, elucidate.

ex·pla·ya·do, –da I. past part. see **explayar** II. adj. HER. displayed with wings outspread (an eagle).

ex·pla·yar tr. to extend, spread out —reflex. FIG. *(dilatarse)* to expatiate, speak at length; FIG. *(irse a divertir)* to relax, unwind; *(confiarse)* to unbosom oneself, confide ♦ **e. a** *or* **con** to confide in.

ex·ple·ti·vo, –va adj. expletive.

ex·pli·ca·ble adj. explicable, explainable.

ex·pli·ca·ción f. explanation ♦ **pedir explicaciones** to demand an explanation • **sin dar explicaciones** without giving a reason.

ex·pli·ca·de·ras f.pl. COLL. way of explaining oneself ♦ **tener buenas e.** to have a knack for explaining things.

ex·pli·car §70 tr. *(hacer comprender)* to explain; *(exponer)* to expound; *(comentar)* to comment on, explain; *(justificar)* to explain, justify; *(enseñar)* to teach —intr. to lecture —reflex. to explain oneself <*¡explíquese usted!* explain yourself!>; to be explained <*esto no se explica fácilmente* this cannot be explained easily>; *(comprender)* to understand <*ahora me lo explico* now I understand it>.

ex·pli·ca·ti·vo, –va adj. explanatory.

ex·plí·ci·ta·men·te adv. explicitly.

ex·plí·ci·to, –ta adj. explicit.

ex·plo·ra·ción f. *(de un territorio)* exploration; *(de minas)* prospecting; MIL. scouting, reconnaissance; TELEV. scanning <*línea de e.* scanning line> ♦ **e. submarina** *(investigaciones)* underwater exploration; *(deporte)* skin diving.

ex·plo·ra·dor, –do·ra I. adj. exploring, exploratory; TELEV. scanning <*haz e.* scanning beam>; MIL. scouting II. m.f. explorer III. m. MIL. scout; MED. probe; TELEV. scanning disk; *(niño)* Boy Scout —f. *(niña)* Girl Scout.

ex·plo·rar tr. *(un terreno)* to explore; *(minas)* to prospect; *(una situación)* to investigate; MED. to probe; MIL. to scout, reconnoiter; TELEV. to scan —intr. to explore.

ex·plo·ra·to·rio, –ria adj. exploratory.

ex·plo·sión f. *(detonación)* explosion, detonation; FIG. *(manifestación)* explosion, outburst <*e. de ira* outburst of anger> ♦ **e. demográfica** population explosion • **hacer e.** to explode • **motor de e.** internal combustion engine.

ex·plo·si·vo, –va I. adj. explosive II. m. *(substancia)* explosive; *(bomba)* bomb ♦ **alto e., e. detonante, e. de gran potencia** *or* **e. rompedor** high explosive —f. PHONET. explosive.

ex·plo·ta·ble adj. workable, exploitable.

ex·plo·ta·ción f. *(operación)* running, operating, working; *(cultivación)* cultivation; *(empresa)* plant <*e. industrial* industrial plant>; exploitation <*la e. de los obreros* the exploitation of the workers> ♦ **en e.** in operation.

ex·plo·ta·dor, –do·ra I. adj. *(operador)* running, operating; *(que abusa)* exploiting II. m.f. *(operador)* operator, cultivator, worker; *(el que abusa)* exploiter.

ex·plo·tar tr. *(operar)* to run, operate; *(una mina)* to work; *(cultivar)* to cultivate; *(sacar provecho de)* to exploit; *(estallar)* to explode —intr. to go off, explode.

ex·po·lia·ción f. plundering, spoliation.

ex·po·lia·dor, –do·ra I. adj. plundering, despoiling II. m.f. plunderer, despoiler.

ex·po·liar tr. to plunder, despoil.

ex·pon·drá, expondría see **exponer**.

ex·po·nen·cial adj. & f. MATH. exponential.

ex·po·nen·te I. adj. explaining, expounding II. m.f. exponent —m. MATH. exponent; *(ejemplo)* example <*un magnífico e.* a magnificent example>; AMER. model, best of its kind <*e. de calidad* the best in quality>.

ex·po·ner §54 tr. *(poner a la vista)* to expose; *(explicar)* to propound, explain; *(proponer)* to put forward; *(declarar)* to state; *(exhibir)* to exhibit; *(arriesgar)* to expose to danger, to risk; *(abandonar)* to abandon; RELIG. to expose; PHOTOG. to expose —reflex. to expose oneself <*exponerse al peligro* to expose oneself to danger>; to run the risk of <*e. a pescar un constipado* to run the risk of catching a cold>.

ex·por·ta·ble adj. exportable.

ex·por·ta·ción f. *(acción de exportar)* exportation, exporting; *(mercancías)* exports; *(artículo de e.)* export (item).

ex·por·ta·dor, –do·ra I. adj. exporting II. m.f. exporter.

ex·por·tar tr. & intr. to export.

ex·po·si·ción f. *(exhibición)* exhibition, show <*e. de modas* fashion show>; *(feria)* fair <*e. universal* world's fair>; *(explicación)* explanation; *(orientación)* exposure <*e. al sol* exposure to the sun>; *(petición)* petition, claim; *(declaración)* exposition, statement; LIT., MUS., RELIG. exposition; PHOTOG. exposure.

ex·po·sí·me·tro m. PHOTOG. exposure meter, light meter.

ex·po·si·ti·vo, –va adj. expositive.

ex·pó·si·to, –ta I. adj. abandoned II. m.f. foundling.

ex·po·si·tor, –to·ra I. adj. expository II. m.f. *(que expone una teoría)* exponent; *(que concurre a una exposición pública)* exhibitor.

ex·prés m. RAIL. express train; MEX. transport company; *(café)* espresso (coffee).

ex·pre·sa·do, –da I. past part. see **expresar** II. adj. above-mentioned.

ex·pre·sa·men·te adv. *(claramente)* clearly, explicitly; *(de propósito)* expressly, specifically; *(rápidamente)* rapidly, swiftly.

ex·pre·sar tr. to express, convey —reflex. to express oneself.

ex·pre·sión f. *(frase)* expression, phrase; *(manifestación)* expression <*la e. del dolor* the expression of sorrow>; *(zumo exprimido)* extract; MATH. expression, term ♦ **expresiones** regards • **reducir a la mínima e.** MATH. to simplify, reduce to the lowest terms; FIG. *(disminuir)* to reduce, diminish.

ex·pre·sio·nis·mo m. ARTS expressionism.

ex·pre·si·va·men·te adv. *(con viveza)* expressively; *(afectuosamente)* affectionately, warmly.

ex·pre·si·vo, –va adj. expressive <*una mirada e.* an expressive glance>; *(afectuoso)* affectionate, warm.

ex·pre·so, –sa I. past part. see **expresar** II. adj. *(especificado)* express, specific; *(directo)* express, direct III. m. RAIL. *(tren)* express train; *(correo)* express mail ♦ **e. aéreo** air express.

ex·pri·mi·ble adj. capable of being pressed *or* squeezed.

ex·pri·mi·dor m. CUL. squeezer, juicer.

ex·pri·mir tr. *(extraer)* to squeeze; *(estrujar)* to squeeze dry; FIG. *(expresar)* to express *or* communicate vividly —reflex. ♦ **e. el cerebro** FIG. to rack one's brains.

ex·pro·pia·ción f. LAW expropriation.

ex·pro·piar tr. LAW to expropriate.

ex·pues·to, –ta I. past part. see **exponer** II. adj. *(peligroso)* dangerous, hazardous; *(vulnerable)* exposed, liable; *(exhibido)* exhibited, on display.

ex·pug·nar tr. MIL. to take by storm.

ex·pul·sar tr. to expel, drive out.

ex·pul·sión f. *(eyección)* ejection, expulsion; SPORT. disarming thrust, sending off.

ex·pur·ga·ción f. *(purificación)* purge, purification; FIG. *(de un libro)* expurgation.

ex·pur·gar §47 tr. *(purificar)* to purge, purify; FIG. *(un libro)* to expurgate.

ex·pur·ga·ti·vo, –va adj. purging, expurgating.

ex·pur·ga·to·rio, –ria I. adj. purging, expurgating II. m. RELIG. index of books (banned by the Roman Catholic Church).

ex·pu·sie·ra, expuso see **exponer.**

ex·qui·si·ta·men·te adv. exquisitely.

ex·qui·si·tez f. [pl. **-te·ces**] exquisiteness.

ex·qui·si·to, –ta adj. *(delicado)* exquisite, delicate; *(delicioso)* delicious, sumptuous.

ex·san·güe adj. MED. exsanguine, anemic.

ex·ta·siar·se §30 reflex. to become ecstatic, go into rapture.

éx·ta·sis f. [pl. **-sis**] *(arrobamiento)* ecstasy, rapture; MED. stasis.

ex·tá·ti·co, –ca adj. *(arrebatado)* ecstatic, enraptured; FIG. *(profundo)* deep, profound.

ex·ta·tis·mo m. state of ecstasy *or* exaltation.

ex·tem·po·ra·nei·dad f. untimeliness, inopportuneness.

ex·tem·po·rá·ne·o, –a adj. untimely, inopportune.

ex·ten·der §50 tr. *(expandir)* to extend, expand, enlarge <*el rey extendió el imperio* the king expanded the empire>; *(ampliar)* to extend, stretch <*extendieron los límites de su poder* they stretched the limits of their power>; *(desdoblar)* to spread out <*e. el mantel* to spread out the tablecloth>; *(exparcir)* to spread <*e. la pintura* to spread the paint>; *(ofrecer)* to offer, extend <*extendió la mano como una señal de amistad* he extended his hand as a sign of friendship>; *(prolongar)* to prolong, extend; *(despachar)* to draw up, issue <*e. un giro* to draw up a bill of exchange>; FIG. *(propagar)* to spread, propagate <*e. una creencia* to spread a belief> —reflex. *(ocupar)* to stretch, extend <*la finca se extiende por ambos lados del río* the farm extends along both sides of the river>; *(durar)* to last <*su reinado se extendió hasta el fin del siglo* his reign lasted

until the end of the century>; *(dilatarse)* to expatiate, speak at length; FIG. *(propagarse)* to spread <*sus ideas se extendían por todo el país* his ideas spread throughout the country>; *(alcanzar)* to extend, range.

ex·ten·di·do, –da I. past part. see **extender** II. adj. *(esparcido)* spread out, extended; *(abierto)* outstretched, open; *(diseminado)* widespread, prevalent.

ex·ten·sa·men·te adv. extensively.

ex·ten·si·bi·li·dad f. extensibility.

ex·ten·si·ble adj. extensible, extendible.

ex·ten·sión f. *(expansión)* extension; *(amplitud)* expanse, stretch; *(dimensión)* extent, size; *(duración)* duration, length; *(importancia)* extent, scope <*la e. del movimiento agrícola* the scope of the agricultural movement>; ELEC., GEOM., GRAM., LOG. extension; AMER., TELEC. extension.

ex·ten·si·vo, –va adj. *(que extiende)* extending; *(flexible)* extendible, extensible; *(grande)* extensive, wide; *(por extensión)* extended <*el sentido e. de una palabra* the extended sense of a word>.

ex·ten·so, –sa I. past part. see **extender** I. adj. extensive, ample, vast ♦ **por e.** at length, in (great) detail.

ex·te·nua·ción f. *(debilitación)* debilitation, weakening; RHET. litotes.

ex·te·nua·do, –da I. past part. see **extenuar** II. adj. debilitated, weakened.

ex·te·nuar §67 tr. to debilitate, weaken.

ex·te·rior I. adj. *(externo)* exterior, outer; *(extranjero)* foreign <*comercio e.* foreign trade> II. m. *(superficie)* exterior, outside; *(apariencia)* personal appearance; *(el extranjero)* foreign countries ♦ **al e.** out, outside • **exteriores** CINEM. exterior shots, exteriors.

ex·te·rio·ri·cé, exteriorice see **exteriorizar.**

ex·te·rio·ri·dad f. *(calidad de externo)* exteriority, externality; *(apariencia)* personal appearance, mien; *(demostración afectiva)* superficiality, shallowness ♦ **exterioridades** pomp, show.

ex·te·rio·ri·za·ción f. externalization, manifestation.

ex·te·rio·ri·zar §04 tr. to express, externalize.

ex·te·rior·men·te adv. externally, outwardly.

ex·ter·mi·na·ble adj. exterminable.

ex·ter·mi·na·ción f. var. of **exterminio.**

ex·ter·mi·na·dor, –do·ra I. adj. exterminating II. m.f. exterminator.

ex·ter·mi·nar tr. *(acabar del todo)* to exterminate, eradicate; *(devastar)* to lay waste (to), devastate.

ex·ter·mi·nio m. *(destrucción)* extermination, eradication; *(devastación)* devastation, ruin.

ex·ter·na·do m. EDUC. day school.

ex·ter·na·men·te adv. externally, outwardly.

ex·ter·no, –na I. adj. *(exterior)* external, outward; GEOM. exterior <*ángulo e.* exterior angle>; EDUC. day (school) <*alumno e.* day school pupil> II. m.f. EDUC. day school pupil.

ex·tien·da, extiende see **extender.**

ex·tin·ción f. *(apagamiento)* extinguishing, extinguishment; *(destrucción)* destruction, obliteration; *(desaparición)* extinction, dying out.

ex·tin·gui·ble adj. extinguishable.

ex·tin·guir §26 tr. *(apagar)* to extinguish, put out; *(destruir)* to wipe out, destroy —reflex. *(apagarse)* to fade, go out; *(desaparecerse)* to become extinct, die out.

ex·tin·ti·vo, –va adj. *(que causa extinción)* extinctive; LAW *(que cancela)* extinguishing.

ex·tin·to, –ta I. past part. see **extinguir** II. adj. *(apagado)* extinguished; *(desaparecido)* extinct; ARG., CHILE late, deceased <*el individuo e.* the deceased (individual)>.

ex·tin·tor I. adj. extinguishing II. m. fire extinguisher.

ex·tir·pa·ción f. extirpation.

ex·tir·pa·dor, –do·ra I. adj. extirpative II. m.f. *(persona)* extirpator —m. AGR. *(aparato)* cultivator.

ex·tir·par tr. *(desarraigar)* to extirpate, uproot; FIG. *(eradicar)* to eradicate, wipe out.

ex·tor·nar tr. MEX. to transfer an entry from debit to credit (in bookkeeping).

ex·tor·sión f. *(despojo)* extortion, exaction; FIG. *(molestia)* harm, trouble.

ex·tor·sio·na·dor, –do·ra I. adj. extortionary II. m.f. extortioner, extortionist.

ex·tor·sio·nar tr. to extort.
ex·tra I. adj. *(notable)* extraordinary, remarkable; *(adicional)* additional, extra ♦ **horas e.** overtime II. prep. ♦ **e. de** COLL. besides, in additon to III. m.f. CINEM., THEAT. *(comparsa)* extra —m. FIG. *(gaje)* extra, gratuity; *(gasto)* extra charge *or* expense; *(comida)* seconds, extra helping.
ex·trac·ción f. *(acción y efecto)* extraction; *(orígenes)* extraction, origin.
ex·trac·tar tr. to abstract, summarize.
ex·trac·ti·vo, –va adj. extractive.
ex·trac·to m. *(compendio)* abstract, summary; *(perfume)* essence; *(substancia concentrada)* extract; LAW *(resumen)* brief, legal abstract ♦ **e. amargo** CHEM. bitter principle • **e. de malta** AGR. malt extract • **e. de Saturno** CHEM. lead acetate • **e. tebaico** opium extract.
ex·trac·tor, –to·ra m.f. extractor.
ex·tra·di·ción f. LAW extradition.
ex·tra·er §72 tr. *(sacar)* to extract; *(hacer salir)* to remove, withdraw; CHEM., MATH. to extract.
ex·tra·hu·ma·no, –na adj. nonhuman, alien.
ex·tra·ju·di·cial adj. extrajudicial.
ex·tra·li·mi·tar·se reflex. to overstep one's power *or* authority.
ex·tra·mu·ros adv. outside (a town or city).
ex·tran·je·ro, –ra I. adj. *(extraño)* alien, foreign; AMER. non-Spanish-speaking II. m.f. *(persona)* foreigner, alien —m. *(otros países)* abroad, foreign countries ♦ **del e.** from abroad • **en** *or* **por el e.** abroad • **estar en el e.** to be abroad • **ir al e.** to go abroad.
ex·tra·ña·men·te adv. strangely, oddly.
ex·tra·ña·mien·to m. *(asombro)* surprise, astonishment; *(destierro)* exile, banishment; *(alejamiento)* alienation, estrangement.
ex·tra·ñar tr. *(desterrar)* to banish, exile; *(privar)* to estrange; *(sentir la novedad)* to find strange, not to be used to <*le extrañan las horas* he is not used to the hours>; *(asombrar)* to surprise; AMER. to miss <*e. a los amigos* to miss one's friends> —reflex. *(maravillarse)* to be surprised *or* astonished; *(desterrarse)* to go into exile.
ex·tra·ñe·za f. *(rareza)* strangeness, oddness; *(cosa rara)* rarity; *(alejamiento)* estrangement, alienation; *(asombro)* surprise, astonishment.
ex·tra·ño, –ña I. adj. *(extranjero)* foreign, alien; *(raro)* strange, odd; *(que no tiene que ver)* extraneous; *(extravagante)* eccentric II. m.f. *(extranjero)* foreigner, alien; *(desconocido)* stranger.
ex·tra·o·fi·cial adj. unofficial, nonofficial.
ex·tra·o·fi·cial·men·te adv. unofficially.
ex·tra·or·di·na·ria·men·te adv. extraordinarily.
ex·tra·or·di·na·rio, –ria I. adj. *(excepcional)* extraordinary, uncommon; *(extraño)* strange, odd II. m. *(correo urgente)* special delivery; *(plato)* extra dish (at a meal); *(periódico)* special edition; *(remuneración)* bonus.
ex·tra·po·la·ción f. extrapolation.
ex·tra·po·lar tr. to extrapolate.
ex·tra·te·rre·no, –na *or* **ex·tra·te·rres·tre** adj. & m.f. extraterrestrial.
ex·tra·te·rri·to·ria·li·dad f. DIPL., LAW extraterritoriality.
ex·tra·va·gan·cia f. *(rareza)* oddness, strangeness; *(excentricidad)* eccentricity ♦ **decir extravagancias** to talk nonsense.
ex·tra·va·gan·te I. adj. *(raro)* odd, strange; *(excéntrico)* eccentric II. m.f. *(persona)* eccentric (person).
ex·tra·ve·nar tr. MED. to bleed, let (blood) flow from the veins; FIG. *(desviar)* to displace —reflex. MED. to flow from the veins (blood).
ex·tra·ver·ti·do, –da I. adj. extroverted, outgoing II. m.f. extrovert, outgoing person.
ex·tra·via·do, –da I. past part. see **extraviar** II. adj. *(apartado)* out-of-the-way, unfrequented; *(perdido)* lost, missing; *(desordenado)* wild, unruly.
ex·tra·viar §30 tr. *(desviar)* to lead astray, misguide; *(perder)* to misplace, lose —reflex. *(perderse)* to be misplaced, get lost; FIG. *(pervertirse)* to go astray; *(equivocarse)* to be mistaken, err.
ex·tra·ví·o m. *(pérdida del camino)* going astray, losing one's way; *(pérdida)* misplacement, loss; FIG. *(desorden)* unruli-

ness, misconduct; *(error)* mistake, error; *(locura)* madness.
ex·tre·ma·da·men·te adv. extremely, exceedingly.
Ex·tre·ma·du·ra f. Extremadura.
ex·tre·mar tr. to carry to an extreme —reflex. to take great pains, exert oneself to the utmost.
ex·tre·ma·un·ción f. RELIG. extreme unction.
ex·tre·me·ño, –ña adj. & m.f. of Extremadura.
ex·tre·mi·dad f. *(punta)* end, tip; *(parte extrema)* extremity; FIG. *(último grado)* border, edge; *(último momento)* brink, verge ♦ **extremidades** ANAT. extremities • **la última e.** the last moment.
ex·tre·mis·mo m. extremism.
ex·tre·mis·ta adj. & m.f. extremist.
ex·tre·mo, –ma I. adj. *(último)* last, ultimate; *(intenso)* extreme <*frío e.* extreme cold>; *(excesivo)* greatest, utmost; *(distante)* far, farthest ♦ **Extremo Oriente** Far East II. m. *(fin)* end, extremity <*el e. de la calle* the end of the street>; *(lado)* side <*el e. del río* the riverside>; extreme <*pasaron de un e. al otro* they went from one extreme to the other>; FIG. *(esmero)* great care; SPORT. wing ♦ **con** *or* **en e.** in the extreme, extremely • **de e. a e.** from one end to the other • **hacer extremos** to gush, be effusive —f. RELIG. extreme unction.
ex·tre·mo·so, –sa adj. *(excesivo)* extreme, excessive; *(cariñoso)* demonstrative, effusive.
ex·trín·se·co, –ca adj. extrinsic.
ex·tro·ver·sión f. extroversion, extraversion.
ex·tro·ver·ti·do, –da I. adj. extroverted, extraverted II. m.f. extrovert, extravert.
e·xu·be·ran·cia f. exuberance, abundance.
e·xu·be·ran·te adj. exuberant, abundant.
e·xu·da·ción f. exudation.
e·xu·da·do, –da I. past part. see **exudar** II. m. exudate, exudation.
e·xu·dar tr. & intr. to exude.
e·xul·ce·ra·ción f. MED. ulceration, chafing.
e·xul·ta·ción f. exultation, rejoicing.
e·xul·tar intr. to exult, rejoice.
e·ya·cu·la·ción f. PHYSIOL. ejaculation.
e·ya·cu·lar tr. PHYSIOL. to ejaculate.
e·yec·ción f. *(deyección)* excretion, elimination; *(extracción)* extraction, removal.

F

f, F f. seventh letter of the Spanish alphabet.
fa m. [pl. **fa**] MUS. fa (fourth tone of the diatonic scale); PERU entertainment, diversion.
fá·bri·ca f. *(fabricación)* making, manufacture; *(factoría)* factory, works; *(edificio)* building, construction; *(construcción de ladrillo o piedra)* brick *or* stone masonry; *(renta)* church building funds; FIG. *(invención)* invention, fabrication; COL. still, alembic ♦ **de f.** CONST. stonework, built of brick *or* stone and mortar • **f. de cerveza** brewery • **f. de conservas** canning plant, cannery • **f. de harina** flour mill • **f. de montaje** *or* **de ensamblaje** assembly plant • **f. de muebles** furniture factory.
fa·bri·ca·ción f. *(manufactura)* making, manufacture; *(construcción)* construction; *(de f. casera)* homemade • **estar en f.** to be in production • **f. en serie** mass production.
fa·bri·ca·dor, –do·ra I. adj. *(que manufactura)* manufacturing, fabricative; *(que inventa)* fabricating, scheming II. m.f. *(fabricante)* manufacturer, maker; *(inventor)* fabricator, inventor; MARIT. constructor.
fa·bri·can·te m. *(manufacturador)* manufacturer, maker; *(dueño)* factory owner.
fa·bri·car §70 tr. *(manufacturar)* to manufacture, make; *(construir)* to build, construct; *(inventar)* to fabricate, invent; *(labrar)* to work ♦ **f. en serie** to mass-produce.
fa·bril adj. manufacturing <*centro f.* manufacturing center>.
fá·bu·la f. *(cuento)* fable, tale; *(leyenda)* fable, legend; *(in-*

vención) lie, fiction; *(objeto de burla)* laughingstock; *(habladuría)* gossip, talk; *(argumento)* plot, story.

fa·bu·lo·sa·men·te adv. *(excesivamente)* fabulously, extremely; *(fingidamente)* falsely.

fa·bu·lo·so, –sa adj. *(imaginario)* fabled, imaginary; *(extraordinario)* fabulous, extraordinary; *(increíble)* incredible; remote, mythical *<tiempos fabulosos* mythical times>.

fa·ca f. large knife (with curved blade).

fac·ción f. *(partido)* faction, party; *(grupo amotinado)* insurgent *or* rebellious group; *(rasgo)* feature, facial feature *<tiene las facciones angulosas* he has angular features>; MIL. *(acción)* combat, battle; duty *<estar de f. de guardia* to be on guard duty>.

fac·cio·na·rio, –ria adj. factional, partisan.

fac·cio·so, –sa I. adj. *(relativo a una facción)* factious; *(rebelde)* rebellious, insurgent II. m.f. POL. *(partidario)* faction member, partisan; *(rebelde)* rebel, insurgent; *(perturbador)* troublemaker, agitator.

fa·ce·ta f. JEWEL. facet, surface (of a gem); ENTOM. facet (of a compound eye); FIG. *(aspecto)* facet, aspect.

fa·cial adj. *(del rostro)* facial, face; *(intuitivo)* intuitive, instinctive.

fá·cil I. adj. *(hacedero)* easy *<este problema es f. de resolver* this problem is easy to solve>; *(sencillo)* simple, easy *<una lección f.* an easy lesson>; *(probable)* likely, probable; *(dócil)* easygoing, docile *<de genio f.* of a docile nature>; *(condescendiente)* easily persuaded, compliant; *(liviana)* loose, of easy virtue ♦ **de puro f.** so easy II. adv. easily.

fa·ci·li·dad f. *(simplicidad)* facility, ease; *(destreza)* ability, aptitude; *(complacencia)* ready complaisance, docility; *(oportunidad)* opportunity, chance ♦ **con la mayor f.** with the greatest of ease • **dar facilidades** to facilitate, make easy • **facilidades** *(comodidades)* facilities, amenities; terms *<grandes facilidades de pago* easy payment terms> • **tener f. de** to be apt to • **tener f. para** to have a gift *or* an aptitude for.

fa·ci·lí·si·mo, –ma adj. very easy, easy as pie.

fa·ci·li·ta·ción f. *(acción de hacer fácil)* facilitation; *(provisión)* provision.

fa·ci·li·tar tr. *(hacer fácil)* to facilitate, make easy; *(proporcionar)* to supply *or* provide (with).

fá·cil·men·te adv. *(sin trabajo)* easily, simply; *(diestramente)* deftly, skillfully.

fa·ci·ne·ro·so, –sa I. adj. *(criminal)* criminal, delinquent; *(malévolo)* wicked II. m.f. *(criminal)* criminal, delinquent; *(malévolo)* wicked person.

fa·cis·tol I. m. *(atril)* lectern, choir desk. —m.f. CARIB., VEN. vain *or* conceited person II. adj. CARIB., VEN. vain, conceited; CUBA, P. RICO joking, teasing.

fa·cón m. ARG., URUG. sheath knife (used by gauchos) ♦ **pelar el f.** ARG., URUG. to unsheathe one's knife.

fac·sí·mil *or* **fac·sí·mi·le** m. facsimile.

fac·ti·ble adj. feasible, practicable.

fac·tor m. FIG. *(elemento)* factor, consideration; *(hacedor)* maker, doer; COM. *(agente)* factor, agent; RAIL. dispatcher; MATH. factor; MIL. victualer, provisions supplier ♦ **f. Rh** BIOCHEM. Rh factor.

fac·to·rí·a f. COM. *(empleo del factor)* factorage, factor's business *or* post; *(oficina del factor)* factor's office, agency; *(establecimiento colonial)* colonial trading post; *(manufactura)* manufacture, manufacturing; AMER. *(fábrica)* plant, factory; ECUAD., PERU foundry, ironworks.

fac·tó·tum m. COLL. *(persona capaz)* factotum; *(entremetido)* busybody; *(agente)* right-hand man.

fac·tu·ra f. *(hechura)* creation, making; COM. invoice, bill; ARG., URUG. baked goods; ECUAD., COM. sales commission ♦ **extender una f.** COM. to make out an invoice • **f. consular** COM. consular invoice • **pasar** *or* **presentar una f.** to send an invoice.

fac·tu·ra·ción f. COM. billing, invoicing; RAIL. checking (of baggage).

fac·tu·rar tr. COM. *(poner en factura)* to invoice, bill; RAIL. to check, deposit (baggage).

fa·cul·tad f. *(potencia)* faculty, inherent power *or* ability; *(virtud)* gift, advantage; PHYSIOL. strength, resistance; *(derecho)* power, right; *(licencia)* license, permission; EDUC. school, college, faculty *<la f. de filosofía y letras* the faculty of philosophy and letters> ♦ **facultades mentales**

mental faculties *or* powers • **tener f. para** to be authorized to.

fa·cul·tar tr. to authorize, empower.

fa·cul·ta·ti·vo, –va I. adj. *(de una facultad mental)* facultative; *(opcional)* optional, facultative; *(profesional)* professional; MED. medical *<un informe f.* a medical report> II. m. MED. physician, doctor.

fa·cun·dia f. *(elocuencia)* eloquence; COLL. *(verbosidad)* gift of gab.

fa·cun·do, –da adj. *(elocuente)* eloquent; *(parlanchín)* talkative.

fa·cha f. *(aspecto)* look, appearance; CHILE arrogance, presumption —m.f. *(adefesio)* sight, mess; COLL. *(fascista)* fascist ♦ **estar hecho una f.** to look terrible *or* a mess • **f. a f.** face to face • **ponerse en f.** MARIT. to lie to; FIG. *(prepararse)* to get ready • **tener buena f.** to look good *or* promising • **tener mala f.** to look bad, have a suspicious look.

fa·cha·da f. *(exterior)* façade, front; *(dimensión)* frontage; COLL. *(apariencia)* façade, show; *(portada)* title page ♦ **con f. a** facing • **hacer f. con** *or* **a** to be opposite, face.

fa·chen·da f. COLL. *(jactancia)* showing off, boasting —m. *(jactancioso)* showoff, boaster.

fa·chen·dis·ta *or* **fa·chen·dón, –do·na** *or* **fa·chen·do·so, –sa** COLL. I. adj. boastful II. m.f. showoff, boaster.

fa·cho·so, –sa adj. *(fachudo)* ridiculous, odd-looking; AMER. elegant; CHILE, MEX. boastful.

fa·e·na f. *(labor)* physical *or* manual labor; *(quehacer)* task, chore; TAUR. series of passes (with the bull); FIG. *(trabajo mental)* mental task; COLL. *(trastada)* dirty trick *<me hizo una f.* she played a dirty trick on me>; CARIB., MEX. overtime work on a plantation; CHILE group of field hands *or* laborers; ECUAD. morning work; ARG. slaughtering of cattle ♦ **estar en plena f.** to be hard at work • **faenas de la casa** household chores, housework.

fa·e·nar tr. ARG. to slaughter and dress (cattle).

fa·e·tón m. phaeton (carriage) ♦ **F.** MYTH. Phaëthon.

fa·got m. MUS. *(instrumento)* bassoon; *(músico)* bassoonist, bassoon player.

fai·sán m. ORNITH. pheasant.

fa·ja f. *(lista)* strip, belt (of cloth, land); *(banda para niños)* swaddling cloth *or* band; *(corsé)* girdle, corset; *(tira de papel)* wrapper (for mailing); *(insignia)* sash; ARCHIT. *(moldura de puertas y ventanas)* window *or* door molding; PHYS. *(banda)* zone, band; HER. fess, fesse; AMER. belt, waistband; MEX., BKB. title label (on spine) ♦ **f. abdominal** abdominal supporter • **f. braga** *or* **pantalón** pantie girdle • **f. de desgarre** AER. ripping panel *or* strip • **f. de frecuencia** RAD. frequency band.

fa·ja·da I. f. AMER. *(acometida)* attack, assault; VEN. trick, ruse II. adj. see **fajado, –da.**

fa·ja·do, –da I. past part. see **fajar** II. adj. AMER. attacked, assaulted III. m. AMER. *(acometida)* attack, beating; VEN. *(chasco)* disillusion, disillusionment —f. see **fajada.**

fa·ja·du·ra f. *(ceñidura con faja)* banding, belting; *(ceñidura con corsé)* girdling; *(envolvimiento con venda)* swathing, bandaging; *(envolvimiento)* wrapping, encircling; *(envolvimiento de un niño)* swaddling; MARIT. tarred covering (for underwater cables); AMER. attack, beating.

fa·ja·mien·to m. *(ceñidura con faja)* banding, belting; *(con corsé)* girdling; *(con venda)* bandaging; *(de un niño)* swaddling; AMER. attack, assault.

fa·jar tr. *(ceñir con faja)* to band, belt; *(poner en corsé)* to girdle, put a girdle on; *(vendar)* to bandage, swathe; *(envolver)* to wrap, put a wrapper on; *(poner la faja a un niño)* to swaddle; AMER. *(acometer)* to attack, assault; *(golpear)* to hit, slap; P. RICO to ask (someone) for a loan ♦ **f. con** *or* **a** to attack, fall on —reflex. to set out *or* continue to do something ♦ **fajarse con** *or* **a** to attack, fall on.

fa·ji·na f. AGR. *(mieses)* shock, rick of sheaves; *(leña)* kindling, fagot of brushwood; MIL. *(toque para retirarse)* call to quarters, taps; *(toque para la comida)* mess call; CONST. *(haz de ramas)* fascine; *(faena)* task, chore; CUBA extra *or* overtime work ♦ **meter f.** COLL. to jabber, ramble on.

fa·jo m. *(atado)* bundle, sheaf; wad, roll *<un f. de billetes* a wad of bills>; AMER. *(trago)* shot, swig (of liquor); MEX. *(cintarazo)* blow; *(cinturón)* man's leather belt ♦ **fajos** swaddling clothes.

fa·jón, –jo·na I. adj. CUBA, P. RICO attacking, assaulting II. m. ARCHIT. plaster border *or* frame (around doors and windows); *(faja grande)* large sash *or* band.

fa·la·cia f. *(engaño)* deceit, deception; *(hábito de engañar)* deceitfulness, falseness; *(error)* fallacy.

fa·lan·ge f. HIST., MIL. phalanx; MIL. *(tropa)* army, troops; ANAT. phalanx, phalange ♦ **la F. (Española)** SP., POL. the Falange.

fa·lan·gis·ta adj. & m.f. Falangist.

fa·laz adj. [pl. **-la·ces**] deceitful *<una persona f.* a deceitful person>; fallacious, deceptive *<una oferta f.* a deceptive offer>.

fa·laz·men·te adv. *(con engaño)* deceitfully; *(de modo falaz)* fallaciously.

fal·ca f. *(alabeo)* warp (in wood); *(cuña)* wedge, chock; MA-RIT. washboard; ARG., BOL. small still; COL. canoe equipped with a roof.

fal·ca·do, –da adj. ARM., HIST. falcated, scythed *<carro f.* scythed chariot>; *(falciforme)* falcate, sickle-shaped.

fal·ci·for·me adj. falciform, sickle-shaped.

fal·da f. *(saya)* skirt *<f. tubo* straight skirt>; ARM. *(hombrera)* brassard, shoulder armor; *(parte de la cintura hacia abajo)* tasse, skirt (of armor); *(carne)* brisket; *(ala de sombrero)* brim, flap; FIG. *(parte inferior de un monte)* foot (of a mountain), lower mountainside; *(regazo)* lap ♦ **aficionado a las faldas** womanizer, woman chaser • **estar pegado** *or* **cosido a las faldas de su madre** FIG., COLL. to be tied to a mother's apron strings • **f. de colina** hillside • **f. de montaña** mountainside • **f. escocesa** kilt • **f. pantalón** culotte *or* divided skirt • **faldas** FIG., COLL. ladies, skirts.

fal·da·men·ta f. *(saya)* skirt (of a garment); *(falda larga)* long *or* full-length skirt.

fal·de·ar tr. to skirt, go around (a hill).

fal·de·llín m. *(falda corta)* short skirt; *(refajo)* underskirt, slip; CARIB., VEN., RELIG. christening *or* baptismal gown.

fal·de·ro, –ra adj. *(de la falda)* lap; *(perro f.* lap dog> ♦ **hombre f.** lady's man • **niño** *or* **niña f.** mother's boy *or* girl.

fal·de·ta f. *(falda pequeña)* small skirt; THEAT. canvas, drape; P. RICO, COLL. man's shirt ♦ **en faldetas** COLL. half-dressed, in shirttails.

fal·dón m. *(falda grande)* large skirt; *(falda suelta)* tail (of a shirt *or* coat); *(saya)* skirt (of a garment); *(piedra de molino)* top millstone (to add weight); ARCHIT. *(de chimenea)* side walls and lintel (of a chimney); *(gablete)* gable; EQUIT. flap, skirt (of a saddle); ARG., RELIG. baptismal gown ♦ **agarrarse** *or* **asirse a los faldones de alguien** to be at someone's coattails *or* heels (seeking help).

fa·len·cia f. *(error)* error, mistake; AMER., COM. bankruptcy, failure.

fa·li·bi·li·dad f. fallibility.

fa·li·ble adj. fallible.

fá·li·co, –ca adj. phallic.

fa·lo m. phallus, penis.

fa·lo·cra·cia f. abuse *or* oppression of women by men.

fal·sa I. f. MUS. *(consonancia redundante)* dissonance; SP. *(desván)* garret, loft; MEX. *(falsilla)* guide lines (for a writing tablet) II. adj. & m. see **falso, –sa.**

fal·sa·men·te adv. falsely.

fal·sa·rio, –ria I. adj. *(que falsifica)* falsifying; *(mentiroso)* lying, untruthful II. m.f. *(falsificador)* falsifier; *(embustero)* liar, dishonest person.

fal·se·a·dor, –do·ra adj. falsifying.

fal·se·a·mien·to m. *(falsificación)* falsifying, falsification; *(de una cerradura)* breaking (of) a lock; *(flaqueamiento)* sagging, weakening; *(torcimiento)* bending, warping.

fal·se·ar tr. *(falsificar)* to falsify; *(contrahacer)* to fake, counterfeit; ARM. *(atravesar)* to pierce *or* split (armor); *(deshacer una cerradura)* to pick (a lock); ARCHIT. to bevel, slant (a surface) —intr. *(flaquear)* to sag, become weak; *(torcerse)* to bend, warp; MUS. to become out of tune (the string of an instrument).

fal·se·dad f. *(falta de verdad)* falseness, falsity; *(hipocresía)* hypocrisy, duplicity; *(mentira)* falsehood, lie.

fal·se·te m. *(corcho)* plug, bung; *(puerta)* small door; MUS. falsetto (voice).

fal·si·fi·ca·ción f. *(falseamiento)* falsification; (law) forgery.

fal·si·fi·ca·dor, –do·ra I. adj. *(falseador)* falsifying; *(que*

copia) forging, counterfeiting; CHEM. adulterating II. m.f. *(falsario)* falsifier; *(copiador)* forger, counterfeiter; CHEM. adulterant.

fal·si·fi·car §70 tr. *(falsear)* to falsify; *(copiar)* to counterfeit, forge; CHEM. to adulterate.

fal·so, –sa I. adj. false, untrue *<un rumor f.* a false rumor>; *(erróneo)* fallacious, unsound *<una teoría f.* an unsound theory>; *(engañoso)* deceitful, false *<un amigo f.* a false friend>; *(falsificado)* counterfeit, fake *<un diamante f.* a fake diamond>; forged *<documentos falsos* forged documents>; *(inexacto)* inexact, inaccurate *<una medida f.* an inaccurate measurement>; *(fingido)* fake, phony *<f. tristeza* fake sadness>; *(vano)* false, unfounded *<esperanzas falsas* false hopes>; MECH. false *<el forro f. de un barco* the false sheathing of a boat>; ZOOL. vicious (said of horses) ♦ **dar un paso en falso** to trip, stumble • **de** *or* **en f.** *(falsamente)* falsely; *(sin firmeza)* superficially • **jurar en f.** to commit perjury • **lo f.** falsehood II. m. SEW. *(refuerzo)* reinforcement, facing; MEX., COLL. false testimony —f. see **falsa.**

fal·ta I. f. *(carencia)* lack, shortage *<hay una f. de recursos naturales en esta región* there is a lack of natural resources in this region>; *(ausencia)* absence; *(deficiencia)* shortcoming, failing; *(defecto)* defect, flaw; *(infracción)* misdemeanor, offense; *(culpa)* fault *<es tu falta* it's your fault>; *(abuso)* breach *<una f. contra la disciplina* a breach of discipline>; *(error)* error, mistake *<una f. de ortografía* a spelling mistake>; *(defecto de peso)* weight shortage; COM. default; SPORT. fault, foul ♦ **a f. de** for lack of, for want of • **caer en f.** to fall into error • **f. de pago** COM. nonpayment • **f. de respeto** disrespect • **hacer f.** *(faltar)* to be lacking, need *<me hacen f. diez dólares* I need ten dollars>; *(ser necesario)* to be necessary *<hace f. añadir más sal* it is necessary to add more salt>; to miss *<me haces falta* I miss you> • **sin f.** without fail • **tomar a f.** to take wrong, misinterpret II. adj. see **falto, –ta.**

fal·tar intr. *(hacer falta)* to lack, need *<nos falta dinero* we need money>; *(carecer de)* to be lacking *<aquí falta agua* water is lacking here>; *(estar ausente)* to be missing *<falta un libro del estante* a book is missing from the shelf>; *(no acudir a)* to be absent, miss *<f. a la clase* to miss the class>; *(no responder)* to fail to function *<la escopeta faltó* the gun failed to function>; *(morir)* to die; *(fallar)* to fail in *<faltó a su deber* he failed in his duty>; *(no cumplir)* to fail to keep, break *<nunca faltaba a una promesa* she never broke a promise>; *(ofender)* to offend, insult *<Jorge me faltó* George insulted me>; *(desmandarse)* to be rude *or* disrespectful *<le faltó a su madre* he was disrespectful to his mother> ♦ **f. a la verdad** to lie, be untruthful • **f. a su lealtad** to be unfaithful • **f. a una cita** to break a date *or* an appointment • **f. en los pagos** COM. to default • **f. mucho para** to be a long way off • **f . . . . para** to be . . . to *<faltan diez minutos para las ocho* it is ten minutes to eight> • **f. poco para** not to be long before *<nos falta poco para terminar* it will not be long before we finish>; to come near *<poco faltó para que lucharan* they came near to fighting> • **f. por** to remain to be *(fallar)* to fail <*falta mucho por hacer* much remains to be done> • **ni f. más ni f. menos** COLL. to be just right • **¡no faltaba más!** COLL. that's the last straw!, that's all we needed! —tr. ARG., MEX., VEN. to be disrespectful to.

fal·to, –ta I. adj. *(carente)* lacking, wanting; *(escaso)* short *<estoy f. de medios* I am short of funds>; *(mezquino)* poor, wretched; *(inexacto)* short *<una libra f.* a short pound>; COL. fatuous, stupid II. f. see **falta.**

fal·tón, –to·na adj. COLL. *(no confiable)* unreliable, undependable; ARG. innocent, simple; CUBA disrespectful, irreverent.

fal·to·so, –sa adj. *(necesitado)* needy; *(incompleto)* incomplete, lacking; AMER. *(informal)* informal, casual; *(irrespetuoso)* disrespectful, rude; COL. quarrelsome, belligerent; PERU unsweetened.

fal·tri·que·ra f. *(bolsillo)* pocket, pouch; *(bolso)* small purse *or* handbag; THEAT. small box (of seats) ♦ **rascarse la f.** COLL. to dig into one's pockets.

fa·lu·cho m. MARIT. felucca, lateen; ARG. *(pendiente)* clover-shaped pendant; *(sombrero)* cocked hat.

fa·lla I. f. *(defecto)* defect, fault; GEOG., MIN. fault; *(cober-*

tura) faille; AMER. *(falta)* fault, failure; *(falta de confianza)* unreliability; ARG., COL. ruffing, trumping (in card games); MEX. baby bonnet **II.** adj. see **fallo, -lla.**

fa·llar¹ tr. LAW to decide, rule on **♦ f. a favor de** to rule in favor of **• f. en contra de** to rule against.

fa·llar² tr. *(decepcionar)* to fail, disappoint <*me falló mi amiga* my friend disappointed me>; *(cartas)* to ruff, trump **♦ f. en cruz** to crossruff —intr. *(frustrarse)* to fail, be unsuccessful; *(no funcionar bien)* to be broken, not to work right; *(perder resistencia)* to fail, give way; *(desilusionar a uno)* to prove unreliable *or* undependable **♦ sin f.** without fail.

fa·lle·ba f. bolt, latch.

fa·lle·cer §17 intr. *(morir)* to die, expire; *(faltar)* to run out, end.

fa·lle·ci·mien·to m. death, demise.

fa·lli·do, -da I. past part. see **fallir II.** adj. *(sin efecto)* vain, frustrated; *(fracasado)* unsuccessful; COM. *(quebrado)* bankrupt; *(incobrable)* uncollectable *or* bad (debt) **III.** m.f. COM. bankrupt.

fa·llir intr. *(faltar)* to run out, end; VEN., COM. to go bankrupt *or* under.

fa·llo¹ I. m. *(sentencia)* ruling, judgment; *(decisión)* decision; *(falta)* error, fault; *(falta de palo)* lack of a card in any particular suit, being void in a suit **♦ tener fallos de memoria** to have lapses in one's memory **II.** adj. see **fallo, -lla.**

fa·llo, -lla I. adj. *(sin cierto palo)* void, lacking a suit (in cards); CHILE, AGR. failed (crop) **II.** m. see **fallo** —f. see **falla.**

fa·ma f. *(renombre)* fame, renown; *(reputación)* reputation, name; *(gloria)* prestige, glory **♦ buena f.** good name *or* reputation **• es f. que** it is rumored *or* reported that **• mala f.** bad name *or* reputation **• tener f.** to be famous *or* well-known.

fa·mé·li·co, -ca adj. starving, famished.

fa·mi·lia f. *(padres e hijos)* family; *(gente de la misma casa)* household; *(hijos)* children, kids; FIG. *(estirpe)* lineage, ancestry; *(servidumbre)* servants, domestics; BIOL. family **♦ de buena f.** well-born **• en f.** with one's family **• la f. política** the in-laws **• La Sagrada F.** RELIG. the Holy Family **• ser como de la f.** to be like one of the family **• venir de f.** to run in the family.

fa·mi·liar I. adj. *(relativo a la familia)* familial, family; *(llano)* familiar, casual; *(conocido)* familiar, well-known; *(corriente)* colloquial, familiar **II.** m. *(pariente)* family member; *(persona de la misma casa)* household member; *(amigo íntimo)* intimate friend, close associate; *(demonio)* familiar, attendant spirit; RELIG. familiar, resident, servant; COL. amulet **♦ F. del Santo Oficio** SP., HIST. Inquisition officer.

fa·mi·li·a·ri·dad f. familiarity.

fa·mi·lia·ri·zar §04 tr. to familiarize, acquaint —reflex. to familiarize oneself with, get to know.

fa·mi·liar·men·te adv. familiarly.

fa·mo·so, -sa adj. *(conocido)* famous; *(ilustre)* celebrated; *(extraordinario)* extraordinary; COLL. *(excelente)* excellent.

fá·mu·la f. COLL. maid, servant.

fá·mu·lo m. COLL. servant.

fa·ná·ti·ca·men·te adv. fanatically.

fa·ná·ti·cé, fanatice see **fanatizar.**

fa·ná·ti·co, -ca I. adj. fanatical, fanatic **II.** m.f. fanatic; *(entusiasta)* fan.

fa·na·tis·mo m. fanaticism.

fa·na·ti·za·dor, -do·ra I. adj. fanaticizing **II.** m.f. person who spreads fanaticism.

fa·na·ti·zar §04 tr. to make fanatical, fanaticize.

fan·dan·go m. *(baile y música)* fandango; FIG., COLL. *(bullicio)* row, uproar.

fan·dan·gue·ro, -ra I. adj. fond of parties *or* of the fandango **II.** m.f. person fond of parties *or* of the fandango.

fa·ne·ga f. AGR. fanega (1.58 bushels in Spain) **♦ f. de tierra** fanega (1.59 acres in Spain).

fan·fa·rre·ar intr. var. of **fanfarronear.**

fan·fa·rria f. COLL. boasting, bragging; MUS. fanfare.

fan·fa·rrón, -rro·na I. adj. COLL. *(jactancioso)* boasting,

bragging; *(presumido)* flashy, showy **II.** m.f. COLL. boaster, braggart **♦ trigo f.** a variety of wheat.

fan·fa·rro·na·da f. *(acción)* boasting, bragging; *(cosa dicha)* boast, brag **♦ decir** *or* **echar fanfarronadas** to boast, brag.

fan·fa·rro·ne·ar intr. to boast, brag.

fan·fa·rro·ne·rí·a f. boasting, bragging.

fan·gal *or* **fan·gar** m. quagmire, mudhole.

fan·go m. *(lodo)* mud, mire; FIG. *(degradación)* degradation.

fan·go·si·dad f. muddiness.

fan·go·so, -sa adj. muddy, miry.

fa·no m. fane, temple (for pagan worship).

fan·ta·se·ar intr. *(soñar)* to daydream, dream; *(imaginar)* to imagine.

fan·ta·sí·a f. *(imaginación)* fantasy, imagination; *(imagen)* fantasy, illusory image; *(cuento)* fantasy, story; MUS. fantasy **♦ de f.** fancy **• por f.** VEN by ear.

fan·ta·sio·so, -sa adj. COLL. conceited, vain.

fan·tas·ma m. *(espectro)* ghost, apparition; *(visión)* vision, illusion; FIG. *(persona seria)* solemn person; *(persona entonada)* conceited person; TELEC. ghost —f. *(espantajo)* scarecrow.

fan·tas·ma·go·rí·a f. phantasmagoria.

fan·tas·ma·gó·ri·co, -ca adj. phantasmagoric.

fan·tas·mal adj. *(espectral)* ghostly, phantasmal.

fan·tás·ti·co, -ca adj. *(imaginario)* fantastic, imaginary; *(irreal)* fantastic, unreal; COLL. *(increíble)* fantastic, incredible.

fan·to·cha·da f. ridiculous action.

fan·to·che m. *(títere)* puppet, marionette; COLL. *(farolón)* boastful nincompoop.

fan·to·che·rí·a f. AMER. tomfoolery.

fa·ra·lá m. [pl. **-la·es**] ruffle, flounce; COLL. *(adorno excesivo)* excessively ornate ruffle *or* flounce.

fa·ra·llón m. *(precipicio)* headland, promontory; MIN. outcrop.

fa·ra·ma·lla I. adj. bamboozling, deceiving **II.** m.f. *(engañador)* bamboozler, deceiver; AMER. boaster, braggart —f. COLL. *(charla artificiosa)* cajolery; *(farfolla)* bauble, trinket.

fa·ra·ma·lle·ro, -ra COLL. **I.** adj. *(engañador)* bamboozling, deceiving; AMER. boasting, bragging **II.** m.f. *(engañador)* bamboozler, deceiver.

fa·ra·ma·llón, -llo·na COLL. adj. & m.f. var. of **faramallero, -ra.**

fa·rán·du·la f. *(profesión)* theater, show business; *(compañía)* troupe of strolling players; FIG., COLL. *(charla)* cajolery.

fa·ran·du·le·ar intr. COLL. to boast, brag.

fa·ran·du·le·ro, -ra I. m.f. THEAT. wandering player *or* comedian; FIG., COLL. *(trapacero)* swindler, trickster **II.** adj. FIG., COLL. *(trapacero)* swindling, tricking; MEX. boastful, bragging.

fa·ra·ón m. *(soberano)* Pharaoh, pharaoh; *(juego de naipes)* faro (card game).

fa·ra·ó·ni·co, -ca adj. Pharaonic, pharaonic.

fa·rau·te m. *(mensajero)* messenger, herald; *(rey de armas)* king-of-arms, herald; THEAT. actor who recites a play's prologue; FIG., COLL. *(entremetido)* busybody, meddler.

far·dar tr. to outfit, dress —intr. COLL. to show off.

far·del m. *(talega)* knapsack; *(pío)* bundle, parcel; FIG., COLL. slob, mess <*ir hecho un f.* to go around looking like a slob>.

far·do m. large bundle *or* parcel.

far·fa·llo·so, -sa adj. stammering, stuttering.

far·fan·te *or* **far·fan·tón** COLL. **I.** adj. boasting, boastful **II.** m. showoff, talkative boaster.

far·fan·to·na·da *or* **far·fan·to·ne·rí·a** f. COLL. boast, brag.

far·fo·lla f. BOT. husk (of corn); COLL. *(faramalla)* bauble, trinket.

far·fu·lla COLL. **I.** m.f. jabberer, gabbler —f. *(barbulla)* jabber, gabble; AMER. boasting, bragging **II.** adj. jabbering, gabbling.

far·fu·lla·dor, -do·ra COLL. **I.** adj. *(barbullón)* jabbering, gabbling; FIG. *(chapucero)* hasty, careless **II.** m.f. *(barbullón)* jabberer, gabbler; FIG. *(chapucero)* hasty *or* careless person.

far·fu·llar COLL. tr. *(barbullar)* to jabber, gabble; FIG. *(cha-*

pucear) to do hastily *or* carelessly —intr. to jabber, gabble.

far·fu·lle·ro, –ra adj. & m.f. var. of **farfullador.**

far·ga·llón, –llo·na COLL. **I.** adj. *(chapucero)* hasty, careless; *(desaliñado)* sloppy, messy **II.** m.f. *(chapucero)* hasty *or* careless person; *(persona desaliñada)* slob, messy person.

fa·ri·ná·ce·o, –a adj. farinaceous.

fa·rin·ge f. ANAT. pharynx.

fa·ri·no·so, –sa adj. floury, mealy.

fa·ri·sai·co, –ca adj. *(de los fariseos)* Pharisaic, Pharisaical; FIG. *(hipócrita)* pharisaic, hypocritical.

fa·ri·se·o m. *(miembro)* Pharisee; FIG. *(hipócrita)* hypocrite, pharisee.

far·ma·céu·ti·co, –ca **I.** adj. pharmaceutical **II.** m.f. pharmacist, druggist.

far·ma·cia f. *(profesión)* pharmacy, pharmaceutics; *(tienda)* drugstore, pharmacy.

fár·ma·co m. medicine, medication.

far·ma·co·lo·gí·a f. pharmacology.

far·ma·co·pe·a f. pharmacopoeia, prescription book.

far·nien·te m. idleness.

fa·ro m. *(torre)* lighthouse; *(señal)* beacon; AUTO. *(linterna)* headlight; FIG. guiding light ♦ **f. trasero** rear light.

fa·rol m. *(linterna)* lantern; *(luz pública)* street lamp; *(luz)* light; *(envite falso)* bluff (in card games); TAUR. cape flourish; FAM. *(fachendoso)* show-off, boaster; ARG. glassed-in balcony, bay window ♦ **adelante con los faroles** keep up the good work • **f. a. la veneciana** Chinese lantern.

fa·ro·la f. *(farol)* streetlight, street lamp; *(fanal)* beacon, large lantern.

fa·ro·le·ar intr. COLL. to boast, brag.

fa·ro·le·rí·a f. COLL. boastfulness.

fa·ro·le·ro, –ra **I.** adj. FIG., COLL. boastful, bragging **II.** m.f. FIG., COLL. boaster, braggart; *(el que cuida de los faroles)* lamplighter; *(el que hace faroles)* lamp maker.

fa·ro·li·llo m. *(lámpara)* small lamp *or* lantern; BOT. Canterbury bell.

fa·rra f. ICHTH. lavaret; AMER., COLL. binge, bash, spree; ARG., URUG. teasing, mockery ♦ **ir de f.** to go on a spree.

fá·rra·go m. hodgepodge, jumble.

fa·rra·guis·ta m.f. confused *or* mixed-up person.

fa·rre·ar intr. AMER. to go on a binge, carouse; ARG., URUG. *(burlarse de alguien)* to make fun of someone, tease someone; ARG. *(malbaratar)* to waste, squander.

fa·rre·ro, –ra *or* **fa·rris·ta** **I.** adj. carousing, reveling **II.** m.f. carouser, reveler.

fa·rro m. AGR. *(cebada)* coarsely ground peeled barley; *(escanda)* spelt wheat.

far·sa f. THEAT. *(comedia)* farce; *(compañía)* company of comic actors; DEROG. *(obra mala)* bad *or* crude play; FIG. *(engaño)* farce, sham.

far·san·te, –ta **I.** m.f. THEAT. comic actor, farceur —m. fake, charlatan **II.** adj. FIG., COLL. fraud, fake.

far·se·ar intr. ARG., C. AMER., CHILE to joke *or* fool around.

far·sis·ta m.f. THEAT. writer of farces, farceur.

fas adv. ♦ **por f. o por nefas** COLL. rightly or wrongly, by hook or by crook.

fas·ces f.pl. fasces.

fas·cí·cu·lo m. ANAT., BKB., BOT. fascicle.

fas·ci·na·ción f. fascination, enchantment.

fas·ci·na·dor, –do·ra adj. fascinating, charming.

fas·ci·nan·te adj. fascinating, charming.

fas·ci·nar tr. *(dominar)* to fascinate, bewitch; *(encantar)* to fascinate, charm; *(engañar)* to deceive.

fas·cis·mo m. POL. fascism ♦ **Fascismo** Fascism.

fas·cis·ta adj. & m.f. fascist, Fascist.

fa·se f. ASTRON., BIOL., ELEC. phase; TECH. stage (of a rocket); FIG. *(etapa)* phase, stage *<las fases de una enfermedad* the stages of an illness>; *(aspecto)* phase, aspect.

fas·ti·diar tr. *(molestar)* to annoy, bother; *(cansar)* to tire, bore; *(perturbar)* to upset, inconvenience —reflex. to get annoyed.

fas·ti·dio m. *(molestia)* annoyance, bother; *(repugnancia)* repugnance; *(aburrimiento)* boredom; FIG. *(asco)* disgust ♦ **¡que f.!** what a nuisance!

fas·ti·dio·so, –sa adj. *(molesto)* annoying, bothersome; *(cargante)* tiresome, tedious.

fas·ti·gio m. *(vértice)* top, apex; FIG. *(cumbre)* pinnacle, summit; ARCHIT. fastigium.

fas·to, –ta **I.** adj. auspicious, happy **II.** m. pomp, splendor ♦ **fastos** *(calendario)* fasti; FIG. *(anales)* annals.

fas·tos m.pl. *(anales)* annals, chronicles; HIST. fasti (Roman calendar).

fas·tuo·sa·men·te *or* **fas·to·sa·men·te** adv. *(lujosamente)* lavishly, splendidly; *(ostentosamente)* ostentatiously.

fas·tuo·si·dad f. pomp, splendor.

fas·tuo·so, –sa *or* **fas·to·so, –sa** adj. *(lujoso)* lavish, splendid; *(ostentoso)* ostentatious.

fa·tal adj. *(inevitable)* fatal; *(funesto)* mournful, unfortunate; *(que causa la muerte)* fatal, deadly, mortal *<un golpe f.* a fatal blow>.

fa·ta·li·dad f. *(destino)* fate, destiny; *(desgracia)* misfortune, calamity.

fa·ta·lis·mo m. PHILOS. fatalism.

fa·ta·lis·ta **I.** adj. fatalistic **II.** m.f. fatalist.

fa·tal·men·te adv. *(desdichadamente)* unfortunately, unhappily; *(inevitablemente)* fatefully, inevitably; *(muy mal)* very badly, wretchedly.

fa·tí·di·co, –ca adj. fatidic, prophetic.

fa·ti·ga f. *(cansancio)* fatigue, weariness; *(trabajo)* tiring *or* strenuous work; PHYSIOL. *(molestia en la respiración)* shortness of breath, shallow breathing; *(náusea)* nausea, uneasy stomach; MECH. fatigue ♦ **dar f.** to trouble, annoy • **f. de combate** MIL. combat fatigue • **f. nerviosa** MED. strain, stress • **f. visual** OPHTHAL. eyestrain • **fatigas** *(dificultades)* difficulties, bother; *(penas)* pains, sorrows.

fa·ti·ga·dor, –do·ra adj. *(que cansa)* fatiguing, tiring; *(molestoso)* annoying, troublesome.

fa·ti·gan·te adj. var. of **fatigoso, –sa.**

fa·ti·gar §47 tr. *(cansar)* to fatigue, tire; *(molestar)* to vex, annoy —reflex. to tire, get tired.

fa·ti·go·so, –sa adj. *(fatigado)* fatigued, tired; *(que cansa)* fatiguing, tiring; COLL. *(cargante)* bothersome, annoying.

fa·tui·dad f. *(destino)* fatuity, fatuousness; *(tontería)* fatuous remark *or* act; *(presunción)* conceit, vanity.

fa·tuo, –tua **I.** adj. *(tonto)* fatuous, foolish; *(presumido)* conceited, vain **II.** m.f. *(tonto)* fool, fatuous person; *(presumido)* vain *or* conceited person.

fau·ces f.pl. ANAT. fauces, gullet ♦ **las f. de la muerte** the jaws of death.

fau·na f. fauna, animal life.

fau·no m. MYTH. faun ♦ **Fauno** Faunus.

faus·to, –ta **I.** adj. fortunate, lucky **II.** m. *(lujo)* luxury; *(esplendor)* splendor, pomp.

fau·tor, –to·ra m.f. abettor, helper.

fau·vis·mo m. ARTS fauvism.

fa·vi·la f. POET. ember.

fa·vor m. *(ayuda)* favor *<hazme un f.* do me a favor>; *(gracia)* favor, grace *<el f. del rey* the favor of the king>; *(amparo)* protection; COL. ribbon; DOM. REP. gift ♦ **a f. de** in favor of, in behalf of • **a f. de la noche** under cover of darkness • **de f.** complimentary, free • **en f. de** in favor of • **por f.** please.

fa·vo·ra·ble adj. favorable.

fa·vo·ra·ble·men·te adv. favorably.

fa·vo·re·ce·dor, –do·ra adj. *(que favorece)* favoring, favorable; flattering, becoming *<un vestido f.* a becoming dress>.

fa·vo·re·cer §17 tr. *(amparar)* to aid, abet; *(apoyar)* to favor, support; *(beneficiar)* to bestow a favor on; AMER. to protect, make safe —reflex. to aid *or* help one another ♦ **favorecerse de** to avail oneself of, fall back on.

fa·vo·re·cien·te adj. *(que favorece)* favoring, favorable; *(que ayuda)* aiding, helping.

fa·vo·ri·tis·mo m. favoritism, partiality.

fa·vo·ri·to, –ta adj. & m.f. favorite.

fa·ya f. TEX. faille.

faz f. [pl. **fa·ces**] *(cara)* face; NUMIS. obverse ♦ **a la f. de** in front of • **f. a f.** face to face • **en f. y en paz** publicly and peacefully • **La Sacra** *or* **Santa F.** RELIG. the Holy Face.

fe f. *(virtud)* faith; *(religión)* faith, religion *<la f. católica* the Catholic faith>; *(creencia)* belief, credence *<esta noticia es digna de f.* this news is worthy of credence>; *(con-*

fianza) trust, confidence *<hay que tener f. en el médico* one must have confidence in one's doctor>; *(palabra de honor)* word of honor *<a f. mía* on my word of honor>; *(seguridad)* assurance, confirmation; *(fidelidad)* fidelity, faithfulness; *(documento)* certificate *<f. de bautismo* baptismal certificate> ♦ **a buena fe** undoubtedly, doubtless • **a fe** or **de fe** truly • **dar fe a** to confirm, certify • **de buena fe** in good faith; from a good source *<lo sé de buena fe* I have it from a good source> • **de mala fe** in bad faith • **fe de erratas** PRINT. errata • **fe pública** legal authority • **hacer fe** to be sufficient proof • **tener fe en** to believe in, have faith in.

fe·al·dad f. *(calidad de feo)* ugliness, hideousness; FIG. *(torpeza)* turpitude, foulness.

fe·a·men·te adv. *(con fealdad)* in an ugly manner, hideously; FIG. *(con torpeza)* basely, foully.

fe·ble adj. *(débil)* feeble, weak; NUMIS. *(deficiente)* deficient in weight or quality.

fe·bre·ro m. February.

fe·bril adj. MED. febrile, feverish; FIG. *(ardiente)* feverish, ardent.

fe·bril·men·te adv. FIG. *(con ardor)* feverishly, ardently; *(con ira)* angrily, vehemently.

fe·cal adj. fecal.

fé·cu·la f. starch.

fe·cu·len·to, -ta I. adj. *(impuro)* feculent, fecal; *(harinoso)* starchy II. m. starch, starchy food.

fe·cu·lo·so, -sa adj. starchy.

fe·cun·da·ble adj. fertile, fecund.

fe·cun·da·ción f. fertilization, fecundation.

fe·cun·da·dor, -do·ra adj. fertilizing, fecundating.

fe·cun·da·men·te adv. fertiley, fruitfully.

fe·cun·dan·te adj. fertilizing, fecundating.

fe·cun·dar tr. *(hacer fecundo)* to make fertile or fruitful; *(engendrar)* to fertilize, fecundate.

fe·cun·da·ti·vo, -va adj. fertilizing, fecundating.

fe·cun·di·dad f. fertility, fecundity; FIG. *(productividad)* fruitfulness, productivity.

fe·cun·di·zar §04 tr. *(hacer fecundo)* to make fertile or fruitful; *(engendrar)* to fertilize, fecundate.

fe·cun·do, -da adj. *(fértil)* fertile, fecund; FIG. abundant, rich.

fe·cha I. f. date *<¿qué f. es hoy?* what is today's date?>; *(día)* day *<el telegrama tardó una f.* the telegram was a day late>; *(momento actual)* now, the present ♦ **a estas fechas** now, by now • **a partir de esta f.** from today or today's date • **con** or **de f. de** dated *<una carta con fecha del 9* a letter dated the ninth> • **f. tope** closing or final date • **hasta la f.** so far, to date • **poner la f. en** to date • **por estas fechas** around this time *<el año pasado vino por estas fechas* last year he came around this time> II. adj. see **fecho, -cha.**

fe·cha·dor m. *(sello para fechar)* dater, date stamp; *(matasellos)* post office canceling stamp, postmark.

fe·char tr. to date, put the date on.

fe·cho, -cha LAW I. adj. done, executed (used in legal documents) II. m. note that certifies the execution of a legal document —f. see **fecha.**

fe·cho·rí·a f. misdeed, misdemeanor.

fe·de·ra·ción f. federation, confederation.

fe·de·ral I. adj. *(federativo)* federal; *(federalista)* federalist II. m.f. federalist, federal.

fe·de·ra·lis·mo m. federalism.

fe·de·ra·lis·ta adj. & m.f. federalist.

fe·de·rar tr. & reflex. to federate, confederate.

fe·de·ra·ti·vo, -va adj. federative, federal.

fe·ha·cien·te adj. authentic, reliable.

fel·des·pa·to m. MIN. feldspar.

fe·li·ci·dad f. *(alegría)* felicity, happiness; *(suerte feliz)* good luck or fortune; *(prosperidad)* prosperity, success ♦ **felicidades** *(enhorabuena)* congratulations; *(deseos amistosos)* best or warm wishes.

fe·li·ci·ta·ción f. congratulations, felicitation.

fe·li·ci·tar tr. *(congratular)* to congratulate, felicitate; *(desear bien)* to wish (someone) well —reflex. *(contentarse)* to be happy or glad; *(congratularse)* to congratulate oneself.

fe·li·grés, -gre·sa m.f. parishioner, church member.

fe·li·gre·sí·a f. *(feligreses)* parish, parishioners; *(parroquía)* parish.

fe·li·no, -na I. adj. *(de gato)* feline; *(gatuno)* feline, catlike II. m. feline.

fe·liz adj. [pl. **-li·ces**] *(alegre)* happy, joyful; *(acertado)* felicitous, apt; *(oportuno)* lucky, fortunate; *(que tiene éxito)* successful.

fe·liz·men·te adv. *(alegremente)* happily, joyfully; *(acertadamente)* felicitously, aptly; *(oportunamente)* fortunately, luckily; *(con éxito)* successfully.

fe·lón, -lo·na I. adj. treacherous, villainous II. m.f. traitor, villain.

fe·lo·ní·a f. treachery, perfidy.

fel·pa f. TEX. plush; FIG., COLL. *(zurra)* beating, thrashing; *(represión)* telling off, scolding ♦ **dar** or **echar una f. a uno** FIG., COLL. to tell someone off.

fel·pa·do, -da I. past part. see **felpar** II. adj. plush.

fel·par tr. TEX. to cover with plush; FIG. *(cubrir)* to carpet, blanket.

fel·pi·lla f. chenille.

fel·po m. mat, rug.

fel·po·so, -sa adj. plush, velvety.

fel·pu·do, -da I. adj. plush, velvety II. m. mat, rug.

fe·me·nil adj. feminine, womanly.

fe·me·ni·no, -na I. adj. *(de mujer)* feminine; BIOL. female; GRAM. feminine II. m. GRAM. feminine.

fe·men·ti·do, -da adj. false, treacherous.

fe·mi·nei·dad f. LAW *(de propiedad)* condition or property belonging to a woman; *(feminidad)* femininity, femaleness.

fe·mi·ni·dad f. *(calidad de femenino)* femininity, feminineness; *(afeminación)* effeminacy.

fe·mi·nis·mo m. feminism.

fe·mi·nis·ta I. adj. feminist, feministic II. m.f. feminist.

fe·mi·ni·za·ción f. feminization.

fé·mur m. ANAT. femur, thighbone.

fe·ne·cer §17 tr. to finish, settle —intr. *(morir)* to die, pass away; *(acabarse)* to come to an end, conclude; *(perecer)* to perish.

fe·ne·ci·mien·to m. *(conclusión)* conclusion, settlement; *(muerte)* death, passing (away); *(fin)* finish, end.

Fe·ni·cia f. Phoenicia.

fe·ni·cio, -cia adj. & m.f. Phoenician.

fé·ni·co, -ca adj. CHEM. phenic, carbolic *<ácido f.* carbolic acid>.

fe·ni·lo m. CHEM. phenyl.

fé·nix f. [pl. **-nix**] MYTH. phoenix; FIG. *(dechado)* phoenix, paragon; BOT. kind of palm.

fe·no·bar·bi·tal m. PHARM. phenobarbital.

fe·nol m. CHEM. phenol.

fe·no·me·nal adj. *(fenoménico)* phenomenal; FIG. *(extraordinario)* phenomenal, extraordinary.

fe·nó·me·no m. *(acontecimiento)* phenomenon, occurrence; FIG. *(monstruo)* freak, monster; *(coloso)* phenomenon, paragon; *(portento)* wonder, marvel.

fe·o, -a I. adj. *(que carece de belleza)* ugly, hideous; *(horroroso)* horrible, disgusting; *(muy serio)* serious, nasty; *(poco decoroso)* unbecoming, indecorous ♦ **dejar f.** to slight, hurt • **más f. que Picio** or **un f. que asusta** as ugly as sin • **quedar f.** to be slighted or offended • **tocarle a uno bailar con la más f.** FIG., COLL. to get the short end of the stick or deal II. adv. AMER. nasty, awful *<huele f.* it smells awful> III. m. COLL. *(desaire)* insult, slight; *(fealdad)* ugliness, hideousness ♦ **hacer un f. a alguien** to slight or offend someone.

fe·ra·ci·dad f. AGR. fertility, fecundity.

fe·ral adj. feral, fierce.

fe·raz adj. [pl. **-ra·ces**] AGR. fertile, fecund.

fé·re·tro m. *(ataúd)* coffin; *(andas)* bier.

fe·ria f. *(mercado)* market; *(exposición)* fair, exhibition; *(fiesta)* fair, carnival; *(descanso)* rest, respite; *(día de fiesta)* holiday; RELIG. feria; MEX., SL. change; C. RICA, SALV. tip, gratuity ♦ **dar ferias** to give a gift.

fe·ria·do adj. ♦ **día f.** holiday.

fe·rial m. *(feria)* fair, market; *(terreno)* fairground.

fe·rian·te I. adj. fair-going, attending a fair II. m.f. *(el que va a la feria)* fairgoer; *(comerciante)* trader, exhibitor.

fe·riar tr. *(comprar)* to buy or purchase (at a fair); *(vender)* to sell *or* exhibit (at a fair); *(regalar)* to give a gift to; AMER. to exchange, barter —intr. to take time off (from work).

fe·ri·no, –na adj. fierce, ferocious ♦ **tos f.** MED. whooping cough.

fer·men·ta·ble adj. fermentable.

fer·men·ta·ción f. fermentation ♦ **f. ácida** acid fermentation • **f. amoniacal** amoniacal fermentation.

fer·men·tar tr. to ferment —intr. CHEM. to ferment; FIG. *(agitarse los ánimos)* to be *or* become excited.

fer·men·ta·ti·vo, –va adj. fermentative.

fer·men·to m. ferment <*f. orgánico* organic ferment>; BIO-CHEM. enzyme; CUL. leaven, leavening ♦ **f. químico** chemical ferment.

fer·mio m. CHEM. fermium.

fe·roz adj. [pl. **-ro·ces**] *(cruel)* ferocious, fierce; FIG., COLL. *(tremendo)* tremendous, terrible, ravenous <*tener un hambre f.* to be ravenous>.

fe·roz·men·te adv. ferociously, fiercely.

fe·rra·do, –da I. past part. see **ferrar** II. adj. METAL. iron-plated, trimmed with iron III. m. SP., AGR. land measure (4 to 6 acres).

fe·rrar §49 tr. METAL. to plate *or* trim with iron.

fe·rra·to m. CHEM. ferrate.

fé·rre·o, –a adj. *(de hierro)* iron, ferrous; FIG. *(duro)* iron, strong; *(severo)* harsh, severe; HIST. Iron Age.

fe·rre·rí·a f. ironworks, foundry.

fe·rre·rue·lo m. short hoodless cape.

fe·rre·te·ar tr. *(labrar con hierro)* to work with iron; *(ferrar)* to plate *or* trim with iron; *(marcar)* to mark with a marking iron.

fe·rre·te·rí·a f. *(ferrería)* ironworks, foundry; *(comercio)* hardware store; *(quincalla)* hardware.

fe·rre·te·ro, –ra m.f. hardware dealer.

fé·rri·co, –ca adj. CHEM. ferric.

fe·rri·ta f. MIN. ferrite.

fe·rro·ca·rril m. railroad, railway ♦ **f. de cremallera** rack railway • **f. funicular** funicular • **f. subterráneo** subway.

fe·rrón m. ironworker, ironmonger.

fe·rro·so, –sa adj. CHEM. ferrous.

fe·rro·via·rio, –ria I. adj. railroad, rail II. m.f. railroad employee.

fér·til adj. *(fecundo)* fertile, fruitful; FIG. *(productivo)* fertile, productive ♦ **f. de** *or* **en** FIG. abundant *or* rich in.

fer·ti·li·cé, fertilice see **fertilizar.**

fer·ti·li·dad f. *(fecundidad)* fertileness, fruitfulness; FIG. *(productividad)* fertility, productivity; *(abundancia)* abundance.

fer·ti·li·za·ción f. fertilization ♦ **f. cruzada** BIOL. cross-fertilization.

fer·ti·li·za·dor, –do·ra adj. fertilizing.

fer·ti·li·zan·te I. adj. fertilizing II. m. fertilizer.

fer·ti·li·zar §04 tr. to fertilize (soil).

fé·ru·la f. BOT. giant fennel; *(palmeta)* rod *or* ruler (for punishment); MED. splint ♦ **estar uno bajo la f. de otro** FIG. to be under someone's thumb *or* domination.

fér·vi·do, –da adj. fervid, fervent.

fer·vien·te adj. fervent, fervid.

fer·vien·te·men·te adv. fervently, fervidly.

fer·vor m. *(calor)* fervor, intense heat; FIG. *(celo)* fervor, zeal.

fer·vo·ro·sa·men·te adv. fervently, fervidly.

fer·vo·ro·so, –sa adj. fervent, fervid.

fes·te·ja·dor, –do·ra *or* **fes·te·jan·te** I. adj. entertaining, feasting II. m. entertainer, host —f. entertainer, hostess.

fes·te·jar tr. *(agasajar)* to entertain, wine and dine; *(celebrar)* to celebrate; *(galantear)* to court, woo; MEX. to beat, thrash —reflex. to enjoy oneself, have a good time.

fes·te·jo m. *(entretenimiento)* entertainment, feast; *(galanteo)* courting, wooing; AMER. celebration, party ♦ **festejos** ublic festivities.

fes·tín m. banquet, feast.

fes·ti·na·ción f. haste, hurry.

fes·ti·nar tr. AMER. to hasten, hurry up; C. AMER. to entertain, wine and dine.

fes·ti·val m. festival <*f. de cine* film festival>.

fes·ti·va·men·te adv. *(alegremente)* festively, joyfully; *(agudamente)* wittily.

fes·ti·vi·dad f. RELIG. feast *or* holy day; *(fiesta)* festivity, celebration; *(regocijo)* rejoicing, merrymaking; *(agudeza)* wit, humor.

fes·ti·vo, –va adj. *(alegre)* festive, joyful; *(agudo)* witty, humorous; RELIG. feast, holy (day).

fes·tón m. *(guirnalda)* festoon, garland; ARCHIT. festoon; SEW. scallops, festoon.

fes·to·ne·ar *or* **fes·to·nar** tr. *(adornar)* to festoon; SEW. to scallop.

fe·tal adj. fetal.

fe·ti·ci·da I. adj. feticidal II. m.f. one who commits feticide.

fe·ti·ci·dio m. feticide.

fe·ti·che m. fetish, fetich.

fe·ti·chis·mo m. fetishism, fetichism.

fe·ti·chis·ta I. adj. fetishistic, fetichistic II. m.f. fetishist, fetichist.

fe·ti·dez f. fetidness, stench.

fé·ti·do, –da adj. fetid, foul-smelling.

fe·to m. fetus.

fe·ú·co, –ca *or* **fe·ú·cho, –cha** adj. COLL. ugly, hideous.

feu·dal adj. feudal, feudalistic.

feu·da·lis·mo m. feudalism.

feu·do m. *(territorio)* feud, fee; *(tributo)* tribute, tithe; FIG. *(vasallaje)* vassalage, fealty ♦ **f. alodial** alodium • **f. franco** freehold.

fez m. [pl. **fe·ces**] fez.

fia·bi·li·dad f. reliability, dependability.

fia·ble adj. reliable, dependable.

fia·do, –da I. past part. see **fiar** II. adj. trusting ♦ **al f.** on credit <*comprar al f.* to buy on credit>.

fia·dor, –do·ra m.f. *(persona)* guarantor; LAW *(afianzador)* bailsman, bailer ♦ **salir f. por** LAW to go bail *or* stand surety for —m. *(presilla)* fastener; TECH. catch; CHILE, ECUAD. chin strap.

fiam·bre I. adj. CUL. (served) cold; COLL. *(sin novedad)* old, stale <*noticia f.* old news>; *(muerto)* dead, pushing up daisies; *(desanimado)* boring, lifeless ♦ **dejar f.** COLL. to kill, do in • **estar hecho f.** COLL. to kick the bucket, drop dead II. m. *(carne fría)* cold cut, delicatessen meat; GUAT., MEX. type of assorted cold plate *or* dish; COLL. *(fiesta aburrida)* boring party, wake; *(cadáver)* corpse ♦ **fiambres variados** assorted cold cuts III. adv. GUAT. (in) cash.

fiam·bre·ra f. *(cesto)* lunch box *or* pail; *(cacerola)* covered casserole; ARG. food storage safe.

fiam·bre·rí·a f. S. AMER. delicatessen.

fian·za f. *(garantía)* guaranty; *(depósito)* security, deposit; *(fiador)* guarantor.

fiar §30 tr. *(garantizar)* to guaranty; *(vender)* to sell on credit; *(confiar)* to entrust; COL. to ask for credit —intr. & reflex. to trust ♦ **fiarse de** *or* **a** to trust in.

fias·co m. fiasco, failure.

fí·at m. [pl. **-ats**] *(mandato)* fiat, decree; *(consentimiento)* consent, approval.

fi·bra f. fiber <*f. animal* animal fiber>; *(de madera)* grain (of wood); FIG. *(vigor)* vigor, energy; MIN. vein; TEX. staple ♦ **f. acrílica** acrylic fiber • **f. artificial** artificial *or* manmade fiber • **f. de vidrio** fiber glass • **f. vegetal** vegetable fiber.

fi·bri·la·do, –da *or* **fi·bri·lar** adj. firbrillated, fibrillar.

fi·bri·na f. BIOCHEM. fibrin.

fi·bro·ce·men·to m. asbestos cement, fibrocement.

fi·bro·ma m. MED. fibroma.

fi·bro·sis f. MED. fibrosis.

fi·bro·so, –sa adj. fibrous.

fí·bu·la f. *(hebilla)* fibula, clasp; ANAT. fibula.

fic·ción f. fiction, invention ♦ **f. de derecho** *or* **legal** LAW legal fiction.

fic·ti·cio, –cia adj. *(fingido)* fictitious, false; *(imaginado)* fictitious, imaginary.

fi·cha f. *(en los juegos)* counter, chip; *(dominó)* domino; *(disco de metal)* token; *(tarjeta)* file *or* index card; AMER., FIG. rogue, rascal; HOND., P. RICO five-cent piece.

fi·char tr. *(apuntar)* to keep (a record) on an index card, to note on an index card; *(en bares, restaurantes)* to keep a tab; (*en fábricas*) to punch (a clock) in *or* out; (*en dominó*) to play (a domino); FIG., COLL. (*cuidarse de*) to keep tabs on (someone) —intr. SPORT. to sign up *or* on; COL. to die.

fi·che·ro m. (*conjunto*) card index, file; (*mueble*) file cabinet.

fi·de·dig·no, –na adj. trustworthy, reliable.

fi·dei·co·mi·sa·rio, –ria LAW I. adj. trust, fiduciary II. m.f. trustee, fiduciary.

fi·de·li·dad f. (*lealtad*) fidelity, faithfulness; (*exactitud*) exactness, accuracy ♦ **alta f.** ELECTRON. high fidelity.

fi·de·o m. CUL. (soup) noodle; FIG., COLL. (*persona delgada*) skinny person, rail ♦ **estar como un f.** COLL. to be as skinny as a rail.

fi·du·cia·rio, –ria I. adj. fiduciary II. m.f. fiduciary, trustee.

fie·bre f. MED. fever; FIG. (*agitación*) fever, intense excitement <*f. política* political fever>; ARG., CHILE (*pícaro*) shrewd person ♦ **bajo f.** in delirium • **f. aftosa** VET. foot-and-mouth disease, hoof-and-mouth disease • **f. amarilla** MED. yellow fever • **f. cerebral** MED. brain fever • **f. del heno** MED. hay fever • **f. láctea** MED. milk fever • **f. palúdica** MED. malaria • **f. reumática** MED. rheumatic fever • **f. tifoidea** MED. typhoid fever • **tener f.** MED. to run a fever *or* a temperature.

fiel I. adj. (*leal*) faithful, loyal <*amigos fieles* faithful friends>; (*constante*) loyal <*ella es f. a las costumbres de su país* she is loyal to the customs of her country>; (*exacto*) exact, accurate <*un relato f.* an accurate account>; (*honrado*) honest, trustworthy <*un criado f.* a trustworthy servant>; (*seguro*) reliable <*un testigo f.* a reliable witness>; (*religioso*) faithful II. m. (*oficial*) public inspector; (*aguja*) needle, pointer (on a scale); (*clavillo*) pin (of scissors) ♦ **los fieles** RELIG. the faithful.

fiel·men·te adv. faithfully, loyally.

fiel·tro m. TEX. felt; (*sombrero*) felt hat.

fie·ra I. f. ZOOL. (*bestia*) wild animal *or* beast; FIG. (*persona irritada*) hothead, ornery person; (*persona cruel*) beast, brute ♦ **estar hecho una f.** FIG. to be hotheaded *or* in a rage • **ser una f. para** FIG. to be a fiend for II. adj. see **fiero, –ra.**

fie·ra·men·te adv. fiercely, ferociously.

fie·re·za f. (*crueldad*) fierceness, ferocity; FIG. (*deformidad*) ugliness, deformity.

fie·ro, –ra I. adj. (*cruel*) fierce, ferocious; (*orgulloso*) haughty, proud; (*grande*) enormous, huge; FIG. (*horroroso*) terrifying, horrifying; MEX., COLL. ugly, hideous II. m. bluff, threat ♦ **echar fieros** to bluster, make threats —f. see **fiera.**

fie·rre, fierro see **ferrar.**

fie·rro m. AMER., AGR. (*marca*) brand, mark (on cattle); (*hierro*) iron; MEX., COLL. coin ♦ **fierros** AMER. tools.

fies·ta f. RELIG. feast, holy day; (*celebración*) party, celebration; (*feriado*) holiday <*f. nacional* national holiday> ♦ **aguar la f.** FIG., COLL. to spoil the fun • **f. de guardar** *or* **de precepto** RELIG. holy day of obligation • **Fiesta de la Raza** Columbus Day • **guardar** *or* **santificar las fiestas** RELIG. to observe the holy days • **hacer f.** to take a holiday • **no estar para fiestas** FIG. to be in no mood for joking • **se acabó la f.** COLL. the party's over.

fies·te·ar intr. AMER. to party, carouse.

fí·ga·ro I. adj. VEN. medium blue II. m. (*barbero*) barber, hairdresser; (*prenda*) short jacket, bolero.

fi·gón m. cheap restaurant.

fi·gu·li·no, –na adj. CERAM. figurine, earthenware.

fi·gu·ra f. (*forma*) figure, form, shape; (*cara*) face, countenance; (*personaje*) figure <*una de las principales figuras del movimiento* one of the principal figures of the movement>; (*actor*) character; (*naipe*) face card; (*mudanza*) figure, step (in dancing); (*símbolo*) sign, symbol <*el cordero pascual era la f. de la Eucaristía* the pascual lamb was the symbol of the Eucharist>; GEOM. figure, diagram; MUS. note; RHET. figure ♦ **f. de dicción** figure of speech • **tener buena f.** to be handsome *or* good-looking —m. (*valentón*) blowhard.

fi·gu·ra·ble adj. imaginable, conceivable.

fi·gu·ra·ción f. (*representación*) figuration, representation;

(*imaginación*) imagination, conception; (*idea*) idea, invention; ARG., role in society.

fi·gu·ra·da·men·te adv. figuratively.

fi·gu·ra·do, –da I. past part. see **figurar** II. adj. (*simbólico*) figurative; MUS. figurate, florid.

fi·gu·ran·te, –ta m.f. THEAT. (*comparsa*) extra, walk-on; FIG. (*persona incidental*) supernumerary.

fi·gu·rar tr. (*representar*) to represent, depict; (*simbolizar*) to allegorize, represent symbolically; (*fingir*) to feign, simulate —intr. (*formar parte*) to figure, be *or* take part; (*ser importante*) to be important *or* notable —reflx. to imagine, figure ♦ **¡figúrate!** just imagine! • **ya me lo figuraba** I thought as much.

fi·gu·ra·ti·vo, –va adj. figurative.

fi·gu·re·ro, –ra I. adj. grimacing II. m.f. (*persona que hace muecas*) grimacer; CERAM. figurine maker *or* merchant.

fi·gu·ri·lla *or* **fi·gu·ri·ta** m.f. COLL. runt, small insignificant person.

fi·gu·rín m. (*dibujo*) fashion plate *or* design; FIG. (*lechuguino*) fashion plate, dandy ♦ **figurines** fashion magazines.

fi·ja I. f. (*bisagra*) large hinge; CONST. (*paleta*) trowel; (*cosa segura*) sure thing, winner; ARG. harpoon ♦ **a la f.** ARG. for sure, for certain II. adj. see **fijo, –ja.**

fi·ja·ción f. (*establecimiento*) fixing, setting; CHEM., PHOTOG., PSYCH. fixation.

fi·ja·do, –da I. past part. see **fijar** II. adj. HER. said of shapes which are pointed at the bottom III. m. PHOTOG. fixer.

fi·ja·dor, –do·ra I. adj. fixing, fixative II. m. CARP., CONST. (*obrero*) pointer; (*líquido para el pelo*) hair spray, setting solution; PAINT., PHOTOG. fixative.

fi·ja·men·te adv. (*con seguridad*) firmly, assuredly; (*atentamente*) fixedly, steadfastly; (*intensamente*) intensely, attentively.

fi·jar tr. (*clavar*) to fix, fasten, secure; (*pegar*) to stick up, put up <*fijaron un anuncio en el tablón* they put an announcement up on the bulletin board>; (*dirigir*) to fix, focus <*fijé la atención en la pantalla* I focused my attention on the screen>; (*precisar*) to fix, set <*fijamos la hora de la cita* we set the time for the appointment>; (*establecer*) to establish <*fijó la residencia en la Ciudad de México* he established residence in Mexico City>; CINEM., PHOTOG. to fix; MAS. to point ♦ **f. los ojos** (*mirar*) to stare; COLL. (*morir*) to die —reflx. (*hacerse estable*) to settle, become fixed <*el dolor se le fijó en la espalda* the pain settled in his shoulder>; (*atender*) to pay attention <*fíjate en lo que digo!* pay attention to what I am saying!>; (*notar*) to notice <*no me fijé en los detalles* I did not notice the details> ♦ **¡fíjate!** just imagine!

fi·je·za f. (*firmeza*) firmness, steadfastness; (*seguridad*) certainty, assuredness; (*persistencia*) persistence, continuance ♦ **mirar con f.** to stare at, look at fixedly • **saber algo con f.** to know something for certain.

Fi·ji Fiji.

fi·jo, –ja I. past part. see **fijar** II. adj. (*firme*) fixed, steady <*la mesa está f.* the table is steady>; (*permanente*) permanent <*un empleado f.* a permanent employee>; (*inmóvil*) stationary, fixed (*una estrella f.* a fixed star>; (*invariable*) fixed, set <*un precio f.* a set price>; (*estable*) stable, steady <*una renta f.* a steady income>; (*de colores*) fast, indelible; CHEM. fixed, nonvolatile ♦ **de f.** certainly, surely III. m. fixed salary —f. see **fija** IV. adv. fixedly, pointedly; PERU certainly.

fi·la f. (*hilera*) file <*f. india* single file>; (*cola*) line, queue; (*línea*) row, tier <*en primera f.* in the first row>; FIG., COLL. (*tirria*) dislike, aversion; SL. (*rostro*) face; MIL. (*rango*) rank ♦ **alistarse en filas** MIL. to sign up, enlist • **cerrar** *or* **estrechar las filas** to close ranks • **en filas** MIL. on active duty *or* service • **llamar a filas** MIL. to call up • **ponerse en f.** to line *or* queue up • **romper filas** MIL. to break ranks • **salir de las filas** to rise from the ranks • **tener f. a uno** COLL. to have something against someone, bear someone a grudge.

fi·lac·te·ria f. phylactery.

Fi·la·del·fia Philadelphia.

fi·la·men·to m. filament.

fi·la·men·to·so, –sa adj. filamentous, filamentary.

fi·lan·tro·pí·a f. philanthropy.

fi·lan·tró·pi·co, –ca adj. philanthropic, philanthropical.
fi·lán·tro·po, –pa m.f. philanthropist.
fi·lar·mo·ní·a f. MUS. love of music.
fi·lar·mó·ni·co, –ca MUS. **I.** adj. philharmonic, fond of music ◆ **orquesta f.** philharmonic (orchestra) **II.** m.f. music lover, philharmonic.
fi·la·te·lia f. philately, stamp collecting.
fi·la·té·li·co, –ca adj. philatelic.
fi·la·te·lis·ta m.f. philatelist, stamp collector.
fi·la·te·ro, –ra **I.** adj. *(verboso)* wordy, verbose; *(embaucador)* fast-talking **II.** m.f. *(hablador)* vervose person; *(embaucador)* fast talker.
fi·le·no, –na adj. COLL. effeminate, dainty.
fi·le·te m. CUL. fillet; *(de lomo)* sirloin; ARCHIT. fillet; EQUIT. snaffle; *(asador)* small roasting spit; TECH. *(del tornillo)* thread (of a screw); *(raya)* band, line.
fi·le·te·ar tr. *(adornar con filetes)* to fillet, decorate with fillets; TECH. *(roscar)* to thread.
fi·lia·ción f. *(descendencia)* filiation; *(enlace)* connection, relationship; *(señas personales)* description; MIL. regimental register.
fi·lial **I.** adj. *(del hijo)* filial; COM. subsidiary, branch **II.** f. COM. *(sucursal)* branch (office); *(subdivisión)* subsidiary.
fi·liar tr. to take down a description of (someone) —reflex. MIL. to enlist, join (up); *(afiliarse)* to join *or* affiliate (with).
fi·li·bus·te·ro m. HIST., POL. filibuster; *(pirata)* pirate, freebooter.
fi·li·for·me adj. filiform, thread-like.
fi·li·gra·na f. *(orfebrería)* filigree; PRINT. watermark; FIG. *(cosa delicada)* delicate object *or* ornamentation; CUBA, BOT. variety of lantana.
fi·li·lí m. [pl. **-lí·es**] COLL. fineness, delicacy.
fi·lí·pi·ca f. philippic, invective.
Fi·li·pi·nas f. (the) Philippines ◆ **las Islas F.** the Philippine Islands.
fi·li·pi·no, –na **I.** adj. Philippine, Filipino **II.** m.f. Filipino.
fi·lis·te·o, –a **I.** adj. HIST. Philistine **II.** m.f. HIST. Philistine —m. FIG. *(hombrón)* giant, big man; FIG., COLL. *(inculto)* boor, Philistine.
film *or* **fil·me** m. CINEM. film, movie.
fil·mar tr. CINEM. to film, shoot (a movie).
fíl·mi·co, –ca adj. CINEM. film, movie, cinematic.
fil·mo·lo·gí·a f. CINEM. film *or* cinema studies.
fi·lo m. *(corte)* cutting edge; *(borde)* edge, dividing line; BIOL. phylum; C. AMER., MEX. hunger ◆ **al f. de la medianoche** at the stroke of midnight • **dar f.** *or* **un f.** *(afilar)* to sharpen; FIG. *(incitar)* to incite, excite • **de f.** COL. resolutely • **f. del viento** direction of the wind • **por f.** exactly • **sacar f.** to sharpen • **tirarse un f. con** CHILE to have an argument with.
fi·lo·lo·gí·a f. philology.
fi·lo·ló·gi·co, –ca adj. philological, philologic.
fi·ló·lo·go, –ga m.f. philologist, philologer.
fi·lón m. MIN. vein, lode; FIG. *(fuente de riquezas)* gold mine.
fi·lo·so, –sa adj. AMER. sharp, sharp-edged; HOND. *(hambriento)* hungry.
fi·lo·so·fa·dor, –do·ra **I.** adj. philosophizing **II.** m.f. philosophizer.
fi·lo·so·fal adj. ◆ **piedra f.** philosopher's stone.
fi·lo·so·far intr. to philosophize.
fi·lo·so·fas·tro m. dilettante philosopher.
fi·lo·so·fí·a f. philosophy.
fi·lo·só·fi·ca·men·te adv. philosophically.
fi·lo·só·fi·co, –ca adj. philosophic, philosophical.
fi·lo·so·fis·mo m. philosophism, sophistry.
fi·ló·so·fo, –fa **I.** adj. *(filosófico)* philosophic, philosophical; *(afilosofado)* pseudo-philosophic **II.** m.f. philosopher.
fi·lo·tec·nia f. love of the arts.
fi·lo·xe·ra f. BOT., ENTOM. phylloxera; COLL. *(borrachera)* drunkenness.
fil·tra·ción f. *(acción de filtrar)* filtration, filtering; FIG. *(malversación)* embezzlement, diverting of funds.
fil·tra·dor, –do·ra **I.** adj. filtering **II.** m.f. *(el que filtra)* filterer —m. *(filtro)* filter.
fil·tran·te adj. *(que filtra)* filtering; *(que se filtra)* disappearing, dwindling.

fil·trar tr. to filter —intr. to filter, pass through —reflex. *(pasarse)* to filter, pass through; *(disminuirse)* to disappear, dwindle <*su dinero se filtraba* his money dwindled>.
fil·tro m. TECH. filter; *(bebedizo)* love potion, philter ◆ **f. de aceite** AUTO. oil filter • **f. de aire** AUTO. air filter • **f. de banda** TELEC. band-pass filter • **f. de gasolina** AUTO. gas filter • **f. de paso alto** *or* **f. superior** TELEC. high-pass filter • **f. de paso bajo** *or* **f. inferior** TELEC. low-pass filter.
fim·bria f. SEW. border *or* hem (of a full-length skirt); ANAT., BOT. fimbria.
fi·mo m. manure, dung.
fin m. *(conclusión)* end, conclusion <*el f. del cuento* the end of the story>; *(extremo)* end <*el f. de la calle* the end of the street>; *(meta)* aim, purpose, end; *(muerte)* death, end ◆ **a f. de** in order to • **a f. de cuentas** in the final analysis • **a f. de que** so that • **a fines de** at the end of <*a fines del mes* at the end of the month> • **al f.** at last, finally • **al f. y al cabo** after all, when all is said and done • **dar f. a** to finish off • **de f.** in the final analysis • **en f.** *(finalmente)* finally; *(en resumen)* in brief, in short; well, well then <*en f., veremos* well, we'll see> • **f. de fiesta** THEAT. grand finale • **f. de semana** weekend • **poner f. a** to finish, put an end to • **por f.** finally, at last • **sin f.** endless • **tener f.** to come to an end • **un sin f.** no end <*un sin f. de problemas* no end of problems>.
fi·na·do, –da **I.** past part. see **finar II.** m.f. deceased, dead person.
fi·nal **I.** adj. final, last, ultimate <*el Juicio F.* RELIG. the Last Judgment> **II.** m. *(fin)* end, ending; MUS. finale —f. SPORT. *(última prueba)* final ◆ **al f.** in *or* at the end.
fi·na·li·dad f. end, purpose, objective.
fi·na·lis·ta m.f. finalist.
fi·na·li·za·ción f. conclusion, finish.
fi·na·li·zar §04 tr. to finish, conclude —intr. to (come to an) end.
fi·nal·men·te adv. finally.
fi·na·men·te adv. *(con finura)* finely, exquisitely; *(cortésmente)* courteously, politely.
fi·nan·cia·ción f. *or* **fi·nan·cia·mien·to** m. financing.
fi·nan·ciar tr. to finance.
fi·nan·cie·ro, –ra **I.** adj. financial **II.** m.f. financier.
fi·nan·zas f.pl. *(hacienda)* finance; *(caudal)* finances.
fi·nar intr. to pass away, die —reflex. to long *or* yearn (for).
fin·ca f. *(propiedad)* (piece of) property, real estate; AMER. farm ◆ **f. mala** COLL. bad lot *or* egg • **f. raíz** real estate • **f. urbana** building.
fin·car §70 tr. P. RICO, AGR. to cultivate, farm —intr. *(adquirir fincas)* to acquire property *or* real estate; to settle, get established <*por fin fincamos en Hermosillo* we finally settled in Hermosillo> AMER. to rest, lie <*el problema finca en su política oficial* the problem rests in their official policy> —reflex. to acquire property *or* real estate.
fi·nés, –ne·sa adj. & m.f. *(habitante)* Finnish —m. *(idioma)* Finnish.
fi·ne·za f. *(cualidad de fino)* fineness, excellence; *(cortesía)* courtesy, politeness; *(amabilidad)* kindness, affection; *(regalo)* gift, present; *(delicadeza)* fine workmanship.
fin·gi·da·men·te adv. feignedly, falsely.
fin·gi·do, –da **I.** past part. see **fingir II.** adj. false, feigned **III.** m.f. feigner, dissembler.
fin·gi·dor, –do·ra **I.** adj. feigning, dissembling **II.** m.f. feigner, dissembler.
fin·gi·mien·to m. feigning, pretense.
fin·gir §32 tr. to pretend, feign <*f. dormir* to pretend to be sleeping>.
fi·ni·qui·tar tr. COM. to close, settle (an account); *(concluir)* to conclude, finish; FIG., COLL. *(matar)* to bump off, rub out.
fi·ni·qui·to m. COM. closing *or* settlement (of an account) ◆ **dar f.** COM. to close *or* settle (an account); FIG. *(concluir)* to finish, wind up.
fi·ni·to, –ta adj. finite.
fin·ja, finjo see **fingir.**
fin·lan·dés, –de·sa **I.** adj. Finnish **II.** m.f. *(habitante)* Finn —m. *(idioma)* Finnish.
Fin·lan·dia f. Finland.
fi·no, –na adj. *(menudo)* fine, slender; *(excelente)* excellent,

of high quality; *(precioso)* precious <*una piedra f.* a precious stone>; *(puro)* pure <*oro f.* pure gold>; *(cortés)* refined, elegant (people); *(de facciones delicadas)* delicate, fine-featured; *(atento)* affectionate, sweet; *(astuto)* astute, shrewd; MARIT. swift (said of sailing vessels).

fi·no·lis COLL. **I.** adj. overly refined, affected **II.** m.f. affected person.

fin·qué, finque see **fincar.**

fin·tar tr. to make a feint —intr. SPORT. to feint.

fi·nu·ra f. *(excelencia)* excellence, fineness; *(urbanidad)* refinement, politeness; *(sutileza)* subtlety, delicacy; *(agudeza)* sharpness, acuteness.

fiord or **fior·do** m. GEOG. fjord, fiord.

fir·ma f. *(nombre)* signature; *(acción de firmar)* signing; COM. firm, company ♦ **f. en blanco** carte blanche.

fir·ma·men·to m. firmament, heavens.

fir·man·te I. adj. signatory **II.** m.f. signer, signatory ♦ **el abajo f.** the undersigned.

fir·mar tr. & reflex. to sign.

fir·me I. adj. *(estable)* firm, stable, steady; *(de colores)* fast, indelible; FIG. *(constante)* steadfast, staunch <*f. en sus propósitos* steadfast in his aims>; *(claro)* clear <*vista f.* clear vision>; COM. firm <*una oferta f.* a firm offer>; MIL. straight <*una columna f.* a straight column> ♦ **de f.** *(con constancia)* hard <*trabajaron de f.* they worked hard>; *(con violencia)* hard, steadily <*llueve de f.* it is raining steadily> • **en f.** final, definitive • **estar en lo f.** to be on firm ground • **¡firmes!** MIL. attention! • **mantenerse f.** to stand firm, hold one's ground • **ponerse f.** to stand firm; MIL. to come to attention **II.** m. foundation, bed **III.** adv. firmly, steadily.

fir·me·men·te adv. firmly.

fir·me·za f. *(solidez)* solidity, stability; FIG. *(entereza)* firmness, resolve.

fir·món, -mo·na I. adj. said of someone who signs another's work **II.** m.f. someone who signs another's work —m. MEX. dummy, figurehead.

fi·ru·le·tes m.pl. AMER. adornments, ornaments.

fis·cal I. adj. *(del fisco)* fiscal, treasury; *(financiero)* fiscal, financial **II.** m. *(tesorero)* treasurer, treasury official; *(abogado)* district attorney, public prosecutor (G.B.); FIG. *(entremetido)* busybody, snooper; AMER. churchwarden.

fis·ca·lí·a f. LAW *(oficio)* post of district attorney; *(oficina)* district attorney's office.

fis·ca·li·cé, fiscalice see **fiscalizar.**

fis·ca·li·za·ción f. *(control)* supervision, overseeing; *(investigación)* investigation, inspection; FIG. *(curioseo)* prying, snooping.

fis·ca·li·za·dor, -do·ra FIG. **I.** adj. prying, snooping **II.** m.f. snooper.

fis·ca·li·zar §04 tr. *(controlar)* to supervise, oversee; *(investigar)* to investigate, inspect; FIG. *(curiosear)* to pry into, snoop; *(criticar)* to criticize, find fault with.

fis·co m. *(tesoro)* public treasury, exchequer (G.B.); VEN. copper coin.

fis·ga f. *(tridente)* fishgig, pronged harpoon; *(burla)* teasing, mocking; GUAT., MEX., TAUR. banderilla ♦ **hacer f. de** to make fun of.

fis·ga·dor, -do·ra I. adj. *(curioso)* prying, snooping; *(burlador)* teasing, mocking; *(pescador)* harpooning, spearing **II.** m.f. *(curioso)* snoop, busybody; *(burlador)* teaser, mocker; *(pescador)* harpooner, spearer.

fis·gar §47 tr. *(pescar)* to spear, harpoon (fish); *(husmear)* to pry into, snoop on —intr. & reflex. to make fun of, mock.

fis·gón, -go·na COLL. **I.** adj. *(curioso)* snooping, prying; *(burlador)* teasing, mocking **II.** m.f. *(curioso)* snooper; *(burlador)* tease, mocker.

fis·go·ne·ar tr. COLL. to snoop or pry habitually.

fi·si·ble adj. fissile.

fí·si·ca I. f. physics ♦ **f. experimental** experimental physics • **f. nuclear** nuclear physics **II.** adj. see **físico, -ca.**

fí·si·ca·men·te adv. physically.

fí·si·co, -ca I. adj. *(corporal)* physical; CUBA, MEX. delicate, finicky **II.** m.f. *(persona)* physicist; ARCH. *(médico)* physician —m. *(apariencia)* physique, appearance —f. see **física.**

fi·sio·cra·cia f. physiocracy.

fi·sió·cra·ta adj. & m.f. physiocrat.

fi·sio·lo·gí·a f. physiology.

fi·sio·ló·gi·co, -ca adj. physiological, physiologic.

fi·si·ó·lo·go, -ga m.f. physiologist.

fi·sión f. PHYS. fission.

fi·sio·te·ra·pia f. MED. physiotherapy.

fi·so·no·mí·a or **fi·sio·no·mí·a** f. *(cara)* physiognomy, face; *(aspecto)* aspect, appearance.

fis·tol m. *(listo)* sly or crafty person; MEX. tie pin.

fís·tu·la f. MED., MUS. fistula; *(conducto)* pipe, tube.

fi·su·ra f. fissure.

fi·to·gra·fí·a f. BOT. phytography, descriptive botany.

fla·be·la·do, -da adj. flabellate, fan-shaped.

flac·ci·dez or **fla·ci·dez** f. flaccidity, flabbiness.

flác·ci·do, -da or **flá·ci·do, -da** adj. flaccid, flabby.

fla·co, -ca I. adj. *(delgado)* thin, lean; FIG. *(sin fuerza)* weak, feeble <*un argumento f.* a weak argument> **II.** m. FIG. *(debilidad de una persona)* weak spot, weakness.

fla·cón, -co·na adj. AMER. skinny, very thin.

fla·cu·cho, -cha adj. COLL. skinny.

fla·cu·ra f. *(delgadez)* thinness, skinniness; *(debilidad)* weakness, feebleness.

fla·ge·la·ción f. flagellation, whipping.

fla·ge·la·do, -da I. past part. of **flagelar II.** adj. flagellate.

fla·ge·la·dor, -do·ra I. adj. flagellating, whipping **II.** m.f. flagellator.

fla·ge·lan·te I. adj. flagellating, whipping **II.** m. RELIG. flagellant ♦ **Flagelante** RELIG. Flagellant.

fla·ge·lar tr. *(azotar)* to flagellate, whip; FIG. *(censurar)* to revile, flay.

fla·ge·lo m. *(azote)* whip, scourge; FIG. *(calamidad)* calamity; ZOOL. flagellum.

fla·gran·cia f. flagrancy.

fla·gran·te adj. *(evidente)* flagrant; POET. flagrant, blazing ♦ **en f. (delito)** in the act, red-handed.

fla·ma f. *(llama)* flame; *(reflejo)* reflection, reverberation (of a flame).

fla·man·te adj. *(brillante)* brilliant, bright; *(nuevo)* brand-new, like new <*ese traje está f.* that suit looks like new>.

fla·me·ar intr. *(llamear)* to blaze, flame; *(ondear)* to flap, flutter <*la vela flamea en el viento* the sail is flapping in the wind> —tr. MED. to sterilize (by burning alcohol).

fla·men·co, -ca I. adj. *(de Flandes)* Flemish; *(agitanado)* flamenco <*un canto f.* a flamenco song>; *(achulado)* cocky <*ponerse f.* to get cocky>; C. AMER., MEX. skinny **II.** m.f. *(habitante)* Fleming ♦ **los flamencos** the Flemish —m. *(idioma)* Flemish; *(cuchillo)* dagger, sheath knife; ORNITH. flamingo.

flá·mu·la f. pennant, streamer.

flan m. CUL. flan, caramel custard.

flan·co m. *(lado)* side, flank; MIL. flank.

Flan·des m. Flanders.

fla·ne·ro m. CUL. custard mold.

flan·que·a·do, -da I. past part. of **flanquear II.** adj. flanked ♦ **f. de** or **por** flanked by.

flan·que·ar tr. MIL. to protect, defend; *(estar al lado)* to flank.

flan·que·o m. flanking.

fla·que·ar intr. *(debilitarse)* to weaken; *(decaer de ánimo)* to lose heart.

fla·que·za f. *(delgadez)* thinness, leanness; *(debilidad)* weakness; FIG. *(fragilidad)* feebleness, frailty.

fla·to m. MED. flatus, gas; AMER. *(tristeza)* sadness, melancholy; C. AMER. *(miedo)* fear, apprehension.

fla·to·so, -sa adj. MED. flatulent; AMER. sad, melancholy.

fla·tu·len·cia f. flatulence.

fla·tu·len·to, -ta adj. flatulent.

flau·ta f. MUS. flute ♦ **entre pitos y flautas** FIG. one thing or another • **f. traversera** MUS. transverse or German flute • **¡la gran f.!** COLL. my God! —m. MUS. flautist, flutist.

flau·ta·do, -da MUS. **I.** adj. flutelike **II.** m. flute (organ stop).

flau·tín m. MUS. *(instrumento)* piccolo; *(músico)* piccolo player.

flau·tis·ta m.f. flautist, flutist.

fla·ves·cen·te adj. flavescent, yellowish.

flé·bil adj. lamentable, deplorable.

fle·bi·tis f. MED. phlebitis.

fle·bo·to·mí·a f. MED. phlebotomy, bloodletting.
fle·co m. (adorno) fringe; (borde desgastado) frayed edge (of cloth); (flequillo) bangs (of hair) ♦ **flecos** gossamer.
flec·tor, –to·ra I. adj. flexural II. m. MECH. flexible joint.
fle·cha f. (saeta) arrow; ARCHIT. (de arco) rise; (aguja) fleche, spire; AUTO. direction indicator; GEOM. sagitta; MEX., P. RICO, MECH. axle ♦ **salir como una f.** to shoot out, fly out like a shot.
fle·cha·dor, –do·ra m.f. archer.
fle·char tr. (estirar el arco) to draw (a bow); (asaetear) to shoot with an arrow; (matar) to kill with an arrow; FIG., COLL. (enamorar) to infatuate, make a hit with; MEX. to gamble recklessly.
fle·cha·zo m. (disparo) arrow shot; (herida) arrow wound; FIG., COLL. (amor) love at first sight.
fle·che·ra f. VEN. (canoa) long canoe; MIL. light war boat.
fle·che·ro m. (arquero) archer, bowman; (fabricante) arrow maker.
fle·je m. (zuncho) iron band or strip (used as barrel hoop); (resorte) iron spring.
fle·ma f. (humor, mucosidad) phlegm; FIG. (serenidad) phlegm, calmness; (torpeza) phlegm, sluggishness.
fle·má·ti·co, –ca adj. phlegmatic, phlegmatical.
fle·mo·so, –sa adj. phlegmatic, phlegmy.
fle·mu·do, –da I. adj. phlegmatic, sluggish II. m.f. phlegmatic or sluggish person.
fle·qui·llo m. bangs (of hair).
fle·ta·dor m. (alquilador) charterer; (embarcador) freighter, freight loader.
fle·ta·men·to m. (alquiler) chartering; (embarco) freighting, freight loading; (contrato) freight charter.
fle·tan·te m. AMER. var. of **fletador**.
fle·tar tr. (alquilar) to charter (a ship or plane); (embarcar) to load; AMER. to hire, rent (animals or vehicles); CHILE, PERU to hurl, unleash (insults or blows) —reflex. CUBA, MEX., COLL. to scram, split; ARG. to crash (a meeting).
fle·te m. (alquiler) charter fee; (carga) freight, cargo; AMER. (transporte) freightage, shipping; (precio de transporte) freightage, shipping fee; ARG., COL. spirited horse; CUBA, PERU high society.
fle·te·ro, –ra I. m. MEX. hauler, freighter; ARG., CHILE, PERU (barquero) boatman, ferryman; ARG. (propietario de carros) owner of vehicles for hire; AMER. (cobrador) fare collector; ECUAD., GUAT. porter, mover —f. CUBA prostitute II. adj. (de alquiler) for hire or rent (vehicles).
fle·xi·bi·li·dad f. flexibility.
fle·xi·bi·li·zar §04 tr. to make flexible, flexibilize.
fle·xi·ble I. adj. (elástico) flexible <cobre f. flexible copper>; FIG. pliant, tractable <una personalidad f. a pliant personality> II. m. ELEC. electric cord.
fle·xión f. (doblamiento) flexion; GRAM. inflection.
fle·xio·nal adj. GRAM. inflectional, flectional.
fle·xor, –xo·ra I. adj. (que dobla) flexing; ANAT. flexor (muscle) II. ANAT. flexor (muscle).
flir·te·ar intr. to flirt.
flir·te·o m. flirt, flirting.
flo·ja·men·te adv. slackly, idly.
flo·je·ar intr. (obrar con flojedad) to slacken, idle; (flaquear) to weaken.
flo·je·dad f. (flaqueza) weakness, debility; FIG. (pereza) laziness, carelessness.
flo·jel m. TEX. nap (of cloth); ORNITH. down.
flo·je·ra f. (pereza) laziness, carelessness.
flo·jo, –ja I. adj. (suelto) loose, slack <una cuerda f. a slack rope>; (fláccido) limp, flabby; (débil) weak, thin <un vino f. a weak wine>; (malo) weak, poor <una novela f. a weak novel>; FIG. (holgazán) lazy, shiftless II. m.f. FIG. idler, loafer; AMER. coward.
flo·que·a·do, –da adj. fringed.
flor f. BOT. flower <f. de la pasión passionflower>; blossom, bloom <en f. in bloom>; (polvo blanco) bloom (on certain fruits); FIG. (parte superior) flower, cream; (frescura) bloom, prime <la f. de la vida the prime of life>; METAL. flowers, powder; (nata de vino) flowers, film (on wine); (piropo) compliment; (parte de piel) grain (of leather); (trampa) card trick; CHILE white spot (on fingernails) ♦ **a f. de** on the surface of, level with • **a f. de agua** (a la superficie) at water level; (inundado) swamped, awash •

andar de f. fragrante FIG., COLL. to be infatuated • **andarse a la f. del berro** FIG. to lead a bohemian life • **como mil flores** or **de mi f.** FIG., COLL. excellent, splendid • **dar en la f.** to get to the point • **dar** or **echar flores** to compliment, flatter • **dar flores secas a** (insultar) to insult; (amenazar) to threaten • **f. artificial** or **de mano** artificial flower • **f. de amor** BOT. amaranth • **f. de cinc** METAL. zinc bloom • **f. de harina** flour meal • **f. de canela** FIG. the best, the tops • **f. de la maravilla** BOT. type of iris • **f. de la Trinidad** BOT. pansy • **f. del embudo** BOT. calla lily • **f. del sol** BOT. sunflower • **f. de lis** BOT. jacobean lily; HER. fleur-de-lis • **f. de Pascua** BOT. poinsettia • **flo·res de cantueso** COLL. trifle, triviality • **flores de muerto** BOT. marigold • **f. y nata** FIG. the cream of the crop.
flo·ra f. BOT. flora.
flo·ra·ción f. BOT. florescence, flowering.
flo·ral adj. floral.
flo·rar intr. to flower, bloom.
flo·re·ar tr. (adornar) to flower, decorate with flowers; (cerner) to sift (flour) —intr. (blandir la espada) to brandish a sword; MUS. to play an arpeggio (on a guitar); FIG., COLL. (echar flores) to pay compliments; FIG. (escoger lo mejor) to pick the best; AMER. to flower.
flo·re·cer §17 intr. (echar flor) to flower, bloom <los árboles florecen cada año the trees bloom each year>; FIG. (prosperar) to thrive, flourish <las artes florecían durante su reinado the arts flourished during his reign> —reflex. (ponerse mohoso) to become or go moldy <se floreció el queso the cheese went moldy>.
flo·re·ci·do, –da I. past part. see **florecer** II. adj. (mohoso) moldy; AMER. flowered.
flo·re·cien·te adj. (que florece) flowering, blooming <campo f. flowering countryside>; FIG. (próspero) thriving, prosperous.
flo·re·ci·mien·to m. flowering, blossoming.
Flo·ren·cia f. Florence.
flo·ren·ti·no, –na adj. & m.f. Florentine.
flo·re·o m. FIG. (conversación vana) chatter, small talk; (dicho frívolo) quip, jest; SPORT. (en la esgrima) flourish (in fencing); MUS. arpeggio (on a guitar); (en la danza) flourish (in dancing).
flo·re·rí·a f. flower or florist's shop.
flo·re·ro, –ra I. adj. FIG. joking, jesting II. m.f. (persona) florist —m. (vaso) (flower) vase; PAINT. flower painting.
flo·res·cen·cia f. CHEM. efflorescence; BOT. florescence, flowering.
flo·res·ta f. (bosque) wood, forest; (sitio ameno) pleasant rural spot; FIG. (antología) collection, anthology.
flo·re·ta f. ARTS flourish (in Spanish dance); (bordadura) leather border (on a girth).
flo·re·ta·zo m. SPORT. foil thrust; MEX., COLL. sponging, cadging (a loan).
flo·re·te I. adj. superfine (sugar or paper) II. m. SPORT. (esgrima) foil fencing; (espadín) foil; TEX. superfine cotton cloth.
flo·rez·ca, florezco see **florecer**.
flo·ri·cul·tor, –to·ra m.f. floriculturist, flower grower.
flo·ri·cul·tu·ra f. floriculture, flower growing.
flo·ri·dez f. FIG. floridity, floweriness.
flo·ri·do, –da adj. (que tiene flores) full of flowers, flowery; FIG. (escogido) choice, select; (ornamentado) flowery, florid (language, style).
flo·ri·pon·dio m. BOT. floripondio; FIG. (adorno) gaudy flower (in printed fabric).
flo·ris·ta m.f. (vendedor) florist; (fabricante) (artificial) flower maker.
flo·ta f. MIL. (buques) fleet; (aviones) squadron; COM. merchant marine; COL. brag, boast; CHILE crowd, throng.
flo·ta·bi·li·dad f. buoyancy, floatability.
flo·ta·ble adj. buoyant, floatable.
flo·ta·ción f. (flotamiento) flotation, floating; FIN. floating (of currency).
flo·ta·dor, –do·ra I. adj. floating, buoyant II. m. (cuerpo) float; MARIT. (batanga) outrigger; MARIT., TECH. (dispositivo del hidroavión) float ♦ **f. de alarma** TECH. boiler float.
flo·ta·du·ra f. or **flo·ta·mien·to** m. flotation, floating.
flo·tan·te adj. (que flota) floating, buoyant; CHILE, COL., COLL. bragging, boastful.

flo·tar intr. *(sostenerse)* to float; FIG. *(oscilar)* to fluctuate.
flo·te ♦ **a flote** afloat • **ponerse** or **salir a flote** FIG. to get back on one's feet.
flo·ti·lla f. MARIT. flotilla; AVIA. small squadron.
fluc·tua·ción f. *(oscilación)* fluctuation, FIG. *(duda)* vacillation, wavering.
fluc·tuan·te adj. fluctuating.
fluc·tuar §67 intr. *(ondear)* to bob, undulate; *(oscilar)* to fluctuate, vary *<precios que fluctúan* fluctuating prices>; FIG. *(estar en peligro)* to be in danger, be at risk; *(dudar)* to vacillate, waver.
fluen·cia f. *(acción)* stream, flow; *(fuente)* source, spring.
fluen·te adj. streaming, flowing.
flui·dez f. fluidity.
flui·di·fi·car §70 tr. to fluidify.
flui·do, –da I. adj. fluid *<el agua es f.* water is fluid>; FIG. *(fluente)* fluid, flowing *<ese autor tiene un estilo f.* that author has a flowing style>; *(inseguro)* in flux; *(corriente)* unobstructed (said of traffic) II. m. *(líquido)* fluid; ELEC. current.
fluir §18 intr. *(correr)* to flow; FIG. *(brotar)* to gush, stream *<las palabras fluían de su boca* words streamed from his mouth>; MED. to flow.
flu·jo m. *(movimiento)* flow, flux; *(marea)* flow, rising tide; FIG. *(abundancia)* flood, stream *<un f. de palabras* a stream of words> MED. flow, discharge; CHEM. flux ♦ **f. de risa** fit of laughter • **f. de sangre** hemorrhage • **f. de vientre** diarrhea • **f. magnético** magnetic flux • **f. y reflujo** ebb and flow.
flú·or m. CHEM. fluorine.
fluo·res·cen·cia f. fluorescence.
fluo·res·cen·te adj. fluorescent.
fluo·ri·za·ción f. fluoridation.
fluo·ros·co·pio m. MED. fluoroscope.
fluo·ru·ro m. CHEM. fluoride.
flu·vial adj. fluvial, river.
flu·vió·me·tro m. fluviometer, fluviograph.
flux m. [pl. **flux**] *(en naipes)* flush (in cards); CARIB. suit ♦ **estar a f. de todo** AMER. to have nothing • **hacer f.** AMER. to squander everything • **tener f.** GUAT. to be lucky.
flu·ya, fluye see **fluir.**
flu·yen·te adj. flowing.
flu·ye·ra, fluyó see **fluir.**
fo·bia f. PSYCH. phobia.
fo·ca f. ZOOL. seal.
fo·cal adj. MATH., PHYS. focal.
fo·co m. MATH., MED., PHYS. focus; FIG. *(centro)* focus, center; *(fuente)* source; *(reflector)* spotlight ♦ **fuera de f.** PHOTOG. out of focus.
fo·fo, –fa adj. *(blando)* soft, spongy; COLL. *(gordo)* flabby.
fo·ga·je m. *(tributo)* hearth money (household tax); METEOROL. hot and stuffy weather; MED. rash, skin eruption; ECUAD. blaze; P. RICO blush, redness (in the face).
fo·ga·ra·da f. sudden blaze or fire.
fo·ga·ta f. *(hoguera)* bonfire; MIL. fougasse (land mine).
fo·gón m. *(cocina)* stove, range; *(de caldera)* firebox; ARM. vent, touchhole; AMER. bonfire.
fo·go·na·du·ra f. MARIT. mast hole; COL. bonfire.
fo·go·na·zo m. powder flash.
fo·go·ne·ro m. stoker, fireman.
fo·go·si·dad f. fire, spirit *<el demagogo habló con gran f.* the demagogue spoke with great fire>.
fo·go·so, –sa adj. fiery, spirited.
fo·gue·ar tr. ARM. to scale (a gun); MIL. to accustom to gunfire (soldiers, horses); FIG. to harden, inure; VET. to cauterize.
fo·gue·o m. MIL. training (for exposure to gunfire) ♦ **de f.** ARM. blank (shell).
fo·ja f. LAW page, leaf (of a brief); AMER. sheet (of paper).
fo·lia·ción f. BOT. foliation; PRINT. foliation, page numbering.
fo·lia·do, –da I. past part. see **foliar**[1] II. adj. BOT. foliate, foliose.
fo·liar[1] tr. PRINT. to foliate, number.
fo·liar[2] adj. BOT. foliar.
fo·lia·tu·ra f. var. of **foliación.**
fo·lí·cu·lar adj. ANAT., BOT. follicular.
fo·li·cu·la·rio m. DEROG. hack, pamphleteer.

fo·lí·cu·lo m. ANAT., BOT. follicle.
fo·lio m. *(hoja)* page, leaf; PRINT. *(título)* running head or title; COL. tip ♦ **de a f.** FIG., COLL. very big, huge • **en f.** PRINT. in folio • **f. de Descartes** GEOM. folium of Descartes.
fo·lio·lar adj. BOT. foliolate.
folk·lo·re m. folklore.
folk·ló·ri·co, –ca adj. *(del folklore)* folk, folkloric; FIG. *(pintoresco)* picturesque, quaint.
fo·lla f. *(mezcla)* mess, jumble; SPORT. chaotic joust; THEAT. revue, variety show.
fo·lla·je m. *(hojas)* foliage; ARCHIT. decoration with a leaf motif; FIG. *(adorno)* tasteless decoration; *(palabrería)* verbiage, verbosity.
fo·llar §19 tr. *(plegar)* to fold into leaves; VULG. *(joder)* to fuck —intr. VULG. to fuck —reflex to break wind or fart silently.
fo·lle·tín m. serial (in a newspaper).
fo·lle·ti·nes·co, –ca adj. *(del folletín)* serial; FIG. *(melodramático)* melodramatic.
fo·lle·to m. pamphlet, brochure.
fo·llón, –llo·na I. adj. *(perezoso)* lazy, indolent; *(jactancioso)* boastful, arrogant II. m. *(cohete)* silent rocket; BOT. shoot (of a tree); COLL. *(persona)* boaster, windbag; *(jaleo)* uproar, commotion; *(lío)* mess; *(ventosidad)* silent fart ♦ **follones** ECUAD. slip, petticoat.
fo·men·ta·ción f. MED. fomentation.
fo·men·ta·dor, –do·ra I. adj. *(instigador)* fomenting; *(promotor)* promoting II. m.f. *(instigador)* fomenter, instigator; *(promotor)* promoter.
fo·men·tar tr. *(calentar)* to warm, incubate; FIG. *(instigar)* to foment, stir up *<f. descontento* to stir up discontent>; *(promover)* to promote, foster *<f. el comercio* to promote trade>; MED. to foment, apply poultices; CUBA, P. RICO to open a business.
fo·men·to m. *(calor)* warmth; *(pábulo)* fuel; FIG. *(auxilio)* promotion, development *<banco de f.* development bank>; MED. fomentation, poultice.
fo·na·ción f. PHONET. phonation, vocalization.
fon·da f. *(posada)* inn; *(restaurante)* restaurant; CHILE, GUAT., SALV. tavern, bar; CHILE refreshment stand; ARG. cheap restaurant.
fon·da·ble adj. MARIT. fit for anchoring (a location).
fon·da·do, –da adj. *(reforzado)* with reinforced heads (a barrel); COL., COLL. rich, loaded.
fon·de·a·de·ro m. MARIT. anchorage.
fon·de·a·do, –da I. past part. see **fondear** II. adj. AMER. rich, wealthy.
fon·de·ar tr. MARIT. *(sondar)* to sound, fathom; *(registrar)* to search (a ship); FIG. *(examinar)* investigate, probe —intr. MARIT. to anchor, drop anchor —reflex. AMER. to get rich.
fon·de·o m. MARIT. *(anclaje)* anchoring; *(registro)* search, searching.
fon·de·ro, –ra m.f. AMER. var. of **fondista.**
fon·di·llo m. rear (end), butt; CHILE underpants, shorts ♦ **fondillos** seat of the pants.
fon·di·llón, –llo·na I. adj. C. AMER., COL. big-bottomed II. m. *(heces)* lees, dregs (in a cask).
fon·dis·ta m.f. *(de una posada)* innkeeper; *(de un restaurante)* restaurant owner.
fon·do m. *(base)* bottom *<al f. de la olla* at the bottom of the pot>; *(hondura)* depth, bed *<f. del río* riverbed>; *(parte más lejos)* rear, back *<me senté al f. del aula* I sat in the back of the classroom>; *(resistencia física)* stamina; *(campo)* ground, background *<el f. de un cuadro* the background of a picture>; *(caudal)* fund *<dio fondos a la causa* he donated funds to the cause>; *(colección)* collection *<un f. de libros* a book collection>; *(residuo)* residue; FIG. *(índole)* character, nature *<ella es de buen f.* she has a good nature>; *(lo principal)* essence, bottom *<llegar al f. de un asunto* to get to the bottom of an affair>; *(reserva)* store, reservoir *<un f. de sabiduría* a reservoir of knowledge>; CHILE, COL. cauldron; C. RICA, HOND. pound (for animals); ARG., PAR. bathroom; C. AMER., MEX. petticoat, underskirt ♦ **a f.** completely, thoroughly • **bajos fondos** scum, dregs • **dar f.** MARIT. to drop anchor; FIG. *(acabar)* to finish, end • **de f.** main, leading *<artículo de f.* leading

article>; long-distance <*carrera de f.* long-distance race> • **doble f.** false bottom • **echar a f.** MARIT. to sink • **en el f.** FIG. at heart, basically • **a f.** abreast <*de dos en f.* two abreast> • **estar con fondos** to have money • **f. de amortización** COM. sinking fund • **f. vitalicio** life annuity • **fondos** COM. funds, capital • **fondos disponibles** COM. ready cash • **fondos públicos** public funds • **irse a f.** MARIT. to sink, founder • **sin f.** bottomless • **sin fondos** COM. bad, bounced <*un cheque sin fondos* a bad check>.

fon·dón, –do·na I. adj. big-bottomed **II.** m. *(heces)* lees, dregs (in a cask); TEX. background of a brocade fabric.

fo·ne·ma m. PHONET. phoneme.

fo·né·ti·co, –ca I. adj. phonetic **II.** f. phonetics.

fo·ne·tis·ta m.f. phonetician, phoneticist.

fó·ni·co, –ca adj. phonic.

fo·no m. CHILE telephone receiver.

fo·no·grá·fi·co, –ca adj. phonographic.

fo·nó·gra·fo m. phonograph, record player.

fo·no·lo·gí·a f. phonology.

fo·no·te·ca f. record library.

fon·ta·nal I. adj. fontal **II.** m. spring, fountain.

fon·ta·ne·rí·a f. *(arte)* plumbing, pipelaying; *(sistema)* plumbing, pipes.

fon·ta·ne·ro, –ra m.f. plumber.

fo·ra·ji·do, –da adj. & m.f. fugitive, outlaw.

fo·ral adj. LAW statutory.

fo·rá·ne·o, –a adj. foreign, alien.

fo·ras·te·ro, –ra I. adj. foreign, alien **II.** m.f. stranger, outsider.

for·cé see **forzar.**

for·ce·jar *or* **for·ce·je·ar** intr. *(hacer fuerza)* to struggle, strive; FIG. *(resistir)* to resist.

for·ce·je·o *or* **for·ce·jo** m. struggle, struggling.

for·ce·ju·do, –da adj. strong, tough.

fór·ceps m. [pl. **-ceps**] SURG. forceps.

fo·ren·se adj. forensic <*medicina f.* forensic medicine>.

fo·re·ro, –ra I. adj. statutory **II.** m. *(dueño)* owner of a leasehold estate; *(arrendatario)* lessee.

fo·res·ta·ción f. forestation, reforestation.

fo·res·tal adj. forest, forestal.

for·ja f. *(fragua)* forge; *(ferrería)* ironworks, foundry; *(forjadura)* forging; *(argamasa)* mortar; COL. small stove.

for·ja·du·ra f. *or* **for·ja·mien·to** m. forging.

for·jar tr. *(martillar)* to forge, hammer; *(fabricar)* to make, form; FIG. *(inventar)* to invent, make up <*forjar embustes* to make up lies>♦ **f. ilusiones** FIG. to build castles in the air —reflex. AMER., COLL. to make a bundle (of money).

for·ma f. *(apariencia)* form <*f. y substancia* form and substance>; *(dimensiones)* shape <*en f. de U* in the shape of a U>; *(silueta)* figure, outline; *(molde)* mold, pattern; *(formato)* format; *(documento)* form, questionnaire; *(manera)* way, method <*no hay f. de cobrar* there is no way to collect>; *(condición física)* shape, condition <*el atleta está en f.* the athlete is in shape>; RELIG. host ♦ **dar f. a** to form, shape • **de f. que** so that, in such a way that • **en debida f.** in due form, duly • **formas sociales** manners, social conventions • **guardar las formas** to keep up appearances • **hacer f.** to line up • **tomar f.** to take form *or* shape.

for·ma·ble adj. formable, malleable.

for·ma·ción f. *(acción de formar)* formation, development; *(educación)* upbringing, rearing; *(instrucción)* education, training; *(brocade)* bullion, braid (in embroidery); MIL. formation.

for·ma·do, –da I. past part. see **formar II.** adj. formed, shaped <*bien f.* well-shaped>; *(desarrollado)* grown (up), developed.

for·mal adj. *(perteneciente a la forma)* formal; *(serio)* correct, proper; *(expreso)* strict, formal <*instrucciones formales* strict instructions>.

for·mal·de·hí·do m. CHEM. formaldehyde.

for·ma·li·cé, formalice see **formalizar.**

for·ma·li·dad f. formality.

for·ma·li·na f. CHEM. formalin, formaline.

for·ma·lis·mo m. formalism.

for·ma·lis·ta I. adj. formalistic **II.** m.f. formalist.

for·ma·li·za·ción f. formalization.

for·ma·li·zar §04 tr. to formalize —reflex. to take offense.

for·mal·men·te adv. formally.

for·mar tr. *(dar forma)* to form; *(moldear)* to shape; *(constituir)* to form, make up <*ocho miembros forman la comisión* eight members make up the commission>; *(criar)* to bring up, rear —intr. MIL. to fall in —reflex. *(tomar forma)* to take form *or* shape; *(desarrollarse)* to develop, grow.

for·ma·ti·vo, –va adj. formative.

for·ma·to m. PRINT. format; *(tamaño)* size.

for·me·ro m. ARCHIT. supporting arch.

for·mi·can·te adj. *(lento)* slow, sluggish; MED. rapid and faint (pulse).

fór·mi·co adj. CHEM. formic.

for·mi·da·ble adj. formidable.

for·mi·do·lo·so, –sa adj. *(miedoso)* very afraid *or* scared; *(espantoso)* frightening, scary.

for·món m. CARP. firmer chisel; *(punzón)* circular punch.

fór·mu·la f. *(modelo)* formula; MED. *(receta)* prescription, formula; CUL. recipe; *(expresión)* formality; CHEM., MATH. formula ♦ **por f.** as a matter of form.

for·mu·lar I. tr. *(expresar)* state, express; *(recetar)* prepare, formulate **II.** adj. formulaic.

for·mu·la·rio I. m. formulary **II.** adj. formulistic.

for·mu·lis·mo m. formulism.

for·mu·lis·ta I. adj. formulistic **II.** m.f. formulist.

for·ni·ca·ción f. fornication.

for·ni·ca·dor, –do·ra I. adj. fornicating **II.** m.f. fornicator.

for·ni·car §70 intr. to fornicate.

for·ni·do, –da adj. robust, strong.

for·ni·tu·ras f. PRINT. type cast to complete a font; ARM., MIL. cartridge belt.

fo·ro m. *(plaza, reunión)* forum; LAW *(corte)* court, tribunal; *(profesión)* bar, legal profession; *(contrato)* contract; *(canon)* rent; THEAT. upstage area ♦ **desaparecer por el f.** to slip away unnoticed • **por tal f.** on such conditions.

fo·rra·je m. *(hierba)* forage, fodder; *(acción de forrajear)* foraging; COLL. *(fárrago)* hodgepodge, mess.

fo·rra·je·ar tr. & intr. to forage.

fo·rrar tr. *(coser)* to line <*el sastre forró al abrigo con seda* the tailor lined the coat with silk>; *(cubrir)* to cover (books, chairs) TECH. to line, cover —reflex. COLL. *(enriquecerse)* to make one's fortune, get rich; AMER. COLL. to stuff oneself (with food).

fo·rro m. lining <*el f. de mi abrigo es de seda* the lining of my coat is silk>; *(cubierta)* cover, covering; MARIT. sheathing; TECH. liner, lining ♦ **de f.** GUAT. besides; CUBA free • **f. d freno** AUTO. brake lining • **ni por el f.** FIG., COLL. not at all.

for·ta·cho, –cha *or* **for·ta·chón, –cho·na** adj. robust, strong.

for·ta·le·ce·dor, –do·ra adj. fortifying.

for·ta·le·cer §17 tr. to fortify.

for·ta·le·ci·mien·to m. *(acción de fortalecer)* fortifying, strengthening; *(defensas)* fortifications, defenses.

for·ta·le·za f. *(vigor)* strength, vigor; *(virtud)* fortitude; *(fortín)* fortress, stronghold; CHILE stench, stink.

for·te I. adv. MUS. forte **II.** interj. MARIT. avast!

for·ti·fi·ca·ción f. fortification.

for·ti·fi·can·te I. adj. fortifying **II.** m. tonic.

for·ti·fi·car §70 tr. MIL. to fortify; *(dar fuerza)* to strengthen, fortify.

for·tín m. *(fuerte)* small, fort; *(refugio)* bunker.

for·tí·si·mo, –ma I. adj. very *or* extremely strong **II.** adv. MUS. fortissimo.

for·tui·ta·men·te adv. fortuitously, by chance.

for·tui·to, –ta adj. fortuitous, chance.

for·tu·na f. *(azar)* fortune, fate; *(suerte)* fortune, luck <*tengo la buena f. de estar sano* I have the good fortune to be healthy>; *(capital)* fortune, wealth <*perdió toda su. f. en la bolsa* he lost all his fortune in the stock market>; *(borrasca)* storm, tempest ♦ **por f.** fortunately • **probar f.** to try one's luck.

for·tu·nón m. COLL. *(suerte)* stroke of luck; *(dineral)* vast fortune, pile of money.

fo·rún·cu·lo m. MED. boil, furuncle.

for·za·da·men·te adv. by force, forcibly.

for·za·do, –da I. past part. see **forzar II.** adj. *(forzoso)* forced, compulsory; *(no espontáneo)* forced, strained <*una sonrisa f.* a forced smile> ♦ **a marchas forzadas** FIG.

double-time, against the clock • **marcha f.** MIL. forced march • **trabajos forzados** LAW hard labor **III.** m. convict; HIST. galley slave.

for·za·dor m. forcer.

for·za·mien·to m. forcing.

for·zar §37 tr. *(violentar)* to force <*f. una puerta* to force a door>; *(entrar)* to force (one's way); *(capturar)* to take *or* capture by force <*el ejército forzó la ciudad* the army took the city by force>; *(violar)* to rape; FIG. *(obligar)* to force, compel <*el profesor nos forzó a que nos quedáramos* the professor forced us to stay>.

for·zo·sa·men·te adv. *(por fuerza)* by force, forcibly; *(ineludiblemente)* unavoidably, inevitably <*f. tendré que estudiar para pasar el examen* inevitably, I will have to study to pass the exam>.

for·zo·so, –sa adj. unavoidable, inevitable.

for·zu·do, –da adj. strong, robust.

fo·sa f. *(sepultura)* grave, tomb; ANAT. fossa ♦ **f. séptica** septic tank • **fosas nasales** ANAT. nostrils.

fo·sar tr. to dig a ditch *or* trench around.

fos·co, –ca I. adj. *(oscuro)* cloudy, gloomy; *(áspero)* sullen, surly **II.** f. haze, mist.

fos·fa·to m. CHEM. phosphate ♦ **f. cálcico** *or* **de cal** calcium phosphate.

fos·fo·re·cer §17 intr. to phosphoresce.

fos·fo·re·ro, –ra m.f. *(vendedor)* match seller —f. *(estuche)* matchbox.

fos·fo·res·cen·cia f. PHYS. phosphorescence.

fos·fo·res·cen·te adj. PHYS. phosphorescent.

fos·fó·ri·co, –ca adj. CHEM. phosphoric.

fós·fo·ro m. CHEM. phosphorus; *(cerilla)* match; COL. percussion cap; MEX., COLL. coffee with brandy.

fos·fo·ro·so, –sa adj. CHEM. phosphorous.

fos·fu·ro m. CHEM. phosphide.

fó·sil I. m. fossil **II.** adj. *(petrificado)* fossil, fossilized; FIG., COLL. *(antiguo)* old, outdated.

fo·si·li·za·ción f. fossilization.

fo·si·li·zar·se §04 reflex. *(convertirse en fósil)* to fossilize, become fossilized; FIG. *(hacerse rígido)* to ossify, become rigid.

fo·so m. *(hoyo)* pit, ditch; THEAT. pit; MIL. moat, trench.

fo·to f. photo, picture ♦ **sacar fotos** to take *or* snap pictures.

fo·to·com·po·si·ción f. PRINT. photocomposition, phototypesetting.

fo·to·co·pia f. photocopy.

fo·to·co·piar tr. to photocopy.

fo·to·e·lec·tri·ci·dad f. photoelectricity.

fo·to·e·léc·tri·co, –ca adj. photoelectric.

fo·to·gé·ni·co, –ca adj. photogenic.

fo·to·gra·ba·do m. photoengraving, photogravure.

fo·to·gra·bar tr. to photoengrave.

fo·to·gra·fí·a f. *(arte)* photography; *(retrato)* photograph, photo, picture; *(taller)* photography studio ♦ **f. aérea** aerial photography • **f. en colores** color photography • **f. instantánea** snapshot.

fo·to·gra·fiar §30 tr. *(retratar)* to photograph; FIG. *(describir)* to describe in detail.

fo·to·grá·fi·co, –ca adj. photographic.

fo·tó·gra·fo, –fa m.f. photographer.

fo·to·li·to m. photolithograph.

fo·to·li·to·gra·fí·a f. *(arte)* photolithography; *(prueba)* photolithograph.

fo·to·me·trí·a f. photometry.

fo·tó·me·tro m. PHYS. photometer.

fo·tón m. PHYS. photon.

fo·to·sen·si·ble adj. photosensitive.

fo·tos·fe·ra f. photosphere.

fo·to·sín·te·sis f. photosynthesis.

fo·to·sin·té·ti·co, –ca adj. photosynthetic.

fo·to·te·ca f. photograph library.

fo·to·ti·po m. phototype.

fo·to·tro·pis·mo m. BOT. phototropism.

frac m. [pl. **fracs** *or* **tra·ques**] tails, formal coat.

fra·ca·sa·do, –da I. past part. see **fracasar II.** adj. failed, unsuccessful **III.** m.f. failure, unsuccessful person.

fra·ca·sar intr. *(fallar)* to fail, be unsuccessful; *(no resultar)* to fall through, fail.

fra·ca·so m. *(malogro)* failure, ruin; *(ruido)* crash (noise).

frac·ción f. *(división)* division, breaking (into parts); *(porción)* fraction, portion; MATH. fraction ♦ **f. continua** MATH. continued fraction • **f. decimal** MATH. decimal fraction • **f. impropia** MATH. improper fraction • **f. propia** MATH. proper fraction.

frac·cio·na·mien·to m. *(división)* division, breaking (into parts); MATH. fractionization; CHEM. fractionation.

frac·cio·nar tr. *(dividir)* to divide, break (into parts); MATH. to fractionize; CHEM. to fractionate.

frac·cio·na·rio, –ria adj. fractional.

frac·tu·ra f. *(rotura)* fracture, break; MED., MIN. fracture ♦ **f. complicada** MED. compound fracture • **f. simple** MED. simple fracture.

frac·tu·rar tr. to fracture, break.

fra·gan·cia f. *(olor)* fragrance, perfume; FIG. *(fama)* good reputation.

fra·gan·te adj. *(oloroso)* fragrant, perfumed; *(flagrante)* flagrant.

fra·ga·ta f. MARIT. frigate; ORNITH. frigate bird ♦ **f. ligera** MARIT. corvette.

frá·gil adj. *(quebradizo)* fragile, breakable; FIG. *(débil)* weak, fragile; *(fugaz)* perishable, fleeting; MEX., COLL. poor, impoverished.

fra·gi·li·dad f. fragility.

frag·men·tar tr. to fragment, break into fragments.

frag·men·ta·rio, –ria adj. fragmentary, fragmented.

frag·men·to m. *(parte)* fragment; *(trozo)* passage, excerpt <*un f. de la novela* a passage from the novel>.

fra·gor m. din, uproar.

fra·go·ro·so, –sa adj. roaring, thunderous.

fra·go·si·dad f. *(espesura)* thickness, density; *(desigualdad)* rough, ruggedness; *(terreno)* rough *or* rugged terrain.

fra·go·so, –sa adj. rough, rugged <*un camino f.* a rugged road>; *(ruidoso)* roaring, thunderous.

fra·gua f. forge, smithy.

fra·gua·do, –da I. past part. see **fraguar II.** m. CONST. setting, hardening.

fra·gua·dor, –do·ra I. adj. scheming, plotting **II.** m.f. schemer, plotter.

fra·guar §10 tr. *(forjar)* to forge (iron); FIG. *(inventar)* to plan, plot —intr. CONST. to set, harden (cement).

frai·le m. RELIG. friar, monk; ARCHIT. hood (of a hearth) ♦ **f. de misa y olla** ignorant *or* simple-minded friar.

frai·le·ro, –ra *or* **frai·les·co, –ca** adj. COLL. monkish, monk-like.

frai·lí·a f. RELIG. regular clergy.

frai·lu·co·n m. DEROG. insignificant friar *or* priest.

frai·lu·no, –na adj. DEROG. monkish, monk-like.

fram·bue·sa f. raspberry.

fram·bue·so m. BOT. raspberry bush.

fran·ca·che·la f. COLL. *(comilona)* feast, spread; *(parranda)* spree, binge.

fran·ca·le·te m. leather strap with a buckle.

fran·ca·men·te adv. frankly, candidly.

fran·cés, –ce·sa I. adj. French ♦ **a la f.** in the French style • **despedirse a la f.** to take French leave **II.** m. *(habitante)* Frenchman; *(idioma)* French —f. Frenchwoman ♦ **los franceses** the French.

Fran·cia f. France.

fran·cio m. CHEM. francium.

fran·cis·ca·no, –na *or* **fran·cis·co, –ca I.** adj. *(religioso)* Franciscan; *(color)* grayish-brown **II.** m.f. Franciscan (monk or nun).

franc·ma·són m. Freemason, Mason.

franc·ma·so·ne·ría f. Freemasonry.

fran·co, –ca I. adj. *(sincero)* frank, candid; *(liberal)* generous, liberal; *(desembarazado)* open, clear <*el camino está f.* the road is clear>; *(exento)* exempt, free <*f. de gastos* expense-free>; COM. free <*f. a bordo* free on board>; *(germánico)* Frankish; *(francés)* Franco- <*franco-español* Franco-Spanish> ♦ **f. de porte** COM. postpaid **II.** m.f. *(germano)* Frank —m. FIN. franc; *(idioma)* Frankish.

fran·có·fi·lo, –la adj. & m.f. Francophile, Francophil.

fran·có·fo·bo, –ba adj. & m.f. Francophobe.

fran·có·fo·no, –na I. adj. Francophone, French-speaking **II.** m.f. Francophone, French-speaking person.

fran·chu·te, –ta m.f DEROG. Frenchy, frog.

fra·ne·la f. TEX. flannel; AMER. undershirt.
fran·go·llar tr. FIG., COLL. to rush, do quickly and carelessly.
fran·go·llo m. *(trigo cocido)* porridge, boiled cereal; *(pienso)* type of cattle feed; FIG., COLL. *(cosa mal hecha)* rushed *or* sloppy job; AMER., P. RICO dessert made from mashed bananas.
fran·ja f. *(adorno)* fringe, border; *(banda)* stripe, band; *(terreno)* strip (of land).
fran·ja·le·te m. leather strap with a buckle.
fran·jar tr. to fringe, trim.
fran·je·a·do, –da I. past part. see **franjear** II. adj. fringed, trimmed.
fran·je·ar tr. to fringe, trim.
fran·que·ar tr. *(eximir)* to exempt <*f. a alguien de un impuesto* to exempt someone from a tax>; *(conceder)* to grant, allow; *(desembarazar)* to clear, open; *(pagar el porte)* to frank (mail); *(liberar)* to free, enfranchise <*Lincoln franqueó a los esclavos en 1863* Lincoln freed the slaves in 1863>; *(atravesar)* to cross, pass through —reflex. *(acceder)* to yield, give in; *(confiar)* to confide <*ella se franqueó con su hermana mayor* she confided in her older sister>.
fran·que·o m. *(de una carta)* franking (of mail); *(liberación)* freeing, enfranchisement.
fran·que·za f. *(veracidad)* frankness; candor; *(exención)* freedom, exemption (from duty or tax); *(generosidad)* generosity.
fran·qui·cia f. exemption (from taxes, etc.) ♦ **f. postal** frank, franking privilege.
fra·que m. var. of **frac**.
fras·co m. *(botellín)* small bottle; *(redoma)* flask, vial; ARM. powder flask.
fra·se f. sentence, phrase ♦ **f. hecha** set phrase *or* expression.
fra·se·ar tr. to phrase (sentences).
fra·se·o m. MUS. phrasing.
fra·se·o·lo·gí·a f. *(estilo)* phrasing, style; *(vocabulario)* phraseology; *(verbosidad)* wordiness, verbosity.
fras·que·ra f. case, box (for bottles) ♦ **f. de fuego** MARIT. fire case *or* chest.
fra·ter·na I. f. reprimand, scolding II. adj. see **fraterno, –na.**
fra·ter·nal adj. brotherly, fraternal.
fra·ter·nal·men·te adv. fraternally.
fra·ter·ni·dad f. brotherhood, fraternity.
fra·ter·ni·zar §04 intr. to fraternize.
fra·ter·no, –na adj. fraternal.
fra·tri·ci·da I. adj. fratricidal II. m.f. fratricide (person).
fra·tri·ci·dio m. fratricide (crime).
frau·de m. fraud.
frau·du·len·cia f. fraud, fraudulence.
frau·du·len·to, –ta adj. fraudulent.
fray m. [contr. of **fraile**] Fra, Brother (used before names).
fra·za·da f. blanket.
fre·cé, frece see **frezar.**
fre·cuen·cia f. *(repetición)* frequency; PHYS. frequency <*alta f.* high frequency> ♦ **con f.** frequently • **f. alterada** ELEC. static, interference • **f. modulada** ELEC. frequency modulation.
fre·cuen·ta·ción f. *(hacer visitas)* frequenting, visiting; *(compañía)* company.
fre·cuen·ta·dor, –do·ra I. adj. frequenting II. m.f. frequenter.
fre·cuen·tar tr. *(visitar)* to frequent, visit; *(conocer)* to keep company (with), see; *(practicar los sacramentos)* to keep the sacraments.
fre·cuen·ta·ti·vo, –va adj. GRAM. frequentative.
fre·cuen·te adj. *(repetido)* frequent, repeated; *(común)* common, habitual.
fre·cuen·te·men·te adv. frequently.
fre·ga·de·ro m. kitchen sink.
fre·ga·do, –da I. past part. see **fregar** II. m. *(lavamiento)* scrubbing; *(restregadura)* scouring, rubbing; FIG., COLL. *(enredo)* mess, tangle; *(pelea)* fracas, fight ♦ **meterse en un f.** to get into a mess III. adj. AMER. stubborn, obstinate.

fre·ga·dor m. *(fregadero)* kitchen sink; *(estropajo)* dishcloth.
fre·ga·du·ra f. *or* **fre·ga·mien·to** m. var. of **fregado.**
fre·gar §52 tr. *(restregar con fuerza)* to scour, scrub; *(lavar)* to wash; FIG., COLL. *(molestar)* to annoy, bother —reflex. to become annoyed *or* bothered.
fre·gón, –go·na I. adj. AMER. *(molesto)* bothersome, annoying; ECUAD., P. RICO *(descarado)* brazen, fresh II. m.f. AMER. *(persona molesta)* pest, annoyance; ECUAD., P. RICO *(descarado)* brazen *or* fresh person —f. scullery maid.
fre·go·te·ar tr. *(fregar repetidas veces)* to wipe *or* clean repeatedly; *(fregar mal)* to give a quick wipe to.
fre·gué see **fregar.**
frei·du·ra f. *or* **frei·mien·to** m. CUL. frying, browning (in a frying pan).
fre·ír §58 tr. CUL. to fry, brown (in a frying pan); COLL. *(matar a tiros)* to kill, shoot; *(fastidiar)* to pester, annoy ♦ **al f. será el reír** COLL. he who laughs last laughs best • **f. a preguntas** to bombard with questions —reflex. COLL. *(desvivirse)* to be excited ♦ **freírse de calor** to be boiling hot.
fre·na·do I. past part. see **frenar** II. m. braking.
fre·nar tr. *(enfrenar)* to bridle (a horse); *(detener)* to brake, apply the brake to; FIG. *(moderar)* to curb, bridle, check.
fre·na·zo m. sudden braking ♦ **dar el f.** to slam on *or* hit the brakes.
fre·ne·sí m. [pl. **-sí·es**] *(delirio)* frenzy.
fre·né·ti·ca·men·te adv. frenetically, frenziedly.
fre·né·ti·co, –ca adj. *(delirante)* frenetic, frenzied; *(colérico)* mad, furious.
fre·ni·llo m. ANAT. frenum; *(hocico)* muzzle, bridle; C. AMER. kite string ♦ **no tener f. en la lengua** to speak one's mind, not to mince words.
fre·no m. EQUIT. bit; MECH. brake; FIG. *(obstáculo)* obstacle, check ♦ **f. de discos** MECH. disc brake • **f. de mano** MECH. hand brake • **f. de tambor** MECH. drum brake • **tascar** *or* **morder el f.** FIG., COLL. to champ at the bit.
fre·no·lo·gí·a f. phrenology.
fren·ta·zo m. *(golpe)* blow with the forehead; MEX. rejection, rebuff.
fren·te f. (anat.) forehead, brow; FIG. *(rostro)* face, countenance; *(cabeza)* head <*con la f. levantada* with one's head held high> ♦ **arrugar la f.** to knit one's brow • **f. a f.** face to face —m. *(parte anterior)* front, front part; *(fachada)* face, façade; *(anverso)* obverse; *(alianza)* front <*f. popular* popular front>; MIL. front <*f. de batalla* battlefront>; METEOROL. front <*f. frío* cold front> ♦ **al f.** *(enfrente)* in front, opposite; COM. carried forward • **al f. de** at the head of, in charge of • **de f.** *(con determinación)* resolutely, without hesitation; head-on <*atacar de f.* to attack head-on>; abreast <*marcharon cuatro de f.* they marched four abreast>; ahead <*se lanzaron de f.* they lunged ahead> • **del f.** COM. brought forward • **en f.** in front, opposite • **formar f.** to form a common cause • **f. a** facing, opposite • **f. por f.** directly opposite • **hacer f. a** *(confrontar)* to face, confront; *(cumplir)* to meet (obligations).
fre·sa f. strawberry; *(fresco)* strawberry, strawberry-colored II. f. BOT. strawberry (plant *or* fruit); DENT. drill; MACH. milling tool.
fres·ca I. f. *(fresco)* cool *or* fresh air; FIG., COLL. *(dicho desagradable)* biting *or* blunt remark ♦ **decir cuatro frescas a uno** to speak one's mind to someone, not mince words with someone • **tomar la f.** to get some fresh air II. adj. see **fresco, –ca.**
fres·ca·chón, –cho·na adj. robust and ruddy, healthy ♦ **viento f.** MARIT. brisk wind.
fres·ca·les m.f. COLL. brazen *or* fresh person.
fres·ca·men·te adv. *(recientemente)* recently, freshly; *(descaradamente)* freshly, cheekily.
fres·co, –ca I. adj. *(frío)* cool; *(nuevo)* fresh <*pan f.* fresh bread>; *(reciente)* fresh, updated <*noticias frescas* updated news>; *(de tela)* cool, light (said of clothing); FIG. *(sano)* fresh, healthy (said of the complexion); *(sereno)* cool, calm; COLL. *(descarado)* fresh, cheeky, impudent ♦ **estar** *or* **quedar f.** COLL. to fail, be disappointed • **hacer f.** to purify • **¡que f.!** what a nerve! II. m. *(frío)* cool, coolness; *(aire)* fresh air <*tomar el f.* to get some fresh air>; ARTS fresco; AMER. cool drink ♦ **al f.** in the open air, in the

fresh air • **echar f. a** AMER. to tell it like it is —f. see **fresca.**

fres·cor m. *(frescura)* freshness, coolness; PAINT. *(color rosado)* pinkness, pink flesh tone.

fres·cu·ra f. *(temperatura)* freshness, coolness; *(fertilidad)* luxuriant verdure *or* foliage; COLL. *(desenfado)* nerve, cheek; FIG. *(chanza)* fresh remark; *(serenidad)* serenity, equanimity; *(descuido)* unconcern, coolness.

fres·no m. BOT. ash (tree *and* wood).

fres·que·ra f. food safe *or* cabinet.

fres·que·rí·a f. AMER. soda shop, refreshment stand.

freu·dia·no, -na adj. & m.f. PSYCH. Freudian.

freu·dis·mo m. PSYCH. Freudianism.

fre·za f. *(estiércol)* dung, dropping; ICHTH. *(desove)* spawning; *(temporada)* spawning season; *(huevos)* spawn; HUNT. hole made by an animal.

fre·za·da f. blanket.

fre·zar §04 intr. *(evacuar el vientre)* to excrete (animals); *(hozar)* to root (an animal); ICHTH. to spawn.

frí·a, frío see **freír.**

fria·ble adj. friable, brittle.

frial·dad f. *(sensación de frío)* coldness, frigidity; *(indiferencia)* indifference, coolness; *(falta de ardor)* lack of passion; *(falta de animación)* dullness, insipidness; MED. *(frigidez)* frigidity; *(impotencia)* impotence; FIG. *(necedad)* nonsense, foolishness ♦ **con f.** coldly, coolly.

frí·a·men·te adv. *(con frialdad)* coldly, coolly; FIG. *(sin gracia)* dully, colorlessly.

fri·á·ti·co, -ca adj. *(friolero)* susceptible to the cold; *(necio)* foolish, silly.

fri·ca·ción f. friction, rubbing.

fri·car §70 tr. to rub.

fri·ca·sé m. CUL. fricassee.

fri·ca·ti·vo, -va adj. & f. PHONET. fricative.

fric·ción f. *(friega)* friction, rubbing; *(masaje)* massage, rubdown; FIG. *(desacuerdo)* friction, discord; MECH. friction ♦ **dar una f.** to give a massage *or* rubdown.

fric·cio·nar tr. *(fricar)* to rub; *(dar masajes)* to massage, rub down.

frie·ga f. *(fricción)* massage, rubdown; COLL. *(fastidio)* bother, annoyance; MEX. scolding, telling off; CUBA thrashing, beating (with a stick); ARG., COL., PERU nonsense, foolishness ♦ **dar friegas** to massage, rub down.

frie·go, friegue see **fregar.**

frie·ra, frió see **freír.**

fri·gi·dai·re m. refrigerator, Frigidaire (trademark).

fri·gi·dez f. *(frialdad)* coldness, frigidity; MED. frigidity, frigidness.

frí·gi·do, -da adj. POET. *(frío)* frigid, cold; MED. frigid.

fri·go·rí·fi·co, -ca I. adj. refrigerator, refrigerating II. m. *(nevera)* refrigerator; *(establecimiento industrial)* cold--storage plant; *(cámara)* locker, cold-storage room.

frí·jol *or* **fri·jol** m. BOT. bean; MEX. joke, jest ♦ **f. colorado** BOT. kidney bean • **f. negro** BOT. black bean • **frijoles** MEX. *(bravatas)* bragging, boasting; *(comida)* food, sustenance.

frí·o, -a I. adj. *(helado)* cold *<la sopa está f.* the soup is cold>; FIG. *(indiferente)* cool, cold *<le dieron un recibimiento f.* they gave him a cold reception>; *(sin gracia)* graceless, insipid ♦ **quedarse f.** FIG. to be left cold; COLL. *(morir)* to die II. m. *(frialdad)* cold, coldness; *(bebida)* cool drink; FIG. *(indiferencia)* coolness, indifference ♦ **coger f.** to catch a cold • **fríos** AMER. malaria; *(helados)* frozen treats • **hacer f.** to be cold *<hace mucho f. hoy* it is very cold today> • **no darle ni f. ni calor** FIG. not to make any difference • **tener f.** to be cold *<tengo f.* I am cold>.

frio·len·to, -ta adj. sensitive to the cold.

frio·le·ra I. f. *(cosa de poco valor)* trifle, bauble; FIG. a mere, only *<tener la f. de cien años de edad* to be a mere 100 years old> II. adj. see **friolero, -ra.**

frio·le·ro, -ra I. adj. sensitive to the cold II. f. see **friolera.**

fri·qué, frique see **fricar.**

fri·sa f. *(tela de lana)* frieze (coarse woolen cloth); MARIT. seal (of a joint); MIL. fraise; ARG., CHILE nap (of felt); DOM. REP., P. RICO blanket, bed throw.

fri·sar tr. TEX. to frieze; *(refregar)* to rub —intr. *(congeniar)* to be compatible, pack (a joint) —intr. *(congeniar)* to be compatible, get

along (with); FIG. *(acercarse)* to be near, approach ♦ **f. con** *or* **en** FIG. to be close to, border on *<su edad frisa en los sesenta* he's close to sixty>.

fri·sio, -sia adj. & m.f. Frisian, Friesian

fri·so m. ARCHIT. frieze; *(faja de pared)* dado, wainscot.

frí·sol *or* **fri·sol** m. BOT. bean.

fri·són, -sona adj. & m.f. Frisian, Friesian —m. *(idioma)* Frisian, Friesian.

fri·ta·da f. CUL. fried dish, fry.

fri·tan·ga f. CUL. fry, fried dish *<f. de pescado* fish fry>; *(fritada mala)* greasy fry.

fri·to, -ta I. past part. see **freír** II. adj. CUL. fried ♦ **estar uno f.** to be at wit's end *or* exasperated III. m. CUL. fried food; VEN. daily bread *or* sustenance.

fri·tu·ra f. CUL. fried food.

fri·vo·li·dad f. frivolity, frivolousness.

frí·vo·lo, -la adj. frivolous.

fron·da f. *or* **fron·de** m. BOT. *(de helecho)* frond (of a fern); *(hoja)* leaf, shoot ♦ **frondas** BOT. foliage, leaves.

fron·do·si·dad f. frondescence, leafiness.

fron·do·so, -sa adj. *(con muchas hojas)* frondose, leafy; *(con mucha vegetación)* luxuriant, lush.

fron·tal I. adj. ANAT. frontal, pertaining to the forehead; *(delantero)* front, frontal II. m. RELIG. frontal (altar curtain); ANAT. frontal bone; AMER. EQUIT. browband, headband.

fron·ta·le·ra f. EQUIT. browband, headband; *(frontil)* yoke pad (for oxen); RELIG. altar frontal adornments.

fron·te·ra I. f. *(confín)* border, frontier; ARCHIT. façade II. adj. see **frontero, -ra.**

fron·te·ri·zo, -za adj. *(contiguo)* border, frontier; *(de enfrente)* facing, opposite.

fron·te·ro, -ra I. adj. facing, opposite II. m. MIL. border commander; *(frentero)* child's protective headband —f. see **frontera** III. adv. in front, opposite.

fron·til m. *(del buey)* yoke pad (for oxen); CUBA, P. RICO, EQUIT. headband, browband.

fron·tis·pi·cio m. ARCHIT. *(fachada)* frontispiece, façade; *(frontón)* pediment, gable; BKB. frontispiece; FIG. *(cara)* face, visage.

fron·tón m. SPORT. *(pared)* front wall of a handball court; *(cancha)* handball court; ARCHIT. pediment, gable.

fro·ta·ción f. rubbing, rub.

fro·ta·dor, -do·ra I. adj. rubbing II. m.f. rubber.

fro·ta·du·ra f. *or* **fro·ta·mien·to** m. *(friega)* rubbing, rub; MECH. friction.

fro·tar tr. to rub —reflex. to rub (together).

fro·te m. rub, rubbing.

fruc·tí·fe·ro, -ra adj. BOT. fructiferous, fruit-bearing; FIG. *(productivo)* fruitful.

fruc·ti·fi·ca·ción f. BOT. fructification.

fruc·ti·fi·ca·dor, -do·ra adj. fructifying.

fruc·ti·fi·can·te adj. fructifying.

fruc·ti·fi·car §70 intr. BOT. to bear *or* produce fruit; FIG. *(producir utilidad)* to prove fruitful *or* productive.

fruc·to·sa f. CHEM. fructose.

fruc·tuo·so, -sa adj. fruitful, productive.

fru·frú m. frou-frou.

fru·gal adj. frugal.

fru·ga·li·dad f. frugality, frugalness.

fru·gal·men·te adv. frugally.

fru·gí·fe·ro, -ra adj. POET. fruit-bearing.

fru·gí·vo·ro, -ra adj. frugivorous, fruit-eating.

frui·ción f. fruition, enjoyment.

fruir §18 intr. to enjoy one's accomplishments *or* possessions.

frui·ti·vo, -va adj. enjoyable, pleasurable.

frun·ce *or* **frun·ci·do** m. SEW. gather, shirr.

frun·ci·mien·to m. SEW. gathering, shirring; FIG. *(enredo)* hoax, scheme ♦ **f. del entrecejo** frown.

frun·cir §35 tr. SEW. to gather, shirr; *(apretar los labios)* to purse (one's lips); *(arrugar la frente)* to frown, knit one's brow; FIG. *(reducir)* to contract, reduce; *(tergiversar)* to twist, distort (the truth) —reflex. to feign modesty.

frus·le·ra I. f. METAL. brass scrapings *or* filings; *(de cobre)* copper scrapings, filings II. adj. see **fruslero, -ra.**

frus·le·rí·a f. *(chuchería)* trifle, trinket; *(nadería)* triviality.

frus·le·ro, –ra I. adj. *(frívolo)* trifling, frivolous **II.** f. see **fruslera.**

frus·tra·ción f. frustration.

frus·tra·do, –da I. past part. see **frustrar II.** adj. *(fracasado)* frustrated, thwarted; *(malogrado)* unsuccessful, failed.

frus·trar tr. to frustrate, thwart —reflex. *(fracasar)* to fail, come to nothing; *(privarse)* to be frustrated.

fru·ta f. BOT. fruit; FIG., COLL. *(resultado)* fruit, result; ARG., BOT. apricot ♦ **f. bomba** CUBA, BOT. papaya • **f. de horno** MEX., CUL. fruit cake • **f. de sartén** CUL. fruit, fritter • **f. prohibida** BIBL., FIG. forbidden fruit • **f. seca** dried fruit.

fru·ta·je m. PAINT. still life (of fruit and flowers).

fru·tal I. adj. fruit *‹árbol f.* fruit tree› **II.** m. fruit tree.

fru·tar intr. BOT. to bear *or* produce fruit.

fru·te·rí·a f. fruit store *or* stand.

fru·te·ro, –ra BOT. **I.** adj. fruit *‹plato f.* fruit dish› **II.** m.f. *(vendedor)* fruit seller *or* merchant —m. *(plato)* fruit bowl *or* plate; *(toalla)* napkin *or* doily covering a fruit dish; PAINT. still life of fruit.

fru·ti·cul·tu·ra f. BOT. fruit growing, cultivation of fruit trees.

fru·ti·lla f. RELIG. rosary bead; ARG., CHILE, BOT. (species of) strawberry.

fru·to m. BOT. fruit; FIG. *(utilidad)* fruit, profit *‹el f. del trabajo* the fuit of labor›; *(resultado)* fruit, result ♦ **dar f.** BOT. to bear *or* produce fruit • **frutos** fruits *‹los frutos de la tierra* the fruits of the earth› • **sacar f.** to derive benefit, profit • **sin f.** *(en vano)* fruitlessly, in vain; *(vano)* fruitless, futile.

fru·ya, fruyo see **fruir.**

fru·ye·ra, fruyó see **fruir.**

fu I. m. hiss, spit (of a cat) **II.** interj. ugh!, phooey! ♦ **hacer f.** COLL. *(huirse)* to dart off, run away; *(despreciar)* to snub • **ni f. ni fa** COLL. so-so, mediocre.

fú·car m. [pl. **-ca·res**] FIG. rich man.

fu·ci·lar intr. *(producirse fucilazos)* to flash (heat lightning); POET. *(fulgurar)* to sparkle, flash.

fu·ci·la·zo m. METEOROL. heat lightning.

fuc·sia f. BOT. fuchsia.

fue·go m. *(combustión)* fire; *(incendio)* fire *‹los bomberos apagaron el f.* the firefighters put out the fire›; *(llama)* flame, heat *‹cocer a f. lento* to cook on a low heat›; *(hogar)* hearth, home; *(fósforo)* light *¿tienes f.?* do you have a light?›; FIG. *(ardor)* heat, passion *‹el f. de la disputa* the heat of the argument›; MARIT. *(faro)* beacon; MIL. *(descarga)* fire, discharge; MED. rash ♦ **a f. lento** *(poco a poco)* slowly, little by little; CUL. on a low flame *or* heat • **a f. y sangre** FIG. mercilessly • **apagar los fuegos del enemigo** MIL. to silence enemy fire • **arma de f.** firearm• **atizar el f.** to poke the fire; FIG. *(agitar la situación)* to stir up trouble, add fuel to the fire • **echar f. por los ojos** FIG. to look daggers • **entre dos fuegos** FIG. between a rock and a hard place • **¡fuego!** MIL. fire!, shoot! • **f. cruzado** MIL. crossfire • **f. fatuo** ignis fatuus, jack-o-lantern • **f. fuerte** blazing fire • **f. graneado** *or* **nutrido** MIL. drumfire, heavy fire • **f. griego** Greek fire • **f. pérsico** MED. shingles • **fuegos artificiales** *or* **pirotécnicos** fireworks • **hacer f.** to fire, shoot • **jugar con f.** FIG. to play with fire • **pegar f.** to set on fire • **romper el f.** to open fire.

fue·gui·no, –na adj. & m.f. GEOG. Fuegian (of Tierra del Fuego).

fuel *or* **fuel oil** m. fuel oil (used for heating).

fue·lle m. *(implemento)* bellows; *(frunce)* pucker, gather; *(pliegue)* accordion pleats; *(cubierta)* folding top *or* hood (of a carriage); RAIL. flexible coupling (between cars); FIG. *(chismoso)* tattletale, gossip; *(pieza plegable)* expandable pocket (of a purse).

fue·lle, fuello see **follar.**

fuen·te f. *(manantial)* spring *‹f. termal* hot spring›; *(aparato)* fountain, water fountain; *(pila)* font *‹f. bautismal* baptismal font›; *(plato)* platter, serving dish (container and contents); *(cabecera)* source, headwater; FIG. *(origen)* source, origin *‹f. fidedigna* from a reliable source›; MED. issue, sore ♦ **beber en buenas fuentes** FIG. to be well-informed • **f. de beber** drinking fountain • **f. de ju-**

ventud FIG. fountain of youth • **f. de ingresos** source of income.

fuer m. [contr. of **fuero**] ♦ **a f. de** as a, like a *‹a f. de hombre de bien* as a good man›.

fue·ra adv. outside *‹hace frío dentro de la casa pero no fuera* it's cold inside the house but not outside›; out *‹Martín está f.* Martin is out› ♦ **¡fuera!** get out! • **f. de** outside of *‹f. de la ciudad* outside of the city›; besides, except for *‹f. de eso, te daré lo que quieres* except for that, I will give you what you want› • **f. de alcance** out of reach • **f. de combate** MIL. out of action • **f. de juego** out of play • **f. de lugar** out of place • **f. de moda** out of fashion • **f. de propósito** irrelevant • **f. de que** aside from the fact that • **f. de sí** FIG. beside oneself • **por f.** on the outside.

fue·ra, fue see **ser²** *or* **ir.**

fue·ra bor·da m. [pl. **fuera borda**] MARIT. outboard (boat *or* motor).

fuer·ce, fuerzo see **forzar.**

fue·ro m. *(jurisdicción)* jurisdiction, power; *(cuerpo de leyes)* code (of laws); *(privilegio)* privilege, exemption ♦ **a f.** according to custom • **de f.** LAW de jure, according to law • **f. externo** *or* **exterior** LAW court of law • **f. interior** FIG. conscience • **fueros** COLL. arrogance, pride.

fuer·te I. adj. strong *‹brazo f.* strong arm›; *(robusto)* vigorous, strong; strong *‹tabaco f.* strong tobacco›; *(fortificado)* fortified; *(intenso)* powerful, forceful *‹un argumento f.* a forceful argument›; *(resistente)* tough, sturdy; *(energético)* energetic; *(valiente)* courageous, strong; *(áspero)* harsh, severe; loud *‹un grito f.* a loud shout›; *(considerable)* great, large *‹una f. cantidad de dinero* a great deal of money›; heavy, rich *‹un almuerzo f.* a heavy lunch›; FIG. *(versado)* well-versed, proficient *‹está f. en la historia* he is well-versed in history›; GRAM. strong (verb) ♦ **plato f.** main dish, entrée **II.** m. *(fortaleza)* fort, fortress; FIG. *(talento)* forte, strong point; MUS. forte **III.** adv. *(fuertemente)* hard *‹le pegó f.* he hit it hard›; *(mucho)* heavily, copiously *‹bebieron f.* they drank heavily›; loudly *‹hablaban f.* they were talking loudly› ♦ **¡mas f.!** louder!, speak up!

fuer·te·men·te adv. hard *‹me apretó f.* he squeezed me hard›; FIG. *(con vehemencia)* vehemently, intensely; loudly *‹hablar f.* to talk loudly›.

fuer·za f. PHYS. *(potencia)* force *‹la f. de la gravedad* the force of gravity›; *(vigor físico)* strength *‹f. muscular* muscular strength›; *(vitalidad)* vigor, energy; *(intensidad)* strength, intensity *‹la f. de un ácido* the strength of an acid›; *(violencia)* force, coercion *‹ceder a la f.* to yield to force›; *(solidez)* solidity, strength *‹la f. de un muro* the strength of a wall›; *(poder)* power *‹la f. del estado* the power of the state›; *(autoridad)* validity, force *‹la f. de un argumento* the force of an argument›; *(valor)* fortitude, courage; *(resistencia)* sturdiness, resistance; *(grupo)* force *‹f. pública* police force›; MECH. power; ELEC. power, current; *(plaza guarnecida)* stronghold, fortress ♦ **a f. de** by dint of • **a la f.** *or* **por f.** by force, forcibly; *(forzosamente)* perforce, necessarily • **a f. viva** by sheer force • **es f.** it is necessary to, one must *‹es f. confesarlo* one must admit› • **f. aérea** MIL. air force • **f. bruta** brute force • **f. centrífuga** PHYS. centrifugal force • **f. centrípeta** PHYS. centripetal force • **f. de la edad** prime of life • **f. disuasoria** deterrent • **f. electromotriz** PHYS. electromotive power • **f. hidráulica** hydraulic power • **f. mayor** act of God, force majeure • **f. salvaje** animal force • **fuerzas armadas** MIL. armed forces • **f. solar** solar power • **f. viva** PHYS. kinetic energy.

fue·ta·zo m. AMER. lash, whiplash.

fue·te m. AMER. whip.

fue·te·ar tr. AMER. to whip, beat with a whip.

fu·ga f. *(huida)* flight, escape; *(ardor)* ardor, impetuosity; *(escape)* leak, leakage; MUS. fugue; *(huida para casarse)* elopement ♦ **darse a la f.** *or* **ponerse en f.** to flee, take (to) flight • **f. de capitales** ECON. flight of capital • **f. de cerebros** brain drain • **f. precipitada** stampede • **poner en f.** to rout, put to flight.

fu·ga·ci·dad f. fugacity, brevity.

fu·ga·da f. gust (of wind).

fu·gar·se §47 reflex. *(huir)* to flee, run away; *(escaparse)* to escape; *(salirse)* leak (out), escape; *(para casarse)* to elope.

fu·gaz adj. [pl. **-ga·ces**] *(pasajero)* fleeting, brief; *(evanescente)* volatile, evanescent; ASTRON. shooting <*estrella f.* shooting star>.

fu·gi·ti·vo, –va **I.** adj. *(que huye)* fugitive, fleeing; *(pasajero)* fleeting, brief **II.** m.f. fugitive, runaway.

fu·gué, fugue see **fugarse.**

fui, fuimos, fuiste see **ser²** *or* **ir.**

fu·la·no, –na m.f. *(no sé cuántos)* so-and-so, what's-his--name; *(persona indeterminada)* John *or* Jane Doe —m. *(tipo)* guy, fellow —f. *(ramera)* whore, prostitute ♦ **(don) f. de tal** John Doe • **Fulano, Zutano Mengano** Tom, Dick, and Harry.

fu·le·ro, –ra adj. COLL. *(chapucero)* rough, shoddy; *(tramposo)* deceitful, tricky.

ful·gen·te adj. brilliant, radiant.

ful·gir §32 intr. *(brillar)* to shine, glow; *(centellear)* to sparkle, glitter.

ful·gor m. *(brillo)* brilliance, radiance; *(centelleo)* sparkle, glitter.

ful·gu·ra·ción f. *(destello)* flash, flashing; MED. lightning stroke.

ful·gu·ran·te adj. *(que fulgura)* flashing, fulgurant; MED. sudden and sharp (pain); FIG. *(rápido)* quick, lightning fast.

ful·gu·rar intr. to flash brilliantly, fulgurate.

ful·gu·ro·so, –sa adj. flashing, fulgurous.

fu·li·gi·no·so, –sa adj. fuliginous, sooty.

ful·ja see **fulgir.**

ful·mi·na·ción f. fulmination.

ful·mi·na·dor, –do·ra **I.** adj. fulminating **II.** m.f. fulminator.

ful·mi·nan·te **I.** adj. *(fulminador)* fulminating; MED. *(grave)* critical, very serious; *(súbito)* fulminant; FIG. *(amenazador)* threatening, menacing <*una mirada f.* a menacing look>; *(que estalla)* exploding, explosive **II.** m. *(explosión)* explosion; ARTIL. *(cápsula)* (percussion) cap.

ful·mi·na·triz adj. [pl. **-tri·ces**] fulminating.

ful·mi·nar tr. *(matar por el rayo)* to strike (and kill) by lightning; *(hacer morir bruscamente)* to strike down *or* dead; *(arrojar)* to throw, hurl; FIG. *(dictar)* to thunder (excommunication, a warning); *(amenazar)* to threaten, menace —intr. to fulminate, explode.

ful·mi·na·to m. CHEM. fulminate.

fu·lle·ar intr. to cheat (at cards).

fu·lle·rí·a f. *(trampa)* cheating (at cards); FIG. *(astucia)* astuteness, guile; COL. presumption, arrogance.

fu·lle·ro, –ra **I.** adj. *(tramposo)* crooked, dishonest (at cards); COLL. *(astuto)* sharp, wily; COL. mischievous (child) **II.** m.f. *(tramposo)* cardsharp, cheat; COLL. *(astuto)* sharpie; COL. rascal (mischievous child).

fu·ma·ble adj. smokable.

fu·ma·da f. *(bocanada)* puff (of smoke); ARG. trick, ruse.

fu·ma·dor, –do·ra **I.** adj. smoking **II.** m.f. smoker.

fu·mar intr. to smoke (tobacco) —tr. to smoke <*f. un pitillo* to smoke a cigarette>; ARG., COLL. to make fun of, trick —reflex. COLL. to squander <*fumarse el salario* to squander one's wages>; COLL. *(faltar)* to skip, cut <*fumarse la clase* to cut class>.

fu·ma·ra·da f. *(de humo)* puff (of smoke); *(de tabaco)* pipeful (of tobacco).

fu·mi·ga·ción f. fumigation.

fu·mi·ga·dor, –do·ra m.f. fumigator (person) —m. fumigator (machine).

fu·mi·gar §47 tr. to fumigate.

fu·mí·ge·no, –na adj. smoking, smoke-producing.

fu·mis·te·rí·a f. *(tienda)* stove *or* heater shop; *(oficio)* stove *or* heater repairing; ARG. joke, prank.

fu·mí·vo·ro, –ra adj. smokeless <*chimenea f.* smokeless chimney>.

fu·mo·so, –sa adj. smoky.

fu·nám·bu·lo, –la m.f. tightrope walker, funambulist.

fun·ción f. *(ejercicio)* function, duty; *(empleo)* position; PHYSIOL. function; THEAT. show, performance <*f. de gala* gala performance>; MATH. function ♦ **en f. de** in terms of • **entrar en funciones** to take office • **f. de tarde** THEAT. matinee.

fun·cio·nal adj. functional, operative.

fun·cio·na·li·dad f. functionality.

fun·cio·na·lis·mo m. functionalism.

fun·cio·na·mien·to m. functioning, operating.

fun·cio·nar intr. to work, run <*este motor no funciona* this engine's not running>.

fun·cio·na·rio, –ria m.f. civil servant, official.

fun·da f. *(cubierta)* cover, case; COL. skirt ♦ **f. de almohada** pillowcase.

fun·da·ción f. *(establecimiento)* foundation, establishment; *(principio)* beginning, origin; *(institución)* foundation, endowment.

fun·da·dor, –do·ra **I.** adj. founding **II.** m.f. founder.

fun·da·men·tal adj. fundamental.

fun·da·men·tar tr. CONST. to lay the foundations of (a building); FIG. *(establecer)* to establish; *(basar)* to base <*f. una opinión en algo* to base an opinion on something>.

fun·da·men·to m. CONST. foundation (of a building); *(base)* foundation, basis; *(seriedad)* seriousness, reliability; *(razón)* reason, ground <*su opinión tiene f.* he has grounds for his opinion>.

fun·dar tr. *(edificar)* to build, raise; *(instituir)* to found, establish; FIG. *(apoyar)* to base, rest <*f. un asunto en los hechos* to base a case on the facts> —reflex. FIG. to be founded *or* based ♦ **fundarse en** FIG. to base one's opinion on, base oneself on.

fun·di·ble adj. fusible.

fun·di·ción f. METAL. *(fusión)* melting, smelting; *(fábrica)* foundry, smeltery; PRINT. font, typeface; *(hierro)* cast iron.

fun·di·do, –da **I.** past part. see **fundir** **II.** adj. *(hecho líquido)* melted, liquefied; *(aparato eléctrico)* burned-out (appliance) **III.** m. CINEM. fade-in *or* fade-out ♦ **f. encadenado** CINEM. dissolve.

fun·di·dor m. foundry worker.

fun·di·llos m.pl. AMER. seat of the pants; MEX. rear (end), backside.

fun·dir tr. METAL. *(derretir)* to melt, smelt; *(moldear)* to cast, mold; *(bombilla)* to burn out (light bulb); *(fusible)* to blow (fuse) —reflex. FIG. *(unirse)* to merge, fuse; AMER. to be ruined, go bankrupt.

fun·do m. LAW rural property farm.

fú·ne·bre adj. *(funerario)* funereal; FIG. *(triste)* mournful, gloomy.

fu·ne·ral adj. & m. funeral ♦ **funerales** funeral, burial.

fu·ne·ra·la adv. ♦ **a la f.** MIL. with inverted weapons • **ojo a la f.** COLL. black eye.

fu·ne·ra·rio, –ria **I.** adj. funeral, funerary **II.** f. funeral home *or* parlor —m. undertaker, mortician.

fu·né·re·o, –a adj. funeral.

fu·nes·to, –ta adj. *(desgraciado)* unfortunate, regrettable; *(fatal)* fatal, ill-fated <*un resultado f.* a fatal outcome>.

fun·gi·ble adj. LAW fungible.

fun·gi·ci·da CHEM. **I.** adj. fungicidal **II.** m. fungicide.

fun·gi·for·me adj. BOT. fungiform, mushroom-shaped.

fun·gir §32 intr. C. AMER., MEX. to act *or* function (as); CUBA *(suplir)* to substitute for, take another's place.

fun·go m. MED. fungus.

fun·go·so, –sa adj. fungous.

fu·ni·cu·lar **I.** adj. funicular **II.** m. cable car.

fun·ja, funjo see **fungir.**

fu·ñi·que **I.** adj. *(inhábil)* awkward, clumsy; *(meticuloso)* fussy **II.** m.f. clumsy *or* awkward person.

fur·cia f. COLL. whore, hooker.

fur·gón f. *(carro)* van, wagon; RAIL. boxcar ♦ **f. de cola** caboose.

fur·go·ne·ta f. van, truck.

fu·ria f. *(ira)* fury, rage; FIG. *(persona muy colérica)* demon; *(agitación)* fury, frenzy <*la f. de los elementos* the frenzy of the elements>; *(prisa)* frenzy, haste ♦ **a toda f.** in frantic haste • **la Furias** MYTH. the Furies • **ponerse como una f.** to become enraged.

fu·ri·bun·do, –da adj. enraged, furious.

fu·rio·sa·men·te adv. furiously, frantically.

fu·rio·so, –sa adj. *(airado)* furious, irate; FIG. *(agitado)* turbulent, raging <*viento f.* raging wind>; *(grande)* tremendous, excessive; *(loco)* crazy, raving.

fu·ror m. *(cólera)* fury, rage; *(locura)* frenzy, fever; *(violencia)* fury, violence ♦ **f. uterino** PSYCH. nymphomania • **hacer f.** to be all the rage.

fur·ti·va·men·te adv. furtively, stealthily.
fur·ti·vo, -va adj. furtive, stealthy.
fu·rún·cu·lo m. MED. boil, furuncle.
fus·co, -ca adj. dark, dusky.
fu·se·la·je m. AVIA. fuselage.
fu·si·ble I. adj. fusible II. m. ELEC. fuse.
fu·sil m. rifle, gun ♦ **f. ametrallador** submachine gun.
fu·si·la·mien·to m. shooting, execution.
fu·si·lar tr. *(matar)* to shoot, execute by shooting; COLL. *(plagiar)* to plagiarize.
fu·si·la·zo m. (rifle) shot.
fu·sión f. *(fundición)* melting, fusion; PHYS. nuclear fusion; COM. merger, amalgamation; FIG. *(unión de intereses)* fusion.
fu·sio·nar intr. to merge, amalgamate.
fus·ta f. *(látigo)* coachman's whip; *(varas)* brushwood, twigs; MARIT. lateen, lateen-rigged boat; TEX. woolen material.
fus·tán m. TEX. fustian; AMER. white petticoat *or* slip.
fus·te m. *(palo)* shaft; FIG. *(importancia)* importance, consequence <*un hombre de poco f.* a man of little importance>; EQUIT. saddle tree; ARCHIT. shaft; ECUAD., VEN. fustian.
fus·ti·ga·ción f. *(azotazo)* whipping, lashing; *(censura)* censure, reprimand.
fus·ti·ga·dor, -do·ra I. adj. *(azotador)* whipping; *(censurador)* censuring II. m.f. *(azotador)* whipper; *(censurador)* censurer.
fus·ti·gar §47 tr. *(azotar)* to whip, lash; FIG. *(criticar)* to censure, reprimand.
fút·bol *or* **fut·bol** m. soccer, football (G.B.) ♦ **f. americano** football.
fut·bo·lín m. table soccer.
fut·bo·lis·ta m.f. soccer player, footballer (G.B.).
fu·te·sa f. trifle, bauble.
fú·til adj. trivial, insignificant.
fu·ti·li·dad f. triviality, insignificance.
fu·tre adj. & m. AMER. dandy.
fu·tu·ra I. f. LAW reversion (right of succession); COLL. *(novia)* fiancée, intended II. adj. see **futuro, -ra**.
fu·tu·ris·mo m. ARTS futurism.
fu·tu·ris·ta adj. & m.f. futurist.
fu·tu·ro, -ra I. adj. future II. m. *(porvenir)* future; COLL. *(novio)* fiancé, intended; GRAM. future —f. see **futura**.
fu·tu·ró·lo·go, -ga m.f. futurologist.

G

g, G f. eighth letter of the Spanish alphabet.
ga·ba·cho, -cha I. adj. *(pirenaico)* Pyrenean; COLL., DEROG. *(francés)* French; COLL. *(desgarbado)* awkward, ungainly; ORNITH. feather-legged (pigeon) II. m.f. *(pirenaico)* Pyrenean; COLL., DEROG. *(francés)* frog, French person —m. *(lenguaje)* Gallicized Spanish.
ga·bán m. overcoat, topcoat.
ga·bar·di·na f. *(tela)* gabardine; *(sobretodo)* raincoat.
ga·ba·rra f. MARIT. barge, lighter.
ga·ba·rro m. VET. *(pepita)* pip (disease of fowl); *(tumor)* tumor (in horse's hoof); TEX. flaw, defect; MIN. nodule; CONSTR. badigeon, filling (in masonry); FIG. *(error)* mistake, error (in accounts); *(incomodidad)* nuisance, annoyance.
ga·ba·zo m. bagasse (sugar-cane pulp).
ga·be·la f. *(impuesto)* tax, duty; FIG. *(carga)* burden; AMER. advantage.
ga·bi·ne·te m. *(cuarto)* study; *(de una mujer)* boudoir; *(muebles)* furniture (for a study); *(laboratorio)* laboratory <*g. de física* physics laboratory>; POL. cabinet; COL. enclosed balcony.
Ga·bón m. Gabon.
ga·bo·nés, -ne·sa adj. & m.f. Gabonese.
ga·ce·la f. ZOOL. gazelle.
ga·ce·ta f. *(periódico)* gazette, journal; COLL. *(chismoso)* gossip, gossip monger; *(diario oficial)* official journal *or* record.

ga·ce·te·ro, -ra m.f. *(vendedor)* news vendor *or* dealer —m. *(periodista)* reporter, journalist.
ga·ce·ti·lla f. JOURN. *(sección)* section of short news items; *(noticia breve)* short news item; *(columna de chismes)* gossip column; *(chismoso)* gossip, gossipmonger.
ga·ce·ti·lle·ro m. JOURN. *(de noticias breves)* writer of short news items; *(de chismes)* gossip columnist.
ga·cha I. f. *(masa blanda)* mush, paste; COL., VEN. bowl ♦ **gachas** *(papilla)* porridge; *(halagos)* cajolery • **hacerse unas gachas** COLL. to get mushy II. adj. see **gacho, -cha**.
ga·che·ta¹ f. *(papilla)* porridge, pap; *(engrudo)* paste.
ga·che·ta² f. spring lever (of latch).
ga·chí f. [pl. **-chís**] SL. girl, chick.
ga·cho, -cha I. adj. *(inclinado)* bowed, bent; *(flojo)* drooping, floppy; ZOOL. with downturned horns (cattle) II. m. AMER. slouch hat ♦ **a gachas** on all fours —f. see **gacha**.
ga·chón, -cho·na adj. COLL. *(gracioso)* charming, sweet; *(mimado)* spoiled (child).
ga·chu·pín AMER. *or* **ga·chu·po** MEX. m. *(inmigrante)* Spanish settler in America; *(español)* Spaniard.
ga·di·ta·no, -na I. adj. of Cádiz II. m.f. native of Cádiz.
ga·do·li·nio m. CHEM. gadolinium.
ga·é·li·co, -ca I. adj. Gaelic II. m.f. Gael —m. *(idioma)* Gaelic.
ga·fa I. f. *(gancho)* hook; *(grapa)* clamp ♦ **gafas** glasses, eyeglasses II. adj. see **gafo, -fa**.
ga·far tr. *(agarrar con las uñas)* to snatch with claws; *(componer con grapas)* to clamp; COLL. *(traer mala suerte)* to jinx, bring bad luck upon.
ga·fe m. COLL. jinx ♦ **ser g.** COLL. to be a jinx, be *or* bring bad luck.
ga·fo, -fa I. adj. MED. claw-handed; AMER. footsore II. f. see **gafa**.
ga·gá I. adj. doting, foolish II. m.f. dotard.
ga·go, -ga adj. AMER. stammering, stuttering.
ga·gue·ar intr. AMER. to stammer, stutter.
ga·gue·ra f. AMER. stammer, stutter.
gai·fa f. MUS. bagpipe <*g. gallega* bagpipe>; *(chirimía)* flageolet; *(organillo)* hurdy-gurdy; FIG., COLL. *(pescuezo)* neck; *(molestia)* nuisance, pain <*fue una g. limpiar mi cuarto ayer* it was a pain to clean my room yesterday>; MEX. good-for-nothing; ARG., DEROG. Galician ♦ **alegre como una g.** happy as a lark.
gai·te·rí·a f. COLL. flashy *or* gaudy clothes.
gai·te·ro, -ra I. adj. COLL. *(bufo)* clownish, buffoonish; *(charro)* flamboyant, gaudy (in dress) II. m.f. *(músico)* bagpiper; *(bufo)* clown, buffoon.
ga·je m. salary ♦ **gajes** salary, wages • **g. del oficio** occupational hazard.
ga·jo m. *(rama)* branch; *(racimo)* bunch (of fruit); *(división)* section <*un g. de naranja* an orange section>; *(punta)* prong, tine; GEOL. spur; BOT. lobe; C. AMER., COL. curl, ringlet (of hair); ARG., HORT. cutting, slip.
ga·jo·so, -sa adj. branched, segmented.
ga·la f. *(vestido)* full dress; *(gracia)* gracefulness, elegance; CUBA, MEX. tip ♦ **de g.** full-dress <*uniforme de g.* full-dress uniform> • **galas** *(adornos)* finery, trappings; *(regalos)* wedding gifts *or* presents • **hacer g. de** *or* **tener a g.** to take pride in, show off.
ga·lác·ti·co, -ca adj. galactic.
ga·lac·ti·ta *or* **ga·lac·ti·tes** f. MIN. galactite.
ga·lai·co, -ca adj. Galician.
ga·lán m. *(hombre bien parecido)* attractive *or* handsome man; *(galante)* gallant, beau; *(pretendiente)* suitor; THEAT. leading man, male lead.
ga·la·na·men·te adv. *(con gala)* smartly; FIG. *(con gracia)* gracefully; *(elegantemente)* elegantly.
ga·lan·ce·te m. *(galán)* handsome young man; THEAT. *(actor)* male juvenile lead.
ga·la·ní·a f. elegance.
ga·la·no, -na adj. *(bien vestido)* spruce, smart; FIG. *(elegante)* elegant; *(gracioso)* graceful; AMER. mottled.
ga·lan·te adj. *(obsequioso)* gallant; *(atento)* attentive, charming; *(amatorio)* flirtatious.
ga·lan·te·a·dor I. adj. flirtatious II. m. gallant, flirt.

ga·lan·te·ar tr. *(cortejar)* to woo, court; *(coquetear)* to flirt with; *(requebrar)* to pay attention to, say nice things to; FIG. *(solicitar con empeño)* to solicit favor.

ga·lan·te·men·te adv. gallantly, politely.

ga·lan·te·o m. *(cortejo)* courting; *(coqueteo)* flirting.

ga·lan·te·rí·a f. *(obsequio)* gallantry; *(cortesanía)* courtesy; *(gracia)* grace, elegance; *(liberalidad)* liberality.

ga·la·nu·ra f. *(elegancia)* elegance, grace; *(gallardía)* self-assurance.

ga·lá·pa·go m. ZOOL. sea turtle; AGR. moldboard (of a plow); *(molde)* tile mold; MED. bandage; METAL. ingot, pig; EQUIT. English saddle; HOND., VEN., EQUIT. sidesaddle.

ga·la·po m. laying top (for rope making).

ga·lar·dón m. reward, prize.

ga·lar·do·nar tr. *(premiar)* to award a prize to; *(recompensar)* to reward, recompense.

ga·la·xia f. ASTRON. galaxy; MIN. galactite.

ga·la·yo m. cliff.

gal·ba·na f. COLL. laziness, sloth.

gal·ba·ne·ar intr. to loaf, idle.

gal·ba·ne·ro, –ra adj. lazy, slothful.

gal·ba·no·so, –sa adj. COLL. lazy, slothful.

ga·le·a·za f. MARIT. galleass (large galley).

ga·lem·bo m. COL., VEN. ORNITH. turkey buzzard.

ga·le·no, –na I. adj. MARIT. soft, gentle (breeze) II. m. COLL. doctor, physician —f. MIN. galena, lead sulfide.

ga·le·ón m. MARIT. galleon.

ga·le·o·te m. MARIT. galley slave.

ga·le·ra f. MARIT., PRINT. galley; *(carro)* covered wagon; *(cárcel de mujeres)* women's prison; *(sala)* hospital ward; CARP. plane; ICHTH. squilla; C. AMER., MEX. shed, lean-to; ARG., CHILE, URUG. top hat; C. RICA slaughterhouse ♦ **condenar a galeras** to condemn to the galleys.

ga·le·ra·da f. *(carga)* wagonload; PRINT. galley, galley proof.

ga·le·rí·a f. *(pieza larga)* gallery; *(museo)* gallery, museum; *(mirador)* gallery; *(bastidor)* curtain rod, valence; FIG. *(vulgo)* gallery, general public.

ga·ler·na f. or **ga·ler·no** m. strong northwest wind.

ga·le·rón m. AMER. popular song and dance; C. RICA shed; MEX. large room.

Ga·les m. Wales.

ga·lés, –le·sa I. adj. Welsh II. m. *(habitante)* Welshman; *(idioma)* Welsh —f. Welshwoman ♦ **los galeses** the Welsh.

gal·ga I. f. *(piedra grande)* boulder, large rock; *(piedra que cae)* rolling stone; TECH. *(muela de molino)* millstone (of an oil press); *(instrumento de medida)* gauge; MED. *(erupción cutánea)* rash; *(cinta de zapato)* shoe ribbon, strap; *(freno)* hub brake (of a wagon); HOND. yellow ant II. adj. see **galgo, –ga.**

gal·go, –ga I. m.f. *(perro)* greyhound ♦ **¡échale un galgo!** some chance!, forget it! —f. see **galga** II. adj. COL. sweet-toothed.

gal·gue·ar intr. ARG., C. AMER. *(tener hambre)* to be starved or famished; *(buscar)* to cast or sniff about (for food).

Ga·lia f. Gaul.

gá·li·bo m. MARIT., TECH. template, pattern; RAIL. *(galga)* gauge; FIG. *(elegancia)* elegance; ARCHIT. perfect proportion.

ga·li·ca·do, –da adj. gallicized, full of gallicisms.

ga·li·ca·no –na adj. RELIG. Gallican; *(galicado)* gallicized.

Ga·li·cia f. GEOG. Galicia.

ga·li·cis·mo m. Gallicism.

Ga·li·le·a f. Galilee.

ga·li·le·o, –a adj. & m.f. Galilean ♦ **el G.** the Galilean, Christ.

ga·li·llo m. ANAT. uvula; COLL. *(gaznate)* gullet, throat.

ga·li·ma·tí·as m. [pl. **-as**] COLL. gibberish, nonsense.

ga·lio m. CHEM. gallium.

ga·lo, –la I. adj. Gallic II. m.f. Gaul —m. *(idioma)* Gaulish.

ga·lo·cha f. wooden or iron clog.

ga·ló·fi·lo, –la adj. & m.f. Francophile.

ga·lón¹ m. *(cinta)* braid, galloon; MIL. stripe, decoration.

ga·lón² m. gallon ♦ **g. inglés** imperial gallon.

ga·lo·ne·ar tr. SEW. to trim with braid, braid.

ga·lo·pan·te adj. *(que galopa)* galloping; MED. galloping.

ga·lo·par intr. ♦ to gallop.

ga·lo·pe m. gallop ♦ **a g. tendido** at full gallop • **ir a** or **al** or **de g.** to gallop, go at a gallop.

ga·lo·pe·ar intr. var. of **galopar.**

ga·lo·pín m. *(pilluelo)* urchin, ragamuffin; *(pícaro)* rascal, rogue; *(galopillo)* scullion, kitchen boy; FIG., COLL. *(hombre taimado)* smart aleck; MARIT. cabin boy.

gal·pón m. AMER. *(cobertizo)* large shed; *(galerón)* slaves' quarters; COL. tileworks, pottery.

gal·va·ni·cé, galvanice see **galvanizar.**

gal·vá·ni·co, –ca adj. PHYS. galvanic.

gal·va·nis·mo m. PHYS. galvanism.

gal·va·ni·za·ción f. PHYS. galvanization.

gal·va·ni·za·do, –da I. past part. of **galvanizar** II. adj. galvanized III. m. galvanization.

gal·va·ni·zar §04 tr. PHYS. to galvanize, electroplate; FIG. *(animar)* to galvanize.

gal·va·nó·me·tro m. PHYS. galvanometer.

ga·lla·da f. CHILE., COLL. bold deed.

ga·llar·da f. *(danza)* galliard (old Spanish dance); PRINT. type size.

ga·llar·de·ar intr. to act with ease and grace.

ga·llar·de·te m. MARIT. streamer, pennant.

ga·llar·dí·a f. *(bizarría)* elegance, charm; *(gracia)* grace; *(valor)* gallantry, bravery.

ga·llar·do, –da adj. *(airoso)* elegant, graceful; *(valiente)* brave, valiant; *(bizarro)* gallant, courageous.

ga·lle·ar intr. *(gritar)* to shout; METAL. to flaw; FIG. *(sobresalir)* to stand out, excel; *(presumir)* to show off; *(fanfarronear)* to brag.

ga·lle·go, –ga I. adj. *(de Galicia)* Galician; S. AMER. Spanish II. m.f. *(habitante de Galicia)* Galician; S. AMER. Spaniard —m. *(idioma)* Galician; *(viento)* northwester; C. RICA fast-swimming reptile.

ga·lle·guis·mo m. Galician word or idiom.

ga·lle·ra f. *(reñidero)* cockpit; *(gallinero)* coop (for gamecocks).

ga·lle·rí·a f. CUBA *(reñidero)* cockpit; *(egoísmo)* egotism, selfishness.

ga·lle·ro m. AMER. *(entusiasta)* cockfighting enthusiast; *(criador)* breeder of gamecocks.

ga·lle·ta f. *(bizcocho de mar)* sea biscuit, hardtack; *(bizcocho)* biscuit, cracker; COLL. *(bofetada)* slap; MIN. type of coal; ARG., BOL., VEN. maté gourd; CHILE coarse bread ♦ **colgar** or **dar la g. a alguien** ARG., COLL. *(despedir)* to fire (an employee); *(un novio)* to dump or jilt someone.

ga·lle·te·ro, –ra I. adj. CHILE flattering, adulatory II. m.f. *(fabricante)* biscuit maker —m. *(recipiente)* cookie jar or tin.

ga·lli·na f. ORNITH. hen, chicken —m.f. FIG. *(cobarde)* chicken, coward ♦ **estar como g. en corral ajeno** FIG., COLL. to be like a fish out of water • **g. ciega** blindman's buff • **g. de agua** or **de río** ORNITH. coot, water hen • **g. pintada** or **de Guinea** ORNITH. guinea hen • **g. sorda** ORNITH. woodcock.

ga·lli·ná·ce·o, –a ZOOL. I. adj. gallinaceous II. f. gallinacean ♦ **gallináceas** Galliformes.

ga·lli·na·zo, –za m. AMER., ORNITH. turkey buzzard.

ga·lli·ne·rí·a f. *(tienda)* poultry shop or market; *(bandada)* flock of hens; FIG. *(cobardía)* cowardice, chickenheartedness.

ga·lli·ne·ro, –ra m.f. chicken vendor —m. *(jaula)* chicken coop, henhouse; COLL. *(sitio ruidoso)* madhouse, noisy place; THEAT. top balcony.

ga·lli·ne·ta f. ORNITH. *(fúlica)* coot; *(chocha)* woodcock; AMER. guinea hen.

ga·lli·to m. FIG. *(fanfarrón)* braggart, showoff; *(persona importante)* notable, celebrity; AMER. bully, aggressive person; AMER., ORNITH. jacana; COL. dart ♦ **g. del rey** ICHTH. blenny.

ga·llo m. ORNITH. cock, rooster; ICHTH. dory; FIG. *(nota falsa)* false note; FIG., COLL. *(jefe)* boss, chief; *(esputo)* spit, spittle; SPORT. bantam (weight); AMER. *(valiente)* cocky person; COL. *(rehilete)* dart, small arrow; CHILE, PERU *(carro)* fire engine; MEX. *(serenata)* serenade; *(ob-*

jeto de segunda mano) secondhand object; PAN. *(cinta)* sash ♦ **alzar el g.** COLL. to brag, mouth off • **andar** *or* **estar de g. bravo** MEX. to be in a bad mood • **comer g.** AMER. to eat crow • **en menos que canta un g.** FIG., COLL. in a jiffy *or* a flash • **g. de pelea** gamecock, fighting cock • **g. de roca** ORNITH. cock-of-the-rock • **g. silvestre** ORNITH. capercaillie • **haber comido g.** MEX. to be in a fighting mood • **ser muy g.** AMER. to be very courageous • **tener mucho g.** to be cocky.

ga·llo·fe·ar intr. to loaf by living on alms.

ga·llo·fe·ro, -ra *o* **ga·llo·fo, -fa** I. adj. *(holgazán)* lazy, idle; *(pordiosero)* begging II. m.f. *(holgazán)* loafer, idler; *(pordiosero)* beggar.

ga·llón m. lawn, turf.

ga·llo·te, -ta adj. C. RICA, MEX., SP. confident, cocky.

ga·ma f. MUS. scale, gamut; FIG. *(escala)* range, gamut.

ga·ma·da adj. ♦ **cruz g.** swastika, gammadion.

gam·ba f. ZOOL. prawn.

gam·ba·do, -da I. past part. see **gambarse** II. adj. CUBA, P.RICO bowlegged.

gam·bar·se reflex. CARIB. to become bowlegged.

gam·be·rro, -rra I. adj. *(libertino)* dissolute, libertine; *(grosero)* vulgar, rowdy II. m.f. *(libertino)* libertine, wanton; *(granuja)* troublemaker, rowdy.

gam·be·ta f. ARTS caper, prance; EQUIT. curvet; ARG., BOL. dodge, duck; ARG., URUG., FIG. dodge, evasion.

gam·be·te·ar intr. ARTS to caper, prance; *(zízaguear)* to zigzag, dodge.

Gam·bia f. Gambia.

gam·bia·no, -na adj. & m.f. Gambian.

ga·me·lla f. *(arco)* bow (of yoke); *(artesa)* large wooden trough; *(camellón)* ridge (between furrows).

ga·me·to m. BIOL. gamete.

gam·ma f. gamma (Greek letter) ♦ **rayos g.** PHYS. gamma rays.

ga·món m. BOT. asphodel.

ga·mo·nal m. *(terreno)* field of asphodels; AMER. cacique, local political boss.

ga·mo·na·lis·mo m. AMER. caciquism.

ga·mu·za f. ZOOL. *(animal)* chamois; *(piel o tejido)* chamois; *(ante)* suede.

ga·na f. *(deseo)* desire, longing <*una gran g. de dormir* a great longing for sleep>; *(apetito)* hunger, appetite ♦ **con ganas** heartily • **darle ganas** *or* **darle la g. de** to feel like <*me dan ganas de jugar* I feel like playing> • **de buena g.** willingly • **de g.** *(con energía)* energetically, eagerly • **de mala g.** unwillingly • **es g.** MEX., COLL. it's a waste of time, there's no chance • **hasta las ganas** MEX. right to the end • **morirse de ganas** FIG. to be dying to • **quedarse con las ganas** to be disappointed, not to get (to) <*me quedé con las ganas de ir* I didn't get to go> • **tener ganas de** to want to, feel like • **sin ganas** unwillingly • **tenerle ganas a alguien** COLL. to have it in for someone.

ga·na·ble adj. gainable.

ga·na·de·rí·a f. AGR. *(ganado)* cattle, livestock; *(cría)* cattle raising; *(raza)* breed, strain (of cattle).

ga·na·de·ro, -ra I. adj. cattle II. m.f. cattle rancher, cattleman.

ga·na·do, -da I. past part. see **ganar** II. m. *(conjunto de animales)* livestock, stock; *(colmena)* hive; FIG., COLL. *(gentío)* mob, horde; AMER. cattle ♦ **g. caballar** AGR. horses • **g. cabrío** AGR. goats • **g. de cerda** *or* **g. porcino** AGR. swine • **g. vacuno** AGR. cattle.

ga·na·dor, -do·ra I. adj. winning, victorious II. m.f. *(el que gana)* winner; *(asalariado)* wage earner.

ga·nan·cia f. *(beneficio)* profit, gain; GUAT., MEX. extra ♦ **g. líquida** *or* **neta** COM. net profit • **g. total** *or* **bruta** COM. gross profit • **ganancias de capital** COM. capital gains • **ganancias y pérdidas** ACC. profit and loss.

ga·nan·cial adj. profit, pertaining to profit.

ga·nan·cio·so, -sa I. adj. *(lucrativo)* profitable, lucrative; *(ganador)* winning II. m.f. winner.

ga·na·pán m. *(trabajador)* laborer, handyman; *(grosero)* lout, uncouth person.

ga·nar tr. *(lograr)* to gain <*el consejero ganó el favor del rey* the counselor gained the favor of the king>; *(llevarse)* to win, get <*gané el premio gordo en la lotería* I won the grand prize in the lottery>; *(recibir)* to earn, make <*gano*

mucho dinero en este puesto I earn a lot of money in this job>; *(triunfar)* to win <*las tropas del rey ganaron la batalla* the king's troops won the battle>; *(conquistar)* to capture, take <*g. la ciudad* to capture the city>; *(vencer)* to beat, defeat <*le gané en ajedrez* I beat him in chess>; *(aventajar)* to surpass <*en destreza te gano* I surpass you in expertise>; *(captar)* to win over <*me ganaron a su lado* they won me over to their side>; *(merecer)* to earn, merit; *(alcanzar)* to reach, arrive at <*g. la frontera* to reach the border> ♦ **g. peso** to gain weight • **g. terreno** to gain ground —intr. to earn <*gana para sólo existir* he earns only enough to live on>; *(triunfar)* to win; *(mejorar)* to improve, advance —reflex. ARG., CHILE to take refuge ♦ **ganarse la gloria** FIG. to go to heaven • **ganarse la vida** to earn one's living.

gan·che·ro m. *(guía)* raftsman; ECUAD. women's saddle horse; CHILE odd-job man —m.f. ARG. assistant, helper.

gan·che·te ♦ **a medio g.** half (completed) • **al g.** from the corner of one's eyes • **de medio g.** AMER. about to fall • COL. **ir de g.** to walk arm in arm.

gan·chi·llo m. *(horquilla)* hairpin; *(aguja)* crochet needle; *(labor)* crochet (work) ♦ **hacer g.** to crochet.

gan·cho m. *(garfio)* hook; *(labor)* crochet; *(del árbol)* snag (of a tree); *(cayado)* crook (staff); *(puñetazo)* hook (punch); FIG., COLL. *(timador)* cajoler; *(rufián)* pimp; *(atractivo)* charm, allure; AMER. hairpin; ARG., GUAT. aid, help; ECUAD., EQUIT. sidesaddle ♦ **echar el g.** FIG. to hook, snare • **hacer g.** ARG., GUAT. to help.

gán·da·ra f. low wasteland.

gan·da·ya f. COLL. loafing, idleness.

gan·di·do, -da adj. AMER. gluttonous, greedy.

gan·din·ga f. MIN. fine washed ore; CUBA, P. RICO liver stew; CUBA laziness, indolence.

gan·du·jar tr. to pleat, fold.

gan·dul, -du·la I. adj. COLL. lazy, shiftless II. m.f. COLL. *(perezoso)* loafer, good-for-nothing —m. BOT. pigeon pea.

gan·du·le·ar intr. to loaf, idle.

gan·du·le·rí·a f. laziness, idleness.

gan·ga f. ORNITH. sand grouse; FIG. *(provecho)* bargain, steal; *(ventaja)* windfall; MIN. gangue; MEX. joke.

gan·glio m. ANAT., MED. ganglion.

gan·go·si·dad f. nasality (of voice).

gan·go·so, -sa adj. nasal, twangy.

gan·gre·na f. MED. gangrene; BOT. corrosive tree disease; FIG. *(corrupción)* rot, corruption.

gan·gre·na·do, -da I. past part. see **gangrenarse** II. MED. gangrenous; FIG. rotten, corrupt.

gan·gre·nar·se reflex. MED. to become gangrenous.

gan·gre·no·so, -sa adj. MED. gangrenous.

gángs·ter m. [pl. **-ters**] gangster, outlaw.

gangs·te·ris·mo m. gangsterism.

gan·gue·ar intr. to speak nasally, speak through one's nose.

gan·gue·o m. nasal tone, twang.

gan·gue·ro, -ra m.f. COLL. bargain hunter.

gán·guil m. MARIT. fishing boat; *(draga)* dump scow.

ga·no·so, -sa adj. desirous, anxious <*están ganosos de conseguir fama* they are anxious to acquire fame>.

gan·sa·da f. FIG., COLL. nonsense, silly act *or* remark.

gan·se·ar intr. COLL. to do *or* say silly things.

gan·so, -sa I. m. ORNITH. gander —f. ORNITH. goose —m.f. FIG. *(torpe)* dummy, dolt; *(rústico)* bumpkin, yokel II. adj. silly, dull-witted.

gan·ta f. PHILIP. liquid measure (equal to three liters).

Gan·te Ghent.

gan·zú·a f. *(instrumento)* picklock; *(ladrón)* picklock, thief; FIG., COLL. *(sonsacador)* cajoler, wheedler (of another's secrets)

ga·ñán m. *(obrero)* farm hand; FIG. *(jayán)* big brute *or* ox.

ga·ña·ní·a f. *(conjunto)* group of farm hands; *(local)* farm hands' living quarters.

ga·ñi·do I. past part. see **gañir** II. m. yelping, howling (of dogs).

ga·ñir §12 intr. *(aullar)* to yelp, howl (dogs); *(graznar)* to croak, caw (birds); COLL. *(resollar)* to wheeze, croak; *(chillar)* to scream, shriek.

ga·ño·te m COLL. throat, gullet ♦ **de g.** COLL. free, gratis.

ga·ño·te·ar tr. COLL. to go without paying, go for free.

ga·ra·ba·te·ar intr. *(echar un garabato)* to hook, grab with a hook; *(escribir)* to scribble, scrawl; FIG., COLL. *(tergiversar)* to beat around the bush —tr. *(escribir)* to scribble, scrawl.

ga·ra·ba·te·o m. *(asimiento)* hooking, grabbing with a hook; *(escritura)* scribbling, scrawling; FIG., COLL. *(tergiversación)* beating around the bush.

ga·ra·ba·to m. *(gancho)* hook, grapple; CUBA *(horca)* pitchfork; *(almocafre)* rake; *(escarabajos)* scribble, scrawl; FIG., COLL. *(gracia)* sex appeal, attractiveness (of women); ARG., BOT. variety of acacia ♦ **garabatos** exaggerated hand gestures.

ga·ra·ba·to·so, -sa adj. scribbled, scrawled.

ga·ra·bi·to m. *(casilla)* market stall; BOL. vagrant, bum.

ga·ra·je m. AUTO. garage.

ga·ra·jis·ta m. AUTO. garage attendant.

ga·ram·bai·na f. *(adorno)* trinket, gaudy ornament ♦ **garambainas** COLL. *(muecas)* airs, mannerisms; *(garabatos)* scribbles, scrawls.

ga·ran·te I. adj. COM. responsible II. m.f. COM. guarantor.

ga·ran·ti·a f. COM. *(aval)* guarantee, warranty; *(fianza)* security, desposit ♦ **garantías constitucionales** constitutional guarantees.

ga·ran·tir §38 tr. *(asegurar)* to guarantee; *(preservar)* to protect, defend.

ga·ran·ti·za·dor, -do·ra I. adj. responsible II. m.f. guarantor.

ga·ran·ti·zar §04 tr. *(responder)* to guarantee, warrant <*g. un coche nuevo* to guarantee a new car>; *(avalar)* to vouch or answer for; FIG. *(asegurar)* to guarantee, assure <*te garantizo que es un hombre honrado* I assure you that he's an honorable man>.

ga·ra·ñón m. *(asno)* stud jackass; C. AMER., MEX. stallion.

ga·ra·pi·ña f. *(helado)* frozen state of (some liquids); *(galón)* braid; CUBA, MEX. pineapple drink.

ga·ra·pi·ñar tr. *(helar)* to freeze (liquids); *(bañar)* to glaze, coat with syrup or sugar.

ga·ra·pu·llo m. *(rehilete)* dart; TAUR. banderilla (barbed dart).

ga·ra·ta f. DOM. REP., P. RICO, COLL. fight, brawl.

ga·ra·tu·ra f. TECH. scraper (used in tanning).

ga·ra·tu·sa f. COLL. *(halago)* compliment, flattery; FENC. thrust.

gar·ban·ce·o m. COLL. daily bread, sustenance.

gar·ban·ce·ro, -ra I. adj. chickpea II. m.f. *(vendedor)* chickpea seller; MEX., DEROG. servant.

gar·ban·zo m. BOT. chickpea; MEX. female servant ♦ **en toda tierra de garbanzos** COLL. everywhere • **g. negro** FIG., COLL. black sheep.

gar·ban·zue·lo m. VET. spavin (disease of horses).

gar·be·ar intr. *(fanfarronear)* to swagger, put on airs; *(robar)* to steal, rob —tr. *(robar)* to steal, rob —reflex. COLL. *(arreglárselas)* to manage, get by; *(pasearse)* to go for a walk.

gar·be·ra f. AGR. shock (of grain).

gar·bí·as m.pl. CUL. fried dish of eggs, herbs and cheese.

gar·bi·llar tr. AGR. to sift, sieve (grain); MIN. to screen, riddle.

gar·bi·llo m. *(zaranda)* sieve; MIN. *(criba)* riddle; *(mineral)* riddled ore.

gar·bi·no m. southwest wind.

gar·bo m. *(gallardía)* elegance, grace; *(atractivo)* attractiveness, stylishness; *(generosidad)* generosity, magnanimity.

gar·bo·sa·men·te adv. *(con elegancia)* elegantly, gracefully; *(generosamente)* generously, magnanimously.

gar·bo·so, -sa adj. *(airoso)* elegant, graceful; *(atractivo)* attractive, stylish; FIG. *(generoso)* generous, magnanimous.

gar·bu·llo m. confusion, uproar.

gar·de·nia f. BOT. gardenia.

gar·du·ño, -ña m.f. COLL. thief, pickpocket —f. ZOOL. marten.

ga·re·te ♦ **ir** or **irse al g.** MARIT. to drift, be adrift; FIG. *(andar sin rumbo)* to drift.

gar·fa f. ZOOL. claw; ELEC. cable clip.

gar·fa·da f. ELEC. clipping, clamping; *(agarrón)* clawing, grabbing (with the claws).

gar·fe·ar intr. to hook, grab with a hook.

gar·fio m. grappling iron, grapple.

gar·ga·je·ar intr. to spit, expectorate (phlegm).

gar·ga·je·o m. spitting, expectoration (of phlegm).

gar·ga·jien·to, -ta I. adj. spitting, expectorating II. m.f. spitter.

gar·ga·jo m. phlegm, spit.

gar·ga·jo·so, -sa adj. var. of gargajiento.

gar·gan·ta f. ANAT. throat, pharynx; *(parte más estrecha)* throat, neck <*la g. de una botella* the neck of a bottle>; *(voz)* (singing) voice <*ese niño tiene buena g.* that boy has a good (singing) voice>; ANAT. *(del pie)* instep; *(desfiladero)* gorge; ARCHIT. gorgerin, necking (of a column); TECH. groove (of a pulley).

gar·gan·ta·da f. gob of spit.

gar·gan·te·ar intr. *(cantar)* to warble, trill.

gar·gan·te·o m. *(quiebro)* warbling, trilling.

gar·gan·ti·lla f. necklace, choker.

gar·gan·tón m. *(collar)* heavy necklace; MEX., EQUIT. halter.

gár·ga·ra f. gargle, gargling ♦ **gárgaras** AMER. gargle (liquid) • **mandar a hacer gárgaras** COLL. to send (someone) packing.

gar·ga·re·ar intr. CHILE var. of gargarizar.

gar·ga·ris·mo m. *(acción)* gargling, gargle; *(líquido)* gargle.

gar·ga·ri·zar §04 intr. to gargle.

gár·gol m. CARP. groove.

gár·go·la f. ARCHIT. gargoyle.

gar·güe·ro or **gar·güe·ro** m. ANAT. windpipe, trachea.

ga·ri·bal·di·no, -na I. adj. HIST. supporting Garibaldi II. m.f. HIST. supporter of Garibaldi —f. garibaldi, smock.

ga·ri·fo, -fa I. adj. *(jarifo)* dapper, elegant; ARG. cheerful, lively; C. RICA, ECUAD., PERU hungry.

ga·ri·ta f. *(casilla)* cabin, box; *(de centinela)* sentry box; *(portería)* porter's offices; *(retrete)* lavatory.

ga·ri·te·ro m. *(dueño)* owner of a gambling house; *(jugador)* gambler; MEX. ticket taker in gambling house.

ga·ri·to m. *(local)* gambling den or house; *(ganancia)* winnings, gambling profits.

gar·la·dor, -do·ra COLL. I. adj. chattering, chatty II. m.f. chatterer.

gar·lar intr. COLL. to chatter, gab.

gar·li·to m. *(de pesca)* fish trap or snare; FIG., COLL. *(trampa)* trap, snare ♦ **caer en el g.** FIG., COLL. to fall into the trap, fall for it • **coger a uno en el g.** FIG., COLL. to catch someone in the act.

gar·lo·pa f. CARP. jack plane.

gar·na·cha¹ f. *(vestidura)* robe, gown (of judge); HOND. assault, attack; MEX. large tortilla.

gar·na·cha² f. AGR. Grenache (grape or wine).

gar·ni·ca f. BOL. very hot pepper.

gar·niel m. leather pouch.

gar·nu·cho m. MEX. rap, fillip.

ga·rra f. ORNITH., ZOOL. claw, talon; FIG., COLL. *(mano)* paw, hand; *(fuerza)* bite, kick <*esa interpretación no tenía ninguna g.* that interpretation did not have any bite to it>; MARIT. hook (of a harpoon); AMER. dried piece of leather; COL. leather bag; MEX. strength ♦ **caer en las garras de alguien** FIG., COLL. to fall into someone's clutches • **como una g.** ARG., COL. very thin, emaciated • **echar la g.** to lay one's hands on • **garras** AMER. tatters, rags • **no hay cuero sin garras** MEX. nothing is perfect.

ga·rra·fa f. carafe, decanter.

ga·rra·fal adj. BOT. large and sweet (said of cherries); COLL. *(muy grande)* huge, enormous <*error g.* an enormous blunder>.

ga·rra·fi·ñar tr. COLL. to grab, snatch.

ga·rra·fón m. *(garrafa)* large carafe; *(damajuana)* demijohn.

ga·rra·pa·ta f. ENTOM. tick, mite; COLL. *(caballo)* nag, worn-out horse.

ga·rra·pa·te·ar intr. to scribble, scrawl.

ga·rra·pa·te·o m. scribble, scrawl.

ga·rra·pa·to·so, -sa adj. scribbled, scrawled (handwriting).

ga·rra·pi·ñar tr. to grab, snatch.

ga·rra·sí m. [pl. **-sí·es**] VEN. cowboy chaps or breeches.

ga·rras·pe·ra f. COL., SP. var. of carraspera.

ga·rre·ar tr. ARG. *(desollar)* to skin the hooves of (a steer); *(robar)* to steal —intr. ARG. to sponge, live off someone else; MARIT. to drag anchor.

ga·rre·te m. AMER. var. of **jarrete**.

ga·rri·do, -da adj. elegant, smart.

ga·rro·cha f. TAUR. lance, goad; SPORT. pole (used in vaulting); MEX. cattle prod; CHILE dart.

ga·rrón m. ORNITH. talon, claw; *(pata)* paw (for hanging dead animal); *(gancho)* stub (of cut tree branch); ARG. hock (of horse).

ga·rro·ta·zo m. blow (given with a club).

ga·rro·te m. *(palo)* club; *(tormento)* garrote; MED. tourniquet; *(abombado)* bulge (of a wall); BOT. cutting; MARIT. fid; MEX. brake ♦ **dar g.** to garrote.

ga·rro·te·ar tr. AMER. to club.

ga·rro·ti·llo m. MED. croup.

ga·rru·cha f. MECH. pulley.

ga·rru·do, -da adj. *(de garras fuertes)* strong-clawed; MEX. muscular, brawny.

ga·rru·lar intr. to chatter, prattle.

ga·rru·le·rí·a f. chatter, prattle.

ga·rru·li·dad f. garrulousness, talkativeness.

gá·rru·lo, –la adj. *(cantor)* noisy, chirping (bird); FIG. *(hablador)* garrulous, talkative; FIG., POET. *(ruidoso)* babbling, murmuring (water).

ga·rú·a *or* **ga·ru·ja** f. AMER. drizzle, fine rain.

ga·ruar §67 intr. AMER. to drizzle.

ga·ru·fa f. ARG., SL. spree, binge.

ga·ru·fe·ar intr. ARG., SL. to go on a spree *or* binge.

ga·ru·lla f. *(uvas)* loose grapes; *(granuja)* rascal, scoundrel; FIG., COLL. *(multitud)* crowd, mob.

ga·ru·lla·da f. FIG., COLL. rowdy bunch, mob.

ga·ru·llo m. COL. din, racket.

gar·za I. f. ORNITH. heron ♦ **g. imperial** purple heron • **g. real** gray heron II. adj. see **garzo, –za**.

gar·zo, –za I. adj. blue, bluish II. m. BOT. agaric —f. see **garza**.

gas m. CHEM., PHYS. gas; *(gasolina)* gasoline ♦ **a todo g.** COLL. full speed • **g. de los pantanos** GEOL. marsh gas • **gases de escape** exhaust fumes • **gases nobles** *or* **raros** CHEM. noble gases • **gases permanentes** *or* **fijos** CHEM. fixed gases. • **g. hilarante** CHEM. laughing gas, nitrous oxide • **g. lacrimógeno** CHEM. tear gas • **g. oil** gas oil, diesel fuel • **g. pobre** CHEM. producer gas • **g. tóxico** MIL. poison gas.

ga·sa f. MED., TEX. gauze; *(de luto)* crepe (for mourning).

gas·cón, –co·na adj. & m.f. Gascon.

Gas·cu·ña f. Gascogne, Gascony.

ga·se·ar tr. *(hacer gaseoso)* to carbonate; *(asfixiar)* to gas, asphyxiate.

ga·se·o·so, –sa I. adj. *(gaseiforme)* gasiform, gaseous; *(que contiene gases)* gaseous II. f. *(bebida)* carbonated beverage.

ga·si·fi·ca·ción f. gasification.

ga·si·fi·ca·dor m. gasifier.

ga·si·fi·car §70 tr. to gasify.

ga·so·duc·to m. gas pipeline.

gas oil *or* **ga·soil** m. AUTO. gas *or* diesel oil.

ga·só·le·o m. AUTO. var. of **gas oil**.

ga·so·li·na f. gasoline, gas.

ga·so·li·ne·ra f. *(lancha)* motorboat; *(tienda)* gas *or* filling station.

gas·ta·ble adj. expendable, spendable.

gas·ta·do, –da I. past part. see **gastar** II. adj. *(debilitado)* worn-out, exhausted; *(usado)* worn, threadbare; *(trillado)* hackneyed, worn-out.

gas·ta·dor, –do·ra I. adj. spendthrift, wasteful II. m.f. *(derrochador)* spendthrift; *(prisionero)* prisoner condemned to hard labor —m. MIL. sapper.

gas·tar tr. *(pagar)* to spend, expend <*gasta mucho dinero en banquetes* he spends a lot of money on banquets>; *(consumir)* to consume, exhaust <*gastó sus fuerzas* he exhausted his efforts>; *(echar a perder)* to wear out <*la niña gastó los zapatos* the little girl wore out her shoes>; *(malgastar)* to waste, squander; *(llevar)* to sport, wear <*g. barba* to sport a beard>; *(poseer)* to have; *(usar)* to use; *(destruir)* to devastate, lay waste to ♦ **gastarlas** COLL. to behave, act <*ya sé cómo las gasta usted* I know how you behave> • **g.**

bromas to play practical jokes —intr. to spend —reflex. *(consumirse)* to be used up, run out; *(deteriorarse)* to wear out; *(debilitarse)* to wear oneself out, become exhausted.

gas·to m. *(desembolso)* expenditure, expense, outlay <*un g. diario de cincuenta pesos* a daily expenditure of fifty pesos>; *(consumo)* use, consumption <*un gran g. de energía* a large consumption of energy>; *(deterioro)* wear and tear; PHYS. volume of flow ♦ **gastos** charges <*gastos bancarios* bank charges>; costs, expenses <*gastos de operación* operating expenses> • **gastos de representación** entertainment allowance • **gastos generales** overhead • **hacer el g. de la conversación** FIG., COLL. to do all the talking.

gas·to·so, –sa adj. spendthrift, wasteful.

gás·tri·co, –ca adj. MED. gastric.

gas·tri·tis f. MED. gastritis.

gas·tro·en·te·ri·tis f. MED. gastroenteritis.

gas·tro·en·te·ro·lo·gí·a f. MED. gastroenterology.

gas·tro·in·tes·ti·nal adj. MED. gastrointestinal.

gas·tro·lo·gí·a f. MED. gastrology.

gas·tro·no·mí·a f. gastronomy.

gas·tro·nó·mi·co, –ca adj. gastronomic, gastronomical.

gas·tró·no·mo, –ma m.f. gastronome, gourmet.

ga·ta f. ZOOL. female cat, tabby; FIG. *(nubecilla)* cloud; BOT. restharrow; CUBA, P. RICO, ICHTH. gata-nosed shark; CHILE crank; MEX. maid, servant girl.

ga·ta·da f. *(acción de gato)* feline action; *(regate)* dodge, sudden turn; FIG. *(astucia)* ruse, trick.

ga·ta·llón, –llo·na COLL. I. adj. rascally, roguish II. m.f. rascal, rogue.

ga·tas ♦ **a. g.** on all fours <*andar a g.* to walk on all fours>; ARG., COLL. hardly, barely.

ga·ta·tum·ba f. COLL. hypocrisy, feigned emotion.

ga·ta·zo m. *(gato)* large cat; COLL. *(engaño)* swindle, trick ♦ **dar g. a** COLL. to swindle.

ga·te·a·do, –da I. past part. see **gatear** II. adj. *(gatuno)* catlike, feline; *(rayado)* striped, streaked III. m. BOT. gateado (wood); *(andar a gatas)* crawling, creeping; *(trepa)* climbing, climb.

ga·te·ar intr. COLL. *(andar a gatas)* to crawl, walk on all fours; *(trepar)* to climb (trees); MEX., COLL. to chase *or* court the female servants —tr. *(arañar)* to scratch, claw; COLL. *(robar)* to swipe, steal.

ga·te·ra f. *(agujero)* cathole; MARIT. hawsehole, cathole —m. COLL. scamp, rogue; BOL. market stallholder.

ga·te·rí·a f. *(gatos)* pack of cats; COLL. *(banda)* gang of hoodlums *or* toughs; *(disimulación)* sham, simulation.

ga·ti·llo m. ARM. *(percusor)* hammer, firing pin; *(disparador)* trigger; DENT. forceps; TECH. clamp; ZOOL. nape (of some animals); FIG., COLL. *(ratero)* petty thief, purse snatcher; CHILE long mane (of horses).

ga·to m. ZOOL. cat, tomcat; *(gancho de hierro)* clamp, vice; *(cric)* jack <*g. hidráulico* hydraulic jack>; COLL. *(portamonedas)* moneybag; *(ahorros)* savings; FIG., COLL. *(ladrón)* sneak thief, cat burglar; *(madrileño)* native of Madrid, Madrilenian; *(hombre astuto)* fox, slyboots; AMER. *(molledo del brazo)* fleshy part of the arm; ARG. folk dance; MEX. *(propina)* tip; *(sirviente)* servant; PERU open-air market; VEN. syphilis ♦ **buscarle tres pies al g.** to complicate matters unnecessarily • **cuatro gatos** COLL. just a few people • **dar g. por liebre** FIG., COLL. to swindle, pull the wool over someone's eyes • **g. cerval** ZOOL. lynx • **g. de algalia** ZOOL. civet • **g. de Angora** Angora cat • **g. encerrado** FIG. something fishy • **g. montés** ZOOL. wildcat • **g. romano** tabby • **g. siamés** Siamese cat • **llevar el g. al agua** FIG. to put to a real test • **no hay gatos** *or* **no hay un g.** COLL. there isn't a soul.

ga·tu·no, –na adj. feline, catlike.

ga·tu·pe·rio m. *(mezcla)* jumble, hodgepodge; FIG., COLL. *(embrollo)* entanglement, intrigue.

gau·cha·da f. COLL. *(acción astuta)* clever *or* neat trick; ARG. favor, good turn.

gau·cha·je m. ARG., CHILE group of gauchos.

gau·ches·co, –ca adj. *(del gaucho)* gaucho; *(parecido al gaucho)* gaucho-like.

gau·chis·mo m. Argentine literary and musical movement concerned with gaucho life.

gau·cho, –cha I. adj. *(del gaucho)* gaucho; AMER., COLL.

shrewd, cunning; ARG., CHILE expert, skilled (in horsemanship); ARG. (*grosero*) crude, uncouth; (*bonito*) handsome II. m. (*habitante de la pampa*) gaucho; AMER. skilled horseman; ECUAD. broad-brimmed straw hat.

gau·de·a·mus m. COLL. celebration, festivity.

gau·sio *or* **gauss** m. PHYS. gauss.

ga·ve·ra f. COL., MEX., VEN. brick *or* tile mold; PERU (*tapia*) adobe wall; (*molde*) adobe wall mold; COL. wooden cooling vat (for cane syrup).

ga·ve·ta f. drawer.

ga·via f. MARIT. (*vela*) (main) topsail; (*cofa*) top, crow's nest; (*jaula*) wooden cage (for madmen); (*zanja*) ditch; ORNITH. seagull, gull.

ga·vial m. ZOOL. gavial, crocodile.

ga·viar intr. CUBA to tassel (said of corn).

ga·vi·lán m. ORNITH. sparrow hawk; (*escritura*) hair stroke, flourish (in penmanship); (*pluma*) nib; (*espada*) quillon; (*aguijada*) iron tip (of goad); BOT. (*flor del cardo*) thistle flower; MED. ingrown nail; ARG., VET. disease of horses.

ga·vi·lla f. AGR. (*cereales*) sheaf of grain; (*sarmientos*) bundle of vines; FIG. (*gente*) gang, band <*g. de ladrones* band of thieves>.

ga·vi·lle·ro m. AGR. stack *or* row of sheaves; COL., ECUAD., VEN. bully, tough; CHILE laborer who loads sheaves.

ga·vión m. MIL., HYDRAUL. (*cestón*) gabion; MIL. (*defensa*) gabionade; FIG., COLL. (*sombrero*) large hat.

ga·vio·ta f. ORNITH. seagull, gull.

ga·yum·ba f. DOM. REP. musical instrument.

ga·za·pa f. COLL. lie, fib.

ga·za·pa·tón m. COLL. blunder.

ga·za·pe·ra f. (*madriguera*) rabbit warren; FIG., COLL. (*pandilla*) unsavory *or* shady gang; (*riña*) brawl, scuffle.

ga·za·pi·na f. COLL. (*junta*) gang (of hoodlums); (*riña*) fight, brawl.

ga·za·po m. ZOOL. young rabbit; FIG., COLL. (*hombre astuto*) shrewd person, sly fox; COLL. (*disparate*) error, slip of the tongue *or* pen; (*mentira*) lie, fib.

ga·za·pón m. gambling den *or* house.

gaz·mo·ña·da *or* **gaz·mo·ñe·rí·a** f. (*pudor*) prudishness, priggishness; (*santurronería*) sanctimoniousness, hypocrisy.

gaz·mo·ñe·ro, –ra *or* **gaz·mo·ño, –ña** I. adj. (*pudoroso*) prudish, priggish; (*santurrón*) unctuous, sanctimonious II. m.f. (*persona pudorosa*) prig, prude; (*santurrón*) sanctimonious person.

gaz·ná·pi·ro, –ra I. adj. simple-minded, dull-witted II. m.f. numbskull, dunce.

gaz·na·ta·da f. blow to the throat; AMER. slap.

gaz·na·te m. (*garguero*) throat, windpipe; (*fruta de sartén*) fritter; MEX. pineapple *or* coconut sweet ♦ **remojar el g.** to wet one's whistle.

gaz·pa·cho m. CUL. gazpacho.

ga·zu·zo, –za I. adj. CHILE hungry, ravenous II. f. COLL. extreme hunger; C. RICA noise, uproar ♦ **tener g.** COLL. to be famished *or* starving.

géi·ser m. geyser.

gel m. CHEM. gel.

ge·la·ción f. CHEM. gelation.

ge·la·ti·na f. CHEM., CUL. gelatin, gelatine.

ge·la·ti·no·so, –sa adj. gelatinous.

gé·li·do, –da adj. POET. gelid, ♦icy.

ge·lig·ni·ta f. CHEM. gelignite.

ge·ma f. MIN. gem, precious stone; BOT. bud, gemma.

ge·me·bun·do, –da adj. groaning *or* moaning loudly.

ge·me·lo, –la adj. & m.f. twin ♦ **gemelos** (*anteojos*) binoculars, field glasses; (*de camisa*) cuff links • **Gemelos** ASTROL., ASTRON. Gemini • **gemelos de teatro** opera glasses.

ge·mi·do I. past part. see **gemir** II. m. moan, groan.

ge·mi·dor, –do·ra adj. moaning, groaning.

ge·mi·na·ción f. (*división*) separation, division; RHET. germination, repetition of one *or* more words.

ge·mi·na·do, –da adj. geminate.

Gé·mi·nis m. ASTROL., ASTRON. Gemini, the Twins.

ge·mir §48 intr. (*quejarse*) to moan, groan; FIG. (*aullar*) to howl, wail (an animal); (*rugir*) to howl (the wind).

gen *or* **ge·ne** m. [pl. **ge·nes**] BIOL. gene.

gen·cia·na f. BOT. gentian.

gen·dar·me m. gendarme, policeman.

gen·dar·me·rí·a f. gendarmerie, gendarmery.

ge·ne·a·lo·gí·a f. genealogy.

ge·ne·a·ló·gi·co, –ca adj. genealogical.

ge·ne·ra·ble adj. generable, capable of being generated.

ge·ne·ra·ción f. generation ♦ **g. espontánea** BIOL. spontaneous generation.

ge·ne·ra·cio·nal adj. generational.

ge·ne·ra·dor, –do·ra I. adj. (*que engendra*) generating, engendering; GEOM. generating II. m.f. (*persona*) generator, engenderer —m. ELEC., MECH. generator —f. (*persona*) generatrix; GEOM. generatrix ♦ **generadores** ANAT. genital organs, genitalia • **g. de gas** gas generator • **g. de señales** RAD. signal generator.

ge·ne·ral I. adj. (*común*) general, usual; (*vago*) general, vague; (*vasto*) vast, broad <*él es un hombre de educación g.* he is a man with a vast education> II. m. MIL., RELIG. general ♦ **en g.** *or* **por lo g.** generally, in general • **g. de brigada** MIL. brigadier general • **g. de división** MIL. major general • **g. en jefe** MIL. commander in chief.

ge·ne·ra·la f. MIL. (*esposa*) general's wife; (*toque*) call to arms.

ge·ne·ra·la·to m. MIL., RELIG. (*grado*) generalship; MIL. (*conjunto*) group of generals in an army.

ge·ne·ra·li·cé, generalice see **generalizar**.

ge·ne·ra·li·dad f. (*calidad de general*) generality, generalness; (*el mayor número*) majority, plurality; (*vaguedad*) generality, vague statement.

ge·ne·ra·lí·si·mo m. MIL. generalissimo, commander in chief.

ge·ne·ra·li·za·ble adj. capable of becoming widespread *or* generalized.

ge·ne·ra·li·za·ción f. (*acción de volver general*) generalization; (*extensión*) widening, expansion.

ge·ne·ra·li·zar §04 tr. (*volver general*) to generalize; (*ampliar*) to widen, expand.

ge·ne·ral·men·te adv. generally.

ge·ne·rar tr. to generate, produce.

ge·ne·ra·ti·vo, –va adj. generative.

ge·ne·ra·triz [pl. **–tri·ces**] I. adj. BOT. pertaining to the thick layers of growth on vegetables; GEOM. generating II. f. BOT. (*crecimiento*) thick layer of growth (on vegetables); GEOM. generatrix; (*procreadora*) engenderer, procreator; ELEC., MECH. generator.

ge·né·ri·ca·men·te adv. generically.

ge·né·ri·co, –ca adj. (*común*) generic, common; GRAM. indicating gender.

gé·ne·ro m. (*tipo*) type, kind <*no me relaciono con ese g. de personas* I don't associate with that type of people>; (*manera*) manner, style; COM. commodity; TEX. fabric, material; BIOL. genus; GRAM. gender; ARTS, LIT. genre ♦ **g. humano** humankind • **géneros de punto** knitwear.

ge·ne·ro·sa·men·te adv. generously.

ge·ne·ro·si·dad f. (*liberalidad*) generosity, liberality; (*magnanimidad*) magnanimity, nobility; (*valor*) valor, courage.

ge·ne·ro·so, –sa adj. (*liberal*) generous, liberal; (*noble*) magnanimous, noble; (*valiente*) brave, courageous; (*fértil*) fertile, abundant; (*de ilustre prosapia*) high-born, of noble ancestry; (*excelente*) excellent, fine.

gé·ne·sis f. [pl. **-sis**] origin, beginning —m. ♦ **G.** BIBL. Genesis.

ge·né·ti·co, –ca I. adj. genetic, genetical II. f. genetics.

ge·nial adj. (*brillante*) brilliant <*una novela g.* a brilliant novel>; COLL. (*agradable*) genial, pleasant; (*característica*) characteristic, typical.

ge·nia·li·dad f. (*rareza*) peculiarity, trait; (*obra*) brilliant *or* inspired work.

ge·nial·men·te adv. (*brillantemente*) brilliantly; (*agradablemente*) genially, pleasantly.

ge·nia·zo m. COLL. bad *or* violent temper.

ge·nio m. (*carácter*) temperament, disposition; (*talento*) genius, talent <*Mozart tenía g. para la música* Mozart had a genius for music>; (*facultad*) genius; (*persona*) genius; (*naturaleza*) peculiarity, nature; MYTH. genie; (*deidad pagaña*) genius, spirit ♦ **de mal g.** bad-tempered.

ge·ni·tal I. adj. BIOL. genital II. m. ANAT. testicle, genital ♦ **genitales** ANAT. genitals, genitalia.

ge·ni·ti·vo, –va I. adj. BIOL. capable of reproducing *or* engendering II. m. GRAM. genitive (case *or* expression).

ge·ni·tor, –to·ra I. adj. engendering, reproductive II. m. procreator, reproducer.

ge·no·ci·dio m. genocide.

ge·no·ti·po m. BIOL. genotype.

Gé·no·va f. Genoa.

ge·no·vés, –ve·sa adj. & m.f. Genoese ♦ los genoveses the Genoese.

gen·te f. people <*hay mucha g. en el mercado* there are a lot of people in the marketplace>; *(nación)* nation, folk; COLL. *(facción)* clan, gang <*yo tengo toda mi g.* I have my whole gang with me>; *(familia)* family, folks; MIL. troops; AMER. decent folk ♦ de g. en g. from generation to generation • g. baja common people • g. bien upper class • g. de bien decent folk • g. de capa parda country folk, rustics • g. de letras well-read people • g. de mar crew, seamen • g. de medio pelo people of limited means • g. de paz MIL. friend (as opposed to foe) • g. de pelo the well-to-do • g. de razón the elite • g. de trato tradespeople • g. de vida airada libertines • g. menuda COLL. kids, small fry • g. perdida *(vagabundos)* tramps, bums; *(ladrones)* crooks • gentes BIBL. Gentiles.

gen·te·ci·lla f. COLL. riffraff, rabble.

gen·til I. adj. RELIG. *(idólatra)* pagan, gentile; *(gracioso)* genteel, polite; *(notable)* remarkable, excellent II. m.f. RELIG. gentile, pagan.

gen·ti·le·za f. *(gracia)* genteelness, gracefulness; *(cortesía)* courtesy, politeness; *(amabilidad)* kindness, goodness; *(bizarría)* dash, stylishness.

gen·til·hom·bre m. [pl. -ti·les·hom·bres] *(buen mozo)* good-looking *or* handsome young man; HIST. *(noble)* gentleman-in-waiting.

gen·ti·li·cio, –cia I. adj. *(relativo a una nación)* pertaining to a certain race *or* people; *(relativo al linaje)* hereditary, genealogical II. m. GRAM. word indicating origin *or* location of a person *or* thing.

gen·ti·li·dad f. *or* gen·ti·lis·mo m. RELIG. *(paganismo)* Gentile religion, paganism; *(conjunto de personas)* (the) Gentiles.

gen·til·men·te adv. *(con gracia)* genteelly, gracefully; *(cortésmente)* courteously, politely; *(amablemente)* kindly, warmly; *(con garbo)* stylishly, dashingly; RELIG. in a Gentile *or* pagan manner.

gen·tí·o m. crowd, mob.

gen·try f. gentry.

gen·tu·za f. riffraff, rabble.

ge·nu·fle·xión f. genuflection, genuflexion.

ge·nui·no, –na adj. genuine.

ge·o·cén·tri·co, –ca adj. geocentric.

ge·o·da f. GEOL. geode.

ge·o·de·sia f. GEOL. geodesy.

ge·o·dé·si·co, –ca adj. GEOL. geodesic, geodetic.

ge·o·fa·gia f. geophagy, geophagia.

ge·o·fí·si·co, –ca I. adj. geophysical II. m.f. geophysicist —f. geophysics.

ge·o·gra·fí·a f. geography ♦ g. botánica geobotany, phytogeography.

ge·o·grá·fi·co, –ca adj. geographic, geographical.

ge·ó·gra·fo, –fa m.f. geographer.

ge·o·lo·gí·a f. geology.

ge·o·ló·gi·co, –ca adj. geological, geologic.

ge·ó·lo·go, –ga m.f. geologist.

ge·o·man·cia f. geomancy.

ge·ó·me·tra m.f. *(matemático)* geometrician, geometer; ZOOL. measuring worm, inchworm.

ge·o·me·trí·a f. *(ciencia)* geometry; *(tratado)* treatise on geometry ♦ g. analítica analytical geometry • g. del espacio solid geometry • g. descriptiva descriptive geometry • g. no-euclidiana non-Euclidian geometry • g. plana plane geometry • g. proyectiva projective geometry.

ge·o·mé·tri·ca·men·te adv. geometrically.

ge·o·mé·tri·co, –ca adj. geometric, geometrical; FIG. *(exacto)* exact, methodical.

ge·o·mor·fí·a *or* ge·o·mor·fo·lo·gí·a f. geomorphology.

ge·o·po·lí·ti·co, –ca I. adj. geopolitical II. f. geopolitics.

ge·o·quí·mi·ca f. geochemistry.

ge·or·gia·no, –na adj. & m.f. GEOG. Georgian.

ge·ór·gi·co, –ca I. adj. AGR., POET. georgic, georgical II. f. ♦ geórgicas POET. georgic.

ge·o·ter·mia f. GEOL. science concerned with geothermic investigation.

ge·o·tér·mi·co, –ca adj. geothermal, geothermic.

ge·ra·nio m. BOT. geranium ♦ g. de rosa rose geranium.

ge·ren·cia f. *(gestión)* management, direction; *(cargo)* managership, directorship; *(oficina)* manager's *or* director's office.

ge·ren·te m. manager, director.

ge·ria·tra m.f. MED. geriatrician, geriatrist.

ge·ria·trí·a f. MED. geriatrics.

ge·riá·tri·co, –ca adj. MED. geriatric.

ge·ri·fal·te m. ORNITH. gyrfalcon, gerfalcon; FIG. *(persona sobresaliente)* outstanding achiever.

ger·ma·nes·co, –ca adj. slang.

ger·ma·ní·a f. *(jerga)* slang of gypsies and thieves; *(amancebamiento)* concubinage.

ger·má·ni·co, –ca adj. & m. Germanic.

ger·ma·nio m. CHEM. germanium.

ger·ma·nis·ta m.f. Germanist, German scholar.

ger·ma·ni·za·ción f. germanization.

ger·ma·ni·zar §04 tr. to germanize.

ger·ma·no, –na I. adj. German, Germanic II. m.f. German.

ger·ma·nó·fi·lo, –la adj. & m.f. Germanophile, Germanophil.

ger·ma·nó·fo·bo, –ba I. adj. relative to fear of Germany *or* German things II. m.f. Germanophobe.

ger·men m. BIOL. germ; FIG. *(origen)* germ, beginnings ♦ g. plasma BIOL. germ plasm *or* plasma.

ger·mi·ci·da BACT. I. adj. germicidal II. m. germicide, germ killer.

ger·mi·na·ción f. BOT., FIG. germination.

ger·mi·na·dor, –do·ra adj. germinating.

ger·mi·nal adj. germinal.

ger·mi·nar intr. BOT., FIG. to germinate.

ge·ron·to·cra·cia f. POL. gerontocracy.

ge·ron·to·lo·gí·a f. MED. gerontology.

ge·ron·tó·lo·go, –ga m.f. MED. gerontologist.

ge·run·dio m. GRAM. *(del español)* present participle; *(del latín)* gerund.

ges·ta f. exploits, heroic deeds (of a person *or* nation) ♦ cantar *or* canción de g. LIT. chanson de geste, epic (poem).

ges·ta·ción f. BIOL. gestation; FIG. *(desarrollo)* gestation, development.

ges·tar tr. to gestate, carry —reflex. to develop, grow.

ges·te·ar intr. *(hacer muecas)* to grimace, make faces; *(hacer ademanes)* to gesture, gesticulate.

ges·ti·cu·la·ción f. *(mueca)* grimace, face; *(ademán)* gesture, gesticulation.

ges·ti·cu·la·dor, –do·ra adj. *(que hace muecas)* grimacing; *(que hace ademanes)* gesturing, gesticulatory.

ges·ti·cu·lar intr. *(hacer muecas)* to grimace, make faces; *(hacer ademanes)* to gesture, gesticulate.

ges·tión f. *(dirección)* administration, management; *(trámite)* step, measure; *(cuasicontrato)* agreement, understanding ♦ hacer gestiones to take steps *or* measures.

ges·tio·nar tr. to take steps *or* measures to obtain.

ges·to m. *(expresión del rostro)* look, facial expression; *(mueca)* grimace, face; *(semblante)* face, visage; *(hecho)* deed, gesture; *(ademán)* gesture, gesticulation ♦ estar de buen g. to be in a good mood *or* good spirits • estar de mal g. to be in a bad mood *or* poor spirits • hacer gestos *(hacer muecas)* to make faces, grimace; *(hacer ademanes)* to gesture, gesticulate • hacer gestos a to look disdainfully at, scorn • poner g. a to scowl at, show displeasure for.

ges·tor, –to·ra COM. I. adj. *(dirigente)* managing, administrative; *(negociador)* negotiating II. m.f. *(gerente)* manager, administrator; *(negociador)* negotiator; *(agente)* agent, business representative.

géy·ser m. geyser.

Gha·na f. Ghana.

gha·nés, –ne·sa adj. & m.f. Ghanaian, Ghanian.

gi·ba f. *(corcova)* hump, hunch; FIG. *(molestia)* nuisance, bother.

gi·bar tr. *(corcovar)* to bend, curve; FIG., COLL. *(molestar)* to annoy, bother.

gi·be·li·no, –na HIST. adj. & m.f. Ghibelline.

gi·bón m. ZOOL. gibbon.

gi·bo·so, –sa I. adj. hunchbacked, gibbous II. m.f. hunchback.

Gi·bral·tar m. GEOG. Gibraltar.

gi·bral·ta·re·ño, –ña I. adj. of Gibraltar II. m.f. native of Gibraltar

gi·ga·bi·tio m. COMPUT. gigabit.

gi·gan·ta f. *(mujer)* giantess; BOT. sunflower.

gi·gan·te I. adj. giant, gigantic II. m. giant.

gi·gan·tes·co, –ca adj. gigantic, huge.

gi·gan·tez f. gigantic size.

gi·gan·tis·mo m. MED. gigantism, giantism.

gi·gan·tón, –to·na m.f. giant (in parades) —m. AMER., BOT. sunflower.

gí·go·lo m. gigolo.

gi·ma, gimo see gemir.

gi·mie·ra, gimió see gemir.

gim·na·sia f. gymnastics ♦ **g. sueca** calisthenics.

gim·na·sio m. SPORT. gymnasium, gym; *(escuela)* high or secondary school.

gim·nas·ta m.f. gymnast.

gim·nás·ti·ca f. var. of **gimnasia.**

gim·nás·ti·co, –ca adj. gymnastic.

gi·mo·te·a·dor, –do·ra I. adj. whining, whimpering II. m.f. whiner, whimperer.

gi·mo·te·ar intr. COLL. to whine, whimper.

gi·mo·te·o m. COLL. whine, whining.

gi·ne·bra¹ f. MUS. early xylophone; *(juego de naipes)* gin (rummy); FIG. *(ruido)* din, uproar; *(confusión)* confusion, bedlam.

gi·ne·bra² f. gin (liquor).

Gi·ne·bra f. Geneva.

gi·ne·brés, –bre·sa or **gi·ne·bri·no, –na** adj. & m.f. Genevan, Genevese.

gi·ne·co·cra·cia f. POL. gynecocracy.

gi·ne·co·lo·gí·a f. MED. gynecology.

gi·ne·có·lo·go, –ga m.f. MED. gynecologist.

gin·gi·vi·tis f. DENT. gingivitis.

gi·ra f. *(excursión)* day trip, outing; *(viaje)* tour.

gi·ra·dis·cos m. [pl. **-cos**] *(tocadiscos)* record player, phonograph; *(plato)* turntable.

gi·ra·do, –da I. past part. see **girar** II. m.f. COM. drawee.

gi·ra·dor, –do·ra m.f. COM. drawer, one who draws money on an account.

gi·ral·da f. weather vane, weathercock.

gi·rán·du·la f. *(cohete)* pinwheel (in fireworks); *(fuente)* fountain, jet; *(candelero)* candle holder, candelabra.

gi·ran·ta f. ARG. SL. tart, hooker.

gi·rar intr. *(dar vueltas)* to revolve, rotate <*la Tierra gira alrededor del Sol* the earth rotates around the sun>; *(moverse alrededor de un eje)* to spin, gyrate; *(torcer)* to turn, veer <*el camino gira a la derecha* the road turns to the right>; FIG. *(desarrollarse)* to revolve, center <*la conversación giraba en torno del nuevo gobierno* the conversation revolved around the new government>; *(negociar)* to do business <*esta empresa gira mucho* this enterprise does a lot of business>; *(enviar)* to wire (money); COM. to draw <*g. contra una cuenta* to draw on an account> ♦ **g. en descubierto** COM. to overdraw —tr. *(rodar)* to rotate, turn; COM. to draw <*g. un cheque* to draw a check>.

gi·ra·sol m. BOT. sunflower; MIN. fire opal, girasol; FIG. *(persona)* social climber, sycophant.

gi·ra·to·rio, –ria adj. turning, rotating.

girl f. chorus girl.

gi·ro m. *(rotación)* revolution, rotation; *(vuelta)* turn; *(acción)* spinning, turning; *(aspecto)* turn <*ese asunto tomó mal g.* that matter took a bad turn>; *(frase)* turn of phrase, expression <*un g. anticuado* an old-fashioned expression>; COM. draft <*g. a la vista* sight draft>; money order <*g. postal* postal money order>; *(negocio)* business, line of business ♦ **andar de mal g.** to be in a bad way • **g. en descubierto** overdraft.

gi·ro·a·vión m. AVIA. gyroplane.

gi·ro·pi·lo·to m. AVIA., MARIT. gyropilot.

gi·ros·co·pio m. PHYS. gyroscope, gyro.

gis m. *(tiza)* chalk; COL. slate pencil.

gi·ta·ne·ar intr. FIG. to wheedle, cajole.

gi·ta·ne·rí·a f. *(reunión)* band or gathering of gypsies; *(gitanada)* gypsy-like actions; *(dicho)* gypsy saying; *(adulación)* wheedling, cajolery.

gi·ta·nes·co, –ca adj. *(de gitano)* gypsy; *(como los gitanos)* gypsy-like.

gi·ta·no, –na I. adj. *(vagabundo)* gypsy; *(adulador)* wheedling, cajoling; *(socaliñero)* sly, crafty II. m.f. *(vagabundo)* gypsy; *(adulador)* wheedler; *(socaliñero)* sly or crafty person.

gla·cia·ción f. GEOL. glaciation.

gla·cial adj. *(helado)* icy, frozen; *(que hace helar)* freezing; FIG. icy, cold <*una mirada g.* an icy stare>.

gla·cial·men·te adv. FIG. icily, coldly.

gla·ciar GEOL. I. m. glacier II. adj. glacial.

gla·dia·dor or **gla·dia·tor** m. HIST. gladiator.

gla·dí·o·lo or **gla·dio·lo** m. BOT. gladiolus.

glan·de m. ANAT. glans penis.

glán·du·la f. ANAT., BOT. gland ♦ **g. endocrina** endocrine or ductless gland • **g. exocrina** exocrine gland • **g. pituitaria** pituitary gland • **g. salivar** salivary gland • **g. sebácea** sebaceous gland • **g. sudorípara** sweat gland • **g. suprarrenal** adrenal gland.

glan·du·lar adj. glandular.

gla·sé m. TEX. glacé (silk).

gla·se·a·do, –da adj. glazed, glossy.

gla·se·ar tr. to glaze.

glau·co, –ca I. adj. BOT. glaucous II. m. ZOOL. sea slug.

glau·co·ma m. MED. glaucoma.

gle·ba f. clod, clump (of earth).

gli·ce·mia f. var. of **glucemia.**

gli·cé·ri·do m. CHEM. glyceride.

gli·ce·ri·na f. CHEM. glycerine, glycerol.

gli·ce·rol m. CHEM. glycerol, glycerin.

gli·ci·na f. BOT. wisteria; CHEM. glycine.

gli·col m. CHEM. glycol.

glíp·ti·ca f. ARTS glyptics.

glo·bal adj. *(de conjunto)* global, overall; COM. total.

glo·bal·men·te adv. as a whole.

glo·bo m. *(esfera)* globe; ASTRON. *(Tierra)* Earth; *(de goma)* balloon ♦ **echar globos** COL. to ponder • **en g.** as a whole • **g. aerostático** aerostat balloon • **g. dirigible** AER. dirigible, airship • **g. ocular** or **del ojo** ANAT. eyeball • **g. sonda** METEOROL. sounding balloon • **g. terráqueo** or **terrestre** globe (model of the earth).

glo·bo·si·dad f. globosity, sphericalness.

glo·bo·so, –sa adj. globose, spherical.

glo·bu·lar adj. globular.

glo·bu·li·for·me adj. globular, globoid.

glo·bu·li·na m. globulin ♦ **g. gama** MED., PHYSIOL. gamma globulin.

gló·bu·lo m. *(cuerpo esférico)* globule; ANAT. corpuscle.

glo·gló m. gurgle, gurgling.

glo·ria f. *(bienaventuranza)* glory; *(honor)* fame, renown; *(esplendor)* splendor, greatness; *(lo que ennoblece)* glory <*la Declaración de Independencia es una de las glorias de la historia americana* the Declaration of Independence is one of the glories of American history>; *(cielo)* heaven <*ganar la g.* to go to heaven>; *(gusto)* enjoyment, pleasure <*su g. es tocar el piano* his pleasure is playing the piano> ♦ **a g.** heavenly, divinely <*esta colonia huele a g.* that cologne smells heavenly> • **estar en la g.** or **en su g.** FIG. to be in seventh heaven • m. RELIG. Gloria.

glo·ria pa·tri m. RELIG. Gloria Patri; MEX., RELIG. paternoster (bead of the rosary) ♦ **de g. p.** cheap, of little value.

glo·riar §30 tr. to glorify —reflex. *(preciarse)* to boast, brag; *(complacerse mucho)* to glory (in).

glo·rie·ta f. *(plaza)* plaza, square; *(cenador)* bower, arbor.

glo·ri·fi·ca·ble adj. glorifiable.

glo·ri·fi·ca·ción f. glorification.

glo·ri·fi·ca·dor, –do·ra I. adj. glorifying II. m.f. glorifier.

glo·ri·fi·car §70 tr. to glorify, praise —reflex. to glory.

glo·rio·sa·men·te adv. gloriously.

glo·rio·so, –sa I. adj. *(digno de gloria)* glorious; *(bendito)* blessed; *(vanidoso)* boastful, conceited II. f. RELIG. The Virgin Mary.

glo·sa f. *(comentario)* gloss, commentary; ACC. note, foot-

glo·sa·dor, –do·ra I. adj. glossing II. m.f. commentator, glossarist.
glo·sar tr. *(añadir glosas)* to gloss, annotate; FIG. *(comentar)* to comment; *(interpretar mal)* to gloss, criticize; COL. to reprimand.
glo·sa·rio m. glossary.
glo·se m. glossing, annotating.
glo·so·pe·da f. VET. foot-and-mouth disease.
glo·tis f. ANAT. glottis.
glo·tón, –to·na I. adj. gluttonous II. m.f. glutton —m. ZOOL. wolverine.
glo·to·na·men·te adv. gluttonously.
glo·to·ne·ar intr. to gormandize, eat gluttonously.
glo·to·ne·rí·a f. gluttony.
glu·ce·mia f. MED. glycemia.
glu·có·ge·no m. PHYSIOL. glycogen.
glu·co·sa f. CHEM. glucose.
glu·glú m. *(del agua)* gurgle (of water); *(del pavo)* gobble, gobbling (of a turkey).
glu·glu·te·ar intr. to gobble (a turkey).
glu·ten m. gluten.
glu·ti·no·so, –sa adj. glutinous, sticky.
gneis m. [pl. **gneis**] GEOL. gneiss.
gnéi·si·co, –ca adj. gneissic.
gno·mo m. gnome.
gno·mon m. gnomon, sundial.
gno·sis f. PHILOS. gnosis.
gnos·ti·cis·mo m. PHILOS. gnosticism.
gnós·ti·co, –ca adj. & m.f. PHILOS. gnostic.
gnu m. ZOOL. gnu.
go·a f. METAL. pig iron, bloom.
go·ber·na·ble adj. governable.
go·ber·na·ción f. *(gobierno)* government; *(territorio)* territory (of the national government) ♦ **Ministerio de la Gobernación** Ministry of the Interior.
go·ber·na·dor I. adj. governing II. m. *(líder)* governor; ARG., ORNITH. cardinal ♦ **g. general** governor general.
go·ber·na·do·ra f. *(líder)* governor; *(esposa del gobernador)* governor's wife.
go·ber·na·lle m. MARIT. rudder.
go·ber·nan·ta f. ARG. governess.
go·ber·nan·te I. adj. ruling, governing II. m.f. *(líder)* ruler, leader; COLL. *(pez gordo)* big shot ♦ **gobernantes** rulers.
go·ber·nar §49 tr. POL. to govern; *(dirigir)* to control <*sus sentimientos gobiernan sus acciones* his feelings control his actions>; *(conducir)* to steer; ARG. to reprimand, scold —intr. MARIT. to steer <*un barco que gobierna bien* a boat that steers easily>.
go·bier·nis·ta adj. AMER., POL. governmental; *(partidario)* partisan.
go·bier·no m. *(dirección)* government, direction; POL. *(autoridad)* government; *(oficio y duración)* governorship; *(edificio)* governor's house; MARIT. *(timón)* rudder; *(manejo)* steering, navigability ♦ **g. de la casa** housekeeping • **g. monárquico** POL. monarchy • **servir de g.** to serve as a guide *or* norm.
go·bio m. ICHTH. gudgeon.
go·ce m. enjoyment, pleasure.
go·cé, goce see **gozar**.
go·do– da I. adj. Gothic II. m.f. HIST. Goth; AMER., DEROG. *(español)* Spaniard; *(conservador)* conservative.
go·fio m. AMER. *(harina)* roasted corn meal; *(pasta)* sweet cake (made with corn meal).
go·fo, –fa adj. *(grosero)* crude, ignorant; PAINT. dwarf (figure).
go·fra·do, –da adj. TECH. corrugated.
gol m. [pl. **gols** *or* **goles**] SPORT. goal ♦ **marcar** *or* **meter un gol** to make *or* score a goal.
go·la f. *(garganta)* gullet, throat; *(adorno)* gorget, ruff; *(gorjal)* gorget; MIL. *(de una fortificación)* gorge; ARCHIT. ogee; MARIT. channel, narrows.
go·le·a·da f. SPORT. high score.
go·le·a·dor, –do·ra m.f. SPORT. goal scorer.
go·le·ar tr. SPORT. to score many goals against (another team) —intr. to score.

go·le·ta f. MARIT. schooner.
golf m. SPORT. golf ♦ **g. miniatura** miniature golf.
gol·fe·rí·a f. *(conjunto)* gang (of urchins); *(acto)* mischief.
gol·fo m. gulf <*el Golfo de México* the Gulf of Mexico>; bay <*el Golfo de Viscaya* the Bay of Biscay> ♦ **el Golfo Pérsico** the Persian Gulf.
gol·fo, –fa m.f. *(pilluelo)* urchin; SP., REG. loafer —f. SP., REG. prostitute.
go·li·lla f. *(cuello)* collar, ruff (worn by magistrates); ARG., BOL., URUG. neckerchief, bandanna; ORNITH. ruff (of rooster); TECH. pipe collar *or* flange; CUBA debt —m. COLL. magistrate.
go·lon·dri·na f. ORNITH. swallow; ICHTH. gurnard, swallow fish; SP., MARIT. motorboat; C. AMER., MEX., BOT. spurge; CHILE moving van ♦ **g. de mar** ORNITH. tern.
go·lon·dri·no m. ORNITH. male swallow; ICHTH. gurnard, swallow fish; FIG. *(vagabundo)* vagrant, bum; MIL. *(desertor)* deserter; MED. boil *or* tumor in the armpit.
go·lo·sa·men·te adv. eagerly, with relish.
go·lo·si·na f. *(manjar agradable)* delicacy, choice food; *(dulce)* candy, sweet; *(deseo)* longing, craving; *(gula)* greediness, gluttony; FIG. *(chuchería)* luxury, frivolity ♦ **amargar la g.** to spoil the pleasure of something.
go·lo·si·nar *or* **go·lo·si·ne·ar** intr. to nibble constantly on sweets.
go·lo·so, –sa I. m.f. *(glotón)* sweet-toothed person II. adj. *(glotón)* sweet-toothed; *(deseoso)* acquisitive, covetous; *(apetitoso)* appetizing, tempting.
gol·pa·zo m. *or* **gol·pa·da** f. heavy *or* violent blow ♦ **golpadas de sangre** streams *or* torrents of blood.
gol·pe m. blow, hit <*el policía le dio un g.* the policeman dealt him a blow>; *(choque)* collision; *(sacudida)* bump; *(latido)* heartbeat, throb; *(explosión)* gust, blast <*un g. de viento* a gust of wind>; *(multitud)* crowd, throng <*un g. de gente* a crowd of people>; *(desgracia)* blow, shock; *(pestillo)* spring lock; SPORT. shot, stroke; FIG. *(sorpresa)* surprise, astonishment; *(gracia)* wit, wittiness; *(ocurrencia)* witty remark; SEW. *(cartera)* pocket flap; CRIMIN. job <*prepararon un g. al banco* they planned a bank job>;- MEX. sledgehammer; VEN. swig ♦ **a golpes** in fits and starts, sporadically • **al g.** AMER. instantly • **dar el g.** COLL. to cause a sensation, make a hit • **de g.** suddenly • **de g. y porrazo** hastily, hurriedly • **de un g.** in one stroke, at one fell swoop • **g. bajo** SPORT. low blow • **g. de estado** coup d'état • **g. de fortuna** *or* **de suerte** stroke of luck • **g. de gracia** coup de grâce, death blow • **g. de mano** coup de main, sudden attack • **g. de pecho** breast beating, great grief • **g. de sol** sunstroke • **g. de tos** coughing fit • **g. de vista** glance, look • **g. en vano** miss, unsuccessful attempt • **g. franco** SPORT. free kick *or* shot • **g. maestro** stroke of genius • **no dar g.** not to do a lick of work • **tener g.** to be amusing <*tiene g. ese chiste* that joke is amusing>.
gol·pe·a·dor, –do·ra I. adj. hitting, striking II. m.f. hitter, striker —m. ARG., CHILE, COL. door knocker.
gol·pe·a·du·ra f. *or* **gol·pe·o** m. *(objetos)* beating, hammering; *(persona)* beating, thrashing.
gol·pe·ar tr. & intr. to beat, strike.
gol·pe·te·ar tr. to pound, pummel.
gol·pe·te·o m. pounding, pummeling.
gol·pi·za f. ECUAD., MEX. beating, thrashing.
go·lle·ta·zo m. *(golpe)* blow on the neck of a bottle; FIG. *(término)* sudden finish (to some business); TAUR. sword thrust (into the bull's neck) ♦ **dar un g. a algo** FIG. to cut something short, put an end to something.
go·lle·te m. *(cuello)* throat, neck; *(de una botella)* neck of a bottle.
go·lle·te·ar tr. COL., VEN. to collar, grab by the neck.
go·ma[1] f. BOT. *(savia)* gum; *(caucho)* rubber; *(pegamento)* glue; *(elástico)* rubber band; MED. gumma ♦ **g. arábiga** BOT. gum arabic • **g. de borrar** eraser • **g. de mascar** chewing gum • **g. laca** shellac.
go·ma[2] f. C. AMER. hangover.
go·mal m. AMER. rubber plantation.
go·me·ro, –ra I. adj. rubber, gum II. m. AMER., BOT. rubber tree; *(productor)* rubber planter; *(obrero)* rubber-plantation worker.
go·mí·fe·ro, –ra adj. gummiferous.

go·mi·na f. hair cream *or* dressing.
go·mo·si·dad f. gumminess, adhesiveness.
go·mo·so, –sa I. adj. *(que tiene goma)* gum, gummy; *(parecido a la goma)* gummy, viscous; C. AMER. hung over II. m. fop, dandy.
gó·na·da f. ANAT. gonad.
gón·do·la f. *(embarcación)* gondola; *(carruaje)* coach, wagon; CHILE, COL. bus.
gon·do·le·ro m. gondolier.
gon·fa·lón f. banner, standard.
gong *or* **gon·go** m. MUS. gong.
gon·go·ris·mo m. LIT. Gongorism, euphuism.
go·no·co·co m. MED. gonococcus.
go·no·rre·a f. MED. gonorrhea.
gor·di·flón, –flo·na *or* **gor·din·flón, –flo·na** COLL. I. adj. chubby, tubby II. m.f. fatty, tub.
gor·do, –da I. adj. *(obeso)* fat, plump; *(abultado)* big; *(graso)* fatty, greasy (said of meat); *(grueso)* thick <*lienzo g.* thick cloth>; *(lo grande)* first <*sacar el premio g.* to win first prize (in a lottery)>; hard <*agua g.* hard water>; FIG., COLL. *(importante)* important; *(enorme)* enormous, huge <*un error g.* an enormous mistake> ♦ **caerle g. a uno** COLL. not to be able to stand someone II. m.f. *(persona)* fat person —m. *(sebo)* fat, suet; *(premio)* first prize (in a lottery) ♦ **armar la g.** COLL. to raise a ruckus • **estar sin una g.** SP., COLL. to be broke.
gor·du·ra f. *(grasa)* fat, grease; *(corpulencia)* obesity, fatness; ARG. cream.
gor·go·jo m. ENTOM. *(insecto)* weevil; *(persona)* midget.
gor·go·ri·te·ar intr. COLL. to warble, trill.
gor·go·ri·tos m.pl. COLL. trills (in singing).
gór·go·ros m.pl. AMER. bubbles.
gor·go·ro·ta·da f. gulp, swallow.
gor·go·te·ar intr. to gurgle, burble.
gor·go·te·o m. gurgling, gurgle.
go·ri·go·ri m. COLL. dirge, funeral chant.
go·ri·la m. ZOOL. gorilla.
gor·ja f. throat, gullet.
gor·jal m. *(de sacerdote)* priest's collar; *(gola)* gorget (on suit of armor).
gor·je·a·dor, –do·ra *or* **gor·je·an·te** adj. warbling, trilling.
gor·je·ar intr. to warble, trill —reflex. COLL. to gurgle (baby).
gor·je·o m. *(quiebro)* warble, trill; *(habla de niños)* gurgling (of baby).
go·rra f. *(sombrero)* cap; *(de bebé)* (baby) bonnet; MIL. busby —m. FIG. *(parásito)* sponger, freeloader ♦ **andar** *or* **vivir de g.** COLL. to sponge, freeload • **de g.** COLL. at another's expense • **pasar la g.** to pass the hat.
go·rre·ar intr. to freeload.
go·rre·ro m. *(fabricante)* cap maker; FIG., COLL. *(gorrón)* sponger, freeloader.
go·rre·ta·da f. tipping of one's cap (in greeting).
go·rrín m. ZOOL. piglet, suckling pig.
go·rri·ne·ra f. pigpen, pigsty.
go·rri·ne·rí·a f. *(porquería)* filth, dirtiness; FIG., COLL. *(acción grosera)* dirty trick.
go·rri·no, –na I. m.f. ZOOL. piglet, suckling pig; FIG. *(persona)* pig, slovenly person II. adj. filthy, piggish.
go·rrión m. ORNITH. sparrow; AMER. hummingbird.
go·rro m. *(sombrero)* cap; *(de niños)* bonnet ♦ **g. de dormir** sleeping cap, nightcap • **g. frigio** liberty cap • **poner el g.** FIG., COLL. *(fastidiar)* to bother, annoy; CHILE to cuckold.
go·rrón m. MECH. pivot, gudgeon; *(guijarro)* smooth round pebble; ENTOM. silkworm that does not finish its cocoon; *(adulador)* flatterer.
go·rrón, –rro·na I. adj. *(que gorrea)* sponging, freeloading; *(egoísta)* selfish, greedy II. m.f. sponger, freeloader.
go·rro·ne·ar intr. to sponge, freeload.
go·rro·ne·rí·a f. *(avaricia)* selfishness, greediness; *(acción de gorronear)* sponging, freeloading.
go·ta f. *(glóbulo)* drop; FIG. *(cantidad)* drop <*sólo bebí una g. de vino* I only drank a drop of wine>; MED. gout; ARCHIT. gutta ♦ **g.** FIG. bit by bit, little by little • **g. caducal** *or* **coral** MED. epilepsy • **g. serena** MED. amaurosis • **sudar la g. gorda** to sweat blood.
go·te·a·do, –da I. past part. see **gotear** II. adj. spotted, stained.

go·te·an·te adj. dripping, trickling.
go·te·ar intr. *(caer)* to drip, trickle; *(dar o recibir)* to give or get in dribs and drabs.
go·te·o m. dripping, trickling.
go·te·ra f. *(gotas de agua)* indoor leaking *or* dripping; *(parte de techo)* rain gutter; *(señal de agua)* drip *or* water mark; *(cenefa)* valance; BOT. disease of trees resulting from seepage ♦ **goteras** FIG. *(achaques)* aches and pains; AMER. outskirts, environs.
go·te·ro m. AMER. eyedropper.
go·te·rón m. *(gota)* large raindrops; ARCHIT. *(canal)* throat.
gó·ti·co, –ca I. adj. Gothic II. m. ARCHIT. Gothic —f. *(escritura)* Gothic (lettering).
go·to·so, –sa I. adj. gouty, suffering from gout II. m.f. person afflicted with gout.
go·zar §04 tr. *(poseer)* to have, enjoy <*g. buena salud* to enjoy good health> —intr. *(disfrutar)* to enjoy, take pleasure in <*gozo de mi copa de rojo* I enjoy my glass of wine> —reflex. *(regocijarse)* to rejoice in <*gozarse en el Señor* to rejoice in the Lord>.
goz·ne m. hinge.
go·zo m. *(alegría)* joy, pleasure; FIG. *(llamarada)* sudden blaze ♦ **gozos** RELIG. hymns of praise.
go·zo·so, –sa adj. joyful, delighted.
gra·ba·ción f. recording ♦ **g. en cinta** tape recording.
gra·ba·do I. past part. see **grabar** II. m. ARTS *(arte, obra)* engraving; *(ilustración)* illustration ♦ **g. al agua fuerte** etching • **g. al agua tinta** aquatint • **g. en cobre** copper plate • **g. en madera** woodcut.
gra·ba·dor, –do·ra m.f. *(persona)* engraver —f. *(magnetófono)* tape recorder.
gra·bar tr. ARTS *(burilar)* to engrave; *(registrar sonidos)* to record, tape; FIG. *(fijar)* to engrave, imprint (in one's mind).
gra·ce·jar intr. COLL. to tell jokes, joke.
gra·ce·jo m. *(donaire)* wit, humor; C. AMER., MEX. clown, joker.
gra·cia f. *(donaire)* charm, grace <*aceptó el premio con g.* he accepted the prize with grace>; *(atractivo)* attractiveness, pleasing quality <*la g. de su rostro* the pleasing quality of her face>; *(beneficio)* favor, kindness <*me concedieron una g.* they granted me a favor>; *(perdón)* forgiveness, pardon; *(buen trato)* good graces <*está en g. cerca del rey* he is in the good graces of the king>; RELIG. grace <*la g. de Dios* the grace of God>; *(agudeza)* witty remark, joke; *(nombre)* name <*dígame usted su g.* tell me your name> ♦ **caer de la g.** to fall out of favor • **caer en g.** to please, find favor • **dar gracias** to give thanks • **de g.** free, gratis • **en g. a** for the sake of *or* benefit of • **gracias** thank you, thanks; MYTH. Graces • **gracias a** thanks to, owing to • **gracias a Dios** thank God • **hacer g.** *(agradar)* to please; *(divertir)* to amuse, strike as funny • **¡maldita la g.!** it's not a bit funny! • **tener g.** to be funny.
gra·cia·ble adj. *(afable)* affable, good-natured; *(fácil de conceder)* easily granted.
grá·cil adj. slender, thin.
gra·ci·li·dad f. slenderness, thinness.
gra·cio·sa·men·te adv. *(con gracia)* gracefully; *(de balde)* gratuitously, free.
gra·cio·so, –sa I. adj. *(encantador)* charming, graceful; *(atractivo)* attractive, pleasing; *(divertido)* amusing, funny; *(gratuito)* free, gratis II. m.f. gracioso, clown; THEAT. fool.
gra·da¹ f. *(peldaño)* step, stair; *(asientos)* tier; MARIT. slipway (for building ships); ECUAD. stairs ♦ **gradas** AMER. atrium.
gra·da² f. AGR. harrow; RELIG. locutory ♦ **g. de cota** AGR. brush harrow • **g. de discos** AGR. disk harrow.
gra·da·ción f. *(progresión)* gradation; RHET. climax.
gra·da·do, –da adj. stepped, with steps.
gra·de·rí·a f. *or* **gra·de·rí·o** m. *(gradas)* tiers, rows (of seats); *(escalera)* (flight of) steps.
gra·dien·te m. METEOROL., PHYS. gradient; AMER. gradient, slope.
gra·di·lla f. *(escalerilla)* stepladder; SCI. test tube holder; CONSTR. brick mold.
gra·do¹ m. *(calidad)* grade, quality; *(nivel)* degree <*en menor g.* to a lesser degree>; *(proximidad)* degree (of kin-

ship); *(fase)* stage, step *<está en el tercer g. de desarrollo* it is in the third stage of development>; *(peldaño)* step, stair; *(título académico)* degree, academic title; *(clase)* class, grade; *(división)* degree *<g. de longitud* degree of longitude>; MIL. rank, grade; GEOM., GRAM. degree; LAW stage of proceedings ♦ **de g. en g.** by degrees, gradually • **en alto g.** to a high degree • **en sumo g.** to the highest degree, exceedingly • **grados** RELIG. minor orders.

gra·do² m. will, liking *<de mal grado* against her will>.

gra·dua·ción f. *(acción de graduar)* graduation; *(proporción de alcohol)* alcoholic strength *or* content; MIL. *(grado)* rank, grading.

gra·dua·do, –da I. past part. see **graduar** II. adj. MIL. breveted; *(dividido en grados)* graduated, scaled III. m.f. EDUC. graduate.

gra·dua·dor m. TECH. gauge, graduator.

gra·dual I. adj. gradual II. m. RELIG. gradual.

gra·dual·men·te adv. gradually, by degrees.

gra·duar §67 tr. *(evaluar)* to gauge, calibrate *<g. el flujo del agua* to calibrate the flow of water>; *(dividir en grados)* to graduate (thermometer, beakers); EDUC. to graduate, confer a degree on; MIL. to confer the rank of *<g. de capitán a un teniente* to confer the rank of captain on a lieutenant> —reflex. to graduate (from school).

grá·fi·ca·men·te adv. graphically.

grá·fi·co, –ca I. adj. *(representativo)* graphic, graphical; *(vivo)* graphic, vivid II. m.f. MATH., SCI. graph, chart.

gra·fi·to m. MIN. graphite, black lead; graffiti.

gra·fo·lo·gí·a f. graphology.

gra·ge·a f. *(confite)* Jordan almond; *(píldora)* sugar-coated pill.

gra·je·ar intr. *(graznar)* to caw (a crow); *(gorjear)* to gurgle (a baby).

gra·jo m. ORNITH. rook, crow; AMER. body odor.

gra·ma f. BOT. Bermuda grass ♦ **g. del norte** couch *or* quitch grass • **g. de olor** vernal grass.

gra·má·ti·ca I. f. *(arte o texto)* grammar ♦ **andar a la g.** COLL. to look out for oneself • **g. parda** COLL. cleverness, shrewdness II. adj. see **gramático, –ca.**

gra·ma·ti·cal adj. grammatical.

gra·má·ti·co, –ca I. adj. grammatical II. m.f. grammarian —f. see **gramática.**

gra·mi·lla f. *(para agramar)* bed of a brake *or* scutcher; ARG., BOT. grass, lawn.

gra·mo m. gram, gramme (G.B.).

gra·mó·fo·no m. gramophone, phonograph.

gra·mo·la f. phonograph.

gran §G21 adj. [contr. of **grande** used before sing. nouns] great, grand *<una gran aventura* a great adventure> —see **grande.**

gra·na¹ f. *(acción)* seeding; *(época)* seeding time; *(semilla)* seed ♦ **dar g.** to go to seed.

gra·na² f. ENTOM. cochineal insect; *(materia colorante)* cochineal; *(color)* scarlet; *(tela)* fine scarlet cloth ♦ **g. de Paraíso** BOT. cardamom • **ponerse rojo como la g.** to turn as red as a beet.

gra·na·da I. f. BOT. pomegranate (fruit); MIL. grenade; ARTIL. shell ♦ **g. de mano** hand grenade • **g. de mortero** mortar shell. II. adj. see **granado, –da.**

Gra·na·da¹ Granada (city).

Gra·na·da² f. Grenada (nation).

gra·na·de·ro m. MIL. grenadier.

gra·na·di·lla f. *(planta y flor)* passionflower; *(fruto)* passion fruit.

gra·na·di·na I. f. *(jarabe)* grenadine; TEX. grenadine; *(tonada)* Andalusian song II. adj. see **granadino, –na¹,²**.

gra·na·di·no, –na¹ I. adj. of Granada II. m.f. native *or* inhabitant of Granada —m. *(flor)* pomegranate flower —f. see **granadina.**

gra·na·di·no, –na² adj. & m.f. Grenadian.

gra·na·do, –da I. past part. see **granar** II. adj. FIG. *(notable)* distinguished, notable; *(experto)* expert; *(alto)* tall, lanky ♦ **lo más g. de** the cream *or* pick of III. m. BOT. pomegranate (tree) —f. see **granada.**

gra·na·dor m. *(criba)* graining sieve; *(lugar)* place where grain is screened.

gra·na·lla f. granulated metal, filings ♦ **g. de carbón** carbon granules.

gra·nar intr. BOT. to go to seed; *(maíz)* to form kernels.

gra·na·te adj. & m. garnet ♦ **g. almandino** MIN. almandine, almandite.

Gran Bretaña f. Great Britain.

gran·de §G21, 22, 24 I. adj. *(enorme)* large, big *<una sala g.* a big room>; *(alto)* tall, big *<un edificio g.* a tall building>; *(elevado)* high, great *<viajaban a gran velocidad* they were traveling at a high speed>; *(considerable)* great *<grandes dificultades* great difficulties>; *(grandioso)* grand, impressive; *(eminente)* great, eminent *<un gran hombre* a great man>; AMER. mature ♦ **en g.** FIG. *(en lujo)* on a grand scale II. m. *(noble)* Spanish grandee —f. ARG., COLL. grand prize (in the lottery).

gran·de·men·te adv. *(muy bien)* grandly, very well; *(en extremo)* extremely, greatly.

gran·de·za f. *(tamaño)* size; *(extensión, magnitud)* bigness, largeness, magnitude; *(nobleza)* greatness, majesty, grandeur; *(dignidad)* grandeeship.

gran·di·lo·cuen·cia f. grandiloquence.

gran·di·lo·cuen·te *or* **gran·dí·lo·cuo, –cua** adj. grandiloquent.

gran·di·llón, –llo·na adj. COLL. overgrown, oversize.

gran·dio·si·dad f. grandeur, magnificence.

gran·dio·so –sa adj. grand, magnificent.

gran·dor m. size, magnitude.

gran·do·te, –ta adj. COLL. very big, huge.

gran·du·llón, –llo·na adj. var. of **grandillón, –llona.**

gra·ne·a·do, –da I. past part. see **granear** II. adj. *(granulado)* granulated, ground; *(punteado)* stippled; MIL. heavy, continuous *<fuego g.* heavy fire> III. m. grain (in leather).

gra·ne·ar tr. *(sembrar)* to sow; *(sacar grano)* to grain; *(puntear)* to stipple; ARG. to give a grain to.

gra·nel ♦ **a g.** COM. *(sin envase)* in bulk, loose; FIG. *(abundantemente)* in abundance.

gra·ne·lar tr. to grain (leather).

gra·ne·ro m. *(sitio)* granary; FIG. *(territorio)* granary, grain-producing region.

gra·ni·cé, granice see **granizar.**

gra·ni·llo m. *(grano)* fine grain; ORNITH. small tumor; FIG. *(utilidad)* profit, gain.

gra·ní·ti·co, –ca adj. granitic, granite.

gra·ni·to m. GEOL. granite; MED. pimple ♦ **echar su g. de sal en** to put one's two cents in.

gra·ni·za·da f. *(copia de granizo)* hailstorm; FIG. *(multitud)* shower, torrent; CHILE, GUAT. iced drink.

gra·ni·za·do I. past part. see **granizar** II. m. iced drink.

gra·ni·zar §04 intr. METEOROL. to hail; FIG. *(caer con fuerza)* to rain, shower.

gra·ni·zo m. METEOROL. hail; FIG. *(abundancia)* hail, torrent.

gran·ja f. *(hacienda)* farm, grange; *(quinta)* country house; *(lechería)* dairy ♦ **g. avícola** chicken *or* poultry farm.

gran·je·ar intr. *(traficar)* to trade, deal; MARIT. to gain *<g. a barlovento* to gain the wind> —tr. FIG. *(conquistar)* to win over, capture; CHILE to swindle —reflex. to gain, win *<granjearse la confianza de* to gain the confidence of>.

gran·je·rí·a f. *(beneficio)* farm earnings; FIG. *(ganancia)* gain, profit.

gran·je·ro, –ra m.f. farmer.

gra·no m. BOT. *(semilla)* grain, seed; BOT. *(fruto)* grain, cereal; *(partícula)* grain, particle *<un g. de sal* a grain of salt>; MED. pimple; *(medida de peso)* grain (weight); *(de la piel)* grain (of a hide); JEWEL. quarter of a carat ♦ **apartar el g. de la paja** FIG., COLL. to separate the wheat from the chaff • **con un g. de sal** FIG. with a grain of salt • **g. malo** ARG., MED. carbuncle • **ir al g.** FIG., COLL. to get down to brass tacks • **no ser g. de anís** FIG., COLL. to be no laughing matter.

gra·no·so, –sa adj. granular, grainy.

gra·nu·ja f. *(uvas)* loose grapes; *(pipa)* seed, pip; COLL. *(granujería)* gang (of urchins) —m. COLL. *(pilluelo)* ragamuffin, street urchin; *(pícaro)* rogue, rascal.

gra·nu·ja·da f. rascality, deviltry.

gra·nu·jien·to, –ta adj. pimply.

gra·nu·lar¹ adj. *(granuloso)* granular, grainy; *(granujiento)* pimply.

gra·nu·lar² tr. to granulate —reflex. MED. to break out in pimples.
grá·nu·lo m. *(grano)* small grain, granule; *(pildorila)* small pill.
gran·zas f.pl. *(ahechaduras)* chaff; *(cerniduras)* siftings, screenings; METAL. dross, slag.
gra·pa f. *(para los papeles)* staple; *(para la madera)* clip, clamp; VET. grapes (cattle disease); ARG. grappa (alcoholic drink).
gra·sa I. f. *(sebo)* fat, grease; *(lubricante)* lubricating oil, grease; *(suciedad)* grease, grime; *(grasilla)* pounce (fine powder); ♦ **criar g.** COLL. to get fat • **g. de ballena** blubber • **g. de pescado** fish oil • **g. para ejes** axle grease • **grasas** METAL. slag • **tener mucha g.** to be very fat II. adj. see **graso, –sa.**
gra·se·ra f. *(vasija)* container for fat or grease; CUL. drip pan.
gra·sien·to, –ta adj. *(grasoso)* greasy, oily; *(sucio)* grimy, greasy.
gra·so, –sa I. adj. *(seboso)* fatty, greasy II. m. fattiness, greasiness —f. see **grasa.**
gra·so·so, –sa adj. greasy, oily.
gra·ta·men·te adv. *(de manera grata)* pleasingly; *(con agrado)* with pleasure; AMER. gratefully.
gra·ti·fi·ca·ción f. *(recompensa)* reward, recompense; *(propina)* tip, gratuity; S. AMER. gratification, satisfaction.
gra·ti·fi·ca·dor, –do·ra I. adj. *(que recompensa)* rewarding; *(que da propina)* tipping; S. AMER. gratifying, rewarding II. m.f. *(que recompensa)* rewarder; *(que da propina)* tipper.
gra·ti·fi·car §70 tr. *(recompensar)* to reward; *(dar una propina)* to tip; *(satisfacer)* to gratify, satisfy ♦ **se gratificará** reward offered.
gra·tin m. CUL. gratin ♦ **al g.** au gratin.
gra·tis adv. gratis, free.
gra·ti·tud f. gratitude.
gra·to, –ta adj. *(placentero)* pleasing, agreeable; *(gratis)* free, gratis; AMER. grateful *<le estoy g. por ello* I am grateful to you for it> ♦ **me es g. anunciar que** I am pleased to announce that.
gra·tui·ta·men·te adv. *(de gratis)* gratuitously, free; FIG. *(arbitrariamente)* gratuitously, groundlessly.
gra·tui·to, –ta adj. *(gratis)* free (of charge); *(arbitrario)* gratuitous, groundless *<afirmación g.* gratuitous remark>.
gra·tu·la·to·rio, –ria adj. congratulatory.
gra·va f. gravel.
gra·va·men m. *(carga)* burden, obligation; *(impuesto)* tax; LAW encumbrance *<libre de g.* free from encumbrances>.
gra·var tr. *(cargar)* to burden, encumber; to tax *<g. los artículos de lujo* to tax luxury items>; *(exigir un impuesto)* to levy, impose (a tax) —reflex. AMER. to get worse.
gra·va·ti·vo, –va adj. burdensome, heavy.
gra·ve adj. FIG. *(serio)* grave, serious (person); *(peligroso)* grave, serious *<una enfermedad g.* a serious illness>; FIG., COLL. *(importante)* important *<un asunto g.* an important matter>; *(bajo)* deep, low (sound); *(pesado)* weighty, heavy; GRAM. paroxytone (accented on the penultimate syllable).
gra·ve·dad f. *(seriedad)* gravity, seriousness; *(importancia)* importance; PHYS. *(ley)* gravity; *(peso)* weight; MUS. depth.
gra·ve·men·te adv. *(con formalidad)* seriously; *(de manera grave)* gravely *<él está g. enfermo* he is gravely ill>.
gra·vi·dez f. pregnancy, gravidity.
grá·vi·do, –da adj. POET. full, loaded; *(preñada)* pregnant.
gra·vi·ta·ción f. PHYS. gravitation.
gra·vi·tan·te adj. gravitating.
gra·vi·tar intr. PHYS. to gravitate ♦ **g. sobre** *(descansar)* to rest on, bear down on; FIG. *(pesar)* to be a burden to, weigh on.
gra·vi·ta·to·rio, –ria or **gra·vi·ta·cio·nal** adj. PHYS. gravitational.
gra·vo·so, –sa adj. *(oneroso)* onerous, burdensome; *(costoso)* costly, expensive.
graz·nar intr. *(chillar)* to squawk; *(cacarear)* to quack (ducks); *(el cuervo)* to caw (crows).
graz·ni·do m. *(chillido)* squawk, squawking; *(del cuervo)*

caw, cawing; *(del pato)* quack, quacking; *(del ganso)* cackle, cackling; FIG., DEROG. *(canto)* yowl, wail.
Gre·cia f. Greece.
gre·co, –ca adj. & m.f. var. of **griego, –ga.**
gre·co·la·ti·no, –na adj. Greco–Latin.
gre·co·rro·ma·no, –na adj. Greco-Roman.
gre·da f. MIN. fuller's earth, clay.
gre·dal I. adj. clayey II. m. clay pit.
gre·do·so, –sa adj. clayey.
gre·ga·rio, –ria adj. *(en compañía de otros)* gregarious; herd, flock *<instinto g.* herd instict>; *(servil)* servile, slavish.
gre·go·ria·no, –na adj. Gregorian.
gre·mial I. adj. *(sindical)* union, trade-union; HIST. guild; S. AMER. trade II. m. *(sindicalista)* union member; HIST. guildsman; RELIG. gremial.
gre·mio m. *(sindicato)* union, trade union; *(asociación)* association, society; HIST. guild, corporation; *(fraternidad)* fraternity, brotherhood.
gren·chu·do, –da adj. disheveled, unkempt.
gre·ña f. *(cabellera)* shock or mop of hair; FIG. *(maraña)* entanglement; MEX. pile of grain to be thrashed ♦ **andar a la g.** COLL. to quarrel, squabble • **en g.** MEX. *(en ramo)* raw (silk); *(sin pulir)* unpolished (silver).
gre·ñu·do, –da I. adj. disheveled, unkempt II. m. shy horse.
gres m. *(arcilla)* potter's clay; stoneware *<vasija de g.* stoneware pot>; GEOL. sandstone.
gres·ca f. *(jaleo)* uproar, hubbub; *(riña)* quarrel, row.
grey f. *(rebaño)* flock, herd; FIG. *(raza)* people, nation; *(fieles)* congregation, flock.
grial m. Grail *<el Santo G.* the Holy Grail>.
grie·go, –ga adj. & m.f. *(habitante)* Greek, Grecian —m. *(idioma)* Greek ♦ **para mí eso es g.** COLL. it's Greek to me.
grie·ta f. *(hendedura)* crack, crevice; MED. chap, crack.
grie·tar·se or **grie·te·ar·se** reflex. *(agrietarse)* to crack; MED. to get chapped; ARTS. to crackle.
gri·fa I. f. COLL. marijuana II. adj. see **grifo, –fa.**
gri·fe·rí·a f. *(llaves para agua)* faucets, spigots; *(tienda)* plumbing shop (where faucets are sold) ♦ **g. sanitaria** bathroom fixtures.
gri·fo I. m. MYTH. griffin, griffon; *(caño)* tap, spigot; *(para marijuana)* roach clip; PERU gas pump II. adj. see **grifo, –fa.**
gri·fo, –fa I. adj. *(crespo)* curly, kinky; PRINT. italic; COL. conceited, stuck-up; COL., MEX. *(borracho)* drunk; *(enojado)* angry, mad; *(intoxicado por la marijuana)* stoned, high II. m. see **grifo** —f. see **grifa.**
gri·tón m. *(grifo)* large faucet or spigot; *(perro)* griffon.
gri·fo·ta m.f. COLL. pot smoker, pothead.
gri·lla f. ENTOM. female cricket; S. AMER. annoyance, bother; COL. row, scuffle.
gri·lle·te m. fetter, shackle.
gri·llo m. ENTOM. cricket; FIG. *(obstáculo)* obstacle, hindrance ♦ **g. cebollero** or **real** ENTOM. mole cricket • **grillos** fetters, shackles.
gri·ma f. *(desazón)* annoyance, disgust; CHILE bit, particle ♦ **dar g.** to grate on one's nerves, annoy • **en g.** COL. alone.
gri·mo·so, –sa adj. annoying.
grin·ga·da f. DEROG. *(acción)* action typical of gringos; *(reunión)* group of gringos.
grin·go, –ga I. adj. *(extranjero)* foreign; *(norteamericano)* Yankee; S. AMER. blond, fair II. m.f. *(extranjero)* foreigner; *(norteamericano)* Yankee; S. AMER. blond, fair-haired person —m. COLL. *(lenguaje)* gibberish ♦ **hablar en g.** to speak gibberish.
gri·ñón m. *(toca)* wimple.
gri·pa f. AMER. flu, influenza.
gri·pal adj. MED. grippy, flu-like.
gri·pe f. MED. grippe, flu ♦ **coger la g.** to catch the flu.
gri·po·so, –sa adj. grippy ♦ **estar g.** to have an attack of the grip, have the flu.
gris I. adj. *(color)* gray; *(triste)* dull, gloomy II. m. *(color)* gray; COLL. *(viento frío)* cold wind; SP., SL. *(agente de policía)* policeman ♦ **hacer g.** COLL. to be brisk (said of weather) • **los grises** SP. riot squad (during Franco regime).

gri·sá·ce·o, -a adj. grayish.
gri·se·o, -a adj. gray.
gris·ma f. AMER. bit, drop.
gri·sú m. MIN. firedamp.
gri·ta f. *(gritería)* outcry, shouting ♦ **dar g. a** COLL. to boo at, hoot at.
gri·tar intr. *(dar gritos)* to shout, scream; *(abuchear)* to jeer, boo —tr. to jeer at, boo <*g. a un mal cantante* to jeer at a bad singer>.
gri·te·rí·a f. *or* **gri·te·rí·o** m. din, uproar.
gri·to m. *(alarido)* shout, scream; *(clamor)* outcry, clamor; ZOOL. cry, call (of a bird or animal) ♦ **a g. pelado** *or* **a voz en g.** at the top of one's lungs, loudly • **al g.** ARG. at once, immediately • **asparse a gritos** FIG. to shout oneself blue *or* hoarse • **dar gritos** to shout, scream • **el último g.** FIG. the latest craze • **estar en un g.** to moan from constant pain • **pedir a gritos** to clamor for • **poner el g. en el cielo** FIG., COLL. to raise the roof.
gri·tón, -to·na adj. COLL. noisy, loud-mouthed.
gro m. TEX. grosgrain.
gro·en·lan·dés, -de·sa I. adj. Greenlandic II. m.f. *(habitante)* Greenlander —m. *(idioma)* Greenlandic.
Gro·en·lan·dia f. Greenland.
grog m. grog, hot toddy.
grog·gy adj. groggy (said of a boxer).
gro·se·lla f. BOT. currant (fruit) ♦ **g. silvestre** gooseberry (fruit).
gro·se·lle·ro m. BOT. currant (plant) ♦ **g. silvestre** gooseberry (plant).
gro·se·ra·men·te adv. *(con descortesía)* discourteously, rudely; *(con ignorancia)* crudely, stupidly; *(con indecencia)* coarsely, indelicately.
gro·se·rí·a f. *(tosquedad)* coarseness, roughness; *(rusticidad)* ignorance, stupidity; *(indecencia)* vulgarity, crudeness; *(descortesía)* discourtesy, rudeness.
gro·se·ro, -ra I. adj. *(basto)* coarse, crude <*¡qué tipo más g.!* what a crude fellow!>; *(descortés)* rude, discourteous; *(rústico)* rustic, unpolished; *(craso)* gross <*error g.* gross error> II. m. boor, ill-bred person.
gro·sor m. thickness.
gro·so mo·do adv. roughly, approximately.
gro·su·ra f. *(grasa)* fat, suet; *(carne)* meat (diet) <*comer g.* to eat meat>; *(de los animales)* extremities and intestines (of animals).
gro·tes·co, -ca I. adj. *(ridículo)* grotesque, outlandish; ARTS grotesque II. m. ARTS grotesque.
grú·a f. *(máquina)* crane, derrick; *(camión de auxilio)* wrecker, tow truck ♦ **g. corrediza**, *or* **oscilante** traveling crane • **g. de auxilio** wrecking crane • **g. de tijera** shears (hoisting device) • **g. fija** stationary crane • **g. flotante** crane ship.
grue·sa I. f. gross (twelve dozen) II. adj. see **grueso, -sa.**
grue·so, -sa I. adj. *(corpulento)* stout, fat <*un hombre g.* a stout man>; *(grande)* big, bulky; *(en grano)* coarse <*sal g.* coarse salt>; *(de grosor)* thick II. m. *(espesor)* thickness; *(parte principal)* bulk <*terminaré el g. del trabajo en casa* I will finish the bulk of the work at home>; *(de escritura)* thick stroke (of a letter); GEOM. depth ♦ **en g.** COM. in bulk, gross —f. see **gruesa.**
gru·jir tr. to trim (glass) with nippers.
gru·lla I. f. ORNITH. crane; MEX. go-getter; ARG., COLL. ugly woman II. adj. see **grullo, -lla.**
gru·llo, -lla I. adj. MEX. *(gris)* dark gray (horse); *(gorrón)* sponging; SP., REG. rustic, boorish II. m. MEX. dark gray horse; ARG. large colt *or* stallion; AMER. peso, dollar —f. see **grulla.**
gru·me·te m. MARIT. cabin boy.
gru·mo m. *(de líquido)* lump; *(de sangre)* clot; *(de leche)* curd; *(de uvas)* bunch, cluster; BOT. bud; ORNITH. wing tip.
gru·mo·so, -sa adj. *(de líquido)* lumpy; *(de sangre)* clotty; *(de leche)* curdy; *(de uvas)* clustered.
gru·ñi·do I. past part. see **gruñir** II. m. *(de un cerdo)* grunt; *(de un perro)* growl; *(de una persona)* grumble, grunt; ♦ **dar gruñidos** to grunt, growl.
gru·ñi·dor, -do·ra I. adj. *(que gruñe)* grunting, growling; FIG. *(refunfuñón)* grouchy, grumpy II. m.f. grouch, grump.

gru·ñir §12 intr. *(un cerdo)* to grunt; *(un perro)* to growl, snarl; *(refunfuñar)* to grumble; *(chirriar)* to creak, squeak.
gru·ñón, -ño·na COLL. I. adj. grouchy, grumpy II. m.f. grouch, grump.
gru·pa f. ZOOL. rump (of a horse) ♦ **montar a la g.** EQUIT. to ride on the pillion.
gru·pe·ra f. EQUIT. *(almohadilla)* pillion (cushion behind the saddle); *(baticola)* crupper ♦ **ir en la g.** EQUIT. to sit behind the rider.
gru·po m. group ♦ **g. de presión** POL. lobby • **g. electrógeno** ELEC. generator • **g. sanguíneo** MED. blood type *or* group.
gru·ta f. grotto, cavern.
gru·yè·re m. Gruyère (cheese).
¡gual! interj. AMER. *(de temor)* oh, dear!; *(de admiración)* well, I'll be!; *(de desprecio)* yuck!
gua·ba f. BOT. guama (fruit); ECUAD., COLL. foot.
gua·ca f. AMER. *(sepultura)* Indian tomb; *(tesoro)* hidden treasure; *(hucha)* money box; C. RICA, CUBA pit (for ripening fruit); PERU, CUL. roasted meat; VEN. *(úlcera)* big sore; *(solterona)* ugly old maid ♦ **hacer g.** AMER. to make a lot of money • **hacer su g.** CARIB., CHILE to make hay while the sun shines • **sacarse la g.** VEN. to get cheated.
gua·cal m. AMER. wooden crate; C. AMER. *(árbol)* calabash tree; *(vasija)* calabash gourd (vessel).
gua·ca·ma·ya, -yo I. adj. P. RICO flashily dressed II. m.f. AMER., ORNITH. macaw; BOT. bladder senna.
gua·ca·mol *or* **gua·ca·mo·le** m. C. AMER., MEX. guacamole.
gua·ca·mo·te m. MEX., BOT. yucca.
gua·car·na·co, -ca I. adj. CHILE, CUBA, ECUAD. foolish, silly; CUBA lanky, long-legged II. m.f. CHILE, CUBA, ECUAD. fool; CUBA long-legged person.
gua·co I. m. BOT. guaco; ORNITH. currasow; AMER. ceramic pottery (found in pre-Columbian tombs); C. RICA, ORNITH. caracara II. adj. AMER. harelipped; MEX. twin.
gua·cha·ra f. CUBA, P. RICO lie; C. RICA MUS. maracas.
gua·che m. COL., VEN. thug, hoodlum; MEX. youngster, kid; COL., MUS. maraca; COL., PERU, BOT. species of cane; MEX. *(persona del interior)* inlander.
gua·cho, -cha I. adj. S. AMER. orphaned; ARG., CHILE, PERU *(borde)* wild (plant); CHILE, PERU *(desparejado)* unmatched, odd (sock) II. m. *(pollo)* chick, baby bird; S. AMER. orphan, foundling; ECUAD. furrow.
gua·dal m. ARG. sandy bog, swamp.
gua·da·ña f. scythe.
gua·da·ñar tr. to scythe, mow.
gua·da·ño m. CUBA, MEX., SP. small harbor boat.
gua·dar·nés m. *(lugar)* harness room; *(mozo)* stable boy; *(armería)* armory.
gua·gua f. *(cosa baladí)* trifle, triviality; S. AMER. *(nene)* baby, infant; CARIB. *(autobús)* bus; CUBA, BOT. chili (plant); ENTOM. orange scale insect; COL., ZOOL. paca (rodent) ♦ **de g.** free, gratis.
guai·ca f. ARG. glass bead; BOL. rosary bead; COL., VEN., BOT. guaiacum.
guai·na m. AMER. youth, young man.
guai·pe m. CHILE rag, cloth.
guai·ra f. PERU, METAL. earthenware smelting furnace; MARIT. triangular sail; C. AMER. Indian panpipe.
gua·ji·ro, -ra I. adj. AMER. rustic, boorish II. m.f. CUBA, DOM. REP. peasant —f. MUS. guajira (peasant song).
gua·jo·lo·te MEX. I. adj. silly, foolish II. m. *(tonto)* fool, simpleton; *(pavo)* turkey.
gual·do, -da I. adj. yellow II. f. BOT. dyer's rocket.
gual·dra·pa f. *(cobertura)* caparison, horse trappings; COLL. *(guiñapo)* tatter, rag.
gua·li·cho *or* **gua·li·chú** m. AMER. evil spirit, devil; ARG. good-luck charm ♦ **tener g.** ARG. to be bewitched.
gua·ma f. COL., VEN., BOT. fruit of the guama tree; COL., FIG. calamity, disaster; C. AMER., COL., VEN. lie, story.
gua·mo m. COL., C. RICA, VEN., BOT. guama (tree); CUBA conch shell.
gua·ná·ba·na f. AMER., BOT. soursop, custard apple (fruit).
gua·ná·ba·no m. AMER., BOT. soursop, custard apple (tree); C. AMER., COL., VEN., COLL. fool, nitwit.
gua·na·ja·da *or* **gua·na·je·rí·a** f. CARIB. foolishness, silliness.

gua·na·jo m. CARIB., COLL. fool, idiot.
guan·do m. AMER. stretcher.
gua·ne·ra f. guano deposit.
guan·go m. ECUAD. *(trenza)* braid worn by Indians; COL. *(racimo)* bunch of bananas; COL., ECUAD. *(fajo)* bundle, bunch; CHILE, ZOOL. field mouse.
gua·no[1] m. guano, fertilizer.
gua·no[2] m. CUBA, BOT. palm tree; AMER., COLL. money, cash.
guan·que m. CHILE, BOT. yam.
guan·ta·da *or* **guan·ta·zo** m. COLL. slap.
guan·te m. *(prenda)* glove; CHILE whip ♦ **arrojar el g.** FIG. to throw down the gauntlet, challenge ● **de g. blanco** formal ● **echar el g. a alguien** COLL. to grab, nab ● **echar un g.** COLL. to pass the hat ● **g. de boxeo** SPORT. boxing glove ● **g. de cirujano** surgeon's glove ● **guantes** tip ● **más suave que un g.** FIG. gentle as a lamb ● **recoger el g.** to pick up the gauntlet, accept a challenge.
guan·te·ar tr. to slap.
guan·te·le·te m. gauntlet.
guan·te·ro, –ra m.f. *(persona)* glover, glove maker —f. AUTO. glove compartment *or* box.
guan·tón m. AMER. var. of **guantada**.
gua·pan·go m. MEX. fandango.
gua·pe·ar intr. COLL. *(ser valiente)* to show courage *or* daring; *(vestirse)* to dress flashily, show off; *(fanfarronear)* to brag, boast.
gua·pe·rí·a f. *(galantería)* gallantry, courage; *(acción valiente)* bold *or* daring action.
gua·pe·tón, –to·na adj. COLL. *(lindo)* very good-looking *or* attractive; *(animoso)* brave, bold; *(ostentoso)* flashy.
gua·pe·za f. COLL. *(bizarría)* boldness, daring; *(ostentación)* flashiness.
gua·po, –pa I. adj. *(lindo)* good-looking, attractive; *(ostentoso)* flashy, boastful; COLL. *(animoso)* brave, daring II. m. *(pendenciero)* bully, troublemaker; COLL. *(galán)* flirt, ladies' man III. interj. honey, sweetheart.
gua·po·te, –ta adj. COLL. *(bonachón)* good-natured, easygoing; *(agraciado)* handsome, pretty.
gua·que·ro, –ra m.f. AMER. hunter of buried treasure; PERU ancient Indian drinking vessel.
gua·ra·ca f. AMER. sling, slingshot.
gua·ra·ca·zo m. COL. sudden blow.
gua·ra·cha f. CARIB., MUS. guaracha (music and dance); CUBA, P. RICO *(diversión)* merrymaking, revelry; *(bulla)* noise, hubbub.
gua·ra·che m. MEX. huarache, sandal.
gua·ra·che·ar intr. CUBA to go on a spree *or* binge.
gua·ra·gua f. CHILE, PERU swing, turn (in dancing); BOL., PERU evasion, indirectness; C. AMER. lie, falsehood ♦ **guaraguas** BOL., CHILE, PERU trinkets, baubles.
gua·rán m. ZOOL. var. of **garañon**.
gua·ran·go, –ga I. m. ECUAD., PERU, BOT. huisache, wild acacia; VEN. divi-divi II. adj. ARG., CHILE boorish, ill-mannered; S. AMER. dirty, filthy.
gua·ran·gue·ar intr. ARG., URUG. to behave boorishly.
gua·ra·ní [pl. **-ní·es**] I. adj. Guarani II. m.f. *(persona)* Guarani —m. *(idioma)* Guarani; PAR. guarani (currency).
gua·ra·nis·mo m. Guarani word *or* expression.
gua·ra·po m. cane liquor.
gua·ra·pón m. AMER. broad-brimmed hat.
gua·ra·que·ar tr. to shoot with a slingshot.
guar·da m.f. *(guardián)* guard, custodian —f. *(guarnición)* guarding; *(tutela)* custody, guardianship; *(cumplimiento)* observance (of a law); *(del abanico)* outside rib (of a fan); *(de la llave)* ward (of a key); *(hoja de papel)* endpaper, flyleaf; PERU ribbing, trimming —m. ARG. bus driver.
guar·da·ba·rre·ra m.f. RAIL. gatekeeper, crossing guard.
guar·da·ba·rros m.pl. fender, mudguard.
guar·da·bos·que m. forest ranger, forester.
guar·da·bri·sa m. *(fanal)* glass shade (for candles); *(parabrisas)* windshield; MEX. screen.
guar·da·ca·de·na m. chain guard (of a bicycle).
guar·da·cos·tas m. [pl. **-tas**] MARIT. coast guard cutter.
guar·da·dor, –do·ra I. adj. *(cuidadoso)* careful, thrifty; *(observante)* observant; *(tacaño)* stingy, miserly II. m.f. *(cuidadoso)* careful person; *(observador)* observer (of

laws); *(avaro)* miser, pennypincher; LAW *(protector)* guardian, protector.
guar·da·es·pal·das m. [pl. **-das**] bodyguard.
guar·da·fan·go m. AMER. var. of **guardabarros**.
guar·da·fre·nos m. [pl. **-nos**] RAIL. brakeman.
guar·da·gu·jas m. [pl. **-jas**] RAIL. switchman.
guar·da·la·do m. rail, railing.
guar·da·me·ta m. SPORT. goalkeeper, goalie.
guar·da·mon·te m. ARM. trigger guard; *(capote)* riding cape *or* cloak; MEX. croup blanket; ARG., BOL. protective strips of leather (hung from the saddle).
guar·da·pe·lo m. locket.
guar·da·pes·ca m. patrol boat.
guar·da·pol·vo m. *(cubierta)* dust cover; *(vestido)* duster; *(tejadillo)* canopy; *(tapa de reloj)* inner lid (of a watch).
guar·da·pun·tas m. [pl. **-tas**] pencil cap.
guar·dar tr. *(vigilar)* to guard, watch over <*las tropas guardaban la ciudad* the troops guarded the city>; *(proteger)* to protect; *(animales)* to keep, tend <*g. carneros* to tend sheep>; *(cumplir)* to keep <*Juan siempre guarda su palabra* John always keeps his word>; *(observar)* to observe, keep <*lo guarda en su bolsillo* she keeps it in her pocket>; *(conservar)* to save, put away <*g. dinero* to save money>; FIG. *(no revelar)* to keep <*g. un secreto* to keep a secret> ♦ **g. cama** to be confined to bed ● **g. silencio** to keep quiet —intr. ♦ **¡guarda!** watch out!, look out! —reflex. *(reservarse)* to keep; *(protegerse)* to be on one's guard ♦ **guardarse de** to take care not to, guard against <*guárdate de derramarlo* take care not to spill it> ● **guardársela** FIG., COLL. to nurse a grudge against someone.
guar·da·rro·pa m. *(cuarto)* cloakroom, checkroom; *(ropero)* wardrobe, closet; *(ropas)* wardrobe (clothes); THEAT. wardrobe keeper; BOT. southernwood —m.f. *(encargado)* cloakroom *or* checkroom attendant.
guar·da·rro·pí·a f. THEAT. *(ropa)* wardrobe; *(accesorios)* props ♦ **de g.** FIG. sham, make-believe.
guar·da·se·llos m. [pl. **-llos**] keeper of the seal.
guar·de·rí·a f. *(empleo)* post of guard *or* warden; *(local)* daycare center, nursery.
guar·dia f. *(tropas)* guard <*g. de honor* honor guard>; *(defensa)* defense, protection; FENC. guard <*en g.* on guard>; MIL. guard, guard duty ♦ **en g.** FIG. on guard ● **g. civil** civil guard ● **g. municipal** city police force —m. *(centinela)* guard, guardsman; *(policía)* policeman ♦ **g. de corps** bodyguard ● **g. marina** MARIT. midshipman.
guar·dián, –dia·na m.f. *(persona que guarda)* guardian, custodian; *(vigilante)* watchman; RELIG. guardian; MARIT. strong hawser.
guar·di·lla[1] f. attic, garret.
guar·di·lla[2] f. SEW. seam binding, welting; *(púa)* largest tooth of a comb.
gua·re·cer §17 tr. to shelter, protect —reflex. to hide, take refuge.
gua·ri·da f. *(de animales)* lair, den; *(refugio)* shelter, refuge; FIG. *(querencia)* haunt, hangout; *(escondite)* hideout.
gua·ris·mo m. number, figure.
guar·ne·ce·dor, –do·ra adj. *(que adorna)* decorating, adorning; *(de vestidos)* trimming, bordering; MAS. plastering.
guar·ne·cer §17 tr. SEW. *(adornar)* to trim, border; *(proveer)* to supply, provide <*g. las tropas con provisiones* to supply the troops with provisions>; JEWEL. *(engastar)* to set; MIL. to garrison; MAS. to plaster; EQUIT. to harness; CUL. to garnish; ARM. to arm (a sword) with a hand guard.
guar·ne·ci·do I. past part. see **guarnecer** II. m. plaster, stucco.
guar·ni·ción f. SEW. *(adorno)* trim, border; JEWEL. *(engaste)* setting; MIL. garrison; EQUIT. harness; CUL. garnish; ARM. guard (of a sword).
guar·ni·cio·nar tr. MIL. to garrison.
gua·ro m. ORNITH. small parrot; C. AMER. tafia, rum; ECUAD., PERU ferry cable.
gua·rre·rí·a f. COLL. *(suciedad)* dirtiness, filth; *(indecencia)* obscenity; *(mala pasada)* dirty trick ♦ **decir guarrerías** to use foul language.
gua·rro, –rra m. ZOOL. hog, swine —f. ZOOL. sow.
gua·sa I. f. COLL. *(pesadez)* slowness, dullness; *(burla)*

joke, jest; CARIB., BOT. guasa tree; CUBA, ICHTH. jewfish ♦ **con** *or* **de g.** jokingly, in jest **II.** adj. see **guaso, ‑sa.**

gua·sa·da f. ARG. vulgarism, coarse word.

guas·ca f. CHILE, PERU whip; AMER. strap, thong ♦ **dar g.** AMER. to whip; ARG., FIG. to persist; PERU to prolong, draw out.

guas·ca·zo m. AMER. lash.

gua·se·rí·a f. ARG., CHILE coarseness, crudeness.

gua·so ‑sa I. m.f. CHILE farmer, peasant; ARG., CUBA, ECUAD. crude *or* coarse person —f. see **guasa II.** adj. ARG., CHILE, ECUAD. crude, coarse.

guas·que·ar tr. AMER. to whip, flog —reflex. ARG. to jump to one side; URUG. to get annoyed without reason.

gua·ta[1] f. TEX. cotton padding *or* batting.

gua·ta[2] f. ARG., CHILE, PERU, COLL. paunch, potbelly; CHILE bulging, warping; CUBA lie; ECUAD. bosom buddy, close friend ♦ **echar g.** CHILE, COLL. to grow rich, prosper.

Gua·te·ma·la f. Guatemala.

gua·te·mal·te·co, ‑ca adj. & m.f. Guatemalan.

gua·tón, ‑to·na adj. CHILE fat, paunchy.

guau m. bow wow (dog's bark).

gua·ya f. lament, lamentation.

gua·ya·ba f. BOT. guava (fruit); *(jalea)* guava jelly *or* preserves; AMER., COLL. *(mentira)* lie; *(muchacha)* pretty young girl.

gua·ya·ba·te m. guava paste.

gua·ya·be·ro, ‑ra AMER. **I.** adj. lying **II.** m.f. *(mentiroso)* liar —f. *(chaquetilla)* lightweight shirt.

gua·ya·bo m. BOT. guava (tree); AMER., COLL. pretty young girl; COL. *(tristeza)* sorrow, grief; *(resaca)* hangover.

Gua·ya·na f. GEOG. Guiana.

gua·yar tr. CARIB. *(rallar)* to grate; *(raspar)* to scrape —intr. to work hard —reflex. P. RICO *(emborracharse)* to get drunk; *(fatigarse)* to get tired.

gua·yo m. CUBA *(rallo)* grater; *(borrachera)* drunkenness; MUS. poor-quality music, caterwauling.

gu·ber·na·men·tal POL. **I.** adj. *(relativo al gobierno)* governmental; *(partidario)* partisan, loyalist **II.** m.f. partisan, loyalist.

gu·ber·na·ti·vo, ‑va adj. POL. governmental.

gu·ber·nis·ta adj. & m.f. POL. partisan, loyalist.

gue·de·ja f. *(cabellera larga)* long hair; ZOOL. (lion's) mane.

gue·de·jón, ‑jo·na *or* **gue·de·jo·so, ‑sa** *or* **gue·de·ju·do, ‑da** adj. long-haired.

Guér·ni·ca GEOG. Guernica.

güe·ro, ‑ra adj. C. AMER., MEX. blond *or* blonde, fair.

gue·rra f. *(combate)* war <*g. civil* civil war>; *(ciencia)* warfare <*g. bacteriológica* germ warfare>; *(discordia)* conflict, hostility; FIG. *(oposición)* contraposition, antithesis ♦ **dar g. a** COLL. to give no peace to • **estar en g.** to be at war • **g. abierta** open warfare • **g. aérea** dogfight • **g. a muerte** a fight to the death • **g. de guerrilla** guerrilla warfare • **g. fría** *or* **de nervios** cold war • **g. santa** holy war, crusade • **hacer la g.** to wage war • **Primera Guerra Mundial** First World War • **Segunda Guerra Mundial** Second World War.

gue·rre·a·dor, ‑do·ra I. adj. warring, fighting **II.** warrior, fighter.

gue·rre·ar intr. *(luchar)* to war, fight; FIG. *(resistir)* to oppose, resist.

gue·rre·ra I. f. MIL. tunic (military jacket) **II.** adj. see **guerrero, ‑ra.**

gue·rre·ro, ‑ra I. adj. *(que guerrea)* warring, fighting; *(belicoso)* bellicose; FIG. *(travieso)* mischievous, annoying **II.** m. *(combatiente)* warrior, fighter; *(soldado)* soldier —f. see **guerrera.**

gue·rri·lla f. MIL. *(modo de guerrear)* guerrilla warfare; *(partida)* band of guerrillas.

gue·rri·lle·ar intr. MIL. to wage guerrilla warfare.

gue·rri·lle·ro m. MIL. guerrilla.

guí·a m.f. guide <*el ciego tenía un g. hábil* the blind man had an able guide>; *(consejero)* adviser <*g. espiritual* spiritual adviser>; FIG. *(director)* director, leader —m. MIL. marker, guide —f. *(faro)* guide <*la estrella polar es la g. del navegante* the polestar is the guide of the navigator>; *(reglamento)* guidepost; *(libro)* guide, manual; directory <*g. telefónica* telephone directory>; *(manillas)* handlebars; *(caballo)* leader, lead horse; *(palo)* stake (for train-

ing vines or trees); COM. customs permit; BOT. leader, guide shoot; MECH. guide; MARIT. guy, guide rope; MIN. leader; MUS. lead voice; COL. check rein ♦ **guías** *(riendas)* reins; *(bigotes)* twisted ends of a moustache.

guia·do, ‑da I. past. part. see **guiar II.** adj. *(acompañado)* guided; *(que tiene permiso)* having a permit ♦ **g. por** guided by.

guia·dor, ‑do·ra I. adj. guiding **II.** m.f. guide.

guiar §30 tr. *(llevar)* to guide, lead; *(conducir)* to guide, drive <*g. un automóvil* to drive a car>; *(mostrar)* to show, direct; FIG. *(aconsejar)* to guide, advise; MARIT. to steer; AVIA. to pilot; AGR. to train (plants) —intr. BOT. to sprout —reflex. to be guided <*los hijos se guían por el ejemplo de sus padres* children are guided by their parents' example>.

gui·ja·rre·ño, ‑ña *or* **gui·je·ño, ‑ña** adj. *(con guijarros)* pebbly, pebbled; FIG. *(robusto)* hardy, robust.

gui·ja·rro m. pebble.

gui·jo m. *(grava)* gravel; MECH. pivot, gudgeon.

guil·da f. guild.

guil·di·via f. rum distillery.

gui·lla·do, ‑da COLL. **I.** past part. see **guillarse II.** adj. crazy, nutty **III.** m.f. crazy *or* nutty person.

gui·llar·se reflex. COLL. *(irse)* to go away, run off; *(chiflarse)* to go crazy *or* nuts.

gui·llo·ti·na f. *(para decapitar)* guillotine; *(para papel)* paper cutter, guillotine.

gui·llo·ti·na·do, ‑da I. past part. see **guillotinar II.** adj. guillotined, beheaded **III.** m.f. guillotined person.

gui·llo·ti·nar tr. *(decapitar)* to guillotine; *(cortar papel)* to cut (with a paper cutter).

guim·ba·le·te m. pump handle.

guin·che *or* **güin·che** m. AMER. winch, hoist.

guin·da f. BOT. sour cherry (fruit).

guin·dar tr. *(colgar)* to hang high, hoist; COLL. *(robar)* to lift, swipe; *(obtener)* to get, land <*guindé el empleo que mis amigos querían* I landed the job that my friends wanted>; *(ahorcar)* to hang, string up (a person); COL. to tie up —reflex. ♦ **guindarse a alguien** CHILE, PERU to kill *or* knock off someone.

guin·di·lla f. BOT. red pepper; SP., COLL., DEROG. cop.

Gui·nea f. Guinea.

Gui·nea·Bis·sau f. Guinea-Bissau.

Gui·nea Ecuatorial f. Equatorial Guinea.

gui·ne·a·no, ‑na adj. of Equatorial Guinea.

gui·ne·o, ‑a adj. & m.f. Guinean —m. CARIB., C. AMER., MEX. variety of banana.

gui·ña·da f. *(pestañeo)* wink; MARIT. lurch, yaw.

gui·ña·dor, ‑do·ra adj. winking.

gui·ña·po m. *(andrajo)* rag, tatter; FIG. *(roto)* slob; *(persona despreciable)* wretch.

gui·ña·po·so, ‑sa adj. ragged, tattered.

gui·ñar tr. to wink —intr. MARIT. to lurch, yaw —reflex. to wink at each other.

gui·ño m. wink ♦ **hacer guiños** to wink.

gui·ñol m. *(teatro)* puppet show; FIG. *(persona)* fool, ridiculous person.

guión m. CINEM., THEAT. script; GRAM. hyphen; *(esquema)* outline, summary; RELIG. *(cruz)* processional cross; *(bandera)* standard, banner; FIG. *(cabecilla)* leader.

guio·nis·ta m.f. scriptwriter.

güi·ra I. f. BOT. calabash (fruit and tree); AMER., COLL. dimit ♦ **dar g.** CHILE to whip (a person) **II.** adj. HOND. cowardly.

gui·ri·gay m. [pl. **‑gays** *or* **‑ga·yes**] COLL. *(lenguaje)* gibberish; *(gritería)* uproar, confusion.

guir·nal·da f. *(adorno)* garland, wreath; BOT. globe amaranth.

güi·ro m. AMER., BOT. gourd, calabash; AMER., MUS. musical instrument made from a gourd; BOL., PERU green corn stalk.

gui·sa f. manner, way ♦ **a g. de** as, for <*usar un palo a g. de bastón* to use a stick as a cane> • **de** *or* **en tal g.** in such a manner *or* way.

gui·sa·do I. past part. see **guisar II.** m. CUL. stew.

gui·san·te m. BOT. pea (plant and seed) ♦ **g. de olor** BOT. sweet pea.

gui·sar tr. CUL. *(cocinar)* to cook, prepare; *(estofar)* to stew; FIG. *(arreglar)* to arrange, prepare.

gui·so m. CUL. *(estofado)* stew; *(plato)* cooked dish.

gui·so·te m. COLL. poorly made stew.

güis·qui m. whiskey.

gui·ta f. *(cuerda)* string, twine; SL. *(dinero)* bucks, cash.

gui·ta·rra f. MUS. guitar; TECH. muller (for gypsum).

gui·ta·rre·ar intr. MUS. to play the guitar.

gui·ta·rre·o m. strumming (of a guitar).

gui·ta·rre·ro, –ra m.f. *(fabricante)* guitar maker; *(vendedor)* guitar seller; *(intérprete)* guitarist.

gui·ta·rri·llo or **gui·ta·rro** m. MUS. small four-string guitar.

gui·ta·rris·ta m.f. guitarist, guitar player.

gui·ta·rrón m. MUS. large guitar; FIG., COLL. *(pícaro)* sly rascal, scoundrel; HOND., ENTOM. large wasp.

gu·la f. gluttony.

gu·lag m. [pl. **-lags**] *(campo de trabajo)* gulag (Russian labor camp); *(régimen)* oppressive political regime.

gul·den m. FIN. gulden, guilder (Dutch monetary unit).

gu·lus·me·ar intr. *(golosinear)* to sniff at what is cooking; *(mordiscar)* to nibble, eat tidbits.

gu·mí·a f. dagger, poignard.

gu·rí, –ri·sa m. ARG. Indian boy —f. Indian girl.

gu·rru·mi·na I. f. COLL. *(idolatría)* uxoriousness (excessive devotion to one's wife); AMER. trifle; ECUAD., GUAT., MEX. annoyance, bother; COL. sadness, melancholy **II.** adj. see **gurrumino, –na.**

gu·rru·mi·no, –na I. adj. *(enclenque)* sickly, puny; BOL., PERU cowardly; HOND. shrewd **II.** m. *(idólatra)* uxorious husband; *(que se deja dominar)* henpecked husband —m.f. C. AMER., MEX. child, youngster; HOND. shrewd person —f. see **gurrumina.**

gu·ru·pié m. AMER. croupier.

gu·sa·ne·ar intr. to swarm, teem.

gu·sa·ne·ra f. *(sitio)* breeding ground for worms; FIG., COLL. *(pasión)* burning passion.

gu·sa·ne·rí·a f. mass of worms.

gu·sa·ni·llo m. ZOOL. small worm; SEW. *(labor)* embroidery; *(hilo)* gold or silver or silk twist ♦ **g. de la conciencia** COLL. remorse • **matar el g.** to take a nip first thing in the morning.

gu·sa·no m. ZOOL. *(lombriz)* worm; ENTOM. *(oruga)* caterpillar; FIG. *(persona)* worm ♦ **g. de la conciencia** FIG. remorse • **g. de luz** ENTOM. glowworm • **g. de seda** ENTOM. silkworm • **matar el g.** ARG., ECUAD., PERU *(beber)* to have a drink; *(satisfacer un deseo)* to satisfy a desire.

gu·sa·no·so, –sa adj. wormy.

gus·ta·ción f. *(acción)* gustation, tasting; *(percepción)* taste.

gus·tar tr. *(probar)* to taste, sample; *(experimentar)* to test, try —intr. to like <*me gustan los pequeñuelos* I like little children>; *(agradar)* to please, be pleasing (to) <*nos gusta verte tan feliz* we are pleased to see you so happy>.

gus·ta·ti·vo, –va adj. gustative, gustatory.

gus·ta·zo m. COLL. great pleasure or delight.

gus·ti·llo m. aftertaste.

gus·to m. *(sentido corporal)* taste, sense of taste <*perdí el g. por el pescado* I lost my taste for fish>; *(sabor)* taste, flavor; *(placer)* pleasure, delight <*lo llamaré con g.* I will call him with pleasure>; *(modo de apreciar)* taste <*de buen g.* in good taste>; *(capricho)* whim, fancy ♦ **a g.** comfortable <*estoy a g. aquí* I feel comfortable here>; *(a voluntad)* at will; CUL. to taste <*añada sal a g.* add salt to taste> • **al g. de uno** to one's taste • **con mucho g.** with pleasure • **dar g. a** to please, gratify • **tener el g. de** to have the pleasure of • **tomar g. a** to take a liking to.

gus·to·sa·men·te adv. *(con placer)* with pleasure, gladly <*lo haré g.* I will do it gladly>.

gus·to·so, –sa adj. *(sabroso)* tasty, savory; *(con placer)* pleased, glad <*g. te lo enviaré* I will be glad to send it to you>; *(agradable)* pleasant, agreeable.

gu·ta·per·cha f. BOT. gutta-percha; *(tela)* cloth (treated with gutta-percha).

gu·tu·ral adj. guttural.

Guy·a·na f. Guyana.

guy·a·nés, –ne·sa adj. & m.f. Guyanese.

H

h, H f. ninth letter of the Spanish alphabet.

ha, has, han see **haber².**

ha·ba f. BOT. *(planta)* fava or broad bean; *(fruto, semilla)* bean <*h. de café* coffee bean>; *(roncha)* swelling (from an insect bite); MIN. nodule; VET. tumor on a horse's palate ♦ **en todas partes se cuecen habas** FIG., COLL. it's the same all over the world • **h. de las Indias** BOT. sweet pea • **son habas contadas** FIG., COLL. it's a sure thing.

Ha·ba·na, La f. Havana.

ha·ba·ne·ro, –ra adj. & m.f. Havanan.

ha·ba·no, –na I. adj. *(de La Habana)* Havanan; *(pardo)* brown **II.** m.f. *(de La Habana)* Havanan —m. *(cigarro)* Cuban cigar.

ha·ber¹ m. COM. credit ♦ **haberes** *(caudal)* assets, property; *(sueldo)* salary, wages; *(tributos)* duties, tributes; FIG. *(cualidades)* good qualities, assets • **h. monedado** hard cash • **tener uno en su h.** to have to one's credit.

ha·ber² §39 §G10 aux. to have <*no hemos comido* we have not eaten> ♦ **h. de** to have to, must <*ellos han de venir* they must come> —impers. ♦ **ha** <*seis años ha murió mi padre* my father died six years ago> • **habidos y por h.** LAW past, present and future • **hay** there is, there are <*hay flores en la mesa* there are flowers on the table> • **hay que** it is necessary <*hay que tener paciencia con ellos* it is necessary to be patient with them> • **no hay de qué** don't mention it, you're welcome • **¿qué hay?** what's up?, what's happening? • **¿qué hay de nuevo?** what's new? • **todo lo habido y por h.** everything imaginable —tr. ARCH. *(poseer)* to have <*h. de mano* to have on hand>; *(alcanzar)* to get one's hands on <*lee cuantos libros puede h.* he reads as many books as he can get his hands on>; *(capturar)* to capture, catch <*el ladrón no ha sido habido* the thief has not been caught> —reflex. to behave, act <*te has habido sin escrúpulos* you have behaved unscrupulously> ♦ **¡allá te las hayas!** that's your problem! • **habérselas con uno** to have it out with someone.

ha·bi·chue·la f. BOT. bean ♦ **h. verde** string bean.

ha·bien·te adj. LAW having, possessing.

há·bil adj. *(capaz)* capable, apt; *(diestro)* clever, skillful; *(adecuado)* suitable, adequate; LAW *(competente)* competent.

ha·bi·li·dad *(capacidad)* capability, aptitude; *(ingeniosidad)* cleverness, skill.

ha·bi·li·do·so, –sa I. adj. able, skillful **II.** m.f. able or skillful person.

ha·bi·li·ta·ción f. *(autorización)* authorization; *(preparación)* setting up; *(facilitación)* provision, supply; COM. financing.

ha·bi·li·ta·do I. past part. of **habilitar II.** m. *(encargado)* paymaster; AMER. businessman financed by another person.

ha·bi·li·ta·dor, –do·ra I. adj. qualifying **II.** m.f. *(autoridad)* qualifier; *(proveedor)* outfitter; COM. *(comanditario)* financial backer.

ha·bi·li·tar tr. *(permitir)* to enable, qualify; *(preparar)* to equip, set up; *(facilitar)* to provide, supply; COM. *(comanditar)* to finance; CUBA to annoy.

há·bil·men·te adv. ably, skillfully.

ha·bi·ta·ble adj. habitable, inhabitable.

ha·bi·ta·ción f. *(domicilio)* residence, dwelling; *(aposento)* room; BOT., ZOOL. habitat.

ha·bi·ta·cio·nal adj. resident, dwelling.

ha·bi·tá·cu·lo m. residence, dwelling.

ha·bi·tan·te m.f. inhabitant.

ha·bi·tar tr. to inhabit, live in.

há·bi·tat m. [pl. **-tats**] habitat.

há·bi·to m. RELIG. habit; *(vestido)* garb, dress; *(costumbre)* habit ♦ **colgar el h.** RELIG. to give up the cloth • **hábitos** RELIG. vestments • **tomar el h.** RELIG. *(monjas)* to take the veil (nuns); *(sacerdotes)* to take holy orders (priests).

ha·bi·tua·ción f. habituation, accustoming.

ha·bi·tual adj. habitual, customary.

ha·bi·tual·men·te adv. habitually, customarily.

ha·bi·tuar §67 tr. to habituate, accustom (to) —reflex. to become accustomed (to), get used to (something).

ha·bla f. *(facultad)* speech, faculty of speech; *(idioma)* language; *(discurso)* speech, talk ♦ **al h.** in communication, in contact <*se puso al h. con su familia* he got in contact with his family>; *(al alcance de la voz)* within speaking distance • **negar** *or* **quitar el h. a** to stop speaking to • **perder el h.** *or* **quedarse sin h.** to be speechless.

ha·bla·do, –da I. past part. of **hablar II.** adj. spoken **III.** f. MEX. gossip ♦ **bien h.** well-spoken • **cine h.** talkies, talking pictures • **mal h.** rude, foul-mouthed.

ha·bla·dor, –do·ra I. adj. *(que habla mucho)* talkative; *(chismoso)* gossipy **II.** m.f. *(charlatán)* talker, chatterbox; *(chismoso)* gossip; MEX. bragger, boaster.

ha·bla·du·rí·a f. *(charla)* idle talk, chatter; *(rumor)* rumor; *(chisme)* gossip.

ha·blan·chín, –chi·na COLL. **I.** adj. *(que habla mucho)* talkative; *(chismoso)* gossipy **II.** m.f. *(charlatán)* talker, chatterbox; *(chismoso)* gossip.

ha·blan·tín, –ti·na COLL. **I.** adj. *(que habla mucho)* talkative; *(chismoso)* gossipy **II.** m.f. *(charlatán)* talker, chatterbox; *(chismoso)* gossip —f. COL. *(charla)* idle talk, chatter.

ha·blar intr. to speak, talk <*ellos hablan en voz alta* they are talking in a loud voice>; FIG. *(tener relaciones)* to go out <*Andrés habló tres años con Bárbara* Andrew went out with Barbara for three years>; *(sonar)* to talk <*Anita hace h. al violín* Anita makes the violin talk> ♦ **estar hablando** to be lifelike (a portrait) • **h. alto** to speak loudly • **h. a tontas y a locas** to talk through one's hat • **h. bajo** to speak softly • **h. bien de** to speak well of • **h. claro** to speak frankly • **h. como un loro** FIG. to chatter • **h. de** to talk about, discuss • **h. en plata** to speak clearly • **h. entre dientes** to mumble, murmur • **h. gordo** to boast, brag • **h. mal de** to speak ill of • **h. más que un papagallo** FIG. to be a chatterbox • **h. por** to speak for, intercede for • **h. por h.** to talk for talking's sake • **h. por los codos** to talk a blue streak • **eso es h.** COLL. now you're talking • **eso es puro h.** COLL. that's baloney! • **¡ni h.!** impossible!, out of the question! —tr. to speak <*hablo francés* I speak French>; *(decir)* to talk, utter <*está hablando disparates* he is talking nonsense>; FIG. *(dar a entender)* to speak of, reveal <*todo habla de su habilidad* everything speaks of his ability> ♦ **hablarlo todo** to tell all —reflex. *(comunicarse)* to speak to one another.

ha·brá, habría see **haber²**.

Habs·bur·go m. Hapsburg.

ha·ca f. small horse, pony.

ha·ce·ci·llo m. BOT. fascicle.

ha·ce·de·ro, –de·ra adj. feasible, practicable.

ha·ce·dor, –do·ra I. adj. making **II.** m.f. *(creador)* creator, maker; *(administrador de hacienda)* administrator (of an estate) —f. PERU woman who makes or sells maize liquor ♦ **el H.** the Creator *or* Maker.

ha·cen·da·do, –da I. past part. of **hacendar II.** adj. landed, property owning **III.** m.f. landowner; AMER. rancher.

ha·cen·dar §49 tr. to give *or* transfer property (to) —reflex. to acquire property, settle down.

ha·cen·dis·ta m. financial expert, economist.

ha·cen·do·so, –sa adj. industrious, hard-working.

ha·cer §40 tr. *(producir)* to make <*mi madre hizo la comida* my mother made the meal>; *(efectuar)* to do <*sus amigos harán lo que puedan* his friends will do what they can>; *(formar)* to form, make <*no hagas un juicio ligero* do not make a hasty judgment>; *(obrar)* to work, perform <*h. un milagro* to work a miracle>; *(realizar)* to make <*hicieron burlas* they made jokes>; *(componer)* to compose, make up; *(arreglar)* to make <*el niño tiene que h. la cama* the boy has to make the bed>; *(causar)* to cause, make; *(obligar)* to make, force <*Ana les hizo salir* Ann forced them to leave>; *(contener)* to contain, hold; *(acostumbrar)* to accustom, condition <*el astronauta hacía el cuerpo a la fatiga* the astronaut conditioned his body to fatigue>; *(representar)* to play the role *or* part of <*h. la reina* to play the part of the queen>; *(igualar)* to make, equal <*tres y tres hacen seis* three and three makes six>; *(suponer)* to suppose *or* assume to be <*le hacía en Ecuador* I assumed him to be in Ecuador>; PHYSIOL. *(expeler)* to evacuate ♦ **h. agua** MARIT. to leak • **h. alarde** to boast, brag • **h. boca** to work up an appetite • **h. brillo** to persist • **h. burla de** to make fun of • **h. cara** *or* **frente a** to face, confront • **h. caso de** *or* **a** to pay attention to • **h. cola** to stand in line • **h. con** *or* **de** to provide *or* supply with <*hicieron a Marta con dinero* they provided Martha with money> • **h. conocer** to make known • **h. daño** to hurt, harm • **h. el amor** to make love • **h. estimación** to estimate • **h. falta** *(faltar)* to be needed *or* lacking <*me hacen falta seis pesos* I need six more pesos>; *(echar de menos)* to be missed <*Cecilia me hace mucha falta* I miss Cecilia very much> • **h. fe** to certify, testify • **h. juego** to match, go together • **hacerla** *or* **hacerlas** to do wrong • **h. la barba** to shave • **h. la guerra** to wage war • **h. la paz** to make peace • **h. mofa de** to mock • **h. pedazos** to smash, break into pieces • **h. presente** to notify • **h. quiebra** to go bankrupt • **h. recados** to run errands • **h. saber** to inform, let know • **h. sombra** to cast a shadow • **h. una apuesta** to place a bet • **h. una maleta** to pack a suitcase • **h. una pregunta** to ask a question • **h. una visita** to pay a visit • **h. uno de las suyas** to be up to one's old tricks —intr. *(importar)* to atter, be relevant <*esto no hace al caso* this is not relevant to the case>; *(corresponder)* to be suitable, fit ♦ **h. de** to act as, serve as <*hago de camarera* I serve as a waitress> • **h. por** *or* **para** to try, strive <*hicimos por llegar a tiempo* we tried to arrive on time> —impers. METEOROL. to be <*hace frío* it is cold>; ago <*hace tres semanas que llegamos* we arrived three weeks ago> ♦ **desde hace** for <*desde hace diez años* for ten years> • **hace mucho** long ago • **hace poco** a little while ago —reflex. *(volverse)* to grow, become <*hacerse viejo* to grow old>; *(convertirse)* to turn into, become <*el vino se hizo vinagre* the wine turned into vinegar>; *(aumentarse)* to grow; *(proveerse)* to provide oneself <*hacerse de dinero* to provide oneself with money>; *(acostumbrarse)* to get used to <*no me hago a vivir solo* I cannot get used to living alone ♦ **hacerse atrás** to move back • **hacerse a un lado** to step aside • **hacerse con** to make off with, get a hold of • **hacerse el sueco** to act dumb • **hacerse la vida** to earn one's living • **hacérsele a uno** to strike, seem <*eso se me hace increíble* that strikes me as incredible>.

ha·cia prep. toward <*viajamos h. Nueva York* we are traveling toward New York>; *(alrededor de)* about, around <*la reunión tendrá lugar h. las ocho* the meeting will take place around eight o'clock> ♦ **h. abajo** downward • **h. acá** here, this way <*venga h. acá* come this way> • **h. adelante** forward • **h. arriba** upward • **h. atrás** backward.

ha·cien·da f. *(finca)* farm, ranch; *(fortuna)* fortune, wealth; AMER. livestock; CUBA corral ♦ **h. pública** public treasury • **haciendas** household chores.

ha·cien·de, haciendo see **hacendar**.

ha·ci·na f. stack, pile <*h. de leña* stack of firewood>; FIG. *(montón)* pile, heap.

ha·ci·na·mien·to m. stacking, piling.

ha·ci·nar tr. *(colocar haces)* to stack, pile; FIG. *(amontonar)* to pile up, accumulate.

ha·cha f. *(herramienta)* ax, axe; *(cuerno del toro)* bull's horn ♦ **de h. y tiza** ARG. tough • **h. de armas** battle-ax • **ser un h.** to be an ace, be outstanding (at something).

ha·char tr. var. of **hachear**.

ha·cha·zo m. *(golpe)* ax blow, stroke with an ax; TAUR. sidelong blow (with a horn); COL. start, shying away (of a horse).

ha·che f. aitch (name of the letter h) ♦ **llámele h.** call it what you like (it's all the same) • **volverse haches y erres** COL. to fall through, fail.

ha·che·ar tr. to ax, hew —intr. to hew with an ax.

ha·che·ro m. *(leñador)* woodcutter, lumberjack; MIL. sapper.

ha·chís m. hashish.

ha·chón m. *(tea)* large torch; *(brasero)* cresset.

ha·da f. fairy ♦ **cuento de h.** fairy tale.

ha·do m. destiny, fate.

haf·nio m. CHEM. hafnium.

ha·ga, hago see **hacer**.

ha·gio·gra·fí·a f. RELIG. hagiography.

Hai·tí m. Haiti.

hai·tia·no, –na adj. & m.f. Haitian.

¡ha·la! interj. hey!, come on!

ha·la·ga·dor, –do·ra adj. *(lisonjero)* flattering; *(adulador)* cajoling.

ha·la·gar §47 tr. *(lisonjear)* to flatter; *(mostrar afecto)* to show affection for; *(agradar)* to please, gratify; *(adular)* to cajole.

ha·la·go m. *(lisonja)* flattery; *(adulación)* cajolery.

ha·la·güe·ño, –ña adj. *(lisonjero)* flattering; *(alentador)* promising <*una oferta h.* promising offer>; *(agradable)* pleasing, gratifying; *(atractivo)* attractive.

ha·lar tr. *(tirar)* to pull toward oneself; MARIT. to haul, tow —intr. MARIT. to pull.

hal·cón m. ORNITH. falcon, hawk.

hal·co·ne·ar intr. FIG. to allure, vamp.

hal·co·ne·rí·a f. falconry, hawking.

hal·co·ne·ro m. falconer, hawker.

hal·da f. *(falda)* skirt; *(harpillera)* sackcloth, burlap (for packing).

ha·li·ta f. MIN. halite, rock salt.

há·li·to m. *(aliento)* breath; *(vapor)* vapor; POET. *(viento suave)* gentle breeze.

ha·li·to·sis f. MED. halitosis, bad breath.

ha·lo m. halo.

ha·ló·ge·no, –na CHEM. I. adj. halogenous II. m. halogen.

hal·te·ra f. SPORT. dumbbell.

hal·te·ro·fi·lia f. SPORT. weightlifting.

hall m. [pl. **halls**] hall, vestibule.

ha·llar tr. *(topar)* to come across, find <*mientras limpiaba mi cuarto hallé una foto de mis padres* while cleaning up my room, I came across a photo of my parents>; *(encontrar)* to find <*el equipo de salvamento halló al niño perdido* the search party found the lost child>; *(averiguar)* to find out; *(notar)* to note <*h. errores en un examen* to note errors on an exam>; *(descubrir)* to discover —reflex. *(encontrarse)* to be, find oneself <*me hallo ahora en Madrid* I am now in Madrid>; *(estar)* to be <*Juan se halla enfermo* John is sick> ♦ **hallarse uno en todo** to have one's hand in everything • **no hallarse** to be uncomfortable, feel out of place.

ha·llaz·go m. *(acción)* finding, discovery; *(objeto)* good find <*ese coche fue un h.* that car was a good find>.

ha·ma·ca f. *(cama)* hammock; *(vehículo)* palanquin; AMER. swing.

ha·ma·car §70 tr. & reflex. AMER. to swing, rock.

ham·bre f. *(apetito)* hunger; *(escasez)* starvation, famine; *(deseo ardiente)* hunger, desire, longing ♦ **h. canina** FIG. ravenous hunger • **matar el h.** FIG. to stave off hunger • **morir** or **morirse de h.** FIG. to be starving, be dying of hunger • **ser más listo que el h.** to be very bright • **tener h.** to be hungry.

ham·bre·ar tr. to make (someone) hungry —intr. to starve, be hungry.

ham·brien·to, –ta I. adj. *(famélico)* starved, hungry; FIG. *(deseoso)* hungry, longing II. m.f. starving or hungry person.

ham·bru·na f. AMER. ravenous hunger.

Ham·bur·go Hamburg.

ham·bur·gués, –gue·sa I. adj. of Hamburg II. m.f. *(persona)* native of Hamburg —f. *(bistec)* hamburger.

ha·mo m. fishhook.

ham·pa f. underworld, low life.

ham·pón I. adj. rowdy, tough II. m. thug, roughneck.

háms·ter m. [pl. **-ters**] ZOOL. hamster.

hand ball m. SPORT. handball.

han·di·cap m. [pl. **-caps**] SPORT. handicap.

han·gar m. AVIA. hangar.

ha·ploi·de adj. BIOL. haploid.

ha·rá, haría see **hacer.**

ha·ra·gán, –ga·na I. adj. lazy, idle II. m. loafer, idler.

ha·ra·ga·ne·ar intr. to be idle, loaf.

ha·ra·ga·ne·rí·a f. laziness, idleness.

ha·ra·pien·to, –ta adj. ragged, tattered.

ha·ra·po m. *(andrajo)* rag, tatter; *(aguardiente)* weak or inferior alcohol, rotgut.

ha·ra·po·so, –sa adj. ragged, tattered.

hard·ware m. COMPUT. hardware.

ha·rén m. harem.

ha·ri·na f. *(trigo molido)* flour; *(cereal molido)* meal <*h. de maíz* corn meal>; FIG. *(polvo)* powder ♦ **estar metido en h.** *(pan)* to be doughy or heavy (said of bread); FIG., COLL.

(estar gordo) to be fat; *(estar absorto)* to be hard at work • **h. de hueso** bone meal • **ser h. de otro costal** FIG., COLL. to be a horse of a different color • **h. lacteada** malted milk powder.

ha·ri·ne·ro, –ra I. adj. flour, of flour <*molino h.* flour mill> II. m. *(persona)* flour dealer; *(receptáculo)* flour bin.

ha·ri·no·so, –sa adj. *(que tiene harina)* floury, farinose; *(farináceo)* farinaceous.

har·mo·ní·a f. var. of **armonía.**

har·ne·ro m. sieve, sifter.

har·pi·lle·ra f. burlap, sackcloth.

har·tar tr. *(saciar el apetito)* to fill, stuff; FIG. *(satisfacer)* to satisfy; *(fastidiar)* to annoy; *(aburrir)* to bore; *(cansar)* to tire, weary.

har·taz·go m. fill, bellyfull ♦ **darse un h. de** *(comer mucho)* to eat one's fill of; FIG. to have had one's fill of <*me di un h. de estudiar* I have had my fill of studying>.

har·to, –ta I. past part. of **hartar** II. adj. *(saciado)* full, satiated; *(cansado)* tired, fed up III. adv. *(bastante)* enough; *(muy)* very.

har·tu·ra f. *(hartazgo)* bellyful, fill; POET. *(abundancia)* abundance, wealth; FIG. *(logro)* gratification, fulfillment.

has·ta §G46 I. prep. until <*estudiamos h. las seis* we studied until six o'clock>; up to, as far as <*caminaron h. la biblioteca* they walked as far as the library> ♦ **h. la vista** or **h. luego** see you, so long • **h. mañana** see you tomorrow • **h. que** until II. adv. even <*h. los criados lo sabían* even the servants knew about it>.

has·tiar §30 tr. *(cansar)* to tire, bore; *(asquear)* to disgust, sicken; *(fastidiar)* to annoy, bother.

has·tí·o m. *(repugnancia)* repugnance, revulsion (to food); FIG. *(fastidio)* annoyance; *(tedio)* boredom, tedium.

ha·te·ar intr. *(recoger)* to gather (one's things together), pack up; AGR. *(dar hatería)* to give provisions (to shepherds).

ha·ti·llo m. small bundle (of one's belongings) ♦ **tomar el h.** FIG., COLL. to leave.

ha·to¹ m. *(porción de ganado)* herd or flock; *(cabaña de pastores)* pastor's hut; *(hatería)* provisions, supplies; FIG. *(banda)* gang, band; *(montón)* lot, bunch; CUBA, VEN. *(hacienda)* cattle ranch.

ha·to² m. everyday clothes, belongings ♦ **liar uno el h.** COLL. to pack one's things.

ha·wai·a·no, –na adj. & m.f. Hawaiian.

hay, haya see **haber².**

Ha·ya f. ♦ **La H.** The Hague.

haz¹ m. [pl. **ha·ces**] *(fardo)* bundle, bunch; *(de leña)* fagot; PHYS. pencil (of light rays) ♦ **haces de rectas** MATH. pencil of lines.

haz² f. [pl. **ha·ces**] *(cara)* face, countenance; FIG. *(de tela)* right side (of cloth) ♦ **a dos haces** FIG. with an ulterior motive • **h. de la tierra** face of the earth • **ser uno de dos haces** FIG. to be two-faced.

haz³ see **hacer.**

ha·za f. plot of arable land.

ha·za·ña f. feat, exploit.

ha·za·ño·so, –sa adj. *(heroico)* heroic; *(valiente)* gallant.

haz·me·rre·ír m. COLL. laughingstock.

he¹ adv. lo, behold ♦ **h. allí** there is or are • **h. aquí** here is or are • **helo aquí** here it is.

he² see **haber².**

heb·dó·ma·da f. *(semana)* hebdomad, week; *(siete años)* seven years.

heb·do·ma·da·rio, –ria I. adj. weekly II. m.f. RELIG. hebdomadary.

he·bi·lla f. buckle, clasp.

he·bra f. SEW. *(hilo)* thread; *(fibra)* fiber; *(filamento)* filament; *(veta)* grain (of wood); FIG. thread <*la h. de un argumento* the thread of a plot>; MIN. vein; POET. hair ♦ **de una h.** CHILE all at once, in one breath • **pegar la h.** to strike up a conversation.

he·brai·co, –ca adj. Hebraic.

he·brai·ís·mo m. Hebraism.

he·brai·zar §06 intr. to Hebraize.

he·bre·o, –a adj. & m.f. *(persona)* Hebrew —m. *(lengua)* Hebrew; DEROG. *(mercader)* merchant.

he·ca·tom·be f. *(sacrificio)* hecatomb; *(matanza)* hecatomb, slaughter; FIG. *(desastre)* disaster.

hec·tá·re·a f. hectare.

héc·ti·co, –ca MED. **I.** adj. consumptive, hectic **II.** f. hectic fever.

hec·to·gra·mo m. hectogram.

hec·to·li·tro m. hectoliter.

hec·tó·me·tro m. hectometer.

he·chi·cé, hechice see **hechizar.**

he·chi·ce·rí·a f. *(brujería)* witchcraft, sorcery; *(hechizo)* spell, charm.

he·chi·ce·ro, –ra **I.** adj. *(mágico)* magic; *(encantador)* enchanting, bewitching **II.** m. *(brujo)* sorcerer, wizard; FIG. *(encantador)* charmer, enchanter —f. *(bruja)* sorceress, witch; FIG. *(encantadora)* charmer, enchantress.

he·chi·zar §04 tr. *(encantar)* to cast a spell on, bewitch; FIG. *(cautivar)* to enchant, charm.

he·chi·zo **I.** adj. *(postizo)* false, imitation; *(fabricado)* made, manufactured; AMER. local, domestic *<producto h.* local product>* **II.** m. *(sortilegio)* spell, enchantment; *(encanto)* charm, fascination; FIG. *(persona)* bewitcher, charmer.

he·cho, –cha **I.** past part. see **hacer** **II.** adj. *(perfecto)* perfect, complete; *(terminado)* done, finished; *(acostumbrado)* accustomed, used to; *(proporcionado)* proportioned *<bien h.* well-proportioned>*; *(maduro)* mature; FIG. *(semejante a)* like *<h. un demonio* like a devil>*; CUL. done, cooked *<muy h.* overcooked>*; SEW. *(ropa)* ready-made ♦ **h. y derecho** complete, perfect, in every respect **III.** m. *(acto)* act, action; *(hazaña)* deed, feat; *(suceso)* event; *(realidad)* fact *<el h. es que* the fact is that>*; *(asunto)* point, matter at hand *<volvamos a h.* let's get back to the point> ♦ **a h.** continuously, without stopping • **a lo h., pecho** let's make the best of it now • **de h.** *(en realidad)* in fact, as a matter of fact; LAW de facto • **h. consumado** fait accompli • **h. de armas** MIL. feat of arms • **Hechos de los Apóstoles** BIBL. Acts of the Apostles.

he·chor, –cho·ra m.f. CHILE malefactor, wrongdoer —m. ARG., VEN., ZOOL. stud donkey.

he·chu·ra f. *(fabricación)* making, creation; *(criatura)* creature, creation; *<somos hechuras de Dios* we are God's creatures>*; *(forma)* shape, form; *(forma del cuerpo)* shape, build; FIG. *(servil)* indebted dependent or subordinate; *(confección)* workmanship, craftsmanship; *(gajes)* fee, charge; CHILE inviting someone to drink ♦ **no tener h.** to be impossible, not to be feasible.

he·der §50 intr. *(apestar)* to stink, reek; FIG. *(enfadar)* to annoy, irritate.

he·dion·dez f. *(hedor)* stench, stink; *(cosa hedionda)* foul-smelling thing.

he·dion·do, –da adj. *(maloliente)* stinking, foul-smelling; FIG. *(repugnante)* repulsive, sickening; *(obsceno)* filthy, obscene; *(molesto)* annoying, insufferable.

he·do·nis·mo m. PHILOS., PSYCH. hedonism.

he·do·nis·ta PHILOS., PSYCH. **I.** adj. hedonistic, hedonic **II.** m.f. hedonist.

he·dor m. stench, stink.

he·ge·lia·nis·mo m. PHILOS. Hegelianism.

he·ge·lia·no, –na adj. & m.f. PHILOS. Hegelian.

he·ge·mo·ní·a f. hegemony.

hé·gi·ra or **hé·ji·ra** f. RELIG. hegira.

he·la·da **I.** f. METEOROL. frost ♦ **h. blanca** or **simple** METEOROL. hoarfrost, rime **II.** adj. see **helado, –da.**

he·la·de·ra f. ARG., PAR., URUG. refrigerator.

he·la·de·rí·a f. ice-cream shop or parlor.

he·la·de·ro, –ra m.f. ice-cream street vendor.

he·la·do, –da **I.** past part. see **helar** **II.** adj. *(muy frío)* very cold *<este vino está bien h.* this wine is very cold>*; FIG. *(atónito)* frozen, dumbfounded *<me quedé h. con la noticia* I was dumbfounded by the news>*; *(desdeñoso)* cold, unfeeling *<un corazón h.* a cold heart>*; BOT. frostbitten, frozen **III.** m. *(manjar)* ice cream; *(sorbete)* sherbet —f. see **helada.**

he·la·dor, –do·ra **I.** adj. freezing **II.** f. ice cream machine.

he·lar §49 tr. *(congelar)* to freeze; FIG. *(dejar pasmado)* to dumbfound, astonish; *(desanimar)* to dispirit, discourage —reflex *(congelarse)* to freeze, become frozen; *(quedarse frío)* to freeze *<en el invierno se hiela uno aquí* in the winter one freezes here>*; BOT. to become frostbitten ♦ **se me heló la sangre** my blood curdled.

he·le·cho m. BOT. fern ♦ **h. arbóreo** tree fern.

he·lé·ni·co, –ca adj. Hellenic, Greek.

he·le·nis·mo m. Hellenism.

he·le·nís·ti·co, –ca adj. Hellenistic.

he·le·ni·zar §04 tr. to Hellenize, make Hellenistic —reflex. to become Hellenized.

he·le·no, –na **I.** adj. Hellenic, Greek **II.** m.f. Hellene, Greek.

hé·li·ce f. GEOM. *(línea)* helix; *(espiral)* spiral, helix; ANAT. helix (of the ear); propeller; ZOOL. snail —m. ♦ **Hélice** ASTRON. Ursa Major, Great Bear.

he·li·coi·dal adj. GEOM. helicoid, spiral.

he·li·cóp·te·ro m. AVIA. helicopter.

he·lio m. CHEM. helium.

he·lio·cén·tri·co, –ca adj. ASTRON. heliocentric, heliocentrical.

he·lio·tro·pis·mo m. BOT. heliotropism.

he·lio·tro·po m. BOT. heliotrope; OPT., SURV. heliostat; MIN. bloodstone, heliotrope.

he·li·puer·to m. AVIA. heliport.

he·má·ti·co, –ca adj. hematic.

he·ma·to·lo·gí·a f. MED. hematology.

he·ma·tó·lo·go m. MED. hematologist.

he·ma·to·ma m. MED. hematoma.

hem·bra f. *(mujer)* woman, female; ZOOL. *(animal femenino)* female; *(cola de caballo)* thin horse tail; BOT. female plant; SEW. *(corchete)* eye; MECH. *(parte hueca que recibe)* female; ELEC. *(enchufe)* socket; *(tornillo)* nut; *(cerradura)* strike (of a lock); *(molde)* hollow mold or form ♦ **h. de cerrojo** or **pestillo** strike plate • **h. del timón** MARIT. gudgeon (of a rudder).

hem·bra·je f. AMER., AGR. female livestock (on a ranch).

hem·bri·lla f. MECH. *(hembra)* female (piece); *(armella)* eyebolt, eyescrew.

he·mi·ci·clo m. *(semicírculo)* semicircle; ARCHIT. hemicycle.

he·mi·ple·jí·a f. MED. hemiplegia.

he·mis·fé·ri·co, –ca adj. hemispheric, hemispherical.

he·mis·fe·rio m. hemisphere ♦ **h. austral** southern hemisphere • **h. boreal** northern hemisphere • **h. cerebral** or **del cerebro** ANAT. cerebral hemisphere • **h. occidental** western hemisphere.

he·mo·fi·lia f. MED. hemophilia.

he·mo·fí·li·co, –ca MED. **I.** adj. hemophilic **II.** m.f. hemophiliac.

he·mo·glo·bi·na f. PHYSIOL. hemoglobin.

he·mo·rra·gia f. MED. hemorrhage ♦ **h. nasal** MED. nosebleed.

he·mo·rrá·gi·co, –ca adj. MED. hemorrhagic.

he·mo·rroi·de f. MED. hemorrhoid ♦ **hemorroides** hemorrhoids, piles.

he·mos see **haber².**

he·mós·ta·to m. MED. hemostat.

he·nal m. hayloft, hay barn.

hen·chi·du·ra f. filling, stuffing.

hen·chi·mien·to m. *(henchidura)* filling, stuffing; *(madera)* wood used to fill holes; *(suelo)* rough floor (in a paper mill).

hen·chir §48 tr. to fill, stuff —reflex. to stuff oneself (with food).

hen·de·du·ra f. crack, cleft.

hen·der §50 tr. *(cortar)* to split, cleave; FIG. *(cortar un fluido)* to cleave, cut through (water or air); *(abrirse paso)* to make or elbow one's way through.

hen·di·du·ra f. crack, cleft.

hen·di·mien·to m. cracking, splitting.

hen·dir §25 tr. AMER. var. of **hender.**

he·ni·fi·car §70 tr. AGR. to hay, make hay (for forage).

he·nil m. hayloft, hay barn.

he·no m. hay ♦ **h. blanco** BOT. velvet grass.

he·ñir §59 tr. CUL. to knead (dough).

he·pá·ti·co, –a **I.** adj. ANAT., BOT., MED. hepatic **II.** m.f. MED. person suffering from liver disease —f. BOT. hepatica, liverwort ♦ **hepáticas** BOT. Hepaticae.

he·pa·ti·tis f. MED. hepatitis.

hep·ta·go·nal adj. heptagonal.

hep·tá·go·no, –na GEOM. **I.** adj. heptagonal **II.** m. heptagon.

he·rál·di·co, –ca I. adj. heraldic **II.** m.f. herald —f. heraldry.

he·ral·do m. herald.

her·bá·ce·o, –a adj. BOT. herbaceous.

her·ba·jar tr. AGR. to put out to pasture, graze —intr. to pasture, graze.

her·ba·je m. AGR. *(pasto)* herbage, pasture; *(derecho)* grazing fee; TEX. waterproof woolen fabric.

her·ba·rio, –ria II. adj. herbal **Ii.** m. *(experto)* herbalist, botanist; *(colección)* herbarium; *(libro)* herbal; ZOOL. rumen.

her·ba·zal m. BOT. grassland, pasture.

her·be·cer §17 intr. BOT. to come up, begin to grow (herbs and grass).

her·bí·vo·ro, –ra ZOOL. **I.** adj. herbivorous, plant-eating **II.** m. herbivore.

her·bo·la·rio, –ria I. adj. COLL. mad, crazy **II.** m. *(comerciante)* herbalist, herb vendor; *(tienda)* herbalist's shop —m.f. COLL. *(loco)* madcap, crazy person.

her·bo·so, –sa adj. herbaceous.

her·cio m. PHYS. hertz.

her·cú·le·o, –a adj. MYTH. Herculean; FIG. herculean.

Hér·cu·les MYTH. Hercules.

he·re·da·ble adj. inheritable.

he·re·dad f. country estate *or* property ♦ **h. residual** *or* **residuaria** LAW residual estate.

he·re·dar tr. BIOL., LAW *(recibir)* to inherit; LAW *(dar)* to bequeath; FIG. *(instituir)* to institute as heir, name in a will.

he·re·de·ro, –ra I. adj. inheriting ♦ **príncipe h.** crown prince **II.** m.f. inheritor —m. heir —f. heiress ♦ **h. forzoso** heir apparent, forced heir • **h. legal** heir at law • **instituir h.** *or* **por h. a** to appoint as one's heir, name in one's will.

he·re·di·ta·rio, –ria adj. BIOL. hereditary; FIG. *(tradicional)* traditional, ancestral.

he·re·je I. adj. CHILE, VEN. excessive, backbreaking <*un trabajo h.* a backbreaking job> **II.** m.f. *(radical)* heretic; *(descarado)* rascal, scoundrel.

he·re·jí·a f. *(opinión no aceptada)* heresy; *(insulto)* injurious expression, insult.

he·ren·cia f. *(patrimonio)* inheritance <*recibir una h.* to receive an inheritance>; FIG. *(tradición)* heritage, tradition; BIOL. heredity ♦ **h. yacente** LAW unclaimed estate, estate in abeyance.

he·ré·ti·co, –ca adj. heretical.

he·ri·da I. f. *(lesión)* wound, injury; FIG. *(ofensa)* wound, offense; *(tormento moral)* torment, anguish <*las heridas espirituales son muy dolorosas* spiritual torments are very painful> ♦ **h. contusa** MED. contusion • **renovar la h.** FIG. to reopen an old wound • **tocar en la h.** FIG. to touch a sore spot **II.** adj. see **herido, –da.**

he·ri·do, –da I. past part. see **herir II.** adj. *(lesionado)* wounded, injured; FIG. *(ofendido)* hurt, offended **III.** m.f. *(persona herida)* wounded or injured person —m. CHILE ditch ♦ **los heridos** the wounded —f. see **herida.**

he·rir §65 tr. *(lesionar)* to wound; *(estropear)* to hurt, offend <*su canto me hiere los oídos* his singing hurts my ears>; FIG. *(ofender)* to offend, insult <*sus insultos me hirieron* his insults offended me>; *(el sol)* to fall or shine on (said of the sun); *(tañer)* to pluck, play (a stringed instrument); *(mover)* to stir, move.

her·ma·fro·di·ta I. adj. hermaphroditic **II.** m.f. hermaphrodite.

her·ma·na·ble adj. *(de hermanos)* fraternal, brotherly; *(de hermanas)* sisterly.

her·ma·na·do, –da I. past part. see **hermanar II.** adj. FIG. *(igual)* identical, matching; *(semejante)* similar, alike; BOT. didymous, twin.

her·ma·na·mien·to m. *(unión)* mating, matching; *(acción de fraternizar)* fraternization.

her·ma·nar tr. *(juntar)* to join, match; *(fraternizar)* to fraternize, treat as a brother; CHILE to pair off, couple —reflex. *(unirse)* to match, be joined or united; *(fraternizarse)* to treat one another as brothers.

her·ma·nas·tro, –tra m. stepbrother —f. stepsister.

her·ma·naz·go m. var. of **hermandad.**

her·man·dad f. *(fraternidad)* brotherhood, fraternity; *(de hermanas)* sisterhood; FIG. *(semejanza)* similarity, likeness; *(amistad)* close friendship; *(liga)* league, alliance ♦ **la Santa H.** SP., HIST. the Holy Brotherhood (medieval Spanish militia).

her·ma·no, –na m. brother <*h. carnal* blood brother>; RELIG. *(religioso)* brother; C. RICA ghost, specter ♦ **h. de leche** foster brother • **h. de madre** *or* **de padre** half brother • **h. gemelo** twin brother • **h. lego** lay brother • **h. mayor** older *or* oldest brother • **h. menor** younger *or* youngest brother • **h. político** brother-in-law • **hermanos siameses** Siamese twins • **medio h.** half brother • **primo h.** first cousin —f. sister <*media h.* half sister>; RELIG. *(religiosa)* sister, nun ♦ **H. de la Caridad** RELIG. Sister of Charity • **h. gemela** twin sister • **h. lega** lay sister • **h. mayor** older *or* oldest sister • **h. menor** younger *or* youngest sister • **h. política** sister-in-law • **prima h.** first cousin —m.f. FIG. *(cosa)* twin, mate.

her·mé·ti·ca·men·te adv. hermetically.

her·me·ti·ci·dad f. *(cerradura perfecta)* airtightness; FIG. *(incomprensibilidad)* impenetrability, incomprehensibleness.

her·mé·ti·co, –ca adj. *(cerrado)* hermetic, airtight; FIG. *(incomprensible)* impenetrable, incomprehensible ♦ **Hermético, –ca** PHILOS. Hermetic.

her·me·tis·mo m. *(incomprensibilidad)* impenetrability, incomprehensibleness; *(reserva)* secrecy, secretiveness.

her·mo·sa·men·te adv. *(con hermosura)* beautifully; FIG. *(con perfección)* perfectly, properly.

her·mo·se·a·mien·to m. beautification, embellishment.

her·mo·se·ar tr. to beautify, make beautiful —intr. to show off one's beauty.

her·mo·so, –sa adj. *(bello)* beautiful, lovely; *(sano)* healthy, robust (said of children); *(despejado)* fine, lovely <*h. tiempo* fine weather>.

her·mo·su·ra f. *(belleza)* beauty, loveliness; *(mujer hermosa)* beauty, beautiful woman.

her·nia f. MED. hernia.

hé·ro·e m. *(campeón)* hero; LIT. *(protagonista)* protagonist, main character; FIG. *(semidiós)* demigod.

he·roi·ca·men·te adv. heroically.

he·roi·ci·dad f. *(calidad de héroe)* heroism; *(hazaña)* heroic deed *or* exploit.

he·roi·co, –ca adj. heroic.

he·ro·í·na f. heroine <*una h. de la literatura y la historia* a heroine of literature and history>; PHARM. heroin.

he·ro·ís·mo m. *(calidad de héroe)* heroism; *(hazaña)* heroic deed *or* exploit.

her·pe m.f. MED. *(erupción)* herpes; *(zona)* zona, shingles.

her·pé·ti·co, –ca MED. **I.** adj. herpetic **II.** m.f. person with herpes.

he·rra·de·ro m. *(acción)* branding of cattle; *(temporada)* branding time *or* season; *(sitio)* branding place.

he·rra·dor, –do·ra m. horseshoer, blacksmith —f. COLL. horseshoer's wife.

he·rra·du·ra f. *(hierro)* horseshoe; *(resguardo)* hoof guard; ZOOL. horseshoe bat ♦ **h. hechiza** horseshoe with fixed nails • **mostrar las herraduras** to take to one's heels.

he·rra·je m. *(quincalla)* hardware, iron fittings; ARG. horseshoe.

he·rra·mien·ta f. *(instrumento)* tool, implement; *(conjunto de instrumentos)* tools, set of tools; TAUR., FIG., COLL. bull's horns; *(dentadura)* grinders, choppers; *(arma)* weapon ♦ **h. cortante** *or* **de corte** cutting tool.

he·rran·za f. S. AMER. horseshoeing.

he·rrar §49 tr. *(clavar)* to shoe, fit with horseshoes; *(marcar)* to brand (cattle); *(guarnecer)* to trim with iron or metal.

he·rrén m. *(foraje)* cattle fodder; *(herrenal)* fodder field *or* pasture.

he·rre·rí·a f. *(fábrica)* ironworks, foundry; *(taller)* smithy, blacksmith's shop; *(oficio)* blacksmithing; FIG. *(ruido)* uproar, din.

he·rre·ro m. *(forjador)* blacksmith, smith; CHILE, P. RICO horseshoer.

he·rre·te m. *(cabo)* metal tag *or* tip; AMER. branding iron.

he·rrín m. rust.

he·rrum·brar tr. to rust.

he·rrum·bre f. *(orín)* rust; *(sabor)* iron taste; BOT. rust, mildew.

he·rrum·bro·so, –sa adj. rusty, rusted.

hertz or **hert·zio** m. PHYS. hertz.

her·vi·de·ro m. PHYS. boiling, ebullition; FIG. (manantial) bubbling spring; (muchedumbre) crowd, swarm.

her·vi·do I. past part. of **hervir** II. m. AMER., CUL. stew.

her·vi·dor m. (utensilio) kettle, boiler; TECH. heating tube or chamber.

her·vir §65 intr. PHYS. to boil, bubble; MARIT., FIG. to surge, become rough (the sea); (excitarse las pasiones) to boil or burn (with emotion) ♦ **h. a fuego lento** to simmer • **h. de** or **en** to seethe or swarm with <hervía de cólera she was seething with anger>; to be consumed with (passion).

her·vor m. PHYS. boiling, ebullition; FIG. (fogosidad) fervor, ardor ♦ **alzar** or **levantar el h.** to come to a boil • **h. de la sangre** MED. skin rash.

her·vo·ro·so, –sa adj. (hirviente) boiling, seething; FIG. (fogoso) fiery, ardent.

he·si·ta·ción f. hesitation, doubt.

he·si·tar intr. to hesitate, doubt.

he·te·ra or **he·tai·ra** f. (cortesana) hetaera (ancient Greek courtesan); FIG. (prostituta) prostitute.

he·te·ro·do·xia f. heterodoxy.

he·te·ro·do·xo, –xa I. adj. heterodox, unorthodox II. m.f. heterodox person.

he·te·ro·ga·mia f. BIOL. heterogamy.

he·te·ró·ga·mo, –ma adj. BIOL., BOT. heterogamous.

he·te·ro·ge·nei·dad f. (calidad de heterogéneo) heterogeneity, heterogeneousness; (mezcla) diversity, variety.

he·te·ro·gé·ne·o, –a adj. (de naturaleza diversa) heterogeneous; FIG. (diferente) dissimilar, different.

he·te·ró·ni·ma f. GRAM. heteronym.

he·te·ro·se·xual adj. & m.f. heterosexual.

he·te·ro·sis f. BIOL. heterosis.

hé·ti·co, –ca I. adj. MED. consumptive, hectic; FIG. (flaco) skinny, emaciated II. m.f. MED. consumptive, person with tuberculosis.

heu·rís·ti·co, –ca I. adj. heuristic, heuristical II. f. heuristics.

he·xa·cor·do m. MUS. (sistema) hexachord; (intervalo) sixth (interval); (lira) lyre of six notes ♦ **h. mayor** MUS. major sixth • **h. menor** MUS. minor sixth.

he·xa·e·dro m. GEOM. hexahedron ♦ **h. regular** cube.

he·xa·go·nal adj. GEOM. hexagonal, six-sided.

he·xá·go·no, –na GEOM. I. adj. hexagonal II. m. hexagon.

he·xá·me·tro, –tra POET. I. adj. hexametrical II. m. hexameter.

he·xa·sí·la·bo, –ba I. adj. PHONET., POET. hexasyllabic, six-syllabled II. m. POET. hexasyllabic verse.

hez f. [pl. **heces**] (poso de licor) lees, sediment; FIG. (cosa vil) scum, dregs ♦ **heces** excrement, feces.

hia·lo·gra·fí·a f. ARTS hyalography.

hia·lo·tec·nia or **hia·lur·gia** f. art of glassmaking.

hia·to m. PHONET., POET. hiatus.

hi·ber·na·ción f. hibernation.

hi·ber·nar intr. ZOOL. to hibernate.

hi·ber·nés, –ne·sa or **hi·bér·ni·co, –ca** adj. & m.f. Hibernian, Irish.

hi·bis·co m. BOT. hibiscus.

hi·bri·da·ción f. hybridization.

hi·bri·dez f. [pl. **-de·ces**] or **hi·bri·dis·mo** m. hybridism, hybridity.

hí·bri·do, –da adj. & m.f. hybrid.

hi·cie·ra, hice see **hacer**.

hi·co m. AMER. clew (cord for suspending a hammock).

hi·dal·ga·men·te adv. nobly, magnanimously.

hi·dal·go, –ga I. adj. (relativo a un noble) noble, of noble blood; FIG. (generoso) noble, magnanimous II. m.f. (noble) noble, person of noble descent —m. NUMIS., MEX. gold piece (equal to ten pesos).

hi·dal·guez or **hi·dal·guí·a** f. (nobleza) nobility; FIG. (generosidad) generosity, magnanimity.

hi·dra f. ZOOL. (pólipo) hydra, freshwater polyp; (culebra) poisonous aquatic snake; FIG. (peligro) hydra, recurring danger ♦ **Hidra** MYTH. Hydra.

hi·dra·ta·ción f. hydration.

hi·dra·ta·do, –da CHEM. I. past part. see **hidratar** II. adj. hydrate, hydrated.

hi·dra·tan·te adj. moisturizing <crema h. moisturizing cream>.

hi·dra·tar tr. CHEM. to hydrate.

hi·dra·to m. CHEM. hydrate ♦ **h. amónico** CHEM. ammonium hydroxide • **h. de calcio** CHEM. calcium hydrate • **h. de carbono** carbohydrate.

hi·dráu·li·ca f. hydraulics.

hi·dria f. hydria (water jug).

hí·dri·co, –ca adj. CHEM. hydric; MED. water <dieta h. water diet>.

hi·dro·a·vión m. hydroplane.

hi·dro·car·bu·ro m. hydrocarbon.

hi·dro·ce·fa·lia f. hydrocephalus, hydrocephaly.

hi·dro·cé·fa·lo, –la adj. hydrocephalous.

hi·dro·di·ná·mi·ca f. PHYS. hydrodynamics.

hi·dro·e·léc·tri·co, –ca adj. hydroelectric.

hi·dró·fi·lo, –la I. adj. absorbent; CHEM. hydrophile; BOT. hydrophilous II. m. ENTOM. hydrophilid.

hi·dro·fo·bia f. MED. hydrophobia, rabies.

hi·dró·fo·bo, –ba I. adj. hydrophobic II. m.f. hydrophobe.

hi·dro·ge·na·ción f. hydrogenation.

hi·dro·ge·na·do, –da I. past part. see **hidrogenar** II. adj. hydrogenous, hydrogenated.

hi·dro·ge·nar tr. to hydrogenate.

hi·dró·ge·no m. CHEM. hydrogen.

hi·dro·gra·fí·a f. hydrography.

hi·dró·li·sis f. hydrolysis.

hi·dro·li·zar §04 tr. & intr. CHEM. to hydrolyze.

hi·dro·lo·gí·a f. hydrology.

hi·dro·ló·gi·co, –ca adj. hydrologic, hydrological.

hi·dró·lo·go, –ga I. adj. hydrologic II. m.f. hydrologist.

hi·dro·me·cá·ni·ca f. PHYS. hydromechanics.

hi·dro·me·trí·a f. hydrometry.

hi·dró·me·tro m. hydrometer.

hi·dro·neu·má·ti·co, –ca adj. hydropneumatic.

hi·dro·pe·sí·a f. MED. dropsy, hydrops.

hi·dró·pi·co, –ca I. adj. MED. dropsical, hydropic; (sediento) extremely thirsty II. m.f. MED. person suffering from dropsy.

hi·dro·pla·no m. MARIT. hydrofoil; AVIA. seaplane.

hi·dro·po·ní·a f. AGR. hydroponics.

hi·dros·fe·ra f. GEOL. hydrosphere.

hi·dro·so·lu·ble adj. water-soluble.

hi·dros·tá·ti·ca f. PHYS. hydrostatics.

hi·dro·tec·nia f. hydraulic engineering.

hi·dro·te·ra·pia f. MED. hydrotherapy.

hi·dro·ter·mal adj. GEOL. hydrothermal.

hi·dro·tro·pis·mo m. BIOL. hydrotropism.

hi·dró·xi·do m. CHEM. hydroxide.

hie·da, hiedo see **heder**.

hie·dra f. BOT. ivy.

hiel f. ANAT., MED. bile, gall; FIG. (amargura) bitterness, gall ♦ **echar la h.** FIG., COLL. to sweat blood, work hard • **hieles** sorrows, troubles.

hie·le, hielo see **helar**.

hie·le·ra f. ECUAD. refrigerator; GUAT. cooler, cooling jar.

hie·lo m. (agua congelada) ice; (helamiento) freezing; FIG. (frialdad) coldness, indifference ♦ **estar hecho un h.** to be freezing cold • **ser más frío que el h.** or **ser como un pedazo de h.** FIG. to be cold as ice.

hie·ma·ción f. (pasar el invierno) wintering; BOT. winter blooming.

hie·na f. ZOOL. hyena; FIG. (persona feroz) beast, brute.

hien·da, hiendo see **hender** or **hendir**.

hie·ra, hiero see **herir**.

hie·rá·ti·ca·men·te adv. hieratically.

hie·rá·ti·co, –ca adj. RELIG. hieratic, sacred; FIG. (estirado) solemn.

hie·ra·tis·mo m. hieratic attitude.

hier·ba f. BOT. grass; herb <hierbas medicinales medicinal herbs>; COLL. (droga) grass, marijuana ♦ **comer su trigo en h.** FIG. to spend money before it is earned, live beyond one's means • **en h.** (verde) green, unripe; FIG. (en potencia) budding, incipient • **h. mate** or **del Paraguay** maté • **hierbas** (años) years <este potro tiene dos hierbas this horse is two years old>; (pastos) pasture, pasturage • **hierbas marinas** algae • **mala h.** BOT. weed; FIG. (muchacho) troublemaker, bad seed • **y otras hierbas** and others, and so forth.

hier·ba·bue·na f. BOT. mint.

hier·bal m. CHILE var. of **herbazal**.

hie·ro·glí·fi·co, –ca adj. & m.f. var. of **Jeroglífico**.

hie·rre, hierro see **herrar**.

hie·rro m. CHEM. iron; (marca) brand; (punta) iron tip, point; FIG. (arma) weapon; CUBA plowing ♦ **de h.** FIG. of iron • **h. colado** or **fundido** cast iron • **h. dulce** soft iron • **h. forjado** wrought iron • **h. galvanizado** galvanized iron • **hierros** irons, shackles.

hier·va, hiervo see **hervir**.

hi·ga f. (amuleto) fist-shaped amulet; (gesto) nose-thumbing; FIG. (desprecio) mockery, derision ♦ **dar una h. a alguien** to thumb one's nose at or make fun of someone • **no dar dos higas por** not to give a damn or two cents about.

hí·ga·do I. m. ANAT. liver ♦ **echar los hígados** FIG., COLL. to break one's back (working) • **hasta los hígados** COLL. with heart and soul • **hígados** FIG., COLL. guts <ese boxeador tiene hígados that boxer has guts> II. adj. C. AMER., CUBA annoying, bothersome.

hi·gie·ne f. hygiene ♦ **h. pública** public hygiene.

hi·gié·ni·ca·men·te adv. hygienically.

hi·gié·ni·co, –ca adj. hygienic.

hi·gie·ni·zar §04 tr. to sanitize, make hygienic.

hi·go m. BOT. fig ♦ **de higos a brevas** FIG. once in a while, once in a blue moon • **h. chumbo** or **de pala** or **de tuna** prickly pear (fruit) • **no dársele a uno un h. de** COLL. not to care a fig or give a damn about.

hi·gró·me·tro m. hygrometer.

hi·gros·có·pi·co, –ca adj. hygroscopic.

hi·gue·ra f. BOT. fig tree ♦ **estar en la h.** FIG., COLL. to be in another world • **h. chumba** or **de Indias** or **de pala** prickly pear • **h. infernal** castor-oil plant.

hi·jas·tro, –tra m.f. stepchild —m. stepson —f. stepdaughter.

hi·jo, –ja m. (niño) son; FIG. (obra) brain child, creation; junior <Mateo Eliseo, h. Matthew Eliseo, junior> ♦ **cada h. de vecino** COLL. every mother's son • **H. de Dios** RELIG. Son of God • **H. del Hombre** RELIG. Son of Man • **h. de puta** VULG. son of a bitch • **h. de su padre** FIG. his father's son • **h. político** son-in-law —f. (niña) daughter ♦ **h. de su madre** FIG. her mother's daughter • **h. política** daughter-in-law; —m.f. (niño) child; (nativo) native <h. de Santiago native of Santiago>; (descendiente) descendant; (querido) dear <sigue este aviso, h. mía follow this advice, my dear> ♦ **h. adoptivo** adopted child • **h. bastardo** or **natural** illegitimate child • **h. de familia** minor • **h. de la cuna** foundling • **h. de leche** foster child • **h. dotado** gifted child • **h. legítimo** or **de bendición** legitimate child • **hijos** children <ella tiene cinco hijos she has five children>; (descendientes) descendants.

hi·jue·la f. SEW. (añadido de un vestido) widening strip or gore (for a dress); (colchón) small mattress; (acequia) small irrigation ditch; (camino) branch (of a road); (correo) rural postal service; RELIG. pall (for covering a chalice); LAW (documento) schedule, inventory (of an inheritance); (bienes) estate; BOT. palm seed; CHILE, PERU subdivision of an estate.

hi·jue·lar tr. CHILE (dividir un fondo) to divide land into parcels; (dar herencia) to give (an heir) his portion of an estate.

hi·la f. (fila) line, row; (acción de hilar) spinning; (tripa delgada) thin gut ♦ **a la h.** single file • **h. de agua** irrigation ditch • **hilas** lint (for dressing wounds).

hi·la·cha f. or **hi·la·cho** m. raveled thread.

hi·la·chen·to, –ta adj. AMER. ragged, tattered.

hi·la·cho·so, –sa adj. ragged, frayed.

hi·la·da f. (hilera) row, line; ARCHIT. course.

hi·la·di·llo m. TEX. (hilo de seda) floss silk; (cinta) narrow ribbon or tape.

hi·la·do m. (acción de hilar) spinning; (hilo) yarn, thread.

hi·la·dor, –do·ra m.f. spinner.

hi·lan·de·rí·a f. (arte de hilar) spinning; (fábrica) spinning mill.

hi·lar tr. (reducir a hilo) to spin; ENTOM. to spin (insects);

FIG. (cavilar) to ponder, consider ♦ **h. delgado** or **muy fino** FIG., COLL. to split hairs.

hi·la·ran·te adj. hilarious, uproarious.

hi·la·ri·dad f. hilarity, laughter.

hi·la·tu·ra f. spinning.

hi·le·ra f. (línea recta) row, file; (hilo) thread, filament; METAL. drawplate, wiredrawer; ARCHIT. ridgepole ♦ **hileras** ZOOL. spinneret.

hi·le·ro m. eddy, current.

hi·lo m. TEX. (hebra) thread; (filamento) filament, fiber; (alambre) fine wire; (tejido) linen; (filo) edge <el h. de una navaja the edge of a knife>; (colgajo) bunch, string <h. de uvas bunch of grapes>; ZOOL. hilum; FIG. (chorro) trickle, thin stream <un h. de sangre a trickle of blood>; (continuación) thread <perdí el h. de la conversación I lost the thread of the conversation> ♦ **a h.** uninterruptedly • **al h.** SEW. along the thread; FIG. (nervioso) on edge • **colgar de un h.** FIG. to hang by a thread • **cortar el h.** FIG. to interrupt • **de h.** straight, directly • **h. de bramante** twine • **h. de cajas** or **de monjas** fine thread • **h. de gallinero** chicken wire • **h. de la vida** FIG. course of life • **h. de perlas** string of pearls • **h. de tierra** ELEC. ground wire • **tener el alma en un h.** FIG. to have one's heart in one's throat, be on pins and needles.

hil·ván m. SEW. (costura a punto largo) basting, tacking; CHILE basting thread.

hil·va·na·do I. past part. see **hilvanar** II. m. SEW. basting, tacking.

hil·va·nar tr. SEW. to baste, tack; FIG., COLL. (hacer con prisa) to throw together, do hastily; FIG. (enlazar) to coordinate.

hi·men m. ANAT. hymen.

hi·me·ne·o m. POET. wedding, nuptials; LIT. epithalamium, wedding song.

ho·mí·ni·do m. ZOOL. hominid.

him·na·rio m. hymnal, hymnbook.

him·no m. hymn ♦ **h. nacional** national anthem.

hin m. whinny, neigh.

hin·ca·da f. AMER. sinking, driving; CHILE, P. RICO genuflection.

hin·ca·du·ra f. sinking, driving.

hin·ca·pié m. planting one's feet ♦ **hacer h. en** FIG., COLL. to insist on, stress.

hin·car §70 tr. (clavar) to sink, drive (in) <h. un clavo to drive a nail>; (apoyar) to brace, plant (against) <h. el pie en la pared to brace one's foot against the wall> ♦ **h. el pico** COLL. to die, kick the bucket —reflex. to sink into ♦ **hincarse de rodillas** to kneel down.

hin·co m. post, stake.

hin·cón m. MARIT. mooring post; (mojón) marker.

hin·cha f. COLL. hatred, enmity ♦ **tener h. a alguien** to have or hold a grudge against someone —m. COLL. fan, supporter.

hin·cha, hincho see **henchir**.

hin·cha·do, –da I. past part. see **hinchar** II. adj. (inflado) inflated, blown up; (lleno) full, filled up; MED. swollen; FIG. (vanidoso) vain, conceited; (pomposo) pompous, turgid (said of style) II. f. COLL. fan.

hin·char tr. (aumentar) to swell <la lluvia hinchó el río the rain swelled the river>; (inflar) to inflate, blow up; FIG. (exagerar) to inflate, exaggerate (a story); MED. to swell —reflex. MED. to swell; (comer) to fill or stuff oneself; FIG. (envanecerse) to become vain or conceited; COLL. (ganar dinero) to line one's pockets (with money) ♦ **hincharse las narices** FIG., COLL. to get one's dander up.

hin·cha·zón f. MED. swelling; FIG. (vanidad) vanity, conceit; (composidad) pomposity, turgidity (of style).

hin·di m. Hindi.

hin·dú adj. & m.f. [pl. **-dú·es**] GEOG. Indian; RELIG. Hindu.

hin·duis·mo m. RELIG. Hinduism.

hi·no·jo¹ m. BOT. fennel ♦ **h. marino** samphire, sea fennel.

hi·no·jo² m. ANAT. knee ♦ **de hinojos** on one's knees, kneeling.

hin·qué, hinque see **hincar**.

hi·ña, hiño see **heñir**.

hi·ñe·ra, hiñera see **heñir**.

hioi·des adj. & m. ANAT., ZOOL. hyoid.

hi·par intr. (tener hipo) to hiccup, have the hiccups; (resollar

los perros) to pant; *(fatigarse)* to wear *or* tire oneself out; *(gimotear)* to whimper, whine ♦ **h. por** FIG. to long *or* yearn to <*estoy hipando por volver allí* I long to return there> • **h. por algo** FIG. to long *or* yearn for something.
hi·pér·bo·la f. GEOM. hyperbola.
hi·pér·bo·le f. RHET. hyperbole.
hi·per·bó·li·ca·men·te adv. hyperbolically.
hi·per·bó·li·co, –ca adj. hyperbolic, hyperbolical.
hi·per·crí·ti·co, –ca I. adj. hypercritical **II.** m.f. hypercritic, severe critic.
hi·pe·res·te·sia f. MED. hyperesthesia.
hi·per·gli·ce·mia *or* **hi·per·glu·ce·mia** f. MED. hyperglycemia.
hi·pe·ri·rri·ta·ble adj. MED. hyperirritable.
hi·per·me·trí·a f. POET. enjambment.
hi·per·me·tro·pí·a f. OPHTHAL. hypermetropy, farsightedness.
hi·per·sen·si·ble adj. hypersensitive.
hi·per·se·xual adj. hypersexual.
hi·per·só·ni·co, –ca adj. hypersonic.
hi·per·ten·sión f. MED. hypertension, high blood pressure.
hi·per·ten·so, –sa adj. MED. hypertensive.
hi·per·ter·mia f. MED. hyperthermia.
hi·per·tro·fia f. MED. hypertrophy.
hi·per·tro·fiar tr. & reflex. MED. to hypertrophy.
hi·per·ven·ti·la·ción f. MED. hyperventilation.
hi·per·vi·ta·mi·no·sis f. MED. hypervitaminosis.
hí·pi·co, –ca adj. horse, equine ♦ **concurso h.** horse show.
hi·pi·do m. whimper, whine.
hi·pis·mo m. horse racing.
hip·no·sis f. MED. hypnosis.
hip·no·te·ra·pia f. MED. hypnotherapy.
hip·no·ti·cé, hipnotice see hipnotizar.
hip·nó·ti·co, –ca adj. & m. hypnotic.
hip·no·tis·mo m. hypnotism.
hip·no·ti·za·ble adj. hypnotizable.
hip·no·ti·za·ción f. hypnotization.
hip·no·ti·za·dor, –do·ra I. adj. hypnotizing **II.** m.f. hypnotist, hypnotizer.
hip·no·ti·zar §04 tr. to hypnotize.
hi·po m. MED. hiccup; FIG. *(ansia)* yearning, longing; *(odio)* grudge, aversion ♦ **quitar el h.** COLL. to astonish, take by surprise • **tener h.** to have (the) hiccups • **tener h. con** *or* **contra** FIG. to have *or* hold a grudge against • **tener h. por** FIG. to yearn for.
hi·po·cen·tro m. GEOL. hypocenter.
hi·po·con·drí·a f. MED. hypochondria.
hi·po·con·dria·co, –ca *or* **hi·po·con·drí·a·co, –ca** MED. **I.** adj. hypochondriac, hypochondriacal **II.** m.f. hypochondriac.
hi·po·con·drio m. ANAT. hypochondrium.
hi·po·crá·ti·co, –ca adj. Hippocratic.
hi·po·cre·sí·a f. hypocrisy.
hi·pó·cri·ta I. adj. hypocritical **II.** m.f. hypocrite.
hi·pó·cri·ta·men·te adv. hypocritically.
hi·po·dér·mi·co, –ca adj. hypodermic ♦ **aguja h.** hypodermic needle.
hi·pó·dro·mo m. racetrack, hippodrome.
hi·po·gli·ce·mia *or* **hi·po·glu·ce·mia** f. MED. hypoglycemia.
hi·po·lo·gí·a f. study of *or* knowledge about horses.
hi·po·pó·ta·mo m. ZOOL. hippopotamus.
hi·po·se·cre·ción f. MED. hyposecretion.
hi·po·so, –sa adj. hiccuping, having hiccups.
hi·pós·ta·sis f. hypostasis.
hi·pos·tá·ti·co, –ca adj. hypostatic.
hi·po·sul·fi·to m. CHEM. hyposulfite.
hi·po·tá·la·mo m. ANAT. hypothalamus.
hi·po·ta·xis f. [pl. **-sis**] GRAM. hypotaxis.
hi·po·te·ca f. mortgage.
hi·po·te·ca·ble adj. mortgageable.
hi·po·te·car §70 tr. to mortgage; FIG. *(comprometer)* to compromise, place in danger <*h. su porvenir* to compromise one's future>.
hi·po·te·ca·rio, –ria adj. FIN. mortgage, hypothecary.
hi·po·ten·sión f. MED. hypotension, low blood pressure.
hi·po·te·nu·sa f. GEOM. hypotenuse.
hi·po·ter·mia f. MED. hypothermia.

hi·pó·te·sis f. [pl. **-sis**] hypothesis.
hi·po·té·ti·ca·men·te adv. hypothetically.
hi·po·té·ti·co, –ca adj. hypothetical.
hi·po·ti·roi·dis·mo m. MED. hypothyroidism.
hi·po·tro·fia f. MED. hypotrophy.
hi·rien·te adj. *(que hiere)* offensive, dangerous (weapon); FIG. *(mordaz)* wounding, cutting (remark).
hi·rie·ra, hirió see herir.
hir·su·to, –ta adj. *(peludo)* hirsute, hairy; *(erizado)* coarse, bristly; FIG. *(brusco)* gruff, rough.
hir·vien·te adj. boiling.
hir·vie·ra, hirvió see hervir.
hi·so·pe·ar tr. RELIG. to sprinkle with holy water.
hi·so·pi·llo m. MED. mouth swab; BOT. winter savory.
his·pá·ni·co, –ca adj. & m.f. Hispanic.
his·pa·ni·dad f. *(cualidad)* Spanishness; *(mundo español)* the Spanish-speaking world ♦ **Día de la H.** Columbus Day.
his·pa·nis·mo m. LING. Hispanicism; *(afición)* interest in *or* love of Spain.
his·pa·nis·ta m.f. EDUC. Hispanist, Hispanicist.
his·pa·no, –na adj. & m.f. Hispanic.
His·pa·no·a·mé·ri·ca f. Spanish *or* Latin America.
his·pa·no·a·me·ri·ca·nis·mo m. Spanish Americanism.
his·pa·no·a·me·ri·ca·nis·ta adj. & m.f. Spanish Americanist.
his·pa·no·a·me·ri·ca·no, –na adj. & m.f. Spanish American.
his·pa·nó·fi·lo, –la I. adj. Hispanophilic **II.** m.f. Hispanophile.
his·pa·no·fo·bia f. Hispanophobia.
his·pa·no·ha·blan·te I. adj. Spanish-speaking **II.** m.f. Spanish-speaking person, Hispanophone.
his·ta·mi·na f. BIOL. histamine.
his·te·rec·to·mí·a f. SURG. hysterectomy.
his·te·ria f. MED. hysteria.
his·té·ri·co, –ca I. adj. *(uterino)* uterine; *(relativo al histerismo)* hysteric, hysterical **II.** m. *(histerismo)* hysteria —m.f. *(persona)* hysteric, hysterical person.
his·te·ris·mo m. MED. hysteria.
his·to·lo·gí·a f. BIOL. histology.
his·tó·lo·go, –ga m. histologist.
his·to·ria f. history; FIG. *(cuento)* story, tale; *(chisme)* gossip, tale <*no me vengas con historias* don't come to me with gossip>; PAINT. history piece, historical painting ♦ **dejarse de historias** to get to the point • **h. antigua** HIST. ancient history • **h. natural** BIOL. natural history • **pasar a la h.** to go down in history.
his·to·ria·do, –da adj. gaudy, ornate; ARTS storied <*un tapiz h.* a storied tapestry>.
his·to·ria·dor, –do·ra m.f. historian.
his·to·rial I. adj. historic, historical **II.** m. *(archivo)* file, dossier; *(reseña personal)* résumé, curriculum vitae.
his·to·riar tr. *(contar)* to tell the story of, narrate; *(escribir)* to chronicle, write the history of; ARTS *(pintar)* to paint, depict (an historical episode); AMER., FIG. to mix up, confuse.
his·tó·ri·ca·men·te adv. historically.
his·to·ri·ci·dad f. historicity.
his·to·ri·cis·mo m. PHILOS. historicism.
his·tó·ri·co, –ca adj. historic, historical.
his·to·rie·ta f. story, anecdote ♦ **historietas ilustradas** *or* **cómicas** comic strips.
his·to·rio·gra·fí·a f. historiography.
his·to·rió·gra·fo m. historiographer.
his·trión, –trio·ni·sa m.f. *(actor)* actor; *(bufón)* clown, mime; *(prestidigitador)* juggler, prestidigitator.
his·trio·nis·mo m. *(oficio)* acting; *(mundo teatral)* theater world, acting profession; *(teatralidad)* histrionics, theatricality.
hi·to, –ta I. adj. *(inmediato)* adjoining (street or house); *(fijo)* fixed, firm **II.** m. *(señal delímite)* boundary marker; *(señal de distancia)* milestone; *(juego)* quoits; FIG. *(blanco)* bull's-eye, target ♦ **a h.** firmly, unwaveringly • **dar en el h.** to hit the nail on the head • **mirar de h. en h.** to stare at, fix one's eyes on.
hi·tón m. square headless nail.
hi·zo see hacer.
ho·ba·chón, –cho·na adj. COLL. fat and lazy.

hob·by m. hobby, pastime.

ho·cé, hoce see **hozar.**

ho·ci·car §70 tr. *(escarbar)* to nuzzle, root; FIG., COLL. *(besuquear)* to smooch —intr. *(golpearse)* to hit one's face (against); FIG., COLL. *(tropezar)* to run into (difficulties); COLL. *(darse por vencido)* to give up; MARIT. to pitch.

ho·ci·co m. ZOOL. muzzle, snout; FIG., COLL. *(boca)* mouth; *(cara)* kisser, puss; *(gesto)* pout, sour face ♦ **caer de hocicos** COLL. to fall flat on one's face • **dar de hocicos** to hit one's face (against something) • **estar de hocicos** SL. to be teed off (angered) • **meter el h. en todo** FIG., COLL. to stick one's nose into everything • **poner h.** COLL. to pout, put on a sour face.

ho·ci·cón, –co·na or **ho·ci·cu·do, –da** adj. ZOOL. big-snouted; COLL., DEROG. *(narigudo)* big-beaked.

ho·ci·qué, hocique see **hocicar.**

ho·ci·no m. TOP. *(angostura)* narrows; *(terreno en una quebrada)* dale.

ho·ci·que·ra f. CUBA, PERU muzzle.

hoc·key m. hockey ♦ **h. sobre hielo** ice hockey.

ho·ga·ño COLL. *(hoy en día)* these days, nowadays; *(en este año)* this year.

ho·gar m. *(de una chimenea)* hearth, fireplace; *(hoguera)* bonfire; FIG. *(casa)* home; *(vida familial)* home or family life.

ho·ga·re·ño, –ña adj. home-loving, domestic.

ho·ga·za f. *(pan grande)* large loaf of bread; *(pan grueso)* coarse bread.

ho·gue·ra f. bonfire.

ho·ja f. BOT. leaf <*este árbol tiene hojas aserradas* this tree has serrate leaves>; BOT. *(pétalo)* petal; *(lámina de papel)* sheet, leaf (of paper); *(lámina de metal)* sheet, foil; *(folio)* leaf, page (of a book); *(documento)* sheet, form; *(cuchilla)* blade <*h. de afeitar* razor blade>; *(parte de puerta)* leaf (of a door); *(parte de ventana)* pane, sheet (of glass); AGR. *(porción de tierra)* strip of fallow land; FIG. *(espada)* sword; *(periódico)* newspaper, sheet ♦ **batir h.** to work metal • **de h. caduca** BOT. deciduous • **de h. perenne** BOT. evergreen • **h. de aluminio** aluminum foil • **h. de estaño** tinfoil • **h. de lata** tin plate • **h. de parra** FIG. fig leaf • **h. de ruta** COM. waybill • **h. de servicios** service record • **h. de vida** résumé • **h. suelta** leaflet, handbill • **h. volante** leaflet, flier • **tener h.** NUMIS. to have a false ring • **volver la h.** *(hojear)* to turn the page; FIG. *(cambiar de tema)* to change the subject; *(empezar nueva vida)* to turn over a new leaf.

ho·ja·la·ta f. tin, tin plate.

ho·ja·la·te·rí·a f. tinsmith's shop.

ho·ja·la·te·ro m. tinsmith.

ho·jal·dra·do, –da adj. CUL. puff, flaky (pastry).

ho·jal·dre m.f. CUL. puff pastry.

ho·ja·ras·ca f. *(hojas secas)* dead or fallen leaves; *(frondosidad)* excessive foliage; FIG. *(cosas inútiles)* rubbish, trash <*lo que me dijo era h.* what he told me was rubbish>.

ho·je·ar tr. *(trashojar)* to skim or leaf (through); —intr. METAL. to peel, flake; *(susurrar)* to rustle (leaves).

ho·jo·so, –sa or **ho·ju·do, –da** adj. leafy.

ho·jue·la f. *(hoja pequeña)* leaflet, small leaf; *(masa frita)* pancake; CUBA, GUAT. puff pastry; *(hollejo de aceituna)* pressed olive skin; *(hoja de metal)* metal leaf or foil; BOT. leaflet, foliole.

¡ho·la! interj. hello!, hi!

ho·lan·da f. TEX. holland, Dutch linen.

Ho·lan·da f. Holland.

ho·lan·dés, –de·sa I. adj. Dutch II. m.f. Dutchman, Hollander —m. *(idioma)* Dutch ♦ **los holandeses** the Dutch.

hol·ga·da·men·te adv. *(con bienestar)* comfortably, easily; *(anchamente)* loosely, amply.

hol·ga·do, –da I. past part. see **holgar** II. adj. *(desocupado)* unemployed, idle; *(ancho)* big, loose (clothing); FIG. *(que vive con bienestar)* comfortable, well-off.

hol·gan·za f. *(descanso)* rest, leisure; *(ociosidad)* laziness, idleness; *(placer)* pleasure, enjoyment.

hol·gar §16 intr. *(descansar)* to rest, relax; *(no trabajar)* not to work, be out of work; *(estar ocioso)* to loaf, be idle; *(estar alegre)* to be happy or glad; *(ser inútil)* to be useless or unnecessary; *(no ajustar)* to be too big, not to fit

(clothes) ♦ **huelga decir que** needless to say • **¡huelgan los comentarios!** no comment. —reflex. *(divertirse)* to have a good time, enjoy (oneself); *(alegrarse)* to be pleased.

hol·ga·zán, –za·na I. adj. lazy, shiftless II. m.f. loafer, loiterer.

hol·ga·za·ne·ar intr. to loaf, be idle.

hol·ga·za·ne·rí·a f. laziness, indolence.

hol·go·rio m. COLL. boisterous merrymaking.

hol·gué see **holgar.**

hol·gu·ra f. *(regocijo)* amusement, enjoyment; *(anchura)* fullness, looseness; *(bienestar)* comfort, affluence <*vivir con h.* to live in comfort>; MECH. *(ajuste de piezas)* play, movement.

hol·mio m. CHEM. holmium.

ho·lo·caus·to m. *(sacrificio)* holocaust, burnt offering; *(víctima)* sacrifice, victim.

ho·lo·gra·fí·a f. holography.

ho·ló·gra·fo, –fa or **o·ló·gra·fo, –fa** I. m. holograph II. adj. holographical.

ho·lo·gra·ma m. hologram.

ho·lla·du·ra f. treading, trampling.

ho·llar §19 tr. *(pisar)* to tread or trample (on); FIG. *(humillar)* to trample on, humiliate.

ho·lle·jo m. BOT. skin, peel (of fruit).

ho·llín m. *(tizne)* soot; FIG. *(riña)* scuffle, row.

ho·lli·nar tr. CHILE to cover with soot.

ho·lli·nien·to, –ta adj. sooty.

hom·bra·da f. manly action.

hom·bre m. *(individuo)* man; *(humanidad)* man, mankind <*la guerra es un vicio del h.* war is a vice of mankind>; COLL. *(esposo)* husband, man; *(juego de naipes)* ombre ♦ **de h. a h.** man-to-man • **¡hombre!** what a surprise!, my goodness! • **¡h. al agua!** man overboard! • **h. bueno** LAW arbiter, referee • **h. de bien** honorable man • **h. de estado** statesman • **h. de letras** man of letters, scholar • **h. del momento** man of the hour • **h. de mar** seaman, sailor • **h. de mundo** man of experience • **h. de negocios** businessman • **h. de paja** FIG. straw man, front • **h. de palabra** man of his word • **h. de pelo en pecho** FIG., COLL. real man • **h. de pro** or **de provecho** worthy man • **h. rana** frogman • **pobre h.** wretch, poor devil • **ser muy h.** to be a real man.

hom·bre·ar[1] intr. COLL. *(echárselas de hombre)* to act in a manly way (said of boys); *(querer igualarse)* to strive to equal; MEX. to work in masculine occupations (said of women) —tr. COL., MEX. to protect, help —reflex. to strive to equal.

hom·bre·ar[2] intr. to push with the shoulders.

hom·bre·ci·llo m. BOT. hop.

hom·bre·ra f. ARM. pauldron, shoulder plate (of armor); *(adorno)* epaulet, epaulette; SEW. shoulder pad.

hom·brí·a f. manliness ♦ **h. de bien** integrity, honesty.

hom·bri·llo m. SEW. yoke (of a shirt).

hom·bro m. ANAT. shoulder <*a hombros* piggyback <*llevé mi hermana a hombros* I carried my sister piggyback> • **arrimar el h.** FIG. *(trabajar)* to put one's shoulder to the wheel; *(ayudar)* to lend a hand • **echar el h.** FIG. to shoulder, take on (responsibility) • **encogerse de hombros** to shrug • **mirar a uno por encima del h.** FIG. to look down on someone • **sobre los hombros** on one's shoulders <*llevaba el bulto sombre los hombros* he carried the package on his shoulders>.

hom·bru·no, –na adj. COLL. manly, masculine <*mujer h.* mannish woman>.

ho·me·na·je m. *(juramento de fidelidad)* homage; *(respeto)* homage, respect; *(acto)* homage, tribute; CHILE gift, favor.

ho·me·na·je·a·do, –da m.f. person to whom homage is paid.

ho·me·na·je·ar tr. to pay homage to.

ho·me·ó·pa·ta I. adj. homeopathic II. m.f. homeopath.

ho·me·o·pa·tí·a f. homeopathy.

ho·me·o·pá·ti·co, –ca adj. homeopathic.

ho·mé·ri·co, –ca adj. Homeric.

ho·mi·ci·da I. adj. homicidal, murderous II. m.f. homicide, murderer.

ho·mi·ci·dio m. homicide, murder.

ho·mi·lí·a f. homily, sermon.

ho·mo m. ANTHR. Homo.
ho·mo·cro·má·ti·co, –ca adj. homochromatic.
ho·mo·e·ro·tis·mo m. homoeroticism, homoerotism.
ho·mo·fi·lia f. homophilia.
ho·mo·fo·ní·a f. MUS., PHONET. homophony.
ho·mó·ga·mo, –ma adj. BOT. homogamous.
ho·mo·ge·nei·dad f. homogeneity.
ho·mo·ge·nei·za·ción f. homogenization.
ho·mo·ge·nei·zar §04 tr. to homogenize.
ho·mo·gé·ne·o, –a adj. homogeneous.
ho·mo·lo·ga·ción f. LAW homologation, confirmation.
ho·mo·lo·gar §47 tr. LAW to homologate, confirm.
ho·mó·lo·go, –ga adj. BIOL., MATH. homologous.
ho·mo·mor·fo, –fa adj. BIOL., BOT. homomorphic, homomorphous.
ho·mo·ni·mia f. homonymy.
ho·mó·ni·mo, –ma I. adj. homonymous **II.** m.f. LING. homonym; (tocayo) namesake.
ho·mo·se·xual adj. & m.f. homosexual.
ho·mo·se·xua·li·dad f. homosexuality.
ho·mún·cu·lo m. homunculus, dwarf.
hon·da I. sling, slingshot **II.** adj. see hondo, –da.
hon·da·men·te adv. (con hondura) deeply; FIG. (profundamente) deeply, profoundly.
hon·da·zo m. shot from a sling.
hon·de·ar tr. MARIT. (sondar) to sound; (desembarcar) to unload a ship.
hon·de·ro m. slinger, person armed with a slingshot.
hon·do, –da I. adj. (profundo) deep <un hoyo h. a deep hole>; (bajo) low; FIG. (intenso) deep, intense <sentí un odio muy h. I felt an intense hatred>; (recóndito) deep, innermost **II.** m. bottom ♦ **de h.** deep, in depth <el pozo tiene cuatro metros de h. the well is four meters deep> —f. see honda.
hon·dón m. (fondo) bottom; (valle) hollow, glen; (ojo de aguja) eye (of a needle).
hon·do·na·da f. ravine, gorge.
hon·du·ra f. depth, profundity ♦ **meterse en honduras** FIG. to get in over one's depth.
Hon·du·ras m. Honduras.
hon·du·re·ño, –na adj. & m.f. Honduran.
ho·nes·ta·men·te adv. (honradamente) honestly, honorably; (decorosamente) decently, decorously; (pudorosamente) modestly.
ho·nes·tar tr. (honrar) to honor, pay respect to; (cohonestar) to gloss over, make excuses for.
ho·nes·ti·dad f. (honradez) honesty, uprightness; (decoro) decency, decorum; (pudor) modesty, reserve; (urbanidad) urbanity, civility.
ho·nes·to, –ta adj. (honrado) honorable, upright; (decoroso) decent, decorous; (pudoroso) modest, virtuous; (razonable) fair, reasonable.
hon·go m. BOT. mushroom; MED. fungus; (sombrero) derby, bowler (hat) ♦ **h. marino** ZOOL. sea anemone • **h. yesguero** BOT. tinder fungus.
ho·nor m. (virtud) honor, integrity; (recato) virtue, chastity; (buena reputación) (good) reputation, prestige; (celebridad) fame, glory ♦ **hacer h. a** to honor • **hacer los honores a** FIG. to do justice to (a meal) • **hacer los honores (de la casa)** to serve (food), do the honors • **honores** (cargo) rank, honors; (título honorario) honorary rank or privilege <tener honores de presidente to be an honorary chairman> • **honores militares** military honors • **tener el h. de** to have the honor of.
ho·no·ra·bi·li·dad f. honorableness, honor.
ho·no·ra·ble adj. honorable.
ho·no·ra·ble·men·te adv. honorably.
ho·no·rar tr. var. of honrar.
ho·no·ra·rio, –ria I. adj. honorary **II.** m. honorarium ♦ **honorarios** fees, emoluments.
ho·no·rí·fi·ca·men·te adv. honorifically.
ho·no·rí·fi·co, –ca adj. (que da honor) honorific <título h. honorific title>; (no oficial) honorary, honorific.
hon·ra f. (estima de la dignidad propia) honor, self-respect; (buena fama) good name, reputation; (pudor) virtue, chastity ♦ **honras** last respects (funeral).
hon·ra·da·men·te adv. honestly, honorably.
hon·ra·dez f. honesty, integrity.

hon·ra·do, –da adj. honest, honorable.
hon·ra·dor, –do·ra I. adj. honoring **II.** m.f. honorer.
hon·rar tr. to honor, respect.
hon·ro·sa·men·te adv. honorably, with integrity.
hon·ro·so, –sa adj. (que da honra) honorable; (decente) decent, proper.
ho·pe·ar intr. (menear la cola) to wag the tail; FIG. (corretear) to run or chase around; VEN. to cry out.
ho·po I. m. (cola) bushy tail; (copete) tuft or shock of hair; (tupé) toupee **II.** interj. COLL. get out! scram!
ho·ra I. f. hour <media h. half an hour>; (momento) time <es h. de cenar it is time for supper>; (legua) league (unit of distance); ASTRON. hour ♦ **a buena h.** in good time, opportunely • **a la h.** on time, punctually • **a primera h.** first thing in the morning • **¿a qué h.?** at what time?, when? • **a todas horas** at all hours • **a última h.** at the last minute; (por la noche) last thing at night • **dar h.** to make an appointment • **dar la h.** to strike <el reloj dio la h. the clock struck> • **de última h.** last-minute • **en h. buena** fortunately • **en h. mala** unfortunately • **h. de comer** mealtime • **h. H** MIL. H hour • **h. legal** standard time • **h. punta** rush hour; ELEC. peak hour • **horas** RELIG. book of hours • **horas canónicas** RELIG. canonical hours • **horas de oficina** office or business hours • **horas extraordinarias** overtime • **horas libres** free time • **horas muertas** wasted time • **la última h.** FIG. time, end, death • **pedir h.** to request an appointment • **poner en hora** to set (a watch or clock) • **por h.** per hour, by the hour • **por horas** by the hours • **¿qué h. es?** what time is it? • **tener las horas contadas** FIG. to be at death's door **II.** adv. now.
ho·ra·da·dor, –do·ra I. adj. drilling, boring **II.** m. (máquina) drill —m.f. (persona) driller.
ho·ra·dar tr. to drill, bore.
ho·ra·do m. (agujero) bore or drill hole; (caverna) cavern, grotto.
ho·ra·rio, –ria I. adj. hourly, horary **II.** m. (mano del reloj) hour hand; (reloj) clock, watch; RAIL. schedule, timetable <h. de los trenes train schedule>; (repartición de tiempo) schedule.
hor·ca f. (aparato de suplicio) gallows, gibbet; AGR. hayfork, pitchfork; (ristra) string (of onions, garlic); P. RICO, VEN., COLL. gift, present ♦ **pasar por las horcas caudinas** FIG. to suffer humiliation.
hor·ca·du·ra f. fork, crotch (of tree trunk).
hor·ca·ja·das ♦ a h. astride, straddling.
hor·ca·jo m. (yugo) yoke, harness (for mules); (confluencia) fork (of rivers); (unión de montañas) junction (of mountains).
hor·car §70 tr. MEX. var. of ahorcar.
hor·co m. string of onions or garlic.
hor·cón m. AGR. (horca) pitchfork; (apoyo) forked pole supporting tree branches; AMER. wooden column supporting ceiling beams.
hor·cha·ta f. orgeat (almond syrup).
hor·da f. horde.
ho·re·ro m. AMER. hour hand (of a clock).
ho·ri·zon·tal adj. & f. horizontal.
ho·ri·zon·tal·men·te adv. horizontally.
ho·ri·zon·te m. (línea) horizon; FIG. (perspectiva) horizon, outlook <ampliar los horizontes to broaden one's horizons>.
hor·ma f. (forma) form, mold; (de zapatero) (shoemaker's) last; (ballesta para zapatos) shoetree; (de sombrero) hat block; CONSTR. dry wall; CUBA, PERU cake mold ♦ **hallar la h. de su zapato** to get what's coming to one.
hor·mi·ga f. ENTOM. ant; MED. formication, itch ♦ **ser una h.** to be industrious or hard-working.
hor·mi·gón m. concrete ♦ **h. armado** reinforced concrete • **h. hidráulico** hydraulic lime mortar • **h. precomprimido** or **pretensado** prestressed concrete.
hor·mi·go·ne·ra f. cement or concrete mixer.
hor·mi·gue·ar intr. (fusanear) to tingle, have pins and needles; FIG. (bullir) to swarm, teem.
hor·mi·gue·o m. (multitud) swarm, throng; (sensación cutánea) tingling, pins and needles.
hor·mi·gue·ro m. ENTOM. anthill; ORNITH. wryneck; FIG. (lugar poblado) anthill, hub of activity; AGR. dried plants burned for fertilizer; AMER., VET. disease of horses.

hor·mi·gui·lla f. COLL. *(picazón)* pins and needles, tingling sensation; FIG., COLL. *(remordimiento)* guilty conscience, remorse.

hor·mi·gui·llo m. VET. founder; *(línea de personas)* human chain; *(picazón)* tingling sensation; AMER., MIN. amalgamation of silver ♦ **parecer tener h.** FIG., COLL. to be jumpy, have ants in one's pants.

hor·mi·gui·ta f. FIG., COLL. industrious *or* diligent person.

hor·mo·na f. PHYSIOL. hormone.

hor·mo·nal adj. PHYSIOL. hormonal.

hor·na·ci·na f. ARCHIT. vaulted niche.

hor·na·chue·la f. hut, hovel.

hor·na·da f. CUL. batch (of baked goods); FIG. *(serie)* group (of people).

hor·na·gue·ar tr. to dig for coal.

hor·na·gue·ro, -ra I. adj. *(amplio)* ample, wide; MIN. coal-bearing II. f. MIN. coal.

hor·na·lla f. PERU large oven; VEN. hearth.

hor·na·za f. MIN. silversmith's furnace; CERAM. yellow glazing.

hor·ne·ar intr. & tr. to bake.

hor·ne·ro, -ra m.f. baker.

hor·ni·lla f. burner <*cocina de cuatro hornillas* four-burner stove>; ORNITH. pigeonhole.

hor·ni·llo m. *(cocina)* stove; MIN. blasthole; MIL. fougasse (land mine) ♦ **h. de atanor** athanor (alchemist's furnace).

hor·no m. CUL. oven <*h. de panadero* baker's oven>; TECH. furnace <*alto h.* blast furnace>; CERAM. kiln; FIG. *(sitio caliente)* oven <*este cuarto es un h.* this room is an oven> ♦ **h. reverbero** TECH. reverberatory furnace • **no está el h. para bollos** FIG., COLL. the time is not ripe.

ho·rós·co·po m. ASTROL. horoscope.

hor·qué, horque see **horcar.**

hor·que·ta f. AGR. pitchfork; *(del árbol)* fork, crotch (of a tree); AMER. fork (in a road); CHILE winnowing fork; ARG. bend (of a river).

hor·qui·lla f. AGR. pitchfork; *(sostén)* forked stake (used as a support); *(alfiler doblado)* hairpin, hair clip; *(de una bicicleta)* fork (of a bicycle).

ho·rren·do, -da adj. horrendous, hideous.

ho·rri·ble adj. horrible, dreadful.

ho·rri·ble·men·te adv. horribly, dreadfully.

ho·rri·dez f. horridness, dreadfulness.

hó·rri·do, -da adj. horrid, dreadful.

ho·rri·fi·car §70 tr. to horrify.

ho·rri·fi·co, -ca adj. horrific, terrifying.

ho·rri·pi·la·ción m. *(erizamiento)* bristling (of the hair); *(repelo)* aversion, dread; MED. horripilation.

ho·rri·pi·lan·te adj. hair-raising, terrifying.

ho·rri·pi·lar tr. *(erizar)* to make one's hair stand on end, give one the creeps <*esa película me horripila* that movie gives me the creeps>; *(horrorizar)* to horrify, terrify.

ho·rrí·so·no, -na adj. horrifying, terrifying (said of noises).

ho·rro, -rra adj. *(libre)* free, enfranchised; *(exento)* free, exempt; *(de baja calidad)* low-quality (tobacco); *(estéril)* infertile (said of livestock).

ho·rror m. *(temor)* horror, terror; *(repulsión)* horror, revulsion; FIG. *(atrocidad)* atrocity, horror; FIG., COLL. *(cantidad)* tons, loads <*ella tiene un h. de blusas* she has tons of blouses>.

ho·rro·ri·zar §04 tr. to horrify, terrify —reflex. to be horrified *or* terrified.

ho·rro·ro·sa·men·te adv. horribly, dreadfully.

ho·rro·ro·so, -sa adj. *(horrible)* horrible, terrifying; COLL. *(feo)* hideous, horrid; *(muy malo)* horrible, terrible.

ho·rru·ra f. filth, dirt ♦ **horruras** MIN. scoria, slag.

hor·ta·li·za f. BOT. vegetable.

hor·te·la·no, -na I. adj. *(del jardín)* garden, of the garden; *(del huerto)* orchard, of the orchard II. m. *(jardinero)* gardener; ORNITH. ortolan.

hor·ten·se adj. *(del jardín)* garden, of the garden; *(del huerto)* orchard, of the orchard.

hor·ten·sia f. BOT. hydrangea.

hor·tí·co·la adj. horticultural.

hor·ti·cul·tor, -to·ra m.f. horticulturist.

hor·ti·cul·tu·ra f. horticulture.

ho·san·na m. RELIG. hosanna.

hos·co, -ca adj. *(obscuro)* dark, gloomy; *(moreno)* dark-skinned, swarthy; *(áspero)* surly, gruff.

hos·pe·da·je m. lodging.

hos·pe·dar tr. to lodge, put up —reflex. to lodge *or* stay (at) <*me hospedé en el hotel* I stayed at the hotel>.

hos·pe·de·rí·a f. *(hotel)* inn, hostel; *(hospedaje)* lodging; RELIG. hospice.

hos·pe·de·ro, -ra m.f. innkeeper.

hos·pi·cia·no, -na m.f. resident of a poorhouse *or* orphanage.

hos·pi·cian·te m.f. AMER. var. of **hospiciano.**

hos·pi·cio m. *(para pobres)* poorhouse; *(para huérfanos)* orphanage; RELIG. hospice.

hos·pi·tal m. hospital ♦ **h. de sangre** MIL. field hospital.

hos·pi·ta·la·rio, -ria adj. *(cordial)* hospitable; *(acogedor)* cozy, inviting; RELIG. of the Hospitalers.

hos·pi·ta·li·cio, -cia adj. hospitable.

hos·pi·ta·li·dad f. *(cordialidad)* hospitality; *(permanencia)* hospital stay.

hos·pi·ta·li·za·ción f. hospitalization.

hos·pi·ta·li·zar §04 tr. to hospitalize.

hos·que·dad f. *(obscuridad)* darkness, gloominess; *(de la piel)* darkness, swarthiness; *(aspereza)* surliness, gruffness.

hos·tal m. var. of **hostería.**

hos·te·le·rí·a f. *(profesión)* hotel management; *(industria)* hotel trade *or* business.

hos·te·le·ro, -ra m.f. innkeeper.

hos·te·rí·a f. inn, hostel.

hos·tia f. *(sacrificio)* sacrifice; CUL., RELIG. wafer; SL. *(golpe)* belt, punch ♦ **darle una h. a alguien** SP., COLL. to give someone a beating • **¡Hostia!** SP., VULG. damn (it)!, Christ!

hos·tia·rio, -ria m. RELIG. *(caja)* wafer box; CUL. *(molde)* wafer mold.

hos·ti·ga·dor, -do·ra FIG. I. adj. harassing, annoying II. m.f. harasser, pest.

hos·ti·ga·mien·to m. *(azotamiento)* whipping, lashing; FIG. *(acosamiento)* harassment.

hos·ti·gar §47 tr. *(azotar)* to whip, lash; FIG. *(acosar)* to harass, pester; *(incitar)* to urge, press <*me hostigan para que estudie más* they urge me to study harder>.

hos·ti·go·so, -sa adj. AMER. cloying, sickening.

hos·til adj. hostile.

hos·ti·li·dad f. hostility ♦ **hostilidades** MIL. hostilities, fighting • **romper las hostilidades** MIL. to begin *or* commence hostilities.

hos·ti·li·zar §04 tr. *(molestar)* to antagonize; MIL. to harass.

ho·tel m. *(hostería)* hotel; *(casa)* house, villa.

ho·te·le·rí·a f. var. of **hostelería.**

ho·te·le·ro, -ra I. adj. hotel <*industria h.* the hotel industry> II. m.f. *(dueño)* hotelkeeper, hotel owner; *(encargado)* hotel manager.

hoy adv. *(en este día)* today <*h. vamos al teatro* today we are going to the theater>; *(en el tiempo presente)* now, nowadays, today <*h. es posible ir a la luna* nowadays it is possible to go to the moon> ♦ **de h. a mañana** at any moment • **de** *or* **desde h. en adelante** from now on, from this day forward • **h. día** *or* **h. en día** now, nowadays • **h. mismo** this very day • **h. por h.** at the present time • **por h.** for now, for the time being.

ho·ya f. *(hoyo)* pit, hole; *(sepultura)* grave; *(remolino)* eddy, whirlpool; ARG. seedbed; GEOG. *(valle)* dale, valley; AMER. river basin.

ho·ya·da f. TOP. depression, hollow (in the land).

ho·yar tr. CHILE, CUBA, AGR. to dig holes (for planting trees).

ho·yo m. *(cavidad)* hole; *(sepultura)* grave; MED. pockmark; SPORT. hole (in golf).

ho·yue·lo m. *(en las mejillas)* dimple; *(en la barbilla)* cleft; *(en el garganta)* depression (at the base of the throat)

hoz f. [pl. **ho·ces**] AGR. sickle.

ho·za·da f. *(golpe)* stroke with a sickle; *(cantidad)* quantity of cereal (cut with one sickle stroke).

ho·za·du·ra f. rooting hole.

ho·zar §04 tr. to root *or* dig (up).

hua·co m. CHILE, PERU ceramic pottery (found in pre-Columbian tombs).

hua·hua m.f. ECUAD, PERU baby, infant.
huai·co m. AMER. *(avalanche)* landslide, avalanche; *(hondonada)* ravine, gorge.
hua·man·ga f. PERU, MIN. alabaster.
huan·ga f. ECUAD. braid (worn by Indians).
huas·ca f. C. AMER. var. of **guasca**.
hua·so, –sa I. m.f. CHILE farmer, peasant; ARG., CUBA, ECUAD. crude person II. adj. ARG., CHILE, ECUAD. rustic, crude.
hua·ta f. TEX. cotton padding *or* batting; ARG., CHILE, PERU *(panza)* potbelly, paunch; CHILE *(pandeo)* bulging, warping; CHILE *or* ECUAD. bosom buddy, close friend; COL. poisonous snake.
huay·co m. PERU landslide.
hu·bie·ra, hubo see **haber²**.
hu·cha f. *(alcancía)* piggy bank; *(arca)* chest (for storage); FIG. *(ahorros)* savings.
hue·bra f. AGR. *(arada)* day's plowing; *(mulas)* team of mules (hired for a day's work); *(barbecho)* fallow (land).
hue·co, –ca I. adj. *(vacío)* hollow <*un leño h.* a hollow log>; *(retumbante)* deep, resonant (sound); *(mullido)* soft, spongy; FIG. *(vacuo)* vacuous, empty; *(vano)* vain, conceited II. m. *(cavidad)* hollow; *(agujero)* hole; *(espacio)* space, interval; FIG., COLL. *(vacante)* vacancy; FIG. *(vacío)* gap, void <*su partida dejó un h. en nuestra empresa* his departure left a gap in our company>; ARCHIT. opening (for a window, door) ♦ **h. de ascensor** elevator shaft.
hue·co·gra·ba·do m. photogravure.
hue·cú m. [pl. **-cú·es**] CHILE bog, swamp.
hue·la, huelo see **oler**.
huel·ga f. *(paro)* strike; AGR. fallow (period); ARCH. *(diversión)* good time, fun ♦ **declararse en h.** to go on strike • **h. de brazos caídos** sit-down strike • **h. de hambre** hunger strike • **h. general** general strike • **h. intermitente** slowdown • **h. patronal** lockout • **h. por solidaridad** sympathy strike • **h. salvaje** wildcat strike.
huel·go, huelgue see **holgar**.
huel·go m. *(aliento)* breath; *(anchura)* room, space; MECH. play.
huel·guis·ta m.f. striker, striking worker.
huel·guís·ti·co, –ca adj. strike, of a strike.
hue·lla f. *(del pie)* footprint; *(de un animal)* track, print; *(vestigio)* trace, mark; *(del escalón)* tread; FIG. *(camino)* footstep <*seguir las huellas de los mayores* to follow in the footsteps of one's elders> ♦ **h. digital** *or* **dactilar** fingerprint.
huel·le, huello see **hollar**.
hue·llo m. *(camino)* track; *(pisada)* tread, step; ZOOL. *(del casco)* sole (of a hoof).
huér·fa·no, –na I. adj. *(sin padres)* orphan, orphaned; FIG. *(sin amparo)* unprotected, defenseless; POET. *(sin hijos)* childless ♦ **h. de** without, devoid of II. m.f. orphan.
hue·ro, –ra adj. *(estéril)* infertile (eggs); FIG. *(vacío)* empty; AMER. *(podrido)* rotten (eggs); MEX. *(rubio)* blond, fair ♦ **salir h.** COLL. to be a dud.
huer·ta f. *(sembrado)* large vegetable garden; *(de árboles)* orchard; SP. *(regadío)* irrigated land.
huer·to m. *(jardín)* vegetable garden; *(de árboles)* orchard.
hue·sa f. grave.
hue·si·llo m. CHILE, PERU dried peach.
hue·so m. ANAT. bone; BOT. pit, stone; FIG. *(cosa difícil)* drudgery, hard work; *(lo inútil)* piece of junk; *(persona desagradable)* pain in the neck, stickler; C. AMER., MEX. *(empleo oficial)* government job; COL. white elephant; ECUAD. mule ♦ **dar** *or* **tropezar en un h.** to hit a snag • **de buen h.** FIG. lucky • **estar en los huesos** FIG. to be nothing but skin and bones • **h. colorado** MEX. northerly wind • **h. de la alegría** funny bone • **h. de la suerte** wishbone • **h. duro de roer** FIG. hard nut to crack • **h. palomo** ANAT. coccyx • **huesos** COLL. hands • **la sin h.** COLL. tongue • **meterse a h. de puerco** MEX. to swagger, show off • **no dejar a uno h. salvo** FIG. to rake over the coals • **soltar la sin h.** FIG. to shoot off one's mouth • **tener los huesos molidos** FIG. to be dead tired.
hue·so·so, –sa adj. bony, osseous.
hués·ped, –pe·da m.f. *(invitado)* guest; BIOL. host —m. *(invitante)* host —f. *(invitante)* hostess.

hues·te f. *(ejército)* army, troop; FIG. *(partidarios)* followers.
hue·su·do, –da adj. bony.
hue·va f. ICHTH. roe.
hue·va·da f. CHILE, MIN. lode; COLL., VULG. *(tontería)* foolish remark.
hue·ve·ra f. ORNITH. oviduct (of birds); *(copa)* eggcup.
hue·vo m. egg <*las yemas de h.* egg yolks>; *(taco de madera)* darning egg; VULG. ball, testicle ♦ **costar un h.** AMER. to cost a fortune • **h. claro** FIG. golden egg • **h. de Colón** *or* **de Juanelo** FIG. something that seems difficult but turns out to be easy • **h. de fraile** MEX. St. Ignatius' bean • **h. duro** hard-boiled egg • **h. escalfado** poached egg • **h. estrellado** *or* **frito** fried egg • **h. huero** infertile egg • **h. oscuro** FIG. rotten egg • **h. pasado por agua** *or* **h. tibio** AMER. soft-boiled egg • **huevos revueltos** *or* **pericos** scrambled eggs • **pensar en los huevos de gallo** C. AMER., COL. to daydream • **tener huevos** to have guts.
hue·vón, –vo·na adj. CUBA, GUAT., MEX., VULG. lazy; CHILE cowardly; CHILE, PERU., VEN. stupid, foolish.
hu·go·no·te, –ta adj. & m.f. Huguenot.
hui·da I. f. *(fuga)* escape; FIG. *(pretexto)* pretext; EQUIT. bolt II. adj. see **huido, –da**.
hui·di·zo, –za *or* **hui·de·ro, –ra** adj. *(fugitivo)* fugitive, fleeing; FIG. *(elusivo)* elusive.
hui·do, –da I. past part. see **huir** II. adj. *(fugitivo)* fugitive, fleeing; *(reservado)* withdrawn III. f. see **huida**.
hui·dor, –do·ra I. adj. fugitive, fleeing II. m.f. fugitive, runaway.
hui·llón, –llo·na AMER. I. adj. cowardly II. m.f. coward.
huin·cha f. BOL., CHILE, PERU *(cinta)* ribbon; CHILE, PERU *(punto de salida)* starting line (in horse racing); CHILE *(para medir)* tape measure ♦ **huinchas** PERU, SPORT. tape (finish line).
huin·che m. AMER. winch.
huir §18 intr. *(escapar)* to escape, run away; FIG. *(evitar)* to avoid, flee from <*h. del pecado* to flee from sin>; *(alejarse)* to slip away <*los años huyen* the years slip away> —reflex. to escape, run away —tr. to avoid, shun.
hu·le m. *(caucho)* rubber; *(tela)* oilcloth; COLL. *(mesa de operaciones)* operating table.
hu·le·ro, –ra AMER. I. adj. rubber <*la industria h.* the rubber industry> II. m.f. rubber gatherer.
hu·lla f. coal ♦ **h. blanca** water power, hydraulic power.
hu·lle·ro, –ra adj. coal, of coal <*la industria h.* the coal industry>.
hu·ma·na·men·te adv. *(con humanidad)* humanely, with humanity; *(según fuerzas humanas)* humanly.
hu·ma·nar tr. to humanize —reflex. *(hacerse humano)* to become human; RELIG. to become man (God); AMER. to condescend.
hu·ma·ni·cé, humanice see **humanizar**.
hu·ma·ni·dad f. *(naturaleza)* humanity, humanness; *(género)* mankind, humanity; *(bondad)* humanity, humaneness; COLL. *(corpulencia)* corpulence ♦ **humanidades** EDUC. humanities.
hu·ma·nis·mo m. humanism.
hu·ma·nis·ta I. m.f. humanist II. adj. humanistic.
hu·ma·nís·ti·co, –ca adj. humanistic.
hu·ma·ni·ta·rio, –ria adj. humanitarian.
hu·ma·ni·ta·ris·mo m. humanitarianism.
hu·ma·ni·zar §04 tr. to humanize —reflex. to become more human, soften.
hu·ma·no, –na I. adj. human; *(benévolo)* humane, benevolent II. m. human, human being.
hu·ma·re·da f. *or* **hu·ma·zo** m. dense smoke.
hu·me·a·da f. AMER. puff of smoke.
hu·me·an·te adj. *(que humea)* smoking, smoky; *(que echa vapor)* steaming.
hu·me·ar intr. *(echar humo)* to smoke; *(echar vapor)* to steam; FIG. *(permanecer)* to smolder <*el enojo humea todavía* anger is still smoldering>; *(presumir)* to become conceited —tr. AMER. to fumigate.
hu·mec·ta·ción f. dampening, moistening.
hu·mec·ta·dor m. humidifier.
hu·mec·tan·te adj. *(que humedece)* moistening, MED. humectant.
hu·mec·tar tr. var. of **humedecer**.

hu·me·dad f. *(calidad de húmedo)* dampness, moisture; METEOROL. humidity ♦ **h. absoluta** METEOROL. absolute humidity • **h. relativa** METEOROL. relative humidity.
hu·me·de·ce·dor m. humidifier.
hu·me·de·cer §17 tr. *(mojar)* to dampen, moisten; METEOROL. to humidify —reflex. *(mojarse)* to become damp *or* moist; METEOROL. to become humid.
hu·me·de·ci·mien·to m. humidification.
hú·me·do, –da adj. *(mojado)* damp, moist; METEOROL. humid.
hu·me·ra f. COLL. drunkenness.
hu·me·ral I. adj. ANAT. humeral II. m. RELIG. humeral veil.
hu·me·ro m. chimney, smokestack.
hú·me·ro m. ANAT. humerus.
hu·mil·dad f. *(virtud)* humility, humbleness; *(de cuna)* humbleness, lowliness (of birth); *(acción)* humble act.
hu·mil·de adj. *(sumiso)* humble, meek; *(bajo)* humble, lowly; *(de poco monto)* modest <*una fortuna h.* a modest fortune>.
hu·mil·de·men·te adv. humbly.
hu·mi·lla·ción f. humiliation.
hu·mi·llan·te adj. humiliating.
hu·mi·llar tr. *(rebajar)* to humble <*h. a un arrogante* to humble an arrogant person>; *(avergonzar)* humiliate; *(bajar la frente)* to bow (one's head) —intr. TAUR. to lower the head —reflex. to humble oneself.
hu·mi·llo m. FIG. pride.
hu·mo m. *(gas)* smoke; *(vapor)* steam ♦ **a h. de pajas** FIG. lightly, without thinking • **bajarle los humos a uno** to put someone in his place • **echar h.** to smoke • **hacerse h.** FIG. to vanish into thin air • **humos** FIG. airs • **tener muchos humos** FIG. to put on airs.
hu·mor m. PHYSIOL. humor; FIG. *(talante)* mood, humor; *(agudeza)* humor, wit ♦ **h. ácueo** PHYSIOL. aqueous humor • **h. vítreo** PHYSIOL. vitreous humor.
hu·mo·ra·do, –da I. adj. ♦ **bien h.** good-humored • **mal h.** bad-humored II. f. *(chiste)* joke; *(capricho)* whim, fancy.
hu·mo·ris·mo m. humor, wit (in writing).
hu·mo·ris·ta I. adj. humorous II. m.f. humorist.
hu·mo·rís·ti·co, –ca adj. humorous.
hu·mo·so, –sa adj. *(lleno de humo)* smoky; *(que echa humo)* smoking.
hu·mus m. GEOL. humus.
hun·di·ble adj. sinkable.
hun·di·do, –da I. past part. see **hundir** II. adj. *(sumido)* sunken, submerged; *(de ojos)* sunken, deep-set; *(mejillas)* hollow, sunken ♦ **h. en los pensamientos** deep in thought.
hun·di·mien·to m. MARIT. *(naufragio)* sinking; *(derrumbe)* cave-in; FIG. *(ruina)* ruin, collapse.
hun·dir tr. *(sumergir)* to sink; FIG. *(confundir)* to confuse <*mis argumentos le hundieron* my arguments confused him>; *(arruinar)* to ruin; *(derrotar)* to defeat; *(clavar)* to plunge (a knife, sword) —reflex. *(sumergirse)* to sink <*el barco se hundió cerca de la costa* the ship sank near the coast>; *(caer)* to fall down, collapse; COLL. *(desaparecer)* to vanish, disappear.
hún·ga·ro, –ra adj. & m.f. Hungarian —m. *(idioma)* Hungarian.
Hun·grí·a f. Hungary.
hu·no, –na I. adj. Hunnish II. m.f. Hun.
hu·ra·cán m. METEOROL. hurricane; FIG. *(vendaval)* gale.
hu·ra·ca·na·do, –da adj. hurricane, of hurricane proportions.
hu·ra·ñí·a f. unsociability.
hu·ra·ño, –ña adj. unsociable.
hur·ga·dor, –do·ra I. adj. poking II. m. poker (tool).
hur·gar §47 tr. *(atizar)* to poke, stir (a fire); *(revolver)* to poke *or* rummage around in; FIG. *(incitar)* to stir, incite.
hur·gón m. poker (tool).
hur·go·ne·ar tr. *(atizar)* to poke, stir (a fire); *(tirar estocadas)* to jab at (with a sword).
hur·gue·te·ar tr. ARG., CHILE to poke *or* rummage around in.
hur·gui·llas m.f. [pl. **-llas**] busybody.
hu·rí f. [pl. **-rí·es**] houri (beautiful woman).
hu·rón, –ro·na m. ZOOL. ferret —m.f. FIG., COLL. *(curioso)* snoop; *(persona huraña)* unsociable person.

hu·ro·ne·ar intr. *(cazar)* to ferret, hunt with a ferret; FIG., COLL. *(curiosear)* to snoop, pry.
hu·ro·ne·ra f. *(madriguera)* ferret hole; FIG., COLL. *(cueva)* hide-out.
¡hu·rra! interj. hurrah!
hu·rra·ca f. ORNITH. magpie; FIG., COLL. *(charlatán)* chatterbox.
hur·ta·di·llas adv. ♦ **a h.** secretly, furtively.
hur·ta·dor, –do·ra I. adj. stealing, thieving II. m.f. thief, robber.
hur·ta·gua f. watering pot.
hur·tar tr. *(robar)* to steal, thieve; *(dar de menos)* to short-change (in weight, measure); FIG. *(erosionar)* to wash away, erode; *(plagiar)* to plagiarize ♦ **h. el cuerpo** to dodge —reflex. to hide.
hur·to m. *(robo)* theft, robbery; *(cosa hurtada)* stolen object.
hu·si·llo m. MECH. *(tornillo)* screw, worm; *(desaguadero)* drain, drainage canal.
hus·ma f. snooping, prying.
hus·me·a·dor, –do·ra FIG. I. adj. snooping, prying II. m.f. snooper.
hus·me·ar tr. *(olfatear)* to scent, smell out; FIG. *(indagar)* to snoop, pry —intr. *(oler mal)* to stink, smell (tainted meat); *(curiosear)* to snoop, pry.
hus·me·o m. *(olfateo)* smelling, FIG. *(fisgoneo)* snooping, prying.
hus·mo m. *(olor)* stench, foul smell ♦ **estar al h.** FIG., COLL. to wait until the time is ripe.
hu·so m. SEW., TEX. spindle; MECH. drum (of a windlass); AER. fuselage ♦ **h. horario** time zone.
hu·ta f. HUNT. hut for concealing hunters.
hu·ya, huyo see **huir**.
hu·yen·te adj. fleeing.
hu·ye·ra, huyó see **huir**.

I

i, I f. tenth letter of the Spanish alphabet ♦ **poner los puntos sobre las íes** FIG., COLL. to dot the i's.
i·ba see **ir**.
I·be·ria f. Iberia.
i·bé·ri·co, –ca *or* **i·be·rio, –ria** adj. Iberian.
i·be·ro, –ra *or* **í·be·ro, –ra** adj. & m.f. Iberian.
I·be·ro·a·mé·ri·ca f. Latin *or* Spanish America.
i·be·ro·a·me·ri·ca·no, –na I. adj. Latin-American, Spanish-American II. Latin *or* Spanish American.
i·bi·cen·co, –ca I. adj. of Ibiza II. m.f. native of Ibiza.
i·bí·dem adv. ibidem.
i·bis f. [pl. **-bis**] ORNITH. ibis.
I·bi·za f. GEOG. Ibiza.
i·cé, ice see **izar**.
ice·berg m. iceberg.
i·co·no m. RELIG. icon.
i·co·no·clas·ta I. adj. iconoclastic II. m.f. iconoclast.
i·co·no·gra·fí·a f. ARTS iconography.
i·co·nó·la·tra I. adj. idol-worshipping II. m.f. iconolater, idol worshipper.
i·co·no·la·trí·a f. iconolatry.
i·co·no·lo·gí·a f. ARTS iconology.
ic·te·ri·cia f. MED. icterus, jaundice.
ic·tio·lo·gí·a f. ichthyology.
ic·tió·lo·go m. ichthyologist.
ic·tio·sau·ro m. ZOOL. ichthyosaurus, ichthyosaur.
i·da I. f. *(acción)* going; *(viaje)* trip; *(huella)* trail, track (of an animal); FIG. *(acometida)* rash *or* impulsive act; SPORT. sally (in fencing) ♦ **en dos idas y venidas** in an nstant • **i. y vuelta** round trip • **idas y venidas** comings and goings II. adj. see **ido, –da**.
i·de·a f. *(concepto)* idea, concept; *(opinión)* idea, opinion <*tiene unas ideas políticas raras* he has some strange political ideas>; *(noción)* idea, notion <*no tengo la menor i.* I don't have the slightest idea>; *(imagen)* image, picture; *(ingenio)* ingenuity, imagination; PHILOS. idea ♦ **cambiar de i.** to change one's mind • **darle a uno la i. de** to get it

into one's head • **hacerse** or **metérsele a uno una i. en la cabeza** FIG., COLL. to get an idea into one's head • **¡ni i.!** COLL. search me! • **no puedes tener i.** you can't imagine • **tener i. de** to intend to.

i·de·a·ción f. PHILOS. ideation.

i·de·al I. adj. *(perfecto)* ideal, perfect; COLL. *(bonito)* lovely, beautiful <*es una casa i.* it's a lovely house> II. m. ideal ♦ **lo i.** the perfect thing.

i·de·a·lis·mo m. PHILOS. idealism.

i·de·a·lis·ta adj. & m.f. idealist.

i·de·a·li·za·ción f. idealization.

i·de·a·li·zar §04 tr. to idealize.

i·de·al·men·te adv. ideally.

i·de·ar tr. *(concebir)* to think up, plan; *(inventar)* to invent, design <*fue ideado por la tecnología moderna* it was designed by modern technology>.

i·de·a·rio m. PHILOS., POL. system of principles, ideology.

i·de·á·ti·co, –ca adj. AMER. *(caprichoso)* whimsical, capricious; *(ingenioso)* ingenious.

í·dem adv. idem, the same.

i·dén·ti·co, –ca adj. identical.

i·den·ti·dad f. identity.

i·den·ti·fi·ca·ble adj. identifiable.

i·den·ti·fi·car §70 tr. to identify —reflex. to identify (oneself) with, be identified with.

i·de·o·gra·fí·a f. ideography.

i·de·o·gra·ma m. ideogram.

i·de·o·lo·gí·a f. ideology.

i·de·o·ló·gi·co, –ca adj. ideological.

i·de·ó·lo·go m. ideologist, ideologue.

i·dí·li·co, –ca adj. idyllic.

i·di·lio m. idyll, idyl.

i·dio·ma m. language, tongue.

i·dio·má·ti·co, –ca adj. idiomatic.

i·dio·sin·cra·sia f. idiosyncrasy.

i·dio·sin·crá·si·co, –ca adj. idiosyncratic.

i·dio·ta I. adj. foolish, idiotic II. m.f. idiot, imbecile.

i·dio·tez f. [pl. **-te·ces**] idiocy.

i·dio·tis·mo m. GRAM. idiom, idiomatic expression; *(ignorancia)* ignorance, folly.

i·dio·ti·zar §04 tr. to turn into an idiot.

i·do, –da I. past part. see **ir** II. adj. AMER. *(ebrio)* drunk, intoxicated; COLL. *(chiflado)* nuts, crazy ♦ **estar i.** FIG. to be miles away, be distracted III. f. see **ida.**

i·dó·la·tra I. adj. idolatrous, idolizing II. m.f. idolater, idolizer

i·do·la·trar tr. to idolize, adore.

i·do·la·trí·a f. idolatry, idolizing.

í·do·lo m. idol.

i·do·nei·dad f. *(aptitud)* aptitude, capacity; *(conveniencia)* suitability, fitness.

i·dó·ne·o, –a adj. *(apto)* capable, apt; *(conveniente)* suitable, fit.

i·gle·sia f. RELIG. *(edificio)* church; *(religión)* Church ♦ **Iglesia Anglicana** Church of England, Anglican Church • **Iglesia Católica** Catholic Church • **i. parroquial** parish church.

i·glú or **i·gloo** m. igloo

íg·ne·o, –a adj. igneous.

ig·ni·ción f. ignition.

ig·no·mi·nia f. ignominy, disgrace.

ig·no·mi·nio·so, –sa adj. ignominious, shameful.

ig·no·ra·ble adj. ignorable.

ig·no·ran·cia f. ignorance.

ig·no·ran·te I. adj. *(que no tiene instrucción)* ignorant, uneducated; *(que no ha sido informado)* uninformed, unaware II. m.f. ignoramus, dunce.

ig·no·ran·tón, –to·na COLL. I. adj. extremely ignorant II. m.f. ignoramus, dunce.

ig·no·rar tr. to be ignorant of, not to know.

ig·no·to, –ta adj. unknown, undiscovered <*tierras ignotas* undiscovered lands>.

i·gual I. adj. *(equivalente)* equal <*dos cantidades iguales* two equal quantities>; *(semejante)* similar, alike <*nuestras esperanzas son iguales* our hopes are similar>; *(mismo)* like <*compraremos algo de i. calidad* we will buy something of like quality>; *(liso)* even, level (terrain) ♦ **darle a uno i.** to be the same to one • **diez iguales** ten all (in

table tennis) • **ir iguales** to be even (in a race) • **ser i. a** *(ser lo mismo)* to be the same as <*eso es i. a mentir* that is the same as lying>; *(igualar)* to be equal to, equal <*dos más dos es i. a cuatro* two plus two equals four> • **serle a uno i. todo** to be all the same to one <*todo me es i.* it's all the same to me> II. m. MATH. equal sign —m.f. *(par)* equal <*mi hermano es mi i. en todo* my brother is my equal in everything> ♦ **al i. que** just like <*Juan, al i. que Carlos, no tiene dinero* John, just like Charles, does not have any money> • **de i. a i.** as an equal <*te hablo de i. a i.* I am speaking to you as an equal> • **i. que** the same as <*cantaremos i. que ayer* we will sing the same as yesterday> • **no tener i.** to have no equal, be unrivaled • **sin i.** unparalleled, unequaled.

i·gua·la f. *(igualación)* equalization; *(ajuste)* agreement, contract; *(estipendio)* stipend; CARP. level.

i·gua·la·ción f. *(iguala)* equalization; FIG. *(arreglo)* agreement; CARP. smoothing, leveling; MATH equating.

i·gua·la·do, –da I. past part. see **igualar** II. adj. ORNITH. with even plumage (said of molting birds); AMER. upstart III. f. SPORT. tied score.

i·gua·la·dor, –do·ra I. adj. equalizing, leveling II. m.f. equalizer, leveler.

i·gua·la·mien·to m. equalization.

i·gua·lar tr. *(hacer igual)* to equalize, make equal; *(allanar)* to smooth (a surface); FIG. *(juzgar igual)* to consider equal, equate; *(comparar)* to compare <*no puedes tú i. tu hijo al mío* you cannot compare your son to mine>; SPORT. to tie (a score). —intr. & reflex. *(ser iguales)* to be equal; SPORT. to be tied ♦ **igualarse a** or **con** to be equal to, be the equal of.

i·gual·dad f. *(equivalencia)* equality; *(semejanza)* similarity, likeness; *(uniformidad)* evenness, levelness (of ground) ♦ **en i. de condiciones** on an equal basis, on equal terms • **i. de ánimo** equanimity.

i·gua·li·ta·rio, –ria adj. & m.f. egalitarian.

i·gua·li·ta·ris·mo m. egalitarianism.

i·gual·men·te adv. *(con igualdad)* equally; *(también)* also, too; *(en la misma manera)* the same, in the same way <*mi hermano se peina i. que yo* my brother combs his hair in the same as I>.

i·gua·na m. ZOOL. iguana; MEX. guitar-like instrument.

i·ja·da f. ANAT. *(de un animal)* flank; *(del hombre)* side; *(dolor)* colic, pain in the side.

i·jar m. var. of **ijada.**

i·la·ción f. *(deducción)* inference; *(enlace de las ideas)* connectedness, cohesiveness (of ideas).

i·le·gal adj. illegal.

i·le·ga·li·dad f. illegality.

i·le·gal·men·te adv. illegally.

i·le·gi·ble adj. illegible.

i·le·gi·ti·mar tr. to make illegitimate.

i·le·gi·ti·mi·dad f. illegitimacy.

i·le·gí·ti·mo, –ma adj. illegitimate.

í·le·on or **í·le·on** m. ANAT. *(intestino)* ileum; *(hueso)* ilium.

i·le·so, –sa adj. unhurt, unscathed <*salió i. del combate* he emerged unscathed from the fighting>.

i·le·tra·do, –da I. adj. uncultured, illiterate II. m.f. illiterate.

i·lia·co, –ca or **i·lí·a·co, –ca** I. adj. ANAT. ileac; HIST. of Ilium (Troy) II. m.f. HIST. native of Ilium, Trojan.

i·lí·ci·to, –ta adj. illicit.

i·li·mi·ta·ble adj. illimitable, limitless.

i·li·mi·ta·do, –da adj. infinite, unlimited.

i·ló·gi·co, –ca adj. illogical.

i·lo·gis·mo m. illogic, illogicality.

i·lo·ta m. HIST. helot, serf.

i·lu·mi·na·ción f. *(acción de iluminar)* illumination; *(alumbrado)* lighting <*i. indirecta* indirect lighting>; FIG. *(realización)* enlightenment (spiritual, mental); ARTS illumination (of a manuscript); PHYS. illumination, illuminance.

i·lu·mi·na·do, –da I. past part. see **iluminar** II. adj. *(alumbrado)* lit (up); FIG. *(realizado)* enlightened III. m.f. *(hereje)* illuminist; *(visionario)* visionary ♦ **los iluminados** the Illuminati.

i·lu·mi·na·dor, –do·ra I. adj. illuminating, illuminative II. m.f. ARTS illuminator of a manuscript.

i·lu·mi·nar tr. *(alumbrar)* to illuminate, light; FIG. *(ilustrar)* to enlighten, illuminate (spiritually, mentally); ARTS to illuminate a manuscript.

i·lu·mi·na·ti·vo, –va adj. illuminating.

i·lu·sión f. *(percepción falsa)* illusion; *(esperanza)* hope, anticipation; *(alegría)* thrill, pleasure ♦ **con i.** hopefully, optimistically ♦ **hacerse la i. de que** to imagine that • **hacerse ilusiones de** to cherish hopes of • **tener i. por** to look forward to.

i·lu·sio·na·do, –da I. past part. see **ilusionar** II. adj. deluded, deceived.

i·lu·sio·nar tr. *(hacer concebir esperanzas)* to build up (someone's) hopes; *(engañar)* to deceive —reflex. *(tener esperanzas)* to have hopes (of); *(alegrarse con)* to be thrilled *or* excited about <*me ilusionan las vacaciones* I'm excited about the vacation>.

i·lu·sio·nis·ta m. illusionist, magician.

i·lu·so, –sa I. adj. deluded, misled II. m.f. dreamer.

i·lu·so·rio, –ria adj. *(engañoso)* illusory, false; LAW *(nulo y sin efecto)* nul and void.

i·lus·tra·ción f. *(aclaración)* illustration, explanation; *(instrucción)* learning, erudition; *(grabado)* picture, illustration; *(revista ilustrada)* illustrated magazine ♦ **la I.** HIST. the Enlightenment.

i·lus·tra·do, –da I. past part. see **ilustrar** II. adj. *(persona)* learned, erudite; *(libro)* illustrated III. m.f. erudite person, savant.

i·lus·tra·dor, –do·ra I. adj. illustrative II. m.f. illustrator, artist.

i·lus·trar tr. *(aclarar)* to illustrate, elucidate; *(hacer famoso)* to make famous <*la teoría de la evolución ilustraba a Darwin* the theory of evolution made Darwin famous>; RELIG. to inspire, illuminate; FIG. *(instruir)* to instruct, enlighten; *(adornar)* to adorn, illustrate (a text).

i·lus·tra·ti·vo, –va adj. illustrative.

i·lus·tre adj. illustrious, distinguished.

i·lus·trí·si·mo, –ma adj. most illustrious ♦ **Su Ilustrísima** His *or* Your Eminence (title applied to bishops).

i·ma·gen f. *(representación)* image; *(semejanza)* image, likeness <*la niña es la misma i. de su madre* the girl is the very image of her mother> *(símbolo)* symbol; TELEV. picture, image ♦ **i. fantasma** TELEV. double image, ghost • **quedarse para vestir imagenes** FIG., COLL. to be an old maid • **ser la i. viva de** FIG. to be the living image of.

i·ma·gi·na·ble adj. imaginable.

i·ma·gi·na·ción f. imagination ♦ **dejarse llevar por la i.** FIG. to let the imagination run away with one • **pasarse por la i.** to occur, cross one's mind <*no me pasó por la i. que tú vendrías hoy* it didn't occur to me that you would be coming today>.

i·ma·gi·nar tr. *(formar una imagen)* to imagine; *(inventar)* to invent; *(suponer)* to suppose, presume —reflex. to imagine.

i·ma·gi·na·rio, –ria I. f. MIL. *(guardia)* reserve guard —m. *(soldado)* barracks sentry *or* guard II. adj. imaginary.

i·ma·gi·na·ti·vo, –va I. f. *(facultad)* imagination; *(sentido común)* common sense II. adj. imaginative.

i·ma·gi·ne·rí·a f. ARTS, RELIG. *(imágenes)* imagery; *(talla o pintura)* carving *or* painting of sacred images; SEW. *(bordado)* embroidery.

i·mán¹ m. RELIG. imam (Moslem priest).

i·mán² m. MIN., PHYS. magnet; FIG. *(atractivo)* charm, magnetism ♦ **i. director** ELEC. control *or* directing magnet • **i. inductor** *or* **del campo** field magnet • **i. laminado** compound magnet.

i·ma·na·ción *or* **i·man·ta·ción** f. magnetization.

i·ma·nar *or* **i·man·tar** tr. magnetize.

im·ba·ti·ble adj. unbeatable, invincible.

im·ba·ti·do, –da adj. unbeaten.

im·be·bi·ble adj. undrinkable.

im·bé·cil I. adj. imbecile, stupid II. m.f. imbecile, idiot.

im·be·ci·li·dad f. imbecility, stupidity.

im·ber·be adj. beardless.

im·bo·rra·ble adj. indelible.

im·bri·ca·ción f. imbrication, overlapping.

im·bri·ca·do, –da *or* **im·bri·can·te** adj. imbricated, overlapping.

im·buir §18 tr. to imbue, inculcate.

im·bun·char tr. CHILE *(embrujar)* to bewitch, cast a spell over; *(estafar)* to defraud, swindle.

im·bun·che m. MYTH. wizard who steals children; CHILE *(maleficio)* spell, hex; *(barullo)* mess, tangle.

i·mi·ta·ble adj. imitable.

i·mi·ta·ción f. imitation ♦ **i. cuero** imitation leather.

i·mi·ta·do, –da I. past part. see **imitar** II. adj. & m.f. fake, artificial <*flores imitadas* artificial flowers>.

i·mi·ta·dor, –do·ra m.f. imitator, mimic.

i·mi·tar tr. to imitate, mimic.

i·mi·ta·ti·vo, –va adj. imitative.

im·pa·cien·cia f. impatience.

im·pa·cien·tar tr. to make (someone) lose patience, irritate —reflex. to lose one's patience, become irritable.

im·pa·cien·te adj. impatient, restless.

im·pa·cien·te·men·te adv. impatiently.

im·pac·to m. *(choque)* impact, shock; FIG. *(repercusión)* impact, repercussion.

im·pa·ga·ble adj. unpayable.

im·pa·ga·do, –da I. adj. unpaid II. m. unpaid bill.

im·pa·go, –ga ARG., CHILE unpaid.

im·pal·pa·bi·li·dad f. impalpability.

im·pal·pa·ble adj. impalpable.

im·par adj. ARITH. odd, uneven; ANAT. unpaired (organ).

im·pa·ra·ble adj. unstoppable.

im·par·cial adj. impartial, objective.

im·par·cia·li·dad f. impartiality, objectivity.

im·par·cial·men·te adv. impartially, objectively.

im·par·ti·ble adj. indivisible.

im·par·tir tr. *(otorgar)* to grant, concede; LAW *(pedir)* to demand, request <*i. auxilio* to request assistance>.

im·pa·si·bi·li·dad f. impassiveness, impassibility.

im·pa·si·ble adj. impassive, stoic.

im·pa·si·ble·men·te adv. impassively.

im·pá·vi·da·men·te adj. fearlessly, dauntlessly.

im·pa·vi·dez f. fearlessness, courage; AMER. audacity, impudence.

im·pá·vi·do, –da adj. fearless, dauntless; AMER. impudent, fresh.

im·pe·ca·ble adj. faultless, impeccable.

im·pe·di·do, –da I. past part. see **impedir** II. adj. crippled, disabled III. m.f. disabled *or* handicapped person.

im·pe·di·men·to m. obstacle, impediment.

im·pe·dir §48 tr. to prevent, obstruct.

im·pe·di·ti·vo, –va adj. preventive, hindering.

im·pe·len·te adj. driving, impelling.

im·pe·ler tr. to drive, impel.

im·pe·ne·tra·bi·li·dad f. impenetrability.

im·pe·ne·tra·ble adj. impenetrable.

im·pe·ni·ten·cia f. impenitence, unrepentance.

im·pe·ni·ten·te I. adj. confirmed, inveterate II. m.f. stubborn *or* intractable person.

im·pen·sa·ble adj. unthinkable, unimaginable.

im·pen·sa·da·men·te adv. inadvertently, unintentionally.

im·pen·sa·do, –da adj. unexpected, fortuitous.

im·pe·pi·na·ble adj. COLL. sure, certain <*eso es i.* that's for sure>.

im·pe·ran·te adj. ruling, dominant.

im·pe·rar tr. to rule, reign.

im·pe·ra·ti·va·men·te adv. imperatively, urgently.

im·pe·ra·ti·vo, –va I. adj. imperative, urgent; GRAM. imperative II. m. GRAM. imperative ♦ **i. categórico** PHILOS. categorical imperative • **imperativos económicos** economic considerations.

im·per·cep·ti·bi·li·dad f. imperceptibility.

im·per·cep·ti·ble adj. imperceptible.

im·per·cep·ti·ble·men·te adv. imperceptibly.

im·per·di·ble m. safety pin.

im·per·do·na·ble adj. unpardonable, inexcusable.

im·pe·re·ce·de·ro, –ra adj. *(duradero)* imperishable, indestructible; FIG. *(inmortal)* immortal.

im·per·fec·ción f. *(desperfecto)* imperfection; *(defecto)* defect, flaw.

im·per·fec·ta·men·te adv. imperfectly, inadequately.

im·per·fec·ti·ble adj. imperfectible.

im·per·fec·to, –ta adj. *(defectuoso)* imperfect, defective; *(incompleto)* incomplete, unfinished; GRAM. imperfect.

im·pe·rial I. adj. imperial II. f. top deck *or* roof (of a coach).

im·pe·ria·lis·mo m. POL. imperialism.

im·pe·ri·cia f. *(torpeza)* unskillfulness; *(incapacidad)* inexperience.

im·pe·rio m. *(mandato)* empire, dominion; *(autoridad)* authority, rule; *(tiempo de duración)* rule, reign; *(estado)* empire; FIG. *(orgullo)* pride.

im·pe·rio·sa·men·te adv. imperiously, masterly.

im·pe·rio·si·dad f. imperiousness.

im·pe·rio·so, –sa adj. *(autoritario)* imperious, overbearing; *(imperativo)* imperative, urgent.

im·per·me·a·bi·li·dad f. impermeability.

im·per·me·a·bi·li·za·ción f. waterproofing.

im·per·me·a·bi·li·zar §04 tr. to make waterproof, waterproof.

im·per·me·a·ble I. adj. impermeable, waterproof II. m. raincoat, mackintosh.

im·per·mu·ta·ble adj. unexchangeable.

im·per·so·nal adj. impersonal.

im·per·so·na·li·zar §04 tr. GRAM. to impersonalize, use impersonally.

im·per·té·rri·to, –ta adj. intrepid, dauntless.

im·per·ti·nen·cia f. *(insolencia)* impertinence, insolence; *(curiosidad)* curiosity.

im·per·ti·nen·te I. adj. *(insolente)* impertinent, insolent; *(irrelevante)* irrelevant, not pertinent; *(molesto)* meddlesome, impertinent II. m.pl. lorgnette, opera glasses (with a long handle).

im·per·ti·nen·te·men·te adv. impertinently.

im·per·tur·ba·bi·li·dad f. imperturbability.

im·per·tur·ba·ble adj. imperturbable.

im·pé·ti·go m. MED. impetigo.

im·pe·tra·ción f. *(obtención)* impetration, obtaining by entreaty; *(súplica)* beseeching; *(solicitación)* impetration.

im·pe·trar tr. *(obtener)* to impetrate, obtain by entreaty; *(suplicar)* to beg for, beseech; *(solicitar)* to impetrate, ask for.

ím·pe·tu m. *(movimiento acelerado)* impetus, impulse; *(violencia)* violence; *(energía)* energy, vigor; *(fogosidad)* impetuosity.

im·pe·tuo·sa·men·te adv. impetuously.

im·pe·tuo·si·dad f. *(ímpetu)* impetus, impulse; *(violencia)* violence; *(fogosidad)* impetuosity.

im·pe·tuo·so, –sa adj. *(violento)* violent; FIG. *(fogoso)* impetuous, impulsive.

im·pí·a·men·te adv. impiously.

im·pi·da, impido see **impedir.**

im·pi·die·ra, impidió see **impedir.**

im·pie·dad f. impiety.

im·pí·o, –a I. adj. impious, irreligious II. m.f. infidel.

im·pla·ca·ble adj. implacable.

im·pla·ca·ble·men·te adv. implacably.

im·plan·ta·ción f. *(establecimiento)* implantation; *(introducción)* introduction; BIOL., MED. implantation.

im·plan·tar tr. *(establecer)* to implant; *(introducir)* to introduce <*i. reformas* to introduce reforms>; BIOL., MED. to implant —reflex. to be *or* become implanted.

im·ple·men·tar tr. AMER. to implement.

im·pli·ca·ción f. *(contradicción)* contradiction; *(complicidad)* implication, complicity; *(consecuencia)* consequence; LOG. inference.

im·pli·can·cia f. *(incompatibilidad)* incompatibility; AMER. legal impediment.

im·pli·can·te adj. implicating.

im·pli·car §70 tr. *(envolver)* to implicate, involve; FIG. *(significar)* to imply, mean —intr. to imply contradiction —reflex. to become involved.

im·pli·ca·to·rio, –ria adj. implicative, implicatory.

im·plí·ci·ta·men·te adv. implicitly.

im·plí·ci·to, –ta adj. implicit.

im·plo·ran·te adj. imploring, entreating.

im·plo·rar tr. to implore, entreat, beg.

im·plo·sión f. PHONET. implosion.

im·plo·si·vo, –va adj. PHONET. implosive.

im·po·lí·ti·ca·men·te adv. impolitely, discourteously.

im·po·lí·ti·co, –ca adj. impolite, discourteous.

im·po·lu·to, –ta adj. unpolluted.

im·pon·de·ra·ble adj. & m. imponderable.

im·po·ne·dor m. imposer, assessor.

im·po·nen·te adj. *(grandioso)* imposing; COLL. *(atractivo)* good-looking.

im·po·ner §54 tr. *(ordenar)* to impose <*i. gravamen* to impose a tax>; *(imputar)* to impute falsely; *(instruir)* to instruct <*le impuse en sus responsabilidades* I instructed him in his responsibilities>; *(informar)* to inform <*me impuso del contenido de la carta* he informed me of the contents of the letter>; *(infundir)* to inspire, instill; PRINT. to impose —reflex. *(ser impuesto)* to be imposed on *or* upon; *(ser necesario)* to be necessary <*se impone que lo hagamos* it is necessary that we do it>; *(obligarse)* to take on <*me impuse esa responsabilidad yo mismo* I took on that responsibility myself> ♦ **imponerse a** to dominate, impose one's authority over.

im·po·ni·ble adj. taxable, subject to tax.

im·po·pu·lar adj. unpopular.

im·po·pu·la·ri·dad f. unpopularity.

im·por·ta·ble adj. importable.

im·por·ta·ción f. COM. importation, importing; *(bienes importados)* imported goods.

im·por·ta·dor, –do·ra I. adj. importing II. m.f. importer.

im·por·tan·cia f. *(valor)* importance, significance; *(autoridad)* authority; *(influencia)* influence ♦ **darse i.** to put on airs • **de i.** of importance, important.

im·por·tan·te adj. important, considerable ♦ **lo i.** the most important thing.

im·por·tar intr. to be important, matter —tr. *(valer)* to cost, be worth; *(introducir en un país)* to import; *(llevar consigo)* to entail.

im·por·te m. amount, cost.

im·por·tu·na·ción f. importuning.

im·por·tu·na·men·te adv. inopportunely.

im·por·tu·nar tr. to importune, bother.

im·por·tu·ni·dad f. *(calidad)* importunity; *(molestia)* importunity, annoyance.

im·por·tu·no, –na adj. *(que no es oportuno)* inopportune; *(enfadoso)* bothersome, annoying.

im·po·si·bi·li·dad f. impossibility.

im·po·si·bi·li·ta·do, –da I. past part. see **imposibilitar** II. adj. *(tullido)* disabled, crippled; *(impedido)* prevented.

im·po·si·bi·li·tar tr. *(prevenir)* to make impossible; *(impedir)* to prevent —reflex. to become disabled *or* crippled.

im·po·si·ble I. adj. *(muy difícil)* impossible; *(inservible)* useless; *(intratable)* intractable, difficult; *(lamentable)* lamentable, sad; AMER. dirty, filthy II. m. impossible ♦ **hacer lo i.** to do the impossible, do the utmost.

im·po·si·ción f. *(acción de imponer)* imposition, burden; *(cantidad)* deposit; *(contribución)* imposition, tax; PRINT., RELIG. imposition.

im·pos·ter·ga·ble adj. unpostponable.

im·pos·tor, –to·ra I. adj. slanderous II. m. impostor, slanderer.

im·pos·tu·ra f. *(engaño)* imposture; *(calumnia)* slander.

im·po·ten·cia f. *(falta de poder)* impotence, powerlessness; MED. impotence.

im·po·ten·te I. adj. *(débil)* impotent, powerless; MED. impotent II. m. impotent man.

im·prac·ti·ca·ble adj. *(irrealizable)* impracticable, unfeasible; *(intransitable)* impassable.

im·pre·ca·ción f. imprecation, curse.

im·pre·car §70 tr. to imprecate, curse.

im·pre·ca·to·rio, –ria adj. imprecatory.

im·pre·ci·sión f. lack of precision, inexactness.

im·pre·ci·so, –sa adj. imprecise, inexact.

im·preg·na·ción f. impregnation.

im·preg·nar tr. to impregnate.

im·pre·me·di·ta·do, –da f. unpremeditated.

im·pren·ta f. *(arte)* printing; *(establecimiento)* printing house, printery; *(impresión)* print; FIG. *(impresos)* press, printed matter.

im·pre·qué, impreque see **imprecar.**

im·pres·cin·di·ble adj. essential, indispensable.

im·pre·sen·ta·ble adj. unpresentable.

im·pre·sión f. print *(edición)* printing; *(tipografía)* typeface; *(obra impresa)* edition; FIG. *(efecto)* impression <*hacer buena i.* to make a good impression>; *(marca)* impression ♦ **i. digital** or **dactilar** fingerprint • **tener la i. de** or **que** FIG. to have the impression that.

im·pre·sio·na·bi·li·dad f. impressionability.

im·pre·sio·na·ble adj. impressionable.

im·pre·sio·nan·te adj. impressive.

im·pre·sio·nar tr. PHOTOG. to expose; FIG. *(causar impresión)* to make an impression on, impress; *(conmover)* to move, touch —reflex. to be impressed, be moved.

im·pre·sio·nis·mo m. ARTS impressionism.

im·pre·sio·nis·ta adj. & m.f. ARTS impressionist.

im·pre·so, –sa I. past part. see **imprimir** II. adj. printed III. m. *(publicación)* publication; *(obra)* book; *(artículo)* article.

im·pre·sor, –so·ra m.f. owner of a printing house or shop —m. printer.

im·pre·vi·si·ble adj. unpredictable, unforeseeable.

im·pre·vi·sión f. lack of foresight, improvidence.

im·pre·vi·sor, –so·ra adj. unforeseeing.

im·pre·vis·to, –ta I. adj. unforeseen, unexpected II. m. something unforeseen ♦ **imprevistos** incidental expenses.

im·pri·mar tr. PAINT. to prime (canvas).

im·pri·má·tur m. imprimatur.

im·pri·mi·ble adj. printable.

im·pri·mir §85 tr. *(publicar)* to print, publish; *(estampar)* to stamp, imprint; *(dejar una huella)* to imprint, leave a print of; FIG. *(hacer impresión)* to impress; *(transmitir)* to transmit, impart.

im·pro·ba·bi·li·dad f. improbability.

im·pro·ba·ble adj. improbable.

im·pro·bi·dad f. improbity, dishonesty.

im·pro·bo, –ba adj. *(sin probidad)* dishonest, corrupt; *(muy duro)* laborious, arduous.

im·pro·ce·den·cia f. *(impropiedad)* inappropriateness; LAW irrelevancy.

im·pro·ce·den·te adj. *(inadecuado)* inappropriate, inadequate; LAW irrelevant.

im·pro·duc·ti·vi·dad f. unproductiveness.

im·pro·duc·ti·vo, –va adj. unproductive.

im·pron·ta f. *(reproducción)* impression; FIG. *(señal peculiar)* stamp, mark.

im·pro·nun·cia·ble adj. unpronounceable.

im·pro·pe·rio m. *(insulto)* insult, taunt ♦ **improperios** ECC. Good Friday lamentations.

im·pro·pia·men·te adv. improperly.

im·pro·pie·dad f. impropriety.

im·pro·pio, –pia adj. *(inadecuado)* inappropriate, unsuitable; *(extraño)* out of place; *(no exacto)* improper, incorrect; MATH. improper.

im·pro·rro·ga·ble adj. unpostponable, that cannot be extended.

im·pro·vi·sa·ción f. improvisation.

im·pro·vi·sa·do, –da I. past part. see **improvisar** II. adj. *(de cosas)* makeshift, improvised; *(de un discurso)* impromptu, extemporaneous; MÚS. improvised.

im·pro·vi·sa·dor, –do·ra improviser.

im·pro·vi·sa·da·men·te adv. suddenly, unexpectedly.

im·pro·vi·sar tr. to improvise; MUS., RHET. to extemporize.

im·pro·vi·so, –sa adj. unexpected, unforeseen ♦ **al** or **de i.** unexpectedly, suddenly.

im·pro·vis·to, –ta adj. unexpected, unforeseen ♦ **coger de i.** to catch unawares • **i. temeraria** LAW negligence.

im·pru·den·cia f. imprudence, indiscretion ♦ **i. temeraria** law negligence.

im·pru·den·te I. adj. imprudent, indiscreet I. m. imprudence.

im·pru·den·te·men·te adv. imprudently.

im·pú·ber or **im·pú·be·ro, –ra** I. adj. below the age of puberty II. m.f. child below the age of puberty.

im·pu·den·cia f. *(desvergüenza)* impudence, shamelessness; *(palabra)* impudence.

im·pú·di·ca·men·te adv. impudently.

im·pu·di·cia or **im·pu·di·ci·cia** f. impudicity, shamelessness.

im·pú·di·co, –ca I. adj. *(desvergonzado)* immodest, shameless; *(deshonesto)* dishonest II. m.f. shameless or dishonest person.

im·pu·dor m. *(desvergüenza)* shamelessness; *(falta de pudor)* impudicity.

im·pues·to I. irreg. past. part. see **imponer** II. m. tax, duty ♦ **i. a las rentas** or **sobre los ingresos** income tax • **i. a las ventas** sales tax • **i. a las herencias** or **de herencias** inheritance tax • **i adicional** ARG. surtax • **i. aduanal** or **de aduanas** customs duty • **i. al consumo** excise tax • **i. arancelario** COL. customs duty • **i. complementario** surtax • **i. de muebles** or **inmobiliario** real-estate tax • **i. real** or **sobre bienes** property tax • **i. sobre incremento del patrimonio** capital-gains tax • **i. sucesorio** or **de sucesión** estate or inheritance tax • **i. suntuario** or **sobre el lujo** luxury tax.

im·pug·na·ble adj. impugnable.

im·pug·na·ción f. refutation, contradiction.

im·pug·na·dor, –do·ra I. adj. impugning II. m.f. impugner, objector.

im·pug·nan·te adj. impugnable.

im·pug·nar tr. *(combatir)* to oppose, contest; *(atacar)* to attack; *(refutar)* to refute, impugn.

im·pul·sar tr. to impel, drive.

im·pul·sión f. impulsion, impulse.

im·pul·si·vi·dad f. impulsiveness.

im·pul·si·vo, –va I. adj. impulsive II. impulsive person, hothead.

im·pul·so m. *(acción)* impulse, drive; *(instigación)* incitement; FIG. *(fuerza)* impulse, prompting.

im·pul·sor, –so·ra I. adj. impelling, driving II. m.f. *(fuerza)* driving force; FIG. *(instigador)* instigator.

im·pu·ne adj. unpunished.

im·pu·ne·men·te adv. with impunity.

im·pu·ni·dad f. impunity.

im·pun·tua·li·dad f. lacking punctuality.

im·pu·ra·men·te adv. *(manchado)* impurely; FIG. *(impúdicamente)* obscenely.

im·pu·re·za f. *(estado)* impurity; FIG. *(mancha)* impure; *(obscenidad)* obscenity.

im·pu·ri·fi·car §70 tr. to make impure, adulterate.

im·pu·ro, –ra adj. *(manchado)* impure; FIG. *(impúdico)* impure, immoral.

im·pu·sie·ra, impuso see **imponer.**

im·pu·ta·ble adj. imputable.

im·pu·ta·ción f. imputation, charge.

im·pu·ta·dor, –do·ra adj. imputing.

im·pu·tar tr. *(atribuir)* to impute, charge with; COM. *(asignar)* to assign.

i·na·bar·ca·ble adj. too wide (to be encompassed).

i·na·bor·da·ble adj. inaccessible, unapproachable.

i·na·bro·ga·ble adj. irrevocable.

i·na·ca·ba·ble adj. interminable, endless.

i·na·ca·ba·do, –da adj. unfinished.

i·nac·ce·si·bi·li·dad f. inaccessibility.

i·nac·ce·si·ble adj. inaccessible.

i·nac·ción f. inaction, inactivity.

i·na·cen·tua·do, –da adj. unaccentuated, unaccented.

i·na·cep·ta·ble adj. unacceptable.

i·na·cos·tum·bra·do, –da adj. unaccustomed.

i·nac·ti·vi·dad f. inactivity.

i·nac·ti·vo, –va adj. inactive.

i·nac·tual adj. AMER. out-of-date, not current.

i·na·dap·ta·ble adj. unadaptable.

i·na·dap·ta·do, –da I. adj. unadapted, maladjusted II. m.f. misfit.

i·na·de·cua·do, –da adj. unsuitable, inadequate.

i·nad·mi·si·ble adj. inadmissible.

i·na·dop·ta·ble adj. unadoptable.

i·nad·ver·ten·cia f. inadvertence, carelessness ♦ **inadvertencias** oversights, errors.

i·nad·ver·ti·da·men·te adv. inadvertently.

i·nad·ver·ti·do, –da adj. *(sin cuidado)* inadvertent, careless; *(no advertido)* unseen, unnoticed.

i·na·go·ta·ble adj. inexhaustible, endless.

i·na·guan·ta·ble adj. unbearable, insufferable.

i·na·lám·bri·co, –ca adj. wireless.

i·nal·can·za·ble adj. unreachable, unattainable.

i·na·lie·na·ble adj. inalienable.

i·na·lie·na·do, –da adj. unalienated.

i·nal·te·ra·bi·li·dad f. unalterability, immutability.

i·nal·te·ra·ble adj. unalterable, immutable.

i·nal·te·ra·do, –da adj. unaltered, unchanged.

i·na·mi·si·ble adj. not likely to be lost.
i·na·mis·to·so, –sa adj. unfriendly, unamiable.
i·na·mo·vi·ble adj. immovable, unremovable ♦ **puesto i.** tenured job or position.
i·na·mo·vi·li·dad f. immovableness, immovability.
i·na·ne adj. inane, pointless.
i·na·ni·ción f. MED. inanition, weakness from lack of food.
i·na·ni·dad f. inanity, emptiness.
i·na·ni·ma·do, –da adj. inanimate, lifeless.
i·na·pa·ga·ble adj. inextinguishable, unquenchable.
i·na·pe·a·ble adj. (incomprensible) incomprehensible, unfathomable; (porfiado) stubborn, obstinate.
i·na·pe·la·ble adj. (sin apelación) unappealable, without appeal; FIG. (inevitable) inevitable, unavoidable.
i·na·pe·ten·cia f. lack of appetite.
i·na·pe·ten·te adj. lacking appetite.
i·na·pla·za·ble adj. unpostponable, urgent.
i·na·pli·ca·ble adj. inapplicable.
i·na·pli·ca·ción f. lack of application, laziness.
i·na·pli·ca·do, –da adj. lazy, slack.
i·na·pre·cia·ble adj. (inestimable) inestimable, invaluable; (imperceptible) imperceptible, inappreciable <una diferencia i. an inappreciable difference>.
i·na·pro·pia·do, –da adj. inappropriate, unsuitable.
i·nap·ti·tud f. inaptitude, incapability.
i·nar·mó·ni·co, –ca adj. inharmonious.
i·na·rru·ga·ble adj. TEX. wrinkle-free, permanent press.
i·nar·ti·cu·la·do, –da adj. inarticulate.
i·na·se·qui·ble adj. (inalcanzable) unattainable, out of reach.
i·na·si·ble adj. ungraspable.
i·na·si·mi·la·ble adj. unassimilable.
i·na·sis·ten·cia f. absence.
i·nas·ti·lla·ble adj. splinterproof.
i·na·ta·ca·ble adj. impregnable, unassailable.
i·na·ten·ción f. inattention.
i·na·ten·to, –ta adj. unattentive, discourteous.
i·nau·di·to, –ta adj. (no oído) unheard-of; FIG. (extraordinario) extraordinary, unprecedented; (monstruoso) monstrous, outrageous.
i·nau·gu·ra·ción f. inauguration, opening.
i·nau·gu·ra·dor, –do·ra I. adj. inaugurating II. m.f. inaugurator.
i·nau·gu·rar tr. to inaugurate, open.
i·na·ve·ri·gua·ble adj. unascertainable.
in·ca adj. & m.f. Inca.
in·cai·co, –ca or **in·cá·si·co, –ca** adj. Inca, Incan.
in·cal·cu·la·ble adj. incalculable.
in·ca·li·fi·ca·ble adj. unspeakable, indescribable.
in·cam·bia·ble adj. (situación) unchangeable; (mercancías) unexchangeable.
in·ca·na·to m. PERU, HIST. period of the Incan empire.
in·can·des·cen·cia f. incandescence.
in·can·des·cen·te adj. incandescent.
in·can·sa·ble adj. untiring, indefatigable.
in·can·sa·ble·men·te adv. untiringly, indefatigably.
in·ca·pa·ci·dad f. (falta de capacidad) incapacity, incompetence; FIG. (rudeza) dullness, stupidity ♦ **i. legal** legal incapacity.
in·ca·pa·ci·ta·do, –da I. past part. see **incapacitar** II. adj. LAW incapacitated, disqualified.
in·ca·pa·ci·tar tr. (hacer incapaz) to incapacitate, render incapable; LAW (declarar ineligible) to incapacitate, declare incapable (as a witness).
in·ca·paz adj. [pl. **-pa·ces**] (sin poder) incapable, unable; (incompetente) incompetent, inept; FIG. (torpe) stupid, foolish; LAW (incapacitado) incapacitated, disqualified; MEX., COLL. unbearable, insufferable.
in·ca·sa·ble adj. unmarriageable.
in·cau·ta·ción f. LAW seizure, confiscation.
in·cau·ta·men·te adv. incautiously, unwarily.
in·cau·tar·se reflex. LAW to seize, confiscate.
in·cau·to, –ta adj. (imprudente) incautious, unwary; (inocente) gullible, naive.
in·cen·diar tr. to set on fire, set fire to —reflex. to catch fire.
in·cen·dia·rio, –ria adj. & m.f. incendiary.

in·cen·dio m. fire, conflagration ♦ **echar** or **hablar incendios** AMER. to curse, swear.
in·cen·sa·ción f. (acción de quemar incienso) incensing, perfuming with incense; FIG. (acción de lisonjear) flattery, cajolery.
in·cen·sar §11 tr. (quemar incienso) to incense, perfume with incense; FIG. (adular) to flatter, cajole.
in·cen·sa·rio m. censer, thurible ♦ **romperle a uno el i. en las narices** COLL. to flatter, butter (someone) up.
in·cen·ti·vo m. incentive, inducement.
in·cer·ti·dum·bre f. uncertainty, doubt.
in·ce·sa·ble or **in·ce·san·te** adj. incessant, uninterrupted.
in·ce·san·te·men·te adv. incessantly, uninterruptedly.
in·ces·to m. incest.
in·ces·tuo·so, –sa I. adj. incestuous I. m.f. person who commits incest.
in·ci·den·cia f. (incidente) incident, occurrence; PHYS. incidence <el ángulo de i. the angle of incidence>; FIG. (consecuencia) consequence, repercussion ♦ **por i.** accidentally, by chance.
in·ci·den·tal I. adj. (incidente) incidental; GRAM. (en paréntesis) parenthetical, parenthetic II. f. GRAM. parenthetical clause.
in·ci·den·tal·men·te adv. incidentally.
in·ci·den·te I. adj. LAW, PHYS. incident II. m. incident, occurrence.
in·ci·dir intr. (incurrir en falta) to fall into fault or error; PHYS. to fall upon, strike; MED. to make an incision ♦ **i. sobre** to influence, affect.
in·cien·se, incienso see **incensar**.
in·cien·so m. (sustancia aromática) incense; FIG. (adulación) adulation, flattery; CUBA, BOT. incense tree.
in·cier·to, –ta adj. (dudoso) uncertain, doubtful; (falso) untrue, false; (no fijo) unstable, unsteady.
in·ci·ne·ra·ble adj. incinerable (said of currency withdrawn from circulation).
in·ci·ne·ra·ción f. incineration, cremation.
in·ci·ne·rar tr. to incinerate, cremate.
in·ci·pien·te adj. incipient, beginning.
in·cir·cun·ci·so, –sa adj. uncircumcised.
in·cir·cuns·cri·to, –ta adj. uncircumscribed, boundless.
in·ci·sión f. (hendedura) incision, cut; POET. caesura.
in·ci·si·vo, –va adj. (cortante) cutting, incisive; FIG. (mordaz) keen, incisive ♦ **diente i.** DENT. incisor.
in·ci·so, –sa I. adj. cut, divided II. m. GRAM. (frase) parenthetical phrase or clause; (coma) comma.
in·ci·ta·ción f. incitement, incitation.
in·ci·ta·dor, –do·ra I. adj. inciting, instigating II. m.f. inciter, instigator.
in·ci·tan·te adj. inciting, instigating.
in·ci·tar tr. to incite, instigate.
in·ci·ta·ti·vo, –va I. adj. inciting II. m. (incitación) incitement —f. LAW mandatory injunction from a higher to a lower court.
in·ci·vil adj. uncivil, rude.
in·ci·vi·li·dad f. incivility, rudeness.
in·ci·vi·li·za·ble adj. uncivilizable.
in·cla·si·fi·ca·ble adj. unclassifiable.
in·cle·men·cia f. inclemency, severity ♦ **a la i.** unsheltered, exposed to the elements.
in·cle·men·te adj. inclement, severe.
in·cli·na·ción f. (del cuerpo) bowing of the head, body; (pendiente) slope, slant; FIG. (tendencia) inclination <siempre tuve una i. hacia el arte I have always had an inclination towards art>; ASTRON., GEOM. inclination; GEOL., MIN. slope.
in·cli·nar tr. (bajar) to bow, lower <i. la cabeza to bow the head>; (desviar) to slant, tilt <i. la silla contra la pared to tilt the chair against the wall>; FIG. (persuadir) to persuade, convince —intr. to resemble, take after —reflex. (doblarse) to bow <el monaguillo se inclinó ante el obispo the altar boy bowed before the bishop>; (desviar) to slant, slope <el camino se inclina a la derecha the road slopes to the right>; (parecerse) to resemble, take after <se inclina a Cervantes it resembles Cervantes>; (estar dispuesto) to be or feel inclined <me inclino a olvidarlo I am inclined to forget it>.
in·cluir §18 tr. to include <el precio incluye todo the price

includes everything>; *(encerrar)* to enclose; *(contener)* to contain; *(insertar)* to insert; *(comprender)* to comprise.
in·clu·se·ro, –ra m.f. COLL. foundling.
in·clu·sión f. *(acción de incluir)* inclusion, including; *(conexión)* relationship, association ♦ **con i. de** including, with the inclusion of.
in·clu·si·va·men·te adv. inclusively, inclusive.
in·clu·si·ve adv. inclusive <*lean desde la página cuatro a la diez i.* read from page four to ten inclusive>; including, included <*todos mis compañeros fueron invitados i. Juan* all my friends were invited, including John>.
in·clu·si·vo, –va adj. inclusive, including.
in·clu·so, –sa I. past part. see **incluir** II. adv. *(inclusivamente)* inclusively; even <*i. le avisé* I even warned him>.
in·clu·ya, incluyo see **incluir.**
in·clu·ye·ra, incluyó see **incluir.**
in·co·a·ción f. commencement, inception.
in·co·ar §38 tr. to commence, initiate.
in·co·a·ti·vo, –va adj. GRAM. inchoative.
in·co·bra·ble adj. irrecoverable, uncollectable.
in·co·er·ci·bi·li·dad f. incoercibility.
in·co·er·ci·ble adj. incoercible.
in·cóg·ni·ta I. f. MATH. *(cantidad desconocida)* unknown quantity <*despejar la i.* to find the unknown quantity>; FIG. *(razón oculta)* hidden motive; *(misterio)* mystery, question II. adj. see **incógnito, –ta.**
in·cóg·ni·to, –ta I. adj. unknown <*regiones incógnitas* unknown regions> ♦ **de i.** incognito <*viajar de i.* to travel incognito> II. m. incognito (one whose identity is disguised or concealed) —f. see **incógnita.**
in·co·he·ren·cia f. incoherence.
in·co·he·ren·te adj. incoherent.
in·co·lo·ro, –ra adj. *(que carece de color)* colorless; FIG. *(sin brillo)* insipid, dull.
in·có·lu·me adj. unharmed, unscathed.
in·com·bi·na·ble adj uncombinable.
in·com·bus·ti·bi·li·dad f. incombustibility.
in·com·bus·ti·ble adj. incombustible, fireproof.
in·co·mes·ti·ble adj. inedible, uneatable.
in·co·mi·ble adj. COLL. uneatable, inedible.
in·co·mo·da·men·te adv. uncomfortably, inconveniently.
in·co·mo·dar tr. to inconvenience, bother —reflex. *(enojarse)* to become angry or vexed; *(preocuparse)* to trouble oneself.
in·co·mo·di·dad f. *(falta de comodidad)* uncomfortableness; *(molestia)* inconvenience, nuisance; *(enfado)* anger, annoyance.
in·co·mo·do m. var. of **incomodidad.**
in·có·mo·do, –da I. adj. uncomfortable, awkward II. m. discomfort, inconvenience.
in·com·pa·ra·ble adj. incomparable, matchless.
in·com·pa·ra·ble·men·te adv. incomparably.
in·com·par·ti·ble adj. unsharable, indivisible.
in·com·pa·si·vo, –va adj. uncompassionate, unsympathetic.
in·com·pa·ti·bi·li·dad f. incompatibility.
in·com·pa·ti·ble adj. incompatible.
in·com·pe·ten·cia f. incompetence.
in·com·pe·ten·te adj. incompetent.
in·com·ple·ta·men·te adv. incompletely.
in·com·ple·to, –ta adj. incomplete, unfinished.
in·com·pren·di·do, –da I. adj. *(no comprendido)* misunderstood; *(no apreciado)* unappreciated, unrecognized II. m.f. misunderstood person.
in·com·pren·si·bi·li·dad f. incomprehensibility.
in·com·pren·si·ble adj. incomprehensible.
in·com·pren·sión f. incomprehension.
in·com·pre·si·ble adj. incompressible.
in·co·mu·ni·ca·ble adj. incommunicable.
in·co·mu·ni·ca·ción f. *(falta de comunicación)* lack of communication; CRIMIN. solitary confinement.
in·co·mu·ni·ca·do, –da I. past part. see **incomunicar** II. adj. *(aislado)* isolated, cut off; CRIMIN. incommunicado, in solitary confinement.
in·co·mu·ni·car §70 tr. *(aislar)* to isolate, cut off; CRIMIN. to put in solitary confinement —reflex. to isolate oneself, shut oneself off.
in·con·ce·bi·ble adj. inconceivable, unimaginable.

in·con·ci·lia·ble adj. irreconcilable.
in·con·clu·so, –sa adj. inconclusive, unfinished.
in·con·cu·so, –sa adj. unquestionable, undeniable.
in·con·di·cio·nal I. adj. unconditional, absolute II. m.f. staunch supporter or follower of a person or ideology.
in·con·di·cio·na·lis·mo m. AMER. servility, subservience.
in·con·di·cio·nal·men·te adv. unconditionally, absolutely.
in·co·ne·xión f. disconnection.
in·co·ne·xo, –xa adj. disconnected, unconnected.
in·con·fe·sa·ble adj. unspeakable, shameful.
in·con·for·me adj. dissatisfied, not in agreement.
in·con·fun·di·ble adj. unmistakable.
in·con·gruen·cia f. incongruousness, incongruity.
in·con·gruen·te adj. incongruous.
in·con·men·su·ra·bi·li·dad f. incommensurability.
in·con·men·su·ra·ble adj. *(inmensurable)* incommensurable, unmeasurable; *(enorme)* enormous, immense.
in·con·mo·vi·ble adj. *(firme)* firm, solid; *(ante amenazas)* unshakable, unyielding.
in·con·mu·ta·bi·li·dad f. incommutability.
in·con·mu·ta·ble adj. *(inmutable)* immutable; *(no conmutable)* incommutable.
in·con·quis·ta·ble adj. *(invencible)* unconquerable, invincible; FIG. *(que no se deja vencer)* unyielding, unbending.
in·cons·cien·cia f. *(pérdida del conocimiento)* unconsciousness; FIG. *(irreflexión)* thoughtlessness, irresponsibility.
in·cons·cien·te I. adj. *(que ha perdido el conocimiento)* unconscious; *(que no tiene consciencia)* unconscious, unaware; FIG. *(irreflexivo)* unthinking, thoughtless II. m. PSYCH. unconscious.
in·cons·cien·te·men·te adv. *(sin consciencia)* unconsciously, unknowingly; *(sin reflexión)* irresponsibly, thoughtlessly.
in·con·se·cuen·cia f. inconsequence, inconsistency.
in·con·se·cuen·te I. adj. inconsistent II. m.f. inconsistent person.
in·con·si·de·ra·ción f. inconsiderateness, thoughtlessness.
in·con·si·de·ra·da·men·te adv. *(sin consideración)* inconsiderately, thoughtlessly; *(atolondradamente)* rashly, impetuously.
in·con·si·de·ra·do, –da I. adj. *(no considerado)* inconsiderate, thoughtless; *(atolondrado)* rash, impetuous II. m.f. *(persona no considerada)* inconsiderate or thoughtless person; *(persona atolondrada)* madcap or reckless person.
in·con·sis·ten·cia f. inconsistency.
in·con·sis·ten·te adj. inconsistent.
in·con·so·la·ble adj. inconsolable, broken-hearted.
in·con·so·la·ble·men·te adv. inconsolably.
in·cons·tan·cia f. changeableness, fickleness.
in·cons·tan·te I. adj. changeable, fickle II. m.f. fickle person.
in·cons·ti·tu·cio·nal adj. LAW unconstitutional.
in·cons·ti·tu·cio·na·li·dad f. LAW unconstitutionality.
in·con·sul·to, –ta adj. AMER. inconsiderate.
in·con·ta·ble adj. *(innumerable)* countless, innumerable; *(que no puede narrarse)* untellable, unrepeatable.
in·con·ta·mi·na·do, –da adj. uncontaminated, unpolluted.
in·con·te·ni·ble adj. uncontainable, irrepressible.
in·con·tes·ta·ble adj. incontestable, unquestionable.
in·con·tes·ta·do, –da adj. uncontested, unquestioned.
in·con·ti·nen·cia f. incontinence.
in·con·ti·nen·te adj. incontinent.
in·con·ti·nen·te or **in·con·ti·nen·ti** adv. instantly, at once.
in·con·tro·la·ble adj. uncontrollable.
in·con·tro·ver·ti·ble adj. incontrovertible, indisputable.
in·con·ven·ci·ble adj. steadfast, unshakable.
in·con·ve·nien·cia f. *(molestia)* inconvenience, trouble; *(incomodidad)* uncomfortableness, discomfort; *(desconformidad)* unsuitability, inappropriateness; *(grosería)* crude remark or action.
in·con·ve·nien·te I. adj. *(molesto)* inconvenient, troublesome; *(inapropiado)* inappropriate, unsuitable; *(grosero)* improper, crude II. m. *(obstáculo)* difficulty, obstacle; *(objeción)* objection; *(desventaja)* disadvantage, drawback ♦ **tener i.** to mind, have an objection, object.
in·con·ver·ti·ble adj. inconvertible.
in·cor·diar tr. COLL. to pester, annoy.

in·cor·dio m. MED. bubo, inflammation; FIG., COLL. *(cosa o persona molesta)* nuisance, pest.

in·cor·po·ra·ble adj. incorporable.

in·cor·po·ra·ción f. *(acción de incorporar)* incorporation, incorporating; *(acción de levantarse)* sitting up.

in·cor·po·ral adj. incorporeal, intangible.

in·cor·po·rar tr. *(unir cosas entre sí)* to incorporate, combine; *(mezclar)* to mix; *(ayudar a sentarse)* to help (someone) sit up —reflex. *(sentarse)* to sit up; *(formar parte de un cuerpo)* to join ♦ **i. a las filas** MIL. to join the ranks.

in·cor·po·rei·dad f. incorporeity.

in·cor·pó·re·o, –a adj. incorporeal.

in·co·rrec·ción f. *(inexactitud)* incorrectness, inaccuracy; *(descortesía)* unseemliness, impropriety.

in·co·rrec·ta·men·te adv. incorrectly, improperly.

in·co·rrec·to, –ta adj. *(inexacto)* incorrect, inaccurate; *(conducta)* incorrect, improper.

in·co·rre·gi·bi·li·dad f. incorrigibility.

in·co·rre·gi·ble adj. incorrigible.

in·co·rrup·ción f. incorruptness.

in·co·rrup·ta·men·te adv. incorruptly.

in·co·rrup·ti·bi·li·dad f. incorruptibility.

in·co·rrup·ti·ble adj. incorruptible.

in·co·rrup·to, –ta adj. *(sin corromperse)* uncorrupted, incorrupt; FIG. *(virgen)* chaste, virginal.

in·cre·di·bi·li·dad f. incredibleness.

in·cre·du·li·dad f. *(escepticismo)* incredulity, skepticism; RELIG. unbelief.

in·cré·du·lo, –la I. adj. *(escéptico)* incredulous, skeptical; RELIG. unbelieving II. m.f. RELIG. unbeliever.

in·cre·í·ble adj. incredible, unbelievable.

in·cre·í·ble·men·te adv. incredibly, unbelievably.

in·cre·men·tar tr. to increase, augment.

in·cre·men·to m. *(aumento)* increase, growth; GRAM. suffix; MATH. increment.

in·cre·pa·ción f. severe rebuke *or* reproach.

in·cre·pan·te adj. rebuking, reproachful.

in·cre·par tr. to rebuke, reprimand.

in·cri·mi·na·ción f. incrimination.

in·cri·mi·nar tr. *(acusar)* to incriminate, accuse; *(exagerar)* to exaggerate a fault *or* crime.

in·cruen·to, –ta adj. bloodless (offering).

in·crus·ta·ción f. *(acción de incrustar)* encrustation, incrustation; GEOL. sinter; TECH. scale; ARTS inlay, inlaying.

in·crus·tar tr. GEOL. to encrust, embed; ARTS to inlay —reflex. *(adherirse)* to become encrusted *or* embedded; FIG. *(grabarse)* to become engraved (in the memory).

in·cu·ba·ción f. incubation.

in·cu·ba·dor, –do·ra I. adj. incubating II. f. incubator.

in·cu·bar tr. & intr. to incubate.

in·cues·tio·na·ble adj. unquestionable, indisputable.

in·cul·car §70 tr. *(infundir en el ánimo)* to inculcate, instill; *(apretar)* to squeeze *or* press together; PRINT. to crowd a line of type —reflex. to be obstinate *or* insistent.

in·cul·pa·bi·li·dad f. innocence, guiltlessness.

in·cul·pa·ción f. LAW inculpation, indictment.

in·cul·pa·do, –da I. past part. see **inculpar** II. adj. & m.f. accused.

in·cul·par tr. to inculpate, indict.

in·cul·qué, inculpe see **inculcar.**

in·cul·ti·va·ble adj. unarable, unfit for cultivation.

in·cul·to, –ta adj. AGR. uncultivated, untilled; FIG. *(sin cultura)* uncultured, uneducated; *(descuidado)* untidy, slovenly.

in·cul·tu·ra f. AGR. lack of cultivation, barrenness; *(falta de cultura)* lack of culture *or* refinement.

in·cum·ben·cia f. incumbency, obligation.

in·cum·bir §38 intr. to be incumbent on, be of concern to <*eso me incumbe a mí* that concerns me>.

in·cum·pli·mien·to m. nonfulfillment.

in·cum·plir tr. to fail to fulfill.

in·cu·na·ble PRINT. I. adj. incunabular II. m. incunabulum, book printed before 1501.

in·cu·ra·bi·li·dad f. incurability, incurableness.

in·cu·ra·ble I. adj. incurable II. m.f. MED. incurably ill person.

in·cu·rrir intr. ♦ **i. en** *(cometer)* to commit an error; *(atraerse)* to incur, bring upon oneself.

in·cur·sión f. MIL. incursion, raid ♦ **i. aérea** MIL. air raid.

in·cur·sio·nar intr. MEX. to penetrate, get through.

in·da·ga·ción f. investigation, inquiry.

in·da·ga·dor, –do·ra I. adj. investigating, inquiring II. m.f. investigator, inquirer.

in·da·gar §47 tr. to investigate, inquire into *or* about.

in·da·ga·to·rio, –ria adj. LAW investigatory.

in·de·bi·da·men·te adv. *(ilegalmente)* illegally, unlawfully; *(desconsideradamente)* unduly, improperly.

in·de·bi·do, –da adj. *(ilegal)* illegal, unlawful; *(desconsiderado)* undue, improper.

in·de·cen·cia f. *(falta de decencia)* indecency, unseemliness; *(acto vituperable)* indecent remark *or* action.

in·de·cen·te adj. *(no decente)* indecent, obscene; FIG. *(miserable)* wretched, miserable.

in·de·cen·te·men·te adv. *(no decentemente)* indecently, obscenely; FIG. *(miserablemente)* wretchedly, miserably.

in·de·ci·ble adj. unspeakable, unutterable.

in·de·ci·sión f. indecision, irresolution.

in·de·ci·so, –sa adj. *(irresoluto)* undecided, hesitant; *(incierto)* indecisive, uncertain; *(vago)* indistinct, vague.

in·de·cla·ra·ble adj. undeclarable.

in·de·cli·na·ble adj. *(obligatorio)* unavoidable, undeclinable; GRAM. indeclinable.

in·de·co·ro·so, –sa adj. indecorous.

in·de·fec·ti·bi·li·dad f. indefectibility.

in·de·fec·ti·ble adj. indefectible, unfailing.

in·de·fec·ti·ble·men·te adv. indefectibly, unfailingly.

in·de·fen·di·ble *or* **in·de·fen·si·ble** adj. indefensible.

in·de·fen·so, –sa adj. *(sin defensa)* defenseless; *(desamparado)* helpless.

in·de·fi·ni·ble adj. indefinable, undefinable.

in·de·fi·ni·da·men·te adv. indefinitely.

in·de·fi·ni·do, –da adj. *(no definido)* undefined; *(indeterminado)* indefinite; GRAM., LOG. indefinite.

in·de·for·ma·ble adj. that keeps its shape.

in·de·le·ble adj. indelible.

in·de·li·be·ra·do, –da adj. indeliberate, unintentional.

in·de·li·ca·do, –da adj. indelicate.

in·dem·ne adj. *(persona)* uninjured, unhurt; *(cosa)* undamaged.

in·dem·ni·dad f. indemnity.

in·dem·ni·za·ción f. *(acción)* indemnification; *(compensación)* indemnity.

in·dem·ni·zar §04 tr. to indemnify, compensate.

in·de·pen·den·cia f. independence.

in·de·pen·den·tis·mo m. POL. independence movement.

in·de·pen·den·tis·ta POL. I. m.f. supporter of an independence movement II. adj. pro-independence.

in·de·pen·dien·te I. adj & m.f. independent II. adv. independently.

in·de·pen·dien·te·men·te adv. *(con independencia)* independently; *(a parte de)* regardless of, irrespective of.

in·de·pen·di·zar·se §04 reflex. to become independent.

in·des·ci·fra·ble adj. undecipherable; FIG. *(impenetrable)* impenetrable.

in·des·crip·ti·ble adj. indescribable.

in·de·se·a·ble adj. & m.f. undesirable.

in·des·truc·ti·ble adj. indestructible.

in·de·ter·mi·na·ble adj. indeterminable, undeterminable.

in·de·ter·mi·na·ción f. indetermination.

in·de·ter·mi·na·do, –da adj. *(indefinido)* indeterminate, indefinite; *(indeciso)* indeterminate, indecisive; MATH. indeterminate; GRAM. indefinite.

in·dex m. index.

In·dia f. India.

in·dia·da f. AMER. *(indios)* group *or* gathering of Indians; *(expresión, acto)* expression *or* act considered typical of Indians.

in·dia·nis·mo m. *(modismo)* idiom from Indian languages; *(estudio)* Indian studies.

in·dia·nis·ta m.f. Indianist.

in·dia·no, –na I. adj. HIST. Spanish-American II. m.f. *(habitante)* Spanish-American; FIG. *(rico)* person returning very wealthy to Europe from Spanish America —f. TEX. printed calico.

in·di·ca·ción f. *(señal)* indication, sign; *(sugerencia)* suggestion <*ir por i. de alguien* to go at someone's suggestion>; *(informe)* directions <*dar una buena i.* to give good directions>; *(instrucción)* direction, instruction <*indicaciones sobre la utilización de un producto* instructions on the use of a product>; *(observación)* remark, observation; CHILE proposal.

in·di·ca·do, –da I. past part. see **indicar II.** adj. *(adecuado)* suitable, good; *(aconsejado)* recommended, advised.

in·di·ca·dor, –do·ra I. adj. indicating, indicatory **II.** m. *(señal)* indicator; CHEM., ECON. indicator ♦ **i. de carretera** road sign • **i. de humo** smoke detector • **i. del nivel de gasolina** fuel gauge • **i. de velocidad** speedometer.

in·di·car §70 tr. *(señalar)* to indicate; *(mostrar)* to show, point out <*nos indicó el camino* he showed us the road>; FIG. *(probar)* to indicate, point to <*esto indica su falta de honor* this indicates his lack of honor>; *(sugerir)* to suggest, imply <*sólo indicaremos los resultados generales* we will only suggest the general results>.

in·di·ca·ti·vo, –va adj. & m. GRAM. indicative.

ín·di·ce I. m. *(general)* table of contents; *(alfabético)* index of a book; *(catálogo)* catalogue of a library; *(indicio)* sign, indication; *(del reloj)* hand of a watch; *(gnomon)* gnomon, style of a sundial; *(coeficiente)* rate <*í. de mortalidad* death rate>; *(cifra)* index <*í. de precios* price index>; ANAT. index finger; CHEM. index, ratio ♦ **Índice** RELIG. Index • **í. cefálico** ZOOL. cephalic index • **í. de compresión** PHYS. compression ratio • **í. de refracción** PHYS. refractive index **II.** adj. ANAT. index.

in·di·cio m. indication, sign ♦ **indicios** clues.

ín·di·co, –ca adj. Indian <*Océano Indico* Indian Ocean>.

in·di·fe·ren·cia f. indifference.

in·di·fe·ren·te adj. indifferent.

in·di·fe·ren·te·men·te adv. indifferently.

in·dí·ge·na I. adj. indigenous, native **II.** m.f. native.

in·di·gen·cia f. indigence, poverty.

in·di·ge·nis·mo m. Indianism (movement in favor of the Indians of the Western Hemisphere).

in·di·ge·nis·ta adj. & m.f. Indianist.

in·di·gen·te I. adj. indigent, poor **II.** m.f. ♦ **los indigentes** the poor, the needy.

in·di·ges·tar·se reflex. *(dar indigestión)* to cause indigestion, give indigestion; *(tener indigestión)* to have indigestion; COLL. *(no agradar)* to dislike.

in·di·ges·tión f. indigestion.

in·di·ges·to, –ta adj. *(no digerible)* indigestible; *(no digerido)* undigested; FIG. *(confuso)* undigested, confused (facts, thoughts); *(desagradable)* unbearable ♦ **estar i.** to have indigestion.

in·dig·na·ción f. indignation.

in·dig·na·men·te adv. despicably, unworthily.

in·dig·nar tr. to anger, infuriate —reflex. to feel indignation, become indignant.

in·dig·ni·dad f. *(carácter)* unworthiness; *(perversidad)* perversity; *(afrenta)* indignity.

in·dig·no, –na adj. *(sin mérito)* unworthy; *(malo)* contemptible, despicable.

ín·di·go m. indigo.

in·di·no adj. COLL. *(descarado)* despicable, contemptible; AMER. *(pillo)* mischievous.

in·di·qué, indique see **indicar**.

in·dio, –dia¹ adj. & m.f. Indian —m. CHEM. indium.

in·dio, –dia² adj. blue.

in·dió·fi·lo, –la adj. & m.f. admirer of Indians.

in·di·rec·ta I. f. hint, insinuation ♦ **lanzar** or **soltar** or **tirar una i.** to hint at, to insinuate. **II.** see **indirecto, –ta.**

in·di·rec·ta·men·te adv. indirectly.

in·di·rec·to, –ta I. adj. indirect **II.** f. see **indirecta.**

in·dis·ci·pli·na f. indiscipline.

in·dis·ci·pli·na·ble adj. untrainable, unmanageable.

in·dis·ci·pli·na·do, –da adj. undisciplined.

in·dis·cre·ción f. indiscretion.

in·dis·cre·ta·men·te adv. indiscreetly.

in·dis·cre·to, –ta I. adj. indiscreet **II.** m.f. indiscreet person.

in·dis·cu·ti·ble adj. indisputable, unquestionable.

in·dis·so·cia·ble adj. inseparable, not dissociable.

in·di·so·lu·bi·li·dad f. indissolubility.

in·di·so·lu·ble adj. indissoluble, undissolvable.

in·dis·pen·sa·ble adj. indispensable.

in·dis·po·ner §54 tr. *(enfermar)* to indispose, upset; FIG. *(malquistar)* to estrange, set against <*le indispusieron con sus viejos amigos* they set him against his old friends> —reflex. *(enfermarse)* to become indisposed, to upset; FIG. *(malquistarse)* to become estranged, fall out <*indisponerse con viejos amigos* to fall out with old friends>.

in·dis·po·ni·bi·li·dad f. unavailability.

in·dis·po·ni·ble adj. unavailable.

in·dis·po·si·ción f. indisposition.

in·dis·pues·to, –ta I. past part. of **indisponer II.** adj. *(enfermo)* indisposed, unwell; *(enfadado)* on bad terms <*está i. con su primo* he is on bad terms with his cousin>.

in·dis·pu·sie·ra, indispuso see **indisponer**.

in·dis·pu·ta·ble adj. indisputable.

in·dis·tin·gui·ble adj. indistinguishable, undistinguishable.

in·dis·tin·ta·men·te adv. *(confusamente)* indistinctly; *(indiferentemente)* indifferently, indiscriminately.

in·dis·tin·to, –ta adj. indistinct.

in·di·vi·dua·ción f. individuation.

in·di·vi·dual I. adj. individual, single <*habitación i.* single room> **II.** m. SPORT. singles <*i. damas* women's singles>.

in·di·vi·dua·li·dad f. individuality.

in·di·vi·dua·lis·mo m. individualism.

in·di·vi·dua·lis·ta I. adj. individualistic **II.** individualist.

in·di·vi·dua·li·za·ción f. individualization.

in·di·vi·dua·li·zar §04 tr. to individualize.

in·di·vi·duar §67 tr. to individuate.

in·di·vi·duo, –dua I. adj. individual **II.** m. *(ser)* individual; *(de una sociedad)* member, fellow; COLL. *(persona indeterminada)* individual; *(uno mismo)* oneself <*cuidar bien de su i.* to take good care of oneself>.

in·di·vi·sa·men·te adv. undividedly.

in·di·vi·si·bi·li·dad f. indivisibility.

in·di·vi·si·ble adj. indivisible.

in·di·vi·sión f. *(falta de división)* indivision; LAW joint ownership.

in·di·vi·so, –sa adj. LAW undivided, joint <*finca i.* joint estate>.

in·do, –da adj. & m.f. Hindu, Indian ♦ **Indo** GEOG. Indus.

in·dó·cil adj. indocile, unruly.

in·do·ci·li·dad f. indocility, unruliness.

in·doc·to, –ta adj. unlearned, uneducated.

in·do·cu·men·ta·do, –da I. adj. *(persona)* undocumented, without any identification papers; *(afirmación)* groundless **II.** m.f. person without identification papers ♦ **es un i.** COLL. he's a duffer.

in·do·chi·no, –na adj. & m.f. Indo-Chinese ♦ **Indochina** Indochina.

in·do·eu·ro·pe·o, –a adj. & m.f. Indo-European.

in·do·ger·má·ni·co, –ca adj. & m.f. Indo-Germanic.

ín·do·le f. *(naturaleza)* nature; *(tipo)* type, kind.

in·do·len·cia f. indolence.

in·do·len·te I. adj. indolent **II.** m.f. idler.

in·do·len·te·men·te adv. indolently, apathetically.

in·do·lo·ro, –ra adj. indolent, painless.

in·do·ma·ble adj. *(animal)* untamable; *(caballo)* unbreakable; *(persona)* uncontrollable; *(inmanejable)* unmanageable; *(pasión, valor)* indomitable.

in·do·mes·ti·ca·ble adj. untamable.

in·dó·mi·to, –ta adj. *(no domado)* untamed; *(no domesticable)* untamable; *(persona)* unruly, unsubmissive; *(carácter)* indomitable.

In·do·ne·sia f. Indonesia.

in·do·ne·sio, –sia adj. & m.f. Indonesian —m. *(idioma)* Indonesian.

In·dos·tán m. Hindustan.

in·dos·tá·ni·co, –ca adj. Hindustani.

in·dos·ta·no, –na adj. & m.f. Hindustani.

in·duc·ción f. induction.

in·du·cir §22 tr. *(deducir)* to induce, infer; *(llevar)* to induce, lead <*i. a error* to lead into error>; ELEC. to induce.

in·duc·ti·vo, –va adj. inductive.

in·duc·tor, –to·ra I. adj. *(que induce)* inducting; ELEC. inductive **II.** m.f. *(persona)* inducer —m. CHEM., ELEC. inductor.

in·du·da·ble adj. indubitable, certain.

in·du·da·ble·men·te adv. undoubtedly, indubitably.

in·du·je·ra, indujo see **inducir**.

in·dul·gen·cia f. indulgence.
in·dul·gen·te adj. indulgent, lenient.
in·dul·gen·te·men·te adv. indulgently, indulgingly.
in·dul·tar tr. *(perdonar)* to pardon; *(exonerar)* to exempt; LAW to pardon, grant amnesty —reflex. BOL. *(entrometerse)* to meddle; CUBA *(salir de una situación difícil)* to escape from a difficult situation.
in·dul·to m. *(perdón)* pardon; *(compasión)* mercy; *(exoneración)* exemption; *(papal)* indult.
in·du·men·ta·ria f. *(estudio)* study of costume; *(vestido)* clothing, garments.
in·du·men·to m. *(vestido)* clothing, garments; BOT. indumentum.
in·dus·tria f. *(producción)* industry <*la i. automotriz* the automobile industry>; *(oficio)* craft, trade; *(inteligencia)* cleverness, skill.
in·dus·trial I. adj. industrial II. m. industrialist.
in·dus·tria·lis·mo m. industrialism.
in·dus·tria·lis·ta adj. pertaining to industrialism.
in·dus·tria·li·za·ción f. industrialization.
in·dus·tria·li·zar §04 tr. to industrialize —reflex. to become industrialized.
in·dus·triar tr. to train, instruct —reflex. to manage, find a way to do something.
in·dus·trio·sa·men·te adv. *(diligentemente)* industriously; *(ingeniosamente)* cleverly, skillfully.
in·dus·trio·so, –sa adj. *(diligente)* industrious; *(ingenioso)* clever, skillful.
in·duz·ca, induzco see **inducir.**
i·né·di·to, –ta adj. unpublished.
i·ne·fa·bi·li·dad f. ineffability.
i·ne·fa·ble adj. ineffable.
i·ne·fa·ble·men·te adv. ineffably.
i·ne·fi·ca·cia f. inefficacy.
i·ne·fi·caz adj. ineffective, inefficacious.
i·ne·je·cu·ción f. nonperformance, nonfulfillment.
i·ne·je·cu·ta·ble adj. *(no realizable)* impracticable, unfeasible; MUS. unplayable, unperformable.
i·ne·le·gi·ble adj. ineligible.
i·ne·luc·ta·ble adj. inevitable, unavoidable.
i·ne·lu·di·ble adj. inevitable, inescapable.
i·ne·na·rra·ble adj. indescribable, inexpressible.
i·nep·cia f. *(necedad)* nonsense, ineptitude, foolishness; AMER. *(incapacidad)* ineptitude, incompetence.
i·nep·ti·tud f. ineptitude.
i·nep·to, –ta I. adj. inept II. m.f. inept person, incompetent.
i·ne·quí·vo·co, –ca adj. unequivocal.
i·ner·cia f. inertia.
i·ner·me adj. *(sin armas)* unarmed, defenseless; BOT., ZOOL. without spines.
i·ner·te adj. inert, lifeless.
i·nes·cru·ta·ble adj. inscrutable.
i·nes·cu·dri·ña·ble adj. inscrutable.
i·nes·pe·ra·da·men·te adv. unexpectedly.
i·nes·pe·ra·do, –da adj. unexpected.
i·nes·ta·bi·li·dad f. instability.
i·nes·ta·ble adj. unstable.
i·nes·ti·ma·ble adj. inestimable, invaluable.
i·nes·ti·ma·do, –da adj. *(subestimado)* underestimated; *(sin tasar)* unestimated, unappraised.
i·ne·vi·ta·ble adj. inevitable.
i·ne·vi·ta·ble·men·te adv. inevitably.
i·ne·xac·ta·men·te adv. inexactly, inaccurately.
i·ne·xac·ti·tud f. inexactness, inaccuracy.
i·ne·xac·to, –ta adj. *(incorrecto)* inexact, inaccurate; *(falso)* untrue.
i·nex·cu·sa·ble adj. inexcusable.
i·nex·haus·to adj. unexhausted.
i·ne·xis·ten·cia f. inexistence, nonexistence.
i·ne·xis·ten·te adj. inexistent, nonexistent.
i·ne·xo·ra·ble adj. inexorable.
i·nex·pe·rien·cia f. inexperience.
i·nex·per·to, –ta *or* **in·ex·pe·ri·men·ta·do, –da** I. adj. inexpert, inexperienced II. m.f. inexperienced person, novice.
i·nex·pia·ble adj. inexpiable.
i·nex·pli·ca·ble adj. unexplainable, inexplicable.
i·nex·pli·ca·ble·men·te adv. inexplicably.

i·nex·plo·ra·do, –da adj. unexplored.
i·nex·plo·ta·ble adj. unexploitable.
i·nex·pre·sa·ble adj. inexpressible.
i·nex·pre·sa·do, –da adj. unexpressed.
i·nex·pre·si·vi·dad f. inexpressiveness, lack of expression.
i·nex·pre·si·vo, –va adj. inexpressive.
i·nex·pug·na·ble adj. *(invencible)* inexpugnable, impregnable; *(que no se puede tomar)* unassailable.
i·nex·ten·si·ble adj. inextensible, unextendible.
i·nex·ten·so, –sa adj. unextended.
i·nex·tin·gui·ble adj. *(que no se apaga)* inextinguishable; FIG. *(que no se aplaca)* unquenchable; *(inagotable)* eternal, perpetual.
i·nex·tir·pa·ble adj. inextirpable, ineradicable.
i·nex·tri·ca·ble adj. inextricable.
in·fa·li·bi·li·dad f. infallibility.
in·fa·li·ble adj. *(inequívoco)* infallible; *(inevitable)* certain, inevitable.
in·fa·li·ble·men·te adv. infallibly.
in·fa·ma·ción f. *(difamación)* defamation, slander; *(desacreditación)* dishonor, discredit.
in·fa·ma·dor, –do·ra I. adj. defamatory, slanderous II. m.f. *(difamador)* defamer, slanderer; *(desacreditador)* discreditor, detractor.
in·fa·man·te adj. defamatory, slanderous.
in·fa·mar tr. *(difamar)* to defame, slander; *(desacreditar)* discreditor, detractor.
in·fa·ma·to·rio, –ria adj. *(difamante)* defamatory, slanderous; *(que desacredita)* discrediting.
in·fa·me I. adj. *(deshonroso)* infamous; FIG. *(odioso)* odious, thankless; *(vil)* vile; *(sucio)* disgusting, dirty <*pocilga i.* disgusting hovel> II. m.f. infamous person.
in·fa·mia f. infamy.
in·fan·cia f. *(período de la vida)* infancy; *(niños)* children; FIG. *(principio)* infancy, beginning stage.
in·fan·ta f. *(niña)* infant, little girl; *(del rey)* infanta, princess.
in·fan·te m. *(niño)* infant, little boy; *(del rey)* infante, prince; MIL. *(soldado)* infantryman; *(del coro)* choirboy.
in·fan·te·rí·a f. infantry ♦ **i. de marina** marines.
in·fan·ti·ci·da I. adj. infanticidal II. m.f. infanticide (criminal).
in·fan·ti·ci·dio m. infanticide (crime).
in·fan·til adj. *(de niños)* infantile; *(aniñado)* infantile, childish.
in·fan·ti·lis·mo m. *(niñería)* childishness; MED. infantilism.
in·far·to m. MED. infarct, infarction.
in·fa·ti·ga·ble adj. indefatigable, untiring.
in·fa·ti·ga·ble·men·te adv. indefatigably, untiringly.
in·fa·tua·ción f. conceit, presumption.
in·fa·tuar §67 tr. to make conceited —reflex. to become conceited.
in·faus·to, –ta adj. *(desgraciado)* unfortunate; *(odioso)* accursed.
in·fec·ción f. infection.
in·fec·cio·so, –sa adj. infectious.
in·fec·ta·do, –da I. past part. see **infectar** II. adj. infected.
in·fec·tar tr. to infect —reflex. to become infected.
in·fec·to, –ta adj. *(inficionado)* infected, contaminated; *(pestilente)* foul.
in·fe·cun·di·dad f. infecundity, sterility.
in·fe·cun·do, –da adj. infecund, sterile.
in·fe·li·ci·dad f. unhappiness, infelicity.
in·fe·liz [pl. **-li·ces**] I. adj. *(desgraciado)* unfortunate, unhappy; *(miserable)* wretched, miserable; COLL. *(bondadoso)* good-hearted II. m.f. *(pobre diablo)* poor devil; COLL. *(persona bondadosa)* good-hearted person.
in·fe·ren·cia f. inference.
in·fe·rior I. adj *(de abajo)* lower <*el labio i.* the lower lip>; *(menor)* inferior <*especies inferiores* inferior species>; *(menos)* less <*uno es i. a dos* one is less than two> II. m. inferior, subordinate.
in·fe·rio·ri·dad f. inferiority.
in·fe·rior·men·te adv. in an inferior way.
in·fe·rir §65 tr. *(deducir)* to infer, deduce; *(ocasionar)* to cause, inflict damage, wound.
in·fer·nal adj. infernal.
in·fes·ta·ción f. infestation.

in·fes·tar tr. to infest; FIG. *(llenar)* to overrun, swamp.

in·fi·cio·nar tr. *(contaminar)* to infect, contaminate; *(envenenar)* to poison, taint; FIG. *(corromper)* to corrupt, pervert —reflex. *(contaminarse)* to become infected, become contaminated; FIG. *(corromperse)* to become corrupted.

in·fi·de·li·dad f. *(traición)* infidelity, unfaithfulness; RELIG. unbelief, disbelief.

in·fiel I. adj. *(falto de fidelidad)* unfaithful; *(desleal)* disloyal, faithless; *(inexacto)* inaccurate, inexact; RELIG. infidel, unbelieving **II.** m.f. RELIG. infidel, unbeliever.

in·fie·ra, infiero see **inferir.**

in·fi·rie·ra, infirió see **inferir.**

in·fier·no m. FIG. *(lugar)* Hell; *(tormento)* hell, torment; *(limbo)* Limbo; FIG. *(demonio)* Devil *<no se deben seguir os consejos del i.* one should not follow the Devil's advice>; *(lugar)* hell *<la guerra es un i.* war is hell>; *(lugar de desorden)* madhouse ♦ **en el quinto i.** FIG., COLL. (out) in the boondocks, in the middle of nowhere • **infiernos** MYTH. Hades.

in·fil·tra·ción f. infiltration.

in·fil·trar tr. & reflex. to infiltrate.

ín·fi·mo, –ma adj. *(muy bajo)* least, lowest; *(peor)* worst.

in·fi·ni·dad f. *(calidad de infinito)* infinity; *(multitud)* an infinity, a lot *<una i. de cosas* a lot of things>; *(muchedumbre)* countless *<una i. de personas* countless people>.

in·fi·ni·te·si·mal adj. infinitesimal.

in·fi·ni·ti·vo, –va adj. & m. GRAM. infinitive.

in·fi·ni·to, –ta I. adj. infinite ♦ **a lo i.** ad infinitum **II.** m. infinite; MATH., PHYS. infinity **III.** adv. infinitely, extremely.

in·fla·ción f. ECON. inflation; FIG. *(engreimiento)* conceit, vanity.

in·fla·cio·na·rio, –ria adj. inflationary.

in·fla·cio·nis·mo m. ECON. inflationism, inflation.

in·fla·cio·nis·ta adj. & m.f. inflationist.

in·fla·dor m. air pump, inflater.

in·fla·ma·bi·li·dad f. inflammability.

in·fla·ma·ble adj. inflammable.

in·fla·ma·ción f. *(ignición)* inflammation, ignition; MED. inflammation.

in·fla·mar tr. *(encender)* to ignite, set on fire; FIG. *(enardecer las pasiones)* to inflame *or* kindle the emotions —reflex. *(encenderse)* to ignite, catch fire; FIG. *(enardecerse)* to become inflamed *or* aroused.

in·fla·ma·to·rio, –ria adj. inflammatory.

in·fla·mien·to m. var. of **inflación.**

in·flar tr *(hinchar un objeto)* to inflate, blow up; FIG. *(envanecer)* to inflate *or* puff up with pride; FIG. *(exagerar)* to exaggerate, inflate —reflex. to become conceited *or* puffed up.

in·fle·xi·bi·li·dad f. inflexibility, rigidity.

in·fle·xi·ble adj. inflexible, rigid.

in·fle·xi·ble·men·te adv. inflexibly.

in·fle·xión f. *(dobladura)* bending, curving; *(voz)* inflection, modulation of the voice; GRAM. inflection; GEOM. inflection of a curve; PHYS. deflection.

in·fli·gir §32 tr. to inflict.

in·fluen·cia f. influence.

in·fluen·ciar tr. to influence.

in·fluen·za f. MED. influenza, flu.

in·fluir §18 intr. to have influence *<el clima influye sobre la arquitectura* climate has an influence on architecture>.

in·flu·jo m. *(influencia)* influence; *(flujo de la marea)* rising tide.

in·flu·yen·te adj. influential.

in·flu·yen·tis·mo m. MEX. the use of personal influence to achieve one's aims.

in·fo·lio m. book in folio form.

in·for·ma·ción f. *(datos)* information, data; LAW *(investigación)* investigation, inquiry; *(noticia)* news report; *(de un empleado)* references ♦ **i. sumaria** LAW summary proceedings • **tratamiento de la i.** COMPUT. data processing.

in·for·ma·dor, –ra I. adj. informing **I.** m.f. informer, informant.

in·for·mal adj. *(de conducta incorrecta)* ill-mannered, ill-behaved; *(poco de fiar)* unreliable, untrustworthy.

in·for·ma·li·dad f. *(mala conducta)* bad manners; *(falta de seriedad)* irresponsibility, unreliability.

in·for·man·te adj. informing.

in·for·mar tr. *(comunicar)* to inform, report; PHILOS. to shape, form —intr. LAW *(investigar)* to investigate, inquire into; LAW *(un abogado)* to plead; *(denunciar)* to inform on a person —reflex. *(enterarse)* to find out, get information.

in·for·má·ti·ca f. COMPUT. data processing.

in·for·ma·ti·vo, –va adj. informative.

in·for·me¹ adj. *(sin forma)* shapeless, formless; *(de forma vaga)* vague, indeterminate.

in·for·me² m. *(noticia)* report, piece of information; LAW *(exposición)* pleading ♦ **informes** *(noticias)* news; *(referencias)* references (of an employee) • **i. a. la prensa** press release.

in·for·mu·la·ble adj. incapable of being formulated.

in·for·tu·na·da·men·te adv. unfortunately.

in·for·tu·na·do, –da I. adj. unfortunate, unlucky **II.** m.f. unfortunate person.

in·for·tu·nio m. misfortune, bad luck.

in·frac·ción f. infraction, transgression.

in·frac·tor, –to·ra I. adj. infringing, transgressing **II.** m.f. transgressor.

in·fra·es·truc·tu·ra f. infrastructure, substructure.

in·fra·gan·ti adv. in the act, red-handed.

in·fra·hu·ma·no, –na adj. subhuman.

in·fran·que·a·ble adj. insurmountable, insuperable.

in·fra·rro·jo, –ja adj. PHYS. infrared.

in·fre·cuen·cia f. infrequency.

in·fre·cuen·te adj. infrequent.

in·frin·gir §32 tr. to infringe, violate.

in·fruc·tí·fe·ro, –ra adj. unfruitful, unprofitable.

in·fruc·tuo·sa·men·te adv. unfruitfully, unprofitably.

in·fruc·tuo·so, –sa adj. fruitless, useless.

ín·fu·la f. RELIG. infula ♦ **ínfulas** airs, conceit *<darse ínfulas* to put on airs>.

in·fu·ma·ble adj. unsmokable (said of tobacco); CUBA., MEX. intolerable, unacceptable.

in·fun·da·do, –da adj. unfounded, groundless.

in·fun·dia f. AMER. var. of **enjundia.**

in·fun·dí·bu·lo m. ANAT. infundibulum.

in·fun·dio m. COLL. lie, false story.

in·fun·dio·so, –sa adj. lying, mendacious.

in·fun·dir tr. *(comunicar un sentimiento)* to instill, arouse (a feeling or emotion); PHARM. to soak, steep.

in·fu·sión f. *(de un sentimiento)* infusion, inspiration (of a feeling); PHARM. *(de un medicamento)* soaking, steeping (of a remedy); *(bebida)* brew, infusion *<la manzanilla es una i. muy buena* chamomile tea is a very fine brew>; RELIG. sprinkling with holy water during baptism.

in·fu·so, –sa I. past part. see **infundir II.** adj. inborn, innate *<ciencias infusas* innate knowledge>.

in·ge·niar tr. to devise, contrive —reflex. to manage, find a way ♦ **ingeniárselas** to manage.

in·ge·nie·rí·a f. engineering.

in·ge·nie·ro m. engineer ♦ **i. agrónomo** agronomist, agricultural engineer • **i. civil** *or* **i. de caminos, canales y puertos** civil engineer • **i. de minas** mining engineer • **i. de montes** forester • **i. eléctrico** electrical engineer • **i. industrial** industrial engineer • **i. mecánico** mechanical engineer • **i. militar** army engineer • **i. naval** naval engineer • **i químico** chemical engineer • **ingenieros** MIL. engineering corps.

in·ge·nio m. *(habilidad)* ingenuity; *(persona)* creative person; *(talento)* talent, skill; *(agudeza)* wit, humor *<es un hombre de i.* he is a man of wit>; *(máquina)* device, apparatus; PRINT. *(guillotina)* paper cutter; AMER. *(plantación)* sugar plantation; *(fábrica)* sugar mill ♦ **afilar** *or* **aguzar el i.** FIG. to sharpen one's wits.

in·ge·nio·sa·men·te adv. ingeniously.

in·ge·nio·si·dad f. ingenuity, ingeniousness, cleverness.

in·ge·nio·so, –sa adj. *(hábil)* ingenious, resourceful; *(agudo)* witty.

in·gé·ni·to, –ta adj. innate, inborn.

in·gen·te adj. huge, enormous.

in·ge·nua·men·te adv. naively, ingenuously.

in·ge·nui·dad f. ingenuousness.

in·ge·nuo, –nua I. adj. ingenuous, naive **II.** m.f. naive *or* ingenuous person.

in·ge·rir §65 tr. to ingest, consume.
in·ges·tión f. ingestion.
In·gla·te·rra f. England.
in·gle f. ANAT. groin.
in·glés, –gle·sa I. adj. English II. m. *(habitante)* Englishman; *(idioma)* English —f. Englishwoman ♦ **los in·gleses** the English.
in·go·ber·na·ble adj. ungovernable.
in·gra·ta·men·te adv. ungratefully.
in·gra·ti·tud f. ingratitude, ungratefulness.
in·gra·to, –ta adj. *(desagradecido)* ungrateful; *(desagradable)* disagreeable, unpleasant; *(que no satisface)* thankless, unrewarding <*una tarea i.* thankless task>.
in·gra·vi·dez f. weightlessness, lightness.
in·grá·vi·do, –da adj. light, weightless.
in·gre·dien·te m. ingredient.
in·gre·sar intr. *(entrar)* to come in, enter; *(hacerse miembro)* to join, become a member of —tr. to deposit, pay a sum —reflex. MEX. to enlist, sign up.
in·gre·so m. *(acción de ingresar)* entrance, entry; *(entrada)* entrance, entryway; *(caudal)* income, revenue ♦ **ingresos** earnings, wages.
in·gui·nal or **in·gui·na·rio, –ria** adj. ANAT. inguinal.
in·há·bil adj. *(incapaz)* unskillful, incompetent; *(inadecuado)* unfit, unsuited <*i. para ser juzgado* incompetent or unfit to stand trial>.
in·ha·bi·li·dad f. *(falta de maña)* unskillfulness; *(ineptitud)* incompetence, ineptitude; *(impedimento para trabajar)* disability, handicap.
in·ha·bi·li·ta·ción f. *(impedimento para trabajar)* incapacitation, disablement; *(pena)* disqualification.
in·ha·bi·li·tar tr. *(declarar inhábil)* to disqualify, debar; *(hacer incapaz)* to disable, make unfit —reflex. to become disabled or incapacitated.
in·ha·bi·ta·ble adj. uninhabitable.
in·ha·bi·ta·do, –da adj. uninhabited, deserted.
in·ha·la·ción f. MED. inhalation.
in·ha·la·dor, –ra I. adj. inhalant II. MED. inhaler.
in·ha·lar tr. MED. to inhale.
in·he·ren·cia f. inherence.
in·he·ren·te adj. inherent.
in·hi·bi·ción f. PHYSIOL., PSYCH. inhibition.
in·hi·bir tr. to inhibit, restrain —reflex. to withdraw (from), stay out (of).
in·hi·bi·to·rio, –ria I. adj. inhibitory, restraining II. f. LAW restraining order.
in·hos·pi·ta·la·rio, –ria adj. inhospitable.
in·hos·pi·ta·li·dad f. inhospitableness, inhospitality.
in·hós·pi·to, –ta adj. var. of **inhospitalario.**
in·hu·ma·ción f. interment, burial.
in·hu·ma·na·men·te adv. inhumanly, cruelly.
in·hu·ma·ni·dad f. inhumanity, cruelty.
in·hu·ma·no, –na adj. *(falto de humanidad)* inhuman, cruel; CHILE filthy.
in·hu·mar tr. to bury, inter.
i·ni·cia·ción f. introduction, initiation.
i·ni·cia·do, –da I. past part. see **iniciar** II. adj. initiated III. m.f. initiate.
i·ni·cia·dor, –ra I. adj. initiating II. m.f. initiator.
i·ni·cial adj. & f. initial.
i·ni·ciar tr. *(admitir)* to initiate, introduce; *(empezar)* to start, begin —reflex. *(instruirse)* to teach oneself; RELIG. to receive holy orders.
i·ni·cia·ti·va f. initiative.
i·ni·cia·ti·vo, –va adj. initiating, initiatory.
i·ni·cio m. beginning.
i·ni·cua·men·te adv. iniquitously.
i·ni·cuo, –cua adj. iniquitous, wicked.
i·ni·gua·la·do, –da adj. peerless, unequaled.
i·ni·ma·gi·na·ble adj. unimaginable, inconceivable.
i·ni·mi·ta·ble adj. inimitable.
i·nin·te·li·gi·ble adj. unintelligible.
i·nin·te·rrum·pi·do, –da adj. uninterrupted.
i·ni·qui·dad f. iniquity, wickedness.
in·je·ren·cia f. meddling, interference.
in·je·rir §65 tr. FIG. to insert, introduce (one thing to another) —reflex. to meddle, interfere.
in·jer·tar tr. AGR., MED. to graft, implant.

in·jer·to m. AGR. graft, scion; MED. graft, transplant.
in·jer·to, –ta I. past part. see **injertar** II. adj. AGR., MED. grafted, implanted III. m. AGR. grafted tree.
in·ju·ria f. *(insulto)* insult, offense; *(daño)* damage, injury.
in·ju·ria·do m. CUBA low grade tobacco.
in·ju·ria·dor, –do·ra m.f. insulting or offensive person.
in·ju·riar tr. *(ofender)* to insult, offend; *(dañar)* to injure, damage.
in·ju·rio·so, –sa adj. injurious, offensive.
in·jus·ta·men·te adv. unjustly.
in·jus·ti·cia f. injustice.
in·jus·ti·fi·ca·ble adj. unjustifiable.
in·jus·ti·fi·ca·do, –da adj. unjustified, unwarranted.
in·jus·to, –ta adj. unjust.
in·ma·cu·la·do, –da adj. spotless, immaculate ♦ **la Inmaculada** the Virgin Mary.
in·ma·du·rez f. immaturity.
in·ma·du·ro, –ra adj. *(fruta)* unripe, green; *(persona)* immature, childish.
in·ma·ne·ja·ble adj. unmanageable.
in·ma·nen·te adj. immanent, inherent.
in·mar·ce·si·ble or **in·mar·chi·ta·ble** adj. unfading, imperishable.
in·ma·te·rial adj. immaterial.
in·ma·te·ria·li·dad f. immateriality.
in·ma·te·ria·lis·mo m. PHILOS. immaterialism.
in·ma·te·ria·li·zar §04 tr. to immaterialize.
in·ma·tu·ro, –ra adj. immature.
in·me·dia·ción f. immediacy ♦ **inmediaciones** environs, outskirts.
in·me·dia·ta·men·te adv. immediately.
in·me·dia·to, –ta adj. *(contiguo)* next to, adjoining <*el cuartio i. es mío* the adjoining room is mine>; *(sin tardanza)* immediately, at once ♦ **de i.** AMER. immediately • **venir** or **llegar a las inmediatas** to get to the core, get to the nitty-gritty.
in·me·jo·ra·ble adj. excellent, unbeatable.
in·me·mo·ra·ble adj. var. of **inmemorial.**
in·me·mo·rial adj. immemorial.
in·men·sa·men·te adv. immensely.
in·men·si·dad f. *(calidad de inmenso)* immensity, vastness; FIG. *(número grande)* vast number.
in·men·so, –sa adj. immense, endless.
in·men·su·ra·ble adj. immeasurable.
in·me·re·ci·da·men·te adv. undeservedly.
in·me·re·ci·do, –da adj. unmerited, undeserved.
in·mer·gir §32 tr. to immerse, submerge.
in·mer·sión f. immersion.
in·mer·so, –sa I. past part. see **inmergir** II. adj. immersed, submerged.
in·mi·gra·ción f. immigration.
in·mi·gra·do, –da I. past part. see **inmigrar** II. adj. & m.f. immigrant.
in·mi·gran·te adj. & m.f. immigrant.
in·mi·grar intr. to immigrate.
in·mi·gra·to·rio, –ria adj. immigrant.
in·mi·nen·cia f. imminence, imminency.
in·mi·nen·te adj. imminent.
in·mis·cuir §18 tr. to mix —reflex. to meddle, interfere.
in·mo·bi·lia·rio, –ria adj. real estate <*agente i.* real estate agent>.
in·mo·de·ra·ción f. immoderation, excess.
in·mo·de·ra·do, –da adj. immoderate, excessive.
in·mo·des·tia f. immodesty.
in·mo·des·to, –ta adj. immodest.
in·mo·la·ción f. immolation, sacrifice.
in·mo·la·dor, –do·ra I. adj. immolating II. m.f. immolator.
in·mo·lar tr. to immolate, sacrifice —reflex. to immolate oneself, sacrifice oneself.
in·mo·ral adj. immoral.
in·mo·ra·li·dad f. immorality.
in·mor·tal adj. immortal.
in·mor·ta·li·dad f. immortality.
in·mor·ta·li·zar §04 tr. to immortalize.
in·mo·vi·ble adj. fixed, immovable.
in·mó·vil adj. immobile, motionless.
in·mo·vi·li·dad f. immobility.

in·mo·vi·li·za·ción f. immobilization; COM. tying up capital.

in·mo·vi·li·zar §04 tr. *(parar)* to immobilize; COM. to tie up capital.

in·mu·da·ble adj. immutable, unchanging.

in·mue·ble I. adj. real <*bienes inmuebles* real estate> II. m. building.

in·mun·di·cia f. *(suciedad)* filth, dirt; FIG. *(impureza)* lewdness, obscenity.

in·mun·do, –da adj. *(sucio)* dirty, filthy; FIG. *(impuro)* indecent, impure.

in·mu·ne adj. MED. immune; *(libre)* free, exempt.

in·mu·ni·dad f. MED. immunity; *(exención)* freedom, exemption.

in·mu·ni·za·ción f. immunization.

in·mu·ni·zar §04 tr. to immunize.

in·mu·no·lo·gí·a f. MED. immunology.

in·mu·ta·bi·li·dad f. immutability.

in·mu·ta·ble adj. immutable.

in·mu·tar tr. to change —reflex. to lose one's composure.

in·na·to, –ta adj. innate, inherent.

in·na·ve·ga·ble adj. MARIT. *(mar o río)* unnavigable; *(barco)* unseaworthy.

in·ne·ce·sa·rio, –ria adj. unnecessary.

in·ne·ga·ble adj. undeniable.

in·no·ble adj. ignoble.

in·no·cuo, –cua adj. var. of **inocuo, –cua.**

in·no·va·ción f. innovation.

in·no·va·dor, –do·ra I. adj. innovative II. m.f. innovator.

in·no·var tr. to innovate.

in·nu·me·ra·ble adj. innumerable, countless.

i·nob·ser·va·ble adj. unobservable.

i·nob·ser·va·do, –da adj. unobserved.

i·nob·ser·van·cia f. inobservance.

i·no·cen·cia f. innocence.

i·no·cen·ta·da f. COLL. *(dicho o hecho sencillo)* naive remark or action; COLL. *(engaño)* naive mistake or blunder; *(broma)* April Fools' joke.

i·no·cen·te adj. & m.f. innocent ♦ **día de los i.** April Fools' Day • **los Inocentes** RELIG. the Innocents.

i·no·cen·te·men·te adv. innocently.

i·no·cen·tón, –to·na I. adj. naive, gullible II. m.f. booby, simpleton.

i·no·cui·dad f. innocuousness, harmlessness.

i·no·cu·la·ble adj. inoculable.

i·no·cu·la·ción f. inoculation.

i·no·cu·la·dor, –do·ra m.f. inoculator.

i·no·cu·lar tr. MED. to inoculate; FIG. *(pervertir)* to contaminate, corrupt.

i·no·cul·ta·ble adj. which cannot be concealed.

i·no·cuo, –cua adj. innocuous, harmless.

i·no·do·ro, –ra I. adj. odorless II. m. toilet, lavatory.

i·no·fen·si·vo, –va adj. inoffensive.

i·no·fi·cio·so, –sa adj. LAW inofficious (testament); AMER. inefficient, useless.

i·nol·vi·da·ble adj. unforgettable.

i·no·pe·ra·ble adj. inoperable.

i·no·pe·ran·te adj. inoperative, inapplicable.

i·no·pi·na·ble adj. indisputable.

i·no·pi·na·da·men·te adv. unexpectedly.

i·no·pi·na·do, –da adj. unexpected, unforeseen.

i·no·por·tu·na·men·te adv. inopportunely.

i·no·por·tu·ni·dad f. inopportuneness, untimeliness.

i·no·por·tu·no, –na adj. inopportune, ill-timed.

i·nor·gá·ni·co, –ca adj. inorganic.

i·no·xi·da·ble adj. inoxidable, rustproof ♦ **acero i.** stainless steel.

in·que·bran·ta·ble adj. unbreakable.

in·quie·ra, inquiero see **inquirir.**

in·quie·ta·men·te adv. uneasily, restlessly.

in·quie·tan·te adj. disquieting, disturbing.

in·quie·tar tr. *(perturbar)* to disturb; *(causar ansia)* to worry, alarm; *(tormentar)* to harass —reflex. to worry.

in·quie·to, –ta adj. *(intranquilo)* restless, fidgety; *(desasosegado)* worried, anxious; GUAT., HOND. inclined, predisposed.

in·quie·tud f. *(agitación)* restlessness, uneasiness; *(aprensión)* uneasiness, apprehension.

in·qui·li·na·je m. var. of **inquilinato.**

in·qui·li·na·to m. *(alquiler)* rental, leasing; *(derecho de ocupación)* tenancy.

in·qui·li·no, –na m.f. *(arrendatario)* tenant; ZOOL. inquiline; CHILE tenant farmer; AMER. occupant.

in·qui·na f. animosity, dislike ♦ **tenerle i. a alguien** to hold a grudge against, have it in for (someone).

in·qui·nar tr. to contaminate.

in·qui·ren·te m. NEOL. inquirer.

in·qui·ri·dor, –do·ra I. adj. inquiring, investigating II. m.f. inquirer, investigator.

in·qui·rir §02 tr. to investigate, probe.

in·qui·si·ción f. *(acción de inquirir)* inquisition, investigation; HIST. Inquisition.

in·qui·si·dor, –do·ra I. adj. inquiring, inquisitive II. m.f. *(que inquiere)* inquirer, investigator —m. HIST. Inquisitor.

in·qui·si·ti·vo, –va adj. inquisitive.

in·sa·cia·bi·li·dad f. insatiability.

in·sa·cia·ble adj. insatiable.

in·sa·cia·ble·men·te adv. insatiably.

in·sa·lu·bre adj. unhealthy, insalubrious.

in·sa·lu·bri·dad f. unhealthiness, insalubrity.

in·sa·na·ble adj. incurable.

in·sa·nia f. insanity, madness.

in·sa·no, –na adj. *(demente)* insane, mad; *(insalubre)* unhealthy.

in·sa·tis·fac·ción f. dissatisfaction.

in·sa·tis·fac·to·rio, –ria adj. unsatisfactory.

in·sa·tis·fe·cho, –cha adj. unsatisfied.

ins·cri·bir §85 tr. *(grabar)* to inscribe, engrave; *(matricular)* to register, enroll; *(anotar)* to enter, record <*inscribí su nombre en la lista de los jubilados* I recorded his name on the list of retirees>; GEOM. to inscribe —reflex. to register, enroll.

ins·crip·ción f. *(acción de inscribir)* inscribing, recording; *(epígrafe)* inscription, engraving; *(apuntamiento)* record, entry; *(matriculación)* registration, enrollment.

ins·cri·to, –ta or **ins·crip·to, –ta** I. past part. see **inscribir** II. adj. *(grabado)* engraved; *(registrado)* inscribed, registered; MATH. inscribed.

in·se·ca·ble adj. *(que no se puede secar)* which cannot be dried; *(que no se puede cortar)* indivisible.

in·sec·ti·ci·da I. adj. insecticidal II. m. insecticide.

in·sec·tí·vo·ro, –ra adj. ZOOL. insectivorous.

in·sec·to m. insect.

in·se·gu·ri·dad j. insecurity.

in·se·gu·ro, –ra adj. insecure.

in·se·mi·na·ción f. insemination ♦ **i. artificial** artificial insemination.

in·sen·sa·tez f. [pl. **-te·ces**] *(estupidez)* senselessness, stupidity; FIG. *(dicho)* foolish remark; *(hecho)* piece of foolishness.

in·sen·sa·to, –ta I. adj. foolish, senseless II. m.f. fool, dolt.

in·sen·si·bi·li·dad f. insensibility, insensitivity.

in·sen·si·bi·li·za·ción f. anesthetization.

in·sen·si·bi·li·za·dor, –do·ra adj. & m.f. anesthetic.

in·sen·si·bi·li·zar §04 tr. to anesthetize.

in·sen·si·ble adj. *(que no se puede sentir)* insensible; FIG *(sin compasión)* callous, unfeeling; *(imperceptible)* imperceptible; *(inconsciente)* anesthetized, unconscious.

in·sen·si·ble·men·te adv. slowly, imperceptibly.

in·se·pa·ra·bi·li·dad f. inseparability.

in·se·pa·ra·ble adj. inseparable.

in·se·pa·ra·ble·men·te adv. inseparably.

in·se·pul·to, –ta adj. unburied.

in·ser·ción f. insertion.

in·ser·tar tr. to insert, attach —reflex. BOT., ZOOL. to be inserted or attached.

in·ser·to, –ta I. past part. see **insertar** II. adj. inserted, attached.

in·ser·vi·ble adj. unusable, unserviceable.

in·si·dia f. trap, snare; *(mala intención)* malice.

in·si·dio·sa·men·te adv. insidiously.

in·si·dio·so, –sa adj. insidious, treacherous.

in·sig·ne adj. famous, illustrious.

in·sig·nia f. badge, emblem.

in·sig·ni·fi·can·cia f. insignificance.

in·sig·ni·fi·can·te adj. insignificant, unimportant.
in·sin·ce·ri·dad f. insincerity.
in·sin·ce·ro –ra adj. insincere.
in·si·nua·ción f. *(acción de insinuar)* insinuation, suggestion; LAW *(derecho)* presentation of an exhibit to a judge; RHET. part of the exordium of a speech.
in·si·nua·dor, –do·ra I. adj. insinuating, suggestive II. m.f. insinuator.
in·si·nuan·te adj. insinuating.
in·si·nuar §67 tr. to insinuate, suggest —reflex. to ingratiate oneself.
in·si·nua·ti·vo, –va adj. insinuating.
in·si·pi·da·men·te adv. insipidly.
in·si·pi·dez f. insipidness.
in·sí·pi·do, –da adj. *(que no tiene sabor)* tasteless, bland; FIG. *(falto de espíritu)* dull, lifeless.
in·sis·ten·cia f. insistence.
in·sis·ten·te adj. insistent.
in·sis·tir intr. to insist ♦ **i. en** to insist on • **i. en que** to insist *or* maintain that.
in·so·bor·na·ble adj. incorruptible.
in·so·cia·bi·li·dad f. unsociability.
in·so·cia·ble adj. unsociable.
in·so·la·ción f. PHOTOG. exposure; MED. sunstroke, overexposure; METEOROL. insolation.
in·so·lar tr. to insolate, expose to the sun —reflex. MED. to get sunstroke.
in·so·len·cia f. *(calidad de insolente)* insolence, arrogance; *(palabra o acción ofensiva)* insolent remark *or* action.
in·so·len·tar tr. to make insolent —reflex. to be insolent.
in·so·len·te adj. insolent, arrogant.
in·so·len·te·men·te adv. insolently.
in·so·li·da·ri·dad f. lack of solidarity.
in·só·li·to, –ta adj. unusual, uncommon.
in·so·lu·bi·li·dad f. insolubility.
in·so·lu·bi·li·zar §04 tr. to make insoluble.
in·so·lu·ble adj. insoluble.
in·so·lu·to, –ta adj. unpaid <*una deuda i.* an unpaid debt>.
in·sol·ven·cia f. insolvency.
in·sol·ven·te adj. & m.f. insolvent.
in·som·ne adj. suffering from insomnia, sleepless.
in·som·nio m. insomnia, sleeplessness.
in·son·da·ble adj. unfathomable.
in·so·no·ri·za·ción f. soundproofing.
in·so·no·ri·zar §04 tr. to soundproof.
in·so·no·ro, –ra adj. soundless.
in·so·por·ta·ble adj. unbearable, intolerable.
in·sos·pe·cha·ble adj. *(sorprendente)* unexpected; *(que no puede ser sospechado)* above suspicion.
in·sos·pe·cha·do, –da adj. unsuspected.
in·sos·te·ni·ble adj. untenable.
ins·pec·ción f. inspection, examination.
ins·pec·cio·nar tr. to inspect, examine.
ins·pec·tor, –to·ra I. adj. inspecting, examining II. m.f. inspector, examiner ♦ **i. de aduanas** customs inspector • **i. de policía** police inspector.
ins·pec·to·rí·a f. CHILE police station.
ins·pi·ra·ción f. *(de ideas)* inspiration; PHYSIOL. *(del aire)* inhalation, breathing.
ins·pi·ra·do, –da I. past part. see **inspirar** II. adj. inspired.
ins·pi·ra·dor, –do·ra I. adj. *(que inspira)* inspiring ANAT. inspiratory II. m.f. inspirer
ins·pi·rar tr. PHYSIOL. to inhale; *(infundir sentimientos ajenos)* to inspire —reflex. to be inspired (by).
ins·pi·ra·ti·vo, –va adj. inspiring, inspirational.
ins·ta·bi·li·dad f. instability.
ins·ta·ble adj. unstable.
ins·ta·la·ción f. *(acción de instalar)* installation; *(fábrica)* plant, installation; *(equipo)* equipment ♦ **i. sanitaria** plumbing.
ins·ta·la·dor, –do·ra I. adj. installing II. m.f. installer, fitter ♦ **i. de cañerías** plumber, pipefitter.
ins·ta·lar tr. *(colocar)* to install; *(poner en un cargo)* to instate, install —reflex. to settle, establish oneself.
ins·tan·cia f. *(petición)* petition, entreaty; LAW *(derecho)* instance <*tribunal de primera i.* court of first instance> ♦ **a i. de** at the request of, upon petition of • **en última i.** as a final resort.

ins·tan·tá·ne·a f. PHOTOG. snapshot.
ins·tan·tá·ne·a·men·te adv. immediately, instantaneously.
ins·tan·tá·ne·o, –ne·a adj. instantaneous.
ins·tan·te m. instant, moment ♦ **a cada i.** constantly, all the time • **al i.** immediately.
ins·tar tr. to urge, press —intr. to be urgent <*insta que sepamos la verdad* it is urgent that we know the truth>.
ins·tau·ra·ción f. *(renovación)* renovation, restoration; *(establecimiento)* establishment, institution.
ins·tau·ra·dor, –do·ra I. adj. *(que establece)* establishing, institutive; *(que restaura)* restorative II. m.f. *(restaurador)* restorer; *(establecedor)* establisher.
ins·tau·rar tr. *(establecer)* to establish, institute; *(restaurar)* to restore.
ins·tau·ra·ti·vo, –va adj. & m. restorative.
ins·ti·ga·ción f. instigation, incitement.
ins·ti·ga·dor, –do·ra I. adj. instigating II. m.f. instigator.
ins·ti·gar §47 tr. to incite, urge.
ins·ti·la·ción f. PHARM. *(de líquidos)* instillation of liquids; FIG. *(de ideas)* instillation, infusion of ideas.
ins·ti·lar tr. PHARM. *(líquidos)* to instill liquids; FIG. *(ideas)* to instill, infuse (ideas).
ins·tin·ti·va·men·te adv. instinctively.
ins·tin·ti·vo, –va adj. instinctive.
ins·tin·to m. instinct ♦ **por i.** by instinct.
ins·ti·tu·ción f. institution ♦ **i. de un heredero** LAW institution *or* appointment of an heir • **instituciones** principles, elements.
ins·ti·tu·cio·nal adj. institutional.
ins·ti·tu·cio·na·li·za·ción f. institutionalization.
ins·ti·tu·cio·na·li·zar §04 tr. to institutionalize.
ins·ti·tuir §18 tr. *(fundar)* to institute, found; *(enseñar)* to teach, instruct.
ins·ti·tu·to m. *(establecimiento)* institute; *(orden religiosa)* religious order; *(escuela)* school <*i. de segunda enseñanza* secondary school>.
ins·ti·tu·tor, –to·ra I. adj. *(que instituye)* founding, instituting; *(que enseña)* teaching II. m.f. *(instituidor)* founder, instituter —m. COL. schoolteacher.
ins·ti·tu·triz f. [pl. **-tri·ces**] governess.
ins·ti·tu·ya, instituyo see **instituir**.
ins·ti·tu·yen·te I. adj. instituting, founding II. m.f. founder, instituter.
ins·ti·tu·ye·ra, instituyó see **instituir**.
ins·truc·ción f. *(enseñanza)* instruction, teaching; *(educación)* education <*i. pública* public education>; *(conocimiento)* learning, knowledge <*un hombre de poca i.* a man of little learning>; *(en derecho)* proceedings; MIL. training, drill ♦ **instrucciones** instructions, directions.
ins·truc·ti·va·men·te adv. instructively.
ins·truc·ti·vo, –va adj. instructive.
ins·truc·tor, –to·ra I. adj. instruction, instructional II. m.f. instructor, trainer.
ins·trui·do, –da I. past part. see **instruir** II. adj. educated, learned.
ins·truir §18 tr. *(enseñar)* to instruct, teach; *(informar)* to inform, tell; SPORT. to train, drill; LAW to investigate, examine a case.
ins·tru·men·ta·ción f. MUS. instrumentation, arrangement.
ins·tru·men·tal adj. MUS. instrumental; LAW documentary <*prueba i.* documentary evidence> II. m. MUS., SURG. instruments; GRAM. instrumental case.
ins·tru·men·tar tr. to orchestrate, arrange.
ins·tru·men·tis·ta m.f. instrumentalist, musician.
ins·tru·men·to m. *(utensilio)* instrument, tool; *(escritura)* document; MUS. instrument <*i. de viento* wind instrument>; FIG. *(medio)* instrument, device.
ins·tru·ya, instruyo see **instruir**.
ins·tru·ye·ra, instruyó see **instruir**.
in·su·bor·di·na·ción f. insubordination.
in·su·bor·di·na·do, –da I. adj. insubordinate, rebellious II. m.f. rebel.
in·su·bor·di·nar tr. to stir up, incite to rebellion —reflex. to rebel.
in·sub·sa·na·ble adj. irreparable, unrepairable.
in·subs·tan·cial I. adj. *(de poca substancia)* insubstantial; FIG. *(trivial)* trite, shallow II. m.f. shallow *or* superficial person.

in·subs·tan·cia·li·dad f. *(falta de substancialidad)* insubstantiality; FIG. *(trivialidad)* triteness, superficiality.
in·subs·tan·cial·men·te adv. insubstantially.
in·subs·ti·tui·ble adj. irreplaceable.
in·su·fi·cien·cia f. *(escasez)* insufficiency, scarcity; *(incompetencia)* inadequacy, incompetence; MED. insufficiency, failure <i. cardíaca heart failure>.
in·su·fi·cien·te adj. *(escaso)* insufficient, inadequate; *(inepto)* incompetent, inept.
in·su·flar tr. to insufflate.
in·su·fri·ble adj. insufferable, intolerable.
ín·su·la f. ARCH. island, isle.
in·su·lar I. adj. island, insular II. m.f. islander.
in·su·la·ri·dad f. insularity.
in·su·li·na f. PHYSIOL. insulin.
in·sul·sez f. *(falta de sabor)* blandness, tastelessness; FIG. *(falta de gracia)* dullness, inanity.
in·sul·so, –sa adj. *(que no tiene sabor)* bland, tasteless; *(insípido)* dull, inane.
in·sul·ta·da f. AMER. insult.
in·sul·ta·dor, –do·ra I. adj. insulting II. m.f. insulter.
in·sul·tan·te adj. insulting, offensive.
in·sul·tar tr. to insult, offend.
in·sul·to m. insult, offense.
in·su·mer·gi·ble adj. unsinkable.
in·su·mi·sión f. disobedience, defiance.
in·su·mi·so, –sa I. adj. defiant, unsubmissive II. m.f. rebel.
in·su·mo m. COM. reinvestment.
in·su·pe·ra·ble adj. insuperable, insurmountable.
in·sur·gen·te adj. & m.f. insurgent.
in·su·rrec·ción f. insurrection.
in·su·rrec·cio·nal adj. insurrectional.
in·su·rrec·cio·nar tr. to incite to insurrection —reflex. to rebel, rise up in arms.
in·su·rrec·to, –ta I. adj. insurrectionary, insurgent II. m.f. rebel, revolutionary.
in·sus·tan·cial adj. var. of **insubstancial.**
in·sus·ti·tui·ble adj. var. of **insubstituible.**
in·tac·to, –ta adj. intact, untouched.
in·ta·cha·ble adj. irreproachable, stainless.
in·tan·gi·bi·li·dad f. intangibility.
in·tan·gi·ble adj. intangible.
in·te·gra·ción f. *(acción de integrar)* integration; MATH. integral calculus.
in·te·gra·dor, –do·ra I. adj. integrating II. m.f. integrator.
in·te·gral I. adj. integral II. f. MATH. integral.
ín·te·gra·men·te adv. integrally.
in·te·gran·te adj. *(que integra)* integrating; *(integral)* integral.
in·te·grar tr. *(componer)* to make up, compose; *(hacer entrar)* to integrate; *(reintegrar)* to reimburse; MATH. to integrate; AMER. to pay ♦ estar integrado por to be composed of.
in·te·gri·dad f. *(rectitud)* integrity, honesty; *(entereza)* wholeness, completeness; *(virginidad)* virginity, maidenhood.
ín·te·gro, –gra adj. *(entero)* whole, complete; FIG. *(honrado)* honest, upright.
in·te·lec·ción f. intellection.
in·te·lec·ti·vo, –va I. adj. intellective II. f. intellect, intelligence.
in·te·lec·to m. intellect, mind.
in·te·lec·tual adj. & m.f. intellectual.
in·te·lec·tua·li·dad f. *(entendimiento)* intellect; *(conjunto de intelectuales)* intelligentsia.
in·te·lec·tua·lis·mo m. intellectualism.
in·te·lec·tua·lis·ta adj. & m.f. intellectualist.
in·te·lec·tua·li·zar §04 intr. to intellectualize.
in·te·lec·tual·men·te adv. intellectually.
in·te·li·gen·cia f. *(facultad de comprender)* intelligence, intellect; *(comprensión)* understanding, knowledge; *(habilidad)* skill, ability <tener i. para las matemáticas to be skilled in math>; *(correspondencia secreta)* intelligence, information ♦ en la i. de que on the understanding that • estar en i. con to be in league with.
in·te·li·gen·te I. adj. intelligent, clever II. m.f. intelligent person.

in·te·li·gi·bi·li·dad f. intelligibility.
in·te·li·gi·ble adj. intelligible.
in·te·li·gi·ble·men·te adv. intelligibly.
in·tem·pe·ran·cia f. intemperance, immoderation.
in·tem·pe·ran·te adj. intemperate, immoderate.
in·tem·pe·rie f. inclemency, bad weather ♦ a la i. outdoors, exposed (to the weather).
in·tem·pes·ti·va·men·te adv. inopportunely.
in·tem·pes·ti·vo, –va adj. inopportune, ill-timed.
in·tem·po·ral adj. *(independiente del tiempo)* nontemporal; *(eterno)* eternal.
in·ten·ción f. *(proyecto)* intention, plan; *(voluntad)* will, wish <el hijo cumplió con las últimas intenciones de su padre the son obeyed his father's last wishes>; FIG. *(instinto dañino)* viciousness in animals ♦ con i. intentionally • cura de primera i. first aid • primera i. frankness, candor • segunda i. underhandedness, duplicity • tener malas intenciones to be up to no good.
in·ten·cio·na·da·men·te adv. intentionally.
in·ten·cio·na·do, –da adj. intentioned.
in·ten·cio·nal adj. intentional.
in·ten·cio·na·li·dad f. intentionality.
in·ten·cio·nal·men·te adv. intentionally.
in·ten·den·cia f. *(cargo)* intendancy; *(división territorial)* intendancy, district; *(oficina)* office of an intendant ♦ i. militar MIL. quartermaster corps.
in·ten·den·te m. intendant ♦ i. del ejército MIL. quartermaster general.
in·ten·sa·men·te adv. intensely.
in·ten·si·dad f. intensity, strength ♦ i. máxima de corriente ELEC. peak current.
in·ten·si·fi·ca·ción f. intensification.
in·ten·si·fi·ca·dor, –do·ra adj. intensifying.
in·ten·si·fi·car §70 tr. to intensify.
in·ten·sión f. var. of **intensidad.**
in·ten·si·vo, –va adj. intensive, intense.
in·ten·so, –sa adj. intense, vivid.
in·ten·tar tr. *(tener intención)* to intend, plan; *(ensayar)* to try, attempt; LAW to institute proceedings ♦ i. un proceso contra to bring a suit against.
in·ten·to m. intent, intention ♦ de i. intentionally, on purpose • i. de suicidio suicide attempt.
in·ten·to·na f. COLL. rash or foolhardy attempt.
ín·ter I. adv. meanwhile II. m. meantime, interim ♦ en el í in the meantime.
in·te·rac·ción f. interaction.
in·te·ra·me·ri·ca·no, –na adj. inter-American.
in·te·ran·di·no, –na adj. inter-Andean.
in·te·ras·tral adj. ASTRON. interstellar.
in·ter·ca·la·ción f. intercalation, interpolation.
in·ter·ca·lar adj. intercalary (day).
in·ter·ca·lar tr. to intercalate, interpolate.
in·ter·cam·bia·ble adj. interchangeable.
in·ter·cam·biar tr. to interchange, exchange.
in·ter·cam·bio m. interchange, exchange.
in·ter·ce·der tr. to intercede.
in·ter·cep·tar tr. *(detener)* to intercept; *(obstruir)* to block, hold up; *(un teléfono)* to tap, wiretap.
in·ter·ce·sión f. intercession, mediation.
in·ter·ce·sor, –so·ra I. adj. interceding II. m.f. intercessor, mediator.
in·ter·co·mu·ni·ca·ción f. intercommunication.
in·ter·co·ne·xión f. interconnection.
in·ter·con·ti·nen·tal adj. intercontinental.
in·ter·cul·tu·ral. adj. intercultural.
in·ter·de·cir §11 tr. to prohibit, interdict.
in·ter·de·pen·den·cia f. interdependence.
in·ter·dic·ción f. prohibition, interdiction.
in·ter·di·gi·tal adj. ZOOL. interdigital.
in·ter·dis·ci·pli·nar or in·ter·dis·ci·pli·na·rio, –ria adj. interdisciplinary.
in·te·rés m. *(provecho)* interest, self-interest <Juan se guía sólo por sus propios intereses John is guided only by his own interests>; COM., FIN. *(utilidad)* interest; FIG. *(valor)* interest <este libro no tiene i. para mí this book has no interest for me> ♦ devengar i. to bear interest • i. acumulado or devengado accrued interest • i. compuesto compound interest • i. dominante controlling interest • i.

público public interest • **i. simple** simple interest • **intereses** possessions, interest • **intereses creados** vested interests • **intereses vencidos** interest due • **sentir** or **tener i. en** to be interested in • **tipo de i.** rate of interest.

in·te·re·sa·do, –da I. past part. see **interesar II.** adj. *(que tienen interés)* interested; *(guiado por el interés)* selfish, mercenary **III.** m.f. interested person or party.

in·te·re·san·te adj. interesting.

in·te·re·sar tr. *(dar parte en un negocio)* to give (someone) an interest in a business; *(inspirar interés)* to interest, arouse interest in; *(afectar)* to affect, afflict (an organ) —intr. to be of interest or concern <*interesó el informe por su brevedad* the report was of interest because of its brevity> —reflex. to be or become interested in <*interesarse por el derecho* to be interested in the law>.

in·te·res·te·lar adj. ASTRON. interstellar.

in·ter·fe·ren·cia f. interference ♦ **interferencias atmosféricas** RAD. atmospheric interference.

in·ter·fe·ren·te adj. PHYS. interfering.

in·ter·fe·rir §65 intr. to interfere.

in·ter·gu·ber·na·men·tal adj. intergovernmental.

in·ter·hu·ma·no, –na adj. interpersonal.

ín·te·rin I. m. interim, meantime <*en el í.* in the meantime> **II.** adv. *(mientras)* while; *(hasta que)* until; *(entretanto)* meanwhile ♦ **por í.** temporarily.

in·te·ri·na·men·te adv. temporarily, provisionally.

in·te·ri·na·to m. AMER. interim; CHILE, HOND. temporary post.

in·te·ri·ni·dad f. *(calidad de interino)* temporariness; *(tiempo que dura un cargo interino)* temporary employment.

in·te·ri·no, –na I. adj. temporary, interim <*una medida i.* an interim measure>; acting <*presidente i.* acting president> **II.** m.f. deputy, substitute.

in·te·rin·su·lar adj. between islands.

in·te·rior I. adj. *(interno)* interior, inner <*patio i.* interior patio>; ECON., POL. *(nacional)* domestic, internal; FIG. *(íntimo)* inner, innermost <*en mis pensamientos interiores* in my innermost thoughts> **II.** m. *(parte interna)* interior, inside; FIG. *(alma)* heart, soul <*sabía la respuesta en su i.* he knew the answer in his heart>; GEOG. interior; SPORT. *(en fútbol)* inside forward ♦ **interiores** *(ropa)* underwear, underclothes; *(entrañas)* entrails.

in·te·rio·ri·dad f. interiority, inwardness ♦ **interioridades** private affairs.

in·te·rior·men·te adv. inside, inwardly.

in·ter·jec·ción f. GRAM. interjection.

in·ter·jec·ti·vo, –va adj. interjectional.

in·ter·lí·ne·a f. *(espacio)* space between lines; *(escritura)* interlineation, interlining; PRINT. lead, leading.

in·ter·li·ne·a·do, –da I. past part. see **interlinear II.** adj. *(escrito)* interlined; PRINT. leaded **III.** m. *(escritura)* interlineation, interlining; PRINT. leading.

in·ter·li·ne·al adj. interlinear.

in·ter·li·ne·ar tr. to interline.

in·ter·lo·cu·tor, –to·ra m.f. interlocutor.

in·ter·me·diar tr. to mediate.

in·ter·me·dia·rio, –ria I. adj. intermediate **II.** m. intermediary.

in·ter·me·dio, –dia I. adj. intermediate **II.** m. *(intervalo)* interval, interim; THEAT. interlude, intermezzo.

in·ter·mi·na·ble adj. interminable, endless.

in·ter·mi·nis·te·rial adj. interministerial.

in·ter·mi·sión f. intermission, interruption.

in·ter·mi·ten·cia f. *(interrupción)* intermittence; MED. intermission (of fever symptoms).

in·ter·mi·ten·te I. adj. intermittent **II.** m. flashing light, traffic signal.

in·ter·na·ción f. *(hospitalización)* hospitalization; *(encerramiento)* internment, confinement.

in·ter·na·cio·nal I. adj. international **II.** f. ♦ **La Internacional** POL. International (socialist organization).

in·ter·na·cio·na·lis·mo m. internationalism.

in·ter·na·cio·na·lis·ta adj. & m.f. POL. internationalist.

in·ter·na·cio·na·li·za·ción f. internationalization.

in·ter·na·cio·na·li·zar §04 tr. to internationalize.

in·ter·na·do I. m. *(escuela)* boarding school; *(alumnos)* boarding students, boarders **II.** adj. see **internado, –da.**

in·ter·na·do, –da I. past. part. see **internar II.** adj. institutionalized **III.** m. see **internado.**

in·ter·na·men·te adv. internally.

in·ter·na·mien·to m. internment.

in·ter·nar tr. *(hospitalizar)* to hospitalize; *(trasladar)* to send inland; *(encerrar)* to confine <*i. en una prisión* to confine in a prison —reflex. *(penetrar)* to penetrate, move inland; *(profundizar)* to study intensely, go deeply into a subject; FIG. *(intimar)* to work one's way into another's confidence.

in·ter·nis·ta m. MED. internist.

in·ter·no, –na I. adj. *(de adentro)* internal <*dolor i.* internal pain>; *(interior)* interior, inside <*patio i.* interior patio>; *(estudiante)* boarding (student) **II.** m.f. boarder, boarding student.

in·te·ro·ce·á·ni·co, –ca adj. interoceanic.

in·ter·pe·la·ción f. *(interrogación)* interpellation; *(ruego)* appeal, plea.

in·ter·pe·lan·te I. adj. *(interrogante)* interrogating; *(suplicante)* appealing, pleading **II.** m.f. *(interrogador)* interpellator; *(suplicante)* appealer.

in·ter·pe·lar tr. POL. *(demandar)* to interpellate; *(preguntar)* to ask; *(rogar)* to appeal, plead.

in·ter·pe·ne·tra·ción f. interpenetration.

in·ter·pla·ne·ta·rio, –ria adj. interplanetary.

in·ter·po·la·ción f. interpolation.

in·ter·po·lar tr. *(intercalar)* to interpolate; *(interrumpir)* to interrupt; MATH. to interpolate.

in·ter·po·ner §54 tr. *(intercalar)* to interpose, put or place between; LAW *(en derecho)* to lodge or file (an appeal); FIG. *(ejercer)* to interpose, exercise <*el senador interpuso su autoridad para conseguir el dinero* the senator interposed his authority to get the money> —reflex. *(intervenir)* to intervene; *(estorbar)* to block, get in the way of <*nada se interpuso en su carrera* nothing got in the way of his career>.

in·ter·po·si·ción f. interposition.

in·ter·pó·si·to, –ta adj. intervening, mediating ♦ **i. persona** LAW *(en derecho)* intermediary, agent; *(tercera persona)* third party.

in·ter·pre·ta·ble adj. interpretable.

in·ter·pre·ta·ción f. interpretation ♦ **i. auténtica** or **legislativa** LAW authentic interpretation • **i. judicial** LAW legal interpretation • **i. restrictiva** LAW limited interpretation • **mala i.** misinterpretation.

in·ter·pre·ta·dor, –do·ra I. adj. interpreting **II.** m.f. interpreter.

in·ter·pre·tar tr. *(explicar)* to interpret; MUS. to perform, sing; THEAT. to play (a role) ♦ **i. mal** to misinterpret.

in·ter·pre·ta·ti·vo, –va adj. interpretative, interpretive.

in·tér·pre·te m.f. *(traductor)* interpreter; *(actor)* actor; *(cantante)* singer.

in·ter·pues·to, –ta I. past part. see **interponer II.** adj. interposed.

in·ter·pu·sie·ra, interpuso see **interponer.**

in·te·rreg·no m. interregnum (period of time between kings).

in·te·rro·ga·ción f. *(acción)* interrogation; *(pregunta)* question; GRAM. question mark.

in·te·rro·ga·dor, –do·ra I. adj. interrogating, questioning **II.** m.f. interrogator.

in·te·rro·gan·te I. adj. interrogating ♦ **punto i.** GRAM. question mark **II.** m. *(pregunta)* question; *(incógnita)* unanswered question <*después de la conferencia quedaron muchas interrogantes* there were many unanswered questions at the end of the lecture>.

in·te·rro·gar §47 tr. to interrogate, question.

in·te·rro·ga·ti·va·men·te adv. *(con interrogación)* interrogatively; *(con duda)* questioningly.

in·te·rro·ga·ti·vo, –va adj. & m. interrogative.

in·te·rro·ga·to·rio m. LAW *(acto)* interrogation, examination; *(pregunta)* interrogatory.

in·te·rro·gue, interrogue see **interrogar.**

in·te·rrum·pir tr. *(suspender)* to interrupt, discontinue <*tuve que i. mis vacaciones* I had to interrupt my vacation>; *(cortar la palabra)* to interrupt <*ella me interrumpió justo cuando yo comenzaba a decirlo* she interrupted me just when I began to say it>; *(obstruir)* to block, obstruct <*los escombros interrumpieron el paso de los bomberos* the debris blocked the path of the firemen>; ELEC. to interrupt, shut off (power).

in·te·rrup·ción f. interruption.

in·te·rrup·tor ELEC. m. *(de pared)* wall switch; *(de circuito)* circuit breaker ♦ **i. auxiliar** booster switch • **i. con fusible** fuse switch • **i. de dos direcciones** two-way switch • **i. de dos posiciones** double-throw switch • **i. de mando** control switch • **i. de palanca acodada** *or* **de volquete** toggle switch • **i. de pie** foot switch • **i. unipolar** single-throw switch.

in·ter·sec·ción f. intersection.

in·ter·si·de·ral adj. ASTRON. interstellar.

in·ters·ti·cio m. interstice, gap.

in·te·rur·ba·no, –na adj. interurban.

in·ter·va·lo m. interval ♦ **a intervalos** at intervals, intermittently.

in·ter·ven·ción f. *(medicación)* intervention, mediation; *(participación)* participation; *(examen de cuentas)* auditing, audit ♦ **i. quirúrgica** SURG. surgical procedure, operation.

in·ter·ven·cio·nis·mo m. POL. interventionism.

in·ter·ven·cio·nis·ta adj. & m.f. POL. interventionist.

in·ter·ve·nir §76 intr. *(participar)* to participate, take part <*me gusta i. en los asuntos de mi vecindario* I like to participate in the affairs of my neighborhood>; *(interceder)* to intervene, mediate; *(interponerse)* to intervene, interfere <*finalmente, la policía tuvo que i.* finally, the police had to intervene>; *(ocurrir)* to happen, occur —tr. *(examinar cuentas)* to audit; *(controlar)* to control; *(vigilar la comunicación)* to tap, wiretap (a telephone); SURG. to operate on.

in·ter·ven·tor, –to·ra I. adj. intervening, participating II. m. government-appointed official who insures that legal procedures are followed.

in·tes·ta·do, –da adj. LAW intestate.

in·tes·ti·nal adj. intestinal.

in·tes·ti·no I. m. ANAT. intestine ♦ **i. ciego** ANAT. caecum • **i. delgado** ANAT. small intestine • **i. grueso** ANAT. large intestine II. adj. see **intestino, –na.**

in·tes·ti·no, –na I. adj. PHYSIOL. internal; POL. domestic, internal <*guerra i.* internal warfare> II. m. see **intestino.**

in·tí m. PERU, FIN. inti (currency worth 1,000 soles).

in·ti·ma *or* **in·ti·ma·ción** f. *(conminación)* ultimatum, warning; *(indicio)* hint, intimation; LAW notice <*i. judicial* judicial notice>.

in·ti·mar tr. *(hacer saber)* to make known, announce; *(mandar)* to order —intr. to become intimate *or* friendly.

in·ti·ma·to·rio, –ria adj. LAW notifying, giving notice.

in·ti·mi·da·ción f. intimidation.

in·ti·mi·dad f. *(amistad)* close friendship *or* relationship <*ese estudiante tiene i. con el profesor* that student has a close relationship with the teacher>; *(vida privada)* privacy <*nadie logra invadir su i.* no one can invade his privacy>; *(cercanía)* intimacy, closeness; *(círculo)* circle of friends, acquaintances ♦ **en la i.** privately • **en la i. de** in the privacy of.

in·ti·mi·dar tr. to intimidate.

ín·ti·mo, –ma I. adj *(interior)* intimate, innermost <*en mis pensamientos íntimos* in my innermost thoughts>; *(esencial)* essential <*la naturaleza í. del hombre* the essential nature of man>; *(estrecho)* intimate, close (relationship, friend); *(privado)* private <*boda i.* private wedding> II. m.f. intimate *or* close friend.

in·ti·tu·lar tr. & reflex. var. of **titular².**

in·to·ca·ble adj. untouchable.

in·to·le·ra·ble adj. intolerable.

in·to·le·ran·cia f. intolerance.

in·to·le·ran·te I. adj. intolerant II. m.f. intolerant person.

in·to·xi·ca·ción f. intoxication.

in·to·xi·car §70 tr. to intoxicate.

in·tra·du·ci·ble adj. untranslatable.

in·tra·mu·ros adv. within the city.

in·tran·qui·li·dad f. *(preocupación)* worry, uneasiness; *(agitación)* restlessness.

in·tran·qui·li·zar §04 tr. to worry, make uneasy.

in·tran·qui·lo, –la adj. *(preocupado)* worried, uneasy; *(agitado)* restless.

in·trans·cen·den·te *or* **in·trans·cen·den·tal** adj. unimportant, insignificant.

in·trans·fe·ri·ble adj. untransferable, nontransferable.

in·tran·si·gen·cia f. intransigence.

in·tran·si·gen·te adj. & m.f. intransigent.

in·tran·si·ta·ble adj. impassable.

in·tran·si·ti·vo, –va adj. GRAM. intransitive.

in·trans·mu·ta·ble adj. intransmutable.

in·tra·ta·ble adj. *(incontrolable)* unmanageable, intractable; FIG. *(insociable)* unsociable; *(grosero)* rude.

in·tra·ve·no·so, –sa adj. MED. intravenous.

in·tre·pi·dez f. intrepidness, boldness.

in·tré·pi·do, –da adj. intrepid, bold.

in·tri·ga f. *(maquinación)* intrigue, scheme; THEAT. plot ♦ **i. secundaria** subplot.

in·tri·ga·do, –da I. past part. see **intrigar** II. adj. intrigued.

in·tri·gan·te I. adj. intriguing II. m.f. scheming.

in·tri·gar §47 intr. & tr. to intrigue.

in·tri·ca·ción f. intricacy, complicatedness.

in·tri·ca·do, –da I. past part. see **intrincar** II. *(complicado)* intricate, complicated; *(denso)* dense <*un bosque i.* a dense wood>.

in·trin·car §70 tr. to complicate, confuse.

in·trín·gu·lis m. [pl. **-lis**] COLL. *(motivo)* ulterior motive; *(dificultad)* snag, difficulty; *(incógnita)* puzzle, mystery.

in·trín·se·ca·men·te adv. intrinsically.

in·trín·se·co, –ca adj. intrinsic.

in·tro·duc·ción f. *(presentación)* introduction <*la i. de una nueva moda* the introduction of a new fashion>; *(inserción)* introduction, insertion; *(prefacio)* introduction, preface; *(preámbulo)* preamble; *(preparación)* introduction <*i. a las matemáticas* introduction to mathematics>; MUS. introduction, overture.

in·tro·du·ci·do, –da I. past part. see **introducir** II. adj. COLL. close, familiar.

in·tro·du·cir §22 tr. *(dar entrada)* to show <*el mayordomo me introdujo en la sala* the butler showed me into the living room>; *(poner)* to put in *or* into, stick in <*el niño introdujo las manos en los bolsillos* the child stuck his hands in his pockets>; *(insertar)* to introduce, insert; FIG. *(presentar)* to introduce <*introdujeron un nuevo modelo* they introduced a new model>; *(ocasionar)* to cause, bring about <*él siempre introduce el desorden cuando entra* he always causes disorder when he enters> —reflex. *(entrar)* to enter, get in; *(entremeterse)* to interfere, meddle.

in·tro·duc·ti·vo, –va adj. introductory.

in·tro·duc·tor, –to·ra I. adj. introductory II. m.f. introducer.

in·tro·mi·sión f. *(intrusión)* meddling, intrusion; LAW intromission.

in·tros·pec·ción f. introspection.

in·tros·pec·ti·vo, –va adj. introspective.

in·tro·ver·sión f. introversion.

in·tro·ver·ti·do, –da I. adj. introverted II. m.f. introvert.

in·tru·sión f. intrusion.

in·tru·so, –sa I. adj. intrusive, meddlesome II. m.f. intruder.

in·tui·ción f. intuition.

in·tuir §18 tr. to intuit, sense.

in·tui·ti·va·men·te adv. intuitively.

in·tui·ti·vo, –va adj. intuitive.

i·nun·da·ción f. *(crecida)* inundation, flooding; *(diluvio)* inundation, flood; FIG. *(abundancia)* flood, stream.

i·nun·dar tr. to inundate, flood.

i·nur·ba·ni·dad f. incivility, impoliteness.

i·nur·ba·no, –na adj. uncivil, impolite.

i·nu·si·ta·do, –da adj. unusual, uncommon.

i·nu·sual adj. unusual, uncommon.

i·nú·til I. adj. *(inservible)* useless <*gasta su dinero en cosas inútiles* he spends his money on useless things>; *(vano)* vain, fruitless <*fue un esfuerzo i.* it was a fruitless effort>; II. m.f. good-for-nothing.

i·nu·ti·li·dad f. *(sin utilidad)* uselessness; *(ineficacia)* fruitlessness, ineffectiveness.

i·nu·ti·li·za·do, –da I. past part. see **inutilizar** II. adj. unused.

i·nu·ti·li·zar §04 tr. *(arruinar)* to ruin, destroy *<el bombardeo inutilizó el aeropuerto* the bombing destroyed the airport>; *(inhabilitar)* to make unusable *<la nieve inutilizó el camino* the snow made the road unusable>; *(sellos)* to cancel (stamps).

i·nú·til·men·te adv. in vain, to no avail *<protestó i. contra la nueva ley* she protested in vain against the new law>.

in·va·dir tr. to invade.

in·va·gi·nar tr. MED. to invaginate.

in·va·li·da·ción f. invalidation, nullification.

in·va·li·dar tr. to invalidate, nullify.

in·va·li·dez f. invalidity.

in·vá·li·do, –da I. adj. MED. invalid, disabled; FIG. *(nulo)* invalid, null II. m.f. MED. invalid, disabled person.

in·va·ria·bi·li·dad f. invariability.

in·va·ria·ble adj. invariable.

in·va·ria·ble·men·te adv. invariably.

in·va·ria·ción f. invariability.

in·va·sión f. invasion.

in·va·sor, –so·ra I. adj. invading II. m.f. invader.

in·vec·ti·va f. invective.

in·ven·ci·ble adj. invincible.

in·ven·ción f. invention.

in·ven·di·ble adj. unsalable.

in·ven·tar tr. *(concebir)* to invent; *(imaginar)* to invent, create *<Cervantes inventó el estilo de la novela actual* Cervantes invented the style of the modern novel>; *(forjar)* to fabricate, make up *<a los niños les gusta i. excusas* children like to make up excuses>.

in·ven·ta·riar §30 tr. to inventory.

in·ven·ta·rio f. inventory ♦ hacer or tomar un i. to make or take an inventory.

in·ven·ti·vo, –va I. adj. inventive II. f. inventiveness.

in·ven·to m. *(invención)* invention; *(creación)* creation; *(engaño)* fabrication; COLL. *(mentira)* lie.

in·ven·tor, –to·ra I. adj. inventive II. m.f. inventor.

in·ver·ná·cu·lo m. greenhouse, hothouse.

in·ver·na·da f. *(temporada)* wintertime, winter; AMER. *(invernadero)* winter pasture (for cattle); *(tiempo del engorde)* wintering (of cattle); VEN. *(aguacero)* downpour.

in·ver·na·de·ro m. *(invernáculo)* greenhouse, hothouse; *(sitio)* winter quarters; *(paraje)* winter pasture (for cattle).

in·ver·nal adj. winter, wintry.

in·ver·nar §49 intr. *(pasar el invierno)* to winter; *(hacer frío)* to be wintry; ZOOL. to hibernate.

in·ver·ni·zo, –za adj. wintry.

in·ve·ro·sí·mil adj. *(improbable)* improbable, unlikely; *(increíble)* unbelievable.

in·ve·ro·si·mi·li·tud f. improbability, unlikeliness.

in·ver·sa·men·te adv. inversely *<la enzima efecta i. el proceso químico* the enzyme inversely affects the chemical process>; *(a la inversa)* conversely.

in·ver·sión f. *(acción)* inversion; CHEM., GRAM., MED. inversion; COM., FIN. investment ♦ i. de capitales COM., FIN. capital investment • i. sexual inversion, homosexuality.

in·ver·sio·nis·ta m.f. COM., FIN. investor.

in·ver·si·vo, –va adj. inversive.

in·ver·so, –sa adj. inverse, inverted *<una imagen i.* an inverted image>; *(opuesto)* opposite ♦ a or por la i. on the contrary.

in·ver·te·bra·do, –da adj. & m. ZOOL. invertebrate.

in·ver·ti·do, –da I. past part. see invertir II. m.f. invert, homosexual.

in·ver·tir §65 tr. *(cambiar sentido)* to invert, reverse; COM., FIN. to invest; *(gastar)* to spend time; MATH. to invert.

in·ves·ti·du·ra f. investiture.

in·ves·ti·ga·ción f. *(indagación)* investigation, inquiry; *(estudio)* research, study.

in·ves·ti·ga·dor, –do·ra I. adj. *(indagador)* investigative, inquiring; *(que experimenta)* researching II. m.f. *(indagador)* investigator; *(científico)* researcher, scholar.

in·ves·ti·gar §47 tr. *(indagar)* to investigate, inquire into; *(estudiar)* to research, study.

in·ves·tir §48 tr. to invest, confer (on).

in·ve·te·ra·do, –da adj. inveterate.

in·ve·te·rar·se reflex. to become inveterate or firmly established.

in·vic·to, –ta adj. undefeated, unbeaten.

in·vier·ne, invierno see invernar.

in·vier·no m. *(estación)* winter; AMER. *(período de lluvia)* rainy season (in the tropics).

in·vier·ta, invierto see invertir.

in·vio·la·bi·li·dad f. inviolability ♦ i. parlamentaria POL. parliamentary immunity.

in·vio·la·ble adj. *(seguro)* inviolable; *(protegido)* impregnable *<una fortaleza i.* an impregnable fortress>.

in·vio·la·do, –da adj. inviolate.

in·vir·tie·ra, invirtió see invertir.

in·vi·si·bi·li·dad f. invisibility, invisibleness.

in·vi·si·ble adj. invisible.

in·vis·ta, invisto see investir.

in·vis·tie·ra, invistió see investir.

in·vi·ta·ción f. invitation.

in·vi·ta·do, –da I. past part. see invitar II. m.f. guest.

in·vi·tar tr. *(convidar)* to invite; FIG. *(inducir)* to invite, induce.

in·vo·ca·ción f. invocation.

in·vo·car §70 tr. to invoke.

in·vo·ca·to·rio, –ria adj. invocatory.

in·vo·lu·cra·do, –da I. past part. see involucrar II. adj. BOT. involucrate.

in·vo·lu·crar tr. *(abarcar)* to involve, implicate; *(divagar)* to introduce digressions in a speech.

in·vo·lun·ta·rio, –ria adj. involuntary.

in·vo·qué, invoque see invocar.

in·vul·ne·ra·ble adj. invulnerable.

in·yec·ción f. injection.

in·yec·ta·ble I. adj. injectable II. m. injectable substance, injection.

in·yec·ta·do, –da I. past part. see inyectar II. adj. flushed, red (cheeks, face) ♦ ojos inyectados bloodshot eyes.

in·yec·tar tr. to inject.

in·yec·tor m. MECH. injector.

io·do m. var. of yodo.

ion m. PHYS. ion.

io·ni·za·ción f. PHYS. ionization.

io·ni·zar §04 tr. PHYS. to ionize.

io·nós·fe·ra f. METEOROL. ionosphere.

io·ta f. iota (Greek letter).

ip·si·lon f. upsilon (Greek letter).

ip·so fac·to adv. LAW ipso facto, by that very fact; *(inmediatamente)* immediately.

ir §41 §G9 intr. to go *<fui con mi padre* I went with my father>; *(moverse)* to move *<iban de un lado a otro* they moved back and forth>; *(caminar)* to walk; *(viajar)* to go, travel *<iremos en coche* we will go by car>; *(dirigirse)* to go, lead *<este sendero va al monasterio* this path leads to the monastery>; *(extenderse)* to go, extend *<la playa va de aquí a San Diego* the beach extends from here to San Diego>; *(diferenciarse)* to differ, be different *<¿cuánto va de ayer a hoy!* how different today is from yesterday!>; *(proceder)* to proceed *<hay que i. con cuidado* it is necessary to proceed with caution>; *(encontrarse)* to do *<¿cómo te va en la clase de inglés?* how are you doing in English class?>; to go *<¿cómo va el asunto?* how is the matter going?>; *(acomodarse)* to suit, become *<a María le va bien ese sombrero* that hat becomes Mary>; *(apostar)* to be at stake, ride *<van cinco pesos a que ellos llegan primero* five pesos are riding on their arriving first>; *(en los naipes)* to lead, go (in cards); to be *<van caminando* they are walking>; to be *<vamos descalzos* we are barefoot>; MATH. to carry *<cinco, y van uno* five, and carry one> ♦ i. a *(estar a punto de)* to be about to *<íbamos a salir cuando llegaron* we were about to leave when they arrived>; to be going to *<voy a comer en casa* I am going to eat at home> • i. adelante to progress, go forward • i. contra la corriente FIG. to go against the current • i. de caza to go hunting • i. de compras to go shopping • i. de mal en peor to go from bad to worse • i. de paseo to go for a walk • i. de pesca to go fishing • i. de veras to be serious • i. de viaje to go on a trip • i. en to concern, affect *<me va el honor en eso* that concerns my honor> • i. por to go for, fetch *<iré por el médico* I will go for the doctor> • ¿quién va? MIL. who goes there? • ¡vaya! *(para expresar sorpresa)* you don't say!, is that so!, what!; what a *<¡vaya memoria!* what a memory!> • ¡vaya con Dios! farewell, God be with you

—reflex. *(moverse)* to go away, leave; *(deslizarse)* to slip <*se le fueron los pies* his feet slipped>; *(morirse)* to die; *(rezumarse)* to ooze, leak; *(evaporarse)* to evaporate; *(desgastarse)* to wear out; *(ventosear)* to break wind ♦ **irse abajo** to topple, collapse • **irse a pique** MARIT. to founder, sink • **irse de** to discard • **vámonos** let's go • **vete a saber** there's no telling.

i·ra f. *(cólera)* anger, wrath; FIG. *(furia)* fury, violence (of the elements) ♦ **llenarse de i.** to become angry.

i·ra·ca f. AMER., BOT. Panama-hat palm.

i·ra·cun·dia f. *(propensión)* irascibility; *(cólera)* ire, wrath.

i·ra·cun·do, –da adj. *(colérico)* irate, angered; *(enojadizo)* irascible.

I·rán m. Iran.

i·ra·ní adj. & m.f. [pl. **-ní·es**] Iranian.

i·ra·nio, -nia adj. & m.f. Iranian —m. *(idioma)* Iranian.

I·raq m. Iraq.

i·ra·quí adj. & m.f. [pl. **-quí·es**] Iraqi ♦ **los iraquíes** the Iraqi.

i·ras·ci·ble adj. irascible.

ir·go, irgue see **erguir.**

ir·guie·ra, irguió see **erguir.**

i·ri·dia·do, –da adj. iridized.

i·ri·dio m. CHEM. iridium.

i·ri·dis·cen·te adj. iridescent.

i·ris m. METEOROL. rainbow; OPHTHAL. iris; MIN. noble opal ♦ **arco i.** rainbow.

i·ri·sa·ción f. iridescence.

i·ri·sar intr. to be iridescent —tr. to cause to be iridescent.

Ir·lan·da f. Ireland ♦ **I del Norte** Northern Ireland.

ir·lan·dés, –de·sa I. adj. Irish II. m. *(habitante)* Irishman; *(idioma)* Irish English —f. Irishwoman ♦ **los irlandeses** the Irish.

i·ro·ní·a f. irony.

i·ró·ni·ca·men·te adv. ironically.

i·ró·ni·co, –ca adj. ironic, ironical.

i·ro·ni·zar §04 tr. *(hablar con ironía)* to ironize, make ironical; *(ridiculizar)* to ridicule, make fun of.

i·ro·qués, –que·sa adj. & m.f. Iroquois.

i·rra·cio·nal adj. irrational.

i·rra·cio·na·li·dad f. irrationality.

i·rra·cio·na·lis·mo m. PHILOS. irrationalism.

i·rra·cio·na·lis·ta adj. & m.f. PHILOS. irrationalist.

i·rra·dia·ción f. irradiation.

i·rra·diar tr. to irradiate.

i·rra·zo·na·ble adj. *(desrazonable)* unreasonable; *(absurdo)* absurd, ridiculous; *(insensato)* senseless.

i·rre·al adj. unreal.

i·rre·a·li·dad f. unreality.

i·rre·a·li·za·ble adj. unrealizable, unattainable.

i·rre·ba·ti·ble adj. irrefutable, indisputable.

i·rre·con·ci·lia·ble adj. irreconcilable.

i·rre·cu·pe·ra·ble adj. irrecoverable, irretrievable.

i·rre·cu·sa·ble adj. unchallengeable, unimpeachable.

i·rre·den·to, –ta adj. unredeemed.

i·rre·du·ci·ble or **i·rre·duc·ti·ble** adj. *(que no se puede reducir)* irreducible; *(inflexible)* inflexible, intransigent.

i·rre·em·pla·za·ble or **i·rrem·pla·za·ble** adj. irreplaceable.

i·rre·fle·xión f. rashness, impetuosity.

i·rre·fle·xi·vo, –va adj. rash, impetuous.

i·rre·for·ma·ble adj. incorrigible, that cannot be reformed.

i·rre·fre·na·ble adj. unrestrainable, uncontrollable.

i·rre·fu·ta·ble adj. irrefutable.

i·rre·gu·lar adj. irregular.

i·rre·gu·la·ri·dad f. irregularity.

i·rre·gu·lar·men·te adv. irregularly.

i·rre·le·van·te adj. irrelevant.

i·rre·li·gión f. irreligion.

i·rre·li·gio·si·dad f. irreligiousness, ungodliness.

i·rre·li·gio·so, –sa I. adj. irreligious, ungodly II. m.f. irreligious or ungodly person.

i·rre·me·dia·ble adj. irremediable.

i·rre·me·dia·ble·men·te adv. irremediably.

i·rre·mi·si·ble adj. unpardonable, irremissible.

i·rre·pa·ra·ble adj. irreparable.

i·rre·pren·si·ble adj. irreprehensible.

i·rre·pri·mi·ble adj. irrepressible.

i·rre·pro·cha·ble adj. irreproachable, faultless.

i·rre·sis·ti·ble adj. irresistible.

i·rre·sis·ti·ble·men·te adv. irresistibly.

i·rre·so·lu·ble adj. *(sin solución)* unsolvable, irresolvable; *(sin resolución)* irresolute, indecisive.

i·rre·so·lu·ción f. irresolution.

i·rre·so·lu·to, –ta I. adj. *(sin resolución)* irresolute, indecisive; *(pendiente)* unresolved II. m.f. irresolute or indecisive person.

i·rres·pe·tuo·so, –sa I. adj. disrespectful II. m.f. disrespectful person.

i·rres·pi·ra·ble adj. unbreathable, irrespirable.

i·rres·pon·sa·bi·li·dad f. irresponsibility.

i·rres·pon·sa·ble adj. & m.f. irresponsible.

i·rres·tric·to, –ta adj. unrestricted.

i·rre·suel·to, –ta adj. unresolved.

i·rre·tro·ac·ti·vi·dad f. LAW nonretroactive principle.

i·rre·ve·la·ble adj. unrevealable.

i·rre·ve·ren·cia f. irreverence.

i·rre·ve·ren·ciar tr. to treat irreverently or with disrespect.

i·rre·ve·ren·te I. adj. irreverent II. m.f. irreverent person.

i·rre·ver·si·ble adj. irreversible.

i·rre·vo·ca·bi·li·dad adj. irrevocability.

i·rre·vo·ca·ble adj. irrevocable.

i·rre·vo·ca·ble·men·te adv. irrevocably.

i·rri·ga·ble adj. irrigable.

i·rri·ga·ción f. irrigation.

i·rri·ga·dor m. irrigator.

i·rri·gar §47 tr. to irrigate.

i·rri·si·ble adj. ridiculous, laughable.

i·rri·sión f. *(mofa)* ridicule, derision; *(hazmerreír)* laughingstock <*ser la i. del pueblo* to be the laughingstock of the town>.

i·rri·so·rio, –ria adj. *(irrisible)* ridiculous, laughable; *(extremadamente bajo)* absurdly or ridiculously low <*un precio i.* a ridiculously low price>.

i·rri·ta·bi·li·dad f. irritability.

i·rri·ta·ble adj. irritable.

i·rri·ta·ción f. *(enfado)* irritation; MED. irritation <*i. de estómago* stomach irritation>; LAW annulment, invalidation.

i·rri·ta·do, –da I. past part. see **irritar** II. adj. irritated.

i·rri·ta·dor, –do·ra I. adj. irritating II. m.f. irritator, irritant.

i·rri·tan·te adj. irritant.

i·rri·tar tr. *(exasperar)* to irritate, exasperate; FIG. *(incitar)* to excite (anger, passion); MED. to irritate.

i·rri·to, –ta adj. LAW null, invalid.

i·rro·gar §47 tr. to cause (damage).

i·rrom·pi·ble adj. unbreakable.

i·rrum·pir intr. *(entrar)* to burst or rush into <*i. en la cocina* to burst into the kitchen>; *(invadir)* to invade.

i·rrup·ción f. *(acometida)* bursting or rushing into; *(invasión)* invasion.

i·sa·be·li·no, –na adj. & m.f. Elizabethan.

I·sa·í·as BIBL. Isaiah.

is·la f. *(tierra)* island; *(casas)* block (of houses); ARG. grove (of trees); CHILE flood plain ♦ **Islas Aleutas** Aleutian Islands • **Islas Baleares** Balearic Islands • **Islas Británicas** British Isles • **Islas Canarias** Canary Islands • **I. del Diablo** Devil's Island • **Islas Filipinas** Philippine Islands • **Islas Malvinas** Falkland Islands • **Is·las Sa·lo·món** Solomon Islands • **Islas Vírgenes** Virgin Islands.

is·lam m. RELIG. Islam.

is·lá·mi·co, –ca adj. RELIG. Islamic, Moslem.

is·la·mis·mo m. RELIG. Islamism.

is·la·mi·ta RELIG. I. adj. Islamic, Moslem II. m.f. Moslem.

is·la·mi·zar §04 intr. to Islamize.

is·lan·dés, –de·sa I. adj. Icelandic II. m.f. *(habitante)* Icelander —m. *(idioma)* Icelandic.

Is·lan·dia f. Iceland.

is·lán·di·co, –ca adj. Icelandic.

is·la·rio m. map or description of islands.

is·le·ño, –ña I. adj. of an island II. m.f. islander.

is·le·ta f. *(isla pequeña)* isle, islet; *(acera)* traffic island.

is·lo·te m. barren isle or islet.

i·so·ba·ra f. METEOROL., PHYS. isobar.

i·só·me·ro, –ra CHEM. I. adj. isomeric II. m. isomer.

i·sós·ce·les adj. GEOM. isosceles.

i·so·tér·mi·co, –ca adj. PHYS. isothermal.

i·so·ter·mo, –ma I. adj. METEOROL., PHYS. isothermal II. f. METEOROL. isotherm.
i·so·tó·pi·co, –ca adj. CHEM. isotopic.
i·só·to·po m. CHEM. isotope.
is·quión m. ischium (lowest bone of pelvis).
Is·ra·el m. Israel.
is·ra·e·lí [pl. **-lí·es**] or **is·ra·e·li·ta** adj. & m.f. Israeli.
is·ra·e·lí·ti·co, –ca adj. Israelite.
ist·me·ño, –ña or **íst·mi·co, –ca** adj. isthmian.
ist·mo m. GEOG. isthmus.
Í·ta·ca f. Ithaca.
I·ta·lia f. Italy.
i·ta·lia·nis·mo m. Italianism.
i·ta·lia·ni·zar §04 tr. to Italianize.
i·ta·lia·no, –na adj. & m.f. Italian —m. (idioma) Italian.
i·tá·li·co, –ca I. adj. (de Italia) Italic; PRINT. italic ♦ **letra i.** italics II. m. Italic (language).
í·tem I. adv. furthermore, moreover, likewise II. m. item, article.
i·te·ra·ción f. iteration, repetition.
i·te·rar tr. to iterate, repeat.
i·te·ra·ti·vo, –va adj. iterative, repetitive.
i·ter·bio m. CHEM. ytterbium.
i·ti·ne·ran·te adj. itinerant.
i·ti·ne·ra·rio, –ria adj. & m. itinerary.
i·trio m. CHEM. yttrium.
i·zar §04 tr. MARIT. to hoist.
iz·quier·da I. f. ANAT. (mano) left hand <*él siempre escribe con la i.* he always writes with his left hand>; (lado) left <*mantente a mi i.* keep to my left>; POL. left, left wing ♦ **a la i.** (dirección) left, to the left <*doblar a la i.* to turn to the left>; (sitio) on the left <*mi casa está a la i.* my house is on the left> • **de la i.** on the left <*la casa de la i. es mía* the house on the left is mine> • **la i.** POL. the left or Left • **por la i.** on the left <*me pasó por la i* he passed me on the left> II. adj. see **izquierdo, –da.**
iz·quier·dis·mo m. POL. leftism.
iz·quier·dis·ta POL. I. adj. leftist, left-wing II. m.f. leftist, left-winger.
iz·quier·do, –da I. adj. (siniestro) left <*ojo i.* left eye>; (zurdo) left-handed; FIG. (torcido) crooked; ZOOL. knock-kneed (said of horse) II. f. see **izquierda.**

J

j, J f. eleventh letter of the Spanish alphabet.
ja·ba f. AMER. cage-like crate; CUBA wicker basket (used by beggars); VEN. (calabaza) hollow gourd; (pobreza) poverty.
ja·ba·do, –da adj. AMER. mottled, parti-colored (fowl); CUBA hesitant, wavering.
ja·bal·cón m. ARCHIT. strut, brace; COL. ravine.
ja·bal·co·nar tr. to support with struts.
ja·ba·lí m. [pl. **-líes**] ZOOL. wild boar.
ja·ba·li·na¹ f. ZOOL. wild sow.
ja·ba·li·na² f. javelin.
ja·bar·de·ar intr. to swarm (said of bees).
ja·bar·di·llo m. (de insectos) swarm, cloud (of buzzing insects); COLL. (multitud de gente) noisy crowd, throng.
ja·bar·do m. (enjambre pequeño) swarm (of bees); (multitud) crowd, throng.
ja·ba·to I. m. ZOOL. young wild boar; COLL. (joven) brash young man II. adj. see **jabato, –ta.**
ja·ba·to, –ta I. adj. CUBA, MEX. rough, uncouth II. m. see **jabato.**
já·be·ga f. (red) dragnet, sweep net; (barco) fishing boat.
ja·be·que¹ m. MARIT. xebec (fishing boat).
ja·be·que² m. COLL. (herida) gash in the face.
ja·bí m. [pl. **-bíes**] (uva) small wild grape; (manzana) small wild apple.
ja·bí² m. [pl. **-bíes**] BOT. quebracho (tree).
ja·bla·de·ra f. CARP. crozer, cooper's tool.
ja·bón m. (para lavar) soap, bar of soap; COLL. (reprensión) tongue-lashing ♦ **dar j. a** FIG., COLL. to soft-soap, flatter • **dar un j. a** FIG., COLL. (regañar) to tell off, rake over the

coals; ARG. to frighten <*el ruido me dio un gran j.* the noise frightened me greatly> • **j. de afeitar** shaving soap • **j. de sastre** soapstone, French chalk • **j. de tocador** or **de olor** toilet soap • **j. en polvo** soap powder • **tener j.** ARG. to be afraid.
ja·bo·na·do, –da I. past part. see **jabonar** II. m. (jabonadura) soaping, lathering; (ropa) laundry, wash —f. AMER. soaping, lathering; ARG., CHILE, MEX., COLL. tongue-lashing.
ja·bo·na·du·ra f. (acción de jabonar) soaping, lathering ♦ **dar una j. a** FIG., COLL. to tell off, rake over the coals <*le voy a dar una j.* I am going to tell him off> • **jabonaduras** soapsuds, lather.
ja·bo·nar tr. (la ropa, el cuerpo) to wash; (la barba) to lather; FIG., COLL. (reprender) to tell off, rake over the coals.
ja·bon·ci·llo m. (jabón) bar of soap; BOT. soapberry (tree and fruit); CHILE shaving soap ♦ **j. de sastre** soapstone, French chalk.
ja·bo·ne·ra I. f. (recipiente) soap dish; BOT. soapwort II. adj. see **jabonero, –ra.**
ja·bo·ne·ro, –ra I. adj. soap <*la industria j.* the soap industry>; TAUR. off-white II. m.f. soapmaker —f. see **jabonera.**
ja·bo·no·so, –sa adj. soapy <*agua j.* soapy water>.
ja·bu·co m. CUBA large straw basket (for transporting eggs).
ja·ca f. (caballito) pony, small horse; ARG. gamecock, fighting cock.
já·ca·ra I. f. (romance) picaresque ballad; (música y danza) merry song and dance; COLL. (juerguistas) group of revelers; (mentira) lie, fib; (molestia) annoyance, bother; (cuento) story, tale ♦ **estar de j.** to be merry, live it up II. adj. see **jácaro, –ra.**
ja·ca·ran·dá m. BOT. jacaranda.
ja·ca·ran·do·so, –sa adj. COLL. merry, lively, carefree.
ja·ca·ré m. AMER., ZOOL. alligator.
ja·ca·re·ar intr. (cantar) to sing merry ballads, go serenading; COLL. (insultar) to be rude or insulting.
ja·ca·re·ro, –ra or **ja·ca·ris·ta** I. adj. merry, lively, carefree II. m.f. (juerguista) merrymaker, reveler; (cantante) singer of merry ballads.
já·ca·ro, –ra I. adj. boastful, swaggering ♦ **a lo j.** boastfully II. m.f. boaster, swaggerer —f. see **jácara.**
já·ce·na f. ARCHIT. girder, main beam.
ja·ce·ri·na f. coat of mail.
ja·cin·to m. BOT. hyacinth, jacinth; MIN. jacinth, zircon ♦ **j. occidental** MIN. topaz • **j. oriental** MIN. ruby.
jaco m. (jamelgo) hack, nag; (cota) short-sleeved coat of mail.
ja·co·bi·no, –na HIST. I. adj. (radical) Jacobinic, radical; (de Jacobo I) Jacobean II. m.f. (radical) Jacobin, radical; (de Jacobo I) Jacobean.
jac·tan·cia f. (alardeo) boast, brag; (arrogancia) boastfulness, arrogance.
jac·tan·cio·so, –sa adj. boastful, arrogant.
jac·tar·se reflex. to boast, brag ♦ **j. de** to boast or brag about.
ja·cu·la·to·rio, –ria I. adj. ejaculatory, brief and fervent II. f. ejaculation, short prayer.
ja·da f. AGR. hoe, spade.
ja·de m. MIN. jade.
ja·de·an·te adj. breathless, panting.
ja·de·ar intr. to pant, gasp.
ja·de·o m. panting, gasping.
ja·diar tr. to hoe, dig with a spade.
ja·ez m. [pl. **-ces**] (arreo) harness; DEROG. (carácter) ilk, kind, sort <*gente de ese j.* that sort of people> ♦ **jaeces** trappings.
ja·guar m. ZOOL. jaguar.
ja·guay m. (aguada) watering trough; PERU pond, reservoir; CUBA liana.
ja·güel m. AMER. pond, reservoir (for watering livestock).
ja·güey m. AMER. (charca) pond, reservoir; BOT. banyan tree.
jai a·lai m. SPORT. jai alai, pelota.
jai·ba I. adj. CUBA, P. RICO, COLL. clever, astute II. f. AMER. (cangrejo) crab; (cámbaro) crayfish.

jai·que m. haik (Moorish hooded cape).

¡ja, ja, ja! interj. ha, ha, ha!

ja·la·pa f. BOT., PHARM. jalap (Mexican plant).

ja·la·pi·na f. jalap resin.

ja·lar tr. COLL. (*tirar*) to pull, haul; PERU to fail, flunk <*jaló el examen* he failed the test>; C. AMER. to make love to; COL., VEN. to do, perform —intr. AMER. to leave, clear out, beat it <*jalaron para su casa* they cleared out for home> —reflex. AMER. to get drunk.

jal·be·gar §47 tr. (*enjalbegar*) to whitewash; COLL. (*afeitar*) to make up (the face).

jal·ca f. PERU elevated place in the mountains.

jal·de or **jal·do, –da** adj. bright yellow.

ja·le·a f. jelly ♦ **hacerse** or **volverse una j.** to go sweet (on), become fond of • **j. de guayaba** guava jelly • **j. de membrillo** quince jelly • **j. real** royal jelly (from bees).

ja·le·a·dor, –do·ra I. adj. cheering, encouraging (by clapping and shouting) II. m.f. cheerer, encourager.

ja·le·ar tr. (*animar*) to encourage (dancers); (*incitar*) to urge on (dogs); AMER. to pester, bother; CHILE to make fun of.

ja·le·o m. (*animación*) clapping and cheering; (*incitación*) urging; (*baile*) popular Andalusian dance; COLL. (*tumulto*) fuss, uproar; (*juerga*) binge, spree; (*mezcolanza*) jumble <*un j. de cifras* a jumble of figures>; C. AMER. courting ♦ **armar un j.** to kick up a fuss • **estar de j.** to have a good time.

ja·li·fa f. Spanish Moroccan governor.

ja·li·fa·to m. territory of a Spanish Moroccan governor.

ja·lis·co, –ca MEX. I. adj. drunk II. m. straw hat.

jal·ma f. packsaddle.

ja·lón[1] m. SURV. (*estaca*) stake, range pole; FIG. (*hito*) milestone; (*etapa*) stage ♦ **j. de mira** SURV. leveling rod.

ja·lón[2] m. AMER., COLL. (*tirón*) pull, tug; (*trecho*) stretch, distance; C. AMER., MEX., COLL. (*trago*) drink, swig.

ja·lo·na·mien·to m. staking or marking out.

ja·lo·nar tr. (*señalar con jalones*) to stake or mark out; FIG. (*marcar*) to mark, dot <*el camino está jalonado de hitos* the road is marked by signposts>.

ja·lo·ne·ar or **ja·lo·te·ar** intr. MEX. (*dar tirones*) to pull, tug; (*regatear*) to haggle.

ja·lo·ne·o or **ja·lo·te·o** m. MEX. (*tirón*) pull, tug; (*regateo*) haggling.

Ja·mai·ca f. Jamaica.

ja·mai·qui·no, –na adj. & m.f. Jamaican.

ja·man·cia f. COLL. food.

ja·mar tr. COLL. to eat.

ja·más §45 adv. never <*j. lo creeré* I'll never believe it>; ever <*el más grande que j. haya visto* the biggest that I have ever seen> ♦ **j. de los jamases** never ever • **nunca j.** never again • **para siempre j.** for ever and ever.

jam·ba f. ARCHIT. jamb (of a door).

jam·ba·je m. (*de una puerta*) door frame; (*de una ventana*) window frame.

jám·bi·co, –ca adj. POET. iambic.

jam·bo·re·e m. jamboree.

ja·mel·go m. nag, hack, jade.

ja·me·te m. TEX. rich silk cloth interwoven with gold or silver thread.

jam·ón m. ham ♦ **j. ahumado** smoked ham • **j. serrano** cured ham • **¡y un j. (con chorreras)!** COLL. nothing doing!, not on your life!

ja·mo·na COLL. I. adj. buxom, plump II. f. buxom (middle-aged) woman ♦ **una mujer j.** a good-looking woman.

ja·mu·gas f.pl. sidesaddle ♦ **ir en j.** to ride sidesaddle.

jan·ga·da f. COLL. (*tontería*) silly remark; COLL. (*trastada*) dirty trick; (*armadía*) raft, float; (*de árboles*) logjam.

jan·se·nis·mo m. RELIG. Jansenism.

Já·nu·ca f. RELIG. Chanukah, Hanukkah.

Ja·pón m. Japan.

ja·po·nés, –ne·sa adj. & m.f. Japanese —m. (*idioma*) Japanese ♦ **los japoneses** the Japanese.

ja·que[1] m. (*ajedrez*) check (in chess) ♦ **dar j.** to check, put in check • **dar j. y mate** to checkmate • **estar en j.** to be in check • **j. al rey** check • **¡j. de aquí!** get out of here!, scram! • **j. mate** checkmate • **tener en j.** FIG. (*amenazar*) to hold a threat over, keep in check; (*hostigar*) to pester, bother.

ja·que[2] m. COLL. (*valentón*) braggart, boaster.

ja·que·ar tr. (*en ajedrez*) to check (in chess); FIG. (*amenazar*) to hold a threat over; (*hostigar*) to pester, bother.

ja·que·ca f. (*migraña*) migraine, migraine headache; COLL. (*molestia*) bother, pain in the neck ♦ **dar una j. a** FIG. to bother, bore to death.

ja·que·co·so, –sa adj. (*con jaqueca*) suffering from migraine headaches; (*fastidioso*) bothersome, tiresome.

ja·que·tón m. COLL. (*valentón*) bully, braggart; (*tiburón*) man-eating shark.

já·qui·ma f. (*del caballo*) headstall; AMER., COLL. drunkenness.

ja·qui·ma·zo m. (*golpe*) blow with the headstall of a halter; FIG., COLL. (*broma pesada*) dirty trick.

ja·qui·món m. AMER. headstall.

ja·ra f. BOT. rockrose; (*arma*) dart, arrow, spear; P. RICO, MEX., COLL. the police, the fuzz; BOL. rest, halt, stop.

ja·ra·be m. syrup ♦ **dar j.** to butter up • **estar hecho un j.** to go sweet on • **j. de arce** maple syrup • **j. de maíz** corn syrup • **j. de pico** FIG., COLL. idle promises, lip service • **j. para la tos** cough syrup • **j. tapatío** popular Mexican folk dance, hat dance.

ja·ra·be·ar tr. to dose (a patient) with medicines —reflex. to take medicinal syrups.

ja·ral m. BOT. bramble, patch of rockroses; FIG. (*cosa intrincada*) thorny question, sticky situation, hornet's nest.

ja·ra·ma·go m. BOT. wall rocket.

ja·ra·mu·go m. small or young fish.

ja·ra·na f. (*divertimiento*) spree, binge; COLL. (*alboroto*) fuss, uproar; CUBA trick, hoax; AMER. (*chanza*) joke, jest; MEX. small guitar; C. AMER. debt ♦ **andar** or **ir de j.** COLL. to go on a binge, carouse • **estar de j.** COLL. to be on a binge, live it up.

ja·ra·ne·ar intr. (*ir de juerga*) to go on a binge; (*divertirse*) to have a good time; AMER. (*estafar*) to swindle, cheat; (*chancear*) to joke, jest; C. AMER. to get into debt.

ja·ra·ne·ro, –ra I. adj. merry, fun-loving; AMER. tricky, dishonest II. m.f. reveler, carouser.

jar·ca f. BOT. acacia.

jar·cia f. or **jar·cias** f.pl. (*cabos y aparejos*) rigging, ropes; (*para pescar*) fishing tackle; (*mezcolanza*) heap, jumble; MEX., CUBA cable, rope ♦ **j. muerta** MARIT. standing rigging.

jar·ciar tr. MARIT. to rig.

jar·dín m. (*terreno*) garden; MARIT. latrine, head; JEWEL. flaw, cloud ♦ **j. botánico** botanical garden • **j. central** (*en béisbol*) center field • **j. colgante** hanging garden • **j. de la infancia** kindergarten • **j. derecho** (*en béisbol*) right field • **j. izquierdo** (*en béisbol*) left field • **j. zoológico** ZOO, zoological garden.

jar·di·na·je m. gardening.

jar·di·ne·ra f. (*para flores*) flower stand or box; (*que cuida un jardín*) gardener; (*transporte*) open carriage or tramcar.

jar·di·ne·rí·a f. gardening.

jar·di·ne·ro m. (*que cuida un jardín*) gardener; (*en béisbol*) outfielder.

ja·re·ta f. (*dobladillo*) casing, hem; MARIT. (*cabo*) cable, rope; (*empalletado*) netting; COLL. chatter ♦ **dar j.** COLL. to chatter.

ja·re·ti·na f. wide hem.

ja·ro·cho, –cha I. adj. uncouth, rude II. m.f. (*insolente*) rude person; MEX. native of Veracruz.

ja·ro·pe m. (*jarabe*) syrup; COLL. (*bebida desagradable*) unpleasant drink.

ja·rra f. (*vasija*) jug, jar, pitcher; (*de leche*) churn; (*de cerveza*) mug, beer mug; (*orden antigua*) ancient Aragonese order ♦ **de** or **en jarra(s)** hands on hips, arms akimbo.

ja·rre·ar tr. (*sacar con jarro*) to draw with a pitcher or jug; FIG. (*llover copiosamente*) to pour, rain cats and dogs.

ja·rre·tar tr. FIG. (*enervar*) to enervate; (*quitar las fuerzas*) to weaken.

ja·rre·te m. ANAT. back of the knee; (*de un animal*) hock.

ja·rre·te·ra f. (*liga*) garter; (*orden militar*) Order of the Garter.

ja·rro m. pitcher, jug ♦ **echar un j. de agua fría a** COLL. to throw cold water on • **llover a jarros** COLL. to rain cats and dogs, to come down in buckets.

ja·rrón m. ARCHIT. urn, vase; *(para flores)* vase.

jas·pe m. MIN. jasper; *(mármol)* veined marble.

jas·pe·a·do, –da I. past part. see **jaspear** II. adj. *(veteado)* marbled, speckled; *(abigarrado)* variegated III. m.f. marbling, speckling.

jas·pe·ar tr. to marble, speckle.

jas·tial m. ARCHIT. façade of an edifice.

ja·to, –ta m.f. calf.

Jau·ja f. utopia, promised land ♦ **¿estamos aquí o en J.?** where do you think you are? • **estar** *or* **vivir en J.** to have it made • **¡esto es J.!** this is the life!

jau·la f. *(para animales)* cage; *(para criminales)* cell, cage; *(embalaje)* crate; *(para niños)* playpen; MIN. cage; P. RICO police car, paddy wagon.

jau·rí·a f. pack (of animals).

ja·va·nés, –ne·sa adj. & m.f. Javanese —m. *(idioma)* Javanese ♦ **los Javaneses** the Javanese.

ja·yán, –ya·na m.f. big strong person, gorilla.

jaz·mín m. BOT. jasmine ♦ **J. del Cabo** *or* **de la India** gardenia.

jazz m. *(música)* jazz.

je·be m. MIN. alum; AMER., BOT. rubber plant; AMER. *(goma elástica)* rubber band; AMER., COLL. rubber, condom.

jeep m. jeep.

je·fa f. boss, chief.

je·fa·tu·ra f. *(dirección)* leadership, management; *(oficina)* headquarters.

je·fe m. *(superior)* boss, chief; *(gerente)* manager; *(líder)* leader; *(cabeza)* head; *(tribu)* chief; *(jurado)* foreman; MIL. commanding officer; PERU police officer ♦ **J. de camareros** *or* **de mozos** headwaiter • **J. de cocina** chef • **J. de día** MIL. officer of the day • **J. de escuadra** MARIT. rear admiral • **J. de estación** RAIL. stationmaster • **J. de estado** POL. chief of state • **J. de estado mayor** MIL. chief of staff • **J. de policía** police chief • **J. de redacción** editor-in-chief • **J. de taller** foreman • **J. de tren** RAIL. conductor • **J. de ventas** sales manager • **J. supremo** *or* **comandante en J.** MIL. commander-in-chief • **ser el J.** FIG. to be the boss.

Je·ho·vá m. Jehovah.

¡je, je, je! interj. hee, hee, hee!

je·jén m. AMER., ENTOM. gnat, mosquito; MEX., FIG. swarm <*un j. de niños* a swarm of children>.

je·me m. *(distancia)* distance between the end of the thumb and the end of the forefinger with the hand extended; FIG., COLL. *(cara)* woman's face.

je·me·que·ar intr. CHILE to whimper, whine.

je·mi·que·ar intr. CHILE to whimper, snivel, whine.

jen·gi·bre m. BOT. ginger (plant and spice).

je·ni·quén m. BOT. henequen (for making rope).

je·ni·za·ro, –ra I. adj. *(híbrido)* mixed, hybrid; MEX. of mixed parentage, of Chinese and Indian parentage II. m. janissary (Turkish soldier).

je·que m. sheik.

je·rar·ca m. hierarch, ruler, high official.

je·rar·quí·a f. hierarchy, rank, scale.

je·rár·qui·co, –ca adj. hierarchical, hierarchic.

je·rar·qui·zar §04 tr. to hierarchize, rank.

jer·bo m. ZOOL. jerboa, mouse.

je·re·mi·a·da f. jeremiad, lamentation.

je·re·mí·as m.f. whiner, complainer ♦ **Jeremías** BIBL. Jeremiah.

je·re·mi·que·ar intr. AMER. to whimper, snivel.

je·re·mi·que·o m. AMER. whimpering, whining.

je·rez m. [pl. **-re·ces**] sherry.

jer·ga¹ f. *(tela)* coarse woolen cloth; *(colchón)* straw mattress; AMER. saddle blanket.

jer·ga² f. *(jerigonza)* slang, jargon; *(galimatías)* gibberish, double talk.

jer·gal adj. slang, slangy.

jer·gón m. *(colchón)* straw mattress; COLL. *(mollejón)* slob, lummox; *(ropa)* ill-fitting garment.

jer·gui·lla f. *(tela)* silk serge; CHILE meat from the neck region of a cow.

je·ri·be·que m. *(mueca)* grimace; *(guiño)* wink, blink.

Je·ri·có f. Jericho.

je·ri·fe m. sherif, sharif.

je·ri·gon·za f. *(jerga)* jargon, slang; *(galimatías)* gibberish; COLL. *(tontería)* foolish action ♦ **andar en jerigonzas** to talk gibberish.

je·rin·ga f. *(para inyecciones)* syringe; COLL. *(molestia)* annoyance, nuisance ♦ **J. de engrase** grease gun • **J. hipodérmica** hypodermic syringe.

je·rin·ga·dor, –do·ra COLL. I. adj. annoying, bothersome II. m.f. pest, nuisance.

je·rin·gar §47 tr. *(inyectar)* to inject, squirt; COLL. *(fastidiar)* to annoy, pester.

je·rin·ga·zo m. *(inyección)* injection, squirt; *(contenido)* injection, syringeful.

je·rin·gón, –go·na adj. AMER. annoying, bothersome.

je·rin·gue·ar tr. AMER. to annoy, pester.

je·rin·gui·lla f. *(jeringa pequeña)* small syringe; BOT. mock orange, syringa.

je·ro·glí·fi·co, –ca I. adj. hieroglyphic II. m. *(carácter)* hieroglyphic, hieroglyph; *(juego)* rebus, picture puzzle.

jer·sey adj. & m. [pl. **-seys** *or* **-seis**] jersey, pullover, sweater.

Je·ru·sa·lén Jerusalem.

je·sui·ta I. adj. Jesuit II. m. RELIG. Jesuit; COLL. *(hipócrita)* hypocrite.

je·su·í·ti·co, –ca adj. jesuitical, jesuitic.

Je·su·cris·to m. Jesus Christ.

Je·sús m. Jesus ♦ **en un J.** COLL. in an instant, in a jiffy • **¡Jesús!** my goodness!; *(al estornudar)* bless you!, Gesundheit • **morir sin decir J.** to drop dead suddenly.

jet m. jet, jet plane.

je·ta f. *(hocico)* snout; *(labios abultados)* thick lips; *(espita)* tap, faucet; COLL. *(cara)* face, mug ♦ **estirar la J.** AMER., COLL. to die, kick the bucket • **poner J.** to make a face, pout.

je·tu·do, –da adj. thick-lipped.

Je·za·bel BIBL. Jezebel.

ji *or* **chi** f. chi (Greek letter).

jí·ba·ro, –ra I. adj. AMER. *(rústico)* rural, rustic; S. AMER. Jivaroan II. m.f. AMER. *(campesino)* peasant, poor farmer; S. AMER. Jivaroan —m. HOND. tall vigorous man.

ji·bia f. ZOOL. *(molusca)* cuttlefish; *(jibión)* cuttlebone.

ji·co·ra f. *(de chocolate)* chocolate cup; AMER. *(güira)* calabash, gourd (fruit); C. AMER., MEX. *(vasija)* calabash cup; MEX., HUM. bald head.

ji·co·te m. AMER., ENTOM. wasp; *(nido)* wasp's nest.

ji·fa f. offal (of slaughtered beasts).

ji·fe·ro, –ra I. adj. *(del matadero)* pertaining to a slaughterhouse; COLL. *(sucio)* dirty, filthy II. m. *(cuchillo)* cleaver, slaughtering knife; *(carnicero)* slaughterer, butcher.

ji·fia f. swordfish.

ji·go·te m. fricassee, braised meat stew.

¡ji, ji, ji! interj. tee, hee, hee!

jil·gue·ro m. ORNITH. goldfinch, linnet.

ji·li·po·lla·da *or* **ji·li·po·llez** f. [pl. **-lle·ces**] SL. *(acción)* stupid thing to do; *(dicho)* stupid thing to say ♦ **esos son jilipolleces** that's a lot of bull • **¡qué j.!** how stupid can you get!

ji·lo·te m. C. AMER., MEX. unripened ear of corn.

ji·mio, –mia adj. & m.f. ZOOL. simian.

jin·da *or* **jin·da·ma** f. COLL. fear, fright.

ji·ne·ta¹ f. ZOOL. genet.

jineta² f. *(lanza corta)* short lance; *(hombrera)* epaulette; *(que cabalga)* horsewoman.

ji·ne·te m. *(cabalgador)* horseman, rider; MIL. cavalryman; *(caballo)* thoroughbred horse; CUBA scrounger, sponger.

ji·ne·te·ar intr. to ride on horseback —tr. AMER. to break in (horses).

jin·glar intr. to swing, rock.

jin·go·ís·mo m. POL. jingoism, extreme patriotism.

jin·go·ís·ta POL. adj. & m.f. jingoist.

jin·jol m. BOT. jujube (berry).

ji·ña f. CUBA human excrement; CHILE trifle, useless object.

ji·par intr. COLL. *(hipar)* to hiccup, hiccough; *(jadear)* to pant, gasp.

ji·pi·do m. COLL. hiccup, hiccough.

ji·pi·ja·pa m. straw hat, Panama hat.

ji·qui·le·te m. BOT. indigo plant.

ji·ra f. *(tira)* strip (of cloth); *(jirón)* shred (of clothing); *(merienda campestre)* picnic; *(excursión)* excursion, outing.

ji·ra·fa f. ZOOL. giraffe; *(del micrófono)* boom (of a microphone).

ji·rón m. *(pedazo)* shred, tatter, piece; SEW. *(ropa)* facing; HER. *(estandarte)* pennant; PERU boulevard, avenue ♦ **hacer jirones** to tear to shreds, tatter.

ji·ro·na·do, -da adj. *(roto)* torn, tattered; HER. divided in gyrons.

ji·to·ma·te m. MEX. variety of tomato.

¡jo! interj. whoa!

Job m. BIBL. Job.

jo·ckey m. jockey.

jo·co·sa·men·te adv. jocosely, amusingly.

jo·co·se·rio, -ria adj. tragicomic.

jo·co·si·dad f. *(gracia)* humor, wit; *(divertimiento)* fun, jocularity; *(chiste)* joke, witticism.

jo·co·so, -sa adj. humorous, witty, amusing.

jo·co·yo·te m. MEX. youngest child (of a family).

jo·cun·di·dad f. jocundity, cheerfulness.

jo·cun·do, -da adj. jocund, cheerful.

jo·der VULG. tr. *(fornicar)* to fuck, screw; *(fastidiar)* to fuck around with; *(estropear)* to fuck up —reflex. *(estropearse)* to get fucked (up); *(irse al diablo)* to go fuck oneself, fuck off.

jo·di·do, -da VULG. I. past part. see **joder** II. adj. *(estropeado)* fucked up; *(maldito)* fucking, damn.

jo·fai·na f. washbasin, washbowl.

jol·go·rio m. merriment, fun ♦ **ir de j.** COLL. to have a good time.

jó·ni·co, -ca I. adj. Ionic, Ionian II. m.f. Ionian.

jo·pe·o m. stroll, walk.

jo·po m. *(mechón)* tuft, shock (of hair); *(rabo)* bushy tail.

¡jo·po! interj. COLL. get out! beat it!

jo·ra f. AMER. type of corn used to make chicha.

jor·dán m. FIG. fountain of youth; *(rejuvenecimiento)* rejuvenation ♦ **ir al j.** FIG., COLL. *(remozarse)* to be rejuvenated; *(convalecer)* to convalesce.

Jor·da·nia f. Jordan.

jor·da·no, -na adj. & m.f. Jordanian.

jor·na·da f. *(viaje)* day's journey, journey, trip; *(día de trabajo)* day's work; workday <una j. de ocho horas an eight-hour workday>; MIL. expedition; FIG. *(vida)* lifetime; *(etapa)* stage; THEAT., ARCH. act; CINEM., TELEV. episode; PRINT. day's print run; CHILE day's wage ♦ **a grandes o largas jornadas** quickly • **de j. entera** full-time work • **de media j.** part-time work.

jor·nal m. *(sueldo)* day's wage; *(día de trabajo)* day's work, workday; SP. *(medida)* land measurement ♦ **a j.** by the day • **j. mínimo** minimum wage.

jor·na·le·ro, -ra m.f. day laborer.

jo·ro·ba f. *(giba)* hump, hunchback; FIG., COLL. *(molestia)* nuisance, bother.

jo·ro·ba·do, -da I. past part. see **jorobar** II. adj. hunchbacked, humpbacked III. m.f. *(giba)* hunchback, humpback; FIG., COLL. *(molestia)* nuisance, bother.

jo·ro·bar tr. FIG., COLL. to bother, pester.

jo·ro·be·ta f. COLL. hunchback, humpback.

jo·ron·go m. MEX. poncho; *(colcha)* bedspread.

jo·ro·po m. COL., VEN. popular folk dance.

jo·rrar tr. to tow, haul (a net).

jo·rro m. dragnet.

Jo·sué m. BIBL. Joshua.

jo·ta¹ f. *(letra)* jay; *(cosa mínima)* iota, bit ♦ **no decir ni j.** FIG., COLL. not to say a word • **no entender ni j.** FIG., COLL. not to understand at all • **sin faltar una j.** without missing a thing, in minute detail.

jo·ta² f. *(baile)* popular Spanish dance and its music; *(sopa)* vegetable soup.

jo·ta³ f. AMER. sandal.

jou·le m. PHYS. joule.

jo·ven I. adj. young, youthful II. m.f. young person, youth.

jo·vial adj. *(alegre)* jovial, merry, cheerful; *(de Júpiter)* Jovian.

jo·via·li·dad f. joviality, merriment.

jo·vial·men·te adv. jovially, cheerfully.

jo·ya f. *(alhaja)* jewel, gem; *(objeto de adorno)* piece of jewelry; *(broche)* jeweled brooch; FIG. *(tesoro)* jewel, gem, treasure; *(regalo)* gift, present; ARCHIT. *(moldura)* astragal, beaded molding ♦ **j. de familia** family heirloom • **joyas** *(de la novia)* trousseau; *(alhajas)* jewelry • **joyas de fantasía** costume jewelry.

jo·yel m. small jewel.

jo·ye·ra f. jewelry box.

jo·ye·ría f. COM. jewelry trade or business; *(tienda)* jewelry store.

jo·ye·ro, -ra m.f. *(lapidario)* jeweler, jeweller (G.B.); *(caja)* jewel case, jewelry box; AMER. goldsmith.

jua·ne·te m. *(pómulo abultado)* prominent cheekbone; MED. bunion; MARIT. topgallant (sail); HOND., COL. hip.

jua·ne·tu·do, -da adj. *(con pómulos)* with prominent cheekbones; MED. suffering from bunions, full of bunions.

ju·bi·la·ción f. retirement <él espera con alegría la j. he is looking forward to retirement>; *(rental)* pension; *(alegría)* jubilation, joy.

ju·bi·la·do, -da I. past part. see **jubilar²** II. adj. *(pensionado)* retired, in retired person; CUBA wise, expert; COL. crazy II. m.f. retired person.

jubilar¹ adj. *(de un aniversario)* jubilee; *(de la jubilación)* pertaining to retirement.

jubilar² tr. *(pensionar)* to retire; FIG., COLL. *(desechar)* to put aside, discard, get rid of —intr. to be jubilant, rejoice —reflex. to retire, go into retirement; *(alegrarse)* to rejoice; GUAT., VEN. to be truant, play hooky; CUBA, MEX. to acquire skill, gain experience; COL. to deteriorate, go to pieces.

ju·bi·le·o m. *(aniversario)* jubilee; FIG. *(idas y venidas)* bustle, comings and goings ♦ **por j.** once in a lifetime.

jú·bi·lo m. jubilation, joy.

ju·bi·lo·so, -sa adj. jubilant, joyful.

ju·bón tr. *(justillo)* jerkin, doublet; *(de mujer)* bodice.

ju·dai·co, -ca adj. Judaic, Jewish.

ju·da·ís·mo m. Judaism.

ju·dai·zar §04 intr. to Judaize.

ju·das m. FIG. *(traidor)* traitor; *(muñeco de paja)* effigy of Judas burnt during Holy Week; MEX. saint's day ♦ **Judas Bibl.** Judas.

ju·de·o·cris·tia·no, -na RELIG. adj. & m.f. Judeo-Christian.

ju·de·ría f. *(barrio)* Jewish quarter, ghetto; *(los judíos)* Jewry.

ju·dí·a f. BOT. bean; *(naipe)* face card (in monte) —m.f. see **judío, -a** ♦ **j. blanca** haricot bean • **j. escarlata** runner bean, kidney bean • **j. verde** green bean, French bean.

ju·di·ca·tu·ra f. *(cargo)* judicature, judgeship; *(mandato)* judge's term of office, judgeship; *(conjunto de jueces)* judiciary.

ju·di·cial adj. judicial, juridical.

ju·di·cial·men·te adv. judicially.

ju·di·cia·rio, -ria adj. judicial.

ju·dí·o, -a I. adj. Jewish II. m.f. Jew —f. Jew, Jewess; see **judía.**

ju·do m. SPORT. judo.

jue·go m. *(recreo)* play, game; *(deporte)* sport; *(cancha)* court, playing field; *(en tenis)* game; *(broma)* fun, jest <lo dijo en j.* he said it in jest>; *(vicio)* gambling, gaming; *(en naipes)* hand (in cards); MECH. play, slack; *(conjunto)* set, service <j. de té tea service>; set, suite <j. de comedor dining room suite>; play <j. de luces en el agua play of lights on the water>; FIG. *(intención)* game, scheme <conozco su j. I know his game> ♦ **a j.** matching, to match <unos zapatos y una bolsa a j.* shoes and a matching purse> • **en j.** in play or at stake <hay mucho dinero en j.* there is a great deal of money at stake> • **fuera de j.** out of play, off-sides • **hacer doble j.** to be two-faced • **hacer j.** to match • **hacer j. de ojos** to flirt • **hacerle el j.** *(ceder⁴a ventaja)* to play into someone's hands; *(cooperar)* to play along with someone • **¡hagan j.!** place your bets! • **j. de azar** or **de suerte** game of chance • **j. de billar** billiards • **j. de bolas** MECH. ball bearing • **j. de damas** checkers, game of checkers • **j. de ingenio** guessing game • **j. de manos** sleight of hand • **j. de naipes** cards, card game • **j. de niños** child's play • **j. de palabras** pun, play on words

• **j. de pelota** ball game • **j. de piernas** SPORT. footwork • **j. limpio** fair play • **juegos** games, exhibitions <*juegos olímpicos* Olympic games> • **juegos malabares** juggling • **j. sucio** foul play• **poner en j.** to put into play *or* at stake • **verle el j.** to know someone's game *or* intentions, be on to someone.

jue·go, juegue see **jugar.**

juer·ga f. COLL. fun, diversion ♦ **correr una j.** *or* **ir de j.** to have fun, live it up.

juer·gue·ar·se reflex. COLL. to live it up, have a good time ♦ **j. de** to make fun of.

juer·guis·ta COLL. I. adj. carousing, boisterous II. m.f. carouser, reveler.

jue·ves m. [pl. -ves] Thursday ♦ **J. Santo** Holy Thursday, Maundy Thursday • **no es cosa del otro j.** FIG. it's nothing special, it's no big deal.

juez m. [pl. **jue·ces**] LAW judge; (*árbitro*) arbitrator, umpire; (*crítico*) critic, arbiter; (*en los deportes*) referee, umpire ♦ **j. arbitrador** arbitrator, umpire • **j. de alzado** *or* **de apelaciones** judge of the court of appeals • **j. de línea** SPORT. linesman • **j. de paz** justice of the peace • **j. de raya** ARG. line judge (at horse races) • **j. municipal** municipal court judge.

ju·ga·da f. (*en el juego*) play, move; FIG. (*treta*) dirty trick ♦ **hacer mala j.** to play a dirty trick.

ju·ga·dor, –do·ra m.f. (*en los juegos*) player; (*en el azar*) gambler ♦ **j. de manos** conjurer, magician • **j. de ventaja** cheater, cardsharp.

ju·gar §42 intr. (*divertirse*) to play, cavort; (*en el azar*) to gamble; (*hacer una jugada*) to make a play; (*en las damas, el ajedrez*) to make a move; (*funcionar*) to work, function <*esta máquina no juega* this machine doesn't work>; MECH. (*tener juego*) to be loose, have slack ♦ **j. a** to play <*jugaron al fútbol* they played soccer> • **j. a la bolsa** COM. to play the (stock) market • **j. con** to play with, toy with • **j. con dos barajas** to be two-faced • **j. sucio** to play dirty —tr. to play <*jugaremos dos partidos* we will play two games>; (*apostar*) to wager, bet; to wield, handle <*jugó la espada* he wielded the sword>; (*hacer juego*) to match, go together; (*mover los miembros*) to move (the limbs); (*tomar parte*) to take part, participate —reflex. (*arriesgar*) to risk, gamble ♦ **jugarse el todo por el todo** to risk everything, play for all or nothing.

ju·ga·rre·ta f. COLL. (*jugada mal hecha*) bad move, bad play; (*trastada*) dirty trick.

ju·glar I. adj. (*de trovadores*) of minstrels; (*chistoso*) comical, witty II. m. (*trovador*) minstrel, troubadour; (*bufón*) jester, buffoon.

ju·gla·res·co, –ca adj. (*de trovadores*) of minstrels; (*de bufones*) of jesters.

ju·gla·ría f. (*de trovadores*) minstrelsy; (*de bufones*) buffoonery.

ju·go m. (*zumo*) juice; CUL. gravy; FIG. (*lo esencial*) essence, substance, pith; PHYSIOL. juice, fluid <*j. gástrico* gastric juice>.

ju·go·si·dad f. (*calidad de jugoso*) juiciness; FIG. (*esencia*) essence, substance.

ju·go·so, –sa adj. (*lleno de jugo*) juicy, full of juice; FIG. (*sustancioso*) essential, substantial.

ju·gué see **jugar.**

ju·gue·te m. (*de un niño*) toy; (*chanza*) joke, jest; THEAT. skit, short play; FIG. toy, plaything <*un j. del viento* a toy of the wind> ♦ **de j.** toy <*tren de j.* toy train>.

ju·gue·te·ar intr. (*divertirse*) to play, cavort; (*jugar con*) to toy with.

ju·gue·te·o m. play, playing.

ju·gue·te·ría f. (*tienda*) toy store; COM. toy business *or* trade.

ju·gue·tón, –to·na adj. playful, frisky.

jui·cio m. (*discernimiento*) judgment, discernment; (*opinión*) judgment, opinion <*a mi j.* in my judgment>; (*razonamiento*) sanity, reason, sound mind; (*sentido común*) sense, common sense; (*cordura*) good sense; (*acción de juzgar*) judgment; LAW (*pleito*) trial; (*sentencia*) sentence, verdict; ASTROL. forecast ♦ **asentar el j.** to come to one's senses • **Día del Juicio** RELIG. Judgment Day• **en el j. de** in the opinion of • **estar en su j.** to be of sound

mind *or* in one's right mind • **estar fuera de j.** to be out of one's mind • **j. de Dios** trial by ordeal • **j. final** *or* **universal** RELIG. Last Judgment, Final Judgment • **pedir en j.** to sue for • **perder el j.** to lose one's mind • **poner en fela de j.** to call into question • **quitarle el j.** to drive someone crazy • **volver al j. de uno** to return to one's senses, to regain consciousness.

jui·cio·sa·men·te adv. judiciously, wisely.

jui·cio·so, –sa adj. judicious, wise.

ju·le·pe m. (*poción*) julep, medicinal drink; (*naipes*) a card game; FIG., COLL. (*reprimenda*) tongue-lashing; AMER. scare, fright <*el ruido nos dio un j.* the noise gave us a scare>; CARIB., MEX. toil, hard work.

ju·le·pe·ar tr. AMER. (*asustar*) to scare, frighten; MEX. to tire, exhaust; COL. to hurry along.

ju·lia·no –na I. adj. Julian <*calendario j.* Julian calendar> II. f. CUL. vegetable soup, julienne.

ju·lio[1] m. July.

ju·lio[2] m. PHYS. joule.

ju·má *or* **ju·ma** f. var. of **jumera.**

ju·ma·do, –da adj. AMER., COLL. drunk, plastered.

ju·mar·se reflex. AMER., COLL. to get drunk.

ju·men·to, –ta m.f. ZOOL. ass, donkey; FIG. (*tonto*) stupid person.

ju·me·ra f. AMER., COLL. drunk, drunken spree ♦ **agarrar una j.** to get drunk, tie one on.

jun·cal[1] m. var. of **juncar.**

jun·cal[2] adj. (*delgado*) slim, willowy; (*guapo*) good-looking.

jun·car m. bed of rushes.

jun·cia f. BOT. sedge ♦ **vender j.** FIG. to brag, boast.

jun·co[1] m. BOT. rush; (*bastón*) cane ♦ **j. de Indias** BOT. rattan • **j. florido** BOT. flowering rush • **j. oloroso** BOT. camel grass.

jun·co[2] m. MARIT. Chinese junk.

jun·gla f. jungle.

ju·nio m. June.

jú·nior m. (*el menor*) junior; RELIG. novice priest.

ju·ní·pe·ro m. BOT. juniper; COL. idiot, fool.

Ju·no MYTH. Juno.

jun·que·ra f. BOT. rush, bulrush.

jun·qui·llo m. BOT. (*flor*) jonquil; (*junco de Indias*) rattan; ARCHIT. (*moldura*) rounded molding.

jun·ta I. f. (*conjunto de personas*) board, junta; (*reunión*) meeting, session; (*unión*) union, junction; CONSTR. joint, scarf; TECH. gasket, washer; MARIT. seam; AMER. junction (of two rivers) ♦ **j. administrativa** administrative council • **j. cardánica** *or* **universal** MECH. universal joint • **j. de educación** board of education • **j. de sanidad** board of health • **j. directiva** board of directors • **j. esférica** ball joint • **j. militar** military junta II. adj. see **junto, –ta.**

jun·ta·men·te adv. together, jointly.

jun·tar tr. (*unir*) to unite, join; (*reunir*) to assemble, gather; to amass, collect <*j. dinero* to amass money>; (*entornar*) to half-close (a door or a window) —reflex. (*reunirse*) to meet, gather; (*asociarse*) to associate with, get together; (*copular*) to mate, copulate; AMER. to live together (out of wedlock) ♦ **juntarse con** to join forces with.

jun·te·ra f. CARP. jointing plane.

jun·to, –ta I. adj. (*unido*) united, joined; (*cercano*) close ♦ **juntos** COL. both II. adv. together, at the same time ♦ **en** *or* **por j.** altogether, all told • **j. a** close to, near • **j. con** along with, together with • **todo j.** at the same time, all together III. f. see **junta.**

jun·tu·ra f. (*punto de unión*) junction, juncture; ANAT. joint; TECH. joint, coupling.

Jú·pi·ter m. ASTRON., MYTH. Jupiter.

ju·ra f. (*juramento*) oath, oath of allegiance; (*ceremonia*) swearing in, administering of an oath.

ju·ra·do I. m. (*tribunal*) jury; (*miembro del tribunal*) juror, juryman; (*de una competición*) panel of judges *or* examiners II. adj. see **jurado, –da.**

ju·ra·do, –da I. past part. see **jurar** II. adj. sworn, under oath III. m. see **jurado.**

ju·ra·men·ta·do, –da I. past part. see **juramentar** II. adj. sworn, under oath.

ju·ra·men·tar tr. to swear in, put under oath —reflex. to be sworn in, take an oath.

ju·ra·men·to m. *(jura)* oath; *(ofensa)* curse, swearword ◆ **bajo j.** under oath • **j. falso** perjury • **j. hipocrático** Hippocratic oath • **prestar j.** to take an oath • **soltar j.** to curse, swear • **tomar j.** to swear in, put under oath.

ju·rar tr. *(prestar juramento)* to swear, take an oath; *(prometer)* to swear, pledge (allegiance) —intr. *(blasfemar)* to swear, curse • **j. en falso** to commit perjury —reflex. ◆ **jurársela a uno** to have it in for someone, swear to get even with someone.

ju·rá·si·co, –ca GEOL. **I.** adj. Jurassic **II.** m. the Jurassic period.

ju·re ◆ **de j.** legally, by right.

ju·rel m. ICHTH. saurel, jack mackerel, yellow jack; AMER. *(miedo)* terror, fright; *(borrachera)* drunkenness.

ju·rí·di·ca·men·te adv. juridically, legally.

ju·ri·di·ci·dad f. lawfulness.

ju·rí·di·co, –ca adj. legal, juridical.

ju·ris·con·sul·to m. jurist, legal expert.

ju·ris·dic·ción f. jurisdiction, authority ◆ **traslado de j.** change of venue.

ju·ris·dic·cio·nal adj. jurisdictional.

ju·ris·pe·ri·cia f. jurisprudence.

ju·ris·pe·ri·to, –ta m.f. legal expert, jurist.

ju·ris·pru·den·cia f. law, jurisprudence; *(precedentes)* case law, legislation.

ju·ris·ta m.f. *(abogado)* jurist, lawyer; *(pensionado)* pensioner; *(dueño)* one who has the right of ownership.

ju·ro m. *(derecho)* right of ownership; *(renta)* pension ◆ **de j.** certainly, surely.

jus·ta **I.** adj. see **justo, –ta** **II.** f. *(torneo)* joust; FIG. *(competencia)* competition, contest.

jus·ta·men·te adv. *(con justicia)* justly, fairly; *(precisamente)* exactly, precisely; very <*ella vivió j. en aquella ciudad* she lived in that very city>.

jus·te·dad f. fairness.

jus·ti·cia f. *(equidad)* justice, fairness; *(castigo)* justice, retribution; *(castigo de muerte)* execution; *(policía)* law, police ◆ **de j.** justly, duly • **hacer j.** to do justice • **ir por j.** or **pedir en j.** to go to court • **tener la j. por su parte** to have justice on one's side • **tomarse la j. por las manos** to take the law into one's own hands.

jus·ti·ciar tr. *(ajusticiar)* to execute (a criminal); *(condenar)* to condemn.

jus·ti·cie·ro, –ra **I.** adj. *(justo)* just, fair; *(riguroso)* strict, severe **II.** m.f. just or righteous person.

jus·ti·fi·ca·ble adj. justifiable.

jus·ti·fi·ca·ción f. *(explicación)* justification; *(prueba)* proof, evidence; PRINT. justification, alignment (of type); THEOL. justification.

jus·ti·fi·ca·do, –da **I.** past part. see **justificar** **II.** adj. justified, just.

jus·ti·fi·ca·dor, –do·ra **I.** adj. justifying **II.** m. PRINT. justification bar.

jus·ti·fi·can·te **I.** adj. justifying **II.** m. voucher.

jus·ti·fi·car §70 tr. *(defender)* to justify, defend; PRINT. to justify, align (type) —reflex. *(explicarse)* to justify or explain oneself; *(probar la inocencia)* to prove one's innocence.

jus·ti·fi·ca·ti·vo, –va adj. justifying.

jus·ti·pre·ciar tr. to appraise, estimate.

jus·ti·pre·cio m. appraisal, estimate.

jus·to, –ta **I.** adj. *(justiciero)* just, fair, right; *(legítimo)* justified, legitimate; *(honrado)* righteous, upright; *(exacto)* exact, precise, correct <*el peso j.* the exact weight>; tight, tight-fitting <*el traje me queda muy j.* the suit is very tight on me> **II.** m.f. just person **III.** adv. *(con justicia)* justly, fairly; *(exactamente)* exactly, precisely; sparingly, tightly <*viven muy j.* they live very sparingly> ◆ **al j.** exactly, precisely.

ju·ve·nil adj. young, youthful.

ju·ven·tud f. *(edad)* youth, early life; *(vigor juvenil)* youthfulness; *(los jóvenes)* young people, the youth.

juz·ga·do, –da **I.** past part. see **juzgar** **II.** adj. judged **III.** m. *(tribunal)* court, tribunal; *(judicatura)* judicature ◆ **j. de circuito** circuit court.

juz·ga·dor, –do·ra **I.** adj. judging **II.** m.f. judge.

juz·gar §47 tr. *(arbitrar)* to judge, pass judgment on; *(considerar)* to judge, consider, believe <*lo juzgo importante* I

consider it important>; *(estimar)* to judge, assess ◆ **a j. por** judging by or from • **j. mal** to misjudge • **j. por las apariencias** to judge by appearances • **juzgue mi sorpresa** imagine my surprise.

K

k, K f. twelfth letter of the Spanish alphabet.

kái·ser m. kaiser, emperor.

ka·ki adj. & m. khaki.

Kam·pu·che·a f. Kampuchea.

Kam·pu·che·a Democrática f. Democratic Kampuchea.

kam·pu·che·a·no, –na adj. & m.f. Kampuchean.

kan or **khan** m. *(príncipe)* khan, ruler; *(caravasar)* khan, caravansery.

ka·na·to m. khanate.

kan·gu·ro m. ZOOL. kangaroo.

kap·pa f. kappa (Greek letter).

ka·ra·te m. karate.

kar·ma f. RELIG. karma.

kar·ting m. go-cart racing.

ka·yac m. kayak.

ke·nia·no, –na adj. & m.f. Kenyan.

Ken·ya m. Kenya.

ke·pí or **ke·pis** m. kepi (military cap).

ker·mes·se f. kermis, church fair.

ke·ro·se·no or **ke·ro·sén** m. kerosene.

ki·butz m. kibbutz, Israeli collective farm.

kif or **ki·fi** m. kif, hashish.

ki·lo m. kilo, kilogram.

ki·lo·ci·clo m. kilocycle.

ki·lo·gra·mo m. kilogram.

ki·lo·li·tro m. kiloliter.

ki·lo·me·trar tr. to measure in kilometers.

ki·lo·me·tra·je m. distance in kilometers.

ki·lo·mé·tri·co, –ca adj. kilometric ◆ **billete k.** rail pass.

ki·ló·me·tro m. kilometer.

ki·lo·tón m. kiloton.

ki·lo·va·tio m. ELEC. kilowatt.

ki·lo·vol·tio m. ELEC. kilovolt.

ki·mo·no m. kimono.

ki·ne·si·te·ra·peu·ta m. masseur —f. masseuse.

ki·ne·si·te·ra·pia f. kinesitherapy, massage.

kios·co m. kiosk.

Ki·ri·ba·ti Kiribati.

ki·rie or **ki·rie e·lei·son** m. RELIG. kyrie, kyrie eleison ◆ **cantar el k.e.** to plead for mercy.

kirsch m. kirsch, cherry brandy.

ki·wi m. ORNITH. kiwi.

kla·xon m. AUTO. horn.

knock-out m. knockout (in boxing)

ko·a·la m. ZOOL. koala.

kol·joz m. kolkhoz, Soviet collective farm.

ko·pek m. FIN. kopeck.

krip·tón m. CHEM. krypton.

Kris·na RELIG. Krishna.

ku·mis m. kumis (fermented drink).

kum·mel m. kümmel (liqueur).

Ku·wait m. Kuwait.

ku·wa·tí adj. & m.f. [pl. **-tí·es**] Kuwaiti.

L

l, L f. thirteenth letter of the Spanish alphabet.

la¹ §G16, 30, 35 **I.** def. art. the <*la maestra* the teacher> ◆ **la que** the one that **II.** pron. her <*la miré* I looked at her>; it <*buscó la cinta y finalmente la encontró* she looked for the ribbon and finally found it>; you <*no la vi a usted en la fiesta, Ana* I didn't see you at the party, Ann>.

la² MUS. la (note).

la·be·rín·ti·co, –ca adj. *(relativo al laberinto)* labyrinthine; FIG. *(enmarañado)* tangled, snarled.

la·be·rin·to m. *(lugar)* labyrinth, maze; FIG. *(cosa enredada)* tangle, maze; ANAT. labyrinth (of the ear); POET. palindrome.

la·bia f. COLL. eloquence, verbal fluency ♦ **tener mucha l.** to have the gift of gab.

la·bial adj. labial.

la·bia·li·zar §04 tr. PHONET. to labialize.

la·bio m. ANAT. lip; FIG. *(borde)* lip, rim; FIG. *(órgano del habla)* lip, mouth ♦ **cerrar** or **sellar los labios** FIG. to keep one's lips sealed • **l. leporino** harelip.

la·bio·den·tal adj. & f. PHONET. labiodental.

la·bio·so, -sa adj. AMER. glib.

la·bor f. *(trabajo)* work <*no pone ningún entusiasmo en su l.* he does not put any enthusiasm into his work>; *(esfuerzo)* work, labor <*esa tarea requiere gran l.* that task requires a lot of work>; *(faena)* task, job <*su l. es limpiar el establo* his task is to clean the stable>; *(productos de tabaco)* tobacco products; AGR. *(labranza)* farm work; *(arada)* plowing; SEW. *(bordado)* embroidery; *(escuela)* sewing school; MIN. excavation; ZOOL. silkworm egg ♦ **labores de aguja** SEW. needlework • **labores domésticas** household chores.

la·bo·ra·ble adj. *(del trabajo)* work, working <*día l.* working day>; AGR. arable, workable <*tierra l.* arable land>.

la·bo·ral adj. labor <*fuerza l.* labor force>; *(técnico)* technical <*enseñanza l.* technical education>.

la·bo·rar tr. *(trabajar)* to work; AGR. *(cultivar)* to cultivate, till; *(arar)* to plow —intr. to scheme.

la·bo·ra·to·rio m. laboratory.

la·bo·re·ar tr. *(trabajar)* to work <*l. la tierra* to work the land>; MIN. to work (a mine) —intr. MARIT. to reeve.

la·bo·re·o m. AGR. farming, cultivation; MIN. mining, excavation.

la·bo·rio·sa·men·te adv. laboriously.

la·bo·rio·si·dad f. laboriousness.

la·bo·rio·so, -sa adj. *(trabajador)* diligent, industrious; *(penoso)* laborious, arduous <*una tarea l.* an arduous task>.

la·bo·ris·mo m. POL. *(partido)* Labor (Party), Labour (G.B.); *(tendencia)* labor movement.

la·bo·ris·ta adj. & m.f. Laborite, Labourite (G.B.).

la·bra f. stone-cutting, engraving.

la·bra·da f. AGR. fallow (land).

la·bra·de·ro, -ra or **la·bra·dí·o, -a** adj. arable, tillable.

la·bra·do, -da I. past part. see **labrar** II. adj. *(forjado)* wrought (said of metal); *(tallado)* carved (said of wood, stone); *(repujado)* tooled (said of leather); AGR. *(cultivado)* cultivated, tilled; *(arado)* plowed; SEW. *(bordado)* embroidered III. m. *(campo)* cultivated or tilled land; *(forjadura)* working (of metals); *(tallado)* carving (of wood, stone); *(repujado)* tooling (of leather); AGR. *(cultivo)* cultivation, tilling; *(arada)* plowing; SEW. *(bordado)* embroidery.

la·bra·dor, -do·ra I. adj. farm, farming II. m.f. *(agricultor)* farmer; *(arador)* plowman; *(campesino)* peasant.

la·bran·tí·o, -a adj. cultivable, tillable.

la·bran·za f. *(cultivo)* cultivation, farming; *(hacienda)* farm; *(tierra)* farmland.

la·brar tr. *(trabajar)* to work (a material); *(metales)* to work (metals); *(tallar)* to carve (wood, stone); *(cuero)* to tool (leather); AGR. *(cultivar)* to cultivate, till; *(arar)* to plow (leather); SEW. *(bordar)* to embroider; FIG. *(causar)* to bring about, cause <*l. la felicidad de alguien* to bring about someone's happiness>; *(edificar)* to build, lay the foundation for <*l. el futuro* to build one's future> —intr. *(trabajar)* to work <*l. en piedra* to work in stone>; *(impresionar)* to make a lasting impression.

la·brie·go, -ga m.f. farm hand or worker.

la·ca f. *(resina)* lac; *(pintura)* lacquer, shellac; *(barniz)* lacquer; *(objeto)* lacquer piece, lacquered object; *(pelo)* hair spray ♦ **l. de uñas** nail polish or varnish.

la·ca·yo m. *(criado)* lackey, valet; *(cintas)* knot of ribbons (worn as an ornament); *(mozo de espuelas)* groom, attendant.

la·cé, lace see **lazar**.

la·ce·a·dor m. AMER. lassoer, roper.

la·ce·ar tr. *(adornar)* to trim with bows; *(atar)* to tie with bow knots; *(disponer la caza)* to drive, round up (game);

(coger con lazo) to trap, snare (game); ARG. to whip with a lasso.

la·ce·ra·ción f. laceration.

la·ce·ran·te adj. lacerating.

la·ce·rar tr. *(magullar)* to lacerate; FIG. *(dañar)* to damage, injure (honor, reputation) —intr. to suffer.

la·ce·ria f. *(pobreza)* misery, want; *(trabajo penoso)* drudgery, toil.

la·ce·rí·a f. *(lazos)* bows; ARCHIT. ornamental bows.

la·ce·ro m. *(laceador)* lassoer, roper; *(de perros)* dogcatcher.

la·cio, -cia adj. *(marchito)* withered, wilted <*flores lacias* wilted flowers>; FIG. *(flojo)* limp, lifeless; *(cabello)* straight, lank (hair).

la·cón m. shoulder of pork.

la·có·ni·ca·men·te adv. laconically.

la·có·ni·co, -ca adj. laconic, terse.

la·co·nis·mo m. laconism, terseness.

la·cra f. *(señal)* mark, scar; FIG. *(defecto)* stain, blemish; GUAT., VEN. *(llaga)* sore, wound; ARG., PERU, P. RICO *(costra)* scab.

la·crar[1] tr. *(una enfermedad)* to strike, afflict (illness); FIG. *(dañar)* to harm, injure —reflex. to be afflicted or stricken (with).

la·crar[2] tr. to seal with wax.

la·cre I. m. *(pasta)* sealing wax; CUBA propolis, beeswax II. adj. red.

la·cri·mal adj. lachrymal, tear.

la·cri·mó·ge·no, -na adj. lachrymatory, tear-producing ♦ **gas l.** tear gas.

la·cri·mo·si·dad f. tearfulness, weepiness.

la·cri·mo·so, -sa adj. *(que tiene lágrimas)* lachrymose, tearful; *(triste)* sorrowful, moving.

lac·ta·ción f. nursing, suckling.

lac·tan·cia f. lactation, nursing period.

lac·tan·te I. adj. nursing, suckling II. m.f. nursling, nursing infant.

lac·tar tr. & intr. to nurse, suckle.

lac·te·a·do, -da adj. lacteal, milky ♦ **harina l.** malted milk.

lác·te·o, -a adj. lacteal, milky ♦ **fiebre l.** MED. milk fever • **Vía Láctea** ASTRON. Milky Way.

lác·ti·co, -ca adj. CHEM. lactic ♦ **ácido l.** lactic acid.

lac·to·sa f. CHEM. lactose.

la·cus·tre adj. lacustrine, of lakes ♦ **vivienda l.** lake dwelling.

la·cho, -cha m.f. CHILE, COLL. *(amante)* lover —m. COLL. *(majo)* dandy —f. ICHTH. anchovy; COLL. *(vergüenza)* shame ♦ **tener poca l.** to be shameless.

la·de·a·do, -da I. past part. see **ladear** II. adj. leaning, tilted (said of plants) III. f. CHILE, COL. *(ladeo)* inclination.

la·de·ar tr. to bend, tilt <*l. el cuerpo a un lado* to bend the body to one side> —intr. to detour —reflex. *(inclinarse)* to lean, tilt; FIG. *(igualarse a algo)* to be even with, be level with; CHILE to fall in love; ARG. to deviate.

la·de·o m. slope, inclination.

la·de·ra f. *(pendiente)* slope; COL. river bank.

la·de·rí·a f. small plateau on a mountain slope.

la·di·lla f. ENTOM. crab louse; BOT. common barley ♦ **pegarse a uno como una l.** FIG., COLL. to stick to someone like a leech.

la·di·no, -na I. adj. *(polígloto)* multilingual, polyglot; AMER. Spanish-speaking (said of Indians); FIG. *(sagaz)* astute, shrewd; C. AMER. mestizo II. m. *(retorromano)* Rhaeto-Romanic; *(judeoespañol)* Ladino, Judeo-Spanish.

la·do m. *(costado)* side <*el l. derecho* the right side>; *(partido)* side <*yo estoy a su l.* I am on his side>; *(línea genealógica)* side <*el l. paterno* on his father's side>; *(sitio)* room <*hazle l.* make room for him>; FIG. *(aspecto)* side, aspect <*hay un nuevo l. en este asunto* there is a new aspect to this matter>; *(camino)* way, road; *(protección)* protection; GEOM. side; MIL. flank; SPORT. end ♦ **al l.** near, close at hand • **al l. de** beside, next to • **a un l.** aside • **dar de l. a alguien** to avoid someone, give someone the cold shoulder • **dejar a un l.** to omit, leave aside • **de un l.** from side to side • **echar a un l.** to cast aside • **hacerse a un l.** to move aside, get out of the way • **l. a l.** side by side • **l. débil** or **flaco** weak spot • **lados** FIG. advisers, aides <*el* *presidente tiene buenos lados* the president has good advisers> • **mirar de l.** to look sideways at • **poner a un l.** to put aside • **ponerse del l. de** to side with someone • **por el l. de** towards, in the direction of • **por otro l.** on the other hand • **por todos lados** on all sides, all around • **por un l.** on the one hand.

la·dra·dor, –ra adj. barking, yelping.

la·drar intr. *(dar ladridos)* to bark; FIG., COLL. *(amenazar)* to growl, snarl; COLL. *(desentonar)* to clash (said of colors).

la·dre·rí·a f. MED. leprosy; VET. cysticercosis.

la·dri·do m. *(perro)* bark, yelp; FIG., COLL. *(crítica)* criticism, censure.

la·dri·lla·do m. brick floor.

la·dri·llal *or* **la·dri·llar** m. brick factory *or* work.

la·dri·llar tr. to brick, pave with bricks.

la·dri·lle·ra f. brick mold.

la·dri·lle·ro m. brick maker.

la·dri·llo m. *(arcilla cocida)* brick; *(azulejo)* tile; FIG. *(tableta)* block, bar <*l. de chocolate* chocolate bar> ♦ **es un l.** it's *or* he's a bore • **l. crudo** adobe.

la·drón, –dro·na I. adj. thievish, thieving II. m.f. *(persona)* thief, robber —m. *(de agua)* sluice gate; *(pavesa)* burnt candle wick; ELEC. *(toma de electricidad)* siphon, tap (of power line); *(enchufe)* multiple socket ♦ **l. de corazones** COLL. lady-killer.

la·dro·ne·ar intr. to go about stealing.

la·dro·ne·ra f. *(refugio)* den of thieves; *(de agua)* sluice gate; *(robo)* theft, robbery; *(alcancía)* money box; MIL. machicolation.

la·dro·ne·rí·o m. larceny, theft.

la·dro·ne·rí·o m. ARG. var. of **ladronesca**.

la·dro·nes·ca f. COLL. gang of thieves.

la·dron·zue·lo, –la m.f. petty thief.

la·ga·ña f. rheum.

la·gar m. wine *or* olive press.

la·ga·re·jo m. small wine press ♦ **hacerse l.** to be bruised (said of grapes).

la·ga·re·ro m. wine *or* olive presser.

la·gar·ta f. ZOOL. female lizard; ENTOM. gypsy *or* tussock moth; FIG., COLL. *(mujer)* crafty *or* shrewd woman.

la·gar·te·ar tr. CHILE to pinion, hold by the arms —intr. to behave shrewdly.

la·gar·te·ra f. lizard hole.

la·gar·ti·ja f. ZOOL. small lizard ♦ **como rabo de l.** FIG., COLL. nervous, fidgety.

la·gar·ti·jo m. ZOOL. small lizard; MEX. sharp dresser.

la·gar·to m. ZOOL. lizard; ANAT. biceps; FIG., COLL. *(hombre astuto)* fox, sly devil; FIG., COLL. *(insignia)* red sword (of the Order of Santiago); AMER. alligator ♦ **¡lagarto!** knock on wood!

la·gar·to·na f. COLL. crafty woman.

la·go m. lake.

la·go·te·ar intr. COLL. to soft-soap.

la·go·te·rí·a f. COLL. soft soap ♦ **hacer lagoterías** COLL. to soft-soap.

la·go·te·ro, –ra I. adj. COLL. soft-soaping II. m.f. soft-soaper.

lá·gri·ma f. tear <*su historia me movió a lágrimas* his story moved me to tears>; BOT. sap; FIG. *(gota)* spot, drop ♦ **beberse las lágrimas** to hold back one's tears • **deshacerse en lágrimas** to burst into tears • **enjugarse las lágrimas** to dry one's eyes *or* tears • **lágrimas** sorrows, troubles • **lágrimas de cocodrilo** FIG. crocodile tears • **lágrimas de Job** BOT. Job's tears • **llorar a l. viva** to cry one's heart out • **ser el paño de lágrimas (de alguien)** to be someone's consolation.

la·gri·mal I. adj. lachrymal II. m. ANAT. lachrymal cáruncle; AGR. rot formed between trunk and tree branch.

la·gri·mar intr. to cry, weep.

la·gri·me·ar intr. *(ojos)* to water, tear; *(persona)* to cry, weep.

la·gri·me·o m. *(ojos)* watering, tearing; *(persona)* tearfulness.

la·gri·mi·lla f. CHILE unfermented grape juice.

la·gri·mo·so, –sa adj. *(ojos)* watery, teary; *(lacrimoso)* tearful, mournful.

la·gu·na f. *(lago)* lagoon; FIG. *(texto)* hiatus, lacuna; *(falta)* gap.

la·gu·na·jo m. puddle, pool.

la·gu·no·so, –sa adj. full of lagoons.

lai·ca·do m. laity.

lai·cal adj. lay, laical.

lai·ca·li·zar §04 tr. CHILE *(secularizar)* to laicize, secularize.

lai·ci·dad f. NEOL. *or* **lai·cis·mo** m. laicism.

lai·co, –ca adj. lay, laical.

la·ís·mo m. GRAM. use of **la** and **las** as indirect objects instead of **le** and **les**.

la·ís·ta adj. GRAM. using **la** and **las** as indirect objects.

la·ja f. *(piedra)* stone slab; MARIT. reef; CHILE, HOND. fine sand (used as abrasive); ECUAD. bank, slope.

la·ma¹ f. *(cieno)* mud, silt; BOT. algae, seaweed; *(tela)* (silver *or* gold) lamé; AMER. slime; BOL., COL. verdigris.

la·ma² m. (Tibetan monk) lama.

la·ma·ís·mo m. RELIG. Lamaism.

lamb·da f. lambda (Greek letter).

lam·ber tr. AMER. *(lamer)* to lick; *(adular)* to fawn on, suck up to.

lam·bis·cón, –co·na MEX. I. adj. fawning, toadying II. m.f. toady, bootlicker.

lam·bis·co·ne·ar tr. MEX., COLL. to suck up to, toady.

lam·bis·co·ne·rí·a f. MEX., COLL. servility, toadying.

lam·bis·que·ar tr. HOND., P. RICO, COLL. to scrounge for sweets (said of children); MEX., COLL. to flatter, suck up to.

la·me·dor, –do·ra I. adj. licking II. m.f. licker —m. *(jarabe)* syrup; FIG. *(halago)* wheedling, cajolery ♦ **dar l.** FIG. to bluff, fool one's opponent.

la·me·du·ra f. lick, licking.

la·men·ta·ble adj. lamentable, deplorable.

la·men·ta·ble·men·te adv. lamentably, deplorably.

la·men·ta·ción f. lamentation, wailing.

la·men·ta·dor, –do·ra I. adj. lamenting, wailing II. m.f. lamenter, wailer.

la·men·tar tr. *(sentir)* to regret, be sorry for <*lamento esta demora* I regret this delay>; *(llorar)* to bewail, bemoan —reflex. to grieve, lament.

la·men·to m. lament.

la·men·to·so, –sa adj. *(que se lamenta)* plaintive, mournful; *(triste)* lamentable, deplorable.

la·me·pla·tos m.f. [pl. -tos] FIG., COLL. *(goloso)* glutton, pig; *(persona que vive de sobras)* scavenger, scrounger.

la·mer tr. *(con la lengua)* to lick; *(tocar suavemente)* to lap <*las olas lamen la orilla* the waves lap the shore>.

la·me·rón, –ro·na I. adj. having a sweet tooth II. m.f. sweet-toothed person.

la·me·ta·da f. *or* **la·me·ta·zo** m. licking, lick.

la·me·tón m. COLL. var. of **lametada**.

la·mi·do, –da I. past part. see **lamer** II. m.f. licking III. adj. FIG. *(flaco)* thin and pale; FIG. *(relamido)* polished, finely finished (style).

lá·mi·na I. f. *(plancha)* lamina, plate; PRINT. engraved plate; *(estampa)* print, engraving; BOT., ZOOL. lamina; FIG. *(figura)* expression II. adj. COL., COLL. sly, roguish.

la·mi·na·ción f. lamination.

la·mi·na·do, –da I. past part. see **laminar²** II. adj. laminated ♦ **hierro l.** sheet metal II. m. lamination.

la·mi·na·dor m. laminator.

la·mi·nar¹ adj. laminar, laminal.

la·mi·nar² tr. to laminate.

la·mi·no·so, –sa adj. laminate.

la·mis·car §70 tr. COLL. to lick greedily.

lam·pa f. CHILE, PERU miner's pick.

lam·pa·ce·ar tr. MARIT. to swab, mop.

lam·pa·la·gua I. f. ARG., CHILE, ZOOL. boa constrictor II. adj. CHILE glutton.

lam·pan·te adj. of lamps ♦ **petróleo l.** kerosene.

lam·par *or* **a·lam·par** intr. to yearn, long, crave.

lám·pa·ra f. *(utensilio)* lamp <*l. de aceite* oil lamp>; *(aparato de alumbrado)* light <*l. eléctrica* electric light>; COLL. *(mancha)* oil spot, grease stain; RAD., TELEV. valve, tube ♦ **atizar la l.** COLL. to refill the glasses • **l. de alcohol** spirit lamp • **l. de arco** arc lamp • **l. de incandescencia** incandescent lamp • **l. de seguridad** safety lamp • **l. de**

soldar blowtorch • **l. de techo** ceiling lamp • **l. fluorescente** fluorescent lamp • **l. neón** neon light • **l. relámpago** PHOTOG. flash lamp • **l. solar** sun lamp.

lam·pa·re·rí·a f. *(fabrica)* lamp factory; *(tienda)* lamp shop *or* store.

lam·pa·ri·lla f. *(lámpara pequeña)* small lamp; *(que se enciende de noche)* night-light; BOT. aspen; COLL. *(aguardiente)* shot of brandy.

lam·pa·rón m. *(aceite)* grease spot *or* stain; MED. scrofula; VET. glanders.

lam·pa·zo m. BOT. burdock; MARIT. swab, mop; COL., COLL. lashing.

lam·pe·ar tr. CHILE to shovel.

lam·pi·ño, –ña adj. *(sin barba)* beardless; *(con poco vello)* hairless; BOT. glabrous.

lam·pión m. large lantern.

lam·pre·a·zo m. COLL. lashing, whipping.

la·na f. *(de oveja)* wool <*la l. de esta oveja es muy suave* this sheep's wool is very soft>; *(tela)* wool (material); MEX., COLL. *(dinero)* bread, bucks; *(mentira)* lie ♦ **cardarle a alguien la l.** FIG., COLL. to tell someone off • **de l.** wool, woolen <*pantalones de l.* wool slacks> • **ir por l. y salir trasquilado** to get more than one bargained for • **l. de acero** steel wool • **l. de vidrio** glass wool —m. C. AMER. *(gentuza)* riffraff; *(tramposo)* swindler.

la·na·do, –da adj. woolly, fleecy.

la·nar adj. wool-bearing ♦ **ganado l.** sheep.

lan·ce m. *(lanzamiento)* cast, throw (of nets, stones); *(pesca)* catch (of fish); *(acontecimiento)* event, occurrence <*un l. imprevisto* an unforeseen event>; *(trance)* predicament, difficult situation <*me hallé en un l.* I found myself in a predicament>; *(jugada)* move (in a game); *(riña)* quarrel, argument; TAUR. pass with the cape; CHILE duck, dodge ♦ **de l.** at a cheap price • **l. apretado** COLL. tight spot, jam • **l. de honor** duel • **l. de fortuna** stroke of luck.

lan·cé, lance see **lanzar**.

lan·ce·a·do, –da I. past part. see **lancear** II. adj. BOT. lanceolate III. f. ARG. lancing, spearing.

lan·ce·ar tr. to lance, spear.

lan·ce·ra f. lance rack (in an armory).

lan·ce·ro m. lancer, pikeman ♦ **lanceros** lancers (dance).

lan·ce·ta m. SURG. lancet; CHILE, MEX., PERU sting.

lan·ci·nan·te adj. stabbing, piercing (pain).

lan·ci·nar tr. to stab, pierce (pain).

lan·cha f. *(embarcación)* boat; *(piedra)* stone slab; *(armadijo)* partridge trap *or* snare; ECUAD. *(niebla)* fog; *(escarcha)* frost ♦ **l. motora** *or* **rápida** motorboat, launch • **l. salvavidas** lifeboat • **l. torpedera** torpedo boat.

lan·cha·da f. boatload.

lan·char m. flagstone quarry.

lan·che·ro m. boatman, ferryman.

lan·chón m. lighter, barge.

lan·da f. moor, heath.

lan·dó m. landau, carriage.

la·ne·rí·a f. wool fabric store.

la·ne·ro, –ra I. adj. woolen II. m. *(negociante)* wool dealer; *(almacén)* wool warehouse.

lan·gos·ta f. ENTOM. locust; ZOOL. lobster.

lan·gos·ti·no *or* **lan·gos·tín** m. ZOOL. crayfish.

lán·gui·da·men·te adv. languidly.

lan·gui·de·cer §17 intr. to languish.

lan·gui·dez f. *(flaqueza)* weakness, feebleness; *(falta de energía)* listlessness, lethargy.

lán·gui·do, –da adj. languid, feeble.

lan·guor m. languor.

la·ni·lla f. *(pelillo)* nap (of cloth); *(tejido)* flannel; *(afeite)* ancient cosmetic.

la·no·li·na f. lanolin.

la·no·so, –sa adj. woolly, fleecy.

lan·ta·ca f. small firearm.

lan·ta·no m. CHEM. lanthanum.

la·nu·do, –da adj. *(que tiene lana)* woolly, fleecy; ECUAD., VEN., FIG. coarse, uncouth.

lan·za I. f. *(arma)* lance, spear; MIL. *(soldado)* lancer; *(boquilla)* nozzle (of a hose) ♦ **correr lanzas** to joust • **estar con la l. en ristre** FIG. to be ready for action • **romper lanzas por** FIG. to defend, fight for • **ser una l.** *or* **ser**

buena **l.** FIG., COLL. to be sharp, be on the ball II. adj. MEX. crafty, deceptive.

lan·za·bom·bas m. [pl. **-bas**] ARTIL. *(de trinchera)* trench mortar; *(de aviones)* bomb release.

lan·za·co·he·tes m. [pl. **-tes**] ARTIL. rocket launcher.

lan·za·da f. *(golpe)* lance thrust; *(herida)* lance wound.

lan·za·de·ra f. TEX. shuttle.

lan·za·dor, –do·ra I. adj. throwing, hurling II. m.f. thrower, pitcher.

lan·za·lla·mas m. [pl. **-mas**] ARM., MIL. flame thrower.

lan·za·mien·to m. throw, throwing ♦ **l. de abastecimientos** MIL. airdrop • **l. del disco** SPORT. discus throwing • **l. de un barco** launching of a ship.

lan·zar §04 tr. *(arrojar)* to throw, hurl <*l. una piedra* to throw a stone>; *(dardos, flechas)* to shoot, fire; *(un proyectil)* to launch (a projectile); *(una bomba)* to drop (a bomb); *(aves)* to release (birds); COLL. *(vomitar)* to vomit, throw up; *(echar)* to put forth <*las plantas lanzan flores en la primavera* plants put forth flowers in the spring>; FIG. *(decir)* to let loose, let out <*l. un grito* to let out a shout>; *(soltar)* to hurl <*l. insultos* to hurl insults>; *(dar a conocer)* to launch <*l. un nuevo producto* to launch a new product>; LAW *(despojar)* to dispossess; *(desalojar)* to evict; SPORT. *(jabalina, disco)* to throw (javelin, discus); *(el peso)* to put (the shot) —reflex. *(arrojarse)* to throw *or* hurl oneself; *(saltar)* to jump; *(asaltar)* to rush, attack; FIG. *(comenzar)* to launch into, embark upon.

lan·za·tor·pe·dos m. [pl. **-dos**] MIL. torpedo tube.

lan·za·zo m. var. of **lanzada**.

la·ña¹ f. clamp.

la·ña² f. BOT. green coconut.

la·ña·dor m. clamper, one who fastens with clamps.

la·ñar tr. *(unir con lañas)* to clamp, fasten with a clamp; *(abrir pescado)* to clean (fish).

la·o *or* **la·o·sia·no, –na** I. adj. Lao, Laotian II. m.f. [pl. **la·o**] *(habitante)* Lao, Laotian —m. *(idioma)* Laotian.

La·o, República Democrática Popular f. Lao People's Democratic Republic.

La·os m. GEOG. Laos.

la·pa¹ f. scum (on liquids).

la·pa² f. ZOOL. limpet; FIG., COLL. *(persona)* leech; VEN. rodent; ECUAD. hat with flattened crown.

la·pa·char m. swamp, marsh.

la·pi·ce·ra f. CHILE penholder; *(portalápiz)* pencil holder; *(lápiz)* pencil; AMER. *(bolígrafo)* ballpoint pen.

la·pi·ce·ro m. *(instrumento)* mechanical pencil; *(lápiz)* pencil; ARG., PERU penholder.

lá·pi·da f. stone tablet *or* marker.

la·pi·da·ción f. *(pedrea)* stoning; *(piedras preciosas)* carving (gems).

la·pi·dar tr. *(matar a pedradas)* to stone to death; AMER. to carve gems.

la·pi·da·rio, –ria I. adj. *(relativo a las piedras preciosas)* lapidary; *(muy conciso)* concise, succinct ♦ **frase l.** memorable phrase II. m. lapidary.

lá·piz m. [pl. **-ces**] *(grafito)* graphite, lead; *(instrumento)* pencil, crayon ♦ **l. de color** colored pencil • **l. de labios** lipstick.

la·po m. COLL. *(bofetada)* slap, swipe; *(trago)* drink, shot; COLL. *(escupitajo)* spit; VEN., COLL. sucker, dupe.

lap·so, –sa I. adj. ARCH. (morally) fallen II. m. *(curso)* lapse, interval; *(error)* lapse, slip.

lap·sus m. lapsus, slip ♦ **l. cálami** slip of the pen • **l. linguae** slip of the tongue.

la·que m. ARG., CHILE, PERU bola.

la·que·ar tr. *(barnizar)* to lacquer, varnish; CHILE to rope with a bola.

lar·dar *or* **lar·de·ar** tr. to baste, lard.

lar·do m. lard, animal fat.

la·res m.pl. HIST. Roman household gods; FIG. *(hogar)* home ♦ **el lar paterno** the family home *or* hearth.

lar·ga I. f. *(billar)* longest billiard cue ♦ **dar largas a** to delay, postpone • **largas** delay, postponement II. adj. see **largo, –ga**.

lar·ga·men·te adv. *(con extensión)* lengthily, at length; FIG. *(cómodamente)* easily, comfortably; FIG. generously, liberally.

lar·gar §47 tr. *(aflojar)* to slacken, let *or* pay out <*l. el cable* to pay out the rope>; *(soltar)* to release, let go <*largaron a los prisioneros* they released the prisoners>; *(despedir)* to fire, dismiss <*l. a un criado* to dismiss a servant>; *(tirar)* to throw, hurl; *(expulsar)* to throw out, expel; COLL. *(decir)* to let out, let fly <*l. una palabrota* to let fly an obscenity>; to deal, land <*le largué una bofetada* I dealt him a blow>; MARIT. to unfurl; COL. to lend, give —reflex. COLL. *(marcharse)* to beat it, scram <*¡lárgate!* beat it!>; MARIT. to set sail, put out to sea; AMER. to begin to <*se largó a llorar* she began to cry>.

lar·go, –ga I. adj. long <*una calle l.* a long street>; *(extenso)* lengthy, long <*una discusión l.* a lengthy discussion>; *(alto)* tall; COLL. *(astuto)* shrewd, astute; *(generoso)* generous; FIG. *(abundante)* abundant, copious <*una cosecha l.* an abundant harvest>; *(muchos)* many <*largos años* many years>; GRAM. long <*vocales largas* long vowels>; MARIT. loose, slack <*un cabo l.* a loose cable> ♦ **a la l.** lengthwise <*una tabla atravesada a la l.* a board crossed lengthwise>; *(con el tiempo)* in the long run <*a la l. lo necesitaremos* in the long run we will need it>; *(poco a poco)* little by little <*a la l. lo acabaré* little by little I will finish it> ♦ **a lo l.** lengthwise <*partir un palo a lo l.* to split a stick lengthwise>; *(por)* along <*a lo l. de la costa* along the coast>; throughout <*a lo l. del año* throughout the year>; *(a lo lejos)* afar <*a lo l. se veía el pueblo* one could see the town from afar>; ♦ **de l.** in formal dress ♦ **l. de manos** heavy-handed ♦ **l. de uñas** COLL. light-fingered ♦ **l. y tendido** COLL. at length **II.** m. *(longitud)* length; MUS. largo ♦ **dar largos a** to put off, postpone ♦ **de l.** long <*la piscina tiene quince pies de l.* the pool is fifteen feet long> ♦ **pasar de l.** to pass by; *(no hacer caso de)* to neglect, ignore —f. see **larga III.** interj. get out! ♦ **¡l. de aquí!** get out of here!

lar·gor m. length.

lar·go·ru·to, –ta or **lar·gu·cho, –cha** adj. lanky, stringy.

lar·gué, largue see **largar**.

lar·gue·a·do, –da adj. striped.

lar·gue·ro I. adj. *(dadivoso)* liberal, generous; AMER. *(hablador)* talkative, verbose **II.** m. *(travesaño)* girder, beam; *(cabezal)* bolster, cushion.

lar·gue·za f. *(liberalidad)* generosity, largesse; *(largura)* length.

lar·gui·ru·cho, –cha adj. COLL. lanky, stringy.

lar·gu·ra f. length.

lar·gu·ru·cho, –cha adj. COLL. lanky, stringy.

la·rin·ge f. ANAT. larynx.

la·rin·gi·tis f. laryngitis.

la·rin·go·lo·gí·a f. MED. laryngology.

lar·va f. [pl. **-vae**] ENTOM. larva.

lar·va·do, –da adj. MED. larvate, larval.

lar·val adj. larval.

las §G16, 30, 35 **I.** def. art. the <*l. piedras* the stones> **II.** pron. them <*¿tienes las monedas? no, no l. tengo* do you have the coins? no, I don't have them>.

las·ca f. chip of stone.

las·car §70 tr. MARIT. to slacken; MEX. to scrape, graze.

las·ci·via f. lasciviousness, lustfulness.

las·ci·vo, –va I. adj. *(lujurioso)* lascivious, lustful; *(juguetón)* frisky, playful **II.** m.f. lascivious or lustful person.

lá·ser m. lasar ♦ **rayo l.** laser beam.

la·si·tud f. lassitude, weariness.

la·so, –sa adj. *(cansado)* tired, weary; *(flojo)* weak, languid; *(sin torcer)* limp (said of thread).

las·qué, lasque see **lascar**.

lás·ti·ma f. *(compasión)* pity, compassion; *(cosa que provoca compasión)* pity, shame; *(quejido)* plaint, lament ♦ **dar l.** to be pitiful ♦ **es l. que** it's a shame that ♦ **llorar lástimas** to feel sorry for oneself ♦ **¡qué l.!** what a shame! ♦ **tener l. de** to feel sorry for.

las·ti·ma·du·ra f. *(daño)* injury; *(herida)* wound.

las·ti·mar tr. *(dañar)* to injure, hurt; *(compadecer)* to feel sorry for, pity; *(agraviar)* to hurt, offend —reflex. *(hacerse daño)* to hurt oneself, injure oneself; *(quejarse)* to complain; *(compadecerse)* to feel sorry.

las·ti·me·ro, –ra adj. sad, pitiful.

las·ti·mo·so, –sa adj. pitiful, deplorable.

las·tra f. flagstone, stone slab.

las·trar tr. MARIT. to ballast; FIG. *(cargar)* to weigh down.

las·tre m. AER., MARIT. ballast; FIG. *(juicio)* judgment, good sense; FIG. *(cosa pesada)* dead weight, burden; *(estorbo)* nuisance; *(piedra)* rubble, gravel.

la·ta f. *(hoja de lata)* tin plate; *(bote)* tin can, can <*una l. de tomates* a can of tomatoes>; *(madero)* small log; *(tablilla para tejas)* roof lath; FIG., COLL. *(persona)* pest, nuisance; VEN. oak staff; ARG. saber; C. AMER., COLL. whippersnapper, upstart ♦ **dar la l.** to bother, annoy ♦ **estar en las latas** C. AMER., COL. to be broke or penniless ♦ **¡qué l.!** what a nuisance!

la·ta·zo m. COLL. bore, bother.

la·te·ar tr. AMER., COLL. to bore (someone), bend someone's ear.

la·ten·te adj. latent, dormant ♦ **calor l.** latent heat.

la·te·ral adj. lateral, side.

la·te·ral·men·te adv. laterally, sideways.

la·te·ro, –ra I. m. tinsmith **II.** adj. annoying, tiresome (person).

lá·tex m. BOT. latex.

la·ti·do m. *(del corazón)* beat, beating (of heart); *(dolor)* throb, throbbing (of pain); *(de los perros)* yelp, yelping (of dogs).

la·tien·te adj. *(pulso)* beating; *(herida)* throbbing; *(perro)* yelping.

la·ti·fun·dio m. latifundium, large estate.

la·ti·fun·dis·mo m. latifundium system.

la·ti·fun·dis·ta m. large landowner.

la·ti·ga·zo m. *(golpe)* whiplash; *(chasquido)* whip-cracking; FIG. *(reprensión)* sharp reprimand; *(daño impensado)* unexpected blow; COLL. *(trago)* drink, snort ♦ **dar latigazos a** to whip, flog ♦ **darse un l.** to have a snort.

lá·ti·go m. *(azote)* horsewhip; *(cuerda)* lashing cord; *(correa)* cinch, strap; COL., ECUAD., PERU whiplash; CHILE *(cuero)* leather strap; *(carreras)* finish (in horseracing); PERU equestrian ♦ **l. de montar** riding crop.

la·ti·gue·a·da f. S. AMER. flogging, whipping.

la·ti·gue·ar intr. *(hacer chasquear el látigo)* to crack the whip; AMER. to flog, whip.

la·ti·gue·o m. crack of the whip.

la·ti·gue·ra f. *(cuerda)* cord, strap; PERU whipping, flogging.

la·ti·gui·llo m. *(látigo)* small whip; BOT. stolon, runner ♦ **de l.** COLL. overacted, hammy.

la·tín m. & adj. Latin ♦ **saber mucho l.** FIG. to be sharp, have a good head on one's shoulders.

la·ti·na·jo m. COLL., DEROG. *(jerga)* Latin-sounding jargon; *(voz latina)* Latin word or phrase ♦ **echar latinajos** to throw Latin phrases into one's speech.

la·ti·ne·ar intr. COLL. to use Latin frequently.

la·ti·ni·cé, latinice see **latinizar**.

la·ti·ni·dad f. *(lengua)* Latin, the Latin tongue; *(pueblos)* the Latin countries, peoples.

la·ti·nis·mo m. Latinism.

la·ti·nis·ta m.f. Latinist.

la·ti·ni·za·ción f. Latinization.

la·ti·ni·zar §04 tr. to latinize —intr. COLL. to sprinkle one's speech with Latin phrases or words.

la·ti·no, –na adj. & m.f. Latin.

La·ti·no·a·mé·ri·ca f. Latin America.

la·ti·no·a·me·ri·ca·no, –na I. adj. Latin-American **II.** m.f. Latin American.

la·tir intr. *(el corazón)* to beat; *(una herida)* to throb; *(un perro)* to yelp; MEX. to have an inkling or a hunch —tr. VEN. to annoy, bother.

la·ti·tud f. *(ancho)* width, breadth; *(extensión)* extent, scope; ASTRON., GEOG. latitude; *(clima)* climate, latitude; FIG. *(libertad)* freedom, latitude.

la·ti·tu·di·nal adj. latitudinal.

la·ti·tu·di·na·rio, –ria adj. & m.f. THEOL. latitudinarian.

la·to, –ta adj. broad, wide <*en el sentido l. de la palabra* in the broad sense of the word>.

la·tón m. *(metal)* brass; BOL., COL. cutlass, saber ♦ **l. de aluminio** aluminum brass ♦ **l. en hojas** or **planchas** sheet brass.

la·to·ne·rí·a f. brassworks.

la·to·ne·ro m. brassworker.

la·to·so, –sa adj. COLL. annoying, bothersome.

la·tro·ci·nio m. robbery, theft.

la·úd m. MUS. lute; MARIT. catboat; ZOOL. striped turtle.
lau·da·ble adj. laudable, praiseworthy.
láu·da·no m. laudanum.
lau·dar tr. LAW to rule, render a verdict on.
lau·da·to·rio, –ria I. adj. laudatory II. f. eulogy.
lau·de f. tombstone.
lau·do m. LAW ruling, verdict.
lau·re·a·do, –da adj. & m.f. laureate.
lau·re·an·do m. graduating student.
lau·re·ar tr. (*coronar*) to crown with laurel; (*premiar*) to honor, reward.
lau·re·dal m. laurel grove.
lau·rel m. BOT. laurel, bay ♦ **dormirse en los laureles** to rest on one's laurels • **laureles** laurels, honors.
lau·ren·cio m. CHEM. lawrencium.
láu·re·o, –a adj. laurel.
lau·ré·o·la *or* **lau·re·o·la** f. (*corona*) laurel wreath *or* crown; (*aureola*) halo, aureola ♦ **l. hembra** BOT. mezereon • **l. macho** BOT. spurge laurel.
la·va f. GEOL. lava.
la·va·ble adj. washable.
la·va·bo m. (*lavamanos*) washstand, wash basin; (*cuarto de aseo*) bathroom, lavatory; RELIG. lavabo.
la·va·ca·ras m.f. [pl. **-ras**] FIG., COLL. toady, bootlicker.
la·va·co·ches m. [pl. **-ches**] car washer.
la·va·da f. washing, laundering.
la·va·de·ro m. (*lavandería*) laundry; (*de un río*) washing place (in a river); MIN. placer.
la·va·do I. past part. see **lavar** II. m. (*lavamiento*) washing, wash; FIG., COLL. (*reprimenda*) talking-to; MED. lavage; PAINT. wash ♦ **l. de cerebro** brainwashing • **l. en seco** dry cleaning.
la·va·dor, –do·ra I. adj. washing II. m.f. (*persona*) washer —m. PHOTOG. washer; ARM. ramrod; GUAT. washstand, sink; AMER., ZOOL. anteater —f. (*máquina*) washing machine, washer; COL. laundress ♦ **l. de platos** dishwasher.
la·va·du·ra f. (*lavamiento*) washing, wash; (*lavazas*) dishwater, dirty water.
la·va·je m. TEX. washing of wool; MED. lavage.
la·va·jo m. watering hole.
la·va·ma·nos m. [pl. **-nos**] washbasin, washbowl.
la·va·mien·to m. (*acción de lavar*) washing; MED. enema.
la·van·da f. BOT. lavender.
la·van·de·ra f. washerwoman, laundrywoman.
la·van·de·rí·a f. laundry, laundromat.
la·van·de·ro m. laundryman, launderer.
la·va·o·jos m. [pl. **-jos**] eyecup.
la·va·pla·tos m. [pl. **-tos**] (*persona o máquina*) dishwasher; CHILE kitchen sink.
la·var tr. (*limpiar*) to wash; FIG. (*purificar*) to wipe away, clean; PAINT. to paint in water colors; MAS. to whitewash; MIN. to wash ♦ **l. el cerebro** to brainwash • **l. en seco** to dry-clean —reflex. to wash, wash oneself ♦ **lavarse las manos de** FIG. to wash one's hands of.
la·va·ti·va f. MED. (*ayuda*) enema; (*aparato*) enema bag, clyster; FIG., COLL. (*molestia*) nuisance, bother.
la·va·to·rio m. (*acción de lavar*) washing; RELIG. (*del Jueves Santo*) Maundy Thursday; (*de la misa*) lavabo; AMER. washstand, washbasin.
la·va·zas f.pl. dirty water, slops.
la·vo·te·ar tr. COLL. to splash *or* sponge oneself.
la·vo·teo m. sponge bath.
la·xa·ción f. *or* **la·xa·mien·to** m. loosening, relaxation.
la·xan·te adj. & m. laxative.
la·xar tr. to loosen, slacken.
la·xa·ti·vo, –va adj. & m. laxative.
la·xi·dad *or* **la·xi·tud** f. laxity, slackness.
la·xo, –a adj. (*flojo*) loose, slack; FIG. (*relajado*) lax, unrestrained.
la·ya¹ f. AGR. spade.
la·ya² f. breed, kind ♦ **eso es de otra l.** FIG. that's a horse of a different color.
la·ya·dor m. AGR. person who digs with a spade.
la·yar tr. AGR. to spade (up), dig with a spade.
la·za·da f. (*nudo*) bowknot; (*lazo*) lasso.
la·zar §04 tr. to lasso, rope.
la·za·re·to m. lazaretto.

la·za·ri·llo m. person who guides the blind.
la·za·ri·no, –na I. adj. leprous II. m.f. leper.
lá·za·ro m. (*pobre*) ragged beggar; ECUAD. leper.
la·za·ro·so, –sa I. adj. leprous II. m.f. leper.
la·zo m. (*lazada*) bow; (*nudo*) knot; (*para sujetar los animales*) lasso, lariat; (*cordel*) lashing rope; (*trampa*) snare, trap; (*en la danza*) figure (in dance); (*de un camino*) bend, turn (in a road); FIG. (*asechanza*) trap; (*vínculo*) bond, tie <*lazos familiares* family ties>; ARCHIT. knot, interlaced design ♦ **l. corredizo** slipknot • **l. de zapato** shoelace.
le §G30, 35 pron. him <*la niña le siguió* the little girl followed him>; you <*no le vi a usted* I didn't see you>; to him, to her, to it, to you <*le dimos un regalo* we gave a present to him>; for him, for her, for it, for you <*le compré una cámara* I bought a camera for her>; from him, from her, from it, from you <*el gobierno le quitó la tierra* the government took his land from him>.
le·al adj. loyal, faithful ♦ **a mi l. saber y entender** to the best of my knowledge.
le·al·men·te adv. loyally, faithfully.
le·al·tad f. loyalty, fidelity.
le·an·dra f. COLL. peseta.
le·bra·da f. CUL. stewed hare.
le·bri·llo m. glazed earthenware pot.
lec·ción f. (*clase*) lesson; (*discurso*) lecture; (*capítulo*) lesson, chapter; (*lectura*) reading; FIG. (*advertencia*) lesson <*sus acciones nos sirven de l.* his actions serve as a lesson to us>; RELIG. lesson, reading (from the Bible) ♦ **dar a uno una l.** FIG. to teach someone a lesson.
lec·ti·vo, –va adj. school ♦ **año l.** school year • **día l.** school day • **tiempo l.** lecture *or* reading time.
lec·tor, –to·ra I. adj. reading II. m.f. (*persona que lee*) reader; RELIG. lector, reader; EDUC. teaching assistant; ELECTRON., COMPUT. reader ♦ **l. de casete** cassette reader.
lec·tu·ra f. (*acción de leer*) reading; (*cosa leída*) reading matter; (*cultura*) culture, literateness; PRINT. pica ♦ **ser una persona de mucha l.** to be well-read.
le·cha·da f. (*de paredes*) whitewash; (*argamasa*) mortar, grout; (*papel*) pulp (for making paper); (*emulsión*) emulsion ♦ **l. de cal** milk of lime.
le·chal I. adj. suckling, nursing (animal); BOT. lactiferous, milky II. m. BOT. milky juice (of plants).
le·char¹ adj. (*lechal*) suckling, nursing; (*que da leche*) milk-producing ♦ **vaca l.** milk *or* milch cow.
le·char² tr. AMER. to milk (cows, goats); C. AMER., MEX. to whitewash.
le·cha·zo m. young lamb.
le·che f. (*bebida*) milk; BOT. milky sap; VULG. semen; S. AMER. luck, good luck ♦ **dientes de l.** milk teeth • **l. condensada** condensed milk • **l. de cabra** goat's milk • **l. de magnesia** milk of magnesia • **l. desnatada** skim milk • **l. de vaca** cow's milk • **l. en polvo** powdered milk • **l. evaporada** evaporated milk • **l. homogeneizada** homogenized milk • **l. pasterizada** pasteurized milk • **mamar una cosa en la l.** FIG. to know something from birth • **tener l. en los labios** FIG. to be wet behind the ears • **tener mala l.** COLL. to be nasty • **tener l.** S. AMER. to be lucky.
le·che·ci·llas f.pl. (*mollejuelas*) sweetbreads; (*asadura*) offal, innards.
le·che·ra f. (*vendedora*) milkmaid, dairymaid; (*recipiente*) milk can; (*jarra*) milk jug; AMER. (*vaca*) milk cow; BOT. spurge ♦ **l. amarga** BOT. milkwort II. adj. see **lechero, –ra**.
le·che·rí·a f. (*tienda*) dairy store; AMER. dairy farm.
le·che·ro, –ra I. adj. (*lechoso*) milky; (*que tiene leche*) milk, dairy <*vaca l.* milk cow>; AMER. (*afortunado*) lucky; (*cicatero*) mean, stingy II. f. see **lechera**.
le·che·rón m. (*vasija*) milk can, milk pail; (*tela*) flannel wrap (for newborn babies); ARG., BOT. gum tree.
le·chi·ga·da f. (*nidada*) brood; (*cría*) litter; (*banda*) gang (of hoodlums).
le·cho m. (*cama*) bed; (*fondo*) bed (of a river, lake); (*capa*) layer, coat; ARCHIT. base; GEOL. bed, layer ♦ **abandonar el l.** FIG. to get up, get out of bed • **l. de roca** GEOL. bedrock.
le·chón m. (*cochinillo*) suckling pig; (*cerdo*) hog; FIG. (*persona*) pig, slob.

le·cho·sa f. BOT. papaya.

le·cho·so, –sa I. adj. *(lácteo)* milky; *(lactífero)* lactiferous, milk-producing (plants) II. m. BOT. papaya tree.

le·chu·ce·ro m. ECUAD., PERU nightwalker, nightowl; PERU *(automóvil)* night taxi; *(chófer)* night taxi driver.

le·chu·ga f. BOT. lettuce; *(cuello)* ruff; *(pliegue)* (in fabric) ♦ **como una l.** fresh as a daisy • **fresco como una l.** brash, cool as a cucumber • **l. romana** romaine lettuce.

le·chu·gui·lla f. BOT. *(lechuga silvestre)* wild lettuce; MEX. *(agave)* variety of agave; HIST. highly starched ruff *or* cuff.

le·chu·gui·na COLL. I. adj. fashionable, elegant II. f. fashionable and elegant young woman.

le·chu·gui·no I. adj. FIG., COLL. fancily dressed II. m. *(lechuga)* small head of lettuce; FIG., COLL. *(muchacho)* callow youth; *(petimetre)* dude, fancy dresser.

le·chu·za f. ORNITH. owl; FIG., COLL. hag, dog.

le·chu·zo m. FIG., COLL. *(el que rocoge dinero)* goon, bill collector; *(hombre feo)* monkeyface, owl.

le·er §43 tr. *(un texto)* to read; FIG. *(enseñar)* to lecture, teach; FIG. *(averiguar)* to interpret ♦ **l. pruebas de imprenta** PRINT. to proofread —intr. *(un texto)* to read; *(enseñar)* to lecture ♦ **l. a primera vista** MUS. to sight-read • **l. entre líneas** FIG. to read between the lines.

le·ga·ción f. legation.

le·ga·do m. *(manda)* legacy, bequest; HIST., RELIG. legate ♦ **l. a látere** RELIG. papal legate.

le·ga·jar tr. AMER. to file.

le·ga·jo m. file, dossier.

le·gal adj. legal, lawful.

le·ga·li·cé, legalice see **legalizar.**

le·ga·li·dad f. legality, lawfulness.

le·ga·lis·ta I. adj. legalistic II. m.f. legalist.

le·ga·li·za·ble adj. which can be legalized.

le·ga·li·za·ción f. *(acción de legalizar)* legalization; *(declaración)* authentication, validation.

le·ga·li·zar §04 tr. *(dar estado legal)* to legalize; *(certificar)* to authenticate, validate.

le·gal·men·te adv. *(según ley)* legally, lawfully; *(lealmente)* faithfully, truly.

lé·ga·mo m. *(cieno)* mud, slime; *(arcilla)* loam.

le·ga·mo·so, –sa adj. muddy.

le·ga·nal m. mud hole.

le·ga·ña f. crusts on the eyelids, rheum.

le·ga·ño·so, –sa adj. crusty-eyed, rheumy.

le·gar §47 tr. *(dejar)* to leave, bequeath; *(enviar)* to delegate; FIG. *(transmitir)* to bequeathe, hand down (culture or ideals).

le·ga·ta·rio, –ria m.f. legatee, heir ♦ **l. universal** general legatee.

le·gen·da·rio, –ria I. adj. legendary II. m. book of legends.

le·gi·ble adj. legible, readable.

le·gión f. MIL. legion; FIG. *(multitud)* legion, multitude ♦ **la Legión Extranjera** the Foreign Legion • **le Legión de Honor** the Legion of Honor.

le·gio·na·rio, –ria I. adj. legionary II. m. legionary, legionnaire.

le·gis·la·ble adj. subject to legislation.

le·gis·la·ción f. legislation.

le·gis·la·dor, –do·ra I. adj. legislative, lawmaking II. m.f. legislator, lawmaker.

le·gis·lar intr. to legislate.

le·gis·la·ti·vo, –va adj. legislative, lawmaking.

le·gis·la·tu·ra f. *(cuerpo legislativo)* legislature, legislative body; *(período)* term *or* session of legislative activity; ARG., MEX., PERU, P. RICO Congress.

le·gis·ta m. *(experto)* legist, specialist in law; *(profesor)* law professor; *(estudiante)* law student; *(abogado)* lawyer ♦ **médico l.** AMER. medical forensic expert.

le·gi·ti·ma·ción f. legitimation, legitimization.

le·gi·ti·ma·dor, –do·ra adj. legitimating.

le·gí·ti·ma·men·te adv. legitimately, rightfully.

le·gi·ti·mar tr. *(certificar)* to legitimize; *(un hijo)* to make legitimate (a child); *(habilitar)* to prepare (for a post).

le·gi·ti·mi·dad f. legitimacy; *(autenticidad)* authenticity (of a product).

le·gí·ti·mo, –ma adj. *(legal)* legitimate, legal; *(cierto)* legitimate, genuine; *(auténtico)* real, authentic <*cuero l.* real leather>; *(válido)* legitimate, valid; *(justo)* just, reasonable.

le·go, –ga I. adj. *(seglar)* lay, secular; *(sin instrucción)* ignorant, uninformed; *(analfabeto)* illiterate ♦ **ser l. en** to know nothing about II. m. layman; RELIG. lay brother.

le·gón m. AGR. hoe.

le·grar tr. MED. *(el hueso)* to scrape (the bone); *(el útero)* to curette.

le·gua f. league ♦ **a la l.** far away, miles away • **l. marina** *or* **marítima** MARIT. marine league • **se ve a la l.** you can see it a mile away.

le·gua·je m. MEX., NIC., PERU distance in leagues; PERU travel subsidy.

le·gué, legue see **legar.**

le·gu·le·yo m. pettifogger, incompetent lawyer.

le·gum·bre f. BOT. legume, pod vegetable <*el garbanzo es una l.* the chick-pea is a legume>; *(verdura)* vegetable.

le·gu·mi·no·so, –sa adj. leguminous.

le·í·ble adj. legible, readable.

le·í·do, –da I. past part. see **leer** II. adj. well-read ♦ **l. y escribido** FIG., COLL. pompous, pretentious III. f. reading <*de una l.* in one reading>.

le·ís·mo m. GRAM. use of *le* as a masculine singular direct object instead of *lo.*

le·ja·ní·a f. *(distancia)* distance; *(paraje lejano)* distant *or* remote place.

le·ja·no, –na adj. distant, remote.

le·jí·a f. *(agua alcalina)* lye; *(detergente)* bleach; FIG., COLL. *(reprimenda)* scolding, reprimand.

le·jos I. adv. *(a gran distancia)* far, far away <*l. de aquí* far away from here>; FIG. *(remoto)* far <*estaba l. de creer eso* I was far from believing that> ♦ **a lo l.** in the distance, far away • **de l.** *(de gran distancia)* from afar, from a distance; *(sin duda)* by far <*él es de l.* *el mejor candidato* he is by far the best candidate> • **desde l.** from afar, from a distance • **ir l.** FIG. to go too far, go a long way • **l. de** *(a gran distancia)* far from, a long way from; FIG. *(en lugar de)* far from <*l. de sufrir, estaba contento* far from suffering, he was happy> • **más l.** farther, further II. m. *(aspecto)* appearance from a distance; PAINT. background; FIG. *(semejanza)* resemblance ♦ **tener buen l.** to look good from a distance.

le·lo, –la I. adj. silly, foolish II. m.f. dolt, ninny ♦ **estar l. por** to be head over heels in love with • **quedarse l.** to be stunned.

le·ma f. *(mote)* motto, slogan; *(nombre falso)* pseudonym; *(argumento)* argument, theme (of a literary work); LOG., MATH. lemma.

lem·nis·co m. ribbon (awarded to winning athletes).

lem·pi·ra m. FIN. lempira (currency of Honduras).

lé·mu·res m.pl. MYTH. lemures; FIG. *(duendes)* ghosts, phantoms.

len adj. flossy, soft (said of thread).

len·ce·rí·a f. *(géneros de lienzo)* linens, linen goods; *(comercio)* linen trade; *(tienda)* dry goods store; *(en un hospital)* linen room; *(ropa blanca)* linen, underwear.

len·ce·ro m. dry goods dealer.

len·dro·so, –sa adj. full of lice *or* nits, lousy.

len·gua f. ANAT. tongue; *(idioma)* tongue, language; *(badajo)* tongue, bell clapper; *(intérprete)* interpreter; CUL. tongue ♦ **andar en lenguas** to be the subject of gossip • **atar la l. a uno** FIG. to tongue-tie • **buscar a uno la l.** FIG. to pick a fight with someone • **con la l. en el palmo** COLL. very eagerly, with one's tongue hanging out • **de l. en l.** by word of mouth • **estar con la l. fuera** FIG. to have one's tongue hanging out • **hablar en lenguas** RELIG. to speak in tongues • **hacerse lenguas de** COLL. to rave about, sing the praises of • **írsele a uno la l.** to talk too much, run off at the mouth • **l. cerval** *or* **de ciervo** BOT. hart's tongue • **l. de buey** BOT. bugloss, oxtongue • **l. de escorpión** *or* **de víbora** COLL. backbiter, gossip • **l. de estropajo** *or* **de trapo** COLL. stammerer • **l. de fuego** tongue of fire, flame • **l. de tierra** promontory, tongue of land • **l. franca** lingua franca • **l. madre** mother tongue, parent language • **l. materna** mother tongue, native language • **l. muerta** dead language • **l. viva** living language • **ligero de l.** indiscreet, loose-tongued • **mala l.** backbiter, gossip • **morderse la l.**

FIG. to bite one's tongue, keep quiet • **sacar la l. a** to stick one's tongue out at • **tirar de la l.** to draw someone out, make someone talk • **trabársele a uno la l.** to become tongue-tied.

len·gua·do m. ICHTH. sole, flounder.

len·gua·je m. language, speech ♦ **l. cifrado** or **convenido** code language.

len·gua·ra·da f. licking, lick.

len·gua·raz [pl. **-ra·ces**] **I.** adj. (políglota) multilingual, polyglot; (deslenguado) foul-mouthed, vulgar; (hablador) talkative, garrulous **II.** m.f. (políglota) polyglot; (persona deslenguada) foul-mouthed or vulgar person; (hablador) chatterbox.

len·guaz adj. [pl. **-gua·ces**] garrulous, loquacious.

len·güe·ta f. (lengua pequeña) small tongue; ANAT. epiglottis; (de una balanza) pointer, needle (of a scale); MUS. reed (of instrument); (barrena) bit, bore; CARP. tongue; ARCHIT. buttress (of a chimney); (zapato) tongue (of shoe); CHILE paper knife; MEX. petticoat flounce; AMER. chatterbox, gossip ♦ **ensambladura de ranura y l.** CARP. tongue-and-groove joint.

len·güe·ta·da f. or **len·güe·ta·zo** m. lick, licking.

len·güe·te·ar intr. AMER. to chatter, rattle on —tr. to lick.

len·güe·te·rí·a f. MUS. reed stops (of an organ).

len·güi·cor·to, -ta adj. COLL. bashful, timid.

len·güi·lar·go, -ga **I.** adj. foul-mouthed **II.** m.f. foul-mouthed person.

len·guón, -guo·na AMER. **I.** adj. gossipy, garrulous **II.** m.f. gossip, chatterbox.

Le·nin·gra·do Leningrad.

le·ni·nis·mo m. POL. Leninism.

le·ni·nis·ta adj. & m.f. POL. Leninist.

le·ni·ti·vo, -va **I.** adj. lenitive, soothing **II.** m. MED. lenitive, palliative.

le·no·ci·nio m. pimping, procuring ♦ **casa de l.** brothel.

len·ta·men·te adv. slowly.

len·te m.f. OPT. lens ♦ **l. de aumento** magnifying glass • **l. de contacto** contact lens • **l. electrónico** electron lens • **lentes** eyeglasses, spectacles • **l. telegráfico** telephoto lens.

len·te·ja f. BOT. lentil; (peso) pendulum disk ♦ **l. de agua** BOT. lesser duckweed.

len·te·jar m. AGR. lentil field.

len·te·jue·la f. sequin, spangle.

len·ti·lla f. contact lens.

len·ti·tud f. slowness.

len·to, -ta **I.** adj. (tardo) slow; MED., PHARM. viscous **II.** adv. ♦ **lento** MUS. lento.

le·ña f. (lumbre) firewood, kindling; FIG., COLL. beating, whipping ♦ **dar l. a alguien** to give someone a beating • **echar l. al fuego** FIG. to add fuel to the fire • **llevar l. al monte** FIG. to carry coals to Newcastle.

le·ña·dor, -do·ra m.f. woodcutter.

le·ña·zo m. COLL. (garrotazo) clubbing, cudgeling; (golpe) blow, wallop.

le·ñe·ra f. woodshed.

le·ño m. (trozo de árbol) log; (madera) wood; FIG., POET. ship; FIG., COLL. idiot, blockhead ♦ **dormir como un l.** FIG., COLL. to sleep like a log.

le·ño·so, -sa adj. woody, ligneous.

le·ón m. ZOOL. lion; AMER. puma; ENTOM. ant lion; ASTRON. Leo ♦ **la parte del l.** FIG. the lion's share • **l. marino** sea lion • **ponerse como un l.** to get furious.

le·o·na f. ZOOL. female lion, lioness.

le·o·na·do, -da adj. reddish-brown, tawny.

le·o·ne·ra f. (jaula) lion cage; FIG., COLL. (casa de juego) gambling den; (cuarto desarreglado) rumpus room, messy room; CHILE, COL. pack (of shady characters); PERU uproar, hullabaloo; ARG., ECUAD., P. RICO detention cell.

le·o·ne·ro, -ra **I.** adj. rowdy, disorderly **II.** m. MEX. place where brawls occur; FIG., COLL. (tablajero) gambler —m.f. (persona que cuida de los leones) lionkeeper.

le·o·nés, -ne·sa adj. & m.f. Leonese.

le·o·ni·no, -na adj. (perteneciente al león) leonine; LAW one-sided (contract).

le·on·ti·na f. JEWEL. watch chain.

le·o·par·do m. ZOOL. leopard.

le·o·tar·do m. leotard.

le·pe m. VEN. (capirotazo) box, slap; (trago) drink of liquor ♦ **saber más que Lepe** or **Lepijo y su hijo** SP. to be very clever or astute.

le·pe·ra·da f. C. AMER., MEX. coarse or vulgar remark.

lé·pe·ro, -ra **I.** adj. C. AMER., MEX. coarse, vulgar; CUBA clever, cunning; ECUAD. bankrupt **II.** m.f. C. AMER., MEX. person of the lowest class; CUBA clever person; ECUAD. bankrupt.

le·po·ri·no, -na adj. ZOOL. leporine ♦ **labio l.** harelip.

le·pra f. MED. leprosy.

le·pro·se·rí·a f. MED. leprosarium, leprosy hospital.

le·pro·so, -sa MED. **I.** adj. leprous **II.** m.f. leper.

ler·da·men·te adv. heavily, sluggishly.

ler·de·ar intr. AMER. to lumber, walk heavily.

ler·do, -da **I.** adj. heavy, sluggish **II.** m.f. dullwitted or obtuse person.

ler·dón m. VET. tumor of a horse's leg.

les §G30, 35 to them, to you <**déles el libro** give the book to them>; for them, for you <**quiero comprarles unos zapatos** I want to buy shoes for you>; from them, from you <**les quitaron la oportunidad** they took the opportunity away from you>.

les·bia·nis·mo m. lesbianism.

les·bia·no, -na or **les·bio, -bia** **I.** adj. (de Lesbos) Lesbian; (homosexual) lesbian **II.** m.f. native of Lesbos —f. (mujer homosexual) lesbian.

le·sión f. MED. lesion, injury; FIG., LAW damage, injury.

le·sio·na·do, -da **I.** past part. see **lesionar** **II.** adj. (herido) injured, wounded; (dañado) damaged, hurt **III.** m.f. ♦ **los lesionados** the wounded.

le·sio·na·dor, -do·ra adj. injuring, damaging.

le·sio·nar tr. (herir) to wound, injure; (dañar) to damage —reflex. to get hurt, get injured.

les·na f. awl.

le·so, -sa adj. (agraviado) injured, wronged; (perturbado) perverted; AMER. silly, stupid ♦ **l. majestad** lese majesty.

Le·so·tho m. Lesotho.

les·te m. MARIT. (sentido) east; (viento) east wind.

le·tal adj. lethal, deadly.

le·ta·ní·a f. RELIG. (oración) litany; (procesión) liturgical procession; FIG. (lista) litany, recital <**una l. de quejas** a litany of complaints>.

le·tár·gi·co, -ca adj. lethargic, sluggish.

le·tar·go m. lethargy, sluggishness.

le·tar·go·so, -sa adj. inducing lethargy.

le·tí·fi·co, -ca adj. gladdening.

le·tón, -to·na **I.** adj. Latvian, Lettish **II.** m.f. (habitante) Latvian, Lett —m. (idioma) Latvian, Lettish.

le·tra f. (signo) letter (of the alphabet); (modo de escribir) handwriting, writing <**l. cursiva** cursive writing>; (sentido) letter, literal meaning <**atarse a la l.** to stick to the literal meaning>; FIG. COLL. (astucia) cunning, shrewdness; PRINT. type; MUS. lyrics, words; COM. draft, bill of exchange ♦ **a la l.** to the letter, literally • **a l. vista** COM. at sight, on sight • **bellas letras** belles-lettres, literature • **dos** or **cuatro letras** COLL. a short note • **l. abierta** COM. letter of credit • **l. a la vista** COM. sight draft • **l. bastardilla** italics • **l. de cambio** COM. bill of exchange • **l. de imprenta** type • **l. de mano** handwriting • **l. de molde** printed letter • **l. gótica** black letter • **l. magnética** laser printing • **l. mayúscula** capital letter • **l. menuda** FIG., COLL. (astucia) cunning, shrewdness; PRINT. fine print • **l. minúscula** lower-case letter • **l. muerta** FIG. dead letter • **l. negrilla** boldface type • **letras** letters, learning • **letras humanas** humanities • **letras sagradas** Scriptures • **primeras letras** primary schooling.

le·tra·do, -da **I.** adj. (instruido) learned, educated; COLL. (presumido) pedantic **II.** m. attorney, lawyer.

le·tre·ro m. (señal) sign; (etiqueta) label.

le·tri·na f. (retrete) latrine, privy; FIG. (cosa sucia) filthy or foul thing.

leu·ce·mia f. MED. leukemia.

leu·co·ci·to m. PHYSIOL. leukocyte.

leu·dar tr. to leaven, add yeast to —reflex. to rise (dough).

le·va f. MARIT. weighing anchor, sailing (a ship); (acción de levarse) leaving, departure; MIL. levy, conscription; MECH. (palanca) lever; (álabe) vane; (rueda) cam; C. AMER., COL. (engaño) trick, scheme; AMER. (prenda de vestir) frock coat ♦ **echar levas** COL. to threaten • **l. de escape** exhaust cam.

le·va·di·zo, –za adj. which can be raised ♦ **puente l.** drawbridge.

le·va·du·ra f. (*fermento*) yeast, leaven; CARP. sawed-off plank; FIG. (*germen*) seed, germ ♦ **l. de cerveza** brewer's yeast • **l. en polvo** baking powder.

le·van·ta·do, –da I. past part. see **levantar** II. adj. FIG. lofty, elevated III. f. rising, getting up.

le·van·ta·dor, –do·ra I. adj. raising, lifting II. m.f. (*persona que levanta*) lifter <*l. de pesos* weight lifter>; (*amotinador*) agitator.

le·van·ta·mien·to m. (*acción*) raising, lifting; (*elevación*) elevation, rise; (*motín*) uprising, rebellion <*l. popular* popular uprising>; MIL. recruitment; GEOL. upheaval ♦ **l. de pesos** weightlifting • **l. topográfico** (land) survey.

le·van·tar tr. (*alzar*) to raise, lift <*ella levantó la mano* she raised her hand>; (*elevar*) to lift up, elevate <*la niña levantó los ojos* the girl lifted her eyes>; (*enderezar*) to straighten up; (*quitar*) to remove <*la criada levantó los manteles* the maid removed the tablecloths>; (*construir*) to raise, erect <*l. una fábrica* to erect a factory>; (*establecer*) to found, set up; (*producir*) to raise <*la piedra levantó un chichón en su frente* the stone raised a bump on his forehead>; (*ahuyentar*) to raise, flush out <*l. la caza* to flush out the game>; (*mudar*) to move; (*suprimir*) to raise, lift <*l. el embargo* to lift the embargo>; (*esforzar*) to raise, uplift <*l. los ánimos* to raise someone's spirits>; (*cortar*) to cut (cards); FIG. (*aumentar*) to raise <*l. la voz* to raise one's voice>; (*ocasionar*) to cause, raise <*su presencia levantó muchas protestas* his presence caused many protests>; (*imputar*) to bring <*l. falsa acusación* to bring a false accusation>; MARIT. to weigh (anchor); MIL. (*reclutar*) to raise (an army); (*deshacer*) to strike, break <*l. el campamento* to break camp> ♦ **l. cabeza** to improve one's condition in life —reflex. (*elevarse*) to rise; (*ponerse de pie*) to stand up, get up; (*salir de cama*) to get out of bed, get up; (*sobresalir*) to stand out; (*sublevarse*) to rebel, rise up; METEOROL. to rise ♦ **levantarse con** to make off with, steal.

le·van·te m. (*oriente*) East, Orient; (*viento*) levanter, easterly Mediterranean wind; GEOG. Spanish Mediterranean coast; C. AMER., P. RICO calumny, slander; CHILE fee paid by woodcutter ♦ **Levante** GEOG. Levant.

le·van·tis·co, –ca adj. restless, turbulent.

le·var tr. MARIT. to weigh (anchor).

le·ve adj. (*ligero*) light; FIG. (*de poca importancia*) slight, trivial.

le·ve·dad f. lightness.

le·ve·men·te adv. (*ligeramente*) lightly, softly; FIG. (*venialmente*) venially, pardonably.

le·vi·ta f. frock coat.

le·vi·ta·ción f. levitation.

le·ví·ti·co, –ca I. adj. BIBL., HIST. Levitical; FIG. (*sacerdotal*) clerical, priestly II. m. BIBL. Leviticus; COLL. (*ceremonial*) ceremony, ritual.

lé·xi·co, –ca I. adj. lexical II. m. (*diccionario*) dictionary, lexicon; (*de un escritor*) vocabulary, lexicon (of a writer).

le·xi·co·gra·fí·a f. lexicography.

le·xi·co·grá·fi·co, –ca adj. lexicographical.

le·xi·có·gra·fo, –fa m.f. lexicographer.

le·xi·co·lo·gí·a f. lexicology.

le·xi·co·ló·gi·co, –ca adj. lexicological.

le·xi·có·lo·go, –ga m.f. lexicologist.

ley f. (*estatuto*) law, statute; (*código*) law, body of laws <*l. mercantil* commercial law>; (*regla*) rule, regulation <*leyes de guerra* rules of war>; (*acto*) act, bill <*l. de congreso* act of Congress>; (*lealtad*) loyalty, devotion; (*religión*) Law <*la l. islámica* Islamic Law>; (*norma*) standard; METAL. fineness ♦ **l. de** on the word of • **al margen de la l.** outside the law • **a toda l.** strictly • **dar la l.** (*servir de modelo*) to serve as an example; (*obligar*) to lay down the law • **de buena l.** sterling, excellent • **de mala l.** crooked, disreputable • **l. adjetiva** procedural law • **l. antigua** Mosaic law • **l. civil** civil law • **l. del embudo** COLL. one-sided law • **l. de prescripción** statute of limitations • **l. de quiebras** bankruptcy law • **l. divina** divine law • **l. escrita**

written law • **l. humana** social law • **l. marcial** martial law • **l. no escrita** unwritten law • **l. sálica** Salic law • **mala l.** ill will • **tener a uno l.** ECUAD. to have ill will towards.

le·yen·da f. (*fábula*) legend, myth; (*de los santos*) life of a saint; (*de una moneda*) legend, inscription (on a coin); (*de un plan*) legend, caption (of a map).

le·ye·ra, leyó see **leer**.

lez·na f. awl.

lí·a f. esparto rope.

liar §30 tr. (*atar*) to tie, bind; (*envolver*) to wrap, wrap up; (*un cigarillo*) to roll (a cigarette); FIG., COLL. (*engañar*) to take in, fool; (*mezclar*) to mix up in, suck into ♦ **liarlas** FIG., COLL. (*huir*) to beat it, scram; (*morir*) to kick the bucket, bite the dust —reflex. (*amancebarse*) to live together, cohabit; FIG., COLL. (*engañarse*) to be taken in; (*mezclarse*) to be mixed up in, be sucked into ♦ **liarse a palos** to come to blows • **liárselas** FIG., COLL. (*huir*) to beat it, scram; (*morir*) to kick the bucket, bite the dust.

li·ba·ción f. libation, drink.

li·ba·nés, –ne·sa adj. & m.f. Lebanese ♦ **los libaneses** the Lebanese.

Lí·ba·no m. Lebanon.

li·bar tr. (*chupar*) to suck (juice from flowers); (*echar*) to pour; (*degustar*) to taste, sip.

li·be·lis·ta m. (*de escritos satíricos*) lampoonist; LAW (*derecho*) libeler.

li·be·lo m. (*escrito satírico*) lampoon; (*infamatorio*) libel; LAW petition ♦ **l. de repudio** written repudiation of a wife by her husband.

li·bé·lu·la f. ENTOM. dragonfly.

li·be·ra·ble adj. which can be liberated.

li·be·ra·ción f. (*acción de libertar*) liberation, freeing; (*recibo*) receipt; (*de una carga*) quittance, release; (*del enemigo*) liberation, deliverance; COL. delivery, childbirth ♦ **l. condicional** parole.

li·be·ra·do, –da I. past part. see **liberar** II. adj. liberated, released.

li·be·ra·dor, –do·ra I. adj. liberating II. m.f. liberator.

li·be·ral I. adj. (*generoso*) liberal, generous; (*progresista*) liberal, progressive II. m. POL. liberal.

li·be·ra·li·dad f. liberality, generosity.

li·be·ra·lis·mo m. POL. liberalism.

li·be·ra·li·za·ción f. liberalization.

li·be·ra·li·zar §04 tr. to liberalize.

li·be·ral·men·te adv. liberally.

li·be·rar tr. (*librar*) to free, liberate; (*de una deuda*) to release, discharge (from an obligation) —reflex. to be released *or* discharged.

li·be·ra·to·rio, –ria adj. releasing, discharging.

Li·be·ria f. Liberia.

li·be·ria·no, –na adj. & m.f. Liberian.

li·bé·rri·mo, –ma adj. absolutely free ♦ **por su l. voluntad** of his own free will.

li·ber·tad f. (*poder de escoger*) liberty, freedom; (*independencia*) independence, freedom; (*exención*) freedom, exemption; (*franqueza*) openness, poise; (*facilidad*) facility, talent; (*derecho*) right, liberty ♦ **en l.** freely • **l. civil** LAW civil liberty • **l. condicional** LAW probation • **l. de comercio** free trade • **l. de conciencia** freedom of worship • **l. de imprenta** *or* **de prensa** freedom of the press • **l. de palabra** freedom of speech • **l. provisional** parole • **libertades** (*inmunidades*) rights; (*maneras*) liberties • **poner en l.** to free, set free • **tomarse libertades** to take liberties.

li·ber·ta·dor, –do·ra I. adj. liberating II. m.f. liberator.

li·ber·tar tr. (*poner en libertad*) to free, liberate; (*salvar*) to save, deliver; (*eximir*) to exempt, release.

li·ber·ta·rio, –ria adj. & m.f. POL. libertarian, anarchist.

li·ber·ti·na·je m. libertinism.

li·ber·ti·no I. adj. libertine II. m.f. (*disoluto*) libertine; (*ateo*) atheist; HIST. child of an emancipated slave (in antiquity).

Li·bia f. Libya ♦ **Jamahiriya Arabe L.** Libyan Arab Jamahiriya.

li·bi·di·no·sa·men·te adv. lustfully.

li·bi·di·no·si·dad f. lustfulness.

li·bi·di·no·so, –sa adj. lustful, libidinous.

li·bi·do m. PSYCH. libido.

li·bio, –bia adj. & m.f. Libyan.

li·bra f. FIN. pound (monetary unit); PHYS. pound (weight) ♦ **Libra** ASTROL., ASTRON. Libra • **l. carnicera** kilogram • **l. esterlina** FIN. pound sterling.

li·bra·co m. COLL. cheap or worthless book.

li·bra·do, –da I. past part see **librar** II. m.f. COM. drawee.

li·bra·dor, –do·ra I. adj. rescuing II. m.f. COM. drawer —m. *(de tienda)* grocer's scoop.

li·bra·mien·to m. *(acción de librar)* rescue, deliverance; COM. draft, bill of exchange.

li·bran·cis·ta m. COM. bearer of a bill of exchange.

li·bran·za f. COM. draft, bill of exchange.

li·brar tr. *(salvar)* to free, deliver; *(confiar)* to place, put (confidence) <*libro la confianza en mis padres*> I place my confidence in my parents>; *(una sentencia)* to pass (sentence); *(un decreto)* to issue (a decree); COM. to draw (a check, letter of credit); LAW *(eximir)* to exempt, release; *(trabar)* to wage <*l. una batalla* to wage a battle> ♦ **¡Dios me libre!** Heaven forbid! —intr. MED. *(parir)* to give birth; *(echar la placenta)* to expel placenta or afterbirth —reflex. *(escapar)* to avoid, escape <*librarse de peligros* to escape danger>.

li·bre adj. *(liberado)* free; *(independiente)* independent; *(soltero)* single, unmarried; *(desembarazado)* clear, open; *(vacante)* free, unoccupied; *(sin trabas)* free, unrestrained <*comercio l.* free trade>; *(atrevido)* free, bold <*es muy l. en el hablar* he is very free in his speech>; *(disoluto)* loose, licentious; *(exento)* free, exempt; *(en la natación)* freestyle ♦ **l. albedrío** free will • **l. cambio** free trade • **l. de** free from • **l. de derechos** duty-free.

li·brea f. *(traje)* livery, uniform; *(clase)* the servants, the help.

li·bre·cam·bio m. free trade or exchange.

li·bre·cam·bis·mo m. free trade (doctrine).

li·bre·cam·bis·ta m.f. free-trade advocate.

li·bre·men·te adv. freely.

li·bre·pen·sa·dor, –do·ra I. adj. freethinking II. m.f. freethinker.

li·bre·pen·sa·mien·to m. freethinking, free thought.

li·bre·rí·a f. *(tienda)* bookstore, bookshop; *(comercio)* book trade; *(oficio)* booksellers, book dealers; *(armario)* bookcase, bookshelf; *(biblioteca)* library ♦ **l. de lance** or **de ocasión** second-hand bookstore.

li·bre·ro m. *(vendedor)* bookseller, book dealer; MEX. bookcase, bookshelf.

li·bre·ta f. *(cuaderno)* notebook; *(agenda)* calendar, appointment book ♦ **l. de ahorros** savings book, passbook • **l. de cheques** checkbook • **l. de direcciones** address book.

li·bre·tis·ta m.f. MUS. librettist.

li·bri·llo m. *(papel de fumar)* packet of cigarette papers; ZOOL. omasum, third stomach (of animals) ♦ **l. de cera** folded wax taper • **l. de oro** or **de plata** booklet of gold or silver sheets.

li·bro m. *(tomo)* book <*l. de consulta* reference book>; *(registro)* register, book; MUS. libretto; DIPL. courier book (designated by color); ZOOL. omasum ♦ **ahorcar** or **hundir los libros** FIG., COLL. to give up studying • **examinar los libros** COM. to audit • **hacer l. nuevo** COLL. to turn over a new leaf • **l. azul** DIPL. blue book • **l. borrador** COM. blotter, daily record • **l. copiador** COM. letter book • **l. de asiento** or **de cuentas** COM. account book • **l. de caballerías** romance of chivalry • **l. de caja** COM. cashbook • **l. de horas** RELIG. Book of Hours • **l. de memoria** memo book • **l. de texto** textbook • **l. diario** COM. journal, daybook • **l. mayor** COM. ledger • **l. en rústica** paperback • **libros sagrados** RELIG. sacred Scriptures • **l. talonario** COM. checkbook.

li·cen·cia f. *(permiso)* license, permission <*lo hicieron sin obtener l.* they did it without getting permission>; *(documento)* license, permit <*l. de conducir* driver's license>; *(libertad excesiva)* license; EDUC. licentiate degree; MIL. discharge ♦ **l. absoluta** MIL. discharge • **l. poética** poetic license • **l. por enfermedad** sick leave.

li·cen·cia·do, –da I. past part. see **licenciar** II. adj. *(presumido)* pompous, pretentious; *(empleado)* dismissed, discharged III. m.f. *(graduado)* university graduate, bachelor (of arts or sciences); COLL. *(estudiante)* student; AMER. lawyer —m. MIL. discharged soldier.

li·cen·cia·mien·to m. MIL. discharge; EDUC. graduation ♦ **l. honroso** MIL. honorable discharge.

li·cen·ciar tr. MIL. to discharge, demobilize; *(dar permiso)* to license, permit; FIG. *(despedir)* to dismiss, discharge; EDUC. to graduate —reflex. EDUC. to graduate <*licenciarse en filosofía* to graduate in philosophy>.

li·cen·cia·tu·ra f. EDUC. *(título)* bachelor's degree; *(acto)* graduation, commencement; *(estudios)* degree program.

li·cen·cio·sa·men·te adv. licentiously, dissolutely.

li·cen·cio·so, –sa adj. licentious, dissolute.

li·ce·o m. HIST. Lyceum; *(sociedad)* lyceum; *(escuela)* grammar or high school.

li·ci·ta·ción f. COM. bid, tender.

li·ci·ta·dor m. COM. bidder.

li·ci·ta·men·te adv. licitly, lawfully.

li·ci·tan·te I. adj. bidding II. m.f. bidder.

li·ci·tar tr. *(ofrecer precio)* to bid for or on; AMER. to auction.

li·ci·ta·to·rio, –ria adj. bidding.

lí·ci·to, –ta adj. licit, legal.

li·ci·tud f. lawfulness, legality.

li·cor m. *(líquido)* liquid; *(bebida alcohólica)* liquor, spirits; *(cordial)* liqueur, cordial; PERU grape brandy.

li·co·re·ra f. liquor tray.

li·co·ris·ta m.f. liquor dealer.

li·cua·ble adj. liquefiable.

li·cua·do·ra f. CUL. mixer, blender.

li·cuar §67 tr. *(volver líquido)* to liquefy; METAL. to liquate.

li·cue·fac·ción f. liquefaction.

li·cur·go, –ga I. adj. FIG. smart, shrewd II. m. legislator.

lid f. *(pelea)* fight, scuffle; FIG. *(disputa)* dispute, argument ♦ **en buena l.** in a fair fight.

lí·der m. *(jefe)* leader, chief; JOURN. editorial, leader (G.B.).

li·de·ra·to or **li·de·raz·go** m. leadership.

li·dia f. fight, battle ♦ **toro de l.** fighting bull.

li·dia·dor, –do·ra m.f. *(luchador)* fighter, combatant —m. *(torero)* bullfighter.

li·dian·te adj. fighting.

li·diar tr. *(torear)* to fight (bulls) —intr. *(luchar)* to fight, battle; *(oponerse a uno)* to oppose, face; *(contender)* to struggle, contend; *(soportar)* to put up with (a nuisance) <*tengo que l. con ese necio* I have to put up with that fool>.

lie·bre f. ZOOL. hare; FIG. *(cobarde)* coward ♦ **levantar la l.** FIG., COLL. to spill the beans, let the cat out of the bag • **l. corrida** MEX. whore • **meter** or **dar gato por l.** to take in, swindle.

Liech·tens·tein Liechtenstein.

lien·ci·llo m. S. AMER. rough cotton cloth.

lien·zo m. *(tela)* linen, canvas; *(pañuelo)* linen handkerchief; PAINT. *(cuadro)* canvas, painting; ARCHIT. *(fachada)* front, façade (of a building); *(pared)* stretch (of a wall); FORT. curtain.

li·ga f. *(jarretera)* garter; *(venda)* band; BOT. *(muérdago)* mistletoe; *(materia viscosa)* birdlime; *(aleación)* alloy; *(confederación)* alliance, league; SPORT. league; *(mezcla)* compound, mixture ♦ **hacer buena** or **mala l. con** to get along well or badly with (someone).

li·ga·ción f. *(acción)* tying, binding; *(enlace)* bond, union; *(liga)* compound, mixture.

li·ga·do I. past part. see **ligar** II. m. PRINT. ligature; MUS. *(modo de tocar)* tie; *(unión de notas)* legato, linked (notes).

li·ga·du·ra f. *(acción)* tying, binding; *(atadura)* tie, bond; FIG. *(traba)* constrictive bond, impediment; MED. *(garrote)* tourniquet; *(de una vena)* ligature; MUS. tie, ligature; MARIT. lashing.

li·ga·men m. undissolved marriage which precludes a second marriage.

li·ga·men·to m. *(ligación)* tying, binding; ANAT. ligament.

li·ga·men·to·so, –sa adj. ligamentous.

li·ga·mien·to m. *(ligación)* tying, tie; *(acuerdo)* concord, unity (of opinion).

li·gar §47 tr. *(atar)* to tie, bind; FIG. *(unir)* to join, link; *(obligar)* to bind, commit <*el convenio nos liga por tres años* the agreement binds us for three years>; METAL. to alloy; MUS. to slur (notes); COL., COLL. to lift, swipe; CUBA to contract in advance (a harvest) —intr. *(en naipes)* to combine cards (of the same suit); ARG. *(tocar)* to fall to; *(entenderse)* to get along well (two people); *(tener suerte)* to be lucky (in cards); C. AMER., MEX. *(mirar)* to stare *or* look at; C. AMER. *(un deseo)* to be fulfilled (said of a desire, wish) —reflex. to unite.

li·ga·zón f. *(unión)* bond, connection; MARIT. futtock.

li·ge·ra·men·te adv. *(de un modo ligero)* lightly; *(de paso)* superficially, in passing.

li·ge·re·za f. *(calidad de ligero)* lightness; *(rapidez)* quickness, swiftness; *(agilidad)* agility, nimbleness; *(acción irreflexiva)* indiscretion; FIG. *(inconstancia)* inconstancy, fickleness.

li·ge·ro, –ra I. adj. *(leve)* light; *(rápido)* quick, swift; *(ágil)* agile, nimble; *(insignificante)* unimportant, insignificant; *(digerible)* light <*comida l.* light meal>; *(tenue)* light <*sueño l.* light sleep>; FIG. *(inconstante)* fickle; SPORT. lightweight ♦ **l. de cascos** FIG., COLL. featherbrained, empty-headed • **l. de dedos** *or* **de manos** light-fingered • **l. de pies** fleet-footed, quick **II.** adv. quickly, swiftly ♦ **a la l.** *(de prisa)* quickly; *(sin reflexión)* without much thought • **de l.** without thinking.

lig·ni·fi·car·se §70 reflex. to lignify, turn into wood.

lig·ni·to m. MIN. lignite, brown coal.

lig·no·so, –sa adj. woody.

li·gón, –go·na I. adj. lucky (at cards) **II.** m. COLL. *(tenorio)* wolf, womanizer —f. COLL. *(coqueta)* flirt.

li·gue m. COLL. *(encuentro)* casual affair; *(persona)* pickup.

li·gué, ligue see **ligar.**

li·gue·ro, –ra adj. of the league.

li·ja I. f. ICHTH. *(pez)* dogfish; *(papel)* sandpaper; CUBA, P. RICO *(presunción)* self-flattery, conceit ♦ **darse l.** to put on airs **II.** adj. MEX., P. RICO shrewd, sharp.

li·ja·do·ra f. sander, sanding machine.

li·jar tr. to sand, sandpaper.

li·la I. f. BOT. lilac; COLL. *(bobo)* fool, dummy **II.** adj. *(morado claro)* lilac-colored; COLL. *(tonto)* foolish, silly.

li·li·pu·tien·se I. adj. lilliputian, tiny **II.** m.f. Lilliputian.

li·ma¹ m. BOT. *(fruto)* lime; *(limero)* lime tree.

li·ma² f. *(herramienta)* file; FIG. *(enmienda)* polishing, refining (of writing); FIG. *(lo que consume)* thing which chips *or* wears away something ♦ **comer como una l.** FIG. to eat like a horse • **l. para las uñas** nail file • **l. sorda** smooth file.

Li·ma f. Lima.

li·ma·co m. ZOOL. slug; VEN. large file.

li·ma·do I. past. part. see **limar II.** m. filing, polishing.

li·ma·du·ra f. filing ♦ **limaduras** filings.

li·ma·lla f. filings.

li·mar tr. *(desbastar)* to file down; FIG. *(pulir)* to polish, refine (writing); *(cercenar)* to pare, trim ♦ **l. asperezas** to smooth disputes.

li·ma·tón m. *(herramienta)* rasp; AMER. roof beam.

lim·bo m. THEOL. limbo; *(vestidura)* border, hem; ASTRON., BOT., MATH. limb; FIG. *(distracción)* daze <*estar en l.* to be in a daze, be miles away>.

li·me·ño, –ña I. adj. of Lima **II.** m.f. native of Lima.

li·me·ro, –ra m.f. lime seller —m. BOT. lime tree.

li·mi·ta·ble adj. limitable.

li·mi·ta·ción f. *(restricción)* limit, restriction; *(distrito)* district.

li·mi·ta·do, –da I. past part. see **limitar II.** adj. FIG. *(poco inteligente)* limited, slow-witted.

li·mi·tar tr. *(delimitar)* to limit, delimit; *(restringir)* to limit, restrict; FIG. *(acortar)* to limit, reduce —intr. to be bounded <*Ecuador limita por el norte con Colombia* Ecuador is bounded on the north by Colombia —reflex. to limit oneself.

li·mi·ta·ti·vo, –va adj. limitative, restrictive.

lí·mi·te I. m. *(frontera)* limit, boundary; FIG. *(término)* limit ♦ **l. de elasticidad** ENGIN. elastic limit **II.** adj. final <*precio l.* final price> ♦ **fecha l.** deadline.

li·mí·tro·fe adj. neighboring, adjoining <*países limítrofes* neighboring countries>.

li·mo m. *(cieno)* mud, slime; AMER. BOT. lime tree.

li·món m. BOT. *(fruto)* lemon; *(árbol)* lemon tree; ARCHIT. string (of staircase); *(de un coche)* shaft ♦ **l. natural** *or* **refresco de l.** lemonade.

li·mo·na·da f. lemonade ♦ **l. de vino** sangría • **l. purgante** citrate of magnesia • **ni chicho ni l.** FIG. neither fish nor fowl.

li·mo·na·do, –da adj. lemon-colored.

li·mo·nar m. BOT. *(sitio)* lemon grove; GUAT. lemon tree.

li·mo·ne·ro, –ra I. adj. shaft (horse) **II.** m.f. *(persona)* lemon seller; *(caballo)* shaft horse —m. BOT. lemon tree —f. shaft (of carriages).

li·mo·si·dad f. *(cieno)* muddiness; DENT. tartar.

li·mo·si·na f. limousine.

li·mos·na f. charity, alms.

li·mos·ne·ar intr. to beg.

li·mos·ne·o m. begging.

li·mos·ne·ro, –ra I. adj. charitable, generous **II.** m.f. *(recolector)* almoner; AMER. beggar —f. alms bag *or* box.

li·mo·so, –sa adj. muddy, slimy.

lim·pia f. *(limpieza)* cleaning; COLL. *(trago)* drink, shot; *(limpiabotas)* bootblack.

lim·pia·ba·rros m. [pl. **-rros**] shoe *or* boot scraper.

lim·pia·bo·tas m. [pl. **-tas**] shoe shiner, bootblack.

lim·pia·chi·me·ne·as m. [pl. **-as**] chimney sweep.

lim·pia·da f. cleaning.

lim·pia·dor, –do·ra I. adj. cleaning **II.** m.f. cleaner (person, substance) —f. cleaning woman *or* lady.

lim·pia·du·ra f. cleaning ♦ **limpiaduras** dirt (from something being cleaned).

lim·pia·ma·nos m. [pl. **-nos**] towel, hand towel.

lim·pia·men·te adv. *(con limpieza)* cleanly; FIG. *(con habilidad)* neatly, skillfully; *(con sinceridad)* sincerely, honestly.

lim·pia·pa·ra·bri·sas m. [pl. **-sas**] AUTO. windshield wiper.

lim·piar tr. *(quitar lo sucio)* to clean, cleanse; FIG. *(purificar)* to clear, exonerate; *(desembarazar)* to clear, rid; BOT. to prune; FIG., COLL. *(robar)* to lift, swipe; *(ganar)* to clean up, make a killing; MEX. to beat, whip; ARG. to kill.

lim·pi·dez f. limpidity.

lím·pi·do, –da adj. POET. limpid.

lim·pie·za f. *(calidad de limpio)* cleanliness; *(acción de limpiar)* cleaning, cleansing; THEOL. virgin birth; FIG. *(pureza)* purity, chastity; *(honradez)* honesty, integrity; *(precisión)* neatness, accuracy; *(destreza)* skill; *(juego)* clean *or* fair play ♦ **l. de bolsa** destitution, pennilessness • **l. de corazón** honesty, rectitude • **l. de manos** honesty, integrity • **l. en seco** dry cleaning.

lim·pio, –pia I. adj. *(sin mancha)* clean, spotless; *(sin mezcla)* pure; *(cantidad)* net; FIG. *(exento)* free, clear; *(aseado)* neat, tidy; *(que ha perdido en el juego)* clean; COLL. *(sin dinero)* cleaned out, broke ♦ **en l.** free and clear, net • **estar** *or* **quedar l.** FIG., COLL. to be broke, be cleaned out **II.** adv. fairly <*jugar l.* to play fair> ♦ **poner en l.** to make a clean copy • **quedar en l.** to become clear • **sacar algo en l.** to understand, get a clear idea (of).

lim·pión m. *(limpiadura)* light cleaning; COLL. *(limpiador)* cleaner, cleaning man; AMER. cleaning rag; C. RICA, VEN. dishrag ♦ **darse un l.** FIG., COLL. to take a bath (fail in one's aims).

li·na·je m. *(familia)* lineage, ancestry; FIG. *(clase)* kind, genre ♦ **el l. humano** humanity, mankind.

li·na·ju·do, –da I. adj. of noble birth **II.** m.f. person of noble ancestry.

li·nar m. flax field.

li·na·za f. BOT. flaxseed, linseed ♦ **aceite de l.** linseed oil.

lin·ce I. m. ZOOL. lynx; FIG. *(persona)* shrewd, discerning person **II.** adj. sharp, discerning <*ojos linces* sharp eyes>.

lin·ce·ar tr. FIG., COLL. to spot, spy (something difficult to see).

lin·cha·mien·to m. lynching.

lin·char tr. to lynch.

lin·da·men·te adv. beautifully, elegantly.

lin·dan·te adj. bordering, adjacent.

lin·dar intr. to border (on), be adjacent (to).

lin·de m.f. boundary, limit.

lin·de·ro, –ra I. adj. bordering **II.** m. edge, border —f. boundary, edge.

lin·de·za f. *(calidad de lindo)* prettiness, loveliness; *(dicho gracioso)* witty remark ♦ **lindezas** insults.

lin·do, –da I. adj. *(bonito)* pretty, lovely; FIG. *(perfecto)* perfect, exquisite **II.** m. COLL. *(hombre presumido)* show-off **III.** adv. ARG. prettily, nicely ♦ **de lo l.** much, a lot.

lin·du·ra f. pretty thing.

lí·ne·a f. line <*l. recta* straight line>; *(renglón)* line <*le* escribí *diez líneas* I wrote him ten lines>; *(vía)* line <*l. férrea* railway line>; *(ecuador)* equator; *(ascendencia)* line, lineage; FIG. *(límite)* line, limit, boundary; *(silueta)* figure, outline; MIL. line; SPORT. line <*l. de meta* goal line>; ELEC. line, cable <*l. telefónica* telephone line> ♦ **en toda la l.** all along the line, completely • **estar en la l.** AMER. to be slim, in shape • **guardar la l.** FIG. to keep one's figure • **l. aérea** airline • **l. de agua** or **de flotación** MARIT. water line • **l. de conducta** or **l. política** policy • **l. de fuego** MIL. firing line • **l. de la tierra** ground line • **l. de montaje** INDUS. assembly line • **l. de partido** POL. party line • **l. de puntos** dotted line • **l. de tiro** line of fire • **l. equinoccial** equator • **l. férrea** railway • **l. telegráfica** telegraph line.

li·ne·al adj. linear.

li·ne·a·men·to or **li·ne·a·mien·to** m. lineament, contour.

li·ne·ar¹ adj. linear.

li·ne·ar² tr. *(tirar líneas)* to draw lines; *(bosquejar)* to outline, sketch.

li·ne·ro, –ra adj. of linen.

lin·fa f. PHYSIOL. lymph.

lin·fá·ti·co, –ca MED. I. adj. lymphatic II. m.f. person suffering from lymphatism.

lin·fo·ci·to m. PHYSIOL. lymphocyte.

lin·go·te m. METAL. ingot, pig (bar) ♦ **l. de primera fusión** or **de arrabio** pig iron • **lingotes de oro** gold bullion.

lin·go·te·ra f. METAL. ingot, pig (mold).

lin·güi·for·me adj. linguiform, tongue-shaped.

lin·güis·ta m.f. linguist.

lin·güís·ti·co, –ca I. adj. linguistic II. f. linguistics.

li·ni·men·to m. PHARM. liniment.

li·no m. BOT. flax; *(de vela)* canvas, sailcloth; *(tela)* linen; ARG., P. RICO flaxseed, linseed.

li·nó·le·o or **li·nó·leum** m. linoleum.

li·nón m. TEX. *(tela engomada)* buckram; *(tela fina)* lawn.

li·no·ti·pia f. PRINT. Linotype (typesetting machine).

li·no·ti·pis·ta m.f. PRINT. Linotype operator.

lin·tel m. ARCHIT. lintel.

lin·ter·na f. *(luz)* lantern; *(de bolsillo)* flashlight; *(lámpara)* lamp, light; ARCHIT. lantern; MECH. lantern wheel or pinion ♦ **l. delantera** AUTO. headlight • **l. mágica** magic lantern • **l. sorda** dark lantern • **l. trasera** AUTO. taillight.

lin·ye·ra m. ARG. *(holgazán)* bum, hobo; *(mochila)* knapsack.

li·ño m. row of trees.

li·ñu·do, –da adj. CHILE woolly, fleecy.

lí·o m. *(cosa atada)* bundle, package; FIG., COLL. *(embrollo)* jam, mess; *(cohabitación)* living together, shacking up ♦ **armar un l.** FIG., COLL. to make a fuss or racket • **hacerse un l.** FIG., COLL. to get into a jam or fix.

lior·na f. FIG., COLL. racket, hullabaloo.

lio·so, –sa adj. COLL. *(embustero)* lying, scheming; *(complicado)* complicated, intricate.

li·pe·güe m. C. AMER. bonus, premium.

lí·pi·do m. CHEM. lipid.

li·pi·ria f. MED. fever and chills.

li·po·so·lu·ble adj. fat-soluble.

li·que·fac·ción f. liquefaction.

li·quen m. BOT., MED. lichen.

li·qui·da·ble adj. liquefiable.

li·qui·da·ción f. *(acción de liquefacer)* liquefaction; COM. *(un negocio)* liquidation; *(cuenta)* settlement; *(venta)* liquidation, clearance sale; FIG. *(eliminación)* liquidation, elimination.

li·qui·da·dor, –do·ra adj. liquidating —m.f. COM. liquidator.

li·qui·dar tr. *(hacer líquido)* to liquefy; COM. *(vender)* to sell off, liquidate; FIG. *(pagar)* to settle, clear (a debt); FIG. *(poner fin)* to resolve, eliminate; COLL. *(matar)* to murder, assassinate.

li·qui·dez f. liquidity.

lí·qui·do, –da I. adj. *(fluido)* liquid; COM. *(disponible)* liquid, ready <*dinero l.* ready cash>; *(sin gravamen)* net; PHONET. liquid II. m. *(fluido)* liquid, fluid; COM. net amount ♦ **l. imponible** taxable income.

li·ra f. MUS. lyre; FIN. lira; POET. *(inspiración)* inspiration, muse; *(arte)* poetry; *(estilo poético)* Spanish poetic form with five verses ♦ **Lira** ASTRON. Lyra.

lí·ri·co, –ca I. adj. lyric, lyrical <*poesía l.* lyric poetry>; FIG. *(lleno de entusiasmo)* lyrical, effusive; ARG., VEN. utopian, impractical II. m. lyric.

li·rio m. BOT. iris ♦ **l. blanco** white or Madonna lily • **l. de agua** calla lily • **l. del valle** lily of the valley.

li·ris·mo m. POET. lyricism; FIG. *(entusiasmo)* lyricism, effusiveness; *(fantasía)* fantasy, daydreaming.

li·rón m. ZOOL. dormouse; BOT. water plantain; FIG. *(persona)* sleepyhead ♦ **dormir como un l.** to sleep like a log.

lis f. BOT. iris ♦ **flor de l.** HER. fleur-de-lis.

li·sa f. ICHTH. striped mullet II. adj. see **liso, –sa.**

li·sa·men·te adv. smoothly, evenly ♦ **lisa y llanamente** openly, frankly.

Lis·bo·a f. Lisbon.

lis·bo·e·ta or **lis·bo·nen·se** I. adj. of Lisbon II. m.f. native of Lisbon.

li·sér·gi·co, –ca adj. CHEM. lysergic (acid).

li·sia·do, –da I. past part. see **lisiar** II. adj. disabled, crippled III. m.f. disabled person, cripple.

li·siar tr. to cripple, disable.

li·so, –sa I. adj. *(igual)* smooth, even; *(llano)* flat; *(sin labrar)* plain, unadorned; AMER., COLL. fresh, nervy ♦ **l. y llano** simple, straightforward II. m. MIN. smooth face (of a rock).

li·son·ja f. flattery.

li·son·je·a·dor, –do·ra I. adj. flattering II. m.f. flatterer.

li·son·je·ar tr. *(adular)* to flatter; FIG. *(deleitar)* to delight, please.

li·son·je·ro, –ra I. adj. *(que lisonjea)* flattering; *(agradable)* pleasing, gratifying II. m.f. flatterer.

lis·ta f. *(enumeración)* list; *(recuento)* roll; *(recuento)* roll call; *(tira)* strip (of cloth); *(raya)* stripe (in cloth) ♦ **l. de comidas** menu, bill of fare • **l. de correos** general delivery • **l. negra** blacklist • **pasar l.** to call roll II. adj. see **listo, –ta.**

lis·ta·do, –da I. adj. striped II. m. striped cloth.

lis·te·ro m. timekeeper (in a factory).

lis·te·za f. smartness, alertness.

lis·tín m. short list.

lis·to, –ta I. adj. *(hábil)* skillful; *(inteligente)* smart, clever; *(preparado)* ready; *(sagaz)* shrewd, cunning ♦ **andar l.** to be careful or cautious • **¿estás l.?** are you ready? • **pasarse de l.** to be too clever for one's own good II. f. see **lista.**

lis·tón I. adj. having a white stripe down the back (said of bulls) II. m. *(cinta)* ribbon; ARCHIT. listel, fillet; CARP. lath, cleat.

lis·to·na·do m. CARP. lathing, lath work.

li·su·ra f. *(igualdad)* smoothness, evenness; FIG. *(sinceridad)* sincerity, candor; *(atrevimiento)* boldness, impudence.

li·te·ra f. *(vehículo)* litter, sedan chair; *(en tren)* berth, bunk.

li·te·ral adj. literal.

li·te·ra·li·dad f. literalness.

li·te·ral·men·te adv. literally.

li·te·ra·ria·men·te adv. literarily.

li·te·ra·rio, –ria adj. literary.

li·te·ra·to, –ta I. adj. well-read, erudite II. m.f. man or woman of letters.

li·te·ra·tu·ra f. literature.

li·ti·ga·ción f. LAW litigation.

li·ti·gan·te adj. & m.f. LAW litigant.

li·ti·gar §47 or **li·ti·giar** tr. LAW to litigate —intr. to contend, dispute.

li·ti·gio m. LAW lawsuit, litigation; *(contienda)* dispute <*las cuestiones en l.* the issues in dispute>.

li·ti·gio·so, –sa adj. LAW litigious.

li·tio m. CHEM. lithium.

li·to·gra·fí·a f. *(arte)* lithography; *(imagen)* lithograph; *(taller)* lithography workshop.

li·to·gra·fiar §30 tr. to lithograph.

li·to·grá·fi·co, –ca adj. lithographic.

li·tó·gra·fo m. lithographer.

li·to·lo·gí·a f. GEOL. lithology.

li·to·ló·gi·co, –ca adj. GEOL. lithological.

li·tó·lo·go m.f. GEOL. lithologist.

li·to·ral adj. & m. littoral, coast.

li·tos·fe·ra f. GEOL. lithosphere.

li·tro m. liter.

li·tua·no, –na adj. & m.f. Lithuanian.
Li·tua·nia f. Lithuania.
li·tur·gia f. RELIG. liturgy.
li·túr·gi·co, –ca adj. liturgical.
liu·dar tr. CHILE., COL., SP. to leaven.
liu·dez f. AMER. laxity.
liu·do, –da adj. *(leudo)* leavened; AMER., FIG. *(laxo)* lax, slack.
li·vian·dad f. *(impudicia)* lewdness, lasciviousness; *(acción desenfrenada)* lewd *or* lascivious act.
li·via·no, –na I. adj. *(ligero)* light; FIG. *(inconstante)* fickle, faithless; *(de poca importancia)* slight, trivial; FIG. *(lascivo)* lewd, lascivious II. f. popular Andalusian song ♦ **livianos** lights (animal parts).
li·vi·dez f. lividity, lividness.
lí·vi·do, –da adj. livid.
li·xi·via·ción f. CHEM. lixiviation.
li·xi·viar tr. CHEM. to lixiviate.
li·za f. *(terreno)* lists, arena (of combat); *(lid)* battle, combat ♦ **entrar en l.** to enter the lists.
li·zo m. TEX. *(de un tejido)* warp thread; *(de un telar)* heddle.
lo §G16, 30, 35, 39 I. def. art. the . . . thing, the . . . part <*lo mejor* the best part>; how <*no puedo creer lo rico que es* I cannot believe how rich he is> ♦ **lo de** the matter of, the business of <*¿y lo de vender la casa?* and the matter of selling the house?> • **lo que** what, which <*no revelarán lo que les dijiste* they will not reveal what you told them> • **lo que es** as to, as for II. pron. it <*no lo creo* I don't believe it>; him <*lo vi* I saw him>; [not translated] <*¿eres estudiante? no, no lo soy* are you a student? no, I am not>.
lo·a f. *(alabanza)* praise; THEAT. prologue (of ancient plays); POET. verse eulogy *or* panegyric ♦ **cantar l.** *or* **hacer l. de** to sing the praises of.
lo·a·ble adj. laudable, praiseworthy.
lo·a·dor, –do·ra I. adj. praising, eulogizing II. m.f. praiser, eulogizer.
lo·ar tr. to praise, laud.
lo·ba f. ZOOL. female wolf; *(vestido)* (ecclesiastical *or* academic) robe, gown; AGR. ridge of earth.
lo·ba·do m. VET. carbuncular tumor.
lo·ba·do, –da adj. BOT., ZOOL. lobed, lobate.
lo·ba·ni·llo m. MED. cyst, wen; BOT. gall.
lo·ba·to m. ZOOL. wolf cub.
lo·be·ar intr. to stalk, lie in wait.
lo·be·ro, –ra I. adj. of wolves, lupine II. m. *(cazador)* wolf trapper; COLL. *(embaucador)* swindler, confidence man —f. wolf range.
lo·bez·no m. ZOOL. wolf cub.
lo·bo[1] m. ZOOL. wolf; ICHTH. loach; FIG., COLL. *(borrachera)* drunk, bender; AMER., ZOOL. coyote ♦ **coger un l.** FIG., COLL. to get drunk as a skunk • **l. cerval** *or* **cervario** ZOOL. lynx • **l. de mar** FIG. old salt, sea dog • **l. de río** ZOOL. coypu (large South American rodent) • **l. marino** ZOOL. seal • **ser lobos de la misma camada** FIG., COLL. to be birds of a feather.
lo·bo[2] m. BOT., ZOOL. lobe.
ló·bre·go, –ga adj. *(obscuro)* dark, somber; FIG. *(triste)* sad, gloomy.
lo·bre·gue·cer §17 tr. to darken <*l. un cuarto* to darken a room> —intr. to grow dark.
lo·bre·guez f. darkness, obscurity.
ló·bu·lo m. ANAT., BOT. lobe, lobule.
lo·bu·no, –na adj. wolflike, lupine.
lo·ca·ción f. rental, leasing.
lo·cal I. adj. local II. m. *(edificio)* premises <*fuera del l.* off the premises>; *(domicilio social)* headquarters; *(lugar)* locale, site.
lo·ca·li·dad f. *(población)* district, locality; *(local)* locale, site; THEAT. *(asiento)* seat; *(billete)* ticket.
lo·ca·lis·mo m. localism.
lo·ca·li·za·ción f. localization.
lo·ca·li·zar §04 tr. *(limitar a un punto)* to localize; *(encontrar)* to locate, find.
lo·ca·men·te adv. crazily, madly.
lo·ca·ta·rio, –ria m.f. tenant, lessee.
lo·ce·rí·a f. pottery shop, china shop.
lo·ce·ro m. pottery seller.

lo·ción f. *(lavadura)* wash, washing; *(producto)* lotion.
lo·co, –ca I. adj. *(demente)* mad, crazy; FIG. *(imprudente)* crazy, reckless; *(extraordinario)* extraordinary, unbelievable ♦ **andar** *or* **volverse l.** to go mad, go crazy • **a locas** *or* **a locas y a tontas** FIG., COLL. without rhyme or reason • **como l.** like crazy, like mad • **estar l. de** *or* **por** to be crazy about, be mad about • **estar l. de atar** *or* **de remate** COLL. to be stark raving mad • **estar l. de contento** COLL. to be wild with joy II. m.f. *(demente)* madman *or* madwoman, lunatic ♦ **cada l. con su tema** FIG. everyone has his own ax to grind • **hacerse el l.** FIG., COLL. to play dumb • **l. rematado** FIG., COLL. raving lunatic.
lo·co·mo·ción f. locomotion.
lo·co·mo·tor, –triz adj. locomotor, locomotive.
lo·co·mo·to·ra f. RAIL. locomotive.
lo·cua·ci·dad f. loquacity.
lo·cuaz adj. [pl. **-cua·ces**] loquacious, talkative.
lo·cu·ción f. *(modo de hablar)* locution, expression; GRAM. phrase <*l. adverbial* adverbial phrase>.
lo·cue·lo, –la COLL. I. adj. harebrained, giddy II. m.f. harebrained *or* giddy young person —f. individual manner of speech.
lo·cu·ra f. *(demencia)* madness, insanity; *(conducta imprudente)* folly, lunacy ♦ **gastar una l.** FIG. to spend a fortune • **hacer locuras** to commit follies.
lo·cu·tor, –to·ra m.f. radio announcer.
lo·cu·to·rio m. *(de visitas)* visiting room; *(de teléfonos)* telephone booth.
lo·da·zal *or* **lo·da·zar** m. quagmire, mudhole.
lo·do m. *(barro)* mud, sludge; MIN. sludge ♦ **arrastrar por el l.** FIG. to drag through the mud • **poner a uno de l.** FIG. to sling mud at someone, smear someone.
lo·do·ñe·ro m. BOT. lignum vitae, guaiacum.
lo·do·so, –sa adj. muddy.
lo·ga·rít·mi·co, –ca adj. MATH. logarithmic.
lo·ga·rit·mo m. MATH. logarithm.
lo·gia f. lodge (of freemasons).
ló·gi·ca I. f. logic II. adj. see **lógico, –ca.**
ló·gi·ca·men·te adv. logically.
ló·gi·co, –ca I. adj. logical II. m.f. logician —f. see **lógica.**
lo·gís·ti·ca I. f. MIL. logistics; PHILOS. symbolic logic II. adj. logistic, logistical.
lo·gos m. PHILOS., THEOL. Logos.
lo·grar tr. *(obtener)* to get, obtain; *(realizar)* to achieve ♦ **dar (algo) por logrado** to take (something) for granted —reflex. to succeed, be successful.
lo·gre·rí·a f. moneylending, usury.
lo·gre·ro, –ra m.f. *(usurero)* moneylender, usurer; *(acaparador)* hoarder, speculator —m. AMER. profiteer.
lo·gro m. *(éxito)* success, achievement; *(lucro)* profit, gain; *(usura)* usury ♦ **prestar a l.** to lend at interest.
lo·ís·mo m. GRAM. use of *lo* as indirect object instead of *le.*
lo·ma f. hillock, knoll.
Lom·bar·dí·a f. GEOG. Lombardy.
lom·bar·do, –da adj. & m.f. Lombard.
lom·bri·ci·da m. MED. vermicide.
lom·bri·gue·ra f. *(agujero)* worm hole; BOT. southernwood.
lom·briz f. [pl. **-bri·ces**] ZOOL. worm, earthworm ♦ **l. intestinal** intestinal worm • **l. solitaria** tapeworm.
lo·me·ar intr. to buck (said of horses).
lo·me·ra f. *(de un caballo)* backstrap; BKB. backhand; ARCHIT. ridgepole.
lo·mien·hies·to, –ta adj. having high haunches (said of horses); FIG., COLL. *(vanidoso)* vain, conceited.
lo·mi·llo m. SEW. cross-stitch; *(de la albarda)* cantle; AMER. saddle pad.
lo·mo m. ANAT. loin; ZOOL. back; CUL. loin; *(de un libro)* spine; AGR. ridge (between furrows); *(de un cuchillo)* back (of a knife) ♦ **lomos** ANAT. ribs • **pasar la mano por el l.** COLL. to pat on the back.
lo·na f. TEX. canvas, sailcloth.
lon·cha f. slice <*una l. de queso* a slice of cheese>.
lon·che m. AMER. lunch.
lon·di·nen·se I. adj. of London II. m.f. Londoner.
Lon·dres m. London.
lon·ga·ni·mi·dad f. longanimity, magnanimity.
lon·gá·ni·mo, –ma adj. magnanimous.

lon·ga·ni·za f. CUL. pork sausage.
lon·ge·vi·dad f. longevity.
lon·ge·vo, –va adj. long-lived.
lon·gi·tud f. *(dimensión)* length; GEOG. longitude ♦ **l. de onda** PHYS. wavelength.
lon·gi·tu·di·nal adj. longitudinal.
lon·gue·ra f. long and narrow strip of land.
lon·ja f. *(tira)* rasher, slice *<una l. de tocino* a slice of bacon>; COM. *(edificio)* marketplace, exchange; ARCHIT. porch, portico; ARG. leather thong *or* strap.
lon·ta·nan·za f. PAINT. background ♦ **en l.** at a distance, far away.
lo·or m. praise.
lo·que·ar intr. to act like a crazy person; FIG. *(alborotar)* to frolic, romp.
lo·que·o m. frolicking, romping.
lo·que·ra f. *(jaula)* padded cell; AMER. madness, insanity.
lo·que·rí·a f. AMER. insane asylum.
lo·que·ro m. asylum guard *or* attendant.
lo·ques·co, –ca adj. COLL. *(alocado)* crazy, nuts; FIG. *(bromista)* joking, comical.
lo·quin·cho, –cha adj. ARG., COLL. half crazy.
lo·ra f. ORNITH. female parrot; AMER. parrot.
Lo·re·na f. GEOG. Lorraine.
lo·ro m. ORNITH. parrot; FIG., COLL. *(mujer)* hag; Chile *(espía)* spy; *(orinal)* bedpan.
los §G16, 30, 35 **I.** def. art. the *<l. actores* the actors> **II.** pron. them *<compré unos zapatos y se l. di a mi hermano* I bought some shoes and gave them to my brother>.
lo·sa f. *(piedra)* slab, stone; *(trampa)* trap, snare ♦ **l. sepulcral** tombstone.
lo·sar tr. to tile.
lo·se·ta f. *(losa)* small slab; *(baldosa)* floor tile; *(trampa)* trap.
lo·te m. *(parte)* lot, share; *(premio)* lottery prize; COM. *(grupo de objetos)* lot; ARG., COLL. imbecile, idiot.
lo·te·ar tr. to divide into lots *or* shares.
lo·te·rí·a f. *(juego público)* lottery, raffle; *(juego casero)* lotto; FIG. *(cosa incierta)* gamble.
lo·te·ro, –ra m.f. lottery ticket seller.
lo·za f. *(barro vidriado)* glazed pottery; *(de la casa)* crockery, china.
lo·za·ne·ar intr. to be vigorous *or* sprightly.
lo·za·ní·a f. *(de las plantas)* lushness, abundance; *(vigor)* vigor, healthiness; *(orgullo)* pride, haughtiness.
lo·za·no, –na adj. *(frondoso)* leafy, luxuriant; FIG. *(robusto)* robust, vigorous.
lú·a f. esparto glove.
lu·bri·ca·ción f. lubrication.
lu·bri·ca·dor, –do·ra adj. lubricating.
lu·bri·can·te I. adj. lubricating **II.** m. lubricant.
lu·bri·car §70 tr. to lubricate.
lu·bri·ci·dad f. lubricity.
lú·bri·co, –ca adj. *(resbaladizo)* slippery, lubricious; FIG. *(lujurioso)* lubricious, lascivious.
lu·bri·fi·can·te I. adj. lubricating **II.** m. lubricant.
lu·bri·fi·car §70 tr. to lubricate.
lu·bri·qué, lubrique see **lubricar.**
lu·ce·ra *or* **lu·cer·na** f. skylight.
lu·ce·ro m. ASTRON. *(astro brillante)* bright star; *(planeta)* Venus; ZOOL. *(de un animal)* white star (on the forehead of an animal); FIG. *(lustre)* splendor, brilliance ♦ **l. del alba** morning star • **l. de la tarde** evening star • **luceros** FIG., POET. the eyes.
lú·ci·da·men·te¹ adv. *(vistosamente)* splendidly, magnificently; *(de modo sobresaliente)* brilliantly.
lú·ci·da·men·te² adv. lucidly, clearly.
lu·ci·dez f. lucidity.
lu·ci·do, –da I. past part. see **lucir II.** adj. *(liberal)* lavish, generous; *(brillante)* splendid, magnificent.
lú·ci·do, –da adj. *(brillante)* bright, shining; FIG. *(inteligente)* brilliant, intelligent.
lu·ci·dor, –do·ra adj. shining, brilliant.
lu·cien·te adj. shining, brilliant.
lu·ciér·na·ga f. ENTOM. glowworm, firefly.
Lu·ci·fer m. RELIG. Lucifer, Satan; ASTRON. Venus, morning star; FIG. *(persona)* wicked and arrogant person.
lu·ci·fe·ri·no, –na adj. satanic.

lu·cí·fe·ro, –ra I. adj. POET. resplendent **II.** m. ASTRON. Venus, morning star; COL. lucifer (friction match).
lu·ci·lo *or* **lu·ci·llo** m. tomb, sarcophagous.
lu·ci·mien·to m. *(brillo)* brilliance, luster; FIG. *(éxito)* success, triumph ♦ **salir (de algo)** *or* **quedar con l.** to come through (something) with flying colors.
lu·cio, –cia I. adj. bright, shiny **II.** m. pool, puddle; ICHTH. pike, luce.
lu·cir §44 intr. *(brillar)* to shine; FIG. *(distinguirse)* to shine, excel *<Mozart lucía en sus estudios musicales* Mozart shone in his musical studies>; *(traer provecho)* to benefit, profit —tr. *(alardear)* to show off, display; *(iluminar)* to illuminate, light up; *(enlucir)* to plaster —reflex. *(vestir bien)* to dress up; *(salir bien)* to come out with flying colors; FIG. *(distinguirse)* to shine, distinguish oneself.
lu·crar tr. to win, obtain —reflex. to gain, profit.
lu·cra·ti·vo, –va adj. lucrative.
lu·cro m. profit, gain.
luc·tuo·so, –sa adj. sad, woeful.
lu·cu·bra·ción f. lucubration, pedantry.
lu·cha f. FIG. *(conflicto)* struggle, conflict; SPORT. wrestling ♦ **l. de clases** class struggle.
lu·cha·dor, –do·ra m.f. *(que lucha)* fighter; SPORT. wrestler.
lu·cha·na f. Vandyke beard.
lu·char intr. FIG. *(pelear)* to fight, struggle; *(disputar)* to argue, quarrel; SPORT. to wrestle.
lú·di·co, –ca *or* **lú·di·cro, –cra** adj. *(del juego)* of games *or* play; *(cómico)* comic, playful.
lu·dir tr. to rub.
lu·dri f. ZOOL. otter.
lú·e *or* **lú·es** f. MED. syphilis.
lue·go §G10 **I.** adv. *(después)* then, afterwards *<l. iremos al cine* then we'll go to the movies>; *(más tarde)* later, later on; *(pronto)* soon *<volveremos l.* we'll come back soon>; COL. from time to time, sometimes; CHILE near ♦ **con tres luegos** COLL. in an instant • **desde l.** of course, naturally • **hasta l.** so long, until later • **l. de** after • **l. que** *or* **l. como** as soon as • **tan l. como** as soon as **II.** conj. therefore *<pienso, l. existo* I think, therefore I am>.
luen·go, –ga adj. long ♦ **luengos años** many long years.
lu·gar m. *(sitio)* place; *(espacio)* room, space *<no hay l. en la cocina* there is no room in the kitchen>; *(pueblo)* town, village; *(pasaje)* passage (in a book); *(tiempo)* time, opportunity *<no hay l. para hacerlo todo* there is no time to do everything>; *(motivo)* motive, reason; *(puesto)* position, office ♦ **en l. de** instead of • **en primer l.** in the first place, first • **l. geométrico** GEOM. locus • **lugares comunes** clichés • **no ha l.** LAW petition denied • **tener l.** to take place, happen.
lu·ga·re·ño, –ña I. adj. of a village **II.** m.f. villager.
lu·gar·te·nen·cia f. lieutenancy.
lu·gar·te·nien·te m. lieutenant.
lú·gu·bre adj. lugubrious, dismal.
luir §18 tr. *(ludir)* to rub; *(redimir)* to redeem, pay off.
lu·jo m. luxury ♦ **artículos de l.** luxury goods • **de l.** de luxe • **vivir a l. asiático** to live like a king.
lu·jo·so, –sa adj. luxurious.
lu·ju·ria f. *(lascivia)* lust, lechery; FIG. *(exceso)* excess.
lu·ju·rian·te adj. lush, luxurious (vegetation).
lu·ju·riar intr. *(persona)* to lust; *(animales)* to mate, copulate.
lu·ju·rio·so, –sa adj. lustful, lascivious.
lum·ba·go m. MED. lumbago.
lum·bar adj. ANAT. lumbar.
lum·bra·da *or* **lum·bra·ra·da** f. bonfire.
lum·bre f. *(luz)* light; *(fuego)* fire; *(mechero)* light *<¿tienes l.?* have you got a light?>; FIG. *(esplendor)* brilliance, splendor; *(de la herradura)* toe (of a horseshoe); ARM. hammer (of a flintlock); *(claraboya)* skylight; VEN. threshold ♦ **a l. de pajas** FIG., COLL. very quickly • **dar l.** to give (someone) a light • **l. del agua** surface of the water • **lumbres** *(yescas)* tinderbox; *(chispas)* sparks.
lum·bre·ra f. *(cuerpo luminoso)* light, luminary; *(en un techo)* skylight; MECH. port, vent; CARP. mouth (of a plane); MARIT. porthole; FIG. *(persona)* luminary; MEX. box (in a bullring) ♦ **l. de admisión** MECH. intake port • **l. de escape** MECH. exhaust port.
lu·men m. PHYS. lumen.

lu·mia f. COLL. prostitute.
lu·mi·na·ria f. RELIG. altar lamp ♦ **luminarias** (decorative) lights.
lu·mi·nis·cen·cia or **lu·mi·nes·cen·cia** f. luminescence.
lu·mi·nis·cen·te or **lu·mi·nes·cen·te** adj. luminescent.
lu·mi·no·sa·men·te adj. luminously.
lu·mi·no·si·dad f. luminosity.
lu·mi·no·so, –sa adj. *(que despide luz)* luminous; FIG. *(excelente)* bright, brilliant (idea).
lu·mi·no·tec·nia f. lighting engineering.
lu·na f. ASTRON. moon; *(vidrio)* plate glass; *(espejo)* mirror; *(lente)* lens; FIG. *(capricho)* notion, wild idea ♦ **estar de buena l.** to be in a good mood • **estar de mala l.** to be in a bad mood • **estar en la l.** to be daydreaming • **l. creciente** crescent moon • **l. de miel** honeymoon • **l. llena** full moon • **l. menguante** waning moon • **l. nueva** new moon • **media l.** half moon; FIG. crescent • **metérsele la l.** FIG., COLL. to act crazy.
lu·na·do, –da adj. lunate, crescent-shaped.
lu·nar[1] m. *(de la piel)* mole, beauty mark; FIG. *(del honor)* stain, blot (on one's honor); *(defecto)* flaw, blemish ♦ **vestido de lunares** polka-dot dress.
lu·nar[2] adj. lunar.
lu·na·re·jo, –ja adj. ARG., CHILE spotted (said of animals).
lu·na·rio, –ria adj. of the lunar month.
lu·ná·ti·co, –ca adj. & m.f. lunatic.
lu·nes m. Monday ♦ **cada l. y cada martes** every day of the week, all the time.
lu·ne·ta f. *(de anteojos)* lens; THEAT. orchestra seat; ARCHIT. *(bocateja)* front tile (of roof); *(bovedilla)* lunette.
lun·far·dis·mo m. Argentinian slang word *or* expression.
lun·far·do, –da ARG. I. m. *(ladrón)* thief, crook; *(caló)* argot, slang II. adj. slang.
lú·nu·la f. ANAT. half-moon of fingernails; GEOM. arc.
lu·pa f. magnifying glass, loupe.
lu·pa·nar m. brothel.
lu·pia f. MED. wen, cyst; HOND. witch doctor.
lu·pi·no, –na I. adj. lupine, wolf-like II. m. BOT. lupine.
lú·pu·lo m. BOT. hops.
lu·que·te m. *(limón o naranja)* lemon *or* orange slice; *(pajuela)* sulfur match.
lu·si·ta·nis·mo m. Portuguese word *or* expression.
lu·si·ta·no, –na or **lu·so, –sa** adj. & m.f. Lusitanian, Portuguese.
lus·tra·bo·tas m. [pl. **-tas**] AMER. shoe shiner, bootblack.
lus·tra·ción f. lustration, purification.
lus·tral adj. lustral, purgative.
lus·trar tr. *(purificar)* to lustrate, purify; *(limpiar)* to polish, shine; *(viajar)* to wander, roam (a country *or* region).
lus·tre m. *(brillo)* luster, shine; FIG. *(esplendor)* splendor, glory; *(betún)* shoe polish; Sp. candy glaze.
lus·trín m. PERU var. of **lustrina**.
lus·tri·na f. TEX. lustring; CHILE shoe polish.
lus·tro m. lustrum, five-year period.
lus·tro·so, –sa adj. lustrous, shiny.
lu·te·cio m. CHEM. lutetium.
lu·te·ra·nis·mo m. RELIG. Lutheranism.
lu·te·ra·no, –na adj. & m.f. Lutheran.
lu·to m. mourning ♦ **ponerse de l.** to go into *or* put on mourning.
lu·xa·ción f. MED. luxation, dislocation.
lu·xar tr. MED. to luxate, dislocate.
Lu·xem·bur·go m. Luxembourg, Luxemburg.
lu·xem·bur·gués, –gue·sa adj. & m.f. Luxembourgian, Luxemburgian.
lu·ya, luyo see **luir**.
lu·ye·ra, luyó see **luir**.
luz f. [pl. **lu·ces**] *(claridad)* light; *(lámpara)* light, lamp *<apague la l.* turn off the lights>; FIG. *(día)* day, daylight; *(guía)* guiding light, luminary; COLL. *(dinero)* money, cash; ARCHIT. window; AUTO. light *<luces traseras* taillights>; PAINT. lighting ♦ **a primera l.** at daybreak • **a todas luces** clearly, from every angle • **dar a l.** PHYSIOL. to give birth; *(publicar)* to publish, print • **de cortos luces** COLL. not very bright • **entre dos luces** at twilight; FIG., COLL. *(borracho)* tipsy • **luces** FIG. enlightenment, learning • **l. cenital** skylight • **l. de Bengala** Bengal light, sparkler • **l. de tráfico** traffic light • **sacar a l.** *(revelar)* to

bring to light; *(publicar)* to bring out, publish • **salir a l.** *(publicarse)* to come out, publish; FIG. *(descubrirse)* to come to light • **ver la l.** FIG. to see the light.
Luz·bel m. Lucifer, Satan.
luz·ca, luzco see **lucir**.

LL

ll, Ll f. fourteenth letter of the Spanish alphabet.
lla·ga f. MED. *(herida)* wound, sore; *(úlcera)* ulcer, sore; FIG. *(daño)* wound, injury; MAS. joint, seam ♦ **poner el dedo en la ll.** to touch on a sore spot.
lla·gar §47 tr. to wound, injure.
lla·ma[1] f. *(fuego)* flame; FIG. *(pasión)* flame, passion ♦ **en llamas** in flames, aflame • **llamas eternas** FIG. eternal flames, hell.
lla·ma[2] f. ZOOL. llama.
lla·ma·da f. *(llamamiento)* call, calling; *(toque)* ring (of a doorbell); *(golpe)* knock (on a door); *(telefónica)* telephone call; *(seña)* reference mark; *(ademán)* gesture, signal; FIG. *(atracción)* call, lure *<la ll. de la selva* the call of the wild>; MIL. call to arms; MEX. cowardice ♦ **ll. al orden** call to order • **ll. de socorro** distress signal.
lla·ma·do I. past part. see **llamar** II. m. AMER. var. of **llamamiento**.
lla·ma·dor, –do·ra m.f. *(persona)* caller; *(mensajero)* messenger —m. *(aldaba)* door knocker; *(timbre)* doorbell.
lla·ma·mien·to m. *(acción)* calling; *(convocación)* call, summons; RELIG. calling, vocation; MED. attraction of bodily humors to one part of the body; LAW *(derecho)* nomination (of an heir) ♦ **ll. a juicio** LAW summons.
lla·mar tr. *(dar voces)* to call; *(convocar)* to call, summon *<me llamó a la sala de espera* he summoned me to the waiting room>; *(telefonear)* to call, telephone *<mi hijo me llamó de Filadelfia* my son called me from Philadelphia>; *(apellidar)* to call *<le llaman Juanito* they call him Johnny>; *(nombrar)* to call *<demostraron lo que llamamos coraje* they demonstrated what we call courage>; *(atraer)* to call, attract *<ll. la atención* to attract attention>; *(suplicar)* to call upon, appeal to ♦ II. **al orden** to call to order • II. **a voces** to shout • II. **por teléfono** to telephone, phone —intr. *(hacer sonar un timbre)* to ring a doorbell; *(tocar a la puerta)* to knock at the door; *(por teléfono)* to call, telephone; *(causar sed)* to make one thirsty ♦ **¿quién llama?** who is it? —reflex. to be called *or* named *<¿cómo se llama?* what's your name?>.
lla·ma·ra·da f. *(fuego)* flare; FIG. *(bochorno)* flush (of the face); *(arrebato)* outburst.
lla·ma·ti·vo, –va adj. showy, flashy.
lla·me·an·te adj. flaming, blazing.
lla·me·ar intr. to flame, blaze.
lla·na I. f. MAS. trowel, float; *(plana de papel)* side (of a piece of paper); *(llanura)* plain II. adj. see **llano, –na**.
lla·na·men·te adv. FIG. simply.
llan·ca f. CHILE, MIN. green-blue copper; *(adorno)* adornment (made with this copper).
lla·ne·ro, –ra m. plainsman —f. plainswoman.
lla·ne·za f. *(familiaridad)* familiarity; FIG. *(sencillez)* simplicity.
lla·no, –na I. adj. *(liso)* flat, even; FIG. *(sencillo)* natural, simple *<los campesinos son gente ll.* peasants are simple people>; *(claro)* clear, evident; *(corriente)* clear, open; *(simple)* simple, plain *<estilo ll.* simple style>; *(estado)* plain, common; GRAM. paroxytone ♦ **a la ll.** simply • **canto ll.** MUS. plainsong • **de ll.** plainly, clearly II. m. GEOG. plain —f. see **llana**.
llan·ta f. *(de una rueda)* rim; AMER. tire.
llan·te·ra f. COLL. weeping, crying.
llan·te·rí·a f. or **llan·te·rí·o** m. AMER. wailing, weeping.
llan·ti·na f. COLL. whimpering, whining.
llan·to m. crying, weeping.
lla·nu·ra f. *(lisura)* flatness, evenness; *(planicie)* plain.
lla·pa f. AMER., MIN. mercury; *(adehala)* extra, lagniappe.
lla·ve f. key *<ll. maestra* master key>; *(grifo)* tap, faucet; ELEC. switch; MECH. wrench; key *<la ll. del reloj* the key of

the clock>; ARM. lock, firing pin; PRINT. *(corchete)* bracket; MUS. clef; SPORT. *(en lucha libre)* lock (in wrestling); FIG. *(solución)* key <*la ll. del éxito* the key to success> ♦ **ama de llaves** housekeeper • **bajo ll.** under lock and key • **echar ll.** to lock • **ll. de bola** *or* **de flotador** ball cock • **ll. de paso** water valve • **ll. de pistón** percussion lock • **ll. inglesa** monkey wrench • **llaves de la Iglesia** RELIG. power of the keys.

lla·ve·ro, –ra m.f. *(persona)* keeper of the keys —m. *(anillo)* key ring ♦ **ll. de cárcel** turnkey, jailer.

lla·vín m. small key.

lle·ga·da f. *(venida)* arrival; SPORT. *(término)* finish <*línea de ll.* finish line>.

lle·gar §47 intr. *(venir)* to arrive, come <*ellos llegarán en abril* they will arrive in April>; *(durar)* to reach, last <*ll. a la vejez* to reach old age>; *(alcanzar)* to reach, extend <*la falda le llega hasta las rodillas* the skirt reaches her knees>; *(ascender)* to amount, come <*la cuenta llegó a quinientas pesetas* the bill came to five hundred pesetas>; *(suceder)* to arrive, come <*llegó el momento de la verdad* the moment of truth arrived> ♦ **ll. a** *(alcanzar)* to arrive at, reach (a destination); to reach (an agreement, understanding); *(lograr)* to manage to <*llegó a controlar la situación* he managed to control the situation> • **ll. a las manos** FIG., COLL. to come to blows • **ll. a saber** to find out • **ll. a ser** to become • **no ll. a** not to be equal to —reflex. *(acercarse)* to move closer, come near; *(ir)* to stop by <*se llegó a la tienda* she stopped by the store> —tr. to move closer, draw closer <*llegó la silla a la mesa* he drew the chair closer to the table>.

lle·na I. f. overflow, flood II. adj. see **lleno, –na.**

lle·nar tr. to fill, fill up <*llene el vaso de vino* fill the glass with wine>; *(ocupar)* to fill, occupy <*él llena el puesto de la persona que se fue* he is filling the position of the person who left>; *(cumplir)* to fulfill, meet <*ll. las condiciones del contrato* to meet the conditions of the contract>; to fill out <*ll. un formulario* to fill out a form>; FIG. *(satisfacer)* to satisfy <*su explicación no me llena* his explanation does not satisfy me>; *(colmar)* to heap <*ll. de insultos* to heap insults on>; ZOOL. to mate, cover —intr. ASTRON. to be full (said of the moon) —reflex. to fill up, be filled <*la sala se llenaba de gente* the room was filling up with people>; COLL. *(hartarse)* to stuff oneself, gorge; *(satisfacerse)* to become full (from eating); FIG., COLL. *(irritarse)* to become annoyed, be fed up.

lle·na·zo m. THEAT. full house.

lle·no, –na I. adj. *(ocupado)* full, filled <*una taza ll. de té* a cup full of tea>; *(redondo)* full <*cara ll.* full face> • **de ll.** *or* **ll. en ll.** fully, completely • **ll. de** full of, filled with II. m. ASTRON. full moon; COLL. *(abundancia)* plenty, abundance; THEAT. full house; FIG. *(perfección)* perfection ♦ **llenos** MARIT. rounded hull —f. see **llena.**

lle·va·de·ro, –ra adj. bearable, tolerable.

lle·va·dor, –do·ra I. adj. carrying II. m.f. carrier.

lle·var tr. *(transportar)* to carry, take <*le llevó flores al hospital* he took flowers to her in the hospital>; *(vestir)* to wear <*lleva medias negras* he is wearing black socks>; *(traer)* to carry, have <*no llevo dinero conmigo* I have no money with me>; *(conducir)* to take, lead <*este camino te llevará a Barcelona* this road will take you to Barcelona>; *(vivir)* to lead <*ll. una vida de perros* to lead a dog's life>; *(encargarse de)* to manage, run <*ella lleva las cuentas de casa* she manages the household accounts>; *(conseguir)* to win, get; *(persuadir)* to win over, persuade; *(tolerar)* to endure, put up with; *(cobrar)* to charge <*no me llevó caro el carnicero* the butcher did not charge me a lot>; *(arrancar)* to tear off, sever <*la metralla le llevó la pierna* the shrapnel severed his leg>; *(pasar)* to have spent, have been <*llevo cinco noches sin dormir* I have spent five nights without sleep>; *(ser mayor)* to be older <*mi hermana me lleva tres años* my sister is three years older than me>; MATH. to carry (addition, multiplication); BOT. to yield, produce ♦ **ll. a cabo** to carry out • **ll. adelante** to go ahead *or* forward with • **llevarla hecha** COLL. to have it all figured out • **ll. la peor parte** to get the worst of it • **ll. las de perder** COLL. to be on the losing end —intr. to lead <*la carretera lleva a la ciudad* the highway leads to the city> —reflex. *(sacar)* to take away, carry off <*se llevó el premio gordo* he

carried off the first prize>; *(robar)* to take <*se llevó el dinero del banco* he took the money from the bank>; *(conseguir)* to get <*se llevó lo que quería* he got what he wanted> ♦ **llevarse bien** to get along well • **llevarse mal** to get along badly.

llo·ra·de·ra f. DEROG. crying for no reason, histrionics.

llo·ra·do, –da I. past part. see **llorar** II. adj. late, deceased.

llo·ra·dor, –do·ra I. adj. crying, weeping II. m.f. cryer, weeper.

llo·ra·due·los m.f. [pl. **-los**] FIG., COLL. crybaby.

llo·ra·mi·co m. crying, weeping.

llo·rar intr. *(derramar lágrimas)* to cry, weep; *(los ojos)* to water, run (the eyes); FIG. *(destilar)* to drip ♦ **ll. a làgrima viva** to cry one's heart out —tr. *(lamentar)* to mourn <*lloramos la pérdida de un gran presidente* we mourn the loss of a great president>; *(sentir mucho)* to regret, bemoan.

llo·re·ra f. COLL. wailing, weeping.

llo·ri·ca m.f. whiner, whimperer.

llo·ri·cón, –co·na I. adj. whining, whimpering II. m.f. whiner, whimperer.

llo·ri·que·ar intr. to whine, whimper.

llo·ri·que·o m. whining, whimpering.

llo·ro m. crying, weeping.

llo·rón, –ro·na I. adj. crying, weeping ♦ **sauce ll.** BOT. weeping willow II. m.f. *(llorador)* weeper; *(lloraduelos)* crybaby —m. *(pluma)* plume —f. *(plañideras)* hired mourner; AMER. spur.

llo·ro·so, –sa adj. *(que ha llorado)* tearful <*ojos llorosos* tearful eyes>; *(triste)* sad, sorrowful.

llo·ve·di·zo, –za adj. leaky, leaking ♦ **agua ll.** rainwater.

llo·ver §78 intr. *(caer agua)* to rain; FIG. *(caer con abundancia)* to rain, shower ♦ **a secas y sin ll.** unexpectedly, without warning • **como llovido** *or* **como llovido del cielo** unexpectedly • **ll. a cántaros** *or* **a chuzos** *or* **a mares** to rain cats and dogs, rain buckets • **llueva o no** rain or shine • **llueve sobre mojado** one thing after another —reflex. to leak.

llo·viz·na f. drizzle.

llo·viz·nar intr. to drizzle.

llue·ca I. adj. broody (said of hens) II. f. broody hen.

llue·va, llue·ve see **llover.**

llu·via f. *(acción)* rain, raining; *(agua)* rain; *(cantidad)* rainfall <*es un país de poca ll.* it is a country with little rainfall>; FIG. *(abundancia)* shower <*ll. de problemas* a shower of problems>; CHILE, NIC. shower, shower bath ♦ **ll. atómica** PHYS. fallout • **ll. de oro** great wealth • **ll. torrencial** torrential rain.

llu·vio·so, –sa adj. METEOROL. rainy, wet (region or season).

M

m, M f. fifteenth letter of the Spanish alphabet.

ma·ca f. *(daño a una fruta)* bruise (on fruit); *(daño leve)* spot, stain; FIG. *(defecto)* defect, flaw; *(engaño)* trick.

ma·ca·bí m. CUBA banana fish.

ma·ca·bro, –bra adj. macabre, funereal.

ma·ca·co, –ca I. adj. AMER. ugly, misshapen; P. RICO foolish, silly II. m. ZOOL. macaque; MEX. bogeyman; HOND. small coin —f. ZOOL. female macaque; CHILE, ENTOM. large coleopteran; COLL. *(borrachera)* drinking spree *or* binge.

ma·ca·dam m. [pl. **-dams**] macadam.

ma·ca·dán m. var. of **macadam.**

ma·ca·gua f. ORNITH. laughing falcon; VEN., ZOOL. poisonous snake; CUBA, BOT. breadfruit tree.

ma·ca·na f. *(arma)* macana (wooden swordlike weapon); *(porra)* club; FIG. *(artículo invendible)* loser, dud (unsaleable item); AMER. *(chapuza)* botched *or* bad job; AMER. *(disparate)* nonsense, foolish thing; *(mentira)* lie, fib; *(broma)* joke.

ma·ca·na·zo m. *(golpe)* blow (with a macana); AMER., COLL. *(disparate)* nonsense, absurdity; *(fastidio)* bother, nuisance.

ma·ca·ne·a·dor, –do·ra adj. ARG. joking, fond of joking.

ma·ca·ne·ar tr. AMER. *(disparatar)* to talk nonsense; *(bromear)* to joke; ARG. to botch, do badly; COL., HOND. to work hard; COL., VEN. to handle (a matter).

ma·ca·ne·o m. ARG. *(disparate)* nonsense, absurdity; *(broma)* joke.

ma·ca·nu·do, –da adj. AMER., COLL. great, terrific.

ma·ca·re·la f. VEN., ICHTH. mackerel.

ma·ca·rrón m. CUL. macaroon ♦ **macarrones** CUL. macaroni; MARIT. stanchions.

ma·ca·rro·na·da f. COL. macaroni dish.

ma·ca·rró·ni·co, –ca adj. COLL. macaronic.

ma·ca·rro·nis·mo m. COLL. macaronic style.

ma·car·se §70 reflex. to spoil, start to rot (fruit).

ma·cé, mace see **mazar**.

ma·ce·ar tr. to hammer, pound —intr. FIG. to insist, go on about.

ma·ce·ra·ción f. *or* **ma·ce·ra·mien·to** m. CUL., PHARM. maceration; FIG. *(mortificación)* mortification.

ma·ce·rar tr. CUL., PHARM. to macerate; FIG. *(mortificar)* to mortify —reflex. to mortify oneself.

ma·ce·ta¹ f. *(mango)* handle (of tools); *(martillo)* stonemason's hammer; AMER. mallet.

ma·ce·ta² f. *(tiesto)* flowerpot; BOT. corymb; CHILE bouquet; MEX., SL. head.

ma·ce·te·ar tr. ARG., COL. to hit with a flowerpot.

ma·ce·te·ro m. flowerpot stand.

ma·ce·tu·do, –da adj. ARG. having short and fat legs.

ma·ci·len·to, –ta adj. emaciated, lean.

ma·ci·zar §04 tr. to fill *or* stop up.

ma·ci·zo, –za I. adj. *(fuerte)* strong, solid; *(sin hueco)* solid; *(fundado)* well-founded, solid II. m. *(masa)* mass; ARCHIT. section of a wall (between two bays); GEOG., GEOL. massif; FIG. *(conjunto de edificios)* block (of buildings); *(agrupación de plantas)* flowerbed.

ma·co·co·a f. COL. melancholy.

ma·co·lla f. bunch, cluster (of plants, flowers, spikes).

ma·co·llar intr. to grow clusters (of flowers or shoots).

ma·co·llo m. HOND. var. of **macolla**.

ma·cón COL. *or* **ma·co·te** ARG. adj. huge, very big.

ma·co·na f. large basket.

ma·cro·bió·ti·co, –ca I. adj. macrobiotic II. f. macrobiotics.

ma·cro·cos·mo m. macrocosm.

ma·cro·e·co·no·mí·a f. macroeconomics.

ma·cro·mo·lé·cu·la f. macromolecule.

ma·cu·co, –ca *or* **ma·cu·cón, –co·na** adj. AMER. big, husky; CHILE, COLL. sly, crafty.

má·cu·la f. *(mancha)* stain, spot; FIG., COLL. *(engaño)* deception, trick; ASTRON. macula; PRINT. mackle, blur.

ma·cu·to m. *(mochila)* knapsack; CUBA, VEN. alms basket.

Mach m. ♦ **número de M.** PHYS. Mach number.

ma·cha f. AMER. mannish woman; C. RICA blond woman; ARG. joke.

ma·cha·ca f. *(instrumento)* crusher, pounder —m.f. FIG. *(persona pesada)* bore, boring person.

ma·cha·ca·de·ra f. crusher, pounder.

ma·cha·ca·dor, –do·ra I. adj. crushing, pounding II. m.f. *(que machaca)* crusher, pounder —f. *(máquina)* crusher, crushing machine.

ma·cha·car §70 tr. to crush, pound —intr. FIG. *(importunar)* to bother, pester; *(insistir)* to insist, go on about ♦ **m. en hierro frío** to bang one's head against a wall.

ma·cha·cón, –co·na I. adj. insistent, tiresome II. m.f. *(pesado)* bore, pest.

ma·cha·co·ne·rí·a f. COLL. insistence.

ma·cha·da f. *(hato)* flock of billy goats; FIG., COLL. *(necedad)* stupidity, foolish remark; *(hombrada)* manly action.

ma·cha·do m. hatchet.

ma·cha·qué, machaque see **machacar**.

ma·cha·que·o m. *(trituración)* crushing, pounding; *(insistencia)* insistence.

ma·che·ta·zo m. blow with a machete.

ma·che·te m. machete.

ma·che·te·ar tr. *(herir)* to wound with a machete; *(talar)* to cut down with a machete (trees, brush) —intr. MARIT. to pitch (a ship); COL. *(porfiar)* to insist, persist; *(vender)* to

sell cheaply; MEX. *(trabajar)* to work; *(empollar)* to study hard.

ma·che·te·ro m. *(desmontador)* cutter, clearer (of a path); *(cortador de caña)* cane-cutter; MEX. *(trabajador)* laborer; *(empollón)* grind (overly dedicated student).

má·chi·ca f. PERU roasted cornmeal.

ma·chie·ga adj. ENTOM. queen <**abeja m.** queen bee>.

ma·chi·hem·bra·do m. CARP. tongue and groove (joint).

ma·chi·na f. *(grúa grande)* crane, derrick; *(martinete)* pile driver.

ma·chis·mo m. machismo, male chauvinism.

ma·chis·ta m. macho, male chauvinist.

ma·cho¹ I. adj. *(masculino)* male; *(fuerte)* strong, tough; *(viril)* manly, virile; FIG. *(necio)* foolish, stupid; BOT., MECH. male II. m. *(animal)* male; *(mulo)* mule; *(parte de corchete)* hook (of a hook and eye); ARCHIT. *(pilar)* buttress, abutment; MECH. pin, plug; ELEC. plug; BOT. male flower; FIG. *(necio)* fool, dolt; COLL. *(fuerte)* he-man; C. RICA, COLL. blond foreigner ♦ **m. cabrío** billy goat • **m. de aterrajar** tap, screw tap.

ma·cho² m. *(mazo grande)* sledgehammer; *(banco de yunque)* anvil block; *(yunque)* square anvil.

ma·chón I. m. ARCHIT. abutment, pilaster II. adj. AMER. mannish woman.

ma·chon·ga f. COL. copper *or* iron pyrite.

ma·cho·rra f. *(hembra estéril)* barren female; *(marimacho)* mannish woman.

ma·cho·ta f. *or* **ma·cho·te** m. *(mazo)* mallet, hammer; MEX., SP., DEROG. mannish woman.

ma·cho·te m. COLL. *(viril)* virile man, he-man; AMER. *(borrador)* rough draft; *(modelo)* model; MEX., MIN. boundary stone ♦ **dárselas de m.** to act like a he-man.

ma·chu·ca·du·ra f. *(golpe)* pounding, beating; *(magullamiento)* bruising, bruise.

ma·chu·car §70 tr. *(golpear)* to pound, beat; *(magullar)* to bruise.

ma·chu·cón m. AMER. var. of **machucadura**.

ma·chu·cho, –cha adj. *(juicioso)* judicious; *(viejo)* elderly, old.

Ma·da·gas·car m. Madagascar.

ma·de·ja f. *(manojillo)* skein (of wool, thread); FIG. *(mata de pelo)* tangle *or* mop of hair; *(perezoso)* loafer, lazy person ♦ **enredar** *or* **enredarse la m.** FIG. to get complicated • **m. sin cuenda** COLL. hopeless mess.

ma·de·ra f. wood <**m. dura** hardwood>; *(de construcción)* timber, lumber; ZOOL. horn; FIG., COLL. flair, knack <**ella tiene m. de oradora** she has a flair for public speaking> ♦ **de m.** wooden, of wood • **m. alburente** sapwood • **m. aserradiza** cut lumber • **m. de raja** split lumber • **m. flotante** driftwood • **m. fósil** lignite • **m. laminada** *or* **contrachapada** plywood • **sangrar la m.** to tap a tree • **tener (buena) m. para** to have what it takes (to accomplish something) • **tocar m.** FIG. to knock on wood.

Madera f. GEOG. Madeira.

ma·de·ra·ble adj. timber-yielding.

ma·de·ra·da f. raft, float.

ma·de·ra·je m. *or* **ma·de·ra·men** m. wooden framework.

ma·de·re·rí·a f. lumberyard.

ma·de·re·ro, –ra I. adj. lumber, timber II. m. *(comerciante)* lumber *or* timber dealer; *(carpintero)* carpenter.

ma·de·ro m. *(pieza de madera)* log, length of timber; FIG. *(persona torpe)* numbskull, blockhead; POET. ship, vessel.

Ma·do·na f. RELIG. Madonna.

ma·dras·tra f. *(madre)* stepmother; FIG. *(molestia)* nuisance, bother.

ma·dra·za f. COLL. doting mother.

ma·dre f. *(mamá)* mother; *(matrona)* matron; RELIG. mother <**m. superiora** mother superior>; COLL. *(anciana)* mother, old woman; ANAT. womb, matrix; *(cauce)* riverbed; *(acequia)* main irrigation ditch; *(cloaca)* main sewer; FIG. *(origen)* mother, cradle; *(causa)* cause; TECH. axle, shaft; *(heces)* mother, dregs; *(de café)* grounds; COL. scab ♦ **m. de leche** wet nurse • **¡m. mía!** my goodness! • **m. patria** mother country, old country • **m. política** mother-in-law • **m. soltera** unwed mother • **sacar de m.** FIG. to provoke, upset • **salirse de m.** *(un río)* to overflow; FIG. to lose control.

ma·dre·per·la f. ZOOL. pearl oyster; *(nácar)* mother-of-pearl.

ma·dre·sel·va f. BOT. honeysuckle.

ma·dri·ga·do, –da adj. COLL. *(práctico)* practical, experienced; *(casada por la segunda vez)* twice-married (woman); *(padreado)* that has sired offspring (an animal).

ma·dri·gue·ra f. ZOOL. *(cuevecilla)* burrow, hole; *(cubil)* den; FIG. *(encondrijo)* hideout, lair.

ma·dri·na f. *(de bautismo)* godmother; *(de boda)* bridesmaid; FIG. *(protectora)* protectress, patroness; *(poste)* prop, post; *(correa)* strap (that yokes two horses); *(yegua)* lead mare; FIG. VEN. lead steer; MARIT. stanchion.

ma·dri·naz·go m. *(acto)* sponsorship; *(título)* role of godmother.

ma·dri·no m. ARG., COL. *(animal)* lead animal; *(árbol)* tree used to fell others.

ma·dro·na f. *(alcantarilla)* main sewer; *(madraza)* doting mother.

ma·dru·ga·da f. *(amanecer)* dawn; *(levantada)* early rising ♦ **a las dos de la m.** at two o'clock in the morning • **de m.** at daybreak, very early.

ma·dru·ga·dor, –do·ra I. adj. *(mañanero)* early-rising; COLL. *(astuto)* clever, astute II. m.f. early riser.

ma·dru·gar §47 intr. *(levantarse temprano)* to get up early; *(ganar tiempo)* to anticipate, be ahead —tr. ARG., MEX., SL. to get the better of (someone) ♦ **a quien madruga, Dios le ayuda** the early bird catches the worm.

ma·dru·gón, –go·na I. adj. early-rising II. m. COLL. early rising (act) ♦ **darse un m.** to get up very early.

ma·du·ra·ción f. maturation, ripening.

ma·du·ra·dor, –do·ra adj. maturing, ripening.

ma·du·ra·men·te adv. maturely, wisely.

ma·du·rar tr. AGR. to ripen, mature; *(problema)* to think out, work out (a problem); MED. to induce suppuration; FIG. *(persona)* to mature —intr. AGR. to ripen, mature; FIG. *(persona)* to mature; MED. to maturate, suppurate (wound, tumor).

ma·du·rez f. AGR. ripeness (of fruit); *(sabiduría)* wisdom, sound judgment; *(edad adulta)* maturity; *(desarrollo completo)* completion, full development.

ma·du·ro, –ra adj. AGR. ripe; *(juicioso)* judicious, wise; *(entrado en años)* mature; MED. ripe (abscess).

ma·es·tra I. f. *(profesora)* teacher, schoolmistress; *(esposa)* teacher's wife; *(escuela)* girls' school; ZOOL. *(abeja)* queen bee; TECH. *(instrumento)* plumb rule; *(listón)* guide line; FIG. *(algo que enseña)* teacher, guide II. adj. see **maestro, –tra.**

ma·es·tran·te m. member of a riding club.

ma·es·tran·za f. *(sociedad)* riding club of Spanish noblemen; MIL. *(almacén)* armory; *(talleres)* arsenal; *(operarios)* arsenal workers; MARIT. navy yard.

ma·es·tre m. MARIT., MIL. master (of a military order, of a merchant ship).

ma·es·tre·ar tr. *(dirigir)* to direct, manage; *(podar)* to prune, trim (vine); TECH. *(alisar)* to smooth (a wall) —intr. to act bossy, to play the master.

ma·es·trí·a f. *(habilidad)* mastery, skill; *(título avanzado)* Master's degree; *(título de maestro)* teaching degree.

ma·es·tro, –tra I. adj. *(perfecto)* master <*obra m.* masterpiece>; *(principal)* main, principal <*cloaca m.* main sewer>; *(amaestrado)* trained <*perro m.* trained dog>; *(perito)* expert, skilled II. m. *(profesor)* teacher; *(perito)* expert, master; *(artesano)* master <*m. sastre* master tailor>; EDUC. master <*m. de artes* master of arts>; MUS. maestro ♦ **m. de capilla** choirmaster • **m. de ceremonias** master of ceremonies • **m. de cocina** chef • **m. de escuela** schoolmaster • **m. de obras** master builder, foreman —f. see **maestra.**

ma·fia f. mafia.

ma·fio·so, –sa I. adj. Mafia of the Mafia. II. m.f. mafioso.

ma·gan·ce·ar intr. CHILE, COL. to loaf about, lead an idle life.

ma·gan·ce·rí·a f. deception, trickery.

ma·gan·cés adj. treacherous, evil.

ma·gan·cia f. CHILE var. of **magancería.**

ma·gan·zón, –zo·na I. adj. AMER., COLL. lazy, idle II. m.f. AMER., COLL. lazybones, loafer.

ma·ga·ña f. *(trampa)* trick, cunning stratagem; ARM. flaw (in the bore of a gun).

ma·gia f. *(arte oculto)* magic; FIG. *(encanto)* magic, enchantment <*la m. de la poesía* the magic of poetry> ♦ **m. blanca** white magic • **m. negra** black magic • **como por arte de m.** as if by magic.

má·gi·co, –ca I. adj. *(de la magia)* magic, magical <*varita m.* magic wand>; *(maravilloso)* marvellous, amazing II. f. *(magia)* magic; *(bruja)* witch, sorceress.

ma·gín m. COLL. imagination, mind.

ma·gis·te·rial adj. magisterial.

ma·gis·te·rio m. *(enseñanza)* teaching; *(profesión)* teaching profession; *(conjunto)* teaching staff; *(pedantería)* pedantry, affected solemnity; CHEM. precipitate.

ma·gis·tra·do m. magistrate.

ma·gis·tral adj. *(del maestro)* magisterial, imposing <*voz m.* magisterial voice>; *(excelente)* skillful, masterful; RELIG. preaching; PHARM. magistral ♦ **canónigo m.** official preacher (of a cathedral).

ma·gis·tral·men·te adv. masterfully.

ma·gis·tra·tu·ra f. magistracy, magistrature.

mag·ma m. GEOL. magma; CHEM. residue.

mag·ná·ni·ma·men·te adv. magnanimously.

mag·na·ni·mi·dad f. magnanimity.

mag·ná·ni·mo, –ma adj. magnanimous.

mag·na·te m. magnate.

mag·ne·sia f. CHEM. magnesia.

mag·ne·sio m. CHEM. magnesium.

mag·ne·ti·cé, magnetice see **magnetizar.**

mag·né·ti·co, –ca adj. PHYS. magnetic, FIG. *(atractivo)* attractive, magnetic.

mag·ne·tis·mo m. PHYS. magnetism; FIG. *(atracción)* attraction, magnetism.

mag·ne·ti·za·ble adj. magnetizable.

mag·ne·ti·za·ción f. magnetization.

mag·ne·ti·zar §04 tr. PHYS. to magnetize; *(hipnotizar)* to hypnotize, mesmerize; FIG. *(atraer profundamente)* to fascinate, mesmerize.

mag·ne·to·fó·ni·co, –ca adj. magnetic ♦ **cinta m.** magnetic tape.

mag·ne·tó·fo·no or **mag·ne·to·fón** m. tape recorder.

mag·ni·ci·dio m. assassination (of an important person).

mag·ni·fi·ca·dor, –do·ra adj. magnifying.

mag·ni·fi·ca·men·te adv. magnificently.

mag·ni·fi·car §70 tr. *(engrandecer)* to magnify, exaggerate; *(ensalzar)* to exalt, glorify; OPT. to magnify, enlarge.

mag·ni·fi·cen·cia f. *(opulencia)* magnificence, splendor; *(generosidad)* generosity.

mag·ni·fi·cen·te adj. magnificent, splendorous.

mag·ní·fi·co, –ca adj. *(hermoso)* magnificent, beautiful; *(excelente)* excellent; *(generoso)* generous.

mag·ni·fi·qué, magnifique see **magnificar.**

mag·ni·tud f. *(tamaño)* magnitude, size; FIG. *(importancia)* importance, order; ASTRON. magnitude; MATH. quantity.

mag·no, –na adj. great, grand <*Alejandro Magno* Alexander the Great>.

mag·no·lia f. BOT. magnolia.

ma·go, –ga I. adj. RELIG. of the Magi, Magian; *(mágico)* magic, magical II. m. *(hechicero)* magician, wizard; *(sacerdote)* magus, sage ♦ **los Reyes Magos** the Three Wise Men, Three Kings.

ma·gro, –gra I. adj. lean, thin. II. m. lean pork.

ma·guey m. BOT. maguey.

ma·gu·lla·du·ra f. or **ma·gu·lla·mien·to** m. bruise, contusion.

ma·gu·llar tr. to bruise, batter.

ma·gu·llón m. AMER. bruise.

ma·ha·ra·já m. maharajah, prince (in India).

ma·ho·me·ta·no, –na adj. & m.f. Mohammedan, Moslem.

ma·ho·me·tis·mo m. Mohammedanism, Islam.

ma·ho·me·tis·ta adj. & m.f. var. of **mahometano, –na.**

ma·ho·me·ti·zar §04 intr. to profess Mohammedanism.

ma·hón m. nankeen (cotton fabric).

mai·ce·na f. cornstarch.

mai·ce·rí·a f. CUBA corn shop.

mai·ce·ro m. COL., ORNITH. ani; CUBA corn seller.

mai·ci·llo m. AMER., BOT. type of sorghum; CHILE *(arena gruesa)* gravel.

mai·ti·nes m.pl. RELIG. matins ♦ **llamar** or **tocar a m.** to call or ring to matins.

ma·íz m. [pl. **-í·ces**] BOT. corn, maize (G.B.) ♦ **m. en mazorca** corn on the cob • **rosetas de m.** popcorn.

mai·zal m. cornfield.

ma·ja I. f. (majadero) pestle; CUBA, COLL. loafer, idler; SP. flashy young woman, flirt II. adj. see **majo, -ja.**

ma·já m. [pl. **-já·es**] CUBA, ZOOL. boa.

ma·ja·da f. (redil) sheepfold; (estiércol) manure, dung; ARG., CHILE flock of sheep.

ma·ja·de·re·ar AMER. tr. to annoy, pester —intr. to be a nuisance or a pest.

ma·ja·de·rí·a f. nonsense, stupid act or remark.

ma·ja·de·ro, -ra I. adj. silly, foolish; II. m.f. silly person, fool —m. (para moler) pestle; (majaderillo) bobbin (for lacemaking).

ma·ja·do m. (cosa triturada) mash, pulp; CHILE, CUL. ground wheat or corn.

ma·ja·dor, -do·ra I. adj. mashing, pounding II. m.f. masher, pounder.

ma·ja·du·ra f. mashing, pounding.

ma·ja·gran·zas m. [pl. **-zas**] COLL. clod, fool.

ma·ja·gua f. CUBA, BOT. magagua (tree); CUBA, COLL. man's sport jacket.

ma·jal m. shoal, school (of fish).

ma·jar tr. to mash, pound <m. algo en un mortero to mash something in a mortar>; FIG., COLL. (molestar) to annoy, bother; (azotar) to beat, flog <m. a alguien a palos FIG. to beat someone up>.

ma·ja·ra or **ma·ja·re·ta** COLL. I. adj. nuts, crazy II. f. nut, crazy person.

ma·jes·tad f. (poder) majesty, sovereignty; (grandeza) grandeur, stateliness ♦ **Su Majestad** Your Majesty.

ma·jes·to·so, -sa adj. var. of **majestuoso.**

ma·jes·tuo·sa·men·te adv. majestically, grandly.

ma·jes·tuo·si·dad f. majesty, grandeur.

ma·jes·tuo·so, -sa adj. majestic, grand.

ma·jo, -ja SP. I. adj. (vistoso) flashy, showy; (bonito) pretty, attractive; (simpático) nice, sweet; smart, well-dressed <ir muy m. to be well-dressed> II. m. gay blade, cocky youth —f. see **maja.**

mal¹ §G21 I. adj. [contr. of **malo** used before m. sing. nouns] bad <mal tiempo bad weather> —see **malo, -la** II. m. (vicio) evil, wrong; (daño) damage, harm; (desgracia) misfortune; (enfermedad) illness, disease; MED. epilepsy ♦ **del m., el menos** the lesser of two evils • **echar a m.** to scorn, despise • **hacer m.** to harm, hurt • **llevar** or **tomar a m.** to be offended, take offense • **m. caduco** MED. epilepsy • **m. de la tierra** homesickness • **m. de mar** seasickness • **m. de montaña** altitude sickness • **m. de ojo** evil eye • **m. de piedra** MED. gallstones • **m. de San Lázaro** MED. elephantiasis • **¡m. haya!** damn! • **parar en m.** to come to a bad end.

mal² §G29 adv. badly, poorly <portarse m. to behave badly>; (desacertadamente) wrongly, incorrectly; (difícilmente) hardly <m. puedo ayudarte I can hardly help you>; (de modo infeliz) badly <la empresa le salió m. the enterprise turned out badly for him> ♦ **de m. en peor** from bad to worse • **m. que bien** willy-nilly, any which way • **menos m.** just as well • **si m. no recuerdo** if I remember correctly.

ma·la·bar m. ♦ **hacer juegos malabares** to juggle.

ma·la·ba·ris·mo m. juggling.

ma·la·ba·ris·ta m. (equilibrista) juggler; CHILE clever thief.

ma·la·ca·te m. (cabrestante) winch, whim; AMER. spindle.

ma·la·con·se·ja·do, -da I. adj. ill-advised II. m.f. ill-advised person.

ma·la·cos·tum·bra·do, -da adj. having bad habits; (malcriado) ill-bred, ill-mannered; (mimado) spoiled.

ma·la·cos·tum·brar·se reflex. to get into bad habits.

ma·la·crian·za f. AMER. bad manners, lack of breeding.

má·la·ga m. Malaga (wine) ♦ **m. añejo** vintage Malaga.

ma·la·gra·de·ci·do, -da adj. AMER. ungrateful, unappreciative ♦ **mostrarse m.** to show a lack of appreciation.

ma·la·gue·ño, -ña I. adj. of or from Malaga II. m.f. native or inhabitant of Malaga —f. MUS. malagueña (popular song and dance of Malaga).

ma·la·men·te adv. (mal) badly, poorly; (de mala fe) wrongly.

ma·lan·dan·za f. misfortune, calamity.

ma·lan·drín, -dri·na I. adj. wicked, evil II. m.f. rascal, scoundrel.

ma·lan·ga CUBA I. adj. COLL. (tímido) timid, cowardly; (torpe) ineffectual, useless II. f. BOT. malanga (root vegetable).

ma·la·pa·ta f. COLL. (mala suerte) bad luck —m.f. (persona) unlucky person.

ma·la·qui·ta f. MIN. malachite.

ma·lar ANAT. I. adj. malar, cheek II. m. malar (cheek bone).

ma·la·ria f. MED. malaria.

ma·la·san·gre I. adj. ill-intentioned, evil-minded II. m. mean or evil-minded person.

Ma·la·sia f. Malaysia.

ma·la·sio, -sia adj. & m.f. Malaysian.

ma·la·som·bra m.f. (persona) bore, boring person; COLL. (mala suerte) bad luck; (falta de gracia) dullness, lack of charm.

ma·la·ve·ni·do, -da adj. incompatible (couple).

ma·la·ven·tu·ra f. misfortune, adversity.

ma·la·ven·tu·ra·do, -da I. adj. ill-fated, unfortunate II. m.f. unfortunate person, poor soul.

ma·la·ven·tu·ran·za f. misfortune, ill fortune.

Ma·la·wi m. Malawi.

ma·la·wia·no, -na adj. & m.f. Malawian.

ma·la·yo, -ya adj. & m.f. Malayan.

mal·ba·ra·ta·dor, -do·ra I. adj. (que malvende) underselling; (malgastador) squandering II. m.f. (que malvende) underseller; (malgastador) squanderer, spendthrift.

mal·ba·ra·tar tr. (malvender) to undersell; (malgastar) to squander.

mal·ba·ra·to m. (malgasto) squandering, waste; (venta) underselling.

mal·ca·ra·do, -da adj. grim-faced.

mal·ca·sa·do, -da adj. (infiel) unfaithful, adulterous; (casado con persona de condición inferior) married to someone below one's station.

mal·ca·sar tr. (ser incompatibles) to mismate, mismatch; (casar con persona de condición inferior) to marry below one's station —reflex. to be mismarried or mismatched.

mal·co·mer intr. to eat poorly.

mal·co·mi·do, -da adj. malnourished, underfed.

mal·con·si·de·ra·do, -da adj. inconsiderate, thoughtless.

mal·con·ten·to, -ta I. adj. (disgustado) discontented, unhappy; (rebelde) malcontent, rebellious II. m.f. (rebelde) malcontent —m. (juego de naipes) card game.

mal·co·ra·zón adj. C. AMER. cruel.

mal·cria·dez or **mal·cria·de·za** f. AMER. bad manners, lack of breeding.

mal·cria·do, -da I. past part. see **malcriar** II. adj. bad-mannered, ill-bred.

mal·criar §30 tr. to spoil, pamper.

mal·dad f. (carácter de malo) wickedness, evil; (acto) evil act ♦ **cometer maldades** to to do evil or wrong.

mal·da·do·so, -sa I. adj. (malo) wicked, evil II. m.f. wicked or evil person.

mal·de·ci·do, -da I. past part. see **maldecir** II. adj. evil, wicked III. m.f. evil person.

mal·de·ci·dor, -do·ra I. adj. (que calumnia) slandering, defaming; (que blasfema) cursing II. m.f. (que calumnia) slanderer; (que blasfema) curser.

mal·de·cir §11 tr. (echar una maldición) to curse, damn; (calumniar) to slander or defame <m. de algo to speak evil of something>; (renegar de) to curse <m. su suerte to curse one's luck> II. intr. to curse.

mal·di·cien·te I. adj. slandering, defaming II. m.f. (calumniador) slanderer, defamer; (detractor) detractor; (persona que maldice) curser.

mal·di·ción I. f. (imprecación) curse, damnation II. interj. damn!, damnation!

mal·di·ga, maldigo see **maldecir.**

mal·di·je·ra, maldijo see **maldecir.**

mal·dis·pues·to, -ta adj. (de mala gana) ill-disposed, reluctant; (enfermo) indisposed, unwell.

mal·di·ta I. f. COLL. (lengua) tongue; CUBA, P. RICO, MED.

boil; P. Rico, Ven. infected insect bite ♦ **soltar uno la m.** to speak one's mind **II.** adj. see **maldito, –ta.**

mal·di·to, –ta I. past part. see **maldecir II.** adj. *(desagradable)* damned, lousy <*esta m. lluvia* this damned rain>; *(de mal carácter)* bad, wicked; theol. damned, condemned ♦ **m. lo que me importa** damned if I care • **no sabe m. la cosa de todo eso** he doesn't know a damned thing about any of this **III. m.** the devil, Satan —f. see **maldita.**

Mal·di·vas f. Maldives.

mal·di·vo, –va adj. & m.f. Maldivian, Maldivan.

ma·le·a·bi·li·dad f. malleability.

ma·le·a·ble adj. malleable.

ma·le·a·do, –da I. past part. see **malear II.** adj. corrupted, perverted.

ma·le·an·te I. adj. *(que pervierte)* vicious, corrupting; *(perverso)* perverse; *(maligno)* malicious, wicked **II.** m.f. *(malhechor)* crook, evildoer.

ma·le·ar tr. *(estropear)* to spoil, ruin; fig. *(pervertir)* to pervert, corrupt —reflex. *(estropearse)* to be ruined; fig. *(pervertirse)* to be perverted *or* corrupted.

ma·le·cón m. sea wall, dike.

ma·le·di·cen·cia f. slander.

ma·le·di·cien·te I. adj. slandering **II.** m.f. slanderer.

ma·le·du·ca·do, –da adj. bad-mannered.

ma·le·fi·cen·cia f. maleficence, evil.

ma·le·fi·cen·te adj. maleficent.

ma·le·fi·ciar tr. *(dañar)* to injure, harm; *(hechizar)* to bewitch, cast a spell on.

ma·le·fi·cio m. spell, curse.

ma·le·fi·co, –ca adj. *(dañino)* maleficent, evil; *(que hace maleficios)* spell-casting, bewitching.

ma·len·ten·di·do m. misunderstanding.

ma·les·tar m. med. malaise, indisposition; fig. *(inquietud)* malaise, uneasiness.

ma·le·ta f. *(de viaje)* suitcase, valise; amer. bundle; arg. saddlebag, knapsack; C. amer., Mex. jerk, creep; P. Rico wicked *or* corrupt person; Col. nuisance, annoyance —m. coll. *(persona torpe)* bungler, incompetent ♦ **hacer la m.** to pack one's bag • **largar** *or* **soltar la m.** chile to kick the bucket, die.

ma·le·te·ro m. *(hacedor o vendedor)* luggage maker *or* seller; *(mozo de estación)* station porter; amer., auto. trunk (of car); ecuad. saddlebag; chile pickpocket.

ma·le·tín m. small suitcase ♦ **m. de grupa** mil. saddlebag.

ma·le·tón m. *(maleta grande)* large suitcase; ecuad. rucksack; col. hunchback, humpback.

ma·le·tu·do, –da adj. amer. hunchbacked, humpbacked.

ma·le·vo·len·cia f. malevolence.

ma·le·vo·len·te adj. var. of **malévolo, –la.**

ma·lé·vo·lo, –la I. adj. malevolent, evil **II.** m.f. malevolent person.

ma·le·za f. *(hierbas)* weeds; *(zarzales)* brambles, underbrush; arg., chile pus.

mal·for·ma·ción f. malformation.

mal·ga·che adj. & m.f. Malagasy.

mal·gas·ta·dor, –do·ra I. adj. spendthrift, wasteful **II.** m.f. spendthrift.

mal·gas·tar tr. to waste, misspend.

mal·ge·nia·do, –da adj. col., peru ill-tempered, irascible.

mal·ge·nio·so, –sa adj. amer. ill-tempered, irritable.

mal·ha·bla·do, –da adj. foul-mouthed, vulgar.

mal·ha·da·do, –da adj. wretched, unfortunate.

mal·ha·ya adj. coll. damned, cursed <*¡m. sea!* damn it!>.

mal·he·chor, –cho·ra I. adj. evil, doing evil **II.** m.f. wrongdoer, evildoer.

mal·he·rir §65 t.r to wound *or* injure badly.

mal·hu·mor m. bad temper, ill humor.

mal·hu·mo·ra·do, –da I. past part. see **malhumorar II.** adj. bad-tempered, peevish.

mal·hu·mo·rar tr. to annoy, irritate.

Ma·lí m. Mali.

ma·li·cia f. *(perversidad)* malice, wickedness; *(disimulo)* slyness, cunning; *(travesura)* mischievousness, naughtiness; coll. *(sospecha)* suspicion.

ma·li·cia·ble adj. *(sospechoso)* suspicious; *(corruptible)* corruptible.

ma·li·ciar·se reflex. *(sospechar)* to be suspicious; *(malear)*

to go bad, become spoiled ♦ **algo me malicio en ese lío** there's something fishy about this business.

ma·li·cio·sa·men·te adv. *(malamente)* maliciously; *(astutamente)* slyly, cunningly.

ma·li·cio·so, –sa I. adj. *(malo)* malicious, wicked; *(astuto)* sly, cunning **II.** m.f. malicious person.

ma·lien·se adj. & m.f. Malian.

ma·lig·na·men·te adv. malignantly.

ma·lig·nar tr. to pervert, corrupt —reflex. to become perverted *or* corrupt.

ma·lig·ni·dad f. malignancy.

ma·lig·no, –na adj. malignant.

ma·lin·ten·cio·na·do, –da I. adj. ill-intentioned **II.** m.f. ill-intentioned person.

mal·man·da·do, –da I. adj. disobedient **II.** m.f. disobedient person.

mal·ma·ri·da·da I. adj. unfaithful, adulterous **II.** f. unfaithful *or* adulterous wife.

mal·mi·ra·do, –da adj. *(malquisto)* disliked, disfavored; *(descortés)* discourteous, inconsiderate.

ma·lo, –la §G21, 24 **I.** adj. bad, poor <*esta tela es de m. calidad* this cloth is of poor quality>; *(perverso)* bad, evil <*un hombre m.* an evil man>; *(dañino)* harmful, bad <*mala influencia* harmful influence>; *(desagradable)* unpleasant, nasty <*pasamos un mal rato* we had an unpleasant time>; *(difícil)* hard, difficult <*el asunto es m. de entender* the matter is difficult to understand>; *(enfermo)* sick, ill <*mi madre está m.* my mother is ill>; *(travieso)* naughty, bad <*ese niño es m.* that child is naughty>; *(deteriorado)* shabby, shoddy <*unos pantalones malos* shabby pants>; *(nocivo)* bad, noxious <*un mal olor* a noxious odor>; coll. *(malicioso)* mean, malicious ♦ **a la m.** amer. by force • **a las malas** *or* **a malas** on bad terms • **de m. gana** reluctantly • **de malas** *(con desgracia)* unlucky, out of luck <*estar de malas* to be out of luck>; *(con mala intención)* with bad intentions; coll. *(molesto)* upset, out of sorts <*hoy estoy de malas* I am out of sorts today> • **lo m. es que** the trouble is . . . • **ponerse m.** to become sick • **por las malas** by force **II.** m. ♦ **el m.** the bad guy, villain; *(Diablo)* the Devil.

ma·lo·ca f. amer. surprise attack, raid; bol., col. maloca (Indian settlement).

ma·lo·gra·do, –da I. past part. see **malograr II.** adj. *(muerto)* having met an untimely death (said of a promising artist); *(frustrado)* frustrated, abortive.

ma·lo·gra·mien·to m. var. of **malogro.**

ma·lo·grar tr. to waste, lose (time, an opportunity); *(estropear)* to spoil, ruin —reflex. *(fracasar)* to fail, come to nothing; *(morir prematuramente)* to come to an untimely end; agr. to fail (crops).

ma·lo·gro m. *(fracaso)* failure; *(fin)* untimely end.

ma·lo·ja f. amer., agr. corn stalks and leaves (used as fodder).

ma·lo·jo m. ven., agr. var. of **maloja.**

ma·lo·lien·te adj. smelly, foul-smelling.

ma·lón m. amer. *(ataque de indios)* surprise Indian attack *or* raid; *(felonía)* dirty trick; *(asalto)* surprise party.

ma·lo·que·ar intr. amer. *(hacer malocas)* to raid, attack (said of Indians); *(sorprender)* to surprise, catch off guard; *(comerciar)* to deal in contraband.

mal·pa·ra·do, –da I. past part. see **malparar II.** adj. damaged, hurt.

mal·pa·rar tr. *(maltratar)* to hurt, harm; *(dañar)* to damage.

mal·pa·ri·da f. woman who has miscarried.

mal·pa·rir intr. to miscarry, have a miscarriage.

mal·par·to m. miscarriage.

mal·pen·sa·do, –da I. adj. evil-minded, malicious **II.** m.f. evil-minded *or* malicious person.

mal·que·rer §55 tr. to bear ill will toward, dislike.

mal·quis·tar tr. to alienate, estrange.

mal·quis·to, –ta I. past part. see **malquerer II.** adj. *(enemistado)* alienated, estranged; *(malmirado)* disliked, unpopular.

mal·sa·no, –na adj. *(poco saludable)* unhealthy, harmful (to one's health); *(enfermizo)* sickly, feeble.

mal·so·nan·te adj. *(que suena mal)* ill-sounding, harsh; *(indecente)* nasty, offensive.

mal·su·fri·do, –da adj. impatient.

mal·ta m. AGR. *(cebada)* malt; *(grano tostado)* toasted grain (used in making beverages); ARG. black beer.

Malta f. Malta.

mal·te·a·do, –da I. past part. see **maltear** II. adj. malted III. m. malting.

mal·te·ar tr. to malt.

mal·tés, –te·sa adj. & m.f. Maltese.

mal·tón, –to·na adj. AMER., COLL. young, baby <*un cordero m.* baby lamb>.

mal·tra·er §72 tr. var. of **maltratar**.

mal·tra·í·do, –da I. past part. see **maltraer** II. adj. AMER. sloppy, disheveled.

mal·tra·ta·mien·to m. maltreatment, mistreatment.

mal·tra·tar tr. *(tratar mal)* to maltreat, mistreat; *(echar a perder)* to spoil, ruin.

mal·tra·to m. var. of **maltratamiento**.

mal·tre·cho, –cha adj. damaged, battered.

mal·tu·sia·nis·mo m. SOCIOL. Malthusianism.

mal·tu·sia·no, –na adj. & m.f. Malthusian.

ma·lu·cho, –cha adj. COLL. out of sorts, under the weather.

ma·lu·ra f. CHILE malaise, indisposition.

mal·va I. f. BOT. *(planta malvácea)* mallow; MEX., COLL. marijuana, weed —m. *(color)* mauve, light violet ♦ m. arbórea *or* loca *or* rósea BOT. rose mallow, hollyhock ♦ haber nacido en las malvas COLL. to be of humble origin • criar malvas COLL. to be pushing up daisies • ser uno como una m. to be obedient, be as meek as a lamb II. adj. mauve, light violet.

mal·va·do, –da I. adj. evil, wicked II. m.f. evildoer, wicked person.

mal·ven·der tr. to sell at a loss, sell off cheap.

mal·ver·sa·ción f. misappropriation, embezzlement.

mal·ver·sa·dor, –do·ra I. adj. embezzling II. m.f. embezzler.

mal·ver·sar tr. to misappropriate, embezzle.

Mal·vi·nas f.pl. Falkland Islands.

mal·vi·vir intr. to live badly.

ma·lla f. *(tejido de red)* mesh, netting; *(de armadura)* mail, chain mail <*cota de m.* coat of mail>; TEX. *(tejido de gimnastas)* stretch fabric, material used in tights; AMER. *(traje de baño)* swimsuit, bathing trunks ♦ hacer m. to knit • m. de alambre wire netting *or* mesh.

ma·llar intr. *(hacer malla)* to make netting *or* mesh; *(enmallarse)* to become enmeshed.

ma·llo m. *(mazo)* mallet, maul; SPORT. *(juego y terreno)* mall, pall mall (game and alley).

Ma·llor·ca f. Majorca.

ma·llor·quín, –qui·na adj. & m.f. Majorcan.

ma·ma f. ZOOL. *(teta)* mamma, mammary gland; COLL. *(madre)* mama, mommy ♦ m. grande AMER. grandmother, grandma, granny.

ma·má f. [pl. **-más**] COLL. mama, mommy ♦ m. abuela Sp. grandma, granny • m. señora AMER. grandma, granny.

ma·ma·ca·llos m. [pl. **-llos**] FIG., COLL. fool, sucker.

ma·ma·da I. f. COLL. *(acción de mamar)* nursing, sucking; *(cantidad de leche tomada)* amount of milk that a child takes in sucking *or* nursing; *(cantidad de tiempo)* amount of time taken in sucking *or* nursing, feeding time; COLL. *(ganga)* cinch, piece of cake; ARG. drinking spree, binge ♦ coger una m. ARG., COLL. to get drunk, go on a drinking spree II. adj. see **mamado, –da**.

ma·ma·de·ra f. *(instrumento para descargar leche)* breast pump; AMER. *(biberón)* baby *or* nursing bottle; *(tetina de biberón)* rubber nipple (of a baby bottle).

ma·ma·do, –da I. past part. see **mamar** II. adj. COLL. *(ebrio)* drunk, sloshed; CUBA *(tonto)* dense, stupid II. m. CUBA child's noisemaker —f. see **mamada**.

ma·ma·dor, –do·ra I. adj. sucking, nursing II. m.f. *(chupador)* nursling, baby who is breast-feeding; COL., CUBA bottle-fed baby.

ma·man·du·rria f. AMER. sinecure.

ma·man·tón, –to·na adj. suckling.

ma·mar tr. *(chupar)* to suckle, nurse; FIG. *(aprender)* to be suckled on, learn (from childhood); COLL. *(tragar)* to wolf, swallow (food); *(conseguir)* to wangle, get <*ella mamó un puesto aunque no tenía el entrenamiento* she wangled a position even though she did not have the training>; *(aprove-*

charse) to milk, take advantage of —intr. to suck, nurse —reflex. COLL. to get drunk *or* smashed ♦ mamarse a alguien AMER., COLL. *(matar)* to knock someone off, do someone in; *(engañar)* to get the better of someone • mamarse el dedo to let oneself be sucked in, be fooled.

ma·ma·rio, –ria adj. ZOOL. mammary.

ma·ma·rra·cha·da f. COLL. *(cuadro malo)* junk, bad painting; *(basura)* junk, rubbish; *(idiotas)* fools, idiots; *(sandez)* stupidity, idiocy.

ma·ma·rra·chis·ta m.f. COLL. dauber, bad artist.

ma·ma·rra·cho m. COLL. *(artes)* bad painting, book, movie, play, etc.; *(basura)* junk, rubbish; *(idiota)* fool, idiot; *(sandez)* stupidity, idiocy; *(espantajo)* fright, sight.

mam·bla f. *(montículo)* mound, hillock; AMER. tumulus, burial mound.

mam·bo m. MUS. mambo (Cuban dance).

ma·me·la f. tip, bonus.

ma·me·lón m. *(colina)* hillock, knoll; ANAT. mammilla, nipple; SURG. mammilla, nipple-like protuberance on scars.

ma·me·lu·co, –ca m. MIL. Mameluke (Egyptian soldier); FIG. *(tonto)* fool, idiot; *(calzones)* union suit; AMER. child's one-piece pajamas —m.f. *(mestizo)* mameluco, Brazilian half-breed.

ma·men·gue ARG. *or* **ma·mer·to, –ta** ECUAD. adj. bashful, awkward.

ma·mey m. BOT. mamey, mammee (tree and fruit).

ma·mí·fe·ro I. adj. mammalian II. m. mammal, mammalian.

ma·mi·la f. ANAT. *(teta de la hembra)* woman's breast around the nipple; *(tetilla del hombre)* nipple (in men); MEX. baby's bottle.

ma·mo·la f. *(caricia)* chuck, pat under the chin; FIG., COLL. *(engaño)* fooling *or* deceit (through kindness).

ma·món, –mo·na I. adj. *(que chupa todavía)* unweaned, still nursing; *(que chupa demasiado)* who nurses a long time, fond of sucking II. m.f. *(bebé que mama todavía)* unweaned baby, baby who still nurses; *(bebé que mama demasiado)* baby who nurses *or* sucks for excessive durations —m. BOT. *(chupón)* shoot, sucker; AMER. *(árbol y fruto de las sapindáceas)* genip; *(papayo)* papaya, papaw (tree and fruit); HOND. stick, club; COLL. *(borracho)* drunkard, drunk —f. *(caricia)* chuck *or* pat under the chin; *(engaño)* deceit, trick; ECUAD. drinking spree, binge.

ma·mo·tre·to m. *(libro de apuntes)* notebook, memo book; COLL. *(legajo grueso)* thick bundle of papers; *(libraco)* large, bulky book; *(armatoste)* monstrosity.

mam·pa·ra f. *(cancel)* movable room divider *or* partition; *(biombo)* screen; PERU glass door.

mam·pa·ro m. MARIT. bulkhead, partition ♦ m. contraincendio fire wall • m. estanco MARIT. watertight bulkhead.

mam·po·rro m. COLL. blow, bump (on the head).

mam·pos·te·rí·a f. CONSTR. rubblework.

mam·pos·te·ro m. CONSTR. mason who does rubblework; *(recaudador)* tithe *or* rent collector.

mam·pues·to, –ta I. adj. CONSTR. *(hilada)* course *or* line of rubblework —m. *(piedra)* rubble, rough stone; ARCHIT. parapet, ledge; AMER. support for aiming a weapon ♦ de m. spare, extra.

ma·mu·jar tr. to nurse intermittently.

ma·mu·llar tr. *(comer o masticar)* to suck in (food); FIG., COLL. *(mascullar)* to mumble, mutter.

ma·mut m. [pl. **-muts**] PALEON. mammoth.

ma·ná m. BIBL. manna; FIG. *(regalo inesperado)* manna, godsend; BOT. manna (dried exudate of certain plants); BOL., PERU nut candy ♦ m. líquido PHARM. sticky sweet purgative.

ma·na·da f. *(hato)* flock, herd; pack <*m. de lobos* pack of wolves>; COLL. *(banda)* gang, bunch; *(manotada)* handful ♦ a manadas COLL. in droves *or* crowds.

ma·na·de·ro, –ra I. adj. flowing, running II. m. *(manantial)* spring, source; *(pastor)* shepherd, herdsman.

Ma·na·gua f. Managua.

ma·na·güen·se adj. & m.f. Managuan.

ma·nan·te adj. flowing, running.

ma·nan·tial I. adj. spring, running <*agua m.* spring water> II. m. *(fontanal)* spring, source; FIG. *(origen)* source, origin.

ma·nan·tí·o, –a adj. flowing, running.

ma·nar tr. to run *or* flow from —intr. *(brotar)* to flow, run; FIG. *(abundar)* to abound in, be full of.

ma·na·tí [pl. **-tí·es**] *o* **ma·na·to** m. ZOOL. manatee, sea cow; *(piel)* manatee hide; AMER. whip (made of manatee hide).

ma·na·za f. large *or* hefty hand.

ma·na·zas [pl. **-zas**] **I.** adj. clumsy, all thumbs **II.** m.f. clumsy person ♦ **ser un m.** to be clumsy, have two left hands.

man·ca·mien·to m. *(acción de mancar)* maiming, disabling; *(falta)* lack, deficiency.

man·car §70 tr. to maim, disable.

man·ca·rrón, –rro·na I. adj. AMER. *(manco)* disabled (person); *(matalón)* worn-out (horse) **II.** m.f. AMER. *(matalón)* nag, worn-out horse; PERU, COLL. *(persona taimada)* stubborn person; CHILE, PERU *(caballón)* dike, levee.

man·ce·ba f. mistress, concubine.

man·ce·bí·a f. *(burdel)* brothel, whorehouse; *(mocedad)* youthful prank *or* carousing.

man·ce·bo m. *(joven)* young man, youth; *(soltero)* bachelor, single man; *(dependiente)* clerk, assistant.

man·ce·ra f. plow handle.

man·ci·lla f. stain, blemish.

man·ci·llar tr. to stain, blemish.

man·ci·par tr. to enslave.

man·co, –ca I. adj. *(de una mano)* one-handed; *(de un brazo)* one-armed; *(sin el uso de un miembro)* maimed, disabled (in an extremity); FIG. *(defectuoso)* defective, imperfect; POET. halting <*verso m.* halting verse> ♦ **no ser manco** COLL. to be important, count **II.** m.f. *(persona con una mano)* one-handed person; *(persona con un brazo)* one-armed person; *(persona sin el uso de un miembro)* person with a disabled extremity; CHILE nag, worn-out horse.

man·co·mu·na·da·men·te *or* **de man·co·mún** adv. jointly, in agreement.

man·co·mu·nar tr. *(unir)* to unite, join; *(combinar)* to combine, pool; LAW *(obligar de mancomún)* to make (two or more parties) jointly liable —reflex. to unite, join together.

man·co·mu·ni·dad f. *(asociación)* association, union; *(comunidad)* community, commonwealth.

man·cor·na f. AMER. pair of matching buttons ♦ **mancornas** AMER. cufflinks.

man·cor·nar §19 tr. *(derribar los cuernos)* to hold down (a steer) by the horns; *(atar con cuerda)* to tie (a steer's) front hoof and horns together (to prevent escape); *(atar los cuernos)* to tie (cattle) together by the horns; FIG., COLL. *(unir)* to tie together, join.

man·cuer·na f. *(pareja)* pair (of oxen) tied together by the horns; PHILIP. pair of prisoners tied together; *(correa)* strap, thong ♦ **mancuernas** MEX. cufflinks.

man·cha f. *(tacha)* stain, spot; *(borrón)* blot, smudge (of ink); *(marca)* spot (on skin, hide); *(trozo)* patch <*una m. de tierra* a patch of land>; FIG. *(infamia)* stain, blot <*una m. en su honra* a blot on his reputation>; ASTRON. sunspot; PAINT. *(boceto)* sketch; ARG., VET. anthrax; SALV. swarm ♦ **cundir** *or* **extenderse como m. de aceite** FIG. to spread like wildfire • **m. solar** ASTRON. sunspot • **sin m.** unblemished.

Mancha, Canal de la GEOG. English Channel.

man·char tr. *(hacer manchas)* to stain; *(ensuciar)* to soil, dirty; FIG. *(deshonrar)* to soil, stain <*m. la honra de la familia* to soil the family's reputation>; PAINT. to daub —reflex. *(hacerse manchas)* to become stained *or* spotted; *(ensuciarse)* to get dirty, become soiled.

man·chón m. *(mancha grande)* large spot *or* stain; AGR. patch of thick vegetation; CHILE muff (for hands).

man·da f. *(oferta)* offer, proposal; *(legado)* legacy, bequest; CHILE, MEX. religious vow.

man·da·de·ro, –ra m.f. messenger, errand boy *or* girl.

man·da·do I. past part. see **mandar II.** m. *(orden)* order, mandate; *(encargo)* task, assignment; *(recado)* errand; COLL. *(puñetazo)* punch, blow ♦ **a su m.** ARG. at your orders.

man·da·más m. [pl. **-más**] COLL. honcho, big shot.

man·da·mien·to m. *(orden)* order, command; BIBL. commandment; LAW writ ♦ **m. de arresto** *or* **de detención** arrest warrant • **m. de embargo** writ of attachment •

mandamientos FIG., COLL. fingers • **mandamientos de la ley de Dios** BIBL. the Ten Commandments.

man·dan·ga f. COLL. *(pachorra)* laziness, indolence; *(cocaína)* cocaine ♦ **mandangas** COLL. nonsense, foolishness.

man·dar tr. *(ordenar)* to order, command <*le mandaron que se fuera* they ordered him to leave>; *(enviar)* to send <*me mandó un paquete* he sent me a package>; *(legar)* to leave, bequeath; *(encargar)* to send <*lo mandamos de emisario* we sent him as an emissary>; AMER. *(dar)* to give, deliver (a blow); *(arrojar)* to throw, hurl ♦ **m. a volar** MEX., COLL. to kill, get rid of • **m. al otro barrio** COLL. to kill, knock off • **m. a paseo** *or* **con viento fresco** COLL. to send packing —intr. *(gobernar)* to be in command, be in charge <*aquí mando yo* I am in charge here> ♦ **¿mande?** MEX. pardon me?, come again? —reflex. *(manejarse)* to get around on one's own <*el enfermo se manda ahora* the patient is getting around on his own now>; ARCHIT. to connect, be connected <*las habitaciones se mandan* the rooms are connected>; AMER. to leave, go away ♦ **mandarse mudar** AMER. to scram, beat it.

man·da·rín m. *(funcionario chino)* mandarin; FIG. petty *or* officious bureaucrat.

man·da·ri·na I. adj. Mandarin **II.** f. *(lengua)* Mandarin; BOT. mandarin (orange).

man·da·ri·no *or* **man·da·ri·ne·ro** m. BOT. mandarin (orange) tree.

man·da·ta·rio m. *(enviado)* agent, mandatary; AMER. leader, chief executive.

man·da·to m. *(orden)* order, command; *(encargo)* charge, trust; DIPL., POL. mandate; LAW *(contrato)* power of attorney; RELIG. maundy ♦ **m. jurídico** LAW court order, injunction.

man·dí·bu·la f. ANAT., ZOOL. jaw, mandible ♦ **reír a m. batiente** to laugh one's head off.

man·dil m. *(delantal)* apron, pinafore; *(bayeta)* cloth for grooming horses; *(red)* fine-meshed fishing net; *(manta de caballo)* horse blanket.

man·di·lón m. FIG., COLL. coward, weakling.

man·din·ga I. adj. Mandingo, black **II.** m. *(persona)* Mandingo, black person; COLL. *(diablo)* devil; ARG. *(revoltoso)* imp, mischievous rogue; *(brujería)* magic, sorcery; C. RICA *(marica)* effeminate man.

man·dio·ca f. BOT. cassava, manioc; *(tapioca)* tapioca.

man·do m. *(autoridad)* authority, power; *(dirección)* command, leadership; POL. term of office (of a governor or president); MECH. control; AUTO. drive ♦ **alto m.** high command ♦ **entregar el m.** to hand over command • **estar al m.** to be in command, be in control • **m. a distancia** remote control • **m. doble** MECH. dual control; AUTO. dual drive • **mandos** TECH. controls • **tablero de mandos** instrument panel • **tomar el m.** to take command *or* control.

man·do·lín m. *or* **man·do·li·na** f. MUS. mandolin.

man·dón, –do·na I. adj. bossy, domineering **II.** m.f. bossy *or* domineering person —m. AMER. foreman (of a mine); CHILE starter (in horse races).

man·dra·che·ro m. owner of a gambling house.

man·dra·cho m. gambling house.

man·dria I. adj. *(cobarde)* cowardly, timid; *(inútil)* useless, worthless **II.** m.f. *(cobarde)* coward; *(necio)* fool, useless person.

man·dril m. ZOOL. mandrill.

man·du·ca f. COLL. food, chow.

man·du·ca·ble adj. COLL. edible, eatable.

man·du·ca·ción f. COLL. eating.

man·du·car §70 tr. & intr. COLL. to eat, chow down.

man·du·ca·to·ria f. COLL. food, chow.

ma·ne·a f. hobble, shackle.

ma·ne·a·dor m. AMER. long strap used for hobbling animals.

ma·ne·ar tr. *(poner maniotas)* to hobble (horses, cattle); *(manejar)* to manage, handle —reflex. MEX. to trip over one's own feet.

ma·ne·ci·lla f. *(broche)* clasp; PRINT. index (mark); *(saetilla del reloj)* hand (of a watch); *(palanquilla)* small handle *or* lever; BOT. tendril.

ma·ne·ja·ble adj. manageable.

ma·ne·jar tr. *(usar)* to handle; *(dirigir)* to run, manage <*m. una inversión* to manage an investment>; EQUIT. to handle (a horse); AMER. to drive (a car) —reflex. (*moverse*) to get or move around; (*comportarse*) to behave —intr. AMER. to drive.

ma·ne·jo m. (*uso*) handling; (*funcionamiento*) running, operation; FIG. (*dirección*) handling, management <*el m. de una empresa es muy difícil* the management of a business is very difficult>; (*maquinación*) machination, trick; EQUIT. horsemanship; AMER. driving (of a car) ♦ **instruc-ciones de m.** directions • **m. doméstico** housekeeping.

ma·ne·ra f. (*modo*) manner, way; (*tipo*) manner, type; (*abertura*) slit (of a skirt); (*bragueta*) fly (of trousers); ARTS (*estilo*) style, manner ♦ **a la m. de** or **a m. de** like, in the manner of • **de alguna m.** somehow, in some way • **de cualquier m.** anyhow, any old way • **de la misma m.** similarly, in the same way • **de mala m.** badly, rudely • **de m. que** so, so that • **de ninguna m.** by no means, in no way • **de otra m.** otherwise • **de tal m.** in such a way • **de todas maneras** at any rate, anyway • **en gran m.** in large measure, greatly • **m. de ser** personality, the way one is • **m. de ver** outlook, point of view • **maneras** manners <*tiene maneras atroces* he has awful manners> • **¡qué m. de . . .!** what a way to . . .! • **sobre m.** exceedingly.

man·flo·ra or **man·flo·ri·ta** adj. (*hermafrodita*) hermaphrodite; AMER. effeminate man.

man·ga f. sleeve <*m. corta* short sleeve>; (*manguera*) hose <*m. de ventilación* air hose>; (*maleta*) portmanteau, valise; (*red*) tubular fishing net; (*tromba de agua*) waterspout; (*colador*) strainer; AER. windsock, wind cone; BOT. mango (fruit and tree); MECH. journal; MARIT. beam, breadth; AMER. (*multitud*) crowd, mob; (*paso estrecho*) narrowing chute (used to corral animals); C. AMER. poncho ♦ **andar m. por hombro** to be disorderly, be a mess • **en mangas de camisa** in shirt sleeves • **estar de m.** COLL. to be in league, be in cahoots • **hacer mangas y capirotes** FIG., COLL. to act impulsively • **m. de agua** METEOROL. cloudburst, squall • **m. de riego** (garden) hose • **m. de viento** METEOROL. tornado, whirlwind • **sin mangas** sleeveless • **tener m. ancha** FIG. to be lenient.

man·ga·jo m. awkward person.

man·ga·na f. lasso.

man·ga·ne·ar tr. (*echar manganas*) to lasso; PERU, VEN. to annoy, bother.

man·ga·ne·so m. CHEM. manganese.

man·ga·ni·lla f. trick, ruse.

man·gan·te COLL. **I.** adj. (*que roba*) stealing; (*pedigüeño*) mooching, sponging **II.** m. (*ladrón*) thief; (*pedigüeño*) moocher, sponger.

man·gan·zón, -zo·na **I.** adj. AMER. lazy, idle **II.** m.f. (*grandulón*) big boy, big girl.

man·gar §47 tr. COLL. (*robar*) to steal, swipe; (*pedir*) to mooch, sponge.

man·glar m. mangrove swamp.

man·gle m. mangrove tree.

man·go¹ m. handle, haft.

man·go² m. BOT. mango (tree and fruit).

man·gón m. (*revendedor*) second-hand dealer; AMER. corral; COL. pasture land.

man·go·na·da f. shove with the arm.

man·go·ne·ar intr. (*entremeterse*) to meddle, pry; COLL. (*mandar*) to boss people about, take charge; AMER. to profit by illicit means; MEX. to steal.

man·go·ne·o m. COLL. (*entremetimiento*) meddling, prying; AMER. graft; MEX., PERU thievery, robbery.

man·go·ne·ro, -ra adj. COLL. meddlesome.

man·go·rre·ro, -ra **I.** adj. (*mal forjado*) crude, rough (knife); COLL. (*que anda entre manos*) passing from hand to hand; FIG. (*inútil*) useless, worthless **II.** f. ARG., BOL. medium-sized knife.

man·gos·ta f. ZOOL. mongoose.

man·go·te m. COLL. (*manga ancha*) wide sleeve; (*manga postiza*) oversleeve.

man·gué, man·gue see **mangar.**

man·gue·ar tr. FIG., COLL. to lure with flattery, cajole; AMER. to flush, startle (game); ARG. to drive into a gangway (cattle); —intr. COL., VEN. to pretend to be working; P. RICO to loaf.

man·gue·ra f. MARIT. (*manga de lona*) pump hose; MARIT.

ventilation duct or shaft; (*manga de riego*) hose, garden hose; (*tromba*) waterspout; ARG. corral.

man·gue·ro m. (*bombero*) fireman; (*tabla*) board for ironing sleeves; MEX. mango (tree).

man·gue·ta f. (*enema*) enema; ARCHIT. beam, tie; (*palanca*) lever; (*tubo de retrete*) U-tube (of a toilet).

man·gui·ta f. case, cover.

man·gui·te·rí·a f. furrier's shop.

man·gui·te·ro f. furrier.

man·gui·to m. (*regalillo*) muff; (*manga de punta*) lace half-sleeve; (*bizcocho*) large ring-shaped cake; (*mangote*) oversleeve; (*manopla*) glove; TECH. sleeve, bushing.

ma·ní m. [pl. **-ní·es** or **-ní·ses**] AMER., BOT. peanut.

ma·ní·a f. (*locura*) mania; (*capricho*) craze, fad; (*costumbre*) habit; COLL. (*tirria*) dislike, aversion ♦ **m. persecutoria** persecution mania or complex • **tenerle m. a alguien** COLL. to dislike someone.

ma·nia·bier·to, -ta **I.** adj. generous, liberal **II.** m.f. generous person.

ma·ní·a·co, -ca **I.** adj. maniac, mad **II.** m.f. maniac.

ma·nia·tar tr. to manacle, handcuff.

ma·niá·ti·co, -ca **I.** adj. maniacal **II.** m.f. maniac.

ma·ni·co·mio m. insane asylum, mental hospital.

ma·ni·cor·to, -ta FIG., COLL. **I.** adj. stingy, tightfisted **II.** m.f. skinflint, miser.

ma·ni·cu·ro, -ra m.f. (*persona*) manicurist —f. (*cuidado*) manicure.

ma·ni·do, -da **I.** past part. see **manir II.** adj. (*podrido*) rotten; FIG. (*gastado*) worn-out, rumpled; (*trillado*) trite, hackneyed <*idea m.* trite idea>; P. RICO full.

ma·nie·ris·mo m. ARTS mannerism.

ma·ni·fes·ta·ción f. (*expresión*) manifestation, expression; (*expresión pública*) demonstration, manifestation.

ma·ni·fes·ta·dor, -do·ra **I.** adj. manifesting, demonstrating **II.** m.f. demonstrator.

ma·ni·fes·tan·te m.f. demonstrator.

ma·ni·fes·tar §49 tr. (*expresar*) to manifest, express; (*anunciar*) to show, reveal; RELIG. to expose (the Holy Eucharist) —intr. to demonstrate —reflex. to reveal oneself.

ma·ni·fies·ta·men·te adv. manifestly, evidently.

ma·ni·fies·to, -ta **I.** past part. see **manifestar II.** adj. manifest, obvious **III.** m. (*llamamiento*) manifest; MARIT. manifest; RELIG. exhibition of the Holy Eucharist.

ma·ni·gua f. or **ma·ni·gual** m. CUBA underbrush, thicket.

ma·ni·gue·ta f. handle, haft.

ma·ni·ja f. (*mango*) handle, haft; (*traba*) hobble, shackle; (*abrazadera de hierro*) clamp, collar.

ma·ni·lar·go, -ga adj. (*de manos largas*) long-handed; FIG., COLL. (*generoso*) generous, openhanded; FIG. (*ladrón*) light-fingered.

ma·ni·lla f. (*pulsera*) bracelet; (*manija*) handle; (*grillete*) handcuff, manacle; (*manecilla de un reloj*) hand (of a watch).

ma·ni·llar m. handlebars (of a bicycle).

ma·ni·o·bra f. (*acto*) handling, operation; FIG. (*artificio*) maneuver, stratagem; MIL. maneuver; MARIT. (*arte*) seamanship; (*aparejos*) rigging, gear ♦ **estar de maniobras** MARIT., MIL. to be on maneuvers • **maniobras** MARIT., MIL. maneuvers; RAIL. shunting.

ma·ni·o·bra·ble adj. maneuverable.

ma·ni·o·brar intr. & tr. to maneuver.

ma·ni·o·ta f. hobble (for horses, cattle).

ma·ni·pu·la·ción f. (*con las manos*) manipulation; COM. handling (of merchandise); FIG. (*maniobra*) act of controlling by artful means.

ma·ni·pu·la·dor, -do·ra **I.** adj. manipulating **II.** m.f. manipulator —m. TELEC. telegraph key.

ma·ni·pu·lar tr. (*manejar*) to manipulate, handle; COM. to manage (a business); (*mercancías*) to handle (merchandise); FIG. (*controlar*) to manipulate, maneuver (to one's advantage).

ma·ni·pu·le·o m. FIG., COLL. (*manipulación*) manipulation, maneuvering; COM. management (of a business).

ma·ni·que·ís·mo m. RELIG. Manichaeism.

ma·ni·quí m. [pl. **-quí·es**] (*armazón de sastre*) dummy, mannequin; (*modelo*) model, mannequin; FIG. (*persona sin carácter*) puppet.

ma·nir tr. CUL. *(ablandar)* to age (meat); *(sobar)* to knead —reflex. to become gamy (meat).

ma·ni·rro·to, –ta I. adj. spendthrift, wasteful II. m.f. spendthrift.

ma·ni·se·ro, –ra m.f. peanut vendor.

ma·ni·tas m. [pl. -tas] handyman.

ma·ni·va·cí·o, –a COLL. empty-handed.

ma·ni·ve·la f. crank.

man·jar m. *(alimento)* food; *(plato)* dish <un m. delicioso a tasty dish>; *(recreo)* recreation, entertainment ♦ **m. blanco** CUL. blancmange.

ma·no¹ f. ANAT. hand; ZOOL. *(pata)* forefoot, front paw; *(trompa del elefante)* elephant's trunk; CUL. foot, trotter; *(del reloj)* hand (of a clock); *(almirez)* pestle, pounder; *(capa)* coat <una m. de barniz a coat of varnish>; *(de papel)* quire (of paper); *(lado)* side <el río está a m. izquierda the river is on the left side>; *(lance)* hand, round <echar una m. de dominó to play a round of dominoes>; *(el primero a jugar)* lead <yo soy m. I am the lead>; FIG., COLL. *(serie)* series, string <le di una m. de palos I dealt him a series of blows>; FIG. *(ayuda)* hand, help <echar una m. to lend a hand>; worker, hired hand <hay que contratar manos we have to hire workers>; *(represión)* reprimand, reproach; *(destreza)* hand, skill; *(influencia)* influence <el tiene m. con el director he has influence with the director>; AMER. *(conjunto)* group of four or five objects; *(accidente)* mishap, accident; *(gajo de plátanos)* bunch (of bananas) ♦ **abrir la m.** FIG. to be more lenient • **a la m.** on hand, at hand • **alzar la m. a** to raise one's hand to, threaten • **a m.** by hand <escrito a m. written by hand>; *(cerca)* at hand, on hand • **a m. airada** violently • **a m. armada** armed, by force • **a m. derecha (izquierda)** on the right (left) side • **a manos llenas** generously, openly • **asentar la m. a** to reprimand, reproach • **bajo m.** underhandedly, secretly • **buena m.** FIG. skill, dexterity • **cargar la m.** to be heavy-handed • **coger a alguien con las manos en la masa** COLL. to catch someone red-handed, catch in the act • **con el corazón en la m.** straight from the heart • **con las manos vacías** empty-handed • **dar la m. a** to shake hands with • **dar la última m. a** FIG. to put the finishing touches on • **darse las manos** *(unirse)* to join hands, unite; *(saludarse)* to shake hands • **dar una m. a** to lend a hand to • **dejar de la m.** to abandon • **de m.** hand <equipaje de m. hand luggage> • **de m. a m.** from hand to hand • **de manos a boca** suddenly, unexpectedly • **de primera m.** firsthand • **de segunda m.** secondhand • **echar m. de** to make use of • **estrechar la m. a** to shake hands with • **ganar a alguien por la m.** to beat someone to it • **hacer lo que está en sus manos** to do everything within one's power • **hecha a m.** handmade • **imponer las manos** RELIG. to lay on hands • **m. a m.** *(juntos)* hand in hand, jointly; *(sin ventaja)* even, on equal terms • **m. de gato** make-up • **m. de obra** labor • **m. derecha** or **diestra** FIG. right-hand man • **m. de santo** FIG. sure cure • **m. oculta** FIG. secret partner • **¡manos a la obra!** let's get to work! • **¡manos arriba!** hands up! • **manos libres** FIG. perquisites • **manos limpias** FIG. integrity, honesty • **manos muertas** LAW mortmain • **meter m. en** COLL., COLL. to interfere, butt in • **pedir la m. a** to ask for someone's hand (in marriage) • **tener algo entre manos** to be working on something • **traer algo entre manos** to be involved in or mixed up in something • **untar la m. a alguien** to grease someone's palm, bribe • **venir a m.** to be convenient • **venir** or **llegar a las manos** to come to blows • **vivir de** or **por sus manos** COLL. to fend for oneself.

ma·no² m. AMER., MEX., COLL. friend, pal.

ma·no·jo m. *(haz)* bundle, bunch; FIG. *(puñado)* handful ♦ **a manojos** abundantly.

ma·no·pla f. ARM. gauntlet; *(látigo)* coachman's whip; *(guante)* mitten; *(para lavarse)* mitten, washcloth; AMER. brass knuckles.

ma·no·se·a·dor, –do·ra I. adj. handling, touching II. m.f. person fond of touching or caressing.

ma·no·se·ar tr. to handle, touch.

ma·no·se·o m. handling, touching.

ma·no·ta·da f. or **ma·no·ta·zo** m. slap, cuff.

ma·no·te·a·do I. past part. see **manotear** II. m. *(golpe)* slapping; *(ademán)* gesticulation.

ma·no·te·ar tr. *(golpear)* to slap, cuff; ARG. to steal —intr. to gesticulate.

ma·no·te·o m. gesticulation.

man·qué, manque see **mancar.**

man·que·ar intr. to be or pretend to be disabled.

man·que·dad or **man·que·ra** f. *(falta de mano o brazo)* lack of hand or arm; FIG. *(defecto)* defect, imperfection.

man·sal·va adv. ♦ **a m.** without any risk.

man·sa·men·te adv. *(con mansedumbre)* meekly, mildly; FIG. *(lentamente)* slowly, gently; *(suavemente)* silently, noiselessly.

man·se·dum·bre f. *(suavidad)* gentleness, mildness; *(de un animal)* tameness.

man·sión f. *(estancia)* stay, sojourn; *(morada)* abode, residence ♦ **hacer m.** to stop over.

man·so, –sa I. adj. *(suave)* gentle, mild; *(domesticado)* tame II. m. bellwether (of a flock); *(casa hacienda)* farmhouse.

man·ta f. *(frazada)* blanket; *(para caballos)* horse blanket; *(mantón)* shawl; COLL. *(paliza)* beating, drubbing; AMER. *(poncho)* poncho; COL., MEX. *(algodón)* coarse cotton cloth; AMER., ICHTH. manta ray; ECUAD. plot, bed (of land) ♦ **a m.** or **a m. de Dios** copiously, plentifully • **m. eléctrica** electric blanket • **tirar la m.** FIG., COLL. to let the cat out of the bag.

man·te·ar tr. *(hacer saltar)* to toss in a blanket; ARG. to rough up (in a gang) —intr. to gad about.

man·te·ca f. *(grasa)* grease, fat; *(de cerdo)* lard; *(de vaca)* butter ♦ **como m.** soft, smooth • **el que asó la m.** FIG., COLL. dodo, nitwit • **m. de cacahuete** peanut butter • **m. de cacao** cocoa butter • **mantecas** fat, blubber <tener buenas mantecas to be a tub of lard>.

man·te·ca·da f. CUL. *(pan)* buttered toast with sugar; *(bollito)* sweet roll.

man·te·ca·do m. CUL. *(bollo)* roll made with lard; *(sorbete)* milk sherbet.

man·te·cón m. FIG., COLL. milksop, mollycoddle.

man·te·co·so, –sa adj. buttery.

man·tel m. *(de la mesa)* tablecloth; *(del altar)* altar cloth ♦ **levantar los manteles** to clear the table.

man·te·le·rí·a f. table linen.

man·te·ne·dor m. president (of a tournament) ♦ **m. de familia** breadwinner.

man·te·nen·cia f. *(acto)* maintenance; *(sostenimiento)* support; *(sustento)* sustenance, food.

man·te·ner §69 tr. *(alimentar)* to feed; *(sustentar)* to maintain, support <m. una familia to support a family>; *(sostener)* to support, hold up; FIG. *(conservar)* to maintain, keep <m. el orden to maintain order>; *(continuar)* to maintain, keep up <m. una conversación to maintain a conversation>; *(afirmar)* to maintain, affirm (opinions, ideas); *(celebrar)* to hold (a tournament, festival) ♦ **m. a distancia** or **a raya** to keep at a distance • **m. en buen uso** to keep in good condition —reflex. *(alimentarse)* to feed oneself; *(sustentarse)* to maintain or support oneself; *(perseverar)* to remain or stand firm <se mantiene en sus creencias he remains firm in his beliefs>; *(permanecer)* to remain, keep oneself ♦ **mantenerse a distancia** to keep one's distance • **mantenerse en sus trece** FIG., COLL. to stick to one's guns • **mantenerse firme** to hold one's ground.

man·te·ni·mien·to m. *(mantenencia)* maintenance; *(sostenimiento)* support; *(sustento)* sustenance, food.

man·te·que·ra I. f. *(persona)* dairymaid, dairy vendor; *(máquina)* butter churn; *(vasija)* butter dish II. adj. see **mantequero, –ra.**

man·te·que·rí·a f. creamery, dairy.

man·te·que·ro, –ra I. m. *(persona)* dairyman; *(vasija)* butter dish —f. see **mantequera** II. adj. butter, of butter <la industria m. the butter industry>.

man·te·qui·lla f. *(manteca de vaca)* butter; *(con azúcar)* butter cream ♦ **m. requemada** browned butter • **m. salada** salted butter.

man·te·qui·lle·ra f. AMER. butter dish.

man·tés, –te·sa COLL. I. adj. rascally, scoundrelly II. m.f. rascal, scoundrel.

man·tie·ne see **mantener.**

man·ti·lla f. *(de una mujer)* mantilla; *(de un niño)* swaddling clothes; *(del caballo)* saddlecloth; PRINT. blanket —m. HOND. coward ♦ **estar en mantillas** *(estar en principios)* to be in infancy, be in embryo (a project); *(ignorar)* to be in the dark, be uninformed (a person) • **salí de mantillas** I wasn't born yesterday.

man·ti·llón, –llo·na I. adj. MEX. dirty, slovenly II. m. AMER. caparison; MEX. scoundrel.

man·ti·sa f. MATH. mantissa.

man·to m. *(capa)* cloak, mantle; *(mantilla)* long mantilla; *(vestidura talar)* robe; *(de la chimenea)* mantel; FIG. *(amparo)* cloak, cover <*lo hicieron bajo el m. de la obscuridad* they did it under the cloak of darkness>; ZOOL. mantle; MIN. layer, stratum; MEX., BOT. bellflower.

man·tón m. *(pañuelo)* shawl; VEN. mantle, cloak ♦ **m. de Manila** embroidered silk shawl.

man·tu·vie·ra, mantuvo see **mantener.**

ma·nua·ble adj. manageable, easy to handle.

ma·nual I. adj. manual <*trabajo m.* manual labor>; *(manejable)* manageable, easy to handle II. m. manual, handbook.

ma·nual·men·te adv. manually, by hand.

ma·nu·brio m. TECH. crank; *(manija)* handle.

ma·nu·fac·tu·ra f. *(fábrica)* factory; *(artículo)* manufactured article; *(fabricación)* manufacture.

ma·nu·fac·tu·rar tr. to manufacture.

ma·nu·fac·tu·re·ro, –ra adj. manufacturing.

ma·nu·mi·sión f. manumission, emancipation.

ma·nu·mi·so, –sa I. past part. see **manumitir** II. adj. freed, emancipated.

ma·nu·mi·tir tr. LAW to manumit, emancipate.

ma·nus·cri·to, –ta I. adj. handwritten II. m. manuscript.

ma·nu·ten·ción f. *(acción de mantener)* maintenance; *(conservación)* conservation.

man·za·na f. BOT. apple; *(cuadra)* block (of buildings); *(de espada)* pommel; COL. hub; AMER., ANAT. Adam's apple ♦ **m. de la discordia** FIG. apple of discord • **m. podrida** FIG. rotten apple • **sano como una m.** FIG., COLL. fit as a fiddle.

man·za·nal m. *(huerto)* apple orchard; *(árbol)* apple tree.

man·za·nar m. apple orchard.

man·za·ne·ra f. BOT. crab apple tree.

man·za·ni·lla f. BOT. chamomile, camomile; *(infusión)* chamomile tea; *(aceituna)* olive; *(adorno)* knob (in the shape of an apple or pine cone); *(barbilla)* point or tip of the chin; *(jerez)* manzanilla ♦ **m. hedionda** BOT. mayweed.

man·za·no m. BOT. apple tree.

ma·ña f. *(habilidad)* skill, dexterity; *(astucia)* craftiness, guile; *(hábito)* bad habit, vice; *(manojo)* bunch, bundle ♦ **darse m. para** to manage or contrive to • **más vale m. que fuerza** brain is better than brawn • **tener m. para** to have a knack for.

ma·ña·na I. f. morning ♦ **a la m. siguiente** the next morning • **ayer por la m.** yesterday morning • **de** or **en** or **por la m.** in the morning • **de la noche a la m.** overnight • **de m.** or **muy de m.** very early (in the morning) • **tomar la m.** AMER. to take a nip in the morning —m. *(futuro)* tomorrow, future <*el m. es incierto* the future is uncertain> II. adv. *(el próximo día)* tomorrow <*lo haremos m.* we will do it tomorrow>; *(en el futuro)* in the future ♦ **a partir de m.** starting tomorrow, as of tomorrow • **hasta m.** see you tomorrow • **m. por la m.** tomorrow morning • **pasado m.** the day after tomorrow.

ma·ña·ne·ar intr. to get up or rise early.

ma·ña·ne·ro, –ra adj. *(madrugador)* early-rising; *(relativo a la mañana)* morning, of morning.

ma·ña·ni·tas f.pl. MEX. serenade (sung at birthdays).

ma·ñe·ar tr. to manage or handle cleverly —intr. to be artful or crafty.

ma·ñe·ro, –ra adj. *(astuto)* clever, shrewd; *(fácil de manejar)* easily manageable; ARG. artful, crafty; CHILE skittish (horse).

ma·ño·co m. *(tapioca)* tapioca; VEN. Indian corn meal.

ma·ño·sa·men·te adv. *(con habilidad)* skillfully, cleverly; *(con astucia)* craftily; *(con malicia)* maliciously.

ma·ño·se·ar intr. CHILE to act with skill and cunning.

ma·ño·so, –sa adj. *(hábil)* skillful, clever; *(astuto)* crafty, cunning; *(que tiene malas mañas)* having bad habits.

mao·ís·mo m. POL. Maoism.

mao·ís·ta adj. & m.f. POL. Maoist.

ma·pa m. map, chart ♦ **desaparecer del m.** to vanish from the face of the earth • **m. acotado** contour map • **m. mudo** blank or skeleton map • **no estar en el m.** FIG., COLL. to be out of this world —f. COLL. cream of the crop, best ♦ **llevarse la m.** to take the cake.

ma·pa·che or **ma·pa·chín** m. ZOOL. raccoon.

ma·pa·mun·di m. GEOG. map of the world, world map; FIG., COLL. *(las nalgas)* fanny, behind.

ma·que m. *(laca)* lacquer; MEX. varnish.

ma·que see **macarse.**

ma·que·ar tr. *(poner laca)* to lacquer; MEX. to varnish —reflex. COLL. to dress up.

ma·que·ta f. ARCHIT. scale model, mock-up; PRINT. dummy.

ma·quí m. CHILE, BOT. maqui.

ma·quia·vé·li·co, –ca adj. Machiavellian.

ma·quia·ve·lis·mo m. Machiavellianism.

ma·qui·lla·je m. *(acción)* making up (of one's face); *(cosmético)* makeup, cosmetics.

ma·qui·llar tr. *(pintar)* to make up (one's face), apply cosmetics to; *(alterar)* to falsify, cover up.

má·qui·na f. *(aparato)* machine <*m. de coser* sewing machine>; *(motor)* engine <*m. de vapor* steam engine>; *(locomotora)* locomotive, engine; LIT., THEAT. machine, deus ex machina; COLL. *(bicicleta)* bike, bicycle; *(automóvil)* car, auto; *(cámara)* camera; FIG. *(proyecto)* project, plan; *(edificio)* edifice, imposing structure; *(autómata)* machine, robot; *(organismo)* machine <*la m. humana* the human machine>; *(sistema)* machine <*la m. del Estado* the machine of the State> ♦ **a toda m.** at full speed • **hecho a m.** machine-made • **m. de escribir** typewriter • **m. de lavar** washing machine • **m. herramienta** machine tool • **m. neumática** air pump • **m. registradora** S. AMER. cash register.

ma·qui·na·ción f. machination, plotting.

ma·qui·na·dor, –do·ra I. adj. plotting, scheming II. m.f. plotter, schemer.

ma·qui·nal adj. mechanical.

ma·qui·nal·men·te adv. FIG. mechanically.

ma·qui·nar tr. to plot, scheme.

ma·qui·na·ria f. *(conjunto de máquinas)* machinery; *(arte de fabricar máquinas)* mechanics; *(mecánica)* applied mechanics.

ma·qui·ni·lla f. small machine or device • **m. de afeitar** or **de seguridad** safety razor • **m. para cortar el pelo** hair clippers.

ma·qui·nis·mo m. INDUS. mechanization; PHILOS. mechanism.

ma·qui·nis·ta m. INDUS. machinist; RAIL. engineer, engine driver; THEAT. stagehand.

mar m. or f. *(agua)* sea <*M. Rojo* Red Sea>; *(marejada)* tide, swell; FIG. *(gran cantidad)* sea, flood <*un m. de lágrimas* a flood of tears> ♦ **alta m.** or **m. ancha** high seas • **arar en el m.** FIG. to labor in vain • **correr a mares** to stream, flow • **hablar de la m.** FIG. to speak of the impossible • **hacerse a la m.** to put out to sea • **la m. de** *(muchos)* loads of, lots of <*la m. de trabajo* loads of work>; *(muy)* very <*él es la m. de tonto* he is very foolish> • **llover a mares** to rain cats and dogs • **M. Adriático** Adriatic Sea • **m. agitado** or **picado** choppy sea • **M. Báltico** Baltic Sea • **m. bravo** rough seas • **m. bonanza** calm seas • **M. Caribe** Caribbean Sea • **m. de fondo** or **de leva** ground swell • **M. de Galilea** Sea of Galilee • **M. de las Antillas** Caribbean sea • **M. Egeo** Aegean Sea • **m. interior** inland sea • **M. Mediterráneo** Mediterranean Sea.

ma·ra·ca f. MUS. maraca; COL., P. RICO, VEN., COLL. dummy, dolt; CHILE prostitute.

ma·ra·ña f. *(maleza)* thicket; BOT. kermes oak; *(enredo)* tangle, mess; FIG. *(embuste)* deception, fraud.

ma·ras·mo m. MED. marasmus; FIG. *(apatía)* apathy; *(estancación)* stagnation, paralysis.

ma·ra·tón m. marathon.

ma·ra·vi·lla f. *(fenómeno)* wonder, marvel; *(asombro)* wonder, astonishment; BOT. *(caléndula)* marigold; *(dondiego* *de día)* morning glory; *(dondiego de noche)* marvel of Peru ♦ **a las mil maravillas** wonderfully, excellently • **a m.** marvellously • **hacer maravillas** to work wonders • **las siete maravillas del mundo** the Seven Wonders of the World • **por m.** rarely, seldom • **venirle a uno de m.** FIG. to be just what the doctor ordered.

ma·ra·vi·llar tr. to amaze, astonish —reflex. to marvel, be amazed ♦ **maravillarse con** *or* **de** to marvel at, be amazed at *or* by.

ma·ra·vi·llo·sa·men·te adv. marvelously, wonderfully.

ma·ra·vi·llo·so, –sa adj. marvelous, wonderful.

mar·be·te m. *(etiqueta)* label, tag; *(orilla)* border, edge.

mar·ca f. *(señal)* mark; *(de ganadería)* brand; *(tipo)* make, brand *¿de qué m. es su auto?* what make is your car?>; *(estampa)* stamp; COM. trademark; *(medidor)* measuring stick, rule; *(medida)* standard (size); *(cicatriz)* mark, scar; SPORT. *(en deportes)* mark, record; MARIT. seamark; GEOG. march, frontier ♦ **de m.** FIG. excellent, outstanding • **de m. mayor** high quality, first-class • **m. de agua** watermark • **m. de fábrica** trademark • **m. registrada** (registered) trademark.

mar·ca·ción f. MARIT. *(acción de marcar)* taking of a ship's bearing; *(orientación)* bearing; AMER. *(hierro)* branding iron; *(acción de marcar)* branding.

mar·ca·da·men·te adv. noticeably, markedly.

mar·ca·do I. past part. see **marcar** II. adj. marked, notable III. m. marking.

mar·ca·dor, –do·ra I. adj. *(que marca)* marking; AMER. branding II. m.f. *(que marca)* marker; *(lápiz)* marker, marking pen; AMER. brander —m. *(de bordado)* embroidery sampler; *(de herrero)* blacksmith's hammer; *(almotacén)* inspector of weights and measures; PRINT. feeder operator; SPORT. scoreboard.

mar·ca·je m. SPORT. scoring.

mar·ca·pa·so *or* **mar·ca·pa·sos** m. MED. pacemaker.

mar·car §70 tr. *(poner marca)* to mark; *(herrar)* to brand (cattle); *(estampillar)* to stamp; *(la ropa)* to label (clothes); *(anotar)* to observe, note; *(indicar)* to say, indicate *<la balanza marca tres kilos* the scale indicates three kilos>; FIG. *(señalar)* to single out (a person); FIG. *(aplicar)* to assign, destine; *(subrayar)* to mark, underline; *(poner el precio)* to mark, price; *(el pelo)* to set (one's hair); *(un número de teléfono)* to dial (a telephone number); PRINT. *(en imprenta)* to feed (paper); SPORT. *(golear)* to score; *(defender)* to guard, cover (an opponent); MARIT. to take (bearings) ♦ **m. el compás** MUS. to keep time • **m. el paso** MIL. to mark time —reflex. SPORT. *(golear)* to score; MARIT. to determine bearings.

mar·cial adj. *(relativo a la guerra)* martial, warlike; *(militar)* military *<porte m.* military bearing>; PHARM. containing iron.

mar·cia·li·dad f. martialness.

mar·cia·no, –na adj. & m.f. ASTRON. Martian.

mar·co m. *(cerco)* frame; FIN. mark (monetary unit); *(peso)* mark (unit of weight); *(patrón)* standard; *(cartabón)* measuring stick (for shoemakers); *(de madera)* standard length of wood; FIG. *(estructura)* framework *<dentro del m. del pensamiento hegeliano* within the framework of Hegelian thought>; SPORT. goal.

mar·cha f. *(movimiento)* march, movement; *(velocidad)* speed, velocity; *(salida)* departure; FIG. *(progresión)* march *<la m. del tiempo* the march of time>; *(curso)* course, progress *<la m. de acontecimientos* the course of events>; MUS. march; MECH. *(funcionamiento)* operation, running ♦ **a largas marchas** quickly, speedily • **a toda m.** at full speed • **dar m. atrás** to go into reverse, reverse • **estar en m.** *(comenzar)* to be underway; *(funcionar)* to be running *or* working (a machine) • **m. atlética** SPORT. walking race • **m. atrás** AUTO. reverse • **m. forzada** MIL. forced march • **m. fúnebre** funeral march • **Marcha Real** Spanish national anthem • **poner en m.** to start (a motor) • **ponerse en m.** to start off (on a trip) • **sobre la m.** on the double.

mar·cha·dor, –do·ra adj. AMER. *(andarín)* walking; *(amblador)* ambling.

mar·cha·mar tr. to mark, stamp (in customs).

mar·cha·me·ro m. customs marker *or* stamper.

mar·cha·mo m. *(de las aduanas)* customs seal *or* stamp;

ARG. tax charged on each head of slaughtered cattle; FIG. *(señal)* mark, stamp.

mar·chan·te, –ta m.f. *(vendedor)* merchant, dealer; *(cliente)* customer, patron.

mar·chan·te·rí·a *or* **mar·chan·tí·a** f. C. AMER., VEN. clientele, customers.

mar·char intr. *(ir)* to go *<marcho a Nueva York* I am going to New York>; *(andar)* to walk; *(moverse)* to move, go; *(funcionar)* to run, work; FIG. *(progresar)* to go, proceed *<todo marcha bien* everything is going well>; *(desenvolverse)* to unfold, develop; MIL. to march; ARG., BOL. to go quickly —reflex. to go (away), leave.

mar·chi·ta·ble adj. perishable, that withers.

mar·chi·ta·mien·to m. withering, wilting.

mar·chi·tar tr. *(secar)* to wither, to wilt; FIG. *(debilitar)* to debilitate, weaken —reflex. *(secarse)* to wither, wilt; *(debilitarse)* to become weak, languish.

mar·chi·tez f. withered *or* wilted condition.

mar·chi·to, –ta adj. withered, wilted.

mar·cho·so, –sa adj. COLL. cheerful, merry.

ma·re·a f. GEOL. tide; *(viento)* sea breeze; FIG. flood; *(rocío)* dew; *(llovizna)* drizzle; *(basura)* litter (washed off the streets); *(orilla)* seashore, beach ♦ **contra viento y m.** against all odds • **m. alta** high tide • **m. baja** low tide • **m. creciente** *or* **entrante** rising tide • **m. menguante** *or* **descendente** low tide.

ma·re·a·do, –da adj. *(malo)* sick; *(en el mar)* seasick; *(bebido)* drunk; *(aturdido)* dizzy.

ma·re·a·mien·to m. seasickness.

ma·re·ar tr. MARIT. to navigate, sail; *(fastidiar)* to annoy, bother —reflex. *(tener náuseas)* to become nauseated; *(en barcos)* to become seasick; *(averiarse)* to become damaged (at sea); AMER. to fade (cloth) ♦ **aguja de m.** compass.

ma·re·ja·da f. MARIT. swell, turbulence (of waves); FIG. *(agitación)* agitation, ferment (of the population).

ma·re·mag·no m. COLL. var. of **mare mágnum.**

ma·re mág·num m. [pl. **ma·re mág·num**] FIG., COLL. *(abundancia)* abundance, profusion; *(confusión)* jumble, mess; *(gentío)* crowd, multitude.

ma·re·mo·to m. seaquake.

ma·re·o m. *(náusea)* sickness, nausea; *(en los barcos)* seasickness; *(en otros vehículos)* motion sickness; FIG., COLL. *(molestia)* headache, nuisance.

mar·fil m. ivory ♦ **m. vegetal** BOT. ivory nut.

mar·fi·la·do, –da NEOL. *or* **mar·fi·le·ño, –ña** adj. POET. ivory, of ivory.

mar·ga f. MIN. marl.

mar·ga·ri·na f. margarine.

mar·ga·ri·ta f. BOT. daisy; *(perla)* margarite, pearl; ZOOL. periwinkle; ECUAD. hyacinth ♦ **echar margaritas a los cerdos** to throw pearls before swine.

mar·gen m. *or* f. *(límite)* margin, border, edge; *(orilla)* bank (of a river); *(nota)* marginal note; FIG. *(amplitud)* leeway, margin *<me dejaron m. en mis trabajos* they gave me leeway in my work>; *(ocasión)* occasion, opportunity; COM. margin ♦ **al m.** *(de papel)* in the margin; FIG. *(afuera)* on the fringe *<vive al m. de la sociedad* he lives on the fringe of society> • **dar m. para** FIG. to give occasion for, give an opportunity for • **m. de error** MATH. margin of error • **m. de ganancias** COM. profit margin.

mar·gi·na·ción f. margination.

mar·gi·na·do, –da I. past part. see **marginar** II. adj. *(que tiene una margen)* marginated; BOT. marginated; FIG. *(apartado)* on the fringe of society III. m.f. FIG. *(persona apartada)* person on the fringe of society.

mar·gi·na·dor, –do·ra m. PRINT. margin stop.

mar·gi·nal adj. marginal.

mar·gi·na·li·dad f. margination.

mar·gi·na·lis·mo m. ECON. marginalism.

mar·gi·na·lis·ta adj. & m.f. ECON. marginalist.

mar·gi·nar tr. *(dejar márgenes)* to marginate, leave a margin on; *(poner notas)* to make marginal notes on; FIG. *(apartar)* to leave out, leave aside.

mar·gue·ra f. marlpit.

ma·ria·no, –na adj. RELIG. Marian, of the Virgin Mary.

ma·rí·as f.pl. ♦ **las tres m.** ASTRON. Orion's Belt.

ma·ri·ca m. COLL., DEROG. *(homosexual)* fairy, queer —f. ORNITH. magpie.

ma·ri·cas·ta·ña f. ♦ **en tiempos de Maricastaña** in days of yore, in the olden days.

ma·ri·cón m. SL., DEROG. *(homosexual)* faggot, gay man; *(pesado)* jerk.

ma·ri·co·na·da f. SL., DEROG. *(acción de maricón)* action typical of gay men; *(mala pasada)* dirty trick.

ma·ri·co·ne·ar intr. SL., DEROG. to act effeminately.

ma·ri·co·ne·o m. SL., DEROG. action typical of gay men.

ma·ri·co·ne·rí·a f. SL., DEROG. *(acción de maricón)* action typical of gay men; *(mala pasada)* dirty trick; *(grupo)* group of gay men.

ma·ri·da·je m. *(vida de los casados)* married life, wedlock; FIG. *(unión)* union, harmony; *(contubernio)* unnatural alliance.

ma·ri·dar intr. *(casar)* to marry, wed; *(vivir juntos)* to live together, cohabit —tr. FIG. to join, unite.

ma·ri·do m. husband, spouse.

ma·ri·gua·na *or* **ma·ri·hua·na** *or* **ma·ri·jua·na** f. marijuana.

ma·ri·ma·cho m. COLL. mannish woman.

ma·ri·man·do·na f. domineering woman.

ma·rim·ba f. *(tambor)* drum; AMER. *(tímpano)* kettledrum; *(xilófono)* marimba, xylophone; ARG. beating, thrashing.

ma·ri·na f. *(costa)* coast; *(náutica)* navigation, seamanship; MIL. navy; PAINT. seascape ♦ **Infantería de Marina** Marine Corps • **m. de guerra** navy • **m. mercante** merchant marine — see **marino, –na.**

ma·ri·nar tr. CUL. to marinate; MARIT. *(tripular)* to man (a ship).

ma·ri·ne·ra I. f. *(blusa)* middy blouse, sailor top; CHILE, ECUAD., PERU marinera (folk dance) ♦ **a la m.** sailor-style II. adj. see **marinero, –ra.**

ma·ri·ne·rí·a f. MARIT. *(profesión)* seafaring, sailoring; *(tripulación)* ship's crew, seamen.

ma·ri·ne·ro, –ra MARIT. I. adj. *(gobernable)* seaworthy; *(marino)* marine, sea; *(marinesco)* sailor, of sailors II. m. *(marino)* sailor, mariner; ZOOL. argonaut, paper nautilus ♦ **m. de agua dulce** landlubber —f. see **marinera.**

ma·ri·no, –na I. adj. marine, sea ♦ **azul m.** navy blue II. m. sailor, mariner —f. see **marina.**

ma·rio·ne·ta f. marionette, puppet.

ma·ri·po·sa I. f. ENTOM. butterfly; CUBA, ORNITH. finch; TECH. *(llave)* butterfly valve; *(tuerca)* butterfly *or* wing nut; *(lamparilla)* night light; ECUAD., MEX., BOT. orchid; CUBA butterfly jasmine; COL., HOND. pinwheel —m.f. FIG., DEROG. fairy, queer II. adj. SPORT. butterfly *<braza m.* butterfly stroke>.

ma·ri·po·se·ar intr. FIG. *(ser inconstante)* to be fickle *or* capricious; *(dar vueltas)* to hover *or* flit about.

ma·ri·po·se·o m. flitting about.

ma·ri·po·són m. COLL. *(galanteador)* Romeo, Don Juan; DEROG. *(homosexual)* pansy, fairy.

ma·ri·qui·ta f. ENTOM. *(coleóptero)* ladybug; *(hemíptero)* firebug; ORNITH. parakeet; ARG. folk dance —m. COLL., DEROG. sissy, pansy.

ma·ri·sa·bi·di·lla f. COLL. bluestocking.

ma·ris·cal m. MIL. marshal; *(herrador)* blacksmith ♦ **m. de campo** field marshal • **m. de logis** quartermaster.

ma·ris·car §70 tr. to gather (shellfish).

ma·ris·co m. ZOOL. shellfish, crustacean.

ma·ris·ma f. salt marsh.

ma·ris·que·ro, –ra m.f. shellfish gatherer.

ma·ris·ta m. & adj. RELIG. Marist.

ma·ri·tal adj. marital.

ma·ri·ta·ta f. CHILE, MIN. *(canal)* trough for collecting metal dust; *(cedazo)* sieve ♦ **maritatas** C. AMER. knickknacks, trinkets.

ma·rí·ti·mo, –ma adj. maritime, sea ♦ **por vía m.** by sea.

mar·mi·ta f. pot, saucepan.

mar·mi·tón m. kitchen helper.

már·mol m. marble ♦ **de m.** FIG. hardhearted, cold.

mar·mo·le·rí·a f. *(conjunto de mármoles)* marbles, marblework; *(obra)* marble; *(taller)* workshop, studio (of marble cutter).

mar·mo·lis·ta m. *(el que labra)* marble cutter, sculptor; *(vendedor)* marble dealer.

mar·mó·re·o, –a adj. marble, marmoreal.

mar·mo·ta f. ZOOL. marmot; FIG. *(dormilón)* sleepyhead; COLL. *(criada)* maid; *(gorra)* worsted cap ♦ **dormir como una m.** to sleep like a log.

ma·ro·me·ar intr. AMER. *(hacer volatines)* to perform on a tightrope; COLL. *(vacilar)* to be a chameleon (change sides easily); *(en una hamaca)* to swing in a hammock.

ma·ro·me·ro m. AMER. tightrope walker; PERU, COLL. opportunist (politician).

ma·ro·mo m. SL. guy.

ma·ro·ni·ta adj. & m.f. Maronite (Lebanese Christian).

mar·qué, marque see **marcar.**

mar·qués m. marquis.

mar·que·sa f. *(persona)* marquise, marchioness; *(sillón)* armchair, easy chair ♦ **m. de vidrio** marquee.

mar·que·sa·do m. marquisate.

mar·que·si·na f. *(cobertizo)* marquee, canopy; *(sillón)* armchair, easy chair.

mar·que·te·rí·a f. *(taracea)* marquetry, inlaid work; *(ebanistería)* cabinet work.

ma·rra·jo, –ja I. adj. *(taimado)* mean, vicious (bulls); FIG. *(hipócrita)* sly, cunning; MEX. stingy, miserly II. m. ICHTH. shark.

ma·rra·mun·cia f. VEN., COLL. flattery, cajolery.

ma·rra·na f. ZOOL. sow; DEROG. *(mujer)* slut; TECH. axle (of a water wheel).

ma·rra·na·da *or* **ma·rra·ne·rí·a** f. FIG., COLL. *(mala pasada)* dirty *or* rotten trick; *(suciedad)* filth, filthiness.

ma·rra·no I. adj. dirty, filthy II. m. ZOOL. pig, hog; FIG., COLL. *(sucio)* pig, slob; *(canalla)* swine; TECH. pressure equalizer; DEROG. converted Jew.

ma·rrar intr. *(errar)* to miss (a shot); *(fallar)* to fail; FIG. *(desviarse)* to go astray *or* wrong.

ma·rra·zo m. *(hacha)* double-bladed ax; MEX. bayonet.

ma·rro m. *(juego de niños)* tag; *(con bolos)* ninepins; *(ladeo)* dodge, swerve; *(falta)* slip, error; MEX. mallet.

ma·rrón I. adj. brown II. m. *(color)* brown; *(castaña)* candied chestnut; COL. paper hair curler; *(martillo)* blacksmith's hammer.

ma·rro·quí adj. & m.f. [pl. **-quí·es**] Moroccan.

ma·rro·qui·ne·rí·a f. morocco (leatherwork).

Ma·rrue·cos m. Morocco.

ma·rru·lle·rí·a *or* **ma·rru·lle·rí·a** f. coaxing, wheedling.

ma·rru·lle·ro, –ra I. adj. conniving II. m.f. conniver, flatterer.

Mar·se·lla f. Marseilles, Marseille.

mar·so·pa *or* **mar·so·pla** f. ZOOL. porpoise.

mar·su·pial adj. & m. ZOOL. marsupial.

mar·ta f. ZOOL. pine marten ♦ **m. cebellina** ZOOL. sable.

mar·ta·gón, –go·na COLL. I. adj. shrewd, astute II. m.f. shrewd *or* astute person.

mar·ta·jar tr. AMER. to crush (corn).

Mar·te m. ASTRON., MYTH. Mars; FIG. *(guerra)* war.

mar·tes m. Tuesday ♦ **cada lunes y cada m.** every day of the week, all the time • **m. de carnaval** *or* **carnestolendas** RELIG. Shrove Tuesday.

mar·ti·lla·da f. hammer blow.

mar·ti·lla·dor, –do·ra I. adj. hammering II. m.f. hammerer.

mar·ti·llar tr. *(golpear)* to hammer; FIG. *(oprimir)* to oppress, torment.

mar·ti·lla·zo m. hard blow of a hammer.

mar·ti·lle·a·dor, –do·ra adj. & m.f. var. of **martillador, –dora.**

mar·ti·lle·ar intr. var. of **martillar.**

mar·ti·lle·o m. hammering.

mar·ti·lle·ro m. AMER. auctioneer.

mar·ti·llo m. *(herramienta)* hammer; *(mallo)* gavel *<m. de subastador* auctioneer's gavel>; ICHTH. hammerhead (shark); FIG. *(establecimiento)* auction house; *(persiguidor)* persecutor; ANAT. malleus, hammer (bone of the ear); SPORT. *(en atletismo)* hammer; MECH. *(del reloj)* hammer (of a clock); MUS. tuning hammer; CARIB., CHILE wing (of a building) ♦ **a macha m.** *(firmemente)* firmly; *(con solidez)* strongly but crudely made • **a m.** by hammering, with a hammer • **m. de fragua** *or* **m. pilón** MECH. drop hammer • **m. neumático** MECH. pneumatic drill • **m. perforador** pneumatic drill.

Mar·ti·ni·ca f. Martinique.
mar·tín pes·ca·dor m. ORNITH. kingfisher.
mar·ti·ne·te[1] m. ORNITH. heron; *(plumas)* heron plumes.
mar·ti·ne·te[2] m. *(macillo)* hammer (of a piano); *(mazo)* drop hammer; *(para clavar estacas)* pile driver; *(cante)* Andalusian song ♦ **m. a vapor** steam hammer • **m. de fragua** trip hammer.
mar·tin·ga·la f. *(en naipes)* martingale (in cards); FIG. *(artimaña)* trick, ploy ♦ **martingalas** breeches worn under armor.
már·tir m.f. martyr.
mar·ti·rio m. martyrdom.
mar·ti·ri·zar §04 tr. *(hacer sufrir martirio)* to martyr, martyrize; FIG. *(atormentar)* to torment.
mar·xis·mo m. POL. Marxism.
mar·xis·mo-le·ni·nis·mo m. POL. Marxism-Leninism.
mar·xis·ta adj. & m.f. POL. Marxist.
mar·zo m. March.
mas §G46 conj. but <*no lo vi, m. lo escuché* I didn't see it, but I heard it> ♦ **m. que** even if, although <*debes irte, m. que no estés listo* you ought to go, even if you aren't ready>.
más §G24, 29 I. adv. more <*m. importante* more important>; most <*la alumna m. inteligente* the most intelligent student>; longer <*durar m.* to last longer>; rather <*m. quiero morir* I would rather die> ♦ **a lo m.** at most, at the most • **a m.** besides, in addition • **a m. de** besides, in addition to • **a m. no poder** as much as possible *or* as can be • **a m. y mejor** a lot, really <*llovía a m. y mejor* it was really raining> • **como el que m.** as much as anyone, as much as the next person • **de m.** too much, extra • **en lo m. mínimo** in the slightest • **en m.** more • **estar de m.** to be superfluous *or* unnecessary • **m. allá** further • **m. bien** rather • **m. de** more than <*m. de cien pesos* more than a hundred pesos> • **m. o menos** more or less • **m. que** more than <*yo sé m. que él* I know more than he>; *(sino)* but, except <*nadie puede hacerlo m. que Carlos* no one can do it except Charles> • **ni m. ni menos** no more, no less • **no m.** only, no more • **no m. que** only • **por m. que** however much, no matter how much • **¿qué m. da?** what difference does it make? • **sin m. ni m.** without further ado II. m. MATH. plus sign ♦ **el m. y el menos** the pros and the cons • **tener sus m. y sus menos** COLL. to have good points and bad points III. prep. plus <*cinco m. ocho son trece* five plus eight is thirteen>.
ma·sa f. *(agregación)* mass; *(volumen)* volume, bulk; *(cuerpo compacto)* lump <*una m. de arcilla* a lump of clay>; *(el pueblo)* people, masses <*la m. popular* the common people>; *(pasta)* dough; FIG. *(muchedumbre)* (the) masses; *(carácter)* nature, disposition; PHYS. mass; ELEC. ground; MAS. mortar; MIL. uniform money; ARG. marzipan candy; ECUAD. puff pastry ♦ **con las manos en la m.** FIG. in the act, redhanded • **en la m. de la sangre** FIG. in one's blood • **en m.** *(todos juntos)* all together, en masse; *(en grande escala)* mass <*protesta en m.* mass protest> • **m. atómica** PHYS. atomic mass • **m. crítica** PHYS. critical mass • **m. de aire** METEOROL. air mass • **m. molecular** PHYS. molecular mass • **producción en m.** mass production.
ma·sa·crar tr. to massacre.
ma·sa·cre m. massacre.
ma·sa·je m. massage.
ma·sa·jis·ta m. masseur —f. masseuse.
ma·sa·to m. AMER. fermented drink made of corn, banana or cassava; COL. dessert made of coconut, corn and sugar; MEX. ground corn (carried when traveling).
mas·ca·da f. AMER. plug, chew (of tobacco); ARG., CHILE *(bocado)* mouthful; ARG. *(utilidad)* profit, gain; MEX. silk neckerchief.
mas·ca·dor, –do·ra I. adj. chewing II. m.f. chewer.
mas·ca·du·ra f. *(acción de mascar)* chewing; HOND. roll, bun.
mas·car §70 tr. *(masticar)* to chew; FIG., COLL. *(mascullar)* to mumble ♦ **m. chocolate** ECUAD. to get bloody (in a fight).
más·ca·ra f. *(careta)* mask; *(traje)* disguise, costume; FIG. *(pretexto)* mask, pretense —m.f. FIG. *(persona)* masker, masquerader ♦ **baile de máscaras** masquerade, masked

ball • **m. antigás** gas mask • **m. de oxígeno** oxygen mask • **quitarse la m.** FIG. to drop one's pretenses.
mas·ca·ra·da f. *(fiesta)* masquerade, masked ball; *(desfile)* masked parade; FIG. *(cosa falsa)* masquerade, charade.
mas·ca·ri·lla f. *(máscara pequeña)* half mask; *(del muerto)* death mask.
mas·ca·rón m. *(máscara grande)* large mask; *(adorno)* sculpted head *or* face (on furniture, fountains) ♦ **m. de proa** MARIT. figurehead.
mas·co·ta f. mascot.
mas·cu·jar tr. COLL. *(mascar mal)* to chew hastily, gulp down; FIG. *(mascullar)* to mumble, mutter.
mas·cu·li·ni·dad f. masculinity.
mas·cu·li·ni·zar §04 tr. to make masculine.
mas·cu·li·no, –na I. adj. BIOL., BOT. male; *(propio de los hombres)* masculine, manly; GRAM. masculine II. m. GRAM. masculine (gender).
mas·cu·llar tr. COLL. to mumble, mutter.
ma·se·ra f. *(artesa)* trough (for kneading dough); ZOOL. large crab.
ma·si·fi·car §70 tr. to extend to the public.
ma·si·lla f. putty.
ma·si·ta f. MIL. cost of uniform (deducted from soldier's pay); AMER. biscuit, pastry.
ma·si·vo, –va adj. *(grande)* massive; mass <*comunicación m.* mass communication>.
ma·són m. Mason, Freemason.
mas·so·ne·rí·a f. Masonry, Freemasonry.
ma·só·ni·co, –ca adj. Masonic.
ma·so·quis·mo m. masochism.
ma·so·quis·ta I. adj. masochistic II. m.f. masochist.
mas·qué, masque see mascar.
mas·ti·ca·ble I. adj. chewy, chewable II. m. chewy caramel.
mas·ti·ca·ción f. chewing, mastication.
mas·ti·car §70 tr. *(triturar)* to chew, masticate; FIG. *(ruminar)* to ponder over, ruminate.
más·til m. MARIT. mast; *(palo)* pole; *(de una pluma)* quill; *(faja)* loincloth, breechcloth (worn by Indians); BOT. stem; MUS. neck (of a stringed instrument) ♦ **m. totémico** totem pole.
mas·tín m. mastiff ♦ **m. danés** Great Dane.
más·ti·que m. mastic.
mas·ti·qué, mastique see masticar.
mas·ti·tis f. MED. mastitis.
mas·to·don·te m. mastodon.
mas·toi·des adj. & f. [pl. -des] ANAT. mastoid.
mas·tuer·zo m. BOT. cress; PERU, ECUAD., BOT. nasturtium; FIG. *(tonto)* dolt, dunce.
mas·tur·ba·ción f. masturbation.
mas·tur·bar tr. & reflex. to masturbate.
ma·ta f. *(arbusto)* bush, shrub; *(pie de una planta)* sprig, tuft; *(campo de árboles)* orchard, grove; *(de pelo)* head of hair; BOT. mastic tree; VEN. copse, thicket; CUBA shrub ♦ **a salto de m.** *(prófugo)* on the run; FIG. hastily, furtively • **m. de la seda** BOT. milkweed • **m. de pelo** head of hair.
ma·ta·cán m. MIL. machicolation; *(veneno)* dog poison; BOT. nux vomica; CONST. large piece of rubble; *(en naipes)* two of clubs; ECUAD. fawn; HOND. fat calf.
ma·ta·can·de·las m. [pl. -las] candle snuffer.
ma·ta·chín m. *(matarife)* butcher; FIG., COLL. *(matón)* bully, troublemaker.
ma·ta·de·ro m. *(de ganado)* slaughterhouse; FIG., COLL. *(trabajo)* drudgery, chore; AMER., COLL. bachelor's pad.
ma·ta·dor, –do·ra I. adj. *(que mata)* killing; COLL. *(penoso)* killing, deadly (work) II. m.f. *(asesino)* killer, murderer —m. *(en naipes)* trump card; TAUR. bullfighter, matador.
ma·ta·du·ra f. VET. sore, gall.
ma·ta·fue·go m. *(aparato)* fire extinguisher; *(bombero)* fireman.
má·ta·las ca·llan·do m.f. COLL. wolf in sheep's clothing.
ma·ta·mo·ros [pl. -ros] I. adj. bragging, blustering II. m. braggart.
ma·ta·mos·cas m. [pl. -cas] fly swatter.
ma·tan·za f. *(acción de matar)* killing, slaughtering; *(de muchas personas)* massacre, slaughter; *(de animales)* slaughtering, butchering; *(época)* slaughtering *or* butchering

season; *(carne del cerdo)* pork (products); FIG., COLL. *(empeño)* determination, persistence.

ma·ta·pe·rra·da f. COLL. high jinks, mischievous prank.

ma·ta·pe·rros m. [pl. **-rros**] COLL. street urchin.

ma·tar tr. *(quitar la vida)* to kill; *(a los animales)* to butcher, slaughter; *(apagar)* to put out, extinguish <*m. el fuego* to put out the fire>; *(echar agua a la cal)* to slake (lime); *(en el juego)* to beat, top (a card); FIG. to pass, kill <*m. el tiempo* to kill time>; *(alterar la salud)* to kill <*el alcohol le está matando* alcohol is killing him>; *(arruinar)* to ruin, break <*m. un proyecto* to ruin a project>; *(incomodar)* to pester, annoy; CARP. to round off, bevel; PAINT. to tone down (colors); METAL. to dull, mat ♦ **estar a m. con** FIG. to be at loggerheads with • **matarlas callando** FIG. to kill with kindness —reflex. *(quitarse la vida)* to kill oneself, commit suicide; to be killed <*su hijo se mató en un accidente* his son was killed in an accident>; FIG. *(acongojarse)* to kill oneself, wear oneself out <*no te mates estudiando* don't wear yourself out studying> —intr. to kill.

ma·ta·ri·fe m. butcher, slaughterer.

ma·ta·rra·tas m. [pl. **-tas**] *(raticida)* rat poison; COLL. *(aguardiente malo)* rotgut, firewater.

ma·ta·sa·nos m. COLL. quack (doctor).

ma·ta·se·llar tr. to cancel, postmark.

ma·ta·se·llos m. [pl. **-llos**] *(instrumento)* canceller; *(marca)* postmark, cancellation.

ma·ta·sie·te m. COLL. braggart, bully.

ma·ta·tí·as m. [pl. **-as**] COLL. moneylender.

ma·ta·zón f. AMER. massacre.

ma·te[1] adj. *(sin brillo)* matte (finish); *(apagado)* dull (sound).

ma·te[2] m. checkmate, mate (in chess) ♦ **dar jaque m.** to checkmate.

ma·te[3] m. AMER., BOT. *(arbusto)* maté tree; *(calabaza)* maté gourd; AMER. *(vasija)* maté pot; *(bebida)* maté; COLL. *(cabeza)* gourd (head) ♦ **hierba** or **yerba m.** maté (tea).

ma·te·ar intr. to drink maté.

ma·te·má·ti·co, –ca I. adj. mathematical II. m.f. mathematician —f. mathematics ♦ **matemáticas** mathematics.

ma·te·ria f. *(substancia)* matter; *(material)* material, substance; FIG. *(asunto)* matter, topic <*hablaremos de esas materias otro día* we will speak about those matters another day>; MED. matter; EDUC. subject ♦ **en m. de** as regards, in the matter of • **entrar en m.** to come to the point, get down to business • **índice de materias** table of contents • **m. colorante** dyestuff • **m. de estado** POL. affair of state • **m. gris** ANAT. gray matter • **m. orgánica** CHEM. organic matter • **m. prima** INDUS. raw material.

ma·te·rial I. adj. material; FIG. *(corpóreo)* physical; *(materialista)* materialistic II. m. *(aparato)* materials, equipment; *(substancia)* material, substance <*hecho de buen m.* made of good material>; *(ingrediente)* ingredient; ARG. adobe.

ma·te·ria·li·dad f. *(calidad de material)* materiality; *(apariencia)* outward appearance.

ma·te·ria·lis·mo m. materialism.

ma·te·ria·lis·ta I. adj. materialistic II. m.f. materialist.

ma·te·ria·li·za·ción f. materialization.

ma·te·rial·men·te adv. materially, physically.

ma·ter·nal adj. maternal.

ma·ter·nal·men·te adv. maternally.

ma·ter·ni·dad f. *(estado)* maternity; *(establecimiento)* maternity hospital.

ma·ter·no, –na adj. *(maternal)* maternal, motherly; maternal <*abuelo m.* maternal grandfather>; *(nativo)* mother, native (language) <*lengua m.* native language>.

ma·te·ro, –ra I. adj. maté-drinking II. m.f. maté drinker.

ma·ti·nal adj. morning, matinal.

ma·tiz m. [pl. **-ti·ces**] *(de color)* shade, tint; FIG. *(aspecto)* shade, nuance (of meaning).

ma·ti·za·ción f. shading.

ma·ti·zar §04 tr. *(juntar distintos colores)* to match, harmonize (colors); *(teñir)* to tint, shade (one color with another); FIG. *(variar)* to vary, introduce variety into <*m. la vóz* to vary one's tone of voice>.

ma·to m. BOT. undergrowth, scrub; VEN., ZOOL. lizard.

ma·to·jo m. BOT. *(mata)* shrub, bush; *(planta)* saltwort.

ma·tón m. COLL. bully.

ma·to·ne·ar intr. COLL. to bully, play the tough guy —tr. C. AMER. to murder.

ma·to·nis·mo m. bullying.

ma·to·rral m. *(maleza)* brushwood, scrub; *(soto)* thicket.

ma·tra·ca f. *(instrumento)* wooden rattle; FIG., COLL. *(burla)* pestering, taunting ♦ **dar la m. a alguien** to pester or taunt someone.

ma·tra·ca·la·da. crowd, mob (of people).

ma·tra·que·ar intr. COLL. *(hacer ruido)* to make noise (with a rattle); *(burlarse)* to pester, taunt.

ma·tra·que·o COLL. *(ruido)* racket, rattling; *(burla)* pestering, taunting.

ma·tre·rí·a f. cunning, shrewdness.

ma·tre·ro, –ra I. adj. *(astuto)* cunning, shrewd; AMER. distrustful, suspicious II. m. AMER. bandit.

ma·triar·ca·do m. matriarchy.

ma·triar·cal adj. matriarchal.

ma·tri·ci·da m.f. matricide (person).

ma·tri·ci·dio m. matricide (crime).

ma·trí·cu·la f. *(lista)* register, list; *(inscripción)* registration, matriculation; *(gente matriculada)* roll; AUTO. registration ♦ **m. de mar** seaman's or mariner's register.

ma·tri·cu·la·ción f. registration.

ma·tri·cu·la·do, –da I. past part. see **matricular** II. adj. *(en escuela, universidad)* enrolled, registered; *(con matrícula)* registered.

ma·tri·cu·lar tr. & reflex. to register, matriculate.

ma·tri·mo·nial adj. matrimonial.

ma·tri·mo·niar intr. to marry, get married.

ma·tri·mo·nio m. *(casamiento)* marriage, matrimony; RELIG. matrimony; COLL. *(marido y mujer)* married couple ♦ **contraer m.** to marry • **fuera del m.** out of wedlock • **m. civil** civil marriage • **m. por poderes** marriage by proxy • **m. rato** unconsummated marriage • **partida de m.** marriage certificate.

ma·triz I. f. [pl. **-tri·ces**] ANAT., PHYSIOL. womb, uterus; *(del talonario)* counterfoil, stub; TECH. *(molde)* mold, die; *(tuerca)* nut; MATH., MIN. matrix II. adj. FIG. *(madre)* mother <*lengua m.* mother tongue>; *(original)* original (draft, copy) ♦ **casa m.** headquarters, main office.

ma·tro·na f. *(madre de familia)* matron; *(partera)* midwife; *(encargada)* matron.

ma·tro·nal adj. matronly.

ma·tun·go, –ga adj. AMER. worn out; ARG., CUBA old, worn out (horse).

ma·tu·rran·ga f. *(treta)* trickery, cajolery.

ma·tu·rran·gue·ro, –ra adj. AMER. tricky, cajoling.

ma·tu·sa·lén m. Methuselah, very old man.

ma·tu·te m. *(acción)* smuggling; *(contrabando)* contraband, smuggled goods; *(garito)* gambling den.

ma·tu·te·ar intr. to smuggle.

ma·tu·te·ro, –ra m.f. smuggler.

ma·tu·ti·no, –na I. adj. morning, matutinal II. m. morning newspaper.

mau·la I. f. *(cosa inútil)* junk, trash; *(retal)* remnant; *(engaño)* trick II. m.f. *(persona inútil)* good-for-nothing; *(estafador)* swindler, cheat; *(mal pagador)* deadbeat, poor payer.

mau·le·ar intr. CHILE to cheat.

mau·le·rí·a f. *(tienda)* remnant shop; *(engaño)* cunning, trickery.

mau·le·ro, –ra m.f. *(vendedor)* remnant seller; *(estafador)* swindler, cheat.

mau·llar §82 intr. to meow, mew.

mau·lli·do or **ma·ú·llo** m. *(voz)* meow, mew; *(acción)* meowing, mewing.

Mau·ri·cio m. Mauritius.

mau·ri·cia·no, –na adj. & m.f. Mauritian.

Mau·ri·ta·nia f. Mauritania.

mau·ri·ta·no, –na adj. & m.f. Mauritanian.

mau·so·le·o m. mausoleum.

má·xi·ma I. f. *(aforismo)* maxim; *(temperatura)* maximum temperature II. adj. see **máximo, –ma.**

má·xi·ma·men·te adv. principally, chiefly.

má·xi·me adv. principally, all the more.

má·xi·mo, –ma I. adj. maximum, greatest <*m. común divi-*

sor greatest common denominator>; highest <*el punto m.* the highest point>; greatest <*el pensador m. de su tiempo* the greatest thinker of his time> **II.** m. maximum ♦ **al m.** to the maximum • **como m.** at the most • **hacer el m.** to do one's utmost —f. see **máxima.**

má·xi·mum m. maximum.

ma·ya I. adj. Maya, Mayan **II.** m.f. *(persona)* Maya, Mayan —m. *(idioma)* Mayan language.

ma·yal m. *(palo de molino)* shaft (for turning a mill); *(desgranador)* threshing flail.

ma·yes·tá·ti·co, –ca adj. majestic.

ma·yo m. *(mes)* May; *(asta adornada)* maypole; *(corona)* love wreath ♦ **mayos** May Day festivals.

ma·yó·li·ca f. majolica ware.

ma·yo·ne·sa f. mayonnaise.

ma·yor §G24 I. adj. *(más grande)* bigger, larger <*la m. parte* the larger part>; *(el más grande)* biggest, largest; *(importante)* greater; *(el más importante)* greatest <*el problema m.* the greatest problem>; *(de más edad)* older, elder <*mi hermano m.* my older brother>; elderly <*un señor m.* an elderly gentleman>; *(el más viejo)* oldest, eldest; *(adulto)* adult, grown-up; *(principal)* major, main <*calle m.* main street>; RELIG. high <*misa m.* high mass>; MUS. major ♦ **al por m.** COM. wholesale • **caza m.** big game hunting • **estado m.** staff (military) • **hacerse m.** to come of age • **m. de edad** of age • **por m.** FIG. summarily **II.** m. *(jefe)* superior, chief ♦ **alzarse a mayores** FIG. to become arrogant • **mayores** elders, ancestors • **m. que** MATH. greater than (sign) —f. LOG. major, major premise.

ma·yo·ral m. *(pastor)* head shepherd; *(cochero)* stagecoach driver; *(capataz)* foreman, overseer; *(mampostero)* rent, tithe collector; AMER. *(cobrador)* trolley conductor.

ma·yo·ra·lí·a f. *(rebaño)* flock; *(sueldo)* salary (of shepherd).

ma·yo·raz·ga f. *(dueña)* female owner (of an entailed estate); *(esposa)* wife of owner (of entailed estate).

ma·yo·raz·go m. *(derecho)* right of primogeniture; *(herencia)* estate inherited by primogeniture; *(heredero)* inheritor of an entailed estate; *(hijo primogénito)* first-born son; COLL. *(primogenitura)* seniority.

ma·yor·do·mí·a f. *(cargo)* stewardship; *(oficina)* majordomo's office.

ma·yor·do·mo m. steward, butler, majordomo; RELIG. churchwarden.

ma·yo·rí·a f. majority ♦ **en la m. de los casos** in most cases • **en su m.** in the main • **m. absoluta** absolute majority • **m. de edad** majority, legal age • **m. relativa** relative majority.

ma·yo·ri·dad f. majority, adult age.

ma·yo·ris·ta I. adj. wholesale **II.** m. *(comerciante)* wholesaler; *(estudiante)* pupil of upper grades (grammar school).

ma·yo·ri·ta·rio, –ria adj. majority <*partido m.* majority party>.

ma·yús·cu·lo, –la I. adj. *(letra)* capital (letter); *(importante)* important, prominent; COLL. *(grande)* enormous, tremendous <*error m.* tremendous mistake> **II.** f. capital letter.

ma·za f. MIL. *(arma)* mace; *(baston ceremonial)* mace; *(utensilio para machacar)* mallet; *(martinete)* drop hammer, pile driver; *(objeto)* object tied to animal's tail or person's clothes (as practical joke); MUS. drumstick; FIG., COLL. *(persona pesada)* bore, pest; AMER. *(cubo de rueda)* hub (of wheel).

ma·za·co·te m. *(barrilla)* soda ash; *(hormigón)* concrete; AMER. *(mezcla)* mixture, mess; FIG., COLL. *(plato mal hecho)* lumpy mess <*el flan se ha hecho un m.* the pudding is a lumpy mess>; *(obra artística fea)* monstrosity, crude work of art; *(persona pesada)* bore, pest.

ma·za·co·tu·do, –da adj. AMER. *(aterronado)* lumpy, dried-out (food); *(feo)* ugly, shapeless (work of art).

ma·za·mo·rra f. AMER. *(gachas)* cornmeal mush, porridge; *(migajas)* biscuit crumbs; *(trozos)* crumbs, bits; MARIT. mess made of biscuit crumbs; VET. blister, sore (on horse's hoof).

ma·za·mo·rre·ro, –ra m.f. *(vendedor)* seller of cornmeal mush; PERU person from Lima.

ma·za·pán m. marzipan.

ma·zar §04 tr. to churn (milk).

ma·za·zo m. blow with a mace or club.

maz·mo·rra f. dungeon.

maz·nar tr. *(amasar)* to knead, squeeze; *(machacar)* to beat (hot iron).

ma·zo m. *(martillo)* mallet, wooden hammer; *(manojo)* bundle, bunch <*m. de llaves* bunch of keys>; *(puñado)* wad (of paper, banknotes); MUS. drumstick; FIG. *(pesado)* bore, annoying person ♦ **a Dios orando y con el m. dando** God helps those who help themselves.

ma·zor·ca f. AGR. *(de maíz)* ear, cob (of corn); *(panoja)* pod (of cacao); *(husada)* spindle; AMER., FIG. authoritarian government, junta.

ma·zor·que·ro m. AMER. terrorist, extremist.

me §G30 pron. me <*me vieron en el jardín* they saw me in the garden>; me, to me <*dame la llave* give me the key>; me, for me <*ella me compró un regalo* she bought a present for me>; from me <*me quitó el pañuelo* he took the handkerchief from me>; myself <*me miré en el espejo* I looked at myself in the mirror>.

me·a·da f. VULG. *(orina)* piss, pee; *(señal)* piss or pee stain ♦ **echar una m.** to take a piss.

me·a·de·ro m. VULG. john, can (toilet).

me·a·dos m.pl. VULG. piss, pee.

me·a·ja f. *(migaja)* crumb; *(moneda)* old Spanish coin.

me·an·dro m. *(curva)* meander, curve; ARCHIT. meander.

me·ar VULG. intr. to piss, pee —reflex. *(orinar)* to piss, pee; *(tener miedo)* to piss or pee in one's pants (be afraid).

Me·ca f. Mecca.

¡me·ca·chis! interj. COLL. darn it!, confound it!

me·cá·ni·ca I. f. *(ciencia)* mechanics; *(mecanismo)* mechanism, works; COLL. *(acción ruin)* despicable act ♦ **m. celeste** astronomy **II.** adj. see **mecánico, –ca.**

me·cá·ni·ca·men·te adv. mechanically.

me·ca·ni·cé, mecanice see **mecanizar.**

me·cá·ni·co, –ca I. adj. *(de la mecánica)* mechanical, machine-operated; *(manual)* manual (labor); *(automático)* automatic, machine-driven; FIG. *(bajo)* mean, servile **II.** m. *(maquinista)* mechanic; *(chófer)* driver —f. see **mecánica.**

me·ca·nis·mo m. *(aparato)* mechanism, working parts; FIG. *(estructura)* structure, workings.

me·ca·ni·za·ción f. mechanization.

me·ca·ni·zar §04 tr. to mechanize.

me·ca·no·gra·fí·a f. typing, typewriting.

me·ca·no·gra·fiar §30 tr. to type.

me·ca·nó·gra·fo, –fa m.f. typist.

me·ca·pal m. C. AMER., MEX. porter's leather harness.

me·ca·pa·le·ro m. C. AMER., MEX. porter, carrier.

me·ca·ta·zo m. C. AMER. *(latigazo)* whiplash; *(trago)* drink, slug (of liquor).

me·ca·te m. AMER. hemp cord, rope.

me·ce·de·ro m. stirrer, swizzle stick.

me·ce·dor, –do·ra I. adj. rocking, swinging **II.** m. *(columpio)* swing; *(paleta)* stirrer (for liquids) —f. rocking chair, rocker.

me·ce·nas m. [pl. **-nas**] patron (of the arts).

me·ce·naz·go m. patronage (of the arts).

me·cer §75 tr. *(cunear)* to rock (a cradle); *(columpiar)* to swing (on a swing); *(balancear)* to move to and fro, sway; *(agitar)* to shake —reflex. to rock < *mecerse en una mecedora* to rock in a rocking chair>; *(columpiarse)* to swing; *(balancearse)* to move to and fro.

me·ci·da f. or **me·ci·mien·to** m. *(de una cuna)* rocking; *(de un columpio)* swinging; *(balanceo)* swaying, to and fro movement.

me·cha f. *(de lámpara)* wick; *(espoleta)* fuse; *(para encender)* match; *(mechón)* lock (of hair); MED., SURG. tent; CUL. strip of bacon (used for larding); MARIT. masthead; TECH. *(del taladro)* drill bit; AMER. joking, kidding; MEX. fear ♦ **a toda m.** at full speed • **aguantar la m.** to grin and bear it • **m. de seguridad** safety fuse.

me·char tr. CUL. to lard (meat).

me·che·ra I. see **mechero II.** f. SL. shoplifter.

me·che·ro m. *(boquilla)* burner, jet <*m. de gas* gas burner>; *(encendedor)* lighter, cigarette lighter; *(canutillo)* wick, holder; *(del candelero)* candle socket (of a candelabra); SL. *(ladrón)* shoplifter; VEN., COLL. joker, cutup ♦ m. **Bunsen** Bunsen burner.

me·chón m. *(mecha grande)* large wick; *(porción de pelo)* lock, tuft (of hair); *(porción de lana)* tuft (of wool).

me·cho·so, -sa *or* **me·chu·do, -da** adj. tousled, uncombed.

me·da·lla f. *(de distinción)* medal; RELIG. medal; *(joya)* medallion ♦ **el reverso de la m.** FIG. the other side of the coin (antithesis).

me·da·llis·ta m.f. medalist.

me·da·llón m. *(medalla grande)* medallion; *(joya)* locket; CUL. pat (of butter).

me·da·nal m. CHILE, URUG. marshy land.

mé·da·no *or* **me·da·no** m. *(duna)* dune, sand dune; *(banco de arena)* sandbank.

me·dia¹ I. f. sock, stocking; *(tiempo)* half past <*las dos y media* half past two> ♦ **m. media** *or* **m. corta** ARG., ECUAD., VEN. ankle-length sock II. adj. see **medio, -dia**.

me·dia² m.pl. mass media.

me·dia·ción f. mediation, arbitration.

me·dia·do, -da I. past part. of **mediar** II. adj. *(medio lleno)* half full; halfway through <*m. la mañana* halfway through the morning> ♦ **a mediados de** halfway through, in the middle of (the month).

me·dia·dor, -do·ra I. adj. mediating, mediative II. m.f. mediator.

me·dia·gua f. sloping roof.

me·dia·lu·na f. *(desjarretadera)* hamstringing *or* hacking knife; *(símbolo musulmán)* crescent, symbol of Islam; CUL. croissant; MIL. demilune.

me·dia·na I. f. GEOM. median II. adj. see **mediano, -na**.

me·dia·na·men·te adv. moderately, fairly.

me·dia·ne·rí·a f. *(pared)* dividing *or* partition wall; AMER. partnership (in farming).

me·dia·ne·ro, -ra I. adj. *(que está en medio)* dividing; *(mediador)* mediating II. m.f. *(intercesor)* mediator; *(vecino)* owner of a house adjacent to another; *(aparcero)* partner (in farming).

me·dia·ní·a f. *(término medio)* halfway mark; *(estado de fortuna)* moderate means; *(persona)* mediocre person, mediocrity; COL. dividing *or* partition wall.

me·dia·no, -na I. adj. *(regular)* average, medium; FIG., COLL. *(mediocre)* mediocre, poor II. f. see **mediana**.

me·dia·no·che f. *(hora)* midnight; CUL. ham sandwich.

me·dian·te I. adj. interceding II. adv. through, by means of ♦ **Dios m.** God willing.

me·diar intr. *(llegar a la mitad)* to get halfway; *(estar en medio)* to be in the middle; *(interponerse)* to intercede, come between; *(transcurrir)* to elapse, go by.

me·dia·tin·ta *or* **me·dia tin·ta** f. halftone.

me·dia·ti·zar §04 tr. *(anexar)* to mediatize; FIG. *(influir)* to influence.

me·dia·to, -ta adj. mediate.

me·di·ca·ción f. *(tratamiento)* medication, medical treatment; *(medicamentos)* medication, medicines.

me·di·ca·men·to m. medicine, medicament.

me·di·car §70 tr. to medicate.

me·di·cas·tro m. *(médico)* quack, medicaster.

me·di·ci·na f. *(ciencia)* medicine, art of healing; *(medicamento)* medicine, medication ♦ **doctor en m.** doctor of medicine.

me·di·ci·nal adj. medicinal, curative.

me·di·ci·nar tr. to treat (with medicine), give medicine to —reflex. to take medicine.

me·di·ción f. measurement, measuring.

mé·di·co, -ca I. adj. medical II. m.f. doctor, physician ♦ **m. de cabecera** family doctor • **m. de apelación** *or* **de consulta** consulting physician • **m. forense** forensic doctor • **m. general** general practitioner.

me·di·cu·cho m. COLL. quack, medicaster.

me·di·da f. measure, measurement <*m. para líquidos* liquid measure>; *(medición)* measuring, measurement; *(recipiente)* measure, measuring device; *(norma)* standard, gauge <*todo depende de la m. en que se juzgue* it all depends on the standard by which one judges>; *(proporción)* proportion, degree <*me pagan a m. de mi trabajo* they pay me in proportion to my work>; *(prevención)* measure, step <*tomó medidas para evitar más problemas* he took steps to

avoid further problems>; *(prudencia)* measure, moderation; POET. measure, meter ♦ **a la m.** to measure, to order <*hecho a la m.* made-to-order> • **a m. del deseo** just as one wanted • **a m. que** as, while • **en la m. en que** insofar as • **en menor m.** to a lesser extent • **pasarse de la m.** to carry things too far • **sin m.** immoderately, in excess.

me·di·dor, -do·ra I. adj. measuring II. m.f. *(persona)* measurer —m. *(instrumento)* measure; AMER. *(contador)* meter (for gas or electricity).

me·die·val adj. medieval.

me·die·va·li·dad f. medievalism.

me·die·va·lis·ta m.f. medievalist.

me·die·vo m. Middle Ages.

me·dio, -dia §G17 I. adj. half <*tres horas y m.* three and a half hours>; *(mediano)* middle, medium < *una persona de talla m.* a person of medium height>; *(central)* middle, midway <*el punto m.* the midway point>; *(regular)* average <*el español m.* the average Spaniard>; MATH. average, mean <*la temperatura m.* the mean temperature> ♦ **m. hermana** half sister • **m. hermano** half brother • **m. luna** half-moon • **m. pasaje** half fare II. m. *(centro)* middle, center; *(ambiente)* environment, medium; *(medida)* measure, step <*procedió adoptando los medios necesarios* he proceeded, taking the necessary measures>; *(medium)* medium, spiritualist; *(moderación)* middle ground; MATH. half *(fraction)*; BIOL. medium; LOG. middle term; SPORT. halfback ♦ **de m. a m.** *(en el centro)* in the middle; *(completamente)* completely, entirely • **de por m.** in between • **en m. de** *(en la mitad)* in the middle; *(sin embargo)* notwithstanding; *(entre tanto)* in the midst of <*en m. de todo eso logró salir bien* in the midst of all that, he managed to come out all right> • **estar de por m.** *(mediar)* to intervene, mediate; *(involucrarse)* to be in the middle, be involved • **m. ambiente** environment • **meterse de por m.** *or* **en m.** to intervene • **por m. de** by means of • **por todos los medios** by all means, at all costs • **quitar de en m.** to get rid of, do away with • **quitarse de en m.** to get out of the way —f. see **media¹** III. adv. half, partially <*m. terminado* half finished> ♦ **a m.** half <*a m. vestir* half-dressed> • **a medias** halfway <*no lo reparó sino a medias* he just repaired it halfway>; *(no del todo)* half <*dormido a medias* half asleep>.

me·dio·cre adj. mediocre.

me·dio·cri·dad f. mediocrity.

me·dio·dí·a m. *(mitad del día)* midday, noon; *(sur)* south.

me·dio·e·val adj. medieval.

me·dio·e·vo m. Middle Ages.

me·di·qué, medique see **medicar**.

me·dir §48 tr. *(mensurar)* to measure; FIG. *(comparar)* to measure, compare; *(moderar)* to weigh <*mide sus palabras cuidadosamente* he weighs his words carefully>; POET. to scan —reflex. *(moderarse)* to be moderate, act with restraint; *(reñir)* to fight, argue.

me·di·ta·bun·do, -da adj. meditative, thoughtful.

me·di·ta·ción f. meditation.

me·di·ta·dor, -do·ra adj. meditating, meditative.

me·di·tar tr. *(pensar)* to meditate, ponder; *(proyectar)* to plan, prepare —intr. to meditate.

me·di·ta·ti·vo, -va adj. meditative.

me·di·te·rrá·ne·o, -a adj. *(rodeado de tierra)* mediterranean, landlocked ♦ **Mediterráneo** GEOG. Mediterranean.

mé·dium m. [pl. **-dium**] medium (spiritualist).

me·dra f. *or* **me·dro** m. *(aumento)* increase, growth; *(mejora)* improvement, progress.

me·drar intr. *(crecer)* to grow, thrive; FIG. *(mejorar)* to improve; *(prosperar)* to prosper, thrive.

me·dro·sa·men·te adv. fearfully, timorously.

me·dro·so, -sa I. adj. *(miedoso)* fearful, timorous; *(que causa miedo)* frightening II. m.f. coward.

me·du·la *or* **mé·du·la** f. ANAT. medulla, marrow; BOT. medulla, pith; FIG. *(esencia)* medulla, essence ♦ **hasta la m.** FIG. to the core • **m. espinal** spinal cord • **m. oblonga** ANAT. medulla oblongata • **m. ósea** bone marrow.

me·du·lar adj. medullary, medullar.

me·du·sa f. ZOOL. medusa, jellyfish.

Me·fis·tó·fe·les Mephistopheles.

me·fi·tis·mo m. mephitis.

me·gá·fo·no m. megaphone.

me·ga·li·to m. ARCHEOL. megalith.
me·ga·lo·cé·fa·lo, –la adj. megalocephalous.
me·ga·lo·ma·ní·a f. PSYCH. megalomania.
me·ga·ló·ma·no, –na PSYCH. I. adj. megalomaniacal
II. m.f. megalomaniac.
me·ga·tón m. PHYS. megaton.
me·ji·ca·no, –na adj. & m.f. Mexican.
Mé·ji·co var. of **México.**
me·ji·lla f. ANAT. cheek.
me·ji·llón m. ZOOL. mussel.
me·jor §G24 I. adj. *(superior)* better <este coche es m. que el
otro this car is better than the other>; best <el m. estudiante de la clase the best student in the class> ♦ **lo m.
posible** as well as possible II. adv. *(más bien)* better
<ella escribe m. que él she writes better than he does>;
(antes) rather <m. morirme que perder la honra I would
rather die than lose my honor> ♦ **a lo m.** maybe, perhaps
• **en el m. de los casos** at best • **m. dicho** rather, more
specifically • **m. que m.** all the better, so much the better
• **tanto m.** better still, so much the better.
me·jo·ra f. *(adelanto)* improvement, betterment; *(aumento)*
increase <m. de sueldo increase in salary>; *(puja)* higher
bid (at an auction); LAW special bequest (to a legal heir).
me·jo·ra·mien·to m. improvement.
me·jo·rar tr. *(poner mejor)* to improve, make better; *(aumentar)* to raise; LAW *(en derecho)* to leave an additional
bequest to (an heir) ♦ **mejorando lo presente** present
company excepted —intr. & reflex. *(ponerse mejor)* to
improve, get better; *(el tiempo)* to clear up (weather); MED.
to improve (said of a patient).
me·jo·rí·a f. *(mejora)* improvement, betterment; *(convalecencia)* improvement (in health); *(ventaja)* advantage.
me·jun·je m. *(mezcla)* mixture; *(enredo)* mess, mix-up; FIG.
(brebaje) potion, brew.
me·la·do m. CUBA, MEX., VEN. thick cane syrup.
me·lan·co·lí·a f. *(tristeza)* melancholy, sadness; MED. mel-
ancholia.
me·lan·có·li·co, –ca I. adj. *(triste)* melancholy, sad; MED.
melancholic II. m.f. *(persona triste)* melancholy person;
MED. melancholiac, melancholic.
me·lan·co·li·zar §04 tr. to make sad, affect with melancholy.
me·la·ni·na f. BIOL. melanin.
me·lar¹ adj. honey-sweet.
me·lar² §49 tr. to boil (cane juice) —intr. to fill the combs
with honey.
me·la·za f. molasses.
mel·co·cha f. taffy.
mel·co·chu·do, –da adj. AMER. soft, flexible.
me·le·na f. *(cabello)* long hair, mop (of hair); *(crin de león)*
mane (of a lion).
me·le·nu·do, –da adj. long-haired, shaggy (of dogs).
me·le·ra f. *(vendedora)* honey vendor (female); *(daño a melones)* bruise (on melons); *(tarro)* honey jar; BOT. bugloss.
me·le·ro I. m. *(vendedor)* honey vendor (male); *(tarro)*
honey jar II. adj. honey <oso m. honey bear>.
me·li·fi·car §70 tr. make honey (bees).
me·lí·fluo, –flua adj. mellifluous, honeyed.
me·lin·dre m. *(fruta de sartén)* honey fritter; *(mazapán)*
sugar-covered marzipan; *(afectación)* affectation, fussiness.
me·lin·dre·ar tr. COLL. to act with affectation.
me·lin·dre·rí·a f. affectation, fussiness.
me·lin·dro·so, –sa or **me·lin·dre·ro, –ra** I. adj. affected,
fussy II. m.f. affected or fussy person.
me·lo·co·tón m. *(fruto)* peach; *(árbol)* peach tree.
me·lo·co·to·nar m. peach orchard.
me·lo·co·to·ne·ro BOT. peach tree.
me·lo·dí·a f. *(canto)* melody, tune; *(calidad)* melody, melo-
diousness.
me·ló·di·co, –ca adj. melodic, tuneful.
me·lo·dio·sa·men·te adv. melodiously.
me·lo·dio·so, –sa adj. melodious, tuneful.
me·lo·dra·ma m. MUS., THEAT. melodrama.
me·lo·dra·má·ti·co, –ca adj. melodramatic, melodramati-
cal.
me·lón m. BOT. melon; COLL. idiot, fool ♦ **catar el m.** FIG.

to get the lay of the land • **m. de agua** watermelon • **m. de
Castilla** cantaloupe.
me·lo·na·da f. foolishness, silly thing ♦ **hacer una m.** to do
something foolish.
me·lo·nar m. melon field or patch.
me·lo·pe·a f. MUS. melopoeia, art of creating melodies;
COLL. *(borrachera)* drunk ♦ **agarrar** or **coger una m.**
COLL. to get loaded or drunk.
me·lo·si·dad f. *(dulzura)* sweetness; *(suavidad)* smoothness; FIG. *(dulce)* sweetness, gentleness.
me·lo·so, –sa adj. *(dulce)* sweet, honeyed; *(suave)* smooth;
FIG. *(dulce)* sweet, gentle.
me·lo·te m. *(melaza)* molasses; SP., CUL. honey preserves.
me·lla f. *(abolladura)* dent (on a metal surface); *(en un filo)*
nick, notch (on a cutting edge); *(en la porcelana)* chip;
(hueco) gap, hole; *(en la dentadura)* gap (in teeth); FIG.
(menoscabo) harm, injury ♦ **hacer m. a** *(impresionar)* to
have an effect upon, impress • **hacer m. en** *(menoscabar a)*
to harm.
me·lla·do, –da I. past part. see **mellar** II. adj. *(en una
superficie de metal)* dented; *(en un filo)* nicked, notched;
(en la porcelana) chipped; *(en la dentadura)* gap-toothed.
me·lla·du·ra f. var. of **mella.**
me·llar tr. *(una superficie de metal)* to dent (a metal surface); *(un filo)* to nick, notch (a cutting edge); *(porcelana)*
to chip (porcelain); FIG. *(menoscabar)* to harm —intr.
(superficie) to become dented or chipped; FIG. *(dañarse)*
to be harmed or injured.
me·lli·zo, –za adj. & m.f. twin (sibling).
me·lli·zos, –zas m.f.pl. twins ♦ **mellizas** handcuffs.
mem·bra·na f. ANAT., BOT. membrane ♦ **m. mucosa** mucous membrane.
mem·bre·te m. *(del remitente)* letterhead; *(del destinatario)*
addressee's name and address; *(anotación)* note, memo.
mem·bre·te·a·do, –da adj. having a letterhead (stationery).
mem·bri·llar m. quince tree orchard.
mem·bri·lle·ro m. quince tree.
mem·bri·llo m. *(árbol)* quince tree; *(fruta)* quince; *(dulce)*
quince jam or jelly.
mem·bru·do, –da adj. robust, muscular.
me·men·to m. RELIG. memento; *(libreta)* memo book,
notebook.
me·mo, –ma I. adj. foolish, simple-minded II. m.f. fool,
simpleton.
me·mo·ra·ble adj. memorable.
me·mo·rán·dum m. [pl. **-rán·dum, -ran·da**] *(nota)* memorandum, memo; *(libreta)* memo book, notebook.
me·mo·rar tr. to remember, recall.
me·mo·ria f. *(facultad)* memory; *(recuerdo)* memory, remembrance <las memorias de la niñez memories of child-
hood>; COM. *(informe)* financial report or statement;
(disertación) thesis, paper; *(monumento)* memorial; COM-
PUT. memory; LAW *(en derecho)* codicil ♦ **borrar de la m.**
to forget completely • **conservar la m. de** to remember •
de m. by heart • **digno de m.** memorable • **en m. de** in
memory of • **falta de m.** forgetfulness • **flaco de m.** forgetful • **hacer m.** de to remember • **irse de la m.** to slip
one's mind • **memorias** *(libro)* memoirs; *(saludos)* regards
• **perder la m.** to lose one's memory • **traer a la m. de uno**
to remind one • **venir a la m.** to come to mind.
me·mo·rial m. *(libreta)* memo book, notebook; *(petición)*
memorial, petition; *(publicación)* publication, bulletin ♦
perder los memoriales COLL. to forget something.
me·mo·rio·so, –sa I. having a good memory II. m.f. person having a good memory.
me·mo·ri·za·ción f. memorization, memorizing.
me·mo·ri·zar §04 tr. to memorize or learn by heart.
me·na f. MIN. ore.
mé·na·de f. MYTH. maenad, bacchante.
me·na·je m. *(hogar)* household furniture and supplies; *(escuela)* school supplies and equipment.
men·ción f. mention ♦ **hacer m. de** to make mention of,
mention • **m. honorífica** honorable mention.
men·cio·nar tr. to mention, name ♦ **sin m.** not to mention.
men·che·vi·que adj. & m.f. POL. Menshevik.
men·da·ci·dad f. *(hábito)* mendacity; *(mentira)* lie.
men·daz [pl. **-da·ces**] I. adj. mendacious, lying II. m.f. liar.
men·de·le·vio m. CHEM. mendelevium.

men·di·can·te I. adj. begging, mendicant ♦ RELIG. **órdenes m.** mendicant orders **II.** m.f. beggar, mendicant.

men·di·ci·dad f. begging, mendicity.

men·di·gar §47 tr. to beg (for) —intr. to beg.

men·di·go, –ga m.f. beggar, mendicant.

men·di·guez f. begging, mendicity.

men·dru·go m. *(de pan)* crust, hunk (of bread); COLL. *(tonto)* idiot, fool.

me·ne·a·dor, –do·ra I. adj. *(que menea)* moving, shaking; *(del rabo)* wagging **II.** m.f. mover, shaker.

me·ne·ar tr. *(mover)* to move; *(agitar)* to shake, wag <*m. la cabeza* to shake one's head>; *(oscilar)* to sway, swing; *(un líquido)* to stir; FIG. *(manejar)* to handle, run (a business) ♦ **peor es menearlo** FIG., COLL. let sleeping dogs lie —reflex. FIG., COLL. to hustle, get a move on ♦ **de no te menees** a hell of <*era un vuelo de no te menees* it was a hell of a flight>.

me·ne·o m. *(movimiento)* movement; *(agitación)* shake (of the head, hands); *(oscilación)* sway, swing; *(un líquido)* stirring; FIG. *(manejo)* handling, running; COLL. *(paliza)* beating, whipping.

me·nes·ter m. *(falta)* need, want; *(ocupación)* occupation, employment <*ir a sus menesteres* to go to one's place of employment>; COLL. *(enseres)* goods, utensils ♦ **haber** or **tener m. de** to need or want (something) • **menesteres** bodily needs • **ser m. que** to be necessary that <*es m. que vengas ahora* it is necessary that you come now>.

me·nes·te·ro·so, –sa I. adj. needy, in need **II.** m.f. needy person.

me·nes·tra f. CUL. stew, soup ♦ **menestras** dried vegetables.

me·nes·tral m. artisan, craftsman.

Men·fis f. Memphis (Egypt).

men·ga·no, –na m.f. so-and-so —m. what's-his-name —f. what's-her-name ♦ **Fulano, M. y Zutano** Tom, Dick, and Harry.

men·gua f. *(disminución)* diminution, decrease; *(falta)* lack; *(pobreza)* poverty; ASTRON. wane, waning (moon); MARIT. fall (of tide); FIG. *(descrédito)* discredit, disgrace; *(intelectual, moral)* decline ♦ **en m. de** to the detriment of.

men·gua·do, –da I. past part. see **menguar II.** adj. *(disminuido)* diminished, decreased; *(cobarde)* cowardly, timid; *(necio)* foolish, silly; *(cicatero)* stingy, miserly **III.** m.f. *(cobarde)* coward, weakling; *(necio)* fool, idiot; *(labores)* drop stitch (knitting).

men·guan·te I. adj. *(que disminuye)* diminishing, decreasing; ASTRON. waning; MARIT. ebb **II.** m. *(disminución)* diminution, decrease; ASTRON. waning; MARIT. ebb; FIG. *(decadencia)* decline, decadence ♦ **cuarto m.** last quarter (of the moon).

men·guar §10 intr. *(disminuir)* to diminish, decrease; ASTRON. to wane; MARIT. to subside, ebb; *(labores de punto)* to decrease (stitching); FIG. *(declinar)* to decline, go downhill —tr. *(disminuir)* to diminish, decrease; *(velocidad)* to reduce (speed); FIG. *(peso, responsabilidad)* to lessen, diminish (burden, responsibility); *(menoscabar)* to detract from <*esto no mengua en nada su fama* this in no way detracts from his reputation>.

men·gue m. COLL. devil.

men·hir m. ARCHEOL. menhir.

me·nin·ge f. ANAT. meninx; *(las meninges)* the meninges.

me·nin·gi·tis f. MED. meningitis.

men·juí m. var. of **benjuí**.

men·jun·je or **men·jur·je** m. var. of **mejunje**.

men·no·ni·ta or **me·no·ni·ta** adj. & m.f. RELIG. Mennonite.

me·no·pau·sia f. MED. menopause.

me·nor §G24 I. adj. less, lesser <*de m. importancia* of lesser importance>; least <*no tengo la m. idea* I don't have the least idea>; younger <*mi hermano m.* my younger brother>; youngest; COLL. *(más pequeño)* smaller; *(el más pequeño)* smallest; MUS., RELIG. minor ♦ **al por m.** COM. retail • **m. de edad** minor, under age • **por m.** in detail, minutely **II.** m. RELIG. Minorite (Franciscan monk); *(joven)* minor, juvenile ♦ **tribunal de m.** juvenile court —f. LOG. minor term.

Me·nor·ca f. Minorca.

me·no·rí·a f. *(subordinación)* subordination; *(edad)* minority (of age).

me·no·ris·ta m. AMER. retailer, retail dealer.

me·nor·quín, –qui·na adj. & m.f. Minorcan.

me·nos §G24, 29 I. adv. less <*ella tiene m. dinero que él* she has less money than he>; least <*Paco es el m. listo de la clase* Frank is the least clever boy in the class>; fewer <*había m. de cincuenta personas en la reunión* there were fewer than fifty people at the meeting> ♦ **al m.** or **a lo m.** at least • **a m. que** unless • **cada vez m.** less and less • **cuanto m. . . . m.** the less . . . the less • **de m.** short <*dos kilos de m.* two kilograms short> • **echar a alguien de m.** to miss someone • **más o m.** more or less • **lo m.** the least • **m. de** less than <*m. de cien dólares* less than one hundred dollars> • **m. que** less than • **ni más ni m.** exactly • **no ser para m.** to be no wonder, little wonder that • **por lo m.** at least • **ser lo de m.** to be the least important thing • **tener a m.** to consider it beneath oneself • **venir a m.** to decline, come down in the world **II.** m. MATH. minus sign ♦ **el más y el m.** the pros and the cons **III.** conj. *(excepto)* but, except <*todo m. eso* all but that> **IV.** prep. MATH. minus <*quince m. siete son ocho* fifteen minus seven is eight>.

me·nos·ca·ba·dor, –do·ra I. adj. *(que reduce)* diminishing, lessening; *(que merma)* damaging, impairing; FIG. *(que desluce)* damaging **II.** m.f. detractor, defamer.

me·nos·ca·bar tr. *(reducir)* to diminish, lessen; *(mermar)* to damage, impair; FIG. *(deslucir)* to damage, tarnish (one's reputation).

me·nos·ca·bo m. *(mengua)* diminishing, lessening; *(daño)* damage; FIG. *(descrédito)* damage (to one's reputation) ♦ **con m. de** to the detriment of.

me·nos·pre·cia·ble adj. despicable, contemptible.

me·nos·pre·cia·dor, –do·ra I. adj. disdainful, contemptuous **II.** m.f. disdainer, scorner.

me·nos·pre·ciar tr. *(despreciar)* to despise, scorn; *(subestimar)* to underestimate, underrate.

me·nos·pre·cia·ti·vo, –va adj. disdainful, contemptuous.

me·nos·pre·cio m. *(desprecio)* contempt, scorn; *(subestimación)* underestimation, underrating; *(falta de respeto)* disrespect ♦ **hacer m. de** to make light of, to scoff at.

men·sa·je m. *(comunicación)* message; *(significado)* intention, message ♦ **m. en clave** coded message.

men·sa·je·rí·a f. *(transporte)* transport service; *(empresa)* transport agency or company ♦ **m. marítima** steamship or shipping line.

men·sa·je·ro, –ra I. adj. messenger, carrier <*paloma mensajera* carrier pigeon> **II.** m.f. messenger, carrier.

men·so, –sa adj. MEX. foolish, stupid.

mens·trua·ción f. MED. menstruation.

mens·trual adj. menstrual.

mens·tru·ar §67 intr. to menstruate.

mens·truo m. menstruation.

men·sual adj. monthly <*revista m.* monthly magazine>.

men·sua·li·dad f. *(salario)* monthly wage; *(pago)* monthly installment.

men·sua·li·zar §04 tr. to pay by the month.

men·sual·men·te adv. monthly.

men·su·ra f. measure, measurement.

men·su·ra·bi·li·dad f. mensurability.

men·su·ra·ble adj. mensurable, measurable.

men·su·ra·dor, –do·ra I. adj. measuring **II.** measurer, meter.

men·su·rar tr. to measure.

men·ta f. BOT. mint; *(sabor)* mint (flavor).

men·ta·do, –da I. past part. see **mentar II.** adj. *(mencionado)* aforementioned, in question; *(famoso)* famous, renowned.

men·tal adj. mental <*cálculo m.* mental calculation>; *(intelectual)* intellectual.

men·ta·li·dad f. mentality, mind ♦ **m. abierta** open mind.

men·tal·men·te adv. *(de la mente)* mentally; *(intelectualmente)* intellectually.

men·tar §49 tr. to name, mention.

men·te f. *(potencia intelectual)* mind, intellect; *(inteligencia)* intelligence; *(pensamiento)* mind <*tener en la m.* to have in mind>; *(propósito)* mind, intention <*tener en m.* to have in mind (to do)>.

men·te·ca·te·rí·a f. *(necedad)* foolishness, nonsense; *(acción)* foolish act; *(comentario)* foolish remark.

men·te·ca·to, –ta I. adj. silly, foolish **II.** m.f. fool, simpleton.

men·tir §65 intr. *(inventar)* to lie, tell lies; *(inducir a error)* to deceive, mislead <*las apariencias mienten* appearances are deceiving>; *(desdecir una cosa)* to belie, contradict.

men·ti·ra f. *(falsedad)* lie, falsehood; *(ficción)* story, tale; *(errata)* error (of a manuscript); *(manchita blanca)* white spot (on a fingernail) ♦ **¡mentira!** that's a lie! • **m. inocente** *or* **piadosa** white lie • **parece m.** it seems unbelievable.

men·ti·ri·ji·llas or **men·ti·ri·llas** ♦ **de m.** in fun, jokingly.

men·ti·rón m. whopping lie, whopper.

men·ti·ro·so, –sa I. adj. *(que miente)* lying; *(engañoso)* deceitful, false; *(lleno de errores)* full of errors *or* misprints (said of a book) **II.** m.f. liar.

men·tís m. denial, refutation (of a statement) ♦ **dar un m. a** to give the lie to.

men·tol m. menthol.

men·to·la·do, –da adj. mentholated.

men·tón m. ANAT. chin.

men·tor m. mentor, counselor.

me·nú m. menu, bill of fare.

me·nu·da·men·te adv. *(de modo menudo)* minutely; *(en detalle)* in detail <*lo describió m.* he described it in detail>.

me·nu·de·ar tr. to do *or* repeat (something) often —intr. *(suceder)* to happen *or* occur often; FIG. *(llover)* to fall, rain; *(contar)* to go into detail about, tell in detail; *(charlar)* to chatter, talk trivialities; COL. to sell by retail; ARG. to increase.

me·nu·den·cia f. *(pequeñez)* minuteness; *(esmero)* meticulousness, exactness; *(fruslería)* trifle ♦ **menudencias** *(de cerdo)* pork products; AMER. *(de res)* offal; *(de ave)* giblets.

me·nu·de·o m. *(repetición)* frequent repetition; *(venta al por menor)* retail ♦ **vender al m.** to sell retail.

me·nu·di·llo m. VET. fetlock joint ♦ **menudillos** giblets.

me·nu·do, –da I. adj. *(pequeño)* small, little; *(sin importancia)* small, insignificant <*problemas menudos* small problems>; *(fino)* fine <*lluvia m.* fine rain>; *(plebeyo)* common, vulgar; *(exacto)* exact, meticulous; *(suelto)* small <*moneda m.* small change>; *(irónico)* fine <*¡en m. lío estamos!* a fine mess we're in!> ♦ **a m.** often, frequently • **por m.** in detail, minutely **II.** m. loose change ♦ **menudos** *(de las reses)* offal; *(de las aves)* giblets; *(moneda)* loose change; *(niños)* little ones, small fry.

me·ñi·que I. adj. *(del dedo)* little, baby (finger); *(pequeño)* tiny **II.** m. little finger, pinkie.

me·ón COLL. **I.** adj. frequently wet (a child) **II.** m.f. *(que mea mucho)* child who wets itself often; *(recién nacido)* newborn, baby.

me·o·llo m. *(médula)* marrow (of bone); *(seso)* brain, gray matter; FIG. *(inteligencia)* brains; *(substancia)* essence, substance ♦ **entrar en el m. del asunto** FIG. to come to the heart of the matter.

me·que·tre·fe m. COLL. pest, loud and obnoxious person.

me·ra·men·te adv. merely, only.

me·rar tr. to mix, combine (two liquids).

mer·ca f. COLL. purchase.

mer·ca·chi·fle m. *(buhonero)* peddler, hawker; *(comerciante)* small-time merchant; DEROG. *(avaro)* shark, money grubber.

mer·ca·de·o m. *(comercio)* trade; *(negocios)* marketing.

mer·ca·de·ar intr. to trade, do business.

mer·ca·der m. merchant, dealer.

mer·ca·de·rí·a f. var. of **mercancía.**

mer·ca·do m. *(feria)* market; *(sitio)* marketplace ♦ **acaparar el m. de** to corner the market in • **m. de cambios** foreign exchange market • **m. de valores** stock market • **m. exterior** foreign *or* overseas market • **m. interior** *or* **nacional** domestic market • **m. negro** black market.

mer·ca·do·tec·nia f. marketing (research).

mer·cal m. *(moneda)* ancient Spanish coin; AMER. tequila.

mer·can·cí·a f. *(artículo)* piece of merchandise, article; *(existencias)* merchandise, goods; *(trato)* trade, commerce.

mer·can·te I. adj. merchant, commercial <*marina m.* merchant marine> **II.** m. merchant, dealer.

mer·can·til adj. *(comercial)* mercantile, commercial; *(codi-*

cioso) mercenary, mercantile ♦ **derecho m.** commercial law • **sociedad m.** trading company.

mer·can·ti·lis·mo m. mercantilism, commercialism.

mer·can·ti·lis·ta I. adj. *(partidario)* mercantilist; LAW expert in commercial law **II.** m.f. *(partidario)* mercantilist; LAW expert in commercial law.

mer·car §70 tr. to purchase, buy.

mer·ced f. *(beneficio)* gift, favor; RELIG. mercy; ARCH. *(título)* grace, worship <*vuestra m.* your grace> ♦ **a la m. de** at the mercy of • **m. a** thanks to • **tenga la m.** please be so kind as.

mer·ce·na·rio, –ria I. adj. *(contratado)* mercenary, hired <*soldado m.* mercenary soldier>; *(codicioso)* mercenary, grasping <*alma m.* mercenary soul> **II.** m. RELIG. Mercedarian; *(soldado)* mercenary; *(obrero)* hired laborer.

mer·ce·rí·a f. notions shop.

mer·ce·ri·za·ción f. *or* **mer·ce·ri·za·do** m. mercerization.

mer·ce·ro, –ra m.f. notions seller.

mer·cu·rial I. adj. METAL. mercurial; ASTRON., MYTH. Mercurial **II.** f. BOT. herb mercury.

mer·cú·ri·co, –ca adj. CHEM. mercuric.

mer·cu·rio m. CHEM. mercury ♦ **Mercurio** ASTRON., MYTH. Mercury • **m. dulce** calomel.

me·re·ce·dor, –do·ra adj. worthy, deserving ♦ **m. de confianza** trustworthy.

me·re·cer §17 tr. *(ser digno de)* to deserve, be worthy of <*m. alabanza* to deserve praise>; *(lograr)* to earn, get <*su comportamiento le mereció una paliza* his behavior earned him a beating> ♦ **m. la pena** to be worthwhile, be worth the trouble —reflex. to be deserving *or* worthy.

me·re·ci·da·men·te adv. deservedly, rightly.

me·re·ci·do I. past part. see **merecer II.** m. just deserts, due <*llevar su m.* to get one's just deserts>.

me·re·ci·mien·to m. merit, worth.

me·re·jo, –ja adj. ECUAD. foolish.

me·ren·dar §49 tr. to eat as a snack, snack on <*merendó un bocadillo* he snacked on a sandwich> —intr. *(tomar la merienda)* to have a snack, have tea —reflex. ♦ **merendarse una cosa** FIG., COLL. to land, get hold of.

me·ren·de·ro m. *(establecimiento)* snack bar, tearoom; *(en el campo)* picnic grounds *or* spot.

me·ren·gar §47 tr. CUL. to whip (milk).

me·ren·gue m. CUL. meringue; MUS. merengue, popular Caribbean dance; *(persona)* weakling, delicate person.

me·ren·gue·ro m. meringue seller; merengue dancer or player.

me·re·triz f. [pl. **-tri·ces**] prostitute, whore.

me·rez·ca, merezco see **merecer.**

me·ri·dia·no, –na I. adj. *(de mediodía)* meridian, midday; ASTRON., GEOG. meridian <*altura m.* meridian altitude> ♦ **ser de una claridad m.** to be crystal clear **II.** m. ASTRON., GEOG. meridian ♦ **primer m.** GEOG. prime meridian —f. *(siesta)* afternoon nap; *(sofá)* chaise longue.

me·ri·dio·nal I. adj. *(del sur de Europa)* southern, meridional; *(en general)* southern, south ♦ **América Meridional** South America **II.** m.f. *(europeo)* meridional; *(en general)* southerner.

me·rien·da f. *(comida ligera)* light lunch, afternoon tea; *(que se lleva)* picnic *or* box lunch ♦ **juntar meriendas** FIG., COLL. to join forces • **m. de negros** confusion, bedlam.

me·rien·de, meriendo see **merendar.**

me·ri·no, –na adj. & m. merino (sheep, wool, cloth).

mé·ri·to m. *(virtud)* merit, worth <*persona de gran m.* person of great merit>; *(valor)* worth, value <*cosa de poco m.* thing of little worth> ♦ **de m.** of merit, notable • **hacer m. de** to mention • **hacer méritos de** *or* **para** to strive to be deserving of.

me·ri·to·rio, –ria I. adj. meritorious **II.** m. unpaid trainee.

mer·lu·za f. ICHTH. hake; COLL. *(borrachera)* drunk, drunken spree.

mer·ma f. *(disminución)* decrease, reduction; *(pérdida)* waste, loss.

mer·mar tr. to reduce, cut down (salary, rations) —intr. *(disminuir)* to decrease, diminish; *(bajar)* to go down (liquid in a vessel).

mer·me·la·da f. *(confitura)* jam, preserves; *(confitura de naranjas)* marmalade.

mer·qué, merque see **mercar.**

me·ro m. ICHTH. grouper.

me·ro, –ra I. adj. *(puro)* mere, pure; GUAT., MEX. *(verdadero)* real; COL., VEN. only, alone *<uno m. de los niños* only one of the children> ♦ **ser el m. malo** to be wickedness itself • **yo m.** I myself II. adv. GUAT., MEX., SALV. exactly, sharp *<a las meras tres de la tarde* at exactly three in the afternoon>.

me·ro·de·a·dor, –do·ra I. adj. marauding II. m.f. marauder.

me·ro·de·ar intr. to maraud, plunder.

me·ro·de·o m. marauding.

mes m. *(período del año)* month; *(sueldo)* monthly salary *<cobrar el m.* to draw one's monthly salary>; *(menstruo)* menses, menstruation ♦ **al** *or* **por m.** by the month • **m. civil** calendar month.

me·sa f. *(mueble)* table; *(junta)* board, council *<m. electoral* electoral board>; *(de una escalera)* landing (of a staircase); GEOG. meseta, plateau; JEWEL. facet, face; FIG. *(comida)* fare, food ♦ **de m.** table *<vino de mesa* table wine> • **levantar** *or* **alzar la m.** to clear the table • **m. de altar** altar • **m. de batalla** sorting table (in a post office) • **m. de billar** billiard table • **m. de noche** night table, nightstand • **m. de operaciones** MED. operating table • **m. de tijera** *or* **de doblar** card table, folding table • **m. redonda** *(en una fonda)* table d'hôte; POL. round table • **poner la m.** to set the table.

me·sa·da f. monthly pay or wages.

me·sa·du·ra f. tearing one's hair.

me·sa·na f. MARIT. *(mástil)* mizzenmast; *(vela)* mizzen.

me·sar tr. tear (one's hair or beard).

mes·cal m. BOT. mescal; *(licor)* mescal.

mes·co·lan·za f. var. of **mezcolanza**.

me·sen·te·rio m. ANAT. mesentery.

me·se·ro, –ra m.f. *(jornalero)* worker receiving monthly wages; MEX. m. *(camarero)* waiter —f. *(camarera)* waitress.

me·se·ta f. *(descanso)* landing (of a staircase); GEOG. plateau.

me·siá·ni·co, –ca adj. messianic.

Me·sí·as m. Messiah.

me·si·lla f. *(mesa pequeña)* small table; *(descanso)* landing (of a staircase); *(de ventana)* ledge, sill ♦ **m. de noche** night table, bedside table • **m. de chimenea** mantelpiece.

mes·me·ris·mo m. mesmerism.

me·so·lí·ti·co adj. Mesolithic.

me·són m. *(hostería)* inn, tavern; CHILE *(mostrador)* counter.

me·són *or* **me·so·trón** m. PHYS. meson, mesotron.

me·so·ne·ro, –ra I. adj. inn II. m.f. innkeeper.

me·sos·fe·ra f. mesosphere.

me·so·zoi·co, –ca adj. & m. GEOL. Mesozoic.

mes·ti·za·je m. *(acción)* miscegenation (esp. between white and Indian races); *(conjunto)* mestizos (collectively).

mes·ti·zar §04 tr. to mix races.

mes·ti·zo, –za I. adj. of mixed parentage II. m.f. mestizo (of white and Indian parentage).

me·su·ra f. *(gravedad)* seriousness, calm; *(cortesía)* courtesy, respect; *(moderación)* moderation, restraint.

me·su·ra·da·men·te adv. prudently, with restraint.

me·su·ra·do, –da I. past part. see **mesurar** II. adj. moderate, circumspect.

me·su·rar tr. to moderate, make moderate.

me·ta f. *(fin)* goal, aim, objective; *(término)* finish (of a race); SPORT. *(guardameta)* goalkeeper.

me·ta·bó·li·co, –ca adj. BIOL. metabolic.

me·ta·bo·lis·mo m. BIOL. metabolism.

me·ta·car·po m. ANAT. metacarpus.

me·ta·fí·si·co, –ca I. adj. metaphysical II. m. metaphysician —f. metaphysics.

me·tá·fo·ra f. metaphor.

me·ta·fó·ri·ca·men·te adv. metaphorically.

me·ta·fó·ri·co, –ca adj. metaphorical, metaphoric.

me·ta·fo·ri·zar §04 tr. to express in metaphors.

me·tal m. metal *(latón)* brass; FIG. *(calidad)* nature, quality; *(timbre)* tone, ring (of voice) ♦ **m. blanco** METAL. nickel or German silver • **m. campanil** bell metal • **m. de imprenta** type metal • **m. en láminas** sheet metal • **m. precioso** precious metal.

me·ta·la·da f. CHILE, MIN. metal contained in a vein.

me·tá·li·co, –ca I. adj. metallic II. m. cash, currency.

me·ta·lí·fe·ro, –ra adj. metal-bearing, metalliferous.

me·ta·li·zar §04 tr. to metalize —reflex. FIG. *(obsesionarse)* to be obsessed with money; *(convertirse en metal)* to become metalized.

me·ta·loi·de m. CHEM. metalloid.

me·ta·lur·gia f. metallurgy.

me·ta·lúr·gi·co, –ca I. adj. metallurgical II. m. metallurgist, metalworker.

me·ta·lur·gis·ta m. metallurgist, metalworker.

me·ta·mór·fi·co, –ca adj. GEOL. metamorphic.

me·ta·mor·fis·mo m. GEOL. metamorphism.

me·ta·mor·fo·se·ar tr. BIOL. to metamorphose.

me·ta·mor·fo·sis *or* **me·ta·mór·fo·sis** f. [pl. **-sis**] BIOL. metamorphosis; FIG. *(transformación)* transformation.

me·ta·no m. CHEM. methane.

me·tás·ta·sis f. MED. metastasis.

me·ta·tar·so m. ANAT. metatarsus.

me·ta·te m. metate (grinding stone).

me·te·dor, –do·ra m.f. *(contrabandista)* smuggler —m. *(paño)* diaper.

me·te·du·ra f. COLL. putting, placing ♦ **m. de pata** blunder, gaffe.

me·te·du·rí·a f. smuggling.

me·tem·psi·co·sis *or* **me·tem·psi·co·sis** f. [pl. **-sis**] PHILOS. metempsychosis, transmigration of souls.

me·te·ó·ri·co, –ca adj. meteoric.

me·te·o·ri·to m. meteorite.

me·te·o·ro *or* **me·té·o·ro** m. meteor.

me·te·o·ro·lo·gí·a f. meteorology.

me·te·o·ro·ló·gi·co, –ca adj. meteorological.

me·te·o·ro·lo·gis·ta *or* **me·te·o·ró·lo·go, –ga** m.f. meteorologist.

me·te·pa·tas m.f. [pl. **-tas**] COLL. blunderer.

me·ter tr. *(introducir)* to put in, insert *<ella metió el dinero en el bolsillo* she put the money in her pocket>; *(de contrabando)* to smuggle in; *(promover)* to start, cause *<m. enredos* to start trouble>; *(causar)* to make *<m. ruido* to make noise>; *(implicar)* to involve, get into *<metió a su hermano en el negocio* he got his brother into the business>; *(apretar)* to squeeze into, squash together; *(apostar)* to stake, wager; COLL. *(dar)* to give, deal (a blow); SEW. to take in; MARIT. to take in (sails) ♦ **m. en cintura** *or* **por vereda** FIG., COLL. to bring into line —reflex. *(entrar)* to get into, enter *<se metieron en el coche* they got into the car>; *(entremeterse)* to intervene, butt in; *(enredarse)* to get mixed up in *<meterse en líos* to get mixed up in a mess>; *(seguir un oficio)* to become *<meterse a fraile* to become a monk>; *(arrojarse)* to attack; AERO. to project, jut out; to flow, empty *<el río se mete en el mar* the river empties into the sea> ♦ **meterse a** *(empezar)* to start; *(hacerse)* to set oneself up as *<él se metió a juez* he set himself up as a judge> • **meterse con** to provoke, annoy • **meterse de** AMER. to become • **meterse en sí mismo** to withdraw into one's shell • **meterse en todo** to meddle.

me·te·te AMER. I. adj. nosy, snoopy II. m. busybody, snoop.

me·ti·cu·lo·so, –sa I. adj. *(medroso)* timid, fearful; *(escrupuloso)* meticulous, finicky II. m.f. meticulous person.

me·ti·do, –da I. past part. see **meter** II. adj. *(abundante)* full *<m. en miel* full of honey>; *(interesado)* involved; AMER. meddlesome ♦ **m. en años** elderly • **m. en sí** withdrawn III. m. *(empujón)* shove; *(puñetazo)* punch, blow; *(metedor)* diaper; SEW. material in seams; FIG., COLL. *(reprensión)* lecture, scolding.

me·ti·lo m. CHEM. methyl.

me·ti·mien·to m. insertion, putting in; FIG., COLL. *(influencia)* influence, pull.

me·tla·pil m. MEX. roller (for grinding corn).

me·tó·di·ca·men·te adv. methodically.

me·tó·di·co, –ca adj. methodical.

me·to·dis·mo m. RELIG. Methodism.

me·to·dis·ta adj. & m.f. RELIG. Methodist.

me·to·di·zar §04 tr. to methodize, systematize.

mé·to·do m. method, technique ♦ **con m.** methodically.

me·to·do·lo·gí·a f. methodology.

me·to·men·to·do m.f. COLL. busybody, meddler.

me·to·ni·mia f. RHET. metonymy.

me·tra·je m. CINEM. footage, length (of a film) ♦ **corto m.** short, short film • **largo m.** full-length or feature film.

me·tra·lla f. ARTIL. (carga) grapeshot, canister shot; (de un proyectil) shrapnel.

me·tra·lla·zo m. ARTIL. discharge (of grapeshot or shrapnel).

me·tra·lle·ta f. ARTIL. submachine gun, tommy gun.

mé·tri·co, –ca I. adj. (relativo al metro) metric <sistema m. metric system>; POET. metrical ♦ **cinta m.** tape measure II. f. metrics.

me·tri·fi·ca·ción f. versification.

me·tro¹ m. (medida) meter, metre (G.B.); (regla) ruler ♦ **m. cuadrado** square meter • **m. cúbico** cubic meter.

me·tro² m. [abbr. of **metropolitano**] subway, underground (G.B.). ♦ **m. aéreo** elevated railway.

me·tró·no·mo m. MUS. metronome.

me·tró·po·li f. (nación) metropolis, mother country; (capital) capital; (iglesia) RELIG. metropolis.

me·tro·po·li·ta·no, –na I. adj. metropolitan II. m. subway, underground (G.B.).

me·xi·ca·nis·mo m. Mexican word or expression.

Mé·xi·co m. Mexico.

me·xi·ca·no, –na adj. & m.f. Mexican.

me·za, mezo see **mecer**.

mez·cal m. BOT. mescal; (licor) mescal.

mez·ca·li·na f. CHEM. mescaline.

mez·cla f. (acción de mezclar) mixing; (combinación) mixture, combination; (de personas) mixture, assortment; (tejido) tweed; CONST. mortar.

mez·cla·ble adj. mixable, miscible.

mez·cla·do, –da I. past part. see **mezclar** II. adj. mixed III. m. tweed.

mez·cla·dor, –do·ra I. adj. mixing, blending II. m.f. (persona) mixer —f. (máquina) mixing machine; CONST. cement mixer.

mez·cla·du·ra or **mez·cla·mien·to** m. mixture, blend.

mez·clar tr. (unir) to mix, blend; (reunir) to mix, mingle; (desordenar) to mix up; (en naipes) to shuffle (cards) —reflex. (unirse) to mix, blend; (reunirse) to mix, mingle (socially); (meterse) to become involved or mixed up (in something).

mez·co·lan·za f. COLL. hodgepodge, jumble.

mez·qui·na·men·te adv. (cruelmente) miserably, meanly; (con avaricia) stingily.

mez·quin·dad f. (avaricia) stinginess, miserliness; (acción tacaña) ill turn, act of meanness.

mez·qui·no, –na I. adj. (pobre) poor, wretched; (avaro) stingy, miserly; (miserable) petty, small; (pequeño) small, tiny II. m. MEX. wart.

mez·qui·ta f. mosque.

mi m. MUS. mi (note).

mí §G30, 34 pron. [used after prepositions] me <lo compró para mí he bought it for me> ♦ **me toca a mí** it's my turn • **¿(y) a mí qué?** so what?

mi, mis §G25 adj. my <mis hermanas my sisters>.

mia·ja f. crumb, bit.

mias·ma m. miasma (emanation).

miau m. meow (of a cat).

mi·ca f. MIN. mica.

mic·ción f. MED. micturition, urination.

mi·ci·fuz m. [pl. **-fu·ces**] COLL. kitty, pussy (cat).

mi·co m. ZOOL. mico, long-tailed monkey; FIG., COLL. (hombre pequeño) runt; (lujurioso) lecher ♦ **dar** or **hacer m. a alguien** to stand someone up • **dejar a uno hecho un m.** to make a monkey out of someone.

mi·co·lo·gí·a f. BOT. mycology.

mi·co·sis f. MED. mycosis.

mi·cra f. micron.

mi·cro m. COLL. mike, microphone.

mi·cro·bio m. microbe.

mi·cro·bio·lo·gí·a f. microbiology.

mi·cro·bús m. AUTO. microbus, minibus.

mi·cro·ce·fa·lia f. microcephaly.

mi·cro·cé·fa·lo, –la adj. microcephalic.

mi·cro·cir·cui·to m. ELECTRON. microcircuit.

mi·cro·ci·ru·gí·a f. microsurgery.

mi·cro·cós·mi·co, –ca adj. microcosmic.

mi·cro·cos·mo or **mi·cro·cos·mos** m. PHILOS. microcosm.

mi·cro·e·co·no·mí·a f. microeconomics.

mi·cro·e·lec·tró·ni·ca f. microelectronics.

mi·cro·fi·cha f. microfiche.

mi·cro·fil·me or **mi·cro·film** m. microfilm.

mi·cró·fo·no m. microphone.

mi·cro·me·trí·a f. micrometry.

mi·cró·me·tro m. micrometer.

mi·crón m. micron.

mi·cro·óm·ni·bus m. microbus, minibus.

mi·cro·on·das f.pl. PHYS. microwaves.

mi·cro·or·de·na·dor m. COMPUT. microcomputer.

mi·cro·or·ga·nis·mo m. BIOL. microorganism.

mi·cro·pla·que·ta f. COMPUT. microchip.

mi·cro·pro·ce·sa·dor m. COMPUT. microprocessor.

mi·cros·có·pi·co, –ca adj. microscopic.

mi·cros·co·pio m. microscope ♦ **m. electrónico** electron microscope.

mi·cro·se·gun·do m. microsecond.

mi·cro·sur·co m. long-playing record, microgroove.

mi·cho, –cha m.f. COLL. kitty, pussycat.

mi·da, mido see **medir**.

mi·die·ra, midió see **medir**.

mie·di·ca COLL. I. adj. cowardly, fearful II. m.f. coward.

mie·di·tis f. COLL. jitters.

mie·do m. (temor) fear, dread; (aprensión) apprehension ♦ **dar m. a** to frighten • **de m.** COLL. (fantástico) great, wonderful; (terrible) awful, terrible • **meterle m. a** to frighten • **m. cerval** intense fear • **morirse de m.** FIG. to be scared to death • **que da** or **mete m.** frightening, fearsome • **tener m.** to be afraid • **tener m. a** or **de** to be afraid of, fear • **tener m. (de) que** to be afraid that <tengo m. (de) que no lleguemos a tiempo I am afraid we will not arrive on time>.

mie·do·so, –sa I. adj. fearful, cowardly II. m. coward.

miel f. (de las abejas) honey; (jarabe) molasses; FIG. (dulzura) honey, sweetness <sus palabras estaban llenas de m. his words were filled with honey> ♦ **dejar a alguien con la m. en los labios** FIG. to cut short someone's enjoyment • **dulce como m.** as sweet as honey • **hacerse de m.** FIG. to be too kind or sweet • **no hay m. sin hiel** FIG. every rose has a thorn • **m. de caña** or **de prima** molasses • **m. sobre hojuelas** FIG. icing on the cake • **panal de m.** honeycomb.

mie·la, mielo see **melar²**.

miel·ga f. BOT. alfalfa; AGR. (bieldo) winnowing fork.

miem·bro m. (parte, socio) member; ANAT. (apéndice) member, limb; (pene) member, penis ♦ **m. viril** ANAT. penis, male member • **m. vitalicio** life member.

mien·ta, miento see **mentir**.

mien·te f. ARCH. thought, mind ♦ **caer en m.** or **en las mientes** to come to mind • **ni por mientes** never • **parar** or **poner mientes en** to reflect upon, consider.

mien·te, miento see **mentar**.

mien·tras I. adv. ♦ **m. más** the more <m. más consigue más quiere the more he gets, the more he wants> • **m. tanto** meanwhile, in the meantime II. conj. (pero) while, whereas <mi casa es pequeña m. la tuya es grande my house is small whereas yours is large>; (durante) while, as long as <m. la huelga duraba while the strike lasted> ♦ **m. que** while.

miér·co·les m. [pl. **-les**] Wednesday ♦ **m. de ceniza** RELIG. Ash Wednesday ♦ **¡imiércoles!** COLL., EUPH. shoot!, darn it!

mier·da f. VULG. shit ♦ **irse a la m.** to go to hell <¡vete a la m! go to hell!> • **es una m.** it isn't worth a damn, it's pure crap.

mies f. AGR. (cereal) grain; (tiempo de la siega) harvest time ♦ **mieses** AGR. grain fields.

mi·ga f. (pedacito) bit, scrap; (del pan) crumb; FIG. (substancia) substance, pith ♦ **hacer buenas** or **malas migas con** FIG., COLL. to get along well or badly with • **migas** CUL. fried bread crumbs.

mi·ga·ja f. (del pan) crumb; (pedacito) scrap, bit ♦ **migajas** FIG. scraps, leftovers • **migaja de pan** bread crumb.

mi·gar §47 tr. (desmenuzar) to crumble; (echar migas) to add crumbs to.

mi·gra·ción f. migration.

mi·gra·ña f. migraine (headache).
mi·gra·to·rio, –ria adj. migratory.
mil §G17 **I.** adj. thousand <*m. flores* a thousand flowers>; *(milésimo)* thousandth; FIG. *(muchos)* thousand, countless <*m. veces* a thousand times> ♦ **a las m. y quinientas** FIG. at the last minute • **m. millones** billion, milliard (G.B.) **II.** m. a thousand, one thousand ♦ **miles** thousands <*miles de ovejas* thousands of sheep>.
mi·la·gro m. RELIG. miracle; *(maravilla)* miracle, wonder; THEAT. miracle play ♦ **hacer milagros** FIG. to work wonders • **vivir de m.** FIG., COLL. to be or stay alive by a miracle.
mi·la·gro·so, –sa adj. miraculous, wondrous.
Mi·lán Milan.
mi·la·nés, –ne·sa adj. & m.f. Milanese.
mi·le·na·rio, –ria I. adj. millenary, millenarian **II.** m. *(período, aniversario)* millennium —m.f. RELIG. millenarian.
mi·le·nio m. millennium.
mi·lé·si·mo, –ma I. adj. thousandth **II.** m. thousandth —f. mill (monetary unit).
mil·ho·jas f. BOT. milfoil, yarrow.
mi·li f. COLL. military service.
mi·li·cia f. *(arte militar)* art of war; *(tropa)* military, soldiery; *(de ciudadanos)* militia; *(servicio militar)* military service ♦ **m. nacional** national guard.
mi·li·cia·no, –na I. adj. military **II.** m. militiaman.
mi·li·co m. AMER., COLL. soldier.
mi·li·gra·mo m. milligram.
mi·li·li·tro m. milliliter.
mi·lí·me·tro m. millimeter.
mi·li·tan·te I. adj. militant **II.** m.f. militant, activist.
mi·li·tan·tis·mo m. militancy.
mi·li·tar[1] **I.** adj. military **II.** m. soldier ♦ **los militares** the military.
mi·li·tar[2] intr. *(como soldado)* to serve (in the military); *(en un partido)* to be active (in a party) ♦ **m. a** or **en favor de** to militate in favor of, lend support to.
mi·li·ta·ra·da f. military uprising.
mi·li·ta·ris·mo m. militarism.
mi·li·ta·ris·ta adj. & m.f. militarist.
mi·li·ta·ri·za·ción f. militarization.
mi·li·ta·ri·zar §04 tr. to militarize.
mi·li·tar·men·te adv. militarily.
mi·lon·ga f. ARG., MUS. milonga (popular song and dance); *(fiesta)* family party; *(enredo)* gossip.
mil·pa f. C. AMER., MEX. cornfield.
mil·pe·ar intr. C. AMER., MEX. *(labrar la tierra)* to till land; MEX. *(brotar)* to sprout (corn).
mil·pe·ro m. MEX. cornfield hand.
mil·piés m. [pl. **-piés**] ENTOM. millipede.
mil·ra·yas m. TEX. striped cloth.
mi·lla f. *(medida inglesa)* mile; MARIT. mile, nautical mile ♦ **m. náutica** nautical mile.
mi·llar m. *(conjunto de mil)* thousand <*un m. de hombres* a thousand men> ♦ **a millares** by the thousands • **millares** thousands, scores.
mi·llón m. million <*un m. de dólares* a million dollars>; FIG. million <*un m. de gracias* a million thanks> ♦ **mil millones** billion, milliard (G.B.) • **tener millones** COLL. to be a millionaire.
mi·llo·na·da f. million, about a million.
mi·llo·na·rio, –ria adj. & m.f. millionaire.
mi·ma·dor, –do·ra adj. pampering, indulgent.
mi·mar tr. *(acariciar)* to caress, fondle; *(consentir)* to pamper, spoil.
mim·bre m. BOT. *(arbusto)* osier; *(varita)* wicker, osier rod.
mim·bre·ar intr. & reflex. to sway.
mim·bre·ra f. *(arbusto)* osier; *(plantío)* osier bed.
mim·bro·so, –sa adj. *(de mimbres)* osier, wicker; *(abundante en mimbreras)* covered with osiers.
mi·me·o·gra·fí·a f. *(acción)* mimeographing; *(copia)* mimeograph.
mi·me·o·gra·fiar §30 tr. to mimeograph.
mi·me·ó·gra·fo m. mimeograph (machine).
mi·me·sis f. mimesis.
mi·mé·ti·co, –ca adj. mimetic.
mi·me·tis·mo m. mimesis, mimicry.

mí·mi·co, –ca I. adj. mimic, imitative **II.** f. THEAT. mime; *(imitación)* imitation, mimicry.
mi·mo m. THEAT. mime; *(caricia)* caressing, fondling; *(de un niño)* pampering, spoiling ♦ **hacerle mimos a alguien** to pamper or indulge someone.
mi·mo·sa f. BOT. mimosa ♦ **m. púdica** or **vergonzosa** mimosa, sensitive plant.
mi·mo·so, –sa adj. *(melindroso)* fussy, finicky; *(mimado)* pampered, spoiled.
mi·na f. *(excavación)* mine; *(galería)* underground passage; FIG. *(fuente)* mine, storehouse <*la enciclopedia es una m. de información* the encyclopedia is a mine of information>; *(empleo)* sinecure; *(de lápiz)* pencil lead; ARM., MIL. mine <*m. terrestre* land mine>; AMER. concubine, mistress.
mi·na·dor, –do·ra I. adj. mining **II.** m. *(ingeniero)* mining engineer; *(obrero)* miner; MIL. miner, sapper; MARIT. minelayer.
mi·nar tr. *(excavar)* to mine; *(cavar lentamente)* to wear away, undermine; FIG. *(buscar)* to mine or search for; *(debilitar)* to undermine, destroy <*m. la salud* to undermine one's health>; MIL. to mine.
mi·na·re·te m. minaret.
mi·ne·ral I. adj. mineral **II.** m. *(substancia)* mineral; *(mena)* ore; *(origen)* source, fountainhead; MEX. mine ♦ **m. de hierro** iron ore.
mi·ne·ra·li·zar §04 tr. to mineralize —reflex. to become mineralized.
mi·ne·ra·lo·gí·a f. mineralogy.
mi·ne·ra·ló·gi·co, –ca adj. mineralogical.
mi·ne·ra·lo·gis·ta m. mineralogist.
mi·ne·rí·a f. *(trabajo)* mining; *(minas)* mines; *(mineros)* miners.
mi·ne·ro, –ra I. adj. mining **II.** m. *(trabajador)* miner; *(propietario)* mine owner; *(mina)* mine; FIG. *(origen)* origin, source; ARG. mouse —f. Sp. mining song.
mi·ner·va f. FIG. *(mente)* mind, intellect; PRINT. platen press; RELIG. procession ♦ **de propia m.** out of one's own head • **Minerva** MYTH. Minerva.
min·ga f. PERU or **min·ga·co** m. CHILE, PERU farm labor performed on holidays in exchange for a meal.
min·gi·to·rio m. urinal.
min·go m. object ball (in billiards) ♦ **coger de m.** to make a scapegoat out of • **poner el m.** COLL. to excel, draw attention.
mi·nia·tu·ra f. miniature.
mi·nia·tu·ris·ta m.f. PAINT. miniaturist.
mi·nia·tu·ri·zar §04 tr. to miniaturize.
mi·ni·fal·da f. miniskirt.
mi·ni·fun·dio m. small farm.
mí·ni·ma f. *(cosa pequeña)* little bit; MUS. half note, minim; METEOROL. minimum temperature —m. see **mínimo, –ma.**
mi·ni·mi·zar §04 tr. to minimize.
mí·ni·mo, –ma I. adj. *(pequeño)* minimum, least; *(minucioso)* minute, minimal **II.** m. RELIG. Minim; *(límite inferior)* minimum; METEOROL. low pressure zone ♦ **al m.** or **a lo más m.** to a minimum • **como m.** at least, at the very least • **en lo más m.** in the slightest • **m. común múltiplo** MATH. lowest common multiple • **m. vital** ECON. subsistence income —f. see **mínima.**
mi·ni·mum m. minimum.
mi·ni·no, –na m.f. COLL. kitty, pussycat.
mi·nio m. CHEM. minium, red lead.
mi·nis·te·rial adj. ministerial.
mi·nis·te·rio m. ministry (post, term, department and office); *(cuerpo de ministros)* cabinet; POL. department ♦ **M. de Agricultura** Department of Agriculture • **M. de Comercio** Department of Commerce • **M. de Hacienda** Treasury Department • **M. de Guerra** Defense Department • **M. de Trabajo** Department of Labor • **M. de Marina** Department of the Navy • **M. de Relaciones Exteriores** State Department.
mi·nis·trar tr. *(servir un oficio)* to hold office; *(dar)* to administer, dispense.
mi·nis·tro m.f. POL. minister, secretary; RELIG. minister <*m. presbiteriano* Presbyterian minister>; DIPL. minister resident; LAW justice ♦ **M. de Agricultura** Secretary of Agriculture • **M. de Comercio** Secretary of Commerce • **m. de**

Dios clergyman • **M. de Hacienda** Secretary of the Treasury • **M. de Guerra** Defense Secretary • **M. de Marina** Secretary of the Navy • **M. de Relaciones Exteriores** Secretary of State • **m. sin cartera** DIPL. minister without portfolio • **primer m.** POL. prime minister.
mi·noi·co, –ca adj. Minoan.
mi·no·ra·ción f. diminution, reduction.
mi·no·rar tr. to diminish, reduce.
mi·no·rí·a or **mi·no·ri·dad** f. minority.
mi·no·ris·ta I. adj. COM. retail II. m. *(clérigo)* minor clergyman; COM. retailer.
mi·no·ri·ta·rio, –ria I. adj. minority II. m.f. member of a minority.
min·tie·ra, mintió see **mentir.**
mi·nu·cia f. small thing, trifle.
mi·nu·cio·sa·men·te adv. thoroughly, minutely.
mi·nu·cio·si·dad f. thoroughness, minuteness.
mi·nu·cio·so, –sa adj. thorough, minute.
mi·nué m. MUS. minuet.
mi·nuen·do m. MATH. minuend.
mi·nús·cu·lo, –la I. adj. *(muy pequeño)* minuscule, tiny; *(insignificante)* insignificant ♦ **letra m.** small or lowercase letter. II. f. small or lowercase letter.
mi·nu·ta f. *(borrador)* rough draft; *(acta)* minutes, record; *(nota)* note, memorandum; *(cuenta)* lawyer's bill or invoice; *(de una comida)* menu, bill of fare.
mi·nu·te·ro m. minute hand (of a clock).
mi·nu·to m. minute ♦ **al m.** right away, at once.
mi·ñan·go m. AMER. small piece.
mí·o, –a §G25, 40 I. adj. mine <*estos libros son míos* these books are mine>; of mine <*un amigo m.* a friend of mine>; my <*¡Dios m.!* my God!>; FIG. *(querido)* my dear <*madre m.* my dear mother> II. pron. mine <*¿dónde está el m.?* where is mine?> ♦ **ésta es la m.** FIG., COLL. this is my big chance • **lo m.** my affair, my business • **los míos** my people, my folks.
mí·o m. kitty (used to call a cat).
mio·pe OPHTHAL. I. adj. myopic, nearsighted II. m.f. myope, myopic person.
mio·pí·a f. OPHTHAL. myopia, nearsightedness.
mi·ra f. ARM., TECH. sight; SURV. leveling rod; FORT. watchtower, lookout; FIG. *(intención)* aim, intention ♦ **con miras a** FIG. with an eye to, with a view to • **estar a la m. de** FIG., COLL. to be on the lookout for • **miras** MIL. prow guns • **poner la m. en** FIG. to aim to, aspire to.
mi·ra·da I. f. look, glance, gaze <*una m. de soslayo* a sidelong glance>; *(apariencia)* look, expression ♦ **echar una m. a** to cast a glance at • **m. fija** stare • **m. perdida** distant look II. adj. see **mirado, –da.**
mi·ra·de·ro m. *(punto de mira)* center of attention, cynosure; *(mirador)* lookout, vantage point.
mi·ra·do, –da I. past part. see **mirar** II. adj. *(circunspecto)* cautious, circumspect; regarded <*mal m.* ill-regarded> ♦ **bien m.** all things considered III. f. see **mirada.**
mi·ra·dor, –do·ra I. adj. looking, watching II. m.f. *(observador)* observer, spectator —m. *(balcón)* balcony, terrace.
mi·rar tr. *(ver)* to look at <*miraron los cuadros* they looked at the pictures>; *(observar)* to watch, observe; *(contemplar)* to gaze at <*m. las estrellas* to gaze at the stars>; FIG. *(reflexionar)* to think about, consider <*mira lo que haces* think about what you are doing>; *(reconocer)* to consider, think of <*lo miran como experto* they think of him as an expert> ♦ **m. bien** or **con buenos ojos** to look with favor on, approve of • **m. de arriba abajo** to look up and down • **m. de hito en hito** to stare at • **m. de reojo** to look askance at • **m. de soslayo** to look sideways at • **m. mal** or **con malos ojos** to disapprove of • **m. por** to look out for, look after <*sólo miran por sus intereses* they only look out for their own interests>; to look out (through) <*miraban por la ventana* they were looking out the window> • **m. por encima** to glance at, look over • **m. por encima del hombro** to look down on —intr. *(ver)* to look; *(observar)* to watch; *(dar a)* to look out on, overlook <*el balcón mira a la plaza* the balcony overlooks the plaza> ♦ **¡mira!** *(como advertencia)* watch out!, be careful!; *(como amenaza)* look here! • **mire** well, let me say this —reflex. to look at oneself <*me miré en el espejo* I looked at myself in the

mirror>; to look at one another <*se miraban con amor* they looked at one another lovingly>; *(tener cuidado)* to be careful, watch out for oneself ♦ **mirarse en ello** to watch one's step • **mirarse unos a otros** to look at each other helplessly.
mi·ra·sol m. BOT. sunflower.
mi·rí·a·da f. myriad.
mi·ri·lla f. *(para observar)* peephole; SURV. target, sight.
mi·ri·ña·que m. *(de falda)* hoopskirt, crinoline (underskirt); *(alhaja)* trinket, bauble; CUBA cotton fabric; VEN. swindle, racket; ARG., RAIL. cowcatcher.
mir·lo m. ORNITH. blackbird; FIG., COLL. *(gravedad)* affected gravity, portentousness ♦ **ser un m. blanco** to be a rare bird.
mi·rón, –ro·na I. adj. nosy, inquisitive II. m.f. *(curioso)* nosy or inquisitive person; *(espectador)* spectator, onlooker.
mi·rra¹ f. BOT. myrrh.
mi·rra² f. VEN. scrap, crumb.
mir·to m. BOT. myrtle.
mi·sa f. RELIG. *(celebración)* Mass; *(sacerdocio)* priesthood ♦ **como en m.** FIG. in a dead silence • **decir m.** to say or celebrate Mass • **m. de difuntos** or **de requiem** Requiem Mass • **m. de gallo** Midnight Mass (celebrated Christmas Eve) • **m. mayor** High Mass • **m. negra** black mass • **m. rezada** Low Mass • **no saber de la m. la media** FIG., COLL. not to know what one is talking about • **oír m.** to hear or attend Mass.
mi·sal I. adj. RELIG. missal II. m. RELIG. missal; PRINT. two-line pica.
mi·san·tro·pí·a f. misanthropy.
mi·san·tró·pi·co, –ca adj. misanthropic.
mi·sán·tro·po m. misanthrope.
mis·ce·lá·ne·o, –a I. adj. miscellaneous II. f. miscellany.
mis·ci·ble adj. miscible, mixable.
mi·se·ra·ble I. adj. *(pobre)* poor, wretched; *(tacaño)* stingy, miserly; *(lastimoso)* miserable, pitiful; *(despreciable)* despicable, vile ♦ **¡miserable de mí!** woe is me! II. m.f. *(pobre)* wretch, unfortunate person; *(tacaño)* miser, skinflint; *(canalla)* cad, scoundrel.
mi·se·ra·ble·men·te or **mi·se·ra·men·te** adv. miserably.
mi·se·re·ar intr. COLL. to pinch pennies.
mi·se·ria f. *(infortunio)* misery, suffering; *(pobreza)* poverty; *(avaricia)* stinginess, miserliness; *(piojos)* lice; FIG., COLL. *(cosa pequeña)* pittance, paltry amount <*me envió una m.* he sent me a pittance> ♦ **estar en la m.** to be down and out.
mi·se·ri·cor·dia f. *(compasión)* compassion, mercy; *(del asiento)* misericord.
mi·se·ri·cor·dio·so, –sa I. adj. compassionate, merciful II. m.f. compassionate or merciful person.
mí·se·ro, –ra adj. wretched, unfortunate.
mi·sia or **mi·siá** f. AMER., COLL. Missis, Missus.
mi·sil m. missile.
mi·sión f. mission.
mi·sio·nal adj. missionary.
mi·sio·nar intr. RELIG. to preach a mission.
mi·sio·ne·ro, –ra adj. & m.f. missionary.
Mi·si·si·pí m. GEOG. Mississippi.
mi·si·va f. missive, letter.
mis·ma·men·te adv. COLL. exactly, precisely.
mis·mí·si·mo, –ma adj. COLL. very, selfsame <*en ese m. día* on that very day>.
mis·mo, –ma adj. *(idéntico)* same <*leí el m. libro* I read the same book>; *(exacto)* very, selfsame <*en ese m. momento* at that very moment>; right <*ahora m.* right now>; self <*yo m.* I myself> ♦ **así m.** *(de esta manera)* in the same way, likewise; *(también)* also • **lo m.** the same thing • **por lo m.** for that reason, for that very reason.
mi·so·gi·nia f. misogyny.
mi·só·gi·no I. adj. misogynistic, misogynous II. m. misogynist, woman hater.
mis·tar tr. to mutter, mumble ♦ **no m.** COLL. to keep mum.
mis·te·rio m. mystery.
mis·te·rio·sa·men·te adv. mysteriously.
mis·te·rio·so, –sa adj. mysterious.
mís·ti·ca f. I. mystical theology II. adj. see **místico, –ca.**
mis·ti·cis·mo m. mysticism.

mís·ti·co, –ca I. adj. mystic, mystical **II.** m.f. mystic —f. see **mística**.

mis·ti·cón, –co·na COLL. **I.** adj. sanctimonious **II.** m.f. sanctimonious person.

mis·ti·fi·ca·ción f. mystification, trick.

mis·ti·fi·car §70 tr. to mystify, trick.

mis·tu·ra f. (mezcla) mixture; BOL. bouquet of flowers.

mis·tu·re·ra f. PERU flower vendor.

mi·ta f. S. AMER. (conscripción) mita (forced labor performed by Indians); PERU (tributo) tax paid by Indians; ARG. cattle transported by train; BOL. coca harvest; CHILE, COLL. turn.

mi·tad f. (una de dos partes) half <la m. de la población half of the population>; (medio) middle <durante la m. de la película during the middle of the movie> ♦ a or en la m. de in the middle of ♦ mi cara m. COLL. my better half (wife) ♦ m. y m. half and half ♦ por la m. in half, in two.

mi·ta·yo, –ya I. adj. ECUAD., DEROG. Indian **II.** m. S. AMER. Indian who worked as conscripted labor.

mí·ti·co, –ca adj. mythical, mythic.

mi·ti·ga·ción f. mitigation.

mi·ti·ga·dor, –do·ra or **mi·ti·gan·te I.** adj. mitigating **II.** m.f. mitigator.

mi·ti·gar §47 tr. to mitigate, alleviate.

mi·ti·ma·es m.pl. PERU, HIST. (colonos) mitimaes (Indians sent by the Incas to colonize new territories); (tropas) Indians who served with Spanish troops.

mi·tin m. [pl. mí·ti·nes] meeting, rally.

mi·to m. (relato) myth; FIG. (leyenda) myth, legend.

mi·to·lo·gí·a f. mythology.

mi·to·ló·gi·co, –ca I. adj. mythological **II.** m. mythologist.

mi·to·lo·gis·ta or **mi·tó·lo·go** m. mythologist.

mi·to·ma·ní·a f. PSYCH. mythomania.

mi·tó·ma·no, –na PSYCH. **I.** adj. mythomaniacal **II.** m.f. mythomaniac.

mi·tón m. mitt (fingerless knitted glove).

mi·to·sis f. BIOL. mitosis.

mi·to·te m. MEX. mitote (Indian dance); AMER. (fiesta) house party; FIG. (melindre) fussiness, fastidiousness; (bulla) rumpus, uproar.

mi·to·te·ar intr. MEX. to fuss.

mi·to·te·ro, –ra AMER., FIG. **I.** adj. (melindroso) fussy, finicky; (bullanguero) rowdy, bosiderous **II.** m.f. (melindroso) finicky person, fussbudget; (bullanguero) rowdy or boisterous person.

mi·tra f. (toca de obispo) miter; FIG. (obispado) bishopric; (arzobispado) archbishopric; (rentas) total revenues of a bishopric or archbishopric.

mi·tra·do, –da I. past part. see **mitrar II.** adj. mitered **III.** m. (obispo) bishop; (arzobispo) archbishop.

mi·trar intr. COLL. to obtain a bishopric.

mix·ti·fi·ca·ción f. mystification, trick.

mix·to, –ta I. adj. (mezclado) mixed; (mestizo) of mixed race **II.** m. (fósforo) match; (substancia inflamable) explosive compound; (tren) mixed freight and passenger train.

mix·tu·ra f. (mezcla) mixture; (pan) mixed-grain bread; PHARM. compound, mixture; BOL., PERU gift of flowers.

mix·tu·rar tr. to mix.

mix·tu·re·ra f. PERU flower vendor.

mne·mó·ni·co, –ca adj. var. of **mnemotécnico, –ca**.

mne·mo·tec·nia or **mne·mo·téc·ni·ca** f. mnemonics.

mne·mo·téc·ni·co, –ca adj. mnemonic.

mo·a·ré m. TEX. moiré.

mo·bi·lia·rio, –ria I. adj. movable (property) **II.** m. furniture, furnishings.

mo·bla·je m. furniture, furnishings.

mo·blar §19 tr. to furnish.

mo·ca f. (café) mocha; ECUAD. mudhole, quagmire.

mo·ca·rro m. SL. snot, mucus.

mo·ca·sín m. moccasin.

mo·ce·ar intr. COLL. (portarse como un mozo) to act like a kid; (correr aventuras) to sow one's wild oats.

mo·ce·dad f. (juventud) youth; (aventura) youthful adventure or prank ♦ mocedades youth <en sus mocedades in her youth>.

mo·ce·tón, –to·na m.f. strapping boy or girl.

mo·ción f. (movimiento) motion, movement; FIG. (inclinación) inclination, tendency; (inspiración) divine inspiration; (proposición) motion, formal proposal ♦ presentar una m. to present or bring forward a motion (in an assembly).

mo·cio·nar tr. AMER. to present a motion, propose.

mo·ci·to, –ta COLL. **I.** adj. (jovencito) very young; SP., REG. single, unmarried **II.** m. (jovencito) youngster, lad —f. (jovencita) young girl, lass —m.f. SP., REG. single or unmarried person.

mo·co m. PHYSIOL. mucus; COLL. snot; FIG. (materia pegajosa) mucilage; (pabilo) snuff (burnt portion of a candlewick); (de una vela) candle drippings; METAL. slag; MARIT. martingale, dolphin striker ♦ a m. de candil by candlelight ♦ limpiarse los mocos to blow one's nose ♦ llorar a m. tendido or a m. y baba FIG., COLL. to cry like a baby ♦ m. de pavo ZOOL. turkey crest; BOT. love-lies-bleeding ♦ no ser m. de pavo FIG., COLL. not to be something to sneeze at.

mo·co·so, –sa I. adj. (que tiene mocos) mucous, mucose; FIG. (malcriado) snotty, bratty; (insignificante) insignificant, unimportant **II.** m.f. FIG. snotty kid, brat.

mo·co·sue·lo, –la I. adj. (malcriado) bratty; (sin experiencia) inexperienced, callow **II.** m.f. (malcriado) brat; (joven) fledgling, callow youth.

mo·cha f. (reverencia) reverent bow (of the head); S. AMER., COLL. head; CUBA type of machete —m. see **mocho, –cha**.

mo·cha·da f. butt, blow with the head.

mo·cha·les adj. [pl. -les] COLL. (loco) crazy, nuts; (enamorado) head-over-heels in love.

mo·char tr. (dar mochadas) to butt, knock one's head against; ARG. to steal, rob; COL., P. RICO (amputar) to amputate; PERU, P. RICO (cortar) to hack or lop off.

mo·cha·zo m. blow with a rifle butt.

mo·che adv. ♦ a troche y m. helter-skelter, pell-mell.

mo·che·ta f. (extremo opuesto al filo) thick or blunt end (of some tools); ARCHIT. (ángulo) quoin (exterior angle of wall); (telar) frame, jamb.

mo·chi·la f. (morral de caminante) pack, knapsack; (morral de cazador) game bag; MIL. provisions, ration; MEX. small case or trunk.

mo·chi·le·ro m. MIL. pack-carrier.

mo·cho, –cha I. adj. (sin punta) blunt, without a point; (sin cuernos) hornless, polled; FIG., COLL. (pelado) shorn, cropped; AMER. mutilated; GUAT., RELIG. lay, laic; MEX. Catholic; GUAT., MEX., POL. conservative **II.** m. (mango) handle; (culata) stock, butt; (caballejo) nag; SALV. ancestor —f. see **mocha**.

mo·da f. style, fashion ♦ a la m. or de m. fashionable, in fashion, chic ♦ a la m. de in the fashion or style of ♦ estar or ser de m. to be in fashion ♦ fuera de m. out of fashion ♦ pasado de m. old-fashioned ♦ pasarse de m. to go out of fashion ♦ ponerse de m. to come into fashion ♦ ser la última m. to be the latest fashion or style.

mo·dal I. adj. modal **II.** m.pl. **modales** manners, behavior.

mo·da·li·dad f. modality, nature.

mo·de·la·do I. past part. see **modelar II.** m. modeling.

mo·de·la·dor, –do·ra ARTS **I.** adj. modeling **II.** m.f. modeler.

mo·de·lar tr. ARTS to model —reflex. to model oneself after someone, emulate.

mo·de·lis·ta m.f. (creador de modelos) modeler, model maker —m. (operario de moldes) person who operates molds (in a factory).

mo·de·lo I. m. (objeto reproducido) model; (representación en pequeña escala) scale model; model <un m. de virtud a model of virtue>; (tipo industrial protegido por patente) industrial model or prototype protected by a patent —m.f. (persona que exhibe las modas) (fashion) model ♦ desfile de modelos fashion show ♦ m. a escala or m. reducido scale model **II.** adj. model, exemplary.

mo·de·ra·ción f. moderation.

mo·de·ra·da·men·te adv. moderately, with or in moderation.

mo·de·ra·do, –da I. past part. see **moderar II.** adj. & m.f. moderate.

mo·de·ra·dor, –do·ra I. adj. moderating **II.** m.f. moderator —m. PHYS. moderator.

mo·de·rar tr. *(templar)* to moderate, regulate; FIG. *(contener)* contain, restrain <*m. las pasiones* to contain one's passions> —reflex. to contain *or* restrain oneself.

mo·der·na·men·te adv. *(recientemente)* recently, lately; *(actualmente)* nowadays, in modern times.

mo·der·ni·cé, modernice see **modernizar.**

mo·der·ni·dad f. modernity, modernness.

mo·der·nis·mo m. modernism ♦ **Modernismo** ARTS, RELIG. Modernism.

mo·der·nis·ta I. adj. modernist, modernistic II. m.f. modernist.

mo·der·ni·za·ción f. modernization.

mo·der·ni·zar §04 tr. to modernize.

mo·der·no, –na I. adj. *(reciente)* modern; HOND. clumsy II. m.f. *(el que vive actualmente)* modern; *(el que es nuevo)* newcomer ♦ **a la moderna** *or* **a lo moderno** in the modern manner *or* fashion.

mo·des·ta·men·te adv. modestly.

mo·des·tia f. modesty.

mo·des·to, –ta I. adj. modest II. m.f. modest person.

mó·di·ca·men·te adv. moderately.

mó·di·co, –ca adj. moderate, reasonable (price).

mo·di·fi·ca·ble adj. modifiable.

mo·di·fi·ca·ción f. modification, alteration.

mo·di·fi·ca·dor, –do·ra I. adj. modifying II. m.f. modifier.

mo·di·fi·car §70 tr. to modify —reflex. to change, become modified.

mo·di·fi·ca·ti·vo, –va adj. modifying.

mo·dis·mo m. GRAM. idiom, idiomatic expression.

mo·dis·ta m.f. dressmaker, modiste.

mo·dis·te·rí·a f. dress shop.

mo·dis·ti·lla f. COLL. *(aprendiza)* apprentice dressmaker, dressmaker's assistant; *(modista inferior)* second-rate dressmaker.

mo·do m. *(manera)* manner, way, mode <*m. de pensar* way of thinking>; GRAM. mood <*m. subjuntivo* subjunctive mood>; MUS. mode <*m. menor* minor mode> ♦ **a** *or* **al m. de** like, in the manner of • **a mi m.** in my own way • **del mismo m.** in the same way • **de m. que** so that • **de ningún m.** by no means • **de todos modos** at any rate, in any case • **en cierto m.** to a certain extent • **m. de ser** character, way of being • **modos** manners <*malos modos* bad manners>.

mo·do·rra f. *(sueño pesado)* drowsiness, heaviness; VET. sturdy, gid.

mo·do·rrar tr. to make drowsy *or* sleepy —reflex. to turn soft, become overripe (fruit).

mo·do·si·dad f. good behavior *or* manners.

mo·do·so, –sa adj. well-behaved, well-mannered.

mo·du·la·ción f. modulation ♦ **m. de amplitud** RAD. amplitude modulation, AM • **m. de fase** phase modulation • **m. de frecuencia** RAD. frequency modulation, FM.

mo·du·la·dor, –do·ra I. adj. modulating II. m.f. modulator.

mo·du·lar tr. & intr. to modulate.

mó·du·lo m. ARCHIT., HYDRAUL., MECH., NUMIS. module; MATH., PHYS. modulus; MUS. *(modulación)* modulation ♦ **m. de aterrizaje** ASTRONAUT. landing module • **m. de elasticidad** PHYS. modulus of elasticity • **m. lunar** ASTRONAUT. lunar module.

mo·fa f. mockery, ridicule ♦ **hacer m. de** to mock, ridicule.

mo·far intr. & reflex. to mock, ridicule ♦ **mofarse de** to mock, ridicule.

mo·fe·ta f. GEOL., MIN. *(gas irrespirable)* blackdamp, chokedamp; *(grisú)* firedamp; ZOOL. skunk, polecat.

mo·fle·te m. COLL. fat *or* chubby cheek.

mo·fle·tu·do, –da adj. COLL. fat-cheeked, chubby-cheeked.

mo·gol, –go·la I. adj. Mongolian II. m.f. *(habitante)* Mongol, Mongolian —m. *(idioma)* Mongolian.

mo·gó·li·co, –ca adj. Mongol, Mongolian.

mo·go·llo I. adj. COL. easy, simple II. m. COL., AGR. very fine bran; CUL. bran bread; SPORT. fluke (shot); CUBA, AGR. cutting of tobacco leaves.

mo·go·llón, –llo·na I. adj. CUBA, ECUAD. sponging, leeching II. m. intrusion, meddling ♦ **comer de m.** to sponge a meal • **de m.** free, for nothing.

mo·go·te m. *(montículo)* knoll, hillock; *(leña)* pile, stack (of firewood); ZOOL. *(cuernas)* budding antlers.

mo·gro·llo m. *(gorrista)* sponger, parasite; COLL. *(descortés)* boor, yokel.

mo·ha·rra f. *(punto de lanza)* spearhead; PERU, TAUR. short spear.

mo·ha·rra·che *or* **mo·ha·rra·cho** m. *(disfrazado)* riduculously disguised person (at a masquerade); FIG., COLL. *(mamarracho)* grotesque figure, scarecrow.

mo·he·cer §17 tr. *(hacer mohoso)* to make moldy *or* mildewed; *(aherrumbrar)* to rust, make rusty —reflex. *(hacerse mohoso)* to become moldy *or* mildewed, mildew; *(aherrumbrarse)* to become rusty, rust.

mo·hín m. grimace, face ♦ **hacer mohines** to grimace, make faces.

mo·hí·no, –na I. adj. *(triste)* sad, melancholy; *(enfadado)* ill-humored, sulky; ZOOL. *(hibrido)* hinny <*mulo m. hinny*>; *(de pelo negro)* black, black-coated II. m.f. ZOOL. *(burdégano)* hinny; *(animal de pelo negro)* black *or* black-coated animal —m. ORNITH. blue magpie —f. *(enojo)* anger, displeasure; *(melancolía)* sadness, melancholy.

mo·ho m. *(hongo)* mold, mildew; *(herrumbre)* rust, corrosion; FIG. *(desidia)* laziness, indolence ♦ **criar m.** *(ponerse mohoso)* to get moldy; *(aherrumbrarse)* to corrode, get rusty • **m. azul** BOT. tobacco mildew • **no criar m.** FIG. to be on the move *or* go.

mo·ho·se·ar·se reflex. AMER. var. of **enmohecerse.**

mo·ho·so, –sa adj. *(lleno de hongos)* moldy, mildewed; *(herrumbroso)* rusty, corroded.

moi·sés m. cradle.

mo·ja·bo·bos m. AMER., METEOROL. var. of **calabobos.**

mo·ja·da I. f. *(acción de mojar)* wetting, drenching; COLL. *(herida)* stab wound; AGR. old Catalonian land measure II. adj. see **mojado, –da.**

mo·ja·do, –da I. past part. see **mojar** II. adj. *(húmedo)* wet, drenched; PHONET. pertaining to a sound formed with the back of the tongue and the palate III. f. see **mojada.**

mo·ja·dor, –do·ra I. adj. *(que moja)* wetting, drenching II. m.f. *(el que moja)* wetter —m. PRINT. moistening tank (for paper); *(esponja)* moistener, sponge.

mo·ja·du·ra f. wetting, drenching.

mo·ján m. COL., VEN. *(ente fabuloso)* imaginary being that protects the fields; COL. *(manantial)* hidden spring of drinking water.

mo·jar tr. *(humedecer)* to wet, make wet; *(empapar)* to drench, soak; to dip <*mojar el pan en aceite* to dip the bread in oil>; FIG., COLL. *(apuñalar)* to stab, stick; P. RICO, COLL. to pay off (bribe) —intr. FIG., COLL. to get mixed up <*no te mojes en ese lío* don't get mixed up in that mess> —reflex. *(humedecerse)* to get wet; CUBA, PERU, P. RICO to profit, benefit.

mo·ja·rra f. ICHTH. mojarra; AMER. small knife.

mo·ja·rri·lla m.f. COLL. good-natured *or* jolly person.

mo·ja·se·llos m. [pl. **-llos**] moistener, sponge (for stamps).

mo·je m. CUL. gravy, juice.

mo·jí m. [pl. **-jíes**] *(bizcocho)* small cake (with marzipan icing); *(bollo)* small bun (for dunking in chocolate).

mo·ji·cón m. *(bizcocho)* small cake (with marzipan icing); *(bollo)* small bun (for dunking in chocolate); COLL. *(puñetazo)* punch in the face.

mo·ji·gan·ga f. *(fiesta de máscaras)* masquerade, costume party; THEAT. farce, comedy; FIG. *(burla)* mockery, joke.

mo·ji·ga·te·rí·a *or* **mo·ji·ga·tez** f. *(hipocresía)* hypocrisy, dissimulation; *(calidad de santurrón)* sanctimoniousness, excessive righteousness.

mo·ji·ga·to, –ta I. adj. *(hipócrita)* hypocritical, dissimulating; *(santurrón)* sanctimonious, overly righteous II. m.f. *(hipócrita)* hypocrite, dissembler; *(santurrón)* sanctimonious *or* overly righteous person.

mo·ji·ne·te m. ARCHIT. *(albardilla)* coping; *(caballete)* ridge, crest (of a rooftop); ARG., CHILE gable.

mo·jo m. CUL. *(salsa)* gravy, juice; BOL. meat and vegetable stew; CUBA rum cocktail.

mo·jón m. *(señal de término)* landmark, boundary marker; *(señal de guía)* milestone, road marker; *(montón)* heap, pile; VULG. *(excremento)* stool, turd.

mo·jo·nar tr. to set up boundary markers around.

mo·jo·ne·ra f. *(sitio donde se ponen mojones)* area where boundary markers are placed; (*serie de mojones*) row of boundary markers.

mo·jo·ne·ro m. appraiser, assessor.

mo·jo·so m. ARG., BOL. large knife (used by the gauchos).

mo·ka m. mocha.

mol m. CHEM. mole, mol.

mo·la f. (*harina de sacrificio*) flour with salt used in sacrificial rites; MED. mole (in the uterus); PAN. (*camisa*) decorative shirt; (*tapiz*) wall hanging ♦ **m. matriz** MED. mole.

mo·lar¹ adj. & m. DENT. molar.

mo·lar² tr. COLL. to taste, sample —intr. COLL. (*lucir*) to shine, succeed; (*presumir*) to brag, boast.

mol·de m. (*objeto hueco*) mold; (*forma*) pattern, model; FIG. (*persona ejemplar*) exemplary person, role model; PRINT. form ready for printing ♦ **de m.** fitting, opportune • **letra de m.** printed letter, print • **venir de m.** or **venir como de m.** to be just what one needs, be just right for someone.

mol·de·a·ble adj. moldable.

mol·de·a·do I. past part. see **moldear** II. m. molding, casting.

mol·de·a·dor, –do·ra I. adj. molding II. m.f. molder.

mol·de·ar tr. CONST. (*moldurar*) to apply molding to; (*sacar el molde*) to mold, shape; (*vaciar*) to cast.

mol·du·ra f. CONST. molding; ECUAD. picture frame.

mo·le I. adj. CUL. soft II. m. MEX., CUL. thick chili sauce —f. (*bulto*) mass, bulk ♦ **m. verde** MEX., CUL. stew of meat and chili and green tomatoes.

mo·lé·cu·la f. molecule ♦ **m. gramo** CHEM. gram molecule.

mo·le·cu·lar adj. molecular.

mo·le·de·ro, –ra I. adj. grindable, millable II. f. (*piedra*) grinding stone; COLL. (*importunación*) nuisance, bother.

mo·le·dor, –do·ra I. adj. (*que muele*) grinding, milling; FIG., COLL. (*pesado*) bothersome, annoying II. m.f. (*persona que muele*) grinder; FIG., COLL. (*pesado*) pest, nuisance —m. TECH. grinder, crusher (in a mill).

mo·le·du·ra f. (*acción de moler*) grinding, milling; FIG., COLL. (*fatiga*) weariness, exhaustion; (*molestia*) bother, nuisance.

mo·le·jón m. (*mollejón*) millstone, grindstone; CUBA rock near the water's surface.

mo·len·de·ro, –ra m.f. (*persona que muele*) grinder, miller —m. CUL. (*de chocolate*) chocolate grinder or maker; C. AMER. grinding table.

mo·le·ño, –ña I. adj. said of rock suitable for making millstones II. f. MIN. fine bread.

mo·ler §78 tr. (*aplastar*) to grind, mill; (*fastidiar*) to annoy, bother; (*cansar*) to exhaust, drain; FIG. (*destruir*) to beat up, cream; CUBA, AGR. to press (sugar cane) ♦ **m. a golpes** or **palos** FIG. to beat to a pulp.

mo·les·tar tr. (*fastidiar*) to bother, annoy; (*interrumpir*) to disturb, disrupt <*no me moleste mientras estoy durmiendo* don't disturb me while I'm sleeping>; (*causar dolor*) to bother, trouble <*sus piernas le molestan cuando anda mucho* his legs bother him when he walks a lot> ♦ **no m.** do not disturb (sign) —reflex. to bother, take the trouble ♦ **no se moleste** don't bother.

mo·les·tia f. (*fastidio*) bother, annoyance; (*incomodidad*) inconvenience, trouble; (*malestar*) discomfort ♦ **si no es m.** if it isn't too much trouble.

mo·les·to, –ta adj. (*fastidioso*) bothersome, annoying <*es una tarea m.* it's an annoying job>; FIG. (*enojado*) bothered, annoyed; (*incómodo*) uncomfortable <*me siento m. aquí* I feel uncomfortable here>; (*inconveniente*) inconvenient, troublesome; awkward <*una situación m.* an awkward situation>.

mo·les·to·so, –sa adj. AMER. var. of **molesto, –ta.**

mo·le·ta f. (*piedra para moler*) muller, millstone; (*aparato para pulir el cristal*) glass polisher.

mo·lib·de·no m. CHEM. molybdenum.

mo·li·cie f. (*blandura*) softness; FIG. (*afición al regalo*) fondness for luxury.

mo·li·do, –da I. past part. see **moler** II. adj. (*aplastado*) ground, milled; FIG. (*derrengado*) beat, worn-out.

mo·lien·da f. (*acción*) grinding, milling; (*cantidad*) batch, quantity ground; (*molino*) mill; (*temporada*) milling season; FIG., COLL. (*fastidio*) annoyance, bore; (*cansancio*) exhaustion.

mo·li·fi·car §70 tr. to mollify, soften.

mo·li·mien·to m. (*acción*) grinding, milling; FIG. (*fatiga*) fatigue, exhaustion.

mo·li·ne·ro, –ra I. adj. milling II. m. miller, grinder —f. (*señora del molinero*) miller's wife; (*encargada*) miller.

mo·li·ne·te m. (*ventilador*) ventilating fan, ventilator; (*juguete de papel*) pinwheel; COL. shift (in the mines); MEX. catherine wheel (firework).

mo·li·ni·llo m. (*instrumento para moler*) mill, grinder; (*palillo*) whisk, beater.

mo·li·no m. (*edificio, máquina*) mill; FIG. (*persona inquieta*) restless person ♦ **m. de viento** windmill • **molinos de viento** FIG. imaginary enemies.

mo·lón, –lo·na adj. COLL. (*lucido*) magnificent, splendid; COLL. (*elegante*) elegant, well-dressed; GUAT., MEX. bothersome.

mo·lon·dro m. COLL. bum, good-for-nothing.

mo·lon·drón m. COLL. (*molondro*) bum, good-for-nothing; VEN. considerable inheritance or amount of money.

mo·lon·que·ar tr. C. AMER., MEX. to beat to a pulp.

mo·lo·te·ra m. C. AMER., CUBA uproar, riot; MEX. (*moño de pelo*) bun, chignon; (*ovillo*) ball (of wool); (*tortilla*) filled corn tortilla; COL., MEX. (*chanchullo*) swindle, racket.

mo·lo·te·ra f. GUAT., HOND. uproar, riot.

mol·tu·ra·ción f. grinding, milling.

mol·tu·ra·dor m. grinder, miller.

mol·tu·rar tr. to grind, mill.

mo·lus·co m. ZOOL. mollusk.

mo·lla f. (*miga de pan*) bread crumb; (*magro de la carne*) lean meat.

mo·llar adj. (*blando*) soft, tender; (*de las carnes*) lean and boneless (meat); (*fácil*) easy, cushy (job).

mo·lle·ar intr. (*ceder una cosa*) to give, yield; (*doblarse una cosa*) to bend.

mo·lle·do m. ANAT. fleshy part (of limbs); (*molla*) bread crumb.

mo·lle·ja f. (*estómago de los aves*) gizzard; (*lechecilla*) sweetbread, thymus gland.

mo·lle·jón m. (*piedra de afilar*) millstone, grindstone; FIG., COLL. (*hombre grueso y flojo*) fat good-for-nothing.

mo·lle·ra f. ANAT. (*cráneo*) crown (of the head); (*fontanela*) fontanelle; FIG. (*seso*) brains, ability ♦ **cerrado de m.** FIG. stupid • **duro de m.** FIG. (*testarudo*) obstinate; FIG. (*torpe*) dense, dull-witted.

mo·lle·ta f. CUL. brown bread.

mo·lle·te m. (*panecillo*) small roll, muffin; (*molledo*) fleshy part (of arms); (*moflete*) fat cheek.

mo·lle·tu·do, –da adj. fat-cheeked.

mo·lliz·nar or **mo·lliz·ne·ar** intr. to drizzle, rain lightly.

mo·me·ar intr. to clown (around).

mo·men·tá·ne·a·men·te adv. (*durante algunos momentos*) momentarily; (*inmediatamente*) immediately, right now.

mo·men·tá·ne·o, –a adj. momentary, temporary.

mo·men·to m. (*tiempo*) moment; (*ocasión*) occasion, time <*no hay m. favorable para hacerlo* there is no good time to do it>; FIG. (*importancia*) importance, consequence <*de poco m.* of little importance>; PHYS. moment <*m. de inercia* moment of inertia> ♦ **a cada m.** continually, at every instant • **a partir de este m.** from this moment (on) • **al m.** immediately, at once • **de m.** at present, for the moment • **de un m. a otro** any moment, from one minute to the next • **dentro de un m.** in a moment • **desde este m.** from this moment (on) • **¡momento!** just a minute! • **m. de fuerza** PHYS. moment • **momentos después** moments later • **por momentos** (*continuadamente*) continually, all the time; (*pronto*) soon.

mo·me·rí·a f. clowning.

mo·mia f. (*cadáver*) mummy; FIG. (*persona seca y delgada*) emaciated person ♦ **estar hecho una m.** to be all skin and bones.

mo·mi·fi·ca·ción f. mummification.

mo·mi·fi·car §70 tr. to mummify II. reflex. to become mummified.

mo·mio, –mia I. adj. lean, thin II. m. (*ganga*) bargain; (*sinecura*) cushy job; (*suplemento*) extra, bonus ♦ **de m.** COLL. free, for nothing.

mo·mo m. funny face.

mo·mos·cle m. MEX. tomb, funeral mound.

mo·na f. ZOOL. *(hembra)* female monkey; *(especie)* Barbary ape, macaque; FIG., COLL. *(mimo)* ape, mimic; *(borrachera)* drunkenness; *(borracho)* drunk (person); *(juego de naipes)* old maid (card game); CHILE mannequin; MEX. coward ♦ **coger** *or* **pillar una m.** FIG., COLL. to get loaded *or* plastered • **dormir la m.** FIG., COLL. to sleep it off (a hangover).
mo·na·cal adj. monastic.
mo·na·ca·to m. monasticism, monkhood.
Mó·na·co m. Monaco.
mo·na·da f. *(gesto)* monkey *or* funny face; *(cosa o persona graciosa)* pretty *or* lovely thing; FIG. *(tontería)* silliness, foolishness; *(halago)* flattery.
mó·na·da f. monad.
mo·na·gui·llo m. acolyte, altar boy.
mo·na·quis·mo f. monasticism, monkhood.
mo·nar·ca m. monarch, sovereign.
mo·nar·quí·a f. monarchy.
mo·nár·qui·co, –ca I. adj. monarchical, monarchic II. m.f. monarchist.
mo·nas·te·rio m. monastery.
mo·nás·ti·co, –ca adj. monastic, monastical.
mon·da f. *(limpieza)* cleaning; *(poda)* pruning, trimming; *(peladura)* peeling, skinning; *(parte podada)* trimmings; *(parte pelada)* peelings, peels; CARIB., COL., MEX. beating, thrashing ♦ **ser la m.** to be great *or* terrific.
mon·da·dien·tes m. [pl. **-tes**] toothpick.
mon·da·dor, –do·ra I. adj. *(podador)* pruning, trimming; *(que pela)* peeling II. m.f. *(podador)* pruner, trimmer; *(pelador)* peeler.
mon·da·du·ra f. *(poda)* pruning, trimming; *(peladura)* peeling; *(parte podada)* pruned branches, trimmings; *(parte pelada)* peelings, peels.
mon·dar tr. *(quitar lo inútil)* to clean, cleanse; *(pelar fruta)* to peel, skin (fruit); *(descascarar nueces)* to shell (nuts); *(podar)* to prune, trim; *(dragar)* to dredge, clean out (a river); *(carraspear)* to clear (one's throat); COLL. *(cortar el pelo)* to cut (someone's hair); FIG. *(quitarle a alguien lo que tiene)* to clean out, fleece (of money) ♦ **m. a alguien a palos** to beat *or* thrash someone II. reflex. ♦ **mondarse de risa** COLL. to laugh one's head off • **mondarse los dientes** to pick one's teeth.
mon·da·ra·jas f.pl. COLL. peelings, peels.
mon·do, –da adj. clean, neat ♦ **m. y lirondo** COLL. unadultered, pure and simple.
mon·don·go m. CUL. tripe; COLL. *(intestinos humanos)* guts, innards; GUAT., P. RICO ridiculous get-up.
mo·ne·ar intr. COLL. *(hacer monadas)* to clown (around); CHILE, MEX., URUG. to boast; VEN. to climb.
mo·ne·da f. *(dinero)* money, coin; *(pieza)* coin; FIN. mint; FIG., COLL. *(caudal)* wealth, money ♦ **acuñar m.** to mint money • **m. corriente** currency • **m. divisionaria** fractional coin • **m. falsa** counterfeit coin • **m. fiduciaria** fiat money • **m. fuerte** hard cash • **m. imaginaria** money of account • **m. sonante** hard money • **m. suelta** loose change • **pagar en la misma m.** FIG. to give someone a taste of his own medicine, give tit for tat.
mo·ne·de·ro m. *(fabricante)* minter, coiner; *(portamonedas)* change purse ♦ **m. falso** counterfeiter.
mo·ne·gas·co, –ca adj. & m.f. Monacan, Monegasque.
mo·ne·rí·a f. *(monada)* cute *or* amusing thing; *(gesto)* funny *or* monkey face; *(tontería)* silliness, foolishness.
mo·ne·ta·rio, –ria I. adj. monetary II. m. coin collection.
mo·ne·ti·za·ción f. monetization.
mo·ne·ti·zar §04 tr. *(amonedar)* to mint, coin; *(dar curso legal)* to monetize.
mon·gol, –go·la adj. & m.f. Mongolian —m. *(idioma)* Mongolian.
Mon·go·lia f. Mongolia.
mon·gó·li·co, –ca I. adj. GEOG. Mongolian; MED. mongoloid II. m.f. *(habitante)* Mongolian; MED. mongoloid.
mon·go·lis·mo m. MED. mongolism, Down's syndrome.
mo·nia·to m. BOT. sweet potato.
mo·ni·ca·co m. VULG. *(monigote)* weakling, shrimp; COL. hypocrite.
mo·ni·go·te *or* **mo·ni·con·go** m. *(de convento)* lay brother; FIG., COLL. *(muñeco ridículo)* rag *or* paper doll; *(pintura mal hecha)* doodle, crude picture, COLL. *(hombre torpe)*

boob, dolt; CUBA, BOT. liana; BOL., CHILE, PERU seminarian.
mo·nín, –ni·na *or* **mo·ni·no, –na** adj. COLL. cute, pretty.
mo·ni·po·dio m. illegal deal *or* dealings.
mo·nís f. trinket, bauble ♦ **monises** COLL. bucks, cash.
mo·nis·mo m. PHILOS. monism.
mo·ni·tor m. *(admonitor)* monitor, adviser; *(entrenador)* trainer; COMPUT., MARIT., MED., TELEV. monitor.
mon·ja f. RELIG. nun; MEX. round sweet bread.
mon·je m. *(fraile)* monk; *(solitario)* recluse, anchorite.
mon·jil I. adj. nun-like, nunnish II. m. *(hábito de monja)* nun's habit; *(traje de luto)* mourning dress.
mon·ji·ta f. ARG. small bird of the Pampas; CHILE white and yellow flowered plant.
mo·no, –na I. adj. COLL. cute, darling; COL., C. RICA reddish (hair) II. m. ZOOL. monkey, ape; FIG. *(imitador)* mimic, ape; COLL. *(tonto)* nincompoop, ninny; *(dibujo)* primitive drawing; *(comodín)* joker (in cards); *(traje)* coveralls; ECUAD., PERU chamberpot; CHILE pile of produce ♦ **estar de monos** to be on bad terms with • **meterle a alguien los monos** COL., CUBA, P. RICO to frighten, put a scare into • **m. aullador** ZOOL. howler monkey • **quedarse hecho un m.** to be made a monkey of • **ser el último m.** to be the least important.
mo·no·a·tó·mi·co, –ca adj. CHEM. monatomic.
mo·no·cor·de m. MUS. monochord, single-string; FIG. *(monótono)* monotonous.
mo·no·cro·mo, –ma adj. monochrome, monochromic.
mo·nó·cu·lo, –la I. adj. monocular, one-eyed II. m. *(lente)* monocle; *(vendaje)* eye patch.
mo·no·cul·ti·vo m. AGR. monoculture.
mo·no·ga·mia f. monogamy.
mo·nó·ga·mo, –ma adj. monogamous.
mo·no·gra·fí·a f. monograph.
mo·no·gra·ma m. monogram, initials.
mo·no·lin·güe adj. monolingual.
mo·no·lí·ti·co, –ca adj. monolithic.
mo·no·li·to m. monolith.
mo·no·lo·gar §47 intr. to soliloquize.
mo·nó·lo·go m. monologue, soliloquy.
mo·no·ma·ní·a f. PSYCH. monomania.
mo·no·pla·no m. AVIA. monoplane.
mo·no·pla·za AVIA. adj. single-seater.
mo·no·po·li·cé, monopolice see **monopolizar.**
mo·no·po·lio m. monopoly.
mo·no·po·lis·ta m.f. monopolist.
mo·no·po·lís·ti·co, –ca adj. monopolistic.
mo·no·po·li·za·ción f. monopolization.
mo·no·po·li·za·dor, –do·ra I. adj. monopolizing II. m.f. monopolizer.
mo·no·po·li·zar §04 tr. to monopolize.
mo·no·si·lá·bi·co, –ca adj. GRAM. monosyllabic.
mo·no·sí·la·bo, –ba GRAM. I. adj. monosyllabic II. m. monosyllable.
mo·no·te m. COLL. dumfounded person.
mo·no·te·ís·mo m. RELIG. monotheism.
mo·no·te·ís·ta RELIG. I. adj. monotheistic II. m.f. monotheist.
mo·no·ti·pia f. PRINT. monotype (process).
mo·no·ti·po m. PRINT. Monotype (machine) (trademark).
mo·nó·to·na·men·te adv. monotonously.
mo·nó·to·ní·a f. monotony.
mo·nó·to·no, –na adj. monotonous.
mo·no·va·len·te adj. CHEM. monovalent, univalent.
mon·ro·ís·mo m. Monroe Doctrine.
mon·se·ñor m. monsignor.
mon·ser·ga f. COLL. *(lenguaje)* gobbledygook, gibberish; *(lata)* pain, nuisance ♦ **dar la m. a alguien** COLL. to annoy *or* pester someone.
mons·truo I. m. monster II. adj. huge, colossal.
mons·truo·si·dad f. monstrosity.
mons·truo·so, –sa adj. monstrous.
mon·ta f. *(acción de montar)* mounting; *(arte de montar)* horseback riding; *(suma)* sum, total; *(acaballadero)* stud farm; MIL. call to mount ♦ **de poca m.** of no account, insignificant —m. URUG. jockey.
mon·ta·car·gas m. [pl. **-gas**] freight elevator.

mon·ta·da f. EQUIT. tongue, groove (of bit); COL. harness, saddle; C. AMER., MEX. mounted police.

mon·ta·do, –da I. past part. see **montar** II. adj. *(que va a caballo)* mounted; *(preparado)* saddled (horse); MECH. assembled (a machine); THEAT. staged III. m. mounted trooper.

mon·ta·dor m. EQUIT. horse block; CINEM. film editor; MECH. assembler, installer ♦ **m. de tuberías** pipefitter.

mon·ta·du·ra f. *(acción de montar)* mounting; EQUIT. harness, saddle; JEWEL. setting.

mon·ta·je m. MECH. assembly, installation; CINEM. montage; ARTIL. mounting; COLL. *(farsa)* sham, put-on ♦ **cadena de m.** assembly line • **m. de cañón** gun mount • **m. de líneas** ELEC. hookup.

mon·tan·te m. *(de una armazón)* upright, strut; *(ventana)* transom; *(listón)* mullion; *(espadón)* broadsword; *(de sostén)* stanchion ♦ **coger el m.** to leave, go away • **meter el m.** to separate two opponents in a fight —f. MARIT. flood tide.

mon·ta·ña f. *(monte)* mountain; FIG. *(amontonamiento)* mountain, heap; *(territorio montañoso)* mountain region ♦ **hacer de todo una m.** FIG. to make a mountain out of a molehill • **La Montaña** region of Santander (Spain) • **m. rusa** rollercoaster • **montañas** highlands.

mon·ta·ñe·ro, –ra m.f. mountaineer, mountain climber.

mon·ta·ñés, –ñe·sa I. adj. *(de una montaña)* mountain, highland; *(de La Montaña)* of Santander (Spain) II. m.f. *(que habite la montaña)* mountain dweller, highlander; *(que habite la Montaña)* inhabitant of Santander (Spain).

mon·ta·ñis·mo m. mountaineering, mountain climbing.

mon·ta·ño·so, –sa adj. mountainous.

mon·ta·pla·tos m. [pl. **-tos**] dumbwaiter.

mon·tar intr. *(subir)* to mount, get on; *(subir a caballo)* to mount a horse; *(cabalgar)* to ride (horseback); FIG. *(importar)* to be important <este asunto monta poco this affair is unimportant> ♦ **m. a caballo** to ride horseback • **m. en** to ride <m. en bicicleta to ride a bicycle> • **m. en cólera** to get angry • **tanto monta** it's all the same, it doesn't matter either way —tr. *(subir)* to mount <m. un caballo to mount a horse>; *(valer)* to mount or amount to <sus cuentas montaron mil dólares his bills mounted to one thousand dollars>; MECH. *(armar)* to assemble, set up (a machine); *(establecer)* to set up <m. un negocio to set up a business>; CINEM. to edit (film); THEAT. to produce (a play); ARM. to cock (a gun); JEWEL. to set; *(acoplar)* to mount (said of animals) ♦ **m. una ofensiva** MIL. to mount an offensive.

mon·ta·raz [pl. **-ra·ces**] I. adj. *(del monte)* mountain, highland; *(salvaje)* savage, wild II. m. forest warden.

mon·ta·rrón m. COL. large forest.

mon·te m. *(montaña)* mount, mountain; *(bosque)* forest, woodland; COLL. *(establecimiento)* pawnshop; FIG., COLL. *(cabello)* mop (of hair); FIG. *(dificultad)* difficulty, problem; *(naipes que quedan)* talon (cards that remain after the deal); *(juego de naipes)* monte (card game); *(banca)* bank (in gambling); AMER. outskirts (of a town); MEX. pasture ♦ **echarse al m.** to take to the hills • **m. alto** forest, woodland (with tall trees) • **m. bajo** brush, brushwood • **m. de Venus** ANAT. mons veneris • **m. pío** assistance fund • **M. de los Olivos** Mount of Olives • **Montes Cantábricos** GEOG. Cantabrian Mountains.

mon·te·ar intr. *(perseguir la caza)* to hunt, give chase; VEN. to chat, gossip.

mon·te·pí·o m. *(casa de empeño)* pawnshop; *(fondo)* fund.

mon·te·ra f. *(de paño)* cloth cap; TAUR. bullfighter's hat; *(de cristales)* skylight; *(del alambique)* lid, cover (of a still); BOL. Indian hat ♦ **ponerse el mundo por m.** not to give a damn what people think.

mon·te·rí·a f. *(caza mayor)* big game; *(arte de cazar)* hunting; CUBA leftover meat; ECUAD. raft.

mon·tés adj. wild, undomesticated.

Mon·te·vi·de·o m. Montevideo.

mon·te·vi·de·a·no, –na I. adj. of Montevideo II. m.f. native of Montevideo.

mon·tí·cu·lo m. knoll, hillock.

mon·to m. amount, total.

mon·tón m. *(acopio)* pile, heap; FIG., COLL. *(mucho)* heaps, lots ♦ **a m.** wholesale, en masse • **a montones** FIG. by the truckload • **del m.** FIG., COLL. ordinary, average • **ser del m.** FIG., COLL. to be one of the herd.

mon·to·ne·ra f. AMER. troop of mounted rebels; COL. stack, pile.

mon·to·ne·ro m. AMER. guerrilla (fighter).

mon·tu·bio, –bia I. m.f. AMER. coastal peasant II. adj. COL., ECUAD., PERU rustic, country.

mon·tu·no, –na adj. *(del monte)* mountain; CHILE, CUBA, VEN. rustic, country; AMER. wild, savage.

mon·tu·ra f. *(cabalgadura)* mount (animal); *(silla)* saddle, mount; *(de una máquina)* assembly, installation; JEWEL. setting (of a jewel); OPT. frame (of eyeglasses).

mo·nu·men·tal adj. monumental, huge.

mo·nu·men·to m. monument.

mon·zón m.f. monsoon.

mo·ña[1] f. *(lazo)* bow, knot; TAUR. *(del toro)* colored ribbons used to identify bull; *(del torero)* black ribbon ornament worn by bullfighter; COL. pride, arrogance; *(muñeca)* mannequin, doll.

mo·ña[2] f. FIG., COLL. drunken binge or spree.

mo·ño m. *(de la mujer)* bun, chignon; *(lazo)* bow, knot; ORNITH. crest (of birds); *(adorno)* trinket; CHILE forelock (of horse); COL. whim, caprice ♦ **agarrarse el m.** FIG., COLL. to pull each other's hair • **estar hasta el m.** FIG., COLL. to be fed up • **hacerse el m.** to comb one's hair • **ponerse moños** FIG., COLL. to put on airs.

mo·ñón, –ño·na adj. *(moñudo)* crested, tufted (said of birds); COL., COLL. sulky, pouty.

mo·ñu·do, –da adj. ORNITH. crested, tufted.

mo·que·ar intr. to snivel, have a runny nose.

mo·que·o m. runny nose.

mo·que·ro m. handkerchief.

mo·que·te m. punch in the face.

mo·que·te·ar intr. to snivel constantly, have a runny nose.

mo·qui·llo m. VET. distemper.

mo·qui·ta f. mucus.

mo·qui·te·ar intr. COLL. to whine, whimper.

mo·qui·te·o m. COLL. whining, whimpering.

mo·ra I. f. LAW delay; BOT. blackberry, mulberry II. adj. see **moro, –ra**.

mo·ra·da I. f. *(casa)* house, dwelling; *(estancia)* stay, sojourn II. adj. see **morado, –da**.

mo·ra·do, –da I. adj. *(violeta)* purple, violet; ARG. cowardly ♦ **pasarlas moradas** FIG., COLL. to have a rough time II. m. purple —f. see **morada**.

mo·ra·dor, –do·ra I. adj. living, residing II. m.f. tenant, resident.

mo·ral I. adj. moral II. f. *(ética)* morals, ethics; *(ánimo)* morale, spirits.

mo·ra·le·ja f. moral (of a story).

mo·ra·li·cé, moralice see **moralizar**.

mo·ra·li·dad f. *(moral)* morality; *(moraleja)* moral ♦ **moralidades** THEAT. morality play.

mo·ra·lis·mo m. moralism.

mo·ra·lis·ta m.f. moralist.

mo·ra·li·za·ción f. moralization.

mo·ra·li·za·dor, –do·ra I. adj. moralizing II. m.f. moralizer, moralist.

mo·ra·li·zar §04 tr. & intr. to moralize.

mo·ral·men·te adv. morally.

mo·rar intr. to live, reside.

mo·ra·to·ria f. LAW moratorium.

mor·bi·dez f. softness, delicateness.

mór·bi·do, –da adj. soft, delicate; MED. morbid.

mor·bi·li·dad o **mor·bi·di·dad** f. MED. morbidity, incidence of disease.

mor·bo m. MED. illness, disease ♦ **m. comicial** epilepsy • **m. gálico** syphilis • **m. regio** jaundice.

mor·bo·si·dad f. MED. morbidity, disease.

mor·bo·so, –sa adj. *(no sano)* morbid; *(enfermo)* sick, diseased.

mor·ci·lla f. CUL. blood pudding or sausage; THEAT., COLL. ad lib, improvisation ♦ **¡que te den morcilla!** COLL. take a walk!, get lost!

mor·ci·lle·ro, –ra m.f. CUL. sausage maker or seller; THEAT., FIG., COLL. ad libber, improviser —f. VEN. annoyance, frustration.

mor·cón m. CUL. large blood pudding; COLL. *(persona gruesa)* short and plump person; *(persona sucia)* slob.

mor·da·ci·dad f. mordacity.

mor·da·ga f. COLL. drunk, binge.

mor·daz adj. [pl. **-da·ces**] *(corrosivo)* corrosive, mordant; *(picante)* burning, pungent (food); FIG. *(punzante)* biting, mordant.

mor·da·za f. *(silencio)* gag; MARIT. hawsehole clamp; TECH. clamp.

mor·de·dor, –do·ra adj. *(que muerde)* biting; FIG. *(satírico)* satirical, caustic.

mor·de·du·ra f. bite.

mor·de·lón, –lo·na adj. COL., VEN. that bites, biting (said of dogs); MEX. bribe-taking, corrupt.

mor·der §78 tr. to bite <*me mordió el perro* the dog bit me>; *(mordiscar)* to nibble (at); *(asir)* to bite, grip; FIG. *(consumir)* to eat away (at), eat into <*el ácido muerde el metal* acid eats into metal>; *(murmurar)* to backbite, disparage; ARTS, PRINT. to etch; AMER. to cheat ♦ **m. el polvo** FIG. to bite the dust —reflex. to bite <*se muerde las uñas* he bites his nails> ♦ **morderse la lengua** FIG. to bite or hold one's tongue • **no morderse la lengua** FIG. to be outspoken —intr. to bite.

mor·di·can·te adj. *(corrosivo)* biting, corrosive; FIG. *(cáustico)* caustic, sarcastic.

mor·di·car §70 tr. to bite, sting.

mor·di·do, –da I. past part. see **morder** II. adj. FIG. diminished, eroded III. f. MEX. bribe.

mor·dien·te I. adj. mordant, biting II. m. *(agua fuerte)* caustic acid; *(de tintorero)* color fixative.

mor·di·mien·to m. bite, biting.

mor·di·qué, mordique see **mordicar.**

mor·dis·car §70 or **mor·dis·que·ar** tr. to nibble.

mor·dis·co m. nibble, bite ♦ **dar** or **pegar un m.** to take a bite (of).

mor·dis·cón m. AMER. big bite.

mo·re·na¹ I. f. loaf of brown bread; II. adj. see **moreno, –na.**

mo·re·na² f. ICHTH. *(pez)* moray; AGR. sheaf, stack (of newly cut corn); GEOL. moraine.

mo·re·no, –na I. adj. *(pardo)* brown; *(tostado)* brown-skinned, dark-skinned; *(pelo)* brown, brunet; FIG., COLL. *(mulato)* mulatto II. m.f. *(negro)* Black, Negro; *(mulato)* mulatto; *(de pelo castaño)* brunet, brunette —f. see **morena¹,².**

mo·re·te·ar intr. AMER. to bruise.

mo·re·tón m. COLL. bruise, black-and-blue mark.

mor·fe·ma m. GRAM. morpheme.

mor·fi·na f. CHEM., PHARM. morphine.

mor·fi·no·ma·ní·a f. MED. morphinomania, addiction to morphine.

mor·fi·nó·ma·no, –na MED. I. adj. addicted to morphine II. m.f. morphine addict.

mor·fo·lo·gí·a f. BIOL., GRAM. morphology.

mor·fo·ló·gi·co, –ca adj. BIOL., GRAM. morphological.

mor·ga·ná·ti·co, –ca adj. morganatic.

mor·gue f. morgue.

mo·ri·bun·do, –da I. adj. moribund, dying II. m.f. dying person.

mo·rir §27 intr. *(fallecer)* to die, pass away; *(extinguirse)* to die, go out <*la lumbre va muriendo* the fire is dying>; *(acabar)* to die <*el día muere* day is dying>; FIG. *(sufrir)* to die <*m. de hambre* to die of hunger>; *(desaparecer)* to die, die out ♦ **m. ahogado** to drown • **m. ahorcado** to be hanged • **m. con las botas puestas** FIG. to die with one's boots on • **m. de frío** to freeze to death • **m. de risa** to die laughing • **m. fusilado** to be shot • **m. vestido** to die violently • **¡muera!** death to . . . !, down with. . . ! —reflex. *(fallecer)* to die; *(extinguirse)* to die, go out; FIG. *(sufrir)* to die <*morirse de risa* to die laughing> ♦ **morirse de aburrimiento** FIG. to be bored to death • **morirse de ganas** to be dying to • **morirse por** FIG. *(estar loco por)* to be crazy about; *(querer)* to be dying to <*me muero por ir a Francia* I am dying to go to France>.

mo·ris·co, –ca I. adj. *(moro)* Moorish, Morisco; CHILE thin, lean II. m.f. Moor, Morisco.

mo·ris·que·ta f. *(ardid)* ruse, trick; AMER. *(mueca)* grimace, face; PHILIP. boiled rice.

mor·la·co, –ca I. adj. sly, cunning II. m.f. *(astuto)* sly fox —m. COLL. *(toro)* fighting bull; AMER. money; COL. nag, old horse.

mor·món, –mo·na m.f. Mormon.

Mor·mo·nis·mo m. Mormonism.

mo·ro, –ra I. adj. *(árabe)* Moorish; *(mahometano)* Moslem; PHILIP. Moro; FIG. *(no bautizado)* unbaptized; *(sin agua)* undiluted (said of wine); *(caballo)* white-stockinged (said of horses) II. m.f. *(árabe)* Moor; *(mahometano)* Moslem; PHILIP. Moro ♦ **m. de paz** peaceable person • **hay moros en la costa** the walls have ears • **hubo moros y cristianos** there was a free-for-all (fight) • **moros y cristianos** AMER., CUL. rice and black beans (together) —f. see **mora.**

mo·ro·cho, –cha adj. AMER., BOT. hard (corn); *(fuerte)* strong, robust; *(moreno de pelo)* brunette; *(moreno de piel)* swarthy, dark-skinned; CHILE shorn to the scalp; ECUAD. hard (coal, wood); VEN. twin.

mo·rón m. hillock, mound.

mo·ron·cho, –cha adj. *(calvo)* bald, hairless; *(pelado)* bare, stripped (of hair, of leaves).

mo·ron·dan·ga f. COLL. collection of junk.

mo·ron·do, –da adj. *(calvo)* hairless; *(pelado)* bare, stripped (of hair, of leaves).

mo·ro·sa·men·te adv. *(lentamente)* slowly; *(con dilación)* tardily.

mo·ro·si·dad f. *(lentitud)* slowness; *(demora)* delay, lateness; *(falta de actividad)* inactivity.

mo·ro·so, –sa adj. *(lento)* slow; *(perezoso)* sluggish, lazy; *(tardío)* late, tardy; FIN. *(retrasado en el pago)* in arrears, delinquent.

mo·rra f. ANAT. crown (of the head); *(juego)* mora (game) ♦ **andar a la m.** to trade blows.

mo·rra·da f. *(golpe)* butt, bump (of two heads); *(bofetada)* slap, blow.

mo·rral m. *(saco de cazador)* game bag; *(mochila)* knapsack; COLL. *(hombre zafio)* boor, rustic.

mo·rre·na f. GEOL. moraine.

mo·rri·llo m. *(cogote de res)* fleshy part of neck (of cattle); COLL. *(cogote grueso)* thick neck; *(canto rodado)* pebble, round stone.

mo·rri·ña f. VET. dropsy; *(tristeza)* sadness, melancholy; *(nostalgia)* homesickness, nostalgia.

mo·rri·ño·so, –sa adj. *(triste)* sad, melancholy; *(raquítico)* weak, rachitic.

mo·rrión m. *(casco antiguo)* morion, helmet; *(gorro militar)* shako.

mo·rris·que·ta f. COL., VEN. face, grimace.

mo·rro m. *(de pistola)* grip, butt (of pistol); *(monte)* knoll, hillock; *(de malecón)* pier, jetty; *(guijarro)* pebble; *(hocico)* snout, nose (of animal) ♦ **beber a m.** to drink straight from the bottle • **estar de morros** to be in a bad mood • **poner morros** to look cross.

mo·rro·co·tu·do, –da adj. COLL. *(importante)* important; *(difícil)* difficult; *(enorme)* enormous, huge; *(magnífico)* magnificent, fabulous; COL. rich, well-off.

mo·rron·go, –ga m.f. COLL. *(gato)* cat, kitty; MEX. servant.

mo·rro·ño·so, –sa adj. C. AMER. *(áspero)* rough, wrinkled; *(egoísta)* mean; PERU weak, sickly.

mo·rru·do, –da adj. *(que tiene hocico)* snouted; *(que tiene labios gruesos)* thick-lipped; ARG. brawny.

mor·sa f. ZOOL. walrus.

mor·se m. Morse code.

mor·ta·ja f. *(sudario)* shroud, winding sheet; AMER. cigarette paper.

mor·tal I. adj. *(sujeto a la muerte)* mortal, subject to death; *(fatal)* mortal, fatal; FIG. *(fuerte)* mortal, deadly <*odio m.* mortal hatred>; *(grave)* mortal <*pecado m.* mortal sin>; *(penoso)* dreadful, awful <*aburrimiento m.* dreadful boredom> II. m. man, mortal.

mor·ta·li·dad f. mortality.

mor·tal·men·te adv. *(de muerte)* mortally, fatally; *(de manera despiadada)* implacably; *(sumamente)* dreadfully, deathly <*una fiesta m. aburrida* a dreadfully boring party>.

mor·tan·dad f. death toll, mortality.

mor·te·ci·no, –na adj. *(muerto naturalmente)* dead (of natural causes); *(apagado)* dying, fading <*luz m.* fading

light>; *(pálido)* dull, pale (color); *(débil)* weak, failing ♦ **hacer la m.** to pretend to be dead, play possum.
mor·te·ra·da f. CUL. any food ground in a mortar; MIL. shot (from a mortar).
mor·te·ro m. ARM., CONST., CUL. mortar; *(bonete)* cap, bonnet.
mor·tí·fe·ro, –ra adj. fatal, lethal.
mor·ti·fi·ca·ción f. *(del cuerpo)* mortification; *(molestia)* annoyance, upset.
mor·ti·fi·ca·dor, –do·ra adj. mortifying.
mor·ti·fi·can·te adj. mortifying.
mor·ti·fi·car §70 tr. MED. *(privar de vitalidad)* to mortify, deaden; *(disciplinar)* to mortify, chastise <*m. la carne* to mortify the flesh>; *(molestar)* to annoy, upset.
mor·tuo·rio, –a I. adj. mortuary, funereal II. m. funeral.
mo·ru·cho, –cha I. adj. COLL. *(moreno)* swarthy, dark-skinned; *(querido)* darling, dear II. m. TAUR. young bull (with tipped horns).
mo·rue·co m. ram, male sheep.
mo·ru·no, –na I. adj. Moorish II. m. CUBA peasant shoe.
mo·sai·co, –ca I. adj. Mosaic, of Moses <*ley m.* Mosaic Law> II. m. mosaic.
mos·ca f. ENTOM. fly; *(barba)* Vandyke beard; *(cebo)* fly (for fishing); COLL. *(dinero)* dough, bread (money); FIG., COLL. *(persona)* pest, pain in the neck; *(molestia)* pain, nuisance (thing) <*será una m. hacer este trabajo* it will be a pain to do this job> ♦ **aflojar** or **soltar la m.** FIG., COLL. to fork out or over, cough up (money) • **cazar moscas** FIG., COLL. to waste time • **estar con** or **tener la m. en la oreja** FIG., COLL. to smell a rat • **m. de burro** or **de mula** ENTOM. horsefly • **m. de España** ENTOM. Spanish fly • **m. muerta** FIG., COLL. hypocrite • **moscas** sparks • **no matar una m.** not to hurt a fly • **papar moscas** FIG. to daydream • **peso m.** lightweight (boxing) • **picarle a uno la m.** FIG. to have a bug in one's ear • **por si las moscas** just in case —m. MEX. stowaway, tramp.
mos·ca·da adj. ♦ **nuez m.** nutmeg.
mos·car·da f. ENTOM. *(moscón)* blowfly, bluebottle; *(huevos)* bee eggs.
mos·car·de·ar intr. *(poner huevos)* to lay eggs (queen bee); *(ser curioso)* to be a busybody, nose around.
mos·car·dón m. *(parásito)* botfly; *(moscón)* blowfly, bluebottle; *(avispón)* hornet; COLL., FIG. *(persona pesada)* pest, nuisance.
mos·car·do·ne·o m. buzz, buzzing.
mos·ca·rrón m. COLL. botfly.
mos·co m. ENTOM. mosquito.
mos·cón m. ENTOM. blowfly, bluebottle; COLL. *(persona pesada)* pest, nuisance.
mos·co·na f. hussy, brazen woman.
mos·co·ne·ar intr. *(zumbar)* to buzz; *(molestar)* to be a nuisance —tr. to annoy, pester.
mos·co·ne·o m. *(zumbido)* buzz, buzzing; *(insistencia)* pestering.
mos·co·vi·ta adj. & m.f. Muscovite —m. MIN. muscovite.
Mos·cú Moscow.
mos·que·a·dor m. *(abanico)* fly swatter; COLL. *(cola de caballo)* switch, tail (of horse).
mos·que·ar tr. *(ahuyentar moscas)* to swat, shoo (flies); FIG. *(responder)* to answer back (with a fresh remark); *(azotar)* to whip —intr. MEX. *(viajar de mosca)* to travel as a tramp, stow away; CUBA *(llenarse de moscas)* to fill up with flies; *(complicarse)* to become complicated; ARG., COL. *(moverse como moscas)* to move like flies —reflex. *(ahuyentar moscas)* to shoo flies; FIG. *(librarse de una molestia)* to rid oneself violently of an annoyance; *(sospechar)* to become suspicious; *(ofenderse)* to take offence.
mos·que·o m. *(moscas)* fly-swatting; *(sospecha)* suspicion; *(resentimiento)* resentment, pique.
mos·que·ro m. *(trampa)* flytrap; AMER. swarm of flies.
mos·que·te m. musket.
mos·que·te·ro m. *(soldado)* musketeer; THEAT. groundling; ARG., BOL. party pooper.
mos·que·tón m. short musket.
mos·quil adj. fly, of flies.
mos·qui·te·ro m. mosquito net.

mos·qui·to m. *(insecto picante)* mosquito; *(mosca pequeña)* gnat, midge; FIG., COLL. *(borrachín)* tippler.
mos·ta·ci·lla f. *(perdigón)* mustard-seed or bird shot; *(abalorio)* glass bead.
mos·ta·cho m. *(bigote)* moustache; COLL., FIG. *(mancha)* spot, blemish (on face); MARIT. bowsprit shroud.
mos·ta·chón m. macaroon.
mos·ta·za f. BOT., CUL. mustard; *(mostacilla)* mustard-seed or bird shot.
mos·te·ar intr. *(destilar mosto)* to produce must; *(echar mosto en cubas)* to put must in vats; *(remostar el vino añejo)* to add must to old wine.
mos·te·la f. AGR. sheaf.
mos·to m. *(zumo)* must; COLL. *(vino)* wine.
mos·tra·do, –da I. past part. see **mostrar** II. adj. accustomed.
mos·tra·dor, –do·ra I. adj. demonstrative, pointing II. m.f. demonstrator —m. *(de tienda)* counter, table top; *(esfera de reloj)* dial, face.
mos·trar §19 tr. *(enseñar)* to show; *(explicar)* to demonstrate, show <*nos mostró cómo hacerlo* he demonstrated to us how to do it>; *(indicar)* to point out; *(expresar)* to show, express (emotions, feelings) —reflex. *(darse a conocer)* to show oneself or prove to be <*se muestra buen profesor* he shows himself to be a good professor>; *(aparecer)* to show oneself, appear <*se mostró en público por primera vez* he appeared in public for the first time>.
mos·tren·co, –ca I. adj. *(sin dueño)* ownerless <*bienes mostrencos* ownerless property>; COLL. *(sin hogar)* homeless, vagabond; *(animal)* stray (animal); *(poco inteligente)* dull, dim-witted; *(gordo)* fat II. m.f. COLL. *(persona ruda)* dolt; *(persona gorda)* fat person.
mo·ta f. TEX. burl, mote (in fabric); *(mancha pequeña)* speck, spot (clothing); FIG. *(defecto ligero)* slight flaw; *(cerro)* hillock, mound; AMER., COLL. marijuana.
mo·te¹ m. *(sentencia enigmática)* riddle, phrase with secret meaning; *(divisa)* device, motto; *(apodo)* nickname; CHILE error; ECUAD. epigraph ♦ **poner m. a alguien** to nickname someone.
mo·te² m. AMER. stewed corn.
mo·te·ar intr. *(salpicar de motas)* to fleck, speckle; PERU *(comer mote)* to eat stewed corn.
mo·te·ja·dor, –do·ra I. adj. labeling II. m.f. labeler.
mo·te·jar tr. to tag, label (someone).
mo·tel m. motel.
mo·te·te m. MUS. motet; AMER. *(cuévano)* pannier, basket; *(lío)* bundle, parcel.
mo·ti·lón, –lo·na I. adj. COLL. hairless II. m.f. *(pelón)* hairless person; *(indio)* Indian from Colombia or Venezuela III. m. COLL. lay brother.
mo·tín m. insurrection, riot.
mo·ti·va·ción f. motivation.
mo·ti·va·dor, –do·ra I. adj. motivating II. m.f. motivator.
mo·ti·var tr. *(causar)* to motivate, cause; *(explicar)* to explain; *(justificar)* justify.
mo·ti·vo, –va I. adj. motive, moving II. m. *(causa)* motive, cause; MUS. *(tema)* motif, theme; ART. *(dibujo)* motif ♦ **motivos** CHILE finickiness • **bajo ningún m.** under no circumstances • **con mayor m.** even more so • **dar m.** to give cause • **no ser m. para** to be no reason to or for • **sin m.** without reason.
mo·to f. COLL. cycle, motorcycle.
mo·to·ci·cle·ta f. motorcycle.
mo·to·ci·clis·mo m. motorcycling.
mo·to·ci·clis·ta I. adj. motorcycle II. m.f. motorcyclist.
mo·to·náu·ti·ca I. adj. motorboat II. f. motorboating.
mo·to·na·ve f. motorboat, motor ship.
mo·tor, –to·ra I. adj. motor II. m. motor engine ♦ **m. auxiliar** AER. booster (engine) • **m. de arranque** AUTO starter • **m. de cilindro en V** AUTO. V-engine • **m. de cohete** AER. rocket engine • **m. de combustión interna** or **de explosión** MECH. internal combustion engine • **m. de reacción** or **de chorro** AER. jet engine • **m. de vapor** MECH. steam engine • **m. diesel** MECH. diesel (engine) • **m. fuera de borda** MARIT. outboard motor • **primer m.** PHILOS. prime mover.
mo·to·ra f. motorboat.
mo·to·ris·ta m.f. *(motociclista)* motorcyclist; *(de automóvil)* motorist.

mo·to·ri·zar §04 tr. to motorize.
mo·to·rre·ac·tor m. jet engine.
mo·to·so, –sa adj. BOL., COLL. dull-edged; PERU *(campesino)* peasant.
mo·triz adj. [pl. **-tri·ces**] motor, driving.
mo·tu pro·prio adv. voluntarily, by one's own will.
mo·ve·di·zo, –za adj. *(que se mueve)* moving, shifting; *(inseguro)* shaky, unfirm; FIG. *(inconstante)* fickle, changeable ♦ **arenas movedizas** quicksand.
mo·ver §78 tr. *(accionar)* to move <*ella quiere m. los muebles* she wants to move the furniture>; *(agitar)* to move about, stir; *(la cabeza)* to shake, nod; MECH. to drive, power <*el vapor mueve la rueda* steam powers the wheel>; *(inducir)* to induce, move; *(en el ajedrez)* to move (a chess piece); FIG. *(incitar)* to incite, provoke <*m. discordia* to provoke discord>; *(conmover)* to excite, stir ♦ **m. a** to move to <*m. a compasión* to move to pity> • **m. cielo y tierra** FIG. to move heaven and earth —intr. ARCHIT. to spring; AGR. to sprout, bud; MED. *(abortar)* to miscarry, have a miscarriage —reflex. to move.
mo·vi·ble adj. *(que puede moverse)* movable; FIG. *(variable)* fickle, variable.
mo·vi·do, –da I. past part. see **mover II.** adj. *(animado)* active, lively (person); *(agitado)* choppy, rough (sea); *(borroso)* fuzzy, blurry (photograph); C. AMER., COL. *(enclenque)* weak, feeble; AMER. *(de cáscara blanda)* soft-shelled (egg).
mó·vil I. adj. *(que puede moverse)* mobile, movable; FIG. *(inestable)* unstable, variable **II.** m. *(motivo)* motive, reason; PHYS. *(cuerpo en movimiento)* moving body; ARTS *(objeto)* mobile.
mo·vi·li·dad f. mobility.
mo·vi·li·za·ción f. mobilization.
mo·vi·li·zar §04 tr. to mobilize.
mo·vi·mien·to m. *(acción de mover)* movement, motion; *(efecto de mover)* move, movement; *(actividad)* activity, movement; *(tendencia)* movement, trend <*un m. político* a political movement>; *(tráfico)* traffic; *(levantamiento)* uprising, upheaval; FIG. *(sentimiento)* feeling; MECH., PHYS. motion <*m. continuo* continuous motion>; ARTS, LIT. movement, action; MUS. *(tiempo)* tempo; *(división)* movement; MIL. movement <*m. de pinza* pincer movement>; COM. activity, movement, fluctuation; ANAT. movement (of the bowels) ♦ **m. perpetuo** PHYS. perpetual motion • **m. sísmico** GEOL. earth tremor • **poner en m.** to put in motion.
mo·za I. f. *(chica)* girl; *(criada)* maid, servant; *(concubina)* mistress; *(pala)* washing paddle (for pounding clothes); *(en naipes)* last hand (in some card games) ♦ **buena m.** good-looking (girl) • **m. de cámara** chambermaid • **m. del partido** FIG. prostitute • **ser una real m.** COLL. to be a doll **II.** adj. see **mozo, –za.**
mo·zal·be·te m. lad, youth.
Mo·zam·bi·que m. Mozambique.
mo·zam·bi·que·ño, –na adj. & m.f. Mozambican.
mo·zá·ra·be I. adj. Mozarabic **II.** m.f. Mozarab.
mo·zo, –za I. adj. *(joven)* young; *(soltero)* single, unmarried **II.** m. *(chico)* boy, young man; *(criado)* servant; *(camarero)* waiter; *(percha)* coat hanger; *(tentemozo)* prop, shore; MIL. conscript ♦ **buen m.** good-looking *or* handsome (young man) • **m. de caballos** stable boy, groom • **m. de cordel** *or* **de cuerda** porter • **m. de espuelas** footman • **m. de hotel** bellboy, bellhop —f. see **moza.**
mo·zue·lo, –la m.f. *(muchacho)* lad; *(muchacha)* girl.
mua·ré m. TEX. moiré, watered silk.
mu·ca·mo, –ma m.f. AMER. servant.
mu·ci·la·go *or* **mu·cí·la·go** m. mucilage.
mu·co·si·dad f. mucosity.
mu·co·so, –sa I. adj. mucous **II.** f. ANAT. mucous membrane.
mú·cu·ra *or* **mu·cu·ra** f. S. AMER. *(vasija)* pitcher, ewer; COL. blockhead, dunce.
mu·cus m. PHYSIOL. mucus.
mu·cha·cha·da f. *(acción propia de niño)* childish prank; *(conjunto de niños)* group of children.
mu·cha·che·ar intr. to act childishly, fool around.
mu·cha·che·rí·a f. var. of **muchachada.**
mu·cha·cho, –cha m.f. *(niño)* child, youngster; FIG., COLL.

(adolescente) youth, kid —m. *(chico)* boy; *(mozo)* houseboy, servant —f. *(chica)* girl; *(moza)* maid, servant.
mu·che·dum·bre f. multitude, crowd.
mu·cho, –cha §G24, 29 **I.** adj. *(abundante)* much, a lot of <*m. agua* a lot of water>; very <*hace m. frío* it is very cold> ♦ **muchos** many, a lot of <*muchos problemas* many problems> <*muchas piedras* a lot of rocks> **II.** pron. a lot <*¿tienes dinero? no, pero mi amiga tiene m.* to you have any money? no, but my friend has a lot> ♦ **muchos** many <*muchos vinieron tarde* many came late> **III.** adv. a lot, much <*ellos trabajan m.* they work a lot>; much <*m. des­pués* much later>; *(largo tiempo)* a long time <*hace m. que viven en Portugal* they have lived in Portugal for a long time> ♦ **ni m. menos** not by a long shot, far from it • **por m. que** however much, no matter how much • **tener en m.** to hold in high regard, think a lot of.
mu·da f. *(cambio)* change, alteration; *(ropa)* change of clothing; *(cambio de pluma)* molting, molt; *(tiempo)* molting season; *(nido)* roost, nest (of a bird of prey); *(de voz)* change of voice ♦ **estar de m.** to have one's voice change.
mu·da·ble adj. *(cambiable)* changeable; *(inconstante)* inconstant, fickle.
mu·da·da f. AMER. change of clothing; ARG., CUBA move, change of address.
mu·dan·za f. *(cambio)* change; *(traslado)* move, moving; *(figura de baile)* figure, movement (in dance); *(inconstancia)* inconstancy, fickleness ♦ **estar de m.** to be moving (to a new address).
mu·dar tr. *(cambiar)* to change <*m. de ropa* to change clothes>; *(trasladar)* to move <*mudó el coche a otro garaje* he moved the car to another garage>; ORNITH., ZOOL. to molt, shed (feathers, skin) ♦ **m. de idea** *or* **de opinión** to change one's mind —reflex. *(cambiarse)* to change <*se mudó la falda* she changed her skirt>; *(trasladarse)* to move <*nos mudamos al campo hoy* we are moving to the country today>.
mu·dez f. *(incapacidad de hablar)* dumbness, muteness; FIG. *(silencio)* silence.
mu·do, –da I. adj. *(que no puede hablar)* mute, dumb; FIG. *(silencioso)* silent, mute; GRAM. silent (letter) **II.** m.f. dumb *or* mute person.
mue·bla·je m. furniture.
mue·ble I. adj. movable **II.** m. piece of furniture ♦ **muebles** furniture.
mue·ble, mueblo see **moblar.**
mue·ble·rí·a f. furniture store.
mue·ca f. face, grimace ♦ **hacer muecas** to make faces.
mue·cín m. RELIG. muezzin.
mue·la f. *(de molino)* millstone; *(de afilar)* grindstone, whetstone; ANAT. molar; *(cerro)* hill, hillock; BOT. vetch ♦ **m. cordal** *or* **de juicio** wisdom tooth.
mue·la, muelo see **moler.**
mue·lle[1] I. adj. *(blando)* soft, tender; *(elástico)* elastic, springy; *(voluptuoso)* luxurious, easy **II.** m. MECH. spring ♦ **m. antagonista** *or* **de retorno** recoil spring • **m. real** mainspring.
mue·lle[2] m. MARIT. pier, wharf, dock; RAIL. loading platform.
mue·ra, muere see **morir.**
muer·da, muerdo see **morder.**
muér·da·go m. BOT. mistletoe.
muér·ga·no m. MUS. *(instrumento)* organ; COL., VEN. *(objeto)* useless *or* worthless object; *(persona)* sloppy *or* unkempt person.
muer·mo m. VET. glanders.
muer·te f. *(fallecimiento)* death; *(homicidio)* murder, homicide; *(pena capital)* death <*lo condenaron a m.* they con­demned him to death>; FIG. *(ruina)* death, ruin <*la m. de un imperio* the death of an empire>; *(esqueleto)* Death, the Grim Reaper ♦ **a m.** to the death <*un duelo a m.* a duel to the death>; *(implacablemente)* to the death, relentlessly <*odiar a m.* to hate relentlessly> • **de mala m.** COLL. crummy, lousy • **de m.** seriously, fatally <*enfermo de m.* fatally ill> • **estar a las puertas de la m.** to be at death's door • **hasta la m.** until death • **m. civil** LAW loss of civil rights.
muer·to, –ta I. past part. see **morir II.** adj. *(difunto)* dead; COLL. *(matado)* killed <*he m. una liebre* I have killed a

rabbit>; FIG. *(apagado)* lifeless; *(marchito)* faded *<color m.* faded color>; *(cansado)* exhausted ♦ **más m. que vivo** FIG. half-dead • **m. de** FIG. dying of *<estoy m. de sed* I am dying of thirst> • **no tener dónde caerse m.** FIG., COLL. to be penniless **III.** m.f. *(difunto)* dead person; *(cadáver)* corpse —m. *(en los naipes)* dummy hand ♦ **cargar con el m.** FIG., COLL. to be left holding the bag • **desenterrar los muertos** FIG. to speak ill of the dead • **echarle a alguien el m.** FIG. to put the blame on • **hacer el m.** to float • **hacerse el m.** FIG. to play possum, play dead • **los muertos** the dead.

mues·ca f. *(corte)* notch, groove; CARP., TECH. mortise; *(en el ganado)* earmark (of cattle).

mues·tra¹ f. *(ejemplo)* sample, specimen *<una m. de tela* a cloth sample>; FIG. *(señal)* sign, indication *<una m. de buena fe* an indication of good faith>; *(modelo)* model, guide; *(letrero)* sign, signboard (over a shop); *(cara del reloj)* dial, face (of a clock); *(en naipes)* turn-up (card turned to indicate trump suit); *(de perros)* set (of a hunting dog); *(exposición artística)* exposition, art show; MIL. review, inspection; MATH. *(en estadística)* sample (in statistics) ♦ **dar muestras de** to show signs of • **pasar m.** MIL. to review, inspect.

mues·tra² f. show, exposition.

mues·tra·rio m. sample book, samples.

mues·tre, muestro see mostrar.

mues·tre·o m. sample, sampling (statistics).

mue·va, mueve see mover.

mu·ga f. *(desove)* spawning; *(fecundación)* fertilization of eggs.

mu·gi·do **I.** past part. see mugir **II.** m. *(de la vaca)* moo, mooing; *(del toro)* bellow, bellowing.

mu·gi·dor, –do·ra *or* **mu·gien·te** adj. *(en una vaca)* mooing, lowing; *(de un toro)* bellowing.

mu·gir §32 intr. *(dar mugidos las vacas)* to moo, low; *(dar mugidos los toros)* to bellow; FIG. *(bramar)* to roar, howl.

mu·gre f. filth, grime.

mu·grien·to, –ta adj. filthy, grimy.

mu·grón m. AGR. *(de la vid)* layer (of vine); *(vástago)* shoot.

mu·gue·te m. BOT. lily of the valley.

mu·ja, mujo see mugir.

mu·jer f. *(hembra)* woman; *(esposa)* wife ♦ **m. de gobierno** housekeeper • **m. de la limpieza** cleaning woman • **m. de su casa** housewife, homemaker • **m. de la vida** *or* **de mal vivir** prostitute • **tomar m.** to take a wife • **tomar por m.** to take (someone) for one's wife.

mu·je·rie·go, –ga **I.** adj. *(mujeril)* feminine, womanly; *(galanteador)* womanizing, philandering **II.** m. (group of) women ♦ **a la m.** EQUIT. sidesaddle • **ser m.** to be a womanizer *or* ladies' man.

mu·je·ril adj. *(feminino)* feminine, womanly; *(afeminado)* effeminate.

mu·la¹ f. ZOOL. female mule ♦ **ser una m.** FIG. to be stubborn as a mule.

mu·la² f. *(calzado)* mule, slipper; *(de los papas)* shoe worn by popes; MEX. *(cojín)* shoulder pad; COLL. *(maula)* junk merchandise; GUAT., HOND., COLL. shame.

mu·la·da f. *(recua)* drove of mules; FIG., COLL. stupidity, stupid act.

mu·la·dar m. *(de basura)* rubbish heap; *(de estiércol)* dungheap; FIG. *(sitio sucio)* dungheap, pigsty.

mu·la·dí adj. & m.f. [pl. **-dí·es**] HIST. Christian Spaniard who converted to Islam.

mu·la·to, –ta **I.** adj. *(de raza mixta)* mulatto; *(de color moreno)* dark, dark-skinned **II.** m.f. *(persona)* mulatto —m. MIN. dark silver ore.

mu·le·ro m. muleteer.

mu·le·ta f. *(para andar)* crutch; FIG. *(sostén)* crutch, support; TAUR. muleta (red cape).

mu·le·te·ro m. *(mozo)* muleteer; TAUR. bullfighter, matador.

mu·le·ti·lla f. *(bastón)* cross-handle cane; SEW. frog, toggle; FIG. *(estribillo)* pet word *or* phrase.

mu·li·llas f.pl. TAUR. mules that drag the dead bull from the ring.

mu·lo m. ZOOL. mule; fig. *(bruto)* brute, beast.

mul·ta f. *(pena pecuniaria)* fine, forfeit; AUTO. parking ticket.

mul·tar tr. to fine *<me multaron en veinte dólares* they fined me twenty dollars>.

mul·ti·ce·lu·lar adj. BIOL. multicellular.

mul·ti·co·lor adj. multicolor.

mul·ti·co·pis·ta f. duplicating machine, copier.

mul·ti·for·me adj. multiform.

mul·ti·la·te·ral adj. multilateral.

mul·ti·mi·llo·na·rio, –ria adj. & m.f. multimillionaire.

mul·ti·na·cio·nal adj. multinational.

múl·ti·ple adj. multiple.

múl·ti·plex adj. ELECTRON., RAD., TELEV. multiplex.

mul·ti·pli·ca·ble adj. multipliable.

mul·ti·pli·ca·ción f. multiplication.

mul·ti·pli·ca·dor, –do·ra **I.** adj. multiplying **II.** m. MATH. multiplier.

mul·ti·pli·can·do adj. & m. MATH. multiplicand.

mul·ti·pli·car §70 tr. & reflex. to multiply.

mul·ti·pli·ci·dad f. muliplicity.

múl·ti·plo, –pla adj. & m. MATH. multiple ♦ **mínimo común m.** lowest common multiple.

mul·ti·po·lar adj. multipolar.

mul·ti·pro·ce·sa·dor adj. & m. COMPUT. multiprocessor.

mul·ti·pro·gra·ma·ción f. COMPUT. multiprogramming.

mul·ti·tud f. multitude.

mul·ti·tu·di·na·rio, –ria adj. multitudinous.

mu·lli·da f. *(para el ganado)* litter, bedding (for animals); *(jergón)* straw mattress.

mu·lli·do, –da **I.** adj. fluffy, soft **II.** m. stuffing, filling (for pillows, cushions).

mu·lli·dor, –do·ra **I.** adj. fluffing, softening **II.** m.f. softener.

mu·llir §13 tr. *(esponjar)* to fluff (up); *(la tierra)* to loosen (dirt, soil); FIG. *(disponer)* to prepare, get ready.

mun·da·nal adj. worldly, mundane.

mun·da·ne·ar intr. to indulge in worldly things.

mun·da·ne·rí·a f. *(calidad)* worldliness; *(acción)* worldly behavior.

mun·da·no, –na adj. *(del mundo)* worldly, mundane; *(que mundanea)* worldly-minded.

mun·de·ar intr. COL. to bum around.

mun·dial **I.** adj. *(del mundo)* world *<guerra m.* world war>; *(universal)* worldwide, universal **II.** m. SPORT. world championship *<mundial de futbol* world soccer championship>.

mun·do m. *(universo)* world; *(tierra)* earth; *(género humano)* world, society; *(agrupación)* world *<el m. de las artes* the art world>; *(baúl)* Saratoga trunk; FIG. *(experiencia)* experience, sophistication *<tener m.* to have experience>; BOT. viburnum, snowball; RELIG. world, secular life ♦ **correr el m.** to travel far and wide • **dar un m. por** FIG., COLL. to give the world for • **desde que el m. es m.** COLL. since time began • **echar al m.** to bring into the world, bring forth • **echarse al m.** FIG. to enter the life of prostitution • **el m. antiguo** the Old World • **el Nuevo M.** the New World • **el otro m.** the other world, the hereafter • **irse al otro m.** FIG. to pass away • **medio m.** FIG., COLL. crowd of people, multitude • **no ser del otro m.** FIG., COLL. to be no big deal • **tener m.** to know one's way around • **Tercer M.** Third World • **todo el m.** everyone, everybody • **venir al m.** FIG. to come into the world, be born • **ver m.** FIG. to travel, see the world.

mu·ni·ción f. MIL. *(pertrechos)* ammunition, munitions; *(bastimentos)* provisions, rations; ARM. *(bala)* shot *<m. menuda* small shot>; *(carga)* charge, load ♦ **m. de fuego** blanks • **municiones de boca** MIL. provisions, rations.

mu·ni·cio·nar tr. *(con armas)* to munition, supply with munitions; *(con bastimentos)* to provision, provide with food *or* rations.

mu·ni·cio·ne·ra f. AMER. cartridge pouch.

mu·ni·ci·pal **I.** adj. municipal **II.** m. *(policía)* policeman; CHILE councilor.

mu·ni·ci·pa·li·dad f. municipality.

mu·ni·ci·pa·li·za·ción f. municipalization.

mu·ni·ci·pa·li·zar §04 tr. to municipalize.

mu·ni·ci·pio m. *(ayuntamiento)* town council, municipality; *(término municipal)* municipality; *(pueblo)* township, district.

mu·ni·fi·cen·cia f. munificence, generosity.

mu·ni·fi·cen·te adj. munificent, generous.
mu·ni·fi·co, –ca adj. munificent, generous.
mu·nir tr. ARG., URUG. to provision, supply.
mu·ñe·ca f. ANAT. wrist; *(juguete)* doll; *(maniquí)* mannequin, dressmaker's dummy; *(trapo)* rag <*m. para barnizar* polishing rag>; FIG., COLL. *(presumida)* conceited girl; *(muchacha bonita)* doll, pretty girl ♦ **menear las muñecas** FIG. to work hard • **m. de trapo** rag doll.
mu·ñe·co m. *(juguete)* doll; *(marioneta)* puppet; FIG., COLL. *(joven afeminado)* sissy.
mu·ñe·que·ra f. wristband.
mu·ñe·que·rí·a f. COLL. foppishness.
mu·ñe·qui·lla f. *(trapo)* polishing rag *or* pad; CHILE young ear of corn.
mu·ñon m. ANAT., SURG. stump (of an amputated limb); ARM. *(del cañón)* trunnion (pin on which a cannon pivots); MECH. gudgeon, wristpin (on which transmission is attached).
mu·ño·ne·ra f. ARM. trunnion plate (of a cannon).
mu·ral I. adj. PAINT. mural <*pintura m.* mural painting>; wall <*mapa m.* wall map> II. m. PAINT. mural.
mu·ra·lis·ta PAINT. I. adj. mural II. m.f. muralist.
mu·ra·lla f. *(fortificación)* wall, rampart; AMER. wall (of a house).
mur·cié·la·go m. ZOOL. bat.
mu·rie·ra, murió see **morir.**
mur·mu·je·ar intr. FIG., COLL. to murmur, mumble.
mur·mu·llo m. *(ruido sordo)* murmur, murmuring; *(de la gente)* murmur; *(del agua)* babbling, gurgle; *(del viento)* sighing, sigh; *(de las hojas)* rustling, rustle; *(queja)* grumble, complaint.
mur·mu·ra·ción f. gossip.
mur·mu·ra·dor, –do·ra I. adj. *(murmurante)* murmuring; *(chismoso)* gossiping II. m.f. gossip.
mur·mu·ran·te adj. murmuring.
mur·mu·rar intr. *(hacer ruido sordo)* to murmur; *(hablar quedo)* to murmur, whisper; *(agua)* to babble, gurgle; *(viento)* to sigh; *(hojas)* to rustle; *(quejar)* to grumble, mutter <*ella siempre murmura cuando no le gusta la comida* she always grumbles when she does not like the meal>; FIG., COLL. to gossip.
mu·ro m. *(pared)* wall; *(muralla)* rampart ♦ **m. del calor** PHYS. heat barrier • **m. del sonido** PHYS. sound barrier.
mu·rrio, –rria COLL. I. adj. blue, sad II. f. the blues.
mu·sa f. muse ♦ **las musas** the liberal arts.
mu·sa·ra·ña f. ZOOL. shrew; FIG. *(animalejo)* vermin; COLL. *(muñeco)* ridiculous puppet, caricature; *(del ojo)* speck (in the eye) ♦ **mirar uno a las musarañas** FIG., COLL. to stare into space • **pensar en las musarañas** FIG., COLL. to let one's mind wander.
mus·co, –ca adj. dark brown.
mus·cu·la·ción f. *(ejercicios)* body building; AMER. musculature.
mus·cu·lar adj. muscular.
mus·cu·la·tu·ra f. musculature.
mús·cu·lo ANAT. m. muscle ♦ **m. cardíaco** myocardium, cardiac muscle • **m. estriado** striated muscle • **m. glúteo** gluteus, gluteal muscle.
mus·cu·lo·so, –sa adj. muscular.
mu·se·li·na f. muslin.
mu·se·o m. museum ♦ **m. de cera** wax museum • **m. de historia natural** museum of natural history.
mu·se·ro·la f. EQUIT. noseband (of a bridle).
mus·go m. BOT. moss ♦ **m. marino** coralline (a red algae).
mus·go·so, –sa adj. mossy, moss-covered.
mú·si·ca I. f. *(arte)* music; *(banda)* band; *(papel)* sheet music; *(obra musical)* musical composition ♦ **irse con la m. a otra parte** FIG., COLL. to get up and go, take one's troubles elsewhere • **m. celestial** FIG., COLL. hot air, drivel • **m. de cámara** chamber music • **m. de fondo** background music • **m. de las esferas** *or* **de los planetas** music of the spheres • **m. electrónica** electronic music • **m. llana** plainsong • **m. ratonera** FIG., COLL. caterwauling • **m. y acompañamiento** FIG., COLL. riff-raff • **m. y letra** words and music • **no entender uno la m.** FIG. to play *or* act dumb • **poner m. a** to set music to, set music II. adj. see **músico, –ca.**
mu·si·cal adj. & m. musical.

mu·si·ca·li·dad f. musicality.
mu·si·ca·li·zar §04 tr. to set to music, set music to.
mu·si·cal·men·te adv. musically.
mu·si·cas·tro m. DEROG. bad musician.
mú·si·co, –ca I. adj. musical II. m.f. *(instrumentista)* musician —m. COL. drunkard, drunk; C. AMER. poor horseman; MEX. hypocrite —f. see **música.**
mu·si·co·lo·gí·a f. musicology.
mu·si·có·lo·go, –ga m.f. musicologist.
mu·si·qui·lla f. COLL. ditty.
mu·si·tar tr. *(susurrar)* to whisper; *(murmurar)* to mumble, mutter.
mus·lo m. ANAT., ZOOL. thigh; *(de pollo)* drumstick, leg (chicken *or* turkey).
mus·tang *or* **mus·tan·go** m. ZOOL. mustang.
mus·tiar·se reflex. to wither, become withered.
mus·tio, –tia adj. *(triste)* sad, gloomy; *(marchito)* withered, wilted; MEX. hypocritical.
mu·sul·mán, –ma·na adj. & m.f. RELIG. Moslem, Muslim.
mu·ta·bi·li·dad f. mutability, changeability.
mu·ta·ble adj. mutable, changeable.
mu·ta·ción f. *(cambio)* mutation, change; THEAT. *(de la escena)* change of scene; METEOROL. *(del tiempo)* change of weather; BIOL. mutation.
mu·ti·la·ción f. mutilation.
mu·ti·la·do, –da I. past part. see **mutilar** II. adj. *(destruido)* mutilated; *(inválido)* disabled III. m.f. disabled person, cripple ♦ **m. de guerra** disabled veteran.
mu·ti·la·dor, –do·ra I. adj. *(que destruye)* mutilating; *(que daña)* disabling II. m.f. mutilator.
mu·ti·lar tr. *(amputar)* to mutilate; *(destruir)* to mutilate, deface <*un loco mutiló la estatua* a crazy man defaced the statue>; *(acortar)* to mutilate, cut up <*los editores mutila­ron su libro* the editors cut up his book>.
mú·ti·lo, –la adj. *(destruido)* mutilated; *(inválido)* disabled.
mu·tis m. THEAT. exit ♦ **hacer m.** *(irse)* to exit, leave; *(callar)* to keep quiet.
mu·tis·mo m. MED. muteness, mutism; *(silencio)* silence.
mu·tual I. adj. mutual II. f. mutual benefit society.
mu·tua·li·dad f. *(calidad)* mutuality; *(corporación)* mutual benefit society.
mu·tua·lis·mo m. *(corporación)* mutual benefit society; BIOL. mutualism.
mu·tua·lis·ta I. adj. *(de una mutualidad)* of a mutual benefit society; BIOL. mutualistic II. m.f. member of a mutual benefit society.
mu·tua·men·te adv. mutually.
mú·tuo, –tua I. adj. mutual II. m. FIN., LAW loan, mutuum.
muy adv. very, quite <*m. alto* very tall>; greatly, quite <*es­toy m. satisfecho* I am quite satisfied>; *(demasiado)* too <*ella es m. joven para ocupar ese puesto* she is too young to occupy that post>; quite a, very much a <*él es m. hombre* he is quite a man> ♦ **m. de noche** late at night • **m. señor mío** Dear Sir (salutation in correspondence) • **ser m. de** to be just like, be very much like <*eso es m. de ella* that is just like her> • **ser m. de su casa** COLL. to be a homebody.
my f. mu (Greek letter).

N

n, N f. *(letra)* sixteenth letter of the Spanish alphabet; X <*la señora N* Madame X>; MATH. *(potencia)* n (indefinite number).
na·bo m. BOT. *(planta)* turnip; *(raíz)* thick root; *(maslo)* stock, root (of a horse's tail); ARCHIT. *(bolo)* newel, newel post; *(eje)* central pillar; MARIT. mast ♦ **n. de Suecia** BOT. Swedish turnip, rutabaga • **n. gallego** BOT. rape.
na·bo·rí m.f. [pl. **-rí·es**] AMER., HIST. free Indian servant.
ná·car m. nacre, mother-of-pearl.
na·ca·ra·do, –da adj. *(perlino)* nacreous, pearly; *(adornado con nácar)* set with mother-of-pearl.
na·ca·ri·no, –na *or* **na·cá·re·o, –a** adj. nacreous.
na·cer §17 intr. *(venir al mundo)* to be born; *(salir del huevo)*

to be hatched; *(germinar)* to sprout, begin to grow; *(florecer)* to bud, blossom; *(los astros)* to rise; *(brotar)* to rise, start to flow; FIG. *(provenir)* to stem *or* originate from <*el vicio nace de la ociosidad* vice stems from idleness>; *(originar)* to originate, be conceived ♦ **al n.** at birth • **n. de pie** FIG., COLL. to be born lucky • **n. para** to be born to <*nació para cantar* he was born to sing> • **volver a n.** to have a narrow escape —reflex. *(brotar)* to sprout, bud; *(abrirse la tela)* to split (seams).

na·ci·do, –da I. past part. see **nacer II.** adj. born <*n. en México* born in Mexico>; *(natural)* inborn, natural ♦ **bien n.** well-born, well-bred • **mal n.** ill-bred, mean • **nacida** née, nee • **n. muerto** stillborn • **recién n.** newborn **III.** m. *(ser humano)* human being; MED. growth, tumor ♦ **ningún n.** nobody • **todos los nacidos** everybody.

na·cien·te I. adj. *(que nace)* nascent; *(inicial)* incipient, initial; *(reciente)* recent, growing <*la n. curiosidad* the growing curiosity>; rising <*el sol n.* the rising sun> **II.** m. Orient, East.

na·ci·mien·to m. *(natal)* birth; *(de pájaros)* hatching; *(de ríos)* source (of water); *(manantial)* spring (of water); *(linaje)* birth, descent, origin; *(natividad)* crèche, Nativity scene ♦ **dar n. a** to give rise to • **de n.** from birth <*sordo de n.* deaf from birth> • **por n.** by birth.

na·ción f. *(patria)* nation, country; *(pueblo)* nation, people ♦ **Naciones Unidas** United Nations.

na·cio·nal I. adj. national, domestic **II.** m.f. *(ciudadano)* national, citizen —m. militiaman.

na·cio·na·li·cé, nacionalice see **nacionalizar.**

na·cio·na·li·dad f. nationality, citizenship ♦ **doble n.** dual citizenship.

na·cio·na·lis·mo m. nationalism.

na·cio·na·lis·ta adj. & m.f. nationalist.

na·cio·na·li·za·ción f. *(expropiación)* nationalization, expropriation; *(naturalización)* naturalization.

na·cio·na·li·zar §04 tr. *(convertir en nacional)* to nationalize; *(naturalizar)* to naturalize —reflex. to become naturalized.

na·cio·nal·so·cia·lis·mo m. POL. National Socialism.

na·cio·nal·so·cia·lis·ta adj. & m.f. National Socialist.

na·co m. ARG., BOL., URUG. chew (of tobacco); ARG. *(susto)* fright, fear; C. AMER. coward.

na·da §G45 **I.** pron. nothing, not anything <*no he visto n.* I have not seen anything> ♦ **a cada n.** AMER. continually, every five minutes • **antes de n.** first, before anything else • **de n.** you're welcome • **n. de** no, none <*n. de quejas* no complaints> • **n. de eso** none of that, not at all • **n. menos** no less, nothing less • **ni n.** COLL. or anything <*no iré ni n.* I will not go or anything> • **no es n.** it's nothing • **no hay n. como** there is nothing like <*no hay n. como un buen libro* there is nothing like a good book> • **por n. del mundo** not for all the world **II.** adv. in no way, not at all <*no es n. extraño* it's not at all strange> **III.** f. *(inexistencia)* nothingness, nothing; *(cosa mínima)* the slightest thing <*una n. le hace llorar* the slightest thing makes him cry>.

na·da·dor, –do·ra I. adj. swimming **II.** m.f. swimmer.

na·dar intr. SPORT. to swim; *(flotar)* to float; FIG. *(abundar)* to swim in <*nado en estos pantalones* I'm swimming in these pants> ♦ **n. de espalda** *or* **de pecho** to do the backstroke *or* breaststroke • **n. en** to have an abundance of • **n. entre dos aguas** to sit on the fence, be undecided.

na·de·rí·a f. insignificant thing, trifle.

na·die §G45 **I.** pron. nobody, no one **II.** m. FIG. a nobody ♦ **no ser n.** to be a nobody • **un don n.** a nobody, an unimportant person.

na·dir m. ASTRON. nadir.

na·do adv. swimming ♦ **a nado** by swimming <*pasó el río a n.* she swam across the river>.

naf·ta f. CHEM. naphtha; AMER. gasoline.

naf·ta·li·na f. CHEM. naphthalene; COLL. *(contra la polilla)* mothballs.

naf·tol m. CHEM. naphthol, naphtol.

na·gual m. MEX. sorcerer, wizard; GUAT., HOND. pet —f. MEX. lie.

na·guas f.pl. COLL. petticoat.

nai·pe m. card, playing card ♦ **barajar los naipes** to shuffle the cards • **castillo de n.** house of cards • **florear el n.** to

stack *or* mark the deck • **n. de figura** face card • **naipes** deck (of cards) • **peinar los naipes** to shuffle thoroughly • **tener buen n.** to be lucky in cards.

nal·ga f. ANAT. buttock ♦ **nalgas** bottom, behind.

nal·ga·da f. *(pernil de cerdo)* ham; *(paliza)* spanking, slap (on the buttocks).

nal·gar adj. ANAT. gluteal, pertaining to the buttocks.

nal·gu·do, –da *or* **nal·gón, –go·na** adj. AMER. having a large behind.

nal·gue·ar intr. to wiggle the behind while walking.

na·na f. COLL. *(abuela)* granny; *(arrullo)* lullaby; AMER. *(niñera)* nanny; *(nodriza)* wet nurse.

nan·quín m. TEX. nankeen.

na·o f. POET. vessel, ship.

na·palm m. CHEM., MIL. napalm.

na·pias f.pl. COLL. noses, snouts.

Ná·po·les Naples.

na·po·li·ta·no, –na adj. & m.f. Neapolitan.

na·ran·ja I. f. BOT. orange; MEX. grapefruit; MIL. cannonball —m. orange (color) ♦ **media n.** FIG., COLL. better half, spouse; ARCHIT. dome • **¡naranjas!** *or* **¡naranjas de la China!** nothing doing! • **n. agria** Seville orange • **n. de ombligo** navel orange • **n. tangerina** *or* **mandarina** tangerine, mandarin orange **II.** adj. orange.

na·ran·ja·da f. orangeade.

na·ran·jal m. orange grove.

na·ran·je·ro, –ra I. adj. orange **II.** m.f. *(vendedor)* orange seller; *(cultivador)* orange grower.

na·ran·jo m. BOT. orange tree; *(madera)* orangewood.

nar·ci·sis·mo m. narcissism.

nar·ci·sis·ta I. adj. narcissistic **II.** m.f. narcissist.

nar·ci·so¹ m. BOT. narcissus.

nar·ci·so² m. MYTH. Narcissus; FIG. narcissist.

nar·co·lep·sia f. MED. narcolepsy.

nar·co·sis f. MED. narcosis.

nar·có·ti·co, –ca adj. & m. MED. narcotic.

nar·co·tis·mo m. MED. narcotism.

nar·co·ti·zan·te adj. & m.f. narcotic.

nar·co·ti·zar §04 tr. to narcotize, drug.

nar·co·tra·fi·can·te m. drug dealer.

nar·do m. BOT. nard, spikenard.

nar·gui·le m. narghile (pipe).

na·ri·gón, –go·na I. adj. COLL. large-nosed **II.** m. COLL. large-nosed person; CUBA *(agujero en un tronco)* hole (in a tree trunk); *(anillo)* nose ring.

na·ri·gu·do, –da adj. large-nosed.

na·riz f. [pl. **-ri·ces**] ANAT. nose; ANAT. *(ventana)* nostril; *(olfato)* sense of smell; FIG. *(aroma)* bouquet (of wine); MECH. socket (of a bolt); *(tajamar)* cutwater (of a bridge); ARM. nozzle (of a retort) ♦ **estar hasta las narices** to have had it up to here, be fed up • **fruncir** *or* **torcer la n. a** COLL. to turn one's nose up at • **hincharse las narices** FIG., COLL. to get angry • **más sonado que las narices** COLL. well-known • **meter las narices en** COLL. to interfere, stick one's nose into • **n. aguileña** aquiline nose • **n. chata** pug nose • **n. perfilada** Grecian nose • **n. respingada** *or* **respingona** snub nose • **¡narices!** COLL. nonsense! • **no ver más allá de las narices** FIG., COLL. not to see past one's nose, to be shortsighted • **sonarse la n.** to blow one's nose • **tener de las narices** COLL. to lead around by the nose.

na·ri·zón adj. COLL. large-nosed.

na·ri·zo·ta f. large ugly nose.

na·rra·ción f. *(narrativa)* narrative, account; *(acción)* narration, recounting ♦ **n. retrospectiva** flashback.

na·rra·dor, –do·ra I. adj. narrative **II.** m.f. narrator.

na·rrar tr. to narrate, relate.

na·rra·ti·vo, –va I. adj. narrative **II.** f. *(narración)* narrative, account; *(habilidad)* narrative skill.

na·rria f. dolly (small cart for moving heavy loads).

nar·val m. ZOOL. narwhal.

na·sal adj. & f. nasal.

na·sa·li·dad f. nasality.

na·sa·li·za·ción f. PHONET. nasalization.

na·sal·men·te adv. nasally.

na·ta I. f. *(crema)* cream; *(capa)* skim (of milk, wine); FIG. *(lo mejor)* (the) cream, (the) best; AMER. scum (of metal)

natas *(crema batida)* whipped cream; *(natillas)* custard II. adj. see **nato, –ta.**
na·ta·ción f. swimming.
na·tal I. adj. *(relativo al nacimiento)* natal, pertaining to birth; *(nativo)* native <*ciudad n.* native city> II. m. *(nacimiento)* birth; *(cumpleaños)* birthday.
na·ta·li·cio adj. & m. birthday.
na·ta·li·dad f. natality, birthrate.
na·ta·to·rio, –ria I. adj. swimming, bathing II. m. swimming pool.
na·ti·llas f.pl. custard.
na·ti·vi·dad f. *(nacimiento)* nativity, birth; RELIG. Nativity scene, crèche; *(Navidad)* Christmas.
na·ti·vis·mo m. nativism.
na·ti·vo, –va I. adj. *(indígeno)* native, indigenous <*país n.* native country>; *(natural)* innate, inborn; MIN. native, pure <*plata n.* native silver> II. m.f. native.
na·to, –ta I. adj. born, natural <*él es un criminal n.* he is a born criminal> II. f. see **nata.**
na·tu·ra f. *(naturaleza)* nature; ANAT. genitals; MUS. major scale ♦ **a** or **de n.** naturally • **contra n.** unnatural.
na·tu·ral I. adj. *(conforme a la naturaleza)* natural <*ley n.* natural law>; *(conforme con la razón)* natural, right; *(sin afectación)* natural, spontaneous; *(nativo)* native, indigenous; *(innato)* innate, native; *(ilegítimo)* illegitimate <*hijo n.* illegitimate son>; MUS. natural ♦ **al n.** naturally, without adornment II. m.f. *(nativo)* native —m. *(carácter)* nature, disposition <*un n. avaro* an avaricious nature>.
na·tu·ra·le·za f. nature <*las leyes de la n.* the laws of nature>; *(carácter)* nature, character <*n. humana* human nature>; *(nacionalidad)* nationality; ANAT. genitals ♦ **contra la n.** against nature, unnatural • **n. muerta** PAINT. still life • **por n.** by nature, naturally.
na·tu·ra·li·dad f. *(calidad de natural)* naturalness; *(sencillez)* ingenuousness; *(nacionalidad)* nationality, citizenship.
na·tu·ra·lis·mo m. naturalism.
na·tu·ra·lis·ta I. adj. naturalistic II. m.f. naturalist.
na·tu·ra·li·za·ción f. naturalization.
na·tu·ra·li·zar §04 tr. *(nacionalizar)* to naturalize, nationalize; *(aclimatar)* to acclimate, adapt —reflex. to be naturalized or nationalized.
na·tu·ral·men·te adv. naturally.
na·tu·ris·mo m. *(doctrina)* naturism; *(desnudismo)* nudism.
na·tu·ris·ta I. adj. naturistic II. m.f. *(partidario de la doctrina)* naturist; *(desnudista)* nudist.
nau·fra·gar §47 intr. *(sumergirse)* to be shipwrecked or wrecked; FIG. *(fracasar)* to fail, flounder <*la empresa naufragó* the enterprise failed>.
nau·fra·gio m. MARIT. shipwreck, wreck; FIG. *(fracaso)* failure, washout.
náu·fra·go, –ga I. adj. shipwrecked, wrecked II. m.f. *(persona)* shipwrecked person —m. ZOOL. shark.
Nau·ru Nauru.
nau·rua·no, –na adj. & m.f. Nauruan.
náu·se·a f. *(basca)* nausea; FIG. *(repugnancia)* nausea, disgust ♦ **dar náuseas** to disgust, nauseate • **sentir náuseas** to feel sick.
nau·se·a·bun·do, –da or **nau·se·ante** adj. nauseous, sickening.
nau·se·ar intr. to feel sick, feel nauseous.
náu·ti·co, –ca I. adj. nautical, maritime ♦ **club n.** yacht club • **deportes náuticos** water sports II. f. navigation.
nau·ti·lo m. ZOOL. nautilus.
na·va f. dell, vale.
na·va·ja f. *(cortaplumas)* jackknife, penknife; ZOOL. razor clam; FIG., COLL. *(crítico)* sharp tongue ♦ **n. de afeitar** razor, shaver • **n. de muelle** or **de resorte** switchblade.
na·va·ja·da f. or **na·va·ja·zo** m. gash or slash (with a switchblade).
na·va·je·ro m. *(estuche)* razor case; *(paño)* razor-cloth; PERU switchblade knife user.
na·val adj. naval, maritime.
Na·va·rra GEOG. Navarre.
na·va·rro, –rra adj. & m.f. Navarrese.
na·ve f. MARIT. ship, vessel <*n. de guerra* battleship>; ARCHIT. nave (in a church) ♦ **n. aérea** airship • **N. de San**

Pedro Roman Catholic Church • **n. espacial** spaceship • **quemar las naves** FIG. to burn one's bridges.
na·ve·ci·lla f. MARIT. small ship; RELIG. navicula, censer.
na·ve·ga·ble adj. navigable.
na·ve·ga·ción f. navigation, sailing ♦ **n. aérea** aerial navigation • **n. costera** coastal navigation • **n. fluvial** river navigation.
na·ve·gar §47 intr. *(viajar)* to travel by boat, sail; MEX. to tolerate, bear; FIG. *(transitar)* to bustle or move about —tr. to navigate, steer.
na·ve·ta f. *(nave pequeña)* small ship; *(gaveta)* drawer (of a desk); RELIG. navicula, censer; ARCHEOL. prehistoric tomb.
Na·vi·dad f. Christmas, Nativity ♦ **¡Feliz Navidad!** Merry Christmas!
na·vi·de·ño, –ña adj. Christmas, of Christmas.
na·vie·ro, –ra I. adj. shipping <*compañia n.* shipping company> II. m.f. ship owner.
na·ví·o m. ship, vessel.
ná·ya·de f. MYTH. naiad.
na·za·re·no, –na or **na·za·re·o, –a** I. adj. *(de Nazaret)* Nazarene; *(judío)* Nazarite II. m.f. *(persona de Nazaret)* Nazarene; *(judío)* Nazarite ♦ **el Nazareno** or **el Divino Nazareno** RELIG. Jesus Christ, the Nazarene.
Na·za·ret Nazareth.
naz·ca, nazco see **nacer.**
na·zi adj. & m.f. Nazi.
na·zis·mo m. POL. Nazism.
ne·bli·na f. mist, fog.
ne·bli·no·so, –sa adj. misty, foggy.
ne·bu·lón m. sly or slippery fellow, smooth operator.
ne·bu·lo·sa I. f. ASTRON. nebula <*n. galáctica* galactic nebula> II. adj. see **nebuloso, –sa.**
ne·bu·lo·si·dad f. *(calidad de nebuloso)* cloudiness, haziness; FIG. *(falta de claridad)* nebulousness, vagueness.
ne·bu·lo·so, –sa I. adj. *(sombrío)* cloudy, nebulous; FIG. *(difícil de entender)* hazy, vague; ASTRON. nebular II. f. see **nebulosa.**
ne·ce·ar intr. COLL. *(decir tonterías)* to talk nonsense, babble; *(hacer pavadas)* to act foolishly.
ne·ce·dad f. foolishness, nonsense ♦ **decir necedades** to babble.
ne·ce·sa·ria·men·te adv. necessarily.
ne·ce·sa·rio, –ria adj. *(preciso)* necessary; *(inevitable)* inevitable; *(útil)* essential, required <*un libro n.* an essential book>.
ne·ce·ser m. *(de tocador)* toilet case, dressing case; *(estuche)* kit <*n. de costura* sewing kit> ♦ **n. de afeitar** shaving kit.
ne·ce·si·dad f. *(obligación)* necessity, need; *(pobreza)* need, poverty; *(menester)* jam, tight spot ♦ **de n.** necessarily, by necessity • **en caso de n.** if necessary • **n. extrema** extreme need, dire straits • **por n.** out of necessity.
ne·ce·si·ta·do, –da I. adj. *(pobre)* needy, poor; *(falto)* in need, lacking II. m.f. needy person.
ne·ce·si·tar tr. *(hacer falta)* to need, want; *(obligar)* to require, necessitate; *(deber)* to have to, need to <*necesitamos escribirlo* we have to write it> —intr. ♦ **n. de** to need, be in need of.
ne·cia·men·te adv. stupidly, foolishly.
ne·cio, –cia I. adj. *(tonto)* ignorant, foolish; *(terco)* stubborn, obstinate; ARG., P. RICO touchy II. m.f. fool ♦ **a necias** foolishly.
ne·cró·fa·go, –ga I. adj. necrophagous, carrion-eating. II. m.f. necrophagous creature.
ne·cro·fi·lia f. necrophilia.
ne·cro·lo·gí·a f. necrology, obituary.
ne·cro·ló·gi·co, –ca adj. necrological.
ne·cró·lo·go, –ga m.f. necrologist.
ne·cro·man·cia f. necromancy, black magic.
ne·cró·po·lis f. [pl. **-lis**] necropolis, cemetery.
ne·cro·sis f. [pl. **-sis**] MED. necrosis, gangrene.
néc·tar m. nectar.
nec·tá·re·o, –a adj. nectarean, nectareous.
nec·ta·ri·na f. nectarine.
ne·er·lan·dés, –de·sa I. adj. of the Netherlands II. m.f. Netherlander.
ne·fa·rio, –ria adj. nefarious, vile.
ne·fas·to, –ta adj. ominous, unlucky.
ne·frí·ti·co, –ca adj. MED. nephritic, renal.

ne·fri·tis f. MED. nephritis.
ne·ga·ble adj. deniable, refutable.
ne·ga·ción f. *(negativa)* negation, denial; *(denegación)* refusal; *(carencia)* total lack; GRAM. negative (particle).
ne·ga·do, –da I. past part. see **negar** II. adj. *(incapaz)* incapable, inept; RELIG. apostate III. m.f. COLL. *(tonto)* dimwit; RELIG. apostate.
ne·gar §52 tr. *(contradecir)* to deny, refute; *(rehusar)* to deny, refuse; *(prohibir)* to prohibit, forbid; *(repudiar)* to disclaim, disavow —intr. COL. to misfire (guns) —reflex. *(rehusar)* to refuse to <*me niego a hablarle* I refuse to speak to him>; *(privarse)* to decline, deny oneself.
ne·ga·ti·va I. f. *(negación)* negation, denial; *(rechazo)* refusal, denial II. adj. see **negativo, –va.**
ne·ga·ti·vi·dad f. negativity, negativeness.
ne·ga·ti·vo, –va I. adj. negative; MATH. negative, minus II. m. PHOTOG. negative —f. see **negativa.**
ne·gli·gé m. negligee.
ne·gli·gen·cia f. *(irresponsabilidad)* negligence, carelessness; *(descuido)* neglect, disregard.
ne·gli·gen·te I. adj. negligent, careless II. m.f. careless person.
ne·go·cia·bi·li·dad f. negotiability.
ne·go·cia·ble adj. negotiable.
ne·go·cia·ción f. *(acción de negociar)* negotiation; COM. *(negocio)* business deal, transaction.
ne·go·cia·do, –da I. past part. see **negociar** II. m. *(departamento)* department, office; *(negocio)* business deal, transaction; AMER. *(negocio ilícito)* shady deal; CHILE establishment, place of business.
ne·go·cia·dor, –do·ra I. adj. negotiating II. m.f. negotiator.
ne·go·cian·te m.f. *(comerciante)* merchant, dealer —m. businessman —f. businesswoman.
ne·go·ciar intr. *(tratar)* to negotiate, discuss; *(comerciar)* to deal, do business —tr. COM., POL. to negotiate.
ne·go·cio m. *(comercio)* business, business concern; *(trabajo)* job, occupation; *(transacción)* transaction, deal; *(utilidad)* profit, return; *(asunto)* affair, concern; ARG., CHILE, URUG. shop, store; P. RICO, PERU, VEN. fact, truth <*el n. es que* the fact is that> ♦ **de negocios** business <*hombre de n.* businessman> • **encargado de negocios** DIPL. chargé d'affaires • **¡mal n.!** nasty business! • **n. redondo** profitable deal • **n. sucio** shady deal.
ne·go·cio·so, –sa adj. diligent, industrious.
ne·gre·ar intr. *(parecer negro)* to appear black; *(tirar a negro)* to turn black, blacken.
ne·gre·cer §17 intr. to turn black, blacken.
ne·gre·rí·a f. AMER. Negroes, Blacks.
ne·gre·ro, –ra I. adj. pertaining to black slaves II. m.f. *(esclavista)* slave trader; FIG. *(explotador)* slave driver.
ne·gri·lla f. PRINT. boldface (type); ICHTH. black conger.
ne·gri·tud f. negritude.
ne·gro, –gra I. adj. *(negruzco)* black; *(oscuro)* dark, black; FIG. *(melancólico)* melancholy, gloomy <*humor n.* melancholy mood>; *(enojado)* furious, angry; *(infeliz)* unlucky, unfortunate ♦ **n. como boca de lobo** *or* **como la pez** pitch-black • **pasarlas negras** to have a hard time • **poner a alguien n.** FIG. to anger someone • **ponerse n.** *(enojarse)* to get angry; *(broncearse)* to get a tan • **ver todo n.** to be pessimistic II. m.f. *(persona)* Black, Negro; AMER. *(querido)* dear, darling —m. *(color)* black —f. MUS. quarter note; HER. sable ♦ **en blanco y n.** in black and white • **n. de humo** lampblack.
ne·groi·de adj. Negroid.
ne·gru·ra f. blackness, darkness.
ne·gruz·co, –ca adj. blackish, dark.
ne·gué see **negar.**
ne·ma f. *(cierre de una carta)* seal, sealing (of a letter) —m. ECUAD. address (of a letter).
né·me·sis f. nemesis.
ne·mo·tec·nia f. mnemonics.
ne·ne, –na f. COLL. *(bebé)* baby, infant; *(querido)* dear, darling; *(villano)* scoundrel, villain.
ne·nú·far m. BOT. water lily.
ne·o·cla·si·cis·mo m. neoclassicism.
ne·o·clá·si·co, –ca I. adj. neoclassic, neoclassical II. m. neoclassicist.

ne·o·co·lo·nia·lis·mo m. neocolonialism.
ne·o·di·mio m. CHEM. neodymium.
ne·o·fas·cis·mo m. POL. neofascism.
ne·o·fas·cis·ta adj. & m.f. neofascist.
ne·ó·fi·to, –ta m.f. neophyte, novice.
ne·o·fo·bia f. fear of innovation *or* change.
ne·o·im·pre·sio·nis·mo m. ARTS neo-impressionism.
ne·o·la·ti·no, –na adj. Romance <*lengua n.* Romance language>.
ne·o·li·be·ra·lis·mo m. neoliberalism.
ne·o·lí·ti·co, –ca I. adj. neolithic II. m.f. neolith.
ne·o·lo·gí·a f. neology.
ne·o·ló·gi·co, –ca adj. neologistic.
ne·o·lo·gis·mo m. neologism.
ne·o·lo·gis·ta *or* **ne·ó·lo·go, –ga** m.f. neologist.
ne·ón m. CHEM. neon.
ne·o·na·to m. newborn baby.
ne·o·pla·tó·ni·co, –ca adj. neo-Platonic.
ne·o·pla·to·nis·mo m. neo-Platonism.
ne·o·pre·no m. neoprene.
ne·o·rre·a·lis·mo m. neorealism.
ne·o·yor·qui·no, –na I. adj. of New York II. m.f. New Yorker.
ne·o·ze·lan·dés, –de·sa I. adj. of New Zealand II. m.f. New Zealander.
Ne·pal m. Nepal.
ne·pa·lés, –le·sa adj. & m.f. Nepalese —m. *(idioma)* Nepalese ♦ **los nepaleses** the Nepalese.
ne·po·te m. privileged relative of the Pope.
ne·po·tis·mo m. nepotism.
nep·tu·nia·no, –na *or* **nep·tú·ni·co, –ca** adj. ASTRON. Neptunian; GEOL. neptunian.
nep·tu·nio m. CHEM. neptunium.
Nep·tu·no m. ASTRON. Neptune.
ne·rei·da f. MYTH. Nereid (sea nymph).
Ne·rón Nero.
ner·va·du·ra f. ARCHIT. rib; BOT., ENTOM. nervation.
ner·vio m. ANAT. nerve <*n. ciático* sciatic nerve>; *(tendón)* tendon, sinew; MUS. string; BOT. rib, vein; BKB. *(de libros)* rib; FIG. *(esencia)* core, guiding principle <*el n. de la teoría* the core of the theory>; *(fuerza)* nerve, guts ♦ **crisparle los nervios a alguien** to get on someone's nerves • **nervios de acero** nerves of steel • **tener los nervios de punta** to be on edge.
ner·vio·sa·men·te adv. nervously.
ner·vio·si·dad f. nervousness, agitation.
ner·vio·sis·mo m. var. of **nerviosidad.**
ner·vio·so, –sa adj. ANAT. nervous <*sistema n.* nervous system>; nerve <*célula n.* nerve cell>; *(el cuerpo)* sinewy, wiry; *(imitable)* nervous, jumpy; FIG. vigorous, energetic ♦ **ponerse n.** to get nervous.
ner·vo·si·dad f. *(agitación)* nervousness, agitation; METAL. flexibility; FIG. *(coherencia)* cogency (of an argument).
ner·vu·do, –da adj. wiry, sinewy, tough.
ne·ta·men·te adv. clearly, distinctly.
ne·to, –ta adj. *(puro)* pure, simple; net <*precio n.* net price>.
neu·má·ti·co, –ca I. adj. pneumatic II. m. AUTO. tire —f. PHYS. pneumatics ♦ **n. de repuesto** spare tire.
neu·mo·ní·a f. MED. pneumonia.
neu·ral·gia f. MED. neuralgia.
neu·rál·gi·co, –ca adj. MED. neuralgic.
neu·ras·te·nia f. MED. neurasthenia.
neu·ras·té·ni·co, –ca adj. & m.f. neurasthenic.
neu·ri·tis f. MED. neuritis.
neu·ro·ci·ru·ja·no, –na m.f. MED. neurosurgeon.
neu·ro·ci·ru·gí·a f. MED. neurosurgery.
neu·ro·lo·gí·a f. MED. neurology.
neu·ro·ló·gi·co, –ca adj. MED. neurological.
neu·ró·lo·go, –ga m.f. MED. neurologist.
neu·ro·na f. ANAT. neuron, neurone.
neu·ró·pa·ta I. adj. neuropathic, neuropathical II. m.f. neuropath.
neu·ro·pa·to·lo·gí·a f. MED. neuropathology.
neu·ro·psi·co·lo·gí·a f. MED. neuropsychology.
neu·ro·psi·quia·tra m.f. neuropsychiatrist.
neu·ro·psi·quia·trí·a f. neuropsychiatry.

neu·ro·sis f. [pl. **-sis**] MED. neurosis ♦ **n. de guerra** shell shock, combat fatigue.
neu·ró·ti·co, –ca adj. & m.f. neurotic.
neu·to·nio m. PHYS. newton.
neu·tral adj. & m.f. neutral.
neu·tra·li·cé, neutralice see **neutralizar.**
neu·tra·li·dad f. neutrality.
neu·tra·lis·mo m. neutralism.
neu·tra·lis·ta I. adj. neutralistic II. m.f. neutralist.
neu·tra·li·za·ción f. neutralization.
neu·tra·li·zan·te I. adj. neutralizing II. m.f. neutralizer.
neu·tra·li·zar §04 tr. to neutralize —reflex. to be neutralized.
neu·tro, –tra I. adj. *(indiferente)* neutral; BIOL. neuter, sexless; GRAM. *(género)* neuter; *(verbos)* intransitive; CHEM., ELEC. neutral II. m. GRAM. neuter.
neu·trón m. neutron.
ne·va·do, –da I. past part. see **nevar** II. adj. *(cubierto de nieve)* snowy, snow-covered; FIG. *(blanco)* snow-white III. m. ECUAD. embroidery —f. snowfall.
ne·var §49 intr. to snow —tr. *(poner blanco)* to whiten, make white; ECUAD. to embroider.
ne·vas·ca f. *(nevada)* snowfall; *(ventisca)* snowstorm, blizzard.
ne·va·zo m. heavy snowfall.
ne·ve·ra f. refrigerator, icebox.
ne·ve·rí·a f. *(tienda donde se vende hielo)* ice shop; MEX. ice cream parlor.
ne·vis·ca f. light snowfall, snow flurry.
ne·vis·car §70 tr. to snow lightly.
ne·vo·so, –sa adj. snowy.
new·ton m. PHYS. newton (unit of force).
new·to·nia·no, –na adj. PHYS. Newtonian.
ne·xo m. nexus, link ♦ **sin n.** unrelated.
ni §G45, 46 conj. neither, nor <*no tomo ni fumo* I neither drink nor smoke> <*ni el uno ni el otro* neither one nor the other>; not even <*ni (siquiera) me hablaron* they did not even speak to me> ♦ **ni que** not even if <*ni que fuera de plomo pesaría tanto* even if it were lead it wouldn't weigh so much>.
ni·be·lun·gos m.pl. MYTH. Nibelungs.
Ni·ca·ra·gua f. Nicaragua.
ni·ca·ra·güen·se adj. & m.f. Nicaraguan.
ni·co·ti·na f. CHEM. nicotine.
nic·tá·lo·pe MED. I. adj. nyctalopic II. m.f. nyctalope.
nic·ta·lo·pí·a f. MED. nyctalopia.
ni·cho m. *(en la pared)* niche, recess; *(tumba)* tomb, vault.
ni·da·da f. *(de huevos)* nest, nestful (of eggs); *(de pájaros)* brood (of birds).
ni·dal m. *(nido)* nest; *(huevo)* nest egg; FIG. *(lugar frecuentado)* hangout, haunt; COLL. *(guarida)* hiding place.
ni·di·fi·car §70 intr. to build a nest, nest.
ni·do m. *(ponedero)* nest; FIG. *(morada)* abode, home; *(guarida)* den, lair <*n. de ladrones* den of thieves>; *(centro)* center, hotbed <*n. de discordias* a hotbed of controversy>; *(agrupación)* nest <*un n. de ametralladoras* a machine gun nest> ♦ **caerse de un n.** FIG., COLL. to be extremely gullible • **patearle el n. a** ARG., URUG. to pull the rug out from under.
ni·do·ro·so, –sa adj. smelling like a rotten egg.
nie·bla f. *(bruma)* fog, mist; *(nube)* cloud; AGR. mildew, blight; FIG. *(confusión)* fog, confusion.
nie·go, niegue see **negar.**
niel or **nie·la·do** m. ARTS niello work.
nie·to, –ta m.f. grandchild —m. grandson —f. granddaughter ♦ **nietos** grandchildren.
nie·va see **nevar.**
nie·ve f. METEOROL. snow; FIG. *(blancura)* whiteness; CUBA, P. RICO water ice ♦ **a punto de n.** stiff • **nieves** snows, snowfall.
Ní·ger m. Niger.
Ni·ge·ria f. Nigeria.
ni·ge·ria·no, –na adj. & m.f. Nigerian.
ni·ge·ri·no, –na adj. of the Niger.
ni·gro·man·cia or **ni·gro·man·cí·a** f. necromancy, black magic.
ni·gro·man·te m.f. necromancer.

ni·gro·mán·ti·co, –ca I. adj. necromantic II. m. necromancer.
ni·gua f. ENTOM. chigger, jigger; GUAT. coward, crybaby ♦ **pegarse como n.** AMER. to stick like glue.
ni·hi·lis·mo m. nihilism.
ni·hi·lis·ta I. adj. nihilistic II. m.f. nihilist.
Ni·lo m. Nile.
ni·lón m. TEX. nylon.
nim·bar tr. to surround with a halo.
nim·bo m. *(aureola)* halo, nimbus; METEOROL. nimbus.
ni·mie·dad f. *(nadería)* trifle, trivial detail; *(exceso)* excess (of care); COLL. *(timidez)* timidity.
ni·mio, –mia adj. *(insignificante)* trivial, insignificant; *(excesivo)* excessive; *(mezquino)* stingy.
nin·fa f. MYTH. nymph; ZOOL. nymph, pupa; ANAT. nympha.
nin·fe·a f. BOT. water lily.
nin·fo m. FIG., COLL. fop, dandy.
nin·fó·ma·na or **nin·fo·ma·ní·a·ca** f. MED., PSYCH. nymphomaniac.
nin·fo·ma·ní·a f. MED., PSYCH. nymphomania.
nin·gún adj. [contr. of **ninguno** used before m. sing. nouns] none, not any —see **ninguno.**
nin·gu·no, –na §G21, 45 I. adj. none, no, not any <*no tengo n. opinión* I have no opinion> ♦ **de n. manera** or **de ningún modo** in no way, by no means • **en n. parte** nowhere II. pron. *(nulo)* none, not any <*no quiero n. de ellos* I do not want any of them>; *(nadie)* no one, nobody.
ni·ña f. & adj. see **niño –na.**
ni·ña·da f. childishness, childish act.
ni·ñe·ar intr. to act like a child.
ni·ñe·rí·a f. *(acción de niños)* childish act; FIG. *(pequeñez)* trifle.
ni·ñe·ro, –ra I. adj. fond of children II. f. nursemaid, nanny, babysitter.
ni·ñez f. *(infancia)* childhood; FIG. *(principio)* infancy, beginning ♦ **segunda n.** second childhood.
ni·ño, –ña I. adj. *(joven)* young, childlike; FIG. *(impulsivo)* immature, childish; *(inexperto)* inexperienced II. m.f. *(muchacho)* child; S. AMER. master (used by servants); CHILE scoundrel —m. *(muchacho)* boy —f. *(muchacha)* girl; *(del ojo)* pupil (of the eye) ♦ **de n.** as a child • **desde n.** from childhood • **niño explorador** Boy Scout • **n. gótico** COLL. showoff • **n. mimado** spoiled child • **n. prodigio** child prodigy • **niños** children.
nio·bio m. CHEM. niobium.
ni·pón, –po·na adj. & m.f. Nipponese, Japanese.
ní·quel m. CHEM. nickel; AMER. nickel; ARG., MEX. money.
ni·que·la·do m. nickeling, nickel-plating.
ni·que·lar tr. to nickel, nickel-plate.
nir·va·na m. RELIG. Nirvana.
nís·pe·ro m. BOT. medlar (tree and fruit).
ni·ti·dez f. *(claridad)* clarity, neatness; *(de fotos)* sharpness.
ní·ti·do, –da adj. *(claro)* clear, neat; *(de fotos)* sharp.
ni·trar tr. to nitrate.
ni·tra·to m. CHEM. nitrate ♦ **n. de potasio** potassium nitrate • **n. de sodio** sodium nitrate.
ní·tri·co, –ca adj. CHEM. nitric.
ni·tri·fi·ca·ción f. CHEM. nitrification.
ni·tri·to m. CHEM. nitrite.
ni·tro m. niter, potassium nitrate.
ni·tro·ce·lu·lo·sa f. CHEM. nitrocellulose.
ni·tro·ge·na·do, –da adj. CHEM. nitrogenous.
ni·tró·ge·no m. CHEM. nitrogen.
ni·tro·gli·ce·ri·na f. CHEM. nitroglycerin.
ni·tro·so, –sa adj. CHEM. nitrous.
ni·vel m. *(altura)* level, height; FIG. *(grado)* level, standard <*n. cultural* cultural level> ♦ **a n.** level • **de alto n.** high-level • **n. de agua** water level • **n. de aire** TECH. spirit level • **n. de vida** standard of living • **n. del mar** sea level • **paso a n.** railroad crossing.
ni·ve·la·ción f. leveling.
ni·ve·la·dor, –do·ra I. adj. leveling II. m.f. leveler.
ni·ve·lar tr. *(igualar)* to make level; SURV. to survey, grade; FIN. *(equilibrar)* to balance (a budget).
ní·ve·o, –a adj. POET. snowy, snow-white.
ni·vo·so, –sa adj. POET. snowy.
Ni·za f. Nice.

no §G45 **I.** adv. no <*¿puedes verlo? no* can you see it? no>; not <*no vengo* I'm not coming> ♦ *¿a qué no?* COLL. do you want to bet? • *¿cómo no?* of course, why not? • **no bien** no sooner • **no más** no more, only; AMER. feel free to <*continúe no más* feel free to continue> • **no obstante** nevertheless, notwithstanding • **no sea que** in case, lest • **no tal** certainly not, no such thing **II.** m. no <*un no definitivo* a definite no> **III.** pref. non <*no intervención* non-intervention>.

no·be·lio m. CHEM. nobelium.

no·bi·lia·rio, –ria I. adj. nobiliary **II.** m. peerage list.

no·ble I. adj. *(aristocrático)* noble, aristocratic; *(elevado)* noble, honorable **II.** m. *(aristócrata)* noble, nobleman; NUMIS. noble —f. noblewoman.

no·ble·men·te adv. nobly.

no·ble·za f. *(aristocracia)* nobility, aristocracy; *(honradez)* nobleness, gentility; *(tela)* fine damask.

no·blo·te, –ta adj. COLL. most noble, unaffectedly generous.

no·ción f. notion, idea ♦ **nociones** slight knowledge <*tengo nociones de algebra* I have a slight knowledge of algebra>.

no·ci·vi·dad f. noxiousness, harmfulness.

no·ci·vo, –va adj. noxious, harmful.

noc·tam·bu·lar tr. to sleepwalk.

noc·tam·bu·lis·mo m. noctambulism, sleepwalking.

noc·tám·bu·lo, –la I. adj. night-wandering **II.** m.f. FIG. night owl.

noc·tur·nal adj. nocturnal.

noc·tur·no, –na I. adj. nocturnal, nightly; FIG. *(triste)* sad, melancholy **II.** m. RELIG. nocturn; MUS. nocturne.

no·che f. *(anochecer)* night, nighttime, evening; *(oscuridad)* darkness; FIG. *(ignorancia)* ignorance, obscurity ♦ **a primera n.** at nightfall, just after dark • **buenas noches** good evening, good night • **cerrar la n.** to become completely dark • **de la n. a la mañana** FIG. suddenly, overnight • **de n.** *(por la noche)* at night; evening, night <*traje de n.* evening gown> • **hacer n.** to spend the night • **esta n.** tonight • **hacerse de n.** to grow dark • **n. cerrada** dark night • **n. toledana** sleepless night • **por la n.** at night • **quedarse a buenas noches** COLL. to be in the dark.

no·che·bue·na f. Christmas Eve.

no·che·vie·ja f. New Year's Eve.

no·do m. ASTRON., MED., PHYS. node.

no·dri·za f. *(persona)* wet nurse; AUTO. vacuum tank.

no·du·lar adj. nodular.

nó·du·lo m. nodule.

No·é BIBL. Noah.

no·gal m. BOT. walnut (tree and wood).

no·ga·li·na f. walnut stain.

no·gue·ra f. var. of **nogal.**

no·gue·ral m. walnut grove.

nó·ma·da *or* **nó·ma·de I.** adj. nomadic **II.** m.f. nomad.

no·más adv. MEX. just, only.

nom·bra·dí·a f. renown, fame.

nom·bra·do, –da I. past part. see **nombrar II.** adj. *(célebre)* renowned, famous; *(sobredicho)* aforementioned.

nom·bra·mien·to m. *(acción de nombrar)* naming; *(nominación)* nomination, appointment; MIL. commission.

nom·brar tr. *(llamar)* to name, mention by name; *(nominar)* to nominate, appoint; MIL. to commission.

nom·bre m. *(designación)* name; *(título)* title; GRAM. noun; FIG. *(renombre)* name, reputation ♦ **de n.** by name; in name only <*presidente de n.* president in name only> • **en n. de** in the name of, by the authority of • **no tener n.** to be unspeakable <*su conducta no tiene n.* his conduct is unspeakable> • **n. artístico** THEAT. stage name; LIT. pen name, nom de plume • **n. común** *or* **apelativo** GRAM. common noun • **n. postizo** alias • **n. propio** GRAM. proper noun • **n. y apellido** full name • **poner n. a** to name • **sin n.** nameless.

no·men·cla·tu·ra f. nomenclature.

no·me·ol·vi·des f. [pl. **-des**] BOT. forget-me-not.

nó·mi·na f. *(lista)* list, roll; COM. payroll.

no·mi·na·ción f. nomination, appointment.

no·mi·na·dor, –do·ra I. adj. nominating **II.** m.f. nominator.

no·mi·nal adj. *(que sólo tiene el nombre)* nominal, titular;

COM. face <*valor n.* face value>; GRAM. nominal, substantival.

no·mi·nar tr. to nominate, appoint.

no·mi·na·ti·vo, –va I. adj. COM. personal, registered; GRAM. nominative **II.** m. GRAM. nominative case.

nó·mi·no m. nominee.

non I. adj. odd, uneven **II.** m. MATH. odd number ♦ **de nones** at odds, idle • **estar** *or* **quedar de n.** to be odd man out • **nones** repeated denial.

no·na I. f. HIST., RELIG. nones **II.** adj. see **nono, –na.**

no·na·da f. trifle, nothing much.

no·na·ge·na·rio, –ria *or* **no·na·gé·si·mo, –ma** adj. & m.f. nonagenarian.

no·na·gé·si·mo, –ma adj. & m. ninetieth.

no·na·to, –ta adj. *(nato mediante la operación cesárea)* not naturally born, born by Caesarian section; FIG. *(no existente)* unborn, nonexistent.

no·no, –na I. adj. ninth **II.** m. *(noveno)* ninth; ARG., URUG., COLL. grandpa —f. grandma; see **nona.**

no·pal m. BOT. prickly pear.

no·que·ar tr. SPORT. to knock out.

no·ra·bue·na f. congratulations.

no·ra·ma·la *or* **no·ra·tal** adv. unfortunately.

nor·des·te *or* **no·res·te I.** adj. northeastern, northeasterly **II.** m. *(dirección)* northeast; *(viento)* northeaster.

nór·di·co, –ca I. adj. *(escandinavo)* Nordic, Norse; *(del norte)* northern **II.** m.f. *(habitante)* Norse —m. *(idioma)* Norse.

no·ria f. AGR. water wheel, chain pump; *(entretenimiento)* Ferris wheel.

nor·ma f. *(modelo)* norm, standard; FIG. *(regla)* rule; CARP., MAS. square.

nor·mal I. adj. *(regular)* normal, standard; GEOM. perpendicular ♦ **escuela n.** teachers training school **II.** f. GEOM. perpendicular.

nor·ma·li·dad f. normality, normalcy.

nor·ma·lis·ta m.f. student teacher.

nor·ma·li·za·ción f. *(acción de normalizar)* normalization; INDUS. standardization.

nor·ma·li·zar §04 tr. *(hacer normal)* to normalize; INDUS. to standardize.

Nor·man·dí·a f. GEOG. Normandy.

nor·man·do, –da adj. & m.f. Norman.

nor·mar tr. to mold, fit —intr. AMER. to set standards.

nor·ma·ti·vo, –va adj. normative.

nor·nor·des·te m. north-northeast.

nor·no·ro·es·te *or* **nor·no·rues·te** m. north-northwest.

no·ro·es·te I. adj. northwestern, northwesterly **II.** m. *(dirección)* northwest; *(viento)* northwester.

nor·te I. adj. northern, northerly **II.** m. *(dirección)* north; *(viento)* north wind; *(polo)* North Pole; *(estrella)* North Star; FIG. *(guía)* guide, lodestar; CUBA, P. RICO drizzle.

Nor·te·a·mé·ri·ca f. GEOG. North America.

nor·te·a·me·ri·ca·no, –na adj. & m.f. American, North American.

nor·te·ño, –ña I. adj. northern **II.** m.f. northerner.

nór·ti·co, –ca adj. northern, northerly.

No·rue·ga f. Norway.

no·rue·go, –ga adj. & m.f. Norwegian —m. *(idioma)* Norwegian.

nos §G8, 30 **I.** pron. us <*ellos n. vieron* they saw us>; us, to us, for us, from us <*él n. vendió la casa* he sold the house to us>; one another, each other <*n. queremos* we love each other>; ourselves <*n. estamos mirando en el espejo* we are looking at ourselves in the mirror> **II.** m.f. we <*n., los representantes* we, the representatives>.

no·so·tros, –tras §G30 pron. we <*n. lo hicimos* we did it>; us, ourselves <*no es para n.* it is not for us>.

nos·tal·gia f. nostalgia, homesickness.

nos·tál·gi·co, –ca I. adj. nostalgic, homesick **II.** m.f. nostalgic *or* homesick person.

no·ta f. *(comentario)* note, observation, commentary; *(apostilla)* note, notation <*n. marginal* marginal note>; *(fama)* note, reputation; *(reparo)* notice, heed; *(calificación)* grade, mark; COM. account; MUS. note; AMER. IOU, promissory note ♦ **dar la n.** to stand out, set the fashion • **de mala n.** with a bad reputation • **de n.** of note, famous • **forzar la n.** to go too far • **n. falsa** MUS. wrong note • **n.**

verbal verbal note • **tomar n. de** to take note of • **tomar notas** to take notes.
no·ta·bi·li·dad f. notability.
no·ta·ble I. adj. *(apreciable)* notable, noteworthy; *(superior)* outstanding, striking **II.** m.f. notable (person).
no·ta·ble·men·te adv. notably.
no·ta·ción f. *(anotación)* note, annotation; ARTS, MATH. notation.
no·tar tr. *(indicar)* to note, point out; *(observar)* to notice, observe; *(apuntar)* to make note of, jot down; *(anotar)* to annotate; *(censurar)* to criticize, censure —reflex. to be seen *or* noticed <*se nota la diferencia* one can see the difference>.
no·ta·rio, –ria m. notary, notary public.
no·ti·cia f. news item, piece of news ♦ **atrasado de noticias** out of date, behind the times • **noticias** news, information • **noticias de última hora** the latest news.
no·ti·ciar tr. to inform, notify.
no·ti·cia·rio m. RAD., TELEV. newscast; CINEM. newsreel.
no·ti·cie·ro, –ra I. adj. news **II.** m.f. JOURN. reporter, journalist; RAD., TELEV. newscaster.
no·ti·ción m. COLL. sensational news.
no·ti·cio·so, –sa I. adj. informed, well-informed **II.** m. AMER. news report.
no·ti·fi·ca·ción f. notification, notice.
no·ti·fi·car §70 tr. to notify, inform.
no·to·ria·men·te adj. notoriously.
no·to·rie·dad f. *(reputación)* notoriety; *(fama)* fame, renown.
no·to·rio, –ria adj. notorious, well-known.
no·va f. ASTRON. nova.
no·va·ción f. LAW novation.
no·va·ta·da f. hazing (in colleges).
no·va·to, –ta COLL. **I.** adj. beginning **II.** m.f. beginner, novice.
no·ve·cien·tos, –tas I. adj. nine hundred <*n. páginas* nine hundred pages>; *(noningentésimo)* nine hundredth **II.** m. nine hundred.
no·ve·dad f. *(calidad de nuevo)* newness; *(innovación)* novelty, innovation; *(cambio)* change, alteration; *(extrañeza)* surprise; *(noticia)* recent event ♦ **no hay n.** nothing is new • **novedades** latest fashions • **sin n.** *(nada nuevo)* as usual, no change; *(bien)* safely, well <*llegó sin n.* he arrived safely>.
no·ve·do·so, –sa adj. novel, new.
no·vel adj. new, inexperienced.
no·ve·la f. LIT. novel, fiction; FIG. *(mentira)* lie, falsehood ♦ **n. policíaca** detective story • **n. por entregas** serial • **n. rosa** love story.
no·ve·la·dor, –do·ra m.f. novelist.
no·ve·lar intr. *(escribir)* to write novels; FIG. *(mentir)* to lie —tr. to novelize.
no·ve·le·rí·a f. *(para novelas)* passion for novels; *(para novedades)* passion for novelties.
no·ve·le·ro, –ra adj. *(amigo de novedades)* fond of novelties; *(aficionado a novelas)* fond of novels; FIG. *(inconstante)* inconstant, fickle.
no·ve·les·co, –ca adj. novelesque.
no·ve·lis·ta m.f. novelist.
no·ve·lís·ti·co, –ca I. adj. novelistic **II.** f. *(estudio)* study of the novel; *(literatura)* novels, fiction.
no·ve·lón m. potboiler (novel).
no·ve·no, –na I. adj. ninth **II.** m. ninth —f. RELIG. novena.
no·ven·ta I. adj. ninety <*el libro tiene n. páginas* the book has ninety pages>; *(nonagésimo)* ninetieth **II.** m. ninety.
no·ven·ta·vo, –va adj. & m. ninetieth.
no·ven·tón, –to·na adj. & m.f. nonagenarian.
no·viaz·go m. *(relaciones amorosas)* courtship; *(compromiso)* engagement, betrothal.
no·vi·cia·do m. RELIG. novitiate; FIG. *(aprendizaje)* apprenticeship.
no·vi·cio, –cia I. adj. beginning, new **II.** m.f. RELIG. novice; FIG. *(aprendiz)* beginner, apprentice.
no·viem·bre m. November.
no·vie·ro, –ra adj. C. AMER., MEX. easily infatuated.
no·vi·lla·da f. *(rebaño)* herd of young bulls; TAUR. bullfight in which only young bulls are used.

no·vi·lle·ro m. *(vaquero)* herdsman who looks after young bulls; TAUR. fighter of young bulls; COLL. *(muchacho)* truant.
no·vi·llo, –lla m. TAUR. young bull; COLL. *(cornudo)* cuckold —f. heifer, young cow ♦ **hacer novillos** COLL. to be truant, play hooky.
no·vio, –via m. *(amigo)* boyfriend; *(prometido)* fiancé; *(recién casado)* groom —f. *(amiga)* girlfriend; *(prometida)* fiancée; *(recién casada)* bride ♦ **novios** *(casados)* newlyweds; *(prometidos)* engaged couple.
no·ví·si·mo, –ma adj. latest, most recent ♦ **novísimos** THEOL. last stages of man.
no·vo·ca·í·na f. PHARM. Novocain (trademark).
nu·ba·da *or* **nu·ba·rra·da** f. METEOROL. downpour, sudden shower; FIG. *(abundancia)* plenty, abundance.
nu·ba·rrón m. large black cloud.
nu·be f. *(cúmulo)* cloud; FIG. *(sombra)* cloud, shadow; *(multitud)* swarm, multitude; MED. *(en los ojos)* cloud, film (on the cornea); JEWEL. flaw ♦ **como caído de las nubes** out of the blue, unexpectedly • **estar en las nubes** to have one's head in the clouds • **n. atómica** atomic cloud • **n. de lluvia** rain cloud • **n. de verano** *(tempestad)* sudden shower; FIG. *(disturbio)* passing annoyance • **por las nubes** sky-high (prices, praise).
nú·bil adj. nubile, marriageable.
nu·bi·li·dad f. nubility.
nu·bla·do, –da I. past part. see **nublar II.** adj. cloudy, overcast **III.** m. METEOROL. storm cloud; FIG. *(desafío)* threat, menace; *(multitud)* swarm, crowd; *(ira)* anger ♦ **descargar el n.** *(llover)* to rain hard, pour; FIG. *(desahogarse)* to vent one's anger.
nu·blar tr. *(cubrirse de nubes)* to cloud, darken; FIG. *(oscurecer)* to cloud, obscure (reason) —reflex. to become cloudy *or* overcast.
nu·bo·si·dad f. cloudiness.
nu·bo·so, –sa adj. cloudy, overcast.
nu·ca f. ANAT. nape (of the neck).
nu·cle·ar adj. BIOL., PHYS. nuclear.
nu·clei·co, –ca adj. BIOCHEM. nucleic.
nú·cle·o m. SCI. nucleus; ELEC. core; BOT. kernel, pit; FIG. *(esencial)* core, essence ♦ **n. de ferrita** COMPUT. ferrite core.
nu·cle·ón m. PHYS. nucleon.
nu·di·llo m. ANAT. knuckle; ARCHIT. plug, dowel.
nu·dis·mo m. nudism.
nu·dis·ta m. nudist.
nu·do m. *(lazo)* knot; ANAT. node, lump; *(centro)* intersection (in roads, communications); BOT. knot (in wood); MARIT. knot (unit of speed); FIG. *(complicación)* snarl, tangle; *(lazo)* bond, tie; *(enredo)* crux, core <*el n. de la trama* the crux of the plot> ♦ **n. corredizo** slipknot, noose • **n. gordiano** Gordian knot • **tener un n. en la garganta** FIG. to have a lump in one's throat.
nu·do·so, –sa adj. knotty, knotted.
nue·ra f. daughter-in-law.
nues·tro, –tra §G25, 40 **I.** adj. our, of ours <*n. coche* our car> **II.** pron. ours, of ours <*el n. es rojo* ours is red> ♦ **los nuestros** our people, our side.
nue·va I. f. news, tidings **II.** adj. see **nuevo, –va.**
Nueva Es·co·cia f. Nova Scotia.
Nueva Gui·ne·a f. New Guinea.
Nueva In·gla·te·rra f. New England.
nue·va·men·te adv. *(de nuevo)* again, anew; *(recientemente)* newly, recently.
Nueva Or·le·áns f. New Orleans.
Nueva York f. New York.
Nueva Ze·lan·dia f. New Zealand.
nue·ve I. adj. nine <*hay n. capítulos en este libro* there are nine chapters in this book>; *(noveno)* ninth ♦ **las n.** nine o'clock **II.** m. nine.
nue·vo, –va I. adj. *(recién hecho)* new <*compré unos zapatos nuevos* I bought some new shoes>; *(otro)* new, another <*compró un n. libro* she bought a new book>; *(original)* novel, fresh <*n. idea* novel idea>; *(recién llegado)* new, newly arrived <*él es n. en la oficina* he is new in the office> ♦ **de n.** again • **N. Mundo** New World • **N. Testamento** New Testament • **¿qué hay de n.?** what's new? **II.** f. see **nueva.**

nuez f. [pl. **nue·ces**] nut; *(del nogal)* walnut; ANAT. Adam's apple; MUS. nut (of a violin); *(en ballestería)* nut, notch (in archery) ♦ **n. moscada** *or* **de especie** nutmeg • **n. vómica** BOT. nux vomica.

nu·li·dad f. *(falta de efecto)* nullity; *(incapacidad)* inability, incompetence; FIG. *(inutilidad)* worthlessness; COLL. *(persona)* useless person.

nu·lo, -la adj. *(sin efecto)* null, void; *(sin mérito)* useless, worthless; *(ninguno)* nil, nonexistent ♦ **n. y sin valor** null and void.

nu·men m. *(inspiración)* inspiration, muse; *(divinidad)* numen, deity.

nu·me·ra·ción f. *acción de numerar)* numeration, numbering; *(números)* numbers, numerals ♦ **n. arábiga** Arabic numerals • **n. romana** Roman numerals.

nu·me·ra·dor m. MATH. numerator.

nu·me·ral adj. numeral.

nu·me·rar tr. *(foliar)* to number; *(contar)* to count, enumerate.

nu·me·ra·rio, -ria I. adj. numerary II. m. cash, currency.

nu·me·ra·ti·vo, -va adj. used for numbering.

nu·mé·ri·ca·men·te adv. numerically.

nu·mé·ri·co, -ca adj. numerical.

nú·me·ro m. *(cuantía)* number; *(signo)* numeral; *(ejemplar)* issue, copy; *(medida)* size (of shoes, gloves); THEAT. number, act ♦ **de n.** regular (member) • **n. arábigo** Arabic numeral • **n. atrasado** back issue • **n. cardinal** cardinal number • **n. complejo** compound number • **n. dígito** digit • **n. entero** whole number • **n. extraordinario** special edition *or* issue • **n. fraccionario** *or* **quebrado** fraction • **n. impar** odd number • **n. ordinal** ordinal number • **n. par** even number • **n. primo** prime number • **n. redondo** round number • **n. romano** Roman numeral • **n. uno** the best, the first • **sin n.** countless, numberless.

nu·me·ro·so, -sa adj. numerous, many.

nu·mis·má·ti·co, -ca I. adj. numismatic II. m.f. numismatist —f. numismatics.

nun·ca §G45 adv. never, not ever ♦ **más que n.** more than ever • **n. jamás** *or* **n. más** never again.

nun·cia·tu·ra f. *(oficio)* nunciature; *(casa)* nuncio's residence.

nun·cio m. RELIG. nuncio; *(mensajero)* messenger; *(señal)* harbinger, herald.

nup·cial adj. nuptial.

nup·cias f.pl. nuptials, wedding.

nu·tra *or* **nu·tria** f. ZOOL. otter.

nu·tri·cio, -cia adj. nutritious.

nu·tri·ción f. nutrition.

nu·tri·do, -da I. past part. see **nutrir** II. adj. *(alimentado)* nourished, fed <*bien n.* well-fed>; FIG. *(abundante)* large, abundant <*una concurrencia muy n.* a large crowd>.

nu·tri·men·to *or* **nu·tri·mien·to** m. nutriment, nourishment.

nu·trir tr. *(alimentar)* to nourish, feed; FIG. *(fortalecer)* to nurture, strengthen.

nu·tri·ti·vo, -va adj. nutritious, nutritive.

ny f. nu (Greek letter).

Ñ

ñ, Ñ f. seventeenth letter of the Spanish alphabet.

ña f. AMER., COLL. dim. of **doña.**

ña·me m. BOT. yam.

ñan·dú m. ORNITH. American ostrich.

ña·ño, -ña I. adj. COL. spoiled, pampered; PERU close, intimate (friend) II. m. ARG., ECUAD. older brother; CHILE dolt, dunce; PERU child, baby.

ña·pa f. AMER. bonus, extra ♦ **de ñ.** to boot, into the bargain.

ña·que m. odds and ends.

ña·to, -ta adj. AMER. snub-nosed; ARG. ugly.

ñe·que I. m. AMER. strength, vigor; C. AMER., MEX. slap, blow II. adj. AMER. strong, vigorous ♦ **hombre de ñ.** FIG., COLL. he-man.

ñe·que·ar intr. ECUAD. to show strength.

ñi·qui·ña·que m. COLL. *(persona)* good-for-nothing; *(cosa)* piece of trash.

ñis·ca f. C. AMER., COL. excrement; AMER. bit, piece.

ño·ñe·rí·a *or* **ño·ñez** f. foolishness, simple-mindedness.

ño·ño, -ña COLL. I. adj. *(apocado)* bashful, timid; *(soso)* dull, inane II. m.f. *(apocado)* bashful *or* timid person; *(soso)* dull *or* inane person.

ño·que *or* **ño·qui** m. CUL. gnocchi.

ñor, ñora AMER., COLL. dim of **señor, señora.**

ñor·bo m. ARG., ECUAD., PERU passionflower.

ñu·do m. ARCH. knot ♦ **al ñ.** ARG. in vain.

O

o, O f. eighteenth letter of the Spanish alphabet.

o §G46 conj. or <*blanco o negro* black or white>; either <*lo harás o de buen grado o por la fuerza* you will do it, either willingly *or* unwillingly> ♦ **o sea** that is to say.

o·a·sis m. [pl. **-sis**] *(en un desierto)* oasis; FIG. *(descanso)* oasis.

ob·ce·ca·ción f. obfuscation, blindness.

ob·ce·ca·da·men·te adv. blindly.

ob·ce·car §70 tr. to obfuscate, blind.

o·be·de·ce·dor, -do·ra I. adj. obedient II. m.f. obeyer.

o·be·de·cer §17 tr. to obey —intr. *(ceder)* to obey; *(responder a)* to respond to <*esta enfermedad obedece al tratamiento* this illness responds to treatment>; *(deberse a)* to be due to, arise from <*su ausencia obedece a varias circunstancias* his absence is due to a number of circumstances> ♦ **hacerse o.** to command obedience.

o·be·de·ci·mien·to m. obedience.

o·be·dien·cia f. obedience ♦ **o. ciega** FIG. blind obedience.

o·be·dien·te adj. obedient.

o·be·dien·te·men·te adv. obediently.

o·be·lis·co m. *(monumento)* obelisk; PRINT. dagger.

o·ber·tu·ra f. MUS. overture.

o·be·si·dad f. obesity.

o·be·so, -sa adj. obese.

ó·bi·ce m. obstacle, impediment.

o·bis·pa·do m. bishopric, episcopate.

o·bis·pal adj. episcopal.

o·bis·po m. *(prelado)* bishop; ICHTH. ray; CUL. blood pudding ♦ **trabajar para el o.** COLL. to work for nothing.

ó·bi·to m. death, demise.

o·bi·tua·rio m. obituary.

ob·je·ción f. objection ♦ **hacer** *or* **levantar una o.** to object, raise an objection • **o. denegada** LAW objection overruled.

ob·je·ta·ble adj. objectionable.

ob·je·tan·te I. adj. objecting II. m.f. objector.

ob·je·tar tr. to object to, raise objections to ♦ **no tener nada que o.** to have no objection *or* objections.

ob·je·ti·va·ción f. objectivization.

ob·je·ti·va·men·te adv. objectively.

ob·je·ti·var tr. to objectify.

ob·je·ti·vi·dad f. objectivity.

ob·je·ti·vis·mo m. *(objetividad)* objectivity; PHILOS. objectivism.

ob·je·ti·vo, -va I. adj. objective II. m. *(meta)* objective, goal; MIL. target; OPT., PHOTOG. objective.

ob·je·to m. *(cosa)* object, thing; *(tema)* subject, theme <*el o. de un discurso* the subject of a speech>; *(fin)* object, aim; GRAM. object ♦ **carecer de o.** to be useless • **con o. de** in order to • **¿con qué o.?** to what end? • **ser o. de** to be the object of • **tener por o.** to be one's aim <*tengo por o. el estudio de la medicina* it is my aim to study medicine>.

ob·je·tor, -to·ra I. adj. objecting II. m.f. objector ♦ **o. de conciencia** MIL. conscientious objector.

o·bla·ción f. oblation, offering.

o·bla·to, -ta RELIG. I. adj. pertaining to an oblate II. m.f. oblate —f. oblation, offering.

o·ble·a f. *(hoja de pegar)* wafer (for sealing letters); PHARM. capsule (for taking medicines); FIG., COLL. *(persona escuálida)* bag of bones, skeleton.

o·bli·cua·men·te adv. obliquely.
o·bli·cui·dad f. obliquity ♦ **o. de la elíptica** ASTRON. obliquity.
o·bli·cuo, –cua adj. *(inclinado)* oblique, slanting; ANAT., GEOM. oblique.
o·bli·ga·ción f. *(imposición)* obligation; *(responsabilidad)* responsibility; *(deber)* duty; LAW *(en derecho)* obligation; FIN. bond ♦ **o. civil** civil obligation • **o. colectiva** joint obligation • **o. de probar** LAW burden of proof • **o. ética** moral obligation • **o. implícita** implied obligation • **o. mancomunada** concurrent obligation • **o. natural** natural obligation • **obligaciones** family obligations • **falter a sus obligaciones** to fail in one's duties • **obligaciones matrimoniales** marital obligations.
o·bli·ga·cio·nis·ta m.f. FIN. bondholder.
o·bli·ga·do, –da I. past part. see **obligar** II. adj. *(obligatorio)* obligatory, compulsory; *(comprometido)* obliged, obligated III. m. *(abastecedor)* town supplier *or* purveyor; MUS. *(pieza)* obligato.
o·bli·gar §47 tr. *(imponer)* to oblige, obligate; FIG. *(compeler)* to force, compel *<su conducta me obligó a salir temprano* his conduct forced me to leave early>; *(favorecer)* to oblige, favor *<nos obligó con su presencia* he favored us with his presence>; *(forzar)* to force *<sólo puedes ponerte los zapatos obligándolos* you can only put on the shoes by forcing them>; *(en derecho)* to pledge as security *or* collateral —reflex. to obligate oneself.
o·bli·ga·to·rie·dad f. compulsoriness.
o·bli·ga·to·rio, –ria adj. obligatory, compulsory.
o·bli·te·ra·ción f. MED. obstruction, occlusion.
o·bli·te·rar tr. MED. to obstruct, occlude.
o·blon·go, –ga adj. oblong, elongated.
ob·nu·bi·la·ción f. *(ofuscamiento)* cloudiness, obfuscation; OPTHAL. cloudiness of vision.
o·bo·e m. MUS. *(instrumento)* oboe; *(músico)* oboist, oboe player.
o·bo·ís·ta m.f. oboist, oboe player.
ó·bo·lo m. *(peso y moneda antiguos)* obolus; FIG. *(cantidad pequeña)* bit, mite; PHARM. one-half scruple, twelve grains.
o·bra f. *(trabajo)* work; *(acción)* action *<poner por o.* to put into action>; ARTS, LIT. work; *(acto)* act *<una o. de misericordia* an act of mercy>; *(labor)* workmanship, labor; *(construcción)* construction site; TECH. hearth (of a kiln) ♦ **de o.** in deed • **o. de arte** work of art • **¡manos a la o.!** let's get to work! • **o. de caridad** charitable deed • **o. de romanos** FIG. huge job • **o. maestra** masterpiece • **o. muerta** MARIT. gunwale, freeboard • **o. pía** charitable institution • **o. prima** shoemaking • **obras públicas** public works • **por o. de** thanks to.
o·bra·dor, –do·ra I. adj. working, laboring II. m.f. *(trabajador)* worker, laborer —m. *(taller)* workshop.
o·bra·je m. *(manufactura)* manufacture; *(fabricación por mano)* handiwork; *(taller)* workshop.
o·brar tr. *(ejecutar)* to handle, work; *(causar efecto)* to work, have an effect; *(edificar)* to construct, build —intr. *(proceder)* to act, proceed; *(evacuar el vientre)* to move one's bowels, have a bowel movement ♦ **o. en** to be in *<la carta obra en manos de Juan* the letter is in John's hands>.
o·bre·rí·a f. *(cargo de obrero)* task of a workman; *(renta de iglesia)* funds for church repairs; *(despacho)* churchwarden's *or* superintendent's office; *(cuidado)* upkeep of a church.
o·bre·ris·mo m. *(movimiento)* labor *or* workers' movement; *(obreros)* labor, workers.
o·bre·ris·ta adj. *(pertaining to)* labor.
o·bre·ro, –ra I. adj. working *<clase o.* working class> ♦ **sindicato o.** labor union II. m.f. *(trabajador)* worker; *(jornalero)* laborer ♦ **o. estacional** seasonal worker • **o. portuario** dockworker.
obs·ce·ni·dad f. obscenity.
obs·ce·no, –na adj. obscene.
obs·cu·re·cer §17 tr. var. of **oscurecer.**
obs·cu·ri·dad f. var. of **oscuridad.**
obs·cu·ro, –ra adj. & m. var. of **oscuro, –ra.**
ob·se·cra·ción f. obsecration, imploring.
ob·se·crar tr. to implore, beseech.
ob·se·cuen·cia f. obsequiousness.
ob·se·cuen·te adj. obedient, compliant.

ob·se·quia·dor, –do·ra I. adj. generous II. m.f. giver, generous person.
ob·se·quiar tr. *(agasajar)* to entertain, regale; *(galantear)* to court, WOO; AMER. to give (something) as a gift, make a present of.
ob·se·quio m. *(agasajo)* attention, kindness; *(regalo)* gift, present; *(galanteo)* courting, wooing; *(cortesía excesiva)* obsequiousness, deference ♦ **deshacerse en obsequios (con alguien)** to lavish attention (on someone) • **en o. de** in honor of, for the sake of • **o. del autor** complimentary copy (of a publication).
ob·se·quio·si·dad f. *(cortesía excesiva)* obsequiousness, deference; *(cortesía)* obligingness, attentiveness.
ob·se·quio·so, –sa adj. *(cortés)* obliging, attentive; *(servil)* obsequious, deferential; MEX. fond of giving gifts, generous with gifts.
ob·ser·va·ble adj. observable, noticeable.
ob·ser·va·ción f. *(acción de observar)* observation, observing; *(nota aclaratoria)* observation, explanatory note *or* remark; *(objeción)* objection ♦ **en** *or* **bajo o.** under observation • **hacer una o.** to make a remark • **o. astronómica** astronomical observation, skywatching • **o. meteorológica** meteorological observation, weather forecasting.
ob·ser·va·dor, –do·ra I. adj. observant, observing II. m.f. observer ♦ **o. de pájaros** birdwatcher • **o. meteorológico** meteorologist, weather forecaster.
ob·ser·van·cia f. *(cumplimiento)* observance; *(acatamiento)* respect, esteem ♦ **poner en o.** to put into effect, enforce.
ob·ser·van·te adj. observant, observing.
ob·ser·var tr. *(guardar y cumplir)* to observe, obey; *(espiar)* to observe, watch; *(notar)* to observe, notice; *(comentar)* to observe, remark.
ob·ser·va·to·rio m. observatory ♦ **o. astronómico** astronomical observatory • **o. meteorológico** meteorological observatory, weather station.
ob·se·sión f. obsession.
ob·se·sio·nan·te adj. obsessive.
ob·se·sio·nar tr. to obsess.
ob·se·si·vo, –va adj. obsessive, obsessional.
ob·se·so, –sa adj. & m.f. obsessive.
ob·si·dia·na f. GEOL. obsidian.
ob·so·les·cen·cia f. obsolescence.
ob·so·le·to, –ta adj. obsolete.
obs·ta·cu·li·zar §04 tr. to obstruct, hinder.
obs·tá·cu·lo m. obstacle ♦ **carrera de obstáculos** steeplechase, obstacle course • **poner obstáculos** to obstruct, hinder; AMER. to object *<puso obstáculos a mis observaciones* he objected to my comments>.
obs·tan·te adj. obstructing ♦ **no o.** nevertheless, however.
obs·tar intr. *(impedir)* to obstruct, hinder; *(oponerse una cosa a otra)* to stand in the way of, prevent.
obs·te·tri·cia f. MED. obstetrics.
obs·té·tri·co, –ca adj. MED. obstetric, obstetrical.
obs·ti·na·ción f. obstinacy, stubbornness.
obs·ti·na·da·men·te adv. obstinately, stubbornly.
obs·ti·na·do, –da I. past part. see **obstinarse** II. adj. obstinate, stubborn.
obs·ti·nar·se reflex. to be *or* become obstinate *or* stubborn.
obs·truc·ción f. obstruction.
obs·truc·cio·nar tr. var. of **obstruir.**
obs·truc·cio·nis·mo m. POL. obstructionism, filibustering.
obs·truc·cio·nis·ta POL. I. adj. obstructionistic II. m.f. obstructionist, filibusterer.
obs·truc·ti·vo, –va adj. obstructive.
obs·truc·tor, –to·ra m.f. obstructor.
obs·truir §18 tr. to obstruct —reflex. to become stopped up *or* obstructed.
ob·ten·ción f. obtaining.
ob·te·ner §69 tr. *(conseguir)* to obtain, get; *(conservar)* to have, keep.
ob·tu·ra·ción f. obturation, plugging.
ob·tu·ra·dor, –triz I. adj. obturating, plugging II. m. *(tapón)* plug, stopper; MED. female contraceptive device; PHOTOG. shutter ♦ **o. de cortina** PHOTOG. roller-blind shutter • **o. de guillotina** PHOTOG. drop shutter • **o. de plano** focal plane shutter.
ob·tu·rar tr. to obturate, stop up.

ob·tu·so, –sa adj. *(romo)* blunt, obtuse; FIG. *(torpe)* dull, obtuse; GEOM. obtuse.

ob·tu·vie·ra, obtuvo see **obtener**.

o·bús m. [pl. **-bu·ses**] ARTIL. *(cañón)* mortar, howitzer; *(proyectil)* shell; *(piececita de cierre)* cap (of an inflatable tire).

ob·viar tr. to obviate, prevent —intr. to stand in the way.

ob·vio, –via adj. obvious, clear.

o·ca f. ORNITH. goose; BOT. oca.

o·ca·sión f. *(oportunidad)* opportunity, occasion; *(motivo)* reason, cause <*no le dé o. para hacer eso* don't give him reason to do that>; *(momento)* occasion, time <*en aquella o. trabajaba en Caracas* at that time I was working in Caracas>; *(circunstancia)* circumstance; *(peligro)* danger, risk; AMER. bargain ♦ **aprovechar una o.** to take advantage of an opportunity • **coger** *or* **tomar la o. por los cabellos** FIG. to seize the opportunity *or* moment • **con o. de** on the occasion of • **de o.** *(de segunda mano)* secondhand; *(de precio reducido)* bargain • **dar o. a** to give rise to • **en cierta o.** once, on a certain occasion • **en la primera o.** at the first opportunity • **en ocasiones** sometimes, at times.

o·ca·sio·na·do, –da I. past part. see **ocasionar** II. adj. *(molesto)* annoying, irritating; *(peligroso)* hazardous, dangerous.

o·ca·sio·na·dor, –do·ra I. adj. occasioning, causing II. m.f. causer, person responsible.

o·ca·sio·nal adj. *(fortuito)* chance, accidental; *(que ocasiona)* occasioning, causing; *(que ocurre de vez en cuando)* occasional.

o·ca·sio·nal·men·te adv. *(casualmente)* by chance, accidentally; *(de vez en cuando)* occasionally.

o·ca·sio·nar tr. *(causar)* to occasion, cause; *(provocar)* to stir up, provoke; *(poner en peligro)* to endanger, jeopardize.

o·ca·so m. *(puesta del sol)* sunset, sundown; *(puesta de un astro)* setting (of a star); *(occidente)* occident, west; FIG. *(decadencia)* decline, end <*el o. de Occidente* the decline of the West>.

oc·ci·den·tal I. adj. western, occidental II. m.f. westerner, occidental.

oc·ci·den·te m. west, occident ♦ **Occidente** West, Occident.

oc·ci·pi·tal ANAT. I. adj. occipital II. m. occipital (bone).

oc·ci·pu·cio m. ANAT. occiput.

oc·ci·so, –sa adj. dead, killed.

o·ce·á·ni·co, –ca I. adj. *(del mar)* oceanic; *(de Oceanía)* Oceanian, Oceanic II. m.f. Oceanian.

o·cé·a·no m. ocean; FIG. *(vasta extensión o cantidad)* ocean, sea ♦ **o. Atlántico** Atlantic Ocean • **o. Índico** Indian Ocean • **o. Pacífico** Pacific Ocean.

o·ce·a·no·gra·fí·a f. oceanography.

o·ce·a·no·grá·fi·co, –ca adj. oceanographic, oceanographical.

o·ce·lo·te m. ZOOL. ocelot.

o·ciar intr. to idle, loaf.

o·cio m. *(cesación del trabajo)* idleness, inactivity; *(diversión)* diversion, pastime; *(tiempo libre)* leisure, free time ♦ **ocios** fruits of one's spare time.

o·cio·sa·men·te adv. *(inútilmente)* pointlessly, uselessly; *(sin ocupación)* idly; *(sin necesidad)* needlessly.

o·cio·si·dad f. idleness ♦ **la o. es la madre de todos los vicios** idleness is the root of all evil.

o·cio·so, –sa I. adj. *(desocupado)* idle; *(inútil)* pointless, useless II. m.f. idler, loafer.

o·clo·cra·cia f. POL. ochlocracy, mob rule.

o·cluir §18 tr. MED. to occlude —reflex. to be *or* become occluded.

o·clu·sión f. occlusion.

o·clu·si·vo, –va adj. & f. GRAM. occlusive.

o·cre m. ocher, ochre ♦ **o. amarillo** yellow ocher • **o. calcinado** *or* **quemado** burnt ocher • **o. rojo** red ocher.

oc·ta·e·dro m. GEOM. octahedron.

oc·ta·go·nal adj. GEOM. octagonal.

oc·tá·go·no, –na GEOM. I. adj. octagonal II. m. octagon.

oc·ta·no m. CHEM. octane <*índice de o.* octane number>.

oc·ta·vo, –va I. adj. eighth II. m. eighth —f. MUS., POET., RELIG. octave.

oc·te·to m. MUS. octet.

oc·to·ge·na·rio, –ria adj. & m.f. octogenarian.

oc·to·gé·si·mo, –ma adj. & m. eightieth.

oc·to·go·nal adj. GEOM. octagonal.

oc·tó·go·no, –na I. adj. GEOM. octagonal II. m. octagon.

oc·tu·bre m. October.

óc·tu·plo, –pla adj. octuple, eightfold.

o·cu·lar I. adj. ocular, pertaining to the eye II. m. eyepiece, ocular.

o·cu·lar·men·te adv. ocularly, visually.

o·cu·lis·ta m.f. oculist.

o·cul·ta·dor, –do·ra I. adj. hiding, concealing II. m.f. *(persona)* hider, concealer —m. PHOTOG. mask.

o·cul·ta·men·te adv. stealthily, secretly.

o·cul·tar tr. *(esconder)* to hide, conceal <*o. algo de alguien* to hide something from someone>; *(callar)* to hush, silence; *(disfrazar)* to disguise, conceal; *(reservar)* to conceal.

o·cul·tis·mo m. occultism.

o·cul·to, –ta adj. *(escondido)* hidden, concealed; *(sobrenatural)* occult ♦ **en o.** secretly.

o·cu·pa·ción f. *(acción de ocupar)* occupation, occupying; *(empleo)* occupation, profession, trade; *(trabajo)* daily activities *or* routine; MIL. occupation; LAW *(modo de adquirir la propiedad)* occupancy.

o·cu·pa·cio·nal adj. occupational, job-related <*enfermedad o.* occupational illness>.

o·cu·pa·do, –da I. past part. see **ocupar** II. adj. *(teléfono, línea)* engaged, busy; *(ciudad, territorio)* occupied; *(seat)* taken <*¿está o. este asiento?* is this seat taken?>.

o·cu·pa·dor, –do·ra I. adj. occupying II. m.f. occupant, occupier.

o·cu·pan·te I. adj. occupying II. m.f. occupant, occupier.

o·cu·par tr. *(apoderarse de)* to occupy, take possession of; *(llenar)* to occupy, fill (space, time); *(habitar)* to occupy, live in <*ellos ocupan la casa a la derecha* they live in the house on the right>; to hold, fill <*ocupó el puesto de ministro* he held the post of minister>; *(emplear)* to employ, give work to; *(encargar)* to occupy, keep busy; *(estorbar)* to bother, annoy <*no le ocupes con los detalles* don't bother him with the details> —reflex. *(emplearse)* to occupy oneself; *(interesarse)* to concern oneself; *(atender a)* to attend, pay attention <*ocuparse de los detalles* to attend to the details>.

o·cu·rren·cia f. *(ocasión)* occurrence, event; *(chiste)* witticism ♦ **o. de acreedores** COM. creditors' meeting • **¡qué o.!** what a thought! • **tener ocurrencias** to be witty.

o·cu·rren·te adj. *(que ocurre)* occurrent, occurring; *(chistoso)* witty, funny.

o·cu·rri·do, –da I. past part. see **ocurrir** II. adj. ECUAD., PERU witty, funny.

o·cu·rrir intr. *(suceder)* to occur, happen; *(acudir)* to go to, show up for <*o. a una cita* to show up for an appointment> ♦ **¿qué ocurre?** what's the matter? —reflex. to occur to, strike <*se me ocurrió que estaba en peligro* it occured to me that I was in danger>.

o·cha·va f. *(octava parte)* eighth; RELIG. octave.

o·cha·va·do, –da adj. octagonal, eight-sided.

o·cha·vón, –vo·na adj. CUBA octoroon.

o·chen·ta I. adj. eighty <*o. pesos* eighty pesos>; *(octogésimo)* eightieth II. m. eighty.

o·chen·ta·vo adj. & m. eightieth.

o·chen·tón, –to·na COLL. adj. & m.f. octogenarian.

o·cho I. adj. eight <*o. metros* eight meters>; *(octavo)* eighth ♦ **las o.** eight o'clock • **o. días** a week II. m. eight.

o·cho·cien·tos, –tas I. adj. eight hundred <*o. habitantes* eight hundred inhabitants>; *(octingentésimo)* eight hundredth II. m. eight hundred.

o·da f. POET. ode.

o·da·lis·ca f. odalisque (female slave or concubine).

o·diar tr. to hate, loathe.

o·dio m. hatred, loathing.

o·dio·sa·men·te adv. odiously, hatefully.

o·dio·si·dad f. *(calidad de odioso)* odiousness, hatefulness; *(odio)* hatred, loathing.

o·dio·so, –sa adj. odious, hateful.

o·di·se·a f. odyssey, adventure ♦ **Odisea** MYTH. Odyssey.

O·di·se·o Odysseus.

o·don·to·lo·gí·a f. MED. odontology, dentistry.

o·don·to·ló·gi·co, –ca adj. MED. odontological, dental.

o·don·tó·lo·go, –ga m.f. MED. odontologist, dentist.

o·do·rí·fe·ro, –ra adj. odoriferous, fragrant.

o·dre m. *(pellejo)* wineskin; FIG., COLL. *(borracho)* drunk, boozer.

o·es·te I. adj. western, westerly II. m. *(dirección)* west; *(viento)* west wind.

o·fen·de·dor, –do·ra I. adj. offending II. m.f. offender.

o·fen·der tr. *(injuriar)* to offend, insult; *(dañar)* to hurt, injure —intr. to be offensive <*este cuadro ofende a la vista* this painting is offensive to the eye> —reflex. to take offense.

o·fen·di·do, –da I. past part. see **ofender** II. adj. offended.

o·fen·sa f. offense.

o·fen·si·vo, –va I. adj. *(persona)* offensive, rude; MIL. offensive II. f. offensive ♦ **tomar la o.** to take the offensive.

o·fen·sor, –so·ra I. adj. offending II. m.f. offender.

o·fe·ren·te I. adj. offering II. m.f. offerer.

o·fer·ta f. *(propuesta)* offer, proposal; COM. bid, tender; *(regalo)* gift, offering ♦ **o. en firme** firm offer • **o. y demanda** supply and demand.

o·fer·tar tr. COM. to tender; AMER. to offer.

o·fer·to·rio m. RELIG. offertory; ANAT. humeral, humerus.

off·set PRINT. adj. & m.f. offset.

o·fi·cial I. adj. official II. m. *(funcionario)* official, officer; *(obrero)* skilled worker; MIL. officer; *(empleado)* clerk, office worker; *(verdugo)* executioner ♦ **o. de guardia** officer of the watch • **o. de sala** LAW actuary • **o. del día** MIL. officer of the day • **o. mayor** chief clerk • **primer o.** head of a department (in a public office); MARIT. first mate.

o·fi·cia·lí·a f. *(empleo)* clerkship (in a public office); *(artesanía)* craftsman status.

o·fi·cia·li·dad f. MIL. officer corps, officers; *(carácter oficial)* official character.

o·fi·cia·li·zar §04 tr. to make official.

o·fi·cial·men·te adv. officially.

o·fi·cian·te m. RELIG. officiant.

o·fi·ciar tr. RELIG. to celebrate (Mass); *(comunicar)* to communicate officially —intr. RELIG. to officiate ♦ **o. de** to act as.

o·fi·ci·na f. *(despacho)* office; *(de farmacia)* laboratory ♦ **horas de o.** business hours • **o. de colocación** employment agency.

o·fi·ci·nes·co, –ca adj. COLL. clerical, bureaucratic.

o·fi·ci·nis·ta m.f. clerk, office worker.

o·fi·cio m. *(ocupación)* labor, work <*o. servil* manual labor>; *(empleo)* office, post; *(artesanía)* trade, craft; *(función)* function, role; *(comunicación)* communiqué, official notice; RELIG. office, service <*o. de difuntos* funeral service> ♦ **artes y oficios** arts and crafts • **buenos oficios** good offices • **de oficio** *(oficialmente)* ex officio, officially; *(de profesión)* by trade • **gajes del o.** occupational hazards • **Santo Oficio** HIST. Holy Office, Inquisition.

o·fi·cio·sa·men·te adj. *(con diligencia)* diligently; *(con complacencia)* obligingly; *(con entremetimiento)* officiously.

o·fi·cio·si·dad f. *(laboriosidad)* diligence, industriousness; *(solicitud)* solicitousness, obligingness; *(importunidad)* officiousness.

o·fi·cio·so, –sa adj. *(laborioso)* hard-working, diligent; *(solícito)* solicitous, obliging; *(importuno)* officious, meddlesome; *(semioficial)* semiofficial ♦ **de fuentes oficiosas** from unofficial sources.

o·fi·dios m.pl. ZOOL. Ophidians.

o·fre·ce·dor, –do·ra I. adj. offering II. m.f. offerer.

o·fre·cer §17 tr. *(presentar)* to offer <*nos ofreció su ayuda* he offered us his help>; *(mostrar)* to offer, present <*esta ventana ofrece un panorama impresionante* this window offers a breathtaking view>; COM. *(dinero)* to offer, bid; RELIG. to offer up, dedicate —reflex. *(entregarse)* to offer oneself, volunteer <*ella se ofreció de secretaria* she offered

herself as a secretary>; *(ocurrir)* to occur, present itself (to someone) <*se me ofrece una idea* an idea occurs to me>.

o·fre·ci·mien·to m. offer, offering.

o·fren·da f. offering, gift.

o·fren·dar tr. to make an offering.

of·tal·mí·a f. MED. ophthalmia.

of·tal·mo·lo·gí·a f. MED. ophthalmology.

of·tal·mó·lo·go m. MED. ophthalmologist.

o·fus·ca·ción f. *or* **o·fus·ca·mien·to** m. *(acción de ofuscar)* blinding, dazzling; FIG. *(confusión)* confusion, bewilderment.

o·fus·car §70 tr. *(cegar)* to blind, dazzle; FIG. *(confundir)* to confuse, bewilder.

o·gro m. ogre.

¡oh! inter. oh!

oh·mio *or* **ohm** m. PHYS. ohm.

o·í·ble adj. audible.

o·í·da f. hearing ♦ **de** *or* **por oídas** by hearsay.

o·í·do I. past part. see **oír** II. m. *(sentido)* hearing, sense of hearing; ANAT. ear <*o. interno* inner ear>; ARM. priming hole, vent; MUS. ear <*ella tiene buen o.* she has a good ear> ♦ **abrir los oídos** FIG. to listen attentively • **aguzar el o.** to prick up one's ears • **al o.** into one's ear <*me lo dijo al o.* he said it into my ear>; *(confidencialmente)* confidentially • **caer en oídos sordos** to fall on deaf ears • **cerrarle a alguien los oídos** FIG. to pull the wool over someone's eyes • **cerrar los oídos a** FIG. to turn a deaf ear to • **dar oídos a** *(escuchar)* to listen to; *(dar crédito a)* to believe, credit • **de o.** MUS. by ear • **duro de o.** hard of hearing • **prestar oídos a** to lend an ear to • **regalarle a alguien el o.** to flatter • **ser todo oídos** FIG. to be all ears.

oi·dor, –do·ra I. adj. hearing II. m.f. *(persona que oye)* hearer —m. HIST. judge.

o·ír §45 tr. *(escuchar)* to hear <*oigo el silbido de un tren* I hear a train whistle>; *(atender)* to listen to, pay attention to; *(entender)* to understand; *(asistir)* to attend <*o. misa* to attend Mass>; LAW to hear ♦ **ahora lo oigo** COLL. that's the first I've heard of it • **como quien oye llover** FIG., COLL. like a brick wall, with a deaf ear • **o. bien** to listen well • **o. hablar de** to hear about • **o., ver y callar** mind one's own business • **¡oye!** *or* **¡oiga!** *(para llamar la atención)* listen!; *(para reprender)* look here!; *(para denotar extrañeza)* the idea!

o·jal m. *(en la ropa)* buttonhole; *(agujero)* hole.

¡o·ja·lá! interj. would to God!, if only <*¡o. vuelva!* if only he would come back!>.

o·je·a·da f. glance, glimpse.

o·je·ar tr. *(mirar)* to eye, look at; *(aojar)* to cast the evil eye on.

o·je·ra f. dark circle *or* ring (under the eyes).

o·je·ri·za f. animosity, grudge.

o·je·ro·so, –sa *or* **o·je·ru·do, –da** adj. having dark circles under the eyes, haggard.

o·je·te m. SEW. eyelet, drawstring hole; COLL., VULG. ass.

o·jia·le·gre adj. COLL. bright-eyed.

o·ji·mo·re·no, –na adj. COLL. brown-eyed.

o·ji·ne·gro, –gra adj. COLL. black-eyed, dark-eyed.

o·ji·tuer·to, –ta adj. cross-eyed.

o·ji·va f. ARCHIT. ogive.

o·ji·zai·no, –na adj. COLL. cross-eyed.

o·ji·zar·co, –ca adj. COLL. blue-eyed.

o·jo m. ANAT. eye; *(agujero)* hole <*o. de la llave* keyhole>; eye <*el o. de una aguja* the eye of a needle>; *(de un puente)* span, arch (of a bridge); *(enjabonada)* soaping, lathering; *(malla)* mesh (of a net); FIG. *(atención)* attention <*pon o. en lo que haces* pay attention to what you are doing>; *(aptitud)* eye <*el tiene buen o.* he has a good eye> ♦ **abrir los ojos** to be on the alert, keep one's eyes open • **abrirle a alguien los ojos** FIG. to open someone's eyes • **a o.** *or* **a o. de buen cubero** roughly, by a rough estimate • **a ojos cerrados** FIG. blindly, with one's eyes closed • **a ojos vistas** visibly, openly • **cerrar los ojos** FIG., COLL. *(dormir)* to sleep; *(morir)* to die; *(arrojarse)* to go ahead blindly • **clavar los ojos en** to stare at • **comerse (algo** *or* **alguien) con los ojos** FIG., COLL. to devour with one's eyes • **con mucho o.** very carefully • **costar un o. de la cara** FIG., COLL. to cost an arm and a leg • **cuatro ojos** DEROG. four-eyes • **dar en los ojos** to be self-evident • **dichosos**

los ojos que te ven COLL. you're a sight for sore eyes • **echar el o. a** to have one's eyes on • **echar un o.** to take *or* have a look • **en un abrir y cerrar de ojos** FIG., COLL. in the twinkling of an eye • **hasta los ojos** FIG., COLL. up to one's eyeballs • **írsele los ojos por** *or* **tras** not to be able to keep one's eyes off of • **mirar con buenos (malos) ojos** to look favorably (unfavorably) on • **¡mis ojos!** *or* **¡ojos míos!** the apple of my eye! • **¡mucho o.!** be careful! • **no pegar o.** not to sleep a wink • **no quitar los ojos de** not to take one's eyes off of • **¡ojo!** look out!, watch out! • **o. avizor** eagle eye • **o. de agua** spring • **o. de buey** BOT. oxeye; *(ventana)* bull's eye (window); MARIT. porthole • **o. de gato** MIN. cat's-eye • **o. de la escalera** ARCHIT. stairwell • **o. de la tempestad** eye of the storm • **o. de vidrio** glass eye • **o. eléctrico** electric eye • **o. morado** black eye • **por o.** an eye for an eye • **ojos rasgados** slanted eyes • **ojos reventones** *or* **saltones** popeyes, bulging eyes • **ojos vivos** sparkling eyes • **pelar el o.** (AMER.) to keep one's eyes peeled, be alert • **saltársele a uno los ojos** FIG. to have one's eyes popping out of one's head • **tener entre ojos** to have a grudge against • **traer entre ojos** to keep one's eye on.

o·jón, –jo·na adj. AMER. big-eyed.

o·jo·so, –sa adj. full of holes (cheese *or* bread).

o·jo·ta f. AMER. sandal.

o·jue·lo m. ♦ **ojuelos** *(ojos)* sparkling *or* laughing eyes; *(anteojos)* glasses, spectacles.

o·la f. *(onda)* wave; FIG. *(aflujo)* wave, upsurge *<una o. de protestas* a wave of protests> ♦ **o. de calor** heat wave • **o. de frío** cold spell.

¡o·le! *or* **¡o·lé!** interj. bravo!, well done!.

o·le·a·da f. *(ola)* big wave; *(embate de ola)* beating of waves; FIG. *(movimiento)* wave, surge *<una o. de gente* a surge of people>; *(cantidad)* wave, large number *<una o. de protestas* a wave of protests>; MEX. run of good luck.

o·le·a·gi·no·so, –sa adj. oily, oleaginous.

o·le·a·je m. *(olas)* surf, waves; *(marejada)* swell.

o·le·an·dro m. BOT. oleander.

o·lei·co, –ca adj. CHEM. oleic.

o·lei·cul·tu·ra f. *(cultivo)* olive growing; *(industria)* olive oil industry.

o·le·i·na f. CHEM. olein.

ó·le·o m. *(aceite)* oil; RELIG. chrism (consecrated oil) ♦ **al ó.** oil *<pintura al ó.* oil painting> • **Los Santos Óleos** the Last Sacraments.

o·le·o·duc·to m. oil pipeline.

o·le·o·mar·ga·ri·na f. oleomargarine.

o·le·o·si·dad f. oiliness.

o·le·o·so, –sa adj. oily.

o·ler §46 tr. *(olfatear)* to smell *<o. las flores* to smell the flowers>; FIG. *(averiguar)* to smell out, uncover; *(inquirir)* to nose *or* pry into —intr. *(tener olor)* to smell; FIG. *(parecer)* to smell of *or* like *<ese hombre huele a soplón* that man smells like an informer> ♦ **no o. bien** FIG. to smell fishy.

o·le·te·ar tr. PERU to pry into.

ol·fa·te·ar tr. *(oler)* to smell, sniff; COLL. *(descubrir)* to get wind of, smell out; *(curiosear)* to pry into; *(caza)* to scent out (game).

ol·fa·te·o m. *(acción de olfatear)* smelling, sniffing; COLL. *(curiosear)* snooping.

ol·fa·ti·vo, –va adj. olfactory.

ol·fa·to m. *(sentido)* sense of smell; FIG. *(intuición)* intuition; *(instinto)* instinct ♦ **el sentido del o.** the sense of smell • **tener o. para los negocios** FIG. to have a good nose for business.

ol·fa·to·rio, –ria adj. olfactory *<nervio olfatorio* olfactory nerve>.

o·lien·te adj. smelling, odorous ♦ **mal o.** bad-smelling, malodorous.

o·li·gar·ca m. oligarch.

o·li·gar·quí·a f. POL. oligarchy.

o·li·gár·qui·co, –ca adj. oligarchic, oligarchical.

o·li·go·po·lio m. ECON. oligopoly.

o·lim·pia·da *or* **o·lim·pí·a·da** f. *(juegos)* Olympic games; *(período)* Olympiad.

o·lím·pi·co, –ca adj. Olympian, Olympic; FIG. *(altivo)* haughty, lofty ♦ **juegos olímpicos** Olympic games.

O·lim·po m. Olympus.

o·lis·car §70 tr. COLL. *(olfatear)* to sniff, smell; FIG. *(curiosear)* to pry into —intr. *(apestar)* to stink, smell bad.

o·lis·que·ar tr. & intr. COLL. var. of oliscar.

o·lis·que·o m. sniffing, smelling.

o·li·va I. adj. olive (color) II. f. *(fruta)* olive (fruit).

o·li·vá·ce·o, –a adj. olivaceous.

o·li·var m. olive grove.

o·li·va·re·ro, –ra adj. olive-growing *<región o.* olive-growing region>; olive *<industria o.* olive industry>.

o·li·vi·cul·tu·ra f. var. of oleicultura.

o·li·vo m. BOT. olive tree, olive; *(color)* olive (color) ♦ **o. y aceituno todo es uno** it's all one and the same.

ol·me·do m. *or* **ol·me·da** f. elm grove.

ol·mo m. BOT. elm, elm tree ♦ **pedir peras al o.** to ask for the impossible.

o·ló·gra·fo, –fa I. adj. holographic. II. m. holograph.

o·lor m. *(sensación)* smell; *(perfume)* smell, odor; *(sospecha)* smell, suspicion; CHILE, MEX. spice ♦ **estar al o.** COLL. to be on the lookout • **tener o. a** to smell of.

o·lo·ri·zar §04 tr. to perfume, scent.

o·lo·ro·so, –sa adj. perfumed, fragrant.

ol·vi·da·di·zo, –za adj. *(desmemoriado)* forgetful, absent-minded; FIG. *(ingrato)* ungrateful ♦ **hacerse el o.** to pretend to forget.

ol·vi·da·do, –da I. past part. see olvidar II. adj. *(desconocido)* forgotten; *(olvidadizo)* forgetful, absent-minded; *(ingrato)* ingrateful.

ol·vi·dar tr. & reflex. *(perder el recuerdo)* to forget; *(dejar)* to leave (behind) *<me olvidé los libros* I forgot the books>; *(omitir)* to leave out *or* off, omit *<olvidaron su nombre del registro* they left his name off the register>; *(descuidar)* to forget, neglect ♦ **olvidarse de** to forget to.

ol·vi·do m. *(desmemoria)* forgetfulness; *(estado)* oblivion *<los planes cayeron en el o.* the plans fell into oblivion>; ♦ **dar al** *or* **en o.** to forget • **echar al** *or* **en o.** to forget • **enterrar en el o.** to cast into oblivion • **poner en el o.** to forget • **sacar del o.** to rescue from oblivion.

o·lla f. *(vasija)* pot, kettle; *(cocido)* stew; *(remolino)* eddy, whirlpool; FIG. *(mezcla)* hodgepodge ♦ **o. de grillos** COLL. madhouse, bedlam • **o. de presión** pressure cooker • **o. podrida** CUL. Spanish stew.

o·llar m. nostril (of a horse).

o·lle·ro, –ra m.f. *(alfarero)* potter; *(negociante)* pottery dealer.

O·mán Oman.

o·ma·ní adj. & m.f. [pl. **–ní·es**] Omani.

om·bli·go m. ANAT. navel; FIG. *(punto central)* center, middle ♦ **encogérsele a uno el o.** FIG., COLL. to get cold feet.

om·bli·gue·ro m. bellyband (for infants).

o·me·ga f. omega (Greek letter).

ó·mi·cron f. omicron (Greek letter).

o·mi·no·so, –sa adj. *(abominable)* abominable, hateful; *(de mal agüero)* ominous, foreboding.

o·mi·sión f. omission, neglect.

o·mi·so, –sa adj. neglectful, careless.

o·mi·tir tr. to omit, leave out.

óm·ni·bus m. omnibus, bus ♦ **tren o.** local train.

om·ni·po·ten·cia f. omnipotence.

om·ni·po·ten·te adj. omnipotent, all-powerful.

om·ni·pre·sen·cia f. omnipresence.

om·ni·pre·sen·te adj. omnipresent.

om·ni·sa·pien·te adj. omniscient, all-knowing.

om·nis·cien·cia f. omniscience.

om·nis·cien·te *or* **om·nis·cio, –cia** adj. omniscient.

om·ní·vo·ro, –ra ZOOL. I. adj. omnivorous II. m. omnivore.

o·mó·pla·to *or* **o·mo·pla·to** m. ANAT. shoulder blade, scapula.

o·na·nis·mo m. onanism.

on·ce I. adj. eleven *<o. días* eleven days>; *(undécimo)* eleventh ♦ **las o.** eleven o'clock II. m. eleven ♦ **hacer** *or* **tomar las o.** AMER. to have a snack.

on·ce·a·vo, –va *or* **on·ce·no, –na** adj. eleventh.

on·co·lo·gí·a f. MED. oncology.

on·da f. *(ola)* wave (of water); *(ondulación)* wave, undulation; *(de la llama)* flicker (of a flame); *(guarnición)* scallop; *(del pelo)* wave, curl (of hair); PHYS. wave ♦ **estar en**

la o. COLL. to be with it • **o. corta** RAD. short wave • **o. de choque** PHYS. shock wave • **o. luminosa** PHYS. light wave • **o. sonora** PHYS. sound wave.

on·de·a·do, –da I. past part. see **ondear** II. adj. wavy, undulating.

on·de·an·te adj. waving, undulating.

on·de·ar intr. *(agua)* to ripple; *(undular)* to wave, flutter; FIG. *(formar ondas)* to undulate —reflex. to swing, sway.

on·de·o m. rippling, waving.

on·di·na f. MYTH. undine, water nymph.

on·do·so, –sa adj. wavy, undulating.

on·du·la·ción f. *(movimiento)* undulation; *(sinuosidad)* winding; *(del cabello)* wave ♦ **o. permanente** permanent wave.

on·du·la·do, –da I. past part. see **ondular** II. adj. wavy, undulating.

on·du·lan·te adj. undulating.

on·du·lar tr. to wave (hair) —intr. to undulate.

o·ne·ro·so, –sa adj. *(molesto)* onerous, troublesome; LAW onerous.

ó·ni·ce m. *or* f. MIN. onyx.

o·ní·ri·co, –ca adj. oneiric (of dreams).

o·ni·ro·man·cia *or* **o·ni·ro·man·cí·a** f. oneiromancy (divination by dreams).

ó·nix f. MIN. onyx.

o·no·más·ti·co, –ca I. adj. onomastic (of names) ♦ **fiesta** *or* **día o.** saint's day II. f. onomastics.

o·no·ma·to·pe·ya f. onomatopoeia.

o·no·ma·to·pé·yi·co, –ca adj. onomatopoeic.

on·to·ge·nia f. BIOL. ontogeny.

on·to·lo·gí·a f. PHILOS. ontology.

on·to·ló·gi·co, –ca adj. PHILOS. ontological.

ONU f. UN, acronym for Organización de las Naciones Unidas.

on·za¹ f. ounce ♦ **o. de oro** Spanish doubloon.

on·za² f. ZOOL. ounce, snow leopard.

on·za·vo adj. & m. eleventh.

o·pa AMER. I. adj. stupid, foolish II. m.f. fool, dolt.

o·pa·ci·dad f. opacity, opaqueness.

o·pa·co, –ca adj. *(no transparente)* opaque; FIG. *(triste)* gloomy.

o·pa·les·cen·cia f. opalescence.

o·pa·les·cen·te adj. opalescent.

o·pa·li·no, –na adj. opaline, opalescent.

ó·pa·lo m. MIN. opal.

op·ción f. *(elección)* option, choice; *(derecho)* option, right.

op·cio·nal adj. optional.

ó·pe·ra f. opera ♦ **o. bufa** comic opera.

o·pe·ra·ble adj. operable.

o·pe·ra·ción f. *(actuación)* operation; COM., FIN. operation, transaction <*o. financiaria* financial transaction>; MATH., MED., MIL. operation ♦ **o. cesárea** MED. Caesarean section • **o. de corazón expuesto** MED. open-heart surgery.

o·pe·ra·cio·nal adj. MIL. operational.

o·pe·ra·do, –da I. past part. see **operar** II. adj. SURG. postoperative III. m.f. SURG. postoperative patient.

o·pe·ra·dor, –do·ra I. adj. operating II. m.f. MECH. operator —m. MED., SURG. surgeon; CINEM. cameraman.

o·pe·ran·te adj. operating, working <*capital o.* working capital>.

o·pe·rar intr. *(obrar)* to operate, work; COM. to deal, do business —tr. SURG. to operate on.

o·pe·ra·rio, –ria m.f. operator, worker.

o·pe·ra·ti·vo, –va adj. operative.

o·pe·ra·to·rio, –ria adj. MED. operative.

o·pér·cu·lo m. ZOOL. operculum.

o·pe·rís·ti·co, –ca adj. operatic.

o·piá·ce·o, –a adj. opiate, containing opium.

o·pia·do, –da adj. opiate, opiated.

o·pia·ta f. opiate.

o·pi·la·ción f. MED. *(obstrucción)* oppilation, obstruction; *(amenorrea)* amenorrhea; *(hidropesía)* dropsy.

o·pi·mo, –ma adj. rich, abundant.

o·pi·na·ble adj. debatable, arguable.

o·pi·nar intr. *(formar opinión)* to think, have an opinion; *(expresar la opinión)* to express an opinion ♦ **o. en** *or* **sobre** to give an opinion on.

o·pi·nión f. opinion ♦ **casarse con su o.** FIG., COLL. to stick to one's opinion.

o·pio m. opium.

o·pió·ma·no m. opium addict.

o·pio·ma·ní·a f. opium addiction.

o·pí·pa·ro, –ra adj. sumptuous, magnificent.

o·po·ner §54 tr. *(contraponer)* to set up *or* put against <*o. el dique a las aguas* to set up the dike against the waters>; *(poner enfrente)* to oppose, put opposite; *(estorbar)* to hinder —reflex. *(opugnar)* to oppose, object to <*el municipio se opuso a nuestros planes* the town council opposed our plans>; *(ser contrario)* to be in opposition to, be contrary <*sus ideas nunca se oponen a las mías* his ideas are never contrary to mine>; *(confrontarse)* to oppose *or* go against each other <*esos candidatos siempre se oponen en un debate* those candidates always oppose each other in a debate>; *(estar enfrente)* to face.

o·po·ni·ble adj. opposable.

o·por·to m. port (wine).

o·por·tu·na·men·te adv. opportunely, conveniently.

o·por·tu·ni·dad f. *(ocasión)* opportunity, chance; *(de una medida)* appropriateness, suitability.

o·por·tu·nis·mo m. opportunism.

o·por·tu·nis·ta adj. & m.f. opportunist.

o·por·tu·no, –na I. adj. *(conveniente)* opportune, timely; *(apropiado)* suitable, fitting; *(ocurrente)* witty II. m.f. witty person.

o·po·si·ción f. *(resistencia)* opposition; *(competición)* competitive examination; ASTRON., POL. opposition.

o·po·si·tar intr. *(oponerse)* to be opposed; *(presentarse a un examen)* to take an examination for a public post.

o·po·si·tor, –to·ra m.f. *(adversario)* opponent; *(candidato)* candidate.

o·pre·sión f. *(de un pueblo)* oppression; *(angustia)* anguish, distress ♦ **o. del pecho** tightness in the chest.

o·pre·si·vo, –va adj. oppressive.

o·pre·so, –sa I. past part. see **oprimir** II. adj. oppressed.

o·pre·sor, –so·ra I. adj. oppressive, tyrannical II. m.f. oppressor, tyrant.

o·pri·men·te adj. oppressing, oppressive.

o·pri·mi·do, –da I. past part. see **oprimir** II. adj. oppressed ♦ **tener el corazon o.** to be sick at heart.

o·pri·mir tr. *(tiranizar)* to oppress, tyrannize; *(apretar)* to press, squeeze.

o·pro·biar tr. to vilify, defame.

o·pro·bio m. shame, disgrace.

o·pro·bio·so, –sa adj. shameful, disgraceful.

op·ta·ción f. assumption (of office).

op·tan·te adj. choosing, selecting.

op·tar tr. *(escoger)* to choose, select; *(presentarse)* to apply (for a job).

op·ta·ti·vo, –va I. adj. *(facultativo)* optional; GRAM. optative II. m. GRAM. optative.

óp·ti·co, –ca I. adj. PHYS. optical II. m. optician —f. PHYS. optics; *(aparato)* stereoscope.

óp·ti·ma·men·te adv. optimally, in the best way.

op·ti·mar tr. to optimize.

op·ti·mis·mo m. optimism.

op·ti·mis·ta I. adj. optimistic II. m.f. optimist.

óp·ti·mo, –ma adj. optimal, best.

op·tó·me·tra m.f. optometrist.

op·to·me·trí·a f. optometry.

o·pues·to, –ta I. past part. see **oponer** II. adj. *(enfrente)* opposite; *(contrario)* opposing, contrary.

o·pug·nar tr. *(atacar)* to attack, assault; FIG. *(contradecir)* to contradict, refute.

o·pu·len·cia f. opulence, abundance.

o·pu·len·to, –ta adj. opulent, abundant.

o·pús·cu·lo m. pamphlet, tract.

o·pu·sie·ra, opuso see **oponer**.

o·que·dal m. forest of tall trees without underbrush.

o·ra conj. *(ahora)* now <*o. de este lado, o. del otro lado* now this way, now the other way>; *(o bien)* either <*o. de día, o. de noche* either by day or by night>.

o·ra·ción f. *(discurso)* speech, oration; RELIG. *(rezo)* prayer; *(hora)* dusk; GRAM. *(frase)* sentence; *(clausula)* clause ♦ **o. adjetiva** *or* **de relativo** GRAM. adjectival clause • **o. adverbial** GRAM. adverbial clause • **o. compuesta** *or*

coordinada GRAM. compound *or* complex sentence • **o. dominical** RELIG. Lord's Prayer, Our Father • **o. simple** GRAM. simple sentence • **o. subordinada** GRAM. subordinate clause • **o. sustantiva** GRAM. noun clause • **oraciones** RELIG. *(toque)* Angelus; *(doctrina)* first part of catechism (taught to children).

o·ra·cio·nal I. adj. GRAM. of a sentence **II.** m. prayer book.

o·rá·cu·lo m. oracle.

o·ra·dor, –do·ra m.f. orator, speaker.

o·ral adj. oral.

o·ral·men·te adv. orally.

o·ran·gu·tán m. ZOOL. orangutan.

o·rar intr. *(hablar)* to speak, make a speech; *(hacer oración)* to pray.

o·ra·te m.f. lunatic, mad person <*casa de orates* lunatic asylum>.

o·ra·to·rio, –ria I. adj. oratory, oratorical **II.** m. *(capilla)* oratory, chapel; MUS. oratorio ♦ **Oratorio** RELIG. Oratory —f. oratory, rhetoric.

or·be m. *(esfera)* orb, sphere; FIG. *(mundo)* world; ICHTH. globefish.

or·bi·cu·lar I. adj. round, circular **II.** m. ANAT. orbicularis, sphincter.

ór·bi·ta f. ASTRON., ANAT. orbit; FIG. *(esfera)* sphere, field.

or·bi·tal adj. orbital.

or·ca f. ZOOL. killer whale, orca.

or·cé, orce see **orzar.**

or·da·lí·as f.pl. HIST. ordeals, trial by ordeal.

or·den m. *(disposición)* order <*o. cronológico* chronological order>; *(sistema)* method, system; *(paz)* order, peace <*el o. público* public order>; *(categoría)* nature, character <*asuntos de o. filosófico* matters of a philosophical nature>; BIOL. order; ARCHIT. order <*o. dórico* Doric order> ♦ **del o. de** on the order of • **de primer o.** of the first order, first-rate • **en o.** in order • **a** with regard to • **llamar al o.** to call to order • **o. de antigüedad** seniority • **o. del día** agenda • **poner en o.** to put in order • **por o.** in its turn —f. *(mandato)* order, command; *(institución)* order <*una o. de caballería* a knightly order>; RELIG. order <*ordenes mayores* major orders>; LAW warrant; COM. order; MIL. order ♦ **a la o. de** at the order of • **a sus órdenes** at your service • **o. de arresto** *or* **de detención** LAW arrest warrant • **o. del día** MIL. order of the day • **o. de registro** LAW search warrant • **o. judicial** LAW court order.

or·de·na·ción f. *(disposición)* order, arrangement; *(acción de disponer)* ordering, arranging; RELIG. ordination ♦ **o. de pagos** controller's office • **o. rural** rural development.

or·de·na·da f. MATH. ordinate.

or·de·na·do, –da I. past part. see **ordenar II.** adj. orderly, methodical.

or·de·na·dor, –do·ra I. adj. ordering, arranging **II.** m.f. *(persona que ordena)* arranger; *(persona que paga)* controller —m. ELECTRON. computer.

or·de·na·mien·to m. *(acción de ordenar)* ordering, arranging; *(ordenanza)* ordinance, law.

or·de·nan·za f. *(reglamento)* regulation, ordinance; *(mandato)* order, command; *(método)* method, order; *(arreglo)* arrangement —m. MIL. orderly; *(empleado)* employee, office worker.

or·de·nar tr. *(poner en orden)* to order, put in order; *(arreglar)* to arrange; *(mandar)* to order, command; *(dirigir)* to direct; RELIG. to ordain; MATH. to arrange (a polynomial) —reflex. RELIG. to be ordained.

or·de·ña·dor, –do·ra I. adj. milking **II.** m.f. *(persona)* milker —f. *(aparato)* milking machine.

or·de·ñar tr. to milk.

or·de·ño m. milking.

or·di·nal adj. ordinal ♦ **número o.** ordinal number.

or·di·na·ria·men·te adv. ordinarily.

or·di·na·riez f. COLL. vulgarity, commonness ♦ **ser de una o.** to be common.

or·di·na·rio, –ria I. adj. *(común)* ordinary, common; *(inculto)* coarse, uncouth <*un chiste o.* a coarse joke>; *(mediocre)* ordinary, mediocre; *(diario)* daily **II.** m. RELIG. Ordinary (bishop); *(correo)* mail, post; *(gastos)* daily household expenses; LAW *(juez)* ordinary (judge) ♦ **de o.**

ordinarily, usually • **o. de la misa** RELIG. Ordinary (of the Mass).

or·di·na·rio·te adj. COLL. very common.

or·di·na·ti·vo, –va adj. ordering, arranging.

o·re·ar tr. to air, ventilate —reflex. to get some air, take a walk.

o·ré·ga·no m. BOT. oregano, wild marjoram.

o·re·ja f. ANAT. ear; *(parte lateral)* flap; *(asa)* handle; *(del sillón)* wing (of an armchair); MECH. lug, flange; FIG. *(chismoso)* gossip, talebearer ♦ **aguzar las orejas** FIG. to prick up one's ears • **apearse por las orejas** *(caerse)* to fall from a horse; FIG. to talk nonsense • **bajar las orejas** FIG. to yield, bow to (in an argument) • **calentar a alguien las orejas** FIG. to pin someone's ears back • **con las orejas caídas** *or* **gachas** crestfallen • **descubrir la o.** FIG. to show one's true colors • **hacer orejas de mercader** FIG. to turn a deaf ear • **mojar a alguien la o.** FIG. to pick a fight with someone.

o·re·ja·no, –na I. adj. unbranded (said of cattle) **II.** m.f. unbranded cattle.

o·re·je·ar intr. *(mover las orejas)* to wiggle the ears (said of animals); FIG. *(obrar con mala gana)* to drag one's feet.

o·re·je·ra f. *(de gorra)* earflap; *(de casco militar)* earpiece; *(de arado)* moldboard (of plow); *(disco)* earring (worn by Peruvian Indians).

o·re·jón, –jo·na I. adj. AMER. *(orejudo)* big-eared; FIG. *(rudo)* coarse, uncouth; HOND. foolish, simple-minded **II.** m. *(tirón de orejas)* tug at the ear; *(fruta)* dried peach *or* apricot half; *(cornudo)* cuckold; HIST. Inca nobleman (name given by Spaniards).

o·re·ju·do, –da adj. big-eared.

o·re·jue·la f. handle.

o·re·o m. *(aire)* breeze, breath of air; *(ventilación)* ventilation, airing.

or·fa·na·to m. orphanage.

or·fan·dad f. *(estado de huérfano)* orphanhood; FIG. *(privación)* abandonment.

or·fe·bre m. *(artífice)* goldsmith *or* silversmith; *(vendedor)* jeweler.

or·fe·bre·rí·a f. *(arte)* gold *or* silver work; *(taller)* gold *or* silver workshop.

or·fe·li·na·to m. orphanage.

ór·fi·co, –ca I. adj. Orphic **II.** f. ♦ **órficas** Orphic festivities.

or·gan·dí m. TEX. organdy.

or·ga·ni·cé, organice see **organizar.**

or·gá·ni·co, –ca adj. organic.

or·ga·ni·gra·ma m. organizational chart.

or·ga·ni·lle·ro, –ra m.f. organ grinder.

or·ga·ni·llo m. barrel organ, hurdy-gurdy.

or·ga·nis·mo m. BIOL. organism; *(organización)* organization, institution.

or·ga·nis·ta m.f. MUS. organist.

or·ga·ni·za·ción f. organization.

or·ga·ni·za·do, –da I. past part. see **organizar II.** adj. organized.

or·ga·ni·za·dor, –do·ra I. adj. organizing **II.** m.f. organizer.

or·ga·ni·zar §04 tr. to organize —reflex. to be organized.

ór·ga·no m. MUS., ANAT. organ; MECH. part, member <*o. de transmisión* driving part>; FIG. *(medio)* medium, agency; *(periódico)* organ, journal ♦ **o. de lengüetas** reed organ • **o. de manubrio** barrel organ.

or·gas·mo m. orgasm.

or·gí·a *or* **or·gia** f. orgy.

or·gia·co, –ca *or* **or·giás·ti·co, –ca** adj. orgiastic.

or·gu·llo m. *(arrogancia)* arrogance, conceit; FIG. *(sentimiento legítimo)* pride • **no caber en sí de o.** *or* **reventar de o.** FIG. to be bursting with pride.

or·gu·llo·sa·men·te adv. proudly.

or·gu·llo·so, –sa I. adj. *(que tiene orgullo)* proud; *(engreído)* conceited, arrogant **II.** m.f. proud person.

o·rien·ta·ción f. *(colocación)* positioning; *(de un edificio)* orientation (of a building); *(consejo)* guidance, direction; MARIT. trimming (of sails); *(inclinación)* orientation <*es un grupo con una o. marxista* it is a group with a Marxist orientation>.

o·rien·ta·dor, –do·ra I. adj. guiding, directing **II.** m.f. guide.

o·rien·tal I. adj. oriental, eastern **II.** m.f. Oriental.

o·rien·ta·lis·mo m. Orientalism.

o·rien·ta·lis·ta m.f. Orientalist.

o·rien·tar tr. *(colocar)* to position <*o. un cañón* to position a cannon>; *(un edificio)* to orient, orientate (a building); *(dirigir)* to direct, guide <*orientó el niño hacia una vocación apropiada* he guided the child towards a suitable vocation>; MARIT. to trim (sails); *(determinar posición)* to orient, orientate —reflex. *(instruirse)* to orient oneself, get one's bearing; *(informar)* to orient, inform (someone); *(encaminar)* to make *or* head (for) <*ellos se orientan hacia la capital* they are heading for the capital>.

o·rien·te m. *(este)* east; *(viento)* east wind; JEWEL. orient (of a pearl) ♦ **Extremo O.** Far East • **Oriente** the Orient • **O. Medio** Middle East.

o·ri·fi·ca·ción f. DENT. *(acción de orificar)* filling (a tooth) with gold; *(oro)* gold filling.

o·ri·fi·car §70 tr. DENT. to fill (a tooth) with gold.

o·ri·fi·ce m. goldsmith.

o·ri·fi·cio m. orifice, opening.

o·ri·gen m. *(principio)* origin, source <*su intervención era el o. de mis problemas.* his intervention was the source of my problems>; *(linaje)* origin, birth <*de o. noble* of noble birth>; *(procedencia)* origin <*de o. mexicano* of Mexican origin>; *(cause)* origin, cause; *(etimología)* derivation (of a word) ♦ **dar o. a** to give rise to • **en su o.** originally.

o·ri·gi·nal I. adj. *(primero)* original, first <*pecado o.* original sin>; *(nuevo)* original, new, novel <*un concepto o.* a novel concept>; *(inventivo)* original, inventive; *(raro)* odd, singular <*su hermano es un tipo o.* his brother is an odd character>; *(auténtico)* original, authentic <*es un boceto o. de Whistler* it is an original sketch by Whistler> **II.** m. *(modelo)* original <*debes sacar copias del o.* you should get copies of the original>; *(manuscrito)* manuscript; *(texto original)* original <*para apreciarlo hay que leerlo en el o.* to appreciate it one must read it in the original>; *(tipo)* character, eccentric.

o·ri·gi·na·li·dad f. *(novedad)* originality, novelty; *(carácter excéntrico)* eccentricity, strangeness.

o·ri·gi·nal·men·te adv. originally.

o·ri·gi·nar tr. to originate, give rise to —reflex. to originate, derive (from).

o·ri·gi·na·ria·men·te adv. originally.

o·ri·gi·na·rio, –ria adj. *(que da origen)* originating, giving rise to; *(que tiene su origen)* coming *or* arising (from).

o·ri·lla f. *(borde)* border, edge; *(del mar)* shore; *(de un río)* bank (of a river) ♦ **a la o.** *or* **a orillas de** by, beside <*a orillas del mar* by the seashore> • **orillas** ARG. outskirts • **salir a la o.** FIG. to come through difficulties.

o·ri·llar tr. FIG. *(concluir)* to settle, wind up; TEX. *(dejar orilla)* to border, edge (cloth); *(guarnecer)* to trim, decorate —intr. to reach the banks *or* shores.

o·ri·llo m. TEX. selvage.

o·rín[1] m. rust.

o·rín[2] m. urine.

o·ri·na f. *or* **o·ri·nes** m.pl. urine.

o·ri·nal m. urinal.

o·ri·nar intr. to urinate —reflex. to wet oneself, wet one's pants.

o·riol m. ORNITH. oriole.

o·riun·dez f. origin (place).

o·riun·do, –da adj. native ♦ **ser o. de** to come from, be native to.

or·la f. TEX., PRINT. border; HER. orle.

or·lar tr. to border, edge.

or·lón m. TEX. Orlon (trademark).

or·me·sí m. TEX. shot silk.

or·na·men·ta·ción f. ornamentation.

or·na·men·tal adj. ornamental.

or·na·men·tar tr. to ornament, adorn.

or·na·men·to m. *(adorno)* ornament, adornment; FIG. *(calidades morales)* moral qualities; ARCHIT. ornamentation, molding ♦ **ornamentos** RELIG. priestly vestments.

or·nar tr. to bedeck, embellish.

or·na·to m. ornament, adornment.

or·ni·to·lo·gí·a f. ornithology.

or·ni·tó·lo·go m.f. ornithologist.

o·ro m. gold; FIG. *(moneda)* gold coin; *(riqueza)* wealth, riches ♦ **como un o.** neat as a pin • **comprar a peso de o.** to buy dearly, pay a fortune for • **chapado de o.** gold-plated • **de o.** gold, golden • **guardar como o. en paño** FIG. to treasure, hold dear • **o. batido** gold leaf • **o. en barras** gold bars, bullion • **o. en polvo** gold dust • **o. negro** FIG. black gold, oil • **oros** suit in Spanish deck of cards.

o·ro·gé·ne·sis f. GEOL. orogenesis, orogeny.

o·ro·gra·fí·a f. GEOL. orography.

o·ron·do, –da adj. *(una vasija)* pot-bellied (vessel); COLL. *(hinchado)* puffed up, self-satisfied; FIG., COLL. *(engreído)* conceited, arrogant.

o·ro·pel m. tinsel.

o·ro·pén·do·la f. ORNITH. golden oriole.

o·ro·ya f. AMER. hanging basket (for crossing rivers).

or·ques·ta f. orchestra.

or·ques·ta·ción f. MUS. orchestration.

or·ques·tal adj. orchestral.

or·ques·tar tr. to orchestrate.

or·quí·de·a f. BOT. orchid ♦ **orquídeas** BOT. Orchidaceae.

or·ti·ga f. BOT. nettle.

or·ti·gal f. BOT. bed of nettles.

or·to m. ASTRON. rise, rising (of sun or star).

or·to·don·cia f. DENT. orthodontia.

or·to·don·tis·ta DENT. **I.** adj. orthodontic **II.** m.f. orthodontist.

or·to·do·xia f. orthodoxy.

or·to·do·xo, –xa adj. orthodox.

or·to·go·nal adj. GEOM. orthogonal.

or·to·gra·fí·a f. GRAM. orthography, spelling ♦ **o. degradada** *or* **en perspectiva** GEOM. linear perspective • **o. geométrica** GEOM. orthogonal *or* orthographic projection.

or·to·grá·fi·co, –ca adj. orthographic.

or·to·pe·dia f. MED. orthopedics.

or·to·pé·di·co, –ca MED. **I.** adj. orthopedic **II.** m.f. orthopedist.

or·to·pe·dis·ta m.f. orthopedist.

o·ru·ga f. ENTOM. caterpillar; AUTO. caterpillar tread.

o·ru·jo m. AGR. residue (of pressed grapes or olives).

or·va·llar intr. to drizzle.

or·va·llo m. drizzle.

or·za f. MARIT. *(acción de orzar)* luffing; *(quilla)* centerboard, sliding keel ♦ **a o.** MARIT. into the wind.

or·zar §04 tr. MARIT. to luff (sail into the wind).

or·zue·lo m. MED. sty; HUNT. trap, snare.

os §G30 pron. you <*os vi en el museo* I saw you in the museum>; you, to you <*os dieron la oportunidad de discutirlo* they gave you the opportunity to discuss it>; for you <*os buscaba un asiento* he was looking for a seat for you>; from you <*os compramos un coche* we bought a car from you>; yourselves <*vosotros os laváis* you wash yourselves>; each other <*vosotros os amáis* you love each other>.

o·sa f. ZOOL. female bear ♦ **O. Mayor, Menor** ASTRON. Ursa Major, Minor.

o·sa·da·men·te adv. boldly, daringly.

o·sa·dí·a f. boldness, audacity.

o·sa·do, –da adj. bold, daring.

o·sa·men·ta f. *(conjunto de huesos)* bones; *(esqueleto)* skeleton.

o·sar intr. to dare.

o·sa·rio m. ossuary, charnel house.

os·ci·la·ción f. *(balanceo)* swing, swinging movement; PHYS. oscillation; FIG. *(vacilación)* vacillation, wavering.

os·ci·la·dor m. PHYS. oscillator.

os·ci·lan·te adj. oscillating.

os·ci·lar intr. *(balancearse)* to swing, move back and forth; PHYS. to oscillate; FIG. *(los precios)* to fluctuate, vary; *(una persona)* to vacillate, waver.

os·ci·la·to·rio, –ria adj. oscillatory.

ós·cu·lo m. kiss.

os·cu·ra·men·te adv. obscurely.

os·cu·ran·tis·mo m. obscurantism.

os·cu·re·cer §17 tr. *(volver oscuro)* to obscure, darken; FIG. *(volver poco inteligible)* to obscure, conceal; *(eclipsar)* to overshadow, eclipse; *(debilitar el brillo)* to tarnish, dim;

PAINT. *(dar sombra)* to shade, shadow —intr. to be getting dark —reflex. *(ponerse oscuro)* to darken, grow dark; *(nublarse)* to become cloudy *or* overcast; FIG., COLL. *(desaparecer)* to disappear, vanish.

os·cu·re·ci·mien·to m. *(acción de volver oscuro)* obscuring, darkening; FIG. *(encubrimiento)* obscuring, concealment; METEOROL. clouding (up).

os·cu·ri·dad f. *(sombra)* darkness, obscurity; FIG. *(imprecisión)* obscurity, haziness (of a text, an idea); *(incertidumbre)* uncertainty; *(humildad)* obscurity <*vivir en o.* to live in obscurity>.

os·cu·ro, –ra I. adj. *(sin luz)* dark; *(desconocido)* obscure <*un poeta o.* an obscure poet>; *(negro)* dark <*ella llevaba una falda o.* she wore a dark skirt>; *(sombrío)* gloomy; FIG. *(confuso)* hazy, unclear; *(incierto)* uncertain; *(nebuloso)* cloudy, overcast ♦ **a oscuras** in the dark • **hacer o.** to become dark • **o. como boca de lobo** pitch-black, pitch-dark • **quedarse a oscuras** to be left in the dark II. m. PAINT. shading.

ó·se·o, –a adj. osseous, bony.

o·sez·no m. ZOOL. bear cub.

o·si·fi·ca·ción f. ossification.

o·si·fi·car·se §70 reflex. to ossify.

os·mio m. CHEM. osmium.

ós·mo·sis *or* **os·mo·sis** f. PHYS. osmosis.

os·mó·ti·co, –ca adj. osmotic.

o·so m. ZOOL. bear; FIG. *(persona insociable)* lone wolf ♦ **hacer el o.** COLL. *(hacer reír)* to clown, play the fool; *(cortejar)* to woo openly • **o. blanco** polar bear • **o. de felpa** teddy bear • **o. gris** grizzly bear • **o. lavador** raccoon • **o. marsupial** koala bear.

os·te·í·tis f. MED. osteitis, bone inflammation.

os·ten·si·ble adj. ostensible.

os·ten·si·vo, –va adj. ostensive.

os·ten·so·rio m. RELIG. ostensory, monstrance.

os·ten·ta·ción f. ostentation.

os·ten·ta·dor, –do·ra I. adj. ostentatious II. m.f. ostentatious person, showoff.

os·ten·tar tr. *(mostrar)* to show; *(hacer gala)* to flaunt, make a show of.

os·ten·ta·ti·vo, –va adj. ostentatious, pretentious.

os·ten·to·so, –sa adj. showy, grandiose.

os·te·o·lo·gí·a f. osteology.

os·te·ó·lo·go, –ga m.f. osteologist.

os·te·o·pa·tí·a f. MED. osteopathy.

os·tra f. ZOOL. oyster ♦ **o. perlera** pearl oyster.

os·tra·cis·mo m. ostracism.

os·tral m. oyster bed.

os·tre·ro, –ra I. adj. oyster <*la industria o.* the oyster industry> II. m.f. *(vendedor)* oyster seller —m. *(ostral)* oyster bed; ORNITH. oystercatcher.

os·tri·cul·tu·ra f. oyster farming.

os·tro·go·do, –da HIST. I. adj. Ostrogothic II. m.f. Ostrogoth.

os·tu·go m. *(rincón)* nook, corner; *(pizca)* bit, pinch.

o·su·do, –da adj. bony.

o·su·no, –na adj. bear-like.

OTAN f. NATO, acronym for Organización del Tratado del Atlántico Norte.

o·te·ar tr. *(desde lugar alto)* to scan, survey (from a height); FIG. *(escudriñar)* to watch, observe.

o·te·ro m. hillock, knoll.

o·ti·tis f. MED. otitis, inflammation of the ear.

o·to·ma·no, –na I. adj. ottoman II. m.f. *(persona)* Ottoman —f. ottoman (backless divan).

o·to·ña·da f. *(estación del año)* autumn; *(pastos)* pasturage.

o·to·ñal adj. autumnal.

o·to·ñar intr. *(pasar el otoño)* to spend the autumn; *(la hierba)* to grow in autumn.

o·to·ño m. autumn, fall.

o·tor·ga·dor, –do·ra I. adj. granting II. m.f. grantor.

o·tor·gar §47 tr. *(consentir)* to grant, give; LAW *(derecho)* to execute, draw up (a deed).

o·to·rri·no·la·rin·go·lo·gí·a f. MED. otorhinolaryngology.

o·tro, –tra §G17 I. adj. *(distinto)* other, another <*¿quieres o. taza de café?* do you want another cup of coffee?>; *(igual)* another <*ella es o. María Callas* she is another Maria Callas> ♦ **o. cosa** something else • **o. vez** again • **por o. parte**

on the other hand II. pron. another one <*no tengo o.* I do not have another one> ♦ **¡otra!** THEAT. encore! • **otros** others • **unos a otros** each other, one another.

o·tro·ra adv. formerly, in olden times.

o·tro·sí I. adv. moreover II. m. LAW each petition made after the principal one.

o·va f. BOT. green alga.

o·va·ción f. ovation.

o·va·cio·nar tr. to applaud, give an ovation to.

o·va·do, –da I. past part. see **ovar** II. adj. *(un ave)* impregnated (said of birds); *(ovalado)* oval, egg-shaped.

o·val *or* **o·va·la·do, –da** adj. oval.

o·va·lar tr. to make oval.

ó·va·lo m. oval.

o·var intr. to lay eggs.

o·vá·ri·co adj. ovarian.

o·va·rio m. ANAT., BOT. ovary; ARCHIT. molding with egg-shaped ornaments.

o·vas f.pl. ICHTH. roe.

o·ve·ja f. ZOOL. ewe, female sheep ♦ **o. descarriada** FIG. lost sheep • **o. negra** FIG. black sheep.

o·ve·je·ro, –ra m. shepherd —f. shepherdess ♦ **perro o.** ARG. sheepdog.

o·ve·ju·no, –na adj. of sheep.

o·ver·tu·ra f. MUS. overture.

o·vi·duc·to m. ANAT. oviduct.

o·vi·for·me adj. oviform, egg-shaped.

o·vi·llar tr. to roll *or* wind —reflex. to roll *or* curl up.

o·vi·llo m. *(de hilo)* ball (of thread); FIG. *(cosa enredada)* tangle, snarl ♦ **hacerse un o.** FIG., COLL. *(acurrucarse)* to curl up; *(embrollarse)* to get tangled up (in words).

o·vi·no, –na adj. ovine, of sheep.

o·ví·pa·ro, –ra I. adj. ZOOL. oviparous II. m.f. oviparous animal.

ov·ni m. UFO, unidentified flying object.

o·vo m. ARCHIT. ovum, egg-shaped ornament.

o·vo·gé·ne·sis f. BIOL. ovogenesis.

o·voi·de *or* **o·voi·de·o, –a** adj. ovoid.

o·vu·la·ción f. BIOL. ovulation.

o·vu·lar I. adj. ovular II. intr. to ovulate.

ó·vu·lo m. BOT., ZOOL. ovule.

o·xe·ar tr. to shoo (birds).

o·xia·ce·ti·lé·ni·co, –ca adj. oxyacetylene.

o·xi·da·ble adj. oxidizable.

o·xi·da·ción f. oxidation.

o·xi·dar tr. & reflex. to oxidize, rust.

ó·xi·do m. CHEM. oxide.

o·xi·ge·na·ción f. CHEM. oxygenation.

o·xi·ge·na·do, –da I. past part. see **oxigenar** II. adj. CHEM. oxygenated ♦ **agua o.** hydrogen peroxide.

o·xi·ge·nar tr. CHEM. to oxygenate —reflex. to breathe fresh air.

o·xí·ge·no m. CHEM. oxygen.

o·xo·nien·se adj. & m.f. Oxonian.

o·yen·te I. adj. hearing, listening II. m.f. *(persona que oye)* hearer, listener; EDUC. auditor ♦ **los oyentes** the audience.

o·ye·ra, oyó see **oír.**

o·zo·na f. var. of **ozono.**

o·zo·nar tr. to ozonize.

o·zo·ni·zar §04 tr. to ozonize.

o·zo·no m. ozone.

P

p, P f. nineteenth letter of the Spanish alphabet.

pa·be·llón m. *(tienda de campaña)* bell tent; *(dosel)* bed canopy; *(colgadura)* hangings, drapings (of altar, throne); *(banderal)* flag, banner; *(edificio)* pavilion, block; *(caseta)* gazebo, hut; MUS. bell (of a wind instrument); MARIT. registration, nationality <*un buque de p. venezolano* a ship of Venezuelan registration>; ANAT. external ear, outer ear; JEWEL. *(tallado)* pavilion (of a precious stone); MIL. stack of rifles; FIG. *(protección)* protection ♦ **arriar p.** to lower the flag • **p. de caza** shooting box • **p. de conciertos** *or* **de música** bandstand.

pa·bi·lo m. *(mecha)* candle wick; *(mecha carbonizada)* snuff, burnt end of a candle wick.

pá·bu·lo m. *(alimento)* food, pabulum; FIG. *(sustento)* support, encouragement ♦ **dar p. a** FIG. to add fuel to the fire, encourage.

pa·ca f. bale, bundle.

pa·ca·na f. BOT. *(árbol)* pecan tree; *(fruto)* pecan nut.

pa·ca·ne·ro or **pa·ca·no** m. AMER., BOT. *(árbol)* pecan tree; *(fruto)* pecan nut.

pa·ca·to, -ta I. adj. timid, mild-mannered II. m.f. timid or quiet person.

pa·cay m. AMER., BOT. *(árbol)* pacay tree; *(fruto)* pacay fruit.

pa·ce·ño, -ña I. adj. of La Paz II. m.f. native of La Paz.

pa·cer §17 intr. to graze (in a pasture) —tr. *(apacentar)* to graze, pasture (animals); *(comer)* to eat away; *(roer)* to gnaw, nibble.

pa·ces f.pl. see **paz.**

pa·cien·cia f. *(conformidad)* patience, forbearance; *(pastelillo)* almond cake ♦ **acabársele** or **agotársele a uno la p.** to lose one's patience • **armarse** or **cargarse de p.** to arm oneself with patience • **llevar** or **tomar algo con p.** to take something calmly, bear something with patience • **perder la p.** to lose one's temper.

pa·cien·cio·so, -sa adj. AMER. very patient.

pa·cien·te I. adj. patient, forbearing II. m.f. MED. *(enfermo)* patient —m. PHILOS. *(sujeto)* patient, recipient of an action.

pa·cien·zu·do, -da adj. very patient.

pa·ci·fi·ca·ción f. pacification.

pa·ci·fi·ca·dor, -do·ra I. adj. pacifying II. m.f. *(persona)* pacifier, peacemaker —m. COL. pacifier (for infants).

pa·ci·fi·ca·men·te adv. peacefully, pacifically.

pa·ci·fi·car §70 tr. *(poner paz)* to pacify, restore peace (in a country); *(reconciliar)* to reconcile, make peace between or among persons; FIG. *(sosegar)* to calm, pacify (tempers) —reflex. to calm down.

pa·cí·fi·co, -ca adj. peaceful, pacific ♦ **coexistencia p.** peaceful coexistence.

Pa·cí·fi·co m. Pacific (Ocean).

pa·ci·fis·mo m. pacifism.

pa·ci·fis·ta adj. & m.f. pacifist.

pa·co m. ZOOL. alpaca, paco; *(guerrillero)* sniper; *(tiro)* sniper shot; AMER., MIN. paco.

pa·co·ti·lla f. *(mercancías)* venture, goods carried by seamen free of freight charges; *(género de calidad inferior)* shoddy goods, junk; AMER. riffraff, rabble ♦ **de p.** shoddy, junky • **hacer su p.** to make a pile, do nicely.

pa·co·ti·lle·ro m. *(vendedor)* seller of shoddy goods; AMER. peddler, hawker.

pac·tar tr. *(convenir)* to agree to or upon; *(estipular)* to stipulate, contract —intr. to come to an agreement, make a pact or agreement ♦ **p. con el diablo** to sell one's soul to the devil.

pac·to m. pact, agreement.

pa·cha·ma·ma f. ARG., BOL., PERU Earth (as a deity).

pa·cha·man·ca f. PERU barbecue (in a covered pit).

pa·chan·ga f. MEX. *(fiesta)* rowdy party; *(baile)* Mexican dance.

pa·chón m. dull fellow, phlegmatic person.

pa·cho·rra f. COLL. slowness, sluggishness.

pa·cho·rra·da f. CUBA, PERU blunder, blooper.

pa·cho·rre·ar intr. AMER. to be slow or sluggish.

pa·cho·rru·do, -da adj. COLL. sluggish, slow.

pa·cho·ta·da f. AMER. blunder, blooper.

pa·chu·cho, -cha adj. *(fruta)* overripe; FIG. weak, soft.

pa·de·cer §17 tr. *(sufrir)* to suffer (from); *(soportar)* to endure, bear; *(ser víctima)* to be the victim of <*padece una equivocación* he is the victim of an error> —intr. *(sufrir)* to suffer; FIG *(recibir daño)* to be damaged ♦ **p. de** to suffer from • **p. del corazón** to have heart trouble.

pa·de·ci·mien·to m. *(sufrimiento)* suffering; *(enfermedad)* ailment, illness.

pa·dras·tro m. *(marido de la madre)* stepfather; *(mal padre)* harsh father; FIG. *(obstáculo)* obstacle, impediment; *(pellejo)* hangnail.

pa·dra·zo m. COLL. overindulgent father.

pa·dre I. m. *(papá)* father; ZOOL. *(macho)* sire; FIG. *(ori-* *gen)* origin, source <*el ocio es el p. de todos los vicios* idleness is the source of all vice>; *(creador)* father, creator <*Cervantes es el p. de la novela moderna* Cervantes is the father of the modern novel>; RELIG. father, priest ♦ **p. de pila** godfather • **p. espiritual** RELIG. confessor • **Padre Eterno** RELIG. Heavenly or Eternal Father, God Almighty • **Padre Nuestro** RELIG. Our Father, Lord's Prayer • **p. político** *(suegro)* father-in-law; *(padrastro)* stepfather • **padres** parents • **Santo Padre** RELIG. *(papa)* Holy Father, Pope; *(doctor de la iglesia)* Father (of the Church) II. adj. terrific, tremendous.

pa·dre·ar intr. *(engendrar)* to breed (animals); *(parecerse al padre)* to resemble one's father.

pa·dre·nues·tro m. [pl. -tros] Lord's Prayer, Our Father ♦ **en un p.** COLL. in the wink of an eye.

pa·dri·llo m. AMER. sire, stallion.

pa·dri·naz·go m. *(cargo de padrino)* godfathership, sponsorship; FIG. *(protección)* favor, patronage.

pa·dri·no m. *(padre de pila)* godfather, sponsor (at child's baptism); *(de boda)* best man, groomsman; *(de desafío)* second (in a duel); FIG. *(patrocinador)* patron, sponsor ♦ **padrinos** godparents.

pa·drón m. *(censo)* census, register; *(dechado)* model, pattern; *(columna)* memorial column or pillar; COLL. *(padrazo)* overindulgent father; FIG. *(nota de infamia)* blemish, blot (on a reputation); AMER. sire, stallion; COL. breeding bull.

pa·dro·te m. COLL. *(padrazo)* overindulgent father; MEX. *(alcahuete)* pimp; *(padre de mancebía)* brothel keeper.

¡paf! interj. bang!, thud!

pa·ga f. *(acción)* payment; *(dinero)* payment, fee; *(sueldo)* earnings, wages; *(expiación)* satisfaction, amends; *(multa)* fine ♦ **buena p.** good pay • **de p.** paying, fee-charging (institution) • **p. extraordinaria** extra pay.

pa·ga·ble adj. payable.

pa·ga·de·ro, -ra I. adj. payable, due II. m. time of payment ♦ **p. a la demanda** or **a la vista** payable on sight • **p. a la entrega** payable on delivery • **p. a plazos** payable in installments.

pa·ga·do, -da I. past part. see **pagar** II. adj. *(cuenta)* paid; *(persona)* hired ♦ **p. de sí mismo** self-satisfied.

pa·ga·dor, -do·ra I. adj. paying II. m.f. *(el que paga)* payer; *(empleado de banco)* teller (in a bank).

pa·ga·men·to or **pa·ga·mien·to** m. payment.

pa·ga·ni·ni m. COLL. sucker, victim.

pa·ga·nis·mo m. paganism, heathenism.

pa·ga·no, -na I. adj. pagan, heathen II. m.f. *(infiel)* pagan, heathen; COLL. *(víctima)* sucker, victim.

pa·gar §47 tr. *(remunerar)* to pay <*p. a los obreros* to pay the workers>; *(satisfacer)* to pay <*p. una deuda* to pay a debt>; *(recompensar)* to repay <*p. un favor* to repay a favor>; FIG. *(sufrir)* to pay for <*pagué las consecuencias de mis acciones* I paid the consequences for my actions> ♦ **a p. a la recepción** COM. cash on delivery • **p. a crédito** or **a plazos** to pay in installments • **p. con la misma moneda** FIG. to give (someone) a taste of their own medicine • **p. el pato** FIG., COLL. to pay the piper • **pagarla** or **pagarlas** FIG. to pay for it • **p. por adelantado** to pay in advance —intr. to pay —reflex. *(aficionarse)* to become fond of; *(ufanarse)* to boast, brag.

pa·ga·ré m. promissory note, IOU.

pá·gi·na f. *(hoja)* page; FIG. *(suceso)* page, event (in life).

pa·gi·na·ción f. pagination.

pa·gi·nar tr. to paginate, number the pages of.

pa·go¹ adj. COLL. paid ♦ **estar p.** to be even, be quits.

pa·go² m. *(entrega)* payment; *(recompensa)* repayment, recompense.

pa·go³ m. *(finca)* estate, property; *(pueblo)* village, town; *(distrito)* district, region.

pa·gué, pague see **pagar.**

pai·la f. *(vasija)* large shallow pan; AMER. frying pan.

pai·pai m. palm fan.

pa·ís m. *(territorio)* country, nation, land; *(región)* region, territory; *(tela de abanico)* paper or cloth backing of fan.

pai·sa·je m. *(terreno)* landscape, countryside; *(cuadro)* landscape.

pai·sa·jis·ta I. adj. landscape II. m.f. landscape painter.

pai·sa·na·je m. *(población)* civil population, civilians; *(calidad)* state of being a compatriot *or* fellow citizen.

pai·sa·no, –na **I.** adj. of the same country or region **II.** m.f. *(campesino)* peasant; *(compatriota)* fellow countryman, compatriot; MIL. civilian —f. *(baile)* country dance; *(compatriota)* fellow countrywoman, compatriot.

Países Bajos m.pl. Netherlands, Low Countries.

pa·ja f. BOT. straw; FIG. *(lo desechable)* deadwood, chaff; *(cosa sin substancia)* rubbish; *(para beber)* (drinking) straw; AMER. faucet, tap ♦ **buscar la p. en el oído** FIG. to look for trouble • **echar pajas** to draw straws • **en un quítame allá las pajas** in the wink of an eye, in a jiffy • **no importar** *or* **no montar una p.** FIG. to be unimportant • **hacerse una p.** VULG. to masturbate, jerk off • **por quítame allá estas pajas** FIG. for no reason, over nothing.

pa·jar m. *(almiar)* haystack; *(cija)* straw loft, barn.

pá·ja·ra f. *(ave)* hen bird; *(cometa)* kite; *(pajarita)* paper bird; FIG. *(mujer)* clever or crafty woman.

pa·ja·re·ar tr. *(ahuyentar)* to scare off, shoo (birds) —intr. *(cazar)* to hunt birds; FIG. *(holgazanear)* to loaf about, loiter; AMER. to shy (a horse); CHILE to be absent-minded.

pa·ja·re·ra f. bird cage.

pa·ja·re·rí·a f. *(bandada)* flock of birds; *(tienda)* bird shop.

pa·ja·re·ro, –ra **I.** adj. *(de los pájaros)* bird; *(chancero)* cheerful, merry; *(chillón)* gaudy, loud (colors); AMER. shy, skittish (horse); VEN. meddlesome; MEX., PERU spirited **II.** m. *(vendedor)* bird seller *(cazador)* fowler, bird catcher; *(avicultor)* bird fancier.

pá·ja·ro m. ZOOL. bird; FIG. *(hombre astuto)* sly fox, crafty devil ♦ **matar dos pájaros de una pedrada** *or* **de un tiro** FIG., COLL. to kill two birds with one stone • **p. bobo** ORNITH. penguin • **p. carpintero** ORNITH. woodpecker • **p. de cuentas** FIG., COLL. big shot, bigwig • **p. del sol** ORNITH. bird of paradise • **p. diablo** ORNITH. European coot • **p. gordo** FIG., COLL. big shot, bigwig • **p. mosca** ORNITH. kingfisher • **tener pájaros en la cabeza** *or* **tener la cabeza llena de pájaros** FIG., COLL. to be featherbrained.

pa·ja·ro·ta *or* **pa·ja·ro·ta·da** f. hoax, canard.

pa·ja·ro·te m. large bird.

pa·ja·rra·co m. *(pájaro)* large ugly bird; FIG., COLL. *(pillo)* shady customer, clever bastard.

pa·ja·za f. leftover straw.

pa·je m. *(criado)* page (knight's attendant); MARIT. cabin boy; FIG. *(mueble)* dressing table; *(familiar)* familiar, servant (to a bishop).

pa·je·ar intr. *(comer)* to feed well, eat a lot of straw (horses); *(conducirse)* to behave, conduct oneself.

pa·je·ro m. straw dealer.

pa·ji·lla f. *(cigarrillo)* cigarette rolled in a corn leaf; *(caña)* drinking straw.

pa·ji·zo, –za adj. *(de paja)* straw, made of straw; *(de color de paja)* straw-colored.

pa·jo·le·ro, –ra adj. COLL. damned, wretched.

pa·jón m. *(paja)* coarse straw; AMER. scrub, stubble.

pa·jo·nal m. AMER. scrub, field of thick stubble.

pa·jo·so, –sa adj. *(lleno de paja)* full of straw; *(como paja)* straw, straw-like; *(de paja)* straw, made of straw.

pa·jo·te m. straw mat used for protecting plants.

pa·jue·la f. *(varilla)* straw taper; BOL. *(fósforo)* match; BOL., COL. *(mondadientes)* toothpick; VEN. mandolin plectrum.

Pa·kis·tán m. Pakistan.

pa·kis·ta·ní adj. & m.f. [pl. **–ní·es**] Pakistani.

pa·la f. *(herramienta)* shovel, spade; *(contenido)* shovelful; *(parte plana)* blade (of a shovel, hoe); *(raqueta)* racquet (for tennis, badminton); *(de ping pong)* (Ping-Pong) paddle; *(de criquet)* bat (for cricket, baseball); *(del remo)* blade (of an oar); *(del curtidor)* fleshing knife (used by tanners); *(del zapato)* vamp (top part of shoe); *(del diente)* flat surface (of teeth); *(chapa de bisagra)* leaf (of a hinge); *(de la hélice)* (propeller) blade; FIG. *(maña)* cunning, craft ♦ **p. mecánica** power shovel.

pa·la·bra f. *(vocablo)* word; *(término)* term; *(facultad de hablar)* speech, faculty of speech; *(elocuencia)* eloquence; *(promesa)* word, promise <ella me dio su p. she gave me her word>; *(derecho)* floor, right to speak <ella tiene la p. she has the floor>; RELIG. Word ♦ **a media p.** FIG. at the least hint • **bajo p.** on one's word of honor • **cogerle la p.**

a alguien to take someone at his word • **conceder** *or* **dar la p. a** to give the floor to • **correr la p.** to pass the word • **cruzar p.** to talk, converse • **cumplir** *or* **mantener su p. uno** to keep one's word • **decir** *or* **tener la última p.** to have the last word • **dejar a alguien con la p. en la boca** to turn one's back on someone who is speaking • **de p.** orally, by word of mouth • **dirigir la p. a** to address, speak to • **empeñar la p.** to pledge one's word • **en dos** *or* **en pocas palabras** in brief • **en otras palabras** in other words • **en una p.** in a word, in short • **escapársele a uno una p.** to let something slip • **faltar a su p.** to go back on one's word • **írsele a uno la p.** COLL. to forget what one was going to say • **medir uno sus palabras** to weigh one's words • **no decir p.** not to say a word • **no tener p.** to be unreliable • **¡palabra!** on my word of honor! • **p. de honor** word of honor • **p. de matrimonio** promise of marriage • **p. divina** *or* **de Dios** RELIG. Word of God • **p. por p.** word for word, verbatim • **palabras** *(texto)* words <en las palabras de Sócrates in the words of Socrates>; *(hechizo)* witch's spell; RELIG. formula (for sacraments) • **palabras mayores** strong language • **pedir la p.** to ask for the floor • **quedarse sin palabras** to be left speechless • **quitarle a alguien la p. de la boca** to take the words right out of someone's mouth • **tomar la p.** to take the floor • **torcer las palabras de alguien** to twist someone's words.

pa·la·bre·ar tr. AMER. to promise to marry (someone) —intr. COLL. *(charlar)* to chat.

pa·la·bre·o m. chatter.

pa·la·bre·rí·a f. *or* **pa·la·bre·rí·o** m. COLL. wordiness, idle chatter.

pa·la·bre·ro, –ra **I.** adj. *(locuaz)* talkative, loquacious; *(no confiable)* unreliable **II.** m.f. *(parlanchín)* chatterbox, talkative person; *(persona poco seria)* unreliable person.

pa·la·bri·ta f. pointed word.

pa·la·bro·ta f. COLL. swearword, dirty word ♦ **decir palabrotas** to swear.

pa·la·ce·te m. manor house, elegant country house.

pa·la·cie·go, –ga adj. *(magnífico)* palatial, magnificent; *(del palacio)* court, palace <costumbres palaciegas court customs>.

pa·la·cio m. *(residencia real)* palace; *(casa magnífica)* mansion ♦ **p. de justicia** courthouse • **p. real** royal palace.

pa·la·da f. *(porción)* shovelful; MARIT. stroke (of an oar).

pa·la·dar m. ANAT. palate, roof of the mouth; FIG. *(gusto)* palate, taste <él tiene un p. refinado he has very discriminating taste>; *(sabor)* taste (of foods).

pa·la·de·ar tr. *(saborear)* to savor, relish; FIG. *(aficionar)* to give (someone) a taste for something —intr. to show a desire to nurse (infant).

pa·la·de·o m. act of savoring *or* relishing.

pa·la·dín *or* **pa·la·di·no** m. *(caballero)* paladin; FIG. *(defensor)* champion, defender.

pa·la·di·no, –na adj. *(público)* public, open; *(obvio)* clear, obvious.

pa·la·dio m. CHEM. palladium.

pa·la·frén m. palfrey (horse).

pa·la·fre·ne·ro m. groom, equerry.

pa·lan·ca f. PHYS. lever; *(utensilio)* crowbar; *(palo)* shaft, pole (used for carrying); *(de la piscina)* diving board, springboard; MARIT. tackle; MECH. lever <p. de mando control lever>; *(fortín)* stockade; FIG., COLL. *(influencia)* pull, influence <aquel hombre tiene mucha p. en el vecindario that man has a lot of influence in the neighborhood> ♦ **p. de cambio** AUTO. gearshift • **p. del timón** AER. rudder bar.

pa·lan·ga·na f. *(jofaina)* washbasin; C. AMER., COL. wooden bowl *or* platter —m. AMER., COLL. *(fanfarrón)* braggart, showoff; *(descarado)* nervy *or* fresh guy.

pa·lan·ga·na·da f. AMER., COLL. bragging, boasting.

pa·lan·ga·ne·ar intr. AMER., COLL. to brag, boast.

pa·lan·ga·ne·ro m. washstand.

pa·lan·que·ar tr. AMER. to lever, pry.

pa·lan·que·ra f. stockade.

pa·lan·que·ro m. *(obrero)* bellows blower (in a forge); CHILE, RAIL. brakeman.

pa·lan·que·ta f. *(palanca)* small lever; *(barra de hierro)* crowbar, jimmy; MARIT. bar shot.

pa·lan·quín m. *(litera)* palanquin, covered litter; MARIT. clew garnet; COLL. *(ganapán)* errand boy, porter.

pa·las·tro m. *(chapa de hierro)* sheet iron; *(chapa de acero)* steel plate; *(planchita)* plate (of a lock).

pa·la·tal adj. & f. ANAT., PHONET. palatal.

pa·la·ta·li·zar §04 tr. PHONET. to palatalize.

pa·la·ti·na·do m. HIST. palatinate.

pa·la·ti·no, –na I. adj. ANAT. palatal, palatine; *(de palacio)* palatine; *(del Palatinado)* of the Palatinate (Germany) II. m. ANAT. palatine bone; *(príncipe)* palatine.

pal·co m. THEAT. *(tablado)* raised platform for spectators; *(aposento privado)* box ♦ **p. de platea** ground-floor *or* parterre box • **p. de proscenio** stage *or* proscenium box • **p. principal** first-tier box.

pa·le·ar tr. *(traspalar)* to shovel; *(aventar)* to winnow.

pa·len·que m. *(estacada)* fence, palisade; *(plaza)* arena; AMER. *(poste)* hitching post; *(lugar bullicioso)* noisy place ♦ **salir al p.** to enter the fray.

pa·le·o·gra·fí·a f. paleography.

pa·le·o·lí·ti·co, –ca adj. & m. paleolithic.

pa·le·ó·lo·go, –ga I. adj. paleological II. m.f. paleologist.

pa·le·on·to·lo·gí·a f. paleontology.

pa·le·on·to·ló·gi·co, –ca adj. paleontologic, paleontological.

pa·le·on·tó·lo·go, –ga m.f. paleontologist.

pa·le·o·zoi·co, –ca adj. & m. Paleozoic.

pa·le·ro, –ra m.f. *(fabricante)* shovel maker; *(obrero)* ditch *or* swamp drainer; MIL. pioneer, sapper; AMER., COLL. *(gancho)* shill, hook (in card games).

Pa·les·ti·na f. Palestine.

pa·les·ti·no, –na adj. & m.f. Palestinian.

pa·les·tra f. *(lugar de lucha)* palestra, gymnasium; FIG. *(lucha)* wrestling; *(campo)* arena ♦ **salir** *or* **saltar a la p.** to enter the fray *or* the arena.

pa·le·ta f. *(pala pequeña)* small shovel *or* spade; *(del pintor)* palette; *(badil)* fire shovel; CUL. *(cucharón)* ladle; *(espátula)* spatula; MAS. *(del albañil)* trowel; ANAT. shoulder blade; MECH. *(álabe)* paddle (of water wheel); *(de la hélice)* blade; *(diente)* front tooth; CHILE bit (of a key); MEX. lollipop.

pa·le·ta·da f. *(contenido de la pala)* shovelful; *(contenido de la llana)* trowelful; *(golpe)* blow with a shovel *or* trovel ♦ **a paletadas** COLL. heaps of, loads of <había libros a paletadas there were loads of books> • **en dos paletadas** in a jiffy, in the wink of an eye.

pa·le·te·ar intr. MARIT. to thrash about with the oars, row without advancing; CHILE, COLL. to be frustrated, be disappointed.

pa·le·te·o m. MARIT. thrashing with oars *or* paddles.

pa·le·ti·lla f. ANAT. *(omóplato)* shoulder blade; *(cartílago)* sternum cartilage; CUL. shoulder (of meat); *(palmatoria)* candlestick.

pa·le·to, –ta COLL. I. adj. peasant, boorish II. m.f. bumpkin, yokel.

pa·le·tó m. coat, greatcoat.

pa·le·tón m. *(de la llave)* bit (of a key); *(diente)* front tooth.

pa·lia f. RELIG. altar cloth.

pa·liar tr. *(encubrir)* to palliate, extenuate; *(aliviar)* to mitigate, alleviate.

pa·lia·ti·vo, –va adj. & m. palliative.

pa·lia·to·rio, –ria adj. palliative.

pa·li·de·cer §17 intr. *(ponerse pálido)* to turn pale, grow pale; *(descolorarse)* to fade (colors); *(oscurecerse)* to wane (daylight); *(apagarse)* to grow dim (light); FIG. *(perder importancia)* to be on the wane.

pa·li·dez f. paleness, pallor.

pá·li·do, –da adj. *(descolorido)* pale, pallid; FIG. *(sin expresión)* pallid, lackluster <estilo p. lackluster style>.

pa·li·du·cho, –cha adj. COLL. pale, palish.

pa·lier m. TECH. bearing.

pa·li·lle·ro m. *(canuto)* toothpick holder; *(portaplumas)* penholder.

pa·li·llo m. *(para agujas)* knitting-needle holder; *(mondadientes)* toothpick; *(bolillo)* bobbin; *(de tambor)* drumstick; FIG. *(palique)* chitchat, small talk ♦ **estar hecho un p.** FIG. to be as thin as a rail • **palillos** *(para comer)* chopsticks; *(en billares)* pins; *(castañuelas)* castanets; TAUR.,

COLL. banderillas • **tocar todas los palillos** FIG. to touch all bases.

pa·limp·ses·to m. palimpsest.

pa·lin·dro·mo, –ma I. adj. palindromic II. m. palindrome.

pa·lio m. *(manto griego)* pallium; *(dosel)* canopy, baldachin; RELIG. pallium; HER. pall ♦ **recibir con** *or* **bajo p.** to receive with great pomp.

pa·li·que m. COLL. chitchat, small talk ♦ **estar de p.** to be chatting, have a chat.

pa·li·que·ar intr. COLL. to chat, have a chat.

pa·li·san·dro m. rosewood.

pa·li·to m. small stick ♦ **pisar el p.** AMER., COLL. to fall into the trap.

pa·li·to·que *or* **pa·li·tro·que** m. *(palito)* small stick; *(escritura)* pothook, stroke (of a pen); TAUR. banderilla.

pa·li·za f. beating, thrashing <darle a alguien una p. to give someone a thrashing> ♦ **ser una p.** to be just awful.

pa·li·za·da f. *(valla)* fence, embankment; *(sitio cercado)* fenced-in enclosure; MIL. stockade, palisade.

pal·ma f. *(de la mano)* palm (of the hand); BOT. *(palmera)* palm, palm tree; *(palmito)* palmetto; *(datilero)* date palm; *(hoja)* palm leaf; FIG. *(victoria)* victory, triumph; VET. palm (of a hoof) ♦ **andar en palmas** FIG. to be applauded • **batir palmas** to applaud • **llevarse la p.** FIG. to carry the day • **p. real** BOT. royal palm • **palmas** applause • **traer en palmas a alguien** FIG. to pamper someone.

pal·ma·da I. f. *(golpe)* slap, pat <dar una p. en el hombro to give a pat on the back>; *(ruido)* hand clap ♦ **dar palmadas** to clap one's hands • **palmadas** applause II. adj. see **palmado, –da.**

pal·ma·do, –da I. adj. *(de forma de palma)* palmate, palmshaped; *(ligado)* webbed (foot) II. f. see **palmada.**

pal·mar[1] I. adj. ANAT. palmar <músculo p. palmar muscle>; *(de un palmo)* one span long; FIG. *(claro)* clear, evident II. m. BOT. palm grove; TECH. card, teasel ♦ **más viejo que un p.** COLL. as old as the hills, as old as Methuselah.

pal·mar[2] intr. COLL. to die, kick the bucket.

pal·ma·rio, –ria adj. obvious, clear.

pal·ma·to·ria f. *(candelero)* candlestick; *(palmeta)* schoolmaster's cane *or* rod.

pal·me·a·do, –da I. past part. see **palmear** II. adj. *(de forma de palma)* palmate, palm-shaped; *(ligado)* webbed (foot).

pal·me·ar intr. *(batir palmas)* to clap (one's hands), applaud —tr. PRINT. to level off, plane down; ARG. to pat, slap.

pal·me·o m. measuring by palms *or* spans.

pal·mer m. TECH. micrometer caliper.

pal·me·ra f. BOT. *(árbol)* palm tree; *(hoja)* palm leaf; *(datilera)* date palm.

pal·me·ral m. palm grove.

pal·me·ro m. *(peregrino)* pilgrim, palmer; ARG., ECUAD., MEX. palm tree.

pal·me·ta f. *(palmatoria)* schoolmaster's cane *or* rod; *(palmetazo)* caning, blow with the cane.

pal·me·ta·zo m. *(golpe)* caning, blow with the cane; *(palmada)* slap, blow.

pal·mi·cho m. AMER., BOT. royal palm.

pal·mi·lla f. *(paño)* woolen cloth; *(plantilla)* inner sole (of shoe).

pal·mí·pe·do, –da ZOOL. I. adj. web-footed II. m. web-footed animal.

pal·mis·ta f. CARIB. palm reader, fortune teller.

pal·mi·ta f. palm marrow ♦ **llevar** *or* **traer a alguien en palmitas** COLL. to wait on someone hand and foot.

pal·mi·tie·so, –sa adj. VET. flat-hoofed (horse).

pal·mi·to m. BOT., CUL. palm heart; FIG. face <buen p. pretty face>.

pal·mo m. span, palm ♦ **crecer a palmos** to shoot up • **dejar a alguien con un p. en las narices** to disappoint someone, let someone down • **p. a p.** little by little, inch by inch.

pal·mo·te·ar intr. to clap (one's hands), applaud.

pal·mo·te·o m. clapping, applause.

pa·lo m. *(vara)* stick, pole; *(bastón)* staff; *(estaca)* stake, post; *(porra)* club, cudgel; *(mango)* stick, handle <p. de escoba broomstick>; *(madera)* wood <p. Brasil Brazilwood>; MARIT. mast, spar; *(golpe)* hit, whack; *(pena capital)* hanging; *(naipes)* suit <p. favorito trump suit>;

PRINT. stroke (of letter); HER. pale; BOT. stalk; P. RICO, VEN., COLL. swig, drink; AMER. tree <*p. de limón* lemon tree> ♦ **dar de palos** to beat, hit • **dar palos de ciego** FIG. to swing wildly • **de tal p., tal astilla** like father, like son • **de p.** wooden • **p. campeche** BOT. logwood • **p. de agua** AMER. downpour • **p. de jabón** BOT. soapbark • **p. de mesana** MARIT. mizzenmast • **p. de rosa** BOT. rosewood • **p. de trinquete** MARIT. foremast • **p. dulce** BOT. licorice root • **p. ensebado** AMER. greased pole • **p. mayor** MARIT. mainmast • **p. santo** BOT. lignum vitae • **palos de golf** golf clubs • **ser un p. de** AMER. to be a remarkable <*el es un p. de hombre* he is a remarkable man>.

pa·lo·ma f. ORNITH. dove, pigeon; FIG. *(persona)* lamb, dear <*el niño era una p.* the child was a lamb>; COLL. *(de camisa)* high collar (of a shirt); *(bebida)* anisette or ouzo with water; HOND. square kite ♦ **p. brava** or **silvestre** stock dove • **p. buchona** pouter pigeon • **p. casera** or **doméstica** domestic pigeon • **p. de moño** or **moñuda** crested pigeon • **p. mensajera** carrier or homing pigeon • **p. torcaz** wood pigeon, ringdove • **p. zurita** rock dove.

pa·lo·mar m. dovecote, pigeon loft.

pa·lo·me·ar intr. *(cazar)* to go pigeon-shooting; *(criar)* to devote a great deal of time to raising pigeons —tr. ECUAD., PERU *(matar)* to shoot dead or down; *(cazar)* to hunt down one by one (one's enemies).

pa·lo·me·o m. PERU act of hunting down enemies one by one.

pa·lo·me·ro m. *(vendedor)* pigeon seller; *(aficionado)* pigeon fancier.

pa·lo·me·ta f. ICHTH. saurel, yellow jack; *(tuerca)* wing or butterfly nut.

pa·lo·mi·lla f. ENTOM. *(paulilla)* grain moth; *(mariposa pequeña)* small butterfly; *(ninfa)* nymph, chrysalis; BOT. *(fumaria)* fumitory; *(onoquiles)* alkanet; ZOOL. back, fore-rump (of horse); MECH. *(palometa)* wing nut, butterfly nut; *(sostén)* wall bracket; *(chumacera)* bearing, axle bearing; AMER., COLL. rabble, riffraff ♦ **palomillas** whitecaps (on waves).

pa·lo·mi·no m. *(cría)* young pigeon; *(uva)* palomino grape (used in sherry); COLL. *(mancha)* stain on a shirttail; *(joven)* callow youth, greenhorn; AMER. white horse.

pa·lo·mi·ta f. *(roseta)* popcorn; *(anís)* anisette and water; AMER. darling.

pa·lo·mo I. adj. AMER. palomino, white (horse) II. m. ORNITH. *(macho)* cock pigeon; *(paloma torcaz)* ring-necked dove; COLL. fool, idiot; AMER. back, fore-rump of horse.

pa·lo·ta·da f. blow with a drumstick ♦ **no dar p.** COLL. *(no acertar)* to get nothing right; *(no hacer nada)* to do nothing, not to do a stroke of work.

pa·lo·te m. MUS. drumstick; *(trazo)* pothook, stroke (in learning to write).

pa·lo·te·ar intr. *(hacer ruido)* to beat sticks together; FIG., COLL. *(discutir)* to bicker, wrangle.

pa·lo·te·o m. bickering, wrangling.

pal·pa·ble adj. *(que se puede tocar)* palpable, touchable; FIG. *(evidente)* palpable, tangible.

pal·pa·ble·men·te adv. palpably, tangibly, obviously.

pal·pa·ción or **pal·pa·du·ra** f. MED. palpation; *(toque)* touching, feeling.

pal·pa·mien·to m. touching, feeling.

pal·par tr. *(tocar)* to touch, feel; *(andar a tientas)* to grope; FIG. *(conocer)* to understand, appreciate <*usted lo palpará algún día* one day you'll understand>; COLL. *(manosear)* to fondle, caress. FIG. to be felt, be perceptible <*se palpaba el descontento* the restlessness could be felt>.

pal·pi·ta·ción f. MED. palpitation, throbbing.

pal·pi·tan·te adj. *(que palpita)* palpitating, throbbing; FIG., COLL. *(interesante)* burning (question, issue).

pal·pi·tar intr. *(temblar)* to palpitate, throb; *(latir)* to beat (heart); FIG. *(emocionarse)* to quiver, be aflutter (with emotion); *(manifestar)* to throb <*en su verso palpita la emoción* his poetry throbs with emotion>.

pál·pi·to m. FIG., COLL hunch, presentiment.

pal·ta f. AMER., BOT. avocado (fruit).

pal·to m. AMER., BOT. avocado tree.

pa·lú·di·co, –ca I. adj. *(pantanoso)* marshy, swampy; MED. malarial II. m.f. MED. person suffering from malaria.

pa·lu·dis·mo m. MED. malaria.

pa·lur·do, –da I. adj. boorish, peasant II. m.f. boor, yokel.

pa·lla f. BOL., CHILE, MIN. *(separación)* extraction of metal from ore; ARG., CHILE improvised song; BOL. palm tree.

pa·lla·du·ra f. AMER. var. of **paya.**

pa·lla·que·ar tr. AMER., MIN. to sort (ore); CHILE *(espigar)* to glean; *(cantar)* to sing improvised songs.

pa·lla·que·ro m. CHILE illegal prospector (of discarded ore).

pa·llar[1] intr. CHILE *(cantar)* to sing improvised songs, sing extemporaneously; *(contar cuentos)* to tell stories —tr. AMER., MIN. to sort (ore).

pa·llar[2] m. CHILE, PERU *(alubia)* lima or butter bean; *(judía)* haricot bean.

pa·me·ma f. COLL. *(aspaviento)* fuss; *(cosa insignificante)* trifle; *(halago)* flattery.

pam·pa I. f. *(llanura)* pampa, plain; CHILE open area (for military exercises) —m.f. ARG. *(indio)* pampean Indian ♦ **a la p.** AMER. in the open air, under the stars • **estar en sus pampas** PERU to be at one's ease • **quedar en p.** to be disappointed II. adj. ARG., BOL., URUG. shady, dishonest (deal); BOL. weak, feeble; ARG. having a white head and a dark-colored body (horse).

pám·pa·na f. BOT. vine leaf.

pám·pa·no m. BOT. *(pimpollo)* tendril, vine shoot; *(hoja)* vine leaf; ICHTH. salp.

pam·pe·a·no, –na AMER. I. adj. from the pampas, pampean II. m.f. inhabitant of the pampas.

pam·pe·ro, –ra I. adj. pampean, of or from the pampas II. m.f. AMER. *(persona)* pampean, native or inhabitant of the pampas; *(viento)* pampero, strong wind (that blows across the pampas).

pam·pi·no, –na CHILE I. adj. of or from the pampas II. m.f. inhabitant of the Chilean pampas.

pam·pi·ta f. PERU, COLL. small field.

pam·pli·na f. BOT. *(álsine)* chickweed; FIG., COLL. *(tontería)* nonsense, foolishness; *(cosa insignificante)* trifle ♦ **p. de agua** BOT. brookweed.

pam·pli·na·da or **pam·plo·na·da** or **pam·pli·ne·rí·a** f. COLL. nonsense, foolishness.

pam·pli·ne·ro, –ra or **pam·pli·no·so, –sa** I. adj. foolish, silly II. m.f. foolish or fussy person.

pam·prin·ga·da f. *(pan)* piece of bread dipped in fat or gravy; COLL. *(sandez)* ridiculous thing or act.

pan m. bread <*p. de centeno* rye bread>; *(pieza)* loaf of bread <*un p. grande* a big loaf of bread>; *(masa)* dough; FIG. cake, loaf <*un p. de jabón* cake of soap>; *(sustento)* bread, food; *(trigo)* wheat; *(hoja de harina)* wafer, host; METAL. leaf, foil <*p. de oro* gold leaf> ♦ **a p. y agua** on bread and water • **con su p. se lo coma** COLL. he asked for it • **contigo p. y cebolla** COLL. for better or for worse • **echar panes** ARG. to boast, brag • **ganarse el p.** to earn a living • **p. ázimo** or **cenceño** unleavened bread • **p. bazo** brown bread • **p. bendito** RELIG. communion bread; FIG. hot cakes <*venderse como p. bendito* to sell like hot cakes> • **p. caliente** AMER., FIG. hot cakes • **p. de maíz** cornbread • **p. de molde** sandwich bread • **panes** grain crops • **p. fermentado** leavened bread • **p. francés** ARG. uproar, din • **p. integral** whole-wheat bread • **p. molido** bread crumbs • **p. tierno** fresh bread • **ser más bueno que el p.** to be kindness itself • **ser p. comido** FIG., COLL. to be a cinch.

pa·na f. corduroy ♦ **p. lisa** velvet.

pa·na·ce·a f. panacea, cure-all.

pa·na·de·rí·a f. *(oficio)* bread-baking (occupation); *(sitio)* bakery, bread shop.

pa·na·de·ro, –ra m.f. baker.

pa·na·di·zo m. MED. felon, whitlow; FIG., COLL. *(persona)* pale and sickly person.

pa·nal m. *(de colmena)* honeycomb; *(dulce)* lemon-flavored syrup.

pa·na·má m. Panama hat.

Pa·na·má m. Panama.

pa·na·me·ño, –ña adj. & m.f. Panamanian.

pa·na·me·ri·ca·no, –na adj. Pan-American.

pa·na·te·la f. long thin spongecake.

pan·ca f. *(barca)* Philippine fishing boat; ARG., BOL., PERU cornhusk.

pan·car·ta f. poster, placard.

pan·cis·ta I. adj. opportunistic (for political expediency) II. m.f. opportunist (in politics).

pán·cre·as m. [pl. **-cre·as**] ANAT. pancreas.

pan·cre·á·ti·co, –ca adj. ANAT. pancreatic.

pan·cro·má·ti·co, –ca adj. PHOTO. panchromatic.

pan·cho, –cha COLL. I. adj. calm, unruffled ◆ **quedarse tan p.** to keep one's cool II. m. belly, paunch.

pan·da m. ZOOL. panda.

pan·de·ar intr. & reflex. *(alabearse la madera)* to warp, bend (wood); *(combarse la pared)* to bulge, sag (wall).

pan·dec·tas f.pl. *(código)* pandect; *(derecho romano)* Pandects (body of Roman law); *(cuaderno)* index book.

pan·de·mo·nio or **pan·de·mó·nium** m. pandemonium.

pan·de·o m. *(alabeo de madera)* warping, bending (of wood); *(forma alabeada)* warp; *(combadura)* bulging, sagging (of a wall); *(forma combada)* bulge, sag.

pan·de·ra·da f. MUS. *(panderos)* collection of tambourines; FIG., COLL. *(necedad)* stupid remark, piece of nonsense.

pan·de·ra·zo m. MUS. blow given on the tambourine.

pan·de·re·ta f. MUS. tambourine ◆ **zumbar la p. a alguien** FIG., COLL. to beat or thrash someone.

pan·de·re·te m. MUS. small tambourine ◆ **tabique de p.** CONSTR. brick partition.

pan·de·re·te·ar intr. to play the tambourine.

pan·de·re·te·o m. *(música)* tambourine playing; *(regocijo)* merrymaking, dancing to the tambourine.

pan·de·re·te·ro, –ra m.f. *(músico)* tambourine player; *(fabricante)* tambourine maker; *(vendedor)* tambourine seller.

pan·de·ro m. MUS. tambourine; FIG., COLL. *(necio)* silly babbler, prattler; *(cometa)* kite.

pan·di·lla f. *(banda)* gang, band <*p. de gamberros* gang of hooligans>; *(grupo de amigos)* group, set; *(grupo exclusivo)* clique, coterie.

pan·di·lle·ro or **pan·di·llis·ta** m. *(miembro)* member of a gang, gangster; *(jefe)* leader of a gang.

pan·dit m. pundit, pandit.

pan·do, –da I. adj. *(que comba)* sagging, bulging (wall); *(alabeado)* warped, bent (wood); *(lento)* slow-moving, slow; FIG. *(pausado)* slow, ponderous II. m. GEOG. plain (between mountains).

pan·dor·ga f. *(cometa)* kite; FIG., COLL. *(mujer)* fat and lazy woman.

pa·ne·ci·llo m. roll, bun ◆ **venderse como panecillos** to sell like hot cakes.

pa·ne·gí·ri·co, –ca I. adj. panegyrical II. m. panegyric.

pa·nel m. ARCHIT. panel (of a door); MARIT. floor board (of deck); PAINT. panel ◆ **paneles** ARCHIT. paneling.

pa·ne·la f. *(bizcocho)* diamond-shaped sponge cake; AMER. brown-sugar loaf; COL., VEN. flatterer.

pa·ne·ra f. *(troje)* granary, barn; *(cesta)* breadbasket.

pa·ne·ro m. *(cesta)* breadbasket; *(esterilla)* small rush mat.

pa·ne·te·la f. *(caldo)* soup made with broth and breadcrumbs; *(cigarro)* panatela, thin cigar.

pan·fi·lis·mo m. extreme kindness.

pán·fi·lo, –la adj. *(cachazudo)* slow, sluggish; *(bobo)* foolish, simple; COLL. pale, wan.

pan·fle·tis·ta m. pamphleteer, satirist.

pan·fle·to m. *(folleto)* pamphlet; AMER. satire, lampoon.

pa·nia·gua·do m. *(criado)* servant; COLL. *(favorecido)* favorite, protégé.

pá·ni·co, –ca I. adj. panic, panicky II. m. panic, fear ◆ **de pánico** wonderful, marvelous.

pa·nie·go, –ga adj. *(que cría trigo)* wheat <*tierra p.* wheatland>; *(que come pan)* bread-loving (person).

pa·ni·fi·ca·ble adj. capable of being made into bread.

pa·ni·fi·ca·ción f. bread-making.

pa·ni·fi·car §70 tr. *(panadear)* to make into bread (flour); *(cultivar)* to convert pasture land into wheat or corn fields.

pa·ni·zo m. *(mijo)* millet; *(maíz)* corn, maize; CHILE, MIN. mineral deposit or bed; *(abundancia)* abundance.

pa·no·cha f. *(panoja)* ear (of corn), CHILE, COL., C. RICA cornmeal pancake; MEX. panocha, brown sugar.

pa·no·ja f. *(mazorca)* ear (of corn); BOT. panicle; *(pescados fritos)* portion of fried fish fastened by the tails; *(colgajo)* bunch of fruit.

pa·no·li or **pa·no·lis** [pl. **-lis**] COLL. I. adj. foolish, silly II. m.f. fool, chump.

pa·no·plia f. panoply.

pa·no·ra·ma m. panorama.

pa·no·rá·mi·co, –ca I. adj. panoramic II. f. CINEM. panorama, view.

pa·no·so, –sa adj. mealy, doughy.

pan·qué or **pan·que·que** m. AMER. pancake.

pan·ta·grué·li·co, –ca adj. Pantagruelian, sumptuous (meal).

pan·ta·le·tas f.pl. AMER. panties, drawers.

pan·ta·lón or **pan·ta·lo·nes** m. *(prenda de hombre)* trousers, pants; *(prenda de mujer)* slacks, trousers; *(ropa interior femenina)* panties, knickers ◆ **llevar** or **ponerse los pantalones** FIG., COLL. to wear the pants in the family • **p. corto** shorts, short pants • **p. vaquero** or **tejano** jeans.

pan·ta·lo·ne·ra f. *(costurera)* trouser maker; MEX. charro pants.

pan·ta·lla f. *(de lámpara)* shade, lamp shade; *(para la lumbre)* fire screen, fireguard; *(telón)* movie screen; *(superficie fluorescente)* screen <*p. de radar* radar screen>; *(cinema)* film <*las estrellas de la p.* film stars>; FIG. *(protección)* screen, shield; *(gancho)* decoy <*servir de p.* to act as a decoy>; AMER. fan ◆ **p. acústica** RAD. baffle.

pan·ta·nal m. marsh, bog.

pan·ta·no m. *(ciénaga)* marsh, bog; *(embalse)* reservoir, dam; FIG. *(atolladero)* difficulty.

pan·ta·no·so, –sa adj. *(cenagoso)* boggy, marshy; FIG. COLL. *(embrollado)* tricky, thorny (problem, case).

pan·te·ís·mo m. PHILOS. pantheism.

pan·te·ís·ta PHILOS. I. adj. pantheistic II. pantheist.

pan·te·ón m. *(templo)* pantheon; *(sepultura)* mausoleum; *(cementerio)* cemetery, graveyard ◆ **p. familiar** family vault.

pan·te·ra f. ZOOL. panther.

pan·tó·gra·fo m. pantograph, instrument for copying.

pan·to·mi·ma f. pantomime.

pan·to·mí·mi·co, –ca adj. pantomimic, pantomimical.

pan·to·mi·mo m. pantomime actor, mime.

pan·to·rra f. COLL. heavy calf (of the leg).

pan·to·rri·lla f. calf (of the leg).

pan·to·rri·lle·ra f. padded stocking.

pan·tu·fla f. or **pan·tu·flo** m. slipper.

pan·za f. COLL. *(barriga)* belly, paunch; ZOOL. rumen (of ruminants); *(de vasija)* belly (of a bowl).

pan·za·da f. *(golpe)* push given with the belly; COLL. *(hartazgo)* bellyful ◆ **darse una p.** *(saciarse)* to gorge oneself (on), have a feast; *(estar harto)* to be fed up (with), to have had a bellyful • **una p. de** a lot of, a bellyful of.

pan·za·zo m. ◆ **darse un p.** to do a bellyflop.

pan·zón, –o·na or **pan·zu·do, –da** adj. paunchy, potbellied.

pa·ñal m. *(lienzo)* diaper; *(faldón)* shirttail ◆ **dejar en pañales a alguien** COLL. to leave someone standing • **estar en pañales** *(ser niño)* to be in diapers; *(ser novato)* to be wet behind the ears, be a novice • **pañales** FIG. early stages, infancy.

pa·ñe·rí·a f. *(tienda)* dry goods store, draper's shop; *(conjunto)* textiles, dry goods.

pa·ñe·ro, –ra I. adj. textile, cloth II. m.f. dry goods dealer, draper.

pa·ño m. *(tela)* cloth, material; *(tejido de lana)* woolen cloth; *(tapiz)* hanging, drapery; SEW. *(ancho de tela)* panel, width; *(mancha en la cara)* liver spot, blemish; *(trapo)* dustcloth, rag; MARIT. sails; MED. compress; CUBA, MEX. plot of land; CUBA fishing net ◆ **conocer el p.** to know one's business • **de p.** THEAT. offstage • **p. de altar** RELIG. altar cloth • **p. de lágrimas** FIG. sympathetic ear, shoulder to cry on • **p. de manos** hand towel • **p. de mesa** tablecloth • **paños** hangings, draperies • **paños calientes** COLL. half measures • **paños menores** underwear, underclothes.

pa·ñol m. MARIT. storeroom, store ◆ **p. de municiones** ammunition room • **p. del agua** water store • **p. del carbón** coal bunker.

pa·ño·le·rí·a f. handkerchief shop.

pa·ño·le·ta f. *(pañuelo)* scarf, fichu; TAUR. *(corbata)* necktie, tie (worn by bullfighters).

pa·ño·lón m. *(mantón)* shawl; *(pañuelo)* large handkerchief.

pa·ño·sa f. COLL. large woolen cape; TAUR. muleta.

pa·ñue·lo m. *(moquero)* handkerchief; *(pañoleta)* scarf ♦ **p. de bolsillo** *or* **de mano** pocket handkerchief • **ser grande como un p.** to be very small *or* tiny • **p. de cuello** neckerchief.

pa·pa¹ m. *(sumo pontífice)* Pope; COLL. *(jefe)* leader, head ♦ **ser más papista que el p.** to be more Catholic than the Pope.

pa·pa² f. BOT. *(patata)* potato; COLL. *(paparrucha)* hoax, false rumor ♦ **p. de caña** *or* **real** Jerusalem artichoke • **p. del aire** yam • **p. dulce** sweet potato • **papas** COLL. *(comida)* food, grub; *(puches)* pap, mush • **no saber ni p. de** COLL. not to know a thing about, not to have a clue about.

pa·pá m. papa, daddy ♦ **Papá Noel** Father Christmas.

pa·pa·co·te m. C. AMER. kite.

pa·pa·da f. double chin.

pa·pa·do m. papacy.

pa·pa·ga·yo m. ORNITH. parrot; ICHTH. rock bass; BOT. *(planta amarantácea)* Joseph's coat; *(planta arácea)* caladium; FIG., COLL. *(parlanchín)* parrot, chatterbox; AMER. kite; ECUAD. poisonous green snake.

pa·pal I. adj. papal II. m. AMER. potato field.

pa·pa·li·na f. *(gorra)* cap that covers the ears; *(cofia)* bonnet ♦ **coger una p.** to get sloshed *or* drunk.

pa·pa·lo·te *or* **pa·pe·lo·te** m. C. AMER., MEX. kite.

pa·pa·mos·cas m. [pl. **-cas**] ORNITH. flycatcher; FIG., COLL. *(bobo)* simpleton, fool.

pa·pa·na·tas m. [pl. **-tas**] COLL. simpleton, ninny.

pa·par tr. *(comer sin mascar)* to eat (soft food) without chewing; COLL. *(comer)* to eat; FIG., COLL. *(no hacer caso)* to pay little attention to ♦ **p. moscas** to gape.

pa·pa·rru·cha f. COLL. *(mentira)* hoax, canard; *(obra sin valor)* worthless piece of work, waste.

pa·pa·rru·cha·da f. hoax, canard.

pa·pa·ya f. papaya (fruit).

pa·pa·yo m. papaya tree.

pa·pel m.ʹ paper <*p. pergamino* parchment paper>; *(hoja)* piece of paper; *(escrito)* paper, writing; *(documento)* paper, document; FIG. *(función)* role, function; THEAT. role, part; COM. security, bond ♦ **hacer buen p.** FIG. to do well, cut a good figure • **hacer el p. de** to act, pretend • **hacer el p. de** to act as, serve as • **hacer mal p.** to do poorly, cut a bad figure • **p. alquitranado** tar paper • **p. biblia** Bible paper, India paper • **p. carbón** carbon paper • **p. cebolla** onionskin • **p. cuadriculado** graph paper • **p. cuché** art paper • **p. de arroz** rice paper • **p. de barba** deckle-edged paper • **p. de calcar** tracing paper • **p. de cartas** note paper, stationery • **p. de China** tissue paper • **p. de estaño** tin foil • **p. de estraza** *or* **de añafea** brown wrapping paper • **p. de filtro** filter paper • **p. de fumar** cigarette paper • **p. de lija** sandpaper • **p. de marca** foolscap • **p. de pagos** stamped paper • **p. de seda** tissue paper • **p. de tornasol** litmus paper • **p. encerado** wax paper • **papeles** *(documentos)* papers, documents; *(identificación)* identification papers • **p. higiénico** toilet paper • **p. matamoscas** flypaper • **p. moneda** paper money • **p. para escribir** writing paper • **p. pautado** *or* **de música** music paper • **p. rayado** lined paper • **p. secante** blotting paper • **p. sellado** stamped paper, official paper • **p. tapiz** wallpaper • **p. vitela** vellum paper.

pa·pe·la·da AMER. farce, charade.

pa·pe·le·ar intr. *(revolver)* to rummage through papers; FIG. *(querer aparentar)* to call or draw attention to oneself.

pa·pe·le·o m. *(acción)* rummaging through papers; *(burocracia)* red tape, paper work.

pa·pe·le·ra I. f. *(mueble)* writing desk; *(fábrica)* paper mill; *(cesto)* wastepaper basket; *(papelería)* pile *or* mass of papers II. adj. see **papelero, -ra.**

pa·pe·le·rí·a f. *(tienda)* stationery store; *(conjunto)* pile *or* mass of papers.

pa·pe·le·ro, -ra I. adj. *(del papel)* paper <*industria p.* paper industry>; FIG., COLL. *(farolero)* pretentious, boastful II. m.f. *(fabricante)* paper manufacturer; *(vendedor)* stationer; FIG., COLL. *(marrullero)* show-off —m. AMER. paper boy, newspaper seller —f. see **papelera.**

pa·pe·le·ta f. *(cédula)* card, slip of paper; *(planilla)* form; *(cucurucho)* paper cone or bag (for candy, snacks); *(ficha)*

index card, file card; *(boletín de voto)* ballot paper, voting paper; *(calificación)* report card, exam report; *(pregunta)* exam question *or* theme (drawn from a hat immediately before the exam); FIG., COLL. *(asunto complicado)* difficult matter, tough job <*menuda p. te ha tocado* that's a tough job you're stuck with>; GUAT. calling card, visiting card ♦ **p. de empeño** pawn ticket.

pa·pe·li·llo *or* **pa·pe·li·to** m. *(trozo)* slip of paper; *(cigarrillo)* cigarette; *(confeti)* confetti; *(paquete)* paper containing a dose of medicine; COL. rouge; P. RICO curl paper, end paper.

pa·pe·lón I. m. *(papel inútil)* piece of wastepaper; *(cartón)* pasteboard, poster board; *(cucurucho)* paper cone or bag; AMER. *(pan de azúcar)* sugar loaf; COL. *(plancha)* blunder, error ♦ **hacer un p.** to make oneself a laughing stock, make a fool of oneself II. adj. see **papelón, -lona.**

pa·pe·lón, -lo·na I. adj. pretentious, showy II. m.f. *(marrullero)* show-off, bluffer —m. see **papelón.**

pa·pe·lo·ne·ar intr. COLL. to boast, show off.

pa·pe·lo·rio *or* **pa·pe·lo·te** *or* **pa·pe·lu·cho** m. worthless scrap of paper.

pa·pe·ra f. MED. goiter ♦ **paperas** MED. mumps.

pa·pe·ro m. saucepan (for preparing baby food).

pa·pi m. COLL. daddy, pop.

pa·pi·la f. ANAT. papilla.

pa·pi·lar adj. ANAT. papillary.

pa·pi·lla f. *(gachas)* pap, soft food; FIG. *(astucia)* guile, deceit ♦ **dar p. a alguien** to deceive someone • **echar la primera p.** to be violently sick, be as sick as a dog • **estar hecho p.** *(estar cansado)* to be exhausted *or* beat; *(estar destrozado)* to be smashed to pieces, be a mess • **hacer p. a alguien** to make mincemeat of someone.

pa·pi·llo·te m. curl paper (for hair).

pa·pi·ro m. papyrus.

pá·pi·ro m. COLL. banknote ♦ **pápiros** COLL. dough, bread.

pa·pi·ro·ta·da f. *or* **pa·pi·ro·ta·zo** m. *(capirote)* flick (of the finger), fillip; AMER. stupid thing, nonsense.

pa·pi·ro·te m. *(capirote)* flick (of the finger), fillip; FIG., COLL. fool, nincompoop.

pa·pis·mo m. papistry, popery.

pa·pis·ta adj. & m.f. papist.

pa·po m. ZOOL. dewlap; ANAT. double chin; MED. goiter.

Pa·pua Nue·va Gui·ne·a f. Papua New Guinea.

pa·que·bo·te m. packet boat, packet.

pa·que·te I. m. *(bulto)* package, parcel; *(caja)* pack, packet <*un p. de cigarillos* a pack of cigarettes>; *(paquebote)* packet boat, packet; COLL. *(hombre)* dandy, fashion plate; *(mentira)* lie; *(conjunto)* parcel, pack <*un p. de niños* a pack of children>; *(lata)* pain, nuisance; *(pasajero)* passenger (in a motorcycle sidecar) II. adj. AMER. smart, elegant, chic.

pa·que·te·rí·a f. *(mercancía)* small goods; *(negocio)* small business, retail trade shop; ARG. affectation, overdressing.

pa·que·te·ro, -ra I. adj. wrapping, packaging II. m.f. *(que hace paquetes)* wrapper, packager; *(repartidor)* distributor of bundles of newspapers to street vendors; CARIB. liar, trickster —m. smuggler.

pa·qui·der·mo, -ma ZOOL. I. adj. pachydermal, pachydermous II. m. pachyderm.

Pa·quis·tán m. var. of **Pakistán.**

pa·quis·ta·ní adj. & m.f. var. of **pakistaní.**

par I. adj. *(igual)* equal; MATH. even; ZOOL. paired II. m. *(dos)* couple <*un p. de huevos* a couple of eggs>; pair <*un p. de pantalones* a pair of pants>; *(yunta)* pair, team (of oxen); *(dignidad)* peer; MATH. even number; ARCHIT. rafter; MECH., PHYS. couple; COM. par ♦ **al p.** *(igualmente)* on a par, equally; *(a un tiempo)* at the same time; COM. at par • **a pares** *or* **en pares** in pairs, by twos • **de p. en p.** wide <*abierto de p. en p.* wide open> • **p. de fuerzas** MECH. couple • **p. galvánico** *or* **voltáico** ELEC. galvanic *or* voltaic couple • **sin p.** without peer *or* equal —f. ♦ **a la p.** *(igualmente)* on a par, equally; *(a un tiempo)* at the same time; COM. at par • **pares** MED. placenta.

pa·ra §G46 prep. □ MOVEMENT TOWARDS towards <*voy p. el sur* I am going towards the south>; for <*salió p. Roma* he left for Rome> □ DESTINATION, PURPOSE for <*el correr es bueno p. la salud* running is good for the health>; for <*los zapatos son p. él* the shoes are for him>; in order to, to

<nos dimos prisa p. llegar a tiempo we hurried in order to arrive on time> □ TIME for, by *<lo terminaremos p. mañana* we will finish it by tomorrow>; about to, on the point of *<estoy p. salir* I am about to leave>; to *<son un cuarto p. las once* it's a quarter to eleven>; for *<vendrá p. mi cumpleaños* she'll come for my birthday> □ COMPARISON for, to *<p. ella el inglés es difícil* English is hard for her>; considering, for *<el castigo fue leve p. lo que hizo* his punishment was light considering what he did>; for *<p. la edad que tiene toca bien el violín* he plays the violin well for his age>* □ ON BEHALF OF for *<estoy pidiendo limosna p. los pobres* I am asking for money for the poor> □ USE [not translated] *<una taza p. café* a coffee cup> *<crema p. afeitar* shaving cream> *<loción p. las manos* hand lotion> □ IDIOMS ♦ **p. con** towards *<no puedo explicar su actitud p. con ustedes* I cannot explain his attitude towards you> • **p. concluir** in conclusion • **p. que** so that, in order that • **¿p. qué?** why *<¿p. qué has venido?* why have you come?>; for what *<¿p. qué sirve esa manija?* what is this handle for?>* • **p. siempre** forever.

pa·ra·bién m. congratulations ♦ **dar el p. a alguien** to congratulate someone.

pa·rá·bo·la f. *(cuento)* parable; GEOM. parabola.

pa·ra·bó·li·co, –ca adj. *(alegórico)* parabolical, allegorical; GEOM. parabolic.

pa·ra·bri·sas m. [pl. **-sas**] windshield, windscreen (G.B.).

pa·ra·ca f. AMER. strong breeze (from the Pacific).

pa·ra·ca·í·das f. [pl. **-das**] parachute.

pa·ra·cai·dis·mo m. parachute jumping, parachuting.

pa·ra·cai·dis·ta I. m.f. *(aficionado)* parachutist; MIL. paratrooper II. adj. parachute.

pa·ra·cho·ques m. [pl. **-ques**] AUTO. bumper, fender.

pa·ra·da I. f. *(acto)* stopping, stop; *(suspensión)* stop, halt; *<había una p. total de trabajo* there was a complete halt of work>; *(sitio)* stop *<p. de autobús* bus stop>; *(fin)* finish, end; *(acaballadero)* stud farm; *(corral)* pen (for cattle); *(tiro de relevo)* relay team (of horses); *(presa)* dam (in a river); *(apuesta)* bet; *(en esgrima)* parry (in fencing); MIL. parade; MUS. pause, break; SPORT. *(en fútbol)* save, stop; AMER. brag, boast ♦ **p. de taxis** taxi or cab stand • **p. en firme** or **en seco** dead stop II. adj. see **parado, –da.**

pa·ra·de·ro m. *(sitio)* whereabouts; *(destino)* destination; *(lugar donde se para)* stopping place; *(domicilio)* home, residence; FIG. *(término)* end *<seguramente tendrá mal p.* he'll surely come to a bad end>; AMER. *(de ferrocarril)* depot, whistle-stop; *(de autobuses)* bus stop ♦ **averiguar el p. de** to ascertain the whereabouts of, locate • **ignorar** or **no saber el p. de algo** or **alguien** not to know where something or someone is.

pa·ra·dig·ma m. paradigm, example.

pa·ra·di·sia·co, –ca or **pa·ra·di·sí·a·co, –ca** adj. paradisiacal, heavenly.

pa·ra·do, –da I. past part. see **parar** II. adj. *(inmóvil)* motionless, stationary; *(detenido)* stopped; *(inactivo)* inactive, idle; *(sin empleo)* unemployed; AMER. standing; CHILE, P. RICO proud, conceited ♦ **salir bien** or **mal p.** to come off well or badly III. m.f. unemployed person ♦ **los parados** the unemployed —f. see **parada.**

pa·ra·do·ja f. paradox.

pa·ra·dó·ji·co, –ca adj. paradoxical.

pa·ra·dor, –do·ra m.f. heavy bettor —m. *(albergue)* inn, roadhouse; *(hotel)* tourist hotel, state hotel.

pa·ra·fi·na f. paraffin.

pa·ra·fi·nar tr. to paraffin, treat with paraffin.

pa·ra·fis·cal adj. FIN. favoring the private sector (taxes).

pa·ra·fra·se·ar tr. to paraphrase.

pa·rá·fra·sis f. [pl. **-sis**] paraphrase.

pa·ra·guas m. [pl. **-guas**] umbrella.

Pa·ra·guay m. Paraguay.

pa·ra·gua·yo, –ya adj. & m.f. Paraguayan.

pa·ra·güe·rí·a f. umbrella shop.

pa·ra·güe·ro, –ra m.f. umbrella maker or seller —m. umbrella stand —f. AMER. umbrella stand.

pa·ra·í·so m. Paradise, Eden; FIG. paradise, heaven; THEAT. top balcony ♦ **p. terrenal** earthly paradise.

pa·ra·je m. *(lugar)* place, spot *<p. desconocido* unknown place>; *(región)* area, region; *(estado)* state, condition *<encontrarse en mal p.* to be in a bad state> ♦ **parajes** *(area)* parts; MARIT. waters.

pa·ra·la·je f. ASTRON. parallax.

pa·ra·le·la·men·te adv. parallel, in parallel.

pa·ra·le·las f.pl. SPORT. parallel bars.

pa·ra·le·lis·mo m. parallelism.

pa·ra·le·lo, –la I. adj. parallel II. m. GEOG. parallel *<el p. treinta y tres* the thirty-third parallel>; *(comparación)* parallel, comparision —f. *(línea)* parallel line; MIL. trench, parallel ♦ **correr p.** to run parallel to • **establecer un p.** to draw a parallel between, compare.

pa·ra·le·lo·gra·mo m. GEOM. parallelogram.

pa·ra·li·cé, paralice see **paralizar.**

pa·rá·li·sis f. [pl. **-sis**] paralysis ♦ **p. cerebral** cerebral palsy • **p. infantil** infantile paralysis, poliomyelitis.

pa·ra·lí·ti·co, –ca adj. & m.f. paralytic.

pa·ra·li·za·ción f. FIG. *(parálisis)* immobilization, paralyzation; COM. *(estancamiento)* stagnation.

pa·ra·li·za·dor, –do·ra or **pa·ra·li·zan·te** adj. paralyzing.

pa·ra·li·zar §04 tr. *(causar parálisis)* to paralyze; FIG. *(estorbar)* to impede, stop —reflex. to become paralyzed.

pa·ra·mé·di·co, –ca adj. paramedical.

pa·ra·men·to m. *(adorno)* ornamental covering; *(gualdrapas)* caparison; ARCHIT. face, surface (of a wall) ♦ **paramentos sacerdotales** RELIG. *(vestiduras)* clerical vestments or robes; *(de altar)* altar hangings.

pa·ra·me·ra f. barren region, wasteland.

pa·rá·me·tro m. GEOM. parameter.

pa·ra·mi·li·tar adj. paramilitary.

pá·ra·mo m. *(terreno desierto)* high barren plain; FIG. *(lugar desamparado)* bleak windswept region; COL., ECUAD. drizzle.

pa·ran·gón m. comparison, parallel ♦ **sin p.** matchless, incomparable.

pa·ran·go·nar tr. *(comparar)* to compare, establish a parallel between (two things); PRINT. to align, justify (type).

pa·ra·nin·fo m. *(padrino de bodas)* best man (at a wedding); *(aula)* assembly hall (of a university).

pa·ra·noi·a f. PSYCH. paranoia.

pa·ra·noi·co, –ca I. adj. paranoid, paranoiac II. m.f. paranoiac.

pa·ra·pe·tar·se reflex. MIL. to defend oneself with parapets; FIG. *(protegerse)* to protect oneself, take cover.

pa·ra·pe·to m. MIL. *(muralla)* parapet, rampart; ARCHIT. *(pretil)* parapet, railing.

pa·ra·ple·ji·a f. MED. paraplegia.

pa·ra·plé·ji·co, –ca adj. & m.f. paraplegic.

pa·ra·psi·co·lo·gí·a f. parapsychology.

pa·rar intr. *(cesar)* to stop, halt *<las actividades de la fábrica pararon* the operations of the factory stopped>; COLL. *(terminar)* to end up *<¿adónde vas a p. con esos preparativos?* where are you going to end up with all those preparations?>; *(alojarse)* to lodge, stay *<pararemos en el hotel más elegante* we will stay in the most elegant hotel>; *(recaer)* to end up, land *<la carta paró en manos de su hija* the letter ended up in the hands of his daughter> ♦ **ir a p.** to end up • **p. en** to end up, result in • **p. en seco** to stop dead • **sin p.** ceaselessly, nonstop • **venir a p.** to end up, result —tr. *(detener)* to stop, halt; *(impedir)* to detain, check; *(prevenir)* to prevent, forestall; *(apostar)* to bet, stake; *(fijar)* to fix, put *<p. mientes en* to fix one's attention on>; HUNT. to point; FENC. to parry, check ♦ **p. la oreja** AMER. to prick up one's ears • **p. los pies a alguien** FIG., COLL. to put someone in his place —reflex. *(detenerse)* to stop; AMER. to stand up; MEX. to get up (out of bed); CUBA, ECUAD., GUAT. to prosper, get rich ♦ **no pararse en barras** to stop at nothing • **pararse a** to stop, pause *<pararse a pensar* to stop to think> • **pararse en** to pay attention to.

pa·ra·rra·yo or **pa·ra·rra·yos** m. [pl. **-yos**] lightning rod or conductor.

pa·ra·si·ta·rio, –ria adj. parasitic, parasitical.

pa·ra·sí·ti·co, –ca adj. parasitic, parasitical.

pa·ra·si·tis·mo m. parasitism.

pa·rá·si·to, –ta I. adj. parasitic, parasitical II. m. BIOL. parasite; FIG. *(persona)* parasite ♦ **parásitos** RAD. interference, static.

pa·ra·si·to·lo·gí·a f. MED. parasitology.

pa·ra·sol m. parasol, sunshade.
pa·ra·ti·foi·de·a f. MED. paratyphoid.
pa·ra·ti·roi·des ANAT. I. adj. parathyroid II. f.pl. parathyroids.
par·ce·la f. *(porción de tierra)* plot, parcel (of land); *(átomo)* particle.
par·ce·la·ble adj. divisible into plots.
par·ce·la·ción f. division into plots, parceling (of land).
par·ce·lar tr. to divide into plots, parcel (land).
par·ce·la·rio, –ria adj. divided into plots *or* parcels.
par·cial I. adj. *(parte de un todo)* part, partial *<pago p.* partial payment>; *(incompleto)* partial, incomplete *<eclipse p.* partial eclipse>; *(injusto)* biased, partial; *(partidario)* partisan II. m. *(partidario)* partisan, follower; *(examen)* periodic exam (given in schools) ♦ **a tiempo p.** part-time.
par·cia·li·dad f. *(prejuicio)* partiality, bias; *(facción)* clique, faction; *(familiaridad)* partiality, special fondness *or* liking.
par·cial·men·te adv. *(en parte)* partially, partly; *(con prejuicio)* partially, one-sidedly.
par·cí·si·mo, –ma adj. *(muy corto)* very sparing; *(muy frugal)* very frugal *or* economical; *(muy moderado)* very moderate; *(muy escaso)* very scanty.
par·co, –ca adj. *(corto)* sparing *<parco en el hablar* sparing in words>; *(frugal)* frugal, economical (in habits); *(moderado)* moderate; *(escaso)* scanty, small (meal); *(mezquino)* mean, small.
par·char tr. ARG., CHIL., MEX. to mend, patch.
par·che m. *(emplasto)* plaster; *(remiendo)* patch; *(piel de tambor)* drumhead; *(tambor)* drum; FIG. *(cosa sobrepuesta)* patch; *(en la pintura)* daub, splotch (of paint) ♦ **pegar un p. a alguien** FIG. to put one over someone.
par·de·ar intr. to look brown *or* gray.
par·de·jón, –jo·na adj. AMER. brownish.
¡par·diez! interj. COLL. good God!, by Jove!
par·do, –da I. adj. *(moreno)* brown *<oso pardo* brown bear>; *(oscuro)* dark, gray (weather); *(apagado)* flat, toneless (voice) II. m.f. AMER. mulatto.
par·dus·co, –ca adj. brownish.
pa·re·ar tr. *(igualar)* to match, pair; *(juntar)* to mate, pair (animals); *(formar pares)* to pair, put in pairs; TAUR. to stick the banderillas in (a bull).
pa·re·cer¹ m. *(opinión)* opinion, view *<a mi p.* in my opinion>; *(aspecto)* appearance, looks ♦ **al p.** apparently, to all appearances • **arrimarse al p. de alguien** to agree with someone's way of thinking, adopt someone's views • **cambiar** *or* **mudar de p.** to change one's mind *or* opinion • **de buen p.** good-looking, nice-looking • **de mal p.** ugly, plain • **p. de peritos** expert opinion • **por el buen p.** to keep up appearances, for form's sake • **ser del p. que** to be of the opinion that • **tomar p. de alguien** to ask for someone's opinion, consult with someone.
pa·re·cer² §17 intr. *(opinar)* to seem *<me parece que no puedes hacerlo* it seems to me that you cannot do it>; *(querer)* to like *<si te parece, saldremos inmediatamente* if you like, we will leave immediately>; *(semejarse)* to resemble, seem like *<esa tela parece lana* that cloth resembles wool>; *(tener cierto aspecto)* to look, appear *<me parece bellísimo el cuadro* the painting looks very beautiful to me>; *(aparecer)* to appear, show up *<el libro no ha parecido todavía* the book has not shown up yet> ♦ **a lo que parece** *or* **al p.** to all appearances, apparently • **así parece** so it seems • **p. mentira** to seem incredible, be hard to believe *<aunque parezca mentira, aprobé el examen* even though it seems incredible, I passed the exam> • **por el bien p.** for appearances' sake —reflex. to resemble one another, look alike *<los niños se parecen mucho* the children look a lot alike> ♦ **parecerse a** to resemble, look like *<se parece a su madre* she resembles her mother>.
pa·re·ci·do, –da I. past part. see **parecer** II. adj. similar, of a certain appearance ♦ **bien p.** good-looking • **mal p.** ugly • **ser p. a** to resemble, be like *<es p. al padre* he resembles his father> III. m. similarity, resemblance.
pa·red f. wall ♦ **darse uno contra la p.** FIG. to knock one's head against the wall • **p. cortina** room divider, partition • **p. maestra** ARCH. main *or* bearing wall • **p. mediana** party wall • **p. por medio** next door • **subirse por las paredes** FIG. to hit the ceiling *or* roof.

pa·re·dón m. large thick wall ♦ **¡al p.!** to the firing squad!
pa·re·ja I. f. *(par)* pair; *(hombre y mujer)* couple; *(dos compañeros)* pair, couple *<p. de amigos* pair of friends>; *(de baile)* dancing partner; *(de juego)* partner in card games; *(guardias)* pair of Civil Guards (in Spain) ♦ **correr parejas** to be on a par, go together • **doble p.** two pairs (poker) • **parejas** two pairs (dice, cards) • **por parejas** two by two, in pairs II. adj. see **parejo, –ja.**
pa·re·jo, –ja I. adj. *(igual)* alike, equal; *(regular)* even, smooth *<una costura p.* an even seam>; *(llano)* flat, level ♦ **ir parejos** to be equal • **por p.** *or* **por un p.** on equal terms, on a par • **van parejos** they're going neck and neck (racehorses) II. m. C. AMER. dancing partner —f. see **pareja** III. adv. S. AMER. *(por igual)* at the same time, together; VEN. *(con frecuencia)* often.
pa·re·ju·ra f. *(semejanza)* similarity, equality; *(igualdad)* evenness.
pa·ren·te·la f. relations, relatives.
pa·ren·tes·co m. *(vínculo consanguíneo)* relationship, kinship; FIG. *(lazo)* tie, bond ♦ **p. espiritual** spiritual bond • **p. político** relationship by marriage.
pa·rén·te·sis m. [pl. **-sis**] *(frase)* parenthesis, parenthetical statement; GRAM. *(signo de puntuación)* parenthesis; FIG. *(suspensión)* break, interruption ♦ **abrir** *or* **cerrar el p.** to open *or* close a parenthetical phrase • **entre p.** in parentheses • **sea dicho entre p.** incidentally.
pa·re·o m. *(unión)* pairing off, matching; *(pájaros)* mating (of birds); *(taparrabos)* sarong.
pa·rez·ca, parezco see **parecer².**
pa·ria m.f. pariah, outcast.
pa·ri·ción f. parturition (of cattle).
pa·ri·da I. adj. who *or* which has recently given birth II. f. woman who has recently given birth.
pa·ri·dad f. *(igualdad)* equality, parity; *(comparación)* comparison, parallel.
pa·ri·de·ra I. adj. prolific, fertile II. f. *(sitio)* parturition place (of cattle); *(acción)* parturition.
pa·rien·te, –ta m.f. relative, relation ♦ **p. consanguíneo** blood relation • **p. político** relative by marriage.
pa·rie·tal I. adj. parietal II. m. ANAT. parietal bone.
pa·ri·gual adj. very similar, very much alike.
pa·ri·hue·las f.pl. stretcher, litter.
pa·rir intr. *(dar a luz)* to give birth; *(aovar)* to lay eggs; FIG. *(salir a luz)* to come to light, become known —tr. *(dar a luz)* to bear, give birth to; FIG. *(causar)* to produce, cause.
Pa·rís m. Paris.
pa·ri·sién *or* **pa·ri·sien·se** *or* **pa·ri·si·no, –na** adj. & m.f. Parisian.
pa·ri·ta·rio, –ria adj. joint *<comisión p.* joint committee>.
par·la·dor, –do·ra I. adj. talkative II. m.f. chatterbox.
par·la·men·tar intr. *(conversar)* to converse, chat; *(conferir)* to parley, confer.
par·la·men·ta·rio, –ria I. adj. parliamentary II. m.f. *(militar)* negotiator; *(diputado)* congressman, member of parliament.
par·la·men·ta·ris·mo m. *(doctrina)* parliamentarianism; *(gobierno)* parliamentary government.
par·la·men·ta·ris·ta adj. & m.f. var. of **parlamentario, –ria.**
par·la·men·to m. *(asamblea)* parliament; *(negociación)* parley, negotiation; *(discurso)* speech, address; *(charla)* chatter; THEAT. long speech.
par·lan·chín, –chi·na I. adj. talkative, chattering II. m.f. chatterbox.
par·lan·te adj. speaking, talking.
par·lar intr. *(hablar)* to talk, speak; *(parlotear)* to chatter, prattle.
par·le·ro, –ra adj. *(locuaz)* talkative, garrulous; *(chismoso)* gossipy; *(que canta)* singing (bird); FIG. *(expresivo)* expressive (eyes); *(ruidoso)* babbling (brook).
par·lo·te·ar intr. COLL. to chatter, prattle.
par·lo·te·o m. COLL. chatter, prattle.
par·na·sia·no, –na adj. & m.f. LIT. Parnassian.
par·na·so m. FIG. *(poetas)* assemblage of poets; *(poesías)* anthology, collection of poems ♦ **Parnaso** MYTH. Mount Parnassus.
pa·ro m. *(suspensión)* stoppage, standstill; *(desempleo)* unemployment; ORNITH. titmouse ♦ **p. estacional** seasonal

unemployment • **p. forzoso** layoff • **p. laboral** strike • **subsidio de p.** unemployment compensation *or* benefits.

pa·ro·dia f. parody.

pa·ro·diar tr. to parody.

pa·ró·di·co, -ca adj. parodical.

pa·ro·dis·ta m.f. parodist.

pa·ro·la f. COLL. *(verbosidad)* loquacity, gift of gab; COLL. *(charla)* long chat —m. CHILE braggart, boaster.

pa·ró·ni·mo, -ma I. adj. paronymous II. m. paronym.

pa·ro·no·ma·sia f. *(semejanza)* paronymy; *(juego de palabras)* paronomasia, play on words.

pa·ro·xis·mo m. MED. paroxysm; FIG. *(exaltación)* paroxysm, exaltation (of feelings).

par·pa·de·ar intr. *(mover los párpados)* to blink, wink; *(temblar)* to flicker, blink (light); *(centellear)* to twinkle, wink (stars).

par·pa·de·o m. *(ojos)* blink, blinking; *(luz)* flicker, blinking; *(stars)* twinkle, twinkling.

pár·pa·do m. eyelid.

par·que m. *(jardín)* park, gardens; *(estacionamiento)* parking lot, car park; MIL. storage depot, park ♦ **p. de atracciones** amusement park, fairground • **p. de bomberos** fire station • **p. nacional** national park • **p. zoológico** ZOO, zoological gardens.

par·qué m. parquet.

par·que·ar tr. AMER. to park (a car).

par·que·o m. AMER. *(acción)* parking; *(lugar)* parking lot.

par·que·dad f. *(prudencia)* frugality, economy; *(templanza)* moderation, temperance; *(escasez)* scantiness, paucity.

par·quí·me·tro m. parking meter.

pa·rra f. *(vid)* grapevine ♦ **hoja de p.** fig leaf (on statues) • **subirse a la p.** COLL. to blow one's stack, hit the ceiling.

pa·rra·fa·da f. COLL. *(charla)* chat, private talk; *(perorata)* speech.

pa·rra·fe·ar intr. COLL. to chat, have a private chat.

pa·rra·fe·o m. COLL. private chat, intimate talk.

pá·rra·fo m. paragraph ♦ **echar un p.** COLL. to have a chat • **hacer p. aparte** to start a new paragraph • **p. aparte** to change the subject.

pa·rral m. *(parra con armazón)* vine arbor; *(viña sin podar)* untrimmed vineyard; *(lugar)* vineyard.

pa·rran·da f. COLL. *(jarana)* party, spree; *(músicos)* band of musicians *or* singers ♦ **andar** *or* **estar de p.** to be out for a good time, be out partying • **irse de p.** to go out partying, go out for a good time.

pa·rran·de·ar intr. COLL. to go out partying.

pa·rran·de·o m. COLL. party, spree.

pa·rran·dis·ta m.f. COLL. reveler, carouser.

pa·rrar intr. to spread out, branch (trees).

pa·rri·ci·da m.f. parricide (person).

pa·rri·ci·dio m. parricide (act).

pa·rri·lla¹ f. earthenware jug.

pa·rri·lla² f. CUL. grill; *(rejilla)* grate, grating (of a furnace); *(sala de fiestas)* party room where food is served.

pa·rri·lla·da f. CUL. dish of grilled fish *or* seafood; ARG. dish of grilled meats.

pá·rro·co I. m. parish priest II. adj. parish *<cura p.* parish priest>.

pa·rro·quia f. *(territorio)* parish; *(habitantes)* parishioners; *(iglesia)* parish church; *(clientela)* customers, clientele.

pa·rro·quial adj. parochial, parish.

pa·rro·quia·no, -na I. adj. parochial, parish II. m.f. *(feligrés)* parishioner; *(cliente)* regular customer, client.

par·si·mo·nia f. *(economía)* frugality, parsimony; *(templanza)* temperance, moderation; *(calma)* deliberateness, calm.

par·si·mo·nio·so, -sa adj. *(sobrio)* frugal, parsimonious; *(tranquilo)* deliberate, unhurried.

par·te f. *(porción)* part, portion; *(cantidad asignada)* part, share *<hizo su p. del trabajo* he did his share of the work>; *(sitio)* place, spot; *(lado)* side; *(facción)* side, faction; COM., LAW party; LIT. part, volume; THEAT. part, role; MUS. part ♦ **a esta p.** ago, past *<de un mes a esta p.* a month ago> • **a partes iguales** in equal shares • **cargar a una p.** to go in one direction, lean to one side • **de mi p.** as far as I'm concerned • **de p. a p.** through and through • **de p. de** *(a nombre de)* in the name of, on behalf of; *(en favor de)* on the side of; *(por orden de)* at the command of

• **¿de p. de quién?** who's calling? • **en alguna p.** somewhere • **en cualquier p.** anywhere • **en gran p.** for the most part • **en ninguna p.** nowhere • **en p.** in part, partly • **en salva sea la p.** COLL. where it hurts most • **en todas partes** everywhere • **hacer su p.** to do one's share • **la mayor p.** the majority • **llevar la mejor p.** to have the upper hand • **no ser p. de** to have nothing to do with • **p. actora** LAW plaintiff • **p. alícuota** MATH. aliquot part • **p. de la oración** GRAM. part of speech • **p. del mundo** continent • **p. por p.** bit by bit • **partes** *(facción)* faction, party; ANAT. genitals • **partes contratantes** LAW contracting parts • **partes pudendas** *or* **vergonzosas** ANAT. private parts • **poner de su p.** to do what one can • **ponerse de p. de** to side with • **por la mayor p.** for the most part • **por mi p.** as far as I am concerned • **por otra p.** on the other hand • **por partes** step by step, systematically • **por todas partes** everywhere • **tener** *or* **tomar p. en** to take part in, participate in • **tomar a mala p.** FIG. to misinterpret, take the wrong way —m. *(escrito)* note; *(despacho)* dispatch, message; *(informe)* report ♦ **dar p.** to report • **dar p. a** to notify, inform • **p. meteorológico** weather report.

par·te·no·gé·ne·sis f. BIOL. parthenogenesis.

Par·te·nón m. Parthenon.

par·te·ra f. midwife.

par·te·ro m. male midwife.

par·ti·ción f. *(reparto)* division, partition (of estate, inheritance); MATH. division.

par·ti·ci·pa·ción f. *(parte)* participation *<p. en un crimen* participation in a crime>; *(contribución)* contribution; *(aviso)* notice *<dar p. de sus propósitos* to give notice of one's intentions>; *(recibo)* part of a lottery ticket; COM. *(acción)* share, interest (in a company); *(inversión)* investment ♦ **p. de boda** wedding invitation • **p. en los beneficios** *or* **en las utilidades** profit sharing.

par·ti·ci·pan·te I. adj. participating, sharing II. m.f. *(que toma parte)* participant, participator; *(que comunica)* informant, notifier; SPORT. entrant, competitor.

par·ti·ci·par tr. *(notificar)* to inform, notify *<le participo a usted mi decisión* I inform you of my decision>; *(proclamar)* to announce *<p. la buena noticia* to announce the good news> —intr. *(tomar parte)* to participate, take part; *(compartir)* to share (in) *<p. en una herencia* to share in an inheritance>; *(poseer acciones)* to have a share in, have an interest in (a company); *(invertir)* to invest.

par·tí·ci·pe I. adj. participating II. m.f. *(colaborador)* participant; *(interesado)* interested party.

par·ti·ci·pio m. GRAM. participle.

par·tí·cu·la f. GRAM., PHYS. particle ♦ **p. alpha** alpha particle • **p. beta** beta particle • **p. subatómica** subatomic particle • **p. V** V-particle.

par·ti·cu·lar I. adj. *(privado)* private *<casa p.* private house>; *(individual)* individual, personal; *(especial)* particular, special *<un talento p.* a special talent>* II. m.f. *(individuo)* individual, private person; *(asunto)* matter, point ♦ **en p.** *(especialmente)* in particular; *(en privado)* privately, in private • **nada de p.** nothing special.

par·ti·cu·la·ri·dad f. *(rasgo)* particularity, peculiarity; *(amistad)* friendship, intimacy.

par·ti·cu·la·ri·zar §04 tr. *(especificar)* to specify, particularize; *(detallar)* to detail, itemize; *(preferir)* to show special favor *or* attention to —reflex. *(distinguirse)* to distinguish oneself, stand out; *(destacarse)* to stand out, be distinguishable *<se particulariza por su hechura* it stands out because of its workmanship>.

par·ti·cu·lar·men·te adv. particularly, in particular.

par·ti·da I. f. *(salida)* departure; *(asiento)* certificate *<p. de bautismo* baptismal certificate>; *(expedición)* party *<p. de caza* hunting party>; *(bando)* band, gang; *(mano de juego)* hand, round; *(apuesta)* wager, bet; FIG. *(muerte)* death; *(proceder)* turn, deed *<una p. serrana* a bad turn>; COM. *(artículo)* entry, item; *(porción)* lot, batch; MIL. detail, squad ♦ **p. de campo** picnic, excursion • **p. de defunción** death certificate ♦ **p. de matrimonio** marriage certificate • **p. de nacimiento** birth certificate • **p. doble** COM. double entry • **p. simple** COM. single entry II. adj. see **partido, -da.**

par·ti·da·rio, -ria I. adj. supporting, partisan II. m.f. *(se-*

guidor) supporter, partisan; AMER. sharecropper —m. *(guerrillero)* guerrilla fighter.

par·ti·dis·mo m. partisanship.

par·ti·dis·ta I. adj. party, partisan *<política p.* party politics>* II. m.f. partisan.

par·ti·do, –da I. past part. see **partir** II. adj. divided; BOT., ENTOM., HER. partite; FIG. *(compartido)* generous, liberal III. m. *(bando)* (political) party, faction; *(amparo)* backing, support; *(convenio)* treaty, pact; *(provecho)* profit, advantage; *(distrito)* district; SPORT. *(competición)* game, match; *(equipo)* team; *(ventaja)* handicap; AMER. *(finca)* small farm; *(crencha)* part (in the hair) ♦ **buen p.** good match (in marriage) • **mal p.** bad match (in marriage) • **sacar p. de** to benefit from • **tomar p.** *(decidir)* to decide; *(ponerse de parte)* to take sides —f. see **partida**.

par·ti·dor m. *(repartidor)* distributor, splitter, cutter *<p. de leña* woodcutter>; *(instrumento)* cleaver, cracker *<p. de nueces* nutcracker>; *(peine)* comb (for parting the hair); MATH. divisor ♦ **p. de tensión** ELEC. voltage divider.

par·ti·du·ra f. part (in hair).

par·tir tr. *(dividir)* to divide, split; to crack *<p. nueces* to crack nuts>; *(romper)* to break, split open; *(repartir)* to share, split; *(acometer)* to attack; MATH. to divide —intr. *(salir)* to leave, depart; *(deducir)* to reckon, start; FIG. *(resolver)* to decide ♦ **a p. de** as of, starting from —reflex. *(marcharse)* to depart, set out; *(dividirse)* to split up, break ♦ **partirse de risa** to die laughing.

par·ti·ti·vo, –va adj. GRAM. partitive.

par·ti·tu·ra f. MUS. score.

par·to m. MED. childbirth, delivery; FIG. *(creación)* creation, brain child.

par·tu·rien·ta f. woman in labor.

par·va f. AGR. unthreshed grain; FIG. *(montón)* heap, pile.

par·va·da f. AGR. heap of unthreshed grain; *(multitud)* large amount, heaps; AMER. flock.

par·ve·dad f. *(pequeñez)* smallness, minuteness; *(corto alimento)* light breakfast (eaten on fast days).

pár·vu·lo, –la I. adj. *(pequeño)* small, little; *(inocente)* innocent, simple II. m.f. small child, tot.

pa·sa I. f. *(uva seca)* raisin; MARIT. channel (between shallows); *(juego)* pass ♦ **estar** or **quedarse hecho una p.** to become all dried up and wrinkled • **p. de Corinto** currant • **p. de Esmirna** sultana (raisin) II. adj. see **paso, –sa**.

pa·sa·ble adj. passable.

pa·sa·ca·lle m. MUS. passacaglia.

pa·sa·da I. f. *(acto)* passage, passing; SEW *(puntada)* stitch; C. AMER. reprimand; VEN. shame; CUBA lesson (learned from experience) ♦ **de p.** *(de paso)* on the way; *(ligeramente)* cursorily, in passing • **mala p.** dirty or mean trick II. adj. see **pasado, –da**.

pa·sa·de·ra f. *(piedra)* stepping stone; MARIT. furling line —m. & adj. see **pasadero, –ra**.

pa·sa·de·ro, –ra I. adj. *(aceptable)* bearable, tolerable; *(mediano)* passable, fair; *(bueno de salud)* fair, reasonably good (health) II. m. stepping stone —f. see **pasadera**.

pa·sa·di·zo m. *(pasillo)* passage, corridor; *(callejón)* alley.

pa·sa·do I. m. *(antigüedad)* past; GRAM. past, preterit; MIL. turncoat, deserter ♦ **lo p., p.** let bygones be bygones II. adj. see **pasado, –da**.

pa·sa·do, –da I. past part. see **pasar** II. adj. past, gone by *<en años pasados* in past years>; *(anterior)* last *<el mes p.* last month>; *(anticuado)* old-fashioned, out-of-date; GRAM. past, preterit; CUL. *(podrido)* rotten, spoiled; *(poco fresco)* stale; *(muy cocido)* overdone; *(huevo)* boiled (egg) ♦ **p. de moda** old-fashioned • **p. la una** after one (o'clock) • **p. mañana** day after tomorrow III. m. see **pasado**.

pa·sa·dor, –do·ra I. adj. passing II. m.f. *(contrabandista)* smuggler —m. *(barra)* bolt *<p. de ventana* window bolt>; *(chaveta)* cotter (pin); *(de pelo)* hairpin; *(de corbata)* tie pin or clip; *(imperdible)* safety pin; *(coladero)* colander, strainer; MARIT. marlinespike ♦ **pasadores** cuff links.

pa·sa·je m. *(acto)* passage; *(derecho)* passage (right to travel); *(vía)* way, route *<el p. a China es bien difícil* the way to China is very difficult>; *(precio)* fare, passage *<¿has pagado el p. a India?* have you paid the fare to India?>; *(pasajeros)* passengers (as a group); LIT., MUS. *(trozo)* passage; *(paso público)* passageway; MUS. *(modula-*

ción) modulation (of key); *(estrecho)* strait, narrow (between two islands); AMER. ticket.

pa·sa·je·ro, –ra I. adj. *(frecuentado)* busy, frequented *<una calle p.* a busy street>; *(transitorio)* passing, fleeting *<sólo sintió una tristeza p.* he only felt a passing sadness>; *(viajero)* traveling ♦ **ave p.** ORNITH. migratory bird II. m.f. passenger, traveler.

pa·sa·ma·no m. *(barandal)* handrail (of banister); MARIT. gangway.

pa·sa·mon·ta·ñas m.pl. balaclava (hat).

pa·san·te I. adj. *(que pasa)* passing; HER. passant II. m.f. *(ayudante)* assistant (of a professional); *(maestro)* tutor, coach; *(empleado)* clerk.

pa·san·tí·a f. *(función de pasante)* assistantship; *(tiempo que dura)* probationary period, apprenticeship.

pa·sa·pa·sa m. sleight of hand, hocus-pocus.

pa·sa·por·tar tr. *(expedir pasaporte)* to issue a passport, provide with a passport; COLL. *(despachar)* to rush off *<p. un trabajo* to rush off a job>; *(mandar)* to pack off *<pasaportó a su hija al campo* he packed off his daughter to the country>; *(acabar)* to deal with, dispatch.

pa·sa·por·te m. *(pase)* passport *<p. mexicano* Mexican passport>; MIL. furlough (document); FIG. *(permiso)* carte blanche, free hand ♦ **dar p. a alguien** to give someone his walking papers.

pa·sa·por·te·ar tr. AMER. to issue a passport, provide with a passport.

pa·sar tr. *(transmitir)* to pass, hand *<pásame la mantequilla, por favor* pass me the butter, please>; *(conducir)* to take or carry across *<p. a los turistas en una barca* to take the tourists across in a ferrry>; *(atravesar)* to cross, go across *<pasaron el río* they crossed the river>; *(ir más allá)* to pass, go beyond *<pasar los límites* to go beyond the limits>; *(enviar)* to send, transmit *<me pasaron un recado* they sent me a message>; *(contrabandear)* to smuggle, slip in *<p. el tabaco* to smuggle tobacco>; *(poner en circulación)* to pass, circulate *<p. un billete falso* to circulate a counterfeit bill>; *(transferir)* to transfer *<le pasarán la tienda* they will transfer the store to him>; MED. to give, pass *<me pasaste el resfriado* you gave me your cold>; *(introducir)* to pass, insert *<pasé el papel por la ranura* I inserted the paper through the slot>; *(tragar)* to swallow; *(colar)* to filter, strain; *(cerner)* to sift; to spend, pass *<pasamos el verano en la playa* we spent the summer at the beach>; *(tolerar)* to tolerate, bear; *(sufrir)* to suffer, undergo *<hemos pasado muchas desgracias* we have undergone many misfortunes>; *(perdonar)* to overlook, pass over *<p. muchas faltas* to overlook many faults>; *(desecar)* to dry in the sun; EDUC. *(aprobar)* to pass *<p. un examen* to pass a test>; *(estudiar)* to study as an assistant; *(enseñar)* to tutor; *(leer)* to read over ♦ **p. de largo** to skim through • **p. en blanco** to omit, leave out • **p. en limpio** to make a clear copy • **p. la noche en blanco** to spend a sleepless night • **p. las de Caín** FIG. to go through hell • **p. lista** to call roll • **pasarlo** to manage, get along • **pasarlo** or **pasarla bien** to have a good time • **pasarlo** or **pasarla mal** to have a bad time • **p. por agua** to soft-boil • **p. por alguien** to pick someone up • **p. por las armas** to shoot, execute • **p. por alto** to omit, leave out —intr. *(moverse)* to pass, go by *<pasé por la biblioteca* I passed by the library>; *(transcurrir)* to go by *<los años pasan* the years go by>; *(entrar)* to come in *<pase usted, por favor* come in, please>; *(ocurrir)* to happen, occur *<¿qué pasó?* what happened?>; *(subsistir)* to get along, get by *<ellos la van pasando con muy poco* they are getting by with very little>; *(durar)* to last, do *<mi abrigo puede p. otro invierno* my overcoat can last another winter>; *(cesar)* to pass, be over *<su cólera pasó* his anger passed>; *(conceder)* to yield, pass *<paso en este asunto* I pass on the matter>; *(morir)* to pass away; *(transferirse)* to pass, be handed down *<los joyas pasan de generación a generación* the jewelry is handed down from generation to generation>; *(extenderse)* to spread; *(ser admitido)* to pass *<los billetes falsos no pasaron* the counterfeit bills did not pass>; *(en el juego)* to pass (in cards) ♦ **hacerse p. por** to pass oneself off as • **p. a** to proceed to • **p. a mejor vida** FIG. to go on to the great beyond • **p. a ser** to become • **p. de** *(exceder)* to exceed, surpass; to be over *<mi tío pasa ya de los ochenta*

my uncle is over eighty years old> • **p. de moda** to go out of fashion • **p. por** *(tener opinión de)* to be considered to be <*pasa por perito en la materia* he is considered to be an expert in the field>; *(detenerse)* to stop by; *(padecer)* to go through, undergo • **p. por encima** FIG. to go over someone's head • **p. sin** to do or go without —reflex. *(moverse)* to pass, go; *(cambiar de partido)* to go over <*el teniente se pasó al enemigo* the lieutenant went over to the enemy>; *(olvidarse)* to forget, slip one's mind <*se me pasó traer el libro* I forgot to bring the book>; *(acabarse)* to pass, be over; *(deslizar)* to pass, run <*se pasó la mano por la frente* she ran her hand across her brow>; *(excederse)* to overdo, go too far; *(filtrarse)* to leak, be porous; CUL. *(echarse a perder)* to go bad; *(estar muy cocido)* to be overcooked; EDUC. to take a test ♦ **pasarse de** to be excessively, be too • **pasarse de la raya** or **pásarsele la mano** to go too far • **pasarse la gran vida** to live it up • **parsarse sin** to go or do without.

pa·sa·re·la f. *(puentecillo)* footbridge; MARIT. gangway, gangplank; THEAT. catwalk.

pa·sa·tiem·po m. pastime, amusement.

pas·ca·na f. S. AMER. *(mesón)* inn, tavern; *(parada)* stop, stage (of a journey).

pas·cua RELIG. *(de la resurrección)* Easter; *(Navidad)* Christmas; *(Epifanía)* Epiphany; *(Pentecostés)* Pentecost; *(fiesta judía)* Passover ♦ **dar las pascuas** to wish (someone) a Merry Christmas • **de Pascuas a Ramos** FIG. once in a blue moon • **estar como unas pascuas** FIG., COLL. to be pleased as Punch, be happy as a lark • **hacer la p.** SL. to mess things up (for someone) • **Pascua florida** RELIG. Easter • **pascuas** RELIG. Christmastide • **santas pascuas** COLL. that's it, that's all there is to it.

pas·cual adj. paschal.

pa·se m. *(permiso)* pass, permit; *(entrada)* pass, free ticket; *(tanda)* showing (of a film); *(finta)* feint (in fencing); SPORT., TAUR. pass; *(pasapasa)* pass (in magic trick); AMER. *(pasaporte)* passport.

pa·se·a·dor, –do·ra I. adj. fond of walking or strolling II. m.f. stroller, promenader.

pa·se·an·te I. adj. strolling II. m.f. stroller, passer-by ♦ **p. en corte** FIG., COLL. idler, loafer.

pa·se·ar intr. *(andar)* to walk, go for a walk; *(a caballo)* to ride (on a horse); *(en coche)* to go for a ride or drive (in a car) ♦ **p. en bicicleta** to bicycle, ride a bicycle • **p. en barco** to boat, travel by boat • **p. en canoa** to canoe —tr. *(hacer andar)* to take for a walk <*paseó a su hija por la calle* he took his daughter for a walk on the street>; FIG. *(exhibir)* to parade, show off —reflex. *(andar)* to walk, go for a walk; *(a caballo)* to ride (on a horse); *(en coche)* to go for a ride or drive (in a car); *(estar ocioso)* to idle, loaf; C. AMER. to become spoiled or ruined.

pa·se·í·llo m. TAUR. opening parade (of bullfighters around the ring).

pa·se·o m. *(caminata)* walk, stroll <*un p. por el bosque* a walk in the park>; *(a caballo)* ride (on a horse); *(en coche)* drive, ride (in a car); *(excursión)* outing, trip; *(paseadero)* walk, promenade; *(avenida)* avenue, street; *(distancia)* short walk <*sólo es un p. al teatro* it's only a short walk to the theater>; *(figura de baile)* figure (in some dances); C. AMER. costumed parade; TAUR. parade (of toreadors before the bullfight) • **dar el p.** COLL. to bump (someone) off, kill • **dar un p.** *(andar)* to walk, go for a walk; *(a caballo)* to ride (on a horse); *(en coche)* to go for a ride or drive (in a car) • **echar** or **mandar a p.** FIG. to send (someone) packing • **ir de p.** *(andar)* to walk, go for a walk; *(viajar)* to go on a trip • **¡vete a p.!** FIG. take a walk, go jump in a lake.

pa·si·cor·to, –ta adj. taking short steps or strides.

pa·si·llo m. *(corredor)* corridor, passage; SEW. *(puntada)* basting stitch; MARIT. gangway; *(paso teatral)* short play, skit; RELIG. reading of the Passion story; AMER. *(estera)* mat; COL. folkloric dance.

pa·sión f. *(emoción)* passion, strong emotion; *(fuerte inclinación)* passion <*tener p. por el arte moderno* to have a passion for modern art>; *(sufrimiento)* passion, suffering <*la p. de Jesucristo* the Passion of Christ> ♦ **tener p. por alguien** to have a passion for someone, be passionately fond of someone.

pa·sio·nal adj. passionate, emotional ♦ **crimen p.** crime of passion.

pa·sio·na·ria f. BOT. passion flower.

pa·si·to I. adv. softly, lightly II. m. short step.

pa·si·vi·dad f. passivity, passiveness.

pa·si·vo, –va I. adj. *(inactivo)* passive; GRAM. passive <*voz p.* passive voice> II. m. COM. liabilities ♦ **p. corriente** or **exigible** current liabilities • **p. eventual** or **contingente** contingent liabilities • **p. fijo** capital liabilities.

pas·ma·do, –da I. past part. see **pasmar** II. adj. COLL. *(atónito)* astounded, astonished; *(helado)* frozen.

pas·mar tr. *(enfriar)* to freeze, chill; FIG. *(dejar atónito)* to stun <*la escena del choque le pasmó* the scene of the accident stunned him>; *(asombrar)* to astound, amaze —reflex. *(enfriarse)* to freeze; MED. to get tetanus or lockjaw; *(descolorarse)* to fade, become dulled (said of colors); FIG. *(atontarse)* to be stunned; *(asombrarse)* to be astounded or amazed; AMER. to become sickly.

pas·ma·ro·ta f. COLL. exaggerated gesture of astonishment.

pas·ma·ro·te m. COLL. dope, fool.

pas·mo m. *(enfriamiento)* chill; MED. tetanus, lockjaw; FIG. *(asombro)* astonishment, amazement; *(maravilla)* wonder, marvel.

pas·mo·sa·men·te adv. astonishingly, amazingly.

pas·mo·so, –sa adj. FIG. astonishing, amazing.

pa·so I. m. step, pace <*dar un p. atrás* to take a step backwards>; *(manera de andar)* walk, gait; EQUIT. gait; *(distancia)* pace; *(acción de pasar)* passing, passage <*el p. del tiempo* the passage of time>; *(travesía)* crossing; *(camino)* passage, way; GEOG. pass; MARIT. strait; *(peldaño)* step, stair; *(huella)* footprint, track; *(pisada)* footstep, footfall <*siento pasos* I hear footsteps>; *(en el baile)* step <*p. de vals* waltz step>; *(licencia)* passage, pass; *(lance)* event, episode; *(apuro)* jam, tight spot; FIG. *(diligencia)* step, measure <*dar los primeros pasos hacia la paz* to take the first steps towards peace>; *(adelanto)* progress; MECH. pitch; ORNITH. migration; SEW. *(puntada)* basting stitch; THEAT. sketch, skit; LIT. passage ♦ **abrir p. a** to make way for • **a buen p.** quickly, rapidly • **a cada p.** at every turn, frequently • **a dos pasos** at a short distance • **a ese p.** at that rate • **aflojar el p.** to slow down • **a grandes pasos** FIG. by leaps and bounds • **alargar** or **apretar el p.** to go faster, speed up • **al p.** in passing, on the way • **al p. que** *(al mismo tiempo)* while, at the same time; at the rate that <*al p. que vas, nunca vas a terminar* at the rate that you are going, you will never finish> • **a p. de carga** FIG. quickly, rashly; MIL. on the double • **a p. de tortuga** FIG. at a snail's pace • **a p. lento** slowly • **a. p. ligero** quickly, rapidly • **a p. llano** smoothly, without difficulty • **a pocos pasos** at a short distance • **ceder el p.** to step aside • **cerrar el p.** to block the way • **cortar el p.** to cut off, obstruct • **de p.** in passing • **llevar el p.** to keep pace, keep step • **mal p.** tight spot, fix • **marcar el p.** to keep time • **¡paso!** make way! • **p. a desnivel** underpass • **p. a dos** pas de deux • **p. a nivel** RAIL. grade crossing • **p. a p.** little by little • **p. de ambladura** EQUIT. amble • **p. de peatones** crosswalk • **p. doble** MUS. march step • **p. largo** stride • **p. libre** free access • **p. ligero** MIL. double time • **p. por p.** step by step • **por sus pasos contados** FIG. step by step, systematically • **salir del p.** to get out of a jam • **salirle al p.** *(salir al encuentro)* to intercept; *(oponer)* to oppose, confront • **seguirle los pasos a alguien** FIG. to keep an eye on, tail • **seguirle los pasos de alguien** FIG. to follow in someone's footsteps • **servidumbre de p.** LAW right of way • **volver sobre sus pasos** to retrace one's steps II. adv. softly, gently III. adj. see **paso, -sa**.

pa·so, –sa I. adj. dried (fruit) ♦ **ciruela pasa** prune • **uvas pasas** rasins II. m. see **paso** —f. see **pasa**.

pa·so·do·ble m. MUS. paso doble (march step).

pa·so·ta m.f. SP., COLL. social and cultural dropout.

pa·so·tis·mo m. SP., COLL. rejection of established social and cultural values.

pas·quín m. *(sátira)* pasquinade, lampoon; *(letrero)* poster, street advertisement; *(periódico)* rag, scandal sheet.

pas·qui·na·da f. pasquinade, lampoon.

pas·ta f. *(masa)* paste; *(para papeles)* binding; PAINT. *(empaste)* impasto; *(galleta)* cookie, biscuit (G.B.); *(de madera)* (wood) pulp; SL. *(dinero)* dough, bread ♦ **de buena**

p. good-natured • **p. de dientes** toothpaste • **pastas** noodles, pasta • **tener p. de** to have the makings of <*tiene p. de buen jugador* he has the makings of a good player>.
pas·ta·flo·ra f. CUL. fine puff pastry.
pas·ta·je m. ARG., COL., GUAT. pasture.
pas·tar tr. to take (cattle) to pasture —intr. to graze, pasture (cattle).
pas·te·ar tr. PERU to spy.
pas·tel m. CUL. cake, pie <*p. de espinacas* spinach pie>; PAINT. pastel (color, drawing, pencil); (*fullería*) cheating (at shuffling cards); FIG., COLL. (*convenio*) shady deal, scheme <*se le descubrió el p.* his little scheme was found out>; (*lío*) mess; BOT. dyer's weed; PRINT. pie, scrambling of type; COL., P. RICO, CUL. dumpling, turnover.
pas·te·le·ar intr. FIG., COLL. to play for time, stall.
pas·te·le·o m. FIG., COLL. playing for time, stalling.
pas·te·le·rí·a f. (*sitio*) pastry shop; (*oficio*) pastry-making.
pas·te·le·ro, –ra m.f. (*repostero*) pastry cook; (*vendedor*) person who sells pastries; FIG., COLL. (*contemporizador*) temporizer, compromiser.
pas·te·lis·ta m.f. pastel painter, pastelist.
pas·te·ri·zar §04 or **pas·teu·ri·zar** §04 tr. to pasteurize.
pas·te·ri·za·ción or **pas·teu·ri·za·ción** f. pasteurization.
pas·ti·che m. pastiche, imitation (of work of art).
pas·ti·lla f. (*dulce*) bar, square (of chocolate); (*de jabón*) bar, cake (of soap); (*tableta*) tablet; (*pasta medicinal*) lozenge, drop <*p. para la tos* cough drop>.
pas·ti·zal m. pasture, grazing land.
pas·to m. (*acto*) pasture, grazing; (*hierba*) pasture, grass; (*sitio*) pasture, grazing land; (*comida*) feed, fodder; FIG. (*alimento*) fuel, food <*la yesca fue p. del fuego* the tinder was food for the fire> • **a p.** abundantly, in abundance • **a todo p.** COLL. freely and excessively • **dar p.** FIG. to be food for, be cause for <*su boda venidera da p. a la murmuración* her upcoming wedding is food for gossip> • **de p.** everyday, everyday • **echar al p.** to put to pasture (cattle).
pas·tor, –to·ra m. (*ovejero*) shepherd, herdsman; (*prelado*) pastor, parish priest ♦ **El Buen Pastor** the Good Shepherd —f. shepherdess.
pas·to·ral I. adj. (*de pastores*) pastoral, of shepherds; (*campestre*) pastoral, rustic; RELIG. pastoral <*anillo p.* pastoral ring> II. f. MUS. pastorale; LIT., RELIG. pastoral.
pas·to·re·ar tr. (*pastar*) to take (cattle) to pasture; FIG. (*cuidar*) to minister to, lead; AMER. to lie in wait for; C. AMER. to spoil, pamper; ARG., URUG. to court, woo.
pas·to·re·o m. shepherding, tending flocks.
pas·to·ril adj. pastoral, of shepherds.
pas·to·si·dad f. (*blandura*) doughiness, pastiness; (*suavidad*) mellowness, richness (of voice); PAINT. pastosity.
pas·to·so, –sa adj. (*blando*) doughy, pasty; (*suave*) mellow, rich (voice); PAINT. impastoed, thickly painted; (*sarroso*) coated (tongue, mouth).
pas·tu·ra·je m.f. (*pasto*) pasture, fodder; (*campo*) pasture, grazing land; LAW grazing rights.
pa·su·do, –da adj. AMER. kinky (hair).
pa·ta I. f. ZOOL. (*pie*) paw, foot; (*pierna*) leg; COLL. (*pierna humana*) leg; (*base*) leg <*las patas de la mesa* the legs of the table>; SEW. (*carterilla*) pocket flap; (*empate*) tie, draw; ORNITH. female duck ♦ **a cuatro patas** on all fours • **a la p. coja** hopscotch • **a la p. la llana** plainly, simply • **andar a p. renca** or **coja** to limp, hobble • **a p.** on foot • **enseñar la p.** FIG. to show one's true colors • **estirar la p.** FIG., COLL. to kick the bucket • **meter la p.** COLL. to put one's foot in it, make a blunder • **p. de banco** COLL. silly remark • **p. de cabra** crowbar • **p. de gallo** BOT. crowfoot; FIG. (*arruga*) crow's-foot • **p. de palo** wooden leg • **patas arriba** (*boca arriba*) upside-down; (*en desorden*) topsy-turvy • **salir** or **ser p.** or **patas** to end in a draw or a tie • **tener mala p.** COLL. to be unlucky II. adj. see **pato, –ta.**
pa·ta·cón m. (*moneda*) patacoon, silver dollar; AMER., COLL. peso, buck; CHILE welt, bruise.
pa·ta·che m. MARIT. tender; ECUAD., PERU (*comida*) food (in general); (*sopa*) soup.
pa·ta·da f. (*puntapié*) kick, stamp; COLL. (*paso*) step; (*huella*) track, footprint ♦ **a patadas** COLL. in abundance, plenty • **dar la p. a alguien** COLL. to give someone the

boot • **darle a alguien una p.** to kick someone • **echar a alguien a patadas** to kick someone out.
pa·ta·grás adj. ♦ **queso p.** AMER. soft cheese.
pa·ta·le·ar intr. (*dar patadas*) to kick; (*pisar*) to stamp (one's feet).
pa·ta·le·o m. (*acción de dar patadas*) kicking; (*acción de pisar*) stamping; (*ruido*) stamping (noise) ♦ **derecho a p.** FIG., COLL. the right to protest.
pa·ta·le·ta f. COLL. tantrum, fit.
pa·tán m. COLL. (*rústico*) rustic, yokel; (*hombre soez*) lout, boor.
pa·ta·ne·rí·a f. COLL. uncouthness, boorishness.
¡pa·ta·plún! interj. var. of **cataplún.**
pa·tas·ca f. S. AMER., CUL. pork and corn stew; PERU quarrel, row.
pa·ta·ta f. BOT. potato ♦ **p. de caña** BOT. Jerusalem artichoke • **patatas fritas** French fries, chips (G.B.) • **p. temprana** new potato.
pa·ta·tal or **pa·ta·tar** m. AGR. potato field.
pa·ta·te·ro, –ra I. adj. potato II. m.f. (*vendedor*) potato seller; COLL. (*oficial*) officer who has risen from the ranks.
pa·ta·tín pa·ta·tán ♦ **que p.** COLL. this and that, and so on and so forth.
pa·ta·tús m. COLL. fainting spell, swoon.
pa·te·a·du·ra f. or **pa·te·a·mien·to** m. COLL. (*pataleo*) stamping, kicking; (*reprensión*) reprimand, scolding.
pa·te·ar tr. COLL. (*pisar*) to kick, stamp; FIG. (*insultar*) to be rude to, treat rudely; (*mostrar desaprobación*) to stamp the feet in disapproval, boo (audience) —intr. COLL. (*dar patadas*) to stamp one's feet <*p. de rabia* to stamp with rage>; AMER. (*ir y venir apresuradamente*) to rush about, chase all over the place (for something); (*cocear*) to kick (gun, horse).
pa·te·na f. RELIG. paten, plate; (*medalla*) medallion worn by peasant women ♦ **limpio como una p.** as neat as a pin, as clean as a whistle.
pa·ten·ta·do I. past part. see **patentar** II. adj. patented.
pa·ten·tar tr. to patent, register.
pa·ten·te I. adj. (*claro*) patent, obvious, clear; COM. patent ♦ **hacer p.** to show clearly, make evident • **letras patentes** LAW letters patent II. f. (*permiso*) grant, warrant; (*licencia*) licence <*p. de chofer* driver's license>; LAW (*de invención*) patent ♦ **p. básica** or **original** or **primitiva** LAW basic patent • **p. de corso** MARIT. letters of marque • **p. de navegación** MARIT. certificate of registration (of a ship) • **p. de sanidad** bill of health • **p. limpia** clean bill of health • **p. pendiente** LAW patent pending • **p. registrada** LAW registered patent.
pa·ten·ti·zar §04 tr. to make evident or patent.
pa·te·o m. COLL. stamping, kicking.
pa·ter·nal adj. paternal, fatherly.
pa·ter·na·lis·mo m. paternalism.
pa·ter·nal·men·te adv. paternally, in a fatherly way.
pa·ter·ni·dad f. (*calidad de padre*) paternity, fatherhood; FIG. (*creación*) authorship.
pa·ter·no, –na adj. paternal <*el abuelo p.* the paternal grandfather>.
pa·te·ro, –ra I. adj. CHILE fawning, flattering; PERU tricky, deceitful II. m. ARG. shed for barnyard fowl; CHILE flatterer; PERU cheat, deceiver.
pa·te·ta m. COLL. (*diablo*) the Devil; (*tullido*) cripple, lame person.
pa·té·ti·ca·men·te adv. pathetically.
pa·té·ti·co, –ca adj. pathetic, touching.
pa·te·tis·mo m. pathos.
pa·tia·bier·to, –ta adj. COLL. bowlegged, bandy-legged.
pa·ti·bu·la·rio, –ria adj. (*del cadalso*) pertaining to the gallows or execution; (*horroroso*) horrifying, harrowing <*rostro p.* horrifying expression>.
pa·tí·bu·lo m. scaffold, gallows.
pa·ti·co·jo, –ja COLL. I. adj. lame, limping II. m.f. cripple, lame person.
pa·ti·di·fu·so, –sa adj. COLL. amazed, dumbfounded.
pa·ti·lla f. (*gatillo*) trigger; MUS. certain position of the fingers (on guitar fret); (*charnela*) chape of a buckle); ARG., BOL. seat, bench ♦ **patillas** (*barba*) sideburns, sidewhiskers; (*rizo*) spitcurls • **Patillas** the Devil • **levantar a alguien de patillas** to get someone's goat, exasperate.

pa·ti·llu·do, –da adj. having long and heavy sideburns.
pa·tín m. *(aparato)* skate; *(hidropedal)* paddle boat; AVIA. skid (of airplane) ♦ **p. de freno** brake shoe • **p. de hielo** *or* **de cuchilla** ice skate • **p. de ruedas** roller skate.
pá·ti·na f. patina.
pa·ti·na·de·ro m. skating rink.
pa·ti·na·dor, –do·ra I. adj. skating II. m.f. skater.
pa·ti·na·je m. *(deporte)* skating; *(resbalo de coche)* skidding ♦ **p. artístico** figure skating • **p. de velocidad** speed skating • **p. sobre hielo** ice skating • **p. sobre ruedas** roller skating.
pa·ti·nar intr. *(deslizarse con patines)* to skate; *(resbalar un vehículo)* to skid (car); *(resbalar voluntariamente)* to slide; *(resbalar sin querer)* to slip; FIG. *(meter la pata)* to blunder, slip up —tr. to give a patina to, coat with a patina.
pa·ti·na·zo m. *(resbalo de coche)* skid (of a car); FIG., COLL. *(planchazo)* blunder, slip.
pa·ti·ne·ta f. *or* **pa·ti·ne·te** m. scooter (child's toy).
pa·ti·ne·jo *or* **pa·ti·ni·llo** m. small patio.
pa·tio m. *(espacio interior)* patio, courtyard; *(cuadrángulo)* quadrangle (of schools); COL., P. RICO *(corral)* yard ♦ **p. de butacas** THEAT. orchestra, parterre • **p. de escuela** *or* **recreo** playground, schoolyard • **p. de maniobras** RAIL. switching yard.
pa·ti·tie·so, –sa adj. *(con las piernas paralizadas)* stiff-legged; FIG., COLL. *(estirado)* stiff, stuck-up; *(aturdido)* paralyzed (with cold, fear) ♦ **dejar p.** to astound, dumbfound • **quedarse p.** to be flabbergasted *or* dumbfounded.
pa·ti·tuer·to, –ta adj. *(tullido)* crippled, crooked-legged; FIG., COLL. *(malhecho)* lopsided, crooked.
pa·ti·zam·bo, –ba I. adj. knock-kneed II. m.f. knock-kneed person.
pa·to I. m. ORNITH. *(ave)* duck; *(pato macho)* drake; AMER. *(bacineta)* bedpan; VULG. *(marica)* faggot, fairy; COLL. *(pelmazo)* bore, drip ♦ **estar hecho un p.** *or* **un p. de agua** to be soaked to the skin • **pagar el p.** COLL. to pay for it, take the rap • **p. flojel** eider duck • **p. real** *or* **silvestre** mallard, wild duck II. adj. see **pato, –ta.**
pa·to, –ta I. adj. ECUAD. *(incauto)* victimized; ARG., COL. *(mirón)* nosy, curious II. m.f. ARG., COL. *(mirón)* busybody, inquisitive person; ECUAD. *(víctima)* victim (of a swindle) ♦ **correr p.** AMER. to be the victim of a swindle *or* robbery —m. see **pato** —f. see **pata.**
pa·to·cha·da f. COLL. blunder, stupid remark.
pa·to·gé·ni·co, –ca adj. MED. pathogenic.
pa·tó·ge·no, –na I. adj. MED. pathogenic II. m. pathogen.
pa·to·je·ar intr. AMER. to waddle (while walking).
pa·to·jo, –ja I. adj. S. AMER. having deformed *or* crooked legs II. m.f. C. AMER. *(chiquillo)* kid, youngster; *(pillo)* street urchin, ragamuffin.
pa·to·lo·gí·a f. MED. pathology.
pa·to·ló·gi·co, –ca adj. MED. pathological.
pa·tó·lo·go, –ga m.f. MED. pathologist.
pa·tón, –to·na adj. COLL. big-footed.
pa·to·so, –sa adj. COLL. boring, dull.
pa·to·ta f. ARG., URUG., COLL. street gang.
pa·to·te·ro m. ARG., URUG., COLL. member of a street gang, young thug.
pa·tra·ña f. COLL. hoax, story.
pa·tra·ñe·ro, –ra I. adj. false II. m.f. fibber, trickster, storyteller.
pa·tra·que·ar tr. CHILE, COLL. to steal, pinch.
pa·tria I. f. homeland, native land ♦ **p. celestial** heaven • **madre p.** motherland • **p. chica** hometown, native region II. adj. see **patrio, –tria.**
pa·triar·ca m. patriarch.
pa·triar·ca·do m. *(dignidad)* patriarchate; *(sistema)* patriarchy.
pa·triar·cal I. adj. patriarchal II. f. *(iglesia)* patriarchal church; *(territorio)* patriarchate.
pa·tri·cia·do m. patriciate.
pa·tri·cio, –cia I. adj. *(romano)* patrician; *(noble)* aristocratic, noble II. m.f. *(noble romano)* patrician; *(noble)* aristocrat, noble.
pa·tri·mo·nial adj. patrimonial.
pa·tri·mo·nio m. patrimony, heritage ♦ **p. forestal** state *or* national forests • **p. nacional** national heritage.

pa·trio, –tria I. adj. *(de la patria)* native, home *<suelo p. native soil>; (del padre)* paternal II. f. see **patria.**
pa·trio·ta m.f. patriot.
pa·trio·te·rí·a f. exaggerated patriotism, jingoism.
pa·trio·te·ro, –ra I. adj. COLL. excessively patriotic, jingoistic II. m.f. jingoist.
pa·trió·ti·ca·men·te adv. patriotically.
pa·trió·ti·co, –ca adj. patriotic.
pa·trio·tis·mo m. patriotism.
pa·tro·ci·na·dor, –do·ra I. adj. sponsoring II. m.f. sponsor, patron.
pa·tro·ci·nar tr. to sponsor, patronize.
pa·tro·ci·nio m. sponsorship, patronage.
pa·trón, –tro·na m.f. *(patrono)* patron *<p. de la ópera* patron of the opera>; *(hostelero)* landlord; RELIG. patron saint —m. *(amo)* master, boss *<el p. dio la libertad a sus esclavos* the master set his slaves free>; MARIT. skipper, captain; *(modelo)* pattern, model; *(unidad de referencia)* standard *<metro p.* standard meter> ♦ **cortado por el mismo p.** FIG. cut of the same cloth, cast in the same mold • **p. oro** ECON. gold standard.
pa·tro·nal adj. *(del patrón)* employers', pertaining to employers *<sindicato p.* employers' association>; *(del santo)* patronal, pertaining to a patron saint.
pa·tro·na·to m. *(protección)* patronage, sponsorship *<bajo el p. de* under the sponsorship of>; *(consejo)* board of trustees, trusteeship; *(organización)* board, council *<p. de turismo* tourist board>; *(patronal)* employers' association; *(fundación)* trust, foundation ♦ **p. de las artes** arts council • **p. de apuestas mutuas** pari-mutuel.
pa·tro·naz·go m. var. of **patronato.**
pa·tro·ní·mi·co, –ca I. adj. patronymic II. m. patronymic, surname.
pa·tro·no, –na m.f. *(jefe)* boss; *(empresario)* owner, employer; *(santo)* patron saint —m. MARIT. *(capitán)* captain, skipper; *(patrocinador)* patron; *(dueño)* landlord, proprietor; *(señor)* lord (of the manor); *(modelo)* model, pattern —f. *(casera)* landlady, proprietress; *(señora)* lady (of the manor).
pa·tru·lla f. *(escuadra)* squad, patrol; FIG. *(cuadrilla)* band, gang.
pa·tru·llar intr. to patrol, go on patrol ♦ **p. por** to patrol *<la policía patrulla por la calle* the police are patrolling the streets>.
pa·tru·lle·ro, –ra I. adj. patrol, patrolling II. m. *(coche)* patrol car; *(buque)* patrol boat; *(avión)* patrol plane.
pa·tu·do, –da adj. COLL. big-footed.
pa·tu·le·a f. COLL. *(soldadesca)* disorderly soldiers; *(muchedumbre)* mob; *(chiquillos)* bunch of unruly children.
pau·lar intr. ♦ **sin p. ni maular** without saying a word.
pau·la·ti·na·men·te adv. little by little, gradually.
pau·la·ti·no, –na adj. slow, gradual.
pau·li·na f. *(carta de excomunión)* letter of excommunication; FIG., COLL. *(represión)* scolding, reprimand; *(carta ofensiva)* poison-pen letter.
pau·pe·ris·mo m. pauperism, poverty.
pau·pe·ri·za·ción f. pauperization.
pau·pé·rri·mo, –ma adj. very poor, poverty-stricken.
pau·sa f. *(interrupción)* pause, break; *(lentitud)* slowness, calm; MUS. rest ♦ **a pausas** at intervals • **con p.** slowly, calmly.
pau·sa·da·men·te adv. slowly, deliberately.
pau·sa·do, –da I. past part. see **pausar** II. adj. slow, deliberate III. adv. slowly, deliberately.
pau·sar tr. to interrupt, make pauses in —intr. *(interrumpirse)* to pause, hesitate; *(retardarse)* to slow down.
pau·ta f. *(regla)* rule, guide; *(rayas)* guidelines (for handwriting); FIG. *(dechado)* model, example *<servir de p. a* to serve as a model for>; *(principio)* guiding principle, norm; MUS. staff; AMER. *(falsilla)* writing guide ♦ **dar** *or* **marcar la p.** FIG. to set the example, lay down the norm *or* guideline.
pau·tar tr. *(rayar)* to trace lines on paper, rule; FIG. *(dar reglas)* to regulate, give directions; MUS. to draw a musical staff on.
pa·va¹ f. ORNITH. *(hembra)* turkey hen; FIG., COLL. *(mujer)* ungainly *or* awkward woman; *(colilla)* cigarette butt; COL., ECUAD., VEN. broad-brimmed straw hat; C. AMER.,

COL. bangs, fringe (hairstyle); BOL., CHILE coarse *or* tasteless joke ♦ **hacer la p.** ARG., PERU to play a joke on • **pelar la p.** to court, woo.

pa·va² f. CHILE urinal; *(fuelle)* furnace bellows; ARG., BOL., PAR. teapot, teakettle.

pa·va·da f *(pavos)* flock of turkeys; FIG., COLL. *(necedad)* stupidity, foolishness.

pa·ve·ar intr. ARG., CHILE *(burlarse)* to play a joke; ARG. *(pelar la pava)* to court, woo; ECUAD., PAN. *(faltar a clase)* to play hooky —tr. COL. to kill treacherously.

pa·ve·rí·a f. ARG., CHILE silliness, stupidity.

pa·ve·ro, –ra I. adj. presumptuous, vain II. m.f. *(criador)* turkey breeder *or* dealer —m. COLL. *(sombrero)* wide-brimmed hat; CHILE practical joker.

pa·ve·sa f. ember, cinder ♦ **estar hecho una p.** COLL. to be exhausted *or* weak, be a shadow of one's former self • **ser una p.** COLL. to be very docile *or* meek.

pá·vi·do, –da adj. frightened, fearful.

pa·vi·men·ta·ción f. *(acción de solar)* flooring; *(revestimiento de una calle)* paving; *(suelo)* floor, flooring; *(superficie transitable)* pavement, paving.

pa·vi·men·tar tr. *(solar)* to floor; *(revestir una calle)* to pave.

pa·vi·men·to m. *(suelo)* floor, flooring; *(superficie transitable)* pavement, paving.

pa·vi·so·so, –sa adj. colorless, dull.

pa·vi·ton·to, –ta adj. stupid, foolish.

pa·vo I. adj. *(soso)* colorless, dull; *(incauto)* unwary, foolish; COL. thin, lean II. m. ORNITH. turkey; FIG. *(hombre soso)* bore, drip; *(hombre incauto)* fool, dope; NUMIS. five-peseta coin; AMER. *(polizón)* stowaway, concealed passenger; *(juego de bailadores)* dancers' step *or* footwork; CARIB. *(reprimenda)* reprimand, rebuke; CHILE type of kite ♦ **comer p.** *(no bailar)* to be a wallflower at a dance; AMER. *(desilusionarse)* to be disillusioned *or* disappointed • **de p.** ECUAD. at someone else's expense, mooching • **edad del p.** awkward age • **ponerse hecho un p.** *or* **subírsele a uno el p.** COLL. to blush, turn as red as a beet • **p. de matorral** ORNITH. brush turkey • **p. marino** ICHTH. peacock fish • **p. real** *or* **ruán** ORNITH. peacock • **p. ruante** HER. strutting peacock • **p. silvestre** ORNITH. wood grouse • **tener p.** to be shy *or* timid.

pa·vón m. ORNITH. peacock; ENTOM. peacock butterfly; METAL. bluing, browning (antirust coating).

pa·vo·na·da I. f. *(paseo)* stroll, short walk <darse una p. to go for a stroll>; *(diversión breve)* brief amusement *or* diversion; FIG. *(ostentación)* ostentation, show II. adj. see **pavonado, –da.**

pa·vo·na·do, –da I. past part. see **pavonar** II. adj. dark blue III. m. METAL. bluing, browning (to prevent rust); *(azul oscuro)* dark blue —f. see **pavonada.**

pa·vo·nar tr. METAL. to blue *or* brown (steel and iron).

pa·vo·ne·ar intr. *(hacer alarde)* to strut, show off; FIG., COLL. to entertain, please —reflex. to strut, show off.

pa·vo·ne·o m. strutting, showing off.

pa·vor m. fright, terror.

pa·vo·ro·sa·men·te adv. frightfully.

pa·vo·ro·so, –sa adj. frightening, terrifying.

pa·vu·ra f. LIT. fright, terror.

pa·ya I. f. ARG., CHILE *(acción de payar)* improvisation of a song; ARG., CHILE *(composición)* improvised song II. adj. see **payo, –ya.**

pa·ya·da f. AMER. improvised song of a traveling minstrel ♦ **p. de contrapunto** AMER. competition among traveling minstrels.

pa·ya·dor m. ARG., CHILE traveling minstrel.

pa·ya·du·ra f. ARG., CHILE var. of **paya.**

pa·yar intr. ARG., CHILE *(cantar payas)* to improvise songs; *(contar cuentos)* to tell stories.

pa·ya·sa·da f. buffoonery, stunt ♦ **hacer payasadas** to fool around.

pa·ya·se·ar intr. AMER. to clown *or* fool (around).

pa·ya·so m. clown, buffoon.

pa·yo, –ya I. adj. *(aldeano)* rustic, boorish; COLL. *(mentecato)* stupid, foolish; ARG., BOL. albino II. m.f. *(rústico)* rustic, peasant; COLL. *(mentecato)* fool, jerk —f. see **paya.**

paz f. [pl. **pa·ces**] *(sin guerra)* peace; *(tratado)* peace treaty <firmaron la p. en octubre they signed the peace treaty in

October>; *(tranquilidad)* peacefulness, tranquility <la p. del bosque le tranquilizó the peacefulness of the forest calmed him>; RELIG. pax (image and ceremony) ♦ **dejar en p.** to leave alone • **descansar en p.** to rest in peace • **estar en p.** *(no guerrear)* to be at peace; *(no deberse nada)* to be even • **hacer las paces** to make peace, make up • **mantener la p.** to keep the peace • **poner en p.** *or* **poner p. entre** to reconcile, make peace between • **p. de la conciencia** peace of mind.

paz·ca see **pacer.**

paz·gua·te·rí·a f. *(simpleza)* foolishness, doltishness; *(mojigatería)* prudishness.

paz·gua·to, –ta I. adj. foolish, doltish II. m.f. *(simple)* fool, dolt; *(mojigato)* prude.

¡pche! *or* **¡pchs!** interj. pshaw!, bah!

pe f. pee (the letter p) ♦ **de pe a pa** from A to Z, from beginning to end.

pe·a f. SL. binge, drinking spree.

pe·a·je m. toll.

pe·a·je·ro, –ra m.f. toll *or* tollbooth collector.

pe·al m. *(pie)* foot (of a stocking); *(polaina de punto)* legging, leg-warmer; FIG., COLL. *(persona torpe)* jerk, dope; AMER. *(pial)* lasso, lariat; C. AMER. *(cuerda)* rope, cord.

pe·a·lar tr. AMER. to lasso, rope.

pe·a·na *or* **pe·a·ña** f. *(sostén)* stand, pedestal; RELIG. altar step *or* platform; COLL. *(pie)* foot.

pe·a·tón m. *(transeúnte)* pedestrian, walker.

pe·a·to·nal adj. pedestrian.

pe·be·te, –ta m. *(sustancia aromática)* incense, joss stick; *(de cohete)* fuse (of fireworks); FIG., COLL. *(cosa maloliente)* smelly thing; MEX. fragrant flower; ARG., VEN. high-grade tobacco —m.f. ARG., URUG. *(niño)* kid, child.

pe·be·te·ro m. incense burner, perfume censer.

pe·bre m.f. CUL. *(salsa)* sauce made with green pepper and garlic; *(pimienta)* (black) pepper.

pe·ca f. freckle.

pe·ca·do I. past part. see **pecar** II. m. RELIG. sin; *(vicio)* sin, vice; *(defecto)* fault, defect <sus pecados son muchos his faults are many> ♦ **de mis pecados** FIG., COLL. of mine <esa hija de mis pecados siempre causa grandes problemas that daughter of mine always causes big problems> • **estar en p.** RELIG. to be in sin, not to be in state of grace • **morir en p.** RELIG. to die unrepentant • **p. contra natura** RELIG. *(sodomía)* sodomy; *(masturbación)* masturbation • **p. mortal** *or* **grave** RELIG. mortal sin • **p. nefando** RELIG. sodomy • **p. original** RELIG. original sin • **siete pecados capitales** RELIG. seven deadly sins.

pe·ca·dor, –do·ra I. adj. sinful, sinning II. m.f. *(transgresor)* sinner ♦ **¡p. de mi!** sinner that I am! —f. COLL. *(prostituta)* prostitute.

pe·ca·mi·no·so, –sa adj. sinful, wicked.

pe·car §47 intr. RELIG. to sin; *(faltar)* to err, transgress <p. contra la ley to transgress the law> ♦ **p. de** to be guilty of <peca de confiado he is guilty of overconfidence>.

pe·ca·rí *or* **pé·ca·ri** m. ZOOL. peccary.

pec·blen·da f. MIN. pitchblende.

pe·ce·ra f. fishbowl, aquarium.

pe·cí·o·lo *or* **pe·cio·lo** m. BOT. petiole.

pé·co·ra f. *(res lanar)* head of sheep ♦ **buena (mala) p.** FIG., COLL. good (wicked) person.

pe·co·so, –sa adj. freckled, freckly.

pec·ti·na f. CHEM. pectin.

pec·to·ral I. adj. ANAT., PHARM. pectoral II. m. *(adorno)* pectoral, chest ornament; PHARM. pectoral; RELIG. *(cruz)* pectoral cross; *(racional)* breastplate (worn by Jewish holy men); SPORT. number (on a player's jersey).

pe·cua·rio, –ria adj. AGR. cattle, livestock.

pe·cu·liar adj. peculiar, characteristic.

pe·cu·lia·ri·dad f. peculiarity.

pe·cu·lio m. LAW peculium; FIG. *(dinero particular)* one's own *or* personal money.

pe·cu·nia f. COLL. money, cash.

pe·cu·nia·ria·men·te adv. *(en dinero efectivo)* in cash; *(económicamente)* pecuniarily, financially.

pe·cu·nia·rio, –ria adj. pecuniary, financial.

pe·cha·da f. CUBA blow to the chest; ARG. *(sablazo)* touch for a loan.

pe·cha·dor m. AMER., COLL. sponger, cadger.
pe·char tr. *(pagar pecho)* to pay (as tax); *(asumir)* to assume, shoulder; AMER., COLL. *(pedir prestado)* to hit *or* touch (someone) for a loan; *(empujar)* to push, shove (with the chest) —intr. ♦ **p. con** to bear, shoulder <*p. con la tarea más complicada* to shoulder the most complicated task>.
pe·che adj. AMER. *(huérfano)* orphaned; *(flaco)* thin, frail.
pe·che·ra I. f. *(parte de la camisa)* shirt front; *(chorrera)* shirt frill, jabot; *(paño para abrigarse)* chest protector; *(petral)* breast strap (of a harness); COLL. *(parte exterior del pecho)* chest; *(pecho de mujer)* breast, bosom; CHILE apron II. adj. see **pechero, -ra.**
pe·che·ro, -ra I. adj. *(que pagaba pecho)* tax-paying; *(plebeyo)* plebeian, common II. m.f. *(que pagaba pecho)* taxpayer; *(plebeyo)* plebeian, commoner —m. *(babero)* bib —f. see **pechera.**
pe·che·rón, -ro·na adj. MEX., COLL. very good *or* fine.
pe·cho¹ m. ANAT. *(tórax)* chest; *(busto)* breast; *(seno)* bosom, breast; ORNITH. breast; *(cuesta)* slope, hill; FIG. *(alma)* heart, breast; *(ánimo)* courage, spirit; *(fuerza de voz)* strength of voice ♦ **abrir el p.** FIG. to unbosom oneself • **p. descubierto** *(sin armas)* defenseless; *(sinceramente)* sincerely, openly • **dar el p.** to suckle, nurse • **de p.** breast-feeding, nursing • **de pechos** leaning <*está de pechos sobre la barandilla* he is leaning on the railing> • **echarse una cosa a pechos** FIG. to put one's heart into something • **entre p. y espalda** COLL. in one's stomach • **hombre de pelo en p.** he-man • **p. arriba** uphill • **poner el p. a** to face, confront • **quedarse con algo en el p.** to hold something back • **sacar el p.** to stick out one's chest • **tomar a pecho** FIG. to take to heart.
pe·cho² m. *(tributo)* feudal tribute *or* tax; FIG. *(contribución)* tax, tribute.
pe·chu·ga f. *(pecho del ave)* breast (of fowl); FIG. *(pecho de persona)* chest, breast; *(cuesta)* slope, incline; AMER. nerve, audacity.
pe·chu·gón, -go·na I. adj. COLL. *(de pecho abultado)* buxom, big-breasted; AMER. nervy, audacious II. m. *(golpe)* blow to the chest; *(tropezón)* collision of persons breast to breast; FIG. *(esfuerzo extremado)* great effort *or* push.
pe·chu·go·na·da f. PERU shamelessness, impudence.
pe·da·go·gí·a f. EDUC. pedagogy, pedagogics.
pe·da·gó·gi·co, -ca adj. EDUC. pedagogic, pedagogical.
pe·da·go·go m. *(perito)* expert in pedagogics; *(maestro de escuela)* schoolteacher, instructor; *(ayo)* tutor; FIG. *(consejero)* advisor, counselor; COLL. *(pedante)* pedant.
pe·dal m. MECH. *(palanca de pie)* (foot) pedal, treadle; MUS. *(mecanismo)* pedal; *(nota sostenida)* pedal (point), sustained note ♦ **dar a los pedales** to pedal • **p. acelerador** AUTO. accelerator (pedal) • **p. de embrague** AUTO. clutch pedal • **p. de freno** AUTO. brake pedal • **p. de sordina** MUS. soft pedal • **p. fuerte** MUS. damper pedal.
pe·da·le·ar intr. to pedal.
pe·da·le·o m. pedaling.
pe·da·ní·a f. AMER. district.
pe·dan·te I. adj. pedantic II. m.f. pedant.
pe·dan·te·rí·a f. *or* **pe·dan·tis·mo** m. pedantry.
pe·dan·tes·co, -ca adj. pedantic.
pe·da·zo m. piece ♦ **a pedazos** in pieces *or* bits • **caerse a pedazos** FIG., COLL. *(deshacerse)* to fall to pieces; *(estar cansadísimo)* to be dead tired, be worn out • **ganarse un p. de pan** to scrape out a living • **hacer pedazos** *(romper)* to break *or* smash into pieces; *(desgarrar)* to tear into pieces • **p. de alcornoque** *or* **de animal** *or* **de bruto** nitwit, blockhead • **p. del alma** *or* **del corazón** FIG. darling, apple of one's eye • **ser un p. de pan** FIG., COLL. to be an angel.
pe·de·ras·ta m. pederast.
pe·de·ras·tia f. pederasty.
pe·der·nal m. MIN. flint; FIG. *(suma dureza)* flintiness, extreme hardness ♦ **duro como el** *or* **un p.** as hard as a rock.
pe·des·tal m. *(podio)* pedestal, foundation; *(peana)* base, stand; FIG. *(fundamento)* base, foundation.
pe·des·tre adj. *(que anda a pie)* pedestrian; SPORT. foot, pertaining to footracing; FIG. *(llano)* pedestrian, commonplace.

pe·di·a·tra *or* **pe·dia·tra** m.f. MED. pediatrician, pediatrist.
pe·dia·trí·a f. MED. pediatrics.
pe·dí·cu·lo m. ANAT., BOT., ZOOL. peduncle.
pe·di·cu·ro, -ra m.f. MED. podiatrist —f. pedicure.
pe·di·do I. past part. see **pedir** II. m. COM. *(encargo)* order; *(petición)* request, petition ♦ **a p. de** at the request of • **a p. del público** by public demand *or* request • **hacer un p.** to place an order • **p. de ensayo** trial order • **p. en firme** guaranteed *or* firm order • **p. por correo** mail order.
pe·di·dor, -do·ra I. adj. *(que pide)* requesting, petitioning; *(exigente)* demanding; *(que pide mucho)* pestering, persistent in asking II. m.f. *(el que pide)* requester, petitioner; *(cliente)* client; *(el que pide con impertinencia)* demanding person, demander; *(el que pide mucho)* pest, nuisance.
pe·di·gre·e *or* **pe·di·gri** m. pedigree.
pe·di·güe·ño, -ña I. adj. persistent, pestering II. m.f. pest, nuisance.
pe·di·lón, -lo·na adj. & m.f. AMER. var. of **pedigüeño, -ña.**
pe·di·men·to m. *(petición)* petition, request; LAW *(escrito)* claim ♦ **a p.** on request.
pe·dir §48 tr. to ask, request <*le pidieron que cerrara la puerta* they asked him to close the door>; to ask for, request <*le pedí diez dólares* I asked him for ten dollars>; *(demandar)* to demand; *(mendigar)* to beg; to order <*pidió una taza de café* he ordered a cup of coffee>; *(necesitar)* to need, require <*la tierra pide abono* the earth needs fertilizer>; *(a una mujer)* to ask (parents) for the hand of (a woman in marriage); COM. *(poner precio)* to ask, charge (a price); *(encargar)* to order (goods) ♦ **a p. de boca** to one's heart's content • **p. disculpas** to apologize • **p. en justicia** LAW to bring a suit, sue • **p. la luna** *or* **p. peras al olmo** FIG. to ask for the moon • **p. la palabra** to ask for the floor • **p. perdón** to beg pardon • **p. prestado** to borrow.
pe·do m. COLL. *(ventosidad)* fart; *(borrachera)* drunk, drunkenness ♦ **estar p.** to be drunk • **p. de lobo** BOT. puffball • **pegarse** *or* **tirarse un p.** to fart.
pe·do·rre·ra I. f. COLL. wind, gas ♦ **pedorreras** tight breeches II. adj. see **pedorrero, -ra.**
pe·do·rre·ro, -ra I. adj. COLL. farting II. m.f. *(persona)* farter —f. see **pedorrera.**
pe·do·rre·ta f. COLL. Bronx cheer, raspberry.
pe·do·rro, -rra COLL. I. adj. farting II. m.f. farter.
pe·dra·da f. *(acción)* throw *or* toss of a stone; *(golpe)* blow with a stone; *(señal)* bruise *or* mark left by a stone; FIG. *(insulto)* barb, insult; *(lazo)* cockade, rosette ♦ **como p. en ojo de boticario** FIG., COLL. in the nick of time, at just the right moment • **matar a pedradas** to stone to death • **pegar una p. a alguien** to throw a stone at someone.
pe·dre·a f. *(acción de apedrear)* stoning, stone-throwing; *(combate)* stone-throwing fight, fight with stones; METEOROL. hailing, hailstorm; FIG., COLL. *(premios)* small prizes (awarded in a lottery).
pe·dre·gal m. stony *or* rocky terrain.
pe·dre·go·so, -sa I. adj. *(lleno de piedras)* rocky, stony; MED. suffering gallstones II. m.f. MED. gallstones sufferer.
pe·dre·jón m. boulder, rock.
pe·dre·ra f. stone quarry *or* pit.
pe·dre·rí·a f. JEWEL. precious stones, gems.
pe·dre·ro m. *(cantero)* stonecutter, quarryman; ARTIL. *(pieza)* stone-hurling mortar; *(hondero)* slinger; HOND. rocky *or* stony terrain.
pe·dris·ca f. METEOROL. *(granizo)* hail; *(granizada)* hailstorm.
pe·dris·co m. METEOROL. hail; *(multitud de piedras)* shower of rocks *or* stones; *(pedrea)* stoning, stone-throwing; *(montón)* heap of small stones.
pe·dri·za f. *(pedregal)* rocky *or* stony terrain; *(valla de piedras)* stone fence *or* wall.
pe·drus·co m. COLL. rough *or* uncut stone.
pe·dún·cu·lo m. BOT., ZOOL. peduncle.
pe·er intr. & reflex. to pass gas, fart.
pe·ga f. *(acción de pegar)* sticking, gluing; *(barniz)* pitch, varnish; COLL. *(chasco)* practical joke, jest; *(zurra)* beating, whipping; *(dificultad)* snag, difficulty; ORNITH. magpie; ICHTH. remora; CHILE contagious period; CUBA job,

task ♦ **de p.** sham, false • **estar en la p.** CHILE to be in one's prime • **p. regorda** ORNITH. shrike.
pe·ga·da f. *(de pelota)* stroke, hit; *(del puño)* punch, blow; COLL. *(buena idea)* good idea; *(good luck)* buena suerte.
pe·ga·di·llo m. *(parche pequeño)* small patch, small plaster; ECUAD., SEW lace, picot ♦ **p. de mal de madre** COLL. pest, nuisance.
pe·ga·di·zo, -za adj. *(que se pega)* sticky, adhesive; *(que se contagia)* catching, contagious; *(que capta la atención)* catchy, infectious; *(parásito)* clinging, parasitic; *(postizo)* false, imitation.
pe·ga·do I. past part. see **pegar II.** adj. ♦ **estar p. en algo** FIG., COLL. to be ignorant about something **III.** m. *(parche)* patch, plaster; CUL. crust, burnt residue.
pe·ga·dor m. MIN. blaster; *(el que pega con cola)* gluer, sticker; *(el que pega carteles)* paperhanger, billposter; *(boxeador)* puncher.
pe·ga·du·ra f. *(acción de pegar)* sticking, gluing; *(unión)* adhesion, joint; COL., ECUAD. trick, fraud.
pe·ga·jo·si·dad f. stickiness, gumminess.
pe·ga·jo·so, -sa adj. *(glutinoso)* sticky, adhesive; *(contagioso)* contagious, catching; FIG., COLL. *(meloso)* sweet, cloying; *(excesivamente meloso)* mushy, gooey; *(sobón)* fresh, randy; *(que atrae)* tempting, alluring; *(cargante)* boring, tiresome.
pe·ga·men·to m. glue, adhesive.
pe·ga·mien·to m. *(acción)* sticking, gluing; *(unión)* adhesion, joint.
pe·ga·pe·ga f. AMER. birdlime; COL., PERU seed which sticks to clothing; CHILE flatterer.
pe·gar §47 tr. *(engomar)* to stick, glue <*p. un anuncio en el tablón* to stick an announcement on the bulletin board>; *(arrimar)* to move closer <*p. el sofá a la pared* to move the sofa closer to the wall>; *(unir)* to fasten, attach; *(coser)* to sew on; *(comunicar)* to get (someone) started <*le pegué la manía de comerse las uñas* I got him started biting his nails>; *(contagiar)* to give, infect; *(golpear)* to hit, beat; to give <*p. un grito* to give a yell> ♦ **no p. ojo** FIG. not to sleep a wink • **p. fuego a** to set fire to • **p. un salto** to jump, give a start • **p. un susto** to frighten • **p. un tiro** to shoot —intr. *(adherir)* to stick, adhere; *(prender)* to catch (fire); *(estar al lado)* to be next to; *(caer bien)* to go together, match; *(tener efecto)* to make an impression; *(tropezar)* to hit, strike <*la pelota pegó en la pared* the ball hit against the wall>; BOT. to take root; MED. to be catching ♦ **p. con** to attack or insult (someone) —reflex. *(unirse)* to stick, adhere; CUL. *(quemarse)* to stick in the pan; FIG. *(meterse)* to tag along, intrude; to pick up <*el vicio de fumar, se le pegó de mí* she picked up the vice of smoking from me> ♦ **pegársele a alguien** FIG., COLL. to deceive or make a fool of someone • **pegársele a uno las sábanas** FIG. to oversleep, sleep in • **pegarse un tiro** to shoot oneself.
pe·ga·ta f. COLL. trick, ruse.
pe·ga·ti·na f. adhesive, sticky substance.
pe·go m. *(fullería)* cheating at cards (by sticking two cards together); FIG., COLL. *(engaño)* trick, ruse ♦ **dar** or **tirar el p.** to trick, deceive.
pe·go·te m. *(emplasto)* sticking plaster; ARTS, LIT., FIG. *(cosa pegajosa)* sticky or gooey mess; *(gorrón)* hanger-on, leech; *(parche)* sloppy patch; COLL. *(guisado espeso)* heavy or thick stew.
pe·go·te·ar intr. COLL. to show up uninvited at mealtime, sponge a meal.
pe·go·te·rí·a f. COLL. sponging (of a meal).
pe·gual m. AMER., EQUIT. cinch, girth.
pe·gué, pegue see **pegar.**
pe·gue·ro m. *(fabricador)* pitch manufacturer; *(comerciante)* pitch dealer.
pe·gu·jal m. *(peculio)* peculium, private property or possession; *(campo pequeño)* small estate or holdings; *(parcela de encargado)* caretaker's parcel (on an estate); ECUAD. poor-quality land.
pe·gu·ja·le·ro, -ra m. *(labrador)* owner of a small farm; *(ganadero)* owner of a small cattle farm.
pei·na f. ornamental comb.
pei·na·da f. COLL. combing ♦ **darse una p.** to comb one's hair.

pei·na·do, -da I. past part. see **peinar II.** adj. *(que se adorna con exceso)* overgroomed, overdecorated; FIG. *(estilo)* highly polished or refined (style) **III.** m. hair style, coiffure.
pei·na·dor, -do·ra I. adj. combing **II.** m.f. *(persona)* hairdresser —m. *(toalla)* towel; *(bata)* bathrobe, peignoir; CHILE, ARG. dressing table —f. wool-combing machine.
pei·na·du·ra f. hairdressing ♦ **peinaduras** combings.
pei·nar tr. *(el cabello)* to comb (hair); *(lana)* to comb, card (wool); *(tocar)* to touch, brush ♦ **p. canas** FIG., COLL. to get old —reflex. to comb one's hair.
pei·ne m. *(para el pelo)* comb; *(para la lana)* card; TEX. reed (of a loom); VEN. snare (for birds); FIG., COLL. *(astuto)* sly or crafty person ♦ **pasarse el p.** to comb one's hair.
pei·ne·ro m.f. *(fabricante)* comb maker; *(vendedor)* comb seller.
pei·ne·ta f. ornamental comb.
pe·je m. *(pez)* fish; FIG., COLL. *(astuto)* sly or crafty person; MEX. fool ♦ **p. araña** stingfish • **p. diablo** scorpion fish.
pe·ji·gue·ra f. COLL. nuisance, annoyance.
Pe·kín or **Pe·quín** m. Peking.
pe·la f. *(peladura)* peeling, stripping; SP., COLL. peseta; AMER. beating, thrashing.
pe·la·da f. *(piel)* pelt, sheepskin (with wool removed); AMER. haircut; COL. blunder; CHILE, COLL. death.
pe·la·de·ra f. MED. alopecia, baldness; CHILE, C. AMER. gossip.
pe·la·de·ro m. *(para pelar cerdos)* place where hogs are scalded; FIG., COLL. *(garito)* gambling den; COL., CHILE barren land, wasteland.
pe·la·do, -da I. past part. see **pelar II.** adj. *(calvo)* bald, hairless; *(con el pelo cortado)* shorn (said of animals, people); *(frutos)* peeled, pared; *(desplumado)* plucked (said of fowl); *(sin carne)* bare, stripped <*un hueso p.* a bare bone>; *(desnudo)* bare, barren <*el campo p.* the barren countryside>; *(sencillo)* direct, straightforward <*un discurso p.* a straightforward speech>; *(número)* round, full <*mil p.* a full one thousand>; FIG. *(pobre)* broke, penniless; AMER. impudent, insolent **III.** m. *(corte de pelo)* haircut; *(peladura)* peeling, paring (of fruits, vegetables); *(esquileo)* shearing <*hacíamos el p. del rebaño una vez al año* we did the shearing of the sheep once a year>; *(de plumas)* plucking (of feathers) —m.f. MEX. *(pobre)* pauper; *(persona grosera)* rude or uncouth person; COL., PAN. child, kid.
pe·la·dor m. peeler, stripper.
pe·la·du·ra f. peeling, stripping.
pe·la·fus·tán m. COLL. good-for-nothing, loafer.
pe·la·ga·llos m. [pl. **-llos**] COLL. bum, tramp.
pe·la·ga·tos m. [pl. **-tos**] COLL. poor devil.
pe·lá·gi·co, -ca adj. pelagic, of open seas.
pe·la·gra f. MED. pellagra.
pe·la·je m. *(pelo)* coat, fur (of an animal); FIG., COLL. *(apariencia)* looks, appearance.
pe·lam·bre m. *(pieles)* batch of hides (for tanning); *(líquido)* lime solution; *(en el cuerpo)* body hair; *(falta de pelo)* baldness; CHILE censure, criticism.
pe·lam·bre·ra f. *(sitio)* liming room (for tanning); *(pelo espeso)* thick hair; MED. baldness.
pe·lam·brón m. AMER. ragamuffin.
pe·la·men m. COLL. var. of **pelambre.**
pe·la·nas m. [pl. **-nas**] COLL. poor devil.
pe·lan·dus·ca f. whore, floozy.
pe·lar tr. *(cortar el pelo)* to cut, shear, crop (hair); *(mondar)* to peel, pare (fruits, vegetables); *(desplumar)* to pluck (feathers); *(quitar la piel)* to strip <*p. un hueso de carne* to strip a bone of meat>; FIG., COLL. *(ganar en el juego)* to clean out <*el tahur me peló en el póker* the gambler cleaned me out in poker>; *(despojar)* to clean out, fleece <*los estafadores pelaron al rústico* the swindlers fleeced the yokel>; FIG. *(despellejar)* to tear down, slur <*sus enemigos le pelan cuando él no está allí* his enemies tear him down when he is not there> ♦ **duro de p.** FIG. hard nut to crack • **p. la pava** FIG., COLL. to court, romance • **p. los ojos** AMER., COLL. to keeps one's eyes peeled —reflex. *(perder el pelo)* to lose one's hair; AMER. to become confused ♦ **pelárselas** COLL. to run like mad • **pelárselas por** to be dying for <*pelárselas por la oportunidad de hacer algo* to be

dying for the opportunity to do something>; to be dying to <*se las pela por cantar* he is dying to sing>.

pel·da·ño m. step (of a staircase); rung (of a ladder).

pe·le·a f. *(riña)* fight, quarrel; *(contienda)* battle, fight; FIG. *(esfuerzo)* struggle, fight (to obtain something) ♦ **p. de gallos** cockfight.

pe·le·a·dor, –do·ra adj. *(que pela)* fighting; *(propenso a pelear)* quarrelsome, pugnacious.

pe·le·ar intr. *(luchar)* to fight, brawl; *(disputar)* to fight, quarrel; *(batallar)* to battle, fight <*los dos ejércitos pelearon por tres días* the two armies battled for three days> ♦ **p. por** to fight or struggle for <*el país pelea por su independencia* the country struggles for its independence> —reflex. *(reñir)* to fight; *(separarse)* to quarrel, fall out <*nos peleamos sobre muchos asuntos* we quarrel over many things>.

pe·le·char intr. *(mudar el pelo)* to shed; *(mudar la pluma)* to molt; *(echar pelos o plumas)* to grow (hair or feathers); FIG., COLL. *(mejorar)* to begin to improve (fortune, health).

pe·le·le m. *(muñeco)* rag doll, puppet; FIG., COLL. *(tonto)* nincompoop; *(traje)* child's pajamas.

pe·le·ón, –o·na I. adj. quarrelsome, pugnacious ♦ **vino p.** cheap wine II. f. see **peleona**.

pe·le·o·na I. f. COLL. quarrel, wrangle II. adj. see **peleón, –o·na**.

pe·le·ro m. AMER. saddle blanket.

pe·le·te·rí·a f. *(oficio)* furriery, fur trade; *(tienda)* fur shop; *(pieles finas)* furs; CUBA shoe store.

pe·le·te·ro m. *(fabricante)* fur maker; *(vendedor)* fur dealer, furrier.

pe·lia·gu·do, –da adj. *(de pelo largo)* long-haired; FIG., COLL. *(difícil)* difficult, tricky; *(hábil)* clever, crafty.

pe·li·ca·no or **pe·lí·ca·no** I. m. ORNITH. pelican; SURG. forceps II. adj. see **pelicano, –na**.

pe·li·ca·no, –na I. adj. gray-haired II. m. see **pelicano**.

pe·lí·cu·la f. *(piel)* skin; *(telilla)* film, pellicle; PHOTOG. film; CINEM. film, movie, motion picture ♦ **de p.** extraordinary, sensational • **echar** or **poner una p.** to show a film • **p. del Oeste** Western • **p. en colores** CINEM. film in color; PHOTOG. color film • **p. hablada** CINEM. talking picture • **p. muda** CINEM. silent movie.

pe·li·grar intr. to be in danger or at risk.

pe·li·gro m. danger, peril ♦ **correr el p. de** to run the risk of • **correr p.** or **estar en p.** to be in danger, run a risk • **fuera de p.** out of danger • **poner en p.** to endanger.

pe·li·gro·si·dad f. dangerousness, danger.

pe·li·gro·so, –sa adj. dangerous, perilous.

pe·li·llo m. *(pelo corto)* short hair; FIG., COLL. *(nadería)* trifle ♦ **echar pelillos a la mar** COLL. to bury the hatchet • **no tener pelillos en la lengua** to speak one's mind, not to mince words • **pararse en pelillos** *(enfadarse)* to be easily offended • **pararse** or **reparar en pelillos** *(preocuparse)* to worry about trifles.

pe·li·llo·so, –sa adj. FIG., COLL. touchy, peevish.

pe·li·rro·jo, –ja I. adj. red-haired, redheaded II. m.f. redhead.

pe·li·rru·bio, –bia I. adj. blond, fair-haired II. m. blond —f. blonde.

pel·ma m.f. COLL. var. of **pelmazo**.

pel·ma·zo m. *(cosa aplastada)* crushed or flattened mass; *(en el estómago)* lump, heavy food (in the stomach); FIG., COLL. *(persona pesada)* bore.

pe·lo m. *(cabello)* hair; *(de la barba)* whisker; *(de cepillo)* bristle; ZOOL. *(piel)* fur, coat; BOT., ORNITH. down; *(filamento)* strand, fiber; ARM. hair trigger; TECH. hairspring; *(del tejido)* nap, pile; *(de la madera)* grain; *(seda)* raw silk; JEWEL. cloud, flaw; FIG. *(nadería)* trifle, nothing ♦ **agarrarse** or **asirse de un p.** FIG. to grasp at straws • **al p.** with the grain or nap; FIG. *(a punto)* just right, pefectly; *(a tiempo)* right on time • **a medios pelos** tipsy, tight • **a p.** with the grain or nap; *(sin aparejo)* bareback; *(sin sombrero)* hatless; FIG. *(a punto)* just right, perfectly; *(a tiempo)* right on time • **contra p.** against the grain or nap; FIG. *(inoportunamente)* inopportunely • **cortar un p. en el aire** FIG. to be as sharp as a tack • **estar hasta los pelos** to be fed up • **hombre de p. en pecho** forceful man • **no tener p. de tonto** FIG., COLL. to be nobody's fool • **no**

tener pelos en la lengua FIG., COLL. to be outspoken, not to mince words • **no verle el p. a alguien** to see neither hide nor hair of someone • **p. arriba** against the grain or nap • **p. de camello** camel hair • **p. de Judas** *(cabello)* red hair; *(persona)* redhead • **pelos y señales** FIG. chapter and verse • **ponérsele a uno los pelos de punta** FIG., COLL. to make one's hair stand on end • **por los pelos** or **por un p.** FIG. by the skin of one's teeth • **tomar a alguien el p.** FIG. to pull someone's leg, tease • **traído por los pelos** farfetched • **venir al p.** *(ser perfecto)* to be just right; *(ser oportuno)* to come in handy, come just in time.

pe·lón, –lo·na I. adj. *(sin pelo)* hairless; *(calvo)* bald; *(pelicorto)* short-haired; FIG., COLL. *(tonto)* stupid, foolish; SP. stingy, miserly; *(sin dinero)* penniless, broke II. m. VEN. mistake, blunder; ARG. smooth-skinned peach —f. see **pelona**.

pe·lo·na I. f. *(alopecia)* alopecia, baldness; COLL. *(muerte)* death II. adj. see **pelón, –lona**.

pe·lo·po·nen·se or **pe·lo·po·ne·sí·a·co, –ca** adj. & m.f. Peloponnesian.

Pe·lo·po·ne·so m. Peloponnesus.

pe·lo·ta f. ball; *(juego)* ball, ball game; *(bola)* ball <*p. de nieve* snowball>; ARM. cannonball; COLL. *(cabeza)* head, noggin; ARG., BOL., URUG. cowhide boat ♦ **en p.** COLL. naked • **estar la p. en el tejado** FIG. to be in the air • **p. base** baseball • **pelotas** VULG. balls • **p. vasca** jai alai • **tener p. por** CUBA, COLL. to have a crush on.

pe·lo·ta·ri m.f. SPORT. pelota or jai alai player.

pe·lo·te·ar tr. to go over, check (an account) —intr. *(jugar)* to kick a ball around; FIG. *(lanzar)* to toss back and forth; *(reñir)* to quarrel, argue.

pe·lo·te·ra f. COLL. brawl, scuffle; AMER. baseball or soccer player.

pe·lo·te·ro m. *(fabricante)* ball maker; COLL. *(riña)* brawl, scuffle; AMER. baseball or soccer player.

pe·lo·ti·lla f. *(de disciplinantes)* ball of wax with embedded glass (used on a whip); SL. *(adulación)* soft soap, flattery —m.f. SL. *(pelotillero)* soft-soaper, flatterer.

pe·lo·ti·lle·ro, –ra I. adj. flattering II. m.f. SL. *(adulón)* soft-soaper, flatterer.

pe·lo·tón m. *(de pelo)* tuft (of hair); MIL. squad <*p. de ejecución* firing squad>; FIG. *(muchedumbre)* crowd; *(en una carrera)* contestants (in a race).

pel·tre m. pewter.

pe·lu·ca f. *(cabellera postiza)* wig; COLL. *(reprensión)* scolding, tongue-lashing.

pe·lu·cón, –co·na m.f. CHILE conservative; ECUAD. bigwig, person of high position.

pe·lu·co·na f. ARCH., COLL. gold doubloon.

pe·lu·che m. TEX. plush.

pe·lu·do, –da I. adj. hairy, shaggy II. m. *(felpudo)* thick mat; ARG., ZOOL. armadillo; ARG. *(borrachera)* drunken spree.

pe·lu·que·rí·a f. *(para hombres)* barber shop; *(para mujeres)* beauty shop or parlor.

pe·lu·que·ro, –ra m.f. *(para hombres)* barber; *(para hombres y mujeres)* hairdresser.

pe·lu·quín m. *(peluca)* small wig; *(bisoñé)* toupee ♦ **ni hablar del p.** COLL. don't even mention it, out of the question.

pe·lu·sa f. *(vello)* down (on plants); *(de telas)* fluff, fuzz; COLL. *(envidia)* jealousy ♦ **tener p.** COLL. to be jealous.

pel·via·no, –na or **pél·vi·co, –ca** adj. ANAT. pelvic.

pel·vis f. [pl. inv.] ANAT. pelvis.

pe·lla f. *(masa redonda)* round mass, lump; BOT. head (of cauliflower); *(manteca del cerdo)* raw lard; FIG., COLL. *(suma de dinero)* sum, amount (of money) ♦ **hacer p.** SL. to play hooky.

pe·lle·ja f. *(piel)* hide, skin; COLL. *(ramera)* whore, prostitute ♦ **salvar la p.** FIG., COLL. to save one's skin.

pe·lle·je·rí·a f. *(curtiduría)* tannery; *(pieles)* skins, hides ♦ **pellejerías** ARG., CHILE trouble, jam.

pe·lle·je·ro, –ra m.f. *(adobador)* tanner, dresser; *(vendedor)* leather dealer.

pe·lle·jo m. *(de un animal)* skin, hide (of an animal); *(de una fruta)* skin, peel (of a fruit); *(de un hombre)* skin (of a man); *(odre)* wineskin; FIG., COLL. *(borracho)* drunk, tippler ♦ **dar el p.** FIG. to give one's life • **perder** or **soltar el**

p. FIG. to lose one's life • **estar en el p. de otro** FIG. to be in another's shoes • **jugarse el p.** FIG. to risk one's neck • **mudar el p.** FIG. to change one's spots • **no caber en el p.** FIG. *(estar gordo)* to be bursting at the seams, be very fat; *(estar contento)* to be bursting at the seams, be overflowing *<el niño no cabe en el p. de alegría* the child is bursting at the seams with joy>; • **no tener más que el p.** FIG. to be as thin as a rail, be skin and bones • **quitar a alguien el p.** FIG. *(matar)* to bump or knock off someone; *(murmurar)* to tear down, slur; *(pelar)* to fleece, clean *<le quitaban el p. en el póker* they fleeced him in poker> • **salvar el p.** FIG. to save one's skin.

pe·lle·ju·do, –da adj. loose-skinned, flabby.

pe·lli·ca f. *(pelleja)* small dressed skin; *(manta)* coverlet (made of fine fur); *(zamarra)* sheepskin jacket.

pe·lli·co m. *(zamarra)* sheepskin jacket; *(abrigo forrado de pieles)* fur-lined jacket.

pe·lli·za·dor, –do·ra I. adj. pinching II. m.f. pincher.

pe·lli·zcar §70 tr. *(apretar)* to pinch; *(asir ligeramente)* to take a pinch of; *(comer un poco)* to nibble.

pe·lli·zco m. *(acción de pellizcar)* pinch; *(pequeña porción)* small portion, FIG. sharp pain ♦ **dar un p. a alguien** to give someone a pinch • **p. de monja** *(con las uñas)* hard pinch; *(dulce)* macaroon.

pe·llón m. *(vellón)* unshorn sheepskin; AMER. saddle pad.

pe·na¹ f. *(castigo)* penalty, punishment; *(aflicción)* sorrow, sadness; *(dolor)* pain, suffering; *(dificultad)* difficulty; COL., MEX., VEN. *(timidez)* shyness, timidity; *(vergüenza)* embarrassment, shame ♦ **a duras penas** with great difficulty • **a penas** hardly, scarcely • **bajo** or **so p. de** under penalty of • **dar p. a** to grieve, pain *<me da p. ver que su condición ha empeorado* it grieves me to see that his condition has worsened> • **pasar la p. negra** FIG. to go through hell • **p. capital** or **de muerte** death penalty • **p. pecuniaria** fine • **penas** PERU ghosts • **penas eternas** hellfire • **¡qué p.!** what a shame! • **valer la p.** to be worthwhile.

pe·na² f. ORNITH. penna, quill feather; MARIT. peak (of lateen yard).

pe·na·ble adj. punishable.

pe·na·cho m. ORNITH. crest, tuft; *(adorno)* plume; FIG. *(de humo)* trail, plume; FIG., COLL. *(soberbia)* arrogance, haughtiness.

pe·na·do, –da I. past part. see **penar** II. adj. *(difícil)* difficult, arduous; *(triste)* sad, grieved III. m.f. convict.

pe·nal I. adj. penal *<código p.* penal code> II. m. penitentiary, prison.

pe·na·li·cé, penalice see **penalizar.**

pe·na·li·dad f. *(pena)* suffering, hardship; LAW penalty, punishment.

pe·na·lis·ta LAW I. adj. specializing in criminal law II. m.f. *(abogado)* criminal lawyer; *(especialista)* specialist in criminal law.

pe·na·li·za·ción f. *(castigo)* sanction; SPORT. penalty.

pe·na·li·zar §04 tr. to penalize.

pe·nar tr. to punish, chastise —intr. *(sufrir)* to suffer; RELIG. to suffer in purgatory ♦ **p. por** to crave or yearn for —reflex. to suffer.

pe·na·tes m.pl. Penates, household gods ♦ **volver a los p.** FIG., COLL. to return home.

pen·ca f. BOT. fleshy leaf; *(azote)* whip; AMER. bunch of bananas; ARG. prickly pear; C. RICA drunken spree; HOND. *(hoja de maíz)* corn leaf; *(chorro de sangre)* gush of blood ♦ **a la pura p.** AMER. naked, nude • **hacerse de pencas** COLL. to hold out, play hard to get.

pen·co m. COLL. *(jamelgo)* hack, nag (worn-out horse); *(tonto)* fool, dope; AMER., BOT. agave; HOND., COLL. bumpkin, yokel.

pen·dan·ga f. *(en naipes)* jack of diamonds; COLL. *(ramera)* prostitute, whore.

pen·de·ja·da f. SL. *(tontería)* foolishness, stupidity; *(cobardía)* cowardliness.

pen·de·jo, –ja SL. I. adj. *(cobarde)* cowardly; *(tonto)* dumb, stupid II. m.f. *(cobarde)* coward; *(tonto)* jerk, dummy —m. *(pelo)* pubic hair.

pen·den·cia f. *(riña)* quarrel, fight; LAW lis pendens, pending lawsuit.

pen·den·ciar intr. to fight, quarrel.

pen·den·cie·ro, –ra I. adj. quarrelsome, belligerent II. m.f. troublemaker.

pen·der intr. *(colgar)* to hang *<el columpio pende del árbol* the swing hangs from the tree>; *(depender)* to depend; FIG. *(estar pendiente)* to be pending.

pen·dien·te I. adj. *(colgante)* hanging; FIG. *(irresoluto)* pending, outstanding *<hay negocios pendientes que debemos resolver* there is pending business that we have to resolve>; *(inclinante)* sloping II. m. *(arete)* earring; *(colgante)* pendant; MIN. top (of a vein) —f. *(cuesta)* slope; *(inclinación del tejado)* pitch, dip (of a roof).

pén·do·la f. *(péndulo)* pendulum; FIG. *(reloj)* pendulum clock; ARCHIT. *(madero)* queen post; *(de un puente)* suspension cable; *(pluma)* pen, quill.

pen·dón m. *(bandera)* banner, pennant; *(estandarte)* standard; FIG., COLL. *(persona alta y desaliñada)* tall and unkempt person; *(mujer licenciosa)* tart, whore; BOT. sprout, shoot.

pen·do·ne·ar intr. COLL. to run around, gallivant.

pen·du·lar adj. pendular, swinging back and forth.

pén·du·lo, –la I. adj. hanging, pendent II. m. pendulum.

pe·ne m. ANAT. penis.

pe·ne·ca m.f. CHILE *(estudiante)* elementary school pupil —f. *(clase)* elementary grade.

pe·ne·tra·bi·li·dad f. penetrability.

pe·ne·tra·ble adj. *(que puede penetrarse)* penetrable; FIG. *(que puede comprenderse)* penetrable, intelligible.

pe·ne·tra·ción f. *(acción de penetrar)* penetration; FIG. *(sagacidad)* insight.

pe·ne·tra·dor, –do·ra adj. FIG. penetrating, acute.

pe·ne·tran·te adj. *(que penetra)* penetrating; FIG. *(inteligencia)* acute, penetrating; *(voz, mirada)* piercing; *(frío)* biting.

pe·ne·trar tr. *(pasar)* to penetrate; *(empapar)* to penetrate, permeate *<un olor desagradable penetró el cuarto* a disagreeable odor permeated the room>; FIG. *(afectar)* to penetrate, pierce *<su dolorosa historia penetró mi corazón* his sad story pierced my heart>; *(comprender)* to fathom, understand *<penetré los motivos de sus acciones* I understood the motives for their actions> —intr. to penetrate, enter *<el ladrón penetró por la ventana* the burglar entered by the window> —reflex. FIG. *(comprender)* to fathom, understand; *(empaparse)* to penetrate, steep oneself *<se penetró de la política de aquella época* she steeped herself in the politics of that period>.

pe·ni·ci·li·na f. PHARM. penicillin.

pe·nín·su·la f. GEOG. peninsula.

pe·nin·su·lar I. adj. GEOG. peninsular II. m.f. inhabitant of a peninsula.

pe·ni·que m. penny (British coin).

pe·ni·ten·cia f. *(sentimiento)* penitence; *(castigo)* penance ♦ **cumplir p.** or **hacer la p.** to do penance.

pe·ni·ten·cia·do, –da I. past part. see **penitenciar** II. adj. HIST. condemned by the Inquisition; AMER. jailed, imprisoned III. m.f. HIST. person condemned by the Inquisition; AMER. prisoner, convict.

pe·ni·ten·cial adj. penitential.

pe·ni·ten·ciar tr. to punish, impose penance on.

pe·ni·ten·cia·rí·a f. *(cárcel)* prison, penitentiary; RELIG. *(tribunal)* penitentiary (tribunal); *(cargo)* office of the Grand Penitentiary.

pe·ni·ten·cia·rio, –ria I. adj. penitentiary II. m. RELIG. penitentiary, confessor.

pe·ni·ten·te adj. & m.f. penitent.

pe·no·so, –sa adj. *(difícil)* difficult, arduous *<una tarea p.* an arduous task>; *(triste)* sad, distressing; FIG. *(afligido)* grieved, distressed.

pen·sa·do, –da I. past part. see **pensar** II. adj. ♦ **bien p.** *(bien reflexionado)* well thought-out (said of plans, ideas); *(con pensamientos favorables)* well-intentioned • **de p.** on purpose, purposely • **el día menos p.** when least expected • **mal p.** *(mal reflexionado)* poorly thought-out (said of plans, ideas); *(con pensamientos malos)* evil-minded • **te·ner p.** to have in mind, intend.

pen·sa·dor, –do·ra I. adj. *(que piensa)* thinking; *(pensativo)* pensive, thoughtful II. m. thinker ♦ **libre p.** freethinker.

pen·sa·mien·to¹ m. *(facultad)* thought; *(idea)* thought,

idea <*su p. es hacerlo rápidamente* his idea is to do it quickly>; FIG. *(sospecha)* suspicion; *(sentencia)* maxim, saying; *(raciocinio)* thought <*el p. platónico es fascinante* Platonic thought is fascinating> ♦ **como el p.** in a flash • **en un p.** in a jiffy • **ni por p.** I wouldn't think of it • **no pasarle por el p.** not to cross one's mind.
pen·sa·mien·to² m. BOT. pansy.
pen·san·te adj. thinking <*un ser p.* a thinking being>.
pen·sar¹ §49 tr. *(considerar)* to think about *or* over, consider <*pensó la respuesta cuidadosamente* he carefully considered the answer>; *(creer)* to think, believe <*pienso que no va a llover hoy* I don't think that it will rain today>; *(intentar)* to think of, intend <*pienso marcharme lo más pronto posible* I intend to leave as soon as possible> ♦ **pensándolo mejor** *or* **bien** on second thought —intr. *(formar ideas)* to think ♦ **p. en** *or* **sobre** to think about • **p. entre sí** *or* **para sí** to think to oneself • **p. mal** to be evil-minded • **¿qué piensas de ...?** what is your opinion about ...? • **sin p.** without thinking, thoughtlessly.
pen·sar² tr. to feed (animals).
pen·sa·ti·vo, –va adj. pensive, thoughtful.
pen·sil I. adj. hanging, dangling II. m. FIG. delightful garden.
pen·sión f. *(en un hotel)* room and board; *(de retiro)* pension, annuity; *(de estudios)* grant, fellowship; *(casa de huéspedes)* boarding house; FIG. *(gravamen)* encumbrance, lien.
pen·sio·na·do, –da I. past part. see **pensionar** II. adj. pensioned III. m.f. *(persona)* pensioner —m. *(colegio)* boarding school.
pen·sio·nar tr. *(conceder una pensión)* to pension; ECUAD. to bother, annoy —reflex. CHILE to be bothered *or* annoyed.
pen·sio·na·rio m. boarder, lodger.
pen·sio·nis·ta m.f. *(persona que disfruta)* pensioner; *(persona que paga)* boarder, lodger.
pen·tá·go·no, –na GEOM. I. adj. pentagonal II. m. pentagon ♦ **Pentágono** the Pentagon (Defense Department).
pen·ta·gra·ma *or* **pen·tá·gra·ma** m. MUS. stave, staff.
pen·tá·me·tro m. POET. pentameter.
pen·ta·teu·co m. BIBL. Pentateuch.
pen·ta·tlón m. SPORT. pentathlon.
pen·te·cos·tés m. RELIG. Pentecost, Whitsuntide.
pen·to·tal m. CHEM. pentothal.
pe·núl·ti·mo, –ma adj. & m.f. penultimate, next to the last.
pe·num·bra f. ASTRON., PHYS. penumbra; PAINT. chiaroscuro.
pe·num·bro·so, –sa adj. penumbral, penumbrous.
pe·nu·ria f. penury, want.
pe·ña f. *(roca)* rock, boulder; *(monte peñascoso)* rocky mountain; *(círculo)* circle, group ♦ **durar por peñas** to last for ages • **ser una p.** FIG. to be hard as stone.
pe·ñas·cal m. rocky place.
pe·ñas·co m. *(piedra)* large rock, crag; ANAT. petrous portion (of temporal bone); TEX. strong silk fabric.
pe·ñas·co·so, –sa adj. rocky, craggy.
pe·ñón m. craggy rock ♦ **p. de Gibraltar** Rock of Gibraltar.
pe·o m. SL. fart.
pe·ón m. *(caminante)* pedestrian; MIL. *(soldado)* foot soldier, infantryman; *(jornalero)* unskilled laborer *or* worker; AMER. farmhand, peon; *(juguete)* top, spinning top; *(en ajedrez)* pawn (in chess); *(en damas)* man, piece (in checkers) ♦ **a p.** COLL. on foot • **p. de brega** TAUR. matador's assistant.
pe·o·na·da f. *or* **pe·o·na·je** m. gang of laborers.
pe·o·nar intr. ARG. to labor.
pe·o·ne·rí·a f. day's labor.
pe·on·za f. spinning top (toy) ♦ **ser una p.** to be restless, be a fidget.
pe·or §G24 I. adj. worse <*éste es p. que el otro* this one is worse than the other>; worst <*soy el p. jugador del equipo* I am the worst player on the team> ♦ **cada vez p.** worse and worse • **y lo que es p.** and what's worse II. adv. worse <*lo hizo p. que ayer* he did it worse than yesterday> ♦ **p. que p.** *or* **tanto p.** worse still III. m.f. worse <*soy el p. de los dos* I am the worse of the two>; worst <*ella es la p. de las bailarinas* she is the worst of the dancers> ♦ **en el p. de los casos** at worst, if worst comes to worst • **lo p.** the

worst thing <*lo p. sería responder* the worst thing would be to answer>.
pe·o·rí·a f. worsening, deterioration.
pe·pa f. AMER. pip, seed; ARG. marble (toy); COL. lie, hoax.
pe·pe·nar tr. C. AMER., MEX. to collect, gather; MIN. to sift (ore).
pe·pi·nar m. cucumber patch.
pe·pi·na·zo m. COLL. explosion, blast.
pe·pi·ni·llo m. cucumber, gherkin.
pe·pi·no m. BOT. cucumber ♦ **no importar un p.** COLL. not to matter a whit.
pe·pi·ta f. BOT. pip, seed; VET. pip; MIN. nugget, lump (of metal).
pe·pi·to m. AMER. fop, dandy; *(bocadillo)* small meat sandwich.
pe·pi·to·ria f. CUL. fricassee (with egg yolk) <*pollo en p.* chicken fricassee>; COLL. *(mezcolanza)* jumble, hodgepodge.
pe·pón, –po·na I. adj. PERU potbellied II. f. see **pepona.**
pe·po·na I. f. large paper doll II. adj. see **pepón, –pona.**
pep·si·na f. BIOCHEM. pepsin, pepsine.
pép·ti·co, –ca adj. peptic.
pe·que m.f. COLL. child, kid.
pe·qué, peque see **pecar.**
pe·que·ñez f. [pl. **-ñe·ces**] *(calidad)* smallness, littleness; *(niñez)* childhood; *(menudencia)* trifle <*no se preocupe por pequeñeces* don't worry yourself with trifles>; FIG. *(mezquindad)* pettiness, meanness ♦ **p. de miras** narrow-mindedness.
pe·que·ñín, –ñi·na I. adj. teeny, tiny. II. m.f. child, tot.
pe·que·ño, –ña §G24 I. adj. *(menudo)* small, little <*compré un coche p.* I bought a small car>; *(corto)* short (in height); *(joven)* small, young <*cuando yo era p.* when I was young>; FIG. *(insignificante)* small, little <*sólo nos queda un problema p.* we only have one small problem left>; *(humilde)* humble, modest ♦ **en p.** in short • **p. burgués** petit bourgeois II. m.f. child ♦ **de p.** as a child.
pe·que·ñue·lo, –la I. adj. tiny, teeny II. m.f. little child, tot ♦ **los pequeñuelos** the little ones, the kiddies.
pe·qui·nés, –ne·sa adj. & m.f. Pekingese, Pekine.
pe·ra I. f. *(fruta)* pear; *(en la barba)* goatee; FIG. *(trabajo fácil)* cushy job; ELEC. pear-shaped switch ♦ **partir peras con** FIG., COLL. to be on friendly terms with • **pedir peras al olmo** COLL. to ask for the moon • **ponerle a alguien las peras al cuarto** COLL. to put the squeeze on someone • **ser la p.** FIG. to be the last straw II. adj. COLL. sharp, elegant.
pe·ral m. pear tree.
pe·ra·le·da f. pear orchard.
per·cal m. TEX. percale.
per·ca·li·na f. TEX. percaline.
per·can·ce m. mishap, setback ♦ **percances del oficio** drawbacks of the job.
per·ca·tar tr. to notice, perceive —reflex. ♦ **percatarse de** to notice, become aware of.
per·ce·be m. ZOOL. goose barnacle; COLL. *(tonto)* fool, dolt.
per·cep·ción f. *(de dinero)* collecting, receiving; *(sensación)* sensation, perception.
per·cep·ti·bi·li·dad f. perceptibility.
per·cep·ti·ble adj. *(que se siente)* perceptible, noticeable; *(que se cobra)* collectable, receivable.
per·cep·ti·vo, –va adj. perceptive.
per·cep·tor, –to·ra I. adj. *(que siente)* perceiving, sensing; *(que cobra)* collecting II. m.f. *(persona que siente)* perceiver, percipient; *(cobrador)* collector, receiver.
per·ci·bir tr. *(distinguir)* to perceive, sense; *(cobrar)* to collect, receive.
per·ci·bo m. collecting, receiving.
per·co·la·dor m. percolator.
per·cu·dir tr. to tarnish, dull —reflex. to become stained (laundry).
per·cu·sión f. percussion.
per·cu·sor m. ARM. firing pin, hammer; *(golpeador)* hitter, striker; MED. plexor.
per·cu·tir intr. *(golpear)* to percuss, strike; MED. to percuss.
per·cu·tor m. ARM. firing pin; *(golpeador)* hitter, striker.
per·cha f. *(madero)* pole, prop; *(mueble)* clothes rack; *(colgador individual)* hanger, coat hanger; *(alcándara)* perch,

roost; *(lazo)* snare; ICHTH. perch; MARIT. headrail; TEX. napping (action).

per·che·ro m. clothes rack.

per·de·dor, –do·ra I. adj. losing II. m.f. loser.

per·der §50 tr. *(dejar de tener)* to lose <*perdió el respeto de sus hijos* he lost the respect of his children>; *(extraviar)* to lose, mislay; *(ser vencido)* to lose <*ellos están perdiendo la batalla* they are losing the battle>; *(no conseguir)* to lose, <*perdí la oportunidad* I missed my chance>; to lose <*ella perdió un hijo en la guerra* she lost a son in the war>; *(arruinar)* to spoil, ruin ♦ **echar a p.** to spoil, ruin ♦ **p. de vista** to lose sight of • **p. el juicio** to lose one's mind • **p. la vista** to lose one's eyesight • **p. terreno** to lose ground • **p. tiempo** to waste time —intr. to lose <*nuestro equipo perdió* our team lost>; *(decaer)* to deteriorate, go downhill; *(desteñirse)* to fade —reflex. *(extraviarse)* to lose, mislay <*se me perdieron los guantes* I lost my gloves>; *(desorientarse)* to get lost, lose one's way <*nos perdimos en la selva* we got lost in the jungle>; *(naufragar)* to be lost at sea, sink; *(desaparecer)* to disappear, fade; FIG. *(conturbarse)* to lose control, lose one's head; *(dejar de ser útil)* to go to waste; *(arruinarse)* to be ruined, go astray ♦ **perderse de vista** to disappear • **perderse por** to be head over heels in love with.

per·di·ble adj. easily lost.

per·di·ción f. *(acción de perder)* loss; FIG. *(ruina moral)* ruin, undoing; RELIG. perdition, damnation; *(disipación)* dissipation, immorality; *(pasión)* unbridled passion.

pér·di·da f. *(privación)* loss, waste <*una p. de tiempo* a waste of time>; *(daño)* damage, harm; *(perdición)* perdition, ruin; COM. wastage ♦ **no tener p.** to be easy to find • **pérdidas y ganancias** profit and loss.

per·di·da·men·te adv. *(con exceso)* madly, desperately; *(inútilmente)* uselessly.

per·di·di·zo, –za adj. COLL. *(una cosa)* lost on purpose; *(una persona)* who gets lost easily ♦ **hacer p.** COLL. to hide • **hacerse el p.** COLL. to sneak off, make oneself scarce • **hacerse p.** COLL. to lose on purpose.

per·di·do, –da I. past part. see **perder** II. adj. *(extraviado)* lost, wasted <*tiempo p.* wasted time>; stray <*una bala p.* a stray bullet>; COLL. *(sucio)* filthy; *(rematado)* confirmed, hardened <*un borracho p.* a confirmed drunkard>; *(incorregible)* incorrigible, dissolute ♦ **estar p. por** to be madly in love with III. m. scoundrel, libertine.

per·di·gón[1] m. ORNITH. young partridge; ARM. small shot.

per·di·gón[2] m. COLL. *(en el juego)* loser (in gambling); *(derrochador)* spendthrift, wastrel; *(alumno)* failed student; *(bolita de moco)* ball of snot.

per·di·gue·ro, –ra I. adj. partridge-hunting II. m. game dealer.

per·dis m. SL. good-for-nothing, rake.

per·diz f. [pl. **-di·ces**] ORNITH. partridge ♦ **p. blanca** rock ptarmigan.

per·dón m. pardon, forgiveness ♦ **con p.** with your permission • **¡perdón!** sorry!, I beg your pardon!

per·do·na·ble adj. pardonable, forgivable.

per·do·na·dor, –do·ra I. adj. pardoning, forgiving II. m.f. pardoner.

per·do·nar tr. *(disculpar)* to pardon, forgive; *(exceptuar)* to exempt, excuse; *(renunciar)* to forego ♦ **no p.** not to miss or overlook.

per·do·na·vi·das m. [pl. **-das**] FIG., COLL. bully, braggart.

per·du·la·rio, –ria I. adj. *(descuidado)* careless, slovenly; *(disoluto)* rakish, dissolute II. m.f. *(descuidado)* careless or slovenly person; *(disoluto)* rake, dissolute person.

per·du·ra·bi·li·dad f. *(de lo eterno)* eternal or everlasting nature; *(de lo duradero)* durability.

per·du·ra·ble adj. *(eterno)* eternal, everlasting; *(duradero)* durable, lasting.

per·du·rar intr. to last.

pe·re·ce·de·ro, –ra I. adj. perishable, mortal II. m. COLL. poverty, want.

pe·re·cer §17 intr. to perish, die —reflex. ♦ **perecerse por** to die for, long for.

pe·re·ci·mien·to m. *(muerte)* death, demise; *(fin)* end, decline.

pe·re·gri·na·ción f. or **pe·re·gri·na·je** m. *(viaje)* peregrination, pilgrimage; FIG. *(vida terrenal)* earthly life.

pe·re·gri·na·men·te adv. *(extraordinariamente)* strangely, curiously; *(primorosamente)* beautifully, splendidly.

pe·re·gri·nan·te I. adj. on a pilgrimage, traveling II. m.f. pilgrim, traveler.

pe·re·gri·nar intr. *(por tierras extrañas)* to travel, journey; *(a un santuario)* to make a pilgrimage.

pe·re·gri·no, –na I. adj. *(que viaja)* traveling; *(en una peregrinación)* on a pilgrimage; ORNITH. migratory; FIG. *(extraño)* strange, peculiar II. m.f. pilgrim.

pe·re·jil m. BOT. parsley; FIG., COLL. *(adorno)* adornment, ornament ♦ **perejiles** titles, decorations.

pe·ren·ce·jo m. so-and-so, what's-his-name.

pe·ren·den·gue m. *(adorno)* cheap ornament; *(pendiente)* earring.

pe·ren·ga·no, –na m.f. so-and-so —m. what's-his-name —f. what's-her-name.

pe·ren·ne adj. perennial.

pe·ren·ne·men·te adv. perennially.

pe·ren·ni·dad f. perpetuity.

pe·ren·to·ria·men·te adv. peremptorily.

pe·ren·to·rie·dad f. *(calidad de perentorio)* peremptoriness; *(urgencia)* urgency.

pe·ren·to·rio, –ria adj. *(un plazo)* strict (time limit); *(terminante)* peremptory; *(apremiante)* urgent, pressing.

pe·re·za f. *(holgazanería)* laziness, indolence; *(lentitud)* slowness, sluggishness; VEN., ZOOL. sloth ♦ **me da p.** I can't be bothered.

pe·rez·ca, pe·rez·co see **perecer**.

pe·re·zo·sa·men·te adv. lazily, indolently.

pe·re·zo·so, –sa I. adj. *(holgazán)* lazy, idle; FIG. *(pesado)* slow, sluggish II. m.f. *(persona)* loafer, idler —m. ZOOL. sloth.

per·fec·ción f. perfection ♦ **a la p.** to perfection, perfectly.

per·fec·cio·na·mien·to m. *(perfección)* perfection, perfecting; *(mejora)* improvement, bettering.

per·fec·cio·nar tr. *(hacer perfecto)* to make perfect, bring to perfection; *(mejorar)* to improve.

per·fec·cio·nis·mo m. perfectionism.

per·fec·cio·nis·ta adj. & m.f. perfectionist.

per·fec·ta·men·te adv. perfectly ♦ **¡perfectamente!** right!, exactly!

per·fec·ti·ble adj. perfectible.

per·fec·to, –ta adj. *(impecable)* perfect; *(excelente)* perfect <*pareja p.* a perfect couple>; *(completo)* perfect, complete <*su p. inocencia* his complete innocence>; GRAM. perfect.

pér·fi·da·men·te adv. perfidiously.

pér·fi·do, –da I. adj. perfidious, treacherous II. m.f. traitor.

per·fil m. *(contorno)* profile, outline; *(sección)* section, cross section; *(línea)* thin stroke (of a letter); PAINT. *(en pintura)* profile; GEOL. cross section; GEOM. section ♦ **de p.** in profile, from the side of <*sólo lo vi de p.* I only saw it from the side> • **medio p.** half profile, three-quarter <*un retrato de medio p. de Lincoln* a three-quarter portrait of Lincoln> • **perfiles** *(retoques)* finishing touches; *(miramientos)* social courtesies ♦ **tomar perfiles** to trace.

per·fi·la·do, –da I. past part. see **perfilar** II. adj. *(de perfil)* in profile; *(rostro)* long and thin (face); *(nariz)* perfect, regular (nose).

per·fi·lar tr. PAINT. to profile; FIG. *(afinar)* to polish, put the finishing touches on —reflex. *(colocarse de perfil)* to show one's profile; FIG. *(tomar forma)* to take shape; COLL. *(aderezarse)* to dress up.

per·fo·ra·ción f. perforation, piercing; MIN. drilling, boring.

per·fo·ra·do I. past part. see **perforar** II. m. perforation.

per·fo·ra·dor, –do·ra I. adj. *(que perfora)* perforating; MIN. boring, drilling II. f. MIN. drill, drilling machine.

per·fo·rar tr. to perforate, pierce; MIN. to drill, bore.

per·fu·ma·de·ro m. cassolette, perfume pan.

per·fu·ma·dor m. *(pulverizador)* perfume atomizer; *(fumigatorio)* perfume pan.

per·fu·mar tr. to perfume —intr. to give off perfume.

per·fu·me m. *(aroma)* perfume, fragrance; *(preparación)* perfume.

per·fu·me·rí·a f. perfumery.

per·fu·me·ro, –ra or **per·fu·mis·ta** m.f. perfumer.

per·ga·mi·no m. *(papel)* parchment, vellum; *(diploma)* diploma; *(documento)* manuscript, document ♦ **pergaminos** FIG., COLL. titles of nobility.

per·ge·ño m. appearance, looks.

pér·go·la f. pergola.

pe·ri·car·dio m. ANAT. pericardium.

pe·ri·car·pio m. BOT. pericarp.

pe·ri·cia f. *(saber)* skill, expertise; *(práctica)* experience, practice.

pe·ri·co m. ORNITH. parakeet; *(en truque)* queen of clubs; MARIT. *(verga)* mizzen topgallant; *(vela)* mizzen topgallant sail; SL. *(bacín)* potty, large chamber pot; COL., ECUAD. drunk; C. RICA compliment; MEX. big talker ♦ **p. entre ellas** COLL. ladies' man • **p. ligero** ZOOL. sloth.

pe·ri·cón, –co·na I. adj. fit for all uses (said of horse or mule) II. m.f. *(caballo o mula)* horse *or* mule fit for all uses —m. *(en el juego)* queen of clubs; *(abanico)* large fan; ARG. popular dance.

pe·ri·co·te m. AMER. large rat.

pe·ri·fe·ria f. MATH. periphery; *(alrededores)* outskirts, periphery (of a city).

pe·ri·fé·ri·co, –ca adj. peripheral.

pe·ri·fo·llo m. BOT. chervil ♦ **perifollos** COLL. ornaments, frills, trimmings.

pe·rí·fra·sis [pl. **-sis**] f. periphrase, circumlocution.

pe·ri·ge·o m. ASTRON. perigee.

pe·ri·he·lio m. ASTRON. perihelion.

pe·ri·lla f. *(adorno)* pear-shaped ornament; *(barbilla)* goatee, imperial; ELEC. switch; *(tirador)* knob, handle; ANAT. ear lobe ♦ **de p.** *or* **perillas** just right • **venir de perillas** COLL. to come in handy, be useful.

pe·rí·me·tro m. GEOM. perimeter.

pe·ri·no·la f. *(juguete)* teetotum; *(adorno)* pear-shaped ornament; COLL. *(mujer)* petite and vivacious woman.

pe·rió·di·ca·men·te adv. periodically.

pe·rio·di·ci·dad f. periodicity.

pe·rió·di·co, –ca I. adj. periodic, periodical II. m. *(diario)* newspaper; *(revista)* periodical.

pe·rio·di·cu·cho m. rag, scandal sheet.

pe·rio·dis·mo m. *(profesión)* journalism; *(periodistas)* journalists.

pe·rio·dis·ta m.f. journalist, reporter.

pe·rio·dís·ti·co, –ca adj. journalistic.

pe·rí·o·do *or* **pe·ri·o·do** m. *(espacio de tiempo)* period, time *<fue un p. de paz>* it was a period of peace>; *(época)* period, age *<el p. isabelino fue una era de grandes creaciones literarias* the Elizabethan period was an era of great literary works>; ASTRON., GRAM., MATH., MED. period; GEOL. age.

pe·ri·pa·té·ti·co, –ca adj. PHILOS. Peripatetic, Aristotelian; FIG., COLL. *(ridículo)* ridiculous, outlandish.

pe·ri·pe·cia f. LIT., THEAT. peripeteia, vicissitude.

pe·ri·plo m. voyage, journey.

pe·ri·pues·to, –ta adj. COLL. dressed *or* dolled up.

pe·ri·que·te m. instant, jiffy.

pe·ri·qui·to m. ORNITH. parakeet.

pe·ris·co·pio m. OPT. periscope.

pe·ris·ti·lo m. ARCHIT. peristyle, colonnade.

pe·ris·to·le f. PHYSIOL. peristole, peristalsis.

pe·ri·ta·ción f. *or* **pe·ri·ta·je** m. expert's work *or* investigation.

pe·ri·to, –ta I. adj. expert, proficient II. m.f. expert.

pe·ri·to·ne·o m. ANAT. peritoneum.

per·ju·di·car §70 tr. *(dañar)* to damage; *(estropear)* to harm, do harm to *<p. la situación financiera a uno* to harm one's financial position>; *(desfavorecer)* not to suit.

per·ju·di·cial adj. harmful, detrimental.

per·jui·cio m. *(daño material)* damage, harm; *(daño moral)* injury, wrong; FIN. loss ♦ **sin p.** LAW without prejudice.

per·ju·rar intr. to commit perjury —reflex. to perjure oneself.

per·ju·rio m. perjury.

per·ju·ro, –ra I. adj. perjured II. m.f. perjurer.

per·la f. *(aljófar)* pearl; PRINT. *(en imprenta)* four-point type; FIG. *(tesoro)* pearl, treasure *<esa niña es una p.* that child is a treasure> ♦ **de perlas** FIG. *(perfectamente)* perfectly; *(de molde)* opportunely • **p. de cultivo** cultured pearl • **venir de perlas** FIG. to come opportunely, come at the right moment.

per·la·do, –da adj. *(forma)* pearl-shaped; *(color)* pearl-colored, pearly; *(cebada)* pearl (barley).

per·le·rí·a f. large quantity of pearls.

per·le·ro, –ra adj. pearl, pertaining to pearls.

per·ma·ne·cer §17 intr. to stay, remain.

per·ma·ne·cien·te adj. *(que permanece)* staying, remaining; *(permanente)* permanent.

per·ma·nen·cia f. *(duración constante)* permanence; *(estancia)* stay, residence.

per·ma·nen·te I. adj. permanent II. f. permanent wave.

per·ma·nen·te·men·te adv. permanently.

per·ma·nez·ca, permanezco see **permanecer.**

per·man·ga·na·to m. CHEM. permanganate.

per·me·a·bi·li·dad f. permeability.

per·me·a·ble adj. permeable.

per·mi·si·ble adj. permissible.

per·mi·sión f. permission, leave.

per·mi·si·vis·mo m. *or* **per·mi·si·vi·dad** f. permissiveness.

per·mi·si·vo, –va adj. permissive.

per·mi·so m. *(autorización)* permission *<nos dio p. para ir al cine* she gave us permission to go to the movies>; *(documento)* permit; MIL. leave, furlough; NUMIS. tolerance (permissible deviation from standard weight of coins) ♦ **con p.** *or* **con su p.** *(perdóneme)* excuse me; *(con su autorización)* with your permission, by your leave *<con su p. me voy ahora* with your permission, I am leaving now> • **p. de conducir** *or* **de conducción** driver's license.

per·mi·ti·do, –da I. past part. see **permitir** II. adj. permitted, allowed.

per·mi·ti·dor, –do·ra I. adj. permitting, allowing II. m.f. permitter.

per·mi·tir tr. *(autorizar)* to permit, allow, let *<me permitió hablar* he let me speak>; *(tolerar)* to allow, tolerate *<permite todo tipo de error* he tolerates all types of error> ♦ **permítame** allow me • **si lo permite el tiempo** weather permitting —reflex. *(estar permitido)* to be permitted *or* allowed *<no se permite el libre cambio en este país* free trade is not permitted in this country>; *(tomar la libertad)* to permit *or* allow oneself, take the liberty of *<me permití una indiscreción pequeña* I allowed myself a little indiscretion>.

per·mu·ta f. *(trueque)* exchange; MATH. permutation.

per·mu·ta·bi·li·dad f. exchangeability; MATH. permutability.

per·mu·ta·ble adj. exchangeable; MATH. permutable.

per·mu·ta·ción f. *(trueque)* exchange, barter; MATH. permutation.

per·mu·tar tr. *(trocar)* to exchange, swap; MATH. to permute.

per·na·da f. *(golpe)* kick.

per·ne·ar intr. *(sacudir las piernas)* to kick; FIG., COLL. *(andar mucho)* to scurry, hustle.

per·ne·ra f. trouser *or* pant leg.

per·nia·bier·to, –ta adj. bowlegged.

per·ni·cio·so, –sa adj. pernicious, harmful.

per·nil m. *(de animal)* haunch and thigh (of an animal); *(de cerdo)* ham; *(de pantalón)* trouser *or* pant leg.

per·no m. *(tornillo)* bolt, pin; *(de un gozne)* knuckle, hook (of a hinge).

per·noc·tar intr. to pass *or* spend the night.

pe·ro¹ m. BOT. *(manzana)* variety of apple; ARG., SP. pear tree.

pe·ro² §G46 I. conj. but *<es bonita p. antipática* she is pretty but disagreeable>; yet *<gana mucho dinero p. siempre está sin blanca* he earns a lot of money yet he is always broke> **II.** m. COLL. *(defecto)* defect, fault; *(dificultad)* snag, objection *<siempre pones peros* you always raise objections> ♦ **no hay p. que valga** COLL. there are no buts about it.

pe·ro·gru·lla·da f. COLL. platitude, trite remark.

pe·ro·gru·lles·co, –ca adj. trite, hackneyed.

pe·ro·gru·llo m. ♦ **verdad de Perogrullo** platitude, truism.

pe·rol m. *(vasija)* pot; *(cacerola)* saucepan.

pe·ro·né m. ANAT. fibula.

pe·ro·ra·ción f. peroration, speech.

pe·ro·rar intr. to perorate, make a speech.

pe·ro·ra·ta f. long-winded speech.

pe·ró·xi·do m. CHEM. peroxide.

per·pen·di·cu·lar GEOM. adj. & f. perpendicular.
per·pen·di·cu·lar·men·te adv. perpendicularly.
per·pe·tra·ción f. perpetration.
per·pe·tra·dor, –do·ra I. adj. perpetrating II. m.f. perpetrator.
per·pe·trar tr. to perpetrate.
per·pe·tua f. BOT. everlasting.
per·pe·tua·ción f. perpetuation.
per·pe·tua·men·te adv. perpetually.
per·pe·tuar §67 tr. to perpetuate —reflex. to be perpetuated.
per·pe·tui·dad f. perpetuity.
per·pe·tuo, –tua adj. (que dura siempre) perpetual, everlasting; (que dura toda la vida) life <cadena p. life imprisonment>.
per·ple·ji·dad f. perplexity.
per·ple·jo, –ja adj. (confuso) perplexed, confused; (que causa confusión) perplexing.
pe·rra I. f. ZOOL. bitch; FIG., COLL. (borrachera) drunk, binge; (moneda) five- or ten-cent piece; (rabieta) tantrum, fit; (obstinación) stubbornness, obstinacy ♦ tener muchas perras COLL. to have lots of cash II. adj. see perro, –rra.
pe·rra·da f. (conjunto de perros) pack of dogs; FIG., COLL. (acción mala) dirty trick.
pe·rra·men·te adv. FIG., COLL. very badly.
pe·rre·ra f. (lugar) dog kennel; (empleo) grind, drudgery; COLL. (mal pagador) bad risk; (rabieta) tantrum, fit; ARG. (perrada) dirty trick; (carro) dogcatcher's wagon; COL. fleabag.
pe·rre·rí·a f. (jauría) pack of dogs; FIG. (mala gente) gang of hoodlums; (expresión de enojo) angry remark; (mala acción) dirty trick.
pe·rre·ro m. (en las iglesias) beadle (who ejects dogs from church); (cuidador) master or keeper of hounds; (a quien le gustan los perros) dog lover.
pe·rri·lla f. SL. (perra chica) little dog; MEX. sty, stye.
pe·rri·llo m. ARM. trigger; (de los frenos) curb (of a bit).
pe·rro, –rra I. m.f. ZOOL. dog; COLL. (arrastrado) dirty dog, scoundrel <el muy p. me burló the dirty dog deceived me> ♦ ¡a otro p. con ese hueso! FIG., COLL. tell it to the Marines! • como perros y gatos FIG. like cats and dogs • de perros lousy, rotten <una vida de perros a rotten life> • echar a perros to misuse, waste • estar para los perros COLL. to be lousy • p. afgano Afghan hound • p. caliente CUL. hot dog • p. cobrador retriever • p. danés Great Dane • p. de aguas or de lanas poodle • p. de casta thoroughbred, pedigreed dog • p. de Terranova Labrador retriever • p. dogo or de presa bulldog • p. faldero lap dog • p. galgo greyhound • p. lebrel whippet • p. lobo wolfhound • p. marino ICHTH. dogfish • p. mastín mastiff • p. mudo raccoon • p. pastor sheep dog • p. pastor alemán German shepherd • p. policía police dog • p. raposero or zorrero foxhound • p. rastrero tracking dog • p. sabueso bloodhound • p. viejo COLL. old hand • tratar a alguien como a un p. FIG., COLL. to treat someone like a dog —f. see perra II. adj. lousy, rotten <suerte p. rotten luck>.
pe·rru·no, –na adj. canine, of dogs.
per·sa adj. & m.f. Persian —m. (idioma) Persian.
per·se·cu·ción f. (tormento) persecution; (seguimiento) pursuit, chase.
per·se·gui·dor, –do·ra I. adj. (que atormenta) persecuting; (que sigue) pursuing, chasing; LAW prosecuting II. m.f. (que atormenta) persecutor; (que sigue) pursuer; LAW prosecutor.
per·se·gui·mien·to m. var. of persecución.
per·se·guir §64 tr. (seguir) to pursue, chase <los cazadores persiguen a la caza the hunters pursue the game>; FIG. (acosar) to persecute <los romanos persiguieron a los primeros cristianos the Romans persecuted the first Christians>; (atormentar) to hound, torment <la tristeza me persigue sadness torments me>; (solicitar) to pester, harass <los niños me persiguieron hasta que compré los helados the children pestered me until I bought them ice cream>; LAW (en derecho) to prosecute.
per·se·ve·ran·cia f. perseverance.
per·se·ve·ran·te adj. persevering.

per·se·ve·rar intr. to persevere.
Per·sia f. GEOG. Persia.
per·sia·na f. TEX. persienne, flowered silk fabric; (celosía) blind <p. veneciana Venetian blind>.
pér·si·co, –ca I. adj. Persian II. m. BOT. peach (tree and fruit).
per·si·ga, persigo see perseguir.
per·sig·nar tr. to cross, make the sign of the cross over —reflex. (santiguarse) to cross oneself; FIG., COLL. (comenzar a vender) to make the first sale of the day.
per·si·guie·ra, persiguió see perseguir.
per·sis·ten·cia f. persistence.
per·sis·ten·te adj. persistent.
per·sis·tir intr. (permanecer) to persist; (continuar) to continue ♦ p. en to persist in.
per·so·na f. (individuo) person; LIT. (personaje) character (in a book, play); GRAM. person <primera p. first person>; (hombre distinguido) personage; THEOL. person ♦ de p. a p. person to person, man to man • en p. in person • p. agente GRAM. agent • p. jurídica or social LAW legal entity, body corporate • personas people • por p. per person, each • tercera p. GRAM. third person; (mediador) third party.
per·so·na·je m. (persona importante) personage, celebrity; LIT. character.
per·so·nal I. adj. personal II. m. (empleados) personnel, staff; SL. (gente) people ♦ p. de tierra AER. ground crew.
per·so·na·li·dad f. (individualidad) personality; (persona notable) personage, public figure; LAW (en derecho) legal status ♦ tener p. to have personality or character.
per·so·na·li·zar §04 tr. (dar carácter personal) to personalize; GRAM. to make personal (an impersonal verb).
per·so·nal·men·te adv. personally.
per·so·nar·se reflex. (reunirse) to meet (with someone); (presentarse) to go, appear (in person); LAW to appear.
per·so·ne·rí·a f. (cargo del personero) representation, procuration; AMER., LAW personality.
per·so·ne·ro m. representative, agent.
per·so·ni·fi·ca·ción f. personification.
per·so·ni·fi·car §70 tr. to personify.
pers·pec·ti·va I. f. (arte) perspective; FIG. (vista) view, scene <mi ventana ofrece una p. magnífica my window offers a magnificent view>; (contingencia) prospect, outlook <una p. positiva a positive outlook>; (apariencia) appearance ♦ p. aérea aerial perspective • p. lineal linear perspective II. see perspectivo, –va.
pers·pec·ti·vo, –va I. adj. perspective II. f. see perspectiva.
pers·pi·ca·cia or **pers·pi·ca·ci·dad** f. perspicacity, sagacity.
pers·pi·caz adj. (agudo) sharp, keen; FIG. shrewd, perspicacious.
pers·pi·cuo, –cua adj. perspicuous, clear.
per·sua·di·dor, –do·ra I. adj. persuasive II. m.f. persuader.
per·sua·dir tr. (inducir a hacer algo) to persuade; (inducir a creer algo) to convince —reflex. to be persuaded or convinced.
per·sua·si·ble adj. plausible, credible.
per·sua·sión f. persuasion.
per·sua·si·vo, –va I. adj. persuasive II. f. persuasiveness.
per·sua·sor, –so·ra I. adj. persuasive II. m.f. persuader, persuasive person.
per·te·ne·cer §17 intr. (ser de) to belong, be <ese dinero pertenece a mí that money belongs to me>; (ser parte) to belong <el anillo perteneció a la colección real de joyas the ring belonged to the royal collection of jewels>; (tocar) to pertain or apply to <esta ley pertenece a todo el mundo this law pertains to everyone>.
per·te·ne·cien·te adj. (referente) referring, pertaining; (de propiedad de) belonging.
per·te·nen·cia f. (derecho) ownership; (posesión) belonging, possession <llevó todas sus pertenencias a California he took all of his belongings to California>; (propiedad) holding, property; MIN. claim (of one square acre) ♦ pertenencias LAW appurtenance (incidental property, privilege or right).
per·te·nez·ca, pertenezco see pertenecer.

pér·ti·ga f. pole ♦ **salto de p.** SPORT. pole vault.
pér·ti·go m. shaft, thill (of a carriage).
per·ti·gue·ar tr. to knock down (fruit from a tree) with a pole.
per·ti·na·cia f. *(terquedad)* stubbornness, obstinacy; FIG. *(persistencia)* persistence, long duration.
per·ti·naz adj. *(obstinado)* obstinate, tenacious; FIG. *(persistente)* persistent.
per·ti·naz·men·te adv. obstinately, tenaciously.
per·ti·nen·cia f. pertinence, relevance.
per·ti·nen·te adj. pertinent, relevant.
per·tre·char tr. MIL. to supply, equip; FIG. *(disponer)* to prepare, arrange —reflex. ♦ **pertrecharse de** or **con** to provide or supply oneself with.
per·tre·chos m.pl. MIL. stores and ammunition; *(instrumentos)* equipment, implements.
per·tur·ba·ción f. perturbation, disturbance; MED. upset, disorder ♦ **p. atmosférica** METEOROL. atmospheric disturbance.
per·tur·ba·dor, –do·ra I. adj. disturbing, upsetting II. m.f. disturber, upsetter.
per·tur·bar tr. *(trastornar)* to disturb, upset; *(desasosegar)* to perturb.
pe·rú m. ♦ **valer un p.** to be worth a fortune.
Pe·rú m. Peru.
pe·rua·nis·mo m. Peruvianism.
pe·rua·no, –na adj. & m.f. Peruvian.
pe·ru·le·ro, –ra I. adj. Peruvian II. m.f. *(peruano)* Peruvian; *(persona que vuelve del Perú)* person who returns from Peru with a fortune —m. *(vasija)* earthenware jar.
per·ver·si·dad f. perversity, wickedness.
per·ver·sión f. perversion, corruption.
per·ver·so, –sa I. adj. *(depravado)* perverse, depraved; *(malo)* evil, wicked II. m.f. *(depravado)* pervert, depraved person; *(persona mala)* evildoer.
per·ver·ti·do, –da I. adj. perverted II. m.f. pervert.
per·ver·ti·dor, –do·ra I. adj. perverting, corrupting II. m.f. perverter, corrupter.
per·ver·ti·mien·to m. perversion, perverting.
per·ver·tir §65 tr. to pervert, corrupt —reflex. to become perverted.
per·vi·ven·cia f. survival, persistence.
per·vi·vir intr. NEOL. to survive, persist.
pe·sa f. weight *<pesas y medidas* weights and measures> ♦ **pesas** SPORT. dumbbells, weights.
pe·sa·car·tas m. [pl. **-tas**] letter scale.
pe·sa·da f. quantity weighed at one time.
pe·sa·da·men·te adv. *(con pesadez)* heavily; FIG. *(de un modo pesado)* annoyingly, irritatingly.
pe·sa·dez f. *(calidad de pesado)* heaviness, weight; FIG. *(impertinencia)* impertinence, insolence; *(sensación)* heaviness, leadenness (of the head, stomach); *(molestia)* annoyance, nuisance; *(lentitud)* slowness, sluggishness; *(aburrimiento)* dullness, tediousness; *(obesidad)* fatness, obesity; PHYS. *(gravedad)* gravity.
pe·sa·di·lla f. nightmare.
pe·sa·do, –da I. past part. see **pesar** II. adj. *(que pesa)* heavy *<llevó el bulto pesado al camión* he carried the heavy package to the truck>; FIG. *(intenso)* deep, sound *<un sueño p.* a deep sleep>; *(cargado)* heavy *<tenía el corazón p.* his heart was heavy>; *(el tiempo)* sultry, oppressive; *(lento)* slow, sluggish; *(torpe)* clumsy, awkward; *(aburrido)* boring, dull *<un profesor p.* a boring teacher>; *(molesto)* annoying, irritating; *(fatigante)* wearisome, tedious; *(difícil)* tough, hard *<un trabajo p.* a tough job>; *(ofensivo)* offensive; *(obeso)* fat, obese ♦ **más p. que un saco de plomo** FIG., COLL. as dull as dishwater.
pe·sa·dor, –do·ra I. adj. weighing II. m.f. weigher.
pe·sa·dum·bre f. *(pesadez)* heaviness, weight; *(pesar)* grief, sorrow; *(desazón)* unpleasantness.
pé·sa·me m. condolence ♦ **dar el p.** to express condolences.
pe·san·te adj. *(que pesa)* weighing, weighty; *(triste)* sad.
pe·san·tez f. PHYS. gravity.
pe·sar¹ m. *(pena)* sorrow, sadness; *(arrepentimiento)* regret *<a mi p.* to my regret> ♦ **a p. de** *(no obstante)* in spite of, despite; against one's will *<a p. suyo* against his will> • **a p. de los pesares** or **a p. de todo** in spite of everything.

pe·sar² tr. *(determinar el peso)* to weigh; to weigh down *<me pesa el fardo* the bundle is weighing me down>; FIG. *(examinar)* to weigh, consider *<p. uno sus palabras* to weigh one's words>; *(agobiar)* to sadden, grieve *<me pesa su enfermedad* his illness saddens me>; COL., VEN. to sell (meat) —intr. *(tener peso)* to weigh *<la caja pesa cinco kilos* the box weighs five kilograms>; to weigh a lot, be heavy *<¡cómo pesa este paquete!* how heavy this package is!>; *(ser importante)* to carry weight, be important ♦ **pese a quien le pese** say what they will, whatever happens.
pe·sa·ro·so, –sa adj. *(arrepentido)* sorry, regretful; *(triste)* sad.
pes·ca f. *(acción)* fishing, angling; *(lo pescado)* catch, haul ♦ **p. costera** or **litoral** coastal fishing • **p. de alta mar** or **de altura** deep-sea fishing • **p. de arrastre** trawling • **p. submarina** underwater fishing.
pes·ca·da f. ICHTH. hake.
pes·ca·de·rí·a f. fish market.
pes·ca·de·ro, –ra m.f. fishmonger.
pes·ca·di·lla f. ICHTH. whiting.
pes·ca·do m. fish (out of water).
pes·ca·dor, –do·ra I. adj. fishing II. m. *(persona)* fisherman; ICHTH. anglerfish —f. fisherwoman.
pes·can·te m. shelf; *(de los cocheros)* driver's or coachman's seat; CONSTR. jib, boom (of a crane); MARIT. davit; THEAT. hoist.
pes·car §70 tr. *(coger peces)* to fish (for); FIG., COLL. *(coger)* to get *<p. una buena reprimenda* to get a good scolding>; *(lograr)* to land *<p. un marido* to land a husband>; *(a un desprevenido)* to catch *<p. a uno en el acto* to catch someone in the act>.
pes·co·ce·ar tr. AMER. to hit on the neck; CHILE to grab by the neck.
pes·co·za·da f. or **pes·co·zón** m. blow on the neck or head.
pes·cue·zo m. *(de un animal)* neck; *(de una persona)* scruff of the neck; FIG. *(vanidad)* pride, haughtiness ♦ **apretar** or **estirar** or **torcer el p. a alguien** FIG., COLL. to wring someone's neck.
pe·se·bre f. rack, manger.
pe·se·bre·ra f. *(conjunto de pesebres)* row of racks or mangers.
pe·se·ro m. AMER. fixed-rate taxi.
pe·se·ta f. FIN. peseta ♦ **cambiar la p.** FIG., COLL. vomit, throw up.
pe·se·te·ro, –ra adj. SP. *(que vale una peseta)* costing a peseta; COLL. *(avaro)* stingy, penny-pinching.
pé·si·ma·men·te adv. badly, terribly.
pe·si·mis·mo m. pessimism.
pe·si·mis·ta I. adj. pessimistic II. m.f. pessimist.
pé·si·mo, –ma adj. very bad, terrible.
pe·so m. *(fuerza)* weight; FIN. peso; *(cosa pesada)* weight; *(balanza)* scale, balance; *(pesa)* counterweight; FIG. *(carga)* weight, burden *<el p. de la culpabilidad* the weight of guilt>; *(importancia)* weight, importance *<su palabra tiene mucho p.* his word carries a lot of weight>; SPORT. shot *<lanzamiento del p.* shot-put> ♦ **a p. de oro** FIG. at exorbitant prices • **caerse una cosa de su propio p.** FIG., COLL. to go without saying, be self-evident • **de p.** FIG. weighty, important • **levantamiento de pesos** SPORT. weightlifting • **levantar en p.** to lift up • **p. absoluto** PHYS. absolute weight • **p. atómico** PHYS. atomic weight • **p. bruto** gross weight • **p. específico** PHYS. density • **p. gallo** SPORT. bantamweight • **p. ligero** or **liviano** SPORT. lightweight • **p. medio** SPORT. middleweight • **p. molecular** PHYS. molecular weight, formula weight • **p. mosca** SPORT. flyweight • **p. muerto** dead weight • **p. neto** net weight • **p. pesado** SPORT. heavyweight • **p. pluma** SPORT. featherweight • **p. semimedio** welterweight • **p. semipesado** SPORT. light heavyweight • **quitarle a alguien un p. de encima** FIG. to take a load off someone's mind.
pes·pi·ta f. GUAT. coquette, flirt.
pes·pun·tar or **pes·pun·te·ar** tr. SEW. to backstitch.
pes·pun·te m. SEW. backstitch.
pes·qué, pesque see **pescar**.
pes·que·rí·a f. *(pesquera)* fishery, fishing ground; *(acción)* fishing.
pes·que·ro, –ra adj. fishing, of fishing.

pes·quis m. SL. brains, sense.
pes·qui·sa f. *(averiguación)* inquiry, investigation —m. ARG., ECUAD. secret police.
pes·qui·sar tr. to investigate, inquire into.
pes·ta·ña f. ANAT. eyelash; *(de una rueda)* rim (of a wheel); *(de un libro)* joint (of a book); *(borde)* edge, border; SEW. *(de una tela)* fringe; BOT. hair; MECH. flange ♦ **no pegar p.** FIG. not to sleep a wink • **p. vibrátil** BIOL. cilium (hairlike protrusion of a cell) • **quemarse las pestañas** FIG., COLL. to burn the midnight oil.
pes·ta·ñe·ar intr. to blink, wink ♦ **sin p.** FIG. without batting an eyelid.
pes·ta·ñe·o m. blinking, winking.
pes·ta·zo m. COLL. stink, smell.
pes·te f. MED. plague <*p. bubónica* bubonic plague>; FIG. *(influencia mala)* pestilence, evil <*hay una p. que amenaza nuestra sociedad* there is a pestilence that threatens our society>; *(persona perniciosa)* menace, evil influence; *(olor)* stench, stink <*la p. de la muerte* the stench of death>; *(exceso)* plague, invasion <*una p. de ratas* a plague of rats>; *(molestia)* nuisance, aggravation <*los niños pueden ser una p.* children can be a nuisance>; CHILE smallpox; COL. cold (illness) ♦ **echar pestes** FIG., FAM. *(tratar mal)* to drag through the mud, heap abuse upon; *(maldecir)* to complain bitterly • **huir de alguien como de la p.** to avoid *or* shun someone like the plague • **p. negra** Black Death • **pestes** offensive words.
pes·ti·fe·ro, –ra I. adj. *(que puede causar peste)* pestiferous; *(que tiene mal olor)* stinking, foul; MED. plague-ridden II. m.f. MED. plague victim.
pes·ti·len·cia f. *(peste)* pestilence, plague; *(olor desagradable)* stench, stink.
pes·ti·len·cial *or* **pes·ti·len·te** adj. *(pestífero)* pestilential, pestiferous; *(que tiene mal olor)* stinking, foul.
pes·ti·llo m. bolt (of a lock).
pes·ti·ño m. CUL. honey-dipped fritter.
pes·to·so, –sa adj. stinking, foul.
pe·su·ña f. var. of **pezuña.**
pe·ta·ca I. f. *(bolsa)* tobacco pouch; *(estuche)* cigar *or* cigarette case; *(baúl)* leather trunk or chest; *(maleta)* suitcase; AMER. lazy person, loafer; C. AMER. hump (on the back); DOM. REP., P. RICO washing trough II. adj. AMER. lazy, idle ♦ **petacas** MEX. buttocks.
pé·ta·lo m. BOT. petal.
pe·tar·de·ar tr. MIL. to blow down with petards; AUTO. to backfire; FIG. *(estafar)* to cheat, swindle.
pe·tar·dis·ta m.f. cheat, swindler.
pe·tar·do m. MIL. petard, bomb; *(cohete)* petard, firecracker; FIG. *(engaño)* fraud, swindle; FIG., COLL. *(mujer fea)* ugly woman ♦ **pegar un p. a alguien** COLL. to hit up someone for money.
pe·ta·te m. *(estera)* sleeping mat; *(de ropa de la cama)* bed roll; COLL. *(de pasajero)* baggage, luggage; *(embustero)* crook, swindler; *(hombre despreciable)* good-for-nothing, scoundrel ♦ **liar el p.** FIG., COLL. *(marcharse)* to hit the road; *(morir)* to kick the bucket.
pe·te·ne·ra f. Andalusian popular song ♦ **salir por peteneras** COLL. to go off on a tangent.
pe·te·ra f. COLL. *(disputa)* brawl, quarrel; *(obstinación)* stubbornness, obstinacy.
pe·ti·ción f. *(demanda)* petition, request; LAW claim, demand ♦ **a p. de** at the request of • **p. de mano** proposal (of marriage).
pe·ti·cio·nar tr. AMER. to petition.
pe·ti·cio·na·rio, –ria *or* **pe·ti·cio·nan·te** AMER. I. adj. petitioning II. m.f. petitioner.
pe·ti·me·tre, –tra m. fop, dandy —f. stylish woman, fashion plate.
pe·ti·so, –sa AMER. I. adj. short, squat II. m. *(caballo)* small horse.
pe·ti·to·rio, –ria I. adj. petitionary II. m. COLL. *(petición enojosa)* tiresome request; PHARM. medicine catalog —f. COLL. petition, request.
pe·to m. *(armadura)* breastplate (of armor); *(de un delantal)* top (of an apron); *(adorno)* stomacher, breast ornament; SPORT., ZOOL. plastron.
pé·tre·o, –a adj. stony, rocky.
pe·tri·fi·ca·ción f. petrification.

pe·tri·fi·car §70 tr. to petrify —reflex. to become petrified.
pe·tro·dó·la·res m.pl. petrodollars.
pe·tro·gli·fo m. petroglyph.
pe·tró·le·o m. petroleum, oil ♦ **p. bruto** *or* **crudo** crude oil • **p. combustible** fuel oil.
pe·tro·le·ro, –ra I. adj. oil, petroleum <*la industria p.* the petroleum industry>; *(incendiario)* incendiary II. m.f. *(incendiario)* incendiary, arsonist; *(vendedor)* petroleum dealer —m. *(buque)* oil tanker.
pe·tro·lí·fe·ro, –ra adj. petroliferous, oil-bearing.
pe·tro·quí·mi·ca f. petrochemistry.
pe·tro·quí·mi·co, –ca adj. petrochemical.
pe·tu·lan·cia f. arrogance, presumptuousness.
pe·tu·lan·te adj. arrogant, presumptuous.
pe·tu·nia f. BOT. petunia.
pe·yo·ra·ti·vo, –va adj. pejorative.
pe·yo·te m. BOT. peyote.
pez¹ m. [pl. **pe·ces**] ICHTH. fish ♦ **estar como el p. en el agua** FIG., COLL. to feel completely at home, be in one's element • **estar p.** FIG., COLL. to be totally ignorant (about something) • **p. austral** ASTRON. Pisces • **p. de San Pedro** ICHTH. dory • **p. espada** ICHTH. swordfish • **p. gordo** FIG., COLL. big shot, bigwig • **p. luna** ICHTH. sunfish • **p. martillo** ICHTH. hammerhead (shark) • **p. mujer** ZOOL. manatee • **p. piloto** ICHTH. pilot fish • **p. reverso** ICHTH. remora • **p. sierra** ICHTH. sawfish • **p. volante** *or* **volador** ICHTH. flying fish • **picar el p.** COLL. to take the bait • **ser un p.** FIG., COLL. to be a dunce.
pez² [pl. **pe·ces**] f. pitch, tar ♦ **p. griega** colophony, rosin.
pe·zón m. BOT. stalk, stem; *(de la teta)* nipple, teat; *(extremo)* point, end.
pe·zo·ne·ra f. *(de eje)* linchpin; *(de mujeres)* nipple shield.
pe·zu·ña f. *(cloven)* hoof.
¡pf! interj. hah!
phi f. phi (Greek letter).
pi f. *(letra)* pi (Greek letter); MATH. pi.
pia·da f. *(de pájaro)* cheep, chirp; FIG., COLL. *(expresión)* borrowed expression *or* saying.
pia·dor, –do·ra *or* **pian·te** adj. cheeping, chirping.
pia·do·sa·men·te adv. *(con lástima)* mercifully, compassionately; *(con devoción)* devoutly, piously.
pia·do·so, –sa adj. *(que compadece)* merciful, compassionate; *(devoto)* pious, devout.
pia·far intr. to paw *or* stamp the ground (a horse).
pia·lar tr. AMER. to snare, trap.
pian, pian *or* **pian, pia·no** adv. COLL. slowly, little by little.
pia·nis·ta m.f. *(músico)* pianist; *(fabricante)* piano maker; *(vendedor)* piano dealer.
pia·nís·ti·co, –ca adj. MUS. piano, pianistic.
pia·no MUS. I. m. piano ♦ **p. de cola** grand piano • **p. de media cola** baby grand • **p. vertical** upright piano II. adv. piano, softly.
pia·no·for·te m. MUS. pianoforte, piano.
piar §30 intr. *(las aves)* to cheep, chirp; COLL. *(pedir)* to beg, whine <*p. por una cosa* to beg *or* whine for something>.
pia·ra f. *(manada de cerdos)* herd (of swine); *(rebaño)* flock (of sheep).
pias·tra f. NUMIS. piaster, piastre.
pi·be, –ba m.f. ARG., URUG., COLL. kid, child.
pi·be·rí·o m. ARG. bunch of kids.
pi·ca¹ f. ARM. pike; MIL. pikeman; TAUR. *(garrocha)* picador's lance *or* goad; *(escoda)* stonemason's hammer; COL. pique, resentment ♦ **poner una p. en Flandes** FIG., COLL. to achieve something difficult.
pi·ca² f. MED. pica (craving for unnatural food).
pi·ca·ce·ro, –ra I. adj. ORNITH. magpie-hunting (hawk) II. f. CHILE, ECUAD., PERU pique, resentment.
pi·ca·cho m. summit, peak.
pi·ca·da I. f. *(picotazo)* peck (with the beak); *(picadura)* bite, sting (of an insect); AMER. narrow trail; ARG. narrow ford; BOL., CHILE, VET. anthrax —adj. see **picado, –da.**
pi·ca·de·ro m. *(para caballos)* ring (for training horses); MARIT. boat skid *or* block; COLL. *(de soltero)* bachelor pad; COL. slaughterhouse.
pi·ca·di·llo m. CUL. chopped meat, hash ♦ **hacer p.** FIG. to make mincemeat of.

pi·ca·do, –da I. past part. see **picar** II. adj. SEW. pricked, perforated; AMER. tipsy, crocked III. m. *(acción de picar)* pricking, perforating; MUS. staccato; AVIA. nose dive —f. see **picada**.

pi·ca·dor m. *(de caballos)* horsebreaker; TAUR. picador; MIN. cutter (miner); CUL. chopping block.

pi·ca·du·ra f. *(acción de picar)* pricking, perforation; *(pinchazo)* bite, sting; *(maca)* bruise, flaw (on fruit); *(tabaco)* cut *or* loose tobacco; DENT. decay, cavity (on a tooth).

pi·ca·flor m. ORNITH. hummingbird; AMER., FIG. flirt, Romeo.

pi·ca·ma·de·ros m. [pl. **-ros**] ORNITH. woodpecker.

pi·ca·na f. ARG., CHILE goad.

pi·ca·ne·ar tr. ARG. to goad.

pi·can·te I. adj. CUL. spicy, highly seasoned; FIG. *(arriesgado)* racy, risqué; *(mordaz)* sharp, biting II. m. FIG. *(mordacidad)* mordacity, bite; CUL. *(calidad)* spiciness; *(guiso)* spicy dish; AMER. hot sauce.

pi·can·te·rí·a f. PERU stall where spicy food is sold.

pi·ca·pe·dre·ro m. stonecutter.

pi·ca·pi·ca f. CUBA, ECUAD. plant with leaves that produce an itch.

pi·ca·plei·tos m. [pl. **-tos**] COLL. *(pleitista)* quarrelsome person; *(abogado)* shyster, pettifogger.

pi·ca·por·te m. *(barrita)* latch; *(llave)* latchkey; *(aldaba)* doorknocker.

pi·car §70 tr. *(punzar)* to prick, puncture; *(agujerear)* to perforate, punch holes in; to punch <p. *los billetes* to punch tickets>; *(la piel)* to pock, pit; SEW. to pink; TAUR. to prick, goad; *(espolear)* to spur; *(morder)* to bite, sting; ICHTH. to bite, take <p. *el cebo* to take the bait>; ORNITH. to peck (at); *(comer)* to pick at, nibble; *(quemar)* to burn, sting <la *pimienta pica la lengua* pepper burns the tongue>; *(cortar)* to chop, mince <p. *la carne* to mince meat>; *(golpear con pico)* to chip (stones); SPORT. to chip (a ball); FIG. *(estimular)* to arouse, pique; *(enojar)* to pique, vex; PAINT. to stipple; MIL. to pursue, harass; MUS. to strike <p. *una nota* to strike a note> —intr. *(escocer)* to itch, prickle <la *lana pica* wool itches>; *(morder)* to sting, bite; *(calentar)* to burn, be hot; FIG. *(ser engañado)* to take the bait; AVIA., ORNITH. to dive; ICHTH. to take the bait, bite ♦ **p. en** *(rayar en)* to border on <eso *pica en descortesía* that borders on rudeness>; to dabble in <ella *pica en la filosofía* she dabbles in philosophy>; to be something of a <él *pica en poeta* he is something of a poet> —reflex. *(agujerearse)* to become moth-eaten; *(echarse a perder)* to rot, decay; *(avinagrarse)* to turn sour (wine); MARIT. to become choppy; FIG. *(irritarse)* to become piqued, get annoyed; *(engrandecerse)* to boast, be proud ♦ **picarse con** to be piqued by, take a liking to • **picarse de** to boast of being, take pride in being.

pí·ca·ra·men·te adv. *(con astucia)* slyly, cunningly; *(de manera traviesa)* mischievously, roguishly; *(con vileza)* meanly, despicably.

pi·car·de·ar intr. *(decir picardías)* to say rude things; *(hacer picardías)* to make mischief —reflex. to go bad, become corrupted.

pi·car·dí·a f. *(acción baja)* dirty trick; *(travesura)* prank, mischief; *(acción deshonesta)* crookedness, dishonesty; *(grupo)* gang of rogues ♦ **picardías** insults.

pi·ca·res·ca I. f. *(pandilla)* gang of rogues; *(vida de pícaro)* rogue's life; LIT. picaresque novel II. adj. see **picaresco, –ca**.

pi·ca·res·co, –ca I. adj. *(relativo a los pícaros)* roguish, mischievous; LIT. picaresque II. f. see **picaresca**.

pí·ca·ro, –ra I. adj. *(bajo)* base, vile; *(astuto)* sly, crafty; FIG. *(malicioso)* wicked, malicious; *(en sentido cariñoso)* rascally, impish II. m.f. *(bribón)* scoundrel, crook; *(astuto)* sly *or* crafty person; FIG. *(malicioso)* villain; *(en sentido cariñoso)* rascal, imp —m. LIT. rogue, vagabond (in a picaresque novel).

pi·ca·rón, –ro·na I. adj. COLL. roguish, mischievous II. m.f. COLL. *(persona)* rogue, rascal —m. CHILE, PERU cruller, fritter.

pi·ca·tos·te m. fried *or* toasted bread.

pi·ca·za I. f. ORNITH. magpie ♦ **p. marina** ORNITH. flamingo II. adj. see **picazo, –za**.

pi·ca·zo I. m. *(golpe)* jab, wound; *(picotazo)* peck, bite II. adj. see **picazo, –za**.

pi·ca·zo, –za I. adj. piebald, black and white (horse) II. m. see **picaza**.

pi·ca·zón f. *(comezón)* itch, itching; FIG., COLL. *(enojo)* annoyance, peevishness; *(inquietud)* anxiety, uneasy feeling.

pi·co m. ORNITH. beak, bill; *(punta)* sharp point, corner, tip; *(de una vasija)* lip, spout; *(herramienta)* pick, pickax; *(cima)* peak, summit; COLL. *(boca)* mouth, trap; *(verbosidad)* gift of gab; GUAT., MEX. kiss; CHILE, VULG. prick, cock ♦ **callar** *or* **cerrar el p.** COLL. to shut one's trap • **darse el p.** COLL. to kiss • **irse del p.** COLL. to shoot off one's mouth • **p. barreno** *or* **p. carpintero** ORNITH. woodpecker • **p. de cigüeña** BOT. cranesbill, geranium • **p. de frasco** *or* **de canoa** ORNITH. toucan • **tener mucho p.** COLL. to have the gift of gab • **tener p. de oro** FIG., COLL. to be silver-tongued • **y p.** odd <veinte *personas y p.* twenty-odd people>; a little after <son *las ocho y p.* it is a little after eight>.

pi·cón, –co·na I. adj. ZOOL. with protruding upper teeth; COLL. *(susceptible)* touchy, peevish II. m. COLL. *(burla)* lampoon, joke; *(carbón)* charcoal for braisers; ICHTH. stickleback.

pi·cor m. itching, smarting.

pi·co·re·to, –ta adj. AMER. chatterbox.

pi·co·ta f. *(suplicio)* pillory; *(juego)* boys' game; *(de una torre)* spire; *(de una montaña)* summit, peak; *(cereza)* bigarreau cherry; MARIT. cheek (of a pump).

pi·co·ta·da f. *or* **pi·co·ta·zo** m. peck, blow with the beak.

pi·co·te·a·do, –da adj. *(que tiene picos)* peaked, having a point; *(cacarañado)* pitted.

pi·co·te·ar tr. *(con el pico)* to peck; FIG. *(comer)* to nibble, pick (at) —intr. EQUIT. to toss its head (a horse); FIG., COLL. *(hablar)* to chatter, jabber —reflex. to quarrel, bicker.

pi·co·te·o m. pecking.

pi·co·te·ro, –ra COLL. I. adj. chatty, gabby II. m.f. chatterbox.

pí·cri·co adj. CHEM. picric.

pic·to·gra·fí·a f. pictography, picture writing.

pic·tó·ri·co, –ca adj. pictorial.

pi·cu·do, –da I. adj. *(puntiagudo)* pointed, peaked; *(hocicudo)* long-snouted, long-nosed; FIG., COLL. *(hablador)* chatty, talkative II. m. *(espetón)* skewer, spit; MEX., ENTOM. weevil.

pi·cha·na CHILE, PERU *or* **pi·chan·ga** COL. f. broom.

pi·chel m. tankard.

pi·chi·ru·che m. CHILE nobody, insignificant person.

pi·chón I. m. ORNITH. young pigeon; FIG., COLL. *(nombre cariñoso)* darling, honey; AMER. novice II. adj. CUBA, COLL. lily-livered, chicken.

pi·da, pido see **pedir**.

pi·die·ra, pidió see **pedir**.

pí·do·la f. leapfrog.

pi·dón, –do·na adj. & m.f. COLL. var. of **pedigüeño, –ña**.

pie m. ANAT. foot; SEW. foot <el *p. de un calcetín* the foot of a sock>; *(base)* base, stand; foot, bottom, end <el *p. de la cama* the foot of the bed>; *(parte final)* foot, bottom <al *p. de la página* at the bottom of the page>; *(medida)* foot <p. *cuadrado* square foot>; *(sedimento)* sediment; *(nota explicativa)* caption, legend; BOT. *(tronco)* trunk; *(tallo)* stem, stalk; *(árbol)* young tree; POET. foot, meter; CHILE down payment ♦ **a cuatro pies** on all fours • **al p. de** *(cerca)* next to, close to; at the foot of <al *p. del olmo* at the foot of the elm tree> • **al p. de la letra** to the letter, literally • **a p.** on foot • **a p. enjuto** *(sin mojarse)* without getting one's feet wet; FIG. *(sin peligro)* without risk; *(sin esfuerzo)* effortlessly • **a p. firme** steadfastly • **a p. juntillas** FIG. firmly, steadfastly • **a p. llano** easily, smoothly • **buscarle tres pies al gato** FIG. to complicate matters, look for trouble • **caer de p.** FIG. to land on one's feet • **con p. derecho** FIG. with the right foot forward, on the right foot • **con pies de plomo** FIG. *(lentamente)* slowly, with feet of lead; *(con prudencia)* warily, cautiously • **dar p.** to give cause, give rise <eso *dio p. a la conversación* that gave rise to the conversation> • **de a p.** foot <soldado *de a p.* foot soldier> • **de p.** *(derecho)* standing, upright; *(en buena salud)* up and about • **dejar a alguien a p.** to leave someone in the lurch • **de pies a cabeza** from head to foot • **echar p. a tierra** to dismount, alight • **en p. de guerra** ready for war • **entrar con buen p.** to get off to a good start • **estar con el p. en el estribo** FIG. to be about to leave • **estar con** or **tener un p. en la sepultura** FIG. to have one foot in the grave • **hacer cosas con los pies** FIG. to make a mess of things • **hacer p.** *(hallar fondo)* to touch bottom; *(estar seguro)* to be on a firm footing, be confident • **írsele los pies a uno** to slip, lose one's footing • **levantarse con el p. izquierdo** to get up on the wrong side of the bed • **nacer de p.** to be born lucky • **no dar p. con bola** to do nothing right • **no tener pies ni cabeza** FIG. to make no sense whatsoever • **perder p.** *(resbalarse)* to slip, lose one's footing; FIG. *(confundirse)* to be out of one's depth • **p. cúbico** cubic foot • **p. de atleta** MED. athlete's foot • **p. de cabra** crowbar • **p. de imprenta** imprint, printer's mark • **p. derecho** upright, vertical prop • **p. forzado** POET. forced meter • **pies planos** MED. flatfeet • **poner pies en polvorosa** to run away, flee • **ponerse de p.** to stand up • **saber de qué p. cojea alguien** FIG. to know someone's weak points • **tomar p.** BOT. to take root.

pie·dad f. RELIG. piety, piousness; *(respeto filial)* respect; *(lástima)* pity, compassion; ARTS Pietà ♦ **mover a alguien a p.** to move someone to pity.

pie·dra f. *(peña)* stone, rock; *(granizo)* hail, hailstone; *(rueda de molino)* millstone, grindstone; MED. stone *<p. biliar* gallstone>; ARM. flint; *(casa cuna)* foundling home; CUBA, P. RICO bore, boring person ♦ **cerrar a p. y lodo** to shut tight • **no dejar p. por mover** to leave no stone unturned • **no dejar p. sobre p.** FIG. to raze, level • **p. afiladera** or **de afilar** whetstone, grindstone • **p. amoladera** or **de amolar** whetstone; FIG. *(base)* cornerstone, basis • **p. angular** CONSTR. cornerstone • **p. azufre** MIN. brimstone, sulfur • **p. berroqueña** MIN. granite • **p. caliza** or **de cal** MIN. limestone • **p. de chispa** ARM. flint • **p. de jabón** MIN. saponite • **p. de Labrador** MIN. labradorite • **p. de la luna** MIN. moonstone • **p. de molino** millstone • **p. de sapo** ARG. mica • **p. de toque** TECH. touchstone; FIG. touchstone, standard • **p. filosofal** philosophers' stone • **p. fundamental** CONSTR. keystone; FIG. *(base)* foundation, basis • **p. huamanga** PERU alabaster • **p. imán** lodestone • **p. infernal** lunar caustic, silver nitrate • **p. lipis** CHEM. copper sulfate • **p. meteórica** meteorite • **p. nefrítica** MIN. nephrite, jade • **p. pómez** pumice stone • **p. preciosa** or **fina** precious stone.

piel f. ANAT. skin; ZOOL. *(sin pelo)* skin, hide; *(con pelo)* fur, pelt; *(cuero)* leather; BOT. peel, skin (of fruit) ♦ **dar** or **soltar la p.** FIG. to kick the bucket • **de p.** *(de cuero)* leather *<valija de p.* leather suitcase>; fur *<abrigo de p.* fur coat>• **p. de cabra** goatskin • **p. de cerdo** pigskin • **p. de foca** sealskin • **p. de gallina** FIG. goose pimples, goose flesh • **p. roja** redskin (American Indian) • **ser de la p. del diablo** FIG., COLL. to be a little devil.

pien·se, pienso see **pensar¹.**

pien·so m. fodder, feed.

pier·da, pierdo see **perder.**

pier·na f. ANAT., ZOOL. leg; *(de un compás)* leg, branch (of a compass); *(de letra)* downstroke (of a letter); *(de una nuez)* lobe (of a nut); ARG. player (in a card game) ♦ **dormir a p. suelta** FIG., COLL. to sleep like a log • **estirar las piernas** FIG. to stretch one's legs, go for a walk.

pier·nas m. [pl. **-nas**] COLL. nobody, insignificant person.

pie·tis·mo m. RELIG. pietism.

pie·za f. *(pedazo)* piece *<una p. de equipaje* a piece of luggage>; *(parte)* piece, part *<una p. de la máquina se rompió* a part of the machine broke>; *(moneda)* piece, coin *<p. de oro* gold coin>; *(objeto labrado)* piece *<es una p. bonita de platería* it is a beautiful piece of silversmithing>; SEW. *(tela)* bolt, roll (of cloth); *(habitación)* room (in a house); *(animal)* head; *(ficha)* piece, man (in chess, checkers); MUS., THEAT. piece ♦ **buena** or **linda p.** FIG., COLL. sly fox • **de una p.** *(sólido)* in one piece, solid; *(honesto)* honest, upright • **dejar de una p.** COLL. to leave speechless • **p. de autos** LAW record of a court case • **p. de convicción** LAW material evidence (used by the prosecution) • **p. de recibo** reception room, parlor • **p. de repuesto** spare part • **p. por p.** FIG. bit by bit • **quedarse de una p.** or **hecho una p.** FIG., COLL. to be left speechless.

pí·fa·no m. *(instrumento)* fife; *(persona)* fife player.

pi·fia f. SPORT. miscue (in pool); FIG., COLL. *(error)* blunder, slip; AMER. joke.

pi·fiar intr. to wheeze (a flautist) —tr. SPORT. to miscue (in pool); COLL. *(cometer una pifia)* to bungle; AMER. to mock.

pig·men·ta·ción f. pigmentation.

pig·men·tar tr. to pigment.

pig·men·to m. pigment.

pig·me·o adj. & m.f. pygmy.

pig·no·ra·ción f. pledging.

pig·no·rar tr. to pledge, pawn.

pi·gri·cia f. *(pereza)* laziness, slothfulness; AMER. trifle.

pi·ja·da f. SL. nonsense.

pi·ja·ma m. pajamas.

pi·jo, –ja COLL. I. adj. foolish II. m.f. *(tonto)* fool —f. VULG. prick, cock.

pi·la f. *(recipiente)* stone or basin; *(de cocina)* sink; *(fuente)* fountain; *(montón)* pile, heap *<una p. de ropa sucia* a pile of dirty clothes>; *(lana)* shorn wool; RELIG. *(de bautismo)* baptismal font; *(de agua bendita)* stoup, holy water font; FIG. *(parroquia)* parish; ENGIN. *(de un puente)* pier (of a bridge); ELEC., PHYS. battery, cell; CUBA faucet, tap ♦ **nombre de pila** Christian or given name • **p. atómica** PHYS. atomic reactor • **p. eléctrica** ELEC. electric cell • **p. galvánica** ELEC. galvanic cell • **p. húmeda** ELEC. wet cell • **p. seca** ELEC. dry cell • **sacar de p.** or **tener en la p.** to be a godparent.

pi·lar¹ m. *(de una fuente)* basin, trough (of a fountain); *(mojón)* milestone; ARCHIT. *(columna)* pillar, column; *(pila de puente)* pier (of a bridge).

pi·lar² tr. to hull or husk (grain).

pi·las·tra f. ARCHIT. pilaster, square column.

pil·ca f. S. AMER. stone wall.

pil·cha f. ARG., CHILE piece of clothing.

pil·che m. PERU wooden cup or bowl.

píl·do·ra f. PHARM. pill; *(contraceptivo)* birth-control pill; FIG., COLL. *(mala noticia)* bitter pill, bad news ♦ **dorar la p.** FIG., COLL. to sugarcoat the pill.

pi·le·ta f. *(pila)* small basin or sink; *(piscina)* swimming pool.

pi·lón¹ m. *(pila)* basin, trough; *(mortero)* pounding mortar; *(pan de azúcar)* sugarloaf; *(pesa móvil)* movable weight (of a steelyard); MEX. tip, gratuity.

pi·lón² m. ARCHIT. pylon.

pi·lon·go, –ga adj. thin, lean.

pi·lo·ta·je m. *(ciencia)* piloting; *(pilotes)* pilings.

pi·lo·tar tr. AVIA., MARIT. to pilot; *(conducir)* to drive.

pi·lo·te m. pile, stake.

pi·lo·te·ar tr. var. of **pilotar.**

pi·lo·to I. m. AVIA. pilot; MARIT. *(navegante)* pilot, helmsman, navigator; *(segundo de un buque)* first mate; FIG. *(guía)* pilot, guide *<yo seré p. para el proyecto* I will be the pilot for the project>; *(luz posterior)* taillight, rear light; *(lámpara indicadora)* pilot lamp; *(llama)* pilot light ♦ **p. automático** AER., AVIA. automatic pilot • **p. de pruebas** AVIA. test pilot • **p. de puerto** MARIT. harbor pilot • **p. práctico** MARIT. coastal pilot II. adj. *(modelo)* pilot, model *<un proyecto p.* a pilot project>.

pil·tra f. SL. bed, sack.

pil·tra·fa f. *(carne)* gristly meat; *(persona)* poor specimen, wretch; AMER. bargain ♦ **piltrafas** scraps.

pil·tre adj. *(alechuguinado)* foppish; CHILE wrinkled, shriveled.

pi·lla·je m. *(robo)* pillage, plunder; MIL. looting.

pi·llar tr. *(robar)* to pillage, plunder; *(coger)* to catch, get caught *<la puerta me pilló el dedo* my finger got caught in the door>.

pi·llas·tre m. COLL. rogue, rascal.

pi·lle·rí·a f. COLL. *(gavilla de pillos)* gang of rascals; *(pillada)* prank, trick.

pi·lle·te or **pi·llín** m. COLL. little scamp, rascal.

pi·llo, –lla COLL. I. adj. roguish, mischievous II. m.f. rogue, scoundrel.

pi·llue·lo, –la I. adj. naughty, mischievous II. m.f. rascal, scamp.

pi·men·tal m. pepper field.

pi·men·te·ro m. BOT. pepper plant; *(vasija)* pepper shaker.

pi·men·tón m. CUL. paprika.

pi·mien·ta f. CUL. pepper (spice) ♦ **sal y p.** FIG., COLL. charm.

pi·mien·to m. BOT. pepper (plant and fruit); *(pimentón)* paprika ♦ **p. chile** chili pepper • **p. morrón** sweet pepper.

pim·pan·te adj. *(bien vestido)* elegant, spruce; *(garboso)* graceful, poised.

pim·pi m. COLL. fool, nincompoop.

pim·pi·ne·la f. BOT. burnet, pimpernel.

pim·po·llo m. *(vástago)* sprout, shoot; *(árbol nuevo)* sapling; *(capullo)* rosebud —m.f. FIG., COLL. *(niño hermoso)* angel, cherub; *(joven)* attractive youth.

pi·na I. f. *(mojón cónico)* conical mound; *(de una rueda)* felly, rim (of a wheel) II. adj. see **pino, –na.**

pi·na·co·te·ca f. art gallery.

pi·ná·cu·lo m. ARCHIT. pinnacle, top; FIG. *(cima)* pinnacle, peak.

pi·na·da, –do adj. BOT. pinnate.

pi·nar m. pine grove.

pin·cel m. *(instrumento)* brush, paintbrush; FIG. *(modo de pintar)* style (of painting); *(pintor)* painter; *(obra)* work, painting.

pin·ce·la·da f. brush stroke ♦ **dar la última p. a** to put the last touches on.

pin·ce·lar tr. ARTS to paint.

pin·ce·la·zo m. var. of **pincelada.**

pin·cha·dis·cos m.f. [pl. **-cos**] disc jockey.

pin·cha·du·ra f. prick, puncture.

pin·char tr. *(picar)* to prick, puncture; FIG. *(irritar)* to tease, annoy; AUTO. to puncture (a tire) ♦ **ni pincha ni corta** FIG., COLL. he has little say —reflex. to give oneself an injection.

pin·cha·ú·vas m. [pl. **-vas**] COLL. *(que roba uvas)* grape-stealer; FIG., COLL. *(hombre despreciable)* good-for-nothing.

pin·cha·zo m. *(picadura)* prick, puncture; *(de un neumático)* puncture, hole (in a tire); *(dicho malicioso)* cutting remark; *(inyección)* injection, shot.

pin·che I. m. *(mozo de cocina)* kitchen boy; COL., ORNITH. house sparrow; *(de un escritorio)* clerk II. adj. MEX. miserable, wretched.

pin·cho m. *(aguijón)* prickle, thorn; *(de aduanero)* sampling stick (of customs agent); *(brocheta)* skewer; *(tapas)* hors d'oeuvres; AMER. hatpin.

pin·don·ga f. COLL. gadabout (woman).

pin·don·gue·ar intr. COLL. to gad about (a woman).

pi·ne·da f. *(plantío)* pine grove or forest.

pin·ga C. AMER., VULG. prick, cock.

pin·ga·jo m. COLL. tatter, rag.

pin·ga·ni·lla f. AMER., COLL. dandy, fop ♦ **en pinganillas** MEX. *(en cuclillas)* squatting, crouching; *(en situación incierta)* in an uncertain position, on tenterhooks.

pin·ga·ni·llo I. m. icicle II. adj. COL., COLL. tubby, chubby; BOL. elegant, well-dressed.

pin·gar §47 intr. *(gotear)* to drip; *(brincar)* to jump, hop (around); *(pender)* to hang.

pin·go m. COLL. *(pingajo)* tatter; *(pendón)* bum, good-for-nothing; ARG., BOL., URUG. fast horse; CHILE, PERU nag, hack; MEX. devil ♦ **pingos** COLL. cheap women's clothes • **andar de p.** FIG., COLL. to gad about (women).

pin·güe adj. *(graso)* greasy, fatty; *(abundante)* abundant, plentiful <*p. ganancias* huge profits>.

pin·güi·no m. ORNITH. penguin.

pi·ni·to m. first step (of a child).

pi·no I. m. BOT. pine (tree); FIG., POET. *(nave)* vessel, boat ♦ **en el quinto p.** in the middle of nowhere • **p. albar** or **royo** or **silvestre** Scotch pine • **p. alerce** larch • **p. carrasco** or **carrasqueño** Aleppo pine • **p. marítimo** or **rodeno** pinaster, cluster pine II. adj. & m. see **pino, –na.**

pi·no, –na I. adj. steep ♦ **en p.** standing, upright II. m. ♦ **pinos** first steps (of a child) —m. see **pino** —f. see **pina.**

pi·nol or **pi·no·le** or **pí·no·le** m. AMER. pinole (roasted corn flour).

pin·ta I. f. *(mancha)* spot, mark; *(adorno)* dot, spot; *(gota)* drop (of liquid); FIG. *(aspecto)* look, appearance <*su cara siempre tiene una p. triste* his face always has a sad look>; *(medida líquida)* pint; MED. typhoid (fever); AMER. *(color)* color (of animals); *(casta)* lineage ♦ **tener p. de** COLL. to look like II. adj. see **pinto, –ta.**

pin·ta·do, –da I. past part. see **pintar** II. adj. *(con pintas)* spotted, mottled; FIG. *(semejante)* exactly like ♦ **como p.** just right • **el más p.** *(el más listo)* the cleverest; *(lo mejor)* the best • **no poder ver (a alguien) ni p.** COLL. not to be able to stand (someone) • **venir como p.** FIG. to suit to a tee, be just right III. m. painting —f. ORNITH. guinea fowl.

pin·ta·mo·nas m.f. [pl. **-nas**] COLL. dauber, amateur painter.

pin·tar tr. *(representar)* to paint <*p. un retrato* to paint a portrait>; *(cubrir con color)* to paint <*p. un cuarto de azul* to paint a room blue>; *(escribir)* to write; FIG. *(describir)* to paint, describe <*el autor pintó una escena desolada de la ciudad* the author painted a bleak picture of the city>; *(exagerar)* to exaggerate ♦ **pintarla** to put on airs —intr. ARTS to paint; *(madurar)* to ripen (said of fruit); COLL. *(demostrarse)* to show or give signs of; *(darse aires)* to put on airs; FIG., COLL. *(importar)* to be important <*ese chico no pinta nada en la clase* that boy is not important at all to the class> —reflex. *(ponerse afeites)* to put on make-up; *(madurar)* to ripen (said of fruit) ♦ **pintárselas solo** FIG. to be made for, be right up one's alley.

pin·ta·rra·jar or **pin·ta·rra·je·ar** tr. COLL. to daub, paint amateurishly —reflex. to put on heavy make-up.

pin·ti·pa·ra·do, –da I. past part. of **pintiparar** II. adj. *(igual)* identical, exactly the same; *(muy a propósito)* just right, ideal, perfect.

pin·ti·pa·rar tr. COLL. *(comparar)* to compare; *(asemejar)* to liken, make alike.

pin·to, –ta I. adj. *(pintado)* spotted, speckled; CUBA roguish, mischievous; VEN. drunk II. f. see **pinta.**

pin·tón, –to·na I. adj. *(de frutas)* ripening, half-ripe (fruit); *(de ladrillos)* half-baked (brick); ARG. slightly drunk, tipsy II. m. ECUAD. half-ripe banana.

pin·tor, –to·ra m.f. m. *(artista)* painter ♦ **p. de brocha gorda** *(de casas)* house painter; *(mal pintor)* bad painter • **p. de paisajes** landscape painter • **p. de retratos** portrait painter.

pin·to·res·co, –ca adj. picturesque.

pin·to·rre·ar tr. COLL. to daub, paint crudely.

pin·tu·ra f. *(arte)* painting; *(cuadro)* painting, picture <*la p. es muy detallada* the painting is very detailed>; *(color)* paint, pigment; FIG. *(descripción)* picture, portrayal <*el primer capítulo es una p. de la vida campestre* the first chapter is a portrayal of country life> ♦ **no poder ver a alguien ni en p.** not to be able to stand the sight of someone • **p. a la acuarela** water color • **p. al fresco** fresco or wall painting • **p. al óleo** oil painting • **p. al pastel** pastel (drawing) • **p. al temple** tempera • **p. de aguazo** or **a la aguada** gouache • **p. de miniatura** miniature painting • **p. figulina** pottery painting • **p. rupestre** cave painting.

pin·tu·re·ro, –ra COLL. I. adj. vain, conceited II. m.f. vain or conceited person.

pin·za f. ZOOL. pincer, claw; SEW. dart; *(para colgar la ropa)* clothespin ♦ **pinzas** *(tenacillas)* tweezers; *(tenazas)* tongs; DENT., SURG. forceps.

pin·zón m. ORNITH. chaffinch ♦ **p. real** bullfinch.

pi·ña f. *(del pino)* pine cone; *(ananás)* pineapple; FIG. *(grupo)* clan, clique; COLL. *(puñetazo)* punch, blow; PHILIP., TEX. piña cloth ♦ **darse de piñas** AMER. to come to blows.

pi·ñal m. AMER. pineapple plantation.

pi·ña·ta f. *(vasija)* piñata; CHILE scramble, scuffle.

pi·ñón[1] m. *(simiente)* pine nut; *(burro)* last mule (in a drove); *(arbusto)* nut pine, piñon; ARM. magazine, catch (on trigger); ORNITH. pinion; CHILE herd ♦ **estar a partir un p. con alguien** to be best friends with someone.

pi·ñón[2] m. MECH. pinion (wheel).

pi·ño·ne·ro I. adj. BOT. stone, nut <*pino p.* nut pine> II. m. ORNITH. bullfinch.

pí·o I. m. *(de aves)* cheeping, chirping (of birds); COLL. *(deseo vivo)* yearning, desire ♦ **no decir ni p.** FIG., COLL. not to say a word II. adj. see **pío, –a.**

pí·o, –a I. adj. *(devoto)* devout, pious; *(compasivo)* merciful, compassionate; *(de beneficencia)* charitable; *(color)* piebald II. m. see **pío.**

pio·cha f. *(joya)* hair ornament; *(flor)* flower made of feathers; MEX. Vandyke beard; *(zapapico)* pickax.

pio·jo m. ENTOM. louse; COL. gambling den ♦ **p. de mar** whale louse ♦ **p. resucitado** COLL. parvenu, upstart.

pio·jo·so, –sa adj. *(lleno de piojos)* lousy; *(sucio)* dirty; FIG. *(miserable)* stingy, mean.

pio·la f. MARIT. houseline, housing; *(juego)* leapfrog; AMER. string, packthread.

pio·ne·ro, –ra m.f. & adj. pioneer.

pio·rre·a f. DENT., MED. pyorrhea.

pi·pa¹ f. *(barrica)* cask, barrel, keg (for wine); *(utensilio para fumar)* pipe (for smoking), tobacco pipe; *(lengüeta)* reed (of a clarion or flute); *(pipiritaña)* pipe (flute made from a green barley stem); *(espoleta)* fuse (of a bomb); AMER. belly ♦ **pasarlo p.** COLL. to have a great deal of fun.

pi·pa² f. pip, seed.

pi·pe·rí·a f. *(pipas)* casks, barrels; MARIT. water tanks.

pi·per·mín m. peppermint.

pi·pe·ta f. pipette.

pi·pí m. ORNITH. pipit, honeycreeper; COLL. *(orina)* wee-wee, pee ♦ **hacer p.** COLL. to make wee-wee, pee.

pi·piar §30 intr. to peep, chirp.

pi·pio·lo m. COLL. *(muchachillo)* youngster; *(principiante)* novice, beginner; CHILE, COLL. liberal (person).

pi·pi·ri·pa·o m. COLL. feast, sumptuous party.

pi·pi·ri·ta·ña f. flute, pipe (made of green cane).

pi·pi·ta·ña f. var. of **pipiritaña**.

pi·pón, –po·na adj. AMER. *(lleno)* full, replete; *(barrigón)* potbellied, paunchy; ARG. large tobacco pipe.

pi·po·rro m. COLL. bassoon.

pi·po·te m. cask, keg.

pi·pu·do, –da adj. COLL. terrific, wonderful.

pi·que¹ m. *(resentimiento)* pique, resentment; *(empeño)* eagerness, zeal *<atacó el problema con un p. contagioso* he attacked the problem with an infectious zeal>; AMER., ENTOM. chigger, chigoe (a type of flea); *(ají)* pepper; ARG. *(senda)* path (in the forest) ♦ **tener un p. con alguien** to hold or have a grudge against someone.

pi·que² MARIT. crotch, crutch.

pi·que³ ♦ **a p.** *(a riesgo)* in danger or in peril; MARIT. sheer, steep (coast, cliff) • **echar a p.** MARIT. to sink (a ship); FIG. *(destruir)* to ruin, destroy *<inversiones malas de capital echaron a p. a la compañía* bad capital investments ruined the company> • **estar a p. de** to be on the verge of • **irse a p.** MARIT. to sink.

pi·qué m. TEX. piqué.

pi·qué, pique see **picar**.

pi·que·ra f. *(de una colmena)* opening in a beehive; *(de un tonel)* bunghole in a cask, cockhole in a barrel; *(alto horno)* outlet of a smelting furnace, taphole in a furnace; *(mechero)* lamp burner, wick in oil lamp; CHILE large earthen jar buried to collect water; CUBA hack stand; MEX. filthy tavern.

pi·que·ro m. MIL. pikeman; ECUAD. miner; CHILE, PERU, ORNITH. booby.

pi·que·ta f. *(zapapico)* pick, pickax; *(herramienta de albañiles)* mason's hammer or pick; CHILE weak wine.

pi·que·ta·zo m. AMER. var. of **picotazo**.

pi·que·te m. *(picadura)* prick, jab; *(aguajero)* small hole or cut; *(jalón)* stake, pole; *(protesta)* picket, protest; MIL. picket, squad; ARG., PAR. corral, pen; COL. picnic; CUBA small band.

pi·ra f. pyre ♦ **ir de p.** FIG., COLL. to play hooky, cut class.

pi·ra·gua f. *(embarcación grande)* pirogue; *(canoa)* canoe; AMER., BOT. anthurium (vine); P. RICO *(artesa)* trough for washing clothes.

pi·ra·güe·ro m. canoeist.

pi·ra·mi·dal adj. pyramidal.

pi·rá·mi·de f. pyramid.

pi·ra·ña f. AMER., ICHTH. piranha.

pi·rar·se reflex. COLL. *(irse)* to take off, leave.

pi·ra·ta I. m. *(ladrón)* pirate; FIG. *(persona cruel)* brute, hardhearted person ♦ **p. aéreo** or **del aire** hijacker II. adj. *(pirático)* piratical, piratic; *(ilegal)* pirate *<grabación p.* pirate recording>.

pi·ra·te·ar intr. *(robar barcos)* to practice piracy, be a pirate; FIG. *(robar)* to steal; *(copiar)* to copy, pirate (a recording).

pi·ra·te·rí·a f. *(robo de barcos)* piracy; FIG. *(robo)* theft ♦ **p. aérea** hijacking.

pi·ra·ya f. AMER. var. of **piraña**.

pir·ca f. S. AMER. dry-stone wall.

pí·ri·co, –ca adj. pertaining to fire or fireworks.

Pi·ri·ne·os m.pl. Pyrenees.

pi·ri·ta f. MIN. pyrites ♦ **p. cobriza** or **de cobre** copper pyrites • **p. de hierro** or **marcial** iron pyrites.

pi·ro·gra·ba·do m. pyrography.

pi·ró·li·sis f. CHEM. pyrolysis.

pi·ro·man·cia or **pi·ro·man·cí·a** f. pyromancy.

pi·ró·ma·no, –na I. adj. pyromaniacal II. m.f. pyromaniac.

pi·rón m. ARG. cassava flour bread (eaten with stew).

pi·ro·pe·ar tr. COLL. to pay flirtatious compliments to, make flattering remarks to.

pi·ro·po m. *(granate)* pyrope, garnet; *(carbúnculo)* carbuncle; COLL. *(requiebro)* flattering remark, compliment ♦ **decir** or **echar piropos** to compliment, make flirtatious remarks.

pi·ro·tec·nia f. pyrotechnics, pyrotechny.

pi·ro·téc·ni·co, –ca I. adj. pyrotechnic, pyrotechnical II. m. pyrotechnist, fireworks maker.

pi·ró·xi·lo m. CHEM. cellulose nitrate, nitrocellulose.

pi·rrar·se reflex. to be crazy about *<me pirran las aceitunas* I'm crazy about olives>.

pí·rri·co, –ca I. adj. Pyrrhic *<una victoria p.* a Pyrrhic victory> II. f. pyrrhic (ancient Greek war dance).

pi·rue·ta f. *(salto)* pirouette (of a dancer); EQUIT. caper (of a horse).

pi·rue·te·ar intr. *(saltar)* to pirouette (a dancer); EQUIT. to caper (a horse).

pi·ru·lí m. [pl. **-lís**] lollipop.

pi·ru·lo m. earthenware pitcher; AMER. slim child.

pis m. COLL. wee-wee ♦ **hacer p.** to pee.

pi·sa f. *(acción)* treading, step; *(aceituna o uva)* batch of olives or grapes for pressing; COLL. *(zurra)* kicking, beating; COL. dance.

pi·sa·da f. *(acción de pisar)* step, footstep; *(huella)* footprint, track ♦ **seguir las pisadas de** FIG. to follow in the footsteps of.

pi·sa·dor, –do·ra I. adj. prancer (horse) II. m. grape treader; COL. lead, halter (for cattle).

pi·sa·du·ra f. var. of **pisada**.

pi·sa·pa·pe·les m. [pl. **-les**] paperweight.

pi·sar tr. *(andar)* to step or walk on *<el niño pisó un clavo* the child stepped on a nail>; *(frutas)* to press (fruit); *(la tierra)* to tamp, pack down (dirt, earth); *(una tela)* to full (cloth); ORNITH. to tread, copulate with (said of male birds); *(cubrir)* to cover; MUS. *(puntear)* to pluck (strings); *(tocar)* to strike (keys); FIG. *(maltratar)* to step or trample *<pisaron su dignidad* they trampled on his dignity> ♦ **andar pisando huevos** FIG. to move or step gingerly —intr. *(estar de arriba)* to be on top of, be one above the other (stories in a building); ARG. to be mistaken or wrong.

pi·sa·ú·vas m. [pl. **-vas**] grape treader.

pi·sa·ver·de m. COLL. dandy.

pis·ca·to·rio, –ria adj. piscatorial, piscatory.

pis·cí·co·la adj. piscicultural.

pis·ci·cul·tu·ra f. pisciculture, fish-breeding.

pis·ci·na f. *(pecina)* fishpond; *(para nadar)* swimming pool; RELIG. piscina ♦ **p. probática** BIBL. tank in which sacrificial victims were washed.

pis·cis m. ASTROL., ASTRON. Pisces.

pis·co m. PERU *(aguardiente)* liquor.

pis·co·la·bis m. [pl. **-bis**] COLL. snack, bite.

pi·so m. *(suelo)* ground; *(de una habitación)* floor *<p. de madera* wooden floor>; *(pavimento)* pavement, surface (of a road, street); *(planta)* floor, story *<el quinto p.* the fifth floor>; *(apartamento)* apartment, flat (G.B.); *(acción)* stepping, walking; *(suela)* sole (of a shoe); MIN. level (in a mine); GEOL. stage; CHILE, PERU *(alfombra)* carpet, rug; CHILE *(taburete)* stool ♦ **p. bajo** first floor, ground floor (G.B.) • **p. principal** second floor, first floor (G.B.) • **primer p.** second floor, first floor (G.B.).

pi·són m. rammer, tamper.

pi·so·ne·ar tr. to ram down, tamp.

pi·so·te·ar tr. *(pisar)* to trample, tread on; FIG. *(oprimir)* to tread on.

pi·so·te·o m. trampling.

pi·so·tón m. COLL. heavy step.

pis·ta f. *(huella)* trail, track <*el cazador perdió la p. del oso* the hunter lost the bear's trail>; *(de carrera)* racetrack, track; *(de bailar)* dance floor; *(de patinar)* (skating) rink; *(para el circo)* ring (of a circus); *(de aterrizaje)* runway, airstrip; FIG. *(indicio)* clue, trail; *(camino)* trail, road ♦ **estar sobre la p.** to be on the trail *or* track • **ponerse a la p.** COLL. to get on the right track • **seguir la p.** FIG. to follow the track, be on the trail.

pis·ta·che·ro m. BOT. pistachio tree.

pis·ta·cho m. pistachio (nut).

pis·tar tr. to crush, pound.

pis·ti·lo m. BOT. pistil.

pis·to m. *(fritada)* vegetable fritter ♦ **darse p.** FIG., COLL. to put on airs.

pis·to·la f. *(arma de fuego)* pistol; *(para pintar)* paint sprayer ♦ **p. ametralladora** submachine gun • **p. de engrase** grease gun.

pis·to·le·ra f. holster.

pis·to·le·ro m. COLL. gunman, gangster.

pis·to·le·ta·zo m. pistol shot.

pis·tón m. TECH. piston; ARM. percussion *or* cartridge cap; MUS. piston (of a brass instrument); AMER. cornet.

pis·to·nu·do, –da adj. COLL. terrific, great.

pi·ta[1] f. BOT. agave, century plant; TEX. pita, thread; *(canica)* (glass) marble ♦ **pedir p.** PERU to beg for mercy.

pi·ta[2] f. hissing, whistling (of displeasure).

pi·ta·da f. *(sonido)* whistle, blow of a whistle; *(salida inoportuna)* inopportune remark; S. AMER. puff (of a cigarette) ♦ **dar una p.** COLL. to boo (in a theater).

pi·ta·gó·ri·co, –ca adj. & m.f. Pythagorean.

pi·tan·ce·ro m. *(persona que reparte)* distributor of dole *or* rations; *(de coro)* superintendent, roll caller (of a choir); *(religioso refitolero)* steward, purveyor (in military order).

pi·tan·za f. *(reparto)* dole, ration; *(estipendo)* stipend; COLL. *(alimento)* daily bread; AMER., COLL. bargain.

pi·tar intr. *(tocar el pito)* to blow a whistle, whistle; *(tener preeminencia)* to have preeminence *or* authority; FIG., COLL. *(ir algo según los deseos de uno)* to go well; *(funcionar)* to work, function; S. AMER. *(fumar)* to smoke ♦ **salir pitando** to go off like a shot, be off like a shot —tr. *(silbar en desaprobación)* to whistle *or* hiss at (in disapproval); pay; COLL. *(arbitrar)* to be the referee of; S. AMER. *(fumar)* to smoke; CHILE *(engañar)* to deceive, make fun of.

pi·ta·rra f. sleep, gummy secretion of the eyes.

pi·ta·rro·so, –sa adj. with sleep in one's eyes.

pi·te·ar intr. AMER. to whistle, blow a whistle.

pi·te·cán·tro·po m. ANTHR. pithecanthropus.

pi·te·jo m. COLL. undertaker.

pi·ti·do m. *(ruido del pito)* whistle, whistling; *(del claxon)* hooting, honking.

pi·ti·lle·ra f. *(cigarrera)* cigarette maker; *(petaca)* cigarette case.

pi·ti·llo m. cigarette.

pi·to[1] m. *(instrumento)* whistle; ENTOM. tick; *(cigarro)* cigarette; *(claxon)* horn (of a car, vehicle); AMER. pipe (for smoking); VULG. prick, cock ♦ **cuando pitos flautas, cuando flautas pitos** COLL. if it's not one thing it's another • **no darle** *or* **importarle a uno un p.** COLL. not to give a damn <*no me importa un p. lo que pasa en las elecciones* I don't give a damn about what happens in the elections> • **no tocar p. en** FIG. to have nothing to do with • **no valer un p.** FIG. to be worthless • **pitos flautos** tomfoolery, foolishness • **ser el p. del sereno** FIG. to be a nobody.

pito[2] m. ORNITH. woodpecker; GUAT., SALV. tree used to shade coffee *or* cocoa plant.

pi·tón[1] m. ZOOL. python.

pi·tón[2] m. *(cuerno)* horn; *(pitorro)* spout; *(protuberancia)* lump, protuberance; *(renuevo del árbol)* shoot; AMER. nozzle; HOND. protruding gutter; CHILE, ECUAD. dibble, dibber; *(clavo)* spike (for mountain climbing).

pi·to·na·zo m. *(golpe)* butt; *(herida)* gore.

pi·to·ni·sa f. HIST., RELIG. pythoness.

pi·to·rre·o m. COLL. *(broma)* joke, mockery; *(alboroto)* fuss.

pi·to·rro m. COLL. spout.

pi·tui·ta·rio, –ria adj. ANAT. pituitary.

pi·tu·so, –sa I. adj. sweet, cute II. m.f. cute child.

pi·vo·te m. TECH. pivot, kingpin; SPORT. pivot.

pí·xi·de f. RELIG. pyx, ciborium; BOT. pyxidium, pyxis.

pi·ya·ma m. var. of pijama.

pi·za·rra f. MIN. slate, shale; *(encerado)* blackboard.

pi·za·rre·ro m. slater, slate cutter.

pi·za·rrín m. slate pencil.

pi·za·rrón m. AMER. *(encerado)* blackboard; SPORT. scoreboard.

pi·za·rro·so, –sa adj. *(abundante en pizarra)* full of slate; *(parecido a la pizarra)* slaty, slate-like.

piz·ca f. COLL. *(porción pequeña)* pinch, small amount; MEX. corn harvest ♦ **ni p.** COLL. at all, not at all <*no hay ni p. de vino* there's no wine at all>.

piz·pe·re·ta *or* **piz·pi·re·ta** adj. COLL. lively (woman).

pla·ca f. *(chapa)* plate <*p. de matrícula* license plate>; *(insignia)* badge; *(conmemorativa)* plaque; *(disco)* record; ELEC., PHOTOG. plate ♦ **p. giratoria** RAIL. turntable.

pla·ce·ar tr. *(vender)* to sell retail, market (provisions); *(publicar)* to publish, make known.

pla·ce·bo m. MED. placebo.

plá·ce·me m. congratulations ♦ **dar el p. a alguien** to congratulate someone.

pla·cen·ta f. BOT., ZOOL. placenta.

pla·cen·te·ro, –ra adj. pleasant.

pla·cer[1] m. *(contento)* pleasure <*halla su p. en ayudar a otros* he finds his pleasure in helping others>; *(diversión)* pleasure, delight <*las placeres del mundo* worldly delights>; *(voluntad)* will, desire ♦ **a p.** as much as one wants.

pla·cer[2] m. MARIT. sandbank; MIN. placer; AMER. pearl fishing ground.

pla·cer[3] §51 tr. to please, gratify <*me place hacerlo* it pleases me to do it>.

pla·ce·ro, –ra I. adj. of the square *or* market place II. m.f. *(tendero)* stallholder, merchant; *(persona ociosa)* loafer, town gossip.

plá·ci·da·men·te adv. placidly.

plá·ci·dez f. placidness, placidity.

plá·ci·do, –da adj. *(quieto)* placid, calm; *(grato)* agreeable, pleasant.

pla·ga f. *(calamidad)* plague, calamity; *(abundancia)* abundance, glut; *(clima)* climatic zone; BOT. blight.

pla·gar §47 tr. *(infestar)* to plague, infest; *(cubrir)* to cover; *(llenar)* to fill <*plagado de dudas* filled with doubts> —reflex. to become infested with, be covered with.

pla·giar tr. to plagiarize.

pla·gia·rio, –ria I. adj. plagiaristic, plagiarizing II. m.f. plagiarist.

pla·gio m. plagiarism.

plan m. *(esquema)* plan, scheme <*el p. de un libro* the plan of a book>; *(proyecto)* plan, project <*el p. durará tres años* the project will last three years>; *(intento)* plan, intention <*no entiendo sus planes* I don't understand her plans>; *(programa)* plan, program <*p. quinquenal* five-year plan>; *(altura)* height, level; FIG., COLL. *(cita)* date <*María siempre tiene muchos planes* Mary always has lots of dates>; MARIT. floor timber; MED. diet; MIN. level; CHILE plain ♦ **en p. de** with the object of, as <*vamos a Peru en p. de turismo* we are going to Peru with the object of touring> • **p. de estudios** curriculum, course of study.

pla·na I. f. *(página)* page, side (of paper); *(ejercicio)* writing exercise (done by children); *(llanura)* plain <*se cultiva trigo en la p.* wheat is grown on the plain>; PRINT. page; MAS. trowel ♦ **a p. y renglón** *(línea por línea)* line for line; FIG. *(ajustado)* just right, perfectly • **cerrar la p.** FIG. to finish, conclude • **corregir** *or* **enmendar la p.** *(criticar)* to find fault (with), criticize; *(exceder)* to surpass, outdo • **de primera p.** front page (of a newspaper). II. adj. see plano, –na.

pla·na·zo m. AMER. blow with the flat of a sword; HOND. thud, bump (of a body hitting the ground).

planc·ton m. BIOL. plankton.

plan·cha f. *(lámina)* plate, sheet (of metal); *(utensilio)* iron <*p. a vapor* steam iron>; *(ropa planchada)* ironing <*pusi-*

mos la p. en el armario we put the ironing in the closet>; *(acto)* ironing (of clothes); COLL. *(error)* blooper, boner <*hacer una p.* to make a blooper>; PRINT. plate; MARIT. gangplank, gangway ♦ **a la p.** CUL. grilled • **hacer la p.** to float on one's back • **p. de blindaje** armor plate • **p. litográfica** PRINT. lithographic plate • **tirarse una p.** COLL. to pull a boner.

plan·cha·da I. f. MARIT. *(puentecillo)* plank, gangplank; ARG., PAR. board, platform for loading and unloading (on the riverbank); AMER., COLL. *(metedura de pata)* blunder, faux pas II. adj. see **planchado, –da.**

plan·cha·do, –da I. past part. of **planchar** II. m. *(acción de planchar)* ironing; *(ropa)* clothes to be ironed —f. see **planchada** III. adj. AMER., COLL. *(sin dinero)* broke, without a cent; GUAT. *(muy elegante)* very elegant, very smart.

plan·cha·dor, –do·ra m.f. ironer, presser.

plan·char tr. *(alisar con una plancha)* to iron, press (clothes); AMER. *(adular)* to flatter.

plan·cha·zo m. COLL. blunder, faux pas.

pla·ne·a·ción f. var. of **planeamiento.**

pla·ne·a·dor m. AER. glider.

pla·ne·a·mien·to m. *(planificación)* planning; AER. gliding.

pla·ne·ar tr. to plan —intr. AER. to glide.

pla·ne·o m. AER. gliding.

pla·ne·ta m. ASTRON. planet —f. RELIG. planeta (short chasuble).

pla·ne·ta·rio, –ria I. adj. planetary II. m. ASTRON. planetarium, orrery; MECH. planet gear *or* differential.

pla·ne·toi·de m. ASTRON. planetoid.

pla·ni·cie f. plain, level ground.

pla·ni·fi·ca·ción f. planning.

pla·ni·fi·ca·dor, –do·ra I. adj. planning II. m.f. planner.

pla·ni·fi·car §70 tr. to plan.

pla·ni·lla f. AMER. *(lista)* list, roll; *(cuadro)* table; *(formulario)* form; MEX. *(papeleta de votos)* voting ballot.

pla·nis·fe·rio m. planisphere.

pla·no, –na I. adj. flat, level, even, smooth II. m. *(superficie)* plane, surface; GEOM. plane; *(plan)* plan, diagram; *(mapa)* map, chart (of a city); CINEM., PAINT. ground <*primer p.* foreground>; *(de una espada)* flat (of a sword); FIG. position, level <*de primer p.* high-level> ♦ **caer de p.** to fall flat • **de p.** clearly, plainly <*hablar de p.* to speak plainly> • **levantar un p.** TOP. to make a survey • **p. de fractura** GEOL. fault plane • **p. de nivel** TOP. datum plane • **p. de sustentación** AVIA. wing • **p. inclinado** MECH. inclined plane • **primer p.** CINEM. close-up shot —f. see **plana.**

plan·ta f. BOT. plant; ANAT. *(del pie)* sole (of the foot); *(diseño)* ground *or* floor plan; *(piso)* floor, story (of a building); *(proyecto)* plan, project; *(lista)* roster *or* list of employees, payroll; *(instalación)* plant <*una p. eléctrica* an electric plant>; *(plantío)* field <*una p. de melones* a field of melons>; *(posición)* stance, position (of feet); GEOM. foot (of a perpendicular) ♦ **buena p.** COLL. good looks • **de nueva p.** *or* **de p.** *(de nuevo)* again; *(desde los cimientos)* from the ground floor • **echar plantas** to bully, swagger • **p. baja** ground floor, first floor (U.S.) • **primera p.** second floor, first floor (G.B.) • **tener buena p.** COLL. to be good-looking.

plan·ta·ción f. *(acción)* planting; *(explotación agrícola)* plantation.

plan·ta·do, –da I. past part. see **plantar** II. adj. planted ♦ **bien p.** FIG., COLL. good-looking • **dejar (a alguien) p.** to stand (someone) up.

plan·ta·dor, –do·ra I. adj. planting II. m.f. *(person)* planter —m. *(herramienta)* dibble, dibber —f. *(máquina)* planter (machine).

plan·tai·na f. BOT. plantain.

plan·tar tr. AGR. to plant, sow (seeds, fields); FIG. *(poner)* to place, put <*planté el niño en el asiento* I put the child in the seat>; *(establecer)* to found, set up <*plantó una colonia cerca del río* he founded a colony near the river>; FIG., COLL. *(dar un golpe)* to plant, land (a blow); *(abandonar)* to jilt, leave <*plantó a su amiga* he jilted his girlfriend> —reflex. *(ponerse de pie)* to plant *or* put oneself <*nos plantamos en la puerta* we planted ourselves in the doorway>; *(resistir)* to stand firm, make a stand <*el senador se planta en cuanto a las elecciones* the senator stands firm with

regard to the elections>; FIG., COLL. *(llegar)* to arrive, reach <*me plantaré en casa en quince minutos* I will reach home in fifteen minutes>; FIG., COLL. *(pararse)* to balk, stop <*el caballo se plantó frente al arroyo* the horse balked at the stream>; *(en naipes)* to stand pat (in cards); C. AMER., COL. to dress up.

plan·te m. *(motín)* mutiny; *(huelga)* strike.

plan·te·a·mien·to m. *(exposición)* exposition, statement; *(propuesta)* proposal; *(establecimiento)* establishment, institution (of a system, reform, etc.); *(enfoque)* setting out, laying out, layout.

plan·te·ar tr. *(exponer)* to expound, set forth; *(tantear)* to try; *(empezar)* to start; *(planear)* to plan, outline; *(establecer)* to establish, institute; *(proponer)* to propose, put forward; *(enfocar)* to set out, lay out.

plan·tel m. *(criadero)* nursery, seedbed; FIG. *(establecimiento educacional)* educational institution, school; *(conjunto)* group, set.

plan·te·o m. var. of **planteamiento.**

plan·ti·fi·car §70 tr. *(establecer)* to establish, institute; COLL. *(golpear)* to land, deal (a blow); FIG. *(colocar)* to plant, place (with strength).

plan·ti·lla f. *(suela interior)* insole, inner sole; *(soleta)* patch (used to repair socks, stockings); TECH. *(patrón)* template; *(plano)* plan, diagram <*nos mostró una p. del proyecto* she showed us a plan of the project>; *(lista)* list *or* roster of employees, payroll; *(de una llanta)* rim (of a carriage wheel); ASTROL. celestial configuration ♦ **p. curva** TECH. French curve • **p. de estarcir** stencil.

plan·tí·o, –a I. adj. *(librado)* planted, cultivated; *(labrantío)* cultivable, ready to be planted II. m. *(acción)* planting; *(lugar)* patch, field (planted); *(plantas)* plants.

plan·tón m. *(pimpollo nuevo)* seedling, sprout (to be transplanted); *(estaca)* scion, cutting (of a plant); *(centinela)* sentry ♦ **estar de p.** *or* **tener p.** FIG., COLL. to be standing around (in one place) a long time, cool one's heels • **dar un p.** to keep (someone) waiting, not turn up.

pla·ñi·de·ra f. hired mourner, weeper.

pla·ñi·de·ro, –ra adj. mournful, plaintive.

pla·ñi·do m. moan, lament.

pla·ñir §12 intr. to moan, lament —reflex. to bemoan, grieve over.

pla·que·a·do, –da adj. veneered.

pla·que·ta f. *(placa pequeña)* plaquette; BIOL. blood platelet.

plas·ma m. ANAT. plasma; MIN. plasma, dark green agate.

plas·mar tr. *(formar)* to shape, mold; *(crear)* to create.

plas·ta f. *(pasta)* paste, soft mass; *(objeto aplastado)* flattened object; FIG., COLL. *(cosa mal hecha)* botch, mess; *(cosa o persona aburrida)* bore.

plas·ti·ci·dad f. plasticity.

plás·ti·co, –ca I. adj. *(moldeable)* plastic, soft ♦ **arte p.** plastic arts II. m. CHEM. *(material moldeable)* plastic (material); *(explosivo)* plastic (explosive) —f. ARTS sculpture, clay modeling.

plas·ti·fi·ca·ción f. *or* **plas·ti·fi·ca·do** m. plasticization.

plas·ti·fi·can·te I. adj. plasticizing, plastifying II. m. plasticizing substance, plasticizer.

plas·ti·fi·car §70 tr. to plasticize, plastify.

pla·ta f. CHEM. silver; FIG. *(moneda)* silver (coin); AMER., FIG. money ♦ **como una p.** bright and shiny • **en p.** FIG. in brief, in a word • **p. labrada** silverware.

pla·ta·for·ma f. *(tablero)* platform; THEAT. *(escenario)* stage; POL. platform, program <*una p. liberal* a liberal platform>; *(vagón)* open wagon; *(estación petrolífera)* drilling rig (in the sea); FIG. *(camino)* steppingstone <*esto me servirá como p. para el dinero* this will serve me as a steppingstone to the money> • **p. continental** GEOG., GEOL. continental shelf • **p. de lanzamiento** AVIA. launching pad.

pla·tal m. AMER., COLL. fortune.

pla·ta·nal *or* **pla·ta·nar** m. banana plantation *or* grove.

pla·ta·na·zo m. C. AMER., VEN. *(caída)* fall; FIG. *(caída de un gobierno)* downfall, collapse (of a government).

pla·ta·ne·ra f. *(platanal)* banana plantation *or* grove; *(vendedora)* banana seller.

pla·ta·ne·ro m. banana tree.

plá·ta·no m. BOT. *(de banano)* banana (tree and fruit); *(ár-*

bol de sombra) plane tree; CARIB., C. AMER. plantain (tree
and fruit) ◊ **p. falso** BOT. sycamore tree.
pla·te·a f. THEAT. *(patio)* orchestra (section); *(palco)* parterre box; ARG. orchestra *or* box seat.
pla·te·a·do, –da I. past part. see **platear** II. adj. *(bañado
de plata)* silver-plated, silvered; *(de color de plata)* silvery,
silver; MEX. rich, wealthy III. m. silver plating.
pla·te·a·du·ra f. silver plating.
pla·te·ar tr. to silver-plate, plate with silver.
pla·te·rí·a f. *(arte)* silversmithing; *(taller)* silversmith's
workshop; *(tienda)* silversmith's shop.
pla·te·ro m. *(artista)* silversmith; *(joyero)* jeweler.
plá·ti·ca f. chat, talk.
pla·ti·car §70 intr. to chat, talk —tr. to talk over *or* about.
pla·ti·llo m. *(plato pequeño)* saucer, small plate *or* dish; *(balanza)* tray, pan (of a scale); MUS. cymbal; CUL. ragout of
meat and vegetables; FIG. *(objeto de chisme)* subject of
gossip ◊ **p. volante** *or* **volador** flying saucer.
pla·ti·na f. PRINT. *(mesa de hierro)* imposing table, imposing stone; *(superficie de la prensa)* platen, bedplate (of the
press on which the form is laid); TECH. plate (of air pump);
(microscopio) stage, slide (of microscope).
pla·ti·na·do m. TECH. platinum plating.
pla·ti·nar tr. to platinize.
pla·ti·no m. CHEM. platinum ◊ **platinos** AUTO. points, contact points.
pla·ti·qué, platique see **platicar.**
pla·to m. plate, dish *<p. sopero* soup dish>; *(contenido)*
plateful, dish; *(comida)* dish *<es un p. típico de los argenti-
nos* it is a typical Argentine dish>; course *<p. fuerte* main
course>; *(de la balanza)* pan, scale; MECH. plate, disk;
ARCHIT. gutta; FIG. *(chisme)* subject of gossip ◊ **comer en
un mismo p.** FIG., COLL. to be close friends • **pagar los
platos rotos** FIG. to pay the consequences • **no haber quebrado un p.** FIG. to be innocent • **p. de segunda mesa**
FIG. second fiddle • **p. giratorio** turntable • **ser p. del
gusto de uno** COLL. to be one's cup of tea.
pla·tó m. CINEM. set, film set.
pla·tó·ni·co, –ca I. adj. PHILOS. Platonist, Platonic; *(ideal,
sin efecto)* platonic II. m.f. PHILOS. Platonist.
pla·tu·do, –da adj. AMER., COLL. rich, wealthy.
plau·si·ble adj. *(admisible)* plausible, admissible; *(laudable)*
commendable, laudable.
pla·ya f. *(ribera arenosa)* beach; AMER. open space, piece of
clear land ◊ **p. de estacionamiento** AMER. parking lot.
pla·ye·ro, –ra I. m.f. *(pescador)* person who sells fish at the
seaside —m. PERU longshoreman, stevedore —f. *(camiseta)* T-shirt II. adj. beach *<sombrero p.* beach hat>.
pla·za f. *(lugar público)* plaza, square; *(mercado)* marketplace, emporium; *(ciudad)* fortified city, stronghold; *(sitio)* space, place, seat *<un avión de cincuenta plazas* an
airplane with fifty seats>; *(empleo)* post, position; MIL.
entry of enlistment; TECH. hearth ◊ **abrir** *or* **hacer p.** to
make room • **ir a la p.** to do the shopping, go shopping •
p. de armas MIL. parade ground • **p. de toros** bullring •
p. fuerte fortress, stronghold • **p. montada** MIL. cavalry
soldier • **sentar p.** MIL. to enlist, join the service.
plaz·ca, plazco see **placer³.**
pla·zo m. *(término)* term, period; *(pago)* installment ◊ **a
corto p.** short-term *<préstamo a corto p.* short-term loan;
(pronto) in the short run *or* term • **a largo p.** long-term
<inversión a largo p. long-term investment>; *(a la larga)*
in the long run • **comprar a plazos** to buy on credit • **en
breve p.** within a short time • **p. de respiro** grace period
• **p. suplementario** extension • **vender a plazos** to sell on
credit.
pla·zo·le·ta f. *(espacio descubierto)* small open space in a
garden *or* walk; *(plazuela)* small square.
pla·zue·la f. small plaza *or* square.
ple·a·mar f. MARIT. high tide *or* water.
ple·be f. *(multitud)* common people, masses; DEROG. *(pueblo
bajo)* plebs.
ple·be·yo, –ya adj. & m.f. plebeian.
ple·bis·ci·tar tr. to submit to a plebiscite.
ple·bis·ci·to m. plebiscite.
plec·tro m. MUS. plectrum, pick; FIG. inspiration.
ple·ga·ble adj. *(que se dobla)* folding, collapsible; *(flexible)*
pliable.

ple·ga·de·ra f. *(cortapapeles)* paperknife; PRINT. folder.
ple·ga·di·zo, –za adj. *(que se dobla)* folding; *(fácil de doblar)* foldable, easy to fold; *(flexible)* pliable, pliant.
ple·ga·do I. past part. see **plegar** II. m. var. of **plegadura.**
ple·ga·dor, –do·ra I. adj. folding II. m.f. *(doblador)*
folder —m. TEX. warp beam (of a silk loom).
ple·ga·du·ra f. *(acción)* folding; *(pliegue)* fold; SEW. pleat.
ple·ga·mien·to m. GEOL. fold.
ple·gar §52 tr. *(hacer pliegues)* to pleat; *(doblar)* to fold;
TEX. to wind (warp) on a warp beam —reflex. *(doblarse)*
to bend, fold; *(someterse)* to submit, yield; *(adherirse)* to
join, adhere.
ple·ga·ria f. *(súplica)* supplication, prayer; *(toque de campanas)* bell call to noon prayers ◊ **hacer plegarias** to implore, beg.
plei·te·ar intr. LAW *(litigar)* to plead, litigate; *(disputar)* to
argue, dispute.
plei·te·sí·a f. *(homenaje)* homage, tribute; ARCH. *(pacto)*
pact, agreement ◊ **rendir p.** to pay homage.
plei·tis·ta I. adj. LAW *(en derecho)* pettifogging, litigious;
(pendenciero) quarrelsome, contentious II. m.f. LAW *(en
derecho)* pettifogger, litigious person; *(aficionado a disputar)* quarrelsome *or* contentious person.
plei·to m. LAW *(causa)* suit, lawsuit; *(disputa)* dispute,
quarrel; *(contienda)* fight, battle ◊ **andar a pleitos** LAW to
be engaged in lawsuits • **contestar el p.** LAW to defend the
suit, oppose the claim • **entablar p.** LAW to bring suit,
bring an action • **estar a p. con** to be at odds with • **ganar
el p.** LAW to obtain a favorable judgment • **p. de acreedores** LAW bankruptcy proceeding • **poner p. a** LAW to sue,
take (someone) to court • **salir con el p.** LAW to win one's
case *or* suit • **ver un p.** LAW to try a case.
ple·na·mar f. var. of **pleamar.**
ple·na·men·te adv. completely, fully.
ple·na·rio, –ria adj. plenary.
ple·ni·lu·nio m. full moon.
ple·ni·po·ten·cia f. full power, unlimited powers.
ple·ni·po·ten·cia·rio, –ria adj. & m.f. plenipotentiary.
ple·ni·tud f. *(totalidad)* plenitude, fullness; *(abundancia)*
abundance, plenty; FIG. prime *<en la p. de la vida* in the
prime of life>.
ple·no, –na I. adj. *(completo)* full, complete *<plenos poderes* full powers>; open *<un pueblo en p. rebelión* a people
in open rebellion> ◊ **a** *or* **en p. vista** in full view • **en p.**
right in the middle of *<en p. calle* right in the middle of
the street> • **en p. día** in broad daylight II. m. COM., FIN.
plenum, joint session.
ple·pa f. COLL. nuisance.
plé·to·ra f. plethora.
ple·tó·ri·co, –ca adj. plethoric.
pleu·ra f. ANAT. pleura.
pleu·re·sí·a f. MED. pleurisy.
ple·xo m. ANAT. plexus ◊ **p. solar** solar plexus.
plie·go m. *(papel doblado)* sheet *or* piece of paper (folded in
half); *(hoja de papel)* sheet *or* piece of paper; *(documento
cerrado)* sealed document; PRINT. signature ◊ **p. de condiciones** list of conditions, specifications.
plie·go, pliegue see **plegar.**
plie·gue m. *(doblez)* fold; GEOL. fold; SEW. pleat.
plin·to m. ARCHIT. plinth; SPORT. horse (for gymnastics).
pli·sa·do I. past part. see **plisar** II. m. *(acción)* pleating;
(efecto) pleat.
pli·sar tr. to pleat.
plo·ma·da f. *(lápiz)* lead pencil; *(plomo colgado)* plumb
(line); MARIT. plumb *or* sounding line; *(perdigonada)* shot
with pellets; *(de una red de pesca)* sinker, lead weight (on
fishing net).
plo·mar tr. to seal with lead (a document).
plo·ma·zo m. shot wound.
plo·me·rí·a f. *(techo de plomo)* lead roofing; *(oficio)* plumbing.
plo·me·ro m. AMER. plumber.
plo·mi·zo, –za adj. leaden.
plo·mo I. m. CHEM. lead; *(peso)* lead weight; *(plomada)*
sinker (in fishing); FIG. *(bala)* bullet; FIG., COLL. *(tabarra)*
bore; ELEC. fuse ◊ **a. p.** *(verticalmente)* vertically, plumb;
FIG. *(justo)* just right II. adj. see **plomo, –ma.**

plo·mo, –ma I. adj. AMER. var. of **plomizo, –za** II. m. see **plomo.**

plo·mo·so, –sa adj. var. of **plomizo, –za.**

plu·guie·ra, plugo see **placer³.**

plu·ma f. ORNITH. feather <*el cardenal tiene plumas rojas* the cardinal has red feathers>; *(conjunto de plumas)* feather, down <*una almohada de p.* a down pillow>; *(pluma para escribir)* quill (for writing); *(estilográfica)* pen; *(adorno)* plume, feather; FIG. *(habilidad)* penmanship, calligraphy; *(escritor)* pen, writer <*ella es una p. estimada* she is a respected pen>; *(profesión)* writing (as a profession); *(estilo)* pen, style <*tiene una p. ingeniosa* he has a witty style>; MECH. derrick; COL. tap, faucet; C. AMER. lie, tale; ARG. prostitute ◆ **al correr de la p.** FIG. without thinking • **dejar correr la p.** *or* **a vuela p.** FIG. to write spontaneously • **peso p.** SPORT. featherweight • **p. fuente** *or* **estilográfica** fountain pen • **p. viva** ORNITH. down • **vivir de la p.** FIG. to live by the pen, live by writing.

plu·ma·da f. pen stroke, flourish.

plu·ma·fuen·te f. AMER. fountain pen.

plu·ma·je m. *(conjunto de plumas)* plumage, feathers; *(adorno)* plume, crest.

plu·ma·zo m. *(colchón)* feather mattress; *(almohada)* feather pillow; *(plumada)* pen stroke, flourish ◆ **de un p.** with one stroke of the pen.

plúm·be·o, –a adj. *(de plomo)* leaden, lead-like; FIG. *(pesado)* leaden, heavy.

plu·me·ar tr. PAINT. to hatch (in), shade (a drawing).

plu·me·rí·a f. *or* **plu·me·ri·o** m. feathers, plumes.

plu·me·ro m. *(para quitar el polvo)* feather duster; *(estuche)* pen box; *(penacho)* plume, crest; AMER. penholder.

plu·mí·fe·ro, –ra I. adj. POET. plumed, feathered II. m.f. COLL. *(chupatintas)* pen-pusher.

plu·mi·lla f. *(pluma pequeña)* small feather; *(de estilográfica)* nib; BOT. plumule.

plu·mis·ta m. clerk, scribe.

plu·món m. ORNITH. down; *(colchón)* feather mattress.

plu·mo·so, –sa adj. feathery.

plu·ral adj. & m. GRAM. plural.

plu·ra·li·cé, pluralice see **pluralizar.**

plu·ra·li·dad f. *(multiplicidad)* plurality; *(mayor número)* majority <*a p. de votos* by a majority of votes>; *(gran número)* large number, multitude.

plu·ra·lis·mo m. pluralism.

plu·ra·lis·ta adj. pluralist.

plu·ra·li·zar §04 tr. to pluralize.

plu·riem·ple·o m. moonlighting (working at a second job).

plu·ri·la·te·ral adj. multilateral, multipartite.

plu·ri·par·ti·dis·ta adj. POL. multiparty.

plus m. bonus.

plus·cuam·per·fec·to m. GRAM. pluperfect, past perfect (tense).

plus·mar·ca f. record <*batir la p.* to beat the record>.

plus·mar·quis·ta m.f. record holder.

plus·va·lí·a f. *(aumento del valor)* appreciation, increased value; ECON. surplus value.

plu·to·cra·cia f. plutocracy.

plu·tó·cra·ta m.f. plutocrat.

plu·to·crá·ti·co, –ca adj. plutocratic.

Plu·tón m. ASTRON., MYTH. Pluto.

plu·to·nio m. CHEM. plutonium.

plu·vial adj. METEOROL. pluvial, rain.

plu·vió·me·tro m. pluviometer, rain gauge.

plu·vio·so adj. rainy, pluvious.

po·bla·ción f. *(acción, habitantes)* population; *(lugar)* locality, district, settlement; *(ciudad)* city, town; *(pueblo)* village.

po·bla·cho m. DEROG. dump, hole (village).

po·bla·da I. f. AMER. *(tumulto)* riot; *(sedición)* rebellion, revolt; *(gentío)* crowd II. adj. see **poblado, –da.**

po·bla·do, –da I. past part. see **poblar** II. adj. *(habitado)* populated, inhabited; FIG. *(lleno de)* full of III. m. *(habitantes)* population; *(villa)* village; *(ciudad)* city; *(pueblo)* town –f. see **poblada.**

po·bla·dor, –do·ra I. adj. *(fundador)* settling, founding; *(residente)* resident, inhabitant II. m.f. *(fundador)* settler, founder; *(habitante)* resident, inhabitant.

po·bla·no, –na I. m.f. AMER. villager; MEX. native of Puebla II. adj. of Puebla, from Puebla (Mexico).

po·blar §19 tr. *(ocupar con gente o animales)* to populate; AGR. to plant; ICHTH. to stock; *(fundar)* to found, settle, colonize —intr. to procreate prolifically, multiply —reflex. *(recibir gente en gran cantidad)* to become populated; *(llenarse)* to fill (with), become crowded; BOT. *(cubrirse de hojas)* to leaf, become covered with leaves.

po·bre I. adj. *(necesitado)* poor, needy <*una familia p.* a poor family>; *(desprovisto)* lacking <*es un cuento p. en ingenio* it is a story lacking in creativeness>; *(estéril)* barren, empty <*vimos un paisaje p.* we saw a barren landscape>; FIG. *(humilde)* poor, humble <*mi p. opinión no vale nada* my humble opinion is worth nothing>; *(desdichado)* poor, unfortunate <*el p. chico se quedó sin familia* the unfortunate boy was left without family>; *(sencillo)* simple ◆ **más p. que Carracuca** *or* **que una rata** COLL. as poor as a church mouse • **p. de** *or* **p. en** lacking (in) <*un desayuno p. de vitaminas* a breakfast lacking (in) vitamins> • **p. de espíritu** poor in spirit • **p. de mí** poor me, woe is me II. m.f. *(necesitado)* poor person; *(desdichado)* poor devil *or* wretch —m. *(mendigo)* beggar, pauper ◆ **los pobres** the poor.

po·bre·men·te adv. *(con pobreza)* poorly, indigently; *(con escasez)* poorly, inadequately <*p. provisto* poorly outfitted>.

po·bre·rí·a f. *or* **po·bre·rí·o** m. var. of **pobretería.**

po·bre·te, –ta I. adj. poor, unfortunate II. m.f. poor devil, unfortunate person.

po·bre·te·ar intr. COLL. to play the poor man.

po·bre·te·rí·a f. *(pobres)* poor people; *(pobreza)* poverty.

po·bre·tón, –to·na I. adj. very poor, wretched II. m.f. very poor person, wretch.

po·bre·za f. *(indigencia)* poverty, indigence <*vivir en la p.* to live in poverty>; *(escasez)* lack, scarcity <*sufrimos de p. de recursos* we suffered from a lack of resources>; *(esterilidad)* barrenness, sterility; FIG. *(mezquindad)* poorness, meanness <*p. de espíritu* poorness of spirit>; RELIG. vow of poverty.

po·ce·ro m. *(cavador de pozos)* well digger.

po·cil·ga f. *(establo)* pigsty, pigpen; FIG., COLL. pigsty, hovel.

po·ci·llo m. *(tinaja)* sump, catch basin; *(jícara para chocolate)* chocolate cup.

pó·ci·ma f. *(cocimiento medicinal)* potion; FIG. *(bebida)* concoction.

po·ción f. PHARM. potion; *(bebida)* concoction, brew.

po·co, –ca §G24, 29 I. adj. little, not much <*hay p. vegetación en esta región* there is little vegetation in this area> ◆ **de p. interés** of little interest • **p. tiempo** short while *or* time • **pocas veces** not very often, rarely • **pocos** few, not many <*hay pocos árboles aquí* there are few trees here> • **ser p. cosa** to be unimportant, be a little thing • **unos pocos** a few <*unos pocos chicos* a few boys> II. m. little, small amount ◆ **dentro de p.** in a short while *or* time, soon • **en p.** about to, on the point of • **otro p.** a little more • **pocos** <*pocos saben la respuesta* few know the answer> • **ser para p.** to be timid, cowardly • **tener en p.** to have a low opinion (of), hold in low esteem • **un poco de** a little, some <*tiene un p. de fama* he has a little fame> III. adv. *(con escasez)* little, not much <*habló p. durante la clase* he spoke little during the class>; *(en corta duración)* not long, a short while *or* time <*tardó p. en terminar* he did not take long to finish>; *(no muy)* not very <*p. amistoso* he is not very friendly; a little <*p. después oí un tiro* a little after I heard a shot> ◆ **a p.** shortly afterwards • **a p. de** shortly after <*a p. de comer fuimos al cine* shortly after eating, we went to the movies> • **de p. más o menos** of little account *or* importance • **hace p.** a short time ago • **p. a p.** little by little, gradually • **p. falta para** *(tiempo)* it is not long before <*p. falta para la época de las lluvias* it is not long before the rainy season>; *(cantidad)* a little more <*p. falta para balancear los pesos* a little more will balance the weight> • **p. más o menos** more or less • **por p.** almost, nearly.

po·che·que·rí·a f. PERU infantile anemia.

po·cho, –cha I. adj. *(descolorido)* discolored, faded; *(demasiado maduro)* overripe; FIG. *(estropeado)* bad, rotten;

(enfermizo) sickly, pale; CHILE chubby, fat; MEX., DEROG. Americanized **II.** m.f. MEX., DEROG. Americanized Mexican.

po·da f. *(acción)* pruning; *(tiempo)* pruning season.
po·da·de·ra f. AGR. pruning knife *or* shears.
po·da·dor, –do·ra I. adj. pruning **II.** m.f. pruner.
po·da·du·ra f. var. of **poda.**
po·dar tr. to prune, trim.
po·den·co, –ca adj. & m.f. spaniel (dog).
po·der¹ m. *(autoridad)* power, authority; *(vigor)* power, might; *(fuerza física)* strength; *(capacidad)* capacity; *(posesión)* power, hands <*tengo en mi p. su carta del once de mayo* I have in my hands your letter of the eleventh of May>; MIL. forces, strength; POL. government; LAW *(autorización)* power of attorney, proxy; MECH. power ♦ **a p. de** by dint of • **a todo p.** with all of one's might • **dar p. a** to empower, authorize • **de p. a p.** hand-to-hand, man-to-man • **estar en p.** to be in power • **p. adquisitivo** purchasing power • **p. ejecutivo** POL. the executive • **p. judicial** POL. the judiciary • **p. legislativo** POL. the legislative branch • **por poderes** by proxy.
po·der² §53 tr. *(lograr)* to be able to <*podremos salir a las ocho* we will be able to leave at eight o'clock>; can <*¿puedes acompañarme?* can you come with me?> —intr. to be able, can <*me gustaría ayudarte pero no puedo* I would like to help you but I am not able to>; to be possible, may <*puede que llueva mañana* it may rain tomorrow> ♦ **a más no p.** *or* **hasta más no p.** for all one's worth, to the utmost • **no p. con** FIG. *(no lograr)* not to be able to handle; *(no soportar)* not to be able to stand • **no p. más** *(estar fatigado)* to be exhausted; *(estar harto)* to be fed up • **no p. menos que** not to be able to help but • **no p. valerse por sí mismo** to be helpless • **no puede ser** that is not possible • **puede ser** maybe • **¿se puede?** may I?, do you mind?
po·der·ha·bien·te m.f. *(que representa)* agent; LAW attorney, proxy.
po·de·rí·o m. power.
po·de·ro·sa·men·te adv. powerfully.
po·de·ro·so, –sa adj. *(fuerte)* powerful; *(rico)* rich, wealthy; *(eficaz)* effective, good.
po·dí·a·tra *or* **po·dia·tra** m. AMER. podiatrist.
po·dia·trí·a f. podiatry.
po·dio m. podium.
po·dó·me·tro m. pedometer.
po·drá, podría see **poder².**
po·dre·dum·bre f. *(corrupción)* corruption; *(putrefacción)* putrefaction; MED. pus.
po·dri·de·ro m. var. of **pudridero.**
po·dri·do, –da I. past part. see **podrir II.** adj. rotten ♦ **estar p. en plata** *or* **de dinero** AMER. to be rolling in money, be stinking rich.
po·drir §84 tr. & reflex. to rot, putrefy.
po·e·ma m. poem ♦ **p. en prosa** prose poem • **p. sinfónico** MUS. symphonic *or* tone poem.
po·e·ma·rio m. book of poems.
po·e·má·ti·co, –ca adj. poetical.
po·e·sí·a f. *(género literario)* poetry; *(poema)* poem.
po·e·ta m. poet.
po·e·tas·tro m. COLL. poetaster.
po·é·ti·ca I. f. poetics **II.** adj. see **poético, –ca.**
po·é·ti·ca·men·te adv. poetically.
po·é·ti·co, –ca I. adj. poetic, poetical **II.** f. see **poética.**
po·e·ti·sa f. poetess.
po·e·ti·zar §04 tr. to poeticize, make poetic —intr. to write poetry, poeticize.
po·gro·mo m. pogrom.
pó·ker m. poker (card game).
po·la·co, –ca I. adj. Polish **II.** m.f. *(habitante)* Pole —m. *(idioma)* Polish.
po·lai·na f. gaiter, legging; ARG., BOL., HOND. annoyance, obstacle.
po·lar adj. *(de los polos)* polar; ELEC. pole.
po·la·ri·dad f. polarity.
po·la·ri·za·ción f. polarization.
po·la·ri·za·dor, –do·ra I. adj. polarizing **II.** m. OPT., PHOTOG. polarizer.

po·la·ri·zar §04 tr. to polarize —intr. to polarize, become polarized.
po·le·a f. MECH. pulley.
po·le·a·da f. ARG. very clear soup ♦ **poleadas** porridge.
po·lé·mi·co, –ca I. adj. polemical, polemic **II.** f. *(arte)* polemics; *(controversia)* polemic.
po·le·mis·ta m.f. polemicist, polemist.
po·le·mi·zar §04 intr. to engage in a polemic, argue.
po·len m. BOT. pollen.
po·li m. SL. cop —f. cops <*¡la p.!* the cops!>.
po·lian·dria f. polyandry.
po·li·cí·a f. *(administración, agentes)* police; *(limpieza)* cleanliness, neatness; *(cortesía)* courtesy, politeness —m. policeman.
po·li·cia·co, –ca *or* **po·li·cí·a·co, –ca** adj. *(de policía)* police; detective <*novela p.* detective novel>.
po·li·cial I. adj. *(de policía)* police; *(de detective)* detective **II.** m. AMER. policeman.
po·li·clí·ni·ca f. MED. polyclinic.
po·li·cro·mí·a f. polychromy.
po·li·cro·mo, –ma adj. polychrome.
po·li·chi·ne·la m. THEAT. punchinello, buffoon.
po·lie·dro m. GEOM. polyhedron.
po·li·fo·ní·a f. MUS. polyphony.
po·li·tó·ni·co, –ca *or* **po·lí·fo·no, –na** adj. polyphonic.
po·li·ga·mia f. polygamy.
po·lí·ga·mo, –ma I. adj. polygamous **II.** m.f. polygamist.
po·lí·glo·to, –ta *or* **po·li·glo·to, –ta** adj. & m.f. polyglot.
po·lí·go·no, –na I. m. GEOM. polygon; MIL. polygon, rifle range ♦ **p. industrial** industrial park **II.** adj. GEOM. polygonal.
po·lí·gra·fo m. *(autor)* writer on a variety of subjects; CRIMIN., MED. polygraph.
po·li·lla f. ENTOM. moth; FIG. *(que destruye)* waster, destroyer.
po·lí·me·ro, –ra I. adj. CHEM. polymeric; BOT. polymerous **II.** m. CHEM. polymer.
po·li·mor·fo, –fa adj. polymorphous.
po·li·ni·za·ción f. BOT. pollination, pollinization.
po·li·no·mio m. MATH. polynomial.
po·lio *or* **po·lio·mie·li·tis** f. MED. polio, poliomyelitis.
pó·li·po m. ZOOL. *(celentéreo)* polyp; *(molusco)* octopus, polypus; MED. polyp, polypus.
po·li·sí·la·bo, –ba I. adj. polysyllabic **II.** m. polysyllable.
po·li·téc·ni·co, –ca adj. polytechnic.
po·li·te·ís·mo m. RELIG. polytheism.
po·li·te·ís·ta RELIG. **I.** adj. polytheistic **II.** m.f. polytheist.
po·lí·ti·ca I. f. *(asuntos de estado)* politics; *(modo de obrar)* policy <*p. monetaria* monetary policy>; *(cortesía)* courtesy, tact **II.** adj. see **político, –ca.**
po·li·ti·cas·tro m. DEROG. politician.
po·li·ti·cé, politice see **politizar.**
po·lí·ti·co, –ca I. adj. *(de asuntos de estado)* political; *(cortés)* courteous, tactful; *(de parentesco)* in-law <*hermana p.* sister-in-law> **II.** m.f. politician —f. see **política.**
po·li·ti·cón, –co·na DEROG. **I.** adj. *(ceremonioso)* excessively ceremonious; *(interesado en política)* devoted to politics **II.** m.f. excessively ceremonious person.
po·li·ti·que·ar intr. COLL. *(hablar de la política)* to talk politics; *(maniobrar)* to politick, maneuver politically.
po·li·ti·que·o m. COLL. political maneuvering.
po·li·ti·que·rí·a f. COLL. var. of **politiqueo.**
po·li·ti·que·ro, –ra m.f. AMER. political maneuverer.
po·li·ti·za·ción f. politicization.
po·li·ti·zar §04 tr. politicize.
po·liu·re·ta·no m. CHEM. polyurethane.
po·li·va·len·te adj. polyvalent, multivalent.
pó·li·za f. *(de seguros)* policy, insurance policy; *(contrato)* contract; *(sello)* stamp; *(de mercancías)* papers.
po·li·zón m. *(persona que embarca)* stowaway; *(ocioso)* bum, hobo.
po·li·zon·te m. DEROG. cop, policeman.
po·lo¹ m. SCI. *(término opuesto)* pole, opposite <*la verdad y la mentira son dos polos* truth and lies are opposites>; *(base)* base, foundation ♦ **p. antártico** *or* **austral** South Pole • **p. ártico** *or* **boreal** North Pole • **p. magnético** magnetic pole • **ser el p. opuesto de** FIG. to be the

polar opposite of • **ser polos opuestos** FIG. to be poles apart.

po·lo² m. SPORT. polo ♦ **p. acuático** water polo.

po·lo³ m. *(helado)* ice cream stick, eskimo pie; *(camisa)* sport shirt.

po·lo·nés, –ne·sa adj. & m.f. var. of **polaco, –ca.**

po·lo·ne·sa f. MUS. polonaise.

Po·lo·nia f. Poland.

po·lo·nio m. CHEM. polonium.

pol·trón, –tro·na I. adj. idle, lazy II. f. *(butaca)* easy chair; DEROG. *(cargo)* sinecure.

pol·tro·ne·ar intr. COLL. to idle, loaf (around).

pol·tro·ne·rí·a f. laziness, idleness.

po·lu·ción f. pollution, contamination.

po·lu·to, –ta adj. soiled, polluted.

pol·va·re·da f. *(nube de polvo)* cloud of dust; FIG. *(alboroto)* rumpus, to-do.

pol·ve·ra f. powder box, compact.

pol·ve·ro m. AMER. cloud of dust; C. AMER. handkerchief.

pol·vo m. *(tierra menuda)* dust; *(substancia pulverizada)* powder; *(porción pequeña)* pinch <*un p. de rapé* a pinch of snuff>; FIG. *(restos humanos)* remains ♦ **en. p.** powdered • **estar hecho p.** *(estar exhausto)* to be exhausted; *(estar desmoralizado)* to be overwhelmed • **hacer morder el p. a uno** FIG. to beat, defeat • **hacer p.** *(romper)* to smash, shatter; *(aniquilar)* to annihilate, pulverize • **limpio de p. y paja** COM. neat, clear; *(sin gravamen)* with no strings attached • **morder el p.** FIG. to bite the dust • **p. cósmico** cosmic dust • **p. de la Madre Celestina** FIG. magic formula • **polvos** cosmetic powder • **sacudir el p.** *(dar golpes)* to beat up; *(impugnar)* to refute.

pól·vo·ra f. *(explosivo)* powder, gunpowder; *(pirotecnia)* fireworks; FIG. *(mal genio)* bad temper; *(viveza)* liveliness, vivacity ♦ **algodón p.** guncotton • **gastar p. en salvas** FIG. to waste time and energy • **no haber inventado la p.** not to be about to set the world on fire • **p. de algodón** guncotton • **p. detonante** or **fulminante** detonating powder • **p. lenta** or **progresiva** slow-burning powder • **ser una p.** FIG. to be a whip • **p. sin humo** smokeless powder • **p. sorda** FIG. snake in the grass.

pol·vo·re·ar tr. to powder, sprinkle.

pol·vo·re·ra f. dust cloud.

pol·vo·rien·to, –ta adj. dusty.

pol·vo·rín m. *(explosivo)* fine gunpowder; *(frasco)* powder flask or horn; *(lugar)* powder magazine; ENTOM. tick; FIG., COLL. *(persona enojadiza)* spitfire, quick-tempered person.

pol·vo·ris·ta m. pyrotechnist, fireworks maker.

po·lla f. *(gallina)* pullet, young hen; *(fúlica)* coot; *(apuesta)* bet, shake; COLL. *(muchacha)* young girl; ARG., BOL. horse race; SL. cock, penis ♦ **p. de agua** water hen.

po·lla·da f. brood, hatch.

po·llas·tre m. *(pollo)* chicken, chick; FIG. kid, youngster; COLL. braggart.

po·llas·tro, –tra m.f. *(pollo)* large chicken —m. FIG., COLL. *(persona astuta)* sly fellow.

po·lla·zón f. brood, hatch.

po·lle·ar intr. to become interested in the opposite sex (adolescents).

po·lle·ra f. *(criadora)* woman poulterer; *(gallinero)* henhouse; *(andador)* baby walker; *(falda interior)* petticoat; AMER. skirt.

po·lle·rí·a f. poultry shop.

po·lle·ro m. poulterer.

po·lli·no, –na m.f. *(asno)* young donkey; FIG., COLL. *(necio)* ass, fool.

po·lli·to, –ta m.f. FIG., COLL. kid, youngster; *(pollo)* chick.

po·llo m. *(cría de aves)* chick; CUL. chicken; FIG., COLL. *(mozo)* boy, youngster; SL. *(gargajo)* spit ♦ **estar hecho un p.** to look young and handsome • **p. pera** COLL. dandy.

po·ma f. *(manzana)* apple; *(perfumador)* cassolette.

po·ma·da f. pomade.

po·mar m. *(huerto)* orchard; *(manzanar)* apple orchard.

po·me·lo m. *(fruta)* grapefruit; *(árbol)* grapefruit tree.

pó·mez adj. ♦ **piedra p.** pumice (stone).

po·mí·fe·ro, –ra adj. pomiferous, apple-bearing.

po·mo m. BOT. pome; *(para licores)* flagon; *(para perfumes)* scent or perfume bottle; *(bola aromática)* pomander; ARM. pommel.

pom·pa f. *(esplendor)* pomp, splendor; *(ostentación)* display, show; *(procesión solemne)* procession, pageant; *(burbuja)* bubble; *(del pavo real)* spread of peacock's tail; MARIT. pump ♦ **pompas fúnebres** funeral.

pom·pe·ar intr. to show off —reflex. *(tratarse con ostentación)* to show off; *(pavonearse)* to swagger, strut about.

Pom·pe·ya f. Pompeii.

pom·pe·ya·no, –na adj. & m.f. Pompeian.

pom·po·sa·men·te adv. *(espléndidamente)* splendidly, with great pomp; *(con arrogancia)* pompously.

pom·po·si·dad f. *(esplendor)* pomp, splendor; *(arrogancia)* pomposity, pompousness.

pom·po·so, –sa adj. *(espléndido)* splendid, magnificent; *(arrogante)* pompous.

pó·mu·lo m. ANAT. *(hueso)* cheekbone; *(mejilla)* cheek.

pon see **poner.**

pon·cha f. AMER. blanket.

pon·cha·da f. AMER. large quantity.

pon·che m. punch (drink).

pon·che·ra f. *(vasija)* punch bowl; AMER. washbasin.

pon·cho I. m. AMER. poncho, cape; MIL. military cape ♦ **estar a p. en algo** ECUAD., PERU to be in the dark about something II. adj. see **poncho, –cha.**

pon·cho, –cha I. adj. *(perezoso)* lazy, indolent; COL. chubby II. m. see **poncho.**

pon·de·ra·ble adj. *(que se puede pesar)* ponderable, weighable; *(digno de ponderación)* worthy of consideration.

pon·de·ra·ción f. *(examinación)* consideration, pondering; *(acción de pesar)* weighing; *(encarecimiento)* excessive praise; *(equilibrio)* balance, equilibrium.

pon·de·ra·do, –da I. past part. see **ponderar** II. adj. prudent, careful.

pon·de·rar tr. *(examinar)* to consider, ponder; *(pesar)* to weigh; *(encarecer)* to overpraise; *(equilibrar)* to balance.

pon·de·ra·ti·vo, –va adj. *(excesivo)* excessive; *(meditativo)* thoughtful, deliberative.

pon·drá, pondría see **poner.**

po·ne·de·ro, –ra I. adj. egg-laying (hen) II. m. nest, hen's nest.

po·ne·dor, –do·ra I. adj. *(que se encabrita)* trained to rear up (a horse); *(ponedero)* egg-laying II. m. bettor, wagerer.

po·nen·cia f. *(cargo)* post of reporter (in an assembly); *(informe)* report; *(trabajo erudito)* paper.

po·nen·te I. adj. reporting II. m.f. reporter (in an assembly).

po·ner §54 tr. *(colocar)* to put, place <*¿dónde pusiste las tijeras?* where did you put the scissors?>; *(disponer)* to set, arrange <*María puso la mesa* Mary set the table>; *(escribir)* to write, set down; *(instalar)* to set up <*p. casa* to set up house>; *(suponer)* to suppose, say <*pongamos que esto es así* let's suppose that this is so>; *(tardar)* to take <*pondrán seis horas en llegar* they will take six hours to arrive>; *(dejar)* to leave <*lo pongo en tus manos* I leave it in your hands>; *(dedicar)* to assign <*lo pusimos a hacer las decoraciones* we assigned him to do the decorations>; *(nombrar)* to name, give <*le pusieron el apodo de Paco* they gave him the nickname of Frank>; ORNITH. to lay; THEAT. to put on <*pondrán una comedia de Lope de Vega* they will put on a play by Lope de Vega>; *(apostar)* to put, stake <*pondré cien pesos a ese caballo* I will put one hundred pesos on that horse>; *(pagar)* to pay, contribute; *(imponer)* to impose, levy; *(exponer)* to put, expose <*sin darme cuenta, puse a Tomás en una situación peligrosa* without realizing it, I put Thomas in a dangerous situation>; *(abusar)* to insult, mistreat <*¡como lo pusieron!* how they insulted him!>; *(causar)* to make, put <*eso lo pondrá de mal humor* that will put him in a bad mood>; *(adaptar)* to set, adjust; *(enviar)* to send <*me puso un telegrama* she sent me a telegram> ♦ **p. al corriente** or **al día** to bring up to date • **p. aparte** or **a un lado** to put aside • **p. conuevo a alguien** *(insultar)* to insult, tell off; *(maltratar)* mistreat • **p. de la parte de uno** to do what one can • **p. en claro** to explain, make clear • **p. en duda** to put in doubt, call into question • **p. en mal a** to speak ill of, run down • **p. en movimiento** to set in motion • **p. en práctica** to put into practice • **p. en ridículo** to ridicule • **p. en venta** to put up for sale • **p. fin a** to put a stop to • **p. manos a la obra** to get to work • **p. miedo** to frighten

• **p. por encima** to prefer • **p. por escrito** to put in writing • **p. por las nubes** FIG. to praise to the skies —intr. OR-NITH. to lay —reflex. *(colocarse)* to put *or* place oneself; *(vestirse)* to put on <*se puso el sombrero* he put on his hat>; *(arriesgarse)* to expose oneself, put oneself <*ponerse en peligro* to put oneself in danger>; ASTRON. to set <*el sol se puso* the sun set>; *(hacerse)* to get, become <*se pusieron furiosos* they became furious>; *(mancharse)* to be covered <*me puse de lodo* I was covered with mud>; *(dedicarse)* to apply oneself ♦ **ponerse a** to begin to • **ponerse al corriente** to bring oneself up to date • **ponerse bien** to get well • **ponerse colorado** to blush • **ponerse de acuerdo** to reach an agreement • **ponerse delante** to get in the way • **ponerse de pie** to stand up • **ponerse en camino** to set out • **ponerse enfermo** to get sick • **ponérsela** GUAT., HOND., MEX., COLL. to get drunk.

pon·go m. ZOOL. orangutan; AMER. Indian servant.
po·nien·te m. *(occidente)* west; *(viento)* west wind.
pon·ta·je *or* **pon·taz·go** f. bridge toll.
pon·ti·fi·ca·do I. past part. see **pontificar** II. m. *(dignidad)* pontificate, papacy; *(tiempo)* papacy.
pon·ti·fi·cal I. adj. pontifical II. m. *(ornamentos)* pontificals; *(libro)* pontifical ♦ **de p.** FIG., COLL. dressed up.
pon·ti·fi·car §70 intr. to pontificate.
pon·tí·fi·ce m. HIST. pontifex (in ancient Rome); RELIG. pontiff ♦ **Sumo Pontífice** Sovereign Pontiff.
pon·ti·fi·cio, –cia adj. pontifical, papal.
pon·tón m. *(barco chato)* pontoon, lighter; *(buque amarrado)* hulk; *(puente)* pontoon bridge; AVIA. float (of a seaplane) ♦ **p. flotante** floating *or* pontoon bridge.
pon·zo·ña f. *(veneno)* poison, venom; FIG. *(doctrina perjudicial)* poison; *(malevolencia)* venom.
pon·zo·ño·so, –sa adj. *(venenoso)* poisonous; FIG. *(perjudicial)* harmful.
po·pa f. MARIT. stern ♦ **a p.** MARIT. astern, abaft ♦ **de p. a proa** FIG. totally, through and through • **viento en p.** smoothly, well <*vamos viento en p.* we are doing well>.
po·po·te m. AMER. (drinking) straw.
po·pu·la·che·rí·a f. cheap popularity.
po·pu·la·che·ro, –ra adj. *(del populacho)* popular, of the masses; *(vulgar)* vulgar, common.
po·pu·la·cho m. masses, populace.
po·pu·lar adj. *(del pueblo)* of the people, people's; *(grato al pueblo)* popular, well-liked; *(coloquial)* colloquial (language); *(música)* folk (music).
po·pu·la·ri·dad f. popularity.
po·pu·la·ri·za·ción f. popularization.
po·pu·la·ri·zar §04 tr. to popularize —reflex. to become popular.
po·pu·lar·men·te adv. popularly.
po·pu·lo·so, –sa adj. populous.
po·pu·rrí m. potpourri.
po·que·dad f. *(escasez)* scantiness, paucity; *(timidez)* timidity; *(fruslería)* trifle.
pó·quer m. poker (card game).
po·qui·to, –ta I. adj. very little ♦ **poquitos** few, very few II. adv. a little, very little III. m. a little bit ♦ **a p.** little by little • **a poquitos** bit by bit, a bit at a time • **p. a poco** little by little.
por §G11 prep. ☐ PLACE by <*pasamos p. el nuevo edificio de correos* we passed by the new post office>; on, along <*caminar p. la calle* to walk along the street>; through <*el ladrón entró p. la ventana* the thief entered through the window>; around <*los niños están jugando p. allí* the children are playing around there>; over <*pasamos p. el puente* we went over the bridge>; around, towards <*esa ciudad está p. el norte, ¿no?* that city is towards the north, isn't it?>; throughout <*la epidemia se extendió p. toda la ciudad* the epidemic extended throughout the city> ☐ TIME for <*estudiaron p. tres horas* they studied for three hours>; around, about <*llegarán p. el diez de mayo* they will arrive around the tenth of May>; in <*p. la tarde* in the afternoon>; at <*p. la noche* at night>; not yet, still to be <*los pisos están p. lavarse* the floors are still to be washed> ☐ AGENT by <*esta novela fue escrita p. Unamuno* this novel was written by Unamuno>; via, by <*envié la carta p. vía aérea* I sent the letter by air mail> ☐ CAUSE, MOTIVE because of, out of <*lo hizo p. necesidad* he did it out of

necessity>; on account of, because of <*dejó de trabajar p. la enfermedad que tenía* he stopped working on account of his illness>; on behalf of, for <*como mi hermana no estaba presente, firmé p. ella* since my sister was not present, I signed for her>; for the sake of, for <*sacrificaron sus vidas p. la patria* they sacrificed their lives for their country>; in order to <*p. no discutir en público* in order not to argue in public>; for <*fui p. el médico* I went for the doctor> ☐ MANNER by, by means of <*nos comunicamos p. señas* we communicated by gestures>; in <*archive estas tarjetas p. orden alfabético* file these cards in alphabetical order>; by, after <*me los comí uno p. uno* I ate them one by one>; as <*lo dio p. perdido* he considered it as lost>; as, for <*la tomé p. esposa* I took her as my wife> ☐ EXCHANGE, RATE for, in exchange for <*te daré mi chaqueta p. la tuya* I will give you my jacket in exchange for yours>; per, a <*los boletos costarán cinco dólares p. persona* the tickets will cost five dollars per person>; by <*vender p. libra* to sell by the pound>; MATH. times <*tres p. cuatro son doce* three times four is twelve> ☐ CONCESSION however, no matter how <*p. cansados que ellos estén* no matter how tired they are> ☐ IDIOMS • **p. acá** *or* **aquí** around here • **p. ahí** *or* **allí** around there • **p. ahora** for the time being, for now • **p. casualidad** perchance • **p. causa de** *or* **p. motivo de** because of • **p. ciento** per cent • **p. cierto** indeed • **p. completo** completely • **p. consiguiente** therefore, consequently • **p. correo** by mail • **p. cuanto** inasmuch as, whereas • **p. cuenta de uno** *(sin ayuda)* by oneself; *(sin requerimiento)* of one's own accord • **p. desgracia** unfortunately • **¡p. Dios!** for Heaven's sake! • **p. docena** by the dozen • **p. donde** because of which • **p. ejemplo** for example • **p. entre** between, among • **p. escrito** in writing • **p. eso** therefore • **p. lo bajo** softly, in a whisper • **p. lo menos** at least • **p. lo tanto** therefore • **p. medio de** through, by means of • **p. otra parte** *or* **p. lo demás** on the other hand • **¿p. qué?** why? • **p. regla general** as a general rule • **p. si** *or* **p. si acaso** in case • **p. sí mismo** by oneself, on one's own • **p. sobre** above • **p. supuesto** of course • **p. todos lados** everywhere • **p. valor de** in the amount of.

por·ca·chón, –cho·na *or* **por·ca·llón, –llo·na** COLL. I. adj. filthy, dirty II. m.f. *(animal)* large pig; *(persona)* pig, filthy person.
por·ce·la·na f. *(loza)* porcelain; *(vajilla)* china, chinaware; *(esmalte)* porcelain enamel; *(color)* porcelain blue.
por·cen·ta·je m. percentage.
por·cen·tual adj. percentage.
por·ci·no, –na I. adj. *(del puerco)* porcine, pig II. m. *(puerco pequeño)* small pig; MED. bump, swelling.
por·ción f. *(parte)* portion, part; *(de comida)* portion, helping (of food) <*sirven porciones abundantes en este restaurante* they serve big portions in this restaurant>; *(cuota)* portion, share, ration <*su p. del dinero fue muy pequeña* his share of the money was very small>; COLL. *(gran cantidad)* lot, large number <*una p. de problemas* a lot of problems>; RELIG. stipend, prebend.
por·che m. *(de una casa)* porch; *(soportal)* arcade.
por·dio·se·ar intr. to beg.
por·dio·se·o m. *or* **por·dio·se·rí·a** f. begging.
por·dio·se·ro, –ra I. adj. begging II. m.f. beggar.
por·fí·a f. *(persistencia)* persistence; *(obstinación)* stubbornness, obstinacy; *(disputa)* dispute, struggle ♦ **a p.** in competition.
por·fia·da·men·te adv. *(persistentemente)* persistently; *(obstinadamente)* stubbornly, obstinately.
por·fia·do, –da I. past part. see **porfiar** II. adj. *(persistente)* persistent; *(obstinado)* stubborn, obstinate III. m.f. stubborn person.
por·fiar §30 intr. *(disputar)* to argue stubbornly; *(hacer instancia)* to persist, insist ♦ **p. en hacer algo** to persist in doing something • **p. en que** to insist that • **p. por hacer algo** to struggle stubbornly to do something.
pór·fi·do m. MIN. porphyry.
por·me·nor m. detail, particular.
por·me·no·ri·zar §04 tr. to detail, describe in detail —intr. to go into detail.
por·no·gra·fí·a f. pornography.
por·no·grá·fi·co, –ca adj. pornographic.

por·nó·gra·fo m. pornographer.

po·ro m. *(intersticio)* interstice; BIOL. pore.

po·ron·go m. AMER. gourd.

po·ro·si·dad f. porousness, porosity.

po·ro·so, –sa adj. porous.

po·ro·to m. AMER., BOT. bean; CUL. bean dish.

por·que conj. *(por causa de que)* because <*trabajo p. quiero comer* I work because I want to eat>; *(para que)* in order that, so that ♦ **p. sí** just because.

por·qué m. *(motivo)* whys and wherefores (of), reason (for), cause (of) <*estudiaremos el p. de la revolución* we will study the reason for the revolution>; COLL. *(cantidad)* share, amount <*tiene un buen p. de dinero* she has a good share of money>.

por·que·rí·a f. *(suciedad)* filth, dirt; *(basura)* junk, garbage; *(grosería)* nastiness, vulgarity; *(jugarreta)* dirty trick; *(cosa de poco valor)* worthless thing, junk; *(comida perjudicial)* unhealthy or junk food ♦ **estar hecho una p.** to be filthy.

por·que·ri·za f. pigsty.

por·que·ri·zo or **por·que·ro** m. swineherd.

po·rra I. f. *(clava)* club, bludgeon; *(de herrero)* sledgehammer; FIG. *(jactancia)* boasting; *(pesado)* bore, pest; *(en un juego)* last player (in a game); THEAT. claque; SP., REG. large fritter ♦ **mandar a la p.** to send packing, send to hell • **¡porra!** damn! II. adj. see **porro, –rra**.

po·rra·da f. *(golpe)* blow; *(golpe con una porra)* blow with a club; FIG., COLL. *(necedad)* nonsense; *(cantidad)* pile, loads <*una p. de cosas* a pile of things>.

po·rra·zo m. *(golpe)* blow; *(golpe con una porra)* blow with a club; *(choque)* bump ♦ **pegarse un p. contra algo** to bump or to bang into something.

po·rri·llo[1] m. mason's hammer.

po·rri·llo[2] adv. ♦ **a p.** galore, in abundance.

po·rro, –rra COLL. I. adj. stupid, thick II. m. *(tonto)* dope, idiot; *(cigarrillo)* joint (marijuana cigarette); cone-shaped drum —f. see **porra**.

po·rrón, –rro·na I. adj. COLL. slow, stupid II. m. *(botijo)* jug; *(salsa)* garlic sauce.

por·ta·a·vio·nes m. [pl. **-nes**] aircraft carrier.

por·ta·ban·de·ra f. flag holder.

por·ta·bom·bas m. [pl. **-bas**] bomb carrier.

por·ta·ca·ja f. drum strap.

por·ta·car·tas m. [pl. **-tas**] mailbag.

por·ta·da I. f. ARCHIT. facade, front; PRINT. *(frontispicio)* title page; *(tapa)* cover; FIG. *(fachada)* facade II. adj. see **portado, –da**.

por·ta·do, –da I. past part. see **portar** II. adj. ♦ **bien p.** *(bien vestido)* well-dressed; *(que se porta bien)* well-behaved ♦ **mal p.** *(mal vestido)* badly dressed; *(que se porta mal)* ill-behaved, rude III. f. see **portada**.

por·ta·dor, –do·ra I. adj. carrying, bearing II. m.f. *(persona que lleva algo)* carrier, bearer —m. *(bandeja)* tray; COM. bearer; MED. carrier.

por·ta·e·qui·pa·jes m. [pl. **-jes**] *(baúl)* trunk (of a car); *(rejilla)* luggage rack.

por·ta·es·tan·dar·te m. standard-bearer.

por·ta·fo·lio m. AMER. briefcase.

por·ta·fu·sil m. sling (for a rifle).

por·tal m. *(zaguán)* entrance hall, vestibule; *(porche de una casa)* porch; *(soportales)* arcade; *(de Navidad)* crèche.

por·ta·lám·pa·ras m. [pl. **-ras**] socket (for a bulb).

por·ta·lá·piz m. [pl. **-lá·pi·ces**] pencil holder.

por·ta·li·bros m. [pl. **-bros**] book straps.

por·ta·lón m. portal, large doorway; MARIT. gangway.

por·ta·man·te·o m. portmanteau, traveling bag.

por·ta·mo·ne·das m. [pl. **-das**] change purse.

por·tan·te m. amble, ambling gait (of a horse) ♦ **tomar el p.** FIG., COLL. to leave, go away.

por·ta·nue·vas m.f. [pl. **-vas**] bearer of news.

por·ta·plu·mas m. [pl. **-mas**] penholder.

por·tar tr. to carry, bear —intr. MARIT. to stand or hold up well (sails and rigging) —reflex. to behave, conduct oneself ♦ **portarse bien** to behave well, behave oneself • **portarse mal** to behave badly, misbehave.

por·ta·rre·tra·tos m. [pl. **-tos**] picture or photograph frame.

por·tá·til adj. portable.

por·ta·vian·das m. [pl. **-das**] *(fiambrera)* lunch box or basket.

por·ta·voz m. [pl. **-vo·ces**] *(bocinal)* megaphone; *(representante)* spokesman; *(representante femenino)* spokeswoman.

por·ta·zo m. slam, bang (of a door) ♦ **dar un p. a alguien** to slam the door in someone's face.

por·te m. carrying, transporting; *(costo)* transport charge; *(de correos)* postage; *(conducta)* behavior, conduct; *(disposición)* bearing, demeanor; *(dimensión)* size, capacity ♦ **p. pagado** postage paid.

por·te·a·dor I. adj. carrying II. m. carrier.

por·te·ar tr. to carry, transport —intr. ARG. to leave, go away.

por·ten·to m. marvel, prodigy.

por·ten·to·so, –sa adj. marvelous, prodigious.

por·te·ño, –ña I. adj. *(bonaerense)* of Buenos Aires; *(de Valparaíso)* of Valparaíso II. m.f. *(bonaerense)* native of Buenos Aires; *(nativo de Valparaíso)* native of Valparaíso.

por·te·o m. carrying, transporting.

por·te·rí·a f. *(pieza del portero)* doorman's or concierge's office; *(empleo del portero)* job of doorman or concierge; *(en un convento)* gatehouse; SPORT. goal.

por·te·ro, –ra m.f. *(conserje)* doorman, concierge; *(de vivienda)* janitor, caretaker; SPORT. goalkeeper.

por·te·zue·la f. *(puerta pequeña)* small door; AUTO. door; SEW. pocket flap.

pór·ti·co m. ARCHIT. *(porche)* portico, porch; *(soportales)* arcade.

por·ti·lla f. *(paso)* gate (in a fence); MARIT. porthole.

por·ti·llo m. *(de muro)* opening, gap; *(postigo)* wicker (small door within a gate); *(puerta)* gate; *(paso angosto)* pass, path (between mountains); FIG. *(mella)* chip (in a plate); *(punto vulnerable)* weak spot; *(posibilidad)* opening (for a solution).

por·tón m. *(puerta grande)* large door; *(del zaguán)* hall or vestibule door.

por·to·rri·que·ño, –ña adj. & m.f. Puerto Rican.

por·tua·rio, –ria adj. port, harbor <*tráfico p.* port traffic>.

Por·tu·gal m. Portugal.

por·tu·gués, –sa adj. & m.f. Portuguese —m. *(idioma)* Portuguese ♦ **los portugueses** the Portuguese.

por·tu·gue·sa·da f. COLL. exaggeration.

por·tu·gue·sis·mo m. Portuguese word or expression.

por·ve·nir m. future ♦ **en el p.** or **lo p.** in the future.

pos adv. ♦ **en p. de** after, in pursuit of.

po·sa·da f. *(mesón)* inn; *(casa de huéspedes)* guest or boarding house; *(hogar)* home, dwelling; *(hospedaje)* lodging, shelter; *(utensilios)* set of dining utensils for traveling ♦ **dar p. a alguien** to give shelter to someone • **Las Posadas** Mexican Christmas ceremony.

po·sa·de·ras f.pl. buttocks, backside.

po·sa·de·ro, –ra m.f. innkeeper.

po·sar intr. *(hospedarse)* to lodge; *(descansar)* to rest; *(pararse las aves)* to perch, alight (birds); PAINT., PHOTOG. to sit, pose (for a portrait) —reflex. *(pararse las aves)* to perch, alight (birds); *(depositarse)* to settle (dust); AVIA. to land —tr. *(soltar)* to put or lay down (a load); *(poner)* to lay, put <*posó su mano en mi hombro* she put her hand on my shoulder>.

pos·da·ta f. postscript.

po·se f. PHOTOG. exposure; *(postura)* pose, posture; *(afectación)* pose, affectation.

po·se·e·dor, –do·ra I. adj. owning, possessing II. m.f. *(dueño)* possessor, owner; holder <*el p. de una marca mundial* the holder of a world record> ♦ **p. de acciones** COM., FIN. stockholder • **p. de obligaciones** COM., FIN. bondholder • **p. de patente** LAW patent holder.

po·se·er §43 tr. *(tener)* to possess, have <*ella posee una buena biblioteca* she has a good library>; *(saber)* to know perfectly, have a mastery of <*posee el inglés* he has a mastery of English>; to hold <*poseyó la marca mundial* he held the world record>; *(obsesionar)* to possess, dominate <*un deseo extraño le poseyó* a strange desire possessed him> —reflex. to control oneself.

po·se·í·do, –da I. past part. see **poseer** II. adj. *(poseso)* possessed (by an evil obsession); FIG. *(loco)* maddened, crazed III. m.f. possessed person.

po·se·sión f. *(propiedad)* possession, property; *(acto de poseer)* possession, ownership; *(del demonio)* possession; AMER. property, estate ♦ **en p. de** in possession of • **posesiones** possessions, personal property • **tomar p. de** to take possession of.

po·se·sio·nar tr. to give possession of —reflex. to take possession of, take over.

po·se·si·vo, –va adj. & m. possessive.

po·se·so, –sa I. past part. see **poseer** II. adj. possessed (by a spirit) III. m.f. possessed person.

po·se·sor, –so·ra adj. & m.f. var. of **poseedor, –dora.**

po·se·so·rio, –ria adj. LAW possessory.

po·se·ye·ra, poseyó see **poseer.**

pos·fe·cha f. postdate.

pos·gra·dua·do, –da I. adj. having a college degree II. m.f. college graduate, postgraduate.

pos·gue·rra f. postwar period.

po·si·bi·li·dad f. *(calidad de posible)* possibility; *(aptitud)* ability, capacity ♦ **posibilidades** *(bienes)* means; *(probabilidades)* chances, possibilities.

po·si·bi·li·tar tr. *(hacer posible)* to make possible, facilitate; *(permitir)* to allow, permit.

po·si·ble I. adj. possible ♦ **de ser p.** if possible • **dentro de** *or* **en lo p.** as far as possible • **hacer p.** to make possible • **hacer (todo) lo p.** to do everything possible • **lo antes p.** as soon as possible II. m.pl. **posibles** means, resources.

po·si·ción f. *(postura)* position, posture; *(condición social)* standing, status; *(sitio)* place, position; MIL. position; SPORT. position, place.

po·si·ti·va·men·te adv. positively.

po·si·ti·vis·mo m. PHILOS. positivism; *(realismo)* realism; *(afición a lo material)* materialism.

po·si·ti·vis·ta I. adj. PHILOS. positivist, positivistic; *(realista)* realistic II. m.f. PHILOS. positivist; *(realista)* realist.

po·si·ti·vo, –va I. adj. positive II. m.f. PHOTOG. positive, print —m. GRAM. positive.

pó·si·to m. *(granero)* public granary; *(asociación)* cooperative, association.

po·si·trón *or* **po·si·tón** m. PHYS. positron.

pos·ma COLL. I. adj. dull, tiresome II. m.f. *(persona)* dull *or* tiresome person —f. *(pesadez)* dullness, tiresomeness.

po·so m. *(sedimento)* sediment, deposit; *(de café)* coffee grounds ♦ **formar p.** to settle (a liquid).

po·so·lo·gí·a f. dosage.

pos·po·ner §54 *(poner detrás)* to place second, put behind; *(diferir)* to postpone, put off.

pos·po·si·ción f. *(aplazamiento)* postponement; *(subordinación)* subordination; GRAM. postposition.

pos·ta f. *(de caballos)* relay, team (of post horses); *(donde se apostaban)* staging post, post; *(tajada)* slice, piece (of meat); *(bala)* small bullet, pellet; *(envite)* stake, bet; ARCHIT. volute ♦ **a p.** on purpose, intentionally.

pos·tal I. adj. postal ♦ **giro p.** money order II. f. postcard, postal card.

post·da·ta f. var. of **posdata.**

post·di·lu·via·no, –na adj. postdiluvian.

pos·te m. *(madero)* post, pole <*p. indicador* signpost>; *(columna)* pillar; SPORT. post <*p. de salida* starting post> ♦ **ser un p.** FIG., COLL. *(ser muy lerdo)* to be very dense; *(estar muy sordo)* to be deaf, be as deaf as a post.

pos·ter·ga·ción f. *(aplazamiento)* postponement; *(relegación)* passing over (for promotion).

pos·ter·gar §47 tr. *(aplazar)* to postpone, defer; *(a un empleo)* to pass over (for promotion).

pos·te·ri·dad f. posterity.

pos·te·rior adj. *(ulterior)* subsequent, later; *(trasero)* posterior, rear, back ♦ **p. a** after, subsequent to.

pos·te·rio·ri·dad f. posteriority ♦ **con p.** later, subsequently • **con p. a** later than, subsequent to.

pos·te·rior·men·te adv. subsequently, later (on).

post·gra·dua·do, –da adj. & m.f. var. of **posgraduado, –da.**

post·gue·rra f. var. of **posguerra.**

pos·ti·go m. *(puerta falsa)* secret *or* hidden door; *(puerta abierta en otra mayor)* wicket (small door in a larger one); *(contraventana)* shutter; *(puerta de ciudad)* postern, side gate (to a city).

pos·ti·llón m. postilion, postboy.

pos·tín m. COLL. *(presunción)* conceit, airs; *(elegancia)* ele-

gance, poshness ♦ **darse p.** COLL. to put on airs • **de p.** COLL. elegant, posh.

pos·ti·zo, –za I. adj. false <*dentadura p.* false teeth>; artificial <*brazo p.* artificial arm>; *(de quitapón)* detachable II. m. hair piece.

post·me·ri·dia·no, –na adj. postmeridian, afternoon.

pos·to·pe·ra·to·rio, –ria adj. MED. postoperative.

pos·tor m. bidder ♦ **mayor** *or* **mejor p.** highest bidder.

pos·tra·ción f. *(acción de postrar)* prostration; *(abatimiento)* exhaustion.

pos·tra·do, –da I. past part. see **postrar** II. adj. prostrate; FIG. overcome, overwhelmed <*p. por la desgracia* overwhelmed by misfortune>.

pos·trar tr. *(humillar)* to prostrate, humiliate; FIG. *(debilitar)* to debilitate, weaken —reflex. *(arrodillarse)* to prostrate oneself, kneel down; *(debilitarse)* to weaken, become debilitated; *(abrumarse)* to be overcome.

pos·tre I. adj. last, final II. m. dessert, sweet ♦ **a la** *or* **al p.** in the end, finally • **llegar a los postres** to come too late.

pos·tre·mo, –ma adj. last, final.

pos·trer [contr. of **postrero** used before m. sing. noun] last, final.

pos·tre·ro, –ra §G21 I. adj. last, final II. m.f. last one.

pos·tri·me·rí·a f. *(último período)* last years, final stages <*en las postrimerías del Renacimiento* in the last years of the Renaissance>; RELIG. death; THEOL. last four stages of man.

pos·tu·la·ción f. *(acción de postular)* postulation; *(colecta)* collection.

pos·tu·la·do I. past part. see **postular** II. m. postulate.

pos·tu·lan·te, –ta I. adj. applying II. m.f. *(solicitante)* applicant; *(de donativos)* collector (for charity); RELIG. postulant, candidate (for admission to an order).

pos·tu·lar tr. *(solicitar)* to apply for; *(pedir una cosa)* to ask for, seek; *(pedir donativos)* to collect (donations); *(ser candidato)* to be a candidate for; RELIG. to postulate —intr. ♦ **p. a** *or* **para** *(solicitar)* to apply; *(ser candidato a)* to be a candidate for <*postula para el consejo municipal* he's a candidate for town council>.

pós·tu·mo, –ma adj. posthumous.

pos·tu·ra f. *(posición)* posture, position; FIG. *(actitud)* posture, attitude; *(opinión)* posture, stand; *(huevo)* egg; *(de huevos)* laying of eggs; *(precio)* fixed price; *(apuesta)* bet, wager; *(pacto)* pact, agreement; *(oferta)* bid.

pos·ven·ta adj. after-sale <*servicio p.* after-sale service>.

po·ta·bi·li·dad f. potability.

po·ta·ble adj. drinkable, potable.

po·ta·je m. *(cocido)* stew, pottage; *(legumbres secas)* dried vegetables; *(bebida)* brew; FIG. *(mezcla)* jumble, muddle.

po·ta·sa f. CHEM. potash.

po·ta·sio m. CHEM. potassium.

po·te m. *(tarro)* pot, jar; *(cazuela)* pan, pot (for cooking); *(cocido)* stew; *(maceta)* flowerpot; FIG., COLL. *(gesto)* pout; AMER. *(lata)* tin, can ♦ **a p.** in abundance • **darse p.** to put on airs.

po·ten·cia f. *(poder)* power, ability; *(fuerza)* power, strength <*la p. del gobierno* the power of the government>; *(autoridad)* authority, control <*p. paterna* paternal authority>; *(posibilidad)* potential, possibility <*existe la p. de una batalla* there exists the potential for a battle>; *(facultad)* faculty; *(nación)* power <*una p. mundial* a world power>; ARM. reach, range; PHILOS. potential; MATH., MECH., PHYS. power ♦ **de p. a p.** as equals • **en p.** potentially • **elevar a la segunda p.** MATH. to raise to the second power, square • **elevar a la tercera p.** MATH. to raise to the third power, cube • **segunda p.** MATH. square • **tercera p.** MATH. cube.

po·ten·cial I. adj. *(que tiene potencia)* potential; GRAM. conditional (tense) II. m. potential ♦ **p. humano** manpower.

po·ten·cia·li·dad f. potentiality, potential.

po·ten·ciar tr. *(comunicar potencia)* to increase the power of; *(facultar)* to make possible.

po·ten·ta·do m. *(soberano)* potentate, sovereign; FIG. *(rico)* tycoon.

po·ten·te adj. *(poderoso)* powerful; *(que puede engendrar)* potent, virile; FIG. *(grande)* big, mighty.

po·tes·tad f. *(poder)* power, authority; *(gobernador)* podesta (Italian magistrate); *(potentado)* potentate ♦ **patria p.** LAW parental authority • **potestades** RELIG. Powers, sixth order of angels.

po·tin·gue m. COLL. concoction.

po·to m. S. AMER. *(trasero)* bottom, backside; *(vasija)* gourd *or* earthenware vessel.

po·tra f. ZOOL. filly, young mare; COLL. hernia, rupture ♦ **tener p.** FIG., COLL. to be lucky.

po·tra·da f. herd of foals.

po·tran·ca f. filly, young mare.

po·tran·co m. colt.

po·tre·ar tr. *(molestar)* to annoy, bother; AMER. to break, tame (a foal); GUAT., PERU to beat, thrash.

po·tre·ro m. *(dehesa)* pasture; AMER. cattle ranch; ARG. playground (in a vacant lot).

po·tri·llo m. colt.

po·tro m. ZOOL. colt; SPORT. horse (for gymnastics); *(aparato para herrar)* stanchion (for branding); *(aparato de tormento)* rack; FIG. *(molestia)* bother, nuisance; COL., ECUAD., MEX. hernia.

po·tro·so, –sa COLL. I. adj. *(hernioso)* ruptured; *(afortunado)* lucky, fortunate II. m.f. person with a hernia.

po·yo m. *(banco)* stone bench; *(derecho)* court fee (paid to a judge).

po·za f. *(charca)* large puddle, pool; *(para enriar el cáñamo)* retting tank.

po·zal m. *(cubo)* bucket, pail (of a well); *(brocal)* curb, rim (of a well); *(pocillo)* catch basin.

po·zo m. *(para sacar agua)* well; *(en un río)* deep pool *or* hole (in a river); *(hoyo profundo)* pit; MARIT. *(sentina)* bilge (lowest inner part of a ship); *(bodega)* hold; MIN. shaft; FIG. *(mina)* well, mine <es un p. de información he is a well of information>; CHILE, COL., VEN. puddle; ECUAD., HOND. spring ♦ **p. airón** *(hoyo profundo)* pit, deep hole; FIG. *(hoyo sin fondo)* bottomless pit • **p. artesiano** artesian well • **p. de petróleo** oil well • **p. negro** cesspool, sump.

po·zue·lo m. catch basin.

prác·ti·ca I. f. practice <aprender con la p. to learn by practice>; *(experiencia)* skill, experience; *(costumbre)* practice <ser p. establecida to be standard practice>; *(método)* method, manner ♦ **en la p.** in practice • **poner en p.** to put into practice • **prácticas** training <prácticas profesionales professional training> II. adj. see **práctico, –ca.**

prac·ti·ca·ble adj. *(que puede practicarse)* practicable; *(transitable)* passable (road).

prác·ti·ca·men·te adv. practically.

prac·ti·can·te I. adj. practicing II. m.f. *(que ejerce una profesión)* practitioner; *(aprendiz)* medical intern; *(auxiliar)* medical assistant; *(de botica)* prescription clerk.

prac·ti·car §70 tr. to practice <p. un baile nuevo to practice a new dance>; *(ejercer)* to practice, exercise (a profession); *(hacer)* to perform, do; *(abrir un agujero)* to make, cut (a hole); SPORT. to play, go in for <p. el béisbol to go in for baseball>.

prác·ti·co, –ca I. adj. practical <conocimiento p. practical knowledge>; *(conveniente)* useful, convenient; *(diestro)* expert, experienced II. m. MARIT. pilot —f. see **práctica.**

pra·de·ra f. meadow.

pra·do m. *(campo)* meadow, field; *(paseo)* promenade ♦ **a p.** out to pasture, grazing • **p. de juego** playground.

Pra·ga f. Prague.

prag·má·ti·co, –ca adj. pragmatic.

prag·ma·tis·mo m. pragmatism.

prag·ma·tis·ta I. adj. pragmatistic II. m.f. pragmatist.

pra·se·o·di·mio m. CHEM. praseodymium.

pre·ám·bu·lo m. *(prólogo)* preamble; *(rodeo)* digression ♦ **gastar preámbulos** to beat around the bush.

pre·ben·da f. RELIG. prebend; FIG., COLL. *(sinecura)* sinecure, cushy job.

pre·ben·da·do m. RELIG. prebendary.

pre·bos·te m. provost.

pre·ca·rio, –ria adj. precarious.

pre·cau·ción f. *(medida)* precaution; *(prudencia)* caution, care ♦ **por p.** as a precaution.

pre·cau·cio·nar·se reflex. to take precautions.

pre·ca·ver tr. *(tomar precauciones)* to guard against, take precautions against; *(impedir)* prevent —reflex. to take

precautions ♦ **precaverse contra** to forestall • **precaverse de** to guard against.

pre·ca·vi·do, –da I. past part. see **precaver** II. adj. cautious, careful.

pre·ce·den·cia f. *(de tiempo, de importancia)* precedence, priority; *(superioridad)* precedence, superiority.

pre·ce·den·te I. adj. preceding, foregoing II. m. precedent ♦ **sentar un p.** to establish *or* set a precedent.

pre·ce·der tr. *(ir adelante)* to precede, go before; FIG. *(tener preferencia)* to take precedence over.

pre·cep·ti·vo, –va I. adj. preceptive, mandatory II. f. precepts, principles.

pre·cep·to m. *(de un arte)* precept, principle; *(orden)* order, rule ♦ **los preceptos del Decálogo** RELIG. the Ten Commandments.

pre·cep·tor, –to·ra m.f. *(maestro particular)* preceptor, tutor; *(profesor)* teacher —f. governess.

pre·ces f.pl. RELIG. prayers, supplications.

pre·ce·sión f. RHET. reticence; ASTRON. precession ♦ **p. de los equinoccios** ASTRON. precession of the equinoxes.

pre·cia·do, –da I. past part. see **preciar** II. adj. *(de valor)* valuable, precious; *(estimado)* esteemed, prized; *(jactancioso)* boastful, conceited.

pre·ciar tr. *(apreciar)* to appreciate, esteem; *(tasar)* to value, appraise —reflex. *(jactarse)* to brag, boast ♦ **preciarse de** to consider *or* think oneself <preciarse de inteligente to consider oneself intelligent>.

pre·cin·ta f. *(en un paquete)* leather strap *or* band; *(en las aduanas)* official stamp *or* seal; MARIT. parceling.

pre·cin·ta·do, –da I. past part. see **precintar** II. adj. sealed III. m. sealing.

pre·cin·tar tr. *(un paquete)* to bind, strap (a package); *(sellar)* to seal, stamp; MARIT. to parcel.

pre·cin·to m. *(de un paquete)* binding, strapping; *(cerramiento)* sealing, closing; *(selladura)* sealing, stamping; LAW official seal; *(ligadura)* strap, tie.

pre·cio m. *(valor pecuniario)* price, cost; FIG. *(valor)* value, worth <es una obra de gran p. it is a work of great worth>; *(sacrificio)* price, cost <el p. de ganar una batalla es la pérdida de vida the cost of winning a battle is the loss of life> ♦ **al p. de** FIG. at the cost of • **alzar el p.** to raise the price • **no tener p.** FIG. to be priceless • **poner a p.** to offer a reward • **poner a p. la cabeza de alguien** to put a price on someone's head • **poner p. a** to put a price on • **p. al contado** cash price • **p. de abertura** FIN. opening price (on stock exchange) • **p. de cierre** FIN. closing price (of stock exchange) • **p. de compra** purchase price • **p. de factura** invoice price • **p. de lista** list price • **p. de mercado** *or* **p. corriente** market price • **p. de venta** selling price • **p. fijo** fixed price • **p. tope** top *or* ceiling price • **p. unitario** *or* **por unidad** unit price • **tener en p.** FIG. to esteem, hold in esteem.

pre·cio·sa·men·te adv. richly, lavishly.

pre·cio·si·dad f. *(valor)* value, preciousness; *(excelencia)* excellence, exquisiteness; *(objeto)* beauty <este vaso es una p. this vase is a beauty>; *(persona)* jewel, darling <su hija es una verdadera p. your daughter is a real jewel>.

pre·cio·sis·mo m. LIT. preciosity, affectation.

pre·cio·so, –sa adj. *(de mucho valor)* precious, valuable <piedra p. precious stone>; *(chistoso)* witty, clever; COLL. *(lindo)* pretty, lovely.

pre·cio·su·ra f. COLL. darling, beauty.

pre·ci·pi·cio m. *(de una montaña)* precipice, cliff; FIG. *(abismo)* abyss <caer al p. to fall into an abyss>; *(ruina)* ruin, downfall.

pre·ci·pi·ta·ción f. *(prisa)* precipitation, haste; METEOROL. precipitation, rain; CHEM. precipitation ♦ **con p.** hastily, hurriedly • **p. radioactiva** (radioactive) fallout.

pre·ci·pi·ta·da·men·te adv. precipitately, hastily.

pre·ci·pi·ta·do, –da I. past part. see **precipitar** II. adj. precipitate, hasty III. m. CHEM. precipitate.

pre·ci·pi·tar tr. *(lanzar)* to hurl, throw <la parada súbita precipitó a los pasajeros en el pasillo the sudden stop threw the passengers into the aisle>; *(apresurar)* to quicken, hasten <p. el paso to quicken one's step>; FIG. *(incitar)* to push; CHEM. to precipitate —reflex. *(darse prisa)* to hurry, rush; FIG. *(arrojarse inconsideradamente)* to rush

headlong <*se está precipitando hacia la destrucción* he is rushing headlong toward destruction>.
pre·ci·pi·to·so, –sa adj. *(resbaladizo)* precipitous, steep; FIG. *(precipitado)* hasty, reckless.
pre·ci·sa·men·te adv. *(justamente)* precisely, exactly; *(especialmente)* specially <*lo compré p. para ti* I bought it specially for you>.
pre·ci·sar tr. *(explicar)* to explain, state clearly; *(fijar)* to fix, set <*p. una fecha* to set a date>; *(obligar)* to force, compel <*precisaron a los presos a hacer una confesión* they forced the prisoners to confess>; *(necesitar)* to need —reflex. to be necessary *or* needed.
pre·ci·sión f. *(necesidad)* necessity, need; *(exactitud)* precision, accuracy; *(claridad)* precision, clarity.
pre·ci·so, –sa adj. *(necesario)* necessary, essential <*es p. tener un coche* it is essential to have a car>; *(fijo)* precise, definite; *(exacto)* exact, accurate; *(claro)* distinct, clear ♦ **cuando sea p.** when necessary • **tener tiempo p. para** to have just enough time for.
pre·ci·ta·do, –da adj. abovementioned, aforementioned.
pre·cla·ro, –ra adj. illustrious, eminent.
pre·co·ci·dad f. precociousness, precocity.
pre·cog·ni·ción f. precognition, foreknowledge.
pre·co·lom·bia·no, –na *or* **pre·co·lom·bi·no, –na** adj. pre-Columbian.
pre·con·ce·bi·do, –da I. past part. see **preconcebir** II. adj. preconceived.
pre·con·ce·bir §48 tr. to preconceive.
pre·co·ni·zar §04 tr. *(alabar)* to praise, commend; *(recomendar)* to recommend, propose; *(aconsejar)* to advise, suggest; RELIG. to preconize.
pre·co·no·cer §17 tr. to know beforehand.
pre·coz adj. [pl. **-co·ces**] *(temprano)* early (fruit); FIG. *(adelantado)* precocious.
pre·cur·sor, –so·ra I. adj. precursory, premonitory II. m.f. precursor, forerunner.
pre·de·ce·sor, –so·ra m.f. predecessor.
pre·de·cir §11 tr. to predict, foretell.
pre·des·ti·na·ción f. predestination.
pre·des·ti·na·do, –da I. past part. see **predestinar** II. adj. THEOL. predestined III. m.f. THEOL. predestinate —m. FIG. *(cornudo)* cuckold.
pre·des·ti·nar tr. to predestine.
pre·de·ter·mi·nar tr. to predetermine.
pré·di·ca f. RELIG. sermon; COLL. *(discurso)* sermon, harangue.
pre·di·ca·ble adj. & m. LOG. predicable.
pre·di·ca·ción f. *(acción de predicar)* preaching; *(sermón)* sermon.
pre·di·ca·de·ras f.pl COLL. preaching ability ♦ **tener buenas p.** to have a talent for preaching.
pre·di·ca·do I. past part. see **predicar** II. m. GRAM., LOG. predicate.
pre·di·ca·dor, –do·ra I. adj. preaching II. m. RELIG. preacher; ENTOM. praying mantis.
pre·di·ca·men·to m. LOG. predicament, category; *(estima)* esteem, regard.
pre·di·car §70 tr. *(publicar)* to proclaim, announce; RELIG. to preach; *(alabar)* to praise, extol; FIG. *(reprender)* to reprove, admonish —intr. to preach ♦ **p. con el ejemplo** to set an example • **p. en el desierto** to preach in the wilderness.
pre·dic·ción f. prediction, forecast.
pre·di·ce see **predecir**.
pre·di·cho, –cha I. past part. see **predecir** II. adj. aforesaid, aforementioned.
pre·di·ga, predigo see **predecir**.
pre·di·je·ra, predijo see **predecir**.
pre·di·qué, predique see **predicar**.
pre·di·lec·ción f. predilection, preference.
pre·di·lec·to, –ta adj. favorite, preferred.
pre·dio m. property, estate ♦ **p. rústico** country property • **p. urbano** city property.
pre·di·rá, prediría see **predecir**.
pre·dis·po·ner §54 tr. to predispose ♦ **p. contra** to prejudice against.
pre·dis·po·si·ción f. predisposition.
pre·do·mi·nan·cia f. predominance.

pre·do·mi·nan·te adj. predominant.
pre·do·mi·nar tr. *(prevalecer)* to predominate *or* prevail over; FIG. *(exceder en altura)* to tower over —intr. to predominate, prevail.
pre·do·mi·nio m. predominance, superiority.
pre·e·mi·nen·cia f. *(superioridad)* pre-eminence, superiority; *(privilegio)* privilege.
pre·e·mi·nen·te adj. pre-eminent.
pre·es·co·lar adj. preschool.
pre·es·ta·ble·ci·do, –da adj. pre-established.
pre·e·xis·ten·cia f. pre-existence.
pre·e·xis·ten·te adj. pre-existing, pre-existent.
pre·e·xis·tir intr. to pre-exist.
pre·fa·bri·ca·ción f. prefabrication.
pre·fa·bri·ca·do, –da I. past part. see **prefabricar** II. adj. prefabricated.
pre·fa·bri·car §70 tr. to prefabricate.
pre·fa·cio m. preface, prologue.
pre·fec·to m. prefect.
pre·fec·tu·ra f. prefecture.
pre·fe·ren·cia f. preference ♦ **de p.** preferably.
pre·fe·ren·te adj. *(que prefiere)* preferring; preferential <*trato p.* preferential treatment>; *(preferible)* preferable; COM. preferred (stock).
pre·fe·ren·te·men·te adv. *(de preferencia)* preferably; *(con prioridad)* preferentially.
pre·fe·ri·ble adj. preferable.
pre·fe·ri·do, –da I. past part. see **preferir** II. adj. preferred, favorite.
pre·fe·rir §65 tr. to prefer.
pre·fi·gu·ra·ción f. prefiguration, foreshadowing.
pre·fi·gu·rar tr. to prefigure, foreshadow.
pre·fi·jar tr. *(fijar antes)* to prearrange, arrange beforehand; GRAM. to prefix.
pre·fi·jo, –ja I. past part. see **prefijar** II. adj. GRAM. prefixed III. m. GRAM. prefix; TELEC. area code.
pre·fi·rie·ra, prefirió see **preferir**.
pre·gón m. *(noticia)* public announcement; *(de vendedor)* street vendor's shout.
pre·go·nar tr. *(publicar)* to proclaim, announce; *(un vendedor)* to hawk, peddle (merchandise); FIG. *(revelar)* to reveal, divulge; *(alabar)* to praise, laud.
pre·go·ne·ro, –ra I. adj. *(anunciador)* announcing, proclaiming; *(revelador)* revealing, divulging II. m.f. *(anunciador)* announcer, proclaimer; *(vendedor)* hawker, peddler —m. *(oficial)* town crier.
pre·gun·ta f. question, query ♦ **andar** *or* **estar** *or* **quedarse a la cuarta p.** FIG., COLL. to be broke *or* penniless • **estrechar a preguntas** to ply with questions • **hacer una p.** to ask a question.
pre·gun·ta·dor, –do·ra I. adj. *(que pregunta)* questioning; *(curioso)* curious, inquisitive II. m.f. *(persona que pregunta)* questioner; *(curioso)* curious *or* inquisitive person.
pre·gun·tar tr. *(hacer una pregunta)* to ask <*me preguntó si había visto a su amiga* he asked me if I had seen his girlfriend>; *(interrogar)* to question <*le preguntaron largamente al candidato sobre los asuntos financieros* they questioned the candidate at length about financial matters> ♦ **p. por** *(pedir noticias)* to ask *or* inquire about; *(llamar)* to ask for (a person) <*preguntan por usted en el teléfono* someone is asking for you on the telephone> —reflex. to wonder, ask oneself.
pre·gun·tón, –to·na COLL. I. adj. nosy, inquisitive II. m.f. nosy *or* inquisitive person.
pre·his·to·ria f. prehistory.
pre·his·tó·ri·co, –ca adj. prehistoric.
pre·in·cai·co, –ca adj. HIST. pre-Incan.
pre·jui·cio m. *(opinión)* prejudice, preconceived idea; *(actitud discriminatoria)* prejudice, bias <*p. racial* racial prejudice>.
pre·juz·gar §47 tr. to prejudge.
pre·la·ción f. priority, precedence <*tener p. sobre* to take precedence over>.
pre·la·do m. RELIG. prelate.
pre·li·mi·nar adj. & m. preliminary.
pre·lu·diar intr. MUS. to warm up (before playing or singing) —tr. MUS. to play a prelude; FIG. to initiate, begin.

pre·lu·dio m. MUS. *(composición)* prelude; *(ensayo)* warm-up; *(introducción)* introduction, prelude.

pre·ma·tu·ra·men·te adv. prematurely.

pre·ma·tu·ro, –ra adj. BIOL. premature; BOT. unripe, out of season; FIG. *(inoportuno)* premature, untimely.

pre·me·di·ta·ción f. LAW premeditation.

pre·me·di·ta·da·men·te adv. deliberately, with premeditation.

pre·me·di·ta·do, –da I. past part. see **premeditar II.** adj. premeditated.

pre·me·di·tar tr. *(proyectar)* to premeditate, plan; LAW to premeditate.

pre·mia·do, –da I. past part. see **premiar II.** adj. *(vencedor)* winning, prize-winning; *(recompensado)* rewarded **III.** m.f. winner, prize winner.

pre·miar tr. *(recompensar)* to reward, recompense; *(en un certamen)* to award a prize to.

pre·mio m. *(recompensa)* reward, recompense; *(en un certamen)* prize, award; COM., FIN. premium; *(demasía)* bonus, premium ♦ **a p.** COM., FIN. at a premium • **p. en efectivo** cash prize • **p. gordo** COLL. jackpot, first prize (in a lottery).

pre·mio·sa·men·te adv. *(con estrechez)* tightly, narrowly; *(con dificultad)* awkwardly, clumsily.

pre·mio·si·dad f. *(estrechez)* tightness; *(molestia)* awkwardness; *(torpeza)* clumsiness.

pre·mio·so, –sa adj. *(apretado)* tight, constricting; *(molesto)* burdensome, onerous; *(apremiador)* pressing, urgent; *(movimiento)* heavy, awkward; *(habla)* slow; *(estilo)* awkward, clumsy; FIG. *(rígido)* rigid, strict.

pre·mi·sa f. LOG. premise.

pre·mi·so, –sa adj. *(prevenido)* foreseen, anticipated; *(enviado con anticipación)* sent in advance; LAW precedent, prior <*p. la autorización* with prior authorization>.

pre·mo·ni·ción f. premonition.

pre·mo·ni·to·rio, –ria adj. MED. premonitory.

pre·mo·rir §27 intr. LAW to predecease.

pre·mu·ra f. urgency, haste.

pre·na·tal adj. prenatal.

pren·da f. *(garantía)* guaranty, pledge; *(de vestir)* garment, article of clothing; FIG. *(señal)* sign, token <*el regalo era una p. de su amistad* the gift was a sign of his friendship>; *(persona amada)* darling, treasure <*amo a mi p.* I love my darling>; S. AMER. jewel, gem ♦ **en p.** as security *or* guaranty • **en p.** *or* **prendas de** as a sign *or* token of • **no soltar p.** to be very discreet • **p. interior** undergarment • **prendas** (good) qualities, virtues.

pren·dar tr. *(dar en garantía)* to pawn, pledge; *(encantar)* to charm, captivate —reflex. to fall in love (with), become fond (of).

pren·de·de·ro *or* **pren·de·dor** m. *(broche)* clasp, hook; JEWEL. pin, brooch; *(para el pelo)* hair ribbon.

pren·der tr. *(asir)* to seize, grasp <*p. el mango* to grasp the handle>; *(aprehender)* to apprehend, capture <*prendieron al ladrón en el banco* they apprehended the thief in the bank>; *(encarcelar)* to imprison, put in prison; *(coger)* to catch <*el clavo prendió su vestido* the nail caught her dress>; *(clavar)* to fix, fasten; AMER. *(con fuego)* to light <*p. el cigarro* to light the cigar>; *(un aparato)* to turn *or* switch on <*prenda la lámpara* turn on the light>; ZOOL. to mate ♦ **p. con alfileres** to pin • **p. fuego a** to set fire to —intr. *(arraigar)* to take root; *(inflamarse)* to catch fire <*prendió la broza durante la sequía* the brush caught fire during the drought>; *(tomar efecto)* to take (effect) <*prendió la vacuna y me curó* the vaccine took (effect) and cured me> —reflex. *(adornarse)* to dress up; DOM. REP., P. RICO to get drunk; COL. to put on one's boots ♦ **prenderse fuego** to catch fire.

pren·de·rí·a f. secondhand shop.

pren·de·ro, –ra m.f. secondhand dealer.

pren·di·do, –da I. past part. see **prender II.** m. *(adorno)* hair clasp; *(patrón)* bobbin lace pattern.

pren·di·mien·to m. *(captura)* apprehension, capture; *(encarcelamiento)* imprisonment; CHILE, MED. constipation; COL., VEN. irritation.

pre·nom·bra·do, –da adj. AMER. aforementioned, aforesaid.

pre·nom·bre m. first *or* given name.

pre·no·tar tr. to note beforehand.

pren·sa f. *(máquina)* press <*p. hidráulica* hydraulic press>; *(imprenta)* printing press; FIG. press <*la p. atacó la última declaración presidencial* the press attacked the latest presidential declaration> ♦ **dar a la p.** PRINT. to publish, print • **entrar en p.** PRINT. to go to press • **meter en p.** PRINT. to go to press; FIG. *(forzar)* to put the squeeze (on someone), force (someone) <*le metí en p. para hacerlo* I put the squeeze on him to do it> • **p. de planchar** *or* **de ropa** clothes press • **p. de uva** winepress • **tener buena (mala) p.** FIG. to have *or* get good (bad) press.

pren·sa·do I. past part. see **prensar II.** m. TEX. luster, sheen.

pren·sa·dor, –do·ra I. adj. pressing **II.** m.f. presser, press operator.

pren·sar tr. to press.

pren·sil adj. prehensile.

pre·nup·cial adj. prenuptial.

pre·ña·do, –da I. past part. see **preñar II.** adj. BIOL. pregnant; FIG. *(abultado)* bulging, sagging (wall); *(cargado)* full, charged **III.** m. BIOL. pregnancy.

pre·ñar tr. BIOL. to impregnate, make pregnant; FIG. *(llenar)* to fill, stuff.

pre·ñez f. BIOL. pregnancy; FIG. *(amenaza)* impending threat.

pre·o·cu·pa·ción f. *(obsesión)* preoccupation <*su p. con el dinero ha llegado a alturas absurdas* his preoccupation with money has reached absurd heights>; *(inquietud)* worry, anxiety <*antes de casarse estaban llenos de preocupaciones* before marrying, they were filled with anxieties>; *(preconcepción)* preconception, prejudice.

pre·o·cu·pa·do, –da I. past part. see **preocupar II.** adj. *(absorto)* preoccupied; *(inquieto)* worried, anxious.

pre·o·cu·par tr. *(absorber)* to preoccupy <*la acumulación de dinero le preocupa hoy día* the accumulation of money preoccupies him nowadays>; *(inquietar)* to worry, concern <*cada problema le preocupa a ella* every problem worries her>; FIG. *(predisponer)* to prejudice, predispose; *(ocupar anteriormente)* to preoccupy, occupy before *or* in advance (of another) —reflex. *(inquietarse)* to worry, be worried <*¡no te preocupes!* don't worry!>; *(cuidarse)* to take care (of) <*yo me preocuparé de eso* I will take care of that> ♦ **preocuparse con** *or* **de** *or* **por** to worry about.

pre·pa·ra·ción f. *(acción de preparar)* preparation, getting ready; PHARM. preparation, compound.

pre·pa·ra·dor, –do·ra I. adj. preparing **II.** m.f. preparer; SPORT. trainer, coach.

pre·pa·ra·mien·to m. var. of **preparación**.

pre·pa·rar tr. to prepare (for), get ready —reflex. to get ready, prepare oneself.

pre·pa·ra·ti·vo, –va I. adj. preliminary, preparatory **II.** m. preparation.

pre·pa·ra·to·rio, –ria adj. preparatory, preliminary.

pre·pon·de·ran·cia f. preponderance, superiority.

pre·pon·de·ran·te adj. preponderant, prevailing.

pre·pon·de·rar intr. FIG. to predominate, prevail.

pre·po·ner §54 tr. to put before, prefer.

pre·po·si·ción f. GRAM. preposition ♦ **p. inseparable** GRAM. prefix.

pre·po·si·cio·nal adj. GRAM. prepositional.

pre·po·ten·cia f. prepotency, great power.

pre·po·ten·te adj. prepotent, predominant.

pre·pu·cio m. ANAT. prepuce, foreskin.

pre·pu·sie·ra, prepuso see **preponer**.

pre·rro·ga·ti·va f. prerogative, privilege.

pre·sa f. *(captura)* capture, seizure; *(cosa apresada)* catch <*la p. del cazador fue muy pequeña* the hunter's catch was very small>; *(en la caza)* prey, quarry; FIG. victim <*p. de las circunstancias* victim of circumstances>; MIL. spoils, booty; MARIT. prize (captured ship); *(dique)* dam; *(conducto)* ditch, channel (for directing water); *(porción)* piece, morsel (of food); ZOOL. fang; ORNITH. claw (of bird of prey) ♦ **hacer p.** *(capturar)* to capture, seize; *(aprovechar)* to take advantage (of an opportunity, situation).

pre·sa·giar tr. to presage, portend.

pre·sa·gio m. *(señal)* presage, omen; *(adivinación)* foreboding, premonition.

pre·sa·go, –ga *or* **pré·sa·go, –ga** adj. presaging, foreboding.

pres·bi·cia f. OPHTHAL. presbyopia, farsightedness.

prés·bi·ta *or* **prés·bi·te** OPHTHAL. adj. farsighted.

pres·bi·te·ria·no, –na adj. & m.f. RELIG. Presbyterian.

pres·bi·te·rio m. presbytery.

pres·bí·te·ro m. presbyter, priest.

pres·cien·cia f. prescience, foreknowledge.

pres·cin·den·cia f. AMER. omission ♦ **con p. de** without.

pres·cin·den·te adj. AMER. independent.

pres·cin·di·ble adj. dispensable, nonessential.

pres·cin·dir intr. *(omitir)* to omit, leave out; *(hacer caso omiso)* to ignore, disregard; *(privarse)* to do without ♦ **prescindiendo de** regardless of.

pres·cri·bir §85 tr. *(ordenar)* to prescribe, set forth; MED. to prescribe —intr. LAW to prescribe.

pres·crip·ción f. LAW, MED. prescription.

pres·cri·to –ta I. past part. see **prescribir** II. adj. prescribed, set forth.

pre·se·lec·ción f. preselection.

pre·sen·cia f. *(hecho de estar presente)* presence; *(figura)* bearing, appearance <*este trabajo necesita una buena p.* this job requires a good appearance> ♦ **en p. de** in the presence of • **hacer acto de p.** to be present, put in an appearance • **p. de ánimo** presence of mind.

pre·sen·cial adj. pertaining to presence ♦ **testigo p.** eyewitness.

pre·sen·ciar tr. to be present at, witness.

pre·sen·ta·ble adj. presentable.

pre·sen·ta·ción f. *(demostración)* presentation, showing; *(exhibición)* exhibition, display <*una p. de unos cuadros de Picasso* an exhibition of some of Picasso's paintings>; *(entrega)* presentation, giving <*la interrupción demoró la p. del premio* the interruption delayed the presentation of the award>; *(introducción)* introduction <*su p. al comité duró unas horas* his introduction to the committee took a few hours>; THEAT. presentation; MED. presentation (position of the fetus at birth); AMER. petition, request.

pre·sen·ta·dor, –do·ra I. adj. presenting II. m.f. presenter; AMER. master of ceremonies (theater, television).

pre·sen·tan·te adj. presenting, introducing.

pre·sen·tar tr. *(mostrar)* to present, show <*p. un libro al público* to present a book to the public>; *(exhibir)* to exhibit, display; *(dar)* to present, give <*queremos p. a usted el Premio Nobel* we wish to give you the Nobel Prize>; *(proponer)* to propose, nominate <*el comité presentó al Señor Márquez para la presidencia* the committee proposed Mister Márquez for the presidency>; *(introducir)* to present, introduce <*mi novia me presentó a sus padres* my fiancée introduced me to her parents>; THEAT. to present (a play); LAW to bring <*p. una demanda contra* to bring action against> ♦ **p. armas** MIL. to present arms • **p. de** *or* **por candidato** to propose as a candidate —reflex. *(mostrarse)* to present oneself <*me presenté ante el prefecto* I presented myself before the prefect>; *(venir)* to show up, appear <*el alumno se presentó al terminar la clase* the student showed up as the class ended>; *(aparecer)* to present itself, appear <*una solución se presentó después de unas horas* a solution presented itself after a few hours>; *(ofrecerse)* to offer oneself *or* one's service <*me le presento como sujeto en su estudio psicológico* I offer my services to you as a subject in your psychological study>; *(introducirse)* to present *or* introduce oneself <*me presenté a los padres de mi novia* I introduced myself to my fiancée's parents>.

pre·sen·te I. adj. *(asistente)* present <*estar p. en* to be present at>; *(actual)* present, current; GRAM. present (tense) ♦ **hacer p.** *(declarar)* to state, declare; *(notificar)* to inform, notify • **tener p.** to remember, keep *or* bear in mind II. m. *(regalo)* present, gift; GRAM. present (tense) ♦ **al p.** now, at present • **hasta el p.** up to the present • **la p.** this letter, the present letter • **lo p.** the present (time) • **los presentes** those present • **mejorando lo p.** present company excepted • **por el** *or* **lo p.** at present II. interj. present, here.

pre·sen·te·men·te adv. at present, now.

pre·sen·ti·mien·to m. presentiment, premonition.

pre·sen·tir §65 tr. to sense, have a presentiment of.

pre·ser·va·ción f. preservation, protection.

pre·ser·va·dor, –do·ra I. adj. *(que preserva)* preserving; *(que protege)* protective II. m.f. preserver.

pre·ser·var tr. to preserve, protect.

pre·ser·va·ti·vo, –va I. adj. preservative II. m. *(remedio)* preservative; *(anticonceptivo)* prophylactic, condom.

pre·si·da·rio m. var. of **presidiario**.

pre·si·den·cia f. *(de una nación)* presidency; *(de una reunión)* chairmanship; *(silla)* chair; *(oficina)* president's office; *(palacio)* presidential palace *or* residence ♦ **ocupar la p.** to take chair (in a meeting).

pre·si·den·cial adj. presidential ♦ **(elecciones) presidenciales** presidential election.

pre·si·den·ta f. *(de una nación u organización)* (woman) president; *(de una reunión)* chairwoman; *(mujer del presidente)* president's wife.

pre·si·den·te m. *(de una nación u organización)* president; *(de una reunión)* chairman; *(del parlamento)* speaker; *(de un tribunal)* presiding judge ♦ **dirigirse al p.** to address the chair.

pre·si·dia·rio m. convict, prisoner.

pre·si·dio m. MIL. garrison; *(cárcel)* prison, penitentiary; *(presos)* prisoners, convicts; *(pena)* hard labor; FIG. *(ayuda)* help, aid.

pre·si·dir tr. *(dirigir)* to preside over, chair; FIG. *(predominar)* to reign over, dominate.

pre·sien·ta, presiento see **presentir**.

pre·si·lla f. *(lazo)* loop, fastener; *(para papeles)* paper clip; SEW. buttonhole stitching; TEX. kind of linen.

pre·sin·tie·ra, presintió see **presentir**.

pre·sión f. pressure ♦ **a p.** pressurized, under pressure • **olla de p.** pressure cooker • **p. arterial** *or* **sanguínea** MED. blood pressure • **p. atmosférica** atmospheric pressure • **p. del aire** *or* **neumática** air pressure.

pre·sio·nar tr. *(apretar)* to press; FIG. *(hacer presión)* to pressure, put pressure on.

pre·so, –sa I. past part. see **prender** II. adj. *(arrestado)* arrested, under arrest; *(recluso)* imprisoned III. m.f. prisoner.

pres·ta·ción f. *(acción)* lending, loaning; *(cosa prestada)* loan; *(aportación)* contribution; *(servicios)* services; service <*p. personal* obligatory communal service>; benefit <*p. por maternidad* maternity benefit> ♦ **p. social** social benefits • **p. de juramento** swearing-in, oath-taking.

pres·ta·di·zo, –za adj. that can be loaned *or* lent.

pres·ta·do I. past part. see **prestar** II. adj. *(dado)* lent; *(tomado)* borrowed; *(dinero)* lent, loaned ♦ **dar p.** to lend • **de p.** as a loan • **pedir** *or* **tomar p.** to borrow.

pres·ta·dor, –do·ra I. adj. lending II. m.f. lender.

pres·ta·men·te adv. quickly, rapidly.

pres·ta·mis·ta m.f. COM. moneylender, pawnbroker.

prés·ta·mo m. *(acción de prestar)* lending; *(acción de tomar prestado)* to borrow; *(empréstito)* loan ♦ **p. a plazo fijo** COM. time loan ♦ **p. a vista** *or* **a la demanda** COM. call *or* demand loan.

pres·tan·cia f. excellence.

pres·tar tr. *(ceder)* to lend, loan; *(ayudar)* to lend, give <*p. ayuda* to lend a hand> ♦ **p. atención** to pay attention • **p. auxilio** *or* **ayuda** to help, assist • **p. juramento** to take the oath • **p. oídos** to lend an ear • **p. paciencia** to show patience • **p. servicio** to be of service *or* assistance • **p. silencio** to keep silent • **p. testimonio** to bear witness —intr. *(ser útil)* to serve, be useful; *(extenderse)* to give, stretch (cloth) —reflex. *(consentir)* to consent; *(ser apto para)* to be suitable (for), lend itself (to); to offer, volunteer <*prestarse a llamar* to offer to call> ♦ **prestarse a discusión** to be debatable.

pres·ta·ta·rio, –ria I. m.f. borrower II. adj. borrowing.

pres·te·za f. promptness, celerity.

pres·ti·di·gi·ta·ción f. prestidigitation, sleight of hand.

pres·ti·di·gi·ta·dor, –do·ra m.f. prestidigitator, magician.

pres·ti·giar tr. to give *or* lend prestige to.

pres·ti·gio m. *(fascinación)* spell, fascination; *(ilusión)* illusion, deception; *(ascendiente)* prestige, good reputation.

pres·ti·gio·so, –sa adj. prestigious.

pres·to, –ta I. adj. *(pronto)* prompt, quick; *(preparado)* ready, prepared; MUS. presto II. adv. promptly, quickly.

pre·su·mi·ble adj. presumable.

pre·su·mi·do, –da I. past part. see **presumir** II. adj. pre-

sumptuous, conceited **III.** m.f. presumptuous *or* conceited person.
pre·su·mir tr. *(suponer)* to presume, suppose; BOL. to court, woo —intr. *(ser presumido)* to think oneself, think one is <*p. uno de listo* to think oneself clever>.
pre·sun·ción f. *(vanidad)* vanity, presumptuousness; *(suposición)* presumption, supposition; LAW presumption.
pre·sun·ta·men·te adv. presumably, presumptively.
pre·sun·ti·vo, –va adj. presumptive, supposed.
pre·sun·to, –ta I. past part. see **presumir II.** adj. presumed, supposed.
pre·sun·tuo·sa·men·te adv. presumptuously, conceitedly.
pre·sun·tuo·si·dad f. presumptuousness, conceit.
pre·sun·tuo·so, –sa I. adj. presumptuous, conceited **II.** m.f. presumptuous *or* conceited person.
pre·su·po·ner §54 tr. *(suponer previamente)* to presuppose; *(hacer un presupuesto)* to estimate, budget.
pre·su·po·si·ción f. *(suposición previa)* presupposition; *(motivo)* motive, cause.
pre·su·pues·tal adj. AMER. budgetary.
pre·su·pues·tar tr. to budget.
pre·su·pues·ta·rio, –ria adj. budgetary.
pre·su·pues·to, –ta I. past part. see **presuponer II.** adj. *(presumido)* presupposed, assumed; *(estimado)* estimated **III.** m. *(motivo)* motive, cause; *(de ingresos y gastos)* budget; *(estimado)* estimate; *(suposición)* supposition, assumption **♦ equilibrar** *or* **nivelar el p.** to balance the budget.
pre·su·pu·sie·ra, presupuso see **presuponer.**
pre·su·ri·zar §04 tr. AER. to pressurize.
pre·su·ro·so, –sa adj. *(rápido)* quick, speedy; *(con prisa)* hurried, in a hurry.
pre·ten·cio·so, –sa adj. pretentious, presumptuous.
pre·ten·der tr. *(buscar)* to seek, strive for <*p. un oficio* to seek an office>; *(intentar)* to try, attempt <*su esposa pretende convencerlo* his wife is trying to convince him>; *(al trono)* to claim, pretend to (a throne); *(a una mujer)* to court, woo (a woman); *(afirmar)* to claim, assert **♦ p. decir** to mean <*¿qué pretende decir este mensaje?* what does this message mean?>.
pre·ten·dien·te, –ta I. adj. *(que reclama)* seeking, claiming; *(al trono)* claiming, pretending to (a throne); *(a una mujer)* courting, wooing **II.** m.f. *(reclamante)* claimant; *(a un puesto)* candidate, aspirant; *(al trono)* claimant, pretender (to the throne) —m. *(a una mujer)* suitor.
pre·ten·sión f. *(aspiración)* aspiration, desire; *(derecho)* pretension, claim; *(vanidad)* pretentiousness, ostentation **♦ sin pretensiones** unpretentious **• tener pretensiones de** to lay claim to **• tener la pretensión de** to intend to, think one is going to <*tiene la p. de sucederme a mí* he thinks he is going to succeed me>.
pre·ten·sio·so, –sa adj. pretentious.
pre·té·ri·to, –ta I. adj. past **II.** m. GRAM. past **♦ p. anterior** GRAM. past anterior **• p. imperfecto** GRAM. imperfect **• p. indefinido** GRAM. preterite, past absolute **• p. pluscuamperfecto** GRAM. pluperfect, past perfect.
pre·ter·na·tu·ral adj. preternatural.
pre·tex·tar tr. to allege *or* claim as a pretext.
pre·tex·to m. pretext, excuse.
pre·til m. *(en un puente)* railing, parapet; AMER. atrium; VEN. stone bench.
pre·tor m. HIST. praetor (Roman magistrate).
pre·to·ria·no, –na I. adj. *(del magistrado)* praetorian; *(del guardia)* Praetorian **II.** m. Praetorian (bodyguard).
pre·u·ni·ver·si·ta·rio m. EDUC. college preparatory program.
pre·va·le·cer §17 intr. *(sobresalir)* to prevail, triumph; BOT. to take root, thrive; FIG. *(prosperar)* to thrive, flourish.
pre·va·le·cien·te adj. prevailing, prevalent.
pre·va·ler §74 intr. to prevail —reflex. **♦ prevalerse de** to avail oneself of, take advantage of.
pre·va·ri·ca·ción f. breach of trust (by a public official).
pre·va·ri·ca·dor, –do·ra I. adj. *(que falta a su deber)* failing in one's duty; *(que pervierte)* corrupting **II.** m.f. *(persona que falta)* one who fails in one's duties; *(pervertidor)* corrupter.
pre·va·ri·car §70 intr. *(faltar a su deber)* to fail in one's

duties, betray one's trust; COLL. *(delirar)* to rave, talk deliriously.
pre·ve·a, preveo see **prever.**
pre·ve·í·a see **prever.**
pre·ven·ción f. *(impedimento)* prevention; *(preparativo)* preparation; *(apresto)* preparedness; *(precaución)* precaution, precautionary measure; *(providencia)* foresight, forethought; *(aviso)* warning; *(prejuicio)* prejudice, bias; *(provisión)* stock, supply; *(de policía)* police station; MIL. *(soldado)* guard; *(cuartel)* guardhouse **♦ a** *or* **de p.** spare, reserve **• tener p. contra alguien** to have a prejudice against someone, be prejudiced against someone.
pre·ven·drá, prevendría see **prevenir.**
pre·ven·ga, prevengo see **prevenir.**
pre·ve·ni·da·men·te adv. beforehand, previously.
pre·ve·ni·do, –da I. past part. see **prevenir II.** adj. *(preparado)* ready, prepared; *(lleno)* filled; *(advertido)* forewarned; *(precavido)* cautious, prudent **♦ hombre p. vale por dos** forewarned is forearmed.
pre·ve·nir §76 tr. *(preparar)* to prepare, make *or* get ready; *(prever)* to foresee, anticipate; *(impedir)* to prevent, forestall; *(avisar)* to forewarn, caution; *(dar prejuicio)* to prejudice, bias; LAW to conduct a preliminary hearing (a case) **♦ p. de** to provide with —reflex. *(disponerse)* to prepare oneself, get ready; *(tomar precauciones)* to take precautions **♦ prevenirse a una cosa** to prepare oneself for something **• prevenirse de** *or* **con algo** to prepare *or* provide oneself with something **• prevenírsele a uno** to occur to one <*se me previene que no le gusta el campo* it occurs to me that she doesn't like the country>.
pre·ven·ti·vo, –va adj. preventive.
pre·ver §77 tr. to foresee, anticipate.
pre·via·men·te adv. previously, beforehand.
pre·vio, –via adj. *(anterior)* previous, former; *(preparatorio)* preliminary, prior <*p. aviso* prior notice>; *(a condición de)* subject to <*p. acuerdo de las partes interesadas* subject to the agreement of the interested parties>; *(después)* after, upon <*p. pago* after *or* upon payment>.
pre·vi·si·ble adj. foreseeable, predictable.
pre·vi·sión f. *(lo que se prevé)* forecast; *(clarividencia)* foresight; *(prudencia)* prudence, precaution; ACC. provision (for contingencies) **♦ p. del tiempo** *or* **meteorológica** weather forecast **• p. social** social security.
pre·vi·si·vo, –va adj. foresighted, prudent.
pre·vi·sor, –so·ra I. adj. foresighted, prudent **II.** foresighted *or* prudent person.
pre·vis·to, –ta I. past part. see **prever II.** adj. *(anticipado)* foreseen, anticipated; *(estipulado)* provided <*p. por la ley* provided by law>.
prez m. honor, glory.
prie·to, –ta adj. *(negro)* dark, swarthy; *(tacaño)* stingy, miserly; *(apretado)* tight.
pri·ma f. COM. *(indemnización)* insurance premium; *(recompensa)* premium, bonus; MUS. treble; RELIG. prime —m.f. see **primo, –ma.**
pri·ma·cí·a f. *(superioridad)* primacy, superiority; RELIG. primacy, primateship.
pri·ma·do m. RELIG. primate.
pri·ma·rio, –ria adj. *(principal)* primary, chief; *(primero)* first; EDUC., ELEC., GEOL. primary.
pri·ma·te m. *(prócer)* important person; ZOOL. primate **♦ primates** ZOOL. Primates.
pri·ma·ve·ra f. *(estación)* spring; *(época)* springtime; BOT. cowslip, primrose; TEX. flowered silk; FIG. *(de la vida)* prime, springtime (of life).
pri·ma·ve·ral adj. vernal, spring, springlike.
pri·mer adj. [contr. of **primero** used before m. sing. nouns] first <*el primer día* the first day> —see **primero, –ra.**
pri·me·ra I. f. AUTO. first gear; HIST. *(juego)* primero (card game) **II.** adj. see **primero, –ra.**
pri·me·ra·men·te adv. first, in the first place.
pri·me·ri·zo, –za I. adj. beginning **II.** m.f. beginner, novice.
pri·me·ro, –ra §G21 **I.** adj. first <*la p. vez* the first time>; first, front <*la p. página* the front page>; *(mejor)* best <*ella es la p. alumna de la clase* she is the best student in the class>; *(fundamental)* primary, basic <*las primeras necesidades* the basic needs>; *(anterior)* former **♦ a p. vista**

at first sight • **de buenas a primeras** all at once, suddenly • **de primera** first-rate, first-class • **de primero** at first • **en primer lugar** in the first place, first of all • **primer actor** THEAT. leading man • **p. actriz** THEAT. leading lady • **p. clase** first class • **p. dama** POL. first lady • **p. edición** first edition • **p. enseñanza** primary school • **primer meridiano** prime meridian • **primer ministro** POL. prime minister • **p. persona** GRAM. first person • **p. piedra** cornerstone • **primeros auxilios** first aid • **primer término** foreground **II.** m.f. first <*Pedro fue el p. en llegar* Peter was the first to arrive>; *(el mejor)* best —f. see **primera III.** adv. first, firstly <*p. haremos un plan* first we will make a plan>; *(más bien)* first, sooner <*p. morir que pedir ayuda* sooner dead than ask for help>.

pri·mi·cia f. *(primer fruto)* first fruits; RELIG. first fruits (offering) ♦ **primicias** FIG. first fruits, early results.

pri·mi·ge·nio, -nia adj. original, primitive.

pri·mi·ti·vis·mo m. primitivism.

pri·mi·ti·vo, -va I. adj. *(original)* primitive, original; ANTHR. primitive, aboriginal **II.** m.f. ANTHR. primitive, aborigene; ARTS primitive.

pri·mo, -ma I. adj. *(primero)* first; *(excelente)* prime, excellent; MATH. prime **II.** m.f. *(pariente)* cousin; FIG., COLL. *(bobo)* fool, dunce ♦ **hacer el p.** FIG., COLL. to be a dupe, be easily taken in • **p. hermano** or **carnal** first cousin • **p. segundo** second cousin —f. see **prima**.

pri·mo·gé·ni·to, -ta adj. & m.f. first-born.

pri·mo·ge·ni·tu·ra f. primogeniture.

pri·mor m. *(exquisitez)* exquisiteness; *(finura)* fineness, delicacy; *(destreza)* skill; COLL. *(cosa exquisita)* exquisite or beautiful thing.

pri·mor·dial adj. primordial.

pri·mo·ro·sa·men·te adv. *(con exquisitez)* beautifully, exquisitely; *(con destreza)* skillfully, finely.

pri·mo·ro·so, -sa adj. *(exquisito)* beautiful, exquisite; *(diestro)* skillful.

prin·ce·sa f. princess.

prin·ci·pa·do m. *(título)* princedom; *(territorio)* princedom, principality; *(primacía)* primacy ♦ **principados** THEOL. principalities.

prin·ci·pal I. adj. *(más importante)* main, principal; *(ilustre)* illustrious, notable; *(esencial)* essential, fundamental; COM. head, chief; GRAM. main (clause); PRINT. first (edition) ♦ **lo p.** the main thing **II.** m. *(piso)* second floor, first floor (G.B.); COM. principal, head; FIN. principal, capital; LAW principal, constituent; MIL. main guard; THEAT. dress circle.

prin·ci·pal·men·te adv. principally, mainly.

prín·ci·pe I. adj. first, original (edition) **II.** m. *(soberano)* prince, sovereign; FIG. master <*los autores príncipes* the old masters> ♦ **p. consorte** prince consort • **p. heredero** crown prince • **p. de Asturias** crown prince of Spain • **p. de las tinieblas** Prince of Darkness, Satan • **príncipes de la Iglesia** princes of the Church, cardinals.

prin·ci·pes·co, -ca adj. princely.

prin·ci·pia·dor, -do·ra I. adj. beginning **II.** m.f. beginner, novice.

prin·ci·pian·ta f. apprentice, novice.

prin·ci·pian·te, -ta I. adj. beginning **II.** m.f. beginner, novice.

prin·ci·piar tr. to begin, start.

prin·ci·pio m. *(comienzo)* beginning, start; *(idea)* principle, idea; *(fundamento)* principle, fundamental <*p. de contradicción* principle of contradiction>; *(rudimento)* rudiment, principle; *(causa primitiva)* source, origin; *(componente)* principle, component, ingredient; *(máxima)* principle, scruple; CUL. entrée ♦ **a p.** or **principios de** at the beginning of (a month) • **al p.** or **a los principios** at first, in or at the beginning • **dar p. a** to start off • **del p. al fin** or **desde el p. hasta el fin** from beginning to end, from start to finish • **en p.** in or on principle • **en un p.** at first, at the beginning • **por p.** on principle • **principios** PRINT. introductory or front matter • **sin principios** unprincipled, unscrupulous • **tener por p.** to make a point of • **tener** or **tomar p. de** to come or spring from, be based on.

prin·gar §47 tr. *(ensuciar)* to get grease on; *(empapar)* to dip or soak in grease or fat; CUL. *(enlardar)* to baste

(meat); FIG., COLL. *(denigrar)* to slander; to involve (in), drag or get (into) <*p. a alguien en un lío* to drag someone into a mess>; COLL. *(herir)* to wound; CHILE *(contagiar)* to give (disease); *(embarazar)* to get (a woman) pregnant —intr. FIG., COLL. *(tomar parte)* to take part, get involved; COLL. *(trabajar)* to work; GUAT., MEX., VEN. to drizzle ♦ **p. en todo** to have many irons in the fire —reflex. *(ensuciarse)* to get grease on, get stained with grease; COLL. *(mezclarse)* to get mixed up (in something illegal).

prin·go·so, -sa adj. greasy, fatty.

prin·gue m.f. *(grasa)* grease, drippings; FIG. *(suciedad)* grease, filth.

prior I. adj. prior, preceding **II.** m. RELIG. prior.

prio·ra f. RELIG. prioress.

prio·ri·dad f. priority.

pri·sa f. *(apuro)* haste, hurry; *(velocidad)* speed; *(urgencia)* urgency; ♦ **a** or **de p.** *(rápidamente)* quickly, fast; *(apresuradamente)* in a hurry, hurriedly • **a toda p.** as quickly as possible • **andar** or **estar de p.** to be in a hurry • **correr** or **dar p.** to be urgent • **dar** or **meter p. a alguien** to rush or hurry someone • **darse p.** to hasten, hurry (up) • **de p. y corriendo** at full speed, in a hurry • **tener p. (por** or **en)** to be in a hurry (to).

pris·co m. BOT. variety of peach.

pri·sión f. *(cárcel)* prison, jail; *(encarcelamiento)* imprisonment, detention; *(acción de prender)* capture, seizure; *(de afecto)* bond, tie ♦ **prisiones** shackles, chains • **p. preventiva** LAW preventive custody or detention • **reducir a p.** to imprison, incarcerate.

pri·sio·ne·ro, -ra m.f. prisoner, captive.

pris·ma m. GEOM., OPT. prism.

pris·má·ti·co, -ca I. adj. prismatic **II.** m.pl. **prismáticos** binoculars.

prís·ti·no, -na adj. pristine, original.

pri·va·ción f. *(acción de privar)* deprivation; *(falta)* privation, lack; *(pérdida)* loss.

pri·va·da·men·te adv. privately, in private.

pri·va·do, -da I. past part. see **privar II.** adj. private, personal ♦ **en p.** in private • **p. de** without, bereft of • **vida p.** privacy **III.** m. protégé, favorite.

pri·var tr. *(despojar)* to deprive, take away; *(prohibir)* to prohibit, forbid <*el médico le privó el tabaco* the doctor forbade him to smoke>; *(quitar el sentido)* to stun, daze —intr. *(tener privanza)* to be in favor <*p. con la reina* to be in the queen's favor>; *(tener aceptación)* to be popular, be in fashion <*este peinado priva mucho ahora* this hairstyle is very popular now> —reflex. to abstain (from), give up.

pri·va·ti·vo, -va adj. *(que causa privación)* privative; *(propio)* particular, personal.

pri·va·ti·za·ción f. privatization.

pri·va·ti·zar §04 tr. to privatize.

pri·vi·le·giar tr. to privilege, favor.

pri·vi·le·gio m. privilege ♦ **p. de invención** patent.

pro m.f. profit, benefit ♦ **¡buena p. le haga!** much good may it do you! • **de p.** noteworthy, of note • **en p. de** pro, in favor of • **en p. y en contra** pro and con.

pro·a f. MARIT. prow, bow ♦ **poner la p. a alguien** FIG. to oppose someone.

pro·ba·bi·li·dad f. probability, likelihood ♦ **probabilidades de vida** life expectancy.

pro·ba·ble adj. *(verosímil)* probable, likely; *(demostrable)* provable.

pro·ba·ble·men·te adv. probably.

pro·ba·do, -da I. past part. see **probar II.** adj. *(demostrado)* proved, demonstrated; *(una persona)* tested, tried; LAW proven.

pro·ba·dor, -do·ra I. adj. *(ensayador)* testing, trying; *(demostrador)* proving, demonstrating **II.** m.f. *(ensayador)* tester —m. *(en una tienda)* fitting room.

pro·ban·za f. LAW proof.

pro·bar §19 tr. *(ensayar)* to test, try, put to the test <*p. su sinceridad* to test one's sincerity>; *(confirmar)* to prove, show; to try on <*p. una camisa* to try on a shirt>; *(saborear)* to taste, try (food) ♦ **p. ventura** to try one's luck —intr. to attempt, try <*p. a nadar un kilómetro* to try to swim a kilometer> ♦ **p. bien** to agree with, suit • **p. de** to taste, try (food) • **p. de todo** to take a taste of everything

• **p. mal** not to agree with, be unsuitable —reflex. to try on (clothing).

pro·ba·to·rio, –ria I. adj. probative, probatory II. f. LAW probatory period.

pro·be·ta f. CHEM. test tube; *(manómetro)* manometer, pressure gauge; MIL. powder tester.

pro·bi·dad f. probity, integrity.

pro·ble·ma m. problem.

pro·ble·má·ti·co, –ca I. adj. problematic, problematical II. f. problems, issues.

pro·bo, –ba adj. upright, honest.

pro·ca·ci·dad f. *(insolencia)* impudence, insolence; *(indecencia)* indecency.

pro·caz adj. [pl. **-ca·ces**] *(insolente)* impudent, insolent; *(indecente)* indecent.

pro·ce·den·cia f. *(origen)* origin, source; *(punto de salida)* origin, point of departure; *(de la conducta)* decency, properness; *(de una idea)* reasonableness, sensibleness; LAW justice, merits (of a claim).

pro·ce·den·te adj. *(que procede)* (coming) from <*el tren p. de Lima* the train from Lima>; LAW admissible; *(sensato)* reasonable, sensible; *(adecuado)* fitting, proper.

pro·ce·der¹ m. conduct, behavior.

pro·ce·der² intr. *(originarse)* to originate in, come from <*todo esto procede de su concepto de la libertad* all this comes from his concept of freedom>; *(ejecutar)* to proceed, go on (to) <*p. a las elecciones* to go on to the elections>; *(ir con orden)* to proceed, go in procession; *(portarse)* to behave, act; *(continuar)* to continue, go on or ahead with; *(ser conveniente)* to be advisable or wise; *(ser apropiado)* to be fitting or appropriate; LAW to be admissible or relevant ♦ **p. contra alguien** to proceed or bring proceedings against someone • **p. con método** to proceed methodically • **p. de consuno** to work in concert.

pro·ce·di·mien·to m. *(método)* method, procedure; *(proceso)* process; LAW proceedings ♦ **p. al carbón** CHEM., METAL. carbon process.

pro·ce·lo·so, –sa adj. POET. stormy, tempestuous.

pró·cer I. adj. *(alto)* tall, lofty; FIG. *(eminente)* eminent, illustrious II. m. eminent or illustrious person.

pro·ce·sa·do, –da I. past part. see **procesar** II. adj. LAW *(del proceso)* procedural, of the proceedings; *(acusado)* accused, indicted III. m.f accused, defendant.

pro·ce·sa·dor m. COMPUT. processor.

pro·ce·sa·mien·to m. LAW prosecution; COMPUT. processing ♦ **p. de datos** COMPUT. data processing.

pro·ce·sar tr. LAW *(formar causa)* to prosecute; *(juzgar)* to try; *(demandar)* to sue; COMPUT. to process.

pro·ce·sión f. *(desfile)* procession, parade; *(acción de proceder)* act of proceeding ♦ **la p. va por dentro** FIG., COLL. still waters run deep • **no se puede repicar y andar en la p.** FIG., COLL. one cannot do two things at once.

pro·ce·so m. process; *(transcurso)* course <*en el p. de una semana* in the course of a week>; ANAT., BOT. process; LAW *(causa criminal)* trial; *(agregado de autos)* proceedings; MED. process, course (of an illness) ♦ **abrir** or **entablar** or **formar p.** to bring suit • **p. ciliar** ANAT. ciliary process • **p. de datos** data processing • **p. verbal** minutes (of a meeting).

pro·cla·ma f. proclamation, announcement ♦ **correr las proclamas** to publish the banns • **proclamas** marriage banns.

pro·cla·ma·ción f. *(proclama)* proclamation, announcement; *(alabanza)* acclamation.

pro·cla·mar tr. *(anunciar)* to proclaim, announce; *(aclamar)* to acclaim, applaud —reflex. to proclaim oneself.

pro·cli·ve adj. inclined, disposed.

pro·cón·sul m. proconsul.

pro·con·su·la·do m. *(cargo)* proconsulate; *(tiempo)* proconsulship.

pro·cre·a·ción f. procreation.

pro·cre·a·dor, –do·ra I. adj. procreant, procreative II. m.f. procreator.

pro·cre·ar tr. to procreate.

pro·cu·ra f. *(poder)* power of attorney, proxy; ARG. search, hunt.

pro·cu·ra·ción f. *(cuidado)* care, diligence (in manage-

ment); *(poder)* power of attorney, proxy; *(cargo)* legal profession; *(oficina)* law office ♦ **por p.** by proxy.

pro·cu·ra·dor, –do·ra I. adj. procuring II. m.f. *(apoderado)* proxy, agent; *(abogado)* attorney, lawyer; RELIG. procurator (of a convent) ♦ **p. a** or **de** or **en Cortes** SP. member of parliament • **p. general** public prosecutor.

pro·cu·ra·du·rí·a f. *(oficio)* legal profession; *(oficina)* law office.

pro·cu·rar tr. *(intentar)* to try, endeavor; *(obtener)* to get, obtain; *(dirigir por otro)* to manage for another; *(ocasionar)* to give, bring —reflex. to get, obtain.

pro·di·gar §47 tr. *(disipar)* to squander, waste; FIG. *(dar con profusión)* to lavish —reflex. to flaunt oneself, show off.

pro·di·gio m. *(persona)* prodigy; *(fenómeno)* wonder, marvel.

pro·di·gio·sa·men·te adv. prodigiously, marvelously.

pro·di·gio·si·dad f. prodigiousness.

pro·di·gio·so, –sa adj. *(maravilloso)* prodigious, wondrous; *(excelente)* excellent, marvelous.

pró·di·go, –ga I. adj. *(malgastador)* prodigal, wasteful; *(muy generoso)* lavish, generous ♦ **hijo p.** prodigal son II. m.f. prodigal, spendthrift.

pro·di·gué, prodigue see **prodigar**.

pro·duc·ción f. *(acción de producir)* production; *(cosa producida)* product; AGR. crop; CINEM. production ♦ **p. automática** automation • **p. en masa** or **en serie** mass production.

pro·du·cen·te adj. *(causativo)* producing, causing; *(productivo)* productive, profitable.

pro·du·ci·ble adj. producible.

pro·du·cir §22 tr. *(causar)* to produce; *(engendrar)* to produce, bear <*el árbol produce buen fruto* the tree bears good fruit>; FIG. *(elaborar)* to produce, manufacture; *(ocasionar)* to cause, bring about; FIN. to bear, yield (interest); LAW to produce (evidence) ♦ **p. en serie** to mass-produce —reflex. *(expresarse)* to express or explain oneself; *(suceder)* to happen, take place; *(aparecer)* to appear.

pro·duc·ti·vi·dad f. productivity.

pro·duc·ti·vo, –va adj. *(que produce mucho)* productive; *(lucrativo)* lucrative, profitable.

pro·duc·to, –ta I. adj. produced II. m. *(cosa producida)* product; CHEM., MATH. product; COM. *(beneficio)* profit, yield; *(ingresos)* proceeds ♦ **p. alimenticio** foodstuff • **p. de desecho** waste product • **p. derivado** or **secundario** by-product • **p. final** end product • **p. nacional bruto** gross national product • **p. neto** COM. net produce • **p. terminado** finished product • **productos agrícolas** farm produce • **productos de consumo** consumer goods.

pro·duc·tor, –to·ra I. adj. productive, producing II. m.f. producer.

pro·du·je·ra, produjo see **producir**.

pro·duz·ca, produzco see **producir**.

pro·e·za f. exploit, feat.

pro·fa·na·ción f. profanation, desecration.

pro·fa·na·dor, –do·ra I. adj. profanatory II. m.f. profaner.

pro·fa·na·men·te adv. profanely.

pro·fa·nar tr. *(maltratar una cosa sagrada)* to profane, desecrate; *(deshonrar)* to dishonor, disgrace.

pro·fa·no, –na I. adj. *(no sagrado)* profane, secular; *(irreverente)* profane, irreverent; *(indecente)* indecent, immodest; *(no iniciado)* uninitiated, lay II. m. layman —f. laywoman.

pro·fe·cí·a f. prophecy.

pro·fe·rir §65 tr. to utter, say.

pro·fe·sar tr. *(ejercer)* to practice, exercise (a profession); *(enseñar)* to teach; *(creer)* to profess, believe in; *(declarar)* to profess, declare; FIG. *(sentir un afecto)* to have, feel; —intr. RELIG. to take vows.

pro·fe·sión f. *(ocupación)* profession, trade; *(declaración)* declaration, avowal ♦ **de p.** by profession or trade • **p. de fe** RELIG. profession or declaration of faith.

pro·fe·sio·nal adj. & m.f. professional.

pro·fe·sio·na·lis·mo m. professionalism.

pro·fe·so, –sa RELIG. I. adj. professed II. m. professed monk —f. professed nun.

pro·fe·sor, –so·ra m.f. *(de escuela)* teacher; *(de universidad)* professor ♦ **p. agregado** or **auxiliar** assistant professor • **p. suplente** substitute teacher.

pro·fe·so·ra·do m. *(cargo)* professorship, teaching position; *(cuerpo docente)* teaching staff, faculty.
pro·fe·ta m. prophet.
pro·fé·ti·co, –ca adj. prophetic.
pro·fe·ti·sa f. prophetess.
pro·fe·ti·zar §04 tr. *(adivinar)* to prophesy; FIG. *(conjeturar)* to forecast, predict.
pro·fie·ra, profiero see **proferir**.
pro·fi·lác·ti·co, –ca MED. **I.** adj. prophylactic, preventive **II.** m. prophylactic, condom —f. prophylaxis, hygiene.
pro·fi·la·xis f. MED. prophylaxis.
pro·fi·rie·ra, profirió see **proferir**.
pró·fu·go, –ga I. adj. fugitive, on the run **II.** m.f. *(fugitivo)* fugitive —m. MIL. draft dodger.
pro·fun·da·men·te adv. profoundly, deeply.
pro·fun·di·dad f. *(hondura)* depth, deepness, profundity; FIG. *(intensidad)* depth, profundity; GEOM. depth, height ♦ **de p.** deep, in depth <*tres pies de p.* three feet deep>.
pro·fun·di·za·ción f. deepening.
pro·fun·di·zar §04 tr. *(cavar)* to deepen, make deeper; FIG. *(estudiar)* to study thoroughly, delve into —intr. to go deeply into a subject.
pro·fun·do, –da I. adj. *(hondo)* deep <*un hoyo p.* a deep pit>; FIG. *(intenso)* profound, intense <*tristeza p.* profound sadness>; *(recóndito)* obscure, difficult <*una teoría p.* a difficult theory>; *(penetrante)* profound, deep <*pensamientos profundos* deep thoughts>; *(sincero)* deep, heartfelt <*una salutación p.* heartfelt greeting> **II.** m. *(profundidad)* depth; POET. *(mar)* deep sea; *(infierno)* hell.
pro·fu·sa·men·te adv. profusely, abundantly.
pro·fu·sión f. profusion, abundance.
pro·fu·so, –sa adj. profuse, abundant.
pro·ge·nie f. progeny, offspring.
pro·ge·ni·tor m. progenitor ♦ **progenitores** *(antepasados)* ancestors; *(padres)* parents.
pro·ge·ni·tu·ra f. *(progenie)* progeny, offspring; *(primogenitura)* primogeniture.
pro·gra·ma m. program ♦ **p. de estudios** curriculum • **p. de urgencia** COLL. crash program • **p. doble** CINEM. double feature • **p. espacial** space program.
pro·gra·ma·ble adj. programmable.
pro·gra·ma·ción f. COMPUT. programming.
pro·gra·ma·dor, –do·ra I. adj. planning, programming **II.** m.f. *(planificador)* planner, programmer; COMPUT. programmer.
pro·gra·mar tr. *(planificar)* to plan, program; COMPUT. to program (a computer).
pro·gre·sar intr. to progress, advance.
pro·gre·sión f. progression ♦ **p. geométrica** geometric progression.
pro·gre·sis·ta adj. & m.f. progressive.
pro·gre·si·va·men·te adv. progressively.
pro·gre·si·vo, –va adj. progressive.
pro·gre·so m. progress ♦ **hacer progresos** to make progress, progress.
pro·hi·bi·ción f. prohibition.
pro·hi·bi·cio·nis·ta m.f. prohibitionist.
pro·hi·bi·do, –da I. past part. see **prohibir II.** adj. prohibited, forbidden ♦ **p. aparcar** or **estacionarse** no parking • **p. la entrada** keep out, no admittance.
pro·hi·bir tr. to prohibit, forbid ♦ **p. a alguien hacer algo** to prohibit someone from doing something, forbid someone to do something ♦ **se prohibe (fumar, estacionar)** no (smoking, parking).
pro·hi·bi·ti·vo, –va or **pro·hi·bi·to·rio, –ria** adj. prohibitive, prohibitory.
pro·hi·jar §81 tr. to adopt.
pro·hom·bre m. *(persona notable)* great man; *(dirigente)* leader.
pró·ji·ma f. COLL. tart, slut.
pró·ji·mo m. *(otra persona)* neighbor, fellow man; *(humanidad)* humanity, mankind; COLL. *(sujeto)* fellow, guy ♦ **amar al p. como a sí mismo** to love one's neighbor as oneself.
pro·le f. progeny, offspring.
pro·le·gó·me·nos m.pl. LIT. prolegomena.
pro·le·ta·ria·do m. proletariat.
pro·le·ta·rio, –ria adj. & m.f. proletarian.

pro·li·fe·ra·ción f. proliferation.
pro·li·fe·rar intr. to proliferate.
pro·lí·fi·co, –ca adj. prolific.
pro·li·ji·dad f. *(pesadez)* prolixity, long-windedness; *(meticulosidad)* meticulousness, thoroughness.
pro·li·jo, –ja adj. *(pesado)* prolix, long-winded; *(meticuloso)* meticulous, thorough.
pro·lo·gar §47 tr. to preface, write a prologue to.
pró·lo·go m. prologue, preface.
pro·lon·ga·ción f. *(acción de prolongar)* prolongation, extension; *(parte prolongada)* extension, continuation.
pro·lon·ga·da·men·te adv. lengthily, at great length.
pro·lon·ga·do, –da I. past part. see **prolongar II.** adj. *(largo)* prolonged, lengthy; *(oblongo)* oblong.
pro·lon·ga·mien·to m. var. of **prolongación**.
pro·lon·gar §47 tr. *(continuar)* to prolong, extend; *(alargar)* to make longer, lengthen —reflex. *(extenderse)* to extend, continue; *(durar más tiempo)* to last longer <*la reunión se prolongó más de lo previsto* the meeting lasted longer than expected>.
pro·me·diar tr. *(dividir en dos partes iguales)* to divide in half; *(sacar el promedio)* to average —intr. *(interceder)* to mediate; *(llegar a la mitad)* to be halfway through, be half over ♦ **al p. el mes** halfway through the month.
pro·me·dio m. *(mitad)* middle; MATH. average, mean ♦ **en** or **por p.** on average • **p. aritmético** arithmetical mean • **p. geométrico** geometric mean.
pro·me·sa f. *(compromiso)* promise, pledge; RELIG. vow; FIG. *(esperanza)* promise, hope ♦ **cumplir (con) una p.** to keep a promise • **faltar a una p.** to break a promise.
pro·me·te·dor, –do·ra I. adj. promising **II.** m.f. promiser.
pro·me·ter tr. to promise, pledge ♦ **p. el oro y el moro** FIG. to promise the moon and stars —intr. to be promising, show promise —reflex. *(esperar)* to expect; *(desposarse)* to become engaged ♦ **prometérselas felices** COLL. to have high hopes.
pro·me·ti·do, –da I. past part. see **prometer II.** adj. *(ofrecido)* promised; *(novios)* engaged, betrothed **III.** m. fiancé —f. fiancée.
pro·me·tio m. CHEM. promethium.
pro·mi·nen·cia f. GEOL. prominence, projection; FIG. prominence.
pro·mi·nen·te adj. prominent, projecting.
pro·mis·cui·dad f. promiscuity, promiscuousness.
pro·mis·cuo, –cua adj. promiscuous.
pro·mi·sión f. promise ♦ **Tierra de P.** Promised Land.
pro·mi·so·rio, –ria adj. promissory.
pro·mo·ción f. *(adelantamiento)* promotion; EDUC. graduating class; SPORT. promotion match ♦ **p. de ventas** sales promotion.
pro·mo·cio·nal adj. promotional.
pro·mo·cio·nar tr. to promote, advance.
pro·mon·to·rio m. GEOG. promontory, headland; FIG. *(bulto)* bulky or unwieldy object.
pro·mo·tor, –to·ra I. adj. *(que promociona)* promoting; *(instigador)* instigating **II.** m.f. *(que promociona)* promoter; *(instigador)* instigator ♦ **p. de la fe** RELIG. devil's advocate • **p. fiscal** public prosecutor.
pro·mo·ve·dor, –do·ra I. adj. *(que promociona)* promoting; *(instigador)* instigating **II.** m.f. *(que promociona)* promoter; *(instigador)* instigator.
pro·mo·ver §78 tr. *(promocionar)* to promote; *(fomentar)* to foster, encourage; *(elevar)* to promote, raise; *(provocar)* to provoke, cause.
pro·mul·ga·ción f. promulgation.
pro·mul·ga·dor, –do·ra I. adj. promulgating **II.** m.f. promulgator.
pro·mul·gar §47 tr. LAW to promulgate, enact; FIG. *(proclamar)* to proclaim, announce.
pro·no, –na adj. *(inclinado)* prone, inclined; *(echado sobre el vientre)* prone, prostrate.
pro·nom·bre m. GRAM. pronoun.
pro·no·mi·nal adj. GRAM. pronominal.
pro·nos·ti·ca·dor, –do·ra I. adj. prognosticative **II.** m.f. prognosticator, forecaster.
pro·nos·ti·car §70 tr. to prognosticate, predict, forecast.
pro·nós·ti·co m. *(predicción)* prognostication, prediction, forecast; *(señal)* prognostic, omen; *(calendario)* almanac;

MED. prognosis ♦ **p. del tiempo** weather forecast • **p. re-servado** MED. guarded prognosis.

pron·ta·men·te adv. *(velozmente)* quickly; *(diligentemente)* promptly.

pron·ti·tud f. *(velocidad)* speed, quickness; *(diligencia)* promptness; *(ingenio)* quickness, sharpness (of mind).

pron·to, –ta I. adj. *(veloz)* quick, rapid, fast; *(diligente)* prompt; quick, speedy <*una p. curación* a speedy recovery>; *(preparado)* ready, prepared; ♦ **p. a** quick to <*p. a enfadarse* quick to anger> II. m. *(impulso)* impulse, sudden feeling; *(movimiento)* start, sudden movement ♦ **tener prontos de enojo** to be quick-tempered III. adv. *(velozmente)* quickly, rapidly; *(diligentemente)* promptly; *(en seguida)* at once, right away; *(dentro de poco)* soon; *(temprano)* early; AMER. suddenly ♦ **al p.** at first • **de p.** *(apresuradamente)* quickly, hastily; *(de repente)* suddenly, all at once • **lo más p. posible** as soon as possible • **por de or el or lo p.** *(por ahora)* for the moment or present; *(al menos)* at least, anyway • **tan p. como** as soon as.

pron·tua·rio m. *(resumen)* summary; *(compendio)* handbook, compendium; AMER., CRIMIN. record, file; *(libro de apuntes)* notebook.

pro·nun·cia·ción f. *(articulación)* pronunciation, articulation; LAW pronouncement, passing (of a judgment) ♦ **p. figurada** phonetic transcription.

pro·nun·cia·do, –da I. past part. see **pronunciar** II. adj. pronounced, marked.

pro·nun·cia·mien·to m. *(golpe de estado)* military coup; LAW pronouncement (of sentence).

pro·nun·ciar tr. *(articular)* to pronounce, articulate; *(decir)* to utter, speak <*no p. ni una palabra* not to utter a single word>; *(discurrir)* to deliver (a speech); LAW to pronounce or pass (judgment) —reflex. *(sublevarse)* to rebel, revolt; *(declararse)* to pronounce or declare oneself.

pro·pa·ga·ción f. *(reproducción)* propagation; FIG. *(difusión)* propagation, spreading; PHYS. propagation ♦ **p. ultrasónica** ACOUS. hypersonic propagation.

pro·pa·ga·dor, –do·ra I. adj. propagating II. m.f. propagator, spreader.

pro·pa·gan·da f. *(de ideas)* propaganda; RELIG. Propaganda; *(publicidad)* advertising, publicity ♦ **hacer p.** to advertise.

pro·pa·gan·dis·ta I. adj. propagandistic II. m.f. propagandist.

pro·pa·gan·dís·ti·co, –ca adj. propagandistic.

pro·pa·gar §47 tr. & reflex. *(reproducir)* to propagate, multiply; FIG. *(difundir)* to propagate, spread.

pro·pa·ga·ti·vo, –va adj. propagative.

pro·pa·lar tr. *(divulgar)* to divulge, reveal (a secret); *(propagar)* to spread.

pro·pa·no m. CHEM. propane.

pro·pa·sar tr. to go beyond, overstep (the limit) —reflex. to go too far, overstep one's authority.

pro·pen·der intr. to tend, be inclined (to or toward).

pro·pen·sión f. *(inclinación)* propensity, inclination; MED. predisposition, susceptibility.

pro·pen·so, –sa adj. inclined, prone ♦ **ser p. a** to be prone to.

pro·pia·men·te adv. *(con propiedad)* properly, correctly; *(realmente)* really, exactly <*no es p. cierto* that's not exactly true> ♦ **p. dicho** strictly speaking.

pro·pi·ciar tr. *(aplacar)* to placate, propitiate; AMER. to sponsor, support; *(favorecer)* to favor.

pro·pi·cia·to·rio, –ria I. adj. propitiatory II. m. RELIG. prie-dieu.

pro·pi·cio, –cia adj. propitious, favorable ♦ **ser p. a** to be inclined or prone to.

pro·pie·dad f. *(pertenencia)* ownership, proprietorship; *(cosa que se posee)* property, possession; *(atributo)* attribute, property <*la incombustibilidad es una p. del asbesto* incombustibility is a property of asbestos>; *(heredad)* estate, property <*es dueño de una gran p.* he's the owner of a great estate>; *(semejanza)* complete accuracy, perfect imitation <*lo pintó con toda p.* he painted it with complete accuracy>; LING. *(rigor)* exactness, correct meaning (of a word); *(oportunidad)* appropriateness, suitability <*la p. de una palabra* the appropriateness of a word> ♦ **de la p. de** belonging to • **hablar con p.** to speak correctly or pre-

cisely • **p. horizontal** cooperative property, ownership of an apartment in a co-op or condominium • **p. industrial** patent rights • **p. inmobiliaria** real estate • **p. intelectual** or **literaria** copyright • **p. particular** private property • **nuda p.** LAW bare ownership • **pertenecer en p.** to rightfully belong to.

pro·pie·ta·rio, –ria I. adj. proprietary II. m. *(amo)* owner, proprietor; *(dueño)* owner; *(terrateniente)* landowner, landlord —f. *(dueña)* owner, proprietress; *(casera)* landlady ♦ **nudo p.** LAW bare owner, owner without usufruct.

pro·pi·le·no m. CHEM. propylene.

pro·pi·lo m. CHEM. propyl.

pro·pi·na f. tip, gratuity ♦ **de p.** COLL. in addition, into the bargain.

pro·pi·nar tr. *(dar a beber)* to treat, buy a drink for; COLL. *(dar)* to give <*p. una paliza* to give a beating>; MED. to prescribe.

pro·pin·cui·dad f. propinquity, proximity.

pro·pio, –pia I. adj. own, one's own <*mató a su p. padre* he killed his own father>; *(original)* own, very <*ésas son sus propias palabras* those are her very words>; *(natural)* own, natural <*su p. pelo* his own hair>; *(mismo)* -self <*el p. interesado debe asistir a la reunión* the interested party himself must attend the meeting>; *(conveniente)* proper, suitable <*no es p. para este caso* it is not suitable for this case>; *(característico)* typical, characteristic <*eso es p. de ella* that is typical of her>; GRAM., MATH. proper ♦ **al p.** properly, precisely; AMER. expressly, on purpose II. m. *(mensajero)* messenger; *(finca)* public land.

pro·pó·le·os m. propolis, bee glue.

pro·po·ne·dor, –do·ra or **pro·po·nen·te** I. adj. proposing II. m.f. proposer, proponent.

pro·po·ner §54 tr. *(sugerir)* to propose, suggest <*p. un plan* to propose a plan>; *(exponer)* to propound, put forward <*p. una teoría* to propound a theory>; *(plantear)* to pose, put up for discussion (a problem, point); *(presentar)* to propose, nominate <*lo propuse para la vacante* I proposed him for the vacant post>; *(opinar)* to move, propose <*propongo que se aplace la sesión* I move that the meeting be postponed>; MATH. to make a proposition —reflex. to intend or propose to do something <*no sé qué te propones* I don't know what you intend to do>.

pro·por·ción f. *(relación entre las cosas)* proportion <*una pena en p. con el delito* a punishment in proportion to the crime>; *(oportunidad)* chance, opportunity; *(tamaño)* size, proportion; MATH. proportion, ratio ♦ **a p. de** according to • **en p. a** in proportion to • **fuera de p.** out of proportion • **guardar p. con** to be in proportion with • **proporciones** proportions, dimensions.

pro·por·cio·na·ble adj. *(que puede distribuirse)* proportionable; *(que puede suministrarse)* which can be provided.

pro·por·cio·na·do, –da I. past part. see **proporcionar** II. adj. *(que guarda proporción)* proportioned, proportionate; *(adecuado)* fitting, commensurate.

pro·por·cio·nal adj. proportional.

pro·por·cio·na·li·dad f. proportionality.

pro·por·cio·nal·men·te adv. proportionally.

pro·por·cio·nar tr. *(distribuir)* to apportion, divide <*p. la carga* to apportion the load>; *(adaptar)* to proportion, adapt <*p. los medios al objeto* to adapt the means to the ends>; *(suministrar)* to furnish, provide —reflex. to get, obtain.

pro·po·si·ción f. *(propuesta)* proposition, proposal; *(moción)* motion, resolution; LOG., MATH., RHET. proposition; GRAM. clause.

pro·pó·si·to m. *(intención)* intention, resolve <*buenos propósitos* good intentions>; *(objetivo)* purpose, aim; *(asunto)* subject matter ♦ **a p.** *(por cierto)* by the way, incidentally; *(útil)* handy, useful <*el cheque me vino muy a p.* the check came in very handy>; *(adecuado)* suitable, appropriate; *(apto)* apt, relevant <*lo que usted dice aquí es muy a p.* what you're saying here is very apt>; *(adrede)* on purpose, deliberately • **a p. de** in regard to, apropos of • **con el p. de** in order to • **con este p.** to this end • **de p.** intentionally, on purpose • **fuera de p.** irrelevant, beside the point • **no venir a p.** to be irrelevant, have nothing to do with the subject.

pro·pues·ta f. *(proposición)* proposal, proposition; *(oferta)* proposal, offer; COM. tender, bid.
pro·pug·na·ción f. defense, advocacy.
pro·pug·nar tr. to defend, advocate.
pro·pul·sar tr. *(repulsar)* to reject, repulse; *(impeler)* to propel, drive forward.
pro·pul·sión f. propulsion, drive ♦ **p. a chorro** *or* **por reacción** AER. jet propulsion • **p. delantera** AUTO. front wheel drive.
pro·pul·sor, –so·ra **I.** adj. propellant, propulsive **II.** m. AER., MARIT. propeller.
pro·pu·sie·ra, propuso see **proponer**.
pro·rra·ta f. quota, share ♦ **a p.** COM. pro rata, proportionally.
pro·rra·te·ar tr. to prorate, divide proportionally.
pro·rra·te·o m. proration, sharing.
pró·rro·ga f. extension, prolongation.
pró·rro·ga·ción f. extension, prolongation; MIL. deferment.
pro·rro·gar §47 tr. *(continuar)* to extend, prolong; *(suspender)* to postpone, defer.
pro·rro·ga·ti·vo, –va adj. prolonging, extending.
pro·rrum·pir intr. *(salir con ímpetu)* to spring *or* burst (forth) <la asistencia prorrumpió en aplausos the audience burst into applause>.
pro·sa f. LIT. prose; FIG. *(aspecto vulgar de las cosas)* prosaicness, ordinariness; *(palabrería)* long-windedness, tediousness ♦ **gastar mucha p.** to waste a lot of hot air • **p. poética** LIT. prose poem.
pro·sa·dor, –do·ra m.f. *(escritor)* prose writer; FIG., COLL. *(hablador)* chatterbox, windbag.
pro·sai·ca·men·te adv. prosaically.
pro·sai·co, –ca adj. prosaic.
pro·sa·ís·mo m. *(falta de armonía)* prosaism; FIG. *(vulgaridad)* prosaic nature.
pro·sa·pia f. ancestry, lineage.
pros·ce·nio m. THEAT. proscenium.
pros·cri·bir §85 tr. *(desterrar)* to exile, banish; *(prohibir)* to proscribe, prohibit, outlaw.
pros·crip·ción f. *(destierro)* exile, banishment; *(prohibición)* proscription, prohibition.
pros·cri·to, –ta **I.** past part. see **proscribir** **II.** adj. exiled **III.** m.f. exile, outlaw.
pro·se·ar intr. ARG., URUG. to chat.
pro·se·cu·ción f. pursuit, pursuance <la p. de una meta the pursuit of a goal>; *(continuación)* continuation.
pro·se·guir §64 tr. *(seguir)* to pursue <p. sus estudios to pursue one's studies>; *(continuar)* to carry on with, continue (with) <proseguiremos nuestra lectura esta tarde we'll continue our reading this afternoon> —intr. ♦ **p. con** *or* **en** to continue (with), go on with.
pro·se·li·tis·mo m. proselytism.
pro·se·li·tis·ta **I.** adj. proselytizing **II.** m.f. proselytizer.
pro·sé·li·to m. proselyte, convert.
pro·sis·ta m.f. prose writer.
pro·so·dia f. GRAM., POET. prosody.
pro·só·di·co, –ca adj. GRAM. orthoepic; POET. prosodic.
pros·pec·ción f. MIN. prospecting; COM. survey, research (of a market).
pros·pec·tar tr. MIN. to prospect; COM. to survey, research (a market).
pros·pec·to m. prospectus, brochure.
prós·pe·ra·men·te adv. prosperously.
pros·pe·rar tr. to make prosperous —intr. to prosper, flourish.
pros·pe·ri·dad f. prosperity.
prós·pe·ro, –ra adj. prosperous.
prós·ta·ta f. ANAT. prostate (gland).
pros·ter·nar·se reflex. to prostrate oneself.
pros·tí·bu·lo m. brothel.
prós·ti·lo adj. & m. ARCHIT. prostyle.
pros·ti·tu·ción f. prostitution.
pros·ti·tuir §18 tr. *(corromper)* to prostitute; FIG. *(deshonrar)* to prostitute, debase —reflex. *(corromperse)* to prostitute oneself, take up prostitution; FIG. *(deshonrarse)* to prostitute *or* debase oneself.
pros·ti·tu·ta f. prostitute.
pro·tac·ti·nio m. CHEM. protactinium.
pro·ta·go·nis·mo m. protagonism.

pro·ta·go·nis·ta m.f. CINEM., LIT., THEAT. protagonist; FIG. *(líder)* champion, leader —m. hero —f. heroine.
pro·ta·go·ni·zar §04 tr. CINEM., THEAT. to play the lead in, star in; FIG. *(hacer un papel principal)* to play a leading role in.
pro·tec·ción f. protection.
pro·tec·cio·nis·mo m. ECON., POL. protectionism.
pro·tec·cio·nis·ta adj. & m.f. ECON., POL. protectionist.
pro·tec·tor, –to·ra *or* **–triz** **I.** adj. *(defensor)* protective, defensive; *(patrocinador)* supporting, patronizing **II.** m.f. *(defensor)* protector, defender; *(patrocinador)* supporter, patron. —f. protectress, patroness.
pro·tec·to·ra·do m. protectorate.
pro·te·ger §34 tr. to protect, defend.
pro·te·gi·do, –da **I.** past part. see **proteger** **II.** adj. protected ♦ **paso p.** right of way **III.** m. protégé —f. protégée.
pro·tei·co, –ca adj. protean, changeable.
pro·te·í·na f. BIOCHEM. protein, proteid.
pró·te·sis f. MED. prosthesis; GRAM. prothesis.
pro·tes·ta f. *(de oposición)* protest; *(declaración)* protestation, declaration.
pro·tes·ta·ción f. *(declaración)* protestation, declaration.
pro·tes·tan·te **I.** adj. *(que protesta)* protesting; RELIG. Protestant **II.** m.f. *(que protesta)* protester; RELIG. Protestant.
pro·tes·tan·tis·mo m. RELIG. Protestantism.
pro·tes·tar tr. *(reclamar)* to protest, object to; *(asegurar)* to affirm, declare; *(la fe)* to profess (faith); COM. to protest (a bill) —intr. to protest, object ♦ **p. contra** to protest against • **p. de** to protest, swear <p. de su inocencia to protest one's innocence>.
pro·tes·to m. *(protesta)* protest, protestation; COM. protest (of a bill).
pro·to·co·lar *or* **pro·to·co·la·rio, –ria** adj. *(relativo al protocolo)* protocolar; FIG. *(ceremonial)* formal.
pro·to·co·lo m. *(registro)* registry, record book; *(de un congreso)* minutes, record (of proceedings); DIPL. protocol.
pro·tón m. PHYS. proton.
pro·to·plas·ma m. BIOL. protoplasm.
pro·to·plas·má·ti·co, –ca *or* **pro·to·plás·mi·co, –ca** adj. BIOL. protoplasmic.
pro·to·ti·po m. prototype.
pro·to·zo·a·rio *or* **pro·to·zo·o** m. ZOOL. protozoan, protozoon.
pro·trác·til adj. protractile.
pro·tu·be·ran·cia f. protuberance, bulge.
pro·tu·be·ran·te adj. protuberant, bulging.
pro·ve·cho m. *(beneficio)* advantage, benefit; *(ganancia)* profit, gain; *(adelantamiento)* progress, advancement ♦ **¡buen p!** COLL. enjoy your meal, hearty appetite • **de ningún p.** of no use • **de p.** *(lucrativo)* profitable, lucrative; *(útil)* useful; *(trabajador)* honest, hardworking • **en p. de** to the benefit of, to the advantage of • **en p. propio** to one's own advantage, for one's own profit • **sacar p. de** *(beneficiarse de)* to benefit from, profit from; *(aprovecharse de)* to take advantage of.
pro·ve·cho·sa·men·te adv. *(beneficiosamente)* profitably; *(ventajosamente)* advantageously.
pro·ve·cho·so, –sa adj. *(beneficioso)* profitable; *(bueno)* beneficial, good <p. para la salud good for one's health>; *(ventajoso)* advantageous.
pro·ve·e·dor, –do·ra m.f. supplier, purveyor.
pro·ve·er §43 tr. *(suministrar)* to provide, furnish <p. de víveres to provide with supplies>; *(disponer)* to decide, resolve (a matter); *(conferir)* to grant, bestow <p. el cargo en el más digno to grant the position to the most worthy>; *(nombrar)* to appoint (a person), fill (a vacancy, post) —intr. LAW to decree, make a ruling —reflex. to provide oneself, supply oneself.
pro·ve·nien·te adj. arising, proceeding.
pro·ve·nir §76 intr. *(proceder)* to arise *or* proceed (from); *(originarse)* to come (from), originate (in) <este vino proviene de la Rioja this wine comes from the Rioja region>.
Pro·ven·za f. Provence.
pro·ven·zal adj. & m.f. Provençal —m. *(idioma)* Provençal.
pro·ver·bial adj. proverbial.

pro·ver·bio m. proverb, adage ♦ **Proverbios** BIBL. Proverbs.

pro·ve·ye·ra, proveyó see **proveer.**

pro·vi·den·cia f. *(disposición)* measure, provision; LAW judgment, ruling ♦ **Providencia** RELIG. Providence • **tomar providencias** to take measures.

pro·vi·den·cial adj. providential.

pro·vi·den·te adj. *(prevenido)* provident, foresighted; *(prudente)* prudent, cautious.

pro·vie·ne see **provenir.**

pro·vin·cia f. province ♦ **en p.** *or* **provincias** outside the capital, in the provinces.

pro·vin·cia·lis·mo m. provincialism.

pro·vin·cia·no, –na adj. & m.f. provincial.

pro·vi·nie·ra, provino see **provenir.**

pro·vi·sión f. *(acción de proveer)* provision, supplying <*un contrato para p. de agua* a contract for provision of water>; *(surtido)* supply, stock <*reponer la p. de lápices* to replenish the pencil supply>; *(medida)* provision, measure; FIN. funds, cover ♦ **p. de boca** food supply • **p. de fondos** FIN. funds • **provisiones** provisions, supplies.

pro·vi·sio·nal adj. provisional, temporary.

pro·vi·sor m. *(proveedor)* supplier, purveyor; RELIG. vicar general; COL. tin jug.

pro·vi·so·rio, –ria adj. AMER. provisional, temporary.

pro·vis·to, –ta I. past part. see **proveer** II. adj. stocked, supplied III. f. ARG., URUG. provisions, food supplies.

pro·vo·ca·ción f. *(incitación)* provocation, incitement; *(insulto)* irritation, insult; *(desafío)* challenge <*responder a una p.* to respond to a challenge>.

pro·vo·ca·dor, –do·ra I. adj. provoking, provocative <*mirada p.* provocative glance> II. m.f. provoker, inciter.

pro·vo·can·te adj. provocative, provoking.

pro·vo·car §70 tr. *(incitar)* to provoke, incite <*p. con gestos* to provoke with gestures>; *(irritar)* to annoy, anger; *(mover)* to move <*p. a risa* to move someone to laugh>; *(despertar)* to rouse, stir up <*p. a cólera* to rouse someone to fury>; *(causar)* to cause, bring about <*su terquedad provocó la disputa* his obstinacy caused the argument>; *(apetecer)* to tempt <*no me provoca salir de compras* I am not tempted to go shopping>; COLL. *(dar ganas de vomitar)* to make sick, make vomit.

pro·vo·ca·ti·vo, –va adj. *(insultante)* provoking, irritating; *(excitante)* provocative, exciting; *(incitante)* inviting, tempting.

pro·xe·ne·ta m. procurer, pimp —f. procuress.

pro·xe·ne·tis·mo m. procuring, pimping.

pró·xi·ma·men·te adv. *(pronto)* soon, before long; *(aproximadamente)* approximately.

pro·xi·mi·dad f. proximity, nearness.

pró·xi·mo, –ma adj. *(cercano)* near, close <*p. a morir* near death>; *(vecino)* nearby, neighboring <*vivía en la casa p.* he lived in the neighboring house>; *(siguiente)* next <*el año p.* next year> ♦ **p. a** *(al lado de)* near to, close to; *(a punto de)* about to, on the point of.

pro·yec·ción f. *(lanzamiento)* projection; CARTOG., GEOM., PHOTOG. *(imagen)* projection; CINEM. *(función)* screening, showing (of film, slides); FIG. *(influencia)* hold, sway ♦ **p. cónica** conic projection • **p. ortogonal** orthogonal *or* orthographic projection.

pro·yec·tan·te adj. projecting.

pro·yec·tar tr. *(lanzar)* to hurl, throw <*p. una bomba* to throw a bomb>; *(planear)* to plan, be thinking of <*proyecto un viaje a Puerto Rico* I'm planning a trip to Puerto Rico>; ARCHIT., TECH. *(trazar)* to design <*p. una casa* to design a house>; *(hacer visible)* to project, cast (light, image); CINEM., PHOTOG. to show, project (film, slides); GEOM. to project.

pro·yec·til m. projectile, missile ♦ **p. antiaéreo** antiaircraft missile • **p. balístico intercontinental** intercontinental ballistic missile • **p. de avión a avión** air-to-air missile • **p. de avión a tierra** air-to-surface missile • **p. dirigido** *or* **teledirigido** guided missile • **p. guiado** *or* **teleguiado** guided missile.

pro·yec·tis·ta m.f. *(planificador)* planner; *(diseñador)* designer.

pro·yec·to, –ta I. adj. GEOM. projected, in perspective II. m. *(plan)* project, plan; ARCHIT., TECH. *(boceto)* design,

plan; *(bosquejo)* draft <*p. de acuerdo* draft agreement> ♦ **en p.** being planned, in the planning stages • **p. de recomendación** draft recommendation • **p. de resolución** draft resolution; FIN. detailed estimate • **p. experimental** pilot project • **p. de ley** bill, proposed law • **tener proyectos** to have plans.

pro·yec·tor, –to·ra I. adj. projecting II. m. *(reflector)* searchlight; CINEM. projector; OPT. condenser; THEAT. spotlight ♦ **p. cinematográfico** CINEM. motion picture *or* movie projector.

pru·den·cia f. *(cuidado)* prudence, caution; *(juicio)* prudence, wisdom.

pru·den·ciar·se reflex. AMER. to control oneself.

pru·den·te adj. *(cuidadoso)* prudent, cautious; *(juicioso)* prudent, wise.

pru·den·te·men·te adv. *(con cuidado)* prudently, cautiously; *(con juicio)* prudently, wisely.

prue·ba f. *(razón)* proof, evidence; *(indicio)* sign, proof; *(ensayo)* sample; *(examen)* test, examination; FIG. *(dificultad)* trial, ordeal; MATH. proof; PRINT. proof; CHEM. test, experiment; PHOTOG. proof, print; LAW proof, evidence; SPORT. qualifying round; SEW. fitting; TECH. test, trial; COM. trial <*a p.* on trial> ♦ **a p. de** -proof <*a p. de balas* bulletproof> • **a p. de agua** waterproof • **a p. de aire** airtight • **a p. de bomba** bombproof • **poner a p.** to put to the test • **p. de fuego** FIG. acid test • **p. de indicios** LAW circumstantial evidence • **p. negativa** PHOTOG. negative • **p. positiva** PHOTOG. print • **pruebas** *(ejercicios acrobáticos)* acrobatics; *(juego de manos)* sleight of hand.

prue·be, pruebo see **probar.**

pru·ri·to m. MED. pruritus, itching; FIG. *(deseo)* urge, itch.

Pru·sia f. Prussia.

pru·sia·no, –na adj. & m.f. Prussian.

pseu·do adj. pseudo, false.

psi f. psi (Greek letter).

psi·co·a·ná·li·sis m. *or* f. psychoanalysis.

psi·co·a·na·lis·ta m.f. psychoanalyst.

psi·co·a·na·lí·ti·co, –ca adj. psychoanalytical.

psi·co·a·na·li·zar §04 tr. to psychoanalyze.

psi·co·dé·li·co, –ca adj. psychedelic.

psi·co·dra·ma m. psychodrama.

psi·co·lo·gí·a f. psychology.

psi·co·ló·gi·co, –ca adj. psychological.

psi·có·lo·go, –ga I. adj. psychological II. m.f. psychologist.

psi·co·me·trí·a f. psychometrics.

psi·co·neu·ro·sis f. [pl. **–sis**] psychoneurosis.

psi·có·pa·ta m.f. MED. psychopath.

psi·co·pa·tí·a f. psychopathy.

psi·co·pá·ti·co, –ca adj. psychopathic.

psi·co·sis f. [pl. **–sis**] psychosis.

psi·co·te·ra·peu·ta I. adj. psychotherapeutic II. m.f. psychotherapist.

psi·co·te·ra·pia f. psychotherapy.

psi·que *or* **psi·quis** f. psyche.

psi·quí·a·tra *or* **psi·quia·tra** m.f. psychiatrist.

psi·quia·trí·a f. psychiatry.

psí·qui·co, –ca adj. psychic.

pso·ria·sis f. MED. psoriasis.

pto·ma·í·na f. BIOCHEM. ptomaine.

pú·a f. *(punta aguda)* sharp point; BOT. spine, thorn; AGR. graft, cutting (of a tree); ZOOL. quill (of porcupine, hedgehog); *(diente de peine)* tooth (of a comb); *(diente de tenedor)* tine, prong (of a fork); *(ganchito)* barb (of a hook, wire); MUS. *(plectro)* pick, plectrum; *(aguja)* needle (of phonograph); S. AMER. *(espolón)* spur (of fighting cock); FIG., COLL. *(persona)* cunning, crafty person; FIG. *(causa de pesar)* sting (of sorrow, remorse).

pú·ber, –be·ra *or* **pú·be·ro, –ra** I. adj. pubescent, adolescent II. m.f. pubescent youth, adolescent.

pu·ber·tad f. puberty, pubescence.

pu·bes·cen·cia f. pubescence, puberty.

pu·bes·cen·te adj. pubescent.

pu·bis m. [pl. **–bis**] ANAT. *(parte inferior del vientre)* pubes, pubic region; *(hueso)* pubis (bone).

pu·bli·ca·ción f. publication.

pu·bli·ca·dor, –do·ra I. adj. publishing II. m.f. publisher.

pú·bli·ca·men·te adv. publicly.

pu·bli·ca·no m. publican (Roman tax collector).

pu·bli·car §70 tr. *(proclamar)* to proclaim, announce; *(divulgar)* to divulge, disclose; *(poner a la venta)* to publish (a book); *(correr las amonestaciones)* to publish (banns).

pu·bli·ci·dad f. *(calidad de público)* publicity, publicness; *(divulgación de anuncios)* publicity, advertising <*agencia de p.* advertising agency>; *(anuncio)* advertisement; TELEV. commercial ♦ **hacer p. por** to advertise.

pu·bli·cis·ta m.f. *(persona versada en derecho)* expert in public law; COM. publicist, press agent.

pu·bli·ci·ta·rio, –ria adj. advertising, publicity.

pú·bli·co, –ca I. adj. *(patente)* public, known <*es p. que* it is known that>; *(no privado)* public, open <*vía p.* public thoroughfare>; *(del pueblo)* general, common <*el bien p.* the common good> ♦ **hacer p.** *(anunciar)* to make public, disclose; *(publicar)* to publish II. m. *(pueblo)* public <*aviso al p.* notice to the public>; *(auditorio)* audience, public; SPORT. *(espectadores)* spectators, crowds; TELEV. viewers; *(lectores)* readers, readership ♦ **dar al p.** *(publicar)* to publish (a book); *(presentar)* to present (a theatrical work) • **en p.** in public, publicly • **p. en general** *or* **gran p.** general public.

pu·bli·qué, publique see publicar.

pu·che·ra f. CUL., COLL. stew.

pu·che·ro m. *(vasija)* pot; CUL. stew; FIG., COLL. *(alimento diario)* daily bread; COLL. *(gesto)* pout ♦ **calentar** *or* **hacer cocer el p.** to keep the pot boiling • **ganarse el p.** FIG., COLL. to earn one's daily bread *or* living • **hacer pucheros** COLL. to pout, pucker up one's face.

pu·ches m.pl. *or* f.pl. porridge, mush.

pu·cho m. S. AMER. *(colilla)* cigarette *or* cigar stub; CHILE, MARIT. cable, rope; S. AMER. *(poco)* trifle, bit; CHILE, ECUAD. youngest child (in a family); ARG. leftover, residue.

pu·den·do, –da adj. shameful, indecent ♦ **partes pudendas** private parts.

pu·di·bun·do, –da adj. *(pudoroso)* modest, bashful; *(gazmoñero)* prudish.

pú·di·co, –ca adj. modest, chaste.

pu·dien·te I. adj. rich, wealthy II. m.f. rich *or* wealthy person ♦ **los pudientes** the rich.

pu·die·ra, pudo see poder².

pu·dor m. *(recato)* modesty, shyness; FIG. *(vergüenza)* shame ♦ **sin p.** shameless.

pu·do·ro·so, –sa adj. *(pudibundo)* modest, shy; *(mojigato)* prudish; *(casto)* chaste.

pu·dri·ción f. putrefaction, rot ♦ **p. roja** plant rot.

pu·dri·de·ro m. *(vertedero)* garbage dump; *(para cadáveres)* temporary vault (for corpses).

pu·dri·mien·to m. putrefaction, rotting.

pu·drir §84 tr. *(descomponer)* to rot, putrefy; FIG. *(molestar)* to annoy, harass —reflex. *(descomponerse)* to rot, decay; FIG. *(molestarse)* to be annoyed *or* harassed ♦ **¡ahí te pudras!** FIG., COLL. to hell with you! • **pudrirse de aburrimiento** FIG. to die of boredom, be bored stiff —intr. to be buried, rot.

pue·bla·da f. S. AMER. rebellion, uprising.

pue·ble, pueblo see poblar.

pue·ble·ri·no, –na I. adj. rural, village; FIG. rustic II. m.f. villager.

pue·blo m. *(población)* town, village; *(conjunto de habitantes)* people, population <*el p. del Caribe* the people of the Caribbean>; *(nación)* people, nation <*tomar un sondaje del p.* to poll the nation>; *(gente común)* (the) common *or* working people ♦ **de pueblos** from the country • **p. bajo** (the) common people • **p. de mala muerte** hick town, backwater.

pue·da, puedo see poder².

puen·te m. bridge <*hay que cruzar un p. para llegar* one must cross a bridge in order to get there>; MUS. bridge; MARIT. *(cubierta)* gun deck; *(plataforma de mando)* bridge; DENT. bridge; ARCHIT. crosspiece, transom ♦ **hacer p.** FIG. to take a long weekend • **p. aéreo** airlift • **p. colgante** suspension bridge • **p. de barcas** *or* **de pontones** pontoon bridge • **p. giratorio** swing bridge • **p. levadizo** drawbridge • **p. para peatones** footbridge.

puer·ca I. f. ZOOL. sow; ENTOM. wood louse; MED. scrofula;

(del gozne) eye (of a hinge); FIG., COLL. *(mujer sucia)* slovenly woman II. adj. see **puerco, –ca.**

puer·ca·da f. AMER. mean *or* base action.

puer·ca·men·te adv. *(con suciedad)* dirtily, filthily; *(con bajeza)* basely, contemptibly; *(asquerosamente)* nastily, disgustingly.

puer·co, –ca I. adj. *(sucio)* dirty, filthy; *(bajo)* base, contemptible; *(asqueroso)* nasty, disgusting II. m. see **puerco** —f. see **puerca.**

puer·co I. m. ZOOL. pig, hog; FIG., COLL. *(hombre)* pig, swine ♦ **echar margaritas a los puercos** FIG., COLL. to throw pearls before swine • **p. de mar** porpoise • **p. espín** porcupine • **p. marino** dolphin • **p. montés** *or* **salvaje** wild boar II. adj. see **puerco, –ca.**

pue·ri·cul·tor, –to·ra m.f. person concerned with child care.

pue·ril adj. puerile, childish.

pue·ri·li·dad f. *(calidad de pueril)* puerility, childishness; *(acción o palabra)* childish action *or* remark; FIG. *(bagatela)* trifle.

pue·ril·men·te adv. puerilely, childishly.

pue·rro m. BOT. leek.

puer·ta f. *(portal)* door <*p. principal* front door>; *(armazón)* gate; *(entrada)* doorway, gateway; FIG. *(camino)* gateway, road <*la virtud es p. de la felicidad* virtue is the gateway to happiness>; SPORT. *(meta)* goal ♦ **abrir la p.** FIG. to open the door to • **a las puertas de la muerte** at death's door • **a p. cerrada** behind closed doors • **cerrar la p. a alguien** FIG. to close the door on someone • **dar a alguien con la p. en las narices** to slam the door in someone's face • **de p. en p.** from door to door • **echar las puertas abajo** to knock the door down • **fuera de puertas** out of doors, outside • **p. accesoria** side door • **p. corredera** *or* **corrediza** sliding door • **p. falsa** *or* **excusada** secret *or* false door • **p. giratoria** revolving door • **p. secreta** hidden doorway • **p. trasera** back door • **p. vidriera** *or* **de vidrio** glass door • **tomar la p.** to leave.

puer·ta·ven·ta·na f. French window.

puer·to m. port, harbor <*p. franco* free port>; *(ciudad)* port, seaport; GEOG. mountain pass; FIG. *(amparo)* shelter, refuge ♦ **p. de arribada** *or* **de escala** port of call • **p. de entrada** port of entry • **p. fluvial** river port • **p. marítimo** seaport • **tomar p.** MARIT. to reach port, make port; FIG. *(refugiarse)* to take refuge.

Puerto Príncipe m. Port-au-Prince.

Puerto Rico m. Puerto Rico.

puer·to·rri·que·ño, –na adj. & m.f. Puerto Rican.

pues I. conj. *(ya que)* since, as <*cómpralo, p. a ti te gusta* buy it, since you like it>; *(porque)* because, for <*no pude verlo bien, p. olvidé las gafas* I couldn't see it too well because I forgot my glasses> ♦ **p. que** since, because II. adv. *(en tal caso)* well, all right <*¿no quieres escucharme? ¡p. te arrepentirás!* you don't want to listen to me? well, you'll regret it!>; *(partícula continuativa)* then <*repito, p., que hace bien* I repeat, then, that he's doing the right thing>; *(así)* so <*p., ¿quién te lo dio?* so, who gave it to you?>; *(partícula enfática)* anyhow, well now <*p., como iba diciendo* well now, as I was saying>; *(¿cómo?)* what?; *(sí)* yes <*¿conque te dijo la verdad? p.* so he told you the truth? yes> ♦ **así, p.** therefore, so therefore • **p. bien** well then • **¡p. claro!** of course!, naturally! • **¿p. qué?** so what?, well, what about it? • **sí p.** *or* **p. sí** yes, of course • **¿y p.?** so?, so what? III. interj. certainly!, yes!

pues·ta I. f. ASTRON. setting; ORNITH. laying; *(apuesta)* bet, stake; ARG. tie, draw ♦ **p. del sol** sunset • **p. en escena** THEAT. staging • **p. en marcha** starting, start II. adj. see **puesto, –ta.**

pues·to, –ta I. past part. see poner II. adj. dressed <*bien p.* well dressed> III. m. *(sitio)* place, position; *(tiendecilla)* stall, booth; *(cargo)* post, position, job; *(acaballadero)* stud farm; MIL. post; HUNT. blind; ARG. cattle station ♦ **p. que** since, as —f. see **puesta.**

¡puf! interj. ugh!, yecch!

pú·gil m. *(gladiador)* pugilist; SPORT. boxer, prizefighter.

pu·gi·la·to m. *(pelea)* fistfight, brawl; SPORT. boxing, pugilism; FIG. *(disputa)* dispute, argument.

pu·gi·lis·ta m. SPORT. boxer, prizefighter.

pu·gna f. *(lucha)* fight, battle; *(oposición)* conflict ♦ **estar en p. con** to clash with.

pug·na·ci·dad f. pugnacity, quarrelsomeness.

pug·nar intr. to fight, struggle ♦ **p. por** to struggle to.

pug·naz adj. pugnacious, aggressive.

pu·ja f. *(esfuerzo)* effort, struggle; *(acción de licitar)* bidding; *(licitación)* bid ♦ **sacar de la p. a alguien** FIG., COLL. to beat *or* outstrip someone.

pu·ja·dor, -do·ra m.f. *(en una subasta)* bidder —m. PAN., MUS. drum.

pu·jan·te adj. strong, vigorous.

pu·jan·za f. strength, vigor.

pu·jar tr. *(aumentar)* to raise (a bid) —intr. *(sobrepujar)* to outbid; *(pugnar)* to struggle, strive; *(balbucir)* to grope for words, stammer; *(vacilar)* to hesitate, falter; FIG., COLL. *(llorar)* to pout, be on the verge of tears ♦ **p. para adentro** AMER. to grin and bear it.

pu·ji·do m. AMER. cry, lament.

pu·jo m. MED. tenesmus; FIG. *(gana incontenible)* irrepressible *or* strong urge <*p. de prorrumpir en risa* a strong urge to burst out laughing>; *(ansia)* longing, yearning; COLL. *(intento)* effort, attempt.

pul·cri·tud f. *(esmero)* neatness, tidiness <*vestirse con p.* to dress neatly>; *(cuidado)* care.

pul·cro, -cra adj. *(esmerado)* neat, tidy; *(bello)* beautiful, exquisite; FIG. *(limpio)* clean, decent.

pul·ga f. ENTOM. flea; *(peón)* tiddlywink ♦ **buscarle a alguien las pulgas** FIG., COLL. to pick a fight with someone, taunt someone • **cada uno tiene su modo de matar pulgas** FIG. everyone has his own way of doing things • **estar con** *or* **tener la p. detrás de la oreja** FIG., COLL. to be uneasy, restless • **hacer de una p. un camello** *or* **un elefante** FIG. to make a mountain out of a molehill • **no aguantar** *or* **sufrir pulgas** FIG. to stand for no nonsense • **p. acuática** *or* **de agua** water flea • **p. del mar** beach flea, sand flea • **sacudirse uno las pulgas** FIG., COLL. to take no notice of annoyances *or* irritations • **tener malas pulgas** FIG. to be touchy *or* bad-tempered • **tener pulgas** FIG. to be jumpy, have ants in one's pants.

pul·ga·da f. inch ♦ **no ceder una p.** COLL. not to give an inch.

pul·gar I. adj. thumb <*dedo p.* thumb> II. m. *(dedo)* thumb; *(viña)* shoot (left on vine).

pul·ga·ra·da f. *(papirote)* flick, fillip (with the thumb); *(pizca)* pinch <*una p. de tabaco* a pinch of tobacco>; *(pulgada)* inch.

pul·gue·ra f. *(sitio)* place full of fleas; BOT. fleawort; *(de ballesta)* notch, nick (of a crossbow).

pul·gui·llas f. COLL. touchy *or* irritable person.

pu·li·dez f. polish, neatness.

pu·li·do, -da I. past part. see **pulir** II. adj. *(metal)* polished, buffed; *(pulcro)* neat, trim; *(refinado)* polished, refined.

pu·li·dor, -do·ra I. adj. polishing II. m. *(instrumento)* polisher; *(para los dedos)* finger protector (used in spinning).

pu·li·men·tar tr. to polish, buff.

pu·li·men·to m. polishing, buffing.

pu·lir tr. *(bruñir)* to polish, put a shine *or* gloss on <*p. el mármol* to polish marble>; *(alisar)* to smooth; *(acabar)* to finish off, put the finishing touches on <*p. una obra de arte* to put the final touches on a work of art>; *(adornar)* to adorn, embellish; FIG. *(perfeccionar)* to perfect, polish <*p. el estilo* to polish one's style>; *(civilizar)* to refine, give polish to (a person); COLL. *(robar)* to lift, pinch; *(vender)* to sell off —reflex. *(afinarse)* to become refined, acquire polish; *(ataviarse)* to dress up, deck oneself out.

pul·món m. ANAT. lung ♦ **p. de acero** iron lung • **p. marino** ZOOL. jellyfish.

pul·mo·nar adj. pulmonary.

pul·mo·ní·a f. MED. pneumonia.

pul·pa f. ANAT., BOT., ZOOL. pulp.

pul·pe·jo m. *(parte carnosa)* fleshy part (of the ear or finger); *(del caballo)* bulb (of a horse's hoof).

pul·pe·rí·a f. AMER. grocery store.

pul·pe·ro m. *(tendero)* grocer, storekeeper; *(pescador)* octopus catcher *or* fisher.

púl·pi·to m. RELIG. pulpit.

pul·po m. ZOOL. octopus.

pul·po·so, -sa adj. pulpy, fleshy.

pul·que m. MEX. pulque (fermented drink).

pul·que·rí·a f. MEX. pulque bar.

pul·sa·ción f. *(acción de pulsar)* pulsation; PHYSIOL. pulsation, beat; MED. stroke ♦ **pulsaciones por minuto** words per minute (typing speed).

pul·sa·dor, -do·ra I. adj. pulsating, beating II. m. push button, buzzer.

pul·sar tr. *(tocar)* to play (an instrument); *(apretar)* to press, push (a button); MED. to take the pulse of; FIG. *(sondear)* to sound out, explore —intr. PHYSIOL. to beat, throb.

púl·sar m. ASTRON. pulsar.

pul·se·ar intr. to arm-wrestle.

pul·se·ra f. JEWEL. bracelet; *(de reloj)* watch band; SURG. wrist bandage ♦ **p. de pedida** engagement bracelet.

pul·so m. ANAT. *(latido)* pulse; *(muñeca)* wrist (pulse point); *(fuerza)* strength of wrist; *(seguridad)* steadiness, steady hand; FIG. *(tiento)* prudence, tact; *(cuidado)* caution, care <*obrar con p.* to proceed with caution>; COL., CUBA bracelet ♦ **a p.** with one's bare hands, all by oneself • **de p.** sensible, prudent • **echar un p.** to Indian wrestle • **p. arrítmico** *or* **irregular** irregular pulse • **p. sentado** steady pulse • **sacar a p.** COLL. to succeed against all odds • **tomar el p. a la opinión** to sound out opinion • **tomarle el p. a alguien** to take someone's pulse.

pu·lu·lan·te adj. pullulating.

pu·lu·lar intr. to pullulate, swarm, teem.

pul·ve·ri·za·ción f. *(de sólidos)* pulverization; *(de líquidos)* atomization.

pul·ve·ri·za·dor m. *(que pulveriza)* pulverizer; *(para pintar)* paint sprayer; *(de perfume)* atomizer, spray.

pul·ve·ri·zar §04 tr. *(reducir a polvo)* to pulverize; to atomize, spray <*p. un perfume* to spray perfume>; FIG. *(demolir)* to smash, destroy —reflex. to pulverize, become pulverized.

pu·lla f. *(palabra grosera)* obscenity; *(expresión aguda)* taunt, gibe; COLL. insinuation <*tirar pullas* to make insinuations>; *(crítica mordaz)* cutting remark; COL. machete.

¡pum! interj. bang!, boom!

pu·ma m. ZOOL. puma, American panther.

pu·na f. S. AMER. *(tierra)* puna (high Andean plateau), MED. puna (mountain sickness).

pun·cé, punce see **punzar.**

pun·ción f. SURG. puncture; *(punzada)* stabbing pain.

pun·do·nor m. honor, integrity.

pun·gir §32 tr. *(picar)* to prick; FIG. *(atormentar)* to prick, torment.

pu·ni·ción f. punishment.

pú·ni·co, -ca adj. HIST. Punic, Carthaginian <*guerras púnicas* Punic Wars>.

pu·ni·ti·vo, -va adj. punitive.

pun·ta f. *(extremo agudo)* point, sharp end <*la p. de una lanza* the point of a spear>; *(extremidad)* tip, end <*la p. de la lengua* the tip of the tongue>; *(cima)* top, apex; *(colilla)* butt, stub <*la p. de un cigarrillo* a cigarette butt>; *(clavo)* small nail; *(buril)* graver, stylus; *(sabor)* sharp taste; FIG. *(algo)* streak, touch <*tiene p. de loco* he has a streak of madness>; ZOOL. *(asta)* horn; *(púa)* point, tine (of an antler); GEOG. point, headland; HUNT. *(parada)* point; HER. point; PRINT. bodkin; MIL. point; AMER. *(ganado)* small herd; *(multitud)* lot, group; VEN. snide remark, barb; ARG. source of a river ♦ **a p. de** by means *or* dint of • **a p. de pistola** at gunpoint • **de p. a cabo** from one end to the other • **de p. en blanco** MIL. in full armor; FIG. to the nines • **de puntas** on tiptoe • **estar hasta la p. de los pelos** COLL. to be fed up • **hacer p.** FIG. to lead, go first • **poner los nervios de p.** to put someone's nerves on edge • **p. de diamante** diamond point • **p. de lanza** spearhead • **p. de París** wire nail • **puntas** needlepoint, needlework • **sacar p. a** *(afilar)* to sharpen; *(criticar)* to find fault with • **tener en la p. de la lengua** FIG. to have on the tip of one's tongue.

pun·ta·da f. SEW. *(punto)* stitch; *(agujero)* stitch hole; FIG. *(dolor)* sharp *or* stabbing pain; *(apunte)* note, memo; *(insinuación)* hint ♦ **no dar p.** COLL. to shoot the breeze, to do nothing.

pun·tal m. ARCHIT. *(madero de sostén)* stay, brace; FIG. *(apoyo)* prop, support; *(elemento principal)* foundation, base; MARIT. depth of hold (of a ship); VEN. snack.

pun·ta·pié m. kick *<dar un p.* to kick> ♦ **echar a puntapiés** to kick out.

pun·te·a·do m. MUS. plucking (of a string); *(línea de puntos)* dotted line; *(acción de puntear)* dotting, stippling.

pun·te·ar tr. MUS. to pluck (a string); *(trazar puntos)* to dot, stipple; COM. *(compulsar)* to check (an account) entry by entry; SEW. to stitch, sew; ARG. to lead, march at the front of —intr. MARIT. to tack.

pun·te·o m. MUS. *(cuerdas)* plucking (of strings); COM. *(compulsa)* checking (items in an account).

pun·te·ra I. f. *(de una media)* toe patch (of stocking); *(de calzado)* toecap (of shoe); COLL. *(puntapié)* kick II. adj. see **puntero, –ra.**

pun·te·rí·a f. *(acción)* aiming; *(dirección)* aim; *(destreza)* skill, marksmanship ♦ **afinar la p.** to aim carefully • **dirigir la p. en** or **hacia** to aim at • **tener buena p.** to be a good shot • **tener mala p.** to be a bad shot.

pun·te·ro, –ra I. adj. outstanding (marksman, leader) II. m. *(vara para señalar)* pointer; *(aguja del reloj)* hand (of a clock); *(de cantero)* stonecutter's chisel; *(punzón de hierro)* metal punch; ARG., COL. leading animal. (of a flock) —f. see **puntera.**

pun·tia·gu·do, –da adj. sharp, pointed.

pun·ti·lla f. *(tachuela)* tack; *(encaje)* lace trim; *(puñal)* dagger; *(plumilla)* nib (of pen); CARP. tracing point; VEN. penknife ♦ **andar de** or **en puntillas** to walk on tiptoe, tiptoe • **dar la p.** FIG. *(rematar)* to finish off; TAUR. to give the coup de grâce • **de** or **en puntillas** on tiptoe.

pun·ti·lla·zo m. COLL. kick; TAUR. coup de grâce.

pun·ti·lle·ro m. TAUR. bullfighter who deals the coup de grâce.

pun·ti·llis·mo m. PAINT. pointillism.

pun·ti·llo m. *(punto pequeño)* small dot; *(nimiedad)* punctilio; MUS. dot (on note); *(pundonor)* honor.

pun·ti·llo·so, –sa adj. punctilious.

pun·to m. *(señal pequeña)* point, dot; *(sitio)* point, spot *<el p. de reunión* the meeting point>; *(ocasión)* point, verge *<ellos están a p. de lograrlo* they are on the verge of accomplishing it>; *(momento)* point, moment *<el p. crítico* the critical moment>; *(asunto)* point, matter *<discutieron el p. en detalle* they discussed the matter in detail>; *(cuestión)* question, point *<p. filosófico* philosophical question>; *(pundonor)* point of honor; *(agujero)* hole, adjusting hole *<hay cinco puntos en este cinturón* there are five holes in this belt>; *(hilo corrido)* run (in stockings); GRAM. dot *<el p. de la i* the dot on the i>; period, full stop (G.B.); PRINT. point; ARM. *(mira)* sight; *(piñón)* catch; SEW. *(puntada)* stitch *<p. por encima* overcast stitch>; *(malla)* mesh; SURG. stitch; *(sitio de taxis)* taxi stand; *(unidad de tanteo)* point (in scoring) *<ganar por puntos* to win on points>; MATH. point *<p. decimal* decimal point>; *(de la pluma)* nib (of a pen); MUS. tone, pitch ♦ **al p.** at once, immediately • **a p.** just in time, opportunely • **a p. de** on the verge of, about to • **a p. fijo** for sure, certainly • **bajar de p.** FIG. to decline, go downhill • **calzar muchos puntos** FIG. to know a great deal • **coger puntos** SEW. to pick up stitches, repair runs (in stockings) • **dar en el p.** to hit the nail on the head • **de medio p.** ARCHIT. semicircular • **de p.** knitted *<calcetines de p.* knitted socks> • **de todo p.** entirely, absolutely • **dos puntos** GRAM. colon • **en p.** on the dot, sharp *<llegaron a las dos en p.* they arrived at two on the dot> • **en su p.** done just right • **hacer p.** to knit • **hasta cierto p.** up to a point • **poner los puntos sobre las íes** COLL. to dot one's i's and cross one's t's • **poner p. final a** FIG. to put a stop to • **p. atrás** SEW. backstitch • **p. cardinal** GEOG. cardinal point • **p. de cruz** SEW. cross-stitch • **p. culminante** climax, high point • **p. de admiración** GRAM. exclamation point • **p. de apoyo** MECH. fulcrum • **p. de arranque** starting point • **p. de cadeneta** SEW. chain stitch • **p. de congelación** freezing point • **p. de costado** MED. stitch, sharp pain • **p. de ebullición** boiling point • **p. de fusión** melting point • **p. de honor** point of honor • **p. de inflamabilidad** CHEM., PHYS. flash point • **p. de interrogación** GRAM. question mark • **p. de observación** observation point • **p. de par-**

tida point of departure • **p. de referencia** reference point • **p. de saturación** saturation point • **p. de vista** point of view, viewpoint • **p. final** GRAM. period • **p. muerto** MECH. dead center; AUTO. neutral; FIG. *(estancamiento)* deadlock, stalemate • **p. por p.** point by point, in detail • **puntos suspensivos** GRAM. suspension points • **p. y aparte** new paragraph • **p. y coma** GRAM. semicolon • **subir de p.** to increase, grow; *(calentarse)* to heat up *<la conversación estaba subiendo de p.* the conversation was heating up> • **y p.** COLL. and that's all.

pun·tua·ción f. GRAM. punctuation, punctuation marks; *(acción de marcar puntos)* scoring; *(calificación)* grade, mark.

pun·tual adj. punctual, prompt *<es muy p.* he is very prompt>; *(preciso)* precise, accurate; *(seguro)* sure, certain.

pun·tua·li·dad f. punctuality, promptness; *(precisión)* accuracy, preciseness.

pun·tua·li·zar §04 tr. *(concretar)* to fix, finalize; *(grabar en la memoria)* to fix in one's mind; *(determinar)* to settle, determine; *(referir detalladamente)* to describe in detail, give a detailed account of; *(perfeccionar)* to perfect, put the finishing touches to.

pun·tual·men·te adv. *(con puntualidad)* punctually, promptly; *(punto por punto)* in detail.

pun·tuar §67 tr. GRAM. to punctuate; *(calificar)* to grade, mark —intr. SPORT. to score points.

pun·za·da f. *(dolor agudo)* sharp or stabbing pain; *(herida)* prick, stab; FIG. *(de conciencia)* pang.

pun·zan·te adj. *(que pincha)* pricking, sharp; *(agudo)* sharp, stabbing (pain); FIG. *(mordaz)* sharp, biting.

pun·zar §04 tr. *(pinchar)* to prick, pierce; MACH. *(agujerear)* to punch (a hole); FIG. *(causar dolor)* to cause a sharp pain; *(atormentar)* to torment.

pun·zón m. *(instrumento para abrir agujeros)* punch, boring tool; *(marca)* punch, stamp; *(buril)* burin; *(cuerno)* horn (of a deer).

pu·ña·da f. punch, blow ♦ **dar de puñadas** to punch, to hit with the fists.

pu·ña·do m. *(porción)* handful, fistful; FIG. *(corta cantidad)* handful, a few *<un p. de gente* a handful of people> ♦ **a puñados** by the handful, lots of.

pu·ñal m. dagger, poniard ♦ **poner el p. en el pecho** FIG. to hold a knife at someone's throat.

pu·ña·la·da f. *(golpe)* stab; FIG. *(sentimiento)* blow, shock; *(dolor físico)* stab of pain ♦ **coser a puñaladas a alguien** COLL. to cut someone to pieces.

pu·ñe·ta f. VULG. masturbation ♦ **¡puñeta!** or **¡qué p.!** hell!, damnation! • **hacer la p.** COLL. *(fastidiar)* to get on someone's nerves, annoy someone; *(estropearlo todo)* to mess things up for someone • **hacer puñetas** VULG. to masturbate • **mandar a alguien a hacer puñetas** COLL. to tell someone to go to hell • **ser la p.** COLL. to be a drag or a bore.

pu·ñe·ta·zo m. punch, blow ♦ **a puñetazos** with one's fists • **dar a alguien de puñetazos** to punch someone • **dar puñetazos en** to pound or hammer on.

pu·ñe·te·rí·a f. COLL. *(menudencia)* trifle; *(molestia)* bother, annoyance.

pu·ñe·te·ro, –ra adj. COLL. *(molesto)* rotten, lousy; *(difícil)* rough, tough; *(malintencionado)* mean.

pu·ñe·te m. *(golpe)* punch, blow; *(pulsera)* bracelet, wristband.

pu·ño m. *(mano cerrada)* fist; *(puñado)* fistful; SEW. cuff, wristband; *(mango)* handle, belt ♦ **apretar los puños** to clench one's fists • **de propio p.** or **de p. y letra de uno** by one's own hand • **meter a alguien en un p.** FIG., COLL. to intimidate someone • **puños** FIG. courage, valor.

pu·pa f. *(en los labios)* cold sore; *(postilla)* scab; *(daño)* harm, hurt (in baby language) ♦ **hacer p. a alguien** to hurt someone.

pu·pi·la f. ANAT. pupil ♦ **tener p.** COLL. to be sharp —m.f. see **pupilo, –la.**

pu·pi·la·je m. *(condición de pupilo)* pupilage, wardship; *(tutela)* tutelage, guardianship; *(casa de huéspedes)* boarding house; *(pago)* fee, board.

pu·pi·lo, –la m.f. *(estudiante)* student (at a boarding school); *(sujeto de un guardián)* ward, pupil; *(huésped)* boarder ♦ **casa de p.** boarding house • **medio pupilo** *(huésped)* boarder who takes only midday meal; *(estudiante)* student who eats lunch at school —f. see **pupila.**

pu·pi·tre m. writing desk.

pu·ra·men·te adv. *(con pureza)* purely, chastely; *(únicamente)* purely, simply.

pu·ré m. [pl. **-rés**] CUL. *(pasta)* purée; *(sopa)* soup <*p. de guisantes* pea soup>.

pu·re·za f. *(calidad de puro)* purity, pureness; FIG. *(castidad)* chastity, virginity; *(inocencia)* innocence.

pur·ga f. *(medicina)* purgative, purge; FIG. *(eliminación)* purge, liquidation (esp. of political opponents).

pur·ga·ción f. *(acción de purgar)* purging, purge; *(purificación)* purification, cleansing; *(expiación)* expiation, atonement; *(menstruación)* period ♦ **purgaciones** COLL. clap, gonorrhea.

pur·ga·mien·to m. var. of **purgación.**

pur·gan·te I. adj. purgative II. m. purgative, laxative.

pur·gar §47 tr. *(eliminar)* to purge, eliminate; *(limpiar)* to cleanse, clean; *(purificar)* to purify; *(a un enfermo)* to purge (a patient); *(expiar)* to expiate, atone; LAW *(desvanecer indicios o sospecha)* to clear oneself of (suspicion); MECH. to drain *or* vent; FIG. to purge, liquidate (a political opponent) —intr. *(pagar un delito)* to pay for one's guilt by serving a prison sentence; RELIG. to suffer in Purgatory —reflex. to take a purgative.

pur·ga·to·rio m. RELIG. Purgatory; FIG. purgatory.

pu·ri·fi·ca·ción f. *(depuración)* purification, purifying; RELIG. purification (of the chalice).

pu·ri·fi·ca·dor, –do·ra I. adj. purifying II. m.f. *(persona que purifica)* purifier —m. RELIG. purificator (cloth).

pu·ri·fi·car §70 tr. *(quitar lo extraño)* to purify; *(limpiar)* to cleanse —intr. to become purified.

Pu·rí·si·ma f. RELIG. the Immaculate Conception ♦ **la P.** the Virgin Mary.

pu·ris·mo m. purism.

pu·ris·ta adj. & m.f. purist.

pu·ri·ta·nis·mo m. RELIG. Puritanism; *(rigorismo)* puritanism, strictness.

pu·ri·ta·no, –na I. adj. RELIG. Puritan; *(estricto)* puritan, puritanical II. m.f. RELIG. Puritan; *(estricto)* puritan.

pu·ro, –ra I. adj. *(sin mezcla)* pure <*oro p.* pure gold>; *(no aguado)* unadulterated <*vino p.* unadulterated wine>; *(casto)* pure, chaste <*joven p.* chaste young woman>; *(incorrupto)* pure, disinterested <*motivo p.* pure motive>; *(despejado)* clear <*cielo p.* clear sky>; *(mero)* sheer, mere <*por p. casualidad* by mere chance>; *(simple)* plain, absolute <*la p. verdad* the absolute truth>; GRAM., LIT. *(correcto)* pure, correct <*estilo p.* pure style>; *(solo)* neat, straight (alcoholic drink); AMER. *(solamente)* only, just <*me queda una p. ración* I have only one ration left> ♦ **a p.** by dint of, by means of • **de p.** out of sheer <*de puro cansado* out of sheer tiredness> II. m. cigar.

púr·pu·ra f. ZOOL. purple (mollusk); *(color)* purple; *(colorante)* purple dye; *(tela)* purple cloth; *(rango)* purple (rank); POET. *(sangre)* blood; MED. purpura.

pur·pú·re·o, –a adj. purple, purple-colored.

pu·ru·len·to, –ta adj. MED. purulent.

pus m. MED. pus.

pu·sie·ra, puso see **poner.**

pu·si·lá·ni·me adj. pusillanimous, faint-hearted.

pu·si·la·ni·mi·dad f. pusillanimity, faint-heartedness.

pús·tu·la f. MED. pustule.

pus·tu·lo·so, –sa adj. MED. pustular, pustulous; *(barroso)* pimply <*cara p.* pimply face>.

pu·ta I. f. VULG. prostitute, whore, streetwalker II. adj. see **puto, –ta.**

pu·ta·da f. COLL. dirty trick.

pu·ta·ti·vo, –va adj. putative, supposed.

pu·te·ar COLL. intr. *(ser prostituta)* to whore, be a prostitute; *(ir con prostitutas)* to go whoring; *(solicitar)* to solicit sexual acts —tr. *(molestar)* to annoy *or* pester.

pu·te·o m. whoring (around); *(molestia)* annoyance, bother.

pu·te·rí·a f. COLL. *(prostitución)* prostitution; *(coquetería)* coquetry; *(provocación)* sexual provocation.

pu·te·río m. COLL. *(grupo)* group of whores; *(prostitución)* prostitution.

pu·te·ro adj. COLL. whoring, debauched.

pu·to, –ta COLL. I. adj. *(fastidioso)* annoying, bothersome; *(malo)* bad, mean; *(astuto)* astute, smart II. m. *(cabrón)* bugger; *(prostituto)* hustler; *(homosexual)* homosexual —f. see **puta.**

pu·tón, –to·na m.f. COLL. cheap whore.

pu·tre·fac·ción f. putrefaction, rotting.

pu·tre·fac·to, –ta adj. rotten, putrid.

pú·tri·do, –da adj. putrid, rotten.

pu·ya f. TAUR. steel point, goad (of a lance); FIG. *(pulla)* dig, gibe; PAN. machete.

pu·yar tr. AMER. to jab *or* goad with a sharp point; C. AMER. to annoy *or* irritate —intr. CHILE, SALV. to work hard; VEN. to sprout (a vegetable).

pu·ya·zo m. TAUR. blow *or* jab with the lance; FIG. *(puya)* gibe, cutting remark.

Q

q, Q f. twentieth letter of the Spanish alphabet.

quan·tum m. [pl. **-ta**] PHYS. quantum ♦ **q. de luz** PHYS. light quantum • **teoría de los quanta** quantum theory.

que §G16, 17, 42, 46 I. rel. pron. that, which <*el coche q. compraron es azul* the car that they bought is blue> <*el libro, q. todavía no he leído, es un gran éxito* the book, which I haven't read yet, is a great success>; who <*los niños, q. jugaban afuera, no vieron nada* the children, who were playing outside, saw nothing>; whom <*los amigos con q. cuento* the friends on whom I am relying> ♦ **el q.** he who, the one who <*el q. se quedó no sabía nada* the one who remained knew nothing>; the one that <*el q. busco es azul* the one that I am looking for is blue> • **la q.** she who, the one who <*¿es ella la q. lo tiene?* is she the one who has it?>; the one that <*ésta es la q. necesito* this is the one that I need> • **las q.** *or* **los q.** those who, the ones who <*soy de los q. lo creen* I am among those who believe it>; the ones that <*¿dónde están los q. compraste?* where are the ones that you bought?> • **lo q.** which <*murió joven, lo q. no le permitió alcanzar fama* he died young, which did not allow him to achieve fame>; what <*no entiendo lo q. dices* I don't understand what you're saying> II. conj. that <*me escribieron que venían* they wrote to me that they were coming>; than <*yo sé más q. tú* I know more than you>; *(porque)* because, since; that <*habla tan rápido q. no lo comprendemos* he speaks so fast that we do not understand him>; and <*justicia pido, q. no gracia* I ask for justice, and not forgiveness>; *(si)* whether <*q. quiera, q. no quiera, lo tiene que hacer* whether he wants to or not, he has to do it>; that <*te pido que salgas* I ask that you leave>; and <*uno habla q. habla pero ella nunca escucha* one talks and talks but she never listens>; [not translated] <*hay mucho q. hacer* there is a lot to do> ♦ **a q.** I bet that • **uno q. otro** one or the other • **yo q. tú** if I were you.

qué §G43 I. adj. which <*¿q. libros necesitan ustedes?* which books do you need?>; what <*¡q. tiempo hace!* what nice weather we're having!> II. pron. what <*¿q. quieres?* what do you want?> III. adv. how <*¡q. precioso!* how lovely!> ♦ **¡a mí q.!** so what!, what is it to me! • **no hay de q.** you're welcome, don't mention it • **¿para q.?** what for? • **¿por q.?** why? • **q. de** *(cuantos)* how many <*¡q. de desgracias sufrieron!* how many misfortunes they suffered!>; what of, what about <*¿y q. de María?* and what about Mary?> • **¡q. hay!** *or* **¿q. tal?** how goes it? • **¿q. pasa?** what's the matter? • **¡q. va!** nonsense!, come on! • **un no sé q.** a certain something • **¿y q.?** so what?

que·bra·cho m. BOT. quebracho.

que·bra·da f. *(desfiladero)* ravine, gorge; *(hendedura)* crack, gap (in the earth); AMER. stream, brook.

que·bra·de·ro m. breaker, splitter ♦ **q. de cabeza** FIG., COLL. headache, pain in the neck.

que·bra·di·zo, –za adj. *(frágil)* brittle, fragile; FIG. *(de salud)* frail, sickly; *(la voz)* cracked; MUS. trilled, trilling; *(quisquilloso)* touchy, sensitive.

que·bra·do, –da I. past part. see **quebrar** II. adj. *(roto)* broken; *(en quiebra)* bankrupt; FIG. *(debilitado)* weak, weakened; *(pálido)* pale, faded; GEOG. rough, uneven (terrain); MED. ruptured, herniated; CUBA full of holes (a tobacco leaf) **III.** m.f. *(en quiebra)* bankrupt person; MED. person with a hernia —m. MATH. fraction; CUBA., MARIT. navigable passage between two reefs ♦ **q. compuesto** compound fraction • **q. decimal** decimal fraction.

que·bra·dor, –do·ra I. adj. breaking **II.** m.f. breaker.

que·bra·du·ra f. *(grieta)* crack, fissure; *(rotura)* break, fracture; MED. *(hernia)* rupture; *(fractura)* fracture.

que·bra·jar tr. to crack.

que·bran·ta·dor, –do·ra I. adj. *(rompedor)* breaking; *(hendedor)* splitting, cracking; *(machacador)* crushing, smashing; FIG. *(debilitante)* weakening **II.** m.f. *(que rompe)* breaker; FIG. *(violador)* offender, violator —m. crusher, crushing machine.

que·bran·ta·mien·to m. *or* **que·bran·ta·du·ra** f. *(rompimiento)* breaking; *(hendimiento)* splitting, cracking; *(acción de machacar)* crushing, smashing; FIG. *(debilitación)* weakening, deterioration; *(violación)* breaking, violation; *(agotamiento)* exhaustion.

que·bran·tar tr. *(romper)* to break <*q. un hueso* to break a bone>; *(hender)* to split, crack; *(machacar)* to crush, smash; FIG. *(forzar)* to force, break <*q. la voluntad de alguien* to break someone's will>; *(debilitar)* to weaken; *(violar)* to break, violate (a law); *(profanar)* to desecrate, defile; *(suavizar)* to tone down (color); *(templar)* to make tepid; *(desanimar)* to lower, crush (spirits); *(molestar)* to annoy, bother; *(mover a lástima)* to move to pity; LAW. to annul, revoke; AMER., EQUIT. to break in (a horse) ♦ **q. la salud** to ruin one's health —reflex. *(romperse)* to break; *(henderse)* to crack, split; FIG. *(perder la salud)* to ruin one's health; *(desanimarse)* to be crushed (in spirit).

que·bran·to m. *(acción de quebrantar)* breaking; FIG. *(agotamiento)* exhaustion; *(debilitación)* weakening, deterioration; *(conmiseración)* commiseration, sympathy; *(pérdida)* loss; *(aflicción)* affliction, sorrow ♦ **q. de fortuna** financial setback.

que·brar §49 tr. *(romper)* to break <*q. un vaso* to break a glass>; *(torcer)* to bend, twist (the body); FIG. *(vencer)* to overcome; *(interrumpir)* to interrupt; *(suavizar)* to soften, tone down (color); *(deslustrar)* to fade (the complexion); ARG., EQUIT. to break in (a horse) —intr. *(debilitar)* to weaken; to break off *or* up <*q. con el novio* to break up with one's boyfriend>; COM. to go bankrupt, fail (a company) —reflex. *(romperse)* to break, be broken; *(hacerse una hernia)* to rupture oneself, get a hernia; FIG. *(ceder moralmente)* to be broken *or* crushed (in spirit); *(deslustrarse)* to become faded (the complexion); ARG. to bend, twist.

que·chu·a *or* **qui·chu·a I.** adj. Quechua, Quechuan **II.** m.f. Quechua (Indian) —m. *(idioma)* Quechua.

que·chuis·mo m. word of Quechuan origin.

que·da f. curfew ♦ **toque de q.** curfew bell *or* signal.

que·da·men·te adv. calmly, softly.

que·dar intr. *(permanecer)* to remain, stay <*el hombre quedó atrás* the man stayed behind>; *(estar)* to be <*el teatro queda muy lejos* the theater is very far away>; *(restar)* to be left <*me quedan cinco dólares* I have five dollars left>; *(acabar)* to be, end up <*quedamos conformes* we are in agreement>; MATH. to be left, leave <*si se quita seis de quince, quedan nueve* six from fifteen leaves nine> ♦ **¿en qué quedamos?** what have we decided?, what shall we do? • **q. atrás** to be left behind; *(no comprender)* to be left behind, not to understand • **q. bien** *(salir bien)* to come out well; FIG. to look good <*ese vestido te queda bien* that dress looks good on you> • **q. en** to agree • **q. mal** to come out badly • **q. por** *(ser considerado como)* to be regarded as <*quedó por valiente* he was regarded as brave>; to remain to be <*el contrato queda por firmar* the contract remains to be signed> —reflex. *(permanecer)* to remain, stay; *(estar)* to be <*se quedó perplejo* he was perplexed>; to become <*quedarse sordo* to become deaf>; *(restar)* to be left <*se quedaron diez libros sin vender* ten books were left unsold>; MARIT., METEOROL. to abate, slacken ♦ **quedarse con** to keep, retain • **quedarse sin** to run out of • **quedarse para vestir santos** COLL. to be an old maid.

que·do, –da I. adj. still, calm **II.** adv. low, softly (voice).

que·ha·ce·res m.pl. chores, tasks.

que·ja f. *(lamento)* moan, groan; *(resentimiento)* grudge; LAW complaint, protest <*presentar una q.* to lodge a complaint>.

que·jar·se reflex. *(gemir)* to moan, groan; *(lamentarse)* to whine, complain ♦ **quejarse de** to complain about.

que·ji·do m. whine, moan, groan ♦ **dar quejidos** to groan.

que·ji·tas m.f. [pl. **-tas**] GUAT., COLL. whiner, complainer.

que·jón, –jo·na adj. querulous, whining.

que·jo·so, –sa adj. annoyed, complaining.

que·jum·bro·so, –sa adj. grumbling, complaining.

que·ma f. *(accion de quemar)* burning; *(incendio)* fire, conflagration; *(liquidación)* clearance sale ♦ **huir de la q.** FIG. to run from danger.

que·ma·de·ro m. *(poste)* stake (for execution); *(incinerador)* incinerator.

que·ma·do, –da I. past part. see **quemar II.** adj. burned, burnt; FIG. *(resentido)* embittered, resentful; *(agotado)* burned out ♦ **q. por el sol** sunburned, sunburnt **III.** m. *(monte)* scorched brushwood; ECUAD. spiked punch.

que·ma·dor, –do·ra I. adj. burning; *(incendiario)* incendiary **II.** m.f. *(incendiario)* arsonist, incendiary —m. *(mechero)* burner <*q. de gas* gas burner>.

que·ma·du·ra f. burn.

que·mar tr. *(arder)* to burn; *(incendiar)* to set on fire, set fire to; *(consumir con fuego)* to burn (up); *(destruir con fuego)* to burn (down); *(chamuscar)* to scorch; *(escaldar)* to scald; *(calentar mucho)* to heat up, make hot; *(secar)* to blight, burn (plants); *(picar)* to burn, sting; *(destilar)* to distill (wine); FIG. *(malbaratar)* to sell cheaply; *(fundir)* to burn out, blow (a fuse); FIG., COLL. *(impacientar)* to annoy, irritate; C. AMER., MEX. to denounce, inform on; CUBA to swindle, cheat; VEN., MEX. to shoot ♦ **q. balas** *or* **cartuchos** to fire shots • **q. las naves** FIG. to burn one's bridges behind one —intr. *(arder)* to burn; *(estar muy caliente)* to be burning hot; *(broncear)* to tan, get tanned —reflex. *(arderse)* to burn, be *or* get burned; to burn oneself <*se quemó con la plancha* she burned herself on the iron>; *(consumir con fuego)* to burn (up); *(destruirse)* to burn (down); *(sentir calor)* to feel hot; *(abrasarse las plantas)* to be blighted *or* burned (plants); *(broncearse)* to get a tan; *(fundirse)* to burn out, blow (a fuse); FIG., COLL. *(estar cerca de encontrar)* to be warm *or* hot (in a game); ARG., CUBA to get depressed; DOM. REP. to get drunk; PERU to step on excrement ♦ **quemarse con** *or* **por algo** FIG. to get annoyed over *or* by something • **quemarse las pestañas** FIG. to burn the midnight oil.

que·ma·rro·pa ♦ **a q.** at pointblank range.

que·ma·zón f. *(quema)* burning; *(calor)* intense heat; FIG., COLL. *(comezón)* itch, itching; *(palabra picante)* cutting remark; *(molestia)* pique, annoyance; ARG. mirage.

que·na f. AMER. Peruvian reed flute.

que·pis m. [pl. **-pis**] MIL. kepi.

que·que m. AMER. cake.

que·re·lla f. *(queja)* complaint, lament; *(disputa)* dispute, quarrel; LAW complaint.

que·re·lla·dor, –do·ra LAW **I.** adj. complaining **II.** m.f. complainant, plaintiff.

que·re·llan·te LAW **I.** adj. complaining **II.** m.f. complainant, plaintiff.

que·rre·llar·se reflex. LAW to lodge a complaint.

que·re·llo·so, –sa I. adj. *(quejica)* querulous; LAW complaining **II.** m.f. LAW complainant, plaintiff.

que·ren·cia f. *(acción de querer)* affection, fondness; *(instinto de los animales)* homing instinct; *(guarida)* den, lair; *(nido)* nest, roost; COLL. *(hogar)* home, nest; TAUR. bull's favorite spot in the ring.

que·ren·cio·so, –sa adj. homing (said of animals).

que·ren·dón, –do·na I. adj. AMER. loving, affectionate **II.** m.f. COLL. darling, sweetheart.

que·rer¹ m. love, affection.

que·rer² §55 tr. *(desear)* to want, desire <*¿quieres otra taza de té?* do you want another cup of tea?>; *(amar)* to love <*te quiero* I love you>; *(resolver)* to want <*quiero subir a la cima* I want to climb to the top>; *(requerir)* to require, need ♦ **como quien no quiere la cosa** offhandedly, casually • **como quiera que** *(de cualquier modo)* however, in whatever way; *(dado que)* since, as • **cuando quiera** at any time • **no q.** to refuse <*no quiso cooperar* he refused to cooperate> • **¿qué más quieres?** COLL. what more do you want? • **q. decir** to mean, signify • **q. es poder** FIG. where there's a will, there's a way • **q. más** to prefer • **quiera que no** like it or not • **sin q.** *(sin intención)* unintentionally; *(por acaso)* by chance —intr. to look as if it is going to <*quiere nevar* it looks as if it is going to snow>.

que·ri·do, –da I. past part. see **querer[2] II.** adj. dear, beloved **III.** f. *(amante)* lover —m.f. COLL. *(amor)* darling, dear <*q. mío* my dear>.

quer·mes m. ENTOM., PHARM. kermes.

que·ro·se·no m. kerosene.

que·rrá, querría see **querer[2].**

que·ru·bín m. cherubim.

que·sa·di·lla f. CUL. *(pastel)* cheesecake; AMER. cornmeal pie filled with cheese.

que·se·ra f. *(fábrica)* cheese factory; *(hacedora)* cheese maker; *(vendedora)* cheese seller; *(molde)* cheese mold; *(plato)* cheese tray.

que·se·rí·a f. cheese store, dairy.

que·se·ro m. *(hacedor)* cheese maker; *(vendedor)* cheese seller.

que·so m. CUL. cheese ♦ **dársela con q. a alguien** FIG., COLL. to put one over on someone, take someone in • **medio q.** SEW. tailor's ironing board • **q. de cerdo** CUL. head cheese • **q. de nata** CUL. cream cheese • **q. fresco** CUL. cottage cheese.

quet·zal m. ORNITH. quetzal; FIN. quetzal (currency of Guatemala).

¡quia! interj. COLL. no kidding!, you don't say!

qui·cial f. *(madero)* hinge pole; *(quicio)* pivot hole.

qui·cio m. pivot hole (of a hinge) ♦ **estar fuera de q.** FIG., COLL. *(una persona)* to be beside oneself; *(una cosa)* to be out of joint, be off kilter • **sacar de q.** FIG., COLL. *(a una persona)* to infuriate, exasperate; *(a una cosa)* to put out of joint or kilter.

qui·ché adj. & m. Quiché (people, language).

qui·chua adj. & m.f. var. of **quechua.**

qui·chuis·mo m. var. of **quechuismo.**

quid m. gist, crux.

quie·bra f. *(rotura)* break, rupture; *(en la tierra)* crack, fissure; *(pérdida)* loss, damage; COM. bankruptcy; *(riesgo)* risk, hazard.

quie·bre, quiebro see **quebrar.**

quie·bro m. *(ademán)* dodge, feint; TAUR. dodge; MUS. trill.

quien §G42 pron. [pl. **quie·nes**] who <*los jefes, quienes estaban ausentes, tenían la información necesaria* the managers, who were absent, had the necessary information>; whom <*la chica de q. hablo se llama Isabel* the girl of whom I am speaking is named Elizabeth>; whomever, he or she who <*q. mal anda mal acaba* whoever lies down with dogs gets up with fleas>.

quién §G43 pron. [pl. **quié·nes**] who <*¿q. es ese chico?* who is that boy?>; whom <*no sé de q. hablas* I do not know of whom you are speaking> ♦ **de q. o de quiénes** whose <*¿de q. es ese libro?* whose book is that?>.

quien·quie·ra pron. [pl. **quie·nes·quie·ra**] whoever, whomever <*q. que sea* whoever it is>.

quie·ra, quiero see **querer[2].**

quie·to, –ta adj. *(inmóvil)* motionless, still; FIG. *(sosegado)* calm, quiet.

quie·tud f. *(inmovilidad)* immobility, motionlessness; FIG. *(sosiego)* calm, tranquility.

qui·ja·da f. ANAT. jawbone, jaw.

qui·jo·ta·da f. quixotism, quixotic action.

qui·jo·te[1] m. *(de la armadura)* cuisse (armor); *(del caballo)* horse's rump or croup.

qui·jo·te[2] m. FIG., LIT. Don Quixote (impractical idealist).

qui·jo·te·rí·a f. quixotism, quixotic nature or action.

qui·jo·tes·co, –ca adj. quixotic.

qui·jo·tis·mo m. *(caballerosidad exagerada)* exaggerated chivalry; *(vanidad ridícula)* ridiculous vanity.

qui·la·te m. JEWEL. carat, karat; FIG. *(excelencia)* excellence, value <*de muchos quilates* of great value>.

quil·ma f. large sack or bag.

qui·lo[1] m. PHYSIOL. chyle ♦ **sudar el q.** FIG., COLL. to sweat blood (work hard).

qui·lo[2] m. kilo, kilogram.

qui·lom·bo m. VEN. hut, shanty; ARG., CHILE, URUG. brothel ♦ **quilombos** VEN., COLL. boondocks.

qui·lla f. MARIT. keel; ORNITH. breastbone, keel ♦ **dar de q.** MARIT. to keel (over).

qui·llay m. ARG., CHILE, BOT. soapbark tree.

qui·llo·tra f. COLL. honey, sweetheart.

qui·llo·trar COLL. tr. *(excitar)* to excite, stimulate; *(cautivar)* to charm, captivate; *(meditar)* to think over, ponder —reflex. *(enamorarse)* to fall in love; *(ataviarse)* to dress up, adorn oneself; *(quejarse)* to complain.

qui·llo·tro m. COLL. *(estímulo)* stimulus, incitement; *(indicio)* sign, symptom; *(enamoramiento)* love affair; *(requiebro)* compliment, sweet nothing; *(amigo)* friend, pal.

quim·ba f. AMER. *(contoneo al andar)* swaying (while walking); *(gallardía)* elegance, charm; COL. hurry, haste; COL., ECUAD., VEN. peasant shoe.

quim·bom·bó m. CUBA, VEN., BOT. okra, gumbo.

qui·me·ra f. MYTH. chimera; FIG. *(ilusión)* chimera, illusion; *(riña)* quarrel, argument.

qui·mé·ri·co, –ca adj. chimerical.

quí·mi·ca f. chemistry ♦ **q. analítica** analytic chemistry • **q. atómica** atomic chemistry • **q. biológica** biochemistry • **q. geológica** geochemistry • **q. industrial** industrial chemistry • **q. inorgánica** inorganic chemistry • **q. nuclear** nuclear chemistry • **q. orgánica** organic chemistry.

quí·mi·ca·men·te adv. chemically.

quí·mi·co, –ca I. adj. chemical ♦ **producto** or **sustancia q.** chemical (substance) **II.** m.f. chemist.

qui·mio·te·ra·pia f. MED. chemotherapy.

qui·mo·no m. kimono, Japanese robe.

qui·na[1] f. string of five numbers (in lotto) ♦ **quinas** *(armas)* Portuguese coat of arms; *(en juegos de dados)* double fives (in backgammon).

qui·na[2] f. BOT. cinchona bark; MED. quinine ♦ **más malo que la q.** COLL. terrible, horrible • **tragar q.** SL. to put up with a lot.

quin·ca·lla f. hardware.

quin·ca·lle·rí·a f. hardware store.

quin·ca·lle·ro, –ra m.f. hardware dealer.

quin·ce I. adj. fifteen <*q. soldados* fifteen soldiers>; *(decimoquinto)* fifteenth ♦ **q. días** fortnight **II.** m. fifteen ♦ **dar q. y raya a** to get the better of, be superior to.

quin·ce·na f. *(quince días)* fortnight, fifteen days; *(paga)* fortnightly pay; MUS. fifteenth.

quin·ce·nal adj. fortnightly, biweekly, semimonthly.

quin·ce·nal·men·te adv. every two weeks.

quin·cua·ge·na·rio, –ria I. adj. *(de cincuenta unidades)* having fifty parts; *(de cincuenta años)* fifty years old **II.** m.f. quinquagenarian (fifty-year-old person).

quin·cua·gé·si·mo, –ma adj. & m. fiftieth —f. RELIG. Quinquagesima, Shrove Sunday.

quin·cha f. AMER. wickerwork; CHILE., PERU wall of reeds and adobe.

quin·dé·ci·mo, –ma adj. & m. fifteenth.

quin·go m. AMER. zigzag.

qui·nie·las f.pl. SPORT. betting against the bank (on football and other games), quinellas.

qui·nien·tos, –tas I. adj. five hundred <*q. vacas* five hundred cows>; *(quingentésimo)* five hundredth **II.** m. five hundred.

qui·ni·na f. CHEM. quinine.

qui·no m. BOT. cinchona (tree and bark).

quin·qué m. hurricane or kerosene lamp.

quin·que·nal adj. five-year, quinquennial <*plan q.* five-year plan>.

quin·que·nio m. quinquennium, five-year period.

quin·qui·na f. BOT. cinchona.

quin·ta I. f. *(casa de campo)* villa, country house; MIL. draft, conscription; *(en los naipes)* quint (in cards); MUS. fifth **II.** adj. see **quinto, –ta.**

quin·ta·e·sen·cia f. quintessence.

quin·tal m. quintal, hundredweight ♦ **q. métrico** 100 kilograms.

quin·tar tr. *(sacar uno de cada cinco)* to take one out of every five; MIL. to draft, conscript; AGR. to plow for the fifth time —intr. *(la luna)* to reach the fifth day (said of the moon); *(en un remate)* to raise the bid by one-fifth.

quin·te·rí·a f. farmhouse.

quin·te·to m. MUS. quintet.

quin·ti·lla f. LIT. five-line stanza.

quin·ti·lli·zos, –zas m.f.pl. quintuplets.

quin·til m. quintile.

quin·to, –ta I. adj. fifth II. m. fifth; MIL. recruit, conscript; CHILE, MEX. five-cent coin —f. see **quinta**.

quin·tu·pli·car §70 tr. to quintuple.

quín·tu·plo, –pla I. adj. quintuple, fivefold II. m. quintuple.

quin·za·vo, –va adj & m. fifteenth.

qui·ña·zo m. AMER. collision, crash.

qui·ñón m. (parte) profit share; (tierra) plot of land; PHILIP. unit of land measurement.

quios·co m. kiosk, pavilion ♦ **q. de música** bandstand • **q. de refrescos** refreshment stand • **q. de periódicos** newsstand.

qui·pe m. BOL., ECUAD., PERU bundle, knapsack.

qui·pos m.pl. CHILE, PERU quipus.

qui·qui·ri·quí m. cock-a-doodle-do.

qui·ró·fa·no m. SURG. operating room.

qui·ro·man·cia f. chiromancy, palmistry.

qui·ro·mán·ti·co, –ca I. adj. chiromantic II. m.f. chiromancer.

quir·quin·cho m. AMER., ZOOL. armadillo.

qui·rúr·gi·co, –ca adj. surgical.

qui·si·co·sa f. COLL. puzzle, riddle.

qui·sie·ra, quiso see **querer**[2].

quis·qui·llo·so, –sa I. adj. (melindroso) fussy, finicky; (susceptible) sensitive, touchy II. m.f. (melindroso) fussy or finicky person; (persona susceptible) touchy or sensitive person.

quis·te m. MED., SURG. cyst.

qui·ta f. LAW acquittance, release (from a debt) ♦ **de q. y pon** detachable, removable.

qui·ta·ción f. (salario) wage, salary; (quita) acquittance, release.

qui·ta·es·mal·te m. nail polish remover.

qui·ta·man·chas m.f. [pl. **-chas**] (persona) cleaner, launderer; (producto) stain or spot remover.

qui·ta·mo·tas m.f. [pl. **-tas**] COLL. bootlicker, flatterer.

qui·ta·nie·ves m. [pl. **-ves**] snowplow.

qui·ta·pe·sa·res m. [pl. **-res**] COLL. comfort, solace.

qui·ta·pón m. headstall ornament (for mules) ♦ **de q.** detachable, removable.

qui·tar tr. (apartar) to take away; (hurtar) to rob of; (restar) to subtract, remove; (abrogar) to annul, repeal; (prohibir) to forbid, prohibit; (impedir) to impede, hinder; (librar) to release, free from; (privar) to deprive of; FENC. to parry ♦ **¡quita!** or **¡quite!** nonsense!, don't give me that! • **q. la mesa** to clear the table • **quitarle a uno las palabras de la boca** to take the words out of one's mouth • **sin q. ni poner** accurately, verbatim —reflex. (irse) to leave, withdraw; to take off <se quitó la chaqueta he took off his jacket>; (una mancha) to come out (said of stains) ♦ **quitarse de encima** to get rid of • **quitarse de en medio** to get out of the way • **quitarse el sombrero** to take one's hat off (in admiration).

qui·ta·sol m. parasol, sunshade.

qui·ta·sue·ño m. COLL. headache, worry.

qui·te m. (acción de quitar) removal; TAUR. movement to distract the bull's attention from a bullfighter in danger; (esgrima) parry (in fencing); COL. dodge ♦ **estar al q.** to avert danger in time.

qui·te·ño, –na I. adj. of Quito II. m.f. native of Quito.

Qui·to m. Quito.

qui·trín m. AMER. two-wheeled open carriage.

qui·zá or **qui·zás** adv. maybe, perhaps.

quó·rum m. quorum.

R

r, R f. twenty-first letter of the Spanish alphabet.

ra·ba·di·lla f. ANAT. coccyx, tailbone; COLL. rump, back (of certain animals).

ra·ba·nal m. AGR. radish bed or patch.

ra·ba·ne·ra I. f. (vendedora) radish seller; FIG., COLL. (mujer grosera) coarse or vulgar woman II. adj. see **rabanero, –ra**.

ra·ba·ne·ro, –ra I. adj. FIG., COLL. (vestido) short (skirt); (grosero) coarse, vulgar II. m. radish seller —f. see **rabanera**.

ra·ba·ni·llo m. BOT. wild radish; FIG. (del vino) sourness (of turning wine).

rá·ba·no m. BOT. radish ♦ **me importa un r.** COLL. I couldn't care less • **r. blanco** horseradish • **r. silvestre** wild radish • **tomar el r. por las hojas** FIG., COLL. to be on the wrong track, be completely mistaken.

ra·be·ar intr. to wag the tail (said of animals).

ra·be·o m. wagging of the tail.

ra·bí m. [pl. **-bí·es**] rabbi, rabbin.

ra·bia f. MED., VET. rabies, hydrophobia <contraer r. to contract rabies>; FIG. (enojo) fury, rage BOT. mildew, plant rot ♦ **cogerle r. a alguien** to get furious with someone • **con r.** S. AMER. extremely, tremendously <es necio con r. he's extremely foolish> • **dar r.** to make furious, infuriate • **que da r.** maddening, infuriating <una experiencia que da r. a maddening experience>; maddeningly, infuriatingly <es entremetido que da r. he's maddeningly nosy> • **tenerle r. a alguien** COLL. to have a grudge against someone, have it in for someone.

ra·biar intr. MED., VET. to have rabies; FIG. (encolerizarse) to be furious or angry, rave <r. contra alguien to be furious with someone> ♦ **a r.** FIG. rabid, extreme <un aficionado de béisbol a r. a rabid baseball fan>; rabidly, extremely <ser anticomunista a r. to be extremely anticommunist> • **hacer r. a alguien** to make someone furious • **me gusta a r.** I'm crazy about it • **que rabia** FIG., COLL. like mad or crazy <duele que rabia it hurts like mad> • **r. de dolor** to be in great pain, suffer extreme pain • **r. de hambre** to be dying of hunger, be famished • **r. de sed** to be dying of thirst • **r. por algo** to long for or be dying for something • **r. por hacer algo** to long or be dying to do something.

rá·bi·co, –ca adj. VET. rabid, rabies <el virus r. the rabies virus>.

ra·bi·cor·to, –ta adj. (un animal) short-tailed; FIG., COLL. (una persona) wearing a short skirt.

ra·bie·ta f. COLL. temper fit, tantrum.

ra·bi·lar·go, –ga I. adj. long-tailed II. m. ORNITH. magpie.

ra·bi·llo m. (cola corta) small tail; (para pantalones) strap, tab; BOT. (de una hoja) leaf stalk; (de una fruta) stem (of a fruit); (cizaña) darnel; AGR. mildew spot (on cereals) ♦ **r. del ojo** corner of the eye.

ra·bí·ni·co, –ca adj. rabbinical, rabbinic.

ra·bi·no m. rabbi, rabbin.

ra·bio·sa·men·te adv. angrily, furiously.

ra·bio·so, –sa I. adj. MED., VET. rabid; FIG. (enojado) furious, enraged; (vehemente) frantic, frenzied; FIG., COLL. (un color) loud, garish; (un sabor) hot, spicy ♦ **r. de ira** FIG. foaming at the mouth, furious II. m.f. MED., VET. animal or person with rabies.

ra·bo m. (cola) tail; FIG., COLL. (cosa que cuelga) tail, train; (ángulo) corner <mirar uno con el r. del ojo to look out of the corner of one's eye>; BOT. stalk, stem; C. AMER., FIG. man <viejo r. verde dirty old man> ♦ **faltar aún** or **estar** or **quedar el r. por desollar** FIG. to have the worst yet to come • **ir uno al r. de otro** to follow adoringly at someone's heels • **irse** or **salir con el r. entre las piernas** FIG., COLL. to leave with one's tail between one's legs • **r. de junco** ORNITH. tropical bird • **r. de zorra** BOT. foxtail • **rabos de gallo** METEOROL. cirrus (cloud).

ra·bón, –bo·na I. adj. (que tiene el rabo corto) short-tailed; (que carece de rabo) tailless; VEN. lacking a handle or hilt (said of a knife) II. f. see **rabona**.

ra·bo·na I. f. CHILE, PERU, MIL. camp follower ♦ **hacer r.** COLL. to play hooky II. adj. see **rabón, –bona**.

ra·bo·ne·ar intr. COLL. to play hooky.

ra·bo·se·ar tr. to rumple, muss.

ra·bo·so, –sa adj. ragged, frayed.

ra·bo·ta·da f. COLL. insult, coarse remark.

ra·bo·te·ar tr. to crop or dock the tail of.

ra·bu·do, –da adj. long-tailed or bushy-tailed.

rá·bu·la m. SL. pettifogger, shyster (lawyer).

ra·cial adj. racial.

ra·ci·mar AGR. tr. to pick the remaining grapes from (the vines) —reflex. to form clusters or bunches.

ra·ci·mo m. BOT. raceme; FIG. (conjunto) bunch, cluster.

ra·cio·ci·na·ción f. ratiocination, reasoning.

ra·cio·ci·nio m. (razón) reason; (razonamiento) reasoning, argument.

ra·ción f. (parte) ration, share; (porción) portion, serving; RELIG. prebend ♦ **a r.** stingily, meanly • **poner a media r.** to put on short rations • **r. de hambre** starvation wages • **r. de reserva** MIL. emergency rations.

ra·cio·nal I. adj. rational, reasonable ♦ **número r.** MATH. rational number II. m. HIST., RELIG. rational, breastplate (worn by high priests).

ra·cio·na·li·cé, racionalice see **racionalizar.**

ra·cio·na·li·dad f. rationality.

ra·cio·na·lis·mo m. PHILOS. rationalism.

ra·cio·na·lis·ta PHILOS. I. adj. rationalist, rationalistic II. m.f. rationalist.

ra·cio·na·li·za·ción f. rationalization.

ra·cio·na·li·zar §04 tr. to rationalize.

ra·cio·nal·men·te adv. rationally.

ra·cio·na·mien·to m. rationing.

ra·cio·nar tr. MIL. to supply with rations; (limitar) to ration.

ra·cis·mo m. racism.

ra·cis·ta adj. & m.f. racist.

ra·cha f. MARIT. squall, gust of wind; FIG., COLL. (período de suerte) streak, run (of luck) ♦ **a rachas** FIG. by fits and starts • **tener una buena** or **una mala r.** FIG., COLL. to have a run of good or bad luck.

ra·da f. MARIT. bay, inlet.

ra·dar m. radar ♦ **r. acústico** sound radar.

ra·dia·ción f. PHYS. radiation; RAD. broadcasting ♦ **r. atmosférica** atmospheric radiation • **r. cósmica** cosmic radiation.

ra·diac·ti·vi·dad f. PHYS. radioactivity.

ra·diac·ti·vo, –va adj. PHYS. radioactive.

ra·dia·do, –da I. past part. see **radiar** II. adj. (formado por rayos) radiated; BOT., ZOOL. radiate; RAD. broadcast, transmitted III. m.pl. ♦ **radiados** ZOOL. radiates.

ra·dia·dor m. radiator.

ra·dial adj. GEOM. radial; AUTO. radial <neumático r. radial tire>; ARG., URUG. radio <locutor r. radio announcer.

ra·dian·te adj. PHYS. radiant <calor r. radiant heat>; FIG. (brillante) radiant, shining.

ra·diar intr. to irradiate —tr. PHYS. to radiate; RAD. to broadcast, transmit; MED. to x-ray; CHILE, COL., P. RICO to cross off a list.

ra·di·ca·ción f. (acción de radicar) taking root; FIG. (de un uso) establishment (of a custom); BOT. rootage; MATH. evolution.

ra·di·cal I. adj. (relativo a la raíz) radical, root; (completo) complete, thoroughgoing; BOT., CHEM., MATH., POL. radical II. m.f. POL. radical; —m. CHEM. radical GRAM., MATH. radical, root.

ra·di·ca·lis·mo m. POL. radicalism.

ra·di·cal·men·te adv. radically.

ra·di·car §70 intr. (arraigar) to take root; (estar) to be, be located <el pueblo radica en el estado de Jalisco the town is located in the state of Jalisco>; (habitar) to live, reside —reflex. (arraigarse) to take root; (domiciliarse) to settle, establish oneself.

ra·dio¹ m. GEOM. radius; FIG. radius <en un r. de diez millas within a radius of ten miles>; (rayo) spoke (of a wheel); ANAT. radius; MECH., MIL. range ♦ **r. de acción** operating range • **r. de giro** AUTO. turning radius • **r. vector** GEOM. radius vector.

ra·dio² m. CHEM. radium.

ra·dio³ f. (aparato, medio) radio, wireless; (radiodifusión) broadcasting —m. (aparato) radio, wireless; COLL. (radiotelegrafista) radio operator; (radiotelegrama) radio, wireless message ♦ **por r.** by radio, on or over the radio.

ra·dio·ac·ti·vi·ad f. var. of **radiactividad.**

ra·dio·ac·ti·vo, –va adj. var. of **radiactivo, –va.**

ra·dio·a·fi·cio·na·do, –da m.f. ham radio operator.

ra·dio·am·pli·fi·ca·dor m. radioamplifier.

ra·dio·car·bo·no m. CHEM. radiocarbon.

ra·dio·com·pás m. radiocompass.

ra·dio·di·fun·dir tr. & intr. RAD. to broadcast.

ra·dio·di·fu·sión or **ra·dio·e·mi·sión** f. RAD. broadcasting.

ra·dio·di·fu·so·ra or **ra·dio·e·mi·so·ra** f. RAD. (broadcasting) station.

ra·dio·e·le·men·to m. radioelement.

ra·dio·es·cu·cha m.f. radio listener.

ra·dio·fa·ro m. AVIA., MARIT. radio beacon.

ra·dio·gra·fí·a f. (técnica) radiography; (imagen) x-ray, radiograph.

ra·dio·gra·fiar §30 tr. to x-ray, radiograph.

ra·dio·gra·ma m. radiogram.

ra·dio·lo·ca·li·za·ción f. RAD. radiolocation.

ra·dio·lo·gí·a f. MED. radiology.

ra·dió·lo·go m.f. radiologist.

ra·dio·me·trí·a f. PHYS. radiometry.

ra·dió·me·tro m. radiometer.

ra·dio·na·ve·ga·ción f. AERO, MARIT. radio navigation.

ra·dio·rre·cep·tor m. RAD. receiver, radio set.

ra·dios·co·pia f. radioscopy.

ra·dio·son·da f. METEOROL. radiosonde.

ra·dio·te·le·fo·ní·a f. radiotelephony.

ra·dio·te·le·fó·ni·co, –ca adj. radiotelephonic.

ra·dio·te·lé·fo·no m. radiotelephone.

ra·dio·te·lé·gra·fo m. radiotelegraph.

ra·dio·te·les·co·pio m. ASTRON. radio telescope.

ra·dio·te·ra·pia f. MED. radiotherapy.

ra·dio·trans·mi·sor m. radio transmitter.

ra·dio·yen·te m.f. radio listener.

ra·di·qué, radique see **radicar.**

ra·dón m. CHEM. radon.

ra·e·du·ra f. (acción de raer) scraping; (parte raída) scrapings.

ra·er §56 tr. (raspar) to scrape, shave; (nivelar) to level; FIG. (extirpar) to extirpate, eradicate; COLL. to wear out (clothes).

rá·fa·ga f. (de viento) gust (of wind); (nube pequeña) small cloud; (de luz) flash (of light); (de ametralladora) burst (of machine-gun fire).

ra·glán m. raglan.

ra·gú m. CUL. ragout.

ra·gua f. AGR. top of sugar cane.

raid m. (incursión) raid; (vuelo) long-distance flight.

ra·í·do, –da I. past part. see **raer** II. adj. (usado) worn, threadbare; (desvergonzado) shameless, impudent.

rai·ga, raigo see **raer.**

rai·gam·bre f. BOT. roots, rootage; FIG. (estabilidad) stability, deep-rootedness; (tradición) tradition, custom <de larga r. of long tradition>.

rai·gón m. (raíz grande) thick root; (de un diente) root of a tooth.

rai·mien·to m. (acción de raer) scraping; (parte raída) scrapings.

ra·íz f. [pl. **ra·í·ces**] ANAT., BOT., GRAM., MATH. root; FIG. (origen) root, origin, source ♦ **a r. de** as a result of, immediately after • **bienes raíces** real estate • **cortar de r.** FIG. to nip in the bud, cut out at the root • **de r.** completely, by the root or roots • **echar raíces** BOT. to root, take root; FIG. (instalarse) to settle (down) • **r. cuadrada** square root • **r. cúbica** cube root • **r. entera** integral root • **r. irracional** or **sorda** irrational root • **sacar de r.** FIG. to cut out or pull up at the roots, wipe out.

ra·ja f. (hendidura) crack; (de madero) splinter, chip; (de melón) slice; COST. slit, vent.

ra·já m. [pl. **-ja·es**] rajah (Indian prince).

ra·ja·de·ra f. cleaver.

ra·ja·di·zo, –za adj. easily split or cracked.

ra·ja·do, –da I. past part. see **rajar** II. adj. (hendido) cracked, split; FIG., COLL. (cobarde) chicken, yellow III. m.f. FIG., COLL. chicken, coward.

ra·ja·du·ra f. split, crack.

ra·jar tr. (dividir) to slice, cut into slices <r. una pera to slice a pear>; (hender) to split, crack; (dar cortes) to chop, cut <r. leña to chop wood>; COL., PERU, P. RICO to crush, defeat; ARG., COLL. to fire, dismiss (a worker) —intr. (hablar mucho) to chatter, jabber; FIG., COLL. (jactarse) to brag, boast —reflex. (henderse) to split, crack; FIG. (faltar a su palabra) to go back on one's word, back out; COLL. (acobardarse) to lose one's nerve, chicken out; C. AMER.

to spend lavishly; ARG., BOL., CARIB. to rush or run off; ARG., COL. to be mistaken; P. RICO, COLL. to get drunk.

ra·je·ta f. (tela) coarse multicolored cloth —m.f. COLL. (persona) chicken, coward.

ra·jón m. (rasguño) rip, tear; CUBA, MEX. (cobarde) chicken; C. AMER. braggart.

ra·le·a f. (linaje) breeding, stock; FIG. (clase) kind, sort; HUNT. prey (of birds).

ra·le·ar intr. (una tela) to become thin or worn; AGR. to yield thin bunches of grapes (said of a grapevine); (una persona) to reveal one's true nature.

ra·len·tí m. CINEM. slow motion.

ra·lo, –la adj. (cabello) thin, sparse; (dientes) widely-spaced; (tela) thin, fine; (aire) rare, thin.

ra·lla·dor m. CUL. grater.

ra·lla·du·ra f. (señal) grater mark; (parte rallada) gratings ♦ **ralladuras de pan** or **de queso** grated bread or cheese.

ra·llar tr. CUL. to grate; COLL. (molestar) to grate on, annoy.

ra·llo m. CUL. grater; (lima) file, rasp; (vasija) earthenware jug.

ra·ma f. BOT. branch, bough; FIG. branch <una r. de la física a branch of physics>; PRINT. chase ♦ **andarse por las ramas** FIG., COLL. to wander off the point, digress • **asirse a las ramas** FIG., COLL. to grab at straws, make excuses • **en r.** (sin elaborar) raw, unfinished <lino en r. raw linen>; BKB. in sheets, unbound.

ra·ma·da f. (ramaje) branches (of a tree); (enramada) arbor, grove.

ra·ma·je m. branches (of a tree).

ra·mal m. (cabo) strand (of a cord); (ronzal) halter (to lead an animal); (de escalera) flight (of stairs); FIG. (ramificación) branch; GEOG. branch (of a mountain range); MIN. secondary shaft; RAIL. branch (line) ♦ **r. de trinchera** MIL. secondary or side trench • **ramales** ARG. bolas.

ra·ma·la·zo m. (golpe) lash, blow; (de viento) gust; FIG. (señal) welt, bruise; (dolor) sharp pain; (pesar inesperado) sudden grief.

ram·bla f. (ramblazo) bed of a torrent; (paseo) avenue, boulevard; TEX. tenter; AMER. dock.

ra·me·ra f. prostitute, streetwalker.

ra·mi·fi·ca·ción f. (división en ramas) ramification, branching; FIG. (subdivisión) branch, subdivision; (consecuencia) repercussion, consequence.

ra·mi·fi·car·se §70 reflex. to ramify, branch off or out.

ra·mi·lle·te m. BOT. umbel, cluster; (ramo de flores) bunch, bouquet (of flowers); FIG. (plato de dulces) dessert platter; (adorno) centerpiece; (colección) collection ♦ **r. de Constantinopla** BOT. sweet William.

ra·mi·lle·te·ro, –ra m.f. (persona) florist, flower seller —m. (maceta) vase.

ra·mo m. (rama pequeña) small branch; (rama cortada) cut branch; (ramillete) bunch, bouquet (of flowers); FIG. (subdivisión) branch, sector ♦ **Domingo de Ramos** Palm Sunday • **tener un r. de locura** FIG., COLL. to have a touch or streak of madness.

ra·món m. (para el ganado) foliage used as cattle fodder; (que resulta de la poda) pruned branches.

ra·mo·ne·ar tr. (los árboles) to prune; (los animales) to browse, graze (said of animals).

ra·mo·ne·o m. pruning.

ra·mo·so, –sa adj. ramose, having many branches.

ram·pa f. (plano inclinado) ramp, slope; MED. cramp; BOL. litter bier ♦ **r. de lanzamiento** ASTRONAUT. launching pad.

ram·plón, –plo·na I. adj. (grosero) vulgar, common; (aburrido) dull, dreary <versos ramplones dull poetry> II. m. calk (of a horseshoe).

ram·plo·ne·rí·a f. vulgarity, commonness.

ram·po·llo m. AGR. cutting.

ra·na f. ZOOL. frog ♦ **no ser r.** FIG., COLL. to be nobody's fool • **r. arbórea** or **de zarzal** ZOOL. tree frog • **r. mugidora** or **toro** ZOOL. bullfrog • **salir r.** FIG., COLL. to turn out badly, be a letdown.

ran·ciar tr. to make rancid —reflex. to turn rancid.

ran·ci·dez or **ran·cie·dad** f. rancidity, rancidness.

ran·cio, –cia I. adj. (comida) rancid, stale; FIG. (antiguo) ancient, antique; (anticuado) old-fashioned II. m. (ranci-

dez) rancidity, staleness; (tocino) rancid bacon; (del paño) greasiness (of cloth).

ran·cio·so, –sa adj. rancid, stale.

ran·che·ar intr. to form a settlement —tr. AMER. to loot.

ran·che·ra f. MEX., PERU, VEN. popular song.

ran·che·rí·a f. settlement, camp.

ran·che·ro m. (cocinero) camp cook; (jefe de un rancho) leader of a settlement; (dueño de un rancho) rancher, farmer.

ran·cho m. AMER. (pastizal) ranch; (granja) farm; P. RICO (cobertizo) shed, shelter; PERU country house; (comida) mess, communal meal; (campamento) camp, settlement; (choza) hut, thatched hut; FIG., COLL. (reunión) meeting, gathering; COLL. (comida mala) swill, bad food; MARIT. (provisión) provisions; (alojamiento) crew's quarters; (cuadrilla) work crew; ARG. straw hat ♦ **alborotar el r.** FIG., COLL. to cause trouble • **asentar el r.** COLL. (parar) to stop for a meal or a rest; FIG., COLL. (organizarse) to settle in, get things organized • **hacer r.** COLL. to make room • **hacer r. aparte** FIG. to go one's own way, go off on one's own • **r. de Santa Bárbara** MARIT. rudder trunk.

ran·da f. lace trimming —m. COLL. pickpocket.

ran·go m. (orden) rank, order; (clase) class; (situación social elevada) high social standing; AMER. pomp, splendor; COL. nag, worn-out horse.

ra·nu·ra f. groove, slot.

ra·pa·ce·rí·a f. childish prank.

ra·pa·ci·dad f. rapacity.

ra·pa·dor, –do·ra I. adj. scraping, shaving II. m.f. (raspador) scraper —m. COLL. (rapabarbas) barber.

ra·pa·du·ra f. (afeitada) shave; (corte de pelo) haircut, tonsure; BOL., CUL. caramel custard; ARG., GUAT., HOND. brown sugar.

ra·pa·mien·to m. var. of **rapadura**.

ra·pan·te adj. (que hurta) stealing, snatching; (que afeita) shaving, scraping; HER. rampant.

ra·pa·piés m. [pl. -piés] firecracker.

ra·pa·pol·vo m. COLL. scolding, dressing-down.

ra·par tr. (la barba) to shave; (el pelo) to crop (hair); FIG., COLL. (hurtar) to steal, snatch.

ra·paz, –pa·za I. m. [pl. -pa·ces] boy, youngster —f. girl, youngster ♦ **rapaces** ORNITH. birds of prey, predators II. adj. rapacious, greedy.

ra·pa·za·da f. childish prank.

ra·pe m. (afeitada) quick shave; COLL. (reprensión) scolding, dressing-down; ICHTH. angler, goosefish ♦ **al r.** close-cropped (hair).

ra·pé I. adj. powdered (tobacco) II. m. tobacco powder, snuff.

rá·pi·da·men·te adv. rapidly, quickly.

ra·pi·dez f. rapidity, speed.

rá·pi·do, –da I. adj. rapid, quick II. m. (tren) express train; (en un río) rapids III. adv. quickly ♦ **¡venga r.!** hurry up!

ra·pi·ña f. robbery, rapine ♦ **ave de r.** ORNITH. bird of prey, raptor.

ra·pi·ñar tr. COLL. to rob, steal.

ra·po·sa f. ZOOL. fox, vixen; FIG., COLL. sly fox.

ra·po·se·ar intr. to use wiles, be cunning.

ra·po·su·no, –na adj. vulpine, foxlike.

rap·so·dia f. POET. rhapsody.

rap·tar tr. to abduct, kidnap.

rap·to m. (arrebato) burst, fit (of anger); (delito) kidnaping, abduction; (éxtasis) rapture, ecstasy; MED. faint, swoon.

rap·tor, –to·ra I. adj. kidnaping II. m.f. kidnaper, abductor.

ra·que I. m. beachcombing II. adj. VEN. thin, slender.

ra·que·ar intr. to go beachcombing.

ra·que·ro, –ra I. adj. piratical II. m. (pirata) pirate; (persona que raquea) beachcomber; (ratero de puertas) dock thief.

ra·que·ta f. SPORT. racket; (para la nieve) snowshoe; BOT. hedge mustard, wall rocket; (en casas de juego) croupier's rake.

ra·quí·de·o, –a adj. ANAT. rachidian.

ra·quí·ti·co, –ca I. adj. MED. rachitic; FIG. (exiguo) skimpy, meager II. m.f. MED. rachitic person.

ra·qui·tis·mo m. or **ra·qui·tis** f. MED. rachitis, rickets.

ra·ra·men·te adv. *(rara vez)* rarely, seldom; *(extrañamente)* strangely, oddly.

ra·re·fac·ción f. rarefaction.

ra·re·za f. *(calidad de raro)* rarity, rareness; FIG. *(peculiaridad)* peculiarity, oddity; *(cosa rara)* rare thing.

ra·ro, –ra adj. *(poco común)* rare, uncommon; *(escaso)* rare, scarce; *(extraño)* strange, odd; *(insigne)* notable, outstanding; CHEM. rare, rarefied (gas) ♦ **rara vez** seldom, rarely.

ras m. ♦ **a r. de** level *or* flush with • **lleno a** *or* **al r.** *(un recipiente)* full to the brim; *(una cucharada)* level (teaspoon) • **r. con r.** level, touching • **volar a r. de tierra** to skim the treetops.

ra·sa f. *(en una tela)* thin *or* threadbare patch (in cloth); GEOG. plateau.

ra·sa·du·ra f. *(arrasamiento)* razing, leveling; AGR. strickling.

ra·san·te I. adj. grazing, (just) touching ♦ **tiro r.** ARTIL. low-angle fire ♦ **vuelo r.** AER. low-level flight II. f. *(de un camino)* slope; RAIL. grade ♦ **cambio de r.** brow of a hill.

ra·sar tr. *(rozar)* to brush, graze; *(arrasar)* to raze, level; AGR. to strickle —reflex. to clear up (said of sky).

ras·ca·cie·los m. [pl. **-los**] skyscraper.

ras·ca·de·ra f. *(rascador)* scraper; COLL. *(almohaza)* currycomb.

ras·ca·dor m. *(para rascar)* scraper; *(en el pelo)* hairpin, hair clip; *(para los fósforos)* striking surface (on a matchbox).

ras·ca·du·ra f. *(acción de rascar)* scratching, scraping; *(rasguño)* scratch.

ras·ca·mien·to m. scratching, scraping.

ras·ca·mo·ño m. hairpin, hair clip.

ras·car §70 tr. *(con la uña)* to scratch; *(raspar)* to scrape —intr. to itch —reflex. *(arañarse)* to scratch, scratch oneself; AMER. to get drunk.

ras·ca·zón f. itching, itch.

ras·cón, –co·na I. adj. sharp, tart (taste) II. m. ORNITH. water rail.

ra·se·ro, –ra I. adj. grazing II. m. AGR. leveler, strickle —f. CUL. spatula ♦ **medir por el mismo r.** FIG., COLL. to treat impartially.

ras·ga·do, –da I. past part. see **rasgar** II. adj. *(desgarrado)* ripped, torn; *(boca)* wide (mouth); *(ojos)* almond-shaped (eyes) III. m. rip, tear.

ras·ga·du·ra f. *(acción de rasgar)* ripping, tearing; *(rasgón)* rip, tear.

ras·gar §47 tr. to rip, tear —reflex. AMER. to die.

ras·go m. *(trazo)* stroke, flourish (of a pen); *(carácter)* trait, characteristic; FIG. *(expresión feliz)* flash, stroke <r. generoso stroke of generosity>; *(acción notable)* feat, deed ♦ **a grandes rasgos** FIG. broadly, in broad strokes • **rasgos** features (of the face).

ras·gón m. rip, tear.

ras·gué, rasgue see **rasgar**.

ras·gue·ar tr. MUS. to strum —intr. to make flourishes (with a pen).

ras·gue·o m. MUS. strumming.

ras·gu·ñar tr. *(arañar)* to scratch; PAINT. to sketch an outline.

ras·gu·ño m. *(arañazo)* scratch; PAINT. sketch.

ra·so, –sa I. adj. *(llano)* flat, level; *(el cielo)* clear, cloudless (sky); *(un asiento)* backless (seat); MIL. private <soldado r. private soldier> ♦ **al r.** in the open air • **cielo r.** ceiling II. m. TEX. satin.

ras·pa f. *(de un pescado)* backbone, spine (of a fish); AGR. beard (of corn or wheat); SP. bunch of grapes; AMER., COLL. dressing-down, reprimand; CUBA burnt residue left in a pot; ARG. petty thief.

ras·pa·di·lla f. PERU, CUL. ice chips flavored with syrup.

ras·pa·do I. past part. see **raspar** II. m. scraping.

ras·pa·dor m. scraper, rasp.

ras·pa·du·ra f. *(acción de raspar)* scratching, scraping; *(lo que se raspa)* scrapings; COLL. *(rapadura)* trim, shave; AMER., CUBA brown sugar.

ras·pa·mien·to m. var. of **raspadura**.

ras·pan·te adj. *(vino)* sharp, acrid; *(abrasivo)* abrasive.

ras·par tr. *(raer ligeramente)* to scrape, scratch (off); *(hur-* *tar)* to steal, rob; AMER. to tell off; *(rasar)* to graze, skim —intr. *(vino)* to be sharp *or* harsh; VEN. to leave, go away.

ras·pe·ar intr. *(la pluma)* to scratch (said of a pen) —tr. to scold, reprimand.

ras·pón m. COL. farmer's straw hat; AMER. *(reprimenda)* dressing-down, scolding; *(desolladura)* scratch, graze ♦ **de r.** in passing.

ras·qué, rasque see **rascar**.

ras·que·te·ar tr. *(caballo)* to brush down, curry; ARG. to scrape.

ras·qui·ña f. itching, itch.

ras·tra f. *(señal)* trail, track; *(narria)* drag, dray (low cart); *(cosa arrastrada)* thing being dragged *or* pulled along; *(ristra)* string of dried fruit *or* vegetables; AGR. *(rastrillo)* rake; *(azada)* hoe; *(grada)* harrow; MARIT. drag, dredge; ARG., URUG. decorative buckle of a gaucho's belt ♦ **a rastras** *(arrastrando)* dragging; FIG. *(del mal grado)* unwillingly, by force • **llevar a rastras** to drag *or* pull (along) • **pescar a la r.** to trawl.

ras·tre·a·dor, –do·ra I. adj. *(que sigue el rastro)* tracking, trailing; MARIT. dragging, dredging; MIL. mine-sweeping II. m. *(que sigue el rastro)* tracker; MARIT. dredge, dredger ♦ **r. de minas** MIL. mine sweeper.

ras·tre·ar tr. *(seguir el rastro)* to track, trail; *(pescar)* to trawl; *(vender carne)* to sell in the market (meat); FIG. *(indagar)* to inquire into; MARIT. to drag, dredge; MIL. to sweep (mines) —intr. *(pescar)* to trawl; AVIA. to fly low, skim the ground; AGR. to rake.

ras·tre·o m. *(seguimiento)* tracking, trailing; *(pesca)* trawling; MARIT. dragging, dredging; AGR. raking ♦ **r. de minas** MIL. mine sweeping.

ras·tre·ro, –ra I. adj. *(que va arrastrando)* dragging, trailing; *(animal)* creeping, crawling; FIG. *(bajo)* vile, despicable; BOT. creeping, trailing ♦ **perro r.** tracker (dog) • **tallo r.** BOT. trailing plant II. m. worker in a slaughterhouse.

ras·tri·lla·da f. *(con el rastrillo)* rakings; AMER. track, trail.

ras·tri·lla·do I. past part. see **rastrillar** II. m. AGR., HORT. raking; TEX. combing, hatcheling.

ras·tri·lla·dor, –do·ra I. adj. AGR., HORT. raking; TEX. combing, hatcheling II. m.f. AGR., HORT. raker; TEX. comber, hatcheler.

ras·tri·lla·je m. AGR., HORT. raking; TEX. combing, hatcheling.

ras·tri·llar tr. TEX. to comb, hatchel; AGR., HORT. to rake; COL. *(un tiro)* to fire (a shot); *(un fósforo)* to strike (a match); ARG. to cock (a pistol).

ras·tri·llo m. AGR., HORT. rake; TEX. comb; MIL. portcullis, iron grating; ARTIL. hammer (of a gunlock); MECH. ward (of a lock or key).

ras·tro[1] m. *(pista)* track, trail; *(carnicería)* wholesale meat market; *(matadero)* slaughterhouse; FIG. *(señal)* sign, trace; *(olor)* scent ♦ **Rastro** SP. Madrid flea market.

ras·tro[2] m. AGR., HORT. rake.

ras·tro·jar tr. AGR. to glean, clear of stubble.

ras·tro·jo m. AGR. *(residuo)* stubble; *(campo segado)* stubble field; AMER. scraps, remains.

ra·su·rar tr. *(afeitar)* to shave; *(raer)* to scrape.

ra·ta f. ZOOL. rat —m. FIG., COLL. *(ratero)* pickpocket, thief ♦ **más pobre que una r.** FIG., COLL. as poor as a church mouse II. adj. see **rato, –ta**.

ra·ta·plán m. rat-tat-tat (sound of a drum).

ra·te·ar[1] tr. to steal, pilfer —intr. *(arrastrarse)* to creep, crawl; AUTO. to stall, die.

ra·te·ar[2] tr. to prorate.

ra·te·o m. proration.

ra·te·rí·a f. stealing, pilfering.

ra·te·ro, –ra I. adj. *(ladrón)* thieving; FIG. *(bajo)* base, vile II. m.f. pickpocket, thief.

ra·ti·fi·ca·ción f. ratification, confirmation.

ra·ti·fi·ca·dor, –do·ra I. adj. ratifying II. m.f. ratifier.

ra·ti·fi·car §70 tr. to ratify, confirm.

ra·ti·fi·ca·to·rio, –ria adj. ratifying, confirming.

ra·to I. m. short time, while ♦ **a cada r.** all the time • **al poco r.** shortly after • **a ratos** from time to time • **a ratos perdidos** at odd moments • **de r. en r.** from time to time • **¡hasta cada** *or* **otro r.!** AMER. so long!, see you soon! • **pasar el r.** to pass the time • **pasar un mal r.** to have a bad time • **un buen r.** *(momento agradable)* a good time;

(mucho tiempo) a good while, quite some time • **un r. (largo)** FIG., COLL. very much, a lot <*me gustó un r. el libro* I liked the book a lot> **II.** adj. see **rato, -ta.**

ra·to, -ta I. adj. LAW unconsummated (marriage) **II.** m. see **rato** —f. see **rata.**

ra·tón m. ZOOL. (male) mouse ♦ **r. almizclero** ZOOL. muskrat • **r. de biblioteca** FIG., COLL. bookworm.

ra·to·nar tr. to nibble, gnaw.

ra·to·ne·ra I. f. *(trampa)* mousetrap; *(agujero)* mousehole; *(madriguera)* nest of mice; ARG. *(ratona)* female mouse; *(casucha)* hovel ♦ **caer en la r.** FIG. to fall into a trap **II.** adj. see **ratonero, -ra.**

ra·to·ne·ro, -ra I. adj. mouselike, ratlike ♦ **música r.** FIG., COLL. raucous music • **perro r.** ratter (dog) **II.** f. see **ratonera.**

ra·to·nes·co, -ca or **ra·to·nil** adj. mouselike or ratlike.

rau·dal m. *(torrente)* torrent, flood; FIG. *(abundancia)* abundance, plenty ♦ **a raudales** in torrents.

rau·do, -da adj. rapid, swift.

ra·vio·les m.pl. CUL. ravioli.

ra·ya¹ f. *(lista)* stripe; *(línea)* line; *(veta)* streak; *(arañazo)* scratch, mark; *(de la palma)* line (on one's palm); *(crencha)* part (in one's hair); *(pliegue)* crease (in trousers); *(frontera)* border, boundary; *(límite)* limit, bounds <*ponerle r. a la situación* to place a limit on the situation>; *(punto)* point (of a score); GRAM., TELEC. dash; ARM. spiral groove; PHYS. line; SPORT. line, mark; AMER. hopscotch; Mex. pay, wages ♦ **a r.** in line • **a rayas** striped • **dar quince y r. a alguien** COLL. to beat someone hands down, run rings around someone • **hacer r.** FIG. to excel, stand out • **hacerse la r.** to part one's hair • **mantener a r. (a alguien)** FIG., COLL. to keep (someone) in his place • **pasarse de la r.** FIG., COLL. to go too far • **poner a r.** to check, hold back • **tener a r.** to keep at bay or in check • **tres en r.** tick-tack-toe.

ra·ya² f. ICHTH. ray, skate.

ra·ya, rayo see **raer.**

ra·ya·do I. past part. see **rayar II.** m. *(conjunto de rayas)* lines, stripes; *(acción de rayar)* striping.

ra·ya·no adj. adjacent, contiguous ♦ **r. en** bordering on.

ra·yar tr. *(trazar líneas)* to line, draw lines on; TEX. *(hacer listas)* to stripe; *(subrayar)* to underline, underscore; *(tachar)* to cross out, strike; *(arañar)* to scratch; COLL. *(pintarrajar)* to scribble on; ARM. *(ranurar)* to rifle —intr. *(lindar)* to border on, be next to <*su finca raya con el bosque* his farm borders on the forest>; *(amanecer)* to dawn, break (the day); *(aparecer)* to appear, come forth (the sun, light); *(arañar)* to scratch; FIG. *(tirar a)* to border or verge on <*esto raya en lo ridículo* this borders on the ridiculous>; *(aproximar)* to be nearly, be approaching <*raya en los cuarenta* he is nearly forty>; *(sobresalir)* to stand out; C. AMER. to spur on a horse; ARG. to stop suddenly (a horse); MEX. *(pagar a los operarios)* to pay workers; *(cobrar)* to collect wages, get paid ♦ **al r. el alba** at the crack of dawn •**r. a gran altura** FIG. to excel, shine —reflex. *(arañarse)* to get scratched; COL. *(colmar los deseos)* to get everything one wants; *(enriquecerse)* to get rich.

ra·ye·ra, rayó see **raer.**

ra·yo m. ray, beam <*r. de luz* ray of light>; *(de sol)* sunbeam, ray of sunlight; *(radio)* spoke (of a wheel); *(descarga de un rayo)* thunderbolt; FIG. *(infortunio)* blow, sudden misfortune; *(dolor)* flash of pain; *(persona pronta)* fast worker, whiz; *(persona aguda)* live wire, sharp or witty person; PHYS. ray <*r. gamma* gamma ray>; METEOROL. *(relámpago)* flash of lightning ♦ **caer como un r.** FIG. to be a bombshell (news) • **como un r.** FIG. like lightning or a shot • **echar rayos y centellas** COLL. to be furious, fume • **r. catódico** ELEC., PHYS. cathode ray • **r. del radio** radio beam • **r. electrónico** PHYS. electron ray • **r. infrarrojo** PHYS. infrared ray • **r. laser** laser (beam) • **r. reflejo** or **refracto** OPT. refracted ray • **rayos cósmicos** cosmic rays • **rayos X** x-rays • **r. textorio** TEX. shuttle • **r. ultravioleta** PHYS. ultraviolet ray.

ra·yón m. or **ra·yo·na** f. TEX. rayon.

ra·yue·la f. *(juego)* pitch and toss; AMER. hopscotch.

ra·za f. *(de personas)* race, ancestry; *(de los animales)* breed ♦ **de pura r.** *(caballos)* thoroughbred; *(perros)* pedigreed •

tener mucha r. PERU, COLL. to have a lot of nerve, be brave.

ra·zón f. *(facultad)* reason, faculty of reasoning; *(explicación)* reason, explanation; *(motivo)* reason, cause, motive; *(justicia)* rightness, fairness; *(recado)* message; *(cómputo)* rate <*a r. de ocho por hora* at a rate of eight an hour>; MATH. ratio, proportion <*r. directa* direct ratio> ♦ **asistirle a uno la r.** to be in the right, have right on one's side • **cargarse de r.** to justify oneself • **con mayor r.** with all the more reason • **con r.** with good reason, rightly so • **con r. o sin ella** right or wrong • **dar la r. a alguien** to agree with or side with someone • **dar r. (de)** to report on, tell about • **dar uno r. de sí** to give an account of oneself • **en r. a** with regard to • **entrar en r.** to come to or see reason • **envolver a alguien en razones** to get someone confused • **meter a alguien en r.** to make someone see reason, talk sense into someone • **no tener r.** to be wrong • **perder la r.** to go out of or lose one's mind • **ponerse en (la) r.** to come to terms, reach an agreement • **por r.** consequently • **privarse de r.** *(volverse loco)* to lose one's senses; *(emborracharse)* to drink oneself senseless • **quitar la r. a alguien** *(no estar de acuerdo)* to disagree with someone; *(probar que alguien se equivoca)* to prove someone wrong • **r. de estado** reason of state • **r. de ser** raison d'être • **r. geométrica** or **por cociente** MATH. geometric ratio, quotient • **r. inversa** MATH. inverse ratio • **r. social** trade or business name • **tener r.** to be right • **tener r. para** to have cause to.

ra·zo·na·ble adj. reasonable, fair.

ra·zo·na·da·men·te adv. rationally.

ra·zo·na·do, -da I. past part. see **razonar II.** adj. reasoned, considered.

ra·zo·na·dor, -do·ra I. adj. reasoning **II.** m.f. reasoner.

ra·zo·na·mien·to m. reasoning.

ra·zo·nar intr. *(pensar)* to reason, think; *(hablar)* to speak —tr. *(explicar)* to explain, give reasons for; *(un problema)* to reason out.

re m. MUS. re, D (second note of the scale).

re·a f. I. (female) defendant **II.** see **reo, -a.**

re·a·brir tr. to reopen.

re·ab·sor·ber tr. to reabsorb.

re·ab·sor·ción f. reabsorption.

re·ac·ción f. reaction ♦ **r. en cadena** CHEM., PHYS. chain reaction • **avión de r.** jet plane.

re·ac·cio·nar intr. to react.

re·ac·cio·na·rio, -ria adj. & m.f. reactionary.

re·a·cio, -cia adj. stubborn, obstinate.

re·ac·ti·va·ción f. *(acción de reactivar)* reactivation; ECON. recovery.

re·ac·ti·var tr. to reactivate.

re·ac·tor m. AER. *(motor)* jet engine; *(avión)* jet plane; PHYS. reactor ♦ **r. nuclear rápido** regenerable fast-breeder reactor.

re·a·dap·ta·ción f. readaptation, readjustment.

re·a·dap·tar tr. to readapt, readjust.

re·ad·mi·sión f. readmission.

re·ad·mi·tir tr. to readmit.

re·a·fir·mar tr. to reaffirm, reassert.

re·a·gru·pa·ción f. regrouping.

re·a·gru·par tr. to regroup.

re·a·jus·tar tr. to readjust.

re·a·jus·te m. readjustment.

re·al¹ adj. *(que existe)* real, actual; *(verdadero)* real, genuine <*problemas reales* real problems> ♦ **lo r.** reality, the real world.

re·al² I. adj. *(del rey)* royal; *(monárquico)* royalist; FIG. *(regio)* fine, excellent; *(bueno)* fine, lovely <*una r. moza* a lovely girl> **II.** m.f. *(monárquico)* royalist —m. *(moneda)* real (small coin); MIL. *(tienda del rey)* king's tent; *(campamento)* army camp ♦ **alzar el r.** or **los reales** MIL. to break camp • **asentar los reales** MIL. to encamp, set up camp • **no tener un r.** COLL. not to have a penny to one's name • **sentar el r.** or **los reales** FIG. to settle down, set up house • **un r. sobre otro** COLL. in cash and in full <*pagar un r. sobre otro* to pay in cash and in full>.

re·al·ce m. *(adorno)* relief, embossment; FIG. *(esplendor)* sparkle, luster; PAINT. highlight ♦ **poner de r.** to highlight, bring out.

re·al·cé, realce see **realzar.**
re·a·len·go, –ga I. adj. *(terreno)* royal, state-owned (land); PERU unencumbered (real estate); P. RICO ownerless (animal) **II.** m. ARG. encumbrance, lien.
re·a·le·za f. majesty, royal dignity.
re·a·li·cé, realice see **realizar.**
re·a·li·dad f. reality, truth ◆ **atenerse a la r.** to stick to facts • **en r.** in fact, actually.
re·a·lis·mo m. ARTS, PHILOS. realism; POL. royalism.
re·a·lis·ta adj. & m.f. *(realidad)* realist; *(monárquico)* royalist.
re·a·li·za·ble adj. attainable, feasible; COM. saleable.
re·a·li·za·ción f. *(ejecución)* realization, execution; *(cumplimiento)* fulfillment; COM. bargain sale; CINEM. production.
re·a·li·za·dor, –do·ra I. adj. realizing, fulfilling **II.** m.f. CINEM., RAD., TELEV. producer.
re·a·li·zar §04 tr. *(cumplir)* to realize, fulfill; *(ejecutar)* to carry out, accomplish; COM. to sell, turn into cash ◆ **r. gestiones** to negotiate —reflex. to come true.
re·al·men·te adv. really, truly.
re·al·qui·lar tr. to sublet, rent again.
re·al·zar §04 tr. SCULP. to set off by relief; FIG. *(dar brillo a)* to heighten, enhance; PAINT., PHOTOG. to enhance, highlight.
re·a·ni·mar tr. to revive, enliven again —reflex. to recover.
re·a·nu·da·ción f. resumption, renewal.
re·a·nu·dar tr. to resume, renew —reflex. to start over, begin again.
re·a·pa·re·cer §17 intr. to reappear.
re·a·pa·ri·ción f. reappearance.
re·a·per·tu·ra f. reopening, resumption.
re·ar·mar tr. & intr. to rearm.
re·ar·me m. MIL. rearmament.
re·a·se·gu·rar tr. to reinsure.
re·a·se·gu·ro m. reinsurance.
re·a·su·mir tr. to resume, take up again.
re·a·ta f. *(fila)* riata, single file (of horse or mules); *(primera mula)* lead mule (of a pack train); *(demás mulas)* additional horses or mules; FIG. *(obediencia)* mindless obedience or following; ECUAD. cotton ribbon or tape ◆ **de r.** single file.
re·a·tar tr. *(atar de nuevo)* to tie again, tie more strongly; *(atar animales)* to tie (animals) single file.
re·a·vi·var tr. to revive, rekindle.
re·ba·ja f. reduction, sale, discount.
re·ba·ja·do, –da I. past part. see **rebajar II.** adj. COM. reduced; MIL. relieved, discharged.
re·ba·ja·mien·to m. reduction.
re·ba·jar tr. *(reducir)* to reduce, lower; FIG. *(humillar)* to diminish, humiliate; ARTS, PHOTOG. to reduce, tone down (a color) —reflex. *(humillarse)* to degrade oneself; MIL. to become discharged ◆ **rebajarse a** to stoop to.
re·bal·sa f. *(agua)* pool (of water); MED. engorgement.
re·bal·sar tr. & intr. to dam, form a pool.
re·bal·se m. *(piscina)* pool; *(presa)* dam.
re·ba·na·da f. slice (of bread).
re·ba·nar tr. to slice, cut into slices.
re·ba·ñe·ra f. grapnel, drag hook.
re·ba·ña·du·ras f.pl. *(sobras)* leftovers, remains; AGR. gleanings.
re·ba·ñar tr. *(comida)* to finish off, eat up; *(el plato)* to wipe clean; FIG. to scrape up or together; AGR. to glean.
re·ba·ño m. herd, flock.
re·ba·sar tr. *(exceder)* to exceed, surpass (a limit, amount); *(en una carrera)* to overtake; MARIT. to sail beyond; AMER. to pass (a car) —intr. to overflow.
re·ba·ti·ble adj. refutable.
re·ba·ti·ña f. scramble, fight ◆ **andar a la r.** to fight over something.
re·ba·tir tr. *(argumento)* to repel, refute; *(an ataque)* to repulse, ward off; *(tentación)* to resist (temptation); COM., MATH. to reduce; CUL. to beat hard, beat again; MIL. to strengthen one's defenses.
re·ba·to m. MIL. *(alarma)* call to arms, alarm; *(ataque)* surprise attack; FIG. *(emoción súbita)* alarm, sudden emotion ◆ **de r.** COLL. suddenly, out of the blue.

re·be·lar·se reflex. *(resistir)* to rebel, resist; FIG. *(amistad)* to withdraw (friendship).
re·bel·de I. adj. *(indócil)* rebellious, unruly; MED. stubborn, resistant; LAW in default **II.** m.f. *(insumiso)* rebel; LAW defaulter.
re·bel·dí·a f. *(insumisión)* rebelliousness, contumacy; LAW in default, in contempt of court.
re·be·lión f. rebellion, violent resistance.
re·ben·ca·zo m. crack or lash (of a whip).
re·ben·que m. *(látigo)* whip; MARIT. lashing, ratline.
re·bién adv. extremely well.
re·blan·de·cer §17 tr. to soften —reflex. to become soft.
re·blan·de·ci·mien·to m. softening.
re·bo·cé, reboce see **rebozar.**
re·bo·llu·do, –da adj. *(gordo)* stocky, heavy-set; JEWEL. in the rough (diamond).
re·bo·ni·to, –ta adj. very good-looking, lovely.
re·bor·de m. border, flange.
re·bor·de·ar tr. to make a flange or border.
re·bo·sa·de·ro m. HYDRAUL. overflow, spillway; CHILE, MIN. large mineral deposits.
re·bo·sa·du·ra f. or **re·bo·sa·mien·to** m. overflow, overflowing.
re·bo·san·te adj. ◆ **r. de** overflowing or bursting with.
re·bo·sar intr. to overflow, spill —reflex. *(derramarse)* to run over; FIG. *(abundar en)* to be brimming with, abound in.
re·bo·ta·du·ra f. *(rebote)* bounce, rebound; FIG. *(molestia)* vexation, annoyance; TEX. napping.
re·bo·tar intr. *(pelota)* to bounce, rebound; *(bala)* to ricochet —tr. to bend back (a nail) —reflex. *(alterarse)* to change color or quality; FIG. *(molestarse)* to become annoyed or irritated.
re·bo·te m. rebound, ricochet ◆ **de r.** on the rebound.
re·bo·zar §04 tr. *(cubrir)* to muffle or cover the face (with a shawl); CUL. to dip (in batter, eggs, or bread crumbs) —reflex. to wrap oneself in a shawl.
re·bo·zo m. *(mantilla)* shawl, mantilla; FIG. *(pretexto)* pretext, excuse ◆ **de r.** underhandedly, secretly • **sin r.** openly, frankly.
re·bro·tar intr. BOT. to sprout.
re·bro·te m. BOT. sprout, shoot.
re·bue·no, –na adj. very good, excellent.
re·bu·far intr. to snort repeatedly or loudly.
re·bu·jar tr. to bundle up, tuck in.
re·bu·ji·na or **re·bu·ji·ña** COLL. uproar, tumult.
re·bu·llir §13 intr. to stir, begin moving —tr. to stir —reflex. to begin moving.
re·bus·ca f. *(acción de rebuscar)* careful search, hunt; *(fruto)* leftover gleanings; FIG. *(desecho)* useless portion of something.
re·bus·ca·do, –da I. past part. see **rebuscar II.** adj. *(persona)* prissy, affected; *(estilo)* pedantic.
re·bus·ca·dor, –do·ra m.f. *(buscador cuidadoso)* meticulous searcher; AGR. gleaner.
re·bus·ca·mien·to m. *(busca)* careful search; *(afectación)* prissiness, affectation.
re·bus·car §70 tr. *(buscar con cuidado)* to search carefully; AGR. to glean.
re·bus·co m. *(busca)* meticulous search; ECUAD. partial cocoa harvest.
re·buz·nar intr. to bray, hee-haw (donkey).
re·buz·no m. braying, hee-hawing.
re·ca·bar tr. *(obtener)* to obtain, succeed in getting; *(pedir)* to request; *(reclamar)* to claim, demand.
re·ca·de·ro, –ra m.f. messenger, deliveryman, errand boy.
re·ca·do m. *(mensaje)* message; *(mandado)* errand <enviar a un r. to send on an errand>; *(provisión)* daily marketing or shopping; *(conjunto)* equipment, materials <r. de escribir writing materials>; PRINT. standing matter; AMER., EQUIT. riding gear, saddle and trappings; NIC., CUL. ground meat filling ◆ **coger** or **tomar un r.** to take a message • **dar r. para** to provide the necessities for • **dejar un r.** to leave a message • **mandar r.** to send word • **recados** P. RICO regards, greetings.
re·ca·er §15 intr. *(volver a caer)* to fall again; MED. to relapse, suffer a relapse; FIG. *(pecar)* to fall into error ◆ **r. en**

to fall to <*la herencia recayó en su hermano menor* the inheritance fell to his younger brother>.

re·ca·í·da f. MED. relapse; FIG. backsliding.

re·ca·lar tr. to saturate, penetrate —intr. MARIT. to sight land; *(bucear)* to swim underwater; S. AMER. to arrive (at a given place).

re·cal·ca·du·ra f. cramming, packing.

re·cal·car §70 tr. *(apretar)* to press, squeeze (in); *(llenar)* to cram, pack; FIG. *(insistir en las palabras)* to emphasize, stress (words) —intr. MARIT. to list —reflex. *(repetirse)* to repeat oneself; COLL. *(arrellanarse)* to sprawl, stretch out ♦ **recalcarse el pie** to sprain one's foot.

re·cal·ci·tran·te adj. recalcitrant, stubborn.

re·cal·ci·trar intr. *(retroceder)* to step back, retreat (in resistance); *(obstinarse)* to balk, resist.

re·ca·len·ta·mien·to m. reheating, overheating.

re·ca·len·tar §49 tr. *(volver a calentar)* to reheat; *(calentar demasiado)* to overheat; FIG. *(una pasión)* to excite (a passion) —reflex. *(frutos)* to spoil, go bad; *(madera)* to rot; FIG. to get excited *or* overheated.

re·cal·qué, recalque see **recalcar.**

re·ca·ma·do I. past part. see **recamar** II. m. SEW. overlay, relief embroidery.

re·ca·mar tr. SEW. to overlay, do relief embroidery on.

re·cá·ma·ra f. *(vestuario)* vestibule, dressing room; FIG., COLL. *(prudencia)* prudence, caution; ARTIL. gun chamber *or* breech; MEX. bedroom.

re·cam·biar tr. *(cambiar de nuevo)* to change again; *(una pieza)* to change, replace (a part); COM. to redraw (an unpaid draft).

re·cam·bio m. *(acción de recambiar)* changing again; *(pieza)* spare part, refill; ♦ **de r.** spare (part).

re·ca·mo m. *(recamado)* overlay, relief embroidery; *(alamar)* tassel, frog closing.

re·can·ca·ni·lla m. *(modo de caminar)* feigned limp; FIG., COLL. *(modo de hablar)* affected manner of speaking.

re·ca·pa·ci·tar tr. to mull over, reconsider.

re·ca·pi·tu·la·ción m. recapitulation, summary.

re·ca·pi·tu·lar tr. to recapitulate, summarize.

re·car·ga·do, –da I. past part. see **recargar** II. adj. *(cargado de nuevo)* reloaded; *(sobrecargado)* overloaded; FIG. heavy, overloaded <*esta semana está recargada de citas* this week is overloaded with appointments>; *(en el adorno)* overdecorated; *(en el vestir)* overdressed.

re·car·gar §47 tr. *(volver a cargar)* to reload; *(aumentar la carga)* to increase (a load); *(sobrecargar)* to overload; *(agravar la condena)* to increase, lengthen (a prisoner's sentence); FIG. *(abrumar)* to overload, overburden; *(adornar a exceso)* to overdecorate; *(vestir a exceso)* to overdress; FIN. *(aumentar un impuesto)* to increase, raise, (a tax); *(volver a cobrar)* to charge again, recharge; *(cobrar más)* to charge extra; *(cobrar demasiado)* to overcharge; TECH. *(reforzar)* to recharge, reload; *(pila)* to recharge —reflex. MED. to run a higher fever.

re·car·go m. *(carga nueva)* additional charge, increase; *(nuevo cargo)* extra load; MED. rise in temperature; MIL. extra service.

re·ca·ta·do, –da I. past part. see **recatar** II. adj. *(cauteloso)* cautious, reserved; *(tímido)* shy, timid; *(pudoroso)* modest, chaste.

re·ca·tar tr. to hide, cover up —reflex. *(mostrar recelo)* to behave prudently *or* chastely; FIG. *(vacilar)* to vacillate, waver.

re·ca·to m. *(cautela)* caution, prudence; *(astucia)* astuteness, discretion; *(modestia)* modesty, chastity.

re·cau·chu·tar tr. AMER. to retread.

re·cau·da·ción f. *(cobranza)* collection (of taxes); *(oficina)* tax office; *(cantidad recaudada)* tax levy, amount collected.

re·cau·da·dor m. tax collector.

re·cau·dar tr. *(impuestos)* to collect, levy (taxes); *(asegurar)* to safeguard, protect; *(cobrar)* to recover (a debt).

re·cau·do m. *(acción de cobrar)* collection, levy (of taxes); *(cuidado)* circumspection, caution; LAW *(caución)* bail, bond; *(fianza)* deposit, security; CARIB., CHILE, MEX. mixed vegetables ♦ **poner a buen r.** to place in safekeeping.

re·ca·ye·ra, recayó see **recaer.**

re·ca·zo m. *(de espada)* guard (of sword); *(de cuchillo)* handle (of a knife); *(de candileja)* saucer (of an oil lamp).

re·cé, rece see **rezar.**

re·ce·lar tr. to suspect, distrust.

re·ce·lo *or* **re·ce·la·mien·to** m. suspicion, distrust.

re·ce·lo·so, –sa adj. suspicious, fearful.

re·cep·ción f. *(acción de recibir)* receiving, reception; *(admisión)* admission, entrance; *(reunión con fiesta)* reception, party; *(en un hotel)* reception, front desk.

re·cep·cio·nis·ta m.f. receptionist.

re·cep·tá·cu·lo m. *(sitio)* receptacle, container; BOT. receptacle; *(refugio)* refuge, shelter.

re·cep·ti·vi·dad f. receptiveness, receptivity.

re·cep·ti·vo, –va adj. receptive.

re·cep·tor, –to·ra I. adj. receiving II. m. ELEC., RAD., TELEC. receiver; BIOL., CHEM., PHYSIOL. receptor; LAW receiver ♦ **r. telefónico** telephone receiver.

re·ce·sión f. ECON. recession, slump.

re·ce·so m. *(separación)* separation, withdrawal; AMER. recess, adjournment ♦ **entrar en r.** to recess (assembly).

re·ce·ta f. PHARM. prescription; CUL. recipe; FIG. formula, secret <*la r. del éxito* the formula for success>.

re·ce·tar tr. MED. to prescribe.

re·ce·ta·rio m. MED. prescription book; PHARM. pharmacopoeia, apothecary's file.

re·cia·men·te adv. vigorously, strongly.

re·ci·bí m. written acknowledgment of receipt.

re·ci·bi·dor, –do·ra I. adj. receiving II. m.f. *(persona)* recipient, receiver —m. *(antesala)* reception room, anteroom; *(vestíbulo)* vestibule, (entrance) hall —f. PERU midwife.

re·ci·bi·mien·to m. *(acción)* receiving; *(recepción)* reception; *(acogida)* welcome, reception; *(antesala)* reception room, anteroom; *(vestíbulo)* vestibule, (entrance) hall; *(sala principal)* main *or* living room; *(fiesta)* reception.

re·ci·bir tr. *(tener)* to receive <*r. una carta* to receive a letter>; *(aceptar)* to receive, accept <*el comité recibió el análisis con gran interés* the committee received the analysis with great interest>; *(admitir visitas)* to receive, entertain (visitors); *(saludar)* to receive, welcome <*r. a alguien con los brazos abiertos* to receive someone with open arms>; *(graduar)* to receive, take (a degree) —intr. *(admitir de visita)* to receive, entertain; RAD. to receive —reflex. ♦ **recibirse de** to graduate *or* qualify as, receive one's degree <*recibirse de ingeniero* to receive one's engineering degree>.

re·ci·bo m. *(acción)* receipt; *(documento)* receipt; *(sala)* reception room ♦ **acusar r.** to acknowledge receipt of • **estar de r.** to be presentable, be ready for visitors.

re·ci·cla·je m. *(de una persona)* retraining, reassignment; *(de una cosa)* recycling.

re·ci·clar tr. to recycle —reflex. to be reassigned.

re·cie·dum·bre f. strength, vigor.

re·cién adv. recently, newly ♦ **r. nacido** newborn.

re·cien·te adj. *(nuevo)* recent; *(moderno)* modern.

re·cien·te·men·te adv. recently, of late.

re·cin·to m. enclosure, area, precincts.

re·cio, –cia adj. *(vigoroso)* vigorous, strong; *(abultado)* bulky, heavy-set; *(tiempo)* harsh, severe; *(lluvia)* hard, heavy; *(veloz)* swift, impetuous ♦ **en lo más r. de** in the thick of, in the dead of.

re·ci·pien·te I. adj. receiving, recipient II. m. *(vasija)* container, vessel (for liquids); *(persona)* recipient.

re·ci·pro·ca·men·te adv. reciprocally, mutually.

re·ci·pro·car §70 tr. *(responder)* to reciprocate; *(hacer corresponder)* to make mutual *or* reciprocal.

re·ci·pro·ci·dad f. reciprocity, mutuality.

re·cí·pro·co, –ca adj. *(mutuo)* reciprocal, mutual; MATH. reciprocal (theorem).

re·ci·ta·ción f. recitation, recital.

re·ci·ta·do I. past part. see **recitar** II. m. MUS. recitative.

re·ci·ta·dor, –do·ra I. adj. reciting II. m.f. reciter.

re·ci·tal m. MUS. recital; LIT. reading.

re·ci·tar tr. to recite, read aloud.

re·ci·ta·ti·vo, –ti·va adj. MUS. recitative.

re·cla·ma·ción f. *(petición)* claim, demand; *(protesta)* protest, complaint; LAW *(oposición)* protest, remonstration ♦ **formular** *or* **hacer una r.** to lodge *or* make a complaint.

re·cla·ma·dor, –do·ra I. adj. claiming <*parte r.* claiming party> II. m.f. claimant.

re·cla·man·te I. adj. claiming II. m.f. claimant, claimer.

re·cla·mar tr. *(pedir)* to claim, demand <*r. lo que uno merece* to claim what one deserves>; *(exigir)* to require, demand; *(clamar)* to clamor for <*la multitud reclamaba que cantara otra canción* the crowd clamored for her to sing another song>; *(recuperar)* to re-claim, recover (one's belongings); HUNT. to call birds; LAW *(buscar)* to look for, seek (a criminal); *(emplazar)* to summon (a witness) —intr. *(protestar)* to protest, complain about <*r. contra una política injusta* to protest against an unfair policy>; LAW to protest, appeal (a decision); POET. to resound ♦ *a r.* MARIT. hoisted taut • *r. en juicio* LAW to appeal —reflex. ORNITH. to call each other (birds).

re·cla·mo m. *(ave amaestrada)* live decoy bird, lure; *(llamada)* birdcall; *(instrumento)* decoy whistle; FIG. *(aliciente)* bait, lure; LAW claim, complaint; COM. advertising slogan; PRINT. catchword, footnote reference mark.

re·cli·na·ción f. reclining.

re·cli·nar tr. *(inclinar)* to lay back, recline; *(apoyar)* to lean *or* rest on —reflex. to lie back, recline.

re·cli·na·to·rio m. *(silla)* recliner, armchair; *(oratorio)* kneeling-stool, prie-dieu.

re·cluir §18 tr. *(encerrar)* to shut in, seclude; *(encarcelar)* to imprison —reflex. to shut oneself in.

re·clu·sión f. *(encierro)* seclusion; *(prisión)* imprisonment.

re·clu·so, –sa I. past part. see **recluir** II. adj. *(encerrado)* secluded; *(preso)* imprisoned III. m.f. prisoner.

re·clu·ta f. recruiting, recruitment —m. *(quinto)* recruit, inductee; ARG. cattle roundup.

re·clu·ta·dor, –do·ra I. adj. recruiting II. m.f. recruiting officer, recruiter.

re·clu·ta·mien·to m. *(acción de reclutar)* recruitment, recruiting; *(conjunto de reclutas)* year's recruits.

re·clu·tar tr. *(alistar reclutas)* to recruit; ARG. to round up (cattle).

re·clu·ya, recluyo see **recluir**.

re·clu·ye·ra, recluyó see **recluir**.

re·co·brar tr. *(recuperar)* to recover, get back; *(reintegrar)* to regain <*r. las fuerzas* to regain strength>; MIL. to recapture —reflex. *(recuperarse)* to recover, recuperate; *(desquitarse)* to get one's money back.

re·co·bro m. recovery, recuperation.

re·co·cer §71 tr. CUL. to recook, to overcook; METAL. to anneal —reflex. to work oneself into a fury, to be overcome by passion.

re·co·chi·ne·ar·se COLL. reflex. *(burlarse)* to make fun of, mock; *(divertirse)* to have fun, enjoy oneself.

re·co·chi·ne·o COLL. m. *(burla)* mockery; *(diversión)* fun, diversion.

re·co·dar¹ intr. & reflex. to rest *or* lean one's elbows (on).

re·co·dar² intr. to wind, twist (a road, a river).

re·co·do m. turn, bend (in a road, in a river); *(ángulo)* angle.

re·co·ge·de·ro m. *(sitio)* collection site; *(instrumento)* dustpan.

re·co·ge·dor, –do·ra I. adj. collecting II. m.f. *(persona)* collector; AGR. harvester —m. AGR. *(rastra)* rake, gleaner; *(recogedero)* dustpan.

re·co·ger §34 tr. *(volver a coger)* to pick up, retrieve <*r. un lápiz del piso* to pick up a pencil from the floor>; to pick up, go for <*r. un paquete en correos* to pick up a package at the post office>; *(juntar)* to collect, gather <*r. datos* to collect information>; *(arreglar)* to pick up, tidy (a room); *(guardar)* to save, put away <*r. dinero* to save money>; *(coleccionar)* to save, collect; *(dar asilo)* to take in, shelter; *(suspender)* to suspend, discontinue; *(encerrar)* to put away, lock up (in an institution); AGR. *(cosechar)* to harvest, gather; EQUIT. to draw up (one's horse); MARIT. to take in (sails); SEW. *(achicar)* to take in; *(acortar)* to shorten; SPORT. to field, stop ♦ *r. agua* to absorb water • *r. las mangas* to roll up one's sleeves —reflex. *(retirarse)* to retire, withdraw; *(irse a casa)* to retire, go home; *(irse a la cama)* to go to bed; *(moderarse)* to cut down (on expenses); FIG. *(ensimismarse)* to withdraw within *or* abstract oneself.

re·co·gi·da I. f. *(acción de juntar)* collecting, gathering; *(re-*

tiro) withdrawal, retirement; *(colección)* pickup, collection <*r. de basura* trash collection>; AGR. harvest, harvesting; ARG., CHILE roundup (of cattle); ARG. *(batida)* raid, sweep II. adj. see **recogido, –da**.

re·co·gi·do, –da I. past part. see **recoger** II. adj. *(apartado)* withdrawn, secluded; *(reservado)* reserved, retiring; *(pequeño)* small; *(tranquilo)* quiet, tranquil; ZOOL. short-trunked (animal) II. m. SEW. tuck, gather —f. *(mujer apartada)* woman secluded in a house of correction *or* retreat — see **recogida**.

re·co·gi·mien·to m. *(acción de juntar)* collecting, gathering; *(retiro)* withdrawal, retirement; *(ensimismamiento)* withdrawal, spiritual absorption; *(residencia)* house of correction *or* retreat; AGR. harvest, harvesting; RELIG. retreat.

re·co·ja, recojo see **recoger**.

re·co·lec·ción f. *(acción de acumular)* collection, gathering; *(resumen)* summary, recapitulation; AGR. harvest, harvesting; RELIG. *(acción)* spiritual absorption, withdrawal; *(casa)* retreat.

re·co·lec·tar tr. *(cosechar)* to gather, harvest; *(colectar)* to collect, gather.

re·co·lec·tor, –to·ra m.f. *(de cosechas)* gatherer, harvester; *(recaudador)* collector (of taxes).

re·co·le·to, –ta I. adj. RELIG. in retreat; *(recogido)* withdrawn, retiring II. m.f. RELIG. recollect.

re·co·men·da·ble adj. *(aconsejable)* recommendable; *(laudable)* commendable.

re·co·men·da·ción f. *(consejo)* recommendation, advice; *(referencia)* reference, introduction; *(súplica)* request.

re·co·men·da·do, –da I. past part. see **recomendar** II. m. protégé —f. protégée.

re·co·men·dar §49 tr. *(aconsejar)* to recommend, advise; *(hablar en favor)* to recommend (a person); *(encargar)* to request.

re·co·men·da·to·rio adj. recommendatory, recommending.

re·co·mer·se reflex. var. of **concomerse**.

re·com·pen·sa f. recompense, reward ♦ *en r. de* in return for, as a reward for.

re·com·pen·sa·ble adj. recompensable, rewardable.

re·com·pen·sar tr. *(conceder recompensa)* to recompense; *(compensar)* to compensate; *(pagar)* to remunerate, pay.

re·com·po·ner §54 tr. *(arreglar)* to repair, fix; COLL. *(acicalar)* to dress *or* doll up; PRINT. to reset.

re·com·po·si·ción f. repair.

re·con·cen·tra·ción f. *(concentración)* concentration; *(ensimismamiento)* withdrawal, self-absorption.

re·con·cen·trar tr. *(reunir)* to concentrate, gather together; FIG. *(disimular)* to hide, conceal (one's feelings) —reflex. *(reunirse)* to become concentrated, gather together; *(ensimismarse)* to withdraw into oneself.

re·con·ci·lia·ble adj. reconcilable.

re·con·ci·lia·ción f. reconciliation.

re·con·ci·lia·dor, –do·ra I. adj. reconciliating II. m.f. reconciler.

re·con·ci·liar tr. to reconcile —reflex. to reconcile, be reconciled.

re·con·co·mio f. COLL. *(sospecha)* suspicion, misgiving; *(deseo)* desire, itch.

re·cón·di·to, –ta adj. recondite, hidden ♦ *en lo más r. de* in the depths *or* the heart of.

re·con·duc·ción f. LAW extension, renewal (of a lease).

re·con·for·tan·te I. adj. comforting II. m. *(consolación)* comfort, consolation; MED. tonic.

re·con·for·tar tr. *(consolar)* to comfort, console; MED. to strengthen, fortify.

re·co·no·cer §17 tr. *(conocer)* to recognize; *(identificar)* to recognize, identify <*se le reconoce por las gafas* you can recognize him by his glasses>; *(aceptar)* to recognize, accept <*no lo reconocen por verdad* they don't accept it as the truth>; *(confesar)* to admit, acknowledge <*r. los errores* to admit one's mistakes>; *(agradecer)* to be grateful for, appreciate; *(registrar)* to search; *(examinar)* to examine; DIPL., POL. to recognize (a nation); MED. to examine; MIL. to reconnoiter; SURV. to survey ♦ *r. la evidencia* to bow to the evidence • *r. los hechos* to face facts • *r. por hijo* to recognize as one's child —reflex. *(dejarse comprender)* to be clear *or* apparent <*ya se reconoce que no vuelve* it's clear that he's not coming back>; *(confesar)* to admit, confess

<reconocerse culpable to admit one's guilt>; *(conocerse uno)* to know oneself.

re·co·no·ci·ble adj. recognizable.

re·co·no·ci·da·men·te adv. *(con gratitud)* gratefully, appreciatively; *(evidentemente)* clearly; *(por confesión)* avowedly.

re·co·no·ci·do, –da I. past part. see **reconocer II.** adj. *(agradecido)* grateful, appreciative; *(aceptado)* recognized, accepted; *(confesado)* confessed, acknowledged.

re·co·no·ci·mien·to m. *(identificación)* recognition, identification; *(confesión)* admission, acknowledgement; *(gratitud)* gratitude, recognition; *(registro)* search, inspection; *(examinación)* examination; DIPL., POL. *(admisión)* recognition; MIL. *(observación)* reconnaissance; SURV. survey ♦ **en r. de** in gratitude for • **r. médico** medical examination or checkup.

re·co·noz·ca, reconozco see **reconocer.**

re·con·quis·ta f. reconquest ♦ **la Reconquista** HIST. the Reconquest (of Spain from Moorish rule).

re·con·quis·tar tr. *(volver a conquistar)* to reconquer; FIG. *(recobrar)* to recover, win back.

re·con·si·de·rar tr. to reconsider.

re·cons·ti·tu·ción f. reconstitution.

re·cons·ti·tuir §18 tr. to reconstitute.

re·cons·ti·tu·yen·te I. adj. reconstituent **II.** m. tonic, restorative.

re·cons·truc·ción f. reconstruction; CONSTR. rebuilding.

re·cons·truir §18 tr. *(volver a construir)* to reconstruct; CONSTR. to rebuild; FIG. *(evocar)* to recall, to reconstruct.

re·con·tar §19 tr. *(volver a contar una cantidad)* to recount, count again; *(volver a narrar)* to retell, tell again.

re·con·ten·to, –ta I. adj. very happy, delighted **II.** m. great happiness, delight.

re·con·ven·ción f. *(reprimenda)* rebuke, reprimand; LAW countercharge, counterclaim.

re·co·pi·la·ción f. *(resumen)* summary, review; *(colección)* compilation, collection.

re·co·pi·la·dor m. compiler.

re·co·pi·lar tr. *(reunir)* to compile; *(resumir)* to summarize.

ré·cord I. m. [pl. **-cords**] record ♦ **batir un r.** to break a record **II.** adj. [pl. **-cord**] record *<una cosecha r.* a record crop>.

re·cor·da·ble adj. memorable.

re·cor·da·ción f. *(acción de recordar)* remembering; *(recuerdo)* memory.

re·cor·dar §19 tr. *(traer a la memoria)* to remember, recall *<r. el pasado* to remember the past>; *(avisar)* to remind *<r. una cita a alguien* to remind someone of an appointment>; *(evocar)* to remind of, bring to mind *<esto me recuerda la casa antigua* this reminds me of the old house>; *(conmemorar)* to commemorate; AMER. to awaken —intr. *(acordarse)* to remember, recall; *(contar los recuerdos)* to reminisce; *(despertar)* to wake up; *(volver en sí)* to revive, come to —reflex. *(despertar)* to wake up; *(conmemorarse)* to be remembered ♦ **recordarse que** to remind oneself that.

re·cor·da·ti·vo, –va I. adj. reminding, reminiscent **II.** m. reminder.

re·cor·da·to·rio m. *(aviso)* memo, reminder; RELIG. memento of deceased used as a bookmark.

re·co·rrer tr. *(caminar)* to tour, travel; *(mirar)* to peruse, to look over; *(reparar)* to overhaul, repair; PRINT. to overrun ♦ **r. el mundo** to see the world • **r. una gran distancia** to cover a lot of ground.

re·co·rri·do I. past part. see **recorrer II.** m. *(viaje)* journey, run; *(espacio)* mileage, distance traveled; *(trayecto)* route, path; *(de cartero, recadero)* route, round; PRINT. overrun; MECH. stroke (of a piston); *(reparación)* repair, overhaul ♦ **r. de aterrizaje** AVIA. landing run, landing strip • **r. de émbolo** MECH. piston travel • **r. de prueba** trial run, dry run.

re·cor·ta·do m. or **re·cor·ta·du·ra** f. var. of **recorte.**

re·cor·tar tr. *(cortar lo sobrante)* to cut, trim; FIG. *(reducir)* to reduce, cut (down); ARTS *(cortar con arte)* cut out (a design); *(dibujar)* to sketch, outline —reflex. to be outlined, stand out *<una sombra que se recorta en la pared* a shadow that is outlined on the wall>.

re·cor·te m. *(acción de recortar)* cutting, trimming; *(de periódico)* newspaper clipping; *(de pelo)* trim (of one's hair); TAUR. dodge ♦ **recortes** cuttings, trimmings.

re·co·ser tr. *(coser de nuevo)* to sew again, sew; *(zurcir)* to mend, darn.

re·co·si·do I. past part. see **recoser II.** m. *(acción de zurcir)* mending; *(zurcido)* mend, darn.

re·cos·tar §19 tr. *(apoyar)* to lean (on); *(inclinar)* to lean, bend —reflex. *(reclinarse hacia atrás)* to lean back, recline; *(acostarse)* to lie down ♦ **recostarse en** or **sobre** to lean on.

re·co·va f. *(comercio)* poultry business; *(mercado)* poultry market; *(jauría)* pack of hunting dogs; AMER. market.

re·co·ve·co m. *(vuelta)* bend (of a stream, road); ARCHIT. nook; FIG. *(rodeo)* cunning, artifice ♦ **recovecos** recesses *<los recovecos del alma* the recesses of the soul> • **sin recovecos** *(franco)* frank, open; *(francamente)* frankly.

re·cre·a·ción f. *(diversión)* recreation, entertainment; *(tiempo para jugar)* recess, break.

re·cre·ar tr. *(divertir)* to entertain, amuse; *(crear de nuevo)* to re-create —reflex. *(entretenerse)* to amuse or entertain oneself; *(gozar)* to enjoy, take pleasure in.

re·cre·a·ti·vo, –va adj. *(divertido)* entertaining, amusing; recreational *<terapia r.* recreational therapy>.

re·cre·cer §17 tr. to increase —intr. *(aumentar)* to increase, grow; *(un río)* to rise, swell; *(volver a suceder)* to recur —reflex. to recover one's spirits.

re·cre·o m. *(diversión)* recreation, amusement; *(tiempo para jugar)* recess, break ♦ **de r.** pleasure *<barco de r.* pleasure boat>.

re·crí·a f. *(cría)* breeding, raising (of animals); THEOL. redemption.

re·criar §30 tr. *(criar)* to breed, raise; THEOL. to redeem.

re·cri·mi·na·ción f. recrimination, reproach.

re·cri·mi·na·dor, –do·ra I. adj. recriminating **II.** m.f. recriminator.

re·cri·mi·nar tr. to recriminate, reproach —intr. to recriminate —reflex. to exchange recriminations, recriminate each other.

re·cri·mi·na·to·rio, –ria adj. recriminatory, recriminative.

re·cru·de·cer §17 intr. & reflex. *(tomar nuevo incremento)* to break out again, recrudesce; *(empeorar)* to worsen.

re·cru·de·ci·mien·to m. *(nuevo incremento)* new outbreak, recrudescence; *(empeoramiento)* worsening.

rec·tal adj. ANAT. rectal.

rec·ta·men·te adv. *(con justicia)* rightly, justly; *(en línea recta)* in a straight line.

rec·tán·gu·lo MATH. **I.** adj. rectangular, right-angled **II.** m. rectangle.

rec·ti·fi·ca·ción f. *(corrección)* rectification, correction; CHEM., ELEC., MATH. rectification.

rec·ti·fi·ca·dor, –do·ra I. adj. rectifying **II.** m. ELEC. rectifier —f. MECH. grinder.

rec·ti·fi·car §70 tr. *(enderezar)* to straighten; *(corregir)* to correct, rectify; CHEM., ELEC., MATH. to rectify; MECH. to resurface; POL. to change (a vote) —intr. to correct oneself.

rec·ti·tud f. *(derechura)* straightness; FIG. *(justicia)* rectitude, honesty.

rec·to, –ta I. adj. *(derecho)* straight *<línea r.* straight line>; *(honrado)* honest, honorable; *(justo)* just, fair; FIG. sound (mind, judgment); GRAM. *(propio)* literal, proper (meaning); ANAT. rectal; GEOM. right (angle) **II.** m. ANAT. *(del intestino)* rectum; *(músculo)* rectus; PRINT. recto (of a page) —f. GEOM. straight line ♦ **r. final** home or final stretch (of a race course) **III.** adv. straight *<seguir r.* to continue straight (down a road)>.

rec·tor, –to·ra I. adj. ruling, governing **II.** m.f. *(de un colegio)* principal, director —m. *(cura)* parish priest; *(de universidad)* president, rector.

rec·to·ra·do m. rectorate.

rec·to·rí·a f. *(oficio)* rectorate; *(oficina)* rector's office.

re·cua f. pack, drove (of pack animals); FIG. gang, crowd.

re·cua·dro m. ARCHIT. panel, compartment; PRINT. box (in a newspaper).

re·cu·bri·mien·to m. *(acción de cubrir)* covering; *(con pintura)* coating (with paint).

re·cu·brir tr. *(cubrir)* to cover; *(pintar)* to coat (with paint).

re·cue·ce see **recocer.**

re·cue·lo m. *(lejía)* strong bleach; *(café recalentado)* reheated coffee.

re·cuen·te, recuento see **recontar**.

re·cuen·to m. *(segunda enumeración)* recount; *(enumeración)* count; *(de votos)* vote count *or* tally ♦ **r. globular** MED. blood count.

re·cuer·de, recuerdo see **recordar**.

re·cuer·do m. *(memoria)* memory, recollection; *(regalo)* momento, souvenir; COL., BOT. climbing plant ♦ **contar los recuerdos** to reminisce • **recuerdos** regards, greetings.

re·cue·ro m. muleteer, pack driver.

re·cues·te, recuesto see **recostar**.

re·cue·za, recuezo see **recocer**.

re·cu·la·da f. *(retroceso)* backward movement; *(de un vehículo)* backing (up), reversing; ARM. recoil; FIG., COLL. *(acción de ceder)* retreating, backing down.

re·cu·lar intr. *(retroceder)* to back up, go backwards; ARM. to recoil; FIG., COLL. *(ceder)* to retreat, back down; MIL. to retreat.

re·cu·lón m. ARG., CHILE *(retroceso)* backward movement; *(de un vehículo)* backing (up), reversing; FIG., COLL. *(acción de ceder)* retreating, backing down ♦ **a reculones** COLL. backwards.

re·cu·pe·ra·ble adj. recoverable, retrievable.

re·cu·pe·ra·ción f. recovery, recuperation.

re·cu·pe·ra·dor, –do·ra I. adj. recovering II. m.f. recoverer.

re·cu·pe·rar tr. *(recobrar)* to recover, recuperate; to regain <*r. el sentido* to regain consciousness>; *(reconquistar)* to win *or* get back; *(compensar una pérdida)* to recoup (a loss); *(compensar el tiempo)* to make up for (lost time); TECH. to reclaim —reflex. to recover, recuperate (health) ♦ **recuperarse de** to recover from (illness, a loss).

re·cu·pe·ra·ti·vo, –va adj. recuperative.

re·cu·rren·te I. adj. *(que recurre)* recurrent; LAW appellant II. m.f. LAW appellant.

re·cu·rrir intr. *(acudir a alguien)* to turn *or* appeal (to); *(valerse de)* to make use (of), resort *or* have recourse (to); *(volver)* to return *or* revert (to); LAW to appeal.

re·cur·so m. *(acción de recurrir)* recourse, resort <*como últi­mo r.* as a last resort>; *(medio)* recourse, means; resource <*recursos naturales* natural resources>; *(retorno)* return; LAW *(apelación)* appeal ♦ **recursos** FIG. expedient • **sin r.** irremediably.

re·cu·sa·ble adj. rejectable, refusable.

re·cu·sa·ción f. *(rechazo)* rejection; LAW challenge.

re·cu·sar tr. *(rechazar)* to reject, refuse; LAW to challenge.

re·cha·cé, rechace see **rechazar**.

re·cha·za·dor, –do·ra I. adj. rejecting, refusing II. m.f. rejecter, refuser.

re·cha·za·mien·to m. rejection <*r. de una teoría anticuada* rejection of an antiquated theory>; *(negativa)* refusal <*r. de una oferta* refusal of an offer>; *(del enemigo)* repulse, repelling (of an enemy); *(negación)* denial.

re·cha·zar §04 tr. *(no admitir)* to reject <*r. el uso de neolo­gismos* to reject the use of neologisms>; *(declinar)* to refuse, turn down <*r. una invitación* to refuse an invitation>; *(repeler)* to resist, repel (an attack); *(empujar)* to push away *or* back; *(no tentarse)* to resist (temptation); *(negar)* to deny; *(reflejar)* to reflect (light).

re·cha·zo m. rejection <*r. de una idea* rejection of an idea>; *(de un arma)* recoil; *(rebote)* rebound; MED. rejection (of a transplant) ♦ **de r.** indirectly, consequently.

re·chi·fla f. *(abucheo)* hissing, booing; *(burla)* derision, mockery.

re·chi·flar tr. to hiss, boo —reflex. to deride, mock.

re·chi·na·dor, –do·ra adj. creaking, squeaky, grating.

re·chi·na·mien·to m. creaking, squeaking, grating.

re·chi·nar intr. *(hacer ruido)* to creak, squeak, grate; *(ludir los dientes)* to grind, gnash (one's teeth); FIG. *(hacer algo a disgusto)* to do something unwillingly —reflex. COL., HOND. to burn, scorch (food).

re·chis·tar intr. to whisper, murmur ♦ **sin r.** without a word *or* murmur (of protest).

re·chon·cho, –cha adj. COLL. chubby, tubby.

re·chu·pe·te COLL. ♦ **de r.** terrific, fabulous <*pasarlo de r.* to have a terrific time>; *(comida)* delicious, scrumptious.

red f. net <*r. de pesca* fishing net>; *(malla)* netting, mesh <*r. de alambre* wire mesh>; *(redecilla)* hairnet; *(de tiendas)* chain (of stores); *(reja)* fence, fencing; FIG. *(engaño)* trick, trap; *(conspiración)* network, ring <*r. de espionaje* spy ring>; RAD., RAIL., TELEC. network, system ♦ **caer en la r.** FIG. to fall for a trick, fall into a trap • **echar** *or* **tender las redes** to cast one's net • **r. barredera** dragnet, trawl • **r. de emisoras** RAD. radio network • **r. de rastreo** RAD. tracking network.

re·dac·ción f. *(escritura)* writing, drafting; *(revisión)* editing; *(oficina)* editorial office; *(personal)* editors, editorial staff.

re·dac·tar tr. *(escribir)* to write, draft; *(revisar)* to edit.

re·dac·tor, –to·ra I. adj. *(que escribe)* writing; *(que revisa)* editing II. m.f. *(escritor)* writer; *(revisor)* editor ♦ **r. jefe** editor in chief.

re·da·da f. *(echada)* casting (of nets); *(pescado)* catch, haul; FIG. *(de la policía)* roundup, dragnet.

re·da·ño m. ANAT. omentum ♦ **redaños** COLL. guts, pluck.

re·de·ci·lla f. *(tejido)* mesh, netting; *(para el pelo)* hairnet; *(bolsa)* string bag; ZOOL. reticulum.

re·de·cir §21 tr. to repeat, say again.

re·de·dor m. surroundings, environs ♦ **al** *or* **en r.** around, surrounding.

re·den·ción f. redemption.

re·den·tor, –to·ra I. adj. redeeming II. m.f. redeemer ♦ **Redentor** RELIG. the Redeemer (Jesus Christ).

re·di see **redecir**.

re·di·ce see **redecir**.

re·di·cho, –cha I. past part. see **redecir** II. adj. COLL. affected, pretentious (in speech).

re·di·ga, redigo see **redecir**.

re·di·je·ra, redijo see **redecir**.

re·dil m. fold, sheepfold ♦ **volver al r.** FIG. to return to the fold.

re·di·mi·ble adj. redeemable.

re·di·mir tr. *(rescatar)* to redeem, liberate; FIN. to redeem; *(librar de una obligación)* to free, exempt (from obligation).

re·di·rá, rediría see **redecir**.

ré·di·to m. COM. yield, interest.

re·di·tua·ble adj. interest-yielding.

re·di·tuar §67 tr. to yield, produce (revenue).

re·do·bla·do, –da I. past part. see **redoblar** II. adj. *(fornido)* stocky, heavy-set; *(fuerte)* resistant; MECH. reinforced ♦ **paso r.** MIL. double time.

re·do·bla·du·ra f. *or* **re·do·bla·mien·to** m. *(acción de redoblar)* redoubling; *(de un clavo)* clinching.

re·do·blar tr. *(intensificar)* to redouble, intensify; *(doblar)* to fold, bend back; *(doblar un clavo)* to clinch; *(repetir)* to repeat, reiterate —intr. to roll, beat (a drum).

re·do·ble m. *(redoblamiento)* redoubling; *(de tambor)* roll, rolling (of a drum).

re·do·ma f. vial, flask.

re·do·ma·do, –da adj. sly, crafty.

re·don·da I. f. *(comarca)* region, district, neighborhood; *(pasto)* pasture; MUS. whole note, semibreve (G.B.) ♦ **a la r.** around II. adj. see **redondo, –da**.

re·don·de·a·do, –da I. past part. see **redondear** II. adj. round, spherical.

re·don·de·ar tr. *(poner redondo)* to make round; FIG. *(sanear)* to clear (of debts); MATH. to round off (a number) —reflex. *(ponerse redondo)* to become round; *(enriquecerse)* to grow rich; FIG. *(librarse de deudas)* to rid oneself of debts.

re·don·del m. COLL. *(círculo)* circle; *(capa)* round cape; TAUR. bull ring, arena.

re·don·dez f. roundness, rotundity ♦ **en la r. de la Tierra** on the face of the Earth.

re·don·di·lla I. f. POET. octosyllabic quatrain II. adj. round <*letra r.* round script>.

re·don·do, –da I. adj. *(circular)* round, circular; *(adehesado)* private (land); FIG. *(claro)* clear, direct; *(total)* complete, all-around <*un éxito r.* an all-around success> ♦ **caer (en) r.** to fall in a heap, collapse • **dar una vuelta** *or* **girar en r.** COLL. to turn around • **en r.** around <*diez pies en r.* ten feet around>; *(directamente)* clearly, flatly • **número r.** round figure • **salir r. (a alguien)** to go well (for someone) • **virar en r.** to veer **II.** m. *(cosa circular)* circle, ring; FIG. *(dinero)* cash, ready money —f. see **redonda.**

re·do·pe·lo m. *(acción)* rubbing against the nap *or* grain; FIG., COLL. *(riña)* scuffle, tussle ♦ **a** *or* **al r.** the wrong way, against the grain.

re·do·rar tr. to gild again.

re·duc·ción f. *(disminución)* reduction, decrease; *(sumisión)* subjugation, subjecting; CHEM., MATH. reduction; SURG. setting (of a bone); AMER. settlement of converted Indians.

re·du·ci·ble adj. reducible.

re·du·ci·do, –da I. past part. see **reducir II.** adj. *(disminuido)* reduced, decreased; *(estrecho)* narrow; *(pequeño)* small, limited <*número r.* small number>; *(confinado)* small, confined <*espacio r.* confined space> ♦ **quedar reducido a** to be reduced to.

re·du·ci·mien·to m. var. of **reducción.**

re·du·cir §22 tr. *(disminuir)* to reduce, decrease <*r. por la mitad* to reduce by half>; *(transformar)* to reduce, convert <*r. a polvo* to reduce to dust>; *(restringir)* to reduce, cut down on (expenses); *(condensar texto)* to reduce, abridge (text); *(sujetar)* to subject, subjugate; *(concentrar)* to reduce, boil down; *(cambiar moneda)* to convert (currency); PAINT. *(ajustar el tamaño)* to reduce to scale; CHEM., LOG., MATH. to reduce; SURG. to set (a bone); MER. to fence (stolen goods) ♦ **r. a la razón** to make see reason • **r. a prisión** to send to prison —reflex. *(disminuirse)* to be reduced *or* decreased; *(restringirse)* to reduce, cut down on (expenses); *(resolverse)* to resolve to *or* do something); *(venir a ser)* to amount to, boil down *or* come down to ♦ **reducirse a la razón** to see reason.

re·duc·to m. MIL. redoubt.

re·duc·tor, –to·ra I. adj. reducing **II.** m. CHEM., ELEC. reducer.

re·du·je·ra, redujo see **reducir.**

re·dun·dan·cia f. redundancy.

re·dun·dan·te adj. redundant.

re·dun·dar intr. *(rebosar)* to overflow; *(resultar)* to redound (to), result (in) ♦ **r. en** to redound to.

re·du·pli·ca·ción f. *(repetición)* reduplication; *(redobladura)* redoubling.

re·du·pli·car §70 tr. *(repitir)* to reduplicate, repeat; *(redoblar)* to redouble, intensify.

re·duz·ca, reduzco see **reducir.**

re·e·di·ción f. reissue, new edition.

re·e·di·fi·ca·ción f. rebuilding, reconstruction.

re·e·di·fi·car §70 tr. to rebuild, reconstruct.

re·e·di·tar tr. to reissue, republish.

re·e·du·car §70 tr. to re-educate.

re·e·lec·ción f. re-election.

re·e·lec·to, –ta I. past part. see **reelegir II.** adj. re-elected.

re·e·le·gir §54 tr. to re-elect.

re·em·bar·car §70 tr. to re-embark, reship.

re·em·bar·que m. re-embarkment, reshipment.

re·em·bol·sa·ble adj. reimbursable, repayable.

re·em·bol·sar tr. to reimburse, repay —reflex. to recover (money).

re·em·bol·so m. reimbursement, repayment ♦ **enviar algo contra r.** to send something cash on delivery *or* C.O.D.

re·em·pla·zan·te I. adj. replacing **II.** m.f. replacement.

re·em·pla·zar §04 tr. to replace, substitute.

re·em·pla·zo m. replacement, substitute.

re·en·car·na·ción f. reincarnation.

re·en·car·nar intr. to reincarnate —reflex. to be reincarnated.

re·en·cuen·tro m. *(de cosas)* collision; MIL. clash, skirmish; SPORT. return match.

re·en·gan·cha·mien·to m. MIL. var. of **reenganche.**

re·en·gan·char tr. & reflex. MIL. to re-enlist.

re·en·gan·che m. MIL. *(acción)* re-enlistment; *(premio)* re-enlistment bonus.

re·en·sa·yar tr. *(probar)* to retest, try again; THEAT. to rehearse again.

re·en·vi·ar §30 tr. *(devolver)* to return, send back; *(reexpedir)* to forward, send on.

re·en·ví·o m. *(devolución)* return, sending back; *(reexpedición)* forwarding.

re·es·tre·no m. CINEM., THEAT. revival.

re·es·truc·tu·ra·ción f. restructuring, reorganization.

re·es·truc·tu·rar tr. to restructure, reorganize.

re·e·xa·mi·nar tr. to re-examine.

re·ex·pe·di·ción f. forwarding, sending on.

re·ex·pe·dir §48 tr. to forward, send on.

re·fac·ción f. *(colación)* snack, refreshment; *(reparación)* repair, renovation; COLL. *(premio)* bonus, premium; CUBA, PERU, P. RICO maintenance *or* upkeep costs.

re·fac·cio·nar tr. AMER. *(reparar)* to repair, renovate; *(financiar)* to finance, give financial assistance to.

re·fa·jo m. underskirt, slip.

re·fec·ción f. *(colación)* snack, refreshment; *(reparación)* repair.

re·fec·to·rio m. refectory, cafeteria, dining hall.

re·fe·ren·cia f. *(narración)* report, account; *(relación)* relationship; *(remisión)* reference; *(sobre una persona)* reference ♦ **por. r.** by hearsay, secondhand.

re·fe·ren·te adj. referring, relating ♦ **r. a** relating to, concerning.

re·fe·rir §65 tr. *(contar)* to relate, tell; *(remitir)* to refer *or* direct (to); *(relacionar)* to refer *or* relate (to) —reflex. to refer (to).

re·fi·lón adv. ♦ **de r.** *(de soslayo)* sideways, obliquely; FIG. *(de pasada)* in passing.

re·fi·na·ción f. refining.

re·fi·na·do, –da I. past part. see **refinar II.** adj. *(fino)* refined, FIG. *(cortés)* refined, polished; *(astuto)* subtle, artful **II.** m. refining.

re·fi·na·dor, –do·ra I. adj. refining **II.** m.f. refiner.

re·fi·na·mien·to m. refinement.

re·fi·nar tr. *(purificar)* to refine, purify; *(perfeccionar)* to refine, polish —reflex. to become refined *or* polished.

re·fi·ne·rí·a f. refinery.

re·fi·no, –na I. adj. extra fine **II.** m. *(refinación)* refining; *(tienda)* market, grocery; MEX. brandy.

re·fi·rie·ra, refirió see **referir.**

re·fi·to·le·ro, –ra I. adj. FIG., COLL. *(entremetido)* meddling, snooping; CUBA, COLL. flattering **II.** m.f. *(encargado del refectorio)* cafeteria supervisor; FIG., COLL. *(entremetido)* snoop, busybody; CUBA, COLL. flatterer.

re·flec·tor, –to·ra I. adj. reflecting **II.** m. OPT. reflector; *(proyector)* spotlight; MIL. searchlight.

re·fle·jar tr. to reflect —reflex. to be reflected.

re·fle·jo, –ja I. adj. PHYS. reflected; PHYSIOL. reflex; GRAM. reflexive **II.** m. PHYS. reflection; PHYSIOL. reflex; *(brillo)* gleam, glint; *(del pelo)* rinse (for the hair) ♦ **r. condicionado** conditioned reflex.

re·fle·xión f. reflection ♦ **sin r.** without thinking, automatically.

re·fle·xio·nar tr. to reflect on, think over —intr. to reflect, think ♦ **r. en** *or* **sobre** to reflect on.

re·fle·xi·vo, –va adj. *(que refleja)* reflecting, reflective; *(que reflexiona)* reflective, thoughtful; GRAM. reflexive.

re·flo·re·cer §17 intr. BOT. to flower *or* bloom again; FIG. *(volver a medrar)* to reflourish, flourish again.

re·flu·jo m. reflux, ebb.

re·fo·ci·la·ción f. enjoyment, delight.

re·fo·ci·lar tr. to enjoy, delight —reflex. to enjoy oneself, be delighted.

re·fo·ci·lo m. enjoyment, delight.

re·for·cé see **reforzar.**

re·fo·res·ta·ción f. AMER. reforestation.

re·for·ma f. *(acción de reformar)* reform <*r. agraria* land reform>; *(modificación)* alteration, improvement ♦ **Reforma** RELIG. Reformation.

re·for·ma·ble adj. reformable.

re·for·ma·ción f. reform, reformation.

re·for·ma·do, –da I. past part. see **reformar II.** adj. *(rehecho)* reformed; *(modificado)* altered; *(mejorado)* improved **III.** m.f. RELIG. Protestant.

re·for·ma·dor, –do·ra I. adj. reforming **II.** m.f. reformer.

re·for·mar tr. *(rehacer)* to reform; *(mejorar)* to correct, improve; *(restaurar)* restore, renovate; *(modificar)* to modify, alter —reflex. *(corregirse)* to reform, mend one's ways; *(contenerse)* to control *or* restrain oneself.

re·for·ma·to·rio I. m. reformatory, reform school **II.** adj. see **reformatorio, –ria.**

re·for·ma·to·rio, –ria I. adj. reformatory, reforming **II.** m. see **reformatorio.**

re·for·mis·ta I. adj. reformist II. m.f. reformist, reformer.

re·for·za·do, –da I. past part. see **reforzar** II. adj. reinforced, strengthened III. m. tape, binding.

re·for·za·dor m. PHOTOG. intensifier, intensifying solution; ELEC. booster.

re·for·zar §37 tr. *(hacer más fuerte)* to reinforce, strengthen; FIG. *(animar)* to cheer up, encourage; ELEC. to boost; PHOTOG. to intensify.

re·frac·ción f. PHYS. refraction.

re·frac·tar tr. PHYS. to refract.

re·frac·ta·rio, –ria adj. PHYS. refractory, heat-resistant; FIG. *(opuesto)* refractory, resistant.

re·frán m. saying, proverb ♦ **como dice** or **según reza el r.** as the saying goes.

re·fra·ne·ro m. collection of proverbs.

re·fre·ga·du·ra f. *(refregamiento)* rubbing, scrubbing; *(señal)* rub mark, abrasion.

re·fre·ga·mien·to m. rubbing, scrubbing.

re·fre·gar §52 tr. *(frotar)* to rub, scrub; FIG., COLL. *(reprochar)* to throw back at ♦ **r. algo a alguien** FIG., COLL. to rub something in.

re·fre·gón m. COLL. *(refregadura)* rubbing, scrubbing; *(señal)* rub mark, abrasion.

re·fre·ír §58 tr. *(freír de nuevo)* to refry; *(freír mucho)* to overfry.

re·fre·na·ble adj. controllable.

re·fre·nar tr. *(sujetar un caballo)* to check, rein in (a horse); FIG. *(contener)* to curb, restrain —reflex. FIG. to restrain oneself.

re·fren·da·ción f. *(firma)* countersignature; *(acción)* countersigning; *(de un pasaporte)* visa, stamp.

re·fren·dar tr. *(firmar)* to countersign, endorse; *(revisar un pasaporte)* to stamp (a passport).

re·fren·da·rio m. countersigner.

re·fren·da·ta f. countersignature.

re·fres·can·te adj. cooling, refreshing.

re·fres·car §70 tr. *(enfriar)* to cool, refresh; *(fortalecer)* to refresh, renew <*un pequeño descanso te refrescará* a short rest will refresh you>; *(repetir una acción)* to repeat; FIG. *(recordar)* to refresh (one's memory); *(mejorar)* to brush up, polish <*r. el italiano* to brush up one's Italian>; *(renovar)* to renew, revive <*r. una vieja costumbre* to revive an old custom> —intr. *(templar)* to become or get cool, cool down; *(tomar fuerzas)* to become refreshed, refresh oneself; *(tomar el fresco)* to take or get some fresh air; *(beber)* to have something to drink, take some refreshment; MARIT. to freshen, increase (the wind); COL. to have an afternoon snack —reflex. *(templarse el calor)* to become or get cool, cool down (weather); *(tomar el fresco)* to get or take some fresh air; *(beber)* to have something to drink, take some refreshment; MARIT. to freshen, increase (the wind).

re·fres·co m. *(alimento)* refreshment, snack; *(bebida)* soft drink ♦ **de r.** again, anew • **refrescos** refreshments.

re·frí·a, refrío see **refreír**.

re·frie·ga f. skirmish, scuffle.

re·frie·go, refriegue see **refregar**.

re·frie·ra, refrió see **refreír**.

re·fri·ge·ra·ción f. *(moderación del calor)* refrigeration; *(de aire)* air conditioning; *(comida)* snack ♦ **r. por agua** water-cooling • **r. por aire** air-cooling.

re·fri·ge·ra·dor, –do·ra I. adj. refrigerating, cooling II. m. or f. refrigerator.

re·fri·ge·ran·te I. adj. refrigerating II. m. *(de alambique)* cooling bath (of a still); CHEM. cooling chamber.

re·fri·ge·rar tr. *(enfriar)* to refrigerate, cool; *(el aire)* to air-condition; *(helar)* to freeze; FIG. *(refrescar)* to refresh.

re·fri·ge·ra·ti·vo, –va adj. refrigerating, cooling.

re·fri·ge·rio m. *(alivio)* relief, comfort; *(alimento)* snack, refreshment.

re·fri·to, –ta I. past part. see **refreír** II. adj. *(frito de nuevo)* refried; *(demasiado frito)* overfried III. m. FIG., COLL. rehash.

re·fuer·ce, refuerzo see **reforzar**.

re·fuer·zo m. *(acción de reforzar)* reinforcement, strengthening; *(sostén)* brace, support; PHOTOG. intensification; SEW. welt ♦ **refuerzos** MIL. reinforcements.

re·fu·gia·do, –da I. past part. see **refugiar** II. adj. & m.f. refugee.

re·fu·giar tr. to shelter, give refuge —reflex. to take refuge or shelter.

re·fu·gio m. *(auxilio)* refuge, shelter; *(andén)* traffic island; FIG. *(asilo)* refuge ♦ **r. antiaéreo** air-raid shelter.

re·ful·gen·cia f. refulgence, brilliance.

re·ful·gen·te adj. refulgent, brilliant.

re·ful·gir §32 intr. to shine brightly.

re·fun·dir tr. METAL. to recast; LIT. *(revisar)* to adapt, revise; FIG. *(reunir)* to bring together, merge (offices).

re·fun·fu·ña·dor, –do·ra I. adj. grumbling, muttering II. m.f. grumbler, grouch.

re·fun·fu·ña·du·ra f. grumble, mutter.

re·fun·fu·ñar intr. to grumble, mutter.

re·fun·fu·ño m. COLL. grumble, mutter.

re·fun·fu·ñon, –ño·na I. adj. grumbling, muttering II. m.f. grumbler, grouch.

re·fu·ta·ble adj. refutable.

re·fu·ta·ción f. refutation, rebuttal.

re·fu·tar tr. to refute, rebut.

re·ga·ble adj. irrigable.

re·ga·de·ra f. *(vasija)* watering can; *(reguera)* irrigation ditch ♦ **estar como una r.** FIG., COLL. to be as crazy as a loon.

re·ga·de·ro m. irrigation ditch.

re·ga·dí·o, –a I. adj. irrigable II. m. irrigated land.

re·ga·dor, –do·ra adj. irrigating, watering.

re·ga·du·ra f. watering, sprinkling.

re·ga·la·do, –da I. past part. see **regalar** II. adj. *(delicado)* dainty, delicate; *(con comodidades)* easy, comfortable; *(barato)* dirt-cheap ♦ **no lo quiero ni r.** I don't want it even as a gift • **vida r.** life of ease.

re·ga·la·dor, –do·ra I. adj. generous, giving II. m.f. *(persona)* giver —m. *(de los boteros)* wineskin scraper.

re·ga·lar tr. *(dar)* to give (as a present), present; *(donar)* to give away; *(deleitar)* to regale, entertain; *(halagar)* to flatter, cajole —reflex. to indulge or regale oneself.

re·ga·lí·a f. *(derecho real)* royal privilege; *(excepción)* privilege, exemption; FIG. *(sueldo)* bonus, perquisite; *(derechos de autor)* royalties; CARIB. gift, present —m. high-quality cigar.

re·ga·liz m. or **re·ga·li·za** f. BOT. licorice.

re·ga·lo m. *(obsequio)* present, gift; *(placer)* joy, pleasure; *(festín)* treat, delicacy (food); *(comodidad)* comfort, ease <*vivir con r.* to live a life of ease> ♦ **dar de r.** to give as a gift.

re·ga·lón, –lo·na adj. COLL. spoiled, pampered ♦ **vida r.** life of ease.

re·ga·ña·dien·tes ♦ **a r.** COLL. grudgingly, reluctantly.

re·ga·ñar intr. *(reñir)* to quarrel, argue; *(amigos)* to fall out; *(novios)* to break off; *(refunfuñar)* to grumble; *(abrirse)* to split open (fruit) —tr. COLL. *(reprender)* to scold, tell off; *(importunar)* to nag.

re·ga·ño m. *(gesto de disgusto)* gesture of annoyance; COLL. *(reprensión)* scolding, telling off.

re·ga·ñón, –ño·na I. adj. grumbling, bad-tempered II. m.f. *(refunfuñón)* grumbler, grouch; *(que importuna)* nag.

re·gar §52 tr. *(echar agua)* to sprinkle, water; *(remojar un terreno)* to irrigate, water; *(limpiar)* to wash or hose down; *(atravesar un río)* to water, wash (said of a river); FIG. *(esparcir)* to scatter, strew; *(bañar)* to bathe (with tears, blood); COLL. *(beber)* to wash down (food).

re·ga·ta¹ f. irrigation ditch.

re·ga·ta² f. MARIT. regatta, boat race.

re·ga·te m. *(del cuerpo)* dodge, duck; FIG., COLL. *(efugio)* dodge, evasion.

re·ga·te·a·dor, –do·ra AMER. I. adj. haggling II. m.f. haggler.

re·ga·te·ar tr. *(negociar)* to haggle over, bargain for; *(vender al menudeo)* to sell at retail; *(dar regates)* to dodge, evade —intr. *(negociar)* to haggle, bargain; *(poner dificultades)* to be difficult; MARIT. to race.

re·ga·te·o m. *(en la compra)* haggling, bargaining; *(regates)* dodging, ducking.

re·ga·te·rí·a f. retailing.

re·ga·tón I. m. tip, ferrule II. adj. see **regatón, –tona**.

re·ga·tón, –to·na COLL. I. adj. haggling II. m.f. haggler —m. see **regatón**.

re·ga·zo m. lap (of a person).

re·gen·cia f. regency.
re·ge·ne·ra·ción f. regeneration.
re·ge·ne·ra·dor, –do·ra I. adj. regenerating **II.** m.f. regenerator.
re·ge·ne·rar tr. to regenerate.
re·gen·tar tr. (dirigir) to manage, direct; (ejercer un cargo) to hold, occupy (a post); FIG. to preside over; COLL. to boss (around).
re·gen·te I. adj. ruling, governing **II.** m.f. (de un estado) regent —m. RELIG. director of studies (in certain orders); (gerente) manager; PRINT. foreman.
re·gen·te·ar tr. to rule, boss.
re·gi·ci·da I. adj. regicidal **II.** m.f. regicide.
re·gi·ci·dio m. regicide.
re·gi·dor, –do·ra I. adj. ruling, governing **II.** m. councilman —f. councilwoman.
ré·gi·men m. (conjunto de reglas) regulations, rules; (modo de regir algo) regime, regimen <un r. severo a severe regimen>; (sistema) system; POL. regime <r. constitucional constitutional regime>; MED. diet, regimen <r. lácteo milk diet>; GRAM. government, regimen; ELEC., MECH. rate, ratio; GEOG. regime, regimen; MECH. speed <r. máximo top or full speed> ♦ **antiguo r.** POL. ancien régime • **estar a r.** to be on a diet • **poner a r.** to put on a diet • **r. del aire** AER. airflow, airstream • **r. de vida** way of life • **r. marioneta** POL. puppet regime or government.
re·gi·men·tar §49 tr. to regiment.
re·gi·mien·to m. (acción de regir) governing, government; (cargo) councilorship; (concejo) council (members); MIL. regiment.
re·gio, –gia adj. (real) royal, regal; FIG. (suntuoso) sumptuous, magnificent; COLL. (fabuloso) great, splendid.
re·gión f. region.
re·gio·nal adj. regional.
re·gio·na·lis·mo m. regionalism.
re·gio·na·li·za·ción f. regionalization.
re·gir §57 tr. (gobernar) to govern, rule; (manejar) to manage, run <r. empresa to manage a business>; GRAM., LAW (gobernar) to govern; GRAM. (pedir) to take <este verbo rige el acusativo this verb takes the accusative>; MED. to keep in good order (the bowels) —intr. (estar vigente) to be in force, apply; (funcionar bien) to function, work; MARIT. (conducir) to steer ♦ **no r.** FIG., COLL. to have a screw loose, be not all there —reflex. ♦ **regirse por** to be guided by, go by.
re·gis·tra·dor, –do·ra I. adj. (que inspecciona) examining, inspecting; (que registra) registering, recording ♦ **caja r.** cash register **II.** m.f. (que inspecciona) examiner, inspector; (que registra) register, recorder —m. (funcionario) recorder, registrar <r. de títulos de propiedad recorder of deeds> —f. (caja) cash register.
re·gis·trar tr. (inspeccionar) to examine, inspect; (copiar en un registro) to register, enter (in a register); (rebuscar) to search, go through <r. la maleta de alguien to search someone's suitcase>; (cachear) to search, frisk <r. a un sospechoso to search a suspect>; (poner registro en un libro) to mark with a book mark; (anotar) to note, write down; (inscribir variables) to note, record <r. un aumento en la natalidad to note an increase in the birth rate>; MUS. to record; PRINT. to register; AMER. to certify, register (mail) —intr. to search <r. en el coche to search in the car> —reflex. (matricularse) to register, enroll; (ocurrir) to happen, occur; (hacerse anotar) to register, record; (comunicarse) to be reported.
re·gis·tro m. (inspección) examination, inspection; (búsqueda) search <r. policíaco police search>; (acción de anotar) registration, recording; (libro) register, record (book); (lista) list, roll <r. electoral electoral roll>; (oficina) registry, registration or record office; (asiento) entry (in a register); (padrón) census list; (pieza de reloj) regulator; (cinta en un libro) bookmark; MUS. (pieza del órgano) (organ) stop; (género de voces) register; (pedal del piano) pedal ; (grabación) recording; PRINT. register <estar en r. to be in register>; TECH. (boca de acceso) manhole; (de calefacción) register, damper (of a heater); (trampilla) inspection plate or hole; ARG., BOL. wholesale textile store ♦ **echar** or **tocar todos los registros** FIG., COLL. to pull out all the stops, use all possible means • **r. civil** registry, hall

of records • **r. de erratas** list of errata • **r. de la propiedad** real estate registry • **r. de la propiedad industrial** trademark registry office • **r. de la propiedad intelectual** copyright registry office • **r. de patentes y marcas** patent office • **r. genealógico** pedigree (of animals).
re·gla f. (para trazar) ruler, rule; (norma) rule, regulation; (modelo) model, (set) pattern; (orden natural) natural order or harmony; (moderación) moderation, restraint; (instrucciones) instructions <reglas para utilizar una computadora instructions for using a computer>; MATH. rule; MED. period; RELIG. rule, order ♦ **en r.** (en orden) in order; (como es debido) by the book • **hacerse una r. de** to make a point of <hacerse una regla de levantarse temprano to make a point of getting up early> • **poner algo en r.** to put something straight • **por r. general** as a rule, usually • **r. áurea** golden rule • **r. de cálculo** MATH. slide rule • **r. de oro** or **de proporción** or **de tres** MATH. rule of three • **r. (en) T** T-square • **r. lesbia** flexible rule (for curved surfaces) • **reglas** MED. (menstrual) period • **reglas de la circulación** traffic regulations • **reglas paralelas** ENGIN. parallel rulers • **salir de r.** FIG. to go too far.
re·gla·je m. (reajuste) adjustment; MIL. correction (of aim); MECH. overhaul.
re·gla·men·ta·ción f. (acción) regulation; (reglas) regulations, rules.
re·gla·men·tar tr. to regulate.
re·gla·men·ta·rio, –ria adj. prescribed, regulation.
re·gla·men·to m. (reglas) regulations, rules; POL. bylaw.
re·glar tr. (rayar) to rule, draw lines on (paper); (regular) to regulate (conduct) —reflex. (templarse) to follow, conform to ♦ **reglarse por** to be guided by.
re·go·ci·jar tr. to delight, gladden, cheer (up) —reflex. to rejoice, be delighted.
re·go·ci·jo m. joy, gladness ♦ **regocijos** festivities.
re·go·de·ar CHILE to skimp, stint —reflex. COLL. (deleitarse) to enjoy, take pleasure in; (bromear) to joke, jest.
re·go·de·o m. delight, pleasure.
re·go·jo m. (de pan) crust (of bread); FIG. (muchacho) runt, small boy.
re·gol·dar §03 intr. SL. to belch, burp.
re·go·na f. large irrigation ditch.
re·gor·de·te, –ta adj. COLL. tubby, plump.
re·gos·tar·se reflex. to acquire a taste for.
re·gos·to m. craving, taste (for more of something).
re·gre·sar tr. AMER. to return, give back —intr. & reflex. AMER. to return, come or go back.
re·gre·sión f. regression, retrogression.
re·gre·si·vo, –va adj. regressive.
re·gre·so m. return, coming back ♦ **estar de r.** to be back.
re·guar·dar·se reflex. to take care of oneself.
re·gué see regar.
re·güel·da, regüeldo see regoldar.
re·güel·do m. SL. belch, burp.
re·gue·ra f. irrigation ditch.
re·gue·ro m. (chorro) trickle, stream; (señal) trail, track; AGR. irrigation ditch ♦ **propagarse como un r. de pólvora** FIG. to spread like wildfire.
re·gu·la·ción f. (acción de ajustar) regulation, adjustment; (control) control <r. de tráfico traffic control> ♦ **r. de la natalidad** or **de los nacimientos** birth control • **r. del volumen** volume control.
re·gu·la·do, –da I. past part. see regular² **II.** adj. (regular) regular, according to rule; (ajustado) regulated, adjusted; (controlado) controlled; (ordenado) arranged, in order.
re·gu·la·dor, –do·ra I. adj. regulating **II.** m. (persona) regulator; CHEM. (neutralizante) regulator, buffer; ELEC. regulator <r. de voltaje voltage regulator>; MECH. regulator, governor; MUS. sign (for crescendo or descrescendo); RAD. button, control knob <r. de volumen volume control>.
re·gu·lar¹ I. adj. (normal) regular; (aceptable) fairly good, fair; (arreglado) orderly, regular; (mediano) ordinary, average; BOT., GEOM., GRAM., MIL., RELIG. regular ♦ **por lo r.** as a rule, generally **II.** adv. COLL. regularly ♦ **estar r.** to be so-so, be OK.
re·gu·lar² tr. (ajustar a regla) to regulate, adjust; (controlar) to control; (ordenar) to put in order.

re·gu·la·ri·dad f. *(conformidad)* regularity ♦ **con r.** regularly.

re·gu·la·ri·za·ción f. regularization.

re·gu·la·ri·za·dor, –do·ra adj. regularizing.

re·gu·la·ri·zar §04 tr. to regularize.

re·gu·lar·men·te adv. *(uniformemente)* regularly; *(comúnmente)* regularly, usually; *(medianamente)* not too badly, fairly well.

re·gu·la·ti·vo, –va adj. regulative.

re·gur·gi·ta·ción f. regurgitation.

re·gur·gi·tar intr. to regurgitate.

re·gus·to m. COLL. aftertaste.

re·ha·bi·li·ta·ción f. *(restablecimiento)* rehabilitation; *(reinstalación)* reinstatement.

re·ha·bi·li·tar tr. *(restablecer)* to rehabilitate; *(reinstalar en un puesto)* reinstate.

re·ha·cer §40 tr. *(volver a hacer)* to redo; *(volver a elaborar)* to remake; *(reparar)* to repair, mend; *(renovar)* to renew, renovate —reflex. MED. to recover; MIL. to rally.

re·he·cho, –cha I. past part. see **rehacer** II. adj. stocky, thickset.

re·hén m. hostage ♦ **quedar en rehenes** to be held hostage.

re·hi·ce, rehiciera see **rehacer**.

re·hi·lar §81 tr. to twist too hard (yarn) —intr. *(temblar)* to quiver, tremble; *(pasar zumbando)* to whiz (an arrow).

re·hi·le·te m. *(flechilla)* dart; TAUR. banderilla; *(volante)* shuttlecock; FIG. *(dicho malicioso)* dig, gibe.

re·hi·le·te·ro m. TAUR. banderillero.

re·hi·zo see **rehacer**.

re·ho·gar §47 tr. CUL. to brown.

re·ho·llar §19 tr. to trample underfoot.

re·ho·yar intr. to redig holes.

re·ho·yo m. deep hole, pit.

re·hui·da f. flight, fleeing.

re·huir §18 tr. *(apartar)* to flee or shrink from; *(rehusar)* to avoid, shun —reflex. to flee or shrink from.

re·hu·me·de·cer §17 tr. to soak, wet through.

re·hun·dir tr. *(hundir)* to sink, submerge; *(ahondar)* to deepen (a hole); FIG. *(gastar)* to waste, squander.

re·hu·sar tr. *(no aceptar)* to refuse, decline; *(negarse)* to refuse <**r. contestar** to refuse to answer>.

re·hu·ya, rehuyo see **rehuir**.

re·hu·ye·ra, rehuyó see **rehuir**.

rei·dor, –do·ra adj. laughing, jolly.

re·im·pre·sión f. *(acción)* reprinting; *(obra)* reprint.

re·im·pre·so, –sa I. past part. see **reimprimir** II. adj. reprinted.

re·im·pri·mir §85 tr. to reprint.

rei·na f. *(noble)* queen; *(dama en ajedrez)* queen (in chess); ENTOM. queen (bee) ♦ **r. de los bosques** BOT. woodruff • **r. de los prados** BOT. meadowsweet.

rei·na·do m. reign, rule.

rei·nan·te adj. *(gobernante)* reigning, ruling; FIG. *(prevaleciente)* prevailing.

rei·nar tr. *(gobernar)* to reign, rule; FIG. *(prevalecer)* to prevail, reign.

re·in·ci·den·cia f. *(recaída)* relapse; CRIMIN. recidivism.

re·in·ci·den·te I. adj. *(que recae)* relapsing; CRIMIN. recidivous II. m.f. CRIMIN. recidivist.

re·in·ci·dir intr. *(recaer)* to relapse; CRIMIN. to repeat an offense.

re·in·cor·po·ra·ción f. reincorporation.

re·in·cor·po·rar tr. to reincorporate.

re·in·gre·sar intr. to re-enter.

rei·no m. kingdom ♦ **r. de los cielos** RELIG. kingdom of heaven.

Reino Unido m. United Kingdom.

Reino Unido de Gran Bretaña e Irlanda del Norte m. United Kingdom of Great Britain and Northern Ireland.

re·ins·ta·la·ción f. *(en un lugar)* reinstallation; *(en un puesto)* reinstatement.

re·ins·ta·lar tr. *(en un lugar)* to reinstall; *(en un puesto)* to reinstate.

re·in·te·gra·ble adj. reimbursable, refundable.

re·in·te·gra·ción f. *(restablecimiento)* restoration, reintegration; *(reembolso)* reimbursement, refund.

re·in·te·grar tr. *(restablecer)* to restore, reintegrate; *(reembolsar)* to reimburse, refund; *(poner pólizas)* to place a

fiscal stamp on —reflex. *(recibir reembolso)* to be paid back, be reimbursed; *(volver)* to return, rejoin <*reintegrarse al equipo* to return to the team>.

re·in·te·gro m. *(restablecimiento)* restoration, reintegration; *(reembolso)* reimbursement, refund; *(pólizas)* fiscal stamps (on a document); *(en la lotería)* return of a stake (in a lottery).

re·ír §58 intr. to laugh <*echarse a r.* to burst out laughing>; FIG. *(burlar de)* to make fun of, laugh at; *(brillar)* to be bright, sparkle (one's eyes) ♦ **r. a carcajadas** to laugh out loud, split one's sides laughing • **r. con ganas** to laugh heartily • **r. con risa de conejo** or **de dientes afuera** to force a laugh or a smile • **r. de** to laugh at • **r. para su capote** to laugh or chuckle to oneself —tr. to laugh at <*r. un chiste* to laugh at a joke> —reflex. *(carcajearse)* to laugh; FIG. *(burlarse de)* to make fun of, laugh at <*reírse de alguien* to make fun of someone>; FIG., COLL. *(abrirse)* to come apart, split (clothing) ♦ **reírse de alguien en su cara** or **en sus barbas** to laugh in someone's face.

rei·te·ra·ción f. reiteration, repetition.

rei·te·rar tr. to reiterate, repeat.

rei·te·ra·ti·vo, –va adj. reiterative, repetitive.

rei·vin·di·ca·ción f. *(reclamación)* claim; LAW replevin, recovery; *(vindicación)* vindication.

rei·vin·di·car §70 tr. *(reclamar)* to claim; LAW to replevy, recover; *(indicar)* to vindicate; *(restablecer)* to restore.

re·ja f. *(del arado)* plowshare; *(cerca)* grille, grating (of a window); FIG. *(labor)* plowing ♦ **dar una r.** AGR. to plow • **estar entre rejas** to be behind bars.

re·je·ro m. railing or grate maker.

re·ji·lla f. *(red de alambre)* grille, lattice; *(celosía)* latticed window; *(tejido de una silla)* wickerwork, canework; *(braserillo)* foot stove, footwarmer; *(armazón de un horno)* fire grate; ELEC., RAD. grid; RAIL. luggage rack ♦ **de r.** wicker, wickerwork <*una mesa de r.* a wicker table> • **r. de pantalla** ELEC., RAD. screen grid • **r. del radiador** AUTO. radiator grille • **r. libre** ELEC., RAD. floating grid.

re·jo m. *(punta)* sharp point, spike; *(aguijón)* sting <*r. de una abeja* bee sting>; *(clavo)* nail, iron pin (used in quoits); *(hierro del cerco)* iron frame (of door); *(vigor)* vigor, strength; *(rebaño)* herd of dairy cows; *(azote)* whip; BOT. radicle; COL. strip of raw leather; ECUAD. milking (of cows).

re·jón m. *(varilla)* spear; *(del trompo)* point (of spinning top); *(garrocha)* goad; TAUR. lance.

re·jo·ne·a·dor m. TAUR. bullfighter on horseback.

re·jo·ne·ar tr. TAUR. to wound with a spear (the bull) —intr. to fight bulls on horseback.

re·jo·ne·o m. TAUR. spearing, lancing (of the bull).

re·jun·tar tr. to collect, gather.

re·ju·ve·ne·cer §17 tr. to rejuvenate —intr. & reflex. to be rejuvenated, rejuvenate.

re·ju·ve·ne·ci·mien·to m. rejuvenation.

re·la·ción f. *(enlace)* relationship, connection; *(trato)* relation <*relaciones públicas* public relations>; *(correspondencia)* relationship, relation <*la r. entre causa y efecto* the relationship between cause and effect>; *(relato)* tale, account; *(ponencia)* report; *(lista)* list; *(partida)* record; GRAM. relation; LAW summary; MATH. ratio <*en una r. de tres a dos* in a ratio of three to two>; *(proporción)* proportion; THEAT. long speech; ARG., URUG. refrain spoken by dancers; MEX. buried treasure ♦ **con** or **en r. a** in relation to • **estar en buenas relaciones con alguien** to be on good terms with someone • **estar en r. con alguien** to be in contact with someone • **guardar r. con algo** to bear relation to something • **hacer r. a** or **sacar a r.** to refer or make reference to • **mantener relaciones con alguien** to keep in touch with someone • **ponerse en r.** to get in touch • **r. jurada** sworn statement • **r. modular** RAD. modular ratio • **relaciones** *(cortejeo)* courting, courtship; *(personas influyentes)* connections, influential friends; *(personas conocidas)* acquaintances • **relaciones comerciales** business connections, trade relations • **relaciones de parentesco** kinship, blood relationship • **relaciones formales** engagement • **tener buenas relaciones** to be well-connected.

re·la·cio·na·do I. past part. see **relacionar** II. adj. *(emparentado)* related; *(concerniente)* concerning, regarding ♦ **r.**

con related to, connected with • **estar bien r.** to have good connections.

re·la·cio·nar tr. *(contar)* to relate, report; *(conectar)* to relate, connect —reflex. *(tener relación)* to be related *or* connected; FIG. *(hacer amistades)* to get acquainted, make friends; *(ponerse en contacto)* to get in touch.

re·la·ja·ción f. *(aflojamiento)* loosening, slackening; *(disminución en la tensión)* easing, relaxation (of tension); *(diversión)* relaxation, amusement; FIG. *(moral)* looseness, laxity; LAW mitigation, reduction (of a penalty); ANAT. relaxing, loosening (of a muscle); MED. hernia, rupture.

re·la·ja·do, –da I. past part. see **relajar** II. adj. *(aflojado)* loose, slack; AMER. *(depravado)* depraved, debauched.

re·la·ja·dor, –do·ra I. adj. relaxing; MED. laxative II. m.f. relaxer.

re·la·ja·mien·to m. var. of **relajación**.

re·la·jar tr. *(aflojar)* to loosen, slacken <**r. una cuerda** to loosen a rope>; *(hacer menos severo)* to relax, slacken (discipline); *(aliviar la tensión)* to ease, relieve (tension); FIG. *(divertir)* to relax, amuse; LAW *(relevar de un voto)* to release (from an obligation); *(aliviar el castigo)* to reduce, make less severe (a penalty); LAW, RELIG. *(entregar un reo)* to deliver (a defendant to a secular court); ANAT. to relax, loosen (up) <**r. un músculo** to relax a muscle>; CUBA, P. RICO, COLL. to mock, make fun of (someone) —reflex. *(aflojarse)* to loosen, slacken (rope); *(hacerse menos severo)* to slacken, become less severe (discipline); FIG. *(divertirse)* to relax, rest; *(viciarse)* to become dissipated, let oneself go; MED. to relax, loosen (up) (a muscle); MED. to sprain <**relajarse la muñeca** to sprain one's wrist>; *(formársele una hernia)* to get a hernia.

re·la·jo m. AMER. *(desorden)* disorder, commotion; *(depravación)* depravity, debauchery; CUBA, P. RICO joke, jest.

re·la·mer tr. to lick —reflex. *(pasarse la lengua)* to lick one's lips *or* chops; FIG. *(pintarse)* to paint one's face; *(gloriarse)* to gloat, brag.

re·la·mi·do, –da I. past part. see **relamer** II. adj. affected, prim.

re·lám·pa·go m. *(fenómeno)* lightning; *(rayo aislado)* flash of lightning; FIG. *(resplandor, cosa rápida)* flash ♦ **como un r.** like lightning, in a flash.

re·lam·pa·gue·an·te adj. flashing, sparkling.

re·lam·pa·gue·ar intr. METEOROL. to flash with lightning; FIG. *(centellar)* to flash, sparkle.

re·lam·pa·gue·o m. METEOROL. lightning; FIG. *(centello)* flash, sparkle.

re·lan·ce m. *(segundo lance)* second chance *or* try; *(suceso)* accident, coincidence; *(en el juego)* second round *or* hand ♦ **de r.** by chance.

re·lan·zar §04 tr. *(rechazar)* to repel, repulse; *(en una elección)* to recast (ballots).

re·lap·so, –sa I. adj. relapsed, backsliding II. m.f. backslider.

re·la·ta·dor, –do·ra I. adj. relating, narrating II. mf. narrator.

re·la·tar tr. *(contar)* to relate, recount; *(narrar)* to narrate, tell; LAW to report.

re·la·ti·va·men·te adv. relatively.

re·la·ti·vi·dad f. relativity.

re·la·ti·vo, –va I. adj. relative ♦ **en lo r. a** with regard to II. m. GRAM. relative.

re·la·to m. *(acción de relatar)* narrating, telling; *(informe)* report, account; *(cuento)* story, narrative, tale.

re·la·tor, –to·ra I. adj. narrating, telling II. m.f. *(de un cuento)* narrator, teller —m. *(en los tribunales)* court reporter; *(ponente)* reporter.

re·le·er §43 tr. to reread, read again.

re·le·ga·ción f. relegation.

re·le·gar §47 tr. to relegate ♦ **r. al olvido una cosa** to cast something into oblivion.

re·len·te m. *(humedad)* night dew; *(frío)* chill (of the night); FIG., COLL. *(descaro)* nerve, brazenness.

re·le·van·te adj. outstanding, notable.

re·le·var tr. *(hacer de relieve)* to emboss, carve in relief; *(exonerar)* to relieve of, release *or* free from <**r. de un gravamen** to relieve of an obligation>; *(absolver)* to absolve, pardon; FIG. *(exaltar)* to praise, exalt; *(reemplazar)* to relieve, remove (from office); MIL. to relieve (from

guard); PAINT. to paint in relief; SPORT. to relay —intr. SCULP. to stand out in relief —reflex. to take turns.

re·le·vo m. *(acto de relevar)* relief, change of the guard; *(soldado)* relief; SPORT. relay <**carrera de relevos** relay race>.

re·le·ye·ra, releyó see **releer**.

re·li·ca·rio m. RELIG. reliquary, shrine; *(medallón)* locket.

re·lie·ve m. ART., PAINT. relief; *(estampado)* embossing; GEOG. relief <**mapa en r.** relief map>; FIG. *(renombre)* prominence, importance <**dar r. a** to give prominence to> ♦ **alto r.** high relief • **bajo r.** bas-relief • **de r.** prominent, important • **en r.** in relief • **estampar en r.** to emboss • **formar r.** to stand out • **medio r.** half relief • **poner en r.** FIG. to emphasize, bring out • **relieves** leftovers, scraps.

re·li·gión f. religion ♦ **entrar en r.** to take vows.

re·li·gio·sa·men·te adv. religiously.

re·li·gio·si·dad f. *(piedad)* religiousness, piety; FIG. *(exactitud)* religiosity, scrupulousness.

re·li·gio·so, –sa I. adj. *(piadoso)* religious, pious; FIG. *(exacto)* conscientious, scrupulous II. m. monk —f. nun.

re·lin·char intr. to whinny, neigh (a horse).

re·lin·cho m. *(del caballo)* whinny, neigh; FIG. *(grito)* whoop, shout (of joy).

re·li·quia f. *(residuo)* relic; MED. malady, lingering ailment ♦ **r. de familia** family heirloom • **reliquias** relics, vestiges.

re·loj m. clock <**r. de pared** wall clock>; *(de pulsera)* watch, wristwatch; TECH. clock, meter ♦ **como un r.** FIG. like clockwork • **contra r.** SPORT. against the clock • **estar como un r.** COLL. to be in good health, be as fit as a fiddle • **marchar como un r.** FIG. to run like clockwork • **r. automático** timer, timing mechanism • **r. de agua** water clock, clepsydra • **r. de arena** hourglass, sandglass • **r. de bolsillo** pocket watch • **r. de caja** *or* **de pie** grandfather's clock • **r. de campana** *or* **de carillón** chiming clock • **r. de cuco** *or* **de cuclillo** cuckoo clock • **r. de la muerte** ENTOM. deathwatch beetle • **r. de longitudes** *or* **marino** marine chronometer • **r. de música** musical clock • **r. de péndulo** pendulum clock • **r. de sol** *or* **solar** sundial • **r. despertador** alarm clock • **relojes** ORNITH. stork's bill • **r. magistral** master *or* standard clock • **r. registrador** time clock.

re·lo·je·rí·a f. *(arte)* watchmaking, clockmaking; *(taller)* watch *or* clock factory; *(tienda)* jewelry store.

re·lo·je·ro, –ra m.f. watchmaker, clockmaker.

re·lu·cien·te adj. shining, glittering.

re·lu·cir §44 intr. *(brillar)* to shine, glitter; FIG. *(destacarse)* to shine, stand out ♦ **sacar a r.** *(mencionar)* to bring up, mention; *(poner en relieve)* to bring out • **salir a r.** to come to light.

re·lum·bran·te adj. dazzling, resplendent.

re·lum·brar intr. to dazzle, sparkle, shine brightly.

re·lum·brón m. *(golpe de luz)* flash, glare; *(oropel)* tinsel ♦ **de r.** FIG. flashy, gaudy.

re·lum·bro·so, –sa adj. dazzling, resplendent.

re·luz·ca, reluzco see **relucir**.

re·lla·nar tr. to level again —reflex. to stretch out in one's chair.

re·lla·no m. *(descansillo)* landing (of a staircase); *(llano)* shelf, terrace (among hills).

re·lle·nar tr. *(volver a llenar)* to refill, replenish; *(llenar completamente)* to fill up; *(henchir)* to fill, stuff; *(llenar un formulario)* to fill out (a form); FIG., COLL. *(dar de comer)* to stuff (with food); CUL. to fill, stuff; SEW. to pad —reflex. FIG., COLL. to stuff oneself.

re·lle·no, –na I. adj. full, stuffed II. m. *(acción)* filling, stuffing; FIG. *(parte superflua)* padding, filler; CUL. filling, stuffing; SEW. padding.

re·ma·cha·do, –da I. past part. see **remachar** II. adj. COL. quiet, reserved III. m. *(con roblón)* riveting; *(del clavo)* clinching.

re·ma·char tr. *(sujetar con roblones)* to rivet; *(machacar)* to clinch; FIG. *(recalcar)* to drive *or* hammer home (a point); *(palabras)* to stress —reflex. COL. to keep still.

re·ma·che m. *(con un roblón)* riveting; *(de un clavo)* clinching; *(roblón)* rivet; COL. stubbornness.

re·ma·dor, –do·ra m.f. rower.

re·ma·llar tr. to mend.

re·ma·nen·te m. remnant, residue; COM. surplus.

re·man·gar §47 tr. to roll or tuck up (sleeves).

re·man·sar·se reflex. to pool, form a pool (water).

re·man·so m. (charca) pool; (agua estancada) backwater; (lugar tranquilo) haven, oasis; FIG. (lentitud) sluggishness.

re·mar intr. MARIT. to row, paddle; FIG. (luchar) to struggle, toil.

re·mar·car §70 tr. to mark again.

re·ma·ta·do, –da I. past part. see rematar II. adj. (sin remedio) utter, hopeless <es un tonto r. he's an utter fool>; LAW convicted.

re·ma·ta·dor, –do·ra m. SPORT. goal scorer (in soccer); ARG., BOL. auctioneer.

re·ma·tar tr. (acabar una cosa) to finish (off), terminate; (agotar) to use up; (matar) to kill or finish off; COM. (hacer remate) to sell off cheap; (subastar) to auction (off); ARCHIT. to top, crown; SEW. to finish off, sew the last stitch; SPORT. to shoot (a goal in soccer); CHILE, EQUIT. to rein in suddenly —intr. (terminar) to end, terminate, come to an end ♦ r. en to end in, come to —reflex. to be finished or destroyed.

re·ma·te m. (fin) end, conclusion; (toque final) finishing touch; ARCHIT. (caballete) crest, ridge <el r. de un tejado the crest of a roof>; (punta) finial (ornamental top); COM. (venta en subasta) sale (at auction); (última puja) highest bid (at auction); (liquidación) closing (of an account); PRINT. vignette; SEW. last stitch; SPORT. shot (in soccer); AMER. auction; MEX., TEX. edge (of a piece of material) ♦ como or para r. to top it all (off), on top of all that • dar or poner r. a FIG. to finish or wind up • de r. (completo) utter, hopeless; (completamente) utterly, hopelessly • por r. finally, in the end.

re·ma·tis·ta m. AMER. auctioneer.

re·me·cer §75 tr. to rock, swing.

re·me·da·dor, –do·ra I. adj. copying, imitating II. m.f. mimic, imitator.

re·me·dar tr. (imitar) to copy, imitate; (burlarse) to mimic, ape.

re·me·dia·ble adj. remediable ♦ fácilmente r. easy to remedy, easily remedied.

re·me·dia·dor, –do·ra I. adj. (que repara) remedial; (que ayuda) helping II. m.f. (ayudante) helper; (consolador) comforter.

re·me·diar tr. (reparar) to remedy, repair; (corregir) to correct; (ayudar) to help, assist; (librar de un riesgo) to save, protect; (evitar) to prevent, avoid; FIG. (resolver) to solve.

re·me·dio m. (medio que repara) remedy, solution; (medicamento) remedy, cure; (enmienda) correction; (ayuda) relief, help; LAW recourse, remedy ♦ como último r. as a last resort • no haber (más) r. to be unavoidable, be no other way • no tener más r. to have no alternative or choice • no tener más r. que hacer algo to have no alternative but to do something • no tener r. to be beyond repair or hope, be hopeless <esta situación no tiene r. this situation is hopeless>; (ser inevitable) to be inevitable • poner r. a to put a stop to, do something about • r. casero household remedy • r. heroico FIG. drastic measure • sin r. (sin falta) without fail; (irremediable) unavoidable, inevitable; (irremediablemente) unavoidably, inevitably.

re·me·do m. (copia) imitation, copy; (parodia) poor imitation, travesty.

re·me·llón, –llo·na adj. COLL. jagged, split.

re·mem·bran·za f. memory, remembrance.

re·mem·brar tr. to remember, recall.

re·me·mo·ra·ción f. remembrance, recollection.

re·me·mo·rar tr. to remember, recall.

re·me·mo·ra·ti·vo, –va adj. commemorative, reminding.

re·men·da·do, –da I. past part. see remendar II. adj. (con remiendos) patched; (con manchas) spotted, patchy.

re·men·dar §49 tr. (reparar) to mend, repair; SEW. to patch, darn; FIG. (corregir) to correct.

re·men·dón, –do·na I. adj. mending, repairing II. m.f. (que repara) mender, repairer; (zapatero) shoemaker, cobbler.

re·me·ro, –ra m.f. rower, paddler.

re·me·sa f. (de dinero) remittance; (de mercancías) shipment, consignment.

re·me·sar tr. (enviar dinero) to remit; (enviar mercancías) to ship, send; (arrancar) to pull or pluck out (hair).

re·me·ter tr. (volver a meter) to put back; (meter más adentro) to tuck in.

re·me·za, remezo see remecer.

re·me·zón m. AMER. mild earthquake.

re·mien·de, remiendo see remendar.

re·mien·do m. (acción de remendar) mending, repairing; FIG. (enmienda) emendation, correction; SEW. (acción) patching; (pedazo) patch; FIG. improvement; ZOOL. spot (on an animal's skin); PRINT. jobwork ♦ a remiendos in bits and pieces, piecemeal • echar un r. FIG. to patch (something) up.

re·mil·ga·do, –da I. past part. see remilgarse II. adj. fussy, affected.

re·mil·gar·se §47 reflex. to behave affectedly.

re·mil·go m. fussiness, affectedness.

re·mi·nis·cen·cia f. reminiscence.

re·mi·ra·do, –da I. past part. see remirar II. adj. (meticuloso) meticulous, cautious; (melindroso) fussy, finicky.

re·mi·rar tr. (volver a mirar) to look at again; (examinar) to look closely at, examine —reflex. (esmerarse) to take pains with; (mirar con deleite) to look at with pleasure.

re·mi·si·ble adj. remissible.

re·mi·sión f. (envío) sending, remittance; (entrega) delivery; (perdón) pardon, forgiveness; (indicación) reference; MED. remission ♦ sin r. without fail.

re·mi·si·vo, –va adj. reference <nota r. reference note>.

re·mi·so, –sa adj. (negligente) careless, remiss; (perezoso) slack, indolent.

re·mi·sor, –so·ra AMER. I. adj. sending, shipping II. m.f. sender, shipper.

re·mi·ten·te I. adj. (que remite) remittent, remitting; MED. remittent II. m.f. sender <devuélvase al r. return to sender>.

re·mi·ti·do I. past part. see remitir II. m. advertisement, announcement (in a newspaper).

re·mi·tir tr. (enviar) to send, transmit; (enviar dinero) to remit (money); (perdonar) to forgive, pardon; (demorar) to put off, postpone; (ceder intensidad) to slacken, diminish; (dejar al juicio de otro) to remit, leave (to someone's judgment) <r. el asunto al gerente to leave the matter to the manager's judgment>; (referir) to refer; COM. to ship, consign; LAW to transfer (a case) —intr. (ceder) to diminish, let up; (hacer referencia a) to refer to —reflex. (atenerse) to yield or defer to, abide by; (referirse) to refer.

re·mo m. (grande) oar; (pequeño) paddle; FIG. (trabajo pesado) stretch of hard work, toil; SPORT. rowing; ANAT. (miembro) limb (of man); (pata) leg (of an animal); ORNITH. wing ♦ a r. y sin sueldo FIG., COLL. working hard for nothing, laboring in vain • a r. y vela FIG., COLL. quickly, efficiently • al r. rowing • andar al r. FIG. to go at it, work hard • ir a r. to row.

re·mo·cé, remoce see remozar.

re·mo·ción f. (acción de remover) removing, removal; (de personal) dismissal (of employees).

re·mo·jar tr. (mojar) to soak, steep; (pan, galleta) to dip, dunk; (celebrar) to celebrate, drink to; AMER. to tip.

re·mo·jo m. (acción de remojar) soaking, steeping; AMER. tip, gratuity ♦ echar en r. FIG., COLL. to put off, let ride • poner en r. to soak.

re·mo·la·cha f. BOT. beet.

re·mo·la·che·ro, –ra I. adj. beet <la industria r. the beet industry> II. m.f. beet grower.

re·mol·ca·dor, –do·ra I. adj. towing, tugging II. m. AUTO. tow truck; MARIT. tugboat.

re·mol·car §70 tr. (arrastrar) to tow, haul; FIG. (convencer) to rope (someone) in.

re·mo·ler §78 tr. (moler mucho) to grind very fine; CHILE, PERU to live it up, have a ball; PERU to exasperate, wear out (patience).

re·mo·li·do I. past part. see remoler II. m. MIN. fine unwashed ore.

re·mo·lien·da f. CHILE, PERU, COLL. binge, spree.

re·mo·li·nar intr. (formar remolinos) to spin, whirl; (amontonarse) to mill, throng.

re·mo·li·ne·ar tr. & intr. to spin, whirl.

re·mo·li·no m. (de agua) whirlpool, eddy; (de aire) whirlwind; (de polvo) whirl, flurry; (de pelo) cowlick; (muche-

dumbre) throng, crowd; *(movimiento)* milling; *(disturbio)* commotion, disturbance.

re·mo·lón I. m. upper tusk (of a wild boar) ♦ **remolones** sharp points (of horses' teeth) **II.** adj. see **remolón, –lona.**

re·mo·lón, –lo·na I. adj. lazy, indolent **II.** m.f. *(holgazán)* loafer, goof-off —m. see **remolón.**

re·mo·lo·ne·ar intr. COLL. to loaf, goof off.

re·mol·que m. *(acción de remolcar)* towing; *(cabo)* tow, towrope; *(vehículo remolcado)* tow, towed vehicle; *(casa remolque)* trailer ♦ **a r.** in tow • **dar r. a** to tow.

re·mol·qué, remolque see **remolcar.**

re·mon·ta f. *(compostura del calzado)* shoe repair; *(remiendo de una prenda)* mending (of clothing); *(parche)* leather patch (on riding breeches); EQUIT. stuffing *or* padding (of a saddle); MIL. *(conjunto de caballos)* supply of remounts (new horses); *(establecimiento)* remount establishment.

re·mon·tar tr. *(componer el calzado)* to repair (shoes); *(echar un remiendo)* to patch (pants); *(superar)* to overcome, surmount; *(elevar)* to elevate, raise; FIG. *(encumbrar)* to honor; HUNT. to frighten away (game); MIL. to remount, supply with new horses; EQUIT. to stuff, pad (a saddle) ♦ **r. el vuelo** to soar —reflex. *(volar muy alto)* to soar; *(subir hasta el origen)* to go back to, date from <*la leyenda se remonta al siglo XIV* the legend dates from the 14th century>; *(refugiarse un cimarrón)* to flee *or* take to the hills (slaves); FIG. *(inspirarse)* to soar <*remontarse en alas de la esperanza* to soar on the wings of hope>; FIN. to amount to.

re·mon·te m. *(compostura)* repair, repairing; *(elevación)* rising; *(vuelo)* soaring; MIL. remounting, supplying with new horses.

re·mo·que·te m. *(puñetazo)* punch, blow with the fist; FIG. *(dicho agudo)* witticism, epigram; COLL. *(galanteo)* courting; SL. *(apodo)* nickname.

ré·mo·ra f. ICHTH. remora; FIG., COLL. *(obstáculo)* hindrance, obstacle.

re·mor·der §78 tr. *(morder)* to bite, gnaw; FIG. *(inquietar)* to trouble, worry ♦ **r. la conciencia** to prey on one's conscience —reflex. to show remorse.

re·mor·di·mien·to m. remorse.

re·mos·que·ar·se reflex. COLL. *(escamarse)* to become suspicious *or* wary; PRINT. to mackle.

re·mo·to, –ta adj. *(lejano)* remote, distant; FIG. *(improbable)* remote, unlikely.

re·mo·ver §78 tr. *(mover)* to move, transfer; *(quitar)* to remove, take away; *(alterar)* to upset, disturb; *(deponer)* to fire, dismiss; *(mezclar)* to stir; *(recuerdos)* to revive, stir up —reflex. to shake, stir.

re·mo·zar §04 tr. *(rejuvenecer)* to rejuvenate, renew; FIG. *(actualizar)* to update, bring up to date —reflex. to be rejuvenated.

rem·pla·zar §04 tr. var. of **reemplazar.**

rem·pu·jar tr. COLL. var. of **empujar.**

rem·pu·jo m. COLL. *(empujón)* pushing, shoving; MARIT. sailmaker's palm.

rem·pu·jón m. COLL. var. of **empujón.**

re·mue·la, remuelo see **remoler.**

re·muer·da, remuerdo see **remorder.**

re·mue·va, remuevo see **remover.**

re·mu·ne·ra·ble adj. remunerable.

re·mu·ne·ra·ción f. remuneration.

re·mu·ne·ra·dor, –do·ra I. adj. *(rentable)* remunerative *(que remunera)* remunerating **II.** m.f. remunerator.

re·mu·ne·rar tr. to remunerate, pay.

re·mu·ne·ra·ti·vo, –va adj. remunerative.

re·mus·gar §47 intr. to suspect, guess.

re·mus·go m. *(sospecha)* suspicion, guess; *(vientecillo)* cold breeze.

re·na·cen·tis·ta I. adj. Renaissance <*estilo r.* Renaissance style> **II.** m.f. expert on the Renaissance.

re·na·cer §17 intr. *(nacer de nuevo)* to be reborn; FIG. *(recobrar fuerzas)* to recover, revive; *(reaparecer)* to reappear.

re·na·ci·mien·to m. rebirth, revival ♦ **Renacimiento** HIST. Renaissance.

re·na·cua·jo m. ZOOL. tadpole, polliwog; FIG., COLL. *(hombrecillo)* shrimp, squirt.

re·nal adj. ANAT. renal.

re·naz·ca, renazco see **renacer.**

ren·ci·lla f. quarrel, fight.

ren·co, –ca I. adj. lame **II.** m.f. lame person.

ren·cor m. rancor, resentment ♦ **guardar r. a alguien** to hold a grudge against someone.

ren·co·ro·so, –sa adj. rancorous, resentful.

ren·da·je m. set of reins *or* bridles.

ren·di·ción f. *(entrega)* surrender; *(sumisión)* submissiveness, submission; *(utilidad)* yield, return.

ren·di·do, –da I. past part. see **rendir II.** adj. *(obsequioso)* obsequious; *(sumiso)* subsmissive, humble <*r. admirador* humble admirer>; *(cansado)* exhausted, worn-out.

ren·di·ja f. crack, split.

ren·di·mien·to m. *(cansancio)* exhaustion; *(sumisión)* submissiveness, submission; *(obsequiosidad)* obsequiousness; *(producto)* yield; *(utilidad)* yield, return; *(funcionamiento)* performance <*r. de un motor* a motor's performance>.

ren·dir §48 tr. *(vencer)* to defeat, overcome; *(sujetar)* to dominate, subect to one's control <*r. un animal al dominio* to subject an animal to one's control>; *(entregar)* to surrender, hand over; *(restituir)* to give back, return; *(producir)* to produce, yield; *(dar utilidad)* to yield; *(dar fruto)* to bear (fruit); *(cansar)* to exhaust, tire out; *(vomitar)* to vomit, throw up; MARIT. to finish (a journey); MIL. *(pasar)* to hand over <*r. la guardia* to hand over the guard>; *(arriar bandera)* to dip (the flag); *(entregar las armas)* to lay down (arms) ♦ **r. cuentas de** to give an explanation *or* account of • **r. culto a** *(venerar)* to worship; *(homenajear)* to pay homage *or* tribute to • **r. examen** to take an examination • **r. homenaje** to pay homage • **r. las gracias** to give *or* say thanks —intr. *(dar utilidad)* to yield, produce, pay (off); AMER. *(expandir)* to swell, expand; *(durar mucho)* to last longer than usual —reflex. *(someterse al vencedor)* to surrender, submit; *(sujetarse)* to yield <*rendirse a la fuerza* to yield to force>; *(cansarse)* to wear oneself out, exhaust oneself; MARIT. to snap, crack (a mast) ♦ **rendirse a la evidencia** to bow before the evidence • **rendirse a la razón** to yield *or* listen to reason.

re·ne·ga·do, –da I. past part. see **renegar II.** adj. *(apóstata)* apostate; FIG., COLL. *(de mal carácter)* gruff, bad-tempered **III.** m.f. *(apóstata)* renegade, apostate; FIG., COLL. *(persona de mal carácter)* gruff *or* bad-tempered person —m. *(juego)* ombre (card game).

re·ne·ga·dor, –do·ra I. adj. swearing, blasphemous **II.** m.f. swearer, blasphemer.

re·ne·gar §52 tr. *(negar mucho)* to deny strongly; *(detestar)* to detest, abhor —intr. RELIG. to apostasize, renounce one's faith; *(blasfemar)* to swear, blaspheme; COLL. *(quejarse)* to grumble, complain ♦ **r. de** to renounce, disown <*r. de la familia* to disown one's family>.

re·ne·gón, –go·na COLL. **I.** adj. swearing **II.** m.f. swearer.

re·ne·gri·do, –da adj. blackish, black.

ren·glón m. *(línea)* line (of words); *(partida)* item ♦ **a r. seguido** FIG., COLL. right after, in short order • **leer entre renglones** to read between the lines.

ren·go, –ga I. adj. lame, crippled **II.** m.f. lame person, cripple.

ren·gue·ar intr. AMER. to limp, hobble.

re·nie·go m. curse, oath.

re·nie·gue, reniego see **renegar.**

re·nio m. CHEM. rhenium.

re·no m. ZOOL. reindeer.

re·nom·bra·do, –da adj. famous, renowned.

re·nom·bre m. *(fama)* fame, renown; *(apodo)* nickname.

re·no·va·ble adj. renewable.

re·no·va·ción f. *(extensión)* renewal; *(restauración)* renovation.

re·no·va·dor, –do·ra I. adj. renewing, restoring **II.** m.f. renewer, restorer.

re·no·var §19 tr. *(extender)* to renew; *(reemplazar)* to replace; *(repetir)* to renew, repeat; *(restaurar)* to renovate, restore; *(decorar)* to redecorate —reflex. to be renewed.

ren·que·ar intr. to limp, hobble.

ren·que·o m. *or* **ren·que·ra** f. AMER. limp.

ren·ta f. *(ingresos)* income, revenue; *(ganancia)* profit, earnings; *(interés)* interest; *(alquiler)* rent; *(que se paga anualmente)* annuity; *(deuda pública)* national debt ♦ **distribución de la r.** distribution of wealth • **r. bruta** gross income • **r. gravable** *or* **imponible** taxable income • **r.**

líquida net income • **r. vitalicia** life annuity • **rentas del trabajo** earned income.

ren·ta·bi·li·dad f. profitability.

ren·ta·ble adj. profitable.

ren·tar tr. *(producir renta)* to yield, produce (income, profit); AMER. *(alquilar)* to rent, let.

ren·tis·ta m.f. *(accionista)* bondholder, holder of Government bonds; *(persona que vive de sus rentas)* independently wealthy person.

re·nuen·cia f. reluctance, unwillingness.

re·nuen·te adj. reluctant, unwilling.

re·nue·ve, renuevo see **renovar.**

re·nun·cia f. *(abandono)* renunciation; *(a un puesto)* resignation (from a post); LAW waiver.

re·nun·cia·ción f. renunciation.

re·nun·cia·mien·to m. renunciation.

re·nun·ciar tr. *(abandonar)* to renounce, give up; *(a un puesto)* to resign (a post); *(no aceptar)* to refuse, reject; *(en naipes)* to renege, revoke (in cards); LAW to waive, drop (a suit).

re·nun·cio m. *(en naipes)* revoke, renounce (in cards); COLL. *(mentira)* lie, contradiction <**coger en r.** to catch in a lie>.

re·ñi·de·ro m. pit (for animal fights) <**r. de gallos** cockpit>.

re·ñi·do, –da I. past part. see **reñir II.** adj. *(enemistado)* on bad terms, at odds <**estar r. con un vecino** to be on bad terms with a neighbor>; *(difícil)* hard-fought, bitter <**una lucha r.** a bitter struggle> ♦ **en lo más r. de la batalla** in the thick of the battle • **r. con** at variance with, contrary to <**r. con la política oficial** contrary to official policy>.

re·ñi·dor, –do·ra adj. *(que regaña)* scolding; *(pendenciero)* quarrelsome.

re·ñi·du·ra f. COLL. scolding, reprimand.

re·ñir §59 intr. *(disputar)* to argue, quarrel; *(enemistarse)* to quarrel, fall out <**r. con su familia** to fall out with one's family>; *(batallar)* to fight, come to blows ♦ **en buena lid** to have a fair fight • **r. por** to fight for or over —tr. *(regañar)* to scold, reprimand; *(llevar a cabo)* to fight, wage <**r. una batalla** to wage a battle>.

re·o, –a I. m.f. *(acusado)* accused, defendant; *(delincuente)* criminal, offender **II.** adj. guilty (of a crime).

re·o·jo ♦ **mirar de r.** *(mirar con disimulo)* to look out of the corner of one's eye; FIG., COLL *(con enfado)* to look askance at.

re·or·de·na·ción f. rearranging, reordering.

re·or·ga·ni·za·ción f. reorganization.

re·or·ga·ni·za·dor, –do·ra I. adj. reorganizing **II.** m.f. reorganizer.

re·or·ga·ni·zar §04 tr. to reorganize.

re·pan·chi·gar·se or **re·pan·ti·gar·se** §47 reflex. to stretch or sprawl out.

re·pa·ra·ble adj. *(remendable)* repairable, reparable <**daño r.** repairable damage>; *(digno de atención)* noteworthy.

re·pa·ra·ción f. *(acción de reparar)* repairing, mending; *(compostura)* repair <**r. de calzado** shoe repair>; *(desagravio)* reparation, amends ♦ **en r.** under repair.

re·pa·ra·dor, –do·ra I. adj. *(que compone)* repairing, repair; *(reparón)* faultfinding, critical; *(que restablece las fuerzas)* restorative, refreshing **II.** m.f. *(que compone)* repairer; *(reparón)* faultfinder, carper —m. repairman.

re·pa·rar tr. *(componer)* to repair, fix, mend; *(notar)* to notice, observe; *(corregir)* to correct; *(desagraviar)* to make amends for <**r. una ofensa** to make amends for an insult>; *(remediar)* to make up for, redress <**reparó el daño que hizo** he made up for the damage he did>; *(evitar un golpe)* to parry, deflect (a blow); *(restablecer las fuerzas)* to restore, refresh <**r. el ánimo a uno** to restore one's spirit>; BOL. to mimic, imitate —intr. *(parar)* to stop; GUAT., MEX. to rear, buck (a horse) ♦ **no r. en nada** to stop at nothing • **r. en** *(considerar)* to pay attention, consider <**repara bien en sus consejos** pay close attenation to her advice>; *(notar)* to notice, observe <**no reparé en su llegada** I didn't notice his arrival> • **r. en detalles** or **en pelillos** to be a stickler for details.

re·pa·ro m. *(remedio)* repair; *(restauración)* restoration; *(objeción)* objection, criticism; *(duda)* misgiving, doubt; *(defensa)* defense, protection; *(mancha)* spot (on the eye or eyelid); MED. remedy, restorative; SPORT. parry (in fencing); GUAT., MEX., SALV., EQUIT. rearing, bucking (of a

horse) ♦ **no andar con reparos** not to hesitate or doubt • **no tener reparos en hacer algo** not to hesitate to do something • **poner reparos (a)** to object (to), find fault (with) • **tirar un r.** GUAT., MEX., SALV., EQUIT. to rear, buck (a horse).

re·pa·rón, –ro·na adj. COLL. faultfinding, critical.

re·par·ti·ble adj. distributable.

re·par·ti·ción f. sharing, division.

re·par·ti·da f. var. of **reparto.**

re·par·ti·dor, –do·ra I. adj. distributing **II.** m.f. *(persona que reparte)* distributor; *(entregador)* deliverer ♦ **r. de la leche** milkman • **r. de periódicos** newspaper boy.

re·par·ti·ja f. var. of **reparto.**

re·par·ti·mien·to m. *(reparto)* sharing, division; *(distribución)* distribution; *(del impuesto)* assessment.

re·par·tir tr. *(dividir)* to share, divide; *(distribuir)* to distribute, hand out; *(entregar)* to deliver; *(colocar en varios sitios)* to space, spread out; COLL. *(bofetadas)* to hand out (blows); THEAT. to cast.

re·par·to m. *(división)* sharing, division; *(distribución)* distribution; *(entrega)* delivery; *(naipes)* deal; CINEM., THEAT. casting.

re·pa·sa·dor m. AMER. dishcloth.

re·pa·sar tr. *(pasar de nuevo)* to go down or along again, pass (by) again <**r. una calle** to go down a street again>; *(examinar de nuevo)* to go over (again), re-examine; *(examinar para corregir)* to check or look over; *(recorrer lo estudiado)* to review, go over <**r. la tarea** to review one's homework>; *(hojear)* to skim (through), glance over; *(volver a explicar)* to explain again, go over (a lesson); *(hacer de nuevo)* to go over (again); *(dar los últimos toques)* to polish (up); *(recoser)* to mend, sew; MECH. to check, overhaul; MIN. to amalgamate (silver ore) —intr. to go down or along again, pass (by) again <**r. por un camino** to go down a road again>.

re·pa·sa·ta f. COLL. scolding, reprimand.

re·pa·so m. *(lectura ligera)* review (of a lesson); *(examinación)* going over, examination; *(remiendo)* mending; COLL. *(repasata)* scolding, reprimand; MECH. check, overhaul ♦ **dar un r. a** to look over or through.

re·pa·te·ar tr. COLL. to bother, annoy.

re·pa·tria·ción f. repatriation.

re·pa·tria·do, –da I. past part. see **repatriar II.** adj. repatriated **III.** m.f. repatriate.

re·pa·triar §30 tr. to repatriate —reflex. to return to one's country.

re·pe·char tr. to go uphill.

re·pe·cho m. short steep incline ♦ **a r.** uphill.

re·pe·lar tr. *(tirar del pelo)* to pull the hair of; *(cortar la hierba)* to clip, crop (grass); FIG. *(cercenar)* to cut (down), trim; EQUIT. to make (a horse) take a short gallop; MEX. to exasperate, irritate.

re·pe·len·te adj. repellent, repulsive.

re·pe·ler tr. *(repugnar)* to repel; *(contradecir)* to reject (an idea); *(resistir)* to repel, shed (water).

re·pe·lo m. *(lo que no va al pelo)* part going against the grain or nap; *(de las uñas)* hangnail; *(en la madera)* cross grain (in wood); FIG., COLL. *(riña)* fight, scuffle; *(repugnancia)* aversion, repugnance.

re·pe·lón m. *(tirón del pelo)* pull of the hair; *(en las medias)* snag, pulled thread (in stocking); *(porción)* small portion; EQUIT. short gallop ♦ **a repelones** COLL. slowly, with effort • **de r.** COLL. swiftly, in passing • **repelones** MIN. flames escaping from a furnace.

re·pen·te m. start, sudden movement ♦ **de r.** suddenly.

re·pen·ti·na·men·te adv. suddenly.

re·pen·ti·no, –na adj. sudden.

re·per·cu·sión f. repercussion.

re·per·cu·tir intr. *(rebotar)* to rebound; *(resonar)* to reverberate, resound ♦ **r. en** to have repercussions on —reflex. to reverberate —tr. MED. to repel.

re·per·to·rio m. repertory, repertoire.

re·pe·ti·ción f. *(acción de repetir)* repetition; *(mecanismo)* repeating mechanism; MUS., THEAT. encore.

re·pe·ti·dor, –do·ra I. adj. repeating **II.** m. *(preceptor)* tutor; TELEC. repeater.

re·pe·tir §48 tr. *(rehacer)* to repeat; *(comer más)* to have a second helping of; *(recitar)* to recite (a lesson); LAW to demand, claim —intr. to repeat (a taste) —reflex. to repeat itself *or* oneself.

re·pe·ti·ti·vo, –va adj. repetitive.

re·pi·car §70 tr. *(sonar)* to ring (bells); *(en naipes)* to repique (in cards); CUL. to mince, chop finely ♦ **r. gordo** COLL. to celebrate in style —intr. *(campanas)* to peal, ring out —reflex. to boast, brag.

re·pin·tar tr. to repaint —reflex. *(afeitarse)* to put on heavy makeup; PRINT. to mackle, blur.

re·pi·que m. *(de campanas)* ringing, pealing (of bells); COLL. *(riña)* squabble, wrangle; *(en naipes)* repique.

re·pi·que·te m. *(de campanas)* lively pealing (of bells); *(riña)* squabble, quarrel; COL. pique, resentment.

re·pi·que·te·ar tr. *(las campanas)* to ring (bells) rapidly; *(tambor)* to beat; FIG. *(golpear)* to drum, tap (on).

re·pi·que·te·o m. *(de campanas)* lively pealing *or* ringing (of bells); FIG. *(de lluvia)* pitter-patter; *(con los dedos)* drumming, tapping.

re·pi·sa f. ARCHIT. bracket, console; *(estante)* shelf.

re·pi·ta, repito see **repetir.**

re·pi·tie·ra, repitió see **repetir.**

re·plan·ta·ción f. *(segunda plantación)* replanting; *(transplantación)* transplanting.

re·plan·tar tr. *(volver a plantar)* to replant; *(transplantar)* to transplant.

re·plan·te·ar tr. *(trazar)* to lay out a ground plan of (a building); *(exponer)* to restate (a problem).

re·plan·te·o s. laying out the ground plan (of a building).

re·ple·ción f. repletion, fullness.

re·ple·gar §52 tr. *(plegar)* to fold over, make folds in; AER. to retract (wheels) —reflex. MIL. to retreat, fall back.

re·ple·to, –ta adj. replete, full ♦ **r. de** crammed full of, packed with.

ré·pli·ca f. *(contestación)* reply, retort; *(copia)* replica, copy; LAW replication ♦ **sin r.** *(cortado)* speechless; *(indiscutiblemente)* unquestionably.

re·pli·car §70 tr. to answer, reply to —intr. *(contestar)* to reply, retort; *(disputar)* to argue, answer back; LAW to answer.

re·pli·cón, –co·na COLL. **I.** adj. argumentative **II.** m.f. argumentative person.

re·plie·go, repliegue see **replegar.**

re·plie·gue m. *(pliegue)* fold, crease; MIL. falling back, retreat.

re·pli·qué, replique see **replicar.**

re·po·bla·ción f. *(de gente)* repopulation; *(de peces)* restocking (with fish) ♦ **r. forestal** reforestation.

re·po·blar §19 tr. *(de gente)* to repopulate; *(de peces)* to restock (with fish); *(de árboles)* to reforest.

re·po·drir §84 tr. & reflex. var. of **repudrir.**

re·po·llo m. BOT. *(col)* cabbage; *(de lechuga)* head (of lettuce).

re·po·llu·do, –da adj. BOT. cabbage-headed; FIG. *(rechoncho)* round, chubby.

re·po·ner §54 tr. *(poner de nuevo)* to put back, reinstate; *(reemplazar)* to replace; *(replicar)* to reply, retort; THEAT. to revive —reflex. *(recuperarse)* to recover (health); *(serenarse)* to calm down.

re·por·ta·je m. JOURN. report, article.

re·por·tar tr. *(reprimir)* to check, curb (a feeling); *(conseguir)* to get, obtain; *(traer)* to bring; PRINT. to transfer (a lithograph) —reflex. to restrain *or* control oneself.

re·por·te m. *(chisme)* rumor, gossip; *(noticia)* news, report; PRINT. transfer.

re·por·te·ro, –ra **I.** adj. reporting **II.** m.f. reporter.

re·po·sa·do, –da **I.** past part. see **reposar** **II.** adj. *(descansado)* rested, relaxed; *(tranquilo)* calm, peaceful.

re·po·sa·piés m. [pl. **-piés**] footrest.

re·po·sar intr. *(descansar)* to rest, relax; *(yacer)* to lie, be buried; *(posarse)* to settle (liquids) —reflex. to settle (liquids).

re·po·si·ción f. *(acción de reemplazar)* replacement, replenishment; MED. recovery; THEAT. revival.

re·po·si·to·rio m. repository.

re·po·so m. rest, repose.

re·pos·te·rí·a f. *(tienda)* pastry *or* confectionery shop; *(despensa)* pantry; *(oficio)* pastry making, confectionery.

re·pos·te·ro m.f. *(pastelero)* pastry cook, confectioner; *(en*

un palacio) king's butler; HER. cloth adorned with a coat of arms.

re·pren·der tr. to scold, reprimand.

re·pren·si·ble adj. reprehensible.

re·pren·sión f. reprehension, reprimand.

re·pren·sor, –so·ra **I.** adj. reproachful **II.** m.f. reproacher, rebuker.

re·pre·sa f. *(acción de represar)* damming, holding back; *(detención del agua)* dam, dike; *(de molino)* millpond; FIG. *(parada)* damming up, stopping.

re·pre·sa·lia f. reprisal, retaliation.

re·pre·sar tr. *(detener agua)* to dam, hold back (water); FIG. *(contener)* to check, hold back; MARIT. to recapture (a ship).

re·pre·sen·ta·ble adj. *(que puede hacerse visible)* representable; THEAT. performable.

re·pre·sen·ta·ción f. *(imagen)* representation, image; *(autoridad)* rank, authority; *(petición)* petition; *(de una nación)* representatives (of a nation); THEAT. performance, production.

re·pre·sen·ta·dor, –do·ra adj. representing.

re·pre·sen·tan·te **I.** adj. representing **II.** m.f. COM., POL. representative; THEAT. actor —f. actress.

re·pre·sen·tar tr. *(volver a presentar)* to present again; *(ser imagen de)* to represent, stand for; *(ser agente de)* to represent, act for; *(declarar)* to state, represent; *(equivaler a)* to represent <*esto representa diez años de trabajo* this represents ten years of work>; FIG. *(aparentar)* to look, appear to be (a certain age); THEAT. to put on, perform —intr. to imagine, picture.

re·pre·sen·ta·ti·vo, –va adj. representative.

re·pre·sión f. repression, control.

re·pre·si·vo, –va adj. repressive.

re·pre·sor, –so·ra **I.** adj. repressing **II.** m.f. represser, repressor.

re·pri·men·da f. reprimand.

re·pri·mir tr. to repress —reflex. to repress *or* stop oneself.

re·pro·ba·ble adj. reprehensible.

re·pro·ba·ción f. censure, reproof.

re·pro·bar §19 tr. to reprove, condemn.

re·pro·ba·to·rio, –ria adj. reprobative, condemning.

ré·pro·bo, –ba adj. & m.f. reprobate.

re·pro·cha·ble adj. reproachable.

re·pro·char tr. to reproach <*r. algo a alguien* to reproach someone for something>.

re·pro·che m. reproach, rebuke.

re·pro·duc·ción f. reproduction.

re·pro·du·ci·ble adj. reproducible.

re·pro·du·cir §22 tr. & reflex. to reproduce.

re·pro·duc·tor, –to·ra **I.** adj. *(que copia)* reproducing; BIOL. reproductive; ZOOL. breeding **II.** m.f. BIOL. reproducer; ZOOL. breeder.

re·prue·be, repruebo see **reprobar.**

rep·ta·ción f. slithering, crawling.

rep·tan·te adj. slithering, crawling; BOT. creeping.

rep·tar intr. to slither, crawl.

rep·til ZOOL. **I.** adj. reptilian, reptile **II.** m. reptile.

re·pú·bli·ca f. republic.

República Cen·tro·a·fri·ca·na f. Central African Republic.

República Do·mi·ni·ca·na f. Dominican Republic.

re·pu·bli·ca·nis·mo m. republicanism.

re·pu·bli·ca·no, –na adj. & m.f. republican.

re·pu·dia·ble adj. repudiable.

re·pu·dia·ción f. repudiation.

re·pu·diar tr. to repudiate; LAW to renounce, relinquish.

re·pu·dio m. repudiation.

re·pu·drir §84 tr. to rot away —reflex. *(pudrirse)* to rot away; FIG., COLL. *(consumirse)* to pine away, eat one's heart out.

re·pue·ble, repueblo see **repoblar.**

re·pues·to m. var. of **recambio.**

re·pues·to, –ta **I.** past part. see **reponer** **II.** adj. *(puesto de nuevo)* replaced, restored; *(apartado)* retired, withdrawn; MED. recovered **III.** m. *(reserva)* stock, supply; *(pieza de recambio)* spare (part); *(mueble)* sideboard ♦ **de r.** spare.

re·pug·nan·cia f. *(antipatía)* repugnance; *(oposición)* opposition, conflict.

re·pug·nan·te adj. repugnant, disgusting, repulsive.

re·pug·nar tr. *(contradecir)* to contradict <*repugnaba todo lo que yo decía* he contradicted everything I said>; *(rehusar)* to do reluctantly —intr. to loathe, detest <*las arañas me repugnan* I detest spiders>.

re·pu·ja·do I. past part. see **repujar** II. m. TECH. repoussé.

re·pu·jar tr. TECH. to do repoussé on.

re·pul·ga·do, –da I. past part. see **repulgar** II. adj. COLL. affected.

re·pul·gar §47 tr. SEW. to hem, overcast.

re·pul·go m. SEW. hem, overcasting; CUL. border (on pastry).

re·pu·li·do, –da I. past part. see **repulir** II. adj. neat, spruce.

re·pu·lir tr. *(pulir)* to polish; *(acicalar)* to smarten *or* dress up —reflex. to dress up.

re·pul·sar tr. to repulse, reject.

re·pul·sión f. *(aversión)* repulsion, repugnance; *(negativa)* rejection.

re·pul·si·vo, –va adj. repulsive.

re·pun·ta f. GEOG. *(cabo)* cape, point; FIG. *(indicio)* sign, indication; FIG., COLL. *(riña)* squabble, quarrel.

re·pun·tar tr. AMER. to round up (cattle) —intr. *(empezar la marea)* to turn (the tide); AMER. to begin to appear; ARG. to round up (cattle) —reflex. *(picarse)* to turn sour (wine); FIG., COLL. *(disgustarse)* to quarrel, fall out.

re·pun·te m. MARIT. turning (of the tide); ARG. *(de ganado)* rounding up (cattle); *(de precios)* price rise.

re·pu·sie·ra, repuso see **reponer**.

re·pu·ta·ción f. reputation.

re·pu·tar tr. *(considerar)* to consider, deem <*le reputan de sabio* he is considered wise>; *(apreciar)* to esteem, appreciate.

re·que·brar §49 tr. *(volver a quebrar)* to break again; *(cortejar)* to flirt with, court; *(lisonjear)* to flatter.

re·que·ma·do, –da I. past part. see **requemar** II. adj. *(quemado)* burned, charred; *(bronceado)* tanned, sunburned.

re·que·mar tr. *(quemar)* to scorch, burn; CUL. to overcook; *(secar)* to wither, parch (plants); *(resquemar)* to burn (the mouth); *(encender la sangre)* to inflame (passions) —reflex. *(quemarse)* to burn, scorch; *(secarse)* to shrivel, become parched (plants); FIG. *(sentirse)* to harbor resentment.

re·que·ri·dor, –do·ra *or* **re·que·rien·te** I. adj. requiring II. m.f. *(persona que requiere)* requirer —m. LAW summons server.

re·que·ri·mien·to m. LAW summons, order, injunction; *(demanda)* request.

re·que·rir §65 tr. *(intimar)* to summon, order; *(solicitar)* to request, ask; *(examinar)* to examine, investigate; *(necesitar)* to require, need; LAW to summon ♦ **r. (de amores)** to court, woo.

re·que·són m. *(queso)* cottage *or* pot cheese; *(cuajada)* curd.

re·que·te·bién adv. COLL. wonderfully, marvelously.

re·quie·bre, requiebro see **requebrar**.

re·quie·bro m. *(lisonja)* compliment, flattery; MIN. crushed ore.

ré·quiem m. MUS., RELIG. requiem.

re·quie·ra, requiero see **requerir**.

re·qui·lo·rio m. COLL. useless formality.

re·quin·tar tr. *(pujar la quinta parte)* to outbid by one-fifth; *(exceder)* to surpass, excel; MUS. to raise *or* lower a fifth; HOND. to begin; AMER. to tighten, squeeze.

re·quin·to m. *(segundo quinto)* second fifth; *(puja)* raise by a fifth (in bidding); *(clarinete)* fife; *(guitarrillo)* small guitar; PERU tribute.

re·qui·rie·ra, requirió see **requerir**.

re·qui·sa f. *(revista)* tour *or* round of inspection; MIL. requisitioning.

re·qui·sar tr. to requisition.

re·qui·si·ción f. MIL. requisition, requisitioning.

re·qui·si·to m. requirement, requisite.

res f. beast, animal ♦ **r. vacuna** head of cattle.

re·sa·ber §62 tr. to know very well.

re·sa·bia·do, –da I. past part. see **resabiar** II. adj. vicious (animals).

re·sa·biar tr. to instill bad habits in —reflex *(adquirir vi-*

cios) to acquire bad habits; *(enfadarse)* to become annoyed.

re·sa·bi·do, –da adj. *(bien conocido)* well-known; *(pedante)* pedantic.

re·sa·bio m. *(vicio)* vice, bad habit; *(mal gusto)* unpleasant aftertaste.

re·sa·brá, resabría see **resaber**.

re·sa·ca f. MARIT. undertow, undercurrent; COM. redraft; FIG., COLL. *(malestar)* hangover.

re·sa·la·do, –da I. past part. see **resalar** II. adj. FIG., COLL. charming, attractive.

re·sa·lar tr. to salt again.

re·sa·lir intr. ARCHIT. to jut out, project.

re·sal·tar intr. *(rebotar)* to bounce, rebound; *(resalir)* to jut out, project; FIG. *(distinguirse)* to stand out, be conspicuous ♦ **hacer r.** to emphasize, stress.

re·sal·to m. *(rebote)* bounce, rebound; *(parte que resale)* projection.

re·sal·vo m. tiller, sapling.

re·sa·nar tr. *(dorar)* to regild, retouch; *(restaurar)* to repair, restore.

re·sar·ci·ble adj. indemnifiable.

re·sar·ci·mien·to m. compensation, indemnification.

re·sar·cir §35 tr. to compensate, indemnify —reflex. ♦ **resarcirse de** to make up for.

res·ba·la·de·ro, –ra I. adj. slippery II. f. chute, slide —m. slippery spot.

res·ba·la·di·zo, –za adj. slippery.

res·ba·la·dor, –do·ra adj. slipping, sliding.

res·ba·la·du·ra f. skid mark.

res·ba·lar intr. *(deslizarse)* to slip, slide; FIG. *(cometer un desliz)* to slip, go astray; AUTO to skid.

res·ba·lón m. *(traspié)* slip, slide; FIG. *(desliz)* slip, error; AUTO. skid.

res·ba·lo·so, –sa I. adj. slippery II. f. ARG. heel-tapping dance.

res·cal·dar tr. var. of **escaldar**.

res·ca·ta·dor, –do·ra I. adj. rescuing II. m.f. rescuer.

res·ca·tar tr. *(recobrar)* to recover, get back; *(pagar por la libertad)* to ransom; *(salvar)* to rescue, save; *(recuperar)* to recover, make up; FIG. *(redimir)* to free, release (from obligation).

res·ca·te m. *(recobro)* recovery, getting back; *(dinero)* ransom money; *(salvación)* rescue, saving; *(recuperación)* recovery, making up; FIN. redemption.

res·cin·di·ble adj. rescindable.

res·cin·dir tr. to rescind, cancel.

res·ci·sión f. rescission, cancellation.

res·col·do m. *(brasa)* embers, hot ashes; FIG. *(escrúpulo)* scruple, misgiving.

re·sé see **resaber**.

re·se·car §70 tr. & reflex. to dry out, parch; BOT. to scorch.

re·sec·ción f. SURG. resection.

re·se·co, –ca adj. *(muy seco)* very dry, parched; *(flaco)* lean, thin.

re·se·llar tr. *(volver a sellar)* to restamp, reseal; *(volver a acuñar)* to recoin.

re·se·llo m. *(de un papel)* restamping, resealing; *(de la moneda)* recoining.

re·sem·brar §49 tr. AGR. to resow.

re·sen·ti·do, –da I. past part. see **resentirse** II. adj. resentful, hurt.

re·sen·ti·mien·to m. resentment, grudge.

re·sen·tir·se §65 reflex. *(sentir malas consecuencias)* to feel the effects of; *(debilitarse)* to be weakened, be impaired; FIG. *(sentirse)* to be resentful, feel hurt ♦ **r. de** *or* **por** to take offense at.

re·se·ña f. MIL. inspection, review; *(descripción)* description, outline; *(relación)* account, report; *(análisis)* review (of a book).

re·se·ñar tr. MIL. to inspect, review; *(describir)* to describe, outline; *(analizar)* to review (a book).

re·se·pa see **resaber**.

re·se·qué, reseque see **resecar**.

re·se·ro m. AMER. herdsman; ARG. livestock dealer.

re·ser·va f. *(provisión)* reserve, stock; *(retención de plaza)* reservation, booking; *(excepción)* reservation <*aprobar algo con ciertas reservas* to approve something with certain

reservations>; *(discreción)* discretion, circumspection; *(cautela)* reserve, reticence; *(terreno)* reserve, preserve <*r. natural* nature reserve>; *(territorio para indígenas)* reservation <*r. de indíos* Indian reservation>; BIOCHEM. reserve <*r. alcalina* alkali reserve>; COM. reserve, reserves <*r. de oro* gold reserves>; MIL. reserve, reserves; RELIG. reservation —m.f. SPORT. reserve ♦ **a r. de** except for • **a r. de que** unless • **con la mayor r.** in the strictest confidence • **de r.** reserve, spare <*tanque de r.* reserve tank> • **r. en metálico** COM. cash reserves • **r. mental** mental reservation • **reservas del excedente** COM. surplus reserves • **sin r.** openly, frankly • **tener algo de** o **en r.** to have something in reserve, have something for an emergency.
re·ser·va·ción f. reservation.
re·ser·va·do, –da I. past part. see **reservar** II. adj. *(que se reserva)* reserved; *(discreto)* discreet, circumspect; *(cauteloso)* reserved, reticent; *(confidencial)* confidential, private III. m. *(lugar)* reserved room *or* area; RAIL. reserved compartment; RELIG. reservation.
re·ser·var tr. *(destinar)* to reserve, set aside <*reservamos el diez por ciento para gastos imprevistos* we set aside ten percent for unforeseen expenses>; *(guardar)* to reserve, save <*reservó la fruta para el desayuno* he saved the fruit for breakfast>; *(retener plaza)* to reserve, book; *(encubrir)* to conceal, hide; *(no comunicar)* to withhold (information); *(dilatar)* to put off, postpone; *(dispensar)* to exempt, exonerate; RELIG. to reserve (the sacrament) —reflex. *(conservarse)* to save oneself, save one's strength; *(cautelarse)* to be wary *or* cautious.
re·ser·vis·ta MIL. I. adj. reserve II. m. reservist.
res·fria·do I. past part. see **resfriar** II. m. *(catarro)* cold <*coger un r.* to catch a cold>; *(destemple)* chill.
res·fria·du·ra f. VET. cold.
res·frian·te I. adj. cooling II. m. cooler (of a still).
res·friar §30 tr. *(enfriar)* to cool, chill; FIG. *(moderar)* to temper, moderate —intr. to cool, turn cold —reflex. MED. to catch a cold; FIG. *(perder el cariño)* to cool, grow cold (affection).
res·guar·dar tr. to defend, protect —reflex. to defend *or* protect oneself; FIG. *(cuidarse)* to be careful, take care.
res·guar·do m. *(guardia)* defense, protection; *(de frontera)* border guard; *(documento)* safeguard, guarantee; *(recibo)* receipt, stub.
re·si·den·cia f. *(morada)* residence; LAW impeachment.
re·si·den·cial adj. residential.
re·si·den·te adj. & m.f. resident.
re·si·dir intr. *(permanecer)* to reside, dwell; FIG. *(consistir)* to reside, lie.
re·si·dual adj. residual.
re·si·duo m. *(sobra)* residue, remnant; MATH. remainder ♦ **residuos** waste, refuse.
re·siem·bra f. AGR. resowing, replanting.
re·siem·bre, resiembro see **resembrar**.
re·sien·ta, resiento see **resentirse**.
re·sig·na·ción f. resignation.
re·sig·nar tr. to resign —reflex. to resign oneself.
re·si·na f. resin.
re·si·na·ción f. extraction of resin.
re·si·no·so, –sa adj. resinous.
re·sin·tie·ra, resintió see **resentirse**.
re·sis·ten·cia f. *(fuerza)* resistance, strength; *(oposición)* resistance, opposition; *(aguante)* endurance, stamina; *(defensa)* resistance; ELEC. resistance <*r. dieléctrica* disruptive strength> ♦ **oponer r.** to resist, put up *or* offer resistance • **R.** HIST. the Resistance • **r. a la torsión** PHYS. torsional strength • **r. de tensión** PHYS. tensile strength • **r. pasiva** passive resistance.
re·sis·ten·te I. adj. *(fuerte)* resistant, strong; *(que opone)* resisting, opposing; BOT. hardy ♦ **hacerse r. (a)** to build p a resistance (to) II. m. HIST. Resistance fighter.
re·sis·ti·ble adj. resistible.
re·sis·ti·dor, –do·ra adj. resistant.
re·sis·tir intr. *(no ceder)* to resist; *(repeler)* to resist, fight off <*r. al asalto* to resist the assault>; *(durar)* to endure, work still <*el tocadiscos resiste todavía* the record player still works> —tr. *(combatir)* to resist, fight against; *(controlar)* to resist <*r. la tentación* to resist temptation>; *(aguantar)* to bear, endure <*no resisto el dolor* I can't bear

the pain>; *(apoyar)* to bear, support <*la columna no resiste el peso* the column can't support the weight> ♦ **r. la mirada de alguien** to stare back at someone —reflex. *(oponerse)* to resist; *(luchar contra)* to struggle, fight against; *(negarse)* to refuse <*me resisto a llamarla* I refuse to call her>.
res·ma f. ream (of paper).
re·so·ba·do, –da adj. trite, hackneyed.
re·so·la·na f. *or* **re·so·la·no** m. *(sitio)* sunny place; *(resol)* sun's glare.
re·so·lu·ble adj. solvable, resolvable.
re·so·lu·ción f. *(decisión)* decision, resolution <*tomar una r.* to make a decision>; *(decreto)* resolution; *(solución)* solution (to a problem); *(valor)* resolution, resolve; MUS. resolution ♦ **en r.** in short.
re·so·lu·to, –ta adj. resolute, determined.
re·so·lu·to·rio, –ria adj. resolute, determined.
re·sol·ver §78 tr. *(solucionar)* to solve, resolve <*r. un problema* to solve a problem>; *(dar solución a)* to settle, resolve <*r. un conflicto* to settle a conflict>; *(descomponer)* to analyze, resolve; *(resumir)* to summarize, sum up; CHEM. to dissolve; MED. to resolve —reflex. *(decidirse)* to resolve, make up one's mind; *(ser solucionado)* to work out, resolve itself <*todo se resolverá con el tiempo* everything will work out in time>; MED. to resolve ♦ **resolverse en** to turn into, end up <*la manifestación se resolvió en un motín violento* the demonstration turned into a violent riot> • **resolverse por** to decide to, decide on *or* in favor of <*se resolvió por quedarse en la ciudad* she decided to stay in the city> —intr. to resolve, decide <*resolvió comprar una casa* she decided to buy a house>.
re·so·lla·de·ro m. CUBA vent, airhole.
re·so·llar §19 intr. *(respirar con ruido)* to snort, breathe heavily; FIG., COLL. *(dar noticia de sí)* to show signs of life, break one's silence ♦ **sin r.** without a word.
re·so·na·ción f. resounding, resonance.
re·so·na·dor I. adj. resounding, resonating II. m. resonator.
re·so·nan·cia f. PHYS. resonance; FIG. *(importancia)* importance, renown ♦ **tener r.** to cause a stir, be a hit.
re·so·nan·te adj. resonant, resounding.
re·so·nar §19 intr. *(repercutir)* to resonate, resound; FIG. *(tener repercusiones)* to have repercussions.
re·so·plar intr. to snort, puff.
re·so·pli·do *or* **re·so·plo** m. puffing, heavy breathing.
re·sor·ber tr. to reabsorb.
re·sor·te m. *(muelle)* spring; *(elasticidad)* springiness, elasticity; FIG. *(medio)* means, resort ♦ **resortes** FIG. strings, connections <*tocar resortes* to pull strings>.
res·pal·dar[1] m. back of a chair.
res·pal·dar[2] tr. *(apuntar)* to sign, endorse (a document); FIG. *(garantizar)* to support, back —reflex. *(arrimarse)* to lean back; VET. to dislocate the backbone (a horse).
res·pal·do m. *(de una silla)* back (of a chair); *(de un papel)* back, verso (of a sheet of paper); *(lo escrito)* endorsement; FIG. *(garantía)* support, backing.
res·pec·ti·va·men·te adv. respectively.
res·pec·ti·vo, –va adj. respective ♦ **en lo r. a** with regard to, as for.
res·pec·to m. respect, relation ♦ **al r.** about the matter • **r. a** *or* **de** with respect to.
rés·ped *or* **rés·pe·de** m. *(de la serpiente)* serpent's tongue; *(de la abeja)* bee's stinger.
res·pe·ta·bi·li·dad f. respectability.
res·pe·ta·ble I. adj. respectable II. m. COLL. audience, public.
res·pe·tar tr. *(tener respeto)* to respect; *(conservar)* to spare, respect.
res·pe·to m. respect, deference ♦ **campar por los respetos de uno** to do as one pleases • **de r.** *(respetable)* respectable, venerable; *(reservado)* extra, spare • **faltar al r.** to be disrespectful • **por r. a** out of consideration for • **respetos** respects ◊ **r. de si mismo** self-respect.
res·pe·tuo·so, –sa adj. *(que manifiesta respecto)* respectful; *(respetable)* respectable.
rés·pi·ce m. COLL *(respuesta seca)* curt reply; *(reprensión)* scolding, tongue-lashing.
res·pin·gar §47 intr. *(sacudirse)* to start, balk (an animal);

SEW. to curl (up) (a garment); FIG., COLL (*resistir*) to balk, do unwillingly.

res·pin·go m. (*sacudida*) start, jump; FIG., COLL. (*movimiento de disgusto*) gesture of impatience *or* unwillingness; CHILE., HOND. curled part of a garment.

res·pin·gón, –go·na *or* **res·pin·go·so, –sa** adj. (*que se sacude*) balky (animal); turned-up <*nariz r.* turned-up nose>.

res·pin·gué, respingue see **respingar**.

res·pi·ra·ble adj. breathable.

res·pi·ra·ción f. PHYSIOL. respiration, breathing; (*aliento*) breath ♦ **r. artifical** artificial respiration.

res·pi·ra·de·ro m. (*abertura*) vent, airhole; (*tronera*) porthole, skylight; (*una cañería*) ventilation shaft; FIG. (*tubo*) snorkel; (*descanso*) breather, rest; COLL. (*nariz*) nose.

res·pi·ra·dor, –do·ra I. adj. (*que respira*) breathing; ANAT. respiratory <*músculos respiradores* respiratory muscles> II. m. (*máquina*) respirator; ANAT. respiratory muscle.

res·pi·rar intr. (*inhalar*) to breathe, respire; (*oler*) to smell; FIG. (*animarse*) to breathe a sigh of relief, breathe again; (*descansar*) to rest, take a breather ♦ **no dejar r. a alguien** FIG. not to give someone a moment's peace, make someone's life miserable • **no poder r.** to be up to one's neck (in work) • **no r.** FIG., COLL. not to breathe a word, say absolutely nothing • **sin r.** (*sin hablar*) without a word; (*sin descansar*) without a rest *or* break, nonstop —tr. (*aspirar*) to breathe (in), inhale <*r. cloroformo* to inhale chloroform>; (*exudar*) to exude <*r. un olor dulce* to exude a sweet smell>; FIG. (*rebosar*) to ooze <*r. desprecio* to ooze contempt>.

res·pi·ra·to·rio, –ria adj. respiratory.

res·pi·ro m. (*respiración*) respiration; (*descanso*) rest, respite; FIG. (*alivio*) respite, break.

res·plan·de·cer §17 intr. (*brillar*) to shine, gleam; FIG. (*sobresalir*) to shine, excel.

res·plan·de·cien·te adj. resplendent, shining.

res·plan·dor *or* **res·plan·de·ci·mien·to** m. (*luz*) light, radiance; (*de llamas*) blaze, glow; FIG. (*brillo*) shine, brilliance; (*esplendor*) splendor; (*afeite*) shiny makeup.

res·pon·de·dor, –do·ra I. adj. answering II. m.f. respondent.

res·pon·der tr. to answer —intr. (*contestar*) to answer, respond to <*r. a una pregunta* to answer a question>; (*corresponder*) to answer, return <*r. a la lealtad con desprecio* to answer loyalty with contempt>; (*replicar*) to answer back, be impudent; (*repetir el eco*) to echo back, answer (an echo); (*surtir efecto*) to perform, produce <*la máquina nueva responde bien* the new machine performs well>; (*reaccionar*) to respond <*el paciente no responde al medicamento* the patient doesn't respond to the medication>; (*armonizar*) to harmonize; (*estar situado*) to face, look towards <*esta ventana responde al sur* this window faces south> ♦ **r. a una descripción** to fit a description • **r. a una necesidad** to meet a need • **r. a una obligación** to honor an obligation • **r. de** (*ser responsable*) to answer for, be responsible for; (*confirmar*) to vouch for • **r. por alguien** to answer for someone, be responsible for someone.

res·pon·dón, –do·na COLL. I. adj. pert, impudent II. m.f. pert *or* impudent person.

res·pon·sa·bi·li·dad f. responsibility ♦ **r. limitada** limited liability.

res·pon·sa·bi·li·zar §04 tr. to make responsible —reflex. to take the responsibility.

res·pon·sa·ble adj. responsible; LAW liable ♦ **hacerse r. de** to assume responsibility for • **la persona r.** the person in charge.

res·pon·sar intr. RELIG. to say prayers for the dead.

res·pon·so m. RELIG. prayer for the dead; COLL. (*regaño*) scolding.

res·pues·ta f. answer, response.

res·que·bra·du·ra f. crack, split.

res·que·bra·ja·di·zo, –za adj. brittle, easily cracked.

res·que·bra·ja·du·ra f. *or* **res·que·bra·ja·mien·to** m. var. of **resquebradura**.

res·que·bra·jar tr. & reflex to crack, split.

res·que·brar §49 intr. to crack, split.

res·que·mor m. (*escozor*) burning, stinging; FIG. (*resentimiento*) resentment; (*remordimiento*) remorse.

res·qui·cio m. (*hendedura*) chink, crack; FIG. (*ocasión*) chance, opportunity; (*posibilidad*) glimmer, ray <*un r. de esperanza* a glimmer of hope>.

res·quie·bre, resquiebro see **resquebrar**.

res·ta f. MATH. (*sustracción*) subtraction; (*residuo*) remainder.

res·ta·ble·cer §17 tr. to reestablish, restore —reflex. to recover, recuperate.

res·ta·ble·ci·mien·to m. (*acción de restablecer*) reestablishment, restoration; MED. recovery.

res·ta·llar intr. to crack (a whip).

res·tan·te I. adj. remaining II. m. remainder.

res·ta·ñar tr. to stanch, stop the flow of (blood).

res·ta·ño m. (*de la sangre*) stanching; (*stancamiento*) stagnation.

res·tar tr. MATH. to subtract; SPORT. to return the serve; FIG. (*quitar*) to take away, remove —intr. (*quedar*) to be left, remain; MATH. to subtract.

res·tau·ra·ción f. restoration.

res·tau·ra·dor, –do·ra I. adj. restoring I. m.f. restorer.

res·tau·ran·te I. adj. restoring II. m.f. (*que restaura*) restorer —m. (*establecimiento*) restaurant.

res·tau·rar tr. to restore.

res·ti·tu·ción f. restitution, return.

res·ti·tui·ble adj. returnable, restorable.

res·ti·tui·dor, –do·ra I. adj. returning, restoring II. m.f. returner, restorer.

res·ti·tuir §18 tr. (*devolver*) to return, restore; (*restaurar*) to restore —reflex. to return, come back.

res·ti·tu·to·rio, –ria adj. LAW restitutive.

res·to m. (*residuo*) rest, remainder; COM. balance, remainder; (*en naipes*) stakes (at cards); MATH. remainder; SPORT. (*jugador*) receiver; (*devolución*) return (of a ball) ♦ **echar el r.** (*apostar todo*) to go for broke, stake all one's money; FIG. (*esforzase*) to do one's utmost, go all out • **r. abierto** with no limit (on stakes) • **restos** CUL. leftovers, scraps; MARIT. wreckage; (*ruinas*) ruins, rubble • **restos de edición** remainders • **restos mortales** mortal remains.

res·to·rán m. restaurant.

res·tre·ga·du·ra f. *or* **res·tre·ga·mien·to** m. hard rubbing *or* scrubbing.

res·tre·gar §52 tr. to rub, scrub.

res·tre·gón m. hard rubbing, scrubbing.

res·tric·ción f. restriction.

res·tric·ti·vo, –va adj. restrictive.

res·trin·gen·te adj. restricting.

res·trin·gir §32 tr. to restrict, limit; MED. to contract —reflex. to cut down on (expenses).

res·tri·ñir §12 tr. (*astringir*) to constrict; (*estreñir*) to constipate.

re·su·ci·ta·dor, –do·ra I. adj. resuscitating II. m.f. resuscitator.

re·su·ci·tar tr. to resuscitate, bring back to life; FIG. to revive, bring back (memories, traditions) —intr. to be resuscitated *or* revived.

re·suel·to, –ta I. past part. see **resolver** II. adj. (*decidido*) resolute, determined; (*diligente*) prompt, diligent.

re·suel·va, resuelvo see **resolver**.

re·sue·lle, resuello see **resollar**.

re·sue·llo m. breathing ♦ **perder el r.** to be out of breath.

re·sue·ne see **resonar**.

re·sul·ta f. result, consequence ♦ **de resultas** as a result of.

re·sul·ta·do, –ta I. past part. see **resultar** II. m. (*efecto*) result, outcome; MATH. answer ♦ **como r.** as a result, in consequence • **dar r.** to produce results • **tener por r.** to have the effect of, lead to.

re·sul·tan·te I. adj. resultant, resulting II. f. MATH., MECH. resultant.

re·sul·tar intr. to be, turn out *or* prove (to be) <*si resulta posible, te acompañaremos* if it turns out to be possible, we'll go with you>; to turn *or* work out <*la investigación no resultó como pronosticaban* the investigation didn't turn out as they predicted>; (*funcionar*) to work (out), be successful <*su idea no resultó* his idea didn't work>; (*salir*) to be <*resultó quemado en el incendio* he was burned in the fire>; (*encontrar*) to find <*ella me resulta muy simpática* I find her very nice>; (*costar*) to cost, come *or* amount to <*los tres tomos resultan por cincuenta dólares* the three volumes come to fifty dollars>; *(valer la pena)* to be worth (it); COLL. *(agradar)* to please <*esta comida no me resulta* this meal doesn't please me>; *(combinar)* to go, look well <*esos zapatos no resultan con ese pantalón* those shoes don't go with those trousers> ♦ **estar resultando** to be beginning <*este tema me está resultando ya aburrido* this topic is beginning to bore me> • **r. de** *(originar)* to result or stem from <*la guerra resultó de la opresión del campesinado* the war resulted from the oppression of the peasantry>; *(ser evidente)* to be evident or follow from <*resulta de ese comentario que no va a volver* it's evident from that remark that he's not coming back> • **r. en** to result in, produce • **r. hacer algo** to be a good idea to do something, be worth it to do something <*resulta reservar una plaza si viajas en el fin de semana* it's a good idea to reserve a seat if you're traveling on the weekend> • **r. que** to turn out that, happen that <*resultó que no pudo venir* it turned out that he couldn't come> • **r. ser** to be turn out or prove (to be).

re·su·men m. *(acción de resumir)* summarizing; *(compendio)* summary, abstract ♦ **en r.** in summary, in short.

re·su·mi·da·men·te adv. briefly, in a word.

re·su·mi·de·ro m. AMER. drain, sewer.

re·su·mir tr. *(condensar)* to summarize, condense; *(contar)* to shorten, abbreviate —reflex. to be summed up ♦ **resumirse en** to amount to, come or boil down to.

re·su·pie·ra, resupo see **resaber.**

re·sur·gi·mien·to m. *(reaparición)* resurgence, reappearance; FIG. *(resucitación)* recovery, revival.

re·sur·gir §32 intr. to reappear.

re·su·rrec·ción f. resurrection.

re·sur·tir intr. to rebound, bounce back.

re·ta·blo m. retable, altarpiece.

re·ta·co m. ARTIL. light shotgun; *(en billar)* short cue (in billiards); COLL. *(persona)* short and heavy-set person.

re·ta·dor, –do·ra I. adj. challenging II. m.f. challenger.

re·ta·guar·dia f. MIL. rear, rear guard.

re·ta·hí·la f. *(serie)* string, series; *(de insultos)* stream, volley.

re·ta·jar tr. *(cortar en redondo)* to cut around; *(cortar la pluma)* to cut the nib (of a quill).

re·tal m. remnant, scrap.

re·ta·ma f. BOT. broom, genista.

re·ta·mal or **re·ta·mar** m. broom field.

re·tar tr. *(desafiar)* to challenge, dare; COLL. *(censurar)* to scold, reprove; ARG., CHILE to insult, abuse.

re·tar·dar tr. to retard, delay.

re·tar·do m. retardation, delay.

re·ta·sar tr. to reappraise.

re·ta·zo m. *(de tela)* remnant, scrap (of cloth); FIG. *(de discurso)* fragment (of a speech).

re·te·jer tr. to weave closely.

re·ten·ción f. *(acción de retener)* retention; *(parte deducida)* deduction, amount withheld.

re·ten·drá, retendría see **retener.**

re·te·ner §69 tr. *(guardar)* to retain, hold; *(recordar)* to remember, retain; *(deducir)* to deduct, withhold —reflex. to control oneself, hold oneself back.

re·te·ni·mien·to m. retention.

re·ten·ti·vo, –va I. adj. retentive, retaining II. f. memory.

re·ti·cen·cia f. *(omisión al hablar)* reticence; RHET. insinuation, innuendo.

re·ti·cen·te adj. hesitant, reticent.

re·tí·cu·la f. OPT. reticle.

re·ti·cu·la·do, –da adj. reticulate.

re·ti·cu·lar adj. reticular.

re·tí·cu·lo m. BIOL. reticulum; OPT. reticle.

re·tie·ne see **retener.**

re·ti·na f. ANAT. retina.

re·ti·ni·tis f. MED. retinitis.

re·tin·te or **re·tin·tín** m. *(de vibración)* ringing; FIG., COLL. *(tonillo)* sarcastic tone of voice.

re·tin·to, –ta adj. dark brown.

re·ti·ra·da f. withdrawal <*la r. de una moneda de la circulación* the withdrawal of a coin from circulation>; *(remoción)* removal; *(sitio)* retreat, refuge; *(jubilación)* retirement; *(terreno)* dry river bed (caused by change in river's course); MIL. *(retreta)* retreat (bugle call); *(retroceso)* re-

treat, withdrawal; DIPL. recall (of an ambassador); FIN. withdrawal; MARIT. ebbing (of the tide) ♦ **batirse en r.** or **emprender una r.** to beat a retreat • **tocar la r.** to sound the retreat.

re·ti·ra·do, –da I. past part. see **retirar** II. adj. *(apartado)* remote, secluded; *(jubilado)* retired; MIL. retired, inactive III. m.f. retired person.

re·ti·rar tr. *(remover)* to remove <*r. los libros del escritorio* to remove the books from the desk>; *(separar)* to move away; *(quitar de la vista)* to take or put away; *(sacar)* to withdraw (from circulation); *(quitar)* to take away <*r. el pasaporte a alguien* to take away someone's passport>; *(retractar)* to retract, take back; *(jubilar)* to retire; DIPL. to withdraw, recall (an ambassador); FIN. to withdraw, take out <*r. diez dólares del banco* to withdraw ten dollars from the bank>; PRINT. to print on the back, back up; SPORT. to withdraw, scratch —reflex. *(apartarse del mundo)* to withdraw, go into seclusion; *(irse para atrás)* to move or draw back; *(jubilarse)* to retire, go into retirement; MARIT. to ebb (the tide); MIL. to retreat, withdraw; SPORT. to withdraw, scratch ♦ **retirarse a dormir** to go to bed • **retirarse ante un peligro** to shrink from danger.

re·ti·ro m. *(retirada)* withdrawal; *(aislamiento)* retirement, seclusion; *(lugar)* retreat, secluded place; *(jubilación)* retirement; *(pensión)* pension; RELIG. retreat ♦ **cobrar el r.** to receive or collect one's pension • **pasar al r.** to retire, to go into retirement • **vivir en el r.** to live in seclusion.

re·to m. *(desafío)* challenge, dare; *(amenaza)* threat.

re·to·ba·do, –da adj. HOND. wild, unruly; AMER. stubborn, obstinate.

re·to·bar tr. CHILE, PERU to bale, pack; AMER. to wrap in leather —reflex. to become angry or irritated.

re·to·bo m. *(desecho)* refuse, junk; AMER. sackcloth.

re·to·car §70 tr. PHOTOG. to retouch, touch up; SEW. to alter; FIG. *(dar la última mano)* to put the finishing touch on.

re·to·cé, retoce see **retozar.**

re·to·mar tr. to take back.

re·to·ñar intr. BOT. to sprout, shoot; FIG. to reappear.

re·to·ño m. BOT. sprout, shoot; FIG., COLL. *(niño)* kid.

re·to·que m. *(acción de retocar)* repeated touching; PHOTOG. retouching, touching up; MED. light case, touch (of illness); SEW. alteration.

re·to·qué, retoque see **retocar.**

re·tor·cer §71 tr. *(torcer)* to wring, twist; *(los bigotes)* to twirl; *(volver un argumento)* to twist, distort (an argument); *(interpretar mal)* to misinterpret, twist —reflex. *(torcerse)* to twist; *(contorcerse)* to writhe, double up.

re·tor·ci·do, –da I. past part. see **retorcer** II. adj. twisted, evil-minded.

re·tor·ci·jón m. var. of **retortijón.**

re·tor·ci·mien·to m. *(torsión)* twisting; *(contorsión)* writhing, contorting.

re·tó·ri·co, –ca I. adj. rhetorical II. m. rhetorician —f. rhetoric ♦ **retóricas** COLL. sophistries.

re·tor·nar tr. *(devolver)* to return, give back; *(hacer retroceder)* to push back —intr. to return, go back.

re·tor·no m. *(acción de retornar)* returning, going back; *(paga)* payment, compensation; *(trueque)* exchange, barter.

re·tor·te·ro m. twirl, rotation ♦ **andar al r.** COLL. to be extremely busy • **traer a alguien al r.** COLL. to keep someone busy.

re·tor·ti·jón m. twisting ♦ **r. de tripas** stomach cramps.

re·tos·ta·do, –da I. past part. see **retostar** II. adj. dark brown.

re·tos·tar §19 tr. *(tostar mucho)* to toast brown; *(volver a tostar)* to toast again.

re·to·zar §04 intr. *(juguetear)* to romp, frolic; FIG. *(agitarse las pasiones)* to be stirred or aroused (passions).

re·to·zo m. romp, frolic.

re·to·zón, –zo·na adj. playful, frolicsome.

re·trac·ción f. retraction.

re·trac·ta·ble adj. retractable.

re·trac·ta·ción f. retractation, recanting.

re·trac·tar tr. *(retirar)* to retract, take back; *(una declaración)* to recant; LAW to redeem —reflex. to retract, recant.

re·trác·til adj. retractile, retractable.
re·tra·er §72 tr. *(volver a traer)* to bring back; *(disuadir)* to dissuade; LAW to redeem —reflex. *(refugiarse)* to take refuge; *(retirarse)* to retreat, withdraw; *(hacer vida retirada)* to live in seclusion.
re·tra·í·do, –da I. past part. see **retraer** II. adj. *(refugiado)* in sanctuary; *(solitario)* solitary, reclusive; FIG. *(poco comunicativo)* aloof, withdrawn.
re·trai·ga, retraigo see **retraer.**
re·trai·mien·to m. *(acción de retraerse)* retreat, withdrawal; *(lugar)* retreat, refuge; *(vida retirada)* seclusion, isolation; *(carácter)* aloofness, reserve.
re·tra·je·ra, retrajo see **retraer.**
re·tran·ca f. *(del arnés)* breeching (of a harness); AMER. brake ♦ **tener mucha r.** to be prudent.
re·trans·mi·sión f. *(de un mensaje recibido)* retransmission; *(segunda difusión)* rebroadcast.
re·trans·mi·tir tr. *(pasar un mensaje)* to pass on, retransmit; *(volver a difundir)* to rebroadcast; TELEC. to relay.
re·tra·sa·do, –da I. past part. see **retrasar** II. adj. *(tren, avión)* late; *(pago, deber)* late, behind; *(persona)* retarded; *(país)* backward.
re·tra·sar tr. *(demorar)* to delay, slow down; *(aplazar)* to postpone, put off; *(un reloj)* to set back —intr. *(ir a menos)* to lag, fall behind; to be slow <*este reloj retrasa* this watch is slow> —reflex. *(demorarse)* to be late *or* delayed; *(irse a menos)* to get *or* fall behind.
re·tra·so m. *(demora)* delay, slowness; FIG. *(subdesarrollo)* underdevelopment, backwardness ♦ **con** *or* **de r.** late.
re·tra·tar tr. PAINT. to paint a portrait of; *(describir)* to portray, depict; PHOTOG. to photograph —reflex. PAINT. to have one's portrait painted; PHOTOG. to have one's photograph taken; FIG. *(reflejarse)* to be reflected.
re·tra·tis·ta m.f. PAINT. portrait painter; PHOTOG. photographer.
re·tra·to m. PAINT. portrait; FIG. *(descripción)* portrait, description; AMER. photograph ♦ **ser el r. vivo de alguien** FIG. to be the living image of someone.
re·tre·che·ro, ~ra adj. COLL. *(astuto)* cunning, crafty; *(atractivo)* attractive, charming; VEN. stingy, miserly.
re·tre·ta f. MIL. retreat (signal); *(fiesta nocturna)* tattoo, evening military parade; AMER. *(retahíla)* series, string; MUS. open-air band concert.
re·tre·te m. toilet, bathroom.
re·tri·bu·ción f. retribution, payment.
re·tri·buir §18 tr. *(pagar)* to pay; *(recompensar)* to reward; AMER. to return, repay (a favor).
re·tri·bu·yen·te adj. repaying, rewarding.
re·tro·ac·ti·vi·dad f. retroactivity.
re·tro·ac·ti·vo, –va adj. retroactive.
re·tro·ce·der intr. *(volver atrás)* turn *or* go back; *(tomar un paso atrás)* to step back, back away; *(bajar el nivel)* to recede, go down (waters); FIG. to look *or* go back (in time); MIL. to withdraw, fall back.
re·tro·ce·so m. *(regresión)* retrocession, backward movement; ARM. recoil; MED. aggravation, worsening (of an illness); MIL. withdrawal; MECH. return (of a typewriter).
re·tro·gra·dar intr. *(volver atrás)* to go backward; ASTRON. to retrograde.
re·tró·gra·do, –da I. adj. *(que retrocede)* retrogressive; ASTRON. retrograde; POL. reactionary II. m.f. POL. reactionary.
re·tro·gre·sión f. retrogression.
re·tro·pro·pul·sión f. AER. jet propulsion.
re·tros·pec·ción f. retrospection.
re·tros·pec·ti·vo, –va I. adj. retrospective II. f. ARTS retrospective.
re·tro·tra·er §72 tr. LAW to antedate.
re·tro·vi·sor m. AUTO. rearview mirror.
re·tru·car §70 intr. *(en el billar)* to kiss (said of billiards) ARG., COLL. to respond, retort.
re·tru·co m. kiss (in billiards).
re·trué·ca·no m. pun, play on words.
re·tru·que m. *(golpe)* kiss (in billiards); ARG. retort.
re·tuer·za, retuerzo see **retorcer.**
re·tues·te, retuesto see **retostar.**
re·tum·ban·te adj. *(sonoro)* resonant, resounding; *(pomposo)* pompous, bombastic.

re·tum·bar intr. *(resonar)* to resonate, resound; *(un cañón)* to boom.
re·tum·bo m. *(acción)* resonance, reverberation; *(ruido)* boom, rumble.
re·tu·vie·ra, retuvo see **retener.**
reú·ma *or* **reu·ma** m. var. of **reumatismo.**
reu·má·ti·co, –ca MED. adj. & m.f. rheumatic.
reu·ma·tis·mo m. MED. rheumatism.
reu·ni·fi·ca·ción f. reunification.
reu·ni·fi·car §70 tr. to reunify.
reu·nión f. *(asamblea)* meeting, gathering; *(después de una separación)* reunion.
reu·nir §60 tr. *(juntar)* to join, unite; FIG. *(agrupar)* to gather, collect; *(tener requisitos)* to fulfill (requirements); *(colectar)* to collect (funds); MIL. to assemble —reflex. *(juntarse)* to join together, unite; *(sostener una reunión)* to meet, hold a meeting; *(encontrarse con)* to meet, get together.
re·vá·li·da f. *(acción)* revalidation; *(examen final)* final examination; *(certificado)* certificate ♦ **r. de bachillerato** EDUC. high school diploma.
re·va·li·da·ción f. *(confirmación)* revalidation; *(renovación)* renewal.
re·va·li·dar tr. *(confirmar)* to revalidate; *(renovar)* to renew —reflex. to take a final examination.
re·va·lo·ri·za·ción f. revaluation.
re·va·lo·ri·zar §04 tr. to revalue.
re·van·cha f. revenge, retaliation.
re·ve·a, reveo see **rever.**
re·ve·la·ción f. revelation.
re·ve·la·do, –da I. past part. see **revelar** II. adj. revealed III. m. PHOTOG. developing.
re·ve·la·dor, –do·ra I. adj. revealing II. m. PHOTOG. developer.
re·ve·lar tr. *(descubrir)* to reveal, disclose; *(mostrar)* to reveal, show; PHOTOG. to develop.
re·ven·de·dor, –do·ra I. adj. reselling II. m.f. *(que revende)* reseller; *(detallista)* retailer ♦ **r. de entradas** ticket scalper.
re·ven·der tr. to resell, retail.
re·ve·nir §76 intr. to return (to an original condition) —reflex. *(encogerse)* to shrink, grow smaller; *(avinagrarse)* to turn sour; *(soltar humedad)* to give off moisture, sweat; *(ponerse correosa)* to become soft *or* runny; FIG., COLL. *(ceder)* to give in.
re·ven·ta f. *(segunda venta)* resale; *(venta al detalle)* retail.
re·ven·ta·de·ro m. *(terreno)* rugged *or* rough ground; FIG., COLL. *(trabajo penoso)* drudgery, grind; CHILE reef *or* rocks where waves break; COL., MEX. bubbling spring.
re·ven·tar §49 intr. *(explotar)* to burst, pop <*el globo reventó en la estratosfera* the balloon burst in the stratosphere>; *(romper un neumático)* to burst, blow (a tire); *(romper olas)* to break (waves); *(brotar)* to burst, gush (a spring); *(estallar una pasión)* to be bursting with <*r. de envidia* to be bursting with envy>; COLL. *(morir)* to kick the bucket, die ♦ **r. de cansancio** to be exhausted • **r. de gordo** to be as fat as a pig • **r. de rabia** to be furious • **r. de risa** to die laughing • **r. por algo** to crave something, be dying for something • **r. por hacer algo** to be dying to do something —tr. *(hacer explotar)* to burst, pop; *(aplastar)* to smash, crush; *(matar un caballo)* to ride to death (a horse); *(fatigar un caballo)* to ride hard, override (a horse); FIG. *(cansar)* to exhaust, work to death; *(causar gran daño)* to ruin, wreck; FIG., COLL. *(molestar)* to annoy, irritate —reflex. *(explotar)* to burst; *(romperse un neumático)* to burst, blow (a tire); *(morirse un caballo)* to die of exhaustion (a horse); FIG. *(cansarse)* to exhaust oneself.
re·ven·tón m. *(explosión)* burst, bursting; *(de un neumático)* blowout, flat tire; *(oleaje)* breaking (of waves); FIG. *(cuesta)* steep slope; *(aprieto)* mess, jam; *(esfuerzo)* all-out effort; AMER., MIN. outcrop; C. RICA shove; CHILE fit, outburst ♦ **dar un r.** to burst • **darse** *or* **pegarse un r.** to knock oneself out, make an all-out effort.
re·ver §77 tr. *(ver de nuevo)* to review, look over; LAW to retry (a case).
re·ver·be·ra·ción f. reflection, reverberation.
re·ver·be·ran·te adj. reverberating.
re·ver·be·rar intr. to be reflected, reverberate.

re·ver·be·ro m. *(reverberación)* reflection, reverberation; *(espejo)* reflector; *(farol)* reflecting lamp; AMER. cooking stove.

re·ver·de·cer §17 intr. *(volver a verdear)* to turn or become green again; FIG. *(recobrar vigor)* to regain vigor, revive.

re·ve·ren·cia f. *(respeto)* reverence, respect; *(saludo)* bow, curtsy ♦ **hacer una r.** to bow, curtsy • **Reverencia** (Your) Reverence.

re·ve·ren·ciar tr. to revere, venerate.

re·ve·ren·dí·si·mo, –ma adj. RELIG. Most Reverend, Right Reverend.

re·ve·ren·do, –da adj. RELIG. reverend; COLL. *(enorme)* huge, enormous.

re·ve·ren·te adj. reverent, respectful.

re·ver·si·bi·li·dad f. reversibility.

re·ver·si·ble adj. reversible.

re·ver·sión f. reversion.

re·ver·so, –sa adj. & m. reverse ♦ **r. de la medalla** FIG., COLL. the opposite side of the coin.

re·ver·ter §50 intr. to overflow.

re·ver·tir §65 intr. to revert.

re·vés m. *(envés)* back, reverse; wrong side <*el r. de una tela* the wrong side of a fabric>; *(bofetada)* backhand slap; FIG. *(desgracia)* reverse, setback; *(cambio de actitud)* change (in behavior or disposition); SPORT. *(jugada)* backhand stroke (in racket sports); *(golpe de espada)* reverse stroke (in fencing); CUBA tobacco weevil ♦ **al r.** *(al contrario)* backwards, in the opposite way; *(con lo de dentro fuera)* inside out, wrong side out; *(con lo de arriba abajo)* upside down; *(viceversa)* vice versa • **al r. de** contrary to • **del r.** *(con lo de arriba abajo)* upside down; *(con lo de dentro fuera)* inside out; *(con lo de delante detrás)* backwards • **volver algo del r.** to turn something around.

re·ve·sa·do, –da adj. *(complicado)* complex, intricate; FIG. *(travieso)* mischievous.

re·ves·ti·mien·to m. covering, coating.

re·ves·tir §48 tr. *(vestir)* to wear; *(cubrir)* to cover, coat; FIG. *(presentar)* to take on, acquire —reflex. *(imbuirse)* to be imbued or carried away; *(engreírse)* to become conceited, put on airs; FIG. *(desarrollar)* to summon up (energy); *(vestirse)* to put on (clothing).

re·vi, revimos see **rever**.

re·vie·jo, –ja adj. very old.

re·vie·ne see **revenir**.

re·vien·te, reviento see **reventar**.

re·vie·ra, revió see **rever**.

re·vier·ta, revierto see **reverter** or **revertir**.

re·vi·nie·ra, revino see **revenir**.

re·vi·rar intr. MARIT. to veer again, retrack.

re·vir·tie·ra, revirtió see **revertir**.

re·vi·sar tr. to revise, check; MECH. to overhaul ♦ **r. las cuentas** to audit accounts.

re·vi·sión f. revision, checking; MECH. overhaul ♦ **r. de cuentas** audit.

re·vi·sio·nis·mo m. revisionism.

re·vi·sio·nis·ta adj. & m.f. revisionist.

re·vi·sor, –do·ra I. adj. revising, checking II. m.f. *(persona que revisa)* reviser, inspector; RAIL. conductor ♦ **r. de cuentas** auditor.

re·vis·ta f. *(periódico)* magazine, journal, review <*r. de modas* fashion magazine>; *(sección de periódico)* section, page <*r. de deportes* sports section>; *(revisión)* inspection, review; MIL. review, inspection; LAW retrial, new trial; THEAT. revue ♦ **pasar r.** *(revisar)* to review, examine carefully; MIL. to review, inspect • **r. comercial** trade magazine • **r. cómica** comic (book) • **r. juvenil** teen magazine • **r. literaria** literary review.

re·vis·ta, revisto see **revestir**.

re·vis·te·ro, –ra m.f. reviewer, critic.

re·vis·tie·ra, revistió see **revestir**.

re·vi·ta·li·zar §04 tr. to revitalize.

re·vi·vi·fi·car §70 tr. to revive, revivify.

re·vi·vir intr. *(resucitar)* to revive, come back to life; FIG. *(renovarse)* to be renewed.

re·vo·ca·ble adj. revocable.

re·vo·ca·ción f. revocation; DIPL. recall (of an ambassador).

re·vo·ca·dor, –do·ra I. adj. revoking, repealing II. m.f.

(persona que revoca) revoker, repealer —m. CONSTR. plasterer.

re·vo·car §70 tr. *(anular)* to revoke, repeal; *(destituir)* to dismiss (from a post); *(disuadir)* to dissuade; *(hacer retroceder)* to repel, push back; *(enlucir)* to plaster, resurface.

re·vo·ca·to·rio, –ria I. adj. revocatory II. f. AMER. revocation (by a judge or public authority).

re·vol·ca·de·ro m. ZOOL. wallow (of animals).

re·vol·car §73 tr. *(derribar)* to knock down or over; FIG., COLL. *(vencer)* to floor, defeat; COLL. *(suspender)* to fail, flunk (an examination) —reflex. to roll <*revolcarse en el suelo* to roll on the ground>; to wallow <*revolcarse en el fango* to wallow in the mud>.

re·vol·cón m. COLL. *(caída)* fall, spill; *(en el suelo)* roll, rolling around; *(en el fango)* wallowing; *(en un examen)* failing, flunking.

re·vo·le·ar intr. ORNITH. to fly around, hover; ARG. to swing a rope or lasso.

re·vo·le·te·ar intr. AMER. var. of **revolotear**.

re·vo·lo·te·ar intr. to flutter or whirl around.

re·vo·lo·te·o m. fluttering, whirling.

re·vol·qué see **revolcar**.

re·vol·ti·jo or **re·vol·ti·llo** m. *(mezcla)* jumble, heap; FIG. *(confusión)* mix-up, mess ♦ **r. de huevos** scrambled eggs.

re·vol·to·so, –sa I. adj. *(alborotador)* troublemaking, agitating; *(travieso)* mischievous, unruly II. m.f. *(alborotador)* troublemaker, agitator; *(rebelde)* rebel; *(niño travieso)* mischievous child.

re·vol·tu·ra f. AMER. mixture.

re·vo·lu·ción f. revolution.

re·vo·lu·cio·nar tr. to revolutionize.

re·vo·lu·cio·na·rio, –ria adj. & m.f. revolutionary.

re·vol·ve·dor, –do·ra I. adj. *(agitante)* agitating; *(inquietante)* disturbing II. m.f. *(alborotador)* agitator, troublemaker —m. CUBA vat, cauldron (in sugar mills); ARG., MEX. cement mixer.

re·vol·ver §78 tr. *(mezclar)* to mix, stir <*r. un líquido* to stir a liquid>; *(agitar)* to shake; *(dar la vuelta a)* to turn over; *(envolver)* to wrap (up); *(volver)* to turn <*r. la cabeza* to turn one's head>; *(dar vuelta entera)* to turn around completely; *(alterar el orden)* to turn upside down, mix up; *(poner en blanco los ojos)* to roll (one's eyes); *(producir náuseas)* to upset, turn (one's stomach); *(registrar)* to rummage or look through; *(discurrir)* to ponder, think over; *(volver a andar)* to retrace one's steps; *(inquietar)* to stir up, rouse <*el atraco revolvió a todo el vecindario* the robbery stirred up the whole neighborhood>; EQUIT. to swing (one's horse) around quickly; COL. to weed ♦ **r. a uno con otro** to set one person against another • **r. la sangre** to make one's blood boil —reflex. *(dar vueltas)* to turn around; *(revolcarse)* to roll <*revolverse en el fango* to roll in the mud>; *(dormir mal)* to toss and turn (in one's sleep); *(volver a andar)* to retrace one's steps; *(moverse)* to move or turn around <*con tantas cajas en el piso, apenas se podía revolver* with so many boxes on the floor, one could hardly turn around>; *(retorcerse)* to writhe, squirm (in pain); *(enturbiarse)* to turn or become cloudy (liquid); ASTRON. to revolve, make a complete revolution; EQUIT. to swing around quickly; MARIT. to get rough (sea); METEOROL. to turn stormy (weather) ♦ **revolverse al enemigo** to turn to face the enemy • **revolverse contra alguien** to turn on or against someone —intr. EQUIT. to swing around quickly ♦ **r. en los bolsillos** to fish in one's pockets • **r. en una maleta** to rummage around in a suitcase.

re·vól·ver m. revolver, pistol.

re·vol·vi·mien·to m. *(revolución)* revolution <*r. de un planeta* revolution of a planet>; *(movimiento)* stirring (of a liquid); *(conmoción)* disturbance, commotion; EQUIT. swinging, turning around.

re·vo·que m. *(acción de enlucir)* plastering, resurfacing; *(material)* plaster, stucco.

re·vo·qué, revoque see **revocar**.

re·vuel·co m. *(caída)* fall, spill; *(en el suelo)* roll, rolling around; *(en el fango)* wallowing.

re·vue·lo m. *(segundo vuelo)* second flight; *(revoloteo)* fluttering; FIG. *(turbación)* stir, commotion; AMER. thrust with the spur (of a fighting cock) ♦ **de r.** lightly, in passing.

re·vuel·que, revuelco see **revolcar**.

re·vuel·ta f. *(motín)* revolt, rebellion; *(vuelta)* turn, bend; *(cambio)* change, alteration; *(riña)* quarrel, dispute.

re·vuel·to, -ta I. past part. see **revolver II.** adj. *(en desorden)* jumbled, disorderly; *(inquieto)* restless, turbulent; *(travieso)* mischievous; FIG. *(enrevesado)* intricate, complicated ♦ **huevos revueltos** scrambled eggs.

re·vuel·va, revuelvo see **revolver**.

rey m. *(monarca)* king, sovereign; *(en juegos)* king; FIG. king *<r. de los animales* the king of beasts> ♦ **a cuerpo de r.** FIG. like a king *<vivir a cuerpo de r.* to live like a king> • **cada uno es r. en su casa** a man's home is his castle • **día de Reyes** Epiphany, Twelfth Night • **lo mismo me da r. que roque** it's all the same to me • **los reyes** the king and queen • **los Reyes Católicos** the Catholic Monarchs (Ferdinand and Isabella) • **ni quito ni pongo r.** FIG., COLL. it's none of my business • **no temer ni r. ni roque** COLL. to be afraid of no one or nothing • **r. de armas** king-of-arms • **r. de Romanos** Holy Roman Emperor • **Reyes magos** the Three Magi *or* Wise Men • **servir al r.** to serve one's country, to be a soldier.

re·yer·ta f. quarrel, wrangle.

re·za·gar §47 tr. *(dejar atrás)* to outstrip, leave behind; *(aplazar)* to put off, postpone —reflex. to lag *or* fall behind.

re·zar §04 tr. RELIG. to say (prayers); COLL. *(decir)* to say —intr. RELIG. to pray; COLL. *(decir)* to say, go *<según reza el refrán* as the saying goes>; *(gruñir)* to grumble, mutter ♦ **r. con** to concern *<esto no reza con él* this does not concern him>.

re·zo m. RELIG. *(oración)* prayer; *(oficio)* office.

re·zon·ga·dor, -do·ra I. adj. grumbling, griping **II.** m.f. grumbler, griper.

re·zon·gar §47 intr. to grumble, gripe.

re·zon·glón, -glo·na adj. grumbling, griping.

re·zon·gue·ro, -ra COLL. **I.** adj. grumbling, griping **II.** m.f. grumbler, griper.

re·zu·mar tr. to ooze, seep —intr. *(contenido)* to ooze, seep (out); *(recipiente)* to leak *<este jarro rezuma* this jug leaks> —reflex. *(salirse)* to ooze, seep (out); to leak *<este jarro se rezuma* this jug leaks>; COLL. *(divulgarse)* to leak out (news).

rí·a f. estuary.

rí·a, río see **reír**.

ria·cho *or* **ria·chue·lo** m. rivulet, stream.

ria·da f. flood, flash flood; FIG. flood, torrent.

ri·be·ra f. *(de un río)* bank, shore (of a river); *(del mar)* shore, seashore.

ri·be·re·ño, -ña *or* **ri·be·ra·no, -na I.** adj. *(de la ribera)* on the bank *or* shore, riparian; *(de un río)* riverside; *(del mar)* shore **II.** shore dweller.

ri·be·ro m. dike, levee.

ri·be·te m. SEW. border, trimming; FIG. *(a un cuento)* addition, embellishment (to a story) ♦ **ribetes** FIG., COLL. touch, streak *<tener ribetes de poeta* to have a touch of the poet>.

ri·be·te·a·do I. past part. see **ribetear II.** adj. edged, trimmed **III.** m. border, trimming.

ri·be·te·a·dor, -do·ra I. adj. edging, trimming **II.** m.f. edger, trimmer.

ri·be·te·ar tr. to border, trim.

ri·ca·cho, -cha *or* **ri·ca·chón, -cho·na** m.f. COLL. moneybags.

ri·ca·men·te adv. *(con abundancia)* richly, opulently; *(muy bien)* excellently, splendidly.

ri·cé, rice see **rizar**.

ri·ci·no m. BOT. castor-oil plant ♦ **aceite de r.** castor oil.

ri·co, -ca I. adj. *(acaudalado)* rich, wealthy; *(fértil)* fertile, rich (land); *(abundante)* abundant *<cosecha r.* abundant crop>; *(magnífico)* luxurious, rich; *(de valor)* valuable, precious; *<joya r.* valuable jewel>; *(sabroso)* delicious, tasty; FIG., COLL. *(simpático)* lovely, adorable ♦ **hacerse r.** to get rich • **r. de** *or* **en** rich in *<una veta r. de oro* a vein rich in gold> **II.** m.f. rich person ♦ **los ricos** the rich • **nuevo r.** nouveau riche.

ric·tus m. rictus, gaping grimace ♦ **r. de dolor** wince of pain.

ri·cu·ra f. deliciousness, tastiness; FIG. darling, cutie.

ri·di·cu·lez f. [pl. **-le·ces**] *(cualidad de absurdo)* ridiculousness, absurdity; *(cosa insignificante)* nothing, trifle.

ri·di·cu·li·zar §04 tr. to ridicule.

ri·dí·cu·lo I. m. *(bolsa)* reticule, woman's handbag **II.** adj. see **ridículo, -la**.

ri·dí·cu·lo, -la I. adj. ridiculous, ludicrous **II.** m. *(ridiculez)* ridiculousness, ridiculous situation ♦ **hacer el r.** to make a fool of oneself • **poner en r.** to make a fool of.

rie·go m. *(irrigación)* irrigation, watering; *(agua)* irrigation water ♦ **boca de r.** hydrant • **r. sanguíneo** ANAT. blood circulation.

rie·go, riegue see **regar**.

riel m. RAIL. rail, track; *(de una cortina)* curtain rod; *(de metal)* ingot, bar ♦ **andar sobre rieles** FIG. to go like clockwork • **r. conductor** RAIL. third rail.

rien·da f. *(correa)* rein; FIG. *(sujeción)* restraint ♦ **a r. suelta** *(con velocidad)* at full *or* top speed; FIG. *(sin sujeción)* freely, without restraint • **aflojar las riendas** FIG. to ease *or* let up, loosen the reins • **dar r. suelta a** to give free rein to • **empuñar las riendas** FIG. to take charge • **falsa r.** EQUIT. checkrein • **riendas** FIG. reins, control *<tomar las riendas del gobierno* to take control of the government> • **tirar (de) la r. a** to tighten the reins on.

rien·te adj. *(que ríe)* smiling, laughing; FIG. *(alegre)* bright, cheerful.

rie·ra, rió see **reír**.

ries·go m. danger, risk ♦ **correr (el) r. de** to run the risk of.

ri·fa f. *(tómbola)* raffle; *(riña)* quarrel, wrangle.

ri·far tr. to raffle —intr. to quarrel, wrangle —reflex. MARIT. to split (a sail).

ri·fi·rra·fe m. COLL. fight, squabble.

ri·fle m. ARM. rifle.

ri·gi·dez f. rigidity, stiffness ♦ **r. cadavérica** rigor mortis.

rí·gi·do, -da adj. rigid, stiff.

ri·gie·ra, rigió see **regir**.

ri·gor m. *(severidad)* rigor, severity; *(precisión)* rigorousness, precision; MED. rigor ♦ **de r.** in fact, in reality • **de r. de rigueur**, obligatory • **ser el r. de las desdichas** FIG. to be born under an unlucky star.

ri·gu·ro·si·dad f. rigorousness.

ri·gu·ro·so, -sa adj. *(severo)* rigorous, severe; *(preciso)* rigorous, precise; *(áspero)* harsh.

ri·ja, rijo see **regir**.

ri·jo·so, -sa adj. *(pendenciero)* quarrelsome; *(sensual)* lustful, sensual; *(inquieto)* restless at the sight of the female (a horse).

ri·ma f. rhyme ♦ **rimas** poems, poetry.

ri·ma·dor, -do·ra I. adj. rhyming **II.** m.f. rhymer, rhymester.

ri·mar intr. & tr. to rhyme.

rim·bom·ban·cia f. *(resonancia)* resonance; *(del estilo)* grandiloquence, bombast.

rim·bom·ban·te adj. *(que resuena)* resounding; *(pomposo)* grandiloquent, bombastic; *(ostentoso)* showy, ostentatious.

rim·bom·bar intr. to resound, echo.

rí·mel m. mascara.

ri·me·ro m. heap, pile.

rin·cón m. *(de paredes)* (inside) corner; *(sitio apartado)* corner, nook; FIG., COLL. *(refugio)* haven, retreat.

rin·co·na·da f. corner.

rin·co·ne·ra f. *(mesa)* corner table; *(armario)* corner cupboard; ARCHIT. wall between corner and window.

rin·da, rindo see **rendir**.

rin·die·ra, rindió see **rendir**.

rin·gla f. *or* **rin·gle** m. *or* **rin·gle·ra** f. COLL. line, row.

rin·gle·ro m. ruled line (on paper).

rin·go·rran·go m. COLL. *(de pluma)* flourish; *(adorno)* frill, bauble.

ri·ni·tis f. MED. rhinitis.

ri·no·ce·ron·te m. ZOOL. rhinoceros.

ri·ña f. quarrel, dispute.

ri·ña, riño see **reñir**.

ri·ñe·ra, riñó see **reñir**.

ri·ñón m. ANAT. kidney; FIG. *(centro)* heart *<en el r. de la provincia* in the heart of the province>; MIN. nodule ♦ **costar un r.** FIG., COLL. to cost a fortune • **pegarse al r.** FIG., COLL. to be very nutritious • **riñones** loins, lower back • **tener el r. bien cubierto** COLL. to be well off *or* be rich • **tener riñones** COLL. to be brave, have guts.

ri·ño·na·da f. ANAT. cortical tissue of the kidney; *(lomo)* loin; CUL. kidney stew ♦ **costar una r.** FIG., COLL. to cost an arm and a leg.

rí·o m. *(corriente)* river; FIG. *(abundancia)* stream, flood <*un r. de cartas de protesta* a flood of letters of protest> ♦ **pescar en** *or* **a r. revuelto** to fish in troubled waters • **r. abajo** downstream • **R. Amazonas** Amazon River • **r. arriba** upstream • **R. de la Plata** River Plate.

ri·pia f. *(tabla delgada)* shingle, lath; *(de un madero)* rough surface (of a log).

ri·piar tr. *(llenar)* to fill with rubble; CUBA to tear to pieces.

ri·pio m. *(residuo)* refuse, residue; *(palabrería inútil)* padding, verbiage; CONSTR. rubble, riprap ♦ **no perder r.** FIG. not to miss a trick.

ri·que·za f. *(abundancia)* wealth, riches; *(opulencia)* richness, opulence; FIG. *(fecundidad)* richness <*r. del vocabulario* richness of vocabulary> ♦ **riquezas** riches • **riquezas naturales** natural resources.

ri·sa f. laugh <*una r. ahogada* a stifled laugh>; laughter <*no hizo caso de la risa de los estudiantes* he took no notice of the students' laughter>; *(lo que mueve a reír)* laugh, joke <*la explicación que dio fue una r.* the explanation he gave was a laugh>; *(hazmerreír)* laughingstock ♦ **caerse** *or* **descoserse** *or* **desternillarse** *or* **reventar de r.** to burst with laughter, split one's sides laughing • **causar r. a alguien** *or* **mover a alguien a r.** to make someone laugh • **contener la r.** to keep a straight face • **cosa de r.** laughing matter • **dar r. a alguien** to make someone laugh • **morirse de r.** to die laughing • **¡qué r.!** how funny! • **r. burlona** *or* **socarrona** mocking laugh • **r. del conejo** forced laugh *or* grin • **ser motivo de r.** to be something to laugh about • **soltar la r.** to burst out laughing • **tener un ataque de r.** to have a fit of laughter • **tomar a r.** to take as a joke.

ris·co m. crag, cliff.

ri·si·ble adj. laughable, ludicrous.

ri·si·ble·men·te adv. laughably, ludicrously.

ri·sión f. COLL. *(burla)* teasing, mockery; *(hazmerreír)* laughingstock.

ri·so·ta·da f. guffaw, horselaugh.

ris·tra f. string <*una r. de ajos* a string of garlic>.

ris·tre m. rest *or* socket (for a lance).

ri·sue·ño, -ña adj. *(que muestra risa)* smiling; FIG. *(agradable)* pleasant; *(favorable)* bright, promising (future).

rít·mi·co, -ca adj. rhythmic.

rit·mo m. rhythm.

ri·to[1] m. rite, ceremony.

ri·to[2] m. CHILE heavy poncho.

ri·tual adj. & m. ritual.

ri·val adj & m.f. rival.

ri·va·li·dad f. rivalry.

ri·va·li·zar §04 intr. to rival, compete.

ri·ve·ra f. brook, stream.

ri·za·do I. past part. see **rizar II.** m. curling (of the hair).

ri·zar §04 tr. *(encrespar)* to curl, crimp (hair); *(formar olas)* to ripple (waves); *(doblar)* to fold, crumple (paper) —reflex. *(pelo)* to curl (up), frizz; *(el mar)* to become choppy.

ri·zo, -za I. adj. *(ensortijado)* curly; TEX. ribbed (velvet) **II.** m. *(mechón)* curl, ringlet; TEX. ribbed velvet; AER. loop ♦ **hacer** *or* **rizar el r.** AER. to loop the loop.

ri·zo·ma m. BOT. rhizome.

ri·zo·so, -sa adj. *(naturally)* curly (hair).

ro interj. rock-a-bye.

ro·a, roo see **roer.**

ro·a·no, -na adj. sorrel, roan (horse).

ro·ba·dor, -do·ra I. adj. robbing, thieving **II.** m.f. robber, thief.

ró·ba·lo *or* **ro·ba·lo** m. ICHTH. bass.

ro·bar tr. *(hurtar)* to rob, steal <*r. la cartera a alguien* to steal someone's wallet>; *(saquear)* to break into, burgle <*r. una casa* to break into a house>; *(raptar)* to abduct, kidnap (children); *(llevar tierra)* to wash away (earth) <*el río roba sus orillas* the river washes away its banks>; *(tomar del monte)* to draw *or* take (cards or dominoes) from the pile; *(redondear)* to round off, smooth (a point); FIG. *(captar la voluntad)* to captivate, steal (away) <*robarle el alma a alguien* to steal away one's soul>.

ro·ble m. BOT. oak; FIG. *(persona)* bulwark, pillar of strength.

ro·ble·dal *or* **ro·ble·do** m. oak grove.

ro·blón m. *(clavo)* rivet; *(teja)* ridge of tiles.

ro·bo m. *(hurto)* robbery, theft; *(en naipes)* draw (in cards).

ro·bus·te·ci·mien·to m. strengthening, fortifying.

ro·bus·te·cer §17 tr. to strengthen, fortify.

ro·bus·tez *or* **ro·bus·te·za** f. robustness, strength.

ro·bus·to, -ta adj. robust, strong.

ro·ca f. GEOL. rock; *(piedra)* stone; FIG. *(cosa dura)* stone, rock <*un corazón de r.* a heart of stone> ♦ **cristal de r.** rock crystal.

ro·ca·lla f. *(fragmentos de roca)* stone chippings; *(abalorio grueso)* large glass bead.

ro·ca·llo·so, -sa adj. rocky, stony.

ro·ce m. *(acción de rozar)* rubbing, friction; *(toque)* touch, contact; FIG. *(trato frecuente)* close contact, familiarity; *(fricción)* friction, animosity.

ro·cé, roce see **rozar.**

ro·cia·da f. *(acción de rociar)* sprinkling, showering; *(rocío)* dew; *(hierba mojada)* dew-drenched grass (fed to horses); FIG. *(abundancia)* shower, hail <*una r. de injurias* a shower of insults>; *(represión severa)* severe reprimand.

ro·cia·dor m. sprinkler, sprayer.

ro·cia·du·ra f. *or* **ro·cia·mien·to** m. sprinkling, spraying.

ro·ciar §30 intr. to fall (said of dew) —tr. *(mojar)* to sprinkle, spray; FIG. *(arrojar)* to scatter, strew.

ro·cín m. *(asno)* donkey, ass; *(caballo de trabajo)* workhorse, nag; FIG., COLL. *(persona ignorante)* clod, dolt; BOL. ox.

ro·ci·nan·te m. worn-out nag.

ro·cí·o m. *(por la mañana)* dew; *(llovizna)* sprinkle, shower; MARIT. spoondrift.

ro·co·so, -sa adj. rocky.

ro·co·te *or* **ro·co·to** m. AMER., BOT. large green pepper.

ro·da·ba·llo m. ICHTH. turbot, flounder; FIG. *(astuto)* shrewd person.

ro·da·do, -da I. adj. *(caballo)* dappled; *(frase)* smooth, flowing (expression); MIN. scattered (ore) **II.** m. ARG., CHILE vehicle, carriage —f. rut, wheel track.

ro·da·dor, -do·ra I. adj. rolling **II.** m. ICHTH. sunfish; AMER., ENTOM. gnat.

ro·da·du·ra f. *(acción de rodar)* rolling; *(estría)* tread (of a wheel).

ro·da·ja f. *(de metal)* disc; *(estrellita)* rowel; *(rueda pequeña)* small wheel; *(de fruta)* slice; CUL. pastry wheel.

ro·da·je m. *(conjunto de ruedas)* wheels, set of wheels; *(impuesto)* vehicle tax; CINEM. filming.

ro·da·mien·to m. bearing <*r. de bolas* ball bearing>.

ro·dan·te adj. *(que rueda)* rolling; CHILE ambling, meandering.

ro·dar §19 intr. *(girar)* to roll <*la canica rueda* the marble rolls>; *(funcionar)* to run <*un camión que rueda bien* a truck that runs well>; *(revolver)* to rotate, turn; *(moverse con ruedas)* to move *or* run (on wheels); *(caer dando vueltas)* to tumble *or* fall (down) <*r. de lo alto* to fall from above>; FIG. *(vagar)* to roam, wander; *(suceder)* to happen in succession; CINEM. to shoot, film; ARG. to stumble (a horse) ♦ **andar rodando** to be scattered about (objects) • **echarlo todo a r.** *(dañar)* to ruin everything; *(abandonar)* to give up • **r. de suelo** AER. to taxi • **r. por el mundo** to roam the world • **r. por** to roll *or* tumble down <*r. por las escaleras* to tumble down the stairs> • **r. por otro** to be at someone's beck and call —tr. *(hacer rodar)* to roll; CINEM. to shoot, film; HOND. to knock down; VEN. to seize.

ro·de·ar intr. *(dar la vuelta)* to go around; *(ir por el camino más largo)* to go by a roundabout way; FIG. *(hablar con rodeos)* to beat around the bush —tr. *(acorralar)* to surround <*los guardias rodearon al ladrón* the guards surrounded the thief>; *(encerrar)* to enclose, surround <*una muralla rodea el jardín* a wall encloses the garden>; *(dar la vuelta)* to go around; AMER. to round up (cattle) ♦ **r. de** to surround with —reflex. *(revolverse)* to toss and turn (in one's sleep); *(volverse)* to turn around ♦ **rodearse de** to surround oneself with <*rodearse de amigos* to surround oneself with friends>.

ro·de·la f. buckler, round shield.

ro·de·o m. *(acción de rodear)* surrounding; *(camino indi-*

recto) roundabout way, long way around; *(regate)* dodge, turn (to escape from someone); *(fiesta)* rodeo; *(reunión de ganado)* (cattle) roundup; *(lugar para ganado)* corral; FIG. *(circunloquio)* evasion, circumlocution; *(subterfugio)* subterfuge ♦ **andar con rodeos** to beat about *or* around the bush • **dar un r.** to go by a roundabout way • **dejarse de rodeos** to stop beating around the bush, come to the point • **sin ambages ni rodeos** directly, bluntly.

ro·de·te m. *(de pelo)* bun, chignon; *(rosca de lienzo)* cloth pad (for carrying loads on the head); *(de cerradura)* ward (of a lock); *(en un coche)* belt wheel; *(rueda hidráulica)* horizontal water wheel.

ro·dez·no m. *(rueda hidráulica)* water wheel; *(en un molino)* cogwheel.

ro·di·lla f. ANAT. knee ♦ **de rodillas** kneeling, on one's knees • **doblar la r.** to go down on one knee • **hincarse** *or* **ponerse de rodillas** to kneel down, go down on one's knees.

ro·di·lla·da f. *or* **ro·di·lla·zo** m. blow with the knee.

ro·di·lle·ra f. *(protección)* knee guard; *(remiendo)* knee patch; *(bolsa)* bagging at the knees.

ro·di·llo m. roller; MECH. *(de una máquina de escribir)* roller, platen; *(de una lavadora)* mangle; CUL. rolling pin.

ro·dio m. CHEM. rhodium.

ro·dri·gón m. *(de una planta)* prop (of a plant); FIG., COLL. *(criado)* chaperon.

ro·e·dor, –do·ra I. adj. gnawing II. m. ZOOL. rodent.

ro·e·du·ra f. *(acción)* gnawing; *(porción roída)* gnawed part.

ro·ent·gen *or* **ro·ent·ge·nio** m. PHYS. roentgen.

ro·er §61 tr. *(con los dientes)* to gnaw <*los ratones roen la madera* the mice gnaw the wood>; *(un hueso)* to pick (a bone); FIG. *(molestar)* to worry, torment; *(gastar)* to gnaw away at, erode <*el agua roe las rocas* the water gnaws away at the rocks>.

ro·gar §16 tr. *(suplicar)* to beg, implore; *(pedir)* to ask, request; *(rezar)* to pray —intr. to pray, plead ♦ **hacerse de r.** to be difficult, play hard to get.

ro·í·do, –da I. past part. see **roer** I. adj. FIG., COLL. stingy, tightfisted.

roi·ga, roigo see **roer**.

ro·je·te m. rouge.

ro·jez f. redness, ruddiness.

ro·ji·zo, –za adj. reddish, ruddy.

ro·jo, –ja I. adj. *(colorado)* red <*tiene el pelo muy r.* she has very red hair>; *(rojizo)* ruddy <*tiene las mejillas rojas* he has ruddy cheeks>; *(rubio)* sandy, reddish blond (hair); POL. red, revolutionary ♦ **mal r.** VET. swine fever • **poner r. a alguien** to make someone blush • **ponerse r.** to blush, turn red • **ponerse r. de ira** to see red, become furious II. m.f. POL. red, revolutionary —m. *(color)* red ♦ **al r. red-hot** • **al r. blanco** white-hot • **calentar** *or* **poner al r. vivo** to make red-hot • **estar al r. vivo** FIG. to be heated *or* tense • **r. cereza** cherry red • **r. de labios** lipstick • **r. de metilo** methyl red • **r. escarlata** scarlet red.

ro·lar intr. MARIT. to veer around; AMER. to pal around (with).

rol·da·na f. MARIT. pulley wheel.

ro·lle·te m. BOL. snout, muzzle; COL., VEN. pad (for carrying loads on the head).

ro·lli·zo, –za I. adj. *(redondo)* round; *(grueso)* chubby, plump II. m. round log.

ro·llo I. m. *(cilindro)* roll <*un r. de cinta adhesiva* a roll of adhesive tape>; *(de escritura)* scroll <*r. de pergamino* parchment scroll>; *(carrete de película)* roll (of film); *(envoltijo)* coil <*r. de cuerda* coil of rope>; MECH., TECH. roller; CUL. rolling pin; FIG. *(carne grasa)* roll *or* layer (of fat); COLL. *(cosa pesada)* bore, drag; *(discurso aburrido)* tedious speech, sermon ♦ **en r.** rolled (up) • **largar el r.** ARG., BOL. to be sick • **soltar el r.** COLL. to go on and on, sermonize II. adj. COLL. boring, tedious.

Ro·ma f. Rome.

ro·ma·na I. f. steelyard II. adj. see **romano, –na**.

ro·man·ce I. adj. Romance (language) II. m. *(lengua moderna)* Romance language; *(castellano)* Spanish (language); LIT. ballad, tale of chivalry; POET. romance (octosyllabic verse with alternating assonant lines) ♦ **en buen r.** in plain *or* clear language • **hablar en r.** FIG. to speak plainly *or* clearly • **r. de gesta** LIT. chanson de geste, epic poem.

ro·man·ce·ar tr. *(traducir)* to translate into Spanish; CHILE to romance, woo.

ro·man·ce·ro, –ra m.f. *(persona)* writer of romances —m. *(colección)* collection of romances.

ro·man·ces·co, –ca adj. novelesque.

ro·man·cis·ta I. adj. writing in Spanish II. m.f. writer in Spanish.

ro·má·ni·co, –ca adj. ARCHIT. Romanesque; PHILOL. Romance.

ro·ma·no, –na I. adj. Roman ♦ **Iglesia Romana** RELIG. Roman Catholic Church • **lechuga r.** romaine lettuce • **números romanos** Roman numerals II. m.f. Roman ♦ **obra de romanos** FIG. Herculean task —f. see **romana**.

ro·man·ti·cis·mo m. ARTS, LIT. romanticism.

ro·mán·ti·co, –ca adj. & m.f. romantic.

rom·bo m. GEOM. rhombus; ICHTH. brill, turbot.

ro·me·o, –a I. adj. Byzantine II. m.f. *(griego)* Byzantine FIG. *(persona enamorada)* lovesick person.

ro·me·ral m. rosemary patch.

ro·me·rí·a f. *(devoción)* pilgrimage; *(fiesta)* festival.

ro·me·ro I. m. BOT. rosemary; ICHTH. whiting, pilot fish II. adj. see **romero, –ra**.

ro·me·ro, –ra I. adj. pilgrim II. m.f. pilgrim —m. see **romero**.

ro·mo, –ma adj. GEOM. obtuse; ANAT. snub-nosed; FIG. dull.

rom·pe·ca·be·zas m. [pl. **-zas**] *(dibujo recortado)* jigsaw puzzle; FIG. *(problema)* riddle *or* difficult puzzle.

rom·pe·de·ra f. blacksmith's iron punch.

rom·pe·de·ro, –ra I. adj. breakable, fragile II. m. ♦ **r. de cabeza** ARG., COLL. problem.

rom·pe·dor, –do·ra I. adj. *(que rompe)* destructive, breaking; COLL. *(que gasta la ropa)* hard on one's clothes II. m.f. *(que rompe)* destructive person, breaker; COLL. *(que gasta la ropa)* one who is hard on clothes.

rom·pe·hie·los m. [pl. **-los**] MARIT. icebreaker, iceboat.

rom·pe·nue·ces m. [pl. **-ces**] nutcracker.

rom·pe·o·las m. [pl. **-las**] breakwater, jetty.

rom·per §85 tr. *(quebrar)* to break, smash <*r. un plato* to break a plate>; *(separar en pedazos)* to tear *or* rip (up) <*r. un papel* to tear a piece of paper>; *(partir)* to break, snap <*r. un cable* to snap a cable>; *(gastar)* to wear out (clothing); *(penetrar)* to pierce, penetrate; FIG. *(interrumpir)* to break, interrupt <*r. el silencio* to break the silence>; *(abrir paso)* to break through <*r. la cerca* to break through the fence>; *(surcar)* to plow, cut through <*el barco rompe el agua* the boat plows the water>; *(quebrantar)* to break <*r. el ayuno* to break a fast>; *(iniciar)* to begin, initiate <*r. las hostilidades* to begin hostilities>; *(cancelar)* to break off, cancel <*r. un compromiso* to break off an engagement>; AGR. to plow, break up (a field); MIL. to break through <*r. la primera línea* to break through the front line>; SPORT. to break (service) ♦ **r. el fuego** MIL. to open fire • **r. el paso** MIL. to break step • **r. filas** MIL. to break ranks, fall out • **r. la cara** *or* **las narices a alguien** to smash someone's face in • **r. la marcha** to lead the way • **r. una lanza por** to fight for, defend • **r.** *(empezar el día)* to break, dawn; *(olas)* to break; *(flores)* to burst (open), bloom ♦ **al r. el alba** at dawn • **al r. el día** at daybreak • **de rompe y rasga** resolute, determined • **r. a** to begin suddenly to <*rompió a cantar* she began suddenly to sing> • **r. con** to break with <*r. con el pasado* to break with the past>; *(perder la amistad)* to end one's friendship with; *(terminar el noviazgo)* to break up *or* off with <*r. con la novia* to break up with one's girlfriend> • **r. en** to burst into <*r. en llanto* to burst into tears> • **r. por** to break through —reflex. *(descomponerse)* to break (down); *(quebrarse)* to break, smash; *(separarse en pedazos)* to tear, rip; *(partirse)* to break, snap; *(gastarse)* to wear out (clothing); MED. to break, fracture ♦ **romperse el alma** *or* **la crisma** FIG. to break one's neck • **romperse la cabeza** *or* **los cascos** FIG. to rack one's brains.

rom·pi·ble adj. breakable.

rom·pien·te m. reef, shoal.

rom·pi·mien·to m. *(ruptura)* break, breaking; *(abertura)* break, opening; *(fin del trato)* break, breaking off <*r. de* *relaciones diplomáticas* break of diplomatic relations>; *(fin de noviazgo)* breakup (of an engagement); FIG. *(riña)* disagreement, quarrel; THEAT. short fore curtain ♦ **r. de hostilidades** outbreak of hostilities.

rom·po·po m. AMER. eggnog, milk punch.

ron m. rum.

ron·ca f. *(bramido)* call of a buck in rutting season; *(época)* rutting season; COLL. *(jactancia)* bullying, swaggering; *(regaño)* reprimand ♦ **echar roncas** COLL. to bully, threaten.

ron·ca·dor, –do·ra I. adj. snoring II. m.f. *(persona)* snorer; ICHTH. grunt, croaker; BOL. large spur.

ron·car §70 intr. *(durmiendo)* to snore; *(gritar)* to bellow, roar; COLL. *(echar roncas)* to bully, threaten; FIG. *(hacer ruido sordo)* to roar (said of the sea, wind).

ron·ce m. COLL. flattery, compliment.

ron·ce·ar intr. *(dilatar)* to dawdle, drag one's feet; *(halagar)* to cajole, bamboozle; MARIT. to sail slowly —tr. ARG., CHILE to lever, move by levering.

ron·ce·rí·a f. *(tardanza)* dawdling; *(halago)* cajolery, bamboozling; MARIT. slow sailing of a ship.

ron·ce·ro, –ra adj. *(perezoso)* dawdling; *(que refunfuña)* grumbling; *(que halaga)* cajoling, bamboozling; MARIT. slow-sailing.

ron·co, –ca I. adj. *(afónico)* hoarse, raw <*voz r.* hoarse voice>; *(áspero)* raucous, harsh <*sonido r.* harsh sound> II. m. CUBA, ICHTH. grunt, croaker.

ron·cón I. m. bagpipe drone II. adj. COL., VEN. bullying, bragging.

ron·cha f. *(herida)* bump, welt; *(cardenal)* bruise; *(rodaja)* slice; COLL. *(estafa)* trickery, cheating.

ron·da f. MUS. strolling musicians, street serenaders; *(tragos)* round (of drinks); *(del policía, sereno)* round, beat; *(deporte)* round; AMER. circle, ring (of people).

ron·da·dor m. *(guardia)* night watchman; MUS. street serenader; ECUAD. reed flute.

ron·da·lla f. MUS. band of strolling musicians; *(cuento)* malicious gossip.

ron·da·na f. TECH. gasket, washer; AMER. pulley wheel.

ron·dar intr. *(vigilar)* to patrol, make rounds; *(dar una serenata)* to court, serenade; *(vagar)* to prowl around; MED. to threaten to relapse —tr. *(dar vueltas)* to hover around <*las mariposas rondan la luz* the butterflies hover around the light>; *(galantear)* to court, serenade; *(asediar)* to pursue.

ron·qué, ronque see **roncar.**

ron·que·ar intr. to speak hoarsely.

ron·que·ra or **ron·quez** f. hoarseness.

ron·qui·do m. *(durmiendo)* snore, snoring; FIG. *(sonido ronco)* roaring, roar.

ron·ro·ne·ar intr. to purr.

Rönt·gen or **Ro·ent·gen** or **Ro·ent·ge·nio** m. PHYS. roentgen (unit of x-ray).

ro·ña f. *(sarna)* rash; *(mugre)* filth, dirt; *(orín)* rust; *(ovejas)* mange, scab; *(corteza de pino)* bark (of pine tree); FIG., COLL. *(tacañería)* meanness, stinginess; C. AMER., CUBA grudge, hostility; COL. cleverness.

ro·ñe·rí·a or **ro·ño·se·ri·a** f. COLL. stinginess.

ro·ñi·ca f. COLL. miser, skinflint.

ro·ño·so, –sa adj. *(sarnoso)* mangy, scabby; *(sucio)* filthy, dirty; *(tacaño)* stingy, miserly; C. AMER. resentful, spiteful.

ro·pa f. *(vestido)* clothes, clothing; *(conjunto)* costume, dress ♦ **a quema r.** *(de cerca)* pointblank, at pointblank range; FIG. *(de improviso)* suddenly, unexpectedly • **hay r. tendida** FIG., COLL. the walls have ears, be careful what you say • **(nadar y) guardar la r.** FIG. to have the best of both worlds • **palparse** or **tentarse la r.** FIG. to consider something carefully (before acting) • **r. blanca** *(sábanas)* linens; *(de mujer)* lingerie; *(de hombre)* underwear • **r. de cama** bed linen • **r. de dormir** bedclothes • **r. dominguera** Sunday best • **r. hecha** ready-made or ready-to-wear clothes • **r. interior** underwear, underclothes • **r. planchada** ironing • **r. sucia** or **lavada** laundry, wash • **r. vieja** COLL. cooked shredded beef.

ro·pa·je m. *(ropas)* clothes, vestments; *(colgaduras)* drapery.

ro·pa·ve·je·ro, –ra m.f. secondhand clothes dealer.

ro·pe·rí·a f. *(oficio)* clothing trade; *(tienda)* clothing store; *(guardarropa)* coat-check room, cloakroom.

ro·pe·ro, –ra m.f. *(vendedor)* clothes dealer; *(guardarropero)* cloakroom attendant —m. *(armario)* closet, wardrobe; *(asociación benéfica)* charity distributing clothing to the poor.

ro·pón m. *(traje)* robe, gown; CHILE, COL. riding skirt.

ro·que m. *(en ajedrez)* tower, rook (in chess); HER. emblazoned tower emblem ♦ **quedarse r.** to fall into a deep sleep.

ro·que·da f. or **ro·que·dal** m. rocky place.

ro·rro m. COLL. *(bebé)* baby, infant; MEX. doll.

ro·sa I. f. BOT. rose; *(adorno)* rose-shaped decoration; *(cosa con forma de rosa)* rose, rosette; *(color)* rose, pink; ANAT. red spot; ARCHIT. rose window; JEWEL. rose-cut diamond ♦ **como las propias rosas** COLL. fine, splendid • **r. albardera** or **de rejalgar** or **montés** BOT. peony • **r. de Jericó** BOT. rose of Jericho • **r. náutica** or **de los vientos** MARIT. compass rose or card • **r. de té** BOT. tea rose • **rosas** popcorn • **verlo todo de color de r.** to see everything through rose-colored glasses II. adj. rose, pink.

ro·sá·ce·o, –a adj. rosy.

ro·sa·do, –da I. adj. *(color)* pink, rosy; *(sabor)* rose-flavored; *(ganado)* roan (livestock); *(vino)* rosé II. m. rosé.

ro·sal m. *(arbusto)* rosebush; AMER. *(jardín)* rose garden.

ro·sa·le·da or **ro·sa·le·ra** f. rose garden.

ro·sa·rio m. RELIG. rosary (prayer, beads); MECH. chain pump, water wheel; FIG. series, string (of misfortunes, events).

ros·bif m. CUL. roast beef.

ros·ca f. *(círculo)* ring, circle; *(vuelta espiral)* thread <*la r. de un tornillo* the thread of a screw>; *(de humo)* ring, smoke ring; CUL. ring, ring-shaped bread; ANAT. roll of fat; AMER. pad (worn on head for carrying loads); ARG., CHILE argument; CHILE *(corro)* circle (of card players) ♦ **hacer la r. (del galgo)** to curl up and go to sleep anywhere • **hacer la r. a alguien** COLL. to flatter someone, suck up to someone • **pasarse de r.** *(no agarrar)* to be stripped (a screw); FIG. *(excederse)* to go too far, overdo it • **r. de Arquímedes** Archimedian screw.

ros·ca·do, –da I. past part. see **roscar** II. adj. screw-shaped III. m. threading (of a screw).

ros·car §70 tr. to thread (screws).

ros·co m. *(pan)* large pastry ring; *(flotador)* flotation ring, livesaver.

ros·cón m. large pastry ring.

ro·se·ta f. *(rosita)* small rose, rosetta; *(mejilla)* rosy cheek; MECH. rosehead, sprinkling nozzle; ARG. spur rowel ♦ **rosetas** popcorn.

ro·se·tón m. ARCHIT. rose window; *(adorno)* large rosetta.

ros·qué, rosque see **roscar.**

ros·que·te m. CUL. large doughnut.

ros·tro m. *(cara)* face, countenance; ZOOL. bill, beak; MARIT. rostrum, beak (of an ancient warship) ♦ **a r. firme** boldly, resolutely • **hacer r.** to face, face up to • **tener r.** FIG., COLL. to have nerve • **torcer el r.** to grimace • **volver uno el r.** to turn one's head away.

ro·ta I. f. *(derrota)* defeat, failure; MIL. rout II. adj. see **roto, –ta.**

ro·ta·ción f. rotation.

ro·ta·ti·vo, –va I. adj. rotary, revolving II. f. MECH. rotary press —m. JOURN. newspaper printed on a rotary press.

ro·ta·to·rio, –ria adj. rotating, rotary.

ro·te·rí·a f CHILE rabble, plebs.

ro·to, –ta I. past part. see **romper** II. adj. *(dañado)* broken; *(quebrado)* broken, smashed; torn, ripped <*una página r.* a torn page>; *(andrajoso)* worn out, ragged; *(arruinado)* destroyed, ruined; FIG. *(licencioso)* dissipated, licentious III. m. *(agujero)* hole; ARG., PERU, DEROG. Chilean; CHILE member of the lowest class; ECUAD. half-breed; MEX. village dandy —f. see **rota.**

ro·ton·da f. rotunda, roundhouse.

ro·tor m. MECH. rotor.

ro·to·so, –sa adj. AMER. ragged, tattered.

ró·tu·la f. ANAT. kneecap; MECH. rounded joint.

ro·tu·la·ción f. labeling, lettering.

ro·tu·la·do I. past part. see **rotular** II. m. sign, label.

ro·tu·la·dor, –do·ra I. adj. labeling, lettering II. m.f. labeling device.

ro·tu·lar tr. to label, letter.

ró·tu·lo m. sign, label ♦ **rótulos** CINEM. titles, subtitles.

ro·tun·do, –da adj. *(redondo)* round; *(sonoro)* resounding; FIG. *(definitivo)* flat, categorical; *(frase)* well-rounded.

ro·tu·ra f. *(rompimiento)* break, fracture; *(en tela)* rip, tear.

ro·tu·ra·ción f. ARG. plowing.

ro·tu·ra·dor, –do·ra I. adj. plowing II. m.f. plower —f. harrow, plow.

ro·tu·rar tr. to break new ground, to plow.

ro·ye·ra, royó see **roer.**

ro·za f. AGR. clearing, cleared ground; *(acción de rozar)* clearing.

ro·za·de·ro m. land being cleared.

ro·za·dor, –do·ra m.f. clearer (of land) —m. VEN. machete.

ro·za·du·ra f. *(frotación)* rubbing; *(señal)* mark, rub; BOT. punk knot; MED. chafed spot, abrasion.

ro·za·gan·te adj. *(vestido)* showy, splendid; *(caballo)* lively, high-spirited.

ro·za·mien·to m. MECH rubbing, friction; AGR. groundclearing; FIG. friction, disagreement.

ro·zar §04 tr. *(frotar)* to rub (against) <*el zapato me roza el dedo gordo* the shoe rubs my big toe>; *(limpiar tierra)* to clear (land); *(raer)* to scrape; *(tocar)* to graze, touch lightly, brush against; *(pacer)* to graze (grass); *(volar a ras de)* to skim; *(ensuciar)* to dirty; FIG. *(rayar en)* to touch or border on <*sus acciones rozan la traición* his actions border on treason>; MED. to chafe —intr. to touch lightly —reflex. *(tropezarse un pie)* to trip over one's own feet; FIG. *(tratarse mucho)* to be close, be on close terms; *(trabarse la lengua)* to stammer, stumble <*rozarse en las palabras* to stumble over one's words>; *(tener conexión con)* to have a connection with ♦ **rozarse con** *(tocarse)* to touch lightly, brush against; FIG. *(mezclarse con)* to rub elbows or mix with.

roz·nar tr. to chew, munch —intr. to bray.

roz·ni·do m. chewing, munching; *(rebuzno)* braying noise.

ro·zo m. ground-clearing.

rua·na I. f. COL., VEN. poncho composed of two equal woolen squares II. adj. see **ruano, –na.**

rua·no, –na I. adj. *(caballo)* roan II. f. see **ruana.**

ru·bé·o·la f. MED. rubella, German measles.

ru·bí m. [pl. **-bí·es**] ruby.

ru·bia I. f. *(mujer)* blonde; BOT. madder plant or root; AUTO. station wagon; SP., COLL. peseta coin II. adj. see **rubio, –bia.**

ru·bi·cán, –ca·na adj. roan.

ru·bi·cun·do, –da adj. ruddy, reddish.

ru·bi·dio m. MIN. rubidium.

ru·bio, –bia I. adj. blond(e), fair ♦ **tabaco r.** Virginia tobacco II. m. blond —f. see **rubia.**

ru·blo m. FIN. ruble.

ru·bor m. *(color)* blush, flush; FIG. *(vergüenza)* embarrassment ♦ **sentir r.** to blush, be embarrassed.

ru·bo·ri·zar·se §04 reflex. to blush, become embarrassed.

ru·bo·ro·so, –sa adj. FIG. embarrassed, red in the face.

rú·bri·ca f. *(sección de periódico)* rubric, section (of a newspaper); *(firma)* signature flourish; *(título)* rubric, title; RELIG. rubric, service instruction ♦ **ser de r.** to be customary.

ru·bri·car §70 tr. *(firmar y sellar)* to sign and seal; FIG. *(dar testimonio)* to subscribe, witness with one's initials.

ru·bro, –bra I. adj. red, ruddy II. m. JOURN. heading, title; ACC. item.

ru·cio, –cia adj. *(gris)* gray (horse); COLL. *(canas)* white-haired (person).

ru·co, –ca adj. AMER. worn-out, useless.

ru·cho m. COLL. donkey, jackass.

ru·da I. f. BOT. rue, goat's rue ♦ **ser más conocido que la r.** to be a household word II. adj. see **rudo, –da.**

ru·de·za f. roughness, rudeness.

ru·di·men·ta·rio, –ria adj. rudimentary, basic.

ru·di·men·to m. *(principio)* rudiment, basic principle; *(libro)* primer; *(esbozo)* preliminary sketch.

ru·do, –da I. adj. *(tosco)* rough, coarse; *(arte)* crude, unpolished; *(tiempo)* severe, harsh; *(condiciones)* hard, difficult; *(tonto)* dull, dimwitted II. f. see **ruda.**

rue·ca f. *(instrumento)* distaff; *(vuelta)* twist, turn.

rue·da f. wheel <*las ruedas de un coche* the wheels of a car>; *(de un mueble)* caster, roller; *(rodaja)* slice; *(corro)* circle, ring (of people); *(suplicio)* rack, wheel (form of torture); *(partida de billar)* threesome at billiards; *(turno)* turn, successive order; ICHTH. sunfish; ORNITH. spread (of peacock's tail) ♦ **comulgar con ruedas de molino** or **tragárselas como ruedas de molino** FIG. to swallow or believe anything • **con** or **de dos ruedas** two-wheeled • **hacer la r. a alguien** FIG. to flatter someone • **hacer r.** to make a circle • **ir sobre ruedas** FIG. to go smoothly • **r. catalina** or **de Santa Catalina** catherine wheel • **r. de alfarero** potter's wheel • **r. de andar** treadwheel • **r. de la fortuna** wheel of fortune • **r. de molino** millstone • **r. de paletas** or **de álabes** paddle wheel • **r. de prensa** or **de periodistas** press conference • **r. de presos** line-up (of suspects) • **r. dentada** cog, cogwheel • **r. hidráulica** or **de agua** water wheel • **r. libre** freewheel.

rue·de, ruedo see **rodar.**

rue·do m. *(acción de rodar)* turn, rotation; *(borde)* edge, border; *(circunferencia)* circumference; *(dobladillo)* hem (of a skirt); *(esterilla)* round mat; TAUR. bullring, arena ♦ **dar la vuelta al r.** TAUR. to go around the bullring receiving applause (a bullfighter) • **echarse al r.** FIG. to enter the fray.

rue·ga, ruego see **rogar.**

rue·go m. petition, request.

ru·fián m. *(chulo)* pimp; *(granuja)* scoundrel, ruffian.

ru·fo, –fa adj. *(rubio)* blond(e); *(bermejo)* red; *(tieso)* curly-haired, stiff; *(vistoso)* showy.

ru·gi·do I. past part. see **rugir** II. m. roar, bellow.

ru·gi·dor, –do·ra or **ru·gien·te** adj. roaring, bellowing.

ru·gir §32 intr. *(bramar)* to roar, bellow; *(crujir)* to howl, rage (storm).

ru·go·si·dad f. wrinkle, rugosity.

ru·go·so, –sa adj. wrinkled, rough.

rui·do m. *(sonido)* noise, sound; *(alboroto)* din, clamor; FIG. *(sensación)* stir ♦ **hacer** or **meter r.** to draw attention, create a stir • **mucho r. y pocas nueces** much ado about nothing • **querer r.** to pick a fight • **quitarse de ruidos** to withdraw from a fight • **r. galáctico** ASTRON., RAD. galactic noise • **sin r.** silently, without a sound.

rui·do·so, –sa adj. noisy, loud; FIG. sensational, smashing.

ruin adj. *(despreciable)* petty, despicable; *(avaro)* mean, stingy; *(animales)* vicious, mean; *(miserable)* poor, miserable; *(raquítico)* puny; CUBA in heat.

rui·na f. *(destrucción)* ruin, decay; *(hundimiento)* downfall, collapse ♦ **estar hecho una r.** FIG. to be a wreck • **ruinas** ruins • **va a ser su r.** it will be his downfall • **vamos a la r.** we are going to wrack and ruin.

ruin·dad f. pettiness, viciousness.

rui·no·so, –sa adj. run-down, dilapidated.

rui·se·ñor m. ZOOL. nightingale.

ru·ja, rujo see **rugir.**

ru·le·ta f. roulette.

ru·lo m. *(cilindro)* roller, rolling pin; CHILE unirrigated land.

Ru·ma·nia f. Rumania, Romania.

ru·ma·no, –na adj. & m.f. Rumanian, Romanian.

rum·ba f. *(baile)* rumba (dance); CHILE heap, pile; CUBA spree, spree.

rum·be·ar intr. AMER. to head for; *(orientarse)* to get one's bearings; *(bailar)* to dance the rumba.

rum·bo m. *(sentido)* direction; FIG. *(pompa)* ostentation, show; *(garbo)* generosity, lavishness; AER., MARIT. course <*cambiar de r.* to change course>; MARIT. *(camino fijo)* rhumb (line); *(abertura)* opening in ship's hull; C. AMER. spree, binge; COL. hummingbird; ARG. cut on the head ♦ **abatir el r.** MARIT. to fall off, fall to leeward • **con r. a** in the direction of, bound for • **corregir el r.** MARIT. to correct the course • **hacer** or **poner r. a** MARIT. to head for • **ir con r. a** to be heading for, be going in the direction of • **marcar el r.** MARIT. to set a course • **perder el r.** FIG. to lose one's bearings • **r. aguja** or **brújula** MARIT. compass course • **r. magnético** AER., MARIT. magnetic bearing •

tomar buen r. FIG. to take a turn for the better (a situation) • **tomar otro r.** FIG. to take a different tack.

rum·bo·so, –sa adj. COLL. (*espléndido*) magnificent, splendid; (*generoso*) magnanimous, generous.

ru·mí m. Roumi (Moslem name for Christians).

ru·mian·te I. adj. ruminant, ruminating **II.** m.pl. **rumiantes** ruminants.

ru·miar tr. (*mascar*) to ruminate, chew the cud; FIG., COLL. (*considerar*) to ruminate, mull over; (*refunfuñar*) to grumble, grouse.

ru·mor m. (*ruido constante*) steady noise, murmur; (*ruido de árboles*) rustle, whisper; (*chismes*) rumor.

ru·mo·re·ar·se or **ru·mo·rar·se** reflex. to be rumored.

ru·na f. rune.

rú·ni·co, –ca adj. runic.

run·rún m. COLL. (*chisme*) rumor, gossip; (*ruido*) noise; (*gato*) purring; ARG., CHILE roar.

ru·pes·tre adj. (*de rocas*) rock; (*de pinturas*) rupestrian, cave (painting).

ru·pia f. FIN. rupee.

rup·tu·ra f. (*acción de romper*) breaking; MED. rupture, fracture; (*de relaciones*) breaking off, breakup.

ru·ral I. (*campestre*) rustic; (*campesino*) rustic, rough **II.** m.f. AMER. peasant, hick.

ru·so, –sa adj. & m.f. Russian —m. (*idioma*) Russian.

rus·ti·ci·dad f. coarseness, rustic quality.

rús·ti·co, –ca I. adj. (*campestre*) rustic, rural; FIG. (*grosero*) rough, gross ♦ **a la** or **en r.** paperback (book edition) **II.** m.f. peasant, hick.

ru·ta f. route, road.

ru·te·nio m. CHEM. ruthenium.

ru·ti·lan·te adj. brilliant, shiny.

ru·ti·lar intr. to shine, sparkle.

ru·ti·na f. routine, habit.

ru·ti·na·rio, –ria I. adj. routine **II.** m.f. FIG. dense, unimaginative person.

Rwan·da m. Rwanda.

rwan·dés, –de·sa adj. & m.f. Rwandese.

S

s, S f. twenty-second letter of the Spanish alphabet.

sá·ba·do m. (*séptimo día*) Saturday; RELIG. Sabbath ♦ **S. de Gloria** or **Santo** Easter Saturday • **s. inglés** Saturday on which one works half a day • **hacer s.** to do the weekly cleaning.

sá·ba·lo m. ICHTH. shad.

sa·ba·na f. AMER. savannah, savanna; CUBA pasture, grazing land ♦ **estar en la s.** VEN., COLL. to be prosperous, be in clover • **ponerse en la s.** VEN., COLL. to become rich overnight.

sá·ba·na f. (*de cama*) sheet, bed sheet; RELIG. altar cloth ♦ **estirarse más de lo que dan de sí las sábanas** to overextend oneself, bite off more than one can chew • **pegársele a uno las sábanas** COLL. to oversleep.

sa·ban·di·ja f. ENTOM. bug, insect; FIG. (*persona*) louse, vermin.

sa·ba·ne·ar intr. AMER. to round up cattle (on the plains).

sa·ba·ne·ro, –ra I. adj. pertaining to a savanna or plain **II.** m.f. (*habitante*) savanna or plain dweller —m. AMER. (*ganadero*) cowboy, cattle drover; C. AMER. (*matón*) bully, troublemaker —f. ZOOL. savanna snake.

sa·ba·ñón m. MED. chilblain ♦ **comer como un s.** COLL. to stuff oneself, eat like a horse.

sa·bá·ti·co, –ca adj. sabbatical.

sa·ba·ti·no, –na I. adj. (*de sábado*) pertaining to Saturday; RELIG. sabbatine **II.** RELIG. Saturday service or mass.

sa·be·dor, –do·ra adj. knowledgeable, aware.

sa·be·lo·to·do m.f. COLL. know-it-all.

sa·ber¹ m. learning, knowledge ♦ **según mi leal s. y entender** to the best of my knowledge.

sa·ber² §62 tr. to know <*ella sabe lo que ocurrió* she knows what happened>; (*tener habilidad*) to know how <*¿sabes cocinar?* do you know how to cook?>; to learn, find out <*supe la noticia demasiado tarde* I learned the news too

late> ♦ **hacer s.** to inform • **¿qué sé yo?** how should I know? • **que yo sepa** as far as I know, to my knowledge • **no s. dónde meterse** COLL. not to know where to hide • **no s. por dónde se anda** COLL. not to know what one is doing • **s. cuántos son cinco** COLL. to know a thing or two • **s. de buena tinta** to have on good authority • **s. de memoria** to know by heart • **sin saberlo yo** without my knowledge • **un no sé qué** a certain something • **véte a s.** your guess is as good as mine • **y no sé qué y no sé cuántos** COLL. and so on and so forth —intr. to know <*el profesor sabe más que yo* the professor knows more than I do>; ARG., ECUAD., PERU to be in the habit of <*él sabe llegar temprano* he is in the habit of arriving early> ♦ **a s.** namely, to wit • **no se sabe** nobody knows • **¿quién sabe?** who knows?, who can tell? • **s. a** to taste like <*esto sabe a fresas* this tastes like strawberries>; FIG. to smack of <*eso sabe a rebelión* that smacks of rebellion> • **s. a gloria** to taste delicious • **s. de** (*conocer*) to know about, be familiar with; to hear from <*hace mucho tiempo que no sabemos de José* we have not heard from Joe in a long time> —reflex. to be known ♦ **sabérselo todo** to know it all.

sa·bia·men·te adv. wisely, judiciously.

sa·bi·do, –da I. past part. see **saber²** **II.** adj. (*conocido*) known; COLL. (*docto*) learned, knowledgeable; COL. lively.

sa·bi·du·rí·a f. (*prudencia*) wisdom; (*conocimiento*) knowledge, learning ♦ **s. popular** folklore, folk wisdom.

sa·bien·das adv. ♦ **a s.** knowingly, consciously.

sa·bi·hon·dez f. COLL. pedantry.

sa·bi·hon·do, –da COLL. **I.** adj. know-it-all, pedantic **II.** m.f. know-it-all, pedant.

sa·bio, –bia I. adj. (*cuerdo*) wise, judicious; (*instruido*) learned, expert; (*instructivo*) instructive; trained <*perro s.* trained dog> **II.** m.f. (*persona prudente*) wise person, sage; (*instruido*) learned person.

sa·bla·zo m. (*golpe*) saber blow; (*herida*) saber wound; FIG., COLL. sponging ♦ **dar un s. a alguien** COLL. to sponge money off someone • **vivir de sablazos** to live by sponging.

sa·ble m. (*arma*) saber, cutlass; (*maña*) sponging; HER. sable, black; CUBA, ICHTH. cutlass fish ♦ **tirar el s.** to fence.

sa·ble·ar intr. COLL. to sponge, cadge.

sa·blón m. coarse sand.

sa·bor m. (*gusto*) taste, flavor; FIG. (*carácter*) flavor, color ♦ **sabores** beads on horse's bit • **con s. a limón** lemon-flavored • **sin s.** tasteless • **tener s. a** to taste of.

sa·bo·re·a·mien·to m. CUL. flavoring, seasoning; (*aprecio*) savoring, relishing.

sa·bo·re·ar tr. (*notar el sabor*) to taste; (*sazonar*) to flavor, season; (*apreciar*) to savor, relish —reflex. to savor, relish.

sa·bo·re·o m. savoring, relishing.

sa·bo·ta·je m. sabotage.

sa·bo·te·a·dor, –do·ra I. adj. sabotaging **II.** m.f. saboteur.

sa·bo·te·ar tr. to sabotage.

sa·bo·te·o m. sabotage.

sa·brá, sabría see **saber²**.

sa·bro·sa·men·te adv. deliciously, tastily.

sa·bro·se·ar·se reflex. C. AMER. to smack one's lips.

sa·bro·se·ra or **sa·bro·su·ra** f. AMER., COLL. delicious or tasty thing.

sa·bro·so, –sa adj. (*delicioso*) delicious, tasty; FIG. (*agradable*) delightful, pleasant; (*picante*) racy, risqué <*un chiste s.* a racy joke>; CUL., COLL. salty; CARIB., MEX., PERU talkative.

sa·bro·són, –so·na adj. COLL. (*sabroso*) delicious, tasty; CARIB., PERU, VEN. talkative.

sa·bue·so m. (*perro*) bloodhound; FIG. (*investigador*) sleuth, bloodhound.

sa·ca¹ f. (*extracción*) extraction, removal; (*exportación*) export; (*copia*) certified copy; AMER. (*ganado*) herd; (*movilización del ganado*) cattle drive.

sa·ca² f. large sack ♦ **s. de correo** mailbag.

sa·ca·bo·ca·dos m. [pl. **-dos**] TECH. punch; (*medio eficaz*) sure way or means (to accomplish something).

sa·ca·bo·tas m. [pl. **-tas**] bootjack.

sa·ca·bu·che m. MUS. *(instrumento)* sackbut; *(músico)* sackbut player; FIG., COLL. *(renacuajo)* shrimp, squirt; MARIT. hand pump.

sa·ca·cla·vos m. [pl. **-vos**] nail puller *or* claw.

sa·ca·cor·chos m. [pl. **-chos**] corkscrew.

sa·ca·da f. *(territorio)* separate territory; AMER. extraction, removal.

sa·ca·di·ne·ro *or* **sa·ca·di·ne·ros** m. [pl. **-ros**] COLL. *(bisutería)* bauble, trinket; *(espectáculo)* gaudy spectacle, sideshow —m.f. *(sablista)* sponger, cadger; *(estafador)* swindler.

sa·ca·dor, –do·ra I. adj. removing, extracting II. m.f. *(que saca)* remover, extractor —m. PRINT. delivery board.

sa·ca·du·ra f. SEW. slash (in a garment); CHILE removal, extraction.

sa·ca·la·gua m. PERU light-skinned mestizo.

sa·ca·li·ña f. *(garrocha)* pointed stick, goad; FIG. *(socaliña)* cunning.

sa·ca·man·chas m.f. [pl. **-chas**] spot *or* stain remover.

sa·ca·mue·las m.f. [pl. **-las**] COLL., MED. dentist; FIG. *(estafador)* charlatan, swindler.

sa·ca·pun·tas m. [pl. **-tas**] pencil sharpener.

sa·car §70 tr. *(extraer)* to take out, extract *<sacó su cartera del bolsillo* he took his wallet out of his pocket>; *(quitar)* to take out, remove *<s. una mancha* to remove a stain>; *(arrancar)* to pull out *<el dentista me sacó la muela* the dentist pulled out my tooth>; *(desenvainar)* to draw, unsheathe (a sword); *(librar)* to bail out *<s. a alguien de un apuro* to bail someone out of a jam>; *(sonsacar)* to get out *<no le puedo s. la información* I cannot get the information out of him>; *(conocer)* to deduce, take it *<de tu expresión, saco que estás preocupado* from your expression, I take it that you are worried>; *(resolver)* to resolve, figure out *<vamos a s. las cuentas* let's figure out the bills>; *(conseguir)* to get, obtain; *(ganar)* to win *<Susana sacó premio en la rifa* Susan won a prize in the raffle>; *(elegir)* to elect; *(adelantar)* to stick out *<s. la lengua* to stick out one's tongue>; *(presentar)* to bring out, come out with *<s. una moda* to come out with a new fashion>; *(publicar)* to publish; *(manifestar)* to bring out *<s. brillo* to bring out a shine>; *(restar)* to subtract *<si a ocho le sacas tres, quedan cinco* if you subtract three from eight, you get five>; *(copiar)* to make *<la secretaria sacará una copia* the secretary will make a copy>; *(fotografiar)* to take *<quiero s. una foto del grupo* I want to take a picture of the group>; *(apuntar)* to take *<s. apuntes* to take notes>; *(aplicar)* to give *<mis amigos me sacaron el apodo "Tito"* my friends gave me the nickname "Tito">; *(citar)* to cite, quote; SPORT. *(la pelota)* to serve, put into play; CHEM. to extract *<s. aceite de las nueces* to extract oil from nuts>; SEW. *(ensanchar)* to let out; C. AMER., ECUAD. *(adular)* to flatter; ECUAD., MEX. *(echar en cara)* to reproach ♦ **s. a bailar** *(invitar)* to ask to dance; FIG., COLL. *(forzar)* to drag in, force to participate • **s. adelante** *(lograr)* to carry out, execute; *(criar)* to rear, bring up • **s. a luz** *(revelar)* to bring to light; *(publicar)* to print, publish • **s. a relucir** to bring up • **s. de quicio** *or* **de sí** to infuriate, drive crazy *<esta situacion me saca de mí* this situation is driving me crazy> • **s. el jugo** FIG. to bleed dry • **s. en claro** to figure out • **s. la cara por** FIG. to defend, stand for • **s. en claro** *or* **en limpo** to get out of, understand • **s. la oreja** ARG. to win by a nose • **sacarle la vuelta a alguien** to avoid someone • **sacarle a alguien los colores** to make someone blush • **s. provecho de** to benefit from • **s. sangre** to make bleed • **s. ventaja** to gain an advantage —reflex. to take off *<sácate el abrigo* take off your coat>.

sa·ca·ri·na f. CHEM. saccharin, saccharine.

sa·ca·ta·pón m. [pl. **-pon·es**] corkscrew.

sa·cer·do·cio m. RELIG. priesthood; FIG. *(consagración)* dedication, devotion (to a task).

sa·cer·do·tal adj. priestly, sacerdotal.

sa·cer·do·te m. priest, clergyman ♦ **s. obrero** worker priest • **sumo s.** high priest.

sa·cer·do·ti·sa f. priestess.

sa·cia·ble adj. satiable.

sa·ciar tr. to satiate, sate ♦ **s. la sed** to quench one's thirst —reflex. to be satiated *or* sated.

sa·cie·dad f. satiation, satiety ♦ **hasta la s.** to the point of satiation.

sa·co m. *(bolsa)* sack, bag (container and contents); ANAT. sac; *(vestidura)* loose-fitting jacket, smock; *(saqueo)* pillage, sack; SPORT. serve, service; MARIT. creek, inlet; AMER. *(chaqueta)* jacket, sports coat; *(bolso de mujer)* handbag ♦ **a sacos** by the ton • **entrar** *or* **meter en s.** to sack, plunder • **no echar en s. roto** COLL. to keep in mind, not to forget • **s. aéreo** ORNITH. air sac *or* cell • **s. terrero** *or* **de arena** MIL. sandbag • **s. de dormir** sleeping bag • **s. de huesos** FIG., COLL. bag of bones • **s. de malicias** FIG., COLL. bag of tricks • **s. de mentiras** FIG. pack of lies • **s. de noche** overnight bag, valise.

sa·cra·men·ta·do, –da RELIG. I. past part. of **sacramentar** II. adj. having received the last sacraments *or* rites.

sa·cra·men·tal I. adj. RELIG. sacramental; FIG. *(ritual)* ritual, ritualistic II. m. member of a Sacramental brotherhood —f. RELIG. Sacramental brotherhood.

sa·cra·men·tar RELIG. tr. *(transubstanciar)* to transubstantiate; *(administrar los sacramentos)* to administer the last sacraments *or* rites to —reflex. to be transubstantiated.

sa·cra·men·to m. RELIG. sacrament ♦ **s. del altar** Sacrament, Eucharist • **recibir los sacramentos** to receive the last sacraments *or* rites.

sa·cri·fi·ca·de·ro m. *(sitio)* place of sacrifice; *(altar)* altar; *(matadero)* slaughterhouse.

sa·cri·fi·ca·dor, –do·ra I. adj. sacrificing II. m.f. sacrificer.

sa·cri·fi·car §70 tr. *(ofrendar)* to sacrifice; *(para el consumo)* to slaughter —reflex. to sacrifice oneself, make a sacrifice.

sa·cri·fi·cio m. *(ofrenda)* sacrifice; *(para el consumo)* slaughter ♦ **s. del altar** *or* **de la misa** RELIG. sacrifice of the mass.

sa·cri·le·gio m. sacrilege.

sa·crí·le·go, –ga I. adj. sacrilegious II. m.f. sacrilegious person.

sa·cris·tán m. RELIG. sacristan, sexton; VEN., COLL. busybody.

sa·cris·tí·a f. *(lugar)* sacristy, vestry; *(cargo)* office of sacristan *or* sexton.

sa·cro, –cra I. adj. *(sagrado)* sacred, holy; ANAT. sacral II. m. ANAT. sacrum.

sa·cro·san·to, –ta adj. sacred, sacrosanct.

sa·cu·di·da f. *(estremecimiento)* shake, shaking; *(tirón)* jerk, tug; *(seísmo)* shock, tremor; *(de una explosión)* blast; FIG. *(cambio)* sudden *or* violent change; FIG. *(emoción)* jolt, shock ♦ **s. eléctrica** electric shock.

sa·cu·di·do, –da I. past part. see **sacudir** II. adj. *(áspero)* unpleasant, surly; *(desenfadado)* determined, resolute; *(movido)* shaken.

sa·cu·di·dor, –do·ra I. adj. shaking, beating II. m.f. shaker, beater —m. *(zorros)* carpet beater, whisk.

sa·cu·di·du·ra f. *or* **sa·cu·di·mien·to** m. *(estremecimiento)* shake, shaking; *(tirón)* jerk, tug.

sa·cu·dir tr. *(agitar)* to shake; *(quitar el polvo)* to dust; *(tirar)* to jerk, tug; *(golpear)* to beat, thrash; *(un ala)* to flap; *(trastornar)* to shake up, jolt; COLL. *(dar dinero)* to cough up, fork out —reflex. *(agitarse)* to shake; *(la ropa)* to shake *or* brush off; COLL. *(dar dinero)* to cough up, fork out.

sa·cu·dón m. AMER. var. of **sacudida**.

sa·char AGR. to weed.

sá·di·co, –ca I. adj. sadistic II. m.f. sadist.

sa·dis·mo m. sadism.

sa·do·ma·so·quis·mo m. sadomasochism.

sa·do·ma·so·quis·ta I. adj. sadomasochistic II. m.f. sadomasochist.

sa·du·ce·o, –a HIST., RELIG. I. adj. Sadducean II. m.f. Sadducee.

sa·e·ta f. *(flecha)* arrow, dart; *(del reloj)* hand (of a clock); *(brújula)* magnetic needle; *(copla)* short song sung in religious ceremonies ♦ **Saeta** ASTRON. Sagitta, the Arrow.

sa·e·ta·da f. *or* **sa·e·ta·zo** m. arrow wound.

sa·e·te·ar tr. to shoot with arrows *or* darts.

sa·e·ti·lla f. *(flecha)* small arrow *or* dart; *(del reloj)* hand (of a clock); *(brújula)* small magnetic needle; BOT. arrowhead.

sa·e·tín m. *(de molino)* millrace, flume; *(clavillo)* brad, tack.

sa·ga f. saga, legend.

sa·ga·ci·dad f. sagacity, sagaciousness.
sa·gaz adj. [pl. **-ga·ces**] *(astuto)* sagacious, astute; *(un perro)* keen-scented.
sa·gaz·men·te adv. sagaciously, wisely.
sa·gi·ta·rio m. *(saetero)* archer, bowman; ASTROL. Sagittarius.
sa·gra·do, –da I. adj. sacred, holy II. m. sanctuary, asylum ♦ **acogerse a s.** to take sanctuary.
sa·gra·rio m. RELIG. *(parte del templo)* shrine, sanctuary; *(para el Santísimo)* tabernacle; *(capilla)* chapel.
sa·gú m. BOT. *(palmera)* sago palm; C. AMER., CUBA arrowroot; *(fécula)* sago (starch).
sa·hu·ma·do, –da I. past part. see **sahumar** II. adj. FIG. *(mejorado)* better (yet), improved; AMER. tipsy, high.
sa·hu·ma·dor m. *(perfumador)* incense burner; *(camilla)* clothes dryer or rack.
sa·hu·ma·du·ra f. var. of **sahumerio**.
sa·hu·mar §82 tr. to perfume with incense —reflex. to become perfumed with incense.
sa·hu·me·rio m. *(acción de sahumar)* perfuming with incense; *(humo)* aromatic smoke; *(materia)* incense, aromatic herbs.
sa·ín m. *(de animal)* animal fat; *(de pescado)* fish oil; *(mugre)* grease, grime.
sai·nar §81 tr. to fatten (animals).
sai·ne·te m. THEAT. one-act farce.
sa·í·no or **sa·hi·no** m. ZOOL. peccary.
sa·ja·du·ra f. incision, cut.
sa·jón, –jo·na adj. & m.f. Saxon.
Sa·jo·nia f. GEOG. Saxony.
sa·kí m. *(bebida)* sake, saki (drink); ZOOL. saki, monkey.
sal¹ f. salt; FIG. *(gracia)* charm, grace; *(agudeza)* wit, wittiness; C. AMER. misfortune, bad luck ♦ **con su s. y pimienta** COLL. wittily • **echar s. a** to salt • **la s. de la vida** FIG. the spice of life • **s. amoníaca** or **amoníaco** CHEM. sal ammoniac, ammonium chloride • **s. de la higuera** or **Epsom** Epsom salt • **s. de mesa** table salt • **s. de nitro** saltpeter • **s. de Saturno** or **de plomo** lead acetate • **sales aromáticas** smelling salts • **sales de baño** bath salts • **s. gema** or **pedrás** rock salt • **s. gorda** or **de cocina** kitchen or cooking salt • **s. marina** sea salt • **tener mucha s.** FIG. to be great fun.
sal² see **salir**.
sa·la f. *(pieza principal)* living room, parlor; *(cuarto grande)* large room, hall; *(teatro)* house, auditorium; MED. hospital ward; LAW *(tribunal)* court, tribunal ♦ **s. capitular** chapter house • **s. de apelaciones** LAW court of appeals • **s. de batalla** sorting room (of post office) • **s. de clase** classroom • **s. de conferencias** lecture or conference hall • **s. de espectáculos** theater, hall • **s. de espera** waiting room • **s. de estar** living room • **s. de fiestas** dance hall, ballroom • **s. de justicia** LAW court of justice • **s. de juntas** COM. boardroom • **s. de lectura** reading room • **s. de lo criminal** LAW criminal court • **s. de mando** control room • **s. de máquinas** engine room • **s. de operaciones** MED. operating theater • **s. de partos** MED. delivery room • **s. de pruebas** fitting room.
sa·la·ci·dad f. salaciousness, lasciviousness.
sa·la·da·men·te adv. wittily, cleverly.
sa·la·de·ro m. *(lugar para salar)* salting house; *(tina)* salting tub; ARG., URUG. large slaughterhouse.
sa·la·do, –da I. past part. see **salar** II. adj. salt, salty *<agua s.* salt water>; salty, salted *<un plato muy s.* a highly salted dish>; FIG. *(gracioso)* witty, amusing; *(atractivo)* attractive, charming; AMER. unlucky, unfortunate; ARG., CHILE expensive • III. m. BOT. saltwort.
sa·la·dor, –do·ra I. adj. salting II. m.f. *(persona que sala)* salter —m. *(saladero)* salting house or room.
sa·la·du·ra f. salting, curing.
sa·la·man·dra f. ZOOL. salamander; *(estufa)* salamander stove ♦ **s. acuática** ZOOL. newt.
sa·la·me m. AMER. salami.
sa·lar tr. *(echar en sal)* to salt, cure; *(sazonar)* to salt, season with salt; COL., ECUAD. to feed salt to cattle; AMER. *(echar a perder)* to spoil, ruin; *(dar mala suerte)* to bring bad luck.
sa·la·rial adj. wage, salary *<aumento s.* wage increase>.
sa·la·riar tr. to pay wages or a salary to.

sa·la·rio m. wage, salary ♦ **s. mínimo** minimum wage • **s. vital** living wage • **s. a destajo** piece rate • **s. por hora** hourly wage.
sa·laz adj. [pl. **-la·ces**] salacious, lascivious.
sa·la·zón f. *(acción de salar)* salting; *(carne salada)* salted meat; *(pescado salado)* salted fish; *(industria)* salting industry; C. AMER., CUBA, COLL. bad luck.
sal·ce·da f. or **sal·ce·do** m. BOT. willow grove.
sal·chi·cha f. CUL. pork sausage.
sal·chi·che·ría f. sausage shop.
sal·chi·che·ro, –ra m.f. *(hacedor)* sausage maker; *(vendedor)* sausage seller.
sal·chi·chón m. CUL. sausage.
sal·dar tr. COM. *(liquidar)* to pay off, settle; *(vender)* to sell off, remainder.
sal·do COM. m. *(liquidación)* payment, settlement; *(cifra final)* balance; *(mercancías)* remnants, remainders; *(venta)* clearance sale ♦ **s. acreedor** or **a favor** credit balance • **s. deudor** or **en contra** debit balance • **s. disponible** available balance, balance in hand.
sal·drá, saldría see **salir**.
sa·le·di·zo ARCHIT. I. adj. salient, projecting II. m. ledge, overhang.
sa·le·gar m. salt lick (for cattle).
sa·le·ro m. *(en la mesa)* saltshaker, saltcellar; *(almacén)* salthouse; *(salegar)* salt lick; FIG., COLL. *(gracia)* wit, charm; *(persona)* witty person; CHILE salt mine or pit.
sa·le·ro·so, –sa adj. COLL. witty, charming.
sal·ga, salgo see **salir**.
sá·li·co, –ca adj. HIST. Salic ♦ **ley s.** Salic law (prohibiting female accession to the throne).
sa·li·da f. *(marcha)* leaving, departure; *(abertura)* exit, outlet; *(publicación)* publication; *(saliente)* projection, protuberance; *(afueras)* environs; FIG. *(escapatoria)* way out, pretext; *(solución)* solution, outcome; *(ocurrencia)* witticism, witty remark; COM. *(venta)* sale; *(posibilidad de venta)* market, outlet; *(transporte)* shipment; *(partida de descargo)* item, entry; MIL. attack, sortie; MARIT. headway; THEAT. entrance; SPORT. start; *(en los naipes)* lead (in cards); ELEC., MECH. outlet ♦ **dar s. a** *(desahogar)* to vent, let out • **s. del sol** ASTRON. sunrise • **s. de tono** FIG. inept remark, faux pas • **s. nula** SPORT. false start • **tener s.** COM. to sell well; ARCHIT., GEOG. to open, lead *<el río tiene s. al mar* the river leads to the sea>.
sa·li·di·zo m. ARCHIT. projection, overhang.
sa·li·do, –da I. past part. see **salir** II. adj. projecting, sticking out ♦ **estar s.** ZOOL. to be in heat.
sa·li·dor, –do·ra adj. CHILE restless, roving; MEX. lively, animated.
sa·lien·te I. adj. ARCHIT. projecting, overhanging; FIG. *(prominente)* salient, outstanding; *(el sol)* rising; *(que se retira)* retiring, outgoing II. m. east; ARCHIT. projection, overhang; MIL. salient.
sa·lí·fe·ro, –ra adj. saliferous.
sa·lín m.
sa·li·na I. f. salt mine or pit ♦ **salinas** salt works II. adj. see **salino, –na**.
sa·li·ne·ra f. salt mine or pit.
sa·li·ni·dad f. salinity, saltiness.
sa·li·no, –na I. adj. saline II. f. see **salina**.
sa·lir §63 intr. to leave *<salimos de la casa a las tres* we left the house at three o'clock>; to go out *<en esta ciudad no es prudente s. por la noche solo* in this city it is not prudent to go out alone at night>; *(partir)* to leave, depart *<pasado mañana saldremos para Grecia* the day after tomorrow we will leave for Greece>; *(librarse)* to get out, escape *<s. de un apuro* to get out of a jam>; *(aparecer)* to come out *<después de la tormenta salió el sol* after the storm the sun came out>; to rise *<el sol salió a las seis* the sun rose at six o'clock>; *(brotar)* to come up *<el maíz sale en abril* the corn comes up in April>; *(proceder)* to emerge, come *<sus ideas salieron de sus estudios con Freud* his ideas emerged from his studies with Freud>; *(desaparecer)* to come out *<la mancha salió* the stain came out>; *(sobresalir)* to jut or stick out; *(mostrarse)* to show *<la culpabilidad le salió a la cara* his guilt showed in his face>; *(publicarse)* to come out *<el periódico sale por la tarde* the newspaper comes out in the afternoon>; *(resultar)* to turn

out to be, prove to be <*el plan salió mal organizado* the plan turned out to be poorly organized>; *(ofrecerse)* to come *or* turn up <*cuando salga la oportunidad* when the opportunity comes up>; *(desembarazarse)* to get rid, dispose <*ya he salido de toda la mercancía* I have already disposed of all of the merchandise>; *(costar)* to cost, come to <*el mantel me salió a cuarenta dólares* the tablecloth cost me forty dollars>; to work out <*no me salen estas cuentas* these accounts are not working out for me>; *(en el juego)* to lead <*s. con un as* to lead with an ace>; *(ir a parar)* to lead <*esta calle sale a la plaza* this street leads to the plaza>; *(parecerse)* to take after, resemble <*esa niña salió a su madre* that little girl takes after her mother>; *(ser elegido)* to be elected; *(en la lotería)* to be drawn; THEAT. to come on, enter ♦ **salga lo que salga** *or* **saliere** COLL. come what may • **s. adelante** to get ahead, do well • **s. bien** to turn out well, succeed • **s. con** to come out with <*él salió con una observación importante* he came out with an important observation>; to go out with, date <*Juan sale con Anita ahora* John is dating Anita now> • **s. del paso** to get out of a jam • **s. mal** to turn out badly, fail • **s. pitando** FIG., COLL. *(echar a correr)* to run out quickly; *(enfadarse)* to blow up, get angry • **s. por** *(defender)* to come out in defense of; *(garantizar)* to back —reflex. to leave <*se salieron del partido* they left the party>; *(derramarse)* to leak; *(rebosar)* to boil over ♦ **salirse con la suya** to get one's own way • **salirse de la regla** to break the rule • **salirse de madre** to overflow (a river) • **salirse del tema** to digress.

sa·li·tra·do, –da adj. saltpetrous.

sa·li·tral I. adj. saltpetrous, nitrous **II.** m. *(yacimiento)* saltpeter bed *or* deposit; *(fábrica)* saltpeter works.

sa·li·tre m. saltpeter, niter.

sa·li·tre·ro, –ra I. adj. saltpetrous **II.** m.f. *(obrero)* saltpeter worker —f. saltpeter bed *or* deposit.

sa·li·tro·so, –sa adj. saltpetrous, nitrous.

sa·li·va f. saliva, spit ♦ **gastar s. en balde** COLL. to waste one's breath, talk in vain • **tragar s.** COLL. to stifle one's feelings.

sa·li·va·ción f. salivation.

sa·li·va·de·ra *or* **sa·li·ve·ra** f. AMER. spittoon, cuspidor.

sa·li·va·jo m. COLL. spit.

sa·li·val *or* **sa·li·var** adj. salivary <*glándula s.* salivary gland>.

sa·li·var intr. PHYSIOL. to salivate; *(escupir)* to spit.

sa·li·va·zo m. COLL. spit, spittle ♦ **arrojar** *or* **echar un s.** to spit.

sa·li·ve·ras f.pl. knobs on a horse's bit.

sa·li·vo·so, –sa adj. salivating excessively.

sal·mis·ta m.f. psalmist.

sal·mo m. psalm.

sal·mo·dia f. RELIG. psalmody; FIG., COLL. *(canto monótono)* monotonous singing, drone.

sal·mo·diar intr. *(recitar salmos)* to sing psalms; FIG., COLL. *(cantar monótonamente)* to sing monotonously, drone.

sal·món m. ICHTH. salmon.

sal·mo·na·do, –da adj. *(parecido al salmón)* salmon-like; *(color)* salmon, salmon-colored.

sal·mue·ra f. brine, pickle.

sa·lo·bre adj. briny, brackish.

sa·lo·bre·ño, –ña adj. saline.

sa·lo·bri·dad f. saltiness, brackishness.

sa·lo·mó·ni·co, –ca adj. Solomonic.

sa·lón m. *(cuarto)* salon, lounge; *(sala grande)* hall <*s. de conferencias* lecture hall>; *(para recibir visitas)* drawing room, parlor; *(galería)* gallery; *(exposición)* exhibition, show; *(tertulia)* salon; *(muebles)* suite of furniture ♦ **s. de actos** *or* **reuniones** *or* **sesiones** assembly hall • **s. de baile** ballroom, dance hall • **s. de belleza** beauty parlor *or* salon • **s. de demostraciones** showroom • **s. de fumar** smoking room • **s. de té** tearoom, tea shop • **s. de ventas** salesroom.

sal·pi·ca·de·ro m. AUTO. dashboard.

sal·pi·ca·du·ra f. *(acción de salpicar)* splashing, spattering; *(salpicón)* splash, spatter.

sal·pi·car §70 tr. *(con un líquido)* to splash, spatter; *(rociar)* to sprinkle; *(motear)* to fleck, dot; FIG. *(pasar de unas cosas a otras)* to touch on without order <*sólo salpicó las

ideas centrales del cuento* he only touched on the story's main ideas>.

sal·pi·cón m. CUL. *(carne picada)* salmagundi, cold hash; FIG., COLL. *(cosa picada)* shredded *or* minced item; *(salpicadura)* splash, spatter; ECUAD. fruit juice ♦ **s. de mariscos** CUL. seafood cocktail.

sal·pi·men·tar §49 tr. CUL. to season with salt and pepper; FIG. *(amenizar)* to spice, make more appetizing.

sal·pi·mien·ta f. CUL. mixture of salt and pepper.

sal·pi·qué, salpique see **salpicar.**

sal·pu·lli·do m. var. of **sarpullido.**

sal·sa f. CUL. sauce, gravy, dressing; FIG. *(sainete)* seasoning <*no hay mejor s. que el hambre* there is no better seasoning than hunger>; COLL. *(gracia)* charm, grace; *(baile)* salsa ♦ **en su propia s.** FIG. in one's element • **s. blanca** white sauce • **s. de San Bernardo** FIG., COLL. hunger • **s. de tomate** tomato sauce, ketchup • **s. inglesa** Worcestershire sauce • **s. mahonesa** *or* **mayonesa** mayonnaise • **s. mayordomo** parsley butter • **s. rubia** brown roux • **s. rusa** Russian dressing • **s. tártara** tartar sauce.

sal·se·ra f. CUL. gravy boat *or* pitcher; PAINT. small saucer (for mixing paints).

sal·se·ro m. CHILE salt vendor.

sal·si·fí m. [pl. **-fí·es**] BOT. salsify, goat's beard ♦ **s. de España** *or* **negro** BOT. black salsify, viper's grass.

sal·ta·ban·co *or* **sal·ta·ban·cos** m.f. *(charlatán)* charlatan, quack; *(jugador de manos)* magician; *(saltimbanqui)* acrobat.

sal·ta·ba·rran·cos m.f. [pl. **-cos**] FIG., COLL. madcap.

sal·ta·de·ro m. *(sitio)* jumping place; *(surtidor de agua)* fountain, jet.

sal·ta·di·zo, –za adj. fragile, brittle.

sal·ta·dor, –do·ra I. adj. jumping, leaping **II.** m.f. *(persona)* jumper, leaper —m. *(comba)* jump rope ♦ **s. de pértiga** *or* **con garrocha** pole vaulter.

sal·ta·mon·tes m. [pl. **-tes**] ENTOM. grasshopper.

sal·tan·te adj. CHILE outstanding, noteworthy.

sal·tar intr. *(brincar)* to jump, leap; *(levantarse)* to jump up; *(dar saltitos)* to hop, skip; *(lanzarse)* to jump, plunge <*s. al agua* to plunge into the water>; to bounce <*la pelota saltó varias veces* the ball bounced several times>; *(brotar)* to gush, spurt up; *(romperse)* to break, burst; *(desprenderse)* to come loose, come off; *(salir con ímpetu)* to bound; *(sobresalir)* to stick out, project; *(ascender)* to be promoted rapidly; FIG. *(enfadarse)* to blow up, explode (in anger) ♦ **s. a la vista** *or* **a los ojos** to be self-evident *or* obvious • **s. de** *(abandonar)* to leave, give up (a job); to jump with <*s. de gozo* to jump with joy> • **s. sobre** to pounce on —tr. *(atravesar)* to jump *or* leap over; *(omitir)* to skip over, leave out; *(en las damas)* to jump (in checkers); MARIT. to loosen, slacken (cables) —reflex. to skip, miss <*saltarse un párrafo* to skip a paragraph>; *(brotar)* to well up <*se le saltaron las lágrimas* tears welled up in his eyes>.

sal·ta·rén m. MUS. dance tune (played on the guitar); ENTOM. grasshopper.

sal·ta·rín, –ri·na adj. *(que salta)* jumping; *(que baila)* dancing; FIG. *(atolondrado)* giddy, reckless.

sal·te·a·do, –da I. past part. see **saltear II.** adj. CUL. sauté.

sal·te·a·dor, –do·ra m. *(bandido)* highwayman —f. *(ladrona)* female robber *or* bandit; *(fulana)* highway robber's wench *or* girl.

sal·te·a·mien·to m. *(robo)* robbery, holdup; *(asalto)* attack, assault.

sal·te·ar tr. *(robar)* to hold up, rob (on the highway); *(atacar)* to assault, attack by surprise; *(hacer algo con interrupciones)* to do (something) in fits and starts, do a little here and a little there; *(sorprender)* to surprise, take by surprise; CUL. *(sofreír)* to sauté, fry lightly.

sal·te·rio m. RELIG. *(libro de salmos)* Psalter, Book of Psalms; *(rosario)* rosary (of 150 beads); MUS. psaltry, psaltery.

sal·tim·ban·co *or* **sal·tim·ban·qui** m. COLL. *(charlatán)* mountebank, charlatan; THEAT. *(titiritero)* puppeteer; *(acróbata)* acrobat, tumbler; *(malabrista)* juggler.

sal·to m. *(brinco)* jump, leap, bound; *(obstáculo)* jump, hurdle; *(despeñadero)* ravine, chasm; *(cascada)* falls, waterfall; *(espacio)* gap; *(omisión)* omission; *(juego)* leapfrog; *(ascenso)* promotion, jump; SPORT. jump <*s. de altura* high jump>; dive <*s. del ángel* swan dive>; MED. palpitation ♦ **al s.** CUBA in cash • **a s. de mata** *(escondiéndose)* hiding, escaping; *(sin recursos)* from hand to mouth • **a saltos** by leaps and bounds • **en un s.** FIG. in a jiffy • **s. de cama** negligée • **s. de carnero** EQUIT. buck • **s. de esquí** ski jump • **s. de la carpa** jackknife dive • **s. de longitud** broad jump • **s. de pértiga** *or* **con garrocha** pole vault • **s. mortal** somersault.

sal·tón, –to·na I. adj. *(que anda a saltos)* jumping, hopping; *(ojos)* protruding, bulging; PERU jumpy, nervous; CHILE, COL., CUL. half-cooked II. m. ENTOM. grasshopper.

sa·lu·bre adj. salubrious, healthful.

sa·lu·bri·dad f. healthfulness.

sa·lud I. f. *(sanidad)* health; *(bienestar)* welfare, wellbeing; RELIG. *(salvación)* salvation ♦ **beber a la s.** to drink to the health of, toast • **estar bien** *or* **mal de s.** to be in good *or* bad health • **gastar s.** to enjoy good health, be in good health• **vender** *or* **verter s.** to be brimming *or* glowing with health II. interj. COLL. *(al estornudar)* (God) bless you!; *(brindis)* cheers!, bottoms up!

sa·lu·da·ble adj. *(sano)* healthy, wholesome; *(provechoso)* beneficial, salutary.

sa·lu·da·dor, –do·ra I. adj. greeting II. m.f. *(persona que saluda)* greeter —m. *(curandero)* charlatan, quack.

sa·lu·dar tr. *(mostrar cortesía)* to greet, salute; MIL. *(honrar)* to salute; *(tirar)* to fire a salute for; MARIT. *(bandera)* to dip the flag to; *(aclamar)* to acclaim, applaud; FIG. *(curar)* to cure by magic *or* quackery ♦ **le saluda atentamente (su seguro servidor)** Yours faithfully *or* truly (at the close of a letter) —intr. MIL. to salute.

sa·lu·do m. *(muestra de cortesía)* greeting, salutation; *(inclinación)* bow; MIL. *(muestra de respeto)* salute ♦ **saludos** regards, best wishes • **atentos saludos** *or* **saludos cordiales** best wishes *or* regards (at the close of a letter).

sa·lu·ta·ción f. salutation, greeting ♦ **S. angélica** RELIG. Hail Mary.

sal·va I. MIL. *(descargas simultáneas)* salvo, volley; *(saludo)* salute; *(salutación)* greeting, salutation; *(aplausos)* salvo, round of applause; *(inspección de la comida)* testing of foods to detect poisons; LAW *(prueba)* ordeal (to prove innocence); *(bandeja)* salver, serving tray; *(juramento)* oath, solemn promise ♦ **hacer la s.** to request the floor for speaking II. adj. see **salvo, –va.**

sal·va·ción f. *(preservación)* salvation, preservation; *(liberación)* deliverance, rescue; RELIG. *(gloria eterna)* salvation, eternal glory.

sal·va·da f. AMER., COLL. good fortune *or* luck.

sal·va·do I. past part. see **salvar** II. m. BOT. bran.

sal·va·dor, –do·ra I. adj. saving II. m.f. savior ♦ **El Salvador** RELIG. the Savior, Jesus Christ.

sal·va·do·re·ño, –na adj. & m.f. Salvadoran.

sal·va·guar·da f. protection, safeguard.

sal·va·guar·dar tr. to safeguard, protect.

sal·va·guar·dia f. *(salvoconducto)* safe-conduct, pass; *(protección)* safeguard, protection —m. guard, guardian.

sal·va·ja·da *or* **sal·va·je·rí·a** f. savagery, brutality.

sal·va·je I. adj. BOT. *(silvestre)* wild, uncultivated; ZOOL. *(no domesticado)* wild, untamed; *(feroz)* savage, ferocious; FIG. *(rudo)* rude, uncouth; *(primitivo)* uncivilized, barbaric; *(necio)* ignorant, stupid; *(sin permiso ni regla)* wildcat, unsanctioned <*huelga s.* wildcat strike> II. m.f. *(bárbaro)* savage; FIG., COLL. *(bruto)* boor, slob; *(necio)* idiot, moron —m. ECUAD., BOT. bromilaceous plant.

sal·va·jis·mo m. savagery.

sal·va·men·to m. *(preservación)* saving, preserving; *(rescate)* deliverance, rescue; *(rescate de peligro)* lifesaving; RELIG. *(salvación)* salvation, redemption; FIG. *(refugio)* refuge, harbor; MARIT. *(rescate)* salvage, salvaging.

sal·var tr. *(librar)* to save, rescue; *(resolver)* to overcome; *(evitar)* to avoid, get around; *(saltar)* to jump over *or* across, clear; *(exceptuar)* to except, exclude <*salvando a los presentes* excluding those present>; *(recorrer)* cover, cross <*el tren salva la distancia en cinco horas*> the train covers the distance in five hours>; LAW to save, prove the innocence of; RELIG. to save ♦ **s. las apariencias** to keep up appearances, save face —reflex. to save oneself, es-

cape; to save one's soul, be saved ♦ **¡sálvese el que pueda!** every man for himself! • **salvarse por los pelos** FIG. to escape by the skin of one's teeth.

sal·va·vi·das I. m. [pl. **-das**] MARIT. *(aparato)* life preserver; *(bote)* lifeboat, life raft; *(boya)* life buoy, lifesaver; *(cinturón)* life belt; AUTO., RAIL. *(quitapiedras)* fender, guard —m.f. *(bañero)* lifeguard, lifesaver II. adj. MARIT. lifesaving <*chaleco s.* life jacket>.

sal·ve I. interj. hail! II. f. RELIG. Salve Regina.

sal·ve·dad f. *(condición)* condition, proviso; *(excepción)* exception, excuse; *(reserva)* reservation, qualification.

sal·via f. BOT. salvia, sage.

sal·vo, –va I. adj. *(ileso)* safe, unharmed; *(rescatado)* saved, rescued; *(omitido)* excepted, omitted ♦ **a s.** safe (and sound), out of danger • **a s. de** safe from • **dejar a s.** *(exceptuar)* to set aside, make an exception of; *(salvaguardar)* to safeguard, spare • **en s.** *(liberado)* in liberty, free; *(sin peligro)* in safety, out of danger • **poner a s.** to rescue, make safe • **ponerse a s.** to reach safety • **sano y s.** safe and sound II. adv. except (for), save, barring ♦ **s. que** unless III. f. see **salva.**

sal·vo·con·duc·to m. *(pase)* safe-conduct, pass; FIG. *(seguridad)* security.

Salz·bur·go Salzburg.

sa·ma·rio m. CHEM. samarium.

sa·ma·ri·ta·no, –na adj. & m.f. Samaritan.

sam·bum·bia f. CUBA drink made from water, cane syrup and peppers; MEX. cordial made from pineapple and sugar; COL. hodgepodge, mess.

Sa·mo·a f. Samoa.

sa·mo·a·no, –na adj. & m.f. Samoan.

sa·mo·var m. samovar.

sam·pán m. sampan (Chinese boat).

san §G21 adj. [contr. of **santo** used before masc. names except for Tomás, Tomé, Toribio, and Domingo] <*San Martín* Saint Martin> —see **santo.**

sa·na·ble adj. curable, healable.

sa·na·lo·to·do m. MED. black plaster; FIG. *(panacea)* cure-all, panacea.

sa·na·men·te adv. *(con sanidad)* healthily, wholesomely; FIG. *(sinceramente)* sincerely, earnestly.

sa·nar tr. to heal, cure —intr. *(enfermedad)* to regain health, recover (from illness); *(herida)* to heal.

sa·na·ti·vo, –va adj. healing, curative.

sa·na·to·rio m. MED. *(para enfermedades crónicas)* sanatorium, sanatarium; *(hospital)* hospital; *(clínica)* clinic.

san·ción f. *(ratificación)* sanction, ratification; *(decreto)* law, decree; *(pena)* penalty, punishment; *(aprobación)* sanction, approval.

san·cio·na·ble adj. sanctionable.

san·cio·na·dor, –do·ra I. adj. sanctioning II. m.f. sanctioner.

san·cio·nar tr. *(ratificar)* to sanction, ratify; *(autorizar)* to sanction, authorize; *(castigar)* to sanction, punish.

san·co·cha·do m. CUL. *(acción de sancochar)* parboiling; PERU stew containing parboiled meat, yucca and bananas.

san·co·char tr. CUL. to parboil (meat).

san·co·cho m. CUL. stew containing parboiled meat, yucca and bananas; CUBA unappetizing dish; C. AMER., FIG. *(lío)* mess, mishmash.

San Cris·tó·bal m. GEOG. St. Kitts; RELIG. Saint Christopher.

sanc·ta·sanc·tó·rum m. RELIG. sanctum sanctorum, holy of holies; FIG. *(misterio)* mystery, secret.

san·da·lia f. sandal.

sán·da·lo m. BOT. *(árbol)* sandalwood; *(planta)* bergamot mint.

san·dez f. [pl. **-de·ces**] *(cualidad)* silliness, foolishness; *(palabra)* silly remark, nonsense.

san·dí·a f. BOT. watermelon.

san·dial *or* **san·diar** m. BOT. watermelon field *or* patch.

san·dio, –dia COLL. I. adj. silly, foolish II. m.f. fool, dolt.

san·dun·ga f. COLL. *(gracia)* wit, charm; CHILE, MEX., PERU din, racket; MEX. dance.

san·dun·gue·ro, –ra adj. COLL. witty, charming.

sa·ne·a·do, –da I. past part. see **sanear** II. adj. LAW unencumbered (wealth).

sa·ne·a·mien·to m. *(mejora)* improvement; *(limpieza)* sanitation; *(corrección)* righting; LAW *(indemnificación)* in-demnification, restitution; COM. *(garantía)* guarantee, warranty; FIN. *(estabilización)* stabilization; *(reorganización de deudas)* reorganization (of debt structure).

sa·ne·ar tr. *(mejorar)* to improve; *(limpiar)* to sanitize, make sanitary; *(corregir)* to right, correct; *(hacer sano)* to make healthy, put on a sound basis *or* footing; LAW *(indemnificar)* to indemnify, restitute; COM. *(garantizar)* to guarantee, warranty; FIN. *(estabilizar)* to stabilize (currency); *(reorganizar)* to reorganize.

sa·ne·drín m. HIST., RELIG. Sanhedrin, Sanhedrim.

san·fa·són m. AMER., COLL. cheek, nerve ♦ **a la s.** AMER., COLL. carelessly, nonchalantly.

san·gra·de·ra f. SURG. lancet; *(vasija)* basin; *(acequia)* gutter, drain; FIG. *(en un caz)* sluice, ditch.

san·gra·du·ra f. ANAT. crook of the elbow; SURG. incision; FIG. *(salida)* sluice, drainage.

san·gran·te adj. bleeding.

san·grar tr. SURG. to bleed, let blood from; *(un terreno)* to drain; *(un árbol)* to tap (a tree); PRINT. to indent; FIG., COLL. *(sacar dinero)* to bleed (someone) dry —intr. to bleed —reflex. SURG. to be bled.

san·gre f. PHYSIOL. blood; FIG. *(linaje)* blood, lineage; *(familia)* family, kindred ♦ **a s. caliente** on the spur of the moment • **a s. fría** in cold blood • **a s. y fuego** by fire and sword, mercilessly • **chupar la s. a alguien** FIG. to be a bloodsucker • **dar sangre** MED. to give blood • **de s. caliente** ZOOL. warm-blooded • **de s. fría** ZOOL. cold-blooded • **echar s.** to bleed • **echar s. por los ojos** FIG. to be furious • **encender** *or* **freír la s. a alguien** FIG., COLL. to infuriate someone • **hacer s.** to draw blood • **llevar en la s.** FIG. to have in one's blood • **mala s.** COLL. bad blood • **no llegar la s. al río** FIG. not to be a serious matter • **pura s.** thoroughbred • **s. azul** blue blood, nobility • **s. de drago** BOT. dragon's blood • **s. fría** sang froid, composure • **s. ligera** AMER. pleasant disposition • **s. pesada** AMER. unpleasant disposition • **s. roja** red blood, arterial blood.

san·gre·gor·da COLL. I. adj. dull, sluggish II. m.f. sluggard.

san·grí·a f. *(extracción de sangre)* bleeding, bloodletting; *(extracción de liquídos)* drainage, draining; *(bebida)* sangria; ANAT. inner part of the elbow; BOT. tap; AGR. drainage ditch *or* channel; METAL. tap; PRINT. *(margen interior)* indentation; FIG. *(gasto continuo)* bleeding, draining; *(hurto)* pilfering, filching.

san·grien·ta·men·te adv. bloodily, cruelly.

san·grien·to, –ta adj. *(que echa sangre)* bloody, bleeding; *(manchado de sangre)* bloodied, blood-stained; *(sanguinario)* sanguinary, bloodthirsty; FIG. *(muy ofensivo)* flagrant, outrageous; POET. *(color)* blood-red.

san·gri·li·via·no, –na adj. COLL. nice, pleasant.

san·gri·pe·sa·do, –da *or* **san·grón, –gro·na** adj. C. AMER., COL., CUBA, COLL. disagreeable, unpleasant.

san·gua·za f. *(sangre)* contaminated blood; FIG. *(de legumbres y frutas)* red juice (of vegetables and fruits).

san·gui·jue·la f. ZOOL. leech, bloodsucker; FIG., COLL. *(parásito)* leech, sponger; *(lapa)* pest, leech.

san·gui·na f. *(lápiz)* red pencil; *(naranja)* blood orange.

san·gui·na·rio, –ria I. adj. bloodthirsty, cruel II. f. MIN. bloodstone.

san·guí·ne·o, –a adj. *(de sangre)* sanguineous, (pertaining to) blood <*grupo sanguíneo* blood group>; *(de color de sangre)* blood-red.

san·guí·no, –na I. adj. *(de color de sangre)* blood-red; *(sanguíneo)* sanguineous, pertaining to blood II. m. BOT. buckthorn.

san·gui·no·len·cia f. bloodiness.

san·gui·no·len·to, –ta adj. *(manchado de sangre)* blood, blood-stained; *(inflamado)* bloodshot <*ojos sanguinolentos* bloodshot eyes>.

san·gui·no·so, –sa adj. *(sanguíneo)* sanguineous, of blood; FIG. *(sanguinario)* bloody, cruel.

sa·ni·dad f. *(salud)* health, healthiness; *(limpieza)* sanitation ♦ **en s.** in perfect health • **s. pública** health department, board of health.

sa·ni·ta·rio, –ria I. adj. sanitary II. m.f. MIL. health officer.

San Jo·sé m. GEOG. San José; RELIG. Saint Joseph.

San Ma·ri·no m. San Marino.

san·ma·ri·nen·se adj. of San Marino.

sa·no, –na adj. *(de buena salud)* healthy, fit; *(saludable)* healthful; *(provechoso)* salutary, wholesome; FIG. *(seguro)* sure, secure; *(en buena condición)* sound, in good condition; *(sin daño)* undamaged, unharmed; *(sin vicio)* wholesome, pure; *(entero)* whole, unbroken; *(sensato)* wise, discreet; *(justo)* just, fair ♦ **cortar por lo s.** to take drastic measures • **s. y salvo** safe and sound.

San Sal·va·dor m. San Salvador.

sáns·cri·to, –ta adj. & m. Sanskrit.

san·se·a·ca·bó COLL. that's the end of it <*no voy y s.* I'm not going and that's the end of it>.

San·ta Lu·cí·a f. Saint Lucia.

san·ta·lu·cen·se adj. & m.f. Saint Lucian.

San·ta Se·de f. Holy See.

san·te·ro, –ra I. adj. image-worshiping II. m.f. *(guardia de un santuario)* keeper of a sanctuary; *(limosnero)* alms collector.

San·tia·go m. GEOG. Santiago; RELIG. Saint James.

san·tia·mén m. COLL. flash, jiffy <*llegamos en un s.* we arrived in a flash>.

san·ti·dad f. sanctity, holiness ♦ **Su S.** RELIG. His Holiness (the Pope).

san·ti·fi·ca·ble adj. sanctifiable.

san·ti·fi·ca·ción f. *(acción de hacer santo)* sanctification, making holy; *(consagración)* consecration, hallowing; *(prácticas)* keeping holy, observance; *(veneración)* veneration, reverence; FIG. *(perdón)* pardon, forgiveness.

san·ti·fi·ca·dor, –do·ra I. adj. sanctifying II. m.f. sanctifier.

san·ti·fi·car §70 tr. *(hacer santo)* to sanctify, make holy; *(consagrar)* to consecrate, hallow; *(venerar)* to revere, venerate; *(practicar)* to observe, keep; FIG. *(perdonar)* to forgive, pardon ♦ **s. el domingo** RELIG. to keep the Sabbath • **santificado sea tu nombre** RELIG. hallowed be thy name.

san·ti·gua·da f. RELIG. *(acción de bendecirse)* making the sign of the cross, crossing oneself; *(seña de la cruz)* sign of the cross ♦ **¡por** *or* **para mi s.!** ARCH. upon my soul, upon my faith.

san·ti·gua·mien·to m. RELIG. making the sign of the cross, crossing oneself.

san·ti·guar §10 tr. RELIG. to make the sign of the cross on, bless; FIG., COLL. *(abofetar)* to slap, smack —reflex. RELIG. *(persignarse)* to cross oneself, make the sign of the cross; FIG., COLL. *(maravillarse)* to marvel, amaze oneself.

san·tí·si·mo, –ma I. adj. most holy II. m. Holy Sacrament.

san·to, –ta §G21 I. adj. *(virtuoso)* holy; *(bendito)* blessed; *(sagrado)* saintly <*una vida s.* a saintly life>; *(inviolable)* sacred, consecrated; *(sencillo)* simple, artless; *(provechoso)* miraculous <*una medicina s.* a miraculous medicine>; COLL. blessed <*esperamos todo el s. día* we waited the whole blessed day> ♦ **S. Oficio** Holy Office (of the Inquisition) • **S. Padre** Holy Father (the Pope) • **s. y bueno** well and good II. m.f. saint <*Santa Teresa* Saint Theresa>; FIG. *(bueno)* saint —m. *(imagen)* image of a saint; *(festividad)* saint's day, name day; COLL. *(estampa)* picture, illustration; MIL. password; CHILE patch ♦ **alzarse con el s. y la limosna** FIG. to make off with everything • **a s. de** because of • **¿a s. de qué?** what on earth for? • **dar el s. y seña** MIL. to give the password • **desnudar a un s. para vestir a otro** FIG. to rob Peter to pay Paul • **írsele a uno el s. al cielo** FIG., COLL. *(distraerse)* to forget what one was about to say, lose one's train of thought; *(asustarse)* to become frightened • **no ser s. de su devoción** to not be keen on • **s. titular** *or* **patrón** patron saint • **tener s. de espaldas** COLL. to be unlucky.

San·to Do·min·go m. GEOG. Santo Domingo; Hispaniola (island); RELIG. Saint Dominic.

san·to·ral m. RELIG. *(libro de las vidas de santos)* book of the lives of the saints; *(libro de coro)* choir book; *(calendario)* calendar of saints' days.

San·to To·mé y Prín·ci·pe m. São Tomé and Principe.

san·tua·rio m. RELIG. temple, sanctuary; FIG. *(asilo)* sanctuary, refuge; *(intimidad)* intimacy, privacy; COL. buried treasure.

san·tu·lón, –lo·na adj. & m.f. var. of **santurrón, –rrona.**

san·tu·rrón, –rro·na I. adj. *(beato)* sanctimonious, affectedly devout; *(hipócrita)* hypocritical **II.** m.f. sanctimonious person, hypocrite.

san·tu·rro·ne·rí·a f. sanctimoniousness, hypocrisy.

San Vi·cen·te y las Gra·na·di·nas Saint Vincent and the Grenadines.

sa·ña f. rage, fury.

sa·ño·so, -sa *or* **sa·ñu·do, -da** adj. enraged, furious.

sa·o m. BOT. mock privet, laburnum; CUBA small savanna with clusters of trees *or* bushes.

sa·pien·cia f. *(sabiduría)* wisdom, knowledge; BIBL. Book of Wisdom, Book of Solomon.

sa·pien·te I. adj. wise, sapient **II.** m.f. wise person.

sa·po m. ZOOL. toad; COLL. *(animalito)* little animal *or* beast; C. AMER., ICHTH. *(pejesapo)* angler, toadfish; FIG., COLL. *(persona torpe)* toad, repulsive *or* disgusting person; CHILE *(suerte)* fluke, stroke of luck; CHILE, MEX., COLL. *(canalla)* scoundrel, rascal ♦ **s. marino** ICHTH. angler, toadfish • **echar sapos y culebras** COLL. to cuss, swear.

sa·po·ná·ce·o, -a adj. saponaceous, soapy.

sa·po·ni·fi·ca·ción f. saponification, making into soap.

sa·po·ni·fi·car §70 tr. to make into soap —reflex. to be made into soap.

sa·po·te m. BOT. sapodilla.

sa·que m. SPORT. *(tenis)* serve, service; *(fútbol)* kickoff; *(raya)* service *or* base line; *(jugador en el tenis)* server; *(jugador en el fútbol)* kicker; AMER. distillery, still ♦ **tener buen s.** FIG., COLL. to be a heavy eater *or* drinker.

sa·qué, saque see **sacar.**

sa·que·a·dor, -do·ra I. adj. sacking, plundering, looting **II.** m.f. sacker, plunderer.

sa·que·a·mien·to m. sacking, plundering.

sa·que·ar tr. to sack, plunder.

sa·que·o m. *(acción de saquear)* sacking, plundering; *(bienes saqueados)* plunder, booty.

sa·que·rí·a f. *(fabricación)* manufacture of sacks; *(conjunto)* sacks.

sa·que·ro, -ra m.f. sack dealer.

sa·que·te m. *(saco pequeño)* small bag *or* sack; ARTIL. *(para cartuchos)* cartridge bag.

sa·ram·pión m. MED. measles.

sa·ra·o m. *(fiesta)* soirée, evening party; COLL. *(jaleo)* shindig.

sa·ra·pe m. MEX. serape, heavy shawl.

sa·ra·sa m. COLL., DEROG. pansy, effeminate man.

sar·cas·mo m. sarcasm.

sar·cás·ti·ca·men·te adv. sarcastically.

sar·cás·ti·co, -ca adj. sarcastic.

sar·có·fa·go m. sarcophagus.

sar·da·na f. sardana (Catalonian dance).

sar·des·co, -ca I. adj. *(caballo o asno)* small (said of horse or donkey); FIG., COLL. *(áspero)* surly, gruff; *(descarado)* shameless, impudent **II.** m. small horse *or* donkey.

sar·di·na f. ICHTH. sardine, pilchard; TAUR., SL. horse in the bullring ♦ **como sardina en lata** *or* **en banasta** COLL., FIG. packed like sardines.

sar·di·nal m. sardine net.

sar·di·ne·ro, -ra I. adj. sardine <*barco s.* sardine boat> **II.** m.f. sardine dealer.

sar·dó·ni·co, -ca adj. sardonic, ironic.

sar·ga¹ f. TEX. serge; PAINT. painted wall fabric.

sar·ga² f. BOT. type of willow.

sar·ga·zo m. BOT. sargasso, gulfweed.

sar·gen·te·ar tr. MIL. to command as a sergeant; FIG. *(dirigir)* to command, lead; FIG., COLL. *(mandar con afectación)* to boss (a person around) —intr. to be bossy.

sar·gen·to m. MIL. sergeant ♦ **s. mayor** MIL. quartermaster-sergeant, sergeant major.

sar·gen·to·na f. COLL. battle-ax, dragon lady (overbearing woman).

sa·ri·lla f. BOT. marjoram.

sar·men·tar §49 intr. AGR. to gather pruned vine shoots.

sar·men·te·ra f. AGR. place where vine shoots are kept.

sar·men·to·so, -sa adj. BOT. sarmentose.

sar·mien·to m. BOT. vine shoot, runner.

sar·na f. MED. itch, scabies; VET. mange ♦ **más viejo que la s.** COLL. as old as the hills.

sar·no·so, -sa I. adj. MED. itchy, scabby; VET. mangy **II.** m.f. MED. person suffering from itch *or* scabies.

sar·pu·lli·do m. MED. rash, skin eruption; *(de la pulga)* flea bite.

sa·rra·ce·no, -na HIST. **I.** adj. Saracenic **II.** m.f. Saracen.

sa·rri·llo m. death rattle.

sa·rro m. *(en las vasijas)* crust, deposit; DENT. tartar; *(en la lengua)* fur, coating (on the tongue); BOT. rust, mildew.

sa·rro·so, -sa adj. *(una vasija)* covered with a deposit *or* crust; DENT. covered with tartar; *(la lengua)* furry, coated (tongue); BOT. rust, mildewy.

sar·ta f. *(cosas en un hilo)* string <*s. de perlas* string of pearls>; FIG. *(serie)* string, series <*s. de mentiras* string of lies>.

sar·tal m. string (of beads).

sar·tén f. CUL. *(vasija)* frying pan, skillet; *(sartenada)* panful, contents of a frying pan ♦ **saltar del s. y caer en las brasas** FIG., COLL. to jump from the frying pan into the fire • **tener la s. por el mango** FIG., COLL. to have the upper hand, run the show.

sar·te·na·da f. CUL. pan *or* panful.

sar·te·na·zo m. *(golpe dado con una sartén)* blow with a frying pan; FIG., COLL. *(porrazo)* hard blow, wallop.

sa·sa·frás m. BOT. sassafras.

sas·tre m. SEW. tailor; THEAT. costumier, costumer ♦ **buen s.** FIG., COLL. well-informed person, someone in the know • **corto s.** FIG., COLL. uninformed person • **s. de señoras** SEW. dressmaker • **traje s.** SEW. woman's tailored suit.

sas·tre·rí·a f. SEW. *(oficio)* tailoring; *(tienda)* tailor's (shop).

Sa·tán *or* **Sa·ta·nás** m. BIBL. Satan, the Devil.

sa·tá·ni·co, -ca adj. BIBL. Satanic; FIG. *(muy perverso)* satanic, fiendish.

sa·ta·nis·mo m. *(culto)* Satanism, Satan-worship; *(carácter satánico)* devilishness, fiendishness.

sa·té·li·te I. adj. ECON., POL. satellite <*país s.* satellite country> **II.** m. ASTRON. satellite; TECH. *(piñón)* loose pinion, planet wheel; ECON., POL. *(nación dependiente)* satellite; FIG., COLL. *(esbirro)* henchman, loyal follower ♦ **s. artificial** ASTRONAUT. satellite.

sa·te·li·zar §04 tr. ASTRONAUT. to place in orbit; POL. to make a satellite of, dominate.

sa·tén *or* **sa·tín** m. TEX. satin.

sa·tín m. satinwood.

sa·ti·na·do, -da I. past part. see **satinar II.** adj. satiny ♦ **papel s.** PRINT. glossy *or* coated paper **III.** m. *(acción de satinar)* glazing, calendering; *(brillo)* gloss, sheen.

sa·ti·nar tr. PRINT., TEX. to calender, glaze; PHOTOG. to burnish.

sá·ti·ra f. satire.

sa·ti·ria·sis f. MED. satyriasis.

sa·tí·ri·ca·men·te adv. satirically.

sa·tí·ri·co, -ca I. adj. *(relativo a la sátira)* satiric, satirical; *(relativo al sátiro)* satyric, satyrical **II.** m.f. satirist.

sa·ti·ri·zan·te adj. satirizing.

sa·ti·ri·zar §04 tr. & intr. to satirize.

sá·ti·ro m. MYTH. satyr; FIG. *(hombre lascivo)* satyr, lecher.

sa·tis·fac·ción f. *(placer)* satisfaction, gratification; *(desagravio)* satisfaction, redress; *(vanagloria)* vanity, conceit ♦ **a s.** satisfactorily • **a s. de** to the satisfaction of • **pedir s.** to demand satisfaction.

sa·tis·fa·cer §40 tr. *(contentar)* to satisfy; *(pagar)* to pay <*s. las deudas* to pay one's debts>; *(saciar)* to satisfy <*s. el hambre* to satisfy one's hunger>; *(cumplir)* to satisfy, meet <*los estudiantes tienen que s. estos requisitos para graduarse* the students have to meet these requirements in order to graduate>; *(dar solución)* to satisfy <*el maestro satisfizo mi curiosidad* the teacher satisfied my curiosity>; *(reparar un daño)* to satisfy, redress; *(premiar)* to compensate, reward —reflex. *(contentarse)* to satisfy oneself; *(vengarse)* to get satisfaction *or* revenge.

sa·tis·fa·cien·te adj. satisfying, satisfactory.

sa·tis·fac·to·rio, -ria adj. satisfactory.

sa·tis·fe·cho, -cha I. past part. see **satisfacer II.** adj. *(contento)* satisfied, content; *(cumplido)* satisfied, met; *(pagado de sí mismo)* smug, self-satisfied ♦ **darse por s. con** to be satisfied *or* content with • **estar** *or* **quedar s.** to be full *or* sated.

sa·tis·fi·cie·ra, satisfice see **satisfacer.**

sa·tis·fi·zo see **satisfacer.**

sa·ti·vo, –va adj. AGR. cultivated <*planta s.* cultivated plant>.

sá·tra·pa m. HIST. satrap; FIG., COLL. (*hombre astuto*) sly fox; (*persona poderosa*) honcho, boss.

sa·tu·ra·ble adj. (*que puede saturarse*) saturable; FIG. (*que puede llenarse*) satiable.

sa·tu·ra·ción f. saturation; FIG. (*hartura*) satiation.

sa·tu·ra·do, –da I. past part. see **saturar** II. adj. (*empapado*) saturated; FIG. (*harto*) satiated.

sa·tu·rar tr. (*empapar*) to saturate; FIG. (*hartar*) to sate, satiate.

sa·tur·nal I. adj. ASTRON., MYTH. Saturnian II. f. ♦ **saturnalias** Saturnalia.

sa·tur·ni·no, –na adj. CHEM., MED. lead, saturnine <*cólico s.* lead colic>; FIG. (*triste*) saturnine, morose.

sa·tur·nis·mo m. MED. saturnism, lead poisoning.

Sa·tur·no m. ASTRON., MYTH. Saturn; CHEM. lead.

sau·ce m. BOT. willow ♦ **s. cabruno** BOT. goat willow • **s. de Babilonia** *or* **llorón** BOT. weeping willow.

sau·ce·da *or* **sau·ce·ra** f. willow grove.

sau·ce·dal m. willow grove.

sau·da·de f. nostalgia.

sau·di·ta adj. & m.f. Saudi.

sau·zal m. BOT. willow grove.

sa·via f. BOT. sap; FIG. (*vigor*) vigor, energy.

sa·xó·fo·no *or* **sa·xo·fón** m. MUS. saxophone.

sa·ya f. (*falda*) skirt; (*enaguas*) petticoat; (*túnica*) tunic.

sa·yal m. sackcloth.

sa·yo m. (*vestido amplio*) smock, frock; (*casaca*) cassock; (*túnica*) tunic ♦ **cortarle a uno un s.** FIG., COLL. to run down, criticize (a person).

sa·yón m. HIST. minister of justice (in the Middle Ages); (*verdugo*) executioner; FIG., COLL. (*hombre feroz*) fierce-looking man.

sa·zón I. adj. AMER. ripe, mature II. f. season <*fruta en s.* fruit in season>; (*condimento*) seasoning, flavoring; AMER. good cooking ♦ **a la s.** at that time, then • **en s.** opportunely, at the right time *or* moment • **fuera de s.** inopportunely, at the wrong time *or* moment.

sa·zo·na·do, –da I. past part. see **sazonar** II. adj. (*sabroso*) seasoned, flavorful; (*maduro*) ripe, mature; FIG. (*ingenioso*) witty, clever.

sa·zo·nar tr. (*dar sabor*) to season, flavor; (*madurar*) to ripen, mature —intr. & reflex. to ripen, mature.

se §§30, 36, 38 reflex. pron. oneself, himself, herself, yourself, itself, themselves, yourselves <*las chicas se están mirando en el espejo* the girls are looking at themselves in the mirror>; to oneself, to himself, to herself, to yourself, to itself, to themselves, to yourselves <*ese viejo se habla a sí mismo* that old man talks to himself>; [to indicate the owner of the direct object of a verb] <*Juan se puso el sombrero* John put on his hat>; [to provide reflex. form to verbs not reflex. in meaning] <*mi tío se murió* my uncle died> —rec. pron. each other, one another <*mis padres se aman* my parents love each other>; to each other, to one another <*ellos se mandaron regalos* they sent presents to one another> —indef. pron. one, they, people <*se dice que la economía mejorará* they say that the economy will improve> —aux. pron. [to give passive meaning to active verbs] <*se venden libros aquí* books are sold here> —pers. pron. [used instead of **le** *or* **les** before **lo, la, los** *or* **las**] to him, to her, to you, to it, to them <*Ana se lo dijo a él* Ann said it to him>; for him, for her, for you, for it, for them <*se la voy a comprar a usted* I am going to buy it for you>; from him, from her, from you, from it, from them <*él se lo robó a ellos* he stole it from them>.

sé see **saber²** *or* **ser².**

se·bá·ce·o, –a adj. sebaceous.

se·bo m. (*para velas*) tallow; (*grasa*) grease, fat; COLL. (*borrachera*) drunkenness; (*gordura*) fat; (*suciedad*) filth, grime; PERU gift asked from godparents by children in baptism.

se·bo·rre·a f. MED. seborrhea.

se·bo·so, –sa adj. (*untado de sebo*) tallowy; (*grasiento*) greasy, fatty; (*sucio*) filthy, grimy.

se·ca I. f. (*sequía*) drought; (*estación*) dry season; MED. (*infarto*) infarction (of a gland); (*período de desecación*)

desquamation (drying period); MARIT. sandbar, sandbank II. adj. see **seco, –ca.**

se·ca·dal m. dry and barren land.

se·ca·de·ro m. drying room.

se·ca·do I. past part. see **secar** II. m. drying.

se·ca·dor m. PHOTOG. dryer; (*para el pelo*) hair dryer; AMER. clothes dryer.

se·ca·do·ra f. clothes dryer.

se·ca·men·te adv. dryly, sarcastically.

se·ca·mien·to m. drying.

se·ca·no m. (*tierra sin riego*) unirrigated land; (*banco de arena*) sandbar; FIG. (*cosa seca*) very dry thing.

se·can·te I. adj. (*que seca*) drying; GEOM. secant; ARG. annoying, irritating II. f. GEOM. secant —m. CHEM. siccative; (*papel*) blotting paper, blotter.

se·car §70 tr. to dry; FIG. (*fastidiar*) to annoy, bother —reflex. (*evaporarse la humedad*) to dry (out) <*la ropa se secó en unas horas* the clothes dried in a few hours>; to dry oneself, dry off; (*ríos y fuentes*) to dry up, run dry; BOT. to wither, wilt; (*enflaquecer*) to waste away; FIG. (*perder la sensibilidad*) to become insensitive.

sec·ción f. (*parte*) section; (*división*) department <*s. de niños* children's department> ♦ **s. transversal** cross section.

sec·cio·nar tr. to section, divide into sections.

se·ce·sión f. secession.

se·ce·sio·nis·ta adj. & m.f. secessionist.

se·co, –ca I. adj. (*árido*) dry; (*desecado*) dried (fruits, wood); (*delgado*) thin, lean; (*corto y brusco*) sharp <*un golpe s.* a sharp blow>; (*apagado*) dull (noise); FIG. (*poco cariñoso*) undemonstrative, impassive <*él siempre era un hombre s.* he always was an undemonstrative man>; (*estricto*) strict; (*sin azúcar*) dry (liquor); (*ronco*) harsh <*una voz s.* a harsh voice>; (*sin adorno*) plain, unadorned; (*falto de amenidad*) dry, laconic ♦ **a palo s.** by itself • **a secas** drily, curtly • **dejar a alguien s.** FIG., COLL. to kill instantly <*lo atropelló el tren y lo dejó s.* the train hit him and killed him instantly>; (*dejar atónito*) to stun <*la noticia me dejó s.* the news stunned me> • **en s.** FIG., COLL. (*bruscamente*) suddenly; (*sin causa*) without cause *or* reason; (*sin medios*) without resources (money); MARIT. high and dry • **limpiar en s.** to dry-clean II. f. see **seca.**

se·co·ya f. BOT. sequoia.

se·cre·ción f. secretion.

se·cre·ta I. f. (*examen*) examination (formerly given in universities); (*sumaria secreta*) secret interrogation; RELIG. secret (prayer); (*excusado*) privy, water closet; SL. (*policía secreta*) secret police —m. SL. member of the secret police II. adj. see **secreto, –ta.**

se·cre·ta·men·te adv. secretly, covertly.

se·cre·tar tr. to secrete.

se·cre·ta·ria f. secretary.

se·cre·ta·rí·a f. (*cargo de un secretario*) secretaryship; (*oficina de un secretario*) secretary's office; (*oficina administrativa*) secretariat ♦ **Secretaría de Estado** State Department.

se·cre·ta·ria·do m. (*oficina*) secretariat; (*cargo*) secretaryship.

se·cre·ta·rio m. (*amanuense*) secretary; ORNITH. secretary bird ♦ **s. municipal** town clerk • **s. particular** private secretary.

se·cre·te·ar intr. COLL. to whisper, talk secretly.

se·cre·te·o m. COLL. whispering.

se·cre·ter m. secretary, writing desk.

se·cre·to I. m. secret <*el s. de la felicidad* the secret of happiness>; (*reserva*) secrecy <*s. profesional* professional secrecy>; (*en muebles*) hidden drawer (in some pieces of furniture); MUS. sounding board, soundboard ♦ **en s.** secretly • **guardar un s.** to keep a secret • **s. a voces** COLL. open secret • **s. de Estado** state secret • **s. de confesión** RELIG. seal of confession II. adj. see **secreto, –ta.**

se·cre·to, –ta I. adj. (*oculto*) secret, covert; (*invisible*) secret, hidden <*una escalera s.* a secret stairway>; (*confidencial*) confidential, private; (*reservado*) secretive <*las personas secretas usualmente no muestran los sentimientos* secretive people usually do not show their feelings> II. m. see **secreto** —f. see **secreta.**

se·cre·tor, –to·ra *or* **se·cre·to·rio, –ria** adj. PHYSIOL. secreting, secretory.

sec·ta f. sect.
sec·ta·rio, –ria adj. & m.f. sectarian.
sec·ta·ris·mo m. sectarianism.
sec·tor m. sector.
sec·to·rial adj. sectorial.
sec·to·ri·za·ción f. sectorization.
se·cuaz [pl. **-cua·ces**] I. adj. partisan II. m.f. *(subalterno)* underling, henchman; *(partidario)* partisan, follower (usually pejorative).
se·cue·la f. consequence, result.
se·cuen·cia f. CINEM., RELIG. sequence.
se·cues·tra·dor, –do·ra I. adj. LAW *(de bienes)* sequestering, sequestrating; *(de una persona)* kidnapping; *(de un vehículo)* hijacking II. m.f. LAW *(de bienes)* sequestrator; *(de personas)* kidnapper; *(de vehículos)* hijacker.
se·cues·trar tr. LAW *(bienes)* to sequester, sequestrate; *(personas)* kidnap, abduct; *(vehículos)* to hijack.
se·cues·tro m. LAW *(de bienes)* sequestration, confiscation; *(de personas)* kidnapping, abduction; *(de vehículos)* hijacking.
se·cu·lar adj. *(seglar)* secular, worldly; *(que sucede cada siglo)* secular; *(muy viejo)* century-old, age-old.
se·cu·la·ris·mo m. secularism.
se·cu·la·ri·za·ción f. secularization.
se·cu·la·ri·zar §04 tr. to secularize.
se·cun·dar tr. to second, support.
se·cun·da·ria·men·te adv. secondarily.
se·cun·da·rio, –ria adj. & m. secondary.
sed f. *(necesidad de beber)* thirst; FIG. *(deseo)* thirst, desire.
se·da f. TEXT. *(tela)* silk; ZOOL. bristle ♦ **como una s.** FIG. *(suave)* as smooth as silk; *(dócil)* as gentle as a lamb • **s. artificial** rayon • **s. azache** low quality silk • **s. conchal** choice silk • **s. cruda** raw silk.
se·da·ción f. *(mitigación)* soothing, calming; MED. sedation.
se·dal m. *(para pescar)* fishing line; SURG. seton.
se·dan·te adj. & m. MED. sedative.
se·dar tr. *(calmar)* to soothe, calm; MED. to sedate.
se·da·ti·vo, –va adj. & m. MED. sedative.
se·de f. RELIG. see; *(del gobierno)* seat (of government); *(de una organización)* headquarters ♦ **Santa S.** RELIG. Holy See • **s. social** head office.
se·den·ta·rio, –ria adj. sedentary.
se·de·rí·a f. *(tejidos)* silks, silk goods; *(negocios)* silk trade or business; *(tienda)* silk shop, drapers.
se·de·ro, –ra I. adj. silk II. m.f. *(comerciante)* silk dealer or seller; *(labrador)* silk weaver.
se·di·ción f. sedition, rebellion.
se·di·cio·so, –sa I. adj. seditious II. m.f. seditionary, rebel.
se·dien·to, –ta adj. *(que tiene sed)* thirsty; FIG. *(árido)* dry, parched (land); FIG. *(deseoso)* thirsty, desirous.
se·di·men·tar tr. to deposit (sediment) —reflex. to settle.
se·di·men·ta·rio, –ria adj. GEOL. sedimentary.
se·di·men·to m. sediment.
se·do·so, –sa adj. silken, silky.
se·duc·ción f. *(acción de seducir)* seduction; *(atractivo)* seductiveness, allure.
se·du·cir §22 tr. *(enamorar)* to seduce; *(cautivar)* to captivate, charm.
se·duc·ti·vo, –va or **se·duc·tor, –to·ra** I. adj. *(que seduce)* seductive; *(fascinante)* fascinating, captivating II. m.f. *(persona que seduce)* seducer; *(persona que encanta)* charmer.
se·far·dí or **se·far·di·ta** I. adj. Sephardic II. m.f. Sephardic Jew, Sephardi ♦ **sefardíes** or **sefarditas** Sephardim.
se·ga·de·ro, –ra I. adj. AGR. ready for harvesting or reaping II. f. sickle.
se·ga·dor, –do·ra II. adj. AGR. mowing, reaping II. m.f. AGR. *(persona)* reaper, harvester —m. ENTOM. daddy longlegs, harvestman —f. AGR. reaper, harvester (machine).
se·gar §52 tr. *(la mies)* to reap, harvest; *(la hierba)* to cut, mow *<él segó el césped* he mowed the lawn>; FIG. *(cortar)* to cut off.
se·glar I. adj. secular II. m. layman —f. laywoman.
seg·men·ta·ción f. segmentation.
seg·men·to m. segment ♦ **s. del émbolo** TECH. piston ring.
se·gre·ga·ción f. segregation.

se·gre·ga·cio·nis·mo m. segregationism.
se·gre·ga·cio·nis·ta adj. & m.f. segregationist.
se·gre·gar §47 tr. *(apartar)* to segregate; MED. *(secretar)* to secrete.
se·gre·ga·ti·vo, –va adj. segregative.
se·gué see **segar**.
se·gui·da I. f. series, succession ♦ **de s.** *(sin interrupción)* continuously, without interruption; *(inmediatamente)* immediately, at once • **en s.** immediately, at once II. adj. see **seguido, –da**.
se·gui·da·men·te adv. *(sin interrupción)* continuously, without interruption; *(después)* next *<s. presentaremos el primer premio* next we will present the first prize>.
se·gui·do, –da I. past part. see **seguir** II. adj. *(continuo)* continuous, successive; *(consecutivo)* consecutive, in a row *<llovió cuarenta días seguidos* it rained for forty consecutive days>; *(directo)* direct, straight ♦ **de s.** continuously, without interruption III. adv. *(inmediatamente)* immediately, at once; AMER. often. IV. f. see **seguida**.
se·gui·dor, –do·ra I. adj. following II. m.f. *(persona que sigue)* follower —m. *(pauta)* guide lines (for writing).
se·gui·mien·to m. *(perseguimiento)* chase, pursuit; *(continuación)* continuation; *(observación)* following, observation.
se·guir §64 §G9 tr. *(caminar detrás)* to follow; *(venir después)* to follow, come after *<el reinado de Juan Carlos siguió a la dictadura de Franco* the reign of Juan Carlos came after Franco's dictatorship>; *(continuar)* to continue, keep *or* go on *<s. hablando* to go on talking>; *(ir en pos)* to pursue; *(perseguir)* to hound, chase; *(espiar)* to follow, watch closely (a suspect); *(caminar)* to follow, go along *<siguieron el río hasta su desembocadura* they followed the river to its mouth>; *(observar)* to follow, watch *<s. los acontecimientos mundiales* to watch world events>; *(adherir)* to follow, adhere to *<yo sigo los principios de Confucio* I follow the principles of Confucio>; *(prestar atención)* to follow, pay attention (to) *<s. un discurso* to follow a speech>; *(emular)* to imitate, emulate *<mi sobrino quiere s. mi estilo de vida* my nephew wants to imitate my lifestyle>; *(estudiar)* to study, take *<sigo medicina* I study medicine>* —intr. *(continuar)* to continue *<todavía sigue en el mismo trabajo* he still continues at the same job>; *(estar de salud)* to feel, do *<¿cómo sigue el enfermo hoy?* how is the patient feeling today?> —reflex. to follow.
se·gún I. prep. according to *<s. este informe* according to this report> II. adv. *(como)* depending on, as *<s. como te comportes, te llevaré al cine* depending on how you behave, I'll take you to the movies>; according to *<el Evangelio s. San Mateo* the Gospel according to Saint Matthew> ♦ **s. y como** or **s. y conforme** *(de igual manera)* just as, exactly as *<lo prepararé s. y conforme a lo que tú me indicas* I shall prepare it exactly as you indicate>; *(de acuerdo a las circunstancias)* depending on the circumstances, maybe.
se·gun·da I. f. *(de cerradura)* double turn (of a lock); *(doble sentido)* double meaning; AUTO. second gear II. adj. see **segundo, –da**.
se·gun·de·ro, –ra I. adj. AGR. second (crop of the year) II. m. second hand (of a watch).
se·gun·di·lla f. call bell (in a convent).
se·gun·do, –da I. adj. second *<febrero es el s. mes del año* February is the second month of the year>; FIG. *(otro)* another *<él es un s. Mozart* he is another Mozart> ♦ **de s. clase** second-class • **de s. mano** secondhand • **s. enseñanza** secondary education • **s. intención** double meaning II. m. second *<hay sesenta segundos en un minuto* there are sixty seconds in a minute>; ASTRON., GEOM. second; *(subjefe)* second-in-comand; *(asistente)* assistant, aide ♦ **sin s.** unequaled, peerless —f. see **segunda**.
se·gun·do·gé·ni·to, –ta adj. & m.f. second-born.
se·gun·dón m. *(segundo hijo)* second son; *(cualquier hijo después del primogénito)* any son born after the first one.
se·gur f. *(hacha)* ax; *(hoz)* sickle.
se·gu·ra·men·te adv. *(ciertamente)* surely, certainly; *(probablemente)* probably.
se·gu·ri·dad f. security, safety *<la s. nacional* national security>; *(certeza)* certainty, assurance; *(confiabilidad)* reliability, trustworthiness; *(fianza)* surety, security ♦ **con toda s.** with absolute certainty • **de s.** safety *<cinturón de*

s. safety belt> • **s. social** social security • **tener la s. de que** to be certain that.

se·gu·ro, –ra I. adj. *(protegido)* secure, safe; *(cierto)* sure, certain <*le espera una muerte s.* a certain death awaits him>; *(confiado)* sure, certain <*estoy s. de que ella viene* I am sure that she is coming>; *(confiable)* reliable, trustworthy; *(firme)* secure, stable ♦ **a buen s.** *or* **de s.** certainly, assuredly • **en s.** in safety, in a safe place • **sobre s.** without risk, safely **II.** m. *(certeza)* certainty, assurance; *(aseguración)* insurance <*s. contra incendio* fire insurance>; ARM. safety catch ♦ **s. contra accidentes** accident insurance • **s. contra desempleo** unemployment insurance • **s. de vida** life insurance • **s. social** social security **III.** adv. certainly, for sure.

seis I. adj. six <*compré s. manzanas* I bought six apples>; *(sexto)* sixth ♦ **las s.** six o'clock **II.** m. six.

seis·cien·tos, –ta I. adj. six hundred <*s. pesos* six hundred pesos>; *(sexcentésimo)* six hundredth **II.** m. six hundred.

se·lec·ción f. selection ♦ **s. biológica** *or* **natural** BIOL. natural selection.

se·lec·cio·na·do, –da I. past part. see **seleccionar II.** adj. SPORT. selected (for a team) **III.** m.f. SPORT. player selected for a team —m. AMER. selection, choice.

se·lec·cio·nar tr. to select, choose.

se·lec·ti·vi·dad f. RAD. selectivity.

se·lec·ti·vo, –va adj. selective.

se·lec·to, –ta adj. select, choice ♦ **selectas** LIT. selections.

se·le·nio m. CHEM. selenium.

se·le·ni·ta f. MIN. selenite.

sel·va f. *(bosque)* forest, woods; *(jungla)* jungle ♦ **S. Negra** Black Forest.

sel·vá·ti·co, –ca adj. *(de las selvas)* forest, woodland; FIG. *(inculto)* rustic, uncouth.

sel·vo·so, –sa adj. forested, wooded.

se·lla·dor, –do·ra I. adj. *(que sella)* sealing; *(que pone sello)* stamping **II.** m.f. *(persona)* stamper; *(instrumento)* seal, signet.

se·llar tr. *(imprimir)* to stamp <*sellé las cartas con el nombre de nuestra compañía* I stamped the cards with our company's name>; *(cerrar)* to seal, close; FIG. *(concluir)* to finish, conclude <*selló el discurso con su humor característico* he concluded the speech with his characteristic humor>.

se·llo m. *(instrumento y marca)* seal, stamp; *(estampilla)* (postage) stamp; FIG. *(carácter distintivo)* stamp <*mi casa muestra el s. de mi personalidad* my house bears the stamp of my personality>; PHARM. cachet ♦ **echar** *or* **poner el s. a algo** to put the finishing touches on something • **s. aéreo** airmail stamp • **s. de correo** *or* **s. postal** postage stamp • **s. fiscal** LAW revenue stamp.

se·má·fo·ro m. semaphore.

se·ma·na f. *(siete días)* week; *(salario semanal)* weekly pay, week's wages ♦ **entre s.** during the week • **s. laboral** working week • **S. Santa** Holy Week.

se·ma·nal adj. weekly.

se·ma·nal·men·te adv. weekly, every week.

se·ma·na·rio, –ria I. adj. weekly **II.** m. weekly publication.

se·ma·ne·ro, –ra I. adj. employed by the week **II.** m.f. worker employed by the week.

se·mán·ti·co, –ca I. adj. semantic **II.** f. semantics.

sem·blan·te m. *(rostro)* face, countenance; FIG. *(apariencia)* appearance, look ♦ **estar de mal s.** to look ill.

sem·blan·te·ar tr. AMER. to look (a person) in the face; MEX. to examine, observe.

sem·blan·za f. biographical sketch *or* profile.

sem·bra·de·ra f. AGR. sower, seeder (machine).

sem·bra·de·ro m. COL. sown field *or* land.

sem·bra·dí·o, –a adj. AGR. arable, ready to be sown.

sem·bra·do I. past part. see **sembrar II.** m. AGR. sown field *or* land.

sem·bra·dor, –do·ra I. adj. sowing, seeding **II.** m.f. *(persona)* sower —f. *(máquina)* seed drill.

sem·bra·du·ra f. AGR. sowing, seeding.

sem·brar §49 tr. *(sementar)* to sow, seed; FIG. *(provocar)* to sow, provoke <*s. discordia* to sow discord>; *(esparcir por el suelo)* to scatter, sprinkle; *(esparcir noticias)* to spread, disseminate.

sem·brí·o m. S. AMER. sown field *or* land.

se·me·jan·te I. adj. *(similar)* similar, alike; *(tal)* such, like

that <*nunca he visto hombre semejante* I have never seen such a man> **II.** m.f. fellow man.

se·me·jan·za f. *(parecido)* similarity, likeness; RHET. simile ♦ **a s. de** like, as.

se·me·jar intr. to resemble, look like —reflex. to resemble one another, look alike ♦ **semejarse a** to look like, resemble.

se·men m. PHYSIOL. semen, sperm; BOT. *(semilla)* seed.

se·men·tal I. adj. AGR., BOT. sowing, seeding; ZOOL. breeding, siring **II.** m. ZOOL. sire.

se·men·tar §49 tr. to seed, sow.

se·men·te·ra f. AGR. sowing, seeding; *(tierra sembrada)* sown field *or* land; *(temporada)* sowing *or* seeding time.

se·men·te·ro m. AGR. *(saco)* seed bag; *(sementera)* seeding, sowing.

se·mes·tral adj. semiannual, biannual.

se·mes·tre m. *(seis meses)* six months, semester; COM. half-yearly payment.

se·mia·ca·ba·do, –da adj. half-finished.

se·miá·ri·do, –da adj. semiarid.

se·miau·to·má·ti·co, –ca adj. semiautomatic.

se·mi·bre·ve f. MUS. whole note, semibreve (G.B.).

se·mi·ca·li·fi·ca·do adj. semiskilled.

se·mi·cir·cu·lar adj. semicircular.

se·mi·cír·cu·lo m. semicircle.

se·mi·cons·cien·te adj. half conscious, semiconscious.

se·mi·con·so·nan·te PHONET. **I.** adj. semiconsonantal **II.** m. semiconsonant.

se·mi·cor·che·a f. MUS. sixteenth note, semiquaver (G.B.).

se·mi·des·nu·do adj. half-naked.

se·mi·diós m. MYTH. demigod.

se·mien·te, semiento see **sementar.**

se·mi·fi·na·lis·ta adj. & m.f. SPORT. semifinalist.

se·mi·lla f. seed.

se·mi·lle·ro m. *(plantación)* seed bed, plot; *(vivero)* nursery; FIG. *(origen)* breeding ground, hotbed.

se·mi·nal adj. seminal.

se·mi·na·rio m. *(escuela)* seminary; *(semillero)* seed bed, plot; *(curso)* seminar ♦ **s. conciliar** theological seminary.

se·mi·na·ris·ta m. seminarian, seminarist.

se·mio·lo·gí·a *or* **se·mió·ti·ca** f. semiology, semiotics.

se·mi·pe·sa·do adj. & m. SPORT. light heavyweight.

se·mi·pre·cio·so, –sa adj. JEWEL. semiprecious.

se·mi·ta I. adj. Semitic **II.** m.f. Semite.

se·mí·ti·co, –ca adj. Semitic.

se·mi·to·no m. MUS. semitone, half tone.

se·mi·vo·cal PHONET. **I.** adj. semivocalic **II.** f. semivowel.

sé·mo·la f. semolina.

sem·pi·ter·no, –na adj. everlasting, eternal.

se·na f. six (on dice) ♦ **senas** double sixes.

Se·na m. Seine.

se·na·do m. *(del gobierno)* senate; FIG. *(reunión)* assembly, gathering.

se·na·dor m. senator.

se·na·to·rio, –ria *or* **se·na·to·rial** adj. senatorial.

sen·ci·lla·men·te adv. simply, plainly.

sen·ci·llez f. *(simplicidad)* simplicity; FIG. *(ingenuidad)* innocence, naïveté; DOM. REP. foolishness, silliness.

sen·ci·llo, –lla I. *(fácil)* simple, easy; *(sin adorno)* simple, plain <*es una casa s.* it is a simple house>; CHEM., PHYS. simple; *(individual)* single <*alquilé un cuarto s. en el hotel* I rented a single room in the hotel>; FIG. *(incauto)* gullible; *(ingenuo)* innocent, naïve **II.** m. AMER. change (money).

sen·da f. *(camino)* path, track; FIG. road, way <*tomar la mala s.* to take the wrong road>.

sen·de·ro m. var. of **senda.**

sen·dos, –das adj. each <*los niños recibieron s. regalos* the children each received a present>.

se·nec·tud f. old age, senescence.

Se·ne·gal m. Senegal.

se·ne·ga·lés, –le·sa adj. & m.f. Senegalese.

se·nes·cen·te adj. senescent, aging.

se·nil adj. senile.

se·no m. *(hueco)* cavity, hollow; *(regazo)* bosom; ANAT. *(pecho)* breast, teat; *(cavidad)* cavity <*senos nasales* sinus cavities>; *(matriz)* womb; FIG. *(adentro)* bosom, womb <*el hijo pródigo volvió al s. de su familia* the prodigal son returned to the bosom of his family>; MATH. sine; ARCHIT. spandrel; MARIT. (*bahía pequeña*) inlet, cove; (*de una vela*) belly (of a sail) ♦ **s. verso** MATH. versed sine.

sen·sa·ción f. (*impresión*) sensation, feeling; (*conmoción*) sensation <*causar s.* to cause a sensation>.

sen·sa·cio·nal adj. sensational.

sen·sa·cio·na·lis·mo m. sensationalism.

sen·sa·cio·na·lis·ta adj. sensationalistic, sensational.

sen·sa·tez f. good sense, prudence.

sen·sa·to, –ta adj. sensible, prudent.

sen·si·bi·li·dad f. (*facultad*) sensibility; (*emotividad*) sensitivity, sensitiveness; (*susceptibilidad*) sensitivity (film, scales).

sen·si·bi·li·za·ción f. sensitization.

sen·si·bi·li·zar §04 tr. to sensitize.

sen·si·ble adj. (*que percibe*) sentient; (*sentimental*) sentimental, sensitive; (*impresionable*) sensitive; (*tangible*) tangible, palpable <*el mundo s.* the tangible world>; (*fácil de observar*) perceptible, noticeable; (*lamentable*) grievous, unfortunate; (*susceptible*) sensitive (film, scales).

sen·si·ble·rí·a f. sentimentality, sentimentalism.

sen·si·ble·ro, –ra adj. overly sentimental.

sen·si·ti·vo, –va adj. (*sensible*) sensitive; (*capaz de sentir*) sentient; (*sensorial*) sense <*órgano s.* sense organ>.

sen·so·rio, –ria *or* **sen·so·rial** I. adj. sensorial, sensory II. m. PHYSIOL. sensorium (part of the brain).

sen·sual adj. (*sensitivo*) sensuous; (*lujurioso*) sensual.

sen·sua·li·dad f. sensuality.

sen·ta·da I. f. (*asentada*) sitting; (*protesta*) sit-in; COL., EQUIT. jerk on the reins II. adj. see **sentado, –da.**

sen·ta·do, –da I. past part. see **sentar** II. adj. (*asentado*) seat, sitting <*estamos sentados en la orquesta* we are seated in the orchestra>; (*establecido*) established, settled; FIG. (*juicioso*) sensible, judicious; BOT. sessile ♦ **dar por s.** to take for granted, assume • **pan s.** stale bread III. f. see **sentada.**

sen·tar §49 tr. (*asentar*) to seat, sit; (*establecer*) to establish, set <*s. precedente* to set a precedent>; COL., ECUAD., EQUIT. to rein (a horse); COL. to crush, squash (someone) —intr. (*caer*) to agree with <*la comida frita no me sienta bien* fried food does not agree with me>; (*quedar*) to fit <*esta falda no me sienta bien* this skirt does not fit me well>; FIG. (*favorecer*) to suit, become <*esos aires no te sientan bien* those airs do not become you>; FIG., COLL. (*agradar*) to please ♦ **s. como anillo al dedo** to fit like a glove —reflex. to sit (down).

sen·ten·cia f. (*refrán*) maxim, axiom; LAW (*juicio*) sentence, judgment; FIG. (*decisión*) ruling, decision ♦ **pronunciar la s.** to pronounce *or* pass sentence • **cumplir la s.** to serve one's sentence • **s. absolutoria** acquittal • **s. condenatoria** guilty verdict • **s. de muerte** death sentence.

sen·ten·cia·dor, –do·ra adj. sentencing, judging.

sen·ten·ciar tr. (*juzgar*) to judge, pass judgment; (*condenar*) to sentence, condemn.

sen·ten·cio·so, –sa adj. (*conceptuoso*) sententious, pithy; (*grave*) grave, serious.

sen·ti·do, –da I. past part. see **sentir²** II. adj. (*sincero*) heartfelt, deeply felt <*un s. pésame* heartfelt condolences>; (*quisquilloso*) sensitive, touchy; GUAT., MEX. cracked, split III. m. (*facultad*) sense <*el s. del olfato* the sense of smell>; (*juicio*) sense, judgment; (*significado*) meaning, sense <*en el s. figurado* in the figurative sense>; (*interpretación*) interpretation <*esta frase tiene various sentidos* this sentence has various interpretations>; feeling <*leyó el poema con mucho s.* he read the poem with a lot of feeling>; (*conciencia*) consciousness <*recobrar el s.* to regain consciousness>; (*dirección*) direction <*en s. contrario* in the opposite direction>; AMER., ANAT. temple ♦ **aguzar el s.** COLL. to prick up one's ears • **con todos los cinco sentidos** FIG. heart and soul • **costar un s.** FIG., COLL. to cost an arm and a leg • **doble s.** double meaning, double-entendre • **en el s. de que** to the effect that • **no tener s.** not to make sense • **perder el s.** to lose consciousness, faint • **poner los cinco sentidos en** FIG. (*dedicarse*) to give one's all to; (*estimar*) to hold dearly • **s. común** common sense • **s. del humor** sense of humor • **sin s.** (*insensato*) senseless, meaningless; (*inconsciente*) unconscious • **tener s.** to make sense.

sen·ti·men·tal adj. sentimental.

sen·ti·men·ta·lis·mo m. sentimentalism, sentimentality.

sen·ti·mien·to m. (*emoción*) sentiment, emotion; (*pesar*) regret, sorrow; (*percepción*) sensitivity, perception; sense <*un s. de responsabilidad* a sense of responsibility>.

sen·ti·na f. MARIT. bilge; FIG. (*cloaca*) sewer, cesspool; (*antro de perdición*) den of iniquity.

sen·tir¹ m. (*sentimiento*) feeling; (*opinión*) opinion, view ♦ **en mi s.** in my opinion.

sen·tir² §65 tr. to feel <*siento el calor del sol en la cara* I feel the heat of the sun on my face>; (*experimentar*) to experience, feel <*s. alegría* to experience joy>; (*oír*) to hear <*sentí pasos* I heard footsteps>; (*lamentar*) to regret, sorry about <*sentimos mucho la muerte de nuestro amigo* we deeply regret the death of our friend>; (*opinar*) to feel, think <*siempre dice lo que siente* he always says what he thinks>; (*presentir*) to sense, perceive <*los animales sienten los cambios del tiempo* animals sense changes in weather>; (*apreciar*) to appreciate, have a feeling for <*ella siente la música en toda su variedad* she appreciates music in all its variety> ♦ **lo siento** I'm sorry —intr. to feel; to regret, be sorry <*dar que s.* to give cause for regret> ♦ **sin s.** inadvertently, without noticing —reflex. (*hallarse*) to feel <*me siento enfermo* I feel sick>; (*juzgarse*) to feel, consider oneself <*Pedro se siente obligado a ayudarlo* Peter feels obligated to help him>; (*doler*) to have a pain <*sentirse de la cabeza* to have a pain in one's head>; (*podrirse*) to begin to rot; AMER. to take offense ♦ **sentirse a sus anchas** to feel at ease • **sentirse como en (su) casa** to feel at home.

se·ña f. (*indicio*) sign, indication; (*señal*) sign, signal <*los dos niños tenían una s. secreta* the two children had a secret signal>; (*marca*) mark; MIL. password ♦ **dar señas de** to show signs of • **hablar por señas** to communicate by gestures • **hacer señas** to signal, make signs • **por más señas** more specifically • **s. mortal** conclusive *or* definite sign • **señas** address • **señas personales** particulars, description.

se·ñal f. (*marca*) sign, mark; (*mojón*) landmark; (*seña*) reminder; (*para libros*) bookmark; (*vestigio*) trace, sign <*el ladrón desapareció sin dejar una s.* the thief disappeared without leaving a trace>; (*prodigio*) mark of distinction; (*aviso*) signal <*s. de peligro* danger signal>; MED. (*cicatriz*) scar; (*síntoma*) symptom; COM. deposit ♦ **dar señales de vida** to show signs of life • **en s. de** as a sign of • **ni s.** not a trace • **s. de cambio** RAIL. switch signal • **s. de la cruz** RELIG. sign of the cross • **s. de líneas** *or* **s. para marcar** TELEC. dial tone • **s. de ocupado** TELEC. busy signal.

se·ña·la·da·men·te adv. (*especialmente*) expressly, especially; (*claramente*) clearly, distinctly.

se·ña·la·do, –da I. past part. see **señalar** II. adj. (*insigne*) outstanding, notable; appointed, fixed <*en el día s.* on the appointed day>.

se·ña·la·mien·to m. (*nombramiento*) appointment; LAW (*en derecho*) designation (of a court proceeding).

se·ña·lar tr. (*poner señal*) to mark, put a mark *or* sign on; (*indicar*) to point (at); (*determinar*) to determine, set <*pronto señalaremos el día para la fiesta* soon we will set the day for the party>; (*dejar cicatriz*) to scar, mark <*el contrincante le señaló con la espada* the opponent marked him with the sword>; (*ganado*) to brand (cattle); (*hacer señal*) to signal; (*nombrar*) to appoint, designate <*el partido me señaló como presidente* the party appointed me president>; (*hacer amago*) to feint; (*tantear*) to add up, total (points in a card game) —reflex. to excel, distinguish oneself.

se·ña·li·za·ción f. (*colocación de señales*) posting of signs; (*señales*) road *or* railway signs.

se·ña·li·zar §04 tr. to place signposts (on roads *or* railways).

se·ñe·ro, –ra adj. (*solitario*) alone, solitary; FIG. (*único*) unique, extraordinary.

se·ñor, –ño·ra §47 I. adj. COLL. (*gran*) really big, hell of a <*me dio una s. bofetada* he dealt me a hell of a blow>; (*noble*) gentlemanly II. m. (*dueño*) master, owner <*el s. de la casa* the master of the house>; (*noble*) noble, lord; (*caballero*) gentleman <*es todo un s.* he's a real gentleman>; Mister <*vi al s. Márquez en el mercado* I saw Mister Márquez in the market>; sir <*siéntese, s.* sit down, sir>; *(esposo)* husband ♦ **el S.** RELIG. the Lord (God) • **muy s. mío** Dear Sir (in correspondence) • **Nuestro S.** RELIG. Our Lord (Jesus Christ) • **¡Señor!** COLL. Good Lord! • **s. mayor** elderly gentleman —f. see **señora.**

se·ño·ra §G47 **I.** f. *(dueña)* lady, mistress <*la s. de la casa* the lady of the house>; *(noble)* lady; Mistress, Mrs. <*aquí viene la s. Martínez* here comes Mrs. Martínez>; madam, ma'am <*buenas tardes, s.* good afternoon, madam>; *(esposa)* wife ♦ **muy s. mía** Dear Madam (in correspondence) • **Nuestra S.** RELIG. Our Lady (Virgin Mary) • **s. de compañía** chaperon • **s. mayor** matron **II.** adj. see **señor, –ñora.**

se·ño·re·ar tr. *(dominar)* to dominate, rule; *(las pasiones)* to master, control (passions); FIG. *(estar superior)* to tower over, be superior to —reflex. to take over, seize <*señorearse de una empresa* to take over a company>.

se·ño·rí·a f. *(dominio)* dominion, control; *(título de un señor)* lordship; *(título de una señora)* ladyship; HIST. seigniory, signory <*la Señoría de Venecia* the Seigniory of Venice>.

se·ño·rial adj. *(propio de señor)* seigniorial, of a lord; *(majestuoso)* majestic, lordly.

se·ño·ril adj. lordly.

se·ño·río m. *(dominio)* dominion, control; *(territorio)* seigniory, domain; *(título)* lordship; *(propiedad)* estate, manor; *(gente de distinción)* gentry, nobility; FIG. *(dignidad)* dignity, solemnity; *(dominio de las pasiones)* self-control, self-restraint.

se·ño·ri·ta §G47 f. *(joven)* young lady; *(antes del apellido)* Miss <*quiero presentarle a la s. Fernández* I would like to introduce to you Miss Fernández>; COLL. *(ama)* miss, mistress.

se·ño·ri·tin·go, –ga m. DEROG. daddy's *or* mama's boy —f. daddy's *or* mama's girl.

se·ño·ri·to m. *(joven)* young man; COLL. *(amo)* master; DEROG. *(ocioso)* playboy, rich kid.

se·ño·rón, –ro·na **I.** adj. lordly, high and mighty **II.** m. great gentleman —f. great lady.

se·ñue·lo m. *(añagaza)* decoy, lure; FIG. *(cebo)* bait, inducement; *(trampa)* trap; AMER. *(buey cabestro)* lead steer; ARG. *(novillos mansos)* young lead bulls; *(madrina de tropilla)* lead mare.

se·pa see **saber².**

sé·pa·lo m. BOT. sepal.

se·pa·ra·ble adj. separable, detachable.

se·pa·ra·ción f. *(acción)* separation; *(división)* division, partition; LAW separation.

se·pa·ra·da·men·te adv. separately.

se·pa·ra·do, –da **I.** past part. see **separar** **II.** adj. separate, separated; *(de un matrimonio dividido)* separated, no longer living together ♦ **por s.** *(separadamente)* separately; *(correos)* under separate cover **III.** m. *(marido)* separated man —f. *(mujer)* separated woman.

se·pa·ra·dor, –do·ra **I.** adj. separating, separative **II.** m.f. *(persona)* separator —m. MECH., TECH. separator; SURG. retractor.

se·pa·rar tr. *(desunir)* to separate, set apart; *(partir)* to divide, split <*s. una palabra en sílabas* to divide a word into syllables>; *(elegir)* to separate, sort <*tenemos que s. las bananas maduras de las verdes* we have to separate the ripe bananas from the unripe ones>; *(apartar)* to separate, break (fighters); *(despedir)* to dismiss, discharge (from a job) —reflex. *(apartarse)* to separate, part company; *(jubilarse)* to retire; LAW *(desistir)* to waive; *(vivir aparte)* to separate (husband and wife).

se·pa·ra·tis·mo m. POL. separatism.

se·pa·ra·tis·ta adj. & m.f. POL. separatist.

se·pe·lio m. burial, interment.

se·pia f. ICHTH. cuttlefish, sepia; PAINT. sepia.

sep·ten·trión m. ASTRON. Ursa Major, Great Bear; GEOG. north.

sep·ten·trio·nal adj. northern, northerly, north <*el polo s.* the North Pole>.

sep·te·to m. MUS. septet.

sép·ti·co, –ca adj. septic.

sep·tiem·bre m. September.

sép·ti·mo, –ma adj. & m. seventh —f. MUS. seventh.

sep·tin·gen·té·si·mo, –ma adj. & m. seven-hundredth.

sep·tua·ge·na·rio, –ria adj. & m.f. septuagenarian.

sep·tua·gé·si·mo, –ma adj. & m. seventieth.

se·pul·cral adj. *(relativo al sepulcro)* sepulchral, pertaining to a grave *or* tomb <*lápida s.* gravestone *or* tombstone>; FIG. *(lúgubre)* gloomy, dismal.

se·pul·cro m. *(tumba)* sepulcher, tomb; ARCHIT. sepulcher, repository for sacred relics ♦ **El Santo S.** RELIG. the Holy Sepulcher • **ser un s.** FIG., COLL. to be as silent as a grave.

se·pul·ta·dor, –do·ra **I.** adj. burying, interring **II.** m.f. gravedigger.

se·pul·tar tr. *(enterrar)* to bury, inter; FIG. *(ocultar)* to conceal, bury —reflex. FIG. to be wrapped up, be buried <*sepultarse en los pensamientos* to be buried in thought>.

se·pul·to, –ta **I.** past part. see **sepultar** **II.** adj. buried, interred.

se·pul·tu·ra f. *(enterramiento)* burial, interment; *(tumba)* grave, tomb ♦ **dar s. a** to bury • **estar con un pie en la s.** to have one foot in the grave.

se·pul·tu·re·ro m. gravedigger.

se·qué, seque see **secar.**

se·que·dad f. *(calidad de seco)* dryness; FIG. *(aspereza)* curtness, dryness.

se·que·dal *or* **se·que·ral** m. dry and barren land.

se·quí·a f. *(temporada seca)* drought, dry season; AMER. thirst.

se·quí·o m. AGR. arid land.

sé·qui·to m. entourage, retinue.

ser¹ m. *(ente)* being; *(esencia)* essence, nature; *(vida)* life, existence ♦ **s. humano** human being • **s. vivo** living creature.

ser² §66 §G11, 13 aux. to be <*el Nuevo Mundo fue descubierto por Colón en 1492* the New World was discovered by Columbus in 1492> —intr. to be ♦ **a** *or* **de no s. por** if it were not for • **a no s. que** unless • **así sea** so be it • **¡cómo es eso!** what do you mean by that! • **¡cómo ha de s.!** what can you expect! • **de no s. así** otherwise • **érase que se era** once upon a time • **es a saber** that is to say, to wit • **es de** it is to be <*es de esperar* it is to be hoped>; *(valer)* to be worth <*es de verse* it is worth seeing> • **no es para menos** COLL. with good reason, rightly so • **no sea que** lest • **o sea** *or* **esto es** that is to say • **o sea que** in other words • **sea como sea** one way *or* the other • **sea lo que sea** be that as it may • **s. de** *(pertenecer)* to belong to <*este libro es de Marta* this book belongs to Martha>; to be made of <*la cadena es de oro* the chain is made of gold>; *(tener origen)* to be *or* come from <*mi madre era de Inglaterra* my mother was from England>; *(formar parte)* to be *or* come from <*el profesor es de la Universidad de Madrid* the professor is from the University of Madrid>; *(suceder)* to become of, happen to <*¿que será de nosotros?* what will become of us?>; *(corresponder)* to be suitable for <*su conducta no es la de un profesional* his conduct is not suitable for a professional> • **s. de lo que no hay** COLL. to be unique, be unequaled • **s. o no s.** to be or not to be • **s. para** to be for, be suited to <*estas manzanas no son para comer* these apples are not for eating> • **siendo así que** since • **soy contigo** *or* **con usted** I'll be right with you • **un sí es, no es** COLL. a bit, somewhat • **ya sea . . . ya sea** either . . . or . . . .

se·rá·fi·co, –ca adj. *(angélico)* seraphic, angelic; RELIG. Franciscan; FIG., COLL. *(humilde)* humble, poor.

se·ra·fín m. *(ángel)* seraph, angel; FIG. *(persona hermosa)* angel, extremely beautiful person.

ser·bio, –bia **I.** adj. Serbian, Serb **II.** m.f. *(habitante)* Serbian, Serb —m. *(idioma)* Serbian.

ser·bo·cro·a·ta adj. & m. Serbo-Croatian.

se·re·na **I.** f. MUS. serenade; *(humedad)* night dew ♦ **a la s.** COLL. in the night air **II.** adj. see **sereno, –na.**

se·re·nar tr. *(calmar)* to calm, make calm; *(aclarar)* to settle, clear (liquors); FIG. *(apaciguar)* to soothe, calm <*la música me ayuda a s. al niño* music helps me soothe the child> —reflex. to become *or* grow calm.

se·re·na·ta f. MUS. *(nocturno)* serenade, serenata; FIG., COLL. *(molestia)* harping, pestering <*dar la s.* to pester>.

se·re·ni·dad f. serenity, calm ♦ **S.** Serenity (title).

se·re·no, –na **I.** adj. *(sosegado)* serene, calm; METEOROL.

clear, cloudless (sky) **II.** m. METEOROL. evening dew; *(guarda)* night watchman ♦ **al sereno** in the night air —f. see **serena.**
se·rial adj. & m. serial ♦ **s. radiofónico** radio serial.
se·ria·men·te adv. seriously, earnestly.
se·riar tr. to place in a series, put in order.
se·rie f. series ♦ **fabricar** or **producir en s.** to mass-produce • **fuera de s.** COLL. out of sight, fantastic.
se·rie·dad f. *(gravedad)* seriousness, gravity; *(comportamiento digno de confianza)* dependability, trustworthiness.
se·ri·gra·fí·a f. ARTS., PRINT. serigraphy, silk-screening.
se·rio, –ria adj. *(grave)* serious, grave; *(concienzudo)* serious, earnest; *(sombrío)* sober, solemn; *(severo)* stern, severe; *(confiable)* reliable, trustworthy ♦ **en s.** *(gravemente)* seriously, gravely; *(sinceramente)* truly, in earnest • **hablar en s.** to be serious, speak seriously • **tomar en s.** to take seriously, believe.
ser·món m. RELIG. sermon; FIG. *(amonestación)* sermon, lecture ♦ **S. de la Montaña** BIBL. Sermon on the Mount.
ser·mo·ne·ar tr. to lecture, scold —intr. to sermonize, preach.
se·ro·so, –sa ANAT. **I.** adj. serous **II.** f. serous membrane.
ser·pen·te·a·do, –da I. past part. see **serpentear II.** adj. serpentine, winding.
ser·pen·te·ar intr. *(culebrear)* to snake, slither; *(encorvarse)* to wind, meander.
ser·pen·te·o m. *(culebreo)* snaking, slithering; *(meandros)* winding, meandering.
ser·pen·tín m. *(del alambique)* coil, worm (of a still); ARTIL. *(gatillo)* serpentine, match holder; *(pieza antigua)* ancient piece of artillery; *(llave)* cock, hammer; MIN. *(piedra)* serpentine ♦ **s. calentador** MECH. heating coil • **s. refrigerante** MECH. cooling coil.
ser·pen·ti·no, –na I. adj. *(de la serpiente)* serpentine, snake-like; FIG. *(ondulado)* winding, snaking **II.** f. *(cinta de papel)* paper streamer; MIN. serpentine.
ser·pien·te f. ZOOL. serpent, snake; FIG. *(diablo)* devil, Satan; COLL. *(persona pérfida)* snake (in the grass) ♦ **s. de anteojo** ZOOL. cobra • **s. cascabel** ZOOL. rattlesnake • **s. de verano** JOURN. sensational and fictitious filler • **s. monetaria** FIN. international monetary regulator.
ser·po·llar intr. BOT. to sprout, put forth shoots.
ser·po·llo m. BOT. sprout, shoot.
se·rra·do, –da adj. *(cortado)* sawed; *(con dientes)* serrated, toothed.
se·rra·dor, –do·ra I. adj. sawing **II.** m.f. sawer, sawyer.
se·rra·du·ras f.pl. CARP. sawdust.
se·rra·llo m. *(harén)* seraglio, harem; FIG. *(burdel)* brothel.
se·rra·ní·a f. mountains, mountain chain.
se·rra·nie·go, –ga adj. mountain, of mountains.
se·rra·no, –na I. adj. *(que habita en una sierra)* mountain-dwelling; *(perteneciente a las sierras)* mountain, of mountains **II.** m.f. *(persona)* mountain-dweller, highlander.
se·rrar §49 tr. to saw.
se·rre·rí·a f. sawmill.
se·rri·jón m. short mountain chain.
se·rrín m. sawdust.
se·rru·cho m. CARP. saw, handsaw; CARIB., ICHTH. sawfish ♦ **al s.** CUBA, COLL. halves, fifty-fifty.
ser·vi·ble adj. serviceable, useful.
ser·vi·cial adj. obliging, diligent.
ser·vi·cial·men·te adv. obligingly, willingly.
ser·vi·cio m. service *<a su s.* at your service>; *(criados)* help, servants; MIL. service, duty *<s. activo* active duty>; *(utilidad)* usefulness; *(orinal)* urinal; *(lavativa)* enema; *(conjunto de vajilla)* service, set *<s. de té* tea service>; *(organización)* service *<s. de correos* postal service>; *(honorario)* service charge; RELIG. service; SPORT. serve, service ♦ **al s. de** in the service of • **en s.** in service • **hacer un flaco s. a** to do a disservice to • **prestar un s.** to perform a service • **s. doméstico** domestic service • **s. militar** military service • **s. público** public service • **servicios** restroom, toilet • **s. secreto** secret service • **servicios sociales** social services.
ser·vi·dor, –do·ra I. adj. serving, attending **II.** m.f. *(criado)* servant, domestic; *(empleado)* employee, worker; *(camarero)* (food) server —m. *(pretendiente)* suitor, wooer;

(orinal) chamber pot; *(utilidad)* utility, usefulness ♦ **s. de usted** your servant, at your service • **su seguro s.** your faithful servant (close of a letter).
ser·vi·dum·bre f. *(esclavitud)* slavery, servitude; *(conjunto)* staff of servants; *(obligación)* obligation; LAW *(derecho)* easement, servitude; FIG. *(represión)* restraint, repression (of one's feelings) ♦ **s. continua** LAW continuous easement • **s. de aguas** LAW water rights • **s. de paso** or **de tránsito** LAW right-of-way.
ser·vil adj. *(de siervo)* servile, slavish; FIG. *(rastrero)* base, abject; *(de un oficio bajo)* menial, servile.
ser·vi·lis·mo m. servility, abjectness.
ser·vil·men·te adv. servilely, abjectly.
ser·vi·lle·ta f. napkin, serviette ♦ **doblar la s.** COLL. to kick the bucket, die • **estar de s. en el ojal** COLL. to be invited out to dinner.
ser·vi·lle·te·ro m. napkin or serviette ring.
ser·vio, –via adj. & m.f. var. of **serbio, –bia.**
ser·vir §48 intr. *(estar al servicio de otro)* to serve *<mi hermano sirve en el ministerio* my brother serves in the ministry>; *(valer)* to serve, be useful *<sus ideas sirvieron de base* his ideas served as a foundation>; *(poner la comida en la mesa)* to serve; MIL. to serve, be in the service; *(en los naipes)* to follow suit (in cards); *(en tenis)* to serve ♦ **no s. para nada** to be useless • **s. de** *(hacer el papel de)* to act or serve as *<s. de guía* to act as a guide>; *(valer)* to be of use • **s. para** to be of use —tr. *(reverenciar)* to serve *<s. a Dios* to serve God>; *(obsequiar)* to oblige, do a favor for; *(llenar el plato)* to serve, wait on; *(dar)* to serve *<mi madre sirvió pescado* my mother served fish>; *(cortejar)* to court, woo —reflex. *(poner comida en el plato)* to serve oneself; *(valerse)* to make use of, use; *(tener a bien)* to be good enough to *<se ha servido ayudarnos* he has been good enough to help us> ♦ **sírvase** please.
ser·vo·fre·no m. power brake.
ser·vo·me·ca·nis·mo m. servomechanism.
ser·vo·mo·tor m. MECH. servomotor.
se·sa·da f. *(de animal)* brains (of an animal); CUL. fried brains.
sé·sa·mo m. BOT. sesame ♦ **¡ábrete, Sésamo!** LIT. Open Sesame!
se·se·ar intr. PHONET. to pronounce the Spanish *c* before *e* or *i* and the *z* as an *s.*
se·sen·ta I. adj. sixty *<mi abuela tiene s. años de edad* my grandmother is sixty years old>; *(sexagésimo)* sixtieth **II.** m. sixty.
se·sen·ta·vo, –va adj. & m. sixtieth.
se·sen·tón, –to·na COLL. adj. & m.f. sixty-year-old, sexagenarian.
se·se·o m. PHONET. pronunciation of the Spanish *c* before *e* or *i* and the *z* as an *s.*
se·se·ra f. ZOOL. brainpan; COLL. *(seso humano)* brains, brain.
ses·ga·da·men·te adv. *(oblicuamente)* slantwise, obliquely; *(al sesgo)* on the bias.
ses·ga·du·ra f. *(oblicuidad)* obliqueness, bias; SEW. *(acción de cortar)* goring, cutting on the bias; *(corte)* cut on the bias; *(tela)* gusset, gore.
ses·gar §47 tr. *(inclinar)* to slant, put askew; SEW. *(cortar)* to cut on the bias.
ses·go, –ga I. adj. *(oblicuo)* oblique, slanted; SEW. *(cortado)* cut on the bias; FIG. *(grave)* stern-faced, solemn; *(torcido)* twisted, wry ♦ **al s.** *(oblicuamente)* slantwise, obliquely; SEW. *(sesgadamente)* on the bias **II.** m. *(inclinación)* slant, slope; SEW. *(corte)* bias; FIG. *(acomodo)* middle road, compromise ♦ **tomar un mal s.** FIG., COLL. to take a turn for the worse.
ses·gué, sesgue see **sesgar.**
se·sión f. *(reunión)* session, meeting; CINEM. showing ♦ **abrir la s.** to open the meeting • **estar en s.** to be in session • **levantar la s.** to adjourn the meeting • **s. espiritista** seance.
se·sio·nar intr. to hold a meeting, be in session.
se·so m. ANAT. brain; FIG. *(prudencia)* sense, good sense *<no tener s.* not to have any sense> ♦ **devanarse los sesos** FIG. to rack one's brains • **perder el s.** FIG. to lose one's mind, go crazy • **sesos** brains • **sorber los sesos a uno** to drive (one) crazy.

ses·te·a·de·ro m. shady resting place (for cattle).
ses·te·ar intr. *(descansar)* to nap, take a siesta; *(el ganado)* to rest in the shade (cattle).
ses·te·o m. *(acción de sestear)* napping, resting; *(siesta)* nap, siesta.
ses·te·ro or **ses·til** m. var. of **sesteadero**.
se·su·do, –da I. adj. *(inteligente)* brainy, intelligent; *(sensato)* sensible, wise II. m.f. *(persona inteligente)* brainy or intelligent person; *(persona sensata)* sensible or wise person.
se·ta f. BOT. mushroom.
se·te·cien·tos, –tas I. adj. seven hundred <*s. libros* seven hundred books>; *(septingentésimo)* seven-hundredth II. m. seven hundred.
se·ten·ta I. adj. seventy <*me prestó s. dólares* he lent me seventy dollars>; *(septuagésimo)* seventieth II. m. seventy.
se·ten·ta·vo, –va adj. & m. seventieth.
se·ten·tón, –to·na COLL. adj. & m.f. seventy-year-old person, septuagenarian.
se·tiem·bre m. September.
sé·ti·mo, –ma adj. & m. seventh.
se·to m. fence, enclosure ♦ **s. vivo** BOT. hedge.
seu·dó·ni·mo, –ma LIT. adj. pseudonymous II. m. pseudonym, pen name.
Se·úl Seoul.
se·ve·ra·men·te adv. *(con rigor)* severely, rigorously; *(inexorablemente)* relentlessly, unsparingly; *(rígidamente)* severely, strictly; *(gravemente)* sternly, gravely; *(duramente)* harshly, severely; *(austeramente)* austerely, severely.
se·ve·ri·dad f. *(rigor)* severity, rigor; *(inexorabilidad)* inexorableness, relentlessness; *(rigidez)* severity, strictness; *(gravedad)* sternness, graveness; *(dureza)* harshness, severity; *(austeridad)* austerity, severity.
se·ve·ro, –ra adj. *(rigoroso)* severe, rigorous; *(inexorable)* unsparing, unyielding; *(rígido)* severe, strict; *(grave)* stern, grave; *(duro)* harsh, severe; *(austero)* austere, severe.
se·xa·ge·na·rio, –ria adj. & m.f. sexagenarian.
se·xa·gé·si·mo, –ma adj. & m. sixtieth.
sex·cen·té·si·mo, –ma adj. & m. six hundredth.
se·xis·mo m. sexism, discrimination based on sex.
se·xis·ta adj. & m.f. sexist.
se·xo m. *(género)* sex <*el s. masculino* the male sex>; *(órgano)* genitals, genitalia ♦ **el bello s.** the fair sex • **el s. débil** the weaker sex • **el s. fuerte** the stronger sex.
sex·tan·te m. GEOM., MARIT. sextant.
sex·te·to m. MUS. sextet.
sex·to, –ta I. adj. sixth II. m. sixth; RELIG. book of canonical decrees; COLL. *(mandamiento)* Sixth Commandment —f. MUS. sixth.
séx·tu·plo, –pla I. adj. sextuple, sixfold II. m. sextuple.
se·xua·do, –da adj. BIOL. sexed, possessing sexual organs.
se·xual adj. sexual, sex <*vida s.* sex life>.
se·xua·li·dad f. sexuality.
Sey·che·lles Seychelles.
si¹ m. MUS. ti (seventh note of the scale).
si² §46 conj. if <*lo compraría si tuviera bastante dinero* I would buy it if I had enough money>; if, whether <*no sabemos si está casado o no* we do not know whether he is married or not>; *(aunque)* although ♦ **como si** as if • **por si acaso** just in case • **si bien** although • **si no** if not, otherwise.
sí¹ §30, 34, 38 pron. oneself, himself, herself, yourself, itself, themselves, yourselves <*ella siempre habla para sí* she always talks to herself> ♦ **dar de sí** *(ser generoso)* to give of oneself; *(alargarse)* to stretch, give • **de por sí** or **en sí** in itself, alone • **de sí** in itself • **fuera de sí** beside oneself • **para sí** to oneself • **por sí y ante sí** of one's own accord • **sí mismo** oneself <*Mateo piensa solo en sí mismo* Matthew thinks only of himself> • **sobre sí** cautiously, on guard.
sí² adv. yes; *(en la votación)* yea, aye; *(ciertamente)* certainly <*ellos sí vendrán* they will certainly come>; so <*creo que sí* I think so> ♦ **por sí o por no** in any case • **sí que** certainly • **sí tal** indeed II. m. [pl. **sí·es**] yes <*un sí categórico* a categorical yes>; *(consentimiento)* consent, per-

mission <*conseguimos el sí del maestro* we got the teacher's permission> ♦ **dar el sí** to say yes, accept.
sia·més, –me·sa I. adj. *(de Tailandia)* Siamese; PHYSIOL. Siamese <*hermanos siameses* Siamese twins> II. m.f. *(habitante)* Siamese —m. *(idioma)* Siamese ♦ **los siameses** the Siamese.
si·ba·ri·ta I. adj. sybaritic II. m.f. sybarite.
si·ba·rí·ti·co, –ca adj. sybaritic, sensuous.
si·be·ria·no, –na adj. & m.f. Siberian.
si·bi·la f. sibyl, prophetess.
si·bi·lan·te adj. & m.f. PHONET. sibilant.
si·bi·li·no, –na adj. sibylline.
si·ca·lip·sis f. pornography.
si·ca·líp·ti·co, –ca adj. pornographic.
si·ci·gia f. ASTRON. syzygy, conjunction of sun and moon.
Si·ci·lia f. GEOG. Sicily.
si·ci·lia·no, –na adj. & m.f. Sicilian.
si·co·a·ná·li·sis m. var. de **psicoanálisis**.
si·co·fan·ta or **si·co·fan·te** f. slanderer.
si·co·lo·gí·a f. var. of **psicología**.
si·có·lo·go, –ga adj. & m.f. var. of **psicólogo, –ga**.
si·có·mo·ro or **si·co·mo·ro** m. BOT. *(árbol exótico)* Egyptian sycamore; *(plátano falso)* sycamore, maple.
si·co·sis f. var. of **psicosis**.
si·co·te·ra·pia f. var. of **psicoterapia**.
si·de·ral or **si·dé·re·o** adj. ASTRON. sidereal, astral.
si·de·rur·gia f. iron and steel industry.
si·de·rúr·gi·co, –ca adj. iron and steel <*industria s.* iron and steel industry>.
si·dra f. alcoholic cider.
si·dre·rí·a f. cider shop.
sie·ga f. AGR. *(acción de segar)* harvesting, reaping; *(temporada)* harvest (time or season); *(cosecha)* harvest, crop.
sie·go, siegue see **segar**.
siem·bra f. AGR. *(acción de sembrar)* sowing, seed-planting; *(temporada)* seedtime, sowing time or season; *(sembrado)* sowed or sown land.
siem·bre, siembro see **sembrar**.
siem·pre adv. *(invariablemente)* always, all the time <*él s. mira el noticiario a las seis de la tarde* he always watches the six o'clock news>; *(por todo tiempo)* always, forever <*s. seremos amigos* we will always be friends>; AMER. surely, certainly ♦ **como s.** as always • **de s.** usual • **para or por s.** forever • **s. jamás** forever and ever • **s. lo mismo** always the same • **s. que** *(cada vez)* every time <*s. que entro en la casa, me quito los zapatos* every time I enter the house, I take off my shoes>; *(a condición de)* provided that • **s. y cuando** as long as, provided that.
siem·pre·vi·va f. BOT. everlasting flower.
sien f. ANAT. temple.
sien·ta, siento see **sentir²** or **sentar**.
sien·te, siento see **sentar** or **sentir²**.
sier·pe f. POET. *(serpiente)* serpent, snake; FIG. *(feo)* ugly-looking person, toad; *(persona feroz)* angry or fierce person; *(cosa que serpentea)* anything that winds or wriggles; BOT. shoot, sprout.
sie·rra f. TECH. *(instrumento)* saw; ICHTH. sawfish; GEOL. mountain range, sierra; PAN., ORNITH. crest, tuft ♦ **s. circular** circular or buzz saw • **s. continua** or **de cinta** band saw • **s. de cadena** chain saw • **s. de cortar metales** hacksaw • **s. de mano** handsaw.
Sie·rra Le·o·na f. Sierra Leone.
sie·rra·le·o·nés, –ne·sa adj. & m.f. Sierra Leonean.
sier·vo, –va I. adj. servile, slavish II. m.f. *(esclavo)* slave; *(esclavo feudal)* serf; *(servidor)* servant ♦ **s. de la gleba** HIST. serf • **s. de Dios** RELIG. servant of the Lord.
sies·ta f. *(calor del mediodía)* hottest part of the day; *(sueño)* afternoon nap ♦ **dormir** or **echar la s.** to take a nap after lunch • **s. del carnero** nap before lunch.
sie·te I. adj. seven <*hay s. días en la semana* there are seven days in a week>; *(séptimo)* seventh ♦ **las s.** seven o'clock II. m. *(número)* seven; CARP. clamp ♦ **más que s.** COLL. a lot.
sí·fi·lis f. MED. syphilis.
si·fi·lí·ti·co, –ca adj. & m.f. MED. syphilitic.
si·fón m. *(tubería)* U-bend, trap (in a drainpipe); *(para trasvasar líquidos)* siphon, syphon; COLL. *(agua gaseosa)* syphon or soda water.

si·fué m. EQUIT. surcingle (strap securing a saddle).

si·ga, sigo see **seguir**.

si·gi·lar tr. *(sellar)* to seal, stamp; FIG. *(ocultar)* to conceal, keep secret.

si·gi·lo m. *(sello)* seal, stamp; FIG. *(secreto)* secret, secrecy; *(discreción)* discretion, prudence.

si·gi·lo·sa·men·te adv. *(en secreto)* secretly, stealthily; *(prudentemente)* prudently, discreetly.

si·gi·lo·so, –sa adj. *(secreto)* secret, secretive; *(prudente)* discreet, prudent.

si·gla f. acronym (word formed from initials).

si·glo m. *(cien años)* century; *(época)* age, era *<el s. del átomo* the atomic age>; FIG. *(mucho tiempo)* ages, long time *<hace siglos que no te veo por aquí* I've not seen you around here for ages>; *(mundo secular)* world, wordly matters, secular life ♦ **en** or **por los siglos de los siglos** forever and ever • **Siglo de las Luces** the Enlightenment • **Siglo de Oro** or **Siglo Dorado** Golden Age.

sig·ma f. sigma (Greek letter).

sig·nar tr. *(firmar)* to sign; RELIG. to make the sign of the cross over, cross —reflex. RELIG. to cross oneself.

sig·na·to·rio, –ria adj. & m.f. signatory.

sig·na·tu·ra f. *(señal)* mark, sign; *(firma)* signature; PRINT. signature, pressmark; *(para clasificar un libro)* catalogue or call number.

sig·ni·fi·ca·ción f. *(significado)* meaning, signification; *(importancia)* significance, importance.

sig·ni·fi·ca·do, –da I. past part. see **significar** II. adj. significant, important III. m. meaning, signification.

sig·ni·fi·ca·dor, –do·ra I. adj. signifying, significant II. m.f. signifier.

sig·ni·fi·can·te adj. significant, meaningful.

sig·ni·fi·car §70 tr. *(querer decir)* to mean, signify; *(hacer saber)* to indicate, make known; *(representar)* to signify, be a sign of —intr. to signify, matter —reflex. to call attention to oneself, distinguish oneself.

sig·ni·fi·ca·ti·vo, –va adj. significative, significant.

sig·no m. *(indicio)* sign *<un s. de locura* a sign of madness>; *(rúbrica)* flourish (of a signature); *(carácter)* mark *<s. de puntuación* punctuation mark>; *(destino)* fate, destiny; ASTRON. sign (of the Zodiac); RELIG. sign of the cross; MATH., MUS. sign ♦ **s. de admiración** exclamation point • **s. de interrogación** question mark • **s. diacrítico** GRAM. diacritical mark • **s. de igual** MATH. equal sign • **s. de más** MATH. plus sign • **s. de menos** MATH. minus sign.

si·guien·te adj. following, next *<el año s.* the next year>.

si·guie·ra, si·guió see **seguir**.

sí·la·ba f. PHONET. syllable ♦ **s. abierta** open syllable • **s. aguda** or **tónica** accented or stressed syllable • **s. átona** unaccented or unstressed syllable • **s. cerrada** or **trabada** closed syllable.

si·la·ba·rio m. spelling book.

si·la·be·ar intr. to syllable.

si·la·be·o m. syllabication.

si·lá·bi·co, –ca adj. syllabic.

sil·ba f. hissing, booing.

sil·ba·dor, –do·ra or **sil·ban·te** I. adj. *(que silba)* whistling; *(que sisea)* hissing, jeering II. m.f. *(persona que silba)* whistler; *(persona que sisea)* hisser, jeerer.

sil·bar intr. *(producir silbos)* to whistle; *(una bala)* to whine, whizz (a bullet); *(sisear)* to hiss, jeer.

sil·ba·ti·na f. AMER. hissing, jeering.

sil·ba·to m. whistle.

sil·bi·do m. *(silbo)* whistle, whistling; *(de una culebra)* hiss, hissing; *(de una bala)* whining, whizzing; MED. wheeze ♦ **s. de oídos** ringing in the ears • **dar un s.** to whistle.

sil·bo m. *(silbido)* whistle, whistling; *(de una culebra)* hiss, hissing; *(de una bala)* whining, whizzing.

sil·bo·so, –sa adj. hissing, booing.

si·len·cia·dor m. *(de arma)* silencer; AUTO. muffler, silencer (G.B.).

si·len·ciar tr. *(pasar en silencio)* to keep silent about; *(ahogar)* to muffle, silence; *(ocultar)* to hush up; *(hacer callar)* to silence, make silent.

si·len·cia·rio, –ria I. adj. observing silence II. m. officer in charge of enforcing silence.

si·len·cio m. *(calma)* silence; MUS. rest ♦ **en s.** in silence • **entregar al s.** to cast into oblivion • **guardar s.** to keep silent • **pasar algo en s.** to keep silent about something, pass over something (in silence) • **reducir al s.** to silence, reduce to silence.

si·len·cio·sa·men·te adv. quietly, silently.

si·len·cio·so, –sa I. adj. quiet, silent II. m. AUTO. muffler, silencer (G.B.).

si·len·te adj. quiet, silent.

síl·fi·de f. sylph.

sil·fo m. MYTH. sylph.

si·li·ca·to m. CHEM. silicate.

sí·li·ce f. CHEM. silica.

si·li·cio m. CHEM. silicon.

si·li·co·na f. CHEM. silicone.

si·li·cua f. BOT. silique, pod.

si·lo m. silo.

si·lo·gis·mo m. LOG. syllogism.

si·lo·gís·ti·co, –ca adj. LOG. syllogistic, syllogistical.

si·lo·gi·zar §04 tr. to syllogize, argue.

si·lue·ta f. silhouette, outline.

sil·va·nos m.pl. MYTH. sylvans (forest deities).

sil·vá·ti·co, –ca adj. var. of **selvático, -co.**

sil·ves·tre adj. rustic, wild.

sil·vi·cul·tor m. forester, silviculturist.

sil·vi·cul·tu·ra f. forestry, silviculture.

sil·vo·so, –sa adj. forested, wooded.

si·lla f. *(asiento)* chair, seat; *(para montar)* saddle; *(sede)* see ♦ **s. curul** curule chair • **s. de la reina** four-hand chair • **s. de manos** sedan chair • **s. de posta** post chaise • **s. de ruedas** wheelchair • **s. de tijera** folding chair • **s. eléctrica** electric chair • **s. giratoria** swivel chair • **s. mecedora** rocking chair • **s. poltrona** easy chair, armchair • **s. turca** ANAT. Turkish saddle.

si·llar m. ARCHIT. ashlar; *(lomo)* horse's back ♦ **s. de concreto** cast stone.

si·lle·rí·a¹ *(conjunto de sillas)* chairs, set of chairs; RELIG. choir stalls; *(taller)* chair shop or factory; *(tienda)* chair store; *(oficio)* chairmaking; ARCHIT. ashlar.

si·lle·rí·a² f. *(fábrica hecha de sillares)* factory made of ashlars; *(conjunto de sillares)* ashlars, building stones.

si·lle·ro, –ra m.f. *(de asientos)* chair maker; *(de sillas de montar)* saddler; MEX. harness keeper; ARG. saddle horse.

si·lle·ta f. *(silla pequeña)* small chair; AMER. chair, seat; *(de los arreos de tiro)* mule chair; *(orinal)* bedpan.

si·lle·ta·zo m. blow with a chair.

si·llín m. *(jamuga)* sidesaddle; *(silla ligera)* light riding saddle; *(de arreos)* harness saddle; *(de bicicleta)* seat, saddle (of a bicycle).

si·llón I. m. *(silla de brazos)* armchair, easy chair; EQUIT. sidesaddle; S. AMER. rocking chair ♦ **s. giratorio** swivel chair • **s. de lona** deck chair • **s. de orejas** wing chair • **s. de ruedas** wheelchair II. adj. AMER. saddle-backed (horse).

si·llo·ne·ro, –ra adj. AMER. easily saddled (said of a horse or mule).

si·ma f. chasm, abyss.

sim·bio·sis f. symbiosis.

sim·bió·ti·co, –ca adj. symbiotic, symbiotical.

sim·bó·li·ca·men·te adv. symbolically.

sim·bó·li·co, –ca adj. symbolic, symbolical.

sim·bo·lis·mo m. symbolism.

sim·bo·lis·ta adj. & m.f. symbolist.

sim·bo·li·za·ción f. symbolization.

sim·bo·li·zar §04 tr. *(ser simbólico de)* to symbolize; *(ser típico de)* to typify.

sím·bo·lo m. symbol, emblem ♦ **s. de prestigio** status symbol • **s. químico** chemical symbol • **s. de la fe** or **de los apóstoles** RELIG. Apostles' Creed.

si·me·trí·a f. symmetry.

si·mé·tri·ca·men·te adv. symmetrically.

si·mé·tri·co, –ca adj. symmetric, symmetrical.

si·mien·te f. *(semilla)* seed; *(germen)* germ; *(semen)* semen, sperm; *(del gusano de seda)* silkworm eggs ♦ **s. de papagayos** BOT. bastard safflower.

si·mies·co, –ca adj. simian, apelike.

sí·mil I. adj. similar, alike II. m. *(semejanza)* similarity, resemblance; *(comparación)* comparison; LIT. simile.

si·mi·lar adj. similar, alike.

si·mi·li·tud f. similitude, similarity.

si·mio, –mia m.f. ZOOL. simian, monkey.
sim·pa·tí·a f. *(afecto)* liking, affection; *(afinidad)* sympathy, affinity; *(amabilidad)* likeableness, congeniality; MED. sympathy ♦ **coger s. a** to take a liking to • **ganarse la s. de** to win the affection of • **inspirar s.** to inspire affection • **tener s. a** *or* **por** to like.
sim·pa·ti·cé, simpatice see **simpatizar.**
sim·pá·ti·co, –ca I. adj. *(amable)* likeable, congenial; ANAT., MUS., PHYS., PHYSIOL. sympathetic II. m. ♦ **gran s.** ANAT. sympathetic nervous system.
sim·pa·ti·zan·te I. adj. sympathizing, supporting II. m.f. sympathizer, supporter.
sim·pa·ti·zar §04 intr. to get along (together) <*no simpatizan para nada* they don't get along at all>.
sim·ple I. adj. *(sin mezcla)* simple; *(que no es doble)* simple, single; *(fácil)* simple, easy <*un trabajo s.* an easy job>; *(sin adornos)* plain, unadorned; *(modesto)* simple, modest; *(tonto)* simple-minded; *(desabrido)* tasteless II. m.f. *(tonto)* simpleton —m. SPORT. singles (in tennis); MED. simple.
sim·ple·men·te adv. *(con sencillez)* simply, plainly; *(sencillamente)* simply.
sim·ple·za f. *(necedad)* simpleness, simplemindedness; *(ingenuidad)* ingenuousness, naïveté ♦ **simplezas** foolish remarks, nonsense.
sim·pli·ci·dad f. *(sencillez)* simplicity, simpleness; *(ingenuidad)* ingenuousness, naïveté.
sim·pli·fi·ca·ble adj. simplifiable.
sim·pli·fi·ca·ción f. simplification.
sim·pli·fi·ca·dor, –do·ra I. adj. simplifying II. m.f. simplifier.
sim·pli·fi·car §70 tr. to simplify.
sim·plis·mo m. simplism, oversimplification.
sim·plis·ta I. adj. simplistic II. m.f. simplifier.
sim·plón, –plo·na *or* **sim·plo·te** COLL. I. adj. simple, naïve II. m.f. simpleton, naïve person.
sim·po·sio *or* **sim·po·sium** m. symposium.
si·mu·la·ción f. simulation, pretense.
si·mu·la·cro m. *(imagen)* simulacrum, image; *(fingimiento)* pretense, sham; *(burla)* mockery; *(representación)* mock-up, mock representation; MIL. war games.
si·mu·la·do, –da I. past part. see **simular** II. adj. simulated, feigned.
si·mu·la·dor, –do·ra I. adj. simulating II. m.f. simulator.
si·mu·lar tr. to simulate, feign.
si·mul·tá·ne·a·men·te adv. simultaneously.
si·mul·ta·nei·dad f. simultaneity.
si·mul·tá·ne·o, –a adj. simultaneous.
si·mún m. simoom, simoon.
sin §G46 prep. without <*él salió s. abrigo* he went out without a coat>; *(fuera de)* besides, not including <*ellos nos cobraron cien dólares s. los gastos de envío* they charged us one hundred dollars, not including the postage>; without <*salieron s. advertirnos* they went out without telling us>; un- <*dejaron mucho s. hacer* they left much undone>; -less <*me quedé s. blanca* I was left penniless> ♦ **s. embargo** however, nevertheless • **s. que** without <*robaron el banco s. que la policía los capturara* they robbed the bank without being caught by the police>.
si·na·go·ga f. RELIG. synagogue.
sin·ce·ra·men·te adv. sincerely.
sin·ce·rar tr. to exculpate, exonerate.
sin·ce·ri·dad f. sincerity ♦ **con toda s.** in all sincerity.
sin·ce·ro, –ra adj. sincere.
sin·cli·nal m. GEOL. syncline.
sín·co·pa f. GRAM. syncope; MUS. syncopation.
sin·co·pa·do, –da I. past part. see **sincopar** II. adj. MUS. syncopated.
sin·co·par tr. GRAM., MUS. to syncopate; FIG. *(abreviar)* to abbreviate, abridge.
sín·co·pe m. GRAM. syncope; MED. syncope, fainting spell ♦ **s. cardíaco** heart attack.
sin·cré·ti·co, –ca adj. syncretic.
sin·cre·tis·mo m. syncretism.
sin·cre·tis·ta I. adj. syncretistic, syncretistical II. m.f. syncretist.
sin·cro·ní·a f. synchrony.
sin·cró·ni·co, –ca adj. synchronic, synchronous.

sin·cro·nis·mo m. synchronism, simultaneity.
sin·cro·ni·za·ción f. synchronization.
sin·cro·ni·zar §04 tr. to synchronize —intr. RAD. to tune in.
sin·di·ca·ción f. *(acción de sindicar)* syndication; *(acusación)* accusation.
sin·di·ca·dor, –do·ra I. adj. *(organizador)* syndicating; *(acusador)* accusing II. m.f. *(organizador)* trade unionist; *(acusador)* accuser.
sin·di·cal adj. union, trade-union <*movimiento s.* trade-union movement>.
sin·di·ca·lis·mo m. unionism, trade unionism.
sin·di·ca·lis·ta I. adj. union, trade-union II. m.f. unionist, trade unionist.
sin·di·ca·li·za·ción f. unionization.
sin·di·ca·li·zar §04 tr. to unionize —reflex. *(formar sindicato)* to form a labor *or* trade union; *(unirse a un sindicato)* to join a labor *or* trade union.
sin·di·car §70 tr. *(formar un sindicato)* to unionize; COM. to syndicate; *(acusar)* to accuse; *(destinar dinero)* to put into trust —reflex. *(formar un sindicato)* to form a labor *or* trade union; *(unirse a un sindicato)* to join a labor *or* trade union.
sin·di·ca·to m. *(de obreros)* labor *or* trade union; COM. syndicate.
sin·di·ca·tu·ra f. COM. post of syndic *or* representative; LAW trusteeship; *(de una quiebra)* receivership.
sín·di·co m. COM. syndic, representative; LAW trustee; *(de una quiebra)* receiver.
sin·di·qué, sindique see **sindicar.**
sín·dro·me m. syndrome.
si·ne·cu·ra f. sinecure.
si·ner·gí·a f. PHYSIOL. synergism, synergy.
sin·fín m. endless number *or* quantity <*hizo un s. de sugerencias* she made an endless number of suggestions>.
sin·fo·ní·a f. MUS. symphony.
sin·fó·ni·co, –ca adj. MUS. symphonic, symphony <*orquesta s.* symphony orchestra>.
Sin·ga·pur m. Singapore.
sin·ga·pu·ren·se adj. & m.f. Singaporean.
sin·gu·lar I. adj. *(único)* single, singular; *(excepcional)* unique, exceptional; *(peculiar)* peculiar, odd II. m. GRAM. singular ♦ **en s.** FIG. in particular.
sin·gu·la·ri·dad f. *(calidad de singular)* singularity; *(carácter excepcional)* uniqueness; *(peculiaridad)* peculiarity.
sin·gu·la·ri·zar §04 tr. *(distinguir)* to distinguish, make stand out; GRAM. to make singular, use in the singular —reflex. to distinguish oneself, stand out.
sin·gu·lar·men·te adv. singularly.
sin·hue·so f. COLL. tongue ♦ **soltar la s.** COLL. to shoot off one's mouth.
si·nies·tra·do, –da I. adj. victimized, injured; HER. sinister II. m.f. victim.
si·nies·tro, –tra I. adj. *(izquierdo)* left <*mano s.* left hand>; left, left-hand <*lado s.* left-hand side>; *(perverso)* sinister, wicked; *(funesto)* fateful, unlucky II. m. *(perversidad)* perversity, bad disposition *or* habit; *(accidente)* disaster, accident —f. left hand; *(lado)* left-hand side.
sin·nú·me·ro m. countless *or* endless number <*un s. de invitados* a countless number of guests>.
si·no[1] m. fate, destiny.
si·no[2] §G46 conj. but <*no llegué el martes s. el jueves* I did not arrive on Tuesday but on Thursday>; *(excepto)* except, save <*nadie lo sabía s. Pedro* no one knew it except Peter> ♦ **no sólo ... s.** not only ... but also <*no sólo es rico s. generoso* he is not only rich but also generous> • **s. que** only that, but that <*no quiero s. que me oigas* I want only that you listen to me>.
si·nó·di·co, –ca adj. RELIG. synodal, synodical; ASTRON. synodical, synodic.
sí·no·do m. RELIG. synod ♦ **Santo S.** RELIG. Holy Synod.
si·no·ja·po·nés, –ne·sa adj. Sino-Japanese.
si·no·lo·gí·a f. Sinology.
si·nó·lo·go, –ga I. adj. Sinological II. m.f. Sinologist.
si·no·ni·mia f. synonymy, synonymity.
si·nó·ni·mo, –ma I. adj. synonymous II. m. synonym.
si·nop·sis f. [pl. **-sis**] synopsis.
si·nóp·ti·co, –ca adj. synoptic, synoptical.

sin·ra·zón f. *(injusticia)* wrong, injustice; *(disparate)* nonsense, absurdity.

sin·sa·bor m. FIG. *(disgusto)* discontent, displeasure; *(pena)* trouble, grief.

sin·tác·ti·co, –ca adj. syntactic.

sin·ta·xis m. [pl. **-xis**] GRAM. syntax.

sín·te·sis f. [pl. **-sis**] synthesis.

sin·té·ti·ca·men·te adv. synthetically.

sin·té·ti·co, –ca adj. synthetic, synthetical.

sin·te·ti·za·dor m. MUS. synthesizer.

sin·te·ti·zar §04 tr. to synthesize.

sin·tie·ra, sintió see **sentir²**.

sin·to·ís·mo m. RELIG. Shinto, Shintoism.

sin·to·ís·ta adj. & m.f. Shintoist.

sín·to·ma m. symptom.

sin·to·má·ti·co, –ca adj. symptomatic.

sin·to·ní·a f. RAD. *(ajuste)* tuning (in); *(tema musical)* musical theme.

sin·to·ni·za·ción f. tuning.

sin·to·ni·za·dor m. tuning knob, tuner.

sin·to·ni·zar §04 tr. to tune (in) ♦ **s. con** to be tuned to.

si·nuo·si·dad f. *(calidad de sinuoso)* sinuosity; *(curva)* curve, bend; *(hueco)* cavity, hollow.

si·nuo·so, –sa adj. *(ondulado)* sinuous, winding; FIG. *(engañoso)* devious, secretive.

si·nu·soi·de f. GEOM. sinusoid.

sin·ver·gon·zón, –zo·na I. adj. shameless, brazen II. m.f. shameless *or* brazen person.

sin·ver·güen·ce·rí·a f. COLL. shamelessness, brazenness.

sin·ver·güen·za I. adj. COLL. shameless, brazen II. m.f. COLL. shameless *or* brazen person.

sin·ver·güen·za·da f. AMER. COLL. dirty trick.

Sión Zion.

sio·nis·mo m. Zionism.

sio·nis·ta adj. & m.f. Zionist.

si·quí·a·tra *or* **si·quia·tra** m.f. MED. psychiatrist.

si·quia·trí·a f. MED. psychiatry.

sí·qui·co, –ca adj. psychic.

si·quie·ra I. conj. *(aunque)* although, even though, if only <*ven a verme, s. por una hora* come and see me, if only for an hour> II. adv. *(por lo menos)* at least <*espéreme diez minutos s.* wait for me for ten minutes at least>; COL. provided that ♦ **ni s.** not even <*ni s. nos miró* he did not even look at us>.

Si·ra·cu·sa Syracuse.

si·re·na f. MYTH. mermaid; FIG. *(mujer seductora)* siren; *(aparato)* siren ♦ **s. de niebla** foghorn • **s. de la playa** bathing beauty.

Si·ria, República Árabe f. Syrian Arab Republic.

si·rin·ga f. S. AMER., BOT. rubber tree; MUS. syrinx, shepherd's flute.

si·rio, –ria adj. & m.f. Syrian.

sir·va, sirvo see **servir**.

sir·vien·ta f. maid, servant.

sir·vien·te I. adj. serving II. m. servant.

sir·vie·ra, sirvió see **servir**.

si·sa¹ f. *(hurto)* petty theft, pilfering; SEW. dart, tapering seam.

si·sa² f. size, sizing.

si·sa·dor, –do·ra I. adj. stealing, pilfering II. m.f. pilferer, thief.

si·sar tr. *(hurtar)* to pilfer, steal; *(una falda)* to dart, take in.

si·se·ar tr. & intr. to hiss, boo.

si·se·o m. hissing, booing.

sís·mi·co, –ca adj. GEOL. seismic.

sis·mo m. earthquake, seism.

sis·mó·gra·fo m. GEOL. seismograph.

sis·mo·lo·gí·a f. GEOL. seismology.

sis·te·ma m. system ♦ **con s.** systematically <*trabajar con s.* to work systematically> • **por s.** as a rule • **s. métrico** *or* **métrico decimal** metric system • **s. nervioso** ANAT. nervous system • **s. periódico** CHEM. periodic system • **s. planetario** *or* **solar** ASTRON. solar system • **s. respiratorio** ANAT. respiratory system.

sis·te·má·ti·ca I. f. systematics II. adj. see **sistemático, –ca**.

sis·te·má·ti·ca·men·te adv. systematically.

sis·te·má·ti·co, –ca I. adj. systematic II. f. see **sistemática**.

sis·te·ma·ti·za·ción f. systematization.

sis·te·ma·ti·zar §04 tr. to systemize, systematize.

sís·to·le f. PHYSIOL. systole.

si·tia·do, –da I. past part. see **sitiar** II. adj. besieged III. m.f. besieged person.

si·tia·dor, –do·ra I. adj. besieging II. m.f. besieger.

si·tial m. seat of honor, high position.

si·tiar tr. MIL. to lay siege, to besiege; FIG. *(rodear)* to surround, hem in.

si·tio m. *(localidad)* site, location; *(lugar)* place <*el libro no está en su s.* the book is not in its place>; *(hacienda)* country estate *or* home; MIL. siege; CUBA small farm; ARG., CHILE building site; COL. town, settlement.

si·to, –ta adj. situated, located.

si·tua·ción f. *(conjunto de circunstancias)* situation, circumstances <*en su s. yo haría la misma cosa* in your situation, I would do the same thing>; *(sitio)* site, location; *(estado)* position <*estar en brillante s.* to be in an excellent position>; *(postura)* position, posture.

si·tua·do, –da I. past part. see **situar** II. m. fixed income.

si·tuar §67 tr. *(poner)* to place, put; *(colocar)* to place, locate; *(asignar dinero)* to assign, set aside (money).

smo·king m. dinner jacket, tuxedo.

snob I. adj. snobbish II. m.f. snob.

sno·bis·mo m. snobbism.

so¹ m. COLL. you ♦ **¡s. tonto!** you idiot!

so² prep. under ♦ **s. capa de** *or* **color de** on the pretense of, under the pretext of • **s. pena de muerte** under pain of death.

¡so! interj. whoa! (to a horse).

so·a·sar tr. CUL. to roast lightly.

so·ba f. *(acción de sobar)* kneading; COLL. *(paliza)* thrashing, beating.

so·ba·co m. ANAT. armpit.

so·ba·de·ro, –ra I. adj. kneadable II. m. fulling mill (for skins).

so·ba·do, –da I. past part. see **sobar** II. adj. CUL. kneaded; *(trillado)* worn, shabby; AMER., COLL. huge, big.

so·ba·dor m. fulling machine.

so·ba·du·ra f. *(amasadura)* kneading; *(de pieles)* fulling.

so·ba·jar *or* **so·ba·je·ar** tr. *(manosear)* to finger, handle; AMER., FIG. to humiliate.

so·ba·je·o m. fingering, handling.

so·ba·que·ra f. *(abertura)* armhole; *(refuerzo)* armhole reinforcement; *(resguardo del vestido)* dress *or* underarm shield; C. AMER., MEX. underarm odor.

so·ba·qui·na f. underarm odor.

so·bar tr. *(manosear)* to knead; to full <*el sobó las pieles* he fulled the skins>; FIG. *(zurrar)* to thrash, beat; *(magrear)* to fondle, paw; *(molestar)* to pester, bother; AMER. to set (bones); CHILE to defeat; ECUAD. to scrub, scour; AMER. to flatter, soft-soap.

so·bar·ba f. *(de la brida)* noseband (of a horse); *(papada)* double chin.

so·bar·ba·da f. *(de un caballo)* sudden checking *or* reining (of a horse); FIG. *(reprensión)* scolding, tongue-lashing.

so·bar·bo m. *(de una rueda hidráulica)* bucket, vane (of a water wheel); TEX. cam (of a fulling mill).

so·be·o m. *(correa)* strap, thong; COLL. *(soba)* fondling, pawing.

so·be·ra·na·men·te adv. *(extremadamente)* extremely, highly; *(con soberanía)* with authority.

so·be·ra·ne·ar tr. to dominate, rule over.

so·be·ra·ní·a f. sovereignty.

so·be·ra·no, –na I. adj. sovereign, supreme <*potencia s.* sovereign power> II. m.f. *(monarca)* sovereign, monarch —m. NUMIS. sovereign.

so·ber·bia I. f. *(orgullo)* pride, arrogance; *(magnificencia)* magnificence, grandeur; *(ira)* anger, fury II. adj. see **soberbio, –bia**.

so·ber·bia·men·te adv. *(orgullosamente)* arrogantly, haughtily; *(magníficamente)* magnificently, superbly.

so·ber·bio, –bia I. adj. *(orgulloso)* arrogant, haughty; FIG. *(magnífico)* magnificent, superb; *(un caballo)* fiery, spirited (horse) II. f. see **soberbia**.

so·bo m. var. of **soba**.

so·bón, –bo·na I. adj. COLL. *(que acaricia mucho)* mushy, overly fond; *(holgazán)* idle, lazy; *(adulador)* fawning, flattering II. m.f. COLL. *(persona que acaricia mucho)* mushy *or* overly fond person; *(holgazán)* idler, loafer; PERU soft-soaper, flatterer.

so·bor·na·ble adj. bribable, venal.

so·bor·na·dor, –do·ra I. adj. bribing II. m.f. briber.

so·bor·nal m. overload.

so·bor·nar tr. to bribe, corrupt.

so·bor·no m. *(acción de sobornar)* bribery, bribing; *(dádiva)* bribe; AMER. extra load, overload ◊ **de s.** AMER. in addition, additional.

so·bra f. excess, surplus ◊ **de s.** superfluous, more than enough • **estar de s.** to be one too many • **sobras** leftovers.

so·bra·da·men·te adv. only too well, more than enough.

so·bra·do, –da I. past part. see **sobrar** II. adj. *(excesivo)* plenty of, more than enough; *(audaz)* bold, brazen; *(rico)* rich, wealthy; CHILE tremendous, huge III. adv. too, excessively IV. m. ARCHIT. attic, garret; ARG. kitchen shelf ◊ **sobrados** CHILE leftovers.

so·bran·te I. adj. *(que sobra)* leftover, remaining; *(excesivo)* excess, surplus II. m. excess, surplus.

so·brar tr. to exceed, surpass —intr. *(estar de más)* to be more than enough *or* too much; *(quedar)* to be left over, remain; *(ser inútil)* to be unnecessary *or* superfluous.

so·bra·sa·da f. sausage from Majorca.

so·bre[1] m. *(cubierta)* envelope; *(sobrescrito)* address (on a letter).

so·bre[2] prep. *(encima)* above, over <*los pájaros volaron s. los verdes campos* the birds flew over the green fields>; *(en)* on, on top of <*ella puso el mantel s. la mesa* she put the tablecloth on the table>; *(superior a)* above, over <*el rango de capitán está s. el de teniente* the rank of captain is above that of lieutenant>; *(acerca de)* about, on <*escribí un ensayo s. los problemas sociológicos* I wrote an essay about the sociological problems>; *(más o menos)* about, around <*vendremos s. las dos* we will come at about two o'clock>; *(además de)* on top of, over <*me dieron cincuenta dólares s. lo acordado* they gave me fifty dollars over what was agreed upon>; *(tras)* on top of, upon <*insulto s. insulto* one insult on top of another>; *(en prenda de)* on, against <*un préstamo s. la finca* a loan on the farm>; on <*un impuesto s. la mercancía importada* a tax on imported goods>; *(de)* in, out of <*seis s. cien* six out of one hundred> ◊ **dar s.** to give onto, face • **s. manera** exceedingly • **s. que** besides • **s. todo** above all, especially.

so·bre·a·bun·dan·cia f. superabundance.

so·bre·a·bun·dan·te adj. superabundant.

so·bre·a·bun·dar intr. to be superabundant *or* overabundant ◊ **s. en** to superabound in.

so·bre·a·li·men·ta·ción f. overfeeding.

so·bre·a·li·men·tar tr. to overfeed.

so·bre·a·ña·dir tr. to add extra.

so·bre·ca·ma f. bedspread.

so·bre·ca·ña f. VET. bony tumor (on a horse's leg).

so·bre·car·ga f. *(exceso de carga)* overload; *(soga)* packing strap; FIG. *(preocupación)* extra burden.

so·bre·car·gar §47 tr. *(cargar demasiado)* to overload, overburden; SEW. to fell (a seam).

so·bre·ce·jo *or* **so·bre·ce·ño** m. frown, scowl.

so·bre·cie·lo m. awning, canopy.

so·bre·cin·cha f. surcingle.

so·bre·co·ger §34 tr. to surprise, catch unawares —reflex. to be surprised.

so·bre·co·gi·mien·to m. surprise, astonishment.

so·bre·co·si·do m. *or* **so·bre·cos·tu·ra** f. SEW. whipstitch.

so·bre·cu·bier·ta f. *(de un objeto)* cover; *(de un libro)* dust jacket.

so·bre·cue·llo m. overcollar.

so·bre·di·cho, –cha adj. aforementioned, above-mentioned.

so·bre·dien·te m. snaggletooth.

so·bre·do·rar tr. *(un metal)* to gild; FIG. *(disimular)* to gloss over.

so·bre·en·ten·der §50 tr. & reflex. var. of **sobrentender**.

so·bre·en·ten·di·do, –da I. past part. see **sobreentender** II. adj. understood, implicit.

so·bre·es·drú·ju·lo, –la adj. var. of **sobresdrújulo, –la.**

so·bre·ex·ci·ta·ción f. overexcitement.

so·bre·ex·ci·tar tr. to overexcite.

so·bre·fal·da f. overskirt.

so·bre·haz f. [pl. **-ha·ces**] *(sobrefaz)* surface, outside; *(cubierta)* cover.

so·bre·hi·la·do I. past part. see **sobrehilar** II. m. SEW. overcast stitch.

so·bre·hi·lar §81 tr. SEW. to overcast, whipstitch.

so·bre·hue·so m. VET. bony tumor; FIG. *(molestia)* trouble, nuisance.

so·bre·hu·ma·no, –na adj. superhuman.

so·bre·jal·ma f. blanket for a packsaddle.

so·bre·lla·ve f. double lock.

so·bre·lle·nar tr. to overfill.

so·bre·lle·var tr. *(ayudar a llevar una carga)* to help carry (a load); FIG. *(ayudar a sufrir)* to comfort; *(resignarse)* to put up with, bear; *(disimular)* to overlook (another's faults).

so·bre·ma·ne·ra adv. excessively, exceedingly.

so·bre·me·sa f. *(tapete)* table cover *or* covering; *(postre)* dessert; *(conversación)* after-dinner conversation ◊ **de s.** after-dinner.

so·bre·na·dar intr. to float.

so·bre·na·tu·ral adj. supernatural.

so·bre·nom·bre m. nickname.

so·bren·ten·der §50 tr. to understand (something implied), infer —reflex. to be understood, go without saying.

so·bre·pa·ga f. *(aumento)* pay raise; *(gratificación)* bonus.

so·bre·pa·sar intr. to exceed, surpass.

so·bre·pe·lliz f. RELIG. surplice.

so·bre·pe·so m. *(obesidad)* overweight, obesity; *(sobrecarga)* overload, extra load.

so·bre·po·ner §54 tr. to superimpose, place on top; *(añadir)* to add —reflex. FIG. *(controlarse)* to control *or* master oneself; *(vencer)* to triumph.

so·bre·pre·cio m. extra charge, surcharge.

so·bre·pro·duc·ción f. overproduction.

so·bre·puer·ta f. ARCHIT. cornice; *(para cortinas)* valance, frame for hanging curtains over a doorway).

so·bre·pues·to, –ta I. past part. see **sobreponer** II. adj. *(puesto encima)* superimposed; SEW. appliqué III. m. SEW. appliqué (work); ARG. honeycomb formed after the hive is full.

so·bre·pu·jar tr. to surpass, outdo.

so·bre·pu·sie·ra, sobrepuso see **sobreponer.**

so·bre·sal·drá, sobresaldría see **sobresalir.**

so·bre·sal·ga, sobresalgo see **sobresalir.**

so·bre·sa·lien·te I. adj. *(saliente)* projecting, overhanging; *(notable)* outstanding <*uno de los sucesos sobresalientes de este año* one of the outstanding events of this year> II. m. *(grado)* highest mark *or* grade —m.f. FIG. *(substituto)* substitute; THEAT. understudy.

so·bre·sa·lir §63 intr. *(resaltar)* to project, jut out; *(sobrepujar)* to excel, be outstanding.

so·bre·sal·tar tr. to frighten, startle —intr. to stand out, be outstanding —reflex. ◊ **sobresaltarse con** *or* **por** to be startled by, to start at.

so·bre·sal·to m. start, fright ◊ **de s.** suddenly, unexpectedly.

so·bre·sa·nar tr. *(una herida)* to heal superficially; FIG. *(un defecto)* to gloss over, cover up.

so·bre·sa·tu·ra·ción f. CHEM. supersaturation.

so·bres·cri·to, –ta m. address (on a letter).

so·bres·drú·ju·lo, –la I. adj. accented on the syllable preceding the antepenult II. m. word accented on the syllable preceding the antepenult.

so·bre·sei·mien·to m. LAW stay (of proceedings) ◊ **s. definitivo** dismissal • **s. libre** nonsuit • **s. provisional** *or* **temporal** temporary stay.

so·bres·tan·te m. supervisor.

so·bres·ti·mar tr. to overestimate.

so·bre·suel·do m. bonus, extra pay.

so·bre·to·do m. overcoat.

so·bre·ve·ni·da f. sudden *or* unexpected occurrence.

so·bre·ve·nir §76 intr. *(venir improvisamente)* to happen *or* occur unexpectedly; *(suceder)* to follow, ensue.

so·bre·vi·vien·te I. adj. surviving II. m.f. survivor.

so·bre·vi·vir intr. to survive.

so·bria·men·te adv. soberly.

so·brie·dad f. sobriety, moderation.

so·bri·no, –na m. nephew —f. niece.

so·brio, –bria adj. *(sin beber)* sober; *(conservador)* sober, moderate.

so·cai·re m. MARIT. lee <*al s.* leeward> ♦ **estar** or **ponerse al s.** FIG. to be protected.

so·ca·li·ña f. cunning, trickery.

so·ca·li·ñar tr. to get by cunning or trickery.

so·ca·li·ñe·ro, –ra I. adj. cunning, crafty II. m.f. cunning or crafty person.

so·ca·pa f. COLL. pretext, pretense ♦ **a s.** surreptitiously.

so·ca·rra f. *(acción de socarrar)* to scorch, singe; *(astucia)* cunning, slyness.

so·ca·rrar tr. to scorch, singe.

so·ca·rre·na f. *(hueco)* hollow, cavity; ARCHIT. space between rafters.

so·ca·rri·na f. COLL. singeing, scorching.

so·ca·rrón, –na I. adj. *(sarcástico)* sarcastic, ironic; *(taimado)* sly, cunning II. m.f. *(person sarcástica)* sarcastic or ironic person; *(persona taimada)* sly or cunning person.

so·ca·rro·ne·rí·a f. *(sarcasmo)* sarcasm, irony; *(astucia)* slyness, cunning.

so·ca·va f. *(acción de socavar)* excavation, digging under; AGR. trench dug around trees to hold irrigation water.

so·ca·va·ción f. undermining, digging under.

so·ca·var tr. *(excavar)* to dig under, excavate; FIG. *(una posición)* to undermine (a position).

so·ca·vón m. *(mina)* gallery, tunnel; *(hundimiento)* cave-in.

so·cia·bi·li·dad f. sociability, friendliness.

so·cia·ble adj. sociable, friendly.

so·cial adj. social.

so·cia·lis·mo m. socialism.

so·cia·lis·ta adj. & m.f. socialist.

so·cia·li·za·ción f. socialization.

so·cia·li·zar §04 tr. to socialize (property).

so·cie·dad f. *(cuerpo social)* society <*la s. feudal* feudal society>; *(asociación)* society, association; COM. company, corporation ♦ **alta** or **buena s.** high society • **formar s.** to associate • **s. anónima** COM. stock company, corporation • **s. comanditaria** or **en comandita** COM. limited partnership • **s. conyugal** LAW joint ownership of property by husband and wife • **s. cooperativa** COM. cooperative partnership • **s. de cartera** COM. investment trust • **s. de control** COM. holding company • **s. de crédito** COM. credit union • **S. de las Naciones** POL. League of Nations • **s. de responsabilidad limitada** COM. limited-liability company • **s. gremial** trade union • **s. mercantil** COM. trading company • **s. regular colectiva** COM. general partnership, copartnership • **s. secreta** secret society.

so·cio, –cia m.f. *(asociado)* member, fellow; *(accionista)* partner, business associate; COLL. *(amigo)* pal, friend ♦ **s. capitalista** COM. financial partner • **s. comanditario** or **pasivo** COM. silent partner • **s. honorario** or **de honor** honorary member • **s. de número** full member.

so·cio·e·co·nó·mi·co, –ca adj. socioeconomic.

so·cio·lo·gí·a f. sociology.

so·cio·ló·gi·co, –ca adj. sociological.

so·ció·lo·go, –ga m.f. sociologist.

so·co, –ca I. adj. CHILE, P. RICO one-armed; C. AMER. drunk II. m. COL. stump (of an amputated limb).

so·co·lor m. pretext, pretense ♦ **s. de** under the pretext of.

so·co·rrer tr. to help, aid.

so·co·rri·do, –da I. past part. see **socorrer** II. adj. *(dispuesto a socorrer)* helpful; *(abastecido)* well-stocked, well-supplied; *(común)* hackneyed, trite.

so·co·rro I. m. *(apoyo)* help, aid; MIL. *(tropas)* reinforcements, relief; *(provisiones)* supplies, provisions II. interj. help! ♦ **puesto de s.** first-aid station • **señal de s.** distress signal.

so·crá·ti·co, –ca adj. & m.f. Socratic.

so·dio m. CHEM. sodium.

So·do·ma m. Sodom.

so·do·mí·a f. sodomy.

so·do·mi·ta I. adj. sodomitical II. m.f. sodomite.

so·ez adj. [pl. **-e·ces**] crude, vulgar.

so·fá m. [pl. **-fás**] sofa.

so·fal·dar tr. *(las faldas)* to truss or tuck up (skirts); FIG. *(descubrir)* to uncover.

so·fí m. [pl. **-fí·es**] HIST. Persian ruler.

so·fión m. *(de enfado)* snort (of anger); *(trabuco)* blunderbuss.

so·fis·ma m. sophism.

so·fis·ta I. adj. sophistic II. m.f. sophist.

so·fis·te·rí·a f. or **so·fí·sti·ca** sophistry.

so·fis·ti·ca·ción f. sophistication.

so·fis·ti·ca·do, –da I. past part. see **sofisticar** II. adj. sophisticated.

so·fis·ti·car §70 tr. *(quitar naturalidad)* to sophisticate; FIG. *(falsificar)* to falsify, doctor.

so·fís·ti·co, –ca adj. sophistic, fallacious.

so·fla·ma f. *(del fuego)* glow, flicker; *(en el rostro)* blush, flush; FIG. *(engaño)* trick, ruse; *(roncería)* flattery, cajolery; *(discurso)* speech, harangue.

so·fla·mar tr. *(engañar)* to trick, bamboozle; *(avergonzar)* to make blush —reflex. to get scorched.

so·fla·me·rí·a f. COLL. bamboozlement.

so·fo·ca·ción f. *(asfixia)* suffocation, smothering; *(ahogo)* choking sensation; FIG. *(disgusto)* embarrassment.

so·fo·ca·dor, –do·ra or **so·fo·can·te** adj. suffocating, stifling.

so·fo·car §70 tr. *(asfixiar)* to suffocate, smother; *(un fuego)* to smother, put out; *(una rebelión)* to suppress, put down; *(avergonzar)* to embarrass, make blush; COLL. *(irritar)* to anger, provoke; *(acosar)* to pester, badger —reflex. *(asfixiarse)* to suffocate, choke; FIG. *(avergonzarse)* to get embarrassed, blush; COLL. *(irritarse)* to get angry or provoked.

so·fo·co m. *(asfixia)* suffocation, smothering; *(ahogo)* choking sensation; FIG. *(disgusto)* embarrassment; COLL. *(enojo)* annoyance, vexation ♦ **pasar un s.** FIG. to suffer an embarrassment.

so·fo·cón m. COLL. *(gran disgusto)* shock; *(enojo)* annoyance, vexation ♦ **darle un s. (a uno)** COLL. to have a fit.

so·fo·qué, sofoque see **sofocar.**

so·fre·ír §58 tr. to fry lightly.

so·fre·na·da f. EQUIT. saccade, sudden check (on the reins); FIG. *(reprimenda)* reprimand, scolding.

so·fre·nar tr. EQUIT. to rein in suddenly, check; FIG. *(reprender)* to reprimand, scold; FIG. *(moderar)* to restrain, control.

so·fri·to I. past part. see **sofreír** II. m. CUL. lightly fried dish.

so·ga f. *(cuerda)* rope; ARCHIT. face (of brick and stone) ♦ **dar s. a alguien** FIG., COLL. to wind someone up, excite someone • **echar la s. tras el caldero** FIG., COLL. to throw the baby out with the bath water • **con la s. al cuello** or **a la garganta** FIG., COLL. with the knife at one's throat.

so·gue·ar tr. AMER. to tie (an animal) with a long rope; COL. to make fun of; CUBA to break, tame.

so·gue·ro m. ropemaker.

so·ja f. BOT. soya, soybean.

so·juz·ga·dor, –do·ra I. adj. subduing, subjugating II. m.f. subduer, subjugator.

so·juz·gar §47 tr. to subdue, subjugate.

sol[1] m. ASTRON. sun; FIG. *(luz)* sun, sunshine, sunlight <*están sentadas al s.* they are sitting in the sun>; *(día)* day; *(joya)* gem, treasure <*Juanito es un s.* Johnny is a treasure>; TAUR. seats on the sunny side of the ring; PERU, FIN. sol (coin) ♦ **adorar el s. que nace** FIG. to jump on the bandwagon • **al ponerse el s.** at sunset • **al salir el s.** at sunrise • **arrimarse al s. que más calienta** FIG. to know on which side one's bread is buttered • **de s. a s.** from sunrise to sunset • **hacer s.** to be sunny • **no dejar a s. ni a sombra a alguien** FIG. to harass, give someone no peace • **s. de las Indias** BOT. sunflower • **tomar el s.** to sunbathe; MARIT. to take the sun's altitude.

sol[2] m. MUS. sol, so (fifth note of the scale).

so·la·cé, solace see **solazar.**

so·la·ce·ar var. of **solazar.**

so·la·do m. or **so·la·du·ra** f. flooring.

so·la·dor m. floorer.

so·la·men·te adv. only ♦ **s. que** provided that.

so·la·na f. *(sitio)* sunny spot; *(en una casa)* solarium, sun room.

so·la·no m. BOT. nightshade; *(viento)* east wind.

so·la·pa f. *(de sobre)* flap; *(de chaqueta)* lapel; FIG. *(pretexto)* pretext ♦ **de s.** stealthily, secretly • **junta de s.** lap joint.

so·la·pa·da·men·te adv. underhandedly, slyly.

so·la·pa·do, –da I. past part. see **solapar** II. adj. underhanded, sly.

so·la·par tr. SEW. to put lapels on; FIG. *(traslapar)* to overlap; FIG. *(ocultar)* to cover up, conceal —intr. to overlap (garment).

so·lar¹ adj. solar, sun <*sistema s.* solar system>.

so·lar² m. *(terreno)* lot, plot; *(terreno bajo construcción)* building site; *(casa solariega)* ancestral home, family seat; FIG. *(linaje)* family, lineage; AMER. backyard; CUBA, PERU tenement.

so·lar³ §19 tr. *(el suelo)* to pave, tile (a floor); *(un calzado)* to sole (a shoe).

so·la·rie·go, –ga adj. *(del patrimonio)* family, ancestral; *(noble)* noble.

so·la·rium or **so·la·rio** m. solarium.

so·laz m. [pl. **-la·ces**] *(descanso)* relaxation, recreation; *(consuelo)* solace, consolation ♦ **a s.** with pleasure, happily.

so·la·zar §04 tr. *(descansar)* to relax, amuse; *(consolar)* to solace, console —reflex. to relax, amuse oneself.

so·la·zo m. COLL. scorching or blazing sunshine.

sol·da·des·co, –ca I. adj. soldierly, soldier-like II. f. rowdy or unruly gang of soldiers.

sol·da·do I. past part. see **soldar** II. m. MIL. soldier; ENTOM. soldier (ant, termite) ♦ **s. primero** private first-class • **s. raso** private • **s. de caballería** cavalryman • **s. de infantería** infantryman • **s. de marina** marine • **s. de Pavia** CUL. fried breaded haddock • **s. de plomo** tin soldier • **s. de sanidad** medical corpsman.

sol·da·dor m. *(obrero)* solderer, welder; *(hierro)* soldering iron; *(soplete)* blow torch.

sol·da·du·ra f. *(acción)* soldering, welding; *(material)* solder; *(juntura)* soldered joint, weld; FIG. *(compostura)* repair, mending • **s. autógena** welding • **s. por arco** arc welding • **s. por puntos** spot-welding.

sol·dar §19 tr. *(pegar)* to solder, weld; FIG. *(unir)* to join, unite; *(componer)* to repair, mend —reflex. *(pegarse)* to join together; FIG. *(sanar)* to knit (bones).

so·le·a·do I. past part. see **solear** II. adj. sunny.

so·le·ar tr. to expose to the sun —reflex. to sunbathe, sun oneself.

so·le·cis·mo m. GRAM., RHET. solecism.

so·le·dad f. *(aislamiento)* solitude; *(sentirse solo)* loneliness; *(lugar)* solitary or lonely place; *(pesar)* grieving, mourning.

so·lem·ne adj. *(grave)* solemn, grave; COLL. *(enfático)* utter, downright <*fue un s. desastre* it was an utter disaster>.

so·lem·ne·men·te adv. solemnly.

so·lem·ni·dad f. solemnity, gravity.

so·lem·ni·zar §04 tr. *(celebrar)* to solemnize, celebrate; *(conmemorar)* to commemorate.

so·le·noi·de m. ELEC. solenoid.

so·ler §78 intr. *(acostumbrar)* to be in the habit of <*Miguel suele levantarse temprano* Michael is in the habit of getting up early>; *(ser frecuente)* to tend to <*suele llover mucho en Londres* it tends to rain a lot in London>.

▲ The most frequent translations of the verb *soler* are the adverbs *usually, frequently, generally,* and *often* <*yo suelo levantarme tarde* I usually get up late> <*suele nevar mucho aquí* it generally snows a lot here>.

so·le·ra f. *(soporte)* crossbeam, stringpiece; *(piedra)* plinth; *(del molino)* lower millstone; *(del horno)* floor (of an oven); *(tradición)* tradition; CHILE curb, curbstone; *(del vino)* lees, mother (of wine) ♦ **vino de s.** aged wine.

so·le·rí·a f. *(cuero)* shoe leather; *(solado)* flooring.

so·le·ta f. *(remiendo)* patch (of a stocking); MEX., CUL. pastry ♦ **picar** or **tomar s.** FIG., COLL. to beat it, run away.

so·le·van·ta·do, –da I. past part. see **solevantar** II. adj. agitated, perturbed.

so·le·van·ta·mien·to m. *(levantamiento)* raising, lifting; *(agitación)* agitation, unrest.

so·le·van·tar tr. *(levantar)* to raise, lift; FIG. *(agitar)* to agitate, stir up.

sol·fa f. MUS. *(solfeo)* sol-fa, solfeggio; *(signos)* musical notation; FIG. music; FIG., COLL. *(zurra)* beating, thrashing ♦ **dar una s.** FIG., COLL. to beat, thrash • **poner en s.** COLL. to ridicule, parody.

sol·fe·ar tr. MUS. to sol-fa; FIG., COLL. *(zurrar)* to beat, thrash; *(reprender)* to reprimand, tell off ♦ **quedar solfeando** HOND. to be ruined.

sol·fe·o m. MUS. sol-fa, solfege; FIG., COLL. *(zurra)* beating, thrashing.

so·li·ci·ta·ción f. *(pedida)* request; *(acción de solicitar)* solicitation.

so·li·ci·ta·dor, –do·ra I. adj. requesting, petitioning II. m.f. petitioner.

so·li·ci·tan·te I. adj. requesting, petitioning II. m.f. petitioner.

so·li·ci·tar tr. *(pedir)* to request, ask for; *(gestionar)* to apply for; *(atraer)* to attract; *(perseguir)* to pursue; *(cortejar)* to court, woo; *(buscar votos)* to solicit, canvass for (votes).

so·lí·ci·to, –ta adj. solicitous, obliging.

so·li·ci·tud f. *(cuidado)* solicitude, care; *(petición)* request; *(instancia)* petition; *(gestión)* application ♦ **a s.** on request • **a s. de** at the request of • **presentar una s.** to submit an application.

só·li·da·men·te adv. solidly.

so·li·dar tr. *(consolidar)* to consolidate; *(solidificar)* to make solid or firm; *(probar)* to prove, back up.

so·li·da·ria·men·te adv. *(con solidaridad)* with solidarity; LAW in solidum.

so·li·da·ri·cé, solidarice see **solidarizar**.

so·li·da·ri·dad f. solidarity ♦ **por s. con** in solidarity with.

so·li·da·rio, –ria adj. *(en común)* common, joint; *(obligatorio)* mutually binding; *(responsable)* jointly responsible or liable; TECH. integral.

so·li·da·ri·zar §04 tr. to make jointly responsible or liable —reflex. *(hacerse solidario)* to become jointly responsible or liable; *(unirse)* to join together, make common cause.

so·li·de·o m. RELIG. skullcap.

so·li·dez f. *(fuerza)* solidity, strength; FIG. *(validez)* soundness; GEOM. volume; TEX. fastness (of color).

so·li·di·fi·ca·ción f. solidification.

so·li·di·fi·car §70 tr. & reflex. to solidify, harden.

só·li·do, –da I. adj. *(denso)* solid; *(fuerte)* strong, firm; FIG. *(válido)* sound; TEX. fast (color); PERU, SP. lonely II. m. MATH., PHYS. solid; NUMIS. solidus (Roman coin).

so·li·lo·quiar intr. to soliloquize, talk to oneself.

so·li·lo·quio m. soliloquy, monologue.

so·lio m. canopied throne.

so·lip·sis·mo m. PHILOS. solipsism.

so·lis·ta m.f. MUS. soloist.

so·li·ta·rio, –ria I. adj. *(solo)* solitary, lone; *(desierto)* solitary, lonely II. m.f. *(ermitaño)* hermit, recluse —m. *(diamante, juego)* solitaire —f. ZOOL. tapeworm.

só·li·to, –ta adj. usual, customary.

so·li·vian·tar tr. *(excitar)* to rouse, stir up; *(irritar)* to irritate; *(preocupar)* to worry —reflex. to become aroused or stirred up.

so·li·viar tr. *(levantar)* to raise, lift; ARG., SL. to lift, steal —reflex. to half rise (from a seated or lying position).

so·lo, –la I. adj. *(sin compañía)* alone, by oneself; *(único)* only, sole; *(aislado)* lonely, all alone ♦ **a solas** alone, by oneself • **café s.** black coffee II. m. ARTS, MUS. solo; *(juego)* solitaire; COLL. *(café)* black coffee.

só·lo adv. only.

so·lo·mi·llo m. CUL. sirloin.

so·lo·mo m. CUL. *(solomillo)* sirloin; *(de cerdo)* loin of pork.

sols·ti·cio m. solstice ♦ **s. de invierno** or **hiemal** winter solstice • **s. de verano** or **vernal** or **de estío** summer solstice.

sol·tar §19 tr. *(aflojar)* to untie, loosen; *(desasir)* to let go of, release <*suelta mi brazo* let go of my arm>; *(liberar)* to free, let or turn loose; *(irrumpir)* to let out, break out in <*el prisionero soltaba gritos de terror* the prisoner let out cries of terror>; *(decir)* to blurt out; *(en tejidos)* to drop (a stitch); COLL. *(evacuar)* to move, loosen (one's bowels) —reflex. *(adquirir soltura)* to become proficient or skilled;

FIG. *(volverse desenvuelto)* to loosen up, lose one's shyness *<la nueva actriz se soltó después del estreno* the new actress loosened up after the opening>; *(empezar)* to begin, start *<su niña se soltó a andar a la edad de nueve meses* his daughter began to walk at the age of nine months>.

sol·te·rí·a f. unmarried state, bachelorhood.

sol·te·ro, –ra I. adj. single, unmarried II. m. bachelor —f. unmarried woman; spinster.

sol·te·rón, –ro·na I. adj. old and unmarried II. m. confirmed bachelor —f. spinster, unmarried woman; COLL. old maid.

sol·tu·ra f. *(aflojamiento)* looseness, slackness; *(seguridad)* confidence, assurance; *(agilidad)* agility, nimbleness; *(al hablar)* fluency; FIG. *(descaro)* brazenness; CRIMIN. release (from prison); MED. diarrhea ♦ **con s.** confidently, with assurance.

so·lu·bi·li·dad f. solubility.

so·lu·bi·li·zar §04 tr. to make soluble.

so·lu·ble adj. CHEM. soluble; *(que se puede resolver)* solvable.

so·lu·ción f. *(acción de disolver)* solution, dissolution; *(explicación)* answer, solution; *(desenlace)* ending, denouement ♦ **s. de continuidad** interruption, break in continuity.

so·lu·cio·nar tr. to solve, resolve.

sol·ven·cia f. *(calidad de solvente)* solvency; FIN. *(pago)* payment, settlement; *(dependabilidad)* dependability, reliability ♦ **s. moral** character.

sol·ven·tar tr. *(arreglar)* to settle; *(resolver)* to solve, resolve.

sol·ven·te I. adj. *(libre de deudas)* solvent; *(responsable)* dependable, reliable II. m. CHEM. solvent.

so·llas·tre m. *(pinche)* kitchen boy, scullion; FIG. *(pícaro)* rascal, rogue.

so·llo·zar §04 intr. to sob.

so·llo·zo m. sob ♦ **estallar** or **prorrumpir en sollozos** to burst into sobs.

so·ma f. coarse flour.

so·ma·lí I. adj. Somalian, Somali II. m.f. [pl. **-lí·es**] Somalian, Somali ♦ **los somalíes** the Somali, the Somalians.

So·ma·lia f. Somalia.

so·man·ta f. COLL. beating, whipping.

so·má·ti·co, –ca adj. somatic, physical.

so·ma·ti·za·ción f. somatization.

so·ma·ti·zar §04 tr. to somatize.

som·bra f. *(obscuridad)* darkness; *(área obscura)* shade; *(imagen)* shadow *<la s. del molino les parecía un monstruo a los niños* the shadow of the windmill seemed like a monster to the children>; *(penumbra)* shade *<a la s. del manzano* in the shade of the apple tree>; *(espectro)* ghost, specter; *(mancha)* spot, stain; *(donaire)* charm; *(falsilla)* guide lines (for writing); FIG. *(ignorancia)* ignorance; *(persona)* shadow; *(protección)* protection *<bajo la s. del rey* under the protection of the king>; *(semejanza)* trace, semblance; CHILE parasol; MEX. awning ♦ **dar s.** to cast a shadow, shade • **hacer s.** *(dar sombra)* to cast a shadow; *(impedir prosperar)* to overshadow, dominate • **poner a la s.** COLL. to put in jail • **sombras chinescas** shadow play • **tener buena s.** FIG., COLL. *(ser simpático)* to be pleasant; *(ser ingenioso)* to be witty; *(ser de buen agüero)* to bring good luck.

som·bra·je m. sunshade, sun screen.

som·bra·jo m. *(para tener sombra)* sunshade, sun screen; COLL. *(sombra)* shadow ♦ **caérsele a uno los palos del s.** COLL. to become discouraged.

som·brar tr. to shade.

som·bre·a·dor, –do·ra adj. *(que produce sombra)* shading; *(de ojos)* eye shadow.

som·bre·ar tr. to shade, throw shadow on.

som·bre·ra·da f. hatful.

som·bre·ra·zo m. COLL. *(saludo)* tip of the hat.

som·bre·re·ra f. *(para señoras)* milliner; *(para hombres)* hatter, hat maker; *(esposa)* hatter's wife; *(caja)* hatbox; ECUAD., PERU, P. RICO hatstand.

som·bre·re·rí·a f. *(fábrica)* hat factory; *(para señoras)* milliner's (shop); *(para hombres)* hatter's (shop).

som·bre·re·ro m. *(para señoras)* milliner; *(para hombres)* hatter, hat maker; ARG., COL. hatstand.

som·bre·re·te m. *(sombrero pequeño)* small hat; *(de chimenea)* cowl, hood (of a chimney); BOT. cap (of a mushroom); TECH. cap, bonnet.

som·bre·ro m. hat *<quitarse el s.* to take off one's hat>; *(tejado)* canopy (of a pulpit); MECH. *(parte superior)* cap; MARIT. drumhead; BOT. cap (of mushrooms); SP., HIST. grandee's privilege of keeping his hat on in the presence of the king ♦ **s. apuntado** cocked hat • **s. castoreño** beaver hat • **s. de canal** or **de teja** RELIG. shovel hat • **s. de copa** top hat • **s. de jipijapa** Panama hat • **s. de muelle** opera hat • **s. de paja** straw hat • **s. de pelo** S. AMER. top hat • **s. de tres picos** or **de tres candiles** three-cornered hat, tricorn • **s. flexible** soft hat, trilby (G.B.) • **s. gacho** slouch hat • **s. hongo** or **de hongo** derby, bowler (G.B.) • **s. jíbaro** C. AMER. straw hat.

som·bri·lla f. parasol.

som·brí·o, –a adj. *(sombreado)* shaded, shady; *(lóbrego)* somber, gloomy; *(obscuro)* dark; FIG. *(de una persona)* somber, sullen.

so·me·ra·men·te adv. superficially, briefly.

so·me·ro, –ra adj. *(de poca profundidad)* shallow; *(superficial)* superficial, shallow; *(breve)* brief, quick.

so·me·ter tr. *(sujetar)* to subdue, put down; *(subordinar)* to subordinate, put under the control of; *(entregar)* to submit, present; to subject or put to *<lo sometieron a una prueba científica* they subjected it to a scientific test> ♦ **s. a prueba** to test, put to the test • **s. a tratamiento** to put under treatment • **s. algo a una autoridad** to refer something to an authority —reflex. *(rendirse)* to yield, surrender; to undergo *<someterse a una operación* to undergo an operation>.

so·me·ti·mien·to m. *(estado)* submission, subjection; *(entrega)* submission, presentation.

som·nam·bu·lis·mo m. sleepwalking, somnambulism.

som·nám·bu·lo, –la I. adj. sleepwalking, somnambulistic II. m.f. sleepwalker, somnambulist.

som·ní·fe·ro, –ra I. adj. somniferous, sleep-inducing II. m. sleeping pill.

som·no·len·cia f. somnolence, sleepiness.

so·mor·gu·jar tr. *(sumergir)* to submerge, plunge —intr. & reflex. to dive, plunge.

so·mor·gu·jo or **so·mor·gu·jón** m. ORNITH. grebe.

so·mor·mu·jar tr. to submerge, plunge.

so·mos see ser².

son¹ m. *(sonido)* sound; FIG. *(noticias)* news, rumor; *(modo)* manner, style *<en s. de guerra* in a warlike manner>; *(motivo)* reason, motive; COLL. *(aire)* tune, song ♦ **a s. de** to the sound of • **¿a s. de qué?** or **¿a qué son?** why?, for what reason? • **bailar al s. que le tocan** FIG., COLL. to adapt to the circumstances • **en s. de** as, like *<en s. de broma* as a joke> • **sin s.** without any reason • **sin ton ni s.** COLL. without rhyme or reason.

son² see ser².

so·na·de·ra f. blowing of the nose.

so·na·do, –da I. past part. see sonar II. adj. *(famoso)* famous, well-known; *(muy divulgado)* talked-about; SL. *(chiflado)* touched, crazy.

so·na·dor, –do·ra I. adj. noise-making II. m.f. *(cosa ruidosa)* noisemaker —m. *(pañuelo)* handkerchief.

so·na·ja f. *(chapa de metal)* metal disk; *(sonajero)* baby's rattle; MEX. MUS. timbrel ♦ **sonajas** MUS. tambourine.

so·na·je·ro m. rattle (baby's toy).

so·nam·bu·lis·mo m. somnambulism, sleepwalking.

so·nám·bu·lo, –la I. adj. somnambulistic, sleepwalking II. m.f. somnambulist, sleepwalker.

so·nan·te I. adj. *(que suena)* sounding; *(que resuena)* resounding; *(sonoro)* sonorous; PHONET. sonant II. m. PHONET. sonant.

so·nar¹ m. TECH. sonar.

so·nar² §19 intr. *(producir sonido)* to sound; *(tintinear)* to ring; *(parecer)* to sound like *<esto me suena a tontería* this sounds like foolishness to me>; *(dar)* to strike (clocks); FIG., COLL. *(mencionarse)* to be mentioned or brought up *<su nombre no suena por estas partes* his name is not mentioned around here>; *(recordar)* to ring a bell, sound familiar *<ese nombre no me suena* that name does not ring a bell with me>; PHONET. to be sounded or pronounced (a letter, syllable) ♦ **como suena** literally —tr. *(hacer que* *suene)* to sound; *(tocar)* to play (an instrument); *(repicar)* to ring (bells); *(limpiar las narices)* to blow (one's nose) —reflex. *(limpiarse las narices)* to blow (one's nose).

son·da f. MARIT. *(acción de sondear)* sounding, fathoming; *(instrumento)* sounding line *or* lead; ASTRONAUT. probe <*s. espacial* space probe>; MED. probe, sound; TECH. drill, bore ♦ **s. acústica** MARIT. sonic depth finder, echo sounder.

son·da·ble adj. soundable, fathomable.

son·dar tr. var. of **sondear**.

son·de·ar tr. MARIT. to sound, fathom; MED. to probe, sound; TECH. to drill, bore; FIG. *(explorar)* to explore, inquire into; *(averiguar)* to sound out <*s. las intenciones de alguien* to sound out someone's intentions>.

son·de·o m. MARIT. sounding, fathoming; MED. probing, sounding; TECH. drilling, boring; METEOROL. wind observation; FIG. *(encuesta)* inquiry, poll.

so·ne·to m. sonnet.

so·ni·do m. sound, noise; PHONET. sound; MED. murmur; FIG. *(noticia)* news ♦ **s. absoluto** MUS. absolute pitch.

so·no·ra·men·te adv. sonorously.

so·no·ri·dad f. sonority, sonorousness.

so·no·ri·za·ción f. PHONET. voicing.

so·no·ri·zar §04 tr. CINEM. to record the sound track of (a film); PHONET. to voice; *(colocar equipos)* to install sound equipment.

so·no·ro, –ra adj. *(perteneciente al sonido)* sound <*onda s.* sound wave>; *(resonante)* sonorous, resonant; PHONET. sonant, voiced.

son·re·ír §58 intr. *(reírse levemente)* to smile; FIG. *(mostrarse favorable)* to smile on <*la fortuna le sonríe* luck smiles on him> —reflex. to smile, give a smile.

son·rien·te adj. smiling.

son·ri·sa f. smile.

son·ro·jar tr. to make blush —reflex. to blush.

son·ro·jo m. *(rubor)* blush, blushing; *(improperio)* offensive word *or* remark.

son·ro·sar tr. to turn pink.

son·ro·se·ar tr. to make pink —reflex. to turn pink, blush.

son·ro·se·o m. blush, blushing.

son·sa·ca f. wheedling, coaxing.

son·sa·ca·dor, –do·ra I. adj. wheedling, coaxing II. m.f. wheedler, coaxer.

son·sa·car §70 tr. *(sacar algo arteramente)* to wheedle, coax; *(solcitar secretamente)* to entice; FIG. *(extraer información)* to worm (information) out of.

son·se·ar intr. AMER. to fool around, act foolishly.

son·so, –sa AMER., COLL. I. adj. silly, foolish II. m.f. ninny, fool.

son·so·ne·te m. *(golpecito)* tap, tapping; *(tono burlador)* mocking tone; *(tono monótono)* monotonous tone, singsong; *(ruido)* din.

so·ña·do, –da I. past part. see **soñar** II. adj. dream, of one's dreams.

so·ña·dor, –do·ra I. adj. dreamy II. m.f. dreamer.

so·ñar §19 tr. & intr. to dream ♦ **¡ni soñarlo!** not on your life!, don't even dream it! • **s. con** to dream of *or* about • **s. con los angelitos** COLL. to have sweet dreams • **s. despierto** to daydream.

so·ño·len·cia f. somnolence, sleepiness.

so·ño·lien·to, –ta adj. *(que tiene sueño)* sleepy, drowsy; *(perezoso)* lazy.

so·pa f. *(comida)* soup <*s. de cebolla* onion soup>; *(pan mojado)* sop (bread) ♦ **andar a** *or* **comer la s. boba** FIG., COLL. to sponge *or* live off someone else • **dar sopas con honda** to excel in many things • **estar** *or* **quedar hecho una s.** to be sopping *or* soaking wet • **s. de verduras** vegetable soup.

so·pa·pe·ar tr. *(dar sopapos)* to slap, hit; FIG., COLL. *(maltratar)* to maltreat.

so·pa·pi·na f. COLL. slapping.

so·pa·po m. *(bofetada)* slap; *(golpe)* punch (on the jaw); TECH. valve, stop valve.

so·par *or* **so·pe·ar** tr. *(pan)* to dip, dunk (bread); BOL. to ink (a pen); ARG. to dunk —reflex. ARG. to butt in.

so·pe·ro, –ra I. adj. soup <*plato s.* soup plate *or* bowl>;

COL. meddling II. m. soup plate *or* bowl —f. soup tureen.

so·pe·sar tr. to heft, test the weight of.

so·pe·te·o m. soaking, dunking.

so·pe·tón m. *(golpe)* slap; *(tostado)* toast soaked in olive oil ♦ **de s.** suddenly, unexpectedly.

so·pi·cal·do m. CUL. thin soup.

so·pla·do, –da I. past part. see **soplar** II. adj. *(demasiado compuesto)* overly neat; FIG., COLL. *(engreído)* stuck-up, conceited; COLL. *(borracho)* smashed, plastered III. m. MIN. deep fissure; *(del vidrio)* glassblowing.

so·pla·dor, –do·ra I. adj. *(que sopla)* blowing; *(que excita)* stirring up II. m. *(de vidrio)* glass blower; *(aventador)* fan, blower; *(abertura)* vent, air hole; ECUAD., GUAT., THEAT. prompter.

so·pla·mo·cos m. [pl. **-cos**] COLL. *(bofetada)* punch (in the nose); MEX. rude remark.

so·plar intr. to blow <*el viento sopló violentamente* the wind blew violently> —tr. *(mover con viento)* to blow (away) <*el viento sopla la hojarasca en el otoño* the wind blows the dead leaves during the fall>; *(apagar)* to blow out <*s. una vela* to blow out a candle>; *(llenar de aire)* to blow up (a balloon); *(abofetear)* to land, deal (punches, blows); FIG. *(sugerir)* to prompt; *(hurtar)* to swipe, steal <*le soplaron el reloj durante la conmoción* they swiped his watch during the commotion>; *(acusar)* to squeal *or* snitch on —reflex. FIG., COLL. to gulp down.

so·ple·te m. blowtorch, blowpipe; MUS. air tube (of bagpipes) ♦ **s. de arena** sandblast • **s. oxiacetilénico** oxyacetylene torch • **s. oxídrico** oxyhydrogen blowpipe • **s. soldador** welding torch.

so·pli·llo m. *(para el fuego)* blowing fan; TEX. gauze.

so·plo m. *(acción)* blowing; *(ráfaga)* gust <*un s. de viento* a gust of wind>; FIG. *(instante)* second, instant <*todas sus pesadillas desaparecieron en un s.* all of his nightmares disappeared in an instant>; FIG., COLL. *(aviso)* tip-off; *(delación)* accusation, denunciation; *(soplón)* snitch, informer.

so·plón, –plo·na I. adj. COLL. informing, squealing II. m.f. COLL. *(delator)* stool pigeon, informer; MEX., COLL. policeman; C. AMER., THEAT. prompter; PERU member of the secret police.

so·pon·cio m. COLL. faint, swoon.

so·por m. MED. sopor; FIG. *(madorra)* sleepiness, drowsiness.

so·po·rí·fe·ro, –ra *or* **so·po·rí·fi·co, –ca** I. adj. *(que mueve al sueño)* sleep-inducing, soporific; COLL. *(pesado)* boring, tiresome II. m. sleeping pill, soporific.

so·por·ta·ble adj. bearable, tolerable.

so·por·ta·dor, –do·ra I. adj. supporting, sustaining II. m.f. supporter, sustainer.

so·por·tar tr. *(sostener)* to support, hold up; FIG. *(sufrir)* to endure, bear.

so·por·te m. *(sostén)* support; *(base)* stand, holder; FIG. *(proveedor)* provider, pillar; COMPUT. memory.

so·pra·no m.f. MUS. soprano.

sor f. RELIG. sister, nun <*s. Elena* Sister Ellen>.

sor·ber tr. *(beber)* to sip, suck; *(aspirar)* to sniff; FIG. *(absorber)* to absorb, soak up; *(tragar)* to swallow (up); MED. to inhale ♦ **s. el seso a uno** FIG., COLL. to be crazy about <*Enrique le sorbe el seso a Elena* Ellen is crazy about Henry> —reflex. to absorb, soak up.

sor·be·te m. CUL. sherbet; MEX. top hat; P. RICO, URUG. straw, drinking straw.

sor·bi·ble adj. which can be sipped.

sor·bo m. sip <*un s. de vino* a sip of wine>; *(acción)* sipping; *(trago)* swallow, gulp.

sor·da·men·te adv. FIG. silently, secretly.

sor·de·ra f. deafness.

sór·di·da·men·te adv. sordidly.

sor·di·dez f. *(suciedad)* squalor; FIG. *(vileza)* sordidness, vileness; *(avaricia)* meannness, miserliness.

sór·di·do, –da adj. *(sucio)* dirty, squalid; FIG. *(vil)* sordid, vile; *(mezquino)* mean, miserly.

sor·di·na f. MUS. damper, mute; *(muelle)* silencer (of a clock) ♦ **a la** *or* **en s.** secretly, surreptitiously.

sor·do, –da I. adj. *(duro de oído)* deaf; *(silencioso)* silent, noiseless; *(apagado)* muffled, dull; FIG. *(insensible)* deaf, indifferent; GRAM. voiceless ♦ **a lo s.** *or* **a sordas** silently, noiselessly • **quedarse s.** to go deaf • **s. como una tapia** stone-deaf **II.** m.f. *(persona)* deaf person; GRAM. surd ♦ **hacerse el s.** to pretend not to hear, turn a deaf ear.

sor·do·mu·dez f. deaf-mutism.

sor·do·mu·do, –da I. adj. deaf-mute, deaf and dumb **II.** m.f. deaf-mute.

sor·go m. sorghum.

sor·na f. FIG. *(mofa)* sarcasm; *(calma)* calmness, deliberation.

so·ro·char·se reflex. AMER., MED. to get mountain sickness; CHILE to blush, redden.

so·ro·che m. AMER. mountain *or* altitude sickness; CHILE *(rubor)* blush, flush; BOL., CHILE, MIN. galena.

sor·pren·den·te adj. *(admirable)* surprising, amazing; *(raro)* unusual, extraordinary.

sor·pren·der tr. *(coger desprevenido)* to surprise, take by surprise; *(asombrar)* to surprise, amaze; FIG. *(descubrir)* to discover, find out ♦ **s. en el hecho** to catch in the act —reflex. to be surprised *or* amazed.

sor·pren·di·do, –da I. past part. see **sorprender II.** adj. *(atónito)* surprised, amazed; *(cogido)* caught; *(descubierto)* discovered.

sor·pre·sa f. *(cosa que sorprende)* surprise; *(asombro)* surprise, amazement ♦ **coger de s.** to take by surprise.

sor·pre·si·vo, –va adj. ARG., C. AMER. *(inesperado)* unexpected; *(sorprendente)* surprising.

so·rros·tra·da f. insolence, impudence.

sor·te·a·ble adj. MIL. eligible for the draft; *(en una rifa)* which can be raffled.

sor·te·a·dor, –do·ra I. adj. drawing lots **II.** m.f. person who draws lots.

sor·te·a·mien·to m. drawing lots.

sor·te·ar tr. *(echar a suertes)* to draw lots for, decide by lot; *(rifar)* to raffle; FIG. *(evitar)* to avoid, dodge; TAUR. to fight clumsily —intr. to draw lots.

sor·te·o m. draw, drawing *<el s. de la lotería* the lottery drawing>; *(rifa)* raffle; FIG. *(acción de evitar)* avoiding, dodging; TAUR. quick pass of the cape ♦ **por s.** by lot.

sor·ti·ja f. *(anillo)* ring; *(de pelo)* curl, ringlet ♦ **s. de sello** signet ring.

sor·ti·le·gio m. *(hechicería)* sorcery, witchcraft; *(hechizo)* spell, charm ♦ **echar un s. a** to cast a spell on.

so·sa I. f. BOT. saltwort; CHEM. soda ♦ **s. cáustica** caustic soda **II.** adj. see **soso, –sa.**

so·se·ga·da·men·te adv. calmly, quietly.

so·se·ga·do, –da I. past part. see **sosegar II.** adj. calm, quiet.

so·se·ga·dor, –do·ra I. adj. calming, quieting **II.** m.f. pacifier, appeaser.

so·se·gar §52 tr. *(apaciguar)* to calm, quiet; FIG. *(aquietar)* to reassure —intr. *(aquietarse)* to calm down; *(descansar)* to rest, repose —reflex. to calm down, become calm.

so·se·ra *or* **so·se·rí·a** f. insipidness, dullness.

so·sie·go m. calmness, tranquility.

sos·la·yar tr. *(poner al soslayo)* to put sideways *or* on a slant; FIG. *(evitar)* to dodge, sidestep.

sos·la·yo, –ya I. adj. slanted, oblique **II.** adv. ♦ **al** *or* **de s.** *(oblicuamente)* obliquely, on a slant; *(de lado)* sideways, sidewise; FIG. *(de pasada)* in passing, hastily • **mirar de s.** to look out of the corner of one's eye (at); FIG. *(desaprobar)* to look askance (at).

so·so, –sa I. adj. *(de poco sabor)* tasteless, insipid; *(sin sal)* unsalted; FIG. *(zonzo)* dull, uninteresting. **II.** f. see **sosa.**

sos·pe·cha f. suspicion.

sos·pe·cha·ble adj. suspicious, suspect.

sos·pe·char tr. to suspect —intr. to be suspicious, suspect *<sospecho de su sinceridad* I am suspicious of his sincerity>.

sos·pe·cho·sa·men·te adv. suspiciously.

sos·pe·cho·so, –sa I. adj. *(desconfiado)* suspicious, distrustful; *(dudoso)* suspicious, suspect **II.** m.f. suspicious person, suspect.

sos·tén see **sostener.**

sos·tén m. *(apoyo)* support; *(acción)* sustenance; *(prenda)* bra, brassiere; FIG. *(protección)* pillar, mainstay; MARIT. steadiness ♦ **s. de familia** breadwinner.

sos·ten·drá, sostendría see **sostener.**

sos·te·ne·dor, –do·ra I. adj. supporting **II.** m.f. supporter.

sos·te·ner §69 tr. to support, hold up *<las vigas sostienen la andamiada* the beams hold up the scaffolding>; *(mantener)* to maintain, keep up; *(defender)* to maintain, uphold *<s. una teoría* to uphold a theory>; FIG. *(sufrir)* to endure, bear; *(apoyar)* to support, back —reflex. to support oneself, hold oneself up; *(mantenerse)* to support oneself; *(continuar)* to continue, remain.

sos·ten·ga, sostengo see **sostener.**

sos·te·ni·do, –da I. past part. see **sostener II.** adj. *(soportado)* supported; *(continuo)* steady, sustained; MUS. sharp **III.** m. MUS. sharp.

sos·te·ni·mien·to m. *(apoyo)* support; *(mantenimiento)* maintenance; *(sustento)* sustenance.

sos·tie·ne see **sostener.**

sos·tu·vie·ra, sostuvo see **sostener.**

so·ta f. *(en naipes)* jack, knave (in cards); *(mujer insolente)* hussy —m. CHILE foreman, overseer.

so·ta·bar·ba f. COLL. beard growing under and around the chin.

so·ta·na[1] f. RELIG. soutane, cassock.

so·ta·na[2] f. COLL. beating, thrashing.

só·ta·no m. *(de un edificio)* basement, cellar; *(del banco)* vault.

so·ta·ven·to m. MARIT. leeward, lee ♦ **a s.** to leeward.

so·te·cha·do m. shed.

so·te·rra·mien·to m. burial.

so·te·rra·ño, –ña I. adj. subterranean, underground **II.** m. underground.

so·te·rrar §49 tr. *(enterrar)* to bury; FIG. *(esconder)* to hide.

so·to m. *(arboleda)* grove; *(matorral)* thicket.

so·tre·ta f. ARG. *(caballo)* nag, useless horse; COLL. *(persona)* idler, useless person.

so·vié·ti·co, –ca adj. & m.f. Soviet.

soy see **ser**[2].

Sri Lanka Sri Lanka.

stan·dard I. adj. standard *<modelo s.* standard model> **II.** m. standard, model ♦ **s. de vida** standard of living.

su, sus §G25 adj. one's, his, her, your, its, their.

sua·ve adj. *(liso)* soft, smooth; *(dulce)* sweet, soft; *(tranquilo)* gentle, mild; *(dócil)* docile, mild; *(moderado)* easy; CHILE, MEX. big, huge.

sua·ve·men·te adv. *(lisamente)* softly, smoothly; *(dulcemente)* softly, sweetly; *(tranquilamente)* gently, mildly.

sua·vi·cé, suavice see **suavizar.**

sua·vi·dad f. *(lisura)* softness, smoothness; *(dulzura)* softness, sweetness; *(tranquilidad)* gentleness, mildness.

sua·vi·za·ción f. softening, smoothing.

sua·vi·za·dor, –do·ra I. adj. softening, smoothing **II.** m. razor strop.

sua·vi·zar §04 tr. *(aguzar)* to soften; *(hacer plano)* to smooth; *(moderar)* to temper, soften —reflex. to soften; *(volver plano)* to become smooth; *(moderarse)* to be tempered *or* softened.

su·ba f. ARG. rise (in prices).

su·ba·cuá·ti·co, –ca adj. subaqueous, underwater.

su·ba·fluen·te m. tributary.

su·bal·ter·no, –na I. adj. *(subordinado)* subordinate, subaltern; *(secundario)* secondary **II.** m.f. subordinate, subaltern.

su·ba·rren·da·dor, –do·ra m.f. subletter, sublessor.

su·ba·rren·da·mien·to m. sublease.

su·ba·rren·dar §49 tr. to sublet, sublease.

su·ba·rren·da·ta·rio, –ria m.f. subtenant, sublessee.

su·ba·rrien·do m. *(contrato)* sublease; *(precio)* sublease rent.

su·bas·ta f. auction ♦ **en s.** for auction • **sacar a s.** to auction, put up for auction • **vender en s.** to auction off, sell at auction.

su·bas·tar tr. to auction, sell at auction.

sub·cla·se f. BOT. subclass.

sub·co·mi·sión f. subcommittee, subcommission.

sub·cons·cien·cia f. subconscious mind.

sub·cons·cien·te I. adj. subconscious **II.** m. subconscious mind.

sub·cu·tá·ne·o, –a adj. subcutaneous.

sub·de·sa·rro·lla·do, –da adj. underdeveloped *<país s.* underdeveloped country>.

sub·di·rec·tor, –to·ra m.f. assistant manager.

súb·di·to, –ta I. adj. subject **II.** m.f. *(de un monarca)* subject; *(ciudadano)* citizen.

sub·di·vi·dir tr. & reflex. to subdivide.

sub·di·vi·sión f. subdivision.

su·bem·ple·o m. underemployment.

su·ben·ten·der §50 tr. to grasp, infer —reflex. to be implied.

su·bes·pe·cie f. BIOL. subspecies.

su·bes·ti·mar tr. *(un valor)* to underestimate, undervalue; *(un caso)* to understate.

sub·gé·ne·ro m. BIOL. subgenus.

sub·go·ber·na·dor, –do·ra m.f. lieutenant governor.

su·bi·ba·ja m. seesaw.

su·bi·da I. f. *(ascensión)* ascent, climb; *(aumento)* raise, increase; *(cuesta)* slope, hill **II.** adj. see **subido, –da.**

su·bi·do, –da I. past part. see **subir II.** adj. *(fuerte)* intense, deep <*rojo s.* deep red>; *(elevado)* high <*precios subidos* high prices>; *(superior)* fine, excellent **III.** f. see **subida.**

su·bi·mien·to m. var. of **subida.**

su·bin·ten·den·te m. assistant superintendent.

su·bir tr. *(escalar)* to climb, go up <*subí la cuesta* I climbed the hill>; *(llevar arriba)* to take *or* carry up <*el botones subió las maletas* the bellboy carried up the suitcases>; *(levantar)* to lift, raise <*suba la cabeza* raise your head>; *(hacer más alto)* to raise <*s. una pared* to raise a wall>; *(aumentar)* to raise <*el carnicero subió el precio de la carne* the butcher raised the price of meat> —intr. *(elevarse)* to rise <*el humo subía* the smoke was rising>; *(ascender)* to go up, come up <*subieron al tercer piso* they went up to the third floor>; *(montar)* to get on *or* into <*sube al coche* get into the car>; *(cabalgar)* to mount <*s. al caballo* to mount a horse>; *(crecer)* to rise, grow <*el río subió a un nivel peligroso* the river rose to a dangerous level>; *(alcanzar)* to come *or* amount to <*la cuenta sube a cincuenta dólares* the bill comes to fifty collars>; *(aumentar)* to rise, increase <*los precios han subido* prices have risen>; FIG. *(ascender en un empleo)* to be promoted, get ahead; *(agravarse)* to get worse <*la fiebre le subió* his fever got worse>; MUS. to raise the pitch ♦ **s. al trono** to ascend to the throne • **s. de punto** increase, grow • **s. de tono** *(intensificarse)* to get louder <*la música subió de tono* the music got louder>; *(acalorarse)* to become heated <*la conversación subió de tono* the conversation became heated> —reflex. *(ascender)* to go up; *(montar)* to get on *or* into <*el niño se subió al tren* the little boy got on the train> ♦ **subírsele a uno a la cabeza** to go to one's head.

sú·bi·ta·men·te adv. suddenly, all of a sudden.

sú·bi·to, –ta I. adj. *(imprevisto)* sudden, unexpected; *(precipitado)* hasty, impetuous ♦ **de s.** suddenly, all of a sudden **II.** adv. suddenly, all of a sudden.

sub·je·fe m. assistant chief *or* manager.

sub·je·ti·vi·dad f. subjectivity.

sub·je·ti·vis·mo m. subjectivism.

sub·je·ti·vo, –va adj. & m. subjective.

sub·jun·ti·vo, –va adj. & m. GRAM. subjunctive.

su·ble·va·ción f. *or* **su·ble·va·mien·to** m. revolt, uprising.

su·ble·var tr. *(agitar)* to incite to rebellion; FIG. *(enojar)* to annoy, irritate —reflex. to revolt, rise in rebellion.

su·bli·ma·ción f. sublimation.

su·bli·ma·do I. past part. see **sublimar II.** m. CHEM. sublimate ♦ **s. corrosivo** CHEM. corrosive sublimate.

su·bli·mar tr. CHEM., PSYCH. to sublimate; *(elevar)* to sublime, exalt —reflex. CHEM., PSYCH. to be sublimated; *(elevarse)* to be sublimed *or* exalted.

su·bli·me adj. sublime, lofty.

sub·ma·ri·no, –na I. adj. submarine, underwater **II.** m. submarine.

sub·o·fi·cial adj. MIL. non-commissioned *or* warrant officer; MARIT. petty officer.

sub·or·den m. BIOL. suborder.

su·bor·di·na·ción f. subordination.

su·bor·di·na·do, –da I. past part. see **subordinar II.** adj. & m.f. subordinate.

su·bor·di·nar tr. to subordinate —intr. to become subordinate.

sub·pro·duc·to m. by-product.

su·bra·ya·do, –da I. past part. see **subrayar II.** adj. *(señalado)* underlined, underscored; PRINT. italicized, in italics **III.** m. *(señalado)* underlining; PRINT. italics.

su·bra·yar tr. *(señalar)* to underline, underscore; PRINT. to italicize, put in italics; FIG. *(poner énfasis)* to emphasize, underline.

su·brep·ti·cio, –cia adj. surreptitious.

su·bro·ga·ción f. LAW subrogation.

su·bro·gar §47 tr. LAW to subrogate.

sub·sa·na·ble adj. *(disculpable)* excusable; *(reparable)* repairable, correctable.

sub·sa·nar tr. *(disculpar)* to excuse; *(reparar)* to repair, correct.

subs·cri·bir §85 tr. *(firmar)* to sign (a document); *(convenir)* to subscribe to, endorse; *(abonar)* to subscribe to (a journal); COM. to underwrite, subscribe —reflex. to subscribe to (a journal).

subs·crip·ción f. subscription.

subs·crip·tor, –to·ra m.f. subscriber.

sub·se·cre·ta·rí·a f. *(oficio)* undersecretaryship; *(oficina)* undersecretary's office.

sub·se·cre·ta·rio, –ria m.f. *(en una oficina)* assistant secretary; *(de un ministro)* undersecretary.

sub·se·cuen·te adj. subsequent.

sub·se·guir §64 intr. & reflex. to follow, come after.

sub·si·diar tr. to subsidize.

sub·si·dia·rio, –ria adj. *(que se da en socorro)* subsidiary; LAW *(en derecho)* ancillary.

sub·si·dio m. *(subvención)* subsidy; *(ayuda)* aid, assistance; COL., ECUAD. worry, anxiety ♦ **s. de enfermo** sick pay • **s. de huelga** strike pay • **s. de natalidad** maternity benefit • **s. de paro** unemployment compensation • **s. de vejez** old-age pension.

sub·si·ga, subsigo see **subseguir.**

sub·si·guien·te adj. subsequent.

sub·si·guie·ra, subsiguió see **subseguir.**

sub·sis·ten·cia f. *(vida)* subsistence; *(provisión)* sustenance.

sub·sis·ten·te adj. subsistent, enduring.

sub·sis·tir intr. *(vivir)* to subsist, live; *(permanecer)* to remain, endure.

subs·tan·cia f. *(materia)* substance, matter; *(esencia)* substance, essence <*la s. de un ensayo* the substance of an essay>; *(jugo)* extract; *(juicio)* judgment, sense; *(valor)* substance, value <*una obra de s.* a work of substance>; PHILOS., THEOL. substance, essence ♦ **en s.** in brief, briefly • **s. gris** ANAT. gray matter.

subs·tan·cia·ción f. *(compendio)* abridgment, condensation; LAW *(en derecho)* substantiation.

subs·tan·cial adj. *(relativo a la substancia)* substantial, material; *(substancioso)* substantial; *(esencial)* essential, fundamental.

subs·tan·cial·men·te adv. *(en substancia)* substantially; *(esencialmente)* essentially.

subs·tan·ciar tr. *(compendiar)* to abridge, condense; LAW *(en derecho)* to substantiate.

subs·tan·cio·so, –sa adj. *(importante)* substantial, important; *(nutritivo)* substantial, nourishing.

subs·tan·ti·va·ción f. GRAM. substantivation, use as a noun.

subs·tan·ti·var tr. GRAM. to substantivate, use as a noun.

subs·tan·ti·vo, –va I. adj. substantive **II.** m. GRAM. substantive, noun.

subs·ti·tu·ción f. substitution, replacement.

subs·ti·tui·ble adj. replaceable.

subs·ti·tui·dor, –do·ra I. adj. substitute, substituting **II.** m.f. substitute.

subs·ti·tuir §18 tr. to substitute, replace.

subs·ti·tu·ti·vo, –va I. adj. substitutive, substitute **II.** m. substitute.

subs·ti·tu·to, –ta m.f. *(persona que substituye a otra)* substitute, replacement; THEAT. understudy.

subs·trac·ción f. *(acción de quitar)* removal, taking away; *(deducción)* deduction; *(robo)* theft; MATH. subtraction.

subs·tra·en·do m. MATH. subtrahend.

subs·tra·er §72 tr. *(quitar)* to remove, take away; *(deducir)* to deduce; *(robar)* to steal; MATH. to subtract —reflex. *(eludir)* to avoid, elude; to get out of <*s. de un compromiso* to get out of an obligation>.

subs·tra·to m. GEOL. substratum; PHILOS. substance, essence.

sub·sue·lo m. GEOL. subsoil; CHILE basement, cellar.

sub·te m. ARG., URUG., COLL. subway.

sub·te·nien·te m. MIL. second lieutenant.

sub·ter·fu·gio m. subterfuge, pretext.

sub·te·rrá·ne·o, –a I. adj. subterranean, underground II. m. (lugar debajo de tierra) underground place; AMER. subway.

sub·tí·tu·lo m. CINEM. subtitle.

su·bur·ba·no, –na I. adj. suburban II. m.f. (persona) suburbanite —m. (tren) suburban train.

su·bur·bio m. (arrabal) suburb; (barrio pobre) slum.

sub·ven·ción f. subsidy, subvention.

sub·ven·cio·nar tr. to subsidize.

sub·ve·nir §76 tr. (proveer) to provide or pay for; (los gastos) to help pay, defray (expenses).

sub·ver·sión f. (acción de subvertir) subversion; (revolución) revolution, overthrow.

sub·ver·si·vo, –va adj. subversive.

sub·ver·tir §65 tr. to subvert, upset.

sub·ya·cen·te adj. subjacent, underlying.

sub·yu·ga·ción f. subjugation.

sub·yu·ga·dor, –do·ra I. adj. (que subyuga) subjugating; FIG. (cautivador) captivating II. m.f. (persona que subyuga) subjugator; FIG. (persona que cautiva) captivator.

sub·yu·gar §47 tr. (avasallar) to subjugate; FIG. (controlar) to master, subdue; FIG. (encantar) to captivate.

suc·ción f. suction.

su·ce·dá·ne·o, –a PHARM. I. adj. substitute II. m. succedaneum, substitute.

su·ce·der intr. (reemplazar) to succeed, follow; (heredar) to be the successor of, inherit; (ocurrir) to happen, occur —reflex. to follow one another.

su·ce·di·do I. past part. see suceder II. m. COLL. event, happening.

su·ce·sión f. succession, series; (al trono) succession; (herederos) issue, heirs; (herencia) inheritance ♦ s. forzosa hereditary succession, forced inheritance • s. intestada intestate succession.

su·ce·si·va·men·te adv. successively ♦ y así s. and so on.

su·ce·si·vo, –va adj. (siguiente) successive, following; (consecutivo) consecutive ♦ en lo s. hereafter, in the future; (en el pasado) thereafter.

su·ce·so m. (acaecimiento) event, occurrence; (transcurso) course, lapse of time); (resultado) result, outcome.

su·ce·sor, –so·ra I. adj. succeeding II. m.f. successor; (heredero) heir.

su·cia·men·te adv. (asquerosamente) dirtily, filthily; FIG. (vilmente) vilely, basely.

su·cie·dad f. (mugre) dirt, filth; (inmundicia) dirtiness, filthiness; FIG. (vileza) vileness, baseness; (acción vil) foul act or remark; (obscenidad) obscenity.

su·cin·ta·men·te adv. succinctly, concisely.

su·cin·to, –ta adj. (dicho en pocas palabras) succinct, concise; (corto) brief, scanty.

su·cio, –cia I. adj. (no limpio) dirty; (asqueroso) filthy; (que se ensucia fácilmente) which dirties easily; (de color confuso) off, dirty <un rojo s. an off red>; FIG. (vil) vile, base; (deshonesto) foul, shady; MED. (de lengua) coated, furred II. adv. dirtily.

su·co, –ca I. adj. ECUAD. blond; PERU orange II. m. (jugo) juice, sap; BOL., VEN. muddy ground.

su·cre m. ECUAD., FIN. sucre (currency).

Su·cre Sucre.

su·cren·se or **su·cre·ño, –ña** I. adj. of Sucre II. m.f. native of Sucre.

sú·cu·bo I. adj. succubine II. m. succubus, demon.

su·cu·cho m. corner, nook.

su·cu·len·cia f. succulence, juiciness.

su·cu·len·to, –ta adj. (sabroso) succulent, juicy; BOT. succulent.

su·cum·bir intr. (rendirse) to succumb, yield; (morir) to succumb, perish; LAW (perder un pleito) to lose a suit.

su·cur·sal I. adj. branch II. f. (oficina) branch (office); (de una empresa) subsidiary.

su·che I. m. ECUAD., PERU, BOT. white frangipani; ARG.

mud; CHILE, DEROG. servile person II. adj. VEN. green, unripe.

sud m. south.

su·da·ción f. sweating.

su·da·de·ro m. (lienzo) handkerchief, sweating cloth; (manta) saddlecloth; (sala) sweating room; (rezumadero) damp place.

Su·dá·fri·ca f. South Africa.

su·da·fri·ca·no, –na adj. & m.f. South African.

Su·da·mé·ri·ca f. South America.

su·da·me·ri·ca·no, –na adj. & m.f. South American.

Su·dán m. Sudan.

su·da·nés, –ne·sa adj. & m.f. Sudanese.

su·dar intr. (transpirar) to sweat, perspire; FIG., COLL. (trabajar) to work hard —tr. (empapar en sudor) to sweat, make sweaty; BOT. to ooze, exude moisture; FIG., COLL. (esforzarse) to work hard for; (pagar) to cough up, shell out ♦ s. la gota gorda to be dripping with sweat.

su·da·rio m. shroud.

su·des·ta·da f. ARG. rainy southeast wind.

su·des·te I. adj. southeastern, southeasterly II. m. southeast; (viento) southeaster.

su·dis·ta m.f. HIST. Confederate, Southerner (in the American Civil War).

su·do·es·te I. adj. southwestern, southwesterly II. m. southwest; (viento) southwester.

su·dor m. (transpiración) sweat, perspiration; (de la pared) sweat, moisture; FIG. (esfuerzo) sweat, toil ♦ sudores MED. sweat treatment • s. frío cold sweat • con el s. de la frente by the sweat of one's brow.

su·do·rí·fe·ro, –ra or **su·do·rí·fi·co, –ca** I. adj. sudoriferous, sudorific II. m. sudorific.

su·do·ro·so, –sa adj. sweaty, sweating.

sud·su·des·te m. south-southeast.

sud·su·do·es·te m. south-southwest.

Sue·cia f. Sweden.

sue·co, –ca I. adj. Swedish II. m.f. (habitante) Swede —m. (idioma) Swedish.

sue·gra f. (madre política) mother-in-law; (del pan) hard crust (of bread).

sue·gro m. father-in-law ♦ suegros parents-in-law, in-laws.

sue·la f. (del calzado) sole; (cuero) tanned leather; (del taco de billar) leather tip (on billiard cue); ARCHIT. socle, base; ICHTH. sole; TECH. washer ♦ suelas sandals • media s. half sole • un pícaro de siete suelas COLL. an out-and-out rascal.

sue·la, suelo see soler.

suel·de, sueldo see soldar.

suel·do m. (salario) salary, pay; NUMIS. solidus (Roman coin) ♦ a s. on a salary.

sue·lo m. (tierra) ground; (terreno) soil, land <s. fértil fertile soil>; (territorio) territory, land; (piso) floor; (pavimento) pavement; (sedimento) sediment (in liquids); FIG. (tierra) earth, world; (fondo) bottom, base; ♦ estar por los suelos FIG., COLL. to be dirt cheap (prices, goods) • s. natal native land, homeland • suelos AGR. leftover grain • venir or venirse al s. (caer) to fall down, collapse; FIG. (fracasar) to fail.

suel·ta I. f. (acción) release, letting loose; EQUIT. fetter (for a horse); (bueyes) relay (of oxen); (sitio) grazing place ♦ dar s. to free, let loose II. adj. see suelto, –ta.

suel·ta·men·te adv. (ágilmente) agilely, nimbly; (espontáneamente) spontaneously; FIG. (impudentemente) impudently.

suel·te, suelto see soltar.

suel·to, –ta I. past part. of soltar II. adj. (libre) loose, free <dejar s. al prisionero to let the prisoner loose>; (separado) loose <escribimos el examen en unas hojas sueltas we wrote the exam on a few loose sheets of paper>; (desatado) untied, undone; (disgregado) runny, watery; (que no hace juego) odd, unmatched; (dinero) loose <no tengo dinero s. I have no loose change>; FIG. (ágil) agile, nimble; (atrevido) daring, loose; (corriente) easy, flowing <estilo s. flowing style>; POET. blank (verse); MED. diarrhetic ♦ cabo s. FIG., COLL. loose end • s. de lengua (charlatán) loose-tongued; (insolente) sharp-tongued • venderse s. (por peso) to be sold by the pound, be sold in bulk; (por *separado)* to be sold singly *or* separately **III.** m. *(artículo)* insert (in a newspaper); *(dinero)* loose change —f. see **suelta.**

sue·ne, sueno see **sonar.**

sue·ñe, sueño see **soñar.**

sue·ño m. *(acto)* sleep <*un s. profundo* a deep sleep>; *(representación)* dream <*sus sueños le recordaron su niñez* his dreams reminded him of his childhood>; *(adormecimiento)* sleepiness, drowsiness; FIG. *(ilusión)* dream, illusion; *(encanto)* dream <*este bebé es un s.* this baby is a dream> ♦ **caerse de s.** FIG. to be falling asleep on one's feet • **dar s.** to make sleepy • **echar un s.** to take a nap • **el s. eterno** FIG. eternal rest *or* peace, death • **entre sueños** FIG. while half asleep • **ni en sueños** *or* **ni por sueños** FIG. not even in one's dreams • **no poder conciliar el s.** not to be able to sleep • **perder el s. por algo** to lose sleep over something • **quitar el s.** to keep awake • **s. dorado** life's dream *or* greatest dream • **s. hecho realidad** FIG. dream come true • **s. pesado** heavy sleep • **tener el s. ligero** *or* **liviano** to be a light sleeper • **tener s.** to be sleepy, feel sleepy.

sue·ro m. MED. serum; *(de la leche)* whey.

suer·te f. *(destino)* fate, lot; *(fortuna)* luck <*tener mala s.* to have bad luck>; *(buena fortuna)* good luck, good fortune <*tuve la s. de encontrarme con ella* I had the good fortune to meet her>; *(condición)* lot, condition <*mejorar la s. del pueblo* to improve the lot of the people>; *(calidad)* quality, class <*de primera s.* first-class>; *(género)* kind, sort <*¿qué s. de vino quieres?* what kind of wine do you want?>; *(casualidad)* lot <*elegir por s.* to choose by lot>; *(manera)* manner, way; *(juego de mano)* magic trick; TAUR. *(etapa)* stage, phase (of a bullfight); *(lance)* skillful maneuver; PRINT. sort; ARG., URUG. lot, plot; PERU lottery ticket ♦ **buena s.** good luck • **caerle** *or* **tocarle a uno en s.** to fall to one's lot • **dar** *or* **traer s.** to bring luck • **de otra s.** otherwise • **de s. que** so that, in a way that • **echar suertes** to cast lots, draw lots • **estar de mala s.** to be out of luck • **estar de s.** to be in luck • **la s. está echada** the die is cast • **mala s.** bad luck • **por s.** *(por casualidad)* by chance; *(por fortuna)* luckily, fortunately • **s. negra** very bad luck • **tener s.** to be lucky • **unirse a la s. de alguien** to throw in one's lot with someone.

suer·te·ro, –ra **I.** adj. AMER., SL. lucky **II.** m.f. PERU lottery ticket seller.

sué·ter m. sweater.

su·fí [pl. **-fí·es**] HIST., RELIG. **I.** adj. Sufic **II.** m.f. Sufi.

su·fi·cien·cia f. *(capacidad)* sufficiency; *(conveniencia)* fitness, suitability; *(aptitud)* competence, ability; COLL. *(presunción)* smugness, cocksureness ♦ **a s.** sufficiently, enough.

su·fi·cien·te adj. *(bastante)* sufficient, enough; *(conveniente)* fitting, suitable; *(presumido)* smug, pedantic.

su·fi·cien·te·men·te adv. sufficiently, enough <*s. grande* big enough>.

su·fi·jo, –ja GRAM. **I.** adj. suffixal, suffixed **II.** m. suffix.

su·fra·gar §47 tr. *(costear)* to pay (for), defray; *(ayudar)* to aid, support —intr. AMER. to vote.

su·fra·gio m. *(derecho)* suffrage, franchise; *(voto)* vote, ballot; *(ayuda)* assistance, aid; RELIG. service for the redemption of souls from Purgatory.

su·fra·gis·mo m. POL. female *or* women's suffrage.

su·fra·gis·ta POL. m.f. suffragist —f. suffragette.

su·fra·gué, sufrague see **sufragar.**

su·fri·ble *or* **su·fri·de·ro, –ra** adj. bearable, endurable.

su·fri·do, –da **I.** past part. see **sufrir** **II.** adj. *(paciente)* long-suffering, patient; FIG., COLL. *(complaciente)* complaisant ♦ **mal s.** *(impaciente)* impatient, rude; *(severo)* severe, harsh **III.** m. FIG., COLL. complaisant husband.

su·fri·dor, –do·ra **I.** adj. suffering **II.** m.f. *(víctima)* sufferer —m. COL., VEN., EQUIT. saddle blanket *or* cloth.

su·fri·mien·to m. *(padecimiento)* suffering; *(tolerancia)* endurance, tolerance.

su·frir tr. *(padecer)* to suffer; *(experimentar)* to undergo, experience; *(soportar)* to bear, endure; *(permitir)* to permit, allow; *(pagar)* to pay, comply with (a penalty) ♦ **s. un examen** EDUC. to take *or* sit for an examination • **s. su calvario** FIG. to carry one's cross —intr. *(padecer)* to suffer, be in pain; *(preocuparse)* to worry, fret ♦ **s. de** to suffer with *or* from.

su·ge·ren·cia f. suggestion, hint.

su·ge·ren·te *or* **su·ge·ri·dor, –do·ra** adj. suggestive, suggesting.

su·ge·rir §65 tr. to suggest, hint.

su·ges·tión f. *(sugerencia)* suggestion, hint; *(acción de sugerir)* suggesting, suggestion.

su·ges·tio·na·ble adj. suggestible, impressionable.

su·ges·tio·nar tr. *(influenciar)* to influence; *(hipnotizar)* to hypnotize —reflex. to undergo hypnosis.

su·ges·ti·vo, –va adj. *(sugerente)* suggestive, evocative; *(interesante)* appealing, alluring.

su·gie·ra, sugiero see **sugerir.**

su·gi·rie·ra, sugirió see **sugerir.**

sui·ci·da **I.** adj. suicidal **II.** m.f. suicide (person).

sui·ci·diar·se reflex. to commit suicide, kill oneself.

sui·ci·dio m. suicide.

Sui·za f. Switzerland.

sui·zo, –za adj. & m.f. Swiss ♦ **los suizos** the Swiss.

su·je·ción f. *(dominación)* subjection, domination; *(ligadura)* fastening, RHET. *(prolepsis)* prolepsis; *(interrogación)* rhetorical question ♦ **con s. a** LAW in accordance with, subject to.

su·je·ta·dor, –do·ra **I.** adj. fastening, binding **II.** m.f. *(objeto que sujeta)* fastener, holder; *(horquilla)* clip —m. *(sostén)* bra, brassière.

su·je·ta·li·bros m. [pl. **-bros**] bookend.

su·je·ta·pa·pe·les m. [pl. **-les**] paper clip *or* clamp.

su·je·tar tr. *(fijar)* to fasten, attach; *(agarrar)* to grasp, seize; *(dominar)* to subject, put under domination; FIG. *(contener)* to restrain, keep in check ♦ **s. con clavos** to nail down • **s. con grapas** to staple —reflex. *(someterse)* to subject oneself, submit; *(agarrarse)* to hang *or* hold on; FIG. *(ajustarse)* to conform, comply.

su·je·to, –ta **I.** past part. see **sujetar** **II.** adj. *(susceptible)* subject *or* liable to; *(dominado)* subject, in subjection; *(fijado)* fastened, attached; *(restringido)* in close check, controlled ♦ **s. a** subject to **III.** m. GRAM., LOG., PHILOS. subject; *(tema)* subject, topic; COLL. *(tipo)* fellow, individual ♦ **buen s.** COLL. good guy.

sul·fa·to m. CHEM. sulfate, sulphate ♦ **s. de cinc** CHEM. zinc sulfate • **s. de magnesio** CHEM. magnesium sulfate • **s. ferroso** *or* **de hierro** CHEM. iron sulfate.

sul·fu·ra·do, –da **I.** past part. see **sulfurar** **II.** adj. CHEM. sulfured, sulfurated; FIG. *(irascible)* irritable, irascible.

sul·fu·rar tr. CHEM. to sulfur, sulfurate; FIG. *(irritar)* to anger, irritate —reflex. FIG. to become infuriated *or* enraged.

sul·fú·ri·co, –ca adj. CHEM. sulfuric, sulphuric.

sul·fu·ro m. CHEM. sulfide, sulfuret ♦ **s. de cinc** CHEM. zinc sulfide.

sul·fu·ro·so, –sa adj. CHEM. sulfurous, sulfur <*agua sulfurosa* sulfur water>.

sul·tán m. sultan.

sul·ta·na f. sultana.

sul·ta·na·do *or* **sul·ta·na·to** m. sultanate.

su·ma **I.** f. *(total)* sum; MATH. *(adición)* addition, adding; *(esencia)* essence, essential point; *(compendio)* compendium, detailed summary; FIG. *(recopilación)* summary ♦ **en s.** in short, to sum up **II.** adj. see **sumo, –ma.**

su·ma·dor, –do·ra **I.** adj. adding **II.** m.f. *(persona)* adder —f. *(máquina)* adding machine.

su·ma·men·te adv. extremely, highly.

su·man·do m. MATH. addend.

su·mar tr. *(resumir)* to add (up); *(totalizar)* to add up to, amount to; FIG. *(compendiar)* to summarize, sum up ♦ **suma y sigue** MATH. *(suma que continúa)* carry forward; COLL. *(hay más)* that's not all, there's more —reflex. to join (in) ♦ **sumarse a** *(añadirse a)* to be added to; *(agregarse a)* to join (a group); *(adherirse a)* to adhere to (an opinion).

su·ma·ria **I.** f. LAW *(proceso escrito)* written proceedings; MIL. indictment **II.** adj. see **sumario, –ria.**

su·ma·ria·men·te adv. summarily, without delay.

su·ma·rio, –ria **I.** adj. *(breve)* summary, brief; LAW summary <*proceso s.* summary proceedings> **II.** m. *(resumen)* summary, abstract; LAW *(acusación)* indictment —f. see **sumaria.**

su·ma·rí·si·mo, –ma adj. LAW swift, expeditious.

su·mer·gi·ble I. adj. submersible, submergible II. m. MA-RIT. submarine, submersible.

su·mer·gir §32 tr. *(meter debajo de agua)* to submerge, immerse; FIG. *(abismar)* to overwhelm, plunge —reflex. to dive, plunge ♦ **sumergirse en** FIG. to become immersed *or* absorbed in.

su·mer·sión f. submergence, immersion.

su·mi·de·ro m. *(alcantarilla)* drain, sewer; PERU, P. RICO *(pozo negro)* cesspool, sump; P. RICO *(tremedal)* quaking bog, quagmire.

su·mi·nis·tra·ble adj. that can *or* should be supplied.

su·mi·nis·tra·ción f. *(suministro)* supplying, providing; *(provisión)* supply, provison.

su·mi·nis·tra·dor, –do·ra I. adj. supplying, providing II. m.f. supplier, provider.

su·mi·nis·trar tr. to supply, provide.

su·mi·nis·tro m. *(acción de suministrar)* supplying, providing; *(provisión)* supply, provision ♦ **suministros** MIL. supplies, provisions • **s. a domicilio** home delivery.

su·mir tr. to sink, submerge —reflex. *(hundirse)* to sink, submerge; FIG. *(en duda, depresión)* to immerse oneself, become immersed.

su·mi·sión f. *(acción de someterse)* submission; *(carácter sumiso)* submissiveness, obsequiousness; *(obediencia)* obedience, compliance; LAW *(renunciación)* renunciation of jurisdiction.

su·mi·so, –sa adj. *(sometido)* submissive, obsequious; *(obediente)* obedient, compliant.

su·mo, –ma I. adj. *(supremo)* greatest, supreme; FIG. *(enorme)* enormous, great ♦ **a lo sumo** at (the) most • **de sumo** completely, entirely II. f. see **suma.**

sun·tua·rio, –ria adj. luxury <*artículo s.* luxury item>.

sun·tuo·sa·men·te adv. sumptuously, lavishly.

sun·tuo·si·dad f. sumptuousness, lavishness.

sun·tuo·so, –sa adj. *(espléndido)* sumptuous, magnificent; *(majestuoso)* stately, majestic.

su·pe·di·ta·ción f. *(subordinación)* subjection, subordination; *(avasallamiento)* subduing, subjugating.

su·pe·di·tar tr. *(sujetar)* to subject, subordinate; *(avasallar)* to subdue, overpower ♦ **estar supeditado a** to be subject to, depend on.

su·pe·ra·ble adj. surmountable, surpassable.

su·pe·ra·bun·dan·cia f. superabundance.

su·pe·ra·bun·dan·te adj. superabundant, plentiful.

su·pe·ra·bun·dar intr. to superabound, be plentiful.

su·pe·ra·ción f. *(vencimiento)* surmounting, overcoming; *(mejoramiento de uno mismo)* self-improvement, self-betterment.

su·pe·ra·li·men·tar tr. *(alimentar demasiado)* to overfeed; MECH. to supercharge.

su·pe·rar tr. *(sobrepujar)* to surpass, exceed; *(vencer dificultades)* to overcome, surmount; *(vencer a una persona)* to outshine, beat ♦ **estar superado** to be over *or* finished —reflex. to better *or* improve oneself.

su·pe·rá·vit m. [pl. **-vit** *or* **-vits**] COM. surplus ♦ **s. reservado** COM. surplus reserves.

su·per·che·rí·a f. fraud, deceit.

su·per·do·ta·do, –da I. adj. exceptionally gifted II. m.f. exceptionally gifted child.

su·pe·re·mi·nen·te adj. supereminent, pre-eminent.

su·pe·res·ti·mar tr. overestimate, overpraise.

su·pe·res·truc·tu·ra f. superstructure.

su·pe·re·ro·ga·ción f. supererogation.

su·per·fi·cial adj. *(relativo a la superficie)* superficial, surface; *(en el cuerpo)* superficial; FIG. *(sin fundamento)* superficial, shallow.

su·per·fi·cia·li·dad f. superficiality.

su·per·fi·cial·men·te adv. superficially.

su·per·fi·cie f. *(parte exterior)* surface; GEOM. *(extensión)* area ♦ **salir a la s.** MARIT. to (come to the) surface, float • **s. de rodadura** AUTO. (tire) tread.

su·per·fi·no, –na adj. superfine, extra fine.

su·per·flui·dad f. *(condición de superfluo)* superfluity, superfluousness; *(cosa superflua)* superfluous item, superfluity.

su·per·fluo, –flua adj. *(que sobra)* superfluous, extra; *(inútil)* needless, unnecessary.

su·per·hom·bre m. superman.

su·pe·rin·ten·den·cia f. *(acción)* direction, management;

(empleo) superintendence; *(oficina)* superintendent's office.

su·pe·rin·ten·den·te m.f. *(encargado)* superintendent; *(supervisor)* supervisor, overseer.

su·pe·rior I. adj. *(de más altura)* upper <*pisos superiores* upper floors>; *(más alto)* higher <*enseñanza s.* higher education>; *(mejor)* better; *(excelente)* superior <*este vino es de una calidad s.* this wine is of a superior quality>; FIG. *(distinguido)* superior; GEOG. upper II. m. superior.

su·pe·rior, –rio·ra I. RELIG. m. superior —f. mother superior II. adj. see **superior.**

su·pe·rio·ri·dad f. *(calidad)* superiority; *(autoridad)* higher authority.

su·pe·rior·men·te adv. superiorly.

su·per·la·ti·vo, –va I. adj. superlative, excellent II. m. GRAM. superlative.

su·per·mer·ca·do m. supermarket.

su·per·nu·me·ra·rio, –ria I. adj. *(que está de más)* supernumerary, extra; MIL. on leave without pay II. m.f. supernumerary.

su·per·po·bla·ción f. overpopulation.

su·per·po·bla·do, –da adj. overpopulated.

su·per·po·ner §54 tr. *(poner encima de)* to superpose, superimpose; FIG. *(anteponer)* to place above *or* before.

su·per·po·si·ción f. superposing, superposition.

su·per·po·ten·cia f. superpower.

su·per·pro·duc·ción f. ECON. overproduction; CINEM. big-budget film.

su·pe·rre·a·lis·mo m. ARTS surrealism.

su·per·só·ni·co, –ca adj. supersonic.

su·pers·ti·ción f. superstition.

su·pers·ti·cio·sa·men·te adv. superstitiously.

su·pers·ti·cio·so, –sa adj. superstitious.

su·per·vi·sar tr. to supervise.

su·per·vi·sión f. supervision.

su·per·vi·sor, –so·ra I. adj. supervising, supervisory II. m.f. supervisor.

su·per·vi·ven·cia f. *(acción de sobrevivir)* survival; LAW *(permiso de renta)* survivorship; FIG. *(vestigio)* vestige, trace of survival.

su·per·vi·vien·te I. adj. surviving II. m.f. survivor.

su·pie·ra, supo see **saber**[2].

su·pi·na·ción f. supination.

su·pi·na·dor, –do·ra ANAT. I. adj. supinating II. m. supinator.

su·pi·no, –na I. adj. supine, face-up ♦ **ignorancia s.** crass ignorance II. m. GRAM. supine.

su·plan·ta·ción f. *(reemplazo)* supplanting, supplantation; *(falsificación)* falsification, forgery.

su·plan·tar tr. *(reemplazar)* to supplant, take the place of; *(falsificar)* to falsify; *(fingir)* to pretend to be.

su·ple·fal·tas m.f. [pl. **-tas**] COLL. fill-in, substitute.

su·ple·men·tal *or* **su·ple·men·ta·rio, –ria** adj. *(agregado)* supplemental, supplementary; GEOM. supplementary (angle).

su·ple·men·to m. *(acción)* supplementing, supplying; GEOM., JOURN., MATH. supplement; RAIL., THEAT. supplementary *or* extra charge.

su·plen·cia f. substitution, replacement.

su·plen·te I. adj. *(que suple)* substitute; SPORT. relief, reserve (player) II. m.f. *(persona que suple)* substitute, replacement; SPORT. relief *or* reserve player; THEAT. understudy.

su·ple·to·rio, –ria adj. supplementary.

sú·pli·ca f. *(ruego)* supplication, plea; *(petición)* request, petition ♦ **a s. de** at the request of, by request of.

su·pli·ca·ción f. *(ruego)* supplication, plea; *(petición)* request, petition; CUL. rolled wafer; LAW *(apelación)* appeal.

su·pli·can·te I. adj. *(que ruega)* entreating, pleading; *(que pide)* requesting, petitioning II. m.f. supplicant, petitioner.

su·pli·car §70 tr. *(rogar)* to supplicate, implore; *(pedir)* to petition, request; LAW *(apelar)* to appeal (a sentence).

su·pli·ca·to·ria f. *or* **su·pli·ca·to·rio** m. LAW letters rogatory.

su·pli·cio m. *(tortura)* torture; *(castigo corporal)* corporal punishment; *(muerte)* capital punishment, execution; *(lu-*

gar) place of torture *or* execution; FIG. (*dolor*) anguish, suffering ♦ **último s.** CRIMIN., LAW death penalty.
su·pli·qué, suplique see **suplicar.**
su·plir tr. (*compensar*) to make up for, supplement; (*reemplazar*) to replace, substitute (for); (*disimular*) to conceal, hide.
su·pon see **suponer².**
su·pon·drá, supondría see **suponer².**
su·po·ner¹ m. COLL. supposition, assumption.
su·po·ner² §54 tr. (*presumir*) to suppose, assume; (*imaginar*) to fancy, imagine; (*traer consigo*) to entail, presuppose <*el proyecto supone grandes gastos* the project entails a considerable outlay> ♦ **ser de s.** to be possible *or* likely • **s. que sí** to suppose so • **suponiendo que** supposing *or* assuming that —intr. to have authority *or* weight.
su·pon·ga, supongo see **suponer².**
su·po·si·ción f. (*conjetura*) supposition, assumption; (*distinción*) authority, distinction; (*mentira*) falsehood, imposture; LOG. supposition.
su·po·si·to·rio m. PHARM. suppository.
su·pra·di·cho, –cha adj. aforesaid, abovementioned.
su·pra·na·cio·nal adj. supranational.
su·pra·rre·a·lis·mo m. ARTS surrealism.
su·pra·rre·nal adj. ANAT. suprarenal <*glándulas suprarrenales* superarenal glands>.
su·pra·sen·si·ble adj. supersensitive.
su·pre·ma I. f. SP., HIST. Supreme Council of the Inquisition II. adj. see **supremo, –ma.**
su·pre·ma·cí·a f. supremacy.
su·pre·mo, –ma I. adj. (*muy alto*) supreme, paramount; (*definitivo*) final, definitive II. m. LAW supreme court —f. see **suprema.**
su·pre·sión f. (*eliminación*) suppression, elimination; (*omisión*) omission, leaving out.
su·pri·mir tr. (*eliminar*) to suppress, eliminate; (*omitir*) to omit, leave out.
su·pues·to, –ta I. past part. see **suponer** II. adj. (*fingido*) assumed, false <*nombre s.* assumed name>; (*que se supone*) supposed, assumed; (*imaginario*) imaginary, fanciful; (*hipotético*) hypothetical ♦ **dar por s.** to take for granted, assume • **esto s.** this being understood • **por s.** of course, naturally • **s. que** (*ya que*) since, granted that; (*si*) if, in the event (that) III. m. assumption, assumption ♦ **en el s. de que** supposing that • **supuestos** data, information • **s. táctico** MIL. military *or* tactical maneuvers.
su·pu·rar intr. PHYSIOL. to suppurate, discharge pus.
su·pu·sie·ra, supuso see **suponer².**
sur I. adj. southern, southerly II. m. (*punto*) south; (*países*) South; (*viento*) souther, south wind, sirocco.
su·ra·me·ri·ca·no, –na adj. & m.f. var. of **sudamericano, –na.**
sur·car §70 tr. AGR. to plow, furrow; (*hacer rayas*) to furrow, groove; MARIT., FIG. to cleave, cut through (water).
sur·co m. (*en la tierra*) furrow, trench; FIG. (*en el rostro*) wrinkle, furrow (of the skin); (*hendedura*) rut, groove ♦ **echarse uno en el s.** COLL. to lie down on the job.
sur·gir §32 intr. (*surtir*) to spurt, shoot up; FIG. (*alzarse*) to arise, appear; MARIT. (*fondear*) to anchor.
Su·ri·na·me Suriname.
su·ri·na·més, –me·sa adj. & m.f. Surinamese ♦ **los surinameses** the Surinamese.
su·ri·pan·ta f. THEAT., COLL. chorine; SL. chorus girl; COLL., DEROG. (*mujer de mal vivir*) tart, slut.
sur·ja, surjo see **surgir.**
sur·me·na·je m. mental strain *or* fatigue.
sur·qué, surque see **surcar.**
su·rre·a·lis·mo m. ARTS, LIT. surrealism.
su·rre·a·lis·ta I. adj. surrealistic II. m.f. surrealist.
sur·ti·de·ro m. conduit, outlet.
sur·ti·do, –da I. past part. see **surtir** II. adj. (*variado*) assorted <*botones surtidos* assorted buttons> III. m. (*variedad*) assortment, selection; (*provisión*) stock, supply.
sur·ti·dor, –do·ra I. adj. providing, supplying II. m. (*proveedor*) provider, supplier; (*chorro*) spout, jet (of water); (*fuente*) fountain ♦ **s. de gasolina** gasoline pump, filling station.
sur·ti·mien·to m. (*surtido*) supply, stock; (*selección*) assortment.

sur·tir tr. (*proveer*) to supply, stock ♦ **s. efecto** to work, have the desired effect • **s. un pedido** to fill an order —intr. (*brotar*) to spout, gush (water) —reflex. to supply oneself.
su·rum·pe m. PERU inflammation of the eyes (caused by reflection from the snow).
¡sus! interj. come on!, keep it up!
sus·cep·ti·bi·li·dad f. susceptibility, sensitivity.
sus·cep·ti·ble *or* **sus·cep·ti·vo, –va** adj. (*capaz de modificación*) susceptible; (*quisquilloso*) sensitive, touchy.
sus·ci·tar tr. (*provocar*) to stir up, provoke <*s. una contienda* to provoke an argument> —reflex. to come up, originate.
sus·cri·bir §85 tr. & reflex. var. of **subscribir.**
sus·crip·ción f. var. of **subscripción.**
sus·crip·tor, –to·ra m.f. var. of **subscriptor, –to·ra.**
su·so·di·cho, –cha adj. aforesaid, abovementioned.
sus·pen·der tr. (*colgar*) to hang; (*interrumpir*) to suspend, interrupt; (*reprobar*) to fail (a student); FIG. (*causar admiración*) to astonish, amaze; (*sancionar*) to suspend <*sus superiores lo suspendieron porque no trabajaba* his superiors suspended him because he did not work>; LAW (*en derecho*) to adjourn.
sus·pen·sión f. (*acción*) suspension; AUTO., CHEM., MUS. suspension; LAW (*en derecho*) adjournment ♦ **s. de fuego** *or* **de hostilidades** cease-fire • **s. de garantías** LAW suspension of constitutional rights • **s. de pagos** COM. suspension of payments.
sus·pen·si·vo, –va adj. suspensive ♦ **puntos suspensivos** ellipsis (punctuation mark).
sus·pen·so, –sa I. past part. see **suspender** II. adj. bewildered, baffled III. m. EDUC. (*nota*) fail, failing mark ♦ **de s.** suspense <*una película de s.* a suspense movie> • **en s.** pending, outstanding • **mantener en s.** to keep in a quandary *or* guessing.
sus·pen·so·res m.pl. AMER. suspenders.
sus·pen·so·rio, –ria I. adj. suspensory II. m. MED. suspensory, truss; SPORT. athletic supporter.
sus·pi·ca·cia f. suspicion, distrust.
sus·pi·caz adj. [pl. **-ca·ces**] suspicious, distrustful.
sus·pi·ra·do, –da I. past part. see **suspirar** II. adj. longed-for, desired.
sus·pi·rar intr. to sigh ♦ **s. por** to long for, desire.
sus·pi·ro m. (*aspiración*) sigh; (*pito*) glass whistle; CUL. ladyfinger; MUS. quarter rest; ARG., CHILE, BOT. morning glory ♦ **dar** *or* **exhalar el último s.** FIG. to breathe one's last.
sus·tan·cia f. var. of **substancia.**
sus·tan·ti·vo, –va adj. & m. var. of **substantivo, –va.**
sus·ten·tá·cu·lo m. support, prop.
sus·ten·ta·dor, –do·ra adj. (*que sustenta*) sustaining, supporting; AER. lifting.
sus·ten·ta·mien·to m. *or* **sus·ten·ta·ción** f. (*alimento*) sustenance, nourishment; (*base*) support; (*afirmación*) maintaining, holding (of an opinion); AER. lift.
sus·ten·tan·te I. adj. sustaining, supporting II. m. ARCHIT. support; (*defensor*) defender (of a thesis).
sus·ten·tar tr. (*alimentar*) to sustain, nourish; (*apoyar*) to support, hold up; (*afirmar*) to maintain, uphold —reflex. (*alimentarse*) to feed *or* nourish oneself; (*mantenerse*) to support oneself ♦ **sustentarse con** *or* **de** to feed on, live off.
sus·ten·to m. (*alimento*) sustenance, food; (*apoyo*) support; (*medios de subsistencia*) livelihood ♦ **ganarse el s.** to earn one's living • **s. principal** mainstay.
sus·ti·tu·ción f. var. of **substitución.**
sus·ti·tuir §18 tr. var. of **substituir.**
sus·ti·tu·to, –ta adj. & m.f. var. of **substituto, –ta.**
sus·to m. (*miedo*) scare, fright; FIG. (*preocupación*) dread; PERU nervous breakdown ♦ **caerse del s.** FIG. to be frightened to death • **darse** *or* **pegarse un s.** to get a scare • **dar un s. al miedo** FIG., COLL. to be as ugly as sin • **dar un s. a alguien** to frighten someone, give someone a scare.
sus·trac·ción f. var. of **substracción.**
sus·tra·er §72 tr. var. of **substraer.**
su·su·rra·dor, –ra I. adj. whispering, murmuring II. m.f. whisperer.
su·su·rran·te adj. (*que susurra*) whispering, murmuring; rustling <*hojas susurrantes* rustling leaves>.

su·su·rrar intr. *(murmurar)* to whisper, murmur; *(rumorear)* to gossip; FIG. *(el agua)* to murmur (water); *(hojas)* to rustle (leaves) —reflex. to be rumored.

su·su·rro m. *(murmullo)* whisper, murmur; FIG. murmur *<el s. del arroyo* the murmur of the brook>; rustling *<el s. de las hojas* the rustling of the leaves>.

su·su·rrón, –rro·na I. adj. whispering, murmuring II. m.f. whisperer, murmurer.

su·til adj. *(tenue)* subtle; *(delicado)* fine, delicate; FIG. *(perspicaz)* clever, sharp.

su·ti·le·za f. *(fineza)* subtlety; *(delicadeza)* fineness, delicateness; FIG. *(agudeza)* cleverness, sharpness; *(instinto)* animal instinct ♦ **s. de manos** manual dexterity.

su·ti·li·dad f. var. of **sutileza**.

su·til·men·te adv. *(con sutileza)* subtly; *(delicadeza)* finely, delicately.

su·tu·ra f. ANAT., BOT., MED. suture.

su·tu·rar tr. to suture, stitch up.

su·yo, –ya §G25, 40 I. adj. his, her, your, their *<la casa s. es elegantísima; la nuestra es bastante fea* their house is very elegant; ours is rather ugly>; of his, of hers, of yours, of theirs *<ese amigo s.* that friend of yours> ♦ **caer de s.** to be self-evident • **de s.** *(naturalmente)* naturally, inherently; *(propiamente)* in itself, per se • **s. afectísimo** yours truly (in closing a letter) II. pron. his, hers, yours, theirs *<mis hermanos no podían encontrar los suyos* my brothers could not find theirs> ♦ **hacer de las suyas** FIG. to be up to one's old tricks • **ir a lo s.** to look after one's own interests • **lo s.** one's share • **los suyos** one's people (friends, family, supporters) • **no ver la s.** to have no way out • **salirse con la s.** FIG., COLL. to get one's way • **ver la s.** to get one's chance.

svás·ti·ca f. swastika.

Swa·zi·lan·dia f. Swaziland.

swa·zi adj. & m.f. Swazi.

T

t, T f. twenty-third letter of the Spanish alphabet.

¡ta! *or* **¡ta·te!** interj. *(eso es)* easy does it!; *(llamada)* knock-knock.

ta·ba f. ANAT. anklebone; COL. vent in a water pipe; MEX. chitchat ♦ **menear t.** ARG. to chat • **tabas** knucklebones (game).

ta·ba·cal m. AGR. tobacco field.

ta·ba·ca·le·ro, –ra I. adj. pertaining to tobacco II. m.f. *(cultivador)* tobacco grower *or* dealer; —f. SP. government tobacco monopoly.

ta·ba·co m. *(planta, hoja y polvo)* tobacco; BOT. black rot ♦ **acabársele a uno el t.** ARG., CHILE to run out of money • **t. de hoja** *or* **en rama** leaf tobacco • **t. de pipa** pipe tobacco • **t. en polvo** snuff.

ta·ba·le·ar tr. to shake —intr. to drum one's fingers.

ta·ba·le·o m. *(sacudida)* shaking; *(movimiento)* fingerdrumming.

ta·ban·co m. COM. mobile food-vending stall; AMER. attic.

tá·ba·no m. ENTOM. gadfly, horsefly.

ta·ba·que·ra I. f. *(caja)* tobacco box *or* pouch; *(pipa)* bowl of a tobacco pipe II. adj. see **tabaquero, –ra**.

ta·ba·que·rí·a f. tobacco store, smoke shop.

ta·ba·que·ro, –ra I. adj. pertaining to tobacco II. m.f. tobacco processor *or* dealer —f. see **tabaquera**.

ta·bar·de·te *or* **ta·bar·di·llo** m. MED. *(tifus)* typhus; *(insolación)* sunstroke; COLL. *(persona pesada)* bore, annoying person.

ta·ba·rra f. COLL. bother, pain in the neck.

ta·ba·rro m. var. of **tábano**.

ta·ber·na f. tavern, inn.

ta·ber·ná·cu·lo m. RELIG. tabernacle.

ta·ber·na·rio, –ria adj. *(de una taberna)* of a tavern; FIG. *(grosero)* vulgar, common.

ta·ber·ne·ro, –ra m.f. bartender, tavernkeeper.

ta·ber·nu·cho, –cha m.f. COLL. dive, run-down bar.

ta·bi·que m. thin wall, partition ♦ **t. de panderete** ARCHIT. brick-on-edge partition • **t. nasal** ANAT. nasal bone.

ta·bla f. CARP. board, plank; *(losa)* slab, tablet *<una t. de mármol* a marble slab>; *(tablón)* bulletin board; *(índice)* index, table of contents; *(lista)* table, list; *(mostrador)* meat counter; *(puesto de carne)* butcher's stall; *(faja de tierra)* strip of land; *(plantel)* garden patch or plot; SEW. panel, gore; JEWEL. flat-cut diamond; PAINT. panel; MATH. table *<t. de multiplicar* multiplication table> ♦ **a raja t.** FIG., COLL. strictly, to the letter • **escapar** *or* **salvarse en una t.** FIG. to narrowly escape • **hacer t. rasa de** to disregard • **t. de armonía** MUS. sounding board • **t. de lavar** washboard • **t. de planchar** ironing board • **t. de río** river bed • **t. de salvación** FIG. last resort • **t. rasa** FIG. tabula rasa • **tablas** *(empate)* tie, draw; RELIG. tables; THEAT. boards, stage; TAUR. good seats (in an arena) • **tablas reales** backgammon board.

ta·bla·da f. ARG. stockyard, cattle yard.

ta·bla·do m. *(tablas)* floorboards; *(plataforma)* wooden platform; THEAT. stage; CRIMIN. execution scaffold; SPORT. wooden target.

ta·bla·je·ro, –ra m.f. *(construcción)* platform builder; *(carnicero)* butcher; *(garitero)* gambler; FIN. tax collector.

ta·bla·o m. SP. stage of flamenco nightclub.

ta·bla·zo m. *(golpe)* blow with a plank; MARIT. shoal.

ta·bla·zón f. boards, planking ♦ **t. de la cubierta** MARIT. deck planks.

ta·ble·a·do, –da I. past part. see **tablear** II. adj. creased, pleated III. m. creases, pleats.

ta·ble·ar tr. CARP. to divide wood into planks; SEW. to divide into pleats.

ta·ble·o m. CARP. planking; SEW. pleating.

ta·ble·ro m. *(tabla)* board, plank; *(en el juego)* board *<t. de ajedrez* chessboard>; *(pizarra)* blackboard; *(mostrador)* counter; *(de sastre)* cutting table; *(casa de juego)* casino, gambling house; CARP. door panel; ELEC. switchboard ♦ **poner** *or* **traer al t.** FIG. to risk, stake • **t. contador** abacus • **t. de dibujo** drawing board • **t. de control** instrument panel; AUTO. dashboard • **tableros** barrier (in a bull ring).

ta·ble·ta f. *(tabla pequeña)* small board; *(pastilla)* tablet, pill ♦ **estar en tabletas** FIG., COLL. to be unsure.

ta·ble·te·a·do m. rattling noise made by boards *or* planks.

ta·ble·te·ar intr. *(ruido)* to make rattling noises with boards; *(disparar)* to fire a machine gun.

ta·ble·te·o m. *(ruido)* rattling noise made by boards; ARTIL. machine-gun fire.

ta·bli·lla f. *(tabla)* small plank; *(para anuncios)* bulletin board; *(en billar)* cushion between side pockets (on billiard table); MED. splint ♦ **tablillas de San Lázaro** wooden rattle (used to request alms) • **tablillas neperianas** MATH. logarithmic tables.

ta·blón m. *(tabla)* large plank; *(para anuncios)* bulletin board; *(borrachera)* COLL. drunkenness; SPORT. trampoline.

ta·bú adj. & m. [pl. **–bú·es**] taboo.

ta·bu·la·dor, –do·ra m.f. tabulator.

ta·bu·lar adj. board-shaped.

ta·bu·re·te m. stool ♦ **taburetes** THEAT. semicircular rows in the pit of a theater.

ta·ca f. *(mueble)* small cupboard; *(mancha)* stain; CHILE edible shellfish.

ta·ca·da f. *(golpe en el billar)* stroke (in billiards); *(carambolas en el billar)* break, run (in billiards); MARIT. wedges.

ta·ca·ñe·ar intr. COLL. to be stingy *or* miserly.

ta·ca·ñe·rí·a f. *(avaricia)* stinginess, miserliness; *(astucia)* cunning.

ta·ca·ño, –na I. adj. *(avaro)* stingy, miserly; *(engañoso)* deceitful, cunning II. m.f. *(avaro)* miser, skinflint; *(engañoso)* cunning *or* crafty person.

ta·ca·zo m. blow, stroke (with a billiard cue).

tá·ci·ta·men·te adv. tactitly, by implication.

tá·ci·to, –ta adj. tacit, implied.

ta·ci·tur·ni·dad f. taciturnity.

ta·ci·tur·no, –na adj. *(callado)* taciturn, silent; *(triste)* melancholy.

ta·co m. *(cuña)* wedge; *(en el billar)* billiard cue; *(canuto)* blowpipe, peashooter; *(de papel)* pad; *(de billetes)* book of tickets; FIG., COLL. *(bocado)* snack, bite; *(trago)* swig of wine; *(lío)* mess, muddle; *(grosería)* swearword; ARM. wad, wadding; *(baqueta)* ramrod; CHILE *(atasco)* obstruction, blockage; *(persona pequeña)* short, stocky person; C. AMER. worry, fear; AMER. heel (of a shoe); MEX. taco ♦ echar *or* soltar tacos FIG., COLL. to swear, curse • hacerse un t. FIG., COLL. to get all mixed up.

ta·cón m. heel (of a shoe).

ta·co·na·zo m. kick, blow with the heel.

ta·co·ne·ar intr. to tap one's heels —tr. CHILE to stuff, fill.

ta·co·ne·o m. heel tapping.

tác·ti·ca I. f. tactic, tactics II. adj. see táctico, -ca.

tác·ti·co, -ca I. adj. tactical II. m.f. tactician —f. see táctica.

tác·til adj. tactile.

tac·to m. *(sentido)* (sense of) touch; *(acción de tocar)* touching; FIG. *(delicadeza)* tact, delicacy ♦ al t. to the touch.

ta·cua·cha f. CUBA con game.

ta·cua·ra f. ARG., BOT. kind of bamboo.

ta·cha¹ f. defect, flaw ♦ poner tachas a to find fault with.

ta·cha² f. large tack.

ta·cha·du·ra f. erasure, deletion.

ta·char tr. *(poner faltas)* to find fault with; *(borrar)* to erase (writing); FIG. *(censurar)* to censure, condemn; LAW to challenge, object to (a witness) ♦ t. de FIG. to accuse of.

ta·che·ro m. AMER. *(en una fábrica de azúcar)* sugar factory worker; *(hojalatero)* tinsmith.

ta·cho m. AMER. *(vasija de metal)* metal bowl; *(para el azúcar)* sugar evaporator; *(hoja de lata)* tin; CHILE casserole; ♦ irse al t. ARG., COLL. to fail, be unsuccessful • t. al *or* de vacío vacuum pan • t. de basura garbage can.

ta·chón m. *(raya)* line (used for crossing out); *(adorno)* trimming, decoration (on clothes); *(clavo)* stud.

ta·cho·nar tr. *(con clavos)* to stud; *(con cintas)* to trim; FIG. *(salpicar)* to dot, stud.

ta·cho·ne·rí·a f. *(con clavos)* studding; *(con cintas)* trimming.

ta·chue·la f. *(clavo pequeño)* tack; COL., CUBA metal pot *or* pan.

ta·fe·tán m. TEX. taffeta ♦ tafetanes FIG. *(banderas)* colors (flag); COLL. *(galas)* (woman's) frills *or* finery • t. inglés PHARM. court *or* sticking plaster.

ta·fia f. AMER. tafia, rum.

ta·fi·le·te m. morocco leather.

ta·fi·le·te·ar tr. to adorn with morocco leather.

ta·fi·le·te·rí·a f. *(arte)* leatherworking; *(tienda)* leather-goods store.

ta·ga·lo, -la adj. & m.f. Tagalog —m. *(idioma)* Tagalog.

ta·ga·ri·no, -na HIST. I. adj. pertaining to Moors living among Christians II. m.f. Moor who lived among Christians.

ta·gar·ni·na f. BOT. golden thistle; COLL. *(cigarro)* cheap cigar.

ta·ga·ro·te m. ORNITH. sparrow hawk; FIG. *(escribiente)* notary's clerk; COLL. *(hidalgo pobre)* genteel pauper; *(hombre alto)* beanpole; C. AMER. *(hombre de pro)* upright *or* honest person; *(mañoso)* crafty *or* cunning person.

ta·gua f. BOT. ivory nut palm; ORNITH. coot ♦ hacer taguas CHILE to dive.

ta·hi·tia·no, -na adj. & m.f. *(persona)* Tahitian —m. *(idioma)* Tahitian.

ta·ho·na f. bakery.

ta·ho·ne·ro, -ra m.f. baker.

ta·húr, -hu·ra I. adj. gambling II. m.f. cardsharp, gambler.

ta·hu·re·rí·a f. *(garito)* gambling house, casino; *(juego)* cardsharping, gambling.

tai·fa f. *(facción)* faction, party; COLL. *(gente de mala vida)* lowlifes.

tai·lan·dés, -de·sa adj. & m.f. Thai, Siamese.

Tai·lan·dia f. Thailand.

tai·ma f. *(astucia)* cunning, craftiness; CHILE sullenness, obstinacy.

tai·ma·do, -da I. adj. *(hipócrita)* sly, hypocritical; *(astuto)* cunning, crafty; CHILE sullen, obstinate II. m.f. *(hipócrita)* hypocrite; *(astuto)* cunning *or* crafty person; CHILE sullen *or* obstinate person.

tai·no, -na adj. & m.f. Taino —m. *(idioma)* Taino.

tai·ta m. *(voz infantil)* child's term of endearment for loved ones; CHILE, ECUAD., COLL. daddy, papa; CUBA term used

to address elderly Black men; COL., COLL. big husky person; ARG. bully.

ta·ja f. *(división)* division, sharing; *(escudo)* shield.

ta·ja·da f. *(porción)* portion, share; *(raja)* slice; COLL. *(ronquera)* hoarseness; *(tos)* cough; SL. *(borrachera)* drunken spree *or* binge ♦ hacer tajadas to cut *or* slash to pieces • sacar t. to benefit *or* profit (from).

ta·ja·de·ra f. *(cuchilla)* chopping knife; *(cortafrío)* cold chisel.

ta·ja·de·ro m. CUL. chopping block *or* board.

ta·ja·do, -da I. past part. see tajar II. adj. *(escarpado)* steep, sheer; COLL. *(borracho)* smashed, plastered; HER. divided (shield).

ta·ja·dor, -do·ra I. adj. cutting, chopping II. m.f. *(persona)* cutter, chopper —m. *(tajo)* cutting *or* chopping board.

ta·ja·du·ra f. *(acción)* cutting, chopping; *(porción)* cut, slice.

ta·ja·mar m. MARIT. cutwater; CHILE dike, seawall; ARG. *(presa)* dam; *(balsa)* pool, pond.

ta·jan·te I. adj. *(cortante)* cutting, sharp; FIG. *(decisivo)* final, definitive; *(categórico)* categorical <una respuesta t. a categorical answer> II. m. butcher.

ta·jar tr. to cut, slice —reflex. COLL. to get drunk.

ta·je·a f. *(atarjea de cañería)* watercourse, channel; *(alcantarilla)* drainpipe.

ta·jo m. *(corte)* cut, gash; *(tarea)* job, task; *(taller)* work, workplace <voy al t. I am going to work>; *(escarpa vertical)* steep cliff; *(filo)* cutting edge; *(de ejecución)* (execution) block; *(con la espada)* slash, slice (with a sword); GEOG. gorge; CUL. cutting board; CHILE, VEN. horse trail.

tal I. adj. *(igual)* such, such a <nunca he visto t. cosa I have never seen such a thing>; *(tanto)* so great a, such a <no es posible que haya cometido t. error it is not possible that he has committed such an error>; *(cierto)* certain <un t. José Gómez te llamó a certain Joseph Gómez called you> ♦ como si t. cosa as if there were nothing to it • t. cual such as <te lo venderé t. cual es I will sell it to you such as it is>; *(uno que otro)* an occasional, a few <no cuento más que con t. cual amigo I rely on only a few friends>; *(pasadero)* so-so, fair • t. vez perhaps, maybe II. pron. such a thing <yo no haría t. I would not do such a thing>; *(alguno)* some, someone ♦ fulano de t. so-and-so • t. para cual COLL. two of a kind • t. por cual a nobody III. adv. thus, so ♦ con t. que provided that • ¿qué t.? COLL. how goes it?

ta·la f. *(de árboles)* cutting down, felling (trees); *(destrucción)* destruction, ruin; *(juego)* tipcat (game); *(palito)* cat, stick (used in tipcat); MIL. tree line fortification; ARG., BOT. hackberry tree.

ta·la·bar·te·rí·a f. saddlery.

ta·la·bar·te·ro m. saddler.

ta·la·dor, -do·ra I. adj. *(que corta)* cutting, felling; *(que destruye)* destroying, ravaging II. m.f. *(cortador)* cutter, feller; *(destruidor)* destroyer, ravager.

ta·la·dra·dor, -do·ra I. adj. drilling, boring II. m.f. *(persona)* driller, borer —f. *(máquina)* drill, boring machine ♦ t. radial MECH. turret drill • t. torneadora MECH. boring and turning machine.

ta·la·drar tr. *(horadar)* to drill, bore; FIG. *(herir los oídos)* to pierce the ears; FIG. *(comprender)* to understand, fathom; COL. to swindle, defraud.

ta·la·dro m. *(taladradora)* drill; *(barrena)* gimlet; *(agujero)* drill hole; ENTOM. shipworm ♦ t. de empuje MECH. push drill • t. de trinquete ratchet drill • t. múltiple gang drill • t. neumático *or* de aire comprimido air drill.

tá·la·mo m. *(lecho conyugal)* nuptial bed; *(alcoba conyugal)* nuptial chamber; ANAT., BOT. thalamus ♦ t. óptico ANAT. optic thalamus.

ta·lán m. ding-dong (sound of a bell).

ta·lan·que·ra f. *(de defensa)* barricade; FIG. *(seguridad)* safety, defense; COL. picket fence.

ta·lan·te m. *(humor)* humor, mood; *(voluntad)* will ♦ hacer algo de buen t. to do something willingly • hacer algo de mal t. to do something unwillingly.

ta·lar¹ I. adj. long, full-length (gown) II. m.pl. MYTH. talaria, winged sandals (of Mercury).

ta·lar² tr. *(un árbol)* to cut down, fell (a tree); *(destruir)* to destroy, devastate.

tal·co m. MIN. talc; PHARM. talcum powder; (material) tinsel.

tal·co·so, –sa adj. talcose, talcous.

ta·le·ga f. (saco) bag, sack; (contenido) bagful, sackful; (para el cabello) hairnet, snood; (pañal) diaper; (dinero) money, wealth; FIG., COLL. (pecados) sins.

ta·le·ga·da f. bagful, sackful.

ta·le·ga·zo m. (golpe) blow with a sack; COLL. (caída) fall.

ta·le·go m. (saco) bag, sack; FIG., COLL. (persona gorda) fat, clumsy person.

ta·len·to m. FIG. (aptitud) talent, aptitude; HIST. talent (ancient weight and coin).

ta·len·to·so, –sa or **ta·len·tu·do, –da** adj. talented, gifted.

ta·lio m. CHEM. thallium.

ta·lión m. talion, retribution ♦ **ley del t.** principle of an eye for an eye.

ta·lis·mán m. talisman, amulet.

tal·mud m. RELIG. Talmud.

tal·mú·di·co, –ca adj. RELIG. Talmudic.

ta·lón m. ANAT., ZOOL. heel; (de zapato) heel (of a sock, shoe); MUS. heel (of a violin bow); ARCHIT. talon (molding); AUTO. flange, rim; (comprobante) coupon, receipt, check (detached from its stub); MARIT. heel (of a boat) ♦ **pisarle a alguien los talones** FIG. to be at someone's heels, follow closely.

ta·lo·na·do, –da I. adj. AMER. with stubs II. f. kick with the heels (given to horses).

ta·lo·na·rio m. (de recibos) receipt book; (de cheques) checkbook.

ta·lo·na·zo m. kick with the heel.

ta·lo·ne·ar intr. COLL. (andar de prisa) to step lively; AMER. to spur on a horse.

ta·lo·ne·ra f. (de calcetines) heel piece; (refuerzo) binding (of pants).

ta·lud m. slope, incline.

ta·lla f. (estatura) stature, height; (medida) size (of clothing); (escultura) wood carving or engraving; (premio) reward, bounty; (en naipes) hand (in cards); FIG. (altura) stature; MED. lithotomy, gallstone removal; ARG., CHILE chitchat; C. AMER. hoax, lie ♦ **tener t. para** to be cut out for.

ta·lla·do, –da I. past part. see **tallar²** II. adj. (madera) carved; (metal) engraved; JEWEL. cut ♦ **bien t.** FIG. well-built III. m. (en madera) carving; (en metal) engraving; JEWEL. cutting.

ta·lla·dor m. (grabador) engraver; MIL. measurer (of recruits); ARG. banker, dealer (in cards).

ta·lla·du·ra f. (en madera) carving; (en metal) engraving; CARP. notch, groove.

ta·llar¹ I. adj. ready for cutting (said of trees) II. m. timber, timberland.

ta·llar² tr. (en naipes) to deal (cards); (en madera) to carve; (en metal) to engrave; JEWEL. to cut; ARTS to sculpt; (de impuestos) to tax; (valuar) to value, appraise; (medir) to measure (a person's height); COLL. (fastidiar) to bother, annoy —intr. ARG., CHILE (charlar) to converse, chat; CHILE (cortejar) to flirt.

ta·lla·rín m. CUL. noodle.

ta·lle m. (de una mujer) figure, shape; (de un hombre) physique, build; (cintura) waist; FIG. (apariencia) looks, appearance; SEW. waist, bodice; CHILE corset.

ta·ller¹ m. (de obreros) shop, workshop; (de artistas) studio, atelier ♦ **t. de reparaciones** AUTO. repair or body shop.

ta·ller² m. cruet stand.

ta·llis·ta m.f. (escultor) sculptor; (grabador) engraver; JEWEL. gem cutter.

ta·llo m. BOT. (de la planta) stalk, stem; (renuevo) sprout, shoot; COL. cabbage.

ta·llu·do, –da adj. (de tallo largo) having a long stalk; FIG. (muy alto) tall, lanky; (de edad madura) middle-aged.

ta·mal m. AMER., CUL. tamale; CHILE package, bundle; AMER., COLL. (intriga) intrigue.

ta·ma·la·da f. MEX. meal of tamales.

ta·ma·le·ro, –ra m.f. tamale vendor.

ta·man·go m. ARG., CHILE crude shoe (worn by gauchos).

ta·ma·ñi·to, –ta adj. confused, abashed ♦ **dejar a alguien t.** to make someone feel small.

ta·ma·ño, –ña I. adj. (tan grande) so large or big, such a

large or big <nunca podremos reembolsar t. deuda we can never repay such a large debt>; (tan pequeño) so small, such a small; (muy grande) very big or wide <abrir tamaños ojos to open one's eyes wide> II. m. (dimensión) size, dimension <¿de qué t. es la caja? what size is the box?>; (volumen) volume, capacity ♦ **del t. de** as large as • **t. natural** life-size.

tá·ma·ra f. BOT. date palm ♦ **támaras** cluster of dates.

ta·ma·rin·do m. BOT. tamarind.

ta·ma·rriz·qui·to, –ta or **ta·ma·rrus·qui·to, –ta** adj. COLL. tiny, teeny.

ta·ma·ru·gal m. CHILE mesquite grove.

ta·ma·ru·go m. CHILE., BOT. mesquite.

tam·ba·le·an·te adj. staggering, tottering.

tam·ba·le·ar intr. to stagger, totter.

tam·ba·le·o m. staggering, tottering.

tam·be·ro, –ra I. adj. ARG. (manso) tame, gentle; (ganado) dairy (said of cattle); S. AMER. pertaining to an inn II. m.f. S. AMER. (dueño de un tambo) innkeeper; ARG., CHILE dairy farmer.

tam·bién adv. (además) also, too; (asimismo) likewise.

tam·bo m. AMER. (parador) roadside inn; ARG. dairy farm; PAR. hitching post.

tam·bor m. MUS. (instrumento) drum; (persona) drummer; ANAT. eardrum; TECH. drum, cylinder; SEW. tambour, embroidery frame; (del revólver) cylinder; (del azúcar) sugar sieve; ARCHIT. tambour; MARIT. capstan; AUTO. brake drum; CUBA burlap; MEX. spring mattress ♦ **a t. batiente** FIG. triumphantly • **t. mayor** drum major.

tam·bo·ra f. MUS. bass drum; AMER. drum, metal container; CUBA lie, hoax.

tam·bo·re·ar intr. to drum (with the fingers).

tam·bo·re·o m. drumming, tapping.

tam·bo·re·te m. MUS. small drum; MARIT. cap (for joining spars).

tam·bo·ril m. MUS. tabor, small drum.

tam·bo·ri·le·ar intr. (el tamboril) to beat; (con los dedos) to drum, tap (with the fingers) —tr. (alabar) to praise, extol; PRINT. to level, plane down (type).

tam·bo·ri·le·o m. beating (of a drum).

tam·bo·ri·le·ro, –ra m.f. drummer.

tam·bo·rín or **tam·bo·ri·no** m. MUS. small tabor or drum.

ta·me·me m. CHILE, MEX., PERU Indian porter.

Tá·me·sis m. Thames.

ta·miz m. [pl. **-mi·ces**] sifter, sieve.

ta·mi·zar §04 tr. (pasar por el tamiz) to sift, sieve; (luz) to filter (light); FIG. (seleccionar) to screen.

ta·mo m. (del lino) lint, fuzz; (de las semillas) grain dust; (debajo de los muebles) dust.

tam·po·co §G45 adv. neither, not either.

tam·pón m. (para entintar) stamp or ink pad; PHARM. tampon.

tam·po·nar tr. to stamp, seal.

tam-tam m. MUS. tom-tom.

tan¹ m. rat-a-tat (sound of a drum).

tan² adv. [contr. of **tanto** used before adj. and adv.] so, as <no soy t. alto como Enrique I am not as tall as Henry> ♦ **t. pronto como** as soon as • **t. siquiera** at least, at the least • **t. sólo** only, merely.

ta·na·gra f. ORNITH. tanager; ARTS figurine.

ta·na·te m. HOND., MEX. leather bag; GUAT. bundle ♦ **cargar con los tanates** C. AMER., FIG., COLL. to pack one's bags.

tan·da f. (turno) turn; (de trabajadores) shift (of workers); (tarea) task, job; (capa) layer <una t. de ladrillos a layer of bricks>; (partida) game (of billiards); COLL. (gran cantidad) lot, bunch; THEAT. performance, show; MEX., COLL. informal group savings plan.

tan·de·o m. distribution of irrigation water by turns.

tan·ga·ni·llas adv. ♦ **en t.** unsteadily, shakily.

tan·gen·te adj. & f. tangent ♦ **irse** or **salir por la t.** FIG., COLL. to go off on a tangent, digress.

Tán·ger Tangier, Tangiers.

tan·gi·ble adj. tangible.

tan·go m. MUS. tango.

tan·gue·ar intr. to tango.

tá·ni·co, –ca adj. CHEM. tannic.

ta·ni·no m. CHEM. tannin.

tan·que m. *(depósito)* tank, reservoir; *(barco)* tanker; MIL. tank.
tan·ta·lio m. CHEM. tantalum.
tan·ta·ran·tán m. *(del tambor)* rat-a-tat-tat (sound of a drum); FIG., COLL. *(golpe)* resounding blow.
tan·te·a·dor, –do·ra m.f. *(persona)* scorekeeper —m. *(marcador)* scoreboard.
tan·te·ar tr. *(calcular)* to do a rough calculation of; *(medir)* to gauge, size up; *(examinar)* to scrutinize, examine closely; *(considerar)* to weigh, consider carefully; *(explorar)* to probe, test; *(sondear)* to sound out; *(en el juego)* to keep score of; *(bosquejar)* to sketch —intr. *(en el juego)* to keep score; *(vacilar)* to feel one's way, grope.
tan·te·o m. *(cálculo)* rough calculation *or* estimate; *(escrutinio)* examination, scrutiny; *(consideración)* careful consideration; *(exploración)* probe, test; *(sondeo)* sounding out; *(en el juego)* score, points ♦ **al t.** roughly, approximately.
tan·to, –ta I. adj. so much <*jamás he visto t. dinero* I have never seen so much money> ♦ **tantas** *or* **tantos** so many, as many **II.** pron. *(eso)* that <*a t. arrastra la codicia* that is what greed leads to>; so much <*comí t.* don't eat so much> ♦ **las tantas** late hour, wee hour ♦ **por (lo) t.** therefore • **t. como** *or* **t. cuanto** as much as • **tantos** so many • **tantos como** *or* **tantos cuanto** as many as **III.** m. *(cierta cantidad)* certain amount; *(ficha)* chip, counter; *(unidad de cuenta)* point (in a game) <*apuntar los tantos* to keep track of the points> ♦ **a tantos de** on a certain date in <*a tantos de junio* on a certain date in June> • **en t.** *or* **entre t.** COLL. in the meantime • **no ser para t.** not to be so bad • **otro t.** the same thing • **t. por ciento** per cent • **y tantos** and some, odd <*mil y tantos* a thousand odd> **IV.** adv. *(de tal modo)* so much <*comí t. que no pude levantarme de la silla* I ate so much that I could not get up from the chair>; so long <*se tardaron t.* they delayed so long>; *(hasta tal grado)* to such an extent; as much <*yo sé t. como tú* I know as much as you> ♦ **t. más** all the more • **t. mejor** all the better • **t. que** so much that.
Tan·za·ni·a, República Unida de f. United Republic of Tanzania.
tan·za·nia·no, –na adj. & m.f. Tanzanian.
ta·ñe·dor, –do·ra m.f. MUS. player (of an instrument).
ta·ñer §68 tr. MUS. *(un instrumento)* to play; *(campana)* to toll —intr. to drum (with the fingers).
ta·ñi·do m. *(de un instrumento)* sound (of an instrument); *(de una campana)* tolling (of a bell).
ta·o·ís·mo m. RELIG. Taoism.
ta·o·ís·ta adj. & m.f. RELIG. Taoist.
ta·pa f. *(cubierta)* top, lid, cover; *(de un libro)* cover (of a book); *(del zapato)* heel lift; *(bocado)* appetizer, hors d'oeuvre (served in a bar) ♦ **levantar la t. de los sesos** FIG., COLL. to blow someone's brains out • **t. de los sesos** COLL. skull.
ta·pa·ba·rro m. CHILE, PERU mudguard.
ta·pa·bo·cas m. [pl. **-cas**] *(bufanda)* scarf, muffler; ARTIL. tampion.
ta·pa·cu·bos m. [pl. **-bos**] AUTO. hubcap.
ta·pa·da f. *(mujer)* veiled woman; MEX. denial.
ta·pa·de·ra f. *(cobertura)* cover, lid; FIG. *(persona)* cover, front.
ta·pa·do I. past part. see **tapar II.** adj. ZOOL. unspotted; COL. stupid, dull **III.** m. AMER. *(tesoro)* buried treasure; *(abrigo)* cloak, cape; COL. barbecue.
ta·pa·dor, –do·ra I. adj. covering **II.** m. *(cubierta)* cover, lid; *(tapón)* plug, stopper.
ta·pa·du·ra f. *(acción de cubrir)* covering up; *(acción de cerrar)* stopping up, plugging up.
ta·pa·gu·je·ros m. [pl. **-ros**] FIG., COLL. *(albañil malo)* inept bricklayer *or* mason; *(sustituto)* substitute, stand-in.
tá·pa·lo m. MEX. shawl, mantle.
ta·pa·mien·to m. var. of **tapadura**.
ta·pan·co m. PHILIP. bamboo awning.
ta·pa·o·jo m. FIG. *(engaño)* swindle; COL., VEN. *(quitapón)* ornamental headstall (on a harness); COL. *(anteojera)* blinders (on a horse).
ta·par tr. *(cubrir)* to cover, cover up; *(cerrar)* to plug up, stop up; *(ocultar)* to block, obstruct (the view); FIG. *(esconder)* to conceal, hide —reflex. to cover oneself up.

ta·pa·ra f. BOT. gourd ♦ **vaciarse como una t.** FIG., COLL. to spill the beans.
ta·pa·ro m. AMER., BOT. gourd tree.
ta·pa·rra·bo m. *(de salvaje)* loincloth; *(de bañador)* bikini.
ta·pe·te m. *(alfombra)* small rug *or* carpet; *(de mesa)* table runner ♦ **estar sobre el t.** FIG. to be under discussion • **poner sobre el t.** FIG. to bring up for discussion • **t. verde** card *or* gambling table.
ta·pia f. *(pared de tierra)* mud *or* adobe wall; *(cerca)* retaining wall ♦ **más sordo que una t.** FIG., COLL. deaf as a post.
ta·pia·dor m. mud wall builder.
ta·pial m. *(molde)* mold for mud walls; *(tapia)* mud wall.
ta·piar tr. *(cerrar con tapias)* to wall in, enclose; FIG. *(cerrar)* to seal, close up.
ta·pi·cé, tapice see **tapizar**.
ta·pi·ce·rí·a f. *(arte de hacer tapices)* tapestry-making; *(arte de tapizar muebles)* upholstery; *(conjunto de tapices)* tapestries; *(tienda del tapicero)* upholsterer's shop.
ta·pi·ce·ro, –ra m.f. *(que hace tapices)* tapestry maker; *(que tapiza muebles)* upholsterer; *(que pone alfombras)* carpet layer.
ta·pio·ca f. CUL. tapioca.
ta·pir m. ZOOL. tapir.
ta·pi·ru·jar·se reflex. COLL. to wrap *or* bundle oneself up.
ta·pis·ca f. C. AMER., MEX., AGR. corn harvest.
ta·pis·car §70 tr. C. AMER., AGR. to harvest corn.
ta·piz m. [pl. **-pi·ces**] tapestry.
ta·pi·zar §04 tr. *(adornar con tapices)* to hang with tapestries; FIG. *(muebles)* to upholster; *(el suelo)* to carpet.
ta·pón m. *(de las botellas)* cork, stopper; *(de tonel)* bung, plug; SURG. tampon ♦ **t. de alberca** *or* **de cuba** COLL. short, fat person • **t. de desagüe** drain plug • **t. de espita** spigot • **t. de rosca** screw-on cap.
ta·po·na·mien·to m. *(de un agujero)* plugging, stopping up; SURG. tamponage, tamponade.
ta·po·nar tr. *(un agujero)* to plug, stop up; SURG. to tampon.
ta·po·na·zo m. pop (of a cork).
ta·po·ne·rí·a f. *(conjunto de tapones)* corks, stoppers; *(fábrica)* cork *or* stopper factory; *(industria)* cork *or* stopper industry.
ta·po·ne·ro, –ra I. adj. cork, stopper <*la industria t.* the cork industry> **II.** m.f. cork *or* stopper maker.
ta·pu·jar·se reflex. COLL. to cover *or* veil one's face (said of a woman).
ta·pu·jo m. *(embozo)* muffler; FIG. *(disimulo)* pretense, deceit.
ta·que·ar tr. AMER., ARTIL. to ram, tamp (a firearm); FIG. *(llenar mucho)* to stuff, cram —intr. ARG., CHILE to tap (with the heels); MEX. to eat tacos.
ta·que·ra f. rack (for billiard cues).
ta·qui·gra·fí·a f. shorthand, stenography.
ta·qui·gra·fiar §30 tr. to write in shorthand, stenograph.
ta·quí·gra·fo, –fa m.f. stenographer.
ta·qui·lla f. *(armario de oficina)* filing cabinet; *(casillero)* pigeonholes, cubbyholes; THEAT. box office; RAIL. ticket office; *(cantidad recaudada)* receipts; ECUAD. small nail, tack; C. RICA bar, tavern ♦ **hacer t.** *or* **tener buena t.** FIG. to be a box-office hit.
ta·qui·lle·ro, –ra I. m.f. RAIL., THEAT. ticket seller *or* agent **II.** adj. CINEM., THEAT., FIG. box-office <*éxito t.* box-office hit>.
ta·qui·me·ca f. COLL. shorthand typist.
ta·ra¹ f. *(peso)* tare; *(defecto)* defect.
ta·ra² f. tally stick.
ta·ra³ f. VEN., ENTOM. green grasshopper; COL., ZOOL. poisonous snake; CHILE, PERU, BOT. divi-divi.
ta·ra·bi·lla f. *(de molino)* millclapper; *(para cerrar puertas)* latch, catch; *(de la sierra)* wooden peg (used to tighten the cord of a frame saw); FIG., COLL. *(persona)* chatterbox; *(palabras desordenadas)* jabber, nonsense; AMER. bull-roarer, rattle.
ta·ra·bi·ta f. *(de la cincha)* tongue (of a belt buckle); S. AMER. rope bridge.
ta·ra·do, –da I. past part. see **tarar II.** adj. *(una mercancía)* defective, damaged; *(una persona)* handicapped.
ta·ram·ba·na m.f. COLL. madcap, scatterbrain.
ta·ran·tín m. C. AMER., CUBA kitchen gadget.

ta·rán·tu·la f. ZOOL. tarantula ♦ **picado de la t.** FIG., COLL. nervous, jumpy.

ta·rar tr. COM. to tare.

ta·ra·re·ar tr. to hum.

ta·ra·re·o m. humming.

ta·ra·ri·ra f. COLL. (*bulla alegre*) noisy merriment; ICHTH. fresh-water fish —m.f. COLL. (*botarate*) noisy person.

ta·ras·ca f. (*figura de dragón*) dragon figure (in Corpus Christi processions); FIG., COLL. (*mujer*) hag, witch; CHILE, C. RICA bigmouth.

ta·ras·ca·da f. (*mordedura*) bite, wound; FIG., COLL. (*respuesta áspera*) rude reply.

ta·ras·car §70 tr. to bite (said of dogs).

tar·dan·za f. (*demora*) delay; (*lentitud*) dalliance.

tar·dar intr. (*demorarse*) to be long, delay <*no tardes en avisarnos* don't delay in informing us>; (*durar*) to take <*el tren tardó tres horas en llegar* the train took three hours to arrive>; (*durar mucho*) to take a long time <*él tardó en contestar* he took a long time to answer>; (*llegar tarde*) to be late ♦ **a más t.** at the latest.

tar·de I. f. afternoon, (early) evening ♦ **buenas tardes** good afternoon • **de t. en t.** now and then II. adv. (*a hora avanzada*) late <*nos acostamos tarde* we went to bed late>; (*fuera de tiempo*) too late <*el médico llegó t.* the doctor arrived too late> ♦ **a la caída de la t.** at dusk • **hacerse t.** to get or grow late • **lo más t.** at the latest • **más vale t. que nunca** better late than never • **por** or **de** or **en la t.** in the afternoon • **t. o temprano** sooner or later.

tar·de·cer §17 intr. (*anochecer*) to grow dark; (*atardecer*) to get late.

tar·dí·a·men·te adv. too late, belatedly.

tar·dí·o, –a adj. (*que sucede después*) late, belated; (*lento*) slow; AGR. late (crop).

tar·do, –da adj. (*lento*) slow; (*retrasado*) late, belated; (*torpe*) slow, dull-witted.

ta·re·a f. task, job ♦ **t. escolar** homework.

ta·ri·fa f. (*tasa*) tariff, rate; (*precio*) fare (on vehicles); (*tabla*) price list.

ta·ri·far tr. to price, apply a tariff or rate to —intr. FIG. to quarrel.

ta·ri·ma f. movable platform, dais.

tar·ja f. (*escudo*) buckler, shield; (*palo*) tally stick; COLL. (*golpe*) bash, blow; ARG., CHILE calling card.

tar·jar tr. (*señalar*) to tally; CHILE to cross out.

tar·je·ta f. card <*t. de identidad* identity card>; (*en un mapa*) heading (on a map); ARCHIT. cartouche, inscribed tablet ♦ **t. de crédito** credit card • **t. de visita** calling card • **t. perforada** punch card • **t. postal** post card.

tar·je·te·ar·se reflex. COLL. to exchange calling cards.

tar·je·te·o m. exchange of calling cards.

tar·je·te·ra f. AMER. card case.

tar·je·te·ro m. card case.

tar·quín m. mud, slime.

tar·qui·no, –na adj. & m.f. ARG. thoroughbred (bull or cow).

ta·rra·ja f. MECH. diestock; VEN. leather tally.

ta·rro m. (*vasija*) jar, pot; MEX. (*vasija de lata*) tin can; CUBA, ZOOL. horn; AMER. top hat.

tar·sa·na f. C. RICA, ECUAD., PERU, BOT. soap bark, quillai bark.

tar·so m. ANAT., ORNITH., ZOOL. tarsus.

tar·ta f. CUL. (*pastel*) tart, pie; (*tartera*) baking pan.

tár·ta·go m. BOT. spurge; FIG., COLL. (*suceso infeliz*) misfortune; (*broma*) practical joke.

tar·ta·je·ar intr. to stutter, stammer.

tar·ta·je·o m. stuttering, stammering.

tar·ta·jo·so, –sa I. adj. stuttering, stammering II. m.f. stutterer, stammerer.

tar·ta·mu·de·ar intr. to stammer, stutter.

tar·ta·mu·de·o m. stammering, stuttering.

tar·ta·mu·dez f. stammering, stuttering.

tar·ta·mu·do, –da I. adj. stammering, stuttering II. m.f. stammerer, stutterer.

tar·tán m. TEX. tartan, scotch plaid.

tár·ta·ro I. m. CHEM., DENT. tartar; VEN., BOT. spurge II. adj. see **tártara, –ra.**

tár·ta·ro, –ra I. adj. Tartar ♦ **bistec t.** CUL. steak tartare • **salsa t.** CUL. tartar sauce II. m.f. Tartar —m. see **tártaro.**

tar·te·ra f. CUL. baking pan; (*fiambrera*) lunch box.

ta·ru·ga·da f. MEX. prank, piece of mischief.

ta·ru·go m. (*clavija de madera*) wooden peg; (*trozo de madera*) wooden block; (*zoquete*) blockhead, dolt; CUBA fright, scare.

ta·rum·ba adj. mixed up, confused ♦ **volverle a alguien t.** COLL. to confuse or rattle someone • **volverse t.** COLL. to get confused or rattled.

ta·sa f. (*valoración*) appraisal, valuation; (*precio*) rate, official price <*t. de interés* rate of interest>; (*norma*) standard, norm ♦ **sin t.** without limit.

ta·sa·ción f. valuation, appraisal.

ta·sa·dor, –do·ra I. adj. appraising II. m.f. appraiser.

ta·sa·je·ar tr. AMER., CUL. to jerk (beef).

ta·sa·jo m. CUL. (*carne seca*) jerked or hung beef; (*pedazo de carne*) piece of meat; COL. tall, thin man.

ta·sa·ju·do, –da adj. AMER. tall and thin.

ta·sar tr. (*poner precio*) to fix or set the price of; (*valorar*) to value, appraise; FIG. (*medir*) to ration; (*reducir*) to limit.

tas·ca f. COLL. (*riña*) fight, quarrel; SL. (*taberna*) dive, bar; (*garito*) gambling house; PERU turbulent coastal waters.

tas·car §70 tr. to scutch, swingle (flax); FIG. (*un animal*) to chomp; ECUAD. to chew ♦ **t. el freno** FIG. to chomp at the bit.

ta·ta f. (*niñera*) nanny, nurse (in babytalk) —m. AMER., COLL. (*papá*) daddy, papa.

ta·ta·ra·bue·lo, –la m. great-great-grandfather —f. great-great-grandmother ♦ **tatarabuelos** great-great-grandparents.

ta·ta·ra·nie·to, –ta m. great-great-grandson —f. great-great-granddaughter ♦ **tataranietos** great-great-grandchildren.

ta·tas f.pl. ♦ **andar a t.** COLL. to toddle.

¡ta·te! interj. (*cuidado*) careful!, watch out!; (*ya comprendo*) I see!, so that's it!

ta·to m. COLL. kid brother.

ta·tua·je m. (*acción de tatuar*) tattooing; (*dibujo*) tattoo.

ta·tuar §67 tr. to tattoo.

tau f. (*letra*) tau (Greek letter); (*cruz*) tau cross.

tau·ma·tur·gia f. thaumaturgy, miracle-working.

tau·ma·tur·go, –ga m.f. thaumaturge, miracle worker.

tau·ri·no, –na adj. taurine, having to do with bulls or bullfighting.

tau·ro·ma·quia f. bullfighting.

tau·to·lo·gí·a f. RHET. tautology.

tau·to·ló·gi·co, –ca adj. tautological.

ta·xa·ti·vo, –va adj. LAW limitative, restrictive.

ta·xi m. taxi, taxicab.

ta·xi·der·mia f. taxidermy.

ta·xí·me·tro m. taximeter.

ta·xis·ta m.f. taxi driver.

ta·xo·no·mí·a f. BIOL. taxonomy.

ta·xo·nó·mi·co, –ca adj. taxonomic, taxonomical.

taz a taz adv. tit for tat.

ta·za f. (*para beber*) cup; (*contenido*) cupful; (*de una fuente*) basin (of a fountain); (*de un retrete*) bowl (of a toilet); (*de una espada*) cup guard (of a sword); CHILE washbasin.

taz con taz adv. even, equal.

ta·zón m. large cup.

te¹ f. (*letra*) tee (letter); CARP. T-square.

te² §G30 pron. you <*te quiero* I love you>; you, to you <*te mandaron una carta* they sent a letter to you>; you, for you <*te compré un regalo* I bought a present for you>; from you <*no le dejes quitarte la pelota* don't let him take the ball from you>; yourself <*cálmate* calm yourself>.

té m. BOT. tea ♦ **t. bailable** tea dance • **t. del Paraguay** BOT. maté.

te·a f. (*antorcha*) torch; MARIT. anchor rope.

te·a·tral adj. theatrical.

te·a·tra·li·dad f. theatricality.

te·a·tro m. ARTS, MIL. theater ♦ **t. de operaciones** MIL. theater of operations • **tener mucho t.** FIG., COLL. to be theatrical or melodramatic.

te·bai·da f. (*desierto*) desert, solitary place; (*soledad*) solitude.

te·ba·no, –na adj. & m.f. Theban.

Te·bas f. Thebes.

te·ca·li m. MEX., MIN. tecali, Mexican onyx.

te·cla f. *(de un instrumento o aparato)* key (of an instrument or machine); FIG. *(materia delicada)* delicate matter ♦ **dar en la t.** COLL. to hit the nail on the head • **tocar una t.** COLL. to pull strings.

te·cla·do m. keyboard.

te·cle·a·do I. past part. see **teclear** II. s. fingering.

te·cle·ar intr. *(tocar las teclas)* to finger a keyboard; FIG., COLL. *(mover los dedos)* to drum with the fingers; *(tocar el piano)* to play the piano; CHILE to be on the verge of death —tr. FIG., COLL. to feel one's way with, approach from various angles (a problem).

te·cle·o m. drumming with the fingers.

tec·ne·cio m. CHEM. technetium.

téc·ni·ca I. f. *(método o habilidad)* technique; *(tecnología)* technology; *(ingeniería)* engineering ♦ **t. electrónica** electronics • **t. hidráulica** hydraulic engineering II. adj. see **técnico, -ca**.

téc·ni·ca·men·te adv. technically.

téc·ni·co, -ca I. adj. technical II. m.f. *(especialista)* technician, expert; *(ingeniero)* engineer ♦ **t. agrícola** agronomist • **t. electricista** electrical engineer —f. see **técnica**.

tec·no·cra·cia f. technocracy.

tec·no·lo·gí·a f. technology.

tec·no·ló·gi·co, -ca adj. technological.

te·co·lo·te m. HOND., MEX., ORNITH. owl; COLL. cop on night shift.

te·co·ma·te *or* **te·co·mal** m. C. AMER. drinking gourd.

tec·tó·ni·co, -ca GEOL. I. adj. tectonic II. f. tectonics.

te·cha·do I. past part. see **techar** II. m. *(techo)* roof, ceiling; *(cobertizo)* shed ♦ **bajo t.** indoors, under cover.

te·cha·dor m. roofer.

te·char tr. to roof.

te·cho m. *(tejado)* roof; *(parte interior)* ceiling; FIG. *(casa)* roof (over one's head); AVIA. ceiling.

te·chum·bre f. *(techo)* roof; *(materials)* roofing.

te·diar tr. to hate, loathe.

te·dio m. *(repugnancia)* repugnance, loathing; *(aburrimiento)* boredom, tedium.

te·dio·so, -sa adj. tedious, boring.

te·gu·men·to m. BOT., ZOOL. tegument.

Te·he·rán Tehran, Teheran.

te·í·na f. CHEM. theine, thein.

te·ís·mo m. RELIG. theism.

te·ja f. tile; *(de la espada)* steel facing (of a sword); MARIT. hollow cut for scarfing ♦ **a toca t.** in cash, for cash.

te·ja·do I. past part. see **techar** II. m. *(techo)* roof ♦ **empezar la casa por el t.** FIG. to put the cart before the horse.

te·ja·ma·ní CUBA *or* **te·ja·ma·nil** MEX. m. shingle, roofing tile.

te·jar¹ m. *(fábrica de tejas)* tile factory *or* works; *(fábrica de ladrillos)* brick factory *or* works.

te·jar² tr. to tile.

te·je·dor, -do·ra I. adj. *(que teje)* weaving; AMER., COLL. scheming, conniving II. m.f. *(persona que teje)* weaver; AMER., COLL. schemer, conniver —m. ENTOM. water strider; ORNITH. weaverbird —f. AMER. stitching machine.

te·je·du·ra f. *(acción de tejer)* weaving; *(textura)* texture, weave.

te·je·ma·ne·je m. *(habilidad)* skill, knack; COLL. *(intriga)* scheme, intrigue.

te·jer intr. *(entrelazar)* to weave, spin; *(hacer punto)* to knit; FIG. *(formar)* to weave, concoct; AMER. to scheme, plot ♦ **t. y destejer** FIG. to blow hot and cold.

te·je·ra *or* **te·je·rí·a** f. tile kiln *or* works.

te·je·ro m. tile maker.

te·ji·do m. *(tela)* cloth, fabric; *(textura)* texture, weave; ANAT., BIOL. tissue ♦ **t. de alambre** wire mesh • **t. de punto** jersey, knit • **t. muscular** muscle tissue.

te·jo m. *(para jugar)* counter, chip; *(juego)* quoits; *(plancha metálica)* metal disk, blank; MEX., TECH. step bearing; BOT. yew tree.

te·jo·lo·te m. MEX. stone pestle.

te·jón¹ m. ZOOL. badger.

te·jón² m. gold ingot *or* disk.

te·jue·la f. *(teja pequeña)* small tile; *(pedazo de barro)* piece of brick; EQUIT. saddletree.

te·jue·lo m. *(tejo pequeño)* small disk; BKB. title plate; TECH. pillow block.

te·la f. *(paño)* cloth, fabric, material; *(membrana)* membrane; *(nata)* film, skin; ANAT. film (over the eye); ENTOM. web <*t. de araña* spider web>; BOT. skin; ARTS *(lienzo)* canvas, painting; FIG. *(materia)* material, stuff <*hay t. de donde cortar* there's plenty of material here to talk about for quite a while> ♦ **poner en t. de juicio** to cast doubt on, call into question • **t. adhesiva** adhesive tape • **t. aislante** electrical tape • **t. metálica** wire netting • **t. mosquitera** mosquito netting.

te·lar m. TEX. loom; THEAT. gridiron; ARCHIT. frame (of a door); BKB. sewing press ♦ **en el t.** FIG. in the making, in the works.

te·la·ra·ña f. ENTOM. spider web, cobweb; FIG. *(cosa de poca importancia)* triviality, trifle ♦ **mirar a las telarañas** FIG. to daydream, be absent-minded • **tener telarañas en los ojos** COLL. to have blinders on.

te·le·co·mu·ni·ca·ción f. telecommunication.

te·le·di·fun·dir tr. to telecast.

te·le·di·fu·sión f. telecast, television broadcast.

te·le·di·ri·gi·do, -da I. past part. see **teledirigir** II. adj. remote control.

te·le·di·ri·gir §32 tr. to guide by remote control.

te·le·fo·na·zo m. COLL. phone call.

te·le·fo·ne·ar tr. to phone, telephone.

te·le·fo·ní·a f. telephony <*t. sin hilos* radio telephony>.

te·le·fó·ni·ca·men·te adv. by phone.

te·le·fó·ni·co, -ca adj. phone, telephone ♦ **cabina t.** phone booth • **central t.** telephone exchange • **guía t.** telephone directory.

te·le·fo·nis·ta m.f. telephone operator.

te·lé·fo·no m. telephone.

te·le·fo·to m. telephoto.

te·le·fo·to·gra·fí·a f. telephotography.

te·le·gé·ni·co, -ca adj. telegenic.

te·le·gra·fí·a f. telegraphy <*t. sin hilos* wireless telegraph>.

te·le·gra·fiar §30 tr. to telegraph, cable.

te·le·grá·fi·co, -ca adj. telegraphic.

te·le·gra·fis·ta m.f. telegrapher, telegraph operator.

te·lé·gra·fo m. telegraph ♦ **hacer telégrafos** COLL. to use sign language • **t. marino** nautical signals • **t. óptico** semaphore.

te·le·gra·ma m. telegram.

te·le·guia·do, -da adj. remote-controlled.

te·le·im·pre·sor m. teleprinter, teletype.

te·le·le m. COLL. swoon, fainting spell.

te·le·me·trí·a f. telemetry.

te·lé·me·tro m. telemeter.

te·le·ob·je·ti·vo m. telephoto lens.

te·le·o·lo·gí·a f. PHILOS. teleology.

te·le·pa·tí·a f. telepathy.

te·le·pá·ti·co, -ca adj. telepathic.

te·le·ra f. *(del arado)* plow pin; *(redil)* sheep pen; *(del carro)* transom, crosspiece; CARP. jaws (of a vise); ARTIL. transom (of a gun carriage); MARIT. rack block; SP. large oval brown loaf (of bread); MEX. whole-wheat bread.

te·les·có·pi·co, -ca adj. telescopic.

te·les·co·pio m. telescope.

te·les·pec·ta·dor, -do·ra m.f. television viewer.

te·le·ti·po m. teletype.

te·le·vi·den·te m.f. television viewer.

te·le·vi·sar tr. to televise.

te·le·vi·sión f. television <*t. en color* color television>.

te·le·vi·sor m. television (set).

te·lex m. telex.

te·li·lla f. TEX. thin camlet; *(en un líquido)* film, skin.

te·lón m. THEAT. curtain; MEX. riddle, conundrum ♦ **t. de acero** POL. Iron Curtain • **t. de boca** THEAT. drop curtain • **t. de fondo** *or* **de foro** backdrop, backcloth • **t. metálico** *or* **de seguridad** THEAT. safety curtain.

te·lú·ri·co, -ca adj. telluric.

te·lu·rio m. CHEM. tellurium.

te·ma m. *(asunto)* subject, topic; *(escrito)* composition, written exercise; *(idea fija)* mania, obsession; *(antipatía)* ill will; MUS. theme, motif; GRAM. stem.

te·ma·rio m. program, agenda.

te·má·ti·co, –ca I. adj. *(del tema)* thematic; *(terco)* obstinate, stubborn **II.** f. subject, theme.

tem·bla·de·ra f. *(acción de temblar)* trembling, shaking; *(vasija)* thin two-handled cup; JEWEL. jewel mounted on a spiral; ICHTH. torpedo fish; BOT. quaking grass; SP., MED. trembling fit; ARG., VET. horse and cattle disease.

tem·bla·de·ral m. ARG. quaking bog.

tem·bla·dor, –do·ra I. adj. trembling, shaking **II.** m.f. *(persona temblorosa)* trembler; RELIG. Quaker —m. VEN., ICHTH. electric eel.

tem·blar §49 intr. *(temblequear)* to tremble, shake; *(tambalear)* to teeter, balance; FIG. *(tener miedo)* to be afraid ♦ **t. de frío** to shiver with cold • **t. de miedo** to quiver with fear.

tem·ble·que m. JEWEL. jewel mounted on a spiral; *(temblón)* trembler (person who shakes); HOND., SP. earthquake.

tem·ble·que·ar intr. COLL. *(temblar)* to tremble, shake; *(fingir temor)* to pretend to shake.

tem·ble·te·ar intr. COLL. var. of **temblequear.**

tem·blón, –blo·na COLL. **I.** adj. trembling, shaking ♦ **álamo t.** BOT. trembling poplar **II.** m.f. trembler, shaker.

tem·blor m. *(agitación)* tremor, trembling; AMER. earthquake ♦ **t. de tierra** earthquake.

tem·blo·ro·so, –sa *or* **tem·blo·so, –sa** adj. tremulous, shaking.

te·me·dor, –do·ra adj. fearful, afraid.

te·mer tr. & intr. to fear, be afraid ♦ **t. a** to be afraid of • **t. por** to fear for.

te·me·ra·ria·men·te adv. rashly, recklessly.

te·me·ra·rio, –ria adj. rash, reckless <*juicio t.* rash judgment>.

te·me·ri·dad f. temerity, recklessness.

te·me·ro·sa·men·te adv. timorously, fearfully.

te·me·ro·so, –sa adj. *(temible)* frightening, fearful; *(tímido)* timid, fearful.

te·mi·ble adj. fearful, frightful.

te·mor m. *(miedo)* fear, dread; *(presunción)* foreboding.

tém·pa·no m. MUS. small drum, kettledrum; *(piel del tambor)* drumhead, drumskin; *(de hielo)* floe, iceberg; *(tapa de tonel)* barrel head; *(corcho)* cork dome (of a beehive) ♦ **t. de hielo** iceberg • **t. de tocino** CUL. side of bacon.

tem·pe·ra·men·tal adj. temperamental.

tem·pe·ra·men·to m. *(naturaleza)* temperament, disposition; *(temperie)* weather; *(conciliación)* conciliation, compromise; MUS. temperament; COL. climate.

tem·pe·ran·cia f. temperance, moderation.

tem·pe·ran·te I. adj. *(calmante)* calming, soothing; MED. sedative; AMER. abstemious **II.** m.f. AMER. teetotaler.

tem·pe·rar tr. *(calmar)* to calm, soothe; *(moderar)* to temper, moderate —intr. AMER. to change climate.

tem·pe·ra·tu·ra f. temperature ♦ **t. absoluta** PHYS. absolute temperature • **tener t.** MED. to have a temperature *or* fever.

tem·pe·rie f. weather (conditions).

tem·pe·ro m. AGR. readiness (of the soil for sowing).

tem·pes·tad f. storm, tempest ♦ **levantar una t.** FIG. to raise a storm (of protest) • **t. de arena** sandstorm • **t. de nieve** snowstorm • **t. en un vaso de agua** FIG. tempest in a teapot.

tem·pes·ti·vo, –va adj. timely, opportune.

tem·pes·tuo·so, –sa adj. tempestuous, stormy.

tem·pla f. ARTS distemper, tempera; CUBA amount of fermented sugar cane juice in a vat.

tem·pla·da·men·te adv. temperately, moderately.

tem·pla·do, –da I. past part. see **templar II.** adj. *(moderado)* moderate, temperate; *(tibio)* warm, lukewarm; *(el clima)* mild, temperate (climate); COLL. *(valiente)* valiant, brave; AMER. *(borracho)* drunk; *(enamorado)* in love; COL., VEN. severe, strict; C. AMER., MEX. clever.

tem·pla·dor, –do·ra I. adj. tempering, moderating **II.** m. MUS. tuning key.

tem·pla·du·ra f. *(moderación)* tempering, moderating; MUS. tuning.

tem·plan·za f. *(sobriedad)* temperance, sobriety; *(moderación)* moderation, restraint; *(del clima)* mildness, temperateness; PAINT. harmony, blending (of colors).

tem·plar tr. *(moderar)* to temper, moderate; *(la temperatura)* to make lukewarm; METAL. to temper; MARIT. to trim to the wind (sails); MUS. to tune; PAINT. to blend (colors); TECH. to tighten, adjust; *(mezclar)* to dilute; FIG. *(mitigar)* to mitigate, moderate; *(apaciguar)* to appease, calm; ECUAD., PERU *(matar)* to kill; C. RICA to beat, hit; COL., ECUAD. *(derribar)* to knock down —intr. to warm up (weather); CUBA to flee, run away —reflex. to be moderate; ECUAD. to face danger; CHILE to fall in love; ECUAD., GUAT., HOND. *(morirse)* to die; AMER. *(embriagarse)* to get drunk.

tem·pla·rio m. HIST., RELIG. Knight Templar, Templar.

tem·ple m. *(tiempo)* weather, atmospheric conditions; *(temperatura)* temperature; *(dureza)* temper (of metals); *(índole)* nature, temper; *(disposición)* mood <*estar de buen t.* to be in a good mood>; *(término medio)* mean, average; *(valentía)* courage, valor; MUS. tuning; ARTS tempera (paint).

tem·ple·te m. *(templo pequeño)* small temple, shrine; *(pabellón)* kiosk, pavilion.

tem·plo m. *(lugar de culto)* temple, shrine; *(iglesia)* church ♦ **como un t.** FIG. huge.

tem·po·ra·da f. *(del año)* season; *(período)* period, time ♦ **de fuera de t.** off-season • **estar de t.** to vacation, spend the season • **por temporadas** off and on • **t. baja** off season • **t. de caza y pesca** open season • **t. de frío** cold spell • **t. de ópera** opera season.

tem·po·ral¹ I. adj. *(pasajero)* temporary, passing; *(secular)* temporal, secular; GRAM. temporal **II.** m. *(tempestad)* storm, tempest; *(lluvia persistente)* rainy weather, rainy spell; CUBA swindler, cheat.

tem·po·ral² ANAT. **I.** adj. temporal **II.** m. temporal bone.

tem·po·ra·li·dad f. temporality ♦ **temporalidades** RELIG. temporalities.

tem·po·ral·men·te adv. *(por algún tiempo)* temporarily; *(seglarmente)* temporally, secularly.

tem·po·rá·ne·o, –ne·a *or* **tem·po·ra·rio, –ria** adj. temporary.

tem·po·re·ro, –ra I. adj. seasonal, temporary **II.** m.f. seasonal *or* temporary worker —f. SP. popular song.

tem·po·ri·zar §04 intr. *(contemporizar)* to temporize; *(matar tiempo)* to pass *or* kill time.

tem·pra·nal AGR. **I.** adj. early-yielding **II.** m. early-yielding land *or* crop.

tem·pra·na·men·te adv. *(temprano)* early; *(prematuramente)* prematurely.

tem·pra·ne·ro, –ra adj. early ♦ **ser t.** to be an early riser.

tem·pra·no, –na I. adj. & adv. early **II.** m. AGR. early crop.

ten see **tener.**

te·na·ce·ar¹ tr. *(torturar)* to torture by tearing the flesh of with pincers; *(sujetar)* to tie down, secure.

te·na·ce·ar² intr. to insist, persist.

te·na·ci·dad f. *(perseverancia)* tenacity, perseverance; METAL. tensile strength.

te·naz adj. [pl. **–na·ces**] *(persistente)* tenacious, persistent; *(pegajoso)* sticky, adhesive.

te·na·za f. *or* **te·na·zas** f.pl. *(herramienta)* pliers, pincers; ZOOL. pincers, claws; MIL. tenail, tenaille; *(del fuego)* tongs; MED. forceps; *(en el juego)* tenace, fourchette; SPORT. scissor hold ♦ **eso no se puede coger ni con tenazas** FIG., COLL. you wouldn't touch it with a ten-foot pole • **movimiento de tenazas** MIL. pincer movement • **tenazas de rizar** curling iron.

te·na·za·da f. *(acción de agarrar)* gripping, grasping (with tongs); FIG. *(bocado)* hard bite.

te·naz·men·te adv. tenaciously.

te·na·zón ♦ **a** *or* **de t.** *(sin fijar la puntería)* blindly, without taking aim; FIG. *(de pronto)* suddenly, without warning.

ten·dal m. *(toldo)* awning; AGR. *(lienzo)* canvas spread to catch ripening olives; ARG. *(para el ganado)* shearing shed; CUBA, ECUAD. *(para el café)* drying floor (for coffee); BOL. *(campo)* flat field; ARG., CHILE, PERU *(multitud)* heap, jumble; CHILE *(puesto)* stall, booth.

ten·da·le·ra f. COLL. jumble, heap.

ten·de·de·ro m. place where clothes are spread to dry.

ten·del m. *(cuerda)* leveling line; *(capa de moretero)* layer of mortar.

ten·den·cia f. tendency, trend.

ten·den·cio·so, –sa adj. tendentious.

ten·den·te adj. tending.

ten·der §50 tr. *(extender)* to spread, spread out; *(alargar)* to stretch out, extend *<me tendió la mano* he extended his hand to me>; *(secar)* to hang out (clothes); to lay *<t. cable* to lay cable>; MAS. to coat (with plaster); CONSTR. to throw, build (a bridge) —intr. to tend, have a tendency —reflex. *(echarse)* to stretch out, lie down; *(en el juego)* to lay one's cards on the table; FIG., COLL. *(descuidarse)* to become careless; AGR. to droop; EQUIT. to gallop.

ten·de·re·te m. COLL. *(tendalero)* place where things are spread out to dry; *(puesto de venta)* stall, stand; *(juego de naipes)* card game.

ten·de·ro, –ra m.f. *(comerciante)* shopkeeper —m. *(fabricante de tiendas)* tent maker.

ten·di·do, –da I. past part. see **tender** II. adj. *(extendido)* stretched *or* spread out; EQUIT. full (gallop) III. m. *(acción)* spreading, stretching; *(encaje)* portion of lace made at one time; *(ropa)* load of wash; *(pan)* batch of bread; TAUR. tier of seats; ARCHIT. slope (of a roof); MAS. coat of plaster; ARG. clear sky.

ten·dien·te adj. AMER. tending.

ten·di·no·so, –sa adj. tendinous, sinewy.

ten·dón m. ANAT. tendon ♦ **t. de Aquiles** Achilles tendon.

ten·drá, tendría see **tener**.

ten·du·cha f. *or* **ten·du·cho** m. DEROG. small, shabby store.

te·ne·bro·si·dad f. darkness, gloom.

te·ne·bro·so, –sa adj. *(sombrío)* dark, gloomy; FIG. *(secreto)* shady, murky; *(oscuro)* obscure, difficult.

te·ne·dor, –do·ra m.f. *(poseedor)* owner, possessor —m. *(utensilio)* fork; COM. bearer, holder ♦ **t. de acciones** stockholder • **t. de la póliza** policyholder • **t. de libros** bookkeeper.

te·ne·du·rí·a f. bookkeeping.

te·nen·cia f. *(posesión)* possession; MIL. lieutenantcy ♦ **t. de alcaldía** deputy mayor's office.

te·ner §69 tr. to have *<tuve una audiencia con el Papa* I had an audience with the Pope>; *(poseer)* to have, possess; *(asir)* to hold, take hold of *<ten el cable* take hold of the rope>; *(contener)* to have, contain *<este libro tiene quince capítulos* this book has fifteen chapters>; *(parar)* to stop, halt; *(pasar)* to have, spend *<tuvimos un mal día* we had a bad day>; *(hospedar)* to have, receive *<no quiero tenerlos en mi casa* I don't want to have them in my home>; *(mantener)* to maintain, sustain; *(considerar)* to consider, deem *<tuvo a menos trabajar en tal cosa* she considered it beneath her to work on anything like that>; to be *<tiene sesenta años de edad* he is sixty years of age>; *(cumplir)* to keep, fulfill ♦ **no tenerlas todas consigo** FIG., COLL. to be worried *or* uneasy • **no t. sobre qué caerse muerto** FIG. not to have a cent to one's name • **t. a bien** to see fit to • **t. calor** to be hot • **t. celos** to be jealous • **t. cuidado** to be careful • **t. en contra** to have (something) against (someone) • **t. en cuenta** to take into account • **t. en mucho** to esteem • **t. en poco** to think little of • **t. éxito** to succeed • **t. frío** to be cold • **t. ganas de** to feel like • **t. hambre** to be hungry • **t. la bondad de** to be kind enough to • **t. la culpa** to be to blame • **t. lugar** to take place • **t. miedo** to be afraid • **t. mucho de** to resemble • **t. para sí** to be of the opinion • **t. por** to consider, think *<lo tengo por sabio* I consider him wise> • **t. presente** to bear in mind • **t. prisa** to be in a hurry • **t. que** to have to, must *<tenemos que hacerlo* we have to do it> • **t. que ver con** to have to do with • **t. razón** to be right • **t. sed** to be thirsty • **t. sueño** to be sleepy • **t. suerte** to be lucky —intr. *(ser rico)* to be well-off —reflex. *(afianzarse)* to steady oneself; *(atenerse)* to stand firm; *(detenerse)* to stop, halt ♦ **tenerse de pie** to stand up, be standing • **tenerse por** to consider oneself • **tenérselas tiesas con alguien** to stand up to someone.

te·ne·rí·a f. tannery.

te·nia f. ZOOL. tenia, tapeworm; ARCHIT. taenia, fillet.

te·ni·da f. *(reunión)* meeting (of a Masonic lodge); CHILE uniform, suit.

te·nien·te I. m. MIL. lieutenant; *(sustituto)* substitute, deputy ♦ **segundo t.** MIL. second lieutenant • **t. de alcalde** deputy mayor • **t. coronel** lieutenant colonel • **t. general** lieutenant general II. adj. *(que tiene)* having, possessing;

BOT. unripe, green (fruit); COLL. *(sordo)* hard of hearing; FIG. *(avaro)* tight-fisted, stingy.

te·nis m. SPORT. tennis; *(campo de tenis)* tennis court ♦ **t. de mesa** Ping-Pong, table tennis.

te·nis·ta m.f. tennis player.

te·nor¹ m. tenor, tone ♦ **a este t.** at this rate • **a. t. de** in accordance with.

te·nor² m. MUS. tenor.

te·no·rio m. FIG. Don Juan, Casanova.

ten·sar tr. to tauten, stretch.

ten·sión f. tension, stress ♦ **t. alta** ELEC. high tension *or* voltage • **t. arterial** MED. blood pressure • **t. superficial** PHYS. surface tension.

ten·so, –sa adj. *(tirante)* tense, taut; FIG. *(nervios, situación)* tense, strained.

ten·sor I. m. *(aparato par tensar)* tension, tightener; TECH. turnbuckle; ANAT. tensor II. adj. see **tensor, –so·ra**.

ten·sor, –so·ra I. adj. tensile II. m. see **tensor**.

ten·ta·ción f. temptation.

ten·tá·cu·lo m. ZOOL. tentacle.

ten·ta·dor, –do·ra I. adj. tempting II. m. tempter ♦ **el T.** the Devil.

ten·tar §49 tr. *(palpar)* to feel, touch; *(seducir)* to tempt, entice; *(intentar)* to try, attempt; *(examinar)* to examine by touch; MED. to probe, palpate ♦ **ir tentando el camino** to feel one's way, grope • **t. a Dios** to tempt fate.

ten·ta·ti·va I. f. attempt, endeavor ♦ **t. de delito** LAW attempted crime II. adj. see **tentativo, –va**.

ten·ta·ti·vo, –va I. adj. tentative II. f. see **tentativa**.

ten·te·mo·zo m. *(puntal)* prop; *(del carro)* pole prop; *(juguete)* tumbler, roly-poly; *(del caballo)* cheek strap (of a harness).

ten·tem·pié m. COLL. *(refrigerio)* snack, bite; *(juguete)* roly-poly, tumbler.

ten·te·ne·lai·re m. *(hijo)* son of a quadroon and a mulatto; ARG., ORNITH. hummingbird —f. daughter of a quadroon and a mulatto.

te·nue adj. *(delgado)* thin, tenuous; *(de poca importancia)* trifling, insignificant; *(sencillo)* simple, natural.

te·nui·dad f. *(poco grosor)* thinness, tenuousness; *(cosa de poco valor)* trifle.

te·ñir §59 tr. *(un vestido)* to dye, tint; PAINT. to darken (a color); FIG. *(imbuir)* to imbue.

te·o·cra·cia f. theocracy.

te·o·crá·ti·co, –ca adj. theocratic.

te·o·do·li·to m. theodolite.

te·o·lo·gal adj. theological, theologic.

te·o·lo·gí·a f. theology ♦ **no meterse en teologías** FIG., COLL. not to get into hot water.

te·o·ló·gi·co, –ca adj. theological, theologic.

te·o·lo·gi·zar §04 tr. to theologize.

te·ó·lo·go, –ga I. adj. theological II. m.f. theologian.

te·o·re·ma m. LOG., MATH. theorem.

te·o·ré·ti·co, –ca adj. theoretical, theoretic.

te·o·rí·a f. theory.

te·ó·ri·ca I. f. theoretics, theory II. adj. see **teórico, –ca**.

te·ó·ri·ca·men·te adv. theoretically.

te·ó·ri·co, –ca I. adj. theoretical II. m.f. *(persona)* theoretician —f. see **teórica**.

te·o·ri·zar §04 tr. to theorize.

te·o·so·fí·a f. theosophy.

te·ó·so·fo, –fa m.f. theosophist.

te·pe m. sod, turf.

te·pe·re·te adj. GUAT. crazy, mad.

te·qui·la f. MEX. tequila.

te·ra·peu·ta m.f. MED. therapist.

te·ra·péu·ti·ca I. f. therapeutics, therapy II. adj. see **terapéutico, –ca**.

te·ra·péu·ti·co, –ca I. adj. therapeutic II. f. see **terapéutica**.

te·ra·pia f. MED. therapy ♦ **t. laboral** *or* **ocupacional** occupational therapy.

ter·bio m. CHEM. terbium.

ter·ce·na f. *(almacén)* tobacco warehouse; ECUAD. butcher shop.

ter·ce·nis·ta m.f. *(tenedor de la tercena)* warehouse keeper; ECUAD. butcher.

ter·cer adj. [contr. of **tercero** used before m. sing. nouns] third <*el t. día* the third day> —see **tercero, –ra.**

ter·ce·ra I. f. *(en los naipes)* tierce (in cards); *(alcahueta)* procuress; MUS. third; AUTO. third gear II. adj. see **tercero, –ra.**

ter·ce·rí·a f. *(mediación)* mediation, arbitration; LAW right of third party; *(alcahuetería)* procuring, pimping.

ter·cer·mun·dis·ta adj. third-worldist.

ter·ce·ro, –ra §G21 I. adj. third <*ella vive en la t. casa a la derecha* she lives in the third house on the right>; *(medianero)* mediating, arbitrating II. m. *(alcahuete)* pimp, procurer; *(mediador)* mediator, arbitrator; LAW third party; RELIG. tertiary; GEOM. third —f. see **tercera.**

ter·ce·rón, –ro·na m. AMER. son of a white and a mulatto —f. daughter of a white and a mulatto.

ter·ce·to m. POET. tercet; MUS. trio.

ter·cia I. f. *(medida)* measurement equal to 11 inches; *(tercio)* third; HIST. forenoon (in ancient Rome); RELIG. tierce (canonical hour); *(en naipes)* tierce (in cards); AGR. third digging II. adj. see **tercio, –cia.**

ter·cia·do, –da I. past part. see **terciar** II. adj. *(azúcar)* brown (sugar); *(toro)* medium-sized (said of a bull); *(atravesado)* crosswise III. m. *(espada)* broadsword; *(cinta)* wide ribbon.

ter·cia·dor, –do·ra I. adj. mediating, arbitrating II. m.f. mediator, arbitrator.

ter·ciar tr. *(dividir)* to divide into three parts; *(sesgar)* to place diagonally across, slant; to carry across one's back <*se terció el bulto* he carried the pack across his back>; AGR. to plow for the third time; AMER. *(aguar)* to water down —intr. *(interponerse)* to mediate, arbitrate; *(participar)* to take part <*t. en una conversación* to take part in a conversation>; *(completar el número)* to fill in, complete the number (of people necessary for an activity); ASTRON. to be in its third day (the moon) —reflex. ◆ **si se tercia** should the opportunity arise.

ter·cia·rio, –ria I. adj. *(tercero)* third; GEOL. Tertiary II. m. GEOL. Tertiary.

ter·cia·zón f. AGR. third plowing.

ter·cio, –cia I. adj. third II. m. *(tercera parte)* third; *(fardo)* bale, pack; TAUR. stage (of a bullfight); MIL. regiment, legion; MARIT. longshoremen's union ◆ **t. de muerte** TAUR. the kill —f. see **tercia.**

ter·cio·pe·lo m. TEX. velvet.

ter·co, –ca adj. *(obstinado)* stubborn, obstinate; ECUAD. cold, aloof.

ter·gi·ver·sa·ción f. twisting, distortion.

ter·gi·ver·sa·dor, –do·ra I. adj. twisting, distorting II. m.f. twister, distorter.

ter·gi·ver·sar tr. to twist, distort.

ter·mal adj. thermal.

ter·mas f.pl. hot baths *or* springs.

ter·mes m. [pl. **termes**] ENTOM. termite.

tér·mi·co, –ca adj. thermic, thermal.

ter·mi·dor m. HIST. Thermidor.

ter·mi·na·ción f. termination, ending.

ter·mi·na·cho m. COLL. *(palabra grosera)* vulgar word; *(término bárbaro)* barbarism.

ter·mi·na·jo m. COLL. vulgar expression.

ter·mi·nal I. adj. terminal II. m. ELEC. terminal —m.f. *(estación)* terminal ◆ **t. aérea** air terminal, airport.

ter·mi·nan·te adj. conclusive, definite.

ter·mi·nan·te·men·te adv. conclusively, definitely.

ter·mi·nar tr. *(poner término a)* to end, terminate; *(acabar)* to complete, finish off —intr. *(tener término)* to end, come to an end; MED. to peak (an illness) ◆ **t. de** *(acabar de)* to have just; *(concluir)* to finish <*terminamos de comer* we finished eating> • **t. en** to end up in <*él va a t. en la cárcel* he is going to end up in jail> • **t. por** to end up <*terminó por marcharse enfadado* he ended up going away angry> —reflex. to end, come to an end.

tér·mi·no m. *(conclusión)* end, finish, conclusion; *(palabra)* term, word; *(límite)* limit, boundary; *(mojón)* landmark, boundary marker; *(distrito)* district, area; *(tiempo determinado)* term, time limit; *(meta)* end, goal; *(condición)* condition, state; ARCHIT., LAW, LOG., MATH. term; PAINT. ground <*primer t.* foreground> ◆ **dar t. a** to finish off • **en buenos términos con** on good terms with • **en propios** términos literally • **en último t.** in the last analysis • **llevar a t.** to carry out • **i 1edios términos** evasions, subterfuges • **poner t. a** to put an end to • **por t. medio** on the average • **t. medio** MATH. average; LOG. middle term; CUL. medium (meat); FIG. *(compromiso)* compromise, middle ground.

ter·mi·no·lo·gí·a f. terminology.

ter·mi·ta m. ENTOM. termite.

ter·mi·te·ro m. termite nest.

ter·mo m. thermos (bottle).

ter·mo·di·ná·mi·ca f. thermodynamics.

ter·mo·e·lec·tri·ci·dad f. thermoelectricity.

ter·mo·e·léc·tri·co, –ca adj. thermoelectric.

ter·mó·gra·fo m. thermograph.

ter·mo·me·trí·a f. PHYS. thermometry.

ter·mo·mé·tri·co, –ca adj. thermometric.

ter·mó·me·tro m. thermometer.

ter·mo·nu·cle·ar adj. thermonuclear <*bomba t.* thermonuclear bomb>.

ter·mo·plás·ti·co, –ca adj. thermoplastic.

ter·mo·quí·mi·ca f. thermochemistry.

ter·mo·rre·gu·la·dor m. thermoregulator, thermostat.

ter·mos·ta·to m. thermostat.

ter·mo·te·ra·pia f. MED. thermotherapy.

ter·na f. *(para un cargo)* list of three candidates for a post; *(en los dados)* pair of three (in dice); *(juego de dados)* set of dice.

ter·na·rio, –ria I. adj. ternary II. m. RELIG. three days' devotion.

ter·ne I. adj. COLL. bullying II. m. COLL. bully; ARG. gaucho knife.

ter·ne·ra f. *(animal)* female calf; *(carne)* veal; ARG. gaucho knife.

ter·ne·ra·je m. AMER. group of calves.

ter·ne·ro m. male calf.

ter·ne·za f. *(ternura)* tenderness, softness; COLL. *(requiebro)* endearment.

ter·no m. *(conjunto de tres cosas)* triad, set of three; *(vestido)* three-piece suit; *(en la lotería)* tern, set of three numbers winning a lottery prize; *(voto)* curse, swearword; PRINT. three printed sheets ◆ **echar ternos** to curse, swear.

ter·nu·ra f. *(calidad de tierno)* tenderness, softness; *(requiebro)* endearment.

ter·que·dad f. *(obstinación)* stubbornness, obstinacy; ECUAD. coldness, aloofness.

te·rra·co·ta f. terra cotta.

te·rra·do m. flat roof *or* terrace.

te·rra·ja f. *(para molduras)* modeling board; *(para tornillos)* diestock.

te·rra·je m. rent on arable land.

te·rra·je·ro m. tenant farmer.

te·rral I. adj. land <*viento t.* land wind> II. m. land wind.

te·rra·mi·ci·na f. PHARM. terramycin.

Te·rra·no·va f. Newfoundland.

te·rra·plén m. embankment, earthwork.

te·rra·ple·nar tr. *(llenar)* to fill up with earth; *(hacer terraplén)* to embank, bank up.

te·rrá·que·o, –a adj. terraqueous, terrestrial <*globo t.* the earth>.

te·rra·te·nien·te m. landowner, landholder.

te·rra·za f. *(balcón)* terrace, balcony; *(azotea)* roof terrace; *(de un café)* terrace, veranda; AGR. terrace.

te·rraz·go m. *(pedazo de tierra)* plot of land; *(renta)* land rent.

te·rraz·gue·ro m. tenant farmer.

te·rre·go·so, –sa adj. full of clods (of earth).

te·rre·mo·to m. earthquake.

te·rre·nal adj. earthly, worldly.

te·rre·no, –na I. adj. *(terrestre)* earthly; *(terrenal)* worldly II. m. *(espacio de tierra)* terrain, ground, land; *(campo)* plot, piece of land; *(suelo)* ground, earth <*t. arcilloso* clayey ground>; GEOL. terrain; SPORT. field; FIG. *(campo de acción)* field, sphere ◆ **ceder t.** to give ground • **ganar t.** FIG. to gain ground • **perder t.** FIG. to lose ground • **preparar el t.** FIG. to pave the way • **reconocer el t.** FIG. to get the lay of the land • **t. conocido** FIG. familiar territory • **t. vedado** FIG. forbidden territory.

té·rre·o, –a adj. *(de tierra)* earthen; *(como la tierra)* earthy.

te·rre·ro, –ra I. adj. *(terrestre)* earthly; *(de tierra)* earth, earthen <*piso t.* earthen floor>; ORNITH. low-flying; EQUIT. low-stepping; FIG. *(humilde)* humble, lowly; P. RICO one-floor, one-story II. m. *(montón)* heap, mound; *(azotea)* terrace; *(blanco)* target, mark; *(plaza)* plaza, square; GEOL. alluvium, deposit.
te·rres·tre adj. terrestrial, earthly.
te·rri·ble adj. terrible, awful.
te·rri·ble·men·te adv. terribly.
te·rrí·co·la m.f. earth dweller, inhabitant of the earth.
te·rrí·fi·co, –ca adj. terrifying, dreadful.
te·rri·to·rial adj. territorial ♦ **código t.** TELEC. area code.
te·rri·to·ria·li·dad f. territoriality.
te·rri·to·rio m. *(de una nación)* territory, region; *(comarca)* district, zone.
te·rrón m. *(de tierra)* clod (of earth); *(de azúcar)* lump (of sugar); *(residuo)* olive residue; FIG., COLL. *(campo pequeño)* plot (of land) ♦ **a rapa t.** completely, to the core • **terrones** COLL. farmland.
te·rror m. terror ♦ **Terror** HIST. Reign of Terror.
te·rro·rí·fi·co, –ca adj. terrifying, dreadful.
te·rro·ris·mo m. terrorism.
te·rro·ris·ta adj. & m.f. terrorist.
te·rro·si·dad f. earthiness.
te·rro·so, –sa adj. *(de tierra)* earthy; *(sucio)* dirty, grimy.
te·rru·ño m. *(tierra)* land, plot; *(terrón)* clod (of earth); *(país)* country, native land.
ter·so, –sa adj. *(limpio)* clear, limpid; *(brillante)* glossy, shiny; FIG. *(estilo)* smooth, flowing (style).
ter·su·ra f. *(de la piel)* smoothness; *(brillo)* shininess, glossiness; FIG. *(del estilo)* smoothness, polish (of style).
ter·tu·lia f. *(reunión)* social gathering, get-together; THEAT. upper gallery (of a theater); ARG. theater seat ♦ **hacer t.** to get together for a chat • **t. literaria** literary circle.
ter·tu·lia·no, –na or **ter·tu·lian·te** I. adj. present at a gathering II. m.f. guest (at a gathering).
ter·tu·liar intr. AMER. to get together for conversation.
te·si·na f. *(tesis de licenciatura)* thesis (bachelor or master level).
te·sis f. [pl. **-sis**] PHILOS. thesis; *(opinión)* theory, opinion ♦ **t. doctoral** EDUC. doctoral thesis.
te·si·tu·ra f. MUS. tessitura; FIG. *(actitud)* attitude, frame of mind.
te·so, –sa I. adj. taut, tense II. m. *(de una colina)* hilltop; *(salida)* bulge (on a flat surface).
te·són m. tenacity, firmness.
te·so·ne·rí·a f. tenacity, persistence.
te·so·ne·ro, –ra adj. tenacious, persistent.
te·so·re·rí·a f. *(oficina)* treasury, treasurer's office; *(cargo)* treasurership.
te·so·re·ro, –ra m.f. COM. treasurer —m. RELIG. custodian (of a church's valuables).
te·so·ro m. *(dinero)* treasure <*t. escondido* hidden treasure>; *(fondos públicos)* treasury; FIG. *(persona o cosa)* treasure, gem <*este niño es un t.* this child is a gem>.
tes·ta f. COLL. *(cabeza)* head; *(frente)* front, face; FIG., COLL. *(inteligencia)* brains, intelligence ♦ **t. coronada** monarch, crowned head.
tes·ta·da f. butt, blow with the head.
tes·ta·do, –da I. past part. see **testar** II. adj. LAW testate.
tes·ta·dor, –do·ra m.f. LAW testator.
tes·ta·fe·rro m. COLL. front, figurehead.
tes·ta·men·ta·rí·a f. *(ejecución)* testamentary execution, testate proceedings; *(sucesión)* estate (of deceased); *(reunión)* meeting of executors; *(documentos)* testamentary documents.
tes·ta·men·ta·rio, –ria I. adj. testamentary II. m. executor —f. executrix.
tes·ta·men·to m. will, testament ♦ **Antiguo T.** BIBL. Old Testament • **Nuevo T.** BIBL. New Testament • **t. cerrado** sealed will • **t. ológrafo** holographic will.
tes·tar intr. to make a will or testament —tr. *(tachar)* to erase; ECUAD. to underscore.
tes·ta·ra·da f. *(golpe)* butt, blow with the head; COLL. *(terquedad)* stubbornness, obstinacy.
tes·ta·ra·zo m. butt, blow with the head; SPORT. header (soccer).

tes·ta·rrón, –rro·na COLL. I. adj. stubborn, pigheaded II. m.f. stubborn or pigheaded person.
tes·ta·rro·ne·rí·a f. COLL. pigheadedness, stubbornness.
tes·ta·ru·dez f. obstinacy, stubbornness.
tes·ta·ru·do, –da I. adj. obstinate, stubborn II. m.f. obstinate or stubborn person.
tes·te m. ANAT. testis, testicle; ARG. wart on the finger.
tes·te·ra f. *(frente)* front, facade; *(en un coche)* forward-facing seat (in a carriage); *(de un caballo)* frontstall, crownpiece (of a harness); *(de un animal)* forehead (of an animal); *(de un horno)* wall (of a furnace).
tes·ti·cu·lar adj. ANAT. testicular.
tes·tí·cu·lo m. ANAT. testicle.
tes·ti·fi·ca·ción f. testimony.
tes·ti·fi·car §70 tr. to testify.
tes·ti·go m.f. witness —m. *(prueba)* proof, evidence; SPORT. *(en una carrera)* baton (passed in a relay race) ♦ **t. de cargo** LAW witness for the prosecution • **t. de descargo** LAW witness for the defense • **t. de Jehová** RELIG. Jehovah's Witness • **t. ocular** or **de vista** eyewitness.
tes·ti·mo·nial adj. testimonial ♦ **testimoniales** pertaining to documentary evidence.
tes·ti·mo·niar tr. to testify to, bear witness to.
tes·ti·mo·nie·ro, –ra I. adj. bearing false witness II. m.f. perjurer, false witness.
tes·ti·mo·nio m. *(testificación)* testimony; *(atestación)* attestation, affidavit; *(muestra)* mark, token ♦ **falso t.** LAW perjury, false evidence.
tes·tos·te·ro·na f. BIOCHEM. testosterone.
tes·tuz m. [pl. **-tu·ces**] *(frente)* forehead (of an animal); *(nuca)* nape (of an animal).
te·ta f. ANAT. *(pecho)* breast; *(de la vaca)* udder; *(pezón)* nipple, teat; *(montículo)* hillock, knoll ♦ **dar la t. a** to suckle, nurse • **niño de t.** suckling infant, babe-in-arms • **quitar la t. a** to wean.
té·ta·nos or **té·ta·no** m. MED. tetanus.
te·tar tr. to suckle, nurse.
te·te·le·me·me m. CHILE, PERU, COLL. fool, nincompoop.
te·te·ra f. *(para el té)* teapot; AMER. nipple (of a baby's bottle).
te·te·ro m. AMER. nipple (of a baby's bottle).
te·ti·lla f. nipple (of a baby's bottle).
te·tón m. stub (of a pruned branch).
te·to·na adj. var. of **tetuda**.
te·tra·é·dri·co, –ca adj. GEOM. tetrahedral.
te·tra·e·dro m. GEOM. tetrahedron.
te·trá·go·no m. GEOM. tetragon.
te·tra·lo·gí·a f. tetralogy.
té·tri·co, –ca adj. somber, gloomy.
te·tu·da adj. large-breasted, large-nippled.
teur·gia f. theurgy.
teu·tón, –to·na I. adj. Teutonic II. m.f. Teuton.
teu·tó·ni·co, –ca I. adj. Teutonic II. m. Teutonic (language).
tex·til adj. & m. textile.
tex·to m. *(contenido)* text; RELIG. text; *(libro)* textbook.
tex·tual adj. textual.
tex·tu·ra f. texture.
tez f. complexion.
te·zon·tle m. MEX., GEOL. volcanic rock.
the·ta f. theta (Greek letter).
ti §G30, 34 pron. you <*lo compré para ti* I bought it for you>; yourself <*hazlo para ti* do it for yourself>.
tí·a f. *(pariente)* aunt; *(a una mujer casada)* lady, missis; COLL. *(mujer cualquiera)* dame, broad; *(ramera)* tart, whore ♦ **cuéntaselo a tu t.** COLL. tell it to the marines • **no hay tu t.** COLL. no use, nothing doing • **t. abuela** great-aunt, grandaunt.
tia·mi·na f. thiamin.
tia·ra f. tiara.
ti·be·rio m. COLL. hullabaloo, uproar.
ti·be·ta·no, –na adj. & m.f. Tibetan.
ti·bia f. ANAT. tibia.
ti·bia·men·te adv. lukewarmly, unenthusiastically.
ti·biar tr. to make lukewarm or tepid —reflex. C. AMER., VEN. to become angry or irritated.
ti·bie·za f. lukewarmness, tepidness.
ti·bio, –bia adj. *(agua)* lukewarm, tepid; FIG. *(poco fervo-*

roso) cool, indifferent; COL., PERU, VEN., COLL. angry, irritated.

ti·bu·rón m. ICHTH. shark; FIG. *(egoísta)* egotistical *or* ruthless person.

tic m. [pl. **tics**] tic, nervous twitch.

ti·co, –ca adj. & m.f. Costa Rican.

tic·tac *or* **tic tac** m. tick-tock, ticking.

tiem·ble, tiemblo see **temblar.**

tiem·po m. *(duración)* time *<matar el t.* to kill time>; *(época)* era, times *<en t. de Napoleón* in the times of Napoleon>; *(ocasión)* time, moment *<se acerca el t. de actuar* the time for action is approaching>; *(oportunidad)* time *<no tengo t. para escribirte* I do not have time to write to you>; *(estación)* time, season; METEOROL. weather *<hace buen t.* it is good weather>; GRAM. tense *<t. compuesto* compound tense>; MUS. time, tempo; MARIT. stormy weather ♦ **alzarse el t.** METEOROL. to clear up • **al mismo t.** at the same time • **al t. que** just as • **andando el t.** in the course of time, as time goes by • **a su t.** in due time • **a t.** in *or* on time • **a un t.** at the same time, simultaneously • **cargarse el t.** METEOROL. to become overcast • **con t.** *(por adelantado)* in advance; *(en el momento oportuno)* in good time • **dar t. al t.** to bide one's time • **de algún t. a esta parte** for some time now • **de t. en t.** from time to time, now and then • **en los buenos tiempos** in the good old days • **en t. del rey que rabió** *or* **de Maricastaña** COLL. in olden times • **fuera de t.** *(inoportunamente)* at the wrong time; AGR. out of season • **ganar t.** to save time • **hacer t.** to mark time • **perder el t.** to waste time • **t. atrás** some time ago • **t. libre** spare time, free time • **t. medio** ASTRON. mean time • **t. verdadero** ASTRON. solar time • **todo el t.** all the time, always.

tien·da f. *(comercio)* store, shop; *(pabellón)* tent; *(toldo)* awning ♦ **batir tiendas** MIL. to strike camp • **t. de abarrotes** *or* **de ultramarinos** grocery store • **t. de campaña** tent • **t. de modas** boutique, dress shop.

tien·da, tiendo see **tender.**

tie·ne see **tener.**

tien·ta f. SURG. probe; TAUR. test of mettle (of young bulls); FIG. *(astucia)* artfulness, cleverness ♦ **a tientas** gropingly • **andar a tientas** FIG. to feel one's way, grope along.

tien·te, tiento see **tentar.**

tien·to m. *(tacto)* touch; *(palo de ciego)* blindman's cane; *(balancín)* balancing pole; *(pulso)* steady hand; FIG. *(prudencia)* caution, care; FIG., COLL. *(golpe)* blow, punch; COLL. *(trago)* swig, belt *<dio un t. a la botella* he took a swig from the bottle>; MUS. preliminary notes, warm-up; PAINT. maulstick; ZOOL. tentacle; ARG. snack; AMER. *(correa)* leather strip ♦ **a t.** *(por el tacto)* by touch; FIG. *(dudosamente)* hesitantly, uncertainly • **con t.** cautiously.

tier·no, –na adj. *(afectuoso)* affectionate, loving; *(blando)* soft; tender *<carne t.* tender meat>; fresh *<pan t.* fresh bread>; *(delicado)* delicate; FIG. *(sensible)* sensitive, touchy; AMER. green, unripe.

tie·rra f. *(planeta)* Earth; land *<viajar por t.* to travel by land>; earth, soil *<t. de batán* fuller's earth>; *(suelo)* ground, earth *<caer a t.* to fall to the ground>; *(patria)* country, soil *<mi t. natal* my native soil>; *(comarca)* land, region; AGR. *(campo)* land *<t. de cultivo* arable land>; ELEC. ground ♦ **besar la t.** COLL. to fall flat • **caer a t.** to fall down • **dar en t. con** to knock down, demolish • **echar por t.** FIG. to wreck, ruin • **echar t. a** hush up, push under the rug • **mover cielo y t.** FIG. to move heaven and earth • **perder t.** to slip, lose one's footing • **poner t. de por medio** to make oneself scarce • **por estas tierras** hereabouts • **t. adentro** inland • **t. del sol de medianoche** Land of the Midnight Sun (Norway) • **t. del sol naciente** Land of the Rising Sun (Japan) • **t. de nadie** no man's land • **T. Prometida** BIBL. Promised Land; FIG. promised land; **t. de Venecia** MIN. yellow ocher • **t. firme** terra firma • **t. negra** *or* **t. vegetal** humus • **t. rara** CHEM. rare earth • **tomar t.** to land • **venir** *or* **venirse a t.** to crumble, collapse • **ver otras tierras** to travel, see the world.

tie·so, –sa I. adj. *(rígido)* rigid, stiff; *(fuerte)* strong, vigorous; *(tirante)* tense, taut; FIG. *(valiente)* brave, courageous; *(estirado)* haughty, arrogant; *(envarado)* formal, stiff; *(terco)* stubborn, obstinate; FIG., COLL. *(muerto)* stiff, dead ♦ **dejar t.** COLL. to kill • **estar t.** to be flat broke

• **tenérselas tiesas** FIG., COLL. to stand firm, hold one's ground **II.** adv. strongly.

ties·to m. *(pedazo de vasija)* piece of pottery *or* earthenware; *(maceta)* flowerpot; CHILE pot, bowl.

tie·su·ra f. *(rigidez)* rigidity, stiffness; FIG. *(gravedad exagerada)* formality, stiffness.

ti·fo m. MED. typhus ♦ **t. asiático** Asiatic cholera • **t. de América** yellow fever • **t. de Oriente** bubonic plague.

ti·foi·de·o, –a adj. **I.** adj. typhoid **II.** f. typhoid fever.

ti·fón m. METEOROL. typhoon.

ti·fus m. MED. typhus; FIG., COLL. *(espectadores)* claque.

ti·gre m. ZOOL. tiger; AMER. jaguar; FIG. *(persona cruel)* cruel *or* bloodthirsty person.

ti·gre·sa f. ZOOL. tigress.

ti·gri·llo m. AMER. wildcat, ocelot.

ti·ja f. stem (of a key).

ti·je·ra f. *(instrumento)* scissors; *(caballo)* sawhorse; *(zanja de desagüe)* drainage ditch; FIG. *(chismoso)* gossip; SPORT. scissors ♦ **cortado por la misma t.** FIG. cut from the same cloth • **de t.** folding *<catre de t.* folding cot> • **echar t.** COLL. to cut to ribbons *or* shreds (by gossiping) • **tijeras** scissors.

ti·je·ra·da f. var. of **tijeretada.**

ti·je·re·ta f. *(tijera pequeña)* small scissors; *(catre)* folding cot; BOT. tendril (of a vine); ENTOM. earwig; ORNITH. scissortail.

ti·je·re·ta·da f. *or* **ti·je·re·ta·zo** m. snip, clip (with scissors).

ti·je·re·te·ar tr. *(con las tijeras)* to snip, clip; FIG., COLL. *(entremeterse)* to butt in, meddle.

ti·je·re·te·o m. *(acción)* snipping, clipping; *(ruido)* snip-snip.

ti·la f. BOT. linden (tree and flower); *(infusión)* linden flower tea; COLL. *(marihuana)* tea, grass (marijuana).

til·dar tr. *(poner acento)* to put a tilde on; *(tachar)* to erase *or* cross out; FIG. *(tratar)* to label, call *<t. a alguien de necio* to call someone a fool>.

til·de m.f. *(sobre la ñ)* tilde; *(acento)* accent; *(tacha)* flaw, blemish —f. *(cosa mínima)* iota, jot ♦ **poner t. a** FIG. to criticize.

ti·lín m. ting-a-ling ♦ **en un t.** *(en un momento)* in a twinkling *or* flash; CHILE, COL. on the verge (of) • **hacer t.** FIG., COLL. to appeal (to someone).

ti·lin·go, –ga adj. ARG. MEX., PERU, COLL. silly, foolish.

ti·lo m. BOT. linden.

ti·ma·dor, –do·ra m.f. swindler, cheat.

ti·mar tr. to swindle, cheat —reflex. COLL. *(hacerse guiños)* to make eyes at one another.

tim·ba f. COLL. *(partida de juego)* hand of cards; *(garito)* gambling den; PHILIP. well bucket; C. AMER., MEX., VEN. stomach, belly; CUBA guava paste.

tim·bal m. MUS. kettledrum; CUL. meat pie.

tim·ba·le·ro, –ra m.f. MUS. kettledrummer.

tim·bi·rim·ba f. COLL. hand of cards; COL. musical instrument.

tim·bra·do, –da I. past part. see **timbrar II.** adj. stamped *<papel t.* stamped paper *or* letterhead>.

tim·brar tr. *(sellar)* to stamp *or* seal; HER. to put a crest on (a coat of arms).

tim·bra·zo m. loud ringing.

tim·bre m. *(sello para estampar)* stamp, seal; *(sello oficial)* tax stamp; *(aparato)* bell, buzzer; *(sonido)* timbre, ring *<un t. metálico* a metallic ring>; HER. *(marca)* crest.

ti·mi·dez f. timidity, bashfulness.

tí·mi·do, –da adj. timid, shy.

ti·mo[1] m. ANAT. thymus.

ti·mo[2] m. COLL. *(estafa)* swindle, trick; *(broma)* practical joke ♦ **dar un t.** FIG., COLL. to swindle, cheat.

ti·món m. MARIT. rudder; AVIA. control stick; AGR. plow beam; *(pértigo)* whippletree; *(varilla del cohete)* rocket stick; FIG. *(dirección)* helm, rudder; AMER. steering wheel ♦ **manejar el t.** FIG. to be at the helm.

ti·mo·ne·ar tr. & intr. MARIT. to steer.

ti·mo·nel m. MARIT. helmsman, steersman.

ti·mo·ne·ra f. ORNITH. rectrix, tail feather; MARIT. wheelhouse, pilothouse.

ti·mo·ne·ro I. adj. beam *<arado t.* beam plow> **II.** m. MARIT. helmsman, steersman.

ti·mo·ra·to, –ta adj. RELIG. God-fearing; *(tímido)* timorous, shy.

tim·pá·ni·co, –ca adj. ANAT., MED. tympanic.

tim·pa·ni·llo m. PRINT. tympan.

tím·pa·no m. MUS. kettledrum; ANAT. eardrum, tympanum; ARCHIT. typanum; PRINT. tympan; *(del tonel)* top (of a barrel) ♦ **tímpanos** timpani.

ti·na f. *(tinaja)* large earthen vat; *(cubo)* tub, vat; *(baño)* bathtub.

ti·na·co m. *(cubo)* wooden tub; AMER. earthenware jar.

ti·na·da f. *(montón de leña)* woodpile; *(cobertizo)* cattle shed.

ti·na·ja f. *(vasija)* large earthen jar; PHILIP. liquid measurement.

ti·na·je·ro m. *(persona)* potter; *(sitio)* stand for earthenware jars.

tin·ca f. BOL. surprise party; CHILE hunch.

tin·car §70 tr. to flick (with the nails) —reflex. CHILE to have a hunch.

tin·gla·do m. *(cobertizo)* shed; *(tablado)* platform; FIG. *(enredo)* trick, ruse; CUBA inclined plane for draining sugar ♦ **conocer el t.** COLL. to know someone's game • **manejar el t.** COLL. to rule the roost.

ti·nie·blas f.pl. *(falta de luz)* darkness, gloom; FIG. *(ignorancia)* darkness, ignorance.

ti·no m. *(habilidad)* skill, knack; *(con un arma)* good aim; FIG. *(juicio)* good judgment ♦ **a buen t.** by guesswork • **a t.** gropingly • **perder el t.** to take leave of one's senses • **sacar de t.** to exasperate, drive crazy • **sin t.** recklessly, immoderately.

tin·qué, tinque see tincar.

tin·ta I. f. *(para escribir)* ink; *(color)* tint, dye; *(acción de teñir)* tinting, dyeing; ZOOL. ink ♦ **a medias tintas** FIG. vaguely • **cargar** *or* **recargar las tintas** to exaggerate • **media t.** ARTS half-tone • **saber de buena t.** FIG., COLL. to have it on good authority • **sudar t.** COLL. to sweat blood • **t. china** India ink • **t. de imprenta** printer's ink • **tintas** hues, colors • **t. simpática** invisible ink II. adj. see **tinto, –ta.**

tin·tar tr. to dye, tint.

tin·te m. *(acción de teñir)* dyeing, tinting; *(colorante)* dye; *(color)* hue, tint; *(de madera)* stain; *(tienda)* dyer's shop; FIG. *(apariencia)* tinge, overtone.

tin·te·ri·lla·da f. C. AMER., CHILE, COL. pettifogging, chicanery.

tin·te·ri·llo m. FIG., COLL. *(chupatintas)* pencil-pusher; AMER. pettifogger, shyster.

tin·te·ro m. *(recipiente)* inkwell, inkstand; *(del caballo)* age mark on horse's tooth; PRINT. ink fountain ♦ **dejarse** *or* **quedársele a uno en el t. una cosa** FIG., COLL. to slip one's mind.

tin·tín *or* **tin·ti·li·ne·o** m. *(de vasos)* clinking (of glasses); *(de campanilla)* jingling, tinkling (of a bell).

tin·ti·nar *or* **tin·ti·ne·ar** intr. *(vasos)* to clink; *(campanilla)* to jingle, tinkle.

tin·ti·ne·o m. var. of tintín.

tin·to, –ta I. past part. see teñir II. adj. *(teñido)* dyed, stained; HOND. wine-colored, dark-red; COL. black (coffee) III. m. *(vino)* red wine; AMER. black coffee —f. see tinta.

tin·to·re·ra f. shark —m.f. see tintorero, –ra.

tin·to·re·rí·a f. *(acción de teñir)* dyeing; *(limpieza en seco)* dry cleaning; *(taller donde se tiñe)* dyer's shop; *(taller donde se limpia en seco)* dry cleaner's shop.

tin·to·re·ro, –ra m.f. *(persona que tiñe)* dyer; *(persona que limpia en seco)* dry cleaner —f. see tintorera.

tin·tu·ra f. *(tinte)* tint, dye; *(afeite)* makeup, cosmetic; PHARM. tincture; FIG. *(noticia ligera)* smattering, slight knowledge ♦ **t. de yodo** PHARM. tincture of iodine.

tin·tu·rar tr. to dye, tint.

ti·ña f. ENTOM. honeycomb moth; MED. scaldhead, ringworm of the scalp; COLL. *(miseria)* misery, poverty.

ti·ña, tiño see teñir.

ti·ñe·ra, tiñó see teñir.

ti·ño·so, –sa I. adj. MED. scabby; FIG., COLL. *(avaro)* stingy, miserly II. m.f. MED. person suffering from ringworm; FIG., COLL. *(avaro)* miser, pennypincher.

tí·o m. *(pariente)* uncle; COLL. *(hombre viejo)* old guy; *(per-*

sona cualquiera) guy, fellow; *(peyorativo)* so-and-so ♦ **el t. del saco** FIG. the bogeyman • **t. abuelo** great-uncle, granduncle • **tíos** aunt and uncle • **Tío Sam** Uncle Sam.

tio·vi·vo m. merry-go-round, carousel.

ti·pa f. BOT. hardwood tree; *(mujer despreciable)* trollop; ARG. wicker basket.

ti·pe·jo, –ja m.f. DEROG. twerp, squirt.

tí·pi·co, –ca adj. typical, characteristic.

ti·pi·fi·car §70 tr. to typify.

ti·ple m. MUS. *(voz)* soprano, treble (voice); *(instrumento)* treble guitar; MARIT. single-piece mast —m.f. MUS. soprano (singer).

ti·po m. *(clase)* type, kind <¿*qué t. de zapatos buscas?* what kind of shoes are you looking for?>; *(modelo)* type, model; *(figura)* figure, physique; COLL. *(persona extraña)* character; *(persona)* guy <¿*quién es ese t.?* who is that guy?>; PRINT. type; COM. rate <*t. de interés* interest rate>.

ti·po·gra·fí·a f. *(arte)* typography, printing; *(lugar)* print shop.

ti·pó·gra·fo, –fa m.f. typographer, typesetter.

ti·po·lo·gí·a f. typology.

ti·quis mi·quis *or* **ti·quis·mi·quis** m.pl. *(escrúpulos)* silly scruples; *(serie)* series <*una t. de versos* a series of verses>; *(cortesías afectadas)* affected manners; *(molestias)* squabbles, spats.

ti·ra f. *(de papel)* strip; *(en un periódico)* comic strip; MARIT. fall ♦ **la t.** SL. heaps, loads • **tiras** CHILE, COLL. rags, clothes.

ti·ra·bo·tas m. [pl. **-tas**] boot hook.

ti·ra·bu·zón m. *(sacacorchos)* corkscrew; FIG. *(de cabello)* corkscrew curl, ringlet; SPORT. twist (on the trampoline) ♦ **sacar con t.** FIG., COLL. to drag something out (of someone).

ti·ra·da I. f. *(lanzamiento)* throw, cast; *(distancia)* distance, stretch; *(serie)* series <*una t. de versos* a series of verses>; PRINT. *(edición)* printing, edition; *(jornada)* day's print run; AMER. boring speech; P. RICO dirty trick ♦ **de una t.** at one stretch • **t. aparte** PRINT. reprint II. adj. see **tirado, –da.**

ti·ra·de·ra f. *(flecha)* long arrow; CUBA ridgeband (of a harness); C. AMER., CUBA, CHILE suspenders.

ti·ra·do, –da I. past part. see tirar II. adj. *(muy barato)* dirt-cheap; *(fácil)* easy as pie; MARIT. long and low (said of a ship); METAL. drawn III. m. METAL. wiredrawing; PRINT. printing, presswork —f. see **tirada.**

ti·ra·dor, –do·ra m. *(de pistola)* marksman, shot <*ser buen t.* to be a good shot>; *(de cajón)* handle, knob; *(de campanilla)* bellpull, rope; METAL. wire drawer; PRINT. pressman; ARG. leather belt (worn by gauchos); *(tiragomas)* catapult —f. markswoman, shot ♦ **t. de oro** METAL. gold-wire drawer.

ti·ra·lí·ne·as [pl. **-as**] m. ruling pen.

ti·ra·ní·a f. tyranny.

ti·ra·ni·ci·da I. adj. tyrannicidal II. m.f. tyrannicide.

ti·ra·ni·ci·dio m. tyrannicide.

ti·rá·ni·co, –ca adj. tyrannical.

ti·ra·ni·zar §04 tr. to tyrannize.

ti·ra·no, –na I. adj. tyrannical II. m.f. tyrant.

ti·ran·te I. adj. *(tenso)* tight, taut; FIG. *(relaciones)* tense, strained II. m. *(de carruaje)* trace (of a harness); *(correa)* strap, tie; ARCHIT. tie beam; TECH. brace, tie rod ♦ **tirantes** suspenders.

ti·ran·tez f. *(de una cuerda)* tenseness, tightness; FIG. *(entre personas)* tension, strain.

ti·rar tr. *(arrojar)* to throw, cast <*t. piedras* to throw stones>; *(desechar)* to throw away, discard; *(derribar)* to knock down <*t. un edificio* to knock down a building>; *(estirar)* to stretch, pull tight <*t. las cuerdas de la guitarra* to stretch the guitar strings>; to draw, elongate <*t. alambre* to draw wire>; *(disparar)* to fire, shoot; *(trazar)* to draw, trace <*t. paralelas* to draw parallel lines>; *(dar)* to give, deal <*le tiré una patada* I gave him a kick>; *(imprimir)* to print <*t. un grabado* to print an engraving>; PHOTOG. to print; FIG. *(disipar)* to waste, squander <*tira el dinero como si nada* he wastes money as if it were nothing>; CUBA, CHILE to haul, transport ♦ **t. a alguien de la lengua** to draw someone out • **tirarla de** FIG. to boast of being <*tirarla de sabio* to boast of being wise> —intr. *(atraer)* to draw, attract <*el imán tira del metal* the magnet attracts metal>; *(traer hacia sí)* to pull <*tiró con todas sus fuerzas he pulled with all his might*>; *(manejar)* to handle <*tira bien a la espada* he handles a sword well>; *(sacar)* to draw, pull out <*tiró de la pistola* he drew his pistol>; *(producir corriente)* to draw <*esta chimenea no tira bien* this chimney does not draw well>; *(torcer)* to turn, go <*t. hacia la izquierda* to turn towards the left>; *(durar)* to last <*los zapatos no tirarán otro año* his shoes will not last another year>; *(aspirar)* to aspire, aim <*él tira para ingeniero* he aspires to be an engineer>; FIG. *(atraer el ánimo)* to have an appeal, draw <*no hay duda de que el terruño siempre tira* there is no doubt that one's native land has an appeal>; *(tender)* to tend, incline; *(parecerse)* to take after, resemble <*ella tira a su madre* she takes after her mother>; *(teñirse)* to have a touch of <*este color tira a rojo* this color has a touch of red>; COLL. *(funcionar)* to work, run <*el coche tira bien* the car runs well> ♦ **a todo t.** at the most • **ir tirando** to get along, manage • **t. de** to pull, draw <*los bueyes tiraban del carro* the oxen were pulling the wagon> • **tira y afloja** give-and-take —reflex. *(arrojarse)* to throw *or* hurl oneself; *(tenderse)* to lie down, stretch out <*tirarse en la cama* to lie down on the bed>; *(pasar)* to spend <*se tiró el día jugando al tenis* he spent the day playing tennis>.

ti·ri·lla f. *(de camisa)* neckband; CHILE rag, tatter.

ti·ri·ta·ña f. *(tela)* thin silk; FIG., COLL. *(cosa insignificante)* trifle, bagatelle.

ti·ri·tar intr. to shiver, shake.

ti·ri·te·ra f. shivering, shaking.

ti·ri·to·na f. COLL. shivers, shakes <*tener la t.* to have the shivers>.

ti·ro m. *(lanzada)* throw, cast; ARM. *(acción)* shooting <*t. al blanco* target shooting>; *(pieza de artillería)* gun, weapon; *(disparo)* shot, discharge; *(estampido)* report <*sonó un t. de cañón* a cannon report sounded>; *(carga)* load, charge; *(alcance)* range <*a t. de fusil* within rifle range; *(trayectoria)* trajectory <*t. sesgado* slanted trajectory>; *(campo)* shooting range *or* gallery; SEW. *(longitud)* length (of cloth); *(anchura)* width from shoulder to shoulder; MIN. shaft; *(caballos)* team (of horses); *(tirante)* trace (of a harness); *(cuerda)* pulley rope; *(corriente de aire)* draft (of air); ARCHIT. flight (of stairs); COLL. *(chut)* shot, kick <*t. a gol* shot at goal>; FIG. *(broma)* prank, trick; *(robo)* theft, robbery; *(daño)* damage, harm; CHILE, MEX., PERU *(canica)* marble; ARG., CHILE *(distancia)* distance, course (of a race) ♦ **al t.** CHILE right away • **a t. de** within reach *or* range of • **a t. limpio** *or* **a tiros** with gunfire • **darse** *or* **pegarse un t.** to shoot oneself • **de a t.** GUAT., MEX. completely • **del t.** CUBA, P. RICO consequently; GUAT. all at once • **de tiros largos** FIG., COLL. dressed to kill • **ni a tiros** COLL. not by a long shot • **salirle a uno el t. por la culata** to backfire • **t. de gracia** coup de grâce, death blow • **tiros** *(correas)* sword belt; ARG. *(tirantes)* suspenders.

ti·roi·des ANAT. adj. & m. thyroid.

ti·rón m. *(acción de tirar)* tug, pull; *(estirón)* yank, jerk; COLL. *(de músculo)* cramp; FIG., COLL. *(distancia grande)* good distance, long stretch; *(atracción)* attraction, pull; *(robo)* purse-snatching ♦ **de un t.** all at once, in one stretch.

ti·ro·ri·ro m. MUS., COLL. sound of reed instruments ♦ **tiroriros** MUS., COLL. reed intruments.

ti·ro·te·ar tr. to snipe *or* fire at —reflex. to exchange fire.

ti·ro·te·o m. firing, shooting.

ti·rria f. COLL. grudge, dislike <*tener t. a* to have a grudge against>.

ti·ru·la·to, -ta adj. COLL. dumbfounded, stupefied.

ti·sa·na f. PHARM. infusion, tisane.

tí·si·co, -ca MED. I. adj. tubercular, consumptive II. m.f. tuberculosis sufferer, consumptive.

ti·sis f. MED. phthisis, tuberculosis.

ti·sú m. TEX. gold *or* silver lamé.

ti·tán m. titan, giant ♦ **Titán** MYTH. Titan.

ti·tá·ni·co, -ca adj. titanic.

ti·ta·nio m. CHEM. titanium.

tí·te·re m. *(marioneta)* puppet, marionette; FIG., COLL. *(presumido)* squirt, twerp; *(tonto)* fool, nincompoop; FIG. *(persona dominada por otra)* puppet, tool ♦ **no dejar t. con**

cabeza FIG. to destroy everything, leave nothing standing • **títeres** puppet show.

ti·te·re·ta·da f. COLL. foolishness, stupidity.

ti·ti·la·ción f. *(temblor)* quivering, shaking; *(de las estrellas)* twinkling, flickering.

ti·ti·la·dor, -do·ra adj. *(tembloroso)* quivering, shaking; *(una estrella)* twinkling, flickering.

ti·ti·lar *or* **ti·ti·le·ar** intr. *(temblar)* to quiver; *(una estrella)* to twinkle, flicker.

ti·ti·le·o m. *(temblor)* quivering, shaking; *(una estrella)* twinkling, flickering.

ti·ti·ri·mun·di m. cosmorama.

ti·ti·ri·tai·na f. COLL. *(de instrumentos)* racket, din (of instruments playing at once); *(bulla)* hullabaloo, uproar.

ti·ti·ri·tar intr. to tremble, shake.

ti·ti·ri·te·ro, -ra m.f. *(titerista)* puppeteer; *(volatinero)* tightrope walker, acrobat.

ti·tu·be·ar intr. *(oscilar)* to stagger, totter; FIG. *(vacilar)* to hesitate, waver; *(farfullar)* to stammer, stutter.

ti·tu·be·o m. *(al andar)* staggering, tottering; FIG. *(vacilación)* hesitation, wavering; *(al hablar)* stammering, stuttering.

ti·tu·la·do, -da I. past part. see titular² II. adj. *(supuesto)* supposed, so-called; *(capacitado)* qualified; *(certificado)* certified III. m.f. titled person.

ti·tu·lar¹ I. adj. *(que tiene título)* titular, official; regular <*el profesor t.* the regular professor> II. m. PRINT. headline, heading —m.f. holder (of a passport, office).

ti·tu·lar² tr. to title, entitle —intr. to receive a title —reflex. EDUC. to receive one's degree.

tí·tu·lo m. *(inscripción)* title; *(encabezado)* caption, heading; *(honor)* title <*el t. de conde* the title of count>; *(noble)* titled person; *(diploma)* diploma, degree; *(división)* section (of a law, etc.); *(causa)* cause, reason; LAW title <*t. de propiedad* deed title>; COM. bond, security <*t. al portador* bearer bond>; CHEM. titer ♦ **a t. de** as, by way of.

ti·za f. chalk.

tiz·na·du·ra f. blackening, smudging.

tiz·na·jo m. COLL. smudge, stain.

tiz·nar tr. *(manchar)* to blacken, smudge; FIG. *(la reputación)* to blacken, stain (reputation) —reflex. ARG., C. AMER. to get drunk.

tiz·ne m.f. soot, grime.

tiz·nón m. smudge, stain.

ti·zón m. *(madera)* half-burned log, firebrand; FIG. *(en la reputación)* stain (on reputation); BOT. smut (on grain); ARCHIT. header.

ti·zo·na f. FIG., COLL. sword.

ti·zo·na·da f. *or* **ti·zo·na·zo** m. *(golpe)* blow with a firebrand; COLL. *(en el infierno)* hellfire.

ti·zo·ne·ar intr. to poke, stir up (a fire).

to·a f. AMER. towrope.

to·a·lla f. towel.

to·a·lle·ro m. towel rack.

to·bi·lle·ra COLL. I. adj. teenage (girl) II. f. teenage girl, bobby soxer ♦ **tobilleras** anklets, bobby socks.

to·bi·llo m. ANAT. ankle.

to·bo·gán m. *(para mercancías)* slide, chute; *(para la nieve)* toboggan.

to·ca f. *(tocado)* hairdo, coiffure; *(sombrero)* hat; *(de religiosa)* wimple ♦ **tocas** compensation given to widow of a deceased employee.

to·ca·ble adj. touchable.

to·ca·dis·cos m. [pl. -cos] record player, phonograph.

to·ca·do I. m. *(peinado)* hairdo, coiffure; *(sombrero)* hat II. adj. see tocado, -da.

to·ca·do, -da I. past part. see tocar II. adj. COLL. touched, crazy <*t. de la cabeza* touched in the head> III. m. see tocado.

to·ca·dor I. m. MUS. player <*t. de guitarra* guitar player>; *(mueble)* dressing table; *(cuarto)* dressing room, boudoir; *(paño)* scarf, kerchief; *(tocado)* hairdo, coiffure; *(neceser)* vanity case; COLL. powder room, ladies' room ♦ **artículos de t.** cosmetics, toiletries II. adj. see tocador, -do·ra.

to·ca·dor, -do·ra MUS. I. adj. playing II. f. player —m. see tocador.

to·can·te adj. touching ♦ **t. a** concerning, with reference to.

to·car¹ §70 tr. to touch <*no toques ese botón* do not touch that button>; *(palpar)* to feel <*lo toqué con el dedo* I felt it with my finger>; *(manosear)* to handle <*no toquen ustedes las mercaderías* do not handle the merchandise>; *(hacer sonar)* to sound <*t. las trompetas* to sound the trumpets>; *(tañer)* to ring, toll ◊ *tocaron las campanas* they rang the bells>; MUS. to play <¿*tocas la guitarra?* do you play the guitar?>; *(tropezar)* to hit, strike <*t. fondo* to hit bottom>; *(estar próximo)* to touch <*nuestra casa toca la suya* our house touches theirs>; *(empezar)* to touch, start <*no ha tocado su comida* he has not touched his food>; FIG. *(conmover)* to touch, affect <*Dios le tocó el corazón* God touched his heart>; *(tratar de)* to touch on, allude to <*tocó la cuestión del dinero* he touched on the question of money>; MIN. *(probar)* to test, try on a touchstone>; MARIT. to touch (bottom); PAINT. to touch up ◊ **t. la diana** MIL. to play reveille • **t. la generala** MIL. to sound the call to arms —intr. *(corresponder)* to be up to, fall to <*me toca a mí darle la noticia* it is up to me to give him the news>; to be one's turn <¿*a quién le toca?* whose turn is it?>; *(conseguir)* to get <*le toca la mitad* he gets half>; *(caer en suerte)* to win <*le tocó el premio gordo* he won the grand prize>; to knock <*t. a la puerta* to knock at the door>; *(rayar en)* to verge, border <*esto toca en la locura* this borders on madness>; *(llegar el momento de)* to be time <*ahora toca pagar* now it is time to pay>; MARIT. to stop, call <*este barco no toca en Barcelona* this ship does not call at Barcelona> ◊ **t. a muerto** to toll the death knell • **t. a rebato** to sound the alarm • **t. a su fin** to be coming to an end • **t. de cerca** to hit home <*es una situación que me toca de cerca* it is a situation that hits home with me>.

to·car² §70 tr. to comb and dress (the hair) —reflex. to cover the head.

to·ca·ta f. MUS. toccata; COLL. *(paliza)* beating, thrashing.

to·ca·yo, -ya m.f. namesake.

to·cé, toce see **tozar**.

to·ci·ne·rí·a f. pork butcher shop.

to·ci·ne·ro, -ra m.f. pork butcher.

to·ci·no m. *(carne)* bacon, salt pork; *(lardo)* lard; *(témpano)* flitch, side (of bacon); *(salto)* quick skip (with a rope); CUBA, BOT. acacia ◊ **t. entreverado** CUL. streaky bacon.

to·co·ma·te m. AMER., BOT. pumpkin.

to·cón, -co·na I. m. stump (of tree or limb) II. adj. COL. bobtailed.

to·cu·yo m. AMER., TEX. coarse cotton cloth.

to·chim·bo m. PERU smelting furnace.

to·cho, -cha I. adj. coarse, boorish II. m. iron ingot.

to·da·bue·na or **to·da·sa·na** f. BOT. St. Johnswort.

to·da·ví·a adv. still <*t. están durmiendo* they are still sleeping>; *(sin embargo)* nevertheless, still <*es malo pero t. lo quiero* he is bad, but I still love him>; *(aún)* even <*él es t. más inteligente que ella* he is even more intelligent than her>; S. AMER. not yet ◊ **t. no** not yet.

to·di·to, -ta adj. COLL. all, the whole <*t. la noche* the whole night>.

to·do, -da I. adj. all <*se comió t. el pan* he ate all the bread>; *(cada)* each, every <*t. delito merece castigo* every crime deserves punishment>; all <*este jardín es t. hierbas* this garden is all weeds>; whole, entire <*t. el universo* the whole universe> ◊ **t. el mundo** everybody • **t. quisque** COLL. everybody II. m. whole <*el t. es mayor que sus partes* the whole is greater than its parts>; all, everything <*t. está listo* everything is ready> ◊ **ante t.** above all, first of all • **así y t.** for all that, just the same • **a t.** at full, at most <*a t. correr* at full speed> • **con t.** nevertheless, still • **del t.** wholly, entirely • **ser el t.** to be the important person • **sobre t.** above all, especially • **todos** everybody, everyone III. adv. all, every inch <*él es t. un hombre* he is every inch a man>.

to·do·po·de·ro·so, -sa adj. all-powerful, almighty ◊ **El Todopoderoso** the Almighty, God.

to·fo m. CHILE refractory clay; MED. tophus, tumor.

to·ga f. *(de los romanos)* toga; *(de los magistrados)* robe, gown.

to·ga·do, -da I. adj. robed II. m.f. attorney ◊ **los togados** the legal profession.

To·go m. Togo.

to·go·lés, -le·sa adj. & m.f. Togolese.

To·kio Tokyo.

tol·da·du·ra f. awning, canopy.

tol·dar tr. to cover with an awning or canopy.

tol·di·llo m. *(silla de manos)* sedan chair; AMER. mosquito netting.

tol·do m. *(cortina)* awning, canopy; AMER. folding hood (of a carriage); ARG. tent, tepee; FIG. *(engreimiento)* haughtiness, conceit.

to·le m. FIG. *(gritería)* hubbub, uproar; *(desaprobación)* clamor, hue and cry ◊ **tomar el t.** FIG. to run away, flee.

to·le·ra·ble adj. tolerable.

to·le·ra·do, -da I. past part. see **tolerar** II. adj. allowed, permissible.

to·le·ran·cia f. tolerance, toleration.

to·le·ran·te adj. tolerant.

to·le·rar tr. *(soportar)* to tolerate, endure; *(condescender)* to be tolerant of; *(permitir)* to allow, permit; *(aguantar)* to tolerate, keep down <*mi estómago no tolera la leche* my stomach cannot tolerate milk>.

to·le·te m. MARIT. thole, tholepin; C. AMER. cudgel, club.

to·le·to·le m. COLL. hubbub, uproar.

to·lon·dro, -dra I. adj. scatterbrained, reckless II. m.f. *(persona)* scatterbrain; m. *(bulto)* bump, swelling.

to·lon·drón, -dro·na I. adj. scatterbrained, reckless II. m.f. *(persona)* scatterbrain; *(chichón)* bump, swelling ◊ **a tolondrones** by fits and starts.

tol·te·ca adj. & m.f. Toltec.

to·lue·no m. CHEM. toluene.

tol·va f. hopper, chute.

tol·va·ne·ra f. dust storm.

to·lli·na f. COLL. beating, licking.

to·llo m. ICHTH. dogfish; *(del ciervo)* loin (of a stag); HUNT. blind; *(atolladero)* quagmire, bog.

to·ma f. *(acción de tomar)* taking; *(conquista)* capture, seizure; *(dosis)* dose <*una t. de quinina* a dose of quinine>; *(entrada)* intake, inlet <*t. de aire* air intake>; *(grifo)* tap, outlet; ELEC. outlet plug; CINEM. take, shot; AMER. *(cauce)* irrigation ditch; *(presa)* dam; GUAT. brook ◊ **t. de conciencia** awareness • **t. de corriente** ELEC. outlet, plug • **t. del sonido** sound recording • **t. de posesión** *(investidura)* inauguration; MIL. occupation, seizure • **t. de tierra** ELEC. ground wire; AVIA. landing, touchdown • **t. de vistas** CINEM. shooting, filming • **t. y daca** give-and-take.

to·ma·de·ro m. *(agarradero)* handle; *(de agua)* tap, outlet (for water).

to·ma·dor, -do·ra I. adj. *(que toma)* taking; *(ratero)* thieving, stealing; *(que bebe)* drinking ◊ **perro t.** retriever (dog) II. m.f. *(persona que toma)* taker; *(ratero)* thief, pickpocket; *(bebedor)* drinker, drunkard; COM. drawee —m. MARIT. gasket.

to·ma·du·ra f. *(toma)* taking; *(cantidad)* portion, quantity (taken at once); MIL. capture, seizure; PHARM. dose ◊ **t. de pelo** hoax, practical joke.

to·ma·jón, -jo·na COLL. I. adj. taking II. m.f. taker.

to·mar tr. to take <*tomó mi consejo* he took my advice>; *(asir)* to take, take hold of <*tomé el libro entre mis manos* I took the book in my hands>; *(aceptar)* to take, accept <*tomaron el dinero que les ofrecí* they took the money that I offered them>; *(recibir)* to take, have <*tomó lecciones de piano* he took piano lessons>; *(ocupar)* to take, occupy <*me tomó mucho tiempo limpiar la casa* it took me a lot of time to clean the house>; *(capturar)* to seize, capture <*las tropas tomaron la ciudad* the troops seized the city>; *(comer)* to eat, have <*tomé el desayuno a las siete* I had breakfast at seven o'clock>; *(beber)* to drink, have <¿*quieres t. una cerveza conmigo?* do you want to have a beer with me?>; *(agarrar)* to take up <*t. la pluma* to take up one's pen>; *(cobrar)* to gain, gather <*t. fuerzas* to gather strength>; *(robar)* to take, steal; *(escoger)* to take, pick <*tome usted uno de estos naipes* pick one of these cards>; *(elegir)* to take <*tomaré estas personas para trabajar conmigo* I will take these people to work with me>; to take, catch <*t. el autobús* to take the bus>; *(usar)* to take, use <*este ejemplo lo tomé del libro* I took this example from the book>; *(interpretar)* to take <*no lo tomo en serio* I do not take it seriously>; *(considerar)* to take, mistake <*lo tomé por el jefe* I mistook him for the boss>; *(adquirir)* to take up, acquire <*t. malas costumbres* to acquire bad habits>; *(emplear)* to take, adopt <*tomaron medidas seve-*

ras they took drastic measures>; *(imitar)* to take on, adopt <*tomó los modales de su hermana mayor* she adopted the manners of her older sister>; *(medir)* to take <*t..la temperatura* to take one's temperature>; *(comprar)* to take, buy <*tomaré dos de éstos y dos de aquéllos* I will take two of these and two of those>; *(alquilar)* to rent <*t. un piso* to rent an apartment>; *(contratar)* to take on, hire <*t. un chófer* to hire a chauffeur>; *(padecer)* to catch <*t. frío* to catch cold>; *(ganar)* to take, win <*t. una baza* to take a trick>; CINEM., PHOTOG. to take, shoot <*t. una escena* to shoot a scene>; COL. to annoy, harass ♦ **t. a bien** to take (something) well • **t. a mal** to take (something) wrong • **t. a pecho** to take to heart • **t. asiento** to take a seat • **t. conciencia** to become aware, realize • **t. el fresco** to take the air • **t. el pelo a alguien** to pull someone's leg • **t. el sol** to sunbathe • **t. en broma** to take as a joke • **t. en cuenta** to take into account *or* consideration • **t. estado** *(casarse)* to marry; RELIG. to take holy orders • **tomarla con alguien** *(criticar)* to pick on someone; *(resentirse)* to have a grudge against someone • **t. la delantera** to take the lead, get ahead • **t. las de Villadiego** COLL. to beat it • **t. nota de** to take note of, notice • **t. parte** to take part, participate • **t. partido** to take sides • **t. por sorpresa** to take by surprise, surprise • **t. posesión de** to take possession of • **t. precauciones** to take precautions • **t. prestado** to borrow • **t. sobre sí** to take on, take upon oneself • **t. tierra** AVIA. to land, touch down —intr. *(encaminarse)* to go, turn <*tomamos por la izquierda* we went to the left> • **¡toma!** really!, fancy that! —reflex. to take <*tomarse libertades con alguien* to take liberties with someone>; *(oxidarse)* to rust, get rusty ♦ **tomarse por** to consider oneself.

to·ma·ta·da f. CUL. fried tomatoes.

to·ma·tal m. AGR. tomato patch *or* field; GUAT. tomato plant.

to·ma·te m. BOT. tomato (fruit and plant); COLL. *(roto)* hole, run (in stockings) ♦ **ponerse como un t.** to become red as a beet • **tener t.** COLL. to be awkward *or* difficult.

to·ma·te·ra f. **I.** BOT. tomato plant; *(persona)* tomato seller; COLL. *(engreimiento)* airs, conceit <*tener t.* to put on airs> **II.** adj. see **tomatero, –ra.**

to·ma·te·ro, –ra I. adj. young and tender (said of a chicken) **II.** m. tomato seller —f. see **tomatera.**

to·ma·vis·tas m. [pl. **-tas**] movie *or* television *or* video camera.

tóm·bo·la f. charity raffle.

to·mi·llo m. BOT. thyme.

to·mis·mo m. THEOL. Thomism.

to·mo m. *(libro)* volume, tome; *(grueso)* volume, bulk; FIG. *(importancia)* importance ♦ **de t. y lomo** FIG., COLL. weighty, important.

to·mó·gra·fo m. MED. scanner.

ton m. ♦ **sin t. ni son** without rhyme *or* reason.

to·na·da f. *(canción)* song, tune; AMER. regional accent.

to·na·di·lle·ro, –ra m.f. writer *or* singer of popular songs.

to·nal adj. MUS. tonal.

to·na·li·dad f. MUS. tonality.

to·nel m. barrel, cask.

to·ne·la·da f. *(peso)* ton; MARIT. barrels, casks.

to·ne·la·je m. MARIT. tonnage, displacement; COM. tonnage dues.

to·ne·le·rí·a f. *(fabricación)* barrelmaking, cooperage; *(taller)* barrel shop, cooperage; MARIT. barrels, casks.

to·ne·le·ro, –ra I. m. barrel maker, cooper **II.** adj. barrel, cask <*la industria t.* the barrel industry>.

ton·ga BOT. **I.** adj. tonka **II.** f. tonka bean.

ton·ga *or* **ton·ga·da** f. *(capa)* layer, covering; CUBA pile, heap; COL. task, job.

Ton·ga f. Tonga.

ton·ga·no, –na adj. & m.f. Tongan.

ton·go m. CHILE, PERU bowler hat; CHILE, SPORT. fixing (a competition) ♦ **hay t. en el combate** the fight has been fixed.

tó·ni·co, –ca I. adj. GRAM., MED. tonic **II.** m. MED. tonic —f. MUS. tonic ♦ **dar la t.** FIG. to set the tone.

to·ni·fi·ca·ción f. toning, strengthening.

to·ni·fi·ca·dor, –do·ra *or* **to·ni·fi·can·te** adj. toning, strengthening.

to·ni·fi·car §70 tr. to tone, strengthen.

to·ni·na f. ICHTH. tuna; ZOOL. dolphin.

to·no m. *(de voz)* tone; *(carácter)* tone <*el t. del ensayo* the tone of the essay>; *(modo de expresarse)* tone; *(color)* tone, shade; PHYSIOL. tone (of muscles); *(vigor)* energy; MUS. *(intervalo)* tone; *(escala)* key <*t. mayor* major key>; *(pieza de instrumento)* slide ♦ **a t.** in tune • **bajar el t.** to tone down • **dar el t.** to set the tone • **darse t.** to put on airs • **de buen t.** stylish, elegant • **de mal t.** crass, vulgar • **fuera de t.** out of place • **subir el t.** *(acalorarse)* to become heated; *(gritar)* to get louder.

ton·su·ra f. hair cutting, tonsure.

ton·su·ra·do I. past part. see **tonsurar II.** m. priest *or* monk (who has been tonsured).

ton·su·rar tr. *(un clérigo)* to tonsure; *(el pelo)* to cut (hair); *(la lana)* to shear (fleece).

ton·ta·da f. nonsense, foolishness.

ton·tai·na *or* **ton·tai·nas** COLL. **I.** adj. silly, dumb **II.** m.f. fool, nitwit.

ton·ta·men·te adv. foolishly, stupidly.

ton·te·ar intr. *(hacer tonterías)* to act foolishly; *(decir tonterías)* to talk foolishly; COLL. *(flirtear)* to flirt.

ton·te·dad *or* **ton·te·ra** f. vars. of **tontería.**

ton·te·rí·a f. *(calidad)* foolishness, stupidity; *(acción)* foolish action; *(dicho)* stupid remark; FIG. *(nadería)* trifle ♦ **decir tonterías** to talk nonsense • **no es ninguna t.** *(va en serio)* it's serious; *(no está nada mal)* it's not bad at all.

ton·ti·lo·co, –ca adj. foolish, harebrained.

ton·to, –ta I. adj. *(necio)* foolish, silly; COL. restless, mischievous • **a tontas y a locas** COLL. any which way, haphazardly **II.** m.f. *(necio)* fool, dolt; COLL. *(payaso)* clown ♦ **hacerse el t.** to play the fool • **t. de capirote** COLL. total fool.

to·ña f. *(juego)* tipcat (game); COLL. *(golpe)* blow, slap; *(borrachera)* drinking binge.

to·pa·cio m. MIN. topaz.

to·pa·da f. butt, blow with the head.

to·pa·dor, –do·ra adj. ZOOL. butting; *(en el juego)* hasty in accepting a bet.

to·par tr. *(chocar)* to bump, bump into; *(encontrar)* to bump into, run into <*topé a un amigo mío en la calle* I ran into a friend of mine in the street>; MARIT. to join, butt; CHILE, PERU to wager, bet —intr. ZOOL. to butt; *(en el juego)* to accept a bet; FIG. *(tropezar)* to run into, encounter <*topamos en muchas dificultades* we encountered many problems>; *(acertar)* to work out well <*veremos si topa* we shall see if it works out well> ♦ **en eso topa la dificultad** FIG. therein lies the difficulty, there's the rub • **t. con** *or* **contra** to bump into, run into <*topé con un poste* I bumped into a post>.

to·pe I. m. *(extremo)* butt, end; *(choque)* collision, bump; FIG. *(riña)* quarrel; *(reyerta)* scuffle; *(límite)* limit, maximum <*hasta el t.* to the limit>; *(dificultad)* snag, difficulty; MECH. stop, catch; AUTO., RAIL. bumper; MARIT. *(de palo)* masthead; *(vigía)* topman, lookout; COL. find, discovery ♦ **al t.** end to end • **estar hasta los topes** *(estar lleno)* to be filled to the brim; FIG. *(estar harto)* to be fed up **II.** m. maximum, top <*precio t.* top price>.

to·pe·ra f. molehill.

to·pe·ta·da f. butt, blow with the head (esp. horned animals).

to·pe·tar *or* **to·pe·te·ar** tr. *(un carnero)* to butt; COLL. *(chocar)* to bump —intr. to bump (into).

to·pe·ta·zo m. butt, bump (with the head).

to·pe·tón m. *(choque)* bump, collision; *(topetada)* butt.

to·pe·tu·do, –da adj. butting.

tó·pi·co, –ca I. adj. topical, local **II.** m. *(tema)* topic, subject; MED. external local application; RHET. commonplace, cliché.

to·po m. ZOOL. mole; FIG., COLL. *(persona torpe)* awkward *or* clumsy person; MEX. gopher; AMER. large pin.

to·po·cho, –cha adj. VEN. chubby, plump.

to·po·gra·fí·a f. topography.

to·po·grá·fi·co, –ca adj. topographical.

to·pó·gra·fo, –fa m.f. topographer.

to·po·lo·gí·a f. topology.

to·po·ni·mia f. toponymy.

to·que m. *(tacto)* touch, touching; *(tañido)* ringing, chime

<*el t. de campanas* the chime of bells>; *(de sirena)* hoot, blast; *(de tambor)* beat; FIG. *(punto esencial)* crux, gist <*aquí está el t. del negocio* here is the crux of the matter>; *(prueba)* test, trial; *(advertencia)* warning; *(golpe)* hit, tap; METAL. assay, assaying; *(piedra)* touchstone; MIL. bugle call; PAINT. touch, dab; BOL. turn ♦ **dar el último t. a** to give the finishing touch to • **darse un t.** ELEC. to get a shock (from static); *(drogas)* to take a toke • **dar un t. a alguien** to put someone to the test • **t. a muerto** death knell • **t. de diana** MIL. reveille • **t. de queda** curfew.

to·qué, toque see **tocar.**

to·que·ar tr. to handle, touch repeatedly.

to·que·o m. handling, touching.

to·qui·lla f. *(pañuelo)* handkerchief; *(bufanda)* scarf; *(adorno)* gauze *or* ribbon trimming (on a man's hat); AMER. straw hat.

to·rá·ci·co, –ca adj. ANAT. thoracic <*caja t.* thoracic cavity>.

to·ra·da f. drove *or* herd of bulls.

to·ral I. adj. *(principal)* main, principal; *(cera)* unbleached (wax) II. m. *(molda)* mold; *(barra de cobre)* copper bar.

tó·rax m. ANAT. thorax.

tor·be·lli·no m. *(viento)* whirlwind; *(agua)* vortex, whirlpool; *(de polvo)* dust storm; FIG. *(de cosas)* whirlwind, rush; FIG., COLL. *(persona)* lively *or* restless person.

tor·caz adj. ♦ **paloma t.** ORNITH. ringdove, wood pigeon.

tor·ca·zo, –za I. adj. COL., COLL. silly, foolish II. m.f. COL., COLL. fool, dunce —f. ORNITH. ringdove, wood pigeon.

tor·ce·de·ro, –ra I. adj. twisted, crooked II. m. twisting apparatus.

tor·ce·dor, –do·ra I. adj. twisting II. m.f. *(que tuerce)* twister —m. *(huso)* spindle; FIG. *(tormento)* torment, annoyance.

tor·ce·du·ra f. *(acción de torcer)* twisting; *(efecto de torcer)* twist; *(vino)* weak wine; MED. sprain.

tor·cer §71 tr. *(dar vueltas a)* to twist, wind <*t. una cuerda* to twist a string>; *(doblar)* to bend <*t. una barra de hierro* to bend an iron bar>; to twist, wrench <*torcerle el brazo a alguien* to twist someone's arm>; *(retorcer)* to contort, screw up <*t. el semblante* to screw up one's face>; MED. to sprain; FIG. *(interpretar mal)* to twist, distort; *(desviar)* to corrupt, pervert —intr. to turn <*el camino tuerce a la izquierda* the road turns to the left> ♦ **no dar el brazo a t.** FIG. to stand firm —reflex. *(estar torcido)* to twist, be twisted; *(doblarse)* to bend, be bent; *(avinagrarse)* to turn sour; *(frustrarse)* to go awry; FIG. *(corromperse)* to go astray.

tor·ci·da I. f. wick II. adj. see **torcido, –da.**

tor·ci·do, –da I. past part. see **torcer** II. adj. *(no recto)* twisted, crooked <*un camino t.* a crooked road>; *(doblado)* bent; FIG. *(corrupto)* crooked, dishonest; C. AMER. unfortunate II. m. CUL. fruit roll; *(vino)* weak wine; TEX. twist —f. see **torcida.**

tor·ci·jón m. MED. stomach cramp; VET. enteritis.

tor·ci·mien·to m. *(acción de torcer)* twisting; FIG. *(circunlocución)* circumlocution.

tor·di·llo, –lla I. adj. dapple-gray (horse) II. m.f. dapple-gray horse.

tor·do I. m. *(caballo)* dapple-gray horse; ORNITH. thrush; ARG., C. AMER., CHILE starling II. adj. dapple-gray (horse).

to·re·a·dor m. TAUR. toreador, bullfighter.

to·re·ar TAUR. to fight (bulls) —tr. *(evitar)* to dodge, sidestep; *(entretener)* to put (someone) off, string along; *(burlarse)* to tease, mock; FIG. *(incomodar)* to pester, harass; ARG. to goad (an animal) —intr. TAUR. to fight bulls.

to·re·o m. TAUR. bullfighting.

to·re·rí·a f. *(toreros)* bullfighters; COLL. *(travesura)* mischief, pranks.

to·re·ro, –ra I. adj. of bullfighting II. m. TAUR. bullfighter.

to·re·te m. ZOOL. young bull; COLL. *(dificultad)* difficulty, problem; *(asunto)* topic of conversation.

to·ril m. TAUR. bull pen.

to·rio m. CHEM. thorium.

to·ri·to m. ARG., PERU, ENTOM. rhinoceros beetle, horn bug;

AMER., BOT. variety of orchid; CHILE awning, shade; CUBA, ICHTH. horned boxfish *or* trunkfish.

tor·men·ta f. METEOROL. storm, tempest; FIG. *(adversidad)* trouble, misfortune; *(de ánimos)* storm, turmoil.

tor·men·to m. *(dolor)* torture, torment; FIG. *(angustia)* anguish, torment.

tor·men·to·so, –sa adj. *(tiempo)* stormy, turbulent; MARIT. storm-tossed (ship).

tor·na f. *(vuelta)* return; *(en una huerta)* weir, dam ♦ **volverle a alguien las tornas** to turn the tables on someone.

tor·na·da f. *(regreso)* return; *(viaje repetido)* return visit.

tor·na·di·zo, –za adj. fickle, changeable.

tor·na·do I. past part. see **tornar** II. m. METEOROL. tornado, hurricane.

tor·na·mien·to m. change, turn.

tor·nar tr. *(devolver)* to return, give back; *(mudar)* to turn, make <*la sangre tornó el agua roja* the blood turned the water red> —intr. to return, go back (to) —reflex. to become, turn into.

tor·na·sol m. BOT. sunflower; CHEM. litmus; *(de una tela)* iridescence, shot effect.

tor·na·so·la·do, –da adj. shot, iridescent.

tor·na·so·lar intr. to be iridescent.

tor·na·trás m.f. [pl. **-trás**] throwback.

tor·na·voz m. [pl. **-vo·ces**] sounding board.

tor·ne·a·dor, –do·ra m.f. *(tornero)* lathe operator —m. *(en un torneo)* participant in a tournament.

tor·ne·a·du·ra f. lathe shavings.

tor·ne·ar[1] tr. to turn (on a lathe) —intr. *(dar vueltas)* to revolve, turn around; FIG. *(en la imaginación)* to ponder, reflect.

tor·ne·ar[2] intr. to participate in a tournament.

tor·ne·o m. HIST. joust, tournament; SPORT. championship, tournament; VET. staggers.

tor·ne·rí·a f. turnery, workshop of lathe operator.

tor·ne·ro, –ra m.f. *(obrero)* lathe operator; Sp. errand boy (in a convent).

tor·ni·lle·ro m. MIL., COLL. deserter.

tor·ni·llo m. *(rosca)* screw; *(torno pequeño)* small lathe ♦ **apretar a alguien los tornillos** FIG. to put the screws to someone • **faltarle un t.** FIG. to have a screw loose • **hacer t.** MIL. to desert • **t. de Arquímedes** Archimedean screw • **t. de banco** vise, clamp • **t. sin fin** worm gear.

tor·ni·que·te m. *(de puerta)* turnstile; SURG. tourniquet; ARG. turnbuckle (of a fence).

tor·nis·cón m. COLL. *(golpe)* slap in the face; AMER., COLL. hard pinch.

tor·no m. *(elevador)* winch, windlass; *(giratorio)* revolving dumbwaiter; CARP. *(prensa)* lathe; *(rodeo)* turn, revolution; *(recodo de río)* turn, bend (in a river); *(freno)* hand brake ♦ **en t. a** around, about • **t. de alfarero** potter's wheel • **t. de banco** vise, clamp • **t. de hilar** spinning wheel.

to·ro[1] m. ZOOL. bull; FIG. *(hombre)* bull, horse; ASTRON. Taurus; CUBA, ICHTH. trunkfish ♦ **coger al t. por los cuernos** FIG., COLL. to take the bull by the horns • **echar a alguien el t.** COLL. to give someone a piece of one's mind • **t. corrido** FIG., COLL. sly dog • **t. de lidia** fighting bull • **toros** bullfight • **ver los toros desde la barrera** FIG., COLL. to be a spectator.

to·ro[2] m. ARCHIT. torus; MATH. torus, tore.

to·ron·ja f. BOT. grapefruit (fruit).

to·ron·jo m. BOT. grapefruit (tree).

tor·pe adj. *(desmañado)* awkward, clumsy; *(necio)* dull-witted, stupid.

tor·pe·de·ar tr. to torpedo.

tor·pe·de·ro m. MARIT. torpedo boat.

tor·pe·do m. ICHTH. torpedo fish, electric ray; MIL. torpedo ♦ **t. de fondo** ground torpedo • **t. flotante** submarine mine.

tor·pe·men·te adv. *(sin destreza)* clumsily, awkwardly; *(lentamente)* slowly, dully.

tor·pe·za f. *(falta de destreza)* clumsiness, awkwardness; *(necedad)* stupidity, slowness ♦ **cometer una t.** to make a blunder.

tór·pi·do, –da adj. torpid, sluggish.

tor·por m. MED. torpor, sluggishness.

to·rra·do m. I. past part. see **torrar** II. toasted chickpea.

to·rrar tr. to toast, roast.

to·rre f. tower <*la T. de Londres* the Tower of London>; *(de ajedrez)* castle, rook; *(villa)* country house; *(de petróleo)* oil derrick; MARIT. turret ♦ **t. albarrana** turret • **t. de control** control tower • **t. del homenaje** keep, donjon • **t. de marfil** FIG. ivory tower • **t. de vigía** observation tower; MARIT. crow's nest.

to·rre·ja f. CUL. French toast; AMER. slice; CHILE slice of lemon.

to·rren·cial adj. torrential.

to·rren·te m. *(de agua)* torrent; *(de sangre)* bloodstream; FIG. *(abundancia)* torrent, avalanche.

to·rren·to·so, –sa adj. torrential.

to·rre·ón m. large fortified tower.

to·rre·ro m. *(de faro)* lighthouse keeper; *(de una casa)* keeper of a villa.

to·rrez·na·da f. CUL. dish of fried bacon.

to·rrez·ne·ro, –ra COLL. **I.** adj. lazy, idle **II.** m.f. loafer.

to·rrez·no m. CUL. fried bacon.

tó·rri·do, –da adj. torrid <*zona t.* torrid zone>.

to·rri·ja f. CUL. French toast.

tor·sión f. torsion ♦ **momento de t.** torque.

tor·so m. ANAT., ARTS torso.

tor·ta f. CUL. cake; FIG. *(masa)* cake; FIG., COLL. *(bofetada)* slap; PRINT. font; C. AMER. omelet; MEX. sandwich ♦ **ni t.** COLL. not a thing • **ser tortas y pan pintado** COLL. to be a cinch, be child's play.

tor·ta·da f. CUL. meat *or* chicken pie; CONSTR. coat of mortar.

tor·ta·zo m. COLL. slap, blow.

tor·te·dad f. blindness in one eye.

tor·te·ra f. CUL. baking pan.

tor·tí·co·lis *or* **tor·ti·co·li** m. MED. stiff neck.

tor·ti·lla f. CUL. omelet, omelette; AMER. tortilla, corn cake ♦ **hacer t. a** FIG., COLL. to flatten, squash • **volverse la t.** FIG., COLL. to turn the tables.

tor·ti·lle·ro, –ra m.f. AMER. tortilla maker *or* seller —f. SL. lesbian.

tór·to·la f. ORNITH. turtledove.

tór·to·lo m. ORNITH. turtledove; FIG., COLL. *(enamorado)* lovebird; COL. fool, nitwit.

tor·tu·ga f. ZOOL. turtle, tortoise.

tor·tuo·si·dad f. tortuosity, tortuousness.

tor·tuo·so, –sa adj. *(sinuoso)* tortuous, winding; FIG. *(solapado)* devious.

tor·tu·ra f. torture, torment.

tor·tu·rar tr. to torture, torment.

tor·va **I.** f. METEOROL. rain *or* snow storm **II.** adj. see **torvo, –va.**

tor·vo, –va **I.** adj. grim, fierce <*mirada t.* grim look> **II.** f. see **torva.**

tor·zal m. *(de seda)* silk twist; FIG. *(de varias cosas)* braid, twist; ARG., CHILE lasso.

tos f. cough, coughing ♦ **acceso de t.** coughing fit • **t. ferina** MED. whooping cough.

tos·ca **I.** f. GEOL. tufa, tuff **II.** adj. see **tosco, –ca.**

tos·co, –ca **I.** adj. *(basto)* rough, crude; *(una persona)* coarse, uncouth **II.** f. see **tosca.**

to·se·go·so, –sa adj. *(tosigoso)* having a chronic cough; *(envenenado)* poisoned.

to·ser intr. to cough ♦ **a. mí nadie me tose** nobody pushes me around • **no hay quien le tosa** he's in a class by himself.

tó·si·go m. *(veneno)* poison; FIG. *(angustia)* anguish, grief.

to·si·go·so, –sa adj. *(envenenado)* poisoned; *(que padece tos)* coughing.

tos·que·dad f. coarseness, crudeness.

tos·ta·da **I.** f. CUL. toast; ARG., COLL. bore, nuisance ♦ **dar** *or* **pegar a alguien la t.** FIG., COLL. to cheat *or* disappoint someone • **no ver la t.** to miss the point **II.** adj. see **tostado, –da.**

tos·ta·de·ro m. place where something is toasted *or* roasted.

tos·ta·do, –da **I.** past part. see **tostar II.** CUL. toasted, roasted; FIG. *(la tez)* tanned, sunburned **III.** m. *(tostadura)* toasting, roasting; ECUAD. toasted maize —f. see **tostada.**

tos·ta·dor, –do·ra **I.** adj. toasting, roasting **II.** m.f. *(persona)* toaster, roaster —m. *(utensilio)* toaster, roaster.

tos·ta·du·ra f. toasting, roasting.

tos·tar §19 tr. CUL. to toast, roast; FIG. *(calentar mucho)* to scorch; *(la piel)* to tan (the skin); COLL. *(azotar)* to tan, thrash —reflex. to become tanned *or* sunburned.

tos·tón m. *(garbanzo)* toasted chickpea; *(tostada mojada en aceite)* toast dripped in oil; *(cosa demasiado asada)* burnt *or* scorched thing; *(cochinillo)* roast suckling pig; COLL. *(cosa pesada)* bore, nuisance; MEX. silver coin ♦ **tostones** CARIB., CUL. fried plantain chips.

to·tal **I.** adj. total, complete **II.** m. total, whole **III.** adv. *(en resumen)* so, in a word <*t., que se fue* so, he left>.

to·ta·li·dad f. totality, whole.

to·ta·li·ta·rio, –ria POL. adj. & m.f. totalitarian.

to·ta·li·ta·ris·mo m. totalitarianism.

to·ta·li·zar §04 tr. to total, add up.

to·tal·men·te adv. totally, completely.

tó·tem m. [pl. **to·tems** *or* **tó·te·mes**] totem.

to·té·mi·co, –ca adj. totemic.

to·te·mis·mo m. totemism.

to·to·pos·te m. C. AMER., CUL. tortilla, corn cake.

to·to·ra f. AMER., BOT. cattail, bulrush.

to·to·ral m. BOT. bulrush bed.

to·tu·ma f. *or* **to·tu·mo** m. AMER., BOT. calabash (tree and fruit).

to·xe·mia f. MED. toxemia.

to·xi·ci·dad f. toxicity.

tó·xi·co, –ca **I.** adj. toxic, poisonous **II.** m. poison.

to·xi·co·lo·gí·a f. toxicology.

to·xi·có·lo·go, –ga m.f. toxicologist.

to·xi·có·ma·no, –na **I.** m.f. drug addict **II.** adj. addicted to drugs.

to·xi·na f. MED. toxin.

to·zu·dez f. stubbornness, obstinacy.

to·zu·do, –da adj. stubborn, obstinate.

to·zue·lo m. back of the neck (of an animal).

tra·ba f. *(liga)* tie, bond; *(para caballos)* hobble, trammel; *(para puertas)* bolt; FIG. *(estorbo)* obstacle, hindrance; LAW distraint, seizure ♦ **poner trabas a** FIG. to put obstacles in the way of.

tra·ba·cuen·ta f. *(error)* mistake, error (in a bill); FIG. *(controversia)* dispute, controversy.

tra·ba·de·ro m. horse's pastern.

tra·ba·do, –da **I.** past part. see **trabar II.** adj. *(un caballo)* with white forefeet; FIG. *(robusto)* strong, vigorous.

tra·ba·du·ra f. *(unión)* joining, union; *(lazo)* bond, tie.

tra·ba·ja·do, –da **I.** past part. see **trabajar II.** adj. *(cansado)* worn-out, tired; *(elaborado)* elaborate, ornate.

tra·ba·ja·dor, –do·ra **I.** adj. hard-working, industrious **II.** m.f. worker, laborer —m. CHILE heron.

tra·ba·jar intr. *(laborar)* to work; *(ganarse la vida)* to work <*t. de carnicero* to work as a butcher>; *(funcionar)* to work, function <*la polea no trabaja* the pulley does not work>; FIG. *(afanarse)* to work at, strive <*ella trabaja por conseguir mejores resultados* she is working at getting better results>; *(torcerse)* to bend, warp; CINEM., THEAT. to act ♦ **hacer t. el dinero** to make one's money work • **poner a t.** to set to work, put to work • **ponerse a t.** to get to work —tr. *(labrar)* to work <*t. madera* to work wood>; AGR. to work, till; *(ejercitar)* to train, work out (horses); FIG. *(molestar)* to work a hardship on; *(hacer trabajar)* to drive, push —reflex. to strive.

tra·ba·je·ra f. COLL. chore, disagreeable task.

tra·ba·jo m. *(labor)* work, labor <*t. manual* manual labor>; *(tarea)* job, task; *(ocupación)* job, work <*ir al t.* to go to work>; *(estudio)* study; *(esfuerzo)* trouble <*tomarse el t. de* to take the trouble to>; PHYS. work ♦ **costar t.** to be hard • **pasar trabajos** to have a hard time • **t. a destajo** piecework • **trabajos** hardships • **trabajos forzados** hard labor.

tra·ba·jo·sa·men·te adv. laboriously.

tra·ba·jo·so, –sa adj. *(difícil)* laborious; FIG. *(defectuoso)* labored; *(enfermizo)* sickly; AMER. *(exigente)* demanding; *(molesto)* bothersome.

tra·ba·len·guas m. [pl. **-guas**] tongue twister, jawbreaker.

tra·bar tr. *(unir)* to join, unite; *(atar)* to bind, fasten; *(asegurar)* to bolt; *(asir)* to grasp, seize; *(una traba a)* to hobble, fetter; *(una sierra)* to set (the teeth of a saw); FIG. *(empezar)* to start up, begin <*t. una conversación* to start up a conversation>; *(enlazar)* to tie together <*t. varios argumentos* to tie together various arguments>; LAW to seize, attach; CUL. to thicken; CUBA, GUAT. to trick, fool ♦ **t. amistad** to strike up a friendship • **t. batalla** to join in battle —intr. *(espesar)* to thicken; *(agarrar)* to take hold —reflex. *(atascarse)* to jam; *(enredarse)* to get tangled up ♦ **trabarse a golpes** FIG. to come to blows • **trabársele a uno la lengua** FIG. to get tongue-tied.

tra·ba·zón m. *(unión)* union, bond; *(consistencia)* thickness, consistency; FIG. *(relación)* relation, connection.

tra·be f. beam, joist.

tra·bi·lla f. *(del pantalón)* foot strap (of pants); *(de cintura)* half belt; *(punto)* dropped stitch.

tra·bón m. *(traba)* hobble, trammel; *(argolla)* hobbling ring; *(de lagar)* cross plank (in an oil mill).

tra·bu·ca f. firecracker.

tra·bu·ca·ción f. *(confusión)* confusion, disorder; *(error)* mistake, blunder.

tra·bu·car §70 tr. *(volcar)* to upset, turn upside down; FIG. *(confundir)* to mix up, confuse; *(interrumpir)* to interrupt (a conversation); *(una palabra)* to mix up (words).

tra·bu·co m. ARM. blunderbuss.

tra·ca f. MARIT. strake; *(petardos)* string of firecrackers.

trá·ca·la f. MEX. trick, fraud.

tra·ca·la·da f. AMER. crowd, mob.

tra·ca·le·ro, –ra MEX., COLL. **I.** adj. cheating, tricky **II.** m.f. cheater, trickster.

tra·ca·mun·da·na f. COLL. *(trueque)* swap, barter; *(alboroto)* hubbub, uproar.

trac·ción f. traction, pulling ♦ **t. delantera** front-wheel drive.

tra·cé, trace see **trazar.**

tra·cio, –cia adj. & m.f. Thracian.

trac·to m. *(de tiempo)* lapse, interval; RELIG. tract.

trac·tor m. tractor ♦ **t. oruga** caterpillar tractor.

trac·to·ris·ta m.f. tractor driver.

tra·di·ción f. *(costumbre)* tradition, custom; LAW delivery.

tra·di·cio·nal adj. traditional.

tra·di·cio·na·lis·mo m. traditionalism.

tra·di·cio·nis·ta m.f. writer of stories relating local customs.

tra·duc·ción f. translation.

tra·du·ci·ble adj. translatable.

tra·du·cir §22 tr. *(una lengua)* to translate; *(expresar)* to express.

tra·duc·tor, –to·ra **I.** adj. translating **II.** m.f. translator.

tra·e·di·zo, –za adj. portable.

tra·e·dor, –do·ra **I.** adj. carrying **II.** m.f. carrier.

tra·er §72 tr. to bring <*traiga los libros a la clase* bring your books to class>; *(llevar)* to wear <*traía un sombrero nuevo* he was wearing a new hat>; *(atraer)* to attract, draw; FIG. *(causar)* to bring about, cause <*esto trae muchos problemas* this brings about many problems>; *(alegar)* to bring forward, adduce <*t. ejemplos* to adduce examples>; *(publicar)* to bring out, carry <*este periódico traía un artículo sobre el escándalo* this newspaper carried an article about the scandal> ♦ **t. a mal** *(maltratar)* to abuse, mistreat; *(molestar)* to annoy, pester • **t. al mundo** to bring into the world • **t. cola** *(tener consecuencias)* to have serious consequences; *(venir acompañado)* to bring a friend along • **t. consigo** to involve, entail • **t. de cabeza** to upset, disturb • **t. entre manos** to plan, be up to • **t. y llevar** to gossip.

trá·fa·go m. *(tráfico)* traffic, trade; *(faena)* work, chore ♦ **tráfagos** ARG. belongings, gear.

tra·fa·gón, –go·na COLL. **I.** adj. hustling, pushing **II.** m.f. hustler (salesperson).

tra·fi·can·te **I.** adj. dealing, trading **II.** m.f. dealer, trader.

tra·fi·car §70 intr. *(hacer comercio)* to deal, trade; COLL. *(viajar)* to bustle about.

trá·fi·co m. *(negocio)* traffic, trade; *(tránsito)* traffic, movement.

tra·ga·de·ras f.pl. *(garganta)* throat; *(credulidad)* gullibility ♦ **tener buenas t.** FIG., COLL. to swallow *or* believe anything.

tra·ga·de·ro m. ANAT. throat, gullet; *(agujero)* gulf, abyss.

tra·ga·dor, –do·ra **I.** adj. *(que traga)* swallowing; *(glotón)* gluttonous **II.** m.f. *(persona que traga)* swallower; *(glotón)* glutton.

tra·ga·hom·bres m. [pl. **-bres**] COLL. bully.

trá·ga·la m. SP., HIST. song sung by Liberal opponents of the Spanish absolutists ♦ **cantarle a alguien el t.** to force someone to eat humble pie.

tra·gal·da·bas m.f. [pl. **-bas**] COLL. glutton.

tra·ga·le·guas m.f. [pl. **-guas**] person who walks a lot.

tra·ga·luz m. [pl. **-lu·ces**] skylight, transom.

tra·ga·ní·quel m. COL. juke box.

tra·gan·te **I.** adj. swallowing **II.** m. SP. flume, millrace; METAL. hopper (of a blast furnace).

tra·gan·tón, –to·na COLL. **I.** adj. gluttonous **II.** m.f. glutton.

tra·gan·to·na f. COLL. *(comilona)* feast, large meal; *(acción de tragar)* gulp, hard swallow; FIG., COLL. *(cosa extraordinaria)* hard pill to swallow.

tra·ga·pe·rras adj. COLL. coin-operated.

tra·gar §47 intr. to swallow —tr. *(ingerir)* to swallow; *(comer)* to devour, eat up; FIG. *(hundirse)* to swallow up <*el mar se tragó el barco* the sea swallowed up the boat>; *(aceptar)* to swallow, fall for; *(soportar)* to stand, stomach <*no trago a ese chico* I cannot stomach that boy>; *(consumir)* to eat up, use up; *(absorber)* to absorb ♦ **tenerse tragada una cosa** FIG. to swallow something hook, line and sinker —reflex. FIG. *(aceptar)* to swallow, fall for; *(soportar)* to stand, stomach.

tra·ga·zón f. COLL. gluttony, voracity.

tra·ge·dia f. tragedy.

trá·gi·co, –ca **I.** adj. tragic **II.** m.f. tragedian.

tra·gi·co·me·dia f. tragicomedy.

tra·gi·có·mi·co, –ca adj. tragicomic.

tra·go m. *(bebida)* drink, shot; *(que se bebe de una vez)* swig, gulp; COLL. *(licor)* liquor, drink; FIG., COLL. *(mal rato)* bad time <*pasar un t. amargo* to have a bad time of it> ♦ **a tragos** bit by bit, little by little • **de un t.** in one shot • **echar un t.** to have a drink.

tra·gón, –go·na adj. & m.f. COLL. gluttonous, greedy.

tra·go·ne·rí·a f. COLL. gluttony, voracity.

tra·gué, trague see **tragar.**

trai·ción f. treason, treachery ♦ **hacer t.** to betray.

trai·cio·nar tr. to betray.

trai·cio·ne·ro, –ra **I.** adj. treacherous, traitorous **II.** m.f. traitor.

tra·í·da **I.** f. bringing, carrying ♦ **t. de agua** water supply **II.** adj. see **traído, –da.**

tra·í·do, –da **I.** past part. see **traer** **II.** adj. worn-out, threadbare ♦ **bien t.** COLL. witty • **t. por los pelos** far-fetched **III.** f. see **traída.**

trai·dor, –do·ra **I.** adj. *(que comete traición)* treasonous, traitorous; *(desleal)* treacherous; *(un caballo)* restive, bad-tempered (horse) **II.** m.f. traitor, betrayer.

trai·ga, traigo see **traer.**

tra·í·lla f. leash.

tra·je m. *(vestido)* dress, gown; *(conjunto)* suit; THEAT. costume ♦ **baile de trajes** costume ball • **t. de baño** bathing suit • **t. de luces** bullfighter's costume.

tra·je·a·do, –da **I.** past part. see **trajear** **II.** adj. dressed, clothed.

tra·je·ar tr. to dress, clothe.

tra·je·ra, trajo see **traer.**

tra·jín m. *(transporte)* transport, carrying; *(trabajo)* work, chores; COLL. *(ajetreo)* comings and goings, hustle and bustle.

tra·ji·nar tr. to carry, transport —intr. COLL. *(ajetrearse)* to bustle about, come and go; CHILE *(registrar)* to search, rummage; *(engañar)* to deceive.

tra·lla f. *(cuerda)* cord, whipcord; *(en el látigo)* snapper (of a whip).

tra·lla·zo m. *(chasquido)* lash *or* crack (of a whip); FIG., COLL. *(represión)* scolding, tongue-lashing.

tra·ma f. *(de un tejido)* weft, woof; FIG. *(intriga)* plot, scheme; *(de una novela)* plot (of a novel); *(en fotograbado)* screen, line screen (in photoengraving); *(flor del olivo)* blossom (of olive trees).

tra·ma·dor, –do·ra **I.** adj. weaving **II.** m.f. weaver.

tra·mar tr. *(un tejido)* to weave; FIG., COLL. *(maquinar)* to hatch, weave (a plot).

tra·mi·ta·ción f. *(de un asunto)* transaction; *(trámites)* procedures, steps.

tra·mi·tar tr. *(un asunto)* to negotiate, transact; *(tomar medidas)* to take the necessary steps.

trá·mi·te m. step, procedure ♦ **trámites** procedures, formalities.

tra·mo m. *(de terreno)* section, stretch (of land); *(de una escalera)* flight (of stairs).

tra·mon·ta·na I. f. *(norte)* north; *(viento)* north wind; FIG. *(vanidad)* vanity, pride ♦ **perder la t.** FIG., COLL. to lose one's head II. adj. see **tramontano –na.**

tra·mon·ta·no, –na I. adj. on the other side of the mountains II. f. see **tramontana.**

tra·mon·tar intr. to go over the mountains.

tra·mo·ya f. THEAT. stage machinery; FIG. *(enredo)* scheme, plot.

tra·mo·yis·ta m.f. THEAT. stagehand; COLL. *(tramposo)* schemer, swindler.

tram·pa f. *(cepo)* trap, snare; *(puerta)* trap door; FIG. *(ardid)* trap, trick; *(portañuela)* fly (of pants); *(deuda)* bad debt ♦ **caer en la t.** FIG. to fall into a trap • **hacer trampas** to cheat.

tram·pe·a·dor, –do·ra COLL. I. adj. cheating, swindling II. m.f cheater, swindler.

tram·pe·ar intr. COLL. *(petardear)* to cheat, swindle; FIG., COLL. *(vivir de su ingenio)* to get by, live by one's wits —tr. COLL. *(engañar)* to trick, deceive.

tram·pe·ro, –ra I. m.f. trapper II. adj. MEX. cheating, swindling.

tram·pi·lla f. *(en el suelo)* trap door, hatch; *(de la carbonera)* door of a coal bin; *(de la braguera)* fly (of pants).

tram·pis·ta COLL. I. adj. cheating, tricking II. m.f. cheater, trickster.

tram·po·lín m. *(del gimnasta)* trampoline; *(del nadador)* diving board; FIG. *(para obtener algo)* springboard.

tram·po·so, –sa adj. I. COLL. cheating, tricking II. m.f. *(engañador)* cheat, swindler; *(en naipes)* cardsharp.

tran·ca f. *(garrote)* cudgel, club; *(de puerta)* bar, crossbar; SL. *(borrachera)* binge, spree; AMER. gate (in a fence) ♦ **coger** or **pegarse una t.** COLL. to get loaded.

tran·ca·da f. *(paso largo)* stride <**en dos trancadas** in a jiffy>; ARG. blow with a stick.

tran·car §70 tr. *(la puerta)* to bar (the door); COL. to resist —intr. *(dar trancos)* to stride; VEN. to lock the door —reflex. to strain, be constipated.

tran·ca·zo m. *(garrotazo)* blow with a stick; FIG., COLL. *(gripe)* flu, gripe.

tran·ce m. *(momento)* moment, juncture; *(apuro)* tight spot, difficulty; *(de la vida)* last moments (of life); *(del médium)* trance ♦ **a todo t.** at all costs • **en t. de muerte** at the point of death • **t. último** or **postrero** or **mortal** last moments (of life).

tran·co m. *(paso largo)* long step, stride; *(umbral)* threshold; AMER. gallop ♦ **a trancos** FIG., COLL. hurriedly and carelessly • **en dos trancos** in a jiffy.

tran·qué, tranque see **trancar.**

tran·que·ar intr. to stride.

tran·que·ra f. *(estacada)* stockade, palisade; AMER. gate.

tran·que·ro m. *(piedra)* lintel; CHILE gate.

tran·qui·li·dad f. tranquility.

tran·qui·li·zan·te MED. I. adj. tranquilizing II. m. tranquilizer.

tran·qui·li·zar §04 tr. to quiet, calm —reflex. to be quieted or calmed.

tran·qui·lo, –la adj. tranquil, quiet ♦ **¡déjala t.!** leave her alone!

tran·qui·lla f. *(pasador)* small peg; FIG. *(en la conversación)* feeler.

tran·qui·llo m. FIG. knack <**coger el t.** to get the knack>.

tran·sac·ción f. COM. transaction; *(acuerdo)* agreement, settlement.

tran·sal·pi·no, –na adj. transalpine.

tran·san·di·no, –na I. adj. trans-Andean II. m. trans-Andean train.

tran·sar intr. AMER. to compromise, settle.

tran·sat·lán·ti·co, –ca I. adj. transatlantic II. m. ocean liner.

trans·bor·da·dor, –do·ra I. adj. transferring II. m. *(puente)* transporter bridge; *(barco)* ferry.

trans·bor·dar tr. to transship, transfer.

trans·bor·do m. transshipment, transfer.

trans·cen·den·cia f. transcendence.

trans·cen·den·tal adj. transcendental.

trans·cen·den·ta·lis·mo m. PHILOS. transcendentalism.

trans·cen·den·te adj. *(que transciende)* transcendent; PHILOS. transcendent, transcendental; MATH. transcendental.

trans·cen·der §50 tr. PHILOS. to transcend.

trans·con·ti·nen·tal adj. transcontinental.

trans·cri·bir §85 tr. to transcribe.

trans·crip·ción f. transcription.

trans·cu·rrir intr. to pass, elapse (said of time).

trans·cur·so m. course <**en el t. de un mes** in the course of a month>.

tran·se·ún·te I. adj. passing, transient II. m.f. *(pasajero)* passerby; *(que reside transitoriamente)* transient.

tran·se·xual adj. & m.f. transsexual.

trans·fe·ren·cia f. transfer, transference.

trans·fe·ri·ble adj. transferable.

trans·fe·ri·dor, –do·ra I. adj. transferring II. m.f. transferrer.

trans·fe·rir §65 tr. *(pasar de un lugar a otro)* to transfer; *(aplazar)* to put off, postpone.

trans·fi·gu·ra·ción f. transfiguration ♦ **Transfiguración** RELIG. Transfiguration.

trans·fi·gu·rar tr. to transfigure —reflex. to be transfigured.

trans·for·ma·ble adj. transformable.

trans·for·ma·ción f. *(cambio)* transformation; SPORT. conversion.

trans·for·ma·dor, –do·ra I. adj. transforming II. m.f. transformer —m. ELEC. transformer.

trans·for·ma·mien·to m. var. of **transformación.**

trans·for·mar tr. *(cambiar)* to transform; FIG. *(mejorar)* to transform, improve; SPORT. to convert —reflex. to be transformed, undergo a transformation.

tráns·fu·ga m.f. or **tráns·fu·go** m. *(fugitivo)* fugitive; *(desertor)* deserter, turncoat.

trans·fun·dir tr. *(líquidos)* to transfuse; FIG. *(noticias)* to spread, transmit.

trans·fu·sión f. transfusion <**t. de sangre** blood transfusion>.

trans·fu·sor, –so·ra I. adj. transfusing II. m.f. transfuser.

trans·gre·dir §38 tr. to transgress, violate.

trans·gre·sión f. transgression, violation.

trans·gre·sor, –so·ra I. adj. transgressing, violating II. m.f. transgressor, violator.

tran·si·be·ria·no, –na I. adj. trans-Siberian II. m. trans-Siberian railway.

tran·si·ción f. transition.

tran·si·do, –da adj. *(angustiado)* torn, wracked; FIG. *(miserable)* miserable, wretched.

tran·si·gen·te adj. accommodating, compromising.

tran·si·gir §32 intr. to compromise, give in ♦ **t. con** to accept, agree to.

tran·sis·tor m. ELEC., RAD. transistor.

tran·si·ta·ble adj. passable <**camino t.** passable road>.

tran·si·tar intr. *(pasar)* to go, pass <**t. por las calles** to go through the streets>; *(viajar)* to travel.

tran·si·ti·va·men·te adv. transitively.

tran·si·ti·vo, –va adj. transitive.

trán·si·to m. *(paso)* transit, passage; *(tráfico)* traffic; *(lugar de parada)* stopping place, stop <**hicimos t. a mitad del viaje** we made a stop in the middle of the trip>; *(corredor)* passageway; *(transición)* transition, change; RELIG. *(muerte)* death, passing; *(fiesta)* Assumption ♦ **de mucho t.** busy <**una calle de mucho t.** a busy street> • **de t.** in transit, passing through.

tran·si·to·ria·men·te adv. transitorily, temporarily.

tran·si·to·rie·dad f. transitoriness, temporariness.

tran·si·to·rio, –ria adj. transitory, temporary.

trans·la·ción f. translation.

trans·li·mi·tar tr. *(límites)* to overstep (the bounds), go too far; MIL. to cross the border of (a country).

trans·li·te·ra·ción f. transliteration.

trans·lu·ci·dez f. translucence, translucency.

trans·lú·ci·do –**da** adj. translucent.

trans·lu·cir·se §44 reflex. *(ser translúcido)* to be translucid; FIG. *(ser evidente)* to be evident, be obvious.

trans·mi·gra·ción f. transmigration.
trans·mi·grar intr. to transmigrate.
trans·mi·si·ble adj. transmissible.
trans·mi·sión f. *(acción de transmitir)* transmission; RAD., TELEV. broadcast ♦ **t. delantera** AUTO. front-wheel drive • **t. del pensamiento** thought transference, telepathy • **transmisiones** MIL. signals <*servicio de transmisiones* signal corps>.
trans·mi·sor, –so·ra I. adj. transmitting II. m. ELEC. transmitter.
trans·mi·tir tr. *(pasar)* to transmit; RAD., TELEV. to broadcast.
trans·mu·ta·ble adj. transmutable.
trans·mu·ta·ción f. transmutation.
trans·mu·tar tr. to transmute —reflex. to be transmuted.
trans·na·cio·nal adj. transnational, multinational.
trans·o·ce·á·ni·co, –ca adj. transoceanic.
trans·pa·ren·cia f. *(calidad de transparente)* transparence, transparency; PHOTOG. transparency, slide.
trans·pa·ren·tar·se reflex. *(verse)* to show through; *(ser transparente)* to be transparent; FIG. *(ser evidente)* to be obvious.
trans·pa·ren·te I. adj. *(un objeto)* transparent; FIG. *(evidente)* transparent, obvious II. m. shade, blind.
trans·pi·ra·ción f. perspiration, sweating.
trans·pi·rar intr. *(sudar)* to perspire, sweat; FIG. *(rezumarse)* to leak out.
trans·plan·tar tr. to transplant.
trans·po·ne·dor, –do·ra I. adj. transplanting II. m.f. transplanter.
trans·po·ner §54 tr. *(mudar de sitio)* to move, transfer; *(trasplantar)* to transplant; *(intercambiar)* to transpose; *(desaparecer)* to disappear behind or around <*los agresores transpusieron la esquina* the assailants disappeared around the corner> —reflex. *(desaparecer)* to disappear, go out of sight; *(el sol)* to set, go down (said of the sun); *(dormitar)* to doze off.
trans·por·ta·ción f. transportation, transport.
trans·por·ta·dor, –do·ra I. adj. transporting II. m.f. transporter —m. MATH. protractor; MECH. conveyor.
trans·por·tar tr. *(llevar)* to transport, carry; MUS. to transpose —reflex. FIG. to get carried away.
trans·por·te m. *(de personas)* transport, transportation <*t. de tropas* troop transport>; COM. transport, freight; *(embarcación)* transport ship; FIG. *(éxtasis)* transport, rapture ♦ **transportes** transport, transportation • **transportes colectivos** or **públicos** public transportation.
trans·por·tis·ta m.f. mover, carrier.
trans·po·si·ción f. transposition.
trans·pu·sie·ra, transpuso see **transponer.**
tran·subs·tan·ciar tr. & reflex. to transubstantiate.
trans·va·sar tr. to decant.
trans·ver·sal I. adj. *(que atraviesa)* transverse, transversal; *(pariente)* collateral (relative) II. m.f. *(pariente)* collateral relative —f. *(calle)* side street.
trans·ver·so, –sa I. adj. transverse II. m. ANAT. transverse muscle.
tran·ví·a m. *(sistema)* tramway; *(coche)* streetcar, trolley.
tran·via·rio, –ria or **tran·vie·ro, –ra** I. adj. streetcar <*red t.* streetcar system> II. m.f. *(empleado)* streetcar worker; *(conductor)* streetcar driver.
tran·za·de·ra f. braid.
tra·pa·ce·ar intr. to cheat.
tra·pa·ce·rí·a f. fraud, swindle.
tra·pa·ce·ro, –ra or **tra·pa·cis·ta** I. adj. cheating, swindling II. m.f. cheater, swindler.
tra·pa·je·rí·a f. rags, tatters.
tra·pa·jo m. rag, tatter.
tra·pa·jo·so, –sa adj. ragged, tattered.
trá·pa·la f. COLL. *(jaleo)* racket, din; *(de caballo)* clattering (of hooves); COLL. *(embuste)* trick, fraud —m.f. COLL. *(hablador)* chatterbox; *(embustero)* liar, cheat.
tra·pa·le·ar intr. COLL. *(mentir)* to lie; *(hablar mucho)* to chatter, jabber.
tra·pa·le·ro, –ra or **tra·pa·lón, –lo·na** adj. COLL. cheating, swindling.
tra·pa·ties·ta f. COLL. racket, uproar.
tra·pa·za f. trick, fraud.

tra·pe m. SEW. interlining; CHILE woven cord.
tra·pe·ar tr. AMER. to mop (the floor).
tra·pe·cio m. GEOM. trapezoid; *(de gimnasia)* trapeze; ANAT. *(músculo)* trapezius; *(hueso)* trapezium.
tra·pe·cis·ta m.f. trapeze artist.
tra·pen·se adj. & m. RELIG. Trappist.
tra·pe·rí·a f. *(trapos)* rags; *(tienda)* old clothing store.
tra·pe·ro, –ra I. m.f. ragpicker II. adj. ♦ **puñalada t.** COLL. stab in the back.
tra·pe·zoi·de m. GEOM. trapezoid; ANAT. trapezium.
tra·pi·che m. *(de aceituna)* olive press; *(de azúcar)* sugar mill; AMER. *(ingenio)* sugar plantation; *(de mineral)* grinding machine.
tra·pi·che·ar intr. COLL. *(ingeniarse)* to contrive, scheme; *(comerciar)* to retail.
tra·pi·che·o m. COLL. trickery, chicanery.
tra·pien·to, –ta adj. ragged, tattered.
tra·pi·llo m. FIG., COLL. *(galán)* suitor without means; *(ahorrillos)* nest egg ♦ **de t.** sloppily dressed.
tra·pí·o m. MARIT. canvas, sails; FIG., COLL. grace, elegance; TAUR. fighting spirit, fine appearance (of bull).
tra·pi·son·da f. COLL. *(jaleo)* hubbub, racket; *(enredo)* scheme, plot; FIG. *(agitación)* choppiness (of the sea).
tra·pi·son·de·ar intr. COLL. *(armar jaleo)* to kick up a rumpus; *(enredar)* to scheme, plot.
tra·pi·son·dis·ta m.f. COLL. *(alborotador)* troublemaker, rowdy; *(enredador)* schemer, plotter.
tra·po m. *(de tela)* rag, tatter; *(para limpiar)* rag, cloth; MARIT. sails; TAUR. muleta ♦ **a todo t.** under full sail • **poner a alguien como un t.** FIG., COLL. to rake someone over the coals • **sacar los trapos a relucir** COLL. to wash one's dirty linen in public • **soltar el t.** COLL. *(echarse a reír)* to burst out laughing; *(echarse a llorar)* to burst out crying • **trapos** clothing.
tra·po·so, –sa adj. ragged, tattered.
tra·que m. *(estallido)* bang, crack; *(guía)* gunpowder fuse ♦ **a todo t.** COLL. continuously, at all times.
trá·que·a or **tra·que·ar·te·ria** f. trachea, windpipe.
tra·que·ar tr. & intr. var. of **traquetear.**
tra·que·o m. *(ruido)* crack, bang (of fireworks); *(agitación)* shaking, jolting.
tra·que·te·ar or **tra·que·ar** intr. *(un cohete)* to go off, explode; *(hacer ruido)* to clatter, rattle; *(agitarse)* to shake, jolt —tr. *(agitar)* to shake; FIG., COLL. *(manosear)* to handle, finger; P. RICO to test, try.
tra·que·te·o m. *(ruido)* bang, crack; *(movimiento)* shaking, rattling, jolting.
tra·qui·do m. crack, bang.
tras[1] I. prep. *(después de)* after <*día t. día* day after day>; *(detrás de)* behind <*caminaban t. un carretón* they walked behind a wagon>; *(además)* besides, in addition <*t. de ser rico, es guapo* in addition to being rich, he is good-looking>; FIG. *(en busca de)* in search of, in pursuit of <*se fue t. la gloria* he went in search of fame> II. m. COLL. behind, backside.
tras[2] m. bang.
tra·sat·lán·ti·co, –ca adj. transatlantic.
tras·cen·den·cia f. PHILOS. transcendence; *(importancia)* importance, significance.
tras·cen·den·tal adj. PHILOS. transcendental; *(que se extiende)* far-reaching; FIG. *(importante)* very important or significant.
tras·cen·den·te adj. transcendent.
tras·cen·der §50 intr. *(oler)* to smell <*el pañuelo de mano trascendía a violeta* the handkerchief smelled of violets>; *(divulgarse)* to transpire, become known; *(extenderse)* to extend, spread.
tras·cen·di·do, –da I. past part. see **trascender** II. adj. keen, perspicacious.
tras·co·lar §19 tr. *(un líquido)* to strain, filter; FIG. *(de un lado a otro)* to pass over.
tras·co·rral m. backyard.
tra·se·char tr. to lie in wait for.
tra·se·ga·du·ra f. decanting.
tra·se·gar §52 tr. *(trastornar)* to mix up, jumble; *(un líquido)* to decant; FIG., COLL. *(beber mucho)* to guzzle.
tra·se·ra I. f. back, rear II. adj. see **trasero, –ra.**
tra·se·ro, –ra I. adj. back, rear II. m. ANAT. behind, bot-

tom; ZOOL. hindquarters, rump ♦ **traseros** COLL. ancestors —f. see **trasera**.
tras·fe·ren·cia f. var. of **transferencia**.
tras·fe·ri·ble adj. var. of **transferible**.
tras·fe·ri·dor, –do·ra adj. & m.f. var. of **transferidor, –dora**.
tras·fon·do m. background.
tras·for·mar tr. var. of **transformar**.
tras·gue·ar intr. to play tricks.
tras·gue·ro, –ra m.f. practical joker.
tras·ho·gue·ro, –ra I. adj. lazy, malingering II. m. (de chimenea) fireback, back plate; (leño) large log.
tras·ho·jar tr. to scan, leaf through.
tras·hu·man·te adj. AGR. transhumant, migrating (to new pastures).
tras·hu·mar intr. to migrate seasonally in search of pastures (said of livestock).
tra·sie·go m. decanting.
tra·sie·go, trasiegue see **trasegar**.
tras·la·ción f. (transporte) transfer, moving; (traducción) translation; RHET. metaphor; MECH., PHYS. translation.
tras·la·da·dor, –do·ra I. adj. transferring, moving II. m.f. transferrer, mover.
tras·la·dan·te adj. transferring, moving.
tras·la·dar tr. (mover) to move, transfer; (a un empleado) to transfer (an employee); (aplazar) to postpone; (traducir) to translate; (copiar) to copy, transcribe —reflex. to move, change residence.
tras·la·do m. (copia) copy, transcript <fiel t. true copy>; (de un empleado) transfer; (cambio de residencia) move, change of residence; LAW communication, notification ♦ **dar t.** to send a copy.
tras·la·par tr. to overlap.
tras·li·mi·tar tr. var. of **translimitar**.
tras·lú·ci·do, –da adj. var. of **translúcido**.
tras·lu·cir·se §44 reflex. var. of **translucirse**.
tras·luz m. (por transparencia) light seen through a transparent body; (reflejado) reflected light ♦ **al t.** against the light.
tras·ma·no m. (en el juego) second hand ♦ **a t.** out of reach.
tras·mi·nar tr. to dig, mine —intr. & reflex. to penetrate, seep through.
tras·mi·tir tr. var. of **transmitir**.
tras·mun·do m. the other world, the hereafter.
tras·mu·tar tr. var. of **transmutar**.
tras·no·cha·da I. f. (anoche) last night; (vela) sleepless night; MIL. attack by night II. adj. see **trasnochado, –da**.
tras·no·cha·do, –da I. past part. see **trasnochar** II. adj. (comida) stale, old (food); (macilento) wan, haggard; (antiguo) stale, trite III. f. see **trasnochada**.
tras·no·cha·dor, –do·ra I. adj. staying up late II. m.f. night owl.
tras·no·char intr. (no acostarse) to stay up all night; (no dormir) to spend a sleepless night —tr. to sleep on, think over.
tra·so·ja·do, –da adj. gaunt, haggard.
tras·pa·lar or **tras·pa·le·ar** tr. (palear) to shovel; FIG. (desplazar) to move, shift.
tras·pa·le·o m. (acción de palear) shoveling; (desplazamiento) moving, shifting.
tras·pa·pe·lar tr. to mislay, misplace —reflex. to get lost, be mislaid.
tras·pa·pe·la·do, –da I. past part. see **traspapelar** II. adj. mislaid, misplaced.
tras·pa·ren·cia f. var. of **transparencia**.
tras·pa·ren·tar·se reflex. var. of **transparentarse**.
tras·pa·ren·te adj. var. of **transparente**.
tras·pa·sa·dor, –do·ra I. adj. transgressing II. m.f. transgressor.
tras·pa·sa·mien·to m. var. of **traspaso**.
tras·pa·sar tr. (perforar) to pierce (with a weapon); (atravesar) to cross, go across <t. el río to cross the river>; (transferir) to transfer <t. la tienda a alguien to transfer the store to someone>; (violar) to break, violate (a law); FIG. to pierce <t. el corazón de dolor to pierce one's heart with pain> —reflex. to go too far <se traspasó en el trato con los otros she went too far in her dealings with others>.
tras·pa·so m. (cesión) transfer, cession; (venta) sale; (lo traspasado) transferred property; (precio) transfer fee;

(ardid) trick, ruse; (infracción) transgression, violation; FIG. (pena) grief, anguish.
tras·pié m. slip, stumble ♦ **dar traspiés** to stumble.
tras·plan·tar tr. BOT., MED. to transplant —reflex. FIG. (cambiar de país) to move, uproot oneself.
tras·plan·te m. BOT., MED. (acción) transplanting; (injerto) transplant.
tras·po·ner §54 tr. var. of **transponer**.
tras·pon·tín or **tras·pun·tín** m. (colchón pequeño) small cushion or pad; COLL. (trasero) seat, backside.
tras·pun·te m. THEAT. prompter.
tras·qui·la f. var. of **trasquiladura**.
tras·qui·la·do I. past part. see **trasquilar** II. m. COLL. priest.
tras·qui·la·dor, –do·ra m.f. clipper, shearer.
tras·qui·la·du·ra f. clipping, shearing.
tras·qui·lar tr. (el pelo) to crop, clip (hair); (el ganado) to shear (sheep); FIG., COLL. (mermar) to cut down, curtail.
tras·qui·li·mo·cho, –cha adj. COLL. clipped, shorn.
tras·qui·lón m. COLL. (trasquiladura) slash, cutting; FIG., COLL. (dinero) ill-gotten gains ♦ **a trasquilones** irregularly, unevenly.
tras·ta·bi·llar intr. to reel, stagger.
tras·ta·bi·llón m. ARG., CHILE slip, stumble.
tras·ta·da f. COLL. prank, dirty trick.
tras·ta·zo m. COLL. whack, blow.
tras·te m. MUS. fret (on guitar); (chisme) thingamajig, whatnot; SP. wine-taster's glass; AMER., COLL. rear, backside ♦ **dar al t. con** COLL. to spoil, wreck • **ir al t.** to fall through.
tras·te·a·do I. past part. see **trastear** II. m. MUS. frets (on instruments).
tras·te·ar intr. (mudar trastos) to move furniture; FIG. (charlar) to converse; C. AMER., Col. to move, change residence —tr. TAUR. to tease (a bull) with a red cape; FIG., COLL. (manejar) to manage, manipulate (a person); MI to strum.
tras·te·o m. TAUR. teasing a bull with a red cape; FIG., COLL. manipulating (people); AMER. moving, changing residence.
tras·te·rí·a f. (trastos) junk, old furniture; FIG., COLL. (trastada) dirty trick.
tras·te·ro, –ra I. adj. junk, storage II. m.f. junk or storage room.
tras·tien·da f. (cuarto) stock room (of a store); FIG., COLL. (astucia) cunning, caution.
tras·to m. (mueble) old piece of furniture; (utensilio) utensil <trastos de cocina kitchen utensils>; (cosa inútil) piece of junk; THEAT. flat, piece of scenery; FIG., COLL. (persona inútil) good-for-nothing ♦ **tirarse los trastos a la cabeza** FIG., COLL. to have a terrible fight • **trastos** (armas) weapons; (utensilios) tools, gear.
tras·to·car §70 tr. to upset, disturb —reflex. to go mad.
tras·tor·na·dor, –do·ra I. adj. upsetting, disturbing II. m.f. upsetter, disturber.
tras·tor·nar tr. (derribar) to turn upside down; (perturbar) to disturb, disrupt; FIG. (inquietar) to disturb, worry; (enloquecer) to drive mad ♦ **trastornarle la mente a alguien** to drive someone mad —reflex. to go mad.
tras·tor·no m. disturbance, upheaval.
tras·tra·bi·llar intr. ECUAD., PERU to stagger, reel.
tras·trás m. COLL. next to last (in children's games).
tras·tro·ca·mien·to m. rearrangement, change.
tras·tro·car §73 tr. to rearrange, change.
tras·true·co or **tras·true·que** m. rearrangement, change.
tra·sun·tar tr. (copiar) to copy, transcribe; (compendiar) to summarize, abridge.
tra·sun·to m. (copia) copy, transcription; (imitación) copy, imitation.
tras·va·sar tr. var. of **transvasar**.
tras·ver·ter §50 intr. to run over, overflow.
tras·vo·lar §19 tr. to fly over.
tra·ta f. slave trade ♦ **t. de blancas** white slavery.
tra·ta·ble adj. sociable, friendly.
tra·ta·do I. past part. see **tratar** II. m. (obra) treatise; (entre gobiernos) treaty; (entre compañías) agreement, contract.
tra·ta·dor, –do·ra I. adj. mediating II. m.f. mediator.
tra·ta·mien·to m. (trato) treatment; (título) title, form of

address; MED. treatment; TECH. treatment, process ♦ **dar t. de** to address as • **t. de la información** COMPUT. data processing.

tra·tan·te m.f. dealer, trader.

tra·tar tr. (manejar) to treat, handle <hay que t. este asunto con cuidado it is necessary to handle this matter carefully>; to treat <no me trates mal do not treat me badly>; (frecuentar) to deal with, have dealings with <no traté a Juan I did not deal with John>; (dar el tratamiento de) to address as <le traté de doña I addressed her as Madame>; (calificar de) to call <le trató de loco she called him crazy>; (comerciar) to handle, manage <t. la venta del negocio to manage the sale of the business>; CHEM. to treat, process; MED. to treat —intr. ♦ **t. con** (relacionarse) to have dealings with • **t. de** (discutir) to deal with, be about <este artículo trata de la economía this article is about the economy>; (procurar) to try to <traté de salir temprano I tried to leave early> • **t. en** to deal in, trade in <t. en lana to trade in wool> —reflex. (cuidarse) to look after oneself, take care of oneself; (relacionarse) to have dealings ♦ **tratarse de** to be about, be a question of <se trata de encontrar una solución it is a question of finding a solution>.

tra·to m. treatment <t. especial preferential treatment>; (título) title, form of address; (relaciones) relationship, dealings; (negocio) trade, commerce; (convenio) deal, agreement ♦ **t. de gentes** social charm • **t. hecho** COLL. it's a deal!

trau·ma m. trauma.

trau·má·ti·co, -ca adj. traumatic.

trau·ma·tis·mo m. MED., PSYCH. traumatism.

trau·ma·ti·zar §04 tr. to traumatize.

tra·ver·sa f. (del carro) transverse bar; MARIT. stay.

tra·vés m. (inclinación) slant, incline; (torcimiento) bend; FIG. (desgracia) misfortune, adversity; SEW. bias; ARCHIT. crossbeam; FORT. traverse ♦ **a** or **al t.** through • **de t.** crosswise, crossways.

tra·ve·sa·ño m. (barra horizontal) crosspiece, strut; (de cama) bolster; CUBA, MEX., RAIL. crosstie.

tra·ve·se·ar intr. (un niño) to romp, cavort; FIG. (discurrir) to converse wittily; (llevar una vida viciosa) to lead a debauched life.

tra·ve·se·ro, -ra I. adj. crosswise II. m. bolster.

tra·ve·sí·a I. f. (camino) crossroad, cross street; (parte de una carretera) part of a highway that goes through a town; (distancia) distance across; (viaje) voyage, crossing; (viento) crosswind; (en el juego) amount of money wagered; FORT. traverse; ARG. arid plain II. adj. see **travesío, -sía.**

tra·ve·sí·o, -a I. adj. (ganado) roving (cattle); (viento) side, lateral (wind) II. m. crossing —f. see **travesía.**

tra·ves·tí or **tra·ves·ti·do** m. transvestite.

tra·ve·su·ra f. (de niño) prank, mischief; FIG. (de genio) wit, sparkle; (acción culpable) caper (criminal act).

tra·vie·sa I. f. (distancia) distance across; (en el juego) raise (on a bet); RAIL. crosstie; ARCHIT. crossbeam, rafter; MIN. transverse gallery II. adj. see **travieso, -sa.**

tra·vie·so, -sa I. adj. (puesto de través) cross, transverse; FIG. (pícaro) mischievous, naughty; (sagaz) shrewd, cunning; (disoluto) dissolute; (en continuo movimiento) lively, animated ♦ **a campo t.** cross-country II. f. see **traviesa.**

tra·yec·to m. (distancia) distance, stretch; (recorrido) route, way.

tra·yec·to·ria f. trajectory, path.

tra·za f. (diseño) design, plan; FIG. (plan) plan; (invención) scheme, trick; (aspecto) appearance, looks; GEOM. trace; VEN., ENTOM. carpet moth ♦ **darse trazas para** to manage or find a way to (do something).

tra·za·do, -da I. past part. see **trazar** II. adj. ♦ **bien t.** good-looking, attractive • **mal t.** unattractive III. m. (diseño) design; (plan) plan; (bosquejo) sketch, outline; (dirección) route; BOL. machete.

tra·za·dor, -do·ra I. adj. planning, designing; ARM. tracer <bala t. tracer bullet> II. m.f. planner, designer —m. CHEM. tracer (isotope).

tra·zar §04 tr. (diseñar) to design; (delinear) to lay out, plot; (bosquejar) to sketch, outline; FIG. (discurrir) to draw up (plans, etc.); (describir) to describe, depict.

tra·zo m. (línea) line <t. rectilíneo straight line>; (diseño) design, plan; (trazado) sketch, outline; (de una letra) stroke; PAINT. fold (in drapery) ♦ **al t.** drawn in outline.

tra·zu·mar·se reflex. to ooze, seep.

tré·be·de f. (parte de una casa) raised part of a house warmed by a fire underneath ♦ **trébedes** trivet, cook's tripod.

tre·be·jar intr. to romp, cavort.

tre·be·jo m. (utensilio) utensil <trebejos de la cocina kitchen utensils>; (juguete) toy, plaything; (de ajedrez) chesspiece.

tré·bol m. BOT. clover, trefoil; ARCHIT. trefoil ♦ **tréboles** clubs (suit of cards).

tre·ce I. adj. thirteen <t. caballos thirteen horses>; (decimotercero) thirteenth II. m. thirteen ♦ **mantenerse** or **seguir en sus treces** FIG., COLL. to stick to one's guns.

tre·cho m. (distancia) distance, stretch; (de tiempo) spell (of time) ♦ **a trechos** (en ciertas partes) in places, in parts; (con interrupción) in stages • **de t. a** or **en t.** (de distancia a distancia) at intervals; (de tiempo en tiempo) every now and then.

tre·fe adj. (flojo) flimsy, weak; (falso) false, fake.

tre·fi·la·do m. wiredrawing.

tre·fi·la·dor m. wiredrawer.

tre·fi·lar tr. to draw, make into wire.

tre·fi·le·rí·a f. (fábrica) wiredrawing factory; (operación) wiredrawing.

tre·gua f. MIL. truce; FIG. (descanso) rest, respite; (pausa) lull, letup ♦ **no dar t.** never to let up.

trein·ta I. adj. thirty <hay t. días en el mes de septiembre there are thirty days in the month of September>; (trigésimo) thirtieth II. m. thirty.

trein·ta·na·rio m. thirty-day period.

trein·ta·vo, -va adj. & m. thirtieth.

trein·te·na f. (treinta unidades) thirty; (treintava parte) thirtieth part.

tre·me·bun·do, -da adj. terrible, dreadful.

tre·me·dal m. quagmire.

tre·men·do, -da adj. (horrendo) terrible, horrible <un espectáculo t. a terrible sight>; (digno de respeto) tremendous, awesome; FIG., COLL. (grandísimo) tremendous, terrible <un disparate t. a terrible blunder> ♦ **tomarlo por** or **a la t.** COLL. to take it very hard, make a big fuss.

tre·men·ti·na f. turpentine ♦ **esencia de t.** oil of turpentine.

tre·mo·lan·te adj. waving, fluttering.

tre·mo·lar tr. (enarbolar) to hoist, raise (a banner); (agitar) to wave (a banner).

tre·mo·li·na f. (del viento) rustling (of the wind); FIG., COLL. (bulla) racket, din ♦ **armar la t.** FIG., COLL. to kick up a rumpus.

tré·mo·lo m. MUS. tremolo.

tre·mor m. tremor.

tré·mu·la·men·te adv. tremulously.

tre·mu·lan·te or **tre·mu·len·to, -ta** adj. trembling, tremulous.

tré·mu·lo, -la adj. (tremulante) trembling; (voz) quivering, shaky; (luz) flickering.

tren m. (ferrocarril) train <t. de recreo excursion train>; (instrumentos) gear, equipment <t. de dragado dredging gear>; (equipaje) baggage, luggage; FIG. (pompa) show, pomp; MIL. convoy; GUAT. bustle, commotion; CUBA absurdity; MEX., URUG. streetcar ♦ **perder el t.** FIG. to miss the boat • **t. correo** mail train • **t. de aterrizaje** AVIA. landing gear • **t. de vida** FIG. way of life • **t. directo** or **expreso** express train • **t. laminador** rolling mill • **t. mixto** passenger and freight train • **t. omnibús** local train • **t. rápido** fast train • **vivir a todo t.** FIG., COLL. to live in style.

tre·na f. MIL. sash; (plata quemada) burnt silver; COLL. (cárcel) clink, jail.

tre·na·do, -da adj. meshed, latticed.

tren·ca f. (de colmena) crosspiece (in a beehive); (de una cepa) main root (of a vine); (abrigo) duffle coat.

tren·cé, trence see **trenzar.**

tren·ci·lla f. braid, trimming.

tren·ci·llar tr. to trim with braid.

tren·ci·llo m. gold or silver hatband.

tren·za f. *(enlace)* braid, plait; ARG. wrestling.
tren·za·de·ra f. braided knot *or* bow.
tren·za·do I. past part. see **trenzar** II. m. *(trenza)* braid, plait; ARTS entrechat; EQUIT. crossover step ♦ **al t.** carelessly, negligently.
tren·zar §04 tr. to braid, plait —intr. ARTS to do an entrechat; EQUIT. to do a crossover step —reflex. S. AMER. to wrestle.
tre·pa f. *(subida)* climb, climbing; SEW. trimming, edging; *(de la madera)* grain (of wood); COLL. *(engaño)* trick, ruse; *(castigo)* whipping, lashing; *(voltereta)* forward roll, somersault.
tre·pa·do, –da I. past part. see **trepar¹,²** II. adj. *(retrepado)* leaning back, reclining; *(un animal)* strong, muscular (animal) III. m. SEW. trimming, edging; *(en un papel)* perforation.
tre·pa·dor, –do·ra I. adj. climbing II. f.pl. ORNITH. climbers, creepers —m. *(sitio)* climbing place ♦ **trepadores** climbing irons.
tre·pa·na·ción f. SURG. trephination.
tre·pa·nar tr. SURG. to trephine.
tré·pa·no m. SURG. trephine; *(perforadora)* drill.
tre·par¹ intr. to climb.
tre·par² tr. *(taladrar)* to drill, bore; SEW. to trim, edge —reflex. to lean backwards.
tre·pi·da·ción f. trepidation.
tre·pi·dan·te adj. shaking, vibrating.
tre·pi·dar intr. *(temblar)* to shake, vibrate; CHILE, PERU to hesitate, waver.
tres I. adj. three <*mi tío me dio t. blusas* my uncle gave me three blouses>; *(tercero)* third ♦ **las t.** three o'clock II. m. *(número)* three; *(naipe)* trey ♦ **como t. y dos son cinco** FIG., COLL. as sure as I am standing here • **t. en raya** tick-tack-toe.
tre·sa·ñal *or* **tre·sa·ñe·jo** adj. three-year-old.
tres·cien·tos, –tas I. adj. three hundred <*t. alumnos* three hundred students>; *(trecientésimo)* three hundredth II. m. three hundred.
tres cuar·tos m. three-quarter-length coat.
tre·si·llo m. *(naipes)* ombre (card game); *(muebles)* three-piece suite (of furniture); *(sortija)* ring with three stones; MUS. triplet.
tres·piés m. [pl. **-piés**] *(trébede)* trivet; *(trípode)* tripod.
tre·ta f. *(ardid)* trick, ruse; SPORT. feint (in fencing); ARG. bad habit ♦ **dar en la t.** to get into the habit.
tre·za·vo, –va adj. & m. thirteenth.
tria·che m. low-grade coffee.
trí·a·da f. triad.
trian·gu·lar adj. triangular.
trián·gu·lo I. adj. triangular II. m. triangle ♦ **t. equilátero** equilateral triangle • **t. escaleno** scalene triangle • **t. esférico** spherical triangle • **t. isósceles** isosceles triangle • **t. rectángulo** right triangle.
triar §30 intr. to swarm in and out of the hive (said of bees) —tr. to select, choose —reflex. TEX. to wear out, become threadbare.
tri·bal adj. tribal.
tri·bu f. tribe.
tri·bual adj. tribal.
tri·bu·la·ción f. tribulation.
tri·bu·na f. *(de un orador)* platform, rostrum; SPORT. bleachers, grandstand; *(en una iglesia)* gallery ♦ **t. del acusado** LAW dock • **t. de la prensa** press box • **t. del jurado** jury box.
tri·bu·nal m. *(lugar)* court, tribunal; *(conjunto de magistrados)* court, bench; *(jueces de exámenes)* board of examiners ♦ **t. de menores** juvenile court.
tri·bu·no m. HIST. tribune; FIG. *(orador)* orator.
tri·bu·ta·ble adj. taxable.
tri·bu·ta·ción f. *(pago)* payment of taxes; *(tributo)* tax, tribute; *(régimen)* tax system.
tri·bu·tar tr. *(tributo)* to pay (taxes); FIG. *(homenaje)* to pay (respect, tribute).
tri·bu·ta·rio, –ria I. adj. *(de los impuestos)* tax <*régimen t.* tax system>; *(un río)* tributary II. m.f. *(que paga impuestos)* taxpayer; *(que paga tributo)* tributary.
tri·bu·to m. *(impuesto)* tribute, tax; *(respeto)* tribute, respect.

tri·cen·te·na·rio m. tricentenary, tricentennial.
tri·cen·té·si·mo, –ma adj. & m. three-hundredth.
trí·ceps adj. & m. [pl. **-ceps**] ANAT. triceps.
tri·ci·clo m. tricycle.
tri·co·lor adj. tricolor, three-colored.
tri·cor·nio I. adj. three-cornered. II. m. three-cornered hat.
tri·cot m. TEX. tricot.
tri·co·to·mí·a f. BOT. trichotomy.
tri·cús·pi·de ADJ. & F. ANAT. tricuspid.
tri·den·te I. adj. tridentate II. m. trident.
tri·di·men·sio·nal adj. three-dimensional.
trie·dro, –dra MATH. I. adj. trihedral II. m. trihedron.
trie·nal adj. triennial.
trie·nio m. triennium.
tri·ful·ca f. METAL. three-lever system (in a foundry); FIG., COLL. *(riña)* scuffle, rumpus <*armar una t.* to kick up a rumpus>.
tri·fur·ca·ción f. trifurcation.
tri·fur·ca·do, –da I. past part. see **trifurcarse** II. adj. trifurcate.
tri·fur·car·se §70 reflex. to divide into three.
tri·gal m. AGR. wheat field.
tri·ga·za adj. of wheat, wheat <*paja t.* wheat chaff>.
tri·gé·mi·no, –na ANAT. I. adj. trigeminal II. m. trigeminal nerve.
tri·gé·si·mo, –ma adj. & m. thirtieth.
tri·gli·cé·ri·do m. BIOCHEM. triglyceride.
tri·go m. BOT. wheat; FIG., COLL. *(dinero)* dough, money ♦ **no ser t. limpio** FIG., COLL. to be dishonest • **t. candeal** white wheat • **t. chamorro** beardless wheat • **t. sarraceno** buckwheat.
tri·go·no·me·trí·a f. trigonometry.
tri·gue·ño, –ña adj. *(tez)* olive-skinned; *(pelo)* dark blond (hair).
tri·gue·ro, –ra I. adj. wheat, of wheat <*campo t.* wheat field> II. m. *(criba)* wheat sieve —m.f. *(comerciante)* wheat merchant.
tri·la·te·ral adj. trilateral.
tri·lá·te·ro, –ra adj. trilateral.
tri·lin·güe adj. trilingual.
tri·lo·gí·a f. trilogy.
tri·lla f. AGR. *(trillo)* thresher; *(acción)* threshing; ICHTH. gurnard, red mullet; CHILE, P. RICO, COLL. thrashing, beating; CUBA path, lane.
tri·lla·de·ra f. AGR. thresher.
tri·lla·do, –da I. past part. see **trillar** II. adj. FIG. *(muy común)* trite, worn-out; *(camino)* beaten, well-worn (path).
tri·lla·dor, –do·ra I. adj. threshing II. f. threshing machine ♦ **t. segadora** AGR. combine.
tri·llar tr. AGR. to thresh; FIG., COLL. *(emplear mucho)* to use frequently; FIG. *(maltratar)* to beat.
tri·lli·zo, –za I. adj. triple II. m.f. triplet.
tri·llo m. AGR. thresher; AMER. path, lane.
tri·llón m. MATH. trillion.
tri·mes·tral adj. trimestral, quarterly.
tri·mes·tral·men·te adv. quarterly, every three months.
tri·mes·tre I. adj. trimestral II. m. *(tres meses)* trimester, quarter; *(pago)* quarterly payment; *(revista)* quarterly.
tri·nar intr. MUS. to trill; ORNITH. to warble; COLL. *(enojarse)* to fume, get furious <*están que trinan* they are fuming>.
trin·ca f. *(grupo de tres)* trio, triad; MARIT. cable, lashing; CHILE pitching pennies ♦ **a la t.** CHILE poor, broke • **t. del bauprés** MARIT. gammoning.
trin·ca·pi·ño·nes m. [pl. **-nes**] COLL. harebrain, scatterbrain.
trin·car §70 tr. *(romper)* to break up, smash; *(sujetar)* to hold down; FIG., SL. *(matar)* to bump off, rub out; *(comer)* to put away (eat); COLL. *(beber)* to put away (drink); *(robar)* to lift, swipe; MARIT. to lash, tie.
trin·cha f. strap.
trin·cha·dor, –do·ra I. adj. carving, slicing II. m.f. *(persona)* carver, slicer —m. *(cuchillo)* carving knife; MEX. trencher, carving board.
trin·chan·te I. adj. carving, slicing II. m. *(persona)* carver; *(tenedor)* carving fork; *(escoda)* stonecutter's hammer.
trin·char tr. *(la carne)* to carve, slice (meat).

trin·che m. AMER. *(tenedor)* carving fork; *(trinchero)* trencher, carving board.

trin·che·ra I. f. MIL. trench; RAIL. cutting; *(abrigo)* trench coat; MEX. sharp instrument ♦ **guerra de trincheras** MIL. trench warfare II. adj. see **trinchero, –ra.**

trin·che·ro, –ra I. adj. carving <*plato t.* carving board> II. m. trencher, carving board —f. see **trinchera.**

trin·che·te m. *(de zapatero)* shoemaker's knife; AMER. (table) knife.

tri·ne·o m. sleigh, sled.

tri·ni·dad f. THEOL. Trinity.

Tri·ni·dad y To·ba·go Trinidad and Tobago.

tri·ni·ta·ria f. BOT. wild pansy, heartsease.

tri·no, –na I. adj. RELIG. triune; *(ternario)* ternary, trine II. m. MUS., ORNITH. trill.

tri·no·mio m. MATH. trinomial.

trin·que m. PERU drink (of liquor).

trin·qué, trinque see **trincar.**

trin·que·ta·da f. MARIT. sailing under the foresail; CUBA, MEX., PERU, COLL. run of bad luck.

trin·que·te m. MARIT. *(palo)* foremast; *(vela)* foresail; SPORT. covered pelota court; MECH. pawl, ratchet; ARG., COLL. tall lanky person ♦ **a cada t.** at every moment • **más fuerte que un t.** COLL. as strong as iron.

trin·quis m. COLL. drink, nip.

trí·o m. trio.

trió·xi·do m. CHEM. trioxide.

tri·pa f. ANAT., ZOOL. gut, intestine; *(panza)* belly, tummy; *(de una vasija)* belly, bulge (of a vessel); *(de cigarro)* tobacco filling ♦ **echar las tripas** FIG., COLL. to retch, vomit • **echar t.** to get a paunch ♦ **hacer de tripas corazón** FIG., COLL. to pluck up one's courage • **llenarse la t.** to eat one's fill • **tener malas tripas** FIG. to be hardhearted • **tripas** ANAT. guts, intestines; BOT. core (of fruit); FIG. *(lo interior)* innards, insides; *(documentos)* file, dossier.

tri·par·ti·ción f. tripartition.

tri·par·tir tr. to divide into three.

tri·par·ti·to, –ta adj. tripartite.

tri·pe·ro, –ra m.f. *(vendedor)* tripe *or* offal merchant —m. COLL. *(abrigo del vientre)* bellyband; *(comilón)* glutton.

tri·pi·ca·lle·ro, –ra m.f. tripe seller.

tri·pi·ca·llos m.pl. CUL. tripe (stew).

tri·ple adj. & m. triple.

tri·pli·ca·ción f. triplication.

tri·pli·ca·do, –da m. triplicate ♦ **por t.** in triplicate.

tri·pli·car §70 tr. to triplicate.

tri·plo, –pla adj. & m. triple.

trí·po·de I. m.f. tripod II. adj. three-legged.

tri·pón, –po·na I. adj. COLL. paunchy, pot-bellied II. m.f. COLL. *(tripudo)* paunchy *or* pot-bellied person; MEX. kid, young goat.

tríp·ti·co m. triptych.

trip·ton·go m. PHONET. triphthong.

tri·pu·do, –da I. adj. paunchy, pot-bellied II. m.f. paunchy *or* pot-bellied person.

tri·pu·la·ción f. AVIA., MARIT. crew ♦ **t. de tierra** AVIA. ground crew.

tri·pu·lan·te m.f. crew member.

tri·pu·lar tr. AVIA., MARIT. to man, provide with a crew; CHILE to mix (liquids).

tri·que m. *(estallido)* bang, crack; AMER. tick-tack-toe; COL. trick, ruse ♦ **a cada t.** at every step • **triques** MEX. things, stuff.

tri·qui·na f. ZOOL. trichina.

tri·qui·no·sis f. MED. trichinosis.

tri·qui·ñue·la f. COLL. trick, ruse ♦ **andar con triquiñuelas** to have tricks up one's sleeve • **triquiñuelas del oficio** tricks of the trade.

tri·qui·tra·que m. *(de un tren)* clickety-clack; *(explosión)* bang, boom; *(cohete)* firecracker ♦ **a cada t.** FIG., COLL. at every step.

tris m. *(ruido)* crack, crunch (noise); FIG. *(instante)* jiffy, trice <*en un t.* in a trice> ♦ **estar en un t. de** *or* **que** FIG., COLL. to be nearly, be within an inch of.

tris·ca f. *(ruido)* crack, crunch; FIG. *(jaleo)* din, racket; CUBA hidden sneer.

tris·ca·dor, –do·ra I. adj. rowdy, boisterous II. m.f. *(per-*

sona) rowdy *or* boisterous person —m. *(para sierras)* saw set.

tris·car §70 tr. *(enredar)* to mix, mingle; FIG. *(una sierra)* to set (a saw) —intr. *(patear)* to stamp, trample; FIG. *(retozar)* to gambol, frisk; COL. to gossip; CUBA to poke fun.

tri·se·car §70 tr. GEOM. to trisect.

tri·sec·ción f. GEOM. trisection.

tris·mo m. MED. trismus.

tris·te I. adj. *(afligido)* sad <*ella está t.* she is sad>; *(melancólico)* melancholy, gloomy <*Juan es un hombre muy t.* John is a very melancholy man>; *(aflictivo)* sad, sorrowful <*noticias tristes* sad news>; *(deplorable)* dismal, miserable <*una vida t.* a miserable life>; *(insuficiente)* miserable, measly; *(doloroso)* sorry, sorry-looking II. m. AMER. sad love song.

tris·te·za f. *(dolor)* sadness, sorrow; AMER., VET. murrain.

tris·tón, –to·na adj. wistful, a little sad.

tris·tu·ra f. sadness.

tri·tón m. MYTH. Triton; ZOOL. newt.

tri·tu·ra·ción f. trituration, crushing.

tri·tu·rar tr. TECH. to triturate; *(moler)* to grind, crush; *(mascar)* to chew; FIG. *(una persona)* to beat up (a person); *(un argumento)* to demolish (an argument).

triun·fa·dor, –do·ra I. adj. triumphant, victorious II. m.f. victor, winner.

triun·fal adj. triumphal <*arco t.* triumphal arch>; *(brillante)* triumphant <*una acogida t.* a triumphant reception>.

triun·fal·men·te adv. triumphantly.

triun·fan·te adj. triumphant.

triun·far intr. MIL. to triumph, win; FIG. *(vencer)* to triumph, succeed; *(en el juego)* to trump, play a trump.

triun·fo m. MIL. *(victoria)* triumph, victory; FIG. *(éxito)* triumph, success; *(naipe)* trump ♦ **en t.** in triumph.

triun·vi·ral adj. triumviral.

triun·vi·ra·to m. triumvirate.

triun·vi·ro m. triumvir.

tri·va·len·te adj. CHEM. trivalent.

tri·vial adj. *(insustancial)* trivial, unimportant; *(común)* trite, common.

tri·via·li·dad f. triviality.

tri·za f. *(pedazo)* piece, shred <*hacer trizas* to tear to pieces>; MARIT. halyard.

tro·ca·ble adj. exchangeable.

tro·ca·mien·to m. barter, exchange.

tro·can·te adj. bartering, exchanging.

tro·cán·ter m. ANAT. trochanter.

tro·car §73 tr. *(cambiar)* to barter, exchange; *(confundir)* to confuse, mix up; *(vomitar)* to vomit; PERU to sell —reflex. to change.

tro·ca·tin·ta f. COLL. mistaken exchange.

tro·cé, troce see **trozar.**

tro·ce·ar tr. to divide into pieces.

tro·ce·o m. *(acción)* cutting up; MARIT. parrel, truss.

tro·cla f. pulley.

tró·co·la f. pulley.

tro·cha f. *(atajo)* shortcut; *(camino)* path, trail; COL., VEN. chore; AMER., RAIL. gauge.

tro·char intr. COL., VEN. to trot.

tro·che·mo·che ♦ **a t.** *or* **a troche y moche** COLL. helter-skelter, pell-mell.

tro·fe·o m. *(señal de victoria)* trophy; *(despojos)* spoils (of war); FIG. *(victoria)* victory, triumph.

tro·glo·di·ta I. adj. *(que habita en las cavernas)* troglodytic, cave-dwelling; FIG. *(bárbaro)* barbarous, cruel; *(comilón)* greedy, gluttonous II. m.f. *(habitante de cavernas)* troglodyte, cave dweller; FIG. *(bruto)* brute; *(comilón)* glutton.

troi·ca f. troika.

troj *or* **tro·je** f. granary, barn.

tro·la f. COLL. *(embuste)* trick, hoax; CHILE *(gajo)* tree branch; *(cosa colgante)* pendant; COL. ham slice.

tro·le m. ELEC. trolley (device).

tro·le·bús m. trolley bus.

tro·le·ro, –ra COLL. I. adj. lying, dishonest II. m.f. liar.

trom·ba f. METEOROL. waterspout ♦ **en t.** FIG. violently, massively.

trom·bón m. MUS. *(instrumento)* trombone; *(músico)* trombonist ♦ **t. de pistones** valve trombone • **t. de varas** slide trombone.

trom·bo·sis f. MED. thrombosis.

trom·pa f. MUS. horn; ZOOL. trunk <*t. de elefante* elephant's trunk>; *(juguete)* large spinning top; ENTOM. proboscis; COLL. *(nariz)* snout, schnozz; *(borrachera)* drunk, drunken spree; TECH. trompe (in a forge); METEOROL. whirlwind; ARCHIT. squinch, arch; ANAT. tube, duct <*t. de Falopio* Fallopian tube> ♦ **t. de caza** hunting horn • **t. de Eustaquio** ANAT. Eustachian tube • **t. gallega** Jew's harp —m. MUS. horn player.

trom·pa·da f. COLL. *(golpe)* blow, punch; FIG., COLL. *(encontrón)* crash, bump.

trom·paz·o m. bump, crash ♦ **darse un t. con la pared** to bump into the wall.

trom·pe·a·dor m. AMER., COLL. puncher, hitter.

trom·pe·ar intr. to spin a top —tr. AMER. to hit, punch.

trom·pe·ta MUS. f. *(instrumento)* trumpet, bugle —m.f. *(persona)* trumpeter, bugler; COLL. *(persona despreciable)* rascal, rogue ♦ **t. de girasol** BOT. sunflower.

trom·pe·ta·da f. COLL. blunder, gaffe.

trom·pe·ta·zo m. *(sonido)* trumpet *or* bugle blast; FIG., COLL. *(trompetada)* blunder, gaffe.

trom·pe·te·ar intr. COLL. to play the trumpet.

trom·pe·te·o m. trumpet playing.

trom·pe·te·rí·a f. MUS. *(de una orquesta)* trumpet section; *(de un órgano)* trumpets.

trom·pe·te·ro m. *(tocador)* trumpeter, trumpet player; *(fabricante)* trumpet maker; ICHTH. boarfish, trumpet fish.

trom·pe·ti·lla f. *(para oír)* ear trumpet; *(cigarro)* cheroot; CUBA, MEX., P. RICO raspberry, Bronx cheer ♦ **de t.** buzzing (said of mosquitoes).

trom·pe·tis·ta m.f. trumpeter, trumpet player.

trom·pi·car §70 tr. *(hacer tropezar)* to trip; FIG., COLL. *(promover)* to promote undeservedly (one person over another) —intr. to trip, stumble.

trom·pi·cón m. *(tropezón)* stumble, trip; COLL. *(mojicón)* punch in the nose ♦ **a trompicones** by fits and starts.

trom·pi·llar tr. & intr. to trip.

trom·pis m. [pl. **-pis**] COLL. punch, blow.

trom·po m. *(juguete)* spinning top; FIG. *(bobo)* dolt, fool; ZOOL. trochid; MECH. pipe-widening tool ♦ **ponerse uno como un t.** FIG., COLL. to stuff *or* gorge oneself.

trom·pón m. *(juguete)* large spinning top; *(golpe)* blow, punch; BOT. narcissus ♦ **a** *or* **de t.** COLL. helter-skelter.

trom·pu·do, –da adj. AMER. thick-lipped.

tro·na·da f. thunderstorm.

tro·na·do, –da I. past part. see **tronar** II. adj. COLL. *(viejo)* old, worn-out; *(sin dinero)* broke, penniless.

tro·na·dor, –do·ra I. adj. *(que truena)* thundering; *(un cohete)* detonating II. f. MEX., BOT. begonia.

tro·nan·te adj. thundering, thunderous.

tro·nar §19 intr. METEOROL. to thunder; *(un cañón)* to thunder, roar; FIG., COLL. *(arruinarse)* to go broke; *(fulminar)* to thunder, fulminate ♦ **estar que t.** to be in a rage • **por lo que pueda t.** just in case • **t. con** to quarrel with, fall out with —tr. C. AMER., MEX. to shoot, kill.

tron·ca f. truncation.

tron·cal adj. trunk, main <*línea t.* trunk line>.

tron·car §70 tr. to truncate.

tron·cé, tronce see **tronzar.**

tron·co m. ANAT., BOT. trunk; GEOM. frustum; *(caballos)* pair, team (of horses); FIG. *(torpe)* dimwit, blockhead; *(linaje)* stock, lineage ♦ **dormir como un t.** FIG. to sleep like a log • **t. de cono** GEOM. truncated cone.

tron·cha f. AMER. *(tajada)* chunk, slice; COLL. *(ganga)* cushy job, sinecure.

tron·char tr. *(un árbol)* to bring down, fell (a tree); FIG. *(romper)* to split, break; *(quitar)* to break off ♦ **troncharse de risa** FIG., COLL. to split one's sides laughing.

tron·cho m. BOT. stem, stalk; COL. chunk, slice.

tro·ne·ra f. MIL. loophole, embrasure; MARIT. porthole; *(ventana)* dormer (window); *(en billar)* pocket (of a pool table) —m.f. COLL. *(persona)* scatterbrain.

tro·ni·do m. *(del trueno)* thunderclap; FIG., COLL. *(de cañón)* boom, roar; *(tronío)* swank, swagger.

tro·no m. *(del rey)* throne; RELIG. tabernacle, shrine ♦ **tronos** RELIG. thrones, seventh choir of angels.

tron·qué, tronque see **troncar.**

tron·quis·ta m. driver, coachman.

tron·zar §04 tr. *(dividir)* to divide, cut up; *(romper)* to break, smash; SEW. to make fine tucks *or* pleats in; FIG. *(cansar)* to wear out, exhaust.

tro·pa f. *(muchedumbre)* troop, crowd; MIL. *(ejército)* army; *(toque)* assembly call; AMER. *(ganado)* herd, drove; *(caravana)* caravan, convoy ♦ **tropas** MIL. troops • **tropas de asalto** MIL. storm troops.

tro·pe·cé see **tropezar.**

tro·pel m. *(desorden)* bustle, confusion; *(prisa)* rush, hurry; *(de cosas)* jumble, hodgepodge ♦ **de** *or* **en t.** in a mad rush.

tro·pe·lí·a f. *(prisa)* rush, confusion; *(ultraje)* outrage, abuse; *(violencia)* violence <*actos de t.* acts of violence>.

tro·pe·za·de·ro m. stumbling place.

tro·pe·za·du·ra f. stumbling.

tro·pe·zar §29 intr. *(dar un traspié)* to stumble, trip; *(encontrar un estorbo)* to trip; FIG. *(cometer un error)* to slip up, go astray; *(reñir)* to quarrel, squabble; COLL. *(encontrar a una persona)* to run *or* bump into ♦ **t. con un hueso** FIG., COLL. to hit a snag —reflex. to interfere, knock one foot against the other (said of horses).

tro·pe·zón, –zo·na I. adj. COLL. interfering, knocking one foot against the other (said of horses) II. m. *(traspiés)* stumble, trip; *(obstáculo)* obstacle, stumbling block; *(desliz)* slip, mistake; CUL. small piece of meat added to stews ♦ **a tropezones** FIG., COLL. by fits and starts.

tro·pe·zo·so, –sa adj. COLL. stumbling, faltering.

tro·pi·cal adj. tropical.

tró·pi·co, –ca I. adj. tropical II. m. tropic ♦ **t. de Cáncer** Tropic of Cancer • **t. de Capricornio** Tropic of Capricorn.

tro·pie·ce, tropiezo see **tropezar.**

tro·pie·zo m. *(obstáculo)* obstacle, stumbling block; *(traspiés)* stumble, trip; FIG. *(desliz)* slip, mistake; *(causa de una culpa)* downfall; *(dificultad)* hitch, snag; *(riña)* argument, quarrel.

tro·pis·mo m. BIOL. tropism.

tro·po m. RHET. trope.

tro·pos·fe·ra f. METEOROL. troposphere.

tro·qué see **trocar.**

tro·quel m. TECH. (stamping) die.

tro·que·lar tr. to coin, mint.

tro·ta·ca·lles m.f. [pl. **-lles**] COLL. gadabout.

tro·ta·da f. *(trote)* trot; *(carrera)* course, distance.

tro·ta·dor, –do·ra adj. trotting.

tro·ta·mun·dos m.f. [pl. **-dos**] globetrotter.

tro·tar intr. *(ir al trote)* to trot; FIG., COLL. *(sin pararse)* to run around, be always on the go.

tro·te m. *(modo de andar)* trot, quick pace; COLL. *(actividad)* bustle, rush; *(apuro)* chore ♦ **al t.** *(trotando)* trotting; *(de prisa)* quickly, in a rush • **de** *or* **para todo t.** COLL. for everyday (wear or use) • **tomar el t.** COLL. to run away • **t. cochinero** COLL. rack, quick trot (of a horse) • **trotes** FIG., COLL. matters, business.

tro·tón, –to·na I. adj. trotting II. m. trotter.

tro·to·ne·rí·a f. steady trot.

tro·va f. POET. ballad.

tro·va·dor, –do·ra I. adj. versifying II. m. *(poeta)* poet; HIST. minstrel, troubador —f. poetess.

tro·va·do·res·co, –ca adj. troubador <*canción t.* troubador song>.

tro·var intr. to write verses *or* poetry —tr. FIG. to misinterpret, misconstrue.

Tro·ya f. HIST. Troy ♦ **ahí** *or* **aquí fue T.** FIG., COLL. that's when it all started • **¡arda Troya!** come what may.

tro·ya·no, –na adj. & m.f. Trojan.

tro·za f. *(de madera)* log; MARIT. parrel truck.

tro·zar §04 tr. *(hacer pedazos)* to break into pieces; *(un árbol)* to cut into logs.

tro·zo m. *(pedazo)* piece, chunk <*t. de madera* chunk of wood>; *(de una obra)* passage, excerpt; MIL. division; MARIT. detail (of a crew) ♦ **t. de retaguardia** MIL. rear guard • **t. de vanguardia** *or* **de San Felipe** advance guard.

tru·car §70 intr. *(hacer el primer envite)* to make the first bet; *(en el billar)* to pocket the ball.

tru·co m. *(habilidad)* trick, knack; *(juego de naipes)* card game; *(en el billar)* pocketing the ball (in pool); *(engaño)* trick, deception; ARG., BOL., CHILE punch, blow ♦ **cogerle el t. a algo** FIG., COLL. to get the hang of something.

tru·cu·len·cia f. truculence, cruelty.
tru·cu·len·to, –ta adj. *(cruel)* cruel, ferocious; *(atroz)* ghastly, atrocious.
tru·cha f. ICHTH. trout; MECH. derrick; C. AMER. stand, kiosk ♦ **t. arco·iris** ICHTH. rainbow trout • **t. asalmonada** ICHTH. salmon trout • **t. de mar** ICHTH. scorpion fish.
tru·che·ro, –ra I. m.f. trout fisher II. adj. containing trout.
tru·chi·mán, –ma·na I. m.f. COLL. *(intérprete)* interpreter; *(persona astuta)* sly fox II. adj. sly, cunning.
true·co m. barter, exchange ♦ **a t.** *or* **en t. de** in exchange for.
true·co, trueque see **trocar**.
true·ne, trueno see **tronar**.
true·no m. METEOROL. thunder; *(de un arma)* shot, report; *(de un cohete)* bang, explosion; COL. firecracker; VEN. wild party, orgy; COLL. *(atolondrado)* reckless youngster ♦ **t. gordo** finale (in fireworks).
true·que m. barter, exchange ♦ **a t.** in exchange for • **true·ques** AMER. change (of currency).
tru·fa¹ f. lie, fib.
tru·fa² f. BOT. truffle.
tru·far¹ intr. to lie, fib.
tru·far² tr. CUL. to stuff with truffles.
tru·hán, –ha·na I. adj. *(pícaro)* scoundrelly, crooked; COLL. *(gracioso)* clownish, buffoonish II. m.f. *(pícaro)* scoundrel, crook; COLL. *(gracioso)* clown, buffoon.
tru·ha·na·da f. *(bribonería)* roguishness, rascality; *(bufonería)* buffoonery, clownishness.
tru·ha·ne·ar intr. *(engañar)* to cheat, trick; COLL. *(decir bufonadas)* to clown, joke.
tru·ha·ne·rí·a f. roguishness, rascality; COLL. *(bufonería)* buffoonery, clownishness.
tru·ha·nes·co, –ca adj. *(bribón)* roguish, crooked; COLL. *(gracioso)* clownish, buffoonish.
tru·jal m. *(para las uvas)* wine press; *(para la aceituna)* olive press; *(molino de aceite)* oil mill; *(tinaja)* vat (used in soapmaking).
tru·ja·mán, –ma·na m.f. *(intérprete)* interpreter —m. *(aconsejador)* counselor, adviser.
tru·ja·ma·ne·ar intr. *(servir de intérprete)* to act as an interpreter; *(trocar géneros)* to exchange goods.
tru·lla f. *(alboroto)* noise, uproar; *(multitud)* crowd; *(llana)* trowel.
trun·ca·do, –da I. past part. see **truncar** II. adj. truncated.
trun·ca·mien·to m. truncation.
trun·car §70 tr. *(cortar)* to truncate, cut short; *(mutilar)* to mutilate; FIG. *(dejar imperfecto)* to leave unfinished.
trun·co, –ca adj. *(truncado)* truncated, cut short; AMER. incomplete.
tru·qué, truque see **trucar**.
tru·sa f. PERU shorts, briefs; CUBA bathing suit ♦ **trusas** trunk hose.
tse-tsé f. ENTOM. tsetse fly.
tú §30, 33 pron. you, thou ♦ **al tú por tú** disrespectfully • **más eres tú** COLL. look who's talking! • **tratar de tú** to address as *tú*, be on friendly terms.
tu, tus §25 adj. your <*tu amigo* your friend>.
tu·ba f. MUS. tuba; PHILIP. tuba (liquor).
tu·ber·cu·li·na f. MED. tuberculin.
tu·bér·cu·lo m. BOT. tuber; MED. tubercle.
tu·ber·cu·lo·sis f. MED. tuberculosis.
tu·ber·cu·lo·so, –sa I. adj. BOT. tuberous; MED. tubercular II. m.f. MED. tuberculosis sufferer.
tu·be·rí·a f. *(serie de tubos)* pipes, tubing; *(tubo)* pipe, tube; *(instalación)* plumbing; *(fábrica)* pipe factory; *(taller)* pipe shop.
tu·be·ro·si·dad f. tuberosity, swelling.
tu·be·ro·so, –sa adj. tuberous, tuberose.
tu·bo m. *(canal)* tube, pipe <*t. de escape* exhaust pipe>; ANAT., ZOOL. tract, canal <*t. digestivo* alimentary canal>; *(recipiente)* tube <*t. de ensayo* test tube>; *(chimenea de lámpara)* lamp chimney ♦ **t. de desagüe** drainpipe • **t. lanzallamas** flame thrower • **t. lanzatorpedos** torpedo tube.
tu·bu·la·do, –da adj. tubular.
tu·bu·lar I. adj. tubular II. m. bicycle tire.
tu·cán m. ORNITH. toucan.
tu·co, –ca I. adj. BOL., ECUAD., P. RICO one-armed,

maimed II. m. ARG., ENTOM. glowworm; HOND. *(fragmento)* piece, fragment; *(tocayo)* namesake; PERU, ORNITH. owl; AMER. stump (of a limb).
tu·des·co, –ca I. adj. German II. m.f. *(alemán)* German; FIG., COLL. *(glotón)* glutton —m. *(capote)* cape, cloak ♦ **comer como un t.** COLL. to eat like a horse.
tue·ca f *or* **tue·co** m. *(tronco)* tree stump; *(oquedad)* hollow (in wood).
tuer·ca f. MECH. nut ♦ **t. de alas** *or* **de mariposa** wing nut.
tuer·ce m. *(torcedura)* twist, twisting; MED. sprain; C. AMER. bad luck, misfortune.
tuer·ce see **torcer**.
tue·ro m. *(leño grueso)* thick log; *(leña)* firewood; COL., GUAT. hide-and-seek.
tuer·to, –ta I. past part. see **torcer** II. adj. *(torcido)* twisted, crooked; *(que no ve con un ojo)* one-eyed III. m.f. *(persona)* one-eyed person —m. *(ofensa)* wrong, injustice ♦ **a tuertas** COLL. backwards • **a t. o a derecho** *or* **a tuertas o a derechas** COLL. rightly or wrongly • **tuertos** MED. postpartum pains.
tuer·za, tuerzo see **torcer**.
tues·te m. toasting.
tues·te, tuesto see **tostar**.
tué·ta·no m. ANAT. marrow; FIG. *(esencia)* essence, core ♦ **estar enamorado hasta los tuétanos** FIG., COLL. to be head over heels in love • **hasta los tuétanos** through and through.
tu·fa·ra·da f. strong smell *or* odor.
tu·fi·llas m.f. [pl. **-llas**] COLL. grouch, crab.
tu·fo¹ m. *(vapor)* fume, vapor; FIG., COLL. *(olor)* stink, stench; *(engreimiento)* conceit, airs.
tu·fo² m. lock of hair (falling over the temples).
tu·gu·rio m. *(choza)* shepherd's hut; FIG. *(habitación pequeña)* small room; *(casucha)* hovel, shack.
tul m. TEX. tulle.
tu·lio m. CHEM. thulium.
tu·li·pa f. *(pantalla)* tulip-shaped lampshade; BOT. small tulip.
tu·li·pán m. BOT. tulip.
tu·lle·cer §17 tr. *(tullir)* to cripple, maim; *(lisiar)* to paralyze —reflex. to be crippled or maimed.
tu·lli·dez f. disablement, paralysis.
tu·lli·do, –da I. past part. see **tullir** II. adj. crippled, disabled.
tu·lli·mien·to m. paralysis, disability.
tu·llir §13 tr. to cripple, maim —reflex. to become crippled or maimed.
tum·ba f. *(sepulcro)* grave, tomb; *(voltereta)* somersault; *(caída)* tumble, fall; *(sacudida)* jolt, lurch; *(cubierta)* arched roof; COL., CUBA, MEX. felling (of trees); ARG., CHILE, URUG. tough meat; CUBA bongo drum.
tum·ba·de·ro m. CUBA, P. RICO *(de árboles)* clearing; CUBA *(burdel)* brothel; VEN. branding yard.
tum·ba·do, –da I. adj. vaulted, arched II. m. ECUAD. ceiling.
tum·ba·ga f. *(liga)* tombac (alloy); *(sortija)* inexpensive ring.
tum·bal adj. tomb, of a tomb.
tum·bar tr. *(derribar)* to knock down, knock over; FIG., COLL. *(suspender)* to fail, flunk; *(atontar)* to knock out <*tanto alcohol nos tumbó* so much alcohol knocked us out> —intr. *(caer)* to fall down; MARIT. to keel over, capsize —reflex. *(echarse a dormir)* to lie down, stretch out; *(abandonar)* to take it easy, let up.
tum·bo m. *(caída)* tumble, fall; *(sacudida)* bump, jolt; *(ondulación)* undulation, roll <*el t. de las olas* the roll of the waves>; *(retumbo)* rumble, boom; FIG. difficulty, setback; COL. jar, bowl ♦ **dar tumbos** to bump, jolt.
tum·bón, –bo·na I. adj. COLL. *(socarrón)* sly, crafty; *(perezoso)* lazy, idle II. m.f. COLL. *(socarrón)* sly *or* crafty person; *(perezoso)* lazy *or* idle person —m. *(coche)* coach with a domed roof; *(cofre)* trunk with an arched lid —f. deck chair, sling chair.
tu·me·fac·ción f. MED. tumefaction, swelling.
tu·me·fac·to, –ta adj. MED. swollen.
tu·mes·cen·cia f. MED. tumescence.
tu·mes·cen·te adj. MED. tumescent.
tu·mor m. MED. tumor <*t. cerebral* brain tumor>.

tú·mu·lo m. *(montecillo)* tumulus, burial mound; *(catafalco)* catafalque; *(sepultura)* tomb.

tu·mul·to m. *(alboroto)* tumult, commotion; *(disturbio)* riot, disturbance.

tu·mul·tuo·so, –sa adj. tumultuous, wild.

tu·na¹ I. f. BOT. prickly pear; GUAT., VEN. drinking binge; COL., GUAT. thorn, thistle II. adj. see **tuno, –na.**

tu·na² I. f. *(vida holgazana)* vagrancy, idleness; *(estudiantina)* group of student minstrels ♦ **correr la t.** COLL. to loaf, bum around II. adj. see **tuno, –na.**

tu·nal m. BOT. *(nopal)* prickly pear; *(sitio)* prickly pear grove.

tu·nan·ta COLL. I. adj. shrewd *or* cunning (woman) II. f. hussy.

tu·nan·ta·da f. dirty trick.

tu·nan·te I. adj. rascally, crooked II. m.f. rascal, crook.

tu·nan·te·ar intr. to be a crook *or* rascal.

tu·nan·te·rí·a f. *(acción)* dirty trick; *(cualidad)* crookedness, roguishness.

tun·co, –ca I. adj. MEX. maimed; HOND. crippled II. m. HOND., MEX. pig, swine.

tun·da f. *(del paño)* shearing (of cloth); COLL. *(azotaina)* whipping, beating.

tun·de·ar tr. to beat, thrash.

tun·di·dor, –do·ra I. adj. shearing, clipping II. m.f. *(persona)* shearer, clipper —f. shearing machine.

tun·di·du·ra f. shearing, clipping.

tun·dir tr. *(el paño)* to shear, clip; FIG., COLL. *(golpear)* to beat, thrash.

tun·dra f. GEOG. tundra.

tu·ne·ar intr. to loaf, bum.

tu·ne·ci·no, –na adj. & m.f. Tunisian.

tú·nel m. tunnel <*t. aerodinámico* wind tunnel>.

tu·ne·rí·a f. roguishness, rascality.

Tú·nez m. Tunisia.

tungs·te·no m. CHEM. tungsten.

tú·ni·ca f. *(traje)* tunic; ANAT., BOT. tunic, tunica.

tú·ni·co m. tunic, gown.

tu·no, –na I. adj. rascally, crooked II. m.f. *(bribón)* rascal, rogue —m. BOT. prickly pear —f. see **tuna¹,².**

tu·pa f. *(acción de tupir)* stuffing, packing; FIG., COLL. *(hartazgo)* bellyful, surfeit; CHILE, BOT. Indian tobacco.

tu·pé m. *(copete)* toupee, hairpiece; FIG., COLL. *(descaro)* nerve, gall.

tu·pi·do, –da I. past part. see **tupir** II. adj. *(espeso)* dense, thick; FIG. *(torpe)* thickheaded, dense; CHILE abundant.

tu·pir tr. *(apretar)* to pack tightly; *(una tela)* to weave closely —reflex. *(hartarse)* to stuff *or* gorge oneself; AMER. to be embarrassed.

tur·ba¹ f. crowd, mob.

tur·ba² f. peat, turf.

tur·ba·ción f. *(emoción)* upset, disturbance; *(desorden)* disorder, confusion.

tur·ba·dor, –do·ra I. adj. disturbing II. m.f. disturber.

tur·ba·mul·ta f. COLL. crowd, mob.

tur·ban·te m. turban.

tur·bar tr. *(descomponer)* to upset, disturb; *(desconcertar)* to embarrass, fluster; *(enturbiar)* to stir up —reflex. to be upset, be disturbed.

túr·bi·do, –da adj. turbid, muddy.

tur·bie·dad f. *(de líquidos)* muddiness, turbidness; FIG. *(oscuridad)* obscurity, opaqueness; *(confusión)* confusion, muddle.

tur·bie·za f. muddiness, turbidness.

tur·bi·na f. TECH. turbine <*t. de vapor* steam turbine>.

tur·bio, –bia I. adj. *(un líquido)* muddy, turbid; FIG. *(un negocio)* shady, crooked; *(agitado)* troubled, turbulent <*un período t.* a turbulent period>; *(vista)* blurred, dim; *(oscuro)* obscure, confused II. m.pl. dregs, sediment.

tur·bión m. *(aguacero)* shower, downpour; FIG. *(multitud de cosas)* shower, torrent.

tur·bo·hé·li·ce *or* **tur·bo·pro·pul·sor** m. TECH. turboprop.

tur·bo·rre·ac·tor m. AER. turbojet.

tur·bu·len·cia f. turbulence.

tur·bu·len·to, –ta adj. turbulent.

tur·ca I. f. COLL. drunken spree ♦ **coger una t.** COLL. to tie one on II. adj. see **turco, –ca.**

tur·co, –ca I. adj. Turkish II. m.f. *(habitante)* Turk —m. *(idioma)* Turkish —f. see **turca.**

tur·gen·cia f. MED. swelling, turgescence.

tur·gen·te adj. turgid.

túr·gi·do, –da adj. turgid.

tu·ris·mo m. *(viajes)* tourism, touring; *(coche)* private car.

tu·ris·ta m.f. tourist.

tu·rís·ti·co, –ca adj. tourist.

tur·nar intr. & reflex. to alternate, take turns.

tur·nio, –nia I. adj. *(bizco)* squint-eyed, cross-eyed; FIG. *(ceñudo)* frowning, scowling II. m.f. *(bizco)* squint-eyed *or* cross-eyed person; FIG. *(persona ceñuda)* frowner, scowler.

tur·no m. *(vez)* turn; *(cuadrilla)* shift; C. AMER. charity raffle ♦ **al t.** by turns • **de t.** duty, on duty <*oficial de t.* duty officer> • **por t.** in turn • **por turnos** by turns • **trabajar por turnos** to work shifts • **t. de día** *or* **de noche** day *or* night shift.

tur·que·sa¹ f. (bullet) mold.

tur·que·sa² f. MIN. turquoise.

tur·quí [pl. **-quíes**] *or* **tur·qui·no, –na** adj. dark blue, indigo.

Tur·quí·a f. Turkey.

tu·rrar tr. CUL. to toast.

tu·rrón m. CUL. nougat; FIG., COLL. *(cargo)* cushy job, sinecure.

tu·rro·ne·rí·a f. candy *or* confectionery store.

tu·ru·la·to, –ta adj. COLL. stunned, dumfounded.

tu·rum·bón m. COLL. bump on the head.

tus m. *or* **¡tus!** interj. here! (to a dog) ♦ **sin decir t. ni mus** COLL. without saying a word.

tu·sa I. f. AMER. *(del maíz)* cornhusk; *(cigarro)* cigar rolled in a cornhusk; *(del caballo)* mane; *(de viruela)* pockmark; *(prostituta)* prostitute II. adj. see **tuso, –sa.**

tu·sar tr. AMER., COLL. to crop, trim (hair).

tu·so, –sa I. m. COLL. dog —f. see **tusa** II. adj. COL. pockmarked; CARIB., SP. short-tailed.

tu·te·ar tr. to address as *tú.*

tu·te·la f. *(de personas)* guardianship, tutelage; *(de territorios)* trusteeship; *(protección)* protection; *(dirección)* guidance ♦ **territorio bajo t.** trust territory • **t. dativa** LAW guardianship by court appointment.

tu·te·lar adj. tutelary, protective.

tu·te·o m. addressing as *tú.*

tu·ti·plén adv. ♦ **a t.** COLL. abundantly, to excess.

tu·tor, –to·ra m.f. *(protector)* guardian, protector —m. HORT. stake, prop.

tu·to·rí·a f. tutelage, guardianship.

tu·triz f. [pl. **-tri·ces**] (female) guardian, protector.

tu·tu·ma f. AMER., BOT. calabash; CHILE bump, swelling.

tu·tu·ru·to, –ta I. adj. AMER. stunned, dumfounded II. m.f. AMER. stunned *or* dumfounded person —f. ARG. rowdy *or* boisterous person; CHILE procuress, madam.

tu·vie·ra, tuvo see **tener.**

tu·yo, –ya §G25, 40 I. adj. yours <*¿es t. el coche?* is the car yours?>; of yours <*un pariente t.* a relative of yours> II. pron. yours <*¿quién tiene el t.?* who has yours?> ♦ **lo t.** your affair, your case • **los tuyos** your people.

U

u, U f. twenty-fourth letter of the Spanish alphabet.

u §G46 conj. [used instead of **o** before words beginning with *o* or *ho*] or <*diez u once* ten or eleven>.

u·bé·rri·mo, –ma adj. *(tierra)* very fertile; *(vegetación)* abundant, luxuriant.

u·bi·ca·ción f. *(sitio)* position, location; *(acción de ubicar)* placing, locating.

u·bi·car §70 intr. to be located *or* situated —tr. AMER. to locate, place; PERU to nominate (candidates) —reflex. ARG. to get hired.

u·bi·cui·dad f. ubiquity.

u·bi·cuo, –cua adj. ubiquitous.

u·bre f. ZOOL. udder.

u·ca·se *or* **u·ka·se** m. ukase, edict.

Ucrania, República Socialista Soviética de f. Ukranian Soviet Socialist Republic.

u·cra·nio, –nia or **u·cra·nia·no, –na** adj. & m.f. Ukranian —m. *(idioma)* Ukranian.

Ud. pron. abbrev. of **usted.**

Uds. pron. abbrev. of **ustedes.**

¡uf! interj. *(cansancio)* whew!; *(repugnancia)* ugh!

u·fa·nar·se reflex. to boast (of), pride oneself (on).

u·fa·ni·a f. pride, vanity.

u·fa·no, –na adj. *(orgulloso)* proud, vain; FIG. *(satisfecho)* satisfied, pleased.

u·fo ♦ **a u.** COLL. at someone else's expense, gratis.

U·gan·da m. Uganda.

u·gan·dés, –de·sa adj. & m.f. Ugandan.

u·jier m. usher, doorkeeper.

úl·ce·ra f. MED. ulcer; BOT. rot.

ul·ce·ra·ción f. ulceration.

ul·ce·rar tr. *(llagar)* to ulcerate; FIG. *(herir moralmente)* to wound, hurt one's feelings —reflex. to ulcerate, fester.

ul·ce·ro·so, –sa adj. ulcerous.

ul·te·rior adj. *(más allá)* ulterior, farther; *(que ocurre después)* later, subsequent.

ul·te·rior·men·te adv. later, subsequently.

ul·ti·ma·ción f. conclusion, completion.

úl·ti·ma·men·te adv. *(por último)* ultimately, finally; *(recientemente)* lately, recently.

ul·ti·mar tr. *(acabar)* to finish, conclude; AMER., COLL. to finish off, kill.

ul·ti·má·tum m. ultimatum.

úl·ti·mo, –ma adj. *(final)* last, final <*la ú. partida de la temporada* the last game of the season>; *(de dos)* latter; *(más reciente)* latest, most recent; *(remoto)* farthest, most remote; *(mejor)* best, finest; *(de abajo)* bottom, last <*la ú. línea de la página* the last line of the page>; *(de arriba)* top, last <*el ú. piso* the top floor>; *(de atrás)* back, last <*la ú. fila* the back row>; FIG. *(definitivo)* last, final <*como ú. remedio* as a last resort>; COM. lowest, bottom <*ú. precio* lowest price> ♦ **a la ú.** up-to-date • **a últimos de** at or towards the end of (a month) • **el ú. grito (de la moda)** FIG. the latest craze • **estar a lo ú. de** to be nearly at the end of, have nearly finished • **estar en las últimas** COLL. *(estar moribundo)* to be on one's last legs, be about to die; *(estar en la miseria)* to be down and out • **llegar el ú.** to arrive last • **por ú.** finally, lastly • **ser el ú. en hacer algo** to be the last to do something.

ul·tra I. adv. besides II. m.f. extremist.

ul·tra·de·re·cha f. POL. far right.

ul·tra·de·re·chis·ta adj. & m.f. POL. far rightist, ultrarightist.

ul·tra·ís·mo m. LIT. ultraism (Spanish and Latin American literary movement).

ul·tra·ís·ta adj. & m.f. LIT. ultraist.

ul·tra·ja·dor, –do·ra I. adj. outrageous, offensive II. m.f. person who outrages or offends.

ul·tra·jan·te adj. outrageous, offensive.

ul·tra·jar intr. to outrage, insult.

ul·tra·je m. outrage, insult.

ul·tra·jo·so, –sa adj. outrageous, offensive.

ul·tra·mar m. overseas country.

ul·tra·ma·ri·no, –na I. adj. overseas II. m.pl. **ultramarinos** *(comestibles)* imported foods; *(tienda)* grocery store.

ul·tra·mo·der·no, –na adj. ultramodern.

ul·tran·za ♦ **a u.** *(a muerte)* to the death; *(resueltamente)* determinedly, unflinchingly.

ul·tra·rro·jo, –ja adj. PHYS. ultrared, infrared.

ul·tra·só·ni·co, –ca adj. ultrasonic.

ul·tra·so·ni·do m. PHYS. ultrasound.

ul·tra·tum·ba f. otherworld, beyond (the grave).

ul·tra·vio·le·ta adj. PHYS. ultraviolet.

u·lu·la·ción f. *(del viento)* howling; *(del búho)* hooting, screeching.

u·lu·lar intr. *(el viento)* to howl; *(un búho)* to hoot, screech.

u·lu·la·to m. *(del viento)* howl, howling; *(del búho)* hoot, hooting.

u·llu·co m. ECUAD., PERU, BOT. ulluco (edible tuber).

um·bi·li·cal adj. ANAT. umbilical ♦ **cordón u.** umbilical cord.

um·bral m. *(de la puerta)* threshold, doorstep; FIG. *(entrada)* threshold, beginning; ARCHIT. lintel ♦ **estar en el u.** to be on the threshold • **pisar el u.** to cross the threshold.

um·brí·o, –brí·a I. adj. shady II. f. shade.

um·bro·so, –sa adj. shady.

un §G17 [contr. of **uno** used before m. sing. and certain f. sing. nouns] I. adj. one <*un chico* one boy> II. indef. art. a, an <*un arma* a weapon>.

u·ná·ni·me adj. unanimous.

u·ná·ni·me·men·te adv. unanimously.

u·na·ni·mi·dad f. unanimity ♦ **por u.** unanimously.

un·ción f. *(acción de ungir)* anointing, unction; RELIG. extreme unction; FIG. *(devoción)* unction, fervor.

un·cir §35 tr. to yoke.

un·dé·ci·mo, –ma adj. & m. eleventh.

un·do·so, –sa adj. wavy, undulating.

un·du·la·ción f. undulation.

un·du·lan·te adj. undulating.

un·du·lar intr. to undulate.

un·du·la·to·rio, –ria adj. undulatory.

un·gi·do m. anointed priest or king.

un·gi·mien·to m. anointing, unction.

un·gir §32 tr. to anoint.

un·güen·to m. unguent, ointment.

un·gu·la·do, –da adj. & m. ZOOL. ungulate.

un·gu·lar adj. ungular, of the nails.

u·ni·ble adj. which can be united or joined.

ú·ni·ca·men·te adv. only, solely.

u·ni·ca·me·ral adj. unicameral.

u·ni·ce·lu·lar adj. BIOL. unicellular.

u·ni·ci·dad f. uniqueness.

ú·ni·co, –ca I. adj. *(solo)* only, sole; FIG. *(extraordinario)* unique, extraordinary II. m.f. only one <*es el ú. que me queda* it's the only one I have left> ♦ **lo ú.** only thing <*¡lo ú. que faltaba!* that's the only thing that was missing!>.

u·ni·cor·nio m. MYTH. unicorn; ZOOL. one-horned rhinoceros; ASTRON. Unicorn ♦ **u. de mar** ICHTH. narwhal.

u·ni·dad f. unity <*la u. regional* regional unity>; MATH., MIL., TECH. unit; *(armonía)* harmony; *(unicidad)* oneness; COLL. *(cada uno)* each (one) <*valen veinte pesos la u.* they cost twenty pesos each>; LIT. unity <*u. de acción* unity of action> ♦ **u. de combate** MIL. combat unit • **u. monetaria** monetary unit • **u. móvil** TELEV. mobile unit.

u·ni·do, –da I. past part. see **unir** II. adj. united, unified.

u·ni·fi·ca·ción f. unification.

u·ni·fi·ca·dor, –do·ra I. adj. uniting, unifying II. m.f. uniter, unifier.

u·ni·fi·car §70 tr. to unite, unify.

u·ni·for·ma·dor, –do·ra adj. standardizing, making uniform.

u·ni·for·mar tr. *(uniformizar)* to make uniform; *(normalizar)* to standardize; *(dar uniforme)* to uniform, make wear a uniform.

u·ni·for·me I. adj. *(igual)* uniform; *(llano)* even, level; *(regular)* steady, even <*ritmo u.* steady rhythm>; *(sin variedad)* plain <*estilo u.* plain style> II. m. uniform ♦ **u. de gala** dress uniform.

u·ni·for·me·men·te adv. uniformly.

u·ni·for·mi·dad f. uniformity.

u·ni·for·mi·zar §04 tr. to make uniform.

u·ni·gé·ni·to, –ta I. adj. only <*hijo u.* only child> II. m. RELIG. Son of God.

u·ni·la·te·ral adj. unilateral.

u·nión f. *(asociación)* union; *(acción de unir)* union, joining; *(armonía)* harmony, unity; *(sindicato)* union <*u. agrícola* agricultural union>; *(conexión)* joint, connection; *(casamiento)* union, marriage; *(concordia)* double finger ring; SURG. closing (of a wound) ♦ **en u. con** with, together with • **u. articulada** MECH. hinged connection.

Unión de Repúblicas Socialistas Soviéticas f. Union of Soviet Socialist Republics.

u·ni·per·so·nal adj. GRAM. unipersonal; *(para una sola persona)* individual, single.

u·nir tr. *(juntar)* to unite, join (together); *(combinar)* to join (together), combine <*u. dos capítulos de un libro en uno* to combine two chapters of a book into one>; *(casar)* to unite (by marriage); *(mezclarse)* to mix; FIG. *(aliar)* to combine <*u. la teoría con la experiencia práctica* to combine theory with practical experience>; COM. to merge, join; MECH., TECH. to join, connect; SURG. to close (a wound) —reflex. *(juntarse)* to unite, join (together); *(encontrarse)* to join, meet; *(casarse)* to marry; *(mezclarse)* to mix; FIG. *(aliarse)* to combine; COM. to merge, join ♦ **unirse a** to join • **unirse en matrimonio** to marry, be united in marriage.

u·ni·se·xo adj. unisex.

u·ní·so·no, -na MUS. **I.** adj. in unison **II.** m. unison, harmony ♦ **al u.** in unison.

u·ni·ta·rio, -ria I. adj. *(no dividido)* unitary, unified; POL. centralist; RELIG. Unitarian **II.** m.f. POL. centralist; RELIG. Unitarian.

u·ni·ver·sal adj. *(general)* universal; FIG. *(del mundo)* world, of the world *<historia u.* world history>.

u·ni·ver·sa·li·dad f. universality.

u·ni·ver·sa·lis·ta adj. & m.f. universalist.

u·ni·ver·sa·li·zar §04 tr. to universalize.

u·ni·ver·sal·men·te adv. universally, all over the world.

u·ni·ver·si·dad f. university.

u·ni·ver·si·ta·rio, -ria I. adj. university *<grado u.* university degree> **II.** m.f. *(profesor)* university teacher *or* professor; *(estudiante)* university student.

u·ni·ver·so, -sa I. adj. universal **II.** m. universe.

u·ní·vo·ca·ción f. having the same meaning.

u·ní·vo·co, -ca adj. *(que tiene el mismo sentido)* having the same meaning; GRAM. homonymic.

un·ja, unjo see **ungir.**

u·no, -na §G17, 21 **I.** m. one **II.** adj. one *<u. cucharada basta* one spoonful is enough>; *(idéntico)* one ♦ **la u.** one o'clock • **u. que otro** a few *<se veía u. que otro pájaro* a few birds were seen> • **unos** *or* **unas** some, a few *<unos estudiantes* some students>; about, approximately *<unos veinte kilómetros de aquí* about twenty kilometers from here> **III.** indef. pron. one *<u. de mis amigos* one of my friends>; one, you *<u. no puede escaparse de aquí* you cannot escape from here>; *(alguien)* someone, somebody *<u. lo hizo* somebody did it> ♦ **cada u.** each one, every one • **de u. en u.** one by one • **u. a otro** *or* **u. con otro** each other, one another *<se miraron u. a otro* they looked at each other> • **u. a u.** *or* **u. por u.** one by one, one at a time • **u. y otro** both • **unos** *or* **unas** some • **unos a otros** each other, one another • **unos cuantos** a few, some • **u. tras otro** one after another **IV.** indef. art. a, an *<necesito u. pluma* I need a pen>.

un·ta·dor, -do·ra I. adj. greasing, oiling **II.** m.f. greaser, oiler.

un·ta·du·ra f. *(con aceite)* greasing, oiling; *(con ungüento)* rubbing; *(aceite)* grease, oil; MED. *(ungüento)* ointment, liniment.

un·tar tr. *(engrasar)* to grease, oil; *(manchar)* to smear *or* cover with *<u. una camisa de tinta* to smear a shirt with ink>; to spread *<u. el pan con mermelada* to spread bread with jam>; MED. to rub, anoint; FIG., COLL. *(sobornar)* to bribe ♦ **u. la mano a alguien** FIG., COLL. to grease someone's palm, bribe —reflex. *(mancharse)* to get smeared, smear oneself; FIG., COLL. *(sacar provecho)* to feather one's nest, take a cut of the profits.

un·to m. *(materia grasa)* grease; *(del animal)* fat; CHILE (shoe) polish; COL., MEX., PERU greasing, smearing ♦ **u. de México** COLL. bribe.

un·tuo·si·dad f. greasiness, oiliness.

un·tuo·so, -sa adj. greasy, oily.

un·tu·ra f. greasing, smearing with ointment.

un·za, unzo see **uncir.**

u·ña f. ANAT. *(de la mano)* nail, fingernail; *(del pie)* nail, toenail; ZOOL. *(garra)* claw; *(pezuña)* hoof; *(del alacrán)* sting; BOT. *(tetón)* stump (of a tree); *(espina)* thorn; MARIT. fluke (of an anchor); MECH. *(garfio)* claw; *(gancho)* hook ♦ **a u. de caballo** at full speed • **comerse las uñas** to bite one's nails; FIG. *(impacientarse)* to be impatient • **largo de uñas** COLL. light-fingered • **sacar las uñas** FIG., COLL. to show one's claws • **ser u. y carne** FIG. to be inseparable, be fast friends • **u. de caballo** BOT. coltsfoot • **u. enterrada** ingrown nail • **u. gata** BOT. restharrow.

u·ña·da *or* **u·ña·ra·da** f. scratch.

u·ñe·ta f. ANAT. small nail; *(cincel)* stonecutter's chisel; CHILE, MUS. plectrum.

u·ñe·ta·zo m. scratch.

u·ñi·du·ra f. yoking.

u·ñir §12 tr. to yoke.

¡u·pa! interj. upsy-daisy (said to children) ♦ **a u.** in arms.

u·par tr. to lift up.

u·ra·lo·al·tai·co, -ca adj. Ural-Altaic.

u·rá·ni·co, -ca adj. CHEM. uranic.

u·ra·nio, -nia I. adj. uranic, celestial **II.** m. CHEM. uranium.

ur·ba·ni·cé, urbanice see **urbanizar.**

ur·ba·ni·dad f. urbanity, politeness.

ur·ba·nis·mo m. urbanism, city planning.

ur·ba·nis·ta I. adj. pertaining to city planning **II.** m.f. city planner.

ur·ba·nís·ti·co, -ca adj. *(de la ciudad)* urban; *(del urbanismo)* city-planning *<proyecto u.* city-planning project>.

ur·ba·ni·za·ción f. *(urbanismo)* urbanization, city planning; *(desarrollo)* development.

ur·ba·ni·za·dor, -do·ra I. adj. urbanizing, developing **II.** m.f. developer.

ur·ba·ni·zar §04 tr. *(civilizar)* to civilize, educate; *(un terreno)* to urbanize, develop ♦ **zona sin u.** undeveloped area.

ur·ba·no, -na adj. *(de la ciudad)* urban; FIG. *(cortés)* urbane, polite.

ur·be f. large city, metropolis.

ur·ca f. MARIT. hooker; ZOOL. orc, killer whale.

ur·di·de·ra f. TEX. warping frame.

ur·di·dor, -do·ra TEX. **I.** adj. warping **II.** m.f. *(persona)* warper —m. *(máquina)* warper, warping frame.

ur·di·du·ra f. TEX. warping.

ur·dim·bre f. TEX. warping; FIG. *(maquinación)* plotting, scheming.

ur·dir tr. TEX. to warp; FIG. *(maquinar)* to scheme, plot.

u·re·a f. BIOCHEM. urea.

u·ré·ter m. ANAT. ureter.

u·re·tra f. ANAT. urethra.

ur·gen·cia f. urgency ♦ **con u.** urgently • **cura de u.** emergency treatment, first aid • **recurso de u.** summary procedure.

ur·gen·te adj. urgent.

ur·gen·te·men·te adv. urgently.

ur·gir §32 intr. to be urgent *or* pressing *<el pedido urge* the request is urgent>.

u·ri·nal adj. urinary.

u·ri·na·rio, -ria I. adj. urinary **II.** m. urinal.

ur·na f. *(vasija)* urn; *(arca)* ballot box; *(caja de cristales)* glass case (for displaying objects) ♦ **acudir** *or* **ir a las urnas** to vote, go to the polls.

u·ro·lo·gí·a f. MED. urology.

u·ró·lo·go, -ga m.f. MED. urologist.

u·rra·ca f. ORNITH. magpie; FIG., COLL. *(persona)* chatterbox.

ur·ti·ca·ria f. MED. urticaria, hives.

u·ru·bú m. [pl. **-bú·es**] ORNITH. urubu, black vulture.

U·ru·guay m. Uruguay.

u·ru·gua·yo, -ya adj. & m.f. Uruguayan.

u·sa·do, -da I. past part. see **usar II.** adj. *(deteriorado)* worn, worn-out; *(de segunda mano)* used, secondhand; *(habituado)* used, accustomed (to something).

u·san·za f. usance, custom.

u·sar tr. *(emplear)* to use, employ *<u. una herramienta* to use a tool>; *(llevar ropa)* to wear (clothing) ♦ **sin u.** unused —intr. *(soler)* to be accustomed (to), be in the habit (of) *<uso nadar todos los días* I'm accustomed to swimming every day>; *(emplear)* to use, make use of *<u. de artimaña* to use trickery> ♦ **u. mal de** to misuse —reflex. *(estar de moda)* to be the custom *or* the fashion; *(estar en uso)* to be used, be in use *<ese método ya no se usa* that method is no longer used>.

us·le·ro m. CUL. rolling pin.

u·so m. *(empleo)* use *<el u. de fibras sintéticas* the use of synthetic fibers>; *(ejercicio)* wear, wearing *<obligar el u. de colores sombríos* to oblige the wearing of somber colors>; *(goce)* exercise, use *<el u. del privilegio hereditario* the exercise of hereditary privilege>; *(moda)* fashion, style; *(costumbre)* custom, practice, usage *<eso va en contra del u. local* that goes against local custom>; *(desgaste)* wear and tear ♦ **al u.** according to custom, as is customary

• **al u. de** in the style *or* fashion of • **de** *or* **para.u. externo** MED. for external use • **deteriorado con el u.** worn, well-used • **en u.** in use • **entrar en los usos** to adopt the customs (of a culture) • **estar en buen u.** to be in good condition • **estar en el u. de la palabra** to have the floor • **estar fuera de u.** to be out of use, be obsolete • **hacer buen u. de** to make good use of, put to good use • **hacer mal u. de** to misuse • **hacer u. de** to use, make use of • **hacer u. de la palabra** to speak, take the floor • **para todo u.** all-purpose • **ser de u.** *(emplearse)* to be used; *(llevarse)* to be worn • **u. de razón** power of reason • **u. y desgaste** wear and tear.

us·ted §G30, 32 pron. you ♦ **de u.** yours • **hablar** *or* **tratar de u.** to use the polite form of address • **ustedes** you, all of you.

u·sual adj. usual, common.

u·sual·men·te adv. usually.

u·sua·rio, –ria LAW I. adj. usufructuary <*derechos usuarios* usufructuary rights> II. m.f. user, usufructuary.

u·su·fruc·to m. LAW usufruct.

u·su·fruc·tuar §67 tr. LAW to hold by usufruct —intr. to be fruitful.

u·su·ra f. *(interés excesivo)* usury, excessive interest; FIG. *(provecho)* profit ♦ **pagar con u.** FIG. to repay many times over.

u·su·ra·rio, –ria adj. usurious.

u·su·re·ar intr. *(dar a usura)* to practice usury; FIG. *(ganar con exceso)* to profiteer.

u·su·re·ro, –ra I. adj. usurious II. m.f. usurer.

u·sur·pa·ción f. usurpation.

u·sur·pa·dor, –do·ra I. adj. usurping II. m.f. usurper.

u·sur·par tr. to usurp.

u·sur·pa·to·rio, –ria adj. usurpatory.

u·ta f. PERU skin disease.

u·ten·si·lio m. utensil, tool.

u·te·ri·no, –na adj. ANAT. uterine ♦ **furor u.** MED. nymphomania.

ú·te·ro m. ANAT. uterus, womb.

ú·til I. adj. *(que puede servir)* useful; *(apto)* fit; working <*día ú.* working day>; LAW lawful, legal (time); MECH. effective, available II. m. tool, utensil ♦ **útiles** equipment, implements • **útiles de pesca** fishing tackle.

u·ti·li·cé, utilice see utilizar.

u·ti·li·dad f. *(calidad de útil)* usefulness, utility; *(provecho)* profit, benefit ♦ **u. bruta** *or* **gruesa** gross profit • **u. de explotación** operating profit • **utilidades** earnings, profits • **utilidades de capital** capital gains • **utilidades impositivas** taxable profits • **utilidades incorporadas** retained income • **utilidades líquidas** net profits.

u·ti·li·ta·rio, –ria adj. & m.f. utilitarian.

u·ti·li·za·ble adj. usable, utilizable.

u·ti·li·za·ción f. utilization.

u·ti·li·za·dor, –do·ra I. adj. using, utilizing II. m.f. user, utilizer.

u·ti·li·zar §04 tr. to use, utilize.

ú·til·men·te adv. usefully.

u·to·pí·a f. utopia.

u·tó·pi·co, –ca adj. & m.f. utopian.

u·va f. BOT. grape; MED. tumor on the uvula ♦ **entrar por uvas** FIG., COLL. to run the risk • **estar de mala u.** to be in a bad mood • **estar hecho una u.** FIG., COLL. to be drunk as a skunk • **u. crespa** *or* **espina** BOT. gooseberry • **u. de raposa** BOT. truelove • **u. lupina** *or* **verga** BOT. monkshood, wolfsbane • **u. marina** BOT. ephedra • **u. moscatel** BOT. muscat grape • **u. pasa** raisin • **u. taminea** BOT. lousewort.

u·va·da f. abundance of grapes.

u·va·te m. grape preserves.

u·ve·ro, –ra I. adj. grape, of grapes <*recolección u.* grape harvest> II. m.f. *(persona)* grape seller —m. BOT. sea grape.

ú·vu·la f. ANAT. uvula.

u·xo·ri·ci·da I. adj. uxoricidal II. m. uxoricide (man who kills his wife).

u·xo·ri·ci·dio m. uxoricide (killing of a wife by her husband).

¡uy! interj. *(sorpresa)* oh!; *(dolor)* ouch!

V

v, V f. twenty-fifth letter of the Spanish alphabet ♦ **v. doble** double-u, w.

va·ca I. f. ZOOL. cow; CUL. beef; *(cuero)* cowhide, leather; *(dinero)* gambling pool ♦ **v. de San Antón** ENTOM. ladybug • **v. lechera** milk cow • **v. marina** ZOOL. manatee, sea cow • **vacas gordas** years of plenty II. adj. see vaco, –ca.

va·ca·ción f. *(descanso)* vacation, holiday; *(suspensión)* recess; *(en un empleo)* vacancy, job opening ♦ **estar de vacaciones** to be on vacation.

va·ca·da f. herd of cows.

va·can·cia f. vacancy, job opening.

va·can·te I. adj. vacant, empty II. f. vacancy, job opening.

va·car §70 intr. *(estar vacante)* to be vacant, empty; *(dejar de trabajar)* to stop working; *(dedicarse)* to devote oneself (to an occupation); *(carecer)* to lack.

va·cia·de·ro m. *(sitio)* dump, rubbish heap; *(conducto)* sewer, drain.

va·cia·do I. past part. see vaciar II. m. *(acción de vaciar)* casting, molding; *(figura)* cast, mold; *(de un depósito)* emptying, draining.

va·cia·mien·to m. emptying.

va·cian·te f. ebb tide.

va·ciar §30 tr. *(dejar vacío)* to empty <*v. una caja* to empty a box>; *(verter)* to drain <*v. una botella* to drain a bottle>; *(fundir)* to cast (a statue); *(sacar filo)* to sharpen, hone; *(ahuecar)* to hollow out; FIG. *(explicar)* to explain, go on at length; *(trasladar)* to copy (out) —intr. to empty, flow <*el río vacía en el mar* the river empties into the sea> —reflex. to empty; FIG., COLL. *(decir indiscretamente)* to blab.

va·cie·dad f. *(tontería)* nonsense, foolishness; *(vacío)* emptiness.

va·ci·la·ción f. *(de un objeto)* swaying, rocking; FIG. *(duda)* hesitation, wavering ♦ **sin v.** unhesitatingly.

va·ci·lan·te adj. *(no fijo)* unsteady, faltering; FIG. *(que duda)* hesitating, wavering; *(luz)* flickering.

va·ci·lar intr. *(moverse una cosa)* to sway, wobble; *(no estar firme)* to be shaky, be unsteady; *(la luz)* to flicker; FIG. *(dudar)* to hesitate, waver; *(la memoria)* to fail, falter; *(tener poca firmeza)* to totter; COLL. *(hablar en broma)* to joke, jest; MEX. to go on a spree ♦ **hacer v.** FIG. to shake beliefs • **sin v.** unhesitatingly.

va·ci·lón, –lo·na AMER., COLL. I. adj. funny, humorous II. m.f. *(persona)* joker —m. MEX. spree.

va·cí·o, –a I. adj. *(falto de contenido)* empty <*estómago v.* empty stomach>; *(desocupado)* empty, vacant <*una sala v.* an empty room>; *(hueco)* hollow; FIG. *(falto)* empty, devoid <*una cabeza v. de ideas* a mind devoid of ideas>; *(sin sentido)* empty, meaningless <*palabras vacías* empty words>; *(vano)* vain, proud; *(ocioso)* lazy, idle; AGR. barren II. m. *(cavidad)* emptiness; *(vacante)* vacancy; *(hueco)* hole, hollow; *(espacio)* empty space, blank; *(ijada)* flank, ribs; FIG. *(falta)* vacuum, void <*su muerte ha dejado un gran v.* his death has left a great void>; PHYS. vacuum ♦ **de v.** empty • **hacer el v. a alguien** FIG., COLL. to give someone the cold shoulder.

va·co, –ca I. adj. vacant, empty <*un empleo v.* a vacant position> II. f. see vaca.

va·cui·dad f. vacuity, emptiness.

va·cu·na f. MED. vaccine; VET. cowpox.

va·cu·na·ción f. MED. vaccination.

va·cu·nar tr. MED. to vaccinate, inoculate; FIG. *(proteger)* to inoculate, make immune.

va·cu·no, –na adj. bovine ♦ **ganado v.** cattle.

va·cuo, –cua I. adj. *(vacío)* vacant, empty; *(frívolo)* vacuous, inane II. m. vacuum, void.

a·de·a·ble adj. *(un río)* fordable; FIG. *(un obstáculo)* surmountable.

va·de·ar tr. *(un río)* to ford, wade across; FIG. *(una dificultad)* to overcome, surmount; *(el ánimo)* to sound out (a person's feelings) —reflex. to behave, conduct oneself.

va·de·mé·cum m. *(libro)* handbook, manual; *(cartera)* satchel, briefcase.

va·do m. *(de un río)* ford; FIG. *(recurso)* solution, remedy ♦

al v. o al puente COLL. one way or the other • **no hallar v.** FIG. to be at an impasse.

va·ga·bun·de·ar intr. to wander, roam.

va·ga·bun·de·o m. vagabondism.

va·ga·bun·de·rí·a *or* **va·ga·bun·dez** f. vagabondism.

va·ga·bun·do, –da I. adj. *(errante)* vagabond, vagrant; FIG. *(en la imaginación)* wandering, roving II. m.f. vagabond, vagrant.

va·ga·men·te adv. vaguely.

va·ga·mun·de·ar intr. var. of **vagabundear.**

va·ga·mun·do, –da COLL. adj. & m.f. var. of **vagabundo, –da.**

va·gan·cia f. *(delito)* vagrancy; *(ociosidad)* laziness, idleness.

va·gan·te adj. *(errante)* roaming; *(suelto)* loose, free.

va·gar¹ §47 intr. *(errar)* to wander, roam; *(andar sin orden)* to drift; *(andar ocioso)* to be lazy *or* idle; *(tener tiempo libre)* to be free, be at leisure.

va·gar² m. *(tiempo libre)* free time, leisure; *(lentitud)* slowness, deliberateness.

va·gi·do m. cry of a newborn.

va·gi·na f. ANAT., BOT. vagina.

va·gi·nal adj. ANAT. vaginal.

va·go, –ga I. adj. *(indeterminado)* vague, indefinite; *(indolente)* lazy, loafing; *(desocupado)* unemployed; *(vagabundo)* vagrant, vagabond; PAINT. blurred; ANAT. vagus ♦ **en v.** *(sin firmeza)* unsteadily; *(al aire)* at nothing *<dar golpe en v.* to swat at nothing>; FIG. *(en vano)* in vain II. m. *(holgazán)* loafer, idler; *(vagabundo)* vagrant, tramp; ANAT. vagus nerve.

va·gón m. RAIL. car, coach; *(para mercancías)* truck, van ♦ **v. cama** sleeping car • **v. de carga** *or* **de mercancías** freight car • **v. de cola** caboose • **v. de equipajes** baggage car • **v. de pasajeros** passenger car • **v. de primera** first-class car • **v. restaurante** restaurant *or* dining car.

va·go·ne·ta f. small wagon *or* cart.

va·gua·da f. lowest part of a valley.

va·gué, vague see **vagar¹.**

va·gue·ar intr. to wander, roam.

va·gue·dad f. *(calidad de vago)* vagueness; *(expresión vaga)* vague remark.

va·gui·do, –da I. adj. dizzy, lightheaded II. m. dizziness.

va·ha·ri·na f. COLL. steam, vapor.

va·he·ar intr. *(exhalar)* to breathe out, exhale; *(echar vapor)* to steam.

va·hí·do m. dizzy spell.

va·ho m. steam, vapor.

vai·na I. f. *(envoltura)* sheath; BOT. pod, husk; MARIT. casing, tabling; AMER., COLL. *(molestia)* nuisance, bother; *(cosa)* thing; COL. stroke of luck II. adj. AMER., COLL. annoying, bothersome.

vai·na·zas m. [pl. **-zas**] COLL. slob.

vai·ni·lla f. BOT., CUL. vanilla; BOT. American heliotrope; SEW. hemstitch.

vai·ni·ta f. AMER. string bean.

vai·vén m. *(entre dos puntos)* oscillation, back-and-forth motion; *(balanceo)* swinging, swaying; FIG. *(cambio)* fluctuation, change; MARIT. three-stranded cable ♦ **vaivenes** FIG. ups and downs.

va·ji·lla f. dishes, tableware ♦ **lavar la v.** to wash the dishes • **v. de plata** silverware • **v. de porcelana** china.

val·drá, valdría see **valer.**

va·le¹ m. *(pagaré)* promissory note, IOU; *(recibo)* receipt; EDUC. gold star; AMER. buddy, pal.

va·le² interj. *(despedida)* adieu!, farewell!; *(de acuerdo)* O.K.

va·le·de·ro, –ra adj. valid.

va·le·dor, –do·ra m.f. *(protector)* protector, defender; MEX. buddy, pal.

va·len·cia f. CHEM. valency, valence ♦ **v. polar** electrovalence, polar valence.

va·len·tí·a f. *(valor)* bravery, valor; *(ánimo)* energy, boldness; *(hazaña heroica)* heroic deed; *(jactancia)* bragging, boastfulness.

va·len·tón, –to·na I. adj. boastful, arrogant II. m.f. braggart.

va·len·to·na *or* **va·len·to·na·da** f. boast, brag.

va·ler §74 I. intr. *(tener valor)* to be worth *<¿cuánto vale ese*

carro? how much is that car worth?>; *(tener mérito)* to be valuable, be of value; *(merecer estimación)* to be worthy *<busco a un hombre que valga* I am looking for a man who is worthy>; *(ser válido)* to be valid *<esta moneda no vale* this coin is not valid>; *(tener autoridad)* to have authority *<el supervisor no vale para esto* the supervisor does not have authority in this matter>; *(servir)* to be useful, be of use *<no le valdrán todas sus palancas* all of his connections will be of no use to him> ♦ **más vale** it is better • **valga lo que valiere** whatever it may be worth, for what it's worth • **¡válgame Dios!** bless my soul! —tr. *(tener un valor de)* to be worth *<el reloj vale cien dólares* the watch is worth a hundred dollars>; *(costar)* to cost, be *<¿cuánto vale?* how much is it?>; *(representar)* to be worth *<una blanca vale dos negras* a half note is worth two quarter notes>; *(amparar)* to protect, defend *<le valió el casco* his helmet protected him>; *(dar)* to give, yield *<esa inversión le valió cien mil pesos* that investment yielded him a hundred thousand pesos>; *(causar)* to cause *<nuestra conducta nos valió muchos disgustos* our conduct caused us a lot of trouble> ♦ **hacer v.** to assert *<hizo v. sus derechos* he asserted his rights> • **v. la pena** to be worthwhile • **v. lo que pesa en oro** FIG. to be worth its weight in gold —reflex. *(lograrse)* to manage *or* fend for oneself ♦ **valerse de** to make use of, avail oneself of II. m. value, worth.

va·le·ria·na f. BOT. valerian.

va·le·ro·si·dad f. bravery, valor.

va·le·ro·so, –sa adj. *(eficaz)* effective, powerful; *(valiente)* valiant, courageous; *(valioso)* valuable, precious.

va·le·tu·di·na·rio, –ria I. adj. valetudinary, sickly II. m.f. valetudinarian, sickly person.

val·ga, valgo see **valer.**

va·lí·a f. *(valor)* value, worth; *(confianza)* confidence, favor *<tener v. con alguien* to be in favor with someone>.

va·li·da·ción f. validation.

va·li·dar tr. to validate.

va·li·dez f. validity.

vá·li·do, –da I. adj. favored, favorite II. m.f. favorite, protégé(e).

vá·li·do, –da adj. *(fuerte)* strong, healthy; *(que vale legalmente)* valid.

va·lien·te I. adj. *(valeroso)* brave, valiant; *(fuerte)* strong, vigorous; *(eficaz)* effective, valid; *(que vale)* valuable; *(excelente)* fine, excellent; FIG., COLL. a fine *<¡v. amigo eres tú!* a fine friend you are!>; *(valentón)* boastful, bragging ♦ **¡v. frío!** it's freezing! II. m. *(valeroso)* brave man; *(valentón)* braggart.

va·li·ja f. *(maleta)* suitcase, valise; *(saco de correo)* mailbag; *(correo)* mail ♦ **v. diplomática** diplomatic pouch.

va·li·je·ro, –ra m.f. *(del correo)* letter carrier; DIPL. courier.

va·li·mien·to m. *(favor)* favor, good graces *<tener v. con alguien* to be in someone's good graces>; *(mérito)* value, merit.

va·lio·so, –sa adj. *(precioso)* valuable, precious; *(rico)* rich, wealthy.

va·lón, –lo·na I. adj. Walloon II. m.f. *(persona)* Walloon —m. *(idioma)* Walloon (dialect) ♦ **valones** knickerbockers, knickers —f. *(cuello)* Vandyke collar; AMER. cropped mane (of horses).

va·lo·nar tr. AMER. to crop a horse's mane.

va·lor m. *(calidad)* value, worth; *(precio)* price, value *<el v. de la propiedad* the price of the property>; *(importancia)* importance, value *<el v. de una acción* the importance of an act>; *(osadía)* audacity, nerve *<tener el v. de negarlo* to have the nerve to deny it>; *(coraje)* courage, valor; MUS., MATH. value ♦ **dar v. a** to attach importance *or* value to • **de v.** valuable • **sin v.** worthless • **v. adquisitivo** purchasing power • **v. comercial** market value • **valores** COM. securities, bonds; *(principios)* values, principles • **valores inmuebles** real estate • **v. nominal** COM. face value.

va·lo·ra·ción f. *(estimación)* valuation, appraisal; *(explotación)* exploitation, use; *(aumento del valor)* appreciation, increasing the value; CHEM. standardization (of a solution).

va·lo·rar tr. *(estimar)* to value, appraise; *(aumentar del valor)* to increase the value of; CHEM. to standardize (a solution).

va·lo·ri·za·ción f. *(estimación)* valuation, appraisal; *(aumento de valor)* raising of the value.

va·lo·ri·za·dor, –do·ra adj. *(evaluador)* evaluating, appraising; *(que aumenta el valor)* raising the value.

va·lo·ri·zar §04 tr. *(evaluar)* to value, appraise; *(aumentar el valor)* to raise the value of.

vals m. MUS. waltz.

va·lua·ción f. valuation, appraisal.

va·lua·dor, –do·ra I. adj. evaluating, appraising II. m.f. appraiser.

va·luar §67 tr. to value, appraise.

val·va f. BOT., ZOOL. valve.

vál·vu·la f. MECH. valve <*v. de admisión* intake valve>; RAD. tube; ANAT., ZOOL. valve <*v. mitral* mitral valve> ♦ **v. de seguridad** safety valve • **v. de escape** FIG., COLL. escape valve.

va·lla f. *(cerca)* fence, barricade; FIG. *(obstáculo)* obstacle, barrier; SPORT. hurdle; CUBA cockpit (for cockfighting); COL. ditch, trench ♦ **v. publicitaria** billboard.

va·lla·dar m. *(cerca)* fence, barricade; FIG. *(obstáculo)* obstacle, barrier.

va·lla·do I. past part. see **vallar** II. m. wall, fence.

va·llar tr. to fence in, enclose.

va·lle m. *(entre montañas)* valley, vale; *(de un río)* river basin ♦ **v. de lágrimas** FIG. vale of tears.

va·mos, van see **ir**.

vam·pi·re·sa f. CINEM. vamp.

vam·pi·ro m. MYTH., ZOOL. vampire.

va·na·dio m. CHEM. vanadium.

va·na·glo·ria f. vainglory, pride.

va·na·glo·riar·se reflex. to boast, brag.

va·na·glo·rio·so, –sa I. adj. *(vano)* vainglorious, proud; *(jactancioso)* boastful, arrogant II. m.f. boastful person, braggart.

va·na·men·te adv. *(inútilmente)* vainly, futilely; *(con vanidad)* vainly, presumptuously; *(tontamente)* idly, foolishly.

van·dá·li·co, –ca adj. HIST. Vandalic; *(del vandalismo)* vandalistic.

van·da·lis·mo m. vandalism.

ván·da·lo, –la m.f. HIST. Vandal; FIG. *(destructor)* vandal.

van·guar·dia f. MIL. vanguard; ARTS, LIT. avant-garde ♦ **ir a la v.** to be in the forefront.

van·guar·dis·mo m. ARTS, LIT. avant-garde movement.

van·guar·dis·ta I. adj. ARTS, LIT. avant-garde II. m.f. ARTS avant-garde artist; LIT. avant-garde writer or poet.

va·ni·dad f. *(inutilidad)* vanity, futility; *(ostentación)* ostentation, pomp; *(ilusión)* illusion; *(orgullo)* vanity, conceit ♦ **vanidades** inanities, foolish remarks.

va·ni·do·so, –sa I. adj. vain, conceited II. m.f. vain or conceited person.

va·ni·lo·cuen·cia f. verbosity.

va·ni·lo·cuen·te adj. verbose.

va·no, –na I. adj. *(inútil)* vain, useless; *(frívolo)* frivolous, inane; *(vanidoso)* vain, conceited ♦ **en v.** in vain, vainly II. m. ARCHIT. window, opening.

va·por m. *(gas)* steam; *(vaho)* vapor; *(vértigo)* vertigo, dizziness; *(desmayo)* faintness; *(buque)* steamer, steamship ♦ **al v.** COLL. *(rápidamente)* swiftly, rapidly; CUL. steamed • **v. de ruedas** paddle steamer • **vapores** MED. hysterics.

va·po·ra·ble adj. vaporizable, volatile.

va·po·rar or **va·po·re·ar** tr. to evaporate.

va·po·ri·za·ción f. vaporization.

va·po·ri·za·dor m. vaporizer.

va·po·ri·zar §04 tr. to vaporize.

va·po·ro·so, –sa adj. *(que despide vapores)* vaporous; FIG. *(estilo)* airy, ethereal; *(tejido)* sheer, diaphanous.

va·pu·le·a·mien·to m. beating, thrashing.

va·pu·le·ar tr. to beat, thrash.

va·pu·le·o m. beating, thrashing.

va·qué, vaque see **vacar**.

va·que·ar intr. ARG. to cover cows (said of bulls).

va·que·rí·a f. *(vacada)* herd of cows; *(establo)* cowshed, barn; *(lechería)* dairy; VEN. cattle-roping.

va·que·ri·zo, –za I. adj. pertaining to cattle II. m.f. cowhand, cowherd —f. winter stable for cattle.

va·que·ro, –ra I. adj. pertaining to cowhands ♦ **pantalón v.** jeans II. m.f. cowhand, cowboy —m. VEN. whip.

va·que·ta f. cowhide, leather.

va·ra f. *(palo)* stick, pole; *(rama)* switch, rod; *(bastón)* staff, cane, wand; BOT. stalk, spike; *(alcándara)* thill,

shaft; *(medida)* linear measurement (.84 meters); MUS. slide (of a trombone); TAUR. *(pica)* pike, lance; *(garrochazo)* thrust with a pike ♦ **v. alta** *(poder)* upper hand, power; *(influencia)* influence **v. de San José** BOT. spikenard, goldenrod.

va·ra·da¹ f. MARIT. beaching, running aground.

va·ra·da² f. SP., AGR. farm labor crew; MIN. *(trabajo)* three months' work; *(pago)* three months' wages.

va·ra·de·ro m. MARIT. shipyard, dry dock.

va·ra·du·ra f. MARIT. beaching, running aground.

va·ral m. *(vara)* long pole; *(del carro)* shaft, thill (of a cart); FIG., COLL. *(persona alta)* beanpole (tall, lanky person).

va·ra·pa·lo m. *(palo)* long thick pole; *(golpe)* blow with a pole; FIG., COLL. *(daño)* blow, setback.

va·rar tr. MARIT. *(botar)* to launch; *(poner en seco)* to beach —intr. MARIT. to run aground; FIG. *(un negocio)* to stall, come to a standstill —reflex. COL., PERU, MARIT. to run aground.

va·ra·se·to m. trellis.

va·ra·zo m. *(golpe)* blow with a stick; TAUR. thrust with a lance.

va·re·a·dor, –do·ra m.f. *(de árboles)* beater (who knocks fruit from trees); *(del ganado)* cowhand, cowherd (who rounds up cattle).

va·re·a·je m. *(de frutos)* knocking down (fruit from trees); TEX. selling by the yard.

va·re·ar tr. *(derribar)* to knock down (fruit from trees); *(dar golpes)* to cudgel, club; *(picar)* to goad (cattle); TEX. to measure or sell by the yard; TAUR. to jab with the lance —reflex. to get thin.

va·re·jón m. *(vara gruesa)* thick pole; AMER. thin pole.

va·re·o m. knocking down (fruit).

va·re·ta f. *(vara pequeña)* small stick; *(para cazar pájaros)* lime-coated twig (for catching birds); *(lista)* stripe (in a fabric); FIG., COLL. *(expresión picante)* cutting remark; *(indirecta)* hint, insinuation ♦ **irse de v.** FIG., COLL. to have diarrhea.

va·re·te·ar tr. to stripe (a fabric).

va·ria·bi·li·dad f. variability.

va·ria·ble I. adj. variable, changeable II. f. MATH. variable.

va·ria·ción f. variation, change ♦ **v. de la aguja** or **magnética** magnetic variation.

va·ria·do, –da I. past part. see **variar** II. adj. varied, diverse.

va·ria·men·te adv. variously, differently.

va·rian·te I. adj. varying, differing II. f. variant, version.

va·riar §30 tr. & intr. to vary, change.

va·ri·ce f. MED. varix, varicose vein.

va·ri·ce·la f. MED. varicella, chicken pox.

va·ri·co·so, –sa MED. I. adj. varicose II. m.f. person suffering from varicose veins.

va·rie·dad f. variety, diversity ♦ **variedades** *(cosas diversas)* miscellany; THEAT. variety show.

va·ri·lla f. *(vara delgada)* rod, wand; *(de un paraguas)* rib (of an umbrella); *(de corsé)* stay, rib; ANAT., COLL. jawbone; *(barra de metal)* metal rod; MEX. peddler's wares; VEN. *(molestia)* nuisance, bother; *(carrera)* trial horse race, heat ♦ **v. de bombeo** pump rod • **v. de pistón** piston rod • **v. de virtudes** or **v. mágica** magic wand • **v. de zahorí** divining rod • **varillas** *(de un cedazo)* frame (of a strainer); COL., MED. tetanus, lockjaw.

va·ri·lla·je m. ribs, ribbing.

va·rio, –ria I. adj. *(que varía)* varied; *(cambiadizo)* varying, changeable ♦ **varios** *(distintos)* various, different; *(unos cuantos)* several II. m.f. ♦ **varios** several, some <*varios piensan que sí* several (people) think so>.

va·rón m. *(hombre)* man, (adult) male; *(niño)* boy, male (child) <*tienen dos hijas y un v.* they have two girls and one boy>; MARIT. rudder tackle ♦ **buen v.** wise man • **santo v.** COLL. plain simple man • **v. de Dios** God-fearing man • **v. del timón** MARIT. rudder pendant.

va·ro·nil adj. *(masculino)* manly, virile; *(relativo a una mujer)* mannish.

va·rra·co m. ZOOL. male hog or boar.

va·rra·que·ar intr. COLL. *(un animal)* to grunt; *(un niño)* to cry, shriek.

Var·so·via f. Warsaw.

var·so·via·no, –na I. adj. of Warsaw II. m.f. native of Warsaw.

va·sa·lla·je m. (servidumbre) vassalage, servitude; FIG. (rendimiento) liege money.

va·sa·llo, –lla I. adj. subordinate, dependent II. m.f. HIST. vassal; (súbdito) subject (of a state).

vas·co, –ca adj. & m.f. Basque —m. (idioma) Basque.

vas·con·ga·do, –da adj. & m.f. Basque.

vas·cuen·ce m. Basque (language).

vas·cu·lar adj. ANAT., BOT. vascular.

va·sec·to·mí·a f. MED. vasectomy.

va·se·li·na f. Vaseline (trademark).

va·si·ja f. vessel, container.

va·so m. (copa) glass <un v. de agua a glass of water>; (contenido) glass, glassful; (jarrón) vase, urn; ZOOL. hoof; BOT. vessel; ANAT. vessel <v. sanguíneo blood vessel>; (bacín) chamber pot; (embarcación) vessel.

vás·ta·go m. BOT. shoot, scion; FIG. (hijo) offspring, scion; MECH. rod, stem; C. RICA, VEN., BOT. banana stalk ♦ **v. del émbolo** MECH. piston rod • **v. de válvula** or **de distribución** valve rod or stem.

vas·te·dad f. vastness.

vas·to, –ta adj. vast, immense.

va·ti·ca·no, –na I. adj. Vatican, of the Vatican II. m. Vatican.

Vaticano, Estado de la Ciudad m. Vatican City State.

va·ti·ci·na·dor, –do·ra I. adj. prophesying II. m.f. prophet.

va·ti·ci·nar tr. to predict, prophesy.

va·ti·ci·nio m. prediction, prophecy.

va·tí·me·tro m. ELEC. wattmeter.

va·tio m. ELEC. watt.

va·tio-ho·ra m. ELEC. watt-hour.

va·ya f. COLL. mockery, banter <dar v. a to make fun of>.

va·ya see ir.

ve f. vee (letter).

ve see ir or ver².

ve·a, veo see ver².

ve·ce·ro, –ra I. adj. (que ejerce un cargo por vez) alternating, taking turns; BOT. biennial II. m.f. (cliente) customer (in a store); (persona que aguarda turno) person awaiting a turn.

ve·ci·nal adj. local.

ve·cin·dad f. (calidad de vecino) nearness, closeness; (vecindario) neighbors; (cercanías) neighborhood, vicinity ♦ **casa de v.** apartment building.

ve·cin·da·rio m. (habitantes) population, inhabitants; (los vecinos) neighbors, neighborhood <lo oyó todo el v. the whole neighborhood heard it>.

ve·ci·no, –na I. adj. (próximo) neighboring, next <mis padres viven en el pueblo v. my parents live in the next town>; FIG. (semejante) similar ♦ **v. a** or **de** near, close to II. m.f. (próximo) neighbor; (residente) resident, inhabitant ♦ **cualquier hijo de v.** anybody, everybody.

vec·tor adj. & m. MATH. vector.

ve·da f. LAW (prohibición) prohibition; HUNT. closed season.

ve·da·do I. adj. forbidden, prohibited II. m. HUNT. game preserve.

ve·dar tr. (prohibir) to prohibit, forbid; (impedir) to prevent, hinder.

ve·di·ja f. (de lana) tuft (of wool); (de pelo) matted lock (of hair); (de humo) spiral (of smoke).

ve·di·jo·so, –sa or **ve·di·ju·do, –da** adj. having matted wool or hair.

ve·e·dor, –do·ra I. adj. prying, curious II. m.f. (entremetido) busybody —m. (inspector) inspector, supervisor.

ve·e·du·rí·a f. (cargo) inspectorship, supervisorship; (oficina) inspector's or supervisor's office.

ve·ga f. (tierra baja y fértil) fertile lowland; CUBA tobacco plantation; CHILE swampy or marshy terrain.

ve·ge·ta·ción f. BOT., MED. vegetation.

ve·ge·tal I. adj. plant, vegetable <reino v. plant kingdom> II. m. plant, vegetable.

ve·ge·tan·te adj. vegetating.

ve·ge·tar intr. to vegetate.

ve·ge·ta·ria·no, –na adj. & m.f. vegetarian.

ve·ge·ta·ti·vo, –va adj. vegetative.

ve·gue·ro, –ra I. adj. lowland, of the plains II. m. (labra-

dor) farmworker; (cigarro) cigar made from a single tobacco leaf.

ve·he·men·cia f. vehemence, passion.

ve·he·men·te adj. vehement, passionate.

ve·hí·cu·lo m. (transporte) vehicle; MED. carrier (of germs).

ve·í·a see ver.

vein·ta·vo, –va adj. & m. twentieth.

vein·te I. adj. twenty <hay v. estudiantes en la clase there are twenty students in the class>; (vigésimo) twentieth ♦ **a las v.** FIG. inopportunely II. m. (número) twenty; CHILE, MEX. twenty-cent piece.

vein·te·na f. twenty, score.

vein·te·ñal adj. twenty-year-long.

vein·ti·cin·co I. adj. twenty-five <v. lápices twenty-five pencils>; (vigésimo quinto) twenty-fifth II. m. twenty-five.

vein·ti·cua·tro I. adj. twenty-four <v. kilómetros twenty-four kilometers>; (vigésimo cuarto) twenty-fourth II. m. twenty-four.

vein·ti·dós I. adj. twenty-two <v. hombres twenty-two men>; (vigésimo segundo) twenty-second II. m. twenty-two.

vein·ti·nue·ve I. adj. twenty-nine <v. mujeres twenty-nine women>; (vigésimo noveno) twenty-ninth II. m. twenty-nine.

vein·tio·cho I. adj. twenty-eight <v. agentes de policía twenty-eight policemen>; (vigésimo octavo) twenty-eighth II. m. twenty-eight.

vein·ti·séis I. adj. twenty-six <v. versos twenty-six verses>; (vigésimo sexto) twenty-sixth II. m. twenty-six.

vein·ti·sie·te I. adj. twenty-seven <v. variedades de té twenty-seven varieties of tea>; (vigésimo séptimo) twenty-seventh II. m. twenty-seven.

vein·ti·tan·tos, –tas adj. (cantidad) about twenty, twenty or so; (del mes) around the twentieth (of the month).

vein·ti·trés I. adj. twenty-three <v. aves twenty-three birds>; (vigésimo tercero) twenty-third II. m. twenty-three.

vein·ti·ún adj. [contr. of veintiuno used before m. nouns] <veintiún hombres twenty-one men> —see veintiuno, –na.

vein·tiu·no, –na I. adj. twenty-one <v. cartas twenty-one letters>; (vigésimo primero) twenty-first II. m. (número) twenty-one —f. (juego) twenty-one (card game).

ve·ja·ción f. (molestia) vexation, annoyance; (insulto) insult, affront.

ve·ja·dor, –do·ra I. adj. (molestador) vexing, annoying; (insultador) insulting II. m.f. (molestador) vexer, annoyer; (insultador) insulter.

ve·ja·men m. (molestia) vexation, annoyance; (insulto) insult, affront; (represión satírica) ridicule, derision.

ve·jan·cón, –co·na COLL. I. adj. very old II. m. old man —f. old woman.

ve·jar tr. to vex, annoy.

ve·ja·to·rio, –ria adj. insulting, humiliating.

ve·jes·to·rio m. DEROG. (persona) old fool; (cosa) old wreck.

ve·je·te COLL. I. adj. old II. m. old man.

ve·jez f. (ancianidad) old age; FIG. (impertinencia) peevishness; (cosa sabida) platitude, trite saying.

ve·ji·ga f. ANAT. bladder; (en la piel) blister ♦ **v. de la bilis** or **de la hiel** ANAT. gall bladder • **v. de perro** BOT. winter cherry • **v. natatoria** ICHTH. swim bladder.

ve·la¹ f. (vigilia) vigil, watch; (trabajo) night shift; (falta de sueño) sleeplessness; (centinela) night watchman, night sentry; (luz) candle <v. de cera wax candle>; MEX. reprimand; C. RICA wake, funeral ♦ **en v.** awake • **estar a dos velas** FIG. to be broke • **no darle a alguien v. en un entierro** FIG. not to give someone a say in the matter • **velas** COLL. snot.

ve·la² f. MARIT. sail; FIG. (barco) sail, boat ♦ **a toda v.** MARIT. under full sail • **barco de v.** sailboat • **buque de v.** sailing ship • **dar, hacer** or **hacerse a la v.** to set sail • **entre dos velas** COLL. three sheets to the wind, drunk • **v. al tercio** MARIT. lugsail • **v. de abanico** MARIT. spritsail • **v. de cruz** MARIT. square sail • **v. de cuchillo** MARIT. staysail • **v. latina** MARIT. lateen sail • **v. mayor** MARIT. mainsail.

ve·la·da I. f. (vela) vigil, watch; (reunión) evening, soirée ♦

quedarse de v. to spend the evening **II.** adj. see **velado, –da.**

ve·la·do, –da I. past part. see **velar²** **II.** adj. *(oculto)* veiled, muffled; *(una voz)* muffled, toneless (voice); *(una imagen)* blurred **II.** f. see **velada.**

ve·la·dor, –do·ra I. adj. watching, guarding **II.** m.f. *(persona que vela)* vigil-keeper —m. *(guarda)* guard, watchman; *(candelero)* candlestick; *(mesita)* pedestal table; *(guardián nocturno)* night watchman; AMER. night table; ARG., PAR., URUG. night-light; MEX. glass lampshade —f. *(lamparilla de dormitorio)* night light; MEX. short thick candle.

ve·la·me or **ve·la·men** m. MARIT. canvas, sails.

ve·lar¹ adj. PHONET. velar.

ve·lar² tr. *(vigilar)* to keep watch over; keep a vigil over; *(cuidar)* to tend, sit up with <*v. a un niño enfermo* to sit up with a sick child>; *(cubrir)* to veil, cover with a veil; FIG. *(esconder)* to veil, hide; *(observar)* to watch (over) —intr. *(no dormir)* to stay awake, stay up; *(trabajar)* to work late; RELIG. to keep vigil ♦ **v. por** FIG. to care for, look after —reflex. PHOTOG. to fade, blur (from overexposure).

ve·la·to·rio m. wake, vigil (for the dead).

ve·lei·dad f. *(deseo vano)* caprice, whim; *(inconstancia)* fickleness, capriciousness.

ve·lei·do·so, –sa adj. fickle, capricious.

ve·le·ro, –ra I. adj. MARIT. swift-sailing **II.** m.f. *(de velas para buques)* sailmaker; *(de velas de cera)* candlemaker —m. *(barco)* sailboat.

ve·le·ta f. METEOROL. weather vane, weathercock; *(de caña de pescar)* float, bob —m.f. FIG., COLL. *(persona inconstante)* weathercock, changeable person.

ve·li·llo m. TEX. embroidered gauze.

ve·lo m. *(prenda)* veil <*v. de novia* bridal veil>; *(humeral)* humeral veil; FIG. *(máscara)* veil, mask; *(pretexto)* pretext, cloak; *(confusión)* confusion ♦ **correr** or **echar un v. sobre algo** to hush something up ♦ **tomar el v.** RELIG. to take the veil, become a nun ♦ **v. del paladar** ANAT. velum, soft palate.

ve·lo·ci·dad f. *(rapidez)* velocity, speed; AUTO. gearbox ♦ **en gran v.** RAIL. by express ♦ **en pequeña v.** RAIL. by freight ♦ **exceso de v.** speeding ♦ **v. angular** angular velocity ♦ **v. de ascensión** AER. climbing speed ♦ **v. de liberación** PHYS. escape velocity ♦ **v. de traslación** MECH. traveling speed ♦ **v. límite** speed limit ♦ **v. máxima** or **tope** or **punta** top speed ♦ **v. sincrónica** ELEC. synchronous speed ♦ **v. unitaria** rate of speed.

ve·lo·cí·me·tro m. speedometer.

ve·lo·cí·pe·do m. velocipede.

ve·lo·cis·ta m.f. SPORT. sprinter.

ve·ló·dro·mo m. SPORT. velodrome, cycle track.

ve·lón m. *(lámpara de aceite)* oil lamp; AMER. thick candle.

ve·lo·ne·ra f. lamp stand.

ve·lo·rio m. *(para difuntos)* wake, vigil; RELIG. taking of the veil (by a nun); ARG. dull party; VEN. roadhouse, inn.

ve·loz adj. [pl. **-lo·ces**] swift, rapid.

ve·lu·di·llo m. TEX. velveteen.

ve·lu·do m. TEX. plush.

ve·lle·ra f. cosmetician who removes unwanted hair.

ve·lli·do, –da adj. downy.

ve·llo m. down, fuzz.

ve·llo·ci·no m. fleece.

ve·llón¹ m. *(lana del carnero)* wool, fleece; *(piel)* sheepskin; *(vedija de lana)* tuft of wool.

ve·llón² m. *(moneda)* copper coin; *(liga)* copper and silver alloy.

ve·llo·rí or **ve·llo·rín** m. TEX. undyed wool broadcloth.

ve·llo·si·dad f. downiness, hairiness.

ve·llo·so, –sa adj. downy, hairy.

ve·llu·do, –da I. adj. hairy, shaggy **II.** m. TEX. velveteen.

ven see **venir.**

ve·na f. ANAT. vein <*v. yugular* jugular vein>; BOT. vein, rib; *(de madera, piedra)* vein, streak; MIN. vein, lode; FIG. *(inspiración)* inspiration; *(impulso)* mood ♦ **darle a uno la v.** FIG. to feel like doing something crazy ♦ **estar en v.** FIG. to be in the mood ♦ **v. cava** ANAT. vena cava ♦ **v. de agua** underground water channel ♦ **v. de loco** mad streak ♦ **v. porta** ANAT. portal vein.

ve·na·blo m. javelin.

ve·na·do m. ZOOL. deer, stag; CUL. venison ♦ **pintar el v.** MEX. to play hooky.

ve·nal adj. venal, mercenary.

ve·na·li·dad f. venality.

ven·ce·de·ro, –ra adj. COM. falling due, payable.

ven·ce·dor, –do·ra I. adj. *(conquistador)* conquering; *(victorioso)* victorious, winning **II.** m.f. *(conquistador)* conqueror; *(ganador)* victor, winner.

ven·ce·jo m. *(lazo)* tie, bond; ORNITH. swift, martin.

ven·cer §75 tr. *(conquistar)* to conquer, vanquish; *(rendir)* to defeat, beat; *(aventajar)* to beat, surpass; *(superar)* to overcome, surmount <*v. un obstáculo* to overcome an obstacle>; *(ser rendido)* to be overcome <*le venció el sueño* he was overcome by sleep>; FIG. *(dominar)* to control, master <*v. las pasiones* to control one's emotions>; *(romper)* to break, snap —intr. *(ganar)* to win, triumph; COM. *(cumplirse un plazo)* to expire; *(una deuda)* to fall due, be payable —reflex. *(controlarse)* to control oneself; *(torcerse)* to bend, incline (under weight); *(romperse)* to collapse; CHILE to get worn-out.

ven·ci·ble adj. conquerable, beatable.

ven·ci·da I. f. ♦ **a la tercera va la v.** *(para exhortar a la perseverancia)* the third time is the charm; *(para amenazar)* three strikes and you're out ♦ **ir de v.** to be about to lose **II.** adj. see **vencido, –da.**

ven·ci·do, –da I. past part. see **vencer** **II.** adj. *(derrotado)* beaten, defeated; COM. *(una deuda)* due, payable; *(cumplido)* expired **III.** m.f. loser —f. see **vencida.**

ven·ci·mien·to m. *(victoria)* victory; *(derrota)* defeat; *(torcimiento)* bend, bending; *(al romperse)* collapse; COM. *(término)* expiration; *(de una deuda)* maturity.

ven·da f. SURG. bandage, dressing; *(de cabeza)* fillet, headband ♦ **tener una v. en los ojos** FIG. to be blindfolded.

ven·da·je¹ m. SURG. bandage, dressing ♦ **v. enyesado** MED. plaster cast.

ven·da·je² m. COM. sales commission; AMER. bonus, premium.

ven·dar tr. to bandage, bind (up) ♦ **v. los ojos** to blindfold.

ven·da·val m. strong wind, gale.

ven·de·de·ra f. saleswoman.

ven·de·dor, –do·ra I. adj. selling **II.** m.f. *(buhonero)* vendor; *(persona que vende)* seller; *(dependiente de tienda)* salesclerk, salesperson ♦ **v. ambulante** peddler.

ven·de·hu·mos m.f. [pl. **-mos**] COLL. influence peddler.

ven·de·ja f. public sale.

ven·der tr. *(ceder)* to sell <*v. el coche* to sell the car>; *(hacer comercio de)* to market; *(sacrificar)* to sell, sell out <*v. la honra* to sell one's honor>; FIG. *(traicionar)* to sell out, betray <*vendió a su amiga* she betrayed her friend> ♦ **v. al contado** to sell for cash ♦ **v. al por mayor** to wholesale, sell wholesale ♦ **v. al por menor** to retail, sell retail ♦ **v. a plazos** to sell on an installment plan ♦ **v. caro** to sell expensive, sell at a high price ♦ **v. la piel del oso antes de cazarlo** FIG. to count one's chickens before they are hatched —reflex. to sell, be sold <*las manzanas se venden por docena* apples are sold by the dozen>; *(dejarse sobornar)* to sell oneself; FIG. *(relevarse)* to give oneself away ♦ **venderse caro** FIG. to play hard to get ♦ **venderse como pan caliente** to sell like hot cakes ♦ **venderse por** to sell for, bring ♦ **se vende** for sale.

ven·di·ble adj. salable.

ven·di·mia f. *(cosecha)* grape harvest; *(año)* vintage; FIG. *(provecho)* profit, gain.

ven·di·mia·dor, –do·ra m.f. grape picker.

ven·di·miar tr. *(las uvas)* to gather, harvest (grapes); FIG. *(un provecho)* to reap unjustly (a profit); FIG., COLL. *(matar)* to kill.

ven·do m. TEX. selvage.

ven·drá, vendría see **venir.**

ven·du·ta f. AMER. auction; CUBA small grocery.

ven·du·te·ro, –ra m.f. AMER. auctioneer.

Ve·ne·cia f. Venice.

ve·ne·cia·no, –na adj. & m.f. Venetian.

ve·ne·no m. *(toxina)* poison, venom; FIG. *(ira)* fury, venom; *(despecho)* spite.

ve·ne·no·si·dad f. poisonousness.

ve·ne·no·so, –sa adj. poisonous, venomous.

ve·ne·ra¹ f. *(concha)* scallop shell; *(insignia)* badge *or* emblem of knighthood.

ve·ne·ra² f. spring, fountain.

ve·ne·ra·ble adj. venerable.

ve·ne·ra·ción f. veneration.

ve·ne·rar tr. to venerate, revere.

ve·né·re·o, –a MED. **I.** adj. venereal **II.** m. venereal disease.

ve·ne·ro m. *(manantial)* spring, fountain; *(de un reloj de sol)* horary line (of a sundial); FIG. *(origen)* source, origin; MIN. seam, vein ♦ **v. de datos** FIG. mine of information.

ve·ne·zo·la·no, –na adj. & m.f. Venezuelan.

Ve·ne·zue·la m. Venezuela.

ven·ga, vengo see **venir**.

ven·ga·dor, –do·ra I. adj. avenging **II.** m.f. avenger.

ven·gan·za f. vengeance, revenge.

ven·gar §47 tr. to avenge —reflex. to avenge oneself ♦ **vengarse de alguien** to take revenge on someone.

ven·ga·ti·vo, –va adj. vengeful, vindictive.

ve·nia f. *(perdón)* pardon, forgiveness; *(permiso)* permission, leave; *(saludo)* greeting, nod; AMER., MIL. salute.

ve·nial adj. venial.

ve·nia·li·dad f. veniality.

ve·nial·men·te adv. venially.

ve·ni·da f. *(llegada)* coming, arrival; *(regreso)* return; *(de un río)* flood; SPORT. attack (in fencing); FIG. *(impetu)* impetuousness, rashness ♦ **idas y venidas** comings and goings.

ve·ni·de·ro, –ra I. adj. coming, future **II.** m.pl. **venideros** heirs, posterity.

ve·nir §76 §G9 intr. to come *<¿vendrás a la fiesta?* will you come to the party?>; *(llegar)* to arrive, come *<vinieron a las seis* they arrived at six o'clock>; *(acercarse)* to come *<ya viene la primavera* spring is coming>; *(ajustarse)* to fit *<esta chaqueta ya no me viene* this jacket no longer fits me>; *(acomodarse)* to suit *<este sombrero me viene mal* this hat does not suit me>; *(tener)* to get *<me vino un dolor de cabeza* I got a headache>; *(proceder)* to come, stem *<esta palabra viene del griego* this word comes from the Greek>; *(inferirse)* to follow *<esta conclusión viene de tal postura* this conclusion follows from such a posture>; *(heredarse)* to come, be inherited *<le vendrá una gran fortuna de su padre* a fortune will come to him from his father>; *(presentarse)* to come, occur *<la idea me vino inesperadamente* the idea occurred to me unexpectedly>; *(producirse)* to grow *<el trigo viene bien en esta región* wheat grows well in this region>; *(suceder)* to end up *<vino a morir* he ended up dying>; *(resultar)* to end up *<viene a ser lo mismo* it ends up being all the same>; to have been *<vengo diciéndolo desde hace cinco meses* I have been saying so for five months> ♦ **en lo por v.** hereafter, in the future • **que viene** next, the coming *<el año que viene* next year> • **v. a la memoria** to come to mind • **v. al caso** to be relevant *or* to the point • **v. al mundo** to come into the world • **v. al pelo** to come in the nick of time • **v. a menos** to come down in the world • **v. en** to decide, resolve • **venga lo que venga** come what may • **venirle ancho a uno** to be too big for one • **ver v.** to see it coming —reflex. to ferment, mature; VULG. to come (sexually) ♦ **venirse abajo** *or* **por tierra** *or* **al suelo** to collapse, fall down.

ve·no·so, –sa adj. venous.

ven·ta f. *(acción de vender)* selling, sale; *(posada)* country inn; CHILE refreshment stand ♦ **servicio de v.** sales department • **v. al contado** cash sale • **v. a crédito** credit sale • **v. al por mayor** wholesale • **v. al por menor** retail • **v. pública** public sale, auction.

ven·ta·da f. blast, gust (of wind).

ven·ta·ja f. *(superioridad)* advantage *<mi hermano tiene la v. de ser alto* my brother has the advantage of being tall>; *(prestación)* benefit *<ventajas sociales* social benefits>; *(en una carrera)* head start, lead; *(provecho)* benefit, profit ♦ **llevar v. a** to be ahead of, have the lead over • **sacar v. a** to be ahead of • **sacar v. de** to take advantage of, profit from.

ven·ta·jo·so, –sa adj. advantageous, profitable.

ven·ta·na f. *(abertura en la pared)* window; *(cerrador)* shut-

ter; ANAT. nostril ♦ **echar** *or* **tirar por la v.** to throw out the window, squander.

ven·ta·na·je m. windows.

ven·ta·nal m. large window.

ven·ta·na·zo m. slamming of a window.

ven·ta·ne·ar intr. COLL. to spend time at the window.

ven·ta·ne·ro, –ra I. adj. fond of flirting through the window **II.** m.f. *(persona que ventanea)* person who flirts through the window —m. *(fabricante)* window maker, glazier.

ven·ta·ni·lla f. *(de un vehículo)* window; *(portilla)* porthole; *(taquilla)* ticket window, box office; ANAT. nostril.

ven·ta·ni·llo m. *(ventana pequeña)* small window; *(mirilla)* peephole; MARIT. porthole.

ven·ta·rrón m. COLL. gale, strong wind.

ven·te·ar intr. to blow (said of the wind) —tr. *(olfatear)* to smell, sniff; *(airear)* to air out; FIG. *(buscar)* to snoop around, pry into —reflex. *(henderse)* to split, crack; ARG., CHILE to go out a lot; *(ventosear)* to break wind.

ven·te·ro, –ra m.f. innkeeper.

ven·ti·la·ción f. ventilation.

ven·ti·la·dor m. fan.

ven·ti·lar tr. *(un lugar)* to ventilate, air out; FIG. *(discutir)* to air, discuss; *(hacer público)* to air, make public —reflex. COLL. to get some fresh air ♦ **ventilárselas** COLL. to take care of oneself.

ven·tis·ca f. blizzard, snowstorm.

ven·tis·car §70 intr. to snow heavily.

ven·tis·co m. blizzard, snowstorm.

ven·tis·co·so, –sa adj. having frequent snowstorms.

ven·tis·que·ar intr. to snow heavily.

ven·tis·que·ro m. *(ventisca)* blizzard, snowstorm; *(altura de un monte)* snowcap; *(helero)* glacier; *(nieve acumulada)* snowdrift.

ven·to·le·ra f. *(golpe de viento)* blast *or* gust of wind; *(molinera)* pinwheel; FIG., COLL. *(vanidad)* vanity, pride; *(pensamiento extravagante)* whim, fancy ♦ **darle a uno la v. de hacer algo** FIG., COLL. to take it into one's head to do something.

ven·to·li·na f. MARIT. light wind, cat's-paw.

ven·to·rri·llo m. *(ventorro)* small inn; *(merendero)* roadhouse; P. RICO neighborhood shop.

ven·to·rro m. DEROG. cheap tavern, dive.

ven·to·sa I. f. MED. cupping glass; ZOOL. sucker; *(abertura)* vent, air hole **II.** adj. see **ventoso, –sa.**

ven·to·se·ar intr. to break wind.

ven·to·si·dad f. MED. gas, flatulence.

ven·to·so, –sa I. adj. windy *<un día v.* a windy day>; *(flatulento)* flatulent, gassy **II.** f. see **ventosa.**

ven·tre·ga·da f. *(camada)* litter, brood; FIG. *(abundancia)* stream, flood (of things at one time).

ven·tre·ra f. *(faja)* bellyband; *(armadura)* stomach plate (of armor); *(del caballo)* cinch.

ven·tri·cu·lar adj. ANAT. ventricular.

ven·trí·cu·lo m. ANAT. ventricle.

ven·trí·lo·cuo, –cua I. adj. ventriloquial, ventriloquistic **II.** m.f. ventriloquist.

ven·tri·lo·quia f. ventriloquism.

ven·tro·so, –sa *or* **ven·tru·do, –da** adj. paunchy.

ven·tu·ra f. *(felicidad)* happiness; *(suerte)* luck, good fortune; *(casualidad)* chance, luck; *(peligro)* danger, risk ♦ **a la v.** *or* **a la buena v.** at random, with no set plan • **decir la buena v. a alguien** to tell someone's fortune • **por v.** as luck would have it • **probar v.** to try one's luck.

ven·tu·ra·do, –da adj. lucky, fortunate.

ven·tu·ran·za f. luck, fortune.

ven·tu·re·ro, –ra I. adj. *(ocioso)* lazy, idle; *(aventurero)* adventurous; *(venturoso)* lucky, fortunate **II.** m.f. adventurer.

ven·tu·ro, –ra adj. future.

ven·tu·ro·so, –sa adj. *(afortunado)* lucky, fortunate; *(exitoso)* successful.

Ve·nus f. ASTRON., MYTH. Venus.

ven·za, venzo see **vencer**.

ver¹ m. *(visión)* vision, sight; *(apariencia)* looks, appearance; *(opinión)* opinion, view *<a mi v.* in my opinion> ♦ **de buen v.** good-looking.

ver² §77 tr. *(percibir)* to see *<¿lo ves en el horizonte?* do you see it on the horizon?>; *(mirar)* to look at, watch <*v. la televisión* to watch television>; *(visitar)* to see, visit <*fui a v. a mi abuela* I went to see my grandmother>; *(averiguar)* to look and see, find out <*vea usted si está Pedro* look and see if Peter is here>; *(examinar)* to examine, look into <*veamos este párrafo* let's examine this paragraph>; *(observar)* to observe, look at; *(comprender)* to see, understand <*ahora veo* now I see>; *(prevenir)* to see, foresee <*veo que va a llover* I see that it is going to rain>; *(conocer)* to know, see <*veo la verdad* I know the truth>; LAW to try, hear (a case) ♦ **a más v.** *or* **hasta más v.** so long ♦ **a v.** let's see, let's have a look ♦ **estar** *or* **quedar en veremos** AMER. to be a long way off, be undecided ♦ **estar por v.** to remain to be seen ♦ **tener que v. con** to have to do with, concern ♦ **veremos** we'll see ♦ **v. venir** to see it coming —reflex. *(ser visto)* to be seen; *(ser obvio)* to be obvious *or* clear; *(mirarse)* to see oneself <*verse en el espejo* to see oneself in the mirror>; *(hallarse)* to find oneself, be <*me veo pobre y sin amigos* I find myself poor and without friends>; *(visitarse)* to see one another; *(encontrarse)* to meet <*verse con los amigos* to meet with friends> ♦ **véase** see (in references) ♦ **vérselas con** COLL. to have to deal with (someone) ♦ **vérselas negras** COLL. to be in a jam ♦ **ya se ve** of course, certainly.

ve·ra f. edge, side ♦ **a la v. de** beside, next to.

ve·ra·ci·dad f. veracity, truthfulness.

ve·ra·na·da f. *(verano)* summer season; ARG. summer pastures.

ve·ra·na·de·ro m. summer pasture.

ve·ra·ne·an·te m.f. summer resident.

ve·ra·ne·ar intr. to summer, spend the summer.

ve·ra·ne·o m. summering, vacationing ♦ **ir de v.** to go on vacation ♦ **lugar de v.** summer resort.

ve·ra·ne·ro, –ra I. m. summer pasture II. adj. summery.

ve·ra·nie·go, –ga adj. *(perteneciente al verano)* summer, summery; FIG. *(ligero)* light, flimsy.

ve·ra·ni·llo m. Indian summer.

ve·ra·no m. summer.

ve·ras f.pl. *(verdad)* truth; *(seriedad)* seriousness, earnestness ♦ **de v.** really, truly.

ve·raz adj. [pl. **-ra·ces**] veracious, truthful.

ver·ba f. loquaciousness, talkativeness.

ver·bal adj. verbal.

ver·bal·men·te adv. verbally.

ver·be·na f. BOT. verbena, vervain; *(fiesta)* festival held on the eve of a saint's day.

ver·bi·gra·cia *or* **ver·bi gra·tia** adv. for example, for instance.

ver·bo m. GRAM. verb; *(voto)* oath, vow ♦ **v. activo** active verb ♦ **v. auxiliar** auxiliary verb ♦ **v. defectivo** defective verb ♦ **v. intransitivo** intransitive verb ♦ **v. neutro** neutral verb ♦ **v. pasivo** passive verb ♦ **v. reflexivo** *or* **reflejo** reflexive verb ♦ **v. transitivo** transitive verb.

ver·bo·rre·a f. COLL. verbosity, wordiness, verbiage.

ver·bo·si·dad f. verbosity, wordiness.

ver·bo·so, –sa adj. verbose, wordy.

ver·dad f. truth <*decir la v.* to tell the truth>; *(veracidad)* veracity, truthfulness ♦ **a decir v.** *or* **a la v.** to tell the truth, to be honest ♦ **bien es v.** *or* **v. es que** it is the truth that ♦ **de v.** *(de veras)* truly, really; *(verdadero)* real <*él es un héroe de v.* he is a real hero> ♦ **¿de v.?** really? ♦ **decirle a alguien cuatro verdades** FIG. to tell it like it is, tell someone a few home truths ♦ **en v.** truly, really ♦ **faltar a la v.** to lie ♦ **la pura v.** the plain truth ♦ **¿no es v.?** isn't that so? ♦ **¿verdad?** is that so? ♦ **v. de Perogrullo** COLL. platitude, truism.

ver·da·de·ro, –ra adj. *(real)* true, real; *(auténtico)* true, genuine; *(veraz)* truthful.

ver·de I. adj. green <*la hierba es v.* grass is green>; *(fresco)* fresh, green <*legumbres verdes* green vegetables>; unseasoned <*leña v.* unseasoned wood>; *(inmaduro)* green, unripe; *(obsceno)* risqué, dirty; *(libertino)* rakish, dirty <*un viejo v.* a dirty old man>; *(incipiente)* incipient, young ♦ **poner v. a uno** to tell someone off ♦ **v. de envidia** green with envy II. m. *(color)* green; *(verdor)* verdure, greenness; *(hierba)* grass; *(follaje)* foliage; *(alcacer)* fresh fodder; *(sabor áspero)* harsh taste (of wine); COL., ECUAD. green banana; ARG., URUG. *(mate)* maté; *(pasto)* pas-

ture; P. RICO countryside ♦ **v. de montaña** MIN. malachite ♦ **v. esmeralda** emerald green ♦ **v. mar** sea green ♦ **v. oliva** olive green.

ver·de·ar intr. *(parecer verde)* to look green; *(las plantas)* to turn green.

ver·de·cer §17 *or* **ver·de·gue·ar** intr. to turn *or* grow green.

ver·de·mar I. adj. sea-green II. m. sea green.

ver·de·te m. CHEM. verdigris.

ver·dín m. *(de las plantas)* verde, fresh green; *(moho)* mold, mildew; *(musgo)* moss; CHEM. verdigris.

ver·di·ne·gro, –gra adj. dark green.

ver·di·no, –na adj. bright green.

ver·di·se·co, –ca adj. half-dried.

ver·dor m. *(color)* greenness, verdancy; FIG. *(fuerza)* strength, vigor (of youth).

ver·do·so, –sa adj. greenish.

ver·du·ga·do m. hoop skirt.

ver·du·gal m. hillside covered with saplings.

ver·du·ga·zo m. blow, lash.

ver·du·go m. BOT. twig, shoot; *(estoque)* rapier; *(azote)* whip, lash; *(verdugón)* welt, bruise; *(ejecutor de la justicia)* executioner; FIG., COLL. *(tormento)* torment, scourge; ORNITH. butcherbird, shrike; ARCHIT. layer of bricks.

ver·du·gón m. *(roncha)* welt, bruise; BOT. shoot, sprout.

ver·du·le·ra f. *(vendedora)* grocer; FIG., COLL. *(rabanera)* fishwife.

ver·du·le·rí·a f. *(tienda)* grocery store; COLL. *(obscenidad)* obscenity.

ver·du·le·ro, –ra m.f. *(vendedor de verduras)* greengrocer —f. FIG., COLL. *(mujer grosera)* fishwife.

ver·du·ra f. *(verdor)* greenness; *(legumbre)* vegetable; *(follaje)* foliage, greenery; *(obscenidad)* obscenity.

ver·dus·co, –ca adj. dark greenish.

ve·re·da f. *(senda)* path, trail; AMER. sidewalk; COL. rural district ♦ **entrar en v.** to fall in line, get in step.

ve·re·dic·to m. LAW verdict.

ver·ga f. ANAT. penis; *(de la ballesta)* steel bow (of a crossbow); MARIT. yard.

ver·ga·jo m. pizzle.

ver·gel m. POET. orchard.

ver·gon·zan·te adj. bashful, shamefaced.

ver·gon·zo·sa·men·te adv. *(ignominiosamente)* shamefully, disgracefully; *(tímidamente)* timidly, bashfully.

ver·gon·zo·so, –sa I. adj. *(ignominioso)* shameful, disgraceful; *(tímido)* shy, bashful II. m.f. *(persona)* shy *or* bashful person —m. ZOOL. armadillo.

ver·güen·za f. *(bochorno)* shame; *(desconcierto)* embarrassment; *(timidez)* shyness, timidity; *(modestia)* modesty; *(oprobio)* disgrace, shame <*él es la v. de su familia* he is the disgrace of his family>; *(honor)* integrity, honor; *(castigo)* public punishment ♦ **darle a uno v.** to be ashamed <*me da v. decírtelo* I am ashamed to tell you> ♦ **no tener v.** to be shameless ♦ **perder la v.** to lose all sense of shame ♦ **¡que v.!** what a disgrace! ♦ **sacar al alguien a la v. pública** to make a public example of someone ♦ **sin v.** shameless ♦ **tener v.** to be ashamed ♦ **vergüenzas** ANAT. private parts.

ve·ri·cue·to m. rugged path.

ve·rí·di·co, –ca adj. *(que dice verdad)* honest, truthful; *(auténtico)* true.

ve·ri·fi·ca·ción f. verification.

ve·ri·fi·ca·dor, –do·ra I. adj. checking, verifying II. m.f. checker, inspector.

ve·ri·fi·car §70 tr. *(la verdad)* to verify, confirm; *(una máquina)* to check, test; *(realizar)* to perform, carry out —reflex. *(tener lugar)* to take place; *(una predicción)* to come true.

ve·ri·fi·ca·ti·vo, –va adj. verificative.

ve·ri·ja f. ANAT. pubes, pubic region; AMER. horse's flanks.

ve·ri·sí·mil adj. var. of **verosímil**.

ve·ris·mo m. ARTS verism, realism.

ver·ja f. *(de una cerca)* railings, rails; *(de una ventana)* grating, grille.

ver·me m. MED. intestinal worm.

ver·mi·ci·da MED. I. adj. vermicidal II. m. vermicide.

ver·mí·fu·go, –ga MED. I. adj. vermifugal, anthelmintic II. m. vermifuge, anthelmintic.

ver·mut *or* **ver·mú** m. *(aperitivo)* vermouth; AMER., CINEM., THEAT. matinée.

ver·ná·cu·lo, –la adj. vernacular.

ver·nal adj. vernal, spring.

ve·ró·ni·ca f. BOT. veronica, speedwell; TAUR. veronica (pass with the cape).

ve·ro·sí·mil adj. probable, likely.

ve·ro·si·mi·li·tud f. probability, likelihood.

ve·rra·co m. ZOOL. (cerdo) male pig, hog; CUBA boar.

ve·rra·que·ar intr. COLL. (gruñir) to grunt; FIG., COLL. (llorar) to shriek, howl.

ve·rra·que·ra f. COLL. (rabieta) crying fit, tantrum; CUBA drunkenness.

ve·rrion·dez f. (de animales) heat, rutting; (de legumbres) witheredness.

ve·rrion·do, –da adj. (animales) in heat, rutting; (legumbres) withered.

ve·rrón m. ZOOL. male pig, hog.

ve·rru·ga f. MED. wart; FIG., COLL. (pesadez) pain in the neck; COLL. (vicio) fault, defect.

ve·rru·go m. COLL. miser, skinflint.

ve·rru·go·so, –sa adj. warty.

ver·sa·do, –da I. past part. see **versar** II. adj. versed, proficient.

ver·sal adj. & f. PRINT. capital.

ver·sa·li·lla or **ver·sa·li·ta** adj. & f. PRINT. small capital.

ver·sar intr. (dar vueltas) to turn or go around; CUBA to versify ♦ **v. sobre** to deal with, be about.

ver·sá·til adj. BOT., ZOOL. versatile; FIG. (cambiante) fickle, changeable.

ver·sa·ti·li·dad f. fickleness, instability.

ver·se·rí·a f. COLL. verses, poems.

ver·si·cu·la·rio m. (de versículos) chanter of versicles; (de los libros de coro) keeper of hymnbooks.

ver·sí·cu·lo m. RELIG. versicle.

ver·si·fi·ca·ción f. versification.

ver·si·fi·ca·dor, –do·ra I. adj. versifying II. m.f. versifier.

ver·si·fi·car §70 intr. & tr. to versify.

ver·sión f. version.

ver·sis·ta m.f. versifier.

ver·so¹ m. (poesía) verse, poetry <*teatro en v.* theater in verse>; (línea) verse, line; (versículo) versicle, verse ♦ **echar versos** MEX. to gab • **v. blanco, suelto** or **libre** free verse, blank verse.

ver·so² m. PRINT. verso.

vér·te·bra f. ANAT. vertebra.

ver·te·bra·do, –da adj. & m. ZOOL. vertebrate.

ver·te·bral adj. vertebral.

ver·te·de·ro m. (desaguadero) drain; (de basura) garbage dump.

ver·te·dor, –do·ra I. adj. emptying, pouring II. m.f. (persona) emptier, pourer —m. (canal) drain; MARIT. bailer; (en una tienda) grocer's scoop.

ver·ter §50 tr. (derramar) to pour, spill; (lágrimas, sangre) to shed; (vaciar) to empty out; (volcar) to turn upside down; (traducir) to translate —intr. to flow.

ver·ti·cal I. adj. vertical, upright II. f. MATH. vertical —m. ASTRON. vertical circle.

ver·ti·ca·li·dad f. verticality.

vér·ti·ce m. ANAT., GEOM. vertex, apex.

ver·tien·te I. adj. flowing II. f. or m. (declive) slope —f. CHILE spring, fountain.

ver·ti·gi·no·si·dad f. vertiginousness.

ver·ti·gi·no·so, –sa adj. vertiginous.

vér·ti·go m. (mareo) vertigo, dizziness; FIG. (locura) temporary madness; (arrebato) rush, frenzy ♦ **tener v.** to feel dizzy.

ver·ti·mien·to m. pouring, emptying.

ve·si·can·te adj. & m. MED. vesicant.

ve·sí·cu·la f. ANAT., BOT., MED. vesicle ♦ **v. biliar** ANAT. gall bladder.

ve·si·cu·lar adj. vesicular.

ves·pe·ral adj. & m. vesperal.

vés·pe·ro m. ASTRON. Vesper, evening star.

ves·per·ti·no, –na I. adj. vespertine II. m. afternoon sermon.

ves·tal adj. & f. vestal.

ves·tí·bu·lo m. (antesala) vestibule, hall; (en un hotel, teatro) lobby, foyer.

ves·ti·do I. past part. see **vestir** II. adj. dressed, clad <*v. de*

negro dressed in black> III. m. (ropa) dress, clothing; (traje) dress; (de hombre) suit ♦ **v. de noche** evening gown.

ves·ti·du·ra f. (prenda de vestir) garment; (ropa) clothes, clothing ♦ **vestiduras** RELIG. vestments.

ves·ti·gio m. vestige, trace.

ves·ti·men·ta f. clothes, garments.

ves·tir §48 tr. (ataviar) to dress, clothe <*vistieron a la novia* they dressed the bride>; (llevar) to wear <*ella vestía un traje rosado* she was wearing a pink suit>; (cubrir) to cover <*v. una puerta de acero* to cover a door with steel>; (proveer con ropa) to clothe <*v. a los pobres* to clothe the poor>; (hacer vestido para) to dress, make clothes for <*este sastre viste a mis hermanos* this tailor dresses my brothers>; FIG. (adornar) to dress up, embellish <*vistió su petición de bellas palabras* he dressed up his request with pretty words>; (disimular) to disguise, cloak ♦ **quedarse para v. santos** FIG., COLL. to be an old maid —intr. (ir vestido) to dress <*ellos visten bien* they dress well>; (lucir) to look good <*la seda viste mucho* silk looks very good> ♦ **v. de** <*él viste de uniforme* he wears a uniform> —reflex. (ataviarse) to dress oneself, get dressed; (ir vestido) to dress <*vestirse a la moda* to dress fashionably>; (cubrirse) to be covered <*el campo se viste de flores* the field is covered with flowers>; FIG. (aparentar) to adopt an attitude <*ella se vistió de importancia* she adopted an attitude of self-importance>.

ves·tua·rio m. (vestido) wardrobe, clothes; THEAT. (trajes) wardrobe, costumes; (donde se visten) dressing room; SPORT. locker room; MIL. uniform.

ve·ta f. (de madera) grain, streak (in wood); MIN. vein, seam; ECUAD. ribbon, band.

ve·ta·do, –da adj. var. of veteado, –da.

ve·tar tr. to veto.

ve·te·a·do, –da I. past part. see **vetear** II. adj. grained, streaked.

ve·te·ar tr. (madera) to grain, streak; ECUAD. to whip.

ve·te·ra·ní·a f. (larga experiencia) long experience; (antigüedad) seniority.

ve·te·ra·no, –na adj. & m.f. veteran.

ve·te·ri·na·rio, –ria I. adj. veterinary II. m.f. (persona) veterinarian —f. veterinary medicine.

ve·to m. veto ♦ **poner el v. a** to veto.

ve·tus·tez f. antiquity, old age.

ve·tus·to, –ta adj. decrepit, ancient.

vez f. [pl. **ve·ces**] time <*te lo dije cuatro veces* I told you four times>; (ocasión) time, occasion <*hay veces que conviene no decir toda la verdad* there are times when it is best not to tell the whole truth>; (turno) turn <*la v. que me tocó no estuve aquí* when it was my turn, I was not here> ♦ **a la v.** at the same time • **a la v. que** while • **alguna que otra v.** once in a while, occasionally • **algunas veces** sometimes • **a su v.** in turn • **a veces** at times, occasionally • **cada v.** every time, each time • **cada v. más** more and more • **cada v. menos** less and less • **cada v. que** whenever, every time that • **de una v.** all at once • **de una v. por todas** once and for all • **de v. en cuando** from time to time, occasionally • **dos veces** twice • **en v. de** instead of • **érase una v.** once upon a time • **hacer las veces de** to stand in for, replace • **muchas veces** often • **otra v.** again • **pocas** or **raras veces** rarely, seldom • **por enésima v.** COLL. for the umpteenth time • **por primera v.** for the first time • **por última v.** for the last time • **repetidas veces** repeatedly, time and again • **tal v.** perhaps, maybe • **toda v. que** since • **una que otra v.** once in a while, occasionally • **una v.** once • **una v. que** once, as soon as.

vi, vimos see ver².

ví·a¹ prep. via <*vamos v. Quito* let's go via Quito>.

ví·a² f. (camino) road, way <*v. pública* public road>; (ruta) route <*v. terrestre* land route>; RAIL. (carril) track, line; ANAT. passage, tract <*vías respiratorias* respiratory tract>; CHEM. process, way <*v. húmeda* wet process>; LAW proceedings <*v. sumaria* summary proceedings>; FIG. (modo) method, way ♦ **en vías de** in the process of • **por v. oral** MED. orally • **v. aérea** airway; (correo) airmail • **V. Crucis** RELIG. Way of the Cross; FIG. (aflicción) ordeal, calvary • **v. de agua** MARIT. leak • **v. de comunicación** channel of communication • **v. férrea** railroad • **v. fluvial** waterway •

V. Láctea ASTRON. Milky Way • **v. marítima** seaway • **v. muerta** RAIL. siding.
via·bi·li·dad f. viability.
via·ble adj. BIOL. viable; *(posible)* viable, feasible.
via·duc·to m. viaduct.
via·ja·dor, –do·ra m.f. traveler.
via·jan·te I. adj. traveling II. m. traveling salesman.
via·jar intr. to travel.
via·je m. *(excursión)* trip, journey; *(libro)* travel guide; *(carga)* load <*un v. de leña* a load of firewood>; COLL. *(ataque)* slash, thrust; *(drogas)* drug trip; TAUR. butt ♦ **¡buen v.!** bon voyage! • **de un v.** AMER. all at once • **ir de v.** to go on a trip, travel • **v. de ida y vuelta** round trip • **v. de novios** honeymoon • **viajes** travel.
via·je·ro, –ra I. adj. traveling II. m.f. traveler.
vial I. adj. road, traffic II. m. tree-lined avenue.
via·li·dad f. highway administration.
vian·da f. *(comida)* food, victuals; CUBA stewed vegetables.
vian·dan·te m.f. *(viajero)* traveler, wayfarer; *(transeúnte)* passerby.
via·rio, –ria adj. pertaining to roads.
viá·ti·co m. *(dietas)* per diem, travel allowance; RELIG. viaticum.
ví·bo·ra f. ZOOL. viper.
vi·bra·ción f. vibration.
vi·bra·do I. past part. see **vibrar** II. adj. TECH. vibrated (cement).
vi·bra·dor, –do·ra I. adj. vibrating II. m. vibrator.
vi·bran·te adj. *(que vibra)* vibrating; *(una voz)* vibrant.
vi·brar tr. *(sacudir)* to vibrate, make quiver; *(una lanza)* to hurl, throw —intr. *(sacudirse)* to vibrate, quiver; FIG. *(sentirse conmovido)* to be moved.
vi·brá·til adj. vibratile.
vi·bra·to·rio, –ria adj. vibratory.
vi·ca·rí·a f. *(oficio y territorio)* vicariate; *(residencia)* vicarage.
vi·ca·rial adj. vicarial.
vi·ca·ria·to m. vicariate.
vi·ca·rio, –ria I. adj. deputy, substitute II. m. vicar.
vi·ce·al·mi·ran·taz·go m. vice-admiralty.
vi·ce·al·mi·ran·te m. vice admiral.
vi·ce·can·ci·ller m. vice chancellor.
vi·ce·can·ci·lle·rí·a f. *(cargo)* vice-chancellorship; *(oficina)* vice-chancellor's office.
vi·ce·cón·sul m. vice consul.
vi·ce·con·su·la·do m. *(cargo)* vice-consulship; *(oficina)* vice-consulate.
vi·ce·ge·ren·cia f. COM. assistant managership; *(del estado)* vicegerency.
vi·ce·ge·ren·te m. COM. assistant manager; *(del estado)* vicegerent.
vi·ce·go·ber·na·dor, –do·ra m.f. vice governor, lieutenant governor.
vi·ce·je·fe m. deputy chief.
vi·ce·pre·si·den·cia f. *(en un país)* vice-presidency; *(en reunión)* vice-chairmanship.
vi·ce·pre·si·den·te m.f. *(en un país)* vice president; *(en reunión)* vice chairman.
vi·ce·se·cre·ta·rí·a f. assistant secretaryship.
vi·ce·se·cre·ta·rio, –ria m.f. assistant secretary.
vi·ce·ver·sa adv. vice versa.
vi·ciar tr. *(contaminar)* to contaminate, pollute <*v. el aire* to pollute the air>; *(pervertir)* to vitiate, corrupt; *(adulterar)* to adulterate; *(falsificar)* to falsify <*v. un manuscrito* to falsify a manuscript>; *(anular)* to vitiate, invalidate; FIG. *(torcer)* to distort, twist <*v. el sentido de una proposición* to distort the meaning of a proposition> —reflex. *(contaminarse)* to become polluted; *(entregarse al vicio)* to become corrupt *or* perverted; *(aficionarse)* to become addicted; *(alabearse)* to warp, become warped.
vi·cio m. *(tendencia a lo malo)* vice, perversion; *(mala costumbre)* bad habit <*ella tiene el v. de fumar* she has the bad habit of smoking>; *(defecto)* defect, flaw; *(alabeo)* warping; *(mimo)* spoiling, overindulgence; BOT. excessive foliage ♦ **de v.** without reason.
vi·cio·so, –sa I. adj. *(defectuoso)* defective, faulty; *(incorrecto)* incorrect; *(depravado)* vicious, depraved; COLL.

(mimado) spoiled, pampered II. m.f. *(persona depravada)* vicious *or* depraved person; *(toxicómano)* drug addict.
vi·ci·si·tud f. vicissitude.
víc·ti·ma f. victim.
vic·ti·ma·rio m. HIST. person who assisted in human sacrifice; AMER. killer, assassin.
vic·to·re·ar tr. to acclaim, cheer.
vic·to·ria f. *(en la guerra)* victory; FIG. *(éxito)* success, triumph; *(coche)* victoria (carriage).
vic·to·ria·no, –na adj. & m.f. HIST. Victorian.
vic·to·rio·so, –sa I. adj. victorious II. m.f. victor.
vi·cu·ña f. vicuña.
vid f. BOT. grapevine.
vi·da f. *(existencia)* life; *(duración)* life, lifetime <*en v. de mi abuelo* in my grandfather's lifetime>; *(sustento)* living, livelihood <*ganarse la v.* to earn one's living>; *(modo de vivir)* life, way of life; *(ser humano)* life, person <*cada v. cuenta* every life counts>; *(biografía)* life story, biography; COLL. dear, darling <*v. mía* my dear>; *(viveza)* vitality, liveliness; *(actividad)* life <*lleno de v.* full of life> ♦ **así es la v.** such is life • **buscarse la v.** FIG. to hustle • **dar la v. por** to give one's life for • **dar mala v. a** to abuse, mistreat • **darse buena v.** to lead the good life, live well • **de por v.** for life, for a lifetime • **echarse a la v.** to become a prostitute • **en la v.** FIG. never • **enterrarse en v.** FIG. to bury oneself alive • **entre la v. y la muerte** at death's door • **escapar con v.** to come out alive • **la otra v.** the hereafter, the next life • **pasar a mejor v.** FIG. to pass away, die • **perder la v.** to lose one's life • **¡por v. de Dios!** come on! • **quitarse la v.** to take one's life • **tener la v. en un hilo** FIG. to be barely alive • **v. de canónigos** FIG. easy life • **v. de perros** COLL. dog's life • **v. eterna** everlasting life • **v. y milagros** FIG. life history • **vivir la v.** FIG. to lead the good life.
vi·den·te I. adj. seeing, sighted II. m.f. seer, prophet.
vi·de·o m.f. video.
vi·de·o·ca·se·te m.f. videocassette.
vi·de·o·dis·co m. videodisc, videodisk.
vi·do·rra f. COLL. life of ease.
vi·dria·do, –da I. past part. see **vidriar** II. adj. glazed III. m. *(barniz)* glaze; *(loza)* glazed earthenware *or* crockery.
vi·driar tr. to glaze, apply a glaze to (pottery, ceramics) —intr. to become glazed.
vi·drie·ra I. f. *(vidrios de colores)* stained glass; *(puerta)* glass door; AMER. showcase, display case II. adj. stained-glass.
vi·drie·rí·a f. *(arte)* glassmaking; *(taller)* glassworks; *(vidriera)* stained glass.
vi·drie·ro, –ra m.f. glazier, glassmaker.
vi·drio m. *(cristal)* glass; *(objeto)* glassware; ARG. windowpane ♦ **pagar los vidrios rotos** FIG., COLL. to take the blame • **v. cilindrado** plate glass • **v. de color** stained glass • **v. tallado** cut glass.
vi·drio·si·dad f. vitreousness, glassiness.
vi·drio·so, –sa adj. *(quebradizo)* brittle, fragile; FIG. *(suelo)* slippery; *(delicado)* tricky, delicate; *(carácter)* touchy, sensitive; *(ojos)* glassy, glazed (eyes).
vie·jo, –ja I. adj. *(anciano)* old, ancient; *(deslucido)* old, worn-out II. m. old man —f. old woman ♦ **viejos** old people, old folks.
Vie·na f. Vienna.
vie·ne see **venir**.
vie·nés, –ne·sa adj. & m.f. Viennese ♦ **los vieneses** the Viennese.
vien·to m. *(brisa)* wind; *(olor)* scent <*el perro tomó el v.* the dog caught the scent>; *(cuerda)* guy, guide rope; ARM. windage; MARIT. course, direction; MUS. wind <*instrumentos de v.* wind instruments>; FIG. *(vanidad)* vanity, conceit; COLL. *(ventosidad)* gas, wind; PAN., P. RICO rheumatism ♦ **a los cuatro vientos** to the four winds, in every direction • **beber los vientos por** FIG. to be crazy about • **contra v. y marea** against all odds, come hell or high water • **corren malos vientos** FIG. an ill wind is blowing • **hacer v.** to be windy • **ir como el v.** to go like the wind • **ir v. en popa** FIG. to go smoothly *or* well • **moverse a todos vientos** FIG. to be fickle • **v. alisio** trade wind • **v. de cola** *or* **v. trasero** AVIA., MARIT. tail wind • **v.**

de proa AVIA., MARIT. head wind • **v. en popa** MARIT. tail wind.

vien·tre m. ANAT. *(abdomen)* stomach, belly; *(matriz)* womb; *(intestino)* bowels <*evacuar el v.* to move one's bowels>; *(bandullo)* guts, entrails; PHYS. loop, bulge; FIG. *(panza)* belly, wide part (of a container) ♦ **bajo v.** lower abdomen.

vier·nes m. [pl. **-nes**] Friday ♦ **cara de v.** FIG., COLL. sad face • **comer de v.** to fast • **Viernes Santo** RELIG. Good Friday.

vier·ta, vierto see **verter.**

Viet Nam or **Viet·nam** m. Viet Nam, Vietnam.

viet·na·mi·ta adj. & m.f. Vietnamese —m. *(idioma)* Vietnamese • **los vietnamitas** the Vietnamese.

vi·ga f. *(madero)* beam, rafter; *(de metal)* girder; *(prensa)* screw press ♦ **estar contando las vigas** FIG. to gaze into space • **v. maestra** main beam • **v. transversal** crossbeam.

vi·gen·cia f. force, effect <*los reglamentos en v.* the regulations in force>.

vi·gen·te adj. in force, in effect.

vi·gé·si·mo, –ma adj. & m. twentieth.

vi·gí·a m. MARIT. watch, lookout —f. *(torre)* watchtower, lookout; *(acción de vigilar)* watch, vigil; MARIT. reef.

vi·gi·lan·cia f. vigilance, watchfulness.

vi·gi·lan·te I. adj. *(que vigila)* vigilant, watchful; *(que vela)* wakeful II. m. *(guarda)* watchman, guard; AMER. policeman.

vi·gi·lar tr. *(cuidar de)* to watch over, guard; *(supervisar)* to supervise —intr. to watch, keep guard ♦ **v. sobre** or **por** to watch over, look after.

vi·gi·lia f. *(vela)* vigil, watch; *(falta de sueño)* sleeplessness; *(trabajo)* night study; *(víspera)* eve; RELIG. *(noche)* vigil, eve; *(misa)* mass for the dead; *(comida con abstinencia)* meatless meal, abstinence <*día de v.* day of abstinence>; MIL. watch, guard.

vi·gor m. *(fuerza)* vigor, strength; *(de una ley)* force, effect <*entrar en v.* to go into force or effect>.

vi·go·rar tr. to strengthen, invigorate.

vi·go·ri·za·dor, –do·ra adj. strengthening, invigorating.

vi·go·ri·zar §04 tr. *(dar vigor)* to strengthen, invigorate; FIG. *(animar)* to encourage.

vi·go·ro·sa·men·te adv. vigorously.

vi·go·ro·si·dad f. vigor, strength.

vi·go·ro·so, –sa adj. vigorous, strong.

vi·gue·rí·a f. girders, beams.

vi·hue·la f. MUS. guitar.

vi·hue·lis·ta m.f. MUS. guitarist.

vil I. adj. vile, despicable II. m.f. vile or despicable person.

vi·la·no m. BOT. burr, down (of a thistle flower).

vi·le·za f. *(calidad)* vileness, baseness; *(acción)* vile or contemptible action.

vi·li·pen·dia·dor, –do·ra I. adj. vilifying, insulting II. m.f. vilifier, insulter.

vi·li·pen·diar tr. to vilify, insult.

vi·li·pen·dio m. vilification, scorn.

vi·li·pen·dio·so, –sa adj. shameful, despicable.

vil·men·te adv. vilely, despicably.

vi·lo adv. ♦ **en v.** FIG. suspended, up in the air.

vi·lor·do, –da adj. lazy, idle.

vi·lor·ta f. *(aro)* wooden ring; *(abrazadera)* iron band or clasp; *(arandela)* washer; *(juego)* game resembling lacrosse; BOT. clematis.

vi·lla f. *(pueblo)* village, hamlet; *(casa)* villa.

vi·lla·na·je m. *(gente villana)* peasants, peasantry; *(condición)* villeinage.

vi·llan·ce·jo or **vi·llan·ce·te** m. var. of **villancico.**

vi·llan·ci·co m. MUS. Christmas carol.

vi·lla·ne·rí·a f. *(vileza)* villainy; *(villanaje)* villeinage.

vi·lla·ní·a f. *(condición)* humble birth; FIG. *(acción)* villainy, despicable act; *(dicho)* coarse remark.

vi·lla·no, –na I. adj. *(que no es noble)* lowly, common; *(paisano)* peasant; FIG. *(grosero)* coarse, rude; *(ruin)* base, wicked II. m.f. *(paisano)* peasant, commoner; *(persona mala)* villain —m. MUS. villanella.

vi·llar m. village, hamlet.

vi·llo·rrio m. DEROG. burg, one-horse town.

vi·na·gre m. *(condimento)* vinegar; FIG., COLL. *(persona)* grouch, sourpuss ♦ **cara de v.** FIG., COLL. sourpuss.

vi·na·gre·ra f. *(vasija)* vinegar bottle; BOT. sorrel; AMER., MED. acidity, heartburn ♦ **vinagreras** cruet.

vi·na·gre·rí·a f. vinegar factory.

vi·na·gre·ro m.f. *(fabricante)* vinegar maker; *(vendedor)* vinegar seller.

vi·na·gre·ta f. CUL. vinaigrette.

vi·na·gro·so, –sa adj. *(parecido al vinagre)* vinegary; FIG., COLL. *(desagradable)* sour, grouchy.

vi·na·je·ra f. RELIG. vessel holding wine or water for the mass.

vi·na·pón m. PERU beer made from corn.

vi·na·rie·go, –ga m.f. viticulturist, grape grower.

vi·na·te·rí·a f. *(tienda)* wine shop; *(comercio)* wine trade.

vi·na·te·ro, –ra I. adj. wine <*la industria v.* the wine industry> II. m.f. *(persona)* wine merchant.

vi·na·zo m. COLL. strong heavy wine.

vin·cu·la·ble adj. LAW entailable.

vin·cu·la·ción f. *(acción de vincular)* linking; *(enlace)* link, tie; LAW entailment.

vin·cu·lar¹ tr. LAW to entail; *(enlazar)* to link, tie; FIG. *(fundar)* to base <*v. sus esperanzas en compromisos vagos* to base one's hopes on vague promises>; *(continuar)* to continue, perpetuate.

vin·cu·lar² adj. linking, connective.

vín·cu·lo m. *(enlace)* link, tie; LAW entailment.

vin·cha f. AMER. headband.

vin·di·ca·ción f. *(venganza)* revenge, vengeance; *(defensa)* vindication.

vin·di·ca·dor, –do·ra I. adj. *(vengador)* avenging; *(defensor)* vindicating II. m.f. *(vengador)* avenger; *(defensor)* vindicator.

vin·di·car §70 tr. *(vengar)* to avenge; *(defender)* to vindicate; LAW *(reivindicar)* to claim, recover.

vin·di·ca·to·rio, –ria adj. vindicatory.

vin·dic·ta f. revenge, vengeance ♦ **v. pública** punishment (for a crime).

vi·ní·co·la I. adj. grape-growing or wine-making II. m. grape grower or winemaker.

vi·ni·cul·tor, –to·ra m.f. grape grower.

vi·ni·cul·tu·ra f. viniculture.

vi·nie·ra, vino see **venir.**

vi·ni·fi·ca·ción f. vinification.

vi·ní·li·co, –ca adj. of vinyl.

vi·ni·lo m. CHEM. vinyl.

vi·no m. wine ♦ **bautizar el v.** FIG., COLL. to water the wine • **dormir el v.** FIG. to sleep it off • **tener mal v.** FIG. to be a bad drunk • **v. abocado** or **embocado** semidry wine • **v. añejo** vintage wine • **v. blanco** white wine • **v. clarete** claret • **v. de coco** fermented coconut milk • **v. de dos orejas** good strong wine • **v. de honor** special wine • **v. de Jerez** sherry • **v. de mesa** table wine • **v. de Oporto** port wine • **v. de pasto** ordinary wine • **v. de postre** dessert wine • **v. espumoso** sparkling wine • **v. generoso** full-bodied wine • **v. peleón** COLL. cheap wine • **v. seco** dry wine • **v. tinto** red wine • **v. verde** new wine.

vi·no·so, –sa adj. *(parecido al vino)* winy, wine-like (color, flavor); *(dado al vino)* winebibbing.

vi·ña f. vineyard ♦ **la v. del Señor** RELIG., FIG. the faithful.

vi·ña·dor m. *(viticultor)* grape grower; *(guarda)* guard of a vineyard.

vi·ña·te·ro, –ra AMER. I. adj. viticultural, grape-growing II. m.f. viticulturist, grape grower.

vi·ñe·do m. vineyard.

vi·ñe·ta f. PRINT. vignette.

vio·la f. *(instrumento)* viola —m.f. *(persona)* violist.

vio·la·ble adj. violable.

vio·lá·ce·o, –a adj. violaceous, violet.

vio·la·ción f. *(de las leyes)* violation, infringement; *(de una mujer)* rape; *(de cosas sagradas)* desecration, profanation.

vio·la·do, –da I. past part. see **violar** II. adj. & m. violet (color).

vio·la·dor, –do·ra I. adj. violating II. m.f. *(de las leyes)* violator —m. *(de una mujer)* rapist.

vio·lar tr. *(las leyes)* to violate, infringe; *(a una mujer)* to rape; *(cosas sagradas)* to desecrate, profane; FIG. *(deslucir)* to spoil, tarnish.

vio·len·cia f. *(fuerza)* violence, force; FIG. *(violación)* rape; FIG., COLL. *(turbación)* embarrassment.

vio·len·tar tr. *(forzar)* to force <*v. una puerta* to force a door>; *(entrar por fuerza)* to break into, enter by force; *(obligar)* to force, persuade forcibly; FIG. *(torcer)* to distort, twist; *(atropellar)* to outrage, infuriate —reflex. to force oneself.

vio·len·to, -ta adj. *(fuerte)* violent <*una tempestad v.* a violent storm>; *(brutal)* violent <*un hombre v.* a violent man>; *(intenso)* intense <*una discusión v.* an intense discussion>; FIG. *(torcido)* distorted, twisted; *(molesto)* awkward, embarrassing <*es v. que me traten así* it is embarrassing to be treated like this>.

vio·le·ta f. & adj. BOT. violet.

vio·lín m. *(instrumento)* violin; *(persona)* violinist ♦ **embolsar el v.** ARG., VEN. to be crushed *or* humiliated • **primer v.** MUS. first violin • **tocar el v.** to play the violin • **tocar v.** S. AMER., FIG. to be a fifth wheel • **v. de Ingrés** avocation, hobby.

vio·li·nis·ta m.f. violinist.

vio·lón m. *(instrumento)* double bass, bass viol; *(persona)* double bass player ♦ **tocar el v.** COLL. to talk through one's hat.

vio·lon·ce·lis·ta *or* **vio·lon·che·lis·ta** m.f. MUS. cellist, violoncellist.

vio·lon·ce·lo *or* **vio·lon·che·lo** m. MUS. cello, violoncello.

vi·pe·ri·no, -na adj. viperine, venomous.

vi·ra·co·cha m. HIST. Spaniard (among the ancient Incans).

vi·ra·da f. *(vuelta)* turn; MARIT. tack.

vi·ra·je m. *(acción de girar)* turning, veering; *(giro)* turn; MARIT. tack; FIG. *(cambio)* turning point; PHOTOG. toning.

vi·rar tr. MARIT. *(de rumbo)* to turn; *(el cabrestante)* to wind (a capstan); PHOTOG. to tone —intr. to turn around ♦ **v. al revés** to turn inside out.

vir·gen I. adj. virgin <*selva v.* virgin forest> II. m.f. virgin ♦ **Virgen** BIBL. Virgin; ASTRON. Virgo • **un viva la Virgen** COLL. a happy-go-lucky *or* devil-may-care type.

vir·gi·nal *or* **vir·gi·ne·o, -a** adj. virginal.

vir·gi·ni·dad f. virginity.

vir·go m. *(virginidad)* virginity; ANAT. hymen ♦ **Virgo** ASTRON. Virgo.

vír·gu·la f. *(vara pequeña)* small rod *or* stick; PRINT. virgule; BACT. cholera bacillus.

vi·ril adj. virile, male.

vi·ri·li·dad f. virility.

vi·ri·po·ten·te adj. *(una mujer)* nubile, marriageable; *(vigoroso)* strong, vigorous.

vi·ro·la f. *(casquillo)* ferrule; ARG. silver disc (for decorating harnesses); *(en la garrocha)* check ring on goads.

vi·ro·len·to, -ta I. adj. *(enfermo)* having smallpox; *(señalado)* pockmarked II. m.f. *(enfermo)* person with smallpox; *(señalado)* pockmarked person.

vi·ro·lo·gí·a f. MED. virology.

vi·ro·te m. *(saeta)* dart; *(hierro)* iron shackle; FIG., COLL. *(persona seria)* stuffed shirt; COL., VEN. fool, dolt.

vi·ro·tis·mo m. COLL. pomposity, pretentiousness.

vi·rrei·na f. vicereine.

vi·rrei·nal adj. viceregal.

vi·rrei·na·to *or* **vi·rrei·no** m. viceroyalty, viceroyship.

vi·rrey m. viceroy.

vir·tual adj. virtual.

vir·tual·men·te adv. virtually.

vir·tud f. *(integridad)* virtue; *(eficacia)* power, ability ♦ **en v. de** by virtue of.

vir·tuo·si·dad f. *or* **vir·tuo·sis·mo** m. virtuosity.

vir·tuo·so, -sa I. adj. virtuous II. m.f. ARTS virtuoso.

vi·rue·la f. MED. *(enfermedad)* smallpox; *(cicatriz)* pockmark ♦ **viruelas locas** MED. chicken pox.

vi·ru·len·cia f. virulence.

vi·ru·len·to, -ta adj. virulent.

vi·rus m. [pl. **-rus**] MED. virus.

vi·ru·ta f. shavings (of wood or metal).

vi·sa f. AMER. visa.

vi·sa·do, -da I. past part. see **visar** II. adj. with visa <*pasaporte v.* passport with visa> III. m. visa.

vi·sa·je m. face, grimace <*hacer visajes* to make faces>.

vi·sar tr. *(un pasaporte)* to visa; *(un documento)* to endorse; ARTIL., SURV. to sight, focus on.

vís·ce·ra f. ANAT. organ ♦ **vísceras** viscera.

vis·ce·ral adj. ANAT. visceral.

vis·co m. birdlime.

vis·co·si·dad f. viscosity.

vis·co·so, -sa adj. viscous, sticky.

vi·se·ra f. *(del casco)* visor; CUBA, P. RICO blinder (on a horse).

vi·si·bi·li·dad f. visibility.

vi·si·ble adj. *(que se puede ver)* visible; COLL. *(decente)* decent, presentable.

vi·si·ble·men·te adv. visibly.

vi·si·go·do, -da HIST. I. adj. Visigothic II. m.f. Visigoth.

vi·si·gó·ti·co, -ca adj. HIST. Visigothic.

vi·si·llo m. window curtain.

vi·sión f. *(vista)* vision, eyesight; *(alucinación)* vision, illusion; FIG., COLL. *(persona)* sight, fright ♦ **quedarse como quien ve visiones** FIG., COLL. to look as though one has seen a ghost • **ver visiones** FIG., COLL. to see things.

vi·sio·na·rio, -ria adj. & m.f. visionary.

vi·sir m. vizier, vizir.

vi·si·ra·to m. vizierate.

vi·si·ta f. *(acción de visitar)* visit, call; *(inspección)* inspection; *(persona)* visitor, caller <*recibir las visitas* to receive visitors>; PERU, P. RICO enema ♦ **hacer una v.** *or* **ir de v.** to pay a visit • **v. de cortesía** *or* **de cumplido** courtesy call • **v. de médico** FIG., COLL. brief visit.

vi·si·ta·ción f. visit, visitation ♦ **Visitación** RELIG. Visitation.

vi·si·ta·dor, -do·ra I. adj. fond of visiting II. m.f. frequent visitor —m. *(inspector)* inspector.

vi·si·tan·te I. adj. visiting II. m.f. visitor, caller.

vi·si·tar tr. *(ir a ver)* to visit, call on; *(examinar)* to inspect —reflex. to visit one another.

vi·si·te·o m. frequent visiting.

vi·si·vo, -va adj. visual.

vis·lum·brar tr. *(ver débilmente)* to glimpse; FIG. *(conjeturar)* to suspect, surmise.

vis·lum·bre f. *(reflejo)* glimmer; FIG. *(sospecha)* glimmer, inkling.

vi·so m. *(reflejo)* sheen, luster; *(destello)* gleam, glint; *(forro)* colored undergarment; *(altura)* rise, height; FIG. *(capa ligera)* thin coat, veneer; *(apariencia)* appearance <*tener v. de verdad* to have the appearance of truth> ♦ **a dos visos** with a double purpose • **de v.** important, prominent • **hacer visos** to shimmer, gleam.

vi·són m. mink ♦ **abrigo de v.** mink coat.

vi·sor m. PHOTOG. viewfinder; ARTIL. sight.

vi·so·rio, -ria I. adj. visual, optic II. m. expert examination *or* inspection.

vís·pe·ra f. eve, day before ♦ **en v. de** on the eve of • **vísperas** RELIG. vespers.

vis·ta I. f. *(visión)* sight, vision; eyesight <*él tiene buena v.* he has good eyesight>; *(aspecto)* appearance, looks; *(panorama)* view, vista; *(cuadro)* view, scene; *(mirada)* eye, eyes <*dirigió la v. a la pantalla* he turned his eyes toward the screen>; *(vistazo)* look, glance; FIG. *(intento)* intent, view <*con v. a* with a view to>; LAW hearing, trial ♦ **aguzar la v.** FIG. to look sharp, keep one's eyes open • **a la v.** COM. at sight, on sight • **a la v. de todos** publicly, in front of everybody • **alzar la v.** to look up • **apartar la v. de** to look away; FIG. *(no hacer caso de)* to turn a blind eye to • **a primera v.** at first sight • **a simple v.** *(de paso)* at a glance; *(con los ojos)* with the naked eye • **a v. de** *(en presencia de)* in front of, in the presence of; *(en consideración de)* in view of, considering • **bajar la v.** to look down • **clavar** *or* **fijar la v. en** to stare at • **comerse** *or* **tragarse con la v.** FIG., COLL. to devour with one's eyes • **conocer de v.** to know by sight • **corto de v.** nearsighted • **en v. de** in view of, considering • **estar a la v.** *(estar a la mira)* to be visible, be within sight; *(ser evidente)* to be obvious *or* evident; *(estar al acecho)* to keep an eye on • **hacerse de la v. gorda** COLL. to turn a blind eye, pretend not to notice • **hasta la v.** so long, good-bye • **írsele la v.** *(desvanecerse)* to faint, swoon; *(marearse)* to become dizzy • **medir con la v.** to size up • **no perder de v. a** not to lose sight of, keep one's eye on • **perder de v.** to lose sight of • **perder la v.** to lose one's sight • **perderse de v.** FIG. to disappear • **saltar a la v.** to hit the eye, be obvious • **segunda** *or* **doble v.** second sight • **v. cansada** tired eyes • **v. de águila** *or* **de lince** eagle eye, hawk eye • **v. de pájaro**

bird's-eye view • **v. doble** MED. double vision • **vistas** *(reunión)* meeting, conference; ARCHIT. *(ventanas)* openings; SEW. collar and cuffs (of a shirt) • **volver la v. atrás** to look back **II.** adj. see **visto, –ta.**

vis·ta, visto see **vestir.**

vis·ta·zo m. glance ♦ **dar un v. a** to take a glance at.

vis·tie·ra, vistió see **vestir.**

vis·to, –ta I. past part. see **ver²** **II.** adj. in view of, considering ♦ **bien v.** acceptable, proper • **es** *or* **está v.** it is commonly accepted • **mal v.** unacceptable, improper • **ni v. ni oído** FIG., COLL. in a flash • **no** *or* **nunca v.** unheard-of • **por lo v.** apparently • **v.** LAW whereas • **v. bueno** approved, O.K. • **v. que** seeing that, since **III.** m. customs inspector —f. see **vista.**

vis·to·sa·men·te adv. brightly, colorfully.

vis·to·si·dad f. brightness, colorfulness.

vis·to·so, –sa adj. bright, colorful.

vi·sual I. adj. visual **II.** f. line of vision *or* sight.

vi·sua·li·za·ción f. visualization.

vi·sua·li·zar §04 tr. to visualize.

vi·tal adj. vital.

vi·ta·li·cio, –cia I. adj. life <*miembro v.* life member> **II.** m. life insurance policy.

vi·ta·li·dad f. vitality.

vi·ta·li·zar §04 tr. to vitalize.

vi·ta·mi·na f. vitamin.

vi·ta·mí·ni·co, –ca adj. vitamin, vitaminic.

vi·te·la f. vellum, parchment.

vi·ti·cul·tu·ra f. viticulture, grape growing.

vi·ti·vi·ní·co·la I. adj. viticultural, vine-growing **II.** m.f. viticulturist, vine grower.

vi·ti·vi·ni·cul·tu·ra f. viticulture.

vi·to·la f. *(para calibrar)* caliper, calipers; *(de puros)* cigar band; FIG. *(aspecto)* appearance.

¡ví·tor! interj. bravo!, hooray!

vi·to·re·ar tr. to cheer, acclaim.

vi·tral m. stained-glass window.

ví·tre·o, –a adj. vitreous.

vi·tri·fi·ca·ción f. vitrification.

vi·tri·fi·car §70 tr. & reflex. to vitrify.

vi·tri·na f. *(caja)* display case; *(de tienda)* shop window.

vi·trió·li·co, –ca adj. vitriolic.

vi·tua·llas f.pl. victuals, provisions.

vi·tua·llar tr. to victual, provision.

vi·tu·pe·ra·ble adj. reprehensible.

vi·tu·pe·ra·ción f. vituperation.

vi·tu·pe·ra·dor, –do·ra I. vituperating, vituperative **II.** m.f. vituperator.

vi·tu·pe·ran·te adj. vituperating, vituperative.

vi·tu·pe·rar tr. to vituperate, censure.

vi·tu·pe·rio m. *(afrenta)* affront; *(insulto)* insult; *(censura)* vituperation, censure; *(vergüenza)* shame, disgrace.

viu·da I. f. *(mujer)* widow; BOT. mourning bride **II.** adj. see **viudo, –da.**

viu·dal adj. of a widow *or* widower.

viu·de·dad f. *(pensión)* widow's pension; *(estado de viudo)* widowerhood; *(estado de viuda)* widowhood.

viu·dez f. *(de viudo)* widowerhood; *(de viuda)* widowhood.

viu·do, –da I. adj. widowed **II.** m. widower —f. see **viuda.**

¡vi·va! interj. long live!, hooray!

vi·vac m. [pl. **-va·ques**] MIL. bivouac. CUBA police station.

vi·va·ci·dad f. *(en las acciones)* vivacity, liveliness; *(del espíritu)* sharpness, keenness; *(de color)* vividness, brightness.

vi·va·men·te adv. *(rápidamente)* rapidly, quickly; *(profundamente)* deeply, keenly.

vi·va·que m. MIL. *(guardia)* guardhouse; *(campo)* bivouac.

vi·var m. *(de conejos)* rabbit warren; *(de peces)* fish hatchery.

vi·va·ra·cho, –cha adj. COLL. vivacious, lively.

vi·vaz adj. [pl. **-va·ces**] *(que vive mucho tiempo)* long-lived; FIG. *(que dura)* persistent, stubborn; *(enérgico)* lively, energetic; *(agudo)* sharp, quick-witted; BOT. perennial.

vi·ven·cia f. PHILOS. (personal) experience.

ví·ve·res m.pl. food, provisions.

vi·ve·ro m. BOT. nursery; *(de peces)* fish hatchery; *(de moluscos)* farm <*v. de ostras* oyster farm>; FIG. *(semillero)* breeding ground; TEX. cloth made in Galicia.

vi·ve·za f. *(vivacidad)* vivacity, liveliness; *(prontitud)* quick-

ness; *(agudeza)* cleverness, sharpness; *(dicho ingenioso)* witty remark; *(brillo)* brightness, vividness; *(gracia)* sparkle, spirit; *(acción inconsiderada)* thoughtless act; *(palabra irreflexiva)* thoughtless remark.

vi·vi·de·ro, –ra adj. habitable, livable.

vi·vi·di·zo m. MEX. sponger, parasite.

ví·vi·do, –da adj. LIT. realistic, true to life.

ví·vi·do, –da adj. vivid, lively.

vi·vi·dor, –do·ra I. adj. *(vivo)* live, living; *(que dura)* long-lived; *(ingenioso)* resourceful, enterprising **II.** m.f. *(ingenioso)* resourceful *or* enterprising person; COLL. *(parásito)* sponger, parasite.

vi·vien·da f. *(lugar)* housing <*escasez de v.* housing shortage>; *(morada)* dwelling; *(casa)* house.

vi·vien·te adj. living.

vi·vi·fi·ca·dor, –do·ra *or* **vi·vi·fi·can·te** adj. vivifying, enlivening.

vi·vi·fi·car §70 tr. to vivify, enliven.

vi·vi·fi·ca·ti·vo, –va adj. vivifying, enlivening.

vi·ví·pa·ro, –ra ZOOL. **I.** adj. viviparous **II.** m.f. viviparous animal.

vi·vir¹ m. life, living ♦ **de mal v.** disreputable, loose-living.

vi·vir² intr. to live <*vivimos en Buenos Aires* we live in Buenos Aires>; FIG. *(durar)* to live, last <*su recuerdo vivirá eternamente* his memory will live forever> ♦ **¿quién vive?** MIL. who goes there? • **saber v.** to know how to live, enjoy life • **¡viva!** hurrah!, long live! <*¡viva el rey!* long live the king!> • **v. al día** to live from hand to mouth • **v. a lo grande** to live it up • **v. de** to live on *or* off <*ella vive de sus rentas* she lives off her investments> • **v. del aire** to live on next to nothing • **v. para ver** to live and learn —tr. to live <*tengo que v. mi vida* I have to live my own life>; *(experimentar)* to experience, go through <*he vivido unos momentos difíciles* I have gone through some difficult moments>.

vi·vi·sec·ción f. vivisection.

vi·vi·sec·tor, –to·ra m.f. vivisector.

vi·vo, –va I. adj. alive, living <*el conejo está v.* the rabbit is alive>; *(intenso)* strong, deep <*un sentimiento v.* a deep feeling>; *(brillante)* vivid, bright <*un color v.* a vivid color>; *(listo)* clever, sharp <*un estudiante v.* a sharp student>; *(astuto)* shrewd, sly; *(perspicaz)* lively, quick <*una inteligencia v.* a quick intelligence>; *(ágil)* lively, vivid <*una imaginación v.* a vivid imagination>; FIG. *(expresivo)* lively, vivid <*una descripción v.* a vivid description>; ARCHIT. sharp <*una arista v.* a sharp edge>; MED. raw <*carne v.* raw skin> ♦ **a lo v.** vividly • **al rojo v.** red-hot • **en v.** TELEC. live • **lo v.** FIG. the raw, the quick <*me hirió en lo v.* he wounded me to the quick> **II.** living person ♦ **los vivos** the living —m. *(borde)* edge, border; SEW. edging, piping; VET. mange, scab; COLL. *(hombre listo)* wise guy.

viz·ca·cha f. ZOOL. viscacha.

viz·con·da·do m. viscountcy.

viz·con·de m. viscount.

viz·con·de·sa f. viscountess.

vo·ca·blo m. word, term.

vo·ca·bu·la·rio m. vocabulary.

vo·ca·bu·lis·ta m.f. lexicographer.

vo·ca·ción f. vocation, calling.

vo·ca·cio·nal adj. vocational.

vo·cal I. adj. vocal **II.** m.f. *(en una junta)* board or committee member —f. PHONET. vowel ♦ **v. breve** short vowel • **v. larga** long vowel.

vo·cá·li·co, –ca adj. PHONET. vocalic.

vo·ca·lis·ta m.f. MUS. vocalist, singer.

vo·ca·li·za·ción f. MUS., PHONET. vocalization.

vo·ca·li·za·dor, –do·ra adj. vocalizing.

vo·ca·li·zar §04 intr. to vocalize.

vo·cal·men·te adv. vocally.

vo·ca·ti·vo m. GRAM. vocative.

vo·ce·a·dor, –do·ra I. adj. loud, vociferous **II.** m.f. *(vocinglero)* loud *or* vociferous person —m. *(pregonero)* town crier; MEX. street hawker (of newspapers).

vo·ce·ar intr. to shout, cry out —tr. *(publicar)* to shout, proclaim; *(llamar a)* to shout to, hail; *(aclamar)* to cheer, acclaim; FIG., COLL. *(ostentar)* to make a fuss about.

vo·ce·o m. shouting, yelling.

vo·ce·rí·a f. *or* **vo·ce·rí·o** m. *(gritería)* shouting, yelling; *(clamor)* clamor, uproar.

vo·ce·ro, –ra m. spokesman —f. spokeswoman.

vo·ci·fe·ra·ción f. vociferation.

vo·ci·fe·ra·dor, –do·ra I. adj. vociferous, vociferating II. m.f. vociferator.

vo·ci·fe·ran·te adj. vociferous, vociferating.

vo·ci·fe·rar tr. & intr. to shout, yell.

vo·cin·gle·o m. *or* **vo·cin·gle·rí·a** f. *(gritería)* shouting, yelling; *(clamor)* clamor, uproar.

vo·cin·gle·ro, –ra I. adj. *(chillador)* screaming, shrieking; *(fanfarrón)* loudmouthed II. m.f. *(chillador)* screamer, shrieker; *(fanfarrón)* loudmouth.

vo·la·da f. *(vuelo corto)* short flight; COL., ECUAD., COLL. trick; MEX. rumor, story; ARG. event, happening ♦ **a las** *or* **en voladas** AMER. in the air, through the air.

vo·la·de·ra f. blade, paddle (of a water wheel).

vo·la·di·zo, –za ARCHIT. I. adj. jutting out, projecting II. m. corbel.

vo·la·do, –da I. past part. see **volar** II. adj. PRINT. superior; COL. furious, angry ♦ **estar v.** FIG., COLL. to be nervous *or* edgy • **hacer algo de v.** FIG. to do something on the run • **v. de genio** AMER. quick-tempered III. m. *(azucarillo)* drink made of syrup, egg white and lemon dissolved in water; ARG., VEN. pleated ruffle *or* flounce; C. AMER. rumor, story.

vo·la·dor, –do·ra I. adj. *(que vuela)* flying; *(rápido)* swift, fleet II. m. *(cohete)* rocket; ICHTH. flying fish; BOT. myrobalan; VEN. kite; C. AMER. pinwheel.

vo·la·du·ra f. explosion, demolition.

vo·lan·das adv. ♦ **en v.** *(por el aire)* in the air; FIG., COLL. *(rápidamente)* rapidly, hastily.

vo·lan·de·ra I. f. *(arandela)* washer; *(de molino)* grindstone, millstone; PRINT. galley slice; FIG. *(mentira)* lie, fib II. adj. see **volandero, –ra.**

vo·lan·de·ro, –ra I. adj. ORNITH. newly fledged, ready to fly; *(suspenso)* hanging, suspended; FIG. *(imprevisto)* accidental, unforeseen; *(vagabundo)* wandering, vagabond II. f. see **volandera.**

vo·lan·di·llas adv. ♦ **en v.** *(por el aire)* in the air; COLL. *(rápidamente)* in a jiffy.

vo·lan·do adv. COLL. quickly, in a flash.

vo·lan·te I. adj. *(que vuela)* flying; FIG. *(sin asiento fijo)* unsettled, wandering II. m. MECH. flywheel; AUTO. steering wheel; *(del reloj)* balance wheel (of a clock); *(papel)* flier, leaflet; *(zoquetillo)* shuttlecock; *(juego)* badminton; SEW. pleated ruffle; *(prensa)* coining press ♦ **ir al v.** to be at the wheel, be driving.

vo·lan·tín, –ti·na I. adj. flying II. m. *(para pescar)* fishing line with several hooks; AMER. *(voltereta)* somersault; CARIB., S. AMER. *(cometa)* small kite; BOL. rocket, firecracker.

vo·lan·tón, –to·na I. adj. ORNITH. newly fledged, ready to fly; ECUAD. wandering, vagabond II. m.f. ORNITH. fledgling; ECUAD. wandering, vagabond.

vo·lar §19 intr. *(moverse por el aire)* to fly <**v. de rama en rama** to fly from branch to branch>; *(ir en avión)* to fly; *(irse volando)* to fly away; FIG. *(ir de prisa)* to fly, rush; *(transcurrir)* to fly <**las horas volaban** the hours flew>; *(desaparecer)* to disappear, vanish; *(divulgarse)* to spread quickly <**la noticia voló por el pueblo** the news spread quickly through the town>; ARCHIT. to jut out, project —tr. *(hacer estallar)* to blow up, explode; *(irritar)* to anger, upset; HUNT. to rouse (game); PRINT. to raise (a letter) —reflex. to fly away; AMER. *(irritarse)* to blow up, get upset.

vo·la·te·rí·a f. HUNT. falconry, hawking; *(aves de corral)* poultry, fowls; ECUAD. fireworks.

vo·lá·til adj. *(que vuela)* flying; CHEM., PHYS. volatile; FIG. *(inconstante)* flighty, fickle.

vo·la·ti·li·zar §04 tr. & reflex. to volatilize.

vo·la·tín, –ti·na m.f. *(volatinero)* tightrope walker, acrobat —m. *(ejercicio)* acrobatic stunt.

vo·la·ti·ne·ro, –ra m.f. tightrope walker, acrobat.

vol·cán m. volcano; FIG. *(persona)* hothead *or* impetuous person; *(peligro)* hidden danger; COL. precipice; ARG., BOL. flood, torrent ♦ **estar sobre un v.** FIG. to be on top of

a volcano, be in imminent danger • **v. apagado** *or* **extinto** extinct volcano.

vol·cá·ni·co, –ca adj. volcanic.

vol·ca·nis·mo m. volcanism, vulcanism.

vol·ca·no·lo·gí·a f. volcanology, vulcanology.

vol·ca·nó·lo·go, –ga m.f. volcanologist, vulcanologist.

vol·car §73 tr. *(derribar)* to knock over, upset; *(verter)* to turn over, overturn; MARIT. to capsize; *(aturdir)* to make dizzy <**ese perfume me vuelca** that perfume makes me dizzy>; FIG. *(persuadir)* to make (someone) change his mind; *(molestar)* to annoy, exasperate —intr. to overturn, turn over —reflex. *(derribarse)* overturn, to turn over; *(entregarse)* to do one's utmost, bend over backwards.

vo·le·a f. *(de carruaje)* swingletree; SPORT. volley.

vo·le·ar tr. SPORT. to volley; AGR. to broadcast, scatter (grain); COL. to beat, strike.

vo·le·o m. SPORT. volley; *(en la danza)* high kick; *(bofetón)* hard slap ♦ **del primer** *or* **de un v.** COLL. quickly, in one stroke • **sembrar a v.** AGR. to broadcast, scatter (seed).

vol·fra·mio m. CHEM. wolfram, tungsten.

vol·fra·mi·ta f. MIN. wolframite.

vo·li·ción f. volition.

vol·qué see **volcar.**

vol·que·te m. tipcart.

vol·tai·co, –ca adj. ELEC. voltaic <**arco v.** voltaic arc>.

vol·ta·je m. ELEC. voltage.

vol·tá·me·tro m. ELEC. voltameter.

vol·tam·pe·rí·me·tro m. ELEC. voltammeter.

vol·tam·pe·rio m. ELEC. volt-ampere.

vol·te·a·dor, –do·ra I. adj. tumbling II. m.f. tumbler, acrobat.

vol·te·ar tr. *(volcar)* to turn over, overturn; *(dar la vuelta a)* to turn around; *(poner al revés)* to turn upside down; *(mudar)* to move; *(construir)* to build (an arch, vault); AMER. *(volver)* to turn <**v. la cabeza** to turn one's head>; *(derribar)* to knock down *or* over —intr. to tumble, do somersaults —reflex. *(volcarse)* to turn over; AMER. to change sides *or* parties.

vol·te·o m. *(acción de voltear)* overturning; *(acrobacia)* tumbling; P. RICO reprimand.

vol·te·re·ta f. *(vuelta en el aire)* somersault; *(en naipes)* turning up a card to determine trumps; FIG. *(cambio)* twist, turnabout (in a situation).

vol·tí·me·tro m. ELEC. voltmeter.

vol·tio m. ELEC. volt.

vol·ti·zo, –za adj. *(torcido)* curled, twisted; FIG. *(cambiante)* fickle, changeable.

vo·lu·bi·li·dad f. volubility.

vo·lu·ble adj. *(rotativo)* voluble, rotating; FIG. *(cambiante)* fickle, changeable; BOT. voluble.

vo·lu·men m. *(capacidad)* volume; *(cuerpo)* bulk; *(libro)* volume, tome ♦ **a todo v.** loud, at full volume.

vo·lu·mé·tri·co, –ca adj. volumetric.

vo·lu·mi·no·so, –sa adj. voluminous.

vo·lun·tad f. *(facultad de determinarse)* will; *(firmeza)* will power <**faltarle la v. de hacerlo** to lack the will power to do it>; *(intención)* intention; *(deseo)* wish, desire; *(cariño)* liking, affection ♦ **a v.** at will • **buena v.** good will • **fuerza de v.** will power • **ganar la v. de alguien** to win someone over • **mala v.** ill will • **tenerle mala v. a alguien** to dislike someone • **última v.** last will and testament, last wish • **v. de hierro** iron will • **v. divina** divine will.

vo·lun·ta·ria·men·te adv. voluntarily.

vo·lun·ta·rie·dad f. *(espontaneidad)* voluntariness; *(capricho)* willfulness, obstinacy.

vo·lun·ta·rio, –ria I. adj. *(que se hace por voluntad)* voluntary, volunteer; *(caprichoso)* willful, obstinate II. m.f. volunteer.

vo·lun·ta·rio·so, –sa adj. *(caprichoso)* willful, obstinate; *(deseoso)* willing, eager.

vo·lup·tuo·sa·men·te adv. voluptuously.

vo·lup·tuo·si·dad f. voluptuousness.

vo·lup·tuo·so, –sa I. adj. voluptuous II. m. voluptuary.

vo·lu·ta f. ARCHIT., ZOOL. volute; FIG. *(espiral)* spiral, volute.

vol·ver §78 tr. to turn <**v. la hoja** to turn the page>; *(dar vuelta)* to turn around; to turn over <**v. el colchón** to turn over the mattress>; to turn inside out <*v. los calcetines* to turn socks inside out>; *(dirigir)* to turn, direct <*volvió los ojos hacia la puerta* she turned her eyes toward the door>; *(devolver)* to return, give back <*le volví el lápiz* I gave him back the pencil>; to return, replace <*¿volviste el libro al estante?* did you return the book to the shelf?>; *(corresponder)* to return, repay <*v. un favor* to return a favor>; *(restablecer)* to return, restore <*volvieron la casa a su estado original* they restored the house to its original condition>; *(dar)* to give <*el dependiente me volvió el cambio* the clerk gave me my change>; *(cerrar)* to close, pull shut <*v. la puerta* to pull the door shut>; *(vomitar)* to throw up, vomit; *(cambiar)* to turn, change; make <*me volvieron loco* they made me crazy>; *(convencer)* to persuade, convince; to reflect <*la pared vuelve la voz* the wall reflects his voice>; *(traducir)* to translate; SPORT. to return (a ball); AGR. to replow ♦ **v. la cara** to turn around • **v. la espalda a alguien** to turn one's back on someone • **v. la esquina** to turn the corner —intr. *(regresar)* to return, go back, come back <*volvimos a casa muy tarde* we returned home very late>; *(torcer)* to turn <*el camino vuelve a la derecha* the road turns to the right>; *(reanudar)* to return, get back <*volvamos a la conversación que teníamos* let's get back to the conversation that we were having> ♦ **v. a** to ... again <*volví a empezar* I began again> • **v. en sí** to come to, come around —reflex. *(darse vuelta)* to turn around; *(hacerse)* to turn, become, go <*volverse religioso* to become religious>; *(agriarse)* to turn, go sour; *(mudar de opinión)* to change one's mind ♦ **volverse atrás** *(desdecirse)* to back down; *(no cumplir)* to back out • **volverse contra** to turn against *or* on • **volverse loco** to go crazy.

vo·mi·ta·dor, –do·ra I. adj. vomiting II. m.f. vomiter.

vo·mi·tar tr. *(regurgitar)* to vomit, regurgitate; FIG. *(emitir)* to belch, spew; *(decir)* to spew, utter; *(un secreto)* to spill (a secret); FIG., COLL. *(restituir)* to cough up, give back (to a rightful owner) —intr. to vomit.

vo·mi·ti·vo, –va MED. adj. & m. vomitive, emetic.

vó·mi·to m. *(acción)* vomiting; *(resultado)* vomit ♦ **provocar a v.** FIG., COLL. to make sick, disgust • **v. de sangre** MED. hemoptysis • **v. negro** MED. yellow fever.

vo·mi·tón, –to·na COLL. I. adj. who vomits frequently (said of a nursing infant) II. f. heavy vomiting.

vo·mi·to·rio, –ria I. adj. MED. vomitory, emetic II. m. MED. vomitory, emetic; HIST. vomitory.

vo·ra·ci·dad f. voracity.

vo·rá·gi·ne f. vortex, whirlpool.

vo·ra·gi·no·so, –sa adj. vortical, turbulent.

vo·raz adj. [pl. **-ra·ces**] voracious.

vór·ti·ce m. *(torbellino)* vortex, whirlpool; *(de un ciclón)* center of a cyclone.

vos §G39 pron. you, thou, ye; S. AMER. you.

vo·se·ar tr. to address as *vos*.

vo·se·o m. use of *vos* in addressing someone.

vo·so·tros, –tras §G30, 33 pl. pron. you, yourselves <*entre v.* among yourselves>.

vo·ta·ción f. *(acción)* voting, balloting; *(voto)* vote; *(conjunto)* votes, vote total.

vo·tan·te I. adj. voting II. m.f. voter.

vo·tar intr. RELIG. to vow, make a vow; *(jurar)* to curse, swear; *(en una elección)* to vote —tr. to vote, pass.

vo·ti·vo, –va adj. votive.

vo·to m. vote <*depositar un v.* to cast a vote>; vow <*v. de castidad* vow of chastity>; *(juramento)* curse, swearword; *(deseo)* wish <*hacemos votos por su mejoría* we send our wishes for her recovery> ♦ **echar votos** to curse, swear • **hacer votos por** to sincerely hope for • **tener v.** to have a vote • **v. de confianza** vote of confidence • **votos** wishes, esires.

voz f. [pl. **vo·ces**] voices <*ella tiene la v. aguda* she has a shrill voice>; *(ruido)* noise, sound <*la v. del mar* the sound of the sea>; *(consejo)* voice <*la v. de la experiencia* the voice of experience>; *(vocablo)* term, expression; <*una v. anticuada* an old-fashioned expression>; MUS. voice, part; GRAM. voice <*v. pasiva* passive voice>; FIG. *(rumor)* story, rumor <*se corrió la v.* the rumor got around>; *(opinión)* opinion <*v. pública* public opinion>; *(facultad de hablar)* say, voice <*tener v.* to have a say>; *(voto)* vote, support ♦ **alzar** *or* **levantar la v.** to raise one's voice • **a**

media v. in a low voice • **a una v.** with one voice, unanimously • **a voces** shouting • **a v. en cuello** at the top of one's voice • **dar voces** to shout • **de viva v.** by word of mouth • **en v. alta** in a loud voice • **llevar la v. cantante** FIG. to be the boss, call the shots • **pedir a voces** to clamor for, cry out for • **tener v. ronca** to be hoarse • **voces** clamor, outcry • **v. activa** GRAM. active voice • **v. cantante** MUS. leading part • **v. del pueblo** voice of the people, vox populi • **v. de mando** MIL. order, command • **v. de trueno** booming voice.

vo·za·rrón m. booming voice.

vuel·co m. upset, overturning ♦ **darle a uno un v. el corazón** FIG., COLL. to skip a beat (said of the heart) • **dar un v.** *(un coche)* to overturn, roll over; *(un barco)* to capsize.

vuel·co, vuelque see volcar.

vue·le, vuelo see volar.

vue·lo m. *(acción de volar)* flying, flight <*el v. del águila* the flight of the eagle>; AVIA. flight <*v. sin escala* nonstop flight>; ORNITH. *(plumas)* flight feathers; *(envergadura)* wingspan, wingspread; SEW. *(amplitud)* flare, fullness (of a skirt); *(adorno)* ruffle; ARCHIT. projection ♦ **al v.** *or* **a v.** *(inmediatamente)* immediately, at once; ORNITH. in flight • **a v. de pájaro** as the crow flies • **cortar los vuelos a alguien** FIG. to clip someone's wings • **de alto v.** big-time, ambitious • **de** *or* **en un v.** quickly, rapidly • **levantar el v.** *(echar a volar)* fly away, take flight; FIG. *(imaginarse)* to let one's imagination go; *(engreírse)* to become arrogant *or* haughty • **tocar a v. las campanas** to ring all the bells at once • **tomar v.** to grow, develop • **v. a vela** gliding • **v. espacial** space flight • **v. nocturno** night flight.

vuel·ta f. *(giro)* turn; *(revolución)* revolution; *(curvatura)* turn, bend, curve <*v. cerrada* sharp curve>; *(devolución)* return, giving back; *(regreso)* return <*te veré a la v.* I will see you upon my return>; *(paseo)* stroll, walk; *(revés)* reverse, back; *(dinero)* change <*quedarse con la v.* to keep the change>; *(repetición)* return, recurrence; *(cambio)* change, alteration; *(paliza)* beating, thrashing; SPORT. lap, round; SEW. *(embozo)* trimming, facing; *(adorno)* ruffle; *(serie de puntadas)* row of stitches; AGR. plowing; ARCHIT. *(bóveda)* vault; *(techo)* ceiling; *(curva)* curve; MUS. ritornello ♦ **a la v.** *(al volver)* on the way back, returning; *(al revés)* on the other side; *(cerca)* around the corner • **a la v. de** after, at the end of <*a la v. de pocos años* after a few years> • **a la v. de la esquina** around the corner • **andar vueltas** to quarrel, argue • **a v. de correo** by return mail • **a vueltas de** besides • **buscarle a alguien las vueltas** FIG. to look for a chance to get someone • **cogerle a alguien las vueltas** FIG. to find out what makes someone tick • **dar cien vueltas a** FIG. to run circles around • **dar la v. a** to turn <*dar la v. a la página* to turn the page> • **darle vueltas a** to turn over in one's mind • **dar vueltas** FIG. to go around in circles • **dar** *or* **darse una v.** *(pasearse)* to take a walk *or* a stroll; *(en auto)* to go for a ride; *(cambiar)* to change, alter • **dar v. a** to turn <*dar v. a la llave* to turn the key> • **dar vueltas** *(girar)* to go around, revolve; *(torcer)* to twist and turn <*la carretera da muchas vueltas* the highway twists and turns a great deal>; *(marearse)* to be in a whirl • **dar vueltas a** to turn • **de ida y v.** round-trip <*un billete de ida y v.* a round-trip ticket> • **déjate de vueltas** COLL. stop beating around the bush • **estar de v.** *(volver)* to be back; COLL. *(saber)* to have been there and back • **media v.** MIL. about-face • **no hay que darle vueltas** FIG. there are no two ways about it • **no tener v. de hoja** COLL. to be undeniable • **poner a alguien de v. y media** COLL. to heap abuse upon someone • **v. de campana** somersault.

vuel·to, –ta I. past part. see volver II. m. AMER. change <*guarde el v.* keep the change> —f. see vuelta.

vuel·va, vuelve see volver.

vues·tro, –tra §G25, 40 poss. adj. *(su)* your <*v. hermano y vuestras hermanas* your brother and (your) sisters>; *(suyo)* yours, of yours <*uno de vuestros parientes* a relative of yours> ♦ **los vuestros** *or* **las vuestras** yours, your own.

vul·ca·nis·mo m. GEOL. volcanism, vulcanism.

vul·ca·ni·zar §04 tr. TECH. to vulcanize.

vul·ca·no·lo·gí·a f. GEOL. volcanology, vulcanology.

vul·gar adj. *(común)* common, ordinary <*el hombre v.* the common man>; *(popular)* popular <*opinión v.* popular

opinion>; *(trivial)* trivial, banal; *(general)* general, lay <*término v.* general term>; *(grosero)* vulgar, coarse; *(hablado)* vulgar, vernacular <*latín v.* Vulgar Latin>.
vul·ga·ri·cé, vulgarice see **vulgarizar.**
vul·ga·ri·dad f. *(de una persona)* vulgarity, commonness; *(trivialidad)* triviality, commonplace.
vul·ga·ris·mo m. vulgarism.
vul·ga·ri·za·ción f. vulgarization, popularization.
vul·ga·ri·za·dor, –do·ra I. adj. popularizing II. m.f. popularizer.
vul·ga·ri·zar §04 tr. *(hacer vulgar)* to vulgarize; *(hacer asequible)* to popularize; *(difundir)* to spread, disseminate —reflex. to become vulgar *or* popularized.
vul·gar·men·te adv. *(groseramente)* vulgarly, coarsely; *(comúnmente)* commonly, popularly.
vul·ga·ta f. BIBL. Vulgate.
vul·go m. common people, masses.
vul·ne·ra·bi·li·dad f. vulnerability.
vul·ne·ra·ble adj. vulnerable.
vul·ne·ra·ción f. *(de una ley)* violation; *(acción de perjudicar)* harming, injuring.
vul·ne·rar tr. *(herir)* to wound; FIG. *(perjudicar)* to harm, injure; *(la ley)* to violate.
vul·pe·ja f. ZOOL. vixen.
vul·va f. ANAT. vulva.
vul·vi·tis f. MED. vulvitis.

W

w, W f. letter which, although not a part of the Spanish alphabet, is used in the spelling of words of foreign origin.
wad m. GEOL., MIN. bog manganese, black ocher.
wa·fle m. CUL. waffle.
wa·fle·ra f. CUL. waffle iron.
wag·ne·ria·no, –na adj. & m.f. MUS. Wagnerian.
wa·gon-lit m. RAIL. sleeping car.
wal·ha·lla m. MYTH. Valhalla.
wal·ki·ria f. MYTH. Valkyrie.
walk-o·ver m. walkover.
wa·rrant m. COM. warrant, receipt.
Wash·ing·ton m. Washington.
wat m. PHYS. watt.
wa·ter-clo·set *or* **wa·ter** m. toilet, water closet.
watt m. var. of **wat.**
week-end m. weekend.
wel·ter m. SPORT. welterweight.
whis·ky m. whiskey.
win·ches·ter m. ARTIL. Winchester (trademark).
wind·surf m. SPORT. windsurfing.
wol·fram *or* **wol·fra·mio** m. METAL. wolfram.

X

x, X f. twenty-sixth letter of the Spanish alphabet.
xan·ta·to m. CHEM. xanthate.
xán·ti·co, –ca adj. CHEM. xanthic.
xan·ti·na f. CHEM. xanthin; BIOCHEM. xanthine.
xa·ra f. RELIG. Moslem law derived from the Koran.
xe·no·fi·lia f. friendliness toward strangers *or* foreigners.
xe·no·fo·bia f. xenophobia.
xe·nó·fo·bo, –ba I. adj. xenophobic II. m.f. xenophobe.
xe·nón m. CHEM. xenon.
xe·ro·co·pia f. photocopy.
xe·ro·co·piar tr. to photocopy.
xe·ro·der·mia f. MED. xerosis.
xe·ró·fi·lo, –la adj. BOT. xerophilous.
xe·ro·gra·fí·a f. xerography.
xe·ro·gra·fiar §30 tr. to make a copy of (by means of xerography).
xe·ro·grá·fi·co, –ca adj. xerographic.
xi f. xi (Greek letter).
xi·le·no m. CHEM. xylene.

xi·ló·fo·no m. MUS. xylophone.
xi·lo·gra·fí·a f. *(arte)* xylography; *(impresión)* xylograph, wood engraving.
xi·loi·de·o, –a adj. xyloid, resembling wood.
xi·lór·ga·no m. MUS. xylophone.

Y

y, Y f. twenty-seventh letter of the Spanish alphabet.
y §G22, 46, 47 conj. and ♦ *¿y bien?* and then?, and what? • **y eso que** although, even though • *¿y qué?* so what?
ya I. adv. *(finalmente)* already <*ya hemos terminado* we have already finished>; *(ahora)* now, nowadays <*ya es famoso* now he is famous>; *(pronto)* soon <*ya nos veremos* we will see each other soon>; *(en seguida)* right away, at once; *(por último)* now <*ya es hora de tomar una decisión* now it is time to make a decision> ♦ **no ya** not only • **si ya** if, as long as • **ya lo creo** of course, naturally • **ya no** no longer • **ya que** since, inasmuch as II. conj. now, at times <*demuestra su talento ya en las artes, ya en las ciencias* she demonstrates her talent at times in the arts, at times in the sciences> III. interj. I see!
yac m. ZOOL. yak.
ya·ca·ré m. AMER., ZOOL. caiman, alligator.
ya·ce·dor m. stable boy (who takes horses out to graze at night).
ya·cen·te I. adj. lying, reclining II. m. MIN. floor of a vein.
ya·cer §79 intr. *(reposar)* to lie, be lying down; *(estar enterrado)* to lie, rest <*aquí yace Enrique Martínez* here lies Henry Martínez>; *(estar)* to be, be located; *(tener trato carnal)* to sleep, lie (with someone); AGR. to graze at night.
ya·cien·te adj. & m. var. of **yacente.**
ya·ci·ja f. *(lecho)* bed; *(tumba)* grave, tomb ♦ **ser de mala y.** FIG. *(dormir mal)* to be a restless sleeper; *(ser mala persona)* to be a ne'er-do-well.
ya·ci·mien·to m. GEOL. bed, deposit ♦ **y. petrolífero** oil field.
yac·tu·ra f. loss, damage.
ya·gua f. VEN., BOT. royal palm; CUBA, P. RICO fibrous tissue of royal palm tree.
ya·gual m. GUAT., HOND., MEX. padded ring (used for carrying loads on the head).
ya·guar m. ZOOL. jaguar.
ya·gu·ré m. AMER., ZOOL. skunk.
yám·bi·co, –ca adj. POET. iambic <*verso i.* iambic verse>.
yam·bo m. POET. iamb.
ya·na·cón, –co·na PERU I. adj. sharecropping II. m.f. sharecropper, tenant farmer.
ya·na·co·na I. adj. working as a servant on a large estate II. m.f. *(criado indio)* Indian servant on a large estate; BOL., PERU sharecropper, tenant farmer.
yan·kee *or* **yan·qui** adj. & m.f. Yankee, American.
ya·pa f. AMER. *(adehala)* bonus, lagniappe; ARG. thick end of a rope; MEX. tip, gratuity.
ya·par tr. AMER. to add a little extra (esp. as an incentive to buy).
ya·ra·ví m. [pl. **-ví·es**] melancholy Indian song.
yar·da f. yard (measurement).
ya·te m. MARIT. yacht.
ya·ya f. PERU, ENTOM. mite; CUBA, P. RICO, BOT. lancewood; COL., COLL. slight injury, boo-boo (babytalk) ♦ **dar y.** CUBA, COLL. to give a beating *or* whipping.
ye f. y (letter).
ye·dra f. BOT. ivy.
ye·gua f. ZOOL. mare; C. AMER. cigar butt.
ye·gua·da f. ZOOL. herd of horses; C. AMER. blunder, foolish remark.
ye·gua·ri·zo, –za I. adj. equine, of horses II. m. ARG. horse keeper, hostler.
ye·güe·rí·a f. herd of horses.
ye·ís·mo m. pronunciation of Spanish *ll* as *y.*
yel·mo m. helmet.
ye·ma f. *(del huevo)* yolk; BOT. bud, shoot; FIG. *(medio)* middle, heart <*la y. del invierno* the middle of winter>; *(lo*

mejor) cream, best part; COLL. (*dificultad*) snag ♦ **y. del dedo** finger tip • **y. mejida** eggnog.

Ye·men m. Yemen.

Yemen Democrático m. Democratic Yemen.

ye·me·ni·ta adj. & m.f. Yemenite.

yen·te I. adj. going **II.** m. ♦ **yentes y vinientes** passersby.

yer·ba f. BOT. grass, herb; S. AMER. maté.

yer·bal m. AMER. (*campo de yerba mate*) field of maté; (*recipiente*) pot for making maté; (*herbazal*) pasture.

yer·ba·te·ro, –ra I. adj. AMER. of maté **II.** m.f. (*curandero*) quack; (*vendedor*) maté seller.

yer·go, yergue see **erguir.**

yer·mar tr. to strip, lay waste (land).

yer·mo, –ma I. adj. (*inculto*) barren, uncultivated; (*inhabitado*) uninhabited, deserted **II.** m. desert, wilderness.

yer·no m. son-in-law.

ye·rra f. AMER. cattle branding.

ye·rre, yerro see **errar.**

ye·rro m. (*falta*) fault, misdeed; (*pecado*) sin; (*error*) mistake, error ♦ **y. de imprenta** typographical error.

yer·to, –ta adj. stiff, rigid ♦ **y. de frío** frozen stiff.

yes·ca f. (*materia que arde*) touchwood, tinder; FIG. (*incentivo*) fuel (of passion); FIG., COLL. (*cosa que da sed*) thirst provoker ♦ **echar una y.** to strike a light • **yescas** tinderbox.

ye·se·ro, –ra I. adj. plaster, of plaster **II.** m. plasterer —f. gypsum pit.

ye·so m. GEOL. gypsum; ARTS, CONSTR. plaster <*y. mate* plaster of Paris>; (*vaciado*) plaster cast; (*tiza*) chalk.

ye·són m. chunk of plaster.

ye·so·so, –sa adj. gypseous, chalky.

yes·que·ro, –ra I. adj. ♦ **cardo y.** BOT. cotton thistle • **hongo y.** BOT. touchwood, tinder fungus **II.** m. (*bolsa*) purse, pouch; (*fabricante*) tinder maker; (*vendedor*) tinder seller; PERU tinderbox; ARG. steel (for striking flint).

yid·dish m. Yiddish.

yo §G30 **I.** pron. I <*yo lo hice* I did it> • **soy yo** it's I *or* me • **yo mismo** I myself **II.** m. ego, self.

yo·da·do, –da adj. iodized.

yo·da·to m. CHEM. iodate.

yó·di·co, –ca adj. CHEM. iodic.

yo·do m. CHEM. iodine.

yo·du·ro m. CHEM. iodide ♦ **y. de plata** silver iodide • **y. mercúrico** mercuric iodine.

yo·ga m. yoga.

yo·gi *or* **yo·ghi** m. yogi.

yo·gur *or* **yo·gurt** m. CUL. yogurt.

yo·la f. MARIT. yawl.

yo·yo m. yo-yo.

y·pe·ri·ta f. CHEM. yperite.

yp·si·lon f. var. of **ípsilon.**

y·ter·bio m. MIN. ytterbium.

y·trio m. MIN. yttrium.

yu·bar·ta f. ZOOL. humpback whale.

yu·ca f. BOT. (*mandioca*) cassava, manioc; (*izote*) yucca; HOND., COLL. bad news; C. AMER. lie.

yu·cal m. BOT. yucca *or* cassava field.

yu·do m. SPORT. judo.

yu·ga·da f. AGR. (*tierra*) day's plowing; (*de bueyes*) yoke (of oxen).

yu·go m. (*arreo*) yoke; FIG. (*opresión*) yoke, oppression; (*carga pesada*) yoke, burden; MARIT. transom ♦ **sacudir el y.** FIG. to throw off the yoke • **y. del matrimonio** marital bond.

Yu·gos·la·via f. Yugoslavia.

yu·gos·la·vo, –va adj. & m.f. Yugoslav, Yugoslavian.

yu·gue·ro m. AGR. plowman.

yu·gu·lar adj. & f. ANAT. jugular.

yun·gas I. f.pl. BOL., CHILE, PERU warm valleys **II.** adj. of the warm valleys.

yun·que m. (*de hierro*) anvil; FIG. (*persona*) patient and persevering person; ANAT. incus, anvil ♦ **estar al y.** COLL. (*trabajar mucho*) to be hard at work; (*en las adversidades*) to bear up, be patient.

yun·to, –ta I. adj. joined, united **II.** adv. close <*arar y.* to plow close> **III.** f. AGR. (*de bueyes*) yoke (of oxen); (*tierra*) day's plowing.

yu·sión f. LAW order, command.

yu·te m. BOT., TEX. jute.

yux·ta·li·ne·al adj. PRINT. line by line, in parallel columns.

yux·ta·po·ner §54 tr. to juxtapose.

yux·ta·po·si·ción f. juxtaposition.

yu·yal m. AMER. weed patch.

yu·yo m. AMER., BOT. weed; CHILE wall rocket; PERU vegetable; COL., ECUAD. herb, condiment; C. RICA foot blister; PERU, FIG., COLL. boob, jerk.

yu·yu·ba f. BOT. jujube.

Z

z, Z f. twenty-eighth letter of the Spanish alphabet.

za·bor·dar intr. MARIT. to run aground.

za·ca·tal m. AMER. pasture.

za·ca·te m. AMER., PHILIP., AGR. fodder, hay.

za·fa·co·ca f. AMER., COLL. fight, squabble.

za·fa·do, –da I. past part. see **zafar II.** adj. ARG. sharp, alert; AMER. shameless, brazen **III.** f. MARIT. unbending, loosening.

za·far tr. MARIT. (*un nudo*) to untie, loosen; (*una vela*) to unbend; (*adornar*) to adorn, deck —reflex. (*de un peligro*) to escape, avoid (a danger); FIG. (*de un compromiso*) to evade, get out of (a commitment); (*de una persona*) to get rid of, get away from (a person); AMER., ANAT. to become dislocated; (*una correa*) to come off, slip off ♦ **zafarse de** to escape from • **zafarse con** COLL. to run off with.

za·fa·rran·cho m. MARIT. clearing the decks; FIG., COLL. (*destrozo*) destruction, havoc; (*riña*) quarrel, rumpus <*armar un z.* to kick up a rumpus> ♦ **z. de combate** MIL., MARIT. clearing for action.

za·fio, –fia adj. crude, coarse.

za·fi·ro m. sapphire.

za·fra¹ f. (*para medidas*) drip can or jar; (*para aceite*) oil can *or* jar.

za·fra² f. (*cosecha*) sugar cane harvest; (*fabricación*) sugarmaking; (*temporada*) sugar cane harvest season; MIN. rubbish, debris.

za·ga f. (*parte posterior*) back, rear; (*carga*) back load; SPORT. back, defense —m. (*en el juego*) last player ♦ **a** *or* **a la** *or* **en z.** behind, in the rear • **no irle uno en z. a otro** FIG. to be just as good as another.

za·gal, –ga·la m. (*mozo*) boy, youth; (*pastor*) shepherd boy —f. (*moza*) girl, lass; (*pastora*) shepherd girl.

za·gual m. paddle (of a canoe).

za·guán m. front hall, vestibule.

za·gua·ne·te m. (*aposento*) royal guardroom; (*guardia*) royal guard.

za·gue·ro, –ra I. adj. (*trasero*) rear, back; (*que va en zaga*) lagging behind **II.** m. (*en fútbol*) back, defense; (*en pelota*) backstop.

za·he·ri·dor, –do·ra I. adj. blaming, criticizing **II.** m.f. blamer, criticizer.

za·he·ri·mien·to m. reproach, dig.

za·he·rir §65 tr. (*criticar*) to criticize, reproach; (*ridiculizar*) to mock, mortify.

za·ho·na·do, –da adj. having front legs of a different color from the body (said of animals).

za·hon·dar tr. to dig —intr. to sink (into the ground).

za·ho·nes m.pl. chaps, leather breeches.

za·ho·rí m. [pl. -**rí·es**] (*adivino*) seer, diviner; FIG. (*persona perspicaz*) perceptive person.

za·hur·da f. (*pocilga*) pigsty; FIG. pigsty, dump.

zai·no, –na adj. (*un caballo*) pure chestnut (horse); (*el ganado vacuno*) pure black (cattle); FIG. (*falso*) false, treacherous ♦ **mirar a lo z.** to look sideways, look out of the corner of one's eye.

Zai·re m. Zaire.

zai·ren·se adj. & m.f. Zairian, Zairean.

za·lá f. [pl. -**la·es**] RELIG. Moslem prayer ♦ **hacer la z. a** FIG., COLL. to butter up, flatter.

za·la·gar·da f. (*emboscada*) ambush, trap; (*pelea*) fight, skirmish; FIG., HUNT. trap, snare; FIG., COLL. (*astucia*) cunning, astuteness; (*alboroto*) rumpus, uproar.

za·la·me·rí·a f. wheedling, cajolery, flattery.

za·la·me·ro, -ra I. adj. coaxing, wheedling II. m.f. coaxer, wheedler, flatterer.

za·le·ma f. salaam.

za·ma·cu·co m. COLL. *(tonto)* fool, ninny; *(hombre solapado)* sly or crafty person; FIG., COLL. drunk, spree.

za·ma·cue·ca f. CHILE, PERU, MUS. folk dance; P. RICO hypocrite.

za·ma·rra f. *(chaqueta)* sheepskin jacket; *(piel)* sheepskin.

za·ma·rre·ar tr. *(sacudir)* to shake; FIG., COLL. *(maltratar)* to push around; FIG. *(en una discusión)* to corner, pin down.

za·ma·rre·o m. *(sacudimiento)* shaking; FIG. *(trato malo)* rough treatment.

za·ma·rro m. *(chaqueta)* sheepskin jacket; *(piel)* sheepskin; FIG., COLL. *(hombre tosco)* boor, lout; C. RICA, VEN. shrewd or cunning person; HOND. rascal, rogue ♦ **zamarros** AMER. chaps.

zam·ba I. f. AMER. *(samba)* samba; ARG. popular dance II. adj. see **zambo, -ba.**

zam·bar·co m. *(correa)* broad breast strap (of a harness); *(cincha)* cinch.

zam·bar·do m. AMER. chance, luck; CHILE *(torpeza)* awkwardness, clumsiness; *(avería)* breakage, damage; *(persona torpe)* awkward or clumsy person.

Zam·be·ze m. Zambezi.

Zam·bia f. Zambia.

zam·bia·no, -na adj. & m.f. Zambian.

zam·bo, -ba I. adj. *(torcido)* bowlegged; AMER. half-Black and half-Indian; CHILE, COL. mulatto II. m.f. *(torcido)* bowlegged person; AMER. half-Black and half-Indian person; CHILE, COL. mulatto —m. ZOOL. spider monkey —f. see **zamba.**

zam·bom·ba f. MUS. zambomba (drum-like folk instrument) ♦ **¡zambomba!** whew!, wow!

zam·bom·ba·zo m. *(golpe)* blow, thump; *(explosión)* explosion; *(ruido)* bang, boom.

zam·bom·bo m. COLL. lout, boor.

zam·bo·ron·dón, -do·na or **zam·bo·ro·tu·do, -da** COLL. I. adj. *(grosero)* crude, uncouth; *(desmañado)* clumsy, awkward II. m.f. *(grosero)* crude or uncouth person; *(desmañado)* clumsy or awkward person.

zam·bra f. *(fiesta morisca)* Moorish festival; *(baile gitano)* Andalusian gypsy dance; COLL. *(algazara)* din, rumpus.

zam·bu·car §70 tr. COLL. to hide, conceal.

zam·bu·lli·da f. *(zambullidura)* dive, plunge; *(en esgrima)* lunge, thrust ♦ **darle a alguien una z.** to duck someone • **darse una z.** to take a dip.

zam·bu·lli·dor, -do·ra I. adj. diving, plunging II. m. COL., ORNITH. dabchick.

zam·bu·lli·du·ra f. or **zam·bu·lli·mien·to** m. dive, plunge.

zam·bu·llir §13 tr. to plunge, duck —reflex. *(meterse en el agua)* to dive, plunge; *(esconderse)* to hide.

zam·bu·llo m. AMER. waste barrel.

zam·bu·qué, zambuque see **zambucar.**

zam·pa·li·mos·nas m.f. [pl. **-nas**] COLL. tramp, bum.

zam·par tr. *(esconder rápidamente)* to hide quickly; *(comer)* to wolf (down), gobble —reflex. to rush, dash (into a room).

zam·pa·tor·tas m.f. [pl. **-tas**] COLL. *(persona glotona)* pig, glutton; *(torpe)* numskull, blockhead.

zam·po·ña f. MUS. reed flute, panpipe; FIG., COLL. *(tontería)* nonsense.

zam·pu·zar §04 tr. to hide quickly.

zam·pu·zo m. hiding, concealing.

za·na·ho·ria f. BOT. carrot; ARG. dummy, nitwit.

zan·ca f. ORNITH. bird's leg; FIG., COLL. *(pierna)* long thin leg (of a person); SP. large pin; *(de una escalera)* stringboard (of a staircase) ♦ **andar en zancas y barrancas** COLL. to stall, invent excuses • **por zancas o barrancas** COLL. by hook or by crook.

zan·ca·da I. f. *(paso largo)* stride ♦ **en dos zancadas** FIG., COLL. in a jiffy. II. adj. see **zancado, -da.**

zan·ca·di·lla f. *(acción de derribar a uno)* tripping; FIG., COLL. *(engaño)* trick; *(trampa)* trap ♦ **armarle z. a alguien** COLL. to set a trap for someone, trip someone up • **echarle la z. a alguien** COLL. to trip someone.

zan·ca·do, -da I. adj. ICHTH. which has spawned (said of salmon) II. f. see **zancada.**

zan·ca·je·ar intr. to rush or dash around.

zan·ca·jo m. *(hueso del talón)* heel bone; *(talón)* heel; *(hueso grande)* long bone; FIG., COLL. *(persona pequeña)* runt, pip-squeak ♦ **ir arrastrando los zancajos** to drag one's heels.

zan·ca·jo·so, -sa adj. *(con los pies torcidos)* bowlegged; *(que lleva calzados rotos)* wearing stockings with torn heels.

zan·ca·rrón m. COLL. *(hueso de la pierna)* leg bone; FIG., COLL. *(hombre viejo)* skinny old man; *(mal profesor)* bad teacher.

zan·co m. stilt <andar en zancos to walk on stilts> ♦ **estar en zancos** FIG., COLL. to be high up, be in a high position.

zan·cón, -co·na adj. COLL. *(zancudo)* lanky, long-legged; AMER. too short (said of a dress).

zan·cu·do, -da I. adj. *(de zancas largas)* long-legged; ORNITH. wading II. f.pl. **zancudas** ORNITH. wading birds —m. AMER., ENTOM. mosquito.

zan·fo·ní·a f. MUS. hurdy-gurdy.

zan·ga·na·da f. COLL. nervy or stupid remark.

zan·gan·don·go, -ga m.f. COLL. *(holgazán)* lazybones; *(desmañado)* clumsy ox.

zan·gan·dun·go, -ga or **zan·gan·du·llo, -lla** m.f. COLL. *(holgazán)* lazybones; *(desmañado)* clumsy ox.

zan·ga·ne·ar intr. COLL. to bum, loaf (around).

zan·ga·ne·rí·a f. bumming, loafing (around).

zán·ga·no f. ENTOM. drone; FIG., COLL. *(holgazán)* sponger, parasite; C. AMER. rascal, rogue.

zan·ga·rre·ar intr. COLL. to strum (a guitar).

zan·ga·rria·na f. VET. staggers; FIG., COLL. *(dolencia)* slight recurring ailment; *(melancolía)* blues, sadness.

zan·ga·ru·llón m. COLL. big lazybones, big good-for-nothing (said of a youth).

zan·go·lo·te·ar tr. COLL. to jiggle, shake —intr. FIG., COLL. to fidget, squirm —reflex. COLL. to rattle, shake (door or window).

zan·go·lo·te·o m. COLL. shaking, rattling.

zan·go·lo·ti·no, -na adj. COLL. babyish, childish <niño z. big baby>.

zan·gón m. COLL. big lazybones, big good-for-nothing (said of a youth).

zan·go·te·ar intr. COLL. to fidget, squirm.

zan·guan·go, -ga I. adj. COLL. lazy, idle II. m.f. *(perezoso)* loafer, bum —f. *(acción de fingir una enfermedad)* faking illness, malingering; *(zalamería)* fawning, wheedling.

zan·ja f. ditch, trench ♦ **abrir las zanjas** to lay the foundations • **zanja de desagüe** drainage channel.

zan·jar tr. *(cavar)* to dig a ditch or trench; FIG. *(aclarar)* to clear up a matter.

zan·jón m. large ditch or trench.

zan·que·a·dor, -do·ra m.f. *(que camina zanqueado)* bowlegged walker; *(que camina mucho)* heavy walker.

zan·que·a·mien·to m. bowlegged walk, waddling.

zan·que·ar intr. *(torcer las piernas al andar)* to walk bowlegged; *(caminar mucho)* to walk a lot, stride along.

zan·qui·va·no, -na adj. COLL. spindle-legged.

za·pa f. *(pala)* spade; *(acción de zapar)* trenching, digging; TECH. shagreen, sharkskin ♦ **piel de z.** shagreen, sharkskin.

za·pa·dor m. MIL. sapper.

za·pa·llo m. AMER., BOT. pumpkin, squash.

za·pa·pi·co m. pickax, mattock.

za·par intr. to sap, mine.

za·pa·rra·da f. COLL. scratch (from a claw).

za·pa·rras·trar intr. to drag or trail one's clothing.

za·pa·rras·tro·so, -sa I. adj. COLL. ragged, shabby II. m.f. bum, tramp.

za·pa·rra·zo m. COLL. scratch (from a claw).

za·pa·ta f. *(calzado)* half boot; MECH. shoe <z. de freno brake shoe>; *(arandela)* washer (of a faucet); MARIT. shoe (of an anchor); ARCHIT. socle.

za·pa·ta·zo m. *(golpe)* blow with a shoe; MARIT. sail-flapping; *(ruido)* bang, thud; *(caballos)* hoofbeats ♦ **dar zapatazos** to stamp one's feet • **mandar a zapatazos** FIG. to tyrannize, rule with an iron hand • **tratar a zapatazos** COLL. to kick around, mistreat.

za·pa·te·a·do m. *(baile)* old Spanish heel-tapping dance; *(taconeo)* footwork.

za·pa·te·a·dor, –do·ra I. adj. tap dancing II. m.f. tap dancer.

za·pa·te·ar tr. *(golpear)* to hit with the shoe; *(bailar)* to tap-dance; FIG., COLL. *(maltratar)* to ill-treat, mistreat —intr. *(bailar)* to tap one's feet; MARIT. to flap (sails) —reflex. FIG. to stand firm.

za·pa·te·o m. *(acción de zapatear)* tapping; *(baile)* tap dancing, heel-tapping; MARIT. flapping (of sails).

za·pa·te·rí·a f. *(taller)* shoemaker's shop; *(tienda)* shoe store; *(oficio)* shoemaking trade ♦ **z. de viejo** cobbler's, shoe repair shop.

za·pa·te·ro, –ra I. adj. underdone, undercooked (vegetables) II. m.f. *(fabricación)* shoemaker; *(venta)* shoe seller; *(remienda)* shoe mender, cobbler; ICHTH. cobbler fish ♦ **quedarse z.** COLL. to get no tricks (cards) • **z., a tus zapatos** mind your own business, stick to what you know.

za·pa·te·ta f. shoe-slap accompanied by a jump in certain dances ♦ **¡zapatetas!** COLL. oh, my!, goodness gracious!

za·pa·ti·lla f. *(pantufla)* house shoe, slipper; *(de baile)* dancing shoe, pump; TAUR. matador's slipper; *(billar)* cue tip; *(esgrima)* button; MECH. washer; MIL., MUS. leather pad; ZOOL. cloven hoof ♦ **z. de la reina** BOT. giant yellow poppy • **poner como una z. china** PERU to tell someone off.

za·pa·to m. shoe ♦ **como tres en un z.** COLL. packed in like sardines • **meter en un z.** FIG. to intimidate • **saber uno donde le aprieta el z.** FIG. to know what is best for oneself • **zapatos papales** overshoes, galoshes.

za·pa·tu·do, –da adj. *(zapatos)* wearing clodhoppers; *(pezuña)* thick-hoofed; CUBA undercooked, underdone; MECH. provided with a washer.

¡za·pe! interj. COLL. *(a un animal)* shoo! scram!; *(en naipes)* denial of request for a card.

za·pe·ar tr. *(un animal)* to shoo or scare away; COLL. *(un jugador)* to deny a request for a card.

za·po·tal m. BOT. sapodilla grove.

za·po·te m. BOT. sapodilla tree or fruit.

za·po·te·co, –ca I. adj. Zapotecan II. m.f. Zapotec.

za·po·te·ro m. BOT. sapodilla tree.

za·qui·za·mí m. [pl. **-mí·es**] *(desván)* attic, garret; *(cuarto incómodo)* hovel, hole.

zar m. czar, tsar.

za·ra·ban·da f. *(baile)* sarabande; *(ruido)* turmoil, tumult.

za·ra·ga·ta f. COLL. *(jaleo)* ruckus, row; CUBA flattery, cajolery.

za·ra·ga·te·ro, –ra I. adj. COLL. rambunctious, quarrelsome II. m.f. troublemaker.

za·ran·da f. *(criba)* sieve, strainer; *(trompo)* spinning top.

za·ran·da·jas f.pl. COLL. trifles, unimportant matters ♦ **entretenerse en z.** to bother with trifles.

za·ran·dar or **za·ran·de·ar** tr. *(cribar)* to sift, winnow; *(colar)* to strain; *(sacudir)* to shake —reflex. to be on the go, wear oneself out —intr. AMER. to walk provocatively.

za·ran·de·o m. *(criba)* sifting, sieving; *(colador)* straining; *(sacudida)* shaking; *(caminada)* coquettish strut; *(prisa)* bustle, rush.

za·ran·de·ro, –ra m.f. sifter.

za·ra·tán m. MED., COLL. breast cancer; HOND., VET. trichina.

za·ra·za f. TEX. chintz, gingham; *(veneno)* homemade poison for vermin.

zar·ce·ño, –ña adj. brambly.

zar·ci·llo m. *(pendiente)* earring; BOT. tendril; *(escardillo)* hoe, rake; ARG. *(ganado)* identification mark on cattle; *(barril)* barrel hoop ♦ **de z.** CHILE arm in arm.

zar·co, –ca adj. *(color)* light blue; ARG. wall-eyed; GUAT. white, Caucasian.

za·ri·güe·ya f. ZOOL. opossum.

za·ri·na f. czarina, tsarina.

za·ris·ta I. adj. czaristic, tsaristic II. m.f. czarist, tsarist.

zar·pa f. *(garra)* claw, paw; *(acción)* pawing; ARCHIT. footing; MARIT. weighing anchor; *(cazcarria)* splash of mud ♦ **echar la z. a algo** COLL. to seize or clutch (something).

zar·pa·da f. pawing, clawing ♦ **dar una z.** to lash out with the claws.

zar·par tr. to raise anchor —intr. to set sail, sail out.

zar·pa·zo m. lash of a claw or paw.

zar·pe m. AMER. splash of mud.

zar·pe·ar tr. AMER. to splash or splatter with mud.

zar·po·so, –sa adj. splattered (with mud).

za·rra·pas·tra f. COLL. splash of mud.

za·rra·pas·tro·so, –sa or **za·rra·pas·trón, –tro·na** I. adj. shabby, ragged II. m.f. ragamuffin, tramp.

zar·za f. BOT. bramble, blackberry bush.

zar·zal m. blackberry or bramble patch.

zar·za·mo·ra f. blackberry.

zar·za·pa·rri·lla f. BOT. sarsaparilla; *(bebida)* sarsaparilla (drink).

zar·zo m. wattle, woven fence; COL. garret.

zar·zo·so, –sa adj. brambly, briery; *(espinoso)* spiny.

zar·zue·la f. MUS., THEAT. Spanish comedy or operetta; SP., CUL. rice and seafood dish.

zar·zue·le·ro or **zar·zue·lis·ta** m. author or composer of zarzuelas.

¡zas! interj. bang!, whack!

za·zo·so, –sa adj. stammering, stuttering.

ze·da f. zee (letter).

ze·di·lla f. *(letra)* cedilla (letter in Old Spanish alphabet); *(signo)* cedilla (diacritic).

ze·nit m. zenith.

ze·ta f. *(letra)* zee; *(letra griega)* zeta (Greek letter).

zi·go·to m. BIOL. zygote.

zi·gu·rat m. ARCHIT. ziggurat.

zig·zag m. zigzag.

zig·za·gue·ar intr. to zigzag, meander.

zig·za·gue·o m. zigzagging, meandering.

Zim·bab·we Zimbabwe.

zim·bab·wen·se adj. & m.f. Zimbabwean.

zinc m. METAL. zinc.

zín·ga·ro, –ra adj. & m.f. gypsy, tzigane.

zi·pi·za·pe m. COLL. row, rumpus.

¡zis, zas! interj. bang! bang!

zó·ca·lo m. ARCHIT. *(de un edificio)* socle; *(pedestal)* plinth; *(parte inferior de una pared)* skirting board; GEOL. shelf; MEX. public square.

zo·ca·te·ar·se intr. to become overripe or mealy (fruit).

zo·ca·to, –ta adj. overripe, mealy (fruit); CUBA stale (bread); COLL. *(zurdo)* left-handed.

zo·co, –ca I. adj. COLL. left-handed, lefty II. m. *(mercado)* Moroccan marketplace; ARCHIT. *(pedestal)* plinth, pedestal.

zo·dia·cal adj. zodiacal.

zo·dia·co or **zo·dí·a·co** m. zodiac.

zoi·lo m. malicious critic.

zo·lo·cho, –cha COLL. I. adj. silly, foolish II. m.f. fool, simpleton.

zom·po, –pa I. adj. *(contrahecho)* crippled, deformed; *(torpe)* clumsy, awkward II. m.f. *(contrahecho)* cripple, deformed person; *(torpe)* clumsy or awkward person.

zo·na f. *(distrito)* zone, district; GEOG. zone <z. templada temperate zone>; MED. zona, shingles; FIG. *(area)* zone, area <z. de influencia zone of influence> ♦ **z. de ensanche** urban development zone • **z. fronteriza** border zone • **z. postal** postal district • **zonas verdes** park areas.

zo·nal adj. zonal.

zon·ce·ra AMER. or **zon·ce·rí·a** f. nonsense, silliness.

zo·ni·fi·ca·ción f. zoning.

zo·ni·fi·car §70 tr. to zone.

zon·zo, –za COLL. I. adj. foolish, silly II. m.f. fool, nitwit.

zo·o m. zoo.

zo·ó·fi·to ZOOL. I. adj. zoophytic, zoophytical II. m. zoophyte.

zo·o·ge·o·gra·fí·a f. zoogeography.

zo·o·gra·fí·a f. zoography.

zo·oi·de adj. & m.f. ZOOL. zooid.

zo·o·lo·gí·a f. zoology.

zo·o·ló·gi·co, –ca adj. zoological ♦ **jardín z.** ZOO.

zo·ó·lo·go, –ga m.f. zoologist.

zoom m. CINEM. *(objetivo)* zoom lens; *(efecto)* zoom effect.

zo·pen·co, –ca COLL. I. adj. dumb, dopy II. m.f. dummy, dope.

zo·pi·lo·te m. AMER., ORNITH. buzzard.

zo·pi·sa f. tar, pitch.

zo·po, –pa I. adj. crippled, deformed II. m.f. cripple, deformed person.
zo·que·ta f. AGR. wooden hand guard.
zo·que·te m. *(de madera)* chunk of wood; FIG. *(de pan)* hunk of bread; FIG., COLL. *(persona pequeña y gorda)* chunky person; *(tonto)* dummy, blockhead.
zo·que·te·ro, –ra I. adj. begging II. m.f. beggar, tramp.
zo·que·tu·do, –da adj. rough, poorly made.
zo·ro·ás·tri·co, –ca adj. & m.f. HIST., RELIG. Zoroastrian.
zo·ro·llo adj. AGR. reaped while unripe (wheat).
zo·rra f. ZOOL. fox; *(hembra)* vixen; FIG. *(astuto)* sly fox, clever person; FIG., COLL. *(prostituta)* whore, prostitute; *(carro)* dray, cart; MEX., COLL. *(borrachera)* drunkenness ♦ **z. de mar** ICHTH. sea fox.
zo·rras·trón, –tro·na I. adj. COLL. crafty, sly II. m.f. cunning person.
zo·rre·ra¹ I. f. *(madriguera)* foxhole; FIG. *(habitación)* smoke-filled room II. adj. see zorrero, –ra.
zo·rre·ra² I. f. COLL. drowsiness, sleepiness II. adj. see zorrero, –ra.
zo·rre·rí·a f. FIG., COLL. craftiness, cunning.
zo·rre·ro, –ra I. adj. *(barco)* heavy-sailing; *(perro)* fox-hunting (dog); *(astuto)* cunning, sly II. m. foxhound.
zo·rri·llo or **zo·rri·no** m. AMER., ZOOL. skunk.
zo·rro m. ZOOL. fox; *(piel)* fox (skin); FIG., COLL. *(astuto)* sly fox, clever person; *(perezoso)* idler, malingerer; AMER. skunk ♦ **hacerse el z.** FIG. to play dumb • **z. azul** blue fox • **z. negro** raccoon • **zorros** duster.
zo·rron·glón, –glo·na I. adj. grumpy, grumbling II. m.f. COLL. grumbler, grump.
zo·rru·no, –na adj. foxlike, vulpine ♦ **oler a z.** FIG., COLL. to smell sweaty.
zor·zal m. ORNITH. thrush; FIG. *(hombre astuto)* sly or cunning person; ARG., BOL., CHILE dullard, simpleton; P. RICO hyperactive boy ♦ **z. marino** ICHTH. black wrasse.
zo·te I. adj. clumsy, dopy II. m.f. COLL. dope, clod.
zo·zo·bra f. *(naufragio)* shipwreck, capsizing; *(hundimiento)* sinking; METEOROL. dangerous weather; FIG. *(perdición)* jeopardy, ruination; *(inquietud)* anxiety, worry <*vivir en una perpetua z.* to fret constantly>.
zo·zo·brar intr. MARIT. *(estar en peligro)* to be in danger; *(hundirse)* to sink, founder; FIG. *(fracasar)* to fail, founder; *(afligirse)* to worry, fret.
zua·vo m. MIL. Zouave.
zue·co m. *(de madera)* clog, wooden shoe; *(de cuero y madera)* leather shoe with wooden sole; COLL. *(persona zurda)* southpaw, lefty.
zu·lú adj. & m.f. Zulu.
zu·llar·se reflex. COLL. *(ensuciarse)* to dirty oneself, defecate; *(ventosearse)* to break wind.
zu·ma·cal or **zu·ma·car** m. sumach field.
zu·ma·que m. BOT. sumac, sumach; COLL. *(vino)* wine ♦ **z. del Japón** BOT. ailanthus, tree of heaven • **z. venenoso** poison sumac, poison ivy.
zum·ba f. *(cencerro)* bell worn by lead animal (in a pack); *(juguete)* bullroarer; FIG. *(broma)* teasing, joking; AMER. beating, thrashing.
zum·ba·dor, –do·ra I. adj. buzzing, humming II. m. *(aparato)* buzzer; AMER. bullroarer.
zum·bar intr. *(un insecto)* to buzz, hum; *(motor)* to purr; *(los oídos)* to ring —tr. COLL. *(golpear)* to deliver (a blow); *(bromear)* to tease; FIG., COLL. *(acercarse a algo)* to be very close to something, be pushing <*ya le zumban los cincuenta años* he's already pushing fifty>; CARIB., COL. to clear out, beat it; AMER. to throw, fling —reflex. COLL. to hit one another, trade blows.

zum·bi·do m. *(de insecto)* buzzing, humming (insects); *(de los oídos)* ringing (ears); *(de un motor)* purring, whirring; COLL. *(golpe)* blow, smack.
zum·bo m. *(ruido)* buzz, hum; COL. gourd, pot.
zum·bón, –bo·na I. adj. *(ruido)* ringing, buzzing; *(burlador)* teasing II. m.f. *(burlador)* joker; ORNITH. pigeon.
zu·mien·to adj. juicy, succulent.
zu·mo m. *(jugo)* juice of a plant or fruit <*z. de tomate* tomato juice>; FIG. *(provecho)* profit, advantage ♦ **sacarle el z. a alguien** to bleed someone dry • **z. de cepas** or **de parras** COLL. wine.
zu·mo·so, –sa adj. juicy, succulent.
zu·na f. RELIG. Sunna, Mohammedan law; *(perfidia)* trickery.
zun·char tr. to fasten with a metal band or strap.
zun·cho m. metal strap or band.
zu·pia f. *(poso)* dregs, sediment; *(vino turbio)* muddy or cloudy wine; FIG. *(cosa de mal aspecto)* something fishy; BOL., VEN. spoiled brandy.
zur·ci·do m. darn, mending ♦ **z. de mentiras** a pack of lies.
zur·ci·dor, –do·ra I. adj. darning II. m.f. darner ♦ **z. de voluntades** pimp, go-between.
zur·ci·du·ra f. *(acción)* darning, mending; *(costura)* mend, darn.
zur·cir §35 tr. *(ropa)* to darn, mend; FIG. *(enlazar)* to join or put together; FIG., COLL. *(mentiras)* to spin a web of lies ♦ **anda y que te zurzan** FIG., COLL. go jump in the lake, go to hell.
zur·de·ra or **zur·de·rí·a** f. left-handedness.
zur·do, –da I. adj. left-handed; MECH. left-handed (screw) II. m.f. left-handed person, southpaw ♦ **a zurdas** *(con la mano izquierda)* with the left hand; COLL. *(al revés)* wrong, backhandedly • **no ser z.** to be agile and clever.
zu·rra f. *(cuero)* tanning, dressing (leather); FIG. *(paliza)* thrashing, tanning; COLL. *(trabajo pesado)* grind, drudgery; *(disputa)* brawl, scuffle.
zu·rra·dor, –do·ra I. adj. tanning II. m.f. tanner (leather).
zu·rra·pa f. *(poso)* dregs, sediment; FIG., COLL. *(cosa despreciable)* nonsense, garbage; COLL. *(joven)* skinny ugly boy ♦ **con zurrapas** COLL. in a base or dirty manner.
zu·rrar tr. to tan, dress (leather); FIG., COLL. *(dar paliza)* to tan (someone's) hide, give a beating; *(reprender)* to give (someone) a tongue-lashing or dressing-down —reflex. *(ensuciarse)* to dirty oneself, soil oneself; *(tener miedo)* to be scared to death.
zu·rriar §30 intr. to rattle, hum.
zu·rri·ban·da f. COLL. *(pelea)* fight, scuffle; *(golpiza)* beating, thrashing.
zu·rri·bu·rri m. COLL. *(canalla)* scum, rogue; *(grupo)* rabble, gang of shady characters; *(jaleo)* tumult, confusion.
zu·rri·do m. *(golpe)* whack, blow; *(ruido)* harsh noise.
zu·rrón m. *(bolsa)* leather bag or pouch; BOT. husk (of fruit); MED. amnion, amniotic bag ♦ **z. de pastor** BOT. shepherd's purse.
zu·rro·na f. COLL. loose woman, tramp.
zu·rro·na·da f. bag, bagful.
zu·rrus·car·se §70 reflex. COLL. to be scared to death, be scared stiff.
zu·ru·llo m. *(cosa blanda)* round lump of soft material; VULG. turd.
zu·ru·pe·to m. COLL. *(corredor de bolsa intruso)* unlicensed broker or agent; *(notario intruso)* unauthorized notary.
zur·za, zurzo see zurcir.
zu·ta·no, –na COLL. m. what's-his-name —f. what's-her-name —m.f. so-and-so.
¡zu·zo! interj. shoo!, scram!

PREFACIO

El *American Heritage Dictionary,* publicado por Houghton Mifflin, es el más innovador e imitado de los diccionarios de lengua inglesa publicados en los Estados Unidos durante las últimas décadas. Su enorme popularidad y su éxito entre los críticos es testimonio del logro de su objetivo principal: registrar con exactitud el uso del inglés de Norteamérica en la forma más accesible.

En el mundo hispánico el nombre de Larousse siempre ha gozado de especial distinción debido a la reconocida autoridad y la enorme circulación de su *Pequeño Larousse ilustrado.* Nuevamente revisado y puesto al día, este diccionario se distingue principalmente por la exactitud de su léxico y por la inclusión del uso y vocabulario de los países hispanoamericanos.

Ahora, Houghton Mifflin y Larousse se han unido para producir el primer diccionario bilingüe importante en muchos años, *The American Heritage Larousse Spanish Dictionary,* basado en el *American Heritage Dictionary* y el *Pequeño Larousse.*

Esta nueva obra se distingue de otras anteriores por varias razones. El uso del inglés en ambas secciones es el de los Estados Unidos, con una cuidadosa indicación en cuanto a los diversos niveles de propiedad. Se han incluido formas y sentidos del uso británico (siempre indicado como tal) que el lector común pudiera encontrar. En cuanto al español, se ha hecho el esfuerzo correspondiente para representar tanto el uso ''pan-hispánico'' como las diversas formas y sentidos utilizados en Hispanoamérica.

Sería arriesgado asegurar que un diccionario está exento de errores. Sin embargo, los lexicógrafos que compilaron el *American Heritage Larousse Spanish Dictionary* han hecho grandes esfuerzos por corregir los errores que se han per-petuado al pasar, por generaciones, de un diccionario a otro. Y como la facilidad en el uso de un diccionario depende tanto de las palabras incluidas como de las excluidas, los responsables de la compilación del presente diccionario han omitido aquellas que a su juicio han dejado de tener vigencia; el espacio así liberado ha sido aprovechado para incluir una generosa porción de palabras técnicas y comerciales más útiles en el mundo contemporáneo.

Como la exactitud depende tanto de los usuarios del diccionario como de quienes lo han compilado, en las entradas múltiples donde se dan varias acepciones, los sinónimos para cada significado aparecen en la lengua de la entrada principal. Así mismo, cuando se ha creído necesario se ha hecho referencia a las secciones gramaticales de la parte introductoria, correspondientes a la entrada. La palabra de cada entrada se ha dividido en sílabas y el género de los sustantivos españoles se ha indicado en la sección inglesa.

En resumen, Houghton Mifflin y Larousse ofrecen aquí una nueva base léxica, una preferencia por el uso angloamericano e hispanoamericano, y una mayor exactitud, modernidad y sensibilidad en cuanto a las necesidades prácticas del usuario.

Edmund L. King, Ph.D.
Walter S. Carpenter, Jr., Professor in the Language, Literature, and Civilization of Spain, Emeritus; Professor of Romance Languages and Literatures, Emeritus Princeton University

Rodolfo Cardona, Ph.D.
University Professor and Professor of Spanish and Comparative Literature Boston University

DIAGRAMA EXPLICATIVO

formas irregulares — gild (gĭld) tr. **gild·ed** o **gilt** (gĭlt), **gild·ing** (to cover with gold) dorar; FIG. (to sugar-coat) dar un falso brillo a.

gild·ing (gĭl'dĭng) s. (process) doradura, dorado; (gold leaf) pan de oro m; (paint) pintura dorada; FIG. (glitter) oropel m. — **acepción**

gill¹ (gĭl) I. s. ICT. agalla, branquia; BOT. laminilla ♦ **gills** ORNIT. (wattle) barba; FAM. (area around the neck) papada • **to look green about** o **around the gills** tener mala cara II. tr. (to catch fish) pescar por las agallas; (to clean fish) limpiar (pescado). — **modismos y usos especiales**

gill² (jĭl) s. EE. UU. cuatro onzas (líquidas); G.B. cinco onzas (líquidas). — **rótulos de región**

gilt (gĭlt) I. pret. y part. p. de **gild** II. adj. dorado III. s. (layer of gold) lámina o chapa de oro; (glitter) brillo; (superficial brilliance) oropel m, falso brillo.

variación ortográfica — gilt-edged (gĭlt'ĕjd') o **gilt-edge** (-ĕj') adj. (having gilded edges) de bordes dorados ♦ **g. securities** FIN. valores de primer orden.

gim·bal (gĭm'bəl, jĭm'-) s. MEC. suspensión de cardán f, soporte cardánico ♦ **gimbals** MARÍT. balancines de la brújula.

gim·crack (jĭm'krăk') **I.** s. baratija, chuchería **II.** adj. mal hecho. — **partes de la oración**

hi·jack (hī'jăk') tr. FAM. (to stop and rob) asaltar (tren, persona); (goods) robarse; (to commandeer) tomar posesión por fuerza de (un vehículo). — **explicación del equivalente**

hi·jack·er (hī'jăk'ər) s. (robber) asaltante mf; (of airplanes) secuestrador m, pirata aéreo.

hi·jack·ing (hī'jăk'ĭng) s. (robbery) asalto; (takeover) secuestro. — **equivalente**

hike (hīk) I. intr. **hiked, hik·ing** (for pleasure) caminar, ir de excursión; (to travel on foot) caminar, ir a pie ♦ **to h. up** subirse, arremangarse <this dress hikes up in the back este vestido se sube por detrás> —tr. aumentar (precios, alquileres) ♦ **to h. up** subir II. s. (long walk) excursión f, caminata; (rise) aumento, subida ♦ **take a h.!** JER. ¡váyase a paseo o a bañar! • **to go on** o **to take a h.** ir de excursión.

hik·er (hī'kər) s. excursionista mf. — **género**

hik·ing (hī'kĭng) s. caminata, excursión a pie f.

pronunciación — hi·lar·i·ous (hī-lâr'ē-əs) adj. (situation, joke) para morirse de risa; (merry) muy divertido.

hi·lar·i·ty (hĭ-lăr'ĭ-tē) s. hilaridad f.

hill (hĭl) s. (elevation) colina, cerro; (heap) montón m; (slope) cuesta ♦ **to be over the h.** FAM. ir cuesta abajo, estar entrado en años. — **rótulo de uso**

plural irregular — hill·bil·ly (hĭl'bĭl'ē) s. [pl. -lies] FAM. campesino, patán m.

hill·ock (hĭl'ək) s. montecillo.

hill·side (hĭl'sīd') s. ladera (de un cerro o colina).

hill·top (hĭl'tŏp') s. cima, cumbre (de un cerro o colina) f.

hill·y (hĭl'ē) adj. **-i·er, -i·est** cerril, montuoso. — **comparativo y superlativo**

hilt (hĭlt) s. puño, mango ♦ **to the h.** (to the limit) hasta las cachas o cuello; (thoroughly) totalmente.

referencia gramatical — him §G29 (hĭm) pron. pers. le, lo <they accepted h. lo aceptaron>; le <they sent h. a letter le mandaron una carta>; él <the letter was addressed to h. la carta iba dirigida a él>. — **ejemplo**

him·self §G37 (hĭm-sĕlf') pron. pers. (reflexively) se <he hit h. se golpeó>; (emphatically) él mismo <he h. couldn't believe it él mismo no podía creerlo>; (after a preposition) sí, sí mismo <he talked about h. habló de sí mismo>; (in person) en persona, personalmente <he will go h. irá él personalmente> ♦ **by h.** solo.

homógrafos — hind¹ (hīnd) adj. trasero, posterior.

hind² (hīnd) s. ZOOL. cierva; ICT. mero. — **rótulo de campo**

hin·der (hĭn'dər) tr. (progress) dificultar; (movement) retardar, obstaculizar; (person) entorpecer, incapacitar; (solution) impedir; (negotiations) obstruir, poner trabas a ♦ **to h. someone from** impedirle a alguien (hacer algo).

hind·er·most (hīn'dər-mōst') adj. var. de **hindmost.** — **variante**

Hin·di (hīn'dē) s. hindi m.

hind·most (hīnd'mōst') adj. (rear) trasero, posterior; (last) último.

hin·drance (hĭn'drəns) s. impedimento, obstáculo.

hind·sight (hīnd'sīt') s. retrospección f, visión retrospectiva. — **género**

parte de la oración — Hin·du (hĭn'dōō) s. & adj. hindú m.

GUÍA PARA EL USO DE ESTE DICCIONARIO

Diseño

El *American Heritage Larousse Spanish Diction-ary* ha sido especialmente diseñado con el fin de proporcionar la mayor claridad, precisión y fa-cilidad de uso al lector. Su objetivo es brindar el equivalente más preciso de una palabra o frase sin que el lector tenga que remitirse a otros vocablos para completar su sentido. Con este fin hemos ideado una combinación de elementos en inglés y en español dentro de cada artículo que, junto con distinciones de orden tipográfico, ayudan a organizar los variados elementos de cada vocablo en una forma coherente y fácil de usar.

Estas características se pueden observar en el diagrama que aparece en la página opuesta. Nótese que la distinción tipográfica entre las pa-labras en inglés y español se mantiene a lo largo de todo el artículo. La palabra inglesa y sus formas irregulares, así como las expresiones de uso co-mún que se incluyen después del rombo, aparecen en letra negrilla. Las palabras en inglés usadas para discriminar los distintos sentidos de un vo-cablo, y los ejemplos, aparecen en cursiva. Todos los elementos en el idioma español, incluyendo los equivalentes, rótulos y traducciones de los ejemplos, aparecen en letra redonda. Esta distin-ción tipográfica ha sido diseñada a fin de ayudar al lector a encontrar rápidamente la información específica que necesita, sin tener que leer la tota-lidad del artículo para ello.

Palabras Guías

En el margen superior de cada página aparecen dos palabras cuya función es ayudar a encontrar la página en la que aparece un vocablo:

| **ideal** | **ill-mannered** | **233** |

La palabra a la izquierda de la línea vertical es la primera en la secuencia de vocablos que aparecen en dicha página. La palabra a la derecha de esta línea indica el último vocablo que aparece en dicha página. En consecuencia, **ideal** y **ill-mannered,** así como todos los vocablos que aparecen alfa-béticamente entre ellos, se pueden encontrar en la página 233.

Vocablos

Las palabras seleccionadas en este diccionario aparecen en orden alfabético. Los vocablos y sus formas irregulares han sido silabeados de acuerdo al *American Heritage Dictionary*. La guía para la pronunciación de los vocablos ha sido basada en el sistema usado por el *American Heritage Dic-tionary,* con modificaciones para ajustar la misma a las necesidades particulares de los lectores bi-lingües. (Véase la Guía para la Pronunciación In-glesa en la página xviii. Una versión concisa de esta Guía aparece al pie de cada página para co-modidad del lector.)

Homógrafos. Las palabras cuya ortografía es idéntica pero cuyos significados son diferentes se incluyen en forma separada, acompañadas de un índice sobrescrito (Diagrama: **hind[1], hind[2]**).

Variantes. Los vocablos que reflejan varia-ciones ortográficas aparecen en este diccionario en su orden alfabético, remitiendo al lector al vo-cablo de ortografía preferida (Diagrama: **hindermost**).

Algunas variaciones de orden menor se indican junto a la forma preferida (Diagrama: **gilt-edged** o **gilt-edge**). Las variaciones ortográficas britá-nicas van precedidas por el rótulo G.B., y remiten al lector al vocablo principal:

hu·mour (hyōō′mər) s. G.B. var. de **humor.**

Formas Irregulares

Cuando el vocablo inglés tiene alguna irregula-ridad, ésta se indica en letra negrilla. En algunos casos aparece precedida por un guión y/o seguida por su pronunciación.

Adjetivos y adverbios. Cuando el compara-tivo y el superlativo se forman con **-er** y **-est,** esta información aparece después de la parte de la ora-ción (Diagrama: **hilly**).

Plurales irregulares. La información referente a la formación de plurales irregulares aparece en corchetes (Diagrama: **hillbilly**).

Verbos irregulares. La ortografía irregular del pretérito, participio pasado y participio presente se indica después de la parte de la oración:

write (rīt) tr. **wrote** (rōt), **writ·ten** (rĭt′n), **writ·ing** . . .

Aun cuando sólo una de las formas es irregular, ofrecemos todas las formas verbales (Diagrama: **gild**). Nótese que cuando el pretérito y el parti-cipio pasado coinciden en forma, la forma irregu-lar aparece solamente una vez (Diagrama: **hike**). Para los verbos de conjugación irregular más fre-cuentes en inglés consulte la lista en la página xii.

Referencias Gramaticales

Ciertos vocablos y sus funciones se explican en detalle en la Gramática que forma parte de este diccionario (págs. v–x). A este fin, han sido iden-tificados con números en letra negrilla, remitiendo al lector a la sección apropiada de la Gramática (Diagrama: **him**).

Rótulos

Los rótulos que se usan en este diccionario han sido diseñados, dentro de lo posible, para que sean inteligibles para los que hablan o inglés o español. La lista completa de rótulos que se usan en la parte inglés-español aparece en la guarda posterior.

Parte de la oración. Los rótulos que determinan la parte de la oración aparecen en letra redonda, después de la pronunciación. Cuando un vocablo tiene más de una función gramatical, éstas han sido separadas por números romanos (Diagrama: **gimcrack**).

Cuando dos partes de la oración tienen el mismo equivalente, los rótulos que designan las partes de la oración han sido unidos por el símbolo & (Diagrama: **Hindu**).

Rótulos de campo, uso y región. Los rótulos que determinan el campo de una actividad, el uso del idioma o que indican origen británico aparecen en letras mayúsculas pequeñas, delante del equivalente que representan (Diagrama: **hind², hill, gill²**).

Cuando un rótulo es aplicable a varias acepciones, éstas aparecen agrupadas consecutivamente, aunque el rótulo no se repita.

Acepciones

Para una mayor precisión en el uso del idioma, las distintas acepciones de cada vocablo han sido separadas por una palabra en inglés que diferencia cada sentido. Estas palabras aparecen en letra cursiva, entre paréntesis, y preceden al equivalente que representan (Diagrama: **gilding**).

En muchos casos estas palabras son un sinónimo aproximado del vocablo principal. En otros, y para mayor claridad, son reemplazadas por una frase prepositiva o por un sujeto u objeto que identifica el significado que se quiere resaltar.

Equivalentes

Como es usual en diccionarios bilingües los vocablos ingleses que aparecen en este libro han sido traducidos, dentro de lo posible, por un equivalente directo en lugar de una definición verbosa (Diagrama: **hijacking**). En muchos casos podrán encontrarse dos equivalentes, separados por una coma, para ilustrar un sentido. Las diferentes acepciones de cada vocablo están separadas por un punto y coma, y van precedidas por otras convenciones, como una palabra en inglés que determina su sentido, rótulo(s) y/o ejemplos.

Los equivalentes guardan una relación gramatical directa con el vocablo inglés, y reflejan el mismo nivel de lenguaje. Para evitar un efecto repetitivo hemos ligado con una *o* en cursiva dos palabras que pueden usarse indistintamente en una frase (Diagrama: **gilt**).

El género de los sustantivos se indica cuando éste no queda clarificado por su terminación o por los adjetivos calificativos que los acompañan (Diagrama: **hiker, hindsight**). Cuándo un equivalente se repite en el artículo, el género no se repite.

Ejemplos

En esta obra hemos incluido miles de ejemplos, en frases y oraciones, cuyo objeto es demostrar al lector el uso idiomático o de contexto de cada vocablo y sus equivalentes. Los ejemplos y sus traducciones aparecen entre corchetes angulares, inmediatamente después de la acepción que ilustran (Diagrama: **him**).

Nótese que el vocablo inglés se abrevia cuando aparece en el ejemplo exactamente como cuando encabeza el artículo. De no ser así, aparece completamente deletreado. Los vocablos compuestos de dos letras solamente (*do, be, it,* etc.) aparecen completamente deletreados a través de toda esta obra.

Explicaciones

En los casos en que un equivalente no transmite el sentido exacto de un vocablo inglés, hemos hallado conveniente ayudar al lector agregando cortas explicaciones que siguen al equivalente, en paréntesis (Diagrama: **hijack**). Estas explicaciones son, generalmente, de tres tipos:

- Palabra(s) o frase opcional que brinda una versión más completa del equivalente:

  back·coun·try . . . s. interior (de un país) *m.*

- Complementos directos o sujetos de verbos:

  ba·by·sit . . . —tr. cuidar (niños).

  school² . . . intr. nadar en cardúmenes (los peces).

- Aclaraciones de ciertos equivalentes que no son de uso frecuente:

  jan·is·sar·y . . . jenízaro (soldado turco).

Modismos y Usos Especiales

Ciertas locuciones, frases verbales, modismos y algunas formas plurales de interés han sido incluidas como artículos suplementarios en la correspondiente parte de la oración. Estos artículos suplementarios van precedidos por un rombo en negrilla (♦) y aparecen en orden alfabético, separados por el símbolo gráfico (•) (Diagrama: **gill¹**). Como en el caso de los ejemplos, el vocablo inglés se abrevia en los artículos suplementarios, salvo que su ortografía varíe, en cuyo caso se deletrea completamente.

Los artículos suplementarios aparecen en negrilla y sus definiciones incluyen, cuando es necesario, todas las convenciones estilísticas usadas en los vocablos: rótulos, explicaciones, etc.

Por regla general, las locuciones y los modismos aparecen en el artículo que corresponde a su palabra principal. Para comodidad del lector en muchos casos las locuciones y modismos más comunes aparecen en más de un vocablo: *to let the cat out of the bag* puede encontrarse bajo **cat** y bajo **bag**.

Empleo de un Vocablo

Al pie de ciertos artículos hemos incluido notas explicativas sobre su empleo. Estas notas explicativas van precedidas por el símbolo gráfico (▲).

NOTAS GRAMATICALES

EL VERBO

G1 El infinitivo

El infinitivo va precedido generalmente por la preposición *to* <*it is important to study* es importante estudiar>. La partícula *to* se omite después de los verbos auxiliares y defectivos, como *may, shall, will, can* y *must* <*we can go now* podemos ir ahora>. *To* se omite también después de verbos que indican percepción <*I saw him leave* lo vi salir> y después de los verbos *let* y *make* <*they let her read it* le permitieron leerlo><*he made me do it* me hizo hacerlo>. También puede omitirse después de *but* y *except* <*she did nothing but laugh* no hizo nada, sino reír>.

El infinitivo puede tener la función de sujeto en una oración <*to err is human* errar es humano> o ser complemento de verbo <*I hope to finish it by tomorrow* espero completarlo para mañana>. También puede ser el complemento de un adjetivo o un adverbio <*it will be easy to do it* será fácil hacerlo>. El infinitivo se puede usar para indicar una obligación <*he wrote to them to explain his position* les escribió para explicarles su punto de vista>.

En términos generales no se acepta que la preposición *to* se separe del infinitivo propiamente dicho. En consecuencia, la oración <*the editor intended to scrutinize the manuscript carefully*> indica un inglés más educado que <*the editor intended to carefully scrutinize the manuscript*>.

G2 El presente indicativo

El tiempo presente se usa para expresar una acción o un estado que existe en la actualidad <*they are in Florida* están en la Florida>. También se usa para expresar una costumbre generalizada <*he always travels by train* siempre viaja por tren>. El presente indicativo puede sustituir, en inglés y en español, al tiempo futuro <*tomorrow I leave for England* mañana parto para Inglaterra>.

La forma enfática del tiempo presente indicativo se forma con el presente del verbo *do* y el infinitivo, y se emplea para dar más énfasis a la acción que se quiere expresar <*I do love her* la amo realmente>.

G3 El pretérito

El tiempo pretérito se usa para expresar una acción o un estado que existió en un momento concreto en el pasado <*he opened the door* abrió la puerta>. Nótese que el pretérito inglés puede traducirse al español por el pretérito o el imperfecto <*he opened the door every morning* abría la puerta todas las mañanas>.

La forma enfática del tiempo pretérito se forma con el pretérito del verbo *do* y el infinitivo, dándose así un énfasis especial a la acción que se quiere expresar <*they did leave on time* realmente salieron a tiempo>.

G4 El futuro

El tiempo futuro se usa para expresar una acción que ocurrirá en el futuro <*we will arrive tomorrow* llegaremos mañana>. El auxiliar *will* se usa con más frecuencia para formar el tiempo futuro que *shall*. *Shall* se usa mayormente en la forma interrogativa, cuando se pide una opinión <*what shall I do? ¿qué haré?*> La frase verbal *to be going to* se usa comúnmente para expresar una acción futura <*we are going to eat dinner at seven* vamos a cenar a las siete>.

G5 El condicional

El condicional es un futuro que depende del tiempo pasado <*I said that I would come* dije que vendría>. También se usa para expresar el modo potencial <*if they offered me the job, I would accept it* si me ofrecieran el puesto, lo aceptaría>.

G6 El imperativo

En inglés el imperativo tiene solamente una forma: la segunda persona, singular o plural <*wait!* ¡espera!, ¡espere!, ¡esperen!, ¡esperad!*> El sujeto *you* es tácito. La forma negativa del imperativo se crea agregando *do not* o *don't* a la orden imperativa <*don't open the door!* ¡no abra la puerta!>.

Otra forma de expresar una orden o sugerencia es usando *let* más el infinitivo. Esta forma se usa principalmente en la primera persona plural, y *let us* se contrae en *let's* <*let's go!* ¡vamos!>.

G7 El subjuntivo

En general el subjuntivo ha caído en desuso en el inglés contemporáneo aunque continúa en uso en oraciones condicionales <*if I were rich, I would buy a yacht* si yo fuera rico, me compraría un yate>.

G8 El gerundio y el participio presente

El gerundio y el participio presente se forman agregando –*ing* al infinitivo <*walking* andando>. En inglés el gerundio es una clase de sustantivo y se puede usar como el sujeto de una oración <*lying is a vice* mentir es un vicio>, o como complemento verbal <*we like skiing* nos gusta esquiar>.

El participio presente se usa con la conjugación del verbo *be* para formar las formas progresivas <*we were studying* estábamos estudiando>. Las formas progresivas expresan una acción que está ocurriendo en el momento al cual uno se refiere. También se pueden usar para referirse a una acción futura <*he is coming tomorrow* viene mañana>.

El participio presente también se puede usar como adjetivo <*a barking dog* un perro que ladra>, o como una cláusula adverbial <*by traveling one learns a lot* viajando se aprende mucho>.

G9 El participio pasado

El participio pasado regular se forma añadiendo –*ed* al infinitivo <*walked* andado>. Se usa con el verbo *have* para formar los tiempos perfectos:

Presente Perfecto <*he has written me a letter* me ha escrito una carta>; Pluscuamperfecto <*we knew that he had arrived* sabíamos que había llegado>; Futuro Perfecto <*he will have gone when you arrive* se habrá ido cuando usted llegue>.

El participio pasado se usa con el verbo *be* para formar la voz pasiva <*the car was stolen* el automóvil fue robado>. También puede tener funciones de adjetivo <*a faded flower* una flor marchita>.

G10 La voz pasiva

La voz pasiva se usa mucho más frecuentemente en inglés que en español; se forma con el verbo *be* y el participio pasado <*the picture was painted by Wyeth* el cuadro fue pintado por Wyeth>. La voz pasiva se usa en inglés en lugar de la forma impersonal hispana "se" <*Spanish is spoken here* aquí se habla español>. La forma pasiva de los tiempos continuos se usa frecuentemente en inglés para expresar una acción que está ocurriendo en el momento en el cual se está hablando <*I waited while the letter was being written* esperé mientras se escribía la carta>.

G11 Verbos auxiliares modales

Un cierto número de verbos auxiliares se denominan modales porque indican la forma o el estado en el que se hace una declaración.

El verbo *be* se usa para formar la voz pasiva y los tiempos progresivos o continuos. El verbo *have* se usa para formar los tiempos perfectos. *Do* se usa para formar oraciones negativas, interrogativas y enfáticas.

Los auxiliares *will* and *shall* se usan para formar el tiempo futuro <*he will eat later* comerá más tarde>. El auxiliar *would* se usa para formar el tiempo condicional <*I would do it* lo haría>.

El auxiliar *should* se usa para expresar una obligación <*you should see a doctor* debes ver a un médico>.

El auxiliar *can* y su pasado *could* se llaman defectivos o anómalos. La forma infinitiva de *can* es *to be able to*. *Can* indica capacidad o habilidad <*we can see it from here* podemos verlo desde aquí>. También se usa para expresar una posibilidad <*it could happen to anyone* podría sucederle a cualquiera>. *Can* también se usa para pedir o dar permiso <*can I go to the movies? Yes, you can go* ¿puedo ir al cine? Sí, puedes ir>.

May y *might* también son denominados auxiliares defectivos modales. Se usan para expresar una posibilidad <*we may arrive early* es posible que lleguemos temprano>. También se usan para pedir o dar permiso <*you may come in now* puede entrar ahora>.

Must es un auxiliar defectivo que se usa para expresar una obligación o necesidad <*they must finish it by Thursday* tienen que terminarlo para el jueves>. También indica una suposición o conjetura <*they must have left early* deben de haber salido temprano>.

El auxiliar *ought* expresa una obligación y se usa con la preposición infinitiva *to* <*we ought to work harder* deberíamos trabajar más duro>.

G12 Verbos impersonales

Verbos impersonales son aquellos que se usan solamente en la tercera persona y con el pronombre neutro *it* <*it is raining* está lloviendo o llueve>. El verbo *be* se usa junto con el adverbio *there* o el pronombre *it* para formar oraciones impersonales <*there are many problems* hay muchos problemas><*it is cold in here* hace frío aquí>.

G13 Contracciones

Las contracciones se usan con gran frecuencia en la conversación diaria. Casi todas las negaciones verbales se expresan con una contracción <*he didn't tell me the secret* no me dijo el secreto>. Algunas de las contracciones más comunes son: *are not = aren't, can not = can't, do not = don't, did not = didn't, does not = doesn't, had not = hadn't, have not = haven't, is not = isn't, should not = shouldn't, was not = wasn't, were not = weren't,* y *will not = won't.*

Las contracciones de los verbos *be, have* y *will* se forman con los pronombres personales: *I am = I'm, he is = he's, she has = she's, they have = they've, you will = you'll,* y *we will = we'll.*

EL SUSTANTIVO

G14 Género

El género se usa para distinguir a personas de distinto sexo. Puede indicarse en inglés por medio de una palabra diferente <*father* padre, *mother* madre>; por la terminación de un sustantivo <*widow* viuda, *widower* viudo>; o por el agregado de una palabra <*bride* novia, *bridegroom* novio>.

El género de los sustantivos abstractos o cosas es tácito o neutro. Existen algunas excepciones, como el sustantivo *boat*, el cual se considera femenino <*as the boat lay in the harbor, the workmen painted her hull* mientras el buque permanecía en el puerto, los trabajadores pintaban su casco>. El género neutro se utiliza cuando se desconoce el sexo de un animal o de un niño <*the baby and its needs* el niño y sus necesidades>.

Algunos sustantivos tienen género común a ambos sexos <*my cousin* mi prima, mi primo>.

G15 Formación del plural

Generalmente el plural se forma agregando –*s* al singular <*land* tierra, *lands* tierras>. El plural de los sustantivos que terminan en –*s*, –*x*, –*sh*, o –*ch* se forma añadiendo –*es* <*kiss* beso, *kisses* besos>. La excepción es cuando la –*ch* final suena como una k <*monarch* monarca, *monarchs* monarcas>.

El plural de los sustantivos que terminan en –*y* precedida por una consonante se forma cambiando la –*y* por –*i*, y añadiendo –*es* <*fly* mosca, *flies* moscas>. El plural de los sustantivos que terminan en –*y* precedida por una vocal, se forma añadiendo –*s* <*day* día, *days* días>.

El plural de los sustantivos que terminan en –*o* precedida por una consonante generalmente se forman añadiendo –*es* <*hero* héroe, *heroes* héroes>. Algunas excepciones son <*halo* aureola, *halos* aureolas><*piano* piano, *pianos* pianos>. El plural de los sustantivos que terminan en –*o* precedida por una vocal se forman añadiendo –*s* <*curio* fruslería, *curios* fruslerías>.

El plural de los sustantivos que terminan en –*f* o –*fe* generalmente se forma cambiando la –*f* por –*v*, y agregando –*es* <*thief* ladrón, *thieves* ladrones>. Algunas excepciones son <*cliff* acantilado, *cliffs* acantilados><*safe* caja fuerte, *safes* cajas fuertes>.

Ciertos sustantivos requieren el cambio de una vocal para formar su plural <*man* hombre, *men* hombres><*woman* mujer, *women* mujeres>. Otros forman su plural de una manera especial <*tooth* diente, *teeth* dientes><*foot* pie, *feet* pies><*mouse* ratón, *mice* ratones><*louse* piojo, *lice* piojos><*goose* ganso, *geese* gansos><*child* niño, *children* niños>.

El plural de los sustantivos compuestos o separados por un guión se forma agregando –*s* a la palabra más importante <*mother-in-law* suegra, *mothers-in-law* suegras><*good-by* adiós, *good-bys* adioses>. El plural de las palabras compuestas formadas por una sola palabra se obtiene añadiendo –*s* <*cupful* taza, *cupfuls* tazas>.

La forma plural de ciertos sustantivos es la misma que la forma singular <*sheep* oveja, ovejas><*deer* ciervo, ciervos>.

G16 El caso posesivo

En inglés el caso posesivo o genitivo se indica con un apóstrofe al final del sustantivo y una –*s* ('s), o, simplemente, con un apóstrofe ('). Para formar el caso posesivo singular, se agrega el apóstrofe y la *s* ('s) <*the dog's tail* la cola del perro>. Si el sustantivo singular termina en –*s*, se agrega solamente el apóstrofe <*for goodness' sake!* ¡por Dios!>. Para formar el caso posesivo plural, se agrega el apóstrofe y la *s* ('s) cuando el plural no termina en –*s* <*the children's manners* el comportamiento de los niños>. Si el sustantivo plural termina en –*s*, se agrega solamente el apóstrofe <*ladies' day* día de damas>.

El caso posesivo se usa para indicar la propiedad de algo <*Mary's book* el libro de María>; fuente de origen <*Robert's birthday present to Mark* el regalo de cumpleaños de Roberto a Marcos>; manufactura o paternidad literaria <*Emily Dickinson's poems* los poemas de Emily Dickinson>; o asociación, conexión, atributo o duración <*an hour's delay* un retraso de una hora>.

G17 El artículo definido

El artículo *the* (el, la, lo, los, las) es invariable, es decir que su forma es la misma en singular como en plural, masculino o femenino. Este artículo se omite en los siguientes casos:

- cuando precede sustantivos generales o abstractos <*do you like music?* ¿te gusta la música?>
- cuando precede títulos <*General San Martín* el general San Martín>
- cuando precede el nombre de lenguas o ciencias <*he likes biology* le gusta la biología><*I do not speak Russian* no hablo el ruso>
- cuando precede las estaciones del año, los días de la semana o ciertas expresiones de tiempo acompañadas de un adjetivo <*summer passed* se fue el verano><*I go to the movies on Sundays* voy al cine los domingos><*until next year* hasta el año que viene>

- cuando precede nombres de ciudades, calles o países <*I live on Sixth Avenue, in New York City* vivo en la Sexta Avenida, en la ciudad de Nueva York><*Canada* el *Canadá*>
- cuando precede el nombre de instituciones como escuelas, iglesias o prisiones <*school will start soon* la escuela comenzará pronto>.

El artículo definido *the* debe usarse en los siguientes casos en inglés, aunque no necesariamente en español:

- cuando precede números ordinales en títulos y fechas <*Henry the Fifth* Enrique Quinto> <*January the sixth* el seis de enero>
- cuando precede adjetivos que se usan como sustantivos colectivos <*the rich* los ricos>
- cuando precede ciertos adverbios <*the more I exercise the better I feel* cuanto más ejercicio hago mejor me siento>.

G18 El artículo indefinido

El artículo indefinido *a* o *an* (un, una) funciona solamente en el singular. Las formas plurales hispanas ''unos, unas'' se traducen al inglés por el adjetivo indefinido *some* <*some beautiful paintings* unos cuadros hermosos>.

A se usa antes de palabras que comienzan con el sonido de una consonante <*a tree* un árbol>, y antes de palabras que comienzan con una *h* aspirada <*a hill* una colina>. La variación *an* se usa con palabras que comienzan con el sonido de una vocal <*an apple* una manzana> y antes de palabras que comienzan con una *h* que no es aspirada <*an hour* una hora>.

El artículo indefinido se usa en los siguientes casos en inglés, aunque no se traduce al español:

- cuando precede a un sustantivo que funciona como predicado, y que no está calificado por un adjetivo <*he was a soldier* era soldado> <*I am a Greek* soy griego>
- cuando precede ciertos adjetivos <*he experienced a certain relief* experimentó cierto alivio> <*I know of a thousand examples* conozco mil ejemplos>
- cuando sigue a palabras como *without, half, such, what* <*without a doubt* sin ninguna duda> <*what a fool!* ¡qué tonto!>
- cuando sigue a ciertos verbos que llevan la conjunción *as* <*he served as a spokesman* era el vocero>
- en expresiones de proporción, relación o razón <*ten miles an hour* diez millas por hora>.

EL ADJETIVO

G19 Concordancia del adjetivo

En inglés los adjetivos son invariables, es decir que su forma es la misma en singular que en plural, masculino o femenino <*a yellow flower* una flor amarilla><*a yellow bird* un pájaro amarillo> <*yellow socks* calcetines amarillos>.

G20 Posición en la oración

El adjetivo generalmente precede al sustantivo que califica <*a good book* un buen libro>. Sin embargo, existen ciertas expresiones en inglés en las que el adjetivo sigue al sustantivo <*from time immemorial* de tiempos inmemoriales><*the heir apparent* el heredero forzoso>. El adjetivo sigue al sustantivo cuando se usa en el predicado de una oración <*his house is old and dirty* su casa es vieja y sucia>. El adjetivo va seguido del sustantivo o por el pronombre *one(s)* en oraciones como <*I want a pink blouse and a white one* quiero una blusa rosa y una blanca>.

G21 Función sustantiva

El adjetivo puede funcionar como sustantivo colectivo cuando va precedido por el artículo definido *the* <*the poor* los pobres>.

G22 El comparativo y superlativo

La forma comparativa de los adjetivos compuestos de una sola sílaba se construye agregando *–r* o *–er;* la forma superlativa, agregando *–st* o *–est* <*high, higher, highest* alto, más alto, el más alto> <*brave, braver, bravest* valiente, más valiente, el más valiente>.

La forma comparativa de los adjetivos de más de una sílaba generalmente se construye usando *more* (o *less*); la forma superlativa, usando *most* (o *least*) <*beautiful, more beautiful, most beautiful* bello, más bello, el más bello>.

Algunos adjetivos de dos o más sílabas, particularmente aquellos que terminan en *–e, –y,* y *–l,* forman el comparativo y superlativo con la terminación *–r* y *–st* <*gentle, gentler, gentlest* suave, más suave, el más suave>. Para formar el comparativo y superlativo de adjetivos que terminan en *–y,* ésta debe cambiarse por *i* antes de agregar las formas comparativas mencionadas <*lovely, lovelier, loveliest* lindo, más lindo, el más lindo>.

Las formas comparativas y superlativas de los siguientes adjetivos son irregulares:

bad, worse, worst malo, peor, el peor
far, farther, farthest lejos, más lejos, el más lejos
good, better, best bueno, mejor, el mejor
late, latter, last tardío, último, el último
many, more, most muchos, más, el más
old, elder, eldest viejo, mayor, el mayor

G23 Adjetivos posesivos

my	mi, mis
your	tu, tus; su, sus (de usted)
her	su, sus (de ella)
his	su, sus (de él)
its	su, sus (neutro)
our	nuestro(s), nuestras(s)
your	vuestro(s), vuestra(s); su, sus (de ustedes)
their	su, sus (de ellos, de ellas)

Los adjetivos posesivos deben coincidir en número y género con el poseedor y no con el objeto que es poseído <*she lost her book* ella perdió su libro><*they lost their money* perdieron su dinero>. Al referirse a las partes del cuerpo o a artículos de ropa el adjetivo posesivo debe utilizarse siempre <*he washed his face* se lavó la cara><*I put on my coat* me puse el abrigo>.

El adjetivo posesivo *whose* se usa para calificar a un sustantivo <*where is the boy whose shoes I found?* ¿dónde está el muchacho cuyos zapatos encontré?>.

G24 Adjetivos demostrativos

Los adjetivos demostrativos *this* (este, esta) y *these* (estos, estas) se refieren a aquello que está relacionado con el locutor en lugar, tiempo o espacio <*this book is mine* este libro es mío>.

Los adjetivos *that* (ese, esa; aquel, aquella) y *those* (esos, esas; aquellos, aquellas) se refieren a aquello que está cerca de la persona a quien se habla en lugar, tiempo o espacio <*do you need those keys?* ¿necesitas esas llaves?>.

G25 Adjetivos interrogativos

El adjetivo interrogativo *what* se usa para pedir información sobre algo <*what kind of dog did you buy?* ¿qué tipo de perro compró?>.

Which se puede utilizar para referirse a cosas o personas <*which blouse did you choose?* ¿cuál blusa escogiste?><*which student won the prize?* ¿cuál alumno ganó el premio?>.

La forma posesiva del adjetivo interrogativo es *whose* <*whose pen is on the table?* ¿de quién es la pluma que está en la mesa?>.

EL ADVERBIO

G26 Formación del adverbio

La mayoría de los adverbios se forman agregando *–ly* al adjetivo correspondiente <*silent, silently* silencioso, silenciosamente>. Los adjetivos que terminan en *–y* deben cambiar su terminación por *–i* antes de agregar el sufijo adverbial <*easy, easily* fácil, fácilmente>. Debe quitársele la *e* a aquellos adjetivos que terminan en *–ue* antes de agregar *–ly* <*true, truly* verdadero, verdaderamente> <*probable, probably* probable, probablemente>. Finalmente, a aquellos adjetivos que terminan en *–ll* se les agrega solamente la *y* <*full, fully* completo, completamente>.

La ortografía de algunos adjetivos y adverbios es invariable <*fast* rápido, rápidamente>.

G27 Posición en la oración

Los adverbios pueden modificar a un adjetivo <*this chapter is very interesting* este capítulo es muy interesante>; o a otro adverbio <*she sings quite well* canta bastante bien>. En estos casos el adverbio precede a la palabra que califica.

Cuando un adverbio modifica a un verbo, generalmente lo sigue en la oración <*they ran slowly* corrían lentamente>. Si el complemento verbal es corto, éste puede colocarse entre el verbo y el adverbio <*he read the letter slowly* leyó la carta lentamente>. Si el verbo se usa con un auxiliar, el adverbio puede colocarse entre el auxiliar y el verbo principal <*she doesn't usually visit us on Wednesdays* no suele visitarnos los miércoles>.

Los adverbios de tiempo usualmente se colocan al final de la oración <*he escaped from prison yesterday* se escapó de la cárcel ayer>. Los adverbios de tiempo indefinido, sin embargo, se colocan antes del verbo <*we often arrive late* a menudo llegamos tarde>.

G28 El comparativo y superlativo

El comparativo y superlativo de los adverbios se forman de la misma manera que el de los adjetivos, agregando *–r* o *–er* y *–st* o *–est* <*soon, sooner, soonest* pronto, más pronto, lo más pronto>. Estas formas también se pueden construir usando *more, most* o *less, least* <*easily, more easily, the most easily* fácilmente, más fácilmente, lo más fácilmente>.

Las formas comparativas y superlativas de los siguientes adverbios son irregulares:

well, better, best bien, mejor, lo mejor
badly, worse, worst mal, peor, lo peor
much, more, most mucho, más, lo más
little, less, least poco, menos, lo menos.

EL PRONOMBRE

G29 Pronombres personales

Número	Persona	Sujeto	Complemento
Singular	primera	*I*	*me*
	segunda	*you*	*you*
	tercera	*he*	*him*
		she	*her*
		it	*it*
Plural	primera	*we*	*us*
	segunda	*you*	*you*
	tercera	*they*	*them*

A diferencia del español el pronombre en inglés debe usarse siempre ya que nunca es tácito. El pronombre precede siempre al verbo <*we turned on the light* encendimos la luz>.

El pronombre de primera persona, singular, *I* (yo) se escribe siempre con mayúscula. *You, they, one,* y *it* se pueden usar como pronombres impersonales en inglés <*you turn left at the corner* se dobla a la izquierda al llegar a la esquina><*they say she's ill* se dice que ella está enferma><*one doesn't say such things* no se dicen tales cosas> <*it isn't possible* no es posible>.

G30 Concordancia del pronombre
El pronombre debe concordar con su antecedente en persona, número y género <*we have ours and you have yours* nosotros tenemos los nuestros y ustedes tienen los suyos>. La mayoría de los pronombres indefinidos son singulares y masculinos o neutros <*everyone has his own way of doing it* cada uno tiene su propia manera de hacerlo>. Esta construcción gramatical presenta un problema en el uso del inglés contemporáneo porque denota una actitud discriminatoria con respecto al otro sexo; es decir, es una forma que da más énfasis a uno de los dos sexos, ignorando al otro. En el ejemplo mencionado, *everyone* puede muy bien incluir mujeres; en consecuencia, el caso posesivo *his* no es exacto. El uso contemporáneo del idioma que ofrece la menor controversia es <*everyone has his or her own way of doing it*>.

G31 Posición del complemento en la oración
En inglés el caso objetivo del pronombre siempre sigue al verbo <*they gave me the message* me dieron el mensaje>. Cuando se usan dos complementos en la oración el directo se coloca antes del indirecto, el cual se expresa con la preposición *to* <*they gave it to me* me lo dieron>. Cuando un verbo y una preposición se usan juntos, el complemento se coloca después del verbo, antes de la preposición <*he threw it away* lo tiró>.

G32 Pronombres posesivos
mine mío(s), mía(s)
yours tuyo(s), tuya(s); suyo(s), suya(s)
hers suyo(s), suya(s)
his suyo(s), suya(s)
its suyo(s), suya(s)
ours nuestro(s), nuestra(s)
yours vuestro(s), vuestra(s); suyo(s), suya(s)
theirs suyo(s), suya(s)

Los pronombres posesivos concuerdan en número y género con la persona a que se refieren <*those shoes are hers* esos zapatos son suyos>. El pronombre posesivo se puede también usar con la preposición *of* <*a friend of mine* un amigo mío>.

G33 Pronombres demostrativos
Los pronombres demostrativos *this* (éste, ésta, esto), *these* (éstos, éstas), *that* (ése, ésa, eso; aquél, aquélla, aquello) y *those* (ésos, ésas; aquéllos, aquéllas) se usan con el pronombre *one(s)* cuando uno se refiere a un antecedente que aparece en una oración anterior <*this book is boring; I prefer that one* este libro es aburrido; prefiero ése>. Cuando el antecedente se menciona en la misma oración, el pronombre *one* no debe usarse <*that is my book* ése es mi libro>.

G34 Pronombres relativos
El pronombre relativo *who* se refiere a personas <*the lady who is speaking* la señora que está hablando>. *Whom* se usa como el caso objetivo de todas las preposiciones, o como el objeto directo de un verbo <*the man with whom you spoke* el hombre con quien tú hablaste> <*the girl whom you saw* la muchacha a quien usted vió>. *Whose* es la forma posesiva de *who* <*the woman whose son died* la mujer cuyo hijo murió>.

El pronombre relativo *which* se usa para referirse a cosas o animales <*the pen which I bought* la pluma que compré>. *Which* también puede utilizarse para referirse a una cláusula completa <*she lost all of her money, which caused her to go insane* perdió todo su dinero, lo cual la volvió loca>.

El pronombre *that* se refiere a personas, animales o cosas <*the novel that he wrote* la novela que él escribió><*she is the woman that I love* es la mujer a quien amo>.

What se refiere a conceptos <*I don't know what you want* no sé lo que quieres>.

El pronombre relativo puede omitirse en el caso objetivo <*the book I read* el libro que leí>.

G35 Pronombres interrogativos
El pronombre interrogativo *who* se refiere a personas <*who is that boy?* ¿quién es ese chico?>. En la conversación diaria *who* puede reemplazar a *whom* en oraciones como <*who did you see?* ¿a quién viste?>, en lugar de <*whom did you see?*>. *Whose* es el pronombre interrogativo posesivo <*whose is that dog?* ¿de quién es ese perro?>.

El pronombre *what* se usa en las formas interrogativas <*what did you say?* ¿qué dijiste?>.

También se usa en expresiones exclamativas <*what a fool!* ¡qué tonto!>.

El pronombre *which* se usa para distinguir entre un grupo de personas o cosas <*which is your house?* ¿cuál es tu casa?><*which of these women is your aunt?* ¿cuál de esas mujeres es tu tía?>.

G36 Pronombres indefinidos

El pronombre indefinido *none* puede ser singular <*none of them has come* ninguno de ellos ha venido> o plural <*there were none on the table* no había ninguno en la mesa>. *All* también puede ser singular <*all is lost* todo está perdido> o plural <*all must die* todos han de morir>.

Los pronombres *either* y *neither* se usan con la preposición *of* y son singulares en número <*either of them will do* cualquiera de los dos servirá> <*neither of them was right* ninguno de los dos tenía razón>. *Both* también puede usarse con la preposición *of*, pero su número es plural <*both of the girls are pretty* ambas chicas son bonitas>.

El pronombre indefinido *some* se usa en oraciones positivas, mientras que *any* se usa en oraciones negativas <*I have some in my pocket* tengo algunos en el bolsillo><*I don't have any* no tengo ninguno>. *Some* y *any* pueden usarse en oraciones interrogativas <*do you need some?* o *do you need any?* ¿necesitas algunos?>.

El pronombre *one* se puede utilizar en inglés como un sujeto impersonal <*one never knows* nunca se sabe>; también se puede utilizar como un artículo definido <*the one that you gave her is broken* el que le diste a ella está roto>.

G37 Pronombres reflexivos

myself me	*oneself* se
yourself te, se	*ourselves* nos
himself se	*yourselves* os, se
herself se	*themselves* se
itself se	

Estos pronombres se usan para indicar que el sujeto y el objeto de la oración son la misma persona o cosa <*she looked at herself in the mirror* se miró en el espejo>. Cuando se usa con la preposición *by* el pronombre reflexivo indica que la acción fue realizada sin la ayuda de nadie <*they did it by themselves* lo hicieron ellos solos>. También puede indicar que la acción fue realizada sola, sin la compañía de nadie <*he went to the museum by himself* fue al museo solo>.

Los pronombres reflexivos también se usan en inglés para dar énfasis al pronombre <*I will come myself* vendré yo mismo>.

G38 Pronombres recíprocos

Los pronombres *one another* y *each other* se usan para indicar que la acción del verbo es recíproca <*they looked at one another* se miraron><*we love each other* nos amamos>.

G39 La negación

La mayoría de las oraciones negativas en inglés se forman con el auxiliar *do* y el adverbio *not* colocado antes del verbo principal <*we do not know his name* no sabemos su nombre>. En oraciones formadas por otros auxiliares, el adverbio *not* se usa por sí solo y se coloca después del auxiliar <*he will not come* no vendrá><*she has not seen him* no lo ha visto>.

Cuando el verbo principal de la oración negativa es *be* y no se requiere ningún auxiliar, *not* se coloca después del verbo <*he is not well* no está bien>. El adverbio *not* se contrae con frecuencia con el auxiliar o el verbo *be* <*I don't want to go* no quiero ir><*she wasn't there* ella no estaba allí>.

Para formar una oración negativa también se pueden utilizar otras palabras negativas, como *nobody*, *nothing* y *nowhere*. En estos casos, el adverbio *not* no se usa ya que en inglés es incorrecto formar oraciones con dos negaciones <*nobody was there* no había nadie><*he had nothing* no tenía nada>.

G40 La forma interrogativa

La forma interrogativa simple se forma, usualmente, colocando el auxiliar *do* antes del sujeto y el verbo principal <*did he go to school?* ¿fue a la escuela?> Cuando el interrogativo se forma con otro verbo auxiliar, éste se coloca antes del sujeto y del verbo <*can I call you tomorrow?* ¿te puedo llamar mañana?>. Cuando el verbo principal no se necesita ningún verbo auxiliar; en este caso, el verbo precede al sujeto <*was your friend at the party?* ¿estaba su amigo en la fiesta?>.

Los pronombres interrogativos *when*, *where*, *what*, *why* y *how* se colocan al principio de la pregunta y no afectan la sintaxis del resto de la oración <*where did you go?* ¿adónde fuiste?> <*what did he say?* ¿qué dijo?>.

Los pronombres interrogativos *who*, *which* y *what* se usan sin auxiliar cuando funcionan como el sujeto de una oración <*who set the table?* ¿quién puso la mesa?><*what is in the closet?* ¿qué hay en el armario?>.

La sintaxis de las oraciones negativas sigue las mismas reglas gramaticales que las de las oraciones afirmativas; el auxiliar precede al sujeto y al verbo principal. El adverbio *not* precede al verbo principal y, usualmente, se contrae con el auxiliar <*didn't you go to church?* ¿no fue a la iglesia?>.

En inglés cualquier oración afirmativa se puede transformar en una pregunta agregando al final de la oración una frase interrogativa. Esta clase de forma interrogativa se usa frecuentemente cuando se espera una confirmación positiva o negativa <*it's raining, isn't it?* está lloviendo, ¿no es verdad?> Si la primera oración es negativa, entonces la frase interrogativa se forma en el caso afirmativo <*he doesn't live here, does he?* no vive aquí, ¿verdad?>.

G41 La conjunción

Las conjunciones copulativas más frecuentes en inglés son: *and* (y), *but* (pero), *for* (ya que, puesto que), *nor* (ni), *or* (o), y *yet* (sin embargo).

Estas conjunciones se usan para unir dos palabras o cláusulas de igual valor gramatical <*they wanted to go but they didn't have the money* querían ir pero no tenían el dinero>. Las conjunciones subordinadas *while*, *than*, *if*, *whether* y *because* se usan para unir una cláusula principal con otra que es dependiente <*we'll pay if you don't have enough money* pagaremos nosotros si no tienen bastante dinero>. La conjunción *that* se omite frecuentemente en inglés <*I told you (that) I would do it* te dije que lo haría>.

VERBOS IRREGULARES

abode	pret. y part. p. de **abide**	flung	pret. y part. p. de **fling**
am	pres. de **be**	forbad(e)	pret. de **forbid**
are	pres. de **be**	forbidden	part. p. de **forbid**
arisen	part. p. de **arise**	foregone	part. p. de **forego**[1]
arose	pret. de **arise**	foresaw	pret. de **foresee**
ate	pret. de **eat**	foreseen	part. p. de **foresee**
awoke	pret. de **awake**	foretold	pret. y part. p. de **foretell**
awoken	part. p. de **awake**	forewent	pret. de **forego**
backbit	pret. y part. p. de **backbite**	forgave	pret. de **forgive**
backbitten	part. p. de **backbite**	forgiven	part. p. de **forgive**
backslid	pret. y part. p. de **backslide**	forgone	part. p. de **forgo.**
backslidden	part. p. de **backslide**	forgot	pret. y part. p. de **forget**
bade	pret. de **bid**	forgotten	part. p. de **forget**
beaten	part. p. de **beat**	forsaken	part. p. de **forsake**
became	pret. de **become**	forsook	pret. de **forsake**
been	part. p. de **be**	forswore	pret. de **forswear**
befallen	part. p. de **befall**	forsworn	part. p. de **forswear**
befell	pret. de **befall**	forwent	pret. de **forgo.**
began	pret. de **begin**	fought	pret. y part. p. de **fight**
begot	pret. y part. p. de **beget**	found	pret. y part. p. de **find**
begotten	part. p. de **beget**	froze	pret. de **freeze**
begun	part. p. de **begin**	frozen	part. p. de **freeze**
beheld	pret. y part. p. de **behold**	gainsaid	pret. y part. p. de **gainsay**
bent	pret. y part. p. de **bend**	gave	pret. de **give**
bereft	pret. y part. p. de **bereave**	gilt	pret. y part. p. de **gild**
besought	pret. y part. p. de **beseech**	girt	pret. y part. p. de **gird**
bespoke	pret. y part. p. de **bespeak**	given	part. p. de **give**
bespoken	part. p. de **bespeak**	gone	part. p. de **go**
bestrewn	part. p. de **bestrew**	got	pret. y part. p. de **get**
bestridden	part. p. de **bestride**	gotten	part. p. de **get**
bestrode	pret. de **bestride**	graven	part. p. de **grave**[3]
betaken	part. p. de **betake**	grew	pret. de **grow**
betook	pret. de **betake**	ground	pret. y part. p. de **grind**
bidden	part. p. de **bid**	grown	part. p. de **grow**
bit	pret. y part. p. de **bite**	had	pret. y part. p. de **have**
bitten	part. p. de **bite**	hamstrung	pret. y part. p. de **hamstring**
bled	pret. y part. p. de **bleed**	heard	pret. y part. p. de **hear**
blent	pret. y part. p. de **blend**	held	pret. y part. p. de **hold**
blest	pret. y part. p. de **bless**	hewn	part. p. de **hew**
blew	pret. de **blow**	hid	pret. y part. p. de **hide**[1]
blown	part. p. de **blow**	hidden	part. p. de **hide**[1]
bode	pret. de **bide**	hove	part. p. de **heave**
bore	pret. de **bear**[1]	hung	pret. y part. p. de **hang**
born(e)	part. p. de **bear**[1]	inlaid	pret. y part. p. de **inlay**
bought	pret. y part. p. de **buy**	is	pres. de **be**
bound	pret. y part. p. de **bind**	kept	pret. y part. p. de **keep**
bred	pret. y part. p. de **breed**	knelt	pret. y part. p. de **kneel**
broke	pret. de **break**	knew	pret. de **know**
broken	part. p. de **break**	known	part. p. de **know**
brought	pret. y part. p. de **bring**	laden	part. p. de **lade**
browbeaten	part. p. de **browbeat**	laid	pret. y part. p. de **lay**[1]
built	pret. y part. p. de **build**	lain	part. p. de **lie**[1]
burnt	pret. y part. p. de **burn**	lay	pret. de **lie**[1]
came	pret. de **come**	leant	pret. y part. p. de **lean**[1]
caught	pret. y part. p. de **catch**	leapt	pret. y part. p. de **leap**
chid	pret. y part. p. de **chide**	learnt	pret. y part. p. de **learn**
chidden	part. p. de **chide**	led	pret. y part. p. de **lead**[1]
chose	pret. de **choose**	left	pret. y part. p. de **leave**[1]
chosen	part. p. de **choose**	lent	pret. y part. p. de **lend**
clad	pret. y part. p. de **clothe**	lit	pret. y part. p. de **light**[1,2]
cleft	pret. y part. p. de **cleave**	lost	pret. y part. p. de **lose**
clove	pret. de **cleave**	made	pret. y part. p. de **make**
cloven	part. p. de **cleave**	meant	pret. y part. p. de **mean**[1]
clung	pret. y part. p. de **cling**	met	pret. y part. p. de **meet**
crept	pret. y part. p. de **creep**	misdid	pret. de **misdo**
crew	pret. de **crow**[2]	misdone	part. p. de **misdo**
dealt	pret. y part. p. de **deal**[1]	mislaid	pret. y part. p. de **mislay**
did	pret. de **do**[1]	misled	pret. y part. p. de **mislead**
done	part. p. de **do**[1]	misspelt	pret. y part. p. de **misspell**
dove	pret. de **dive**	misspent	pret. y part. p. de **misspend**
drank	pret. de **drink**	mistaken	part. p. d **mistake**
drawn	part. p. de **draw**	mistook	pret. de **mistake**
dreamt	pret. y part. p. de **dream**	misunderstood	pret. y part. p. de **misunderstand**
drew	pret. de **draw**		
driven	part. p. de **drive**	mown	part. p. de **mow**[2]
drove	pret. de **drive**	outbidden	part. p. de **outbid**
drunk	part. p. de **drink**	outdid	pret. de **outdo**
dug	pret. y part. p. de **dig**	outdone	part. p. de **outdo**
dwelt	pret. y part. p. de **dwell**	outgrew	pret. de **outgrow**
eaten	part. p. de **eat**	outgrown	part. p. de **outgrow**
fallen	part. p. de **fall**	outran	pret. de **outrun**
fed	pret. y part. p. de **feed**	outshone	pret. y part. p. de **outshine**
fell	pret. de **fall**	outwore	pret. de **outwear**
felt	pret. y part. p. de **feel**	outworn	part. p. de **outwear**
fled	pret. y part. p. de **flee**	overate	pret. de **overeat**
flew	pret. de **fly**[1]	overbore	pret. de **overbear**
flown	part. p. de **fly**[1]	overborne	part. p. de **overbear**

overcame	pret. de **overcome**
overdid	pret. de **overdo**
overdone	part. p. de **overdo**
overdrawn	part. p. de **overdraw**
overdrew	pret. de **overdraw**
overeaten	part. p. de **overeat**
overgrew	pret. de **overgrow**
overgrown	part. p. de **overgrow**
overheard	pret. y part. p. de **overhear**
overhung	pret. y part. p. de **overhang**
overlaid	pret. y part. p. de **overlay**
overran	pret. de **overrun**
overridden	part. p. de **override**
overrode	pret. de **override**
oversaw	pret. de **oversee**
overseen	part. p. de **oversee**
overshot	pret. y part. p. de **overshoot**
overslept	pret. y part. p. de **oversleep**
overtaken	part. p. de **overtake**
overthrew	pret. de **overthrow**
overthrown	part. p. de **overthrow**
overtook	pret. de **overtake**
paid	pret. y part. p. de **pay**
partaken	part. p. de **partake**
partook	pret. de **partake**
proven	part. p. de **prove**
ran	pret. de **run**
rang	pret. de **ring**[2]
rebuilt	pret. y part. p. de **rebuild**
redid	pret. de **redo**
redone	part. p. de **redo**
re-laid	pret. y part. p. de **re-lay**
remade	pret. y part. p. de **remake**
rent	pret. y part. p. de **rend**
repaid	pret. y part. p. de **repay**
reran	pret. de **rerun**
retold	pret. y part. p. de **retell**
rewound	pret. y part. p. de **rewind**
rewritten	part. p. de **rewrite**
rewrote	pret. de **rewrite**
ridden	part. p. de **ride**
risen	part. p. de **rise**
riven	part. p. de **rive**
rode	pret. de **ride**
rose	pret. de **rise**
rung	part. p. de **ring**[2]
said	pret. y part. p. de **say**
sang	pret. de **sing**
sank	pret. de **sink**
sat	pret. y part. p. de **sit**
saw	pret. de **see**[1]
sawn	part. p. de **saw**[1]
seen	part. p. de **see**[1]
sent	pret. y part. p. de **send**
sewn	part. p. de **sew**
shaken	part. p. de **shake**
shaven	part. p. de **shave**
shod	pret. y part. p. de **shoe**
shone	pret. y part. p. de **shine**
shook	pret. de **shake**
shorn	part. p. de **shear**
shot	pret. y part. p. de **shoot**
shown	part. p. de **show**
shrank	pret. de **shrink**
shriven	part. p. de **shrive**
shrove	pret. de **shrive**
shrunk	pret. y part. p. de **shrink**
shrunken	part. p. de **shrink**
slain	part. p. de **slay**
slept	pret. y part. p. de **sleep**
slew	pret. de **slay**
slid	pret. y part. p. de **slide**
slung	pret. y part. p. de **sling**
slunk	pret. y part. p. de **slink**
smelt	pret. y part. p. de **smell**
smitten	part. p. de **smite**
smote	pret. y part. p. de **smite**
sold	pret. y part. p. de **sell**
sought	pret. y part. p. de **seek**
sown	part. p. de **sow**[1]
spat	pret. y part. p. de **spit**[1]
sped	pret. y part. p. de **speed**
spelt	pret. y part. p. de **spell**[1]
spent	pret. y part. p. de **spend**
spilt	pret. y part. p. de **spill**[1]
spoilt	pret. y part. p. de **spoil**
spoke	pret. de **speak**
spoken	part. p. de **speak**
sprang	pret. de **spring**
sprung	pret. y part. p. de **spring**
spun	pret. y part. p. de **spin**
stank	pret. de **stink**
stole	pret. de **steal**
stolen	part. p. de **steal**
stood	pret. y part. p. de **stand**
stove	pret. y part. p. de **stave**
strewn	part. p. de **strew**
stricken	part. p. de **strike**
stridden	part. p. de **stride**
striven	part. p. de **strive**
strode	pret. de **stride**
strove	pret. de **strive**
struck	pret. y part. p. de **strike**
strung	pret. y part. p. de **string**
stuck	pret. y part. p. de **stick**
stung	pret. y part. p. de **sting**
stunk	pret. y part. p. de **stink**
sunburnt	pret. y part. p. de **sunburn**
sung	pret. y part. p. de **sing**
sunk	pret. y part. p. de **sink**
sunken	part. p. de **sink**
swam	pret. de **swim**
swept	pret. y part. p. de **sweep**
swollen	part. p. de **swell**
swore	pret. de **swear**
sworn	part. p. de **swear**
swum	part. p. de **swim**
swung	pret. y part. p. de **swing**
taken	part. p. de **take**
taught	pret. y part. p. de **teach**
thought	pret. y part. p. de **think**
threw	pret. de **throw**
thriven	part. p. de **thrive**
throve	pret. de **thrive**
thrown	part. p. de **throw**
told	pret. y part. p. de **tell**
took	pret. de **take**
tore	pret. de **tear**[1]
torn	part. p. de **tear**[1]
trod	pret. y part. p. de **tread**
trodden	part. p. de **tread**
unbent	pret. y part. p. de **unbend**
unbound	pret. y part. p. de **unbind**
underbidden	part. p. de **underbid**
undergone	part. p. de **undergo**
undersold	pret. y part. p. de **undersell**
understood	pret. y part. p. de **understand**
undertaken	part. p. de **undertake**
undertook	pret. de **undertake**
underwent	pret. de **undergo**
underwritten	part. p. de **underwrite**
underwrote	pret. de **underwrite**
undid	pret. de **undo**
undone	part. p. de **undo**
unwound	pret. y part. p. de **unwind**
upheld	pret. y part. p. de **uphold**
was	pret. de **be**
waylaid	pret. y part. p. de **waylay**
went	pret. de **go**
wept	pret. y part. p. de **weep**
were	pret. de **be**
withdrawn	part. p. de **withdraw**
withdrew	pret. de **withdraw**
withheld	pret. y part. p. de **withhold**
withstood	pret. y part. p. de **withstand**
woke	pret. de **wake**[1]
woken	part. p. de **wake**[1]
won	pret. y part. p. de **win**
wore	pret. de **wear**[1]
worn	part. p. de **wear**[1]
wound	pret. y part. p. de **wind**[2,3]
wove	pret. de **weave**
woven	part. p. de **weave**
written	pret. de **write**
wrote	pret. de **write**
wrung	pret. y part. p. de **wring**

NÚMEROS, PESOS Y MEDIDAS

Cardinal	Ordinal		Cardinal	Ordinal		Cardinal	Ordinal
0 zero		10	ten	tenth	20	twenty	twentieth
1 one	first	11	eleven	eleventh	21	twenty-one	twenty-first
2 two	second	12	twelve	twelfth	22	twenty-two	twenty-second
3 three	third	13	thirteen	thirteenth	30	thirty	thirtieth
4 four	fourth	14	fourteen	fourteenth	40	forty	fortieth
5 five	fifth	15	fifteen	fifteenth	50	fifty	fiftieth
6 six	sixth	16	sixteen	sixteenth	60	sixty	sixtieth
7 seven	seventh	17	seventeen	seventeenth	70	seventy	seventieth
8 eight	eighth	18	eighteen	eighteenth	80	eighty	eightieth
9 nine	ninth	19	nineteen	nineteenth	90	ninety	ninetieth

	Cardinal	Ordinal
100	one hundred	one hundredth
101	one hundred one	one hundred first
123	one hundred twenty-three	one hundred twenty-third
200	two hundred	two hundredth
300	three hundred	three hundredth
400	four hundred	four hundredth
500	five hundred	five hundredth
600	six hundred	six hundredth
700	seven hundred	seven hundredth
800	eight hundred	eight hundredth
900	nine hundred	nine hundredth
1000	one thousand	one thousandth
1001	one thousand one	one thousand first
2023	two thousand twenty-three	two thousand twenty-third
1 000 000	one million	one millionth
1 000 000 000	one billion	one billionth
1 000 000 000 000	one trillion	one trillionth

TABLA DE CONVERSIÓN MÉTRICA

Multiplique los	por	para obtener	Multiplique los	por	para obtener
Longitud					
millimeters	0.04	inches	inches	25	millimeters
centimeters	0.4	inches	inches	2.5	centimeters
meters	3.3	feet	feet	30.5	centimeters
meters	1.1	yards	yards	0.9	meters
kilometers	0.6	miles	miles	1.6	kilometers
Superficie					
centimeters^2	0.16	inches^2	inches^2	6.5	centimeters^2
meters^2	1.2	yards^2	yards^2	0.8	meters^2
kilometers^2	0.4	miles^2	miles^2	2.6	kilometers^2
hectares	2.5	acres	acres	0.4	hectares
Peso y Masa					
grams	0.035	ounces	ounces	28.3	grams
kilograms	2.2	pounds	pounds	0.45	kilograms
tons (1000 kg)	1.1	short tons	short tons (2000 lbs)	0.9	metric tons
Volumen					
milliliters	0.03	fluid ounces	fluid ounces	30	milliliters
liters	2.1	pints	pints	0.47	liters
liters	1.06	quarts	quarts	0.95	liters
liters	0.26	gallons	gallons	3.8	liters
meters^3	35	feet^3	feet^3	0.03	meters^3
meters^3	1.3	yards^3	yards^3	0.76	meters^3

ABREVIATURAS MÁS USADAS EN INGLÉS

AA Alcoholics Anonymous.
A.B. *Lat.* Artium Baccalaureus (Bachelor of Arts).
ABA American Bar Association.
ABM antiballistic missile.
ac *o* **AC** alternating current.
a.c. *o* **a/c** air conditioning.
acct. account; accountant.
ACLU American Civil Liberties Union.
A.D. *Lat.* anno Domini (in the year of the Lord).
adm. administration.
Adm. admiral; admiralty.
AEC Atomic Energy Commission.
AFB air force base.
AFDC Aid to Families with Dependent Children.
AFL American Federation of Labor.
AFL-CIO American Federation of Labor and Congress of Industrial Organizations.
AK Alaska.
a.k.a. also known as.
AL Alabama.
alt. 1. altitude **2.** alternate.
am *o* **AM** amplitude modulation.
A.M. 1. ante meridiem **2.** *Lat.* Artium Magister (Master of Arts).
AMA *o* **A.M.A.** American Medical Association.
Amex American Stock Exchange.
amt. amount.
anon. anonymous.
AP *o* **A.P.** Associated Press.
APO *o* **A.P.O.** Army Post Office.
appt. appointment.
Apr. April.
apt. apartment.
AR Arkansas.
A/R accounts receivable.
ASAP as soon as possible.
assn. *o* **assoc.** association.
asst. assistant.
attn. attention.
atty. *o* **att.** attorney.
Aug. August.
AV *o* **A.V.** audio-visual.
ave. *o* **Ave.** avenue.
avg. average.
AZ Arizona.

B.A. *Lat.* Baccalaureus Artium (Bachelor of Arts).
BBB Better Business Bureau.
B.C. before Christ.
bd. ft. board foot.
bldg. building.
blvd. boulevard.
B/R bills receivable.
bros. brothers.
B.S. Bachelor of Science.
BSA Boy Scouts of America.
B.Sc. Bachelor of Science.
bsh. bushel.
Btu British thermal unit.

c *o* **c.** cup.
c. *o* **C.** century.
C celsius.
CA California.
cal calorie (small).

Cal calorie (large).
Capt. captain.
Card. Cardinal.
CARE Cooperative for American Relief Everywhere.
CB *o* **C.B.** citizen's band.
cc 1. cubic centimeter **2.** carbon copy.
CD 1. *o* **C/D** certificate of deposit **2.** *o* **C.D.** civil defense.
Cdr. commander.
CDT *o* **C.D.T.** Central Daylight Time.
cf. confer (compare).
cg centigram.
cgs. *o* **CGS** centimeter-gram-second.
ch. *o* **chap.** chapter.
CIA Central Intelligence Agency.
CIO Congress of Industrial Organizations.
cl centiliter.
cm centimeter.
Cmdr. commander.
co. *o* **Co.** company.
CO 1. Colorado **2.** *o* **c.o.** commanding officer **3.** *o* **C.O.** conscientious objector.
c/o *o* **c.o.** care of.
COD *o* **C.O.D.** cash on delivery.
Col. colonel.
COLA cost-of-living adjustment.
Comr. commissioner.
cont. continue; continued.
corp. corporation.
CP Communist Party.
CPA *o* **C.P.A.** certified public accountant.
CPI consumer price index.
CPR cardiopulmonary resuscitation.
cps characters per second.
Cpt. captain.
CPU central processing unit.
CRT cathode-ray tube.
CST *o* **C.S.T.** Central Standard Time.
CT Connecticut.
cu. *o* **cu** cubic.
cwt. hundredweight.
cyl. cylinder.

D.A. 1. *o* **DA** district attorney **2.** Doctor of Arts.
D&C dilatation and curettage.
DAR Daughters of the American Revolution.
dB decibel.
dc *o* **DC** direct current.
DCM Distinguished Conduct Medal.
D.D. *Lat.* Divinitatis Doctor (Doctor of Divinity).
D.D.S. Doctor of Dental Science.
DE Delaware.
Dec. December.
D.Ed. Doctor of Education.
Dem. Democratic; Democrat.
dept. 1. department **2.** deputy.
dg decigram.
D.H. Doctor of Humanities.
diam. *o* **dia.** diameter.
dir. director.
div. division.
DJ disc jockey.
dkg dekagram.
dkm dekameter.
dl deciliter.

D.Lit *o* **D.Litt.** *Lat.* Doctor Litterarum (Doctor of Letters *or* Literature).
dm decimeter.
D.M.D. *Lat.* Dentariae Medicinae Doctor (Doctor of Dental Medicine).
DMZ demilitarized zone.
DOA *Med.* dead on arrival.
DOD Department of Defense.
DOS disk operating system.
doz. dozen.
DP 1. data processing **2.** *o* **D.P.** displaced person.
D.Ph. *o* **D.Phil.** Doctor of Philosophy.
DPT diphtheria, pertussis, tetanus (vaccine).
dr dram.
Dr. 1. doctor **2.** drive (in street names).
DSC Distinguished Service Cross.
DSM Distinguished Service Medal.
DSO Distinguished Service Order.
DST *o* **D.S.T.** daylight-saving time.
DT *o* **D.T.** daylight time.
dz. dozen.

E *o* **E.** east.
ea. each.
ed. edited; editor; edition.
Ed.M. *Lat.* Educationis Magister (Master of Education).
EDT *o* **E.D.T.** Eastern Daylight Time.
E.E. electrical engineering.
EEC European Economic Community.
EEG electroencephalogram.
e.g. *Lat.* exempli gratia (for example).
EKG electrocardiogram.
EMT emergency medical technician.
enc. *o* **encl.** enclosed; enclosure.
EPA Environmental Protection Agency.
ER emergency room.
ERA Equal Rights Amendment.
ESL English as a second language.
ESP extrasensory perception.
Esq. Esquire (title).
EST *o* **E.S.T.** Eastern Standard Time.
est. established.
ETA *o* **e.t.a.** estimated time of arrival.
et al. *Lat.* et alii (and others).
ETD *o* **e.t.d.** estimated time of departure.
eV electron volt.
Exc. Excellency.
exec. executive.

F Fahrenheit.
FAA Federal Aviation Administration.
FBI *o* **F.B.I.** Federal Bureau of Investigation.
fc foot-candle.
FCC Federal Communications Commission.
FDA Food and Drug Administration.
FDIC Federal Deposit Insurance Corporation.
Feb. February.
fed. federal.
ff. 1. folios **2.** following.
FHA Federal Housing Administration.
FICA Federal Insurance Contributions Act.
fl fluid.

FL Florida.
fl dr fluid dram.
fl oz fluid ounce.
FM *o* **fm** frequency modulation.
f.o.b. *o* **F.O.B.** free on board.
Fri. Friday.
ft foot.
FTC Federal Trade Commission.
ft-lb foot-pound.
FY fiscal year.

GA Georgia.
gal. gallon.
Gen. general.
GHQ general headquarters.
GHZ Gigahertz.
GI *o* **G.I.** Government Issue.
gm gram.
GMT *o* **G.M.T.** Greenwich mean time.
GMW gram-molecular weight.
GNP gross national product.
GOP *o* **G.O.P.** Grand Old Party (Republican).
Gov. governor.
govt. government.
G.P. *o* **GP** general practitioner.
GPA grade-point average.
gr. wt. gross weight.

hdqtrs. headquarters.
HEW (Department of) Health, Education, and Welfare.
HI Hawaii.
H.M. Her *o* His Majesty.
HMO health maintenance organization.
HMS Her *o* His Majesty's Ship.
Hon. Honorable (title).
HOPE Health Opportunity for People Everywhere.
hp horsepower.
HQ *o* **h.q.** headquarters.
hr hour.
H.R.H. Her *o* His Royal Highness.
hrs. hours.
HS *o* **H.S.** high school.
ht height.
HUD *o* **H.U.D.** Housing and Urban Development.
hwy. highway.
Hz hertz.

IA *o* **Ia.** Iowa.
ibid. *Lat.* ibidem (in the same place).
ICBM intercontinental ballistic missile.
ICC Interstate Commerce Commission.
ID 1. Idaho **2.** *o* **I.D.** identification.
i.e. *Lat.* id est (that is).
IFR instrument flight rules.
IL Illinois.
IMF International Monetary Fund.
IN Indiana.
Inc. incorporated.
intl. *o* **int.** international.
inv. invoice.
I/O input/output.
IQ *o* **I.Q.** intelligence quotient.
IRA 1. Individual Retirement Account **2.** *o* **I.R.A.** Irish Republican Army.
IRBM Intermediate Range Ballistic Missile.
IRS Internal Revenue Service.
ISBN International Standard Book Number.
IUD intrauterine device.
IV intravenous; intravenously.

Jan. January.
J.D. *Lat.* Jurum Doctor (Doctor of Laws).
JP *o* **J.P.** justice of the peace.
jr. *o* **Jr.** junior.

Jul. July.
Jun. June.

k 1. karat **2.** kilo–.
kc kilocycle.
kcal kilocalorie.
kg kilogram.
KHz kilohertz.
KKK *o* **K.K.K.** Ku Klux Klan.
km kilometer.
kmph kilometers per hour.
KS Kansas.
kW kilowatt.
kWh kilowatt-hour.
KY *o* **Ky.** Kentucky.

l liter.
LA *o* **La.** Louisiana.
L.A. *o* **LA** Los Angeles.
lat. latitude.
lb. *Lat.* libra (pound).
LC Library of Congress.
lcd *o* **l.c.d.** lowest common denominator.
LCD liquid crystal display.
LCM least (lowest) common multiple.
LED light-emitting diode.
l.h. *o* **LH** left hand.
lit. literature; literally.
Lit.D. *o* **Litt.D.** *Lat.* Litterarum Doctor (Doctor of Letters *or* Literature).
LL.D. *Lat.* Legum Doctor (Doctor of Laws).
lm lumen.
LMT local mean time.
LNG liquified natural gas.
loc. cit. *Lat.* loco citato.
long. longitude.
LP long-playing (record).
LPG liquefied petroleum gas.
LPN *o* **L.P.N.** licensed practical nurse.
LSAT Law School Admissions Test.
Lt. lieutenant.
ltd. *o* **Ltd.** limited.

m 1. meter **2.** mass.
MA Massachusetts.
M.A. *Lat.* Magister Artium (Master of Arts).
M.A.Ed. Master of Arts in Education.
Maj. major.
Mar. March.
M.A.T. Master of Arts in Teaching.
max. maximum.
mb millibar.
M.B.A. Master of Business Administration.
mc millicurie.
Mc megacycle.
MC Medical Corps.
M.C. *o* **m.c.** master of ceremonies.
MD *o* **Md.** Maryland.
M.D. *Lat.* Medicinae Doctor (Doctor of Medicine).
mdse. merchandise.
ME *o* **Me.** Maine.
M.Ed. Master of Education.
M.F.A. Master of Fine Arts.
mfg. manufacturing; manufactured.
mfr. manufacturer; manufactured.
mg milligram.
Mgr. *o* **mgr.** manager.
mgt. management.
MI Michigan.
mi. mile.
MIA missing in action.
min. 1. minimum **2.** *o* **min** minute.
misc. miscellaneous.
mkt. market.
ml milliliter.
MLA *o* **M.L.A.** Modern Language Association.

M.L.S. Master of Library Science.
mm millimeter.
MN Minnesota.
MO *o* **Mo.** Missouri.
mo. month.
mol wt molecular weight.
Mon. Monday.
mos. months.
MP *o* **M.P.** military police.
M.P. Member of Parliament.
mpg *o* **m.p.g.** miles per gallon.
mph *o* **m.p.h.** miles per hour.
ms millisecond.
MS 1. Mississippi **2.** multiple sclerosis.
ms. *o* **MS.** *o* **ms** manuscript.
msec millisecond.
MSG monosodium glutamate.
Msgr. Monseigneur; Monsignor.
mss. *o* **MSS.** *o* **mss** manuscripts.
MST *o* **M.S.T.** Mountain Standard Time.
M.S.W. Master of Social Welfare.
MT 1. Montana **2.** *o* **M.T.** Mountain Time.
mt. *o* **Mt.** mount; mountain.
m.t. *o* **M.T.** metric ton.
mV millivolt.
mW milliwatt.
MW megawatt.

N *o* **N.** north.
NA *o* **n/a** not applicable.
NAACP National Association for the Advancement of Colored People.
NASA National Aeronautics and Space Administration.
NATO North Atlantic Treaty Organization.
n.b. *o* **N.B.** nota bene.
NC *o* **N.C.** North Carolina.
NCO noncommissioned officer.
ND *o* **N.D.** North Dakota.
NE 1. Nebraska **2.** *o* **N.E.** New England **3.** northeast.
NEA National Education Association.
NH *o* **N.H.** New Hampshire.
NIH National Institute of Health.
NJ *o* **N.J.** New Jersey.
NLRB *o* **N.L.R.B.** National Labor Relations Board.
NM *o* **N.M.** New Mexico.
no. number.
Nov. November.
NOW National Organization for Women.
N.P. notary public.
NRA National Rifle Association.
NRC Nuclear Regulatory Commission.
NSF National Science Foundation.
nt. wt. net weight.
NV Nevada.
NW northwest.
NY *o* **N.Y.** New York.
NYSE New York Stock Exchange.
NYC *o* **N.Y.C.** New York City.

OAS Organization of American States.
OCS Officer Candidate School.
Oct. October.
OEO Office of Economic Opportunity.
OH Ohio.
OK Oklahoma.
OMB Office of Management and Budget.
op. cit. *Lat.* opere citato (in the work cited).
OPEC Organization of Petroleum Exporting Countries.
OR *o* **Or.** Oregon.
O.R. *o* **OR** operating room.

org. organization; organized.
o.t. *o* **O.T. 1.** occupational therapy **2.** overtime.
oz *o* **oz.** ounce.

p. 1. page **2.** per.
PA 1. *o* **Pa.** Pennsylvania **2.** public address (system).
PAC political action committee.
pat. patent.
patd. patented.
PBX *o* **P.B.X.** private branch (telephone) exchange.
PC personal computer.
PCB polychlorinated biphenyl.
pd. paid.
PDT *o* **P.D.T.** Pacific Daylight Time.
Pfc *o* **Pfc.** private first class.
pg. page.
Phar.D. *Lat.* Pharmaciae Doctor (Doctor of Pharmacy).
Ph.D. *Lat.* Philosophiae Doctor (Doctor of Philosophy).
pkg. *o* **pkge.** package.
pkwy. parkway.
Pl. place (in street names).
PLO Palestine Liberation Organization.
P.M. 1. *o* **p.m.** post meridiem **2.** Prime Minister.
PO *o* **P.O.** *o* **p.o. 1.** petty officer **2.** post office.
POE *o* **P.O.E.** port of entry.
pop. population.
POW *o* **P.O.W.** prisoner of war.
pp. pages.
ppd. 1. postpaid **2.** prepaid.
P.P.S. *o* **p.ps** *Lat.* post postscriptum (additional postscript).
pr. pair.
PR 1. Puerto Rico **2.** public relations.
Pres. President.
Prof. professor.
P.S. *o* **p.s. 1.** postscript **2.** public school.
PSAT Preliminary Scholastic Aptitude Test.
psf *o* **p.s.f.** pounds per square foot.
psi *o* **p.s.i.** pounds per square inch.
PST *o* **P.S.T.** Pacific Standard Time.
pt. part.
P.T. *o* **PT** Pacific Time.
PT part-time.
PTA *o* **P.T.A.** Parent-Teacher Association.
PVC polyvinyl chloride.
pvt. *o* **Pvt.** private.
pwr. power.
PX Post Exchange.

Q.E.D. *Lat.* quot erat demonstrandum (which was to be demonstrated).
QMG Quartermaster General.
qt *o* **qt.** quart.
q.v. *Lat.* quod vide (which see).

r *o* **R 1.** radius **2.** *Elec.* resistance.
RAF *o* **R.A.F.** Royal Air Force.
RAM random-access memory.
R&B rhythm and blues.
R&D research and development.
RC 1. Red Cross **2.** Roman Catholic.
rept. receipt.
RD rural delivery.
Rd. *o* **rd.** road.
RDA recommended daily allowance.
recd. *o* **rec'd.** received.
reg. registered.
Rep. Republican.
Rev. reverend (title).
RFD *o* **R.F.D.** rural free delivery.

r.h. *o* **RH** right hand.
RI *o* **R.I.** Rhode Island.
R.I.P. *Lat.* requiescat in pace (may he *o* she rest in peace).
RN *o* **R.N. 1.** registered nurse **2.** Royal Navy.
ROM read-only memory.
ROTC Reserve Officers' Training Corps.
rpm *o* **r.p.m** revolutions per minute.
rps *o* **r.p.s** revolutions per second.
RR rural route.
R.R. 1. railroad **2.** Right Reverend.
R.S.V.P. *o* **r.s.v.p.** *French* repondez s'il vous plait (please reply).
rte. route.

S *o* **S.** south.
SAC Strategic Air Command.
SALT Strategic Arms Limitations Talks.
SAM surface-to-air-missile.
SASE self-addressed stamped envelope.
SAT Scholastic Aptitude Test.
Sat. Saturday.
SBN Standard Book Number.
SC *o* **S.C.** South Carolina.
SD *o* **S.D. 1.** South Dakota **2.** standard deviation.
SDI Strategic Defense Initiative.
SE southeast.
SEATO Southeast Asia Treaty Organization.
sec second.
SEC Securities and Exchange Commission.
secy. secretary.
Sen. Senate; Senator.
Sept. *o* **Sep.** September.
SF science fiction.
Sgt. sergeant.
SIDS sudden infant death syndrome.
S.J. Society of Jesus.
S.J.D. *Lat.* Scientiae Juridicae Doctor (Doctor of Juridical Science).
S.M. *Lat.* Scientiae Major (Master of Science).
soc. society.
SOP standard operating procedure.
SPCA Society for the Prevention of Cruelty to Animals.
sq. square.
Sr. *o* **sr.** senior.
SRO standing room only.
S.S. *o* **SS** steamship.
ST standard time.
st. *o* **St.** street.
St. saint.
s.t. short ton.
std. standard.
STP standard temperature and pressure.
Sun. Sunday.
supt. *o* **Supt.** superintendent.
sw short wave.
SW southwest.

t 1. ton **2.** troy (system of weights).
t. teaspoon; teaspoonful.
T. tablespoon; tablespoonful.
TB *o* **T.B.** tuberculosis.
tbs. *o* **tbsp.** tablespoon; tablespoonful.
temp. 1. temperature **2.** temporary.
TESOL teachers of English to speakers of other languages.
Th.D. *Lat.* Theologiae Doctor (Doctor of Theology).
Thurs. *o* **Thur.** Thursday.
TM trademark.

TN Tennessee.
tsp. teaspoon; teaspoonful.
Tues. *o* **Tu.** Tuesday.
TX Texas.

U. university.
U.A.R. United Arab Republic.
UAW United Automobile Workers.
uhf *o* **UHF** ultrahigh frequency.
U.K. United Kingdom.
UMW United Mine Workers.
UN *o* **U.N.** United Nations.
UNESCO United Nations Educational, Scientific, and Cultural Organization.
UNICEF United Nations International Children's Emergency Fund.
UPI *o* **U.P.I.** United Press International.
USAF United States Air Force.
USCG United States Coast Guard.
USDA United States Department of Agriculture.
USIA United States Information Agency.
USMC United States Marine Corps.
USN United States Navy.
USO United Service Organizations.
USS United States Ship.
usu. usually.
UT Utah.

V 1. velocity **2.** volt **3.** volume.
v. verse
v. *o* **V.** *Lat.* vide (see).
VA *o* **Va.** Virginia.
V.A. *o* **VA** Veterans' Administration.
VAT value-added tax.
VD *o* **V.D.** venereal disease.
VDT video display terminal.
VFR visual flight rules.
VFW Veterans of Foreign Wars.
vhf *o* **VHF** very high frequency.
VI Virgin Islands.
VISTA Volunteers in Service to America.
viz. *Lat.* videlicet (namely).
vol. volume.
VP *o* **V.P.** Vice President.
vs. versus.
VT Vermont.

W *o* **W.** west.
W watt.
WA Washington.
WAC Women's Army Corps.
WAF Women in the Air Force.
WATS Wide-Area Telephone Service.
w.c. water closet.
Wed. Wednesday.
WH watt-hour.
WHO World Health Organization.
whse. warehouse.
whsle. wholesale.
WI Wisconsin.
wk. 1. week **2.** work.
w/o without.
WP word processing; word processor.
wpm *o* **w.p.m** words per minute.
wt. weight.
WV West Virginia.
WWI *o* **W.W.I** World War I.
WWII *o* **W.W.II** World War II.
Wy *o* **Wyo.** Wyoming.

yd yard (measurement).
YMCA *o* **Y.M.C.A.** Young Men's Christian Association.
yr. 1. year **2.** your.
YWCA *o* **Y.W.C.A.** Young Women's Christian Association.

ZPG zero population growth.

LA ORTOGRAFÍA DEL INGLÉS

El alfabeto inglés

El alfabeto inglés consta de 26 letras. Éstas son las mismas que las del alfabeto español, excepto que la *ch, ll, ñ* y *rr* no constituyen letras independientes. La *k* y la *w*, que se usan sólo en vocablos extranjeros en español, se consideran parte íntegra del alfabeto inglés.

a	(ā)	n	(ĕn)
b	(bē)	o	(ō)
c	(sē)	p	(pē)
d	(dē)	q	(kyoo)
e	(ē)	r	(är)
f	(ĕf)	s	(ĕs)
g	(jē)	t	(tē)
h	(āch)	u	(yoo)
i	(ī)	v	(vē)
j	(jā)	w	(dŭb′əl-yoo)
k	(kā)	x	(ĕks)
l	(ĕl)	y	(wī)
m	(ĕm)	z	(zē)

El uso de las mayúsculas y la puntuación

Las mayúsculas se emplean con más frecuencia en inglés que en español. Además de emplearse al principio de una oración y con nombres propios, se emplean en inglés con los nombres de los días de la semana y con los meses del año <*Monday* lunes><*March* marzo>. El pronombre personal de la primera persona tambien se escribe con mayúscula <*I* yo>. Se emplea la mayúscula con los adjetivos de nacionalidad y los nombres de los idiomas <*the French government* el gobierno francés><*I am studying Spanish* estudio español>. La mayúscula también se emplea con los adjetivos que denotan la religión <*a Catholic church* una iglesia católica>. Adjetivos derivados de nombres propios se escriben con mayúscula en inglés <*Freudian psychology* la psicología freudiana>.

Los signos de puntuación se usan en inglés así como en español con unas excepciones. Los puntos de interrogación y de admiración no se usan al principio de la oración <*what did you say?* ¿qué dijiste?><*what a fool!* ¡qué tonto!>. Las comillas (" ") se usan en vez del guión (—) para marcar el diálogo. La puntuación usada en los números es distinta de la española. En inglés se usa un punto en vez de una coma de decimales: 6.84 en vez de 6,84. Para dividir números grandes se usa una coma en inglés: 8,439,621 en vez de 8.439.621.

Variaciones ortográficas

Entre el inglés norteamericano y el británico hay varias diferencias. Por ejemplo:

* en los EE. UU. se usa *–or* en vez del británico *–our* <*color, colour*>
* en los EE. UU. se usa *–old* en vez de *–ould* <*mold, mould*>
* en los EE. UU. se usa *–er* en vez de *–or* <*adviser, advisor*>
* en los EE. UU. se usa *–er* en vez de *–re* <*theater, theatre*>; en algunas excepciones los norteamericanos conservan *–re* <*ogre, acre, massacre*>
* en los EE. UU. se usa *–ence* en vez del británico *–ense* <*defence, defense*>
* en los EE. UU. ciertas consonantes se escriben simple, mientras que en el inglés británico se escriben doble <*traveler, traveller; worshiped, worshipped; wagon, waggon*>
* en los EE. UU. se suprime la *e* en la escritura de ciertas palabras del inglés británico <*judgment, judgement; ax, axe*>
* en los EE. UU. los diptongos del origen griego y latino se simplifican mientras que los ingleses conservan la ortografía original <*hemoglobin, haemoglobin; esophagus, oesophagus*>

GUÍA PARA LA PRONUNCIACIÓN INGLESA

En la lengua española existen sólo cinco sonidos de vocal. En el inglés, en cambio, una misma vocal puede tener hasta cinco sonidos distintos.

Debido a la complejidad de la pronunciación inglesa, esta parte del Diccionario indica, entre paréntesis, la pronunciación aproximada de cada vocablo. Esta transcripción fonética, que es una versión simplificada del Alfabeto Fonético Internacional, consiste en una serie de símbolos fonéticos, cada uno de los cuales equivale a un sonido solamente.

En el cuadro que se ofrece a continuación figuran los símbolos fonéticos que representan los sonidos del idioma inglés, junto con ejemplos de palabras inglesas en las que ocurren estos sonidos.

En los casos en que los sonidos son similares a los del español, se dan también ejemplos de palabras en este idioma. Para los sonidos que existen solamente en el inglés se explica cómo los hispanohablantes pueden lograr la articulación aproximada de estos sonidos. Una versión concisa de esta Guía aparece al pie de cada página para comodidad del lector.

A diferencia del español, muchas palabras en inglés tienen más de un acento tónico. El acento tónico primario se indica con una marca en letra negrilla (′) al final de la sílaba acentuada. El acento tónico secundario se indica en letra redonda (′), también al final de la sílaba. Por ejemplo: **rainwater** (rān′wô′tər).

Símbolo	Ejemplo inglés	Ejemplo español	Sonido aproximado
ă	pat	—	entre la *a* y la *e*
ā	pay, mate	rey	
âr	care, hair	—	parecido a *ea* en *brea*, articulado con la *r* que le sigue
ä	father	año	
b	bib	boca, hombre	
ch	church	chico	
d	deed, milled	dar	
ĕ	pet, feather	el	
ē	bee, me, piece	mil	
f	fife, phase, rough	fama	
g	gag	gato	
h	hat	joya	
hw	which	juez, juicio	
ĭ	pit	—	entre la *i* y la *e*
ī	pie, by	aire	
îr	pier, dear, mere	—	entre *ía* en *día* e *íe* en *fíe*
j	judge	—	entre la *y* inicial y la *ch*
k	kick, cat, pique	casa	
kw	quick	cuan, cuido	
l	lid, needle	luz	
m	mum	muy	
n	no, sudden	no	
ng	thing	inglés	
ŏ	pot, swat	la	
ō	toe, go, boat	solo	
ô	caught, paw, for	corre	
oi	noise, boy	oigo	
o͝o	took	—	parecido a la *u* en *uno*, pero menos prolongado
o͞o	boot, suit	uno	
ou	out, cow	auto	
p	pop	pan	
r	roar	—	entre la *r* en *quiero* y la *rr* en *barro*, pero con la punta de la lengua elevada y retrocediendo hacia el paladar, sin tocarlo
s	sauce	sapo	
sh	ship, dish	—	parecido a la *ch*, pero más suave; se asemeja al silbido *sshhh!* con que se pide silencio
t	tight, stopped	tu	
th	thin, path	—	parecido a la *z* en *brazo*, según se pronuncia en Castilla
th	this, bathe	—	parecido a la *d* en *cada;* se asemeja al sonido anterior, pero es más largo y sonorizado
ŭ	cut, rough	—	parecido a una *o* que tira a la *a*
yo͞o	use, few	ciudad	
ûr	urge, term, firm, word, heard	—	parecido a una *e* que tira a la *o* y que se pronuncia articulada con la *r* que le sigue
v	valve	—	parecido a la *v* de *varón*
w	with	cual, hueco	
y	yes	yo	
z	zebra, xylem	mismo	
zh	vision, pleasure, garage	—	parecido a la *ll* o la *y* inicial, según la pronunciación de los argentinos y uruguayos
ə	about, item, edible, gallop, circus	—	parecido a una *e* muy breve que tira a la *i*
ər	butter	—	parecido a una *e* muy breve que se articula con la *r* que le sigue

A

a, A (ā) s. [pl. **a's, A's**] *(letter)* primera letra del alfabeto inglés; *(grade)* la calificación más alta; MÚS. la *m* ♦ **A flat, major, minor, sharp** MÚS. la bemol, mayor, menor, sostenido • **from A to Z** FAM. de cabo a rabo, de pe a pa.

a §G18 (ə, ā) art. indef. [ú. antes de sonido consonate] un <*a book* un libro>; a, por, cada, el <*two dollars a barrel* dos dólares el barril>; mismo <*two of a kind* dos de la misma clase>; un tal <*a Mr. Brown called today* un tal Sr. Brown llamó hoy>.

a·back (ə-băk') adv. por sorpresa, de improviso ♦ **to be taken a.** quedar desconcertado • **to take a.** desconcertar.

ab·a·cus (ăb'ə-kəs) s. [pl. **-cus·es** o **ab·a·ci** (ăb'ə-sī')] *(computing device)* ábaco; ARQ. ábaco.

a·baft (ə-băft') MARÍT. I. adv. en popa, hacia la popa II. prep. detrás de.

ab·a·lo·ne (ăb'ə-lō'nē) s. ZOOL. oreja marina.

a·ban·don (ə-băn'dən) I. tr. *(to desist)* abandonar; *(to desert)* desertar, dejar; *(to give up)* renunciar a ♦ **to a. oneself to** entregarse a, abandonarse a II. s. abandono, desenfreno.

a·ban·doned (ə-băn'dənd) adj. *(deserted)* abandonado, desierto; *(unrestrained)* perdido.

a·ban·don·ment (a-băn'dən-mənt) s. abandono.

a·base (ə-bās') tr. **a·based, a·bas·ing** rebajar, humillar.

a·base·ment (ə-bās'mənt) s. degradación *f,* humillación *f.*

a·bash (ə-băsh') tr. *(to make ashamed)* avergonzar; *(to disconcert)* desconcertar.

a·bate (ə-bāt') tr. **a·bat·ed, a·bat·ing** disminuir, aminorar —intr. menguar, amainar <*the wind is abating* el viento está amainando>.

a·bate·ment (ə-bāt'mənt) s. disminución *f.*

ab·ba·cy (ăb'ə-sē) s. [pl. **-cies**] RELIG. abadía (dignidad o jurisdicción).

ab·bess (ăb'ĭs) s. RELIG. abadesa.

ab·bey (ăb'ē) s. [pl. **-beys**] RELIG. abadía, convento.

ab·bot (ăb'ət) s. RELIG. abad *m.*

ab·bre·vi·ate (ə-brē'vē-āt') tr. **-at·ed, -at·ing** *(to make shorter)* abreviar, resumir; *(to reduce)* abreviar.

ab·bre·vi·a·tion (ə-brē'vē-ā'shən) s. abbreviación *f,* abreviatura.

ab·di·cate (ăb'dĭ-kāt') tr. & intr. **-cat·ed, -cat·ing** abdicar, renunciar.

ab·di·ca·tion (ăb'dĭ-kā'shən) s. abdicación *f,* renuncia.

ab·do·men (ăb'də-mən, ăb-dō'-) s. abdomen *m,* vientre *m.*

ab·dom·i·nal (ăb-dŏm'ə-nəl) adj. abdominal.

ab·duct (ăb-dŭkt') tr. *(to kidnap)* secuestrar, raptar; ANAT., FISIOL. abducir (un miembro o parte del cuerpo).

ab·duc·tion (ăb-dŭk'shən) s. *(kidnapping)* rapto, secuestro; ANAT., FISIOL. abducción *f.*

ab·duc·tor (ăb-dŭk'tər) s. *(kidnapper)* raptor *m,* secuestrador *m;* ANAT., FISIOL. abductor *m.*

a·be·ce·dar·i·an (ā'bē-sē-dâr'ē-ən) I. s. *(learner)* persona que aprende el abecedario; *(novice)* novicio, novato II. adj. *(of the alphabet)* alfabético; *(arranged alphabetically)* ordenado alfabéticamente; *(elementary)* rudimentario, elemental.

a·bed (ə-běd') adv. en cama, acostado.

A·bel (ā'bəl) s. BÍBL. Abel.

ab·er·rant (ă-běr'ənt) adj. aberrante.

ab·er·ra·tion (ăb'ə-rā'shən) s. aberración *f.*

a·bet (əbĕt') tr. **a·bet·ted, a·bet·ting** incitar, instigar (a cometer un delito) ♦ **to aid and a.** ser cómplice de.

a·bet·tor o **a·bet·ter** (ə-bět'ər) s. *(instigator)* instigador *m;* *(accomplice)* cómplice *mf.*

a·bey·ance (ə-bā'əns) s. suspensión *f* ♦ **in a.** en suspenso • **estate in a.** DER. bienes relictos yacentes.

ab·hor (ăb-hôr') tr. **-horred, -hor·ring** aborrecer, detestar.

ab·hor·rence (ăb-hôr'əns) s. aborrecimiento, odio ♦ **to hold in a.** aborrecer, detestar.

ab·hor·rent (ăb-hôr'ənt) adj. aborrecible, detestable.

a·bid·ance (ə-bīd'ns) s. permanencia, continuidad *f* ♦ **a. by** acatamiento de, cumplimiento de.

a·bide (ə-bīd') tr. **a·bode** (ə-bōd') o **a·bid·ed, a·bid·ing** *(to wait)* esperar, aguardar; *(to tolerate)* tolerar, soportar —intr. *(to remain)* permanecer, continuar; *(to reside)* morar, habitar ♦ **to a. by** cumplir con, acatar.

a·bid·ing (ə-bī'dĭng) adj. *(enduring)* constante, duradero; *(obedient)* obediente, respetuoso ♦ **law-a.** respetuoso de las leyes.

a·bil·i·ty (ə-bĭl'ĭ-tē) s. [pl. **-ties**] *(skill)* capacidad *f,* habilidad *f; (talent)* talento, aptitud *f.*

ab·ject (ăb'jěkt') adj. *(contemptible)* abyecto, vil; *(wretched)* miserable.

ab·jure (ăb-jōōr') tr. **-jured, -jur·ing** abjurar, retractarse bajo juramento de.

ab·la·tive (ăb'lə-tĭv) adj. & s. GRAM. ablativo.

a·blaze (ə-blāz') adj. *(on fire)* ardiente, encendido; FIG. *(beaming)* inflamado.

a·ble (ā'bəl) adj. **a·bler, a·blest** capaz, hábil ♦ **to be a. to** poder, ser capaz (de).

a·ble-bod·ied (ā'bəl-bŏd'ēd) adj. sano, fuerte.

able-bodied seaman MARÍT. marinero de primera.

a·bloom (ə-blōōm') adj. en flor, floreciente.

ab·lu·tion (ə-blōō'shən) s. ablución *f* ♦ **ablutions** FAM. lavabo.

a·bly (ā'blē) adv. hábilmente, diestramente.

ab·ne·gate (ăb'nĭ-gāt') tr. **-gat·ed, -gat·ing** abnegar.

ab·ne·ga·tion (ăb'nĭ-gā'shən) s. abnegación *f.*

ab·nor·mal (ăb-nôr'məl) adj. anormal.

ab·nor·mal·i·ty (ăb'nôr-măl'ĭ-tē) s. [pl. **-ties**] anormalidad *f.*

a·board (ə-bôrd') I. adv. a bordo ♦ **all a.!** F.C. ¡pasajeros al tren! • **to go a.** embarcarse, ir a bordo II. prep. a bordo de <*life a. ship* la vida a bordo del buque>.

a·bode (ə-bōd') I. un pret. y part. p. de **abide** II. s. morada, residencia.

a·bol·ish (ə-bŏl'ĭsh) tr. abolir, eliminar.

a·bol·ish·ment (ə-bŏl'ĭsh-mənt) s. abolición *f,* eliminación *f.*

ab·o·li·tion (ăb'ə-lĭsh'ən) s. *(act, state)* abolición *f,* eliminación *f;* HIST. la abolición de la esclavitud (en EE. UU.).

ab·o·li·tion·ist (ăb'ə-lĭsh'ə-nĭst) s. abolicionista *mf.*

A-bomb (ā'bŏm') s. bomba atómica.

a·bom·i·na·ble (ə-bŏm'ə-nə-bəl) adj. abominable, detestable.

a·bom·i·nate (ə-bŏm'ə-nāt') tr. **-nat·ed, -nat·ing** abominar, detestar.

a·bom·i·na·tion (ə-bŏm'ə-nā'shən) s. abominación *f.*

ab·o·rig·i·nal (ăb'ə-rĭj'ə-nəl) s. & adj. aborigen *mf,* indígena *mf.*

ab·o·rig·i·ne (ăb'ə-rĭj'ə-nē) s. aborigen *mf,* indígena *mf.*

a·bort (ə-bôrt') intr. MED. abortar; FIG. *(to fall through)* malograrse —tr. abortar.

a·bor·ti·fa·cient (ə-bôr'tə-fā'shənt) adj. & s. abortivo.

a·bor·tion (ə-bôr'shən) s. MED. aborto; FIG. *(failure)* aborto, fracaso.

a·bor·tion·ist (ə-bôr'shə-nĭst) s. abortista *mf,* profesional que hace abortos *mf.*

a·bor·tive (ə-bôr'tĭv) adj. *(causing abortion)* abortivo; FIG. *(unsuccessful)* fracasado, frustrado.

a·bound (ə-bound') intr. abundar.

a·bout (ə-bout') I. prep. *(relating to)* acerca de, sobre <*stories a. animals* cuentos sobre animales>; *(in the nature of)* con respecto a <*something odd a. his accent* algo curioso con respecto a su acento>; *(concerning)* por <*crazy a. sweets* loco por los dulces>; *(approximately)* a eso de, alrededor de <*a. ten o'clock* alrededor de las diez>; *(on all sides of)* alrededor de, a la redonda; *(near to)* cerca de, en torno de ♦ **how a. that!** ¡qué te parece! • **how a. you?** ¿y tú? • **to be a. to** estar a punto de II. adv. *(approximately)* aproximadamente, casi <*a. two days* aproximadamente dos días>; *(all around)* aquí y allá, por todas partes <*great waves tossed the ship a.* las olas grandes sacudían al barco por todas partes>; *(in the reverse direction)* en la dirección opuesta ♦ **all a.** por todas partes • **to be up and a.** estar levantado (de la cama).

a·bout-face (ə-bout'fās') I. s. *(turn)* media vuelta; *(change)* cambio de opinión o conducta II. intr. **-faced, -fac·ing** *(to* turn) dar media vuelta; FIG. *(to change)* cambiar de opinión *o* conducta.

a·bove (ə-bŭv′) **I.** adv. *(higher place)* en lo alto, encima; *(earlier part of a text)* más arriba ♦ **a. all** sobre todo • **from a.** desde lo alto, desde el cielo **II.** prep. *(over)* sobre, por encima de <*seagulls hovered a. the waves* las gaviotas revoloteaban sobre las olas>; *(greater than)* superior a <*last week's spending was a. normal* los gastos de la semana pasada fueron superiores a lo normal> ♦ **a. and beyond** mucho más allá de **III.** adj. precitado, antedicho <*the a. figures* los números precitados> **IV.** s. *(the top)* lo alto, (la más) alta autoridad <*the instructions come from a.* las instrucciones provienen de la más alta autoridad>; *(stated earlier)* lo dicho, lo anterior.

a·bove·board (ə-bŭv′bôrd′) **I.** adj. franco, abierto **II.** adv. francamente.

a·bove-men·tioned (ə-bŭv′mĕn′shənd) adj. anteriormente citado, de referencia <*the a. example* el ejemplo de referencia>.

ab·ra·ca·dab·ra (ăb′rə-kə-dăb′rə) s. *(magic word)* abracadabra *m*; *(jargon)* jerga, galimatías *m*.

a·brade (ə-brād′) tr. **a·brad·ed, a·brad·ing** raer, desgastar.

a·bra·sion (ə-brā′zhən) s. MED. abrasión *f*; TEC. desgaste *m*; GEOL. erosión *f*.

a·bra·sive (ə-brā′sĭv) adj. & s. abrasivo.

a·breast (ə-brĕst′) adv. en una línea ♦ **to be a. of** *o* **with** *(to keep up with)* correr parejo con; *(to be up-to-date with)* estar al corriente de • **two a.** en fila de a dos.

a·bridge (ə-brĭj′) tr. **a·bridged, a·bridg·ing** *(to condense)* abreviar, condensar; *(to curtail)* privar (de un derecho).

a·bridg·ment *o* **a·bridge·ment** (ə-brĭj′mənt) s. *(act)* abreviación *f*, condensación *f*; *(synopsis)* compendio, resumen *m*.

a·broad (ə-brôd′) adv. *(not in one's land)* en el extranjero, fuera del país; *(widely)* en todas partes *o* direcciones ♦ **there is a rumor a. that** corre un rumor que.

ab·ro·gate (ăb′rə-gāt′) tr. **-gat·ed, -gat·ing** abrogar, revocar.

ab·ro·ga·tion (ăb′rə-gā′shən) s. abrogación *f*, revocación *f*.

a·brupt (ə-brŭpt′) adj. *(brusque)* abrupto, brusco; *(unexpected)* inesperado, repentino; *(very steep)* escarpado.

a·brupt·ly (ə-brŭpt′lē) adv. bruscamente, repentinamente.

a·brupt·ness (ə-brŭpt′nĭs) s. brusquedad *f*.

ab·scess (ăb′sĕs) MED. **I.** s. absceso **II.** intr. formar un absceso.

ab·scis·sa (ăb-sĭs′ə) [pl. **-scis·sas** *o* **-scis·sae** (-sĭs′ē)] s. GEOM. abscisa.

ab·scond (ăb-skŏnd′) intr. esconderse, ocultarse.

ab·sence (ăb′səns) s. ausencia, falta.

ab·sent I. adj. (ăb′sənt) *(not present)* ausente; *(not existent)* no existente; *(absorbed in thought)* abstraído, distraído **II.** tr. (ăb-sĕnt′) ausentarse de ♦ **to a. oneself from** ausentarse de, no presentarse a.

ab·sen·tee (ăb′sən-tē′) s. ausente *mf.*

absentee ballot s. voto por correspondencia (de persona ausente).

ab·sen·tee·ism (ăb′sən-tē′ĭz′əm) s. absentismo, ausentismo.

ab·sent-mind·ed (ăb′sənt-mīn′dĭd) adj. distraído.

ab·sent-mind·ed·ly (ăb′sənt-mīn′dĭd-lē) adv. distraídamente.

ab·sent-mind·ed·ness (ăb′sənt-mīn′dĭd-nĭs) s. distracción *f.*

ab·sinthe *o* **ab·sinth** (ăb′sĭnth′) s. BOT. ajenjo; *(liquor)* licor de ajenjo *m.*

ab·so·lute (ăb′sə-lōōt′) **I.** adj. *(complete)* absoluto; *(pure)* puro, sin mezcla; *(unconditional)* incondicional, total <*a. confidence* confianza total>; *(unrestricted)* sin restricción, autocrático <*a. monarchy* monarquía autocrática>; FÍS. absoluto **II.** s. lo absoluto.

absolute alcohol s. alcohol puro.

absolute ceiling s. AER. altura máxima, techo teórico *o* absoluto.

absolute pitch s. MÚS. *(sound)* tono *o* sonido absoluto; *(ability)* oído absoluto.

absolute scale s. FÍS. escala de temperatura Kelvin *o* absoluta.

absolute zero s. FÍS. cero absoluto.

ab·so·lu·tion (ăb′sə-lōō′shən) s. absolución *f*, perdón *m.*

ab·so·lut·ism (ăb′sə-lōō′tĭz′əm) s. absolutismo, autocracia.

ab·so·lut·ist (ăb′sə-lōō′tĭst) s. & adj. absolutista *mf*, autócrata *mf.*

ab·solve (əb-zŏlv′) tr. **-solved, -solv·ing** *(of sin)* absolver; *(of obligation)* eximir, dispensar; *(of guilt)* exculpar, exonerar.

ab·sorb (əb-sôrb′) tr. *(to soak in)* absorber; *(to take in)* asimilar, incorporar; *(to muffle)* amortiguar; *(to take up)* ocupar <*the work absorbs all of my time* el trabajo me ocupa todo el tiempo>.

ab·sorbed (əb-sôrbd′) adj. absorto, abstraído.

ab·sorb·en·cy (əb-sôr′bən-sē) s. absorbencia.

ab·sorb·ent (əb-sôr′bənt) adj. & s. absorbente *m.*

ab·sorp·tion (əb-sôrp′shən) s. *(act)* absorción *f*; *(mental concentration)* concentración *f*, ensimismamiento.

ab·stain (ăb-stān′) intr. ♦ **to a. from** abstenerse de.

ab·stain·er (ăb-stā′nər) s. *(non-drinker)* abstemio; *(non-voter)* persona que se abstiene de votar.

ab·ste·mi·ous (ăb-stē′mē-əs) adj. abstinente.

ab·sten·tion (ăb-stĕn′shən) s. abstención *f*, abstinencia.

ab·sti·nence (ăb′stə-nəns) s. abstinencia, continencia.

ab·sti·nent (ăb′stə-nənt) adj. abstemio.

ab·stract I. adj. (ăb′străkt′) abstracto ♦ **a. number** número abstracto **II.** s. (ăb′străkt′) *(summary)* sumario, resumen *m*; *(essence)* extracto, resumen analítico ♦ **in the a.** en abstracto **III.** tr. (ăb-străkt′) *(to remove)* extraer, quitar; *(to pilfer)* hurtar, robar; *(to consider theoretically)* abstraer; *(to summarize)* resumir, compendiar.

ab·stract·ed (ăb-străk′tĭd) adj. abstraído, ensimismado.

ab·strac·tion (ăb-străk′shən) s. *(process)* abstracción *f*, separación *f*; *(idea)* idea *o* concepto abstracto; *(absent-mindedness)* distracción *f*, descuido.

ab·strac·tion·ism (ăb-străk′shə-nĭz′əm) s. arte abstracto.

ab·strac·tive (ăb-străk′tĭv) adj. abstractivo.

ab·struse (ăb-strōōs′) adj. abstruso.

ab·surd (əb-sûrd′) adj. absurdo, ridículo.

ab·surd·i·ty (əb-sûr′dĭ-tē) s. [pl. **-ties**] absurdo, ridiculez *f.*

ab·surd·ly (əb-sûrd′lē) adv. absurdamente, ridículamente.

a·bu·li·a (ə-bōō′lē-ə, ə-byōō′-) s. PSIC. abulia, carencia de voluntad.

a·bu·lic (ə-bōō′lĭk, ə-byōō′-) adj. PSIC. abúlico.

a·bun·dance (ə-bŭn′dəns) s. abundancia.

a·bun·dant (ə-bŭn′dənt) adj. abundante.

a·buse I. (ə-byōōz′) tr. **a·bused, a·bus·ing** *(to misuse)* abusar de; *(to hurt)* maltratar, ultrajar; *(to berate)* insultar, injuriar **II.** s. (ə-byōōs′) *(misuse)* abuso; *(corruption)* corrupción *f*, corruptela; *(maltreatment)* maltrato; *(sexually)* violación *f*; *(insult)* insulto, improperio.

a·bus·er (ə-byōō′zər) s. abusador *m.*

a·bu·sive (ə-byōō′sĭv) adj. *(abusing)* abusivo; *(insulting)* injurioso, insultante.

a·but (ə-bŭt′) intr. **a·but·ted, a·but·ting** ♦ **to a. on** *o* **against** terminar en, descansar en • **to a. upon** lindar con —tr. lindar con <*the shed abuts the barn* el establo linda con el granero>.

a·but·ment (ə-bŭt′mənt) s. *(limit)* linde *m*, confín *m*; CARP. empalme *m*; ARQ., CONSTR. estribo, contrafuerte *m.*

a·but·tal (ə-bŭt′l) s. linde *m*, confín *m.*

a·bys·mal (ə-bĭz′məl) adj. *(unfathomable)* abismal, profundo; FIG. *(wretched)* malísimo, pésimo.

a·byss (ə-bĭs′) s. *(bottomless chasm)* abismo; FIG. *(hell)* profundidad *f*, infierno.

a·bys·sal (ə-bĭs′əl) adj. abisal, abismal.

a·ca·cia (ə-kā′shə) s. BOT. acacia.

ac·a·deme (ăk′ə-dēm′) s. ámbito universitario.

ac·a·de·mi·a (ăk′ə-dē′mē-ə) s. el mundo académico.

ac·a·dem·ic (ăk′ə-dĕm′ĭk) **I.** adj. *(of a school)* académico, universitario; *(liberal or classical)* relativo a las humanidades; *(speculative)* especulativo, teórico **II.** s. catedrático.

academic freedom s. libertad de enseñanza *f.*

ac·a·de·mi·cian (ăk′ə-də-mĭsh′ən, ə-kăd′ə-) s. académico.

ac·a·dem·i·cism (ăk′ə-dĕm′ĭ-sĭz′əm) s. academicismo, academismo.

a·cad·e·my (ə-kăd′ə-mē) s. [pl. **-mies**] academia.

ā rey / ä año / b boca / ch chico / d dar / ĕ el / ē mil / g gato / h joya / hw juez / ī aire / k casa / kw cuan /

a·can·thus (ə-kăn'thəs) s. [pl. **-thus·es** o **-thi** (-thī')] ARQ., BOT. acanto.

ac·a·rid (ăk'ə-rĭd) s. ZOOL. acárido, ácaro.

ac·a·roid resin (ăk'ə-roid') s. BOT. resina acaroidea.

ac·a·rus (ăk'ər-əs) s. [pl. **-ri** (-rī')] ZOOL. ácaro, arador m.

ac·cede (ăk-sēd') intr. **-ced·ed, -ced·ing** (to assent to) consentir en, acceder a <I acceded to her request accedí a su pedido>; (to come into office) subir a, ascender a (un trono, presidencia).

ac·ced·ence (ăk-sēd'ns) s. consentimiento, acuerdo.

ac·cel·er·ate (ăk-sĕl'ə-rāt') tr. **-at·ed, -at·ing** acelerar, apresurar —intr. apresurarse, darse prisa.

ac·cel·er·a·tion (ăk-sĕl'ə-rā'shən) s. aceleración f, aceleramiento.

ac·cel·er·a·tive (ăk-sĕl'ə-rā'tĭv) adj. acelerador

ac·cel·er·a·tor (ăk-sĕl'ə-rā'tər) s. AUTO. acelerador m; QUÍM. catalizador m; FÍS. acelerador de partículas.

ac·cel·er·om·e·ter (ăk-sĕl'ə-rŏm'ĭ-tər) s. FÍS. acelerómetro.

ac·cent (ăk'sĕnt') I. s. GRAM., MAT., MÚS. acento; (style of pronunciation) pronunciación f, dejo (propio de otro idioma, región); POÉT. énfasis m, inflexión f ♦ **written a.** acento ortográfico II. tr. (to stress) acentuar; (to accentuate) recalcar.

ac·cen·tu·ate (ăk-sĕn'chōō-āt') tr. **-at·ed, -at·ing** acentuar, dar énfasis a.

ac·cen·tu·a·tion (ăk-sĕn'chōō-ā'shən) s. acentuación f.

ac·cept (ăk-sĕpt') tr. (to receive) aceptar; (to receive with favor) admitir, dar acogida a; COM. aceptar.

ac·cept·a·bil·i·ty (ăk-sĕp'tə-bĭl'ĭ-tē) s. aceptabilidad f.

ac·cept·a·ble (ăk-sĕp'tə-bəl) adj. aceptable, admisible.

ac·cep·tance (ăk-sĕp'təns) s. (act) aceptación f; (reception) (buena) acogida; (approval) aprobación f; COM. aceptación.

ac·cep·ta·tion (ăk'sĕp-tā'shən) s. (meaning) acepción f, significado (de una palabra); (acceptance) aceptación f, acogida.

ac·cept·ed (ăk-sĕp'tĭd) adj. (received) aceptado; (widely used) corriente, normal; (recognized) reconocido.

ac·cess (ăk'sĕs') s. (passage) acceso, entrada; (permission) permiso (de entrada, uso); MED. acceso, ataque m ♦ **to give a. to** dar entrada a.

ac·ces·sa·ry (ăk-sĕs'ə-rē) s. & adj. var. de **accessory.**

ac·ces·si·bil·i·ty (ăk-sĕs'ə-bĭl'ĭ-tē) s. accesibilidad f.

ac·ces·si·ble (ăk-sĕs'ə-bəl) adj. accesible, asequible ♦ **a. to** (open to) susceptible a (adulación, influencia); (capable of) capaz de (compasión).

ac·ces·sion (ăk-sĕsh'ən) I. s. (attainment) accesión f, ascenso (de dignidad, rango); (addition) ampliación f, expansión f; (of property) incremento del valor de la propiedad; (assent) consentimiento, accesión; (access) acceso, entrada; (outburst) arrebato, furor repentino II. tr. catalogar (en orden de adquisición).

ac·ces·so·ry (ăk-sĕs'ə-rē) s. [pl. **-ries**] (adjunct) accesorio; (in law) cómplice mf ♦ **a. after the fact** DER. encubridor (de un delito) • **a. before the fact** instigador (de un delito) II. adj. accesorio, adjunto.

ac·ci·dence (ăk'sĭ-dəns) s. GRAM. estudio de accidentes (de las palabras).

ac·ci·dent (ăk'sĭ-dənt) s. (mishap) accidente m; (chance) casualidad f; LÓG. accidente; TOP. desigualdad (del terreno) f ♦ **by a.** por casualidad.

ac·ci·den·tal (ăk'sĭ-dĕn'tl) I. adj. accidental, casual II. s. MÚS. accidental m.

ac·ci·den·tal·ly (ăk'sĭ-dĕn'tl-ē) adv. (by chance) por casualidad; (unintentionally) sin querer.

accident insurance s. seguro de accidentes y muerte accidental, seguro contra lesiones y muerte accidentales.

ac·claim (ə-klām') I. tr. aclamar, ovacionar II. s. aclamación f, ovación f.

ac·cla·ma·tion (ăk'lə-mā'shən) s. aclamación f, aprobación unánime f.

ac·clam·a·to·ry (ə-klăm'ə-tôr'ē) adj. aclamatorio.

ac·cli·mate (ə-klī'mĭt, ăk'lə-māt') tr. & intr. **-mat·ed, -mat·ing** aclimatar(se).

ac·cli·ma·tion (ăk'lə-mā'shən) s. aclimatación f, adaptación f.

ac·cli·ma·ti·za·tion (ə-klī'mə-tĭ-zā'shən) s. aclimatación f, adaptación f.

ac·cli·ma·tize (ə-klī'mə-tīz') tr. & intr. **-tized, -tiz·ing** aclimatar(se).

ac·cliv·i·ty (ə-klĭv'ĭ-tē) s. [pl. **-ties**] cuesta, pendiente f.

ac·co·lade (ăk'ə-lād', -läd') s. (embrace) abrazo; (approval) aprobación f, elogio; (of a knight) acolada, espaldarazo.

ac·com·mo·date (ə-kŏm'ə-dāt') tr. **-dat·ed, -dat·ing** (to oblige) hacer un favor a, complacer <I shall try to a. you haré lo posible para complacerle>; (to supply with) proveer de, surtir de; (to have space for) tener espacio para, dar cabida a; (to adapt) amoldar, ajustar a; (to reconcile) reconciliar, avenir —intr. adaptarse.

ac·com·mo·dat·ing (ə-kŏm'ə-dā'tĭng) adj. (obliging) solícito, servicial; (adaptable) acomodadizo.

ac·com·mo·da·tion (ə-kŏm'ə-dā'shən) s. (act) acomodación f; (convenience) favor m, servicio; (compromise) reconciliación f, avenencia; FISIOL. adaptación f, ajuste m.

ac·com·mo·da·tive (ə-kŏm'ə-dā'tĭv) adj. complaciente, servicial.

ac·com·pa·ni·ment (ə-kŭm'pə-nē-mənt) s. (complement) acompañamiento, accesorio; MÚS. acompañamiento.

ac·com·pa·nist (ə-kŭm'pə-nĭst) s. MÚS. acompañante mf.

ac·com·pa·ny (ə-kŭm'pə-nē) tr. **-nied, -ny·ing** acompañar, ir con —intr. MÚS. acompañar, tocar el acompañamiento musical.

ac·com·plice (ə-kŏm'plĭs) s. cómplice mf.

ac·com·plish (ə-kŏm'plĭsh) tr. lograr, realizar.

ac·com·plished (ə-kŏm'plĭsht) adj. (completed) consumado, realizado; (skilled) competente; (sophisticated) instruido, culto.

ac·com·plish·ment (ə-kŏm'plĭsh-mənt) s. realización f, logro.

ac·cord (ə-kôrd') I. tr. (to cause to agree) acordar, armonizar; (to grant) conceder, otorgar —intr. avenirse, concordar <his ideas a. with mine sus ideas concuerdan con las mías> II. s. acuerdo, convenio ♦ **in a. with** de acuerdo con • **of one's own a.** de propia voluntad.

ac·cor·dance (ə-kôr'dns) s. acuerdo f, conformidad f ♦ **in a. with** de conformidad con.

ac·cord·ing·ly (ə-kôr'dĭng-lē) adv. (correspondingly) en conformidad; (consequently) en consecuencia, por consiguiente.

according to prep. conforme a, según.

ac·cor·di·on (ə-kôr'dē-ən) I. s. MÚS. acordeón m II. adj. (said of folders) plegadizo; (said of pleats) plisado.

ac·cor·di·on·ist (ə-kôr'dē-ə-nĭst) s. MÚS. acordeonista mf.

ac·cost (ə-kôst') tr. abordar, dirigirse a.

ac·count (ə-kount') I. s. (narrative) relato, informe m; (explanation) explicación f, motivo; (worth) monta, importancia <a man of little a. un hombre de poca importancia>; COM. cuenta ♦ **accounts** COM. estado de cuenta, factura • **accounts payable** TEN. cuentas a pagar • **accounts receivable** TEN. cuentas a cobrar • **by all accounts** según el decir o la opinión general • **to settle accounts with** FIG. ajustar cuentas con • **charge a.** COM. cuenta corriente • **joint a.** COM. cuenta indistinta • **on a.** COM. a cuenta • **on a. of** a causa de, por • **on no a.** de ninguna manera • **on one's own a.** por cuenta propia • **to call to a.** pedir cuentas a • **to give an a. of** (oneself) dar buena cuenta de (sí) • **to take a. of** o **to take into a.** tomar en cuenta II. tr. (to regard) estimar, considerar; (to note) explicar, dar razón de.

ac·count·a·bil·i·ty (ə-koun'tə-bĭl'ĭ-tē) s. [pl. **-ties**] responsabilidad f.

ac·count·a·ble (ə-koun'tə-bəl) adj. (answerable) responsable (por); (explicable) justificable.

ac·count·an·cy (ə-koun'tən-sē) s. contaduría, contabilidad f.

ac·count·ant (ə-koun'tənt) s. contador m, contable mf.

account executive s. (salesman) agente vendedor m; (in advertising) persona responsable por el manejo de las campañas publicitarias de sus clientes.

ac·count·ing (ə-koun'tĭng) s. contabilidad f.

ac·cou·ter·ment (ə-kōō'tər-mənt) s. MIL. equipaje m, atavío

♦ **ac·cou·ter·ments** MIL. pertrechos, equipo; *(trappings)* adornos, atavío.

ac·cou·tre·ment (ə-kōō'tər-mənt, -trə-mənt) s. G.B. var. de **accoutrement**.

ac·cred·it (ə-krĕd'ĭt) tr. *(to credit with)* acreditar, reconocer; *(to supply with credentials)* acreditar, dar credenciales (diplomáticas).

ac·cred·i·ta·tion (ə-krĕd'ĭ-tā'shən) s. EDUC. autorización *f*; DIPL. acreditación *f*.

ac·cred·it·ed (ə-krĕd'ĭ-tĭd) adj. autorizado, reconocido.

ac·cre·tion (ə-krē'shən) s. *(growth)* crecimiento, acrecentamiento; GEOL., MIN. acreción *f*; DER. acrecencia.

ac·cru·al (ə-krōō'əl) s. incremento, acumulación *f*.

ac·crue (ə-krōō') intr. **-crued, -cru·ing** *(to accumulate)* acumularse; *(to proceed)* proceder, resultar <*benefits that a. from scientific research* beneficios que resultan de la investigación científica>.

ac·cul·tur·ate (ə-kŭl'chə-rāt') tr. & intr. **-at·ed, -at·ing** ANTROP. transformar(se) o adaptar(se) por asimilación cultural.

ac·cul·tur·a·tion (ə-kŭl'chə-rā'shən) s. aculturación *f*.

ac·cu·mu·late (ə-kyōōm'yə-lāt') tr. & intr. **-lat·ed, -lat·ing** acumular(se), amontonar(se).

ac·cu·mu·la·tion (ə-kyōōm'yə-lā'shən) s. acumulación *f*.

ac·cu·mu·la·tive (ə-kyōōm'yə-lā'tĭv, -lə-tĭv) adj. acumulativo.

ac·cu·mu·la·tor (ə-kyōōm'yə-lā'tər) s. *(person)* acumulador *m*; G.B., AUTO. acumulador (de electricidad), batería.

ac·cu·ra·cy (ăk'yər-ə-sē) s. exactitud *f*, precisión *f*.

ac·cu·rate (ăk'yər-ĭt) adj. exacto, preciso.

ac·curs·ed (ə-kûr'sĭd, ə-kûrst') o **ac·curst** (ə-kûrst') adj. *(doomed)* condenado, maldito; *(hateful)* odioso, infausto.

ac·cu·sa·tion (ăk'yə-zā'shən) s. *(act, allegation)* acusación *f*; FOR. cargo, imputación *f*.

ac·cu·sa·tive (ə-kyōō'zə-tĭv) adj. & s. GRAM. acusativo.

ac·cu·sa·to·ri·al (ə-kyōō'zə-tôr'ē-əl) adj. acusatorio.

ac·cuse (ə-kyōōz') tr. **-cused, -cus·ing** acusar.

ac·cused (ə-kyōōzd') adj. acusado, inculpado ♦ **the a.** FOR. el acusado, el inculpado.

ac·cus·er (ə-kyōō'zər) s. acusador *m*.

ac·cus·tom (ə-kŭs'təm) tr. & intr. acostumbrar(se).

ac·cus·tomed (ə-kŭs'təmd) adj. acostumbrado, habitual ♦ **a. to** acostumbrado a.

ace (ās) I. s. as (de naipes, dados, dominó, tenis, aviación) *m*; FAM. *(expert)* as (persona que se estaca en una profesión o campo) ♦ **a. in the hole** FAM. as de reserva (idea o plan importante que se reserva para un momento oportuno) II. tr. **aced, ac·ing** FAM. *(to score well)* recibir la calificación más alta (en un examen, prueba); *(to outdo)* superar a otros en una competencia.

a·ceph·a·lous (ā-sĕf'ə-ləs) adj. ZOOL. acéfalo, sin cabeza; *(without a leader)* acéfalo.

a·cerb (ə-sûrb') adj. acerbo, amargo.

ac·er·bate (ăs'ər-bāt') tr. **-bat·ed, -bat·ing** exasperar, irritar.

a·cer·bi·ty (ə-sûr'bĭ-tē) s. [pl. **-ties**] *(sourness)* acerbidad *f*, acritud *f*; FIG. *(sharpness)* aspereza.

ac·et·al·de·hyde (ăs'ĭ-tăl'də-hīd') s. QUÍM. acetaldehído, aldehído.

ac·e·tate (ăs'ĭ-tāt') s. QUÍM. acetato.

a·ce·tic (ə-sē'tĭk) adj. QUÍM. acético.

ac·e·tone (ăs'ĭ-tōn') s. QUÍM. acetona.

ac·e·tyl (ăs'ĭ-tl, ə-sĕt'l) s. QUÍM. acetilo.

a·cet·y·lene (ə-sĕt'l-ēn') s. QUÍM. acetileno ♦ **a. torch** soplete oxiacetilénico.

a·ce·tyl·sal·i·cyl·ic acid (ə-sĕt'l-săl'ĭ-sĭl'ĭk) s. QUÍM. ácido acetilsalicílico, aspirina.

ache (āk) I. intr. **ached, ach·ing** doler <*my head aches* me duele la cabeza> ♦ **to a. for** FIG. anhelar, ansiar II. s. dolor *m*.

a·chiev·a·ble (ə-chēv'ə-bəl) adj. realizable, factible.

a·chieve (ə-chēv') tr. **a·chieved, a·chiev·ing** llevar a cabo, ejecutar —intr. alcanzar su objetivo, tener éxito.

a·chieve·ment (ə-chēv'mənt) s. *(act)* ejecución *f*, realización *f*; *(accomplishment)* logro, hazaña.

a·chiev·er (ə-chē'vər) s. persona que alcanza su objetivo.

A·chil·les (ə-kĭl'ēz) s. MITOL. Aquiles ♦ **Achilles' heel** talón de Aquiles • **Achilles' tendon** tendón de Aquiles.

ach·ro·mat·ic (ăk'rə-măt'ĭk) adj. *(neutral)* incoloro; ÓPT. acromático.

a·chro·ma·tism (ā-krō'mə-tĭz'əm) s. acromatismo *m*.

ac·id (ăs'ĭd) I. s. QUÍM. ácido; JER. *(drug)* LSD II. adj. *(of an acid)* ácido; *(sour)* agrio; *(biting)* mordaz, punzante.

ac·id-fast (ăs'ĭd-făst') adj. a prueba de ácidos.

a·cid·ic (ə-sĭd'ĭk) adj. ácido.

a·cid·i·fi·er (ə-sĭd'ə-fī'ər) s. QUÍM. substancia acidificante.

a·cid·i·fy (ə-sĭd'ə-fī') tr. & intr. **-fied, -fy·ing** acidificar(se), acedar(se).

a·cid·i·ty (ə-sĭd'ĭ-tē) s. acidez *f*.

ac·id·ly (ăs'ĭd-lē) adv. FIG. mordazmente, cáusticamente.

acid test s. FIG. prueba decisiva (de calidad, mérito).

a·cid·u·late (ə-sĭj'ə-lāt') tr. & intr. **-lat·ed, -lat·ing** acidular(se), avinagrar(se).

a·cid·u·lous (ə-sĭj'ə-ləs) adj. acídulo, cáustico.

ac·knowl·edge (ăk-nŏl'ĭj) tr. **-edged, -edg·ing** *(to admit)* admitir, confesar; *(to recognize)* reconocer; *(to express thanks)* agradecer; *(to report receipt of)* acusar recibo de; DER. atestiguar, certificar.

ac·knowl·edged (ăk-nŏl'ĭjd) adj. reconocido.

ac·knowl·edg·ment o **ac·knowl·edge·ment** (ăk-nŏl'-ĭj-mənt) s. *(confession)* admisión *f*, confesión *f*; *(recognition)* reconocimiento; *(thanks)* agradecimiento; *(receipt)* acuse de recibo *m*; DER. certificación *f*.

ac·me (ăk'mē) s. cumbre *f*, cima.

ac·ne (ăk'nē) s. acné *m*.

ac·o·lyte (ăk'ə-līt') s. RELIG. acólito, monaguillo; FIG. *(follower)* seguidor *m*.

a·corn (ā'kôrn', ā'kərn) s. BOT. bellota.

a·cous·tic (ə-kōō'stĭk) o **a·cous·ti·cal** (-stĭ-kəl) adj. acústico.

acoustic nerve s. ANAT. nervio auditivo.

a·cous·tics (ə-kōō'stĭks) s. FÍS. [ú. con v. sing.] acústica (ciencia); [ú. con v. pl.] acústica (calidad sonora).

ac·quaint (ə-kwānt') tr. familiarizar, poner al corriente ♦ **to a. with** poner al corriente de • **to be** o **become acquainted** conocerse (uno al otro) • **to be acquainted with** conocer, estar al corriente de.

ac·quain·tance (ə-kwān'təns) s. *(knowledge)* conocimiento <*I have some a. with Spanish* tengo algo de conocimiento de español>; *(person)* conocido.

ac·quain·tance·ship (ə-kwān'təns-shĭp') s. relaciones *f*, trato.

ac·quaint·ed (ə-kwān'tĭd) adj. *(known)* conocido; *(informed)* enterado.

ac·qui·esce (ăk'wē-ĕs') intr. **-esced, -esc·ing** consentir, asentir.

ac·qui·es·cence (ăk'wē-ĕs'əns) s. aquiescencia, aprobación *f*.

ac·qui·es·cent (ăk'wē-ĕs'ənt) adj. condescendiente, conforme.

ac·quire (ə-kwīr') tr. **-quired, -quir·ing** adquirir, obtener.

acquired immune deficiency syndrome s. MED. síndrome de inmunodeficiencia adquirida *m*, SIDA.

ac·qui·si·tion (ăk'wĭ-zĭsh'ən) s. adquisición *f*, obtención *f*.

ac·quis·i·tive (ə-kwĭz'ĭ-tĭv) adj. codicioso, ávido.

ac·quis·i·tive·ness (ə-kwĭz'ĭ-tĭv-nĭs) s. codicia, avidez *f*.

ac·quit (ə-kwĭt') tr. **-quit·ted, -quit·ting** *(to absolve)* absolver, exculpar; *(to clear)* exonerar, relevar; *(to repay)* pagar ♦ **to a. oneself** portarse, conducirse.

ac·quit·tal (ə-kwĭt'l) s. absolución *f*, descargo.

ac·quit·tance (ə-kwĭt'ns) s. comprobante de pago *m*, recibo.

a·cre (ā'kər) s. acre *m*.

a·cre·age (ā'kər-ĭj) s. superficie en acres *f*.

ac·rid (ăk'rĭd) adj. acre, cáustico.

ac·rid·ness (ăk'rĭd-nĭs) s. *(harshness)* acritud *f*, acrimonia; FIG. *(mordancy)* mordacidad *f*, causticidad *f*.

ac·ri·mo·ni·ous (ăk'rə-mō'nē-əs) adj. acrimonioso, cáustico.

ac·ri·mo·ny (ăk'rə-mō'nē) s. acrimonia, mordacidad *f*.

ac·ro·bat (ăk'rə-băt') s. acróbata *mf*.

ac·ro·bat·ic (ăk'rə-băt'ĭk) adj. acrobático.

ac·ro·bat·ics (ăk'rə-băt'ĭks) s. acrobacia.

ac·ro·nym (ăk'rə-nĭm') s. siglas *f.*

ac·ro·pho·bi·a (ăk'rə-fō'bē-ə) s. acrofobia, vértigo de las alturas.

a·crop·o·lis (ə-krŏp'ə-lĭs) s. acrópolis *f*, ciudadela.

a·cross (ə-krôs') I. prep. *(through)* por, a través de *<a. the plains* a través de las praderas>; *(on the other side of)* al otro lado de, en el otro lado de *<a hill a. the valley* una colina en el otro lado del valle>; *(from one side to the other)* a(l) través, por, de un lado a otro *<the man walked a. the street* el hombre cruzó de un lado a otro de la calle> II. adv. *(on the other side)* a través, del otro lado *<at this speed we shall soon be a.* a esta velocidad pronto estaremos del otro lado>; *(from one side to the other)* de una parte a otra, de ancho *<the pool is twenty feet a.* la piscina tiene veinte pies de ancho>; *(crosswise)* transversalmente, en cruz ♦ **to come** *o* **run a.** encontrarse con • **to go a.** atravesar, cruzar.

▲ En los casos en que la preposición *across* sigue a un verbo, ésta no se traduce literalmente ya que el verbo la incluye implícitamente *<the man walked across the street* el hombre cruzó la calle>; "de lado a lado" está sobreentendido.

a·cross-the-board (ə-krôs'thə-bôrd') adj. general, para todos.

a·cros·tic (ə-krô'stĭk) s. POÉT. acróstico.

a·cryl·ic (ə-krĭl'ĭk) I. adj. QUÍM. acrílico II. s. *(paint)* pintura acrílica; *(fiber)* fibra acrílica.

act (ăkt) I. tr. *(to perform)* representar, hacer el papel de; *(to pose as)* hacer el papel de ♦ **to a. as** actuar como, actuar en lugar de • **to a. as if** hacer como que • **to a. on** guiarse por • **to a. like** portarse como • **to act on** *o* **upon** influir en, obrar sobre —intr. *(to do something)* actuar, hacer algo; *(to perform in a role)* hacer un papel, actuar ♦ **to a. up** portarse mal II. s. *(action)* acto, hecho; *(deed)* acción *f*; *(performance)* número *<a juggling a.* un número de malabarismo>; *(division of play)* acto; *(pretense)* simulación *f*, fingimiento; *(a law)* ley *f*, decreto ♦ **Acts of the Apostles** BÍBL. Hechos de los Apóstoles • **to catch in the a.** coger con las manos en la masa • **to get into the a.** FAM. introducirse en el asunto • **to put on an a.** simular, fingir.

act·ing (ăk'tĭng) I. adj. interino, suplente *<the a. director* el director interino> II. s. TEAT. actuación *f.*

ac·tin·i·um (ăk-tĭn'ē-əm) QUÍM. actinio.

ac·tion (ăk'shən) s. *(acting)* acción *f*, hecho; *(motion)* operación *f*, movimiento; *(activity)* actividad *f*, acción *<firemen sprang into a.* los bomberos se pusieron inmediatamente en acción>; TEAT. argumento, trama; *(effect)* influencia, efecto *<the corrosive a. of acid on metal* el efecto corrosivo del ácido sobre el metal>; MEC. mecanismo, funcionamiento; MIL. batalla, acción de guerra *f* ♦ **actions** conducta • **to bring an a. against** DER. entablar juicio contra • **to put out of a.** destrozar, inutilizar • **to take a.** tomar medidas.

ac·ti·vate (ăk'tə-vāt') tr. **-vat·ed, -vat·ing** *(to make active)* activar, agitar; QUÍM. acelerar (una reacción); FÍS. hacer radioactiva (una substancia).

ac·ti·va·tion (ăk'tə-vā'shən) s. FÍS., QUÍM. activación *f.*

ac·tive (ăk'tĭv) adj. *(in action)* activo, en movimiento; *(energetic)* enérgico, vigoroso ♦ **a. duty** *o* **service** MIL. servicio activo • **a. voice** GRAM. voz activa • **to play an a. part in** colaborar activamente en • **to take an a. interest in** interesarse vivamente por.

ac·tiv·ism (ăk'tə-vĭz'əm) s. POL. activismo.

ac·tiv·ist (ăk'tə-vĭst) adj. & s. activista *mf*, militante *mf.*

ac·tiv·i·ty (ăk-tĭv'ĭ-tē) s. [pl. **-ties**] *(state)* actividad *f*; *(occupation)* ocupación *f.*

act of God s. DER. obra de Dios, hecho imprevisible *o* inevitable.

ac·tor (ăk'tər) s. TEAT. actor *m.*

ac·tress (ăk'trĭs) s. TEAT. actriz *f.*

ac·tu·al (ăk'chōō-əl) adj. *(real)* real, verdadero *<it was not a dream but an a. occurrence* no fue un sueño sino un hecho verdadero>; *(current)* actual, presente *<inflation is one of the worst a. conditions* la inflación es una de las peores condiciones actuales>.

ac·tu·al·i·ty (ăk'chōō-ăl'ĭ-tē) s. [pl. **-ties**] realidad *f.*

ac·tu·al·i·za·tion (ăk'chōō-ə-lĭ-zā'shən) s. realización *f.*

ac·tu·al·ize (ăk'chōō-ə-līz') tr. **-ized, -iz·ing** *(to realize)* realizar; *(to describe)* describir vívidamente.

ac·tu·al·ly (ăk'chōō-ə-lē) adv. *(really)* en realidad, realmente.

ac·tu·ar·y (ăk'chōō-ĕr'ē) s. [pl. **-ies**] FIN. actuario de seguros.

ac·tu·ate (ăk'chōō-āt') tr. **-at·ed, -at·ing** *(to motivate)* activar, impulsar; *(to put into motion)* poner en movimiento, hacer funcionar.

a·cu·i·ty (ə-kyōō'ĭ-tē) s. [pl. **-ties**] acuidad *f*, agudeza (de los sentidos).

a·cu·men (ə-kyōō'mən) s. perspicacia, ingenio.

ac·u·punc·ture (ăk'yə-pŭngk'chər) s. MED. acupuntura.

a·cute (ə-kyōōt') adj. *(sharp)* agudo; *(sensitive)* sagaz, perspicaz ♦ **a. accent** GRAM. acento agudo • **a. angle** GEOM. ángulo agudo.

a·cute·ly (ə-kyōōt'lē) adv. agudamente.

a·cute·ness (ə-kyōōt'nĭs) s. *(sharpness)* agudeza; *(perspicacity)* perspicacia; MED. carácter agudo (de una enfermedad).

ad (ăd) s. FAM. anuncio, publicidad *f.*

ad·age (ăd'ĭj) s. adagio, proverbio.

Ad·am (ăd'əm) s. BÍBL. Adán.

ad·a·mant (ăd'ə-mənt) I. s. mineral impenetrable *m* II. adj. inexorable, inflexible.

ad·a·man·tine (ăd'ə-măn'tēn', -tīn') adj. MIN. diamantino; FIG. *(unyielding)* inflexible.

ad·a·mant·ly (ăd'ə-mənt-lē) adv. firmemente, inflexiblemente.

Ad·am's apple (ăd'əmz) s. ANAT. nuez de la garganta *f.*

a·dapt (ə-dăpt') tr. & intr. adaptar(se), acomodar(se).

a·dapt·a·bil·i·ty (ə-dăp'tə-bĭl'ĭ-tē) s. adaptabilidad *f*, flexibilidad *f.*

a·dapt·a·ble (ə-dăp'tə-bəl) adj. adaptable, acomodable.

ad·ap·ta·tion (ăd'ăp-tā'shən) s. *(act)* adaptación *f*; CINEM., TEAT., TELEV. adaptación, versión *f.*

a·dapt·er *o* **a·dap·tor** (ə-dăp'tər) s. *(person)* adaptador *m*; ELEC. adaptador, enchufe múltiple *m.*

a·dap·tive (ə-dăp'tĭv) adj. capaz de adaptación.

add (ăd) tr. *(to join)* añadir, agregar; *(to find the sum of)* sumar ♦ **to a. insult to injury** añadir ofensa al daño • **to a. up** sumar • **to a. up to** *(to amount to)* subir a, ascender a; FIG. *(to mean)* venir a ser, equivaler a —intr. *(to be an addition)* aumentar, acrecentar *<this adds to my pleasure* esto acrecienta mi placer>; *(to find a sum)* sumar ♦ **to a. up** FAM. tener sentido.

ad·dend (ăd'ĕnd', ə-dĕnd') s. MAT. sumando.

ad·den·dum (ə-dĕn'dəm) s. [pl. **-da** (-də)] addenda *m*, apéndice *m.*

add·er¹ (ăd'ər) s. ELECTRÓN. sumador *m.*

ad·der² (ăd'ər) s. víbora, culebra.

ad·dict I. tr. (ə-dĭkt') dedicar(se), entregar(se) ♦ **addicted to** dedicado a, entregado a II. s. (ăd'ĭkt) *(drug user)* adicto a las drogas); *(fanatic)* fanático.

ad·dic·tion (ə-dĭk'shən) s. *(vice)* vicio; *(liking)* afición *f.*

ad·dic·tive (ə-dĭk'tĭv) adj. que forma hábito.

adding machine s. sumadora.

ad·di·tion (ə-dĭsh'ən) s. *(adding)* adición *f*; MAT. suma ♦ **in a.** además, también.

ad·di·tion·al (ə-dĭsh'ə-nəl) adj. adicional, suplementario.

ad·di·tion·al·ly (ə-dĭsh'ə-nə-lē) adv. adicionalmente, además.

ad·di·tive (ăd'ĭ-tĭv) adj. & s. aditivo.

ad·dle (ăd'l) tr. **-dled, -dling** enturbiar, confundir —intr. *(to become rotten)* pudrirse; *(to become confused)* confundirse.

ad·dress I. s. (ə-drĕs', ăd'rĕs) *(on an envelope)* dirección *f*, señas; *(formal speech)* discurso, alocución *f*; *(behavior)* modales *m*, conducta ♦ **a. book** libreta de direcciones • **addresses** galanteras, atenciones • **home a.** (dirección de) domicilio II. tr. (ə-drĕs') *(to speak to)* dirigirse a, dirigir la palabra a; *(to give a speech to)* dar un discurso *o* alocución a; *(an envelope, letter)* dirigir (una carta), poner las señas a; *(to consign)* consignar ♦ **to a. oneself to** emprender (una tarea), aplicarse a • **to a. someone as** dar a alguien el tratamiento de.

ad·dress·ee (ăd'rĕ-sē', ə-drĕs'ē') s. destinatario.

ad·duce (ə-dōōs', ə-dyōōs') tr. **-duced, -duc·ing** aducir, alegar.

ad·duc·tor (ə-dŭk'tər) s. ANAT. aductor (músculo) *m.*

ad·e·noi·dal (ăd'n-oid'l) adj. *(glandular)* adenoideo; *(nasal)* gangoso.

ad·e·noids (ăd'n-oidz') s.pl. MED. vegetaciones adenoideas *f.*

a·dept I. adj. (ə-dĕpt') perito II. s. (ăd'ĕpt') experto.

a·dept·ness (ə-dĕpt'nĭs) s. pericia, habilidad *f.*

ad·e·qua·cy (ăd'ĭ-kwə-sē) s. suficiencia.

ad·e·quate (ăd'ĭ-kwĭt) adj. *(appropriate)* adecuado; *(sufficient)* suficiente.

ad·here (ăd-hîr') intr. **-hered, -her·ing** *(to stick together)* pegarse; *(to be loyal to)* adherirse; *(to follow closely)* ceñirse.

ad·her·ence (ăd-hîr'əns) s. *(condition)* adherencia, pegajosidad *f; (devotion)* adhesión *f.*

ad·her·ent (ăd-hîr'ənt) I. adj. *(sticky)* adhesivo, pegajoso; BOT. adherente II. s. adherente *mf*, partidario.

ad·he·sion (ăd-hē'zhən) s. *(attachment)* adhesión *f;* MED. adherencia.

ad·he·sive (ăd-hē'sĭv) I. adj. adhesivo, pegajoso II. s. adhesivo.

ad·he·sive·ness (ăd-hē'sĭv-nĭs) s. adherencia.

adhesive tape s. cinta adhesiva.

ad·i·pose (ăd'ə-pōs') I. adj. adiposo, grasiento II. s. tejido adiposo.

ad·ja·cen·cy (ə-jā'sən-sē) s. adyacencia, contigüidad *f.*

ad·ja·cent (ə-jā'sənt) adj. adyacente, contiguo.

ad·jec·ti·val (ăj'ĭk-tī'vəl) adj. adjetival, del adjetivo.

ad·jec·tive (ăj'ĭk-tĭv) s. GRAM. adjetivo.

ad·join (ə-join') tr. *(to be next to)* estar contiguo a, lindar con; *(to attach to)* juntar, unir —intr. colindar, estar contiguo.

ad·join·ing (ə-joi'nĭng) adj. contiguo, colindante.

ad·journ (ə-jûrn') tr. suspender, levantar (una sesión) —intr. *(to suspend)* aplazar (una sesión); *(to move)* cambiarse <they adjourned to the next room se cambiaron al cuarto vecino>.

ad·journ·ment (ə-jûrn'mənt) s. *(closing)* suspensión *f*, clausura; *(transfer)* traslación *f.*

ad·judge (ə-jŭj') tr. **-judged, -judg·ing** DER. *(to decide)* juzgar, fallar; *(to award)* adjudicar; *(to consider)* considerar (un caso).

ad·ju·di·cate (ə-jōō'dĭ-kāt') tr. **-cat·ed, -cat·ing** DER. juzgar, fallar.

ad·ju·di·ca·tion (ə-jōō'dĭ-kā'shən) s. DER. sentencia, fallo.

ad·ju·di·ca·tor (ə-jōō'dĭ-kā'tər) s. DER. juez *m,* árbitro.

ad·junct (ăj'ŭngkt') I. s. *(person)* adjunto, ayudante *mf; (thing)* adjunto, añadidura; GRAM. adjunto II. adj. *(said of a person)* adjunto; *(auxiliary)* auxiliar, subordinado.

ad·ju·ra·tion (ăj'ə-rā'shən) s. solicitud solemne *f.*

ad·jure (ə-jōōr') tr. **-jured, -jur·ing** *(to command)* ordenar *o* mandar bajo juramento solemne; *(to appeal to)* suplicar, conjurar.

ad·just (ə-jŭst') tr. *(to fit)* ajustar; *(to fix)* arreglar; *(to regulate)* regular; *(to adapt)* adaptar; *(to correct)* corregir; COM. liquidar, ajustar (reclamo) ♦ **to a. oneself to** ajustarse a —intr. ajustarse.

ad·just·a·ble (ə-jŭs'tə-bəl) adj. ajustable.

ad·just·ed (ə-jŭs'tĭd) adj. *(fitted)* ajustado; *(fixed)* arreglado; *(regulated)* regulado; *(adapted)* adaptado; *(corrected)* corregido.

ad·just·er *o* **ad·jus·tor** (ə-jŭs'tər) s. MEC. regulador *m;* COM. ajustador, liquidador de reclamos) *m.*

ad·just·ment (ə-jŭst'mənt) s. *(fitting)* ajuste *m; (fixing)* arreglo; *(correction)* corrección *f;* COM. ajuste, liquidación (de una cuenta) *f.*

ad·ju·tant (ăj'ə-tnt) s. MIL. ayudante *m,* asistente *m; (assistant)* asistente *mf;* ZOOL. *(stork)* marabú *m.*

ad lib (ăd lĭb') adv. de manera improvisada.

ad·lib (ăd-lĭb') I. tr. & intr. **-libbed, -lib·bing** improvisar II. s. FAM. improvisación *f* III. adj. improvisado.

ad·min·is·ter (ăd-mĭn'ĭ-stər) tr. *(to manage)* administrar, manejar; *(to dispense)* administrar, dar (últimos ritos, medicina); *(to allot)* suministrar, proveer ♦ **to a. an oath to** tomar juramento a • **to a. to** ayudar, cuidar (de una persona) —intr. administrar, actuar como administrador.

ad·min·is·trate (ăd-mĭn'ĭ-strāt') tr. **-trat·ed, -trat·ing** *(to manage)* administrar; *(as a remedy)* suministrar.

ad·min·is·tra·tion (ăd-mĭn'ĭ-strā'shən) s. *(management)* administración *f*, manejo; *(of a government)* dirección *f*, gobierno; *(of medicine, rites)* administración ♦ **the A.** el gobierno (en EE. UU.).

ad·min·is·tra·tive (ăd-mĭn'ĭ-strā'tĭv, -strə-tĭv) adj. administrativo.

ad·min·is·tra·tor (ăd-mĭn'ĭ-strā'tər) s. *(executive)* administrador *m,* ejecutivo; *(director)* director.

ad·mi·ra·ble (ăd'mər-ə-bəl) adj. admirable.

ad·mi·ral (ăd'mər-əl) s. *(rank, officer)* almirante *m; (ship)* buque almirante *m;* ENTOM. ninfa.

ad·mi·ral·ty (ăd'mər-əl-tē) s. [pl. **-ties**] almirantazgo.

ad·mi·ra·tion (ăd'mə-rā'shən) s. *(wonder)* admiración *f; (object)* maravilla.

ad·mire (ăd-mīr') tr. **-mired, -mir·ing** *(with wonder)* admirar; *(with praise)* elogiar.

ad·mir·er (ăd-mīr'ər) s. *(one who admires)* admirador *m, (suitor)* enamorado, pretendiente *m; (enthusiast)* amante *mf,* aficionado (al arte, música).

ad·mir·ing·ly (ăd-mīr'ĭng-lē) adv. con admiración.

ad·mis·si·bil·i·ty (ăd-mĭs'ə-bĭl'ĭ-tē) s. admisibilidad *f.*

ad·mis·si·ble (ăd-mĭs'ə-bəl) adj. admisible, aceptable.

ad·mis·sion (ăd-mĭsh'ən) s. *(act)* admisión *f; (fee)* entrada; *(access)* ingreso (al foro, universidad); *(acknowledgment)* admisión, concesión *f* ♦ **a. fee** cuota de inscripción, matrícula.

ad·mit (ăd-mĭt') tr. **-mit·ted, -mit·ting** *(to let in)* admitir, dar entrada a <this ticket admits two people este boleto le da entrada a dos personas>; *(to accept)* recibir, dar entrada; *(to acknowledge)* confesar, reconocer; *(to concede)* conceder, aceptar —intr. *(to allow)* permitir, dejar lugar <that problem admits of no solution ese problema no deja lugar a ninguna solución>; *(to afford access)* dar entrada (a un lugar).

ad·mit·tance (ăd-mĭt'ns) s. *(admission)* admisión *f; (permission to enter)* acceso, (derecho de) entrada.

ad·mit·ted·ly (ăd-mĭt'ĭd-lē) adv. reconocidamente, concedido que.

ad·mix (ăd-mĭks') tr. & intr. mezclar(se), agregar(se).

ad·mix·ture (ăd-mĭks'chər) s. *(act)* mixtura, mezcla; *(addition)* aditivo, agregado.

ad·mon·ish (ăd-mŏn'ĭsh) tr. *(to reprove)* amonestar, reprender; *(to caution)* advertir, prevenir; *(to warn)* poner sobre aviso; *(to exhort)* exhortar.

ad·mo·ni·tion (ăd'mə-nĭsh'ən) s. *(reproof)* admonición *f,* amonestación *f; (warning)* advertencia; *(advice)* consejo.

ad·mon·i·to·ry (ăd-mŏn'ĭ-tôr'ē) adj. *(showing reproof)* de admonestación, de represión; *(showing counsel)* de advertencia, de consejo.

a·do (ə-dōō') s. *(fuss)* bulla, alboroto; *(trouble)* lío, dificultad *f.*

a·do·be (ə-dō'bē) CONSTR. I. s. *(brick)* adobe *m,* ladrillo sin cocer; *(clay)* arcilla adobina; *(house)* casa de adobe II. adj. de adobe.

ad·o·les·cence (ăd'l-ĕs'əns) s. adolescencia.

ad·o·les·cent (ăd'l-ĕs'ənt) s. & adj. adolescente *mf.*

A·don·is (ə-dŏn'ĭs, ə-dō'nĭs) s. MITOL. Adonis ♦ **a.** joven hermoso.

a·dopt (ə-dŏpt') tr. *(as one's own)* adoptar <to a. a child adoptar a un niño>; *(to take up)* tomar, aceptar; *(to take on)* adoptar, asumir <to a. an air of importance asumir un aire de importancia>.

a·dopt·a·ble (ə-dŏp'tə-bəl) adj. adoptable.

a·dopt·ed (ə-dŏp'tĭd) adj. *(a child)* adoptivo; *(assumed)* adoptado.

a·dop·tion (ə-dŏp'shən) s. adopción *f.*

ā rey / ä año / b boca / ch chico / d dar / ĕ el / ē mil / g gato / h joya / hw juez / ī aire / k casa / kw cuan /

a·dop·tive (ə-dŏp'tĭv) adj. adoptivo <*a. parents* padres adoptivos>.

a·dor·a·ble (ə-dôr'ə-bəl) adj. *(lovable)* adorable; *(charming)* encantador.

ad·o·ra·tion (ăd'ə-rā'shən) s. adoración *f.*

a·dore (ə-dôr') tr. **a·dored, a·dor·ing** adorar.

a·dorn (ə-dôrn') tr. adornar, decorar.

a·dorn·ment (ə-dôrn'mənt) s. adorno, decoración *f.*

ad·re·nal (ə-drē'nəl) ANAT. **I.** adj. adrenal, suprarrenal **II.** s. glándula suprarrenal.

a·dren·a·line (ə-drĕn'ə-lĭn) s. BIOQUÍM. adrenalina.

A·dri·at·ic Sea (ā'drē-ăt'ĭk) s. Mar Adriático.

a·drift (ə-drĭft') adv. & adj. a la deriva, sin dirección.

a·droit (ə-droit') adj. diestro, hábil.

a·droit·ness (ə-droit'nĭs) s. destreza, habilidad *f.*

ad·sorb (ăd-sôrb') tr. adsorber.

ad·sor·bent (ăd-sôr'bənt) adj. & s. adsorbente *m.*

ad·sorp·tion (ăd-sôrp'shən) s. adsorción *f.*

ad·u·late (ăj'ə-lāt') tr. **-lat·ed, -lat·ing** adular, lisonjear.

ad·u·la·tion (ăj'ə-lā'shən) s. adulación *f,* lisonja.

a·dult (ə-dŭlt', ăd'ŭlt') **I.** s. adulto, persona mayor **II.** adj. adulto, mayor.

a·dul·ter·ant (ə-dŭl'tər-ənt) **I.** adj. adulterante, adulterador **II.** s. substancia adulterante.

a·dul·ter·ate (ə-dŭl'tə-rāt') tr. **-at·ed, -at·ing** adulterar.

a·dul·ter·a·tion (ə-dŭl'tə-rā'shən) s. adulteración *f.*

a·dul·ter·er (ə-dŭl'tər-ər) s. adúltero.

a·dul·ter·ess (ə-dŭl'tər-ĭs) s. adúltera.

a·dul·ter·ous (ə-dŭl'tər-əs) adj. adúltero.

a·dul·ter·y (ə-dŭl'tə-rē) s. [pl. **-ies**] adulterio.

a·dult·hood (ə-dŭlt'hŏŏd) s. edad adulta.

ad·um·brate (ăd'əm-brāt', ə-dŭm'-) tr. **-brat·ed, -brat·ing** *(to outline)* bosquejar, esbozar; *(to foreshadow)* presagiar.

ad va·lo·rem (ăd' və-lôr'əm) adj. COM. ad valorem, con arreglo al valor.

ad·vance (ăd-văns') **I.** tr. **-vanced, -vanc·ing** *(to move forward)* avanzar, adelantar <*to a. the troops* avanzar las tropas>; *(to propose)* proponer, presentar <*to a. a plan* presentar un plan>; *(to further)* fomentar, promover; *(to promote)* promover a, ascender a; *(to hasten)* adelantar <*to a. the completion date* adelantar la fecha de terminación>; *(to increase)* aumentar; *(to lend)* adelantar, anticipar ♦ **to a. on someone** acercarse a alguien de modo amenazador —intr. *(to move forward)* avanzar <*the troops advanced toward the city* las tropas avanzaron hacia la ciudad>; *(to improve)* hacer progresos; *(to rise)* elevarse, subir (valor, posición) **II.** s. *(forward movement)* avance *m,* adelanto; *(progress)* progreso; *(increase)* alza, aumento (de valor, precio); *(loan)* anticipo, préstamo ♦ **advances** propuesta amorosa **III.** adj. adelantado, anticipado ♦ **a. guard** MIL. avanzada, vanguardia • **a. payment** adelanto, anticipo • **in a.** por anticipado, de antemano <*make arrangements in a.* hagan planes por anticipado>.

ad·vanced (ăd-vănst') adj. *(higher level)* avanzado, superior; *(ahead)* adelantado; *(far along)* avanzado <*an a. stage of illness* un estado avanzado de enfermedad>; *(progressive)* progresista <*a. ideas* ideas progresistas>; *(very old)* avanzado, maduro (en años).

ad·vance·ment (ăd-văns'mənt) s. *(act)* avance *m;* *(improvement)* adelanto; *(development)* progreso <*the a. of science* el progreso de la ciencia>; *(promotion)* ascenso.

ad·vanc·er (ăd-văn'sər) s. promotor *m,* impulsor *m.*

ad·van·tage (ăd-văn'tĭj) **I.** s. *(factor)* ventaja <*having a car is always an a.* tener un automóvil es siempre una ventaja>; *(gain)* provecho, partido; *(superiority)* ventaja <*they had an a. over us* ellos tenían una ventaja sobre nosotros> ♦ **to one's a.** para ventaja *o* provecho propio • **to take a. of** *(to make use of)* aprovechar, valerse de; *(to exploit)* abusarse de, engañar **II.** tr. **-taged, -tag·ing** favorecer, beneficiar.

ad·van·ta·geous (ăd'văn-tā'jəs) adj. ventajoso, provechoso.

ad·vent (ăd'vĕnt') s. advenimiento, llegada ♦ **A.** RELIG. adviento, advenimiento (de Cristo).

Ad·vent·ism (ăd'vĕn'tĭz'əm) s. RELIG. adventismo.

Ad·vent·ist (ăd'vĕn'tĭst) s. RELIG. adventista *mf.*

ad·ven·ti·tious (ăd'vĕn-tĭsh'əs) adj. *(by chance)* adventicio, accidental; BIOL., BOT. adventicio.

ad·ven·ture (ăd-vĕn'chər) **I.** s. *(enterprise)* aventura; *(experience)* peripecia, suceso; *(business venture)* aventura, riesgo ♦ **an a. story** historia de aventuras **II.** tr. & intr. **-tured, -tur·ing** aventurar(se), arriesgar(se).

ad·ven·tur·er (ăd-vĕn'chər-ər) s. aventurero.

ad·ven·tur·ous (ăd-vĕn'chər-əs) adj. *(audacious)* audaz, emprendedor; *(reckless)* temerario, arrojado; *(risky)* arriesgado.

ad·verb (ăd'vûrb') s. GRAM. adverbio.

ad·ver·bi·al (ăd-vûr'bē-əl) adj. GRAM. adverbial.

ad·ver·sar·y (ăd'vər-sĕr'ē) s. [pl. **-ies**] adversario, enemigo.

ad·verse (ăd-vûrs', ăd'vûrs') adj. *(antagonistic)* adverso, desfavorable <*a. criticism* crítica desfavorable>; *(opposing)* opuesto, contrario.

ad·verse·ly (ăd-vûrs'lē) adv. adversamente, desfavorablemente.

ad·ver·si·ty (ăd-vûr'sĭ-tē) s. [pl. **-ties**] adversidad *f,* infortunio.

ad·vert[1] (ăd-vûrt') intr. referirse, aludir <*the chairman adverted to the problem* el presidente aludió al problema>.

ad·vert[2] (ăd'vûrt) s. G.B., FAM. anuncio, publicidad *f.*

ad·ver·tise (ăd'vər-tīz') tr. **-tised, -tis·ing** COM. anunciar; *(to make known)* divulgar ♦ **to a. for** buscar por medio de avisos —intr. COM. poner un anuncio, hacer publicidad.

ad·ver·tise·ment (ăd'vər-tīz'mənt, ăd-vûr'tĭs-) s. anuncio, publicidad *f.*

ad·ver·tis·er (ăd'vər-tī'zər) s. anunciante *mf,* anunciador *m.*

ad·ver·tis·ing (ăd'vər-tī'zĭng) s. publicidad *f,* propaganda *f.*

ad·vice (ăd-vīs') s. *(counsel)* consejo; *(opinion)* opinión *f* ♦ **advices** noticias • **a piece of a.** un consejo • **to take a.** seguir el consejo.

ad·vis·a·bil·i·ty (ăd-vī'zə-bĭl'ĭ-tē) s. conveniencia.

ad·vis·a·ble (ăd-vī'zə-bəl) adj. aconsejable, prudente.

ad·vise (ăd-vīz') tr. **-vised, -vis·ing** *(to counsel)* dar consejo a, aconsejar <*the doctor advised me to rest* el médico me aconsejó reposo>; *(to suggest)* recomendar, sugerir <*I a. you to take the bus* te sugiero que tomes el autobús>; *(to notify)* informar, notificar <*to a. someone of a decision* notificar a alguien una decisión> ♦ **to a. on** ser asesor en • **to a. with** consultar —intr. dar consejo, orientar.

ad·vised (ăd-vīzd') adj. aconsejado ♦ **to keep a.** mantener al corriente.

ad·vis·ed·ly (ăd-vī'zĭd-lē) adj. *(prudently)* prudentemente, en forma bien pensada; *(deliberately)* deliberadamente, adrede.

ad·vise·ment (ăd-vīz'mənt) s. deliberación *f,* consideración *f* ♦ **to take under a.** someter a consideración.

ad·vis·er *o* **ad·vi·sor** (ăd-vī'zər) s. *(one who advises)* consejero, asesor *m;* *(tutor)* tutor *m* ♦ **legal a.** asesor legal.

ad·vi·so·ry (ăd-vī'zə-rē) **I.** adj. consultivo, asesor <*an a. committee* un comité asesor> **II.** s. [pl. **-ries**] recomendación *f,* aviso de precaución *f* <*a traveler's a.* aviso de precaución para viajeros>.

ad·vo·ca·cy (ăd'və-kə-sē) s. [pl. **-cies**] apoyo, promoción (de una causa o idea) *f.*

ad·vo·cate (ăd'və-kāt') **I.** tr. **-cat·ed, -cat·ing** abogar por, apoyar (causa, idea) **II.** s. (-kĭt, -kāt') *(supporter)* defensor *m,* partidario; G.B. *(lawyer)* abogado.

adz *o* **adze** (ădz) s. azuela.

Ae·ge·an Sea (ĭ-jē'ən) s. Mar Egeo.

ae·gis (ē'jĭs) s. MITOL. égida; FIG. *(sponsorship)* patrocinio, tutela ♦ **under the a. of** bajo el patrocinio de.

Ae·o·li·an (ē-ō'lē-ən) adj. & s. HIST. eolio, eólico.

aer·ate (âr'āt') tr. **-at·ed, -at·ing** QUÍM. gasear (un líquido); MED. oxigenar (la sangre); *(to air)* ventilar, airear.

aer·a·tion (â-rā'shən) s. *(act)* aireación *f,* ventilación *f;* *(for carbonated drinks)* gasificación *f;* MED. oxigenación *f.*

aer·a·tor (âr'ā'tər) s. aparato para la aeración.

aer·i·al (âr'ē-əl) **I.** adj. *(of the air)* aéreo, de aire; *(lofty)* etéreo, vaporoso **II.** s. antena.

aer·i·al·ist (âr'ē-ə-lĭst) s. volatinero, equilibrista (de la cuerda floja, trapecio) *mf.*

aerial ladder s. escalera plegable *o* extensible (usada por los bomberos).

aer·ie (âr′ē, îr′ē) s. [pl. **-ies**] ORNIT. *(nest)* aguilera, nido de ave de rapiña; FIG. *(house)* casa construida en una altura.
aer·o·bat·ics (âr′ə-băt′ĭks) s. [ú. con v. sing. o pl.] acrobacia aérea.
aer·o·bic (â-rō′bĭk) adj. BIOL. aeróbico.
aer·o·bics (â-rō′bĭks) s. [ú. con v. sing. o pl.] entrenamiento físico riguroso que combina elementos de calistenia con movimientos de danza.
aer·o·drome (âr′ə-drōm′) s. G.B. var. de **airdrome**.
aer·o·dy·nam·ic (âr′ō-dī-năm′ĭk) adj. aerodinámico.
aer·o·dy·nam·ics (âr′ō-dī-năm′ĭks) s. [ú. con v. sing.] aerodinámica.
aer·o·naut (âr′ə-nôt′) s. AVIA. aeronauta *mf.*
aer·o·nau·tic (âr′ə-nô′tĭk) o **aer·o·nau·ti·cal** (-tĭ-kəl) adj. aeronáutico.
aer·o·nau·tics (âr′ə-nô′tĭks) s. [ú. con v. sing.] aeronáutica.
aer·o·plane (âr′ə-plān′) s. G.B. var. de **airplane**.
aer·o·sol (âr′ə-sôl′) s. aerosol *m.*
aerosol bomb s. bomba de aerosol, vaporizador *m.*
aer·o·space (âr′ō-spās′) I. s. región que incluye la atmósfera y el espacio exterior II. adj. aeroespacial <*a. vehicle* vehículo aeroespacial>.
aer·o·stat (âr′ō-stăt′) s. aeróstato, globo aerostático.
aer·y (âr′ē, îr′ē) s. var. de **aerie**.
aes·thete (ĕs′thēt′) s. esteta *mf.*
aes·thet·ic (ĕs-thĕt′ĭk) adj. estético.
aes·thet·ics (ĕs-thĕt′ĭks) s. [ú. con v. sing.] estética.
a·far (ə-fär′) adv. lejos, distante ♦ **from a.** de lejos.
af·fa·bil·i·ty (ăf′ə-bĭl′ĭ-tē) s. afabilidad *f.*, amabilidad *f.*
af·fa·ble (ăf′ə-bəl) adj. afable, amable.
af·fair (ə-fâr′) s. *(business)* asunto, actividad *f.*; *(event)* incidente *m*, episodio; *(liaison)* amorío; *(gathering)* acontecimiento social ♦ **affairs** asuntos personales • **business affairs** asuntos de negocios • **world affairs** situación mundial.
af·fect¹ I. tr. (ə-fĕkt′) *(to have an influence on)* afectar, influir en <*climatic conditions a. people's way of living* las condiciones climatéricas influyen en el modo de vivir de la gente>; *(to move)* afectar, conmover <*the news of the latest flood affected me greatly* las noticias sobre la última inundación me afectaron mucho> II. s. (ăf′ĕkt′) PSIC. sentimiento, emoción *f.*
af·fect² (ə-fĕkt′) tr. *(to feign)* fingir, simular <*they affected ignorance of the new rules* simularon ignorar las nuevas reglas>; *(to prefer)* gustar de, preferir.
af·fec·ta·tion (ăf′ĕk-tā′shən) s. afectación *f.*, amaneramiento.
af·fect·ed¹ (ə-fĕk′tĭd) adj. *(acted upon)* afectado; *(moved)* conmovido, impresionado; *(infected)* infectado, aquejado.
af·fect·ed² (ə-fĕk′tĭd) adj. *(assumed)* afectado; *(mannered)* amanerado, lleno de afectación; *(inclined)* inclinado, dispuesto.
af·fect·ing (ə-fĕk′tĭng) adj. *(moving)* sensible, conmovedor; *(pathetic)* patético, lastimoso; *(false)* fingido.
af·fec·tion (ə-fĕk′shən) s. *(feeling)* afecto, cariño; *(condition)* afección *f.*; *(tendency)* inclinación *f.*, propensión *f.*
af·fec·tion·ate (ə-fĕk′shə-nĭt) adj. afectuoso, cariñoso.
af·fec·tive (ə-fĕk′tĭv) adj. afectivo, emotivo.
af·fi·ance (ə-fī′əns) tr. **-anced, -anc·ing** dar palabra de casamiento.
af·fi·ant (ə-fī′ənt) s. DER. deponente *mf*, declarante *mf.*
af·fi·da·vit (ăf′ĭ-dā′vĭt) s. DER. afidávit *m*, declaración jurada.
af·fil·i·ate (ə-fĭl′ē-āt′) I. tr. **-at·ed, -at·ing** afiliar, asociar ♦ **to a. oneself with** afiliarse a —intr. afiliarse, asociarse II. s. (-ĭt, -āt′) socio, asociado.
af·fil·i·a·tion (ə-fĭl′ē-ā′shən) s. afiliación *f.*
af·fin·i·ty (ə-fĭn′ĭ-tē) s. [pl. **-ties**] *(attraction)* afinidad *f.*; *(resemblance)* semejanza, analogía; *(relationship)* parentesco; BIOL., QUÍM. afinidad.
af·firm (ə-fûrm′) tr. *(to assert)* afirmar, aseverar; *(to confirm)* confirmar, ratificar —intr. DER. dar testimonio, testificar.
af·fir·ma·tion (ăf′ər-mā′shən) s. *(assertion)* afirmación *f*, aserción *f.*; DER. declaración *f.*
af·fir·ma·tive (ə-fûr′mə-tĭv) I. adj. afirmativo II. s. afirmativa.

affirmative action s. EE. UU. acción afirmativa (determinada a favorecer a ciertos grupos, esp. las minorías).
af·fix I. tr. (ə-fĭks′) *(to fasten)* sujetar; *(to attach)* pegar, adherir; *(to add)* poner <*t a. a signature to a document* poner la firma a un documento>; *(to append)* agregar, añadir <*to a. a postscript* añadir una posdata> II. s. (ăf′ĭks′) *(something added)* agregado, añadidura, añadido; GRAM. afijo.
af·flict (ə-flĭkt′) tr. afligir, acongojar ♦ **to be afflicted with** padecer de, sufrir de.
af·flic·tion (ə-flĭk′shən) s. *(grief)* aflicción *f*; *(suffering)* sufrimiento; *(misfortune)* desgracia.
af·flu·ence (ăf′lŏō-əns) s. *(riches)* riqueza; *(abundance)* abundancia; *(opulence)* opulencia; *(a flowing toward)* afluencia, corriente *f.*
af·flu·ent (ăf′lŏō-ənt) I. adj. *(rich)* rico; *(opulent)* opulento; *(abundant)* abundante; *(flowing freely)* afluente, corriente II. s. afluente (río) *m.*
af·ford (ə-fôrd′) tr. *(able to spend money)* tener con qué comprar, tener los recursos para <*can we a. a new car?* ¿tenemos con qué comprar un automóvil nuevo?>; *(to spare)* poder disponer de, tener la libertad de <*I can a. one hour for lunch* puedo disponer de una hora para el almuerzo>; *(to risk)* afrontar <*we cannot a. such risk* no podemos afrontar tal riesgo>; *(to provide)* proporcionar, dar <*reading this story will a. great pleasure* leer esta historia nos dará un enorme placer>; *(to furnish)* proveer de, suplir <*our garden affords a great supply of fresh vegetables* nuestro huerto nos provee de un gran surtido de vegetales frescos>.
af·ford·a·ble (ə-fôr′də-bəl) adj. *(within one's means)* que se puede comprar; *(that can be given)* que se puede dar.
af·fray (ə-frā′) s. refriega, riña.
af·fri·cate (ăf′rĭ-kĭt) s. FONÉT. africada (consonante).
af·front (ə-frŭnt′) I. tr. *(to insult)* afrentar, insultar; *(to confront)* confrontar, enfrentar II. s. afrenta, insulto.
Af·ghan (ăf′găn′) adj. & s. afgano ♦ **a.** manta o cubrecama tejido.
Af·ghan·i·stan (ăf-găn′ĭ-stăn′) s. Afganistán *m.*
a·field (ə-fēld′) adv. *(off the track)* fuera del camino, descarriado; *(away from home)* lejos de casa; *(to or on a field)* en o al campo ♦ **far a.** muy lejos.
a·fire (ə-fīr′) adj. & adv. *(on fire)* ardiendo, en llamas; FIG. *(involved)* intensamente interesado.
a·flame (ə-flām′) adj. & adv. en llamas, ardiendo; FIG. *(excited)* inflamado.
a·float (ə-flōt′) adj. & adv. *(floating)* a flote, flotando; *(at sea)* a bordo; *(flooded)* inundado (cubierta de un barco); FIG. *(free of difficulty)* a flote <*he could not keep the business a.* no pudo mantener el negocio a flote>; *(in circulation)* en circulación, corriente.
a·flut·ter (ə-flŭt′ər) adj. *(in a flutter)* revoloteando; *(nervous)* nervioso, agitado.
a·foot (ə-fŏōt′) adj. & adv. *(on foot)* a pie, andando; *(in progress)* en marcha, en movimiento.
a·fore·men·tioned (ə-fôr′mĕn′shənd) adj. mencionado, citado.
a·fore·said (ə-fôr′sĕd′) adj. antedicho, susodicho.
a·fore·thought (ə-fôr′thôt′) adj. premeditado, con premeditación.
a·foul of (ə-foul′) prep. enredado con, en líos con ♦ **to run a.** enredarse con, meterse en líos con.
a·fraid (ə-frād′) adj. asustado, atemorizado ♦ **to be a.** tener miedo • **to be a. of** tener miedo de o a • **to be a. that** temer que.
a·fresh (ə-frĕsh′) adv. de nuevo, otra vez.
Af·ri·ca (ăf′rĭ-kə) s. África *m.*
Af·ri·can (ăf′rĭ-kən) adj. & s. africano.
Af·ri·kaans (ăf′rĭ-känz′) s. afrikaans.
Af·ri·ka·ner (ăf′rĭ-kä′nər) s. afrikánder.
Af·ro (ăf′rō) I. s. [pl. **-ros**] estilo de peinado II. adj. al estilo africano.
Af·ro-A·mer·i·can (ăf′rō-ə-mĕr′ĭ-kən) I. adj. afroamericano II. s. negro norteamericano.
aft (ăft) adj. & adv. MARÍT. a popa, en popa, hacia popa.
af·ter (ăf′tər) I. prep. *(behind in place, order)* después de, detrás de <*you come a. me in line* usted viene después de

mí en esta línea>; *(following)* tras <*day a. day* día tras día>; *(in search of)* en pos, tras <*the dog ran a. the rabbit* el perro salió corriendo tras el conejo>; *(about)* acerca de, por <*your aunt asked a. you* su tía preguntó por Ud.>; *(at the end of)* después de, al cabo de <*a. one hour* al cabo de una hora>; *(later than)* y <*it's a quarter a.* two son las dos y cuarto> ♦ **a. all** al fin y al cabo • **a. much trouble** tras mucha dificultad • **named a.** llamado como, llamado así en honor a • **to be a. someone** perseguir a alguien **II.** conj. después (de) que <*we shall eat a. he leaves* comeremos después que él parta> **III.** adv. *(afterward)* después <*before and a.* antes y después>; *(behind)* atrás **IV.** adj. *(subsequent)* siguiente, próximo; MARÍT. de popa.

af·ter·birth (ăf'tər-bûrth') s. MED. secundinas, placenta.

af·ter·bur·ner (ăf'tər-bûr'nər) s. AER. quemador auxiliar (para motores de turborreacción) *m.*

af·ter·care (ăf'tər-kâr') s. MED. asistencia postoperatoria, terapia de la convalecencia.

af·ter·ef·fect (ăf'tər-ĭ-fĕkt') s. efecto posterior, consecuencia.

af·ter·glow (ăf'tər-glō') s. *(light)* resplandor (esp. crepuscular) *m*; FIG. *(feeling)* sensación de bienestar *f.*

af·ter·hours (ăf'tər-ourz') adj. *(late)* tarde (después del horario normal); *(late night)* de trasnoche (bar, discoteca).

af·ter·im·age (ăf'tər-ĭm'ĭj) s. imagen consecutiva *o* accidental.

af·ter·life (ăf'tər-līf') s. vida venidera.

af·ter·mar·ket (ăf'tər-mär'kĭt) s. COM., FIN. mercado secundario.

af·ter·math (ăf'tər-măth') s. consecuencias, resultados.

af·ter·noon (ăf'tər-nōōn') s. tarde *f* ♦ **a. nap** siesta • **good a.!** ¡buenas tardes!

af·ter·pains (ăf'tər-pānz') s.pl. MED. dolores después del parto *m.*

af·ter·shave (ăf'tər-shāv') s. loción para después de afeitarse *f.*

af·ter·taste (ăf'tər-tāst') s. *(taste)* dejo, resabio; FIG. *(impression)* sabor *m*, impresión *f.*

af·ter·thought (ăf'tər-thôt') s. idea tardía, reflexión *f.*

af·ter·ward (ăf'tər-wərd) *o* **af·ter·wards** (-wərdz) adv. después, luego ♦ **long a.** mucho tiempo después.

af·ter·world (ăf'tər-wûrld') s. el otro mundo, el más allá *m.*

a·gain (ə-gĕn') adv. *(another time)* otra vez, nuevamente; *(on the other hand)* por otra parte <*he might go, and then a. he might not* puede ser que él vaya, por otra parte, puede ser que no> ♦ **a. and a.** *o* **time and a.** una y otra vez, repetidamente • **as much a.** otro tanto más • **never a.** nunca más • **now and a.** de vez en cuando.

▲ En algunos casos el adverbio *again* no se traduce literalmente ya que algunos verbos en español llevan implícitos el sentido reiterativo <*would you do it again?* ¿lo volverías a hacer?> <*he left home, but went back again* él se fue de su casa, pero retornó>.

a·gainst (ə-gĕnst') prep. *(in opposition to)* en contra de, contra <*to row a. the current* remar en contra de la corriente>; *(in contrast to)* en contraste con, sobre <*dark colors a. a light background* colores oscuros sobre un fondo claro>; *(as a defense from)* como protección contra <*wear gloves a. the cold* usa guantes como protección contra el frío>; *(in preparation for)* en preparación para <*squirrels store up nuts a. the winter* las ardillas acumulan nueces en preparación para el invierno>; *(for)* por <*to trade one thing a. another* canjear una cosa por otra> ♦ **a. the grain** *(paper, fabric)* contra la dirección de la fibra; FIG. *(displeasing)* de forma desagradable, de mal grado.

a·gape (ə-gāp') adv. & adj. boquiabierto.

a·gar (ā'gär, ä'gär) *o* **a·gar-a·gar** (ā'gär-ā'gär, ä'gär-ä'gär) s. BIOL. agar agar *m.*

ag·ate (ăg'ĭt) s. MIN. ágata; *(a marble)* canica (de ágata o imitación); IMPR. tipo de 5½ puntos.

a·gave (ə-gä'vē) s. BOT. agave *mf*, pita.

age (āj) **I.** s. edad *f* <*what is your a.?* ¿cuál es su edad?>; *(era)* época, era <*the a. we live in* la era en que vivimos> ♦ **at my a.** a mi edad • **golden a.** edad de oro, siglo de oro • **mental a.** edad mental • **middle a.** edad mediana • **of a.** mayor de edad • **old a.** vejez, senectud • **to act one's a.**

portarse según la edad de uno • **to come of a.** llegar a la mayoría de edad • **under a.** menor de edad **II.** tr. & intr. aged, ag·ing envejecer(se), madurar(se).

ag·ed (ā'jĭd) adj. *(old)* envejecido, anciano; (ājd) *(of the age of)* de la edad de, de <*a person a. twenty* una persona de veinte años>; *(mature)* maduro, sazonado.

age·ing (ā'jĭng) s. G.B. var. de **aging**.

age·less (āj'lĭs) adj. *(not old)* eternamente joven; *(existing forever)* perenne, eterno.

age·long (āj'lông') adj. eterno, de siempre.

a·gen·cy (ā'jən-sē) s. [pl. **-cies**] *(a means)* medio, acción *f*; *(business)* agencia; *(governmental department)* ministerio, dependencia gubernamental.

a·gen·da (ə-jĕn'də) s. [ú. con v. sing.] agenda, temario.

a·gent (ā'jənt) s. *(representative)* agente *mf*, representante *mf*; *(a means)* instrumento, medio; *(chemical substance)* agente *m*, factor *m*; *(of government)* agente, funcionario.

age of consent s. DER. edad *f* en que el consentimiento propio adquiere validez, edad núbil.

age-old (āj'ōld') adj. antiquísimo.

ag·glom·er·ate (ə-glŏm'ə-rāt') **I.** tr. & intr. **-at·ed, -at·ing** aglomerar(se), amontonar(se) **II.** adj. (-ər-ĭt) aglomerado **III.** s. (-ər-ĭt) aglomerado, conjunto; GEOL. aglomerado.

ag·glom·er·a·tion (ə-glŏm'ə-rā'shən) s. aglomeración *f*, amontonamiento.

ag·glu·ti·nate (ə-glōōt'n-āt') tr. & intr. **-nat·ed, -nat·ing** aglutinar(se).

ag·glu·ti·na·tion (ə-glōōt'n-ā'shən) s. aglutinación *f.*

ag·gran·dize (ə-grăn'dīz', ăg'rən-) tr. **-dized, -diz·ing** *(to enlarge)* agrandar; *(to magnify)* engrandecer; *(to exaggerate)* exagerar; *(to exalt)* exaltar, ensalzar.

ag·gran·dize·ment (ə-grăn'dĭz-mənt, -dīz'-) s. *(enlargement)* agrandamiento; *(exaltation)* exaltación *f.*

ag·gra·vate (ăg'rə-vāt') tr. **-vat·ed, -vat·ing** *(to worsen)* agravar, empeorar; *(to annoy)* irritar, exasperar.

aggravated assault s. DER. asalto con intención de crimen.

ag·gra·va·tion (ăg'rə-vā'shən) s. *(worsening)* agravación *f*, empeoramiento; *(annoyance)* irritación *f*, exasperación *f.*

ag·gre·gate (ăg'rĭ-gĭt, -gāt') **I.** adj. agregado, colectivo **II.** s. agregado, totalidad *f* ♦ **in the a.** en total, en conjunto **III.** tr. (-gāt') **-gat·ed, -gat·ing** *(to gather)* agregar, unir; *(to total up to)* sumar, ascender a.

ag·gre·ga·tion (ăg'rĭ-gā'shən) s. agregado, colección *f.*

ag·gress (ə-grĕs') intr. *(to attack)* agredir; *(to start a quarrel)* iniciar una pelea *o* disputa.

ag·gres·sion (ə-grĕsh'ən) s. *(assault)* agresión *f*, ataque *m*; *(hostile action)* acto de hostilidad.

ag·gres·sive (ə-grĕs'ĭv) adj. *(hostile)* agresivo, ofensivo; *(assertive)* emprendedor, dinámico.

ag·gres·sive·ly (ə-grĕs'ĭv-lē) adv. *(with hostility)* agresivamente; *(assertively)* dinámicamente.

ag·gres·sor (ə-grĕs'ər) s. agresor *m.*

ag·grieve (ə-grēv') tr. **-grieved, -griev·ing** *(to distress)* apenar, afligir; *(to injure)* lastimar, dañar.

ag·grieved (ə-grēvd') adj. *(distressed)* apenado, afligido; *(offended)* ofendido; DER. dañado, agraviado.

a·ghast (ə-găst') adj. espantado, horrorizado.

ag·ile (ăj'əl, ăj'īl') adj. *(active)* ágil, ligero; *(mentally alert)* ágil, listo.

a·gil·i·ty (ə-jĭl'ĭ-tē) s. agilidad *f*, ligereza.

ag·ing (ā'jĭng) s. *(maturity)* envejecimiento, madurez *f*; *(process)* añejamiento.

ag·i·tate (ăj'ĭ-tāt') tr. **-tat·ed, -tat·ing** *(to excite physically)* agitar; *(to upset)* inquietar, perturbar —intr. excitar la opinión pública, agitar.

ag·i·tat·ed (ăj'ĭ-tā'tĭd) adj. agitado, inquieto.

ag·i·ta·tion (ăj'ĭ-tā'shən) s. agitación *f*, perturbación *f.*

ag·i·ta·tor (ăj'ĭ-tā'tər) s. agitador *m*, instigador *m.*

ag·it·prop (ăj'ĭt-prŏp') s. POL. agitación *f* y propaganda (comunista).

a·glit·ter (ə-glĭt'ər) adj. & adv. reluciente, brillante.

a·glow (ə-glō') adj. & adv. resplandeciente ♦ **a. with** radiante de.

ag·nos·tic (ăg-nŏs'tĭk) s. & adj. agnóstico.

ag·nos·ti·cism (ăg-nŏs'tĭ-sĭz'əm) s. agnosticismo.

a·go §G3 (ə-gō') adj. & adv. hace <*two years a.* hace dos años> ✦ **a long time a.** hace mucho tiempo • **how long a.?** ¿cuánto tiempo hace?

a·gog (ə-gŏg') I. adj. ansioso, anhelante II. adv. ansiosamente, con vivo interés.

ag·o·nize (ăg'ə-nīz') intr. **-nized, -niz·ing** (to struggle) hacer grandes esfuerzos; (to anguish) atormentarse (por una duda, decisión); (to be in agony) agonizar —tr. atormentar, angustiar.

ag·o·ny (ăg'ə-nē) s. [pl. **-nies**] (anguish) agonía, angustia; (dying) agonía.

ag·o·ra (ăg'ə-rə) s. HIST. ágora, plaza pública (en la Grecia antigua).

ag·o·ra·pho·bi·a (ăg'ə-rə-fō'bē-ə) s. PSIC. agorafobia, aversión a los espacios abiertos o públicos.

a·gou·ti (ə-gōō'tē) s. [pl. **-tis** o **-ties**] ZOOL. agutí m.

a·grar·i·an (ə-grâr'ē-ən) adj. agrario.

a·grar·i·an·ism (ə-grâr'ē-ə-nĭz'əm) s. agrarismo.

a·gree (ə-grē') intr. **a·greed, a·gree·ing** (to accede) consentir, acceder a <he agreed to accompany us accedió a acompañarnos>; (to match) corresponder a, concordar <the copy agrees with the original la copia concuerda con el original>; (to come to terms) avenirse, ponerse de acuerdo <they all agreed on the terms of the contract todos se avinieron a las condiciones del contrato>; (to concur) estar de acuerdo, coincidir <I agree with your opinion estoy de acuerdo con su opinión>; (to be suitable) sentar bien a <spicy food does not a. with him la comida muy condimentada no le sienta bien a él>; GRAM. concordar <the subject and verb must a. in number el sujeto y el verbo deben concordar en número> —tr. quedar en <he agreed that we should go quedó en que iríamos> ✦ **don't you a.?** ¿no le parece?

a·gree·a·ble (ə-grē'ə-bəl) adj. (pleasant) agradable; (willing to agree) complaciente; (in accord) conforme, de acuerdo.

a·gree·a·bly (ə-grē'ə-blē) adv. (pleasantly) agradablemente; (compatibly) compatiblemente.

a·greed (ə-grēd') adj. convenido, entendido.

a·gree·ment (ə-grē'mənt) s. (accord) concordancia, conformidad f; (treaty) acuerdo, pacto; GRAM. concordancia ✦ **by mutual a.** de común acuerdo • **in a. with** de acuerdo con • **to enter into an a.** firmar un contrato.

ag·ri·busi·ness (ăg'rə-bĭz'nĭs) s. producción y distribución de productos y maquinarias agrícolas.

ag·ri·cul·tur·al (ăg'rĭ-kŭl'chər-əl) adj. agrícola, agrario ✦ **a. college** escuela de agricultura.

ag·ri·cul·ture (ăg'rĭ-kŭl'chər) s. agricultura.

ag·ri·cul·tur·ist (ăg'rĭ-kŭl'chər-ĭst) s. (farmer) agricultor m; (expert) (ingeniero) agrónomo.

ag·ro·nom·ics (ăg'rə-nŏm'ĭks) s. var. de **agronomy.**

a·gron·o·mist (ə-grŏn'ə-mĭst) s. agrónomo.

a·gron·o·my (ə-grŏn'ə-mē) s. agronomía.

a·ground (ə-ground') adv. & adj. MARÍT. varado, encallado.

a·gue (ā'gyōō) s. MED. (fever) fiebre palúdica, fiebre intermitente f; (chill) escalofrío.

ah (ä) interj. ¡ah!, ¡ayh!

a·ha (ä-hä') interj. ¡ajá!

a·head (ə-hĕd') adv. (at or to the front) delante, al frente, adelante; (in advance) por adelantado, por anticipado <to get tickets you have to phone a. para conseguir boletos tiene que telefonear por adelantado> ✦ **a. of** antes que, antes de <he arrived a. of us llegó antes que nosotros> • **go a.!** ¡adelante! • **to be a. of** llevar ventaja a • **to get a.** progresar, adelantar.

a·hem (ə-hĕm') interj. ¡ejem!

a·hoy (ə-hoi') interj. MARÍT. ¡ah! <a. there! ¡ah del barco!> ✦ **ship a.!** ¡barco a la vista!

aid (ād) I. tr. & intr. ayudar, auxiliar II. s. ayuda, auxilio ✦ **first a.** primeros auxilios • **to come to the a. of** acudir en ayuda de • **with the a. of** con la ayuda de.

aide (ād) s. asistente mf, ayudante mf.

aide-de-camp (ād'dĭ-kămp') s. [pl. **aides-de-camp**] MIL. ayudante de campo m, edecán m.

AIDS (ādz) s. MED. SIDA, síndrome de inmunodeficiencia adquirida m.

ail (āl) intr. sufrir, estar enfermo —tr. afligir, doler.

ai·le·ron (ā'lə-rŏn') s. AVIA. alerón m.

ail·ing (ā'lĭng) adj. enfermizo, achacoso.

ail·ment (āl'mənt) s. dolencia, enfermedad f.

aim (ām) I. tr. apuntar <he aimed at the lion but missed apuntó al león pero falló> —intr. (a weapon) apuntar; (to aspire) aspirar, proponerse <we a. at a better education aspiramos a una educación mejor>; (to intend) proponerse II. s. (of a weapon) puntería, apunte m; (purpose) objetivo, meta ✦ **to take accurate a.** afinar la puntería • **to take a. at** apuntar a.

aim·less (ām'lĭs) adj. sin objeto, a la deriva.

aim·less·ly (ām'lĭs-lē) adv. a la ventura, a la deriva.

ain't (ānt) FAM. contr. de **am not, is not, are not, has not,** y **have not.**

▲ La contracción ain't no está aceptada como una expresión formal del idioma inglés. Al contrario, su uso refleja un nivel de lenguaje pobre e inculto. A veces entre personas cultas se usa para provocar humor, causar un impacto o algún otro efecto especial.

air (âr) I. s. (gas) aire m; (breeze) brisa; (atmosphere) atmósfera; (aura) apariencia, aspecto; MÚS. aire, tonada ✦ **airs** aires, afectación • **by a.** (mail) por avión, por vía aérea; (persons) en avión • **in the open a.** al aire libre, a la intemperie • **there's something in the a.** se está tramando algo • **to be on the a.** RAD., TELEV. estar emitiéndose (un programa) • **to clear the a.** FIG. aclarar las cosas • **to take the a.** tomar el fresco • **to vanish into thin a.** desaparecer por completo • **to walk on a.** FIG. estar bañado de agua de rosas • **up in the a.** incierto, no resuelto II. tr. (to hang out to dry) orear; (to ventilate) ventilar, airear; (to circulate) hacer público, divulgar.

air base s. AVIA. base aérea.

air bladder s. ZOOL. vejiga natatoria.

air·boat (âr'bōt') s. embarcación propulsada por una hélice montada en la popa de la misma.

air·borne (âr'bôrn') adj. AVIA. (by aircraft) aerotransportado, por avión; (flying) volando, en el aire; (pollen, seeds) llevado por el aire.

air brake s. freno de aire comprimido, freno neumático.

air·brush o **air brush** (âr'brŭsh') s. aerógrafo.

air command s. MIL. comando aéreo.

air-con·di·tion (âr'kən-dĭsh'ən) tr. acondicionar el aire, climatizar.

air conditioner s. acondicionador de aire m.

air conditioning s. (coolness) aire acondicionado; (system) sistema de acondicionamiento del aire m.

air-cool (âr'kōōl') tr. enfriar por aire.

air corridor s. corredor aéreo, pasillo aéreo.

air cover s. MIL. apoyo aéreo, protección aérea.

air·craft (âr'krăft') s. [pl. **aircraft**] nave aérea.

aircraft carrier s. portaaviones m.

air cushion s. (inflatable cushion) colchón de aire m, cojín neumático; (air spring) amortiguador de aire m.

air·drome (âr'drōm') s. aeródromo.

air·drop (âr'drŏp') I. s. AVIA. suministro por paracaídas II. tr. & intr. **-dropped, -drop·ping** lanzar(se), dejar(se) caer (desde un aeroplano).

air-dry (âr'drī') I. tr. **-dried, -dry·ing** secar al aire II. adj. seco.

air express s. expreso aéreo, sistema aéreo del transporte de carga.

air·fare (âr'fâr') s. tarifa aérea, precio del pasaje de avión.

air·field (âr'fēld') s. AVIA. campo de aterrizaje, campo de aviación.

air·flow (âr'flō') s. corriente de aire (natural o provocada por cuerpos en movimiento como trenes, carros, aviones) f.

air·foil (âr'foil') s. AVIA. superficie sustentadora.

air force s. MIL. fuerza aérea.

air freight s. carga aérea, flete por avión m.

air gun s. pistola o carabina de aire comprimido.

air·hole (âr'hōl') s. (vent) respiradero; AER. bache m, bolsa o pozo de aire.

air·i·ly (âr'ə-lē) adv. (nonchalantly) ligeramente, alegremente; (delicately) delicadamente, gentilmente.

air·i·ness (âr'ē-nĭs) s. (lightness) ligereza, liviandad f; (delicacy) delicadeza, gentileza.

air·ing (âr'ĭng) s. (exposure to air) ventilación f, oreo; (dis-

cussion) ventilación (de ideas, opiniones); *(exercising)* paseo (para tomar el aire); *(broadcast)* transmisión *f.*

air lane s. ruta aérea.

air·less (âr′lĭs) adj. sin aire, sofocante.

air letter s. carta aérea.

air·lift (âr′lĭft′) I. s. MIL. puente de aerotransporte *m*, puente aéreo II. tr. transportar por vía aérea.

air·line (âr′līn′) s. aerolínea, compañía de aviación.

air·lin·er (âr′lī′nər) s. avión de pasajeros *m*, aeronave *f.*

air lock s. *(sealed chamber)* esclusa de aire, esclusa neumática; *(air bubble)* burbuja de aire.

air·mail (âr′māl′) I. tr. enviar por vía aérea II. adj. de vía aérea <*an a. stamp* una estampilla de vía aérea> ♦ **by a.** por vía aérea.

air·man (âr′mən) s. [pl. **-men**] MIL. soldado de la fuerza aérea; *(aviator)* aviador *m.*

air mass s. METEOR. masa de aire.

air mattress s. colchón de aire *m.*

air·plane (âr′plān′) s. AVIA. avión *m*, aeroplano.

air pocket s. bache *m*, pozo de aire.

air·port (âr′pôrt′) s. AVIA. aeropuerto, aeródromo.

air·proof (âr′prōōf′) I. adj. hermético II. tr. hacer hermético.

air pump s. bomba neumática, bomba de aire.

air raid s. MIL. ataque aéreo, incursión aérea.

air rifle s. rifle *m o* escopeta de aire comprimido.

air sac s. BIOL., ORNIT. bolsa de aire.

air·ship (âr′shĭp′) s. aeronave *f*, dirigible *m.*

air·sick (âr′sĭk′) adj. mareado (en un viaje aéreo).

air·sick·ness (âr′sĭk′nĭs) s. mareo (en un viaje aéreo).

air·space (âr′spās′) s. espacio aéreo (propio de un país o el que ocupa una formación militar en maniobra).

air speed s. AER. velocidad de un aparato aéreo en el aire *f.*

air·strip (âr′strĭp′) s. pista de aterrizaje.

air·tight (âr′tīt′) adj. herméticamente cerrado, hermético.

air-to-air missile (âr′tə-âr′) s. mísil de avión a avión *m.*

air-to-sur·face missile (âr′tə-sûr′fĭs) s. mísil de avión a superficie (tierra o mar) *m.*

air·waves (âr′wāvz′) s.pl. RAD., TELEV. ondas hertzianas *o* electromagnéticas.

air·way (âr′wā′) s. MIN. *(passageway)* conducto de ventilación *m*; AVIA. *(route)* aerovía, línea aérea.

air·wor·thy (âr′wûr′*th*ē) adj. AVIA. en condiciones de vuelo.

air·y (âr′ē) adj. **-i·er, -i·est** *(of the air)* aéreo, de la atmósfera; *(breezy)* bien ventilado; *(immaterial)* etéreo; *(delicate)* diáfano, ligero; *(light-hearted)* alegre, vivaz.

aisle (īl) s. ARQ. *(of a church)* nave lateral *f*; *(passageway)* pasillo.

a·jar[1] (ə-jär′) adv. & adj. entornado, entreabierto.

a·jar[2] (ə-jär′) adv. & adj. discorde, en desacuerdo con <*a. with the times* en desacuerdo con la época>.

a·kim·bo (ə-kĭm′bō) adj. & adv. en jarras, en asas ♦ **with arms a.** con los brazos en jarras.

a·kin (ə-kĭn′) adj. *(related)* consanguíneo, emparentado; *(similar)* parecido, semejante.

al·a·bas·ter (ăl′ə-băs′tər) s. MIN. alabastro; *(color)* color alabastro.

a·lack (ə-lăk′) interj. ¡ay!, ¡ay de mí!

a·lac·ri·ty (ə-lăk′rĭ-tē) s. *(eagerness)* alacridad *f*, vivacidad *f*; *(speed)* presteza, prontitud *f.*

a·larm (ə-lärm′) I. s. *(fear)* alarma, temor *m*; *(device)* mecanismo *o* señal de alarma; MIL. rebato ♦ **to sound the a.** *(to warn)* dar la alarma; MIL. tocar a rebato II. tr. *(to frighten)* alarmar, inquietar; *(to warn)* dar la alarma.

alarm clock s. (reloj) despertador *m.*

a·larm·ing (ə-lär′mĭng) adj. alarmante, inquietante.

a·larm·ist (ə-lär′mĭst) s. alarmista *mf.*

a·las (ə-lăs′) interj. ¡ay!, ¡ay de mí!

alb (ălb) s. RELIG. alba.

al·ba·core (ăl′bə-kôr′) s. [pl. **albacore** *o* **-cores**] ICT. albacora, bonito.

Al·ba·ni·a (ăl-bā′nē-ə) s. Albania.

Al·ba·ni·an (ăl-bā′nē-ən) adj. & s. *(inhabitant, language)* albanés *m.*

al·ba·tross (ăl′bə-trôs′) s. [pl. **albatross** *o* **-tross·es**] ORNIT. albatros *m*; FIG. *(burden)* pena, sufrimiento.

al·be·it (ôl-bē′ĭt) conj. aunque, no obstante, si bien.

al·bi·nism (ăl′bə-nĭz′əm) s. albinismo.

al·bi·no (ăl-bī′nō) s. [pl. **-nos**] albino.

al·bum (ăl′bəm) s. álbum *m.*

al·bu·men (ăl-byōō′mən) s. BIOQUÍM. albumen *m*; *(albumin)* albúmina.

al·bu·min (ăl-byōō′mĭn) s. BIOQUÍM., BOT. albúmina.

al·che·mist (ăl′kə-mĭst) s. alquimista *mf.*

al·che·my (ăl′kə-mē) s. alquimia.

al·co·hol (ăl′kə-hôl′) s. QUÍM. alcohol *m*; *(liquor)* bebida alcohólica.

al·co·hol·ic (ăl′kə-hô′lĭk) I. adj. *(from alcohol)* alcohólico; *(condition)* alcohólico, alcoholizado II. s. bebedor alcoholizado.

al·co·hol·ism (ăl′kə-hô′lĭz′əm) s. alcoholismo.

al·cove (ăl′kōv′) s. *(of a room)* trasalcoba; *(in a garden)* glorieta, cenador *m.*

al·de·hyde (ăl′də-hīd′) s. QUÍM. aldehído.

al·der (ôl′dər) s. BOT. aliso.

al·der·man (ôl′dər-mən) s. [pl. **-men**] concejal *m*, regidor *m.*

ale (āl) s. ale (cerveza espesa y amarga) *f.*

a·le·a·to·ry (ā′lē-ə-tôr′ē) adj. de suerte, de azar.

ale·house (āl′hous) s. cervecería, taberna.

a·lem·bic (ə-lĕm′bĭk) s. alambique *m*, destilador *m.*

a·lert (ə-lûrt′) I. adj. *(watchful)* alerta, vigilante; *(intelligent)* alerta, listo II. s. *(warning signal)* alarma; *(duration of alert)* estado de alarma ♦ **to be on the a.** estar sobre aviso III. tr. *(to warn)* alertar; *(to make aware of)* poner sobre aviso.

Al·ex·an·dri·a (ăl′ĭg-zăn′drē-ə) s. Alejandría.

Al·ex·an·dri·an (ăl′ĭg-zăn′drē-ən) adj. & s. alejandrino.

al·ex·an·drine *o* **Al·ex·an·drine** (ăl′ĭg-zăn′drĭn) s. & adj. POÉT. alejandrino.

al·fal·fa (ăl-făl′fə) s. BOT. alfalfa, mielga.

al·ga (ăl′gə) s. [pl. **-gae** (-jē)] alga.

al·ge·bra (ăl′jə-brə) s. álgebra.

al·ge·bra·ic (ăl′jə-brā′ĭk) adj. algebraico.

Al·ge·ri·a (ăl-jîr′ē-ə) s. Argelia.

Al·ge·ri·an (ăl-jîr′ē-ən) adj. & s. argelino.

al·gid (ăl′jĭd) adj. álgido, muy frío.

Al·giers (ăl-jîrz′) s. Argel.

al·gin (ăl′jĭn) s. BIOQUÍM. algina.

ALGOL (ăl′gŏl′) s. COMPUT. lenguaje algorítmico.

al·go·rithm (ăl′gə-rĭ*th*′əm) s. MAT. algoritmia, algoritmo.

al·go·rith·mic (ăl′gə-rĭ*th*′mĭk) adj. MAT. algorítmico.

a·li·as (ā′lē-əs) I. s. alias *m*, seudónimo II. adv. alias, conocido por <*Pérez, a. Jaguar* Pérez, conocido por Jaguar>.

al·i·bi (ăl′ə-bī′) I. s. [pl. **-bis**] DER. coartada, alibí *m*; FAM. *(excuse)* excusa, pretexto II. intr. **-bied, -bi·ing** FAM. excusarse.

a·lien (āl′yən) I. adj. *(foreign)* extranjero; *(unfamiliar)* ajeno, extraño; *(against)* ajeno, contrario <*lying is a. to his nature* mentir es contrario a su naturaleza> II. s. *(foreign resident)* extranjero; *(stranger)* forastero; CIENC. FIC. *(being)* ser de otro planeta III. tr. transferir.

al·ien·a·ble (āl′yə-nə-bəl) adj. DER. alienable, enajenable.

al·ien·ate (āl′yə-nāt) tr. **-at·ed, -at·ing** *(to estrange)* alienar, enajenar; *(to keep away)* alejar <*political scandals a. many young people from politics* los escándalos políticos alejan a muchos jóvenes de la política>; DER. enajenar, traspasar.

al·ien·a·tion (āl′yə-nā′shən) s. *(isolation)* alienación *f*, enajenación *f*; *(mental state)* alienación, enajenación mental; DER. alienación, traspaso.

a·li·form (ā′lə-fôrm′, ăl′ə-) adj. aliforme.

a·light[1] (ə-līt′) intr. **a·light·ed** *o* **a·lit** (ə-lĭt′), **a·light·ing** *(to come down)* descender, posarse <*a bird alit on the branch* un pájaro se posó en la rama>; *(to dismount)* bajar, apearse.

a·light[2] (ə-līt′) adj. *(lighted)* iluminado <*her eyes were a. with joy* sus ojos estaban iluminados por la alegría>; *(burning)* ardiendo, en llamas.

a·lign (ə-līn′) tr. alinear, poner en línea ♦ **to a. oneself with** ponerse del lado de —intr. alinearse.

a·lign·ment (ə-līn′mənt) s. alineación *f*, alineamiento.

a·like (ə-līk′) I. adj. semejante, parecido II. adv. igualmente, de la misma forma o manera <*they dress and walk a.* se visten y caminan de la misma manera>.

al·i·ment (ăl'ə-mənt) s. *(food)* alimento, comida; *(sustenance)* sustento.

al·i·men·ta·ry (ăl'ə-mĕn'tə-rē) adj. *(nutritional)* alimental, alimentario; *(nourishing)* alimenticio.

alimentary canal s. ANAT. canal alimenticio.

al·i·men·ta·tion (ăl'ə-mĕn-tā'shən) s. *(act)* alimentación *f*; *(sustenance)* sustento, alimentación.

al·i·mo·ny (ăl'ə-mō'nē) s. [pl. **-nies**] DER. pensión (por divorcio o separación) *f*.

a·line (ə-līn') tr. **a·lined, a·lin·ing** alinear, poner en línea.

a·lit (ə-lĭt') pret. y part. p. de **alight¹**.

a·live (ə-līv') adj. *(living)* con vida, vivo; *(active)* en uso, funcionando; *(lively)* animado, activo ♦ **a. to** FIG. despierto para, sensible a (posibilidades, ideas) • **a. with** rebosante de, lleno de • **to be a.** estar vivo, vivir • **to be a. and kicking** FIG. estar vivito y coleando • **to come a.** FIG. cobrar vida.

al·ka·li (ăl'kə-lī') s. [pl. **-lis** o **-lies**] QUÍM. álcali *m*.

alkali metal s. QUÍM. metal alcalino.

al·ka·line (ăl'kə-līn, -līn') adj. alcalino.

al·ka·lin·i·ty (ăl'kə-lĭn'ĭ-tē) s. QUÍM. alcalinidad *f*.

al·ka·lize (ăl'kə-līz') o **al·ka·lin·ize** (-lə-nīz') tr. & intr. **-lized, -liz·ing** o **-ized, -iz·ing** alcalizar(se), alcalinizar(se).

al·ka·loid (ăl'kə-loid') s. QUÍM. alcaloide *m*.

al·kyl (ăl'kəl) s. QUÍM. alcohilo, alquilo.

all §G36 (ôl) I. adj. *(the total extent of)* todo, todos <*a. the time* todo el tiempo>; *(any whatsoever)* cualquier, todo <*proven beyond a. doubt* comprobado más allá de toda duda> ♦ **and a. that** y otras cosas por el estilo • **it's a. done** todo está hecho, está terminado • **of a. things!** ¡imagínate! II. pron. todo, todos, todo el mundo, cada uno <*a. aboard the ship speak Spanish* todos a bordo hablan español> ♦ **above a.** sobre todo, ante todo • **after a.** después de todo, al fin y al cabo • **a. in a.** en resumen • **a. of us** todos nosotros, nosotros todos • **a. told** en conjunto, considerado todo • **at a.** siquiera algo; del todo <*she is not at a. sure* ella no está segura del todo> • **not at a.** nada, en absoluto; *(you're welcome)* no hay de qué (como respuesta a gracias) III. s. todo <*he lost his a. in the fire* perdió todo lo que poseía en el incendio> ♦ **that's a.** eso es todo, nada más IV. adv. *(completely)* enteramente, completamente <*she's a. wrong* está completamente equivocada>; *(exclusively)* exclusivamente, solamente <*the cake is a. for him* la torta es solamente para él>; DEP. *(apiece)* por cada bando, por bando <*a score of five a.* cinco puntos por bando> ♦ **a. along** siempre, desde el principio • **a. around** por todas partes • **a. at once** de repente, de golpe • **a. but** casi • **a. in** JER. agotado, rendido • **a. of a sudden** de repente, inesperadamente • **a. over** *(finished)* terminado; *(everywhere)* por todas partes • **a. right** satisfactorio, bueno • **a. that** tan <*she's not a. that bright* ella no es tan lista> • **a. the better** (*o* **worse**) tanto mejor (*o* peor) • **a. too** demasiado, muy • **a. too soon** demasiado pronto.

▲ Cuando el pronombre *all* se refiere a "todo" (cosas), se usa con un verbo en singular: *all is not lost.* Cuando se refiere a "todos, cada uno" (personas, cosas), se usa con un verbo en plural: *all members were present; all items have been inspected.*

Al·lah (ăl'ə, ä'lə) s. RELIG. Alá.

all-A·mer·i·can (ôl'ə-mĕr'ĭ-kən) adj. típicamente norteamericano, que representa lo mejor de EE. UU.

all-a·round (ôl'ə-round') adj. *(comprehensive)* completo; *(versatile)* versátil.

al·lay (ə-lā') tr. *(to lessen)* disminuir, reducir; *(to calm)* calmar, aquietar.

all clear s. señal que indica que el peligro de un ataque aéreo ha terminado.

al·le·ga·tion (ăl'ĭ-gā'shən) s. *(act)* alegación *f*; *(plea)* argumento (sin pruebas); DER. alegato, alegación.

al·lege (ə-lĕj') tr. **-leged, -leg·ing** *(to declare)* alegar; *(to affirm)* afirmar; *(to assert without proof)* argumentar (sin pruebas).

al·leged (ə-lĕjd', ə-lĕj'ĭd) adj. alegado, supuesto.

al·leg·ed·ly (ə-lĕj'ĭd-lē) adv. supuestamente.

al·le·giance (ə-lē'jəns) s. lealtad *f*, fidelidad *f* ♦ **to swear a. to** jurar lealtad a.

al·le·gor·ic (ăl'ĭ-gôr'ĭk) o **al·le·gor·i·cal** (-ĭ-kəl) adj. alegórico.

al·le·go·rize (ăl'ĭ-gə-rīz') tr. & intr. **-rized, -riz·ing** alegorizar.

al·le·go·ry (ăl'ĭ-gôr'ē) s. [pl. **-ries**] alegoría.

al·le·lu·ia (ăl'ə-lōō'yə) interj. ¡aleluya!

al·ler·gen (ăl'ər-jən) s. MED. alérgeno.

al·ler·gic (ə-lûr'jĭk) adj. alérgico.

al·ler·gist (ăl'ər-jĭst) s. MED. alergista *mf*.

al·ler·gy (ăl'ər-jē) s. [pl. **-gies**] alergia ♦ **a. attack** ataque de alergia.

al·le·vi·ate (ə-lē'vē-āt') tr. **-at·ed, -at·ing** aliviar, mitigar.

al·le·vi·a·tion (ə-lē'vē-ā'shən) s. alivio.

al·ley (ăl'ē) s. [pl. **-leys**] *(street)* callejón *m*, callejuela; *(path)* pasillo, camino; *(in bowling)* bolera ♦ **blind a.** callejón sin salida • **up one's a.** lo de uno (en actividad o conocimiento).

alley cat s. gato callejero.

al·ley·way (ăl'ē-wā') s. callejón *m*.

all fours s. FAM. extremidades *f* ♦ **on a.** a gatas, en cuatro patas.

al·li·ance (ə-lī'əns) s. *(pact)* alianza, unión *f*; *(relationship)* relación *f*; *(affinity)* afinidad *f*.

al·lied (ə-līd', ăl'īd') adj. *(joined)* aliado, confederado; *(similar)* afín, relacionado.

Al·lies (the) (ăl'īz', ə-līz') s.pl. MIL., POL. los aliados.

al·li·ga·tor (ăl'ĭ-gā'tər) s. caimán (animal, cuero) *m*; *(tool)* rastra.

alligator pear s. aguacate *m*, palta.

all-im·por·tant (ôl'ĭm-pôr'tnt) adj. de suma importancia.

al·lit·er·ate (ə-lĭt'ə-rāt') intr. & tr. **-at·ed, -at·ing** formar aliteración (en).

al·lit·er·a·tion (ə-lĭt'ə-rā'shən) s. aliteración *f*.

al·lit·er·a·tive (ə-lĭt'ə-rā'tĭv, -ər-ə-tĭv) adj. aliterado.

al·lo·cate (ăl'ə-kāt') tr. **-cat·ed, -cat·ing** destinar, asignar.

al·lo·ca·tion (ăl'ə-kā'shən) s. asignación *f*, reparto.

al·lo·cu·tion (ăl'ə-kyōō'shən) s. alocución *f*, discurso.

al·lo·path (ăl'ə-păth') s. MED. alópata *mf*.

al·lop·a·thy (ə-lŏp'ə-thē) s. MED. alopatía.

al·lot (ə-lŏt') tr. **-lot·ted, -lot·ting** *(to apportion)* asignar, distribuir; *(to allocate)* destinar <*to a. three weeks to a project* destinar tres semanas para un proyecto>.

al·lot·ment (ə-lŏt'mənt) s. *(act)* distribución *f*; *(object, quantity)* lote *m*, porción *f*.

all-out (ôl'out') adj. *(maximum)* extremo, máximo <*she made an a. effort to be accepted* ella hizo un esfuerzo máximo para que la aceptaran>; *(complete)* completo, total.

all over adv. *(everywhere)* por todos lados <*I searched a. for you* te busqué por todos lados>; *(in all respects)* en todo sentido <*she is her grandmother a.* ella es su abuela en todo sentido>.

all-o·ver (ôl'ō'vər) adj. que cubre toda la superficie.

al·low (ə-lou') tr. *(to permit)* dejar, permitir <*please, a. me to finish* por favor, permítame terminar>; *(to give)* conceder, dar <*his father allows him ten dollars a week* su padre le da diez dólares por semana>; *(to set aside)* dar, poner aparte <*let's a. one hour to discuss this matter* pongamos aparte una hora para discutir este asunto>; *(to provide)* asignar, aprobar <*the city allowed the funds in case of emergency* la ciudad aprobó los fondos en caso de emergencia>; *(to admit)* confesar, admitir <*I a. that some mistakes have been made* admito que se han cometido algunos errores>; *(to discount)* deducir, descontar <*he allowed me twenty dollars on my old typewriter* me descontó veinte dólares por entregar mi máquina de escribir vieja> ♦ **after allowing for** después de considerar • **a. me** permítame (como expresión de cortesía) • **to a. for** tener en cuenta, tomar en consideración • **to a. of** permitir, admitir • **to a. oneself** permitirse, darse el gusto de.

al·low·a·ble (ə-lou'ə-bəl) adj. admisible, permisible.

al·low·ance (ə-lou'əns) s. *(permission)* permiso, autorización *f*; *(rebate)* reducción *f*, rebaja; *(money)* estipendio, dinero de bolsillo (que se da a los niños en EE. UU.); *(dimensions, weight)* tolerancia (en tamaño, peso); *(pay-*

ment) asignación *f*, pago ♦ **to make a. for** tener en cuenta, tomar en consideración • **to make allowances for** ser condescendiente con (una persona).

al·loy I. s. (ăl'oi', ə-loi') METAL., QUÍM. aleación *f*; *(mixture)* mezcla II. tr. (ə-loi') METAL., QUÍM. alear; FIG. *(to debase)* alterar, deteriorar.

all-pur·pose (ôl'pûr'pəs) adj. de uso múltiple.

all right adv. *(satisfactory)* satisfactorio, bueno; *(without error)* correcto, acertado; *(without injury)* ileso, sin daño; *(very well)* muy bien; *(yes)* sí; *(in agreement)* de acuerdo.

all-right (ôl'rīt') adj. JER. *(dependable)* responsable, digno de confianza; *(good)* bueno, excelente.

all-round (ôl'round') adj. var. de **all-around.**

All Saints' Day s. RELIG. día de Todos los Santos *m*.

All Souls' Day s. RELIG. día de difuntos *m*.

all-spice (ôl'spīs') s. pimienta de Jamaica, pimienta inglesa (árbol, fruto).

all-star (ôl'stär') adj. de primeras figuras.

all-time (ôl'tīm') adj. nunca visto, nunca alcanzado *<an a. high* un alza nunca alcanzada>.

al·lude (ə-lōōd') intr. **-lud·ed, -lud·ing** aludir, referirse.

al·lure (ə-lōōr') I. tr. **-lured, -lur·ing** atraer, fascinar II. s. atracción *f*, fascinación *f*.

al·lur·ing (ə-lōōr'ĭng) adj. atractivo, fascinante.

al·lu·sion (ə-lōō'zhən) s. *(mention)* alusión *f*; *(reference)* referencia indirecta.

al·lu·sive (ə-lōō'sĭv) adj. alusivo.

al·lu·vi·al (ə-lōō'vē-əl) adj. GEOL. aluvial, de aluvión.

al·lu·vi·um (ə-lōō'vē-əm) s. [pl. **-vi·ums** *o* **-vi·a** (-vē-ə)] GEOL. aluvión *m*.

al·ly I. tr. (ə-lī', ăl'ī') **-lied, -ly·ing** *(to unite)* unir, aliar; *(to associate)* emparentar, hacer alianza con ♦ **to a. oneself with** aliarse con —intr. unirse, aliarse II. s. (ăl'ī', ə-lī') [pl. **-lies**] aliado.

al·ma mat·er (ăl'mə mä'tər) s. la universidad donde uno se ha recibido.

al·ma·nac (ôl'mə-năk', ăl'-) s. calendario, almanaque *m*.

al·might·y (ôl-mī'tē) I. adj. *(all-powerful)* potente, todopoderoso; FAM. *(great)* enorme, imponente II. s. ♦ **the A.** RELIG. el Todopoderoso.

al·mond (ä'mənd, ăm'ənd) s. *(tree)* almendro; *(nut)* almendra.

al·most (ôl'mōst', ōl-mōst') adv. casi, por poco.

alms (ämz) s.pl. limosna, caridad *f*.

alms·house (ämz'hous') s. casa de beneficencia, asilo de pobres.

al·oe (ăl'ō) s. BOT. áloe *m*, alcíbar *m* ♦ **aloes** [ú. con v. sing.] MED. áloe, alcíbar.

a·loft (ə-lôft') I. adv. *(high)* en lo alto; *(in the air)* en el aire; *(in flight)* en vuelo; MARÍT. *(in the rigging)* en la arboladura II. prep. arriba de *<birds perching a. the telephone pole* pájaros posados arriba del poste telefónico>.

a·lone (ə-lōn') I. adj. *(unaccompanied)* solo *<are you a. in the house?* ¿estás solo en casa?>; *(only)* sólo *<God a. knows* sólo Dios sabe>; *(with nothing added)* solamente, en sí mismo *<New York City a. has over seven million people* la ciudad de Nueva York en sí misma tiene más de siete millones de personas> ♦ **let a.** sin mencionar, mucho menos *<he can hardly support himself, let a. somebody·else* apenas puede mantenerse a sí mismo, mucho menos a otra persona> • **to leave** *o* **let a.** no molestar, dejar en paz • **to stand a.** ser único II. adv. sólo, solamente *<he did the job for money a.* hizo el trabajo solamente por el dinero>.

a·long (ə-lông') I. adv. *(in line with)* a lo largo *<trees growing a. the river* árboles creciendo a lo largo del río>; *(forward)* adelante; *(together)* junto con *<one thing a. with another* una cosa junto con otra>; *(with one)* consigo *<bring your parents a.* traiga a sus padres consigo>; FAM. *(advanced)* avanzado *<the evening was well a.* era avanzada la tarde> ♦ **all a.** desde el principio • **a. about** FAM. a eso de *<a. about midnight* a eso de la medianoche> • **a. with** junto con, conjuntamente con • **to get a. with someone** llevarse bien con alguien • **to go a. with** *(to accompany)* acompañar; JER. *(to accept)* aceptar, estar conforme con (idea, plan) II. prep. *(by the length of)* a lo largo de, paralelo a *<to walk a. a river* caminar paralelo a la costa

de un río>; *(in accordance with)* de acuerdo con *<to think a. certain lines* pensar de acuerdo con ciertas ideas>; *(during)* en el curso de, mientras *<we met a. the way* nos encontramos mientras íbamos>.

a·long·shore (ə-lông'shôr') adv. a lo largo de la costa, a la orilla ♦ **to come a.** MARÍT. atracar.

a·long·side (ə-lông'sīd') I. adv. *(along the side)* a lo largo, al lado; MARÍT. al costado, de costado II. prep. *(by the side of)* junto a, a lo largo de; MARÍT. al costado de.

a·loof (ə-lōōf') I. adj. distante, reservado II. adv. lejos, a distancia ♦ **to keep** *o* **to stand a. from** mantenerse apartado de.

a·loof·ness (ə-lōōf'nĭs) s. reserva, indiferencia.

a·loud (ə-loud') adv. en voz alta, con voz fuerte.

alp (ălp) s. montaña elevada (esp. una de los Alpes).

al·pac·a (ăl-păk'ə) s. ZOOL. alpaca (animal, piel, tela) ♦ **an a. suit** un traje de alpaca.

al·pha (ăl'fə) s. alfa ♦ **a. and omega** alfa y omega • **a. particle** FÍS. partícula alfa • **a. ray** FÍS. rayo alfa.

al·pha·bet (ăl'fə-bĕt') s. *(letters)* alfabeto, abecedario; *(rudiments)* rudimentos (de ciencia, técnica).

al·pha·bet·i·cal (ăl'fə-bĕt'ĭ-kəl) *o* **al·pha·bet·ic** (-bĕt'ĭk) adj. alfabético.

al·pha·bet·i·za·tion (ăl'fə-bĕt'ĭ-zā'shən) s. alfabetización *f*.

al·pha·bet·ize (ăl'fə-bĭ-tīz') tr. **-ized, -iz·ing** alfabetizar.

al·pha·nu·mer·ic (ăl'fə-nōō-mĕr'ĭk, -nyōō-) adj. alfanumérico.

al·pine (ăl'pīn') adj. alpino.

al·pin·ism (ăl'pə-nĭz'əm) s. alpinismo.

al·pin·ist (ăl'pə-nĭst) s. alpinista *mf*.

Alps (ălps) s. Alpes *m*.

al·read·y (ôl-rĕd'ē) adv. ya *<I have a. finished* ya he terminado>.

al·right (ôl-rīt') adv. FAM. var. de **all right.**

Al·sace (ăl'săs', ăl-săs') s. Alsacia.

Al·sace-Lor·raine (ăl'săs'lə-răn', ăl'săs'-) s. Alsacia Lorena.

Al·sa·tian (ăl-sā'shən) I. adj. alsaciano II. s. *(inhabitant, language)* alsaciano; *(dog)* perro lobo.

al·so (ôl'sō) I. adv. también, además *<this dress is pretty and a. inexpensive* este vestido es bonito y además barato>.

al·so-ran (ôl'sō-răn') s. FAM. *(horse)* caballo que no figura (en una carrera); *(candidate)* candidato vencido (en una elección); *(failure)* fracasado, nulidad *f*.

al·tar (ôl'tər) s. altar *m*.

altar boy s. monaguillo.

al·tar·piece (ôl'tər-pēs') s. retablo.

al·ter (ôl'tər) tr. *(to modify)* alterar, cambiar; *(a garment)* arreglar; FAM. *(an animal)* castrar —intr. cambiarse, transformarse.

al·ter·a·ble (ôl'tər-ə-bəl) adj. alterable, variable.

al·ter·a·tion (ôl'tə-rā'shən) s. *(modification)* alteración *f*, cambio; *(of a dress)* arreglo.

al·ter·cate (ôl'tər-kāt') intr. **-cat·ed, -cat·ing** altercar, disputar.

al·ter·ca·tion (ôl'tər-kā'shən) s. altercado, disputa.

al·ter e·go (ôl'tər ē'gō) s. PSIC. alter ego *m*, otro yo; *(inseparable friend)* persona de absoluta confianza.

al·ter·nate (ôl'tər-nāt') I. intr. **-nat·ed, -nat·ing** alternar *<the rainy season alternates with the dry season* la época lluviosa se alterna con la seca> —tr. alternar *<they alternated swimming and rowing* ellos alternaban la natación con el remo> II. adj. (-nĭt) *(substitute)* sustituto, alterno *<an a. plan* un plan alterno>; *(every other)* alterno; BOT., GEOM. alterno II. s. (-nĭt) sustituto, suplente *mf*.

al·ter·nate·ly (ôl'tər-nĭt-lē) adv. alternativamente, por turno.

alternating current s. ELEC. corriente alterna.

al·ter·na·tion (ôl'tər-nā'shən) s. alternación *f*, turno.

al·ter·na·tive (ôl-tûr'nə-tĭv, ăl-) I. s. alternativa ♦ **to have no a.** no tener otra alternativa, no tener mas remedio II. adj. alternativo.

al·ter·na·tor (ôl'tər-nā'tər, ăl'-) s. ELEC. alternador *m*.

al·though (ôl-thō') conj. aunque, si bien, aún cuando.

al·tim·e·ter (ăl-tĭm'ĭ-tər) s. AER. altímetro.

al·tim·e·try (ăl-tĭm'ə-trē) s. AER., TOP. altimetría.

---

al·ti·tude (ăl'tĭ-tōōd', -tyōōd') s. GEOG. altitud *f*; elevación *f*; ASTRON., GEOM. altura.
altitude sickness s. MED. mal de altura, puna.
al·to (ăl'tō) adj. & s. [pl. **-tos**] MÚS. contralto.
al·to·geth·er (ŏl'tə-gĕth'ər) adv. *(entirely)* enteramente, del todo <*the noise faded away a.* el sonido desapareció del todo>; *(all told)* en total <*a. one hundred people came* en total vinieron cien personas>; *(on the whole)* en suma <*a. I'm sorry it happened* en suma, lamento que eso haya sucedido> ◆ **in the a.** FAM. en cueros.
al·tru·ism (ăl'trōō-ĭz'əm) s. altruismo.
al·tru·is·tic (ăl'trōō-ĭs'tĭk) adj. altruista.
al·um (ăl'əm) s. QUÍM. alumbre *m*.
a·lu·mi·na (ə-lōō'mə-nə) s. QUÍM. alúmina.
a·lu·min·i·um (ăl'yə-mĭn'ē-əm) s. G.B. var. de **aluminum.**
a·lu·mi·nize (ə-lōō'mə-nīz') tr. **-nized**, **-niz·ing** cubrir con aluminio *o* pintura de aluminio.
a·lu·mi·num (ə-lōō'mə-nəm) s. QUÍM. aluminio.
a·lum·na (ə-lŭm'nə) s. [pl. **-nae** (-nē')] ex-alumna (graduada).
a·lum·nus (ə-lŭm'nəs) s. [pl. **-ni** (-nī')] ex-alumno (graduado).
al·ve·o·lar (ăl-vē'ə-lər) adj. ANAT., FONÉT. alveolar.
al·ve·o·lus (ăl-vē'ə-ləs) s. [pl. **-li** (-lī')] ANAT., ENTOM. alvéolo.
al·ways (ŏl'wāz, -wēz) adv. *(invariably)* siempre; *(forever)* para siempre <*we will be friends a.* seremos amigos para siempre>.
am (ăm, əm) primera persona sing. del pres. indic. de **be.**
a.m. *o* **A.M.** (ā'ĕm') I. adv. de la mañana II. s. *(morning)* mañana <*in the a.m.* en la mañana>.
a·mal·gam (ə-măl'gəm) s. QUÍM. amalgama, aleación *f*; *(mixture)* mezcla.
a·mal·ga·mate (ə-măl'gə-māt') tr. & intr. **-mat·ed**, **-mat·ing** QUÍM. amalgamar(se); FIG. *(to mix)* mezclar(se); COM. *(to merge)* unir(se).
a·mal·ga·ma·tion (ə-măl'gə-mā'shən) s. QUÍM. amalgamación *f*, aleación *f*; COM. fusión *f*.
am·a·ranth (ăm'ə-rănth') s. BOT. amaranto; *(color)* púrpura oscuro.
am·a·ryl·lis (ăm'ə-rĭl'ĭs) s. amarilis *f*.
a·mass (ə-măs') tr. acumular, amontonar.
am·a·teur (ăm'ə-tûr', -ə-chŏŏr') I. s. *(aficionado)* aficionado, amateur *mf*; *(athlete)* amateur; *(beginner)* principiante *mf*; *(unskillful person)* chapucero II. adj. amateur.
am·a·teur·ish (ăm'ə-tûr'ĭsh, -ə-chŏŏr'-) adj. amateur.
am·a·teur·ism (ăm'ə-tûr'ĭz'əm, -ə-chŏŏr'-) s. amateurismo.
am·a·tive (ăm'ə-tĭv) adj. amatorio, apasionado.
am·a·to·ry (ăm'ə-tôr'ē) adj. amoroso, amatorio.
a·maze (ə-māz') I. tr. **a·mazed**, **a·maz·ing** asombrar, sorprender II. s. POÉT. asombro, sorpresa.
a·mazed (ə-māzd') adj. *(astonished)* asombrado; *(surprised)* sorprendido; *(perplexed)* perplejo.
a·maze·ment (ə-māz'mənt) s. *(astonishment)* asombro; *(surprise)* sorpresa; *(perplexity)* perplejidad *f*.
a·maz·ing (ə-mā'zĭng) adj. *(astonishing)* asombroso; *(surprising)* sorprendente; *(marvelous)* maravilloso.
Am·a·zon (ăm'ə-zŏn', -zən) I. adj. amazónico II. s. MITOL. amazona; *(river)* Amazonas *m* ◆ **a.** *(strong woman)* amazona.
Am·a·zo·ni·an (ăm'ə-zō'nē-ən) adj. MITOL. amazónica ◆ **a.** amazónicas (díc. de las mujeres).
am·a·zon·ite (ăm'ə-zə-nīt') s. MIN. amazonita.
am·bas·sa·dor (ăm-băs'ə-dər) s. DIPL. embajador *m*; *(representative)* enviado, representante *mf* ◆ **a. at large** embajador viajero • **a. extraordinary** embajador en misión extraordinaria • **a. plenipotentiary** embajador plenipotenciario.
am·bas·sa·do·ri·al (ăm-băs'ə-dôr'ē-əl) adj. de embajador.
am·bas·sa·dor·ship (ăm-băs'ə-dər-shĭp') s. embajada *(cargo)*.
am·ber (ăm'bər) I. s. JOY. ámbar *m*, succino *m*; *(color)* color de ámbar ◆ **an a. necklace** un collar de ámbar II. adj. ambarino.
am·ber·gris (ăm'bər-grĭs, -grēs') s. ámbar gris *m*.
am·bi·ance *o* **am·bi·ence** (ăm'bē-əns) s. ambiente *m*.

am·bi·dex·trous (ăm'bĭ-dĕk'strəs) adj. *(using both hands)* ambidextro; *(adroit)* habilidoso; *(deceitful)* falso.
am·bi·ent (ăm'bē-ənt) adj. ambiente.
am·bi·gu·i·ty (ăm'bĭ-gyōō'ĭ-tē) s. [pl. **-ties**] ambigüedad *f*.
am·big·u·ous (ăm-bĭg'yōō-əs) adj. *(vague)* ambiguo, vago; *(uncertain)* indefinido, incierto.
am·big·u·ous·ness (ăm-bĭg'yōō-əs-nĭs) s. ambigüedad *f*.
am·bi·tion (ăm-bĭsh'ən) s. ambición *f*, afán *m*.
am·bi·tious (ăm-bĭsh'əs) adj. *(full of ambition)* ambicioso; *(striving)* emprendedor, afanoso; *(grand)* grandioso.
am·biv·a·lence (ăm-bĭv'ə-ləns) s. ambivalencia.
am·biv·a·lent (ăm-bĭv'ə-lənt) adj. ambivalente.
am·ble (ăm'bəl) I. intr. **-bled**, **-bling** *(to stroll)* deambular, andar despreocupadamente; EQUIT. amblar II. s. EQUIT. ambladura; *(leisurely pace)* paseo.
am·bro·sia (ăm-brō'zhə) s. ambrosía.
am·bu·lance (ăm'byə-ləns) s. ambulancia.
ambulance chaser s. FAM. abogado propenso a obtener clientes por cualquier medio, picapleitos.
am·bu·lant (ăm'byə-lənt) adj. ambulante.
am·bu·late (ăm'byə-lāt') intr. **-lat·ed**, **-lat·ing** deambular, pasear.
am·bu·la·to·ry (ăm'byə-lə-tôr'ē) I. adj. ambulante, ambulatorio II. s. [pl. **-ries**] deambulatorio, galería.
am·bus·cade (ăm'bə-skād') I. s. emboscada, celada II. tr. **-cad·ed**, **-cad·ing** emboscar, tender una celada a.
am·bush (ăm'bŏŏsh') I. s. emboscada, celada II. tr. emboscar, tender una celada a.
a·me·ba (ə-mē'bə) s. var. de **amoeba.**
a·me·bic (ə-mē'bĭk) adj. var. de **amoebic.**
a·me·lio·rate (ə-mēl'yə-rāt') tr. & intr. **-rat·ed**, **-rat·ing** mejorar(se), aliviar(se).
a·me·lio·ra·tion (ə-mēl'yə-rā'shən) s. mejora, alivio.
a·men (ā-mĕn', ä-mĕn') interj. RELIG. amén.
a·me·na·bil·i·ty (ə-mē'nə-bĭl'ĭ-tē, ə-mĕn'ə-) s. [pl. **-ties**] *(responsiveness)* receptibilidad *f*; *(responsibility)* responsabilidad *f*.
a·me·na·ble (ə-mē'nə-bəl, ə-mĕn'ə-) adj. *(responsive)* receptivo; *(accountable)* responsable (frente a la ley) ◆ **to be a. to** estar dispuesto a.
a·mend (ə-mĕnd') tr. *(to improve)* mejorar; *(to correct)* corregir, rectificar; *(to revise)* enmendar; POL. poner adición a una constitución con provisiones más específicas —intr. enmendarse, reformarse.
a·mend·ment (ə-mĕnd'mənt) s. *(improvement)* mejora, reforma; *(correction)* corrección; *(alteration)* enmienda; POL. *(addition to a constitution)* enmienda.
a·mends (ə-mĕndz') s.pl. indemnización *f*, reparación *f* ◆ **to make a. for** dar satisfacción por.
a·men·i·ty (ə-mĕn'ĭ-tē, ə-mē'nĭ-) s. [pl. **-ties**] *(agreeableness)* amenidad *f*, afabilidad *f*; *(comfort)* comodidad ◆ **amenities** *(civilities)* modales; *(courtesies)* cortesías; *(comfort)* comodidades.
A·mer·i·ca (ə-mĕr'ĭ-kə) s. los Estados Unidos ◆ **the Americas** América.
A·mer·i·can (ə-mĕr'ĭ-kən) adj. & s. *(of the Americas)* americano; *(of U.S.A.)* norteamericano, estadounidense *mf*.
A·mer·i·ca·na (ə-mĕr'ĭ-kă'nə, -kän'ə, -kā'nə) s.pl. colección de artículos y artefactos relacionados con el folklore, la geografía *o* la historia de EE. UU.
American eagle s. águila calva.
American Indian s. indio americano.
A·mer·i·can·ism (ə-mĕr'ĭ-kə-nĭz'əm) s. americanismo.
A·mer·i·can·ize (ə-mĕr'ĭ-kə-nīz') tr. & intr. **-ized**, **-iz·ing** americanizar(se).
American plan s. habitación con pensión completa (en los hoteles).
am·er·i·ci·um (ăm'ə-rĭsh'ē-əm) s. QUÍM. americio.
Am·er·ind (ăm'ə-rĭnd') *o* **Am·er·in·di·an** (ăm'ə-rĭn'dē-ən) s. amerindio, indio americano.
a·mi·a·bil·i·ty (ā'mē-ə-bĭl'ĭ-tē) s. amabilidad *f*.
a·mi·a·ble (ā'mē-ə-bəl) adj. *(good-natured)* amable, amistoso; *(congenial)* ameno, agradable.
a·mi·a·bly (ā'mē-ə-blē) adv. amablemente.

ã rey / ä año / b boca / ch chico / d dar / ĕ el / ē mil / g gato / h joya / hw juez / ī aire / k casa / kw cuan /

am·i·ca·ble (ăm′ĭ-kə-bəl) adj. amigable, amistoso.
a·mid (ə-mĭd′) prep. en medio de, entre, rodeado por.
a·mid·ships (ə-mĭd′shĭps′) o **a·mid·ship** (-shĭp′) adv. MA-RÍT. en medio del barco.
a·midst (ə-mĭdst′) prep. var. de **amid.**
a·mi·no acid (ə-mē′nŏ, ăm′ə-nŏ′) s. BIOQUÍM. aminoácido.
a·miss (ə-mĭs′) **I.** adj. fuera de orden, mal <*I find nothing a.* no encuentro nada mal> **II.** adv. equivocadamente, mal ♦ **to be a.** estar fuera de lugar <*a little love would not be a.* un poco de amor no estaría fuera de lugar> • **to go a.** salir mal • **to take a.** tomar a mal, interpretar mal <*don't take it a. if she corrects you* no lo tomes a mal si ella te corrige>.
am·i·ty (ăm′ĭ-tē) s. [pl. **-ties**] *(friendship)* amistad *f*; *(between nations)* concordia.
am·me·ter (ăm′mē′tər) s. ELEC. amperímetro.
am·mo (ăm′ō) s. MIL. munición *f.*
am·mo·nia (ə-mōn′yə) s. QUÍM. *(gas)* amoníaco; *(ammonium hydroxide)* hidróxido de amonio, agua amoniacal.
am·mo·ni·ac (ə-mō′nē-ăk′) adj. QUÍM. amónico, amoniacal.
ammonia water s. QUÍM. agua amoniacal.
am·mo·ni·um (ə-mō′nē-əm) s. QUÍM amonio.
ammonium chloride s. QUÍM. cloruro de amonio.
am·mu·ni·tion (ăm′yə-nĭsh′ən) s. ARM. municiones *f*; FIG. *(reasons)* argumentos <*the president's speech gave new a. to the opposition* el discurso del presidente le dio nuevos argumentos a la oposición>.
am·ne·sia (ăm-nē′zhə) s. amnesia.
am·ne·si·ac (ăm-nē′zē-ăk′, –zhē-) s. & adj. amnésico.
am·nes·ty (ăm′nĭ-stē) **I.** s. [pl. **-ties**] amnistía, indulto **II.** tr. **-tied, -ty·ing** indultar.
am·ni·ot·ic (ăm′nē-ŏt′ĭk) o **am·ni·on·ic** (-on′ĭk) adj. MED. amniótico.
a·moe·ba (ə-mē′bə) s. [pl. **-bas** o **-bae** (-bē)] ameba.
a·moe·bic (ə-mē′bĭk) adj. amébico, amíbico.
amoebic dysentery s. MED. disentería amibiana.
a·mok (ə-mŭk′, ə-mŏk′) adv. var. de **amuck.**
a·mong (ə-mŭng′) o **a·mongst** (ə-mŭngst′) prep. *(surrounded by)* en medio de, entre <*a. friends* entre amigos>; *(between one another)* uno con otro, entre <*the children quarreled a. themselves* los niños discutían entre ellos>.
a·mor·al (ā-môr′əl) adj. amoral.
a·mo·ral·i·ty (ā′mə-răl′ĭ-tē) s. amoralidad *f.*
am·o·rous (ăm′ər-əs) adj. *(full of love)* amoroso; *(in love)* enamoradizo.
a·mor·phous (ə-môr′fəs) adj. *(shapeless)* amorfo, informe; *(unclear)* vago, general.
am·or·ti·za·tion (ăm′ər-tĭ-zā′shən, ə-môr′tĭ-) s. amortización *f.*
am·or·tize (ăm′ər-tīz′, ə-môr′tīz′) tr. **-tized, -tiz·ing** amortizar.
a·mount (ə-mount′) **I.** s. cantidad *f*, monto **II.** intr. *(to add up)* subir a, sumar, ascender a <*the loss from the flood amounts to ten million dollars* la pérdida ocasionada por la inundación asciende a diez millones de dólares>; *(to be equivalent)* ser igual a, (venir a) ser lo mismo que <*keeping what belongs to another amounts to stealing* quedarse con lo que es ajeno es lo mismo que robar>.
am·per·age (ăm′pər-ĭj, ăm′pîr′ĭj) s. ELEC. amperaje *m.*
am·pere (ăm′pîr′) s. ELEC. amperio.
am·per·sand (ăm′pər-sănd′) s. el signo "&" que significa *and.*
am·phet·a·mine (ăm-fĕt′ə-mēn′, -mĭn) s. FARM. anfetamina.
am·phib·i·an (ăm-fĭb′ē-ən) **I.** s. ZOOL. anfibio; *(vehicle)* vehículo anfibio **II.** adj. anfibio.
am·phib·i·ous (ăm-fĭb′ē-əs) adj. anfibio.
am·phi·the·a·ter (ăm′fə-thē′ə-tər) s. anfiteatro.
am·pho·ra (ăm′fər-ə) s. [pl. **-pho·rae** (-fə-rē′) o **-pho·ras**] ánfora.
am·ple (ăm′pəl) adj. **-pler, -plest** *(spacious)* espacioso, amplio; *(large)* grande, generoso <*an a. reward* una recompensa generosa>; *(abundant)* copioso, abundante; *(adequate)* suficiente, adecuado.
am·pli·fi·ca·tion (ăm′plə-fĭ-kā′shən) s. *(act)* amplificación *f*, ampliación *f*; *(of an idea, thought)* explicación *f*, aclaración *f*; ELECTRÓN., FÍS. amplificación.

am·pli·fi·er (ăm′plə-fī′ər) s. amplificador *m*, ampliador *m*; ELECTRÓN., FÍS. amplificador.
am·pli·fy (ăm′plə-fī′) tr. **-fied, -fy·ing** *(to increase)* aumentar, ampliar; *(to expand)* desarrollar, comentar sobre; ELECTRÓN., FÍS. amplificar —intr. explayarse.
am·pli·tude (ăm′plĭ-tōod′, -tyōod′) s. *(magnitude)* amplitud *f*, extensión *f*; *(abundance)* abundancia; ASTRON., FÍS., RAD. amplitud.
amplitude modulation s. RAD. modulación de amplitud *f.*
am·ply (ăm′plē) adv. ampliamente.
am·poule o **am·pule** (ăm′pōol′, -pyōol′) s. FARM. ampolla, ampolleta.
am·pu·tate (ăm′pyə-tāt′) tr. **-tat·ed, -tat·ing** CIR. amputar.
am·pu·ta·tion (ăm′pyə-tā′shən) s. amputación *f.*
am·pu·tee (ăm′pyə-tē′) s. amputado.
a·muck (ə-mŭk′) adv. frenéticamente, furiosamente ♦ **to run a.** abandonarse a la furia, correr a ciegas.
am·u·let (ăm′yə-lĭt) s. amuleto, talismán *m.*
a·muse (ə-myōoz′) tr. **a·mused, a·mus·ing** *(to entertain)* entretener, distraer; *(to cause to laugh)* divertir ♦ **to a. one-self** divertirse, entretenerse.
a·muse·ment (ə-myōoz′mənt) s. *(pastime)* entretenimiento, pasatiempo; *(laughter)* diversión *f*, risa <*his joke caused a lot of a.* su broma causó mucha risa>.
a·mus·ing (ə-myōo′zĭng) adj. entretenido, divertido.
am·yl (ăm′əl) s. QUÍM. amilo.
amyl alcohol s. QUÍM. alcohol amílico.
an §G18 (ən, ăn) art. indef. [ú. antes de sonido vocal] un, una <*an egg* un huevo> <*an hour* una hora>.
An·a·bap·tist (ăn′ə-băp′tĭst) s. RELIG. anabaptista *mf.*
a·nach·ro·nism (ə-năk′rə-nĭz′əm) s. anacronismo.
a·nach·ro·nis·tic (ə-năk′rə-nĭs′tĭk) adj. anacrónico.
an·a·con·da (ăn′ə-kŏn′də) s. ZOOL. anaconda.
a·nae·mi·a (ə-nē′mē-ə) s. var. de **anemia.**
a·nae·mic (ə-nē′mĭk) adj. var. de **anemic.**
an·aer·o·bic (ăn′ə-rō′bĭk) adj. BIOL., BOT. anaerobio.
an·aes·the·sia (ăn′ĭs-thē′zhə) s. var. de **anesthesia.**
an·a·gram (ăn′ə-grăm′) s. anagrama *m* ♦ **anagrams** juego de anagramas.
a·nal (ā′nəl) adj. ANAT. anal.
an·al·ge·si·a (ăn′əl-jē′zē-ə) s. MED. analgesia.
an·al·ge·sic (ăn′əl-jē′zĭk) s. & adj. analgésico.
an·a·log (ăn′ə-lôg′) s. var. de **analogue.**
analog computer s. computadora analógica.
an·a·log·i·cal (ăn′ə-lŏj′ĭ-kəl) o **an·a·log·ic** (-ĭk) adj. analógico.
a·nal·o·gist (ə-năl′ə-jĭst) s. persona que razona por medio de analogías.
a·nal·o·gize (ə-năl′ə-jīz′) tr. **-gized, -giz·ing** explicar algo usando analogías —intr. pensar en forma analógica.
a·nal·o·gous (ə-năl′ə-gəs) adj. análogo, semejante.
an·a·logue (ăn′ə-lôg′) s. *(analogy)* palabra o cosa análoga; BIOL. órgano análogo.
a·nal·o·gy (ə-năl′ə-jē) s. [pl. **-gies**] *(correspondence)* analogía, semejanza <*there is an a. between the human heart and a pump* existe una analogía entre el corazón humano y una bomba>; *(correlation)* correlación *f* <*don't make an incorrect a. between the British and Roman empires* no hagas una correlación incorrecta entre los imperios británico y romano>.
an·al·pha·bet·ic (ăn-ăl′fə-bĕt′ĭk) adj. & s. analfabeto.
a·nal·y·sand (ə-năl′ĭ-sănd′) s. persona que está en tratamiento psicoanalítico.
an·a·lyse (ăn′ə-līz′) tr. G.B. var. de **analyze.**
a·nal·y·sis (ə-năl′ĭ-sĭs) s. [pl. **-ses** (-sēz′)] QUÍM. análisis *m*; *(critical study)* estudio (crítico); PSIC. psicoanálisis *m.*
an·a·lyst (ăn′ə-lĭst) s. *(one who analyzes)* analista *mf*; PSIC. psicoanalista *mf*, analista.
an·a·lyt·ic (ăn′ə-lĭt′ĭk) o **an·a·lyt·i·cal** (-ĭ-kəl) adj. analítico.
an·a·lyt·ics (ăn′ə-lĭt′ĭks) s. [ú. con v. sing.] LÓG. analítica.
an·a·lyze (ăn′ə-līz′) tr. **-lyzed, -lyz·ing** *(to examine)* analizar; PSIC. psicoanalizar.
an·a·lyz·er (ăn′ə-lī′zər) s. analizador *m.*
an·aph·ro·dis·i·a (ăn-ăf′rə-dĭz′ē-ə) s. anafrodisia.
an·ar·chic (ăn-är′kĭk) o **an·ar·chi·cal** (-kĭ-kəl) adj. anárquico.

---

ng inglés / ŏ la / ō bou / ô corre / oi oigo / ōo uno / ou auto / yōo ciudad / w hueco / y yo / z mismo

an·ar·chism (ăn′ər-kĭz′əm) s. POL. anarquismo.
an·ar·chist (ăn′ər-kĭst) s. anarquista *mf.*
an·ar·chis·tic (ăn′ər-kĭs′tĭk) adj. anárquico.
an·ar·chy (ăn′ər-kē) s. [pl. **-chies**] POL. anarquía.
a·nath·e·ma (ə-năth′ə-mə) s. [pl. **-mas**] RELIG. anatema *m;* FIG. *(curse)* persona *o* cosa odiada, anatema <*his name is a. to me* su nombre es anatema para mí>.
a·nath·e·ma·tize (ə-năth′ə-mə-tīz′) tr. **-tized, -tiz·ing** RELIG. anatemizar; FIG. *(to curse)* maldecir.
an·a·tom·i·cal (ăn′ə-tŏm′ĭ-kəl) *o* **an·a·tom·ic** (-tŏm′ĭk) adj. ANAT. anatómico.
a·nat·o·mist (ə-năt′ə-mĭst) s. anatomista *mf.*
a·nat·o·mize (ə-năt′ə-mīz′) tr. **-mized, -miz·ing** *(to dissect)* anatomizar, disecar; FIG. *(to analyze)* analizar.
a·nat·o·my (ə-năt′ə-mē) s. [pl. **-mies**] BIOL. *(structure)* anatomía; *(treatise)* tratado de anatomía; *(dissection)* disección *f; (skeleton)* esqueleto; *(analysis)* análisis (de obra, crimen) *m; (body)* cuerpo humano.
an·ces·tor (ăn′sĕs′tər) s. antepasado.
an·ces·tral (ăn-sĕs′trəl) adj. ancestral.
an·ces·try (ăn′sĕs′trē) s. [pl. **-tries**] *(lineage)* linaje *m; (race)* casta, raza.
an·chor (ăng′kər) I. s. MARÍT. ancla, áncora; FIG. *(pillar)* soporte *m,* pilar *m;* RAD., TELEV. locutor *m,* anunciador *m* ♦ **at a.** anclado • **to cast a.** echar anclas • **to weigh a.** levar anclas, zarpar II. tr. asegurar, sujetar <*let's a. the tent with spikes* sujetemos la carpa con escarpios> —intr. MARÍT. anclar, fondear.
an·chor·age (ăng′kər-ĭj) s. MARÍT. ancladero, fondeadero; *(action)* anclaje *m; (fee)* derecho de anclaje.
an·cho·rite (ăng′kə-rīt′) s. RELIG. anacoreta *m,* ermitaño.
an·chor·man (ăng′kər-măn′) s. [pl. **-men** (-mĕn′)] RAD., TE-LEV. locutor *m,* anunciador *m.*
an·chor·wom·an (ăng′kər-wōŏm′ən) s. [pl. **-wom·en** (-wĭm′ĭn)] RAD., TELEV. locutora, anunciadora.
an·cho·vy (ăn′chō′vē, ăn-chō′vē) s. [pl. **anchovy** *o* **-vies**] anchoa ♦ **a. paste** pasta de anchoas.
an·cient (ăn′shənt) I. adj. *(very old)* antiguo, vetusto; *(venerable)* venerable II. s. anciano ♦ **the ancients** *(peoples)* los antiguos, los antepasados; *(culture)* la antigüedad.
an·cil·lar·y (ăn′sə-lĕr′ē) adj. & s. [pl. **-ies**] subordinado, auxiliar *mf.*
and §G41 (ənd, ən, ănd) conj. y, e <*a long a. happy life* una vida larga y feliz> <*thoughts a. ideas* pensamientos e ideas>; de, a <*try a. find it* trata de encontrarlo> <*go a. see* anda a ver>.
An·da·lu·sian (ăn′də-lōŏ′zhən) adj. & s. andaluz *m.*
An·de·an (ăn′dē-ən) adj. andino.
An·des (ăn′dēz) s. Andes *m.*
and·i·ron (ănd′ī′ərn) s. morillo.
an·dro·gen (ăn′drə-jən) s. BIOL. andrógeno.
an·drog·e·nous (ăn-drŏj′ə-nəs) adj. andrógeno.
an·drog·y·nous (ăn-drŏj′ə-nəs) adj. andrógino.
an·droid (ăn′droid′) s. androide *m,* robot *m.*
An·drom·e·da (ăn-drŏm′ī-də) s. ASTRON., MITOL. Andrómeda.
an·ec·do·tal (ăn′ĭk-dōt′l) adj. anecdótico.
an·ec·dote (ăn′ĭk-dōt′) s. anécdota.
an·ec·dot·ic (ăn′ĭk-dŏt′ĭk) *o* **an·ec·dot·i·cal** (-ĭ-kəl) adj. anecdótico.
a·ne·mi·a (ə-nē′mē-ə) s. MED. anemia.
a·ne·mic (ə-nē′mĭk) adj. anémico.
a·ne·mom·e·ter (ăn′ə-mŏm′ī-tər) s. METEOR. anemómetro.
a·nem·o·ne (ə-nĕm′ə-nē) s. BOT. anémona ♦ **sea a.** ICT. actinia, anémona marina.
an·es·the·sia (ăn′ĭs-thē′zhə) s. MED. anestesia.
an·es·the·si·ol·o·gist (ăn′ĭs-thē′zē-ŏl′ə-jĭst) s. anestesiólogo.
an·es·the·si·ol·o·gy (ăn′ĭs-thē′zē-ŏl′ə-jē) s. MED. anestesiología.
an·es·thet·ic (ăn′ĭs-thĕt′ĭk) s. & adj. anestésico.
a·nes·the·tist (ə-nĕs′thĭ-tĭst) s. MED. anestesista *mf.*
a·nes·the·tize (ə-nĕs′thĭ-tīz′) tr. **-tized, -tiz·ing** anestesiar.
an·eu·rysm *o* **an·eu·rism** (ăn′yə-rĭz′əm) s. MED. aneurisma *m.*
a·new (ə-nōŏ′, ə-nyōŏ′) adv. *(again)* nuevamente, de nuevo;

(differently) de un modo nuevo, en forma diferente <*in each generation love is born a.* en cada generación el amor resurge en forma diferente>.
an·frac·tu·ous (ăn-frăk′chōŏ-əs) adj. anfractuoso, sinuoso.
an·gel (ăn′jəl) s. RELIG. ángel *m;* FIG., FAM. ángel <*my father is an a.* mi padre es un ángel>.
an·gel·fish (ăn′jəl-fĭsh′) s. [pl. **angelfish** *o* **-fish·es**] ICT. angelote *m.*
an·gel·ic (ăn-jĕl′ĭk) *o* **an·gel·i·cal** (-ĭ-kəl) adj. angélico, angelical.
an·ger (ăng′gər) I. s. ira, enojo II. tr. & intr. airar(se), enojar(se).
an·gi·na (ăn-jī′nə, ăn′jə-) s. MED. angina.
an·gle¹ (ăng′gəl) intr. **-gled, -gling** DEP. pescar con caña ♦ **to a. for** FIG., FAM. ir a la pesca de.
an·gle² (ăng′gəl) I. s. GEOM. ángulo; *(corner)* esquina, codo; *(point of view)* ángulo, punto de vista <*let's examine the problem from a new a.* examinemos el problema desde un punto de vista diferente>; *(plan)* plan <*he had a hidden a. to get what he wanted* él tenía un plan secreto para conseguir lo que quería> ♦ **at an a.** en ángulo • **at right angles** en ángulo recto II. tr. **-gled, -gling** *(to move)* poner *o* mover en ángulo; FIG. *(to bias)* dar un punto de vista parcial a (reporte, noticias) —intr. doblar *o* moverse en ángulo.
angle bracket s. IMPR. corchete *m o* paréntesis *m* angular (< >).
angle iron s. hierro angular, ángulo.
an·gler (ăng′glər) s. *(fisherman)* pescador (de caña y anzuelo) *m; (a schemer)* maquinador *m,* intrigante *mf;* ICT. alacrán marino *m,* pejesapo.
an·gler·fish (ăng′glər-fĭsh′) s. [pl. **anglerfish** *o* **-fish·es**] ICT. alacrán marino, pejesapo *m.*
an·gle·worm (ăng′gəl-wûrm′) s. lombriz *f.*
An·gli·can (ăng′glĭ-kən) adj. & s. RELIG. anglicano.
Anglican Church s. RELIG. Iglesia Anglicana.
An·gli·can·ism (ăng′glĭ-kə-nĭz′əm) s. RELIG. anglicanismo.
An·gli·cism *o* **an·gli·cism** (ăng′glĭ-sĭz′əm) s. FILOL. anglicismo; *(quality)* cualidad *f o* carácter *m* típicamente inglés.
An·gli·cist (ăng′glĭ-sĭst) s. anglicista *mf,* especialista en lingüística inglesa *mf.*
An·gli·cize *o* **an·gli·cize** (ăng′glĭ-sīz′) tr. & intr. **-cized, -ciz·ing** anglicanizar, hacer inglés.
an·gling (ăng′glĭng) s. DEP. pesca con caña.
An·glo (ăng′glō′) s. [pl. **-glos**] FAM. angloamericano.
An·glo-A·mer·i·can (ăng′glō-ə-mĕr′ĭ-kən) adj. & s. angloamericano.
An·glo·phile (ăng′glə-fīl′) *o* **An·glo·phil** (-fīl) s. & adj. anglófilo.
An·glo·phobe (ăng′glə-fōb′) s. & adj. anglófobo.
An·glo·phone (ăng′glə-fōn′) s. anglófono.
An·glo-Sax·on (ăng′glō-săk′sən) adj. & s. anglosajón *m.*
An·go·la (ăng-gō′lə) s. Angola.
An·go·lan (ăng-gō′lən) adj. & s. angoleño.
an·gri·ly (ăng′grə-lē) adv. con enojo, con ira.
an·gry (ăng′grē) adj. **-gri·er, -gri·est** *(incensed)* enojado, enfadado; *(menacing)* borrascoso, amenazador <*a. clouds* nubes amenazadoras>; MED. inflamado ♦ **to be a. at** *o* **about (something)** estar enojado por (algo) • **to be a. with (someone)** estar enojado con (alguien) • **to make (someone) a.** enojar (a alguien).
angst (ängkst) s. angustia, ansiedad *f.*
ang·strom (ăng′strəm) s. FÍS. angstróm *m.*
an·guish (ăng′gwĭsh) I. s. angustia, congoja II. tr. & intr. angustiar(se), acongojar(se).
an·guished (ăng′gwĭsht) adj. angustiado, acongojado.
an·gu·lar (ăng′gyə-lər) adj. *(having angles)* angular; *(gaunt)* anguloso.
an·gu·lar·i·ty (ăng′gyə-lăr′ĭ-tē) s. [pl. **-ties**] angularidad *f,* angulosidad *f* ♦ **angularities** recodos, esquinas.
an·gu·late (ăng′gyə-lĭt, -lāt′) I. adj. angulado, anguloso II. tr. & intr. (-lāt′) **-lat·ed, -lat·ing** doblar(se) en ángulo.
an·hy·dride (ăn-hī′drīd′) s. QUÍM. anhídrido.
an·hy·drous (ăn-hī′drəs) adj. QUÍM. anhidro.
an·il (ăn′ĭl) s. BOT. añil (planta, color, tintura) *m.*
an·ile (ăn′īl′, ā′nīl′) adj. caduca, vieja.

ã rey / ä año / b boca / ch chico / d dar / ĕ el / ē mil / g gato / h joya / hw juez / ī aire / k casa / kw cuan /

an·i·line *o* **an·i·lin** (ăn′ə-lĭn) s. QUÍM. anilina.
aniline dye s. color *m o* tintura de anilina.
an·i·ma (ăn′ə-mə) s. alma, espíritu *m*
an·i·mad·ver·sion (ăn′ə-măd-vûr′zhən) s. *(act)* animadversión *f,* animosidad; *(remark)* reprobación *f,* reproche *m.*
an·i·mal (ăn′ə-məl) **I.** s. ZOOL. animal *m;* FIG. *(brute)* animal, bruto **II.** adj. ZOOL. animal; *(sensual)* sensual, carnal.
an·i·mal·cule (ăn′ə-măl′kyōōl) s. animáculo (animal microscópico).
animal husbandry s. zootecnia, cría de animales domésticos.
an·i·mal·ism (ăn′ə-mə-lĭz′əm) s. animalismo.
an·i·mal·is·tic (ăn′ə-mə-lĭs′tĭk) adj. como animal, de animal.
an·i·mal·i·ty (ăn′ə-măl′ĭ-tē) s. *(characteristics)* animalidad *f;* *(animal kingdom)* reino animal.
animal kingdom s. reino animal.
animal magnetism s. *(hypnotism)* hipnotismo, mesmerismo; *(magnetic presence)* magnetismo animal; *(sensualism)* sensualismo, atractivo animal.
an·i·mate (ăn′ə-māt′) **I.** tr. **-mat·ed, -mat·ing** *(to fill with life)* animar, dar vida a; *(to enliven)* infundir vida a, vivificar; *(to encourage)* alentar, infundir ánimo *o* valor; CINEM. animar (dibujos) **II.** adj. (-mĭt) animado, viviente.
an·i·mat·ed (ăn′ə-mā′tĭd) adj. *(filled with activity)* animado, vivaz; *(moving)* animado, que se mueve ♦ **a. cartoon** CINEM. dibujos animados.
an·i·ma·tion (ăn′ə-mā′shən) s. *(act)* animación *f,* *(liveliness)* vivacidad *f,* espíritu *m;* CINEM. *(art, process)* animación; *(cartoon)* película de dibujos animados ♦ **suspended a.** BIOL. muerte aparente.
an·i·ma·tor *o* **an·i·mat·er** (ăn′ə-mā′tər) s. animador *m;* *(of cartoons)* dibujante *m,* animador *m.*
an·i·mism (ăn′ə-mĭz′əm) s. FILOS, RELIG. animismo.
an·i·mos·i·ty (ăn′ə-mŏs′ĭ-tē) s. [pl. **-ties**] animosidad *f,* hostilidad.
an·i·mus (ăn′ə-məs) s. *(intention)* ánimo, intención *f;* *(animosity)* animosidad *f,* aversión *f.*
an·i·on (ăn′ī′on) s. QUÍM., FÍS. anión *m,* ion negativo.
an·ise (ăn′ĭs) s. BOT. anís *m.*
an·i·seed (ăn′ĭ-sēd′) s. BOT. anís *m,* simiente de anís *f.*
an·i·sette (ăn′ĭ-sĕt′) s. anisete *m,* licor de anís *m.*
an·kle (ăng′kəl) s. tobillo.
an·kle·bone (ăng′kəl-bōn′) s. ANAT. hueso del tobillo, taba.
an·klet (ăng′klĭt) s. *(ornament)* ajorca para el tobillo; *(socks)* media tobillera.
an·ky·lose (ăng′kə-lōs′) tr. & intr. **-losed, -los·ing** MED. anquilosar(se).
an·nals (ăn′əlz) s.pl. *(records)* anales *m;* *(history)* crónica; *(journal)* anales *m,* actas *f.*
an·nat·to (ə-nä′tō) s. [pl. **-tos**] BOT. *(tree, seeds)* onoto, bija; *(dyestuff)* bijol *m.*
an·neal (ə-nēl′) tr. TEC. recocer, templar (cristal, metales); FIG. *(to temper)* endurecer, fortalecer (el espíritu).
an·ne·lid (ăn′ə-lĭd) adj. & s. ZOOL. anélido.
an·nex **I.** tr. (ə-nĕks′) *(to incorporate)* anexar, anexionar; *(to add to)* agregar, añadir **II.** s. (ăn′ĕks′) *(building)* pabellón *m,* ala (de un edificio); *(appendix)* anexo, anejo.
an·nex·a·tion (ăn′ĭk-sā′shən) s. anexión *f,* unión *f.*
an·ni·hi·late (ə-nī′ə-lāt′) tr. **-lat·ed, -lat·ing** aniquilar, reducir a la nada.
an·ni·hi·la·tion (ə-nī′ə-lā′shən) s. aniquilación *f,* aniquilamiento.
an·ni·hi·la·tor (ə-nī′ə-lā′tər) s. aniquilador *m.*
an·ni·ver·sa·ry (ăn′ə-vûr′sə-rē) s. [pl. **-ries**] aniversario ♦ **a. party** fiesta de aniversario.
an·no·tate (ăn′ə-tāt′) tr. **-tat·ed, -tat·ing** *(to gloss)* anotar —intr. poner notas.
an·no·ta·tion (ăn′ə-tā′shən) s. anotación *f,* nota.
an·no·ta·tor (ăn′ə-tā′tər) s. anotador *m,* comentador *m.*
an·nounce (ə-nouns′) tr. **-nounced, -nounc·ing** anunciar, declarar.
an·nounce·ment (ə-nouns′mənt) s. anuncio, declaración *f.*
an·nounc·er (ə-noun′sər) s. *(promulgator)* anunciador *m;* RAD., TELEV. anunciador, locutor *m.*

an·noy (ə-noi′) tr. *(to irritate)* molestar, irritar; *(to bother)* fastidiar —intr. ser molesto.
an·noy·ance (ə-noi′əns) s. *(irritation)* molestia, irritación *f;* *(bother)* fastidio.
an·noy·ing (ə-noi′ĭng) adj. molesto, irritante.
an·nu·al (ăn′yōō-əl) **I.** adj. anual **II.** s. *(yearbook)* publicación anual *f,* anuario; BOT. planta anual.
an·nu·al·ly (ăn′yōō-ə-lē) adj. anualmente, cada año.
annual ring s. BOT. capa cortical, anillo de corteza.
an·nu·i·tant (ə-nōō′ĭ-tənt) s. censualista *mf,* rentista *mf.*
an·nu·i·ty (ə-nōō′ĭ-tē, -nyōō′) s. [pl. **-ties**] FIN. *(annual payment)* anualidad *f;* *(income for life)* renta vitalicia.
an·nul (ə-nŭl′) tr. **-nulled, -nul·ling** *(to nullify)* anular, invalidar; *(to cancel)* cancelar.
an·nu·lar (ăn′yə-lər) adj. anular, en forma de anillo ♦ **a. eclipse** ASTRON. eclipse anular.
an·nul·ment (ə-nŭl′mənt) s. *(invalidation)* anulación *f,* invalidación *f;* *(cancellation)* cancelación *f.*
an·nun·ci·ate (ə-nŭn′sē-āt′) tr. **-at·ed, -at·ing** anunciar, proclamar.
an·nun·ci·a·tion (ə-nŭn′sē-ā′shən) s. anunciación *f,* anuncio.
an·nun·ci·a·tor (ə-nŭn′sē-ā′tər) s. *(announcer)* anunciador *m;* ELEC. indicador *m,* anunciador (de llamadas telefónicas).
an·ode (ăn′ōd) s. ELEC., FÍS. ánodo.
an·o·dize (ăn′ə-dīz′) tr. **-dized, -diz·ing** FÍS., QUÍM. anodizar.
an·o·dyne (ăn′ə-dīn′) adj. & s. MED. anodino, calmante *m.*
a·noint (ə-noint′) tr. *(to apply oil to)* untar; RELIG. ungir.
a·noint·ment (ə-noint′mənt) s. RELIG. unción *f,* ungimiento *m.*
a·nom·a·lous (ə-nŏm′ə-ləs) adj. anómalo, irregular.
a·nom·a·ly (ə-nŏm′ə-lē) s. [pl. **-lies**] anomalía, irregularidad *f.*
a·non (ə-nŏn′) adv. *(again)* luego, otra vez; ANT. *(soon)* pronto, en seguida.
an·o·nym (ăn′ə-nĭm′) s. *(person)* anónimo; *(pseudonym)* seudónimo.
an·o·nym·i·ty (ăn′ə-nĭm′ĭ-tē) s. anonimato.
a·non·y·mous (ə-nŏn′ə-məs) adj. anónimo.
a·noph·e·les (ə-nŏf′ə-lēz′) s. ENTOM. anofeles *m.*
an·o·rec·tic (ăn′ə-rĕk′tĭk) *o* **an·o·ret·ic** (-rĕt′ĭk) *o* **an·o·rex·ic** (-rĕk′sĭk) MED. **I.** adj. falto de apetito **II.** s. persona que sufre de anorexia.
an·o·rex·i·a (ăn′ə-rĕk′sē-ə) s. MED. anorexia.
an·oth·er §G38 (ə-nŭ*th*′ər) **I.** adj. *(additional)* otro <*may I have a. glass of milk, please?* ¿me podrías dar otro vaso de leche, por favor?>; *(different)* diferente, distinto <*show me a. kind* muéstreme otra clase distinta>; *(changed)* distinto, cambiado <*he's been a. person since he got that job* es una persona distinta desde que consiguió ese trabajo>; *(more)* adicional, más <*we need a. two men* necesitamos dos hombres más>; *(equal to)* igual que, otro <*he thinks he is a. Caruso* él se cree otro Caruso> ♦ **a. time** más tarde, más adelante **II.** pron. *(a different one)* otro <*this pen doesn't write, please give me a.* esta pluma no escribe; por favor, dame otra>; *(an additional one)* otro más, uno más <*she ate an apple and then asked for a.* comió una manzana y luego pidió una más> ♦ **one a.** uno a otro, unos a otros.
an·swer (ăn′sər) **I.** s. *(reply)* respuesta, contestación *f;* *(solution)* solución *f,* resultado; *(reason)* explicación *f,* razón *f;* FOR. réplica, contestación a la demanda ♦ **to know all the answers** FIG. saberlo todo **II.** intr. *(to respond)* dar contestación, responder; *(to suffice)* servir; *(to match)* corresponder <*a car answering to that description* un automóvil que corresponde a esa descripción> ♦ **to a. back** responder con insolencia —tr. *(to reply to)* responder a, contestar a; *(to respond correctly to)* resolver, solucionar (problema, enigma); *(to correspond to)* corresponder a ♦ **a. for** *(a person)* responder por, respaldar; *(to be liable)* ser responsable por ♦ **to a. to the name of** responder al nombre de, tener por nombre.
an·swer·a·ble (ăn′sər-ə-bəl) adj. *(accountable)* responsable <*you are a. for him* tú eres responsable por él>; *(solvable)* contestable, soluble.

---

answering machine s. contestador automático (de teléfono).

answering service s. servicio que interrumpe las llamadas telefónicas y toma recados para el número llamado.

answer phone s. G.B. contestador automático (de teléfono).

ant (ănt) s. hormiga.

ant·ac·id (ănt-ăs'ĭd) adj. & s. antiácido.

an·tag·o·nism (ăn-tăg'ə-nĭz'əm) s. antagonismo, rivalidad *f.*

an·tag·o·nist (ăn-tăg'ə-nĭst) s. antagonista *mf*, rival *mf.*

an·tag·o·nis·tic (ăn-tăg'ə-nĭs'tĭk) adj. antagónico, hostil.

an·tag·o·nize (ăn-tăg'ə-nīz') tr. **-nized, -niz·ing** *(to provoke hostility)* provocar la hostilidad de; *(to annoy)* contrariar.

Ant·arc·tic (ănt-ärk'tĭk, -är'tĭk) I. adj. antártico ♦ **A. Circle** círculo (polar) antártico II. s. ♦ **the A.** la Antártida.

Ant·arc·ti·ca (ănt-ärk'tĭ-kə, -är'tĭ-) s. Antártida.

an·te (ăn'tē) I. s. *(stake)* apuesta inicial (en póker); JER. *(share)* cuota, pago II. tr. **-ted** *o* **-teed, -te·ing** *(to bet)* apostar (en póker); JER. *(to pay)* pagar.

ant·eat·er (ănt'ē'tər) s. oso hormiguero.

an·te·bel·lum (ăn'tē-běl'əm) adj. EE. UU., HIST. antes de la guerra civil.

an·te·cede (ăn'tĭ-sēd') tr. & intr. **-ced·ed, -ced·ing** anteceder, antecede (a), preceder (a).

an·te·ce·dence (ăn'tĭ-sēd'ns) s. antecedencia, precedencia.

an·te·ce·dent (ăn'tĭ-sēd'nt) I. adj. antecedente II. s. GRAM., LÓG., MAT. antecedente *m* ♦ **antecedents** antepasados.

an·te·cham·ber (ăn'tē-chām'bər) s. antecámara, antesala.

an·te·date (ăn'tĭ-dāt') I. tr. **-dat·ed, -dat·ing** preceder, anteceder (en tiempo); *(predate)* antedatar II. s. antedata.

an·te·di·lu·vi·an (ăn'tĭ-də-lōō'vē-ən) adj. antediluviano; FIG. *(antiquated)* anticuado, muy viejo.

an·te·lope (ăn'tl-ōp') s. [pl. **antelope** *o* **-lopes**] antílope (animal, piel) *m.*

an·te·me·rid·i·an (ăn'tē-mə-rĭd'ē-ən) adj. antemeridiano, matutino.

an·ten·na (ăn-těn'ə) s. [pl. **-ten·nae** (-těn'ē)] ZOOL. antena; RAD. [pl. **-nas**] antena.

an·te·pe·nul·ti·mate (ăn'tē-pĭ-nŭl'tə-mĭt) I. adj. antepenúltimo II. s. GRAM. antepenúltima sílaba.

an·te·ri·or (ăn-tîr'ē-ər) adj. anterior.

an·te·room (ăn'tē-rōōm', -rōōm') s. antesala, sala de espera.

an·them (ăn'thəm) s. *(hymn)* himno; RELIG. antífona, motete *m.*

an·ther (ăn'thər) s. BOT. antera, borlilla.

ant·hill (ănt'hĭl') s. hormiguero (en forma de montículo).

an·thol·o·gist (ăn-thŏl'ə-jĭst) s. antólogo.

an·thol·o·gize (ăn-thŏl'ə-jīz') tr. **-gized, -giz·ing** compilar, recopilar.

an·thol·o·gy (ăn-thŏl'ə-jē) s. [pl. **-gies**] antología.

an·thra·cite (ăn'thrə-sīt') s. antracita.

an·thrax (ăn'thrăks') s. MED., VET. ántrax *m.*

an·thro·po·cen·tric (ăn'thrə-pə-sěn'trĭk) adj. FILOS. antropocéntrico.

an·thro·poid (ăn'thrə-poid') adj. & s. antropoideo.

an·thro·po·log·ic (ăn'thrə-pə-lŏj'ĭk) *o* **an·thro·po·log·i·cal** (-ĭ-kəl) adj. antropológico.

an·thro·pol·o·gist (ăn'thrə-pŏl'ə-jĭst) s. antropólogo.

an·thro·pol·o·gy (ăn'thrə-pŏl'ə-jē) s. antropología.

an·thro·po·mor·phism (ăn'thrə-pə-môr'fĭz'əm) s. antropomorfismo.

an·thro·po·mor·phous (ăn'thrə-pə-môr'fəs) adj. antropomorfo.

an·ti (ăn'tī, -tē) s. FAM. persona que está en contra de un grupo, plan, propuesta *o* práctica.

an·ti·a·bor·tion (ăn'tē-ə-bôr'shən) adj. que se opone al aborto.

an·ti·air·craft (ăn'tē-âr'krăft') adj. antiaéreo.

an·ti·A·mer·i·can (ăn'tē-ə-měr'ĭ-kən) adj. antiamericano.

an·ti·bac·te·ri·al (ăn'tē-băk-tîr'ē-əl) adj. MED. antibacteriano, antibactérico.

an·ti·bal·lis·tic missile (ăn'tē-bə-lĭs'tĭk) s. MIL. proyectil antibalístico.

an·ti·bi·ot·ic (ăn'tē-bī-ŏt'ĭk) s. & adj. MED. antibiótico.

an·ti·bod·y (ăn'tĭ-bŏd'ē) s. [pl. **-ies**] BIOQUÍM. anticuerpo.

an·tic (ăn'tĭk) I. s. *(caper)* travesura; *(prank)* jugarreta II. adj. extravagante.

an·ti·christ (ăn'tĭ-krīst') s. TEO. anticristo.

an·tic·i·pate (ăn-tĭs'ə-pāt') tr. **-pat·ed, -pat·ing** *(to foresee)* anticipar, prever; *(to forestall)* adelantarse, anticiparse a <*to a. a point in an argument* anticiparse a un punto en una discusión>; *(to prevent)* impedir, prevenir <*I always try to a. problems* siempre trato de prevenir los problemas>.

an·tic·i·pa·tion (ăn-tĭs'ə-pā'shən) s. *(act)* anticipación *f*; *(expectation)* expectación *f*, esperanza ♦ **in a.** anticipadamente, de antemano.

an·tic·i·pa·to·ry (ăn-tĭs'ə-pə-tôr'ē) adj. anticipante.

an·ti·cler·i·cal (ăn'tē-klěr'ĭ-kəl) adj. anticlerical.

an·ti·cler·i·cal·ism (ăn'tē-klěr'ĭ-kə-lĭz'əm) s. anticlericalismo.

an·ti·cli·mac·tic (ăn'tē-klī-măk'tĭk) adj. decepcionante.

an·ti·cli·max (ăn'tē-klī'măks') s. anticlímax, decepción *f.*

an·ti·cline (ăn'tĭ-klīn') s. GEOL. anticlinal *m.*

an·ti·co·ag·u·lant (ăn'tē-kō-ăg'yə-lənt) s. & adj. FARM. anticoagulante *m.*

an·ti·co·lo·ni·al·ist (ăn'tē-kə-lō'nē-ə-lĭst) s. & adj. anticolonialista *mf.*

an·ti·com·mu·nist (ăn'tē-kŏm'yə-nĭst) s. & adj. anticomunista *mf.*

an·ti·cy·clone (ăn'tē-sī'klōn') s. METEOR. anticiclón *m.*

an·ti·de·pres·sant (ăn'tē-dĭ-prěs'ənt) s. FARM. antidepresivo.

an·ti·dote (ăn'tĭ-dōt') s. antídoto.

an·ti·es·tab·lish·ment (ăn'tē-ĭ-stăb'lĭsh-mənt) adj. que es hostil a los principios sociales, políticos o económicos convencionales.

an·ti·freeze (ăn'tĭ-frēz') s. anticongelante *m.*

an·ti·gen (ăn'tĭ-jən) s. MED. antígeno.

an·ti·he·ro (ăn'tĭ-hîr'ō) s. [pl. **-roes**] LIT. protagonista *m* que es todo lo contrario del héroe clásico.

an·ti·his·ta·mine (ăn'tē-hĭs'tə-mēn', -mĭn) s. FARM. antihistamínico.

an·ti·in·flam·ma·tory (ăn'tē-ĭn-flăm'ə-tôr'ē) adj. antiinflamatorio.

an·ti·in·fla·tion·ar·y (ăn'tē-ĭn-flā'shə-něr'ē) adj. antiinflacionista.

an·ti·knock (ăn'tĭ-nŏk') s. antidetonante *m.*

An·til·les (ăn-tĭl'ēz) s. Antillas ♦ **Greater A.** Antillas Mayores • **Lesser A.** Antillas Menores (con excepción de las Bahamas).

an·ti·mag·net·ic (ăn'tē-măg-nět'ĭk) adj. antimagnético.

an·ti·ma·lar·i·al (ăn'tē-mə-lâr'ē-əl) FARM. I. adj. antipalúdico II. s. droga antipalúdica.

an·ti·mat·ter (ăn'tĭ-măt'ər) s. FÍS. antimateria.

an·ti·mo·ny (ăn'tə-mō'nē) s. QUÍM. antimonio.

an·ti·nu·cle·ar (ăn'tē-nōō'klē-ər, -nyōō'-) adj. antinuclear.

An·ti·och (ăn'tē-ŏk') s. Antioquía.

an·ti·ox·i·dant (ăn'tē-ŏk'sĭ-dnt) s. QUÍM. antioxidante *m.*

an·ti·par·ti·cle (ăn'tē-pär'tĭ-kəl) s. FÍS. antipartícula.

an·ti·pa·thet·ic (ăn-tĭp'ə-thět'ĭk) adj. *(averse)* averso, contrario; *(causing antipathy)* antipático.

an·tip·a·thy (ăn-tĭp'ə-thē) s. [pl. **-thies**] antipatía, aversión *f.*

an·ti·per·son·nel (ăn'tē-pûr'sə-něl') adj. MIL. antipersonal.

an·ti·per·spi·rant (ăn'tē-pûr'spər-ənt) s. *(perspiration suppressant)* antisudoral *m*; *(deodorant)* desodorante *m.*

an·tip·o·des (ăn-tĭp'ə-dēz') s.pl. antípodas *f.*

an·ti·pol·lu·tion (ăn'tē-pə-lōō'shən) adj. contra la contaminación (del aire, agua).

an·ti·py·ret·ic (ăn'tē-pī-rět'ĭk) adj. & s. FARM. antipirético.

an·ti·quar·i·an (ăn'tĭ-kwâr'ē-ən) s. anticuario.

an·ti·quar·y (ăn'tĭ-kwěr'ē) s. [pl. **-ies**] anticuario.

an·ti·quate (ăn'tĭ-kwāt') tr. **-quat·ed, -quat·ing** anticuar.

an·ti·quat·ed (ăn'tĭ-kwā'tĭd) adj. *(obsolete)* anticuado; *(aged)* añoso, viejo.

an·tique (ăn-tēk') I. adj. *(ancient)* antiguo; *(archaic)* arcaico, primitivo; *(old)* viejo, anticuado II. s. antigüedad *f*, antigualla III. tr. **-tiqued, -tiqu·ing** dar aspecto de antigüedad a.

an·tiq·ui·ty (ăn-tĭk'wĭ-tē) s. [pl. **-ties**] antigüedad *f*, tiempos antiguos ♦ **antiquities** antigüedades.

an·ti·rust (ăn'tē-rŭst') adj. & s. antioxidante *m.*

ã rey / ä año / b boca / ch chico / d dar / ĕ el / ē mil / g gato / h joya / hw juez / ī aire / k casa / kw cuan /

an·ti-Sem·ite (ăn'tē-sĕm'īt') s. antisemita *mf.*
an·ti-Se·mit·ic (ăn'tē-sə-mĭt'ĭk) adj. antisemítico, antisemita.
an·ti-Sem·i·tism (ăn'tē-sĕm'ĭ-tĭz'əm) s. antisemitismo.
an·ti·sep·tic (ăn'tĭ-sĕp'tĭk) I. adj. *(germ-free)* antiséptico; *(clean)* limpio; *(austere)* austero II. s. antiséptico.
an·ti·se·rum (ăn'tĭ-sîr'əm) s. [pl. **-rums** *o* **-ra** (-rə)] BIOQUÍM. antisuero.
an·ti·skid (ăn'tē-skĭd') adj. antideslizante.
an·ti·slav·e·ry (ăn'tē-slā'və-rē, -slāv'rē) adj. en contra de la esclavitud, antiesclavista.
an·ti·so·cial (ăn'tē-sō'shəl) adj. antisocial.
an·ti·spas·mod·ic (ăn'tē-spăz-mŏd'ĭk) adj. & s. FARM. antiespasmódico.
an·ti·sub·ma·rine (ăn'tē-sŭb'mə-rēn') adj. antisubmarino.
an·ti·tank (ăn'tē-tăngk') adj. MIL. antitanque.
an·ti·ter·ror·ism (ăn'tē-tĕr'ə-rĭz'əm) s. antiterrorismo.
an·ti·theft device (ăn'tē-thĕft') s. dispositivo *o* sistema antirrobo *m.*
an·tith·e·sis (ăn-tĭth'ĭ-sĭs) s. [pl. **-ses** (-sēz')] antítesis *f,* oposición *f,* contraste *m.*
an·ti·thet·i·cal (ăn'tĭ-thĕt'ĭ-kəl) adj. *(marked by antithesis)* antitético; *(directly opposed)* opuesto, contrario.
an·ti·tox·ic (ăn'tē-tŏk'sĭk) adj. FARM. antitóxico.
an·ti·tox·in (ăn'tē-tŏk'sĭn) s. FARM. antitoxina.
an·ti·trust (ăn'tē-trŭst') adj. contra los monopolios, antimonopolio.
an·ti·ven·in (ăn'tē-vĕn'ən) s. contraveneno.
ant·ler (ănt'lər) s. asta, mogote *m.*
an·to·nym (ăn'tə-nĭm') s. GRAM. antónimo.
an·trum (ăn'trəm) s. [pl. **-tra** (-trə)] ANAT. cavidad *f.*
Ant·werp (ănt'wûrp') s. Amberes.
a·nus (ā'nəs) s. ANAT. ano.
an·vil (ăn'vĭl) s. ANAT., MEC. yunque *m.*
anx·i·e·ty (ăng-zī'ĭ-tē) s. [pl. **-ties**] *(apprehension)* ansiedad *f,* ansia; *(angst)* ansiedad, angustia; *(eagerness)* anhelo, afán *m.*
anx·ious (ăngk'shəs) adj. *(worried)* ansioso, inquieto; *(eager)* deseoso, anhelante.
anx·ious·ly (ăngk'shəs-lē) adj. *(worried)* ansiosamente; *(uneasily)* inquietamente; *(eagerly)* anhelosamente.
an·y §G36 (ĕn'ē) I. adj. *(one)* cualquier *<take a. book you want* tome cualquier libro que le guste>; *(some)* algún *<do you have a. doubt?* ¿tienes alguna duda?>; [en oraciones negativas solamente] algún, ningún *<I do not have a. question* no tengo ninguna pregunta *o* no tengo pregunta alguna *<there isn't a. reason* no hay ninguna razón *o* no hay razón alguna>; [en el sentido partitivo, el adjetivo *any* generalmente no se traduce] *<have you got a. change?* ¿tienes cambio?> *<is there a. mail for me?* ¿hay correo para mí?>; *(every)* cualquiera, todo *<we must avoid a. contact* debemos evitar todo contacto> *<a. form of injustice is unacceptable* cualquier forma de injusticia es inaceptable> ✦ **a. minute** de un momento a otro, pronto • **at a. cost** a toda costa • **at a. rate** de todas maneras, de todos modos • **at a. time** *(any time)* a cualquier hora, en cualquier momento; *(ever)* alguna vez *<did you at a. time think you'd make it?* ¿pensaste alguna vez que lo lograrías?> • **in a. case** en todo caso, de todos modos II. pron. alguno, cualquiera *<I'd eat another apple, have you got a. left?* comería otra manzana, ¿te queda alguna?> *<take a. you like* toma cualquiera que te guste>; [en oraciones negativas solamente] ninguno, ninguna *<I don't recognize a. of them* no reconozco a ninguno de ellos> ✦ **if a.** si los hay *<freight charges, if a., will be added to the invoice* los gastos de flete, si los hay, se agregarán a la factura> III. adv. algo, de algún modo *<do you feel a. better?* ¿te sientes algo mejor?>; [en oraciones negativas solamente] nada, para nada *<I still don't feel a. better* todavía no me siento nada mejor> *<it didn't bother me a.* no me molestó para nada>; [el adverbio *any* no se traduce en oraciones negativas *o* interrogativas cuando refuerza el sentido de otro adverbio] *<I can't run a. faster* no puedo correr más rápido> *<don't do it a. more* no lo hagas más> ✦ **a. longer** más tiempo, todavía • **not . . . a. more** no . . . más, ya no *<I am not young a. more* ya no soy joven más>.

an·y·bod·y (ĕn'ē-bŏd'ē) I. pron. cualquiera, quienquiera, todo el mundo, cualquier persona *<a. could do it* cualquiera podría hacerlo>; [en oraciones interrogativas] alguien, alguno *<did you see a.?* ¿viste a alguien?>; [en oraciones negativas] ninguno, nadie *<I didn't see a.* no vi a nadie> II. s. alguien *m,* personaje (persona de importancia) *m.*
an·y·how (ĕn'ē-hou') adv. *(even so)* de todas maneras, de todos modos *<it was raining, but I walked to the house a.* llovía, pero caminé hasta la casa de todos modos>; *(carelessly)* descuidadamente, de cualquier manera, de cualquier modo.
an·y·more (ĕn'ē-môr') adv. [en oraciones negativas] nunca más, ya más, ya no *<I don't run a.* ya no corro más>; [en oraciones interrogativas] aún, todavía *<do you run a.?* ¿corres todavía?>.
an·y·one (ĕn'ē-wŭn') pron. consulte **anybody.**
an·y·place (ĕn'ē-plās') adv. consulte **anywhere.**
an·y·thing (ĕn'ē-thĭng') I. pron. [en oraciones interrogativas] algo, alguna cosa *<are you doing a. now?* ¿estás haciendo algo ahora?>; [en ciertas oraciones negativas] nada, ninguna cosa *<I can't see a.* no veo nada>; [en oraciones afirmativas] cualquier cosa, todo lo que *<take a. you like* toma todo lo que quieras> ✦ **a. else?** ¿algo más?, ¿alguna otra cosa? • **like a.** FAM. a más no poder II. adv. algo parecido a, como *<is she a. like her mother?* ¿es ella como su mamá?> ✦ **a. but** para nada, todo menos *<he's a. but bright* él es todo menos inteligente *o* él no es inteligente para nada>.
an·y·time (ĕn'ē-tīm') adv. a cualquier hora, en cualquier momento.
an·y·way (ĕn'ē-wā') adv. *(at any rate)* de cualquier manera, de cualquier modo; *(just the same)* lo mismo, de todos modos *<the roads were slippery but we drove a.* las carreteras estaban resbalosas pero manejamos lo mismo>.
an·y·ways (ĕn'ē-wāz') adv. FAM. var. de **anyway.**
an·y·where (ĕn'ē-hwâr') adv. [en oraciones afirmativas] dondequiera, a *o* en cualquier sitio, a *o* en cualquier parte *<I can meet you a. you say* nos podemos encontrar dondequiera que tú digas>; [en oraciones negativas] en, a, *o* por ninguna parte, en, a, *o* por ningún lado *<I'm not going a.* yo no voy a ninguna parte>; [en oraciones interrogativas] en algún lugar, en alguna parte *<do you see him a.?* ¿lo ves en alguna parte?> ✦ **a. else** [en oraciones afirmativas] en cualquier otro sitio; [en oraciones negativas] en ningún otro sitio *o* parte *<you won't find anything better a. else* no encontrará nada mejor en ninguna otra parte> • **a. from** FAM. entre *<you can save a. from five to ten dollars* puedes ahorrar entre cinco y diez dólares>.
an·y·wise (ĕn'ē-wīz') adv. de cualquier modo.
A-OK *o* **A-o·kay** (ā'ō-kā') adj. & adv. perfecto, excelente.
A-one *o* **A-1** (ā'wŭn') adj. FAM. de primera clase, excelente.
a·or·ta (ā-ôr'tə) s. [pl. **-tas** *o* **-tae** (-tē)] ANAT. aorta.
a·pace (ə-pās') adv. rápidamente, velozmente.
a·part (ə-pärt') I. adv. *(at a distance)* aparte, a distancia *<they stood three feet a. from one another* se pararon a tres pies de distancia uno de otro>; *(to either side)* a un lado; *(in separate pieces)* separadamente ✦ **a. from** aparte de, con la excepción de • **to come a.** desprenderse, desunirse • **to fall a.** *(to crumble)* caerse a pedazos, descomponerse; FIG. *(to break down)* venirse abajo, quedar moralmente destrozado • **to keep a.** apartar, separar • **to take a.** desarmar, desmontar • **to tear a.** despedazar, destrozar • **to tell a.** distinguir, diferenciar • **to stand a.** *(to be isolated)* mantenerse apartado; *(to excel)* distinguirse • **to set a.** reservar, poner a un lado II. adj. aparte, separado.
apart from prep. *(with the exception of)* aparte de, con la excepción de; *(besides)* además de.
a·part·heid (ə-pärt'hīt', -hāt') s. política de segregación racial (esp. en África del Sur).
a·part·ment (ə-pärt'mənt) s. *(residence)* departamento, apartamento; *(room)* cuarto, habitación *m.*
apartment house s. casa *o* edificio de departamentos.
ap·a·thet·ic (ăp'ə-thĕt'ĭk) adj. apático, indiferente.
ap·a·thy (ăp'ə-thē) s. apatía, indiferencia.
ape (āp) I. s. ZOOL. mono; FIG. *(imitator)* imitador *m,* imita-

---

ng **inglés** / ŏ **la** / ō **bou** / ô **corre** / oi **oigo** / ōō **uno** / ou **auto** / yōō **ciudad** / w **hueco** / y **yo** / z **mismo**

monos *mf*; FAM. *(oaf)* persona torpe **II.** tr. **aped, ap·ing** imitar, remedar.

ape-man (ăp'măn') s. [pl. **-men** (-měn')] hombre mono.

Ap·en·nines (ăp'ə-nīnz') s. GEOG. Apeninos.

a·pé·ri·tif (ä-pěr'ī-tēf') s. aperitivo.

ap·er·ture (ăp'ər-chər) s. *(opening)* abertura; ÓPT. abertura.

a·pex (ā'pĕks') s. [pl. **a·pex·es** *o* **a·pi·ces** (ā'pĭ-sēz', ăp'ĭ-)] *(vertex)* ápice *m*, cima; GEOM. vértice *m*.

a·phaer·e·sis (ə-fĕr'ĭ-sĭs) s. GRAM. aféresis *f*.

a·pha·sia (ə-fā'zhə) s. MED. afasia.

a·phid (ā'fĭd, ăf'ĭd) s. ENTOM. áfido, afidio, pulgón *m*.

aph·o·rism (ăf'ə-rĭz'əm) s. aforismo, refrán *m*.

aph·ro·dis·i·ac (ăf'rə-dĭz'ē-ăk') adj. & s. afrodisíaco.

a·pi·ar·y (ā'pē-ĕr'ē) s. [pl. **-ies**] ENTOM. abejar *m*, colmenar *m*.

a·pi·ces (ā'pĭ-sēz', ăp'ĭ-) un pl. de **apex**.

a·pi·cul·ture (ā'pĭ-kŭl'chər) s. ENTOM. apicultura.

a·piece (ə-pēs') adv. por cabeza, cada uno <*we got two tickets a.* conseguimos dos boletos cada uno>.

ap·ish (ā'pĭsh) adj. *(apelike)* simiesco; *(imitative)* imitador; *(silly)* tonto.

APL (ā'pē-ĕl') s. COMPUT. lenguage APL *m*.

a·plomb (ə-plŏm', ə-plŭm') s. aplomo, confianza en sí mismo.

A·poc·a·lypse (ə-pŏk'ə-lĭps') s. BÍBL. Apocalipsis *m* ♦ **a.** revelación.

a·poc·a·lyp·tic (ə-pŏk'ə-lĭp'tĭk) adj. apocalíptico.

a·poc·o·pe (ə-pŏk'ə-pē) s. GRAM. apócope *m*.

A·poc·ry·pha (ə-pŏk'rə-fə) s. [ú. con v. sing. o pl.] BÍBL. libros apócrifos ♦ **a.** escritos *o* libros de dudosa autenticidad.

a·poc·ry·phal (ə-pŏk'rə-fəl) adj. apócrifo.

ap·o·gee (ăp'ə-jē) s. ASTRON. apogeo.

a·po·lit·i·cal (ā'pə-lĭt'ĭ-kəl) adj. apolítico.

A·pol·lo (ə-pŏl'ō) s. MITOL. Apolo ♦ **a.** joven hermoso.

a·pol·o·get·ic (ə-pŏl'ə-jĕt'ĭk) adj. lleno de disculpas.

a·pol·o·get·i·cal·ly (ə-pŏl'ə-jĕt'ĭ-kə-lē) adv. excusándose, disculpándose.

a·pol·o·get·ics (ə-pŏl'ə-jĕt'ĭks) s. [ú. con v. sing.] TEO. apologética.

ap·o·lo·gi·a (ăp'ə-lō'jē-ə) s. apología, justificación *f* o defensa formal.

a·pol·o·gist (ə-pŏl'ə-jĭst) s. apologista *mf*.

a·pol·o·gize (ə-pŏl'ə-jīz') intr. **-gized, -giz·ing** disculparse, excusarse ♦ **to a. for** disculparse por *o* de • **to a. to** disculparse con.

a·pol·o·gy (ə-pŏl'ə-jē) s. [pl. **-gies**] *(statement)* apología, disculpa; *(formal defense)* discurso de defensa *o* justificación; *(substitute)* substituto inadecuado ♦ **to offer one's apologies** presentar sus excusas, disculparse.

ap·o·plec·tic (ăp'ə-plĕk'tĭk) adj. apoplético.

ap·o·plex·y (ăp'ə-plĕk'sē) s. MED. apoplejía.

a·port (ə-pôrt') adv. MARÍT. a babor.

a·pos·ta·sy (ə-pŏs'tə-sē) s. [pl. **-sies**] apostasía.

a·pos·tate (ə-pŏs'tāt', -tĭt) **I.** s. apóstata *mf* **II.** adj. de apostasía.

a·pos·ta·tize (ə-pŏs'tə-tīz') intr. **-tized, -tiz·ing** apostatar.

a·pos·tle (ə-pŏs'əl) s. propagador de una doctrina *m* ♦ **A.** BÍBL. apóstol • **Apostles' Creed** RELIG. Credo de los Apóstoles.

a·pos·to·late (ə-pŏs'tə-lāt') s. RELIG. apostolado.

ap·os·tol·ic (ăp'ə-stŏl'ĭk) adj. BÍBL., RELIG. apostólico ♦ **a. succession** sucesión apostólica.

Apostolic See s. RELIG. Sede Apostólica.

a·pos·tro·phe¹ (ə-pŏs'trə-fē) s. GRAM. apóstrofo.

a·pos·tro·phe² (ə-pŏs'trə-fē) s. RET. apóstrofe *m*.

a·poth·e·car·y (ə-pŏth'ĭ-kĕr'ē) s. [pl. **-ies**] boticario, farmacéutico.

ap·o·them (ăp'ə-thĕm') s. GEOM. apotema.

a·poth·e·o·sis (ə-pŏth'ē-ō'sĭs, ăp'ə-thē'ə-sĭs) s. [pl. **-ses** (-sēz')] apoteosis *f*, glorificación *f*.

ap·o·the·o·size (ə-pŏth'ē-ə-sīz', ə-pŏth'ē-ə-sīz') tr. **-sized, -siz·ing** exaltar, glorificar.

Ap·pa·la·chi·ans (ăp'ə-lā'chē-ənz, -lăch'ē-) s.pl. GEOG. Apalaches *m*.

ap·pall (ə-pôl') tr. pasmar, asombrar.

ap·pall·ing (ə-pô'lĭng) adj. pasmoso, asombroso.

ap·pa·ra·tus (ăp'ə-rā'təs, -răt'əs) s. [pl. **apparatus** *o* **-tus·es**] *(system)* aparato; *(equipment)* equipo; *(device)* instrumento; FIG. *(political organization)* aparato, mecanismo (político); FISIOL. aparato.

ap·par·el (ə-păr'əl) **I.** s. *(garments)* ropa, indumentaria; *(decoration)* atavío, adorno **II.** tr. *(to clothe)* vestir; *(to embellish)* ataviar, adornar.

ap·par·ent (ə-păr'ənt) adj. *(seeming)* aparente; *(perceptible)* evidente, claro.

ap·par·ent·ly (ə-păr'ənt-lē) adv. *(seemingly)* aparentemente, por lo visto; *(obviously)* evidentemente, claramente.

ap·pa·ri·tion (ăp'ə-rĭsh'ən) s. *(specter)* aparición *f*, fantasma; *(unusual sight)* visión *f*.

ap·peal (ə-pēl') **I.** s. *(urgent request)* exhortación *f*, súplica; *(a call for)* llamada; *(petition)* petición *f*, instancia; *(attraction)* atracción *f*, encanto; DER. apelación *f*, recurso ♦ **without a.** DER. sin recurso, inapelable **II.** intr. ♦ **to a. to** exhortar a, suplicar a; DER. *(law)* recurrir a, apelar a; *(to be attractive)* atraer, tener atractivo para —tr. DER. llevar a un tribunal superior.

ap·peal·ing (ə-pē'lĭng) adj. *(imploring)* suplicante, implorante; *(attractive)* atrayente.

ap·pear (ə-pîr') intr. *(to come into view)* aparecer, asomarse; *(to come into existence)* salir a luz, publicarse; *(to seem to be)* parecer, lucir <*she appears tired* ella parece cansada>; *(to seem likely)* parecer <*it appears that we will get the house* parece que conseguiremos la casa>; *(on the stage)* actuar, presentarse; *(in court)* comparecer, responder.

ap·pear·ance (ə-pîr'əns) s. *(act)* aparición *f*; *(presentation)* presentación *f*; *(looks)* aspecto, apariencia; *(pretense)* pretensión *f*, simulación *f* ♦ **appearances** apariencias, exterioridad • **to keep up appearances** guardar las apariencias • **to put in an a.** hacer acto de presencia, dejarse ver.

ap·pease (ə-pēz') tr. **-peased, -peas·ing** *(to calm)* apaciguar, pacificar; *(to relieve)* aplacar, mitigar.

ap·pease·ment (ə-pēz'mənt) s. apaciguamiento, pacificación *f*.

ap·peas·er (ə-pē'zər) s. pacificador *m*, reconciliador *m*.

ap·pel·lant (ə-pĕl'ənt) DER. **I.** adj. de apelación **II.** s. apelante *mf*.

ap·pel·late (ə-pĕl'ĭt) adj. DER. de apelación ♦ **a. court** DER. tribunal de apelación.

ap·pel·la·tion (ăp'ə-lā'shən) s. *(title)* título; *(name)* nombre *m*; *(naming)* denominación *f*.

ap·pend (ə-pĕnd') tr. anexar, adjuntar.

ap·pend·age (ə-pĕn'dĭj) s. anexo, adjunto; ANAT. apéndice *m*.

ap·pen·dant (ə-pĕn'dənt) **I.** adj. *(affixed)* anexo, adjunto; *(attendant)* acompañante, adjunto; DER. *(subsidiary)* accesorio **II.** s. *(appendage)* apéndice *m*, añadidura; DER. accesorio.

ap·pen·dec·to·my (ăp'ən-dĕk'tə-mē) s. [pl. **-mies**] CIR. apendectomía.

ap·pen·di·ces (ə-pĕn'dĭ-sēz') un pl. de **appendix**.

ap·pen·di·ci·tis (ə-pĕn'dĭ-sī'tĭs) s. MED. apendicitis *f*.

ap·pen·dix (ə-pĕn'dĭks) s. [pl. **-dix·es** *o* **-di·ces** (-dī-sēz')] apéndice (de un libro) *m*; ANAT. apéndice.

ap·per·cep·tion (ăp'ər-sĕp'shən) s. PSIC. apercepción *f*.

ap·per·tain (ăp'ər-tān') intr. pertenecer, corresponder.

ap·pe·tite (ăp'ĭ-tīt') s. *(hunger)* apetito; *(urge)* apetito, apetencia.

ap·pe·tiz·er (ăp'ĭ-tī'zər) s. aperitivo.

ap·pe·tiz·ing (ăp'ĭ-tī'zĭng) adj. apetitoso, gustoso.

ap·plaud (ə-plôd') intr. aplaudir —tr. *(to clap)* aplaudir; *(to praise)* elogiar, aplaudir <*we a. your decision* aplaudimos tu decisión>.

ap·plause (ə-plôz') s. *(with the hands)* aplauso, aclamación *f*; *(praise)* aplauso, aprobación *f*.

ap·ple (ăp'əl) s. *(tree)* manzano; *(fruit)* manzana ♦ **a. of one's eye** la niña de los ojos de uno • **a. pie** CUL. pastel de manzana.

ap·ple·jack (ăp'əl-jăk') s. aguardiente de manzana *m*.

ap·ple-pol·ish (ăp'əl-pŏl'ĭsh) intr. JER. adular, chupar medias.

ă rey / ä año / b boca / ch chico / d dar / ĕ el / ē mil / g gato / h joya / hw juez / ī aire / k casa / kw cuan /

ap·ple·sauce (ăp′əl-sôs′) s. CUL. compota de manzana; JER. *(nonsense)* tontería, disparate *m.*

ap·pli·ance (ə-plī′əns) s. artefacto, aparato ♦ **household a.** aparato electrodoméstico.

ap·pli·ca·bil·i·ty (ăp′lĭ-kə-bĭl′ĭ-tē, ə-plĭk′ə-) s. aplicabilidad *f,* pertinencia.

ap·pli·ca·ble (ăp′lĭ-kə-bəl, ə-plĭk′ə-) adj. aplicable, pertinente.

ap·pli·cant (ăp′lĭ-kənt) s. aspirante *mf,* candidato.

ap·pli·ca·tion (ăp′lĭ-kā′shən) s. *(act)* aplicación *f; (method)* modo de empleo, uso; *(relevance)* correspondencia, pertinencia; *(diligence)* atención *f,* esmero; *(request)* solicitación *f,* petición *f; (form)* solicitud *f,* formulario.

ap·pli·ca·tor (ăp′lĭ-kā′tər) s. aplicador *m.*

ap·plied (ə-plīd′) adj. aplicado <*a. science* ciencia aplicada>.

ap·pli·qué (ăp′lĭ-kā′) COST. **I.** s. aplicado, aplicación *f* **II.** adj. aplicado **III.** tr. **-quéd, -qué·ing** decorar con aplicado ♦ **a. lace** encaje de aplicación.

ap·ply (ə-plī′) tr. **-plied, -ply·ing** aplicar <*to a. ointment to the skin* aplicar untura a la piel>; *(to allocate)* destinar, asignar (fondos) ♦ **to a. for** solicitar, pedir (empleo, admisión) • **to a. to** *(to refer to)* referirse a, ser relativo a; *(to make application to)* dirigirse a, acudir (por ayuda, asistencia) • **to a. oneself to** aplicarse a, dedicarse a (tarea) —intr. ser pertinente, concernir.

ap·point (ə-point′) tr. *(to designate)* nombrar, designar; *(to set)* fijar, determinar; *(to furnish)* equipar, amueblar.

ap·point·ed (ə-poin′tĭd) adj. *(designated)* nombrado, designado; *(furnished)* equipado, amueblado.

ap·point·ee (ə-poin′tē′, ăp′oin-) s. persona designada.

ap·point·ive (ə-poin′tĭv) adj. electivo.

ap·point·ment (ə-point′mənt) s. *(act)* nombramiento, designación *f; (post)* puesto, cargo; *(date)* cita, compromiso ♦ **appointments** *(furnishings)* equipo, mobiliario • **a. book** agenda de compromisos.

ap·por·tion (ə-pôr′shən) tr. *(to divide)* prorratear; *(to assign)* asignar.

ap·por·tion·ment (ə-pôr′shən-mənt) s. *(act)* distribución *f,* reparto; POL. asignación *f,* prorrateo.

ap·pose (ă-pōz′) tr. **-posed, -pos·ing** *(to juxtapose)* yuxtaponer, poner lado a lado; *(to apply)* añadir a, aplicar a <*the official seal was apposed to the document* se aplicó el sello oficial al documento>.

ap·po·si·tion (ăp′ə-zĭsh′ən) s. *(juxtaposition)* yuxtaposición *f;* GRAM. *;* BIOL., MIN. aposición, adición *f.*

ap·pos·i·tive (ə-pŏz′ĭ-tĭv) s. GRAM. apositivo.

ap·prais·al (ə-prā′zəl) s. *(act)* evaluación *f,* estimación *f; (valuation)* tasación *f.*

ap·praise (ə-prāz′) tr. **-praised, -prais·ing** evaluar, tasar.

ap·prais·er (ə-prā′zər) s. tasador *m.*

ap·pre·cia·ble (ə-prē′shə-bəl) adj. apreciable, considerable.

ap·pre·cia·bly (ə-prē′shə-blē) adv. sensiblemente, perceptiblemente.

ap·pre·ci·ate (ə-prē′shē-āt′) tr. **-at·ed, -at·ing** *(to recognize)* apreciar, reconocer; *(to value)* valuar, estimar; *(to be thankful)* agradecer <*I a. your help* le agradezco su ayuda>; *(to realize)* darse cuenta de <*I a. your problems* me doy cuenta de sus problemas>; *(to raise in value)* valorizar, aumentar de valor —intr. valorizarse, subir de precio *o* valor.

ap·pre·ci·a·tion (ə-prē′shē-ā′shən) s. *(recognition)* apreciación *f,* reconocimiento; *(gratitude)* gratitud *f,* agradecimiento; *(a rise in value)* valorización *f,* subida.

ap·pre·cia·tive (ə-prē′shə-tĭv, -shē-ā′tĭv) adj. apreciativo, agradecido.

ap·pre·hend (ăp′rĭ-hĕnd′) tr. *(to arrest)* aprehender, arrestar; *(to understand)* comprender, entender; *(to fear)* temer, recelar —intr. comprender.

ap·pre·hen·si·ble (ăp′rĭ-hĕn′sə-bəl) adj. comprensible, entendible.

ap·pre·hen·sion (ăp′rĭ-hĕn′shən) s. *(dread)* aprensión *f,* temor *m; (arrest)* aprehensión *f,* captura; *(understanding)* percepción *f,* comprensión *f.*

ap·pre·hen·sive (ăp′rĭ-hĕn′sĭv) adj. aprensivo, temeroso.

ap·pren·tice (ə-prĕn′tĭs) **I.** s. aprendiz *m* <*an a. carpenter*

aprendiz de carpintero>; *(beginner)* novicio, principiante *mf* **II.** tr. **-ticed, -tic·ing** poner de aprendiz.

ap·pren·tice·ship (ə-prĕn′tĭs-shĭp′) s. aprendizaje *m.*

ap·prise (ə-prīz′) tr. **-prised, -pris·ing** *(to appraise)* tasar; *(to notify)* informar, notificar.

ap·proach (ə-prōch′) **I.** intr. aproximarse, acercarse —tr. *(to come near to)* aproximarse a, acercarse a; *(to approximate)* parecerse a, compararse con <*what approaches the joy of singing?* ¿qué otra cosa se compara con la alegría de cantar?>; *(to make overtures to)* abordar, hacer propuestas a; *(to begin to work on)* abordar, emprender (tarea, asunto) **II.** s. *(act)* acercamiento; *(access)* acceso, vía de entrada; *(overture)* proposición *f,* propuesta; *(method)* método, enfoque (de un asunto, situación) *m.*

ap·proach·a·ble (ə-prō′chə-bəl) adj. *(accessible)* accesible, alcanzable; *(friendly)* accesible, abordable.

ap·proach·ing (ə-prō′chĭng) adj. *(upcoming)* venidero, próximo; *(coming closer)* que se acerca.

ap·pro·ba·tion (ăp′rə-bā′shən) s. *(praise)* elogio, alabanza; *(passage of bill)* aprobación *f,* sanción (de un proyecto de ley) *f.*

ap·pro·pri·ate (ə-prō′prē-ĭt) **I.** adj. apropiado, adecuado **II.** tr. (-āt′) **-at·ed, -at·ing** *(to set apart)* destinar, consignar; *(to usurp)* apropiarse de, adueñarse de.

ap·pro·pri·ate·ly (ə-prō′prē-ĭt-lē) adv. apropiadamente, convenientemente.

ap·pro·pri·ate·ness (ə-prō′prē-ĭt-nĭs) s. propiedad *f,* conveniencia.

ap·pro·pri·a·tion (ə-prō′prē-ā′shən) s. *(act)* apropiación *f; (allocation)* asignación *f.*

ap·prov·al (ə-prōō′vəl) s. *(consent)* aprobación *f,* consentimiento; *(sanction)* sanción *f,* confirmación *f* ♦ **on a.** *(for examination)* a prueba; COM. previa aceptación.

ap·prove (ə-prōōv′) tr. **-proved, -prov·ing** *(to endorse)* aprobar, consentir; *(to sanction)* sancionar, ratificar <*a treaty approved by the Senate* un tradado ratificado por el senado> —intr. dar su aprobación, aprobar <*I don't a. of what you're going to do* yo no apruebo lo que vas a hacer>.

ap·prov·ing·ly (ə-prōō′vĭng-lē) adj. con aprobación, con consentimiento.

ap·prox·i·mate (ə-prŏk′sə-mĭt) **I.** adj. *(near)* aproximado, aproximativo; *(very like)* próximo, cercano **II.** tr. & intr. (-māt′) **-mat·ed, -mat·ing** aproximar(se), acercar(se).

ap·prox·i·mate·ly (ə-prŏk′sə-mĭt-lē) adv. aproximadamente.

ap·prox·i·ma·tion (ə-prŏk′sə-mā′shən) s. aproximación *f.*

ap·pur·te·nance (ə-pûr′tn-əns) s. accesorio ♦ **appurtenances** *(gear)* equipo, accesorios; DER. anexidades.

ap·pur·te·nant (ə-pûr′tn-ənt) adj. DER. auxiliar, anexo; *(incident to)* accesorio, propio de.

a·pri·cot (ăp′rĭ-kŏt′, ā′prĭ-) **I.** s. *(tree)* albaricoquero, damasco; *(fruit)* albaricoque *m; (color)* color damasco **II.** adj. de color albaricoque *o* damasco.

A·pril (ā′prəl) s. abril *m* ♦ **A. showers** lluvias de abril.

April fool s. inocente *mf,* persona que es víctima de las bromas que se hacen el primer día de abril.

April Fools' Day s. día de los Inocentes (el primer día de abril).

a·pron (ā′prən) **I.** s. *(garment)* delantal *m,* mandil *m;* MAQ. placa de protección; AVIA. pista (delante de los hangares); TEAT. proscenio ♦ **to be tied to (a mother's) a. strings** estar dominado por (la madre) **II.** tr. resguardar, abrigar.

ap·ro·pos (ăp′rə-pō′) **I.** adj. adecuado, oportuno **II.** adv. a propósito <*a., where were you last night?* ¿a propósito, dónde estabas anoche?> **III.** prep. a propósito de, respecto a.

apse (ăps) s. ARQ. ábside *m.*

apt (ăpt) adj. *(suitable)* apropiado, conveniente; *(fitting)* acertado, atinado; *(inclined)* propenso, inclinado; *(smart)* listo.

APT (ā′pē-tē′) s. COMPUT. lenguaje APT *m.*

ap·ti·tude (ăp′tĭ-tōōd′, -tyōōd′) s. *(talent)* aptitud *f,* capacidad *f; (intelligence)* inteligencia ♦ **a. test** prueba de aptitud.

apt·ly (ăpt′lē) adv. *(suitably)* convenientemente; *(fittingly)* atinadamente; *(ably)* capazmente.

---

ng inglés / ŏ la / ō bou / ô corre / oi oigo / ōō uno / ou auto / yōō ciudad / w hueco / y yo / z mismo

apt·ness (ăpt′nĭs) s. *(suitability)* lo conveniente, lo apropiado; *(capability)* capacidad *f*, aptitud *f*.

aq·ua (ăk′wə, ä′kwə) s. [pl. **aq·uae** (ăk′wē, ä′kwī′) *o* **aq·uas**] FARM. solución acuosa; *(color)* color aguamarina.

Aqua Lung s. marca registrada de un aparato de respiración subacuática.

aq·ua·ma·rine (ăk′wə-mə-rēn′, ä′kwə-) s. MIN. aguamarina; *(color)* color aguamarina.

aq·ua·plane (ăk′wə-plān′, ä′kwə-) s. acuaplano, hidropatín *m*.

aq·ua·relle (ăk′wə-rĕl′, ä′kwə-) s. PINT. acuarela.

a·quar·i·um (ə-kwâr′ē-əm) s. [pl. **-i·ums** *o* **-i·a** (-ē-ə)] acuario.

A·quar·i·us (ə-kwâr′ē-əs) s. ASTROL. Acuario.

a·quat·ic (ə-kwŏt′ĭk, ə-kwăt′-) I. adj. acuático, acuátil II. s. BOT. planta acuática; ZOOL. animal acuático ♦ **aquatics** deportes acuáticos.

aq·ua·tint (ăk′wə-tĭnt′, ä′kwə-) I. s. *(process)* acuatinta; *(etching)* grabado al acuatinta II. tr. grabar al acuatinta.

aq·ue·duct (ăk′wĭ-dŭkt′) s. ING. *(conduit)* acueducto; ANAT. *(passage)* conducto.

a·que·ous (ā′kwē-əs, ăk′wē-) adj. *(watery)* acuoso, ácueo; GEOL. sedimentario.

aq·ui·fer (ăk′wə-fər) s. GEOL. roca acuífera.

aq·ui·line (ăk′wə-līn′, -lĭn) adj. aguileño, aquilino.

Aq·ui·taine (ăk′wĭ-tān′) s. Aquitania.

Ar·ab (ăr′əb) I. s. *(inhabitant)* árabe *mf*; *(horse)* caballo árabe II. adj. árabe.

ar·a·besque (ăr′ə-bĕsk′) I. s. ARTE. arabesco; *(ballet)* posición plástica en ballet II. adj. ARTE. arabesco, arábigo.

A·ra·bia (ə-rā′bē-ə) s. Arabia.

A·ra·bi·an (ə-rā′bē-ən) adj. & s. árabe *mf* ♦ **A. Desert** GEOG. desierto de Arabia.

Ar·a·bic (ăr′ə-bĭk) I. adj. árabe, arábigo ♦ **A. numeral** número arábigo II. s. arábigo, (lengua) árabe.

ar·a·ble (ăr′ə-bəl) adj. arable, cultivable.

a·rach·nid (ə-răk′nĭd) s. ENTOM. arácnido.

Ar·a·go·nese (ăr′ə-gə-nēz′) adj. & s. aragonés *m*.

ar·bi·ter (är′bĭ-tər) s. árbitro.

ar·bi·trage (är′bĭ-träzh′) s. arbitraje *m*.

ar·bi·trar·i·ly (är′bĭ-trâr′ə-lē) adv. arbitrariamente.

ar·bi·trar·i·ness (är′bĭ-trĕr′ē-nĭs) s. arbitrariedad *f*.

ar·bi·trar·y (är′bĭ-trĕr′ē) adj. *(whimsical)* arbitrario; *(despotic)* despótico.

ar·bi·trate (är′bĭ-trāt′) tr. & intr. **-trat·ed, -trat·ing** arbitrar.

ar·bi·tra·tion (är′bĭ-trā′shən) s. arbitraje *m*.

ar·bi·tra·tor (är′bĭ-trā′tər) s. arbitrador *m*, árbitro.

ar·bor¹ (är′bər) s. enramada, pérgola.

ar·bor² (är′bər) s. MEC. árbol *m*, eje *m*.

ar·bo·re·al (är-bôr′ē-əl) adj. arbóreo.

ar·bo·res·cent (är′bə-rĕs′ənt) adj. arborescente.

ar·bo·re·tum (är′bə-rē′təm) s. jardín botánico, vivero.

ar·bor·vi·tae (är′bər-vī′tē) s. BOT. árbol de la vida *m*, tuya; ANAT. árbol de la vida.

ar·bour (är′bər) s. G.B. var. de **arbor**¹.

ar·bu·tus (är-byōō′təs) s. BOT. madroño, arborio.

arc (ärk) I. s. arco II. intr. **arced** (ärkt) *o* **arcked, arc·ing** (är′kĭng) *o* **arck·ing** formar arco.

ar·cade (är-kād′) s. ARQ. *(arch)* arcada; *(roofed passageway)* galería.

Ar·ca·di·a (är-kā′dē-ə) *o* **Ar·ca·dy** (är′kə-dē) s. Arcadia.

ar·ca·na (är-kā′nə) un pl. de **arcanum**.

ar·cane (är-kān′) adj. *(secret)* arcano, secreto; *(esoteric)* esotérico.

ar·ca·num (är-kā′nəm) s. [pl. **-na** (-nə) *o* **-nums**] *(mystery)* arcano, misterio; *(elixir)* elixir *m*.

arch¹ (ärch) I. s. ARQ. arco, empeine *m* ♦ **fallen arches** pies planos II. tr. *(to cause to curve)* enarcar, arquear; *(to span)* atravesar —intr. arquearse, formar un arco.

arch² (ärch) adj. *(principal)* principal; *(mischievous)* astuto, pícaro.

ar·chae·o·log·i·cal (är′kē-ə-lŏj′ĭ-kəl) adj. arqueológico.

ar·chae·ol·o·gist (är′kē-ŏl′ə-jĭst) s. arqueólogo.

ar·chae·ol·o·gy (är′kē-ŏl′ə-jē) s. arqueología.

ar·cha·ic (är-kā′ĭk) adj. *(ancient)* arcaico; *(antiquated)* anticuado; *(outmoded)* desusado.

ar·cha·ism (är′kē-ĭz′əm, -kā-) s. arcaísmo, frase *o* voz arcaica.

ar·cha·ize (är′kē-īz′, -kā-) tr. **-ized, -iz·ing** arcaizar, llenar (una lengua) de arcaísmos —intr. usar arcaísmos.

arch·an·gel (ärk′ān′jəl) s. TEO. arcángel *m*.

arch·bish·op (ärch-bĭsh′əp) s. RELIG. arzobispo.

arch·bish·op·ric (ärch-bĭsh′əp-rĭk) s. arzobispado.

arch·dea·con (ärch-dē′kən) s. RELIG. archidiácono, arcediano.

arch·di·o·cese (ärch-dī′ə-sĭs, -sēz′) s. RELIG. archidiócesis *f*, arquidiócesis *f*.

arch·duch·ess (ärch-dŭch′ĭs) s. archiduquesa.

arch·duch·y (ärch-dŭch′ē) s. [pl. **-ies**] archiducado.

arch·duke (ärch-dōōk′, -dyōōk′) s. archiduque *m*.

arched (ärcht) adj. arqueado, enarcado.

arch·en·e·my (ärch-ĕn′ə-mē) s. [pl. **-mies**] enemigo acérrimo, el mayor enemigo ♦ **the A.** Satanás.

ar·che·ol·o·gy (är′kē-ŏl′ə-jē) s. var. de **archaeology.**

arch·er (är′chər) s. DEP. arquero (de arco y flecha).

arch·er·y (är′chə-rē) s. *(sport)* tiro de arco y flecha; *(troop)* tropa de arqueros.

ar·che·type (är′kĭ-tīp′) s. arquetipo, prototipo.

arch·fiend (ärch-fēnd′) s. archienemigo, el enemigo mayor *m* ♦ **the A.** el diablo, Satanás.

Ar·chi·me·des (är′kĭ-mē′dēz) s. Arquímedes.

arch·ing (är′chĭng) s. arqueo.

ar·chi·pel·a·go (är′kə-pĕl′ə-gō′) s. [pl. **-goes** *o* **-gos**] *(islands)* archipiélago; *(sea)* mar poblado de islas.

ar·chi·tect (är′kĭ-tĕkt′) s. *(designer)* arquitecto; FIG. *(planner)* artífice *mf*.

ar·chi·tec·ton·ics (är′kĭ-tĕk-tŏn′ĭks) s. [ú. con v. sing.] arquitectura.

ar·chi·tec·tur·al (är′kĭ-tĕk′chər-əl) adj. arquitectónico.

ar·chi·tec·ture (är′kĭ-tĕk′chər) s. *(art)* arquitectura; *(structure)* obra arquitectónica; *(style)* estilo arquitectónico.

ar·chi·val (är-kī′vəl) adj. de archivos, de archivar.

ar·chive (är′kīv′) s. archivo.

ar·chi·vist (är′kə-vĭst, -kī-) s. archivista *mf*.

arch·priest (ärch-prēst′) s. RELIG. arcipreste *m*.

arch·way (ärch′wā′) s. ARQ. arcada, pasaje abovedado.

ar·ci·form (är′sə-fôrm′) adj. arqueado, curvado.

arcked (ärkt) un pret. y part. p. de **arc**.

arc lamp s. lámpara de arco, voltaico arco.

arc·tic (ärk′tĭk, är′tĭk) adj. frígido, glacial ♦ **A.** GEOL. del Ártico, ártico • **A. Circle** círculo (polar) ártico.

ar·dent (är′dnt) adj. ardiente, vehemente.

ar·dor (är′dər) s. ardor *m*, pasión *f*.

ar·dour (är′dər) s. G.B. var. de **ardor**.

ar·du·ous (är′jōō-əs) adj. *(difficult)* arduo; *(strenuous)* penoso; *(steep)* escarpado (ladera, escalera).

ar·du·ous·ness (är′jōō-əs-nĭs) s. dificultad *f*, rigor *m*.

are¹ (är) segunda persona singular y plural del pres. indic. de **be**.

are² (âr, är) s. unidad de superficie agraria equivalente a 100m² *f*.

ar·e·a (âr′ē-ə) s. *(region)* zona, región *f*; *(section)* sección *f*, zona; GEOM. área, superficie *f*; *(scope)* área <*in the a. of finance* en el área de las finanzas>.

area code s. prefijo telefónico (para llamadas de larga distancia).

ar·e·al (âr′ē-əl) adj. de un área *o* superficie.

a·re·na (ə-rē′nə) s. *(center part)* arena, pista; *(auditorium)* estadio (de eventos deportivos); *(field)* área, campo <*the political a.* el campo político>.

aren't (ärnt, är′ənt) contr. de **are not.**

Ar·gen·ti·na (är′jən-tēn′ə) s. Argentina.

ar·gen·tine (är′jən-tīn′, -tēn′) I. adj. plateado, argentino II. s. *(silver)* plata; *(silvery metal)* metal plateado.

Ar·gen·tine (är′jən-tēn, -tīn) *o* **Ar·gen·tin·i·an** (är′jən-tīn′ē-ən) adj. & s. argentino ♦ **the Argentine** la Argentina.

ar·gon (är′gŏn′) QUÍM. argón *m*, argo.

Ar·go·naut (är′gə-nôt′) s. MITOL. Argonauta *m* ♦ **a.** ICT. argonauta, nautilo.

ā rey / ä año / b boca / ch chico / d dar / ĕ el / ē mil / g gato / h joya / hw juez / ī aire / k casa / kw cuan /

ar·go·sy (är'gə-sē) s. [pl. **-sies**] HIST. buque mercante grande *m.*

ar·got (är'gō, -gət) s. *(specialized vocabulary)* argot *m;* vocabulario (especializado); *(slang)* lunfardo.

ar·gu·a·ble (är'gyōō-ə-bəl) adj. discutible, disputable.

ar·gue (är'gyōō) tr. **-gued, -gu·ing** *(to debate)* argüir, presentar <*the lawyer argued his case* el abogado presentó su caso>; *(to contend)* razonar, argumentar; *(to persuade)* persuadir, convencer <*he argued me into going* me convenció a que fuera> —intr. *(to give reasons)* argumentar, argüir (en favor o en contra de algo); *(to dispute)* disputar, discutir <*they spent hours arguing* pasaron horas discutiendo>.

ar·gu·ment (är'gyə-mənt) s. *(debate)* discusión *f,* debate *m; (quarrel)* pelea, disputa; *(contention)* razonamiento, argumento <*his a. was based on recent facts* su argumento se basaba en hechos recientes>; *(summary)* resumen *m,* sumario.

ar·gu·men·ta·tion (är'gyə-mĕn-tā'shən) s. *(act)* argumentación *f; (reasoning)* raciocinio; *(debate)* debate *m.*

ar·gu·men·ta·tive (är'gyə-mĕn'tə-tĭv) adj. *(disputatious)* discutidor, disputador; *(characterized by argument)* argumentativo.

ar·gyle *o* **ar·gyll** (är'gīl') s. *(pattern)* diseño de rombos; *(socks)* calcetines con diseño de rombos *m.*

a·ri·a (ä'rē-ə) s. MÚS. *(melody)* melodía, aire *m; (solo)* aria.

ar·id (är'ĭd) adj. *(dry)* árido, seco; *(dull)* insulso, insípido.

a·rid·i·ty (ə-rĭd'ĭ-tē) s. aridez *f,* sequedad *f.*

Ar·ies (âr'ēz', âr'ē-ēz') s. ASTROL. Aries *m.*

a·right (ə-rīt') adv. correctamente, rectamente.

a·rise (ə-rīz') intr. **a·rose** (ə-rōz'), **a·ris·en** (ə-rĭz'ən), **a·ris·ing** *(to get up)* levantarse, ponerse en pie; *(to ascend)* ascender, elevarse <*a mist arose from the lake* una niebla se elevó del lago>; *(to originate)* surgir, originarse <*myths arose in order to explain natural occurrences* los mitos se originaron para explicar los hechos naturales>; *(to result)* resultar, provenir.

a·ris·en (ə-rĭz'ən) part. p. de **arise.**

a·ris·toc·ra·cy (ăr'ĭ-stŏk'rə-sē) s. [pl. **-cies**] *(nobility)* aristocracia, nobleza; *(ruling class)* gobierno aristócrata; *(higher class)* clase aristocrática.

a·ris·to·crat (ə-rĭs'tə-krăt', ăr'ĭs-) s. *(member)* aristócrata *mf,* noble *mf; (oligarch)* oligarca *r.f.*

a·ris·to·crat·ic (ə-rĭs'tə-krăt'ĭk, ăr'ĭs-) adj. aristocrático.

Ar·is·to·te·li·an (ăr'ĭ-stə-tē'lē-ən) adj. FILOS. aristotélico.

Ar·is·tot·le (ăr'ĭ-stŏt'l) s. Aristóteles.

a·rith·me·tic (ə-rĭth'mĭ-tĭk) s. aritmética.

ar·ith·met·ic (ăr'ĭth-mĕt'ĭk) *o* **ar·ith·met·i·cal** (-ĭ-kəl) adj. aritmético.

ark (ärk) s. arca, barcaza ♦ **A. of the Covenant** RELIG. arca de la Alianza • **Holy A.** RELIG. cofre que contiene la tora en las sinagogas.

arm[1] (ärm) s. ANAT. brazo; ZOOL. brazo, pata delantera; *(of a dress)* manga ♦ **a. in a.** tomados del brazo, de bracete • **babe in arms** niño de pecho • **to keep at arm's length** FIG. mantener a distancia prudencial • **with open arms** con los brazos abiertos.

arm[2] (ärm) I. s. *(weapon)* arma ♦ **arms race** POL. carrera de armamentos • **to be up in arms** *(to rebel)* alzarse en armas; *(to be indignant)* poner el grito en el cielo • **to bear arms** MIL. llevar las armas, servir como soldado • **to lay down one's arms** rendir las armas • **to present arms** MIL. presentar armas • **to take up arms** MIL. tomar las armas II. tr. *(to supply with arms)* armar; *(to fortify)* fortalecer; *(to provide with)* armar.

ar·ma·da (är-mä'də, -mā'-) s. MARÍT. armada, flota.

ar·ma·dil·lo (är'mə-dĭl'ō) s. [pl. **-los**] armadillo.

ar·ma·ment (är'mə-mənt) s. MIL. armamento, armas ♦ **armaments** armas, armamento.

ar·ma·ture (är'mə-chōōr', -chər) s. ELEC. armadura; ARM., BIOL. armadura; ESCULT. armazón *f.*

arm·band (ärm'bănd') s. brazalete *m,* brazal *m.*

arm·chair (ärm'châr') I. s. sillón *m,* butaca II. adj. ♦ **a. politician** político de café.

armed (ärmd) adj. armado, provisto de armas.

armed forces s.pl. fuerzas armadas.

Ar·me·ni·a (är-mē'nē-ə) s. Armenia.

Ar·me·ni·an (är-mē'nē-ən) s. & adj. armenio.

arm·ful (ärm'fōōl') s. [pl. **-fuls**] brazada.

arm·hole (ärm'hōl') s. COST. sisa, sobaquera.

ar·mi·stice (är'mĭ-stĭs) s. armisticio, tregua.

arm·let (ärm'lĭt) s. *(band)* brazalete *m; (of sea)* brazo.

ar·moire (ärm-wär', är'mər) s. armario, ropero.

ar·mor (är'mər) I. s. *(covering)* armadura, coraza; MIL. *(metal plating)* blindaje *m; (armored vehicles)* vehículos blindados II. tr. blindar, acorazar.

ar·mor-clad (är'mər-klăd') adj. acorazado, blindado.

ar·mored (är'mərd) adj. MIL. *(covered)* acorazado, blindado; *(equipped)* blindado (un batallón).

ar·mor·er (är'mər-ər) s. *(of armors)* armero; *(of weapons)* fabricante de armas *mf;* MIL. *(soldier)* soldado que cuida *o* repara armas ligeras.

ar·mo·ri·al (är-môr'ē-əl) I. adj. heráldico II. s. armorial *m.*

armor plate s. plancha de blindaje, coraza.

ar·mor·y (är'mə-rē) s. [pl. **-ies**] *(storehouse)* armería, arsenal *m; (headquarters)* cuartel *m; (factory)* fábrica de armas.

ar·mour (är'mər) s. G.B. var. de **armor.**

arm·pit (ärm'pĭt') s. ANAT. axila.

arm·rest (ärm'rĕst') s. brazo de un sillón.

ar·my (är'mē) s. [pl. **-mies**] MIL. ejército; FIG. *(multitude)* muchedumbre *f,* multitud *f* ♦ **the Army** el Ejército • **an a. officer** un oficial del ejército.

a·ro·ma (ə-rō'mə) s. aroma *m,* fragancia.

ar·o·mat·ic (ăr'ə-măt'ĭk) I. adj. aromático, fragante II. s. planta *o* substancia aromática.

a·ro·ma·tize (ə-rō'mə-tīz') tr. **-tized, -tiz·ing** aromatizar.

a·rose (ə-rōz') pret. de **arise.**

a·round (ə-round') I. adv. *(in all directions)* por todos lados, en derredor; *(in the opposite direction)* en la dirección contraria; *(here and there)* por aquí, por allá; *(in circumference)* a la redonda, de circunferencia <*the tree measures three feet a.* el árbol mide tres pies de circunferencia>; FAM. *(approximately)* cerca, aproximadamente ♦ **all a.** por todos lados • **the other way a.** al contrario, al revés • **to come a.** *(to visit)* venir de visita; *(to come to)* volver en sí; FIG. *(to change one's mind)* aceptar ahora algo que se rechazó antes • **to get a.** *(to go places)* viajar, ir a lugares; *(to become known)* divulgarse, propalarse (noticia, rumor) • **to have been a.** tener experiencia, haber corrido mundo II. prep. *(about)* cerca de, alrededor de <*a. the year 1450* alrededor del año 1450>; *(encircling)* alrededor de; *(here and there)* por todos lados, en torno de <*the reporter looked a. the room* el reportero miró en torno del cuarto>; *(on the farther side of)* a la vuelta de <*the house a. the corner* la casa a la vuelta de la esquina>.

a·round-the-clock (ə-round'thə-klŏk') adj. continuamente, a toda(s) hora(s).

a·rous·al (ə-rou'zəl) s. despertar (de un deseo, esp. sexual) *m.*

a·rouse (ə-rouz') tr. **a·roused, a·rous·ing** *(to awaken)* despertar; *(to stir up)* estimular, incitar —intr. despertarse.

ar·peg·gi·o (är-pĕj'ē-ō) s. [pl. **-os**] MÚS. arpegio.

ar·raign (ə-rān') tr. *(before a court)* hacer comparecer; *(to charge)* denunciar, acusar <*he arraigned the foreign policy as not being logical* acusó a la política exterior de no ser lógica>.

ar·raign·ment (ə-rān'mənt) s. DER. acusación *f.*

ar·range (ə-rānj') tr. **-ranged, -rang·ing** *(to put in order)* organizar, ordenar; *(to settle upon)* fijar, señalar (fechas, convenios); *(to plan)* planear, preparar; MÚS. adaptar, arreglar ♦ **to a. with** llegar a un acuerdo con • **to a. for** hacer arreglos *o* tomar medidas para —intr. *(to agree)* acordar, convenir en <*can we a. to meet this evening* ¿podemos convenir en encontrarnos esta noche?>.

ar·range·ment (ə-rānj'mənt) s. *(act, result)* arreglo <*the a. of flowers is an art* el arreglo de flores es un arte>; *(order)* disposición *f,* orden *m* <*alphabetical a.* orden alfabético>; *(agreement)* convenio, arreglo; MÚS. arreglo, adaptación *f* ♦ **arrangements** planes, medidas.

ar·rang·er (ə-rān'jər) s. persona que planea, arregla, *o* prepara algo; MÚS. músico que transcribe para otros instrumentos *o* que hace arreglos musicales.

ar·rant (ăr'ənt) adj. notorio, consumado.

ar·ray (ə-rā') **I.** tr. *(to arrange)* formar (soldados, tropa); *(to adorn)* adornar (con lujo) **II.** s. *(formation)* formación (soldados, caballería) *f*; *(large group)* multitud *f* <*an a. of deadly weapons* una multitud de armas mortíferas>; *(attire)* vestimenta lujosa; COMPUT., MAT. ordenación *f*.

ar·ray·al (ə-rā'əl) s. MIL. formación *f*, orden *m* del campo de batalla; *(impressive display)* conjunto, serie *f o* colección impresionante *f*; *(elegant attire)* atavío, vestido lujoso; MAT. ordenación *f*, matriz *f*.

ar·rears (ə-rîrz') s.pl. atraso de pagos ♦ **to be in a.** estar atrasado en pagos de deuda.

ar·rest (ə-rĕst') tr. *(to halt)* detener, parar <*the drug arrested the progress of the disease* el medicamento detuvo el progreso de la enfermedad>; *(to seize)* arrestar, detener; *(to engage)* atraer, cautivar <*the first chapter arrested the reader's attention* el primer capítulo cautivó la atención del lector> **II.** s. *(seizure)* arresto, detención *f*; *(device)* interrupción *f*, paro ♦ **under a.** detenido, arrestado.

ar·rest·ing (ə-rĕs'tĭng) adj. llamativo, impresionante.

ar·rhyth·mi·a (ə-rĭth'mē-ə) s. MED. arritmia.

ar·riv·al (ə-rī'vəl) s. llegada, arribo ♦ **new a.** recién llegado.

ar·rive (ə-rīv') intr. **-rived, -riv·ing** *(to reach a place)* llegar; *(by boat)* arribar; *(to reach a goal)* alcanzar, lograr (un objetivo); FIG., FAM. *(to make it)* tener éxito, llegar <*a singer who has truly arrived* un cantante que realmente ha llegado> ♦ **to a. at** llegar a (conclusión, objetivo).

ar·ro·gance (ăr'ə-gəns) s. arrogancia, altivez *f*.

ar·ro·gant (ăr'ə-gənt) adj. arrogante, altivo.

ar·ro·gate (ăr'ə-gāt') tr. **-gat·ed, -gat·ing** ♦ **to a. to oneself** arrogarse, atribuirse.

ar·row (ăr'ō) s. *(weapon)* flecha, saeta; *(sign)* señal de dirección *f*, flecha.

ar·row·head (ăr'ō-hĕd') s. *(tip)* punta de flecha; BOT. sagitaria.

ar·row·root (ăr'ō-rōōt', -rŏŏt') s. arrurruz (planta y almidón) *m*.

ar·se·nal (är'sə-nəl) s. *(place)* arsenal (de armas) *m*; *(stock)* surtido *o* abastecimiento de armas; FIG. *(supply)* arsenal, caudal *m*.

ar·se·nic (är'sə-nĭk) s. & adj. QUÍM. arsénico.

ar·son (är'sən) s. incendio premeditado.

ar·son·ist (är'sə-nĭst) s. incendiario.

art (ärt) s. *(creativity)* arte *m*; *(skill)* destreza, técnica ♦ **a. museum** museo de arte • **arts** maña, astucia.

ar·te·fact (är'tə-făkt') s. var. de **artifact.**

ar·te·ri·al (är-tîr'ē-əl) adj. arterial.

ar·te·ri·o·scle·ro·sis (är-tîr'ē-ō-sklə-rō'sĭs) s. MED. arteriosclerosis *f*, arterioesclerosis *f*.

ar·ter·y (är'tə-rē) s. [pl. **-ies**] ANAT. arteria; *(highway)* arteria.

ar·te·sian well (är-tē'zhən) s. pozo artesiano.

art·ful (ärt'fəl) adj. *(skillful)* ingenioso, diestro; *(clever)* artificioso, disimulado; *(deceitful)* mañoso, artero.

ar·thrit·ic (är-thrĭt'ĭk) adj. & s. artrítico.

ar·thri·tis (är-thrī'tĭs) s. artritis *f*.

ar·thro·pod (är'thrə-pŏd') s. ZOOL. artrópodo.

ar·ti·choke (är'tĭ-chōk') s. alcaucil *m*, alcachofa ♦ **Jerusalem a.** aguaturma, tupinambo.

ar·ti·cle (är'tĭ-kəl) **I.** s. *(item)* artículo, objeto; *(clause)* cláusula; *(essay)* artículo; GRAM. artículo ♦ **a. of clothing** prenda de vestir • **a. of faith** RELIG. artículo de fe • **articles and conditions** COM. pliego de condiciones • **articles of incorporation** COM. estatutos de una sociedad anónima • **definite a.** GRAM. artículo definido • **indefinite a.** GRAM. artículo indefinido • **leading a.** PERIOD. artículo de fondo **II.** tr. **-cled, -cling** articular, distribuir en artículos ♦ **to a. an apprentice** COM. colocar de aprendiz bajo contrato.

ar·tic·u·late (är-tĭk'yə-lĭt) **I.** adj. *(speaking)* que habla; *(clear speech or writing)* inteligible, claro; BIOL. articulado **II.** tr. *(-lāt')* **-lat·ed, -lat·ing** *(to enunciate)* articular, enunciar <*he articulated his words clearly* enunció sus palabras claramente>; *(to form a joint)* articular —intr. articular, enunciar.

ar·tic·u·la·tion (är-tĭk'yə-lā'shən) s. *(enunciation)* articula-

ción *f*, enunciación *f*; *(jointing)* articulación; BOT., ZOOL. articulación.

ar·ti·fact (är'tə-făkt') s. *(instrument)* artefacto; *(archaeological discovery)* resto(s).

ar·ti·fice (är'tə-fĭs) s. *(stratagem)* artificio, estratagema; *(trickery)* engaño; *(skill)* arte *m*, ingeniosidad *f*.

ar·tif·i·cer (är-tĭf'ĭ-sər) s. *(craftsman)* artífice *mf*, artesano; *(inventor)* inventor *m*, creador *m*.

ar·ti·fi·cial (är'tə-fĭsh'əl) adj. *(manmade)* artificial, sintético; *(affected)* afectado, fingido.

ar·ti·fi·ci·al·i·ty (är'tə-fĭsh'ē-ăl'ĭ-tē) s. artificialidad *f*, afectación *f*.

ar·ti·fi·cial·ly (är'tə-fĭsh'ə-lē) adv. *(not naturally)* artificialmente; *(affectedly)* afectadamente.

ar·til·ler·y (är-tĭl'ə-rē) s. MIL. artillería.

ar·til·ler·y·man (är-tĭl'ə-rē-mən) s. [pl. **-men**] MIL. artillero.

ar·ti·san (är'tĭ-zən, -sən) s. artesano, artífice *mf*.

art·ist (är'tĭst) s. *(creator)* artista *mf*; FAM. *(expert)* maestro, experto.

ar·tiste (är-tēst') s. artista (esp. el cantante o bailarín profesional) *mf*.

ar·tis·tic (är-tĭs'tĭk) adj. artístico.

art·ist·ry (är'tĭ-strē) s. arte *mf*, talento artístico.

art·less (ärt'lĭs) adj. *(naive)* sencillo, ingenuo; *(natural)* natural, sencillo; *(lacking art)* desmañado, torpe; *(uncultured)* tosco, ordinario.

art·mo·bile (ärt'mə-bēl') s. remolque *m* que se usa en una exhibición de arte ambulante.

art song s. canción lírica.

art·sy-craft·sy (ärt'sē-krăft'sē) adj. FAM. pseudo-artístico, afectadamente artístico.

art·work (ärt'wûrk') s. ARTE. artesanía; IMPR. *(illustrative elements)* ilustraciones y decoraciones que acompañan a un texto; *(mechanicals)* ilustraciones y texto preparados para ser fotografiados por el impresor.

art·y (är'tē) adj. **-i·er, -i·est** FAM. ostentosamente artístico.

Ar·y·an (âr'ē-ən) adj. & s. ario.

as (ăz, əz) **I.** adv. *(equally)* así de, tan <*it won't be easy to find someone as nice* no será fácil encontrar alguien tan bueno>; *(for example)* (tal) como <*some animals, as dogs and cats, eat meat* algunos animales, como los perros y los gatos, comen carne> ♦ **as . . . as** tan . . . como <*as strong as an ox* tan fuerte como un buey> • **as far as I'm concerned** en cuanto a mí respecta • **as far as I know** que yo sepa • **as good as** prácticamente <*the car looks as good as new* el automóvil luce prácticamente nuevo> **II.** conj. *(to the same degree)* igual que, como <*sweet as sugar* dulce como el azúcar>; *(while)* al mismo tiempo que, mientras <*she sang as she worked* ella cantaba mientras trabajaba>; *(because)* ya que, porque <*he stayed home as he was ill* él se quedó en su casa porque estaba enfermo>; *(though)* a pesar de que, aunque <*brave as they were the danger made them afraid* eran valientes el peligro los asustaba> ♦ **as from** a partir de • **as it to** como para • **as it were** por así decirlo • **as though** como si • **as to** en cuanto a • **as yet** hasta ahora **III.** prep. *(in the same manner)* lo mismo que, como <*we will fight as men* pelearemos como hombres>; *(in the role of)* en carácter de, como <*he was sent as a peacemaker* lo enviaron como conciliador> ♦ **as a rule** por regla general • **as for** en cuanto a • **as for** en cuanto a mí> **IV.** pron. *(which)* que <*do the same things as I do* haz las mismas cosas que yo hago>; *(a fact that)* como <*she is very careful, as her work shows* ella es muy cuidadosa, como lo demuestra su trabajo> ♦ **as much** (tanto) eso <*I might have guessed as much* yo hubiera podido imaginarme (todo) eso> • **such as** tal como.

as·bes·tos (ăs-bĕs'təs, ăz-) s. MIN. asbesto, amianto ♦ **a. cement** fibrocemento.

as·cend (ə-sĕnd') intr. *(to rise)* elevarse, remontarse <*the balloon ascended rapidly* el globo se elevó rápidamente>; *(to slope upwards)* ascender, subir <*the road ascended near the village* el camino subía cerca del pueblo> —tr. *(to climb)* subir (escalera, montaña); *(to assume)* subir a, ascender a (trono).

as·cen·dance o **as·cen·dence** (ə-sĕn'dəns) s. ascendiente *m*, predominio.

as·cen·dan·cy *o* **as·cen·den·cy** (ə-sĕn′dən-sē) s. ascendiente *m,* predominio.

as·cen·dant *o* **as·cen·dent** (ə-sĕn′dənt) I. adj. *(rising)* ascendiente; *(dominant)* ascendiente, predominante II. s. *(dominance)* predominio; ASTROL. ascendente *m.*

as·cend·ing (ə-sĕn′dĭng) adj. que sube, ascendente.

as·cen·sion (ə-sĕn′shən) s. ascensión *f* ♦ **A.** RELIG. la ascención (del Señor).

as·cent (ə-sĕnt′) s. *(act)* subida, ascención *f; (in rank)* ascenso; *(upward slope)* cuesta, pendiente *f.*

as·cer·tain (ăs′ər-tān′) tr. determinar, comprobar.

as·cet·ic (ə-sĕt′ĭk) I. s. asceta *mf* II. adj. ascético, austero.

as·cet·i·cism (ə-sĕt′ĭ-sĭz′əm) s. ascetismo.

as·cor·bic acid (ə-skôr′bĭk) s. QUÍM. ácido ascórbico, vitamina C.

as·cot (ăs′kət, -kŏt′) s. corbata (a la inglesa), chalina.

as·cribe (ə-skrīb′) tr. **-cribed, -crib·ing** *(to attribute)* atribuir, imputar; *(to assign)* adscribir, aplicar.

a·sea (ə-sē′) adv. hacia *o* en el mar, en alta mar.

a·sep·sis (ə-sĕp′sĭs) s. MED. asepsia.

a·sep·tic (ə-sĕp′tĭk) adj. MED. aséptico; FIG. *(impassive)* impasible, seco *<an a. tone of voice* un tono de voz seco*>.*

a·sex·u·al (ā-sĕk′shōō-əl) adj. asexual, asexuado.

ash¹ (ăsh) s. ceniza.

ash² (ăsh) s. BOT. fresno.

a·shamed (ə-shāmd′) adj. avergonzado ♦ **to be a.** darle vergüenza a uno *<she was a. to admit it* le daba vergüenza de admitirlo*>.*

ash can s. *(receptacle)* bote de basura *m,* cubo de basura; JER. *(depth charge)* carga de profundidad (contra submarinos).

ash·en (ăsh′ən) adj. pálido, ceniciento.

a·shore (ə-shôr′) adv. MARÍT. a tierra, en tierra ♦ **to go a.** bajar a tierra, desembarcar • **to run a.** varar, encallar.

ash·ram (ăsh′rəm) s. comunidad religiosa (que practica el hinduismo).

ash·tray (ăsh′trā′) s. cenicero.

Ash Wednesday s. RELIG. miércoles de ceniza *m.*

ash·y (ăsh′ē) adj. **-i·er, -i·est** ceniciento.

A·sia (ā′zhə) s. Asia ♦ **A. Major** Asia Mayor • **A. Minor** Asia Menor.

A·sian (ā′zhən) adj. & s. asiático.

A·si·at·ic (ā′zhē-ăt′ĭk, ā′zē-) adj. & s. asiático.

a·side (ə-sīd′) I. adv. *(to one side)* al lado, a un lado *<step a.* hágase a un lado*>; (apart)* de lado, aparte *<joking a.* bromas aparte*>* ♦ **to cast** *o* **throw a.** echar a un lado • **to put a.** *(to disregard)* poner de lado (temores, ansias); *(to reserve)* reservar, poner aparte (para un futuro) II. s. TEAT. aparte *m; (digression)* digresión *f.*

aside from prep. excepto, a no ser por *<a. a miracle nothing can save us* a no ser por un milagro, nada nos puede salvar*>.*

as if conj. como si *<you speak a. you were angry* hablas como si estuvieras enojado*>.*

as·i·nine (ăs′ə-nīn′) adj. *(of an ass)* asnal; FIG. *(stupid)* estúpido, necio.

ask (ăsk) tr. *(to put a question to)* preguntar *<he asked me my age* me preguntó mi edad*>; (to inquire)* pedir; *(to request)* solicitar, rogar; *(to demand)* exigir *<to a. too much of a child* exigir demasiado de un niño*>; (to invite)* invitar *<I asked her to the party* la invité a la fiesta*>; (to beg)* suplicar ♦ **to a. a favor** pedir un favor • **to a. after** preguntar por *<he asked after your health* preguntó por tu salud*>* • **to a. a question** hacer una pregunta • **to a. for** *(to request)* pedir (informes, instrucciones); *(to inquire)* preguntar por —intr. *(to inquire)* preguntar por *<they asked about you* preguntaron por tí*>; (to make a request)* pedir *<he asked for help* pidió ayuda*>* ♦ **to a. for it** FAM. buscársela • **to be had for the asking** basta pedirlo para conseguirlo.

a·skance (ə-skăns′) adv. de reojo, de soslayo; *(with suspicion)* con recelo, con desconfianza.

a·skew (ə-skyōō′) I. adj. ladeado, torcido II. adv. oblicuamente, sesgadamente.

a·slant (ə-slănt′) I. adv. sesgadamente, oblicuamente II. adj. ladeado, inclined.

a·sleep (ə-slēp′) I. adj. *(sleeping)* dormido; *(inactive)* inactivo; *(numb)* entumecido, adormecido; *(dead)* muerto II. adv. durmiendo ♦ **to fall a.** quedarse dormido.

as long as conj. *(since)* ya que *<a. you have offered, I accept* ya que lo has ofrecido, acepto*>; (on the condition that)* siempre y cuando *<we will cooperate a. we are notified on time* cooperaremos siempre y cuando nos lo notifiquen a tiempo*>; (while)* mientras *<a. you both shall live* mientras vosotros dos viváis*>.*

a·slope (ə-slōp′) I. adv. diagonalmente, en declive II. adj. inclinado, en pendiente.

a·so·cial (ā-sō′shəl) adj. *(not gregarious)* que evita la compañía de otros, solitario; *(self-centered)* egoísta, indiferente.

asp (ăsp) s. ZOOL. áspid *m,* áspide *m,* víbora venenosa.

as·par·a·gus (ə-spăr′ə-gəs) s. espárrago.

as·pect (ăs′pĕkt′) s. *(air)* aspecto; *(appearance)* apariencia; *(facet)* cara, superficie *f;* ASTROL. aspecto.

as·pen (ăs′pən) s. BOT. álamo temblón.

as·per·ate (ăs′pə-rāt′) tr. **-at·ed, -at·ing** asperezar, poner áspero *o* tosco.

as·per·i·ty (ă-spĕr′ĭ-tē) s. [pl. **-ties**] *(roughness)* aspereza, rugosidad *f; (irritability)* aspereza, rudeza.

as·per·sion (ə-spûrs′zhən) s. difamación *f,* calumnia.

as·phalt (ăs′fôlt′) I. s. asfalto ♦ **a. highways** carreteras de asfalto II. tr. asfaltar.

as·phyx·i·a (ăs-fĭk′sē-ə) s. asfixia.

as·phyx·i·ate (ăs-fĭk′sē-āt) tr. & intr. **-at·ed, -at·ing** asfixiar(se), sofocar(se).

as·phyx·i·a·tion (ăs-fĭk′sē-ā′shən) s. asfixia, sofocación *f.*

as·pic (ăs′pĭk) s. CUL. gelatina (de carne, pescado o tomate).

as·pi·rant (ăs′pər-ənt, ə-spīr′-) I. s. aspirante *mf,* pretendiente *mf* II. adj. aspirante.

as·pi·rate (ăs′pə-rāt′) I. tr. **-rat·ed, -rat·ing** FONÉT., MED. aspirar II. s. (-pər-ĭt) FONÉT. aspiración *f* III. adj. (-pər-ĭt) FONÉT. aspirado.

as·pi·ra·tion (ăs′pə-rā′shən) s. FONÉT., MED. aspiración *f; (desire)* anhelo, deseo; *(goal)* aspiración.

as·pi·ra·tor (ăs′pə-rā′tər) s. aspirador *m.*

as·pire (ə-spīr′) intr. **-pired, -pir·ing** *(to desire)* aspirar, ambicionar *<to a. to be an actress* ambicionar a ser una actriz*>;* ANT., FIG. *(to soar)* elevarse, subir.

as·pi·rin (ăs′pər-ĭn) s. FARM. aspirina.

ass¹ (ăs) s. asno, burro.

ass² (ăs) s. VULG. *(the buttocks)* culo, nalgas *f; (anus)* ano; *(coitus)* cogida.

as·sail (ə-sāl′) tr. asaltar, atacar, acometer.

as·sail·ant (ə-sā′lənt) s. asaltante *mf,* agresor *m.*

as·sas·sin (ə-săs′ĭn) s. asesino.

as·sas·si·nate (ə-săs′ə-nāt′) tr. **-nat·ed, -nat·ing** *(to murder)* asesinar; *(to destroy)* destruir, dañar *<to a. a person's character* destruir la reputación de una persona*>.*

as·sas·si·na·tion (ə-săs′ə-nā′shən) s. asesinato.

as·sault (ə-sôlt′) I. s. *(attack)* asalto, ataque *m; (criticism)* ultraje *m;* DER. *(law)* asalto (físico y violento); *(rape)* violación *f* II. tr. & intr. asaltar, atacar.

assault and battery s. DER. asalto y agresión *f.*

as·say I. s. (ăs′ā′, ă-sā′) *(of gold)* aquilatamiento; *(of metals)* ensaye *m* II. tr. (ă-sā′, ăs′ā′) ensayar (metales o aleación).

as·say·er (ă-sā′ər) s. ensayista (de substancias o metales) *mf.*

as·sem·blage (ə-sĕm′blĭj) s. *(of people)* asamblea; *(collection)* conjunto, colección *f;* MEC. ensamblaje *m,* montaje *m;* ARTE. collage *m.*

as·sem·ble (ə-sĕm′bəl) tr. **-bled, -bling** *(to gather)* congregar, reunir; MEC. ensamblar, montar —intr. congregarse, reunirse.

as·sem·bler (ə-sĕm′blər) s. ensamblador *m,* montador *m.*

as·sem·bly (ə-sĕm′blē) s. [pl. **-blies**] *(act)* congregación *f,* reunión *f; (meeting)* asamblea, congreso; MEC. *(fitting)* montaje *m,* ensamblaje *m;* MIL. asamblea, toque de llamada *m.*

assembly language s. COMPUT. lenguaje ensamblador *m.*

assembly line s. línea de montaje.

---

as·sent (ə-sĕnt′) I. intr. asentir, convenir II. s. asentimiento, aprobación f.

as·sert (ə-sûrt′) tr. *(to affirm)* asertar, afirmar; *(to maintain)* mantener, hacer valer ♦ **to a. oneself** imponerse, hacer valer uno sus derechos.

as·ser·tion (ə-sûr′shən) s. aserción f, afirmación f.

as·ser·tive (ə-sûr′tĭv) adj. asertivo, positivo.

as·ser·tive·ness (ə-sûr′tĭv-nĭs) s. acometividad f, agresividad f.

as·sess (ə-sĕs′) tr. *(to impose a tax)* gravar, multar; *(to evaluate)* evaluar, juzgar ♦ **to a. at** *(to appraise)* avaluar o tasar en.

as·sess·a·ble (ə-sĕs′ə-bəl) adj. *(appraisable)* tasable, valorable; *(said of taxes, fines)* gravable.

as·sess·ment (ə-sĕs′mənt) s. *(appraisal)* evaluación f, tasación f; *(amount assessed)* tasa.

as·ses·sor (ə-sĕs′ər) s. *(official)* tasador (de impuestos) m; *(adviser)* asesor m.

as·set (ăs′ĕt′) s. *(item)* posesión f, bien m; FIG. *(advantage)* ventaja ♦ **assets** COM., DER. bienes, activo • **a. in hand** activo disponible • **fixed a.** activo fijo.

as·sev·er·ate (ə-sĕv′ə-rāt′) tr. **-at·ed, -at·ing** aseverar, afirmar.

as·sev·er·a·tion (ə-sĕv′ə-rā′shən) s. aseveración f, afirmación f.

as·si·du·i·ty (ăs′ĭ-dōō′ĭ-tē) s. asiduidad f, perseverancia.

as·sid·u·ous (ə-sĭj′ōō-əs) adj. asiduo, perseverante.

as·sign (ə-sīn′) I. tr. *(to designate)* asignar, designar; *(to appoint)* designar, nombrar; *(to allot)* asignar, señalar (una tarea); *(to ascribe)* atribuir, indicar; DER. transferir, traspasar; MIL. asignar, destinar II. s. DER. cesionario, beneficiario.

as·sign·a·ble (ə-sīn′ə-bəl) adj. asignable; *(attributable)* atribuible; *(transferable)* transferible.

as·sig·na·tion (ăs′ĭg-nā′shən) s. *(act)* asignación f, designación f; *(date)* cita (amorosa).

as·sign·ee (ə-sī′nē′, ăs′ə-nē′) s. DER. *(transferee)* cesionario, beneficiario; *(representative)* apoderado.

as·sign·ment (ə-sīn′mənt) s. *(act)* asignación f; *(task)* tarea, deber m; *(position)* puesto, cargo; *(document)* escritura de cesión; DER. cesión f, traspaso.

as·sign·or (ə-sī′nôr′, ə-sī′nər) s. DER. cedente mf, transferidor m.

as·sim·i·late (ə-sĭm′ə-lāt′) tr. & intr. **-lat·ed, -lat·ing** asimilar(se).

as·sim·i·la·tion (ə-sĭm′ə-lā′shən) s. *(act)* asimilación f, absorción f; FISIOL. asimilación; FONÉT. asimilación; SOCIOL. integración f, adopción f (de características foráneas) f.

as·sist (ə-sĭst′) I. tr. asistir, auxiliar —intr. *(to aid)* asistir, auxiliar; *(to attend)* asistir II. s. ayuda, auxilio.

as·sis·tance (ə-sĭs′təns) s. asistencia, ayuda. ♦ **to be of a. to** ayudar a • **to come to someone's a.** acudir en auxilio de alguien.

as·sis·tant (ə-sĭs′tənt) s. & adj. ayudante mf, auxiliar m.

assistant professor s. profesor auxiliar o adjunto.

as·sis·tant·ship (ə-sĭs′tənt-shĭp′) EDUC. ayudantía.

as·so·ci·ate (ə-sō′shē-āt′, -sē-) I. tr. **-at·ed, -at·ing** *(to bring together)* asociar; *(to join)* juntar, unir; *(to relate)* asociar, relacionar ♦ **to a. oneself with** participar uno en, plegarse a —intr. *(to join in)* asociarse, unirse; *(to keep company)* juntarse, tratarse II. s. (-ĭt, -āt′) *(partner)* socio, consocio; *(companion)* compañero III. adj. (-ĭt, -āt′) asociado, adjunto.

associate professor s. profesor adjunto.

as·so·ci·a·tion (ə-sō′sē-ā′shən, -shē-) s. *(act)* asociación f; *(organized body)* asociación, organización f.

as·so·ci·a·tive (ə-sō′shē-ā′tĭv, -sē-, -shə-tĭv) adj. asociativo, de asociación.

as·so·nance (ăs′ə-nəns) s. FONÉT., POÉT. asonancia.

as·so·nant (ăs′ə-nənt) adj. & s. asonante.

as·sort (ə-sôrt′) tr. clasificar, ordenar —intr. cuadrar, concordar.

as·sort·ed (ə-sôr′tĭd) adj. *(various)* surtido, variado; *(classified)* clasificado; *(matched)* juntado, unido.

as·sort·ment (ə-sôrt′mənt) s. *(act)* clasificación f, arreglo; *(variety)* surtido, colección variada.

as·suage (ə-swāj′) tr. **-suaged, -suag·ing** *(to ease)* aliviar, mitigar; *(to satisfy)* satisfacer, saciar; *(to calm)* calmar, aplacar.

as·suage·ment (ə-swāj′mənt) s. alivio, mitigación f.

as·sum·a·ble (ə-sōō′mə-bəl) adj. asumible.

as·sume (ə-sōōm′) tr. **-sumed, -sum·ing** *(to take on)* asumir, adoptar (actitud); *(to undertake)* encargarse de, asumir; *(to ascend to)* asumir, tomar (el poder); *(to arrogate)* arrogarse (un derecho); *(to feign)* fingir, simular; *(to suppose)* presumir, suponer <*I assumed you knew it* supuse que tú lo sabías>.

as·sumed (ə-sōōmd′) adj. *(pretended)* simulado, fingido; *(taken for granted)* supuesto, presunto.

as·sum·ing (ə-sōō′mĭng) adj. pretensioso, arrogante.

as·sump·tion (ə-sŭmp′shən) s. *(act)* asunción f, toma (del poder); *(supposition)* suposición f, conjetura ♦ **A.** RELIG. la Asunción (de la Virgen).

as·sur·ance (ə-shōōr′əns) s. *(act)* aseveración f, afirmación f; *(guarantee)* garantía, promesa; *(certainty)* certeza, seguridad f; *(self-confidence)* aplomo.

as·sure (ə-shōōr′) tr. **-sured, -sur·ing** *(to dispel doubts)* asegurar; *(to convince)* convencer; *(to reassure)* tranquilizar; *(to ensure)* asegurar, garantizar.

as·sured (ə-shōōrd′) adj. *(made certain)* seguro, cierto; *(self-confident)* confiado, seguro (de sí mismo).

as·sur·ed·ly (ə-shōōr′ĭd-lē) adv. *(certainly)* seguramente, ciertamente; *(with self-confidence)* confiadamente, seguro de uno mismo.

As·syr·i·a (ə-sîr′ē-ə) s. HIST. Asiria.

As·syr·i·an (ə-sîr′ē-ən) adj. & s. *(inhabitant, language)* asirio.

a·stat·ic (ā-stăt′ĭk) adj. FÍS., MED. astático, inestable.

as·ter (ăs′tər) s. BIOL., BOT. áster m.

as·ter·isk (ăs′tə-rĭsk′) I. s. asterisco II. tr. marcar con asterisco.

a·stern (ə-stûrn′) adv. MARÍT. *(toward the rear)* a popa, de popa; *(backwards)* hacia atrás ♦ **a. of** MARÍT. detrás de.

as·ter·oid (ăs′tə-roid′) I. s. ASTRON. asteroide m; ICT. estrella de mar II. adj. asteroide, de forma de estrella.

as·the·ni·a (ăs-thē′nē-ə) s. MED. astenia, debilidad general f.

asth·ma (ăz′mə, ăs′-) s. asma.

asth·mat·ic (ăz-măt′ĭk, ăs′-) adj. & s. asmático.

as·tig·mat·ic (ăs′tĭg-măt′ĭk) adj. OFTAL. astigmático.

a·stig·ma·tism (ə-stĭg′mə-tĭz′əm) s. OFTAL. astigmatismo.

a·stir (ə-stûr′) adj. *(moving about)* activo, en movimiento; *(out of bed)* levantado, despierto.

a·ston·ish (ə-stŏn′ĭsh) tr. asombrar, sorprender.

a·ston·ish·ing (ə-stŏn′ĭ-shĭng) adj. asombroso, pasmoso.

a·ston·ish·ment (ə-stŏn′ĭsh-mənt) s. asombro, estupefacción f.

a·stound (ə-stound′) tr. maravillar, sorprender.

a·strad·dle (ə-străd′l) I. adv. a horcajadas II. prep. a horcajadas sobre.

as·tra·khan (ăs′trə-kăn′, -kən) s. astracán (piel, tela) m.

as·tral (ăs′trəl) adj. ASTRON., BIOL. astral.

a·stray (ə-strā′) adv. por mal camino ♦ **to go a.** extraviarse • **to lead a.** descarriar.

as·trict (ə-strĭkt′) tr. constreñir, restringir (esp. por obligaciones morales o legales).

a·stride (ə-strīd′) I. prep. *(over)* a horcajadas sobre; *(spanning)* de un lado al otro de II. adv. a horcajadas.

astride of prep. a horcajadas sobre.

as·tringe (ə-strĭnj′) tr. **-tringed, -tring·ing** constreñir, restringir.

as·trin·gen·cy (ə-strĭn′jən-sē) s. *(act)* astringencia; FIG. *(austerity)* austeridad f, severidad f.

as·trin·gent (ə-strĭn′jənt) I. adj. *(styptic)* astringente, astrictivo; FIG. *(harsh)* áspero, severo II. s. astringente m.

as·tro·dome (ăs′trə-dōm′) s. AVIA. cúpula (de una aeronave, usada para observación); DEP. estadio encerrado bajo tejado translúcido.

as·trol·o·ger (ə-strŏl′ə-jər) s. astrólogo.

ā rey / ä año / b boca / ch chico / d dar / ĕ el / ē mil / g gato / h joya / hw juez / ī aire / k casa / kw cuan /

as·tro·log·ic (ăs'trə-lŏj'ĭk) o **as·tro·log·i·cal** (-ĭ-kəl) adj. astrológico.
as·trol·o·gy (ə-strŏl'ə-jē) s. astrología.
as·tro·naut (ăs'trə-nôt') s. astronauta *mf*, cosmonauta *mf*.
as·tro·nau·tics (ăs'trə-nô'tĭks) s. [ú. con v. sing.] astronáutica.
as·tron·o·mer (ə-strŏn'ə-mər) s. astrónomo.
as·tro·nom·i·cal (ăs'trə-nŏm'ĭ-kəl) o **as·tro·nom·ic** (-ĭk) adj. ASTRON. astronómico; FIG. (*immense*) astronómico.
as·tron·o·my (ə-strŏn'ə-mē) s. astronomía.
as·tro·phys·i·cist (ăs'trō-fĭz'ĭ-sĭst) s. astrofísico.
as·tro·phys·ics (ăs'trō-fĭz'ĭks) s. [ú. con v. sing.] astrofísica.
as·tute (ə-stōōt', ə-styōōt') adj. astuto, sagaz.
a·sun·der (ə-sŭn'dər) adv. (*in pieces*) en pedazos, en dos; (*apart*) en partes, en pedazos.
a·sy·lum (ə-sī'ləm) s. (*institution*) asilo, hospicio; (*refuge*) refugio, amparo; POL. protección *f*, asilo.
a·sym·met·ric (ā'sĭ-mĕt'rĭk) o **a·sym·met·ri·cal** (-rĭ-kəl) adj. asimétrico.
a·sym·me·try (ā-sĭm'ĭ-trē) s. asimetría.
at (ăt, ət) prep. en <*at right angles* en ángulo recto>; a <*at noon* al mediodía>; por <*to be angry at something* estar enfadado por algo>; de <*don't laugh at me!* ¡no te rías de mí!>; en casa de <*I'll be at Diane's for the next hour or so* estaré en casa de Diana durante la próxima hora, más o menos> ♦ **at a distance** a lo lejos • **at a loss** perplejo, dudoso • **at best** en el mejor de los casos, cuando mejor • **at ease** (*comfortable*) tranquilo, cómodo; MIL. ¡descanso! • **at first** al principio, inicialmente • **at hand** a mano, a la mano • **at large** (*in general*) en general; (*plenipotentiary*) plenipotenciario • **at last** por último, por fin • **at least** como mínimo, por lo menos • **at length** (*completely*) en su totalidad; (*time*) largo y tendido • **at most** a lo sumo, cuando más • **at night** de *a,* por la noche • **at no time** nunca, jamás • **at once** a la vez, inmediatamente • **at peace** en paz • **at play** jugando • **at present** actualmente, en la actualidad • **at sea** (*sailing*) en el mar, navegando; FIG. (*uncertain*) incierto, perplejo • **at that** (*as it is*) sin más, así <*we simply didn't understand one another and we left it at that* simplemente no nos entendíamos y lo dejamos así>; (*additionally*) más aún, además <*she is a skater and a good one at that* es patinadora, y una muy buena además> • **at worst** en el peor de los casos.
at·a·vism (ăt'ə-vĭz'əm) s. atavismo.
at·a·vis·tic (ăt'ə-vĭs'tĭk) adj. atávico.
ate (āt) pret. de **eat.**
at ease s. MIL. descanso (posición u orden).
at·el·ier (ăt'l-yā') s. (*workshop*) taller *m*; (*studio*) estudio de un artista.
a·the·ism (ā'thē-ĭz'əm) s. ateísmo.
a·the·ist (ā'thē-ĭst) s. ateo.
a·the·is·tic (ā'thē-ĭs'tĭk) o **a·the·is·ti·cal** (-tĭ-kəl) adj. ateístico, ateísta.
A·the·ni·an (ə-thē'nē-ən) adj. & s. ateniense *mf*.
Ath·ens (ăth'ənz) s. Atenas.
ath·er·o·scle·ro·sis (ăth'ə-rō-sklə-rō'sĭs) s. MED. aterosclerosis *f*, ateroesclerosis *f*.
a·thirst (ə-thûrst') adj. sediento <*a. for freedom* sediento de libertad>.
ath·lete (ăth'lēt') s. atleta *m*, deportista *mf*.
athlete's foot s. MED. pie de atleta, tiña podal.
ath·let·ic (ăth-lĕt'ĭk) adj. (*of athletes*) atlético; (*strong*) fuerte, robusto.
ath·let·ics (ăth-lĕt'ĭks) s. (*sports*) [ú. con v. pl.] atletismo, actividades atléticas; (*program*) [ú. con v. sing.] atletismo, entrenamiento.
athletic supporter s. DEP. suspensorio masculino.
at-home (ət-hōm') s. recepción (en una casa particular) *f*.
a·thwart (ə-thwôrt') I. adv. de través, transversalmente II. prep. (*across*) a través de; (*against*) contra, en oposición a.
a·tilt (ə-tĭlt') adj. & adv. inclinado.
At·lan·tic (ăt-lăn'tĭk) adj. atlántico, del océano Atlántico.
Atlantic Ocean s. océano Atlántico.
At·lan·tis (ăt-lăn'tĭs) s. Atlántida.
at·las (ăt'ləs) s. atlas (colección de mapas) *m*.

at·mos·phere (ăt'mə-sfîr') s. FÍS., METEOR. atmósfera; (*surroundings*) medio ambiente, atmósfera.
at·mos·pher·ic (ăt'mə-sfĕr'ĭk, -sfîr'-) adj. atmosférico.
atmospheric pressure s. FÍS. presión atmosférica.
a·toll (ăt'ôl', ā'tôl') s. GEOG. atolón *m*.
at·om (ăt'əm) s. FÍS., QUÍM. átomo; FIG. (*iota*) átomo.
atom bomb s. bomba atómica.
a·tom·ic (ə-tŏm'ĭk) adj. atómico.
atomic age s. era atómica.
atomic bomb s. bomba atómica.
atomic energy s. energía atómica.
at·o·mic·i·ty (ăt'ə-mĭs'ĭ-tē) s. QUÍM., FÍS. atomicidad *f*, valencia.
atomic mass s. FÍS. masa atómica.
atomic number s. FÍS. número atómico.
atomic reactor s. reactor atómico.
atomic weight s. FÍS. peso atómico.
at·om·ism (ăt'ə-mĭz'əm) s. FILOS., SOCIOL. atomismo.
at·om·ize (ăt'ə-mīz') tr. -ized, -iz·ing FIG. (*to spray*) atomizar, pulverizar; FÍS. atomizar; MIL. bombardear con bombas atómicas.
at·om·iz·er (ăt'ə-mī'zər) s. atomizador *m*, vaporizador *m*.
atom smasher s. FÍS. acelerador de partículas atómicas *m*.
a·to·nal (ā-tō'nəl) adj. MÚS. atonal.
a·to·nal·i·ty (ā'tō-năl'ĭ-tē) s. MÚS. atonalidad *f*.
a·tone (ə-tōn') intr. **a·toned, a·ton·ing** dar reparación, expiar ♦ **to a. for** dar reparación por, expiar.
a·tone·ment (ə-tōn'mənt) s. expiación *f*, reparación *f*.
a·ton·ic (ā-tŏn'ĭk) I. adj. FONÉT. átono; MED. atónico, débil II. s. GRAM. palabra, sílaba o sonido átono.
a·top (ə-tŏp') I. adv. encima II. prep. encima de, sobre.
a·tri·um (ā'trē-əm) s. [pl. **a·tri·a** (ā'trē-ə) o -ums] ARQ. atrio, patio interior; ANAT. atrio, aurícula.
a·tro·cious (ə-trō'shəs) adj. atroz, abominable.
a·troc·i·ty (ə-trŏs'ĭ-tē) s. [pl. -ties] atrocidad *f*.
at·ro·phy (ăt'rə-fē) I. s. [pl. -phies] atrofia II. tr. & intr. -phied, -phy·ing atrofiar(se).
at·ro·pine (ăt'rə-pēn', -pĭn') o **at·ro·pin** (-pĭn') s. QUÍM. atropina.
at·tach (ə-tăch') tr. (*to affix*) ligar, juntar, sujetar; FIG. (*to ascribe*) dar, atribuir (importancia, significado); (*to seize*) embargar, incautar —intr. ♦ **to a. to** (*to adhere*) unirse a; (*to go with*) pertenecer.
at·tach·a·ble (ə-tăch'ə-bəl) adj. (*connectable*) que se puede unir o conectar; (*seizable*) embargable, incautable.
at·ta·ché (ăt'ə-shā', ă-tă'shā') s. DIPL. agregado.
attaché case s. portafolio, maletín *m*.
at·tached (ə-tăcht') adj. adherido, adjunto ♦ **a. to** encariñado con, apegado a.
at·tach·ment (ə-tăch'mənt) s. (*act*) enlace *m*, unión *f*; (*tie*) atadura, lazo; (*affection*) cariño, afición *f*; MEC. acoplamiento; DER. embargo, incautación *f*.
at·tack (ə-tăk') I. tr. (*to assail*) atacar, agredir; FIG. (*to undertake*) abordar, acometer (tarea, problema); MED. (*to beset*) atacar, aquejar —intr. ir al ataque II. s. (*assault*) ataque *m*, agresión *f*; MED. ataque.
at·tack·er (ə-tăk'ər) s. agresor *m*, asaltante *mf*.
at·tain (ə-tān') tr. (*to accomplish*) lograr, conseguir; (*to arrive at*) llegar a, alcanzar —intr. ♦ **to a. to** alcanzar, llegar a <*he attained to the desired position* él llegó a la posición deseada>.
at·tain·a·ble (ə-tā'nə-bəl) adj. (*feasible*) lograble; (*reachable*) alcanzable.
at·tain·der (ə-tān'dər) s. (*outlawry*) proscripción *f*, muerte civil *f*; ANT. (*dishonor*) mancha, tacha.
at·tain·ment (ə-tān'mənt) s. logro, realización *f* ♦ **attainments** conocimientos, habilidades.
at·tar (ăt'ər) s. aceite esencial (esp. de ciertas rosas) *m*.
at·tempt (ə-tĕmpt') I. tr. (*to try*) intentar, tratar de II. s. (*try*) intento, prueba; (*attack*) ataque *m*, atentado.
at·tend (ə-tĕnd') tr. (*to be present at*) atender, asistir a; (*to accompany*) acompañar; (*to wait upon*) asistir, servir; (*to take care of*) atender, cuidar ♦ **to a. to** prestar atención a, ocuparse de —intr. (*to be present*) atender, asistir; (*to serve*) servir, atender.
at·ten·dance (ə-tĕn'dəns) s. asistencia, concurrencia.

at·ten·dant (ə-těn'dənt) I. s. *(help)* encargado, mozo; *(companion)* acompañante *mf* II. adj. concomitante, concurrente.
at·ten·tion (ə-těn'shən) s. *(concentration)* atención *f*; *(attentiveness)* cuidado <*do it with your full a.* hazlo con mucho cuidado>; *(notice)* atención <*it has come to our a.* ha llegado a nuestra atención>; *(courtesy)* cortesía <*she treats me with a lot of a.* me trata con mucha cortesía>; *(service)* servicio (en restaurante, hotel); MIL. posición de firmes *f* <*he brought the soldiers to a.* puso los soldados en posición de firmes>; MED. asistencia, cuidado ♦ **attention!** MIL. ¡firmes! • **attentions** cortesías, atenciones • **to pay a.** (to) prestar atención (a) • **to stand at a.** MIL. cuadrarse.
at·ten·tive (ə-těn'tĭv) adj. *(observant)* atento; *(courteous)* atento, considerado.
at·ten·tive·ly (ə-těn'tĭv-lē) adv. *(mindfully)* cuidadosamente, con atención; *(considerately)* atentamente, cortésmente.
at·ten·tive·ness (ə-těn'tĭv-nĭs) s. *(care)* cuidado, atención *f*; *(thoughtfulness)* atención *f*.
at·ten·u·ate (ə-těn'yoo-āt') I. tr. & intr. **-at·ed, -at·ing** atenuar(se), disminuir(se) II. adj. (-ĭt) *(reduced)* atenuado, disminuido; BOT. asaetada, lanceolada.
at·ten·u·a·tion (ə-těn'yoo-ā'shən) s. *(act)* atenuación *f*, disminución *f*; MEC. amortiguamiento.
at·test (ə-těst') tr. *(to affirm)* atestiguar, dar fe de; *(to supply evidence)* certificar, testificar; *(to put under oath)* juramentar —intr. ♦ **to a. to** dar fe de.
at·tes·ta·tion (ăt'ě-stā'shən)) s. *(affirmation)* atestación *f*; *(testimony)* testimonio.
at·tes·tor (ə-těs'tər) s. testigo *mf*, certificador *m*.
at·tic (ăt'ĭk) s. *(top floor)* desván *m*, guardilla; ARQ. ático.
At·tic (ăt'ĭk) I. adj. ático (del Ática, de Atenas) II. s. *(inhabitant, language)* ático.
At·ti·ca (ăt'ĭ-kə) s. Ática.
at·tire (ə-tīr') I. tr. **-tired, -tir·ing** ataviar, vestir II. s. *(clothing)* atavío, vestido; HER. *(antlers)* astas de venado.
at·ti·tude (ăt'ĭ-tood', -tyood') s. *(position)* actitud *f*, postura; *(mental state)* actitud, disposición *f*; AER. *(orientation)* posición *f*.
at·ti·tu·di·nal (ăt'ĭ-tood'n-əl, -tyood'-) adj. de la actitud.
at·tor·ney (ə-tûr'nē) s. [pl. **-neys**] abogado, apoderado.
attorney at law s. abogado.
attorney general s. [pl. **attorneys general**] fiscal general *m*, procurador general *m*.
at·tract (ə-trăkt') tr. *(to draw near)* atraer, traer hacia sí; *(to allure)* atraer, llamar (la atención) —intr. atraer, ejercer atracción.
at·trac·tion (ə-trăk'shən) s. FÍS. atracción *f*, magnetismo; *(allure)* atractivo, atracción; *(entertainment)* atracción, espectáculo.
at·trac·tive (ə-trăk'tĭv) adj. atractivo, atrayente.
at·trac·tive·ness (ə-trăk'tĭv-nĭs) s. atractivo, encanto.
at·trib·ute (ə-trĭb'yoot) I. tr. **-ut·ed, -ut·ing** atribuir II. s. (ăt'rə-byoot') *(quality)* atributo, cualidad *f*; *(characteristic)* característica, atributo; GRAM. atributo.
at·tri·bu·tion (ăt'rə-byoo'shən) s. *(act)* atribución *f*; *(attribute)* atributo, cualidad *f*.
at·trib·u·tive (ə-trĭb'yə-tĭv) GRAM. I. s. atributo II. adj. atributivo.
at·tri·tion (ə-trĭsh'ən) s. *(friction)* fricción *f*, roce *m*; *(diminution)* desgaste *m*, agotamiento; *(personnel reduction)* reducción (en el número del personal por retiro, renuncia o muerte) *f*.
at·tune (ə-toon', ə-tyoon') tr. **-tuned, -tun·ing** MÚS. afinar; FIG. *(to bring into harmony)* adaptar, armonizar.
a·twit·ter (ə-twĭt'ər) adj. tembloroso, trémulo.
a·typ·i·cal (ā-tĭp'ĭ-kəl) adj. anormal, que no es típico.
au·burn (ô'bərn) I. s. color castaño II. adj. castaño.
auc·tion (ôk'shən) I. s. subasta, remate *m* II. tr. subastar, rematar.
auc·tion·eer (ôk'shə-nîr') I. s. subastador *m*, rematador *m* II. tr. subastar, rematar.
au·da·cious (ô-dā'shəs) adj. *(bold)* audaz, osado; *(insolent)* atrevido, descarado.
au·dac·i·ty (ô-dăs'ĭ-tē) s. [pl. **-ties**] *(boldness)* audacia, osadía; *(insolence)* atrevimiento, descaro.

au·di·bil·i·ty (ô'də-bĭl'ĭ-tē) s. audibilidad *f*.
au·di·ble (ô'də-bəl) adj. audible, oíble.
au·di·ence (ô'dē-əns) s. *(public)* auditorio, público; *(formal hearing)* audiencia.
au·di·o (ô'dē-ō') I. adj. RAD. de frecuencia audible II. s. RAD., TELEV. transmisión *f* o recepción del sonido *f*.
audio frequency s. FÍS., RAD. audiofrecuencia, frecuencia auditiva.
au·di·o·phile (ô'dē-ə-fīl') s. diletante de las reproducciones musicales *mf*.
au·di·o·typ·ing (ô'dē-ō-tī'pĭng) s. dictado de mecanografía tomado directamente de una cinta grabada.
au·di·o·vi·su·al (ô'dē-ō-vĭzh'oo-əl) adj. audiovisual ♦ **a. aids** material audiovisual.
au·dit (ô'dĭt) I. s. COM. auditoría, intervención (de cuentas) *f* II. tr. COM. examinar, verificar; EDUC. ser oyente de (una clase).
au·di·tion (ô-dĭsh'ən) I. s. audición *f* II. tr. dar audición a, probar a —intr. actuar en una audición (de prueba).
au·di·tive (ô'dĭ-tĭv) adj. auditivo.
au·di·tor (ô'dĭ-tər) s. *(listener)* oidor *m*, oyente *mf*; COM. auditor *m*, interventor *m*; EDUC. alumno libre.
au·di·to·ri·um (ô'dĭ-tôr'ē-əm) s. [pl. **-ri·ums** o **-ri·a** (-ē-ə)] *(theater)* sala, anfiteatro; *(hall)* auditorio, auditorium *m*.
au·di·to·ry (ô'dĭ-tôr'ē) adj. auditorio, auditivo.
au·ger (ô'gər) s. CARP. barrena *m*, taladro; MIN. barreno, sonda.
aught (ôt) s. cero.
aug·ment (ôg-měnt') tr. & intr. aumentar(se), acrecentar(se).
aug·men·ta·tion (ôg'měn-tā'shən) s. aumento.
aug·men·ta·tive (ôg-měn'tə-tĭv) I. adj. aumentador, aumentivo; GRAM. aumentativo II. s. GRAM. aumentativo.
aug·ment·ed (ôg-měn'tĭd) adj. MÚS. aumentada (intervalo).
au·gur (ô'gər) I. s. *(seer)* vidente *mf*, adivino; HIST. augur *m* II. tr. & intr. augurar, pronosticar ♦ **to a. ill** ser de mal agüero • **to a. well** ser de buen agüero.
au·gu·ry (ô'gyə-rē) s. [pl. **-ries**] augurio, presagio.
au·gust (ô-gŭst') adj. *(majestic)* augusto, majestuoso; *(venerable)* venerable.
Au·gust (ô'gəst) s. agosto.
Au·gus·tine (ô'gə-stēn', ô-gŭs'tĭn) s. Agustín.
Au·gus·tin·i·an (ô'gə-stĭn'ē-ən) RELIG. I. adj. *(of the order)* agustino; *(of the doctrine)* agustiniano II. s. agustino.
auk (ôk) s. ORNIT. alca.
aunt (ănt, änt) s. tía.
au·ra (ôr'ə) s. *(invisible breath)* aura, emanación *f*; FIG. *(air)* aura, aire *m*.
au·ral (ôr'əl) adj. auricular, auditivo.
au·re·ole (ôr'ē-ōl') s. aureola, halo.
au·ri·cle (ôr'ĭ-kəl) s. ANAT. aurícula.
au·ric·u·lar (ô-rĭk'yə-lər) adj. ANAT. auricular; *(spoken into the ear)* dicho al oído.
au·rif·er·ous (ô-rĭf'ər-əs) adj. aurífero.
au·ro·ra (ə-rôr'ə) s. METEOR. aurora; POÉT. alba, aurora; FIG. *(beginning)* origen *m*, principio ♦ **a. australis** aurora austral • **a. borealis** aurora boreal.
aus·cul·ta·tion (ô'skəl-tā'shən) s. MED. auscultación *f*.
aus·pice (ô'spĭs) s. *(patronage)* auspicio; *(divination)* adivinación *f*, predicción *f* ♦ **under the auspices of** bajo los auspicios de.
aus·pi·cious (ô-spĭsh'əs) adj. propicio, favorable.
aus·tere (ô-stîr') adj. austero.
aus·ter·i·ty (ô-stěr'ĭ-tē) s. [pl. **-ties**] austeridad *f*, severidad *f*.
Aus·tral·a·sia (ô'strə-lā'zhə) s. Australasia.
Aus·tra·li·a (ô-strāl'yə) s. Australia.
Aus·tra·lian (ô-strāl'yən) adj. & s. australiano.
Aus·tri·a (ô'strē-ə) s. Austria.
Aus·tri·an (ô'strē-ən) adj. & s. austríaco.
au·tar·chy (ô'tär'kē) s. [pl. **-chies**] POL. autarquía, autocracia; *(autarky)* ECON. POL. autarquía, independencia económica.
au·tar·ky (ô'tär'kē) s. [pl. **-kies**] ECON. POL. autarquía, independencia económica.
au·then·tic (ô-thěn'tĭk) adj. *(bona fide)* auténtico, fidedigno; *(genuine)* genuino; *(legal)* autorizado, legalizado.

ã rey / ä año / b boca / ch chico / d dar / ě el / ē mil / g gato / h joya / hw juez / ī aire / k casa / kw cuan /

au·then·ti·cate (ô-thĕn'tĭ-kāt') tr. **-cat·ed, -cat·ing** autenticar, autentificar.
au·then·ti·cat·ed (ô-thĕn'tĭ-kā'tĭd) adj. autenticado, autentificado.
au·then·ti·ca·tion (ô-thĕn'tĭ-kā'shən) s. autenticación *f*, autentificación *f.*
au·then·tic·i·ty (ô'thĕn-tĭs'ĭ-tē) s. autenticidad *f.*
au·thor (ô'thər) **I.** s. *(writer)* autor *m; (originator)* creador *m* **II.** tr. escribir.
au·thor·ess (ô'thər-ĭs) s. autora.
au·thor·i·tar·i·an (ə-thôr'ĭ-târ'ē-ən) **I.** adj. autoritario, dictatorial **II.** s. dictador *m*, déspota *mf.*
au·thor·i·tar·i·an·ism (ə-thôr'ĭ-târ'ē-ə-nĭz'əm) s. FILOS., POL. autoritarismo.
au·thor·i·ta·tive (ə-thôr'ĭ-tā'tĭv) adj. *(official)* autorizado; *(dictatorial)* autoritario.
au·thor·i·ty (ə-thôr'ĭ-tē) s. [pl. **-ties**] *(power)* autoridad *f*, poder *m; (authorization)* autorización *f*, facultad *f; (expert)* experto, perito ♦ **on good a.** de buena tinta.
au·thor·i·za·tion (ô'thər-ĭ-zā'shən) s. autorización *f*, permiso.
au·thor·ize (ô'thə-rīz') tr. **-ized, -iz·ing** *(to empower)* autorizar, facultar; *(to approve)* aprobar; *(to justify)* justificar (por uso o costumbre).
au·thor·ized (ô'thə-rīzd) adj. autorizado.
au·thor·ship (ô'thər-shĭp') s. *(profession)* profesión de autor *f; (source)* paternidad literaria.
au·tism (ô'tĭz'əm) s. PSIC. autismo.
au·tis·tic (ô-tĭs'tĭk) adj. PSIC. autista.
au·to (ô'tō) s. FAM. automóvil *m*, auto.
au·to·bi·o·graph·ic (ô'tō-bī'ə-grăf'ĭk) *o* **au·to·bi·o·graph·i·cal** (-ĭ-kəl) adj. autobiográfico.
au·to·bi·og·ra·phy (ô'tō-bī-ŏg'rə-fē) s. [pl. **-phies**] autobiografía.
au·to·bus (ô'tō-bŭs') s. [pl. **-bus·es** *o* **-bus·ses**] autobús *m*, ómnibus *m.*
au·toc·ra·cy (ô-tŏk'rə-sē) s. [pl. **-cies**] POL. autocracia, dictadura.
au·to·crat (ô'tə-krăt') s. autócrata *mf*, déspota *mf.*
au·to·crat·ic (ô'tə-krăt'ĭk) adj. POL. autocrático, despótico.
au·to·di·dact (ô'tō-dī'dăkt) s. autodidacto.
au·to·gen·e·sis (ô'tō-jĕn'ĭ-sĭs) s. BIOL. autogénesis *f*, generación espontánea.
au·to·gi·ro (ô'tō-jī'rō) s. [pl. **-ros**] AER. autogiro.
au·to·graph (ô'tə-grăf') **I.** s. autógrafo, firma ♦ **a. collection** colección de autógrafos • **a. hunter** cazador de autógrafos **II.** tr. autografiar, firmar.
au·to·gy·ro (ô'tō-jī'rō) s. var. de **autogiro.**
au·to·hyp·no·sis (ô'tō-hĭp-nō'sĭs) s. autohipnosis *f.*
au·to·im·mune (ô'tō-ĭ-myōōn') adj. BIOL., MED. autoinmune.
au·to·in·tox·i·ca·tion (ô'tō-ĭn-tŏk'sĭ-kā'shən) s. MED. autointoxicación *f.*
au·to·load·ing (ô'tō-lō'dĭng) adj. ARM. semiautomático.
Au·to·mat (ô'tə-măt') s. marca registrada de restaurantes de servicio automático operado con monedas.
au·to·mate (ô'tə-māt') tr. & intr. **-mat·ed, -mat·ing** automatizar(se).
au·to·mat·ic (ô'tə-măt'ĭk) **I.** adj. automático **II.** s. arma automática.
automatic pilot s. piloto automático.
automatic pistol s. pistola automática.
automatic rifle s. fusil ametrallador *m.*
au·to·ma·tion (ô'tə-mā'shən) s. INDUS. automación *f*, automatización *f.*
au·tom·a·ti·za·tion (ô-tŏm'ə-tĭ-zā'shən) s. INDUS. automación *f*, automatización *f.*
au·tom·a·tize (ô-tŏm'ə-tīz') tr. **-tized, -tiz·ing** automatizar.
au·tom·a·ton (ô-tŏm'ə-tən, -tŏn') s. [pl. **-tons** *o* **-ta** (-tə)] autómata *mf.*
au·to·mo·bile (ô'tə-mō-bēl') s. automóvil *m*, carro ♦ **a. engine** motor de automóvil • **a. accident** accidente de automóvil.
au·to·mo·tive (ô'tə-mō'tĭv) adj. *(self-moving)* automotor, automotriz; *(of vehicles)* automovilístico.
au·to·nom·ic (ô'tə-nŏm'ĭk) adj. *(independent)* indepen-

diente, autonómico; *(spontaneous)* espontáneo; FISIOL. autónomo.
au·ton·o·mous (ô-tŏn'ə-məs) adj. autónomo, independiente.
au·ton·o·my (ô-tŏn'ə-mē) s. [pl. **-mies**] autonomía, independencia.
au·top·sy (ô'tŏp'sē, ô'təp-) s. [pl. **-sies**] autopsia.
au·to·sug·ges·tion (ô'tō-səg-jĕs'chən) s. autosugestión *f.*
au·to·work·er (ô'tō-wûr'kər) s. trabajador de la industria automovilística *m.*
au·tumn (ô'təm) s. otoño.
au·tum·nal (ô-tŭm'nəl) adj. otoñal, de otoño.
aux·il·ia·ry (ôg-zĭl'yə-rē, -zĭl'ə-rē) **I.** adj. *(helping)* auxiliar; *(additional)* adicional, suplementario **II.** s. [pl. **-ries**] *(assistant)* auxiliar *mf*, asistente *mf*; GRAM. verbo auxiliar ♦ **auxiliaries** MIL. tropas auxiliares.
auxiliary verb s. GRAM. verbo auxiliar.
a·vail (ə-vāl') **I.** tr. beneficiar, ayudar ♦ **to a. oneself of** aprovecharse de, valerse de —intr. valer, servir **II.** s. beneficio, ventaja ♦ **of** *o* **to no a.** en vano.
a·vail·a·bil·i·ty (ə-vā'lə-bĭl'ĭ-tē) s. disponibilidad *f.*
a·vail·a·ble (ə-vā'lə-bəl) adj. disponible, obtenible ♦ **to make a. to** poner a la disposición de.
av·a·lanche (ăv'ə-lănch') s. *(slide)* avalancha, alud *m*; FIG. *(large amount)* avalancha, torrente *m.*
a·vant-garde (ä'vänt-gärd') **I.** s. vanguardia **II.** adj. de vanguardia.
av·a·rice (ăv'ər-ĭs) s. avaricia, codicia.
av·a·ri·cious (ăv'ə-rĭsh'əs) adj. avaricioso, avaro.
av·a·tar (ăv'ə-tär') s. RELIG. avatar *m*, encarnación *f.*
a·venge (ə-vĕnj') tr. & intr. **a·venged, a·veng·ing** vengar(se).
a·veng·er (ə-vĕn'jər) s. vengador *m.*
av·e·nue (ăv'ə-nōō', -nyōō') s. *(thoroughfare)* avenida *f*, FIG. *(means)* medios, camino.
a·ver (ə-vûr') tr. **a·verred, a·ver·ring** *(to declare)* afirmar, declarar; DER. *(to justify)* establecer prueba de.
av·er·age (ăv'ər-ĭj) **I.** s. promedio, término medio, media ♦ **on an** *o* **on the a.** por término medio, como promedio **II.** adj. *(of average)* medio, de término medio <*a. cost* costo medio>; *(not exceptional)* común, ordinario **III.** tr. **-aged, -ag·ing** *(to compute)* calcular el promedio de; *(to obtain)* hacer *o* alcanzar un promedio de <*this car averages 150 kilometers per hour* este automóvil alcanza un promedio de 150 kilómetros por hora>; *(to prorate)* prorratear —intr. alcanzar un promedio de, ser de un promedio de.
a·verse (ə-vûrs') adj. *(having aversion)* opuesto, contrario; BOT. apartado, separado (del tallo) ♦ **to be a. to** oponerse a.
a·ver·sion (ə-vûr'zhən) s. *(dislike)* aversión *f*, antipatia; *(repugnance)* repugnancia.
a·vert (ə-vûrt') tr. *(to turn away)* desviar, apartar (mirada, pensamientos); *(to prevent)* prevenir (peligro, desastre).
a·vi·an (ä'vē-ən) adj. aviar (perteneciente a las aves).
a·vi·ar·y (ä'vē-ĕr'ē) s. [pl. **-ies**] aviario, pajarera.
a·vi·a·tion (ä'vē-ā'shən, ăv'ē-) s. aviación *f* ♦ **a. cadet** cadete de aviación • **a. show** desfile aéreo.
a·vi·a·tor (ä'vē-ā'tər, ăv'ē-) s. aviador *m*, piloto.
a·vi·a·trix (ä'vē-ā'trĭks, ăv'ē-) s. aviadora.
a·vi·cul·ture (ä'vĭ-kŭl'chər, ăv'ĭ-) s. avicultura, cría de aves.
av·id (ăv'ĭd) adj. *(eager)* ávido, ansioso; *(greedy)* codicioso; *(ardent)* entusiasta.
a·vid·i·ty (ə-vĭd'ĭ-tē) s. *(eagerness)* ansia; *(greed)* avidez *f*, codicia; *(affinity)* afinidad *f*; QUÍM. fuerza (de un ácido, base).
A·vi·gnon (ä'vēn-yōN') s. Aviñón.
a·vi·on·ics (ä'vē-ŏn'ĭks, ăv'ē-) s. [ú. con v. sing.] electrónica de la aviación *f.*
av·o·ca·do (ăv'ə-kä'dō, ä'və-) s. [pl. **-dos**] aguacate *m*, palta ♦ **a. salad** ensalada de aguacate.
av·o·ca·tion (ăv'ō-kā'shən) s. *(hobby)* pasatiempo, distracción *f*; ANT. *(profession)* trabajo, profesión *f.*
a·void (ə-void') tr. *(to shun)* evitar; *(to evade)* eludir, huir de; *(to refrain from)* abstenerse de; *(to invalidate)* anular, invalidar.

a·void·a·ble (ə-voi'də-bəl) adj. *(that can be avoided)* evitable, eludible; *(voidable)* anulable, revocable.

a·void·ance (ə-void'ns) s. *(act)* el evitar, evitación; *(invalidation)* anulación *f*, revocación *f*.

av·oir·du·pois (ăv'ər-də-poiz') s. FÍS. sistema de pesas y medidas (basado en la libra); FAM. *(weight)* peso, gordura (de un persona).

avoirdupois weight s. COM. sistema de pesas y medidas usado en los países de habla inglesa.

a·vouch (ə-vouch') tr. *(to guarantee)* garantizar, responder; *(to assert)* afirmar, declarar; *(to acknowledge)* reconocer, confesar.

a·vow (ə-vou') tr. *(to acknowledge)* reconocer; *(to admit)* admitir; *(to confess)* confesar.

a·vow·al (ə-vou'əl) s. *(acknowledgment)* reconocimiento; *(admission)* admisión *f*.

a·vowed (ə-voud') adj. reconocido, declarado.

a·vun·cu·lar (ə-vŭng'kyə-lər) adj. avuncular, de tío.

a·wait (ə-wāt') tr. & intr. esperar, aguardar.

a·wake (ə-wāk') I. tr. **a·woke** (ə-wōk'), **a·waked, a·wak·ing** *(to awaken)* despertar (del sueño); FIG. *(to stir)* despertar, traer a la memoria —intr. *(to wake up)* despertar(se) (del sueño); *(to realize)* darse cuenta (de), tomar conciencia (de) II. adj. *(not asleep)* despierto; *(alert)* alerta, vigilante.

a·wak·en (ə-wā'kən) tr. & intr. despertar(se).

a·wak·en·ing (ə-wā'kə-nĭng) s. despertar *m*.

a·ward (ə-wôrd') I. tr. *(to grant)* conceder, asignar; *(to adjudge)* adjudicar, otorgar; *(to bestow)* conferir II. s. *(decision)* decisión *f*, fallo; *(prize)* premio, recompensa.

a·ware (ə-wâr') adj. *(having cognizance)* consciente; *(knowing)* percatado de *o* que ♦ **to be a. of** *o* **that** tener conciencia de *o* que • **to become a. of** enterarse de, percatarse de.

a·ware·ness (ə-wâr'nĭs) s. *(cognizance)* conciencia; *(knowledge)* conocimiento.

a·wash (ə-wŏsh') adj. & adv. *(level with water)* a flor de agua; *(flooded)* inundado; *(floating)* flotante.

a·way (ə-wā') I. adv. *(far)* lejos, a lo lejos; *(from a given place)* lejos de, a <*the store is only one mile a. from here* la tienda está sólo a una milla de aquí>; *(continuously)* constantemente, sin parar; *(aside)* en el sentido opuesto, hacia el otro lado <*he glanced a.* echó una mirada hacia el otro lado> ♦ **far a.** lejos • **right a.** inmediatamente • **to do a. with** *(to get rid of)* deshacerse de; *(to kill)* matar • **to get a.** escaparse • **to get a. with** *(with impunity)* salir airoso o impunidad; FAM. *(to succeed)* salir airoso • **to give a.** *(as presents)* regalar; *(to get rid of)* deshacerse de; *(to reveal)* revelar, delatar • **to put a.** *(to keep in a place)* guardar, poner en su sitio; FIG. *(to save)* ahorrar; FAM. *(to place in confinement)* encerrar, meter (en un manicomio, cárcel) • **to run a.** fugarse, escaparse • **to send a.** *(to dismiss)* echar, despedir; *(to dispatch)* enviar, expedir • **to take a.** *(to carry off)* llevarse; *(to subtract)* restar II. adj. *(absent)* ausente; *(at a distance)* distante, lejano.
▲ El adverbio *away* no se traduce literalmente en los casos en los cuales el verbo español lo incluye implícitamente. Algunos de esos casos son <*to get away* escaparse>, <*to go away* irse>, y <*to run away* fugarse>.

awe (ô) I. s. temor *m* o admiración reverente *f* ♦ **to fill with a.** *(to fill with wonder)* llenar de admiración; *(to intimidate)* asustar, impresionar • **to stand in a. of** temer a, admirar a II. tr. **awed, aw·ing** infundir temor o admiración reverente.

a·weigh (ə-wā') adj. MARÍT. pendiente (ancla) ♦ **anchors a.!** ¡levanten anclas!

awe·some (ô'səm) adj. pasmoso, asombroso.

awe·some·ness (ô'səm-nĭs) s. pasmo, asombro.

awe·struck (ô'strŭk') *o* **awe·strick·en** (ô'strĭk'ən) adj. pasmado, asombrado.

aw·ful (ô'fəl) adj. *(terrible)* pavoroso, temible; *(dreadful)* detestable; *(enormous)* enorme, tremendo.

aw·ful·ly (ô'fə-lē) adv. *(terribly)* pavorosamente, terriblemente; *(dreadfully)* detestablemente; *(great)* muchísimo, muy <*it's a. good* es muy bueno>.

aw·ful·ness (ô'fəl-nĭs) s. *(horror)* horror *m*; *(atrocity)* atro-

cidad *f*; *(enormity)* enormidad *f* <*the a. of the crime* la enormidad del crimen>.

a·while (ə-hwīl') adv. un rato, algún tiempo.

awk·ward (ôk'wərd) adj. *(clumsy)* torpe, desmañado; *(embarrassing)* embarazoso, incómodo; *(requiring tact)* delicado, difícil (situación, asunto); *(shape, object)* inconveniente, difícil de manejar.

awk·ward·ness (ôk'wərd-nĭs) s. *(clumsiness)* torpeza; *(uncomfortableness)* incomodidad *f*.

awl (ôl) s. lezna, punzón *m*.

awn (ôn) s. BOT. arista, cañamiza.

awn·ing (ô'nĭng) s. toldo, marquesina.

a·woke (ə-wōk') pret. de **awake.**

a·wok·en (ə-wō'kən) G.B. part. p. de **awake.**

a·wry (ə-rī') I. adv. *(askew)* de soslayo; *(amiss)* erradamente, incorrectamente ♦ **to go a.** salir mal II. adj. sesgado, torcido.

ax *o* **axe** (ăks) I. s. [pl. **ax·es** (ăk'sĭz)] hacha ♦ **to get the a.** JER. ser despedido • **to have an a. to grind** FAM. tener intereses personales II. tr. **axed, ax·ing** cortar (con un hacha).

ax·el (ăk'səl) s. DEP. salto en el aire de una vuelta y media (en el patinaje sobre hielo).

ax·es (ăk'sēz') pl. de **axis.**

ax·i·al (ăk'sē-əl) adj. axial, del eje.

ax·il·la (ăk-sĭl'ə) s. [pl. **-il·lae** (-sĭl'ē)] axila, sobaco.

ax·il·lar·y (ăk'sə-lĕr'ē) I. adj. ANAT. axilar, de la axila II. s. [pl. **-ies**] ORNIT. pluma axilar.

ax·i·om (ăk'sē-əm) s. *(maxim)* axioma, máxima; LÓG., MAT. axioma.

ax·i·o·mat·ic (ăk'sē-ə-măt'ĭk) *o* **ax·i·o·mat·i·cal** (-ĭ-kəl) adj. axiomático, evidente.

ax·is (ăk'sĭs) s. [pl. **ax·es** (ăk'sēz')] eje *m* ♦ **a. of rotation** GEOM. eje de rotación • **the earth's a.** el eje terrestre.

ax·le (ăk'səl) s. MEC. eje *m*, árbol *m*.

ax·le·tree (ăk'səl-trē') s. MEC. árbol *m*, eje *m*.

ax·o·lotl (ăk'sə-lŏt'l) s. ZOOL. ajolote *m*.

ax·on (ăk'sŏn') *o* **ax·one** (-sōn') s. ANAT. axón *m*, neuroeje *m*.

a·ya·tol·lah (ī'ə-tō'lə, -tŏl'ə) s. RELIG. líder religioso islámico de la secta chiíta.

aye[1] *o* **ay** (ī) I. s. voto a favor ♦ **the ayes** los que votan a favor II. adv. sí.

aye[2] *o* **ay** (ā) adv. siempre ♦ **for a.** para siempre.

a·zal·ea (ə-zāl'yə) s. BOT. azalea.

az·i·muth (ăz'ə-məth) s. acimut *m*, azimut *m*.

A·zores (ā'zôrz) s.pl. Azores *f*.

Az·tec (ăz'tĕk') s. & adj. azteca *mf*.

az·ure (ăzh'ər) I. s. *(color)* azul celeste *m*; HER. azur *m*, azul oscuro II. adj. azul celeste.

az·ur·ite (ăzh'ə-rīt') s. MIN. azurita, malaquita azul.

B

b, B (bē) s. [pl. **b's, B's**] segunda letra del alfabeto inglés; MÚS. si *m* ♦ **B flat, major, minor, sharp** MÚS. si bemol, mayor, menor, sostenido.

baa (bă, bä) I. intr. balar II. s. balido.

bab·ble (băb'əl) I. intr. **-bled, -bling** *(to prattle)* barbotar, mascullar; *(to chatter)* parlotear; *(a brook)* murmurar, susurrar —tr. *(to prattle)* farfullar; *(to blurt out)* revelar II. s. *(prattle)* barboteo; *(chatter)* parloteo; *(murmur)* murmullo, susurro.

babe (bāb) s. *(baby)* criatura, infante *m*; *(naive person)* persona inocente; JER. *(girl)* monada, belleza.

ba·boon (bă-bōōn') s. ZOOL. *(monkey)* babuino, mandril *m*; *(boor)* patán *m*.

ba·by (bā'bē) I. s. [pl. **-bies**] *(infant)* bebé *m*, nene *m*; *(youngest child)* benjamín *m*; *(animal)* cachorro; *(bird)* pichón *m*; *(childish person)* niño <*he is such a b.* es tan niño>; JER. *(girl)* monada, belleza; *(special interest)* creación *f*, niña de los ojos <*that idea was his b.* esa idea era la niña de sus ojos> ♦ **b. brother, sister** hermanito, hermanita • **b. carriage** cochecito de niños • **b. face** FAM. persona de facciones infantiles • **b. talk** balbuceo, habla de los niños II. tr. **-bied, -by·ing** mimar, consentir.

ba·by·hood (bā′bē-hōŏd′) s. (primera) infancia, niñez *f.*

ba·by·ish (bā′bē-ĭsh) adj. infantil, de niño.

Bab·y·lon (băb′ə-lŏn′) s. Babilonia.

Bab·y·lo·ni·an (băb′ə-lō′nē-ən) I. adj. HIST. (of Babylon) babilónico, babilonio; FIG. (luxurious) babilónico II. s. HIST. (inhabitant, language) babilonio.

ba·by-sit (bā′bē-sĭt′) intr. **-sat** (-săt′), **-sit·ting** cuidar niños —tr. cuidar (niños).

baby sitter s. niñera empleada por hora.

bac·ca·lau·re·ate (băk′ə-lôr′ē-ĭt) s. EDUC. (degree) bachillerato; (speech) discurso de despedida.

bac·ca·rat (bä′kə-rä′, băk′ə-) s. bacará *m.*

bac·cha·nal (băk′ə-năl′) I. s. (bacchante) bacante *f*; (celebration) bacanal *f*, juerga; (reveler) juerguista *mf*, parrandero ♦ **bacchanals** bacanales II. adj. báquico.

bac·cha·na·lia (băk′ə-nāl′yə) s. [pl. **bacchanalia**] bacanal *f*, parranda.

bac·cha·na·lian (băk′ə-nāl′yən) I. adj. báquico II. s. juerguista *mf*, parrandero.

bac·chant (bə-kănt′) s. (priest) sacerdote de Baco *m*; (votary) devoto de Baco; (reveler) juerguista *m*, parrandero.

Bac·chus (băk′əs) s. MITOL. Baco.

bach·e·lor (băch′ə-lər) s. (single man) soltero; EDUC. (degree) bachillerato; (graduate) bachiller *m* ♦ **B. of Arts** EDUC. bachiller en filosofía y letras • **b. party** despedida de soltero • **B. of Science** EDUC. bachiller en ciencias.

bach·e·lor·hood (băch′ə-lər-hōŏd′) s. soltería, estado de soltero.

bach·e·lor's-but·ton (băch′ə-lərz-bŭt′n) s. BOT. aciano.

bac·il·lar·y (băs′ə-lĕr′ē) o **ba·cil·lar** (bə-sĭl′ər, băs′ə-lər) adj. (rod-shaped) baciliforme; BACT. bacilar.

ba·cil·lus (bə-sĭl′əs) s. [pl. **-cil·li** (-sĭl′ī′)] BACT. bacilo.

back (băk) I. s. (of human beings) espalda; (of animals) lomo, espinazo; (spine) columna vertebral; (reverse side) envés *m*, revés *m*; (of coins, checks) dorso, reverso; (of chairs) respaldo, espaldar *m*; (of books) lomo; DEP. (sports) defensa, zaga ♦ **at the b. of** detrás de, en la parte de atrás de • **b. to b.** (touching) espalda con espalda; (consecutively) uno detrás del otro • **behind someone's b.** a espaldas o por detrás de alguien • **in b. of** detrás de • **on one's b.** postrado, en cama • **to get off someone's b.** FAM. dejar de molestar a alguien <get off my b.! ¡deja de molestarme!> • **to get one's b. up** enojarse, picarse • **to have at the b. of one's mind** tener presente • **to have** o **to carry on one's b.** llevar a cuestas • **to know like the b. of one's hand** conocer como la palma de la mano • **to scratch someone's b.** FIG. hacer un favor a alguien • **to turn one's b. on** volver la espalda a, abandonar • **with one's b. to the wall** entre la espada y la pared II. adv. (backward) atrás, hacia atrás; (to a former place) de vuelta, de regreso <they are b. están de vuelta> ♦ **as far b. as** ya en <as far b. as 1970 ya en 1970> • **b. and forth** de acá para allá • **in b. of** detrás de, tras de • **to answer b.** replicar, rebatir • **to come b.** volver, regresar • **to go b.** regresar, retornar • **to go on one's word** desdecirse, faltar a una promesa • **to go b. and forth** ir y venir • **to hold b.** (to control) detener(se), refrenar(se); (to hide) esconder, ocultar • **to pay someone b.** (to repay) devolverle dinero a alguien; (to avenge oneself) pagarle a alguien con la misma moneda • **to put b.** poner en su lugar • **to send b.** (person) hacer volver (a una persona); (to return) devolver (una cosa) • **to set b.** (to hinder) detener, entorpecer (desenvolvimiento); (a clock) atrasar (un reloj) • **years b.** años atrás, hace años III. adj. (in the rear) de atrás, posterior; (remote) apartado, lejano; (overdue) atrasado <b. rent renta atrasada> IV. tr. (to move backward) mover hacia atrás; (vehicle) dar marcha atrás a, hacer retroceder a; (to strengthen) reforzar, respaldar (con un forro o respaldo); (to support) respaldar, apoyar; (to bet on) apostar a o por ♦ **to bet on the wrong horse** FIG., FAM. escoger mal • **b. up** (vehicle) mover hacia atrás, dar marcha atrás; (to support) respaldar, apoyar; (to justify) justificar con pruebas; (to guarantee) respaldar (fondos); (to finance) financear, cos-

tear • **to b. water** MARÍT. ciar —intr. moverse hacia atrás, retroceder ♦ **to b. away** alejarse retrocediendo • **to b. down** ceder, echarse atrás • **to b. out** (vehicle) salir dando marcha atrás; (to withdraw) retractarse, volverse atrás • **to b. up** o **off** retroceder.

back·ache (băk′āk′) s. dolor de espalda *m.*

back·bite (băk′bīt′) tr. **-bit** (-bĭt′), **-bit·ten** (-bĭt′n), **-bit·ing** calumniar, hablar mal de —intr. murmurar.

back·board (băk′bôrd′) s. (of a bed, chair) respaldo, espaldar *m*; (reinforcement) tabla de refuerzo.

back·bone (băk′bōn′) s. (spine) espinazo, columna vertebral; (determination) carácter *m*, firmeza; (support) pilar *m*, piedra angular <agriculture is the b. of the economy la agricultura es la piedra angular de la economía>.

back·break·ing (băk′brā′kĭng) adj. agobiador, agotador.

back·coun·try (băk′kŭn′trē) s. interior (de un país) *m.*

back·date (băk′dāt′) tr. **-dat·ed, -dat·ing** antedatar.

back door s. puerta de atrás, puerta de servicio.

back·drop (băk′drŏp′) s. TEAT. telón de fondo o de foro *m*; (setting) marco, trasfondo.

back·er (băk′ər) s. (supporter) partidario; (sponsor) patrocinador *m*, promotor *m*; (bettor) apostador *m.*

back·fire (băk′fīr′) I. s. (fire) contracandela, contrafuego; AUTO. petardeo, explosión *f* II. intr. **-fired, -fir·ing** AUTO. petardear, explotar; (scheme) salir al revés ♦ **to b. on someone** salirle a alguien el tiro por la culata.

back·for·ma·tion (băk′fôr-mā′shən) s. FILOL. (word) derivado regresivo; (process) derivación regresiva.

back·gam·mon (băk′găm′ən) s. chaquete *m.*

back·ground (băk′ground′) s. ARTE. (of a picture) fondo, trasfondo; (unobtrusive position) fondo, segundo plano; (circumstances) trasfondo, antecedentes *m*; (past) pasado; (education) formación *f*; (experience) experiencia; (knowledge) conocimientos *m.*

back·hand (băk′hănd′) I. s. DEP. (stroke) revés *m*; (handwriting) escritura inclinada hacia la izquierda II. adv. de revés III. tr. DEP. golpear de revés.

back·hand·ed (băk′hăn′dĭd) adj. (stroke) dado con el revés de la mano; (handwriting) inclinado hacia la izquierda; (roundabout) ambiguo, indirecto.

back·ing (băk′ĭng) s. (reinforcement) refuerzo; (support) respaldo (moral, económico).

back·lash (băk′lăsh′) s. (motion) contragolpe *m*, sacudida; (reaction) reacción *f* <a b. of indignation una reacción de indignación>; MEC. juego.

back·less (băk′lĭs) adj. (chair) sin espaldar; (dress) sin espalda.

back·list (băk′lĭst′) s. catálogo de libros publicados.

back·log (băk′lôg′) I. s. (log) leño trasero (de un fuego); (reserve) reserva, provisión *f*; (accumulation) acumulación (de trabajo, pedidos) *f* II. tr. & intr. **-logged, -log·ging** acumular(se), amontonar(se).

back number s. (issue) número atrasado (de una publicación); FAM. (person) persona anticuada; (thing) antigualla.

back·pack (băk′păk′) I. s. mochila II. intr. ir de excursión (llevando mochila) —tr. llevar (en una mochila).

back·pack·er (băk′păk′ər) s. mochilero.

back·rest (băk′rĕst′) s. respaldo (de un asiento).

back seat s. (of a vehicle) asiento de atrás; FAM. (subordinate position) posición inferior o de poca monta *f.*

back-seat driver (băk′sēt′) s. FAM. (passenger) pasajero que irrita al conductor con sus indicaciones; (busybody) persona entremetida.

back·side (băk′sīd′) s. FAM. trasero, nalgas.

back·slap (băk′slăp′) tr. & intr. **-slapped, -slap·ping** dar palmadas en la espalda, demostrar efusiva buena voluntad.

back·slide (băk′slīd′) intr. **-slid** (-slĭd′), **-slid** o **-slid·den** (-slĭd′n), **-slid·ing** reincidir (en el pecado, delito).

back·slid·er (băk′slīd′ər) s. reincidente *mf.*

back·space (băk′spās′) intr. **-spaced, -spac·ing** hacer retroceder (el carro de una máquina de escribir).

back·spin (băk′spĭn′) s. DEP. efecto.

back·stage I. adv. (băk′stāj′) TEAT. entre bambalinas, entre bastidores; FIG. (privately) entre bastidores II. adj.

(băk'stāj') TEAT. de bastidores; FIG. *(private)* clandestino, secreto.

back stairs s. escalera de servicio.

back·stairs (băk'stârz') o **back·stair** (-stâr') adj. furtivo, clandestino.

back·stay (băk'stā') s. MARÍT. estay *m*, traversa; FIG. *(support)* soporte *m*.

back·stitch (băk'stĭch') COST. I. s. pespunte *m* II. tr. pespuntear.

back·stop (băk'stŏp') I. s. DEP. red o valla para retener la pelota II. tr. **-stopped, -stop·ping** *(a ball)* servir de red o valla a; *(to support)* reforzar; *(to substitute for)* sustituir, suplir (en caso de emergencia).

back·street (băk'strēt') adj. furtivo, clandestino.

back·stretch (băk'strĕch') s. DEP. pista opuesta a la recta final.

back·stroke (băk'strōk') DEP. s. *(backhand)* revés *m*; *(in swimming)* brazada de espalda.

back swept (băk'swĕpt') adj. inclinado hacia atrás.

back talk s. impertinencia(s).

back·track (băk'trăk') intr. *(to go back)* retroceder, desandar; *(to reverse position)* volverse atrás.

back-up (băk'ŭp') I. s. *(reserve)* reserva; *(substitute)* sustituto, suplente *mf*; *(spare)* repuesto; *(support)* respaldo, apoyo; *(clog, accumulation)* acumulación *f*, atascamiento; MÚS. *(accompaniment)* acompañamiento II. adj. *(standby)* suplente, de reserva; *(spare)* de repuesto (copia, material).

back·ward (băk'wərd) o **back·wards** (-wərdz) I. adv. *(back)* hacia atrás, para atrás <*to look b.* mirar para atrás>; *(with one's back leading)* de espaldas <*to fall b.* caerse de espaldas>; *(in reverse order)* al revés, al contrario <*they do everything b.* lo hacen todo al revés>; *(worse)* hacia atrás, de mal en peor ♦ **to bend over b.** esforzarse al máximo, hacer todo lo posible • **to know backwards and forwards** saberse al dedillo II. adj. *(toward the back)* hacia atrás; <*a b. look* una mirada hacia atrás>; *(motion)* de retroceso; *(with one's back leading)* de espaldas; *(reverse)* al revés, inverso; *(unprogressive)* atrasado (país, época); *(retarded)* retrasado; *(shy)* tímido.
▲ Como adverbio, las formas *backward* y *backwards* son intercambiables. Como adjetivo, úsase solamente *backward*.

back·ward·ness (băk'wərd-nĭs) s. *(in progress)* atraso; *(in development)* retraso; *(shyness)* timidez *f*.

back·wards (băk'wərdz) adv. consulte **backward**.

back·wash (băk'wŏsh') s. *(flow)* contracorriente (de agua, aire) *f*; *(aftermath)* consecuencias, repercusiones *f*.

back·wa·ter (băk'wô'tər) s. *(water)* agua estancada; *(place)* lugar atrasado <*a cultural b.* un lugar culturalmente atrasado>.

back·woods (băk'wŏŏdz') s.pl. *(wild region)* monte *m*, selva; *(remote area)* lugar apartado.

back·woods·man (băk'wŏŏdz'mən) s. [pl. -men] rústico.

back yard o **back·yard** (băk'yärd') s. traspatio ♦ **in one's own b.** FIG. en las puertas de uno.

ba·con (bā'kən) s. tocino ♦ **to bring home the b.** FAM. traer el sustento a la casa.

bac·te·ri·a (băk-tîr'ē-ə) pl. de **bacterium**.

bac·te·ri·al (băc-tîr'ē-əl) adj. bacteriano.

bac·te·ri·cide (băk-tîr'ĭ-sīd') s. bactericida *m*.

bac·te·ri·ol·o·gist (băk-tîr'ē-ŏl'ə-jĭst) s. bacteriólogo.

bac·te·ri·ol·o·gy (băk-tîr'ē-ŏl'ə-jē) s. bacteriología.

bac·te·ri·um (băk-tîr'ē-əm) s. [pl. -ri·a (-ē-ə)] bacteria.

bad §G22 (băd) I. adj. **worse** (wûrs), **worst** (wûrst) *(poor)* malo, inferior; *(evil)* malo, malvado; *(unfavorable)* malo (suerte, tiempo); *(upsetting)* malo <*b. news* malas noticias>; *(improper)* malo, incorrecto <*b. manners* malos modales>; *(defective)* malo, defectuoso; *(check)* sin fondos; *(naughty)* malo, desobediente <*a b. boy* un niño desobediente>; *(harmful)* malo, perjudicial <*tobacco is b. for your health* el tabaco es perjudicial para la salud>; *(severe)* fuerte <*a b. cold* un catarro fuerte>; *(rotten)* malo, podrido; *(great)* fantástico, formidable ♦ **from b. to worse** de mal en peor • **not b.** FAM. no está mal, bastante bien • **to be a b. apple** o **a b. egg** JER. ser un tipo malo, ser un mal sujeto • **to feel b.** *(to feel ill)* sentirse mal; *(to feel*

sorry)* sentir, lamentar • **to go b.** echarse a perder • **too b.!** *(how unfortunate!)* ¡qué lástima!; *(tough!)* ¡mala suerte! II. s. lo malo III. adv. FAM. *(wrong)* mal; *(very much)* mucho <*it hurts b.* me duele mucho> ♦ **to be b. off** FAM. estar mal (esp. de dinero).

bad blood s. mala sangre, encono.

bade (băd, bād) un pret. de **bid**.

badge (băj) s. *(insignia)* distintivo; *(armband)* brazalete *m*; *(award)* condecoración *f*; *(symbol)* emblema *m*.

badg·er (băj'ər) I. s. ZOOL. tejón (animal y piel) *m* II. tr. importunar, molestar.

bad·i·nage (băd'n-äzh') s. broma, chacota.

bad·lands (băd'lăndz') s.pl. páramo, pedregal *m*.

bad·ly §G28 (băd'lē) adv. *(wrong)* mal; *(very much)* mucho, con urgencia <*I need it b.* lo necesito con urgencia>; *(seriously)* gravemente, de gravedad <*b. wounded* herido de gravedad> ♦ **to take something b.** tomar a mal algo.

bad·min·ton (băd'mĭn'tən) s. DEP. volante *m*.

bad·mouth o **bad-mouth** (băd'mouth') tr. JER. hablar pestes de, poner por los suelos.

bad·ness (băd'nĭs) s. *(wickedness)* maldad *f*; *(naughtiness)* desobediencia, travesura.

bad-tem·pered (băd'těm'pərd) adj. *(permanently)* de mal genio; *(occasionally)* de mal humor, malhumorado.

baf·fle (băf'əl) I. tr. **-fled, -fling** *(to bewilder)* confundir, desconcertar; *(to foil)* eludir, impedir; *(to deflect)* desviar; *(to stop)* detener II. s. *(deflector)* deflector *m*; RAD. pantalla acústica.

baf·fle·ment (băf'əl-mənt) s. *(perplexity)* confusión *f*, desconcierto; *(deflection)* desviación *f*.

baf·fling (băf'lĭng) adj. *(bewildering)* desconcertante; *(thwarting)* obstaculizador.

bag (băg) I. s. *(container, content)* bolsa; *(sack)* saco; *(purse)* bolso, cartera; *(suitcase)* valija, maletín *m*; ANAT., ZOOL. *(pouch)* bolsa (de los ojos, canguro); *(in clothing)* bolsa, pliegue suelto; *(animals killed)* caza ♦ **b. and baggage** *(with all of one's belongings)* con todos los bártulos; *(entirely)* totalmente • **bags** equipaje • **in the b.** JER. en el bolsillo, seguro • **to leave someone holding the b.** FAM. *(to leave with nothing)* dejar a alguien con las manos vacías; *(to place the blame on)* echar el muerto a alguien • **to let the cat out of the b.** FAM. dejar escapar el secreto o la liebre II. tr. **bagged, bag·ging** *(to put into a bag)* meter en una bolsa; *(to hunt)* cazar; FAM. *(to capture)* coger, pescar —intr. *(to hang)* formar bolsas; *(to bulge)* abultarse.

bag·a·telle (băg'ə-těl') s. *(trifle)* bagatela, nadería; *(billiards)* billar inglés *m*.

ba·gel (bā'gəl) s. panecillo en forma de rosca.

bag·ful (băg'fŏŏl') s. [pl. -fuls] bolsa, saco.

bag·gage (băg'ĭj) s. *(luggage)* equipaje *m*, maletas; MIL. *(equipment)* bagaje *m*; FIG. *(ideas)* bagaje; *(slut)* descarada.

bag·gage·mas·ter (băg'ĭj-măs'tər) s. jefe de equipajes *m*.

bag·gy (băg'ē) adj. **-gi·er, -gi·est** *(bulging)* abultado; *(loose)* holgado, bombacho.

Bagh·dad (băg'dăd') s. Bagdad.

bag·man (băg'mən) s. [pl. -men] JER. *(collector)* recaudador (de dinero mal habido) *m*; G.B. *(salesman)* vendedor ambulante *m*.

bag·pipe (băg'pīp') s. MÚS. gaita.

bah (bä, bă) interj. ¡bah!

Ba·ha·mas (bə-hä'məz) s.pl. Bahamas.

Ba·ha·mi·an (bə-hä'mē-ən) adj. & s. bahamés.

Bah·rain o **Bah·rein** (bä-rān') s. Bahrein.

bail[1] (bāl) I. s. DER. *(security)* fianza, caución *f*; *(bondsman)* fiador *m* ♦ **out on b.** en libertad bajo fianza • **to go b. for** salir fiador por, dar fianza por • **to jump b.** JER. escapar estando bajo fianza II. tr. dar fianza o caución por ♦ **to b. out** DER. *(to release)* poner en libertad bajo fianza; *(to extricate)* sacar de apuros.

bail[2] (bāl) I. tr. MARÍT. achicar (el agua de un bote) —intr. achicar (agua) ♦ **to b. out** *(to parachute)* saltar en paracaídas; JER. *(of an enterprise)* zafarse, salirse.

bail[3] (bāl) *(of a pail)* asa, agarradera; *(of a wagon)* soporte del toldo de una carreta *m*.

bail·ee (bā-lē') s. DER. depositario.

ã rey / ä año / b boca / ch chico / d dar / ĕ el / ē mil / g gato / h joya / hw juez / ī aire / k casa / kw cuan /

33

bailer | **Baltic**

bail·er (bā′lər) s. achicador *m.*
bail·iff (bā′lĭf) s. DER. alguacil (de un juzgado) *m;* G.B. *(overseer)* administrador *m,* mayordomo.
bail·i·wick (bā′lə-wĭk′) s. DER. alguacilazgo; *(forte)* jurisdicción *f,* competencia.
bail·ment (bāl′mənt) s. DER. *(posting of bail)* afianzamiento; *(delivery of goods)* entrega de bienes.
bail·or (bā′lər, bā-lôr′) s. DER. fiador *m,* fianza.
bail·out (bāl′out′) s. COM. rescate financiero.
bails·man (bālz′mən) s. [pl. -men] DER. fiador *m,* fianza.
bait (bāt) I. s. DEP. *(lure)* cebo, carnada; *(enticement)* señuelo ♦ **to take the b.** FIG. tragarse el anzuelo II. tr. DEP. *(to place bait in)* poner el cebo en (anzuelo, trampa); *(to lure)* atraer, tentar; *(to torment)* atormentar, hostigar; *(to tease)* tomar el pelo a.
baize (bāz) s. bayeta ♦ **green b.** tapete verde de las mesas de juego.
bake (bāk) I. tr. baked, bak·ing CUL. cocer en el horno, hornear; *(to dry)* secar; *(to harden)* endurecer —intr. cocerse II. s. *(process)* cocción (al horno) *f; (gathering)* asado.
bak·er (bā′kər) s. *(of bread)* panadero; *(of pastry)* repostero; *(oven)* horno portátil.
baker's dozen s. docena de fraile.
bak·er·y (bā′kə-rē) s. [pl. -ies] *(of bread)* panadería; *(of pastry)* repostería, pastelería.
bak·ing (bā′kĭng) s. *(process)* cocción *f; (amount)* hornada.
baking powder s. levadura en polvo, polvo de hornear.
baking soda s. QUÍM. bicarbonato de sodio.
bal·ance (bāl′əns) I. s. *(scale)* balanza; *(equilibrium)* equilibrio *<to lose one's b.* perder el equilibrio>; TEN. *(equality)* balance *m; (difference)* saldo *<the b. of the account* el saldo de la cuenta>; FAM. *(remainder)* resto; *(harmony)* armonía (de proporciones, colores); *(sanity)* juicio, serenidad *f;* MAT., QUÍM. igualdad *f* ♦ **b. due** TEN. saldo deudor • **off b.** *(unstable)* en desequilibrio; *(off guard)* desprevenido • **on b.** a fin de cuentas, en líneas generales • **to be in the b.** estar en la balanza • **to throw off b.** FIG. desconcertar II. tr. -anced, -anc·ing *(to weigh)* pesar; *(to consider)* pesar, contrastar; *(to bring into equilibrium)* balancear, equilibrar; *(to counterbalance)* compensar, contrarrestar; TEN. *(to compute)* cuadrar; *(to reconcile)* equilibrar *<to b. the budget* equilibrar el presupuesto>; *(to settle)* saldar; MAT., QUÍM. igualar ♦ **to b. the books** TEN. pasar balance —intr. *(to come into equilibrium)* equilibrarse; TEN. *(account)* cuadrar; *(to sway)* balancearse.
balance beam s. DEP. barra fija.
bal·anced (bal′ənst) adj. balanceado, equilibrado.
balance sheet s. TEN. balance *m.*
balance wheel s. MEC. volante compensador *m.*
bal·bo·a (băl-bō′ə) s. FIN. balboa (unidad monetaria panameña).
bal·co·ny (băl′kə-nē) s. [pl. -nies] *(of a house)* balcón *m; (of a theater)* galería, paraíso.
bald (bôld) adj. -er, -est *(hairless)* calvo; *(tire)* desgastado; *(blunt)* categórico, sin rodeos ♦ **to go b.** quedarse calvo.
bald eagle s. ORNIT. águila de cabeza blanca; *(symbol)* ave heráldica de EE. UU.
bal·der·dash (bôl′dər-dăsh′) s. disparates *m.*
bald·faced (bôld′fāst′) adj. descarado, desvergonzado.
bald·head·ed (bôld′hĕd′ĭd) adj. calvo.
bald·ing (bôl′dĭng) adj. FAM. que se está quedando calvo.
bald·ness (bôld′nĭs) s. *(lack of hair)* calvicie *f; (bluntness)* franqueza.
bald·pate (bôld′pāt′) s. *(person)* calvo; ORNIT. lavanco.
bale (bāl) I. s. bala, fardo II. tr. baled, bal·ing embalar, enfardar.
Bal·e·ar·ic (băl′ē-ăr′ĭk) I. adj. baleárico, balear *<the B. Islands* las (Islas) Baleares> II. s. balear *mf.*
ba·leen (bə-lēn′) s. ZOOL. barba de ballena, ballena (lámina).
bale·ful (bāl′fəl) adj. *(malignant)* maléfico, malsano; *(ominous)* ominoso, funesto.
balk (bôk) I. intr. *(to stop)* detenerse, plantarse; *(to refuse)* negarse, oponerse *<he balked at a compromise* se opuso a

un arreglo> —tr. impedir, frustar II. s. *(hindrance)* obstáculo, impedimento.
Bal·kan (bôl′kən) adj. balcánico, de las Balcanes.
Bal·kans (bôl′kənz) s.pl. Balcanes *m.*
balk·y (bô′kē) adj. -i·er, -i·est *(horse)* repropio; *(person)* reacio.
ball¹ (bôl) I. s. *(sphere)* bola *<crystal b.* bola de cristal>; *(of wool)* ovillo; DEP. *(in baseball, tennis)* pelota; *(in soccer, basketball)* pelota, balón *m; (in billiards, bowling)* bola; MIL. *(projectile)* bala, proyectil *m; (cannonball)* bala de cañón; ANAT. *(of the hand)* pulpejo; *(of the eye)* globo; *(of the foot)* eminencia metatarsiana del pie ♦ **balls** JER., VULG. pelotas, cojones • **to be on the b.** JER. no dejar pasar una, estar atento • **to play b.** FAM. *(to cooperate)* cooperar, entrar en el juego • **to start the b. rolling** poner las cosas en movimiento II. tr. *(to form into a ball)* hacer una bola de; JER., VULG. *(a person)* chingarse a, cogerse a ♦ **to b. (something) up** enredar, embrollar (algo) —intr. *(thing)* hacerse una bola; JER., VULG. *(person)* chingar, coger.
ball² (bôl) s. baile de etiqueta *m* ♦ **to have a b.** JER. divertirse mucho, pasarla muy bien.
bal·lad (băl′əd) s. *(poem)* balada, romance *m; (music, song)* balada, copla.
bal·lad·eer (băl′ə-dîr′) s. romancero, trovador *m.*
ball and chain s. grillo con bola (para sujetar a los presos).
ball-and-sock·et joint (bôl′ən-sŏk′ĭt) s. MEC. articulación de rótula *f.*
bal·last (băl′əst) I. s. *(in boats, balloons)* lastre *m; (for railroads)* balasto; FIG. *(stabilizing force)* firmeza, estabilidad *f* II. tr. *(boat, balloon)* lastrar; *(railroad)* balastar; FIG. *(character)* dar firmeza a.
ball bearing s. MEC. *(bearing)* cojinete (de bolas) *m; (ball)* balín *m,* bola de rodamiento.
ball cock s. MEC. grifo *o* llave *f* de flotante.
bal·le·ri·na (băl′ə-rē′nə) s. bailarina (de ballet).
bal·let (bă-lā′, băl′ā′) s. *(dance, music)* ballet *m; (group)* compañía de ballet.
ball game s. DEP. *(game)* juego, partido de béisbol; FAM. *(competition)* competencia, juego ♦ **to be a different b.** FIG. ser otra cosa.
bal·lis·tic (bə-lĭs′tĭk) adj. balístico.
ballistic missile s. MIL. proyectil balístico.
bal·lis·tics (bə-lĭs′tĭks) s. [ú. con v. sing.] balística.
ball lightning s. METEOR. relámpago esférico.
bal·loon (bə-lōōn′) I. s. *(for flying)* globo (aerostático); *(toy)* globo; *(in cartoons)* bocadillo II. intr. *(to ride)* montar en globo; *(to swell)* hincharse, inflarse; *(to increase)* aumentar rápidamente —tr. hinchar, inflar.
bal·loon·ist (bə-lōō′nĭst) s. aeronauta *mf,* ascensionista *mf.*
bal·lot (băl′ət) I. s. POL. *(sheet of paper)* papeleta (electoral); *(voting)* votación *f; (electoral ticket)* candidaturas, lista de candidatos; *(votes cast)* votos emitidos; *(franchise)* sufragio, derecho al voto ♦ **b. box** urna electoral II. intr. *(to vote)* votar; *(to draw lots)* sortear.
ball·park *o* **ball park** (bôl′pärk′) s. DEP. estadio ♦ **in the b.** FAM. aproximada.
ball-point pen (bôl′point′) s. bolígrafo.
ball·room (bôl′rōōm′, -rōōm′) s. salón de baile *m.*
bal·ly·hoo (băl′ē-hōō′) FAM. I. s. [pl. -hoos] *(advertising)* bombo, propaganda exagerada; *(uproar)* alboroto, jaleo II. tr. -hooed, -hoo·ing dar mucho bombo *o* propaganda a.
balm (bäm) s. *(resin, ointment)* bálsamo; BOT. melisa, citronela; *(comfort)* bálsamo, alivio.
balm·y (bä′mē) adj. -i·er, -i·est *(balm-like)* balsámico; *(fragrant)* fragante; *(soothing)* balsámico; *(pleasant)* agradable, suave (clima, brisa); JER. *(silly)* chiflado, tocado.
ba·lo·ney (bə-lō′nē) s. [pl. -neys] FAM. *(bologna)* salchicha Bologna; *(nonsense)* disparates *m; (lies)* cuentos de camino.
bal·sa (bôl′sə) s. BOT. balsa (árbol y madera); *(raft)* balsa.
bal·sam (bôl′səm) s. *(resin, ointment)* bálsamo; BOT. *(tree)* abeto balsámico; *(plant)* balsamina.
balsam fir s. BOT. abeto balsámico.
Bal·tic (bôl′tĭk) adj. báltico.

ng inglés / ŏ la / ō bou / ô corre / oi oigo / ōō uno / ou auto / yōō ciudad / w hueco / y yo / z mismo

Baltic Sea s. Mar Báltico.
bal·us·ter (băl′ə-stər) s. ARQ. balaustre *m*.
bal·us·trade (băl′ə-strād′) s. ARQ. balaustrada.
bam·boo (băm-bōō′) s. [pl. **-boos**] BOT. *(tree)* bambú *m*; *(stem)* caña (de bambú).
bam·boo·zle (băm-bōō′zəl) tr. **-zled, -zling** FAM. engatusar, embaucar.
ban (băn) I. tr. **banned, ban·ning** *(to prohibit)* prohibir, proscribir; *(to exclude)* proscribir, excluir II. s. *(prohibition)* prohibición *f*, proscripción *f*; *(censure)* desaprobación (pública) *f*; RELIG. excomunión *f* ♦ **to put a b. on** prohibir, proscribir.
ba·nal (bə-nắl′, -năl′, bā′nəl) adj. banal, trivial.
ba·nal·i·ty (bə-năl′ĭ-tē) s. banalidad *f*, trivialidad *f*.
ba·nan·a (bə-năn′ə) s. BOT. *(tree)* plátano, banano; *(fruit)* plátano, banana ♦ **to go bananas** JER. chiflarse.
band¹ (bănd) I. s. *(strip of material)* banda, faja; *(of paper)* tira, faja; *(stripe)* franja, lista; *(of cigars)* anillo, vitola; *(wedding ring)* alianza, anillo (de compromiso); *(strip of fabric)* cinta (de vestido, sombrero); *(collar)* tirilla de camisa; *(of land)* faja; TEC. *(clasp)* abrazadera; FÍS. *(of light)* haz *m*; RAD. banda II. tr. *(to bind)* fajar, atar; *(to put a band on)* poner una banda a; *(to mark)* marcar.
band² (bănd) I. s. *(of people)* banda, cuadrilla; *(of animals)* banda; MÚS. *(military band)* banda; *(jazz band)* orquesta; *(rock group)* conjunto II. tr. & intr. ♦ **to b. together** agrupar(se), juntar(se).
band·age (băn′dĭj) I. s. venda, vendaje *m* II. tr. **-aged, -aging** vendar.
Band-Aid (bănd′ād′) s. marca registrada de una pequeña venda adhesiva.
ban·dan·na *o* **ban·dan·a** (băn-dăn′ə) s. pañuelo grande.
band·box (bănd′bŏks′) s. sombrerera, caja de sombreros.
ban·de·role *o* **ban·de·rol** (băn′də-rōl′) s. banderola.
ban·dit (băn′dĭt) s. bandido, bandolero ♦ **one-armed b.** FAM. (máquina) tragaperras.
ban·dit·ry (băn′də-trē) s. bandidaje *m*, bandolerismo.
band·mas·ter (bănd′măs′tər) MÚS. director de una banda *m*.
ban·do·leer *o* **ban·do·lier** (băn′də-lîr′) s. MIL. bandolera, cartuchera.
band saw s. CARP. sierra continua (de motor).
bands·man (băndz′mən) s. [pl. **-men**] músico (de banda).
band·stand (bănd′stănd′) s. MÚS. quiosco de orquesta.
band·wag·on (bănd′wăg′ən) s. carro, carroza ♦ **to get** *o* **jump on the b.** FAM. *(to join a trend)* seguir la moda; *(to side with the winners)* arrimarse al que lleva la batuta.
ban·dy (băn′dē) I. tr. **-died, -dy·ing** *(to toss)* pasarse, tirar (de un lado a otro); *(to exchange)* intercambiar (insultos, golpes) ♦ **to b. about** pelotear II. adj. *(bent)* curvado, arqueado; *(legs)* zambo.
ban·dy-leg·ged (băn′dē-lĕg′ĭd) adj. patizambo.
bane (băn) s. *(cause of ruin)* ruina, perdición *f*; *(poison)* veneno ♦ **to be the b. of someone's existence** hacerle la vida imposible a alguien.
bane·ful (băn′fəl) adj. pernicioso, nocivo.
bang¹ (băng) I. s. *(explosion)* detonación *f*, estallido; *(loud slam)* golpe *m*, golpetazo; FAM. *(burst of action)* energía, ímpetu *m* <he started off with a b. comenzó con ímpetu>; JER. *(thrill)* emoción *f*, excitación *f* II. tr. *(to bump)* golpear, dar golpes; *(to slam)* cerrar de un golpetazo (puerta, ventana); *(to handle violently)* golpear; VULG. *(to screw)* joder, chingar ♦ **to be all banged up** *(thing)* estar todo escachado; *(person)* estar todo magullado —intr. *(to explode)* detonar, explotar; *(to make a loud noise)* dar un golpetazo; *(to crash)* estrellarse, chocar ♦ **to b. away** *(guns)* tronar sin cesar; *(to assail)* acosar (a preguntas); *(to work)* trabajar sin descanso III. adv. exactamente, justo en IV. interj. *(shot)* ¡pum!; *(blow)* ¡zas!
bang² (băng) s. ♦ **bangs** cerquillo, flequillo.
Bang·la·desh (băng′glə-dĕsh′) s. Bangladesh.
ban·gle (băng′gəl) s. esclava, ajorca.
bang-up (băng′ŭp′) adj. JER. formidable, excelente.
ban·ish (băn′ĭsh) tr. *(to exile)* exiliar, desterrar; *(to deport)* deportar; *(to cast out)* echar fuera, ahuyentar.

ban·ish·ment (băn′ĭsh-mənt) s. *(exile)* exilio, destierro; *(ban)* proscripción *f*.
ban·is·ter (băn′ĭ-stər) s. *(handrail)* barandilla; *(baluster)* balaustre *m*.
ban·jo (băn′jō) s. [pl. **-jos** *o* **-joes**] MÚS. banjo.
bank¹ (băngk) I. s. *(of a river)* ribera, orilla; *(hillside)* loma, cuesta; *(of clouds)* masa (de niebla, nubes); *(of snow)* montón *m*; AVIA. inclinación lateral *f*; *(of a pool table)* banda ♦ **banks** MARÍT. bajío, banco (de arena) II. tr. *(to embank)* terraplenar, cubrir *(el fuego)*; *(a road)* peraltar; AVIA. inclinar, ladear (un avión) —intr. *(to rise)* apilarse, amontonarse; AVIA. inclinarse, ladearse.
bank² (băngk) I. s. COM. banco; *(in gambling)* banca; *(for storage)* banco <eye b. banco de ojos> II. tr. depositar en un banco —intr. COM. *(to have an account)* tener cuenta; *(to operate a bank)* dedicarse a la banca ♦ **to b. on** contar con, confiar en.
bank³ (băngk) I. s. *(row)* hilera, fila; *(elevators)* grupo de ascensores; *(keys)* teclado; *(galley bench)* banco (en una galera); ELEC. batería (de alternadores, transformadores) II. tr. poner en fila, formar hileras de.
bank account COM. cuenta bancaria.
bank·book (băngk′bŏŏk′) s. COM. libreta de banco.
bank·er (băng′kər) s. COM. banquero.
bank·ing (băng′kĭng) s. COM. *(occupation)* banca; *(bank business)* operaciones bancarias.
bank note s. COM. billete de banco *m*.
bank·roll (băngk′rōl′) I. s. *(roll of bills)* fajo de billetes; FAM. *(ready cash)* dinero en el banco, fondos II. tr. costear, financiar.
bank·rupt (băngk′rəpt′) I. s. COM. quebrado, insolvente *mf* II. adj. COM. *(insolvent)* insolvente; *(ruined)* arruinado; *(lacking)* falto, carente ♦ **to go b.** COM. declararse en quiebra, quebrar III. tr. COM. *(to make bankrupt)* hacer quebrar; *(to ruin)* arruinar.
bank·rupt·cy (băngk′rəpt-sē) s. [pl. **-cies**] quiebra, bancarrota.
ban·ner (băn′ər) I. s. *(flag)* bandera, estandarte *m*; *(newspaper headline)* titular a toda plana *m* II. adj. excelente, sobresaliente.
ban·nis·ter (băn′ĭ-stər) s. var. de **banister**.
banns (bănz) s.pl. amonestaciones *f* ♦ **to publish** *o* **put up the b.** correr las amonestaciones • **to forbid the b.** FIG. prohibir las bodas.
ban·quet (băng′kwĭt) I. s. banquete *m* II. tr. & intr. banquetear.
ban·quette (băng-kĕt′) s. *(bench)* banqueta tapizada (colocada contra una pared); MIL., FORT. *(platform)* banqueta.
ban·tam (băn′təm) s. I. s. ZOOL. gallina enana; FIG. *(person)* gallito II. adj. *(diminutive)* diminuto, pequeño; FIG. *(aggressive)* agresivo.
ban·tam·weight (băn′təm-wāt′) s. DEP. peso gallo.
ban·ter (băn′tər) I. s. broma, burla II. tr. burlarse de, embromar a —intr. burlar, bromear.
ba·o·bab (bā′ō-băb′) s. BOT. baobab *m*.
bap·tism (băp′tĭz′əm) s. RELIG. bautismo.
bap·tis·mal (băp-tĭz′məl) adj. bautismal, de bautismo.
Bap·tist (băp′tĭst) s. RELIG. bautista *mf* ♦ **b.** bautista (persona que bautiza) • **John the B.** BÍBL. San Juan Bautista.
bap·tis·ter·y *o* **bap·tis·try** (băp′tĭ-strē) s. [pl. **-ies** *o* **-tries**] RELIG. baptisterio, bautisterio.
bap·tize (băp-tīz′) tr. **-tized, -tiz·ing** RELIG. *(to christen)* bautizar; *(to cleanse)* purificar; *(to name)* dar nombre a.
bar¹ (bär) I. s. *(rod)* barra; *(of gold)* lingote *m*; *(lever)* palanca; *(of a prison)* barrote *m*; *(of soap)* pastilla (de jabón); *(of chocolate)* tableta; *(of color)* raya, franja; *(obstacle)* obstáculo; *(tavern)* bar *m*; *(counter)* mostrador *m*; MARÍT. banco (de arena, grava); DER. *(tribunal)* tribunal *m*; *(legal profession)* abogacía; *(lawyers)* cuerpo de abogados; MÚS. *(line)* barra; *(measure)* compás *m* ♦ **behind bars** entre rejas • **prisoner at the b.** DER. acusado II. tr. **barred, bar·ring** *(to fasten)* cerrar con barras; *(to obstruct)* obstruir; *(to exclude)* excluir; *(to prohibit)* prohibir; *(to mark)* rayar III. prep. excepto ♦ **b. none** sin excepción.
bar² (bär) s. FÍS. bar (unidad de presión) *m*.
barb (bärb) I. s. *(sharp point)* púa; *(of arrow, fishhook)*

lengüeta; *(cutting remark)* observación mordaz *f*; BOT. barbas; ORNIT. barba **II.** tr. poner púas *o* lengüetas a.
Bar·ba·di·an (bär-bā'dē-ən) adj. & s. barbadense *mf.*
Bar·ba·dos (bär-bā'dōs) s. Barbados.
bar·bar·i·an (bär-bâr'ē-ən) s. & adj. bárbaro, salvaje *mf.*
bar·bar·ic (bär-bâr'ĭk) adj. *(uncivilized)* bárbaro; *(savage)* salvaje.
bar·ba·rism (bär'bə-rĭz'əm) s. *(act)* barbarie *f*; GRAM. barbarismo.
bar·bar·i·ty (bär-bâr'ĭ-tē) s. [pl. **-ties**] *(brutal act)* barbaridad *f*, barbarie *f*; *(crudeness)* ordinariez *f.*
bar·ba·rous (bär'bər-əs) adj. *(uncivilized)* bárbaro; *(brutal)* brutal.
bar·be·cue (bär'bĭ-kyōō') **I.** s. *(grill)* parrilla; *(meat)* barbacoa, parrillada; *(gathering)* festín de barbacoa *m* **II.** tr. **-cued, -cu·ing** asar a la parrilla.
barbed (bärbd) adj. *(having barbs)* con púas; *(cutting)* mordaz <*b.* criticism crítica mordaz>.
barbed wire s. alambre de púas *m.*
bar·bell (bär'bĕl') s. DEP. barra con pesas, haltera.
bar·ber (bär'bər) **I.** s. barbero, peluquero **II.** tr. *(to shave)* afeitar; *(to cut hair)* cortar el pelo —intr. ser barbero.
bar·ber·shop (bär'bər-shŏp') s. barbería, peluquería.
bar·bi·tal (bär'bĭ-tôl') s. FARM. barbital *m.*
bar·bi·tu·rate (bär-bĭch'ər-ĭt) s. QUÍM. barbitúrico.
bar·ca·role *o* **bar·ca·rolle** (bär'kə-rōl) s. barcarola.
bard (bärd) s. poeta, bardo.
bare¹ (bâr) **I.** adj. **bar·er, bar·est** *(naked)* desnudo; *(head)* descubierto; *(feet)* descalzo; *(undisguised)* descubierto, a la vista; *(empty)* desprovisto, vacío; *(plain)* puro, sencillo <the *b.* truth la pura verdad>; *(mere)* mínimo <the *b.* necessities las necesidades mínimas> ♦ **to lay b.** revelar, poner al descubierto **II.** tr. **bared, bar·ing** *(to make bare)* desnudar; *(to strip of covering)* desenfundar, destapar; *(to unsheathe)* desenvainar; *(to reveal)* revelar.
bare² (bâr) ANT. pret. de **bear¹.**
bare·back (bâr'băk') adv. & adj. montado a pelo, en pelo.
bare·faced (bâr'fāst') adj. *(beardless)* imberbe; *(unconcealed)* sin máscara; *(shameless)* descarado (mentira).
bare·foot (bâr'fŏŏt') *o* **bare·foot·ed** (-fŏŏt'ĭd) adv. & adj. descalzo.
bare·hand·ed (bâr'hăn'dĭd) adj. & adv. *(with bare hands)* sólo con las manos; *(without weapons)* desarmado.
bare·head·ed (bâr'hĕd'ĭd) adj. & adv. con la cabeza descubierta.
bare·ly (bâr'lē) adv. *(hardly)* apenas; *(scantily)* escasamente.
bar·gain (bär'gən) **I.** s. *(agreement)* pacto, convenio; *(favorable price)* ganga <at that price the car was a *b.* a ese precio el auto era una ganga> ♦ **to drive a hard b.** negociar duramente • **into the b.** por añadidura • **to strike a b.** llegar a un acuerdo **II.** intr. *(to negotiate)* negociar, pactar; *(to haggle)* regatear ♦ **to b. for** *o* **on** esperar —tr. trocar, cambiar.
bar·gain·ing (bär'gə-nĭng) s. *(haggling)* regateo; *(negotiation)* negociación *f.*
barge (bärj) **I.** s. MARÍT. *(flat-bottomed boat)* barcaza, gabarra; *(of a flag officer)* lancha oficial; *(pleasure boat)* embarcación de recreo *f* **II.** tr. **barged, barg·ing** llevar en barcaza —intr. ♦ **to b. in** entremeterse • **to b. into** *(to intrude)* entremeterse; *(to burst into)* irrumpir en.
bar graph s. gráfico de líneas (esp. verticales).
bar·hop (bär'hŏp') intr. **-hopped, -hop·ping** ir de bar en bar.
bar·ite (bär'īt' s. MIN. barita.
bar·i·tone (bär'ĭ-tōn') s. MÚS. barítono.
bar·i·um (bär'ē-əm) s. QUÍM. bario.
bark¹ (bärk) **I.** s. *(of a dog)* ladrido; *(of a gunshot)* estampido; FAM. *(of a cough)* tos *f* ♦ **his b. is worse than his bite** perro que ladra no muerde **II.** intr. *(to utter a bark)* ladrar; FAM. *(to cough)* toser ♦ **to b. up the wrong tree** FIG. equivocarse —tr. FIG. ladrar <he barked out the orders ladró las órdenes>.
bark² (bärk) **I.** s. BOT. corteza **II.** tr. descortezar (un árbol).

bar·keep·er (bär'kē'pər) *o* **bar·keep** (-kēp') s. *(owner)* tabernero, dueño de un bar; *(bartender)* barman *m.*
bark·er (bär'kər) s. FAM. *(in fairgrounds)* pregonero, gritón (en una feria) *m.*
bar·ley (bär'lē) s. BOT. cebada.
bar·ley·corn (bär'lē-kôrn') s. BOT. grano de cebada.
bar·maid (bär'mād') s. camarera, cantinera.
bar·man (bär'mən) s. [pl. **-men**] barman *m.*
bar mitz·vah (bär mĭts'və) **I.** s. *(boy)* joven judío de trece años que asume sus responsabilidades morales y religiosas; *(ceremony)* ceremonia en la que se consagra a un joven de trece años **II.** tr. **-vahed, -vah·ing** confirmar (a un joven de trece años en sus responsabilidades morales y religiosas).
barn (bärn) s. *(for grain)* granero; *(for livestock)* establo.
bar·na·cle (bär'nə-kəl) s. ZOOL. *(crustacean)* percebe *m*; *(goose)* barnacla.
barn·storm (bärn'stôrm') intr. *(to travel about)* recorrer el campo dando conferencias y discursos *o* representando obras teatrales; *(to appear at fairs)* presentarse en una feria haciendo acrobacias en avión *o* en paracaídas.
barn swallow s. ORNIT. golondrina norteamericana.
barn·yard (bärn'yärd') **I.** s. corral *m* **II.** adj. de corral.
bar·o·gram (bär'ə-grăm') s. METEOR. barograma *m.*
bar·o·graph (bär'ə-grăf') s. METEOR. barógrafo.
ba·rom·e·ter (bə-rŏm'ĭ-tər) s. FÍS. barómetro; *(indicator)* barómetro <sales are an economic *b.* las ventas son un barómetro de la economía>.
bar·o·met·ric (bär'ə-mĕt'rĭk) *o* **bar·o·met·ri·cal** (-rĭ-kəl) adj. barométrico.
ba·rom·e·try (bə-rŏm'ĭ-trē) s. la medición barométrica.
bar·on (bär'ən) s. *(nobleman)* barón *m*; *(magnate)* magnate *m*, potentado.
bar·on·age (bär'ə-nĭj) s. *(rank)* baronía; *(list)* lista de lores; *(peers)* los pares del reino.
bar·on·ess (bär'ə-nĭs) s. baronesa.
bar·on·et (bär'ə-nĭt, bär'ə-nĕt') s. baronet *m.*
ba·ro·ni·al (bə-rō'nē-əl) adj. *(of a baron)* de barón; *(stately)* majestuoso, señorial.
bar·on·y (bär'ə-nē) [pl. **-ies**] baronía.
ba·roque (bə-rōk') **I.** adj. ARTE. barroco; *(ornate)* extravagante, recargado **II.** s. barroco.
bar·rack (bär'ək) tr. acuartelar.
bar·racks (bär'əks) s.pl. [ú. con v. pl. *o* sing.] MIL. cuartel *m*, barraca; *(building)* caserón *m.*
bar·ra·cu·da (bär'ə-kōō'də) s. [pl. **barracuda** *o* **-das**] ICT. barracuda.
bar·rage (bə-räzh') **I.** s. MIL. *(protective fire)* cortina de fuego; *(missile discharge)* andanada, descarga; FIG. *(burst)* andanada **II.** tr. **-raged, -rag·ing** MIL. *(to fire at)* tender una cortina de fuego contra; *(to discharge against)* barrer con una andanada; FIG. *(to overwhelm)* bombardear, abrumar.
bar·ra·try (bär'ə-trē) s. [pl. **-tries**] DER. tendencia a ocasionar pleitos infundados.
bar·rel (bär'əl) s. *(container, content)* barril *m*, tonel *m*; *(of a gun)* cañón (de un arma de fuego) *m*; MAQ. *(cylindrical part)* cubo, tambor *m* ♦ **to be a b. of fun** FIG. ser divertidísimo • **to be over a b.** FIG. estar con el agua al cuello **II.** tr. entonelar, embarrilar —intr. JER. moverse a gran velocidad.
bar·rel·house (bär'əl-hous') s. taberna de mala muerte.
bar·ren (bär'ən) **I.** adj. *(sterile)* estéril, infecundo; *(desertlike)* árido, yermo; *(unproductive)* infructuoso, vano; *(lacking in)* falto de, desprovisto **II.** s. ♦ **barrens** tierra yerma, páramo.
bar·rette (bə-rĕt') s. pasador *m*, broche para el cabello *m.*
bar·ri·cade (bär'ĭ-kād') **I.** s. barricada, barrera **II.** tr. **-cad·ed, -cad·ing** levantar barricadas.
bar·ri·er (bär'ē-ər) s. *(fence)* barrera, valla; *(obstacle)* impedimento, obstáculo.
barrier reef s. barrera de coral.
bar·ring (bär'ĭng) prep. salvo, excepto.
bar·ri·o (bär'ē-ō') s. [pl. **-os**] *(district)* barrio; *(neighborhood)* barriada de personas de habla española en EE. UU.
bar·ris·ter (bär'ĭ-stər) s. G.B., DER. abogado.

bar·room (bär'rōōm', -rŏŏm') s. bar *m*.

bar·row (bär'ō) s. *(wheelbarrow)* carretilla; ARQUEOL. *(grave mound)* túmulo.

bar·tend·er (bär'těn'dər) s. camarero de bar, barman *m*.

bar·ter (bär'tər) I. intr. & tr. trocar, cambiar II. s. trueque *m*, cambio.

bar·y·cen·ter (bär'ĭ-sĕn'tər) s. FÍS. baricentro.

bas·al (bā'səl) adj. *(fundamental)* fundamental, básico; MED. basal.

basal metabolism s. BIOL. metabolismo basal.

ba·salt (bə-sôlt') s. MIN. basalto.

bas·cule bridge (bās'kyōōl) s. puente basculante *o* levadizo.

base¹ (bās) I. s. *(foundation)* base *f*; *(basis)* base, fundamento; *(chief ingredient)* base <*a paint with an oil b.* una pintura con base de aceite>; GEOM., MIL., QUÍM. base; ARQ. basa; GRAM. raíz *f*; ELECTRÓN. terminal *f* ♦ **to be off b.** estar equivocado II. adj. de la base III. tr. **based, bas·ing** ♦ **to b. on** *o* **upon** basar en *o* sobre.

base² (bās) adj. **bas·er, bas·est** *(vile)* ruin; *(lowly)* bajo, humilde; *(said of metals)* inferior, de baja ley.

base·ball (bās'bôl') s. DEP. *(game)* béisbol *m*; *(ball)* pelota (de béisbol).

base·board (bās'bôrd') s. ARQ. zócalo.

base·born (bās'bôrn') adj. *(of humble birth)* de humilde cuna, plebeyo; *(illegitimate)* bastardo, ilegítimo; *(contemptible)* bajo, despreciable.

base·less (bās'lĭs) adj. infundado.

base level GEOG. nivel de base *m*, punto máximo de erosión.

base·line (bās'lĭn') s. *(measurement line)* línea que sirve de patrón; *(in tennis)* línea de fondo *o* de saque.

base·ment (bās'mənt) s. *(cellar)* sótano; *(foundation)* cimientos.

ba·ses (bā'sēz') pl. de **basis**.

bash (bāsh) I. tr. FAM. *(to strike)* golpear (fuertemente) II. s. FAM. *(blow)* golpazo, porrazo; JER. *(party)* fiesta.

bash·ful (bāsh'fəl) adj. tímido, encogido.

ba·sic (bā'sĭk) I. adj. *(essential)* básico, fundamental; *(elementary)* básico; QUÍM., GEOL. básico II. s. base *f*, fundamento.

BA·SIC (bā'sĭk) s. COMPUT. BASIC (lenguaje de computadoras) *m*.

ba·si·cal·ly (bā'sĭk-lē) adv. básicamente, fundamentalmente.

ba·sic·i·ty (bā-sĭs'ĭ-tē) s. QUÍM. basicidad *f*.

ba·si·fy (bā'sə-fī') tr. **-fied, -fy·ing** QUÍM. hacer básico.

bas·il (băz'əl, bā'zəl) s. BOT. albahaca.

ba·sil·i·ca (bə-sĭl'ĭ-kə) s. ARQ., RELIG. basílica.

bas·i·lisk (băs'ə-lĭsk') s. basilisco.

ba·sin (bā'sĭn) s. *(container, content)* palangana, jofaina; *(washbowl)* pila, pileta; MARÍT. dársena; GEOG. depresión *f*, cuenca.

ba·sis (bā'sĭs) s. [pl. **-ses** (-sēz')] *(foundation)* base *f*, fundamento <*the b. of the agreement* la base del acuerdo>; *(standard)* base; *(chief component)* elemento principal ♦ **on the b.** de en base a.

bask (băsk) intr. *(in the sun)* tomar el sol, asolearse; *(to enjoy)* gozar, complacerse.

bas·ket (băs'kĭt) s. *(container, content)* cesta, canasta; *(in basketball)* canasta, cesto.

bas·ket·ball (băs'kĭt-bôl') s. DEP. *(game)* baloncesto; *(ball)* pelota.

bas·ket·ful (băs'kĭt-fōōl') s. [pl. **-fuls**] cestada, canastada.

bas·ket·ry (băs'kĭ-trē) s. *(craft)* cestería; *(baskets)* las cestas.

bas·ket·weave (băs'kĭt-wēv') s. tejido esterilla.

Basque (băsk) I. adj. vasco II. s. *(inhabitant)* vasco; *(language)* vasco, vascuence *m*.

bas-re·lief (bä'rĭ-lēf') s. bajo relieve.

bass¹ (băs) s. [pl. **bass** *o* **bass·es**] ICT. róbalo.

bass² (bās) s. MÚS. *(voice)* bajo; *(instrument)* contrabajo, bajo.

bass clef (bās) s. MÚS. clave de fa *f*.

bass drum (bās) s. MÚS. bombo.

bas·set (băs'ĭt) s. ZOOL. perro basset.

bass horn (bās) s. MÚS. tuba, bombardón *m*.

bas·si·net (băs'ə-nĕt') s. cuna.

bas·so (băs'ō) s. MÚS. bajo.

bas·soon (bə-sōōn') s. MÚS. fagot *m*, bajón *m*.

bast (băst) s. BOT. líber *m*.

bas·tard (băs'tərd) I. s. *(illegitimate child)* bastardo; JER. *(mean person)* canalla II. adj. *(illegitimate)* ilegítimo; *(spurious)* espurio; *(hybrid)* híbrido.

baste (bāst) tr. **bast·ed, bast·ing** *(to sew)* hilvanar, bastear; CUL. lardear; *(to thrash)* zurrar, apalear; *(to berate)* regañar.

bast·ing (bā'stĭng) s. *(loose stitching)* hilvanado, hilván *m*; CUL. acto de lardear.

bas·tion (băs'chən) s. MIL. bastión *m*; FIG. *(stronghold)* baluarte *m*.

bat (băt) I. s. *(cudgel)* garrote *m*, palo; *(blow)* garrotazo, palo; DEP. *(for baseball)* bate *m*; *(racket)* raqueta; ZOOL. murciélago; JER. *(spree)* juerga ♦ **right off the b.** FAM. inmediatamente, sin vacilar ♦ **to be as blind as a b.** ser más ciego que un topo • **to be at b.** DEP. estar bateando *o* al bate • **to go to b. for** FAM. sacar la cara por • **to have bats in the belfry** JER. estar chiflado, estar mal de la azotea II. tr. **bat·ted, bat·ting** *(to hit)* dar un palo a, golpear; DEP. batear, golpear; *(to wink)* pestañear ♦ **not to b. an eye** no pestañear, permanecer imperturbable • **to b. around** FAM. discutir mucho, pelotear sobre un asunto *o* tópico —intr. DEP. *(to hit)* batear; *(to take one's turn)* tocar a uno batear ♦ **to b. around** vagar.

batch (băch) s. CUL. hornada; *(lot)* partida, lote *m*; *(group)* grupo, tanda.

bate (bāt) tr. **bat·ed, bat·ing** *(to moderate)* moderar, disminuir; *(to subtract)* sustraer, reducir.

bat·ed (bā'tĭd) adj. ♦ **with b. breath** con aliento entrecortado *o* pasmado.

bath (băth, bäth) s. [pl. **baths** (băthz, bäthz)] *(soaking)* baño <*to take a b.* tomar un baño>; *(bathtub)* bañera; *(bathroom)* cuarto de baño; *(coating)* baño (de pintura, chocolate) ♦ **baths** casa de baños.

bathe (bāth) intr. **bathed, bath·ing** bañarse —tr. *(to wet)* bañar; *(to wash)* lavar; *(to flood)* inundar <*lights bathed the stage* las luces inundaron el escenario>.

ba·thet·ic (bə-thĕt'ĭk) adj. que pasa de lo sublime a lo trivial.

bath·house (băth'hous', bäth'-) s. *(public baths)* casa de baños; *(changing rooms)* casilla, vestidor (en un balneario) *m*.

bath·ing (bā'thĭng) s. baño, baños.

bathing suit s. traje de baño *m*.

ba·thos (bā'thŏs') s. LIT. caída de lo sublime a lo trivial; *(triteness)* trivialidad *f*.

bath·robe (băth'rōb', bäth'-) s. bata (de baño), albornoz *m*.

bath·room (băth'rōōm', -rŏŏm', bäth'-) s. cuarto de baño.

bath·tub (băth'tŭb', bäth'-) s. bañera.

bath·y·scaph (băth'ĭ-skăf') *o* **bath·y·scaphe** (-skăf') s. MARÍT. batiscafo.

ba·tik (bə-tēk', băt'ĭk) s. batik (método javanés de teñido de telas) *m*.

ba·tiste (bə-tēst', bă-) s. COST., TEJ. batista.

ba·ton (bə-tŏn', băt'n) s. MÚS. batuta; *(symbol)* bastón (de mando) *m*; DEP. posta (de carreras) *m*.

bats (băts) adj. JER. chiflado, tocado.

bat·tal·ion (bə-tăl'yən) s. MIL. batallón *m*; FIG. *(large number)* ejército.

bat·ten¹ (băt'n) intr. *(to get fat)* cebarse, engordar; *(to thrive)* vivir, enriquecerse.

bat·ten² (băt'n) s. *(floorboard)* listón *m*; MARÍT. verga II. tr. poner listones a, asegurar con listones.

bat·ter¹ (băt'ər) tr. *(to beat)* golpear (repetidamente), apalear; *(to damage)* deteriorar, estropear —intr. batir, golpear.

bat·ter² (băt'ər) s. CUL. pasta; DEP. bateador *m*.

bat·ter·ing-ram *o* **battering ram** (băt'ər-ĭng-răm') s. ariete *m*.

bat·ter·y (băt'ə-rē) s. [pl. **-ies**] ELEC. batería, pila; MIL. batería; FIG. *(group)* batería; DER. *(beating)* agresión *f*, asalto.

ā rey / ă año / b boca / ch chico / d dar / ĕ el / ē mil / g gato / h joya / hw juez / ī aire / k casa / kw cuan /

bat·ting (băt′ĭng) s. DEP. batea; *(stuffing)* guata, algodón en láminas *m*.
bat·tle (băt′l) I. s. *(combat)* batalla, combate *m*; *(struggle)* lucha <*a political b.* una lucha política> II. intr. & tr. **-tled, -tling** combatir, luchar.
bat·tle-ax o **bat·tle-axe** (băt′l-ăks′) s. *(weapon)* hacha (de combate); FAM. *(shrew)* arpía.
battle cry s. *(shout)* grito de guerra; *(slogan)* lema *m*.
bat·tle·field (băt′l-fēld′) s. campo de batalla.
bat·tle·front (băt′l-frŭnt′) s. frente de batalla *m*.
bat·tle·ground (băt′l-ground′) s. campo de batalla.
bat·tle·ment (băt′l-mənt) s. ARQ. almenaje *m*, almena.
battle royal s. [pl. **battles royal**] MIL. batalla campal; *(fight to the finish)* lucha a muerte; *(altercation)* zafarrancho, riña.
bat·tle·ship (băt′l-shĭp′) s. acorazado.
bat·ty (băt′ē) adj. **-ti·er, -ti·est** JER. chiflado, tocado.
bau·ble (bô′bəl) s. chuchería, baratija.
baud (bôd) s. COMPUT. baudio (unidad de velocidad en la transmisión electrónica).
baulk (bôk) v. & s. var. de **balk**.
baux·ite (bôk′sīt′) s. MIN. bauxita.
bawd (bôd) s. *(madam)* patrona de un burdel; *(prostitute)* ramera.
bawd·i·ness (bô′dē-nĭs) s. obscenidad *f*, indecencia.
bawd·y (bô′dē) adj. **-i·er, -i·est** obsceno, indecente.
bawd·y·house (bô′dē-hous′) s. burdel *m*, lupanar *m*.
bawl (bôl) I. intr. *(to cry)* llorar; *(to shout)* gritar, chillar —tr. gritar, vociferar ♦ **to b. out** *(to reprimand)* regañar; *(to shout out)* gritar II. s. chillido, grito.
bay¹ (bā) s. GEOG. bahía.
bay² (bā) s. ARQ. intercolumnio, crujía; *(window)* vano, hueco; *(in a barn)* pajar *m*.
bay³ (bā) I. s. *(horse)* bayo; *(color)* color bayo II. adj. bayo.
bay⁴ (bā) I. s. aullido, ladrido ♦ **to keep at b.** mantener a raya II. intr. & tr. ladrar (a), aullar (a).
bay⁵ (bā) s. BOT. laurel *m*.
bay·ber·ry (bā′bĕr′ē) s. [pl. **-ries**] BOT. baya del laurel.
bay leaf s. BOT., CUL. hoja de laurel seca usada en cocina.
bay·o·net (bā′ə-nĕt′) s. MIL. I. s. bayoneta II. tr. pasar a la bayoneta.
bay window s. ARQ. ventana saledíza; FAM. *(paunch)* barriga.
ba·zaar o **ba·zar** (bə-zär′) s. *(market)* bazar *m*, mercado oriental; *(sale)* venta benéfica.
ba·zoo·ka (bə-zōō′kə) s. bazuca *m*.
be §G11, 13 (bē) intr. I. ser ⬜ CUALIDAD, CARACTERÍSTICA, DESCRIPCIÓN <*Mary is good* María es buena> <*ice is cold* el hielo es frío> ⬜ HORA DEL DÍA, FECHAS, EXPRESIONES IMPERSONALES <*what time is it? it's three o'clock* ¿qué hora es? son las tres> <*yesterday was the 15th of July* ayer fue el 15 de julio> <*it is possible* es posible> ⬜ ORIGEN, CONSTRUCCIÓN, POSESIÓN <*I am a Colombian* soy colombiano> <*it is solid gold* es de oro macizo> <*is this glove yours?* ¿es tuyo este guante?> ⬜ VOZ PASIVA <*this road was built by the local government* este camino fue construido por el gobierno local> II. estar ⬜ POSICIÓN, SITIO <*where is the library?* ¿dónde está la biblioteca?> <*Buenos Aires is in Argentina* Buenos Aires está en la Argentina> ⬜ ESTADO, CONDICIÓN <*the children are happy today* los niños están contentos hoy> <*my coffee is cold* mi café está frío> III. tener, hacer, haber, quedarse ⬜ EDAD, SENSACIÓN FÍSICA <*the boy is six years old* el niño tiene seis años> <*I am cold* tengo frío> ⬜ TIEMPO, TEMPERATURA <*it is sunny* hay sol> <*it is cold today* hace frío hoy> ⬜ REACCIÓN INMEDIATA <*she was speechless* se quedó sin palabras> ⬜ USADO CON THERE <*there are tickets for ten people* hay localidades para diez personas> IV. haber de, ir a, tener que, deber [cuando el verbo *be* va seguido de otro verbo en infinitivo que expresa una obligación] <*what are we to do?* ¿qué vamos a hacer?> <*how am I to know?* ¿cómo he de saberlo?> <*you are to leave immediately* tienes que o debes partir inmediatamente> V. EXPRESIONES IDIOMÁTICAS ♦ **as it were** por así decirlo • **be that as it may** sea como fuere • **so be it** así sea • **to be in** estar <*is the doctor*

in? ¿está el médico?> • **to be off** *(to leave)* irse; *(to be mistaken)* estar equivocado • **to be out** no estar <*the doctor is out* el médico no está> • **to be out of** FAM. no tener, quedarse sin <*I'm out of cigarettes* me he quedado sin cigarrillos> • **to be right** tener razón • **to be up** haberse levantado (de la cama) <*are you up?* ¿te levantaste?>; *(to be finished)* estar terminado, acabarse <*your time is up* se te acabó el tiempo>.
beach (bēch) I. s. playa II. tr. MARÍT. varar.
beach·comb·er (bēch′kō′mər) s. *(person)* persona que frecuenta las playas; *(wave)* ola ancha.
beach·head (bēch′hĕd′) s. MIL. *(position)* cabeza de playa; *(foothold)* posición *f*.
bea·con (bē′kən) I. s. *(lighthouse)* faro; *(signal fire)* almenara; AVIA., MARÍT. *(light)* baliza; *(radio transmitter)* radiofaro; *(signal)* faro, guía *m* II. tr. & intr. AVIA., MARÍT. balizar.
bead (bēd) I. s. *(of a necklace)* cuenta, abalorio; *(drop)* gota <*a b. of dew* una gota de rocío>; *(bubble)* burbuja; MIL. punto de mira (de una pistola, fusil); ARQ. moldura ♦ **beads** *(necklace)* collar; *(rosary)* rosario • **to draw a b. on** tomar puntería, apuntar a II. tr. adornar con cuentas o abalorios —intr. formarse en gotas <*sweat beaded on his brow* el sudor formaba gotas en su frente>.
bead·ing (bē′dĭng) s. *(beads)* abalorios, cuentas; COST. *(ornament)* adorno (de canutillos, mostacilla); *(lace)* encaje calado; ARQ. moldura
bea·dle (bēd′l) s. *(of a parish)* pertiguero; *(of a school)* bedel *m*; *(of a law court)* alguacil *m*.
bead·work (bēd′wûrk′) s. COST. adorno (de canutillos, mostacilla); ARQ. *(molding)* reborde (en forma de cuentas) *m*.
bead·y (bē′dē) adj. **-i·er, -i·est** *(bead-like)* de forma de abalorio; COST. con adornos de canutillos, mostacilla o abalorios ♦ **b. eyes** ojos pequeños y brillantes.
bea·gle (bē′gəl) s. ZOOL. beagle *m*.
beak (bēk) s. ORNIT. pico; *(point)* punta; FAM. *(nose)* nariz *f*.
beak·er (bē′kər) s. *(cup)* vaso o taza de boca ancha; QUÍM. vaso de precipitación.
beam (bēm) I. s. *(of light)* haz *m*, rayo; ARQ. *(support)* viga; *(reinforcement)* tablón *m*, madero; MARÍT. manga, ancho máximo; TEJ. enjulio de telar; *(of an engine)* balancín *m*; *(of a plow)* timón *m*, cama (del arado); *(of a balance)* astil *m*; RAD. onda dirigida ♦ **broad in the b.** ancho de caderas • **to be on the b.** AER. *(on course)* seguir el haz del radiofaro; FAM. *(on the right track)* estar sobre la pista II. tr. emitir, dirigir —intr. *(to shine)* destellar, irradiar; *(to smile)* sonreír radiantemente, rebosar de felicidad.
bean (bēn) I. s. BOT. *(legume)* habichuela, judía, frijol *m*; *(seed)* haba, semilla; *(of coffee, cocoa)* grano; JER. *(head)* coco ♦ **beans** JER. pizca, jota <*they don't know beans about the market* ellos no saben ni una jota sobre el mercado> • **to spill the beans** FAM. descubrir el pastel II. tr. JER. pegar en el coco.
bean·bag (bēn′băg′) s. bolsita con frijoles secos usado por los niños para jugar.
bean curd s. queso de soja.
bean·ie (bē′nē) s. FAM. gorro pequeño sin visera.
bean·pole (bēn′pōl′) s. *(vine support)* rodrigón de frijoles *m*; JER. *(person)* persona larguirucha.
bean sprout s. BOT., CUL. brote de frijol germinado *m*.
bean·stalk (bēn′stôk′) s. BOT. tallo de la planta de frijoles.
bear¹ (bâr) tr. **bore** (bôr), **borne** o **born** (bôrn), **bear·ing** *(to support)* aguantar, sostener; *(to carry)* cargar, llevar; *(to display)* tener, llevar <*the proclamation bore the imperial seal* la proclama llevaba el sello imperial>; FIG. *(to harbor)* sentir, guardar <*to b. a grudge* guardar un rencor>; *(to conduct)* comportarse, conducirse <*she bore herself with dignity* se condujo con dignidad>; *(to assume)* asumir, hacerse cargo de <*to b. the costs* hacerse cargo de los gastos>; *(to admit of)* admitir, dar lugar a <*the accident bears two explanations* el accidente da lugar a dos explicaciones>; *(to endure)* sufrir, aguantar; *(to give birth to)* parir, dar a luz; *(to yield, produce)* producir <*to b. results* producir resultados>; *(to give)* dar <*she bore him a son* le dio un

hijo>; *(to push)* empujar, impeler ◆ **to b. arms** *(to carry weapons)* portar armas; MIL. servir como soldado • **to b. down on** abrumar, pesar sobre • **to b. in mind** tener en cuenta, recordar • **to b. mention** merecer mencionarse • **to b. off** llevarse • **to b. out** confirmar, corroborar • **to b. with** tolerar, tener paciencia con • **to b. witness** atestiguar, testimoniar —intr. *(to produce)* producir, rendir; *(to pressure)* ejercer presión, pesar; *(to go)* mantenerse sobre <*b. right after the sign* manténgase sobre la derecha después de la señal de tráfico> ◆ **to b. away** MARÍT. cambiar de rumbo • **to b. down** esforzarse <*you'll have to b. down to pass the exam* tendrás que esforzarte para aprobar el examen> • **to b. on** *o* **upon** referirse a, relacionarse con • **to b. up** resistir • **to bring to b.** hacer uso de, aplicar <*he brought his experience to b. in the negotiations* aplicó su experiencia en las negociaciones>.
▲ Los participios pasados del verbo *bear* son *born* y *borne.* En su forma verbal, *born* se utiliza solamente en la voz pasiva, refiriéndose a nacimientos <*the child was born on August 1* el niño nació el primero de agosto>. En todas las otras acepciones del verbo *bear,* el participio pasado que debe usarse es *borne.*
bear² (bâr) s. ZOOL. oso; *(clumsy man)* hombre torpe *m*; FIN. bajista *mf.*
bear·a·ble (bârʹə-bəl) adj. soportable, tolerable.
beard (bîrd) s. *(hair)* barba; BOT. arista.
beard·ed (bîrʹdĭd) adj. *(having a beard)* barbudo; BOT. con aristas; ASTRON. barbato (cometa).
bear·er (bârʹər) s. *(carrier)* porteador *m*; *(of message, check)* portador *m*; *(porter)* maletero; BOT. árbol fructífero.
bear·ing (bârʹĭng) s. *(poise)* porte *m*; *(relationship)* relación *f* <*this has no b. on my situation* esto no tiene relación con mi situación>; MEC. *(machine part)* cojinete *m*; *(support)* soporte *m*; ARQ. sotabanco, soporte *m*; AER., MARÍT. dirección *f*, rumbo; HER. blasón *m*, figura (en un escudo de armas) ◆ **bearings** orientación • **to get one's bearings** orientarse • **to lose one's bearings** desorientarse.
bear·ish (bârʹĭsh) adj. *(clumsy)* torpe, desmañado; *(surly)* huraño; COM. *(tending to lower prices)* bajista, con tendencia a la baja (mercado); *(pessimistic)* pesimista.
bear·skin (bârʹskĭn´) s. *(hide)* piel de oso *m*; MIL. sombrero militar de piel ◆ **b. rug** alfombra de piel de oso.
beast (bēst) s. *(animal)* bestia, animal *m*; *(vile person)* bestia, bruto.
beast·ly (bēstʹlē) I. adj. **-li·er, -li·est** *(bestial)* bestial, brutal; *(nasty)* detestable, repugnante II. adv. G.B. sumamente <*a b. hot month* un mes sumamente caluroso>.
beast of burden s. bestia de carga.
beat (bēt) I. tr. **beat, beat·en** (bētʹn) *o* **beat, beat·ing** *(to hit)* golpear, sacudir; *(to flog)* pegar, aporrear; *(to pound)* batir, azotar <*the waves b. the breakwater* las olas azotaban la escollera>; *(to hammer into shape)* batir, martillar; CUL. batir; *(to flap)* batir (las alas); *(to outdo)* llegar antes que <*I b. him to the elevator* llegué al ascensor antes que él>; *(to defeat)* vencer, derrotar; *(to avoid)* eludir, evitar; *(to surpass)* sobrepasar, superar a <*nothing beats a home-cooked meal* nada supera a una comida hecha en casa>; JER. *(to perplex)* confundir, dejar perplejo; MÚS. *(to sound)* tocar (tambor); *(to mark time, rhythm)* marcar, llevar ◆ **b. it!** ¡lárgate!, ¡márchate! • **to b. a retreat** batirse en retirada • **to b. back** repeler, hacer retroceder a • **to b. black and blue** FAM. moler a palos, acardenalar • **to b. down** *(to haggle over)* regatear; *(to overcome)* superar, vencer; *(to knock down)* derribar <*he beat down the door* derribó la puerta> • **to b. off** rechazar (ataque, asaltante) • **to b. one's brains out** FIG., FAM. romperse la cabeza —intr. *(to hit)* golpear, caer con violencia; *(to throb)* latir, pulsar; *(to emit sound)* resonar, redoblar (tambores); CUL. batir; *(to hunt)* mover la maleza para levantar la caza, dar una batida; MARÍT. barloventear ◆ **to b. around the bush** FIG., FAM. andarse con rodeos • **to b. down on** azotar (el sol), caer a cántaros (la lluvia) • **to b. off** JER., VULG. masturbarse II. s. *(blow)* golpe *m*; *(throb)* latido, pulsación *f*; *(tempo)* compás *m*, ritmo; *(route)* ronda; FÍS. batimiento III. adj. FAM. rendido, deslomado.
beat·en (bētʹn) adj. *(much used)* trillado; *(vanquished)* ven-

cido, batido; *(worn-out)* cansado, abatido; METAL. golpeado, batido <*b. gold* oro batido> ◆ **off the b. path** *o* **track** fuera de lo común, poco usual.
beat·er (bēʹtər) s. CUL. batidora; *(in hunting)* batidor *m*, ojeador *m.*
be·a·tif·ic (bē´ə-tĭfʹĭk) adj. beatífico.
be·at·i·fi·ca·tion (bē-ăt´ə-fĭ-kā´shən) s. beatificación *f.*
be·at·i·fy (bē-ătʹə-fī´) tr. **-fied, -fy·ing** beatificar.
beat·ing (bēʹtĭng) s. *(thrashing)* paliza; *(defeat)* derrota; *(of the heart)* latido; *(pulsation)* pulsación *f.*
be·at·i·tude (bē-ătʹĭ-tōōd´, -tyōōd´) s. RELIG. beatitud *f.*
beat·nik (bētʹnĭk) s. beatnik *mf.*
beau (bō) s. [pl. **beaus** *o* **beaux** (bōz)] *(suitor)* pretendiente *m*, novio; *(dandy)* dandy *m*, petimetre *m.*
Beau·fort scale (bōʹfərt) s. FÍS. escala de Beaufort.
beaut (byōōt) s. JER. maravilla.
beau·te·ous (byōōʹtē-əs) adj. bello, hermoso.
beau·ti·cian (byōō-tĭshʹən) s. cosmetólogo.
beau·ti·fi·ca·tion (byōō´tə-fĭ-kā´shən) s. embellecimiento.
beau·ti·ful (byōōʹtə-fəl) adj. bello, hermoso.
beau·ti·ful·ly (byōōʹtə-fə-lē) adj. *(attractively)* bellamente, hermosamente; *(very well)* espléndidamente, maravillosamente.
beau·ti·fy (byōōʹtə-fī´) tr. **-fied, -fy·ing** embellecer, hermosear —intr. embellecerse.
beau·ty (byōōʹtē) s. [pl. **-ties**] *(quality)* belleza, hermosura; *(person, thing)* belleza; *(feature)* el mejor, lo gracioso <*the b. of the story* lo mejor del cuento> ◆ **that was a (real) b.!** ¡que golpe más bueno!
beauty contest s. concurso de belleza.
beauty parlor *o* **beauty salon** s. salón de belleza *m.*
beaux (bōz) un pl. de **beau.**
bea·ver (bēʹvər) s. ZOOL. castor (animal y piel) *m.*
be·calm (bĭ-kämʹ) tr. MARÍT. *(to render motionless)* dejar parado por falta de viento; *(to soothe)* calmar, serenar.
be·came (bĭ-kāmʹ) pret. de **become.**
be·cause (bĭ-kôzʹ, -kŭzʹ) conj. porque.
because of prep. a causa de, con.
beck (bĕk) s. seña con la cabeza ◆ **at someone's b. and call** al servicio de alguien.
beck·on (bĕkʹən) I. tr. *(to summon)* hacer señas; *(to entice)* atraer, llamar —intr. *(to summon)* hacer señas; *(to be enticing)* atraer II. s. seña.
be·cloud (bĭ-kloudʹ) tr. oscurecer.
be·come (bĭ-kŭmʹ) intr. **-came** (-kāmʹ), **-come, -com·ing** *(to grow to be)* llegar a ser; *(to come to be)* hacerse, ponerse <*he became very angry* se puso muy enojado> ◆ **b. of** ser, hacerse <*what has b. of George?* ¿qué se ha hecho de Jorge?> —tr. *(to be suitable for)* quedar bien, sentar bien; *(to look good on)* quedar bien, sentar a uno bien <*that dress becomes you* ese vestido te queda bien>.
be·com·ing (bĭ-kŭmʹĭng) adj. *(suitable)* apropiado, conveniente; *(attractive)* que sienta bien.
bed (bĕd) I. s. *(furniture)* cama, lecho; *(lodging)* alojamiento, hospedaje *m*; *(in a garden)* macizo (de flores); *(roadbed)* afirmado, firme (de una carretera) *m*; CUL. *(layer)* cama; *(rock mass)* veta, yacimiento II. tr. **bed·ed, bed·ding** *(to put up)* alojar, dar cama a; *(to put to bed)* acostar, poner en la cama; *(to plant)* plantar, sembrar (en un macizo); *(to arrange in layers)* poner en capas sobrepuestas; *(to embed)* fijar, asentar; *(to have sex with)* tener relaciones sexuales con —intr. *(to go to bed)* acostarse; GEOL. depositarse en capas *o* estratos.
bed and board s. *(at a hotel)* pensión completa; *(at someone's home)* techo, hogar *m.*
be·daub (bĭ-dôbʹ) tr. *(to smear)* embadurnar; *(to ornament)* adornar burdamente.
be·daz·zle (bĭ-dăzʹəl) tr. **-zled, -zling** deslumbrar.
bed·bug (bĕdʹbŭg´) s. ENTOM. chinche *f.*
bed·cham·ber (bĕdʹchăm´bər) s. alcoba, dormitorio.
bed·clothes (bĕdʹklōthz´) s.pl. ropa de cama.
bed·ding (bĕdʹĭng) s. *(bedclothes)* ropa de cama; *(litter)* cama, lecho (para animales); *(foundation)* asiento, fundamento; GEOL. estratificación *f.*
be·deck (bĭ-dĕkʹ) tr. *(to embellish)* engalanar, adornar lla-

ã rey / ä año / b boca / ch chico / d dar / ĕ el / ē mil / g gato / h joya / hw juez / ī aire / k casa / kw cuan /

mativamente; *(to cover)* llenar (de adornos, condecoraciones).

be·dev·il (bĭ-dĕv′əl) tr. *(to annoy)* fastidiar, dificultar; *(to bewitch)* embrujar, endemoniar.

be·dew (bĭ-dōō′) tr. regar, rociar.

bed·fel·low (bĕd′fĕl′ō) s. *(bedmate)* compañero de cama; FIG. *(associate)* socio.

bed·lam (bĕd′ləm) s. *(uproar)* algarabía, alboroto; ANT. *(asylum)* casa de locos.

bed linen s. ropa de cama.

bed of roses s. lecho de rosas.

Bed·ou·in (bĕd′ōō-ĭn) adj. & s. beduino.

bed·pan (bĕd′păn′) s. orinal *m,* chata.

bed·post (bĕd′pōst′) s. pilar de la cama *m.*

bed·rid·den (bĕd′rĭd′n) o **bed·rid** (-rĭd′) adj. postrado en cama.

bed·rock (bĕd′rŏk′) s. *(bottom)* fondo; *(principle)* fundamento, principio; MIN. roca de fondo, roca firme.

bed·roll (bĕd′rōl′) s. lecho portátil que se enrolla.

bed·room (bĕd′rōōm′, -rŏŏm′) I. s. dormitorio, alcoba II. adj. *(dealing with sexual relations)* de alcoba <*a b. comedy* una comedia de alcoba>; *(inhabited by commuters)* residencial.

bed sheet s. sábana.

bed·side (bĕd′sīd′) I. s. cabecera II. adj. de cabecera, de noche <*a b. table* una mesita de noche>.

bedside manner s. comportamiento de un médico *o* enfermera ante el enfermo.

bed·sore (bĕd′sôr′) s. MED. úlcera por decúbito.

bed·spread (bĕd′sprĕd′) s. cubrecama *m,* colcha.

bed·spring (bĕd′sprĭng′) s. resorte *m,* somier *m.*

bed·stead (bĕd′stĕd′) s. cuja (armazón de la cama).

bed·time (bĕd′tīm′) s. hora de acostarse.

bedtime story s. historia que se cuenta a los niños al acostarlos.

bed·wet·ting (bĕd′wĕt′ĭng) s. MED. enuresis nocturna.

bee (bē) s. *(insect)* abeja; FAM. *(gathering)* reunión *f; (contest)* concurso ♦ **to have a b. in one's bonnet** estar obsesionado con una idea.

beech (bēch) s. BOT. haya (árbol y madera).

beech·nut (bēch′nŭt′) s. BOT. nuez de haya *f,* hayuco.

beef (bēf) I. s. [pl. **beeves** (bēvz)] *(animal)* res *f; (meat)* carne de res *f;* FAM. *(brawn)* musculatura, fuerza muscular; JER. *(complaint)* [pl. **beefs**] queja ♦ **to have a b.** quejarse II. intr. JER. quejarse —tr. ♦ **to b. up** JER. reforzar, fortalecer.

beef·eat·er (bēf′ē′tər) s. *(yeoman)* soldado de caballería de la guardia real inglesa; *(warder)* guardián de la Torre de Londres *m.*

beef·steak (bēf′stāk′) s. bistec *m,* biftec *m.*

beef·y (bē′fē) adj. **-i·er, -i·est** *(resembling beef)* carnoso, como de carne de res; *(brawny)* fornido, musculoso.

bee·hive (bē′hīv′) s. colmena.

bee·keep·er (bē′kē′pər) s. apicultor *m.*

bee·keep·ing (bē′kē′pĭng) s. apicultura, cría de abejas.

bee·line (bē′līn′) s. línea recta.

Be·el·ze·bub (bē-ĕl′zə-bŭb′) s. RELIG. Belcebú *m.*

been (bĭn) part. p. de **be.**

beep (bēp) I. s. sonido agudo II. intr. & tr. sonar con sonido agudo.

beep·er (bē′pər) s. dispositivo de llamada (por medio de un sonido agudo).

beer (bîr) s. cerveza ♦ **dark b.** cerveza negra • **draft b.** cerveza de barril • **light b.** cerveza dorada.

bees·wax (bēz′wăks′) s. cera.

beet (bēt) s. BOT. remolacha.

bee·tle (bēt′l) I. s. escarabajo II. adj. prominente (frente).

beeves (bēvz) un pl. de **beef.**

be·fall (bĭ-fôl′) intr. & tr. **-fell** (-fĕl′), **-fall·en** (-fô′lən), **-fall·ing** acontecer a, suceder a.

be·fit (bĭ-fĭt′) tr. **-fit·ted, -fit·ting** convenir.

be·fit·ting (bĭ-fĭt′ĭng) adj. *(suitable)* conveniente; *(proper)* apropiado.

be·fog (bĭ-fŏg′) tr. **-fogged, -fog·ging** *(to obscure)* oscurecer, envolver en niebla; *(to confuse)* confundir, desconcertar.

be·fore (bĭ-fôr′) I. adv. *(earlier)* antes <*come at eleven, not*

b. venga a las once, no antes>; *(in the past)* anteriormente, ya una vez <*I have read that book b.* he leído ese libro ya una vez>; *(ahead)* delante <*we went b. to show them the way* íbamos delante para mostrarles el camino> II. prep. *(earlier than)* antes de <*they left b. midnight* se fueron antes de medianoche>; *(in front of)* delante de <*we stopped b. the house* nos detuvimos delante de la casa>; *(awaiting)* ante <*they have a great future b. them* tienen un gran futuro ante ellos>; *(in the presence of)* ante <*to sing b. a big audience* cantar ante un gran público>; *(under consideration)* ante <*the case b. the court* el caso presentado ante el tribunal> III. conj. *(in advance)* antes de que <*b. he went* antes de que él fuera>; *(rather than)* antes que <*I would die fighting b. betraying my country* yo moriría peleando antes que traicionar a mi patria>.

be·fore·hand (bĭ-fôr′hănd′) adv. *(earlier)* antes <*we should do it b.* lo debiéramos hacer antes>; *(in anticipation)* de antemano <*to prepare b.* preparar de antemano>.

be·foul (bĭ-foul′) tr. *(to soil)* ensuciar, embadurnar; *(to speak badly of)* manchar, calumniar a alguien.

be·friend (bĭ-frĕnd′) tr. entablar amistad con.

be·fud·dle (bĭ-fŭd′l) tr. **-dled, -dling** confundir, dejar atónito.

beg (bĕg) tr. **begged, beg·ging** *(to ask for charity)* mendigar; *(to entreat)* suplicar, rogar ♦ **to b. the question** dar por sentado lo que queda por probar —intr. *(to solicit alms)* pedir limosna; *(to petition)* suplicar, implorar <*to b. for mercy* implorar clemencia> ♦ **to b. off** disculparse.

be·gan (bĭ-găn′) pret. de **begin.**

be·get (bĭ-gĕt′) tr. **-got** (-gŏt′), **-got·ten** (-gŏt′n) o **-got, -get·ting** *(to father)* engendrar, procrear; FIG. *(to produce)* engendrar, causar.

beg·gar (bĕg′ər) I. s. *(one who begs)* mendigo, pordiosero; *(pauper)* indigente *mf; (rascal)* bribón *m* II. tr. empobrecer ♦ **b. description** superar descripción.

beg·gar·ly (bĕg′ər-lē) adj. mísero, pobre.

beg·gar·y (bĕg′ə-rē) s. *(penury)* miseria, penuria; *(state)* mendicidad *f; (beggars)* mendigos.

be·gin (bĭ-gĭn′) intr. **-gan** (-găn′), **-gun** (-gŭn′), **-gin·ning** *(to commence)* empezar, comenzar; *(to arise)* surgir ♦ **to b. by** empezar por • **to b. with** *(first)* para empezar; *(to start with)* empezar con —tr. comenzar, empezar.

be·gin·ner (bĭ-gĭn′ər) s. *(initiator)* originador *m,* iniciador *m; (novice)* principiante *mf,* novato.

be·gin·ning (bĭ-gĭn′ĭng) s. *(start)* comienzo, principio; *(source)* origen *m,* causa primera ♦ **beginnings** albores, comienzos • **b. with** a partir de • **from b. to end** desde el principio hasta el final • **in the b.** al principio.

be·gone (bĭ-gôn′) interj. ¡fuera de aquí!, ¡fuera!

be·go·nia (bĭ-gōn′yə) s. BOT. begonia.

be·got (bĭ-gŏt′) pret. y un part. p. de **beget.**

be·got·ten (bĭ-gŏt′n) un part. p. de **beget.**

be·grime (bĭ-grīm′) tr. **-grimed, -grim·ing** tiznar, ensuciar.

be·grudge (bĭ-grŭj′) tr. **-grudged, -grudg·ing** *(to envy)* envidiar; *(to give reluctantly)* escatimar, dar de mala gana.

be·guile (bĭ-gīl′) tr. **-guiled, -guil·ing** *(to deceive)* engañar, burlar; *(to charm)* encantar, seducir.

be·gun (bĭ-gŭn′) part. p. de **begin.**

be·half (bĭ-hăf′, -hȁf′) s. *(benefit)* beneficio; *(interest)* interés *m; (favor)* favor *m* ♦ **for, on b. of** para, para <*in b. of the poor* para los pobres> • **on b. of** en nombre de.

be·have (bĭ-hāv′) intr. **-haved, -hav·ing** *(to function)* funcionar; *(to act)* portarse, comportarse; *(to conduct oneself properly)* portarse bien —tr. *(to conduct oneself well)* comportarse *o* portarse bien; *(to act)* portarse, comportarse.

be·hav·ior (bĭ-hāv′yər) s. *(conduct)* comportamiento, conducta; *(functioning)* funcionamiento.

be·hav·ior·al (bĭ-hāv′yər-əl) adj. de comportamiento, de conducta.

behavioral science s. ciencias sociales que estudian el comportamiento humano.

be·hav·ior·ism (bĭ-hāv′yə-rĭz′əm) s. PSIC. behaviorismo.

be·hav·ior·ist (bĭ-hāv′yə-rĭst′) s. adepto de la teoria del behaviorismo.

be·hav·iour (bĭ-hāv′yər) s. G.B. var. de **behavior.**

be·head (bĭ-hĕd') tr. decapitar, descabezar.
be·held (bĭ-hĕld') pret. y part. p. de **behold.**
be·he·moth (bĭ-hē'məth) s. *(animal)* behemot *m; (something enormous)* monstruo.
be·hest (bĭ-hĕst') s. *(order)* orden *f,* mandato; *(request)* petición *f* ♦ **at the b. of** a instancias *o* petición de.
be·hind (bĭ-hīnd') I. adv. *(toward the rear)* atrás, detrás; *(in a former place)* atrás <*the woman he left b.* la mujer que él dejó atrás>; *(in arrears)* atrasado; *(below standard)* a la zaga <*she fell b. the class* ella quedó a la zaga de la clase>; *(slow)* con retraso <*the clock is running b.* el reloj anda con retraso> II. prep. *(in back of)* detrás de <*he sat b. her* él se sentó detrás de ella>; *(beyond)* detrás de, tras; *(in a prior place)* atrás; *(later than)* después de <*the boat left b. schedule* el barco salió después de la hora>; *(less advanced than)* por debajo de; *(underlying)* detrás de; *(serving to support)* detrás <*the directors are b. the plan* los directores están detrás del plan>; *(in pursuit of)* atrás, tras III. s. FAM. trasero, nalgas.
be·hold (bĭ-hōld') tr. **-held** (-hĕld'), **-hold·ing** mirar, contemplar —interj. ¡mirad!, he aquí.
be·hold·en (bĭ-hōl'dən) adj. ♦ **to be b. to someone** estar obligado con alguien.
be·hoove (bĭ-hōōv') tr. **-hooved, -hoov·ing** *(to be a good idea for)* convenir; *(to befit)* corresponder —intr. *(to be fitting)* convenir; *(to be necessary)* ser menester.
beige (bāzh) s. & adj. beige *m.*
be·ing (bē'ĭng) s. *(existence)* existencia; *(entity)* ser *m,* ente *m; (person)* ser <*he is a solitary b.* él es un ser solitario>; *(nature)* naturaleza <*violence is a part of his b.* la violencia es parte de su naturaleza>; FILOS. *(essence)* esencia del existir ♦ **for the time b.** por el momento • **human b.** ser humano • **the Supreme Being** RELIG. el Ser Supremo • **to bring into b.** to engender, engendrar, procrear; *(to produce)* realizar; *(to create)* crear.
bel (bĕl) s. FÍS. belio, bel *m.*
be·la·bor (bĭ-lā'bər) tr. *(to beat)* golpear, apalear; *(to scold)* regañar, reñir; *(to harp on)* extenderse (sobre un tema).
be·la·bour (bĭ-lā'bər) tr. G.B. var. de **belabor.**
be·lat·ed (bĭ-lā'tĭd) adj. atrasado, tardío.
be·lay (bĭ-lā') I. tr. *(in mountain climbing)* asegurar; *(to cause to stop)* detener; MARÍT. amarrar —intr. *(to be made secure)* amarrarse, asegurarse; *(to stop)* detenerse II. s. agarradero, asidero.
belaying pin s. MARÍT. cabilla.
belch (bĕlch) I. intr. & tr. *(to burp)* eructar; FIG. *(to expel)* arrojar, vomitar II. s. eructo.
be·lea·guer (bĭ-lē'gər) tr. MIL. sitiar, cercar; FIG. *(to beset)* llenar (de problemas, dificultades).
bel·fry (bĕl'frē) s. [pl. **-fries**] campanario.
Bel·gian (bĕl'jən) adj. & s. belga *mf.*
Bel·gium (bĕl'jəm) s. Bélgica.
be·lie (bĭ-lī') tr. **-lied, -ly·ing** *(to misrepresent)* representar mal; *(to refute)* desmentir, contradecir; *(to disappoint)* frustrar, defraudar (esperanzas).
be·lief (bĭ-lēf') s. *(conviction)* creencia, fe *f; (confidence)* confianza; *(opinion)* opinión *f;* RELIG. credo, fe.
be·liev·a·ble (bĭ-lē'və-bəl) adj. creíble, digno de crédito.
be·lieve (bĭ-lēv') tr. **-lieved, -liev·ing** creer —intr. *(to have faith)* creer, tener fe; *(to trust)* confiar; *(to be in favor of)* ser partidario de <*to b. in charity* ser partidario de la caridad> ♦ **to make b.** aparentar, fingir.
be·liev·er (bĭ-lē'vər) s. creyente *mf.*
be·lit·tle (bĭ-lĭt'l) tr. **-tled, -tling** *(to minimize)* minimizar; *(to disparage)* menospreciar, despreciar.
Be·lize (bə-lēz') s. Belice *m.*
bell (bĕl) I. s. *(instrument)* campana; *(handbell)* campanilla; *(of a door)* timbre *m; (of animals)* esquila, cencerro; *(of collar)* cascabel *m;* BOT. corola acampanada; MARÍT. *(stroke)* campanada; *(time)* media hora (de guardia) ♦ **sound as a b.** en perfecta salud • **to ring a b.** *(to evoke)* sonar; *(to play)* tocar (una campana, un timbre) • **with bells on** FAM. con mucho gusto ♦ **to put a bell on** poner un cencerro *o* un cascabel (a un animal); *(to shape)* acampanar ♦ **to b. the cat** poner el cascabel al gato

—intr. *(to flare)* acampanarse; *(to toll)* tocar timbre *o* campana.
bel·la·don·na (bĕl'ə-dŏn'ə) s. belladonna.
bell-bot·tom (bĕl'bŏt'əm) adj. acampanado <*b. trousers* pantalones acampanados>.
bell·boy (bĕl'boi') s. botones *m,* paje *m.*
bell buoy s. MARÍT. boya de campana.
belle (bĕl) s. belleza, mujer bella ♦ **the b. of the ball** la mujer más bella del baile.
bell·flow·er (bĕl'flou'ər) s. BOT. campánula, campanilla.
bell·hop (bĕl'hŏp') s. botones *m,* paje *m.*
bel·li·cose (bĕl'ĭ-kōs') adj. belicoso, agresivo.
bel·lig·er·ence (bə-lĭj'ər-əns) *o* **bel·lig·er·en·cy** (-ən-sē) s. beligerancia, hostilidad *f.*
bel·lig·er·ent (bə-lĭj'ər-ənt) I. adj. beligerante, hostil II. s. beligerante (nación en guerra) *mf.*
bell jar s. fanal *m,* campana de cristal.
bell·man (bĕl'mən) s. [pl. **-men**] pregonero.
bel·low (bĕl'ō) I. intr. *(to roar)* bramar, rugir; *(to shout)* vociferar, rugir —tr. vociferar, gritar a voz en cuello II. s. bramido, rugido.
bel·lows (bĕl'ōz) s. [ú. con v. sing. o pl.] fuelle *m,* barquín *m.*
bell pepper s. pimiento dulce, chile dulce *m.*
bell-shaped (bĕl'shāpt') adj. acampanado.
bell tower s. campanario.
bell·weth·er (bĕl'wĕth'ər) s. *(animal)* manso líder de rebaño; *(leader)* cabecilla *mf,* jefe *m.*
bel·ly (bĕl'ē) I. s. [pl. **-lies**] *(abdomen)* abdomen *m,* vientre *m; (stomach)* estómago; *(uterus)* útero; *(bulge)* comba, protuberancia; FAM. *(tummy)* panza, barriga; FIG. *(bottom side)* panza <*the b. of a plane* la panza de un avión>; *(appetite)* apetito, ganas *f;* MARÍT. *(bulging part)* bolso, seno (de una vela) II. intr. & tr. **-lied, -ly·ing** inflar(se), hinchar(se).
bel·ly·ache (bĕl'ē-āk') I. s. *(pain)* dolor de barriga *o* de vientre *m;* JER. *(complaint)* queja II. intr. **-ached, -ach·ing** JER. quejarse, lamentarse.
bel·ly·band (bĕl'ē-bănd') s. *(for horses)* cincha; *(for babies)* faja, ombliguero.
bel·ly·but·ton (bĕl'ē-bŭt'n) s. FAM. ombligo.
belly flop s. panzazo, panzada ♦ **to do a b.** dar un panzazo.
bel·ly·ful (bĕl'ē-fōōl') s. FAM. panzada, hartazgo.
belly laugh s. carcajada, risotada.
be·long (bĭ-lông') intr. *(to have a proper place)* deber estar <*the table belongs here* la mesa debe estar aquí>; *(to go well together)* ir bien; *(to fit into a group)* estar en su ambiente ♦ **to b. to** *(to be owned by)* pertenecer a, ser de; *(to be a member of)* ser miembro de; *(to be part of)* corresponder a.
be·long·ings (bĭ-lông'ĭngz) s.pl. efectos personales *m,* pertenencias.
be·lov·ed (bĭ-lŭv'ĭd, -lŭvd') adj. & s. querido, amado.
be·low (bĭ-lō') I. adv. *(beneath)* abajo; *(downstairs)* abajo; *(farther down)* más abajo; *(in hell)* en el infierno; *(on earth)* aquí abajo; *(in a lesser rank)* por debajo de; MARÍT. en una cubierta inferior II. prep. *(beneath)* debajo de; *(lower than)* por debajo de <*b. sea level* por debajo del nivel del mar>; *(lower in degree)* inferior a, bajo <*temperatures b. zero* temperaturas bajo cero>; *(unworthy)* indigno de.
belt (bĕlt) I. s. *(garment)* cinturón *m,* cinto; *(encircling route)* carretera de circunvalación; *(seat belt)* cinturón de seguridad; JER. *(punch)* golpe *m; (reaction)* emoción viva, conmoción *f; (drink)* trago de licor fuerte; TEC. *(chain)* correa de transmisión; *(reinforcing material)* banda, faja (reforzada de una llanta); GEOG. *(region)* zona, región *f* ♦ **to hit below the b.** golpear bajo *o* de forma ilícita • **to tighten one's b.** apretarse el cinturón • **to be under one's b.** estar en poder de uno II. tr. *(to gird)* rodear; *(to attach)* ceñir; *(to strike)* pegar con una correa, azotar; JER. *(to punch)* golpear, asestar un golpe; *(to sing)* cantar (con voz chillona).
belt·ing (bĕl'tĭng) s. *(belts)* correaje *m; (material)* material para correas *o* cinturones *m.*
belt tightening s. FIG. disminución de gastos *f.*

be·lu·ga (bə-lōō′gə) s. ZOOL. *(white whale)* beluga; *(sturgeon)* esturión blanco.

be·moan (bĭ-mōn′) tr. *(to lament)* lamentar, plañir; *(to mourn over)* llorar por; *(to express pity for)* tener piedad de —intr. plañir, lamentarse.

be·muse (bĭ-myōōz′) tr. **-mused, -mus·ing** *(to confuse)* pasmar, causar estupefacción; *(to preoccupy)* preocupar.

bench (bĕnch) I. s. *(seat)* banco, banqueta; *(workbench)* banco de trabajo; MARÍT. *(thwart)* travesaño, asiento (en un bote); DER. *(place)* asiento de los jueces, estrado; *(office of the judge)* judicatura, magistratura; *(court)* tribunal m; GEOL. *(terrace)* banco (de arena), arrecife m; *(shelf of ground)* desnivel m; G.B. *(in Parliament)* escaño II. tr. *(to furnish)* proveer de bancos; *(to seat)* sentar en un banco.

bench mark o **bench·mark** (bĕnch′märk′) s. TOP. cota de referencia ♦ **benchmark** punto de referencia.

bench warrant s. DER. auto de detención.

bend (bĕnd) I. tr. **bent** (bĕnt), **bend·ing** *(the head)* inclinar; *(the knee)* doblar; *(one's back)* encorvar; *(a bow)* armar; *(to curve)* doblar, plegar; *(to deflect)* desviar; *(to subdue)* doblegar, hacer acatar <*he bent her to his will* la hizo acatar a su voluntad>; *(to concentrate on)* concentrarse en, dedicarse a; MARÍT. amarrar, envergar (vela, cable) —intr. *(to curve)* doblarse; *(to crook)* curvarse; *(to swerve)* desviarse, torcer; *(to stoop)* encorvarse; *(to sag)* combarse ♦ **to b. back** doblarse hacia atrás • **to b. over backwards** hacer el mayor esfuerzo posible II. s. *(curve)* curva; *(turn)* vuelta, recodo; *(sag)* combadura; MARÍT. *(knot)* nudo ♦ **bends** [ú. con v. sing. o pl.] parálisis que afecta a los bucedores • **to go around the b.** volverse loco.

bend·er (bĕn′dər) s. FAM. borrachera, juerga.

be·neath (bĭ-nēth′) I. prep. *(below)* debajo de; *(lower than)* por debajo de; *(unworthy)* indigno de II. adv. *(below)* abajo; *(underneath)* debajo.

Ben·e·dic·tine (bĕn′ĭ-dĭk′tĭn) adj. & s. RELIG. benedictino.

ben·e·dic·tion (bĕn′ĭ-dĭk′shən) s. *(blessing)* bendición f; *(blessedness)* gracia.

ben·e·fac·tion (bĕn′ə-făk′shən) s. *(act)* obra de beneficiencia; *(gift)* donación f.

ben·e·fac·tor (bĕn′ə-făk′tər) s. benefactor m, bienhechor m.

ben·e·fac·tress (bĕn′ə-făk′trĭs) s. benefactora, bienhechora.

be·nef·ic (bə-nĕf′ĭk) adj. benéfico, benefactor.

ben·e·fice (bĕn′ə-fĭs) s. RELIG. beneficio.

be·nef·i·cence (bə-nĕf′ĭ-səns) s. *(benevolence)* beneficencia, caridad f; *(act)* acto de caridad; *(gift)* donación f.

be·nef·i·cent (bə-nĕf′ĭ-sənt) adj. benéfico, benefactor.

ben·e·fi·cial (bĕn′ə-fĭsh′əl) adj. *(advantageous)* beneficioso, provechoso; DER. usufructuario.

ben·e·fi·ci·ar·y (bĕn′ə-fĭsh′ē-ĕr′ē) s. [pl. **-ies**] *(recipient)* beneficiario; RELIG. beneficiado.

ben·e·fit (bĕn′ə-fĭt) I. s. *(profit)* beneficio, provecho; *(advantage)* ventaja <*he has the b. of being taller* tiene la ventaja de ser más alto>; *(payment)* subsidio, asistencia <*social security benefits* asistencia del seguro social>; *(service)* beneficio <*fringe benefits* beneficios adicionales>; *(fund-raiser)* beneficio ♦ **for the b. of** en beneficio de • **to be of b. to** ser beneficioso para, redundar en provecho de • **to give someone the b. of the doubt** no juzgar a alguien por anticipado II. tr. beneficiar —intr. ♦ **to b. by** o **from** sacar provecho de.

be·nev·o·lence (bə-nĕv′ə-ləns) s. *(good will)* benevolencia; *(kindly act)* acto de caridad.

be·nev·o·lent (bə-nĕv′ə-lənt) adj. *(kindly)* benévolo, bondadoso; *(charitable)* caritativo; *(philanthropic)* de beneficencia.

Ben·gal (bĕn-gôl′) s. Bengala m.

Ben·gal·ese (bĕn′gə-lēz′) adj. & s. [pl. **Bengalese**] bengalí mf ♦ **the B.** los bengalíes.

be·night·ed (bĭ-nī′tĭd) adj. *(overtaken by night)* anochecido, oscurecido; FIG. *(unenlightened)* ignorante.

be·nign (bĭ-nīn′) adj. *(kind, gentle)* benigno; *(beneficial)* benigno, favorable; MED. benigno.

be·nig·nant (bĭ-nĭg′nənt) adj. *(kindly)* benigno, bondadoso; *(favorable)* favorable, beneficioso.

Be·nin (bə-nēn′) s. Benin.

Be·nin·ese (bĕn′ĭ-nēz′) adj. & s. [pl. **Beninese**] beninés m ♦ **the B.** los benineses.

ben·i·son (bĕn′ĭ-zən, -sən) s. bendición f.

bent (bĕnt) I. pret. y part. p. de **bend** II. adj. *(crooked)* doblado, torcido; *(stooped)* encorvado; *(determined)* resuelto, empeñado <*he was b. on going to the theater* estaba empeñado en ir al teatro> III. s. *(tendency)* inclinación f, tendencia; ING. pilón transversal m.

be·numb (bĭ-nŭm′) tr. *(to make numb)* entumecer; *(to stupefy)* entorpecer, embotar.

Ben·ze·drine (bĕn′zĭ-drēn′) s. FARM. marca registrada de anfetamina.

ben·zene (bĕn′zēn′) s. QUÍM. benceno.

ben·zine (bĕn′zēn′) o **ben·zin** (-zĭn) s. QUÍM. *(ligroin)* bencina; *(benzene)* benceno.

ben·zo·caine (bĕn′zə-kān′) s. FARM., MED. benzocaíne.

be·queath (bĭ-kwēth′, -kwēth′) tr. legar.

be·quest (bĭ-kwĕst′) s. legado.

be·rate (bĭ-rāt′) tr. **-rat·ed, -rat·ing** *(to scold)* reprender, regañar; *(to condemn)* censurar.

Ber·ber (bûr′bər) I. adj. beréber, berberisco II. s. *(inhabitant, language)* beréber m.

be·reave (bĭ-rēv′) tr. **-reaved** o **-reft** (-rĕft′), **-reav·ing** *(to deprive)* separar (por la muerte), privar <*bereaved of his mother and father* separado de la madre y el padre por la muerte>; *(to leave desolate)* desconsolar, desolar ♦ **the bereaved** los deudos del difunto.

be·reave·ment (bĭ-rēv′mənt) s. *(grief)* luto, duelo; *(loss)* pérdida (de un ser querido).

be·reft (bĭ-rĕft′) adj. *(deprived)* privado <*b. of his dignity* privado de su dignidad>; *(lacking)* desprovisto; *(bereaved)* desolado.

be·ret (bə-rā′, bĕr′ā′) s. boina.

berg (bûrg) s. iceberg m, témpano de hielo.

ber·i·ber·i (bĕr′ē-bĕr′ē) s. MED. beriberi m.

ber·ke·li·um (bər-kē′lē-əm) s. QUÍM. berkelio.

Ber·lin (bər-lĭn′) s. Berlín.

ber·ry (bĕr′ē) s. [pl. **-ries**] BOT. *(fruit)* baya; *(dry kernel)* grano (de café, cebada); *(fish egg)* hueva.

ber·serk (bər-sûrk′) adj. *(violent)* vesánico, furioso; *(deranged)* loco ♦ **to go b.** volverse loco.

berth (bûrth) I. s. *(bunk)* litera; MARÍT. *(bed)* cama; *(stateroom)* camarote m; *(at a wharf)* atracadero; *(sea room)* espacio para maniobrar; *(employment)* puesto, colocación f; *(parking space)* estacionamiento ♦ **to give a wide b. to** no acercarse a, evitar II. tr. *(a ship)* atracar; *(a passenger)* acomodar —intr. MARÍT. atracar.

be·ryl·li·um (bə-rĭl′ē-əm) s. QUÍM. berilio.

be·seech (bĭ-sēch′) tr. **-sought** (-sôt′) o **-seeched, -seech·ing** suplicar, implorar.

be·set (bĭ-sĕt′) tr. **-set, -set·ting** *(to assail)* asediar, atacar; *(to harass)* asediar, acosar <*b. by doubts* acosado por las dudas>; *(to surround)* rodear; INY. *(to stud)* engastar.

be·side (bĭ-sīd′) prep. *(next to)* junto a, al lado de; *(in comparison with)* comparado con, al lado de <*a small contribution b. yours* una contribución pequeña al lado de la tuya>; *(except for)* aparte de; *(not relevant to)* lejos de, fuera de ♦ **to be b. oneself** estar fuera de sí • **to be b. the point** no venir al caso.

be·sides (bĭ-sīdz′) I. adv. *(in addition)* además, también; *(moreover)* además <*I was bored, and b. it was late* estaba aburrido y, además, era tarde>; *(otherwise)* por otro lado, aparte de eso II. prep. *(in addition to)* además de; *(except)* aparte de, fuera de.

be·siege (bĭ-sēj′) tr. **-sieged, -sieg·ing** *(to lay siege to)* asediar, sitiar; *(to hem in)* rodear, cercar; *(to harass)* asediar, abrumar ♦ **to be besieged with (calls, requests)** haber recibido un torrente de (llamadas, peticiones).

be·smear (bĭ-smîr′) tr. *(to bedaub)* embarrar; *(to defile)* ensuciar, mancillar.

be·smirch (bĭ-smûrch′) tr. *(to soil)* ensuciar, embadurnar; *(to dishonor)* ensuciar, manchar.

be·sought (bĭ-sôt′) un pret. y part. p. de **beseech.**

be·speak (bĭ-spēk') tr. **-spoke** (-spōk'), **-spo·ken** (-spō'kən) o **-spoke, -speak·ing** (to indicate) indicar, revelar; (to foretell) presagiar, anunciar.

be·spec·ta·cled (bĭ-spĕk'tə-kəld) adj. con anteojos, que lleva gafas.

be·spoke (bĭ-spōk') pret. y un part. p. de **bespeak.**

be·spo·ken (bĭ-spō'kən) un part. p. de **bespeak.**

be·sprin·kle (bĭ-sprĭng'kəl) tr. **-kled, -kling** salpicar.

best (bĕst) [superl. de **good**] I. adj. (most excellent or desirable) mejor <the b. solution la mejor solución>; (largest) mayor <the b. part of the journey la mayor parte del viaje> ♦ **b. man** padrino (de una boda) • **to know what is b. for one** saber lo que más le conviene a uno II. adv. (in the best way) mejor; (most) más <what do you like to eat b.? ¿qué es lo que más le gusta comer?> ♦ **had b.** mejor sería, más vale que <you had b. get out of here más vale que te vayas de aquí> • **to know b.** saber lo que conviene más III. s. (choice) mejor m, lo mejor m <the b. of the lot lo mejor del lote>; (one's major effort) todo lo que puede hacer (uno) <I am doing my b. estoy haciendo todo lo que uedo>; (regards) buenos deseos, mejores votos <give her my b. dale mis mejores votos> • **at b.** en el mejor de los casos, a lo más • **for the b.** lo mejor cuando todo sea dicho • **to do one's b.** hacer lo mejor que uno puede • **to make the b. of it** salir de un mal negocio lo mejor posible • **to the b. of my recollection** que yo sepa, que yo recuerde IV. tr. vencer, ganar.

bes·tial (bĕs'chəl) adj. bestial.

bes·ti·al·i·ty (bĕs'chē-ăl'ĭ-tē) s. [pl. **-ties**] bestialidad f.

be·stir (bĭ-stûr') tr. ♦ **to b. oneself** rebullirse, moverse.

be·stow (bĭ-stō') tr. (to confer) otorgar, conceder; (to give) otorgar, entregar; (praise) colmar de.

be·stow·al (bĭ-stō'əl) s. otorgamiento.

be·strew (bĭ-strōō') tr. **-strewed, -strewed** o **-strewn** (-strōōn'), **-strew·ing** (to scatter) esparcir, desparramar; (to lie scattered) salpicar, cubrir <bestrewn with flowers salpicado de flores>.

be·stride (bĭ-strīd') tr. **-strode** (-strōd), **-strid·den** (-strĭd'n), **-strid·ing** (a horse) montar (a horcajadas); (a chair) sentarse a horcajadas en; (to stand on) estar parado a caballo sobre; (to step over) cruzar (de una zancada); (to tower over) dominar, alzarse sobre.

best seller s. libro de gran éxito, best seller m.

bet (bĕt) I. s. apuesta ♦ **to be a sure b.** ser cosa segura II. tr. **bet** o **bet·ted, bet·ting** (to wager) apostar; (to maintain) asegurar, estar seguro ♦ **I b. . . .** FAM. a que . . ., seguro que . . . —intr. (to make a bet) apostar; (to gamble) jugar ♦ **I b.!** FAM. ¡ya lo creo! • **you b.!** FAM. ¡claro!, ¡por supuesto!

be·ta (bā'tə, bē'-) s. (Greek letter) beta; FÍS (particle) partícula beta.

be·take (bĭ-tāk') tr. **-took** (-tōōk), **-tak·en, -tak·ing** ♦ **to b. oneself** (to go to) trasladarse a; ANT. (to commit oneself to) entregarse a.

beta ray s. FÍS. rayo beta.

beta rhythm s. FÍS., MED. ritmo beta, onda beta.

beth·el (bĕth'əl) s. RELIG. (holy place) lugar sagrado; (chapel) capilla para marineros.

Beth·le·hem (bĕth'lə-hĕm') s. Belén.

be·to·ken (bĭ-tō'kən) tr. (to indicate) indicar, demostrar; (to portend) presagiar, anunciar.

be·took (bĭ-tōōk') pret. de **betake.**

be·tray (bĭ-trā') tr. (to be a traitor to) traicionar; (to inform on) delatar, denunciar; (a promise) violar; (to divulge) revelar (secreto, trama); (unintentionally) traicionar, delatar <his voice betrayed his fears su voz delató sus temores>; (to deceive) traicionar, defraudar (confianza, esperanzas).

be·tray·al (bĭ-trā'əl) s. (treason) traición f; (by an informant) delación f, denuncia; (divulgation) revelación f; (deception) traición f, defraudación f.

be·troth (bĭ-trōth') tr. (to promise in marriage) prometer en matrimonio; (to promise to marry) prometer matrimonio a.

be·troth·al (bĭ-trō'thəl) s. desposorios, compromiso matrimonial.

be·trothed (bĭ-trōthd') s. prometido, novio.

bet·ter (bĕt'ər) [comp. de **good**] I. adj. (superior) mejor, superior; (preferable) más apropiado, preferible; (larger) mayor <I will be away the b. part of the week estaré ausente la mayor parte de la semana> ♦ **b. half** FAM. media naranja, cara mitad • **to be b. to** valer más, ser mejor • **to be no b. than** no ser más que <he's no b. than a fool no es más que un tonto> II. adv. mejor <try to do it b. next time trata de hacerlo mejor la próxima vez>; (more) más <it is b. than a mile from here to the station es más de una milla de aquí a la estación>; (to a greater extent) en mayor grado, mejor ♦ **all the b.** o **so much the b.** tanto mejor • **b. and b.** cada vez mejor • **b. late than never** más vale tarde que nunca • **b. off** (more affluent) más rico, en mejor posición económica; (in a more favorable condition) en mejores condiciones • **had b.** sería mejor que, más vale que <we had b. go más vale que nos vayamos> • **the sooner the b.** cuanto antes mejor • **to get b.** (to improve) mejorar; (to regain health) recobrarse, mejorar • **to go one b.** (to offer) hacer una oferta más atractiva, ofrecer más; (to improve) hacer mejor todavía • **to think b. of** reconsiderar, volver a considerar III. tr. (to improve) mejorar, adelantar; (to exceed) superar —intr. mejorarse, ponerse mejor IV. s. el mejor ♦ **betters** superiores • **for b. or worse** en la fortuna como en la desventura • **to get the b. of** superar, vencer.

bet·ter·ment (bĕt'ər-mənt) s. mejora, mejoramiento.

bet·tor (bĕt'ər) s. apostador m, apostante mf.

be·tween (bĭ-twēn') I. prep. entre ♦ **b. now and then** de aquí a entonces • **b. the devil and the deep blue sea** entre la espada y la pared • **b. you and me** entre nosotros, en confianza II. adv. en medio, de por medio ♦ **far b.** a grandes intervalos • **in b.** mientras tanto.

be·twixt (bĭ-twĭkst') adv. ♦ **b. and between** entre una cosa y otra.

bev·el (bĕv'əl) I. s. (surface) bisel m; (rule) falsa escuadra II. tr. biselar —intr. inclinarse.

bev·eled (bĕv'əld) adj. biselado.

bev·er·age (bĕv'ər-ĭj) s. bebida.

bev·y (bĕv'ē) s. [pl. **-ies**] (of birds) bandada; (of animals) manada; (of people) grupo.

be·wail (bĭ-wāl') tr. lamentar, lamentarse de.

be·ware (bĭ-wâr') I. tr. **-wared, -war·ing** tener cuidado con —intr. tener cuidado ♦ **b. of** cuidado con <b. of the dog cuidado con el perro> II. interj. ¡cuidado!

be·wil·der (bĭ-wĭl'dər) tr. desconcertar, dejar perplejo.

be·wil·der·ment (bĭ-wĭl'dər-mənt) s. desconcierto, perplejidad f.

be·witch (bĭ-wĭch') tr. (to put a spell on) hechizar, embrujar; (to fascinate) hechizar, fascinar.

be·witch·ment (bĭ-wĭch'mənt) s. hechizo.

be·yond (bē-ŏnd', bĭ-yŏnd') I. prep. (greater than) más allá, fuera de <that house is b. his means esa casa está fuera de sus posibilidades>; (past) después de ♦ **b. belief** increíble • **b. description** indescriptible • **b. dispute** incontestable • **b. doubt** fuera de duda • **b. help** sin remedio • **b. measure** inmenso • **it's b. me** no alcanzo a comprender II. adv. más lejos, más allá.

Bhu·tan (bōō-tän') s. Bután.

Bhu·tan·ese (bōō'tə-nēz') adj. & s. [pl. **Bhutanese**] butanés m.

bi·an·nu·al (bī-ăn'yōō-əl) adj. semestral.

bi·as (bī'əs) I. s. (tendency) inclinación f, tendencia f; (prejudice) prejuicio; (partiality) preferencia, preocupación f; COST. (cut) bies m, sesgo <on the b. al bies>; ELECTRÓN. voltaje de polarización m II. tr. predisponer, influenciar ♦ **to be biased** ser parcial.

bi·ax·i·al (bī-ăk'sē-əl) adj. biáxico.

bib (bĭb) I. s. (for children) babero, babador m; (of an apron) peto, pechera II. tr. **bibbed, bib·bing** tomarse, beber —intr. empinar el codo.

bib and tucker s. ♦ **to be in one's b.** FAM. llevar la mejor ropa que uno tiene.

Bi·ble (bī'bəl) s. Biblia ♦ **b.** biblia, evangelio <the b. of French cooking la biblia de la cocina francesa>.

Bib·li·cal o **bib·li·cal** (bĭb'lĭ-kəl) adj. bíblico.

bib·li·og·ra·pher (bĭb'lē-ŏg'rə-fər) s. bibliógrafo.

ā rey / ä año / b boca / ch chico / d dar / ĕ el / ē mil / g gato / h joya / hw juez / ī aire / k casa / kw cuan /

bib·li·o·graph·ic (bĭb′le-ə-grăf′ĭk) o **bib·li·o·graph·i·cal** (-ĭ-kəl) adj. bibliográfico.
bib·li·og·ra·phy (bĭb′lē-ŏg′rə-fē) s. [pl. **-phies**] bibliografía.
bib·li·o·phile (bĭb′lē-ə-fīl′) s. bibliófilo.
bib·u·lous (bĭb′yə-ləs) adj. *(fond of liquor)* bebedor; *(absorbent)* absorbente.
bi·cam·er·al (bī-kăm′ər-əl) adj. POL. bicameral.
bi·car·bon·ate (bī-kär′bə-nāt′) s. bicarbonato ♦ **b. of soda** bicarbonato de sosa • **sodium b.** bicarbonato sódico o de sodio.
bi·cen·ten·a·ry (bī′sĕn-tĕn′ə-rē) s. [pl. **-ries**] bicentenario.
bi·cen·ten·ni·al (bī′sĕn-tĕn′ē-əl) adj. & s. bicentario.
bi·ceps (bī′sĕps) s. [pl. **biceps** o **-ceps·es** (-sĕp′sĭz)] ANAT. bíceps *m.*
bick·er (bĭk′ər) I. intr. reñir, disputar II. s. riña, disputa.
bi·con·cave (bī′kŏn-kāv′) adj. bicóncavo.
bi·con·vex (bī′kŏn-vĕks′) adj. biconvexo.
bi·cus·pid (bī-kŭs′pĭd) I. adj. bicúspide II. s. ODONT. premolar *m.*
bi·cy·cle (bī′sĭk′əl) I. s. bicicleta II. intr. **-cled, -cling** *(to ride)* montar en bicicleta; *(to travel)* ir en bicicleta.
bi·cy·clist (bī′sĭk′lĭst) s. ciclista *mf.*
bid (bĭd) I. tr. **bade** (băd, bād) o **bid, bid·den** (bĭd′n) o **bid, bid·ding** *(to order)* ordenar, mandar; *(to utter a greeting)* dar <*to b.* good morning dar los buenos días>; *(to invite or summon)* invitar, convidar; *(in bridge)* declarar; *(to offer)* hacer una oferta, licitar ♦ **to b. farewell** o **goodbye to** decir adiós a —intr. *(to make an offer)* hacer una oferta; *(to strive)* hacer un esfuerzo II. s. *(offer)* licitación *f.*, oferta; *(invitation)* invitación *f.*; *(in bridge)* declaración *f.*; *(trump)* comodín *m.*; *(effort)* esfuerzo, tentativa.
▲ El pretérito y el participio pasado *bid* se usan en casos referentes a licitaciones y juegos de cartas. Para todos los otros casos, úsase *bade* y *bidden.*
bid·den (bĭd′n) un part. p. de **bid.**
bid·der (bĭd′ər) s. *(at a sale)* postor *m* <*the highest b.* el mejor postor>; *(in cards)* declarante *mf.*
bid·ding (bĭd′ĭng) s. *(command)* mandato, orden *f* <*at the b. of his king* por orden de su rey>; *(summons)* mandata, llamado; *(at an auction)* oferta; *(in cards)* declaración *f.*
bid·dy (bĭd′ē) s. [pl. **-dies**] ZOOL. gallina; JER. vieja chacharera.
bide (bīd) intr. & tr. **bid·ed** o **bode** (bōd), **bid·ed, bid·ing** aguardar, esperar ♦ **to b. one's time** aguardar el momento oportuno.
bi·en·ni·al (bī-ĕn′ē-əl) I. adj. bienal II. s. *(festival)* bienal *f*; *(plant)* planta bienal.
bier (bĭr) s. féretro.
biff (bĭf) JER. I. tr. dar un sopapo o un porrazo a II. s. sopapo, porrazo.
bi·fo·cal (bī-fō′kəl) adj. bifocal.
bi·fo·cals (bī-fō′kəlz) s.pl. anteojos o lentes bifocales *m.*
bi·fur·cate (bī′fər-kāt′) I. intr. **-cat·ed, -cat·ing** bifurcarse, dividirse en dos II. adj. bifurcado.
bi·fur·ca·tion (bī′fər-kā′shən) s. bifurcación *f.*
big (bĭg) I. adj. **big·ger, big·gest** *(large)* gran, grande; *(great in intensity)* fuerte, intenso; *(grown-up)* mayor <*my b. brother* mi hermano mayor>; *(pregnant)* encinta, embarazada; *(important)* importante, influyente; *(momentous)* de gran significado, trascendental; *(loud)* fuerte, resonante; *(bountiful)* generoso, magnánimo; FAM. *(boastful)* jactancioso, fanfarrón II. adv. *(boastful)* jactanciosamente, pomposamente; *(with success)* en gran forma, con mucho éxito ♦ **to be b. on** FAM. ser entusiasta de <*he's b. on tennis* es entusiasta del tenis> • **to make it b.** tener gran éxito.
big·a·mist (bĭg′ə-mĭst) s. bígamo.
big·a·mous (bĭg′ə-məs) adj. bígamo.
big·a·my (bĭg′ə-mē) s. [pl. **-mies**] bigamia.
big bang theory s. ASTRON. teoría del origen del cosmos en una gran explosión.
big brother s. hermano mayor ♦ **B.** brazo omnipotente de un gobierno autoritario.
big game s. DEP. *(in hunting)* caza mayor; JER. *(objective)* peces gordos.
big·head (bĭg′hĕd′) s. FAM. hinchazón *f*, vanidad *f.*

big-heart·ed (bĭg′här′tĭd) adj. generoso, que es todo corazón.
big·horn (bĭg′hôrn′) s. ZOOL. carnero salvaje de las Montañas Rocosas.
big house s. JER. jaula, cárcel *f.*
big league s. DEP. *(association)* liga mayor (profesional); FIG. *(big time)* nivel importante *m* <*the promotion put him in the b.* el ascenso lo colocó en un nivel importante>.
big-mouth (bĭg′mouth′) s. JER. *(loudmouth)* gritón *m*; *(gossip)* hablador *m*, chismoso; *(boaster)* bocón *m.*
big·ness (bĭg′nĭs) s. *(size)* grandor *m*; *(importance)* grandeza.
big·no·ni·a (bĭg-nō′nē-ə) s. BOT. bignonia.
big·ot (bĭg′ət) s. *(sectarian)* sectario, persona llena de prejuicios; *(intolerant person)* intolerante *mf.*
big·ot·ed (bĭg′ə-tĭd) adj. *(sectarian)* sectario, lleno de prejuicios; *(intolerant)* intolerante.
big·ot·ry (bĭg′ə-trē) s. *(sectarianism)* sectarismo; *(intolerance)* intolerancia.
big shot s. JER. pez gordo (persona importante).
big-time (bĭg′tīm′) JER. de los grandes, de mucho éxito <*a b. gambler* un jugador de los grandes>.
big top s. FAM. *(circus tent)* tienda mayor de un circo; *(circus)* circo.
big wheel s. JER. pez gordo.
big·wig (bĭg′wĭg′) s. FAM. grande *m*, pez gordo.
bike (bīk) I. s. *(bicycle)* bici *f*, bicicleta; *(motorcycle)* moto *f*, motocicleta II. intr. **biked, bik·ing** *(to bicycle)* montar en bici; *(to motorcycle)* manejar una moto.
bik·er (bī′kər) s. motociclista *mf.*
bi·ki·ni (bĭ-kē′nē) s. bikini *f.*
bi·lat·er·al (bī-lăt′ər-əl) adj. bilateral.
bil·ber·ry (bĭl′bĕr′ē) s. [pl. **-ries**] BOT. arándano (planta y fruto).
bile (bīl) s. *(fluid)* bilis *f*; *(ill temper)* mal genio.
bile duct s. ANAT. conducto biliar.
bilge (bĭlj) I. s. MARÍT. *(of a hull)* sentina; *(bilge water)* agua de sentina; *(of a barrel)* barriga; JER. *(stupid talk)* disparates *m* II. intr. **bilged, bilg·ing** MARÍT. *(to leak)* hacer agua (por la sentina); *(to swell)* hincharse.
bil·i·ar·y (bĭl′ē-ĕr′ē) adj. FISIOL. biliar, biliario.
bi·lin·gual (bī-lĭng′gwəl) I. adj. bilingüe II. s. persona bilingüe.
bil·ious (bĭl′yəs) adj. bilioso.
bilk (bĭlk) I. tr. *(to swindle)* estafar, defraudar; *(debts)* evadir; *(to thwart)* defraudar, frustrar; *(to elude)* escabullirse a, burlar II. s. *(swindler)* estafador *m*, defraudador *m*; *(swindle)* estafa, defraudación *f.*
bill¹ (bĭl) I. s. *(invoice)* cuenta, factura; *(list)* lista (de platos, artículos); *(program)* programa *m*; *(poster)* cartel *m* <*post no bills* prohibido fijar carteles>; *(handbill)* volante *m*; *(bank note)* billete *m* <*a ten-dollar b.* un billete de diez dólares>; *(bill of exchange)* letra (de cambio); *(proposed law)* proyecto de ley; DER. *(formal statement)* demanda ♦ **to fill the b.** satisfacer todos los requisitos • **to foot the b.** FAM. *(in a restaurant, shop)* pagar; *(in business)* correr con los gastos II. tr. *(a customer)* pasar la cuenta a <*we will b. you next week* le pasaremos la cuenta la semana que viene>; *(expenses, goods)* facturar; TEAT. *(a performance)* anunciar en la cartelera; *(to promote)* anunciar, promocionar.
bill² (bĭl) I. s. *(beak)* pico; *(visor)* visera; *(anchor part)* uña del ancla II. intr. ORNIT. *(to touch beaks)* acariciarse con el pico ♦ **to b. and coo** arrullarse, acariciarse.
bill·board (bĭl′bôrd′) s. cartelera.
bill·er (bĭl′ər) s. *(clerk)* facturador *m*; *(machine)* máquina facturadora.
bil·let (bĭl′ĭt) I. s. MIL. *(lodging)* alojamiento en recintos civiles; *(written order)* boleta (de alojamiento); FAM. *(job)* empleo II. tr. MIL. alojar.
bill·fold (bĭl′fōld′) s. billetera, cartera.
bil·liard (bĭl′yərd) I. s. carambola II. adj. de billar (bola, mesa).
bil·liards (bĭl′yərdz) s. [ú. con v. sing.] billar *m.*
bill·ing (bĭl′ĭng) s. CINEM., TEAT., TELEV. *(order)* orden de

---

importancia en un reparto; *(advertising)* publicidad *f* ♦ **billings** facturación.

bil·lion (bĭl'yən) s. EE. UU. mil millones *m*; G.B. billón *m*.

bil·lion·aire (bĭl'yə-nâr') s. & adj. billonario.

bill of attainder s. HIST., DER. pena de ejecución y muerte civil.

bill of exchange s. COM. letra de cambio.

bill of fare s. lista de platos, menú *m*.

bill of goods s. consignación de mercadería *f* ♦ **to sell (someone) a b.** FAM. engañar.

bill of health s. MARÍT. carta de sanidad (de un buque) ♦ **a clean b.** FAM. visto bueno (de estado físico, salud).

bill of lading s. COM. conocimiento de embarque.

bill of rights s. declaración de derechos *f* ♦ **B.** las primeras diez enmiendas a la constitución de EE. UU.

bill of sale s. COM. boleto de compra y venta.

bil·low (bĭl'ō) **I.** s. *(wave)* oleada, ola; *(surge)* torrente, oleada (de gente, risa); *(of smoke)* ola **II.** intr. *(sea)* encresparse, levantarse; *(sails)* encresparse, hincharse.

bil·low·y (bĭl'ō-ē) adj. ondulante, encrespado.

bil·ly club (bĭl'ē) s. porra, bastón (de policía) *m*.

billy goat s. FAM. macho cabrío.

bi·met·al·lism (bī-mĕt'l-ĭz'əm) s. FIN. bimetalismo (sistema monetario).

bi·mod·al (bī-mōd'l) adj. que posee dos métodos estadísticos.

bi·month·ly (bī-mŭnth'lē) **I.** adj. *(every two months)* bimestral, bimestre; *(twice a month)* bimensual, quincenal **II.** adv. *(every two months)* bimestralmente; *(twice a month)* bimensualmente, quincenalmente **III.** s. [pl. **-lies**] *(published every two months)* publicación bimestral *f*; *(published semimonthly)* publicación bimensual *o* quincenal.

bin (bĭn) s. *(box)* cajón *m*; *(container)* recipiente *m*, compartimiento.

bi·na·ry (bī'nə-rē) adj. binario.

binary digit s. COMPUT. dígito binario.

binary numeration system s. COMPUT., MAT. sistema de numeración binaria *m*.

binary operation s. COMPUT., MAT. operación binaria.

bind (bīnd) **I.** tr. **bound** (bound), **bind·ing** *(to tie)* amarrar, atar; *(to gird)* liar, ceñir; *(one's hair)* recogerse; *(to bandage)* vendar; *(morally, legally)* obligar, comprometer a <*I am bound to follow their policies* me he comprometido a seguir sus normas>; *(to unite)* ligar, vincular <*we are bound to him by gratitude* nos ligan a él lazos de agradecimiento>; *(to make irrevocable)* ratificar (compra, convenio); *(to indenture)* contratar *o* poner como aprendiz; *(to fasten together)* unir; *(to harden)* endurecer (cemento, fango); *(a mix)* aglutinar; *(a book)* encuadernar, empastar; *(sheaves)* atar, agavillar; *(to put a border on)* ribetear; *(to constipate)* estreñir ♦ **to be bound up with** FIG. estar ligado *o* relacionado con • **to b. over** DER. poner bajo fianza *o* **to b. up** amarrar, atar —intr. *(to be tight)* apretar; *(to harden)* endurecerse; *(a mix)* aglutinarse; *(engine, gears)* fundirse; *(a contract)* tener fuerza obligatoria **II.** s. lazo ♦ **to be in a b.** FAM. estar en un aprieto *o* un apuro.

bind·er (bīn'dər) s. *(bookbinder)* encuadernador *m*; *(fastener)* atadura; *(notebook cover)* carpeta; *(magazine cover)* cubierta; *(for a mix)* aglutinante *m*; DER. *(payment)* garantía, depósito; *(contract)* contrato provisional.

bind·er·y (bīn'də-rē) s. [pl. **-ies**] taller de encuadernación *m*.

bind·ing (bīn'dĭng) **I.** s. *(action, fastener)* atadura; *(of a book)* encuadernación *f*; *(strip)* ribete *m* **II.** adj. *(tight)* apretado, ceñido; *(compulsory)* obligatorio; *(promise)* que compromete a uno.

binge (bĭnj) s. JER. parranda ♦ **to go on a (shopping, eating) b.** darse un banquete (comprando, comiendo).

bin·go (bĭng'gō) s. [pl. **-gos**] bingo, lotería casera ♦ **b.!** JER. ¡pum!, ¡zas!

bin·oc·u·lar (bə-nōk'yə-lər, bī-) **I.** adj. binocular **II.** s. ♦ **binoculars** gemelos, prismáticos.

bi·no·mi·al (bī-nō'mē-əl) **I.** adj. MAT. binomio; BIOL. binario **II.** s. MAT. binomio.

bi·o·chem·i·cal (bī'ō-kĕm'ĭ-kəl) adj. bioquímico.

bi·o·chem·ist (bī'ō-kĕm'ĭst) s. bioquímico.

bi·o·chem·is·try (bī'ō-kĕm'ī-strē) s. bioquímica.

bi·o·de·grad·a·ble (bī'ō-dĭ-grā'də-bəl) adj. biodegradable, que se descompone naturalmente.

bi·o·feed·back (bī'ō-fēd'băk') s. MED. biorreacción *f*.

bi·o·gen·e·sis (bī'ō-jĕn'ĭ-sĭs) s. BIOL. biogénesis *f*.

bi·og·ra·pher (bī-ŏg'rə-fər) s. biógrafo.

bi·o·graph·i·cal (bī'ə-grăf'ĭ-kəl) *o* **bi·o·graph·ic** (-grăf'ĭk) adj. biográfico.

bi·og·ra·phy (bī-ŏg'rə-fē) s. [pl. **-phies**] biografía.

bi·o·log·i·cal (bī'ə-lŏj'ĭ-kəl) *o* **bi·o·log·ic** (-lŏj'ĭk) adj. biológico.

biological clock s. BIOL. mecanismo biológico que determina las funciones periódicas.

biological warfare s. MIL. guerra biológica *o* bacteriológica.

bi·ol·o·gist (bī-ŏl'ə-jĭst) s. biólogo.

bi·ol·o·gy (bī-ŏl'ə-jē) s. biología.

bi·o·mass (bī'ō-măs') s. BIOL. biomasa.

bi·ome (bī'ōm) s. ECOL. flora y fauna (de una sola región ecológica).

bi·o·met·rics (bī'ō-mĕt'rĭks) s. [ú. con v. sing.] biometría (estudio estadístico).

bi·on·ics (bī-ŏn'ĭks) s. [ú. con v. sing.] BIOL., ELECTRÓN. biónica, diseño de sistemas.

bi·ont (bī'ŏnt') s. BIOL. organismo.

bi·o·phys·i·cist (bī'ō-fĭz'ī-sĭst) s. biofísico.

bi·o·phys·ics (bī'ō-fĭz'ĭks) s. [ú. con v. sing.] biofísica.

bi·op·sy (bī'ŏp'sē) s. [pl. **-sies**] MED. biopsia.

bi·o·rhythm (bī'ō-rĭth'əm) s. ritmo *o* ciclo biológico.

bi·o·sci·ence (bī'ō-sī'əns) s. ciencia natural.

bi·o·scope (bī'ə-skōp') s. proyector cinematográfico antiguo.

bi·o·syn·the·sis (bī'ō-sĭn'thĭ-sĭs) s. BIOQUÍM. biosíntesis *f*.

bi·o·tin (bī'ə-tĭn) s. BIOQUÍM. biotina.

bi·par·ti·san (bī-pär'tĭ-zən) adj. POL. bipartidista, de dos partidos.

bi·par·tite (bī-pär'tīt') adj. *(having two parts)* bipartido; *(treaty)* bipartito.

bi·ped (bī'pĕd') s. & adj. bípedo.

bi·plane (bī'plān') s. biplano.

bi·po·lar (bī-pō'lər) adj. *(of two poles)* bipolar; *(contradictory)* antípoda, antitético.

bi·ra·cial (bī-rā'shəl) adj. de dos razas.

birch (bûrch) **I.** s. *(tree, wood)* abedul *m*; *(rod)* vara de abedul (para azotar) **II.** tr. azotar.

bird (bûrd) **I.** s. ORNIT. *(small)* pájaro; *(large)* ave *f* <*a b. of prey* un ave de rapiña>; *(game)* caza de pluma; *(clay pigeon)* plato de tiro; *(in badminton)* volante *m*; JER. *(rocket)* bólido, cohete *m*; *(individual)* pájaro, bicho <*an odd b.* un pájaro raro>; G.B., JER. *(woman)* chica, muchacha ♦ **birds of a feather** FAM. lobos de la misma camada • **early b.** madrugador • **for the birds** cosa de bobos • **to kill two birds with one stone** matar dos pájaros de un tiro **II.** intr. *(to watch)* observar pájaros; *(to hunt)* cazar pájaros.

bird·bath (bûrd'băth', -bäth') s. pila de baño para pájaros.

bird·brain (bûrd'brān') s. JER. cabeza de chorlito *mf*.

bird·cage (bûrd'kāj') s. *(small)* jaula (de pájaros); *(large)* pajarera.

bird·call (bûrd'kôl') s. *(bird's song)* canto; *(device)* reclamo.

bird dog s. perro perdiguero.

bird·house (bûrd'hous') s. *(aviary)* pajarera, aviario; *(nesting place)* nidal *m*.

bird·ie (bûr'dē) s. FAM. pajarito, pajarillo.

bird·lime (bûrd'līm') **I.** s. liga **II.** tr. cazar con liga.

bird of paradise s. ave del paraíso *m*, pájaro del sol.

bird·seed (bûrd'sēd') s. alpiste *m*.

bird's-eye (bûrdz'ī') **I.** s. BOT. primavera; *(fabric)* ojo de perdiz **II.** adj. ♦ **a b. view** una vista panorámica.

bird watcher s. observador de pájaros *m*.

birth (bûrth) s. *(beginning of existence)* nacimiento; *(beginning)* nacimiento, origen *m*; *(ancestry)* ascendencia, linaje *m*; MED. parto ♦ **by b.** de nacimiento • **to give b. to** *(child)* dar a luz a; *(situation)* dar origen a.

birth certificate s. partida de nacimiento.

birth control s. control de la natalidad *m*.

birth·day (bûrth'dā') s. cumpleaños ♦ **b. party** fiesta de

---

cumpleaños • **b. present** regalo de cumpleaños • **on one's (15th, 25th) b.** al cumplir los (15, 25) años.
birthing room s. cuarto de hospital en donde se efectúan los partos naturales.
birth·mark (bûrth'märk') s. lunar *m,* mancha de nacimiento.
birth·place (bûrth'plās') s. *(place of birth)* lugar de nacimiento *m; (place of origin)* lugar de origen.
birth·rate (bûrth'rāt') s. índice de natalidad *m.*
birth·right (bûrth'rīt') s. *(privilege)* derechos de nacimiento; *(of a first-born)* derechos de primogenitura; *(patrimony)* patrimonio.
birth·stone (bûrth'stōn') s. piedra preciosa correspondiente al mes de nacimiento.
bis·cuit (bĭs'kĭt) s. [pl. **-cuits** o **biscuit**] *(bread)* bizcocho, panecillo; G.B. *(cookie, cracker)* galletita; *(color)* beige; *(pottery)* biscuit *m.*
bi·sect (bī-sĕkt') tr. GEOM. *(a figure)* bisecar; *(to divide)* dividir en dos —intr. bifurcarse.
bi·sec·tion (bī-sĕk'shən) s. GEOM. *(of a figure)* bisección *f; (division)* división en dos *f.*
bi·sec·tor (bī-sĕk'tər) s. GEOM. bisector *m,* bisectriz *f.*
bi·sex·u·al (bī-sĕk'shōō-əl) I. adj. bisexual II. s. persona bisexual.
bi·sex·u·al·i·ty (bī-sĕk'shōō-ăl'ĭ-tē) s. bisexualidad *f.*
bish·op (bĭsh'əp) s. *(clergyman)* obispo; *(in chess)* alfil *m.*
bish·op·ric (bĭsh'ə-prĭk) s. obispado.
bis·muth (bĭz'məth) s. QUÍM. bismuto.
bi·son (bī'sən) s. bisonte *m.*
bis·tro (bĕ'strō, bĭs'trō) s. [pl. **-tros**] taberna, bar *m.*
bi·sul·fate (bī-sŭl'fāt') s. QUÍM. bisulfato.
bit¹ (bĭt) s. *(piece)* pedacito, trocito; *(amount)* poco <*this one is a b. cheaper* éste es un poco más barato>; *(moment)* ratito, momento; FAM. *(matter)* asunto; *(coin)* moneda; TEAT. *(routine)* número; *(episode)* escena; *(role)* papel secundario **♦ a b. of advice** un consejo • **a good b.** bastante • **b. by b.** poco a poco • **bits and pieces** cosas sueltas • **every b. a (man, soldier)** (hombre, soldado) de pies a cabeza • **not a b.** en absoluto • **the whole b.** FAM. todo • **to blow to bits** hacer pedazos *o* añicos • **to do one's b.** poner de la parte de uno • **two bits** veinticinco centavos.
bit² (bĭt) s. *(drill)* broca, barrena; *(cutting edge)* filo; *(of a key)* paletón *m; (of a bridle)* freno, bocado II. tr. **bit·ted, bit·ting** *(a horse)* poner el freno a; *(to check)* refrenar.
bit³ (bĭt) s. COMPUT. bit *m,* bitio (unidad binaria).
bit⁴ (bĭt) pret. y un part. p. de **bite.**
bitch (bĭch) I. s. *(female)* hembra; *(dog)* perra; *(fox)* zorra; JER. *(spiteful woman)* zorra, arpía; *(lewd woman)* perra, puta; *(complaint)* queja; *(annoyance)* jodienda **♦ son of a b.** hijo de puta II. intr. JER. quejarse.
bitch·y (bĭch'ē) adj. **-i·er, -i·est** *(ill-humored)* malhumorado; *(malicious)* malicioso, mal intencionado; *(spiteful)* rencoroso.
bite (bīt) I. tr. **bit** (bĭt), **bit·ten** (bĭt'n) *o* **bit, bit·ing** *(with the teeth)* morder; *(insects, snakes)* picar; *(to cut into)* cortar, penetrar; *(to grab)* morder, agarrar *(herramienta, ancla); (to corrode)* morder, comerse; *(to cause to prickle)* picar, escocer; *(wind)* cortar **♦ to b. at** tirar dentelladas a • **to b. down on** cerrar los dientes contra • **to b. off** arrancar de un mordisco • **to b. the bullet** apretar los dientes y aguantar • **to b. the dust** morder el polvo —intr. *(with the teeth)* morder <*the dog does not b.* el perro no muerde>; *(insects, birds)* picar; *(to grab)* agarrarse *(neumáticos, ancla); (to prickle)* picar, escocer; *(wind)* cortar; *(to take the bait)* picar *(pez)* II. s. *(act)* mordisco, dentellada; *(wound)* mordedura; *(sting)* *(prickling sensation)* escozor *m; (in fishing)* picada; *(mouthful)* mordisco, bocado; *(grip)* agarre *m; (in etching)* mordedura (del ácido) **♦ to have a b. to eat** FAM. comer algo, tomar un piscolabis • **to have b.** ser incisivo *o* penetrante.
bit·ing (bī'tĭng) adj. *(wind)* cortante, penetrante; *(taste)* picante; *(incisive)* incisivo, penetrante; *(sarcastic)* mordaz.
bit·ten (bĭt'n) un part. p. de **bite.**
bit·ter (bĭt'ər) I. adj. **-er, -est** *(in taste)* amargo; *(pain)* penetrante, agudo; *(weather)* malísimo, glacial; *(wind, cold)*

cortante, penetrante; *(hard to accept)* duro, amargo <*it was a b. pill to swallow* fue una píldora amarga de pasar>; *(fierce)* encarnizado, implacable; *(painful)* doloroso, penoso; *(cry, tears)* amargo; *(resentful)* resentido, amargado <*a b. man* un hombre amargado> II. s. **♦ bitters** biter *m.*
bitter end s. **♦ to the b.** *(to stay)* hasta el final; *(to fight)* hasta vencer *o* morir.
bit·ter·ly (bĭt'ər-lē) adv. *(with a bitter taste)* amargo; *(in a bitter way)* amargamente, con amargura; *(fiercely)* implacablemente.
bit·ter·ness (bĭt'ər-nĭs) s. *(of taste)* amargura; *(of weather)* severidad *f,* dureza; *(fierceness)* encarnizamiento, implacabilidad *f; (anguish)* amargura, pena; *(resentment)* resentimiento, rencor *m.*
bit·ter·root (bĭt'ər-rōōt') s. BOT. planta portulacácea norteamericana de raíz comestible.
bit·ter·sweet (bĭt'ər-swēt') adj. agridulce.
bit·u·men (bĭ-tōō'mən, -tyōō'-) s. betún *m.*
bi·tu·mi·nous (bĭ-tōō'mə-nəs, -tyōō'-) adj. bituminoso **♦ b. coal** carbón bituminoso.
bi·va·lent (bī-vā'lənt) adj. bivalente.
bi·valve (bī'vălv') s. & adj. ZOOL., BOT. bivalvo.
biv·ou·ac (bĭv'ōō-ăk') I. s. vivaque *m,* vivac *m* II. intr. **-acked, -ack·ing** vivaquear, acampar.
bi·week·ly (bī-wēk'lē) I. adj. *(every two weeks)* quincenal; *(twice a week)* bisemanal II. adv. *(every two weeks)* quincenalmente; *(twice a week)* dos veces por semana III. s. [pl. **-lies**] revista quincenal.
bi·year·ly (bī-yîr'lē) I. adj. *(every two years)* bienal; *(twice a year)* semestral II. adv. *(every two years)* bienalmente; *(twice a year)* semestralmente.
bi·zarre (bĭ-zär') adj. *(appearance, style)* extravagante; *(incident)* extraño.
blab (blăb) I. tr. **blabbed, blab·bing** *(to reveal)* soltar, descubrir *(secreto)* —intr. *(to tell secrets)* soltar el secreto, descubrir el pastel; *(to chatter)* chismosear II. s. *(person)* chismoso, hablador *m; (chatter)* charloteo, cotorreo.
blab·ber (blăb'ər) I. intr. cotorrear II. s. *(chatter)* cotorreo; *(person)* cotorra, chismoso.
blab·ber·mouth (blăb'ər-mouth') s. JER. cotorra, correvedile *m.*
black (blăk) I. s. *(color)* negro; *(mourning clothes)* luto <*to wear b.* estar de luto>; *(darkness)* oscuridad *f* **♦ B. o b.** *(person)* negro • **to be in the b.** COM. estar haciendo ganancias II. adj. **-er, -est** *(color)* negro; *(gloomy)* sombrío, deprimente; *(wicked)* perverso, malvado; *(sullen)* hosco, ceñudo; *(without milk)* solo, negro *(café); (dirty)* negro, sucio **♦ B. o b.** *(Negroid)* negro III. tr. *(to make black)* ennegrecer; *(to polish)* embetunar **♦ to b. out** MIL. apagar las luces; *(to go unconscious)* perder el conocimiento; *(to undergo a blackout)* producir *o* causar un apagón; FIG. *(to prohibit)* censurar, bloquear *(noticias).*
black-and-blue (blăk'ən-blōō') adj. FAM. amoratado.
black and white s. *(writing)* escritura; *(picture)* fotografía en blanco y negro **♦ in b.** por escrito.
black-and-white (blăk'ən-hwīt') adj. *(partially black and white)* blanco y negro; *(unequivocal)* inequívoco <*a b. answer* una respuesta inequívoca>.
black art s. magia negra.
black·ball (blăk'bôl') I. s. bola negra II. tr. dar *o* echar bola negra.
black belt s. *(in judo, karate)* cinta negra; *(in a city, state)* distrito de población negra.
black·ber·ry (blăk'bĕr'ē) s. [pl. **-ries**] *(plant)* zarza; *(fruit)* zarzamora.
black·bird (blăk'bûrd') s. mirlo.
black·board (blăk'bôrd') s. pizarra, pizarrón *m.*
black box s. ELECTRÓN. *(circuit)* caja negra; AVIA. *(recorder)* registrador de vuelo *m.*
black·en (blăk'ən) tr. *(to make black)* ennegrecer; *(to darken)* oscurecer; *(to defame)* mancillar, difamar —intr. *(to become black)* ennegrecerse; *(to darken)* oscurecerse.
black eye s. *(bruise)* ojo morado; *(bad name)* mala fama **♦ to give someone a b.** poner un ojo morado a alguien
black fly s. jején *m.*
black·head (blăk'hĕd') s. espinilla, grano.

black hole s. ASTRON. agujero negro.
black·ing (blăk′ĭng) s. *(lampblack)* negro de humo; *(polish)* betún negro.
black·jack (blăk′jăk′) s. *(bludgeon)* cachiporra; *(game)* veintiuna.
black·list (blăk′lĭst′) I. s. lista negra II. tr. poner en la lista negra.
black lung s. MED. neumoconiosis *f.*
black magic s. magia negra, nigromancia.
black·mail (blăk′māl′) I. s. chantaje *m* II. tr. chantajear.
black·mail·er (blăk′mā′lər) s. chantajista *mf.*
black market s. mercado negro, estraperlo.
black·ness (blăk′nĭs) s. *(black color)* negrura; *(darkness)* oscuridad *f*; *(of feelings)* maldad.
black nightshade s. hierba mora.
black·out (blăk′out′) s. *(of illumination)* apagón *m*; *(of consciousness)* desmayo; *(of memory)* pérdida de la memoria; *(suppression)* bloqueo, supresión *f.*
black pepper s. pimienta negra.
Black Power s. POL. Poder Negro (movimiento de la población negra norteamericana).
black sheep s. FIG. oveja negra.
black·smith (blăk′smĭth′) s. herrero.
black tie s. *(tie)* corbata negra de lazo; *(dress code)* smoking *m.*
black·top (blăk′tŏp′) I. s. asfalto II. tr. -topped, -top·ping asfaltar.
black widow s. ENTOM. viuda negra.
blad·der (blăd′ər) s. *(sac)* vejiga (de animal, superficie); BOT. vesícula.
blade (blād) s. *(of a tool, weapon)* hoja; *(sword)* hoja, espada; *(of a razor)* hoja, cuchilla, *(of an ice skate)* cuchilla; *(of an oar)* pala; *(of a propeller, fan)* aleta; *(of windshield wiper)* goma; *(of the shoulder)* paleta; *(of grass)* brizna; *(of a leaf)* limbo; *(of a windmill)* aspa; *(young man)* galán *m.*
blah (blä) JER. I. s. pamplinas ♦ **to get the blahs** desanimarse II. adj. aburrido, tedioso.
blain (blān) s. llaga, ampolla.
blame (blām) I. tr. blamed, blam·ing *(to accuse)* echar la culpa, culpar; *(to censure)* culpar, reprochar ♦ **to be to b. for** tener la culpa de • **to b. something on** echar la culpa de algo a • **to have only oneself to b. (for)** ser uno el único culpable (de) II. s. *(guilt)* culpa; *(censure)* reproche *m*, censura ♦ **to put the b. on** echar la culpa a.
blame·less (blām′lĭs) adj. libre de culpa, inocente.
blame·wor·thy (blām′wûr′thē) adj. -thi·er, -thi·est censurable, culpable.
blanch (blănch) tr. *(to bleach)* blanquear; *(to scald)* escaldar; *(to make pale)* hacer palidecer —intr. palidecer.
bland (blănd) adj. -er, -est *(gentle)* blando, suave; *(soothing)* suave; *(balmy)* templado, benigno; *(dull)* insulso.
blan·dish (blăn′dĭsh) tr. persuadir con halagos, engatusar.
blan·dish·ment (blăn′dĭsh-mənt) s. lisonja, zalamería.
blank (blăngk) I. adj. -er, -est *(unused)* en blanco (papel, casete); *(wall)* liso; *(expressionless)* sin expresión; *(bewildered)* desconcertado, perplejo; *(empty)* vacío (memoria, años); *(fruitless)* inútil <b. efforts esfuerzos inútiles>; *(complete)* absoluto <a b. refusal una negativa absoluta> ♦ **to go b.** quedarse en blanco II. s. *(empty space)* vacío; *(in a document)* espacio en blanco; *(document)* formulario (en blanco); *(cassette)* casete en blanco *m*; *(gun cartridge)* cartucho de salvas o de fogueo; *(lottery ticket)* billete no premiado; TIP. raya ♦ **to draw a b.** no saber qué decir o contestar III. tr. borrar.
blank check s. *(check)* cheque en blanco *m*; *(carte blanche)* carta blanca.
blan·ket (blăng′kĭt) I. s. *(covering)* manta, frazada; *(layer)* manto, capa <a b. of snow un manto de nieve> ♦ **to throw a wet b. on** echar un jarro de agua fría a • **wet b.** aguafiestas II. adj. general, comprensivo III. tr. *(a person)* tapar con una manta o frazada; *(a surface)* cubrir con un manto o una capa; *(to suppress)* tapar, acallar; RAD. bloquear, producir interferencia en; *(to spread)* difundir por toda una área (noticias, propaganda).
blank verse s. verso blanco o suelto.

blare (blâr) I. intr. blared, blar·ing resonar, sonar estruendosamente —tr. proclamar, pregonar II. s. estruendo.
blar·ney (blär′nē) s. FAM. labia.
bla·sé (blä-zā′) adj. hastiado, indiferente ♦ **to be b. about** demostrar indiferencia por.
blas·pheme (blăs-fēm′) tr. -phemed, -phem·ing blasfemar contra, maldecir —intr. blasfemar.
blas·phe·mous (blăs′fə-məs) adj. blasfemo, blasfematorio.
blas·phe·my (blăs′fə-mē) s. [pl. -mies] blasfemia.
blast (blăst) I. s. *(gust)* ráfaga <a b. of air una ráfaga de aire>; *(of sand, water)* flujo, chorro; *(explosion)* explosión *f*, voladura; *(explosive)* carga explosiva, barreno; *(explosion effect)* onda de choque; FAM. *(verbal outburst)* explosión, estallido; JER. *(wild party)* alboroto; MÚS. toque *m*, soplido (de un instrumento) ♦ **at full b.** a todo vapor II. tr. *(to blow up)* hacer volar, bombardear; FIG. *(to smash)* hacer añicos, acabar con (las esperanzas); *(to open)* abrir, perforar (con barrenos); FAM. *(to criticize)* criticar, infamar —intr. *(to blow up)* volar, explotar; *(to sound off)* sonar fuerte y repentinamente; FAM. *(to criticize)* criticar; AGR. *(to wither)* añublarse, marchitarse ♦ **to b. away** disparar repetidamente • **to b. off** despegar.
blast·ed (blăs′tĭd) adj. FAM. condenado, maldito.
blast furnace s. METAL. alto horno.
blast·off o **blast-off** (blăst′ôf′) s. AER. lanzamiento, disparo.
blat (blăt) tr. blat·ted, blat·ting decir o hablar sin consideración —intr. balar.
bla·tan·cy (blāt′n-sē) s. [pl. -cies] *(loudness, showiness)* estridencia; *(obviousness)* evidencia.
bla·tant (blāt′nt) adj. *(loud, showy)* chillón, estridente; *(obvious)* patente, evidente <a b. error una equivocación patente>.
blath·er (blăth′ər) I. intr. decir disparates II. s. disparates *m.*
blaze¹ (blāz) I. s. *(flame)* llamarada; *(glare)* resplandor *m*; *(fire)* incendio, fuego; *(display)* llamarada, alarde *m* <a b. of color una llamarada de color>; *(outburst)* llamarada, arranque *m* <in a b. of anger en un arranque de ira> II. intr. blazed, blaz·ing *(to burn)* llamear, arder <a fire was blazing in the hearth el fuego ardía en el hogar>; *(to shine)* arder, resplandecer; *(to flare up)* encenderse, estallar ♦ **blazing with (lights, colors)** resplandeciente de (luces, colores) • **to b. away** disparar continuamente • **to b. up** *(to burn)* arder con más vigor; *(to burst out)* encenderse, estallar —tr. encender, inflamar.
blaze² (blāz) I. s. *(on an animal)* lucero, estrella; *(on a tree)* marca, punto de referencia II. tr. blazed, blaz·ing marcar, poner puntos de referencia en ♦ **to b. a trail** abrir un camino.
blaze³ (blāz) tr. blazed, blaz·ing proclamar, pregonar.
blaz·er (blā′zər) s. chaqueta deportiva.
bla·zon (blā′zən) I. tr. *(a coat of arms)* blasonar; *(to adorn)* decorar, adornar; *(to proclaim)* pregonar II. s. *(coat of arms, description)* blasón *m*; *(display)* boato, ostentación *f.*
bla·zon·ry (blā′zən-rē) s. [pl. -ries] HER. *(art, coat of arms)* blasón *m*; *(display)* boato, ostentación *f.*
bleach (blēch) I. tr. *(to make colorless)* decolorar, descolorar <to b. one's hair decolorarse el cabello>; *(to make white)* blanquear; *(clothes)* blanquear —intr. descolorarse II. s. *(chemical)* decolorante *m*; *(for clothes)* lejía.
bleach·er (blē′chər) s. *(chemical)* decolorante *m*; *(for clothes)* lejía ♦ **bleachers** gradas.
bleak (blēk) adj. -er, -est *(barren)* desolado; *(cold)* frío, crudo; *(dreary)* triste, sombrío; *(cheerless)* frío (saludo, bienvenida); *(not encouraging)* poco prometedor.
blear (blîr) tr. *(the eyes)* nublar, empañar; *(to blur)* nublar, volver borroso.
blear·y (blîr′ē) adj. -i·er, -i·est *(eyes)* nublado; *(blurred)* borroso; *(exhausted)* agotado, exhausto.
blear·y-eyed (blîr′ē-īd′) adj. *(with bleary eyes)* con los ojos nublados; *(dull-witted)* de pocas luces.
bleat (blēt) I. s. *(sheep's cry)* balido; *(whine)* gemido II. intr. *(to baa)* balar; *(to whine)* gemir —tr. decir entre gemidos.

bleed (blĕd) **I.** intr. **bled** (blĕd), **bleed·ing** *(to lose blood)* sangrar, perder sangre; *(to be wounded)* derramar sangre (en una batalla); *(to feel grief)* sufrir <*my heart bleeds for you* mi corazón sufre por ti>; *(to exude)* exudar, perder savia; *(to discolor)* desteñirse; FIG., JER. *(to pay)* pagar mucho; IMPR. hacer sangre, ensancharse ♦ **to b. to death** morir desangrado —tr. *(to take blood from)* desangrar a, sacar sangre a; *(to draw off)* sangrar (líquidos, gases); JER. *(to extort money from)* desplumar a; BOT. sangrar, resinar ♦ **to b. someone white** *o* **dry** FAM. esquilmar a alguien, chuparle la sangre a alguien **II.** s. IMPR. borde impreso *m*, corte *m*.

bleed·er (blĕ′dər) s. *(hemophiliac)* hemofílico; *(bloodletter)* sangrador *m*; TEC. válvula de escape.

bleed·ing (blĕ′dĭng) **I.** s. *(bloodletting)* sangría; *(hemorrhage)* hemorragia **II.** adj. *(losing blood)* sangrante; *(compassionate)* compasivo <*a b. heart* un corazón compasivo>; G.B., JER. *(confounded)* maldito.

bleep (blēp) **I.** s. sonido electrónico agudo **II.** tr. hacer un sonido agudo.

blem·ish (blĕm′ĭsh) **I.** tr. *(to stain)* manchar; *(to spoil)* estropear; *(to taint)* manchar, mancillar **II.** s. *(stain)* mancha; *(imperfection)* defecto; *(taint)* mancha, tacha.

blench (blĕnch) intr. retroceder, acobardarse.

blend (blĕnd) **I.** tr. **blend·ed** *o* **blent** (blĕnt), **blend·ing** *(to mix)* mezclar; *(to harmonize)* combinar, armonizar (estilos, colores) —intr. *(to mix)* mezclarse; *(to become one)* entremezclarse (aguas, colores); *(to harmonize)* armonizar, hacer juego **II.** s. *(mixture)* mezcla; *(combination)* combinación *f*.

blend·er (blĕn′dər) s. *(person)* mezclador *m*; *(appliance)* licuadora, batidora.

blent (blĕnt) un pret. y part. p. de **blend**.

bless (blĕs) tr. **blessed** *o* **blest** (blĕst), **bless·ing** RELIG. *(to sanctify)* bendecir; *(to glorify)* bendecir, alabar <*b. the Lord* alabado sea el Señor> ♦ **b. my soul!** *o* **b. me!** ¡válgame Dios!, ¡bendito sea Dios! • **God b. you!** *(blessing)* ¡que Dios te bendiga!; *(after sneezing)* ¡Jesús!, ¡salud! • **to b. with** conceder la dicha de, dotar de.

bless·ed (blĕs′ĭd) adj. RELIG. *(holy)* bendito; *(hallowed)* santo, santísmo <*the B. Trinity* la Santísima Trinidad>; *(beatified)* beato; *(fortunate)* bienaventurado; *(bringing happiness)* dichoso, feliz <*a b. event* un feliz acontecimiento>; JER. *(cursed)* maldito, condenado ♦ **not a b. thing** FAM. nada en absoluto.

Blessed Virgin s. RELIG. Santísima Virgen.

bless·ing (blĕs′ĭng) s. RELIG. *(act)* bendición *f*; *(favor)* bendición, dicha <*what a b.!* ¡qué dicha!>; *(gift)* don *m*; *(boon)* ventaja <*the blessings of progress* las ventajas del progreso>; *(approval)* consentimiento, aprobación *f*; *(grace)* bendición de la mesa.

blest (blĕst) **I.** un pret. y part. p. de **bless II.** adj. var. de **blessed**.

blew (blōō) pret. de **blow**[1].

blight (blīt) **I.** s. BOT. *(disease)* añublo, tizón *m*; FIG. *(plague)* plaga; *(decay)* ruina, decadencia **II.** tr. arruinar, destruir (cosecha, esperanzas).

blimp (blĭmp) s. AER. dirigible no rígido.

blind (blīnd) **I.** adj. **-er, -est** *(sightless)* ciego, no vidente; *(without visibility)* a ciegas <*b. navigation* navegación a ciegas>; *(without preparation)* sin preparación, confuso; *(insensitive)* ciego, insensible; *(not based on reason)* sin razón, ciego <*b. faith* fe ciega>; *(illegible)* ilegible; *(hidden)* oculto <*b. turn* una curva escondida>; *(closed at one end)* sin salida <*b. alley* callejón sin salida> ♦ **b. as a bat** ciego como un topo • **b. in one eye** tuerto • **b. with** ciego de (odio, pasión) • **the b.** los ciegos **II.** s. *(screen)* biombo; *(window shade)* celosía, persiana; *(hide-out)* escondrijo; *(subterfuge)* subterfugio **III.** adv. a ciegas ♦ **b. drunk** borracho como una cuba **IV.** tr. *(to make sightless)* cegar; *(to dazzle)* deslumbrar; FIG. *(to deprive of judgment)* enceguecer; *(to deprive of light)* oscurecer.

blind date s. FAM. cita concertada entre dos personas que no se conocen.

blind·er (blīn′dər) s. ♦ **blinders** anteojeras.

blind·fold (blīnd′fōld′) **I.** tr. *(a person)* vendar los ojos a; *(the eyes)* poner una venda en **II.** s. venda **III.** adj. *(with eyes covered)* con los ojos vendados; *(reckless)* ciego.

blind·ing (blīn′dĭng) adj. *(dazzling)* cegador, deslumbrante; *(snow, smoke)* cegador, que ciega.

blind·ly (blīnd′lē) adv. ciegamente, a ciegas.

blind·man's buff (blīnd′mănz) s. gallinita ciega.

blind·ness (blīnd′nĭs) s. ceguera.

blind spot s. *(on the retina)* punto ciego; *(in visibility)* ángulo muerto; *(subject)* punto flaco; RAD. zona de mala recepción.

blink (blĭngk) **I.** intr. *(eyes)* parpadear, pestañear; *(light)* parpadear; *(signal)* brillar intermitentemente; FIG. *(to back down)* ceder, echarse atrás —tr. *(the eyes)* abrir y cerrar, guiñar; *(to ignore)* no querer ver, pasar por alto ♦ **to b. an eye** hacer la vista gorda • **to b. at** *(a light, surprise)* parpadear a causa de; *(a fact)* no querer ver, pasar por alto • **without blinking an eye** sin mostrar ninguna emoción **II.** s. *(winking)* parpadeo, pestañeo; *(glance)* vistazo; *(gleam)* destello ♦ **on the b.** JER. descompuesto.

blink·er (blĭng′kər) s. *(of an automobile)* intermitente *m*; AVIA., MARÍT. señal intermitente *f*; JER. *(eye)* ojo ♦ **blinkers** *(goggles)* gafas protectoras; *(blinders)* anteojeras.

blink·ing (blĭng′kĭng) **I.** s. parpadeo **II.** adj. *(flickering)* parpadeante; *(intermittent)* intermitente; G.B., JER. *(damned)* maldito.

blip (blĭp) s. *(on a radar)* cresta de eco; *(interruption)* corte del sonido *m*.

bliss (blĭs) s. dicha, felicidad *f* ♦ **eternal** *o* **heavenly b.** bienaventuranza • **to be b.** FAM. ser divino *o* maravilloso.

bliss·ful (blĭs′fəl) adj. dichoso, feliz.

blis·ter (blĭs′tər) **I.** s. *(on the skin)* ampolla; *(on a plant)* verruga; *(on a surface)* ampolla, burbuja **II.** tr. *(the skin, a surface)* ampollar, levantar ampollas en; *(to reprove)* criticar —intr. ampollarse.

blis·ter·ing (blĭs′tər-ĭng) adj. *(hot)* abrasador; *(harsh)* desollador, feroz (palabras); *(fast-paced)* forzado.

blithe (blīth) adj. **blith·er, blith·est** *(cheerful)* jovial, alegre; *(carefree)* despreocupado.

blithe·some (blīth′səm, blīth′-) adj. jovial, alegre.

blitz (blĭts) s. MIL. *(offensive)* ataque relámpago *m*; *(air raid)* bombardeo aéreo; *(campaign)* ataque, acometida.

blitz·krieg (blĭts′krēg′) s. MIL. *(offensive)* guerra relámpago; *(effort)* ataque *m*, acometida.

bliz·zard (blĭz′ərd) s. *(storm)* ventisca; FIG. *(torrent)* torrente *m*, abundancia.

bloat (blōt) **I.** tr. *(to inflate)* hinchar, inflar; *(to make vain)* envanecer; *(to cure)* ahumar, curar (pescado) —intr. hincharse, inflarse.

blob (blŏb) **I.** s. *(mass)* masa informe; *(of color)* mancha **II.** tr. **blobbed, blob·bing** salpicar.

bloc (blŏk) s. POL. bloque *m*.

block (blŏk) **I.** s. *(large piece)* bloque *m*, trozo; *(supporting piece)* soporte *m*; *(executioner's block)* tajo; *(auction stand)* plataforma (de subastas); *(wooden mold)* molde *m*, horma (de sombrero); *(of ice)* témpano; *(in printing)* plancha, estampa; *(pulley)* polea; POL. bloque; *(of a city)* cuadra, manzana; *(street)* calle *f*, cuadra; *(of an anvil)* cepo (de yunque); *(of paper)* bloc de papel *m*; *(blocking)* bloque, impedimento; *(obstacle)* obstrucción *f*, obstáculo; JER. *(head)* coco, cabeza; DEP., MED., PSICOL. bloqueo, obstrucción; MEC. bloque (de cilindro *o* de motor) ♦ **to be on the b.** estar en venta *o* en remate **II.** tr. *(to shape into a block)* dar forma de bloque a; *(to reinforce)* reforzar, calzar; *(to shape)* conformar, dar forma a (sombrero); *(to obstruct)* bloquear, obstruir (tráfico, avance); *(to sketch)* esbozar, delinear; MED., PSICOL. obstruir, interrumpir —intr. DEP. bloquear, obstruir.

block·ade (blŏ-kād′) **I.** s. bloqueo, asedio **II.** tr. **-ad·ed, -ad·ing** bloquear, asediar.

block·ade-run·ner (blŏ-kād′rŭn′ər) s. *(ship)* barco que rompe un bloqueo; *(person)* persona que rompe un bloqueo.

block·age (blŏk′ĭj) s. obstrucción *f*.

block and tackle s. MEC. aparejo de poleas.

block·bust·er (blŏk′bŭs′tər) s. *(bomb)* bomba masivamente destructora; FIG. éxito impresionante.

block·head (blŏk'hĕd') s. FAM. alcornoque *m*, zoquete *m*.
block·house (blŏk'hous') s. FORT. blocao.
bloke (blōk) s. G.B., FAM. tipo, fulano.
blond (blŏnd) s. & adj. **-er, -est** rubio.
blonde (blŏnd) I. adj. **blond·er, blond·est** rubia, blonda (mujer) II. s. rubia.
blood (blŭd) I. s. BIOL. sangre *f*; *(juice)* jugo, zumo; *(life-blood)* alma; *(bloodshed)* derrame de sangre *m*; *(temperament)* sangre, temperamento; *(lineage)* sangre, linaje *m*; *(kinship)* parentesco; *(dandy)* petimetre *m* ♦ **in cold b.** a sangre fría • **new b.** FIG. sangre nueva II. tr. encarnar (perros) III. adj. *(horse)* de pura sangre; *(animal)* de pura raza.
blood bank s. MED. banco de sangre.
blood bath s. carnicería, matanza.
blood brother s. hermano de sangre.
blood count s. MED. recuento globular.
blood·cur·dling (blŭd'kûrd'lĭng) adj. espeluznante.
blood·ed (blŭd'ĭd) adj. *(with a given kind of blood)* de sangre *<a cold-blooded animal* un animal de sangre fría>; *(thoroughbred)* de pura sangre.
blood group s. MED. grupo sanguíneo.
blood·guilt (blŭd'gĭlt') s. culpable de homicidio.
blood·hound (blŭd'hound') s. sabueso.
blood·less (blŭd'lĭs) adj. *(without blood)* exangüe; *(anemic)* pálido, anémico; *(without bloodshed)* sin derramamiento de sangre; *(dull)* insípido desanimado.
blood·let·ting (blŭd'lĕt'ĭng) s. *(bleeding)* sangría, flebotomía; *(draining away)* sangría; *(bloodshed)* derramamiento de sangre *f*.
blood·line (blŭd'līn') s. *(descent)* genealogía; *(pedigree)* pedigrí *m*.
blood·mo·bile (blŭd'mə-bēl') s. equipo móvil de extracción de sangre.
blood poisoning s. envenenamiento de la sangre.
blood pressure s. tensión arterial *f*, presión sanguínea.
blood relation s. consanguíneo.
blood·shed (blŭd'shĕd') s. derramamiento de sangre.
blood·shot (blŭd'shŏt') adj. inyectado de sangre.
blood·stain (blŭd'stān') I. s. mancha de sangre II. tr. ensangrentar.
blood·stream (blŭd'strēm') s. corriente sanguínea.
blood·suck·er (blŭd'sŭk'ər) s. sanguijuela.
blood test s. análisis de sangre *m*.
blood·thirst·y (blŭd'thûr'stē) adj. sanguinario, sediento de sangre.
blood type s. tipo sanguíneo.
blood vessel s. vaso sanguíneo.
blood·y (blŭd'ē) I. adj. **-i·er, -i·est** *(with blood)* sangriento, ensangrentado; *(cruel)* cruel, encarnizado; *(red)* sanguinolento; G.B., JER. *(vile)* maldito, infame *<b. dog!* ¡perro infame!>* II. adv. G.B., JER. muy, sumamente III. tr. **-ied, -y·ing** ensangrentar.
bloom (blōōm) I. s. *(flower)* flor *f <in b.* en flor>; *(flowering)* florecimiento; *(period)* floración *f*; *(freshness)* frescura, lozanía; BOT. vello, pelusa II. intr. *(to flower)* florecer; *(to flourish)* prosperar.
bloom·ers (blōō'mərz) s.pl. pantalones bombachos (de mujer), calzón bombacho.
bloom·ing (blōō'mĭng) adj. *(flowering)* floreciente; G.B., JER. *(bloody)* maldito.
bloop·er (blōō'pər) s. *(in baseball)* voleo alto y débil; FAM. *(clumsy mistake)* metida de pata.
blos·som (blŏs'əm) I. s. *(flower)* flor *f*; *(flowering)* florescencia, floración *f* ♦ **in b.** en flor II. intr. *(to bloom)* florecer; *(to flourish)* florecer, prosperar.
blot (blŏt) I. s. mancha, tacha II. tr. **blot·ted, blot·ting** *(to stain)* manchar; *(to disgrace)* difamar; *(to dry)* secar (con papel secante) ♦ **to b. out** *(to cancel)* suprimir; *(to erase)* borrar —intr. *(to make stains)* emborronarse; *(to become stained)* mancharse (de tinta).
blotch (blŏch) I. s. *(blot)* mancha; *(pimple)* grano II. tr. & intr. *(to blot)* cubrir(se) de manchas; *(to be covered with pimples)* cubrirse de granos.
blotch·y (blŏch'ē) adj. **-i·er, -i·est** *(spotted)* lleno de manchas; *(said of the skin)* enrojecido.

blot·ter (blŏt'ər) s. *(paper)* secante *m*, papel secante *m*; *(register)* registro.
blotting paper s. papel secante *m*.
blouse (blous, blouz) I. s. *(woman's shirt)* blusa; *(smock)* guardapolvo, blusón *m*; MIL. guerrera II. intr. & tr. **bloused, blous·ing** colgar holgadamente.
blou·son (blou'sŏn', blōō'zŏn') s. blusón *m*.
blow¹ (blō) I. intr. **blew** (blōō), **blown** (blōn), **blow·ing** *(wind, air)* soplar; *(with the mouth)* soplar; *(with bellows)* afollar; *(to sound)* tocar, hacer sonar soplando; *(to pant)* resollar, jadear; *(to burst out)* quemarse (los fusibles); *(to burst)* explotar; *(like a whale)* resoplar; JER. *(to boast)* fanfarronear; FAM. *(to leave)* irse, largarse *<I'm going to b. this town* me voy a largar de este pueblo> ♦ **to b. in** FAM. llegar inesperadamente • **to b. off** *(steam)* escaparse el vapor; *(a boiler, locomotive)* evacuar vapor • **to b. out** *(to be extinguished)* apagarse por causa del viento; *(tire)* estallar, reventarse; ELEC. *(fuse)* fundirse, quemarse • **to b. over** *(storm)* disiparse, pasar; *(scandal)* olvidarse • **to b. up** *(wind)* surgir; *(storm)* venirse; *(to explode)* explotar; *(to inflate)* reventarse; inflarse, hincharse; *(to explode with anger)* encolerizarse —tr. *(wind)* soplar; *(air from the mouth)* soplar, echar; *(air, smoke)* echar; *(the nose)* sonarse; *(glass)* soplar; *(to put out of breath)* dejar sin aliento; *(electric fuse)* fundir; *(to waste)* malgastar; JER., VULG. *(to perform fellatio upon)* mamar, chupar ♦ **to b. away** *(lint, dust)* soplar; *(the wind)* arrastrarse, llevarse • **to b. down** *(to topple)* derribar • **to b. off** *(to remove)* quitar; *(to destroy)* volar • **to b. off steam** FIG. desahogarse emocionalmente • **to b. one's trumpet** *o* **horn** FIG. alabarse a sí mismo • **to b. out** *(to extinguish)* soplar, apagar; *(tire)* reventar; ELEC. *(fuse)* fundir, quemar • **to b. over** *(to topple)* derribar; *(to surprise)* sorprender • **to b. up** *(to destroy)* volar, hacer saltar; *(to inflate)* inflar; FOTOG. ampliar II. s. *(blast of air)* soplido, soplo; *(storm)* tormenta.
blow² (blō) s. *(hit)* golpe *m*; *(calamity)* desgracia; *(unexpected attack)* ataque repentino; *(setback)* revés *m* ♦ **to come to blows** agarrarse a puñetazos.
blow-by-blow (blō'bī-blō') adj. detallado *<a b: description* una descripción detallada>.
blow-dry·er (blō'drī'ər) s. secador de cabello *m*.
blow·er (blō'ər) s. *(bellows)* fuelle *m*; *(fan)* ventilador *m*; JER. *(braggart)* fanfarrón *m*; G.B., JER. *(telephone)* teléfono.
blow·gun (blō'gŭn') s. *(for hunting)* cerbatana; *(for painting)* pistola.
blow·hard (blō'härd') s. JER. fanfarrón *m*, jaquetón *m*.
blow·hole (blō'hōl') s. respiradero.
blown (blōn) part. p. de **blow¹**.
blow·out (blō'out') s. *(of a tire)* reventón *m*, pinchazo; *(escape)* salida, escape *m*; JER. *(large party)* gran festín *m*, comilona.
blow·pipe (blō'pīp') s. *(blowtorch)* soplete *m*; *(blowgun)* cerbatana; *(blowtube)* caña de vidriero.
blow·torch (blō'tôrch') s. soplete *m*, lámpara de soldar.
blow·up (blō'ŭp') s. *(explosion)* explosión *f*; *(of temper)* estallido de ira; FOTOG. ampliación *f*.
blow·y (blō'ē) adj. **-i·er, -i·est** ventoso.
blub·ber (blŭb'ər) I. intr. lloriquear, gimotear —tr. decir llorando, expresar entre llantos II. s. *(weeping)* lloriqueo, gimoteo; *(whale fat)* grasa de ballena; *(body fat)* grasa (en el cuerpo).
bludg·eon (blŭj'ən) I. s. cachiporra, maza II. tr. *(to hit)* aporrear; *(to threaten)* intimidar.
blue (blōō) I. s. *(color)* azul *m*; *(bluing)* azul, azulete *m*; *(the sea)* mar *m*, océano; *(the sky)* cielo • **blues** MIL. uniforme de la marina estadounidense; *(melancholy)* melancolía • **out of the b.** de repente II. adj. **blu·er, blu·est** *(of the color blue)* azul; *(purplish)* azulado, amoratado; *(gloomy)* tristón, melancólico; *(risqué)* indecente, verde *<a b. joke* un chiste verde> ♦ **once in a b. moon** una vez cada muerte de obispo III. tr. & intr. **blued, blu·ing** azular(se).
Blue·beard (blōō'bîrd') s. Barba Azul.
blue·bell (blōō'bĕl') s. BOT. campánula, campanilla.

blue·ber·ry (blōō'bĕr'ē) s. [pl. **-ries**] BOT. arándano.
blue·bird (blōō'bûrd') s. ORNIT. azulejo.
blue blood s. *(noble descent)* sangre azul *f*; *(aristocrat)* aristócrata *mf*, noble *mf*.
blue·bot·tle (blōō'bŏt'l) s. ENTOM. moscarda, mosca azul.
blue chip s. FIN. *(stock)* acción selecta (por su estabilidad); *(valuable asset)* bien de mucho valor *m*.
blue·col·lar (blōō'kŏl'ər) adj. de obreros.
blue·grass (blōō'grăs') s. BOT. hierba azulada; MÚS. música folklórica del sur de EE. UU.
blue·jack·et (blōō'jăk'ĭt) s. marinero.
blue jay (jā) s. ORNIT. arrendajo.
blue jeans s.pl. pantalones vaqueros.
blue·pen·cil (blōō'pĕn'səl) tr. *(to correct)* corregir (con lápiz azul); *(to censure)* censurar.
blue·print (blōō'prĭnt') I. s. FOTOG. cianotipo, copia azul; *(plan)* proyecto detallado II. tr. FOTOG. copiar en cianotipo; *(to plan)* planear.
blue ribbon s. cinta azul (primer premio).
blue·rib·bon (blü'rĭb'ən) adj. selecto (jurado, panel).
blues (blōōz) s. [ú. con v. sing. o pl.] *(melancholy)* melancolía; MÚS. jazz melancólico.
blue·stock·ing (blōō'stŏk'ĭng) s. marisabidilla.
bluff¹ (blŭf) I. tr. engañar ♦ **to b. someone into thinking that** hacer creer a alguien que —intr. farolear, aparentar II. s. *(act)* engaño, farol *m*; *(braggart)* farolero, fanfarrón *m* ♦ **to call someone's b.** desenmascarar.
bluff² (blŭf) I. s. *(cliff)* acantilado; *(promontory)* promontorio; *(river bank)* ribera escarpada II. adj. **-er, -est** *(steep)* escarpado; *(brusque)* brusco.
bluff·er (blŭf'ər) s. fanfarrón *m*, farolero.
blu·ing (blōō'ĭng) s. añil *m*, azulete *m*.
blu·ish (blōō'ĭsh) adj. azulado.
blun·der (blŭn'dər) I. s. error craso, metida de pata II. intr. *(to move clumsily)* andar a tropezones, moverse torpemente; *(to err)* cometer un error craso —tr. meter la pata ♦ **to b. away** dejar escapar (secreto, oportunidad).
blunt (blŭnt) I. adj. **-er, -est** *(not sharp)* desafilado; *(frank)* franco; *(brusque)* brusco; *(dull)* torpe, lerdo II. tr. *(to make less sharp)* desafilar, embotar; *(to weaken)* embotar, entorpecer —intr. desafilarse.
blunt·ly (blŭnt'lē) adv. *(frankly)* francamente; *(brusquely)* bruscamente.
blur (blûr) I. tr. **blurred, blur·ring** *(to make hazy)* empañar, nublar; *(to stain)* manchar, emborronar; *(to dim)* obscurecer —intr. *(to become hazy)* empañarse; *(to dim)* ponerse borroso II. s. *(smudge)* borrón *m*, manchón *m*; *(haziness)* borrosidad *f*, nebulosidad *f*.
blurb (blûrb) s. *(publicity notice)* propaganda; *(in a drawing)* subtítulo.
blur·ry (blûr'ē) adj. **-ri·er, -ri·est** confuso, borroso.
blurt (blûrt) tr. ♦ **to b. out** dejar escapar, decir impulsivamente.
blush (blŭsh) I. intr. *(to flush)* ruborizarse, sonrojarse; *(to become red)* enrojecer ♦ **to b. at** avergonzarse de II. s. *(flush)* rubor *m*, sonrojo; *(color)* color rosado.
blush·er (blŭsh'ər) s. *(person)* persona que se sonroja; *(make-up)* colorete *m*.
blush·ing (blŭsh'ĭng) adj. ruborizado, sonrojado.
blus·ter (blŭs'tər) I. intr. *(wind)* bramar, soplar con ráfagas violentas; *(to boast)* echar bravatas; *(to shout)* vociferar —tr. intimidar con amenazas II. s. *(wind)* ráfaga violenta; *(confusion)* tumulto; *(boasting)* fanfarronada.
blus·ter·y (blŭs'tə-rē) adj. *(gusty)* borrascoso; *(boastful)* fanfarrón.
bo·a (bō'ə) s. ZOOL. boa *f*; *(scarf)* boa (prenda) *m*.
boar (bôr) s. *(male pig)* verraco; *(wild pig)* jabalí *m*.
board (bôrd) I. s. *(slab of lumber)* madero; *(plank)* tabla; *(playing surface)* tablero; *(book cover)* tapa, cartón de tapa (de un libro) *m*; *(table)* mesa; *(meals)* comida, pensión *f*; *(authoritative body)* junta, consejo de administración); ELEC. *(panel)* cuadro, tablero ♦ **above b.** honesto, sin reservas • **boards** TEAT. tablas, escenario • **on b.** MA-RÍT., AVIA. a bordo • **to go by the b.** *(to be ignored)* ser ignorado *u* olvidado; *(to be ruined)* frustarse II. tr. *(to house and furnish with meals)* dar hospedaje con comida;

(to go on a ship, airplane) embarcar(se) en ♦ **to b. up** tapar con tablas —intr. hospedarse con comida.
board·er (bôr'dər) s. *(in a house)* huésped *m*, pensionista *mf*; *(in a school)* interno.
board·ing·house (bôr'dĭng-hous') s. pensión *f*, casa de huéspedes.
boarding school s. internado.
board of trade s. junta de comercio.
board·walk (bôrd'wôk') s. *(at a beach)* paseo entablado (en las playas); *(sidewalk)* acera de madera.
boast (bōst) I. intr. jactarse, alardear ♦ **to b. of** *o* **about** jactarse de, hacer alarde de • **to be nothing to b. about** no ser cosa para jactarse —tr. ostentar II. s. jactancia, alarde *m*.
boast·ful (bōst'fəl) adj. jactancioso.
boast·ing (bō'stĭng) s. jactancia, vanagloria.
boat (bōt) I. s. *(small craft)* bote *m*, barca; *(ship)* barco, buque *m*; *(dish)* salsera ♦ **to be in the same b.** FIG. estar en la misma situación II. intr. navegar —tr. *(to transport)* transportar en barco; *(to place)* poner a bordo.
boat·house (bōt'hous') s. cobertizo para botes.
boat·ing (bō'tĭng) s. paseo en bote.
boat·man (bōt'mən) s. [pl. **-men**] botero, lanchero.
boat·swain (bō'sən) s. MARÍT. contramaestre *m*.
bob¹ (bŏb) I. s. *(movement)* sacudida, movimiento brusco; *(tap)* golpecito; *(of a plumb line)* plomo, peso; *(float)* flotador *m*, corcho (de pescador); *(lock)* rizo; *(haircut)* corte de pelo corto *m*; *(tail)* cola cortada (del caballo); *(bobsled)* bobsleigh *m* II. intr. **bobbed, bob·bing** *(to move)* balancearse <*a log bobbing on the water* un tronco balanceándose en el agua>; *(to bow)* hacer una reverencia ♦ **to b. up** surgir, presentarse ; *(to move)* mover, menear (de arriba abajo); *(to tap)* dar un golpe ligero.
bob² (bŏb) s. [pl. **bob**] G.B., JER. chelín *m*.
bob·ber (bŏb'ər) s. flotador *m*, corcho (de pescador).
bob·bin (bŏb'ĭn) s. *(spool)* bobina, carrete *m*; *(trimming)* bolillo.
bobbin lace s. COST. encaje de bolillos *m*.
bob·ble (bŏb'əl) I. intr. moverse, sacudirse —tr. dejar caer II. s. falla, error *m*.
bob·by (bŏb'ē) s. [pl. **-bies**] G.B., FAM. policía *mf*.
bobby pin s. horquilla, pasador *m*.
bobby socks *o* **bobby sox** (bŏb'ē sŏks) s.pl. calcetines cortos, medias cortas.
bob·by·sox·er (bŏb'ē-sŏk'sər) s. jovencita (adolescente).
bob·cat (bŏb'kăt') s. gato montés, lince *m*.
bob·sled (bŏb'slĕd') DEP. I. s. trineo de balancín, bobsleigh *m* II. intr. **-sled·ded, -sled·ding** ir en trineo.
bob·tail (bŏb'tāl') s. *(tail)* cola cortada; *(animal)* animal rabicorto.
bode¹ (bōd) tr. **bod·ed, bod·ing** presagiar ♦ **to b. well (ill)** ser de buen (mal) agüero.
bode² (bōd) un pret. de **bide**.
bod·ice (bŏd'ĭs) s. COST. *(fitted part)* cuerpo; *(vest)* corpiño; ANT. *(corset)* corsé *m*.
bod·ied (bŏd'ēd) adj. de cuerpo <*strong-bodied* de cuerpo fuerte>.
bod·i·less (bŏd'ē-lĭs) adj. incorpóreo.
bod·i·ly (bŏd'l-ē) I. adj. corporal, físico II. adv. *(physically)* corporalmente, físicamente; *(as a whole)* en pleno.
bod·ing (bō'dĭng) I. s. presagio, presentimiento II. adj. presagioso, ominoso.
bod·kin (bŏd'kĭn) s. *(for making holes)* punzón *m*; *(for ribbon)* pasacintas *m*; *(hairpin)* horquilla.
bod·y (bŏd'ē) I. s. [pl. **-ies**] *(of man, animal)* cuerpo; *(trunk)* torso, tronco; *(corpse)* cadáver *m*, cuerpo; *(part of garment)* cuerpo (de vestido, abrigo); *(entity)* corporación *f*, cuerpo; *(organization)* organización *f*, organismo; *(group)* grupo, conjunto <*we walked out in a b.* nos fuimos en grupo>; *(number)* número <*a large b. of employees* un gran número de empleados>; *(main part)* parte principal; *(frame)* bastidor; *(mass)* masa <*a b. of water* una masa de agua>; *(consistency)* consistencia, espesor (de salsa, vino) *m*; DER. recopilación *f*, colecccíon (de leyes) *f*; ARQ. cuerpo; *(of church)* nave *f*; AVIA. fuselaje *m*; MARÍT. casco; ASTRON., FÍS., GEOM. cuerpo; AUTO. carrocería; TIP. cuerpo

(de la letra de imprenta); MÚS. caja de resonancia; MIL. cuerpo (de ejército) ♦ **to keep b. and soul together** tener lo justo para vivir, subsistir **II.** tr. **-ied, -y·ing** *(to give body to)* dar cuerpo a, encarnar; FIG. *(to give form to)* representar, simbolizar (idea, concepto).
body corporate s. DER. persona jurídica, corporación *f.*
bod·y·guard (bŏd′ē-gärd′) s. guardaespaldas *m.*
body politic s. entidad política.
body snatcher s. ladrón de cadáveres *m.*
body work s. AUTO. reparación de carrocerías *f.*
bog (bŏg) **I.** s. pantano, ciénaga **II.** tr. & intr. **bogged, bog·ging** ♦ **to b. down** empantanar(se), atascar(se).
bo·gey (bō′gē) s. [pl. **-geys**] *(goblin)* duende *m;* *(ghost)* espectro, fantasma; *(in golf)* recorrido normal aproximado.
bog·ey·man (bōōg′ē-măn′) s. [pl. **-men** (-mĕn′)] FAM. cuco, coco.
bog·gle (bŏg′əl) intr. **-gled, -gling** sobresaltarse ♦ **to b. at** vacilar ante —tr. sobresaltar ♦ **it boggles the mind** es de volverse loco.
bog·gy (bŏ′gē) adj. **-gier, -giest** pantanoso, cenagoso.
bo·gus (bō′gəs) adj. falso, fraudulento.
bo·gy (bō′gē) s. [pl. **-gies**] *(hobgoblin)* espectro, fantasma; *(worry)* preocupación *f,* inquietud *f.*
Bo·he·mi·an (bō-hē′mē-ən) adj & s. bohemio.
boil¹ (boil) **I.** intr. *(liquids)* hervir; *(to cook)* cocer; *(to be excited)* hervir, bullir ♦ **to b. down** reducirse • **to b. over** *(to overflow)* salirse, rebosar (al hervir); FIG. *(to rage)* enfurecerse, explotar de rabia —tr. *(a liquid)* hacer hervir; *(to cook)* cocer, hervir, herventar; *(an egg)* pasar por agua ♦ **to b. down** reducir • **to b. down to** reducirse a **II.** s. *(ebullition)* punto de ebullición *f,* hervor *m* ♦ **to bring to a b.** calentar hasta que hierva • **to come to a b.** comenzar a hervir.
boil² (boil) s. MED. furúnculo, divieso.
boil·er (boi′lər) s. *(of a heating system)* caldera; *(storage tank)* tanque de agua caliente *m.*
boil·er·plate (boi′lər-plāt′) s. acero para calderas.
boil·ing (boi′lĭng) **I.** adj. hirviente **II.** s. ebullición *f,* hervor *m.*
boiling point s. *(temperature)* punto de ebullición; FAM. *(temper)* límite de la paciencia *m.*
bois·ter·ous (boi′stər-əs) adj. *(noisy)* bullicioso; *(stormy)* tempestuoso, turbulento.
bold (bōld) adj. **-er, -est** *(courageous)* valiente; *(audacious)* audaz; *(impudent)* descarado; *(distinct)* marcado, pronunciado; *(steep)* escarpado ♦ **in b. face** IMPR. en negritas.
bold·face (bōld′fās′) IMPR. **I.** s. negrita **II.** tr. **-faced, -fac·ing** imprimir en negritas.
bold-faced (bōld′fāst′) adj. *(impudent)* descarado; IMPR. en negritas.
bold·ly (bōld′lē) adv. *(audaciously)* audazmente; *(impudently)* descaradamente.
bo·le·ro (bə-lâr′ō) s. [pl. **-ros**] COST., MÚS. bolero.
bo·li·var (bŏl′ə-vär, bŏl′ə-vər) s. FIN. bolívar (unidad monetaria venezolana) *m.*
Bo·liv·i·a (bə-lĭv′ē-ə) s. Bolivia.
Bo·liv·i·an (bə-lĭv′ē-ən) adj. & s. boliviano.
boll (bōl) s. BOT. vaina, cápsula.
bo·lo·gna (bə-lō′nē) s. salchicha de Bolonia.
Bo·lo·gna (bə-lōn′yə) s. Bolonia.
bo·lo·ney (bə-lō′nē) s. var. de baloney y bologna.
Bol·she·vik (bōl′shə-vĭk′, bŏl′-) s. [pl. **-viks** *o* **-vi·ki** (-vē′kē)] bolchevique *mf.*
Bol·she·vism *o* **bol·she·vism** (bōl′shə-vĭz′əm, bŏl′-) s. HIST., POL. bolchevismo.
bol·ster (bōl′stər) **I.** s. cabezal *m,* travesaño **II.** tr. *(to support)* apoyar; *(to strengthen)* reforzar; *(to hearten)* animar.
bolt¹ (bōlt) **I.** s. CARP., MEC. *(threaded pin)* tornillo, perno; *(fastener)* cerrojo, pestillo; *(bar)* pasador *m;* *(of a rifle)* cerrojo de fusil; *(roll of cloth)* rollo *o* pieza de tela; *(sudden dash)* salto brusco *o* rápido; *(thunderbolt)* rayo, centella; *(arrow)* saeta, flecha (de ballesta) ♦ **a b. from the blue** FIG. suceso inesperado, acontecimiento imprevisto • **b. and nut** perno y tuerca **II.** tr. *(to lock)* echar el cerrojo a, cerrar con pestillo; *(to bar)* atrancar; *(to fasten)* sujetar con tornillos *o* pernos; *(to gulp)* engullir, tragar sin masti-

car; POL. retirar el apoyo a (partido) —intr. *(to dash off)* largarse, salir rápidamente; *(to run away)* dispararse, desbocarse <*the horse bolted at the sight of the car* el caballo se desbocó cuando vio el automóvil>; POL. irse, retirar el apoyo a (partido) ♦ **to b. in** entrar de repente • **to b. off** fugarse, huir • **to b. out** salir de repente • **to b. past** pasar como un rayo.
bolt² (bōlt) tr. cerner, tamizar.
bomb (bŏm) **I.** s. *(weapon)* bomba; JER. *(failure)* fracaso, fiasco ♦ **b. shelter** refugio contra bombardeos • **the b.** la bomba nuclear **II.** tr. bombardear —intr. *(to drop bombs)* arrojar bombas; JER. *(to fail)* fracasar.
bom·bard I. tr. (bŏm-bärd′) *(to bomb)* bombardear; FIG. *(to harass)* abrumar, acosar **II.** s. (bŏm′bärd′) MIL. bombarda.
bom·bar·dier (bŏm′bər-dîr′) s. MIL. bombardero.
bom·bard·ment (bŏm-bärd′mənt) s. bombardeo.
bom·bast (bŏm′băst′) s. *(speech)* discurso grandilocuente; *(writing)* escrito grandilocuente.
bom·bas·tic (bŏm-băs′tĭk) adj. grandilocuente, ampuloso.
bombed (bŏmd) adj. JER. borracho.
bomb·er (bŏm′ər) s. bombardero.
bomb·ing (bŏm′ĭng) s. bombardeo.
bomb-proof (bŏm′prōōf′) adj. a prueba de bombas.
bomb·shell (bŏm′shĕl′) s. *(bomb)* bomba; FIG. *(surprise)* bomba.
bomb·sight (bŏm′sīt′) s. AER., MIL. visor de bombardeo *m.*
bo·na fide (bō′nə fīd′, fī′dē) adj. *(sincere)* de buena fe, seria <*a b. offer* una oferta de buena fe>; *(authentic)* genuino, auténtico.
bo·nan·za (bə-năn′zə) s. bonanza, mina.
bon·bon (bŏn′bŏn′) s. confite *m,* caramelo.
bond (bŏnd) **I.** s. *(fastener)* lazo, atadura; FIG. *(tie)* vínculo, unión *f;* DER. *(bail)* fianza, garantía; *(bondsman)* fiador *m;* FIN. bono, obligación *f;* *(certificate of debt)* bono, título de una deuda; *(insurance contract)* contrato, obligación *f;* QUÍM. grado de afinidad, enlace *m* ♦ **bonds** *(shackles)* cadenas; FIG. *(tie)* lazo, encadenamiento moral • **in b.** en depósito, afianzado • **municipal bonds** obligaciones municipales • **treasury bonds** bonos del tesoro • **under b.** bajo fianza **II.** tr. *(to join securely)* ligar estrechamente, unir; *(to mortgage)* hipotecar; *(to furnish surety for)* afianzar, dar fianza a; *(to place under guarantee)* afianzar (un empleado, mercaderías) —intr. unirse, pegarse.
bond·age (bŏn′dĭj) s. *(slavery)* esclavitud *f;* *(subjugation)* dominación *f.*
bond·ed (bŏn′dĭd) adj. COM. *(guaranteed)* garantizado; *(deposited)* depositado bajo fianza.
bonded warehouse s. depósito de artículos bajo fianza.
bond·hold·er (bŏnd′hōl′dər) s. obligacionista *mf,* tenedor de bonos *m.*
bond·ing (bŏn′dĭng) s. ANTROP. nexo, lazos afectuosos entre individuos socialmente relacionados.
bond paper s. papel de hilo *m.*
bond·ser·vant (bŏnd′sûr′vənt) s. esclavo, siervo.
bonds·man (bŏndz′mən) s. [pl. **-men**] *(guarantor)* fiador *m,* garante *mf;* *(bondservant)* esclavo.
bone (bōn) **I.** s. *(of the body)* hueso; *(of fish)* espina; *(of corset)* ballena ♦ **to feel it in one's bones** tener el presentimiento de algo • **to have a b. to pick with someone** FAM. tener alguna queja de alguien • **to make no bones of** *o* **about** no andarse con rodeos • **to the b.** hasta el hueso <*he cut his finger to the b.* se cortó el dedo hasta el hueso>; FIG. *(to the limit)* al máximo, completamente **II.** tr. **boned, bon·ing** *(to debone meat)* deshuesar; *(to debone fish)* quitar las espinas a; *(to stiffen garments)* poner ballenas a, emballenar —intr. ♦ **to b. up on** JER. estudiar duro.
bone china s. porcelana translúcida.
bone-dry (bōn′drī′) adj. completamente seco.
bone meal s. harina de huesos.
bone of contention s. manzana de la discordia.
bon·er (bō′nər) s. FAM. *(mistake)* desatino, disparate *m;* *(blunder)* metedura de pata.
bon·fire (bŏn′fīr′) s. fogata, hoguera.
bon·go drums (bŏng′gō) s.pl. MÚS. bongó.
bon·ho·mie (bŏn′ə-mē′) s. afabilidad *f,* bondad *f.*

bo·ni·to (bə-nē′tō) s. [pl. **bonito** o **-tos**] ICT. bonito.
bon·net (bŏn′ĭt) s. *(hat)* toca, sombrero (de mujer); *(cap)* gorra escocesa; *(metal plate)* sombrerete *m*, casquete *m*; G.B. *(of a car)* capó.
bo·nus (bō′nəs) s. *(reward)* gratificación *f*; *(earnings)* beneficio; *(dividend)* dividendo extraordinario.
bon·y (bō′nē) adj. **-i·er, -i·est** *(osseous)* óseo, huesoso; *(thin)* flaco; *(angular)* huesudo; *(full of bones)* espinoso.
boo (bōō) **I.** s. [pl. **boos**] abucheo, rechifla **II.** interj. ¡bú! **III.** intr. & tr. **booed, boo·ing** abuchear (a), rechiflar (a).
boob (bōōb) s. FAM. *(fool)* bobalicón *m*; JER. *(breast)* teta.
boo-boo (bōō′bōō) s. [pl. **-boos**] JER. *(blunder)* metida de pata; *(mistake)* error *m*; *(injury)* nana, pupa.
boob tube s. JER. televisión *f*.
boo·by (bōō′bē) s. FAM. *(fool)* bobalicón *m*; JER. *(breast)* teta.
booby prize s. premio al peor.
booby trap s. *(trap)* engañabobos *m*, trampa; MIL. trampa explosiva.
boo·dle (bōōd′l) s. JER. *(counterfeit)* dinero falsificado, moneda falsa; *(bribe)* soborno.
boog·ie-man o **boog·y·man** (bōōg′ē-măn′, bōō′gē-) s. [pl. **-men** (-mĕn′)] FAM. fantasma, cuco.
boog·ie-woog·ie (bōōg′ē-wōō′gē) s. MÚS. estilo de jazz.
book (bŏŏk) **I.** s. *(volume)* libro; *(tome)* tomo; *(notebook)* libreta; COM., TEN. libro de asiento; TEAT. libreto; *(record of bets)* registro (de apuestas) ♦ **b. of matches** carterilla de fósforos • **b. review** reseña o crítica literaria • **books** COM., TEN. los libros • **like a b.** bien, a fondo <*I can read him like a b.* lo conozco a fondo> • **the Book** o **the Good Book** la Biblia • **to go by the b.** proceder según las reglas • **to make b. on** aceptar apuestas sobre • **to throw the b. at someone** JER. castigar severamente **II.** tr. *(on the police blotter)* asentar, registrar; *(a hotel, seats)* reservar, hacer reservación de; *(entertainers)* contratar (artistas); *(to register)* anotar en un libro, inscribir ♦ **to be booked up** *(hotel, restaurant)* estar completo; *(to have no tickets available)* no haber localidades; *(to have another engagement)* tener otro compromiso.
book·bind·er (bŏŏk′bīn′dər) s. encuadernador *m*.
book·bind·er·y (bŏŏk′bīn′də-rē) s. [pl. **-ies**] taller de encuadernación *m*.
book·bind·ing (bŏŏk′bīn′dĭng) s. encuadernación *f*.
book·case (bŏŏk′kās′) s. estantería para libros.
book·end o **book end** (bŏŏk′ĕnd′) s. sujetalibros *m*.
book·ie (bŏŏk′ē) s. FAM. corredor de apuestas *m*.
book·ing (bŏŏk′ĭng) s. *(engagement)* contratación (de artistas) *f*; *(reservation)* reservación *f*, reserva.
book·ish (bŏŏk′ĭsh) adj. *(of books)* libresco; *(studious)* libresco, estudioso; *(pedantic)* pedante.
book jacket s. forro, cubierta de libro.
book·keep·er (bŏŏk′kē′pər) s. tenedor de libros *m*, contable *mf*.
book·keep·ing (bŏŏk′kē′pĭng) s. teneduría de libros, contabilidad *f*.
book·let (bŏŏk′lĭt) s. folleto.
book·mak·er (bŏŏk′mā′kər) s. *(printer)* impresor *m*; *(binder)* encuadernador *m*; *(bookie)* corredor de apuestas *m*.
book·mark (bŏŏk′märk′) s. señal *f* o marcador de libro *m*.
book·mo·bile (bŏŏk′mō-bĕl′) s. biblioteca ambulante.
Book of Common Prayer s. Libro de Oración Común (liturgia anglicana).
book·plate (bŏŏk′plāt′) s. ex libris *m*.
book·rack (bŏŏk′răk′) s. *(bookshelf)* estante para libros *m*; *(bookrest)* atril *m*.
book review s. reseña, crítica.
book·sell·er (bŏŏk′sĕl′ər) s. librero, vendedor de libros *m*.
book·shelf (bŏŏk′shĕlf′) s. [pl. **-shelves** (-shĕlvz′)] estante para libros *m*, anaquel *m*.
book·shop (bŏŏk′shŏp′) s. librería.
book·stall (bŏŏk′stôl′) s. *(in open air)* quiosco, puesto de libros; *(booth)* caseta (para libros).
book·store (bŏŏk′stôr′) s. librería.
book·worm (bŏŏk′wûrm′) s. *(larva)* polilla (que roe los libros); FIG. *(person)* ratón de biblioteca *m*.

boom¹ (bōōm) **I.** s. *(explosion)* estampido, trueno; *(increase)* auge *m* **II.** intr. *(to thunder)* tronar, retumbar; *(to flourish)* estar en auge —tr. *(to roar)* hacer tronar, hacer retumbar; *(to prosper)* hacer prosperar rápidamente.
boom² (bōōm) s. *(spar)* botalón *m*, botavara; *(jib)* aguilón *m*, pescante (de grúa); *(barrier)* cadena de troncos flotantes; CINEM., RAD. jirafa, brazo (de micrófono).
boo·mer·ang (bōō′mə-răng′) **I.** s. *(curved stick)* bumerang *m*; FIG. *(action)* bumerang, acción contraproducente *f* **II.** intr. ser contraproducente.
boon (bōōn) s. *(blessing)* bendición *f*; *(favor)* favor *m*.
boon·docks (bōōn′dŏks′) s.pl. JER. *(wilderness)* selva, jungla; FIG. *(backwoods)* los quintos infiernos.
boon·dog·gle (bōōn′dô′gəl) FAM. **I.** s. trabajo pagado innecesario **II.** intr. **-gled, -gling** trabajar innecesariamente y cobrar.
boor (bōōr) s. patán *m*.
boor·ish (bōōr′ĭsh) adj. tosco, rudo.
boost (bōōst) **I.** tr. *(to lift)* alzar, levantar; FIG. *(to increase)* elevar, aumentar; *(to encourage)* fomentar, ayudar **II.** s. *(push)* impulso, ayuda; *(increase)* incremento, aumento.
boost·er (bōō′stər) s. ELEC. elevador de voltaje *m*; RAD. amplificador de antena *m*; *(promoter)* promotor *m*, impulsor *m* ♦ **b. rocket** ASTRONÁUT. cohete acelerador • **b. shot** MED. inyección de refuerzo.
boot (bōōt) **I.** s. *(footgear)* bota, botín *m*; *(sheath)* cubierta, envoltura *f*; *(torture device)* calceta; FAM. *(kick)* puntapié *m*, patada; G.B. *(trunk)* portaequipajes *m*; MIL. recluta de marina *m* ♦ **to b.** FAM. además • **to bet your boots** jugarse la cabeza • **to get the b.** FAM. ser despedido del empleo **II.** tr. *(to fit boots on)* calzar; *(to kick)* dar puntapié a, patear; JER. *(to fire)* despedir, echar (de un empleo.)
boot camp s. MIL. campamento de entrenamiento de reclutas.
boo·tee (bōō′tē) s. calzado de punto (para bebés) *m*.
booth (bōōth) s. [pl. **booths** (bōōthz)] *(compartment)* cabina <*telephone b.* cabina telefónica>; *(stand)* puesto, quiosco.
boo·tie (bōō′tē) s. var. de **bootee**.
boot·leg (bōōt′lĕg′) **I.** tr. & intr. **-legged, -leg·ging** contrabandear **II.** s. *(goods)* contrabando; *(of a boot)* caña **III.** adj. de contrabando.
boot·leg·ger (bōōt′lĕg′ər) s. contrabandista (esp. de licores) *mf*.
boot·lick (bōōt′lĭk′) tr. & intr. adular, hacer la pelotilla.
boot·lick·er (bōōt′lĭk′ər) s. adulón *m*.
boot·strap (bōōt′străp′) s. oreja, tirante (de bota) *m* ♦ **by one's bootstraps** por sí mismo, sin ayuda ajena.
boo·ty (bōō′tē) s. [pl. **-ties**] *(plunder)* botín *m*; *(loot)* presa; *(prize)* premio, recompensa.
booze (bōōz) FAM. **I.** s. *(drink)* bebida alcohólica; *(spree)* borrachera **II.** intr. **boozed, booz·ing** beber, emborracharse.
booz·er (bōō′zər) s. FAM. bebedor, borrachín *m*.
bop¹ (bŏp) FAM. **I.** tr. **bopped, bop·ping** golpear, pegar **II.** s. golpe *m*, puñetazo.
bop² (bŏp) s. MÚS. estilo de jazz.
bo·rac·ic (bə-răs′ĭk) adj. var. de **boric**.
Bor·deaux (bôr-dō′) s. Burdeos.
bor·der (bôr′dər) **I.** s. *(boundary)* frontera, límite *m*; *(edge)* borde *m*, orilla; *(design)* orla, ribete *m* **II.** tr. *(to edge)* bordear; *(to adjoin)* limitar con, lindar con; COST. ribetear —intr. ♦ **to b. on** o **upon** *(to adjoin)* lindar con, tocar; *(to approach)* aproximarse a, rayar en.
bor·der·land (bôr′dər-lănd′) s. *(land)* zona fronteriza; *(indefinite area)* zona imprecisa.
bor·der·line o **border line** (bôr′dər-līn′) **I.** s. *(boundary)* frontera; *(indefinite area)* zona imprecisa **II.** adj. dudoso <*a b. case* un caso dudoso>.
bore¹ (bôr) **I.** tr. **bored, bor·ing** *(to drill)* taladrar, barrenar; *(to burrow)* perforar —intr. *(to drill)* taladrar, barrenar; *(to advance)* abrirse paso **II.** s. *(hole)* agujero; *(diameter)* diámetro interior; *(caliber)* calibre *m*; *(tool)* taladro, barreno; ARM. *(of a barrel)* ánima, alma.
bore² (bôr) **I.** tr. **bored, bor·ing** aburrir, cansar **II.** s. *(person)* pesado, pelmazo; *(thing)* lata, pesadez *f*.
bore³ (bôr) pret. de **bear¹**.

---

ng inglés / ŏ la / ō bou / ô corre / oi oigo / ōō uno / ou auto / yōō ciudad / w hueco / y yo / z mismo

bo·re·al (bôr′ē-əl) adj. boreal, septentrional.
bore·dom (bôr′dəm) s. aburrimiento.
bor·er (bôr′ər) s. *(tool)* barrena, taladro; *(person)* perforador *m*, taladrador *m*; *(machine)* perforadora; *(insect)* barrenillo.
bo·ric (bôr′ĭk) adj. QUÍM. bórico.
bo·ride (bôr′īd′) s. QUÍM. boruro.
bor·ing (bôr′ĭng) I. s. taladrado, perforación *f* ♦ **borings** viruta II. adj. aburrido, pesado.
born (bôrn) I. un part. p. de **bear**[1] ♦ **to be b.** *(to come into life)* nacer <*I was b. in Argentina* nací en la Argentina>; *(to originate)* originarse <*the Republican Party was b. in 1854* el partido republicano se originó en 1854> II. adj. nato <*a b. artist* un artista nato>; de nacimiento <*he is Russian-born* es ruso de nacimiento> ♦ **a b. fool** un tonto de nacimiento • **a b. liar** un mentiroso innato • **in all my b. days** FAM. en toda mi vida.
born-a·gain (bôrn′ə-gĕn′) adj. RELIG. nacido otra vez, renacido.
borne (bôrn) un part. p. de **bear**[1].
bo·ron (bôr′ŏn′) s. QUÍM. boro.
bor·ough (bûr′ō) s. *(town, municipality)* municipio; *(district)* distrito.
bor·row (bôr′ō) tr. *(to receive on loan)* tomar prestado; *(to use)* apropiarse (de); *(to take)* tomar; MAT. tomar prestado (al restar) —intr. tomar un préstamo.
bor·row·er (bôr′ō-ər) s. prestatario.
bor·row·ing (bôr′ō-ĭng) s. *(loan)* préstamo; FIG. *(adoption)* adopción *f*.
bosh (bŏsh) s. FAM. *(nonsense)* necedades *f*, galimatías *m*; TEC. *(of a furnace)* talaje *m*.
bo's'n *o* **bos'n** (bō′sən) s. var. de **boatswain**.
bos·om (boʊz′əm, boʊ′zəm) s. *(chest)* pecho, seno; *(breasts)* pechos, senos; *(of a garment)* pecho, pechera; FIG. *(heart)* seno ♦ **b. buddy** FAM. amigo del alma.
Bos·po·rus (bŏs′pər-əs) *o* **Bos·pho·rus** (-fər-) s. Bósforo.
boss[1] (bôs) I. s. *(employer)* patrón *m*; *(supervisor)* supervisor *m*, capataz *m*; *(leader)* jefe *m* II. tr. *(to supervise)* dirigir, supervisar; *(to command)* mandar ♦ **to b. around** mandonear —intr. mandar III. adj. JER. inmejorable.
boss[2] (bôs) I. s. *(protuberance)* bulto, protuberancia; *(stud)* bollón *m*, tachón *m*; *(in a roof)* almohadilla, crucería; *(of a shaft)* árbol *m*; *(in a book)* bullón *m* II. tr. abollonar, tachonar.
boss·y[1] (bô′sē) adj. **-i·er, -i·est** mandón, dominante.
boss·y[2] (bô′sē) s. [pl. **-ies**] FAM. *(cow)* vaca; *(calf)* ternero.
bo·sun (bō′sən) s. var. de **boatswain**.
bo·tan·i·cal (bə-tăn′ĭ-kəl) *o* **bo·tan·ic** (-tăn′ĭk) adj. botánico.
bot·a·nist (bŏt′n-ĭst) s. botánico.
bot·a·ny (bŏt′n-ē) s. botánica.
botch (bŏch) I. tr. chapucear II. s. chapucería.
both §G36 (bōth) I. pron. ambos, los dos <*if one is guilty, b. are* si uno es culpable, ambos lo son> ♦ **b. of them** ambos, los dos • **b. of us** nosotros dos • **b. of you** vosotros dos II. adj. ambos, los dos <*b. houses are similar in their architecture* ambas casas son similares en su arquitectura> ♦ **to have it b. ways** sacar ventaja de una manera u otra III. conj. . . . . y . . . además <*he is b. strong and healthy* él es fuerte y sano además>.
both·er (bŏth′ər) I. tr. & intr. *(to annoy)* molestar(se), fastidiar(se); *(to worry)* preocupar(se) ♦ **to b. about** *o* **with** *(to take the trouble)* molestarse por; *(to worry)* preocuparse por *o* de II. s. *(annoyance)* molestia, fastidio; *(worry)* preocupación *f*.
both·er·some (bŏth′ər-səm) adj. molesto, fastidioso.
Bot·swa·na (bŏt-swä′nə) s. Botswana.
bot·tle (bŏt′l) I. s. *(container, content)* botella; *(flask)* frasco, pomo; *(for a baby)* biberón *m* ♦ **to hit the b.** JER. beber, tomar con exceso II. tr. **-tied, -tling** embotellar, envasar ♦ **to b. up** *(to repress)* reprimir, contener; *(to seal)* sellar.
bottled gas s. gas envasado.
bot·tle·neck (bŏt′l-nĕk′) s. *(of a bottle)* cuello; FIG. *(obstruction)* embotellamiento.
bot·tler (bŏt′lər) s. embotellador *m*.

bot·tom (bŏt′əm) I. s. *(lowest, deepest part)* fondo; *(last place)* final <*he is at the b. of the list* está al final de la lista>; *(of a boat)* quilla; *(foot)* pie *m*; *(of sea, river)* lecho, fondo; *(underlying cause)* meollo, base *f* <*to get to the b. of the matter* llegar al meollo del asunto>; *(seat of a chair)* asiento; *(of pants)* fondillos; *(hem, cuff)* bajo; FAM. *(buttocks)* trasero, nalgas *f* ♦ **b. dollar** *(lowest price)* precio más bajo; *(one's last dollar)* el último peso que tiene uno • **bottoms** *(of pajamas)* pantalones; GEOG. hondonada II. tr. *(to provide with a foundation)* hacer una base a; *(to provide with an underside)* poner fondo a; *(to ground)* fundamentar, basar <*the theory is bottomed on questionable assumptions* la teoría se funda en suposiciones dudosas> —intr. *(to be grounded)* fundamentarse, basarse; MARÍT. tocar fondo.
bot·tom·land (bŏt′əm-lănd′) s. tierra baja a lo largo de un río.
bot·tom·less (bŏt′əm-lĭs) adj. sin fondo, insondable.
bottom line s. FIN. *(balance)* balance *m*; *(main point)* quid *m*.
bot·u·lism (bŏch′ə-lĭz′əm) s. MED. botulismo.
bou·gain·vil·lea *o* **bou·gain·vil·lae·a** (boʊ′gən-vĭl′ē-ə, -vĭl′yə) s. BOT. buganvilla.
bough (bou) s. BOT. rama.
bought (bôt) pret. y part. p. de **buy**.
bou·gie (boʊ′zhē) s. *(candle)* vela; MED. *(implement)* sonda; *(suppository)* supositorio.
bouil·lon (boʊl′yŏn′) s. caldo.
boul·der (bōl′dər) s. canto rodado.
boul·e·vard (boʊl′ə-värd′, boʊl′ə-) s. bulevar *m*.
bounce (bouns) I. intr. **bounced, bounc·ing** rebotar; *(to bound enthusiastically)* saltar, dar brincos <*the child bounced into the room* el niño entró saltando en la habitación>; COM., FAM. *(to be returned)* ser rechazado ♦ **to b. back** recuperarse —tr. *(to cause to rebound)* hacer rebotar; JER. *(to expel)* sacar, echar; *(to fire)* poner de patitas en la calle, despedir II. s. *(leap)* salto, brinco; *(rebound)* rebote *m*; *(reflection)* reflexión *f*; *(springiness)* elasticidad *f*; *(liveliness)* vigor *m*, vitalidad *f*.
bounc·er (boun′sər) s. JER. persona encargada de echar a los alborotadores.
bounc·ing (boun′sĭng) adj. robusto, fuerte.
bounc·y (boun′sē) adj. **-i·er, -i·est** *(elastic)* elástico, flexible; *(lively)* vivo, exuberante; *(up and down)* que rebota, que salta.
bound[1] (bound) I. intr. *(to spring)* saltar; *(to leap)* dar brincos, avanzar a saltos; *(to rebound)* rebotar II. s. *(leap)* salto, brinco; *(bounce)* rebote *m*.
bound[2] (bound) I. s. ♦ **bounds** *(limit)* límite <*his joy knew no bounds* su alegría no tenía límite>; *(boundary)* fronteras • **out of bounds** DEP. fuera de la cancha; *(beyond limits)* fuera de los límites (usuales, legales, de seguridad); *(prohibited)* prohibido II. tr. *(to delimit)* deslindar, señalar los límites de; *(to border)* lindar con.
bound[3] (bound) I. pret. y part. p. de **bind** II. adj. *(tied)* atado, amarrado; *(certain)* seguro <*if you continue searching you are b. to find the answer* si continúas en tu búsqueda es seguro que encontrarás la respuesta>; *(obliged)* obligado; *(put in a cover)* encuadernado; FAM. *(resolved)* resuelto, determinado; *(constipated)* estreñido; *(united)* ligado, vinculado ♦ **b. up in** absorbido por, entregado a • **b. up with** estrechamente relacionado con • **it is b. to happen** tiene forzosamente que ocurrir.
bound[4] (bound) adj. destinado, encaminado ♦ **to be b. for** dirigirse a, ir con destino a.
bound·a·ry (boun′də-rē) s. [pl. **-ries**] límite *m*, frontera.
bound·less (bound′lĭs) adj. ilimitado, infinito.
boun·te·ous (boun′tē-əs) adj. *(generous)* generoso; *(abundant)* abundante, copioso.
boun·ti·ful (boun′tə-fəl) adj. *(generous)* generoso; *(plentiful)* abundante, copioso.
boun·ty (boun′tē) s. [pl. **-ties**] *(generosity)* generosidad *f*; *(gift)* regalo; *(reward)* recompensa, gratificación *f*.
bou·quet (bō-kā′, bōō-) s. *(of flowers)* ramo, ramillete *m*; *(of wine)* aroma *m*, buqué *m*.
bour·bon (bûr′bən) s. whisky de maíz *m*.

ã rey / ä año / b boca / ch chico / d dar / ĕ el / ē mil / g gato / h joya / hw juez / ī aire / k casa / kw cuan /

bour·geois (bŏŏr-zhwä′) s. & adj. burgués m.
bour·geoise (bŏŏr-zhwäz′) s. burguesa.
bour·geoi·sie (bŏŏr′zhwä-zē′) s. burguesía.
bout (bout) s. *(contest)* combate m; *(spell)* ataque (de una enfermedad) m; *(period of time)* rato, momento.
bou·tique (bŏŏ-tēk′) s. tienda pequeña de artículos de moda.
bo·vine (bō′vīn′) I. adj. ZOOL. *(of a cow)* bovino, vacuno; FIG. *(dull)* lento II. s. bovino.
bow¹ (bou) s. MARÍT. *(section)* proa; *(person)* remero de proa.
bow² (bou) I. intr. *(to stoop)* inclinarse, doblegarse <*he bowed beneath the load* se doblegó bajo la carga>; *(to nod)* saludar, inclinar la cabeza; *(to bend the knee)* doblar la rodilla, hacer una reverencia; *(to incline the body)* inclinarse; *(to submit)* someterse, ceder ♦ **to b. out** retirarse, renunciar —tr. *(the head, body)* inclinar; *(the knee)* doblar; *(to convey)* indicar con una reverencia <*they bowed their thanks* indicaron su agradecimiento con una reverencia>; *(to escort deferentially)* acompañar respetuosamente a; *(to overburden)* doblegar II. s. *(obeisance)* reverencia; *(greeting)* saludo; *(sign of respect)* señal f de respeto o reconocimiento.
bow³ (bō) I. s. *(weapon)* arco; *(archer)* arquero; *(bowknot)* lazo; *(curve)* arco, curva; *(rainbow)* arco iris; *(oxbow)* collera de yugo; MÚS. arco II. tr. & intr. *(to bend)* arquear(se), doblar(se); MÚS. tocar (con un arco).
bowd·ler·ize (bōd′lə-rīz′) tr. expurgar (un escrito).
bow·el (bou′əl) s. intestino ♦ **bowels** entrañas.
bow·er·y (bou′ə-rē) I. s. ♦ **B.** calle y sector de Manhattan, en la ciudad de Nueva York, frecuentados por desvalidos y vagabundos II. adj. *(leafy)* frondoso; *(shady)* sombrío.
bow·ing (bō′ĭng) s. MÚS. manera de usar el arco.
bowl¹ (bōl) s. *(dish)* fuente f, cuenco; *(cup)* tazón m; *(washbasin)* palangana, jofaina; *(fountain basin)* pila; *(of a spoon)* paleta; *(of a pipe)* tabaquera, cazoleta; *(toilet)* taza; *(river basin)* cuenca; *(outdoor theater)* anfiteatro; DEP. estadio.
bowl² (bōl) I. s. *(ball)* bola (de bolos); *(throw)* jugada, tiro ♦ **bowls** bochas, bolos II. intr. *(to play)* jugar a los bolos; *(to move)* deslizarse <*the bus bowled along the road* el autobús se deslizaba por la carretera> —tr. *(to throw)* lanzar, tirar (la bola); *(to make a score)* hacer (tantos) ♦ **to b. over** *(to knock over)* derribar; *(to astound)* pasmar.
bow·leg·ged (bō′lĕg′ĭd) adj. patizambo, estevado.
bowl·er¹ (bō′lər) s. jugador de bolos m.
bowl·er² (bō′lər) s. G.B. *(hat)* sombrero hongo, bombín m.
bow·line (bō′lĭn) s. MARÍT. bolina (de una vela); *(knot)* nudo marinero.
bowl·ing (bō′lĭng) s. bolos m.
bowling alley s. bolera.
bow·man¹ (bō′mən) s. [pl. **-men**] arquero.
bow·man² (bou′mən) s. [pl. **-men**] remero de proa.
bow tie (bō) s. corbata de lazo.
box¹ (bŏks) I. s. *(case)* caja; *(large case)* cajón m; *(small case)* estuche m; *(pigeonhole)* casilla; *(rectangle)* casilla, cuadro <*place an x in the correct b.* ponga una x en la casilla correspondiente>; *(in a theater)* palco; *(in a vehicle)* compartimiento; *(stall)* casilla de una cuadra; *(of a carriage)* pescante m; *(guardhouse)* garita, caseta; *(in baseball)* cuadrado del bateador; *(enclosed printed matter)* recuadro; *(for the mail)* casilla, apartado; *(chest)* cofre m, arca; FIG. *(awkward situation)* aprieto, apuro II. tr. *(to put in a box)* meter en una caja, poner en un estuche; IMPR. encerrar en un recuadro ♦ **to b. in** encajonar • **to b. up** *(to surround)* encerrar; *(to pack up)* empaquetar.
box² (bŏks) I. s. bofetada, cachete m II. tr. *(to hit with the hand)* abofetear; *(to hit with the fist)* dar un puñetazo; DEP. boxear —intr. DEP. boxear.
box·car (bŏks′kär′) s. F.C. furgón m.
box·er (bŏk′sər) s. DEP. boxeador m, púgil m; *(dog)* bóxer m.
box·ing (bŏk′sĭng) s. DEP. boxeo, pugilato; *(wrapping)* embalaje m, envase m.
boxing glove s. DEP. guante de boxeo m.

box office s. taquilla, boletería ♦ **a b. success** un éxito de taquilla.
box spring s. colchón de resortes m, somier m.
box stall s. casilla para un caballo.
box·wood (bŏks′wŏŏd′) s. BOT. boj (árbol y madera) m.
box·y (bŏk′sē) adj. **-ier, -iest** achaparrado.
boy (boi) I. s. *(child)* niño; *(youth)* muchacho; *(servant)* muchacho, sirviente m; *(messenger)* mensajero; FAM. *(fellow)* muchacho, amigo <*he is going out with the boys* se va de parranda con los amigos> II. interj. ¡chico!, ¡hombre!
boy·cott (boi′kŏt′) I. tr. boicotear II. s. boicot m.
boy·friend o **boy friend** (boi′frĕnd′) s. FAM. *(sweetheart)* novio, enamorado; *(friend)* amigo.
boy·hood (boi′hŏŏd′) s. niñez f, infancia.
boy·ish (boi′ĭsh) adj. *(childlike)* infantil; *(youthful)* juvenil.
Boy Scout s. (niño) explorador.
bo·zo (bō′zō) s. [pl. **-zos**] JER. *(fellow)* sujeto, tipo; *(fool)* tonto, bobo.
bra (brä) s. sostén m, corpiño.
brace (brās) I. s. *(clamp)* abrazadera, laña; *(reinforcement)* refuerzo; *(beam)* tirante m, puntal m; *(stay)* riostra; *(truss)* braguero; *(orthopedic support)* aparato ortopédico; *(rope)* braza; *(connected staves)* corchete m; *(handle)* manija; *(bracket)* llave f, corchete m; *(posture)* postura rígida; *(of a drill)* berbiquí m; *(pair)* par <*a b. of pigeons* un par de palomas> ♦ **braces** ODONT. aparato de ortodoncia; G.B. *(suspenders)* tirantes m, tiradores m (para el pantalón) II. tr. **braced, brac·ing** *(to support)* apuntalar, reforzar; *(to hold steady)* asegurar; *(to invigorate)* fortificar, vigorizar; MARÍT. bracear; IMPR. *(to put brackets on)* poner llave ♦ **to b. oneself for** prepararse para (golpe, noticia) —intr. prepararse ♦ **to b. up** cobrar ánimo, animarse.
brace·let (brās′lĭt) s. brazalete m, pulsera.
brac·er (brā′sər) s. FAM. bebida estimulante f, reconstituyente m; ARM. brazal m.
bra·ce·ro (brə-sâr′ō) s. [pl. **-ros**] bracero, peón mexicano que entra a los EE. UU. con permiso temporario de trabajo.
brac·ing (brā′sĭng) I. adj. fortificante, vigorizante II. s. TEC. *(propping)* apuntalamiento; *(reinforcement)* refuerzo.
brack·en (brăk′ən) s. BOT. *(fern)* helecho; *(area)* helechal m.
brack·et (brăk′ĭt) I. s. *(support)* soporte m, escuadra; *(of a lamp)* brazo; *(of a roof)* ménsula; *(shelf)* repisa; *(classification)* categoría, grupo; *(square symbol)* corchete m; *(angular symbol)* paréntesis angular m II. tr. *(to support)* sujetar, asegurar con un soporte; *(to enclose)* poner entre corchetes; *(to group together)* agrupar, clasificar.
brack·ish (brăk′ĭsh) adj. *(saline)* salino, salobre; *(unpalatable)* desabrido.
bract (brăkt) s. BOT. bráctea.
brad (brăd) s. puntilla, clavito.
brag (brăg) I. intr. **bragged, brag·ging** jactarse, alardear —tr. jactarse de, hacer alarde de II. s. *(boast)* jactancia, alarde m; *(boaster)* fanfarrón m, jactancioso.
brag·ga·do·ci·o (brăg′ə-dō′sē-ō′, -shē-ō′) s. [pl. **-os**] *(boaster)* fanfarrón m, jactancioso; *(boast)* fanfarronada, jactancia.
brag·gart (brăg′ərt) s. & adj. fanfarrón m, jactancioso.
brag·ger (brăg′ər) s. fanfarrón m, jactancioso.
Brah·ma (brä′mə) s. RELIG. Brahma (dios hindú) m.
Brah·man (brä′mən) s. RELIG. brahmán m, brahmín m.
Brah·man·ism (brä′mə-nĭz′əm) s. RELIG. brahmanismo.
Brah·min (brä′mĭn) s. RELIG. brahmán m.
braid (brād) I. tr. *(to plait)* trenzar; *(to decorate)* galonear; *(to weave)* trenzar, entrelazar II. s. *(plait)* trenza; *(trim)* galón m.
Braille o **braille** (brāl) s. Braille (escritura en relieve) m.
brain (brān) I. s. ANAT. cerebro; FAM. *(intelligent person)* cerebro, genio ♦ **brains** CUL. sesos; *(intelligence)* inteligencia, cabeza; FAM. *(organizer)* cerebro • **to beat** o **to rack one's brains** devanarse los sesos • **to blow someone's brains out** levantar la tapa de los sesos a alguien II. tr. *(to smash in)* aplastar el cráneo a; JER. *(to hit on the head)* romper la crisma a.
brain child s. FAM. invento, creación f.
brain·less (brān′lĭs) adj. estúpido, descabellado.

---

ng inglés / ŏ la / ō bou / ô corre / oi oigo / ŏŏ uno / ou auto / yŏŏ ciudad / w hueco / y yo / z mismo

brain·storm (brān'stôrm') s. *(mental disturbance)* acceso de locura; *(clever idea)* inspiración *f*, idea genial.

brain trust s. grupo de consejeros.

brain·wash (brān'wŏsh') tr. FIG. lavar el cerebro.

brain·wash·ing (brān'wŏsh'ĭng) s. FIG. lavado de cerebro.

brain wave s. FISIOL. onda cerebral; FIG. *(inspiration)* idea genial, inspiración súbita *f*.

brain·y (brā'nē) adj. **-i·er, -i·est** FAM. inteligente, listo.

braise (brāz) tr. **braised, brais·ing** CUL. dorar a fuego lento en cazuela tapada.

brake (brāk) I. s. *(device)* freno; FIG. *(restraint)* freno <*to put a b. on* poner freno a> II. tr. **braked, brak·ing** frenar —intr. aplicar *o* echar el freno.

brake band s. cinta de freno.

brake drum s. tambor de freno *m*.

brake lining s. guarnición de freno *f*, forro del freno.

brake shoe s. zapata de freno.

bram·ble (brăm'bəl) s. BOT. zarzamora, cambrón *m*.

bran (brăn) s. salvado, afrecho.

branch (brănch) I. s. BOT. rama; *(division)* ramo, rama <*biology is a b. of science* la biología es una rama de la ciencia>; *(office)* sucursal *f*, agencia; *(of a family)* rama; *(of a candlestick, river)* brazo; *(creek)* arroyo; COMPUT. transferencia condicional; AUTO., F.C. ramal *m*, bifurcación *f* II. intr. *(trees)* echar ramas; *(to spread out)* ramificarse; *(to bifurcate)* bifurcarse; COMPUT. bifurcarse ♦ **to b. out** FIG. ampliar el campo de operaciones, extender las actividades.

bran·chi·a (brăng'kē-ə) s. [pl. **-chi·ae** (-kē-ē)] ZOOL. branquia, agalla.

branch office s. sucursal *f*.

brand (brănd) I. s. *(trademark)* marca (de fábrica); *(style)* modo, manera <*his novel b. of singing* su novedoso modo de cantar>; *(type)* clase *f*, tipo; *(branding iron)* hierro de marcar; *(stigma)* marca infamante, estigma; *(firebrand)* tea, tizón *m*; ANT., POÉT. *(sword)* acero, espada II. tr. *(with a hot iron)* marcar, herrar; *(to trademark)* poner la marca a; *(to stigmatize)* calificar de, tildar de.

brand·ing (brăn'dĭng) s. herradero, hierra.

branding iron s. hierro de marcar.

bran·dish (brăn'dĭsh) I. tr. *(to wave)* blandir, esgrimir; *(to flaunt)* hacer alarde de, ostentar **II.** s. ademán provocativo, movimiento desafiante.

brand-new (brănd'nōō', -nyōō') adj. flamante.

bran·dy (brăn'dē) s. [pl. **-dies**] *(cognac)* coñac *m*; *(distilled spirits)* aguardiente *m*.

brash (brăsh) adj. **-er, -est** *(rash)* impetuoso; *(impudent)* descarado, insolente.

brass (brăs) s. *(metal)* latón *m*, cobre *m*; FAM. *(effrontery)* descaro, insolencia; G.B., JER. *(money)* plata, pasta ♦ **brasses** MÚS. cobres, metales ♦ **top b.** JER. peces gordos.

brass hat s. MIL., JER. oficial de estado mayor *m*.

bras·siere (brə-zîr') s. sostén *m*, corpiño.

brass knuckles s.pl. manopla.

brass tacks s.pl. FIG., FAM. ♦ **to get down to b.** ir al grano.

brass·y (brăs'ē) adj. **-i·er, -i·est** *(of brass)* de latón; *(said of color)* de color de cobre; *(sound)* metálico; *(flashy)* llamativo, chillón; FAM. *(impudent)* desvergonzado, descarado.

brat (brăt) s. niño malcriado, mocoso.

brat·tle (brăt'l) I. intr. **-tled, -tling** traquetear II. s. traqueteo.

bra·va·do (brə-vä'dō) s. [pl. **-does** *o* **-dos**] bravata, baladronada.

brave (brāv) I. adj. **brav·er, brav·est** *(courageous)* valiente, bravo; *(splendid)* magnífico, espléndido <*a b. performance* una magnífica actuación>; ANT. *(excellent)* bravo, excelente II. s. *(Indian warrior)* guerrero indio; *(courageous person)* valiente *mf* III. tr. **braved, brav·ing** *(to face)* arrostrar, afrontar; *(to defy)* desafiar.

brave·ly (brāv'lē) adv. *(courageously)* valientemente, bravamente; *(splendidly)* magníficamente, espléndidamente.

brav·er·y (brā'və-rē) s. [pl. **-ies**] valentía, valor *m*.

bra·vo (brä'vō, brä-vō') interj. ¡bravo!

bra·vu·ra (brə-vōōr'ə, -vyōōr'ə) s. *(performance)* ejecución brillante *f*; *(manner)* arrojo, brío.

brawl (brôl) I. s. *(quarrel)* pelea, disputa; JER. *(party)* fiesta ruidosa II. intr. pelear, disputar.

brawl·er (brô'lər) s. peleador *m*, camorrista *mf*.

brawn (brôn) s. *(muscles)* músculos; *(strength)* fuerza muscular; G.B. *(headcheese)* queso de cerdo.

brawn·y (brô'nē) adj. **-i·er, -i·est** musculoso.

bray¹ (brā) I. s. *(of a donkey)* rebuzno; *(sound)* sonido ronco II. intr. rebuznar ♦ **to b. out** sonar roncamente —tr. decir con voz ronca.

bray² (brā) tr. *(to crush)* triturar, moler; *(to ink)* entintar.

braze¹ (brāz) tr. **brazed, braz·ing** *(to decorate)* adornar con bronce; *(to harden)* endurecer.

braze² (brāz) tr. **brazed, braz·ing** TEC. soldar (en fuerte).

bra·zen (brā'zən) I. adj. *(impudent)* descarado; *(resonant)* bronco; *(brassy)* de latón II. tr. ♦ **to b. out** afrontar descaradamente.

bra·zier (brā'zhər) s. brasero.

Bra·zil (brə-zĭl') Brasil *m*.

Bra·zil·ian (brə-zĭl'yən) adj. & s. brasileño.

Brazil nut s. nuez del Brasil *f*.

bra·zil·wood (brə-zĭl'wōōd') s. palo brasil.

breach (brēch) I. s. *(of a law)* violación *f*, infracción *f*; *(of a promise)* incumplimiento; *(hole)* brecha, abertura; *(estrangement)* ruptura, rompimiento (de relaciones); *(leap)* salto (de una ballena); *(of waves)* rompimiento; ANT. *(wound)* desgarramiento II. tr. *(to make a hole)* abrir una brecha en; *(to violate)* violar, quebrantar —intr. saltar fuera del agua (la ballena).

breach of promise s. DER. incumplimiento de un compromiso.

bread (brĕd) I. s. *(food)* pan *m*; JER. *(money)* plata, pasta ♦ **to break b.** *(to eat)* hincar el diente; *(to share)* compartir la comida II. tr. CUL. empanar.

bread and butter s. FAM. pan de cada día *m*.

bread-and-but·ter (brĕd'n-bŭt'ər) adj. corriente <*a b. job* un trabajo corriente>; *(expressing gratitude)* de agradecimiento.

bread·bas·ket (brĕd'băs'kĭt) s. *(basket)* panera; FIG. *(region)* granero; JER. *(stomach)* panza, barriga.

bread·board (brĕd'bôrd') s. tabla para cortar pan.

bread crumb s. *(bit)* migaja de pan; CUL. pan rallado.

bread·fruit (brĕd'frōōt') s. *(tree)* árbol del pan *m; (fruit)* fruto del árbol del pan.

bread line s. cola para recibir alimentos gratis.

bread·stuff (brĕd'stŭf') s. *(bread)* pan *m; (flour)* harina; *(grain)* cereales *m*, granos.

breadth (brĕdth) s. *(dimension)* anchura, ancho; *(scope)* extensión *f*, envergadura; *(openness)* liberalidad *f*; COST. *(width)* paño, ancho de tela.

breadth·wise (brĕdth'wīz') *o* **breadth·ways** (-wāz') I. adv. a lo ancho II. adj. de ancho.

bread·win·ner (brĕd'wĭn'ər) s. sostén de la familia *m*.

break (brāk) I. tr. **broke** (brōk), **bro·ken** (brō'kən), **break·ing** *(to smash)* romper <*the boy broke the window* el niño rompió la ventana>; *(to crack)* quebrar, fracturar; *(to damage)* estropear, descomponer; *(to put an end to)* romper <*the owner broke the strike by hiring new personnel* el dueño rompió la huelga tomando nuevo personal>; *(to disobey)* infringir, violar (ley, precepto); *(to interrupt abruptly)* interrumpir, romper <*a cry broke the silence* un grito rompió el silencio>; *(to fail to keep)* romper (cita, compromiso); *(to call off)* cancelar; *(to tame)* domar, amansar (caballos); *(to destroy the completeness of)* truncar, deshacer (juego de libros, muebles); *(to lessen in force)* amortiguar, parar (golpe, caída); *(to weaken morally)* abatir, destrozar (moralmente); *(to make bankrupt)* arruinar, causar quiebra *o* bancarrota; *(to reduce in rank)* degradar <*the sergeant was broken for neglect of duty* al sargento lo degradaron por abandono de sus obligaciones>; *(to reduce money to smaller units)* cambiar (un billete); *(to surpass)* batir, quebrar (un record); *(to make known)* dar, comunicar (noticias); *(to decipher)* descifrar, resolver; *(to invalidate)* anular, invalidar (testamento); ELEC. interrumpir, cortar ♦ **to b. down** *(to analyze)* detallar, pormenorizar; *(to destroy)* derrumbar ♦ **to b. for** hacer una pausa para <*can we b. for lunch?* ¿podemos hacer una pausa para almorzar?> • **to b. ground** *(in construction)* comenzar a construir un edificio; *(to lead the way)* abrir el camino • **to b. in** *(to make comfortable)* amoldar *(zapatos)*; *(to train)* entrenar • **to b. into** *(to enter)* entrar forzadamente (con intención de robar, dañar); *(to interrupt)* interrumpir; *(to begin suddenly)* prorrumpir en, echarse a • **to b. off** *(to detach)* romper, separar; *(to suspend)* suspender, discontinuar *(sesión, discusión)* • **to b. one's back** romperse el alma • **to b. oneself of a habit** quitarse una costumbre, librarse de un hábito • **to b. one's neck** *(physical sense)* desnucarse; *(to do the utmost)* romperse el alma • **to b. open** abrir forzando, forzar • **to b. out** abrir (esp. champaña) • **to b. someone's heart** partirle el corazón a alguien • **to b. the bank** hacer saltar la banca (en juegos de azar) • **to b. the ice** romper el hielo • **to b. up** *(to crumble)* desmenuzar; *(to put an end to)* acabar, terminar; *(to upset)* quebrantar, apesadumbrar; *(with laughter)* hacer morir de risa • **to b. (up) with** romper con (una relación) —intr. *(to shatter)* romperse <*glass breaks easily* el vidrio se rompe fácilmente>; *(to come apart)* partirse; *(to become unusable)* estropearse, descomponerse <*the typewriter broke* se descompuso la máquina de escribir>; *(to decline abruptly)* ceder, bajar <*his fever broke* le bajó la fiebre>; *(to disperse)* dispersarse (la multitud); *(to dash suddenly)* arrancar, echarse a correr; *(to dawn)* apuntar, rayar (el día); *(to appear suddenly)* emerger; *(to be crushed)* partirse, romperse <*his heart broke when she died* se le partió el corazón cuando ella murió>; *(to change in pitch)* fallar (la voz); *(to come suddenly)* estallar <*the storm broke within five minutes* a los cinco minutos estalló la tormenta>; *(to become weak)* debilitarse, decaer; *(to become bankrupt)* quebrar, arruinarse; *(to stop)* quebrarse, interrumpirse; *(to burst)* abrirse, reventarse (abscesos, granos); *(to become known)* divulgarse, revelarse; COM. bajar (los precios); DEP. separarse (los púgiles) ♦ **to b. away** *(to withdraw)* separarse; *(to escape)* escaparse; *(to start suddenly)* arrancar, arremeter • **to b. away from** romper con, abandonar (partido político, costumbres) • **to b. down** *(to malfunction)* averiarse, descomponerse; *(to become weak)* debilitarse, desmejorarse; *(to become distressed)* abatirse, derrumbarse (moralmente); *(to begin to cry)* prorrumpir en llanto • **to b. even** salir sin ganar o perder • **to b. in** *(to enter)* entrar forzadamente (con intención de robar, dañar); *(to burst in)* irrumpir; *(to interrupt)* interrumpir • **to b. loose** *(to become detached)* soltarse, desprenderse; *(to escape)* escaparse; *(to happen suddenly)* desencadenarse (tormenta), FIG., JER. *(to go on a spree)* desmandarse • **to b. off** *(to become detached)* soltarse, desprenderse; *(to stop)* pararse, detenerse <*he broke off in the middle of his speech to clear his throat* se detuvo en la mitad del discurso para aclararse la garganta> • **to b. out** *(to escape)* escaparse; *(to spring up)* estallar <*a fire broke out in our building* estalló un incendio en nuestro edificio>; *(to develop a rash)* salirle a uno (sarpullido, manchas) • **to b. through** atravesar, abrirse paso • **to b. up** *(to end)* acabarse, terminarse (partido, reunión); *(to split up)* separarse (una relación); *(to scatter)* dispersarse, levantarse <*the fog is breaking up* se está levantando la niebla> **II. s.** *(act)* ruptura, rompimiento; *(fracture)* fractura; *(crack)* grieta, raja; *(gap)* abertura; *(opening in clouds)* claro (en las nubes); *(change)* cambio, interrupción *f*; *(pause)* intervalo, pausa; *(sudden dash)* salida, arrancada; *(escape)* fuga, evasión *f*; *(marked change)* cambio (de tiempo); FAM. *(unexpected occurrence)* coyuntura, casualidad *f* <*a lucky b.* una coyuntura feliz>; POÉT. cesura, pausa; COM. baja (de precios, valores); MÚS. *(in singing)* gallo, nota falsa; *(solo)* solo, improvisación (en jazz) *f*; DEP. separación (de los boxeadores) *f*; IMPR. puntos suspensivos; ELEC. interrupción, corte *m* ♦ **at the b. of day** al amanecer • **to give someone a b.** dar una oportunidad a alguien • **to take a b.** descansar • **without a b.** parar.

break·a·ble (brā′kə-bəl) adj. quebradizo, frágil ♦ **breakables** objetos frágiles.

break·age (brā′kĭj) s. *(act)* rotura, rompimiento; *(quantity)* objetos rotos *m*; *(loss)* daños de rotura *m*; *(allowance)* indemnización por objetos rotos *f*.

break·down (brāk′doun′) s. *(malfunction)* avería, desperfecto; *(interruption)* interrupción *f*; *(failure)* fracaso; *(collapse)* colapso, depresión <*nervous b.* depresión nerviosa>; *(analysis)* análisis *m*; *(outline)* clasificación *f*; *(detail)* desglose *m* <*b. of costs* desglose de los costos>; ELEC. corte *m*; QUÍM. descomposición *f*.

break·er (brā′kər) s. *(person)* rompedor *m*, quebrador *m*; *(machine)* quebrantador *m*, trituradora; *(electric switch)* interruptor automático; *(wave)* cachón *m*.

break·fast (brĕk′fəst) **I. s.** desayuno **II. intr.** desayunar, tomar el desayuno.

break-in (brāk′ĭn′) s. *(entry)* allanamiento, entrada forzada (con fines ilícitos); *(training)* aprendizaje *m*; *(testing period)* periodo de prueba.

breaking point s. punto de ruptura, punto límite.

break·neck (brāk′nĕk′) adj. *(dangerous)* peligroso, arriesgado; *(rapid)* rápido.

break·through (brāk′thrōō′) s. *(penetration)* penetración *f*; *(achievement)* adelanto, progreso; MIL. ruptura.

break·up (brāk′ŭp′) s. *(separation)* separacion *f*; *(division)* división *f*; *(disintegration)* desintegración *f* <*the b. of a union* la desintegración de un sindicato>.

break·wa·ter (brāk′wô′tər) s. rompeolas *m*.

breast (brĕst) **I. s.** *(upper body)* pecho; *(of a woman)* pecho, seno; ZOOL. *(udder)* teta; *(of a fowl)* pechuga; FIG. *(bosom)* pecho; *(heart)* corazón *m*; *(of a hill)* repecho; ARM. *(breastplate)* peto ♦ **to beat one's b.** darse golpes de pecho • **to make a clean b. of it** confesar (algo) **II. tr.** *(to face)* arrostrar, afrontar; *(to advance)* abrirse paso entre.

breast·bone (brĕst′bōn′) s. esternón *m*.

breast-feed (brĕst′fēd′) tr. **-fed** (-fĕd′), **-feed·ing** amamantar, dar el pecho a.

breast stroke s. DEP. brazada de pecho.

breast·work (brĕst′wûrk′) s. FORT. parapeto.

breath (brĕth) s. *(air)* respiración *f*, aliento; *(breathing)* respiración; *(ability to breathe)* resuello <*running fast made him lose his b.* el correr ligero le hizo perder el resuello>; *(inhalation)* inhalación *f*; *(exhalation)* exhalación *f*; *(of an animal)* hálito; *(light breeze)* soplo (de aire); *(respite)* respiro, pausa; *(hint)* indicio <*a b. of suspicion hung around him* un indicio de sospecha flotaba a su alrededor>; FIG., POÉT. *(moment)* momento, instante *m* ♦ **b. of life** soplo de vida • **in one b.** de un tirón, de una vez • **in the same b.** al mismo tiempo, en el mismo tiempo • **last b.** último suspiro • **to be out of b.** estar o quedar sin aliento • **to be short of b.** estar corto de resuello, faltarle el aire a uno • **to catch one's b.** recobrar el aliento • **to gasp for b.** jadear • **to get one's b. back** recobrar el aliento • **to hold one's b.** contener el aliento • **to save one's b.** ahorrar palabras • **to take one's b. away** *(to leave breathless)* dejar sin resuello; *(to astonish)* dejar pasmado • **under one's b.** en voz baja • **to waste one's b.** gastar saliva en balde.

breathe (brĕth) intr. **breathed**, **breath·ing** *(to inhale)* respirar; *(to live)* respirar, vivir; *(to blow)* soplar suavemente; *(to give out)* emitir, emanar; *(to pause)* respirar, descansar —tr. *(to inhale)* respirar; *(to impart)* infundir, insuflar <*to b. life into a portrait* infundir vida a un retrato>; *(to exhale)* dar, emitir; *(to whisper)* susurrar, decir <*I did not b. a word* no dije ni una palabra>; *(to allow to rest)* dar una tregua a ♦ **to b. in** inhalar, aspirar • **to b. one's last** exhalar el último suspiro • **to b. out** exhalar.

breath·er (brē′thər) s. FAM. respiro, pausa.

breath·ing (brē′thĭng) s. *(respiration)* respiración *f*; GRAM. *(mark)* espíritu *m* ♦ **b. space** respiro, pausa.

breath·less (brĕth′lĭs) adj. *(without breath)* sin aliento, falto de aliento; *(dead)* sin vida, exánime; *(panting)* jadeante; *(amazed)* sin resuello, pasmado; *(stifling)* sofocante; *(exciting)* intenso.

breath·tak·ing (brĕth′tā′kĭng) adj. *(amazing)* asombroso; *(exciting)* emocionante; *(impressive)* impresionante, imponente <*a b. landscape* un paisaje impresionante>.

breath·y (brĕth′ē) adj. **-i·er**, **-i·est** velado (voz, sonido).

bred (brĕd) pret. y part. p. de **breed**.

breech (brēch) s. *(buttocks)* nalgas, trasero; *(of a pulley)* rabera; *(of a firearm)* recámara, culata ♦ **breeches** (brĭch′ĭz) *(knee breeches)* calzones; FAM. *(trousers)* pantalones.

---

ng inglés / ŏ la / ō bou / ô corre / oi oigo / ōō uno / ou auto / yōō ciudad / w hueco / y yo / z mismo

breech·cloth (brĕch′klôth′) *o* **breech·clout** (-klout′) s. taparrabo.

breech·load·er (brĕch′lō′dər) s. arma de retrocarga.

breed (brēd) **I.** tr. **bred** (brĕd), **breed·ing** *(to procreate)* procrear; *(to engender)* engendrar, producir; *(to raise)* criar *<he makes a living breeding dogs* se gana la vida criando perros>; *(to crossbreed)* cruzar; *(to graft)* injertar; *(to rear)* criar, educar *<he was born and bred a Catholic* nació y se educó católico> —intr. *(to procreate)* procrear, reproducirse; *(to originate)* engendrarse **II.** s. *(strain)* raza; *(type)* casta, especie f.

breed·er (brē′dər) s. *(person)* criador m; *(animal)* reproductor m, semental m.

breeder reactor s. FÍS. reactor reproductor m.

breed·ing (brē′dĭng) s. *(ancestry)* raza, descendencia; *(background)* clase f; *(training)* crianza f, educación f; *(reproduction)* cría, reproducción f.

breeze (brēz) **I.** s. *(wind)* brisa; G.B., FAM. *(commotion)* alboroto; FAM. *(easy task)* paseo, papa *<the climb was a b.* la subida fue un paseo> **II.** intr. **breezed, breez·ing** *(to blow)* soplar débilmente; FAM. *(to do effortlessly)* despachar, hacer fácilmente ♦ **to b. in** entrar alegremente ♦ **to b. through** hojear, repasar por encima.

breeze·way (brēz′wā′) s. pasaje (abierto a los costados y techado, entre dos edificios) m.

breez·y (brē′zē) adj. **-i·er, -i·est** *(windy)* ventoso; *(lively)* alegre, jovial; *(not serious)* despreocupado.

Brem·en (brĕm′ən, brā′mən) s. Brema.

breth·ren (brĕth′rən) s. ANT. pl. de **brother.**

Bret·on (brĕt′n) adj. & s. *(inhabitant, language)* bretón m.

breve (brēv) s. FONÉT., MÚS. breve f.

bre·vi·ar·y (brē′vē-ĕr′ē, brĕv′ē-) s. [pl. **-ies**] breviario.

brev·i·ty (brĕv′ĭ-tē) s. brevedad f.

brew (brōō) **I.** tr. *(beer)* fabricar, elaborar (esp. cerveza); *(to boil)* preparar, hacer (esp. té); *(to devise)* tramar, urdir —intr. *(to make beer)* fabricar cerveza; *(to be imminent)* formarse, amenazar *<a storm brewing in the distance* una tormenta amenazando a lo lejos> **II.** s. *(beverage)* brebaje m, infusión f; FAM. *(beer)* cerveza.

brew·er (brōō′ər) s. cervecero.

brewer's yeast s. levadura de cerveza.

brew·er·y (brōō′ə-rē) s. [pl. **-ies**] cervecería.

brew·ing (brōō′ĭng) s. *(of tea)* infusión f; *(of beer)* ocupación *o* procedimiento de hacer cerveza.

bri·ar (brī′ər) s. BOT. *(shrub)* brezo, zarza; *(pipe)* pipa de madera de brezo.

bribe (brīb) **I.** s. soborno ♦ **to take bribes** dejarse sobornar **II.** tr. **bribed, brib·ing** sobornar.

brib·er·y (brī′bə-rē) s. [pl. **-ies**] soborno.

bric-a-brac (brĭk′ə-brăk′) s. *(curiosities)* curiosidades f; *(knickknacks)* baratijas.

brick (brĭk) **I.** s. CONSTR. ladrillo; *(bricklike object)* pedazo, trozo; *(of gold)* lingote m; *(of ice)* bloque m **II.** tr. *(to construct with bricks)* hacer de ladrillos; *(to pave)* enladrillar; *(to close with brick)* tapiar con ladrillos.

brick·bat (brĭk′băt′) s. *(piece of brick)* trozo de ladrillo; *(criticism)* crítica cortante, pulla.

brick·lay·er (brĭk′lā′ər) s. albañil m.

brick·work (brĭk′wûrk′) s. enladrillado, ladrillos m.

bri·dal (brīd′l) **I.** s. boda, casamiento **II.** adj. nupcial ♦ **b. gown** traje de boda.

bride (brīd) s. novia, desposada.

bride·groom (brīd′grōōm′, -grŏŏm′) s. novio, desposado.

brides·maid (brīdz′mād′) s. dama de honor.

bridge (brĭj) **I.** s. *(structure)* puente m; *(of the nose)* caballete m; *(of an instrument)* puente; MARÍT., ODONT. puente ♦ **suspension b.** puente colgante ♦ **to burn one's bridges** quemar las naves **II.** tr. **bridged, bridg·ing** *(to build)* tender un puente sobre; *(to span)* extenderse a través de *<his life bridged three generations* su vida se extendió a través de tres generaciones> ♦ **to b. the gap** *(to reach an understanding)* salvar las diferencias; *(to satisfy a need)* llenar un vacío.

bridge² (brĭj) s. *(card game)* bridge m.

bridge·work (brĭj′wûrk′) s. *(dental bridge)* puente m; *(construction)* construcción de puente f.

bridg·ing (brĭj′ĭng) s. ARQ. puntales m.

bri·dle (brīd′l) **I.** s. *(harness)* brida; *(restraint)* freno **II.** tr. **-dled, -dling** *(to put a bridle on)* embridar; *(to restrain)* refrenar, dominar —intr. *(to bristle)* erguirse desdeñosamente; *(to take offense)* picarse *<she bridled at the criticism* se picó por la crítica>.

bridle path s. camino de herradura.

brief (brēf) **I.** adj. **-er, -est** *(in time, duration)* breve; *(in length)* corto *<a b. skirt* una falda corta>; *(succinct)* conciso; *(curt)* brusco **II.** s. *(short statement)* informe m; *(summary)* sumario, resumen m; DER. expediente m ♦ **briefs** calzoncillos • **in b.** en resumen, en pocas palabras **III.** tr. *(to give instructions)* dar instrucciones; *(to inform)* informar; *(to summarize)* resumir.

brief·case (brēf′kās′) s. portafolio, cartera.

brief·ing (brē′fĭng) s. *(act)* reunión de información f; *(information)* información f.

brief·ly (brēf′lē) adv. *(in a short time)* brevemente; *(succinctly)* concisamente; *(in short)* en resumen, en pocas palabras.

bri·er (brī′ər) s. var. de **briar.**

brig (brĭg) s. MARÍT. *(ship)* bergantín m; MIL., FAM. *(prison)* calabozo.

bri·gade (brĭ-gād′) s. brigada.

brig·a·dier (brĭg′ə-dîr′) s. MIL. general de brigada m.

brigadier general s. [pl. **brigadier generals**] MIL. general de brigada m.

brig·and (brĭg′ənd) s. bandido, bandolero.

brig·an·tine (brĭg′ən-tēn′) s. bergantín m.

bright (brīt) **I.** adj. **-er, -est** *(shining)* brillante, resplandeciente; *(intense)* subido, vivo *<a b. red* un rojo subido>; *(sunlit)* luminoso; *(quick-witted)* ingenioso *<he made a b. remark* hizo un comentario ingenioso>; *(smart)* inteligente, despierto; *(happy)* alegre; *(promising)* prometedor, brillante **II.** s. ♦ **brights** AUTO. luces altas *o* de carretera **III.** adv. brillantemente.

bright·en (brīt′n) tr. *(to make bright)* aclarar, iluminar; *(to make happy)* alegrar, animar —intr. *(to become bright)* aclararse, iluminarse; *(to become happy)* alegrarse, animarse.

bright·ness (brīt′nĭs) s. *(quality)* claridad f, brillantez f; *(degree)* intensidad luminosa, luminosidad f.

bril·liance (brĭl′yəns) *o* **bril·lian·cy** (-yən-sē) s. brillo, brillantez (de luz, color, inteligencia) f.

bril·liant (brĭl′yənt) **I.** adj. *(shining)* brillante; *(vivid)* vivo; *(inventive)* genial; *(successful)* arrollador, clamoroso **II.** s. *(gem)* brillante m.

bril·lian·tine (brĭl′yən-tēn′) s. *(hair-dressing)* brillantina; *(fabric)* brillantina, percalina de lustre.

brim (brĭm) **I.** s. *(of a cup)* borde m; *(of a hat)* ala; *(shore)* orilla **II.** tr. **brimmed, brim·ming** llenar hasta el tope —intr. estar lleno hasta el tope ♦ **to b. over** desbordarse, rebosar.

brim·ful (brĭm′fŏŏl′) adj. lleno hasta el tope.

brine (brīn) **I.** s. *(salty water)* salmuera; *(ocean water)* agua de mar; *(sea)* mar mf **II.** tr. **brined, brin·ing** poner en salmuera.

bring (brĭng) tr. **brought** (brôt), **bring·ing** *(to take with oneself)* traer *<I brought you these flowers* te traje estas flores>; *(to escort, carry)* conducir, llevar; *(to yield)* producir, rendir *<diamonds always b. high prices* los diamantes siempre rinden buenos precios>; *(to persuade)* persuadir, convencer *<the president was brought to accept the plan* lo convencieron al presidente para que aceptara el plan>; *(to put forward)* hacer, formular *<to b. charges* formular cargos> ♦ **brought forward** COM. suma y sigue • **to b. about** *(to effect)* efectuar, realizar *<to b. about a change* realizar un cambio>; *(to cause)* causar, provocar • **to b. around** *(to restore to consciousness)* revivir, hacer volver en sí; *(to persuade)* convencer, persuadir • **to b. back** *(to return)* devolver *<did she b. back your camera?* ¿te devolvió la cámara?>; *(to call to mind)* hacer recordar, traer (a la mente); *(to cause to return)* traer de vuelta • **to b. before** encomendar a, someter a • **to b. down** *(to lower)* bajar, hacer bajar; *(to cause to fall)* tumbar, abatir; *(to overthrow)* derribar • **to b. down the house** tirar abajo el teatro con

aplausos • **to b. forth** *(to bear)* producir (frutos); *(to reveal)* poner de manifiesto, deparar • **to b. forward** COM. llevar un saldo a otra cuenta; *(to cite as evidence)* poner de manifiesto; *(to present)* presentar • **to b. home** demostrar *o* dar a entender claramente <*her eloquence helped her b. the idea home* su elocuencia le ayudó a demostrar claramente su idea> • **to b. home the bacon** FAM. ganar el pan • **to b. in** *(to introduce)* presentar, introducir (queja, cuenta); *(to show in)* hacer entrar, hacer pasar; *(to harvest)* recoger; *(to make money)* rendir, producir; DER. *(to announce officially)* pronunciar <*the jury brought in the verdict of guilty* el jurado pronunció el veredicto de culpable>; *(to arrest)* arrestar • **to b. into play** poner en juego • **to b. off** *(to carry out successfully)* conseguir, lograr hacer <*he brought off a good business deal* logró hacer un buen arreglo comercial> • **to b. on** ocasionar, causar <*his bad cold brought on pneumonia* su resfrío fuerte le causó neumonía> • **to b. oneself to** resignarse a • **to b. out** *(to offer to the public)* presentar; *(to society)* presentar en sociedad (a una debutante); *(to highlight)* hacer resaltar, poner de manifiesto (cualidades); *(to reveal)* revelar, mostrar • **to b. suit** DER. entablar un pleito • **to b. to** *(to revive)* reanimar, hacer volver en sí • **to b. to bear** aplicar, utilizar <*he brought his influence to bear* utilizó su influencia> • **to b. to light** revelar, sacar a la luz • **to b. to mind** recordar • **to b. to terms** hacer ceder, obligar a convenir • **to b. together** reconciliar • **to b. up** *(to care for in childhood)* criar, educar; *(to suggest for action, discussion)* plantear, traer a colación; *(to vomit)* vomitar • **to b. upon oneself** buscarse, acarrearse.
brink (brĭngk) s. *(edge)* borde *m*; *(margin)* margen *f* ♦ **on the b. of** a punto de <*on the b. of jumping* a punto de saltar>.
brink·man·ship (brĭngk′mən-shĭp′) s. POL. política arriesgada.
brin·y (brī′nē) I. adj. **-i·er, -i·est** salobre, salado II. s. FAM. el mar.
bri·o (brē′ō) s. brío, vigor *m*.
bri·quette *o* **bri·quet** (brĭ-kĕt′) s. briqueta, comprimido de carbón.
brisk (brĭsk) adj. **-er, -est** *(energetic)* enérgico, vigoroso; *(invigorating)* estimulante; *(sharp)* frío <*a b. greeting* un recibimiento frío>; *(zestful)* sabroso <*a b. tea* un té sabroso>.
bris·ket (brĭs′kĭt) s. falda (de una res).
bris·tle (brĭs′əl) I. s. cerda II. intr. **-tled, -tling** *(to react angrily)* erizarse; *(to have one's hair stand up)* ponerse los pelos de punta ♦ **to b. with** estar lleno *o* erizado de —tr. *(to stiffen)* erizar, poner de punta; *(to put bristles on)* poner cerdas a; *(to disturb)* agitar.
bris·tly (brĭs′lē) adj. *(with bristles)* cerdoso; *(stiff)* erizado.
Brit·ain (brĭt′n) s. Gran Bretaña.
Bri·tan·nia (brĭ-tăn′yə) s. Britania ♦ **b.** britannia (amalgama de metales).
britch·es (brĭch′ĭz) s.pl. FAM. pantalones *m* ♦ **too big for one's b.** FAM. arrogante, engreído.
Brit·i·cism (brĭt′ĭ-sĭz′əm) s. expresión inglesa propia de Inglaterra (a diferencia de EE. UU.).
Brit·ish (brĭt′ĭsh) I. adj. británico, inglés II. s. [ú. con v. pl.] inglés *m* ♦ **the B.** los ingleses.
Brit·ish·er (brĭt′ĭ-shər) s. británico, inglés *m*.
British Isles s. GEOG. Islas Británicas.
British thermal unit s. unidad de calor británica.
Brit·ish·ism (brĭt′ĭ-shĭz′əm) s. var. de **Briticism**.
British thermal unit s. unidad térmica británica.
Brit·on (brĭt′n) s. británico.
Brit·ta·ny (brĭt′n-ē) s. Bretaña.
brit·tle (brĭt′l) I. adj. **-tler, -tlest** *(fragile)* quebradizo, frágil; *(snappish)* irritable II. s. caramelo de nueces.
broach (brōch) I. s. *(tool)* escariador *m*; *(spit)* espetón *m*, brocheta; *(of a drill)* mecha, broca; *(brooch)* broche *m* II. tr. *(to begin to discuss)* abordar, sacar a colación <*to b. a subject* abordar un tema>; *(to announce)* dar a conocer; *(a cask)* espitar; *(a hole)* escariar.
broad (brôd) I. adj. **-er, -est** *(wide)* ancho; *(spacious)* extenso, amplio; *(clear)* pleno <*in b. daylight* en pleno día>; *(general)* general; *(essential)* esencial, principal <*the b.*

outline of the problem los rasgos esenciales de la cuestión>; *(obvious)* evidente, claro <*a b. clue* un indicio evidente>; *(tolerant)* liberal, de miras amplias; *(open)* abierto, jovial <*a b. smile* una sonrisa jovial>; *(strong)* marcado, pronunciado <*a b. accent* un acento marcado>; FONÉT. abierto II. s. *(broad part)* parte ancha, ancho; JER. *(woman)* mina, fulana III. adv. plenamente, completamente.
broad·cast (brôd′kăst′) I. tr. **-cast** *o* **-cast·ed, -cast·ing** RAD. emitir, radiar; TELEV. transmitir, televisar; *(to make known)* difundir, divulgar; AGR. *(to sow)* sembrar a voleo —intr. RAD. emitir, radiar un programa; TELEV. transmitir, televisar un programa II. s. RAD., TELEV. *(transmission)* transmisión *f*, emisión *f*; *(program)* programa *m* III. adj. *(by radio)* radiodifundido; *(by television)* televisado; *(scattered)* difundido.
broad·cast·er (brôd′kăs′tər) s. RAD., TELEV. *(person)* locutor *m*; *(station)* estación radiodifusora *o* de televisión.
broad·cast·ing (brôd′kăs′tĭng) s. *(by radio)* radiodifusión *f*; *(by television)* transmisión *f*, difusión *f*.
broad·cloth (brôd′klôth′) s. *(woolen cloth)* paño fino de lana; *(cotton)* paño de tejido denso.
broad·en (brôd′n) tr. & intr. ensanchar(se), ampliar(se).
broad jump s. DEP. salto de longitud.
broad·loom (brôd′lōōm′) I. adj. tejido en telar ancho II. s. alfombra ancha.
broad·ly (brôd′lē) adv. *(in general)* en general; *(widely)* ampliamente.
broad·mind·ed (brôd′mīn′dĭd) adj. tolerante, comprensivo.
broad·side (brôd′sīd′) I. s. *(of a ship)* costado; *(guns)* batería del costado; *(firing)* andanada, descarga; FIG. *(verbal attack)* andanada, retahíla (de insultos); IMPR. pliego suelto II. adv. de costado.
broad·spec·trum (brôd′spĕk′trəm) adj. de aplicaciones múltiples.
Broad·way (brôd′wā′) I. s. Broadway (calle de Nueva York y centro teatral de esa ciudad) II. adj. de Broadway.
bro·cade (brō-kād′) I. s. brocado II. tr. **-cad·ed, -cad·ing** decorar con brocado.
broc·co·li (brŏk′ə-lē) s. brécol *m*, brócoli *m*.
bro·chette (brō-shĕt′) s. broqueta, asador *m*.
bro·chure (brō-shŏŏr′) s. folleto.
broc·o·li (brŏk′ə-lē) s. var. de **broccoli**.
brogue (brōg) s. *(heavy shoe)* zapato grueso; *(accent)* acento regional (esp. el irlandés).
broil¹ (broil) I. tr. *(to cook)* cocinar a la parrilla; FIG. *(to expose to heat)* asar, tostar —intr. asarse, tostarse II. s. asado *o* carne asada a la parrilla.
broil² (broil) I. s. *(brawl)* pelea; *(argument)* discusión *f*, disputa II. intr. pelearse.
broil·er (broi′lər) s. *(grill)* parrilla; *(oven)* horno; *(chicken)* pollo tierno (para asar).
broke (brōk) I. pret. de **break** II. adj. JER. pelado, sin un centavo.
bro·ken (brō′kən) I. part. p. de **break** II. adj. *(shattered)* roto; *(out of order)* roto; *(violated)* violado, quebrantado; *(spoken imperfectly)* chapurreado, mal pronunciado; *(weakened)* decaído, quebrantado <*b. health* salud quebrantada>; *(overwhelmed)* abatido; *(tamed)* domado, amansado (caballo); *(interrupted)* interrumpido <*b. sleep* sueño interrumpido>; *(bankrupt)* en bancarrota; *(not continuous)* quebrado <*b. line* línea quebrada>; *(not complete)* incompleto <*a b. set of books* una colección incompleta de libros>; *(uneven)* desparejo, accidentado (terreno); *(subdued)* sumiso <*a b. spirit* un espíritu sumiso>; *(crushed)* destrozado <*a b. heart* un corazón destrozado>.
bro·ken-down (brō′kən-doun′) adj. *(infirm)* decrépito; *(out of order)* roto.
bro·ken-heart·ed (brō′kən-här′tĭd) adj. con el corazón destrozado.
bro·ker (brō′kər) COM. I. s. *(agent)* agente *mf*, comisionista *mf*; *(stockbroker)* corredor de bolsa *m* II. tr. gestionar negocios ajenos.
bro·ker·age (brō′kər-ĭj) s. COM. corretaje *m*.

bro·mide (brō'mīd') s. QUÍM. bromuro; FIG. *(platitude)* trivialidad *f*; *(bore)* pelmazo.
bro·mine (brō'mēn') s. QUÍM. bromo.
bron·chi (brŏng'kī) pl. de **bronchus.**
bron·chi·a (brŏng'kē-ə) pl. de **bronchium.**
bron·chi·al (brŏng'kē-əl) adj. bronquial.
bronchial tube s. bronquio.
bron·chi·tis (brŏng-kī'tĭs) s. bronquitis *f.*
bron·chi·um (brŏng'kē-əm) s. [pl. **-chi·a** (-kē-ə)] bronquio.
bron·cho·pneu·mon·ia (brŏng'kō-nōō-mōn'yə, -nyōō-) s. bronconeumonía.
bron·chus (brŏng'kəs) s. [pl. **-chi** (-kī)] ANAT. bronquio.
bron·co (brŏng'kō) s. [pl. **-cos**] mustango, potro cerril.
bron·to·saur (brŏn'tə-sôr') o **bron·to·sau·rus** (-sôr'əs) s. ZOOL. brontosaurio.
bronze (brŏnz) I. s. *(alloy, artwork)* bronce *m*; *(color)* color de bronce *m* II. adj. *(made of bronze)* de bronce; *(color)* bronceado III. tr. **bronzed, bronz·ing** broncear.
brooch (brōch, brōoch) s. broche *m.*
brood (brōod) I. s. *(young birds)* nidada; *(children)* progenie *f*, prole *f* II. tr. *(to incubate)* empollar, incubar; *(to protect)* proteger, amparar —intr. *(to incubate)* empollar; *(to ponder)* cavilar ♦ **to b. on** *u* **over** cernerse sobre III. adj. de cría.
brood·er (brōo'dər) s. *(thinker)* pensador *m*, meditador *m*; *(hen)* gallina clueca; *(enclosure)* incubadora.
brook¹ (brōok) s. arroyo.
brook² (brōok) tr. tolerar, aguantar.
brook·let (brōok'lĭt) s. arroyuelo.
broom (brōom, brōom) I. s. *(brush)* escoba; BOT. retama, hiniesta II. tr. barrer.
broom·stick (brōom'stĭk', brōom'-) s. palo de escoba.
broth (brôth) s. [pl. **broths** (brôths, brô*th*z)] CUL. caldo.
broth·el (brŏth'əl) s. burdel *m*, lupanar *m.*
broth·er (brŭ*th*'ər) s. *(sibling)* hermano; *(fellow man)* compañero; *(friend)* amigo; *(comrade)* camarada *m*; *(colleague)* colega *m*; *(fellow member)* compañero; RELIG. hermano.
broth·er·hood (brŭ*th*'ər-hōod') s. *(bond)* hermandad *f*, fraternidad *f*; *(fellowship)* asociación *f*, sociedad *f*; *(guild)* gremio, sindicato; *(confraternity)* cofradía, hermandad.
broth·er·in·law (brŭ*th*'ər-ĭn-lô') s. [pl. **broth·ers·in·law**] cuñado, hermano político.
broth·er·ly (brŭ*th*'ər-lē) adj. fraternal, fraterno.
brought (brôt) pret. y part. p. de **bring.**
brou·ha·ha (brōo'hä-hä') s. alboroto, tumulto.
brow (brou) *(eyebrow)* ceja; *(forehead)* frente *f*; *(facial expression)* rostro, semblante *m*; *(of a hill)* cresta.
brow·beat (brou'bēt') tr. **-beat, -beat·en** (-bēt'n), **-beat·ing** *(to intimidate)* intimidar; *(to domineer)* tiranizar.
brown (broun) I. s. narrón *m*, castaño II. adj. **-er, -est** *(color)* marrón; *(hair)* castaño; *(skin)* moreno; *(suntanned)* tostado (por el sol) III. tr. & intr. *(to tan in the sun)* tostar(se); CUL. dorar(se).
brown bear s. oso pardo.
brown·ie (brou'nē) s. *(sprite)* duende *m*; *(cake)* bizcocho de chocolate y nueces ♦ **B.** niña exploradora.
brown·out (broun'out') s. apagón parcial *m.*
brown rice s. arroz integral *m.*
brown·stone (broun'stōn') s. *(sandstone)* piedra arenisca; *(house)* casa de piedra arenisca.
brown sugar s. azúcar rubia *o* morena.
browse (brouz) I. intr. **browsed, brows·ing** *(in a place)* curiosear; *(a book)* hojear un libro; *(on leaves, shoots)* pacer —tr. *(to look through)* mirar, curiosear; *(to nibble)* mordisquear; *(to graze)* pacer II. s. pasto.
bruise (brōoz) I. s. *(contusion)* magulladura, contusión (en la piel) *f*; *(damage)* daño, machucadura (en la fruta); *(injury)* herida II. tr. **bruised, bruis·ing** *(to injure)* magullar, contusionar (la piel); *(to damage)* dañar, machucar (la fruta); *(to crush)* aplastar, triturar; *(to hurt)* herir (los sentimientos) —intr. *(to be injured)* magullarse; *(to feel injured)* sentirse herido.
bruis·er (brōo'zər) s. JER. matón *m.*
bruit (brōot) tr. difundir, divulgar (noticia).
brunch (brŭnch) s. combinación de desayuno y almuerzo.

bru·net (brōo-nĕt') adj. & s. moreno.
bru·nette (brōo-nĕt') adj. & s. morena.
brunt (brŭnt) s. fuerza, impacto (de ataque, crítica) ♦ **to bear the b. of** llevar el peso de.
brush¹ (brŭsh) I. s. *(for brushing)* cepillo; *(broom)* escoba; *(paintbrush)* brocha; *(of an artist)* pincel *m*; *(brushing)* cepillado; *(bushy tail)* cola peluda; *(skirmish)* escaramuza, encuentro; *(graze)* roce *m*; ELEC. escobilla II. tr. *(to use a brush)* cepillar, pasar el cepillo a; *(to apply with a brush)* untar con una brocha; *(to paint)* pintar con brocha *o* pincel; *(to remove)* quitar con el cepillo, barrer <to b. the crumbs off the table barrer las migajas de la mesa>; *(to graze against)* rozar al pasar ♦ **to b. off** *o* **aside** *(to dismiss)* hacer caso omiso de <he brushed aside the charges hizo caso omiso de los cargos>; *(to get rid of)* sacarse de encima • **to b. up** repasar, retocar • **to b. up on** refrescar los conocimientos de —intr. pasar rozando.
brush² (brŭsh) s. maleza.
brushed (brŭsht) adj. peinado.
brush fire s. incendio de matorrales.
brush·ing (brŭsh'ĭng) s. cepillado.
brush·off (brŭsh'ôf') s. FAM. despedida brusca.
brush stroke s. *(with a large brush)* brochazo; *(with an artist's brush)* pincelada.
brush·wood (brŭsh'wōod') s. *(cut)* ramitas de árbol caídas *o* cortadas; *(undergrowth)* maleza.
brush·work (brŭsh'wûrk') s. PINT. *(brush stroke)* pincelada; *(technique)* técnica de pincel.
brusque *o* **brusk** (brŭsk) adj. brusco.
Brus·sels (brŭs'əlz) s. Bruselas.
Brussels sprout s. col de Bruselas *f.*
brut (brōot) adj. seco (vino).
bru·tal (brōot'l) adj. *(bestial)* brutal, bestial; *(cruel)* cruel, salvaje; *(harsh)* crudo.
bru·tal·i·ty (brōo-tăl'ĭ-tē) s. [pl. **-ties**] *(brutal conduct)* brutalidad *f*, bestialidad *f*; *(cruelty)* crueldad *f*; *(harshness)* crudeza; *(brutal act)* acto brutal.
bru·tal·ize (brōot'l-īz') tr. **-ized, -iz·ing** *(to make brutal)* embrutecer; *(to treat brutally)* tratar brutalmente, brutalizar.
brute (brōot) I. s. *(beast)* bestia; *(person)* salvaje *mf*, bestia *mf* II. adj. *(instinctive)* bruto; *(lacking reason)* brutal; *(cruel)* cruel, salvaje; *(gross)* grosero, tosco.
brut·ish (brōo'tĭsh) adj. *(like a brute)* bruto; *(lacking reason)* brutal; *(cruel)* cruel; *(sensual)* sensual.
bub·ble (bŭb'əl) I. s. *(in a liquid)* burbuja; *(soap bubble)* pompa de jabón; *(dome)* campana de vidrio; *(fantasy)* ilusión *f* ♦ **to blow bubbles** hacer pompas de jabón • **to burst someone's b.** desengañar a alguien II. intr. **-bled, -bling** *(to make bubbles)* burbujear; *(to flow)* murmurar (arroyo) —tr. hacer burbujear ♦ **to b. over with** rebosar de, desbordar de.
bubble chamber s. FÍS. cámara de burbujas.
bubble gum s. chicle de globo *m.*
bub·bly (bŭb'lē) I. s. [pl. **-blies**] FAM. champán *m* II. adj. **-bli·er, -bli·est** *(effervescent)* efervescente, espumoso; *(lively)* alegre.
bub·by (bōob'ē, bōo'bē) s. [pl. **-bies**] JER. teta, pecho.
bu·bon·ic plague (bōo-bŏn'ĭk, byōo-) s. MED. peste bubónica.
buc·cal (bŭk'əl) adj. bucal.
buc·ca·neer (bŭk'ə-nîr') s. bucanero, filibustero.
Bu·cha·rest (bōo'kə-rĕst', byōo'-) s. Bucarest.
buck¹ (bŭk) I. s. ZOOL. *(male)* macho; *(deer)* ciervo, gamo; *(rabbit)* conejo macho; FAM. *(youth)* joven despierto; *(fop)* petimetre *m* II. intr. *(to rear and kick)* encabritarse y corcovear (caballo, mulo); *(to butt)* embestir con la cabeza; *(to jolt)* dar sacudidas; *(to balk)* resistirse; FAM. *(to strive)* esforzarse ♦ **to b. up** FAM. animarse —tr. *(to unseat)* derribar; *(to butt against)* topar; *(to oppose)* oponerse III. adj. MIL. raso.
buck² (bŭk) s. JER. dólar *m.*
buck·a·roo *o* **buck·er·oo** (bŭk'ə-rōo') s. [pl. **-roos** *o* **-oos**] vaquero.
buck·board (bŭk'bôrd') s. carro.
buck·et (bŭk'ĭt) I. s. *(pail)* cubo, balde *m*; *(of waterwheel)* cangilón *m*; *(scoop)* pala ♦ **to kick the b.** FIG., FAM. estirar

la pata • **to rain buckets** llover a cántaros **II.** tr. *(to put in a bucket)* echar en un cubo; *(to carry in a bucket)* llevar en un cubo; *(to ride)* cabalgar duro sin descansar —intr. *(to move fast)* moverse a trompicones; *(to hustle)* darse prisa.

buck·et·ful (bŭk'ĭt-fool) s. cubo (contenido) ♦ **by the b.** FIG. en gran cantidad, a cántaros.

bucket seat s. asiento de automóvil deportivo.

buck·le¹ (bŭk'əl) **I.** s. hebilla ♦ **belt b.** hebilla de cinturón **II.** tr. & intr. **-led, -ling** abrochar(se) ♦ **to b. down to** dedicarse con empeño a.

buck·le² (bŭk'əl) **I.** intr. **-led, -ling** *(to bend)* combarse; *(to collapse)* derrumbarse; *(to surrender)* rendirse —tr. combar **II.** s. comba.

buck·shot (bŭk'shŏt') s. perdigón m, posta.

buck·skin (bŭk'skĭn') s. *(suede)* ante m, cabritilla; *(horse)* caballo (del color del ante).

buck·tooth (bŭk'tooth') s. [pl. **-teeth** (-tēth')] diente saliente m.

buck·wheat (bŭk'hwēt') s. trigo sarraceno, alforfón m.

bu·col·ic (byoo-kŏl'ĭk) **I.** adj. *(pastoral)* bucólico, pastoril; *(rural)* rural, campestre **II.** s. POÉT. bucólica.

bud (bŭd) **I.** s. *(shoot)* brote m, yema; *(undeveloped flower)* capullo ♦ **in the b.** en cierne o ciernes • **to nip in the b.** cortar de raíz **II.** intr. **bud·ded, bud·ding** *(to produce buds)* echar brotes o capullos; *(to grow from a bud)* brotar; FIG. *(to bloom)* florecer; *(to be like a bud)* estar en ciernes —tr. *(to cause to bud)* hacer echar brotes o capullos; *(to graft a bud)* injertar.

Bud·dha (boo'də, bood'ə) s. Buda m.

Bud·dhism (boo'dĭz'əm, bood'ĭz'-) s. budismo.

bud·ding (bŭd'ĭng) adj. FIG. en cierne <a b. actor un actor en cierne>.

bud·dy (bŭd'ē) s. [pl. **-dies**] FAM. *(comrade)* compañero, compadre m; *(friend)* amigo.

budge (bŭj) intr. **budged, budg·ing** *(to move)* moverse un poco; FIG. *(to yield)* ceder —tr. *(to move)* mover un poco; FIG. *(to cause to yield)* hacer ceder.

budg·et (bŭj'ĭt) **I.** s. presupuesto **II.** tr. presupuestar, hacer un presupuesto.

budg·et·ar·y (bŭj'ĭ-tĕr'ē) adj. presupuestario.

buff¹ (bŭf) **I.** s. *(leather)* cuero; *(color)* color de ante m; *(instrument)* pulidor m ♦ **in the b.** en cueros **II.** adj. de color del ante **III.** tr. *(to polish)* pulir; *(to dye)* teñir de color ante.

buff² (bŭf) s. FAM. entusiasta mf, aficionado.

buf·fa·lo (bŭf'ə-lō') **I.** s. [pl. **-loes** o **-los** o **buffalo**] ZOOL. búfalo, bisonte m **II.** tr. **-loed, -lo·ing** JER. *(to intimidate)* intimidar; *(to confuse)* confundir.

buff·er¹ (bŭf'ər) s. pulidor m.

buff·er² (bŭf'ər) **I.** s. *(shock absorber)* amortiguador m; *(intercessor)* intercesor m; QUÍM. regulador m **II.** tr. QUÍM. tratar (una solución) con un regulador.

buf·fet¹ (bə-fā', boo-) s. *(sideboard)* aparador m; *(restaurant)* cantina, buffet m.

buf·fet² (bŭf'ĭt) **I.** s. bofetada **II.** tr. *(to slap)* abofetear; *(to strike)* golpear; *(to rough)* zarandear —intr. abrirse paso con dificultad o a golpes.

buf·foon (bə-foon') s. bufón m, payaso.

buf·foon·er·y (bə-foo'nə-rē) s. bufonada, payasada.

bug (bŭg) **I.** s. *(insect)* insecto, bicho; FAM. *(bacterium)* microbio; *(defect)* defecto, falla (en un sistema); JER. *(enthusiast)* entusiasta mf, loco por <she is a T.V. b. es una loca por la televisión>; *(microphone)* micrófono oculto **II.** intr. **bugged, bug·ging** salirse hacia afuera, resaltar <his eyes bugged out with fear se le salían los ojos del miedo> —tr. JER. *(to pester)* fastidiar, importunar; *(to install a bug)* instalar un micrófono oculto en.

bug·a·boo (bŭg'ə-boo') s. [pl. **-boos**] *(bugbear)* cuco, fantasma m; *(worry)* pesadilla, preocupación f.

bug·bear (bŭg'bâr') s. *(dread)* terror m, pavor m; *(specter)* espectro, fantasma m; *(bogie)* cuco, coco.

bug·ger (bŭg'ər) **I.** s. JER. *(low person)* bribón m; *(fellow)* tipo, sujeto; VULG. *(sodomite)* sodomita m **II.** tr. JER., VULG. cometer sodomía con —intr. cometer sodomía.

bug·gy¹ (bŭg'ē) s. [pl. **-gies**] *(horse-drawn carriage)* calesa; *(baby carriage)* coche de niño m.

bug·gy² (bŭg'ē) adj. **-gi·er, -gi·est** *(infested with bugs)* lleno de bichos; JER. *(crazy)* loco, chiflado.

bug·house (bŭg'hous') s. JER. manicomio.

bu·gle (byoo'gəl) **I.** s. bugle m **II.** intr. **-gled, -gling** tocar el bugle.

build (bĭld) **I.** tr. **built** (bĭlt), **build·ing** *(to construct)* construir; *(buildings)* construir, edificar; *(monuments)* erigir; *(fire)* preparar; *(to give form to)* formar, hacer; *(to develop)* desarrollar; *(to ground)* fundamentar, basar ♦ **to b. on** o **upon** *(building)* levantar sobre; *(trust)* contar con, confiar en • **to b. up** *(from parts)* montar, armar; *(theory, method)* elaborar; *(collection)* hacer, reunir; *(image, reputation)* crear; *(sales, business)* aumentar; *(health)* fortalecer —intr. *(houses)* construirse; *(to be a builder)* ser constructor, construir; *(to develop)* elaborar ♦ **to b. up** *(to increase)* aumentar; *(to intensify)* intensificarse, ir en aumento **II.** s. *(of a person)* talle m, figura; *(of an object)* estructura, forma.

build·er (bĭl'dər) s. *(one that builds)* constructor m; *(contractor)* contratista m.

build·ing (bĭl'dĭng) s. *(structure)* edificio, casa; *(construction)* construcción f ♦ **b. lot** solar, terreno.

building site s. *(before construction)* solar m, terreno; *(under construction)* obra.

building trade s. industria de la construcción.

build-up o **build·up** (bĭld'ŭp') s. *(increase)* aumento; MIL. *(of troops)* concentración f, acumulación f; FAM. *(publicity)* publicidad f, propaganda ♦ **arms b.** MIL. incremento bélico.

built (bĭlt) pret. y part. p. de **build.**

built-in (bĭlt'ĭn') adj. *(not movable)* empotrado <a b. closet un ropero empotrado>; *(built inside)* interior, incorporado; *(as an integral part)* que es parte integral.

built-up (bĭlt'ŭp') adj. *(made up of parts)* ensamblado, compuesto; *(filled with buildings)* urbanizado.

bulb (bŭlb) s. *(stem)* bulbo, cebolla; *(tuber)* tubérculo; *(lamp)* bombilla; ANAT. bulbo.

bul·bous (bŭl'bəs) adj. *(protuberant)* protuberante; *(tuberous)* bulboso.

Bul·gar (bŭl'gär', bool'-) s. búlgaro (habitante).

Bul·gar·i·a (bŭl-gâr'ē-ə, bool-) s. Bulgaria.

Bul·gar·i·an (bŭl-gâr'ē-ən, bool-) adj. & s. *(inhabitant, language)* búlgaro.

bulge (bŭlj) **I.** s. *(protuberance)* protuberancia; *(in a wall)* pandeo; *(increase)* alza, aumento **II.** intr. & tr. **bulged, bulg·ing** hinchar(se), abultar.

bulg·ing (bŭl'jĭng) **I.** adj. *(swollen)* hinchado; *(protuberant)* saltón **II.** s. hinchazón f, abultamiento.

bulg·y (bŭl'jē) adj. protuberante, abultado.

bulk (bŭlk) **I.** s. *(volume)* volumen m, tamaño; *(corpulence)* corpulencia; *(thickness)* grosor m, espesor m; *(the largest part)* la mayor parte; MARÍT. *(cargo)* carga; *(hold)* bodega ♦ **in b.** *(loose)* a granel, suelto; *(in large amounts)* en grandes cantidades **II.** intr. *(to increase)* aumentar ♦ **to b. large** ser importante —tr. *(to cause to swell)* hinchar; *(to pile)* amontonar.

bulk·head (bŭlk'hĕd') s. MARÍT. mamparo; MIN. tabique m, muro de contención.

bulk·y (bŭl'kē) adj. **-i·er, -i·est** *(massive)* voluminoso; *(unwieldy)* pesado.

bull¹ (bool) **I.** s. *(male of bovine)* toro; *(of other animals)* macho; *(man)* hombre fuerte m, toro; *(buyer)* alcista (en la bolsa) m; JER. *(nonsense)* tontería, sandez f ♦ **B.** ASTROL. Tauro • **to shoot the b.** JER. charlar, parlotear **II.** tr. COM. jugar al alza con ♦ **to b. one's way** abrirse paso —intr. COM. *(to rise)* subir (precio de valores); *(to push)* abrirse paso **III.** adj. *(male)* macho; *(strong)* fuerte ♦ **a b. market** COM. un mercado en alza • **b. neck** cuello de toro.

bull² (bool) s. RELIG. bula.

bull·dog (bool'dôg') **I.** s. buldog m, dogo **II.** adj. tenaz, firme **III.** tr. **-dogged, -dog·ging** derribar un novillo tomándolo por los cuernos.

bull·doze (bool'dōz') tr. **-dozed, -doz·ing** *(to clear, dig up)* nivelar o excavar con una excavadora; FAM. *(to bully)* intimidar ♦ **to b. one's way into** abrirse paso a empujones entre • **to b. down** derribar con una excavadora.

bull·doz·er (bŏŏl'dō'zər) s. *(tractor)* excavadora; JER. *(bully)* valentón *m.*

bul·let (bŏŏl'ĭt) s. *(projectile)* bala; *(cartridge)* cartucho.

bul·le·tin (bŏŏl'ĭ-tn) I. s. *(periodical)* boletín *m;* *(statement)* parte *m,* comunicado II. tr. dar a conocer mediante boletín *o* comunicado.

bulletin board s. tablero de anuncios.

bul·let·proof (bŏŏl'ĭt-prōōf') I. adj. a prueba de balas II. tr. construir a prueba de balas.

bull·fight (bŏŏl'fīt') s. corrida de toros.

bull·fight·er (bŏŏl'fī'tər) s. torero.

bull·finch (bŏŏl'fĭnch') s. ORNIT. pinzón real *m,* piñonero.

bull·frog (bŏŏl'frŏg') s. rana toro, rana mugidora.

bull·head·ed (bŏŏl'hĕd'ĭd) adj. testarudo, terco.

bull·horn (bŏŏl'hôrn') s. megáfono eléctrico.

bul·lion (bŏŏl'yən) s. *(gold)* oro en lingotes *o* barras; *(silver)* plata en lingotes *o* barras.

bull·ish (bŏŏl'ĭsh) adj. *(like a bull)* semejante a un toro; *(bullheaded)* testarudo; *(optimistic)* optimista; FIN. en alza.

bull·necked (bŏŏl'nĕkt') adj. de cuello corto y grueso.

bul·lock (bŏŏl'ək) s. *(steer)* buey *m,* toro castrado; *(young bull)* novillo.

bull·pen (bŏŏl'pĕn') s. *(for bulls)* toril *m;* *(for prisoners)* celda temporaria de una comisaría.

bull·ring (bŏŏl'rĭng') s. *(stadium)* plaza de toros; *(ring)* ruedo, redondel *m.*

bull session s. FAM. tertulia.

bull's eye *o* **bull's-eye** (bŏŏlz'ī') s. *(target)* blanco; *(shot)* acierto, tiro acertado; FIG. *(success)* acierto, exito total; *(window)* ojo de buey; *(lens)* lente planoconvexa; *(porthole)* portilla ♦ **to hit the b.** dar en el blanco.

bull·shit (bŏŏl'shĭt') VULG. I. s. mierda, porquería II. tr. **-shit, -shit·ting** dar mierda, mentir.

bull terrier s. bulterrier (perro) *m.*

bull·whip (bŏŏl'hwĭp') I. s. látigo (de cuero) II. tr. **-whipped, -whip·ping** azotar.

bul·ly (bŏŏl'ē) I. s. [pl. **-lies**] *(cruel person)* abusador *m;* ANT. *(ruffian)* malhechor *m* II. tr. **-lied, -ly·ing** intimidar, amedrentar —intr. abusar III. adj. FAM. excelente, formidable IV. interj. ¡bien!, ¡bravo!

bul·rush (bŏŏl'rŭsh') s. BOT. anea, espadaña.

bul·wark (bŏŏl'wərk, bŭl'-) I. s. *(rampart)* baluarte *m,* bastión *m;* *(defense)* baluarte, defensa; *(breakwater)* rompeolas *m* ♦ **bulwarks** MARÍT. borda II. tr. *(to fortify)* fortificar (con bastiones); *(to defend)* defender; *(to protect)* proteger.

bum (bŭm) I. s. *(hobo)* vagabundo, linyera *m;* *(loafer)* vago, holgazán *m;* *(incompetent)* pobre tipo; G.B., FAM. *(buttocks)* trasero II. intr. **bummed, bum·ming** *(to loaf)* vagabundear, vagar; *(to sponge)* gorronear, sablear —tr. *(to sponge)* gorronear, sablear III. adj. FAM. *(worthless)* sin valor, inútil; *(of poor quality)* de mala calidad, malo; *(sore)* dolorido.

bum·ble (bŭm'bəl) intr. **-bled, -bling** *(to mumble)* hablar con torpeza; *(to behave)* obrar con torpeza —tr. chapucear.

bum·ble·bee (bŭm'bəl-bē') s. abejón *m,* abejorro.

bump (bŭmp) I. tr. *(to collide with)* chocar contra; *(to knock against)* golpear contra; *(to displace)* desplazar; FAM. *(to oust)* quitar el puesto ♦ **b. into** tropezarse con, tropezarse con • **to b. off** JER. matar, despachar —intr. *(to knock)* chocar contra; *(to jolt)* moverse a sacudidas II. s. *(collision)* choque *m,* topetón *m;* *(swelling)* hinchazón *f,* chichón *m;* *(protuberance)* protuberancia, bulto; *(in a road)* bache *m.*

bump·er¹ (bŭm'pər) s. *(of a car)* parachoques *m;* *(protective device)* defensa, amortiguador de golpes *m.*

bump·er² (bŭm'pər) I. s. *(vessel)* vaso (lleno hasta el borde); *(something large)* enormidad *f* II. adj. abundante <*a b. crop* una cosecha abundante>.

bump·kin (bŭmp'kĭn) s. *(yokel)* patán *m,* palurdo *m;* MARÍT. *(spar)* pescante *m.*

bump·tious (bŭmp'shəs) adj. presuntuoso, engreído.

bump·y (bŭm'pē) adj. **-i·er, -i·est** *(uneven)* desigual, accidentado; *(jolty)* agitado, sacudido ♦ **b. road** camino lleno de baches • **b. ride** paseo zarandeado.

bun (bŭn) s. *(bread)* bollo, panecillo; *(hair)* moño.

bunch (bŭnch) I. s. *(of grapes)* racimo; *(of flowers)* ramillete *m,* ramo; *(of sheep)* rebaño; *(of hair)* mechón *m;* *(handful)* montón *m,* puñado; FAM. *(of people)* grupo <*a b. of friends* un grupo de amigos>; *(swelling)* bulto II. tr. *(to gather)* agrupar, juntar; *(to form into a bunch)* atar en un manojo; *(to put in folds)* fruncir —intr. *(to group)* juntarse, agruparse; *(to protrude)* abultar.

bun·dle (bŭn'dl) I. s. *(of objects)* bulto, fardo; *(of papers)* legajo, fajo; *(of reeds)* haz *m,* manojo; *(package)* paquete *m;* JER. *(large sum)* montón de dinero *m* II. tr. **-dled, -dling** *(to tie)* atar; *(to wrap)* envolver; *(to hustle)* mandar sin perder tiempo; *(to dress warmly)* arropar bien, abrigar bien —intr. *(to leave hastily)* salir volando; *(to share a bed)* acostarse juntos con la ropa puesta ♦ **to b. up** arroparse, abrigarse.

bung (bŭng) I. s. *(stopper)* tapón *m,* bitoque *m;* *(bunghole)* piquera, boca de tonel II. tr. taponar (con bitoque).

bun·ga·low (bŭng'gə-lō') s. chalé *m,* bungalow *m.*

bun·gle (bŭng'gəl) I. tr. & intr. **-gled, -gling** chapucear II. s. chapucería.

bun·ion (bŭn'yən) s. juanete *m.*

bunk¹ (bŭngk) I. s. *(bed)* litera; FAM. *(place)* lugar para dormir II. intr. *(to sleep in a bunk)* dormir en una litera; *(to sleep in rough quarters)* dormir en un improvisado ♦ **to b. with** parar con.

bunk² (bŭngk) s. JER. tontería, sandez *f.*

bun·ker (bŭng'kər) I. s. MARÍT. pañol del carbón *m,* bonera; MIL. *(shelter)* refugio subterráneo, bunker *m* II. tr. meter en la carbonera.

bunk·house (bŭngk'hous') s. barraca.

bun·ny (bŭn'ē) s. [pl. **-nies**] FAM. conejo, conejito.

Bun·sen burner (bŭn'sən) s. lámpara *o* mechero de Bunsen.

bunt·ing (bŭn'tĭng) s. *(cloth)* tela para banderas *o* colgaduras; *(flags)* banderas.

buoy (bŏŏ'ē, boi) I. s. MARÍT. *(float)* boya; *(life preserver)* salvavidas *m* II. tr. MARÍT. *(to mark)* aboyar, señalar con boyas; *(to keep afloat)* mantener a flote; FIG. *(to hearten)* animar, alentar <*the news buoyed him up* las noticias lo alentaron>.

buoy·an·cy (boi'ən-sē, bŏŏ'yən-) s. *(capacity)* flotabilidad *f,* capacidad de flote *f;* FÍS. *(force)* empuje (de un líquido) *m;* *(recuperative ability)* capacidad de recuperación de un revés; *(cheerfulness)* optimismo.

buoy·ant (boi'ənt, bŏŏ'yənt) adj. *(able to float)* boyante, flotante; *(animated)* animado; *(cheerful)* optimista.

bur (bûr) s. & v. var. de **burr¹,².**

bur·ble (bûr'bəl) I. s. *(sound)* borboteo; *(of speech)* farfulla II. intr. **-bled, -bling** *(to bubble)* borbotar, borbollar; *(to speak)* farfullar, hablar atropelladamente.

bur·den¹ (bûr'dn) I. s. *(load)* carga; *(encumbrance)* carga, peso <*her debts are a b.* sus deudas son una carga>; *(responsibility)* responsabilidad *f;* MARÍT. *(amount of cargo)* arqueo, capacidad de carga *f;* *(weight)* peso de la carga de un buque ♦ **the b. of proof** la carga de la prueba II. tr. *(to load)* cargar; FIG. *(to oppress)* agobiar.

bur·den² (bûr'dn) s. MÚS. *(refrain)* estribillo; *(accompaniment)* acompañamiento del contrabajo; *(idea, theme)* idea *o* tema central *m.*

bu·reau (byŏŏr'ō) s. [pl. **-reaus** *o* **-reaux** (-ōz)] *(dresser)* tocador *m;* *(government department)* departamento (del gobierno); *(office)* oficina; *(business)* agencia <*a travel b.* una agencia de viajes>; G.B. *(desk)* escritorio.

bu·reau·cra·cy (byŏŏ-rŏk'rə-sē) s. [pl. **-cies**] burocracia.

bu·reau·crat (byŏŏr'ə-krăt') s. burócrata *mf.*

bu·reau·crat·ic (byŏŏr'ə-krăt'ĭk) adj. burocrático.

bu·rette *o* **bu·ret** (byŏŏ-rĕt') s. QUÍM. bureta, probeta.

bur·geon (bûr'jən) I. intr. *(to sprout)* brotar; *(to flourish)* florecer II. s. brote *m,* retoño.

burg·er (bûr'gər) s. FAM. *(hamburger)* hamburguesa; *(sandwich)* bocadillo, emparedado.

---

burgh·er (bûr'gər) s. *(middle-class person)* burgués *m*; *(citizen)* ciudadano.

bur·glar (bûr'glər) s. ladrón *m*.

burglar alarm s. alarma antirrobo.

bur·glar·ize (bûr'glə-rīz') tr. **-ized, -iz·ing** robar (en casa, tienda).

bur·glar·proof (bûr'glər-prōof') adj. contra robo, antirrobo.

bur·gla·ry (bûr'glə-rē) s. [pl. **-ries**] robo con allanamiento de morada.

bur·gle (bûr'gəl) tr. **-gled, -gling** FAM. robar (en casa, tienda).

Bur·gun·dy (bûr'gən-dē) s. [pl. **-dies**] *(region)* Borgoña; *(wine)* borgoña ♦ **b.** color vino tinto.

bur·i·al (bĕr'ē-əl) s. entierro ♦ **b. ground** cementerio, camposanto.

burl (bûrl) **I.** s. *(nub)* mota (en una tela); BOT. nudo (en un árbol) **II.** tr. TEJ. desmotar.

bur·lap (bûr'lăp') s. arpillera.

bur·lesque (bər-lĕsk') **I.** s. *(parody)* parodia, farsa; *(vaudeville)* espectáculo de variedades; *(mockery)* burla **II.** tr. **-lesqued, -lesqu·ing** parodiar **III.** adj. burlesco.

bur·ley (bûr'lē) s. [pl. **-leys**] tabaco de color claro.

bur·ly (bûr'lē) adj. **-li·er, -li·est** fuerte, robusto.

Bur·ma (bûr'mə) s. Birmania.

Bur·mese (bər-mēz') adj. & s. [pl. **Burmese**] *(inhabitant, language)* birmano ♦ **the B.** los birmanos.

burn (bûrn) **I.** tr. **burned** o **burnt** (bûrnt), **burn·ing** *(to set on fire)* quemar <*to b. wood* quemar leña>; *(to destroy with fire)* incendiar; *(to injure)* quemar, abrasar <*he burned his hand* se quemó la mano>; *(to sting)* quemar <*the pepper burned my mouth* el pimiento me quemó la boca>; *(to use as fuel)* quemar (combustible); *(to harden, glaze by fire)* cocer (ladrillos); *(to expend)* gastar <*athletes b. a lot of energy* los atletas gastan muchas energías>; *(to cauterize)* cauterizar; *(to brand)* herrar (animales); JER. *(to anger)* irritar, exasperar; *(to cheat out of)* embaucar; QUÍM. calcinar ♦ **to b. a hole in one's pocket** FIG. quemarle a uno en el bolsillo • **to b. away** quemar lentamente hasta consumirlo • **to b. in** marcar a fuego • **to b. into** *(to eat its way into)* quemar; *(to make an indelible impression on)* grabar en • **to b. one's bridges** FIG. quemar las naves • **to b. oneself out** FIG., JER. agotarse, gastarse (uno) • **to b. out** quemar • **to b. the candle at both ends** FIG. vivir una vida agitada • **to b. the midnight oil** FIG. quemarse las pestañas o cejas • **to b. to a crisp** achicharrar (carne, tostadas) • **to b. to the ground** reducir a cenizas • **to b. up** *(to consume)* consumir; *(to devour)* devorar <*this car burns up the miles* este automóvil devora las millas>; FIG., FAM. *(to enrage)* enfurecer, indignar —intr. *(to be on fire)* quemarse, arder; *(to be destroyed by fire)* consumirse; *(to give off light)* estar encendido (luz); *(to give off heat)* quemar, abrasar; JER. *(to be electrocuted)* morir en la silla eléctrica; *(with fever)* arder; *(with strong emotions)* consumirse; CUL. *(to be scorched)* quemarse ♦ **to b. away** quemarse, consumirse por el fuego • **to b. down** quemarse por completo • **to b. out** *(to cease to burn)* consumirse, apagarse <*don't let the fire b. out* no dejes que se apague el fuego>; *(fuse)* quemarse, fundirse • **to b. up** *(to go up in flames)* quemarse o consumirse completamente <*the papers burned up* se quemaron completamente los papeles>; *(to become angry)* enfurecerse, indignarse • **to b. up with** arder de **II.** s. *(injury)* quemadura; *(firing)* cocedura (de ladrillos); *(sunburn)* quemadura de sol; *(brand)* marca de hierro candente.

burn·er (bûr'nər) s. quemador *m*, mechero.

burn·ing (bûr'nĭng) adj. *(hot)* ardiente, abrasador; *(passionate)* ardiente <*a b. desire* un deseo ardiente>; *(urgent)* urgente; *(heated)* candente (cuestión, problema).

bur·nish (bûr'nĭsh) **I.** tr. *(to polish)* pulir, bruñir; *(to rub)* lustrar (con un aparato) **II.** s. brillo, lustre *m*.

bur·noose o **bur·nous** (bər-nōos') s. albornoz *m*.

burn·out (bûrn'out') s. *(failure)* extinción *f*; *(exhaustion)* agotamiento ♦ **to suffer b.** agotarse.

burnt (bûrnt) un pret. y t part. p. de **burn.**

burp (bûrp) **I.** s. eructo **II.** intr. eructar —tr. hacer eructar (a un niño).

burr¹ (bûr) **I.** s. *(tool)* taladro; *(dentist's drill)* fresa; *(roughness)* rebaba; *(of plants)* parte espinosa; *(plant)* planta espinosa; *(protuberance)* nudo (en un árbol); *(nettlesome person)* lapa, persona pegajosa **II.** tr. *(to form a burr on)* formar una rebaba en; *(to remove)* quitar la rebaba de.

burr² (bûr) s. TEC. *(washer)* arandela; *(blank)* agujero en una chapa de metal.

bur·ro (bûr'ō, bōōr'ō) s. [pl. **-ros**] burro, asno.

bur·row (bûr'ō) **I.** s. *(hole)* madriguera; *(of a rabbit)* conejera **II.** intr. *(to dig)* hacer una madriguera; *(to hide)* amadrigarse, meterse en una madriguera; *(to move)* avanzar; *(to search)* buscar —tr. *(to make by burrowing)* cavar, excavar; *(to dig a burrow in)* hacer una madriguera en; ANT. *(to hide)* esconder.

bur·sa (bûr'sə) s. ANAT. bolsa, saco.

bur·sar (bûr'sər) s. COM. tesorero.

bur·si·tis (bər-sī'tĭs) s. MED. bursitis *f*.

burst (bûrst) **I.** intr. **burst, burst·ing** *(to break open)* estallar, reventarse; *(to break out)* romperse; *(to explode)* explotar; *(to fly apart suddenly)* volar(se); *(to be very full)* rebosar <*the silos are bursting with wheat* los silos rebosan de trigo> ♦ **to b. in** interrumpir <*to b. in with questions* interrumpir con preguntas> • **to b. into bloom** brotar • **to b. open** abrirse violentamente • **to b. out** *(to exclaim)* exclamar; *(to emerge)* surgir; *(to leave suddenly)* salir corriendo; *(to bloom)* brotar; *(to explode)* reventar; *(to yield to emotions)* romper a, echarse a <*she b. out crying when she heard the news* se echó a llorar cuando recibió la noticia> —tr. *(to shatter)* reventar <*to b. a balloon* reventar un globo>; *(to force open)* romper ♦ **to b. in** irrumpir en, entrar violentamente en • **to b. into** *(to appear suddenly)* entrar violentamente en, irrumpir en; *(to give way from emotion)* desatarse en (lágrimas, insultos) • **to b. upon** irrumpir en • **to b. with** *(to give sudden expression)* reventar de (risa, impaciencia); *(to be full of)* rebosar de (sentimientos) **II.** s. *(bursting)* reventón *m*; *(explosion)* explosión *f*; *(outburst)* estallido <*a b. of laughter* un estallido de risa>; *(of a weapon)* ráfaga, andanada ♦ **b. of activity** explosión de actividad • **b. of anger** arranque o arrebato de cólera • **b. of applause** salva de aplausos • **b. of energy** explosión de energía.

Bu·run·di (bōō-rōōn'dē) s. Burundi.

bur·y (bĕr'ē) tr. **-ied, -y·ing** *(to conceal)* enterrar <*to b. a bone* enterrar un hueso>; *(to inter)* sepultar, enterrar; *(to hide)* esconder, ocultar; *(to absorb)* absorber, sumergir <*he buried himself in his work* se sumergió en su trabajo>; *(to abandon)* dejar, abandonar ♦ **to b. the hatchet** FIG. hacer las paces.

bus (bŭs) **I.** s. [pl. **bus·es** o **bus·ses**] *(motor vehicle)* autobús *m*, ómnibus *m*; FAM. *(automobile)* automóvil grande; *(cart)* mesa de ruedas **II.** tr. **bused, bus·ing** o **bussed, bus·sing** transportar en autobús —intr. viajar en autobús.

us·boy (bŭs'boi') s. ayudante de camarero *m*.

bush¹ (bōōsh) **I.** s. *(shrub)* arbusto; *(thicket)* maleza; *(land)* matorral *m*; *(backland)* región alejada de población; *(lock)* mecha; *(fox's tail)* cola de zorro **II.** intr. crecer (como un arbusto) —tr. poner arbustos en ♦ **to beat around** o **about the b.** FIG. andar con rodeos.

bush² (bōōsh) tr. MEC. forrar, encasquillar.

bushed (bōōsht) adj. FAM. agotado, hecho polvo.

bush·el (bōōsh'əl) s. *(unit of volume)* medida de áridos (35,24 litros en EE. UU.; G.B. 36,37 litros); *(container)* recipiente (de estas medidas) *m*; FAM. *(great deal)* montón *m*.

bush·ing (bōōsh'ĭng) s. MEC. *(lining)* forro, casquillo; *(bearing)* cojinete *m*.

Bush·man (bōōsh'mən) s. [pl. **-men**] bosquimano ♦ **b.** hombre montaraz.

bush·whack (bōōsh'hwăk') intr. *(to make one's way through)* abrirse paso en la maleza; *(to travel)* andar por el bosque —tr. tender una emboscada.

bush·y (bōōsh'ē) adj. **-i·er, -i·est** *(full of bushes)* breñoso, lleno de arbustos; *(thick)* tupido, espeso.

bus·i·ly (bĭz'ə-lē) adj. diligentemente, afanosamente.

busi·ness (bĭz'nĭs) s. *(occupation)* oficio, ocupación *f*; *(es-*

tablishment) comercio, negocio; *(firm)* firma, empresa; *(volume of trade)* negocios; *(commercial policy)* práctica comercial; *(one's concern)* asunto, cosa <*that is not your b.* eso no es cosa tuya>; *(responsibility)* deber *m*; *(matter)* asunto, cuestión *f*; FAM. *(scolding)* regaño ♦ **b. school** escuela de comercio • **to give someone the b.** JER. *(to upbraid)* halar las orejas; *(to treat roughly)* propinar una paliza • **to mean b.** no andar con juegos, hablar *o* actuar en serio.

busi·ness·like (bĭz′nĭs-līk′) adj. *(methodical)* metódico, sistemático; *(earnest)* serio, formal.

busi·ness·man (bĭz′nĭs-măn′) s. [pl. **-men** (-měn′)] hombre de negocios *m*, comerciante *m*.

busi·ness·wom·an (bĭz′nĭs-wŏŏm′ən) s. [pl. **-wom·en** (-wĭm′ĭn)] mujer de negocios *f*, comerciante *f*.

bus·ing (bŭs′ĭng) s. transporte de niños en autobús a escuelas de otros barrios para lograr la integración racial.

busk (bŭsk) s. ballena de corsé.

bus·kin (bŭs′kĭn) s. *(boot)* borceguí *m*; HIST. coturno.

bus·man (bŭs′mən) s. [pl. **-men**] conductor de ómnibus *m*.

bus·man's holiday (bŭs′mənz) s. vacaciones en las que uno sigue haciendo la misma actividad laboral.

bus·ses (bŭs′ĭz) un pl. de **bus**.

bus·sing (bŭs′ĭng) s. var. de **busing**.

bus stop s. parada de ómnibus.

bust¹ (bŭst) s. *(breast)* busto, pecho (de mujer); *(sculpture)* busto.

bust² (bŭst) FAM. **I.** tr. *(to smash)* reventar, romper; *(to break up)* acabar con; *(to tame)* amansar (un caballo); *(to cause to become bankrupt)* llevar a la quiebra; *(to demote)* degradar; *(to punch)* pegar, dar un puñetazo a; *(to arrest)* arrestar —intr. *(to break)* reventar, romperse; *(to become bankrupt)* quebrar **II.** s. *(flop)* chasco, fracaso; *(bankruptcy)* quiebra; *(time of depression)* época de depresión económica; *(punch)* trompada, puñetazo; *(spree)* parranda, juerga; *(arrest)* arresto; *(raid)* redada, batida.

bus·tle (bŭs′əl) **I.** intr. **-tied, -tling** apresurarse **II.** s. bullicio, animación *f*.

bust·y (bŭs′tē) adj. **-i·er, -i·est** FAM. pechugona.

bus·y (bĭz′ē) **I.** adj. **-i·er, -i·est** *(occupied)* atareado, ocupado; *(crowded with activity)* animado, concurrido; *(meddlesome)* entrometido, oficioso; *(in use)* ocupado *(teléfono)* **II.** tr. & intr. **-ied, -y·ing** mantener(se) ocupado.

bus·y·bod·y (bĭz′ē-bŏd′ē) s. [pl. **-ies**] entremetido.

busy signal s. TEL. señal de ocupado.

but §G1, 41 (bŭt, bət) **I.** conj. *(on the other hand)* pero, mas <*you may go, b. you must be back early* puedes ir, pero debes regresar temprano>; *(rather)* sino <*it is not intelligence but experience that he needs* no es inteligencia sino experiencia que le hace falta>; *(nevertheless)* no obstante, sin embargo <*he felt something bad was going to happen, b. he went ahead anyway* él sintió que algo malo iba a suceder, no obstante siguió adelante>; *(except)* excepto <*I would never have heard of him b. that my grandmother once met him* nunca hubiera sabido nada de él, excepto que mi abuela lo conoció una vez> ♦ **b. then** pero por otra parte • **cannot (help) b.** no poder menos que <*I could not help b. laugh* no pude menos que reír> • **none b.** solamente **II.** adv. *(just)* nada más que, solamente <*this is b. one case in many* éste es nada más que un caso entre muchos> ♦ **all b.** casi • **to do nothing b.** no hacer más que <*I do nothing b. work* no hago más que trabajar> **III.** prep. menos, excepto <*I used to work every day b. Sundays* yo solía trabajar todos los días excepto los domingos> ♦ **b. for** a no ser por <*b. for you I would have failed the exam* a no ser por tí habría reprobado el examen> **IV.** s. pero <*there are no buts about it* no hay peros que valgan>.

bu·tane (byōŏ′tān′) s. QUÍM. butano.

butch·er (bŏŏch′ər) **I.** s. *(slaughterer)* matarife *m*; *(meat seller)* carnicero; *(killer)* hombre sanguinario, carnicero; FAM. *(botcher)* chapucero **II.** tr. *(to slaughter)* matar (animales); *(to murder)* asesinar, matar sanguinariamente; FAM. *(to botch)* chapucear.

butch·er·y (bŏŏch′ə-rē) s. [pl. **-ies**] *(trade)* oficio de carni-

cero; *(slaughterhouse)* matadero; *(carnage)* matanza; *(shop)* carnicería; *(botch)* chapucería.

but·ler (bŭt′lər) s. mayordomo.

butt¹ (bŭt) **I.** tr. *(to ram)* embestir; *(to hit)* topar, dar un topetazo ♦ **to b. in** *o* **into** FAM. entremeterse en —intr. *(to strike)* embestir; *(to hit)* dar un topetazo; *(to project out)* sobresalir **II.** s. *(blow)* topetazo; *(push)* embestida.

butt² (bŭt) **I.** tr. *(to attach)* empalmar; *(to abut)* colindar —intr. estar empalmado **II.** s. TEC. *(butt joint)* junta a tope; *(butt hinge)* bisagra.

butt³ (bŭt) s. *(object of ridicule)* hazmerreír *m*, objeto de bromas; *(target)* blanco ♦ **butts** campo de tiro al blanco.

butt⁴ (bŭt) s. *(thicker end)* extremo más grueso; *(of a rifle)* culata; *(cigarette end)* colilla; *(stub)* cabo; JER. *(cigarette)* rubio, pitillo; FAM. *(buttocks)* trasero.

butte (byōŏt) s. cerro *o* monte aislado, otero.

but·ter (bŭt′ər) **I.** s. *(from milk)* mantequilla; *(paste)* pasta, mantequilla; *(vegetable fat)* mantequilla, manteca; FAM. *(flattery)* adulación *f*, halago **II.** tr. untar con mantequilla ♦ **to b. up** FIG. adular, lisonjear.

but·ter·cup (bŭt′ər-kŭp′) s. BOT. ranúnculo, botón de oro *m*.

but·ter·fat (bŭt′ər-făt′) s. grasa *o* nata de la leche.

but·ter·fin·gered (bŭt′ər-fĭng′gərd) adj. FAM. torpe.

but·ter·fin·gers (bŭt′ər-fĭng′gərz) s. FAM. persona torpe.

but·ter·fly (bŭt′ər-flī′) s. [pl. **-flies**] *(insect)* mariposa; *(person)* persona frívola; DEP. *(swimming stroke)* mariposa ♦ **to have butterflies in one's stomach** tener cosquillas en el estómago.

but·ter·milk (bŭt′ər-mĭlk′) s. suero de la leche.

but·ter·nut (bŭt′ər-nŭt′) s. *(tree)* nogal ceniciento; *(nut)* nuez de Cuba *f*.

but·ter·scotch (bŭt′ər-skŏch′) s. caramelo.

but·ter·y (bŭt′ə-rē) adj. *(of butter)* mantecoso; FIG. *(flattering)* zalamero.

but·tock (bŭt′ək) s. nalga ♦ **buttocks** trasero.

but·ton (bŭt′n) **I.** s. *(fastener)* botón *m*; *(switch)* botón, pulsador *m*; *(badge)* insignia, distintivo; *(globule)* glóbulo de metal (que queda después de soldar); *(bud)* botón, yema; JER. *(of the chin)* punta de la barbilla; DEP. botón (en la punta del florete) ♦ **on the b.** FAM. correcto, exacto **II.** tr. *(to fasten)* abotonar, abrochar; *(to decorate)* poner botones a *o* en —intr. abotonarse, abrocharse.

but·ton·hole (bŭt′n-hōl′) **I.** s. *(slit)* ojal *m*; G.B. *(boutonniere)* flor en el ojal *f* **II.** tr. **-holed, -hol·ing** *(to make)* hacer un ojal; *(to sew)* coser con punto de ojal; *(to detain)* retener (a alguien y obligarlo a escuchar).

but·ton·hook (bŭt′n-hōŏk′) s. abotonador *m*, abrochador *m*.

but·tress (bŭt′rĭs) **I.** s. *(structure)* contrafuerte *m*, botarel *m*; *(support)* apoyo, sostén *m*; *(of a hill)* estribación *f* **II.** tr. reforzar, apoyar.

bux·om (bŭk′səm) adj. *(plump)* rollizo; ANT. *(lively)* alegre; *(obedient)* obediente.

buy (bī) **I.** tr. **bought** (bôt), **buy·ing** *(to purchase)* comprar, adquirir; FAM. *(to bribe)* sobornar <*members of the jury had been bought* miembros del jurado habían sido sobornados>; FIG., FAM. *(to believe)* creer, aceptar <*if you say it, I'll b. it* si tú lo dices, yo lo acepto> ♦ **to b. a pig in a poke** JER. comprar algo sin saber exactamente qué es • **to b. into** COM. comprar cantidades importantes de acciones de (una empresa) • **to b. off** sobornar • **to b. on credit** comprar al fiado • **to b. out** COM. comprar la parte de • **to b. up** acaparar —intr. hacer compras **II.** s. *(purchase)* compra; FAM. *(bargain)* ganga ♦ **a good b.** una buena compra, ganga.

buy·er (bī′ər) s. *(customer)* comprador *m*; *(purchasing agent)* agente comprador *m*.

buyer's market s. ECON. mercado favorable al comprador, mercado a bajo precio.

buzz (bŭz) **I.** intr. *(to hum loudly)* zumbar; *(to whisper excitedly)* cuchichear, susurrar; *(to murmur)* murmurar; *(to bustle)* ajetrearse; *(with a buzzer)* tocar el timbre ♦ **to b. off** FAM. largarse —tr. *(to cause to buzz)* hacer zumbar; FAM. *(to fly)* volar muy cerca de; *(to murmur)* murmurar; *(to signal with a buzzer)* llamar con un timbre; FAM. *(to*

---

telephone) telefonear, dar un telefonazo **II.** s. *(drone)* zumbido; *(murmur)* murmullo; FAM. *(telephone call)* telefonazo.

buz·zard (bŭz′ərd) s. buitre *m.*

buzz·er (bŭz′ər) s. timbre *m.*

buzz saw s. sierra circular.

by¹ §G37 (bī) **I.** prep. *(authorship)* por *<a novel written by Cervantes* una novela escrita por Cervantes>; *(means)* en *<we will go by plane* iremos en avión>; *(via)* por *<he went by the main road* fue por la carretera principal>; *(measure)* por *<eggs are sold by the dozen* los huevos se venden por docena>; *(with the sanction of)* por *<I swear by God that it is true* juro por Dios que es cierto>; *(cause)* por *<the house was destroyed by the fire* la casa fue destruida por el fuego>; MAT. *(multiplication, division)* por *<multiply two by two* multiplique dos por dos>; *(rate)* *<they pay me by the hour* me pagan por hora>; *(origin)* de *<French by birth* francés de nacimiento>; *(from)* de *<he has a child by a previous wife* tiene un hijo de una esposa anterior>; *(time)* de *<by night* de noche>; *(next to)* junto a, cerca de *<let's sit by the fire* sentémonos junto al fuego>; *(according to)* según, de acuerdo con *<to play by the rules* jugar de acuerdo con las reglas>; *(not later than)* *<finish it by noon* termínalo para el mediodía>; *(after)* a *<day by day* día a día>; *(direction)* cuarta a *<north by northwest* norte cuarta al noroeste>; *(during)* durante, de *<the sun shines by day* el sol brilla de día> ◆ **by all means** *(without fail)* sin falta; *(certainly)* por supuesto *<may I have another piece? by all means!* ¿puedo servirme otra porción? ¡por supuesto!>* • **by any means** cueste lo que cueste • **by chance** por casualidad • **by degrees** gradualmente • **by far** con mucho • **by hand** *(not using machinery)* a mano; *(via messenger)* por mensajero • **by heart** de memoria • **by hook or by crook** FAM. de una manera u otra • **by itself** *(without any help)* por sí solo; *(unto itself)* de por sí • **by means of** mediante, por medio de • **by nature** por naturaleza • **by no means** de ningún modo • **by now** ahora, ya • **by oneself** *(alone)* solo, a solas; *(without help)* solo, sin ayuda • **by proxy** por poder • **by the by** de paso, a propósito • **by the way** de paso, entre paréntesis • **by this time** *(hour)* a esta hora; *(point)* a estas alturas • **to go by** guiarse por, regirse por • **to know by name** conocer de nombre • **to stand by (someone)** *(to be faithful to)* ser fiel a; *(to defend)* defender **II.** adv. *(nearby)* cerca, al lado de; *(aside)* a un lado, aparte ◆ **by and by** *(soon)* pronto; *(after a while)* más tarde • **by and large** en términos generales • **by reason of** a causa o fuerza de • **by then** para entonces • **close by** muy cerca • **to go by** pasar de largo • **to stand by** estar listo o pronto • **to stop by** hacer una visita. ▲ La preposición *by* no se traduce cuando precede a un gerundio que indica una manera o un método *<by studying you will learn* estudiando usted aprenderá> *<she did it by working hard* lo logró trabajando fuerte>.

by² (bī) s. var. de **bye.**

by-and-by (bī′ən-bī′) s. *(future occasion)* ocasión futura; *(hereafter)* en el futuro, con el tiempo.

bye (bī) s. aspecto secundario ◆ **by the b.** incidentalmente.

bye-bye (bī′bī′) interj. FAM. ¡adiós!, ¡hasta luego!

Bye·lo·rus·sia (byĕl′ō-rŭsh′ə) s. Bielorrusia.

Bye·lo·rus·sian (byĕl′ō-rŭsh′ən) adj. & s. bielorruso.

by·gone (bī′gôn′) **I.** adj. pasado *<b. days* días pasados> **II.** s. cosa pasada ◆ **to let bygones be bygones** olvidar lo pasado.

by·law (bī′lô′) s. *(statute)* estatuto; *(regulations)* reglamento; *(of a city)* ordenanza municipal.

by-line o **by·line** (bī′līn′) **I.** s. renglón *m* con el nombre del autor (al comienzo de un artículo periodístico) **II.** intr. **-lined, -lin·ing** firmar un artículo.

by-pass o **by·pass** (bī′păs′) **I.** s. *(road)* carretera de circunvalación; *(detour)* desvío, desviación; *(pipe)* tubo de desviación, tubo de paso; ELEC. derivación *f* ◆ **coronary b.** MED. desviación coronaria **II.** tr. *(to avoid)* evitar; *(to ignore)* pasar por alto; *(to change the direction of)* desviar, evitar pasar por.

by-play (bī′plā′) s. TEAT. juego escénico secundario.

by-prod·uct (bī′prŏd′əkt) s. *(secondary product)* subproducto, derivado; *(side effect)* efecto secundario.

by·road (bī′rōd′) s. carretera secundaria.

by·stand·er (bī′stăn′dər) s. *(spectator)* espectador *m*, persona presente; *(onlooker)* curioso.

byte (bīt) s. COMPUT. byte *m*, octeto (grupo de bits).

by·way (bī′wā′) s. *(byroad)* carretera secundaria; *(field of study)* campo de investigación secundario *u* olvidado.

by·word (bī′wûrd′) s. *(proverb)* refrán *m*, proverbio; *(type)* prototipo; *(object of contempt)* objeto de escarnio; *(nickname)* sobrenombre, apodo.

Byz·an·tine (bĭz′ən-tēn′) adj. & s. bizantino.

By·zan·ti·um (bĭ-zăn′shē-əm) s. Bizancio.

C

c, C (sē) s. [pl. **c's, C's**] tercera letra del alfabeto inglés; MÚS. do ◆ **C flat, major, minor, sharp** MÚS. do bemol, mayor, menor, sostenido.

cab (kăb) s. *(taxicab)* taxi *m*; *(cabriolet)* cabriolé de alquiler *m*; *(cabin of vehicle)* cabina.

ca·bal (kə-băl′) **I.** s. *(scheme)* cábala, intriga; *(conspiratorial group)* camarilla **II.** intr. **-balled, -bal·ling** conspirar, intrigar.

cab·a·la (kăb′ə-lə, kə-bä′-) s. RELIG. cábala.

cab·a·ret (kăb′ə-rā′) s. *(nightclub)* cabaret *m*; *(show)* espectáculo.

cab·bage (kăb′ĭj) s. *(plant)* col *f*, berza; JER. *(money)* dinero de papel.

cab·ba·la (kăb′ə-lə, kə-bä′-) s. var. de **cabala.**

cab·by o **cab·bie** (kăb′ē) s. [pl. **-bies**] FAM. taxista *mf*, conductor de taxi *m.*

cab·driv·er (kăb′drī′vər) s. taxista *mf*, conductor de taxi *m.*

cab·in (kăb′ĭn) s. *(small house)* barraca, choza; *(of a ship)* camarote *m*; *(of a plane)* cabina.

cabin boy s. MARÍT. grumete *m.*

cabin class s. MARÍT. segunda clase.

cabin cruiser s. yate de recreo *m.*

cab·i·net (kăb′ə-nĭt) s. *(cupboard)* armario; *(showcase)* vitrina ◆ **C.** consejo o gabinete de ministros.

cab·i·net·mak·er (kăb′ə-nĭt-mā′kər) s. ebanista *mf.*

cab·i·net·work (kăb′ə-nĭt-wûrk′) s. ebanistería.

ca·ble (kā′bəl) **I.** s. *(rope, wire)* cable *m*; *(cablegram)* cablegrama *m*, cable; *(television)* televisión por cable *f* **II.** tr. **-bled, -bling** *(to send a cablegram to)* enviar un cable a; *(to send by cablegram)* cablegrafiar —intr. enviar un cable.

cable car s. funicular *m.*

ca·ble·gram (kā′bəl-grăm′) s. cablegrama *m.*

ca·ble·vi·sion (kā′bəl-vĭzh′ən) s. televisión por cable *f.*

ca·boo·dle (kə-bōōd′l) s. FAM. montón *m*, conjunto ◆ **the whole c.** *(things)* el montón entero, todo el conjunto; *(persons)* toda la banda.

ca·boose (kə-bōōs′) s. F.C. furgón de cola *m.*

cab·o·tage (kăb′ə-täzh′) s. MARÍT. cabotaje *m.*

cab·stand (kăb′stănd′) s. parada de taxis.

ca·ca·o (kə-kā′ō, -kä′ō) s. [pl. **-os**] cacao (árbol y semilla).

cach·a·lot (kăsh′ə-lŏt′, -ə-lō′) s. ZOOL. cachalote *m.*

cache (kăsh) **I.** s. *(hole)* escondite *m*, escondrijo; *(hidden goods)* reserva escondida **II.** tr. **cached, cach·ing** guardar en un escondrijo.

ca·chet (kă-shā′) s. *(seal)* sello; FIG. *(mark)* sello, cachet *m* *<a profession with a c. of prestige* una profesión con un sello de prestigio>; *(capsule)* cápsula, sello.

cack·le (kăk′əl) **I.** intr. **-led, -ling** *(of hens)* cacarear; *(to laugh)* reírse estridentemente —tr. decir como cacareando **II.** s. *(of hens)* cacareo; *(laughter)* risa estridente; *(chatter)* cháchara.

ca·coph·o·nous (kə-kŏf′ə-nəs) adj. cacofónico.

ca·coph·o·ny (kə-kŏf′ə-nē) s. [pl. **-nies**] cacofonía.

cac·tus (kăk′təs) s. [pl. **-ti** (-tī′) o **-tus·es**] cactus *m*, cacto.

cad (kăd) s. desvergonzado, sinvergüenza *m.*

ca·dav·er (kə-dăv′ər) s. cadáver *m.*

ca·dav·er·ous (kə-dăv′ər-əs) adj. cadavérico.

---

ng inglés / ŏ **la** / ō **bou** / ô **corre** / oi **oigo** / ōō **uno** / ou **auto** / yōō **ciudad** / w **hueco** / y **yo** / z **mismo**

cad·die (kăd′ē) DEP. I. s. [pl. **-dies**] caddy *m* II. intr. **-died, -dy·ing** servir de caddy.

cad·dy¹ (kăd′ē) s. [pl. **-dies**] cajita para el té.

cad·dy² (kăd′ē) s. & v. var. de **caddie**.

ca·dence (kād′ns) o **ca·den·cy** (kād′n-sē) s. [pl. **-denc·es** o **-den·cies**] cadencia.

ca·det (kə-dĕt′) s. MIL. cadete *m*.

cadge (kăj) tr. & intr. **cadged, cadg·ing** FAM. gorronear.

cad·mi·um (kăd′mē-əm) s. QUÍM. cadmio.

cad·re (kăd′rē) s. cuadro.

ca·du·ce·us (kə-dōō′sē-əs, -dyōō′-) s. [pl. **-ce·i** (-sē-ī′)] caduceo.

Cae·sar (sē′zər) s. HIST. César ♦ **c.** dictador.

Cae·sar·e·an o **Cae·sar·i·an** (sī-zâr′ē-ən) s. MED. cesárea, operación cesárea.

Caesarean section o **caesarean section** s. MED. cesárea, operación cesárea.

ca·fé o **ca·fe** (kă-fā′) s. café *m*, cafetería.

caf·e·te·ri·a (kăf′ĭ-tîr′ē-ə) s. cafetería, restaurante de autoservicio *m*.

caf·feine o **caf·fein** (kă-fēn′) s. QUÍM. cafeína.

caf·tan (kăf′tăn′) s. caftán *m*, túnica.

cage (kāj) I. s. (*enclosure*) jaula II. tr. **caged, cag·ing** enjaular.

cag·ey o **cag·y** (kā′jē) adj. **-i·er, -i·est** (*wary*) cauteloso; (*crafty*) astuto.

ca·hoots (kə-hōōts′) s.pl. FAM. confabulación *f*, connivencia ♦ **to be in c. with** FAM. estar en connivencia con.

cai·man (kā′mən) s. ZOOL. caimán *m*.

Cain (kān) s. BÍBL. Caín; (*murderer*) asesino ♦ **to raise C.** armar jaleo, armar barullo.

cairn (kârn) s. montón de piedras (como señal) *m*.

Cai·ro (kī′rō) s. El Cairo.

cais·son (kā′sŏn′, -sən) s. (*box*) cajón *m*, campana (para trabajar bajo el agua); MARÍT. (*camel*) camello; (*lock*) compuerta de dique; MIL. (*box*) cajón de municiones; (*cart*) furgón de municiones *m*.

ca·jole (kə-jōl′) tr. **-joled, -jol·ing** engatusar.

Ca·jun (kā′jən) s. natural del estado de Luisiana de ascendencia francesa.

cake (kāk) I. s. (*pastry*) pastel *m*; (*without filling*) bizcocho; (*with filling*) tarta; (*pancake*) torta, panqueque *m*; (*patty*) croqueta; (*bar*) pastilla <a *c. of soap* una pastilla de jabón>; (*piece*) pedazo <a *c. of ice* un pedazo de hielo> ♦ **to take the c.** FAM. ser el colmo, llevarse la palabra II. tr. & intr. **caked, cak·ing** endurecer(se).

cal·a·bash (kăl′ə-băsh′) s. BOT. (*vine, fruit*) calabaza; (*tree*) güira; (*bowl*) totumo.

cal·a·boose (kăl′ə-bōōs′) s. JER. calabozo.

cal·a·mine (kăl′ə-mīn′) s. QUÍM. calamina.

ca·lam·i·tous (kə-lăm′ĭ-təs) adj. calamitoso.

ca·lam·i·ty (kə-lăm′ĭ-tē) s. [pl. **-ties**] calamidad *f*, desastre *m*.

cal·cic (kăl′sĭk) adj. QUÍM. cálcico.

cal·ci·fy (kăl′sə-fī′) tr. & intr. **-fied, -fy·ing** calcificar(se).

cal·ci·mine (kăl′sə-mīn′) I. s. CONSTR. encalado II. tr. **-mined, -min·ing** encalar, blanquear.

cal·ci·um (kăl′sē-əm) s. QUÍM. calcio.

calc·spar o **calc-spar** (kălk′spär′) s. MIN. calcita.

cal·cu·la·ble (kăl′kyə-lə-bəl) adj. (*countable*) calculable; (*dependable*) fiable.

cal·cu·late (kăl′kyə-lāt′) tr. **-lat·ed, -lat·ing** (*to compute*) calcular, computar; (*to evaluate*) determinar; (*to make for a purpose*) hacer a propósito; (*to intend*) tener la intención de; (*to think*) creer —intr. (*to make a computation*) hacer cálculos; (*to guess*) suponer ♦ **to c. on** contar con.

cal·cu·lat·ed (kăl′kyə-lā′tĭd) adj. (*counted*) calculado; (*deliberate*) deliberado, intencional.

cal·cu·lat·ing (kăl′kyə-lā′tĭng) adj. calculador.

cal·cu·la·tion (kăl′kyə-lā′shən) s. (*computation*) cálculo, cómputo; (*deliberation*) cálculo, deliberación *f*.

cal·cu·la·tor (kăl′kyə-lā′tər) s. (*person*) calculador *m*; (*device*) calculadora.

cal·cu·lus (kăl′kyə-ləs) s. [pl. **-li** (-lī′) o **-lus·es**] MAT., MED. cálculo.

Cal·cut·ta (kăl-kŭt′ə) s. Calcuta.

cal·dron (kôl′drən) s. caldera.

cal·en·dar (kăl′ən-dər) I. s. (*of days*) calendario; (*list*) lista, registro; (*schedule*) agenda II. tr. poner en un calendario o en una agenda.

cal·en·der (kăl′ən-dər) I. s. MEC. calandria II. tr. calandrar.

cal·ends (kăl′əndz) s. [pl. **calends**] HIST. calendas, primer día de cada mes.

calf¹ (kăf, käf) s. [pl. **calves** (kăvz, kävz)] (*of cows*) becerro, ternero; (*of mammals*) cría; (*leather*) piel de becerro *f*.

calf² (kăf, käf) s. [pl. **calves** (kăvz, kävz)] ANAT. pantorrilla.

calf·skin (kăf′skĭn′, käf′-) s. piel de becerro *f*.

cal·i·ber (kăl′ə-bər) s. calibre *m*.

cal·i·brate (kăl′ə-brāt′) tr. **-brat·ed, -brat·ing** (*guns, cylinders*) calibrar; (*thermometer*) graduar.

cal·i·bra·tion (kăl′ə-brā′shən) s. (*of guns, cylinders*) calibración *f*; (*of a thermometer*) graduación *f*.

cal·i·bra·tor (kăl′ə-brā′tər) s. TEC. calibrador *m*.

cal·i·bre (kăl′ə-bər) s. G.B. var. de **caliber**.

cal·i·ces (kăl′ĭ-sēz′, kāl′ĭ-) pl. de **calix**.

cal·i·co (kăl′ĭ-kō′) s. [pl. **-coes** o **-cos**] (*cloth*) calicó; (*animal*) animal pinto.

ca·lif (kăl′ĭf, kāl′ĭf) s. var. de **caliph**.

Cal·i·for·nia (kăl′ə-fôr′nyə) s. California.

Cal·i·for·nian (kăl′ə-fôr′nyən) adj. & s. californiano.

cal·i·for·ni·um (kăl′ə-fôr′nē-əm) s. QUÍM. californio.

cal·i·per (kăl′ə-pər) s. (*instrument*) compás de calibre *m*, calibrador *m*; (*vernier caliper*) calibrador micrométrico ♦ **calipers** calibrador.

ca·liph (kăl′ĭf, kāl′ĭf) s. califa *m*.

ca·liph·ate (kăl′ĭ-fāt′, kāl′ĭ-) s. califato *m*.

cal·is·then·ics (kăl′ĭs-thĕn′ĭks) s. [ú. con v. sing. o pl.] calistenia.

ca·lix (kā′lĭks, kāl′ĭks) s. [pl. **ca·li·ces** (kā′lĭ-sēz′, kāl′ĭ-)] RELIG. cáliz *m*.

calk (kôk) v. var. de **caulk**.

call (kôl) I. tr. (*to cry out*) llamar; (*to proclaim*) proclamar, pregonar; (*to send for*) llamar, hacer venir <*c. the doctor* llama al médico>; (*to convene*) convocar, citar; (*to summon to a vocation*) llamar <*he was called to the priesthood* fue llamado al sacerdocio>; (*to awaken*) llamar, despertar <*c. me at three o'clock* despiértame a las tres>; (*to telephone*) telefonear, llamar a; (*to lure*) reclamar a <a *device to c. the ducks* un aparato para reclamar a los patos>; (*to name*) llamar, nombrar; (*to consider*) considerar, juzgar <*I c. that fair* lo considero razonable>; (*to label*) calificar (de); (*to declare*) declarar <*the union called a strike* el sindicato declaró una huelga>; (*to forecast*) pronosticar, predecir <*he called the outcome of the election* predijo el resultado de la elección>; COM. (*to demand repayment of*) pedir el reembolso de (préstamo, deuda) ♦ **to c. back** (*to retract*) revocar, anular; (*to ask to return*) hacer volver; (*to return a telephone call*) volver a llamar • **to c. down** FAM. (*to scold*) regañar, reñir; (*to invoke*) invocar • **to c. forth** hacer surgir • **to c. in** (*to summon*) hacer venir, llamar; (*to withdraw*) retirar de circulación; COM. (*to demand payment of*) pedir el reembolso de • **to c. in** o **into question** poner en tela de juicio • **to c. in** FIG. hacer entrar en juego • **to c. it a day** FAM. poner fin a las labores del día • **to c. it quits** FAM. parar • **to c. off** (*to cancel*) cancelar; (*to put an end to*) parar, suspender • **to c. one's own** (*to claim*) llamar suyo; (*to possess*) poseer, disponer de • **to c. one-self** llamarse • **to c. out** (*to summon into action*) convocar a la acción; (*to shout*) llamar; (*to challenge*) desafiar, retar (a duelo) • **to c. (someone) names** insultar (a alguien) • **to c. together** convocar, reunir • **to c. to account** (*to demand an explanation of*) pedir cuentas; (*to scold*) censurar, regañar • **to c. to mind** evocar, traer a la memoria • **to c. to order** llamar al orden • **to c. the bar** recibir de abogado • **to c. the roll** pasar lista • **to c. attention** hacer notar o reparar en <*he called my attention to the problem* me hizo reparar en el problema> • **to c. up** (*by telephone*) llamar a, telefonear; MIL. llamar a las armas —intr. (*to telephone*) hacer una llamada (telefónica), llamar; (*to visit*) hacer una visita; (*to yell*) llamar, gritar; ORNIT., ZOOL. reclamarse ♦ **to c. again** venir otra vez, volver • **to c. at** pasar por (casa, oficina de alguien); MARÍT. hacer escala en • **to c.**

back volver a llamar por teléfono • **to c. for** *(to go and get)* ir a buscar, ir a recoger <*the cab called for her at the hotel* el taxi la fue a recoger al hotel>; *(to need)* requerir, necesitar <*the recipe calls for two eggs* la receta requiere dos huevos> • **to c. on** *o* **upon** *(to visit)* visitar a, ir a ver a <*we must c. on our new neighbors* debemos ir a ver a nuestros nuevos vecinos>; *(to appeal)* solicitar, recurrir a <*he called upon his friends for help* recurrió a sus amigos para que lo ayudaran>; *(to invoke from above)* invocar • **to c. out** exclamar, gritar **II.** s. *(shout)* llamada; *(appeal)* llamada, llamamiento; ORNIT., ZOOL. reclamo, canto; *(expression)* seña, señal *f*; *(signal)* toque (de trompeta, tambor) *m*; *(telephone communication)* llamada telefónica; *(short visit)* visita (corta) <*the doctor made five calls today* el doctor hizo cinco visitas hoy>; *(summons)* llamamiento, convocatoria; *(invitation)* invitación *f*; RELIG. *(vocation)* vocación *f*, llamamiento; COM. opción de compra *f*; FIG. *(reason)* derecho, por qué <*you have no c. to meddle in other people's affairs* tú no tienes por qué meterte en los asuntos de los demás>; COM. *(demand)* demanda, pedido <*there isn't much c. for inkwells today* no hay gran demanda de tinteros hoy en día>; *(claim)* exigencia ♦ **a close c.** peligro que se evita por muy poco • **c. button** botón de llamada • **collect c.** llamada telefónica a cobrar, conferencia de cobro revertido • **on c.** *(on duty)* de guardia; COM. a vista, a solicitud • **port of c.** MARÍT. puerto de escala • **to pay a c. on** hacer visita a • **within c.** al alcance de la voz.
call·back (kôl'băk') s. COM. llamada para la devolución de un producto al fabricante (para corregir un defecto).
call·er (kô'lər) s. *(by telephone)* persona que llama; *(visitor)* visita, visitante *mf*.
call girl s. FAM. prostituta.
cal·lig·ra·pher (kə-lĭg'rə-fər) s. calígrafo.
cal·lig·ra·phy (kə-lĭg'rə-fē) s. caligrafía.
call·ing (kô'lĭng) s. *(call)* llamado, llamamiento; *(vocation)* vocación *f*; *(occupation)* profesión *f*.
calling card s. tarjeta de visita.
cal·li·o·pe (kə-lī'ə-pē) s. MÚS. órgano de vapor ♦ **C.** MITOL. Calíope.
cal·li·per (kăl'ə-pər) s. var. de **caliper.**
call loan s. COM. préstamo pagadero a petición.
call money s. COM. dinero pagadero a petición.
cal·los·i·ty (kə-lŏs'ĭ-tē) s. [pl. **-ties**] *(callousness)* dureza; *(insensitivity)* insensibilidad *f*; *(callus)* callo, callosidad *f*.
cal·lous (kăl'əs) **I.** adj. *(toughened)* encallecido, calloso; FIG. *(unfeeling)* insensible **II.** intr. FISIOL. *(to develop a hard surface)* encallecerse; FIG. *(to harden)* hacerse insensible.
cal·low (kăl'ō) adj. **-er, -est** *(inexperienced)* inexperto; *(immature)* inmaturo; *(unfledged)* implume, sin plumas.
call rate s. COM. tipo de interés aplicado a préstamos pagaderos a petición.
call-up (kôl'ŭp') s. MIL. llamada a filas.
cal·lus (kăl'əs) **I.** s. [pl. **-lus·es**] BOT., MED. callo **II.** intr. encallecerse.
calm (käm) **I.** adj. **-er, -est** sereno, tranquilo **II.** s. *(serenity)* calma, tranquilidad *f*; METEOR. calma **III.** tr. & intr. aplacar(se), calmar(se).
calm·a·tive (kä'mə-tĭv, kăl'mə-) adj. & s. calmante *m*, sedante *m*.
calm·ness (käm'nĭs) s. tranquilidad *f*.
ca·lor·ic (kə-lôr'ĭk) adj. & s. calórico.
cal·o·rie (kăl'ə-rē) s. FÍS., FISIOL. caloría.
cal·o·rim·e·try (kăl'ə-rĭm'ĭ-trē) s. FÍS. calorimetría.
cal·u·met (kăl'yə-mĕt') s. pipa de la paz.
ca·lum·ni·ate (kə-lŭm'nē-āt') tr. **-at·ed, -at·ing** calumniar.
cal·um·ny (kăl'əm-nē) s. [pl. **-nies**] calumnia.
cal·va·ry (kăl'və-rē) s. [pl. **-ries**] calvario ♦ **C.** RELIG. Calvario.
calve (kăv, käv) intr. & tr. **calved, calv·ing** *(to give birth)* parir (la vaca); *(to detach)* desprenderse (una parte de un glaciar *o* un iceberg).
calves (kăvz, kävz) pl. de **calf.**
Cal·vin (kăl'vĭn) s. Calvino.
Cal·vin·ism (kăl'vĭ-nĭz'əm) s. RELIG. calvinismo.
Cal·vin·ist (kăl'vĭ-nĭst) s. & adj. RELIG. calvinista *mf*.

ca·lyx (kā'lĭks, kăl'ĭks) s. [pl. **ca·lyx·es** *o* **ca·ly·ces** (kā'lĭ-sēz', kăl'ĭ-)] ANAT., BOT. cáliz *m*.
cam (kăm) s. MEC. leva.
ca·ma·ra·der·ie (kä'mə-rä'də-rē) s. compañerismo, camaradería.
cam·ber (kăm'bər) **I.** s. *(arch)* curvatura; *(of a road)* peralte *m*; AUTO. inclinación *f* **II.** tr. & intr. combar(se), arquear(se).
cam·bi·um (kăm'bē-əm) s. BOT. cambium *m*.
Cam·bo·di·a (kăm-bō'dē-ə) s. Camboya.
Cam·bo·di·an (kăm-bō'dē-ən) adj. & s. camboyano.
came (kăm) pret. de **come.**
cam·el (kăm'əl) s. MARÍT., ZOOL. camello.
ca·mel·lia (kə-mēl'yə) s. BOT. camelia.
camel's hair s. pelo de camello.
cam·e·o (kăm'ē-ō') s. [pl. **-os**] *(engraving)* camafeo; *(role)* papel de actor invitado *m*.
cam·er·a (kăm'ər-ə) s. FOTOG. cámara *o* máquina fotográfica; CINEM., TELEV. cámara; *(camera obscura)* cámara obscura; *(of a judge)* cámara de juez ♦ **in c.** DER. en sesión secreta, a puerta cerrada.
cam·er·a·man (kăm'ər-ə-măn') s. [pl. **-men** (-mən)] CINEM., TELEV. cameraman *m*.
Cam·er·oon, United Republic of (kăm'ə-rōōn') s. República Unida de Camerún.
Cam·er·oon·i·an (kăm'ə-rōō'nē-ən) adj. & s. camerunés *m*.
cam·i·sole (kăm'ĭ-sōl') s. cubrecorsé *m*.
cam·o·mile (kăm'ə-mīl') s. var. de **chamomile.**
cam·ou·flage (kăm'ə-fläzh', -fläj') **I.** s. camuflaje *m* **II.** tr. & intr. **-flaged, -flag·ing** camuflar.
camp¹ (kămp) **I.** s. *(group of shelters)* campo <*concentration c.* campo de concentración>; *(for the army, for recreation)* campamento; *(group)* campo, facción *f*; *(military life)* vida militar **II.** intr. & tr. acampar.
camp² (kămp) **I.** s. *(affectation)* afectación frívola; *(behavior)* conducta afectada y frívola; *(banality)* banalidad *f*, superficialidad *f* **II.** adj. afectado **III.** intr. actuar *o* comportarse de manera estrafalaria y ridícula.
cam·paign (kăm-pān') **I.** s. campaña **II.** intr. hacer una campaña.
cam·paign·er (kăm-pā'nər) s. *(fighter)* luchador *m*; *(propagandist)* propagandista *mf* ♦ **old c.** MIL. veterano.
cam·pa·ni·le (kăm'pə-nē'lē) s. [pl. **-les** *o* **-li** (-lē)] ARQ. campanil *m*, campanario.
camp·er (kăm'pər) s. *(person)* campista *mf*; *(vehicle)* caravana.
camp·fire (kămp'fīr') s. *(fire)* hoguera de campamento; *(meeting)* reunión alrededor de una hoguera *f*.
camp follower s. *(peddler)* vivandero; *(prostitute)* prostituta; *(follower)* seguidor *m*.
camp·ground (kămp'ground') s. acampada, camping *m*.
cam·phor (kăm'fər) s. QUÍM. alcanfor *m*.
camp·ing (kăm'pĭng) s. camping *m* <*I love to go c.* me encanta ir de camping>.
camp meeting s. RELIG. reunión religiosa al aire libre *f*.
camp·site (kămp'sīt') s. acampada, camping *m*.
cam·pus (kăm'pəs) s. [pl. **-pus·es**] ciudad universitaria.
cam·shaft (kăm'shăft') s. MEC. árbol de levas *m*.
can¹ §G11 (kăn, kən) aux. [pret. **could** (kōōd)] *(to be able to)* poder <*I c. run* puedo correr>; *(to know how to)* saber <*she c. sew and cook* ella sabe coser y cocinar>; *(to have the right to)* poder <*anyone c. cross the street here* cualquiera puede cruzar la calle aquí>; *(to be allowed to)* tener permiso para, poder <*you c. eat your dessert now* puedes comer el postre ahora>.
can² (kăn) **I.** s. *(tin)* lata (recipiente y contenido); *(large container)* tacho, cubo <*a garbage c.* un cubo de basura>; JER. *(jail)* chirona, cárcel *f*; *(toilet)* retrete *m*, excusado; *(buttocks)* nalgas; MIL. *(depth charge)* carga de profundidad; *(destroyer)* destructor *m* **II.** tr. **canned, can·ning** *(to preserve)* enlatar, conservar en lata; JER. *(to fire)* despedir <*he was canned from his job* lo despidieron del trabajo>; *(to record)* grabar ♦ **c. it!** JER. ¡a callar!, ¡basta!
Ca·naan (kā'nən) s. Canaán.
Can·a·da (kăn'ə-də) s. Canadá *m*.
Ca·na·di·an (kə-nā'dē-ən) adj. & s. canadiense *mf*.

ca·nal (kə-năl′) I. s. canal m II. tr. construir un canal.
can·a·li·za·tion (kăn′ə-lĭ-zā′shən) s. canalización f.
Canal Zone s. Zona del Canal de Panamá.
ca·nard (kə-närd′) s. bulo, patraña.
ca·nar·y (kə-nâr′ē) s. [pl. **-ies**] (bird) canario; JER. (informer) soplón m; (wine) vino de Canarias; (yellow) amarillo canario.
Canary Islands s. Islas Canarias, Canarias.
can·cel (kăn′səl) I. tr. to annul) anular, cancelar; (to cross out) suprimir, tachar; (to stamp) matar (un sello); (to offset) compensar, contrarrestar; MAT. cancelar, eliminar (factores, coeficientes) —intr. anularse, eliminarse II. s. cancelación f, anulación f.
can·cel·la·tion (kăn′sə-lā′shən) s. (canceling) cancelación f, anulación f; (mark) tachadura; (of a stamp) matasellos.
can·cer (kăn′sər) s. MED. cáncer m ♦ C. ASTROL. Cáncer.
can·cer·ous (kăn′sər-əs) adj. canceroso.
can·de·la (kăn-děl′ə) s. FÍS. candela.
can·de·la·brum (kăn′dl-ä′brəm) s. [pl. **-bra** (-brə) o **-brums**] candelabro.
can·des·cent (kăn-děs′ənt) adj. candente, incandescente.
can·did (kăn′dĭd) I. adj. (frank) franco; (impartial) imparcial; (not posed) espontáneo II. s. fotografía espontánea.
can·di·da·cy (kăn′dĭ-də-sē) s. [pl. **-cies**] candidatura.
can·di·date (kăn′dĭ-dāt′) s. candidato.
can·died (kăn′dēd) adj. escarchado, almibarado.
can·dle (kăn′dl) I. s. (taper) vela, bujía; FÍS. candela ♦ not to hold a c. to no llegar ni a la suela del zapato de II. tr. **-dled, -dling** examinar a contraluz (un huevo).
can·dle·foot (kăn′dl-fŏŏt′) s. FÍS. unidad luminosa.
can·dle·hold·er (kăn′dl-hōl′dər) s. candelero, palmatoria.
can·dle·light (kăn′dl-līt′) s. (light) luz de una vela f, FIG. (dusk) atardecer m, crepúsculo.
Can·dle·mas (kăn′dl-məs) s. RELIG. Candelaria.
can·dle·pow·er (kăn′dl-pou′ər) s. candela (intensidad luminosa).
can·dle·stick (kăn′dl-stĭk′) s. candelero, palmatoria.
can·dor (kăn′dər) s. (frankness) sinceridad f, franqueza; (impartiality) imparcialidad f.
can·dy (kăn′dē) s. [pl. **-dies**] (sweet) caramelo; (bonbon) bombón m II. tr. & intr. **-died, -dy·ing** escarchar(se).
candy store s. confitería.
cane (kān) I. s. (stem) vara; (stick) bastón m; (plant) caña; (furniture material) mimbre m; (sugar cane) caña de azúcar II. tr. **caned, can·ing** (to make) tejer con mimbre; (to repair) poner (asiento de mimbre); (to beat) golpear con una vara.
cane·brake (kān′brāk′) s. cañaveral m.
cane sugar s. azúcar de caña m.
ca·nine (kā′nīn′) I. adj. canino II. s. (animal) animal canino; (tooth) diente canino.
can·is·ter (kăn′ĭ-stər) s. (container) lata; MIL. (cylinder) bote de metralla m.
can·ker (kăng′kər) I. s. (sore) úlcera en la boca; BOT., VET. cancro; FIG. (spreading corruption) cáncer m II. tr. & intr. MED. ulcerar(se); FIG. (to decay) corromper(se).
can·ker·ous (kăng′kər-əs) adj. ulceroso.
canker sore s. MED. úlcera en la boca.
can·ker·worm (kăng′kər-wûrm′) s. especie de oruga.
can·na·bis (kăn′ə-bĭs) s. BOT. cáñamo índico.
canned (kănd) adj. (in a can) enlatado; (preserved) en conserva; FAM. (taped) grabado.
canned heat s. bombona (de alcohol, petróleo).
can·ner·y (kăn′ə-rē) s. [pl. **-ies**] fábrica de conservas.
can·ni·bal (kăn′ə-bəl) s. caníbal m, antropófago.
can·ni·bal·ism (kăn′ə-bə-lĭz′əm) s. canibalismo, antropofagia.
can·ni·bal·is·tic (kăn′ə-bə-lĭs′tĭk) adj. caníbal, antropófago.
can·ni·bal·ize (kăn′ə-bə-līz′) tr. **-ized, -iz·ing** (to remove parts from) recuperar las piezas servibles de (avión, tanque); (to deprive) utilizar el personal de una organización en otra.
can·ning (kăn′ĭng) s. enlatado.
can·non (kăn′ən) ARM. I. s. [pl. **-non** o **-nons**] cañón m II. tr. cañonear.

can·non·ade (kăn′ə-nād′) I. tr. & intr. **-ad·ed, -ad·ing** cañonear II. s. cañoneo.
can·non·ball o **cannon ball** (kăn′ən-bôl′) s. bala de cañón.
can·non·eer (kăn′ə-nîr′) s. MIL. artillero.
cannon fodder s. FIG. carne de cañón f.
can·non·ry (kăn′ən-rē) s. [pl. **-ries**] (artillery) artillería f, (fire) fuego de artillería.
cannon shot s. (ammunition) bala de cañón; (shot) cañonazo; (range) alcance de un cañón m.
can·not (kăn′ŏt′, kə-nŏt′) forma negativa de **can**[1].
can·ny (kăn′ē) adj. **-ni·er, -ni·est** (shrewd) astuto; (cautious) cauto.
ca·noe (kə-nōō′) I. s. canoa II. tr. **-noed, -noe·ing** llevar en canoa —intr. ir en canoa.
ca·noe·ing (kə-nōō′ĭng) s. DEP. piragüismo.
can·on[1] (kăn′ən) s. DER. canon m; RELIG. (calendar) calendario eclesiástico.
can·on[2] (kăn′ən) s. RELIG. (member of a chapter) canónigo.
ca·ñon (kăn′yən) s. var. de **canyon**.
ca·non·i·cal (kə-nŏn′ĭ-kəl) o **ca·non·ic** (-ĭk) adj. RELIG. canónico; FIG. (authorized) ortodoxo.
can·on·i·za·tion (kăn′ə-nĭ-zā′shən) s. RELIG. canonización f.
can·on·ize (kăn′ə-nīz′) tr. **-ized, -iz·ing** RELIG. (to declare a saint) canonizar; (approve) aprobar.
canon law s. RELIG. derecho canónico, canon m.
can opener s. abrelatas m.
can·o·py (kăn′ə-pē) I. s. [pl. **-pies**] (cloth covering) dosel m; (awning) toldo; ARQ. (structure) doselete m; FIG. (of leaves, stars) bóveda; AVIA. cubierta movible de la cabina; (of a parachute) casquete m II. tr. **-pied, -py·ing** endoselar.
cant[1] (kănt) I. s. (slant) inclinación f, (corner) esquina (de un edificio); (slanted surface) plano inclinado II. tr. (to tilt) inclinar; (to bevel) biselar; (to swerve) cambiar de dirección repentinamente —intr. (to slant) inclinarse, ladearse; MARÍT. escorar (el barco).
cant[2] (kănt) I. s. (whine) quejido, gemido; (trivial statement) tópico, trivialidad f, (insincere talk) hipocresía; (slang of thieves) germanía; (jargon) jerga II. intr. (to whine) hablar quejosamente; (to moralize) moralizar; (to use special jargon) hablar en jerga.
can't (kănt) contr. de **cannot**.
Can·ta·bri·an (kăn-tā′brē-ən) I. adj. cantábrico, cántabro II. s. cántabro (habitante).
can·ta·loupe o **can·ta·loup** (kăn′tl-ōp′) s. BOT. cantalupo, melón (cantalupo).
can·tan·ker·ous (kăn-tăng′kər-əs) adj. FAM. malhumorado, pendenciero.
can·ta·ta (kən-tä′tə) s. MÚS. cantata.
can·teen (kăn-tēn′) s. (store, cafeteria) cantina; (flask) cantimplora.
can·ter (kăn′tər) I. s. EQUIT. medio galope II. intr. ir a medio galope —tr. hacer ir al caballo a medio galope.
Can·ter·bur·y (kăn′tər-bĕr′ē) s. Canterbury, Cantorbery.
can·ti·cle (kăn′tĭ-kəl) s. cántico.
can·ti·le·ver (kăn′tl-ē′vər, -ěv′ər) I. s. ARQ., TEC. ménsula II. tr. construir con una ménsula.
can·to (kăn′tō) s. [pl. **-tos**] LIT. canto (de un poema épico).
can·ton (kăn′tən, -tŏn′) s. (Swiss) cantón m; (French) distrito.
Can·ton (kăn′tŏn′) s. Cantón.
can·tor (kăn′tər) s. RELIG. (soloist) solista (de una sinagoga) m; (precentor) chantre m.
can·vas (kăn′vəs) s. (fabric) lona; ARTE. (painting) lienzo m; (sails) velas, velamen m; (tent) tienda, carpa (de circo); (for embroidery) cañamazo; DEP. (in wrestling) lona.
can·vass (kăn′vəs) I. tr. (to solicit) solicitar (votos, suscripciones); (to poll) hacer una encuesta; (to scrutinize) escudriñar, examinar —intr. (to solicit) solicitar votos; (to examine) examinar; (to discuss) discutir (detalladamente) II. s. (solicitation) solicitación (de votos, pedidos) f, (survey) encuesta; (examination) examen m; (discussion) discusión f.
can·vass·er (kăn′və-sər) s. (solicitor) solicitante (de votos, pedidos) mf; (counter) escrutador m.

can·yon (kăn′yən) s. GEOG. cañón *m*, desfiladero.
cap (kăp) **I.** s. *(hat)* gorro, gorra; *(coif)* cofia; *(of cardinal)* capelo; *(mortarboard)* birrete *m*; *(cover)* tapa; *(limit)* tope *m*; ARQ. capitel *m*; *(of a fungus)* sombrerete *m*; *(percussion cap)* cápsula, pistón *m*; *(explosive charge)* pistón **II.** tr. **capped, cap·ping** *(to put a head covering on)* poner una gorra; *(to put a cover on)* poner una tapa; *(to cover)* cubrir; *(to complete)* terminar; *(to surpass)* sobrepasar, superar ♦ **to c. off** culminar.
ca·pa·bil·i·ty (kā′pə-bĭl′ĭ-tē) s. [pl. **-ties**] capacidad *f*, aptitud *f* ♦ **capabilities** capacidad en potencia.
ca·pa·ble (kā′pə-bəl) adj. *(able)* capaz; *(open to)* susceptible de.
ca·pa·cious (kə-pā′shəs) adj. espacioso, de gran cabida.
ca·pac·i·tance (kə-păs′ĭ-tns) s. ELEC. capacitancia.
ca·pac·i·tor (kə-păs′ĭ-tər) s. ELEC. condensador *m*.
ca·pac·i·ty (kə-păs′ĭ-tē) s. [pl. **-ties**] *(volume)* capacidad *f*, cabida; *(maximum content)* capacidad máxima; *(maximum production)* rendimiento máximo; *(ability)* capacidad; *(role)* calidad *f* <in the c. of teacher en calidad de maestro>; DER., ELEC. capacidad ♦ **c. house** TEAT. lleno, completo • **to fill to c.** llenar completamente, llenar hasta el tope.
ca·par·i·son (kə-păr′ĭ-sən) s. *(for horse)* caparazón *m*; *(ornamental clothing)* galas.
cape¹ (kāp) s. GEOG. cabo.
cape² (kāp) s. *(garment)* capa.
Cape of Good Hope s. Cabo de Buena Esperanza.
ca·per¹ (kā′pər) **I.** s. *(leap)* brinco; *(prank)* travesura; JER. *(plot)* conspiración criminal *f* **II.** intr. brincar.
ca·per² (kā′pər) s. BOT. *(shrub)* alcaparro; *(bud)* alcaparra.
Cape Verde (vûrd) s. Cabo Verde *m*.
Cape Verd·e·an (vûr′dē-ən) adj. & s. caboverdiano.
cap gun s. pistola de fulminante.
cap·il·lar·i·ty (kăp′ə-lăr′ĭ-tē) s. [pl. **-ties**] FÍS. capilaridad *f*.
cap·il·lar·y (kăp′ə-lĕr′ē) ANAT. **I.** s. [pl. **-ies**] vaso capilar **II.** adj. capilar.
cap·i·tal¹ (kăp′ĭ-tl) **I.** s. *(city)* capital *f*; *(center)* capital <Paris is the c. of fashion París es la capital de la moda>; *(material wealth)* capital *m*, caudal *m*; *(assets)* capital *m*; *(net worth)* capital social *m*; IMPR. *(upper-case letter)* mayúscula **II.** adj. *(foremost)* capital, primordial <a decision of c. importance una decisión de importancia capital>; *(excellent)* excelente, magnífico; *(involving death)* capital; GRAM. mayúscula.
cap·i·tal² (kăp′ĭ-tl) s. ARQ. capitel (de columna) *m*.
capital account s. TEN. cuenta de capital.
capital assets s. TEN. activo fijo.
capital expenditure s. TEN. inversión de capital *f*.
capital gain s. FIN. ganancias sobre el capital.
capital goods s. ECON. bienes de equipo *m*.
cap·i·tal·ism (kăp′ĭ-tl-ĭz′əm) s. capitalismo.
cap·i·tal·ist (kăp′ĭ-tl-ĭst) s. capitalista *mf*.
cap·i·tal·is·tic (kăp′ĭ-tl-ĭs′tĭk) adj. capitalista.
cap·i·tal·i·za·tion (kăp′ĭ-tl-ĭ-zā′shən) s. ECON., FIN. capitalización *f*; GRAM. uso de letras mayúsculas.
cap·i·tal·ize (kăp′ĭ-tl-īz′) tr. **-ized, -iz·ing** FIN. capitalizar; GRAM. escribir con mayúscula —intr. ♦ **to c. on** aprovechar, sacar provecho de.
capital letter s. GRAM. letra mayúscula.
capital levy s. impuesto sobre el capital.
cap·i·tal·ly (kăp′ĭ-tl-ē) adv. admirablemente.
capital punishment s. DER. pena de muerte, pena capital.
capital stock s. FIN. capital social *m*.
cap·i·tol (kăp′ĭ-tl) s. capitolio ♦ **C.** Capitolio.
Capitol Hill s. Congreso de los EE. UU.
ca·pit·u·late (kə-pĭch′ə-lāt′) intr. **-lat·ed, -lat·ing** capitular, rendirse.
ca·pit·u·la·tion (kə-pĭch′ə-lā′shən) s. *(surrender)* capitulación *f*, rendición *f*; *(summary)* recapitulación *f*, resumen *m*.
ca·pon (kā′pŏn′) s. capón *m*, pollo castrado.
cap·ping (kăp′ĭng) s. TEC. capsulado.
cap pistol s. pistola de fulminante.
ca·price (kə-prēs′) s. capricho, antojo.

ca·pri·cious (kə-prĭsh′əs, -prē′shəs) adj. caprichoso, antojadizo.
Cap·ri·corn (kăp′rĭ-kôrn′) s. ASTROL. Capricornio.
cap screw s. tornillo de casquete cuadrado, tornillo de cabeza.
cap·size (kăp′sīz′) intr. **-sized, -siz·ing** volcar —tr. hacer volcar.
cap·stan (kăp′stən) s. *(hoist)* cabrestante *m*; ELECTRÓN. espiga (de una grabadora).
cap·stone (kăp′stōn′) s. ARQ. albardilla; FIG. *(culmination)* culminación *f*.
cap·su·lar (kăp′sə-lər) adj. capsular.
cap·sule (kăp′səl, -sōol) **I.** s. ANAT., AVIA., FARM. cápsula; *(summary)* resumen breve *m* **II.** tr. **-suled, -sul·ing** *(to enclose)* meter en una cápsula; *(to summarize)* resumir.
cap·tain (kăp′tən) **I.** s. capitán *m* **II.** tr. capitanear.
cap·tion (kăp′shən) **I.** s. *(explanation)* pie *m*, leyenda; CINEM. subtítulo; *(heading)* encabezamiento; DER. *(of a document)* indicación de origen *f* **II.** tr. *(to title)* encabezar; *(to explain)* poner una leyenda.
cap·tious (kăp′shəs) adj. *(carping)* criticón, reparón; *(deceptive)* capcioso, insidioso.
cap·ti·vate (kăp′tĭ-vāt′) tr. **-vat·ed, -vat·ing** cautivar, fascinar.
cap·ti·va·tion (kăp′tĭ-vā′shən) s. encanto, fascinación *f*.
cap·ti·va·tor (kăp′tĭ-vā′tər) s. cautivador *m*, fascinador *m*.
cap·tive (kăp′tĭv) **I.** s. cautivo **II.** adj. *(confined)* cautivo; *(captivated)* cautivado, fascinado ♦ **c. audience** personas en una situación que les obliga a escuchar *o* ver algo.
cap·tiv·i·ty (kăp-tĭv′ĭ-tē) s. [pl. **-ties**] cautividad *f*, cautiverio.
cap·tor (kăp′tər) s. capturador *m*.
cap·ture (kăp′chər) **I.** tr. **-tured, -tur·ing** *(to seize)* capturar; *(to win)* ganar; *(to grasp)* captar **II.** s. *(seizure)* captura; *(catch)* presa; *(prize)* premio.
cap·u·chin (kăp′yə-chĭn, kə-pyōō′-) s. *(cloak)* capuchón *m*; *(monkey)* capuchino ♦ **C.** RELIG. capuchino.
car (kär) s. *(automobile)* automóvil *m*, carro; *(coach)* coche *m*, vagón (de tren) *m*; *(tramcar)* tranvía *m*; *(elevator car)* caja, jaula; *(platform)* barquilla (de globo).
ca·rafe (kə-răf′) s. garrafa.
car·a·mel (kăr′ə-məl) s. *(candy)* caramelo; *(burnt sugar)* azúcar quemado.
car·a·pace (kăr′ə-pās′) s. ZOOL. caparazón *m*.
car·at (kăr′ət) s. JOY. quilate *m*.
car·a·van (kăr′ə-văn′) s. caravana.
car·a·van·sa·ry (kăr′ə-văn′sə-rē) s. [pl. **-ries**] posada para caravanas.
car·a·vel (kăr′ə-věl′) s. MARÍT. carabela.
car·a·way (kăr′ə-wā′) s. BOT. *(plant)* alcaravea; *(seed)* carvi *m*.
car barn *o* **car·barn** (kär′bärn′) s. depósito de tranvías *o* autobuses.
car·bide (kär′bīd′) s. QUÍM. carburo.
car·bine (kär′bīn′, -bēn′) s. ARM. carabina.
car·bi·neer (kär′bə-nîr′) s. MIL. carabinero.
car·bo·hy·drate (kär′bō-hī′drāt′) s. QUÍM. carbohidrato, hidrato de carbono.
car·bon (kär′bən) s. QUÍM. carbono; *(paper)* papel carbón *m*; *(copy)* copia (hecha con papel carbón); ELEC. carbón *m*.
carbon 14 s. FÍS., QUÍM. carbono 14 (isótopo radioactivo) *m*.
car·bon·ate (kär′bə-nāt′) QUÍM. **I.** tr. **-at·ed, -at·ing** *(to aerate)* carbonatar; *(to carbonize)* carbonizar **II.** s. carbonato.
carbonated water s. gaseosa.
car·bon·a·tion (kär′bə-nā′shən) s. QUÍM. carbonización *f*.
carbon black s. QUÍM. negro de carbón.
carbon copy s. copia hecha con papel carbón; FIG., FAM. *(duplicate)* réplica.
carbon cycle s. BOT., QUÍM. ciclo del carbono (en la naturaleza).
carbon dating s. FÍS. determinación de la edad (por el método del carbono 14).
carbon dioxide s. QUÍM. bióxido de carbono, anhídrido carbónico.

car·bon·ic acid (kär-bŏn'ĭk) s. ácido carbónico.
car·bon·if·er·ous (kär'bə-nĭf'ər-əs) adj. QUÍM. carbonífero.
car·bon·i·za·tion (kär'bə-nĭ-zā'shən) s. QUÍM. carbonización f.
carbon monoxide s. QUÍM. monóxido de carbono.
carbon paper s. papel carbón m.
Car·bo·run·dum (kär'bə-rŭn'dəm) s. QUÍM. carborundo (marca registrada de carburo de silicio).
car·bun·cle (kär'bŭng'kəl) s. MED. carbunco, carbunclo; MIN. carbúnculo, rubí m.
car·bu·ret (kär'bə-rāt', -rĕt', -byə-) tr. QUÍM. carburar, combinar con carbono.
car·bu·re·tion (kär'bə-rā'shən, -byə-) s. TEC. carburación f.
car·bu·re·tor (kär'bə-rā'tər, -byə-) s. TEC. carburador m.
car·bu·ret·tor (kär'bə-rĕt'ər, -byə-) s. G.B. var. de **carburetor**.
car·cass (kär'kəs) s. *(dead body)* res muerta f, cadáver m; FAM. *(body)* cuerpo; *(framework)* armazón m, esqueleto.
car·cin·o·gen (kär-sĭn'ə-jən) s. MED. agente cancerígeno.
car·cin·o·gen·ic (kär'sə-nə-jĕn'ĭk) adj. MED. cancerígeno.
car·ci·no·ma (kär'sə-nō'mə) s. [pl. **-mas** o **-ma·ta** (-mə-tə)] MED. carcinoma m.
card¹ (kärd) I. s. *(playing card)* naipe m, carta; *(greeting card)* tarjeta; *(post card)* postal f, tarjeta postal; *(identification card)* tarjeta de identificación, carnet de identidad m; *(membership card)* carnet m; DEP. *(program)* programa m; *(of a compass)* rosa náutica, rosa de los vientos; FAM. *(comic person)* tipo gracioso o excéntrico ♦ **cards** [ú. con v. sing. o pl.] cartas, naipes • **house of cards** castillo de naipes • **it's in the cards** está escrito • **pack of cards** mazo de naipes • **punch c.** tarjeta perforada • **to have a card** o **an ace up one's sleeve** tener un plan secreto, traerse un as entre manos • **to hold all the cards** tener todos los triunfos en la mano • **to play one's cards right** actuar de la manera más ventajosa para uno • **to play one's last c.** jugarse la última carta • **to put one's cards on the table** poner las cartas sobre la mesa • **to show one's cards** FIG. mostrar las cartas II. tr. *(to catalogue)* poner o registrar en una ficha; FAM. *(to check)* comprobar la edad de.
card² (kärd) TEJ. I. s. carda, cardencha II. tr. cardar.
card·board (kärd'bôrd') s. cartón m.
card catalog s. fichero.
car·di·ac (kär'dē-ăk') MED. I. adj. *(of the heart)* cardiaco, cardíaco; *(of the cardia)* del cardias II. s. cardiaco, cardíaco.
car·di·gan (kär'dĭ-gən) s. COST. chaqueta de punto, rebeca.
car·di·nal (kär'dn-əl) I. adj. *(primary)* cardinal, esencial; *(deep red)* purpúreo II. s. ORNIT., RELIG. cardenal m; *(deep red)* púrpura; *(number)* número cardinal.
cardinal number s. número cardinal.
cardinal point s. punto cardinal.
cardinal sin s. RELIG. pecado capital.
cardinal virtue s. virtud cardinal f.
car·di·o·gram (kär'dē-ə-grăm') s. MED. cardiograma m.
car·di·ol·o·gist (kär'dē-ŏl'ə-jĭst) s. cardiólogo.
car·di·ol·o·gy (kär'dē-ŏl'ə-jē) s. MED. cardiología.
car·di·o·pul·mo·nar·y resuscitation (kär'dē-ō-pŏŏl'mə-nĕr'ē) s. resucitación cardiopulmonar f.
car·di·o·vas·cu·lar (kär'dē-ō-văs'kyə-lər) adj. ANAT. cardiovascular.
card·sharp (kärd'shärp') o **card·sharp·er** (-shär'pər) s. fullero, tahúr m.
card·sharp·ing (kärd'shär'pĭng) s. fullería.
care (kâr) I. s. *(worry)* inquietud f, preocupación f <*he doesn't have a c. in the world* él no tiene una preocupación en la vida>; *(grief)* desasosiego, pena; *(responsibility)* responsabilidad f, cargo <*this matter is in my c.* este asunto está a mi cargo>; *(caution)* cuidado <*to drive with c.* manejar con cuidado>; *(custody)* cuidado <*she was busy with the c. of her baby* estaba muy ocupada con el cuidado del niño>; *(supervision)* cargo, custodia f; *(attentiveness)* esmero, detenimiento <*you should study the matter with c.* deberías estudiar el asunto con detenimiento> ♦ **(in) c. of** o **c/o** para entregar a • **to take c.** tener cuidado • **to take c. not to** guardarse de, cuidarse de no • **to take c. of** *(person)*

cuidar de, encargarse de; *(thing)* ocuparse de; *(expenses)* correr con • **to take c. of itself** resolverse por sí mismo • **to take c. of oneself** *(to treat well)* cuidarse a sí mismo; *(to support)* mantenerse a sí mismo • **under (someone's) care** a cargo de (alguien) II. intr. **cared, car·ing** *(to be concerned)* inquietarse, preocuparse <*I c. about her health* me preocupa su salud>; *(to mind)* importar <*I don't c. if you borrow my car* no me importa si tomas prestado mi automóvil> ♦ **I couldn't c. less** FAM. me importa un pito, me importa un pepino • **to c. for** *(to look after)* cuidar; *(to love)* querer, tener afecto por <*you know I c. for you* tú sabes que te quiero>; *(to like)* apetecer, querer <*would you c. for a cup of tea?* ¿quiere una taza de té?> • **to c. to** tener ganas de, querer <*would you c. to sit down? ¿quiere usted sentarse?*> —tr. *(to wish)* interesarle a uno <*we don't c. to attend* no nos interesa ir>; *(to be concerned)* preocuparle a uno <*I don't c. a bit what he thinks* no me preocupa para nada lo que piensa él>.
ca·reen (kə-rēn') I. intr. *(to lurch)* dar bandazos; MARÍT. inclinarse —tr. MARÍT. *(to tilt)* ladear; *(to lean)* inclinar, volcar (un bote para limpiarlo); *(to repair)* carenar II. s. MARÍT. carena, carenadura f.
ca·reer (kə-rîr') I. s. *(profession)* carrera, profesión f; *(course)* curso (de la vida); *(speed)* avance rápido, ímpetu m II. intr. correr a toda velocidad, precipitarse.
ca·reer·ist (kə-rîr'ĭst) s. arribista mf.
care·free (kâr'frē') adj. despreocupado.
care·ful (kâr'fəl) adj. *(cautious)* cauteloso, prudente; *(conscientious)* cuidadoso, meticuloso; *(solicitous)* atento; *(anxious)* lleno de preocupaciones ♦ **to be c.** tener cuidado.
care·less (kâr'lĭs) adj. *(negligent)* descuidado, negligente; *(thoughtless)* imprudente; *(unconcerned)* indiferente; *(unstudied)* espontáneo; *(cheerful)* alegre.
care·less·ness (kâr'lĭs-nĭs) s. *(negligence)* descuido, negligencia; *(indifference)* indiferencia.
ca·ress (kə-rĕs') I. s. caricia II. tr. acariciar.
car·et (kär'ĭt) s. IMPR. signo de intercalación.
care·tak·er (kâr'tā'kər) s. *(custodian)* guardián m, vigilante m; *(of a residence)* portero.
care·worn (kâr'wôrn') adj. agobiado por las inquietudes.
car·fare (kär'fâr') s. precio de trayecto.
car·go (kär'gō) s. [pl. **-goes** o **-gos**] carga, cargamento ♦ **c. boat** buque de carga.
car·hop (kär'hŏp') s. camarero en un restaurante donde se sirve a los clientes en su automóvil.
Car·ib (kär'əb) s. caribe mf.
Car·ib·be·an (kär'ə-bē'ən, kə-rĭb'ē-) adj. & s. caribe m ♦ **C. Sea** Mar Caribe.
car·i·bou (kär'ə-bōō') s. [pl. **caribou** o **-bous**] ZOOL. caribú m.
car·i·ca·ture (kär'ĭ-kə-chŏŏr') I. s. caricatura II. tr. **-tured, -tur·ing** caricaturizar.
car·i·ca·tur·ist (kär'ĭ-kə-chŏŏr'ĭst) s. caricaturista mf.
car·ies (kâr'ēz) s. [pl. **caries**] MED. caries f.
car·il·lon (kär'ə-lŏn') I. s. MÚS. carillón m II. intr. **-lonned, -lon·ning** repicar.
car·load (kär'lōd') s. *(capacity)* carga máxima; *(weight)* carga mínima que se beneficia de tarifa reducida.
Car·lo·vin·gian (kär'lə-vĭn'jən) adj. & s. HIST. carolingio, carlovingio.
Car·mel·ite (kär'mə-līt') s. RELIG. carmelita m.
car·min·a·tive (kär-mĭn'ə-tĭv, kär'mə-nā'-) adj. & s. MED. carminativo.
car·mine (kär'mĭn, -mīn') s. & adj. carmín m.
car·nage (kär'nĭj) s. carnicería, matanza f.
car·nal (kär'nəl) adj. *(sensual)* carnal, sensual; *(worldly)* mundano.
carnal knowledge s. cópula, ayuntamiento carnal.
car·na·tion (kär-nā'shən) s. BOT. clavel m.
car·ni·val (kär'nə-vəl) s. *(celebration)* carnaval m; *(amusement)* feria, parque de atracciones m.
car·ni·vore (kär'nə-vôr') s. BOT., ZOOL. carnívoro.
car·niv·o·rous (kär-nĭv'ər-əs) adj. carnívoro.
carn·y (kär'nē) s. [pl. **-nies**] JER. *(carnival)* feria; *(person)* artista de feria mf.

ã rey / ä año / b boca / ch chico / d dar / ĕ el / ē mil / g gato / h joya / hw juez / ī aire / k casa / kw cuan /

car·ob (kăr′əb) s. BOT. *(tree)* algarrobo; *(bean)* algarroba.
car·ol (kăr′əl) I. s. villancico II. tr. cantar —intr. *(to sing)* cantar villancicos; *(to warble)* cantar alegremente.
Car·o·lin·gian (kăr′ə-lĭn′jən) adj. & s. HIST. carolingio, carlovingio.
car·om (kăr′əm) I. s. *(billiard)* carambola; *(collision)* rebote *m* II. intr. *(to collide)* rebotar; *(to make a billiard shot)* hacer carambola.
car·o·tene (kăr′ə-tēn′) s. QUÍM. caroteno.
ca·rot·id (kə-rŏt′ĭd) s. & adj. ANAT. carótida.
ca·rous·al (kə-rou′zəl) s. jarana, juerga.
ca·rouse (kə-rouz′) I. s. juerga, jarana II. intr. **-roused, -rous·ing** *(to drink)* beber excesivamente; *(to revel)* ir de juerga.
car·ou·sel (kăr′ə-sĕl′) s. carrusel *m*, tiovivo.
carp¹ (kärp) intr. quejarse ♦ **to c. at** criticar.
carp² (kärp) s. ICT. carpa.
car·pel (kär′pəl) s. BOT. carpelo.
car·pen·ter (kär′pən-tər) I. s. carpintero ♦ **c. ant** ENTOM. hormiga carpintera II. tr. & intr. carpintear.
car·pen·try (kär′pən-trē) s. carpintería.
car·pet (kär′pĭt) I. s. alfombra, tapiz *m* ♦ **to be on the c.** *(to be under discussion)* estar sobre el tapete, estar en discusión; *(to be reprimanded)* estar recibiendo una regañina II. tr. alfombrar.
car·pet·bag (kär′pĭt-băg′) s. maleta hecha de alfombra.
car·pet·bag·ger (kär′pĭt-băg′ər) s. HIST. *(northerner)* norteño que iba al sur para sacar provecho político o económico (en EE. UU.); POL. *(politician)* político que no es del distrito que representa.
car·pet·ing (kär′pĭ-tĭng) s. *(carpets)* alfombrado; *(fabric)* tejido para alfombras.
carp·ing (kär′pĭng) adj. criticón.
car·pool (kär′pool′) I. s. convenio entre varias personas para viajar cada día en el automóvil de una de ellas II. tr. llevar en automóvil por turno.
car·port (kär′pôrt′) s. cobertizo para automóviles.
car·rel (kăr′əl) s. cubículo de estudio (en una biblioteca).
car·riage (kăr′ĭj) s. *(vehicle)* carruaje *m*, coche *m*; *(perambulator)* cochecito de niño; *(posture)* porte, presencia; MIL. *(frame)* cureña (de cañón); MEC. *(moving part)* carro; COM. *(transport)* transporte *m*; *(cost)* costo de transporte, porte; G.B. coche, vagón (de tren) *m*.
carriage trade s. FAM. clientela adinerada.
car·ri·er (kăr′ē-ər) s. *(transporter)* portador *m*, transportador *m*; *(person in business)* transportista *mf*; MEC. *(mechanism)* conductor *m*, portador *m*; MED. portador (de una enfermedad contagiosa) ♦ **c. pigeon** paloma mensajera.
car·ri·on (kăr′ē-ən) s. carroña.
car·rot (kăr′ət) s. BOT. zanahoria (planta y tubérculo).
car·rot·y (kăr′ə-tē) adj. *(orange-red)* de color zanahoria; *(red-haired)* pelirrojo.
car·ry (kăr′ē) I. tr. **-ried, -ry·ing** *(to move)* llevar <*he carried the boxes into the house* llevó las cajas adentro de la casa>; *(to transport)* llevar, transportar; *(to serve as a conduit)* llevar, conducir; *(to have with one)* llevar, portar <*I never c. much money* nunca llevo mucho dinero>; *(to support)* mantener, sostener; *(to transmit)* transmitir <*mosquitoes c. malaria* los mosquitos transmiten la malaria>; *(to be pregnant with)* estar embarazada con, llevar; *(to have in stock)* tener surtido de, tener en existencia; *(to entail)* llevar aparejado, acarrear <*this crime should c. a heavier penalty* este crimen debería acarrear un castigo más severo>; *(to contain)* contener, entrañar; *(to win over)* conquistar a, capturar a; *(to win)* ganar <*the Republican candidate car­ried the election* el candidato republicano ganó la elec­ción>; *(to pass)* aprobar (una moción); *(to extend)* prolongar, extender; *(to impel)* mover, impulsar <*hard work carried him far in his career* el trabajo duro lo im­pulsó mucho en su carrera>; *(to print)* publicar <*all the papers carried that story* todos los periódicos publicaron esa historia>; *(to broadcast)* transmitir <*her speech was carried on radio and television* su discurso fue transmitido por radio y televisión>; *(to hold one's body)* llevar <*she carried her head high* llevaba la cabeza erguida>; MAT. llevarse; TEN. llevar, transferir (suma, saldo) ♦ **to c. a torch**

for FIG. estar enamorado de ● **to c. a tune** cantar afinado ● **to c. along** arrastrar ● **to c. arms** llevar armas ● **to c. away** *(to excite)* arrobar, entusiasmar <*he was carried away by the book* estaba entusiasmado con el libro> ● **to c. back** FIG. recordar, hacer recordar ● **to c. forward** TEN. llevar, transportar a (columna, cuenta); *(to progress with)* llevar adelante <*the new government carried forward the program* el nuevo gobierno llevó adelante el programa> ● **to c. insurance** tener póliza de seguro, estar asegurado ● **to c. off** *(to win)* llevarse (premio, galardón); *(to kill)* matar <*the epidemic carried off thousands* la epidemia mató a millares>; *(to complete)* realizar, llevar a cabo ● **to c. on** *(to engage in)* mantener, sostener (conversación, correspondencia); *(to conduct)* dirigir, asumir el manejo (de empresa, asuntos) ● **to c. oneself** *(to behave)* portarse, comportarse; *(to hold oneself)* andar, moverse ● **to c. out** *(to accomplish)* realizar, llevar a cabo; *(to get done)* cumplir ● **to c. over** TEN. pasar a otra columna o página; *(to keep until later)* guardar, tener para más tarde ● **to c. something too far** FIG. llevar algo al exceso, excederse ● **to c. the day** triunfar, salir victorioso ● **to c. through** *(to complete)* completar, llevar a cabo; *(to sustain)* sostener <*my faith carried me through the ordeal* mi fe me sostuvo en la prueba> ● **to c. weight** FIG. ser de peso o influencia —intr. *(to be passed)* ganar, aprobarse <*the proposal car­ried by a wide margin* la propuesta se aprobó por un am­plio margen>; *(to extend)* llegar, extenderse <*the smoke carried for miles* el humo se extendía por millas>; *(to project)* oírse, proyectarse <*a voice that carries well* una voz que se proyecta bien> ♦ **c. on!** ¡siga!, ¡continúe! ● **to c. on** *(to continue)* seguir, continuar; *(to misbehave)* portarse mal; FAM. *(to have a love affair)* tener una aventura ● **to c. over** conservarse <*habits which have carried over from the past* hábitos que se conservan del pasado> II. s. [pl. **-ries**] *(portage)* transporte *m*; *(range)* alcance *m*.
car·ry·all (kăr′ē-ôl′) s. *(bag)* bolsa grande, maletín *m*; *(carriage)* coche de un solo caballo *m*.
carrying charge s. COM. recargo.
car·ry·o·ver (kăr′ē-ō′vər) s. *(part left over)* remanente *m*; TEN. *(sum)* suma o saldo anterior.
car·sick (kär′sĭk′) adj. mareado.
cart (kärt) I. s. *(horse-drawn)* carro; *(handcart)* carretilla, carro de mano; *(trolley)* carrito II. tr. *(to carry in a cart)* acarrear; *(to lug)* arrastrar ♦ **to c. away** o **off** llevar.
cart·age (kär′tĭj) s. acarreo, porte *m*.
carte blanche (kärt blänsh′, blänch′) s. carta blanca.
car·tel (kär-tĕl′) s. COM. cártel *m*.
Car·te·sian (kär-tē′zhən) adj. & s. FILOS. cartesiano.
Car·thage (kär′thĭj) s. Cartago.
Car·tha·gin·i·an (kär′thə-jĭn′ē-ən) adj. & s. cartaginés *m*, cartaginense *mf*.
car·ti·lage (kär′tl-ĭj) s. ANAT. cartílago.
cart·load (kärt′lōd′) s. carretada ♦ **by cartloads** a carretadas.
car·tog·ra·pher (kär-tŏg′rə-fər) s. cartógrafo.
car·tog·ra·phy (kär-tŏg′rə-fē) s. cartografía.
car·ton (kär′tn) I. s. caja de cartón II. tr. embalar en una caja de cartón.
car·toon (kär-toon′) s. *(caricature)* caricatura; *(joke)* chiste *m*; *(comic strip)* tira humorística, historieta; *(film)* dibujos animados *m*; ARTE. *(preliminary sketch)* cartón *m*.
car·toon·ist (kär-too′nĭst) s. caricaturista *mf*.
car·tridge (kär′trĭj) s. ARM., FOTOG. cartucho; *(small removable unit)* pieza intercambiable; RAD. *(phonograph pickup)* elemento captador, componente de la aguja *m*; *(cassette)* casete *m*; *(ink refill)* repuesto.
cartridge belt s. cartuchera.
cartridge clip s. cargador *m*, peine (de balas) *m*.
cart·wheel (kärt′hwēl′) s. *(wheel)* rueda de carreta; *(acrobatics)* voltereta lateral; JER. *(coin)* moneda.
cart·wright (kärt′rīt′) s. CARP. carretero.
carve (kärv) tr. **carved, carv·ing** *(to cut up)* partir, trinchar; *(to parcel out)* dividir, repartir; *(to fashion by cutting)* tallar, cincelar; *(to engrave)* grabar; *(to decorate by carving)* adornar con diseños tallados ♦ **to c. out** labrar, recortar —intr. *(to sculpt)* esculpir; *(to slice)* trinchar carne.

carv·ing (kär′vĭng) s. talla, escultura.
car·y·at·id (kăr′ē-ăt′ĭd) s. [pl. **-ids** o **-i·des** (-ĭ-dēz′)] ARQ. cariátide f.
Cas·a·no·va (kăz′ə-nō′və, kăs′-) s. tenorio.
cas·cade (kă-skād′) I. s. (waterfall) cascada, salto de agua; FIG. (torrent) chorro, torrente m; ELEC. conexión en cascada f II. intr. **-cad·ed, -cad·ing** caer en forma de cascada.
case¹ (kās) I. s. (instance) caso <in this c. en este caso>; (example) ejemplo; (matter) cuestión f <a c. of honor una cuestión de honor>; (condition) condición f, estado; (argument) argumento; MED. (of disease, disorder) caso; (patient) paciente mf; DER. (action) causa, pleito; GRAM. caso; FAM. (odd person) caso <he is a real c. él es realmente un caso> • **a c. in point** un ejemplo, un caso pertinente • **in any c.** en todo caso, en cualquier caso • **in c. of** en caso de • **in no c.** de ningún modo • **in that c.** en tal caso • **in the c. of** en cuanto a, en lo que se refiere a • **it is not a c. of** no se trata de • **it is not the c.** no es ése el caso, no es cierto eso • **that being the c.** siendo así, si ése es el caso • **the c. in point** el caso en cuestión • **to bring a c. against** poner un pleito a • **to make one's c.** probar la tesis de uno • **to put forward a c.** presentar argumentos convincentes • **to put** o **state one's c.** presentar uno los argumentos • **to rest one's c.** terminar uno el alegato • **to state the c.** exponer los hechos II. tr. **cased, cas·ing** JER. espiar, campanear.
case² (kās) I. s. (box) caja; (hard protective covering) estuche m; (soft protective covering) funda; (set) juego, par m <a c. of pistols un par de pistolas>; ARQ. (framework) bastidor m, marco; IMPR. (storage tray) caja de imprenta II. tr. **cased, cas·ing** (to package) empacar, embalar; (to enclose in a hard case) poner en un estuche; (to sheathe) enfundar.
case·hard·en (kās′här′dn) tr. METAL. cementar; FIG. (to make insensitive) insensibilizar, endurecer.
case history s. MED. hoja clínica, historia clínica; SOCIOL. antecedentes m, historial m.
ca·sein (kā′sēn′) s. QUÍM. caseína.
case·ment (kās′mənt) s. (frame) marco de ventana; (window) ventana batiente.
case study s. monografía sobre un problema médico o social.
case·work (kās′wûrk′) s. SOCIOL. estudio de los antecedentes personales o familiares.
cash (kăsh) I. s. (money) efectivo; COM. (payment) pago al contado II. tr. hacer efectivo, cobrar • **to c. in** (to change into cash) convertir en efectivo; (to make money) ganar dinero; JER. (to die) morirse • **to c. in on** aprovecharse de, sacar partido de.
cash·book (kăsh′bŏŏk′) s. TEN. libro de caja.
cash·box (kăsh′bŏks′) s. COM. caja.
cash crop s. AGR. cultivo destinado a la venta.
cash·ew (kăsh′ōō) s. BOT. anacardo.
cash flow s. COM. flujo de efectivo.
cash·ier¹ (kă-shîr′) s. COM. cajero.
ca·shier² (kă-shîr′) tr. despedir (esp. como castigo).
cashier's check s. COM. cheque de caja m, cheque de la gerencia.
cash·mere (kăzh′mîr′, kăsh′-) s. TEJ. cachemira.
cash register s. COM. caja registradora.
cas·ing (kā′sĭng) s. (cover) cubierta, envoltura; (intestine) tripa (de embutido); (frame) marco (de puerta o ventana); (pipe) tubo.
ca·si·no (kə-sē′nō) s. [pl. **-nos**] casino.
cask (kăsk) s. barril m, tonel m.
cas·ket (kăs′kĭt) s. (coffin) ataúd m; (small box) joyero, estuche m.
cas·sa·va (kə-sä′və) s. (plant) mandioca; (flour, bread) cazabe m.
cas·se·role (kăs′ə-rōl′) s. cazuela, cacerola.
cas·sette (kə-sĕt′, kă-) s. (of film) cartucho; (of magnetic tape) casete mf.
cas·sock (kăs′ək) s. sotana.
cast (kăst) I. tr. **cast, cast·ing** (to hurl) tirar, arrojar; (to molt) mudar, cambiar (piel, plumas); (to drop) soltar,

echar <to c. anchor echar el ancla>; (to throw on the ground) tumbar, derribar; (to deposit) echar, depositar <to c. a vote depositar un voto>; (to direct) volver, dirigir <she c. her eyes on the speaker dirigió la mirada hacia el orador>; (to project) proyectar (luz, sombra); (to throw) tirar <to c. the dice tirar los dados>; CINEM., TEAT. (to play) hacer el reparto de; (roles) repartir (papeles); (actors) asignar (una parte a un actor); (in hunting) husmear (un sabueso); METAL. (to melt) fundir; METAL., TEC. (to mold) moldear; (to devise) idear; (to add up) sumar; ASTROL. (to forecast) hacer (horóscopos); (to warp) combar; IMPR. (to stereotype) estereotipar; (to electroplate) electrotipar; MA-RÍT. (to turn) hacer virar ♦ **the die is cast** FIG. la suerte está echada • **to c. a glance** o **an eye at** echar una mirada o una ojeada a • **to c. aside** o **away** desechar, descartar • **to c. a spell on** hechizar, encantar • **to c. doubt on** o **upon** poner en duda • **to c. down** (to lower) bajar (los ojos); (to dishearten) desanimar • **to c. light on** FIG. esclarecer • **to c. lots** echar suertes, sortear • **to c. off** (to abandon) abandonar; (to rid of) desechar • **to c. out** echar fuera, arrojar • **to c. up** (to raise) levantar; (to add up) sumar —intr. (for fish) echar el sedal; (to add up) sumar; (to forecast) pronosticar; (to take shape) hacerse al molde ♦ **to c. about** buscar, estar buscando • **to c. off** MARÍT. desamarrar, soltar las amarras; (in knitting) terminar una vuelta • **to c. on** empezar una hilera II. s. (act) tirada, lanzamiento; (of dice) tirada; (of snake) piel f, pellejo; (calculation) cálculo; (of color) tinte m; (appearance) apariencia; (arrangement) arreglo, disposición f; (type) clase f, tipo; (tendency) tendencia; METAL., TEC. (mold) molde f, forma; (product) pieza fundida; MED. (squint) ligero estrabismo; (rigid dressing) enyesadura; CINEM., TEAT. reparto.
cas·ta·nets (kăs′tə-nĕts′) s.pl. MÚS. castañuelas.
cast·a·way (kăst′ə-wā′) adj. & s. (shipwrecked) náufrago; (outcast) paria mf.
caste (kăst) s. casta.
cast·er (kăs′tər) s. TÉC. vaciador m; (wheel) ruedecilla; (for salt) salero; (for pepper) pimentero; (stand) convoy, vinagrera.
cas·ti·gate (kăs′tĭ-gāt′) tr. **-gat·ed, -gat·ing** (to punish) castigar; (to rebuke) reprobar, censurar.
cas·ti·ga·tion (kăs′tĭ-gā′shən) s. (punishment) castigo; (rebuke) reprobación f, censura.
Cas·tile (kă-stēl′) s. GEOG. Castilla.
Cas·til·ian (kă-stĭl′yən) adj. & s. castellano.
cast·ing (kăs′tĭng) s. METAL. (process) fundición f; (object) pieza fundida; TEAT. (selection of actors) reparto.
casting vote s. voto de calidad, voto decisivo.
cast iron s. METAL. hierro fundido o colado.
cast-i·ron (kăst′ī′ərn) adj. (of cast iron) de hierro fundido; (rigid) férreo, rígido.
cas·tle (kăs′əl) I. s. (building) castillo; (in chess) torre f, roque m II. tr. & intr. **-tled, -tling** enrocar (al rey).
cast-off (kăst′ôf′) s. (reject) persona o cosa desechada, desecho; IMPR. cálculo tipográfico, cálculo de espacio.
cast-off (kăst′ôf′) adj. desechado.
cas·tor¹ (kăs′tər) s. (substance) castóreo; (hat) sombrero de castor; (fabric) castor m.
cas·tor² (kăs′tər) s. (wheel) ruedecilla; (for salt) salero; (for pepper) pimentero; (stand) convoy, vinagrera.
castor oil s. FARM., MED. aceite de ricino m.
cas·trate (kăs′trāt′) tr. **-trat·ed, -trat·ing** (to geld, spay) castrar, capar; (to weaken) emascular.
cas·tra·tion (kă-strā′shən) s. castración f, capadura.
ca·su·al (kăzh′ōō-əl) I. adj. (accidental) casual, fortuito; (occasional) que ocurre de vez en cuando; (indifferent) indiferente, despreocupado; (without formality) informal; (not dressy) informal, de sport <c. clothes ropa de sport>; (superficial) superficial II. s. temporero.
ca·su·al·ly (kăzh′ōō-əl-ē) adv. (accidentally) casualmente; (by the by) de paso, sin darle importancia; (informally) informalmente, de sport.
ca·su·al·ty (kăzh′ōō-əl-tē) s. [pl. **-ties**] (accident) accidente m, desastre m; (victim) muerto; MIL. baja.
ca·su·ist (kăzh′ōō-ĭst) s. casuista mf.
ca·su·ist·ry (kăzh′ōō-ĭ-strē) s. FILOS. casuística.

ã rey / ä año / b boca / ch chico / d dar / ĕ el / ē mil / g gato / h joya / hw juez / ī aire / k casa / kw cuan /

cat (kăt) s. ZOOL. *(pet)* gato; *(feline)* felino; *(fur)* piel de gato *f*; *(whip)* azote de nueve ramales *m*; *(catfish)* bagre *m*; *(spiteful woman)* arpía, pécora; JER. *(guy)* tipo, individuo; MARÍT. *(cathead)* serviola, pescante *m*; *(catboat)* laúd *m* ♦ **to let the c. out of the bag** revelar un secreto, irse de la lengua.

ca·tab·o·lism (kə-tăb′ə-lĭz′əm) s. MED. catabolismo.

cat·a·clysm (kăt′ə-klĭz′əm) s. cataclismo.

cat·a·clys·mic (kăt′ə-klĭz′mĭk) *o* **cat·a·clys·mal** (-məl) adj. catastrófico.

cat·a·combs (kăt′ə-kōmz′) s.pl. catacumbas.

cat·a·falque (kăt′ə-fălk′, -fôlk′) s. catafalco.

Cat·a·lan (kăt′l-ăn′) **I.** adj. catalán, de Cataluña **II.** s. *(inhabitant, language)* catalán *m*.

cat·a·lep·sy (kăt′l-ĕp′sē) s. MED. catalepsia.

cat·a·logue *o* **cat·a·log** (kăt′l-ôg′) **I.** s. catálogo **II.** tr. **-logued, -logu·ing** *o* **-loged, -log·ing** catalogar —intr. hacer un catálogo.

Cat·a·lo·nia (kăt′l-ōn′yə) s. GEOG. Cataluña.

Cat·a·lo·nian (kăt′l-ō′nyən) adj. & s. catalán *m*.

ca·tal·y·sis (kə-tăl′ĭ-sĭs) s. QUÍM. catálisis *f*.

cat·a·lyst (kăt′l-ĭst) s. QUÍM. catalizador *m*.

cat·a·lyt·ic (kăt′l-ĭt′ĭk) adj. catalítico.

catalytic converter s. AUTO. convertidor catalítico.

cat·a·lyze (kăt′l-īz′) tr. **-lyzed, -lyz·ing** QUÍM. catalizar.

cat·a·ma·ran (kăt′ə-mə-răn′) s. MARÍT. catamarán *m*.

cat·a·pult (kăt′ə-pŭlt′, -pŏolt′) **I.** s. *(mechanism)* catapulta; *(slingshot)* tirador *m*, tiragomas *m* **II.** tr. catapultar —intr. lanzarse violentamente.

cat·a·ract (kăt′ə-răkt′) s. catarata.

ca·tarrh (kə-tär′) s. MED. catarro.

ca·tas·tro·phe (kə-tăs′trə-fē) s. catástrofe.

cat·a·stroph·ic (kăt′ə-strŏf′ĭk) adj. catastrófico.

cat·a·ton·ic (kăt′ə-tŏn′ĭk) adj. MED. catatónico.

cat·call (kăt′kôl′) s. silbido, silbatina.

catch (kăch, kĕch) **I.** tr. **caught** (kôt), **catch·ing** *(to grab)* coger, agarrar <*c. the ball with both hands* agarra la pelota con las dos manos>; *(to capture)* prender, capturar <*the policeman caught the thief* el policía prendió al ladrón>; *(to hunt)* cazar; *(to fish)* pescar; *(to go aboard)* alcanzar, tomar (avión, tren); *(to entangle)* engancharse <*I caught my sweater on the fence* me enganché el suéter en la verja>; *(to pinch)* cogerse, agarrarse con <*she caught her finger in the door* se agarró el dedo con la puerta>; *(to hit)* pegar, dar <*the punch caught me in the jaw* el puñetazo me dió en la mandíbula>; *(to contract)* coger, contraer <*to c. a cold* contraer un resfrío>; FIG. *(to surprise)* coger desprevenido, sorprender <*mother caught me just as I was hiding her present* mamá me sorprendió justo cuando estaba escondiendo su regalo>; *(to become imbued with)* contagiarse de; *(to understand)* entender, captar; *(to capture)* captar, reproducir; FAM. *(to see)* ver <*I'll c. it on the news tonight* lo veré esta noche en el noticiario>; *(to go to see)* ir a ver <*let's c. a movie* vamos a ver una película> ♦ **to c. fire** encenderse, prenderse • **to c. hold of** agarrarse a, asirse a • **to c. it** FAM. ganarse una paliza *o* reprimenda • **to c. one's breath** recobrar el aliento • **to c. one's fancy** antojársele a uno • **to c. one's eye** atraer la atención de uno • **to c. oneself** *(to check oneself)* contenerse; *(to realize)* darse cuenta <*she caught herself daydreaming* se dió cuenta que estaba fantaseando> • **to c. red-handed** agarrar con las manos en la masa • **to c. sight of** vislumbrar, avistar • **to c. up on** *o* **with** ponerse al día *o* al corriente en cuanto a • **to c. up with** alcanzar <*I caught up with him at the corner* lo alcancé en la esquina> —intr. *(to become fastened, hooked)* engancharse; *(to be entangled)* enredarse; *(to hold)* agarrar, enganchar <*the bolt does not c.* el cerrojo no engancha>; *(to spread)* agarrar, ser contagioso; *(to burn)* prender fuego, encenderse <*the charcoal won't c.* el carbón no se enciende> ♦ **to c. on** *(to understand)* comprender; *(to become aware)* caer en la cuenta; *(to become popular)* hacerse *o* volverse muy popular • **to c. up** ponerse al día *o* al corriente **II.** s. *(act)* cogida; *(lock)* cerradura; *(bolt)* pestillo; *(latch)* pasador *m*; *(in hunting)* presa; *(in fishing)* pesca; *(capture)* captura, FIG., FAM.

(trick) truco, trampa; *(something, someone worth catching)* buen partido.

catch·all (kăch′ôl′, kĕch′-) s. *(container)* caja para guardar trastos.

catch·er (kăch′ər, kĕch′-) s. DEP. receptor *m*, catcher *m*.

catch·ing (kăch′ĭng, kĕch′-) adj. *(infectious)* contagioso; *(attractive)* atractivo; *(fascinating)* fascinante.

catch·ment (kăch′mənt, kĕch-) s. *(catching)* captación de agua *f*; *(basin)* embalse para captar el agua de varias vertientes *m*; *(volume of water)* cantidad de agua embalsada *f*.

Catch-22 (kăch′twĕn-tē-tŏo′, kĕch′-) s. paradoja.

catch·up (kăch′əp, kĕch′-) s. var. de **ketchup.**

catch·word (kăch′wûrd′, kĕch′-) s. *(phrase)* lema *m*, slogan *m*; IMPR. *(first word)* reclamo.

catch·y (kăch′ē, kĕch′ē) adj. **-i·er, -i·est** *(attractive)* atractivo; *(easy to remember)* pegadizo; *(tricky)* capcioso.

cat·e·chism (kăt′ĭ-kĭz′əm) s. catecismo.

cat·e·chist (kăt′ĭ-kĭst) s. catequista *mf*.

cat·e·chize (kăt′ĭ-kīz′) tr. **-chized, -chiz·ing** RELIG. *(to teach)* catequizar; *(to question)* preguntar.

cat·e·chu·men (kăt′ĭ-kyŏo′mən) s. RELIG. catecúmeno.

cat·e·gor·i·cal (kăt′ĭ-gôr′ĭ-kəl) *o* **cat·e·gor·ic** (-ĭk) adj. categórico.

cat·e·go·ri·za·tion (kăt′ĭ-gər-ĭ-zā′shən) s. categorización *f*, clasificación *f*.

cat·e·go·rize (kăt′ĭ-gə-rīz′) tr. **-rized, -riz·ing** clasificar.

cat·e·go·ry (kăt′ĭ-gôr′ē) s. [pl. **-ries**] categoría.

cat·e·na·tion (kăt′n-ā′shən) s. encadenamiento.

ca·ter (kā′tər) intr. proveer *o* abastecer de comida *o* servicios ♦ **to c. to** intentar satisfacer los deseos de.

cat·er-cor·nered (kăt′ər-kôr′nərd, kăt′ē-) *o* **cat·er-cor·ner** (-nər) **I.** adj. diagonal **II.** adv. diagonalmente, en diagonal.

ca·ter·er (kā′tər-ər) s. encargado de banquetes.

ca·ter·ing (kā′tər-ĭng) s. servicio de comidas *o* banquetes.

cat·er·pil·lar (kăt′ər-pĭl′ər) s. ENTOM. oruga.

cat·er·waul (kăt′ər-wôl′) **I.** intr. *(to meow)* maullar; FIG. *(to screech)* chillar; *(to quarrel)* pelearse **II.** s. *(meow)* maullido; *(screech)* chillido.

cat·fish (kăt′fĭsh′) s. [pl. **catfish** *o* **-fish·es**] ICT. siluro, bagre *m*.

cat·gut (kăt′gŭt′) s. *(cord)* cuerda de tripa; CIR. catgut *m*.

ca·thar·sis (kə-thär′sĭs) s. [pl. **-ses** (-sēz′)] catarsis *f*.

ca·the·dral (kə-thē′drəl) s. & adj. catedral *f*.

cath·e·ter (kăth′ĭ-tər) s. MED. catéter *m*.

cath·ode (kăth′ōd′) s. ELECTRÓN. cátodo.

cathode ray s. FÍS. rayo catódico.

cath·ode-ray tube (kăth′ōd-rā′) s. FÍS. tubo de rayos catódicos.

cath·o·lic (kăth′ə-lĭk) **I.** adj. *(universal)* general, universal; *(liberal)* liberal ♦ **C.** RELIG. católico **II.** s. ♦ **C.** RELIG. católico.

Catholic Church s. RELIG. Iglesia Católica.

Ca·thol·i·cism (kə-thŏl′ĭ-sĭz′əm) s. catolicismo.

ca·thol·i·cize (kə-thŏl′ĭ-sīz′) tr. **-cized, -ciz·ing** catolizar.

cat·i·on (kăt′ī′ən) s. FÍS. catión *m*.

cat·kin (kăt′kĭn′) s. BOT. amento, inflorescencia colgante.

cat·like (kăt′līk′) adj. *(feline)* felino.

cat·nap (kăt′năp′) **I.** s. siesta corta **II.** intr. **-napped, -napping** echar una siesta corta.

cat·nip (kăt′nĭp′) s. BOT. nébeda.

cat-o'-nine-tails (kăt′ə-nīn′tālz) s. látigo de nueve colas.

cat·sup (kăt′səp, kăch′əp, kĕch′-) s. var. de **ketchup.**

cat·tail (kăt′tāl′) s. BOT. anea, espadaña.

cat·tle (kăt′l) s. ganado vacuno.

cat·tle·man (kăt′l-măn′) s. [pl. **-men** (-mən)] ganadero.

cattle prod s. picana eléctrica, aguijón eléctrico (para controlar al ganado).

cat·ty (kăt′ē) adj. **-ti·er, -ti·est** *(catlike)* gatuno, felino; FIG. *(spiteful)* malicioso, rencoroso.

cat·ty-cor·nered (kăt′ē-kôr′nərd) adj. & adv. var. de **cater-cornered.**

cat·walk (kăt′wôk′) s. ARQ. pasadizo, pasarela.

Cau·ca·sian (kô-kā′zhən) s. & adj. caucáseo, caucásico.

cau·cus (kô′kəs) **I.** s. [pl. **-cus·es** *o* **-cus·ses**] *(for elections)* reunión electoral *f*; G.B. *(committee)* comité *m* **II.** intr. celebrar reunión electoral.

cau·dal (kôd'l) adj. ANAT., ZOOL. caudal.

caught (kôt) pret. y part. p. de **catch**.

caul (kôl) s. ANAT. *(of intestines)* redaño, omento; *(of a fetus)* amnios *m*.

caul·dron (kôl'drən) s. var. de **caldron**.

cau·li·flow·er (kô'lĭ-flou'ər) s. BOT. coliflor *f*.

caulk (kôk) tr. MARÍT. calafatear; *(to fill in)* rellenar, tapar (grietas).

caus·al (kô'zəl) adj. causal.

cau·sal·i·ty (kô-zăl'ĭ-tē) s. [pl. **-ties**] causalidad *f*.

cau·sa·tion (kô-zā'shən) s. causalidad *f*.

caus·a·tive (kô'zə-tĭv) adj. & s. causativo.

cause (kôz) **I.** s. *(causation)* causa; *(reason)* motivo, razón *f* <there is no c. for alarm no hay motivo para alarmarse>; *(crusade)* causa <to fight for a c. luchar por una causa>; DER. *(lawsuit)* causa, pleito **II.** tr. **caused, caus·ing** *(to bring about)* causar, provocar; *(to make)* hacer <he caused her to cry hizo que ella llorara>.

cause·way (kôz'wā') s. *(roadway)* calzada, carretera elevada; *(embankment)* terraplén *m*.

caus·tic (kô'stĭk) adj. & s. cáustico.

cau·ter·i·za·tion (kô'tər-ĭ-zā'shən) s. cauterización *f*.

cau·ter·ize (kô'tə-rīz') tr. **-ized, -iz·ing** cauterizar.

cau·tion (kô'shən) **I.** s. *(carefulness)* cautela, precaución *f*; *(warning)* advertencia **II.** tr. *(to warn)* advertir, prevenir de; *(to reprimand)* amonestar.

cau·tion·ar·y (kô'shə-nĕr'ē) adj. *(preventive)* preventivo; *(admonitory)* admonitorio; *(exemplary)* aleccionador.

cau·tious (kô'shəs) adj. cauteloso, precavido.

cav·al·cade (kăv'əl-kād') s. *(of horses)* cabalgata; FIG. *(procession)* desfile *m*.

cav·a·lier (kăv'ə-lîr') **I.** s. caballero **II.** adj. *(disdainful)* arrogante; *(carefree)* desenvuelto.

cav·al·ry (kăv'əl-rē) s. [pl. **-ries**] caballería.

cav·al·ry·man (kăv'əl-rē-mən) s. [pl. **-men**] MIL. soldado de caballería.

cave (kāv) **I.** s. cueva, caverna **II.** intr. **caved, cav·ing ♦ to c. in** *(to collapse)* hundirse, derrumbarse; *(to yield)* acceder, ceder.

ca·ve·at (kăv'ē-ăt', kä'vē-ät') s. DER. advertencia, amonestación *f*.

cave dweller s. cavernícola *mf*, troglodita *mf*.

cave-in (kāv'ĭn') s. hundimiento, socavón *m*.

cave man s. ANTROP. *(cave dweller)* cavernícola *m*; FAM. *(brute)* troglodita *m*.

cav·ern (kăv'ərn) s. caverna.

cav·ern·ous (kăv'ər-nəs) adj. cavernoso.

cav·i·ar o **cav·i·are** (kăv'ē-är', kä'vē-) s. caviar *m*.

cav·il (kăv'əl) **I.** intr. & tr. poner reparos (a) **II.** s. reparo, quisquilla.

cav·i·ty (kăv'ĭ-tē) s. [pl. **-ties**] *(hole)* cavidad *f*, hueco; *(in a tooth)* caries *f*.

ca·vort (kə-vôrt') intr. *(to caper)* corvetear; *(to frolic)* juguetear.

caw (kô) ORNIT. **I.** s. graznido **II.** intr. graznar.

cay (kē, kā) s. GEOG., GEOL. cayo.

cay·enne pepper (kī-ĕn') s. pimienta del ají o chile.

cay·man (kā'mən) s. var. de **caiman**.

Cay·man (kī-män', kā'mən) o **Cay·mans** (kī-mänz', kā'mənz) s. (Islas) Caimanes.

cease (sēs) **I.** tr. **ceased, ceas·ing** *(to end)* terminar; *(to discontinue)* suspender **♦ c. fire!** MIL. ¡alto el fuego! —intr. cesar **II.** s. cese **♦ without c.** incesantemente.

cease-fire (sēs'fīr') s. MIL. suspensión de fuego *f*.

cease·less (sēs'lĭs) adj. incesante, continuo.

ce·dar (sē'dər) s. BOT. cedro (árbol y madera).

cede (sēd) tr. **ced·ed, ced·ing** ceder.

ce·dil·la (sĭ-dĭl'ə) s. cedilla.

ceil·ing (sē'lĭng) s. *(upper surface)* cielo raso, techo; AER. altura máxima, techo; *(limit)* tope *m*, límite *m*.

cel·e·brant (sĕl'ə-brənt) s. celebrante *mf*.

cel·e·brate (sĕl'ə-brāt') tr. **-brat·ed, -brat·ing** *(to commemorate)* festejar, conmemorar; *(a mass)* celebrar; *(to extol)* exaltar, alabar —intr. celebrar, festejar.

cel·e·brat·ed (sĕl'ə-brā'tĭd) adj. célebre, famoso.

cel·e·bra·tion (sĕl'ə-brā'shən) s. celebración *f*.

ce·leb·ri·ty (sə-lĕb'rĭ-tē) s. [pl. **-ties**] celebridad *f*.

ce·ler·i·ty (sə-lĕr'ĭ-tē) s. celeridad *f*.

cel·er·y (sĕl'ə-rē) s. [pl. **-ies**] BOT. apio.

ce·les·tial (sə-lĕs'chəl) adj. *(of the sky)* celeste; *(divine)* celestial.

celestial navigation s. navegación astronómica.

cel·i·ba·cy (sĕl'ə-bə-sē) s. celibato.

cel·i·bate (sĕl'ə-bĭt) adj. & s. célibe *mf*.

cell (sĕl) s. *(room)* celda; BIOL., ELEC., POL. célula.

cel·lar (sĕl'ər) s. *(basement)* sótano; *(of wines)* bodega.

cel·lo (chĕl'ō) s. [pl. **-los**] violoncelo.

cel·lo·phane (sĕl'ə-fān') s. celofán *m*.

cel·lu·lar (sĕl'yə-lər) adj. celular.

cel·lule (sĕl'yōōl) s. BIOL. celulilla.

cel·lu·loid (sĕl'yə-loid') s. QUÍM. celuloide *m*.

cel·lu·lose (sĕl'yə-lōs') s. BOT. celulosa.

Cel·si·us (sĕl'sē-əs, -shəs) s. Celsio, centígrado.

Celt (kĕlt, sĕlt) s. HIST. celta *mf*.

Celt·ic (kĕl'tĭk, sĕl'-) **I.** s. *(language)* celta *m* **II.** adj. céltico.

ce·ment (sĭ-mĕnt') **I.** s. *(for construction)* cemento; *(glue)* pegamento; FIG. *(bond)* vínculo **II.** tr. *(to bind)* unir con cemento; *(to glue)* pegar; *(to cover)* revestir de cemento; FIG. *(to strengthen)* cimentar, reforzar —intr. pegarse.

cement mixer s. CONSTR. hormigonera, mezclador de cemento *m*.

cem·e·ter·y (sĕm'ĭ-tĕr'ē) s. [pl. **-ies**] cementerio, camposanto.

cen·o·taph (sĕn'ə-tăf') s. cenotafio, monumento.

cen·ser (sĕn'sər) s. incensario.

cen·sor (sĕn'sər) **I.** s. censor *m* **II.** tr. censurar.

cen·so·ri·ous (sĕn-sôr'ē-əs) adj. censurador.

cen·sor·ship (sĕn'sər-shĭp') s. censura.

cen·sur·a·ble (sĕn'shər-ə-bəl) adj. censurable.

cen·sure (sĕn'shər) **I.** s. censura, reprensión *f* **II.** tr. **-sured, -sur·ing** censurar, reprender.

cen·sus (sĕn'səs) s. censo.

cent (sĕnt) s. FIN. centavo, céntimo.

cen·taur (sĕn'tôr') s. MITOL. centauro.

cen·ta·vo (sĕn-tä'vō) s. [pl. **-vos**] FIN. centavo.

cen·te·nar·i·an (sĕn'tə-nâr'ē-ən) s. centenario (persona).

cen·ten·a·ry (sĕn-tĕn'ə-rē, sĕn'tə-nĕr'ē) adj. & s. [pl. **-ries**] centenario (cien años).

cen·ten·ni·al (sĕn-tĕn'ē-əl) adj. & s. centenario (fiesta).

cen·ter (sĕn'tər) **I.** s. *(middle)* centro, medio; *(axis)* eje *m*; GEOM. centro; *(focus)* centro; ELEC., GEOL. núcleo; ANAT. centro <nerve c. centro nervioso>; DEP. centro **II.** tr. *(to place in the middle)* centrar, centralizar; FIG. *(to concentrate)* concentrar; DEP. centrar —intr. concentrarse **♦ to c. at, in** o **on** centrarse en, girar alrededor de.

center of gravity s. FÍS. centro de gravedad.

cen·ter·piece (sĕn'tər-pēs') s. *(decoration)* centro de mesa (adorno); FIG. foco o núcleo principal.

cen·tes·i·mal (sĕn-tĕs'ə-məl) adj. centesimal.

cen·tes·i·mo (sĕn-tĕs'ə-mō') s. [pl. **-mos**] FIN. centésimo.

cen·ti·grade (sĕn'tĭ-grād') adj. centígrado.

cen·ti·gram (sĕn'tĭ-grăm') s. centigramo.

cen·ti·li·ter (sĕn'tə-lē'tər) s. centilitro.

cen·time (sän'tēm, sĕn'-) s. FIN. céntimo.

cen·ti·me·ter o **cen·ti·me·tre** (sĕn'tə-mē'tər, sän'-) s. centímetro.

cen·ti·mo (sĕn'tə-mō') s. [pl. **-mos**] FIN. céntimo.

cen·ti·pede (sĕn'tə-pēd') s. ENTOM. ciempiés *m*.

cen·tral (sĕn'trəl) **I.** adj. *(middle)* central, céntrico; *(important)* central **♦ c. nervous system** sistema nervioso central **II.** s. *(telephone exchange)* central telefónica.

Central African Republic s. República Centroafricana.

Central America s. América Central, Centroamérica.

Central American adj. & s. centroamericano.

cen·tral·ism (sĕn'trə-lĭz'əm) s. POL. centralidad *f*, centralismo.

cen·tral·i·ty (sĕn-trăl'ĭ-tē) s. posición central *f*.

cen·tral·i·za·tion (sĕn'trə-lĭ-zā'shən) s. centralización *f*.

cen·tral·ize (sĕn'trə-līz') tr. & intr. **-ized, -iz·ing** centralizar(se).

ã rey / ä año / b boca / ch chico / d dar / ĕ el / ē mil / g gato / h joya / hw juez / ī aire / k casa / kw cuan /

cen·tre (sĕn′tər) s. G.B. var. de **center.**
cen·tric (sĕn′trĭk) adj. céntrico, central.
cen·trif·u·gal (sĕn-trĭf′yə-gəl, -trĭf′ə-) adj. centrífugo.
cen·tri·fuge (sĕn′trə-fyōōj′) I. s. centrifugadora II. tr.
-fuged, -fug·ing centrifugar.
cen·trip·e·tal (sĕn-trĭp′ĭ-tl) adj. centrípeto.
cen·trism (sĕn′trĭz′əm) s. POL. centrismo.
cen·trist (sĕn′trĭst) s. POL. centrista *mf.*
cen·tu·ri·on (sĕn-tŏŏr′ē-ən, -tyŏŏr′-) s. HIST., MIL. centurión
m.
cen·tu·ry (sĕn′chə-rē) s. [pl. **-ries**] *(time)* siglo, centuria;
HIST. centuria (del ejército romano) ♦ **c. plant** maguey,
agave.
ce·phal·ic (sə-făl′ĭk) adj. ANAT. cefálico.
ce·ram·ic (sə-răm′ĭk) s. *(clay)* arcilla, barro; *(porcelain)*
porcelana ♦ **ceramics** [ú. con v. sing.] cerámica.
ce·re·al (sîr′ē-əl) s. cereal *m.*
cer·e·bel·lum (sĕr′ə-bĕl′əm) s. [pl. **-bel·lums** o **-bel·la** (-bĕl′-
ə)] ANAT. cerebelo.
cer·e·bra (sĕr′ə-brə, sə-rē′-) un pl. de **cerebrum.**
cer·e·bral (sĕr′ə-brəl, sə-rē′-) adj. cerebral.
cerebral cortex s. ANAT. corteza cerebral.
cerebral palsy s. parálisis cerebral *f.*
cer·e·brate (sĕr′ə-brāt′) intr. **-brat·ed, -brat·ing** pensar, reflexionar.
cer·e·bro·spi·nal (sĕr′ə-brō-spī′nəl) adj. cerebroespinal.
cer·e·brum (sĕr′ə-brəm, sə-rē′-) s. ANAT. [pl. **-brums** o **-bra**
(-brə)] cerebro.
cere·cloth (sîr′klôth′) o **cer·e·ment** (sĕr′ə-mənt, sîr′mənt) s.
mortaja encerada.
cer·e·mo·ni·al (sĕr′ə-mō′nē-əl) I. adj. ceremonial II. s.
ceremonial *m,* rito.
cer·e·mo·ni·ous (sĕr′ə-mō′nē-əs) adj. ceremonioso.
cer·e·mo·ny (sĕr′ə-mō′nē) s. [pl. **-nies**] ceremonia.
Ce·res (sîr′ēz) s. *(asteroid)* Ceres *m;* *(goddess)* Ceres *f.*
ce·ri·um (sîr′ē-əm) s. QUÍM. cerio.
cer·tain (sûr′tn) adj. *(fixed)* cierto, determinado <*to get together at a c. time* reunirse a cierta hora>; *(inevitable)* seguro, inevitable; *(confident)* seguro <*we are c. that they will
come* estamos seguros de que vendrán>; *(indisputable)* indudable; *(some)* algunos, ciertos <*c. players are not training* ciertos jugadores no se entrenan>; *(particular)* tal <*a
c. Mr. Smith* un tal Mr. Smith> ♦ **for c.** por cierto, ciertamente ♦ **to make c.** asegurarse.
cer·tain·ly (sûr′tn-lē) adv. *(surely)* cierto, *(of course)* desde
luego, por supuesto <*c. not!* ¡por supuesto que no!>;
(without fail) sin falta, seguro.
cer·tain·ty (sûr′tn-tē) s. [pl. **-ties**] *(sureness)* certeza, certidumbre *f;* *(fact)* cosa segura.
cer·ti·fi·a·ble (sûr′tə-fī′ə-bəl) adj. certificable.
cer·tif·i·cate (sər-tĭf′ĭ-kĭt) I. s. *(document)* certificado, partida <*a birth c.* partida de nacimiento>; *(verification)* certificado (de estudios); *(degree)* diploma *m,* título II. tr.
(-kāt′) **-cat·ed, -cat·ing** dar un certificado.
certificate of deposit s. COM. certificado de depósito.
cer·ti·fi·ca·tion (sûr′tə-fĭ-kā′shən) s. *(act)* certificación *f;*
(document) certificado.
cer·ti·fied (sûr′tə-fīd′) adj. certificado.
certified check s. cheque certificado.
certified mail s. correo certificado.
certified public accountant s. contador público titulado.
cer·ti·fy (sûr′tə-fī′) tr. & intr. **-fied, -fy·ing** certificar, atestiguar.
cer·ti·tude (sûr′tĭ-tōōd′, -tyōōd′) s. certidumbre *f,* certeza.
ce·ru·men (sə-rōō′mən) s. cerumen *m,* cera de los oídos.
cer·vi·cal (sûr′vĭ-kəl) adj. ANAT. cervical.
cer·vix (sûr′vĭks) s. [pl. **cer·vix·es** o **cer·vi·ces** (-vĭ-sēz′)]
(neck) cerviz *f;* *(of the uterus)* cuello del útero.
Ce·sar·e·an o **Ce·sar·i·an** (sĭ-zâr′ē-ən) s. var. de **Caesarean.**
ce·si·um (sē′zē-əm) s. QUÍM. cesio.
ces·sa·tion (sĕ-sā′shən) s. cesación *f,* cese *m.*
ces·sion (sĕsh′ən) s. cesión *f.*
cess·pool (sĕs′pōōl′) s. *(sewer)* pozo negro; FIG. *(filthy
place)* cloaca, sentina.
ce·ta·ce·an (sĭ-tā′shən) adj. & s. ZOOL. cetáceo.

Cey·lon (sĭ-lŏn′) s. Celián *m.*
Cey·lon·ese (sē′lə-nēz′, sā′lə-) adj. & s. [pl. **Ceylonese**] cingalés *m.*
Chad (chăd) s. Chad *m.*
Chad·i·an (chăd′ē-ən) adj. & s. chadiano.
chafe (chāf) I. tr. **chafed, chaf·ing** *(to abrade)* desgastar,
raer; *(to rub)* raspar, rozar; *(to annoy)* irritar, exacerbar;
(to warm) frotar —intr. *(to become worn)* desgastarse,
raerse; *(to rub)* rozarse; *(to become annoyed)* irritarse, enfadarse <*he chafed at the delay* se enfadó por la demora>
II. s. *(wear)* desgaste *m,* roce *m;* *(annoyance)* irritación *f,*
enfado; *(rubbing)* rozadura.
chaff (chăf) I. s. *(of wheat)* ahechaduras, barcia; *(of other
grains)* granzas; *(straw)* paja (cortada); *(worthless matter)*
paja, broza; *(banter)* chanza, zumba II. tr. zumbar, chasquear.
chafing dish s. escalfador *m,* calientaplatos *m.*
cha·grin (shə-grĭn′) I. s. *(disappointment)* desilusión *f;*
(grief) pesadumbre *f,* contrariedad *f* II. tr. *(to disappoint)*
desilusionar; *(to grieve)* apesadumbrar, contrariar.
chain (chān) I. s. cadena II. tr. encadenar.
chain gang s. cadena de presidiarios, cuadrilla de presos.
chain mail s. ARM. cota de mallas.
chain reaction s. reacción en cadena *f.*
chain saw s. sierra de cadena.
chain-smoke (chān′smōk′) intr. & tr. **-smoked, -smok·ing**
fumar un cigarrillo tras otro.
chain smoker s. fumador que enciende un cigarrillo tras
otro *m.*
chain store s. sucursal de una cadena de tiendas *f.*
chair (châr) I. s. *(furniture)* silla; *(chairman)* presidente *m;*
(chairmanship) presidencia; *(in a university)* cátedra; *(sedan chair)* silla de manos; FAM. *(electric chair)* silla eléctrica; F.C. *(block)* cojinete de riel *m* II. tr. *(to seat)*
asentar; *(to install in office)* instalar en oficio (presidente,
autoridad); *(to preside over)* presidir; G.B. *(to carry aloft)*
llevar en triunfo.
chair lift s. telesilla (para esquiadores).
chair·man (châr′mən) I. s. [pl. **-men**] presidente *m* II. tr.
-manned, -man·ning presidir.
chair·man·ship (châr′mən-shĭp′) s. presidencia.
chair·per·son (châr′pûr′sən) s. presidente *m,* presidenta.
chair·wom·an (châr′wŏŏm′ən) s. [pl. **-wom·en** (-wĭm′ĭn)]
presidenta.
chaise longue (shāz lông′) s. [pl. **chaise longues** o **chaises
longues** (shāz lông′)] meridiana, tumbona.
chal·ced·o·ny (kăl-sĕd′n-ē) s. [pl. **-nies**] MIN. calcedonia.
cha·let (shă-lā′) s. chalet *m,* chalé *m.*
chal·ice (chăl′ĭs) s. cáliz *m.*
chalk (chôk) I. s. MIN. creta; *(for blackboards)* tiza II. tr.
marcar, escribir (con tiza) ♦ **to c. up** *(to earn)* anotarse,
apuntarse <*to c. up a victory* apuntarse una victoria>; *(to
credit)* acreditarse, poner a cuenta de <*c. it up to experience* ponlo a cuenta de la experiencia>.
chalk·board (chôk′bôrd′) s. pizarrón *m,* pizarra.
chalk·y (chô′kē) adj. **-i·er, -i·est** *(said of earth)* cretáceo,
grietoso; *(said of water)* calcáreo.
chal·lenge (chăl′ənj) I. s. *(dare)* desafío, reto; *(dispute)*
cuestionamiento; *(stimulus)* estímulo, incentivo; MIL. alto,
quién vive *m;* DER. *(objection)* recusación *f,* objeción *f*
II. tr. **-lenged, -leng·ing** *(to dare)* desafiar, retar; *(to contest)* cuestionar, disputar; *(to stimulate)* estimular; MIL.
(to shout) dar el quién vive; DER. *(to object)* recusar, objetar.
chal·leng·er (chăl′ən-jər) s. desafiador *m,* retador *m.*
chal·leng·ing (chăl′ən-jĭng) adj. *(defiant)* desafiante, de
desafío; *(exacting)* arduo, difícil; *(stimulating)* estimulante.
cham·ber (chām′bər) I. s. cámara ♦ **chambers** despacho
(de un juez) II. tr. poner en una cámara.
cham·ber·lain (chām′bər-lən) s. *(steward, officer)* cham-
belán *m;* *(treasurer)* tesorero; RELIG. camarlengo.
cham·ber·maid (chām′bər-mād′) s. camarera, criada.
chamber music s. música de cámara.
chamber of commerce s. cámara de comercio.
chamber pot s. orinal *m.*

cha·me·leon (kə-mēl'yən) s. ZOOL. camaleón *m*; FIG. *(person)* camaleón.

cham·ois (shăm'ē) s. [pl. **chamois**] ZOOL. gamuza.

cham·o·mile (kăm'ə-mīl') s. BOT. camomila, manzanilla.

champ[1] (chămp) tr. & intr. tascar ♦ **to c. at the bit** FIG. tascar el freno, impacientarse.

champ[2] (chămp) s. FAM. campeón *m*.

cham·pagne (shăm-pān') s. champaña *m*, champán *m*.

cham·pi·on (chăm'pē-ən) I. s. *(winner)* campeón *m*; FIG. *(defender)* defensor *m*, paladín *m* II. tr. abogar por, ser el paladín de III. adj. excelente.

cham·pi·on·ship (chăm'pē-ən-shĭp') s. *(competition)* campeonato; *(advocacy)* defensa.

chance (chăns) I. s. *(accident)* casualidad *f* <*by c.* por casualidad>; *(fortuity)* azar *m* <*game of c.* juego de azar>; *(luck)* suerte *f*; *(opportunity)* oportunidad *f* <*give me a c. to explain* déme la oportunidad de explicarlo>; *(possibility)* posibilidad *f* <*not to stand a c.* no tener posibilidad alguna>; *(risk)* riesgo <*to take a c.* correr un riesgo> ♦ **by any c.** por casualidad II. intr. **chanced, chanc·ing** suceder, acaecer —tr. *(to risk)* arriesgar; *(to try)* probar <*to c. one's luck* probar fortuna> ♦ **to c. on** *o* **upon** encontrarse *o* toparse con III. adj. casual, fortuito <*a c. meeting* un encuentro casual>.

chan·cel (chăn'səl) s. presbiterio, antealtar *m*.

chan·cel·ler·y (chăn'sə-lə-rē, -slə-rē) s. [pl. **-ies**] cancillería.

chan·cel·lor (chăn'sə-lər) s. POL. canciller *m*; *(of a university)* rector *m*.

Chancellor of the Exchequer s. ministro de Hacienda (en Gran Bretaña).

chan·cer·y (chăn'sə-rē) s. [pl. **-ies**] DER. *(court)* tribunal *m*, juzgado; *(office of public records)* archivo; *(chancellery)* cancillería.

chan·cre (shăng'kər) s. MED. chancro.

chanc·y (chăn'sē) adj. **-i·er, -i·est** *(uncertain)* incierto; *(risky)* arriesgado, peligroso.

chan·de·lier (shăn'də-lîr') s. araña, candelabro colgante.

chan·dler (chănd'lər) s. *(candlemaker)* cerero, velero; *(dealer)* proveedor *m*.

chan·dler·y (chănd'lə-rē) s. [pl. **-ies**] *(candle shop)* cerería; *(supplier's business)* proveeduría.

change (chānj) I. tr. **changed, chang·ing** *(to make different)* cambiar <*let's c. the subject* cambiemos de tema>; *(to switch)* cambiar <*they changed seats* cambiaron de asiento>; *(to alter)* cambiar, alterar; *(to transform)* transformar, convertir <*irrigation changed the desert to fertile land* la irrigación convirtió el desierto en tierra fértil>; *(to trade)* trocar, permutar; *(to exchange for)* cambiar de <*to c. one's name* cambiar de nombre>; *(to lay aside)* cambiar (de plan, método); *(to exchange)* cambiar (dinero); *(clothes, coverings)* mudar, cambiar ♦ **to c. color** *(act)* mudar de color; *(to blush)* ruborizarse; *(to turn pale)* palidecer • **to c. gear** *(automobile)* cambiar de velocidad; *(objective)* cambiar de objectivo • **to c. hands** cambiar de manos *o* de dueño • **to c. key** MÚS. cambiar de tono • **to c. one's position** *(to better)* mejorar; *(to get married)* casarse • **to c. one's mind** cambiar de opinión *o* parecer • **to c. one's tune** cambiar de tono *o* actitud —intr. *(to vary)* cambiar <*the scenery is beginning to change now* el paisaje está empezando a cambiar ahora>; *(to become different)* convertirse, volverse <*the ice is changing to water* el hielo se está volviendo agua>; *(to transfer)* transbordarse, hacer transbordo; *(voice)* cambiar, hacerse grave ♦ **to c. off** turnarse, alternarse • **to c. over** cambiar II. s. *(act)* cambio; *(substitution)* substitución *f*, relevo; *(of clothing)* muda; *(money)* cambio, vuelto; *(coins)* suelto, moneda suelta ♦ **a c. for the better** un cambio beneficioso • **c. of heart** arrepentimiento • **for a c.** para variar • **keep the c.** quédese con el vuelto.

change·a·ble (chān'jə-bəl) adj. *(alterable)* cambiable; *(inconstant)* variable.

change·less (chānj'lĭs) adj. inmutable, invariable.

change·ling (chānj'lĭng) s. niño cambiado por otro.

change of life s. menopausia.

change·o·ver (chānj'ō'vər) s. cambio, alteración *f*.

chang·er (chăn'jər) s. *(device)* cambiador *m*; FIN. cambiante *mf*, cambista *mf*.

chan·nel (chăn'əl) I. s. *(passage)* canal *m*; *(riverbed)* cauce *m*, lecho; *(tube)* tubo, conducto; *(groove)* ranura; RAD., TELEV. canal *m*, estación *f* II. tr. *(to set in a course)* canalizar; *(to groove)* estriar, ranurar.

chan·nel·ize (chăn'ə-līz') tr. **-ized, -iz·ing** canalizar, encauzar.

chant (chănt) I. s. *(song)* canto; *(psalm)* cántico, salmodia; *(monotonous call)* canto II. tr. cantar —intr. RELIG. salmodiar.

chant·er (chăn'tər) s. *(person)* cantor *m*, cantante *mf*; *(pipe)* caramillo (de la gaita).

chan·te·relle (shăn'tə-rĕl', shän'-) s. BOT. mízcalo.

chan·ti·cleer (chăn'tĭ-klîr', shăn'-) s. gallo.

Cha·nu·kah (KHä'nə-kə, hä'-) s. RELIG. Januca.

cha·os (kā'ŏs') s. caos *m*, confusión *f*.

cha·ot·ic (kā-ŏt'ĭk) adj. caótico, confuso.

chap[1] (chăp) I. tr. & intr. **chapped, chap·ping** paspar(se) II. s. grieta, paspadura.

chap[2] (chăp) s. FAM. *(fellow)* tipo, muchacho.

chap·ar·ral (shăp'ə-răl') s. chaparral *m*.

chap·book (chăp'bŏŏk') s. libro de cordel.

chap·el (chăp'əl) s. *(church)* capilla; *(religious service)* servicio religioso; *(association)* gremio de impresores.

chap·er·on *o* **chap·er·one** (shăp'ə-rōn') I. s. carabina, acompañante de señoritas *mf* II. tr. **-oned, -on·ing** hacer de carabina con, acompañar (a una señorita).

chap·lain (chăp'lĭn) s. RELIG. capellán *m*.

chap·let (chăp'lĭt) s. *(garland)* guirnalda; RELIG. *(of a rosary)* cinco décadas del rosario; *(string of beads)* collar *m*; ARQ. *(molding)* moldura, astrágalo.

chaps (chăps, shăps) s.pl. zahones *m*, chaparreras.

chap·ter (chăp'tər) s. *(of a book)* capítulo; *(branch)* sección (de una organización) *f*; RELIG. *(passage)* capítulo; *(of canons)* cabildo.

char (chär) I. tr. & intr. **charred, char·ring** *(to scorch)* chamuscar(se); *(to reduce to coal)* carbonizar(se) II. s. carbón de leña *m*.

char·ac·ter (kăr'ək-tər) s. *(nature)* carácter *m*; LIT. *(person)* personaje *m*; *(reputation)* reputación *f*; *(personage)* personaje; FAM. *(individual)* tipo; IMPR. tipo ♦ **in c.** característico.

char·ac·ter·is·tic (kăr'ək-tə-rĭs'tĭk) I. adj. característico II. s. característica.

char·ac·ter·i·za·tion (kăr'ək-tər-ĭ-zā'shən) s. caracterización *f*.

char·ac·ter·ize (kăr'ək-tə-rīz') tr. **-ized, -iz·ing** caracterizar.

cha·rade (shə-rād') s. charada, acertijo.

char·coal (chär'kōl') I. s. *(fuel)* carbón de leña *m*, carbón vegetal; DIB. *(pencil)* carboncillo; *(drawing)* carboncillo, dibujo al carbón; *(color)* color carbón *m* II. tr. dibujar con carboncillo.

chard (chärd) s. BOT. acelga.

charge (chärj) I. tr. **charged, charg·ing** *(to entrust)* encargar, encomendar <*they charged her with the task of supervising the beginners* le encomendaron la tarea de supervisar a los principiantes>; DER. *(to instruct)* ordenar, instruir <*the judge charged the jury to arrive at a verdict* el juez instruyó al jurado a que llegase a un veredicto>; *(to accuse)* acusar; *(a price)* pedir, cobrar <*she charges ten dollars for a haircut* ella cobra diez dólares por un corte de pelo>; *(to postpone payment)* cargar <*c. it to my account, please* cárguelo a mi cuenta, por favor>; MIL. *(to attack)* atacar, acometer; ARM. *(to load)* cargar; *(to saturate)* impregnar, saturar <*the air was charged with perfume* el aire estaba saturado de perfume>; ELEC. cargar —intr. *(to attack)* atacar, ir a la carga; COM. cobrar II. s. *(management)* cargo, dirección *f* <*he is in c. of this experiment* él está a cargo de este experimento>; *(obligation)* obligación *f*, responsabilidad *f*; *(someone, something)* cargo, custodia; *(burden)* carga, peso; *(cost)* costo, precio <*delivery c.* costo del envío>; *(tax)* impuesto, gravamen *m*; *(load)* carga, ataque *m*; *(explosive)* carga; FÍS. carga ♦ **admission c.** entrada • **free of c.** gratis • **in c. of** encargado de • **to appear on a c. of** DER. comparecer acusado de • **to be in c.** ser el encargado • **to bring charges against** DER. hacer acusaciones contra • **to reverse the charges** TEL. cobrar al número llamado, hacer una llamada de cobro revertido • **to take c.** asumir el mando • **to take c. of** encargarse de, hacerse cargo de.

charge·a·ble (chär'jə-bəl) adj. *(to an account)* que se puede cargar (a una cuenta); DER. acusable, imputable.

charge account s. COM. cuenta de crédito.

char·gé d'af·faires (shär-zhā' də-fâr') s. [pl. **char·gés d'af·faires** (-zhā', -zhāz')] DIPL. encargado de negocios.

charg·er (chär'jər) s. MIL. *(person)* cargador *m*; *(horse)* caballo de batalla; ELEC. cargador.

char·i·ot (chär'ē-ət) s. cuadriga, carro de batalla.

char·i·o·teer (chär'ē-ə-tîr') s. auriga *m*, cochero.

cha·ris·ma (kə-rīz'mə) s. *(attraction)* carisma; RELIG. carisma.

char·is·mat·ic (kăr'īz-măt'īk) adj. carismático.

char·i·ta·ble (chăr'ī-tə-bəl) adj. caritativo, benéfico.

char·i·ty (chăr'ī-tē) s. [pl. **-ties**] *(benevolence)* caridad *f*, beneficencia; *(institution)* beneficencia, institución benéfica; *(alms)* limosna.

char·la·tan (shär'lə-tn) s. charlatán *m*, farsante *m*.

char·ley horse (chär'lē) s. FAM. calambre *m*.

charm (chärm) I. s. *(attraction)* encanto; *(amulet)* amuleto ♦ **like a c.** como por encanto II. tr. *(to fascinate)* encantar; *(to beguile)* seducir <*he charmed them into doing it his way* los sedujo para que lo hicieran a su manera>; *(to bewitch)* embrujar, hechizar —intr. *(to fascinate)* ejercer fascinación; *(to use spells)* practicar hechicería.

charm·er (chär'mər) s. *(charming person)* persona encantadora; *(of snakes)* encantador *m*; *(sorcerer)* hechicero.

charm·ing (chär'mĭng) adj. encantador.

char·nel house (chär'nəl) s. osario.

chart (chärt) I. s. *(table, graph)* cuadro; *(map)* mapa *m*, carta de navegación II. tr. *(to make a chart of)* hacer un cuadro de; *(to plan)* trazar.

char·ter (chär'tər) I. s. POL. carta; *(of an organization)* estatutos; *(lease)* fletamento ♦ **c. flight** vuelo fletado II. tr. POL. otorgar una carta; *(to organize)* establecer los estatutos de; *(to rent)* fletar.

chartered accountant s. G.B. contador público.

char·ter·house (chär'tər-hous') s. RELIG. cartuja.

charter member s. socio fundador.

char·wom·an (chär'wŏom'ən) s. [pl. **-wom·en** (-wĭm'ĭn)] G.B. criada, empleada de limpieza.

char·y (châr'ē) adj. **-i·er, -i·est** *(wary)* cauteloso; *(shy)* tímido; *(sparing)* parco.

chase[1] (chās) I. tr. **chased, chas·ing** *(to pursue)* perseguir; *(to hunt)* cazar, dar caza; *(to follow)* ir detrás de, perseguir ♦ **to c. after** perseguir a • **to c. away** *o* **off** ahuyentar • **to c. out** echar fuera —intr. *(to pursue)* perseguir; *(to rush about)* ir corriendo <*he chased after them* se fué corriendo trás ellos> II. s. *(pursuit)* persecución *f*; G.B. *(game preserve)* coto de caza; *(hunting right)* permiso *o* derecho de caza ♦ **the c.** *(sport)* la cacería; *(quarry)* caza, presa.

chase[2] (chās) I. s. *(groove)* ranura, estría; *(of a gun)* caña II. tr. **chased, chas·ing** *(to emboss)* repujar; *(to groove)* ranurar, acanalar.

chas·er (chā'sər) s. *(pursuer)* perseguidor *m*; FAM. *(drink)* bebida ligera (que se toma después de una fuerte).

chasm (kăz'əm) s. *(cleft, difference)* abismo; *(hiatus)* ruptura.

chas·sis (shăs'ē, chăs'ē) s. [pl. **chassis** (-ēz)] chasis *m*, armazón *f*.

chaste (chāst) adj. **chast·er, chast·est** casto.

chas·ten (chā'sən) tr. *(to chastise)* castigar; *(to restrain)* disciplinar; *(to refine)* pulir, depurar.

chas·tise (chăs-tīz') tr. **-tised, -tis·ing** castigar.

chas·ti·ty (chăs'tĭ-tē) s. castidad *f*.

chastity belt s. HIST. cinturón de castidad *m*.

chas·u·ble (chăz'ə-bəl, chăzh'ə-) s. RELIG. casulla.

chat (chăt) I. intr. **chat·ted, chat·ting** charlar, platicar II. s. *(conversation)* charla, plática; ORNIT. culiblanco.

chat·tel (chăt'l) s. *(article)* bien mueble *m*; *(slave)* esclavo.

chattel mortgage s. hipoteca prendaria, hipoteca sobre bienes muebles.

chat·ter (chăt'ər) I. intr. *(to jabber)* parlotear, chacharear; *(to rattle)* castañetear, rechinar —tr. *(to utter)* parlotear, chacharear II. s. *(talk)* parloteo, cháchara; *(rattle)* castañeteo.

chat·ter·box (chăt'ər-bŏks') s. charlatán *m*, parlanchín *m*.

chat·ty (chăt'ē) adj. **-ti·er, -ti·est** *(informal)* familiar; *(talkative)* parlanchín.

chauf·feur (shō'fər, shō-fûr') I. s. chofer *o* chófer *m*, conductor *m* II. tr. conducir, manejar.

chau·vin·ism (shō'və-nīz'əm) s. chauvinismo, patriotería.

chau·vin·ist (shō'və-nĭst) s. chauvinista *mf*, patriotero.

chau·vin·is·tic (shō'və-nĭs'tĭk) adj. chauvinista, patriotero.

cheap (chēp) I. adj. **-er, -est** *(inexpensive, easy)* barato; *(inferior)* de mala calidad; *(tawdry)* charro; *(mean)* bajo, vil ♦ **dirt c.** baratísimo • **to feel c.** sentirse rebajado II. adv. **-er, -est** barato.

cheap·en (chē'pən) tr. & intr. *(to make cheaper)* abaratar(se); *(to degrade)* rebajar(se), degradar(se).

cheap·ly (chēp'lē) adv. barato, a bajo precio ♦ **c. made** de baja calidad.

cheap·ness (chēp'nĭs) s. *(price)* bajo precio; *(quality)* mala calidad; *(lowness)* bajeza; *(stinginess)* tacañería.

cheap·skate (chēp'skāt') s. JER. tacaño, mezquino.

cheat (chēt) I. tr. *(to swindle)* defraudar, estafar; *(to deceive)* engañar, burlar —intr. *(in a game)* hacer trampa; *(to copy)* copiar; FAM. *(to be unfaithful)* ser infiel (sexualmente) II. s. *(swindler)* tramposo; *(trick)* trampa; *(swindle)* estafa.

cheat·er (chē'tər) s. tramposo.

cheat·ing (chē'tĭng) I. adj. *(deceiving)* tramposo; *(fraudulent)* fraudulento II. s. trampa.

check (chĕk) I. s. *(abrupt halt)* parada, detención *f*; *(brake)* freno; *(obstacle)* obstáculo, impedimento; *(control)* comprobación *f*, inspección *f*; *(test)* examen *m*, chequeo; *(mark)* marca, señal *f*; *(ticket)* talón *m*, contraseña; *(bill)* cuenta (de restaurante); *(gambling chip)* ficha; *(bank draft)* cheque *m*; *(pattern)* cuadros; *(square)* cuadro; *(fabric)* tela a cuadros; *(in chess)* jaque *m* ♦ **to act as a c. on** *(to restrain)* refrenar; *(to verify)* verificar • **to keep** *o* **to hold in c.** tener a raya, tener controlado II. interj. *(in chess)* ¡jaque!; FAM. *(agreed)* ¡de acuerdo! III. tr. *(to halt)* detener, parar; *(to restrain)* refrenar, contener; *(to control)* contener, reprimir <*to c. one's anger* reprimir la ira>; *(to be an obstacle)* impedir, estorbar; *(to reprimand)* reprender; *(to rebuff)* rechazar; *(to test)* examinar, controlar; *(to verify)* verificar; *(to put a check on)* marcar, chequear; *(to deposit for safekeeping)* depositar (valijas, prendas); *(in chess)* dar jaque a; *(baggage)* facturar; *(to square)* cuadricular ♦ **c. it out!** JER. ¡mire esto!, ¡observe! • **to c. against** chequear, cotejar • **to c. off** marcar *o* identificar (uno por uno), chequear • **to c. out** FAM. comprobar • **to c. up on** comprobar, verificar • **to c. with** *(to compare)* comparar *o* cotejar con; *(to consult with)* consultar con —intr. *(to halt)* detenerse, pararse; *(to agree)* corresponder, concordar <*these two lists c.* estas dos listas concuerdan>; *(to determine accuracy)* comprobar, averiguar <*he phoned to c. on his departure* telefoneó para averiguar la hora de partida>; *(in chess)* dar jaque ♦ **to c. in** *o* **into** registrarse (en un hotel) • **to c. out** pagar la cuenta y marcharse de un hotel.

check·book (chĕk'bŏok') s. chequera, talonario de cheques.

checked (chĕkt) adj. *(checkered)* a cuadros; *(restrained)* controlado.

check·er (chĕk'ər) I. s. *(pattern)* cuadros; *(square)* cuadro; *(examiner)* verificador *m*; *(cashier)* cajero; *(in the game)* pieza del juego de damas ♦ **checkers** damas II. tr. *(to mark)* marcar con cuadros, escaquear; *(to variegate)* jaspear.

check·er·board (chĕk'ər-bôrd') s. tablero de damas.

check·ered (chĕk'ərd) adj. *(checked)* cuadriculado, a cuadros; FIG. *(varied)* variado; *(uneven)* con altibajos.

checking account s. cuenta corriente, cuenta de cheques.

check list s. lista de control, lista de verificación.

check·mate (chĕk'māt') I. tr. **-mat·ed, -mat·ing** *(in chess)* dar jaque y mate; *(to defeat)* vencer, frustrar II. s. *(in chess)* jaque y mate *m*; *(defeat)* derrota absoluta.

check-out (chĕk'out') s. *(cashier)* caja; *(exit)* salida (de hotel, supermercado, biblioteca); *(test)* prueba; *(inspection)* inspección *f.*
check·point (chĕk'point') s. lugar de inspección *m.*
check·rein (chĕk'rān') s. EQUIT. gamarra, engallador *m.*
check·room (chĕk'rōōm', -rŏŏm') s. *(cloakroom)* guardarropa *m; (for luggage)* consigna.
checks and balances s.pl. POL. sistema de equilibrio de poderes (en un gobierno constitucional) *m.*
check·up (chĕk'ŭp') s. *(examination)* examen *m,* revisión *f; (physical)* reconocimiento médico general.
cheek (chĕk) I. s. *(of the face)* mejilla; *(impudence)* desfachatez *f,* descaro *m* ♦ **c. to c.** mejilla a mejilla • **c. by jowl** codo con codo II. tr. FAM. tratar con descaro.
cheek·bone (chĕk'bōn') s. ANAT. pómulo, malar *m.*
cheek·y (chē'kē) adj. **-i·er, -i·est** descarado, caradura.
cheep (chēp) I. s. gorjeo, piada II. tr. & intr. piar.
cheer (chîr) I. tr. *(to make happy)* animar, alegrar; *(to encourage)* alentar; *(to shout)* vitorear, ovacionar ♦ **to c. on** animar, alentar • **to c. up** alegrar, animar —intr. *(to become cheerful)* animarse, alegrarse; *(to applaud)* aplaudir ♦ **c. up!** ¡ánimo!, ¡anímate! II. s. *(gaiety)* alegría, ánimo; *(shout)* grito de aclamación, hurra ♦ **cheers!** ¡salud!
cheer·ful (chîr'fəl) adj. *(happy)* alegre, animado; *(good-humored)* de buen humor.
cheer·ful·ness (chîr'fəl-nĭs) s. alegría, buen humor *m.*
cheer·i·ly (chîr'ə-lē) adv. alegremente, de buen humor.
cheer·i·o (chîr'ē-ō') G.B. interj. *(hello)* hola; *(good-by)* chao.
cheer·lead·er (chîr'lē'dər) s. persona que alienta y dirige los vivas en una encuesta deportiva.
cheer·less (chîr'lĭs) adj. triste.
cheer·y (chîr'ē) adj. **-i·er, -i·est** alegre, animado.
cheese (chēz) s. queso.
cheese·burg·er (chēz'bûr'gər) s. hamburguesa con queso.
cheese·cake *o* **cheese cake** (chēz'kāk') s. CUL. torta de queso, quesadilla; JER. *(photographs)* fotografías de mujeres semidesnudas.
cheese·cloth (chēz'klôth') s. estopilla.
chees·y (chē'zē) adj. **-i·er, -i·est** *(like cheese)* caseoso, como queso; *(cheap)* vulgar, de pacotilla.
chee·tah (chē'tə) s. ZOOL. onza, leopardo cazador.
chef (shĕf) s. cocinero, jefe de cocina *m.*
chem·i·cal (kĕm'ĭ-kəl) I. adj. químico *<c. engineer* ingeniero químico> II. s. sustancia química.
chemical bond s. QUÍM. enlace químico, afinidad química.
chemical engineering s. ingeniería química.
Chemical Mace s. marca registrada de un producto químico usado como arma defensiva.
chemical warfare s. guerra química.
che·mise (shə-mēz') s. camisa (de mujer).
chem·ist (kĕm'ĭst) s. *(scientist)* químico; G.B. *(pharmacist)* farmacéutico.
chem·is·try (kĕm'ĭ-strē) s. [pl. **-tries**] química.
che·mo·ther·a·py (kē'mō-thĕr'ə-pē) s. MED. quimioterapia.
cheque (chĕk) s. G.B. cheque *m.*
cher·ish (chĕr'ĭsh) tr. *(to love)* querer, amar; *(to hold dear)* apreciar, estimar; FIG. *(to keep fondly in mind)* abrigar (ideas, esperanzas).
cher·ry (chĕr'ē) I. s. [pl. **-ries**] BOT. *(tree)* cerezo; *(fruit)* cereza; *(color)* color rojo cereza *m* II. adj. de color rojo cereza.
cher·ub (chĕr'əb) s. [pl. **cher·u·bim** (chĕr'ə-bĭm', -yə-bĭm')] RELIG. querubín *m; (child)* angelito.
che·ru·bic (chə-rōō'bĭk) adj. querúbico.
cher·vil (chûr'vəl) s. BOT. perifollo, cerafolio.
chess (chĕs) s. ajedrez *m.*
chess·board (chĕs'bôrd') s. tablero de ajedrez.
chess·man (chĕs'măn') s. [pl. **-men** (-mĕn')] pieza de ajedrez, trebejo.
chess player s. ajedrecista *mf.*
chest (chĕst) s. ANAT. pecho; *(box)* caja; *(coffer)* cofre *m;* arca *m; (trunk)* baúl *m; (dresser)* cómoda.
ches·ter·field (chĕs'tər-fēld') s. *(overcoat)* abrigo de vestir; *(sofa)* sofá *m.*
chest·nut (chĕs'nət) I. s. BOT. *(tree, wood)* castaño; *(nut)*

castaña; *(reddish brown)* color castaño; *(horse)* zaino; *(joke)* chiste gastado; *(something trite)* refrito II. adj. castaño, marrón.
chest·y (chĕs'tē) **-i·er, -i·est** s. FAM. *(having a large chest)* de pecho grande; *(conceited)* engreído.
chev·ron (shĕv'rən) s. MIL. galón *m.*
chew (chōō) I. tr. masticar, mascar ♦ **to c. out** regañar, reprender • **to c. over** rumiar, meditar *<to c. the problem over* rumiar el problema> • **to c. someone's ear off** dar lata • **to c. the fat** conversar, parlotear —intr. *(to masticate)* masticar; *(to meditate)* meditar sobre; FAM. *(tobacco)* mascar tabaco II. s. *(mastication)* masticación *f; (of tobacco)* mascada.
chew·ing (chōō'ĭng) s. masticación *f.*
chewing gum s. chicle *m,* goma de mascar.
chew·y (chōō'ē) adj. *(meat, vegetables)* fibroso, duro; *(sweets)* que se pega a los dientes.
chi (kī) s. ji (letra griega) *f.*
chic (shēk) I. s. elegancia, distinción *f* II. adj. **-er, -est** chic, elegante.
Chi·ca·go (shĭ-kä'gō, -kô'-) s. Chicago.
chi·ca·ner·y (shĭ-kä'nə-rē, chĭ-) s. [pl. **-ies**] trapacería, argucia.
Chi·ca·no (chĭ-kä'nō, shĭ-) s. & adj. chicano.
chick (chĭk) s. *(chicken)* polluelo; *(child)* niño, pollito; JER. *(girl)* chavala, jovencita.
chick·en (chĭk'ən) I. s. gallina, pollo II. adj. FAM. miedoso, cobarde III. intr. ♦ **to c. out** acobardarse.
chicken feed s. JER. bagatela, suma insignificante.
chick·en-heart·ed (chĭk'ən-här'tĭd) adj. cobarde, miedoso.
chicken pox s. MED. varicela.
chick·pea (chĭk'pē') s. BOT. garbanzo.
chic·o·ry (chĭk'ə-rē) s. achicoria.
chide (chīd) intr. & tr. **chid·ed** *o* **chid** (chĭd,) **chid·ed** *o* **chid** *o* **chid·den** (chĭd'n,) **chid·ing** regañar, reprender.
chief (chēf) I. s. jefe *m* II. adj. principal.
chief justice s. *(of a court)* presidente del tribunal *m; (of the Supreme Court)* presidente de la Corte Suprema.
chief·ly (chēf'lē) I. adv. *(especially)* sobre todo; *(mainly)* principalmente II. adj. de jefe.
chief of staff s. jefe del estado mayor *m.*
chief of state s. jefe de estado *m,* primer mandatario.
chief·tain (chēf'tən) s. cacique *m,* caudillo.
chif·fon (shĭ-fŏn') s. TEJ. chifón *m,* gasa.
chig·ger (chĭg'ər) s. ENTOM. pique *m,* nigua.
chil·blain (chĭl'blān') s. MED. sabañón *m.*
child (chīld) s. [pl. **chil·dren** (chĭl'drən)] *(young person)* niño; *(fetus)* feto; *(baby)* bebé *m; (offspring)* hijo; FIG. *(product)* fruto, producto *<this project is a c. of her imagination* este proyecto es un producto de su imaginación> ♦ **with c.** embarazada, encinta.
child abuse s. abuso infantil, maltrato de niños.
child·bear·ing (chīld'bâr'ĭng) s. maternidad *f.*
child·birth (chīld'bûrth') s. parto, alumbramiento.
child·hood (chīld'hŏŏd') s. niñez *f,* infancia.
child·ish (chīl'dĭsh) adj. infantil, pueril.
child·less (chīld'lĭs) adj. sin hijos.
child·like (chīld'līk') adj. infantil.
child neglect s. abandono de la niñez, desamparo infantil.
chil·dren (chĭl'drən) pl. de **child.**
child's play s. FIG. juego de niños, actividad de fácil ejecución *f.*
chil·e (chĭl'ē) s. var. de **chili.**
Chil·e (chĭl'ē, chē'lā) s. Chile *m.*
Chil·e·an (chĭl'ē-ən, chĭ-lā'ən) adj. & s. chileno.
chil·i (chĭl'ē) s. [pl. **-ies**] BOT. chile *m,* ají *m.*
chill (chĭl) I. s. *(temperature)* frío; *(sensation)* escalofrío; *(damper)* enfriamiento ♦ **to catch a c.** resfriarse ♦ **to take the c. off** calentar, templar II. adj. frío III. tr. *(to cool)* enfriar; *(to refrigerate)* refrigerar; METAL. templar —intr. *(to become cold)* enfriarse; METAL. templarse.
chill·er (chĭl'ər) s. historia escalofriante.
chill·i·ness (chĭl'ē-nĭs) s. frialdad *f.*
chill·ing (chĭl'ĭng) I. s. refrigeración *f* II. adj. *(cold)* frío; *(frightening)* escalofriante, de terror; *(discouraging)* frío.

ā rey / ä año / b boca / ch chico / d dar / ĕ el / ē mil / g gato / h joya / hw juez / ī aire / k casa / kw cuan /

chill·y (chĭl'ē) adj. **-i·er**, **-i·est** *(cold)* frío; FIG. *(unfriendly)* frío, poco amistoso ♦ **to be c.** *(weather)* hacer o estar fresco; *(person)* tener escalofrío.
chime (chīm) I. s. *(bell)* carillón *m*; FIG. *(accord)* armonía, concordancia ♦ **chimes** carillón II. intr. **chimed, chim·ing** *(to ring)* repicar, sonar; FIG. *(to agree)* armonizar, concordar ♦ **to c. in** intervenir (en una conversación) —tr. *(to ring)* tocar (campanas); *(a clock)* dar (la hora).
chi·me·ra (kĭ-mîr'ə, kī-) s. quimera.
chi·mer·i·cal (kĭ-měr'ĭ-kəl, -mîr'-, kī-) o **chi·mer·ic** (-měr'ĭk, -mîr'-) adj. quimérico.
chim·ney (chĭm'nē) s. [pl. **-neys**] *(flue)* chimenea; *(of a lamp)* tubo de vidrio.
chim·ney·piece (chĭm'nē-pēs') s. repisa de una chimenea.
chimney sweep s. deshollinador *m*.
chimp (chĭmp) s. FAM. chimpancé *m*.
chim·pan·zee (chĭm'păn-zē') s. ZOOL. chimpancé *m*.
chin (chĭn) I. s. ANAT. barbilla, mentón *m* ♦ **c. deep** o **up to the c.** FIG. hasta el cuello • **to keep one's c. up** no desanimarse II. tr. **chinned, chin·ning** ♦ **to c. oneself** hacer flexiones en la barra tocándola con la barbilla —intr. JER. parlotear.
chi·na (chī'nə) s. *(ceramic)* china; *(porcelain)* porcelana; *(crockery)* loza.
Chi·na (chī'nə) s. China.
Chi·na·town (chī'nə-toun') s. barrio chino.
chin·chil·la (chĭn-chĭl'ə) s. ZOOL. chinchilla (animal y piel); *(cloth)* paño grueso de lana.
Chi·nese (chī-nēz') I. adj. chino II. s. [pl. **Chinese**] *(inhabitant, language)* chino ♦ **the C.** los chinos.
Chinese puzzle s. *(puzzle)* rompecabezas chino; FIG. *(problem)* rompecabezas *m*.
chink¹ (chĭngk) I. s. grieta II. tr. *(to crack)* agrietar; *(to fill cracks in)* tapar rajaduras.
chink² (chĭngk) I. s. tintín *m*, sonido metálico II. tr. & intr. retiñir, tintinear.
Chink (chĭngk) s. DESPEC. chino.
chintz (chĭnts) s. TEJ. zaraza.
chintz·y (chĭnt'sē) adj. **-i·er**, **-i·est** FAM. de oropel.
chip (chĭp) I. s. *(small piece)* pedacito; *(splinter)* astilla; *(of wood, metal)* viruta; *(in china)* desportilladura; *(in a knife)* mella; *(in gambling)* ficha; ELECTRÓN. *(silicon square)* placa, cubo ♦ **a c. off the old block** de tal palo, tal astilla • **chips** CUL. patatas fritas • **in the chips** JER. forrado de dinero • **the chips are down** JER. la suerte está echada • **to cash in one's chips** FAM. estar listo para irse o morir • **to have a c. on one's shoulder** guardar rencor, estar resentido II. tr. **chipped, chip·ping** *(to splinter)* hacer astillas; *(to chop)* picar, cortar; *(to chisel)* cincelar, cepillar ♦ **to c. off** desportillar —intr. *(china)* desportillarse; *(a knife)* mellarse; *(wood)* astillarse ♦ **to c. in** *(to contribute)* contribuir; *(to bet)* apostar.
chip·munk (chĭp'mŭngk') s. ZOOL. ardilla listada.
chip·per (chĭp'ər) adj. FAM. animado, jovial.
chi·rop·o·dy (kĭ-rŏp'ə-dē, shĭ-) s. MED. quiropodia.
chi·ro·prac·tor (kī'rə-prăk'tər) s. MED. quiropráctico.
chirp (chûrp) I. s. *(of birds)* gorjeo; *(of crickets)* chirrido II. intr. & tr. *(a bird)* gorjear; *(a cricket)* chirriar.
chir·rup (chûr'əp, chĭr'-) I. int. & tr. chirriar II. s. chirrido.
chis·el (chĭz'əl) I. s. TEC. cincel *m* II. tr. TEC. cincelar; FAM. *(to cheat)* estafar —intr. TEC. trabajar con el cincel ♦ **to c. in** entrometerse.
chis·el·er (chĭz'ə-lər) s. *(one who chisels)* cincelador *m*; FAM. *(swindler)* tramposo, estafador *m*.
chit (chĭt) s. vale *m*, cuenta.
chit·chat (chĭt'chăt') s. charla, cháchara.
chit·ter·lings o **chit·lins** (chĭt'lĭnz) s. CUL. mondongo, tripas (de cerdo).
chiv·al·rous (shĭv'əl-rəs) adj. caballeresco, caballeroso.
chiv·al·ry (shĭv'əl-rē) s. [pl. **-ries**] caballerosidad *f*.
chive (chīv) s. BOT. cebolleta, cebollino ♦ **chives** hojas de cebolleta.
chlo·rate (klôr'āt') s. QUÍM. clorato.
chlo·ric (klôr'ĭk) adj. QUÍM. clórico.
chlo·ride (klôr'īd') s. QUÍM. cloruro.

chlo·ri·nate (klôr'ə-nāt') tr. **-nat·ed, -nat·ing** QUÍM. clorinar, tratar con cloro.
chlo·ri·na·tion (klôr'ə-nā'shən) s. QUÍM. tratamiento con cloro.
chlo·rine (klôr'ēn') s. QUÍM. cloro.
chlo·ro·form (klôr'ə-fôrm') I. s. QUÍM. cloroformo II. tr. anestesiar con cloroformo, cloroformizar.
chlo·ro·phyll o **chlo·ro·phyl** (klôr'ə-fĭl') s. clorofila.
chock (chŏk) I. s. *(wedge)* calza, cuña; MARÍT. *(fitting)* choque *m* II. tr. calzar III. adv. completamente, al máximo.
chock-a-block (chŏk'ə-blŏk') adj. atestado, apiñado.
chock-full (chŏk'fŏŏl', chŭk'-) adj. repleto, colmado.
choc·o·late (chô'kə-lĭt, chŏk'lĭt) I. s. chocolate *m* II. adj. *(made of chocolate)* de chocolate; *(color)* de color chocolate.
choice (chois) I. s. *(selection)* elección *f*, selección *f*; *(option)* opción *f*; *(variety)* surtido, variedad *f*; *(alternative)* alternativa ♦ **by c.** por gusto • **the c. of** lo mejor de • **to have no c.** no tener alternativa • **to make a c.** escoger, elegir II. adj. **choic·er, choic·est** escogido, superior.
choir (kwīr) s. ARQ., MÚS. coro.
choir·boy (kwīr'boi') s. MÚS., RELIG. niño de coro.
choir·mas·ter (kwīr'măs'tər) s. MÚS. director de coro *m*; RELIG. maestro de capilla.
choke (chōk) I. tr. **choked, chok·ing** *(to strangle)* estrangular; *(to suffocate)* sofocar; *(to asphyxiate)* asfixiar, ahogar; *(to suppress)* reprimir, contener <to c. back tears contener las lágrimas>; *(to clog)* atorar, atascar; *(to jam)* taponar, obturar; AUTO. ahogar, obturar ♦ **to c. down** *(to eat)* tragar; *(to suppress)* ahogar (llanto, sentimientos) • **to c. off** cortar o terminar abruptamente • **to c. up** obstruir, atascar —intr. *(to suffocate)* sofocarse, asfixiarse; *(to clog)* atorarse, obstruirse ♦ **to c. up** FAM. *(to get emotional)* emocionarse; *(to be unable to function)* turbarse II. s. *(act)* sofocación *f*, ahogo; AUTO. regulador de aire *m*.
chok·er (chō'kər) s. *(necklace)* gargantilla; *(collar)* cuello alto; *(fur)* estola.
chol·er (kŏl'ər, kō'lər) s. ira, cólera.
chol·er·a (kŏl'ər-ə) s. MED. cólera *m*.
chol·er·ic (kŏl'ə-rĭk, kə-lěr'ĭk) adj. colérico.
cho·les·ter·ol (kə-lěs'tə-rôl') s. QUÍM. colesterol *m*.
chomp (chŏmp) tr. & intr. ronzar, mascar haciendo ruido.
choose (chōōz) I. tr. **chose** (chōz), **cho·sen** (chō'zən), **choos·ing** *(to select)* elegir, escoger; *(to prefer)* preferir; *(to want)* desear, querer <I c. to go yo quiero ir> —intr. querer <he did as he chose hacía lo que quería>.
choos·ing (chōō'zĭng) s. elección *f*, selección *f*.
choos·y (chōō'zē) adj. **-i·er**, **-i·est** FAM. quisquilloso.
chop (chŏp) I. tr. **chopped, chop·ping** *(to cut)* cortar; *(to mince)* picar; DEP. dar efecto a ♦ **to c. at** hacer cortes en • **to c. down** talar • **to c. up** cortar en trozos —intr. MARÍT. chapotear II. s. *(cut)* corte *m*, tajo; *(blow)* golpe *m*; *(meat)* chuleta; MARÍT. chapoteo.
chop·per (chŏp'ər) s. *(ax)* hacha; *(of wood)* leñador *m*; FAM. *(helicopter)* helicóptero; ELEC. interruptor *m* ♦ **choppers** JER. dientes (postizos).
chop·ping (chŏp'ĭng) s. tajo, hachazo.
chopping block s. tajo (de cocina).
chop·py (chŏp'ē) adj. **-pi·er**, **-pi·est** picado, agitado.
chops (chŏps) s.pl. *(lips)* labios *m*; *(mouth)* boca; *(jaw)* quijada, mandíbula ♦ **to lick one's c.** relamerse.
chop·sticks (chŏp'stĭks') s.pl. palillos chinos.
cho·ral (kôr'əl) adj. & s. MÚS. coral *f*.
cho·rale (kə-răl') s. MÚS. coral *m*.
chord¹ (kôrd) s. MÚS. acorde *m*; *(string)* cuerda; FIG. *(feeling)* fibra, cuerda sensible.
chord² (kôrd) s. ANAT., GEOM., MÚS. cuerda.
chore (chôr) s. quehacer *m*, faena.
cho·re·o·graph (kôr'ē-ə-grăf') tr. hacer la coreografía de —intr. trabajar como coreógrafo.
cho·re·og·ra·pher (kôr'ē-ŏg'rə-fər) s. coreógrafo.
cho·re·og·ra·phy (kôr'ē-ŏg'rə-fē) s. coreografía.
cho·ris·ter (kôr'ĭ-stər) s. *(singer)* corista *mf*.
chor·tle (chôr'tl) I. intr. **-tled, -tling** reír entre dientes II. s. risa ahogada.

---

cho·rus (kôr'əs) **I.** s. [pl. **-rus·es**] MÚS., TEAT. *(composition, performance)* coro; MÚS., POÉT. *(refrain)* estribillo, refrán *m* ♦ **in c.** al unísono **II.** tr. & intr. cantar en coro.
chorus girl s. TEAT. corista.
chose (chōz) pret. de **choose.**
cho·sen (chō'zən) **I.** part. p. de **choose II.** adj. & s. elegido, escogido.
chow¹ (chou) o **chow chow** (chou'chou') s. *(dog)* perro chino.
chow² (chou) **I.** s. FAM. *(food)* comida **II.** intr. ♦ **to c. down** comer.
chow·der (chou'dər) s. CUL. sopa de pescado.
chrism (krĭz'əm) s. RELIG. crisma *m.*
Christ (krīst) s. RELIG. Cristo.
chris·ten (krĭs'ən) tr. bautizar.
Chris·ten·dom (krĭs'ən-dəm) s. cristiandad *f.*
chris·ten·ing (krĭs'ə-nĭng) s. bautismo, bautizo.
Chris·tian (krĭs'chən) adj. & s. cristiano ♦ **C. name** nombre de pila.
Chris·ti·an·i·ty (krĭs'chē-ăn'ĭ-tē, krĭs'tē-) s. *(religion)* cristianismo; *(Christendom)* cristiandad *f.*
Chris·tian·ize (krĭs'chə-nīz') tr. **-ized, -iz·ing** cristianizar —intr. convertirse al cristianismo.
Christ·like (krīst'līk') adj. como Cristo.
Christ·mas (krĭs'məs) s. RELIG. Navidad *f* ♦ **Merry C.!** ¡Feliz Navidad!, ¡Felices Pascuas (de Navidad)!
Christmas Eve s. Nochebuena.
Christ·mas·tide (krĭs'məs-tīd') s. Navidades *m*, Pascuas.
Christmas tree s. árbol de Navidad *m.*
chro·mat·ic (krō-măt'ĭk) adj. cromático.
chro·ma·tog·ra·phy (krō'mə-tŏg'rə-fē) s. FÍS., QUÍM. cromatografía.
chrome (krōm) **I.** s. cromo **II.** tr. **chromed, chrom·ing** cromar.
chro·mi·um (krō'mē-əm) s. QUÍM. cromo.
chro·mo·some (krō'mə-sōm') s. BIOL. cromosoma *m.*
chron·ic (krŏn'ĭk) adj. crónico.
chron·i·cle (krŏn'ĭ-kəl) **I.** s. crónica **II.** tr. **-cled, -cling** hacer la crónica de.
Chron·i·cles (krŏn'ĭ-kəlz) s.pl. BÍBL. Crónicas.
chron·o·graph (krŏn'ə-grăf', krō'nə-) s. cronógrafo.
chron·o·log·i·cal (krŏn'ə-lŏj'ĭ-kəl) o **chron·o·log·ic** (-lŏj'ĭk) adj. cronológico.
chro·nol·o·gy (krə-nŏl'ə-jē) s. [pl. **-gies**] cronología.
chro·nom·e·ter (krə-nŏm'ĭ-tər) s. cronómetro.
chro·nom·e·try (krə-nŏm'ĭ-trē) s. cronometría.
chrys·a·lid (krĭs'ə-lĭd) s. ENTOM. crisálida.
chrys·a·lis (krĭs'ə-lĭs) s. ENTOM. crisálida.
chry·san·the·mum (krĭ-săn'thə-məm, -zăn'-) s. BOT. crisantemo.
chub·by (chŭb'ē) adj. **-bi·er, -bi·est** rechoncho.
chuck¹ (chŭk) **I.** tr. *(to pat)* hacer la mamola, golpear en la barbilla ♦ **to c. out** *(to discard)* tirar; *(to eject)* echar, expulsar **II.** s. *(pat)* mamola; *(throw)* tiro.
chuck² (chŭk) s. CUL. *(beef)* paletilla; TEC. *(clamp)* mandril *m.*
chuck·hole (chŭk'hōl') s. FAM. bache *m.*
chuck·le (chŭk'əl) **I.** intr. **-led, -ling** reírse entre dientes; *(to cluck)* cloquear **II.** s. risita, risa ahogada.
chuck wagon s. carreta en que se prepara y se sirve la comida en el campo.
chug (chŭg) **I.** s. traqueteo **II.** intr. **chugged, chug·ging** traquetear.
chum (chŭm) **I.** s. compañero, compinche *m* **II.** intr. **chummed, chum·ming** ser buen compañero.
chum·my (chŭm'ē) adj. **-mi·er, -mi·est** amistoso.
chump (chŭmp) s. FAM. tonto, bobalicón *m.*
chunk (chŭngk) s. *(piece)* pedazo corto y grueso; *(amount)* cantidad grande *f.*
chunk·y (chŭng'kē) adj. **-i·er, -i·est** *(thick)* corto y grueso; *(stocky)* fornido; *(in chunks)* en pedazos.
church (chûrch) **I.** s. *(building, congregation)* iglesia; *(Mass)* misa <*after c.* después de la misa> **II.** adj. *(of the church)* de la iglesia; *(ecclesiastical)* eclesiástico.
church·go·er (chûrch'gō'ər) s. devoto (que va a misa regularmente).

church·man (chûrch'mən) s. [pl. **-men**] *(clergyman)* clérigo; *(parishioner)* feligrés *m.*
Church of England s. RELIG. iglesia anglicana.
church·yard (chûrch'yärd') s. *(yard)* patio de la iglesia; *(cemetery)* cementerio, camposanto.
churl (chûrl) s. *(boor)* patán *m*; *(miser)* tacaño.
churl·ish (chûr'lĭsh) adj. *(boorish)* maleducado; *(miserly)* tacaño.
churn (chûrn) **I.** s. mantequera **II.** tr. CUL. *(to whip)* batir (leche), hacer (mantequilla); *(to shake)* agitar, revolver ♦ **to c. out** producir en profusión —intr. CUL. *(to make butter)* hacer mantequilla; *(to shake)* agitarse, revolverse.
chute (shoot) s. *(ramp)* rampa; *(slide)* tobogán *m*; *(waterfall)* salto de agua; *(pipe)* conducto; FAM. *(parachute)* paracaídas *m.*
chut·ney (chŭt'nē) s. condimento picante hecho de frutas, especias y hierbas aromáticas.
ci·bo·ri·um (sĭ-bôr'ē-əm) s. [pl. **-bo·ri·a** (-bôr'ē-ə)] RELIG. *(altar canopy)* ciborio; *(receptacle)* copón *m.*
ci·ca·da (sĭ-kä'də, -kä'-) s. [pl. **-das** o **-dae** (-dē)] ENTOM. cigarra.
cic·a·trix (sĭk'ə-trĭks, sĭ-kä'trĭks) s. [pl. **cic·a·tri·ces** (sĭk'-ə-trī'sēz, sĭ-kä'trī-sēz')] cicatriz *f.*
cic·e·ro·ne (sĭs'ə-rō'nē) s. [pl. **-nes** o **-ni** (-nē)] guía *mf*, cicerone *mf.*
Cid, The (sĭd, sēd) s. HIST., LIT. el Cid.
ci·der (sī'dər) s. sidra.
ci·gar (sĭ-gär') s. cigarro, puro.
cig·a·rette o **cig·a·ret** (sĭg'ə-rĕt') s. cigarrillo.
cil·i·a (sĭl'ē-ə) pl. de **cilium.**
cil·i·ar·y (sĭl'ē-ĕr'ē) adj. ANAT. ciliar.
cil·i·um (sĭl'ē-əm) s. [pl. **-i·a** (-ē-ə)] BIOL. cilio.
cinch (sĭnch) **I.** s. EQUIT. *(girth)* cincha; FAM. *(sure thing)* certidumbre; *(easy thing)* cosa fácil; *(grip)* apretón *m* **II.** tr. EQUIT. *(to saddle)* cinchar; FAM. *(to make certain)* asegurar.
cin·cho·na (sĭng-kō'nə, sĭn-chō'-) s. BOT. *(tree)* chinchona, quino; *(bark)* quina.
cin·der (sĭn'dər) s. carbonilla ♦ **cinders** cenizas.
cinder block s. CONSTR. bloque de cenizas *m.*
Cin·der·el·la (sĭn'də-rĕl'ə) s. LIT. Cenicienta.
cin·e·ma (sĭn'ə-mə) s. *(theater)* cine *m*, cinema *m*; *(film)* película, filme *m*; *(industry)* cine, cinematografía.
cin·e·mat·ic (sĭn'ə-măt'ĭk) adj. fílmico.
cin·e·ma·tog·ra·phy (sĭn'ə-mə-tŏg'rə-fē) s. cinematografía.
cin·e·rar·i·um (sĭn'ə-râr'ē-əm) s. [pl. **-i·a** (-ē-ə)] nicho para urna cineraria.
cin·na·mon (sĭn'ə-mən) **I.** s. BOT. *(tree)* canelo, cinamomo; *(spice)* canela; *(color)* color canela *m* **II.** adj. de color canela.
ci·pher (sī'fər) **I.** s. *(number)* cifra; MAT. *(zero)* cero; FIG. *(nonentity)* cero a la izquierda **II.** intr. hacer un cálculo —tr. *(to encipher)* cifrar; *(to calculate)* calcular.
cir·ca (sûr'kə) prep. hacia, alrededor de <*c. 1400* hacia 1400>.
cir·cle (sûr'kəl) **I.** s. *(curve)* círculo; *(circumference)* circumferencia; *(circuit)* circuito; *(orbit)* órbita; *(under the eyes)* ojera; *(turn)* vuelta; *(tier)* hemiciclo; *(cycle)* ciclo; *(group)* círculo <*a sewing c.* un círculo dedicado a la costura>; *(sphere)* esfera, medio <*in high circles* en altas esferas>; *(repetition)* círculo <*vicious c.* círculo vicioso>; GEOG. círculo <*the Arctic Circle* el círculo polar ártico> ♦ **circles** medios, esferas <*well-informed circles* medios bien informados> • **to come full c.** volver al punto de partida • **to go around in circles** *(to roam)* dar vueltas; *(to discuss)* estar en un círculo vicioso **II.** tr. **-cled, -cling** *(to enclose)* cercar, rodear; *(to draw a circle around)* hacer un círculo alrededor de <*c. the correct response* haga un círculo alrededor de la respuesta correcta>; *(to turn)* dar la vuelta a; *(to revolve around)* girar alrededor de —intr. dar vueltas.
cir·cuit (sûr'kĭt) **I.** s. *(circle)* circuito; *(journey)* gira; ELEC., RAD. circuito; ASTRON. revolución *f*, vuelta; FOR. distrito, jurisdicción *f* **II.** intr. & tr. dar la vuelta (a).
circuit breaker s. ELEC. cortacircuitos, interruptor automático.
circuit court s. tribunal de distrito *m.*

ã rey / ä año / b boca / ch chico / d dar / ĕ el / ē mil / g gato / h joya / hw juez / ī aire / k casa / kw cuan /

cir·cu·i·tous (sər-kyōō'ĭ-təs) adj. indirecto.
circuit rider s. ANT. predicador ambulante m.
cir·cuit·ry (sûr'kĭ-trē) s. ELEC. sistema de circuitos m.
cir·cu·lar (sûr'kyə-lər) adj. & s. circular f.
cir·cu·lar·ize (sûr'kyə-lə-rīz') tr. -ized, -iz·ing anunciar por circulares.
circular saw s. sierra circular.
cir·cu·late (sûr'kyə-lāt') intr. -lat·ed, -lat·ing circular —tr. (to distribute) circular; (to disseminate) hacer circular, divulgar.
cir·cu·lat·ing (sûr'kyə-lā'tĭng) adj. circulante.
cir·cu·la·tion (sûr'kyə-lā'shən) s. circulación f.
cir·cu·la·tor (sûr'kyə-lā'tər) s. (distributor) distribuidor m; (disseminator) divulgador m.
cir·cu·la·to·ry (sûr'kyə-lə-tôr'ē) adj. circulatorio.
circulatory system s. ANAT. aparato circulatorio.
cir·cum·cise (sûr'kəm-sīz') tr. -cised, -cis·ing circuncidar.
cir·cum·cised (sûr'kəm-sīzd') adj. circunciso.
cir·cum·ci·sion (sûr'kəm-sĭzh'ən) s. circuncisión f.
cir·cum·fer·ence (sər-kŭm'fər-əns) s. circunferencia.
cir·cum·flex (sûr'kəm-flĕks') I. s. acento circunflejo II. adj. circunflejo.
cir·cum·lo·cu·tion (sûr'kəm-lō-kyōō'shən) s. circunlocución f, circunloquio.
cir·cum·nav·i·gate (sûr'kəm-năv'ĭ-gāt') tr. -gat·ed, -gat·ing circunnavegar.
cir·cum·scribe (sûr'kəm-skrīb') tr. -scribed, -scrib·ing (to encircle) circunscribir, circundar; (to restrict) restringir, limitar.
cir·cum·spect (sûr'kəm-spĕkt') adj. circunspecto.
cir·cum·spec·tion (sûr'kəm-spĕk'shən) s. circunspección f.
cir·cum·stance (sûr'kəm-stăns') I. s. (factor) circunstancia; (incident) incidente m, acontecimiento; (detail) detalle m; (ceremony) ceremonia ♦ **circumstances** situación, posición • **under** o **in the circumstances** en estas circunstancias, bajo o debido a las circunstancias • **under no circumstances** de ninguna manera, bajo ningún concepto II. tr. -stanced, -stanc·ing situar.
cir·cum·stan·tial (sûr'kəm-stăn'shəl) adj. (incidental) circunstancial; (detailed) circunstanciado.
circumstantial evidence s. DER. pruebas circunstanciales, pruebas indirectas.
cir·cum·vent (sûr'kəm-vĕnt') tr. (to avoid) evitar; (to skirt) circundar; (to entrap) embaucar.
cir·cum·ven·tion (sûr'kəm-vĕn'shən) s. (act of avoiding) acción de circundar; (entrapment) engaño.
cir·cum·vo·lu·tion (sûr'kəm-vō-lōō'shən) s. circunvolución f.
cir·cus (sûr'kəs) s. circo.
cirque (sûrk) s. GEOL. circo, depresión natural f.
cir·rho·sis (sĭ-rō'sĭs) s. MED. cirrosis f.
cir·ri (sĭr'ī') pl. de **cirrus**.
cir·ro·cu·mu·lus (sîr'ō-kyōōm'yə-ləs) s. METEOR. cirrocúmulo.
cir·rus (sîr'əs) s. [pl. **cir·ri** (sĭr'ī')] BOT., METEOR, ZOOL. cirro.
cis·tern (sĭs'tərn) s. (for water) cisterna, aljibe m; ANAT. cisterna.
cit·a·del (sĭt'ə-dəl) s. FORT. (fortress) ciudadela; FIG. (bulwark) baluarte m.
ci·ta·tion (sī-tā'shən) s. (quotation) cita; DER. (summons) citación f; MIL. (commendation) mención f.
cite (sīt) tr. cit·ed, cit·ing (to quote) citar; DER. (to summon) citar; MIL. (to commend) mencionar.
cit·i·fied (sĭt'ĭ-fīd') adj. acostumbrado a la vida urbana.
cit·i·zen (sĭt'ĭ-zən) s. ciudadano.
cit·i·zen·ry (sĭt'ĭ-zən-rē) s. ciudadanos.
cit·i·zen·ship (sĭt'ĭ-zən-shĭp') s. ciudadanía.
cit·ric (sĭt'rĭk) adj. cítrico <c. acid ácido cítrico>.
cit·ron (sĭt'rən) s. (tree) cidro; (fruit) cidra; (rind) cáscara confitada de fruta cítrica.
cit·ro·nel·la (sĭt'rə-nĕl'ə) s. BOT. citronela; (oil) aceite de citronela m.
cit·rus (sĭt'rəs) BOT. I. adj. cítrico ♦ **c. fruits** agrios, cítricos II. s. [pl. **-rus·es** o **citrus**] árbol cítrico.
cit·y (sĭt'ē) s. [pl. **-ies**] (town) ciudad f; (municipality) municipalidad f, ayuntamiento.

city hall s. ayuntamiento, municipalidad f.
city manager s. administrador municipal m.
city slicker s. FAM. capitalino.
civ·et (sĭv'ĭt) s. ZOOL. civeta; QUÍM. civeto, algalia (perfume).
civ·ic (sĭv'ĭk) adj. cívico.
civ·ics (sĭv'ĭks) s. [ú. con v. sing.] estudio del gobierno civil.
civ·il (sĭv'əl) adj. (of citizens) civil; (civilized) civilizado; (polite) cortés; (domestic) interno, civil <c. war guerra civil>; (of citizen's rights) civil <c. law ley civil>.
civil defense s. defensa civil (contra ataque enemigo).
civil disobedience s. resistencia pasiva (contra un gobierno o una ley).
civil engineer s. ingeniero civil.
ci·vil·ian (sĭ-vĭl'yən) I. s. civil m, paisano II. adj. civil, de paisano.
ci·vil·i·ty (sĭ-vĭl'ĭ-tē) s. [pl. **-ties**] urbanidad f, civilidad f.
civ·i·li·za·tion (sĭv'ə-lĭ-zā'shən) s. civilización f.
civ·i·lize (sĭv'ə-līz') tr. -lized, -liz·ing civilizar.
civil law s. derecho civil.
civil liberty s. libertad ciudadana.
civil marriage s. matrimonio civil.
civil rights s.pl. derechos civiles.
civil servant s. empleado público.
civil service s. administración pública.
clack (klăk) I. intr. (to rattle) castañetear (superficies, dientes); (to chatter) chacharear; (to cackle) cloquear II. s. (sound) castañeteo; (chatter) cháchara.
clad¹ (klăd) tr. **clad, clad·ding** revestir de metal (otro metal).
clad² (klăd) un pret. y part. p. de **clothe**.
claim (klām) I. tr. (to demand) reclamar, reivindicar; (to assert) afirmar, sostener; (to deserve) merecer, requerir (atención, estudio) II. s. (demand) reclamación f, reivindicación f; (assertion) afirmación f; (right) derecho, título; MIN. concesión f, denuncio; DER. demanda, petición f.
claim·ant (klā'mənt) s. DER. demandante mf; (to a position) pretendiente mf.
clair·voy·ance (klâr-voi'əns) s. clarividencia.
clair·voy·ant (klâr-voi'ənt) adj. & s. clarividente mf.
clam (klăm) I. s. ZOOL. almeja; FAM. (person) chiticalla mf; (clamp) grapa, grampa II. intr. **clammed, clam·ming** pescar almejas ♦ **to c. up** callarse como un muerto.
clam·bake (klăm'bāk') s. picnic (en que se cuecen almejas) m; FAM. (party) fiesta bulliciosa.
clam·ber (klăm'bər) I. intr. subir gateando II. s. subida a gatas.
clam·my (klăm'ē) adj. -mi·er, -mi·est (damp) frío y húmedo; (sticky) viscoso, pegajoso.
clam·or (klăm'ər) I. s. clamor m II. tr. & intr. clamar.
clam·or·ous (klăm'ər-əs) adj. clamoroso.
clam·our (klăm'ər) s. & v. G.B. var. de **clamor**.
clamp (klămp) I. s. TEC. grapa; (brace) abrazadera; CARP. cárcel f; ELEC. borne m II. tr. (to grasp) engrapar, sujetar con abrazadera; FIG. (to grasp) agarrar firmemente ♦ **to c. down on** FAM. apretar las clavijas a.
clam·shell (klăm'shĕl') s. ZOOL. concha de almeja; (bucket) cucharón de almeja m, cucharón de doble pala.
clan (klăn) s. clan m.
clan·des·tine (klăn-dĕs'tĭn) adj. clandestino.
clang (klăng) I. intr. sonar con sonido metálico —tr. hacer sonar, tañer II. s. (sound) sonido metálico; (of bells) tañido.
clan·gor (klăng'ər) I. s. (sound) sonido metálico; (noise) estruendo II. intr. sonar con sonido metálico.
clank (klăngk) I. s. ruido metálico II. intr. hacer un ruido metálico.
clan·nish (klăn'ĭsh) adj. (of a clan) de clan; (exclusive) exclusivo.
clans·man (klănz'mən) s. [pl. **-men**] miembro de un clan.
clap¹ (klăp) I. intr. **clapped, clap·ping** (to applaud) dar palmadas, aplaudir; (to bang together) golpearse ♦ **to c. shut** cerrarse de golpe —tr. (to applaud) aplaudir; (to tap) dar una palmada a ♦ **to c. in jail** FAM. meter en la cárcel • **to c. together** FAM. improvisar II. s. (applause) aplauso; (tap)

palmada; *(bang)* estampido, ruido seco; *(a slap)* cachetada, bofetada.

clap² (klăp) s. JER. gonorrea.

clap·board (klăb'ərd, klăp'bôrd') I. s. ARQ. chilla, tablilla ♦ **c. house** casa hecha de tablillas II. tr. forrar de chillas o tablillas.

clap·per (klăp'ər) s. *(person)* persona que aplaude; *(of a bell)* badajo ♦ **clappers** MÚS. claquetas.

clap·ping (klăp'ĭng) s. *(applause)* aplausos; *(in time)* palmadas.

clap·trap (klăp'trăp') s. charlatanería, palabrería.

claque (klăk) s. claque *f.*

clar·et (klăr'ĭt) s. & adj. *(wine)* clarete *m;* *(color)* burdeos.

clar·i·fi·ca·tion (klăr'ə-fĭ-kā'shən) s. clarificación *f,* aclaración *f.*

clar·i·fy (klăr'ə-fī') tr. & intr. **-fied, -fy·ing** *(a problem)* clarificar(se), aclarar(se); *(a liquid)* clarificar(se).

clar·i·net (klăr'ə-nĕt') s. MÚS. clarinete *m.*

clar·i·net·ist o **clar·i·net·tist** (klăr'ə-nĕt'ĭst) s. clarinetista *mf.*

clar·i·on (klăr'ē-ən) I. s. MÚS. clarín *m;* *(sound)* toque de clarín *m* II. adj. estentóreo, sonoro.

clar·i·ty (klăr'ĭ-tē) s. claridad *f.*

clash (klăsh) I. intr. *(to collide)* chocar, entrechocarse; *(to conflict)* chocar, estar en conflicto —tr. hacer chocar con estruendo II. s. *(noise)* estruendo; *(collision)* choque *m;* *(conflict)* desacuerdo, conflicto.

clasp (klăsp) I. s. *(device)* cierre *m;* *(on a belt)* hebilla; *(hug)* abrazo; *(of the hands)* apretón *m* II. tr. *(to hook)* abrochar, enganchar; *(to hug)* abrazar; *(to clutch)* agarrar; *(the hand)* estrechar, apretar.

clasp knife s. navaja de muelle.

class (klăs) I. s. *(group)* clase *f* <*working c.* clase obrera>; *(kind)* clase, tipo; *(caliber)* categoría <*to be of the same c.* ser de la misma categoría>; *(of students)* clase; *(graduates)* promoción *f* <*c. of 1986* promoción de 1986>; *(quality)* clase <*first c.* primera clase>; FAM. *(style)* clase, distinción *f* <*she really has c.* ella sí tiene clase>; BIOL. clase II. tr. clasificar.

class action s. DER. proceso en que el demandante representa un grupo de personas con intereses similares.

class-con·scious (klăs'kŏn'shəs) adj. con conciencia de clase social.

class consciousness s. conciencia de clase social.

clas·sic (klăs'ĭk) I. adj. *(outstanding)* clásico; *(typical)* clásico, típico <*a c. German maneuver* una típica maniobra alemana> II. s. clásico <*The Iliad is a c.* La Ilíada es un clásico> ♦ **classics** los clásicos.

clas·si·cal (klăs'ĭ-kəl) adj. clásico.

clas·si·cism (klăs'ĭ-sĭz'əm) s. clasicismo.

clas·si·cist (klăs'ĭ-sĭst) s. clasicista *mf.*

clas·si·fi·ca·tion (klăs'ə-fĭ-kā'shən) s. clasificación *f.*

clas·si·fied (klăs'ə-fīd') adj. *(arranged)* clasificado; *(limited)* restringido; *(secret)* secreto.

classified advertisement s. anuncio clasificado, anuncio por palabras.

clas·si·fy (klăs'ə-fī') tr. **-fied, -fy·ing** *(to arrange)* clasificar; *(to restrict)* restringir.

class·mate (klăs'māt') s. compañero de clase.

class·room (klăs'rōōm', -rŏōm') s. aula, sala de clase.

class struggle s. lucha de clases.

class·y (klăs'ē) adj. **-i·er, -i·est** JER. elegante, de mucho postín.

clat·ter (klăt'ər) I. intr. *(to rattle)* traquetear, trapalear; *(to chatter)* charlotear —tr. hacer sonar estruendosamente II. s. *(rattle)* traqueteo; *(chatter)* charloteo; *(disturbance)* conmoción *f;* *(din)* estruendo.

clause (klôz) s. GRAM. oración *f;* *(of a document)* cláusula *f.*

claus·tro·pho·bi·a (klô'strə-fō'bē-ə) s. claustrofobia.

claus·tro·pho·bic (klô'strə-fō'bĭk) adj. claustrofóbico.

clav·i·chord (klăv'ĭ-kôrd') s. MÚS. clavicordio.

clav·i·cle (klăv'ĭ-kəl) s. ANAT. clavícula.

cla·vier (klə-vîr', klă'vē-ər) s. teclado.

claw (klô) I. s. ZOOL. garra; *(of cat)* uña; *(of a crustacean)* tenaza, pinza; TEC. garfio, gancho ♦ **c. hammer** martillo sacaclavos II. tr. & intr. arañar.

clay (klā) s. CERÁM. arcilla; *(mud)* barro; FIG. *(human body)* barro.

clay pigeon s. DEP. plato (de tiro al blanco).

clean (klēn) I. adj. **-er, -est** *(unsoiled)* limpio <*a c. room* un cuarto limpio>; *(unadulterated)* puro <*c. water* agua pura>; *(well-proportioned)* bien proporcionado, inmaculado <*the c. lines of a fine piece of furniture* las líneas inmaculadas de un mueble de calidad>; *(adroit)* diestro, hábil; *(unencumbered)* despejado; *(complete)* completo, radical <*a c. break with tradition* un corte radical con la tradición>; *(legible)* legible; *(blank)* en blanco; *(morally pure)* puro, sin mancha; *(decent)* decente; *(fair)* limpio <*a c. fighter* un boxeador limpio>; JER. *(unarmed)* desarmado; *(free from narcotics)* limpio de drogas; *(innocent)* inocente (de sospechas) ♦ **c. as a whistle** limpio como una patena • **to make a c. breast of it** confesar de plano II. adv. *(in a clean manner)* limpiamente; FAM. *(entirely)* por completo, completamente <*I c. forgot* se me olvidó completamente> ♦ **to come c.** confesarlo todo III. tr. *(to tidy)* limpiar; *(to empty)* vaciar; CUL. *(meat)* quitar la grasa a; *(vegetables)* pelar; *(fish)* escamar y abrir ♦ **to c. out** *(to drive out)* expulsar, expeler; *(to empty out)* dejar vacío, vaciar; *(to use up)* agotar; FAM. *(to leave penniless)* sacarle hasta el último centavo a • **to c. up** *(to tidy up)* limpiar a fondo; *(to dispose of)* terminar con, acabar con; *(to eradicate)* erradicar, extirpar • **to c. up after someone** limpiar las cosas sucias dejadas por otro —intr. *(to tidy up)* limpiar; *(to tidy oneself)* limpiarse ♦ **to c. house** FIG. poner las cosas en orden • **to c. up** *(to wash up)* lavarse; FAM. *(to make a profit)* ganarse una fortuna, llenarse los bolsillos.

clean-cut (klēn'kŭt') adj. *(sharp)* nítido, definido; *(clear)* claro; *(clean)* limpio; *(wholesome)* sano.

clean·er (klē'nər) s. *(person)* tintorero, lavandero; *(substance)* quitamanchas *m.*

clean·ing (klē'nĭng) s. limpieza ♦ **dry c.** limpieza en seco.

clean·li·ness (klĕn'lē-nĭs) s. limpieza, aseo.

cleanse (klĕnz) tr. **cleansed, cleans·ing** limpiar, purificar.

cleans·er (klĕn'zər) s. *(person)* limpiador *m;* *(product)* producto para la limpieza.

clean-shav·en (klēn'shā'vən) adj. bien afeitado.

cleans·ing (klĕn'zĭng) I. s. *(of a wound)* limpieza; *(purifying)* purificación *f* II. adj. limpiador.

cleansing cream s. desmaquillador *m.*

clean·up (klēn'ŭp') s. *(cleaning)* limpieza general o a fondo; *(profit)* gran ganancia; *(elimination)* eliminación *f,* erradicación *f.*

clear (klîr) I. adj. **-er, -est** *(limpid)* claro; *(cloudless)* despejado, limpio; *(transparent)* transparente, diáfano <*c. air* aire diáfano>; *(flawless)* sin defectos; *(unblemished)* terso <*a c. complexion* un cutis terso>; *(unobstructed)* libre, despejado <*a c. view* una vista despejada>; *(evident)* claro, evidente <*a c. case of cheating* un caso evidente de fraude>; *(distinct)* claro <*a c. voice* una voz clara>; *(certain)* seguro <*are you c. about your plan?* ¿estás seguro acerca de tus planes?>; *(absolute)* absoluto; *(untroubled)* limpio, tranquilo <*my conscience is c.* tengo la conciencia limpia>; *(net)* neto, en limpio <*he earns a c. fifteen thousand dollars* gana quince mil dólares neto>; *(empty)* vacío ♦ **as c. as day** más claro que el agua • **as c. as mud** claro • **c. of** libre de • **c. profit** beneficio neto • **the coast is c.** no hay moros en la costa • **to be c. on** tener una idea muy clara de • **to make oneself c.** explicar claramente o con claridad • **to want to make it c. that** querer dejar claro o sentado que II. adv. *(clearly)* claro, con claridad; FAM. *(completely)* completamente ♦ **to speak loud and c.** hablar fuerte y claramente • **to stand c.** mantenerse aparte III. tr. *(to make light)* aclarar; *(to scatter)* dispersar; *(to unobstruct)* despejar; *(to disentangle)* desenredar; *(to open)* abrir <*to c. the way* abrir el camino>; *(to remove)* quitar <*to c. the snow from the road* quitar la nieve de la carretera>; *(to jump)* saltar; *(to pass over)* pasar por encima de, salvar; *(to pass under)* pasar sin rozar por debajo de; *(the throat)* aclararse; *(to purify)* limpiar, depurar; *(wine)* clarificar; *(conscience)* descargar, aliviar; *(suspicion, blame)* limpiar; *(to acquit)* absolver, probar la inocencia de; *(to clarify)* aclarar; *(to*

ā rey / ä año / b boca / ch chico / d dar / ĕ el / ē mil / g gato / h joya / hw juez / ī aire / k casa / kw cuan /

approve) aprobar; AVIA. *(to give clearance)* autorizar; *(to net)* ganar, obtener una ganancia líquida; *(a check)* compensar; *(debt)* liquidar, pagar; *(mortgage)* satisfacer; *(customs)* sacar de la aduana ♦ **to c. away** quitar • **to c. off** liquidar • **to c. out** *(to empty)* vaciar, desocupar; *(to clean)* limpiar; *(to rid of)* echar; COM. *(to sell)* liquidar • **to c. the air** aclarar las cosas • **to c. the table** levantar la mesa • **to c. up** *(to tidy up)* ordenar, sacar estorbos de; *(to clean)* limpiar; *(to dispel)* disipar; *(to resolve)* aclarar —intr. *(to become lighter)* aclararse; *(sky)* despejarse; *(crowd)* dispersarse; *(goods)* venderse; *(ship)* zarpar; *(impurities)* limpiarse, depurarse; *(clearing-house)* pasar; *(customs requirements)* satisfacer los requisitos de la aduana ♦ **to c. off** irse, largarse • **to c. out** *(person)* irse, largarse; *(ship)* despacharse y salir • **to c. through** pasar por, ser aprobado por • **to c. up** *(sky)* despejarse; *(symptom)* desaparecer **IV.** s. claro, espacio libre ♦ **in the c.** *(from burden)* libre de preocupaciones; *(out of danger)* fuera de peligro; *(blameless)* fuera de sospecha.

clear·ance (klîr′əns) s. *(removal)* despejo; *(clearing)* luz *f*, espacio libre; *(sale)* liquidación *f*, saldo; *(space)* espacio, margen *m*; *(permission)* paso, permiso; *(by customs)* despacho; *(by security)* acreditación *f*; COM. *(of a check)* compensación *f*.

clear-cut (klîr′kŭt′) adj. *(clear)* claro, bien definido; *(evident)* patente, obvio.

clear-eyed (klîr′īd′) adj. perspicaz.

clear·ing (klîr′ĭng) s. claro (en un bosque).

clear·ing-house o **clear·ing·house** (klîr′ĭng-hous′) s. oficina de compensación.

clear·ly (klîr′lē) adv. *(with clarity)* claramente; *(evidently)* evidentemente; *(of course)* por supuesto.

clear·ness (klîr′nĭs) s. claridad *f*.

clear-sight·ed (klîr′sī′tĭd) adj. *(keen-sighted)* de vista penetrante; *(perceptive)* penetrante, perspicaz.

cleat (klēt) **I.** s. *(support)* travesaño, listón *m*; *(wedge)* calce *m*, cuña; MARÍT. *(fastening device)* cornamusa; *(on shoes)* clavo, tapón *m* **II.** tr. *(to support)* enlistonar; *(to wedge)* calzar; *(to tie)* atar (a una cornamusa).

cleav·age (klē′vĭj) s. *(act, state)* hendidura, división *f*; BIOL. segmentación *f*; MIN. crucero; FAM. *(of breasts)* escote *m*.

cleave¹ (klēv) tr. **cleft** (klĕft) o **cleaved** o **clove** (klōv), **cleft** o **cleaved** o **clo·ven** (klō′vən), **cleav·ing** *(to split)* partir, hender; *(to cut through)* abrirse (camino); *(to pierce)* perforar, penetrar ♦ **to c. to** sér fiel a —intr. *(to split)* partirse, henderse; *(to pass)* abrirse paso.

cleave² (klēv) intr. **cleaved** o **clove** (klōv), **cleaved**, **cleav·ing** *(to adhere)* adherirse, pegarse; FIG. *(to be faithful)* ser fiel.

cleav·er (klē′vər) s. cuchillo o hachuela (de carnicero).

clef (klĕf) s. MÚS. clave *f*.

cleft (klĕft) **I.** pret. y part. p. de **cleave¹** **II.** adj. *(split)* hendido, partido; BOT. hendido **III.** s. *(crack)* grieta, fisura; *(indentation)* hendidura.

cleft palate s. ANAT. fisura palatina.

clem·a·tis (klĕm′ə-tĭs) s. BOT. clemátide *f*, hierba de los lazarosos.

clem·en·cy (klĕm′ən-sē) s. [pl. **-cies**] *(mercy)* clemencia, indulgencia; *(mildness)* benignidad *f*.

clem·ent (klĕm′ənt) adj. *(merciful)* clemente, indulgente; *(benign)* bueno, benigno <c. weather buen tiempo>.

clench (klĕnch) **I.** tr. *(to grip)* apretar, sujetar firmemente; *(to squeeze)* cerrar, apretar (puño, dientes); *(to clinch)* remachar **II.** s. apretón *m*.

cler·gy (klûr′jē) s. [pl. **-gies**] RELIG. clero.

cler·gy·man (klûr′jē-mən) s. [pl. **-men**] clérigo.

cler·ic (klĕr′ĭk) RELIG. **I.** s. clérigo **II.** adj. clerical.

cler·i·cal (klĕr′ĭ-kəl) **I.** adj. *(of an office)* de oficina; RELIG. clerical, eclesiástico **II.** s. RELIG. clérigo, sacerdote *m* ♦ **clericals** vestidura eclesiástica.

clerk (klûrk) **I.** s. *(office worker)* oficinista *mf*, empleado de oficina; DER. *(record keeper)* escribano, amanuense *mf*; *(salesperson)* vendedor *m*, dependiente *mf*; RELIG. clérigo **II.** intr. trabajar como empleado de oficina.

clev·er (klĕv′ər) adj. **-er**, **-est** *(alert)* listo, despierto; *(bright)*

inteligente; *(quick-witted)* ingenioso; *(dexterous)* diestro, hábil.

clev·er·ness (klĕv′ər-nĭs) s. *(skill)* habilidad *f*, destreza; *(intelligence)* inteligencia.

clev·er·ly (klĕv′ər-lē) adv. *(skillfully)* hábilmente, ingeniosamente; *(intelligently)* inteligentemente.

clew (klōo) **I.** s. *(of thread)* ovillo; MARÍT. *(of a sail)* puño **II.** tr. hacer un ovillo, enrollar.

cli·ché (klē-shā′) s. cliché *m*, clisé *m*.

click (klĭk) **I.** s. *(sound)* chasquido, ruidito seco; *(pawl)* trinquete *m*, retén *m*; FONÉT. sonido implosivo, chasquido **II.** intr. *(to produce a click)* chasquear, hacer un ruidito seco; JER. *(to succeed)* tener éxito <they clicked with the audience tuvieron éxito con el público>; *(to get along)* entenderse, llevarse bien <they clicked from the moment they met se llevaron bien desde el momento que se conocieron> —tr. chasquear.

cli·ent (klī′ənt) s. cliente *mf*.

cli·en·tele (klī′ən-tĕl′, klē′-) s. clientela.

cliff (klĭf) s. acantilado, precipicio.

cliff dweller s. HIST. troglodita *mf*; FIG. persona que vive en un gran edificio de apartamentos.

cliff·hang·er (klĭf′hăng′ər) s. FAM. *(melodrama)* melodrama de suspenso *m*; *(contest)* competencia que no se resuelve hasta el último momento.

cli·mac·tic (klī-măk′tĭk) o **cli·mac·ti·cal** (-tĭ-kəl) adj. culminante.

cli·mate (klī′mĭt) s. *(weather)* clima *m*; *(region)* zona meteorológica; *(atmosphere)* ambiente *m*, atmósfera <a c. of fear una atmósfera de miedo>.

cli·mat·ic (klī-măt′ĭk) s. climático.

cli·ma·tol·o·gy (klī′mə-tŏl′ə-jē) s. climatología.

cli·max (klī′măks′) **I.** s. *(culmination)* punto culminante, culminación *f*; LIT., RET. clímax *m*; *(orgasm)* orgasmo **II.** tr. llevar al punto culminante —intr. culminar.

climb (klīm) **I.** tr. *(to go up)* subir, trepar; *(to scale)* escalar —intr. *(to ascend)* subir, ascender <he climbed to the highest level of the company él subió hasta el nivel más alto de la compañía>; *(to slope up)* subir <the road climbed to the hills el camino subía hacia las sierras>; *(a plant)* trepar ♦ **c. down** descender, bajar <he climbed down the mountain descendió de la montaña> **II.** s. subida, ascenso.

climb·er (klī′mər) s. *(scaler)* escalador *m*; *(mountaineer)* alpinista *mf*; FIG., FAM. *(arriviste)* arribista *mf*; *(plant)* enredadera, planta trepadora.

climb·ing (klī′mĭng) **I.** adj. trepador **II.** s. *(alpinism)* alpinismo; FIG. *(opportunism)* arribismo.

clime (klīm) s. POÉT. clima *m*.

clinch (klĭnch) **I.** tr. *(to fasten)* remachar (clavo, tornillo); *(to secure)* afianzar, asegurar; *(to settle)* decidir, concluir (asunto, negocio); MARÍT. *(to fasten)* entalingar, atar (con medio nudo); *(to win)* ganar <he clinched the title ganó el título> —intr. *(to be secured)* estar afianzado; DEP. *(to hold)* luchar cuerpo a cuerpo (en boxeo); JER. *(to embrace)* abrazarse (enamorados) **II.** s. TEC. *(of a nail)* remache *f*; *(conclusion)* conclusión (de asunto, negocio) *f*; DEP. *(hold)* lucha cuerpo a cuerpo, forcejeo (en boxeo); MARÍT. *(knot)* entalingadura, medio nudo; JER. *(embrace)* abrazo apasionado.

clinch·er (klĭn′chər) s. *(person)* remachador *m*; *(nail)* remache *m*; *(tool)* remachadora; FAM. *(argument)* argumento decisivo.

cling (klĭng) **I.** intr. **clung** (klŭng), **cling·ing** *(to hold fast)* asirse, agarrarse <monkeys c. to branches los monos se agarran de las ramas>; *(to remain close)* apegarse <to c. to friends apegarse a los amigos>; *(to stick)* pegarse, ceñirse; *(to hold on)* aferrarse <to c. to old ideas aferrarse a viejas ideas> **II.** s. pavía, albérchigo.

clin·ic (klĭn′ĭk) s. clínica.

clin·i·cal (klĭn′ĭ-kəl) adj. MED. clínico; *(objective)* objetivo, analítico <a c. attitude una actitud objetiva>.

cli·ni·cian (klī-nĭsh′ən) s. MED. clínico.

clink¹ (klĭngk) **I.** intr. tr. sonar metálicamente, tintinear —tr. hacer sonar metálicamente, tintinear **II.** s. sonido metálico, tintineo; G.B. trino (de ciertos pájaros).

clink² (klĭngk) s. JER. *(jail)* prisión *f*, cárcel *f*.

---

clink·er (klǐng'kər) I. s. TEC. *(residue)* escoria, residuo incombustible; *(mistake)* falta, error *m* II. intr. escorificar, convertir en escoria.

clip¹ (klǐp) I. tr. **clipped, clip·ping** *(to cut)* cortar, recortar; *(to shorten)* acortar; *(to trim)* cortar, podar; *(to curtail)* abreviar; *(to shear)* esquilar (ovejas). FAM. *(to hit)* golpear, pegar <*to c. on the mouth* pegar en la boca>; *(to overcharge)* estafar —intr. *(to cut)* cortar, recortar ♦ **to c. along** ir a buen paso II. s. *(cut)* corte *m*, recorte *m*; *(shearing)* esquileo; *(wool)* lana de esquileo; FAM. *(blow)* golpe; *(pace)* paso rápido ♦ **clips** tijeras.

clip² (klǐp) I. s. *(fastener)* broche *m*, sujetador *m*; *(for paper)* sujetapapeles *m*; *(cartridge frame)* cargador (de cartuchos) *m* II. tr. **clipped, clip·ping** *(to fasten)* sujetar; *(to block)* obstaculizar ilícitamente (en fútbol americano).

clip·board (klǐp'bôrd') s. tablilla con sujetapapeles.

clip joint s. JER. restaurante *o* cabaret que cobra precios exagerados *m*.

clip·per (klǐp'ər) s. *(person)* cortador *m*, trasquilador *m*; *(for shearing)* esquiladora; MARÍT. clíper *m* ♦ **clippers** maquinilla para cortar el pelo • **nail clippers** cortaúñas.

clip·ping (klǐp'ǐng) s. *(cutting)* recorte *m*, corte (periódico, cabello) *m*; *(shearing)* esquileo (de ovejas).

clique (klēk, klǐk) s. pandilla, camarilla.

clit·o·ris (klǐt'ər-ǐs) s. ANAT. clítoris *m*.

cloak (klōk) I. s. capa, manto II. tr. *(to cover)* encapotar; *(to conceal)* encubrir, disimular.

cloak-and-dag·ger (klōk'ən-dăg'ər) adj. *(of adventure)* de capa y espada; *(of spies)* de espionaje.

cloak·room (klōk'rōōm', -rōōm') s. guardarropa *m*, ropería.

clob·ber (klǒb'ər) tr. JER. *(to hit)* golpear; *(to defeat)* dar una paliza, derrotar abrumadoramente.

clock (klŏk) I. *(timepiece)* reloj (de pie, de mesa) *m*; *(chronometer)* cronómetro II. tr. tomar el tiempo de, cronometrar.

clock·wise (klŏk'wīz') adv. & adj. en el sentido de las agujas del reloj.

clock·work (klŏk'wûrk') s. mecanismo de relojería ♦ **like c.** con precisión, como un reloj.

clod (klŏd) s. *(of dirt)* terrón *m*, gleba; *(dolt)* simplón *m*, bobo.

clod·hop·per (klŏd'hŏp'ər) s. patán *m*, paleto ♦ **clodhoppers** zapatones.

clog (klŏg) I. s. *(obstacle)* traba, obstáculo; *(fetter)* traba; *(wooden shoe)* zueco II. tr. **clogged, clog·ging** *(to obstruct)* obstruir, trabar; *(to impede)* impedir; *(to hamper)* estorbar —intr. *(to become obstructed)* obstruirse, taparse (una cañería); *(to coagulate)* coagularse; *(to dance)* zapatear, bailar un zapateado.

clois·ter (kloi'stər) I. s. *(monastery)* monasterio, convento; *(reclusion)* reclusión monástica, claustro; ARQ. *(walkway)* cláustro II. tr. enclaustrar, recluir.

clois·tered (kloi'stərd) adj. *(confined)* enclaustrado; *(monastic)* monástico.

clomp (klŏmp) intr. andar pesada y ruidosamente.

clone (klōn) BIOL. I. s. clon *m* II. tr. & intr. **cloned, clon·ing** reproducir(se) asexualmente.

clop (klŏp) s. sonido producido por el casco de un caballo.

close I. adj. (klōs) **clos·er, clos·est** *(near)* cercano; *(closely associated)* cercano <*a c. relative* un pariente cercano>; *(united)* unido <*the two brothers are very c.* los dos hermanos son muy unidos>; *(intimate)* íntimo <*c. friends* amigos íntimos>; *(similar)* parecido, similar; *(compact)* compacto, tupido <*a c. weave* un tejido tupido>; *(tight)* reñido <*a c. election* unas elecciones reñidas>; *(almost equal)* casi igual, casi parejo; *(like an original)* fiel, exacto <*a c. copy* una copia fiel>; *(rigorous)* detenido, minucioso <*a very c. analysis* un análisis muy minucioso>; *(full)* mucho, total <*he paid c. attention* prestó su total atención>; *(shut)* cerrado; *(enclosed)* cercado, encerrado; *(tight-fitting)* apretado, ajustado <*c. garments* ropa apretada>; *(stuffy)* cargado, pesado; *(lacking fresh air)* mal ventilado; *(restricted)* de acceso limitado, exclusivo; *(confining)* estrecho; *(strict)* estricto <*c. supervision* supervisión estricta>; *(secluded)* oculto; *(reticent)* reservado; *(stingy)* apretado, tacaño; *(difficult to obtain)* restringido; *(scarce)*

escaso; GRAM. cerrado ♦ **a c. resemblance** un gran parecido • **at c. range** a quemarropa, de cerca • **c. combat** MIL. combate cuerpo a cuerpo • **c. quarters** lugar estrecho II. tr. (klōz) **closed, clos·ing** *(to shut)* cerrar <*who closed the window?* ¿quién cerró la ventana?>; *(to fill)* tapar <*to c. the cracks with plaster* tapar las grietas con yeso>; *(to obscure)* obstruir, tapar (la vista); *(to conclude)* concluir <*to c. a letter* concluir una carta>; *(to seal)* cerrar <*the deal will be closed tomorrow* el trato se cerrará mañana>; *(to wrap up)* cerrar, clausurar; *(session)* levantar; COM. *(to terminate an account)* cerrar, liquidar; *(to unite)* juntar; *(to diminish)* disminuir, acortar <*to c. the distance* acortar la distancia>; *(to enclose)* encerrar ♦ **to c. down** cerrar definitivamente • **to c. in** rodear, cercar • **to c. out** *(account)* saldar; *(to sell)* liquidar, vender en liquidación • **to c. ranks** MIL. cerrar filas • **to c. up** cerrar definitivamente • **to c. up shop** *(to shut down)* cerrar el negocio; *(to cease activities)* cesar toda actividad —intr. *(to become shut)* cerrarse <*the door closed* se cerró la puerta>; *(to discontinue operation)* cerrar <*the store closes at six* la tienda cierra a las seis>; *(to come to an end)* terminarse, concluirse; *(to agree)* ponerse de acuerdo; *(to come together)* cerrarse <*his arms closed around her* sus brazos se cerraron en torno a ella> ♦ **to c. down** clausurarse, cerrarse definitivamente • **to c. in** *(to surround)* rodear; *(to draw near)* acercarse; *(the night)* acercarse, caer • **to c. out** liquidar • **to c. up** *(to shut)* cerrar; *(opening)* taparse; *(wound)* cerrarse, cicatrizarse; *(to fall silent)* callarse, quedar callado III. s. (klōz) *(conclusion)* final *m*, conclusión *f*; *(place)* recinto ♦ **at the c. of the day** a la caída de la tarde • **to bring (something) to a c.** terminar (algo) IV. adv. (klōs) cerca ♦ **c. at hand** a mano • **c. by** muy cerca • **c. to** muy cerca de, junto a • **c. together** muy juntos • **to come c.** acercarse • **to get c. to** acercarse a.

close call (klōs) s. FAM. escape difícil *m* ♦ **to have a c.** FAM. casi escaparse.

closed (klōzd) adj. *(shut)* cerrado, clausurado; *(blocked)* cerrado, obstruido; *(restricted)* exclusivo, reservado; *(enclosed)* limitado, con límites; *(finished)* vedado (temporada, caza); *(narrow)* estrecha <*a c. mind* una mente estrecha>.

closed-cir·cuit television (klōzd'sûr'kǐt) s. televisión en circuito cerrado *f*.

closed corporation s. COM. sociedad anónima cuyos dignatarios son dueños de todas las acciones.

close·down (klōz'doun') s. cierre (de un negocio, fábrica).

closed shop s. establecimiento que contrata solamente a miembros sindicados.

close-fist·ed (klōs'fǐs'tǐd) adj. tacaño.

close·ly (klōs'lē) adv. *(near)* cerca, de cerca; *(intimately)* íntimamente, estrechamente <*it is c. related to this matter* se relaciona estrechamente con este asunto>; *(exactly)* con fidelidad, con exactitud; *(attentively)* atentamente; *(tightly)* apretadamente; *(densely)* densamente.

close-mouthed (klōs'mouthd', -moutht') adj. taciturno, poco comunicativo.

close·ness (klōs'nǐs) s. *(nearness)* cercanía, proximidad *f*; *(intimacy)* intimidad *f*; *(of a copy, translation)* fidelidad *f*, exactitud *f*; *(exclusivity)* exclusividad *f*; *(tightness)* apretadura; *(density)* densidad (de personas, edificios) *f*.

close-out (klōz'out') s. COM. liquidación *f*.

close shave (klōs) s. JER. escape milagroso.

clos·et (klŏz'ǐt) I. s. *(cabinet)* armario, ropero; *(private room)* gabinete *m* II. tr. encerrar.

close-up (klōs'ŭp') s. FOTOG. primer plano.

clos·ing (klō'zǐng) s. *(act)* cierre *m*; *(conclusion)* conclusión *f*; COM. *(of a deal)* cierre; *(liquidation)* liquidación (de una cuenta, negocio) *f* ♦ **c. remarks** observaciones finales • **in c.** para concluir o terminar.

closing price s. FIN. cotización de cierre *f*.

clo·sure (klō'zhər) s. *(closing)* cierre *m*; *(conclusion)* conclusión *m*.

clot (klŏt) I. s. coágulo II. intr. **clot·ted, clot·ting** coagularse, cuajarse —tr. coagular, cuajar.

cloth (klôth) s. [pl. **cloths** (klôths, klôthz)] *(material)* tela,

paño; *(strip)* trapo; *(tablecloth)* mantel ♦ **the c.** FIG. el clero.
cloth·bound (klôth′bound′) adj. LIT. encuadernado en tela.
clothe (klōth) tr. **clothed** o **clad** (klăd), **cloth·ing** vestir, arropar.
clothes (klōthz) s.pl. ropa, vestimenta.
clothes·horse (klōthz′hôrs′) s. *(frame)* tendedero; FIG. *(person)* persona que presta excesiva atención a la vestimenta.
clothes·line (klōthz′līn′) s. cuerda para tender ropa.
clothes·pin (klōthz′pĭn′) s. pinza para tender ropa.
cloth·ier (klōth′yər) s. COM. pañero, ropero.
cloth·ing (klō′thĭng) s. ropa, indumentaria.
clo·ture (klō′chər) POL. **I.** s. clausura **II.** tr. **-tured, -tur·ing** clausurar.
cloud (kloud) **I.** s. *(water vapor)* nube *f*; *(mass)* nube (de polvo, humo); *(swarm)* nube, multitud *f* <*c. of locusts* nube de langostas>; *(shadow)* sombra (de tristeza, melancolía); JOY. *(blemish)* nube, sombra; *(milkiness)* nebulosidad (en vidrio, líquido) *f* ♦ **in the clouds** *(distracted)* en las nubes, distraído; *(unreal)* imaginario, irreal • **on c. nine** FAM. contentísimo • **under a c.** *(under suspicion)* bajo sospecha; *(melancholy)* melancólico, deprimido **II.** tr. *(to make cloudy)* nublar; *(to darken)* oscurecer; *(to make gloomy)* deprimir, entristecer; *(to discredit)* oscurecer —intr. nublarse ♦ **to c. over** o **up** nublarse.
cloud·burst (kloud′bûrst′) s. aguacero, tromba de agua.
cloud·i·ness (klou′dē-nĭs) s. *(of the sky)* nubosidad *f*, nebulosidad *f*; *(of a liquid)* turbulencia; *(indistinctness)* nebulosidad, vaguedad *f*.
cloud·less (kloud′lĭs) adj. METEOR. sin nubes, despejado.
cloud·y (klou′dē) adj. **-i·er, -i·est** *(overcast)* nublado; *(vague)* nebuloso, vago; *(gloomy)* sombrío; *(of a liquid)* turbio.
clout (klout) **I.** s. *(blow)* bofetada, golpe *m*; FAM. *(influence)* poder *m*, influencia; DEP. *(target)* blanco (en tiro de arco) **II.** tr. abofetar.
clove[1] (klōv) s. BOT. *(tree)* clavero; *(spice)* clavo de especia; *(of garlic)* diente *m*.
clove[2] (klōv) un pret. de **cleave**[1,2].
clo·ven (klō′vən) un part. p. de **cleave**[1].
cloven hoof s. pezuña hendida.
clo·ver (klō′vər) s. BOT. trébol *m* ♦ **to be in c.** vivir como un rey.
clo·ver·leaf (klō′vər-lēf′) s. [pl. **-leafs** o **-leaves** (-lēvz′)] AUTO. cruce en trébol (en las carreteras) *m*.
clown (kloun) **I.** s. *(jester)* payaso, bufón *m*; *(boor)* patán *m*, grosero **II.** intr. payasear, bufonear.
clown·ish (klou′nĭsh) adj. *(like a clown)* de payaso; *(rude)* grosero.
cloy (kloi) tr. & intr. *(to surfeit)* empalagar; FIG. *(to sicken)* saciar, hartar.
cloy·ing (kloi′ĭng) adj. empalagoso.
club (klŭb) **I.** s. *(cudgel)* porra, maza; DEP. *(stick)* palo (de golf, hockey); *(in cards)* trébol *m*; *(association)* asociación *f*, club *m* ♦ **clubs** bastos, bastones (en los naipes españoles) **II.** tr. **clubbed, club·bing** *(to beat)* dar garrotazos, aporrear; *(to hit)* golpear (con la culata) —intr. ♦ **to c. together** reunirse.
club car s. F.C. coche salón *m*.
club·foot (klŭb′fŏŏt′) s. pie deforme *m*.
club·house (klŭb′hous′) s. sede (de un club) *f*, club *m*.
club soda s. agua de Seltz, soda.
cluck (klŭk) **I.** s. *(sound)* cloqueo; FAM. *(person)* estúpido, tonto **II.** intr. cloquear —tr. llamar con cloqueo.
clue (klōō) **I.** s. *(hint)* pista; *(evidence)* indicio; *(indication)* indicación (en crucigramas) *f* ♦ **I haven't a c.** no tengo ni idea **II.** tr. **clued, clue·ing** o **clu·ing** dar una pista, dar información ♦ **to c. someone in** ponerle a alguien al tanto de la situación.
clump (klŭmp) **I.** s. *(lump)* masa; *(trees)* grupo (de árboles); *(sound)* ruido sordo **II.** intr. *(to tramp)* andar con pisadas fuertes; *(to lump)* agruparse —tr. agrupar.
clum·si·ness (klŭm′zē-nĭs) s. torpeza.
clum·sy (klŭm′zē) adj. **-si·er, -si·est** *(awkward)* torpe; *(unwieldy)* incómodo; *(unrefined)* crudo.
clung (klŭng) pret. y part. de **cling.**
clunk (klŭngk) **I.** s. *(thump)* sonido sordo; *(blow)* golpe

fuerte *m*; *(person)* estúpido, tonto **II.** intr. *(to move)* moverse, avanzar <*to c. along* avanzar haciendo ruido>; *(to strike)* dar un golpe (fuerte) —tr. golpear fuerte.
clus·ter (klŭs′tər) **I.** s. *(group)* grupo; *(bunch)* racimo, ramo; *(band)* manada, caterva (de animales) **II.** tr. & intr. agrupar(se), amontonar(se), arracimar(se).
clutch (klŭch) **I.** tr. *(to grasp)* agarrar, asir —intr. ♦ **to c. at** agarrarse a **II.** s. *(claw, hand)* garra; *(grasp)* apretón (de manos, brazo) *m*; MEC. embrague *m* ♦ **clutches** FIG. garras • **in the c.** en situación crítica.
clut·ter (klŭt′ər) **I.** s. *(bunch)* montón *m*; *(mess)* desorden *m*; *(clatter)* estrépito, ruido **II.** tr. *(to litter)* esparcir desordenadamente —intr. *(to move)* moverse atropelladamente.
coach (kōch) **I.** s. *(carriage)* coche *m*, carruaje *m*; *(automobile)* coche, carro; *(bus)* ómnibus *m*, autocar *m*; *(passenger car)* vagón de pasajeros *m*; *(accommodation)* clase económica, segunda clase; *(trainer)* entrenador *m*, director técnico; *(tutor)* maestro particular **II.** tr. *(to tutor)* dar lecciones suplementarias; *(to provide expert answers)* asesorar; *(to train)* entrenar; *(to transport)* transportar, llevar —intr. *(to teach)* dar lecciones suplementarias; *(to train)* entrenar; *(to ride)* andar, viajar.
coach class s. clase económica, segunda clase.
coach·ing (kō′chĭng) s. *(training)* entrenamiento; *(tutoring)* clases suplementarias *f*.
coach·man (kōch′mən) s. [pl. **-men**] cochero.
co·ac·tion (kō-ăk′shən) s. acción conjunta.
co·ad·ju·tant (kō-ăj′ə-tənt) **I.** adj. coadyuvante **II.** s. ayudante *m*, auxiliar *mf*.
co·ad·ju·tor (kō′ə-jōō′tər) s. auxiliar *mf* ♦ **bishop c.** obispo auxiliar.
co·ag·u·lant (kō-ăg′yə-lənt) s. coagulante *m*.
co·ag·u·late (kō-ăg′yə-lāt′) tr. & intr. **-lat·ed, -lat·ing** coagular(se).
co·ag·u·la·tion (kō-ăg′yə-lā′shən) s. coagulación *f*.
coal (kōl) **I.** s. MIN. carbón *m*, hulla; *(charcoal)* carbón vegetal; *(ember)* ascua, brasa ♦ **c. mine** mina de carbón • **hard c.** antracita, hulla seca ♦ **soft c.** carbón bituminoso o blando • **to carry coals to Newcastle** echar agua en el mar • **to rake over the coals** reprender, retar (severamente) **II.** tr. & intr. abastecer(se) de carbón.
co·a·lesce (kō′ə-lĕs′) intr. **-lesced, -lesc·ing** *(to fuse)* fundirse; *(to unite)* unirse.
co·a·les·cence (kō′ə-lĕs′əns) s. fundición *f*, unificación *f*.
coal·field (kōl′fēld′) s. *(region)* cuenca carbonífera; *(deposit)* yacimiento de carbón.
co·a·li·tion (kō′ə-lĭsh′ən) s. coalición *f*.
coal tar s. alquitrán de hulla *m*.
coarse (kôrs) adj. **coars·er, coars·est** *(inferior)* basto, corriente; *(uncouth)* vulgar, grosero; *(rough)* áspero, tosco; *(grainy)* granular, granoso.
coarse-grained (kôrs′grănd′) adj. *(rough)* grueso, basto (fibra, grano); *(crude)* crudo, grosero.
coars·en (kôr′sən) intr. *(to become rough)* volverse tosco; *(to become vulgar)* volverse grosero o burdo —tr. *(to roughen)* volver basto; *(to make vulgar)* vulgarizar.
coarse·ness (kôrs′nĭs) s. *(of quality)* tosquedad *f*; *(of manners)* grosería; *(of a surface, skin)* aspereza.
coast (kōst) **I.** s. *(shore)* costa; *(coastline)* costa, litoral *m*; *(slope)* pendiente *f*, cuesta (deslizadiza); *(glide)* deslizamiento ♦ **the c. is clear** no hay moros en la costa **II.** intr. *(to slide)* deslizarse; *(to move without power)* rodar sin impulso (en bicicleta, automóvil); *(to sail)* costear; *(to wander)* errar, vagar —tr. costear.
coast·al (kō′stəl) adj. costero.
coast·er (kō′stər) s. *(ship)* barco de cabotaje; *(sled)* trineo, tobogán *m*; *(mat)* posavasos; *(tray on wheels)* mesita rodante (para bebidas).
coast guard s. MARÍT. *(service)* guardacostas *m*, servicio costanero; *(person)* guardacostas *mf*.
coast·line (kōst′līn′) s. costa, litoral *m*.
coat (kōt) **I.** s. *(overcoat)* abrigo, sobretodo; *(suit coat)* saco, chaqueta; *(fur)* piel *f*, pelo (de animal); *(layer)* mano *f*, capa (de pintura, barniz); *(coating)* baño, revestimiento ♦ **to turn (one's) c.** *(to change sides)* pasarse al otro

bando; *(to betray)* traicionar **II.** tr. *(to dress)* vestir con chaqueta *o* abrigo; *(to cover)* cubrir, revestir; *(to paint)* dar una mano *o* capa; *(to plate)* bañar (en oro, plata).

coat·ed (kō'tĭd) adj. *(covered)* cubierto, bañado; IMPR. cuché *m.*

coat·ing (kō'tĭng) s. *(layer)* capa, mano (de pintura, barniz) *f*; *(covering)* baño, revestimiento (de oro, plata); *(cloth)* tela *o* paño (para abrigos).

coat of arms s. [pl. **coats of arms**] HER. escudo de armas.

coat of mail s. [pl. **coats of mail**] ANT., ARM. cota de malla.

coat·tail (kōt'tāl') s. faldón (de un frac) *m* ♦ **on someone's coattails** a base del éxito de otra persona.

co·au·thor (kō-ô'thər) **I.** s. coautor *m*, colaborador *m* **II.** tr. escribir en colaboración con otra persona.

coax (kōks) tr. *(to wheedle)* engatusar; *(to persuade)* instar, persuadir.

co·ax·i·al (kō-ăk'sē-əl) adj. coaxial.

coaxial cable s. TELEV. cable coaxial *m.*

coax·ing (kōk'sĭng) **I.** s. *(persuasion)* persuasión *f*; *(wheedling)* engatusamiento **II.** adj. *(wheedling)* engatusador; *(persuasive)* persuasivo.

cob (kŏb) s. *(of corn)* elote *m*, mazorca; *(male swan)* cisne macho; *(horse)* jaca.

co·balt (kō'bôlt') s. QUÍM. cobalto.

cob·ble¹ (kŏb'əl) **I.** tr. **-bled, -bling** empedrar con adoquines **II.** s. adoquín *m.*

cob·ble² (kŏb'əl) tr. **-bled, -bling** remendar (calzado).

cob·bler (kŏb'lər) s. zapatero; *(fruit pie)* tarta de fruta; *(drink)* bebida helada de vino y frutas.

cob·ble·stone (kŏb'əl-stōn') s. piedra redonda ♦ **c. pavement** empedrado.

CO·BOL *o* **Co·bol** (kō'bôl') s. COMPUT. COBOL (lenguaje de programación) *m.*

co·bra (kō'brə) s. ZOOL. cobra.

cob·web (kŏb'wĕb') s. telaraña ♦ **cobwebs** confusión, desorden.

co·ca (kō'kə) s. BOT. coca.

co·caine *o* **co·cain** (kō-kān') s. QUÍM. cocaína.

coc·cyx (kŏk'sĭks) s. [pl. **coc·cy·ges** (-sĭ-jēz')] ANAT. cóccix *m*, coxis *m.*

cock¹ (kŏk) **I.** s. *(rooster)* gallo; *(male bird)* gallo, macho; *(weather vane)* veleta en forma de gallo; *(leader)* jefe *m*, líder *m*; *(faucet)* grifo, llave *f*; ARM. *(hammer)* martillo; *(tilt of a hat)* inclinación *f*, ángulo; VULG. *(penis)* pene *m* **II.** tr. ARM. amartillar; *(a hat)* inclinar (hacia arriba); *(to prepare to hit)* alzar, levantar <he cocked his fists alzó los puños> —intr. ARM. amartillarse; *(to stick up)* levantarse (orejas, cejas) **III.** adj. macho <c. sparrow gorrión macho>.

cock² (kŏk) AGR. **I.** s. montón de heno *m* **II.** tr. amontonar.

cock·ade (kŏ-kād') s. escarapela.

Cock·aigne (kŏ-kān') s. tierra imaginaria de vida cómoda y lujosa.

cock·a·ma·mie *o* **cock·a·ma·my** (kŏk'ə-mā'mē) adj. JER. *(valueless)* de calidad inferior; *(ludicrous)* absurdo.

cock-and-bull story (kŏk'ən-bool') s. FAM. patraña, cuento increíble.

cock·a·too (kŏk'ə-tōo') s. ORNIT. cacatúa.

cock·er·el (kŏk'ər-əl) s. gallo joven.

cock·er spaniel (kŏk'ər) s. perro cócker, pachón inglés *m.*

cock·eyed (kŏk'īd') adj. *(cross-eyed)* bizco; JER. *(crooked)* oblicuo, torcido; *(foolish)* absurdo, ridículo; *(drunk)* borracho.

cock·fight (kŏk'fīt') s. pelea de gallos.

cock·fight·ing (kŏk'fī'tĭng) **I.** adj. de la pelea de gallos **II.** s. pelea de gallos.

cock·i·ness (kŏk'ē-nĭs) s. *(cheek)* descaro, frescura; *(cocksureness)* presunción *f*, engreimiento.

cock·le (kŏk'əl) **I.** s. *(mollusk)* berberecho; *(boat)* cascarón de nuez *m*; *(wrinkle)* arruga ♦ **the cockles of one's heart** las entretelas del corazón **II.** intr. & tr. **-led, -ling** ondular(se) ligerísimamente.

cock·le·shell (kŏk'əl-shĕl') s. *(shell)* concha de berberecho; *(boat)* barqueta.

cock·ney (kŏk'nē) s. [pl. **-neys**] *(dialect)* lenguaje propio de los barrios bajos de Londres; *(person)* habitante de los barrios bajos de Londres.

cock·pit (kŏk'pĭt') s. *(arena)* cancha, redondel *m*; *(in airplane)* cabina del piloto; *(in ships)* caseta.

cock·roach (kŏk'rōch') s. ZOOL. cucaracha.

cocks·comb (kŏks'kōm') s. ZOOL. *(comb)* cresta de gallo; BOT. cresta de gallo; *(fop)* petimetre *m*, fatuo.

cock·sure (kŏk'shoor') adj. demasiado seguro.

cock·tail (kŏk'tāl') s. cóctel *m.*

cock·y (kŏk'ē) adj. **-i·er, -i·est** FAM. presumido, engreído.

co·co (kō'kō) **I.** s. BOT. *(tree)* coco, cocotero; *(fruit)* coco **II.** adj. de coco.

co·coa (kō'kō) s. cacao.

co·co·nut *o* **co·coa·nut** (kō'kə-nət) s. BOT. coco.

coconut palm s. BOT. cocotero.

co·coon (kə-kōon') s. capullo.

cod (kŏd) s. [pl. **cod** *o* **cods**] ICT. bacalao, bagadejo.

co·da (kō'l) s. MÚS. coda.

cod·dle (kŏd'l) tr. **-dled, -dling** *(to cook)* cocer a fuego lento; *(to pamper)* mimar, consentir.

code (kōd) **I.** s. *(laws, rules)* código; *(signals)* código; *(cipher)* clave *f*, cifra ♦ s. TEL. prefijo, código territorial • **Morse c.** alfabeto Morse **II.** tr. **cod·ed, cod·ing** *(laws, rules)* codificar; *(a message)* cifrar.

co·de·fend·ant (kō'dĭ-fĕn'dənt) s. DER. coacusado.

co·deine (kō'dēn') s. FARM., QUÍM. codeína.

co·dex (kō'dĕks') s. [pl. **co·di·ces** (kō'dĭ-sēz', kŏd'ĭ-)] códice *m.*

cod·fish (kŏd'fĭsh') s. [pl. **codfish** *o* **-fish·es**] bacalao.

codg·er (kŏj'ər) s. FAM. vejete *m.*

co·di·ces (kō'dĭ-sēz', kŏd'ĭ-) pl. de **codex.**

cod·i·cil (kŏd'ĭ-sĭl) s. DER. codicilo.

cod·i·fi·ca·tion (kŏd'ə-fĭ-kā'shən, kō'də-) s. codificación *f.*

cod·i·fi·er (kŏd'ə-fī'ər, kō'də-) s. codificador *m.*

cod·i·fy (kŏd'ə-fī') tr. **-fied, -fy·ing** codificar.

co·di·rec·tion (kō'dĭ-rĕk'shən, -dī'-) s. CINEM. codirección *f.*

cod-liv·er oil (kŏd'lĭv'ər) s. aceite de hígado de bacalao *m.*

co·ed *o* **co-ed** (kō'ĕd') s. FAM. **I.** s. alumna de una universidad mixta **II.** adj. de ambos sexos, coeducacional.

co·ed·u·ca·tion *o* **co-ed·u·ca·tion** (kō-ĕj'ə-kā'shən) s. coeducación *f*, enseñanza mixta.

co·ed·u·ca·tion·al *o* **co-ed·u·ca·tion·al** (kō-ĕj'ə-kā'shə-nəl) adj. mixto, coeducacional.

co·ef·fi·cient (kō'ə-fĭsh'ənt) adj. MAT. coeficiente *m.*

co·e·qual (kō-ē'kwəl) adj. & s. igual *mf.*

co·erce (kō-ûrs') tr. **-erced, -erc·ing** *(to compel)* coaccionar, obligar.

co·er·cion (kō-ûr'zhən) s. *(compulsion)* coacción *f*; DER. *(restraint)* coerción *f.*

co·er·cive (kō-ûr'sĭv) adj. coercitivo.

co·e·val (kō-ē'vəl) adj. & s. coetáneo.

co·ex·ist (kō'ĭg-zĭst') intr. coexistir.

co·ex·is·tence (kō'ĭg-zĭs'təns) s. coexistencia.

co·ex·is·tent (kō'ĭg-zĭs'tənt) adj. coexistente.

co·ex·ten·sive (kō'ĭk-stĕn'sĭv) adj. coextenso.

cof·fee (kō'fē) s. café *m* ♦ **coffee cup** taza de café.

coffee house *o* **cof·fee·house** (kō'fē-hous') s. café *m*, cafetería.

coffee mill s. molinillo de café.

cof·fee·pot (kō'fē-pŏt') s. cafetera.

coffee shop s. café *m*, cafetería.

coffee table s. mesa de café, mesa de centro.

coffee tree s. BOT. cafeto.

cof·fer (kō'fər) s. cofre *m*, caja de valores ♦ **coffers** tesorería, fondos.

cof·fer·dam (kō'fər-dăm') s. HIDRÁUL. ataguía.

cof·fin (kō'fĭn) **I.** s. *(box)* ataúd *m*, féretro; *(hoof)* casco (de un caballo) **II.** tr. poner en un ataúd.

cog (kŏg) s. MEC. diente (de rueda dentada) *m*; FAM. *(subordinate)* eslabón *m.*

co·gen·er·a·tion (kō-jĕn'ə-rā'shən) s. ING. generación eléctrica mediante la energía de escape.

co·gent (kō'jənt) adj. profundamente pensado.

cog·i·tate (kŏj'ĭ-tāt') intr. & tr. **-tat·ed, -tat·ing** reflexionar, meditar.

cog·i·ta·tion (kŏj'ĭ-tā'shən) s. reflexión *f*, meditación *f.*

ă rey / ä año / b boca / ch chico / d dar / ĕ el / ē mil / g gato / h joya / hw juez / ī aire / k casa / kw cuan /

co·gnac (kōn′yăk′, kŏn′-) s. coñac *m.*

cog·nate (kŏg′nāt′) I. adj. DER. cognado; GRAM. afín; *(analogous)* similar II. s. DER. cognado; GRAM. palabra afín.

cog·ni·tion (kŏg-nĭsh′ən) s. *(faculty)* cognición *f; (knowledge)* percepción *f.*

cog·ni·tive (kŏg′nĭ-tĭv) adj. FILOS. cognoscitivo.

cog·ni·zance (kŏg′nĭ-zəns) s. *(knowledge)* conocimiento; DER. *(jurisdiction)* jurisdicción *f,* competencia ♦ **to take c. of** tener en cuenta.

cog·ni·zant (kŏg′nĭ-zənt) adj. enterado, informado ♦ **to be c. of** saber.

cog·no·men (kŏg-nō′mən) s. [pl. **-mens** *o* **-nom·i·na** (-nŏm′-ə-nə)] *(surname)* apellido; *(nickname)* apodo.

cog railway s. ferrocarril de cremallera *m.*

cog·wheel (kŏg′hwēl′) s. TEC. rueda dentada.

co·hab·it (kō-hăb′ĭt) intr. cohabitar.

co·hab·i·ta·tion (kō-hăb′ĭ-tā′shən) s. cohabitación *f.*

co·here (kō-hîr′) intr. **-hered, -her·ing** adherirse, *(to stick together)* pegarse; *(to be logical)* tener coherencia, ser coherente.

co·her·ence (kō-hîr′əns, -hĕr′-) *o* **co·her·en·cy** (-ən-sē) s. *(sticking)* adherencia; *(logical connection)* coherencia.

co·her·ent (kō-hîr′ənt, -hĕr′-) adj. *(sticking together)* adherido; *(logically connected)* coherente; FÍS. cohesivo.

co·he·sion (kō-hē′zhən) s. cohesión *f.*

co·he·sive (kō-hē′sĭv) cohesivo.

co·hort (kō′hôrt′) s. *(group)* cohorte *f,* banda; FAM. *(companion)* socio, compañero.

coif (koif) s. *(cap)* cofia; *(coiffure)* tocado, peinado.

coif·fure (kwä-fyŏor′) s. tocado, peinado.

coil (koil) I. s. *(of rope)* rollo; *(ring)* anillo, vuelta (de un rollo); *(of pipe)* serpentín *m;* ELEC. bobina, carrete *m* II. tr. enrollar, enroscar —intr. *(to wind itself up)* enrollarse, enroscarse; *(to move spirally)* serpentear.

coin (koin) I. s. moneda ♦ **to toss** *o* **flip a c.** echar a cara o cruz II. tr. acuñar ♦ **to c. a phrase** inventar una frase.

coin·age (koi′nĭj) s. *(act)* acuñación *f; (money)* moneda; *(system)* sistema monetario; *(of words, phrases)* invención *f,* creación *f.*

co·in·cide (kō′ĭn-sīd′) intr. **-cid·ed, -cid·ing** coincidir.

co·in·ci·dence (kō-ĭn′sĭ-dəns) s. *(identicalness)* coincidencia; *(chance)* casualidad *f <by c.* por casualidad>.

co·in·ci·dent (kō-ĭn′sĭ-dənt) adj. coincidente ♦ **c. with** acorde con.

co·in·ci·den·tal (kō-ĭn′sĭ-dĕn′təl) adj. *(identical)* coincidente; *(accidental)* casual, fortuito.

coin·er (koi′nər) s. *(of coins)* acuñador *m; (counterfeiter)* falsificador de moneda *m; (inventor)* inventor *m,* creador *m.*

co·i·tus (kō′ĭ-təs, kō-ē′-) *o* **co·i·tion** (kō-ĭsh′ən) s. coito.

coke¹ (kōk) I. s. MIN. coque *m* II. tr. & intr. **coked, cok·ing** convertir(se) en coque, coquizar(se).

coke² (kōk) s. JER. cocaína.

co·la (kō′lə) s. BOT. cola; *(drink)* gaseosa con extracto de cola.

col·an·der (kŭl′ən-dər, kŏl′-) s. colador *m,* escurridor *m.*

cold (kōld) I. adj. **-er, -est** *(chilly)* frío; *(unemotional)* frío, desapasionado; *(impassive)* impasible <a c. audience un público impasible>; *(objective)* objetivo <c. logic lógica objetiva>; *(bare)* mero <that is the c. truth es la mera verdad>; *(gloomy)* deprimente <a c. decor una decoración deprimente>; *(aloof)* frío, indiferente <a c. person una persona indiferente>; *(sexually frigid)* frígido; *(said of a color)* frío; FAM. *(unconscious)* inconsciente, sin conocimiento <he fell down c.* cayó sin conocimiento>; *(dead)* frío, tieso <he is c. in his grave está tieso en la tumba>; JER. *(not stolen)* legal; *(unprepared)* sin preparación <to enter a game c.* entrar en un juego sin preparación>; *(completely mastered)* al dedillo <the actor had his lines down c.* el actor sabía su papel al dedillo> ♦ **c. comfort** poco consuelo • **c. snap** *o* **spell** ola de frío • **in c. blood** a sangre fría • **to be c.** *(object)* estar frío; *(person)* tener frío; *(weather)* hacer frío • **to throw c. water on** echar un jarro de agua fría a II. adv. *(totally)* completamente <he was c.* sober estaba completamente sobrio>; *(without preparation)*

sin preparación, en seco <they took the exam c. and passed tomaron el examen sin preparación y lo pasaron> ♦ **to blow hot and c.** vacilar, cambiar sucesivamente de parecer III. s. *(lack of warmth)* frío; MED. catarro, resfriado ♦ **out in the c.** en la estacada • **to catch a c.** refriarse, coger un resfriado • **to have a c.** tener catarro, estar resfriado.

cold-blood·ed (kōld′blŭd′ĭd) adj. *(cruel)* cruel, despiadado; *(emotionless)* impasible; *(murder)* a sangre fría; ZOOL. de sangre fría.

cold chisel s. cortahierro, cortafrío.

cold cream s. crema para el cutis.

cold cuts s.pl. CUL. fiambres *m.*

cold feet s. JER. miedo <he got c. le dio miedo>.

cold frame s. cajonera en frío.

cold front s. METEOR. frente frío.

cold-heart·ed (kōld′här′tĭd) adj. insensible, indiferente.

cold·ness (kōld′nĭs) s. *(low temperature)* frío; *(lack of heat)* frialdad *f; (of emotion)* frialdad.

cold pack s. MED. compresa fría; *(canning process)* envasado en frío.

cold-shoul·der (kōld′shōl′dər) tr. FAM. *(to treat with indifference)* tratar con indiferencia; *(to snub)* desairar, desdeñar.

cold shoulder s. FAM. indiferencia, frialdad *f* ♦ **to give someone the c.** tratar a alguien con indiferencia.

cold sore s. MED. fuegito, afta (labial).

cold storage s. almacenamiento en frío ♦ **to put in c.** FIG. postergar indefinidamente.

cold turkey s. FAM. ♦ **to go c.** abandonar algo total y repentinamente • **to talk c.** hablar francamente, hablar sin rodeos.

cold war s. guerra fría.

cold wave s. METEOR. *(sudden cold)* ola de frío; *(hair-setting process)* ondulación permanente del cabello (al frío) *f.*

cole (kōl) s. BOT. *(rape)* colza, nabo; *(cabbage)* col *f.*

co·lec·to·my (kə-lĕk′tə-mē) s. [pl. **-mies**] CIR. colectomía.

cole·slaw (kōl′slô′) s. ensalada de col.

col·ic (kŏl′ĭk) s. MED. cólico.

col·i·se·um (kŏl′ĭ-sē′əm) s. coliseo.

co·li·tis (kō-lī′tĭs) s. MED. colitis *f.*

col·lab·o·rate (kə-lăb′ə-rāt′) intr. **-rat·ed, -rat·ing** colaborar.

col·lab·o·ra·tion (kə-lăb′ə-rā′shən) s. *(cooperation)* colaboración *f; (treason)* colaboracionismo.

col·lab·o·ra·tion·ist (kə-lăb′ə-rā′shə-nĭst) s. colaboracionista *mf.*

col·lab·o·ra·tive (kə-lăb′ə-rā′tĭv, -ər-ə-) adj. dispuesto a colaborar, de colaboración.

col·lab·o·ra·tor (kə-lăb′ə-rā′tər) s. *(associate)* colaborador *m; (traitor)* colaboracionista *mf.*

col·lage (kə-läzh′) s. ARTE. collage *m,* montaje *m.*

col·la·gen (kŏl′ə-jən) s. BIOQUÍM. colágeno.

col·lapse (kə-lăps′) I. intr. **-lapsed, -laps·ing** *(to fall down)* caerse, derrumbarse; *(to fold)* plegarse; MED. *(to break down)* enfermarse súbitamente, tener un colapso —tr. hacer derrumbar II. s. *(cave-in)* colapso, derrumbe; *(breakdown)* colapso.

col·laps·i·ble *o* **col·laps·a·ble** (kə-lăp′sə-bəl) adj. plegable.

col·lar (kŏl′ər) I. s. *(of a garment)* cuello; *(necklace)* collar *m,* gargantilla; *(animal collar)* collar; *(part of a harness)* collera (de animal de tiro); BIOL. *(band)* collar; MEC. collar, collarín *m* II. tr. *(an animal)* poner un collar; FAM. *(to seize)* agarrar, detener <the police collared the thief la policía agarró al ladrón>.

col·lar·bone (kŏl′ər-bōn′) s. ANAT. clavícula.

col·late (kə-lāt′, kŏl′āt, kō′lāt′) tr. **-lat·ed, -lat·ing** *(to compare)* colacionar, cotejar; *(pages)* ordenar.

col·lat·er·al (kə-lăt′ər-əl) I. adj. *(adjacent)* colateral; *(parallel)* paralelo; *(coinciding)* coincidente; *(concomitant)* concomitante; *(corroborating)* corroborante; *(subordinate)* subordinado; *(guaranteed)* con garantía de pago <a c. loan un préstamo con garantía de pago>; *(related)* emparentado colateralmente II. s. COM., FIN. prenda, hipoteca <do you have c. to secure the loan?* ¿tiene usted una prenda para garantizar el préstamo?>; *(relative)* pariente colateral *mf.*

---

col·la·tion (kə-lā′shən) s. *(comparison)* colación *f*, cotejo; *(order)* ordenamiento; *(meal)* colación, refrigerio.

col·league (kŏl′ēg′) s. colega *mf*.

col·lect (kə-lĕkt′) I. tr. *(to gather)* juntar, reunir; *(to accumulate)* coleccionar (sellos, insectos); *(payments)* recaudar ♦ **to c. oneself** controlarse —intr. *(to gather)* juntarse; *(payments)* recaudar II. adj. & adv. TEL. a pagar por el recibidor, de cobro revertido.

col·lect·ed (kə-lĕk′tĭd) adj. *(composed)* recogido, sosegado; *(assembled)* reunido, recogido ♦ **c. works** obras completas.

col·lect·i·ble *o* **col·lect·a·ble** (kə-lĕk′tə-bəl) adj. cobrable.

col·lec·tion (kə-lĕk′shən) s. *(group)* colección *f*; *(accumulation)* acumulación *f*; *(series)* colección, serie *f*; *(compilation)* compilación *f*, recopilación *f*; *(of money due)* cobranza, cobro; *(of taxes)* recaudación *f*; *(donation)* colecta.

col·lec·tive (kə-lĕk′tĭv) I. adj. colectivo II. s. cooperativa.

collective bargaining s. negociaciones colectivas.

collective farm s. granja cooperativa.

collective noun s. GRAM. sustantivo colectivo.

col·lec·tiv·ism (kə-lĕk′tə-vĭz′əm) s. colectivismo.

col·lec·tiv·ist (kə-lĕk′tə-vĭst) s. colectivista *mf*.

col·lec·tiv·i·za·tion (kə-lĕk′tə-vĭ-zā′shən) s. colectivización *f*.

col·lec·tiv·ize (kə-lĕk′tə-vīz′) tr. **-ized, -iz·ing** colectivizar.

col·lec·tor (kə-lĕk′tər) s. ELEC., ELECTRÓN., MEC. colector *m*; *(of taxes)* recaudador *m*; *(of bills)* cobrador *m*; *(of stamps, paintings)* coleccionista *mf*.

col·lege (kŏl′ĭj) s. *(university)* universidad *f*; *(division)* facultad *f* <*the Law C. of the University of Buenos Aires* la Facultad de Derecho de la Universidad de Buenos Aires>; *(campus)* ciudad universitaria *f*; *(association)* asociación (de dentistas, ingenieros) *f*; RELIG. colegio.

College of Cardinals s. Colegio de Cardenales.

col·le·gian (kə-lē′jən) s. estudiante universitario.

col·le·giate (kə-lē′jĭt) *o* **col·le·gi·al** (-jē-əl) adj. *(of a college, students)* universitario; RELIG. colegial.

col·lide (kə-līd′) intr. **-lid·ed, -lid·ing** *(to crash)* chocar; *(to conflict)* estar en conflicto.

col·lie (kŏl′ē) s. perro pastor escocés.

col·lier (kŏl′yər) s. G.B. *(miner)* minero de carbón; *(ship)* barco carbonero.

col·lier·y (kŏl′yə-rē) s. [pl. **-ies**] mina de carbón.

col·li·sion (kə-lĭzh′ən) s. choque *m*; *(conflict)* conflicto.

col·loid (kŏl′oid′) s. & adj. QUÍM. coloide *m*.

col·loid·al (kə-loid′l) adj. coloidal.

col·lo·qui·al (kə-lō′kwē-əl) adj. coloquial, familiar.

col·lo·qui·al·ism (kə-lō′kwē-ə-lĭz′əm) s. *(style)* estilo familiar; *(expression)* expresión familiar *f*.

col·lo·qui·um (kə-lō′kwē-əm) s. [pl. **-qui·ums** *o* **-qui·a** (-kwē-ə)] *(informal meeting)* coloquio; *(seminar)* conferencia, coloquio.

col·lo·quy (kŏl′ə-kwē) s. [pl. **-quies**] coloquio.

Co·los·sians (kə-lŏsh′ənz) s. BÍBL. Colosenses *m*.

col·lude (kə-lōōd′) intr. **-lud·ed, -lud·ing** confabularse, conspirar.

col·lu·sion (kə-lōō′zhən) s. colusión *f*, confabulación *f*.

co·logne (kə-lōn′) s. colonia (perfume).

Co·logne (kə-lōn′) s. Colonia.

Co·lom·bi·a (kə-lŭm′bē-ə) s. Colombia.

Co·lom·bi·an (kə-lŭm′bē-ən) adj. & s. colombiano.

co·lon¹ (kō′lən) s. [pl. **-lons**] GRAM. dos puntos.

co·lon² (kō′lən) s. [pl. **-lons** *o* **-la** (-lə)] ANAT. colon *m*.

co·lon³ (kə-lōn′) s. [pl. **-lon** *o* **-lo·nes** (-lō′nās′)] FIN. colón (unidad monetaria de Costa Rica y El Salvador) *m*.

colo·nel (kûr′nəl) s. MIL. coronel *m*.

co·lo·ni·al (kə-lō′nē-əl) I. adj. *(of a colony)* colonial; *(colonizing)* colonizador II. s. colono.

co·lo·ni·al·ism (kə-lō′nē-ə-lĭz′əm) s. colonialismo.

co·lo·ni·al·ist (kə-lō′nē-ə-lĭst) s. & adj. colonialista *mf*.

col·o·nist (kŏl′ə-nĭst) s. *(colonizer)* colonizador *m*; *(inhabitant)* colono.

col·o·ni·za·tion (kŏl′ə-nĭ-zā′shən) s. colonización *f*.

col·o·nize (kŏl′ə-nīz′) tr. **-nized, -niz·ing** colonizar, poblar

—intr. *(to found)* establecer una colonia; *(to settle in)* establecerse en una colonia.

col·o·niz·er (kŏl′ə-nī′zər) s. colonizador *m*.

col·on·nade (kŏl′ə-nād′) s. ARQ. columnata.

col·o·ny (kŏl′ə-nē) s. [pl. **-nies**] colonia.

col·o·phon (kŏl′ə-fŏn′) s. IMPR. colofón *m*, pie de imprenta *m*.

col·or (kŭl′ər) I. s. *(hue)* color *m* <*primary colors* colores primarios>; *(shade)* matiz *m*; *(dye)* color, tinte *m*; *(complexion)* color (de la cara); *(blush)* rubor *m*; *(racial complexion)* color; *(appearance)* apariencia, aspecto; *(picturesque detail)* color, colorido; ARTE. colorido, tono; MÚS. color, colorido ♦ **colors** *(flag)* bandera, estandarte <*the regimental colors* el estandarte del regimiento>; *(badge)* insignia <*school colors* insignia del colegio>; *(opinion)* opinión <*he stuck to his colors* mantuvo su opinión>; *(character)* carácter *m* <*he showed his true colors* mostró su verdadero carácter>; *(flag salute)* saludo a la bandera • **c. bearer** abanderado, portaestandarte • **c. photography** cromofotografía, fotografía en colores • **c. plate** placa *o* grabado a color • **c. rinse** enjuague de color • **c. television** televisión en color • **fast c.** color que no destiñe • **in c.** en colores • **in full c.** a todo color • **off c.** *(colorless)* descolorido; *(sick)* indispuesto; *(joke)* verde • **to change c.** mudar de color • **to lose c.** palidecer • **with flying colors** *(ship)* con banderas desplegadas; FIG. *(successfully)* con mucho éxito II. tr. *(to give color to)* colorear; *(to paint)* pintar; *(to dye)* teñir; *(to distort)* alterar, desvirtuar; *(to embellish)* embellecer; *(to modify)* modificar; *(to influence)* influir en —intr. *(to become colored)* colorearse; *(to change color)* cambiar de color; *(to blush)* sonrojarse, ruborizarse.

col·or·a·tion (kŭl′ə-rā′shən) s. *(pattern)* coloración *f*; *(beliefs)* ideario.

color bearer s. abanderado.

col·or·blind (kŭl′ər-blīnd′) adj. OFTAL. daltoniano.

col·or·blind·ness (kŭl′ər-blīnd′nĭs) s. OFTAL. daltonismo.

col·ored (kŭl′ərd) I. adj. *(having color)* coloreado, de color; *(non-Caucasian)* de color; *(of mixed race)* de sangre mezclada; *(biased)* tendencioso <*his opinions are c.* sus opiniones son tendenciosas> II. s. persona de color.

col·or·fast (kŭl′ər-făst′) adj. de color fijo, que no destiñe.

col·or·ful (kŭl′ər-fəl) adj. *(vivid)* de gran colorido; *(exciting)* animado; *(picturesque)* pintoresco (personaje).

color guard s. escolta de bandera.

col·or·ing (kŭl′ər-ĭng) s. *(coloration)* coloración *f*; *(dye)* colorante *m*; *(appearance)* coloración, colorido.

col·or·less (kŭl′ər-lĭs) adj. *(without color)* incoloro, sin color; *(pallid)* descolorido, pálido; *(dull)* soso, aburrido.

color line s. FIG. barrera racial.

co·los·sal (kə-lŏs′əl) adj. colosal.

co·los·sus (kə-lŏs′əs) s. [pl. **-los·si** (-lŏs′ī′) *o* **-los·sus·es**] coloso.

co·los·to·my (kə-lŏs′tə-mē) s. [pl. **-mies**] CIR. colostomía.

co·los·trum (kə-lŏs′trəm) s. calostro, primera leche después del parto.

col·our (kŭl′ər) s. G.B. var. de **color**.

colt (kōlt) s. *(horse)* potro; *(youth)* mozuelo; *(beginner)* novato.

colt·ish (kōl′tĭsh) adj. *(frisky)* retozón, juguetón; *(youthful)* juvenil.

Co·lum·bus (kə-lŭm′bəs) s. Colón ♦ **C. Day** Día de la Hispanidad *o* de la Raza (12 de octubre).

col·umn (kŏl′əm) s. columna.

col·um·nist (kŏl′əm-nĭst) s. columnista *mf*.

co·ma (kō′mə) s. MED. coma *m*.

co·ma·tose (kō′mə-tōs′, kŏm′ə-) adj. MED. comatoso.

comb (kōm) I. s. *(for the hair)* peine *m*; *(currycomb)* almohaza; *(for textiles)* carda; ORNIT. *(crest)* cresta; *(honeycomb)* panal *m* II. tr. *(to arrange hair)* peinar; *(to card)* cardar; *(to search)* registrar (detalladamente) —intr. *(to break)* romperse <*the waves combed violently* las olas rompieron violentamente>.

com·bat I. tr. (kəm-băt′, kŏm′băt′) *(to fight against)* pelear contra; *(to oppose in battle)* dar batalla; *(to oppose)* combatir; *(to resist)* resistir —intr. *(to engage in fighting)*

ã **rey** / ä **año** / b **boca** / ch **chico** / d **dar** / ĕ **el** / ē **mil** / g **gato** / h **joya** / hw **juez** / ī **aire** / k **casa** / kw **cuan** /

combatir; (to contend) contender; (to struggle) luchar **II.** s. (kŏm-băt') (battle) combate m; (strife) lucha.

com·bat·ant (kəm-băt'nt, kŏm'bə-tnt) s. & adj. combatiente m.

combat fatigue s. fatiga de combate.

com·bat·ive (kəm-băt'ĭv) adj. combativo, belicoso.

comb·er (kō'mər) s. (of wool) cardador m; (wave) ola encrespada.

com·bi·na·tion (kŏm'bə-nā'shən) s. (union) combinación f; (alliance) alianza; (association) asociación f; (lock code) combinación; (article of clothing) combinación; (mix) mezcla.

combination lock s. cerradura de combinación.

com·bine I. tr. (kəm-bīn') **-bined, -bin·ing** (to unite) combinar; (to mix) mezclar —intr. (to become united) combinarse; (to coalesce) fundirse; (to join forces) unirse; (to mix) mezclar **II.** s. (kŏm'bīn') (harvester) segadora; (association) asociación f <the farmers' c. la asociación de labradores>; (mix) mezcla; (combination) combinación f.

com·bined (kəm-bīnd') adj. (mixed) combinado, compuesto; (united) unido; (effort) conjunto, colectivo; MIL. (operation) combinado.

com·bo (kŏm'bō) s. [pl. **-bos**] MÚS. conjunto; JER. (combination) combinación f.

com·bus·ti·ble (kəm-bŭs'tə-bəl) **I.** adj. (flammable) combustible; (ardent) impetuoso, fogoso **II.** s. combustible m.

com·bus·tion (kəm-bŭs'chən) s. combustión f.

combustion chamber s. cámara de combustión.

come (kŭm) **I.** intr. **came** (kām), **come, com·ing** (to move toward) venir <can you c. to my house? ¿puedes venir a mi casa?>; (to approach) aproximarse, acercarse; (to arrive at) llegar <we finally came to a mutual understanding finalmente llegamos a un entendimiento mutuo>; (to reach) llegar <the dress came to her knees el vestido le llegaba a las rodillas>; (to result) resultar, suceder <this comes of your carelessness esto sucede por tu falta de cuidado>; (to originate) proceder, venir de <that girl comes from a good family esa niña viene de una buena familia>; (to amount to) ascender a <his expenses came to more than his income sus gastos ascendieron a más que sus ingresos>; (to available) venir <these shoes c. in all sizes estos zapatos vienen en todas las medidas>; (to cost) costar <the good things in life c. high en la vida las cosas buenas cuestan caro>; VULG. (to experience orgasm) tener un orgasmo, venirse ♦ c. hell or high water JER. caigan rayos o centellas • c. what may pase lo que pase ♦ how c.? FAM. ¿cómo es posible? • to c. about (to happen) suceder, ocurrir; MARÍT. virar • to c. across (to find) encontrarse con; (to be understood) ser comprendido • to c. after (to follow) venir después de; (to pursue) venir en busca de • to c. alive cobrar vida • to c. along (to accompany) venir, acompañar; (to progress) progresar • to c. apart separarse, desunirse • to c. around o round (to turn around) cambiar de dirección; MARÍT. virar; (to visit) hacer una visita; (to regain consciousness) volver en sí; (to recover) reponerse; (to yield) ceder • to c. at atacar • to c. away (to leave) irse, retirarse; (to become separated) desprenderse • to c. back (to return) volver; (to respond) replicar; (to be recalled) volver a la mente o memoria • to c. before (to precede) preceder; (to arrive before) llegar antes; DER. (to appear) comparecer ante (juez, tribunal) • to c. between interponerse entre • to c. by (to pass near) pasar junto a; (to visit) hacer una visita; (to obtain) obtener, lograr • to c. clean JER. confesarlo todo • to c. down (to descend) bajar; (to collapse) desplomarse, derrumbarse; (to fall) caerse; (to deteriorate) venir a menos • to c. down on o upon (to collapse) caer encima <the wall came down on his head la pared le cayó sobre la cabeza>; (to reproach) reprochar • to c. down to reducirse a <the discussion finally came down to the subject of money la conversación finalmente se redujo al asunto del dinero> • to c. down with FAM. caer enfermo con • to c. easy costar poco esfuerzo, resultar fácil <math comes easy to me las matemáticas me resultan fáciles> • to c. first (to precede) preceder, venir primero; (to take priority) ser lo más importante • to c. forth (to appear) aparecer, hacer su aparición; (to step forward) adelantarse • to c. forward

ofrecerse, presentarse • to c. in (to enter) entrar; (to arrive) llegar <my horse came in second mi caballo llegó segundo>; (to fit in) figurar, entrar • to c. in for FAM. recibir • to c. in handy FAM. resultar útil u oportuno • to c. into heredar, recibir (herencia, dinero) • to c. into one's own FIG. hacer valer los derechos o méritos de uno • to c. into play FIG. entrar en juego • to c. into sight o view aparecer, asomar • to c. into the world FIG. nacer, venir al mundo • to c. near (to approach) acercarse; FAM. (to almost do) faltar poco para <she came near committing suicide faltó poco para que ella se suicidara> • to c. next venir después (de), seguir • to c. of age llegar a la mayoría de edad • to c. off (to become loose) soltarse, separarse; (to acquit oneself) salir (bien, mal) <he came off badly at the meeting él no salió bien en la conferencia>; (to happen) suceder, tener lugar <the party came off last Friday la fiesta tuvo lugar el viernes pasado>; (to result) resultar <my meeting with him did not c. off as I expected mi reunión con él no resultó como esperaba>; (to succeed) tener éxito, salir bien • to c. on TEAT. salir a escena; (to present oneself) presentarse <he comes on as a true professional él se presenta como un verdadero profesional> • to c. one's way FAM. caerle a uno <the chance to go to France came my way unexpectedly la oportunidad de ir a Francia me cayó inesperadamente> • to c. on to FAM. tirarse a • to c. out salir <she came out and told them to be quiet salió y les dijo que se callaran>; (to be published) salir, publicarse; (to debut) debutar, ser presentado en sociedad; (to result) resultar <everything came out fine todo resultó bien>; (to attend) asistir <how many people came out for the wedding? ¿cuánta gente asistió a la boda?>; (to declare oneself) pronunciarse, declararse <the committee came out in favor of the new law el comité se declaró a favor de la nueva ley>; (to be removed) salir, quitarse <the spot on the carpet came out la mancha en la alfombra salió>; (to become known) salir a la luz, revelarse <the truth came out during the trial la verdad se reveló durante el juicio>; (to bloom) florecer • to c. out with (to disclose) revelar, publicar <the government came out with a new tax el gobierno publicó un nuevo impuesto>; (to offer) salir con, ofrecer <the company is coming out with a new line of hats la compañía está ofreciendo una nueva línea de sombreros>; FAM. (to say) saltar con, soltar (comentario, maldición) • to c. over (to happen) sobrevenir, invadir <strange feelings came over her all of a sudden unos sentimientos muy extraños la invadieron de repente>; FAM. (to pay a visit) venir <she came over to see me vino a ver>; (to change sides) pasarse a <he came over to our side of the argument se pasó a nuestro lado de la disputa> • to c. through (to do what is wanted) cumplir <I asked for his help and he came through le pedí que me ayudara y él cumplió>; (to become manifest) expresarse, manifestarse <his ideas never came through clearly sus ideas nunca se manifestaron claramente>; (to endure) pasar por, salir de <he came through the fight without a scratch salió de la pelea sin un rasguño> • to c. through with JER. cumplir con • to c. to (to regain consciousness) recobrar los sentidos, volver en sí; (to cross one's mind) ocurrírsele <her name came to me all of a sudden se me ocurrió su nombre de repente>; (to amount to) reducirse a <all of his efforts came to nothing todos sus esfuerzos se redujeron a nada>; (to manage to) llegar a, lograr <how did you c. to do that all by yourself? ¿cómo lograste hacer eso solo?>; MARÍT. (to turn) orzar; (to stop) detenerse • to c. to a halt detenerse • to c. to a head FIG. madurar, definirse • to c. to an end acabarse, llegar al fin • to c. to a point rematar o acabar en punta • to c. to blows FAM. venirse a las manos, llegar a golpes • to c. together reunirse, juntarse • to c. to grips with FAM. afrontar, habérselas con • to c. to light FIG. salir a la luz, descubrirse • to c. to mind venir a la memoria • to c. to one's senses FIG. recobrar la razón o los sentidos • to c. to pass suceder, ocurrir • to c. to terms llegar a un acuerdo • to c. to the point venir al caso, ir al grano • to c. to the rescue acudir en ayuda • to c. true realizarse • to c. under (to be classified under) clasificarse entre, figurar entre; (to be subject to) caer bajo, estar sometido a (poder, influencia) • **to c. undone** deshacerse • **to c. up** *(to ascend)* subir; *(to arise)* presentarse, surgir *<the same problem came up repeatedly* el mismo problema surgió repetidas veces>; *(to emerge)* brotar; *(to be mentioned)* ser mencionado *<that idea never came up in our discussion* esa idea nunca fue mencionada en nuestra conversación> • **to c. up against** tropezar con, dar con • **to c. up to** *(to equal)* igualar, estar a la altura de *<your work does not c. up to hers* tu trabajo no está a la altura del de ella>; *(to reach a height)* llegar hasta; *(to approach)* acercarse a, abordar *<she came up to him and asked him a question* ella se le acercó y le hizo una pregunta> • **to c. up with** sugerir, proponer • **to c. within** entrar dentro de, estar dentro de • **when it comes to** cuando se trata de *<when it comes to money, you can't count on him* cuando se trata de asuntos de dinero, no se puede contar con él> **II.** interj. ¡venga!, ¡ven! ♦ **c. again!** repítalo, ¿cómo? • **c. in!** ¡adelante!, ¡pase! • **c. off it!** FAM. ¡déjate de tonterías!, ¡no me vengas con eso! • **c. now!** ¡vamos!, ¡no es para tanto! • **c. on!** FAM. *(hurry up!)* ¡date prisa!, ¡apúrate!; *(you're kidding!)* ¡no me digas! **III.** s. VULG. acabada, leche *f.*

come·back (kŭm′băk′) s. *(return)* retorno, reaparición *f;* *(retort)* réplica, respuesta ingeniosa ♦ **to make a c.** restablecerse, reaparecer.

co·me·di·an (kə-mē′dē-ən) s. *(joker)* cómico; *(actor)* comediante *m.*

co·me·dic (kə-mē′dĭk) adj. *(funny)* cómico; *(comedy)* de comedia.

co·me·di·enne (kə-mē′dē-ĕn′) s. *(joker)* cómica; *(actress)* comedianta.

come·down (kŭm′doun′) s. *(downfall)* bajón *m,* perdida de rango; *(in self-esteem)* humillación *f;* *(disappointment)* revés *m.*

com·e·dy (kŏm′ĭ-dē) s. [pl. **-dies**] comedia.

comedy of manners s. TEAT. comedia de costumbres.

come-hith·er (kŭm-hĭth′ər) adj. seductor, sugestivo.

come·ly (kŭm′lē) adj. **-li·er, -li·est** atractivo.

come-on (kŭm′ŏn′) s. *(incentive)* aliciente *m,* incentivo; FAM. *(proposition)* invitación (sexual) *f.*

com·er (kŭm′ər) s. *(arrival)* persona que llega *<the first c.* el primero en llegar>; FAM. *(rising star)* persona prometedora.

co·mes·ti·ble (kə-mĕs′tə-bəl) adj. & s. comestible *m.*

com·et (kŏm′ĭt) s. ASTRON. cometa *m.*

come·up·pance (kŭm-ŭp′əns) s. FAM. castigo merecido.

com·fort (kŭm′fərt) **I.** tr. *(to hearten)* confortar; *(to console)* consolar; *(to relieve)* aliviar **II.** s. *(well-being)* confort *m;* *(relief)* alivio; *(assistance)* asistencia *<to give c. to the enemy* dar asistencia al enemigo>; *(consolation)* consuelo; *(ease)* comodidad *f <the c. of his own bed* la comodidad de su propia cama> • **to be a c.** ser un consuelo.

com·fort·a·ble (kŭm′fər-tə-bəl) adj. *(easy)* confortable, cómodo; FAM. *(sufficient)* suficiente, adecuado.

com·fort·a·bly (kŭm′fər-tə-blē) adv. *(easily)* confortablemente, cómodamente; FAM. *(sufficiently)* suficientemente.

com·fort·er (kŭm′fər-tər) s. *(consoler)* consolador *m;* *(quilt)* edredón *m;* G.B. *(scarf)* bufanda.

comfort station s. excusado público, servicio.

com·fy (kŭm′fē) adj. **-fi·er, -fi·est** FAM. cómodo, confortable.

com·ic (kŏm′ĭk) **I.** adj. cómico **II.** s. *(person)* cómico; *(book)* revista de historietas ilustradas ♦ **comics** tiras cómicas.

com·i·cal (kŏm′ĭ-kəl) adj. cómico.

comic opera s. ópera cómica, ópera bufa.

comic strip s. tira cómica.

com·ing (kŭm′ĭng) **I.** adj. *(next)* venidero, próximo; FAM. *(promising)* prometedor **II.** s. venida, llegada.

com·ing-out (kŭm′ĭng-out′) s. FAM. debut *m,* presentación en sociedad *f.*

com·ma (kŏm′ə) s. GRAM. coma.

com·mand (kə-mănd′) **I.** tr. *(to control)* mandar; *(to give orders)* ordenar; *(to have authority over)* mandar; *(to rule)* regir; *(to have at one's disposal)* disponer de, poseer; *(to deserve)* infundir *<his bravery commanded respect* su valor infundió respeto>; *(to exact)* exigir; *(to overlook)* dominar *<a mountain commanding the valley* una montaña que

domina el valle> —intr. *(to give commands)* dar órdenes; *(to exercise authority)* mandar, estar en control **II.** s. *(act)* mando; *(order)* orden *f;* *(authority)* mandato, mando; *(mastery)* dominio *<the c. of four languages* el dominio de cuatro idiomas>; MIL. *(jurisdiction)* comando ♦ **at one's c.** a la disposición de uno • **c. headquarters** centro de comando • **c. performance** función pedida por un monarca • **c. post** puesto de mando • **high c.** alto mando • **to be in c. of** estar al mando de • **to take c.** tomar el mando • **under the c. of** al mando de.

com·man·dant (kŏm′ən-dănt′, -dänt′) s. MIL. comandante *m.*

com·man·deer (kŏm′ən-dîr′) tr. *(to conscript)* reclutar por la fuerza; *(to confiscate)* requisar, confiscar; FAM. *(to seize)* apoderarse de.

com·mand·er (kə-măn′dər) s. *(leader)* jefe *m;* MARÍT. capitán de fragata *m;* MIL. comandante *m;* *(in knightly or fraternal orders)* comendador *m.*

commander in chief s. [pl. **commanders in chief**] MIL. comandante en jefe *m.*

com·mand·ing (kə-măn′dĭng) adj. *(in command)* que está al mando; *(impressive)* imponente; *(dominating)* dominante.

commanding officer s. MIL. jefe *m,* comandante *m.*

com·mand·ment (kə-mănd′mənt) s. *(command)* orden *f;* RELIG. mandamiento.

com·man·do (kə-măn′dō) s. [pl. **-dos** *o* **-does**] MIL. comando.

com·mem·o·rate (kə-mĕm′ə-rāt′) tr. **-rat·ed, -rat·ing** conmemorar.

com·mem·o·ra·tion (kə-mĕm′ə-rā′shən) s. conmemoración *f.*

com·mem·o·ra·tive (kə-mĕm′ər-ə-tĭv′, -rā′-) **I.** adj. conmemorativo **II.** s. objeto *o* acto conmemorativo.

com·mence (kə-mĕns′) tr. & intr. **-menced, -menc·ing** comenzar.

com·mence·ment (kə-mĕns′mənt) s. *(start)* comienzo, principio; *(ceremony)* ceremonia de entrega de diplomas.

com·mend (kə-mĕnd′) tr. *(to praise)* elogiar, alabar; *(to recommend)* recomendar; *(to entrust)* encomendar, confiar.

com·mend·a·ble (kə-mĕn′də-bəl) adj. digno de elogio, loable.

com·men·da·tion (kŏm′ən-dā′shən) s. *(praise)* elogio, alabanza; *(recommendation)* recomendación *f;* *(citation)* mención *f.*

com·men·da·to·ry (kə-mĕn′də-tôr′ē) adj. laudatorio, elogioso.

com·men·sal (kə-mĕn′səl) adj. & s. comensal *m.*

com·men·su·ra·ble (kə-mĕn′sər-ə-bəl, -shər-) adj. *(measurable)* conmensurable; *(fitting)* proporcionado.

com·men·su·rate (kə-mĕn′sər-ĭt, -shər-) adj. *(proportionate)* proporcionado; *(commensurable)* conmensurable.

com·ment (kŏm′ĕnt′) **I.** s. *(annotation)* comentario; *(remark)* observación *f;* *(gossip)* comentario **II.** intr. comentar, observar.

com·men·tar·y (kŏm′ən-tĕr′ē) s. [pl. **-ies**] comentario ♦ **commentaries** *(exegesis)* exégesis *f;* *(memoir)* memoria.

com·men·tate (kŏm′ən-tāt′) tr. & intr. **-tat·ed, -tat·ing** comentar.

com·men·ta·tor (kŏm′ən-tā′tər) s. *(annotator)* comentarista *mf;* *(announcer)* locutor *m.*

com·merce (kŏm′ərs) s. *(business)* comercio; *(social exchange)* trato; *(sexual intercourse)* ayuntamiento carnal.

com·mer·cial (kə-mûr′shəl) **I.** adj. comercial **II.** s. RAD., TELEV. anuncio.

commercial bank s. banco comercial.

com·mer·cial·ism (kə-mûr′shə-lĭz′əm) s. comercialismo, mercantilismo.

com·mer·cial·ize (kə-mûr′shə-līz′) tr. **-ized, -iz·ing** comercializar.

commercial paper s. documento *o* instrumento negociable.

commercial traveler s. viajante de comercio *m.*

com·mie (kŏm′ē) s. FAM. rojo, comunista *mf.*

com·min·gle (kə-mĭng′gəl) tr. & intr. **-gled, -gling** mezclar(se).

ă rey / ä año / b **boca** / ch **chico** / d **dar** / ĕ **el** / ē **mil** / g **gato** / h **joya** / ′hw **juez** / ī **aire** / k **casa** / kw **cuan** /

com·mis·er·ate (kə-mĭz′ə-rāt′) tr. & intr. **-at·ed, -at·ing** compadecer(se), apiadar(se) ♦ **to c. with** compadecerse de.
com·mis·er·a·tion (kə-mĭz′ə-rā′shən) s. conmiseración *f,* compasión *f.*
com·mis·sar (kŏm′ĭ-sär′) s. comisario.
com·mis·sar·i·at (kŏm′ĭ-sâr′ē-ĭt) s. *(government department)* comisaría; MIL. intendencia; *(food supply)* aprovisionamiento de alimentos.
com·mis·sar·y (kŏm′ĭ-sĕr′ē) s. [pl. **-ies**] *(store)* economato; *(delegate)* comisario, delegado.
com·mis·sion (kə-mĭsh′ən) **I.** s. *(act)* comisión *f; (task)* misión *f; (authorization)* autorización *f; (official group)* delegación *f; (percentage)* comisión <*a c. of five per cent* una comisión del cinco por ciento>; *(perpetration)* perpetración *f,* ejecución *f;* MIL. *(conferral of rank)* nombramiento; *(rank)* grado (de oficial, en las fuerzas armadas) ♦ **in c.** *(ship, airplane)* en servicio activo; *(in usable condition)* usable • **out of c.** *(ship, airplane)* fuera de servicio; *(not operating)* descompuesto, averiado; *(person)* fuera de servicio • **to put out of c.** *(to retire)* jubilar, retirar del servicio; *(to ruin)* arruinar, inutilizar; FAM. *(to finish off)* poner fuera de combate, acabar con • **to work on c.** trabajar a comisión **II.** tr. MIL. *(to grant a commission to)* nombrar <*he was commissioned captain* lo nombraron capitán>; *(to order)* encargar, mandar a hacer <*to c. a painting* mandar a hacer un cuadro>; *(ship)* poner en servicio.
commissioned officer s. MIL. oficial *m;* MARÍT. alférez *m.*
com·mis·sion·er (kə-mĭsh′ə-nər) s. *(member)* miembro de una comisión; *(official)* comisario.
com·mit (kə-mĭt′) tr. **-mit·ted, -mit·ting** *(to make, perform)* cometer, hacer <*to c. an error* cometer un error>; *(to perpetrate)* cometer <*to c. a crime* cometer un crimen>; *(to entrust)* encomendar <*I c. it to your good will* lo encomiendo a tu buena voluntad>; *(to jail)* encarcelar; *(to institutionalize)* internar; *(to dispose of)* entregar <*the document was committed to the flames* el documento fue entregado a las llamas>; *(to refer to a committee)* someter a una comisión ♦ **to c. oneself** comprometerse • **to c. suicide** suicidarse • **to c. to memory** aprender de memoria • **to c. to paper** *o* **writing** consignar por escrito.
com·mit·ment (kə-mĭt′mənt) s. *(pledge)* compromiso; *(assignment)* cometido; *(institutionalization)* internamiento, reclusión *f; (court order)* auto de prisión; *(obligation)* obligación *f; (of a bill)* devolución a una comisión *f.*
com·mit·tal (kə-mĭt′l) s. *(pledge)* compromiso; *(entrusting)* encargo; *(confinement)* confinamiento, reclusión *f; (pledging)* obligación *f,* cometido; *(burial)* entierro.
com·mit·tee (kə-mĭt′ē) s. *(group of people)* comité *m,* comisión *f; (trustee)* curador *m.*
com·mode (kə-mōd′) s. *(chest of drawers)* cómoda; *(washbowl)* palanganero; *(toilet)* retrete *m; (chair)* silla retrete.
com·mo·di·ous (kə-mō′dē-əs) adj. *(spacious)* espacioso, amplio; ANT. *(suitable)* cómodo, conveniente.
com·mod·i·ty (kə-mŏd′ĭ-tē) s. [pl. **-ties**] mercancía, mercadería.
com·mo·dore (kŏm′ə-dôr′) s. MARÍT. comodoro.
com·mon (kŏm′ən) **I.** adj. **-er, -est** *(joint)* común <*common interests* intereses comunes>; *(public)* público <*the c. good* el bien público>; *(widespread)* general <*c. knowledge* de conocimiento general>; *(frequent)* usual, frecuente <*a c. occurrence* un caso frecuente>; *(ordinary)* ordinario; *(average)* común, general <*the c. spectator* el espectador común>; *(mediocre)* mediocre; *(second-rate)* inferior; *(vulgar)* vulgar, ordinario <*c. manners* modales ordinarios>; GRAM. común ♦ **c. ground** tema de interés mutuo • **in c.** en común • **to have a lot in c.** tener muchos intereses en común **II.** s. *(land)* ejido, campo comunal; DER. *(right)* derecho conjunto ♦ **commons** *(people)* vulgo, populacho; G.B. comunes • **Commons** G.B. Cámara de los Comunes.
com·mon·age (kŏm′ə-nĭj) s. derecho de pasto en un terreno comunal.
com·mon·al·ty (kŏm′ə-nəl-tē) *o* **com·mon·al·i·ty** (kŏm′-ə-năl′ĭ-tē) s. [pl. **-ties**] *(common people)* vulgo, pueblo; *(corporation)* corporación *f; (entire group)* comunidad *f,* conjunto.

common carrier s. transportista *m.*
common cold s. MED. resfriado, catarro.
common denominator s. MAT. común denominador *m; (trait)* denominador común.
com·mon·er (kŏm′ə-nər) s. plebeyo.
common factor s. factor común *m.*
common fraction s. MAT. fracción ordinaria.
common law s. DER. derecho consuetudinario.
com·mon-law marriage (kŏm′ən-lô′) s. DER. matrimonio consensual.
Common Market s. Mercado Común.
common multiple s. MAT. múltiple común *m.*
common noun s. GRAM. sustantivo *o* nombre común *m.*
com·mon·place (kŏm′ən-plās′) **I.** adj. común, ordinario **II.** s. lugar común *m.*
common sense s. sentido común.
common stock s. COM., FIN. acciones ordinarias.
com·mon·wealth (kŏm′ən-wĕlth′) s. *(people)* comunidad *f; (state)* república ♦ **C. of Nations** Comunidad de Naciones.
com·mo·tion (kə-mō′shən) s. *(disturbance)* disturbio; *(hubbub)* alboroto; *(mental turmoil)* conmoción *f.*
com·mu·nal (kə-myōō′nəl, kŏm′yə-) adj. comunal.
com·mu·nal·ism (kə-myōō′nə-lĭz′əm, kŏm′yə-nə-) s. POL. confederación de comunas *f; (theory)* teoría de propiedad comunal.
com·mune¹ (kə-myōōn′) intr. **-muned, -mun·ing** *(to communicate)* comunicarse, compartir pensamientos y sentimientos; RELIG. comulgar.
com·mune² (kŏm′yōōn′, kə-myōōn′) s. POL. municipio, comuna; *(community)* vivienda colectiva.
com·mu·ni·ca·ble (kə-myōō′nĭ-kə-bəl) adj. *(transmissible)* comunicable; *(communicative)* comunicativo; *(contagious)* contagioso.
com·mu·ni·cant (kə-myōō′nĭ-kənt) **I.** s. RELIG. comulgante *m; (informer)* informante **II.** adj. comunicante.
com·mu·ni·cate (kə-myōō′nĭ-kāt′) tr. **-cat·ed, -cat·ing** *(to convey)* comunicar; *(to transmit a disease)* contagiar —intr. *(to relate)* comunicarse; REL. comulgar.
com·mu·ni·ca·tion (kə-myōō′nĭ-kā′shən) s. *(transmission)* comunicación *f; (message)* mensaje *m,* comunicación *f* ♦ **communications** comunicaciones.
communications satellite s. satélite de comunicación *m.*
com·mu·ni·ca·tive (kə-myōō′nĭ-kā′tĭv, -kə-tĭv) adj. comunicativo.
com·mu·ni·ca·tor (kə-myōō′nĭ-kā′tər) s. persona *o* cosa comunicadora.
com·mun·ion (kə-myōōn′yən) s. comunión *f* ♦ **C.** RELIG. comunión *f.*
com·mu·ni·qué (kə-myōō′nĭ-kā′) s. comunicado oficial.
com·mu·nism (kŏm′yə-nĭz′əm) s. comunismo.
com·mu·nist (kŏm′yə-nĭst) s. & adj. comunista *mf.*
com·mu·nis·tic (kŏm′yə-nĭs′tĭk) adj. comunista.
com·mu·ni·ty (kə-myōō′nĭ-tē) s. [pl. **-ties**] *(locality)* comunidad *f; (society as a whole)* sociedad *f; (local inhabitants)* vecindario.
community center s. centro social.
community chest s. fondo para beneficencia pública.
community property s. DER. *(joint estate)* bienes gananciales *m; (public property)* bienes comunales.
com·mu·nize (kŏm′yə-nīz′) tr. **-nized, -niz·ing** *(property)* convertir en propiedad comunal; *(to make communist)* volver comunista.
com·mut·a·ble (kə-myōō′tə-bəl) adj. *(exchangeable)* conmutable, intercambiable; DER. *(penalty)* conmutable.
com·mu·ta·tion (kŏm′yə-tā′shən) s. *(exchange)* conmutación *f,* intercambio; *(travel)* viajes diarios; DER., ELEC. conmutación *f.*
commutation ticket s. billete de abono *m.*
com·mu·ta·tive (kŏm′yə-tā′tĭv, kə-myōō′tə-tĭv) adj. conmutativo.
com·mu·ta·tor (kŏm′yə-tā′tər) s. ELEC. conmutador *m.*
com·mute (kə-myōōt′) **I.** tr. **-mut·ed, -mut·ing** *(to exchange)* conmutar, intercambiar; DER. *(a penalty)* conmutar —intr. viajar diariamente al lugar en que se trabaja **II.** s. viaje diario.

---

com·mut·er (kə-myōō'tər) s. persona que viaja diariamente (esp. al trabajo).

Com·o·ros (kŏm'ə-rōz) s. Comores f.

com·pact¹ **I.** adj. (kəm-păkt', kŏm'păkt') *(packed together)* compacto; *(compressed)* comprimido; *(concise)* conciso <a c. narration un relato conciso> **II.** tr. (kəm-păkt') *(to compress)* comprimir; *(to compose)* componer, preparar **III.** s. (kŏm'păkt') *(for make-up)* polvera; *(automobile)* automóvil compacto o pequeño.

com·pact² (kŏm'păkt') s. pacto, convenio.

com·pac·tor (kəm-păk'tər, kŏm'păk'-) s. compresor de basura m.

com·pan·ion (kəm-păn'yən) s. *(comrade)* compañero; *(assistant)* acompañante mf; *(one of a set)* compañero.

com·pan·ion·a·ble (kəm-păn'yə-nə-bəl) s. sociable.

com·pan·ion·ship (kəm-păn'yən-shĭp') s. compañerismo, camaradería.

com·pan·ion·way (kəm-păn'yən-wā') s. MARÍT. escalera de cámara.

com·pa·ny (kŭm'pə-nē) s. [pl. **-nies**] *(business)* compañía, empresa; *(group)* grupo <a c. of athletes un grupo de atletas>; *(companions)* compañía <he is in good c. está en buena compañía>; *(guest)* invitado <we have c. for dinner tenemos invitados para la cena>; *(companionship)* compañerismo; *(in theater)* compañía; MARÍT. tripulación f; MIL. compañía ♦ **to keep c. with** *(to associate)* asociarse con; *(to court)* cortejar, galantear ♦ **to keep someone c.** hacerle compañía a alguien • **to part c.** separarse.

com·pa·ra·bil·i·ty (kŏm'pər-ə-bĭl'ĭ-tē) o **com·pa·ra·ble·ness** (kŏm'pər-ə-bəl-nĭs) s. comparabilidad f.

com·pa·ra·ble (kŏm'pər-ə-bəl) adj. comparable.

com·par·a·tive (kəm-păr'ə-tĭv) **I.** adj. *(involving comparison)* comparativo; *(literature, studies)* comparado; *(relative)* relativo <c. prosperity prosperidad relativa> ♦ **c. literature** EDUC. literatura comparada **II.** s. GRAM. comparativo.

com·pare (kəm-pâr') **I.** tr. **-pared, -par·ing** *(to liken)* comparar; *(to examine)* comparar; GRAM. formar el comparativo de ♦ **as compared with** comparado con —intr. poderse comparar **II.** s. ♦ **beyond c.** incomparable, sin igual.

com·par·i·son (kəm-păr'ĭ-sən) s. comparación f ♦ **by c.** en comparación.

com·part·ment (kəm-pärt'mənt) s. compartimiento.

com·part·men·tal·ize (kŏm'pärt-mĕn'tl-īz', kəm-pärt'-) tr. **-ized, -iz·ing** dividir en compartimientos.

com·pass (kŭm'pəs) **I.** s. *(magnetic needle)* brújula, compás m; *(circumference)* perímetro, circuito <outside the c. of the fence fuera del perímetro de la cerca>; *(space)* espacio, recinto; *(scope)* alcance m; MÚS. extensión f ♦ **c.** o **compasses** GEOM. compás **II.** tr. *(to circle)* dar la vuelta a; *(to surround)* circundar, rodear; *(to understand)* captar, concebir; *(to achieve)* conseguir, lograr; *(to plot)* tramar, maquinar **III.** adj. circular, redondo.

com·pas·sion (kəm-păsh'ən) s. compasión f.

com·pas·sion·ate (kəm-păsh'ə-nĭt) adj. compasivo.

com·pat·i·bil·i·ty (kəm-păt'ə-bĭl'ĭ-tē) s. compatibilidad f.

com·pat·i·ble (kəm-păt'ə-bəl) adj. compatible.

com·pa·tri·ot (kəm-pā'trē-ət) s. compatriota mf.

com·peer (kŏm'pîr', kəm-pîr') s. *(equal)* igual m, par m; *(companion)* compañero.

com·pel (kəm-pĕl') tr. **-pelled, -pel·ling** *(to force)* compeler, obligar; *(to exact)* exigir, requerir; *(respect)* imponer.

com·pel·ling (kəm-pĕl'ĭng) adj. *(compulsory)* compulsivo, obligatorio; *(commanding)* irresistible; *(voice)* autoritario; *(evidence)* incontestable; *(need)* apremiante.

com·pen·di·ous (kəm-pĕn'dē-əs) adj. compendioso, sucinto.

com·pen·di·um (kəm-pĕn'dē-əm) [pl. **-di·ums** o **-di·a** (-dē-ə)] s. compendio, sinopsis f.

com·pen·sate (kŏm'pən-sāt') tr. **-sat·ed, -sat·ing** *(to counterbalance)* compensar; *(to pay)* remunerar; *(to reimburse)* indemnizar —intr. ♦ **to c. for** compensar.

com·pen·sa·tion (kŏm'pən-sā'shən) s. *(act)* compensación f; *(payment)* remuneración f; *(for a loss)* indemnización f <workers' c. indemnización obrera>; BIOL. compensación.

com·pen·sa·tor (kŏm'pən-sā'tər) s. compensador m.

com·pen·sa·to·ry (kəm-pĕn'sə-tôr'ē) adj. compensatorio.

com·pete (kəm-pēt') intr. **-pet·ed, -pet·ing** competir ♦ **to c. in** concursar o tomar parte en (una carrera, partido).

com·pe·tence (kŏm'pĭ-tns) s. *(of a person, court)* competencia; *(means)* subsistencia.

com·pe·tent (kŏm'pĭ-tnt) s. competente.

com·pe·ti·tion (kŏm'pĭ-tĭsh'ən) s. competencia ♦ **the c.** nuestros competidores.

com·pet·i·tive (kəm-pĕt'ĭ-tĭv) adj. *(price)* competitivo; *(person)* competidor; *(spirit)* de competencia ♦ **c. examination** oposiciones.

com·pet·i·tive·ness (kəm-pĕt'ĭ-tĭv-nĭs) s. *(of prices)* carácter competitivo; *(of a person)* espíritu de competencia.

com·pet·i·tor (kəm-pĕt'ĭ-tər) s. competidor m.

com·pi·la·tion (kŏm'pə-lā'shən) s. compilación f, recopilación f.

com·pile (kəm-pīl') tr. **-piled, -pil·ing** compilar, recopilar.

com·pil·er (kəm-pī'lər) s. compilador m, recopilador m.

com·pla·cen·cy (kəm-plā'sən-sē) o **com·pla·cence** (-səns) s. *(gratification)* complacencia; *(smugness)* satisfacción de sí mismo f.

com·pla·cent (kəm-plā'sənt) adj. satisfecho o pagado de sí mismo.

com·plain (kəm-plān') intr. *(to gripe)* quejarse <to c. about a headache quejarse de un dolor de cabeza>; DER. *(to make an accusation)* quejarse, presentar una denuncia; *(to make a claim)* reclamar.

com·plain·ant (kəm-plā'nənt) s. DER. demandante mf.

com·plain·er (kəm-plā'nər) s. quejón m.

com·plaint (kəm-plānt') s. *(plaint)* queja; *(grievance)* motivo de queja; *(claim)* reclamación f; DER. *(accusation)* acusación f; *(suit)* demanda.

com·plai·sance (kəm-plā'səns) s. voluntad de complacer f.

com·plai·sant (kəm-plā'sənt) adj. complaciente.

com·ple·ment (kŏm'plə-mənt) **I.** s. *(completion)* complemento; MARÍT. *(crew)* dotación f; GEOM., GRAM. complemento **II.** tr. complementar.

com·ple·men·ta·ry (kŏm'plə-mĕn'tə-rē) adj. complementario.

com·plete (kəm-plēt') **I.** adj. **-plet·er, -plet·est** *(whole)* completo <a c. meal una comida completa>; *(entire)* entero, todo <the c. afternoon la tarde entera>; *(concluded)* terminado, acabado; *(thorough)* total; *(utter)* verdadero, completo <a c. fool un verdadero idiota>; *(accomplished)* consumado **II.** tr. **-plet·ed, -plet·ing** *(to finish)* completar, llevar a cabo; *(a form)* llenar; *(to conclude)* terminar, acabar.

com·plete·ness (kəm-plēt'nĭs) s. carácter completo ♦ **for the sake of c.** para que no falte nada.

com·ple·tion (kəm-plē'shən) s. *(conclusion)* terminación f; *(execution)* realización f ♦ **to be near c.** estar al terminarse.

com·plex **I.** adj. (kəm-plĕks', kŏm'plĕks') *(composite)* compuesto; *(intricate)* intrincado, complejo; *(complicated)* complicado; GRAM. compuesta (oración, palabra) **II.** s. (kŏm'plĕks') *(whole)* complejo <the urban c. el complejo urbano>; *(repressed problem)* complejo <an inferiority c. un complejo de inferioridad>; FAM. *(obsession)* obsesión f, complejo <he has a c. about eyes él tiene una obsesión con los ojos>.

complex fraction s. MAT. fracción compuesta.

com·plex·ion (kəm-plĕk'shən) s. *(skin)* cutis m, tez f; *(character)* aspecto, carácter m.

com·plex·i·ty (kəm-plĕk'sĭ-tē) s. [pl. **-ties**] complejidad f.

complex number s. MAT. número complejo.

com·pli·ance (kəm-plī'əns) o **com·pli·an·cy** (-ən-sē) s. *(with an order)* acatamiento, obediencia; *(tendency to yield)* conformidad f, docilidad f ♦ **in c. with** conforme a.

com·pli·ant (kəm-plī'ənt) adj. *(obedient)* obediente, dócil; *(helpful)* acomodaticio.

com·pli·cate (kŏm'plĭ-kāt') tr. & intr. **-cat·ed, -cat·ing** complicar(se).

com·pli·cat·ed (kŏm'plĭ-kā'tĭd) adj. complicado.

com·pli·ca·tion (kŏm'plĭ-kā'shən) s. complicación f.

com·plic·i·ty (kəm-plĭs'ĭ-tē) s. [pl. **-ties**] complicidad f.

com·pli·ment (kŏm'plə-mənt) **I.** s. *(praise)* elogio; *(honor)*

honor *m*; *(flattery)* piropo; *(courtesy)* cumplido ♦ **compliments** *(regards)* saludos <*extend my compliments to your parents* saludos a sus padres>; *(congratulations)* felicidades, enhorabuena • **to pay a c.** to elogiar • **to take it as a c. that** ser un honor para uno que • **with the compliments of** obsequio de, de parte de II. tr. *(to praise)* elogiar; *(to congratulate)* felicitar ♦ **to c. someone with** obsequiar a alguien.

com·pli·men·ta·ry (kŏm'plə-mĕn'tə-rē) adj. *(praising)* elogioso, halagador; *(free)* de cortesía; *(ticket)* de favor.

com·ply (kəm-plī') intr. **-plied, -ply·ing** *(with an order)* acatar, obedecer <*to c. with the regulations* acatar los reglamentos>; *(with a request)* acceder.

com·po·nent (kəm-pō'nənt) I. s. *(element)* componente *m*; *(part)* elemento II. adj. *(constituent)* componente, constituyente; *(system)* de elementos.

com·port (kəm-pôrt') tr. ♦ **to c. oneself** comportarse —intr. ♦ **to c. with** concordar con.

com·port·ment (kəm-pôrt'mənt) s. comportamiento, conducta.

com·pose (kəm-pōz') tr. **-posed, -pos·ing** *(to create)* componer; *(to constitute)* componer, integrar; *(to reconcile)* componer, arreglar; IMPR. componer ♦ **to be composed of** estar integrado por • **to c. oneself** sosegarse, tranquilizarse —intr. componer.

com·posed (kəm-pōzd') adj. sosegado, tranquilo.

com·pos·er (kəm-pō'zər) s. MÚS. compositor *m*.

com·pos·ite (kəm-pŏz'ĭt) I. adj. compuesto II. s. *(structure, material)* compuesto; BOT. *(plant)* compuesto.

composite photograph s. fotografía de superposición.

com·po·si·tion (kŏm'pə-zĭsh'ən) s. *(arrangement)* composición *f*; *(mixture)* combinación *f*; *(work, essay)* composición; *(settlement)* arreglo.

com·pos·i·tor (kəm-pŏz'ĭ-tər) s. IMPR. cajista *mf*.

com·post (kŏm'pōst') s. *(fertilizer)* mantillo, abono; *(mixture)* compuesto, combinación *f*.

com·po·sure (kəm-pō'zhər) s. compostura, serenidad *f*.

com·pound¹ I. tr. (kəm-pound') *(to combine)* componer; *(to mix)* mezclar, combinar; *(to settle)* arreglar, ajustar; *(interest)* calcular cumulativamente; *(to add to)* agravar <*to c. the difficulties* agravar las dificultades> —intr. *(to combine)* combinarse, mezclarse; *(to agree)* arreglarse, ajustarse II. adj. (kŏm'pound', kəm-pound') compuesto III. s. (kŏm'pound') *(combination)* compuesto; GRAM. palabra compuesta.

com·pound² (kŏm'pound') s. conglomerado encerrado de residencias.

compound fracture s. MED. fractura complicada.

compound interest s. FIN. interés compuesto o cumulativo.

com·pre·hend (kŏm'prĭ-hĕnd') tr. *(to understand)* comprender, entender; *(to comprise)* comprender, incluir.

com·pre·hen·si·ble (kŏm'prĭ-hĕn'sə-bəl) adj. comprensible, inteligible.

com·pre·hen·sion (kŏm'prĭ-hĕn'shən) s. comprensión *f*, entendimiento.

com·pre·hen·sive (kŏm'prĭ-hĕn'sĭv) I. adj. *(wide)* amplio, general; *(view)* de conjunto; *(research)* global; *(understanding)* comprensivo; *(charge)* total, que lo incluye todo; *(insurance)* a todo riesgo II. s. ♦ **comprehensives** EDUC. exámenes generales.

com·press I. tr. (kəm-prĕs') *(to press together)* comprimir; *(to shorten)* condensar II. s. (kŏm'prĕs') MED. *(pad)* compresa; *(machine, plant)* embaladora de algodón.

com·pressed (kəm-prĕst') adj. comprimido.

compressed air s. aire comprimido.

com·press·i·ble (kəm-prĕs'ə-bəl) adj. compresible, comprimible.

com·pres·sion (kəm-prĕsh'ən) s. compresión *f*.

com·pres·sor (kəm-prĕs'ər) s. TEC. compresor *m*.

com·prise (kəm-prīz') tr. **-prised, -pris·ing** *(to include)* comprender, incluir; *(to consist of)* constar de.

com·pro·mise (kŏm'prə-mīz') I. s. *(settlement)* compromiso, acuerdo; *(concession)* concesión *f*; *(combination)* término medio II. tr. **-mised, -mis·ing** *(to settle)* componer; *(to endanger)* poner en peligro; *(reputation)* compro-

meter —intr. *(to yield)* hacer concesiones, transigir; *(to reach agreement)* llegar a un arreglo.

com·pro·mis·ing (kŏm'prə-mī'zĭng) adj. *(accommodating)* transigente, acomodaticio; *(detrimental)* comprometedor.

comp·trol·ler (kən-trō'lər) s. var. de **controller.**

com·pul·sion (kəm-pŭl'shən) s. *(coercion)* compulsión *f*, obligación *f*; *(impulse)* impulso ♦ **to feel a c. to** sentirse obligado o impelido • **under c.** por obligación, a la fuerza.

com·pul·sive (kəm-pŭl'sĭv) adj. *(desire)* incontrolable; *(talker, eater)* obsesivo, que no se puede controlar; *(drinker, gambler)* empedernido.

com·pul·so·ry (kəm-pŭl'sə-rē) adj. *(coercive)* compulsorio, coercitivo; *(required)* obligatorio.

com·punc·tion (kəm-pŭngk'shən) s. *(qualm)* compunción *f*; *(remorse)* remordimiento ♦ **without c.** sin escrúpulo.

com·put·a·ble (kəm-pyōō'tə-bəl) adj. computable, calculable.

com·pu·ta·tion (kŏm'pyōō-tā'shən) s. *(act)* cálculo; *(result)* cómputo, cálculo.

com·pute (kəm-pyōōt') I. tr. **-put·ed, -put·ing** computar, calcular II. s. computación *f*.

com·put·er (kəm-pyōō'tər) s. computadora, ordenador *m*.

com·put·er·ize (kəm-pyōō'tə-rīz') tr. **-ized, -iz·ing** *(information)* computarizar; *(a business office)* instalar computadoras en ♦ **to be computerized** hacerse por computadoras.

com·put·er·ized (kəm-pyōō'tə-rīzd') adj. computadorizado.

computer language s. lenguaje de máquina *m*.

com·rade (kŏm'rād') s. camarada *mf*, compañero.

com·rade·ship (kŏm'rād-shĭp') s. camaradería, compañerismo.

con¹ (kŏn) I. adv. contra ♦ **pro and c.** a favor y en contra II. s. ♦ **pros and cons** los pros y los contras.

con² (kŏn) tr. **conned, con·ning** *(to peruse)* examinar, estudiar detenidamente; *(to memorize)* aprender de memoria.

con³ (kŏn) JER. I. tr. **conned, con·ning** *(to swindle)* estafar, timar; *(to dupe)* engañar II. s. estafa.

con⁴ (kŏn) s. JER. preso, presidiario.

con·cat·e·nate (kən-kăt'n-āt') tr. **-nat·ed, -nat·ing** concatenar, concadenar.

con·cave (kŏn-kāv') adj. cóncavo.

con·cav·i·ty (kŏn-kăv'ĭ-tē) s. [pl. **-ties**] concavidad *f*.

con·ca·vo-con·vex (kŏn-kā'vō-kŏn-vĕks') adj. concavoconvexo.

con·ceal (kən-sēl') tr. *(to hide)* ocultar; *(a crime)* encubrir.

con·ceal·ment (kən-sēl'mənt) s. *(act)* ocultación *f*; *(of a crime)* encubrimiento; *(place)* escondite *m*.

con·cede (kən-sēd') tr. **-ced·ed, -ced·ing** *(to admit)* conceder, reconocer; *(to give)* conceder, otorgar —intr. hacer una concesión, transigir.

con·ceit (kən-sēt') s. *(vanity)* vanidad *f*, presunción *f*; *(witticism)* agudeza; *(metaphor)* concepto.

con·ceit·ed (kən-sē'tĭd) adj. vanidoso, engreído.

con·ceiv·a·ble (kən-sē'və-bəl) adj. concebible, imaginable.

con·ceive (kən-sēv') tr. **-ceived, -ceiv·ing** *(child)* concebir; *(to imagine)* concebir, imaginar; *(to understand)* entender —intr. concebir ♦ **to c. of** concebir.

con·cen·trate (kŏn'sən-trāt') tr. & intr. **-trat·ed, -trat·ing** concentrar(se) ♦ **to c. on** concentrar(se) en II. s. QUÍM. concentrado.

con·cen·tra·tion (kŏn'sən-trā'shən) s. concentración *f*.

concentration camp s. campo de concentración.

con·cen·tric (kən-sĕn'trĭk) o **con·cen·tri·cal** (-trĭ-kəl) adj. concéntrico.

con·cept (kŏn'sĕpt') s. concepto.

con·cep·tion (kən-sĕp'shən) s. *(of an embryo, idea)* concepción *f*; *(plan)* proyecto; *(idea)* concepto, idea <*to have no c. of* no tener ni idea de>.

con·cep·tu·al (kən-sĕp'chōō-əl) adj. conceptual.

con·cep·tu·al·ize (kən-sĕp'chōō-ə-līz') tr. **-ized, -iz·ing** conceptuar —intr. formar conceptos.

con·cern (kən-sûrn') I. tr. *(to be about)* referirse a, tratar de; *(to affect)* concernir a, afectar <*the decision concerns us all* la decisión nos afecta a todos>; *(to be the affair of)* concernir a, ser asunto de; *(to involve)* involucrar, implicar <*they were concerned in the matter* estuvieron involucrados en el asunto>; *(to trouble)* preocupar ♦ **as concerns en lo que concierne a** • **as far as one is concerned** por lo que a uno se refiere • **to c. oneself with** ocuparse de, interesarse por • **to whom it may c.** a quien corresponda **II.** s. *(affair)* asunto <*that is their c.* eso es asunto suyo>; *(interest)* interés *m*; *(worry)* preocupación *f*; COM. *(company)* empresa ♦ **those concerned** los interesados • **to be of no c.** carecer de importancia.

con·cerned (kən-sûrnd′) adj. *(interested)* interesado; *(worried)* preocupado.

con·cern·ing (kən-sûr′nĭng) prep. concerniente a, referente a.

con·cert I. s. (kŏn′sûrt′) *(performance)* concierto; *(agreement)* acuerdo, concierto ♦ **in c. with** de concierto con, de común acuerdo con **II.** tr. & intr. (kən-sûrt′) concertar(se).

con·cert·ed (kən-sûr′tĭd) adj. conjunto, combinado.

con·cer·ti (kən-chĕr′tē) un pl. de **concerto.**

con·cer·ti·na (kŏn′sər-tē′nə) s. MÚS. concertina.

con·cer·tize (kŏn′sər-tīz′) intr. **-tized, -tiz·ing** MÚS. dar conciertos.

con·cer·to (kən-chĕr′tō) s. [pl. **-tos** o **-ti** (-tē)] MÚS. concierto.

con·ces·sion (kən-sĕsh′ən) s. concesión *f.*

con·ces·sion·aire (kən-sĕsh′ə-nâr′) o **con·ces·sion·er** (-sĕsh′ə-nər) s. concesionario.

conch (kŏngk, kŏnch) s. [pl. **conchs** (kŏngks) o **conch·es** (kŏn′chĭz)] *(mollusk)* caracol marino; *(shell)* caracola.

con·cil·i·ate (kən-sĭl′ē-āt′) tr. **-at·ed, -at·ing** *(to placate)* conciliar; *(to make consistent)* reconciliar.

con·cil·i·a·tion (kən-sĭl′ē-ā′shən) s. *(appeasement)* conciliación *f*; *(reconciliation)* reconciliación *f.*

con·cil·i·a·tor (kən-sĭl′ē-ā′tər) s. mediador *m.*

con·cil·i·a·to·ry (kən-sĭl′ē-ə-tôr′ē) adj. conciliatorio.

con·cise (kən-sīs′) adj. conciso, sucinto.

con·ci·sion (kən-sĭzh′ən) o **con·cise·ness** (kən-sīs′nĭs) s. concisión *f.*

con·clave (kŏn′klāv′) s. cónclave *m.*

con·clude (kən-klōōd′) tr. & intr. **-clud·ed, -clud·ing** *(to close)* concluir, terminar; *(to decide)* concluir, resolver.

con·clu·sion (kən-klōō′zhən) s. *(close, decision)* conclusión *f*; *(of a treaty)* cierre *m*, firma ♦ **in c.** en conclusión, en suma • **to bring to a c.** concluir, terminar.

con·clu·sive (kən-klōō′sĭv) adj. concluyente, decisivo.

con·coct (kən-kŏkt′) tr. *(food, drink)* confeccionar, preparar; *(to invent)* fabricar; *(to plan)* fraguar.

con·coc·tion (kən-kŏk′shən) s. *(act)* confección *f*, preparación *f*; *(brew)* brebaje *m*; *(invention, lie)* fabricación *f.*

con·com·i·tant (kən-kŏm′ĭ-tnt) adj. concomitante.

con·cord (kŏn′kôrd) s. *(accord)* concordia; *(treaty)* tratado de paz; GRAM. concordancia.

con·cor·dance (kən-kôr′dns) s. *(concord)* concordancia; *(index)* concordancias.

con·cor·dant (kən-kôr′dnt) adj. *(agreeing)* concordante, concorde; *(harmonious)* armonioso.

con·cor·dat (kən-kôr′dăt′) s. RELIG. concordato.

con·course (kŏn′kôrs′) s. *(throng)* concurrencia, multitud *f*; *(flowing together)* confluencia; *(for passengers)* salón *m*, vestíbulo; *(thoroughfare)* avenida.

con·crete (kŏn-krēt′) **I.** adj. *(real)* concreto; *(solid)* concreto, sólido; *(made of concrete)* de concreto o hormigón **II.** (kŏn′krēt′) CONSTR. concreto, hormigón *m* ♦ **reinforced c.** concreto *u* hormigón armado **III.** tr. **-cret·ed, -cret·ing** CONSTR. revestir de concreto *u* hormigón.

concrete mixer s. CONSTR. concretera, hormigonera.

con·crete·ness (kŏn-krēt′nĭs) s. concreción *f.*

con·cre·tion (kən-krē′shən) s. concreción *f.*

con·cu·bi·nage (kŏn-kyōō′bə-nĭj) s. concubinato.

con·cu·bine (kŏng′kyə-bīn′) s. concubina.

con·cu·pis·cence (kŏn-kyōō′pĭ-səns) s. concupiscencia.

con·cu·pis·cent (kŏn-kyōō′pĭ-sənt) adj. concupiscente, lascivo.

con·cur (kən-kûr′) intr. **-curred, -cur·ring** *(to agree)* convenir, estar de acuerdo; *(to cooperate)* colaborar; *(to coincide)* concurrir, coincidir.

con·cur·rence (kən-kûr′əns) s. *(agreement)* acuerdo; *(coin-*

cidence) concurrencia, coincidencia; *(cooperation)* colaboración *f.*

con·cur·rent (kən-kûr′ənt) adj. concurrente.

con·cus·sion (kən-kŭsh′ən) s. *(shock)* concusión *f*, sacudida; *(injury)* conmoción cerebral *f.*

con·demn (kən-dĕm′) tr. *(to convict, sentence)* condenar; *(to deplore)* condenar, desaprobar; *(to declare uninhabitable)* declarar inhabitable; *(to declare unfit)* declarar inservible; *(to appropriate)* confiscar.

con·dem·na·ble (kən-dĕm′nə-bəl) adj. condenable, censurable.

con·dem·na·tion (kŏn′dĕm-nā′shən) s. *(blame)* condenación *f*; *(punishment)* condena.

con·dem·na·to·ry (kən-dĕm′nə-tôr′ē) adj. condenatorio.

con·demned (kən-dĕmd′) adj. condenado.

con·den·sa·tion (kŏn′dĕn-sā′shən) s. *(process)* condensación *f*; *(condensate)* condensado; *(synopsis)* versión condensada.

con·dense (kən-dĕns′) tr. & intr. **-densed, -dens·ing** condensar(se).

condensed milk s. leche condensada.

con·dens·er (kən-dĕn′sər) s. condensador *m.*

con·de·scend (kŏn′dĭ-sĕnd′) intr. *(to deign)* condescender, dignarse <*she condescended to call* se dignó llamar>; *(to be patronizing)* comportarse condescendientemente.

con·de·scend·ing (kŏn′dĭ-sĕn′dĭng) adj. condescendiente.

con·de·scen·sion (kŏn′dĭ-sĕn′shən) s. condescendencia.

con·di·ment (kŏn′də-mənt) s. condimento.

con·di·tion (kən-dĭsh′ən) **I.** s. *(state)* condición *f*, estado <*to arrive in good c.* llegar en buen estado>; *(health)* estado de salud; FAM. *(ailment)* enfermedad *f*, problemas *m* <*a heart c.* problemas del corazón>; *(rank, prerequisite)* condición; *(provision)* condición, estipulación *f*; GRAM. oración condicional *f* ♦ **conditions** condiciones, circunstancias <*poor driving conditions* malas condiciones para manejar> • **on c. that** a condición que • **on one c.** con una condición • **to be in no c.** no estar en condiciones de • **to keep in c.** mantenerse en forma **II.** tr. *(to make conditional)* condicionar, determinar; *(to stipulate)* estipular; *(to make fit)* preparar, poner en condiciones; *(by exercising)* poner en forma; *(to adapt)* acostumbrar, adaptar; *(air)* acondicionar.

con·di·tion·al (kən-dĭsh′ə-nəl) **I.** adj. *(not absolute)* condicional; GRAM. condicional, potencial ♦ **to be c. on** depender de **II.** s. GRAM. condicional *m*, potencial *m.*

con·di·tioned (kən-dĭsh′ənd) adj. *(dependent, trained)* condicionado; *(physically fit)* en forma; *(prepared)* preparado; *(air)* acondicionado.

con·di·tion·er (kən-dĭsh′ə-nər) s. acondicionador *m* ♦ **air c.** acondicionador de aire.

con·di·tion·ing (kən-dĭsh′ə-nĭng) s. acondicionamiento ♦ **air c.** aire acondicionado.

con·do·lence (kən-dō′ləns) s. condolencia, pésame *m* ♦ **please accept my condolences** le acompaño en sus sentimientos • **to offer condolences to** dar el pésame a.

con·dom (kŏn′dəm, kŭn′-) s. condón *m*, preservativo.

con·do·min·i·um (kŏn′də-mĭn′ē-əm) [pl. **-ums**] s. *(sovereignty)* condominio; *(apartment)* condominio, propiedad horizontal *f.*

con·do·na·tion (kŏn′də-nā′shən) s. condonación *f*, perdón *m.*

con·done (kən-dōn′) tr. **-doned, -don·ing** condonar, perdonar.

con·dor (kŏn′dôr) s. cóndor *m.*

con·duce (kən-dōōs′, -dyōōs′) intr. **-duced, -duc·ing** ♦ **c. to** conducir a.

con·du·cive (kən-dōō′sĭv, -dyōō′-) adj. ♦ **c. to** *(leading to)* conducente a; *(favorable to)* propicio para.

con·duct I. tr. (kən-dŭkt′) *(to direct)* dirigir (negocio, orquesta); *(to carry out)* llevar a cabo, hacer <*to c. an investigation* llevar a cabo una investigación>; *(to escort)* conducir, llevar; *(a tour)* servir de guía a; ELEC., FÍS. conducir ♦ **to c. oneself** conducirse, comportarse —intr. *(to lead)* conducir; MÚS. dirigir **II.** s. (kŏn′dŭkt′) *(behavior)* conducta, comportamiento; *(management)* dirección *f.*

con·duc·tance (kən-dŭk′təns) s. ELEC. conductancia.

con·duc·tion (kən-dŭk′shən) s. ELEC., FÍS. conducción *f.*
con·duc·tiv·i·ty (kŏn′dŭk-tĭv′ĭ-tē) s. conductividad *f,* conductibilidad *f.*
con·duc·tor (kən-dŭk′tər) s. *(of a train, bus)* conductor *m,* cobrador *m; (of an orchestra)* director *m;* (guide) guía *m;* (lightning rod) pararrayos; ELEC., FÍS. conductor.
con·duc·tress (kən-dŭk′trĭs) s. *(of a train, bus)* conductora, cobradora; (guide) guía *f; (of an orchestra)* directora.
con·duit (kŏn′dĭt, -dōō-ĭt) s. (channel) conducto; (pipe) tubo.
cone (kōn) s. (figure) cono; (for ice cream) barquillo, cucurucho; BOT., FISIOL. cono.
con·fab I. s. (kŏn′făb′) charla, plática II. intr. (kən-făb′) **-fabbed, -fab·bing** charlar, platicar.
con·fab·u·late (kən-făb′yə-lāt′) intr. **-lat·ed, -lat·ing** confabular, charlar.
con·fect (kən-fĕkt′) tr. *(to put together)* confeccionar, preparar; (fruits) confitar.
con·fec·tion (kən-fĕk′shən) s. (act) confección *f;* (sweet) confitura.
con·fec·tion·er (kən-fĕk′shə-nər) s. confitero, repostero.
con·fec·tion·er·y (kən-fĕk′shə-nĕr′ē) s. [pl. **-ies**] (sweets) confituras; (shop) confitería, repostería.
con·fed·er·a·cy (kən-fĕd′ər-ə-sē) s. [pl. **-cies**] (league) confederación *f; (conspiracy)* complot *m* ♦ **C.** EE. UU., HIST. Confederación.
con·fed·er·ate (kən-fĕd′ər-ĭt) I. s. (ally) confederado; *(accomplice)* cómplice *mf* ♦ **C.** EE. UU., HIST. confederado, sudista II. adj. confederado III. tr. & intr. (-ə-rāt′) **-at·ed, -at·ing** confederar(se).
con·fed·er·a·tion (kən-fĕd′ə-rā′shən) s. confederación *f.*
con·fer (kən-fûr′) tr. **-ferred, -fer·ring** *(to bestow)* conferir, otorgar —intr. conferir, consultar <*c. with them first* consulten con ellos primero>.
con·fer·ee (kŏn′fə-rē′) s. (participant) participante en una conferencia *mf; (of an honor)* recipiente *mf.*
con·fer·ence (kŏn′fər-əns) s. (assembly) conferencia, congreso; (meeting) reunión *f; (consultation)* consulta; DEP. liga deportiva.
conference room s. sala de conferencias *o* de reuniones.
con·fer·ra·ble (kən-fûr′ə-bəl) adj. que se puede conferir.
con·fer·ral (kən-fûr′əl) s. concesión *f,* otorgamiento.
con·fess (kən-fĕs′) tr. confesar —intr. *(to admit)* confesar; RELIG. (to tell one's sins) confesarse ♦ **to c. to** confesar.
con·fessed (kən-fĕst′) adj. declarado.
con·fes·sion (kən-fĕsh′ən) s. confesión *f.*
con·fes·sion·al (kən-fĕsh′ə-nəl) I. adj. confesional II. s. RELIG. confesionario.
con·fes·sor (kən-fĕs′ər) s. RELIG. (priest) confesor *m; (sinner)* penitente *mf.*
con·fet·ti (kən-fĕt′ē) s.pl. [ú. con v. sing.] confeti *m.*
con·fi·dant (kŏn′fĭ-dănt′, -dänt′) s. confidente *mf.*
con·fi·dante (kŏn′fĭ-dănt′, -dänt′) s. confidente *f.*
con·fide (kən-fīd′) tr. **-fid·ed, -fid·ing** confiar (secreto, objeto) —intr. confiar ♦ **to c. in** confiar en.
con·fi·dence (kŏn′fĭ-dəns) s. (trust, assurance) confianza; *(secret)* confidencia, secreto ♦ **in c.** en confianza • **to be in the c. of** tener trato íntimo con • **to place one's c. in** confiar en • **to take someone into one's c.** confiarse a alguien.
confidence game s. estafa, fraude *m.*
confidence man s. estafador *m.*
con·fi·dent (kŏn′fĭ-dənt) s. (certain) confiado, seguro <*the team is c. of victory* el equipo está seguro de la victoria>; *(self-assured)* confiado, seguro de sí mismo; (tone, manner) de confianza, de seguridad.
con·fi·den·tial (kŏn′fĭ-dĕn′shəl) adj. *(secret)* confidencial, privado; *(trusted, intimate)* de confianza.
con·fi·den·ti·al·i·ty (kŏn′fĭ-dĕn′shē-ăl′ĭ-tē) s. carácter confidencial *o* privado.
con·fid·ing (kən-fī′dĭng) adj. confiado.
con·fig·u·ra·tion (kən-fĭg′yə-rā′shən) s. configuración *f.*
con·fine (kən-fīn′) I. tr. **-fined, -fin·ing** *(to shut in)* confinar, recluir; *(to restrict)* restringir, limitar <*c. your answers to one sentence* limítense a responder con una sola oración> ♦ **to be confined to bed** tener que guardar cama —intr.

confinar, lindar II. s. (kŏn′fīn′) ♦ **confines** confines, límites.
con·fine·ment (kən-fīn′mənt) s. (seclusion) confinamiento, reclusión *f; (restriction)* restricción *f,* limitación *f; (to bed)* obligación de guardar cama *f; (lying-in)* parto ♦ **in solitary c.** CRIMIN. incomunicado.
con·firm (kən-fûrm′) tr. *(to verify)* confirmar; *(to approve)* ratificar; RELIG. confirmar.
con·firm·a·ble (kən-fûr′mə-bəl) adj. que se puede confirmar.
con·fir·ma·tion (kŏn′fər-mā′shən) s. (verification) confirmación *f; (approval)* ratificación *f;* RELIG. confirmación.
con·firmed (kən-fûrmd′) adj. (verified) confirmado; (approved) ratificado; (inveterate) habitual, inveterado; *(chronic)* crónico.
con·fis·cate (kŏn′fĭ-skāt′) tr. **-cat·ed, -cat·ing** confiscar.
con·fis·ca·tion (kŏn′fĭ-skā′shən) s. confiscación *f.*
con·fla·gra·tion (kŏn′flə-grā′shən) s. conflagración *f,* incendio.
con·flict I. s. (kŏn′flĭkt) conflicto ♦ **to be in c. with** estar en pugna con • **to come into c.** chocar II. intr. (kən-flĭkt′) *(to clash)* oponerse; *(to differ)* contradecirse.
con·flict·ing (kən-flĭk′tĭng) adj. (clashing) opuesto; *(differing)* contradictorio.
conflict of interest s. conflicto de intereses.
con·flu·ence (kŏn′flōō-əns) s. confluencia.
con·flu·ent (kŏn′flōō-ənt) I. adj. confluente II. s. GEOG. tributario.
con·form (kən-fôrm′) intr. *(to be similar)* conformarse, concordar; *(to standards)* ajustarse; *(to rules)* ajustarse, someterse —tr. ajustar.
con·form·a·ble (kən-fôr′mə-bəl) adj. (submissive) conforme; GEOL. concordante ♦ **c. to** conforme a.
con·form·ance (kən-fôr′məns) s. conformidad *f.*
con·for·ma·tion (kŏn′fər-mā′shən) s. (structure) conformación *f; (adaptation)* ajuste *m,* sometimiento.
con·form·ist (kən-fôr′mĭst) s. conformista *mf.*
con·for·mi·ty (kən-fôr′mĭ-tē) s. [pl. **-ties**] conformidad *f* ♦ **in c. with** conforme a.
con·found (kən-found′) tr. *(to bewilder)* confundir, desconcertar; *(to confuse)* confundir, mezclar; *(to damn)* maldecir ♦ **c. it!** ¡maldito sea!
con·found·ed (kən-foun′dĭd) adj. (confused) confundido, desconcertado; *(damned)* maldito, condenado.
con·front (kən-frŭnt′) tr. *(to face)* enfrentar, hacer frente a <*he confronted his accuser* enfrentó al que lo acusaba>; *(to place before)* presentar; *(to encounter)* encontrar <*to c. new difficulties* encontrar nuevas dificultades>; *(dangers)* arrostrar; *(to arise)* presentarse, surgir.
con·fron·ta·tion (kŏn′frən-tā′shən) s. confrontación *f.*
con·fuse (kən-fyōoz′) tr. **-fused, -fus·ing** *(to disconcert, to mix up)* confundir; *(to blur)* confundir, complicar <*to c. the issue* complicar las cosas>.
con·fused (kən-fyōozd′) adj. (bewildered) confundido, desconcertado; *(disordered)* confuso.
con·fus·ing (kən-fyōo′zĭng) adj. (bewildering) confuso, desconcertante; *(disordered)* confuso.
con·fu·sion (kən-fyōo′zhən) s. confusión *f* ♦ **to be in c.** *(to be bewildered)* estar confundido *o* desconcertado; *(to be disordered)* estar en desorden.
con·fute (kən-fyōot′) tr. **-fut·ed, -fut·ing** confutar, refutar.
con game s. JER. estafa, fraude *m.*
con·geal (kən-jēl′) intr. & tr. *(to freeze)* congelar(se); *(to coagulate)* coagular(se).
con·ge·la·tion (kŏn′jə-lā′shən) s. (freezing) congelación *f; (coagulation)* coagulación *f.*
con·gen·ial (kən-jēn′yəl) adj. (kindred) similar, afín; *(compatible)* compatible; *(sociable)* afable, simpático; *(suitable)* agradable, apropiado.
con·ge·ni·al·i·ty (kən-jē′nē-ăl′ĭ-tē) s. (kindredness) similaridad *f,* afinidad *f; (sociability)* afabilidad *f,* simpatía.
con·gen·i·tal (kən-jĕn′ĭ-tl) adj. congénito, de nacimiento.
con·ger o **con·ger eel** s. ICT. congrio.
con·gest (kən-jĕst′) tr. & intr. *(to overfill)* atestar(se), abarrotar(se); MED. (with blood) congestionar(se) ♦ **to be con-**

congested | conscript

gested MED. estar constipado • **to be congested with** estar abarrotado o lleno de.

con·gest·ed (kən-jĕs′tĭd) adj. *(by traffic, blood)* congestionado; *(by population)* superpoblado; *(chest, nose)* constipado.

con·ges·tion (kən-jĕs′chən) s. *(overcrowding)* congestión f, acumulación f; MED. *(with blood, mucus)* congestión, constipación f ♦ **traffic c.** congestión de tránsito.

con·ges·tive (kən-jĕs′tĭv) adj. congestivo.

con·glom·er·ate (kən-glŏm′ə-rāt′) **I.** tr. & intr. **-at·ed, -at·ing** conglomerar(se) **II.** s. (-ər-ĭt) COM., GEOL. conglomerado **III.** adj. (-ər-ĭt) conglomerado.

con·glom·er·a·tion (kən-glŏm′ə-rā′shən) s. *(process, state)* conglomeración f; *(collection)* acumulación f.

Con·go (kŏng′gō) s. Congo.

Con·go·lese (kŏng′gə-lēz′) adj. & s. *(inhabitant, language)* congoleño, congolés m.

con·grat·u·late (kən-grăch′ə-lāt′) tr. **-lat·ed, -lat·ing** felicitar, dar la enhorabuena ♦ **to c. oneself** congratularse.

con·grat·u·la·tion (kən-grăch′ə-lā′shən) s. felicitación f, congratulación f ♦ **congratulations!** ¡felicidades!, ¡enhorabuena!

con·grat·u·la·to·ry (kən-grăch′ə-lə-tôr′ē) adj. de felicitación.

con·gre·gate (kŏng′grĭ-gāt′) intr. & tr. **-gat·ed, -gat·ing** congregar(se), reunir(se).

con·gre·ga·tion (kŏng′grĭ-gā′shən) s. *(gathering)* congregación f, reunión f; RELIG. *(worshipers)* feligreses m; *(order)* congregación.

con·gre·ga·tion·al (kŏng′grĭ-gā′shə-nəl) adj. de la congregación.

con·gre·ga·tion·al·ism (kŏng′grĭ-gā′shə-nə-lĭz′əm) s. congregacionalismo.

con·gress (kŏng′grĭs) s. congreso ♦ **C.** POL. Congreso.

con·gres·sion·al (kən-grĕsh′ə-nəl) adj. del congreso.

congressional district s. EE. UU. distrito electoral (para la Cámara de Representantes).

Congressional Record s. EE. UU. actas de sesiones del Congreso.

con·gress·man (kŏng′grĭs-mən) s. [pl. **-men**] EE. UU. diputado de la Cámara de Representantes.

con·gress·wom·an (kŏng′grĭs-wŏŏm′ən) s. [pl. **-wom·en** (-wĭm′ĭn)] EE. UU. diputada de la Cámara de Representantes.

con·gru·ence (kŏng′grōō-əns, kən-grōō′-) o **con·gru·en·cy** (-ən-sē) s. congruencia.

con·gru·ent (kŏng′grōō-ənt, kən-grōō′-) adj. congruente.

con·gru·i·ty (kən-grōō′ĭ-tē) s. [pl. **-ties**] congruencia.

con·gru·ous (kŏng′grōō-əs) adj. congruo, congruente.

con·ic (kŏn′ĭk) o **con·i·cal** (-ĭ-kəl) **I.** adj. cónico **II.** s. GEOM., MAT. sección cónica.

conic section s. GEOM., MAT. sección cónica.

con·i·fer (kŏn′ə-fər, kō′nə-) s. BOT. conífera.

co·nif·er·ous (kə-nĭf′ər-əs) adj. BOT. conífero.

con·jec·tur·al (kən-jĕk′chər-əl) adj. conjetural.

con·jec·ture (kən-jĕk′chər) **I.** s. conjetura **II.** tr. **-tured, -tur·ing** conjeturar —intr. hacer conjeturas.

con·join (kən-join′) tr. & intr. unir(se), juntar(se).

con·joint (kən-joint′) adj. conjunto.

con·ju·gal (kŏn′jə-gəl) adj. conyugal.

con·ju·gate (kŏn′jə-gāt′) **I.** tr. & intr. **-gat·ed, -gat·ing** conjugar(se) **II.** adj. (-gĭt) *(joined)* conjugado; GRAM. congénere.

con·ju·ga·tion (kŏn′jə-gā′shən) s. conjugación f.

con·junct (kən-jŭngkt′, kŏn′jŭngkt′) adj. conjunto, unido.

con·junc·tion (kən-jŭngk′shən) s. conjunción f ♦ **in c. with** en combinación o conjuntamente con.

con·junc·tive (kən-jŭngk′tĭv) **I.** adj. conjuntivo **II.** s. conjunción f.

con·junc·ti·vi·tis (kən-jŭngk′tə-vī′tĭs) s. OFTAL. conjuntivitis f.

con·junc·ture (kən-jŭngk′chər) s. coyuntura.

con·jure (kŏn′jər, kən-jōōr′) tr. **-jured, -jur·ing** conjurar, suplicar ♦ **to c. away** conjurar, exorcizar • **to c. up** *(to summon)* invocar; *(to cause to appear)* hacer aparecer por arte de magia; *(to evoke)* evocar —intr. hacer juegos de manos.

con·jur·er o **con·jur·or** (kŏn′jər-ər) s. mago.

conk (kŏngk) FAM. **I.** s. *(head)* coco; *(nose)* narices f, hocico; *(blow)* golpe m **II.** tr. golpear en el coco —intr. ♦ **to c. out** *(to break down)* romperse, fastidiarse; *(to pass out)* caerse redondo, desmayarse.

con man s. JER. estafador m.

con·nect (kə-nĕkt′) tr. *(to join)* conectar, unir; *(to associate)* vincular, relacionar <there is no reason to c. the two events no hay motivo para vincular los dos sucesos>; *(by telephone)* comunicar, poner en comunicación; ELEC. *(an appliance, wire)* conectar —intr. *(to become joined)* unirse; *(to communicate)* comunicarse (habitaciones, lagos); *(buses, trains)* hacer combinación.

con·nect·ed (kə-nĕk′tĭd) adj. *(joined together)* conectado; *(semantically, socially)* relacionado; *(related)* emparentado; ELEC. enchufado, conectado ♦ **to be well-connected** estar bien relacionado.

connecting rod s. MEC. biela.

con·nec·tion (kə-nĕk′shən) s. *(act)* conexión f; *(association)* vínculo, relación f; *(contact)* enchufe m, relación <he relies on his connections cuenta con sus relaciones>; *(relative)* pariente m; *(buses, trains)* combinación f; ELEC., TEL. conexión ♦ **in c. with** en relación con • **in this c.** a este respecto, a propósito de esto.

con·nec·tive (kə-nĕk′tĭv) **I.** adj. conectivo **II.** s. GRAM. nexo.

connective tissue s. BIOL. tejido conectivo.

con·nec·tor o **con·nect·er** (kə-nĕk′tər) s. MEC. conectador m; ELEC. hilo de conexión.

con·nex·ion (kə-nĕk′shən) s. G.B. var. de **connection**.

conning tower s. MARÍT. *(of a ship)* torre de mando f; *(of a submarine)* torre.

con·niv·ance (kə-nī′vəns) s. connivencia.

con·nive (kə-nīv′) intr. **-nived, -niv·ing** *(to feign ignorance)* hacer la vista gorda, consentir; *(to conspire)* intrigar, conspirar.

con·niv·er (kə-nī′vər) s. intrigante mf, conspirador m.

con·niv·ing (kə-nī′vĭng) adj. confabulador.

con·nois·seur (kŏn′ə-sûr′) s. conocedor m, experto.

con·no·ta·tion (kŏn′ə-tā′shən) s. connotación f.

con·note (kə-nōt′) tr. **-not·ed, -not·ing** *(to suggest)* connotar; *(to involve)* implicar, entrañar.

con·nu·bi·al (kə-nōō′bē-əl, -nyōō′-) adj. connubial, conyugal.

con·quer (kŏng′kər) tr. *(land, nation)* conquistar; *(enemy, disease)* vencer —intr. vencer, triunfar.

con·quer·or (kŏng′kər-ər) s. *(conquistador)* conquistador m; *(victor)* vencedor m.

con·quest (kŏng′kwĕst′) s. conquista.

con·san·guin·e·ous (kŏn′săng-gwĭn′ē-əs) adj. consanguíneo.

con·science (kŏn′shəns) s. conciencia ♦ **in all c.** en conciencia, en justicia • **to have a guilty c.** sentirse culpable • **to have something on one's c.** tener un peso en la conciencia, tener un cargo de conciencia • **with a clear c.** con la conciencia limpia.

conscience money s. dinero dado para quedar con la conciencia tranquila.

conscience-strick·en (kŏn′shəns-strĭk′ən) adj. arrepentido, con remordimientos de conciencia.

con·sci·en·tious (kŏn′shē-ĕn′shəs) adj. concienzudo, escrupuloso.

con·sci·en·tious·ness (kŏn′shē-ĕn′shəs-nĭs) s. escrupulosidad f.

conscientious objector s. objetor de conciencia m.

con·scious (kŏn′shəs) adj. *(awake)* consciente; *(aware)* consciente <to be c. of ser consciente de>; *(intentional)* intencional, deliberado <a c. effort un esfuerzo deliberado> ♦ **to become c.** volver en sí • **to become c. of** darse cuenta de.

con·scious·ly (kŏn′shəs-lē) adv. conscientemente.

con·scious·ness (kŏn′shəs-nĭs) s. *(awareness)* conciencia; MED. conocimiento.

con·script MIL. **I.** tr. (kən-skrĭpt′) reclutar, alistar **II.** s.

(kŏn′skrĭpt′) recluta *m*, conscripto III. adj. (kŏn′skrĭpt′) conscripto, alistado.

con·scrip·tion (kən-skrĭp′shən) s. conscripción *f*, reclutamiento.

con·se·crate (kŏn′sĭ-krāt′) tr. **-crat·ed, -crat·ing** consagrar.

con·se·crat·ed (kŏn′sĭ-krā′tĭd) adj. consagrado.

con·se·cra·tion (kŏn′sĭ-krā′shən) s. consagración *f*.

con·sec·u·tive (kən-sĕk′yə-tĭv) adj. consecutivo.

con·sen·su·al (kən-sĕn′shōō-əl) adj. consensual.

con·sen·sus (kən-sĕn′səs) s. consenso ♦ **c. of opinion** opinión *o* consenso general.

con·sent (kən-sĕnt′) I. intr. consentir II. s. consentimiento ♦ **by mutual c.** de mutuo acuerdo.

con·se·quence (kŏn′sĭ-kwĕns′) s. *(result)* consecuencia; *(significance)* significación *f*, importancia ♦ **in c.** por consiguiente.

con·se·quent (kŏn′sĭ-kwĕnt′) I. adj. consecuente, consiguiente II. s. GRAM., LÓG., MAT. consecuente *m*.

con·se·quen·tial (kŏn′sĭ-kwĕn′shəl) adj. *(resulting)* consecuente, consiguiente; *(significant)* de consecuencia, importante; *(arrogant)* altivo, pomposo.

con·se·quent·ly (kŏn′sĭ-kwĕnt′lē) adv. consecuentemente, por consiguiente.

con·ser·van·cy (kən-sûr′vən-sē) s. [pl. **-cies**] conservación *f*, preservación *f*.

con·ser·va·tion (kŏn′sər-vā′shən) s. conservación *f*, preservación *f*.

con·ser·va·tion·ist (kŏn′sər-vā′shə-nĭst) s. conservacionista *mf*.

con·ser·va·tism (kən-sûr′və-tĭz′əm) s. POL. conservadurismo.

con·ser·va·tive (kən-sûr′və-tĭv) I. adj. *(traditional)* conservador; *(moderate)* moderado <*a c. estimate* un cálculo moderado>; *(cautious)* prudente II. s. *(person)* conservador *m*; *(preservative)* preservativo.

con·ser·va·tor (kən-sûr′və-tər, kŏn′sər-vā′tər) s. *(protector)* protector *m*, defensor *m*; DER. tutor *m*.

con·ser·va·to·ry (kən-sûr′və-tôr′ē) s. [pl. **-ries**] *(for plants)* invernadero; *(school)* conservatorio.

con·serve (kən-sûrv′) I. tr. **-served, -serv·ing** conservar, preservar II. s. (kŏn′sûrv′) conserva, mermelada.

con·sid·er (kən-sĭd′ər) tr. *(to think over)* considerar, pensar; *(to believe)* juzgar, estimar; *(to bear in mind)* tener *o* tomar en cuenta; *(to show consideration for)* considerar; *(to examine)* examinar ♦ **all things considered** considerando todos los puntos • **to c. oneself** considerarse —intr. considerar, reflexionar.

con·sid·er·a·ble (kən-sĭd′ər-ə-bəl) I. adj. considerable II. s. FAM. cantidad considerable *f*.

con·sid·er·ate (kən-sĭd′ər-ĭt) adj. considerado, atento.

con·sid·er·a·tion (kən-sĭd′ə-rā′shən) s. *(careful thought)* consideración *f*; *(thoughtfulness)* consideración, miramiento; *(high regard)* estimación *f*; respeto; *(payment)* retribución *f*, gratificación *f* ♦ **after due c.** después de un detenido examen • **in c. of** en consideración a, en reconocimiento de • **out of c. for** por respeto a • **to take into c.** tomar en consideración • **under c.** en consideración.

con·sid·ered (kən-sĭd′ərd) adj. considerado ♦ **it is my c. opinion that** estoy convencido de que.

con·sid·er·ing (kən-sĭd′ər-ĭng) I. prep. considerando, teniendo en cuenta II. adv. FAM. considerándolo bien, después de todo.

con·sign (kən-sīn′) tr. COM. consignar; *(to entrust)* confiar.

con·sign·ee (kŏn′sī-nē′, kən-sī′nē′) s. COM. consignatario.

con·sign·ment (kən-sīn′mənt) s. COM. consignación *f* <*on c.* en consignación>.

con·sig·nor (kŏn′sī-nôr′, kən-sī′-) s. COM. consignador *m*.

con·sist (kən-sĭst′) intr. *(to be made up of)* consistir, componerse <*the city consists of seven districts* la ciudad consiste de siete distritos>; *(to lie in)* consistir, radicar <*its beauty consists in its simplicity* su belleza consiste en su sencillez>.

con·sis·ten·cy (kən-sĭs′tən-sē) s. [pl. **-cies**] *(coherence)* coherencia; *(compatibility)* conformidad *f*, acuerdo; *(firmness)* firmeza; *(texture)* consistencia.

con·sis·tent (kən-sĭs′tənt) adj. *(coherent)* coherente; *(com-*

patible) de acuerdo; *(firm)* firme; *(uniform in texture)* consistente.

con·sis·to·ry (kən-sĭs′tə-rē) s. [pl. **-ries**] RELIG. consistorio; *(counsel)* asamblea, congreso.

con·so·la·tion (kŏn′sə-lā′shən) s. consolación *f*, consuelo ♦ **c. prize** premio de consolación.

con·sole¹ (kən-sōl′) tr. **-soled, -sol·ing** consolar.

con·sole² (kŏn′sōl′) s. *(cabinet)* gabinete (de radio o televisor) *m*; MÚS. consola; ELEC., MEC. mesa de control, tablero de mando; ARQ. ménsula.

con·sol·i·date (kən-sŏl′ĭ-dāt′) tr. & intr. **-dat·ed, -dat·ing** *(to strengthen)* consolidar(se); *(to compress)* comprimir(se); *(to merge)* fusionar(se).

con·sol·i·da·tion (kən-sŏl′ĭ-dā′shən) s. *(act)* consolidación *f*; COM. fusión *f*.

con·sol·i·da·tor (kən-sŏl′ĭ-dā′tər) s. persona que consolida.

con·so·nance (kŏn′sə-nəns) s. *(accord, rhyme)* consonancia; GRAM., MÚS. consonancia.

con·so·nant (kŏn′sə-nənt) I. s. GRAM. consonante *f* II. adj. MÚS. consonante; *(in accordance)* conforme, de acuerdo.

con·so·nan·tal (kŏn′sə-năn′tl) adj. consonántico, de consonantes.

con·sort I. s. (kŏn′sôrt′) *(spouse)* consorte *mf*; *(partner)* socio, asociado; MARÍT. escolta II. tr. (kən-sôrt′) asociar, juntar —intr. *(to associate)* asociarse; *(to be in agreement)* estar de acuerdo.

con·sor·ti·um (kən-sôr′shē-əm) s. [pl. **-ti·a** (-shē-ə)] COM. consorcio.

con·spic·u·ous (kən-spĭk′yōō-əs) adj. *(noticeable)* destacado, evidente; *(visible)* visible; *(remarkable)* conspicuo ♦ **to be c.** destacar(se) • **to be c. by one's absence** brillar uno por su ausencia.

con·spic·u·ous·ness (kən-spĭk′yōō-əs-nĭs) s. *(obviousness)* evidencia; *(strikingness)* carácter llamativo.

con·spir·a·cy (kən-spîr′ə-sē) s. [pl. **-cies**] conspiración *f*.

con·spir·a·tor (kən-spîr′ə-tər) s. conspirador *m*.

con·spir·a·to·ri·al (kən-spîr′ə-tôr′ē-əl) adj. de conspirador, misterioso.

con·spire (kən-spīr′) intr. **-spired, -spir·ing** conspirar —tr. maquinar, tramar.

con·sta·ble (kŏn′stə-bəl, kŭn′-) s. *(peace officer)* alguacil *m*; HIST. *(officer)* condestable *m*; G.B. *(policeman)* policía *m*, guardia *m*.

con·stab·u·lar·y (kən-stăb′yə-lĕr′ē) I. s. [pl. **-ies**] *(police)* policía *f*; *(armed force)* fuerza armada II. adj. policial.

con·stan·cy (kŏn′stən-sē) s. *(persistence)* constancia; *(faithfulness)* fidelidad *f*, lealtad *f*; *(changelessness)* invariabilidad *f*.

con·stant (kŏn′stənt) I. adj. *(persistent)* constante; *(faithful)* fiel, leal; *(changeless)* invariable II. s. constante *f*.

Con·stan·ti·no·ple (kŏn′stăn′tə-nō′pəl) s. Constantinopla.

con·stel·la·tion (kŏn′stə-lā′shən) s. constelación *f*.

con·ster·na·tion (kŏn′stər-nā′shən) s. consternación *f*.

con·sti·pate (kŏn′stə-pāt′) tr. **-pat·ed, -pat·ing** MED. estreñir.

con·sti·pa·tion (kŏn′stə-pā′shən) s. MED. estreñimiento.

con·stit·u·en·cy (kən-stĭch′ōō-ən-sē) s. [pl. **-cies**] POL. *(voters)* electorado; *(district)* distrito electoral.

con·stit·u·ent (kən-stĭch′ōō-ənt) I. adj. *(component)* constituyente, constitutiva; POL. *(electoral)* electoral; *(constitution)* constituyente <*c. assembly* asamblea constituyente> II. s. *(component)* componente *m*; *(client)* poderante *mf*; *(voter)* elector *m*.

con·sti·tute (kŏn′stĭ-tōōt′, -tyōōt′) tr. **-tut·ed, -tut·ing** *(to compose, establish)* constituir; *(to appoint)* nombrar.

con·sti·tu·tion (kŏn′stĭ-tōō′shən, -tyōō′-) s. *(setting up)* constitución *f*, establecimiento; *(physical make-up)* constitución; POL. *(document)* constitución; *(statutes)* estatutos.

con·sti·tu·tion·al (kŏn′stĭ-tōō′shə-nəl, -tyōō′-) I. adj. constitucional II. s. caminata, paseo (para conservar la salud).

con·sti·tu·tion·al·ism (kŏn′stĭ-tōō′shə-nə-lĭz′əm, -tyōō′-) s. constitucionalismo.

con·sti·tu·tion·al·i·ty (kŏn′stĭ-tōō′shə-năl′ĭ-tē, -tyōō′-) s. constitucionalidad *f*.

constitutional monarchy s. monarquía constitucional.

con·strain (kən-strān') tr. *(to oblige)* constreñir, compeler; *(to confine)* encerrar; *(to restrict)* restringir.

con·strained (kən-strānd') adj. *(forced)* forzado <*a c. smile* una sonrisa forzada>; *(confined)* encerrado ♦ **to feel c. to** ver la necesidad de.

con·straint (kən-strānt') s. *(coercion)* constreñimiento, coacción *f*; *(restriction)* restricción *f*, limitación *f*; *(of feelings)* represión *f*; *(embarrassment)* molestia.

con·strict (kən-strĭkt') tr. & intr. *(to contract)* estrechar(se), encoger(se); *(to compress)* comprimir(se).

con·stric·tion (kən-strĭk'shən) s. constricción *f*.

con·stric·tive (kən-strĭk'tĭv) adj. constrictivo.

con·stric·tor (kən-strĭk'tər) s. *(muscle)* constrictor *m*; ZOOL. boa constrictora.

con·struct (kən-strŭkt') tr. construir.

con·struc·tion (kən-strŭk'shən) s. *(building)* construcción *f*; *(structure)* estructura; *(interpretation)* interpretación *f* ♦ **under c.** en construcción.

con·struc·tive (kən-strŭk'tĭv) adj. *(helpful, structural)* constructivo; DER. inferido, implícito.

con·struc·tor (kən-strŭk'tər) s. constructor *m*.

con·strue (kən-strōō') tr. **-strued, -stru·ing** *(to interpret)* interpretar; GRAM. construir —intr. *(to interpret)* GRAM. tener construcción, prestarse al análisis.

con·sul (kŏn'səl) s. DIPL., HIST. cónsul *m*.

con·su·lar (kŏn'sə-lər) adj. consular.

con·su·late (kŏn'sə-lĭt) s. consulado.

consul general s. [pl. **consuls general**] cónsul general *m*.

con·sult (kən-sŭlt') tr. & intr. consultar.

con·sult·ant (kən-sŭl'tənt) s. *(advisor)* asesor *m*, consultor *m*; MED. especialista *mf*.

con·sul·ta·tion (kŏn'səl-tā'shən) s. consultación *f*, consulta.

con·sul·ta·tive (kən-sŭl'tə-tĭv) adj. consultivo, asesor.

con·sult·ing (kən-sŭl'tĭng) s. consultor, asesor.

con·sum·a·ble (kən-sōō'mə-bəl) **I.** adj. consumible, de consumo **II.** s. COM. artículo de consumo.

consumable resources s.pl. recursos de consumo.

con·sume (kən-sōōm') tr. **-sumed, -sum·ing** *(to eat)* comerse; *(to drink)* beberse; *(to destroy)* consumir <*fire consumed the building* el fuego consumió el edificio>; *(to use up)* consumir; *(to take)* tomar (tiempo, esfuerzo) ♦ **to be consumed with** estar muerto de, estar consumido por —intr. consumirse.

con·sum·er (kən-sōō'mər) s. consumidor *m*.

consumer goods s.pl. bienes de consumo *m*.

con·sum·er·ism (kən-sōō'mə-rĭz'əm) s. movimiento de protección al consumidor.

consumer price index s. índice de precios de consumo *m*.

con·sum·mate **I.** tr. (kŏn'sə-māt') **-mat·ed, -mat·ing** consumar **II.** adj. (kən-sŭm'ĭt) consumado.

con·sum·ma·tion (kŏn'sə-mā'shən) s. *(completion)* consumación *f*; *(of a goal)* culminación *f*.

con·sump·tion (kən-sŭmp'shən) s. *(act)* consumo, consumisión *f*; ECON. consumo; MED. consunción *f*, tisis *f*.

con·sump·tive (kən-sŭmp'tĭv) **I.** adj. *(consuming)* consuntivo; MED. hético, tísico **II.** s. MED. tísico.

con·tact (kŏn'tăkt) **I.** s. *(touch)* contacto; *(connection)* relación *f* <*he has a lot of contacts* tiene muchas relaciones>; *(lens)* lente de contacto *mf* ♦ **to come in c. with** entrar en contacto con, tratar • **to get in c. with** ponerse en contacto con **II.** tr. *(to bring together)* poner en contacto; FAM. *(to communicate with)* ponerse en contacto —intr. *(to be together)* estar en contacto; *(to come together)* ponerse en contacto **III.** adj. de contacto <*c. sports* deportes de contacto>; MED. transmitido por contacto.

contact lens s. lente de contacto *mf*.

contact print s. FOTOG. copia por contacto.

con·ta·gion (kən-tā'jən) s. *(of a disease)* contagio; *(contamination)* contaminación *f*; FIG. *(influence)* contagio.

con·ta·gious (kən-tā'jəs) adj. contagioso, infeccioso.

con·ta·gious·ness (kən-tā'jəs-nĭs) s. contagiosidad *f*.

con·tain (kən-tān') tr. *(to hold)* contener; *(to include)* contener, abarcar; *(to control)* contener <*she could not c. her laughter* no pudo contener la risa>; MAT. ser divisible por ♦ **to c. oneself** contenerse.

con·tain·er (kən-tā'nər) s. *(receptacle)* recipiente *m*; *(package)* envase *m*; COM. *(for goods)* contenedor *m*.

con·tain·er·i·za·tion (kən-tā'nər-ĭ-zā'shən) s. COM. embalaje en contenedor *m*.

con·tain·er·ize (kən-tā'nə-rīz') tr. **-ized, -iz·ing** COM. embalar en contenedor.

container ship s. buque de carga (en contenedores) *m*.

con·tain·ment (kən-tān'mənt) s. contención *f*, represión *f*.

con·tam·i·nant (kən-tăm'ə-nənt) s. contaminador *m*, contaminante *m*.

con·tam·i·nate (kən-tăm'ə-nāt') tr. **-nat·ed, -nat·ing** contaminar.

con·tam·i·na·tion (kən-tăm'ə-nā'shən) s. contaminación *f*.

con·tem·plate (kŏn'təm-plāt') tr. **-plat·ed, -plat·ing** *(to look at)* contemplar; *(to ponder)* contemplar, considerar; *(to have in mind)* pensar, proyectar <*she was contemplating suicide* estaba pensando suicidarse>; *(to expect)* contar con <*they did not c. this possibility* no contaban con esta posibilidad> —intr. *(to meditate)* meditar; RELIG. contemplar.

con·tem·pla·tion (kŏn'təm-plā'shən) s. *(gazing)* contemplación *f*; *(meditation)* meditación *f*; *(intention)* intención *f*, perspectiva.

con·tem·pla·tive (kən-tĕm'plə-tĭv, kŏn'təm-plā'-) adj. contemplativo.

con·tem·po·ra·ne·ous (kən-tĕm'pə-rā'nē-əs) adj. contemporáneo.

con·tem·po·rar·y (kən-tĕm'pə-rĕr'ē) adj. & s. [pl. **-ies**] contemporáneo, coetáneo.

con·tempt (kən-tĕmpt') s. *(disdain)* desprecio, desdén *m*; DER. desacato <*c. of court* desacato al juez> ♦ **beneath c.** despreciable • **to hold in c.** despreciar.

con·tempt·i·ble (kən-tĕmp'tə-bəl) adj. despreciable, desdeñable.

con·temp·tu·ous (kən-tĕmp'chōō-əs) adj. despreciativo, desdeñoso.

con·tend (kən-tĕnd') intr. *(to fight)* contender, luchar; *(to compete)* competir, rivalizar; *(to argue)* argüir, disputar —tr. mantener, sostener <*I c. that she is mistaken* mantengo que ella está equivocada>.

con·tend·er (kən-tĕn'dər) s. *(competitor)* competidor *m*; *(rival)* contendiente *mf*.

con·tent¹ (kŏn'tĕnt') s. *(material contained)* contenido; *(meaning)* significado; *(proportion)* contenido, proporción *f* (de alcohol, proteína) ♦ **contents** contenido, materia.

con·tent² (kən-tĕnt') **I.** adj. *(satisfied)* contento, satisfecho; *(resigned)* resignado, conforme ♦ **to be c. with** contentarse con, conformarse con **II.** tr. contentar, satisfacer **III.** s. satisfacción *f* ♦ **to one's heart's c.** hasta saciarse.

con·tent·ed (kən-tĕn'tĭd) adj. contento, satisfecho.

con·ten·tion (kən-tĕn'shən) s. *(conflict)* contienda, disputa <*in c.* en disputa>; *(rivalry)* competencia, rivalidad *f*; *(assertion)* argumento, punto de vista.

con·ten·tious (kən-tĕn'shəs) adj. contencioso, pendenciero.

con·tent·ment (kən-tĕnt'mənt) s. contentamiento, satisfacción *f*.

con·ter·mi·nous (kən-tûr'mə-nəs) adj. limítrofe.

con·test **I.** s. (kŏn'tĕst') *(struggle)* contienda, lucha; *(competition)* competencia, concurso **II.** tr. (kən-tĕst') *(to compete for)* contender; *(to challenge)* cuestionar, impugnar —intr. contender, competir.

con·test·a·ble (kən-tĕs'tə-bəl) adj. discutible, cuestionable.

con·tes·tant (kən-tĕs'tənt) s. *(rival)* rival *mf*, contendiente *mf*; *(participant)* concursante *mf*.

con·text (kŏn'tĕkst') s. contexto ♦ **out of c.** fuera de contexto.

con·tex·tu·al (kən-tĕks'chōō-əl) adj. según el contexto.

con·ti·gu·i·ty (kŏn'tĭ-gyōō'ĭ-tē) s. [pl. **-ties**] contigüidad *f*.

con·tig·u·ous (kən-tĭg'yōō-əs) adj. contiguo, colindante.

con·ti·nence (kŏn'tə-nəns) s. continencia.

con·ti·nent (kŏn'tə-nənt) **I.** adj. continente **II.** s. GEOG. continente *m* ♦ **the C.** la Europa continental.

con·ti·nen·tal (kŏn'tə-nĕn'tl) **I.** adj. continental ♦ **C.** europeo ♦ **c. breakfast** desayuno completo **II.** s. ♦ **C.** europeo (habitante).

continental divide s. GEOG. divisoria continental.

---

continental shelf s. GEOG. plataforma continental.
con·tin·gen·cy (kən-tĭn'jən-sē) s. [pl. **-cies**] contingencia.
con·tin·gent (kən-tĭn'jənt) I. adj. *(likely)* contingente, eventual; *(dependent)* dependiente de, subordinado a; *(accidental)* fortuito, accidental ♦ **to be c. on** depender de II. s. *(eventuality)* contingencia; *(delegation)* contingente *m*.
con·tin·u·a (kən-tĭn'yōō-ə) un pl. de **continuum**.
con·tin·u·al (kən-tĭn'yōō-əl) adj. continuo.
con·tin·u·ance (kən-tĭn'yōō-əns) s. *(continuation)* continuación *f*, prolongación *f*; *(permanence)* permanencia; *(duration)* duración *f*; DER. *(postponement)* aplazamiento.
con·tin·u·a·tion (kən-tĭn'yōō-ā'shən) s. continuación *f*.
con·tin·ue (kən-tĭn'yōō) intr. **-ued, -u·ing** *(to go on)* continuar, seguir; *(to last)* prolongarse, durar; *(to remain)* seguir, quedarse; *(to resume)* continuar, proseguir ♦ **to be continued** continuará —tr. *(to prolong)* prolongar; *(to develop)* desarrollar; *(to maintain)* mantener; *(to resume)* continuar; DER. *(to postpone)* aplazar.
con·tin·ued (kən-tĭn'yōōd) adj. *(continuous)* continuo; *(continual)* continuado.
con·ti·nu·i·ty (kŏn'tə-nōō'ĭ-tē, -nyōō'-) s. [pl. **-ties**] *(continuation)* continuidad *f*; CINEM., RAD., TELEV. guión *m*.
con·tin·u·ous (kən-tĭn'yōō-əs) adj. continuo.
con·tin·u·um (kən-tĭn'yōō-əm) s. [pl. **-u·a** (-yōō-ə) o **-u·ums**] continuo.
con·tort (kən-tôrt') tr. torcer, retorcer —intr. desfigurarse, demudarse (el rostro).
con·tor·tion (kən-tôr'shən) s. contorsión *f*.
con·tor·tion·ist (kən-tôr'shə-nĭst) s. contorsionista *mf*.
con·tour (kŏn'tōōr') I. s. *(outline)* contorno; TOP. curva de nivel ♦ **contours** superficie curva, curvatura II. tr. *(to outline)* contornear, perfilar; *(to build)* construir según los accidentes del terreno.
contour map s. TOP. mapa o plano topográfico, mapa acotado.
con·tra·band (kŏn'trə-bănd') s. contrabando.
con·tra·bass (kŏn'trə-bās') s. MÚS. contrabajo.
con·tra·bas·soon (kŏn'trə-bə-sōōn') s. MÚS. contrafagot *m*.
con·tra·cep·tion (kŏn'trə-sĕp'shən) s. contracepción *f*.
con·tra·cep·tive (kŏn'trə-sĕp'tĭv) adj. & s. contraceptivo, anticonceptivo.
con·tract I. s. (kŏn'trăkt') *(agreement)* contrato; *(document)* contrato; *(betrothal)* capitulaciones *f*; *(in bridge)* contrato; JER. *(murder assignment)* contrato para asesinar <there is a c. on him hay un contrato para asesinarlo> ♦ **under c.** bajo contrato II. tr. (kən-trăkt') *(to agree to)* contratar; *(to acquire)* contraer <to c. obligations contraer obligaciones>; *(to shrink)* contraer, encoger; MED. coger, contraer; GRAM. contraer —intr. *(to reach an agreement)* hacer un contrato; *(to shrink)* contraerse, encogerse.
contract bridge s. bridge contrato *m*.
con·trac·tile (kən-trăk'təl, -tīl') adj. contráctil.
con·tract·ing (kən-trăk'tĭng) I. adj. *(of a contract)* contratante, contrayente; *(shrinking)* contractivo, contráctil II. s. contratación *f*.
con·trac·tion (kən-trăk'shən) s. contracción *f*.
con·trac·tor (kən-trăk'tər, kən-trăk'-) s. COM. contratista *mf*; ANAT. músculo que se contrae.
con·trac·tu·al (kən-trăk'chōō-əl) adj. contractual.
con·tra·dict (kŏn'trə-dĭkt') tr. & intr. contradecir(se).
con·tra·dic·tion (kŏn'trə-dĭk'shən) s. contradicción *f*.
con·tra·dic·to·ry (kŏn'trə-dĭk'tə-rē) adj. contradictorio.
con·tra·dis·tinc·tion (kŏn'trə-dĭ-stĭngk'shən) s. contraste *m*.
con·trail (kŏn'trāl') s. AER. estela de condensación.
con·tra·in·di·cate (kŏn'trə-ĭn'dĭ-kāt') tr. **-cat·ed, -cat·ing** contraindicar.
con·trap·tion (kən-trăp'shən) s. artefacto.
con·tra·pun·tal (kŏn'trə-pŭn'tl) adj. MÚS. de contrapunto.
con·tra·ri·e·ty (kŏn'trə-rī'ĭ-tē) s. [pl. **-ties**] contrariedad *f*, oposición *f*.
con·trar·i·ness (kŏn'trĕr'ē-nĭs, kən-trâr'-) s. *(opposition)* contrariedad *f*; *(willfulness)* testarudez *f*, terquedad *f*.
con·trar·i·wise (kŏn'trĕr'ē-wīz', kən-trâr'-) adv. *(on the contrary)* al contrario; *(opposite)* al revés.

con·trar·y (kŏn'trĕr'ē) I. adj. *(opposed)* contrario, opuesto; *(adverse)* adverso; *(ornery)* testarudo, terco II. s. [pl. **-ies**] lo contrario, lo opuesto ♦ **on the c.** al contrario, por el contrario • **quite the c.!** ¡todo lo contrario! • **to the c.** en contra, en contrario III. adv. contrariamente ♦ **c. to** en contra de.
con·trast I. tr. (kən-trăst') hacer contrastar, poner en contraste —intr. contrastar II. s. (kŏn'trăst') contraste *m* ♦ **in c.** por contraste • **in c. to** a diferencia de.
con·trast·y (kŏn'trăs'tē) adj. FOTOG. con muchos contrastes (de luz).
con·tra·vene (kŏn'trə-vēn') tr. **-vened, -ven·ing** *(to go against)* contravenir; *(to oppose)* oponerse a; DER. *(to infringe on)* contravenir.
con·tra·ven·tion (kŏn'trə-vĕn'shən) s. contravención *f*.
con·trib·ute (kən-trĭb'yōōt) tr. **-ut·ed, -ut·ing** *(to donate)* contribuir; *(an article)* escribir (para); *(information)* aportar —intr. *(to donate)* contribuir; *(to assist)* contribuir, cooperar; PERIOD. colaborar.
con·tri·bu·tion (kŏn'trĭ-byōō'shən) s. *(donation)* contribución *f*; *(article)* colaboración *f*.
con·trib·u·tor (kən-trĭb'yə-tər) s. contribuidor *m*, colaborador *m*.
con·trib·u·to·ry (kən-trĭb'yə-tôr'ē) adj. contribuyente, cooperante.
con·trite (kən-trīt', kŏn'trīt') adj. contrito, arrepentido.
con·tri·tion (kən-trĭsh'ən) s. contrición *f*, arrepentimiento.
con·tri·vance (kən-trī'vəns) s. *(invention)* invento; *(artifact)* artefacto; *(resourcefulness)* ingenio.
con·trive (kən-trīv') tr. **-trived, -triv·ing** *(to devise)* inventar, idear; *(to plan)* planear; *(to manage)* conseguir (hacer algo) —intr. *(to scheme)* maquinar; *(to plan)* formar planes.
con·trived (kən-trīvd') adj. artificial.
con·trol (kən-trōl') I. tr. **-trolled, -trol·ling** *(to direct)* controlar, dirigir; *(to restrain)* controlar, regular; *(to verify)* verificar, comprobar; *(to drive)* conducir ♦ **to c. oneself** dominarse II. s. *(authority)* control *m*, autoridad *f*; *(restraint)* restricción *f*, dominio; *(standard)* testigo, control ♦ **beyond our c.** fuera de nuestro control • **birth c.** control de la natalidad • **controls** mandos, controles • **remote c.** mando a distancia, control remoto • **to be in c.** tener el mando • **to be out of c.** estar fuera de control • **to be under c.** estar bajo control • **to get out of c.** desmandarse • **to lose c. of** perder control de • **to lose c. of oneself** perder el control.
con·trol·la·ble (kən-trō'lə-bəl) adj. *(manageable)* controlable, manejable; *(verifiable)* verificable, comprobable.
con·trol·ler (kən-trō'lər) s. *(device)* regulador *m*, control *m*; AVIA. controlador *m*; *(comptroller)* interventor *m*.
con·trol·ling (kən-trō'lĭng) adj. *(prevailing)* predominante; *(decisive)* determinante.
controlling interest s. FIN. *(ownership)* mayoría de acciones; *(owners)* accionistas principales *mf*.
control stick s. AVIA. palanca de mando.
control tower s. AER. torre de control o de mando *f*.
con·tro·ver·sial (kŏn'trə-vûr'shəl, -sē-əl) adj. *(disputable)* polémico, discutible; *(disputatious)* discutidor.
con·tro·ver·sy (kŏn'trə-vûr'sē) s. [pl. **-sies**] controversia, polémica.
con·tro·vert (kŏn'trə-vûrt', kŏn'trə-vûrt') tr. *(to contradict)* contradecir, rebatir; *(to debate)* controvertir, debatir.
con·tu·ma·cious (kŏn'tə-mā'shəs) adj. contumaz.
con·tu·sion (kən-tōō'zhən, -tyōō'-) s. contusión *f*.
co·nun·drum (kə-nŭn'drəm) s. *(riddle)* adivinanza, acertijo; *(problem)* enigma *m*.
con·va·lesce (kŏn'və-lĕs') intr. **-lesced, -lesc·ing** convalecer.
con·va·les·cence (kŏn'və-lĕs'əns) s. convalecencia *f*.
con·va·les·cent (kŏn'və-lĕs'ənt) adj. & s. convaleciente *m*.
con·vec·tion (kən-vĕk'shən) s. *(transmittal)* conducción *f*, transmisión *f*; FÍS., METEOR. convección *f*.
con·vec·tor (kən-vĕk'tər) s. estufa de convección.
con·vene (kən-vēn') intr. **-vened, -ven·ing** reunirse —tr. *(to convoke)* convocar; *(to summon)* citar.
con·ven·ience (kən-vēn'yəns) s. *(suitability)* conveniencia;

(comfort) comodidad *f; (advantage)* ventaja; *(useful device)* dispositivo útil; G.B. *(lavatory)* baño ♦ **at your c.** cuando guste • **at your earliest c.** tan pronto como le sea posible.

con·ven·ient (kən-vēn′yənt) adj. *(suitable)* conveniente; *(favorable)* oportuno; *(handy)* útil, ventajoso; *(comfortable)* cómodo.

con·vent (kŏn′vənt) s. convento.

con·ven·tion (kən-vĕn′shən) s. *(assembly)* convención *f; (agreement)* convenio, pacto; *(custom)* costumbre *f*, regla convencional.

con·ven·tion·al (kən-vĕn′shə-nəl) adj. *(conformist)* convencional; *(accepted)* normal, corriente; *(war, weapons)* clásico.

con·ven·tion·al·i·ty (kən-vĕn′shə-năl′ĭ-tē) s. [pl. **-ties**] convencionalismo.

con·ven·tion·eer (kən-vĕn′shə-nîr′) s. convencionista *mf.*

con·verge (kən-vûrj′) intr. **-verged, -verg·ing** converger, convergir —tr. hacer converger *o* convergir.

con·ver·gence (kən-vûr′jəns) *o* **con·ver·gen·cy** (-jən-sē) s. [pl. **-genc·es** *o* **-gen·cies**] convergencia.

con·ver·gent (kən-vûr′jənt) adj. convergente.

con·ver·sant (kən-vûr′sənt, kŏn′vər-) adj. ♦ **c. with** versado en, familiarizado con.

con·ver·sa·tion (kŏn′vər-sā′shən) s. conversación *f* ♦ **to make c.** dar conversación, platicar.

con·ver·sa·tion·al (kŏn′vər-sā′shə-nəl) adj. *(person)* locuaz, hablador; *(tone)* familiar; *(method)* de conversación.

con·ver·sa·tion·al·ist (kŏn′vər-sā′shə-nə-lĭst) s. conversador *m*, hablador *m.*

con·verse¹ I. intr. (kən-vûrs′) **-versed, -vers·ing** conversar, platicar II. s. (kŏn′vûrs′) conversación *f*, plática.

con·verse² I. adj. (kən-vûrs′, kŏn′vûrs′) inverso, contrario II. s. (kŏn′vûrs′) *(opposite)* lo opuesto, lo contrario; LÓG. proposición recíproca, conversa.

con·verse·ly (kən-vûrs′lē) adv. a la inversa.

con·ver·sion (kən-vûr′zhən) s. *(transformation)* conversión *f*, transformación *f*; DER. apropiación ilícita; DEP., LÓG., PSIC., RELIG. conversión, transformación.

con·vert I. tr. (kən-vûrt′) *(to transform)* convertir, transformar; *(to exchange)* convertir, cambiar; DER. apropiarse ilícitamente; DEP. convertir, transformar; LÓG., PSIC., RELIG. convertir —intr. *(to change)* convertirse; DEP. transformar un ensayo, lograr un tanto II. s. (kŏn′vûrt′) RELIG. converso.

con·vert·er *o* **con·ver·tor** (kən-vûr′tər) s. TEC. convertidor *m*; ELÉC. transformador *m.*

con·vert·i·bil·i·ty (kən-vûr′tə-bĭl′ĭ-tē) s. convertibilidad *f.*

con·vert·i·ble (kən-vûr′tə-bəl) I. adj. convertible II. s. AUTO. descapotable *m*, automóvil convertible *m.*

con·vex (kŏn′vĕks′, kən-vĕks′) adj. convexo.

con·vex·i·ty (kən-vĕk′sĭ-tē) s. [pl. **-ties**] convexidad *f.*

con·vex·o·con·cave (kŏn-vĕks′ō-kŏn-kāv′) adj. convexoconcavo.

con·vey (kən-vā′) tr. *(to carry)* transportar, llevar; *(to transmit)* transmitir; *(to impart)* impartir, comunicar; *(to suggest)* dar a entender; DER. transferir, ceder.

con·vey·ance (kən-vā′əns) s. *(means)* transporte *m; (transmission)* transmisión *f*; DER. *(transfer)* cesión *f*, traspaso; *(deed)* escritura de traspaso.

con·vey·er *o* **con·vey·or** (kən-vā′ər) s. *(transporter)* transportador *m; (belt)* cinta transportadora; DER. cedente *mf.*

con·vict I. tr. (kən-vĭkt′) declarar culpable, condenar II. s. (kŏn′vĭkt′) *(guilty person)* convicto; *(prisoner)* presidiario.

con·vic·tion (kən-vĭk′shən) s. DER. condena; *(act of convincing)* convencimiento; *(strong belief)* convicción *f* ♦ **to carry c.** *(statement)* ser convincente; *(person)* expresarse con convicción.

con·vince (kən-vĭns′) tr. **-vinced, -vinc·ing** convencer.

con·vinc·ing (kən-vĭn′sĭng) adj. convincente.

con·viv·i·al (kən-vĭv′ē-əl) adj. *(sociable)* sociable; *(festive)* jovial, festivo.

con·vo·ca·tion (kŏn′və-kā′shən) s. *(act)* convocación *f; (assembly)* asamblea.

con·voke (kən-vōk′) tr. **-voked, -vok·ing** convocar.

con·vo·lute (kŏn′və-lōōt′) I. adj. *(coiled)* enrollado; *(intri-*

cate) intrincado, complicado II. tr. & intr. **-luted, -lut·ing** enrollar(se).

con·vo·lut·ed (kŏn′və-lōō′tĭd) adj. *(coiled)* enrollado; *(intricate)* intrincado, complicado.

con·vo·lu·tion (kŏn′və-lōō′shən) s. *(contortion)* enrollamiento, tortuosidad *f*; ANAT. circunvolución *f.*

con·voy I. tr. (kən-voi′) escoltar, convoyar II. s. (kŏn′voi′) convoy *m.*

con·vulse (kən-vŭls′) tr. **-vulsed, -vuls·ing** convulsionar ♦ **to be convulsed with laughter** estar muerto de risa —intr. padecer convulsiones.

con·vul·sion (kən-vŭl′shən) s. MED. convulsión *f; (laughter)* ataque de risa *m.*

con·vul·sive (kən-vŭl′sĭv) adj. convulsivo.

coo (kōō) I. s. arrullo II. intr. arrullar.

cook (kŏŏk) I. tr. *(to prepare)* cocinar, guisar; *(to treat by heat)* cocer ♦ **to c. up** FAM. *(to fabricate)* inventar; *(to plot)* tramar —intr. *(to undergo cooking)* cocinarse, guisarse; *(to prepare food)* cocinar; FAM. *(to happen)* suceder, pasar <*what's cooking?* ¿qué pasa?> II. s. cocinero.

cook·book (kŏŏk′bŏŏk′) s. libro de cocina.

cook·er (kŏŏk′ər) s. *(stove)* cocina, hornillo; *(pot)* olla <*pressure c.* olla de presión>.

cook·er·y (kŏŏk′ə-rē) s. *(art)* arte culinaria, cocina; *(place)* cocina.

cook·ie (kŏŏk′ē) s. var. de **cooky.**

cook·ing (kŏŏk′ĭng) I. s. *(act)* cocción *f; (method)* cocina <*Italian c.* cocina italiana> II. adj. de cocina.

cook·out (kŏŏk′out′) s. comida cocinada al aire libre.

cook·y (kŏŏk′ē) s. [pl. **-ies**] galletita, bizcochito.

cool (kōōl) I. adj. **-er, -est** *(moderately cold)* fresco <*c. weather* tiempo fresco>; *(said of clothes)* fresco <*a c. blouse* una blusa fresca>; *(calm)* tranquilo, sereno; *(unenthusiastic)* frío, indiferente <*a c. greeting* un saludo frío>; *(impudent)* descarado, audaz; *(color)* fresco, frío; JER. *(excellent)* fenomenal; FAM. *(full)* la friolera de, nada menos que <*they lost a c. million* perdieron la friolera de un millón de dólares> ♦ **as c. as a cucumber** más fresco que una lechuga • **to keep c.** no perder la calma • **to play it c.** tomarlo con calma II. tr. & intr. *(to make, become cool)* refrescar(se), enfriar(se); *(to moderate, abate)* apaciguar(se), serenar(se) ♦ **c. it!** JER. ¡cálmate! • **to c. off** *(to get colder)* refrescarse; *(to calm down)* calmarse, tranquilizarse; *(to lose enthusiasm)* perder el entusiasmo, entibiarse • **to c. one's heels** estar esperando mucho tiempo, hacer antesala larga III. s. fresco, frescor *m* ♦ **in the c.** al fresco • **to lose one's c.** perder la serenidad.

cool·ant (kōō′lənt) s. líquido refrigerante.

cool·er (kōō′lər) s. *(cooling device)* enfriador *m; (refrigerator)* refrigerador *m; (drink)* refresco; JER. *(prison)* chirona, calabozo.

cool-head·ed (kōōl′hĕd′ĭd) adj. sereno, tranquilo.

coo·lie (kōō′lē) s. coolí *m*, culí *m.*

cool·ing (kōō′lĭng) adj. refrescante.

cooling system s. *(of a refrigerator)* sistema de refrigeración *m; (of an engine)* sistema de enfriamiento.

cool·ly (kōōl′lē) adv. *(coldly)* friamente; *(calmly)* tranquilamente; *(with detachment)* indiferentemente.

cool·ness (kōōl′nĭs) s. *(temperature)* frescor *m*, fresco; *(calmness)* calma, serenidad *f; (lack of enthusiasm)* frialdad *f.*

coon (kōōn) s. ZOOL. mapache *m*; JER., DESPEC. *(Negro)* negro.

coop (kōōp) I. s. *(for poultry)* gallinero; JER. *(jail)* cárcel *f*, chirona ♦ **to fly the c.** fugarse, escaparse II. tr. ♦ **to c. up** encerrar, enjaular.

co-op (kō′ŏp′) s. FAM. cooperativa.

coo·per (kōō′pər) I. s. barrilero, cubero II. tr. & intr. fabricar barriles.

coo·per·age (kōō′pər-ĭj) s. tonelería, cubería.

co·op·er·ate (kō-ŏp′ə-rāt′) intr. **-at·ed, -at·ing** cooperar.

co·op·er·a·tion (kō-ŏp′ə-rā′shən) s. cooperación *f.*

co·op·er·a·tive (kō-ŏp′ər-ə-tĭv, -ə-rā′-) I. adj. *(joint)* cooperativo; *(helpful)* servicial II. s. cooperativa.

co-opt (kō-ŏpt′) tr. *(to elect)* elegir por votación colectiva;

(to appoint) nombrar sumariamente; *(to appropriate)* apropiar; *(to win over)* ganar (por asimilación).

co·or·di·nate (kō-ôr′dn-ĭt) **I.** s. *(equal)* igual *mf*, semejante *mf*; MAT. coordenada **II.** adj. *(equal)* igual, semejante; *(coordinated)* coordinado; MAT. coordenado **III.** tr. & intr. (-āt′) **-nat·ed, -nat·ing** coordinar(se).

co·or·di·nat·ing (kō-ôr′dn-ā′tĭng) adj. coordinador.

co·or·di·na·tion (kō-ôr′dn-ā′shən) s. coordinación *f.*

co·or·di·na·tor (kō-ôr′dn-ā′tər) s. coordinador *m.*

coot (kōōt) s. ORNIT. negreta, fúlica; FIG. *(idiot)* bobalicón *m*, memo.

cop¹ (kŏp) s. TEJ. canilla, husada; ANT. *(summit)* cima, cumbre *f.*

cop² (kŏp) **I.** s. FAM. policía *m* **II.** tr. **copped, cop·ping** JER. *(to steal)* robar; *(to seize)* capturar, prender ♦ **to c. a plea** FAM. declararse culpable de un delito menos grave a cambio de no ser acusado de otro peor • **to c. out** JER. echarse atrás.

co·pa·cet·ic (kō′pə-sĕt′ĭk) adj. FAM. excelente.

co·part·ner (kō-pärt′nər) s. consocio, copartícipe *mf.*

co·part·ner·ship (kō-pärt′nər-shĭp′) s. copropiedad *f*, asociación *f.*

co·pa·set·ic (kō′pə-sĕt′ĭk) adj. var. de **copacetic.**

cope¹ (kŏp) intr. arreglárselas FAM. *(to strive)* arreglárselas, dar abasto <to c. with studies and work arreglárselas para estudiar y trabajar>; *(to face up)* enfrentarse, hacer frente <to c. with a bad situation hacer frente a una mala situación>.

cope² (kŏp) **I.** s. *(cloak)* capa, manto; RELIG. *(cape)* capa pluvial; ARQ. *(vault)* bóveda, cúpula; *(coping)* albardilla, coronamiento **II.** tr. **coped, cop·ing** *(to dress)* vestir con una capa; ARQ. *(to vault)* poner una bóveda; *(a wall)* poner albardilla.

Co·pen·ha·gen (kō′pən-hā′gən, -hä′-) s. Copenhague.

cop·i·er (kŏp′ē-ər) s. *(machine)* copiadora; *(person)* copiador *m*, copista *mf.*

co·pi·lot (kō′pī′lət) s. copiloto.

cop·ing (kō′pĭng) s. ARQ. albardilla.

co·pi·ous (kō′pē-əs) adj. *(abundant)* copioso, abundante; *(wordy)* prolijo, florido.

co·plain·tiff (kō-plān′tĭf) s. DER. codemandante *mf.*

co·pla·nar (kō-plā′nər) adj. GEOM. coplanario.

cop-out (kŏp′out′) JER. s. *(surrender)* rendición *f*, resignación *f*; *(person)* persona que rehusa comprometerse.

cop·per¹ (kŏp′ər) **I.** s. QUÍM. cobre *m*; *(coin)* cobre (moneda); G.B. *(pot)* caldera **II.** tr. revestir de cobre **III.** adj. *(of copper)* cobre, cobreño; *(color)* cobrizo.

cop·per² (kŏp′ər) s. JER. policía *m.*

cop·per·head (kŏp′ər-hĕd′) s. ZOOL. víbora norteamericana.

cop·per·y (kŏp′ər-ē) adj. cobrizo.

copse (kŏps) s. bosquecillo, soto.

cop·ter (kŏp′tər) s. FAM. helicóptero.

cop·u·la (kŏp′yə-lə) s. GRAM., LÓG. cópula.

cop·u·late (kŏp′yə-lāt′) intr. **-lat·ed, -lat·ing** copularse.

cop·u·la·tion (kŏp′yə-lā′shən) s. copulación *f*, cópula.

cop·y (kŏp′ē) **I.** s. [pl. **-ies**] *(reproduction)* copia, imitación *f*; *(specimen)* ejemplar *m*; IMPR. original *m*, material *m* ♦ **to make a c. of** copiar, sacar una copia de • **to make good c.** PERIOD. ser tema interesante • **rough c.** borrador **II.** tr. **-ied, -y·ing** *(to make a copy of)* copiar, sacar en limpio; *(to imitate)* imitar —intr. *(to make a reproduction)* hacer una copia; *(to cheat)* copiar (en un examen); *(to reproduce)* reproducirse, ser reproducible.

cop·y·cat (kŏp′ē-kăt′) s. FAM. imitador *m*, remedador *m.*

cop·y·ed·it (kŏp′ē-ĕd′ĭt) tr. corregir (un manuscrito).

copy editor s. redactor *m*, corrector de originales *m.*

cop·y·read·er (kŏp′ē-rē′dər) s. *(editor)* corrector de manuscrito *m*; PERIOD. redactor de mesa *m.*

cop·y·right (kŏp′ē-rīt′) **I.** s. derechos de autor, propiedad literaria **II.** adj. protegido por los derechos de autor **III.** tr. registrar como propiedad literaria.

cop·y·writ·er (kŏp′ē-rī′tər) s. redactor de textos publicitarios *m.*

co·quette (kō-kĕt′) s. coqueta.

co·quet·tish (kō-kĕt′ĭsh) adj. coquetón.

cor·al (kôr′əl) **I.** s. coral *m* **II.** adj. coralino, de coral.

coral reef s. arrecife de coral *m.*

cord (kôrd) **I.** s. *(rope)* cuerda; *(wire)* cordón *m*; FIG. *(binding)* lazo, vínculo; TEJ. *(fabric)* pana; *(of wood)* cuerda (medida de leña) ♦ **cords** FAM. pantalones de pana • **spinal c.** médula espinal, espina dorsal • **umbilical c.** cordón umbilical • **vocal c.** cuerda vocal **II.** tr. *(to bind)* encordonar; *(to measure)* medir o amontonar en cuerdas (leña).

cord·age (kôr′dĭj) s. *(ropes)* cordaje *m*; MARÍT. jarcias; *(measurement)* cantidad de cuerdas (de leña) *f.*

cor·dial (kôr′jəl) **I.** adj. amable, amistoso **II.** s. cordial *m.*

cor·dial·i·ty (kôr-jăl′ĭ-tē) s. amabilidad *f.*

cord·less (kôrd′lĭs) adj. *(having no cord)* sin cable; *(battery-powered)* a baterías, a pilas.

cor·do·ba (kôr′də-bə) s. FIN. córdoba (unidad monetaria de Nicaragua) *m.*

cor·don (kôr′dn) **I.** s. cordón *m* **II.** tr. acordonar.

cor·do·van (kôr′də-vən) s. cordobán *m.*

cor·du·roy (kôr′də-roi′) s. pana ♦ **corduroys** pantalones de pana.

cord·wood (kôrd′wŏŏd′) s. haz de leña *m.*

core (kôr) **I.** s. *(heart)* corazón *m*, médula; *(center)* núcleo, foco <a c. of resistance un núcleo de resistencia>; BOT. corazón, hueso (de frutas); ELECTRÓN. núcleo magnético; METAL. macho, ánima (de molde); MIN. muestra de sondaje, testigo ♦ **to the c.** FIG. hasta la médula **II.** tr. **cored, cor·ing** quitar el corazón de.

core dump s. COMPUT. vuelco de la memoria.

co·re·spon·dent (kō′rĭ-spŏn′dənt) s. DER. cómplice del demandado en un divorcio *m.*

Cor·fu (kôr′fōō, -fyōō) s. Corfú.

co·ri·an·der (kôr′ē-ăn′dər) s. BOT. coriandro, cilantro.

Cor·inth (kôr′ĭnth) s. Corinto.

Co·rin·thi·an (kô-rĭn′thē-ən) adj. & s. corintio ♦ **Corinthians** BÍBL. Corintios.

cork (kôrk) **I.** s. *(bark)* corcho; *(stopper)* tapón *m*, corcho; *(float)* flotador *m*, corcho ♦ **to blow one's c.** explotar, enojarse **II.** tr. encorchar, taponar.

cork·age (kôr′kĭj) s. recargo que se paga en un restaurante por consumir una botella que no es de la casa.

cork·er (kôr′kər) s. *(machine)* encorchadora, máquina de taponar; FAM. *(character)* tipo formidable; *(lie)* mentira grande.

cork·screw (kôrk′skrōō′) **I.** s. tirabuzón *m*, sacacorchos *m* **II.** adj. en espiral, en caracol **III.** tr. & intr. *(to wind)* serpentear, girar en espiral.

cork-tipped (kôrk′tĭpt′) adj. con boquilla de corcho.

cork·y (kôr′kē) adj. *(like cork)* como el corcho; *(lively)* vivaz.

cor·mo·rant (kôr′mər-ənt) s. ORNIT. cormorán *m*, cuervo marino; *(person)* ave de rapiña *m.*

corn¹ (kôrn) s. maíz *m* <c. on the cob maíz en la mazorca>; *(grain)* grano <a pepper c. un grano de pimienta>; FAM. *(whiskey)* whisky de maíz *m*; JER. *(something mawkish)* cosa sensiblera; G.B. *(wheat)* trigo.

corn² (kôrn) s. MED. callo, callosidad *f.*

corn·ball (kôrn′bôl′) JER. **I.** s. patán *m* **II.** adj. sensiblero.

Corn Belt s. región maicera de los EE. UU.

corn·cob (kôrn′kŏb′) s. *(ear)* mazorca; *(pipe)* pipa hecha de mazorca.

corn·crib (kôrn′krĭb′) s. granero.

cor·ne·a (kôr′nē-ə) s. ANAT. córnea.

corned beef s. carne salada de res, carne en conserva.

cor·ner (kôr′nər) **I.** s. *(exterior angle)* esquina; *(interior angle)* rincón *m*; *(intersection)* esquina; *(predicament)* aprieto, apuro; FIG. *(place)* región *f*, rincón (de país, ciudad); *(guard)* cantonera, rinconera; *(monopoly)* monopolio, acaparamiento; ANAT. rabillo (del ojo); *(commissure)* comisura (de los labios) ♦ **around the c.** a la vuelta de la esquina • **in a c.** en un aprieto • **out of the c. of one's eye** con el rabillo del ojo • **the four corners of the earth** las cinco partes del mundo • **to cut corners** *(to go directly)* tomar atajos; *(to economize)* reducir gastos • **to drive someone into a c.** arrinconar o acorralar a alguien • **to turn the c.** doblar la esquina; *(to improve)* pasar el punto crítico II. tr. *(to trap)* arrinconar, acorralar; *(to monopolize)* monopolizar, acaparar —intr. *(to make an angle)* formar esquina; *(to turn)* doblar una esquina, tomar una curva.

cor·nered (kôr′nərd) adj. *(having corners)* angulado, esquinado; *(trapped)* arrinconado, acorralado.

cor·ner·stone o **corner stone** (kôr′nər-stōn′) s. piedra angular.

cor·net s. MÚS. (kôr-nĕt′) corneta; *(cone)* (kôr′nĭt) cucurucho, barquillo; *(headdress)* (kôr′nĭt) toca.

corn flakes s.pl. copos de maíz.

corn flour s. harina de maíz.

corn·flow·er (kôrn′flou′ər) s. BOT. aciano, liebrecilla.

corn·husk (kôrn′hŭsk′) s. vaina de maíz.

cor·nice (kôr′nĭs) s. ARQ. cornisa.

corn·meal o **corn meal** (kôrn′mēl′) s. harina de maíz

corn pone s. CUL. pan de maíz *m.*

corn·stalk o **corn stalk** (kôrn′stôk′) s. tallo del maíz.

corn·starch (kôrn′stärch′) s. maicena, almidón de maiz *m.*

cor·nu·co·pi·a (kôr′nə-kō′pē-ə) s. cornucopia, cuerno de la abundancia.

corn whiskey s. whisky de maíz *m.*

corn·y (kôr′nē) adj. **i·er, -i·est** *(old-fashioned)* pasado de moda; *(mawkish)* sensiblero; *(not funny)* demasiado obvio *<a c. joke* un chiste demasiado obvio>.

co·rol·la (kə-rŏl′ə, -rō′lə) s. BOT. corola.

cor·ol·lar·y (kôr′ə-lĕr′ē) I. s. [pl. **-ies**] *(proposition)* corolario; *(consequence)* consecuencia, resultado II. adj. consecuente.

co·ro·na (kə-rō′nə) s. [pl. **-nas** o **-nae** (-nē)] corona.

cor·o·nar·y (kôr′ə-nĕr′ē) adj. & s. [pl. **-ies**] coronario.

coronary thrombosis s. MED. trombosis coronaria.

cor·o·na·tion (kôr′ə-nā′shən) s. coronación *f.*

cor·o·ner (kôr′ə-nər) s. pesquisidor (que investiga la causa de un fallecimiento) *m.*

cor·o·net (kôr′ə-nĕt′) s. *(crown)* corona; *(diadem)* diadema.

cor·po·ra (kôr′pər-ə) pl. de **corpus.**

cor·po·ral¹ (kôr′pər-əl) adj. corporal, físico.

cor·po·ral² (kôr′pər-əl) s. MIL. cabo.

corporal punishment s. castigo corporal.

cor·po·rate (kôr′pər-ĭt) adj. *(incorporated)* constituido en sociedad; *(of a corporation)* corporativo; *(collective)* colectivo; *(combined)* combinado.

cor·po·ra·tion (kôr′pə-rā′shən) s. COM. corporación *f,* sociedad anónima.

cor·po·ra·tive (kôr′pər-ə-tĭv, -pə-rā′tĭv) adj. corporativo.

cor·po·re·al (kôr-pôr′ē-əl) adj. *(bodily)* corpóreo; *(material)* material, tangible.

corps (kôr) s. [pl. **corps**] MIL. *(unit)* cuerpo; *(professional group)* cuerpo *<diplomatic c.* cuerpo diplomático> ♦ **c. de ballet** cuerpo de ballet • **Peace C.** EE. UU. Cuerpo de Paz.

corpse (kôrps) s. cadáver *m.*

cor·pu·lence (kôr′pyə-ləns) s. corpulencia, gordura.

cor·pu·lent (kôr′pyə-lənt) adj. corpulento, gordo.

cor·pus (kôr′pəs) s. [pl. **-po·ra** (-pər-ə)] *(body)* cuerpo; *(capital)* capital *m;* *(collection)* cuerpo, recopilación (de escritos) *f.*

cor·pus·cle (kôr′pə-səl) s. corpúsculo.

cor·pus·cu·lar (kôr-pŭs′kyə-lər) adj. corpuscular.

cor·ral (kə-răl′) I. s. corral *m* II. tr. **-ralled, -ral·ling** *(to pen up)* acorralar, encerrar; FAM. *(to seize)* capturar, conseguir.

cor·rect (kə-rĕkt′) I. tr. *(to make right)* corregir; *(to admonish)* reprender; *(to remedy)* subsanar, remediar; *(to adjust)* ajustar, rectificar —intr. *(to amend)* hacer correcciones; *(to compensate)* hacer ajustes ♦ **to stand corrected** confesar que uno se equivocó II. adj. correcto ♦ **to be c.** tener razón.

cor·rect·a·ble o **cor·rect·i·ble** (kə-rĕk′tə-bəl) adj. capaz de corrección, corregible.

cor·rec·tion (kə-rĕk′shən) s. *(act)* corrección *f;* *(punishment)* castigo; *(adjustment)* ajuste *m,* rectificación *f;* FIN. *(decline)* corrección, declinación (en la bolsa) *f.*

cor·rec·tion·al (kə-rĕk′shə-nəl) adj. correccional.

cor·rec·tive (kə-rĕk′tĭv) I. adj. correctivo II. s. medida correctiva, remedio.

cor·rect·ness (kə-rĕkt′nĭs) s. *(propriety)* corrección *f;* *(accuracy)* exactitud *f.*

cor·rec·tor (kə-rĕk′tər) s. corrector *m.*

cor·re·late (kôr′ə-lāt′) I. tr. **-lat·ed, -lat·ing** correlacionar, poner en correlación —intr. estar en correlación II. adj. & s. correlativo.

cor·re·la·tion (kôr′ə-lā′shən) s. correlación *f.*

cor·rel·a·tive (kə-rĕl′ə-tĭv) I. adj. correlativo II. s. *(correlate)* correlativo; GRAM. palabra correlativa.

cor·re·spond (kôr′ĭ-spŏnd′) intr. *(to agree)* corresponder, convenir; *(to be equivalent)* equivaler; *(to write)* escribirse, comunicarse por carta.

cor·re·spon·dence (kôr′ĭ-spŏn′dəns) s. correspondencia ♦ **c. course** curso por correspondencia.

cor·re·spon·dent (kôr′ĭ-spŏn′dənt) I. s. *(writer)* corresponsal *mf;* *(correlative)* cosa correspondiente II. adj. correspondiente.

cor·re·spon·ding (kôr′ĭ-spŏn′dĭng) adj. correspondiente.

cor·ri·dor (kôr′ĭ-dər, -dôr′) s. *(hallway)* pasillo, corredor *m;* GEOG. corredor.

cor·rob·o·rate (kə-rŏb′ə-rāt′) tr. **-rat·ed, -rat·ing** corroborar, confirmar.

cor·rob·o·ra·tion (kə-rŏb′ə-rā′shən) s. corroboración *f,* confirmación *f.*

cor·rob·o·ra·tive (kə-rŏb′ə-rā′tĭv, -ər-ə-) adj. corroborativo.

cor·rode (kə-rōd′) tr. & intr. **-rod·ed, -rod·ing** corroer(se).

cor·ro·sion (kə-rō′zhən) s. corrosión *f.*

cor·ro·sive (kə-rō′sĭv) I. adj. corrosivo II. s. sustancia corrosiva.

cor·ru·gate (kôr′ə-gāt′) tr. & intr. **-gat·ed, -gat·ing** estriar(se) (chapa, hierro).

cor·ru·gat·ed (kôr′ə-gā′tĭd) adj. *(cardboard)* corrugado, estriado; *(metal)* acanalado.

cor·ru·ga·tion (kôr′ə-gā′shən) s. *(act)* ondulado; *(groove)* estrías.

cor·rupt (kə-rŭpt′) I. adj. *(depraved)* corrompido, depravado; *(dishonest)* corrupto, venal; *(decaying)* contaminado, podrido; *(containing errors)* alterado, lleno de errores II. tr. *(to subvert)* corromper; *(to bribe)* sobornar; *(to pervert)* pervertir; *(to contaminate)* contaminar; *(to alter)* alterar —intr. corromperse.

cor·rupt·er (kə-rŭp′tər) s. corruptor *m,* pervertidor *m.*

cor·rupt·i·ble (kə-rŭp′tə-bəl) adj. corruptible.

cor·rupt·ing (kə-rŭp′tĭng) adj. corruptor.

cor·rup·tion (kə-rŭp′shən) s. corrupción *f.*

cor·rup·tive (kə-rŭp′tĭv) adj. corruptivo.

cor·rupt·ness (kə-rŭpt′nĭs) s. corruptela, venalidad *f.*

cor·sage (kôr-säzh′, -säj′) s. *(bouquet)* ramillete *m;* *(bodice)* cuerpo.

cor·sair (kôr′sâr′) s. *(pirate)* corsario, pirata *m;* *(ship)* corsario, barco pirata.

corse·let o **cors·let** (kôr′slĭt) s. MIL. coselete *m.*

cor·set (kôr′sĭt) s. corsé *m.*

Cor·si·ca (kôr′sĭ-kə) s. Córcega.

Cor·si·can (kôr′sĭ-kən) adj. & s. corso.

cor·tege o **cor·tège** (kôr-tĕzh′) s. cortejo, séquito.

cor·tex (kôr′tĕks′) s. [pl. **-ti·ces** (-tĭ-sēz′) o **-tex·es**] corteza.

cor·ti·cal (kôr′tĭ-kəl) adj. ANAT. cortical.

cor·ti·ces (kôr′tĭ-sēz′) un pl. de **cortex.**

cor·ti·sone (kôr′tĭ-sōn′, -zōn′) s. FARM. cortisona.

cor·run·dum (kə-rŭn′dəm) s. MIN. corindón *m.*

cor·vette (kôr-vĕt′) s. corbeta.

co·ry·za (kə-rī′zə) s. MED. coriza, catarro nasal.

co·se·cant (kō-sē′kănt′) s. MAT. cosecante *f.*

co·sign o **co·sign** (kō′sīn′) tr. *(to sign)* firmar junto con otro *u* otros; FIN. *(to endorse)* avalar.

co·sig·na·to·ry (kō-sĭg′nə-tôr′ē) s. [pl. **-ries**] cosignatario.

co·sign·er (kō′sī′nər) s. cosignatario.

co·sine (kō′sīn′) s. MAT. coseno.

cos·met·ic (kŏz-mĕt′ĭk) s. & adj. cosmético.

cos·me·tol·o·gy (kŏz′mĭ-tŏl′ə-jē) s. cosmética.

cos·mic (kŏz′mĭk) adj. cósmico.

cosmic ray s. ASTRON., FÍS. rayo cósmico.

cos·mog·o·ny (kŏz-mŏg′ə-nē) s. [pl. **-nies**] cosmogonía.

101

cos·mog·ra·phy (kŏz-mŏg′rə-fē) s. [pl. **-phies**] cosmografía.
cos·mol·o·gy (kŏz-mŏl′ə-jē) s. [pl. **-gies**] cosmología.
cos·mo·naut (kŏz′mə-nôt′) s. cosmonauta *mf*, astronauta *mf*.
cos·mo·pol·i·tan (kŏz′mə-pŏl′ĭ-tn) adj. & s. cosmopolita *mf*.
cos·mop·o·lite (kŏz-mŏp′ə-līt′) s. cosmopolita *mf*.
cos·mos (kŏz′məs) s. cosmos *m*.
Cos·sack (kŏs′ăk′) s. & adj. cosaco.
cost (kôst) **I.** s. *(expense)* costo, coste *m*, costa <*c. of living* costo de vida>; *(price)* precio, coste ♦ **at all costs** *o* **at any c.** cueste lo que cueste • **at c.** a precio de costo • **at the c. of** a costa de • **costs** *(expenses)* gastos; *(risks)* riesgos; DER. costas **II.** intr. **cost, cost·ing** costar —tr. calcular el costo de.
cost accountant s. COM. contador de costos *m*.
cos·tal (kŏs′təl) adj. ANAT. costal, de la costilla.
co·star *o* **co-star** (kō′stär′) **I.** s. actor de uno de los papeles estelares *m* **II.** intr. **-starred, -star·ring** ♦ **costarring** con • **to c. with** figurar en un papel estelar con.
Cos·ta Ri·ca (kŏs′tə rē′kə, kô′stə) s. Costa Rica.
Costa Ri·can (rē′kən) adj. & s. costarriqueño, costarricense *mf*.
cos·tive (kŏs′tĭv) adj. *(constipated)* estreñido, estíptico; *(stingy)* tacaño; *(sluggish)* lerdo.
cost·ly (kôst′lē) adj. **-li·er, -li·est** *(expensive)* caro; *(valuable)* valioso; *(entailing loss)* costoso.
cost-plus (kôst′plŭs′) s. COM. costo de producción más una utilidad fija.
cos·tume I. s. (kŏs′tōōm′, -tyōōm′) *(style of dress)* traje *m*; *(fashion)* atuendo; *(disguise)* máscara, disfraz *m* ♦ **c. ball** baile de disfraces • **costumes** TEAT. vestuario **II.** tr. (kŏ-stōōm′, -styōōm′) **-tumed, -tum·ing** *(to dress)* vestir; *(to disguise)* disfrazar.
cos·tum·er (kŏs′tōō′mər, -tyōō′-) *o* **cos·tum·i·er** (kŏ-stōō′mē-ā′, styōō′-) s. *(seller)* mascarero; *(tailor)* sastre de teatro *m*.
co·sy (kō′zē) adj. var. de **cozy**.
cot¹ (kŏt) s. catre *m*.
cot² (kŏt) s. choza, casa de campo.
co·tan·gent (kō-tăn′jənt) s. MAT. cotangente *f*.
cote (kŏt) s. *(for sheep)* redil *m*; *(dovecote)* palomar *m*; REG. *(cottage)* cabaña.
co·ten·ant (kō-tĕn′ənt) s. coinquilino.
co·ter·ie (kō′tə-rē) s. *(group)* tertulia; *(clique)* camarilla, peña.
co·ter·mi·nous (kō-tûr′mə-nəs) adj. limítrofe.
co·til·lion (kō-tĭl′yən) s. cotillón *m*.
cot·tage (kŏt′ĭj) s. casa de campo, chalet *m*.
cottage cheese s. requesón *m*, cuajada.
cot·ter (kŏt′ər) s. MEC. chaveta.
cotter pin s. pasador de chaveta m.
cot·ton (kŏt′n) **I.** s. *(plant)* algodón *m*, algodonero; *(fiber, cloth)* algodón ♦ **c. fabric** tela de algodón • **c. industry** industria algodonera **II.** intr. ♦ **to c. to** FAM. sentirse atraído por.
cotton candy s. algodón de azúcar *m*.
cotton gin s. AGR. desmotadora.
cot·ton·seed (kŏt′n-sēd′) s. [pl. **cottonseed** *o* **-seeds**] semilla de algodón.
cot·ton·tail (kŏt′n-tāl′) s. ZOOL. liebre de cola blanca *f*.
cot·ton·wood (kŏt′n-wōōd′) s. BOT. álamo de Virginia.
cotton wool s. *(raw cotton)* algodón en rama *m*; G.B. *(absorbent cotton)* algodón absorbente.
cot·ton·y (kŏt′n-ē) adj. *(fluffy)* algodonoso; *(nappy)* velloso.
cot·y·le·don (kŏt′l-ēd′n) s. BOT. cotiledón *m*.
couch (kouch) **I.** s. *(sofa)* sofá *m*; *(bed)* lecho **II.** tr. *(to lie down)* recostar; *(a spear)* poner en ristre; *(to phrase)* expresar, formular <*he couched the complaint tactfully* expresó su queja discretamente> —intr. ANT. *(to lie down)* recostarse; *(to lurk)* acechar.
cou·gar (kōō′gər) s. puma *m*.
cough (kôf) **I.** intr. toser —tr. ♦ **to c. up** *(to expel)* escupir; JER. *(to produce)* soltar **II.** s. tos *f*.
cough drop s. pastilla para la tos.
could §G11 (kōōd) pret. de **can¹**.

could·n't (kōōd′nt) contr. de **could not**.
cou·lee (kōō′lē) s. *(ravine)* barranco; *(of lava)* corriente de lava *f*.
cou·lomb (kōō′lŏm′, -lōm′) s. ELEC. culombio.
coun·cil (koun′səl) s. *(assembly)* consejo, junta; *(of church officials)* concilio ♦ **city** *o* **town c.** concejo municipal • **c. member** POL. consejero.
coun·cil·man (koun′səl-mən) s. [pl. **-men**] concejal *m*.
coun·cil·or *o* **coun·cil·lor** (koun′sə-lər) s. consejero.
coun·cil·wo·man (koun′səl-wōōm′ən) s. [pl. **-wom·en** (-wĭm′ĭn)] concejala.
coun·sel (koun′səl) **I.** s. *(advice)* consejo; *(consultation)* consulta; *(plan)* plan *m*; DER. *(attorney)* abogado; *(adviser)* asesor jurídico ♦ **c. for the defense** DER. abogado defensor • **c. for the prosecution** DER. fiscal • **to keep one's own c.** guardar secreto • **to take c.** consultar, asesorarse **II.** tr. aconsejar —intr. consultar.
coun·sel·or *o* **coun·sel·lor** (koun′sə-lər) s. *(adviser)* consejero; *(consultant)* asesor *m*; *(lawyer)* abogado.
coun·sel·or-at-law (koun′sə-lər-ət-lô′) s. [pl. **counselors-at-law**] abogado.
count¹ (kount) **I.** tr. *(to enumerate)* contar; *(to include)* contar, tener en cuenta <*ten dogs, counting the puppies* diez perros, teniendo en cuenta los cachorros>; *(to deem)* considerar ♦ **to c. against** ir en contra de, pesar contra • **to c. for** valer por, equivaler a • **to c. in** incluir • **to c. on** *o* **upon** contar con, confiar en • **to c. out** excluir • **to c. up** contar • **to c. up to** ascender a, sumar —intr. *(to recite numbers)* contar <*c. by tens* cuente de diez en diez>; *(to have importance)* tener importancia, valer <*his opinions don't c.* sus opiniones no tienen ninguna importancia>; *(to keep time)* llevar el compás ♦ **to c. down** contar hacia atrás, contar al revés **II.** s. *(act)* cuenta; *(number)* cómputo, cálculo; *(totality)* total *m*, suma; *(charge)* cargo ♦ **to keep c. of** llevar la cuenta de • **to lose c. of** perder la cuenta de.
count² (kount) s. conde *m*.
count·a·ble (koun′tə-bəl) adj. contable, contadero.
count·down (kount′doun′) s. cuenta atrás.
coun·te·nance (koun′tə-nəns) **I.** s. semblante *m*, cara ♦ **to be out of c.** estar desconcertado • **to give c. to** sancionar • **to keep one's c.** contenerse **II.** tr. **-nanced, -nanc·ing** sancionar, aprobar.
coun·ter¹ (koun′tər) **I.** adj. contrario, opuesto **II.** s. *(opposite)* lo contrario, lo opuesto; *(in boxing, fencing)* contragolpe *m*, contra ♦ **the c. to** lo contrario de **III.** tr. *(a blow)* contrarrestar; *(to oppose)* oponerse a, contrariar; *(to respond)* replicar, contestar —intr. contraatacar **IV.** adv. de modo contrario ♦ **to go** *o* **to run c. to** ir en contra de.
count·er² (koun′tər) s. *(of a shop)* mostrador *m*; *(of a bank)* ventanilla; *(of a kitchen)* tablero, mesa; *(chip, token)* ficha ♦ **over the c.** FIN. *(transaction)* mediante un corredor de bolsa; *(drugs)* sin receta • **under the c.** por debajo del tapete.
count·er³ (koun′tər) s. *(enumerator)* contador *m*.
coun·ter·act (koun′tər-ăkt′) tr. *(to check)* contrarrestar; *(to oppose)* contrariar.
coun·ter·at·tack I. s. (koun′tər-ə-tăk′) contraataque *m* **II.** intr. & tr. (koun′tər-ə-tăk′) contraatacar.
coun·ter·bal·ance I. s. (koun′tər-băl′əns) contrapeso **II.** tr. (koun′tər-băl′əns) **-anced, -anc·ing** contrapesar.
coun·ter·charge I. s. (koun′tər-chärj′) DER. *(charge)* reconvención *f*; MIL. contraataque *m* **II.** tr. (koun′tər-chärj′) **-charged, -charg·ing** *(to charge)* reconvenir; MIL. contraatacar.
coun·ter·check I. s. (koun′tər-chĕk′) *(check)* contrarresto; *(crosscheck)* comprobación adicional *f* **II.** tr. (koun′tər-chĕk′) *(to check)* contrarrestar; *(to crosscheck)* comprobar de nuevo.
coun·ter·claim I. s. (koun′tər-klām′) DER. contrademanda **II.** tr. (koun′tər-klām′) contrademandar.
coun·ter·clock·wise (koun′tər-klŏk′wīz′) adv. & adj. en sentido contrario a las agujas del reloj, de derecha a izquierda.
coun·ter·cul·ture (koun′tər-kŭl′chər) s. contracultura, anticultura.

ng inglés / ŏ la / ō bou / ô corre / oi oigo / ōō uno / ou auto / yōō ciudad / w hueco / y yo / z mismo

coun·ter·es·pi·o·nage (koun'tər-ĕs'pē-ə-näzh') s. contraespionaje *m.*

coun·ter·feit (koun'tər-fīt') **I.** tr. *(to forge)* falsificar, contrahacer; *(to feign)* simular, fingir **II.** adj. *(money)* contrahecho, falso; *(jewel)* falso; *(feigned)* simulado, fingido **III.** s. *(imitation)* falsificación *f*, imitación *f*; *(money)* moneda falsa.

coun·ter·feit·er (koun'tər-fīt'ər) s. *(forger)* falsificador (de dinero) *m*; *(faker)* simulador *m*, falso.

coun·ter·foil (koun'tər-foil') s. talón (de un cheque) *m.*

coun·ter·in·sur·ance (koun'tər-ĭn-shŏŏr'əns) s. contraseguro.

coun·ter·in·tel·li·gence (koun'tər-ĭn-tĕl'ə-jəns) s. contraespionaje *m.*

coun·ter·ir·ri·tant (koun'tər-îr'ĭ-tnt) s. MED. contrairritante *m.*

coun·ter·mand **I.** tr. (koun'tər-mănd') contramandar, contraordenar **II.** s. (koun'tər-mănd') contramandato, contraorden *f.*

coun·ter·march MIL. **I.** s. (koun'tər-märch') contramarcha **II.** intr. (koun'tər-märch') contramarchar.

coun·ter·mea·sure (koun'tər-mĕzh'ər) s. contramedida.

coun·ter·move (koun'tər-mōōv') s. contramaniobra.

coun·ter·of·fen·sive (koun'tər-ə-fĕn'sĭv) s. MIL. contraofensiva.

coun·ter·pane (koun'tər-pān') s. colcha, cubrecama *m.*

coun·ter·part (koun'tər-pärt') s. *(opposite number)* colega equivalente *mf*; *(of a set)* pareja; *(double)* doble *m*; *(complement)* complemento.

coun·ter·plot (koun'tər-plŏt') **I.** s. contracomplot *m* **II.** intr. **-plot·ted, -plot·ting** conspirar.

coun·ter·point (koun'tər-point') s. contrapunto.

coun·ter·poise (koun'tər-poiz') **I.** s. *(weight, influence)* contrapeso; *(equilibrium)* equilibrio **II.** tr. **-poised, -pois·ing** contrapesar.

coun·ter·pro·duc·tive (koun'tər-prə-dŭk'tĭv) adj. contraproducente.

coun·ter·pro·pos·al (koun'tər-prə-pō'zəl) s. contrapropuesta.

coun·ter·ref·or·ma·tion (koun'tər-rĕf'ər-mā'shən) s. contrarreforma.

coun·ter·rev·o·lu·tion (koun'tər-rĕv'ə-lōō'shən) s. contrarrevolución *f.*

coun·ter·rev·o·lu·tion·ar·y (koun'tər-rĕv'ə-lōō'shə-nĕr'ē) adj. & s. [pl. **-ies**] contrarrevolucionario.

coun·ter·sign (koun'tər-sīn') **I.** tr. refrendar **II.** s. *(signature)* refrendata, firma avaladora; *(password)* contraseña.

coun·ter·sig·na·ture (koun'tər-sĭg'nə-chər) s. refrendata, aval *m.*

coun·ter·sink (koun'tər-sĭngk') MEC. **I.** s. *(hole)* agujero avellanado; *(tool)* avellanador *m* **II.** tr. **-sunk** (sŭngk'), **-sink·ing** avellanar.

coun·ter·spy (koun'tər-spī') s. [pl. **-spies**] contraespía *mf.*

coun·ter·vail (koun'tər-vāl') tr. *(to counteract)* contrarrestar; *(to offset)* compensar.

coun·ter·weigh (koun'tər-wā') tr. contrapesar.

coun·ter·weight (koun'tər-wāt') s. contrapeso.

count·ess (koun'tĭs) s. condesa.

count·ing (koun'tĭng) s. cuenta, contaje *m.*

count·ing·house (koun'tĭng-hous') s. COM. oficina de contabilidad.

count·less (kount'lĭs) adj. incontable, innumerable.

coun·tri·fied (kŭn'trĭ-fīd') adj. rústico.

coun·try (kŭn'trē) s. [pl. **-tries**] *(land)* país *m*, tierra <*Spain was the c. of the Goths* España era la tierra de los godos>; *(rural area)* campo <*to live in the c.* vivir en el campo>; *(nation)* país, nación *f*; *(homeland)* patria; DER. *(jury)* jurado.

country and western s. EE. UU. estilo de música popular.

country club s. club de actividades deportivas y sociales *m.*

country estate s. finca, heredad *f.*

country house s. casa de campo, quinta.

coun·try·man (kŭn'trē-mən) s. [pl. **-men**] *(compatriot)* compatriota *mf*; *(inhabitant)* ciudadano; *(rustic)* campesino.

country music s. EE. UU. estilo de música popular.

coun·try·side (kŭn'trē-sīd') s. campo, paisaje *m.*

coun·try·wom·an (kŭn'trē-wŏŏm'ən) s. [pl. **-wom·en** (-wĭm'-ĭn)] *(compatriot)* compatriota, paisana; *(inhabitant)* habitante *f*; *(rustic)* campesina.

coun·ty (koun'tē) s. [pl. **-ties**] condado, distrito.

county seat s. capital del condado *f*, cabeza de distrito.

coup (kōō) s. *(masterstroke)* golpe maestro; *(coup d'état)* golpe (de estado).

coup d'é·tat (kōō' dā-tä') s. POL. golpe de estado *m.*

coup de grâce (kōō' də gräs') s. golpe de gracia *m.*

coupe (kōōp) s. automóvil de dos puertas.

cou·pé (kōō-pā') s. cupé *m.*

cou·ple (kŭp'əl) **I.** s. *(pair)* par *m*, pareja; *(of spouses)* matrimonio, pareja; *(two people)* pareja; *(several)* par, unos cuantos <*a c. of days* un par de días>; par **II.** tr. **-pled, -pling** *(to join)* juntar; *(to marry)* unir, casar; *(sexually)* acoplar; ELEC., TEC. acoplar —intr. *(to join)* juntarse; *(sexually)* acoplarse.

cou·pler (kŭp'lər) s. ELEC. acoplador *m*; *(for railroad cars)* empalme *m.*

cou·plet (kŭp'lĭt) s. pareado.

cou·pling (kŭp'lĭng) s. *(copulating)* acoplamiento; F.C. *(coupler)* empalme *m*; ELEC., TEC. *(connection)* acoplamiento.

cou·pon (kōō'pŏn', kyōō'-) s. *(certificate)* cupón *m*, vale *m*; *(blank)* solicitud *f*; *(for payments)* talón *m.*

cour·age (kûr'ĭj) s. coraje *m*, valor *m* ♦ **to have the c. of one's convictions** obrar según los principios de uno • **to take c.** animarse.

cou·ra·geous (kə-rā'jəs) adj. valiente.

cou·ri·er (kŏŏr'ē-ər) s. correo, cosario.

course (kôrs) **I.** s. *(progress)* curso, transcurso <*during the c. of the deliberations* durante el transcurso de las deliberaciones>; *(duration)* transcurso <*in the c. of a year* en el transcurso de un año>; *(direction)* dirección *f*, rumbo <*the c. of a ship* el rumbo de un barco>; *(flow)* curso; *(trajectory)* trayectoria, recorrido; *(mode of action)* proceder *m*, línea de conducta <*he followed the best c. and waited* siguió la mejor línea de conducta y esperó>; *(development)* marcha, desarrollo; *(way, means)* camino, vía; *(part of a meal)* plato <*the main c.* el plato fuerte>; *(curriculum)* programa *m*; *(unit of a curriculum)* curso, asignatura <*a French c.* un curso de francés>; DEP. *(racetrack)* pista; *(in golf)* campo; ARQ. *(layer of material)* hilada; MARÍT. *(sail)* vela baja; *(heading)* rumbo, derrotero ♦ **c. of action** línea de acción • **c. of treatment** tratamiento, cura • **in due c.** a su debido tiempo • **matter of c.** cosa común y corriente, cosa de cajón • **of c.** por supuesto, claro • **of c. not** por supuesto que no, claro que no • **to change c.** cambiar de rumbo • **to take** o **run its c.** seguir a su curso, llegar a su debido fin **II.** tr. **coursed, cours·ing** *(to traverse)* atravesar, recorrer; *(to hunt)* cazar con perros —intr. *(to proceed)* encaminarse; *(to flow)* correr.

court (kôrt) **I.** s. *(courtyard)* patio; *(alley)* callejón sin salida *m*; *(palace)* palacio; *(retinue)* corte *f*; DER. *(tribunal)* tribunal *m*, corte; *(courthouse)* juzgado, corte; *(session)* audiencia <*open c.* audiencia pública>; *(playing area)* cancha ♦ **c. jester** bufón de la corte • **c. order** orden judicial • **juvenile c.** tribunal de menores • **to pay c. to** *(to flatter)* adular; *(to woo)* hacer la corte a, cortejar • **to settle out of c.** llegar a un arreglo • **to take to c.** llevar a los tribunales **II.** tr. *(to fawn)* adular; *(to woo)* requebrar, enamorar; *(to seek)* buscar, procurar <*to c. success* buscar el éxito>; *(to invite)* ir en busca de, exponerse a <*to c. danger* ir en busca del peligro> —intr. hacer la corte.

cour·te·ous (kûr'tē-əs) adj. *(polite)* cortés, atento; *(considerate)* atento.

cour·te·san (kôr'tĭ-zən) s. cortesana.

cour·te·sy (kûr'tĭ-sē) s. [pl. **-sies**] *(behavior)* cortesía; *(remark)* cumplido <*to exchange courtesies* cambiar cumplidos> ♦ **out of c.** por cortesía • **to do someone the c. of** o **the c. to** tener la amabilidad de.

court·house (kôrt'hous') s. palacio de justicia, tribunales *m.*

court·i·er (kôr'tē-ər) s. cortesano.

court·ing (kôr'tĭng) s. cortejo, galanteo.

court·li·ness (kôrt'lē-nĭs) s. *(urbanity)* cortesanía, urbanidad *f*; *(elegance)* elegancia.

ã rey / ä año / b boca / ch chico / d dar / ĕ el / ē mil / g gato / h joya / hw juez / ī aire / k casa / kw cuan /

court·ly (kôrt′lē) adj. **-li·er, -li·est** *(stately)* cortés; *(elegant)* distinguido, elegante.
court-mar·tial (kôrt′mär′shəl) **I.** s. [pl. **courts-martial**] consejo de guerra, tribunal militar *m* **II.** tr. procesar *o* juzgar en consejo de guerra.
court of appeals s. DER. tribunal de apelación *m*.
court·room (kôrt′rōōm′, -rōōm′) s. sala de justicia.
court·ship (kôrt′shĭp′) s. *(act)* corte *f*; *(period)* noviazgo.
court·yard (kôrt′yärd′) s. patio.
cous·in (kŭz′ĭn) s. primo ♦ **first c.** primo hermano • **second s.** primo segundo.
couth (kōōth) adj. pulido, refinado.
co·va·lence (kō-vā′ləns) s. QUÍM. covalencia.
co·va·lent bond (kō-vā′lənt) s. QUÍM. enlace covalente *m*.
co·var·i·ant (kō-vâr′ē-ənt) adj. FÍS., MAT. covariante.
cove (kōv) s. *(bay)* abra, cala; *(cave)* cueva; *(gap)* abra; ARQ. moldura convexa.
cov·en (kŭv′ən) s. reunión de brujas *f*.
cov·e·nant (kŭv′ə-nənt) **I.** s. *(agreement)* convenio, pacto; *(contract)* contrato; BÍBL. alianza **II.** tr. prometer (en un convenio) —intr. hacer un convenio *o* pacto.
cov·er (kŭv′ər) **I.** tr. *(to place upon)* cubrir; *(to overlay)* cubrir, revestir <to c. a wall with cement revestir una pared de cemento>; *(to put a covering on)* tapar; *(to put a wrapper around)* forrar <to c. a book forrar un libro>; *(to sheathe)* poner el forro a; *(to clothe)* cubrir, tapar <c. your ears tápate las orejas>; *(to extend over)* abarcar, ocupar una extensión de; *(to conceal)* cubrir, ocultar; *(to hush up)* ocultar, encubrir; *(to protect)* cubrir, proteger; *(to insure)* asegurar; *(to compensate for)* compensar; *(to defray)* cubrir <to c. all expenses cubrir todos los gastos>; *(to embrace)* cubrir, abarcar; *(to deal with)* tratar <the book does not c. such matters el libro no trata esos asuntos>; *(to report)* informar sobre; *(to traverse)* cubrir, recorrer; *(to work in)* cubrir, ocuparse de; *(to hold within aim)* encañonar, vigilar (con un arma); *(a bet)* igualar, igualar; DEP. *(to guard)* cubrir; ZOOL. *(to copulate)* cubrir; *(to incubate)* empollar ♦ **to c. oneself with glory** cubrirse de gloria • **to c. one's tracks** tapar las huellas • **to c. over** cubrir por completo • **to c. the ground** *(distance)* recorrer a buen paso; *(task)* desempeñar bien una tarea • **to c. up** *(to cover completely)* cubrir por completo; *(to conceal)* disimular, encubrir —intr. cubrir; FAM. *(to substitute)* cubrir el puesto <can you c. for me tonight? ¿puedes cubrir mi puesto esta noche?>; *(to hide)* encubrir, servir de pantalla **II.** s. *(something that covers)* cubierta; *(lid)* tapa; *(sheath)* funda, forro; *(jacket)* cubierta, forro; *(of a magazine)* portada; *(bedspread)* cobertor *m*, sobrecama; *(of a parcel)* envoltura; *(pretense)* pretexto, excusa; *(shelter)* refugio; *(protection)* amparo; *(underbrush)* guarida; *(hiding place)* escondite *m*; *(table setting)* cubierto; *(envelope)* sobre *m*; *(funds)* fondos ♦ **covers** ropa de cama • **to break c.** salir del escondite • **to take c.** refugiarse, ponerse a cubierto • **under c.** *(under a roof)* bajo techo, a cubierto; *(operating secretly)* cubiertamente, clandestinamente • **under separate c.** por separado, aparte.
cov·er·age (kŭv′ər-ĭj) s. *(of a subject)* tratamiento; *(in the news)* reportaje *m*; *(of insurance policy)* riesgos incluidos, protección *f*; *(for liabilities)* fondos.
cov·er·alls (kŭv′ər-ôlz′) s.pl. mono.
cover charge s. precio de entrada *o* del cubierto.
covered wagon s. carromato, carretón de toldo *m*.
cover girl s. modelo fotográfica *f*.
cov·er·ing (kŭv′ər-ĭng) s. *(for protection)* cubierta; *(wrapping)* envoltura; *(clothing)* ropa; *(layer)* capa <a c. of leaves una capa de hojas>.
cov·er·let (kŭv′ər-lĭt) s. colcha, sobrecama.
cover letter s. carta adjunta *o* explicatoria.
cov·ert (kŭv′ərt, kō-vûrt′) **I.** adj. *(sheltered)* cobijado; *(furtive)* disimulado, furtivo; *(secret)* secreto **II.** s. *(shelter)* cobija; *(underbrush)* matorral *m*; ORNIT. cobertera.
cov·er-up *o* **cov·er·up** (kŭv′ər-ŭp′) s. encubrimiento, ocultamiento.
cov·et (kŭv′ĭt) tr. codiciar.
cov·et·ous (kŭv′ĭ-təs) adj. codicioso.

cov·ey (kŭv′ē) s. [pl. **-eys**] ORNIT. *(flock)* nidada (de perdices); *(group)* grupo.
cow¹ (kou) s. ZOOL. *(of cattle)* vaca; *(of other animals)* hembra; JER. *(woman)* lechona.
cow² (kou) tr. intimidar, atemorizar.
cow·ard (kou′ərd) s. cobarde *mf*.
cow·ard·ice (kou′ər-dĭs) s. cobardía.
cow·ard·ly (kou′ərd-lē) **I.** adj. cobarde **II.** adv. cobardemente.
cow·bell (kou′bĕl′) s. cencerro.
cow·boy (kou′boi′) s. vaquero ♦ **c. boots** botas de vaquero.
cow·catch·er (kou′kăch′ər, -kĕch′-) s. F.C. rastrillo delantero, quitapiedras *m*.
cow·er (kou′ər) intr. encogerse de miedo.
cow·girl (kou′gûrl′) s. vaquera.
cow·hand (kou′hănd′) s. vaquero.
cow·herd (kou′hûrd′) s. vaquero.
cow·hide (kou′hīd′) s. *(leather)* cuero *o* piel *f* de vaca; *(whip)* látigo de cuero.
cowl (koul) s. *(of a monk)* capucha; *(of a chimney)* sombrerete *m*; AVIA. capota.
cow·lick (kou′lĭk′) s. mechón (de pelo) *m*.
cowl·ing (kou′lĭng) s. AVIA. capota.
cow·man (kou′măn′) s. [pl. **-men** (-mĕn′)] *(owner)* ganadero; *(cowboy)* vaquero.
co-work·er (kō′wûr′kər) s. compañero de trabajo.
cow·poke (kou′pōk′) s. FAM. vaquero.
cow pony s. caballo ganadero.
cow·pox (kou′pŏks′) s. VET. vacuna.
cow·punch·er (kou′pŭn′chər) s. FAM. vaquero.
cow·ry *o* **cow·rie** (kou′rē) s. [pl. **-ries**] ICT. cauri (caracol marino).
cow·slip (kou′slĭp′) s. BOT. primavera, prímula.
cow town s. pueblo de la zona ganadera.
cox·comb (kŏks′kōm′) s. *(dandy)* petimetre *m*; ANT. *(cap)* gorro de bufón.
cox·swain (kŏk′sən, -swān′) s. timonel *m*.
coy (koi) adj. **-er, -est** *(shy)* reservado, tímido; *(demure)* remilgado, gazmoño; *(evasive)* evasivo, esquivo.
coy·ness (koi′nĭs) s. *(shyness)* timidez *f*; *(affectation)* afectación *f*, gazmoñería.
coy·o·te (kī-ō′tē, kī′ōt′) s. ZOOL. coyote *m*.
co·zi·ly (kō′zə-lē) adv. *(warmly)* acogedoramente; *(comfortably)* cómodamente.
co·zi·ness (kō′zē-nĭs) s. *(comfort)* comodidad *f*; *(privacy)* intimidad *f*.
co·zy (kō′zē) **I.** adj. **-zi·er, -zi·est** *(warm)* caliente; *(comfortable)* cómodo ♦ **to play it c.** JER. actuar con cautela **II.** intr. **-zied, -zy·ing** ♦ **to c. up to** FAM. arrimarse a **III.** s. [pl. **-zies**] cubretetera.
crab¹ (krăb) **I.** s. *(crustacean)* cangrejo; *(louse)* ladilla; *(hoist)* grúa ♦ **C.** ASTROL. cangrejo • **to catch a c.** dar un golpe en falso con el remo **II.** intr. **crabbed, crab·bing** *(to catch)* pescar cangrejos; *(to move)* moverse oblicuamente.
crab² (krăb) **I.** s. refunfuñón *m*, cascarrabias *mf* **II.** intr. **crabbed, crab·bing** FAM. refunfuñar —tr. FAM. *(to ruin)* estropear; *(to criticize)* refunfuñar contra.
crab apple s. BOT. *(tree)* manzano silvestre; *(fruit)* manzana silvestre.
crab·bed (krăb′ĭd) adj. *(irritable)* refunfuñón, de malas pulgas; *(intricate)* enredado.
crab·by (krăb′ē) adj. **-bi·er, -bi·est** refunfuñón, de malas pulgas.
crab·grass (krăb′grăs′) s. BOT. garranchuelo.
crack (krăk) **I.** intr. *(to break)* <the eggs cracked se rompieron los huevos>; *(to make a snapping sound)* restallar <the whip cracked el látigo restalló>; *(to snap one's fingers)* chasquear (los dedos); *(to pop)* crujir <his knuckles cracked sus nudillos crujieron>; *(to split)* rajarse, agrietarse; *(to splinter)* astillarse; *(the voice)* cascarse, quebrarse; *(to break down)* romperse; *(to fail)* fallar; FAM. *(to have a breakdown)* sufrir un colapso; *(to go mad)* chiflarse, volverse loco; QUÍM. *(to decompose)* fraccionarse ♦ **to c. down** tomar medidas enérgicas • **to c. up** *(to wreck)* estrellarse, hacerse pedazos; *(physically)* sufrir un colapso, agotarse; *(mentally)* perder la razón, enloquecer; *(to laugh)*

morirse de risa • **to get cracking** FAM. poner manos a la obra —tr. *(to snap)* restallar; *(to cause to snap)* chasquear (esp. los dedos); *(to pop)* hacer crujir (esp. los nudillos); *(to split)* rajar, agrietar; *(to splinter)* astillar; *(to break)* romper, partir; *(to strike)* pegar, golpear; *(to break open)* forzar <*to c. a safe* forzar una caja fuerte>; *(to split open)* cascar (esp. nueces); *(to uncap)* abrir, destapar; *(to decipher)* descifrar; FAM. *(to tell)* contar, gastarse; *(to cause to have a breakdown)* hacer sufrir un colapso a; QUÍM. *(to decompose)* fraccionar • **to c. a window open** abrir un poquito una ventana • **to c. up** *(to wreck)* estrellar, hacer pedazos; *(to cause amusement)* hacer morir de risa; *(to praise)* elogiar, pintar <*he was not as smart as he was cracked up to be* él no era tan listo como lo pintaban> **II.** s. *(of a whip)* restallido; *(of the fingers)* chasquido; *(of the knuckles)* crujido; *(of a firearm)* estallido; *(split)* rajadura, grieta; *(slit)* rendija; *(blow)* golpe *m*, porrazo; *(of the voice)* gallo; *(chance)* oportunidad *f*; *(witty remark)* salida, chiste *m*; *(sarcastic remark)* pulla; *(instant)* instante *m*, momento • **at the c. of dawn** al romper el alba • **to fall through the cracks** ser pasado por alto • **to take a c. at** probar, intentar **III.** adj. *(skillful)* experto; *(first-rate)* de primera, excelente.

crack·brain (krăk′brān′) s. FAM. chiflado, tocado.
crack·down (krăk′doun′) s. medidas represivas.
cracked (krăkt) adj. *(broken)* cuarteado, agrietado; FAM. *(insane)* chiflado, loco.
crack·er (krăk′ər) s. *(biscuit)* galleta; *(firecracker)* petardo.
crack·er-bar·rel (krăk′ər-băr′əl) adj. rústico, tosco.
crack·er·jack (krăk′ər-jăk′) JER. **I.** adj. maravilloso **II.** s. maravilla.
crack·ing (krăk′ĭng) **I.** s. QUÍM. craqueo, fraccionamiento **II.** adj. extraordinario.
crack·le (krăk′əl) **I.** intr. **-led, -ling** *(to pop)* crepitar, chisporrotear; *(to become cracked)* agrietarse; FIG. *(to be vivacious)* rebozar vivacidad —tr. *(to crush)* hacer crujir; *(to crack)* agrietar **II.** s. *(act, sound)* crepitación *f*, chisporroteo; *(crackling)* crujido; *(cracks)* rayado, rayadura; *(pottery, glassware)* objeto rayado o estriado.
crack·ling (krăk′lĭng) s. crepitación *f*, traqueteo • **cracklings** chicharrones.
crack·pot (krăk′pŏt′) s. chiflado, excéntrico.
crack·up (krăk′ŭp′) s. *(collision)* choque *m*; *(of an airplane)* caída; *(breakdown)* colapso (físico, nervioso).
Crac·ow (krăk′ou′, krä′kou′) s. Cracovia.
cra·dle (krād′l) **I.** s. *(bed, period)* cuna, basada; *(of a phone)* horquilla, gancho; *(for a mechanic)* camilla; MED. arco; MIN. criba • **to rob the c.** FAM. salir o casarse con una persona muy joven **II.** tr. **-dled, -dling** *(to place in)* poner en la cuna; *(in one's arms)* mecer en los brazos; *(to support)* sostener; *(to care for)* criar; MIN. pasar por la criba.
cra·dle·song (krād′l-sông′) s. nana, canción de cuna *f*.
craft (krăft) s. *(skill)* habilidad *f*, arte *m*; *(guile)* habilidad, astucia; *(trade)* oficio; *(guild)* gremio; *(boat)* nave *f*, embarcación *f*; *(airplane)* avión *m*.
craft·i·ness (krăf′tē-nĭs) s. *(shrewdness)* astucia, maña; ANT. *(dexterity)* habilidad *f*, ingenio.
crafts·man (krăfts′mən) s. [pl. **-men**] *(artisan)* artesano; *(maker)* artífice *m*.
crafts·man·ship (krăfts′mən-shĭp′) s. *(work)* artesanía; *(skill)* habilidad *f*, arte *m*; *(finish)* remate *m*, hechura.
craft·y (krăf′tē) adj. **-i·er, -i·est** hábil, astuto.
crag (krăg) s. risco, peñasco.
crag·gy (krăg′ē) adj. **-gi·er, -gi·est** *(having crags)* peñascoso; *(steep)* escarpado.
cram (krăm) **I.** tr. **crammed, cram·ming** *(to stuff)* empujar, meter a la fuerza; *(to overfill)* abarrotar, llenar hasta los topes; *(with food)* atiborrarse de —intr. *(with food)* atiborrarse, atracarse; FAM. *(for an exam)* estudiar a última hora **II.** s. *(crush)* aglomeración *f*; FAM. *(study)* estudio de última hora.
cramp¹ (krămp) **I.** s. MED. calambre *m* • **cramps** retortijones **II.** tr. *(muscles)* dar calambre en; *(stomach)* dar retortijones en —intr. acalambrarse.
cramp² (krămp) **I.** s. *(iron)* grapa; *(clamp)* torno, cárcel *f*;

(limitation) restricción *f* **II.** tr. *(to hold together)* engrapar; *(to restrict)* restringir • **to c. one's style** JER. cortar los vuelos a uno **III.** adj. apretado.
cramped (krămpt) adj. *(crowded)* apretado, apiñado; *(difficult)* incómodo, estrecho <*in c. circumstances* en circunstancias incómodas>; *(illegible)* ilegible, indescifrable.
cram·pon (krăm′pŏn′) s. • **crampons** *(for lifting)* garfio; DEP. *(for climbing)* trepadores.
cran·ber·ry (krăn′běr′ē) s. [pl. **-ries**] BOT. arándano (arbusto y fruto).
crane (krān) **I.** s. ORNIT. grulla; *(for hoisting)* grúa **II.** tr. **craned, cran·ing** *(to hoist)* levantar con una grúa; *(to stretch)* estirar —intr. estirar el cuello.
cra·ni·a (krā′nē-ə) un pl. de **cranium**.
cra·ni·al (krā′nē-əl) adj. craneal, craneano.
cra·ni·um (krā′nē-əm) s. [pl. **-ni·ums** o **-ni·a** (-nē-ə)] cráneo.
crank (krăngk) **I.** s. *(handle)* manivela; MEC. *(crankshaft)* cigüeñal *m*; *(verbal conceit)* juego de palabras; FAM. *(grouch)* cascarrabias *mf*; *(eccentric)* excéntrico, chiflado **II.** tr. MEC. *(start)* arrancar (un motor) dando vueltas a la manivela; *(to bend)* acodar; *(to provide with a handle)* poner una manivela a FIG. producir como si fuera una máquina <*he cranked out book after book* producía libro tras libro como si fuera una máquina> • **to c. up** FIG. poner en movimiento, echar a andar <*to c. up a publicity campaign* echar a andar una campaña de publicidad> —intr. MEC. *(to turn a crank)* dar vueltas a una manivela; *(to wind)* dar vueltas.
crank·case (krăngk′kās′) s. MEC. cárter del cigüeñal *m*.
crank·i·ness (krăng′kē-nĭs) s. *(irritability)* irritabilidad *f*, mal humor *m*; *(eccentricity)* excentricidad *f*; *(whim)* capricho, manía; *(craziness)* chifladura.
crank·shaft (krăngk′shăft′) s. MEC. cigüeñal *m*.
crank·y (krăng′kē) adj. **-i·er, -i·est** *(irritable)* quisquilloso, malhumorado; *(odd)* estrafalario, caprichoso; *(crooked)* tortuoso.
cran·ny (krăn′ē) s. [pl. **-nies**] grieta.
crap¹ (krăp) JER., VULG. **I.** s. *(excrement)* mierda; *(nonsense)* porquería, disparates *m*; *(lies)* cuentos; *(rubbish)* porquería • **to take a c.** cagar **II.** intr. **crapped, crap·ping** cagar.
crap² (krăp) **I.** s. mala tirada (en los dados) **II.** intr. **crapped, crap·ping** • **to c. out** *(in dice)* hacer una mala tirada; FAM. *(to get tired)* cansarse.
crape (krāp) **I.** s. *(fabric)* crespón *m*, crepé *m*; *(band)* crespón de luto **II.** tr. **craped, crap·ing** vestir con crespón.
craps (krăps) s.pl. [ú. con v. sing. o pl.] dados • **to shoot c.** jugar a los dados.
crap·shoot·er (krăp′shoo′tər) s. jugador de dados *m*.
crap·u·lence (krăp′yə-ləns) s. crápula.
crash (krăsh) **I.** intr. *(to fall)* caer; *(to smash)* estrellarse, chocar; *(to break)* romperse, hacerse pedazos; *(to resound)* retumbar, estallar; *(to burst in)* entrar violentamente, irrumpir; *(to go bankrupt)* quebrar; *(to fail)* fracasar; JER. *(to go to sleep)* irse a dormir —tr. *(to drop)* hacer caer; *(to smash)* estrellar, hacer chocar; *(to break)* romper, hacer pedazos; FAM. *(to join without invitation)* colarse, zamparse (en una fiesta) **II.** s. *(noise)* estrépito; *(collision)* choque *m*, colisión *f*; AVIA. caída, accidente *m*; COM. *(failure)* ruina, quiebra (de un negocio) **III.** adj. FAM. *(intensive)* intensivo <*a c. course* un curso intensivo>; AVIA. de emergencia <*a c. landing* aterrizaje de emergencia>.
crash dive s. MARÍT. sumersión de emergencia *f*.
crash helmet s. casco protector.
crash·ing (krăsh′ĭng) adj. *(total)* completo, absoluto; *(stunning)* impresionante, rotundo <*a c. success* un triunfo rotundo>.
crash-land (krăsh′lănd′) intr. AVIA. hacer un aterrizaje forzoso.
crass (krăs) adj. **-er, -est** craso, burdo.
crate (krāt) **I.** s. *(container)* cajón *m*; FAM. *(vehicle)* cacharro **II.** tr. **crat·ed, crat·ing** poner en un cajón.
cra·ter (krā′tər) s. cráter *m*.
cra·vat (krə-văt′) s. corbata.
crave (krāv) tr. **craved, crav·ing** *(to desire)* desvivirse por,

---

ã rey / ä año / b boca / ch chico / d dar / ĕ el / ē mil / g gato / h joya / hw juez / ī aire / k casa / kw cuan /

desear ardientemente; *(to require)* morirse por; *(to beg)* implorar, suplicar —intr. ♦ **to c. for** morirse por.

cra·ven (krā'vən) adj. & s. cobarde *mf.*

crav·ing (krā'vĭng) s. *(yearning)* deseo ardiente, anhelo; *(during pregnancy)* antojo.

craw (krô) s. buche *m.*

craw·fish (krô'fĭsh') **I.** intr. FAM. echarse atrás **II.** s. [pl. **crawfish** *o* **-fish·es**] var. de **crayfish.**

crawl (krôl) **I.** intr. *(to creep)* arrastrarse, reptar; *(baby)* gatear; *(to inch)* avanzar a paso de tortuga; *(to act in servile manner)* arrastrarse, humillarse; *(to shiver)* erizarse; DEP. nadar estilo crol ♦ **to be crawling with** hervir de, estar lleno de • **to c. up** trepar **II.** s. *(action)* arrastramiento; *(fish pen)* corral *m;* DEP. crol *m* ♦ **at a c.** a paso de tortuga.

crawl·er (krô'lər) s. *(insect)* larva; *(tractor)* tractor oruga *m.*

crawl·y (krô'lē) adj. **-ier, -iest** horripilante, espeluznante.

cray·fish (krā'fĭsh') s. [pl. **crayfish** *o* **-fish·es**] ICT. *(freshwater crustacean)* cangrejo de río, ástaco *m;* *(lobster)* langosta.

cray·on (krā'ŏn') **I.** s. *(stick)* pastel *m;* *(drawing)* pastel, dibujo al pastel **II.** tr. dibujar al pastel.

craze (krāz) **I.** tr. **crazed, craz·ing** *(to derange)* enloquecer, volver loco; *(to crackle)* agrietar —intr. *(to go insane)* enloquecer(se), volverse loco; *(to crackle)* agrietarse **II.** s. *(fashion)* moda; *(fad)* furor *m;* *(crackle)* grieta fina.

crazed (krāzd) adj. *(deranged)* loco; *(crackled)* agrietado.

cra·zi·ness (krā'zē-nĭs) s. locura.

cra·zy (krā'zē) adj. **-zi·er, -zi·est** *(insane)* loco; *(foolish)* de locos, disparatado ♦ **like c.** FAM. como loco • **to be c. about** *(to be in love with)* estar loco por; *(to like)* estar loco con • **to go c.** volverse loco.

crazy quilt s. *(quilt)* centón *m,* colcha de retazos; *(hodgepodge)* mezcolanza.

cream sauce s. *(quilt)* salsa bechamel, besamela.

creak (krēk) **I.** intr. *(to squeak)* crujir; *(metal parts)* chirriar **II.** s. *(squeak)* crujido; *(of metal parts)* chirrido.

creak·y (krē'kē) adj. **-i·er, -i·est** *(squeaky)* que cruje, que suena; *(metal parts)* chirriante; *(dilapidated)* desvencijado.

cream (krēm) **I.** s. *(milk fat)* crema, nata; *(color)* color crema; *(food, cosmetics)* crema <*cold c.* crema para el cutis> ♦ **the c. of the crop** la flor y nata, lo mejor • **whipped c.** (crema) chantillí **II.** intr. *(to form cream)* hacer nata; *(to froth)* hacer espuma —tr. *(to skim)* descremar, desnatar; *(to remove)* llevarse lo mejor de; *(to beat)* batir; *(to apply to face)* poner crema en; JER. *(to defeat)* hacer polvo, aplastar.

cream cheese s. queso crema *o* de nata.

cream·er (krē'mər) s. *(pitcher)* jarrita para la nata; *(separator)* desnatadora.

cream·er·y (krē'mə-rē) s. [pl. **-ies**] lechería y quesería.

cream of tartar s. CUL., QUÍM. cremor tártaro.

cream puff s. *(pastry)* pastelito de crema; JER. *(sissy)* mariquita *m.*

cream sauce s. salsa bechamel, besamela.

cream·y (krē'mē) adj. **-i·er, -i·est** cremoso.

crease (krēs) **I.** s. *(fold)* pliegue *m;* *(of trousers)* filo, raya; *(wrinkle)* arruga **II.** tr. **creased, creas·ing** *(to fold)* plegar; *(to press)* hacer el filo *o* la raya a; *(to wrinkle)* arrugar —intr. arrugarse.

cre·ate (krē-āt') tr. **-at·ed, -at·ing** *(to originate)* crear; *(to cause)* producir, causar; *(to appoint)* crear, nombrar.

cre·a·tion (krē-ā'shən) s. *(act, product)* creación *f;* *(garment)* confección *f,* diseño ♦ **the c.** el mundo, el cosmos.

cre·a·tive (krē-ā'tĭv) adj. *(capable of creating)* creador; *(original)* original; *(constructive)* constructivo ♦ **c. writing** EDUC. composición literaria.

cre·a·tiv·i·ty (krē'ā-tĭv'ĭ-tē) s. *(ability)* facultad creadora; *(originality)* originalidad *f.*

cre·a·tor (krē-ā'tər) s. creador *m* ♦ **C.** el Creador, Dios.

crea·ture (krē'chər) s. *(living being)* criatura; *(product)* obra, producto <*a c. of one's imagination* producto de la imaginación>; *(animal)* bestia, bicho ♦ **poor c.!** ¡el pobre!

creature comfort s. comodidad material *f.*

crèche (krĕsh) s. *(nativity)* pesebre *m,* nacimiento *m;* G.B. *(nursery)* guardería.

cre·dence (krēd'ns) s. crédito, fe *f* <*to give c. to* dar crédito a>.

cre·den·tial (krĭ-dĕn'shəl) s. credencial *f* ♦ **credentials** credenciales.

cred·i·bil·i·ty (krĕd'ə-bĭl'ĭ-tē) s. *(plausibility)* credibilidad *f,* lausibilidad *f;* *(reliability)* crédito.

cred·i·ble (krĕd'ə-bəl) adj. *(plausible)* creíble, plausible; *(reliable)* digno de crédito.

cred·it (krĕd'ĭt) **I.** s. *(belief)* crédito, creencia <*to give c. to* dar crédito a>; *(reputation)* crédito, buena fama; *(pride)* orgullo, honor *m* <*he is a c. to his family* es el orgullo de su familia>; *(merit)* mérito; *(recognition)* reconocimiento <*to get c. for* recibir reconocimiento por>; *(influence)* influencia; COM. *(solvency)* crédito <*I have c. at the gas station* tengo crédito en la gasolinera>; *(time for payment)* crédito, plazo; TEN. *(deduction for amount due)* crédito; *(righthand side of an account)* haber *m* <*debit and c.* debe y haber> ♦ **credits** CINEM. títulos de crédito • **on c.** a crédito, a plazos • **to give c.** COM. dar crédito, conceder crédito; *(recognition)* reconocer el mérito, dar reconocimiento; *(justice)* hacer justicia; *(name)* reconocer, nombrar (a autor, obra) • **to give someone c. for** reconocer los méritos de alguien • **to take c. for** atribuirse el mérito de **II.** tr. *(to believe in)* dar crédito a, creer; *(to give recognition for)* otorgar reconocimiento; *(to attribute to)* atribuir; TEN. *(to enter as credit)* abonar en cuenta; *(to make an entry in)* poner en el haber de ♦ **to c. (someone) with** *(to attribute)* atribuir (a alguien) el mérito de; *(to mention)* reconocer (como autor, creador).

cred·it·a·ble (krĕd'ĭ-tə-bəl) adj. *(praiseworthy)* encomiable, loable; *(credible)* digno de crédito; COM. solvente.

credit bureau s. COM. agencia que investiga la solvencia de los que solicitan crédito.

credit card s. COM. tarjeta de crédito.

credit line s. *(in a publication)* nota de reconocimiento de fuentes; *(credit)* límite de crédito *m.*

cred·i·tor (krĕd'ĭ-tər) s. COM. acreedor *m.*

credit rating s. COM. límite de crédito, solvencia máxima.

credit union s. COM. asociación de crédito *f,* banco cooperativo.

cre·do (krē'dō, krā'-) s. [pl. **-dos**] credo.

cre·du·li·ty (krĭ-dōō'lĭ-tē, -dyōō'-) s. credulidad *f.*

cred·u·lous (krĕj'ə-ləs) adj. crédulo.

creed (krēd) s. credo.

creek (krēk, krĭk) s. *(stream)* riachuelo, arroyo; G.B. *(inlet)* cala ♦ **up the** *o* **a c.** FAM. en apuros, en un aprieto.

creel (krēl) s. nasa.

creep (krēp) **I.** intr. **crept** (krĕpt), **creep·ing** *(to slide along the ground)* arrastrarse, deslizarse; *(to crawl)* gatear; *(to move cautiously)* avanzar con cautela; *(to move slowly)* ir a paso de tortuga; *(to tingle)* sentir hormigueo; *(to shiver)* ponérsele la piel de gallina <*it made my flesh c.* me hizo poner la piel de gallina>; BOT. trepar ♦ **to c. by** pasar lentamente • **to c. in** entrar cautelosa *o* furtivamente • **to c. out** salir cautelosa *o* furtivamente • **to c. up on someone** acercarse a alguien sigilosamente **II.** s. *(sliding)* arrastramiento, deslizamiento; *(crawling)* gateamiento; *(in the skin)* hormigueo; JER. *(obnoxious person)* desgraciado, cretino; METAL. *(flow)* movimiento lento; GEOL. deslizamiento ♦ **creeps** FAM. escalofrío, pavor <*the howl of the wind gave me the creeps* el silbido del viento me llenó de pavor>.

creep·er (krē'pər) s. *(animal)* animal rastrero; *(plant)* enredadera; *(grapnel)* rastrillo de dragado ♦ **creepers** *(for ice)* ramplones; *(for climbing)* trepadores.

creep·y (krē'pē) adj. **-i·er, -i·est** FAM. horripilante, espeluznante.

cre·mate (krē'māt', krĭ-māt') tr. **-mat·ed, -mat·ing** incinerar.

cre·ma·tion (krĭ-mā'shən) s. cremación *f,* incineración *f.*

cre·ma·to·ri·um (krē'mə-tôr'ē-əm) s. [pl. **-i·ums** *o* **-i·a** (-ē-ə)] crematorio.

cre·ma·to·ry (krē'mə-tôr'ē) s. [pl. **-ries**] & adj. crematorio.

cren·e·lat·ed *o* **cren·el·lat·ed** (krĕn'ə-lā'tĭd) adj. almenado.

Cre·ole (krē'ōl') s. & adj. criollo ♦ **c.** lengua criolla.

cre·o·lized language (krē'ə-līzd') s. lengua criolla.

cre·o·sol (krē′ə-sôl′) s. QUÍM. creosol *m.*

cre·o·sote (krē′ə-sōt′) s. QUÍM. creosota.

crepe *o* **crêpe** (krāp) s. *(fabric)* crespón *m*, crepé *m; (band)* crespón de luto; *(paper)* papel crepé *o* de China *m; (rubber)* crepé; *(pancake)* hojuela, panqueque *m.*

crepe paper s. papel crepé, papel de China.

crep·i·tate (krĕp′ĭ-tāt′) intr. **-tat·ed, -tat·ing** crepitar.

crept (krĕpt) pret. y part. p. de **creep.**

cres·cen·do (krə-shĕn′dō) s. [pl. **-dos** *o* **-di** (-dē)] MÚS. crescendo.

cres·cent (krĕs′ənt) **I.** s. *(moon)* luna creciente; *(emblem, roll)* medialuna; *(semicircle)* semicírculo **II.** adj. creciente.

cress (krĕs) s. BOT. berro.

crest (krĕst) **I.** s. *(tuft)* cresta; *(on a helmet)* penacho, cimera; *(of a wave)* cresta; *(summit)* cresta, cumbre *f; (climax)* apogeo, cumbre; HER. *(device)* timbre *m;* ARQ. cumbrera **II.** tr. *(a mountain)* llegar hasta la cumbre de; *(to top)* coronar —intr. encresparse.

crest·ed (krĕs′tĭd) adj. coronado.

crest·fall·en (krĕst′fô′lən) adj. alicaído, abatido.

Crete (krēt) s. Creta.

cre·tin (krēt′n) s. cretino.

cre·tin·ism (krēt′n-ĭz′əm) s. cretinismo.

cre·tonne (krĭ-tŏn′, krē′tŏn′) s. TEJ. cretona.

cre·vasse (krĭ-văs′) s. grieta, fisura (esp. de glaciar).

crev·ice (krĕv′ĭs) s. grieta, rajadura.

crew[1] (krōō) s. *(personnel)* personal *m*, tripulación *f;* MIL. *(of a gun)* dotación *f; (of oarsmen)* remeros *f; (of workers)* equipo; *(gang)* cuadrilla; DEP. remo.

crew[2] (krōō) un pret. de **crow**[2].

crew cut s. pelado al cepillo.

crib (krĭb) **I.** s. *(baby's bed)* cuna; *(corn granary)* granero, silo de maíz; *(manger)* pesebre *m; (stable)* cuadra; *(cottage)* choza, casucha; *(wicker basket)* cesto, canasto; FAM. *(petty theft)* ratería; *(plagiarism)* plagio; *(in exam)* chuleta; MIN. entibación *f* **II.** tr. cribbed, crib·bing *(to confine)* enjaular, encerrar; *(to furnish with a crib)* poner una cuna en; FAM. *(to plagiarize)* plagiar; *(to steal)* birlar —intr. FAM. *(in exam)* usar una chuleta; *(to cheat)* copiarse.

crick[1] (krĭk) s. *(in the back)* lumbago; *(in the neck)* tortícolis *f.*

crick·et[1] (krĭk′ĭt) s. ENTOM. grillo.

crick·et[2] (krĭk′ĭt) s. DEP. críquet *m* ♦ **it's not c.** FAM. no es jugar limpio, eso es jugar sucio.

crick·et·er (krĭk′ĭ-tər) s. DEP. jugador de críquet *m.*

cri·er (krī′ər) s. pregonero ♦ **town c.** pregonero público.

crime (krīm) s. *(violation, injustice)* crimen *m; (crime rate)* criminalidad *f.*

crim·i·nal (krĭm′ə-nəl) **I.** s. criminal *mf* **II.** adj. *(guilty, disgraceful)* criminal; *(penal)* penal <*c. record* antecedentes penales>.

crim·i·nal·i·ty (krĭm′ə-năl′ĭ-tē) s. [pl. **-ties**] criminalidad *f.*

criminal law s. derecho penal.

crim·i·nate (krĭm′ə-nāt′) tr. **-nat·ed, -nat·ing** DER. *(to incriminate)* criminar; *(to condemn)* condenar.

crim·i·nol·o·gist (krĭm′ə-nŏl′ə-jĭst) s. criminalista *mf.*

crim·i·nol·o·gy (krĭm′ə-nŏl′ə-jē) s. criminología.

crimp (krĭmp) **I.** tr. *(cloth)* plisar; *(hair)* rizar, encrespar; *(to wave)* ondular; *(to mold)* dar forma a **II.** s. *(hair)* pelo rizado; *(of wool)* ovillos ♦ **to put a c. in** obstruir, poner trabas a.

crim·son (krĭm′zən) **I.** adj. & s. carmesí *m* **II.** tr. teñir de carmesí —intr. sonrojarse.

cringe (krĭnj) intr. **cringed, cring·ing** *(to shrink back)* encogerse, acobardarse; *(to fawn)* humillarse, arrastrarse.

crin·kle (krĭng′kəl) **I.** intr. **-kled, -kling** *(to wrinkle)* arrugarse; *(to ripple)* rizarse, ondularse; *(to rustle)* crujir —tr. *(to wrinkle)* arrugar; *(to ripple)* rizar, ondular; *(to rustle)* hacer crujir **II.** s. *(wrinkle)* arruga; *(ripple)* rizo, ondulación *f; (rustle)* crujido.

crin·o·line (krĭn′ə-lĭn) s. TEJ. *(fabric)* crinolina; *(petticoat)* miriñaque *m.*

crip·ple (krĭp′əl) **I.** s. lisiado, cojo **II.** tr. **-pled, -pling** *(to maim)* lisiar, tullir; *(to damage)* inutilizar; *(to hinder)* estropear.

---

cri·sis (krī′sĭs) s. [pl. **-ses** (-sēz′)] crisis *f.*

crisp (krĭsp) **I.** adj. **-er, -est** *(crunchy)* tostado, crujiente; *(fresh)* fresco; *(invigorating)* vivificante; *(animated)* animado; *(curt)* seco; *(precise)* preciso, claro; *(curly)* rizado **II.** tr. *(food)* tostar, volver crujiente; *(to curl)* rizar —intr. *(food)* tostarse, ponerse crujiente; *(to curl)* rizarse.

crisp·y (krĭs′pē) adj. **-i·er, -i·est** *(crunchy)* tostado, crujiente; *(fresh)* fresco; *(invigorating)* vivificante; *(curly)* rizado.

criss·cross (krĭs′krôs′) **I.** tr. *(to mark)* rayar, sombrear; *(to traverse)* entrecruzar —intr. entrecruzarse **II.** s. *(pattern)* entrecruzamiento; *(hatching)* sombreado **III.** adj. entrecruzado **IV.** adv. en cruz.

cri·te·ri·on (krī-tîr′ē-ən) s. [pl. **-te·ri·a** (-tîr′ē-ə) *o* **-te·ri·ons**] criterio.

crit·ic (krĭt′ĭk) s. crítico.

crit·i·cal (krĭt′ĭ-kəl) adj. *(analytical)* crítico <*c. essay* ensayo crítico>; *(faultfinding)* criticón; *(grave)* crítico, grave ♦ **in c. condition** MED. grave ♦ **to be c. of** criticar.

crit·i·cal·ly (krĭt′ĭ-kə-lē) adv. *(gravely)* gravemente, seriamente <*he was c. injured* fue gravemente herido>; *(by critics)* críticamente.

critical mass s. FÍS. masa crítica.

critical point s. FÍS. punto crítico.

crit·i·cism (krĭt′ĭ-sĭz′əm) s. crítica.

crit·i·cize (krĭt′ĭ-sīz′) tr. & intr. **-cized, -ciz·ing** criticar.

cri·tique (krĭ-tēk′) s. crítica.

crit·ter (krĭt′ər) s. FAM. *(creature)* bicho, animal *m;* REG. *(domestic animal)* cabeza de ganado.

croak (krōk) **I.** s. *(of frog)* croar *m*, canto; *(of crow)* graznido; *(of person)* gruñido **II.** intr. *(frog)* croar, cantar; *(crow)* graznar; *(person)* gruñir; JER. *(to die)* estirar la pata —tr. *(to utter)* decir gruñendo; JER. *(to kill)* despachar.

Cro·a·tia (krō-ā′shə) s. Croacia.

cro·chet (krō-shā′) **I.** intr. & tr. tejer a ganchillo **II.** s. croché *m*, ganchillo.

cro·ci (krō′sī′) un pl. de **crocus.**

crock (krŏk) s. *(earthenware)* vasija de barro; JER. *(nonsense)* tontería.

crocked (krŏkt) adj. JER. hecho una uva, borracho.

crock·er·y (krŏk′ə-rē) s. vajilla de barro, loza.

croc·o·dile (krŏk′ə-dīl′) s. ZOOL. *(reptile)* cocodrilo; *(leather)* piel de cocodrilo *f.*

crocodile tears s.pl. lágrimas de cocodrilo.

cro·cus (krō′kəs) s. [pl. **-cus·es** *o* **-ci** (-sī′)] BOT. *(plant)* azafrán *m; (for polishing)* azafrán de Marte.

croft (krôft) s. G.B. *(field)* parcela; *(farm)* finca en arrendamiento.

crone (krōn) s. arpía.

cro·ny (krō′nē) s. [pl. **-nies**] compinche *mf*, amigote *m.*

crook (krōōk) **I.** s. *(hook)* gancho; *(shepherd's staff)* cayado; *(crosier)* báculo; *(curve)* curva, ángulo; *(of river, path)* recodo; *(of leg)* corva; FAM. *(thief)* tramposo, ladrón *m* **II.** tr. & intr. doblar(se).

crook·ed (krōōk′ĭd) adj. *(bent)* doblado; *(not straight)* torcido; *(winding)* tortuoso; *(curved)* curvo; *(nose)* corvo; *(back)* encorvado; FAM. *(dishonest)* tramposo.

crook·ed·ness (krōōk′ĭd-nĭs) s. *(sinuosity)* sinuosidad *f;* FAM. *(dishonesty)* falta de honradez.

croon (krōōn) **I.** intr. *(to hum)* canturrear; *(for entertainment)* cantar de modo sentimental **II.** s. canturreo.

croon·er (krōō′nər) s. cantante sentimental.

crop (krŏp) **I.** s. *(produce)* cultivo <*they had planted five different crops* habían sembrado cinco cultivos distintos>; *(harvest)* cosecha; *(group)* cosecha, acopio <*a c. of new ideas* una cosecha de ideas nuevas>; *(haircut)* pelado corto; *(whip)* fusta; *(handle of a whip)* mango (de una fusta); ORNIT. buche *m* **II.** tr. **cropped, crop·ping** *(to cut off the stems of)* cortar las ramas de, podar; *(to cut off the top of)* recortar la punta de; *(to cut very short)* cortar muy corto (esp. el pelo); *(to clip)* desmochar (esp. las orejas de un animal); *(to harvest)* cosechar; *(to cause to grow)* cultivar —intr. *(to plant)* sembrar; *(to grow)* hacer un cultivo; *(to yield)* rendir ♦ **to c. up** surgir, presentarse inesperadamente.

ā rey / ä año / b boca / ch chico / d dar / ĕ el / ē mil / g gato / h joya / hw juez / ī aire / k casa / kw cuan /

crop·per¹ (krŏp'ər) s. *(of animals)* esquilador *m*; *(sharecropper)* aparcero.

crop·per² (krŏp'ər) s. ♦ **to come a c.** fracasar totalmente.

crop rotation s. AGR. rotación de cultivos *f.*

cro·quette (krō-kĕt') s. CUL. croqueta.

cross (krôs) **I.** s. cruz *f*; *(sign)* cruz; *(burden)* cruz, pena <*to bear one's c.* llevar su propia cruz>; *(pipe fitting)* cruceta; *(mixture)* mezcla <*a novel that is a c. between melodrama and satire* una novela que es una mezcla de melodrama y sátira>; JER. *(swindle)* estafa; BIOL. *(crossbreed)* híbrido; *(crossbreeding)* cruce *m*, cruzamiento ♦ **to make the sign of the c.** RELIG. hacer la señal de la cruz **II.** tr. *(to go over)* cruzar, atravesar; *(to eliminate)* tachar <*to c. names off a list* tachar nombres de una lista>; *(to make a line across)* hacer un trazo horizontal a, cruzar; *(in handwriting)* poner el palito a <*c. your t's* pon el palito a la te>; *(to mark with a cross)* marcar con una cruz; *(to place crosswise)* cruzar <*she crossed her legs* cruzó las piernas>; *(to encounter)* cruzarse con; FAM. *(to oppose)* contrariar; BIOL. cruzar ♦ **to c. one's arms** cruzarse de brazos • **to c. one's mind** ocurrírsele a uno, pasarle por la mente • **to c. over** atravesar • **to c. swords** batirse, contender —intr. *(to intersect)* cruzarse; *(to go over)* cruzar, atravesar; BIOL. cruzarse ♦ **to c. over** pasar de un lado a otro, ir al otro lado **III.** adj. *(intersecting)* transversal <*a c. street* una calle transversal>; *(contrary)* contrario, opuesto; *(angry)* de mal humor; *(reciprocal)* recíproco; BIOL. cruzado ♦ **to get c.** enfadarse **IV.** adv. de modo atravesado.

cross·bar (krôs'bär') s. *(of wood)* travesaño; *(of metal)* barra; *(of door)* tranca.

cross·beam (krôs'bēm') s. ARQ. viga transversal, travesaño.

cross·bones (krôs'bōnz') s. ♦ **skull and c.** calavera.

cross·bow (krôs'bō') s. ballesta.

cross·breed (krôs'brēd') BIOL. **I.** tr. & intr. **-bred** (-brĕd'), **-breed·ing** cruzar(se) **II.** s. híbrido.

cross·breed·ing (krôs'brē'dĭng) s. cruzamiento, hibridación *f.*

cross·coun·try (krôs'kŭn'trē) adj. *(across country)* a campo traviesa; *(across the nation)* a través del país ♦ **c. race** DEP. cros, carrera a campo traviesa.

cross·cur·rent (krôs'kûr'ənt) s. contracorriente *f.*

cross·cut (krôs'kŭt') **I.** tr. & intr. cortar transversalmente **II.** s. *(cut)* corte transversal *m*; *(short cut)* atajo; MIN. crucero.

cross·ex·am·i·na·tion (krôs'ĭg-zăm'ə-nā'shən) s. DER. repregunta, interrogatorio.

cross·ex·am·ine (krôs'ĭg-zăm'ĭn) tr. **-ined, -in·ing** DER. repreguntar, interrogar.

cross·ex·am·in·er (krôs'ĭg-zăm'ə-nər) s. DER. interrogador *m*, examinador *m.*

cross·eye (krôs'ī') s. bizquera.

cross·eyed (krôs'īd') adj. bizco.

cross·fer·til·i·za·tion (krôs'fûr'tl-ĭ-zā'shən) s. BIOL. fecundación cruzada.

cross·fer·til·ize (krôs'fûr'tl-īz') tr. & intr. **-ized, -iz·ing** BIOL. fecundar(se) por fecundación cruzada.

cross·fire (krôs'fīr') s. fuego cruzado.

cross·grained (krôs'grānd') adj. *(wood)* de vetas cruzadas; *(troublesome)* difícil.

cross hair s. ÓPT. retículo.

cross·hatch (krôs'hăch') tr. DIB. sombrear, rayar.

cross·ing (krô'sĭng) s. *(intersection)* cruce *m*; *(on a road)* cruce, paso de peatones; F.C. *(over tracks)* paso a nivel; *(at a river)* paso, vado; ARQ. crucero.

cross·o·ver (krôs'ō'vər) s. *(place)* cruce *m*, paso; F.C. *(track)* empalme *m*; BIOL. cruzamiento.

cross·piece (krôs'pēs') s. CONSTR., TEC. travesaño.

cross·pol·li·na·tion (krôs'pŏl'ə-nā'shən) s. BOT. polinización cruzada.

cross·pur·pose (krôs'pûr'pəs) s. objetivo opuesto ♦ **to be at cross-purposes** no entenderse.

cross·ques·tion (krôs'kwĕs'chən) DER. **I.** tr. repreguntar, interrogar **II.** s. repregunta, interrogación *f.*

cross·ref·er·ence (krôs'rĕf'ər-əns) s. remisión *f*, referencia.

cross·road (krôs'rōd') s. via transversal *f* ♦ **crossroads** [ú. con v. sing.] encrucijada.

cross section s. *(representation)* sección *f* o corte transversal *m*; *(sample)* muestra representativa.

cross·stitch (krôs'stĭch') s. TEJ. punto cruzado.

cross·talk (krôs'tôk') s. ELECTRÓN., TEL. interferencias.

cross·tie (krôs'tī') s. F.C. traviesa.

cross·town (krôs'toun') adj. que atraviesa la ciudad (a lo ancho).

cross·tree (krôs'trē') s. MARÍT. cruceta.

cross·walk (krôs'wôk') s. cruce *m*, paso de peatones.

cross·way (krôs'wā') s. vía transversal.

cross·wind (krôs'wĭnd') s. viento de costado.

cross·wise (krôs'wīz') o **cross·ways** (-wāz') adv. al través, transversalmente.

cross·word puzzle (krôs'wûrd') s. crucigrama *m.*

crotch (krŏch) s. *(of branches)* horquilla; *(of legs)* entrepiernas.

crotch·et (krŏch'ĭt) s. *(hook)* gancho pequeño; *(whim)* capricho; MÚS. negra.

crotch·et·y (krŏch'ĭ-tē) adj. caprichoso.

crouch (krouch) intr. *(to stoop)* agacharse, acuclillarse; *(to cringe)* rebajarse, humillarse.

croup¹ (krōop) s. MED. crup *m*, garrotillo.

croup² (krōop) s. grupa (del caballo).

crou·pi·er (krōo'pē-ər) s. crupier *m.*

crow¹ (krō) s. *(bird)* cuervo; *(crowbar)* pata de cabra ♦ **as the c. flies** en línea recta • **to eat c.** FAM. besar la correa, humillarse.

crow² (krō) **I.** intr. **crowed** o **crew** (krōo), **crow·ing** *(rooster)* cantar; *(infant)* gorjear ♦ **to c. over** cantar, jactarse de **II.** s. *(of a rooster)* canto; *(of an infant)* gorjeo.

crow·bar (krō'bär') s. pata de cabra, palanca.

crowd (kroud) **I.** s. *(throng)* multitud *f*, muchedumbre *f*; *(mob)* gentío; *(populace)* populacho, vulgo; *(spectators)* público; *(clique)* grupo, gente *f*; *(of things)* montón *m* ♦ **to follow the c.** hacer lo que todos • **to rise above the c.** sobresalir, destacarse **II.** intr. apiñarse, amontonarse ♦ **to c. into** *(a theater)* atestar; *(a car)* apiñarse dentro —tr. *(to shove)* apretujar, empujar; *(to force together)* apiñar, amontonar; *(to fill)* atestar, llenar; FAM. *(to pressure)* apremiar ♦ **to c. someone out** quitar o empujar a alguien.

crowd·ed (krou'dĭd) adj. *(full)* lleno, muy concurrido; *(cramped)* apretado, apiñado.

crown (kroun) **I.** s. *(of a monarch)* corona; *(coin)* corona; *(of the head)* corona, coronilla; *(of a hat)* copa; *(of a mountain)* cima, cumbre *f*; *(of a bird)* copete *m*, cresta; *(highest quality)* cima; *(of a tooth)* corona; *(of a tree)* copa; *(achievement)* coronación *f*, coronamiento ♦ **the C.** la Corona **II.** tr. *(to put a crown on)* coronar; *(to reward)* coronar, premiar; *(to form the top of)* rematar; *(to consummate)* coronar, rematar; *(a tooth)* poner una corona a; *(in checkers)* coronar; FAM. *(to hit)* dar un cocotazo a ♦ **to c. it all** para rematar.

crown colony s. colonia de la corona británica.

crown·ing (krou'nĭng) s. ARQ. coronamiento, remate *m*; *(enthronement)* coronación *f*; MED. coronamiento.

crown prince s. príncipe heredero.

crow's·foot (krōz'fŏŏt') s. [pl. **-feet** (-fēt')] COST. puntada de tres picos ♦ **crow's-feet** *(wrinkles)* patas de gallo.

crow's·nest (krōz'nĕst') s. *(on a ship)* cofa de vigía; *(lookout)* torre de vigía *f.*

cru·ces (krōo'sēz') un pl. de **crux.**

cru·cial (krōo'shəl) adj. crucial, decisivo.

cru·ci·ble (krōo'sə-bəl) s. crisol *m.*

cru·ci·fied (krōo'sə-fīd') adj. crucificado.

cru·ci·fix (krōo'sə-fĭks') s. RELIG. crucifijo.

cru·ci·fix·ion (krōo'sə-fĭk'shən) s. crucifixión *f.*

cru·ci·form (krōo'sə-fôrm') adj. cruciforme.

cru·ci·fy (krōo'sə-fī') tr. **-fied, -fy·ing** *(on a cross)* crucificar; *(to torment)* martirizar.

crud (krŭd) s. JER. *(filth)* costra de mugre; *(person)* basura *mf.*

crude (krōod) adj. **crud·er, crud·est** *(raw)* crudo; *(fruit)* verde; *(vulgar)* ordinario, grosero; *(unrefined)* tosco, basto; *(blunt)* sin rodeos, áspero; MIN. crudo, bruto II. s. MIN. crudo, petróleo crudo.

crude·ness (krōōd′nĭs) s. *(rawness)* crudeza; *(vulgarity)* ordinariez *f*, grosería; *(lack of refinement)* tosquedad *f*, bastedad *f*; *(bluntness)* aspereza.

crude oil s. petróleo bruto.

cru·di·ty (krōō′dĭ-tē) s. var. de **crudeness**.

cru·el (krōō′əl) adj. **-er, -est** cruel, despiadado.

cru·el·ty (krōō′əl-tē) s. [pl. **-ties**] crueldad *f.*

cru·et (krōō′ĭt) s. *(for vinegar)* vinagrera; *(for oil)* aceitera.

cruise (krōōz) I. intr. **cruised, cruis·ing** *(to sail)* navegar; *(as a tourist)* hacer un crucero; *(to travel about)* circular; *(at a cruising speed)* ir a velocidad de crucero ♦ **to c. for** FAM. circular en busca de —tr. *(to cross)* cruzar, atravesar; *(to travel about)* circular por II. s. crucero.

cruis·er (krōō′zər) s. *(warship)* crucero; *(motorboat)* yate con camarotes *m*; *(police car)* patrullero.

cruis·ing (krōō′zĭng) adj. de crucero <*c. speed* velocidad de crucero>.

crumb (krŭm) I. s. *(of baked goods)* miga, migaja; *(bit)* migaja, pizca; *(inner portion of bread)* miga II. tr. *(to crumble)* desmigajar; *(to bread)* empanar.

crum·ble (krŭm′bəl) tr. & intr. **-bled, -bling** *(bread)* desmigajar(se); *(to disintegrate)* desmoronar(se).

crum·bly (krŭm′blē) adj. **-bli·er, -bli·est** desmoronadizo.

crum·my *o* **crumb·y** (krŭm′ē) adj. **-mi·er, -mi·est** *o* **-i·er, -i·est** *(miserable)* malísimo; *(cheap)* de poca categoría.

crum·pet (krŭm′pĭt) s. G.B. panecillo blando.

crum·ple (krŭm′pəl) tr. **-pled, -pling** arrugar, estrujar —intr. *(to shrivel)* arrugarse, estrujarse; *(to collapse)* desplomarse.

crunch (krŭnch) I. tr. *(food, stones)* triturar; *(to tread)* hacer crujir —intr. crujir II. s. *(act)* trituración *f*; *(noise)* crujido *m*; FAM. *(crisis)* aprieto, crisis *f*; *(shortage)* escasez *f.*

crunch·y (krŭn′chē) adj. *(said of snow, ice)* crujiente; *(said of food)* crocante.

cru·sade (krōō-sād′) I. s. cruzada, campaña ♦ **C.** HIST. cruzada II. intr. **-sad·ed, -sad·ing** hacer una cruzada ♦ **to c. for** hacer campaña a favor de.

cru·sad·er (krōō-sā′dər) s. cruzado.

crush (krŭsh) I. tr. *(to squash)* aplastar; *(to squeeze)* exprimir, prensar (uvas, azúcar); *(to crumple)* estrujar, arrugar (ropa, papel); *(to hug forcefully)* apretar (en un abrazo); *(to grind)* triturar, moler; *(to crowd)* apretujar, apiñar; *(to suppress)* aplastar (enemigo, rebelión); *(to overwhelm)* abrumar, agobiar <*debt was crushing him* las deudas lo agobiaban> —intr. *(to squash)* aplastarse; *(to crowd together)* apretujarse II. s. *(crushing)* aplastamiento; *(crowd)* multitud *f*, aglomeración *f*; *(beverage)* exprimido; *(infatuation)* enamoramiento ♦ **to have a c. on someone** FAM. perder la chaveta por alguien.

crush·er (krŭsh′ər) s. trituradora, quebrantadora.

crust (krŭst) I. s. *(of baked goods)* corteza; *(covering)* costra, capa; *(in bottles)* sarro; *(layer)* corteza; *(shell)* carapacho; *(scab)* costra, postilla; JER. *(gall)* desfachatez *f*, frescura ♦ **the upper c.** FIG. lo más selecto II. tr. & intr. encostrar(se).

crus·ta·cean (krŭ-stā′shən) s. & adj. crustáceo.

crust·y (krŭs′tē) adj. **-i·er, -i·est** *(bread)* de corteza dura; *(surface)* costroso; *(surly)* áspero, brusco.

crutch (krŭch) s. MED. muleta; *(leg rest)* soporte *m*; ARQ. *(for a wall)* puntal *m*; FIG. *(prop)* soporte, sostén *m* <*to use drugs as a c.* usar las drogas como sostén>.

crux (krŭks, krōōks) s. [pl. **crux·es** *o* **cru·ces** (krōō′sēz′)] *(crucial moment)* punto crítico; *(central feature)* quid *m* <*the c. of an argument* el quid de un razonamiento>; *(puzzle)* enigma *m*, problema enigmático ♦ **C.** ASTRON. Cruz.

cru·zei·ro (krōō-zâr′ō) s. [pl. **-ros**] FIN. cruzeiro (unidad monetaria del Brasil).

cry (krī) I. intr. **cried, cry·ing** *(to weep)* llorar; *(to shout)* gritar; *(animals)* aullar ♦ **to c. for joy** llorar de alegría ♦ **to c. out** exclamar, gritar —tr. *(to utter loudly)* gritar, decir a gritos; *(to announce in public)* pregonar; *(to beg for)* implorar, pedir <*to c. forgiveness* implorar perdón> ♦ **to c. down** menospreciar • **to c. havoc** dar la alarma • **to c. oneself to sleep** llorar hasta quedarse dormido • **to c. out**

exclamar, gritar • **to c. over spilled milk** lamentarse por lo que no tiene remedio • **to c. up** exaltar, poner por las nubes II. s. [pl. **cries**] *(shout)* grito; *(weeping)* llanto; *(entreaty)* petición *f*; *(peddler's call)* pregón *m* ♦ **a far c. from** muy distante de, muy diferente de • **in full c.** en plena persecución • **to have a good c.** llorar a lágrima viva.

cry·ba·by (krī′bā′bē) s. [pl. **-bies**] llorón *m.*

cry·ing (krī′ĭng) I. s. *(weeping)* llanto; *(shouting)* gritería, gritos II. adj. inmenso, espantoso <*a c. shame* una inmensa vergüenza>.

cry·o·gen (krī′ə-jən) s. criógeno (refrigerante).

cry·o·stat (krī′ə-stăt′) s. FÍS. criostato.

crypt (krĭpt) s. cripta.

cryp·tic (krĭp′tĭk) *o* **cryp·ti·cal** (-tĭ-kəl) adj. *(enigmatic)* enigmático, misterioso; *(occult)* oculto; BIOL. *(coloring)* simulador.

cryp·to·gam (krĭp′tə-găm′) s. BOT. criptógama.

cryp·to·gram (krĭp′tə-grăm′) s. criptograma *m.*

cryp·tog·ra·phy (krĭp-tŏg′rə-fē) s. criptografía.

crys·tal (krĭs′təl) I. s. cristal *m* ♦ **as clear as c.** claro como el agua II. adj. *(transparent)* cristalino; *(made of crystal)* de cristal.

crystal ball s. bola de cristal.

crystal gazing s. *(divination)* adivinación *f* por medio de la bola de cristal; *(prediction)* predicción *f.*

crys·tal·line (krĭs′tə-lĭn, -līn′) adj. *(made of crystal)* cristalino, de cristal; *(clear)* cristalino, transparente.

crys·tal·li·za·tion (krĭs′tə-lĭ-zā′shən) s. cristalización *f.*

crys·tal·lize (krĭs′tə-līz′) tr. & intr. **-lized, -liz·ing** cristalizar(se).

crys·tal·lized (krĭs′tə-līzd′) adj. cristalizado.

crys·tal·log·ra·phy (krĭs′tə-lŏg′rə-fē) s. cristalografía.

cub (kŭb) s. *(animal)* cachorro; *(novice)* principiante *mf*, novato ♦ **C.** *o* **C. Scout** explorador más joven (de los Boy Scouts).

Cu·ba (kyōō′bə) s. Cuba.

Cu·ban (kyōō′bən) adj. & s. cubano.

cub·by·hole (kŭb′ē-hōl′) s. *(room)* cuchitril *m*, cubículo; *(compartment)* compartimiento; *(cupboard)* armario pequeño.

cube (kyōōb) I. s. cubo ♦ **sugar c.** terrón de azúcar II. tr. **cubed, cub·ing** MAT. cubicar, elevar al cubo; *(to measure)* medir en unidades cúbicas; *(to cut)* cortar en forma de cubo.

cube root s. MAT. raíz cúbica.

cu·bic (kyōō′bĭk) adj. cúbico.

cu·bi·cle (kyōō′bĭ-kəl) s. *(room)* cubículo; *(compartment)* compartimiento.

cu·bi·form (kyōō′bə-fôrm′) adj. de forma cúbica.

cub·ism (kyōō′bĭz′əm) s. ARTE. cubismo.

cub·ist (kyōō′bĭst) s. ARTE. cubista *mf.*

cu·bit (kyōō′bĭt) s. ANT. codo (medida).

cuck·old (kŭk′əld, kōōk′-) I. s. cornudo II. tr. poner los cuernos a.

cuck·oo (kōō′kōō, kōōk′ōō) I. s. [pl. **-oos**] ORNIT. *(bird)* cuco, cuclillo; *(call)* cucú *m* II. tr. **-ooed, -oo·ing** repetir una y otra vez III. adj. loco, chiflado.

cuckoo clock s. reloj de cuco *m.*

cu·cum·ber (kyōō′kŭm′bər) s. BOT. pepino ♦ **cool as a c.** fresco como una lechuga.

cud (kŭd) s. ZOOL. bolo alimenticio ♦ **to chew the c.** rumiar.

cud·dle (kŭd′l) I. tr. & intr. **-dled, -dling** abrazar(se), acurrucar(se) II. s. abrazo.

cud·dly (kŭd′lē) adj. **-dli·er, -dli·est** *(person, animal)* mimoso; *(thing)* que da ganas de abrazarlo.

cudg·el (kŭj′əl) I. s. garrote *m*, bastón *m* ♦ **to take up the cudgels for** salir en defensa de II. tr. golpear con un garrote *o* bastón ♦ **to c. one's brains** devanarse los sesos.

cue¹ (kyōō) I. s. *(in billiards)* taco; *(braid)* trenza, cola de caballo II. tr. **cued, cu·ing** *(a ball)* golpear con el taco; *(hair)* trenzar.

cue² (kyōō) I. s. TEAT. *(signal)* pie *m*, señal *f*; *(reminder)* señal ♦ **to take one's c. from** guiarse por, seguir el ejemplo de II. tr. **cued, cu·ing** TEAT. dar el pie *o* la señal a ♦ **to c.**

---

in TEAT. *(to insert)* introducir, dar entrada a; *(to fill in)* poner al tanto.
cue ball s. mingo, bola blanca.
cuff¹ (kŭf) s. *(of a sleeve)* puño; *(of trousers)* bajos, vuelta ♦ **cuffs** esposas • **off the c.** FAM. de improviso • **on the c.** FAM. al fiado, a plazos.
cuff² (kŭf) **I.** tr. abofetear **II.** s. bofetada.
cuff links s.pl. gemelos, yugos.
cui·rass (kwĭ-răs′) s. MIL., ZOOL. coraza.
cui·sine (kwĭ-zēn′) s. cocina, arte culinario.
cu·li·nar·y (kyōō′lə-nĕr′ē, kŭl′ə-) adj. culinario.
cull (kŭl) **I.** tr. *(to select)* entresacar, seleccionar; *(to gather)* recoger, coger ♦ **to c. out** sacar, separar **II.** s. desecho.
cul·mi·nate (kŭl′mə-nāt′) intr. **-nat·ed, -nat·ing** culminar.
cul·mi·na·tion (kŭl′mə-nā′shən) s. culminación *f.*
cul·pa·bil·i·ty (kŭl′pə-bĭl′ĭ-tē) s. culpabilidad *f.*
cul·pa·ble (kŭl′pə-bəl) adj. culpable.
cul·prit (kŭl′prĭt) s. *(accused)* acusado; *(offender)* culpable *mf.*
cult (kŭlt) s. *(worship, admiration)* culto; *(sect)* secta.
cult·ist (kŭl′tĭst) s. fanático, devoto.
cul·ti·va·ble (kŭl′tə-və-bəl) adj. cultivable.
cul·ti·vate (kŭl′tə-vāt′) tr. **-vat·ed, -vat·ing** *(to till, grow)* cultivar; *(to develop)* cultivar <to c. a friendship cultivar una amistad>; BIOL. cultivar, criar.
cul·ti·vat·ed (kŭl′tə-vā′tĭd) adj. culto, refinado.
cul·ti·va·tion (kŭl′tə-vā′shən) s. *(act, state)* cultivo; *(refinement)* cultura, refinamiento.
cul·ti·va·tor (kŭl′tə-vā′tər) s. cultivador *m.*
cul·tur·al (kŭl′chər-əl) adj. cultural.
cul·ture (kŭl′chər) **I.** s. *(civilization, works)* cultura <Greek c. la cultura griega>; *(refinement)* cultura, refinamiento; AGR., BIOL. cultivo **II.** tr. **-tured, -tur·ing** AGR., BIOL. cultivar.
cul·tured (kŭl′chərd) adj. *(person)* culto, refinado; *(pearl)* cultivado, de cultivo.
culture medium s. BIOL. caldo de cultivo.
cul·vert (kŭl′vərt) s. alcantarilla.
cum (kōōm, kŭm) prep. con ♦ **c. laude** con honor.
cum·ber (kŭm′bər) **I.** tr. *(to burden)* agobiar; *(to hamper)* embarazar, entorpecer **II.** s. embarazo, molestia.
cum·ber·some (kŭm′bər-səm) adj. *(unwieldy)* embarazoso, entorpecedor; *(bulky)* abultado, voluminoso; *(troublesome)* embarazoso, difícil.
cum·brous (kŭm′brəs) adj. embarazoso, incómodo.
cum·in (kŭm′ĭn) s. BOT. comino (planta y semilla).
cum·mer·bund (kŭm′ər-bŭnd′) s. faja (de traje de etiqueta).
cum·quat (kŭm′kwŏt) s. var. de **kumquat.**
cu·mu·late (kyōōm′yə-lāt′) tr. & intr. **-lat·ed, -lat·ing** cumular(se), acumular(se).
cu·mu·la·tion (kyōōm′yə-lā′shən) s. cumulación *f*, acumulación *f.*
cu·mu·la·tive (kyōōm′yə-lā′tĭv, -lə-tĭv) adj. *(effect, interest)* acumulativo; DER. *(evidence)* cumulativo; *(voting)* plural.
cu·mu·li (kyōōm′yə-lī′) pl. de **cumulus.**
cu·mu·lo·nim·bus (kyōōm′yə-lō-nĭm′bəs) s. [pl. **-bus·es** o **-bi** (-bī′)] METEOR. cumulonimbo.
cu·mu·lus (kyōōm′yə-ləs) s. [pl. **-li** (-lī′)] *(cloud)* cúmulo; *(pile)* cúmulo; *(pile)* cúmulo, acumulación *f.*
cu·ne·i·form (kyōō′nē-ə-fôrm′, kyōō-nē′-) **I.** adj. cuneiforme **II.** s. *(writing)* escritura cuneiforme; *(bone)* cuneiforme *m.*
cun·ning (kŭn′ĭng) **I.** adj. *(crafty)* astuto, taimado; *(masterful)* hábil, ingenioso <c. workmanship artesanía ingeniosa>; *(cute)* mono, precioso **II.** s. *(craftiness)* astucia; *(mastery)* habilidad *f*, ingenio.
cunt (kŭnt) s. VULG. coño, concha.
cup (kŭp) **I.** s. *(container, content)* taza; *(trophy)* copa; *(chalice)* cáliz *m*; *(hollow)* hoyo; *(of a brassiere)* copa; *(athletic supporter)* protector *m*; *(bones)* cavidad *f*; *(of a flower)* cáliz, FIG. *(suffering)* cáliz ♦ **c. of tea** gusto <that's not my c. of tea eso no es de mi gusto> • **in one's cups** FAM. borracho, bebido **II.** tr. **cupped, cup·ping** *(to put in a cup)* poner en una taza o copa; *(to shape like a cup)* ahuecar.

cup·bear·er (kŭp′bâr′ər) s. copero.
cup·board (kŭb′ərd) s. *(cabinet)* aparador *m*, armario; *(closet)* alacena.
cup·cake (kŭp′kāk′) s. bizcochito redondo.
cup·ful (kŭp′fōōl′) s. [pl. **-fuls**] taza.
Cu·pid (kyōō′pĭd) s. MITOL. Cupido.
cu·pid·i·ty (kyōō-pĭd′ĭ-tē) s. codicia, avaricia.
cu·po·la (kyōō′pə-lə) s. ARQ. *(dome)* cúpula; *(tower)* linterna.
cup·ping (kŭp′ĭng) s. MED. aplicación de ventosas *f.*
cu·pric (kōō′prĭk, kyōō′-) adj. QUÍM. cúprico.
cur (kŭr) s. *(mongrel)* perro cruzado; *(person)* perro, canalla *m.*
cur·a·bil·i·ty (kyōōr′ə-bĭl′ĭ-tē) s. curabilidad *f.*
cur·a·ble (kyōōr′ə-bəl) adj. curable.
cu·ra·cy (kyōōr′ə-sē) s. [pl. **-cies**] RELIG. curato.
cu·ra·re (kōō-rä′rē) s. BOT. curare *m.*
cu·ras·sow (kōōr′ə-sô′, kyōōr′-) s. ORNIT. guaco.
cu·rate (kyōōr′ĭt) s. RELIG. *(priest)* cura *m*; *(assistant)* coadjutor *m.*
cu·ra·tive (kyōōr′ə-tĭv) **I.** adj. curativo **II.** s. cura, remedio.
cu·ra·tor (kyōō-rā′tər, kyōōr′ə-) s. conservador (de un museo) *m.*
curb (kûrb) **I.** s. *(of a street)* bordillo, orilla de la acera; *(restraint)* freno, restricción *f*; *(flange)* reborde *m*; *(of bridle)* barbada **II.** tr. refrenar, restringir.
curb·stone (kûrb′stōn′) s. bordillo, orilla de la acera.
curd (kûrd) **I.** s. cuajada, requesón *m* **II.** intr. & tr. cuajar(se).
cur·dle (kûr′dl) tr. & intr. **-dled, -dling** cuajar(se) ♦ **to c. one's blood** FIG. helarle la sangre a uno.
cure (kyōōr) **I.** s. *(recovery, treatment)* cura; *(remedy)* remedio; *(of food)* cura, curación *f*; RELIG. *(curacy)* curato **II.** tr. **cured, cur·ing** *(to heal)* curar; *(to remedy)* remediar, poner remedio a; *(food)* curar; *(rubber)* vulcanizar —intr. curarse.
cure-all (kyōōr′ôl′) s. *(for diseases)* curalotodo; *(for evils)* panacea.
cure·less (kyōōr′lĭs) adj. incurable.
cu·ret·tage (kyōōr′ĭ-täzh′) s. CIR. raspado.
cur·few (kûr′fyōō) s. *(period)* queda; *(signal)* toque de queda *m.*
cu·ri·a (kōōr′ē-ə, kyōōr′-) s. [pl. **cu·ri·ae** (kōōr′ē-ē′, kyōōr′-)] HIST. *(of Rome)* curia (romana); *(medieval council)* curia, asamblea; *(royal court)* corte real de justicia *f* ♦ **C.** RELIG. Curia (católica).
cu·rie (kyōōr′ē) s. FÍS. curio, curie *m* (unidad de radiactividad).
cu·ri·o (kyōōr′ē-ō′) s. [pl. **-os**] curiosidad *f*, baratija.
cu·ri·os·i·ty (kyōōr′ē-ŏs′ĭ-tē) s. [pl. **-ties**] *(inquisitiveness)* curiosidad *f*; *(novelty)* curiosidad, rareza.
cu·ri·ous (kyōōr′ē-əs) adj. *(inquisitive)* curioso; *(odd)* curioso, raro ♦ **to be c. to** tener deseos de.
cu·ri·um (kyōōr′ē-əm) s. QUÍM. curio.
curl (kûrl) **I.** tr. *(to twist)* rizar <to c. one's hair rizarse el pelo>; *(to wind)* enrollar; *(the lips)* fruncir —intr. *(to form ringlets)* rizarse; *(to wind)* enrollarse; *(lips)* fruncirse; *(path)* serpentear; *(smoke)* formar volutas ♦ **to c. up** hacerse un ovillo, acurrucarse **II.** s. *(ringlet)* riza, crespo; *(of smoke)* voluta.
curl·er (kûr′lər) s. *(something that curls)* rizador *m*; *(hair roller)* rulo, bigudí *m.*
curl·i·cue (kûr′lĭ-kyōō′) s. rasgo, plumada.
curl·i·ness (kûr′lē-nĭs) s. ensortijamiento, rizado.
curl·y (kûr′lē) adj. **-i·er, -i·est** *(hair)* rizado, crespo; *(wood)* de vetas onduladas.
cur·mudg·eon (kər-mŭj′ən) s. cascarrabias *mf.*
cur·rant (kûr′ənt) s. BOT. *(shrub)* grosellero; *(fruit)* grosella; *(dried grape)* pasa de Corinto.
cur·ren·cy (kûr′ən-sē) s. [pl. **-cies**] *(money)* moneda, dinero (corriente); *(use)* vigencia, boga ♦ **foreign c.** FIN. divisas, moneda extranjera.
cur·rent (kûr′ənt) **I.** adj. *(present-day)* actual <our c. problems nuestros problemas actuales>; *(in progress)* corriente, en curso; *(magazine issue)* último; *(money)* corriente; *(accepted)* corriente, generalizado (opinión, cre-

encia); *(in use)* vigente, en boga ♦ **c. events** actualidades
• **c. liabilities** COM. pasivo exigible II. s. *(flow)* corriente
(de aire, agua) *f; (tendency)* curso, dirección *f <the c. of
events* el curso de los acontecimientos>; ELEC. corriente ♦
alternating c. ELEC. corriente alterna • **direct c.** ELEC.
corriente continua.
current assets s.pl. COM. activo realizable *o* disponible.
cur·rent·ly (kûr′ənt-lē) adv. *(now)* actualmente, en la actualidad; *(commonly)* corrientemente, de modo generalizado.
cur·ric·u·lum (kə-rĭk′yə-ləm) s. [pl. **-la** (-lə) *o* **-lums]** EDUC.
programa de estudios *m.*
curriculum vi·tae (vī′tē) s. currículo, historial profesional
m.
cur·ri·er (kûr′ē-ər) s. zurrador *m.*
cur·ry¹ (kûr′ē) tr. **-ried, -ry·ing** *(a horse)* almohazar; *(hides)*
zurrar ♦ **to c. favor with** congraciarse con, adular a.
cur·ry² (kûr′ē) s. [pl. **-ries]** CUL. *(powder)* cari *m*, pimienta
de la India; *(sauce)* salsa de cari.
curse (kûrs) I. s. *(invocation, evil)* maldición *f; (scourge)*
desgracia, calamidad *f <poverty is a great c.* la pobreza es
una inmensa desgracia>; *(obscenity)* mala palabra, grosería; RELIG. anatema *m*, excomunión *f* II. tr. **cursed** *o* **curst**
(kûrst), **curs·ing** *(to damn)* maldecir; *(to afflict)* desgraciar, afligir; *(to swear at)* insultar a; RELIG. anatematizar,
excomulgar ♦ **to be cursed with** *(an ailment)* padecer de;
(an evil) tener la desgracia de —intr. decir malas palabras *o* groserías ♦ **to c. at** insultar a.
curs·ed (kûr′sĭd, kûrst) adj. maldito.
curs·ing (kûr′sĭng) I. adj. maldiciente, blasfemador II. s.
maldición *f*, blasfemia.
cur·sive (kûr′sĭv) I. adj. cursiva II. s. letra cursiva.
cur·sor (kûr′sər) s. COMPUT. cursor *m.*
cur·so·ry (kûr′sə-rē) adj. superficial, rápido.
curst (kûrst) I. un pret. y part. p. de **curse** II. adj. var. de
cursed.
curt (kûrt) adj. **-er, -est** *(brusque)* brusco, seco; *(concise)*
conciso, lacónico.
cur·tail (kər-tāl′) tr. *(to abbreviate)* cortar; *(to reduce)* reducir.
cur·tail·ment (kər-tāl′mənt) s. *(abbreviation)* acortamiento,
corte *m; (reduction)* reducción *f.*
cur·tain (kûr′tn) I. s. *(in a window)* cortina; *(cover)* cortina
(de fuego, humo); TEAT. *(drape)* telón *m; (time)* hora de
subir el telón; FORT. cortina ♦ **behind the c.** FIG. entre
bambalinas, por debajo del tapete • **curtains** JER. fin •
Iron C. POL. cortina de hierro ♦ **to draw the c. over** *o* **on**
correr un velo sobre • **to raise the c. on** poner al descubierto II. tr. *(a window)* poner cortinas en; *(to cover)* velar, encubrir ♦ **to c. off** separar con cortinas.
curtain call s. TEAT. llamada a escena (para recibir ovación).
curt·ness (kûrt′nĭs) I. s. *(brusqueness)* sequedad *f*, brusquedad *f; (conciseness)* concisión *f*, laconismo.
curt·sy (kûrt′sē) I. s. [pl. **-sies]** reverencia II. intr. **-sied,
-sy·ing** hacer una reverencia.
cur·va·ceous (kûr-vā′shəs) adj. curvilíneo, con muchas
curvas.
cur·va·ture (kûr′və-chŏŏr′, -chər) s. *(curve)* curvatura; *(of
the spine)* encorvamiento.
curve (kûrv) I. s. curva ♦ **curves** JER. curvas (del cuerpo)
II. intr. **curved, curv·ing** *(surface)* doblarse; *(road)* curvear, doblar; *(ball)* curvear —tr. doblar.
curved (kûrvd) adj. *(line, road)* curvo, curvado; *(bent)* doblado, torcido.
cur·vi·lin·e·ar (kûr′və-lĭn′ē-ər) *o* **cur·vi·lin·e·al** (-əl) adj.
curvilíneo.
cush·ion (kŏŏsh′ən) I. s. *(pad)* cojín *m*, almohadilla; *(shock
absorber)* colchón *m*, amortiguador *m; (of billiard table)*
banda; *(for lacemaking)* almohadilla; *(mitigator)* resguardo, protección *f <a c. against unemployment* un resguardo contra el desempleo> II. tr. *(a chair)* poner un
cojín *o* una almohadilla en; *(to pad)* acolchonar, acolchar;
(an impact) amortiguar; *(to hide)* tapar, sofocar; *(to mitigate)* resguardar, proteger.
cush·y (kŏŏsh′ē) adj. **-i·er, -i·est** JER. fácil, cómodo *<a c. job*
un trabajo cómodo>.

cusp (kŭsp) s. *(point)* cúspide *f; (of the moon)* cuerno; ARQ.,
GEOM. cúspide, vértice *m.*
cus·pid (kŭs′pĭd) s. ODONT. diente canino, colmillo.
cus·pi·dor (kŭs′pĭ-dôr′) s. escupidera.
cuss (kŭs) FAM. I. intr. decir malas palabras *o* groserías
—tr. maldecir ♦ **to c. out** insultar a II. s. *(invocation)*
maldición *f; (obscenity)* mala palabra, grosería; *(person)*
majadero.
cuss·ed (kŭs′ĭd) adj. FAM. *(cursed)* maldito; *(vexatious)*
majadero, empecinado.
cuss·ed·ness (kŭs′ĭd-nĭs) s. majadería, empecinamiento.
cus·tard (kŭs′tərd) s. natilla ♦ **caramel c.** flan.
custard apple s. BOT. anón *m*, anona (árbol y fruto).
cus·to·di·al (kŭ-stō′dē-əl) I. s. RELIG. custodia II. adj. de la
custodia.
cus·to·di·an (kŭ-stō′dē-ən) s. *(caretaker)* custodio, guardián *m; (janitor)* conserje *m.*
cus·to·dy (kŭs′tə-dē) s. [pl. **-dies]** *(of children)* custodia;
(care) cuidado; *(imprisonment)* detención *f* ♦ **to be in c.**
estar detenido • **to take into c.** detener, arrestar.
cus·tom (kŭs′təm) I. s. *(tradition, habit)* costumbre *f; (patronage)* clientela; DER. derecho consuetudinario ♦ **customs** [u. con v. sing.] *(duty)* derechos de aduana; *(agency)*
aduana *<to go through customs* pasar la aduana> II. adj.
(goods) hecho a gusto del comprador, especial; *(clothes)* a
la medida; *(person)* que trabaja por encargo.
cus·tom·ar·i·ly (kŭs′tə-mâr′ə-lē) adv. *(according to custom)*
acostumbradamente; *(ordinarily)* normalmente.
cus·tom·ar·y (kŭs′tə-mĕr′ē) adj. *(usual)* acostumbrado, de
costumbre; DER. *(law)* consuetudinario ♦ **to be c.** ser costumbre, acostumbrarse.
cus·tom-built (kŭs′təm-bĭlt′) adj. fabricado a gusto del
comprador.
cus·tom·er (kŭs′tə-mər) s. *(patron)* cliente *mf*; FAM. *(individual)* tipo, individuo.
cus·tom·house *o* **custom house** (kŭs′təm-hous′) s.
aduana.
cus·tom·ize (kŭs′tə-mīz′) tr. **-ized, -iz·ing** preparar a gusto
del comprador.
cus·tom-made (kŭs′təm-mād′) adj. hecho a gusto del comprador.
cut (kŭt) I. tr. **cut, cut·ting** *(to incise)* cortar; *(to sever)* cortar; *(to slice)* cortar *<why don't you c. the bread?* ¿por qué
no cortas el pan?>; *(to divide)* dividir, repartir; *(to clip)*
cortar *<to c. one's hair* cortarse el pelo>; *(to mow)* cortar
<to c. the grass cortar la hierba>; *(to harvest)* segar; *(to
fell)* talar; *(teeth)* salir *<the baby is cutting teeth* le están
saliendo los dientes al niño>; *(stone)* tallar, labrar; *(to
carve)* tallar, grabar; *(to dig)* abrir, excavar; *(to cross)*
cruzar, atravesar; *(cards)* cortar (naipes); *(size)* reducir,
acortar; *(time)* abreviar; *(prices)* reducir, rebajar; *(to dilute)* diluir; *(to dissolve)* disolver *<soap cuts grease* el jabón disuelve la grasa>; *(to hurt feelings)* lastimar, herir;
(to stop) parar *<to c. the engine* parar el motor>; *(to quit)*
dejarse de, acabar con *<c. the noise!* ¡acaben con el
ruido!>; *(to record)* grabar (un disco); COST. cortar; CI-
NEM., TELEV. *(to terminate)* cortar; *(to edit)* montar; FAM.
(classes, school) fumarse, faltar a *<to c. a class* fumarse
una clase> ♦ **to c. a caper** hacer cabriolas • **to c. across**
(to cross) cortar por; *(to do away with)* derribar *<this issue
cuts across ideological differences* este asunto derriba las
diferencias ideológicas> • **to c. a fine figure** FAM. ser elegante • **to c. a long story short** para ser breve • **to c. back**
(to shorten) recortar; *(to reduce)* reducir, disminuir • **to c.
corners** *(to simplify)* simplificar; *(to economize)* economizar • **to c. down** JER. *(to kill)* matar; *(expenses)* reducir;
(prices) rebajar; *(a tree)* talar • **to c. down to size** desinflar las pretensiones de • **to c. no ice** FAM. no tener influencia • **c. it out!** ¡basta ya! • **to c. off** *(to sever)* cortar;
(to amputate) amputar; *(to shut off)* parar; *(to block)* aislar, bloquear; *(to obstruct)* obstruir, tapar (esp. la vista);
(to break off) romper (esp. negociaciones); *(to disinherit)*
desheredar • **to c. one's losses** cortar por lo sano • **to c.
one's teeth on** iniciarse en, ejercitarse en • **to c. out** *(to
remove)* cortar, tranchar; *(to reshape)* recortar; *(to deprive)* privar de; *(to exclude)* excluir; *(to delete)* suprimir;

(to stop) dejar de <*I have to c. out smoking* tengo que dejar de fumar> • **to cut short** *(to stop)* cortar en seco <*I c. short his explanations* corté en seco sus explicaciones>; *(to abbreviate)* abreviar, acortar • **to c. someone in** incluir a alguien en, hacer a alguien participar en • **to c. the mustard** FAM. hacer lo que se espera de uno • **to c. to the bone** reducir al mínimo • **to c. up** *(into pieces)* cortar en pedazos, partir; *(to destroy)* destrozar —intr. *(to separate)* cortar <*you did not c. deep enough* no cortaste lo suficientemente hondo>; *(to allow cutting)* cortarse <*butter cuts easily* la mantequilla se corta fácilmente>; *(teeth)* salir; *(to injure)* cortar; *(to change direction)* virar, doblar <*to c. to the left* virar a la izquierda>; *(to go directly)* cortar <*he c. across the field* cortó por el campo>; *(cards)* cortar • **to be c. out for** estar hecho para <*I'm not c. out for this sort of work* no estoy hecho para este tipo de trabajo> • **to c. back** hacer reducciones • **to c. both ways** FIG. tener doble filo • **to c. down** reducir lo sobrante • **to c. in** *(a line of people)* colarse; *(a line of cars)* meterse delante; *(a conversation)* interrumpir; ELEC. conectarse • **to c. loose** JER. *(to flee)* escaparse; *(to let go of restraints)* hablar o actuar sin cuidarse • **to c. off** *(to stop)* pararse; *(to break off)* romperse • **to c. out** FAM. largarse, irse • **to c. up** hacer diabluras **II.** s. *(slit)* corte *m*; *(gash)* tajo; *(notch)* muesca; *(deletion)* corte <*a c. in the speech* un corte en el discurso>; *(reduction)* reducción *f*; *(discount)* rebaja; *(of cards)* corte; FAM. *(share)* tajada, parte *f*; *(absence)* falta, inasistencia; *(style)* corte; JOY. talla; IMPR. grabada; CINEM., TELEV. corte, interrupción *f* ♦ **a c. above** un poco mejor que • **short c.** atajo.
cut-and-dried (kŭt′ən-drīd′) adj. *(prearranged)* preconcebido; *(routine)* rutinario.
cu·ta·ne·ous (kyōō-tā′nē-əs) adj. cutáneo.
cut·back (kŭt′băk′) s. reducción *f*.
cute (kyōōt) adj. **cut·er, cut·est** *(pretty)* mono, lindo; *(contrived)* afectado ♦ **to get c. with** hacerse el listo con.
cute·ness (kyōōt′nĭs) s. *(grace)* gracia, encanto; *(prettiness)* lindura, monería.
cu·tes (kyōō′tēz′) un pl. de **cutis.**
cut·ey (kyōō′tē) s. var. de **cutie.**
cut glass s. cristal tallado.
cu·ti·cle (kyōō′tĭ-kəl) s. cutícula.
cut·ie (kyōō′tē) s. [pl. **-ies**] JER. monada.
cu·tis (kyōō′tĭs) s. [pl. **-tes** (-tēz′) o **-tis·es**] ANAT. cutis *m*, piel *f*.
cut·lass o **cut·las** (kŭt′ləs) s. MIL. sable *m*.
cut·ler (kŭt′lər) s. cuchillero.
cut·ler·y (kŭt′lə-rē) s. *(instruments)* instrumentos cortantes; *(tableware)* cubiertos; *(occupation)* cuchillería.
cut·let (kŭt′lĭt) s. CUL. chuleta.
cut·off (kŭt′ôf′) s. *(limit)* límite *m*; *(short cut)* atajo; *(cutting off)* corte *m*; *(device)* obturador *m*.
cut·out (kŭt′out′) s. *(piece)* recorte *m*; *(figure)* figura recortada; ELEC. interruptor *m*.
cut-rate (kŭt′rāt′) adj. rebajado, de descuento.
cut·ter (kŭt′ər) s. *(in tailoring)* cortador *m*; *(of stones)* tallista *mf*; *(device)* cortadora; MARÍT. cúter *m* ♦ **coast guard c.** guardacostas.
cut·throat (kŭt′thrōt′) **I.** s. *(murderer)* degollador *m*; *(criminal)* asesino **II.** adj. *(cruel)* cruel, sanguinario; *(competition)* despiadado, implacable.
cut·ting (kŭt′ĭng) **I.** s. *(clipping)* recorte *m*; *(excavation)* paso; *(editing)* desglose *m*; AGR. esqueje *m*, rampollo **II.** adj. *(tool, wind)* cortante; *(remark)* mordaz.
cut·tle·bone (kŭt′l-bōn′) s. jibión *m*.
cut·tle·fish (kŭt′l-fĭsh′) s. [pl. **cuttlefish** o **-fish·es**] jibia.
cut·up (kŭt′ŭp′) s. FAM. bromista *mf*.
cut·wa·ter (kŭt′wô′tər) s. tajamar *m*.
cy·a·nide (sī′ə-nīd′) o **cy·a·nid** (-nĭd) s. QUÍM. cianuro.
cy·ber·net·ics (sī′bər-nĕt′ĭks) s. [u. con v. sing.] cibernética.
cy·cla·mate (sī′klə-māt′, sĭk′lə-) s. QUÍM. ciclamato.
cy·cla·men (sī′klə-mən, sĭk′lə-) s. BOT. ciclamen *m*.
cy·cle (sī′kəl) **I.** s. *(period, series)* ciclo; *(orbit)* órbita; *(bike)* bicicleta; *(motorcycle)* motocicleta **II.** intr. **-cled, -cling** *(to occur)* ocurrir cíclicamente; *(to go)* ir en bicicleta o motocicleta.

cy·clic (sī′klĭk, sĭk′lĭk) o **cy·cli·cal** (sī′klĭ-kəl, sĭk′lĭ-kəl) adj. cíclico.
cy·cling (sī′klĭng) DEP. **I.** s. ciclismo **II.** adj. ciclista <*c. competition* competencia ciclista>.
cy·clist (sī′klĭst) s. *(bicycle rider)* ciclista *mf*; *(motorcycle rider)* motociclista *mf*.
cy·clone (sī′klōn′) s. ciclón *m*.
Cy·clops (sī′klŏps′) s. [pl. **Cy·clo·pes** (sī-klō′pēz′)] MITOL. cíclope *m*.
cy·clo·ram·a (sī′klə-răm′ə, -rä′mə) s. ciclorama *m*.
cy·clo·thy·mia (sī′klə-thī′mē-ə) s. PSIC. ciclotimia.
cy·clo·tron (sī′klə-trŏn′) s. FÍS. ciclotrón *m*.
cyg·net (sĭg′nĭt) s. ORNIT. pichón de cisne *m*.
cyl·in·der (sĭl′ən-dər) s. cilindro ♦ **hydrogen c.** balón de hidrógeno.
cylinder head s. MEC. cabeza o culata del cilindro.
cy·lin·dri·cal (sə-lĭn′drĭ-kəl) o **cy·lin·dric** (-drĭk) adj. cilíndrico.
cym·bal (sĭm′bəl) s. címbalo, platillo.
cyn·ic (sĭn′ĭk) s. & adj. cínico.
cyn·i·cal (sĭn′ĭ-kəl) adj. cínico.
cyn·i·cism (sĭn′ĭ-sĭz′əm) s. cinismo.
cy·no·sure (sī′nə-shōōr′, sĭn′ə-) s. centro de atracción.
cy·press (sī′prəs) s. BOT. ciprés *(árbol y madera)* *m*.
Cyp·ri·an (sĭp′rē-ən) adj. & s. chipriota *mf*.
Cy·prus (sī′prəs) s. Chipre.
cyst (sĭst) s. *(growth)* quiste *m*; *(sac)* vesícula.
cys·tic (sĭs′tĭk) adj. MED. enquistado; *(of the bladder)* cístico.
cystic fibrosis s. MED. fibrosis cística.
cys·ti·tis (sĭ-stī′tĭs) s. MED. cistitis *f*.
cy·tol·o·gy (sī-tŏl′ə-jē) s. BIOL. citología.
cy·to·plasm (sī′tə-plăz′əm) s. BIOL. citoplasma *m*.
czar (zär) s. zar *m*.
czar·e·vitch (zär′ə-vĭch′) s. zarevitz *m*.
cza·ri·na (zä-rē′nə) o **cza·rit·za** (zä-rĭt′sə, -rēt′-) s. zarina.
Czech (chĕk) adj. & s. *(inhabitant, language)* checo, checoslovaco.
Czech·o·slo·vak (chĕk′ə-slō′väk′, -văk′) o **Czech·o·slo·va·ki·an** (-slō-vä′kē-ən, -väk′ē-ən) adj. & s. *(inhabitant, language)* checoslovaco.
Czech·o·slo·va·ki·a (chĕk′ə-slō-vä′kē-ə, -väk′ē-ə) s. Checoslovaquia.

D

d, D (dē) s. [pl. **d's, D's**] cuarta letra del alfabeto inglés; MÚS. re *m* ♦ **D flat, major, minor, sharp** MÚS. re bemol, mayor, menor, sostenido.
dab[1] (dăb) **I.** tr. **dabbed, dab·bing** dar toques a, retocar suavemente —intr. golpear rápida y ligeramente **II.** s. *(bit)* pizca; *(light blow)* golpe ligero.
dab[2] (dăb) s. ICT. platija.
dab·ber (dăb′ər) s. IMPR. bala, tampón *m*.
dab·ble (dăb′əl) tr. **-bled, -bling** salpicar —intr. *(to splash)* chapotear; *(to do superficially)* interesarse superficialmente.
dab·bler (dăb′lər) s. diletante *mf*.
dace (dās) s. ICT. albur *m*, lencisco.
dachs·hund (däks′hōōnt′) s. perro tejonero, perro salchicha.
Da·cron (dā′krŏn′, dăk′rŏn′) s. TEJ. dacrón *(marca registrada)* *m*.
dad (dăd) s. FAM. papá *m*.
dad·dy (dăd′ē) s. [pl. **-dies**] FAM. papacito, papito.
daddy long·legs (lông′lĕgz′) s. ENTOM. *(arachnid)* segador *m*; *(crane fly)* típula.
da·do (dā′dō) s. [pl. **-does**] ARQ. *(of a pedestal)* dado, neto; *(of a wall)* friso, rodapié *m*; *(groove)* estría.
daf·fo·dil (dăf′ə-dĭl′) s. BOT. narciso.
daf·fy (dăf′ē) adj. **-fi·er, -fi·est** FAM. chalado, chiflado.
daft (dăft) adj. **-er, -est** *(crazy)* loco; *(foolish)* tonto.

dag·ger (dăg′ər) s. *(knife)* daga, puñal *m*; IMPR. *(obelisk)* obelisco, cruz *f.*

da·go (dā′gō) s. [pl. **-gos** *o* **-goes**] DESPEC. español *m*, portugués *m*, *o* italiano de tez morena.

da·guerre·o·type (də-gâr′ə-tīp′) s. FOTOG. daguerrotipo.

dahl·ia (dăl′yə, däl′-) s. BOT. dalia.

dai·ly (dā′lē) I. adj. diario, cotidiano II. adv. diariamente, cada día III. s. [pl. **-lies**] diario, periódico.

daily double s. apuesta combinada ganada en un mismo día.

dain·ti·ly (dān′tl-ē) adv. delicadamente.

dain·ti·ness (dān′tē-nĭs) s. delicadeza.

dain·ty (dān′tē) adj. **-ti·er, -ti·est** *(exquisite)* exquisito; *(delicate)* delicado; *(refined)* refinado; *(affected)* remilgado.

dai·qui·ri (dī′kə-rē, dăk′ə-) s. [pl. **-ris**] daiquirí (cóctel de ron, jugo de lima y azúcar) *m.*

dair·y (dâr′ē) s. [pl. **-ies**] *(store)* lechería; *(on a farm)* vaquería, tambo; *(products)* productos lácteos.

dairy cattle s.pl. vacas lecheras.

dairy farm s. granja lechera.

dair·y·man (dâr′ē-mən) s. [pl. **-men**] lechero.

da·is (dā′ĭs) s. tarima, estrado.

dai·sy (dā′zē) s. [pl. **-sies**] BOT. margarita.

dale (dāl) s. valle *m.*

dal·li·ance (dăl′ē-əns) s. *(dawdling)* gandulería; *(flirtation)* coqueteo.

dal·ly (dăl′ē) tr. **-lied, -ly·ing** *(to flirt)* coquetear; *(to waste time)* gandulear; *(to play)* entretenerse —tr. perder (tiempo).

Dal·ma·tian (dăl-mā′shən) s. perro dálmata.

dal·ton·ism (dôl′tə-nĭz′əm) s. MED. daltonismo.

dam¹ (dăm) I. s. *(barrier)* presa; *(reservoir)* embalse *m* II. tr. **dammed, dam·ming** embalsar, represar.

dam² (dăm) s. madre (de animales cuadrúpedos) *f.*

dam·age (dăm′ĭj) I. s. *(injury)* daño, lesión *f*; MEC. *(impairment)* avería, desperfecto; FIG. *(harm)* perjuicio; FAM. *(cost)* costo ♦ **damages** DER. daños y perjuicios II. tr. & intr. **-aged, -ag·ing** dañar(se), estropear(se).

Da·mas·cus (də-măs′kəs) s. Damasco.

dam·ask (dăm′əsk) I. s. *(fabric)* damasco; *(steel)* acero damasquino II. tr. *(to damascene)* damasquinar III. adj. *(damascene)* adamascado, damasquino; *(deep-pink)* de color rosa de Damasco.

dame (dām) s. *(matron)* señora, dama; *(woman)* mujer *f*; JER. *(broad)* hembra; G.B. *(title)* dama.

damn (dăm) I. tr. *(to condemn)* condenar; *(to ruin)* arruinar, echar a perder; *(to swear at)* maldecir —intr. maldecir II. interj. ♦ **d!** *o* **d. it!** ¡maldito sea!, ¡maldición! III. s. ♦ **I don't give a d.** no me importa un comino • **it's not worth a d.** no vale un comino IV. adj. maldito *<this d. elevator* este maldito ascensor> V. adv. muy *<it's d. cheap* es muy barato>.

dam·na·ble (dăm′nə-bəl) adj. *(deserving condemnation)* condenable; *(odious)* detestable.

dam·na·tion (dăm-nā′shən) I. s. *(condemnation)* condenación *f*; RELIG. *(perdition)* perdición *f*, condenación al castigo eterno II. interj. ¡maldición!

damned (dămd) I. adj. **-er, -est** *(detestable)* condenado, maldito; RELIG. *(condemned)* condenado, réprobo; FAM. *(huge)* espantoso, tremendo II. adv. FAM. muy, sumamente III. s. ♦ **the d.** RELIG. los condenados, los réprobos.

damp (dămp) I. adj. **-er, -est** húmedo, ligeramente mojado II. s. *(moisture)* humedad *f*; MIN. *(gas)* mofeta, grisú *m*; *(discouragement)* desánimo, desaliento III. tr. *(to moisten)* humedecer; *(to smother)* sofocar, apagar; *(to discourage)* desanimar, desalentar; FÍS. *(to lessen)* amortiguar.

damp·en (dăm′pən) tr. *(to moisten)* humedecer; FIG. *(to depress)* deprimir, disminuir (ardor, celo) —intr. humedecerse.

damp·er (dăm′pər) s. TEC. compuerta de tiro; FÍS. amortiguador *m*; MÚS. sordina ♦ **to put a d. on** desanimar, apagar (entusiasmo, ánimo).

damp·ness (dămp′nĭs) s. humedad *f.*

dam·sel (dăm′zəl) s. damisela.

dam·son (dăm′zən) s. BOT. *(tree)* ciruelo damasceno; *(fruit)* ciruela damascena.

dance (dăns) I. intr. **danced, danc·ing** bailar; FIG. *(to leap)* saltar, brincar —tr. hacer bailar II. s. *(steps)* baile *m*, danza; *(party)* baile.

danc·er (dăn′sər) s. *(one who dances)* bailador *m*, danzante *mf*; *(of flamenco)* bailaor *m*; *(professional)* bailarín *m.*

danc·ing (dăn′sĭng) I. s. baile *m* II. adj. de baile *<d. school* escuela de baile>.

dan·de·li·on (dăn′dl-ī′ən) s. BOT. diente de león *m.*

dan·der (dăn′dər) s. FAM. cólera, rabia ♦ **to get someone's d. up** hacer que alguien rabie.

dan·di·fy (dăn′də-fī′) tr. **-fied, -fy·ing** elegantizar afectadamente.

dan·dle (dăn′dl) tr. **-dled, -dling** *(to rock)* mecer; *(to pamper)* mimar.

dan·druff (dăn′drəf) s. caspa.

dan·dy (dăn′dē) I. s. [pl. **-dies**] *(fop)* dandi *m*, petimetre *m* II. adj. **-di·er, -di·est** *(excellent)* excelente; *(elegant)* elegante.

Dane (dān) s. danés *m*, dinamarqués *m.*

dan·ger (dān′jər) s. peligro, riesgo.

dan·ger·ous (dān′jər-əs) adj. peligroso, arriesgado.

dan·gle (dăng′gəl) intr. **-gled, -gling** *(to sway)* pender, balancearse; *(to hang)* colgar —tr. *(to sway)* balancear en el aire; *(to hang)* colgar.

Dan·iel (dăn′yəl) s. BÍBL. Daniel.

Dan·ish (dā′nĭsh) I. adj. danés, dinamarqués II. s. *(language)* danés *m*, dinamarqués *m*; CUL., FAM. pastelillo con fruta *o* con frutos secos.

dank (dăngk) adj. **-er, -est** malsano y húmedo.

Dan·ube (dăn′yōōb) s. Danubio.

dap·per (dăp′ər) adj. *(stylish)* atildado, apuesto; *(active)* vivaracho.

dap·ple (dăp′əl) I. s. mancha moteada II. tr. **-pled, -pling** motear III. adj. moteado, manchado.

Dar·da·nelles (där′dn-ĕlz′) s. Dardanelos.

dare (dâr) I. intr. **dared, dar·ing** osar, atreverse —tr. *(to face)* arrostrar, hacer frente; *(to challenge)* retar, desafiar ♦ **I d. say** me parece probable II. s. desafío, reto.

dare·dev·il (dâr′dĕv′əl) adj. & s. atrevido, temerario.

dar·ing (dâr′ĭng) I. adj. temerario, audaz II. s. *(audacity)* temeridad *f*, audacia; *(boldness)* atrevimiento, osadía.

dark (därk) I. adj. **-er, -est** *(without light)* oscuro, sin luz; *(dim)* opaco, gris; *(said of a color)* oscuro; *(complexion)* moreno, morocho; *(threatening)* amenazador; *(deep)* profundo (sonido, voz); *(dismal)* triste; *(evil)* siniestro; *(unknown)* desconocido, misterioso; *(secret)* secreto, oculto; *(ignorant)* ignorante II. s. *(darkness)* oscuridad *f*, tinieblas *f*; *(nightfall)* anochecer *m*, noche *f*; PINT. *(shade)* sombra ♦ **to be in the d.** no estar informado.

Dark Ages s.pl. HIST. Alta Edad Media, Edad de las Tinieblas.

dark·en (där′kən) tr. & intr. oscurecer(se); FIG. *(to sadden)* entristecer(se).

dark horse s. FIG., DEP. participante desconocido; POL. candidato con un apoyo inesperado.

dark·ness (därk′nĭs) s. oscuridad *f.*

dark·room (därk′rōōm′, -rōōm′) s. FOTOG. cuarto oscuro.

dar·ling (där′lĭng) I. s. *(loved one)* querido, amado; *(favorite)* favorito, predilecto II. adj. *(beloved)* querido, amado; FAM. *(charming)* encantador, adorable.

darn¹ (därn) COST. I. tr. zurcir —intr. hacer zurcidos II. s. zurcido.

darn² (därn) I. interj. ¡maldición! II. adj. maldito III. adv. FAM. muy IV. tr. & intr. maldecir.

darned (därnd) I. adj. maldito II. adv. muy, sumamente.

darn·ing (där′nĭng) s. COST. zurcido.

darning needle s. *(needle)* aguja de zurcir; ENTOM., FAM. *(dragonfly)* libélula.

dart (därt) I. intr. correr, lanzarse —tr. lanzar, arrojar II. s. *(projectile)* dardo, saeta; *(sting)* aguijón *m*; *(movement)* movimiento rápido; COST. *(tuck)* pinza ♦ **darts** [ú. con v. sing.] dardos (juego).

dart·board (därt′bôrd′) s. blanco (para dardos).

Dar·win·ian (där′wĭn′ē-ən) adj. darviniano.

Dar·win·ism (där′wĭ-nĭz′əm) s. darvinismo.

Dar·win·ist (där′wĭ-nĭst) s. darvinista *mf.*

ã rey / ä año / b boca / ch chico / d dar / ĕ el / ē mil / g gato / h joya / hw juez / ī aire / k casa / kw cuan /

dash (dăsh) **I.** tr. *(to mash)* estrellar, romper; *(to hurl)* tirar; *(to splash)* salpicar; *(to do hastily)* hacer rápidamente *<he dashed off a letter* escribió una carta rápidamente>; *(to sprinkle)* salpicar; *(to mix)* mezclar; *(to frustrate)* frustrar; *(to abash)* avergonzar —intr. ♦ **to d. by** pasar corriendo • **to d. in** entrar corriendo • **to d. on** ir de prisa • **to d. out** salir corriendo **II.** s. *(blow)* golpe (rápido) *m*; *(splash)* salpicadura; *(bit)* pizca; *(rush)* prisa; PINT. *(stroke)* pincelada; DEP. *(race)* carrera corta; *(verve)* brío; *(drive)* empuje *m*; GRAM., IMPR. *(mark)* raya; TELEG. raya (en Morse); AUTO. *(dashboard)* tablero de instrumentos ♦ **at a d.** de un golpe • **to cut a d.** FAM. causar sensación • **to make a d. at** precipitarse sobre • **to make a d. for** precipitarse hacia • **to make a d. for it** echarse a correr, huir.
dash·board (dăsh'bôrd') s. AUTO. tablero de instrumentos, salpicadero.
dash·ing (dăsh'ĭng) adj. *(audacious)* audaz, arrojado; *(elegant)* elegante.
das·tard·li·ness (dăs'tərd-lē-nĭs) s. cobardía.
das·tard·ly (dăs'tərd-lē) adj. *(cowardly)* cobarde; *(vicious)* vil, ruin.
da·ta (dā'tə, dăt'ə) s.pl. [ú. con v. sing. o pl.] *(information)* información *f*, datos; COMPUT. *(numerical information)* datos.
data bank *o* **da·ta·bank** (dā'tə-băngk', dăt'ə-) s. COMPUT. *(data base)* base de datos *f*; *(organization)* banco de datos, centro de información.
data base *o* **da·ta·base** (dā'tə-bās', dăt'ə-) s. COMPUT. base de datos *f*.
data carrier s. TEC. portador de información *m*.
data processing s. COMPUT. *(science)* informática, tratamiento de la información; *(process)* procesamiento de datos.
data processor s. COMPUT. ordenador *m*, computadora.
data set s. COMPUT. *(series)* colección de artículos de información *f*; *(modem)* modem (modulador/demodulador) *m*.
date[1] (dāt) **I.** s. *(time)* fecha; *(epoch)* época, período; *(appointment)* cita, compromiso; *(companion)* acompañante *mf* ♦ **to be out-of-d.** estar atrasado, ser anticuado • **to be up-to-d.** estar al día • **to this d.** hasta la fecha **II.** tr. **dat·ed, dat·ing** *(to place in time)* fechar; *(to go out with)* salir con; *(to betray the age of)* revelar la edad de —intr. *(to place in time)* fechar; *(to become old-fashioned)* volverse anticuado; *(to go out)* salir (en una cita) *<I d. a lot* yo salgo mucho> ♦ **to d. back to** remontar(se) a *<that book dates back to the Middle Ages* ese libro se remonta al Medioevo> • **to d. from** datar de.
date[2] (dāt) s. *(tree)* datilero; *(fruit)* dátil *m*.
dat·ed (dā'tĭd) adj. *(bearing a date)* fechado; *(out-of-date)* pasado de moda, anticuado.
date·line (dāt'līn') s. PERIOD. fecha y lugar de origen.
date line s. GEOG. meridiano de cambio de fecha.
date palm s. BOT. palmera datilera.
date stamp s. fechador *m*.
da·tive (dā'tĭv) GRAM. adj. & s. dativo.
da·tum (dā'təm, dăt'əm) s. [pl. **-ta** (-tə)] *(fact)* dato; TOP. [pl. **-tums**] línea de referencia.
da·tu·ra (də-tōŏr'ə, -tyŏŏr'ə) s. BOT. datura, estramonio.
daub (dôb) **I.** tr. *(to cover)* revestir; *(to smear)* embadurnar; *(to paint)* pintarrajear —intr. pintarrajear **II.** s. *(coating)* revestimiento, capa; *(smear)* mancha; *(crude painting)* mamarracho.
daub·er (dô'bər) s. *(whitewasher)* embadurnador *m*; *(painter)* pintamonas *mf*.
daugh·ter (dô'tər) s. hija.
daugh·ter-in-law (dô'tər-ĭn-lô') s. [pl. **daugh·ters-in-law**] nuera, hija política.
daunt (dônt) tr. *(to intimidate)* intimidar; *(to dishearten)* desanimar, desalentar.
daunt·less (dônt'lĭs) adj. intrépido.
dau·phin (dô'fĭn) s. HIST. delfín *m*.
dau·phin·ess (dô'fĭ-nĭs) *o* **dau·phine** (dô-fēn') s. HIST. delfina.
dav·en·port (dăv'ən-pôrt') s. *(sofa)* sofá grande *m*, sofá cama *m*; G.B. *(desk)* escritorio pequeño.
dav·it (dăv'ĭt, dā'vĭt) s. MARÍT. pescante *m*.

daw·dle (dôd'l) intr. **-dled, -dling** *(to delay)* andar despacio, demorarse; *(to loiter)* haraganear, holgazanear —tr. ♦ **to d. away** perder, malgastar.
daw·dler (dôd'lər) s. *(lazy person)* holgazán *m*; *(slow walker)* persona lenta *o* rezagada.
dawn (dôn) **I.** s. *(morning)* amanecer *m*, alba; FIG. *(beginning)* albor *m*, alborada **II.** intr. *(to become light)* amanecer, alborear; FIG. *(to emerge)* amanecer, nacer ♦ **it dawned on me** caí en la cuenta.
day (dā) s. *(period)* día *m*; *(of work)* jornada; *(epoch)* época ♦ **d. in, d. out** día trás día • **d. off** día franco • **d. of reckoning** día de ajuste de cuentas • **every other d.** cada dos días • **Holy D.** fiesta religiosa • **it's all in a day's work** son gajes del oficio • **the d. after** al día siguiente • **the d. after tomorrow** pasado mañana • **the d. before . . .** la víspera de . . . • **the d. before yesterday** anteayer • **these days** hoy en día *<these days food is expensive* hoy en día la comida está cara> • **to call it a d.** dar por acabado, retirarse (de carrera, trabajo) • **to carry the d.** triunfar, llevarse la palma • **to have had one's d.** haber pasado de moda • **to have seen better days** haber conocido días mejores, haber estado en mejores condiciones • **to save for a rainy d.** ahorrar para momentos difíciles.
day bed s. sofá cama *m*.
day·book (dā'bŏŏk') s. TEN. diario; *(diary)* diario.
day·break (dā'brāk') s. amanecer *m*, alba.
day care s. cuidado de niños durante el día ♦ **day-care center** guardería.
day·dream (dā'drēm') **I.** s. ensueño, ilusión *f* **II.** intr. **-dreamed** *o* **-dreamt** (-drĕmt'), **-dream·ing** soñar despierto, ilusionarse.
day·dream·er (dā'drē'mər) s. soñador *m*.
day laborer s. jornalero, peón *m*.
day letter s. telegrama *m*.
day·light (dā'līt') s. *(light of day)* luz del día *f*; *(dawn)* amanecer *m*, alba; *(daytime)* día *m*; FIG. *(understanding)* comprensión *f* ♦ **to scare the daylights out of someone** FAM. asustar mucho a alguien • **to see d.** llegar a comprender.
day·light-sav·ing time (dā'līt-sā'vĭng) s. hora de verano.
day·long (dā'lông') **I.** adj. que dura todo el día **II.** adv. todo el día.
day nursery s. guardería infantil.
Day of Atonement s. RELIG. Día de la Expiación *m*.
Day of Judgment s. RELIG. Día del Juicio *m*.
days (dāz) adv. de día.
day school s. EDUC. externado, colegio de externos.
day·spring (dā'sprĭng') s. aurora, alba.
day·time (dā'tīm') s. día *m*.
day-to-day (dā'tə-dā') adj. *(daily)* cotidiano; *(a day at a time)* al día.
daze (dāz) **I.** tr. **dazed, daz·ing** *(to stun)* aturdir; *(to dazzle)* deslumbrar **II.** s. aturdimiento, atolondramiento.
daz·zle (dăz'əl) **I.** tr. & intr. **-zled, -zling** deslumbrar **II.** s. deslumbramiento.
daz·zling (dăz'lĭng) **I.** adj. deslumbrante, deslumbrador **II.** s. deslumbramiento.
D-day (dē'dā') s. HIST. día en el que las fuerzas aliadas invadieron Francia durante la Segunda Guerra Mundial; FIG. *(date)* fecha en la que se realizará *u* ocurrirá algo importante.
DDT (dē'dē-tē') s. insecticida (marca registrada) *m*.
dea·con (dē'kən) s. RELIG. diácono.
dea·con·ess (dē'kə-nĭs) s. RELIG. diaconisa.
dea·con·ry (dē'kən-rē) s. [pl. **-ries**] RELIG. diaconado, diaconato.
de·ac·ti·vate (dē-ăk'tə-vāt') tr. **-vat·ed, -vat·ing** *(to make inactive)* desactivar; MIL. pasar a la reserva.
dead (dĕd) **I.** adj. *(no longer alive)* muerto; *(doomed)* condenado; *(inanimate)* exánime, inerte; *(exhausted)* agotado; *(numb)* indiferente, insensible; *(barren)* estéril; *(motionless)* estancado; *(quiet)* tranquilo; *(obsolete)* anticuado; *(dull)* triste, aburrido; *(abrupt)* repentino, en seco; *(said of sounds, voice)* sordo; *(desolate)* desolado, desierto; *(extinct)* extinto, apagado; *(said of a ball)* sin rebote; *(said of certainty, quietness)* completo, absoluto;

(exact) exacto, certero; DEP. *(out of play)* fuera de juego; ELEC. *(lacking connection)* sin corriente, desconectado; *(discharged)* descargado **II.** s. muerto ♦ **the d.** los muertos • **the d. of night** plena noche • **the d. of winter** pleno invierno **III.** adv. *(absolutely)* completamente, absolutamente <*d. right* absolutamente correcto>; *(exactly)* exactamente, justo <*d. in the center* justo en medio>.

dead-air space (dĕd′âr′) s. espacio sin ventilación.

dead·beat (dĕd′bēt′) **I.** adj. ELEC., RAD. aperiódico **II.** s. JER. *(sponger)* gorrón *m*; *(loafer)* holgazán *m*.

dead center s. MEC. punto muerto.

dead duck s. JER. persona destinada a la derrota.

dead·en (dĕd′n) tr. *(to lessen the force of)* amortiguar; *(to alleviate)* calmar, aliviar; *(to make soundproof)* insonorizar —intr. *(sound, blow)* amortiguarse; *(vitality)* disminuir.

dead-end (dĕd′ĕnd′) adj. *(closed)* sin salida; *(without opportunity)* sin porvenir; FAM. *(of the slums)* barriobajero.

dead end s. callejón sin salida *m*.

dead·eye (dĕd′ī′) s. MARÍT. vigota; JER. *(marksman)* tirador seguro.

dead·fall (dĕd′fôl′) s. *(trap)* trampa; *(mass)* montón de árboles y maleza *m*.

dead·head (dĕd′hĕd′) **I.** s. FAM. gorrón *m* **II.** tr. mover un vehículo sin pasajeros ni carga.

dead heat s. DEP. empate *m*.

dead letter s. carta no reclamada.

dead·line (dĕd′līn′) s. *(time limit)* fecha tope, plazo; *(in a prison)* línea vedada.

dead·li·ness (dĕd′lē-nĭs) s. efecto *o* carácter mortífero.

dead load s. peso muerto.

dead·lock (dĕd′lŏk′) **I.** s. estancamiento **II.** tr. & intr. estancar(se).

dead·ly (dĕd′lē) **I.** adj. -**li·er**, -**li·est** *(lethal)* mortífero; *(implacable)* implacable, mortal; *(destructive)* devastador; *(absolute)* absoluto; *(accurate)* certero; FAM. *(dull)* aburrido, pesado **II.** adv. extremadamente.

deadly nightshade s. BOT. belladona.

deadly sin s. RELIG. pecado capital.

dead·ness (dĕd′nĭs) s. *(lifelessness)* falta de vida; *(of a limb)* entumecimiento.

dead·pan (dĕd′păn′) JER. **I.** s. cara impasible, semblante inexpresivo **II.** adj. inexpresivo, impasible **III.** adv. de forma impasible.

dead reckoning s. AVIA., MARÍT. estima.

Dead Sea s. GEOG. Mar Muerto.

dead weight s. peso muerto.

dead·wood (dĕd′wŏŏd′) s. BOT. *(wood)* rama muerta; *(person, thing)* persona *o* cosa inútil.

deaf (dĕf) adj. sordo.

deaf-and-dumb (dĕf′ən-dŭm′) s. & adj. sordomudo.

deaf·en (dĕf′ən) tr. *(to make deaf)* ensordecer; *(to make soundproof)* aislar contra el ruido.

deaf·en·ing (dĕf′ə-nĭng) adj. ensordecedor.

deaf-mute *o* **deaf mute** (dĕf′myōōt′) s. & adj. sordomudo.

deaf·ness (dĕf′nĭs) s. sordera.

deal¹ (dēl) **I.** tr. dealt (dĕlt), **deal·ing** *(to apportion)* repartir; *(to distribute)* distribuir; *(a blow)* asestar; *(cards)* dar, repartir —intr. *(cards)* dar, repartir ♦ **to d. in** comerciar en • **to d. with** *(in business)* tratar con; *(to meet a situation)* enfrentarse con; *(to resolve)* resolver (dificultad); *(to treat)* tratar de *o* sobre; *(to take action)* ocuparse de, encargarse de; *(to punish)* castigar **II.** s. *(agreement)* arreglo, convenio; *(in cards)* reparto; *(hand)* mano *f*; *(turn to distribute cards)* turno; FAM. *(treatment)* trato, tratamiento; *(sale)* negocio, transacción *f*; POL. *(program)* programa *m*, plan *m* ♦ **a good d.** *o* **a great d.** mucho, una gran cantidad • **big d.!** ¡gran cosa! • **it's a d.!** ¡trato hecho! • **to make a big d. out of nothing** FAM. hacer un escándalo por nada.

deal² (dēl) s. *(board)* tablón *m*, madero; *(wood)* pino, abeto.

deal·er (dē′lər) s. *(merchant)* negociante *mf*, traficante *mf*; *(in cards)* banquero.

deal·er·ship (dē′lər-shĭp′) s. COM. *(franchise)* concesión *f*; *(business)* negocio.

deal·ing (dē′lĭng) s. comportamiento, trato ♦ **dealings**

COM. *(business)* transacciones, negocios; *(relations)* relaciones, trato.

dealt (dĕlt) pret. y part. p. de **deal**.

dean (dēn) s. DIPL., EDUC. decano; RELIG. deán *m*.

dean·ship (dēn′shĭp′) s. EDUC. decanato; RELIG. deanato, deanazgo.

dear (dîr) **I.** adj. -**er**, -**est** *(loved)* querido; *(esteemed)* estimado; *(precious)* valioso; *(costly)* costoso, caro; *(eager)* ardiente, sincero; *(in salutations)* querido <*D. Paul* Querido Pablo>, muy . . . mío (nuestro) <*D. Sir* Muy señor mío>, estimado <*D. Sir* Estimado señor mío (nuestro)> **II.** adv. *(costly)* caro; *(fondly)* con cariño **III.** s. *(an endearing person)* encanto; *(darling)* querido.

dear·ly (dîr′lē) adv. *(costly)* caro; *(fondly)* con cariño; *(very much)* mucho.

dearth (dûrth) s. *(lack)* escasez *f*; *(famine)* hambre *f*.

dear·y (dîr′ē) s. FAM. querido.

death (dĕth) s. *(fact of dying)* muerte *f*; *(cause of dying)* causa de muerte; FIG. *(end)* fin *m*, extinción *f*; *(execution)* ejecución *f*, ajusticiamiento ♦ **to be bored to d.** estar muerto de aburrimiento • **to do to d.** *(to kill)* matar, asesinar; *(to do)* repetir hasta el aburrimiento • **to put to d.** *(to kill)* matar; *(to execute)* ejecutar.

death·bed (dĕth′bĕd′) s. *(bed)* lecho de muerte; *(last hours)* últimos momentos.

death·blow (dĕth′blō′) s. golpe mortal *m*.

death certificate s. certificado *o* partida de defunción.

death duty s. G.B. impuesto sobre sucesiones.

death·less (dĕth′lĭs) adj. inmortal.

death·ly (dĕth′lē) **I.** adj. *(deathlike)* cadavérico; *(of silence)* sepulcral; *(fatal)* fatal, mortífero **II.** adv. *(as if dead)* como un muerto; *(extremely)* muy.

death mask s. mascarilla.

death penalty s. DER. pena de muerte.

death rate s. índice de mortalidad *m*.

death rattle s. estertor de la muerte.

death row s. ♦ **to be on d.** estar en capilla (los condenados a muerte).

death's-head (dĕths′hĕd′) s. calavera.

death·trap (dĕth′trăp′) s. *(place)* lugar peligroso; *(situation)* situación peligrosa.

death warrant s. DER. orden de ejecución *f*.

death·watch (dĕth′wŏch′) s. *(vigil)* velatorio; *(guard)* guardia de un condenado a muerte.

de·ba·cle (dĭ-bä′kəl, -băk′əl) s. *(disaster)* desastre *m*, fracaso; MIL. *(defeat)* derrota.

de·bar (dē-bär′) tr. -**barred**, -**bar·ring** excluir, prohibir.

de·bark (dĭ-bärk′) tr. & intr. desembarcar.

de·bar·ka·tion (dē′bär-kā′shən) s. *(of people)* desembarco; *(of cargo)* desembarque *m*.

de·base (dĭ-bās′) tr. -**based**, -**bas·ing** *(to devalue)* desvalorizar; *(to degrade)* degradar, rebajar.

de·base·ment (dĭ-bās′mənt) s. *(degradation)* degradación *f*; *(falsification)* adulteración *f*.

de·bat·a·ble (dĭ-bā′tə-bəl) adj. discutible.

de·bate (dĭ-bāt′) **I.** tr. & intr. -**bat·ed**, -**bat·ing** *(to deliberate)* deliberar, discutir; *(to argue)* discutir, debatir **II.** s. *(discussion)* discusión *f*, debate *m*; *(deliberation)* deliberación *f*; *(argumentation)* debate.

de·bat·er (dĭ-bā′tər) s. polemista *mf*.

de·bauch (dĭ-bôch′) **I.** tr. *(to corrupt)* corromper, pervertir; *(to seduce)* seducir —intr. pervertirse **II.** s. *(dissipation)* libertinaje *m*; *(orgy)* orgía.

de·bauch·ee (dĭ-bô′chē′, dĕb′ə-shē′) s. libertino, disoluto.

de·bauch·er·y (dĭ-bô′chə-rē) s [pl. -**ies**] *(dissipation)* disolución *f*, libertinaje *m*; *(corruption)* corrupción *f*.

de·ben·ture (dĭ-bĕn′chər) s. FIN. *(debt certificate)* obligación *f*; *(bond)* bono sin garantía prendaria; *(certificate)* certificado de aduanas.

de·bil·i·tate (dĭ-bĭl′ĭ-tāt′) tr. -**tat·ed**, -**tat·ing** debilitar.

de·bil·i·ta·tion (dĭ-bĭl′ĭ-tā′shən) s. debilitación *f*.

de·bil·i·ty (dĭ-bĭl′ĭ-tē) s. [pl. -**ties**] debilidad *f*.

deb·it (dĕb′ĭt) **I.** s. TEN. *(entry)* débito; *(left side)* debe *m*, pasivo ♦ **d. balance** saldo deudor **II.** tr. cargar en cuenta.

deb·o·nair *o* **deb·o·naire** (dĕb′ə-nâr′) adj. *(charming)* agraciado, alegre; *(elegant)* elegante, garboso.

de·brief (dē-brēf') tr. someter a un interrogatorio (después de cumplida una misión).

de·brief·ing (dē-brē'fĭng) s. interrogatorio (efectuado después de una misión).

de·bris o **dé·bris** (də-brē', dā-) s. *(remains)* escombros *m*, desechos *m*; GEOL. detrito, deyección *f.*

debt (dĕt) s. *(something owed)* deuda; *(obligation)* obligación *f*; RELIG. *(sin)* pecado ♦ **to be in someone's d.** estar en deuda con alguien • **to run into d.** contraer deudas.

debt·or (dĕt'ər) s. *(person)* deudor *m*; RELIG. *(sinner)* pecador *m.*

de·bug (dē-bŭg') tr. **-bugged, -bug·ging** *(to remove insects)* extirpar insectos de; ELECTRÓN. anular un dispositivo electrónico secreto; COMPUT. suprimir errores.

de·bunk (dē-bŭngk') tr. FAM. desenmascarar (falsedad, exageración).

de·but o **dé·but** (dā-byōō') **I.** s. *(first appearance)* estreno, debut *m*; *(coming out)* presentación en sociedad *f* **II.** intr. FAM. debutar.

deb·u·tante o **dé·bu·tante** (dĕb'yōō-tänt', dā'byōō-) s. debutante *f*, joven que hace su presentación en sociedad *f.*

dec·ade (dĕk'ād') s. *(ten years)* decenio, década; *(group of ten)* decena.

de·ca·dence (dĭ-kād'ns, dĕk'ə-dns) s. decadencia, declinación *f.*

de·ca·den·cy (dĭ-kād'n-sē, dĕk'ə-dn-) s. decadencia.

de·ca·dent (dĭ-kād'nt, dĕk'ə-dnt) adj. & s. decadente *mf.*

dec·a·gon (dĕk'ə-gŏn') s. GEOM. decágono.

dec·a·gram (dĕk'ə-grăm') s. decagramo.

dec·a·he·dron (dĕk'ə-hē'drən) s. [pl. **-drons** o **-dra** (-drə)] GEOM. decaedro.

de·cal (dē'kăl') s. calcomanía.

de·cal·ci·fy (dē-kăl'sə-fī') tr. **-fied, -fy·ing** MED. descalcificar.

de·cal·co·ma·ni·a (dē-kăl'kə-mā'nē-ə) s. calcomanía.

dec·a·li·ter (dĕk'ə-lē'tər) s. decalitro.

Dec·a·logue o **Dec·a·log** (dĕk'ə-lôg') s. BÍBL. Decálogo.

dec·a·me·ter (dĕk'ə-mē'tər) s. decámetro.

de·camp (dĭ-kămp') intr. FAM. *(to go away)* largarse; MIL. decampar, levantar el campo.

de·cant (dĭ-kănt') tr. decantar.

de·cant·er (dĭ-kăn'tər) s. *(bottle)* garrafa, jarra; TEC. *(vessel)* decantador *m.*

de·cap·i·tate (dĭ-kăp'ĭ-tāt') tr. **-tat·ed, -tat·ing** decapitar, degollar.

de·cap·i·ta·tion (dĭ-kăp'ĭ-tā'shən) s. decapitación *f*, degollación *f.*

de·cap·i·ta·tor (dĭ-kăp'ĭ-tā'tər) s. degollador *m.*

de·car·bon·ate (dē-kär'bə-nāt') tr. **-at·ed, -at·ing** QUÍM. descarbonatar.

de·cath·lon (dĭ-kăth'lŏn) s. DEP. decatlón *m.*

de·cay (dĭ-kā') **I.** intr. *(to decompose)* descomponerse; *(a tooth)* cariarse; *(to rot)* pudrirse; *(to disintegrate)* desintegrarse; *(to deteriorate)* deteriorarse; *(to fall into ruin)* decaer, arruinarse; *(health)* decaer, debilitarse **II.** s. *(decomposition)* descomposición *f*; *(of a tooth)* caries *f*; *(rot)* putrefacción *f*; *(of health)* debilitamiento; *(of morals)* decadencia.

de·cease (dĭ-sēs') **I.** intr. **-ceased, -ceas·ing** morir, fallecer **II.** s. muerte *f*, fallecimiento.

de·ceased (dĭ-sēst') adj. & s. difunto.

de·ce·dent (dĭ-sēd'nt) s. DER. difunto.

de·ceit (dĭ-sēt') s. *(deception)* engaño; *(fraud)* fraude *m*, superchería; *(falseness)* falsedad *f.*

de·ceit·ful (dĭ-sēt'fəl) adj. *(deceiving)* engañoso; *(lying)* mentiroso; *(false)* falso.

de·ceive (dĭ-sēv') tr. & intr. **-ceived, -ceiv·ing** engañar.

de·ceiv·er (dĭ-sē'vər) s. embustero.

de·cel·er·ate (dē-sĕl'ə-rāt') tr. **-ated, -at·ing** disminuir la velocidad de —intr. ir más despacio, decelerar.

de·cel·er·a·tion (dē-sĕl'ə-rā'shən) s. deceleración *f*, disminución de la velocidad *f.*

De·cem·ber (dĭ-sĕm'bər) s. diciembre *m.*

de·cen·cy (dē'sən-sē) s. [pl. **-cies**] decencia, decoro.

de·cen·ni·al (dĭ-sĕn'ē-əl) **I.** adj. decenal **II.** s. *(a tenth anniversary)* décimo aniversario.

de·cent (dē'sənt) adj. *(proper)* decente; *(modest)* decoroso; *(adequate)* aceptable, adecuado <a d. salary un sueldo adecuado>; *(good)* bueno <a d. fellow un buen tipo>; FAM. *(dressed)* vestido <are you d.? ¿estás vestido?>.

de·cent·ly (dē'sənt-lē) adv. decentemente.

de·cen·tral·i·za·tion (dē-sĕn'trə-lĭ-zā'shən) s. descentralización *f.*

de·cen·tral·ize (dē-sĕn'trə-līz') tr. **-ized, -iz·ing** descentralizar.

de·cep·tion (dĭ-sĕp'shən) s. *(deceit)* engaño; *(fraud)* fraude *m*, superchería.

de·cep·tive (dĭ-sĕp'tĭv) adj. engañoso.

de·cep·tive·ness (dĭ-sĕp'tĭv-nĭs) s. apariencia engañosa.

dec·i·are (dĕs'ē-âr') s. deciárea.

dec·i·bel (dĕs'ə-bĕl') s. FÍS. decibel *m*, decibelio.

de·cide (dĭ-sīd') tr. **-cid·ed, -cid·ing** *(to settle)* decidir; *(to resolve)* resolver ♦ **to d. on** o **upon** decidir, optar por —intr. decidir.

de·cid·ed (dĭ-sī'dĭd) adj. *(resolute)* decidido, resuelto; *(definite)* claro, indudable.

de·cid·u·ous (dĭ-sĭj'ōō-əs) adj. BOT., ZOOL. caduco.

dec·i·gram (dĕs'ĭ-grăm') s. decigramo.

dec·i·li·ter (dĕs'ə-lē'tər) s. decilitro.

dec·i·mal (dĕs'ə-məl) s. & adj. MAT. decimal *m.*

decimal point s. MAT. coma.

dec·i·mate (dĕs'ə-māt') tr. **-mat·ed, -mat·ing** diezmar.

dec·i·ma·tion (dĕs'ə-mā'shən) s. acción de diezmar *f.*

dec·i·me·ter (dĕs'ə-mē'tər) s. decímetro.

de·ci·pher (dĭ-sī'fər) tr. descifrar.

de·ci·pher·a·ble (dĭ-sī'fər-ə-bəl) adj. descifrable.

de·ci·sion (dĭ-sĭzh'ən) s. *(judgment)* decisión *f*; DER. *(verdict)* fallo ♦ **to make** o **take a d.** tomar una decisión.

de·ci·sive (dĭ-sī'sĭv) adj. decisivo, concluyente.

de·ci·sive·ness (dĭ-sī'sĭv-nĭs) s. firmeza, resolución *f.*

deck¹ (dĕk) **I.** s. MARÍT. cubierta; *(of cards)* baraja ♦ **to clear the d.** FAM. prepararse para la acción **II.** tr. *(to furnish with a deck)* poner una cubierta a; JER. *(to knock down)* tumbar <he decked him with a punch lo tumbó con un puñetazo>.

deck² (dĕk) tr. adornar, engalanar ♦ **to d. oneself out** emperifollarse.

deck chair s. tumbona.

deck hand s. MARÍT. marinero (de cubierta).

deck·house (dĕk'hous') s. MARÍT. caseta de cubierta.

de·claim (dĭ-klām') tr. & intr. declamar.

dec·la·ma·tion (dĕk'lə-mā'shən) s. declamación *f.*

de·clam·a·to·ry (dĭ-klăm'ə-tôr'ē) adj. declamatorio.

de·clar·a·ble (dĭ-klâr'ə-bəl) adj. que se puede declarar.

de·clar·ant (dĭ-klâr'ənt) s. DER. declarante *mf.*

dec·la·ra·tion (dĕk'lə-rā'shən) s. declaración *f.*

Declaration of Independence s. HIST. Declaración de Independencia (de EE. UU.) *f.*

de·clar·a·tive (dĭ-klâr'ə-tĭv) o **de·clar·a·to·ry** (-tôr'ē) adj. declaratorio.

de·clare (dĭ-klâr') tr. **-clared, -clar·ing** *(to state)* declarar; *(to proclaim)* proclamar; *(at customs, in bridge)* declarar —intr. hacer una declaración ♦ **to d. against** o **for** pronunciarse en contra de o a favor de.

de·clas·si·fy (dē-klăs'ə-fī') tr. **-fied, -fy·ing** anular la clasificación confidencial de.

de·clen·sion (dĭ-klĕn'shən) s. GRAM. declinación *f*, desinencia; *(slope)* declive *m*, inclinación *f*; *(deterioration)* decadencia, deterioro.

dec·li·na·tion (dĕk'lə-nā'shən) s. *(sloping)* declive *m*; *(deterioration)* decadencia; *(refusal)* rechazo, negativa; *(deviation)* desviación *f*; ASTRON., FÍS. declinación *f.*

de·cline (dĭ-klīn') **I.** intr. **-clined, -clin·ing** *(to refuse)* rehusar, negarse; *(to slope downwards)* inclinarse; *(to condescend)* condescender; *(to deteriorate)* deteriorarse; *(health)* debilitarse, decaer; *(prices)* bajar; *(sun, moon)* ponerse; *(day)* acabarse —tr. *(to refuse)* rehusar, rechazar; *(to incline)* inclinar; GRAM. declinar **II.** s. *(decrease)* disminución *f*; *(deterioration)* deterioro; *(refusal)* negativa; *(of prices)* descenso; *(of sun, moon)* ocaso; *(downward slope)* pendiente *f.*

de·clin·ing (dĭ-klī'nĭng) adj. declinante <*d. health* salud declinante>.

de·cliv·i·ty (dĭ-klĭv'ĭ-tē) s. [pl. **-ties**] declive *m*, pendiente *f*.

de·coc·tion (dĭ-kŏk'shən) s. *(boiling)* decocción *f*, cocimiento; *(extract)* extracto.

de·code (dē-kōd') tr. **-cod·ed, -cod·ing** descifrar, descodificar.

de·cod·er (dē-kō'dər) s. descifrador (persona *o* máquina que descifra) *m*.

de·cod·ing (dē-kō'dĭng) s. desciframiento, descodificación *f*.

de·col·late¹ (dĭ-kŏl'āt') tr. **-lat·ed, -lat·ing** decapitar, degollar.

de·col·late² (dĕk'ə-lāt', dē-kŏ'-) tr. **-lat·ed, -lat·ing** separar (copias).

dé·colle·tage (dā'kŏl-täzh') s. escote *m*.

de·col·o·nize (dē-kŏl'ə-nīz') tr. **-nized, -niz·ing** descolonizar.

de·com·pose (dē'kəm-pōz') tr. **-posed, -pos·ing** *(to separate)* separar, descomponer; *(to cause to rot)* hacer podrir —intr. *(to disintegrate)* descomponerse, desintegrarse; *(to rot)* podrirse.

de·com·po·si·tion (dē-kŏm'pə-zĭsh'ən) s. *(disintegration)* descomposición *f*; *(putrefaction)* putrefacción *f*.

de·com·press (dē'kəm-prĕs') tr. descomprimir.

de·com·pres·sion (dē'kəm-prĕsh'ən) s. descompresión *f*.

decompression sickness s. MED. aeroembolismo, enfermedad de Caisson *f*.

de·com·pres·sor (dē'kəm-prĕs'ər) s. descompresor *m*.

de·con·ges·tant (dē'kən-jĕs'tənt) s. descongestionante *m*.

de·con·tam·i·nate (dē'kən-tăm'ə-nāt') tr. **-nat·ed, -nat·ing** descontaminar.

de·con·tam·i·na·tion (dē'kən-tăm'ə-nā'shən) s. descontaminación *f*.

de·con·trol (dē'kən-trōl') ECON., POL. I. tr. **-trolled, -trol·ling** librar de control (gubernamental) II. s. anulación del control (gubernamental) *f*.

dé·cor *o* **de·cor** (dā'kôr') s. *(style)* decoración *f*; TEAT. *(scenery)* escenografía, decorado.

dec·o·rate (dĕk'ə-rāt') tr. **-rat·ed, -rat·ing** *(to adorn)* decorar; *(with medals)* condecorar.

dec·o·ra·tion (dĕk'ə-rā'shən) s. *(decor)* decoración *f*; *(medal)* condecoración *f*.

dec·o·ra·tive (dĕk'ər-ə-tĭv, -ə-rā'-) adj. decorativo, ornamental.

dec·o·ra·tor (dĕk'ə-rā'tər) s. decorador *m*.

dec·o·rous (dĕk'ər-əs, dĭ-kôr'-) adj. decoroso.

de·co·rum (dĭ-kôr'əm) s. decoro.

de·coy I. s. (dē'koi') señuelo, reclamo II. tr. (dĭ-koi') atraer con señuelo.

de·crease I. intr. & tr. (dĭ-krēs') **-creased, -creas·ing** disminuir, reducir II. s. (dē'krēs') disminución *f*.

de·creas·ing (dĭ-krē'sĭng) adj. decreciente, menguante.

de·cree (dĭ-krē') I. s. *(edict)* decreto, edicto; DER. *(order)* sentencia II. tr. **-creed, -cree·ing** decretar —intr. promulgar un decreto.

dec·re·ment (dĕk'rə-mənt) s. *(decrease)* decremento, disminución *f*; COMPUT., MAT. decremento.

de·crep·it (dĭ-krĕp'ĭt) adj. decrépito.

de·crep·i·tude (dĭ-krĕp'ĭ-tōōd', -tyōōd') s. decrepitud *f*.

de·cre·scen·do (dā'krə-shĕn'dō) MÚS. I. s. & adj. [pl. **-dos**] decrescendo II. adv. con decrescendo.

de·crim·i·nal·i·za·tion (dē-krĭm'ə-nə-lĭ-zā'shən) s. legalización *f*.

de·crim·i·nal·ize (dē-krĭm'ə-nə-līz') tr. **-ized, -iz·ing** legalizar.

de·cry (dĭ-krī') tr. **-cried, -cry·ing** *(to censure)* despreciar, criticar; *(to depreciate)* desvalorizar.

ded·i·cate (dĕd'ĭ-kāt') tr. **-cat·ed, -cat·ing** *(energy, book)* dedicar; *(building)* inaugurar; RELIG. *(church)* consagrar.

ded·i·cat·ed (dĕd'ĭ-kā'tĭd) I. pret. *y* part. p. de **dedicate** II. adj. COMPUT. especializado (en una sola actividad).

ded·i·ca·tion (dĕd'ĭ-kā'shən) s. *(commitment)* dedicación *f*; *(inscription)* dedicatoria; *(ceremony)* inauguración *f*.

de·duce (dĭ-dōōs', -dyōōs') tr. **-duced, -duc·ing** deducir, inferir.

de·duct (dĭ-dŭkt') tr. *(to subtract)* restar, substraer; *(to deduce)* deducir, inferir.

de·duct·i·ble (dĭ-dŭk'tə-bəl) adj. deducible.

de·duc·tion (dĭ-dŭk'shən) s. *(discount)* deducción *f*, descuento; LÓG. deducción, conclusión *f*.

de·duc·tive (dĭ-dŭk'tĭv) adj. deductivo.

deed (dēd) I. s. *(act)* acto; *(action)* acción *f*, hecho; *(feat)* proeza; DER. *(title)* escritura, título de propiedad II. tr. DER. traspasar por escritura.

deem (dēm) tr. considerar, juzgar.

deep (dēp) I. adj. **-er, -est** *(in depth)* profundo, de profundidad; *(thick)* de espesor <*the wall is two feet d.* la pared tiene dos pies de espesor>; *(wide)* de ancho; FIG. *(distant)* distante, alejado; *(recondite)* recóndito; *(inscrutable)* inescrutable, impenetrable; *(mysterious)* misterioso; *(shrewd)* astuto, sagaz; *(serious)* grande, gran <*to be in d. trouble* estar metido en un gran lío>; *(in thought, meditation)* absorto; *(feelings)* intenso, profundo; *(colors)* subido, intenso; *(voice)* grave, profundo; MÚS. bajo, grave ♦ **d. down** en el fondo • **d. in debt** cargado de deudas • **to be in d. water** estar en honduras, verse en dificultades • **to go off the d. end** FIG. ponerse histérico II. adv. *(deeply)* profundamente, en lo más hondo ♦ **d. into the night** hasta muy entrada la noche III. s. *(depth)* profundidad *f*; *(immensity)* inmensidad *f*, abismo; *(the most intense part)* lo más intenso *o* profundo <*the d. of night* lo más profundo de la noche>; POÉT. el mar.

deep·en (dē'pən) tr. & intr. hacer(se) más profundo, ahondar(se).

Deep-freeze (dēp'frēz') s. marca registrada de un congelador ♦ **to put in d.** FIG. postergar indefinidamente.

deep-fry (dēp'frī') tr. **-fried, -fry·ing** freír por inmersión en aceite.

deep·ly (dēp'lē) adv. *(in depth)* profundamente, hondamente; *(greatly)* sumamente, en sumo grado <*d. offended* ofendido en sumo grado>; *(gravely)* gravemente, seriamente <*d. implicated* seriamente comprometido>.

deep-root·ed (dēp'rōō'tĭd, -rōōt'ĭd) adj. profundamente arraigado.

deep-sea (dēp'sē') adj. de mar profundo, de alta mar.

deep-seat·ed (dēp'sē'tĭd) adj. profundamente arraigado.

deep-set (dēp'sĕt') adj. *(firmly implanted)* arraigado profundamente; *(eyes)* hundidos.

deep space s. espacio interplanetario *o* intergaláctico.

deer (dîr) s. [pl. **deer**] ciervo, venado.

deer·skin (dîr'skĭn') s. gamuza.

de·es·ca·late (dē-ĕs'kə-lāt') tr. & intr. **-lat·ed, -lat·ing** disminuir (intensidad, frecuencia).

de·es·ca·la·tion (dē-ĕs'kə-lā'shən) s. disminución *f* (en intensidad, frecuencia) *f*.

de·face (dĭ-fās') tr. **-faced, -fac·ing** *(to disfigure)* desfigurar; *(to mutilate)* mutilar; *(to efface)* borrar (inscripción).

de fac·to (dĭ făk'tō, dā) adv. & adj. de facto, de hecho.

def·a·ma·tion (dĕf'ə-mā'shən) s. difamación *f*, calumnia.

de·fam·a·to·ry (dĭ-făm'ə-tôr'ē) adj. difamatorio, calumnioso.

de·fame (dĭ-fām') tr. **-famed, -fam·ing** difamar, calumniar.

de·fault (dĭ-fôlt') I. s. *(of obligation)* incumplimiento; *(of duty)* descuido, negligencia; *(absence)* abandono <*the player won by d.* el jugador ganó por abandono>; DER. contumacia II. intr. *(to fail to do)* dejar de cumplir, faltar a un compromiso; DER. estar en rebeldía; DEP. dejar de presentarse —tr. *(obligation)* no cumplir; DER. perder un caso por contumacia; DEP. dejar de presentarse a.

de·fault·er (dĭ-fôl'tər) s. COM. deudor moroso; DER. rebelde *mf*.

de·feat (dĭ-fēt') I. tr. *(to beat)* derrotar, vencer; *(to thwart)* frustrar II. s. *(loss)* derrota; *(failure)* fracaso; *(frustration)* frustración *f*.

de·feat·ism (dĭ-fē'tĭz'əm) s. derrotismo.

de·feat·ist (dĭ-fē'tĭst) s. derrotista *mf*.

def·e·cate (dĕf'ĭ-kāt') intr. **-cat·ed, -cat·ing** defecar —tr. QUÍM. *(to clarify)* depurar, purificar; *(to void feces)* defecar.

def·e·ca·tion (dĕf'ĭ-kā'shən) s. FISIOL. defecación *f*, evacuación *f*; QUÍM. defecación, purificación *f*.

ã rey / ä año / b boca / ch chico / d dar / ĕ el / ē mil / g gato / h joya / hw juez / ī aire / k casa / kw cuan /

de·fect I. s. (dē′fĕkt′) defecto, desperfecto II. intr. (dĭ-fĕkt′) desertar, pasarse a otra banda *o* país.

de·fec·tion (dĭ-fĕk′shən) s. defección *f,* deserción *f.*

de·fec·tive (dĭ-fĕk′tĭv) I. adj. *(faulty)* defectuoso; GRAM. *(said of verb)* defectivo; *(subnormal)* deficiente II. s. PSIC. *(person)* persona anormal; GRAM. *(verb)* verbo defectivo.

de·fec·tor (dĭ-fĕk′tər) s. desertor *m.*

de·fence (dĭ-fĕns′) s. & v. G.B. var. of **defense.**

de·fend (dĭ-fĕnd′) tr. *(to protect)* defender; *(to justify)* justificar; *(to maintain)* sostener (posición, tesis); DER. *(to represent)* defender —intr. hacer una defensa.

de·fen·dant (dĭ-fĕn′dənt) s. DER. acusado, demandado.

de·fend·er (dĭ-fĕn′dər) s. defensor *m.*

de·fend·ing (dĭ-fĕn′dĭng) adj. defensor.

de·fense (dĭ-fĕns′) I. s. *(protection)* defensa, protección *f;* PSIC. *(mechanism)* mecanismo de defensa; DER. defensa II. tr. **-fensed, -fens·ing** DEP. marcar (al adversario).

de·fense·less (dĭ-fĕns′lĭs) adj. indefenso, sin defensa.

de·fense·less·ness (dĭ-fĕns′lĭs-nĭs) s. vulnerabilidad *f.*

defense mechanism s. PSIC. mecanismo de defensa.

de·fen·si·ble (dĭ-fĕn′sə-bəl) adj. defendible.

de·fen·sive (dĭ-fĕn′sĭv) adj. defensivo, de defensa.

de·fer (dĭ-fûr′) tr. **-ferred, -fer·ring** *(to postpone)* posponer, postergar; MIL. *(to delay induction)* otorgar una prórroga a —intr. *(to procrastinate)* postergar; *(to delay)* demorar; *(to yield)* deferir, remitirse.

def·er·ence (dĕf′ər-əns) s. deferencia, consideración *f.*

def·er·en·tial (dĕf′ə-rĕn′shəl) adj. deferente, respetuoso.

de·fer·ment (dĭ-fûr′mənt) s. *(postponement)* aplazamiento; MIL. prórroga.

de·fer·ra·ble (dĭ-fûr′ə-bəl) adj. diferible, aplazable.

de·fer·ral (dĭ-fûr′əl) s. var. de **deferment.**

de·ferred (dĭ-fûrd′) adj. *(postponed)* diferido, aplazado; COM. diferido (pago, activo).

de·fi·ance (dĭ-fī′əns) s. desafío, reto.

de·fi·ant (dĭ-fī′ənt) adj. *(provoking)* provocador; *(challenging)* desafiante.

de·fi·cien·cy (dĭ-fĭsh′ən-sē) s. [pl. **-cies**] deficiencia, carencia.

de·fi·cient (dĭ-fĭsh′ənt) adj. deficiente, carente.

def·i·cit (dĕf′ĭ-sĭt) s. déficit *f.*

deficit spending s. ECON. gasto deficitario.

de·file¹ (dĭ-fīl′) tr. **-filed, -fil·ing** *(to dirty)* ensuciar; *(to pollute)* contaminar; *(to corrupt)* corromper; *(to sully)* mancillar; *(to desecrate)* profanar; *(to rape)* violar.

de·file² (dĭ-fīl′) I. intr. **-filed, -fil·ing** MIL. desfilar II. s. GEOL. desfiladero; MIL. desfile *m.*

de·fil·er (dĭ-fī′lər) s. *(contaminator)* contaminador *m,* corruptor *m;* *(desecrator)* profanador *m,* violador *m.*

de·fin·a·ble (dĭ-fī′nə-bəl) adj. definible.

de·fine (dĭ-fīn′) tr. **-fined, -fin·ing** *(to state the meaning of)* definir; *(to specify)* definir, especificar; *(to describe)* describir; *(to explain)* explicar; *(to delineate)* delinear —intr. definir.

def·i·nite (dĕf′ə-nĭt) adj. *(limited)* definido; *(certain)* definitivo; *(explicit)* claro, explícito; *(precise)* preciso; *(categoric)* categórico; GRAM. definido, determinado.

definite article s. GRAM. artículo determinado *o* determinado.

def·i·nite·ly (dĕf′ə-nĭt-lē) I. adv. *(certainly)* definitivamente; *(explicitly)* claramente; *(categorically)* categóricamente II. interj. ¡por supuesto!, ¡desde luego!

def·i·ni·tion (dĕf′ə-nĭsh′ən) s. *(precise meaning)* definición *f;* *(of power, authority)* limitación *f;* FOTOG., TELEV. definición, nitidez *f.*

de·fin·i·tive (dĭ-fĭn′ĭ-tĭv) adj. definitivo.

de·fin·i·tive·ly (dĭ-fĭn′ĭ-tĭv-lē) adv. definitivamente, decisivamente.

de·flate (dĭ-flāt′) tr. **-flat·ed, -flat·ing** *(to release air from)* desinflar; *(pride, confidence)* rebajar; FIN. *(currency)* desvalorizar —intr. desinflarse.

de·fla·tion (dĭ-flā′shən) s. *(deflating)* desinflamiento; FIN. *(of currency)* deflación *f.*

de·fla·tor (dĭ-flā′tər) s. ECON. índice de deflación *m.*

de·flect (dĭ-flĕkt′) tr. & intr. desviar(se).

de·flec·tion (dĭ-flĕk′shən) s. desviación *f.*

de·flec·tor (dĭ-flĕk′tər) s. FÍS. deflector *m.*

de·flow·er (dē-flou′ər) tr. desflorar.

de·fo·cus (dē-fō′kəs) OPT. I. tr. desenfocar II. s. desenfoque *m.*

de·fog (dē-fôg′) tr. **-fogged, -fog·ging** desempañar.

de·fo·li·ant (dē-fō′lē-ənt) s. QUÍM. defoliante *m.*

de·fo·li·ate (dē-fō′lē-āt′) tr. & intr. **-at·ed, -at·ing** BOT. deshojar(se).

de·fo·li·a·tion (dē-fō′lē-ā′shən) s. BOT. defoliación *f.*

de·for·est (dē-fôr′ĭst) tr. desmontar, desforestar.

de·form (dĭ-fôrm′) tr. & intr. deformar(se), desfigurar(se).

de·for·ma·tion (dē′fôr-mā′shən, dĕf′ər-) s. *(of the body)* deformación *f;* *(of the face)* desfiguración *f;* FÍS. deformación.

de·formed (dĭ-fôrmd′) adj. *(misshapen)* deforme, desfigurado; *(changed)* deformado.

de·for·mi·ty (dĭ-fôr′mĭ-tē) s. [pl. **-ties**] deformidad *f.*

de·fraud (dĭ-frôd′) tr. defraudar, estafar.

de·fraud·er (dĭ-frô′dər) s. defraudador *m,* estafador *m.*

de·fray (dĭ-frā′) tr. sufragar, costear.

de·fray·al (dĭ-frā′əl) s. pago, subvención de gastos *f.*

de·frock (dē-frŏk′) tr. RELIG. expulsar de una orden religiosa.

de·frost (dē-frôst′) tr. & intr. deshelar(se), descongelar(se).

de·frost·er (dē-frô′stər) s. descongelador *m.*

de·frost·ing (dē-frô′stĭng) s. descongelación *f.*

deft (dĕft) adj. **-er, -est** hábil, diestro.

deft·ness (dĕft′nĭs) s. habilidad *f,* destreza.

de·funct (dĭ-fŭngkt′) adj. difunto.

de·fuse (dē-fyōōz′) tr. **-fused, -fus·ing** quitar la espoleta a; *(hostility)* templar, minorar.

de·fy (dĭ-fī′) tr. **-fied, -fy·ing** *(to confront)* enfrentar; *(to challenge)* desafiar; *(to resist)* resistir.

de·gen·er·a·cy (dĭ-jĕn′ər-ə-sē) s. [pl. **-cies**] *(degeneration)* degeneración *f;* *(perversion)* perversión sexual *f.*

de·gen·er·ate (dĭ-jĕn′ər-ĭt) I. adj. & s. degenerado II. intr. (-ə-rāt′) **-at·ed, -at·ing** degenerar.

de·gen·er·a·tion (dĭ-jĕn′ə-rā′shən) s. degeneración *f.*

de·gen·er·a·tive (dĭ-jĕn′ər-ə-tĭv) adj. degenerativo, degenerante.

deg·ra·da·tion (dĕg′rə-dā′shən) s. *(process)* degradación *f;* *(degeneration)* degeneración *f;* QUÍM. descomposición *f.*

de·grade (dĭ-grād′) tr. **-grad·ed, -grad·ing** *(to debase)* degradar; *(in value, quality)* rebajar; QUÍM. descomponer(se).

de·grad·ed (dĭ-grā′dĭd) adj. *(in rank, honor)* degradado; *(in value)* rebajado; *(depraved)* depravado.

de·grad·ing (dĭ-grā′dĭng) adj. degradante.

de·gree (dĭ-grē′) s. *(unit of measurement)* grado; *(progression)* grado; *(level)* nivel *m,* categoría; *(amount)* grado; EDUC. *(title)* título ♦ **by degrees** gradualmente, poco a poco • **doctor's d.** doctorado • **to a certain d.** *o* **to some d.** hasta cierto punto • **to a d.** *(to a great extent)* sumamente; *(a little)* un poco • **to take a d. in** licenciarse en • **to the highest d.** en sumo grado.

de·gres·sion (dĭ-grĕsh′ən) s. descenso gradual.

de·hu·man·i·za·tion (dē-hyōō′mə-nĭ-zā′shən) s. deshumanización *f.*

de·hu·man·ize (dē-hyōō′mə-nīz′) tr. **-ized, -iz·ing** deshumanizar.

de·hu·mid·i·fi·ca·tion (dē′hyōō-mĭd′ə-fĭ-kā′shən) s. deshumidificación *f,* desecación *f.*

de·hu·mid·i·fy (dē′hyōō-mĭd′ə-fī′) tr. **-fied, -fy·ing** deshumedecer, desecar.

de·hy·drate (dē-hī′drāt′) tr. & intr. **-drat·ed, -drat·ing** deshidratar(se).

de·hy·dra·tion (dē′hī-drā′shən) s. deshidratación *f.*

de·hy·dro·ge·na·tion (dē′hī-drŏj′ə-nā′shən, dē-hī′drə-jə-) s. QUÍM. deshidrogenación *f.*

de·hyp·no·tize (dē-hĭp′nə-tīz′) tr. **-tized, -tiz·ing** deshipnotizar.

de·ice (dē-īs′) tr. **-iced, -ic·ing** descongelar, deshelar.

de·ic·er (dē-ī′sər) s. *(compound)* descongelador *m;* AVIA. dispositivo antihielo.

de·i·cide (dē′ĭ-sīd′) s. *(god killing)* deicidio; *(god killer)* deicida *mf.*

de·i·fi·ca·tion (dē′ə-fĭ-kā′shən) s. deificación *f.*

de·i·fy (dē'ə-fī') tr. **-fied, -fy·ing** deificar; FIG. *(to idealize)* idealizar.

deign (dān) tr. dignarse a <*d. to answer* dignarse a dar una respuesta> —intr. dignarse.

de·ism (dē'ĭz'əm) s. —RELIG. deísmo.

de·i·ty (dē'ĭ-tē) s. [pl. **-ties**] *(god)* deidad *f*; *(divinity)* divinidad *f* ♦ **D.** Dios.

de·ject (dĭ-jĕkt') tr. desanimar.

de·ject·ed (dĭ-jĕk'tĭd) adj. desanimado, deprimido.

de·jec·tion (dĭ-jĕk'shən) s. *(depression)* depresión *f*, abatimiento; MED. *(of feces)* deyección *f*.

de ju·re (dē joor'ē, dā yoor'ā) adj. & adv. de derecho, de ley.

dek·a·me·ter (dĕk'ə-mē'tər) s. var. de **decameter**.

de·lay (dĭ-lā') I. tr. *(to postpone)* postergar; *(to defer)* diferir; *(to make late)* retrasar, demorar; *(to hinder)* estorbar; *(to hold up)* entretener —intr. *(to procrastinate)* demorarse; *(to linger)* tardar II. s. *(act)* demora; *(postponement)* postergación *f*; *(time)* retraso, atraso <*the train will arrive with a five minute d.* el tren llegará con cinco minutos de atraso>.

de·lay·ing (dĭ-lā'ĭng) adj. dilatorio.

de·lec·ta·ble (dĭ-lĕk'tə-bəl) adj. deleitable, delicioso.

del·e·gate (dĕl'ĭ-gāt', -gĭt) I. s. *(representative)* delegado; *(deputy)* diputado; *(agent)* agente *mf* II. tr. (-gāt') **-gat·ed, -gat·ing** *(to authorize)* delegar; *(to entrust)* comisionar.

del·e·ga·tion (dĕl'ĭ-gā'shən) s. delegación *f*.

de·lete (dĭ-lēt') tr. **-let·ed, -let·ing** tachar, suprimir.

del·e·te·ri·ous (dĕl'ĭ-tîr'ē-əs) adj. deletéreo, nocivo.

de·le·tion (dĭ-lē'shən) s. tachadura, supresión *f*.

del·i (dĕl'ē) s. [pl. **-is**] FAM. fiambrería.

de·lib·er·ate I. adj. (dĭ-lĭb'ər-ĭt) *(intentional)* deliberado, a propósito; *(premeditated)* premeditado; *(slow)* pausado II. intr. & tr. (dĭ-lĭb'ə-rāt') **-at·ed, -at·ing** *(to consider)* deliberar; *(to reflect)* reflexionar.

de·lib·er·ate·ly (dĭ-lĭb'ər-ĭt-lē) adv. deliberadamente, a propósito.

de·lib·er·a·tion (dĭ-lĭb'ə-rā'shən) s. *(debate)* deliberación *f*; *(thoughtfulness)* reflexión *f*; *(slowness)* lentitud *f*.

de·lib·er·a·tive (dĭ-lĭb'ə-rā'tĭv, -ər-ə-) adj. deliberante, deliberativo.

del·i·ca·cy (dĕl'ĭ-kə-sē) s. [pl. **-cies**] *(exquisiteness)* delicadeza, finura; *(daintiness)* primura; *(fine food)* manjar *m*, gollería; *(tact)* delicadeza, tacto; *(accuracy)* precisión *f*.

del·i·cate (dĕl'ĭ-kĭt) adj. *(exquisite)* delicado, fino; *(dainty)* primoroso; *(frail)* frágil; *(considerate)* delicado, considerado; *(requiring tact)* delicado, difícil <*a d. subject* un tema delicado>; *(fine in touch)* fino, suave; *(accurate)* de precisión <*a d. instrument* un instrumento de precisión>; *(subtle)* sutil.

del·i·ca·tes·sen (dĕl'ĭ-kə-tĕs'ən) s. fiambrería.

de·li·cious (dĭ-lĭsh'əs) adj. delicioso.

de·light (dĭ-līt') I. s. *(pleasure)* deleite *m*; *(person, thing)* encanto ♦ **to find** *o* **take d. in** encontrar deleite en II. tr. & intr. *(to please)* deleitar(se); *(to charm)* encantar.

de·light·ed (dĭ-lī'tĭd) adj. encantado.

de·light·ful (dĭ-līt'fəl) adj. delicioso, encantador.

de·lim·it (dĭ-lĭm'ĭt) tr. delimitar.

de·lim·it·er (dĭ-lĭm'ĭ-tər) s. COMPUT. símbolo delimitador *(de una unidad de información)*.

de·lin·e·ate (dĭ-lĭn'ē-āt') tr. **-at·ed, -at·ing** *(to outline)* delinear; *(to sketch)* bosquejar; *(to depict)* describir, pintar.

de·lin·e·a·tion (dĭ-lĭn'ē-ā'shən) s. *(outline)* delineación *f*; *(sketch)* bosquejo, esbozo; *(description)* descripción *f*.

de·lin·quen·cy (dĭ-lĭng'kwən-sē) s. [pl. **-cies**] *(failure)* delincuencia; *(misdeed)* delito.

de·lin·quent (dĭ-lĭng'kwənt) I. adj. COM. moroso, retrasado (en el pago) II. s. delincuente *mf*.

del·i·quesce (dĕl'ĭ-kwĕs') intr. **-quesced, -quesc·ing** licuarse.

de·lir·i·ous (dĭ-lîr'ē-əs) adj. delirante.

de·lir·i·ous·ness (dĭ-lîr'ē-əs-nĭs) s. condición delirante *f*.

de·lir·i·um (dĭ-lîr'ē-əm) s. [pl. **-iums** *o* **-i·a** (-ē-ə)] delirio, desvarío.

delirium tre·mens (trē'mənz) s. MED. delírium tremens *m*.

de·liv·er (dĭ-lĭv'ər) tr. *(to rescue)* rescatar, liberar; MED. *(to*

midwife) partear; *(to distribute)* repartir; *(to hand over)* entregar; *(to send)* dar, propinar <*to d. a blow to the jaw* propinar un golpe a la mandíbula>; *(to throw)* arrojar; *(to pronounce)* dar <*he delivered a lecture* dio una conferencia>; *(to get)* conseguir <*he delivered the votes* consiguió los votos> ♦ **d. us from evil** líbranos del mal ▪ **to d. oneself of an opinion** opinar —intr. *(to fulfill)* cumplir <*the senator delivered on his promise* el senador cumplió con su promesa> ♦ **we d.** entregamos a domicilio.

de·liv·er·a·ble (dĭ-lĭv'ər-ə-bəl) adj. remitible.

de·liv·er·ance (dĭ-lĭv'ər-əns) s. *(delivery)* entrega; *(freeing)* liberación *f*; DER. *(verdict)* veredicto.

de·liv·er·er (dĭ-lĭv'ər-ər) s. *(liberator)* liberador *m*, salvador *m*; COM. repartidor *m*.

de·liv·er·y (dĭ-lĭv'ə-rē) s. [pl. **-ies**] *(act, object)* entrega; *(release)* liberación *f*; *(rescue)* rescate *m*; *(parturition)* parto; *(style)* elocución *f*; DEP. *(throwing form)* forma, estilo.

de·liv·er·y·man (dĭ-lĭv'ə-rē-măn') s. [pl. **-men** (-mən)] repartidor *m*.

dell (dĕl) s. valle pequeño.

de·louse (dē-lous') tr. **-loused, -lous·ing** despiojar, espulgar.

del·phin·i·um (dĕl-fĭn'ē-əm) s. BOT. delfinio, espuela de caballero.

del·ta (dĕl'tə) s. *(of a river)* delta *m*; *(Greek letter)* delta *f*.

delta wing s. AER. ala en forma de delta.

del·toid (dĕl'toid') s. & adj. ANAT., GEOM. deltoides *m*.

de·lude (dĭ-lōōd') tr. **-lud·ed, -lud·ing** engañar, despistar.

del·uge (dĕl'yōōj) I. tr. **-uged, -ug·ing** *(to inundate)* inundar; *(to overwhelm)* abrumar, inundar II. s. *(flood)* inundación *f*; *(downpour)* diluvio; *(overwhelming rush)* avalancha, alud *m* ♦ **D.** BÍBL. el Diluvio.

de·lu·sion (dĭ-lōō'zhən) s. *(deception)* engaño; *(illusion)* ilusión *f*, concepto falso; MED. delirio, alucinación *f* ♦ **delusions of grandeur** delirio de grandeza.

de·lu·sive (dĭ-lōō'sĭv) adj. *(deceiving)* engañoso; *(illusory)* ilusorio, falso.

de luxe *o* **de·luxe** (dĭ-lōōks', -lŭks') I. adj. de lujo, lujoso II. adv. con todo lujo.

delve (dĕlv) intr. **delved, delv·ing** indagar, hurgar.

de·mag·net·ize (dē-măg'nĭ-tīz') tr. **-ized, -iz·ing** desmagnetizar, desimantar.

dem·a·gog (dĕm'ə-gôg', -gŏg') s. var. de **demagogue**.

dem·a·gog·ic (dĕm'ə-gŏj'ĭk, -gŏg'-) adj. demagógico.

dem·a·gogue (dĕm'ə-gôg', -gŏg') s. demagogo.

dem·a·gogu·er·y (dĕm'ə-gŏg'ə-rē, -gŏg'ə-) s. demagogia.

de·mand (dĭ-mănd') I. tr. *(to ask for)* reclamar, exigir; *(to ask to be informed of)* demandar; *(to require)* requerir <*this matter demands great attention* este asunto requiere mucha atención>; *(to insist on)* insistir en; DER. demandar —intr. formular una demanda II. s. *(request)* pedido, solicitud *f*; *(claim)* reclamación *f*; *(requirement)* necesidad *f*; COM. demanda ♦ **on d.** *(on presentation)* a presentación; *(by request)* a petición ▪ **supply and d.** la oferta y la demanda ▪ **to be in d.** ser solicitado, ser popular.

demand deposit s. COM. depósito a la vista.

de·mand·ing (dĭ-măn'dĭng) adj. *(exigent)* exigente; *(exhausting)* agotador; *(absorbing)* absorbente.

demand loan s. COM. préstamo reembolsable a la vista.

demand note s. COM. letra pagadera a la vista.

de·mar·cate (dĭ-mär'kāt') tr. **-cat·ed, -cat·ing** demarcar.

de·mar·ca·tion *o* **de·mar·ka·tion** (dē'mär-kā'shən) s. demarcación *f*.

de·mean[1] (dĭ-mēn') tr. portarse, comportarse.

de·mean[2] (dĭ-mēn') tr. rebajar ♦ **to d. oneself** rebajarse.

de·mean·or (dĭ-mē'nər) s. comportamiento.

de·mean·our (dĭ-mē'nər) s. G.B. var. de **demeanor**.

de·ment·ed (dĭ-mĕn'tĭd) adj. demente, loco.

de·men·tia (dĭ-mĕn'shə) s. MED. demencia.

dementia prae·cox (prē'kŏks') s. MED. demencia precoz.

de·mer·it (dĭ-mĕr'ĭt) s. *(fault)* demérito, desmerecimiento; *(a mark)* nota de reprobación.

dem·i·god (dĕm'ē-gŏd') s. semidiós *m*.

dem·i·john (dĕm'ē-jŏn') s. damajuana, garrafón *m*.

de·mil·i·ta·rize (dē-mĭl'ĭ-tə-rīz') tr. **-rized, -riz·ing** MIL. desmilitarizar.

de·mise (dǐ-mīz′) **I.** s. *(death)* fallecimiento, defunción *f*; DER. *(of an estate)* traspaso (de bienes); POL. *(of authority)* transmisión (del poder) *f* **II.** tr. **-mised, -mis·ing** DER. *(by lease)* traspasar (por contrato); *(by will)* legar; POL. *(sovereignty)* transmitir (el poder) —intr. *(to die)* fallecer; DER. *(by will)* transmitirse por herencia o sucesión.

de·mis·sion (dǐ-mǐsh′ən) s. dimisión *f*, abdicación *f*.

dem·i·tasse (dĕm′ē-tăs′, -täs′) s. tacita de café.

de·mo·bil·i·za·tion (dē-mō′bə-lǐ-zā′shən) s. MIL. desmovilización *f*.

de·mo·bil·ize (dē-mō′bə-līz′) tr. MIL. desmovilizar.

de·moc·ra·cy (dǐ-mŏk′rə-sē) s. [pl. **-cies**] democracia.

dem·o·crat (dĕm′ə-krăt′) s. demócrata *mf* ♦ **D.** miembro del partido demócrata de EE. UU.

dem·o·crat·ic (dĕm′ə-krăt′ĭk) adj. democrático ♦ **D.** POL. del partido demócrata en EE. UU.

Democratic Kampuchea s. Kampuchea Democrática.

Democratic Party s. EE. UU., POL. partido demócrata.

Democratic Yemen s. Yemen Democrático.

de·moc·ra·ti·za·tion (dǐ-mŏk′rə-tǐ-zā′shən) s. POL. democratización *f*.

de·moc·ra·tize (dǐ-mŏk′rə-tīz′) tr. **-tized, -tiz·ing** POL. democratizar.

dem·o·graph·ic (dĕm′ə-grăf′ĭk, dē′mə-) adj. demográfico.

dem·o·graph·ics (dĕm′ə-grăf′ĭks, dē′mə-) s. [ú. con v. pl.] datos demográficos.

de·mog·ra·phy (dǐ-mŏg′rə-fē) s. demografía.

de·mol·ish (dǐ-mŏl′ĭsh) tr. *(to tear down)* demoler, derribar; *(to destroy)* destruir.

dem·o·li·tion (dĕm′ə-lĭsh′ən, dē′mə-) s. *(tearing down)* demolición *f*; *(destruction)* destrucción *f*.

de·mon (dē′mən) s. *(devil)* demonio, diablo; *(force)* demonio <*driven by the d. of avarice* impulsado por el demonio de la avaricia>; *(spirit)* espíritu *m*; *(skillful person)* genio; *(zealot)* fanático, fiera; MITOL. *(inferior divinity)* dios menor *m*.

de·mon·e·ti·za·tion (dē-mŏn′ǐ-tǐ-zā′shən) s. ECON. desmonetización *f*.

de·mo·ni·ac (dǐ-mō′nē-ăk′) o **de·mo·ni·a·cal** (dē′mə-nī′ə-kəl) adj. *(possessed)* endemoniado; *(fiendish)* demoniaco.

de·mon·ic (dǐ-mŏn′ĭk) adj. demoniaco.

de·mon·stra·ble (dǐ-mŏn′strə-bəl) adj. demostrable.

dem·on·strate (dĕm′ən-strāt′) tr. **-strat·ed, -strat·ing** *(to make evident)* demostrar, probar <*he demonstrated to me that he was right* me demostró que tenía razón>; *(to show)* mostrar; *(to manifest)* manifestar (sentimientos, opinión) —intr. protestar, hacer una demostración.

dem·on·stra·tion (dĕm′ən-strā′shən) s. *(proof)* demostración *f*, prueba; *(illustration)* demostración <*a d. of how well the product works* una demostración de lo bien que funciona el producto>; *(show of feelings)* demostración, expresión *f*; *(rally)* manifestación *f*.

dem·on·stra·tive (dǐ-mŏn′strə-tǐv) **I.** adj. *(serving to prove)* demostrativo; *(expressive)* expresivo, efusivo; GRAM. demostrativo **II.** s. GRAM. demostrativo.

dem·on·stra·tor (dĕm′ən-strā′tər) s. *(sample)* modelo de muestra; *(person)* manifestante *mf*.

de·mor·al·ize (dǐ-môr′ə-līz′) tr. **-ized, -iz·ing** *(to debase)* corromper; *(to dishearten)* desmoralizar, desalentar; *(to confuse)* confundir.

de·mote (dǐ-mōt′) tr. **-mot·ed, -mot·ing** degradar, rebajar de categoría.

de·mo·tion (dǐ-mō′shən) s. degradación *f*, descenso (de rango, categoría).

de·mur (dǐ-mûr′) intr. **-murred, -mur·ring** *(to object)* hacer objeciones; *(to delay)* demorar; DER. alegar excepción perentoria **II.** s. *(objection)* objeción *f*; *(delay)* demora.

de·mure (dǐ-myŏŏr′) adj. **-mur·er, -mur·est** *(modest)* recatado; *(coy)* remilgado.

den (dĕn) s. *(lair)* cubil *m*, madriguera; *(hide-out)* escondrijo, guarida; *(study room)* estudio.

de·na·tion·al·i·za·tion (dē-năsh′ə-nə-lǐ-zā′shən) s. DER. desnacionalización *f*.

de·na·tion·al·ize (dē-năsh′ə-nə-līz′) tr. **-ized, -iz·ing** desnacionalizar.

de·nat·u·ral·ize (dē-năch′ər-ə-līz′) tr. **-ized, -iz·ing** GEOG., POL. desnaturalizar.

de·na·ture (dē-nā′chər) tr. **-tured, -tur·ing** desnaturalizar.

de·ni·al (dǐ-nī′əl) s. *(refusal)* negativa; *(disavowal)* desaprobación *f*; *(rejection)* rechazo; *(self-denial)* abnegación *f*; DER. denegación *f*.

den·i·grate (dĕn′ĭ-grāt′) tr. **-grat·ed, -grat·ing** denigrar.

den·i·gra·tion (dĕn′ĭ-grā′shən) s. denigración *f*.

den·im (dĕn′ĭm) s. TEJ. mahón *m*, dril de algodón *m* ♦ **denims** vaqueros.

den·i·zen (dĕn′ĭ-zən) s. *(resident)* habitante *mf*, residente *mf*; BOT., ZOOL. habitante.

Den·mark (dĕn′märk′) s. Dinamarca.

de·nom·i·na·tion (dǐ-nŏm′ə-nā′shən) s. *(designation)* denominación *f*, clasificación *f*; *(of currency)* valor *m*, denominación; RELIG. *(sect)* secta, creencia.

de·nom·i·na·tion·al (dǐ-nŏm′ə-nā′shə-nəl) adj. RELIG. sectario.

de·nom·i·na·tor (dǐ-nŏm′ə-nā′tər) s. denominador *m*.

de·no·ta·tion (dē′nō-tā′shən) s. *(indication)* indicación *f*, denotación *f*; *(meaning)* significado.

de·no·ta·tive (dē-nō′tə-tǐv, dē′nō-tā′-) adj. revelador.

de·note (dǐ-nōt′) tr. **-not·ed, -not·ing** *(to indicate)* indicar; *(to mean)* significar; *(to mark)* denotar.

dé·noue·ment o **de·noue·ment** (dā′nōō-mäN′) s. desenlace *m*, solución *f*.

de·nounce (dǐ-nouns′) tr. **-nounced, -nounc·ing** *(to accuse)* denunciar, acusar; *(to speak against)* denunciar; *(to criticize)* censurar, criticar.

de·nounce·ment (dǐ-nouns′mənt) s. *(accusation)* denuncia; *(criticism)* censura, crítica.

dense (dĕns) adj. **dens·er, dens·est** denso; *(dark)* obscuro <*d. shadows* sombras obscuras>; *(deep)* profundo <*the densest part of the woods* lo más profundo del bosque>; FAM. *(stupid)* estúpido; FOTOG. opaco.

den·si·tom·e·ter (dĕn′sǐ-tŏm′ǐ-tər) s. FOTOG. densitómetro.

den·si·ty (dĕn′sǐ-tē) s. [pl. **-ties**] densidad *f*; FAM. *(stupidity)* estupidez *f*.

dent (dĕnt) **I.** s. *(depression)* abolladura, mella; *(progress)* avance *m*, progreso **II.** tr. & intr. abollar(se), mellar(se).

den·tal (dĕn′tl) **I.** adj. dental **II.** s. GRAM. consonante dental *f*.

dental floss s. hilo dental.

dental hygienist s. higienista dental *mf*.

dental plate s. dentadura postiza.

den·ti·frice (dĕn′tə-frĭs) s. dentífrico.

den·tine (dĕn′tēn) o **den·tin** (-tĭn) s. ANAT. dentina, esmalte (de los dientes) *m*.

den·tist (dĕn′tĭst) s. dentista *mf*, odontólogo.

den·tist·ry (dĕn′tĭ-strē) s. odontología.

den·ti·tion (dĕn-tĭsh′ən) s. dentición *f*.

den·ture (dĕn′chər) s. dentadura postiza.

de·nu·cle·ar·ize (dē-nōō′klē-ə-rīz′, -nyōō′-) tr. **-ized, -iz·ing** eliminar las armas nucleares.

de·nude (dǐ-nōōd′, -nyōōd′) tr. **-nud·ed, -nud·ing** *(to strip)* desnudar; GEOL. *(to wear)* denudar, desgastar.

de·nun·ci·a·tion (dǐ-nŭn′sē-ā′shən, -shē-) s. *(accusation)* denuncia; *(criticism)* censura, crítica.

de·ny (dǐ-nī′) tr. **-nied, -ny·ing** *(to declare untrue)* negar; *(to reject)* rechazar; *(not to permit)* denegar, decir no a; *(to repudiate)* repudiar; *(to refuse)* negar <*I d. you my friendship* te niego mi amistad> ♦ **to d. oneself** privarse de.

de·o·dor·ant (dē-ō′dər-ənt) s. desodorante *m*.

de·o·dor·ize (dē-ō′də-rīz′) tr. **-ized, -iz·ing** desodorizar.

de·o·dor·iz·er (dē-ō′də-rī′zər) s. desodorante *m*.

de·ox·i·dize (dē-ŏk′sĭ-dīz′) tr. **-dized, -diz·ing** QUÍM. desoxidar, desoxigenar.

de·ox·y·ri·bo·nu·cle·ic acid (dē-ŏk′sē-rī′bō-nōō-klē′ĭk) s. BIOQUÍM. ácido desoxirribonucleico.

de·part (dǐ-pärt′) intr. *(to leave)* marcharse, irse; *(to deviate)* desviarse, apartarse; *(to die)* morir —tr. ♦ **to d. this world** pasar a mejor vida.

de·part·ed (dǐ-pär′tǐd) adj. *(bygone)* pasado; *(dead)* muerto, difunto ♦ **the d.** los difuntos.

de·part·ment (dǐ-pärt′mənt) s. *(division)* departamento, servicio (en una organización); *(in a college)* departamento, facultad *f*; FIG., FAM. *(sphere of activity)* esfera de actividad, competencia <*that is not my d.* eso no es de mi competencia> ◆ **D. of Justice** Ministerio de Justicia • **D. of Labor** Ministerio de Trabajo • **D. of State** Departamento de Estado (en EE. UU.).

de·part·men·tal (dē'pärt-měn'tl) adj. departamental.

de·part·men·tal·ize (dē'pärt-měn'tl-īz') tr. **-ized, -iz·ing** dividir en departamentos.

department store s. tienda grande, gran almacén *m*.

de·par·ture (dĭ-pär'chər) s. *(act)* partida, salida; *(deviation)* desviación *f*; *(start)* comienzo.

de·pend (dĭ-pěnd') intr. ◆ **to d. on** *o* **upon** *(to rely on)* depender de <*I d. on my family for my money* dependo de mi familia para mi dinero>; *(to trust)* confiar en, fiar <*you can d. on his judgment* puedes confiar en su juicio>; *(to count on)* contar con <*can we d. on your help?* ¿podemos contar con tu ayuda?> • **to d. on one's work for a living** vivir de su trabajo • **you can d. on it!** ¡puedes estar seguro!

de·pend·a·bil·i·ty (dĭ-pěn'də-bĭl'ĭ-tē) s. *(of a person)* seriedad *f*, confianza; *(of a machine)* seguridad de funcionamiento *f*.

de·pend·a·ble (dĭ-pěn'də-bəl) adj. *(trustworthy)* digno de confianza, de confianza; *(reliable)* seguro.

de·pend·ence *o* **de·pend·ance** (dĭ-pěn'dəns) s. *(support)* dependencia; *(subservience)* subordinación *f*, sumisión *f*; *(trust)* confianza ◆ **d. on** *o* **upon** *(reliance)* dependencia de; *(trust)* confianza en.

de·pend·en·cy *o* **de·pend·an·cy** (dĭ-pěn'dən-sē) s. [pl. **-cies**] dependencia.

de·pend·ent *o* **de·pend·ant** (dĭ-pěn'dənt) I. adj. ◆ **d. on** *o* **upon** dependiente de, subordinado a II. s. persona a cargo.

dependent clause s. GRAM. cláusula subordinada.

de·per·son·al·ize (dē-pûr'sə-nə-līz') tr. **-ized, -iz·ing** despersonalizar.

de·pict (dĭ-pĭkt') tr. representar, pintar.

de·pic·tion (dĭ-pĭk'shən) s. representación *f*, descripción *f*.

de·pil·a·to·ry (dĭ-pĭl'ə-tôr'ē, -tôr'ē) I. adj. depilatorio II. s. [pl. **-ries**] crema depilatoria.

de·plane (dē-plān') intr. **-planed, -plan·ing** bajar *o* desembarcar del avión.

de·plete (dĭ-plēt') tr. **-plet·ed, -plet·ing** agotar, reducir.

de·ple·tion (dĭ-plē'shən) tr. agotamiento, reducción *f*.

de·plor·a·ble (dĭ-plôr'ə-bəl) adj. deplorable, lamentable.

de·plore (dĭ-plôr') tr. **-plored, -plor·ing** *(to regret deeply)* deplorar, lamentar; *(to disapprove)* desaprobar.

de·ploy (dĭ-ploi') tr. & intr. MIL. desplegar(se).

de·ploy·ment (dĭ-ploi'mənt) s. MIL. despliegue *m*.

de·po·lar·ize (dē-pō'lə-rīz') tr. **-ized, -iz·ing** ELEC., FÍS. despolarizar.

de·po·nent (dĭ-pō'nənt) I. adj. GRAM. deponente II. s. GRAM. verbo deponente; DER. declarante *mf*, testigo.

de·pop·u·late (dē-pŏp'yə-lāt') tr. **-lat·ed, -lat·ing** despoblar.

de·pop·u·la·tion (dē-pŏp'yə-lā'shən) s. despoblación *f*.

de·port (dĭ-pôrt') tr. *(to expel)* deportar, expulsar; *(to behave)* portarse, comportarse.

de·por·ta·tion (dē'pôr-tā'shən) s. deportación *f*, expulsión *f*.

de·port·ee (dē'pôr-tē') s. deportado.

de·port·ment (dĭ-pôrt'mənt) s. comportamiento, conducta.

de·pose (dĭ-pōz') tr. **-posed, -pos·ing** *(to remove from office)* deponer, destituir; *(to dethrone)* destronar; DER. *(to testify)* deponer, atestiguar —intr. testificar.

de·pos·it (dĭ-pŏz'ĭt) I. tr. *(to put down)* depositar; GEOG., QUÍM. *(to make layers)* depositar, sedimentar; COM. *(to secure)* dar de garantía *o* de seña; *(as initial payment)* dar de entrada; *(to bank)* depositar, ingresar —intr. GEOG., QUÍM. depositarse, sedimentarse II. s. COM. *(for safekeeping)* depósito; *(payment)* pago, entrada; *(down payment)* seña.

dep·o·si·tion (dĕp'ə-zĭsh'ən) s. *(removal from office)* deposición *f*, destitución *f*; DER. *(testimony)* declaración *f*, testimonio; *(deposit)* depósito.

de·pos·i·tor (dĭ-pŏz'ĭ-tər) s. depositador *m*, depositante *mf*; COM. cuentacorrentista (en un banco) *mf*.

de·pos·i·to·ry (dĭ-pŏz'ĭ-tôr'ē) s. [pl. **-ries**] *(storehouse)* depositaria, almacén *m*; *(person)* depositario.

de·pot (dē'pō, dĕp'ō) s. *(station)* estación (de ferrocarril, autobús) *f*; *(warehouse)* almacén *m*, depósito; MIL. *(barracks)* cuartel *m*.

dep·ra·va·tion (dĕp'rə-vā'shən) s. depravación *f*, perversión *f*.

de·prave (dĭ-prāv') tr. **-praved, -prav·ing** depravar, pervertir.

de·praved (dĭ-prāvd') adj. depravado, pervertido.

de·prav·i·ty (dĭ-prăv'ĭ-tē) s. [pl. **-ties**] depravación *f*.

dep·re·cate (dĕp'rĭ-kāt') tr. **-cat·ed, -cat·ing** *(to disapprove)* desaprobar; *(to belittle)* menospreciar.

dep·re·ca·tion (dĕp'rĭ-kā'shən) s. *(disapproval)* desaprobación *f*; *(scorn)* menosprecio, desdén *m*.

dep·re·ca·to·ry (dĕp'rĭ-kə-tôr'ē, -tôr'ē) *o* **dep·re·ca·tive** (-kā'tĭv) adj. deprecatorio, deprecativo.

de·pre·ci·ate (dĭ-prē'shē-āt') tr. **-at·ed, -at·ing** *(to devalue)* depreciar, desvalorar; *(to belittle)* despreciar, menospreciar —intr. depreciarse, desvalorarse.

de·pre·ci·a·tion (dĭ-prē'shē-ā'shən) s. *(devaluation)* depreciación *f*, desvalorización *f*; *(disparagement)* desprecio, menosprecio.

dep·re·da·tion (dĕp'rĭ-dā'shən) s. depredación *f*, pillaje *m*.

de·press (dĭ-prěs') tr. *(to dispirit)* deprimir, desanimar; *(to press down)* deprimir, presionar; *(to lower)* bajar; *(to weaken)* debilitar; *(to reduce)* reducir.

de·pres·sant (dĭ-prěs'ənt) adj. & s. MED. calmante *m*, sedante *m*.

de·pressed (dĭ-prěst') adj. *(dispirited)* deprimido, desanimado; BOT., ZOOL. deprimido; ECON. *(period)* de depresión; *(economy)* deprimido.

de·press·ing (dĭ-prěs'ĭng) adj. deprimente.

de·pres·sion (dĭ-prěsh'ən) s. *(a hollow)* cavidad *f*, hueco; ECON., MED. depresión *f*.

de·pres·sive (dĭ-prěs'ĭv) adj. *(depressing)* deprimente; *(of depression)* depresivo.

de·pres·sor (dĭ-prěs'ər) s. depresor *m*.

de·pres·sur·i·za·tion (dē-prěsh'ər-ĭ-zā'shən) s. FÍS. descompresión *f*.

de·pres·sur·ize (dē-prěsh'ə-rīz') tr. **-ized, -iz·ing** descomprimir.

dep·ri·va·tion (dĕp'rə-vā'shən) s. privación *f*.

de·prive (dĭ-prīv') tr. **-prived, -priv·ing** privar.

de·prived (dĭ-prīvd') adj. pobre, necesitado.

de·pro·gram (dē-prō'grăm') tr. **-grammed, -gram·ming** contrarrestar los efectos de una indoctrinación (esp. religiosa).

depth (dĕpth) s. *(downward measurement)* profundidad *f*; *(most intense part)* lo más profundo <*in the d. of despair* en lo más profundo de la desesperación>; *(severest part)* lo más recio <*in the d. of winter* en lo más recio del invierno>; *(deteriorated condition)* estado de deterioro; *(intellectual complexity)* profundidad, complejidad *f*; *(understanding)* alcance *m*; *(richness)* intensidad *f*, densidad *f* <*the d. of the colors in the painting* la intensidad de los colores del cuadro>; *(lowness in pitch)* profundidad <*the d. of his voice* la profundidad de su voz> ◆ **in d.** a fondo • **depths** *(lowest part)* lo más hondo; *(farthest part)* lo más recóndito.

depth charge s. ARM., MARÍT. carga de profundidad.

dep·u·ta·tion (dĕp'yə-tā'shən) s. diputación *f*, delegación *f*.

dep·u·tize (dĕp'yə-tīz') tr. **-tized, -tiz·ing** diputar, delegar —intr. sustituir.

dep·u·ty (dĕp'yə-tē) s. [pl. **-ties**] *(delegate)* delegado, comisionado; *(assistant)* asistente *m*, suplente *mf*; POL. *(legislator)* diputado.

de·rail (dē-rāl') tr. hacer descarrilar —intr. descarrilar.

de·rail·ment (dē-rāl'mənt) s. descarrilamiento.

de·range (dĭ-rānj') tr. **-ranged, -rang·ing** *(to disturb)* perturbar; *(to throw into disorder)* desordenar; *(to make insane)* enloquecer.

de·ranged (dĭ-rānjd') adj. loco, trastornado.

de·range·ment (dĭ-rānj'mənt) s. *(disorder)* desorden *m*, desarreglo; MED. trastorno (mental).

der·by (dûr'bē) s. [pl. **-bies**] *(horse race)* derby *m*; *(open race)* carrera, competencia; *(hat)* sombrero hongo.

ã rey / ä año / b **boca** / ch **chico** / d **dar** / ĕ **el** / ē **mil** / g **gato** / h **joya** / hw **juez** / ī **aire** / k **casa** / kw **cuan** /

de·reg·u·late (dē-rĕg′yə-lāt′) tr. **-lat·ed, -lat·ing** quitar las reglamentaciones de.

der·e·lict (dĕr′ə-lĭkt′) **I.** s. *(person)* vago; MARÍT. *(ship)* derrelicto **II.** adj. *(remiss)* negligente, remiso; *(abandoned)* abandonado (propiedad).

der·e·lic·tion (dĕr′ə-lĭk′shən) s. *(abandonment)* abandono; *(neglect)* negligencia.

de·ride (dĭ-rīd′) tr. **-rid·ed, -rid·ing** burlarse de, mofarse de.

de·ri·sion (dĭ-rĭzh′ən) s. burla, mofa.

de·ri·sive (dĭ-rī′sĭv, -rĭs′ĭv) o **de·ri·so·ry** (dĭ-rī′sə-rē) adj. *(mocking)* burlón, mofador; *(ridiculous)* irrisorio.

der·i·va·tion (dĕr′ə-vā′shən) s. derivación *f.*

de·riv·a·tive (dĭ-rĭv′ə-tĭv) **I.** adj. derivado **II.** s. GRAM., QUÍM. derivado; MAT. derivada.

de·rive (dĭ-rīv′) tr. **-rived, -riv·ing** *(to deduce from)* derivar; *(to obtain)* sacar, obtener; QUÍM. derivar —intr. derivar, resultar.

der·ma (dûr′mə) o **derm** (dûrm) o **der·mis** (dûr′mĭs) s. ANAT. dermis *f.*

der·ma·ti·tis (dûr′mə-tī′tĭs) s. MED. dermatitis *f.*, dermitis *f.*

der·ma·tol·o·gist (dûr′mə-tŏl′ə-jĭst) s. dermatólogo.

der·ma·tol·o·gy (dûr′mə-tŏl′ə-jē) s. MED. dermatología.

der·ma·to·sis (dûr′mə-tō′sĭs) s. [pl. **-ses** (-sēz′)] MED. dermatosis *f.*

der·o·gate (dĕr′ə-gāt′) tr. **-gat·ed, -gat·ing** menospreciar —intr. ♦ **to d. from** *(to detract from)* disminuir.

der·o·ga·tion (dĕr′ə-gā′shən) s. *(disparagement)* menosprecio; DER. derogación *f.*

de·rog·a·to·ry (dĭ-rŏg′ə-tôr′ē) o **de·rog·a·tive** (-tĭv′) adj. *(disparaging)* despectivo, despreciativo; DER. derogatorio.

der·rick (dĕr′ĭk) s. *(crane)* grúa, malacate *m*; *(of an oil well)* torre de perforación *f.*

der·ring-do (dĕr′ĭng-dōō′) s. valor *m*, intrepidez *f.*

der·vish (dûr′vĭsh) s. RELIG. derviche *m.*

de·sal·i·nate (dē-săl′ə-nāt′) tr. **-nat·ed, -nat·ing** desalar, desalinizar.

de·salt (dē-sôlt′) tr. desalar.

de·scend (dĭ-sĕnd′) intr. *(to come down)* descender; *(to pass by inheritance)* transmitirse por herencia; *(to lower oneself)* rebajarse, decaer; *(to descend upon)* caer encima de, acometer —tr. descender, bajar.

de·scen·dent o **de·scen·dant** (dĭ-sĕn′dənt) s. & adj. descendiente *mf.*

de·scent (dĭ-sĕnt′) s. *(act)* descenso; *(incline)* declive *m*; *(lineage)* descendencia; *(attack)* embestida; FIG. *(decline)* decadencia; DER. sucesión *f*, transmisión por herencia *f.*

de·scribe (dĭ-skrīb′) tr. **-scribed, -scrib·ing** describir.

de·scrip·tion (dĭ-skrĭp′shən) s. *(representation)* descripción *f*; *(a type)* clase *f*, tipo.

de·scrip·tive (dĭ-skrĭp′tĭv) adj. descriptivo.

de·scrip·tor (dĭ-skrĭp′tər) s. COMPUT. descriptor *m.*

de·scry (dĭ-skrī′) v. **-scried, -scry·ing** tr. *(to discern)* discernir; *(to make out)* divisar, descubrir.

des·e·crate (dĕs′ĭ-krāt′) tr. **-crat·ed, -crat·ing** profanar.

des·e·cra·tion (dĕs′ĭ-krā′shən) s. profanación *f.*

de·seg·re·gate (dē-sĕg′rĭ-gāt′) intr. & tr. **-gat·ed, -gat·ing** eliminar la segregación racial (en).

de·sen·si·tize (dē-sĕn′sĭ-tīz′) tr. **-tized, -tiz·ing** desensibilizar, insensibilizar.

de·sen·si·tiz·er (dē-sĕn′sĭ-tī′zər) s. FISIOL., MED. desensibilizante *m*; FOTOG. desensibilizador *m.*

des·ert¹ (dĕz′ərt) s. desierto ♦ **d. heat** calor desértico.

de·sert² (dĭ-zûrt′) s. *(something deserved)* merecido <*he received his just deserts* se llevó su merecido>; *(state)* merecimiento.

de·sert³ (dĭ-zûrt′) tr. *(to abandon)* abandonar; MIL. desertar de —intr. desertar.

de·sert·er (dĭ-zûr′tər) s. desertor *m.*

de·ser·tion (dĭ-zûr′shən) s. MIL. deserción *f*; DER. *(abandonment)* abandono, desamparo.

de·serve (dĭ-zûrv′) tr. & intr. **-served, -serv·ing** merecer(se).

de·served (dĭ-zûrvd′) adj. merecido.

de·serv·ing (dĭ-zûr′vĭng) **I.** adj. digno, meritorio **II.** s. mérito, merecimiento.

des·ic·cate (dĕs′ĭ-kāt′) tr. & intr. **-cat·ed, -cat·ing** desecar(se).

de·sign (dĭ-zīn′) **I.** tr. *(to invent)* idear, concebir; *(to prepare plans)* diseñar; *(to draw)* diseñar, dibujar; *(to intend)* planear, proyectar —intr. hacer diseños **II.** s. *(model)* diseño, modelo; *(drawing)* dibujo; ARQ. plano; *(project)* proyecto; *(intention)* propósito, intención *f* ♦ **by d.** intencionalmente • **to have designs on** poner las miras en.

de·sign·ed·ly (dĭ-zī′nĭd-lē) adv. a propósito, intencionalmente.

des·ig·nate (dĕz′ĭg-nāt′) **I.** tr. **-nat·ed, -nat·ing** *(to appoint)* designar, nombrar; *(to characterize)* describir; *(to name)* denominar; *(to specify)* indicar **II.** (-nĭt) adj. designado, nombrado.

des·ig·na·tion (dĕz′ĭg-nā′shən) *(act)* designación *f*; *(appointment)* nombramiento; *(denomination)* denominación *f.*

de·sign·er (dĭ-zī′nər) s. diseñador *m.*

de·sign·ing (dĭ-zī′nĭng) **I.** adj. intrigante, maquinador **II.** s. *(of fashion)* creación *f*; *(of machines)* diseño.

de·sir·a·bil·i·ty (dĭ-zīr′ə-bĭl′ĭ-tē) s. *(pleasing aspect)* atractivo, aspecto apetecedor; *(advisability)* conveniencia.

de·sir·a·ble (dĭ-zīr′ə-bəl) adj. deseable.

de·sire (dĭ-zīr′) **I.** tr. **-sired, -sir·ing** desear, anhelar **II.** s. *(wish)* deseo, anhelo; *(request)* petición *f*; *(sexual appetite)* deseo sexual.

de·sir·ous (dĭ-zīr′əs) adj. deseoso.

de·sist (dĭ-zĭst′) intr. dejar de hacer algo ♦ **to d. from** desistir de.

desk (dĕsk) s. *(in an office)* escritorio; *(at school)* pupitre *m*; *(counter)* mostrador *m*, mesa.

des·o·late **I.** adj. (dĕs′ə-lĭt) desolado **II.** tr. (dĕs′ə-lāt′) **-lat·ed, -lat·ing** *(to destroy)* desolar, asolar; *(to depopulate)* despoblar; *(to forsake)* abandonar; *(to distress)* desconsolar.

des·o·la·tion (dĕs′ə-lā′shən) s. desolación *f.*

de·spair (dĭ-spâr′) **I.** s. desesperación *f* **II.** intr. desesperar(se).

des·patch (dĭ-spăch′) v. & s. var. de **dispatch.**

des·per·a·do (dĕs′pə-rä′dō) s. [pl. **-does** o **-dos**] forajido, bandolero.

des·per·ate (dĕs′pər-ĭt) adj. *(reckless)* desesperado; *(grave)* crítico, muy grave; *(urgent)* apremiante.

des·per·ate·ly (dĕs′pər-ĭt-lē) adv. desesperadamente.

des·per·a·tion (dĕs′pə-rā′shən) s. desesperación *f.*

des·pi·ca·ble (dĕs′pĭ-kə-bəl, dĭ-spĭk′ə-) adj. odioso, vil.

de·spise (dĭ-spīz′) tr. **-spised, -spis·ing** despreciar.

de·spite (dĭ-spīt′) **I.** prep. a pesar de, no obstante **II.** s. *(malice)* despecho; *(insult)* insulto.

de·spoil (dĭ-spoil′) tr. *(to deprive of)* despojar; *(to plunder)* expoliar, saquear.

de·spoil·er (dĭ-spoi′lər) s. expoliador *m*, saqueador *m.*

de·spo·li·a·tion (dĭ-spō′lē-ā′shən) s. expoliación *f.*

de·spon·den·cy (dĭ-spŏn′dən-sē) o **de·spon·dence** (-dəns) s. desánimo, desesperanza.

de·spon·dent (dĭ-spŏn′dənt) adj. desanimado, desesperanzado.

des·pot (dĕs′pət) s. déspota *mf.*

des·pot·ic (dĭ-spŏt′ĭk) adj. despótico.

des·pot·ism (dĕs′pə-tĭz′əm) s. despotismo.

des·sert (dĭ-zûrt′) s. CUL. postre *m.*

de·sta·bi·lize (dē-stā′bə-līz′) tr. **-lized, -liz·ing** desestabilizar, desequilibrar.

de·sta·lin·i·za·tion (dē-stä′lĭ-nĭ-zā′shən) s. POL. desestalinización *f.*

des·ti·na·tion (dĕs′tə-nā′shən) s. destino.

des·tine (dĕs′tĭn) tr. **-tined, -tin·ing** destinar ♦ **destined for** con destino a.

des·ti·ny (dĕs′tə-nē) s. [pl. **-nies**] destino, sino.

des·ti·tute (dĕs′tĭ-tōōt′, -tyōōt′) adj. indigente, necesitado ♦ **d. of** desprovisto de, carente de.

des·ti·tu·tion (dĕs′tĭ-tōō′shən, -tyōō′-) s. *(poverty)* indigencia, miseria; *(lack)* carencia.

de·stroy (dĭ-stroi′) tr. *(to ruin)* destruir; *(to kill)* matar; *(to render ineffective)* anular.

de·stroy·er (dĭ-stroi′ər) s. *(person)* destructor *m*; MARÍT. destructor.

de·struct (dĭ-strŭkt′, dē′strŭkt′) s. AER. destrucción deliberada de un vehículo espacial después del lanzamiento.

de·struc·ti·bil·i·ty (dĭ-strŭk′tə-bĭl′ĭ-tē) s. destructibilidad *f.*

de·struc·ti·ble (dĭ-strŭk′tə-bəl) adj. destructible.

de·struc·tion (dĭ-strŭk′shən) s. destrucción *f.*

de·struc·tive (dĭ-strŭk′tĭv) adj. destructivo, destructor ♦ **d. of** *o* **to** perjudicial para.

de·struc·tor (dĭ-strŭk′tər) s. *(incinerator)* incinerador de basura *m*; *(explosive)* dispositivo destructor de cohetes.

de·sul·fur·i·za·tion (dē-sŭl′fər-ĭ-zā′shən) s. QUÍM. desulfuración *f.*

des·ul·to·ry (dĕs′əl-tôr′ē) adj. *(disconnected)* inconexo; *(disordered)* desordenado; *(random)* esporádico, intermitente.

de·tach (dĭ-tăch′) tr. *(to separate)* separar, desprender; MIL. destacar.

de·tach·a·ble (dĭ-tăch′ə-bəl) adj. *(separable)* separable; *(parts)* amovible, desmontable.

de·tached (dĭ-tăcht′) adj. *(separate)* separado, independiente; *(loose)* suelto; *(aloof)* indiferente, despreocupado.

de·tach·ment (dĭ-tăch′mənt) s. *(separation)* separación *f*, desprendimiento; *(impartiality)* imparcialidad *f*, objetividad *f*; *(aloofness)* indiferencia, despreocupación *f*; MIL. destacamiento.

de·tail (dĭ-tāl′, dē′tāl′) I. s. *(particular)* detalle *m*, pormenor *m*; MIL. destacamento II. tr. detallar, pormenorizar; MIL. destacar.

detailed (dĭ-tāld′, dē′tāld′) adj. detallado, minucioso.

de·tain (dĭ-tān′) tr. *(to delay)* retardar, demorar; *(to confine)* detener, arrestar.

de·tain·ment (dĭ-tān′mənt) s. detención *f*, arresto.

de·tect (dĭ-tĕkt′) tr. *(to note)* advertir; *(to perceive)* percibir; detectar; RAD. demodular.

de·tect·a·ble *o* **de·tect·i·ble** (dĭ-tĕk′tə-bəl) adj. perceptible.

de·tec·tion (dĭ-tĕk′shən) s. *(discovery)* descubrimiento; TEC. detección *f*; RAD. demodulación *f.*

de·tec·tive (dĭ-tĕk′tĭv) s. detective *mf* ♦ **a d. story** una novela policial.

de·tec·tor (dĭ-tĕk′tər) s. *(person)* descubridor *m*; *(device)* detector *m.*

de·tent (dĭ-tĕnt′) s. trinquete *m.*

dé·tente (dā-tänt′) s. POL. distensión *f.*

de·ten·tion (dĭ-tĕn′shən) s. *(delay)* retraso, demora; *(confinement)* detención *f*, arresto.

detention home s. CRIMIN. cárcel provisional para delincuentes juveniles *f.*

de·ter (dĭ-tûr′) tr. **-terred, -ter·ring** *(to prevent)* impedir; *(to discourage)* desanimar, disuadir.

de·ter·gent (dĭ-tûr′jənt) s. detergente *m.*

de·te·ri·o·rate (dĭ-tîr′ē-ə-rāt′) tr. **-rat·ed, -rat·ing** deteriorar, empeorar —intr. *(to worsen)* desmejorar, empeorar; *(to degenerate)* degenerar.

de·te·ri·o·ra·tion (dĭ-tîr′ē-ə-rā′shən) s. *(worsening)* deterioro, empeoramiento; *(degeneration)* degeneración *f.*

de·ter·min·a·ble (dĭ-tûr′mə-nə-bəl) adj. determinable.

de·ter·mi·nant (dĭ-tûr′mə-nənt) I. s. *(factor)* factor determinante *m*; MAT. determinante *m* II. adj. determinante, decisivo.

de·ter·mi·nate (dĭ-tûr′mə-nĭt) adj. *(given)* determinado; *(final)* definitivo.

de·ter·mi·na·tion (dĭ-tûr′mə-nā′shən) s. *(decision)* determinación *f*; *(firmness of purpose)* resolución *f*; DER. *(ruling)* decisión *f*, fallo.

de·ter·mine (dĭ-tûr′mĭn) tr. **-mined, -min·ing** determinar —intr. decidir.

de·ter·mined (dĭ-tûr′mĭnd) adj. *(resolute)* determinado; *(decided)* decidido, convenido.

de·ter·min·er (dĭ-tûr′mə-nər) s. *(person)* persona que determina; GRAM. vocablo determinativo.

de·ter·min·ing (dĭ-tûr′mĭ-nĭng) adj. decisivo, concluyente.

de·ter·min·ism (dĭ-tûr′mə-nĭz′əm) s. FILOS. determinismo.

de·ter·rence (dĭ-tûr′əns) s. disuasión *f.*

de·ter·rent (dĭ-tûr′ənt) I. s. agente disuasivo, medida repre-

siva II. adj. *(preventive)* impeditivo; *(restrictive)* restrictivo, represivo.

de·test (dĭ-tĕst′) tr. detestar, aborrecer.

de·test·a·ble (dĭ-tĕs′tə-bəl) adj. detestable, aborrecible.

de·tes·ta·tion (dē′tĕ-stā′shən) s. *(abhorrence)* aborrecimiento, execración *f*; *(thing)* objeto de aborrecimiento.

de·throne (dē-thrōn′) tr. **-throned, -thron·ing** destronar.

det·o·nate (dĕt′n-āt′) tr. **-nat·ed, -nat·ing** hacer detonar —intr. detonar.

det·o·na·tion (dĕt′n-ā′shən) s. detonación *f.*

det·o·na·tor (dĕt′n-ā′tər) s. detonador *m.*

de·tour (dē′tŏor′, dĭ-tŏor′) I. s. desvío, desviación *f* II. tr. & intr. desviar(se).

de·tox MED., FAM. I. tr. (dē-tŏks′) **-toxed, -tox·ing** desintoxicar II. s. (dē′tŏks′) sección de desintoxicación *f.*

de·tox·i·fi·ca·tion (dē-tŏk′sə-fĭ-kā′shən) s. MED. desintoxicación *f.*

de·tox·i·fy (dē-tŏk′sə-fī′) tr. **-fied, -fy·ing** MED. desintoxicar.

de·tract (dĭ-trăkt′) intr. detraer, disminuir <*rust detracts from the car's value* la herrumbre disminuye el valor del auto> —tr. distraer, distraer.

de·trac·tion (dĭ-trăk′shən) s. detracción *f*, difamación *f.*

de·trac·tor (dĭ-trăk′tər) s. detractor *m.*

de·train (dē-trān′) tr. hacer bajar de un tren —intr. bajar de un tren.

det·ri·ment (dĕt′rə-mənt) s. detrimento, perjuicio.

det·ri·men·tal (dĕt′rə-mĕn′tl) adj. perjudicial, dañino.

de·tri·tus (dĭ-trī′təs) s. [pl. **-tus**] GEOL. detrito.

deuce[1] (dōos, dyōos) s. *(in cards, dice)* dos *m*; *(in tennis)* cuarenta iguales.

deuce[2] (dōos, dyōos) s. FAM. diablos, demonios <*where the d. were you?* ¿dónde diablos estabas?>.

deuc·ed (dōo′sĭd, dyōo′-) adj. endemoniado, maldito.

deu·te·ri·um (dōo-tîr′ē-əm, dyōo-) s. QUÍM. deuterio, hidrógeno pesado.

Deu·ter·on·o·my (dōo′tə-rŏn′ə-mē, dyōo′-) s. BÍBL. Deuteronomio.

deut·sche mark *o* **deut·sche·mark** (doi′chə-märk′) s. FIN. marco alemán.

de·val·u·ate (dē-văl′yōo-āt′) tr. **-at·ed, -at·ing** devaluar, desvalorizar.

de·val·u·a·tion (dē-văl′yōo-ā′shən) s. devaluación *f*, desvalorización *f.*

de·val·ue (dē-văl′yōo) v. var. de **devaluate**.

dev·as·tate (dĕv′ə-stāt′) tr. **-tat·ed, -tat·ing** devastar, asolar; FIG., FAM. *(to overwhelm)* abrumar.

dev·as·tat·ing (dĕv′ə-stā′tĭng) adj. devastador, asolador.

dev·as·ta·tion (dĕv′ə-stā′shən) s. devastación *f*, asolación *f.*

de·vel·op (dĭ-vĕl′əp) tr. *(potentialities)* desarrollar, desenvolver; *(muscles, beliefs)* fortalecer, robustecer; *(plan, plot)* revelar, desarrollar; *(expertise, ability)* formar <*years of practice d. an expert* años de práctica forman un experto>; *(industry, education)* activar, fomentar; *(resources)* aprovechar, explotar; *(land)* urbanizar; *(taste, liking)* adquirir, tomar; *(habit, disease)* contraer, incubar; MIL. desplegar; MAT., QUÍM. desarrollar, extender; MÚS. elaborar, desarrollar; FOTOG. revelar —intr. *(to grow)* desarrollarse, crecer; *(to advance)* avanzar, progresar; *(to appear gradually)* aparecer, mostrarse; *(to be disclosed)* descubrirse, revelarse; *(to evolve)* evolucionar, progresar.

de·vel·op·er (dĭ-vĕl′ə-pər) s. CONSTR. urbanizador *m*; FOTOG. revelador *m.*

de·vel·op·ing (dĭ-vĕl′ə-pĭng) adj. en desarrollo, en vías de desarrollo <*d. nations* países en vías de desarrollo>.

de·vel·op·ment (dĭ-vĕl′əp-mənt) s. *(act)* desarrollo; *(exploitation)* aprovechamiento; *(event)* acontecimiento, suceso; *(of real estate)* urbanización *f*; FOTOG. revelado.

de·vel·op·men·tal (dĭ-vĕl′əp-mĕn′tl) adj. *(producing growth)* de desarrollo; *(experimental)* experimental.

de·vi·ance (dē′vē-əns) *o* **de·vi·an·cy** (-ən-sē) s. desviación *f.*

de·vi·ant (dē′vē-ənt) I. s. desviacionista *mf*, persona aberrante II. adj. desviacionista, aberrante.

de·vi·ate I. intr. (dē′vē-āt′) **-at·ed, -at·ing** desviarse, apartarse de las normas sociales —tr. desviar II. s. (dē′vē-ĭt) desviacionista *mf*, persona aberrante.

de·vi·a·tion (dē′vē-ā′shən) s. *(act)* desviación *f*; *(deviant be-*

havior) inversión (sexual) *f;* FIG. *(departure)* alejamiento (de la verdad); AVIA., MARÍT. *(deflection)* desviación.

de·vice (dǐ-vīs′) s. *(scheme)* estratagema *m,* ardid *m;* TEC. *(mechanism)* dispositivo, aparato; LIT. *(contrivance)* recurso; HER. divisa.

dev·il (dĕv′əl) **I.** s. *(evil spirit)* diablo, demonio; *(person)* diablo; *(printer's devil)* aprendiz de imprenta *m; (toothed machine)* máquina de deshilachar ♦ **a d. of (something)** (algo) del diablo *<a d. of a problem* un problema del diablo> • **between the d. and the deep blue sea** entre la espada y la pared **II.** tr. *(to tear up)* deshilachar; *(to annoy)* fastidiar, molestar; CUL. condimentar mucho —intr. trabajar de aprendiz de imprenta ♦ **the D.** TEO. el diablo, Satanás • **devil's advocate** abogado del diablo • **poor d.** pobre diablo • **the d.!** FAM. ¡diablos!, ¡rayos! • **to give the d. his due** dar a cada uno lo suyo, reconocer los méritos a *<we may not like them, but we must give the d. his due* tal vez no nos caigan bien, pero debemos reconocer sus méritos>.

dev·il·ish (dĕv′ə-lĭsh) **I.** adj. *(diabolic)* diabólico, malvado; *(mischievous)* travieso; FAM. *(excessive)* infernal **II.** adv. sumamente.

dev·il-may-care (dĕv′əl-mā-kâr′) adj. *(reckless)* temerario, imprudente; *(carefree)* despreocupado.

dev·il·ment (dĕv′əl-mənt) s. diablura, travesura.

dev·il·try (dĕv′əl-trē) *o* **dev·il·ry** (-əl-rē) s. [pl. **-tries** *o* **-ries**] *(mischief)* diablura; *(cruelty)* crueldad *f; (wickedness)* maldad *f; (witchcraft)* brujería, magia negra.

de·vi·ous (dē′vē-əs) adj. *(sinuous)* tortuoso, sinuoso; *(erring)* errado, descarriado; *(not straightforward)* taimado, solapado.

de·vi·ous·ness (dē′vē-əs-nǐs) s. tortuosidad *f.*

de·vise (dǐ-vīz′) **I.** tr. **-vised, -vis·ing** *(to conceive)* idear, concebir; *(to contrive)* trazar, tramar; DER. *(to give by will)* legar (bienes raíces). **II.** s. DER. legado, testamento (de bienes raíces).

de·vi·sor (dǐ-vī′zər) s. DER. testador (de bienes inmuebles) *m.*

de·vi·tal·ize (dē-vīt′l-īz′) tr. **-ized, -iz·ing** debilitar, minar la vitalidad de.

de·void (dǐ-void′) adj. desprovisto, carente *<a novel d. of wit* una novela carente de gracia>.

de·voir (dəv-wär′) s. *(civility)* amabilidad *f,* cortesía; *(duty)* deber *m.*

de·vol·a·til·ize (dē-vŏl′ə-tl-īz′) tr. **-ized, -iz·ing** extraer las sustancias volátiles de.

dev·o·lu·tion (dĕv′ə-lōō′shən, dē′və-) s. *(transfer)* transmisión *f; (of authority)* delegación (de poderes) *f;* BIOL. *(degeneration)* degeneración *f.*

de·volve (dǐ-vŏlv′) tr. **-volved, -volv·ing** *(to pass on)* transmitir, transferir; *(to delegate)* delegar —intr. *(to be passed on)* transmitirse, transferirse ♦ **to d. upon** transmitirse a, incumbir a.

de·vote (dǐ-vōt′) tr. **-vot·ed, -vot·ing** dedicar, consagrar.

de·vot·ed (dǐ-vō′tǐd) adj. *(loving)* afectuoso, cariñoso; *(dedicated)* dedicado, consagrado; *(ardent)* fervoroso.

dev·o·tee (dĕv′ə-tē′) s. devoto.

de·vo·tion (dǐ-vō′shən) s. *(affection)* devoción *f,* afecto; *(piety)* devoción, fervor *m* ♦ **devotions** RELIG. oraciones, rezos.

de·vo·tion·al (dǐ-vō′shə-nəl) **I.** adj. devoto, piadoso **II.** s. oficio religioso breve.

de·vour (dǐ-vour′) tr. devorar, engullir.

de·vour·ing (dǐ-vou′rǐng) adj. devorador.

de·vout (dǐ-vout′) adj. **-er, -est** *(pious)* devoto, piadoso; *(sincere)* sincero; *(earnest)* fervoroso.

de·vout·ness (dǐ-vout′nǐs) s. devoción *f,* piedad *f.*

dew (dōō, dyōō) **I.** s. rocío **II.** tr. rociar.

dew point s. punto de condensación.

Dew·ar flask (dōō′ər, dyōō′-) s. LAB. frasco de Dewar.

dew·drop (dōō′drŏp′, dyōō′-) s. gota de rocío.

Dew·ey decimal system (dōō′ē, dyōō′ē) s. sistema decimal de Dewey *m.*

DEW line (dōō, dyōō) s. estaciones de radar de defensa antiaérea (en EE. UU. y Canadá).

dew·y (dōō′ē, dyōō′ē) adj. **-i·er, -i·est** *(moist)* rociado, ba-

ñado de rocío; *(resembling dew)* de rocío; POÉT. *(refreshing)* refrescante; *(pure)* puro, virginal.

dex·ter·i·ty (dĕk-stĕr′ĭ-tē) s. *(adroitness)* destreza, habilidad *f; (cleverness)* agilidad mental *f.*

dex·ter·ous (dĕk′stər-əs) *o* **dex·trous** (-strəs) adj. *(adroit)* diestro, hábil; *(clever)* ágil, listo.

dex·trose (dĕk′strōs′) s. QUÍM. dextrosa.

di·a·be·tes (dī′ə-bē′tīs) s. MED. diabetes *f.*

di·a·bet·ic (dī′ə-bĕt′ĭk) adj. & s. MED. diabético.

di·a·bol·ic (dī′ə-bŏl′ĭk) *o* **di·a·bol·i·cal** (-ĭ-kəl) adj. diabólico.

di·a·crit·ic (dī′ə-krĭt′ĭk) **I.** adj. GRAM., MED. diacrítico **II.** s. GRAM. signo diacrítico.

di·a·crit·i·cal mark (dī′ə-krĭt′ĭ-kəl) s. GRAM. signo diacrítico.

di·a·dem (dī′ə-dĕm′) **I.** s. *(crown)* diadema; *(royalty)* realeza **II.** tr. adornar con una diadema.

di·ag·nose (dī′əg-nōs′) tr. **-nosed, -nos·ing** MED. diagnosticar —intr. hacer un diagnóstico.

di·ag·no·sis (dī′əg-nō′sĭs) s. [pl. **-ses** (-sēz′)] *(act)* diagnosis *f; (conclusion)* diagnóstico.

di·ag·nos·tic (dī′əg-nŏs′tĭk) adj. diagnóstico.

di·ag·o·nal (dī-ăg′ə-nəl) adj. & s. diagonal *f.*

di·a·gram (dī′ə-grăm′) **I.** s. *(plan, drawing)* diagrama *m; (sketch)* esquema *m; (graph)* gráfico **II.** tr. **-grammed, -gram·ming** representar con un diagrama.

di·al (dī′əl) **I.** s. *(of a scale, clock)* esfera, cuadrante *m; (sundial)* cuadrante *m,* reloj de sol *m;* RAD., TELEV. *(panel)* dial *m; (knob)* botón selector *m;* TEL. *(disk)* disco **II.** tr. RAD., TELEV. *(to select)* sintonizar; TEL. marcar (un número) —intr. RAD., TELEV. hacer sintonía; TEL. marcar un número.

di·a·lect (dī′ə-lĕkt′) s. dialecto.

di·a·lec·tic (dī′ə-lĕk′tĭk) *o* **di·a·lec·ti·cal** (-tĭ-kəl) FILOS. **I.** s. dialéctica ♦ **dialectics** dialéctica **II.** adj. dialéctica.

di·a·lec·ti·cian (dī′ə-lĕk-tĭsh′ən) s. FILOL. dialectólogo; FILOS. dialéctico.

dialing tone s. G.B., TEL. tono para marcar.

di·a·logue *o* **di·a·log** (dī′ə-lôg′) s. diálogo.

dial tone s. TEL. tono para marcar.

di·al·y·sis (dī-ăl′ĭ-sĭs) s. [pl. **-ses** (-sēz′)] BIOQUÍM. diálisis *f.*

di·am·e·ter (dī-ăm′ĭ-tər) s. GEOM. diámetro.

di·a·met·ri·cal (dī′ə-mĕt′rĭ-kəl) *o* **di·a·met·ric** (-rĭk) adj. *(of a diameter)* diametral, del diámetro; *(contrary)* opuesto *<d. views* opiniones opuestas>.

di·a·mond (dī′ə-mənd) s. *(jewel)* diamante *m; (rhombus)* rombo; *(in cards)* diamante; DEP. *(infield)* cuadrado de las bases (en béisbol); *(field)* campo de béisbol ♦ **d. ring** sortija de diamantes.

di·a·per (dī′pər, dī′ə-pər) **I.** s. *(for babies)* pañal *m; (pattern)* motivo romboidal; *(cloth)* lienzo adamascado **II.** tr. *(a baby)* poner el pañal a; *(to decorate)* adornar con un motivo de rombos.

di·aph·a·nous (dī-ăf′ə-nəs) adj. diáfano.

di·a·phragm (dī′ə-frăm′) s. diafragma *m.*

di·a·rist (dī′ə-rĭst) s. diarista *mf,* persona que lleva un diario.

di·ar·rhe·a *o* **di·ar·rhoe·a** (dī′ə-rē′ə) s. MED. diarrea.

di·a·ry (dī′ə-rē) s. [pl. **-ries**] diario.

Di·as·po·ra *o* **di·as·po·ra** (dī-ăs′pər-ə) s. BÍBL., HIST. Diaspora ♦ **d.** dispersión de un pueblo homogéneo.

di·a·spore (dī′ə-spôr′, -spōr′) s. MIN. diásporo.

di·as·to·le (dī-ăs′tə-lē) s. FISIOL. diástole *f.*

di·a·ton·ic (dī′ə-tŏn′ĭk) adj. MÚS. diatónico.

di·a·tribe (dī′ə-trīb′) s. RET. diatriba.

dice (dīs) **I.** s.pl. [sing. **die**] dados **II.** intr. **diced, dic·ing** jugar a los dados —tr. perder (dinero) jugando a los dados; *(to decorate)* adornar con cuadritos; CUL. *(to cut up)* picar en cubitos.

dic·er (dī′sər) s. *(gambler)* jugador de dados *m;* CUL. *(utensil)* aparato para picar en cubitos.

dic·ey (dī′sē) adj. **-i·er, -i·est** *(risky)* arriesgado; *(chancy)* azaroso.

di·chlo·ride (dī-klôr′īd′) s. QUÍM. bicloruro.

di·chog·a·mous (dī-kŏg′ə-məs) adj. BOT. dicógamo.

di·chot·o·my (dī-kŏt′ə-mē) s. [pl. **-mies**] dicotomía.

dick¹ (dĭk) s. JER. sabueso, detective *m.*
dick² (dĭk) s. VULG. *(penis)* polla, pinga; JER., G.B. *(guy)* tipo.
dick·ens (dĭk′ənz) s. diablo, demonio.
Dick·en·si·an (dĭ-kĕn′zē-ən) adj. perteneciente a la obra *o* a los personajes de Charles Dickens.
dick·er (dĭk′ər) intr. *(to bargain)* regatear; *(to barter)* hacer trueques —tr. *(to trade)* trocar.
dick·ey *o* **dick·ie** *o* **dick·y** (dĭk′ē) s. [pl. **-eys** *o* **-ies**] *(blouse front)* camisola; *(shirt front)* peto postizo; *(collar)* cuello postizo; *(bib)* babero; *(donkey)* burro; *(bird)* pajarito; *(forward seat)* pesante *m*; *(rear seat)* asiento auxiliar trasero.
Dic·ta·belt (dĭk′tə-bĕlt′) s. marca registrada de una cinta plástica para dictáfonos.
Dic·ta·phone (dĭk′tə-fōn′) s. dictáfono (marca registrada).
dic·tate I. tr. (dĭk′tāt′, dĭk-tāt′) **-tat·ed, -tat·ing** *(to say aloud)* dictar; *(to impose)* imponer —intr. *(to issue orders)* mandar, dar órdenes II. s. (dĭk′tāt′) mandato, orden *f* ♦ **dictates** dictados *<the d. of conscience* los dictados de la conciencia>.
dic·ta·tion (dĭk-tā′shən) s. dictado.
dic·ta·tor (dĭk′tā′tər) s. POL. dictador *m.*
dic·ta·to·ri·al (dĭk′tə-tôr′ē-əl) adj. dictatorial.
dic·ta·tor·ship (dĭk-tā′tər-shĭp′) s. POL. dictadura.
dic·tion (dĭk′shən) s. dicción *f.*
dic·tion·ar·y (dĭk′shə-nĕr′ē) s. [pl. **-ies**] diccionario.
dic·tum (dĭk′təm) s. [pl. **-ta** (-tə) *o* **-tums**] *(pronouncement)* dictamen *m*; *(maxim)* máxima, dicho.
did (dĭd) pret. de **do¹.**
di·dac·tic (dī-dăk′tĭk) *o* **di·dac·ti·cal** (-tĭ-kəl) adj. didáctico.
did·dle¹ (dĭd′l) tr. **-dled, -dling** timar, embaucar —intr. malgastar el tiempo.
did·dle² (dĭd′l) tr. & intr. **-dled, -dling** menear(se).
did·n't (dĭd′nt) contr. de **did not.**
die¹ (dī) intr. **died, dy·ing** *(to expire)* morir, fallecer; *(to lose force)* apagarse, disminuir; *(to become extinct)* extinguirse, desaparecer.
die² (dī) s. [pl. **dies**] MAQ. *(for stamping)* cuño, troquel *m*; *(for casting)* matriz *f*, molde *m*; *(for punching)* punzón *m*, buril *m*; [pl. **dice**] *(for gambling)* dado; *(cube)* cubito.
die-hard *o* **die·hard** (dī′härd′) s. intransigente *mf*, testarudo.
di·er·e·sis *o* **di·aer·e·sis** (dī-ĕr′ĭ-sĭs) s. [pl. **-ses** (-sēz′)] GRAM. diéresis *f.*
die·sel (dē′zəl) s. vehículo de motor diesel.
diesel engine s. motor diesel *m.*
di·et¹ (dī′ĭt) I. s. *(usual food)* dieta, alimentación *f*; *(regulated food)* dieta, régimen *m* II. intr. estar a dieta *o* régimen.
di·et² (dī′ĭt) s. POL. dieta.
di·e·tar·y (dī′ĭ-tĕr′ē) adj. dietético.
di·et·er (dī′ĭ-tər) s. persona que hace dieta.
di·e·tet·ic (dī′ĭ-tĕt′ĭk) adj. dietético.
di·e·tet·ics (dī′ĭ-tĕt′ĭks) s. [ú con v. sing.] MED. dietética.
di·e·ti·tian *o* **di·e·ti·cian** (dī′ĭ-tĭsh′ən) s. MED. dietista *mf.*
dif·fer (dĭf′ər) intr. disentir, no estar de acuerdo *<I d. with you* no estoy de acuerdo con usted> ♦ **to d. from** diferir con, ser diferente de.
dif·fer·ence (dĭf′ər-əns) s. *(condition)* diferencia; *(disagreement)* desacuerdo, discrepancia; MAT. *(remainder)* diferencia, resta ♦ **it makes no d.** da lo mismo, da igual • **what d. does it make?** ¿qué más da? • **what's the d.?** ¿qué importa?
dif·fer·ent (dĭf′ər-ənt) adj. diferente, distinto.
dif·fer·en·tial (dĭf′ə-rĕn′shəl) I. adj. *(of a difference)* diferencial; *(distinctive)* característico II. s. *(amount of difference)* índice diferencial *m*; MAT. diferencial *f.*
differential calculus s. MAT. cálculo diferencial.
differential gear s. MAQ. engranaje diferencial.
dif·fer·en·ti·ate (dĭf′ə-rĕn′shē-āt′) tr. & intr. **-at·ed, -at·ing** diferenciar(se), distinguir(se).
dif·fer·en·ti·a·tion (dĭf′ə-rĕn′shē-ā′shən) s. diferenciación *f.*
dif·fi·cult (dĭf′ĭ-kəlt) adj. difícil.
dif·fi·cul·ty (dĭf′ĭ-kəl-tē) s. [pl. **-ties**] dificultad *f* ♦ **difficulties** apuros, problemas.

dif·fi·dence (dĭf′ĭ-dns) s. timidez *f*, falta de confianza en sí mismo.
dif·fi·dent (dĭf′ĭ-dnt) adj. tímido, falto de confianza en sí mismo.
dif·fract (dĭ-frăkt′) tr. & intr. FÍS. difractar(se).
dif·frac·tion (dĭ-frăk′shən) s. FÍS. difracción *f.*
dif·fuse I. tr. & intr. (dĭ-fyōōz′) **-fused, -fus·ing** difundir(se), esparcir(se) II. adj. (dĭ-fyōōs′) *(scattered)* difuso, esparcido; *(wordy)* difuso.
dif·fu·sion (dĭ-fyōō′zhən) s. difusión *f.*
dig (dĭg) I. tr. **dug** (dŭg), **dig·ging** *(to excavate)* cavar; *(the ground)* remover; *(a hole, a well)* hacer, abrir; *(coal, minerals)* extraer, sacar; *(to look for)* buscar; *(to force down)* clavar, hincar *<the batter dug his feet into the ground* el bateador hincó los pies en la tierra>; *(to prod against)* hundir *<he dug the gun into his back* le hundió la pistola en la espalda>; JER. *(to understand)* comprender *<can you d. what the man is saying?* ¿comprendes lo que dice el socio?>; *(to like)* gustar, volverse loco por; *(to notice)* fijarse en *<did you d. that outfit?* ¿te fijaste en ese traje?> ♦ **to d. in** enterrar • **to d. into** clavar, hundir • **to d. out** *(treasure)* extraer; *(facts)* sacar a la luz; *(to find)* encontrar • **to d. up** *(treasure)* desenterrar; *(facts)* descubrir —intr. *(to excavate)* cavar; *(to work hard)* romperse el lomo ♦ **to d. in** *(to dig holes)* hacer huecos; *(to entrench oneself)* atrincherarse; FAM. *(to begin to eat)* atacar II. s. *(prod)* golpe *m*; *(with the elbow)* codazo; *(gibe)* pulla, indirecta; ARQUEOL. excavación *f* ♦ **digs** G.B., FAM. *(lodgings)* alojamiento.
di·gest I. tr. (dī-jĕst′, dī-) *(food)* digerir; *(to organize)* clasificar; FIG. *(to comprehend)* asimilar —intr. digerirse II. s. (dī′jĕst′) compendio, sinopsis *f.*
di·gest·i·bil·i·ty (dī-jĕs′tə-bĭl′ĭ-tē, dī-) s. digestibilidad *f.*
di·gest·i·ble (dī-jĕs′tə-bəl, dī-) adj. digestible, digerible; FIG. *(comprehensible)* asimilable.
di·ges·tion (dī-jĕs′chən, dī-) s. BIOL. digestión *f*; FIG. *(understanding)* asimilación *f.*
di·ges·tive (dī-jĕs′tĭv, dī-) adj. & s. digestivo.
digestive system s. ANAT. aparato digestivo.
dig·ger (dĭg′ər) s. *(person)* cavador *m*; *(tool)* azadón *m*; *(machine)* excavadora.
dig·ging (dĭg′ĭng) s. excavación *f.*
dig·gings (dĭg′ĭngz) s.pl. mina, lugar de excavaciones *m.*
digit (dĭj′ĭt) s. ANAT. dedo; MAT. dígito.
dig·i·tal (dĭj′ĭ-tl) adj. digital.
digital clock s. reloj numérico.
digital computer s. computadora digital.
dig·i·tal·is (dĭj′ĭ-tăl′ĭs) s. FARM. digitalina; BOT. digital *f*, dedalera.
dig·i·tal·ize (dĭj′ĭ-tl-īz′) tr. **-ized, -iz·ing** MED. tratar con digitalina.
dig·it·ize (dĭj′ĭ-tīz′) tr. **-ized, -iz·ing** MAT., TEC. dar valor numérico a, cifrar.
dig·ni·fied (dĭg′nə-fīd′) adj. digno, decoroso.
dig·ni·fy (dĭg′nə-fī′) tr. **-fied, -fy·ing** *(to give honor to)* dignificar, honrar; *(to add importance to)* realzar.
dig·ni·tar·y (dĭg′nĭ-tĕr′ē) s. [pl. **-ies**] dignatario.
dig·ni·ty (dĭg′nĭ-tē) s. [pl. **-ties**] dignidad *f*, honor *m.*
di·graph (dī′grăf′) s. FONÉT. dígrafo.
di·gress (dī-grĕs′, dī-) intr. divagar, hacer una digresión.
di·gres·sion (dī-grĕsh′ən, dī-) s. digresión *f.*
di·gres·sive (dī-grĕs′ĭv, dī-) adj. digresivo, inconexo.
dike¹ (dīk) I. s. *(embankment)* dique *m*, represa; *(barrier)* barrera; *(causeway)* terraplén *m*; *(channel)* canal *m*, zanja II. tr. **diked, dik·ing** proteger con un dique.
dike² (dīk) s. JER. marimacho *f*, lesbiana.
di·lap·i·dat·ed (dĭ-lăp′ĭ-dā′tĭd) adj. desmoronado, desvencijado.
di·lap·i·da·tion (dĭ-lăp′ĭ-dā′shən) s. dilapidación *f*, desmoronamiento.
dil·a·ta·tion (dĭl′ə-tā′shən, dī′lə-) s. FÍS., MED. dilatación *f*, expansión *f.*
di·late (dī-lāt′) tr. & intr. **-lat·ed, -lat·ing** dilatar(se), expandir(se).
di·la·tion (dī-lā′shən) s. dilatación *f*, expansión *f.*
di·la·tor (dī-lā′tər) s. dilator *m.*

dil·a·to·ry (dĭl′ə-tôr′ē) adj. dilatorio.
dil·do *o* **dil·doe** (dĭl′dō) s. [pl. **-dos** *o* **-does**] VULG. consolador *m.*
di·lem·ma (dĭ-lĕm′ə, dī-) s. dilema *m.*
dil·et·tante (dĭl′ĭ-tänt′) s. & adj. diletante *mf*, aficionado.
dil·i·gence (dĭl′ə-jəns) s. *(assiduity, care)* diligencia; *(stagecoach)* diligencia.
dil·i·gent (dĭl′ə-jənt) adj. diligente.
dill (dĭl) s. BOT., CUL. eneldo.
dil·ly (dĭl′ē) s. [pl. **-lies**] FAM. joya, perla <*that joke is a d.* ese chiste es una joya>.
dil·ly-dal·ly (dĭl′ē-dăl′ē) intr. **-lied, -ly·ing** *(to dawdle)* perder el tiempo; *(to vacillate)* vacilar.
dil·u·ent (dĭl′yŏŏ-ənt) adj. & s. diluyente *m.*
di·lute (dĭ-lŏŏt′, dī-) I. tr. **-luted, -lut·ing** *(to thin)* diluir, desleír; FIG. *(to weaken)* debilitar, atenuar II. adj. *(thinned)* diluido; FIG. *(weak)* debilitado, atenuado.
di·lu·tion (dī-lŏŏ′shən, dī-) s. dilución *f.*
di·lu·vi·al (dī-lŏŏ′vē-əl) *o* **di·lu·vi·an** (-ən) adj. diluvial, diluviano.
dim (dĭm) I. adj. **dim·mer, dim·mest** *(dark)* oscuro; *(lights)* bajo, débil; *(color)* opaco, deslustrado; *(outline)* borroso, desdibujado; *(sight)* turbio, nublado; *(memory)* lejano, vago; *(view)* sombrío, pesimista; *(person)* lerdo, de pocas luces ♦ **to take a d. view of** *(to doubt)* considerar con pesimismo; *(to disapprove of)* ver de modo poco favorable II. tr. **dim·med, dim·ming** *(room)* oscurecer; *(lights)* bajar; *(color)* volver más opaco; *(outline)* borrar, desdibujar; *(sight)* enturbiar, nublar; *(memory)* borrar, empañar; AUTO. bajar —intr. *(room)* oscurecerse; *(lights)* perder intensidad; *(color)* volverse más opaco; *(outline)* borrarse, desdibujarse; *(sight)* enturbiarse, nublarse; *(memory)* borrarse, empañarse.
dime (dĭm) s. moneda de diez centavos (en EE. UU.).
dime novel s. LIT. novela barata, melodrama *m.*
di·men·sion (dĭ-mĕn′shən, dī-) I. s. dimensión *f* II. tr. dar dimensiones a.
di·men·sion·al (dĭ-mĕn′shə-nəl, dī-) adj. dimensional.
dime store s. tienda de baratijas.
di·min·ish (dĭ-mĭn′ĭsh) tr. *(to reduce)* disminuir, reducir; *(to degrade)* degradar —intr. disminuir.
diminishing returns s.pl. ECON. utilidad decreciente *f.*
dim·i·nu·tion (dĭm′ə-nŏŏ′shən, -nyŏŏ′-) s. disminución *f.*
di·min·u·tive (dĭ-mĭn′yə-tĭv) I. adj. *(tiny)* diminuto; GRAM. diminutivo II. s. GRAM. diminutivo.
di·min·u·tive·ness (dĭ-mĭn′yə-tĭv-nĭs) s. pequeñez *f.*
dim·mer (dĭm′ər) s. ELEC. regulador *o* reductor de luz *m* ♦ **dimmers** AUTO. *(parking lights)* luces de estacionamiento; *(low beams)* luces bajas *o* de cruce.
dim·ness (dĭm′nĭs) s. *(darkness)* oscuridad *f*; *(faintness)* debilidad *f.*
dim-out (dĭm′out′) s. apagón parcial (como defensa antiaérea) *m.*
dim·ple (dĭm′pəl) I. s. *(on the face)* hoyuelo; *(in a surface)* depresión *f*, hendidura II. tr. **-pled, -pling** formar hoyuelos —intr. tener hoyuelos.
dim·wit (dĭm′wĭt′) s. JER. mentecato, alcornoque *m.*
dim·wit·ted (dĭm′wĭt′ĭd) adj. JER. mentecato, de pocas luces.
din (dĭn) s. *(noise)* estrépito; *(of a crowd)* clamoreo, alboroto.
di·nar (dĭ-när′) s. FIN. dinar *m.*
dine (dīn) intr. **dined, din·ing** *(in the evening)* cenar; *(in general)* comer —tr. ♦ **to wine and d. someone** festejar a alguien.
din·er (dī′nər) s. *(person)* comensal *mf*; *(railroad car)* coche *m o* vagón restaurante *m*; *(restaurant)* restaurante popular *m.*
di·nette (dī-nĕt′) s. *(room)* comedor pequeño; *(furniture)* juego de comedor pequeño.
ding (dĭng) I. s. tintineo II. intr. sonar, repicar —tr. machacar, repetir insistentemente.
ding-dong (dĭng′dông′) I. s. talán talán (de campanas) *m* II. adj. reñido. III. intr. repiquetear.
din·ghy (dĭng′ē) s. [pl. **-ghies**] MARÍT. bote (de remo) *m.*

din·gi·ness (dĭn′jē-nĭs) s. *(sordidness)* sordidez *f*; *(dirtiness)* suciedad *f.*
din·gy (dĭn′jē) adj. **-gi·er, -gi·est** *(squalid)* sórdido; *(dirty)* sucio; *(worn)* deslustrado.
dining car s. F.C. coche comedor *m*, vagón restaurante *m.*
dining hall s. refectorio.
dining room s. comedor *m.*
din·ky (dĭng′kē) adj. **-ki·er, -ki·est** FAM. diminuto, insignificante.
din·ner (dĭn′ər) s. *(in the evening)* cena; *(at noon)* comida (principal); *(formal meal)* banquete *m.*
dinner jacket s. smoking *m*, chaqueta formal.
di·no·saur (dī′nə-sôr′) s. PALEON. dinosaurio.
dint (dĭnt) I. s. *(force)* fuerza; *(dent)* abolladura II. tr. abollar.
di·o·cese (dī′ə-sĭs, -sēs′) s. RELIG. diócesis *f.*
di·ode (dī′ōd′) s. ELEC. diodo.
Di·o·nys·i·ac (dī′ə-nĭs′ē-ăk′) adj. dionisiaco, dionisíaco.
di·op·ter *o* **di·op·tre** (dī-ŏp′tər) s. ÓPT. dioptría.
di·o·ram·a (dī′ə-răm′ə, -rä′mə) s. ARTE. diorama *m.*
di·ox·ide (dī-ŏk′sīd′) s. QUÍM. dióxido.
di·ox·in (dī-ŏk′sĭn) s. QUÍM. compuesto venenoso presente en ciertos herbicidas.
dip (dĭp) I. tr. **dipped, dip·ping** *(to dunk)* bañar, mojar; *(to immerse)* sumergir, meter <*he dipped his hand in the fish tank* metió la mano en la pecera>; *(to plate)* enchapar; *(to scoop)* sacar; *(the flag)* saludar con; *(to lower)* inclinar, bajar <*he dipped his head to avoid the branch* bajó la cabeza para esquivar la rama> —intr. *(to plunge)* sumergirse, zambullirse; *(to have a swim)* darse un chapuzón; *(to put the hand into)* meter la mano; *(to drop out of sight)* hundirse, descender; *(to dabble)* meterse; *(to slope downward)* bajar, inclinarse hacia abajo; *(prices)* bajar; *(a book)* hojear; GEOL. buzar; AVIA. bajar en picado ♦ **to d. into** meterse en, ocuparse superficialmente en ♦ **to d. into one's savings** echar mano a los ahorros II. s. *(immersion)* inmersión *f*; *(swim)* chapuzón *m*; *(liquid)* baño; *(container)* cazo; *(candle)* vela de sebo; *(slope)* pendiente *f*, declive *m*; *(downward course)* bajada, caída; *(magnetic dip)* inclinación de la aguja magnética *f*; *(hollow)* hondonada, depresión *f*; *(in a road)* badén *m*; CUL. salsa; AVIA. bajón *m*; GEOL. buzamiento ♦ **to take a d.** darse un chapuzón.
di·phen·yl (dī-fĕn′əl, -fē′nəl) s. QUÍM. difenilo.
diph·the·ri·a (dĭf-thîr′ē-ə, dĭp-) s. MED. difteria.
diph·thong (dĭf′thông′, dĭp′-) s. GRAM. diptongo.
di·plex (dī′plĕks′) adj. RAD., TELEG. diplex, de transmisión doble.
di·plo·ma (dĭ-plō′mə) s. diploma *m.*
di·plo·ma·cy (dĭ-plō′mə-sē) s. [pl. **-cies**] diplomacia.
dip·lo·mat (dĭp′lə-măt′) s. diplomático.
dip·lo·mat·ic (dĭp′lə-măt′ĭk) adj. diplomático.
diplomatic corps s. cuerpo diplomático.
diplomatic immunity s. inmunidad diplomática.
dip needle s. FÍS. aguja de inclinación.
di·pole (dī′pōl′) s. ELECTRÓN., FÍS. dipolo.
dip·per (dĭp′ər) s. *(ladle)* cazo, cucharón *m* ♦ **D.** ASTRON. *(Big Dipper)* Osa Mayor; *(Little Dipper)* Osa Menor.
dip·so·ma·ni·a (dĭp′sə-mā′nē-ə) s. dipsomanía.
dip·so·ma·ni·ac (dĭp′sə-mā′nē-ăk′) s. dipsomaníaco, dipsómano.
dip·stick (dĭp′stĭk′) s. indicador de nivel *m.*
dip·tych (dĭp′tĭk) s. ARTE. díptico.
dire (dīr) adj. **dir·er, dir·est** *(terrible)* terrible, espantoso; *(extreme)* extremo <*d. poverty* extrema pobreza> ♦ **to be in d. need of** necesitar urgentemente.
di·rect (dĭ-rĕkt′, dī-) I. tr. *(to manage)* dirigir; *(to control)* dirigir, gobernar; *(to command)* mandar, ordenar <*they directed him to answer* le ordenaron que contestara>; *(to guide)* dirigir, orientar; CINEM., MÚS., TEAT. dirigir ♦ **to d. one's attention to** fijarse en —intr. dirigir II. adj. *(straight)* directo; *(candid)* franco; *(immediate)* directo <*d. sunlight* la luz directa del sol>; *(lineal)* directo; *(literal)* literal, textual ♦ **the d. opposite** exactamente lo contrario III. adv. directamente.
direct current s. ELEC. corriente continua.
di·rec·tion (dĭ-rĕk′shən, dī-) s. *(directing)* dirección *f*; *(or-*

der) orden *f* ♦ **in the d. of** en la dirección de, con rumbo a • **directions** instrucciones.

di·rec·tion·al (dĭ-rĕk'shə-nəl, dī-) adj. direccional.

direction finder s. RAD. radiogoniómetro, antena indicadora de dirección.

di·rec·tive (dĭ-rĕk'tĭv, dī-) **I.** s. *(guideline)* directiva; *(order)* orden *f* **II.** adj. directivo.

di·rect·ly (dĭ-rĕkt'lē, dī-) adv. *(straight)* directamente; *(exactly)* exactamente; *(instantly)* inmediatamente, al instante.

direct object s. GRAM. complemento directo.

di·rec·tor (dĭ-rĕk'tər, dī-) s. director *m.*

di·rec·tor·ship (dĭ-rĕk'tər-shĭp', dī-) s. cargo de director, dirección *f.*

di·rec·tor·ate (dĭ-rĕk'tər-ĭt, dī-) s. *(office)* dirección *f;* *(board)* junta directiva, directorio.

di·rec·to·ry (dĭ-rĕk'tə-rē, dī-) s. [pl. **-ries**] *(telephone)* guía telefónica; *(of rules)* libro *o* manual de instrucciones *m;* *(directors)* directorio, junta directiva ♦ **d. assistance** información telefónica.

direct tax s. impuesto directo.

dire·ful (dīr'fəl) adj. terrible, espantoso.

dirge (dûrj) s. *(lament)* endecha; *(mournful music, poem)* canto fúnebre.

dir·i·gi·ble (dĭr'ə-jə-bəl, dĭ-rĭj'ə-) s. AER. dirigible *m.*

dirk (dûrk) **I.** s. puñal *m,* daga *f.* **II.** tr. apuñalar.

dirn·dl (dûrn'dl) s. vestido tirolés.

dirt (dûrt) s. *(soil)* tierra; *(grime)* suciedad *f,* mugre *f;* *(filth)* suciedad; *(gossip)* chisme *m;* *(smut)* porquería; *(excrement)* excremento; MIN. lodo ♦ **to treat someone like d.** tratar a alguien como un trapo.

dirt bike s. AUTO. motocicleta para caminos de tierra.

dirt-cheap (dûrt'chēp') adj. & adv. FAM. baratísimo, tirado.

dirt farmer s. FAM. labrador pobre *m,* chacarero.

dirt·y (dûr'tē) **I.** adj. **-i·er, -i·est** *(soiled)* sucio; *(obscene)* verde *<a d. old man* un viejo verde*>;* *(malicious)* vil; *(language)* grosero; *(demanding)* difícil; *(clouded)* sucio, turbio; *(stormy)* malo *<what d. weather!* ¡qué tiempo más malo!*>* ♦ **d. language** groserías • **d. trick** mala jugada • **to give someone a d. look** mirar a alguien con mala cara **II.** tr. **-ied, -y·ing** *(to make dirty)* ensuciar; *(to tarnish)* manchar —intr. *(to become dirty)* ensuciarse; *(to become tarnished)* mancharse.

dirty pool s. JER. jugarreta.

dirty tricks s.pl. FAM. *(espionage)* espionaje *m;* *(behavior)* mala jugada.

dirty word s. *(obscenity)* taco, mala palabra; *(expression)* insulto.

dirty work s. trabajo pesado *o* desagradable.

dis·a·bil·i·ty (dĭs'ə-bĭl'ĭ-tē) s. [pl. **-ties**] *(incapacity)* incapacidad *f,* invalidez *f;* *(handicap)* desventaja; DER. *(disqualification)* incapacidad.

dis·a·ble (dĭs-ā'bəl) tr. **-bled, -bling** *(to incapacitate)* incapacitar; *(to cripple)* lisiar; DER. *(to disqualify)* incapacitar.

dis·a·bled (dĭs-ā'bəld) adj. *(incapacitated)* incapacitado; *(crippled)* lisiado, inválido; *(broken down)* averiado *<a d. truck* un camión averiado*>* ♦ **the d.** los inválidos.

dis·a·ble·ment (dĭs-ā'bəl-mənt) s. *(incapacity)* incapacidad *f; (loss)* pérdida.

dis·a·buse (dĭs'ə-byōōz') tr. **-bused, -bus·ing** sacar de un error a, desengañar a.

dis·ad·van·tage (dĭs'əd-văn'tĭj) **I.** s. *(handicap)* desventaja, inconveniente *m; (damage)* detrimento ♦ **to be at a d.** estar en situación desventajosa • **to put at a d.** poner en situación desventajosa • **to the d. of** en detrimento de **II.** tr. **-taged, -tag·ing** perjudicar.

dis·ad·van·taged (dĭs'əd-văn'tĭjd) **I.** adj. desvalido **II.** s. ♦ **the d.** los desvalidos.

dis·ad·van·ta·geous (dĭs-ăd'vən-tā'jəs) adj. desventajoso, desfavorable.

dis·af·fect (dĭs'ə-fĕkt') tr. indisponer, enemistar.

dis·af·fect·ed (dĭs'ə-fĕk'tĭd) adj. desafecto.

dis·af·fec·tion (dĭs'ə-fĕk'shən) s. desafección *f,* desafecto.

dis·af·fil·i·ate (dĭs'ə-fĭl'ē-āt') tr. **-at·ed, -at·ing** desasociar.

dis·a·gree (dĭs'ə-grē') intr. **-greed, -gree·ing** *(to dissent)* no estar de acuerdo, estar en desacuerdo; *(to be different)* dis-

crepar *<our conclusions d.* nuestras conclusiones discrepan*>;* *(to be bad for)* sentar mal *<fried food disagrees with me* la comida frita me sienta mal*>;* *(to quarrel)* reñir.

dis·a·gree·a·ble (dĭs'ə-grē'ə-bəl) adj. desagradable.

dis·a·gree·a·bly (dĭs'ə-grē'ə-blē) adv. desagradablemente.

dis·a·gree·ment (dĭs'ə-grē'mənt) s. *(lack of agreement)* desacuerdo; *(difference)* disconformidad *f; (quarrel)* riña.

dis·al·low (dĭs'ə-lou') tr. *(to prohibit)* prohibir; *(to reject)* rechazar, denegar; DEP. anular.

dis·al·low·ance (dĭs'ə-lou'əns) s. *(prohibition)* prohibición *f; (rejection)* rechazo; DEP. anulación *f.*

dis·ap·pear (dĭs'ə-pîr') intr. desaparecer ♦ **the disappeared** los desaparecidos • **to d. without a trace** desaparecer sin dejar huellas.

dis·ap·pear·ance (dĭs'ə-pîr'əns) s. desaparición *f.*

dis·ap·point (dĭs'ə-point') tr. *(not to satisfy)* decepcionar, desilusionar; *(to fail)* decepcionar, defraudar *<he did not d. his parents* no defraudó a sus padres*>.*

dis·ap·point·ed (dĭs'ə-poin'tĭd) adj. *(not satisfied)* decepcionado; *(in love)* desengañado.

dis·ap·point·ing (dĭs'ə-poin'tĭng) adj. decepcionante.

dis·ap·point·ment (dĭs'ə-point'mənt) s. *(dissatisfaction)* desilusión *f,* decepción *f; (in love)* desengaño.

dis·ap·prov·al (dĭs'ə-prōō'vəl) s. desaprobación *f.*

dis·ap·prove (dĭs'ə-prōōv') tr. **-proved, -prov·ing** desaprobar —intr. desaprobar, estar en contra ♦ **to d. of** no gustarle a uno.

dis·arm (dĭs-ärm') tr. *(of weapons)* desarmar; FIG. *(to win)* desarmar, cautivar —intr. *(of weapons)* desarmar(se); *(to lay down arms)* deponer las armas.

dis·ar·ma·ment (dĭs-är'mə-mənt) s. desarme *m.*

dis·arm·ing (dĭs-är'mĭng) adj. FIG. que desarma, cautivante *<a d. smile* una sonrisa cautivante*>.*

dis·ar·range (dĭs'ə-rānj') tr. **-ranged, -rang·ing** desarreglar, desordenar.

dis·ar·range·ment (dĭs'ə-rānj'mənt) s. desarreglo, desorden *m.*

dis·ar·ray (dĭs'ə-rā') **I.** s. *(confusion)* desarreglo, desorden *m; (of a dress)* desaliño **II.** tr. desarreglar, desordenar.

dis·as·sem·ble (dĭs'ə-sĕm'bəl) tr. **-bled, -bling** desarmar, desmontar.

dis·as·sem·bly (dĭs'ə-sĕm'blē) s. MEC. desarme *m,* desmontaje *m.*

dis·as·so·ci·ate (dĭs'ə-sō'shē-āt', -sē-) tr. **-at·ed, -at·ing** disociar, desasociar.

dis·as·so·ci·a·tion (dĭs'ə-sō'shē-ā'shən, -sē-) s. disociación *f.*

dis·as·ter (dĭ-zăs'tər) s. desastre *m.*

disaster area s. POL. zona de desastre.

disaster dump s. COMPUT. vuelco por error irreversible.

dis·as·trous (dĭ-zăs'trəs) adj. desastroso.

dis·a·vow (dĭs'ə-vou') tr. *(knowledge)* desconocer; *(faith, friends)* renegar de; *(responsibility)* negarse a aceptar.

dis·a·vow·al (dĭs'ə-vou'əl) s. *(denial)* negación *f; (repudiation)* repudio; *(disapproval)* desaprobación *f.*

dis·band (dĭs-bănd') tr. & intr. *(to dissolve)* disolver(se); *(to disperse)* dispersar(se).

dis·bar (dĭs-bär') tr. **-barred, -bar·ring** DER. excluir del foro, expulsar del colegio de abogados.

dis·bar·ment (dĭs-bär'mənt) s. DER. exclusión del foro *f,* expulsión del colegio de abogados *f.*

dis·be·lief (dĭs'bĭ-lēf') s. incredulidad *f.*

dis·be·lieve (dĭs'bĭ-lēv') tr. **-lieved, -liev·ing** no creer —intr. ser incrédulo.

dis·be·liev·er (dĭs'bĭ-lē'vər) s. incrédulo.

dis·be·liev·ing (dĭs'bĭ-lē'vĭng) adj. incrédulo.

dis·burs·a·ble (dĭs-bûr'sə-bəl) adj. desembolsable.

dis·bur·sal (dĭs-bûr'səl) s. desembolso.

dis·burse (dĭs-bûrs') tr. **-bursed, -burs·ing** desembolsar.

dis·burse·ment (dĭs-bûrs'mənt) s. desembolso.

disc (dĭsk) s. disco.

dis·card I. tr. (dĭs-kärd') *(to reject)* descartar; *(to throw away)* desechar, botar; *(to abandon)* renunciar a; *(a card)* descartar —intr. descartarse **II.** s. (dĭs'kärd') *(act, card)* descarte *m; (thing)* desecho.

disc brake s. AUTO. freno de disco, freno de plato.

dis·cern (dĭ-sûrn', -zûrn') tr. *(to distinguish)* discernir, vislumbrar; *(to perceive)* percibir —intr. hacer distinciones.
dis·cern·i·ble (dĭ-sûr'nə-bəl, -zûr'-) adj. *(distinguishable)* discernible; *(perceptible)* perceptible.
dis·cern·ing (dĭ-sûr'nĭng, -zûr'-) adj. *(discriminating)* discernidor, discerniente; *(perceptive)* perspicaz.
dis·cern·ment (dĭ-sûrn'mənt, -zûrn'-) s. *(discrimination)* discernimiento; *(perspicacity)* perspicacia.
dis·charge I. tr. (dĭs-chärj') **-charged, -charg·ing** descargar; *(soldiers)* licenciar; *(patients)* dar de alta; *(employees)* despedir; *(odor, scent)* despedir, desprender; *(pus)* arrojar; *(arm)* disparar, descargar; *(duty)* desempeñar, ejecutar; *(promise)* cumplir, cumplir con; *(debt)* saldar; *(prisoner)* librar, poner en libertad; *(order)* anular; *(jury)* disolver; *(color)* desteñir; ELEC. descargar; ARQ. distribuir el peso, aligerar —intr. *(weight, burden)* descargarse; *(arm)* dispararse; *(waste, contents)* vaciarse, verter; *(color)* correrse, desteñirse; ELEC. descargarse II. s. (dĭs'chärj') *(act)* descarga; *(shooting)* disparo, descarga; *(emission)* escape m; *(secretion)* secreción f; *(flow)* flujo; *(acquittal)* descargo, exoneración f; *(performance)* desempeño, cumplimiento; *(dismissal)* despido; *(from a hospital)* alta; *(pus)* pus m; *(of soldiers)* licenciamiento; *(of prisoners)* liberación f; ELEC. descarga.
dis·charg·er (dĭs-chär'jər) s. ELEC. descargador m; ARM. disparador m.
dis·ci·ple (dĭ-sī'pəl) s. discípulo.
dis·ci·pli·nar·i·an (dĭs'ə-plə-nâr'ē-ən) I. s. ordenancista mf II. adj. disciplinario.
dis·ci·pli·nar·y (dĭs'ə-plə-nĕr'ē) adj. disciplinario.
dis·ci·pline (dĭs'ə-plĭn) I. s. *(behavior, order)* disciplina; *(punishment)* castigo; *(knowledge)* disciplina II. tr. **-plined, -plin·ing** *(to control, train)* disciplinar; *(to punish)* castigar.
disc jockey s. RAD. animador (de un programa de discos) m; *(of a disco)* montadiscos mf.
dis·claim (dĭs-klām') tr. *(to reject)* rechazar; DER. renunciar a —intr. DER. renunciar.
dis·claim·er (dĭs-klā'mər) s. *(denial)* denegación f; *(repudiation)* repudiación f; *(rectification)* rectificación f; DER. renuncia.
dis·close (dĭs-klōz') tr. **-closed, -clos·ing** divulgar, revelar.
dis·clo·sure (dĭs-klō'zhər) s. divulgación f, revelación f.
dis·co (dĭs'kō) s. *(night club)* discoteca; *(dance)* baile de discoteca m.
dis·col·or (dĭs-kŭl'ər) tr. & intr. descolorar(se), desteñir(se).
dis·col·or·a·tion (dĭs-kŭl'ə-rā'shən) s. descoloramiento.
dis·com·bob·u·late (dĭs'kəm-bŏb'yə-lāt') tr. **-lated, -lat·ing** FAM. confundir, trastornar.
dis·com·fit (dĭs-kŭm'fĭt) I. tr. *(to frustrate)* frustrar; *(to defeat)* derrotar; *(to disconcert)* desconcertar II. s. *(frustration)* frustración f; *(defeat)* derrota; *(discomfort)* desconcierto.
dis·com·fi·ture (dĭs-kŭm'fĭ-chŏŏr', -chər) s. *(frustration)* frustración f; *(defeat)* derrota; *(discomfort)* desconcierto.
dis·com·fort (dĭs-kŭm'fərt) I. s. *(pain)* molestia, dolor m; *(distress)* malestar m; *(worry)* preocupación f; *(annoyance)* incomodidad f II. tr. *(to bother)* molestar; *(to worry)* preocupar; *(to annoy)* incomodar.
dis·com·mode (dĭs'kə-mōd') tr. **-mod·ed, -mod·ing** incomodar, molestar.
dis·com·pose (dĭs'kəm-pōz') tr. **-posed, -pos·ing** *(to perturb)* perturbar; *(to disorder)* desordenar, desarreglar.
dis·com·po·sure (dĭs'kəm-pō'zhər) s. *(agitation)* desconcierto, agitación f; *(disorder)* desorden m, confusión f.
dis·con·cert (dĭs'kən-sûrt') tr. *(to bewilder)* desconcertar; *(to perturb)* perturbar.
dis·con·form·i·ty (dĭs'kən-fôr'mĭ-tē) s. [pl. **-ties**] ANT. disconformidad f; GEOL. discordancia.
dis·con·nect (dĭs'kə-nĕkt') tr. *(to separate)* separar; ELEC., TEL. desconectar <*the operator disconnected us* el operador nos desconectó>.
dis·con·nect·ed (dĭs'kə-nĕk'tĭd) adj. *(unconnected)* desconectado; *(unrelated)* sin conexión, sin relación; *(illogical)* inconexo, ilógico.
dis·con·nec·tion (dĭs'kə-nĕk'shən) s. desconexión f.

dis·con·so·late (dĭs-kŏn'sə-lĭt) adj. *(inconsolable)* desconsolado; *(cheerless)* deprimente <*a d. landscape* un paisaje deprimente>.
dis·con·tent (dĭs'kən-tĕnt') I. s. descontento, desagrado II. adj. descontento III. tr. descontentar, desagradar.
dis·con·tent·ed (dĭs'kən-tĕn'tĭd) adj. descontento.
dis·con·tent·ment (dĭs'kən-tĕnt'mənt) s. descontento.
dis·con·tin·u·ance (dĭs'kən-tĭn'yŏŏ-əns) s. *(discontinuation)* descontinuación f; DER. suspensión (de un pleito) f.
dis·con·tin·u·a·tion (dĭs'kən-tĭn'yŏŏ-ā'shən) s. discontinuidad f, cesación f.
dis·con·tin·ue (dĭs'kən-tĭn'yŏŏ) tr. & intr. **-ued, -u·ing** discontinuar(se), suspender(se).
dis·con·ti·nu·i·ty (dĭs-kŏn'tə-nŏŏ'ĭ-tē, -nyŏŏ'-) s. *(lack of continuity)* discontinuidad f; *(interruption)* interrupción f; *(in ideas)* falta de ilación.
dis·con·tin·u·ous (dĭs'kən-tĭn'yŏŏ-əs) adj. discontinuo, interrumpido.
dis·cord (dĭs'kôrd') s. *(dissension)* discordia, disensión f; MÚS. disonancia.
dis·cor·dance (dĭ-skôr'dns) s. *(nonconformity)* discordancia; *(dissent)* discordia, disensión f; MÚS. disonancia.
dis·cor·dant (dĭ-skôr'dnt) adj. *(conflicting)* discordante, discorde; MÚS. disonante.
dis·co·theque *o* **dis·co·thèque** (dĭs'kə-tĕk') s. discoteca.
dis·count (dĭs'kount') I. tr. *(to reduce)* descontar, rebajar; *(to disregard)* descontar, dar poca importancia a; *(to anticipate)* descontar, dar por cierto; FIN. descontar —intr. FIN. descontar letras de cambio II. s. descuento, rebaja.
dis·count·a·ble (dĭs'koun'tə-bəl) adj. COM. descontable.
dis·count·er (dĭs'koun'tər) s. COM., FIN. persona que hace descuentos.
discount rate s. COM., FIN. tasa de descuento.
discount store s. tienda de rebajas.
dis·cour·age (dĭ-skûr'ĭj) tr. **-aged, -ag·ing** *(to dishearten)* desanimar, desalentar; *(to hinder)* no fomentar, impedir <*inflation discourages saving* la inflación no fomenta el ahorro> ♦ **to d. from** *(to advise against)* recomendar que no; *(to dissuade from)* hacer desistir de, disuadir que no.
dis·cour·age·ment (dĭ-skûr'ĭj-mənt) s. desaliento, desánimo.
dis·cour·ag·ing (dĭ-skûr'ə-jĭng) adj. desalentador, desanimador.
dis·course I. s. (dĭs'kôrs') *(formal discussion)* discurso, disertación f; *(conversation)* conversación f, plática II. intr. (dĭ-skôrs') **-coursed, -cours·ing** conversar, platicar ♦ **to d. on** disertar sobre.
dis·cour·te·ous (dĭs-kûr'tē-əs) adj. descortés, desatento.
dis·cour·te·sy (dĭs-kûr'tĭ-sē) s. [pl. **-sies**] descortesía.
dis·cov·er (dĭ-skŭv'ər) tr. *(to learn of, find)* descubrir; *(to realize)* darse cuenta de.
dis·cov·er·er (dĭ-skŭv'ər-ər) s. descubridor m.
dis·cov·er·y (dĭ-skŭv'ə-rē) s. [pl. **-ies**] descubrimiento.
dis·cred·it (dĭs-krĕd'ĭt) I. tr. *(to disbelieve)* no dar crédito a, poner en duda; *(to disparage)* desprestigiar, desacreditar II. s. *(doubt)* duda; *(disrepute)* desprestigio, descrédito ♦ **to be a d. to** deshonrar a • **to be to the d. of** ir en descrédito de.
dis·creet (dĭ-skrēt') adj. discreto.
dis·creet·ness (dĭ-skrēt'nĭs) s. discreción f.
dis·crep·an·cy (dĭ-skrĕp'ən-sē) *o* **dis·crep·ance** (-skrĕp'əns) s. [pl. **-cies** *o* **-anc·es**] discrepancia.
dis·crep·ant (dĭ-skrĕp'ənt) adj. discrepante.
dis·crete (dĭ-skrēt') adj. *(unconnected)* separado, inconexo; *(different)* distinto.
dis·cre·tion (dĭ-skrĕsh'ən) s. *(quality)* discreción f; *(careful behavior)* prudencia; *(judgment, choice)* juicio, opción f ♦ **at one's d.** al albedrío de uno, al gusto de uno • **at the d. of** a juicio de, según el deseo de.
dis·cre·tion·ar·y (dĭ-skrĕsh'ə-nĕr'ē) adj. discrecional.
dis·crim·i·nate (dĭ-skrĭm'ə-nāt') intr. & tr. **-nat·ed, -nat·ing** discriminar, distinguir ♦ **to d. against** discriminar en contra de • **to d. from** discriminar de.
dis·crim·i·nat·ing (dĭ-skrĭm'ə-nā'tĭng) adj. *(discriminatory)* discriminatorio; *(distinctive)* distintivo; *(perceptive)* discerniente; *(selective)* exigente.

---

dis·crim·i·na·tion (dǐ-skrǐm'ə-nā'shən) s. *(prejudice)* discriminación *f*; *(perception)* discernimiento; *(distinction)* distinción *f*.

dis·crim·i·na·to·ry (dǐ-skrǐm'ə-nə-tôr'ē) adj. *(discriminatory)* discriminatorio (ley, conducta); *(distinctive)* distintivo; *(perceptive)* discerniente; *(selective)* exigente.

dis·cur·sive (dǐ-skûr'sǐv) adj. *(digressive)* digresivo, divagante; *(logical)* lógico.

dis·cus (dǐs'kəs) s. [pl. **-cus·es**] DEP. disco.

dis·cuss (dǐ-skǔs') tr. *(to talk over)* hablar de, hablar sobre; *(to discourse on)* discutir, tratar.

dis·cus·sion (dǐ-skǔsh'ən) s. *(conversation)* discusión *f*; *(discourse)* disertación *f* ♦ **to be under d.** estar en discusión • **to come up for d.** ser sometido a discusión • **a subject for d.** un tema de discusión.

dis·dain (dǐs-dān') I. tr. *(to scorn)* desdeñar, menospreciar; *(to be unwilling)* no dignarse <I d. to answer no me digno a contestar> II. s. desdén *m*, menosprecio.

dis·dain·ful (dǐs-dān'fəl) adj. desdeñoso.

dis·ease (dǐ-zēz') s. enfermedad *f*.

dis·eased (dǐ-zēzd') adj. enfermo.

dis·em·bark (dǐs'ěm-bärk') tr. & intr. desembarcar.

dis·em·bar·ka·tion (dǐs-ěm'bär-kā'shən) *o* **dis·em·bark·ment** (dǐs'ěm-bärk'mənt) s. *(of people)* desembarco; *(of goods)* desembarque *m*.

dis·em·bod·ied (dǐs'ěm-bǒd'ēd) adj. incorpóreo.

dis·em·bod·i·ment (dǐs'ěm-bǒd'ē-mənt) s. separación *f o* liberación *f* del cuerpo.

dis·em·bod·y (dǐs'ěm-bǒd'ē) tr. **-ied, -y·ing** separar del cuerpo.

dis·em·bow·el (dǐs'ěm-bou'əl) tr. desentrañar, destripar.

dis·en·chant (dǐs'ěn-chǎnt') tr. desencantar, desilusionar.

dis·en·chant·er (dǐs'ěn-chǎn'tər) s. desencantador *m*.

dis·en·chant·ment (dǐs'ěn-chǎnt'mənt) s. desilusión *f*, desencanto.

dis·en·cum·ber (dǐs'ěn-kǔm'bər) tr. librar (de impedimento, estorbo).

dis·en·fran·chise (dǐs'ěn-frǎn'chīz') tr. **-chised, -chis·ing** POL. privar de derechos civiles; COM. quitar una concesión.

dis·en·fran·chise·ment (dǐs'ěn-frǎn'chǐz'mənt) s. POL. suspensión de los derechos civiles *f*; COM. suspensión de una concesión.

dis·en·gage (dǐs'ěn-gāj') tr. & intr. **-gaged, -gag·ing** *(to uncouple)* desenganchar(se); *(to free)* soltar(se); *(of gears)* desengranar(se); MIL. retirar(se); AUTO. *(of the clutch)* desembragar(se); *(to separate)* separar(se).

dis·en·gaged (dǐs'ěn-gājd') adj. *(free)* desembarazado, libre; *(loose)* suelto; *(detached)* desenvuelto; AUTO. desembragado.

dis·en·gage·ment (dǐs'ěn-gāj'mənt) s. *(separation)* separación *f*; MIL. retirada de las tropas; AUTO. desembrague *m*, desengranaje *m*.

dis·en·tan·gle (dǐs'ěn-tǎng'gəl) tr. & intr. **-gled, -gling** *(to unravel)* desenredar(se), desenmarañar(se); *(to solve)* resolver(se).

dis·en·tomb (dǐs'ěn-tōōm') tr. exhumar, desenterrar.

dis·en·twine (dǐs'ěn-twīn') tr. **-twined, -twin·ing** *(to unravel)* desenredar(se); *(to untwist)* destorcer(se).

dis·e·qui·lib·ri·um (dǐs-ē'kwə-lǐb'rē-əm, -ěk'wə-) s. desequilibrio.

dis·es·tab·lish (dǐs'ǐ-stǎb'lǐsh) tr. separar la iglesia del estado.

dis·fa·vor (dǐs-fā'vər) I. s. *(disapproval)* desaprobación *f*, desagrado ♦ **to fall into d.** caer en desgracia II. tr. *(not to favor)* desfavorecer; *(to disapprove)* desaprobar.

dis·fig·u·ra·tion (dǐs-fǐg'yə-rā'shən) s. desfiguración *f*.

dis·fig·ure (dǐs-fǐg'yər) tr. **-ured, -ur·ing** *(to deform)* desfigurar; *(to make ugly)* afear.

dis·fig·ure·ment (dǐs-fǐg'yər-mənt) s. var. de **disfiguration**.

dis·fran·chise (dǐs-frǎn'chīz') tr. **-chised, -chis·ing** POL. privar de derechos civiles; COM. quitar una concesión.

dis·gorge (dǐs-gôrj') tr. **-gorged, -gorg·ing** *(to vomit)* devolver, vomitar; *(to discharge)* descargar, derramar —intr. derramarse, vaciarse.

dis·grace (dǐs-grās') I. s. *(loss of honor)* deshonra; *(ignominy)* ignominia II. tr. **-graced, -grac·ing** deshonrar.

dis·grace·ful (dǐs-grās'fəl) adj. vergonzoso.

dis·grun·tle (dǐs-grǔn'tl) tr. **-tled, -tling** disgustar, contrariar.

dis·grun·tled (dǐs-grǔn'tld) adj. *(discontented)* descontento, disgustado; *(crossed)* contrariado.

dis·guise (dǐs-gīz') I. s. disfraz *m* II. tr. **-guised, -guis·ing** disfrazar.

dis·gust (dǐs-gǔst') tr. *(to sicken)* repugnar, asquear; *(to offend)* indignar II. s. repugnancia.

dis·gust·ed (dǐs-gǔs'tǐd) adj. *(sickened)* asqueado, repugnado; *(irritated)* irritado.

dis·gust·ing (dǐs-gǔs'tǐng) adj. *(sickening)* repugnante; *(repellent)* repulsivo.

dish (dǐsh) I. s. *(container, serving)* plato; FAM. *(like)* gusto <golf is not my d. el golf no es de mi gusto>; RAD., TELEV. disco (de antena) II. tr. *(to serve)* servir (comida, bebida); *(to hollow)* ahuecar, hacer cóncavo; G.B. *(to ruin)* arruinar ♦ **to d. out** repartir, dar (consejos, golpes).

dis·har·mo·ny (dǐs-här'mə-nē) s. *(discord)* discordia, falta de armonía; MÚS. disonancia.

dish·cloth (dǐsh'klôth') s. repasador *m*, trapo de fregar.

dis·heart·en (dǐs-här'tn) tr. desanimar, desalentar.

di·shev·el (dǐ-shěv'əl) tr. *(hair)* despeinar; *(clothes)* desaliñar, desarreglar.

di·shev·eled *o* **di·shev·elled** (dǐ-shěv'əld) adj. desaliñado, desarreglado.

dis·hon·est (dǐs-ǒn'ǐst) adj. *(said of people)* deshonesto, deshonrado; *(fraudulent)* fraudulento.

dis·hon·es·ty (dǐs-ǒn'ǐ-stē) s. [pl. **-ties**] *(lack of integrity)* deshonestidad *f*, falta de honradez; *(fraud)* fraude *m*.

dis·hon·or (dǐs-ǒn'ər) I. s. *(loss of honor)* deshonra; *(shame)* vergüenza; COM. rechazo (de cheque, giro) II. tr. *(to bring disgrace upon)* deshonrar; COM. rechazar.

dis·hon·or·a·ble (dǐs-ǒn'ər-ə-bəl) adj. deshonroso.

dish·pan (dǐsh'pǎn') s. barreño, paila para fregar platos.

dish·rag (dǐsh'rǎg') s. trapo de fregar.

dish·ware (dǐsh'wâr') s. juego de platos (de mesa), loza.

dish·wash·er (dǐsh'wǒsh'ər) s. *(persona, máquina)* lavaplatos *m*.

dish·wa·ter (dǐsh'wô'tər) s. agua de fregar platos.

dis·il·lu·sion (dǐs'ǐ-lōō'zhən) I. tr. desilusionar II. s. desilusión *f*.

dis·il·lu·sion·ment (dǐs'ǐ-lōō'zhən-mənt) s. desilusión *f*.

dis·in·cen·tive (dǐs'ǐn-sěn'tǐv) s. falta de incentivo.

dis·in·cli·na·tion (dǐs-ǐn'klə-nā'shən) s. *(reluctance)* desgana, *(aversion)* aversión *f*.

dis·in·clined (dǐs'ǐn-klīnd') adj. maldispuesto.

dis·in·fect (dǐs'ǐn-fěkt') tr. desinfectar.

dis·in·fec·tant (dǐs'ǐn-fěk'tənt) s. & adj. desinfectante *m*.

dis·in·fla·tion (dǐs'ǐn-flā'shən) s. FIN. deflación *f*.

dis·in·fla·tion·ar·y (dǐs'ǐn-flā'shə-něr'ē) adj. deflacionista, deflacionario.

dis·in·for·ma·tion (dǐs-ǐn'fər-mā'shən) s. información incorrecta (para despistar).

dis·in·gen·u·ous (dǐs'ǐn-jěn'yōō-əs) adj. insincero, falso.

dis·in·her·it (dǐs'ǐn-hěr'ǐt) tr. desheredar.

dis·in·te·grate (dǐs-ǐn'tǐ-grāt') tr. & intr. **-grat·ed, -grat·ing** desintegrar(se).

dis·in·te·gra·tion (dǐs-ǐn'tǐ-grā'shən) s. desintegración *f*.

dis·in·ter (dǐs'ǐn-tûr') tr. **-terred, -ter·ring** *(exhume)* desenterrar, exhumar; *(to expose)* exponer.

dis·in·ter·est (dǐs-ǐn'tər-ǐst) s. desinterés *m*.

dis·in·ter·est·ed (dǐs-ǐn'trǐ-stǐd) adj. *(impartial)* desinteresado, imparcial; *(indifferent)* indiferente, desinteresado.

dis·in·ter·me·di·a·tion (dǐs-ǐn'tər-mē'dē-ā'shən) s. FIN. proceso de préstamos directos (sin intervención de bancos).

dis·in·ter·ment (dǐs'ǐn-tûr'mənt) s. desenterramiento, exhumación *f*.

dis·in·vest·ment (dǐs'ǐn-věst'mənt) s. FIN. disminución del capital invertido *f*.

dis·join (dǐs-join') tr. & intr. desunir(se), separar(se).

dis·joint (dǐs-joint') I. tr. & intr. *(to dislocate)* dislocar(se); *(to disarticulate)* desarticular(se); *(to separate)* separar(se) II. adj. MAT. sin elementos comunes, disjunto.

dis·joint·ed (dǐs-join'tǐd) adj. *(dislocated)* dislocado; *(dis-*

articulated) desarticulado; *(incoherent)* incoherente, inconexo.

dis·junc·tion (dĭs-jŭngk′shən) s. *(act)* disyunción *f*, separación *f*; LÓG. disyunción.

dis·junc·tive (dĭs-jŭngk′tĭv) I. adj. disyuntivo, separativo II. s. GRAM. conjunción disyuntiva; LÓG. proposición disyuntiva.

disk (dĭsk) I. s. disco II. tr. AGR. arar con arado de discos.

disk·ette (dĭ-skĕt′) s. COMPUT. disco.

disk pack s. COMPUT. pila *o* lote de discos *m*.

dis·lik·a·ble *o* **dis·like·a·ble** (dĭs-lī′kə-bəl) adj. antipático, odioso.

dis·like (dĭs-līk′) I. tr. **-liked, -lik·ing** tener aversión a, no gustarle a uno II. s. antipatía, aversión *f*.

dis·lo·cate (dĭs′lō-kāt′) tr. **-cat·ed, -cat·ing** *(bones)* dislocar, descoyuntar; *(things)* trastornar, desarreglar.

dis·lo·ca·tion (dĭs′lō-kā′shən) s. *(disarticulation)* dislocación *f*, desarticulación *f*; MED. dislocación; *(disruption)* trastorno, desarreglo.

dis·lodge (dĭs-lŏj′) tr. **-lodged, -lodg·ing** desalojar, echar fuera —intr. mudarse, trasladarse.

dis·lodge·ment *o* **dis·lodg·ment** (dĭs-lŏj′mənt) s. desalojamiento.

dis·loy·al (dĭs-loi′əl) adj. desleal.

dis·loy·al·ty (dĭs-loi′əl-tē) s. [pl. **-ties**] deslealtad *f*.

dis·mal (dĭz′məl) adj. *(sad)* triste; *(depressing)* deprimente; *(dreadful)* terrible, espantoso.

dis·man·tle (dĭs-măn′tl) tr. **-tled, -tling** *(to tear down)* desmantelar; *(to disassemble)* desarmar.

dis·mast (dĭs-măst′) tr. MARÍT. desarbolar.

dis·may (dĭs-mā′) I. tr. *(to upset)* consternar; *(to dishearten)* desalentar II. s. *(consternation)* consternación *f* <*to witness in d.* presenciar con consternación>; *(discouragement)* desaliento.

dis·mem·ber (dĭs-mĕm′bər) tr. desmembrar.

dis·mem·ber·ment (dĭs-mĕm′bər-mənt) s. desmembramiento.

dis·miss (dĭs-mĭs′) tr. *(from employment)* despedir; *(officials)* destituir; *(to allow to leave)* dejar ir, dar permiso para retirarse; *(an assembly)* disolver; *(to reject)* desechar, descartar; *(to dispel)* alejar (de la mente); MIL. *(to discharge)* licenciar; DER. *(a claim)* desestimar, declarar sin lugar.

dis·miss·al (dĭs-mĭs′əl) s. *(of employees)* despido; *(of officials)* destitución *f*; *(of an assembly)* disolución *f*; *(of an idea)* abandono; MIL. licenciamiento; DER. desestimación *f*.

dis·mount (dĭs-mount′) tr. & intr. desmontar(se).

dis·o·be·di·ence (dĭs′ə-bē′dē-əns) s. desobediencia.

dis·o·be·di·ent (dĭs′ə-bē′dē-ənt) adj. desobediente.

dis·o·bey (dĭs′ə-bā′) tr. & intr. desobedecer.

dis·or·der (dĭs-ôr′dər) I. s. *(confusion)* desorden *m*; *(public disturbance)* desorden, disturbio; MED. *(ailment)* trastorno II. tr. *(to disarrange)* desordenar; MED. *(to derange)* trastornar.

dis·or·dered (dĭs-ôr′dərd) adj. *(disarranged)* desordenado; *(deranged)* trastornado.

dis·or·der·ly (dĭs-ôr′dər-lē) adj. *(disarranged)* desordenado; *(unruly)* alborotador.

disorderly conduct s. DER. conducta escandalosa.

dis·or·gan·i·za·tion (dĭs-ôr′gə-nĭ-zā′shən) s. desorganización *f*.

dis·or·gan·ize (dĭs-ôr′gə-nīz′) tr. **-ized, -iz·ing** desorganizar.

dis·o·ri·ent (dĭs-ôr′ē-ĕnt′) tr. desorientar.

dis·o·ri·en·ta·tion (dĭs-ôr′ē-ən-tā′shən) s. desorientación *f*.

dis·own (dĭs-ōn′) tr. *(not to recognize)* desconocer, no reconocer como suyo; *(to repudiate)* repudiar.

dis·par·age (dĭ-spăr′ĭj) tr. **-aged, -ag·ing** *(to belittle)* menospreciar; *(to discredit)* desacreditar.

dis·par·age·ment (dĭ-spăr′ĭj-mənt) s. *(belittlement)* menosprecio; *(discredit)* descrédito.

dis·par·ag·ing (dĭ-spăr′ĭ-jĭng) adj. menospreciativo.

dis·pa·rate (dĭs′pər-ĭt) adj. dispar, desigual.

dis·par·i·ty (dĭ-spăr′ĭ-tē) s. [pl. **-ties**] disparidad *f*, desigualdad *f*.

dis·pas·sion·ate (dĭs-păsh′ə-nĭt) adj. *(devoid of passion)* desapasionado; *(unbiased)* imparcial.

dis·patch (dĭ-spăch′) I. tr. *(to send off)* despachar, enviar <*to d. a message* enviar un mensaje>; *(to complete promptly)* despachar; *(to kill)* despachar, matar II. s. *(sending off)* despacho, envío; *(speed)* diligencia; *(execution)* liquidación *f*; PERIOD., POL. despacho; MIL. parte *m*.

dis·patch·er (dĭ-spăch′ər) s. *(sender)* expedidor *m*; *(of trains, buses)* jefe de control de circulación *m*; COMPUT. seleccionador de tareas *m*.

dis·pel (dĭ-spĕl′) tr. **-pelled, -pel·ling** disipar.

dis·pen·sa·ble (dĭ-spĕn′sə-bəl) adj. prescindible.

dis·pen·sa·ry (dĭ-spĕn′sə-rē) s. [pl. **-ries**] dispensario.

dis·pen·sa·tion (dĭs′pən-sā′shən) s. *(distribution)* reparto, distribución *f*; *(exemption)* dispensa, exención *f*; TEO. designio divino, acto providencial.

dis·pense (dĭ-spĕns′) tr. **-pensed, -pens·ing** *(to distribute)* dispensar, distribuir; *(medicines)* dispensar; *(to administer)* administrar, aplicar (leyes, ordenanzas); *(to exempt)* dispensar, eximir.

dis·pens·er (dĭ-spĕn′sər) s. dispensador *m*.

dis·per·sal (dĭ-spûr′səl) s. dispersión *f*.

dis·perse (dĭ-spûrs′) tr. & intr. **-persed, -pers·ing** dispersar(se).

dis·per·sion (dĭ-spûr′zhən) s. dispersión *f*.

di·spir·it (dĭ-spĭr′ĭt) tr. desalentar, desanimar.

di·spir·it·ed (dĭ-spĭr′ĭ-tĭd) adj. desalentado, desanimado.

dis·place (dĭs-plās′) tr. **-placed, -plac·ing** *(to move)* desplazar; *(to dislodge)* desalojar; *(to dismiss)* destituir; *(to supplant)* substituir, suplantar; FÍS. desplazar.

displaced person s. persona expatriada, expatriado (a causa de una guerra).

dis·place·ment (dĭs-plās′mənt) s. *(movement)* desplazamiento; *(dismissal)* destitución *f*; *(substitution)* reemplazo, sustitución *f*; FÍS., MARÍT., QUÍM. desplazamiento.

displacement ton s. MARÍT. tonelada de desplazamiento.

dis·play (dĭ-splā′) I. tr. *(to exhibit)* exhibir, mostrar; *(to show off)* ostentar, hacer alarde de; *(to unfurl)* desplegar, lucir II. s. *(a showing)* exhibición *f*; *(demonstration)* demostración *f*; *(exposition)* exposición *f*; *(show)* despliegue *m*; *(ostentation)* ostentación *f*; COMPUT. representación visual *f*.

dis·please (dĭs-plēz′) tr. & intr. **-pleased, -pleas·ing** desagradar, disgustar.

dis·pleas·ing (dĭs-plē′zĭng) adj. desagradable.

dis·pleas·ure (dĭs-plĕzh′ər) s. desagrado, disgusto.

dis·port (dĭ-spôrt′) tr. ♦ **to d. oneself** entretenerse, retozar.

dis·pos·a·ble (dĭ-spō′zə-bəl) adj. *(available)* disponible; *(discardable)* desechable.

dis·pos·al (dĭ-spō′zəl) s. *(placement)* disposición *f*, colocación *f*; *(discarding)* eliminación *f*, desecho; *(settlement)* resolución *f*; *(sale)* venta; *(transfer)* traspaso ♦ **at your d.** a su disposición • **garbage d.** aparato triturador para la eliminación de basura.

dis·pose (dĭ-spōz′) tr. **-posed, -pos·ing** *(to place)* disponer, colocar; *(to incline)* volver propenso a ♦ **to d. of** *(by ridding of)* despachar, deshacerse de; *(by attending to)* despachar, resolver; *(by selling)* vender; *(by destroying)* despachar, destruir; *(by discarding)* desechar, deshacerse de; *(by eating)* comer, consumir —intr. disponer.

dis·posed (dĭ-spōzd′) adj. dispuesto.

dis·po·si·tion (dĭs′pə-zĭsh′ən) s. *(mood)* disposición *f*, carácter *m*; *(tendency)* predisposición *f*; *(inclination)* inclinación *f*, propensión *f*; *(arrangement)* disposición, colocación *f*; *(settlement)* disposición ♦ **at the d. of** a la disposición de.

dis·pos·sess (dĭs′pə-zĕs′) tr. *(of property)* desposeer, privar de; *(to evict)* desahuciar, expulsar.

dis·pos·ses·sion (dĭs′pə-zĕsh′ən) s. desposeimiento, privación *f*; *(eviction)* desahucio, expulsión *f*.

dis·proof (dĭs-prōōf′) s. refutación *f*.

dis·pro·por·tion (dĭs′prə-pôr′shən) I. s. desproporción *f* II. tr. desproporcionar.

dis·pro·por·tion·ate (dĭs′prə-pôr′shə-nĭt) adj. desproporcionado.

dis·prove (dĭs-prōōv′) tr. **-proved, -prov·ing** refutar.

dis·put·a·ble (dĭ-spyo͞o′tə-bəl, dĭs′pyə-) adj. disputable, discutible.

dis·pu·tant (dĭ-spyo͞o′nt) adj. & s. disputador *m*.

dis·pu·ta·tion (dĭs′pyə-tā′shən) s. *(argument)* disputa, discusión *f*; *(debate)* debate *m*.

dis·pu·ta·tious (dĭs′pyə-tā′shəs) adj. disputador, discutidor.

dis·pute (dĭ-spyo͞ot′) I. tr. **-put·ed, -put·ing** *(to debate)* disputar, debatir; *(to argue)* discutir, reñir; *(to doubt)* cuestionar, poner en duda; *(to contest for)* disputar, competir por; *(to oppose)* oponerse a, rechazar —intr. *(to debate)* disputar, debatir; *(to argue)* discutir, reñir; *(to quarrel)* pelear II. s. *(debate)* disputa, debate *m*; *(quarrel)* pelea.

dis·qual·i·fi·ca·tion (dĭs-kwŏl′ə-fĭ-kā′shən) s. *(act)* descalificación *f*; *(incapacity)* incapacidad *f*.

dis·qual·i·fy (dĭs-kwŏl′ə-fī′) tr. **-fied, -fy·ing** *(to declare unqualified)* descalificar; *(to incapacitate)* incapacitar.

dis·qui·et (dĭs-kwī′ĭt) I. tr. inquietar, preocupar II. s. *(restlessness)* inquietud *f*; *(worry)* preocupación *f*.

dis·qui·e·tude (dĭs-kwī′ĭ-to͞od′, -tyo͞od′) s. inquietud *f*, preocupación *f*.

dis·qui·si·tion (dĭs′kwĭ-zĭsh′ən) s. RET. disquisición *f*.

dis·re·gard (dĭs′rĭ-gärd′) I. tr. no hacer caso de, no prestar atención a II. s. desatención *f*, negligencia.

dis·re·mem·ber (dĭs′rĭ-mĕm′bər) tr. FAM. no poder recordar —intr. olvidar.

dis·re·pair (dĭs′rĭ-pâr′) s. mal estado, falta de arreglo ♦ **to fall into d.** *(machinery)* descomponerse; *(a house)* caer en ruina.

dis·rep·u·ta·ble (dĭs-rĕp′yə-tə-bəl) adj. *(not respectable)* de mala fama, desacreditado; *(sloppy)* de mala presencia.

dis·re·pute (dĭs′rĭ-pyo͞ot′) s. mala fama, descrédito ♦ **to bring into d.** desprestigiar • **to fall into d.** desprestigiarse, desacreditarse.

dis·re·spect (dĭs′rĭ-spĕkt′) I. s. falta de respeto, descortesía II. tr. faltar el respeto.

dis·re·spect·ful (dĭs′rĭ-spĕkt′fəl) adj. irrespetuoso, descortés.

dis·robe (dĭs-rōb′) tr. & intr. **-robed, -rob·ing** desvestir(se), desnudar(se).

dis·rupt (dĭs-rŭpt′) tr. *(to upset)* perturbar, trastornar; *(to interrupt)* interrumpir, obstruir; *(to rupture)* romper; *(to disorganize)* desorganizar.

dis·rup·tion (dĭs-rŭp′shən) s. *(upset)* perturbación *f*, trastorno; *(interruption)* interrupción *f*, obstrucción *f*; *(disorganization)* desorganización *f*.

dis·rup·tive (dĭs-rŭp′tĭv) adj. *(upsetting)* perturbador; *(interfering)* interruptor, obstructor.

dis·sat·is·fac·tion (dĭs-săt′ĭs-făk′shən) s. insatisfacción *f*, descontento.

dis·sat·is·fied (dĭs-săt′ĭs-fīd′) adj. *(discontent)* insatisfecho, descontento; *(disappointed)* decepcionado.

dis·sat·is·fy (dĭs-săt′ĭs-fī′) tr. **-fied, -fy·ing** *(to fail to satisfy)* no satisfacer, no contentar; *(to disappoint)* decepcionar.

dis·sect (dĭ-sĕkt′, dī-) tr. *(to cut apart)* disecar; *(to analyze)* analizar minuciosamente.

dis·sec·tion (dĭ-sĕk′shən, dī-) s. *(cutting apart)* disecación *f*, disección *f*; *(analysis)* análisis minucioso.

dis·sem·ble (dĭ-sĕm′bəl) tr. **-bled, -bling** *(to conceal)* disimular, encubrir; *(to feign)* simular, fingir —intr. disimular.

dis·sem·i·nate (dĭ-sĕm′ə-nāt′) tr. & intr. **-nat·ed, -nat·ing** diseminar(se), difundir(se).

dis·sem·i·na·tion (dĭ-sĕm′ə-nā′shən) s. diseminación *f*, difusión *f*.

dis·sen·sion (dĭ-sĕn′shən) s. disensión *f*, discordia.

dis·sent (dĭ-sĕnt′) I. intr. disentir, discordar II. s. *(dissension)* disención *f*, discordancia; RELIG. *(nonconformity)* disidencia.

dis·sent·er (dĭ-sĕn′tər) s. disidente *mf*.

dis·ser·ta·tion (dĭs′ər-tā′shən) s. *(discourse)* disertación *f*; *(thesis)* tesis *f*.

dis·ser·vice (dĭs-sûr′vĭs) s. perjuicio, daño.

dis·si·dence (dĭs′ĭ-dns) s. disidencia, disensión *f*.

dis·si·dent (dĭs′ĭ-dnt) adj. & s. disidente *mf*.

dis·sim·i·lar (dĭ-sĭm′ə-lər) adj. disímil, distinto.

dis·sim·i·lar·i·ty (dĭ-sĭm′ə-lăr′ĭ-tē) s. [pl. **-ties**] *(difference)* disimilitud *f*, desemejanza; *(distinction)* distinción *f*.

dis·sim·i·la·tion (dĭ-sĭm′ə-lā′shən) s. disimilación *f*.

dis·sim·u·late (dĭ-sĭm′yə-lāt′) tr. & intr. **-lat·ed, -lat·ing** disimular.

dis·si·pate (dĭs′ə-pāt′) tr. **-pat·ed, -pat·ing** *(to diffuse)* disipar, desvanecer; *(to break up)* dispersar <*to d. the crowd* dispersar a la muchedumbre>; *(to squander)* disipar, derrochar —intr. *(to diffuse)* disiparse, desvanecerse; *(to break up)* dispersarse; *(to indulge)* darse a los placeres.

dis·si·pat·ed (dĭs′ə-pā′tĭd) adj. *(dissolute)* disipado, disoluto; *(squandered)* disipado, derrochado.

dis·si·pa·tion (dĭs′ə-pā′shən) s. *(diffusion)* disipación *f*, desvanecimiento; *(dispersion)* dispersión *f*; *(waste)* derroche *m*, desperdicio; *(dissoluteness)* disipación, libertinaje *m*.

dis·so·ci·ate (dĭ-sō′shē-āt′, -sē-) tr. & intr. **-at·ed, -at·ing** disociar(se).

dis·so·ci·a·tion (dĭ-sō′sē-ā′shən, -shē-) s. disociación *f*.

dis·so·lute (dĭs′ə-lo͞ot′) adj. disoluto, disipado.

dis·so·lute·ly (dĭs′ə-lo͞ot′lē) adv. disolutamente, disipadamente.

dis·so·lu·tion (dĭs′ə-lo͞o′shən) s. *(termination)* disolución *f*, disipación *f*; *(disintegration)* desintegración *f*; *(annulment)* anulación *f*, disolución.

dis·solv·a·ble (dĭ-zŏl′və-bəl) adj. *(soluble)* soluble; *(dispersible)* desintegrable, dispersable.

dis·solve (dĭ-zŏlv′) I. tr. **-solved, -solv·ing** *(to make liquid)* disolver; *(to disintegrate)* desintegrar; *(to terminate)* terminar, disolver; DER. *(to annul)* anular, rescindir —intr. *(to become liquid)* disolverse; *(to disintegrate)* desintegrarse; *(to disperse)* dispersarse; *(to terminate)* terminarse, disolverse; *(to melt into)* deshacerse <*the child dissolved into tears* el niño se deshizo en lágrimas>; CINEM. *(to fade)* hacer un fundido II. s. CINEM. fundido.

dis·so·nance (dĭs′ə-nəns) s. *(discord)* desacuerdo, discordancia; MÚS. disonancia.

dis·so·nant (dĭs′ə-nənt) adj. *(discordant)* discordante; MÚS. disonante.

dis·suade (dĭ-swād′) tr. **-suad·ed, -suad·ing** disuadir, desaconsejar.

dis·sua·sion (dĭ-swā′zhən) s. disuasión *f*.

dis·sua·sive (dĭ-swā′sĭv) adj. disuasivo.

dis·sym·met·ric (dĭs′ĭ-mĕt′rĭk) o **dis·sym·met·ri·cal** (-rĭ-kəl) adj. disimétrico.

dis·taff (dĭs′tăf′) s. *(staff)* rueca; *(woman's work)* quehaceres femeninos; *(women)* las mujeres.

distaff side s. línea femenina, rama femenina de la familia.

dis·tance (dĭs′təns) I. s. *(time, space)* distancia; *(range)* alcance *m*; *(stretch)* trecho, tirada; *(far horizon)* lontananza, lejanía; *(coolness)* frialdad *f*, reserva; MÚS. intervalo ♦ **d. race** carrera de distancia o de fondo • **it is a good d. away** está bastante lejos • **keep one's d.** guardar las distancias, mantener cierta reserva • **within walking d.** suficientemente cerca como para ir andando II. tr. **-tanced, -tanc·ing** *(to place at a distance)* alejar; *(to outdistance)* dejar atrás.

dis·tant (dĭs′tənt) adj. *(far off)* distante, alejado; *(in relationship)* lejano; *(aloof)* reservado, frío.

dis·taste (dĭs-tāst′) s. aversión *f*.

dis·taste·ful (dĭs-tāst′fəl) adj. desagradable, de mal gusto.

dis·tem·per¹ (dĭs-tĕm′pər) I. s. *(of dogs)* moquillo; *(of people)* malestar *m*, destemplanza; *(ill humor)* malhumor *m*; *(disturbance)* desorden *m* II. tr. poner de malhumor.

dis·tem·per² (dĭs-tĕm′pər) PINT. I. s. pintura al temple II. tr. pintar al temple.

dis·tend (dĭ-stĕnd′) tr. & intr. *(to expand)* distender(se); *(to swell)* hinchar(se).

dis·ten·tion o **dis·ten·sion** (dĭ-stĕn′shən) s. *(expansion)* distensión *f*; *(swelling)* hinchazón *f*.

dis·till (dĭ-stĭl′) tr. & intr. destilar.

dis·til·late (dĭs′tə-lāt′, dĭ-stĭl′ĭt) s. QUÍM. destilado.

dis·til·la·tion (dĭs′tə-lā′shən) s. destilación *f*.

dis·till·er (dĭ-stĭl′ər) s. destilador *m*.

dis·till·er·y (dĭ-stĭl′ə-rē) s. [pl. **-ies**] destilería *f*.

dis·tinct (dĭ-stĭngkt′) adj. *(different)* distinto, diferente;

ã rey / ä año / b boca / ch chico / d dar / ĕ el / ē mil / g gato / h joya / hw juez / ī aire / k casa / kw cuan /

(clear) claro, preciso; *(unquestionable)* marcado, indudable.

dis·tinc·tion (dĭ-stĭngk′shən) s. distinción *f* ♦ **to gain d.** distinguirse • **with d.** con (nota de) sobresaliente, con mérito.

dis·tinc·tive (dĭ-stĭngk′tĭv) adj. distintivo, característico.

dis·tinct·ly (dĭ-stĭngkt′lē) adv. *(differently)* de otro modo; *(clearly)* claramente; *(unquestionably)* indudablemente.

dis·tin·guish (dĭ-stĭng′gwĭsh) tr. & intr. distinguir(se) ♦ **to d. oneself** distinguirse, descollar.

dis·tin·guish·a·ble (dĭ-stĭng′gwĭ-shə-bəl) adj. distinguible, discernible.

dis·tin·guished (dĭ-stĭng′gwĭsht) adj. *(elegant)* distinguido, elegante; *(eminent)* notable, eminente.

dis·tort (dĭ-stôrt′) tr. *(to contort)* distorsionar, deformar; *(to misrepresent)* tergiversar, alterar.

dis·tor·tion (dĭ-stôr′shən) s. *(deformation)* distorsión *f*, deformación *f*; *(misrepresentation)* tergiversación *f*, alteración *f*; ELEC., ÓPT. distorsión.

dis·tract (dĭ-străkt′) tr. *(to divert)* distraer; *(to bewilder)* aturdir, turbar.

dis·trac·tion (dĭ-străk′shən) s. *(diversion)* distracción *f*; *(amusement)* diversión *f*; *(frenzy)* frenesí *m*.

dis·traught (dĭ-strôt′) adj. *(worried)* aturdido, turbado; *(crazed)* desequilibrado, demente.

dis·tress (dĭ-strĕs′) I. s. *(grief)* aflicción *f*, pena; *(anxiety)* ansiedad *f*; *(pain)* dolor *m*; *(severe strain)* agotamiento mental; *(danger)* peligro; DER. *(seizure)* embargo II. tr. *(to grieve)* afligir; DER. embargar.

dis·tressed (dĭ-strĕst′) adj. *(afflicted)* afligido; *(anguished)* angustiado; *(weak)* extenuado, agotado; *(in distress)* en peligro; *(poor)* en apuros.

dis·tress·ing (dĭ-strĕs′ĭng) adj. angustioso.

distress signal s. señal de socorro *f*.

dis·trib·u·tar·y (dĭ-strĭb′yə-tĕr′ē) s. [pl. **-ies**] brazo desaguadero de un río.

dis·trib·ute (dĭ-strĭb′yət) tr. **-ut·ed, -ut·ing** *(to dispense)* distribuir, repartir; *(to classify)* clasificar; IMPR. distribuir.

dis·trib·ut·ed (dĭ-strĭb′yə-tĭd) adj. distribuido estadísticamente.

dis·tri·bu·tion (dĭs′trə-byōō′shən) s. *(apportionment)* distribución *f*, reparto; *(classification)* clasificación *f*; IMPR. distribución.

dis·trib·u·tive (dĭ-strĭb′yə-tĭv) I. adj. distributivo II. s. GRAM. adjetivo distributivo.

distributive property s. MAT. propiedad de una operación distributiva *f*.

dis·trib·u·tor (dĭ-strĭb′yə-tər) s. distribuidor *m*.

dis·trict (dĭs′trĭkt) I. s. *(area)* región *f*, comarca; *(of a city)* zona, barrio; POL. *(division)* distrito, partido II. tr. dividir en distritos.

district attorney s. fiscal de un distrito judicial *mf*.

district court s. DER. tribunal federal *m*.

dis·trust (dĭs-trŭst′) I. s. desconfianza, recelo II. tr. *(to mistrust)* desconfiar de; *(to suspect)* sospechar.

dis·trust·ful (dĭs-trŭst′fəl) adj. *(mistrustful)* desconfiado, receloso; *(suspicious)* sospechoso.

dis·turb (dĭ-stûrb′) tr. *(to alter)* perturbar, alterar; *(to upset)* turbar, trastornar; *(to interrupt)* interrumpir; *(to bother)* molestar; *(to disarrange)* desordenar; *(to agitate)* mover, remover (agua, nieve).

dis·tur·bance (dĭ-stûr′bəns) s. *(act)* perturbación *f*, alteración *f*; *(worry)* trastorno; *(interruption)* interrupción *f*; *(bother)* molestia; *(disorder)* desorden *m*; *(public disorder)* disturbio, alboroto; *(dysfunction)* desequilibrio, problema *m* <*an emotional d.* un desequilibrio mental>.

dis·un·ion (dĭs-yōōn′yən) s. desunión *f*.

dis·u·nite (dĭs′yōō-nīt′) tr. & intr. **-nit·ed, -nit·ing** desunir(se), separar(se).

dis·u·ni·ty (dĭs-yōō′nĭ-tē) s. [pl. **-ties**] desunión *f*.

dis·use (dĭs-yōōs′) s. desuso.

ditch (dĭch) I. s. *(trench)* zanja; *(for irrigation)* acequia; *(for drainage)* canal *m*; *(of a road)* cuneta; *(moat)* foso (de castillo, fortificación) ♦ **the D.** G.B. el Canal de la Mancha • **to the last d.** hasta el final II. tr. *(to dig)* cavar zanjas en; *(a vehicle)* meter en la cuneta; FAM. *(to discard)* abandonar.

dith·er (dĭth′ər) s. *(excitement)* nerviosismo, agitación *f*; *(indecision)* estado de indecisión.

dit·to (dĭt′ō) I. s. [pl. **-tos**] *(same as above)* ídem *m*; *(punctuation mark)* comillas (para indicar la repetición de la palabra en la línea más arriba); *(copy)* copia, duplicado II. adv. ídem, del mismo modo III. tr. **-toed, -to·ing** *(to duplicate)* sacar un duplicado de; *(to repeat)* repetir.

dit·ty (dĭt′ē) s. [pl. **-ties**] cancioncita.

ditty bag s. bolsa para guardar cosas pequeñas.

di·u·ret·ic (dī′ə-rĕt′ĭk) adj. & s. MED. diurético.

di·ur·nal (dī-ûr′nəl) adj. *(daily)* diario; *(daytime)* diurno.

di·va·gate (dī′və-gāt′, dĭv′ə-) intr. **-gat·ed, -gat·ing** *(to wander)* vagar; *(to digress)* divagar.

di·van (dī-văn′) s. diván *m*.

dive (dīv) I. intr. **dived** *o* **dove** (dōv), **dived, div·ing** *(from a springboard)* saltar; *(to go headfirst)* zambullirse, tirarse al agua; *(a submarine)* sumergirse; *(professionally)* bucear (un buzo); *(airplane)* bajar en picado; *(to plummet)* caer verticalmente; *(to lunge)* tirarse; *(to plunge into)* lanzarse, meterse de lleno —tr. *(airplane)* hacer bajar en picado a; *(submarine)* sumergir II. s. *(in swimming)* salto; *(leading headfirst)* zambullida; *(of an airplane)* picado; *(of a submarine)* inmersión *f*, sumersión *f*; *(drop)* caída, baja; JER. *(bar)* garito, tugurio.

dive-bomb (dīv′bŏm′) tr. bombardear en picada.

dive-bomb·er (dīv′bŏm′ər) s. AVIA. bombardero de ataque en picada.

div·er (dī′vər) s. DEP. *(platform jumper)* saltador (de trampolín) *m*; *(underwater)* buzo, buceador *m*; ORNIT. *(loon)* somorgujo.

di·verge (dī-vûrj′, dĭ-) intr. **-verged, -verg·ing** *(to branch out)* divergir; *(to deviate)* desviarse, salirse de lo normal; *(to differ)* diferir —tr. desviar.

di·ver·gence (dī-vûr′jəns, dĭ-) *o* **di·ver·gen·cy** (-jən-sē) s. [pl. **-genc·es** *o* **-gen·cies**] divergencia.

di·ver·gent (dī-vûr′jənt, dĭ-) adj. divergente.

di·vers (dī′vərz) adj. diversos, varios.

di·verse (dī-vûrs′, dī-) adj. *(unlike)* diferente, distinto; *(varied)* variado; *(diversified)* diverso.

di·ver·si·fi·ca·tion (dī-vîr′sə-fī-kā′shən, dī-) s. diversificación *f*.

di·ver·si·fy (dī-vûr′sə-fī′, dī-) tr. & intr. **-fied, -fy·ing** diversificar(se).

di·ver·sion (dī-vûr′zhən, dī-) s. *(detour)* desviación *f*; *(distraction)* distracción *f*; *(entertainment)* diversión *f*, entretenimiento; MIL. diversión.

di·ver·sion·ar·y (dī-vûr′zhə-nĕr′ē, dī-) adj. de diversión.

di·ver·si·ty (dī-vûr′sĭ-tē, dī-) s. [pl. **-ties**] *(difference)* diversidad *f*; *(variety)* variedad *f*.

di·vert (dī-vûrt′, dī-) tr. *(to turn aside)* desviar; *(to distract)* distraer; *(to entertain)* divertir, entretener.

Di·ves (dī′vēz′) s. hombre rico.

di·vest (dī-vĕst′, dĭ-) tr. *(to strip)* quitar; *(to deprive)* deprivar; *(to dispossess)* desposeer.

di·ves·ti·ture (dī-vĕs′tĭ-chər) s. despojo, desposeimiento.

di·vide (dī-vīd′) I. tr. **-vid·ed, -vid·ing** *(to separate)* dividir, partir; *(to classify)* clasificar; *(to disunite)* desunir, apartar; *(to apportion)* repartir, distribuir; MAT. dividir —intr. dividirse II. s. divisoria ♦ **the Great D.** los Montes Rocosos (en EE. UU.).

di·vid·ed (dī-vī′dĭd) adj. *(separated in parts)* dividido; *(separated by distance)* separado; BOT. seccionado ♦ **d. highway** carretera con barrera divisoria.

div·i·dend (dĭv′ĭ-dĕnd′) s. COM., MAT. dividendo.

di·vid·er (dī-vī′dər) s. *(separator)* divisor *m*; *(partition)* separación *f*, tabique *m*; MAT. divisor ♦ **dividers** compás de punta seca.

div·i·na·tion (dĭv′ə-nā′shən) s. *(foretelling)* adivinación *f*; *(guess)* adivinanza; *(presentiment)* corazonada.

di·vine¹ (dī-vīn′) I. adj. **-vin·er, -vin·est** divino II. s. *(clergyman)* eclesiástico, clérigo; *(theologian)* teólogo.

di·vine² (dī-vīn′) tr. **-vined, -vin·ing** adivinar —intr. *(to practice divination)* ser adivino; *(to guess)* adivinar.

divine right s. derecho divino.

div·ing (dī′vĭng) s. DEP. *(jump)* clavado, salto (de trampolín); *(underwater)* buceo.

---

diving bell s. campana de buzo.

diving board s. trampolín m.

diving suit s. escafandra, traje de buzo m.

divining rod s. varilla de zahorí (para buscar agua o minerales).

di·vin·i·ty (dĭ-vĭn′ĭ-tē) s. [pl. **-ties**] *(divineness)* divinidad f; *(theology)* teología ♦ **D.** Dios.

di·vis·i·ble (dĭ-vĭz′ə-bəl) adj. *(dividable)* divisible; *(separable)* separable.

di·vi·sion (dĭ-vĭzh′ən) s. *(distribution, category)* división f; *(disagreement)* división; *(partition)* separación f, tabique m; *(section)* sección f, departamento; LÓG., MAT., POL. división.

division of labor s. ECON. división del trabajo f.

division sign s. MAT. signo de la división.

di·vi·sive (dĭ-vī′sĭv) adj. divisivo.

di·vi·sive·ness (dĭ-vī′sĭv-nĭs) s. divisibilidad f.

di·vi·sor (dĭ-vī′zər) s. MAT. divisor m.

di·vorce (dĭ-vôrs′) I. s. divorcio II. tr. **-vorced, -vorc·ing** *(to separate)* divorciar; *(to shed one's spouse)* divorciarse de.

di·vor·cé (dĭ-vôr′sā′, -sē′) s. divorciado.

di·vor·cée (dĭ-vôr′sā′, -sē′) s. divorciada.

di·vulge (dĭ-vŭlj′) tr. **-vulged, -vulg·ing** divulgar, revelar (un secreto).

Dix·ie (dĭk′sē) s. estados del sur de EE. UU.

Dix·ie·land (dĭk′sē-lănd′) s. MÚS. jazz típico de Nueva Orleans.

diz·zi·ness (dĭz′ē-nĭs) s. *(giddiness)* mareo; *(from height, speed, or illness)* vértigo.

diz·zy (dĭz′ē) I. adj. **-zi·er, -zi·est** *(giddy)* mareado; *(bewildered)* aturdido, confundido; *(vertiginous)* vertiginoso <*d. speed* velocidad vertiginosa>; FAM. *(foolish)* lelo, bobo II. tr. **-zied, -zy·ing** *(to make giddy)* marear; *(from height, speed, or illness)* dar vértigo; *(to bewilder)* aturdir, confundir.

Dji·bou·ti (jĕ-bōō′tē) s. Djibouti.

DNA (dē′ĕn-ā′) s. BIOQUÍM. ácido desoxirribonucleico.

do¹ §G11 (dōō) I. tr. **did** (dĭd), **done** (dŭn), **do·ing** *(to execute)* hacer; *(to carry out)* hacer, cumplir con <*to do one's duty* cumplir con el deber de uno>; *(to produce)* hacer, producir; *(to tidy up)* arreglar, limpiar; *(to wash)* fregar, limpiar; *(justice, homage)* rendir, tributar; *(to work as)* dedicarse a <*I do gardening* me dedico a la jardinería>; *(to work out by studying)* hacer, preparar <*do lesson number ten for tomorrow* preparen la lección número diez para mañana>; *(to study)* estudiar <*I am doing engineering* estoy estudiando ingeniería>; *(to play the role of)* hacer de, desempeñar el papel de; *(to cook)* cocinar <*is this steak done?* ¿está cocinado (suficientemente) este bistec?>; *(to render)* hacer <*to do something for someone* hacer algo por alguien>; *(to present a play)* representar <*the Comédie Française did "La Voix humaine"* la Comedia Francesa representó "La voz humana">; *(said of nails, hair)* hacerse, arreglarse <*women do their hair and nails before going to a party* las mujeres se arreglan el cabello y las uñas antes de ir a una fiesta>; *(to write)* escribir, preparar <*he's doing a book on whales* está preparando un libro sobre las ballenas>; *(to work)* trabajar en <*the gardener is doing the rosebushes* el jardinero está trabajando en los rosales>; *(to cover)* hacer <*I can do a mile in four minutes* yo puedo hacer una milla en cuatro minutos>; *(to tour)* ver, recorrer <*we did three cities in two days* recorrimos tres ciudades en dos días>; *(to meet the needs of)* convenir, venir bien <*this room will do us very nicely* este cuarto nos vendrá muy bien>; *(to decorate)* decorar; FAM. *(to serve time)* cumplir una condena de <*he did six years in Alcatraz* cumplió una condena de seis años en Alcatraz>; JER. *(to swindle)* estafar, engañar ♦ **to do again** volver a hacer, hacer de nuevo • **to do a number on** JER. *(to confuse)* confundir o estafar; *(to make fun of)* mofarse de • **to do away with** *(to do without)* suprimir; *(to abolish)* abolir; FAM. *(to kill)* matar • **to do for** servir de <*this kitchen table will do me for a desk* esta mesa de cocina me servirá de escritorio> • **to do in** JER. *(to kill)* matar, liquidar; *(to ruin)* arruinar <*a dishonest cashier can do you in pretty quickly* un cajero deshonrado te puede arruinar

bien pronto>; *(to exhaust)* agotar, cansar • **to do one credit** decir mucho en favor de uno • **to do (one) good** sentarle bien, hacer bien (a uno) <*a walk after dinner will do us good* una caminata después de la cena nos hará bien> • **to do one's best** hacer todo lo posible, hacer cuanto uno puede • **to do one's thing** hacer lo que a uno más le gusta • **to do over** *(to do again)* volver a hacer; FAM. *(to redecorate)* redecorar • **to do the trick** JER. surtir efecto • **to do time** FAM. cumplir una condena • **to do up** *(laces)* atarse; *(buttons)* abrocharse; *(to wrap up)* envolver, empaquetar • **to do with** *(to get along on)* conformarse con <*I do with very little money* me conformo con muy poco dinero>; *(to find desirable)* venirle a uno (muy) bien <*we could do with a nap* nos vendría muy bien una siesta> • **what can I do for you?** ¿en qué puedo serle útil?, ¿en qué puedo servirle? —intr. *(to behave)* conducirse, comportarse; *(to strive)* obrar, actuar; *(to fare)* andar, irle a uno <*to be doing well at school* irle a uno bien en la escuela>; *(to feel)* encontrarse, sentirse <*how are you doing?* ¿cómo te encuentras?>; *(to serve the purpose)* servir <*this coat will do for another season* este tapado me servirá para otra temporada> ♦ **how do you do?** ¿cómo está usted? • **nothing doing!** JER. ¡nada de eso!, ¡ni hablar! • **that will do!** ¡basta ya! • **that will never do** o **that won't do** *(it is improper)* eso no se hace, eso es inaceptable; *(it is inconvenient)* eso no conviene, eso no es conveniente • **to be done** estar terminado <*the ironing is done* el planchado está terminado> • **to be done for** FAM. *(to be doomed)* estar muerto o desahuciado; *(to be ruined)* estar arruinado o echado a perder • **to be well-done** CUL. *(foods in general)* estar bien cocido, asado o frito; *(meat)* muy hecho • **to do well by** tratar bien • **to do badly** irle mal <*because of his illness, he is doing badly* por su enfermedad, le está yendo mal> • **to do or die** vencer o morir • **to do well** prosperar, pasarlo bien • **to do without** pasar sin, prescindir de • **to make do with** arreglárselas con <*I will make do with these boots for another season* me las arreglaré con estas botas por otra temporada> —aux. [usado en interrogaciones] <*do you think it's funny?* ¿crees que eso es gracioso?>; [usado en negaciones] <*I don't think it's funny* no lo encuentro gracioso>; [usado en inversiones] <*never did I say it was funny* nunca dije que fuera gracioso>; [usado como énfasis] <*do behave* pórtate bien <*I did ask you to behave* te pedí que te portaras bien> <*I do like it this way* me gusta de esta manera>; [como substituto de una frase] <*I asked you to behave, didn't I?* te pedí que te portaras bien, ¿nó?> <*do you understand me? Yes, I do* ¿me entiendes? sí> <*she behaves well, doesn't she?* ella se porta bien, ¿verdad?> II. s. [pl. **do's** o **dos**] *(party)* fiesta <*the staff put on a great do at Christmas* el personal hizo una gran fiesta para Navidad> ♦ **the do's and don'ts** lo que se debe y lo que no se debe hacer.

do² (dō) s. [pl. **dos**] MÚS. do.

do·a·ble (dōō′ə-bəl) adj. factible, realizable.

doc·ile (dŏs′əl, -īl′) adj. dócil.

do·cil·i·ty (dŏ-sĭl′ĭ-tē) s. docilidad f.

dock¹ (dŏk) I. s. MARÍT. *(wharf)* muelle m; *(basin)* dársena; *(between two piers)* dique m; *(for trucks, cars)* andén m II. tr. *(ship)* hacer entrar en dársena; *(spacecraft)* acoplar —intr. *(ship)* atracar al muelle; *(spacecraft)* acoplarse.

dock² (dŏk) I. s. ZOOL. *(tail)* maslo; VET. *(stump)* muñón de cola m II. tr. VET. *(to cut)* cercenar, cortar (la cola); *(to fine)* multar, castigar con una multa; *(to deduct)* descontar (de un salario).

dock³ (dŏk) s. DER. *(defendant's stand)* banquillo del acusado.

dock·age (dŏk′ĭj) s. MARÍT. *(charge)* muellaje m, derechos de atraque m; *(facilities)* dársena; *(docking)* entrada al dique, atraque m.

dock·et (dŏk′ĭt) I. s. *(agenda)* agenda, orden del día m; *(label)* rótulo, marbete m; DER. sumario de causas II. tr. *(in an agenda)* incluir en una agenda; DER. asentar en el registro de sumarios de causas.

dock·hand (dŏk′hănd′) s. estibador m, trabajador portuario.

dock·ing (dŏk′ĭng) s. MARÍT. atracamiento; ASTRONÁUT. acoplamiento.

dock·work·er (dŏk′wûr′kər) s. MARÍT. estibador *m*, trabajador portuario.

dock·yard (dŏk′yärd′) s. *(shipbuilding yard)* astillero; *(naval yard)* arsenal *m*.

doc·tor (dŏk′tər) I. s. *(physician)* médico, doctor *m*; *(university graduate)* doctor II. tr. *(to treat)* tratar, atender; *(to repair)* remendar, componer; *(to falsify)* adulterar —intr. practicar la medicina, ser médico.

doc·tor·al (dŏk′tər-əl) adj. doctoral.

doc·tor·ate (dŏk′tər-ĭt) s. doctorado.

doc·tri·naire (dŏk′trə-nâr′) s. & adj. doctrinario.

doc·trine (dŏk′trĭn) s. doctrina.

doc·u·ment (dŏk′yə-mənt) I. s. documento II. tr. documentar, probar con documentos.

doc·u·men·tal (dŏk′yə-mĕn′tl) adj. de documentos.

doc·u·men·ta·ry (dŏk′yə-mĕn′tə-rē) adj. & s. [pl. **-ries**] documental *m*.

doc·u·men·ta·tion (dŏk′yə-mĕn-tā′shən) s. documentación *f*.

dod·der (dŏd′ər) intr. *(to shake)* temblar, temblequear; *(to move feebly)* andar con pasos vacilantes.

dod·der·ing (dŏd′ər-ĭng) adj. senil.

dodge (dŏj) I. tr. **dodged, dodg·ing** *(to move aside)* esquivar; *(by cunning)* evadir, eludir —intr. *(to move aside)* echarse a un lado; *(to practice cunning)* andar con argucias o rodeos II. s. *(quick move)* regate *m*, esguince *m*; *(evasive plan)* evasiva; *(stratagem)* argucia, truco.

dodg·er (dŏj′ər) s. *(trickster)* trampista *mf*, tramposo; *(handbill)* anuncio o cartel pequeño.

do·do (dō′dō) s. [pl. **-does** o **-dos**] ORNIT. ave extinta de la isla Mauricio; FAM. *(fogy)* vejestorio; *(stupid person)* bobo.

doe (dō) s. [pl. **does** o **doe**] *(female deer)* gama; *(female kangaroo)* cangura.

do·er (dōō′ər) s. *(agent)* agente *mf*, realizador *m*; *(active person)* persona activa.

does (dŭz) tercera persona sing. del pres. indic. de **do¹**.

doe·skin (dō′skĭn′) s. *(pelt)* piel de gamo *f*, ante *m*; *(soft fabric)* tejido fino de lana.

does·n't (dŭz′ənt) contr. de **does not**.

doff (dŏf) tr. *(to take off)* sacarse, quitarse; *(one's hat)* quitarse; *(discard)* tirar, desechar.

dog (dŏg) I. s. *(animal)* perro; *(male animal)* macho; *(contemptible person)* perro, canalla *mf*; *(for gripping)* cabezal *m*; FAM. *(fellow)* tipo <*he's a lucky d.* es un tipo de suerte>; *(fiasco)* bomba, desastre *m* <*that play was some d.* esa obra de teatro fue un tremendo desastre> ◆ **dogs** JER. pies *m*, patas II. tr. **dogged, dog·ging** *(to track)* perseguir (como un perro); *(to follow)* seguir.

dog·catch·er (dŏg′kăch′ər) s. cazador de perros *m*, perrero.

dog days s.pl. canícula.

doge (dōj) s. HIST. dux *m*.

dog-ear (dŏg′îr′) I. s. esquina o punta doblada de una página II. tr. doblar la esquina o punta de.

dog-eared (dŏg′îrd′) adj. sobado (libro, página).

dog-eat-dog (dŏg′ĕt-dŏg′) adj. atrozmente competitivo.

dog·face (dŏg′fās′) s. JER., MIL. soldado de la infantería de EE. UU. en la Segunda Guerra Mundial.

dog·fight (dŏg′fīt′) s. *(brawl)* refriega; MIL. combate aéreo reñido.

dog·ged (dŏg′ĭd) adj. *(inflexible)* inflexible; *(willful)* testarudo; *(stubborn)* terco, obstinado.

dog·ged·ly (dŏ′gĭd-lē) adv. inflexiblemente.

dog·ged·ness (dŏ′gĭd-nĭs) s. inflexibilidad *f*.

dog·ger·el (dŏg′ər-əl) s. versos ramplones, coplas de ciego.

dog·gy bag (dŏ′gē) s. receptáculo para llevarse los restos de comida de un restaurante.

dog·gone (dŏg′gôn′) s. FAM. maldito.

dog·grel (dŏg′rəl) s. var. de **doggerel**.

dog·house (dŏg′hous′) s. caseta de perro ◆ **in the d.** JER. en desgracia.

do·gie o **do·gy** (dō′gē) s. [pl. **-gies**] becerro sin madre.

dog·ma (dŏg′mə) s. [pl. **-mas** o **-ma·ta** (-mə-tə)] FILOS., TEO. dogma *m*.

dog·mat·ic (dôg-măt′ĭk) adj. dogmático.

dog·ma·tism (dôg′mə-tĭz′əm) s. dogmatismo.

dog·ma·tist (dôg′mə-tĭst) s. dogmatizador *m*.

dog officer s. perrero.

do-good·er (dōō′gŏŏd′ər) s. FAM. bienhechor *m*.

dog paddle s. brazada con los brazos y piernas bajo el agua.

dog sled o **dog sledge** s. trineo tirado por perros.

dog tag s. placa de identificación para perros y, en EE. UU., para militares.

dog-tired (dôg′tīrd′) adj. rendido.

dog-trot (dôg′trŏt′) s. trote suave *m*, trote lento.

dog·wood (dôg′wŏŏd′) s. BOT. cornejo, sanguiñuelo.

doi·ly o **doy·ly** o **doy·ley** (doi′lē) s. [pl. **-lies** o **-leys**] tapete *m*.

do·ing (dōō′ĭng) s. *(act)* hecho, obra <*it was not of his d.* no fue obra de él>; *(effort)* esfuerzo <*it's a task that will take some d.* es una tarea que requerirá bastante esfuerzo> ◆ **doings** *(actions)* hechos, obras; *(social events)* fiestas; *(activities)* actividades.

do-it-your·self (dōō′ĭt-yər-sĕlf′) adj. FAM. diseñado para ser hecho por uno mismo.

dol·drums (dōl′drəmz′, dôl′-) s.pl. [ú. con v. sing.] *(inactivity)* estancamiento, inactividad *f*; *(listlessness)* decaimiento, depresión *f*; MARÍT. calmas ecuatoriales.

dole¹ (dōl) I. s. *(distribution)* distribución *f*, reparto; *(alms)* limosna; G.B. *(relief payments)* subsidio de paro ◆ **to be on the d.** estar acogido al paro II. tr. **doled, dol·ing** dar limosna ◆ **to d. out** repartir, distribuir en pequeñas cantidades.

dole² (dōl) s. ANT. pesar *m*, aflicción *f*.

dole·ful (dōl′fəl) adj. triste.

do-lit·tle (dōō′lĭt′l) s. & adj. perezoso.

doll (dŏl) I. s. *(toy, child, woman)* muñeca; *(darling)* encanto II. intr. & tr. ◆ **to d. (oneself) up** JER. emperifollar(se).

dol·lar (dŏl′ər) s. FIN. dólar *m* ◆ **to bet one's bottom d.** JER. *(to bet)* apostar hasta el último centavo; *(to be sure)* apostarse la cabeza.

dollar cost averaging s. FIN. inversión fija de una cantidad de dólares en la bolsa de valores.

dollar diplomacy s. diplomacia del dólar.

dollar sign s. signo del dólar.

dol·ly (dŏl′ē) I. s. [pl. **-lies**] *(toy)* muñeca; *(platform)* carretilla; *(for thumping clothes)* batidor *m*; *(locomotive)* pequeña locomotora; MEC. *(tool)* aguantadora, contrarremachadora; CINEM., TELEV. travelín *m*, plataforma rodante II. intr. **-lied, -ly·ing** ◆ **to d. in** CINEM., TELEV. acercarse o alejarse la cámara.

do·lor·ous (dō′lə-rəs, dŏl′ə-) adj. doloroso, penoso.

dol·phin (dŏl′fĭn, dôl′-) s. *(mammal)* delfín *m*; *(fish)* dorado.

dolt (dōlt) s. tonto, idiota *mf*.

do·main (dō-mān′) s. *(territory)* dominio; *(field)* campo; FÍS. *(region)* región de imantación uniforme *f*; MAT. *(set)* dominio; DER. *(right)* dominio.

dome (dōm) I. s. *(shape)* bóveda, cima; ARQ. *(roof)* cúpula, domo; POÉT. *(mansion)* mansión *f*, edificio majestuoso; JER. *(head)* coco II. tr. **domed, dom·ing** *(to cover)* cubrir con una cúpula; *(to shape)* dar forma de cúpula —intr. *(to swell)* abombarse; *(to rise)* elevarse en forma de cúpula.

do·mes·tic (də-mĕs′tĭk) I. adj. *(of the household)* doméstico; *(of home life)* hogareño, casero; *(tame)* doméstico; ECON. *(not foreign)* nacional, del país II. s. *(servant)* doméstico, sirviente *m*; *(product)* producto nacional o del país ◆ **domestics** *(products)* productos nacionales o del país; *(linens)* ropa blanca.

do·mes·ti·cate (də-mĕs′tĭ-kāt′) tr. **-cat·ed, -cat·ing** *(to train)* domesticar, amansar; *(to naturalize)* aclimatar; *(to make domestic)* volver casero.

do·mes·ti·ca·tion (də-mĕs′tĭ-kā′shən) s. *(of animals)* domesticación *f*; *(of plants)* aclimatación *f*.

do·mes·tic·i·ty (dō′mĕ-stĭs′ĭ-tē) s. [pl. **-ties**] *(of animals)* domesticidad *f*; *(home life)* vida casera ◆ **domesticities** asuntos domésticos.

---

ng inglés / ŏ la / ō bou / ô corre / oi oigo / ōō uno / ou auto / yōō ciudad / w hueco / y yo / z mismo

domestic science s. economía doméstica.
dom·i·cile (dŏm′ĭ-sīl′, dŏ′mĭ-) I. s. domicilio II. tr. **-ciled, -cil·ing** domiciliar —intr. residir.
dom·i·nance (dŏm′ə-nəns) o **dom·i·nan·cy** (-nən-sē) s. dominación f.
dom·i·nant (dŏm′ə-nənt) I. adj. dominante II. s. (character) rasgo dominante; (species) especie dominante f; MÚS. dominante.
dom·i·nate (dŏm′ə-nāt′) tr. & intr. **-nat·ed, -nat·ing** dominar.
dom·i·na·tion (dŏm′ə-nā′shən) s. dominación f ♦ **dominations** RELIG. dominaciones.
dom·i·neer (dŏm′ə-nîr′) tr. & intr. dominar, tiranizar.
Dom·i·ni·ca (dŏm′ə-nē′kə) s. Dominica.
Do·min·i·can (də-mĭn′ĭ-kən) adj. & s. (of the Dominican Republic) dominicano; RELIG. dominico.
Dominican Republic s. República Dominicana.
do·min·ion (də-mĭn′yən) s. dominio ♦ **D.** dominio británico • **dominions** RELIG. dominaciones.
dom·i·no[1] (dŏm′ə-nō′) s. [pl. **-noes** o **-nos**] (robe) dominó, disfraz con capucha m; (cape) capa con capucha.
dom·i·no[2] (dŏm′ə-nō′) s. [pl. **-noes** o **-nos**] dominó (ficha) ♦ **dominoes** o **dominos** [ú. con v. sing.] dominó (juego).
domino theory s. teoría del efecto producido en cadena.
don[1] (dŏn) s. (Spanish gentleman) caballero, hidalgo; G.B. (head) catedrático ♦ **D.** don, señor.
don[2] (dŏn) tr. **donned, don·ning** (to put on) ponerse; (to assume) asumir.
do·nate (dŏ′nāt′) tr. **-nat·ed, -nat·ing** donar.
do·na·tion (dō-nā′shən) s. (act) donación f; (gift) donativo.
do·na·tor (dō′nā′tər) s. donador m, donante mf.
done (dŭn) I. part. p. de **do**[1] II. adj. (finished) terminado, hecho; CUL. (cooked) cocido, hecho ♦ **d.!** ¡convenido!, ¡trato hecho! • **d. for** FAM. (exhausted) agotado, rendido; (doomed) vencido • **d. with** acabado, terminado • **well-d.** CUL. bien cocido o hecho • **well d.!** ¡muy bien!
don·jon (dŏn′jən, dŭn′-) s. torre del homenaje f.
don·key (dŏng′kē, dŭng′-) s. [pl. **-keys**] burro, asno.
do·nor (dō′nər) s. donador m, donante mf.
do-noth·ing (dōō′nŭth′ĭng) I. adj. que no hace hada II. s. (idler) perezoso; (lazy person) persona sin iniciativa.
don't (dŏnt) contr. de **do not**.
do·nut (dō′nət) s. var. de **doughnut**.
doo·dad (dōōd′ dăd′) s. FAM. chuchería.
doo·dle (dōōd′l) FAM. I. intr. **-dled, -dling** garabatear, hacer garabatos (distraídamente) II. s. garabato.
doo·hick·ey (dōō′hĭk′ē) s. [pl. **-eys**] FAM. chuchería.
doom (dōōm) I. s. (destiny) destino; (ruin) ruina, perdición f; (death) muerte f; (sentence) sentencia; RELIG. (Last Judgment) juicio final II. tr. (to destine) destinar; (to condemn) condenar.
doom·say·er (dōōm′sā′ər) s. pesimista mf.
dooms·day (dōōmz′dā′) s. día del juicio final m.
door (dôr) s. puerta ♦ **behind closed doors** a puerta cerrada • **next d. to** (at the house next to) en o de la casa de al lado; (almost) casi • **to close the d. upon** cerrar la puerta a • **to knock the d. down** echar la puerta abajo • **to lay at the d. of** FIG. echar la culpa a • **to lie at one's d.** FIG. recaer sobre uno • **to show to the d.** acompañar hasta la puerta • **to slam the d.** (to close the door) dar un portazo; (to reject) cerrar la puerta • **to slam the d. in someone's face** dar a alguien con la puerta en las narices.
door·bell (dôr′bĕl′) s. timbre (de la puerta) m.
door·jamb (dôr′jăm′) s. jamba de puerta.
door·keep·er (dôr′kē′pər) s. portero.
door·knob (dôr′nŏb′) s. perilla o pomo (de la puerta).
door·man (dôr′măn′) s. portero.
door·mat (dôr′măt′) s. felpudo, estera.
door·nail (dôr′nāl′) s. clavo de puerta ♦ **dead as a d.** completamente muerto.
door·sill (dôr′sĭl′) s. umbral m.
door·step (dôr′stĕp′) s. escalón de la puerta m ♦ **at one's d.** FIG. cerca de uno.
door·stop (dôr′stŏp′) s. (wooden strip) tope de puerta m; (to keep a door open) retenedor de puerta m.

door-to-door (dôr′tə-dôr′) adj. de puerta en puerta ♦ **d. salesperson** persona que vende a domicilio.
door·way (dôr′wā′) s. puerta, entrada.
dope (dōp) I. s. (lubricant) lubricante m; (varnish) barniz m; FAM. (narcotic) narcótico, droga; JER. (stupid person) tonto, idiota mf; (information) informes m o datos (de naturaleza personal) II. tr. **doped, dop·ing** FAM. (to drug) narcotizar, drogar ♦ **to d. out** (to figure out) calcular, deducir —intr. drogarse.
dop·ey o **dop·y** (dō′pē) adj. **-i·er, -i·est** JER. (drugged) drogado; (lethargic) atontado, aletargado; (stupid) tonto.
Do·ric (dôr′ĭk) s. & adj. dórico.
dorm (dôrm) s. FAM. (room) dormitorio; (building) residencia para estudiantes.
dor·man·cy (dôr′mən-sē) s. BIOL. (of plants) estado latente; (of animals) letargo.
dor·mant (dôr′mənt) adj. (inactive) inactivo, durmiente; (of an animal) en estado letárgico; (of a plant) en estado latente.
dor·mer (dôr′mər) s. ventana vertical de buhardilla.
dor·mi·to·ry (dôr′mĭ-tôr′ē) s. [pl. **-ries**] (room) dormitorio; (building) residencia.
dor·mouse (dôr′mous′) s. ZOOL. lirón m.
dor·sal (dôr′səl) adj. dorsal.
dorsal fin s. ICT. aleta dorsal.
do·ry[1] (dôr′ē) s. [pl. **-ries**] esquife de fondo plano m.
do·ry[2] (dôr′ē) s. [pl. **-ries**] ICT. pez de San Pedro m.
dos·age (dō′sĭj) s. FARM., MED. (determination) dosificación f, posología f; (amount) dosis f.
dose (dōs) I. s. (quantity) dosis f; JER. (disease) enfermedad venérea (esp. gonorrea) II. tr. **dosed, dos·ing** MED. (to treat) medicinar; (to divide) dosificar.
do·sim·e·ter (dō-sĭm′ĭ-tər) s. FÍS., MED. dosímetro.
do·sim·e·try (dō-sĭm′ĭ-trē) s. MED. dosimetría.
dos·si·er (dŏs′ē-ā′) s. expediente m.
dot[1] (dŏt) I. s. (mark) punto; (symbol of multiplication) signo de multiplicación; (amount) pequeña cantidad; TELEG. (in Morse) punto; MÚS. (mark) puntillo; MAT. (decimal point) punto de decimal ♦ **d. on the d.** FAM. (on time) a la hora; (exactly) exactamente; en punto • **three dots** puntos suspensivos II. tr. **dot·ted, dot·ting** (to mark) poner el punto a; (to form with) puntear, dibujar una cosa con puntos; (to scatter) salpicar.
dot[2] (dŏt, dō) s. dote mf.
dot·age (dō′tĭj) s. chochez f.
dot·ard (dō′tərd) s. viejo o vieja chocha.
dote (dŏt) intr. chochear ♦ **d. on** adorar.
dot product s. FÍS., MAT. producto escalar.
dot·ty (dŏt′ē) adj. **-ti·er, -ti·est** chiflado.
dou·ble (dŭb′əl) I. adj. (twofold) doble, duplo; (ambiguous) doble, ambiguo; (accommodating two) doble, para dos <a d. sleeping bag una bolsa de dormir para dos>; (folded) doblado; BOT. doble <d. chrysanthemums crisantemos dobles> ♦ **d. entry** TEN. partida doble II. s. (increased twofold) doble m, duplo; (duplicate) duplicado, copia; (fold) doblez m, pliegue m; (bet) apuesta combinada; CINEM., TEAT. (understudy) substituto; (stunt person) doble mf ♦ **doubles** DEP. dobles • **on o at the d.** FAM. con toda rapidez; MIL. a paso ligero III. tr. **-bled, -bling** (to make twice as great) doblar, duplicar; (to fold in two) doblar, plegar; (to add another layer to) poner doble; (to repeat) redoblar ♦ **to be doubled up with pain** retorcerse de dolor • **to d. back** doblar • **to d. up** hacer doblarse (en dos) —intr. (to increase twofold) doblarse, duplicarse; TEAT. doblar ♦ **to d. as** hacer las veces de, servir como • **to d. back** (to reverse direction) volver uno sobre sus pasos • **to d. for** sustituir a • **to d. up** (from pain) doblarse en dos; (to curl up) acurrucarse; (to share) compartir la misma habitación o cama • **to d. up with laughter** desternillarse de risa IV. adv. (doubly) doble, doblemente; (two together) dos juntos <we will be sleeping d. tonight dormiremos los dos juntos esta noche> ♦ **d. or nothing** doble o nada.
double agent s. espía que trabaja para dos potencias enemigas mf, espía doble.
dou·ble-bar·reled (dŭb′əl-băr′əld) adj. (of double effect) de doble efecto; ARM. (of a gun) de dos cañones.

double bass s. MÚS. contrabajo, violón m.
double bassoon s. contrafagot m.
double bed s. cama doble.
double boiler s. cacerola doble (usada para el baño de María).
dou·ble-breast·ed (dŭb′əl-brĕs′tĭd) adj. COST. cruzado.
dou·ble-check (dŭb′əl-chĕk′) tr. & intr. verificar por segunda vez.
double chin s. papada.
dou·ble-cross (dŭb′əl-krôs′) JER. I. tr. traicionar (a un cómplice) II. s. traición f.
dou·ble-cross·er (dŭb′əl-krô′sər) s. JER. traidor m.
double date s. cita doble (de dos parejas).
dou·ble-deal·er (dŭb′əl-dē′lər) s. (cheat) embustero; (traitor) traidor m.
dou·ble-deck·er (dŭb′əl-dĕk′ər) s. (bus) omnibus de dos pisos m; (ship) navío de dos cubiertas; (sandwich) emparedado doble.
dou·ble-dig·it (dŭb′əl-dĭj′ĭt) adj. de dos dígitos.
dou·ble-edged (dŭb′əl-ĕjd′) adj. de dos filos, de doble filo.
double feature s. CINEM. programa doble (con dos películas) m.
double jeopardy s. DER. juzgamiento de una persona por segunda vez.
dou·ble-joint·ed (dŭb′əl-join′tĭd) adj. de articulaciones dobles.
double knit s. TEJ. material de tejido doble m.
dou·ble-park (dŭb′əl-pärk′) tr. & intr. estacionar en doble fila.
dou·ble-quick (dŭb′əl-kwĭk′) I. adj. rapidísimo II. s. MIL. paso ligero o rápido III. intr. MIL. marchar a paso ligero o rápido.
dou·ble-space (dŭb′əl-spās′) intr. & tr. **-spaced, -spac·ing** escribir a máquina con doble espacio.
double standard s. normas de conducta doble (esp. para el hombre y la mujer).
dou·blet (dŭb′lĭt) s. (pair) pareja; HIST. (jacket) casaca, jubón m; GRAM. (word) doblete m ◆ **doublets** doblete, parejo (en juegos de dados).
double take s. reacción tardía.
double talk s. (gibberish) galimatías, tonterías; (ambiguous language) lenguaje ambiguo o de doble sentido.
double time s. (wage) paga doble (por horas extra de trabajo); MIL. (step) paso ligero; MÚS. (rhythm) compás binario.
double vision s. OFTAL. visión doble f, diplopia.
dou·bloon (dŭ-blōōn′) s. NUMIS. doblón español m.
dou·bly (dŭb′lē) adv. (twice) doblemente; (in duplicate) por duplicado.
doubt (dout) I. tr. (to be skeptical about) dudar; (to mistrust) poner en tela de juicio; (to distrust) desconfiar de —intr. no decidirse, dudar II. s. (uncertainty) duda; (lack of trust) desconfianza ◆ **beyond d.** fuera de duda • **in d.** dudoso • **no d.** sin duda, indudablemente.
doubt·er (dou′tər) s. escéptico.
doubt·ful (dout′fəl) adj. (uncertain) dudoso; (ambiguous) ambiguo; (irresolute) indeciso.
doubt·ful·ness (dout′fəl-nĭs) s. duda.
doubt·less (dout′lĭs) I. adj. seguro II. adv. (certainly) sin duda, indudablemente; (probably) probablemente.
douche (dōōsh) I. s. (jet of water) ducha, irrigación f; (instrument) ducha, irrigador m II. tr. & intr. **douched, douch·ing** duchar(se), irrigar(se).
dough (dō) s. (mixture) masa, pasta; JER. (money) dinero, plata.
dough·boy (dō′boi′) s. (bread dough) bolita de pasta frita; FAM., MIL. (soldier) soldado de infantería de EE. UU. de la Primera Guerra Mundial.
dough·nut (dō′nət) s. rosquilla, buñuelo.
dough·ty (dou′tē) adj. **-ti·er, -ti·est** valeroso, valiente.
dough·y (dō′ē) adj. **-i·er, -i·est** pastoso.
dour (dōōr, dour) adj. (stern) severo; (obstinate) obstinado; (sullen) hosco, agrio.
douse (dous) tr. **doused, dous·ing** (to immerse) sumergir; (to drench) empapar, mojar; (to extinguish) extinguir —intr. empaparse.

dove[1] (dŭv) s. ORNIT. paloma; FIG. (pacifist) pacifista mf.
dove[2] (dōv) un pret. de **dive**.
dove·tail (dŭv′tāl′) I. s. CARP. cola de milano II. tr. CARP. ensamblar o machihembrar a cola de milano; (to connect) encajar —intr. encajar.
dov·ish (dŭv′ĭsh) adj. (innocent) columbino, inocente; (pacifist) pacifista.
dow·a·ger (dou′ə-jər) s. (widow) viuda con viudedad; (elderly woman) señora mayor.
dow·dy (dou′dē) I. adj. **-di·er, -di·est** (shabby) desaliñado, andrajoso; (old-fashioned) pasado de moda II. s. [pl. -dies] mujer desaliñada.
dow·el (dou′əl) I. s. clavija II. tr. sujetar o alinear con clavijas.
dow·er (dou′ər) I. s. (property) viudedad f; (dowry) dote f II. tr. asignar viudedad.
down[1] (doun) I. adv. (downward) abajo, hacia abajo <from the top d. de arriba hacia abajo>; (away from this place) allá <d. at the shore allá en la playa>; (in writing) por escrito, COM. (in advance) como adelanto ◆ **d. and out** (without money) sin un real, pobrísimo; (in boxing) fuera de combate • **d. below** abajo • **face d.** boca abajo • **further d.** más abajo • **up and d.** de arriba abajo II. adj. descendente, que va hacia abajo <a d. escalator una escalera mecánica que va hacia abajo>; (at a reduced level) reducido; (sick) enfermo <d. with the flu enfermo con la gripe>; (depressed) deprimido; COM. (said of payment) inicial, a cuenta ◆ **to be d. on** tenerle tirria o inquina a III. prep. abajo <d. the hill cuesta abajo> ◆ **d. the centuries** a través de los siglos • **d. the road** más abajo IV. s. descenso, caída ◆ **ups and downs** altibajos V. tr. (motion) bajar, derribar; (food) tragar, engullir; (liquids) vaciar de un trago; (an airplane) derribar —intr. bajar, descender.
▲ En algunos casos el adverbio down no se traduce separadamente; su sentido está dado por el verbo propiamente dicho <to write down escribir, anotar> <to go down ir> <to cut down recortar, rebajar>.
down[2] (doun) s. (feathers) plumón m; (soft substance) pelusa, vello.
down-at-heel (doun′ət-hēl′) o **down-at-the-heel** (-ət-thə-hēl′) adj. (worn) gastado; (slovenly) desaliñado, desaseado.
down·beat (doun′bēt′) I. s. MÚS. señal f inicial del director de una orquesta; FAM. (depression) depresión f II. adj. pesimista, sombrío.
down·cast (doun′kăst′) adj. (depressed) abatido, desalentado; (downward) hacia abajo, bajo <d. glance mirada baja>; (inclined) inclinado, descendente.
down·er (dou′nər) s. JER. (tranquilizer) tranquilizante m; (experience) experiencia o acontecimiento que deprime.
down·fall (doun′fôl′) s. (ruin) ruina; (of rain) chaparrón m, caída de lluvia; (of snow) caída de nieve, nevada.
down·fall·en (doun′fô′lən) adj. arruinado.
down·grade (doun′grād′) I. s. (slope) bajada, pendiente f; (downward trend) descenso II. tr. **-grad·ed, -grad·ing** disminuir (de categoría, importancia).
down·heart·ed (doun′här′tĭd) adj. descorazonado, abatido.
down·hill (doun′hĭl′) I. adv. cuesta abajo II. adj. inclinado, en declive.
down·play (doun′plā′) tr. minimizar (significado, importancia).
down·pour (doun′pôr′) s. chaparrón m, aguacero.
down·range (doun′rānj′) adv. MIL. a cierta distancia del lugar de lanzamiento (de un misil).
down·right (doun′rīt′) I. adj. (complete) absoluto, completo; (forthright) franco, categórico II. adv. (thoroughly) completamente; (categorically) categóricamente.
Down's syndrome (dounz) s. MED. mongolismo.
down·stage (doun′stāj′) TEAT. I. adv. al frente del escenario, hacia el proscenio II. s. frente del escenario m, proscenio.
down·stairs (doun′stârz′) I. adv. & adj. (lower floor) en o del piso de abajo; (main floor) en o de la planta baja II. s.pl. planta baja.
down·stream (doun′strēm′) I. adv. agua o río abajo II. adj. en dirección de la corriente.

---

ng inglés / ŏ la / ō bou / ô corre / oi oigo / ōō uno / ou auto / yōō ciudad / w hueco / y yo / z mismo

down·stroke (doun'strōk') s. *(line)* trazo hacia abajo (en la escritura); MEC. carrera descendente de un pistón.

down·swing (doun'swĭng') s. DEP., MEC. gira hacia abajo; COM. *(falling off)* bajón en la actividad comercial o económica *m.*

down·time (doun'tīm') s. período de inactividad (de la maquinaria de una fábrica).

down-to-earth (doun'tə-ûrth') adj. práctico, realista.

down·town (doun'toun') I. adv. hacia o en el centro de una ciudad. II. adj. del centro III. s. centro de una ciudad.

down·trend (doun'trĕnd') s. tendencia descendente.

down·trod·den (doun'trŏd'n) adj. *(stepped on)* pisoteado; *(oppressed)* oprimido, esclavizado.

down·turn (doun'tûrn') s. COM., FIN. baja, bajón *m.*

down·ward (doun'wərd) I. adv. *(descending)* hacia abajo; *(more recently)* desde II. adj. descendente.

down·wards (doun'wərdz) adv. *(descending)* hacia abajo; *(in time)* hacia una época posterior.

down·wind (doun'wĭnd') adv. & adj. de o a sotavento, a favor del viento.

down·y (dou'nē) adj. -i·er, -i·est *(covered with down)* cubierto de plumón; *(soft)* aterciopelado, suave.

dow·ry (dou'rē) s. pl. -ries *(money, property)* dote *f*; *(talent)* dote natural *m*, don *m.*

dowse (douz) intr. **dowsed, dows·ing** buscar agua o minerales con una varilla divinatoria.

Dow theory (dou) s. FIN. teoría de pronosticación en la bolsa de valores (establecida por Charles H. Dow).

dox·ol·o·gy (dŏk-sŏl'ə-jē) s. pl. -gies RELIG. doxología.

doy·en (doi-ĕn') s. decano.

doy·enne (doi-ĕn') s. miembro femenino más antiguo de un grupo.

doze (dōz) I. intr. **dozed, doz·ing** dormitar ♦ **to d. off** dormirse, echar una cabezada II. s. sueño ligero, cabezada.

doz·en (dŭz'ən) I. s. pl. **doz·en** o **doz·ens** docena ♦ **baker's d.** docena de fraile • **dozens of times** FIG. miles de veces II. adj. docena de.

drab[1] (drăb) I. adj. **drab·ber, drab·best** *(brownish)* pardusco, pardo; *(dull)* deslustrado, ordinario; *(monotonous)* monótono, gris (vida, existencia) II. s. *(cloth)* sayal *m*; *(color)* color pardo.

drab[2] (drăb) s. prostituta, ramera.

drab·ness (drăb'nĭs) s. *(monotony)* monotonía; *(shabbiness)* desaliño.

drach·ma (drăk'mə) s. FIN. dracma.

dra·co·ni·an (drə-kō'nē-ən) adj. draconiano.

draft (drăft, dräft) I. s. *(air current)* corriente de aire *f*; *(of a chimney)* tiro; *(of a drawing, plan)* bosquejo; *(of a document)* borrador *m*; *(of a writing)* versión *f*; *(blueprint)* plano; *(gulp)* trago; MIL. *(conscription)* servicio militar, quinta; MARÍT. calada; COM. giro, letra de cambio ♦ **on d.** de barril II. tr. *(a bill)* hacer un anteproyecto de; *(a drawing)* esbozar; *(a writing)* hacer un borrador de; *(to compose)* redactar <to d. a speech redactar un discurso>; MIL. *(to induct)* llamar al servicio militar, reclutar III. adj. *(said of a horse)* de tiro; *(said of beer)* de barril.

draft board s. MIL. junta de reclutamiento.

draft·ee (drăf-tē', dräf-) s. MIL. recluta *m*, conscripto.

draft·ing (drăf'tĭng, dräf'-) s. dibujo (mecánico o arquitectónico).

drafts·man (drăfts'mən, dräfts'-) s. dibujante *m*, diseñador *m.*

draft·y (drăf'tē, dräf'-) adj. -i·er, -i·est que tiene corrientes de aire.

drag (drăg) I. tr. **dragged, drag·ging** *(to haul)* arrastrar; *(river, lake)* dragar, rastrear; *(to bring forcibly)* llevar de los pelos <we always have to d. him to the dentist siempre tenemos que llevarlo de los pelos al dentista>; *(to prolong)* alargar interminablemente ♦ **to d. along** arrastrar • **to d. in** *(someone)* hacer entrar a la fuerza; *(a subject)* traer de los pelos • **to d. out** sacar —intr. arrastrar(se); *(to trail)* arrastrarse; *(to lag behind)* rezagarse; *(to pass slowly)* hacerse interminable, no acabar nunca; JER. *(to draw on a cigarette)* dar una pitada ♦ **to d. on** hacerse interminable, no acabar nunca II. s. *(act)* arrastre *m*; *(harrow)* grada; *(hook)* rastra; *(drawback)* estorbo; *(resistance)* resistencia al avance; JER. *(bore)* pesado; *(puff)* chupada, pitada; *(street)* calle *f*; *(road)* carretera ♦ **in d.** JER. vestido de mujer (un hombre, o viceversa).

drag·ger (drăg'ər) s. bote de pesca que arrastra las redes *m.*

drag·gle (drăg'əl) tr. **-gled, -gling** manchar de barro —intr. *(to dirty)* mancharse de barro; *(to straggle)* rezagarse.

drag·gy (drăg'ē) adj. -gi·er, -gi·est *(listless)* aburrido; JER. *(tiresome)* pesado.

drag·net (drăg'nĕt') s. *(net)* red barredera; *(roundup)* pesquisa.

drag·on (drăg'ən) s. *(animal)* dragón *m*; *(person)* fiera.

drag·on·fly (drăg'ən-flī') s. ENTOM. libélula.

dra·goon (drə-gōōn') I. s. MIL. dragón *m* II. tr. coaccionar.

drag race s. carrera de automóviles de aceleración.

drain (drān) I. tr. *(to draw off)* drenar, desaguar; *(to drink)* beber; *(to empty)* vaciar; *(to exhaust)* agotar —intr. *(to draw off)* desaguarse, desecarse; *(to become empty)* vaciarse II. s. *(conduit)* desagüe *m*, desaguadero; *(something that exhausts)* desgaste *m* ♦ **down the d.** malgastado, por la ventana <to throw money down the d. tirar dinero por la ventana>.

drain·age (drā'nĭj) s. *(emptying)* drenaje *m*; *(artificial system)* alcantarillado; *(natural system)* cuenca.

drain·er (drā'nər) s. *(for water, sewage)* escurridero; *(for dishes)* escurreplatos; *(colander)* colador *m.*

drain·pipe (drān'pīp') s. caño de desagüe.

drake (drāk) s. ZOOL. pato (macho).

dram (drăm) s. *(weight)* dracma (unidad de peso); *(small drink)* traguito, copita; *(a bit)* pizca, triza.

dra·ma (drä'mə, drăm'ə) s. *(play)* drama *m*; *(play production)* arte escénico.

Dram·a·mine (drăm'ə-mēn') s. FARM. dramamina (marca registrada).

dra·mat·ic (drə-măt'ĭk) adj. dramático.

dra·mat·ics (drə-măt'ĭks) s.pl. [ú. con v. sing. o pl.] *(exaggerated behavior)* histrionismo; TEAT. arte dramático, teatro.

dram·a·tist (drăm'ə-tĭst, drä'mə-) s. dramaturgo.

dram·a·ti·za·tion (drăm'ə-tĭ-zā'shən, drä'mə-) s. escenificación *f*, dramatización *f.*

dram·a·tize (drăm'ə-tīz', drä'mə-) tr. **-tized, -tiz·ing** *(for the stage)* escenificar; *(to present in a dramatic way)* dramatizar.

dram·a·turge (drăm'ə-tûrj', drä'mə-) s. TEAT. dramaturgo.

drank (drăngk) cf. **drink.**

drape (drāp) I. tr. **draped, drap·ing** *(to adorn)* adornar con colgaduras; *(to cover)* cubrir <I draped a towel around my shoulders me cubrí los hombros con una toalla>; *(to arrange in loose folds)* drapear; *(to hang limply)* colgar; *(to rest limply)* echar <he draped his legs over the chair echó las piernas encima de la silla> —intr. caer II. s. caída ♦ **drapes** cortinas.

drap·er (drā'pər) s. G.B. pañero.

drap·er·y (drā'pə-rē) s. pl. -ies *(cloth)* paños; *(fabrics)* telas; G.B. *(business)* pañería, mercería ♦ **draperies** cortinas.

dras·tic (drăs'tĭk) adj. drástico.

draught (drăft, dräft) s., v., & adj. G.B. var. de **draft.**

draughts (drăfts, dräfts) s. G.B. juego de damas.

draw (drô) I. tr. **drew** (drōō), **drawn** (drôn), **draw·ing** *(to ull)* tirar de, halar; *(to lead)* conducir, llevar <she drew us into the room nos condujo a la habitación>; *(curtains, drapes)* correr; *(to cause to flow)* sacar <a pump drawing water una bomba que saca agua>; *(to inhale)* aspirar, tomar; *(to displace water)* calar, tener un calado de; *(to pull out)* sacar <the man drew a pistol el hombre sacó una pistola>; *(to attract)* atraer; *(to induce to act)* incitar, conducir; *(to provoke)* provocar; suscitar <they drew enemy fire provocaron el fuego del enemigo>; *(to infer)* sacar <I drew the wrong conclusion saqué una conclusión equivocada>; *(salary)* cobrar; *(document)* redactar; *(cards)* robar; *(game, contest)* empatar; *(to stretch taut)* tensar; *(a line)* trazar; *(to formulate)* formular, hacer <to d. a comparison hacer una comparación>; ARTE. dibujar; COM. *(interest)* ganar, devengar <the account does not d. interest la

ā rey / ä año / b boca / ch chico / d dar / ě el / ē mil / g gato / h joya / hw juez / ī aire / k casa / kw cuan /

cuenta no devenga interés>; *(to withdraw money)* sacar, retirar; *(to use a check)* girar, extender ♦ **to d. a blank** *(to fail to find)* no encontrar nada; *(to fail to remember)* no recordar nada • **to d. attention** llamar la atención • **to d. blood** sacar sangre, hacer sangrar • **to d. down** mermar, consumir • **to d. in** esbozar, hacer un croquis de • **to d. lots** echar suertes • **to d. out** *(conversation)* sacar conversación a; *(information)* sonsacar; *(to prolong)* prolongar, alargar • **to d. straws** echar pajas • **to d. together** unir, juntar • **to d. the line** trazar un límite • **to d. up** *(to write)* redactar, preparar; *(to halt)* parar —intr. *(to proceed)* avanzar; *(to contract)* encogerse; *(to pour)* vaciarse; *(to take in air)* tirar; *(to pull out a weapon)* sacar el arma; *(to call upon a supply)* servirse, hacer uso; CINEM., TEAT. ser popular, venderse; COM. *(to use a fund)* girar; DEP. *(to tie)* empatar; ARTE. *(to sketch)* dibujar ♦ **to d. away** apartarse • **to d. back** echarse para atrás • **to d. near** acercarse • **to d. on** *(to get near)* aproximarse, acercarse; *(to take from)* recurrir a • **to d. up** pararse II. s. *(pull)* tiro, tracción *f*; *(attraction)* atracción *f*; *(air intake)* tiro; *(lottery, lots)* sorteo; *(tie)* empate *m*.

draw·back (drô'băk') s. *(disadvantage)* desventaja; *(shortcoming)* inconveniencia; COM. reintegro de derechos de aduana.

draw·bridge (drô'brĭj') s. *(rising)* puente levadizo; *(pivoting)* puente giratorio.

draw·er (drô'ər) s. *(storage place)* cajón *m*, gaveta; *(sketcher)* dibujante *mf*; COM. librador *m*, girador *m* ♦ **drawers** *(women's)* bombachas; *(men's)* calzoncillos.

draw·ing (drô'ĭng) s. ART. dibujo; *(sketch)* bosquejo, diagrama *m*; *(lottery)* lotería, sorteo.

drawing account s. TEN. cuenta de adelantos.

drawing board s. tablero de dibujo.

drawing card s. atracción *f*, atractivo <*Caruso was a great d.* Caruso era un gran atractivo>.

drawing pen s. tiralíneas *m*.

drawing room s. *(room)* salón *m*; *(reception)* recepción *f*; *(in a train)* compartimiento.

drawl (drôl) I. intr. arrastrar las palabras, hablar lentamente —tr. pronunciar lentamente II. s. voz cansina.

drawn (drôn) part. p. de **draw**.

draw·string (drô'strĭng') s. *(cord)* cordón *m*; *(ribbon)* lazo.

dray (drā) I. s. carretón *m*, carro II. tr. acarrear, carretear.

dray·age (drā'ĭj) s. *(transport)* acarreo, carretaje *m*; *(charge)* precio de acarreo.

dread (drĕd) I. s. *(fear)* pavor *m*, terror *m*; *(anticipation)* aprensión *f*; ANT. *(awe)* temor *m* II. tr. *(to fear)* temer, tener terror de; *(to anticipate)* anticipar (con temor) —intr. tener mucho temor *o* terror III. adj. espantoso, terrible.

dread·ful (drĕd'fəl) adj. espantoso, terrible.

dread·nought (drĕd'nôt') s. MARÍT. acorazado.

dream (drēm) I. s. *(sleep)* sueño; *(reverie)* sueño, ensueño; *(trance)* sueño; *(hope)* sueño, esperanza; *(beautiful thing)* belleza, sueño <*the Alps are a d.* los Alpes son un sueño> II. intr. dreamed *o* dreamt (drĕmt), dream·ing *(to daydream)* imaginar, fantasear; *(to have a deep aspiration)* soñar con, aspirar a <*he dreams of being a lawyer* aspira a ser abogado> —tr. soñar; *(to pass idly)* pasar soñando ♦ **to d. of** soñar con • **to d. up** hallar, inventar <*to d. up a solution* inventar una solución>.

dream·er (drē'mər) s. soñador *m*.

dream·land (drēm'lănd') s. país de los sueños *m* ♦ **to be in d.** estar soñando.

dreamt (drĕmt) un pret. y part. p. de **dream**.

dream·world (drēm'wûrld') s. mundo de ensueños.

dream·y (drē'mē) adj. -i·er, -i·est *(dreamlike)* como un sueño, de ensueño; *(soothing)* tranquilizante, sereno; *(daydreaming)* soñador; FAM. *(wonderful)* maravilloso, precioso <*my girlfriend is d.* mi novia es maravillosa>.

drea·ri·ness (drîr'ē-nĭs) s. *(bleakness)* aspecto lúgubre, tristeza; *(gloom)* melancolía; *(boredom)* aburrimiento.

drea·ry (drîr'ē) adj. -ri·er, -ri·est *(bleak)* deprimente, melancólico; *(gloomy)* tenebroso, desapacible; *(barren)* pelado; *(uninteresting)* monótono, aburrido.

dredge¹ (drĕj) I. s. *(for harbors)* draga, rastra; *(for shellfish)* red barredera, brancada II. tr. **dredged, dredg·ing** *(harbors)* dragar, rastrear; *(to fish)* pescar con una brancada ♦ **to d. up** desenterrar —intr. dragar.

dredge² (drĕj) tr. **dredged, dredg·ing** CUL. *(with sugar)* espolvorear (con azúcar); *(with flour)* enharinar.

dredg·er (drĕj'ər) s. MARÍT. draga; CUL. espolvoreador *m*.

dregs (drĕgz) s.pl. *(residue)* poso, heces *f*; FIG. *(trash)* escoria <*the d. of society* la escoria de la sociedad>.

drench (drĕnch) tr. *(to wet)* empapar; *(to fill)* saturar, inundar; VET. dar un purgante a.

dress (drĕs) I. s. *(clothing)* vestido, traje *m*; *(apparel)* vestimenta, ropa II. tr. *(to put clothes on)* vestir; *(to decorate)* decorar, adornar; *(hair)* peinar, arreglar; *(wounds)* curar; *(garden)* cultivar; *(food)* aderezar, condimentar ♦ **dressed to kill** vestida muy elegantemente • **dressed to the nines** de punta en blanco —intr. *(to put clothes on oneself)* vestirse; MIL. alinearse ♦ **to d. down** regañar • **to d. up** vestirse de etiqueta, vestirse bien III. adj. *(for semiformal wear)* de vestir <*in offices men wear d. shirts* en las oficinas los hombres usan camisas de vestir>; *(calling for formal clothes)* de etiqueta <*a d. reception* una recepción de etiqueta>.

dress ball s. baile de gala, baile de etiqueta *m*.

dress code s. reglamento de la vestimenta.

dress designer s. COST. diseñador de moda *m*.

dress·er¹ (drĕs'ər) s. *(well-dressed person)* persona que viste bien; TEAT. ayuda de cámara.

dress·er² (drĕs'ər) s. *(bureau)* cómoda, tocador *m*; *(cupboard)* aparador *m*, armario.

dress·ing (drĕs'ĭng) s. *(act)* acto de vestir; *(manure)* abono; MED. vendajes *m*, hilas; CUL. *(sauce)* aliño, salsa; *(stuffing)* relleno.

dressing gown s. bata, salto de cama.

dressing room s. *(in a theater)* camerino, camarín *m*; *(in a house)* sala de vestir, tocador *m*.

dressing table s. tocador *m*, coqueta.

dress·mak·er (drĕs'mā'kər) s. modista *mf*, costurera.

dress·mak·ing (drĕs'mā'kĭng) s. costura (arte y oficio).

dress rehearsal s. ensayo general, ensayo final.

dress suit s. traje de etiqueta *m*.

dress·y (drĕs'ē) adj. -i·er, -i·est elegante.

drew (drōo) pret. de **draw**.

drib·ble (drĭb'əl) I. intr. -bled, -bling *(to trickle)* gotear, escurrir gota a gota; *(to drool)* babear, babosear; *(in soccer)* gambetear; *(in basketball)* hacer dribling, driblear —tr. *(to trickle)* escurrir gota a gota; *(in soccer)* gambetear; *(in basketball)* driblear II. s. *(trickle)* goteo, hilo <*a d. of blood* un hilo de sangre>; *(small quantity)* gota, pizca; *(in soccer)* gambeta; *(in basketball)* dribling *m*.

drib·let (drĭb'lĭt) s. *(drop)* gota (minúscula); *(small amount)* cantidad pequeña, pizca.

drier (drī'ər) s. *(appliance)* secador *m*; *(machine)* secadora; *(clothes rack)* tendedero; *(dish rack)* escurreplatos; *(substance)* desecante *m*, secante *m*.

drift (drĭft) I. intr. *(to be carried off course)* ir a la deriva; *(to be carried by water, air)* ser arrastrado por la corriente; *(to roam)* vagar, vagabundear; *(to accumulate)* amontonarse, apilarse —tr. llevar, arrastrar II. s. *(flotsam)* lo llevado por una corriente; *(tendency)* tendencia; *(deviation)* deriva, desviación *f*; *(of sand, snow)* pila, montón *m*; *(direction)* dirección *f*, rumbo <*the d. of the conversation* el rumbo de la conversación>; GEOL. terreno de acarreo; MARÍT. dirección ♦ **to get the d.** FAM. entender, comprender.

drift·er (drĭf'tər) s. trotamundos *mf*, vagabundo.

drift·wood (drĭft'wŏod') s. madera flotante.

drill¹ (drĭl) I. s. *(tool)* torno, taladro; *(for oil prospecting)* perforadora, trépano; *(machine)* taladradora; *(exercises)* ejercicios repetitivos (de enseñanza, adiestramiento); *(monkey)* dril *mf*; *(mollusk)* molusco gasterópodo; *(cloth)* dril *m*, tela cruda (de algodón *o* lino) II. intr. & tr. *(act)* taladrar, perforar; *(to bore a well)* perforar; *(to exercise)* ejercitar; *(to train)* adiestrar; *(to teach)* enseñar por medio de repetición.

drill² (drĭl) AGR. I. s. *(furrow)* surco, hilera; *(tool)* sembradora mecánica II. tr. sembrar *o* plantar en hileras.

drill·ing (drĭl'ĭng) I. s. *(boring)* perforación *f*; *(exercise)*

ejercicio; *(training)* instrucción *f*, adiestramiento **II.** adj. para barrenado.
drill press s. prensa taladradora.
drink (drĭngk) **I.** tr. & intr. **drank** (drăngk), **drunk** (drŭngk), **drink·ing** beber, tomar <*I never d. tea* nunca tomo té> ♦ **to d. in** *(to take in)* devorar; *(to soak up)* absorber • **to d. like a fish** beber como una esponja • **to d. oneself into** beber hasta alcanzar un estado de • **to d. someone under the table** FAM. aguantar más la bebida que alguien • **to d. to** brindar por, beber a la salud de • **to d. up** FAM. bebérselo todo, terminar una bebida **II.** s. *(beverage)* bebida; *(excessive drinking)* bebida <*d. will be the death of you* la bebida será tu perdición>; *(liquor)* bebida, copa; *(swallow)* trago, buche *m* ♦ **soft d.** refresco, bebida no alcohólica • **strong d.** bebida alcohólica • **to take to d.** darse a la bebida • **to give someone a d.** dar de beber a alguien.
drink·a·ble (drĭng′kə-bəl) **I.** adj. potable, bebible **II.** s. FAM. bebida.
drink·er (drĭng′kər) s. bebedor *m*.
rink·ing (drĭng′kĭng) s. *(act)* beber *m*; *(habit)* bebida <*to have a d. problem* tener un problema con la bebida>.
drinking water s. agua potable.
drip (drĭp) **I.** tr. **dripped, drip·ping** echar (a gotas) —intr. gotear **II.** s. *(drop)* gota; *(sound of drops)* goteo, goteadero; ARQ. goterón *m*; JER. *(bore)* pelma *m*, pesado.
drip-dry (drĭp′drī′) **I.** adj. que seca rápidamente sin arrugas al estar colgado **II.** intr. **-dried, -dry·ing** secarse rápidamente sin arrugas al estar colgado.
drip·ping (drĭp′ĭng) **I.** s. goteo ♦ **drippings** CUL. *(juices)* jugo, grasa (de un asado) **II.** adv. completamente <*d. wet* completamente mojado>.
drive (drīv) **I.** tr. **drove** (drōv), **driv·en** (drĭv′ən), **driv·ing** *(a vehicle)* conducir, guiar; *(passengers)* llevar; *(distance)* recorrer; *(to push)* empujar; *(to force to work)* hacer trabajar; *(to compel)* forzar, obligar; *(a nail)* clavar; *(a machine)* hacer funcionar, accionar; *(a stake)* hincar; *(to put in)* introducir, meter ♦ **to d. away** alejar, apartar • **to d. back** *(to push back)* hacer retroceder; *(to take in a car)* acompañar en coche • **to d. in** clavar • **to d. off** alejar, apartar • **to d. out** *(to drive away)* echar; *(to force to come out)* hacer salir —intr. *(a vehicle)* conducir, guiar; *(to travel by car)* ir en coche; *(rain, snow)* golpear, azotar ♦ **to d. at** insinuar, querer decir • **to d. away** irse en coche • **to d. back** regresar en coche • **to d. by** pasar por • **to d. on** seguir el camino • **to d. through** pasar (por) **II.** s. *(act)* conducción *f*, manejo; *(ride)* vuelta en coche; *(journey)* viaje *m*; *(roadway)* carretera, autopista; *(campaign)* campaña; *(vigor)* vigor *m*, energía; *(push)* empuje *m*, agresividad *f*; MEC. transmisión *f*; AUTO. tracción *f*; PSIC. impulso, urgencia <*homicidal d.* impulso homicida>; MIL. ofensiva, ataque vigoroso ♦ **d. belt** correa de transmisión • **to go for a d.** dar una vuelta en coche.
drive-in (drīv′ĭn′) s. lugar que atienda a los clientes sin que se bajen del automóvil (cine, restaurante, banco).
driv·el (drĭv′əl) **I.** intr. *(to slobber)* babosear, babear; *(to talk nonsense)* decir tonterías, bobear —tr. decir balbuceando **II.** s. *(saliva)* baba; *(nonsense)* boberías.
driv·en (drĭv′ən) **I.** part. p. de **drive II.** adj. ♦ **a d. person** una persona compulsiva • **d. snow** nieve amontonada por el viento.
driv·er (drī′vər) s. chofer *mf*, conductor *m*.
drive shaft s. eje de transmisión *m*.
drive-up (drīv′ŭp′) adj. con acceso para automovilistas (restaurante, banco).
drive·way (drīv′wā′) s. camino de entrada.
driv·ing (drī′vĭng) **I.** adj. *(impelling)* impulsor, motriz <*d. force* fuerza motriz>; *(violent)* violento; *(energetic)* enérgico, activo; AUTO. de conducción **II.** s. *(act)* acción de conducir *f*; *(motoring)* automovilismo; DEP. golpe inicial (en golf) *m*.
driz·zle (drĭz′əl) **I.** intr. **-zled, -zling** lloviznar, garuar —tr. rociar, salpicar **II.** s. llovizna, garúa.
droll (drōl) adj. **-er, -est** *(amusing)* cómico, gracioso; *(odd)* extraño, raro.
drom·e·dar·y (drŏm′ĭ-dĕr′ē, drŭm′-) s. [pl. **-ies**] dromedario.

drone[1] (drōn) s. *(bee)* zángano, abejón *m*; *(loafer)* haragán *m*, perezoso; *(aircraft)* aeroplano de control remoto.
drone[2] (drōn) **I.** intr. **droned, dron·ing** *(to buzz)* zumbar; *(to speak)* hablar monótonamente —tr. decir en forma monótona **II.** s. *(buzz)* zumbido; MÚS. *(bagpipe)* roncón de gaita *m*; *(tone)* tono sostenido.
drool (drōol) **I.** intr. *(to salivate)* babosear, babear; *(to show desire)* caérsele la baba; *(to talk nonsense)* decir tonterías, bobear —tr. decir balbuceando **II.** s. *(saliva)* baba, saliva; *(silly talk)* tonterías.
droop (drōop) **I.** intr. *(to hang)* inclinarse, doblarse; *(trees, eyelids)* caerse; *(flowers)* marchitarse; *(head)* inclinarse; *(shoulders)* encorvarse, estar encorvado; *(to become exhausted)* debilitarse; *(to become dejected)* desanimarse, decaerse **II.** s. *(of trees, eyelids)* caída; *(of shoulders)* encorvamiento, encorvadura; *(of the head)* inclinación *f*.
droop·ing (drōo′pĭng) adj. *(sloping)* inclinado; *(sagging)* bajo, caído; *(said of shoulders)* encorvado; FIG. *(fallen)* abatido, lánguido.
drop (drŏp) **I.** s. *(of a liquid)* gota; *(trace)* poco, pizca <*not a d. of pity* ni una pizca de compasión>; *(earring)* arete *m*, pendiente *m*; *(candy)* pastilla <*cough d.* pastilla para la tos>; *(fall)* bajada, caída; *(height of fall)* altura; *(difference in levels)* desnivel *m*; *(in prices)* baja; *(in value, quality)* disminución *f*; *(slope)* pendiente *f*, declive *m*; *(abyss)* precipicio; *(by parachute)* lanzamiento; *(for messages)* buzón *m*; TEAT. telón *m*; ELECTRÓN. conexión de terminal *f* ♦ **a d. in the bucket** una gota de agua en el mar • **drops** MED. gotas **II.** tr. **dropped, drop·ping** *(to drip)* caer en gotas, gotear; *(to fall)* caer a tierra, desplomarse; *(wind)* disminuir, amainar; *(temperature, prices)* bajar; *(value, quality)* disminuir; *(conversation)* terminarse; *(to die)* morir de repente; *(to faint)* desmayarse, desvanecerse ♦ **to d. behind** quedarse atrás • **to d. in** *o* **by** pasar (por casa de alguien) • **to d. off** *(leaves)* caer; *(part)* caerse, desprenderse; *(to diminish)* disminuir; *(to die)* morir • **to d. out** *(to let go of)* dejar caer; *(to omit)* omitir; *(to stop participating)* dejar de participar —tr. *(to let fall)* dejar caer, soltar; *(to let go of)* soltar; *(a liquid)* echar gota a gota; *(a letter)* echar; *(a friend)* dejar; *(conversation)* interrumpir; *(plan)* abandonar; *(work)* dejar inconcluso; *(stitch)* dejar escapar; *(syllable)* omitir, suprimir; *(passenger)* dejar; *(habit)* dejar de; *(hint)* soltar; *(voice, prices)* bajar; *(bombs)* lanzar; *(to parachute)* lanzar o tirar en paracaídas ♦ **to d. someone a line** poner unas líneas a alguien.
drop hammer s. martinete *m*, martillo de fragua *m*.
drop-in (drŏp′ĭn′) s. *(person)* persona que hace una visita informal; *(social event)* reunión informal *f*.
drop·let (drŏp′lĭt) s. gotita.
drop letter s. carta que se echa y entrega desde la misma oficina de correos.
drop-off (drŏp′ôf′) s. *(slope)* bajada escarpada; *(decrease)* disminución significativa.
drop·out (drŏp′out′) **I.** s. *(student)* estudiante que abandona sus estudios *mf*; *(from society)* persona que rechaza a la sociedad; COMPUT. aberración por defecto *f*.
drop·per (drŏp′ər) s. gotero, cuentagotas *m*.
drop·ping (drŏp′ĭng) s. caída ♦ **droppings** excremento de animales.
drop·sy (drŏp′sē) s. MED. hidropesía.
dross (drŏs) s. TEC. *(residue)* escoria; FIG. *(chaff)* desperdicio.
drought (drout) *o* **drouth** (drouth) s. *(dry period)* sequía, seca; FIG. *(dearth)* escasez *f*.
drove[1] (drōv) pret. de **drive**.
drove[2] (drōv) s. *(herd)* manada; FIG. *(crowd)* multitud *f*, gentío ♦ **in droves** a manadas.
drov·er (drō′vər) s. *(of cattle, mules)* arriero, vaquero; *(of sheep)* pastor *m*.
drown (droun) **I.** intr. *(to die)* ahogarse **II.** tr. *(to kill)* ahogar; *(to flood)* anegar; FIG. *(to suppress)* ahogar (penas, ruido).
drowse (drouz) **I.** tr. **drowsed, drows·ing** adormecer —intr. estar medio dormido, estar adormecido **II.** s. adormecimiento, somnolencia.

drows·i·ness (drou′zē-nĭs) s. *(sleepiness)* somnolencia, modorra; FIG. *(sluggishness)* pereza.
drows·y (drou′zē) adj. **-i·er, -i·est** *(sleepy)* soñoliento; *(sluggish)* amodorrado.
drub (drŭb) I. tr. **drubbed, drub·bing** *(to thrash)* apalear, pegar (con un palo); *(to defeat)* derrotar por completo ♦ **to d. something into someone** meter algo en la cabeza de alguien —intr. golpear la tierra, apisonar II. s. golpe con un palo m.
drub·bing (drŭb′ĭng) s. *(thrashing)* paliza, zurra; *(defeat)* derrota severa.
drudge (drŭj) I. s. esclavo del trabajo II. intr. **drudged, drudg·ing** ser esclavo del trabajo.
drudg·er·y (drŭj′ə-rē) s. [pl. **-ies**] trabajo, faena pesada y aburrida.
drug (drŭg) I. s. *(medicine)* droga, medicamento; *(narcotic)* droga, narcótico II. tr. **drugged, drug·ging** *(to medicate)* dar medicamento; *(to give a narcotic)* drogar, narcotizar; *(to mix with a narcotic)* poner una droga en.
drug addict s. narcómano, drogadicto.
drug addiction s. narcomanía, toxicomanía.
drug·gist (drŭg′ĭst) s. farmacéutico, boticario.
drug·store *o* **drug store** (drŭg′stôr′) s. farmacia, botica.
dru·id *o* **Dru·id** (drōō′ĭd) s. HIST. druida (sacerdote de los celtas) m.
drum (drŭm) I. s. *(cylinder)* cilindro, tambor m; *(barrel)* barril m, tonel m; *(of a revolver)* tambor, cilindro; MÚS. tambor; ANAT. tímpano ♦ **drums** MÚS. batería II. intr. & tr. **drummed, drum·ming** tocar el tambor; *(to tap rhythmically)* tamborilear con, golpetear con ♦ **to d. something into someone's head** meterle a alguien algo en la cabeza • **to d. out** echar, expulsar • **to d. up** conseguir.
drum·beat (drŭm′bēt′) s. toque del tambor m.
drum·fire (drŭm′fīr′) s. MIL. fuego graneado.
drum major s. MÚS. tambor mayor (de una banda) m.
drum memory s. COMPUT. memoria en tambor magnético.
drum·mer (drŭm′ər) s. MÚS. baterista mf, tambor mf; *(salesman)* viajante de comercio m.
drum·stick (drŭm′stĭk′) s. *(stick)* baqueta, palillo; CUL. *(thigh)* muslo.
drunk (drŭngk) I. part. p. de **drink** II. adj. *(drunken)* ebrio, borracho; FIG. *(overcome by emotion)* embriagado, ebrio <*d. with love* ebrio de amor> ♦ **to get d.** emborracharse III. s. *(drunkard)* borracho; *(bout)* juerga.
drunk·ard (drŭng′kərd) s. borracho.
drunk·en (drŭng′kən) adj. *(intoxicated)* borracho, bebido; *(of drunkards)* de borrachos <*a d. brawl* pelea de borrachos>; *(of intoxication)* de embriaguez <*d. state* estado de embriaguez>.
drunk·en·ness (drŭng′kən-nĭs) s. embriaguez f, borrachera.
drupe (drōōp) s. BOT. drupa.
dry (drī) I. adj. **dri·er, dri·est** *o* **dry·er, dry·est** *(lacking moisture)* seco; *(arid)* árido, seco <*d. climate* clima seco>; *(rainless)* sin lluvia, seco <*a d. April* un abril seco>; *(without milk)* seca <*a d. cow* una vaca seca>; *(lacking a discharge)* seca <*a d. cough* una tos seca>; *(thirsty)* sediento <*I am d.* estoy sediento>; *(said of wine)* seco; *(said of toast)* sin mantequilla; *(boring)* aburrido, pesado; *(said of wit, style)* agudo, satírico; *(county, state)* prohibicionista; *(without inspiration)* sin inspiración ♦ **as d. as dust** *(very dry)* muy árido; *(boring)* aburrido • **d. land** tierra firme • **the d. facts** los hechos concretos • **to run d.** secarse, agotarse II. tr. **dried, dry·ing** *(to make dry)* secar; *(to desiccate)* desecar, deshidratar ♦ **to d. out** secar • **to d. up** secar completamente —intr. secarse, desecarse ♦ **d. up!** ¡cállate la boca! • **to d. out** FIG. dejar de beber • **to d. up** *(to lose moisture)* desecarse; FIG., FAM. *(to shut up)* callarse.
dry cell s. ELEC. elemento seco, celda seca.
dry-clean (drī′klēn′) tr. limpiar en seco.
dry cleaner s. tintorero ♦ **dry cleaner's** tintorería, tinte.
dry cleaning s. limpieza en seco.
dry dock s. dique seco, carenero.
dry-dock (drī′dŏk′) tr. & intr. MARÍT. carenar(se), encarenar(se).
dry·er (drī′ər) s. *(appliance)* secador m; *(machine)* secadora;

(clothes rack) tendedero; *(dish rack)* escurreplatos; *(substance)* desecante m, secante m.
dry fly s. mosca artificial flotante (para pesca).
dry goods s. mercería, lencería.
dry ice s. hielo seco, hielo carbónico.
dry·ing (drī′ĭng) adj. desecante, secante.
dry mea·sure s. FÍS. sistema de medidas para áridos m.
dry·ness (drī′nĭs) s. sequedad f.
dry rot s. putrefacción (de la madera) f.
dry run s. práctica, simulacro.
D.T.'s (dē-tēz′) s. JER. delírium tremens m.
du·ad (dōō′ăd′, dyōō′-) s. pareja, par m.
du·al (dōō′əl, dyōō′-) I. adj. dual, doble II. s. GRAM. número dual.
du·al·ism (dōō′ə-lĭz′əm, dyōō′-) s. dualismo, dualidad f.
du·al·i·ty (dōō-ăl′ĭ-tē, dyōō′-) s. [pl. **-ties**] dualidad f.
du·al-pur·pose (dōō′əl-pûr′pəs, dyōō′-) adj. de doble propósito, de doble función.
dub[1] (dŭb) I. tr. **dubbed, dub·bing** *(to knight)* armar, hacer caballero; *(to honor)* titular, honrar con un nuevo título; *(to nickname)* apodar; *(leather)* alisar; *(wood)* desbastar; CUL. *(to dress)* aderezar, aliñar; JER. *(in golf)* golpear mal (la pelota) II. s. JER. chambón m.
dub[2] (dŭb) tr. **dub·bed, dub·bing** MÚS., RAD. mezclar; CINEM. doblar.
dub·bing (dŭb′ĭng) s. CINEM. doblaje m.
du·bi·ous (dōō′bē-əs, dyōō′-) adj. *(doubtful)* dudoso, incierto; *(suspicious)* sospechoso, cuestionable; *(irresolute)* indeciso.
Dub·lin (dŭb′lĭn) s. Dublín.
duc·at (dŭk′ət) s. FIN., HIST. *(coin)* ducado; JER. *(ticket)* boleto de entrada.
duch·ess (dŭch′ĭs) s. duquesa.
duch·y (dŭch′ē) s. [pl. **-ies**] ducado (territorio).
duck[1] (dŭk) s. *(drake)* pato; *(female duck)* pata; *(food)* pato, carne de pato f; JER. *(person)* tipo raro ♦ **like water off a duck's back** FAM. como si nada • **to take to something like a d. to water** adaptarse fácilmente a algo.
duck[2] (dŭk) I. tr. *(to crouch)* agachar; *(to dodge)* eludir, evadir; *(to dive)* zambullir —intr. *(to lower)* agacharse; *(to move swiftly)* escaparse; *(to dive)* zambullirse ♦ **to d. out** desaparecer • **to d. out on** eludir II. s. *(lowering)* agachada; *(plunge)* zambullida.
duck·ling (dŭk′lĭng) s. patito, anadón m ♦ **an ugly d.** un patito feo.
duck·y (dŭk′ē) adj. **-i·er, -i·est** JER. *(charming)* precioso; *(wonderful)* maravilloso.
duct (dŭkt) s. *(passage)* conducto, tubo; ANAT. *(canal)* canal m, conducto; ELEC. *(tube)* tubo.
duc·tile (dŭk′təl, -tīl′) adj. dúctil.
dud (dŭd) s. FAM. *(bomb)* bomba o granada que no estalla; *(failure)* desastre m, calamidad f ♦ **duds** FAM. *(clothes)* trapos, ropa; *(belongings)* posesiones.
dude (dōōd, dyōōd) s. FAM. *(city man)* hombre de ciudad m; *(dandy)* petimetre m; JER. *(guy)* tipo, tío.
dude ranch s. rancho o estancia para turistas.
dudg·eon (dŭj′ən) s. cólera, enojo ♦ **in high d.** muy enojado.
due (dōō, dyōō) I. adj. *(payable)* pagadero; *(owed as a debt)* sin pagar <*the amount still d.* la cantidad aún sin pagar>; *(just)* debido, merecido <*d. esteem* debido aprecio>; *(sufficient)* suficiente <*we have d. cause to honor him* tenemos motivo suficiente para honrarlo> ♦ **d. date** vencimiento • **to be d.** *(to be expected)* esperarse <*he is d. at your house tomorrow* se espera que llegue a tu casa mañana>; *(to be scheduled)* deber <*the plane is d. to arrive at five o'clock sharp* el avión debe llegar a las cinco en punto> • **to be d. to** deberse <*his hesitancy was d. to fear* su indecisión se debía al miedo> • **to become** *o* **to fall d.** vencer II. s. *(comeuppance)* merecido; *(reward)* recompensa ♦ **dues** cuota III. adv. derecho hacia <*d. west* derecho hacia el oeste>.
du·el (dōō′əl, dyōō′-) I. s. duelo II. intr. batirse en duelo.
du·el·er (dōō′ə-lər, dyōō′-) *o* **du·el·ist** (-lĭst) s. duelista m.
due process s. DER. proceso legal correspondiente.
du·et (dōō-ĕt′, dyōō-) s. MÚS., TEAT. dueto, dúo.

due to prep. debido a, a causa de.

duff¹ (dŭf) s. CUL. budín *m*, pudín *m*.

duff² (dŭf) s. *(vegetable matter)* humus *m*, mantillo; *(coal)* cisco.

duff³ (dŭf) s. JER. nalgas, trasero.

duf·fel *o* **duf·fle** (dŭf'əl) s. *(fabric)* muletón *m*; *(camping equipment)* equipo para campamento.

duffel bag s. bolsa de lona.

duf·fer (dŭf'ər) s. FAM. *(dope)* zoquete *m*; JER. *(peddler)* buhonero.

dug¹ (dŭg) s. *(teat)* teta; *(udder)* ubre *f*.

dug² (dŭg) pret. y part. p. de **dig**.

dug·out (dŭg'out') s. *(boat)* piragua; MIL. *(shelter)* trinchera.

duke (dook, dyook) s. duque *m*.

dukes (dooks, dyooks) s.pl. JER. puños ♦ **put** *o* **stick up your d.!** JER. ¡ponte en guardia!

dul·cet (dŭl'sĭt) adj. suave, dulce.

dul·ci·mer (dŭl'sə-mər) s. MÚS. dulcémele *m*, salterio.

dull (dŭl) I. adj. **-er, -est** *(stupid)* tonto, torpe; *(slow to learn)* duro de comprensión; *(insensitive)* lento, embotado; *(blunt)* desafilado, romo; *(not intense)* sordo <a d. ache un dolor sordo>; *(boring)* aburrido, tedioso; *(sluggish)* flojo <a d. day at the stock exchange un día flojo en la Bolsa>; *(not vivid)* opaco, apagado; *(cloudy)* nublado, gris; *(not loud)* apagado, sordo II. tr. & intr. *(to blunt)* desafilar(se), enromar(se); *(to mitigate)* aliviar(se) (dolor); *(to devitalize)* embotar(se) (sentidos); *(to darken)* oscurecer(se); *(to muffle)* amortiguar(se), apagar(se).

dull·ard (dŭl'ərd) s. estúpido, idiota *mf*.

dull·ness *o* **dul·ness** (dŭl'nĭs) s. *(lack of sharpness)* embotamiento; *(of senses)* embotamiento, insensibilidad *f*; *(stupidity)* torpeza, estupidez *f*; *(lifelessness)* falta de vida; *(sadness)* tristeza, depresión *f*; *(flatness)* monotonía, insipidez *f*.

du·ly (doo'lē, dyoo'-) adv. *(properly)* correctamente, debidamente; *(punctually)* puntualmente, al debido tiempo.

dumb (dŭm) adj. **-er, -est** *(mute)* mudo; FAM. *(stupid)* tonto, estúpido ♦ **the d.** los mudos ♦ **to be struck d.** quedarse mudo *o* sin habla ♦ **to strike someone d.** dejar a alguien sin habla *o* mudo.

dumb·bell (dŭm'bĕl') s. DEP. *(weight)* pesas; JER. *(dolt)* estúpido, tonto.

dumb·found (dŭm'found') v. var. de **dumfound**.

dumb show s. pantomima ♦ **by d.** por señas.

dumb·wait·er (dŭm'wā'tər) s. *(elevator)* montaplatos; *(table)* mesita de servicio.

dum·dum bullet (dŭm'dŭm') s. bala de expansión.

dum·found (dŭm'found') tr. pasmar, asombrar.

dum·my (dŭm'ē) I. s. [pl. **-mies**] FAM. *(dolt)* tonto, bobo; *(puppet)* muñeco, títere *m*; *(mannequin)* maniquí *m*; *(front)* testaferro; IMPR. *(model)* maqueta II. adj. falso, ficticio <a d. corporation una corporación ficticia> III. intr. **-mied, -my·ing** ♦ **to d. up** FAM. callarse.

dummy variable s. MAT. variable (que puede reemplazarse por otra variable de cualquier valor) *f*.

dump (dŭmp) I. tr. *(to throw away)* tirar; *(to get rid of)* deshacerse de <to d. toxic waste deshacerse de los deshechos tóxicos>; *(to empty)* vaciar, descargar; COM. *(to unload)* inundar el mercado con; COMPUT. imprimir (información) —intr. *(to fall)* desplomarse; *(to unload)* descargar II. s. *(refuse site)* vertedero, muladar *m*; *(depot)* depósito; *(pile)* pila, montón *m*; JER. *(unkept place)* pocilga, tugurio <that hotel is a real d. ese hotel es una verdadera pocilga>.

dump·ing (dŭm'pĭng) s. *(unloading)* descarga; COM. inundación del mercado *f*.

dump·ling (dŭm'plĭng) s. CUL. *(dough)* bola de masa cocida; *(dessert)* fruta envuelta en masa y asada.

dumps (dŭmps) s.pl. depresión *f* ♦ **to be down in the d.** estar deprimido.

dump truck s. volquete *m*.

dump·y (dŭm'pē) adj. **-i·er, -i·est** *(squat)* gordo, rechoncho; *(depressed)* deprimido.

dun¹ (dŭn) I. tr. **dunned, dun·ning** apremiar (a un deudor)

II. s. *(demand)* petición de reembolso *f*; *(person)* acreedor fastidioso.

dun² (dŭn) s. *(color)* pardo; *(horse)* caballo pardo.

dunce (dŭns) s. FAM. zopenco, burro.

dunce cap *o* **dunce's cap** s. orejas de burro.

dune (doon, dyoon) s. duna ♦ **d. buggy** automóvil para andar sobre dunas.

dung (dŭng) I. s. estiércol *m* II. tr. estercolar, abonar.

dun·ga·ree (dŭng'gə-rē') s. mahón (tela) *m* ♦ **dungarees** pantalones vaqueros.

dun·geon (dŭn'jən) s. *(prison)* calabozo, mazmorra; ARQ., HIST. *(donjon)* torre del homenaje *f*.

dung·hill (dŭng'hĭl') s. *(manure pile)* pila *o* montón *m* de estiércol; *(foul place)* lugar asqueroso.

dunk (dŭngk) I. tr. *(to dip food)* ensopar, remojar (pan, galletas); *(to immerse)* sumergir, hundir; DEP. *(in basketball)* encestar —intr. *(to submerge)* bañarse; DEP. *(in basketball)* meter cesto II. s. *(dip)* baño; DEP. *(shot)* cesta, cesto.

du·o (doo'ō, dyoo'ō) s. [pl. **-os**] FAM. *(pair)* pareja; MÚS. dúo.

du·o·dec·i·mal (doo'ə-dĕs'ə-məl, dyoo'-) I. adj. duodecimal II. s. duodécimo.

duodecimal system s. MAT. sistema de numeración duodecimal *m*.

du·o·dec·i·mo (doo'ə-dĕs'ə-mō', dyoo'-) s. *(page size)* página en dozavo; *(book)* libro en dozavo.

du·o·de·num (doo'ə-dē'nəm, dyoo'-) s. [pl. **-na** (-nə) *o* **-nums**] ANAT. duodeno.

dupe (doop, dyoop) I. s. FAM. *(gullible person)* primo; *(tool)* títere *m* II. tr. **duped, dup·ing** embaucar, engañar.

du·plex (doo'plĕks, dyoo'-) I. adj. *(double)* doble; ELECTRÓN. dúplex II. s. *(apartment)* apartamento de dos pisos; *(house)* casa de dos viviendas.

du·pli·cate (doo'plĭ-kĭt, dyoo'-) I. s. duplicado, copia ♦ **in d.** por duplicado II. tr. (doo'plĭ-kāt', dyoo'-) **-cat·ed, -cat·ing** *(to copy)* copiar; *(to reproduce)* multicopiar, reproducir; *(to repeat)* repetir; *(to double)* doblar III. adj. *(copy)* duplicado; *(double)* doble.

du·pli·ca·tion (doo'plĭ-kā'shən, dyoo'-) s. *(act)* duplicación *f*; *(replica)* réplica, copia.

du·pli·ca·tor (doo'plĭ-kā'tər, dyoo'-) s. máquina de hacer copias.

du·plic·i·ty (doo-plĭs'ĭ-tē, dyoo-) s. [pl. **-ties**] *(deception)* engaño; *(state)* doblez *f*, duplicidad *f*.

du·ra·bil·i·ty (door'ə-bĭl'ĭ-tē, dyoor'-) s. durabilidad *f*.

du·ra·ble (door'ə-bəl, dyoor'-) adj. duradero.

durable goods s.pl. productos no perecederos.

du·ra·tion (doo-rā'shən, dyoo-) s. duración *f*.

du·ress (doo-rĕs', dyoo-) s. *(coercion)* coerción *f*; DER. coerción, coacción *f*.

dur·ing (door'ĭng, dyoor'-) prep. durante.

dusk (dŭsk) I. s. crepúsculo ♦ **at d.** al atardecer, al anochecer II. tr. & intr. oscurecer(se).

dusk·y (dŭs'kē) adj. **-i·er, -i·est** *(shadowy)* oscuro, fusco; *(dark)* negruzco, moreno.

dust (dŭst) I. s. *(powder)* polvo; *(cloud)* polvareda; *(remains)* restos, polvo II. tr. *(to clean)* limpiar el polvo de; *(to cover)* empolvar, rociar con polvo; *(to sprinkle)* espolvorear —intr. limpiar el polvo ♦ **to bite the d.** morirse • **to let the d. settle** dejar que se calme la situación.

dust·bin (dŭst'bĭn') s. G.B. basurero.

dust·cloth (dŭst'klôth') s. *(duster)* trapo (para limpiar); *(cover)* guardapolvo.

dust cover s. *(of a turntable)* funda; *(dust jacket)* sobrecubierta.

dust·er (dŭs'tər) s. *(cloth)* trapo (para limpiar); *(with feathers)* plumero; *(smock)* guardapolvo; *(shaker)* espolvoreador *m*.

dust·i·ness (dŭs'tē-nĭs) s. polvo, condición polvorienta.

dust·ing (dŭs'tĭng) s. *(cleaning)* limpieza de polvo; *(covering)* capa de polvo; G.B., FAM. *(thrashing)* paliza, tunda.

dust jacket s. sobrecubierta.

dust·man (dŭst'mən) s. G.B. barrendero, basurero.

dust·pan (dŭst'păn') s. pala para la basura, recogedor de polvo *m*.

ā rey / ä año / b boca / ch chico / d dar / ĕ el / ē mil / g gato / h joya / hw juez / ī aire / k casa / kw cuan /

dust·y (dŭs′tē) adj. -i·er, -i·est *(powdery)* polvoriento; *(covered with dust)* cubierto de polvo; *(like dust)* de polvo, en polvo.

Dutch (dŭch) I. adj. holandés II. s. [pl. **Dutch**] *(inhabitant)* holandés *m* ♦ **the D.** los holandeses III. adv. ♦ **to go D.** o **D. treat** FAM. pagar cada uno por lo suyo, ir a medias.

Dutch door s. puerta de dos paneles.

Dutch·man (dŭch′mən) s. holandés *m*.

Dutch oven s. *(iron pot)* olla o caldero de hierro; *(for roasting)* parrilla; *(brick oven)* horno de ladrillos.

Dutch treat s. pago a escote.

Dutch uncle s. FAM. crítico o mentor severo.

du·te·ous (dōō′tē-əs, dyōō′-) adj. obediente.

du·ti·a·ble (dōō′tē-ə-bəl, dyōō′-) adj. DER. imponible, sujeto a derechos aduaneros.

du·ti·ful (dōō′tĭ-fəl, dyōō′-) adj. concienzudo, cumplidor.

du·ty (dōō′tē, dyōō′-) s. [pl. **-ties**] *(obligation)* deber *m*, obligación *f*; *(function)* función *f*; *(tax)* impuesto, arancel (de aduana) *m*; MIL. guardia ♦ **duty-bound** obligado • **in the line of d.** en cumplimiento del deber • **out of a sense of d.** por cumplido, para cumplir • **to be on d.** estar de servicio • **to be off d.** estar libre, no estar de servicio • **to do** o **carry out one's d.** cumplir con su deber • **to make it one's d.** obligarse a.

du·ty-free (dōō′tē-frē′, dyōō′-) adj. & adv. exento de derechos de aduana.

du·ty-paid (dōō′tē-pād′, dyōō′-) adj. con los derechos de aduana pagados.

dwarf (dwôrf) I. s. [pl. **dwarfs** o **dwarves** (dwôrvz)] enano; ASTRON. estrella enana II. tr. *(stunt)* impedir o arrestar el crecimiento; *(to make small)* achicar, empequeñecer III. adj. enano *<a d. pine* un pino enano*>*.

dwarf·ish (dwôr′fĭsh) adj. enano.

dwarves (dwôrvz) un pl. de **dwarf.**

dwell (dwĕl) I. tr. & intr. **dwelt** (dwĕlt) o **dwelled, dwell·ing** *(to reside)* morar, residir; *(to exist)* persistir, existir *<there dwells in us* persiste en nosotros*>* ♦ **to d. on** *(to pay special attention to)* detenerse en, insistir en; *(to expatiate)* extenderse en, dilatarse sobre II. s. COMPUT. apertura y cierre.

dwell·er (dwĕl′ər) s. morador *m*, habitante *mf*.

dwell·ing (dwĕl′ĭng) s. *(residence)* residencia, morada; *(expatiation)* disertación *f*.

dwelt (dwĕlt) un pret. y part. p. de **dwell.**

dwin·dle (dwĭn′dl) tr. & intr. **-dled, -dling** disminuir, menguar.

dy·ad (dī′ăd′) I. s. *(pair)* par *m*, pareja; BIOL. díade *f*; QUÍM. díada II. adj. bipartido, bivalente.

dye (dī) I. s. tintura, tinte *m* ♦ **color-fast d.** color sólido II. tr. & intr. **dyed, dye·ing** teñir(se), colorar(se).

dyed-in-the-wool (dīd′ĭn-thə-wōōl′) adj. TEJ. teñido en rama; FIG. *(extreme)* acérrimo *<a d. communist* un comunista acérrimo*>*.

dye·ing (dī′ĭng) I. part. pres. de **dye** II. s. *(dye)* tinte *m*, tintura; *(process)* teñido.

dye·er (dī′ər) s. tintorero.

dye·stuff (dī′stŭf′) s. tinte *m*, colorante *m*.

dy·ing (dī′ĭng) adj. *(about to die)* moribundo, a punto de morir; *(final)* último *<d. words* últimas palabras*>*; *(fading)* agonizante, mortecino ♦ **the d.** los agonizantes.

dyke (dīk) s. DESPEC., JER. lesbiana.

dy·nam·ic (dī-năm′ĭk) o **dy·nam·i·cal** (-ĭ-kəl) adj. dinámico.

dy·nam·ics (dī-năm′ĭks) s. [ú. con v. sing. o pl.] dinámica.

dy·na·mism (dī′nə-mĭz′əm) s. dinamismo.

dy·na·mite (dī′nə-mīt′) I. s. dinamita II. tr. **-mit·ed, -mit·ing** JER. estupendo, maravilloso.

dy·na·mo (dī′nə-mō′) s. [pl. **-mos**] *(generator)* dínamo *f*, dínamo *m*; FIG. *(person)* dínamo, persona enérgica.

dy·na·mom·e·ter (dī′nə-mŏm′ĭ-tər) s. FÍS. dinamómetro.

dy·na·mo·tor (dī′nə-mō′tər) s. ELEC., MEC. dinamotor *m*.

dy·nas·tic (dī-năs′tĭk) adj. dinástico.

dy·nas·ty (dī′nə-stē) s. [pl. **-ties**] dinastía.

dy·na·tron (dī′nə-trŏn′) s. ELEC. dinatrón *m*.

dyne (dīn) s. FÍS. dina.

dys·en·ter·y (dĭs′ən-tĕr′ē) s. MED. disentería.

dys·func·tion (dĭs-fŭngk′shən) s. MED., PSIC., SOCIOL. disfunción *f*.

dys·lex·i·a (dĭs-lĕk′sē-ə) s. MED. dislexia.

dys·lex·ic (dĭs-lĕk′sĭk) adj. disléxico.

dys·pep·sia (dĭs-pĕp′shə) s. MED. dispepsia, indigestión *f*.

dys·pep·tic (dĭs-pĕp′tĭk) adj. & s. MED. dispéptico.

dys·tro·phy (dĭs′trə-fē) o **dys·tro·phi·a** (dĭ-strō′fē-ə) s. MED. distrofia.

E

e, E (ē) s. [pl. **e's, E's**] quinta letra del alfabeto inglés; MÚS. mi *m* ♦ **E flat, major, minor, sharp** MÚS. mi bemol, mayor, menor, sostenido.

each (ēch) I. adj. cada *<e. contestant won something* cada concursante ganó algo*>* ♦ **e. and every one** todos sin excepción II. pron. cada uno *<e. of the contestants won something* cada uno de los concursantes ganó algo*>* ♦ **e. for himself** cada cual por su cuenta, cada cual por su lado • **to e. his own** cada uno con su gusto III. adv. por persona, cada uno *<it will cost us fifteen dollars e.* nos costará quince dólares cada uno*>*.

▲ Cuando el sujeto de la oración comienza con el pronombre *each* ésta se considera singular. En consecuencia, el verbo y los pronombres que la forman deben usarse también en singular *<each of the teachers has a style of his own* cada uno de los maestros tiene un estilo propio*>*. Cuando *each* sigue a un sujeto en plural, el verbo y los pronombres de la oración deben mantenerse en el plural *<the teachers e. have their own style* cada uno de los maestros tiene un estilo propio*>*.

each other §G38 pron. uno a otro, mutuamente *<we enjoy helping e.* nos gusta ayudarnos mutuamente*>*.

▲ El pronombre *each other* a menudo se traduce al español como "nos", "os", o "se", según el sujeto. El sentido de reciprocidad se entiende por el contexto y, si hace falta, alguna expresión aclaratoria *<they love each other* (ellos) se aman (una al otro)*>*.

ea·ger (ē′gər) adj. -er, -est *(avid)* ansioso, ávido *<e. to learn* ávido por aprender*>*; *(desirous)* deseoso, ardiente *<an e. look* una mirada ardiente*>* ♦ **to be e. for something** ansiar o anhelar algo.

eager beaver s. FAM. persona de exagerado afán o entusiasmo.

ea·ger·ness (ē′gər-nĭs) s. *(avidity)* ansia, anhelo; *(impatience)* impaciencia.

ea·gle (ē′gəl) s. ORNIT. águila; *(coin)* moneda antigua de oro (en EE. UU.).

ear¹ (îr) s. ANAT. oreja; *(organ of hearing)* oído *<inner e.* oído interno*>*; *(handle)* oreja, asa; IMPR. oreja ♦ **to be all ears** ser todo oídos, estar completamente atento • **to be up to one's ears in** estar abrumado de o empeñado hasta las orejas • **to fall on deaf ears** caer en saco roto • **to give an e. to** prestar atención a • **to go in one e. and out the other** entrar por un oído y salir por el otro • **to have a good e. (for)** tener un buen oído (para) • **to have someone's e.** tener la atención de alguien, gozar de la confianza de • **to keep** o **have one's e. to the ground** mantenerse alerta o al corriente • **to listen with half an e.** escuchar a medias • **not to believe one's ears** no dar crédito a los oídos • **to play by e.** tocar de oído • **to play it by e.** improvisar sobre la marcha • **to prick up one's ears** aguzar el oído • **to turn a deaf e.** no prestar atención, hacerse el sordo.

ear² (îr) I. s. BOT. espiga, mazorca II. intr. espigar.

ear·ache (îr′āk′) s. dolor de oído *m*.

ear·drum (îr′drŭm′) s. ANAT. tímpano.

ear·flap (îr′flăp′) s. orejera.

ear·ful (îr′fōōl′) s. FAM. *(talk)* raudal de chismes *m*; *(scolding)* regaño, admonición *f*.

earl (ûrl) s. conde (en G.B.) *m*.

earl·dom (ûrl′dəm) s. condado (dignidad, territorio).

ear lobe s. ANAT. lóbulo de la oreja.

ear·ly (ûr'lē) **I.** adj. **-li·er, -li·est** *(before usual)* temprano; *(first)* primero <*in the e. stages* en las primeras etapas>; *(quick)* rápido, pronto; *(premature)* temprano, prematuro <*an e. death* una muerte prematura>; *(primitive)* primitivo, primero ♦ **at an e. age** a temprana edad • **at an e. date** en fecha cercana • **at the earliest** lo más pronto, como muy pronto • **at your earliest convenience** con la mayor brevedad • **e. riser** madrugador • **e. show** primera función • **to be in one's e. (thirties)** tener poco más de (treinta) años **II.** adv. **-li·er, -li·est** *(soon)* temprano, pronto; *(before)* antes <*come one hour e.* llegue una hora antes>; *(in advance)* con tiempo, con anticipación; *(prematurely)* prematuramente, joven <*she died e.* ella murió joven> ♦ **as e. as** ya en • **as e. as possible** lo más pronto posible, cuanto antes • **bright and e.** muy temprano • **e. in** al principio de, a principios de • **e. in the morning** de madrugada, por la mañanita • **e. on** pronto.

early bird s. FAM. *(early riser)* madrugador m; *(early arrival)* persona que llega temprano ♦ **the e. catches the worm** al que madruga Dios le ayuda.

ear·mark (îr'märk') **I.** s. *(on an animal)* marca en la oreja; *(characteristic)* marca característica, señal f **II.** tr. poner una señal en, marcar ♦ **to be earmarked for** estar reservado para.

ear·muff (îr'mŭf') s. orejera.

earn (ûrn) tr. *(to make)* ganar; *(to deserve)* ganarse, merecer; *(to acquire)* obtener, conseguir ♦ **to e. a living** ganarse la vida • **to e. interest** devengar interés.

ear·nest¹ (ûr'nĭst) adj. *(determined)* resuelto; *(devoted)* dedicado; *(sincere)* sincero; *(serious)* serio <*in e.* en serio>; *(important)* importante.

ear·nest² (ûr'nĭst) s. *(deposit)* arras, caparra; *(token)* señal f, prenda.

earn·ings (ûr'nĭngz) s.pl. *(salary)* salario, sueldo; COM. *(income)* ingresos; *(profits)* utilidades f, ganancias.

ear·phone (îr'fōn') s. *(hearing aid)* audífono; *(of a telephone)* auricular m.

ear·ring (îr'rĭng) s. pendiente m, arete m.

ear·shot (îr'shŏt') s. ♦ **within e.** al alcance del oído.

ear·split·ting (îr'splĭt'ĭng) adj. *(deafening)* ensordecedor; *(shrill)* estridente.

earth (ûrth) **I.** s. *(planet)* tierra; *(soil)* tierra, suelo; *(world)* mundo <*the whole e. watched* el mundo entero vio>; RELIG. tierra; ELEC. tierra; QUÍM. tierra (rara) ♦ **down to e.** sensato, realista • **E.** ASTRON. Tierra • **to come back to e.** volver a la realidad • **to move heaven and e.** mover cielo y tierra • **to run to e.** *(animal)* acosar o cazar hasta su madriguera; *(person)* encontrar por fin • **on e.** diablo, demonios <*who on e. is he?* ¿quién diablo es él?> **II.** tr. *(to hound)* acosar, acorralar; AGR. acollar, enterrar; ELEC. conectar a tierra —intr. guarecerse, esconderse.

earth·bound o **earth-bound** (ûrth'bound') adj. *(stuck in the earth)* apegado a la tierra; *(unimaginative)* prosaico, inculto; *(earthward)* que se dirige hacia la tierra; *(terrestrial)* terrestre.

earth·en (ûr'thən, -thən) adj. *(earthy)* de tierra; *(clayey)* de barro; *(earthly)* terrenal.

earth·en·ware (ûr'thən-wâr', -thən-) **I.** s. loza **II.** adj. de barro.

earth·ling (ûrth'lĭng) s. *(inhabitant)* habitante del planeta Tierra m; *(human being)* ser humano; *(worldly person)* persona mundana; CIENC. FIC. terrícola mf.

earth·ly (ûrth'lē) adj. *(secular)* mundanal, terreno; *(materialistic)* terrenal, mundano; FAM. *(conceivable)* concebible, posible ♦ **no e. reason** ninguna razón • **to be of no e. use** no servir para nada.

earth·quake (ûrth'kwāk') s. terremoto, temblor m.

earth·shak·ing (ûrth'shā'kĭng) adj. FIG. importantísimo, de enormes consecuencias.

earth·ward (ûrth'wərd) adv. & adj. hacia la tierra.

earth·work (ûrth'wûrk') s. MIL. *(embankment)* terraplén m; CONSTR. movimiento de tierras.

earth·worm (ûrth'wûrm') s. lombriz f, gusano.

earth·y (ûr'thē) adj. **-i·er, -i·est** *(earthen)* terroso, térreo; *(worldly)* mundano; *(unrefined)* vulgar, tosco.

ear·wax (îr'wăks') s. cerumen m, cera de los oídos.

ear·wig (îr'wĭg') **I.** s. ENTOM. tijereta **II.** tr. **-wigged, -wigging** tratar de ejercer influencia sobre (alguien) con cuchicheos.

ease (ēz) **I.** s. *(comfort)* comodidad f; *(relief)* alivio, desahogo; *(naturalness)* naturalidad f, desenvoltura; *(facility)* facilidad f, soltura; *(affluence)* afluencia, abundancia; *(calmness)* sosiego, tranquilidad f ♦ **at e.** *(comfortable)* cómodo; MIL. en posición de descanso, ¡descanso! • **to feel at e.** sentirse cómodo • **to feel ill at e.** sentirse molesto o inquieto • **to put at e.** poner cómodo • **to stand at e.** descansar • **with e.** fácilmente, sin esfuerzo **II.** tr. **eased, eas·ing** *(to alleviate)* aliviar, mitigar; *(to relieve pressure)* aligerar, descargar; *(to relieve tension)* relajar; *(to loosen)* aflojar ♦ **to e. in** o **into** hacer entrar con cuidado • **to e. up on someone** tratar a alguien con menos rigor —intr. *(to mitigate)* mitigarse, calmarse; *(to relax)* relajarse (tensión) ♦ **to e. up** bajar, disminuir.

ea·sel (ē'zəl) s. caballete m.

ease·ment (ēz'mənt) s. *(relief)* alivio; DER. *(right)* servidumbre f.

eas·i·ly (ē'zə-lē) adv. *(without difficulty)* fácilmente; *(without doubt)* fácilmente, holgadamente; *(possibly)* muy probablemente.

eas·i·ness (ē'zē-nĭs) s. *(ease)* facilidad f; *(comfort)* comodidad f; *(calmness)* tranquilidad f; *(gracefulness)* soltura.

east (ēst) **I.** s. este m, oriente m ♦ **the E.** *(the Orient)* el Oriente; *(in U.S.)* el este (de EE. UU.) • **the Far E.** el Lejano Oriente • **the Near E.** el Cercano Oriente • **the Middle E.** El Oriente Medio **II.** adj. del este, oriental **III.** adv. al este, hacia el este.

East Berlin s. Berlín Oriental m, Berlín Este.

east·bound (ēst'bound') adj. con rumbo al este.

east by north I. s. este cuarta al nordeste m **II.** adj. del este cuarta al nordeste **III.** adv. a o hacia el este cuarta al nordeste.

east by south I. s. este cuarta al sudeste m **II.** adj. del este cuarta al sudeste **III.** adv. a o hacia el este cuarta al sudeste.

Eas·ter (ē'stər) s. RELIG. Pascua de Resurrección; *(period)* Semana Santa <*I'll be on vacation at E.* estaré de vacaciones en Semana Santa>; *(Easter Sunday)* domingo de Pascua o de Resurrección.

Easter egg s. huevo de Pascua.

Easter Island s. Isla de Pascua.

Easter lily s. BOT. azucena.

east·er·ly (ē'stər-lē) **I.** adj. que viene del este, oriental **II.** s. [pl. **-lies**] este m, viento que sopla del este **III.** adv. desde o hacia el este.

Easter Monday s. RELIG. lunes de Pascua de Resurrección m.

east·ern (ē'stərn) adj. oriental, del este ♦ **E.** GEOG. de la región oriental.

east·ern·er o **East·ern·er** (ē'stər-nər) s. *(inhabitant of the east)* oriental m; *(from eastern U.S.)* habitante del este (de EE. UU.) m.

Eastern Hemisphere s. Hemisferio Oriental.

east·ern·most (ē'stərn-mōst') adj. más oriental, más al este.

Eastern Standard Time s. hora oficial del este (de EE. UU.).

Eas·ter·tide (ē'stər-tīd') s. RELIG. tiempo de Pascua.

East Germany s. República Democrática Alemana, Alemania Oriental.

East Indies s.pl. Indias Orientales.

East Pakistan s. Paquistán Oriental m.

east·ward (ēst'wərd) **I.** adv. hacia el este **II.** adj. oriental, que va al este **III.** s. este m.

eas·y (ē'zē) **I.** adj. **-i·er, -i·est** *(simple)* fácil <*an e. task* un trabajo fácil>; *(free from worry)* tranquilo; *(comfortable)* cómodo; *(socially at ease)* desenvuelto; *(easygoing)* natural; *(smooth)* claro, sencillo <*an e. style* un estilo sencillo>; *(not strict)* suave, leve; *(wanton)* desordenado <*she leads an e. life* lleva una vida desordenada>; *(readily persuaded)* fácil de convencer; *(unhurried)* lento, pausado ♦ **an e.** su buen <*it cost an e. five hundred dollars* costó sus buenos quinientos dólares> • **to be e. to get along with** ser fácil congeniar con • **to be on e. street** vivir acomodado

II. adv. **-i·er, -i·est** fácilmente ♦ **e. does it** con calma, sin agitarse • **to go e. on** FAM. *(to use moderately)* moderarse con, usar con moderación; *(to be lenient to)* no tratar con mucha severidad • **to take it e.** FAM. *(to relax)* descansar; *(to stay calm)* no agitarse; *(to refrain from worrying)* tomar las cosas con calma, no preocuparse; *(to go slow)* ir despacio, no apurarse.

easy chair s. sillón *m.*

eas·y-go·ing *o* **eas·y-go·ing** (ē'zē-gō'ĭng) adj. *(unconcerned)* despreocupado; *(free)* desenvuelto; *(lax)* descuidado, relajado; *(tolerant)* tolerante, clemente; *(undemanding)* sereno, poco exigente.

easy street *o* **Easy Street** s. ♦ **to be on e.** JER. disfrutar de una situación acomodada.

eat (ēt) tr. **ate** (āt), **eat·en** (ēt'n), **eat·ing** *(to consume)* comer; *(to devour)* tragar, devorar; *(to corrode)* corroer; JER. *(to annoy)* molestar, fastidiar ♦ **to e. away (at, through)** corroer, carcomer • **to e. breakfast** tomar el desayuno, desayunar • **to e. crow** aceptar la derrota • **to e. dinner** tomar la cena, cenar • **to e. humble pie** retractarse • **to e. into** *(to corrode)* corroer, carcomer; *(to use up)* gastar, desgastar • **to e. lunch** tomar el almuerzo, almorzar • **to e. one's heart out** consumirse con (amargura, anhelo) • **to e. one's words** retractarse, tragarse las palabras • **to e. someone out of house and home** comer mucho • **to e. up** *(to devour)* comerselo todo; *(to use up)* consumir, gastar; *(to be credulous)* creer sin crítica; *(to enjoy)* deleitarse en • **what's eating you?** ¿qué mosca te ha picado? —intr. comer, alimentarse ♦ **to e. like a horse** comer como un caballo, comer excesivamente • **to e. out** comer fuera (de casa) • **to have someone eating out of one's hand** poder manejar a alguien como uno quiere.

eat·a·ble (ē'tə-bəl) **I.** adj. *(edible)* comible; *(palatable)* comestible **II.** s. ♦ **eatables** comestibles, alimentos.

eat·en (ēt'n) part. p. de **eat.**

eat·er (ē'tər) s. *(person who eats)* comedor *m*; *(big eater)* comilón *m*; G.B. *(fruit)* fruta de mesa.

eat·er·y (ē'tə-rē) s. [pl. **-ies**] FAM. *(diner)* fonda; *(restaurant)* restaurante pequeño.

eat·ing (ē'tĭng) **I.** s. *(act)* acción de comer *f*; *(food)* comida **II.** adj. de *o* para comer.

eats (ēts) s.pl. JER. comida, alimento.

eaves (ēvz) s.pl. ARQ. alero, tejaroz *m.*

eaves·drop (ēvz'drŏp') intr. **-dropped, -drop·ping** escuchar disimulada *o* secretamente.

eaves·drop·per (ēvz'drŏp'ər) s. persona que escucha disimulada *o* secretamente.

ebb (ĕb) **I.** s. *(tide)* menguante *f*, reflujo; FIG. *(decline)* decadencia, caída ♦ **e. and flow** MARÍT. flujo y reflujo; FIG. *(ups and down)* los altibajos • **the e. of life** FIG. la vejez • **to be at a low e.** FIG. tener poca energía **II.** intr. MARÍT. menguar, bajar; FIG. *(to decline)* decaer, declinar.

ebb tide s. MARÍT. marea menguante.

eb·on·y (ĕb'ə-nē) **I.** s. [pl. **-ies**] BOT. ébano (madera y árbol) **II.** adj. negro.

e·bul·lience (ĭ-bŏol'yəns, ĭ-bŭl'-) s. *(effervescence)* ebullición *f*, efervescencia; FIG. *(enthusiasm)* exaltación *f*, entusiasmo.

e·bul·lient (ĭ-bŏol'yənt, ĭ-bŭl'-) adj. *(boiling)* hirviente; FIG. *(lively)* entusiasta; *(bubbly)* burbujeante.

eb·ul·li·tion (ĕb'ə-lĭsh'ən) s. *(act)* ebullición *f*, hervor *m*; FIG. *(outburst)* arrebato.

ec·cen·tric (ĭk-sĕn'trĭk) **I.** adj. *(not normal)* excéntrico, extravagante; GEOM., MEC. excéntrico **II.** s. *(person)* excéntrico; MEC. excéntrica.

ec·cen·tric·i·ty (ĭk'sĕn-trĭs'ĭ-tē) s. [pl. **-ties**] excentricidad *f.*

Ec·cle·si·as·tes (ĭ-klē'zē-ăs'tēz') s. BÍBL. Eclesiastés.

ec·cle·si·as·tic (ĭ-klē'zē-ăs'tĭk) **I.** adj. RELIG. eclesiástico **II.** s. eclesiástico, clérigo.

ec·cle·si·as·ti·cal (ĭ-klē'zē-ăs'tĭ-kəl) adj. eclesiástico.

Ec·cle·si·as·ti·cus (ĭ-klē'zē-ăs'tĭ-kəs) s. BÍBL. Eclesiástico.

ech·e·lon (ĕsh'ə-lŏn') **I.** s. MIL. *(formation)* escalón *m*; *(rank)* grado, clase *f*; *(level)* nivel *m*; ÓPT. difracción en escalones *f* **II.** tr. & intr. escalonar(se).

ech·o (ĕk'ō) **I.** s. [pl. **-oes**] *(sound)* eco; FIG. *(repetition)* eco, repetición *f*; *(sympathy)* resonancia, acogida favor-

able; AER., ELECTRÓN., MÚS., POÉT. eco ♦ **e. chamber** cámara de resonancia **II.** tr. **-oed, -o·ing** *(to resound)* hacer eco; *(to repeat)* repetir; *(to imitate)* imitar —intr. producir eco, resonar <*his footsteps echoed in the dark* sus pasos resonaron en la oscuridad>.

ech·o·car·di·o·gram (ĕk'ō-kär'dē-ə-grăm') s. cardiograma obtenido por sonido ultrasónico.

ech·o·lo·ca·tion (ĕk'ō-lō-kā'shən) s. BIOL., ELEC. ecolocación *f.*

é·clat (ā-klä') s. *(brilliance)* brillo; *(success)* éxito clamoroso; *(acclamation)* aclamación *f.*

e·clec·tic (ĭ-klĕk'tĭk) adj. & s. ecléctico.

e·clec·ti·cism (ĭ-klĕk'tĭ-sĭz'əm) s. eclecticismo.

e·clipse (ĭ-klĭps') **I.** s. ASTRON. eclipse *m*; FIG. *(downfall)* eclipse **II.** tr. **e·clipsed, e·clips·ing** ASTRON. eclipsar; FIG. *(to outshine)* eclipsar, superar en brillantez.

e·clip·tic (ĭ-klĭp'tĭk) s. ASTRON. eclíptica.

e·co·log·i·cal (ĕk'ə-lŏj'ĭ-kəl, ē'kə-) adj. ecológico.

e·col·o·gist (ĭ-kŏl'ə-jĭst) s. ecólogo.

e·col·o·gy (ĭ-kŏl'ə-jē) s. ecología.

e·con·o·met·rics (ĭ-kŏn'ə-mĕt'rĭks) s.pl. [ú. con v. sing.] econometría *f.*

ec·o·nom·ic (ĕk'ə-nŏm'ĭk, ē'kə-) adj. económico.

ec·o·nom·i·cal (ĕk'ə-nŏm'ĭ-kəl, ē'kə-) adj. *(economic)* económico; *(thrifty)* frugal.

ec·o·nom·ics (ĕk'ə-nŏm'ĭks, ē'kə-) s. [ú. con v. sing.] *(science)* economía; *(profitability)* rentabilidad *f.*

e·con·o·mist (ĭ-kŏn'ə-mĭst) s. economista *mf.*

e·con·o·mize (ĭ-kŏn'ə-mīz') intr. **-mized, -miz·ing** economizar ♦ **to e. on** economizar en —tr. economizar.

e·con·o·my (ĭ-kŏn'ə-mē) **I.** s. [pl. **-mies**] economía *f* **II.** adj. económico <*e. car* automóvil económico>.

economy class s. clase económica *o* turista.

e·co·sys·tem (ĕk'ə-sĭs'təm, ē'kə-) s. ECOL. ecosistema *m.*

ec·ru (ĕk'rōo, ā'krōo) adj. de color crudo, amarillento.

ec·sta·sy (ĕk'stə-sē) s. [pl. **-sies**] *(delight)* éxtasis *m*; *(rapture)* rapto, arrebato.

ec·stat·ic (ĕk-stăt'ĭk) adj. extático.

ec·to·plasm (ĕk'tə-plăz'əm) s. BIOL. ectoplasma *m*; *(in spiritism)* efluvio.

Ec·ua·dor (ĕk'wə-dôr') s. Ecuador *m.*

Ec·ua·dor·i·an (ĕk'wə-dôr'ē-ən) adj. & s. ecuatoriano.

ec·u·men·i·cal (ĕk'yə-mĕn'ĭ-kəl) *o* **ec·u·men·ic** (-mĕn'ĭk) adj. ecuménico, universal.

ec·u·me·nism (ĕk'yə-mə-nĭz'əm, ĭ-kyōo'-) s. RELIG. ecumenismo.

ec·ze·ma (ĕk'sə-mə, ĭg-zē'-) s. MED. eczema *m*, eccema *m.*

E·den (ēd'n) s. BÍBL. edén *m.*

ed·dy (ĕd'ē) **I.** s. [pl. **-dies**] *(whirlpool)* remolino; *(countercurrent)* contracorriente *f* **II.** intr. **-died, -dy·ing** arremolinarse, remolinar —tr. remolinar.

e·del·weiss (ā'dəl-vīs') s. BOT. edelweiss (planta alpina) *m.*

e·de·ma (ĭ-dē'mə) s. BOT., MED. edema *m.*

edge (ĕj) **I.** s. *(cutting side)* filo, corte *m*; *(ridge)* borde *m*; *(boundary)* linde *m*, límite *m*; *(shoreline)* borde, orilla; *(outskirts)* afueras; *(margin)* margen *m*; *(angle)* ángulo, arista; *(blunt edge)* canto (moneda, libro); *(farthest part)* extremidad *f*, punta; *(trimming)* orilla, ribete *m*; FIG. *(sharpness)* filo, mordacidad *f*; FAM. *(advantage)* ventaja, superioridad *f* ♦ **on e.** de canto • **to be on e.** tener los nervios de punta, estar tenso • **to be on the cutting** *o* **leading e. of** estar en el puesto de avanzada • **to be on the e. of** estar al borde *o* al punto de • **to have an e. on** *o* **over** llevar una ventaja a • **to set one's teeth** *o* **nerves on e.** FIG. dar dentera, ponerle a uno los pelos de punta • **to take the e. off** *(to blunt)* embotar; *(the appetite)* acallar **II.** tr. **edged, edg·ing** *(to sharpen)* afilar; *(to border)* bordear; *(to trim)* ribetear ♦ **to e. someone out** vencer por un margen pequeño • **to e. towards** mover *o* adelantar poco a poco —intr. andar *o* moverse cautelosamente.

edge·wise (ĕj'wīz') *o* **edge·ways** (-wāz') adv. *(on end)* de filo *o* de canto; *(sideways)* sesgadamente, de lado ♦ **not to be able to get a word in e.** no poder meter baza.

edg·ing (ĕj'ĭng) s. *(edge)* borde *m*; *(trimming)* orla, ribete *m.*

edg·y (ĕj'ē) adj. **-i·er, -i·est** *(tense)* nervioso, tenso; *(sharp)* afilado, agudo; *(clear)* nítido, claro.
ed·i·ble (ĕd'ə-bəl) I. adj. comestible, comible II. s. comestible *m*.
e·dict (ē'dĭkt') s. edicto.
ed·i·fi·ca·tion (ĕd'ə-fĭ-kā'shən) s. *(instruction)* edificación *f*, instrucción *f*; *(enlightenment)* esclarecimiento.
ed·i·fice (ĕd'ə-fĭs) s. edificio.
ed·i·fy (ĕd'ə-fī') tr. **-fied, -fy·ing** *(to instruct)* edificar; *(to enlighten)* esclarecer.
Ed·in·burgh (ĕd'n-bûr'ə) s. Edimburgo.
ed·it (ĕd'ĭt) tr. *(to prepare text)* redactar; *(to correct)* corregir; *(to take out)* quitar, suprimir; *(to revise)* preparar para la imprenta; *(a publication)* dirigir; CINEM. hacer el montaje, montar.
ed·it·ing (ĕd'ĭ-tĭng) s. *(of text)* redacción *f*; *(correction)* corrección *f*, revisión *f*; *(of newspaper)* dirección *f*; *(of film)* montaje *m*.
e·di·tion (ĭ-dĭsh'ən) s. *(publication)* edición *f* <*a pocket e.* edición de bolsillo>; *(number of copies)* tiraje *m*, tirada *f*; FIG. versión *f* <*he is a smaller e. of his father* es una versión en pequeño de su padre>.
ed·i·tor (ĕd'ĭ-tər) s. *(supervisor)* redactor jefe *m*, director *o* jefe de redacción *m*; *(of textbooks, films)* editor *m*; *(commentator)* editorialista *mf*; CINEM. *(film cutter)* montador *m*.
ed·i·to·ri·al (ĕd'ĭ-tôr'ē-əl) I. s. editorial *m*, artículo de fondo II. adj. editorial, de redacción ♦ **e. staff** redacción.
ed·i·to·ri·al·ize (ĕd'ĭ-tôr'ē-ə-līz') intr. **-ized, -iz·ing** escribir editoriales *o* artículos de fondo.
editor in chief s. [pl. **editors in chief**] jefe de redacción *m*, redactor en jefe *m*.
ed·i·tor·ship (ĕd'ĭ-tər-shĭp') s. dirección *f*, redacción *f*.
ed·u·ca·ble (ĕj'ə-kə-bəl) adj. educable.
ed·u·cate (ĕj'ə-kāt') tr. **-cat·ed, -cat·ing** *(to teach)* educar, enseñar; *(to train)* entrenar; *(an animal)* amaestrar.
ed·u·cat·ed (ĕj'ə-kā'tĭd) adj. *(cultured)* culto, cultivado; *(schooled)* educado, instruido; *(informed)* informado; *(trained)* amaestrado (animal).
ed·u·ca·tion (ĕj'ə-kā'shən) s. *(act)* educación *f*, enseñanza; *(knowledge)* educación, cultura; *(training)* entrenamiento.
ed·u·ca·tion·al (ĕj'ə-kā'shə-nəl) adj. *(relating to education)* docente; *(imparting knowledge)* educativo.
ed·u·ca·tive (ĕj'ə-kā'tĭv) adj. educativo, instructivo.
ed·u·ca·tor (ĕj'ə-kā'tər) s. *(teacher)* educador *m*; *(pedagogue)* pedagogo.
Ed·ward·i·an (ĕd-wär'dē-ən) adj. eduardiano.
eel (ēl) s. [pl. **eel** *o* **eels**] ICT. anguila.
e'er (âr) contr. de **ever**.
ee·rie *o* **ee·ry** (îr'ē) adj. **-ri·er, -ri·est** *(creepy)* horripilante, espeluznante; *(scary)* espantoso, pavoroso; *(weird)* extraño; *(mysterious)* sobrenatural, misterioso.
ef·face (ĭ-fās') tr. **-faced, -fac·ing** borrar <*time effaced the memory* el tiempo borró el recuerdo> ♦ **to e. oneself** comportarse sin llamar la atención.
ef·fect (ĭ-fĕkt') I. s. *(result)* resultado, consecuencia; *(influence)* efecto; *(impression)* impresión *f*, efecto ♦ **effects** *(belongings)* bienes, pertenencias • **for e.** para causar efecto, para impresionar • **in e.** *(in fact)* efectivamente, en realidad; *(virtually)* casi, prácticamente; *(in operation)* en vigor, vigente • **or words to that e.** o algo por el estilo • **personal effects** efectos personales • **sound effects** efectos sonoros • **special effects** efectos especiales • **to be in e.** estar vigente • **to go into e.** entrar en vigor • **to have no e.** no dar resultado • **to no e.** inútilmente, sin resultado • **to take e.** *(medication)* surtir efecto; *(laws, schedule)* entrar en vigor, tener efecto • **to that e.** por el estilo, en el mismo sentido (palabras) II. tr. efectuar, realizar.
ef·fec·tive (ĭ-fĕk'tĭv) I. adj. *(efficacious)* efectivo, eficaz; *(striking)* impresionante; *(operative)* vigente; MIL. disponible, efectivo II. s. MIL. efectivos.
ef·fec·tive·ness (ĭ-fĕk'tĭv-nĭs) s. *(efficiency)* eficacia, (effect) efecto.
ef·fec·tu·al (ĭ-fĕk'chōō-əl) adj. eficaz.
ef·fec·tu·ate (ĭ-fĕk'chōō-āt') tr. **-at·ed, -at·ing** efectuar, realizar.

ef·fem·i·na·cy (ĭ-fĕm'ə-nə-sē) s. afeminación *f*, afemimiento.
ef·fem·i·nate (ĭ-fĕm'ə-nĭt) adj. afeminado.
ef·fer·ent (ĕf'ər-ənt) adj. FISIOL. eferente.
ef·fer·vesce (ĕf'ər-vĕs') intr. **-vesced, -vesc·ing** *(to bubble)* estar en efervescencia; *(to be vivacious)* bullir, hervir.
ef·fer·ves·cence (ĕf'ər-vĕs'əns) s. *(act, condition)* efervescencia; *(vivacity)* vivacidad *f*.
ef·fer·ves·cent (ĕf'ər-vĕs'ənt) adj. *(bubbly)* efervescente; *(vivacious)* vivaz.
ef·fete (ĭ-fēt') adj. *(infertile)* estéril; *(worn-out)* exhausto, gastado; *(decadent)* decadente; *(overrefined)* refinadísimo, remilgado.
ef·fi·ca·cious (ĕf'ĭ-kā'shəs) adj. eficaz.
ef·fi·ca·cy (ĕf'ĭ-kə-sē) s. eficacia.
ef·fi·cien·cy (ĭ-fĭsh'ən-sē) s. [pl. **-cies**] *(effectiveness)* eficacia, eficiencia; FAM. *(apartment)* apartamento de un cuarto con cocina y baño; MEC. rendimiento.
ef·fi·cient (ĭ-fĭsh'ənt) adj. *(effective)* eficaz, eficiente; MEC. de buen *o* gran rendimiento ♦ **e. cause** causa eficiente.
ef·fi·gy (ĕf'ə-jē) s. [pl. **-gies**] efigie *f*.
ef·flo·resce (ĕf'lə-rĕs') intr. **-resced, -resc·ing** BOT. florecer; QUÍM. eflorecerse.
ef·flo·res·cence (ĕf'lə-rĕs'əns) s. BOT. florecimiento, florecencia; QUÍM. eflorecencia.
ef·flu·ence (ĕf'lōō-əns) s. emanación *f*, efluvio.
ef·flu·ent (ĕf'lōō-ənt) I. adj. efluente II. s. chorro.
ef·flu·vi·um (ĭ-flōō'vē-əm) s. [pl. **-vi·a** (-vē-ə) *o* **-vi·ums**] *(emanation)* efluvio, emanación *f*; *(aura)* irradiación *f*.
ef·fort (ĕf'ərt) s. *(exertion)* esfuerzo; *(achievement)* obra, producto; *(attempt)* tentativa ♦ **to make an e.** hacer un esfuerzo • **to spare no e.** hacer todo lo posible.
ef·fort·less (ĕf'ərt-lĭs) adj. fácil, sin esfuerzo.
ef·fron·ter·y (ĭ-frŭn'tə-rē) s. [pl. **-ies**] descaro, desvergüenza.
ef·ful·gence (ĭ-fŏŏl'jəns, ĭ-fŭl'-) s. resplandor *m*, refulgencia.
ef·ful·gent (ĭ-fŏŏl'jənt, ĭ-fŭl'-) adj. resplandeciente, refulgente.
ef·fuse (ĭ-fyōōz') tr. & intr. **-fused, -fus·ing** *(to pour out)* derramar(se); *(to disseminate)* diseminar(se).
ef·fu·sion (ĭ-fyōō'zhən) s. *(act)* efusión *f*; *(of feelings)* efusión, desahogo; MED. derrame *m*.
ef·fu·sive (ĭ-fyōō'sĭv) adj. efusivo.
e·gad (ĭ-găd') interj. ¡pardiez!
e·gal·i·tar·i·an (ĭ-găl'ĭ-târ'ē-ən) I. adj. igualitario, de la doctrina de la igualdad social II. s. partidario de la igualdad social.
egg (ĕg) I. s. *(food)* huevo; BIOL. óvulo; JER. *(fellow)* tío, tipo ♦ **bad e.** JER. calavera • **fried e.** huevo frito • **good e.** JER. buen tipo • **hard-boiled e.** huevo duro • **poached e.** huevo escalfado • **scrambled eggs** huevos revueltos • **soft-boiled e.** huevo pasado por agua • **to kill the goose that laid the golden e.** matar la gallina de los huevos de oro • **to lay an e.** *(animals)* poner un huevo; FAM. *(to fail)* fracasar completamente • **to put all one's eggs in one basket** jugárselo todo en una carta • **to walk** *o* **tread on eggs** andar con extremo cuidado • **with e. on one's face** pasando vergüenza II. tr. CUL. arrebozar, rebozar ♦ **to e. someone on** incitar a alguien.
egg·beat·er (ĕg'bē'tər) s. batidor de huevos *m*.
egg·head (ĕg'hĕd') s. JER. *(intellectual)* intelectual *mf*; *(theorist)* científico.
egg·nog (ĕg'nŏg') s. ponche (de leche, huevos y licor) *m*, ronpopo.
egg·plant (ĕg'plănt') s. berenjena.
egg·shell (ĕg'shĕl') s. *(shell)* cascarón *m*, cáscara de huevo; *(color)* blanco amarillento.
egg white s. clara de huevo.
e·go (ē'gō, ĕg'ō) s. [pl. **e·gos**] *(self)* yo, ego; *(egotism)* egoísmo.
e·go·cen·tric (ē'gō-sĕn'trĭk, ĕg'ō-) adj. egocéntrico.
e·go·cen·tric·i·ty (ē'gō-sĕn-trĭs'ĭ-tē, ĕg'ō-) s. egocentrismo.
e·go·ism (ē'gō-ĭz'əm, ĕg'ō-) s. *(self-interest)* egoísmo; *(egotism)* egotismo.

e·go·ist (ē'gō-ĭst, ĕg'ō-) s. *(selfish person)* egoísta *mf*; *(egotist)* egotista *mf*, ególatra *mf.*

e·go·is·tic (ē'gō-ĭs'tĭk, ĕg'ō-) *o* **e·go·is·ti·cal** (-tĭ-kəl) adj. egoísta.

e·go·ma·ni·a (ē'gō-mā'nē-ə, ĕg'ō-) s. preocupación obsesiva *o* patológica con el ego.

e·go·tism (ē'gə-tĭz'əm, ĕg'ə-) s. egotismo.

e·go·tist (ē'gə-tĭst, ĕg'ə-) s. *(self-important person)* egotista *mf*; *(egoist)* egoísta *mf.*

e·go·tis·tic (ē'gə-tĭs'tĭk) *o* **e·go·tis·ti·cal** (-tĭ-kəl) adj. *(selfish)* egoísta; *(self-important)* egotista.

ego trip s. JER. satisfacción del ego *f*, cumplido ♦ **what an e.!** ¡qué agradable *o* halago! • **to be on an e.** tener una experiencia muy halagadora *o* agradable, sentirse satisfecho de sí mismo.

e·gre·gious (ĭ-grē'jəs) adj. *(atrocious)* atroz; *(blatant)* flagrante; *(extraordinary)* extraordinario.

e·gress (ē'grĕs') s. salida.

e·gret (ē'grĭt, ĕg'rĭt) s. ORNIT. airón *m*, garceta.

E·gypt (ē'jĭpt) s. Egipto.

E·gyp·tian (ĭ-jĭp'shən) adj. & s. egipcio.

eh (ā, ĕ) interj. eh *<he's a shrewd one, eh?* es astuto, ¿eh?>.

ei·der·down (ī'dər-doun') s. edredón *m.*

eight (āt) I. s. *(number)* ocho; *(boat)* bote de a ocho *m* ♦ **e. o'clock** las ocho II. adj. ocho.

eight ball s. bola negra (de billar que lleva el número ocho) ♦ **to be behind the e.** FAM. estar en apuros.

eight·een (ā-tēn') s. & adj. dieciocho, diez y ocho.

eight·eenth (ā-tēnth') I. s. *(place)* dieciocho; *(part)* dieciochavo, dieciochava parte II. adj. *(place)* décimoctavo; *(part)* dieciochavo.

eighth (ātth) s. & adj. octavo.

eight hundred s. & adj. ochocientos.

eighth note s. MÚS. corchea.

eight·i·eth (ā'tē-ĭth) I. s. *(place)* ochenta; *(part)* ochentavo, octogésima parte II. adj. octogésimo.

eight·y (ā'tē) s. & adj. ochenta *m.*

eight·y-one (ā'tē-wŭn') s. & adj. ochenta y uno.

Ein·stein·i·an (īn-stī'nē-ən) adj. de Einstein.

ein·stein·i·um (īn-stīn'ē-əm) s. QUÍM. einstenio.

ei·ther §G36 (ē'thər, ī'thər) I. pron. uno u otro, cualquiera de los dos *<you can wear e. of the coats* puedes ponerte cualquiera de los dos abrigos>; [en oraciones negativas] ni uno ni otro, ninguno de los dos *<I don't like e. of them* no me gusta ninguno de los dos> II. conj. o . . . o *<e. we go now, or we remain here forever* o nos vamos ahora o nos quedamos aquí para siempre>; III. adj. uno u otro, cualquiera de los dos *<you can take e. coat* puedes tomar cualquiera de los dos abrigos>; [en oraciones negativas] ni uno ni otro, ninguno de los dos *<I don't like e. one* no me gusta ninguno de los dos>; *(both)* ambos *<she had rings on e. hand* tenía anillos en ambas manos> IV. adv. tampoco *<if you don't go, I won't e.* si tú no vas, yo tampoco>.

e·jac·u·late (ĭ-jăk'yə-lāt') I. tr. **-lat·ed, -lat·ing** FISIOL. eyacular, expeler; *(to exclaim)* exclamar, proferir de repente —intr. eyacular II. s. (-lĭt) eyaculación *f*, semen eyaculado.

e·jac·u·la·tion (ĭ-jăk'yə-lā'shən) s. *(act)* eyaculación *f*; *(exclamation)* exclamación *f*; *(prayer)* jaculatoria.

e·ject (ĭ-jĕkt') tr. *(to throw out)* expeler, expulsar (persona); *(to evict)* desahuciar —intr. AVIA. eyectar, expeler (un piloto).

e·jec·tion (ĭ-jĕk'shən) s. *(dismissal)* expulsión *f*; AER., ARM. eyección *f.*

ejection seat s. asiento eyectable *o* lanzable, asiento proyectable.

e·jec·tor (ĭ-jĕk'tər) s. MEC. eyector *m*; ARM. eyector, expulsor *m.*

eke (ēk) tr. **eked, ek·ing** hacer durar, escatimar ♦ **to e. out** suplir para que sea apenas suficiente • **to e. out a living** ganarse la vida a duras penas.

el *o* **El** (ĕl) s. FAM. ferrocarril elevado.

e·lab·o·rate (ĭ-lăb'ər-ĭt) I. adj. *(detailed)* detallado, esmerado; *(intricate)* intrincado, complicado II. tr. (-ə-rāt') **-rat·ed, -rat·ing** *(to create)* elaborar; *(to work out)* desarrollar

—intr. explicarse ♦ **to e. on** explayarse, explicar con más detalles.

e·lab·o·ra·tion (ĭ-lăb'ə-rā'shən) s. *(of a project)* elaboración *f*; *(explanation)* explicación *f.*

e·lapse (ĭ-lăps') intr. **e·lapsed, e·laps·ing** transcurrir, pasar (el tiempo).

e·las·tic (ĭ-lăs'tĭk) I. adj. *(stretchable)* elástico; *(flexible)* flexible II. s. *(fabric)* elástico; *(rubber band)* goma elástica.

e·las·tic·i·ty (ĭ-lă-stĭs'ĭ-tē) s. *(condition, property)* elasticidad *f*; *(flexibility)* flexibilidad *f.*

e·late (ĭ-lāt') I. tr. **e·lat·ed, e·lat·ing** regocijar, alborozar II. adj. regocijado, alborozado.

e·lat·ed (ĭ-lā'tĭd) adj. contento, alborozado.

e·la·tion (ĭ-lā'shən) s. regocijo, alegría.

el·bow (ĕl'bō') I. s. *(of people)* codo; *(of animals)* codillo; *(bend)* recodo, curva II. tr. *(to jab)* dar un codazo; *(to make one's way)* abrirse paso a codazos —intr. abrirse paso a codazos.

elbow grease s. FAM. energía física, trabajo.

el·bow·room (ĕl'bō-rōom', -rōm') s. *(ample space)* espacio suficiente; *(leeway)* libertad *f o* campo de acción.

eld·er (ĕl'dər) I. adj. mayor *<an e. sister* una hermana mayor> ♦ **the E.** el Viejo • **to be (two) years (his) e.** ser (dos) años mayor que (él) II. s. *(old person)* mayor *m <to respect one's elders* tener respeto a los mayores>; *(leader)* anciano (del pueblo); RELIG. anciano.

eld·er·ly (ĕl'dər-lē) adj. mayor (de edad), entrado en años ♦ **the e.** la gente mayor de edad.

eld·est (ĕl'dĭst) adj. mayor *<my e. brother* mi hermano mayor>.

El Dorado (ĕl'də-rä'dō) s. Eldorado.

e·lect (ĭ-lĕkt') I. tr. & intr. elegir II. adj. *(chosen)* escogido, selecto; POL. electo *<president-elect* presidente electo>♦ **the e.** RELIG. los elegidos.

e·lec·tion (ĭ-lĕk'shən) s. *(choice)* elección *f*; *(for public office)* elecciones ♦ **e. returns** *o* **results** resultados electorales • **e. time** período electoral • **to hold an e.** convocar elecciones.

e·lec·tion·eer (ĭ-lĕk'shə-nîr') POL. intr. *(to work actively)* hacer campaña electoral; *(to canvass)* solicitar votos (en una campaña electoral).

e·lec·tive (ĭ-lĕk'tĭv) I. adj. *(electoral)* electivo, electoral; *(optional)* elegible, opcional II. s. asignatura *o* materia electiva, curso electivo.

e·lec·tor (ĭ-lĕk'tər) s. *(person)* elector, votante; *(of the Electoral College)* miembro del colegio electoral (de EE. UU.).

e·lec·tor·al (ĭ-lĕk'tər-əl) adj. electoral.

e·lec·tor·ate (ĭ-lĕk'tər-ĭt) s. POL. *(qualified voters)* electorado; *(district)* distrito electoral.

e·lec·tric (ĭ-lĕk'trĭk) *or* **e·lec·tri·cal** (-trĭ-kəl) I. adj. FÍS. eléctrico; FIG. *(thrilling)* excitante, emocionante II. s. tranvía *m o* ferrocarril eléctrico.

electrical engineering s. ingeniería eléctrica, electrotecnia.

electric cell s. ELEC. pila eléctrica.

electric chair s. silla eléctrica.

electric charge s. ELEC. carga eléctrica.

electric current s. ELEC. corriente eléctrica.

electric eel s. ICT. anguila eléctrica.

electric eye s. ELECTRÓN. ojo eléctrico, célula fotoeléctrica.

electric field s. ELEC. campo eléctrico.

electric guitar s. MÚS. guitarra eléctrica.

e·lec·tri·cian (ĭ-lĕk-trĭsh'ən) s. electricista *mf.*

e·lec·tric·i·ty (ĭ-lĕk-trĭs'ĭ-tē) s. electricidad *f.*

electric lamp s. ELEC. lámpara eléctrica.

electric light s. ELEC. luz eléctrica.

electric motor s. ELEC. motor eléctrico, electromotor *m.*

e·lec·tri·fi·ca·tion (ĭ-lĕk'trə-fĭ-kā'shən) s. electrificación *f.*

e·lec·tri·fy (ĭ-lĕk'trə-fī') tr. **-fied, -fy·ing** *(to equip)* electrizar, electrificar; FIG. *(to excite)* excitar, electrizar.

e·lec·tro·car·di·o·gram (ĭ-lĕk'trō-kär'dē-ə-grăm') s. MED. electrocardiograma *m.*

e·lec·tro·car·di·o·graph (ĭ-lĕk'trō-kär'dē-ə-grăf') s. MED. electrocardiógrafo.

e·lec·tro·cute (ĭ-lĕk'trə-kyōot') tr. **-cut·ed, -cut·ing** electrocutar.

---

e·lec·trode (ĭ-lĕk′trōd′) s. ELEC. electrodo.
e·lec·tro·dy·nam·ics (ĭ-lĕk′trō-dī-năm′ĭks) s. [ú. con v. sing.] FÍS. electrodinámica.
e·lec·tro·en·ceph·a·lo·graph (ĭ-lĕk′trō-ĕn-sĕf′ə-lə-grăf′) s. MED. electroencefalógrafo.
e·lec·trol·y·sis (ĭ-lĕk-trŏl′ĭ-sĭs) s. FÍS., QUÍM. electrólisis f; MED. tratamiento electrolítico.
e·lec·tro·lyte (ĭ-lĕk′trə-līt′) s. FÍS., QUÍM. electrólito.
e·lec·tro·lyt·ic cell (ĭ-lĕk′trə-lĭt′ĭk) s. FÍS., QUÍM. célula o cuba electrolítica.
e·lec·tro·mag·net (ĭ-lĕk′trō-măg′nĭt) s. FÍS., ELEC. electroimán m.
e·lec·tro·mag·net·ic (ĭ-lĕk′trō-măg-nĕt′ĭk) adj. electromagnético.
electromagnetic field s. FÍS. campo electromagnético.
e·lec·tro·mag·net·ism (ĭ-lĕk′trō-măg′nĭ-tĭz′əm) s. ELEC., FÍS. electromagnetismo.
e·lec·tro·me·chan·i·cal (ĭ-lĕk′trō-mĭ-kăn′ĭ-kəl) adj. TEC. electromecánico.
e·lec·trom·e·ter (ĭ-lĕk′trŏm′ĭ-tər) s. ELEC., FÍS. electrómetro.
e·lec·tro·mo·tive force (ĭ-lĕk′trō-mō′tĭv) s. ELEC., FÍS. fuerza electromotriz.
e·lec·tron (ĭ-lĕk′trŏn′) s. FÍS., QUÍM. electrón m.
e·lec·tro·neg·a·tive (ĭ-lĕk′trō-nĕg′ə-tĭv) adj. ELEC., FÍS., QUÍM. electronegativo.
electron gun s. FÍS. lanzador de electrones m, cañon electrónico.
e·lec·tron·ic (ĭ-lĕk-trŏn′ĭk) adj. electrónico, de la electrónica.
electronic flash s. ELECTRÓN., FOTOG. flash electrónico.
electronic music s. ACÚS. música electrónica.
e·lec·tron·ics (ĭ-lĕk-trŏn′ĭks) s. [ú. con v. sing.] electrónica.
electron microscope s. FÍS. microscopio electrónico.
electron volt s. FÍS. electrón-voltio, voltio electrónico.
e·lec·tro·plate (ĭ-lĕk′trə-plāt′) tr. **-plat·ed, -plat·ing** galvanizar o platear (por electrodeposición).
e·lec·tro·pos·i·tive (ĭ-lĕk′trō-pŏz′ĭ-tĭv) adj. ELEC., FÍS., QUÍM. electropositivo.
e·lec·tro·shock (ĭ-lĕk′trō-shŏk′) s. MED. electrochoque m.
e·lec·tro·stat·ic (ĭ-lĕk′trō-stăt′ĭk) adj. ELEC., FÍS. electrostático.
electrostatic precipitation s. ELEC. precipitación electrostática.
e·lec·tro·ther·mal (ĭ-lĕk′trō-thûr′məl) adj. ELEC. electrotérmico.
e·lec·tro·type (ĭ-lĕk′trə-tīp′) I. s. ELEC., IMPR. electrotipo, galvano; (electrotypy) electrotipia II. tr. **-typed, -typ·ing** electrotipar, galvanotipar.
e·lec·tro·va·lence (ĭ-lĕk′trō-vā′ləns) o **e·lec·tro·va·len·cy** (-lən-sē) s. FÍS., QUÍM. electrovalencia.
el·e·gance (ĕl′ĭ-gəns) o **el·e·gan·cy** (-gən-sē) s. elegancia.
el·e·gant (ĕl′ĭ-gənt) adj. (graceful) elegante; (refined) refinado; (excellent) excelente.
el·e·gi·ac (ĕl′ə-jī′ək, ĭ-lē′jē-ăk′) o **el·e·gi·a·cal** (ĕl′ə-jī′ə-kəl) I. adj. (of an elegy) elegíaco; (mournful) triste, apenado II. s. POÉT. poesía o dístico elegiaco.
el·e·gist (ĕl′ə-jĭst) s. autor de elegías m.
el·e·gize (ĕl′ə-jīz′) intr. **-gized, -giz·ing** escribir elegías —tr. escribir una elegía para.
el·e·gy (ĕl′ə-jē) s. [pl. **-gies**] POÉT. elegía.
el·e·ment (ĕl′ə-mənt) s. (part) elemento, parte f; (portion) algo <an e. of truth algo de verdad>; (factor) factor m; (environment) elemento; MAT., QUÍM., FÍS. elemento ♦ **ele·ments** elementos • **the elements** (weather) los elementos; RELIG. especies eucarísticas • **to be in** (o out of) **one's e.** estar uno en (o fuera de) su elemento.
el·e·men·tal (ĕl′ə-mĕn′tl) adj. (of an element) a o de los elementos; (fundamental) elemental.
el·e·men·ta·ry (ĕl′ə-mĕn′tə-rē) adj. elemental.
elementary particle s. FÍS. partícula elemental o fundamental.
elementary school s. escuela primaria.
el·e·phant (ĕl′ə-fənt) s. ZOOL. elefante m.
el·e·phan·ti·a·sis (ĕl′ə-fən-tī′ə-sĭs) s. MED. elefantiasis f, elefancia.

el·e·phan·tine (ĕl′ə-făn′tēn′, -tīn′) adj. (of an elephant) elefantino; (huge) enorme, inmenso; (clumsy) torpe.
el·e·vate (ĕl′ə-vāt′) tr. **-vat·ed, -vat·ing** (to raise) elevar, alzar; (to increase) subir, aumentar; (to edify) elevar, levantar; (to elate) regocijar ♦ **to e. someone to** ascender a alguien a.
el·e·vat·ed (ĕl′ə-vā′tĭd) I. adj. (raised) elevado; FIG. (exalted) elevado, exaltado; (elated) alborozado II. s. FAM. ferrocarril elevado.
elevated railway s. ferrocarril elevado.
el·e·va·tion (ĕl′ə-vā′shən) s. (act) elevación f; (height) elevación f, altura; (exaltation) elevación, exaltación f; GEOG., TOP. altitud f.
el·e·va·tor (ĕl′ə-vā′tər) s. (in a building) elevador m, ascensor m; (on a farm) elevador; AVIA. timón de profundidad m.
el·ev·en (ĭ-lĕv′ən) s. & adj. once m ♦ **e. o'clock** las once.
el·ev·enth (ĭ-lĕv′ənth) I. s. (place) undécimo, onceno; (part) onzavo, undécima parte II. adj. (place) undécimo, onceno; (part) onzavo.
eleventh hour s. FIG. último momento <they were rescued at the e. los rescataron en el último momento>.
elf (ĕlf) s. [pl. **elves** (ĕlvz)] (creature) duende m; (child) elfo, diablillo.
elf·in (ĕl′fĭn) adj. (of an elf) de duende, semejante a un duende; (fairylike) mágico; (mischievous) travieso.
elf·ish (ĕl′fĭsh) adj. (of elves) de duende; (supernatural) mágico; FIG. (mischievous) travieso.
e·lic·it (ĭ-lĭs′ĭt) tr. (to bring out) sonsacar, sacar; (to obtain) obtener; (to evoke) evocar; (to cause) provocar.
e·lide (ĭ-līd′) tr. **e·lid·ed, e·lid·ing** FONÉT. elidir; (to eliminate) anular, suprimir.
el·i·gi·bil·i·ty (ĕl′ĭ-jə-bĭl′ĭ-tē) s. eligibilidad f.
el·i·gi·ble (ĕl′ĭ-jə-bəl) adj. (qualified) elegible; (acceptable) aceptable, adecuado.
e·lim·i·nate (ĭ-lĭm′ə-nāt′) tr. **-nat·ed, -nat·ing** eliminar.
e·lim·i·na·tion (ĭ-lĭm′ə-nā′shən) s. eliminación f.
e·lim·i·na·to·ry (ĭ-lĭm′ə-nə-tôr′ē) adj. eliminatorio.
e·li·sion (ĭ-lĭzh′ən) s. GRAM. elisión f; POÉT. omisión f.
e·lite o **é·lite** (ĭ-lēt′, ā-lēt′) s. élite f, minoría selecta.
e·lit·ism o **é·lit·ism** (ĭ-lē′tĭz′əm, ā-lē′-) s. gobierno o dominio de una élite o minoría selecta.
e·lit·ist (ĭ-lē′tĭst, ā-lē′-) I. adj. de una élite o minoría selecta II. s. persona de una minoría selecta.
el·ix·ir (ĭ-lĭk′sər) s. elixir m.
E·liz·a·be·than (ĭ-lĭz′ə-bē′thən) adj. elisabetiano, isabelino.
elk (ĕlk) s. [pl. **elks** o **elk**] ZOOL. alce m.
ell (ĕl) s. ANT. medida de longitud inglesa (equivalente a cuarenta y cinco pulgadas).
el·lipse (ĭ-lĭps′) s. GEOM. elipse f.
el·lip·sis (ĭ-lĭp′sĭs) s. [pl. **-ses** (-sēz′)] GRAM. elipsis f; IMPR. puntos suspensivos.
el·lip·soid (ĭ-lĭp′soid′) s. GEOM. elipsoide m.
el·lip·tic (ĭ-lĭp′tĭk) o **el·lip·ti·cal** (-tĭ-kəl) adj. GEOM., GRAM. elíptico.
elm (ĕlm) s. BOT. olmo.
el·o·cu·tion (ĕl′ə-kyōō′shən) s. (style) elocución f; (art) declamación f.
el·o·cu·tion·ist (ĕl′ə-kyōō′shə-nĭst) s. declamador m, orador m.
e·lon·gate (ĭ-lông′gāt′) I. tr. & intr. **-gat·ed, -gat·ing** extender(se), alargar(se) II. adj. (lengthened) extendido, alargado; (slender) delgado.
e·lon·ga·tion (ĭ-lông′gā′shən) s. extensión f, alargamiento f.
e·lope (ĭ-lōp′) intr. **e·loped, e·lop·ing** (with a lover) fugarse con un amante; (to run away) escaparse, huir.
e·lope·ment (ĭ-lōp′mənt) s. fuga.
el·o·quence (ĕl′ə-kwəns) s. elocuencia.
el·o·quent (ĕl′ə-kwənt) adj. elocuente.
El Sal·va·dor (ĕl săl′və-dôr′) s. El Salvador.
else (ĕls) adj. & adv. ♦ **all e.** o **everything e.** todo lo demás • **anybody e.** o **anyone e.** (anybody) cualquier otro, cualquier otra persona; (somebody) alguien más <is anybody e. coming? ¿viene alguien más?>; [después de una negación] ningún otro, nadie más <I don't see anyone e. there no veo a ningún otro allí> • **anything e.** cualquier otra cosa, algo

más <*have you anything e. to add?* ¿tienes algo más que agregar?>; [después de una negación] ninguna otra cosa, nada más • **anywhere e.** *(place)* en cualquier otra parte; *(direction)* a cualquier otro lugar, a cualquier otra parte; [después de una negación] a ningún otro lugar, a ninguna otra parte <*I am not going anywhere e.* no voy a ningún otro lugar>; en ningún otro lugar, en ninguna otra parte <*you won't find a better price anywhere e.* no encontrará un precio mejor en ningún otro lugar> • **everyone e.** todos los demás • **everywhere e.** *(place)* en todas partes; *(direction)* a todas partes • **how e.?** ¿de qué otro modo?, ¿de qué otra manera? • **much e.** mucho, muchas cosas • **nobody e.** o **no one e.** nadie más, ningún otro • **nothing e.** nada más • **nowhere e.** *(place)* en ningún otro lugar, en ninguna otra parte; *(direction)* a ningún otro lugar, a ninguna otra parte • **or e.** si no <*remind me of it tomorrow or e. I'll forget* recuérdamelo mañana, si no me olvido>; si no . . . <*you'd better show up on time tomorrow, or e.* mejor será que llegues a hora mañana, si no . . . > • **somebody e.** o **someone e.** otro, otra persona • **something e.** *(something different)* otra cosa; *(something additional)* otra cosa, algo más <*I want something e. but I don't know what* quiero algo más pero no sé que>; FAM. algo especial <*you're something e.!* ¡tú eres algo especial!> • **somewhere e.** *(place)* en otra parte; *(direction)* a otra parte • **what e.** ¿qué más? • **where e.?** *(place)* ¿en qué otro sitio?; *(direction)* ¿a qué otro sitio? • **who e?** ¿quién más?

else·where (ĕls′hwâr′) adv. *(to a different place)* a otra parte, a otro lado; *(in a different place)* en otra parte, en otro lado.

e·lu·ci·date (ĭ-lŏo′sĭ-dāt′) tr. **-dat·ed, -dat·ing** elucidar, poner en claro.

e·lude (ĭ-lŏod′) tr. **e·lud·ed, e·lud·ing** *(to avoid)* eludir, esquivar; *(to evade)* evadir; *(to escape from)* escapar de; *(to escape understanding)* escapársele a uno.

e·lu·sive (ĭ-lŏo′sĭv) adj. *(evasive)* evasivo; *(tending to escape)* esquivo, escurridizo; *(hard to describe)* difícil de describir.

elves (ĕlvz) pl. de **elf.**

E·ly·sian (ĭ-lĭzh′ən) adj. *(of Elysium)* elíseo; FIG. *(blissful)* paradisíaco.

'em (əm) pron. FAM. contr. de **them.**

e·ma·ci·ate (ĭ-mā′shē-āt′) tr. **-at·ed, -at·ing** *(face)* demacrar; *(body)* adelgazar, enflaquecer.

e·ma·ci·a·tion (ĭ-mā′shē-ā′shən, -sē-) s. *(of the face)* demacración *f*; *(of the body)* adelgazamiento.

em·a·nate (ĕm′ə-nāt′) intr. **-nat·ed, -nat·ing** *(to come from)* proceder de, emanar de; *(to originate)* originarse.

em·a·na·tion (ĕm′ə-nā′shən) s. *(act)* emanación *f*; *(effluence)* efluencia, efluvio; QUÍM. gas *m.*

e·man·ci·pate (ĭ-măn′sə-pāt′) tr. **-pat·ed, -pat·ing** emancipar, liberar ♦ **to become emancipated** emanciparse.

e·man·ci·pa·tion (ĭ-măn′sə-pā′shən) s. emancipación *f*, liberación *f.*

e·man·ci·pa·tor (ĭ-măn′sə-pā′tər) s. emancipador *m.*

e·mas·cu·late (ĭ-măs′kyə-lāt′) tr. **-lat·ed, -lat·ing** *(to castrate)* emascular, castrar; *(to weaken)* debilitar, disminuir; *(to make effeminate)* afeminar.

em·balm (ĕm-bäm′) tr. *(a corpse)* embalsamar; *(a memory)* conservar, preservar; *(a fragrance)* perfumar.

em·balm·er (ĕm-bä′mər) s. embalsamador *m.*

em·bank·ment (ĕm-băngk′mənt) s. *(of dirt)* terraplén *m*; *(process)* proceso de terraplenar.

em·bar·go (ĕm-bär′gō) I. s. [pl. **-goes**] *(of ships, trade)* embargo; *(restriction)* restricción *f*; *(prohibition)* prohibición *f* II. tr. **-goed, -go·ing** embargar.

em·bark (ĕm-bärk′) tr. *(passengers)* embarcar —intr. embarcarse ♦ **to e. for** embarcarse con rumbo a • **to e. on** *(to board)* embarcarse en; *(to start)* lanzarse a, aventurarse a.

em·bar·ka·tion (ĕm′bär-kā′shən) s. *(of people)* embarco; *(of goods)* embarque *m.*

em·bar·rass (ĕm-băr′əs) tr. *(to disconcert)* desconcertar, poner en un apuro; *(to humiliate)* humiliar, mortificar a; *(to cause trouble for)* poner en aprieto; *(to complicate)* complicar, dificultar; *(to hinder)* estorbar, embarazar ♦ **to be embarrassing** ser molesto o embarazoso • **to be** o **feel**

embarrassed pasar un apuro, sentirse molesto o avergonzado.

em·bar·rass·ing (ĕm-băr′əs-ĭng) adj. *(disconcerting)* desconcertante; *(troublesome)* molesto; *(causing embarrassment)* embarazoso.

em·bar·rass·ment (ĕm-băr′əs-mənt) s. *(shame)* vergüenza, turbación *f*; *(trouble)* embarazo, estorbo; *(confusion)* desconcierto.

em·bas·sy (ĕm′bə-sē) s. [pl. **-sies**] embajada.

em·bat·tled (ĕm-băt′ld) adj. asediado.

em·bed (ĕm-bĕd′) tr. & intr. **-bed·ded, -bed·ding** *(to fix in a surrounding mass)* implantar(se), incrustar(se); *(to enclose snugly)* encajar(se), empotrar(se); FIG. *(to fix)* plantar(se), fijar(se).

em·bel·lish (ĕm-bĕl′ĭsh) tr. *(to beautify)* embellecer, hermosear; *(to adorn)* adornar; *(to add)* añadir detalles a.

em·bel·lish·ment (ĕm-bĕl′ĭsh-mənt) s. *(adornment)* embellecimiento, adornamiento; *(ornamentation)* ornamento.

em·ber (ĕm′bər) s. ascua, brasa ♦ **embers** ascuas.

em·bez·zle (ĕm-bĕz′əl) tr. **-zled, -zling** *(to misappropriate)* malversar; *(to steal)* desfalcar.

em·bez·zle·ment (ĕm-bĕz′əl-mənt) s. malversación *f*, desfalco *f.*

em·bez·zler (ĕm-bĕz′lər) s. malversador *m*, desfalcador *m.*

em·bit·ter (ĕm-bĭt′ər) tr. amargar, agriar.

em·bla·zon (ĕm-blā′zən) tr. HER. blasonar; *(to make resplendent)* esmaltar con colores brillantes; *(to exalt)* ensalzar, alabar.

em·blem (ĕm′bləm) s. emblema *m.*

em·blem·at·ic (ĕm′blə-măt′ĭk) o **em·blem·at·i·cal** (-ĭ-kəl) adj. *(of an emblem)* emblemático; *(symbolic)* simbólico.

em·bod·i·ment (ĕm-bŏd′ē-mənt) s. personificación *f.*

em·bod·y (ĕm-bŏd′ē) tr. **-ied, -y·ing** *(to incarnate)* encarnar; *(to personify)* personificar; *(to include)* incluir.

em·bold·en (ĕm-bōl′dən) tr. dar ánimo a, alentar.

em·bo·lism (ĕm′bə-lĭz′əm) s. MED. embolia; ASTRON. embolismo.

em·bo·lus (ĕm′bə-ləs) s. [pl. **-li** (-lī′)] MED. émbolo.

em·boss (ĕm-bôs′) tr. *(to mold in relief)* grabar en relieve; *(leather, silver)* repujar; *(to ornament)* adornar, embellecer.

em·brace (ĕm-brās′) I. tr. **-braced, -brac·ing** *(to hug)* abrazar; *(to comprise)* abarcar, comprender; *(to adopt)* adoptar, abrazar <*to e. a cause* abrazar una causa>; *(to accept eagerly)* aprovechar, aprovecharse de (oportunidad) —intr. abrazarse II. s. *(hug)* abrazo; FIG. *(acceptance)* adopción *f*, aceptación *f.*

em·brac·er (ĕm-brā′sər) s. DER. cohechador *m*, sobornador *m.*

em·broi·der (ĕm-broi′dər) tr. COST. bordar; FIG. *(to embellish)* embellecer, adornar —intr. COST. hacer bordado.

em·broi·der·er (ĕm-broi′dər-ər) s. bordador *m*, recamador *m.*

em·broi·der·y (ĕm-broi′də-rē) s. [pl. **-ies**] COST. bordado, recamado; *(ornamentation)* adorno.

em·broil (ĕm-broil′) tr. *(to entangle)* embrollar, enredar; *(to confuse)* confundir.

em·broil·ment (ĕm-broil′mənt) s. *(entanglement)* embrollo; *(confusion)* confusión *f.*

em·bry·o (ĕm′brē-ō′) I. s. [pl. **-os**] BIOL., BOT. embrión *m* II. adj. *(incipient)* incipiente; *(rudimentary)* embrionario, rudimentario.

em·bry·ol·o·gist (ĕm′brē-ŏl′ə-jĭst) s. MED. embriólogo.

em·bry·ol·o·gy (ĕm′brē-ŏl′ə-jē) s. BIOL. embriología.

em·bry·on·ic (ĕm′brē-ŏn′ĭk) o **em·bry·o·nal** (ĕm-brī′ə-nəl) adj. BIOL. embrionario, del embrión; *(incipient)* incipiente; *(rudimentary)* rudimentario.

em·cee (ĕm′sē′) FAM. I. s. maestro de ceremonias, animador *m* II. tr. **-ceed, -cee·ing** servir de maestro de ceremonias en —intr. actuar de maestro de ceremonias.

e·mend (ĭ-mĕnd′) tr. enmendar, corregir.

e·men·date (ē′mĕn-dāt′) tr. **-dat·ed, -dat·ing** enmendar, corregir.

e·men·da·tion (ē′mĕn-dā′shən) s. enmienda, corrección *f.*

em·er·ald (ĕm′ər-əld) I. s. MIN. esmeralda II. adj. esmeraldino, de color esmeralda.

Emerald Isle s. GEOG. Irlanda ♦ **the E.** la verde Erín.

e·merge (ĭ-mûrj′) intr. **e·merged, e·merg·ing** *(to come into sight)* emerger, surgir; *(to become known)* aparecer; FIG. *(to rise from obscurity)* surgir.

e·mer·gence (ĭ-mûr′jəns) s. *(act)* surgimiento, salida; BOT. *(outgrowth)* prominencia; SOCIOL., BIOL. *(appearance)* aparición f.

e·mer·gen·cy (ĭ-mûr′jən-sē) s. [pl. **-cies**] *(crisis)* emergencia; MED. caso de urgencia; *(straits)* aprieto, apuro; *(need)* necesidad urgente f ♦ **e. exit** salida de emergencia • **e. landing** aterrizaje forzoso.

emergency brake s. AUTO. freno de emergencia.

e·mer·gent (ĭ-mûr′jənt) adj. *(coming into existence)* emergente; *(issuing forth)* saliente, naciente; *(urgent)* urgente.

e·mer·i·tus (ĭ-mĕr′ĭ-təs) adj. emérito.

e·mer·sion (ĭ-mûr′zhən) s. *(emergence)* surgimiento, salida; ASTRON. emersión f, reaparición f; BIOL., FÍS. emergencia, salida.

em·er·y (ĕm′ə-rē) s. MIN. esmeril m.

emery board s. lima de uñas.

emery cloth s. tela de esmeril.

e·met·ic (ĭ-mĕt′ĭk) adj. & s. emético, vomitivo.

em·i·grant (ĕm′ĭ-grənt) s. & adj. emigrante m.

em·i·grate (ĕm′ĭ-grāt′) intr. **-grat·ed, -grat·ing** emigrar.

em·i·gra·tion (ĕm′ĭ-grā′shən) s. emigración f.

em·i·nence (ĕm′ə-nəns) o **em·i·nen·cy** (-nən-sē) s. [pl. **-cies**] eminencia ♦ **His E.** RELIG. Su Eminencia.

em·i·nent (ĕm′ə-nənt) adj. *(renowned)* eminente; *(prominent)* elevado; *(distinguished)* distinguido; *(noteworthy)* notable, ilustre.

eminent domain s. DER. dominio eminente.

e·mir (ĭ-mîr′, ā′mîr′) s. emir m.

e·mir·ate (ĭ-mîr′ĭt) s. emirato.

e·mis·sar·y (ĕm′ĭ-sĕr′ē) s. [pl. **-ies**] emisario, enviado.

e·mis·sion (ĭ-mĭsh′ən) s. *(act)* emisión f, emanación f; COM. emisión (de valores).

e·mit (ĭ-mĭt′) tr. **e·mit·ted, e·mit·ting** *(to discharge)* emitir, despedir; *(to express)* expresar, emitir; *(currency, stock)* emitir.

e·mol·lient (ĭ-mŏl′yənt) adj. & s. emoliente m.

e·mol·u·ment (ĭ-mŏl′yə-mənt) s. emolumento, remuneración f.

e·mote (ĭ-mōt′) intr. **e·mot·ed, e·mot·ing** FAM. actuar.

e·mo·tion (ĭ-mō′shən) s. emoción f.

e·mo·tion·al (ĭ-mō′shə-nəl) adj. *(affective)* emocional <*e. tension* tensión emocional>; *(moving)* emotivo, conmovedor <*an e. scene* una escena conmovedora>; *(sensitive)* emotivo <*an e. person* una persona emotiva>.

e·mo·tion·al·ism (ĭ-mō′shə-nə-lĭz′əm) s. sentimentalismo.

e·mo·tion·al·ize (ĭ-mō′shə-nə-līz′) tr. **-ized, -iz·ing** dar un carácter emocional a.

e·mo·tion·less (ĭ-mō′shən-lĭs) adj. falto de emoción.

e·mo·tive (ĭ-mō′tĭv) adj. emotivo.

em·pan·el (ĕm-păn′əl) v. var. de **impanel.**

em·pa·thize (ĕm′pə-thīz′) intr. **-thized, -thiz·ing** ♦ **to e. with** identificarse con.

em·pa·thy (ĕm′pə-thē) s. empatía, identificación f.

em·per·or (ĕm′pər-ər) s. *(ruler)* emperador m; ZOOL. pavón m ♦ **e. moth** mariposa nocturna grande.

em·pha·sis (ĕm′fə-sĭs) s. [pl. **-ses** (-sēz′)] *(special attention)* énfasis m; *(intensity)* intensidad f, insistencia f; GRAM. *(stress)* acentuación f, acento.

em·pha·size (ĕm′fə-sīz′) tr. **-sized, -siz·ing** *(to stress)* enfatizar, hacer hincapié en; GRAM. acentuar, poner el acento en.

em·phat·ic (ĕm-făt′ĭk) adj. *(with emphasis)* enfático; *(strongly marked)* enérgico; *(striking)* marcado; *(definite)* categórico, decidido; GRAM. acentuado.

em·phy·se·ma (ĕm′fĭ-sē′mə) s. MED. enfisema m.

em·pire (ĕm′pīr′) s. imperio.

em·pir·i·cal (ĕm-pîr′ĭ-kəl) o **em·pir·ic** (-pîr′ĭk) adj. empírico.

em·pir·i·cism (ĕm-pîr′ĭ-sĭz′əm) s. FILOS. empirismo.

em·place (ĕm-plās′) tr. **-placed, -plac·ing** *(to place in position)* instalar, colocar; MIL. emplazar.

em·place·ment (ĕm-plās′mənt) s. *(placement)* emplaza-

miento, colocación f; *(location)* posición f, ubicación f; MIL. emplazamiento.

em·ploy (ĕm-ploi′) I. tr. *(to use)* emplear, usar; *(to spend)* dedicar (tiempo, dinero); *(to hire)* emplear, contratar ♦ **to be employed** tener empleo II. s. empleo ♦ **in the e. of** empleado por, al servicio de.

em·ploy·ee (ĕm-ploi′ē′) s. empleado.

em·ploy·er (ĕm-ploi′ər) s. empleador m.

em·ploy·ment (ĕm-ploi′mənt) s. *(work)* empleo, trabajo; *(profession)* ocupación f, profesión f.

em·po·ri·um (ĕm-pôr′ē-əm) s. [pl. **-ri·ums** o **-ri·a** (-ē-ə)] emporio.

em·pow·er (ĕm-pou′ər) tr. DER. autorizar, dar poder; *(to enable)* autorizar, habilitar.

em·press (ĕm′prĭs) s. emperatriz f.

em·presse·ment (än′prĕs-män′) s. cordialidad f.

emp·ti·ness (ĕmp′tē-nĭs) s. *(nothingness)* vacío; *(of a person, words)* vacuidad f.

emp·ty (ĕmp′tē) I. adj. **-ti·er, -ti·est** *(containing nothing)* vacío; *(vacant)* vacío, desocupado; *(unpopulated)* desierto <*the streets were e.* las calles estaban desiertas>; *(vain)* vano, hueco; *(idle)* ocioso <*e. hours* horas ociosas>; *(hungry)* vacío; *(devoid)* desprovisto, falto <*e. of pity* falto de piedad> II. tr. **-tied, -ty·ing** *(to vacate)* vaciar; *(to move out of)* dejar vacío, desalojar; *(to unload)* descargar —intr. *(to become empty)* vaciarse; *(to become vacant)* desocuparse, quedarse vacío; *(a river)* desembocar, desaguar III. s. [pl. **-ties**] envase vacío.

emp·ty-hand·ed (ĕmp′tē-hăn′dĭd) adj. con las manos vacías.

emp·ty-head·ed (ĕmp′tē-hĕd′ĭd) adj. sin nada en la cabeza, frívolo.

em·py·re·al (ĕm′pī-rē′əl, ĕm-pîr′ē-əl) adj. *(empyrean)* empíreo; *(celestial)* celestial; *(sublime)* sublime.

em·py·re·an (ĕm′pī-rē′ən, ĕm-pîr′ē-ən) s. & adj. empíreo.

em·u·late (ĕm′yə-lāt′) tr. **-lat·ed, -lat·ing** *(to imitate)* emular, imitar; *(to compete)* competir.

em·u·la·tion (ĕm′yə-lā′shən) s. emulación f.

em·u·la·tor (ĕm′yə-lā′tər) s. emulador m, émulo.

e·mul·si·fi·ca·tion (ĭ-mŭl′sə-fĭ-kā′shən) s. FOTOG., QUÍM. emulsificación f.

e·mul·si·fy (ĭ-mŭl′sə-fī′) tr. **-fied, -fy·ing** FOTOG., QUÍM. emulsionar, emulsificar.

e·mul·sion (ĭ-mŭl′shən) s. FOTOG., QUÍM. emulsión f.

en·a·ble (ĕn-ā′bəl) tr. **-bled, -bling** *(to make able)* capacitar; *(to make possible)* posibilitar, permitir; DER. autorizar, habilitar.

en·act (ĕn-ăkt′) tr. *(to make into law)* promulgar; *(to decree)* decretar; TEAT. representar.

en·act·ment (ĕn-ăkt′mənt) s. *(of a law)* promulgación f, sanción f; *(of a statute)* estatuto, norma; *(of a play)* representación f.

e·nam·el (ĭ-năm′əl) I. s. esmalte m II. tr. esmaltar.

e·nam·el·ing (ĭ-năm′ə-lĭng) s. esmaltado, esmalte m.

e·nam·el·ware (ĭ-năm′əl-wâr′) s. utensilios de hierro esmaltado.

en·am·or (ĭ-năm′ər) tr. *(to infatuate)* enamorar; *(to charm)* encantar; *(to captivate)* cautivar.

en·camp (ĕn-kămp′) tr. & intr. MIL. acampar(se).

en·camp·ment (ĕn-kămp′mənt) s. MIL. campamento.

en·cap·su·late (ĕn-kăp′sə-lāt′) tr. & intr. **-lat·ed, -lat·ing** encerrar(se) en una cápsula.

en·case (ĕn-kās′) tr. **-cased, -cas·ing** *(to enclose)* encerrar; *(to box up)* encajonar; *(to cover)* cubrir.

en·case·ment (ĕn-kās′mənt) s. encajonamiento.

en·ceph·a·li·tis (ĕn-sĕf′ə-lī′tĭs) s. MED. encefalitis f.

en·ceph·a·lo·gram (ĕn-sĕf′ə-lō-grăm′) s. MED. encefalograma m.

en·ceph·a·lon (ĕn-sĕf′ə-lŏn′) s. [pl. **-la** (-lə)] ANAT. encéfalo, cerebro.

en·chain (ĕn-chān′) tr. encadenar.

en·chant (ĕn-chănt′) tr. *(to charm)* encantar; *(to bewitch)* hechizar.

en·chant·er (ĕn-chăn′tər) s. *(charmer)* persona encantadora; *(sorcerer)* hechicero.

en·chant·ing (ĕn-chăn′tĭng) adj. encantador.

ā rey / ä año / b boca / ch chico / d dar / ĕ el / ē mil / g gato / h joya / hw juez / ĭ aire / k casa / kw cuan /

en·chant·ment (ĕn-chănt'mənt) s. *(bewitchment)* encantamiento, hechicería; *(charm)* encanto.

en·chant·ress (ĕn-chăn'trĭs) s. *(charmer)* mujer encantadora, seductora; *(sorceress)* encantadora, bruja.

en·ci·pher (ĕn-sī'fər) tr. cifrar, poner en cifra.

en·cir·cle (ĕn-sûr'kəl) tr. **-cled, -cling** *(to circumscribe)* rodear, circundar; MIL. *(to surround)* envolver.

en·clave (ĕn'klāv', ŏn'-) s. enclave *m.*

en·close (ĕn-klōz') tr. **-closed, -clos·ing** *(to surround)* rodear, circundar; *(to close in)* encerrar; *(to insert)* incluir, adjuntar; *(to fence in)* cercar, vallar ♦ **enclosed herewith** encontrará adjunto.

en·clo·sure (ĕn-klō'zhər) s. *(act)* encierro; *(enclosed terrain)* cercado, vallado; *(enclosed document)* carta adjunta, documento anexo; *(fence)* cerco, valla.

en·code (ĕn-kōd') tr. **-cod·ed, -cod·ing** codificar, poner en código.

en·co·mi·um (ĕn-kō'mē-əm) s. [pl. **-mi·ums** *o* **-mi·a** (-mē-ə)] elogio, encomio.

en·com·pass (ĕn-kŭm'pəs) tr. *(to surround)* rodear, circundar; *(to envelop)* envolver; *(to include)* incluir, abarcar.

en·core (ŏn'kôr') I. s. repetición *f,* bis *m* II. tr. **-cored, -cor·ing** pedir la repetición de III. interj. ¡otra!, ¡bis!

en·coun·ter (ĕn-koun'tər) I. s. *(meeting)* encuentro; *(confrontation)* encuentro hostil, choque *m* II. tr. *(to come upon)* encontrar, tropezar con; MIL. enfrentarse con —intr. enfrentarse, confrontarse.

en·cour·age (ĕn-kûr'ĭj) tr. **-aged, -ag·ing** *(to hearten)* animar, alentar; *(to embolden)* fortalecer; *(to foster)* fomentar, estimular.

en·cour·age·ment (ĕn-kûr'ĭj-mənt) s. *(courage)* ánimo, aliento; *(incentive)* incentivo.

en·cour·ag·ing (ĕn-kûr'ə-jĭng) adj. alentador, halagüeño.

en·croach (ĕn-krōch') intr. *(to intrude on)* inmiscuirse en, meterse en; *(to trespass)* violar, invadir <*to e. on someone's land* invadir la propiedad de alguien>.

en·croach·ment (ĕn-krōch'mənt) s. *(intrusion)* intromisión *f,* intrusión *f; (inversion)* usurpación *f.*

en·crust (ĕn-krŭst') tr. incrustar.

en·crus·ta·tion (ĕn'krŭ-stā'shən) s. incrustación *f.*

en·crypt (ĕn-krĭpt') tr. *(to encode)* codificar, poner en código; COMPUT. *(to scramble)* deformar (una señal) para hacerla ininteligible *o* secreta.

en·cum·ber (ĕn-kŭm'bər) tr. *(to overburden)* sobrecargar; *(to impede)* impedir; *(to weigh down)* gravar, abrumar <*to e. with obligations* abrumar con obligaciones>.

en·cum·brance (ĕn-kŭm'brəns) s. *(impediment)* obstáculo, impedimento; DER. *(lien)* gravamen *m,* carga.

en·cyc·li·cal (ĕn-sĭk'lĭ-kəl) s. RELIG. encíclica.

en·cy·clo·pe·di·a *o* **en·cy·clo·pae·di·a** (ĕn-sī'klə-pē'dē-ə) s. enciclopedia.

en·cy·clo·pe·dic *o* **en·cy·clo·pae·dic** (ĕn-sī'klə-pē'dĭk) adj. enciclopédico.

en·cy·clo·pe·dist *o* **en·cy·clo·pae·dist** (ĕn-sī'klə-pē'dĭst) s. enciclopedista *mf.*

end (ĕnd) I. s. *(tip)* extremo, punta <*the e. of a log* el extremo de un tronco>; *(boundary)* límite *m,* extremo; *(conclusion)* fin *m,* final *m* <*the e. of a day* el fin de un día>; *(outcome)* conclusión *f,* desenlace *m; (death)* fin, muerte *f; (goal)* finalidad *f,* propósito *m* <*to this end* con este propósito>; *(responsibility)* parte *f,* aspecto <*I take care of the business e. of this company* me ocupo de la parte financiera de esta compañía>; *(destruction)* destrucción *f* ♦ **at the e. of** al cabo de, al final de • **at loose ends** en desorden • **e. to e.** punta con punta • **for days on end** día tras día • **from e. to e.** de un extremo al otro, de punta a punta • **in the e.** al fin, al final • **odds and ends** restos, sobrante • **on e.** *(upright)* de pie, derecho; *(nonstop)* sin parar, continuamente; *(hair)* de punta, erizado • **the e. justifies the means** el fin justifica los medios • **to be at wit's e.** no saber qué hacer • **to bring to an e.** llevar a su fin, terminar • **to come to an e.** llegar a su fin, terminarse • **to get the short e. of the stick** FIG., FAM. jorobarse, salir mal parado • **to go off the deep e.** FIG., FAM. perder la chaveta • **to make ends meet** cubrir las necesidades con el dinero que se tiene • **to meet one's e.** encontrar la muerte • **to never**

hear the e. of something FAM. no dejarle a uno olvidar algo • **to no e.** en vano, inútilmente • **to put an e. to** poner fin a • **to reach its e.** llegar a su fin • **to stand on e.** ponerse de punta (el cabello) • **to what end?** ¿con qué finalidad? II. tr. *(to finish)* acabar, concluir; *(to destroy)* destruir ♦ **to e. it all** acabar con la vida —intr. *(to cease)* terminar(se), acabar(se); *(to die)* morir(se) ♦ **to e. up** terminar, ir a parar <*your toys ended up in the garage* tus juguetes fueron a parar al garaje>.

en·dan·ger (ĕn-dān'jər) tr. *(to risk)* arriesgar; *(to imperil)* poner en peligro.

en·dan·gered (ĕn-dān'jərd) adj. en peligro de extinción.

en·dear (ĕn-dîr') tr. *(to make beloved)* hacerse querer *o* apreciar; ANT. *(to increase)* encarecer.

en·dear·ing (ĕn-dîr'ĭng) adj. atractivo, encantador.

en·dear·ment (ĕn-dîr'mənt) s. *(affection)* cariño, afecto; *(expression)* expresión *o* frase cariñosa; *(caress)* caricia.

en·deav·or (ĕn-dĕv'ər) I. s. *(effort)* esfuerzo, empeño; *(attempt)* intento, tentativa II. intr. *(to try)* intentar; *(to strive)* esforzarse.

en·dem·ic (ĕn-dĕm'ĭk) I. adj. endémico II. s. ECOL. endemia.

end·game (ĕnd'gām') s. *(ending part)* final (de juego) *m; (in chess)* final (de partida).

end·ing (ĕn'dĭng) s. *(conclusion)* conclusión *f,* fin *m; (of a story)* desenlace *m,* final *m; (of a word)* desinencia, terminación *f.*

en·dive (ĕn'dīv', ŏn'dēv') s. BOT. escarola, endibia.

end·less (ĕnd'lĭs) adj. *(interminable)* interminable; *(infinite)* infinito; *(incessant)* incesante; *(continuous)* continuo.

end·most (ĕnd'mōst') adj. último, lo más lejos *o* remoto.

en·do·car·di·um (ĕn'dō-kär'dē-əm) s. [pl. **-di·a** (-dē-ə)] ANAT. endocardio.

en·do·crine (ĕn'də-krĭn, -krīn') ANAT. I. adj. endocrino II. s. glándula endocrina.

endocrine gland s. ANAT. glándula endocrina, glándula de secreción interna.

en·do·cri·nol·o·gy (ĕn'də-krī-nŏl'ə-jē) s. FISIOL. endocrinología.

en·dog·a·my (ĕn-dŏg'ə-mē) s. endogamia.

en·dog·e·nous (ĕn-dŏj'ə-nəs) adj. endógeno.

en·do·mor·phic (ĕn'də-môr'fĭk) adj. FISIOL., MIN. endomórfico.

en·dorse (ĕn-dôrs') tr. **-dorsed, -dors·ing** COM. *(a check)* endosar; *(to guarantee)* avalar; *(to support)* apoyar, respaldar; *(to acknowledge)* acusar recibo de (con una firma); *(to approve)* aprobar, sancionar.

en·dors·ee (ĕn-dôr-sē') s. COM. endosatorio, endosado.

en·dorse·ment (ĕn-dôrs'mənt) s. COM. *(act, signature)* endoso; *(approval)* aprobación *f; (support)* respaldo, apoyo; *(guarantee)* aval *m; (amendment)* enmienda.

en·dors·er (ĕn-dôr'sər) s. COM. endosador *m,* endosante *mf.*

en·do·skel·e·ton (ĕn'dō-skĕl'ĭ-tn) s. ANAT., ZOOL. endoesqueleto, neuroesqueleto.

en·do·sperm (ĕn'də-spûrm') s. BOT. endoesperma.

en·do·ther·mic (ĕn'də-thûr'mĭk) *o* **en·do·ther·mal** (-məl) adj. QUÍM. endotérmico.

en·dow (ĕn-dou') tr. *(to donate)* donar; *(with talent)* dotar; ANT. *(with a dowry)* dotar (a una hija).

en·dow·ment (ĕn-dou'mənt) s. *(act)* dotación *f; (donation)* donación *f,* fundación *f; (natural gift)* dote *m,* don *m.*

end·pa·per *o* **end paper** (ĕnd'pā'pər) s. IMPR. guarda.

end·point (ĕnd'point') s. GEOM., QUÍM. punto final.

end product s. producto final.

end reaction s. QUÍM. reacción final *f.*

end table s. mesa pequeña colocada al lado de un sofá.

en·due (ĕn-dōō', -dyōō') tr. **-dued, -du·ing** *(with a quality)* dotar; *(with a garment)* poner.

en·dur·a·ble (ĕn-dōōr'ə-bəl, -dyōōr'-) adj. *(tolerable)* tolerable; *(bearable)* soportable, aguantable.

en·dur·ance (ĕn-dōōr'əns, -dyōōr'-) s. resistencia, aguante *m.*

en·dure (ĕn-dōōr', -dyōōr') tr. **-dured, -dur·ing** *(to resist)* resistir, aguantar; *(to tolerate)* tolerar —intr. *(to hold out)* aguantarse, resistir; *(to last)* durar, perdurar <*nature's* *beauty will e. forever* la belleza de la naturaleza durará por siempre>.

en·dur·ing (ĕn-dŏŏr'ĭng, -dyŏŏr'-) adj. *(lasting)* perdurable, duradero; *(chronic)* crónico; *(unresolved)* constante; *(long-suffering)* sufrido.

end·wise (ĕnd'wīz') o **end·ways** (-wāz') adv. *(upright)* de punta, de pie; *(end foremost)* con la punta al frente; *(lengthwise)* longitudinalmente; *(end to end)* extremo con extremo, unido por los extremos.

en·e·ma (ĕn'ə-mə) s. MED. enema, lavativa.

en·e·my (ĕn'ə-mē) s. [pl. **-mies**] & adj. enemigo, adversario.

en·er·get·ic (ĕn'ər-jĕt'ĭk) adj. enérgico, vigoroso.

en·er·get·ics (ĕn'ər-jĕt'ĭks) s. [ú. con v. sing.] FÍS. energética.

en·er·gize (ĕn'ər-jīz') tr. **-gized, -giz·ing** *(to give energy to)* dar energía a, vigorizar; *(to activate)* activar, estimular; ELEC. *(to charge)* excitar —intr. desplegar *u* obrar con energía.

en·er·gy (ĕn'ər-jē) s. [pl. **-gies**] *(vigor)* energía, vitalidad *f; (determination)* determinación *f,* resolución *f;* FÍS. *(work)* energía.

energy level s. FÍS. nivel de energía *m.*

en·er·vate I. tr. (ĕn'ər-vāt') **-vat·ed, -vat·ing** *(to weaken)* debilitar; *(to depress)* deprimir II. adj. (ĭ-nûr'vĭt) debilitado, enervado.

en·fee·ble (ĕn-fē'bəl) tr. **-bled, -bling** debilitar, enervar.

en·fold (ĕn-fōld') tr. *(to envelop)* envolver; *(to surround)* rodear; *(to embrace)* abrazar.

en·force (ĕn-fôrs') tr. **-forced, -forc·ing** DER. *(to force compliance with)* hacer cumplir, hacer respetar; *(to impose)* imponer; *(to compel)* exigir, obligar; *(to give force to)* dar fuerza a, reforzar.

en·force·a·ble (ĕn-fôr'sə-bəl) adj. *(said of a law)* aplicable; *(said of a contract)* ejecutorio; *(that can be enforced)* que se puede hacer cumplir.

en·force·ment (ĕn-fôrs'mənt) s. *(act)* aplicación *f,* ejecución *f; (putting into effect)* entrada en vigor.

en·forc·er (ĕn-fôr'sər) s. persona que hace cumplir.

en·fran·chise (ĕn-frăn'chīz') tr. **-chised, -chis·ing** *(the right to vote)* otorgar el derecho al voto; *(to free)* libertar, manumitir, liberar.

en·gage (ĕn-gāj') tr. **-gaged, -gag·ing** *(to employ)* emplear, tomar al servicio de uno; *(to reserve)* contratar, reservar <*to e. a room* reservar una habitación>; *(to engross)* absorber, cautivar <*studying engages her attention for hours* el estudio cautiva su atención por horas>; *(to promise)* comprometer, empeñar; MIL. *librar o trabar combate* <*to e. the enemy* trabar combate con el enemigo>; *(to win over)* captar, atraer (a alguien); *(to entangle)* enredar, embrollar; MEC. *(to mesh)* engranar, embragar —intr. *(to be obligated to)* comprometerse, obligarse (a pagar, ayudar); *(to agree)* ponerse *o* estar de acuerdo; MIL. trabarse en combate; MEC. engranar, encajarse ♦ **to e. in** *(to occupy oneself with)* ocuparse en; *(to participate)* tomar parte en.

en·gaged (ĕn-gājd') adj. *(employed)* empleado; *(busy)* ocupado; *(reserved)* contratado; *(betrothed)* comprometido; *(involved in conflict)* combatiente; *(in gear)* engranado; *(meshed)* endentado; ARQ. embebido, empotrado ♦ **to be e.** *(to be busy)* estar ocupado; *(to be betrothed)* estar comprometido ♦ **to get e.** prometerse.

en·gage·ment (ĕn-gāj'mənt) s. *(obligation)* compromiso, obligación *f; (betrothal)* esponsales *m,* compromiso (de matrimonio); *(contract)* contratación *f,* contrata; *(appointment)* cita, compromiso; *(employment)* empleo; MIL. batalla, combate *m;* MEC. engranaje *m.*

en·gag·ing (ĕn-gā'jĭng) adj. *(appealing)* atractivo; *(charming)* encantador.

en·gen·der (ĕn-jĕn'dər) tr. *(to give rise to)* engendrar, producir; *(to procreate)* procrear —intr. engendrarse.

en·gine (ĕn'jĭn) s. FÍS., MEC. máquina, motor *m;* F.C. locomotora.

engine block s. AUTO., MEC. bloque de cilindros *m.*

en·gi·neer (ĕn'jə-nîr') I. s. TEC. ingeniero; F.C. maquinista *m,* mecánico; MIL. ingeniero, soldado; FIG. *(artificer)* artífice *mf,* autor *m* II. tr. *(to build)* construir, edificar; *(to maneuver)* maniobrar, maquinar.

en·gi·neer·ing (ĕn'jə-nîr'ĭng) s. ingeniería.

Eng·land (ĭng'glənd) s. Inglaterra.

Eng·lish (ĭng'glĭsh) I. adj. inglés II. s. inglés *m* ♦ **e.** DEP. efecto (esp. lateral) ♦ **in plain E.** claramente, con palabras sencillas ♦ **the E.** los ingleses ♦ **the King's E.** *o* **the Queen's E.** (el) inglés correcto III. tr. traducir al inglés.

English Channel s. Canal de la Mancha *m.*

Eng·lish·man (ĭng'glĭsh-mən) s. [pl. **-men**] inglés *m.*

Eng·lish·wom·an (ĭng'glĭsh-wŏŏm'ən) s. [pl. **-wom·en** (-wĭm'ĭn)] inglesa.

en·gorge (ĕn-gôrj') tr. **-gorged, -gorg·ing** *(to devour)* devorar; *(to gorge)* engullir, comer con glotonería; MED. *(to congest)* congestionar —intr. comer con ansia y voracidad.

en·graft (ĕn-grăft') tr. AGR. *(to graft in)* injertar; *(to establish)* establecer firmemente; *(ideas)* inculcar.

en·grain (ĕn-grān') v., adj., & s. var. de **ingrain.**

en·grave (ĕn-grāv') tr. **-graved, -grav·ing** *(to carve)* tallar; *(to etch)* grabar; *(to print)* imprimir con plancha grabada; FIG. *(to impress permanently)* grabar.

en·grav·er (ĕn-grā'vər) s. grabador *m.*

en·grav·ing (ĕn-grā'vĭng) s. IMPR. grabado.

en·gross (ĕn-grōs') tr. *(the attention)* absorber, cautivar; *(goods)* acaparar; *(a document)* transcribir formalmente.

en·gross·ing (ĕn-grō'sĭng) adj. absorbente.

en·gulf (ĕn-gŭlf') tr. *(to surround)* rodear; *(to swallow up)* tragarse.

en·hance (ĕn-hăns') tr. **-hanced, -hanc·ing** *(to make greater)* acrecentar, aumentar; *(to intensify)* dar realce a, realzar.

en·hance·ment (ĕn-hăns'mənt) s. *(increase)* acrecentamiento, aumento; *(of flavor, beauty)* realce *m.*

e·nig·ma (ĭ-nĭg'mə) s. enigma *m.*

en·ig·mat·ic (ĕn'ĭg-măt'ĭk) *o* **en·ig·mat·i·cal** (-ĭ-kəl) adj. enigmático.

en·join (ĕn-join') tr. *(to command)* mandar, ordenar; *(to impose)* imponer; DER. *(to prohibit)* prohibir.

en·join·der (ĕn-join'dər) s. DER. mandato.

en·joy (ĕn-joi') tr. *(to experience joy)* gozar, disfrutar; *(to be pleasing to)* gustar a <*she enjoys reading* a ella le gusta leer>; *(to benefit from)* gozar de ♦ **e. your meal!** ¡buen provecho!, ¡buen apetito! ♦ **to e. oneself** divertirse, pasarlo bien.

en·joy·a·ble (ĕn-joi'ə-bəl) adj. *(pleasant)* agradable, encantador; *(amusing)* divertido.

en·joy·ment (ĕn-joi'mənt) s. *(act, state)* placer *m,* goce *m; (use)* uso, usufructo.

en·large (ĕn-lärj') tr. **-larged, -larg·ing** *(to make bigger)* agrandar; *(to add to)* aumentar; *(to magnify)* magnificar; *(to expand)* ensanchar; FOTOG. ampliar —intr. *(to get bigger)* agrandarse; *(to expound upon)* explayarse sobre.

en·large·ment (ĕn-lärj'mənt) s. *(in size)* agrandamiento, aumento; *(expansion)* expansión *f;* FOTOG. ampliación *f;* MED. dilatación *f.*

en·larg·er (ĕn-lär'jər) s. FOTOG. ampliadora.

en·light·en (ĕn-līt'n) tr. *(to edify)* iluminar, ilustrar; *(to instruct)* instruir; *(to inform)* aclarar, explicar.

en·light·ened (ĕn-līt'nd) adj. *(cultured)* culto, ilustrado; *(well-informed)* bien informado; *(spiritually)* iluminado.

en·light·en·ment (ĕn-līt'n-mənt) s. iluminación *f,* ilustración *f* ♦ **the E.** la Ilustración.

en·list (ĕn-lĭst') tr. MIL. reclutar, alistar; *(to engage)* ganar el apoyo *o* cooperación de; *(to secure)* obtener, conseguir —intr. MIL. alistarse, enrolarse; *(to participate)* participar, meterse.

enlisted man s. MIL. soldado de tropa.

en·list·ment (ĕn-lĭst'mənt) s. reclutamiento, alistamiento.

en·liv·en (ĕn-lī'vən) tr. *(to make lively)* alegrar; *(to animate)* animar.

en·mesh (ĕn-mĕsh') tr. *(to entangle)* enredar, enmarañar; *(to catch)* coger en una red.

en·mi·ty (ĕn'mĭ-tē) s. [pl. **-ties**] *(hostility)* enemistad *f; (antagonism)* antagonismo.

en·no·ble (ĕn-nō'bəl) tr. **-bled, -bling** ennoblecer.

en·no·ble·ment (ĕn-nō'bəl-mənt) s. ennoblecimiento.

en·nui (ŏn-wē') s. *(listlessness)* lasitud *f; (boredom)* aburrimiento.

ã **rey** / ä **año** / b **boca** / ch **chico** / d **dar** / ĕ **el** / ē **mil** / g **gato** / h **joya** / hw **juez** / ī **aire** / k **casa** / kw **cuan** /

e·nor·mi·ty (ĭ-nôr'mĭ-tē) s. [pl. **-ties**] *(size)* enormidad *f*; *(wickedness)* atrocidad *f*, monstruosidad *f*.

e·nor·mous (ĭ-nôr'məs) adj. *(immense)* enorme, inmenso; ANT. *(atrocious)* atroz.

e·nough (ĭ-nŭf') **I.** adj. bastante, suficiente ♦ **to be e.** ser suficiente, bastar **II.** adv. bastante, suficientemente <*did you eat e.?* ¿comiste suficientemente?> ♦ **curiously e.** lo curioso es que • **oddly e.** por raro que parezca • **sure e.** en efecto • **well e.** bastante bien **III.** s. lo bastante, lo suficiente ♦ **e. and some to spare** de sobra, de más • **e. is e.** basta y sobra • **it is e. to drive you mad** es para volverse loco • **to have had e.** *(to be satisfied with)* estar satisfecho; *(to be tired of)* estar harto <*I've had e. of this nonsense* estoy harto de estas tonterías>; *(to become tired)* empezar a cansarse <*tell me when you've had e.* díme en cuanto te empieces a cansar> **IV.** interj. ¡basta! ♦ **e. of this!** ¡basta ya!

en·quire (ĕn-kwīr') v. var. de **inquire**.

en·rage (ĕn-rāj') tr. **-raged, -rag·ing** enfurecer, encolerizar.

en·rapt (ĕn-răpt') adj. *(enraptured)* arrebatado, embelesado; *(enthralled)* cautivado.

en·rap·ture (ĕn-răp'chər) tr. **-tured, -tur·ing** arrebatar, embelesar.

en·rich (ĕn-rĭch') tr. *(to make rich)* enriquecer; *(to fertilize)* fertilizar, abonar.

en·rich·ment (ĕn-rĭch'mənt) s. *(act, state)* enriquecimiento; *(of the soil)* fertilización *f*, abono.

en·robe (ĕn-rōb') tr. **-robed, -rob·ing** vestir ricamente.

en·roll o **en·rol** (ĕn-rōl') tr. *(to register)* registrar, inscribir; *(a student)* matricular; *(to roll up)* enrollar; *(to wrap up)* envolver —intr. inscribirse, alistarse.

en·roll·ment o **en·rol·ment** (ĕn-rōl'mənt) s. *(in a list)* inscripción *f*; *(in school)* matriculación *f*; *(record)* registro.

en·sconce (ĕn-skŏns') tr. **-sconced, -sconc·ing** *(to settle)* acomodar, establecer cómodamente <*to e. oneself in an armchair* establecerse cómodamente en un sillón>; *(to conceal)* ocultar, esconder.

en·sem·ble (ŏn-sŏm'bəl) s. *(group)* conjunto; *(outfit)* conjunto; MÚS. conjunto, grupo musical; TEAT. compañía.

en·shrine (ĕn-shrīn') tr. **-shrined, -shrin·ing** *(to enclose)* guardar en un relicario; *(to cherish)* conservar religiosamente.

en·shroud (ĕn-shroud') tr. *(to shroud)* amortajar; *(to conceal)* ocultar.

en·sign (ĕn'sən, ĕn'sīn') s. *(military flag)* bandera nacional, pabellón *m*; (ĕn'sən) *(officer)* alférez *m*.

en·slave (ĕn-slāv') tr. **-slaved, -slav·ing** esclavizar.

en·slave·ment (ĕn-slāv'mənt) s. esclavitud *f*.

en·snare (ĕn-snâr') tr. **-snared, -snar·ing** entrampar.

en·sue (ĕn-sōō') intr. **-sued, -su·ing** *(to follow)* seguir(se); *(to result)* resultar.

en·su·ing (ĕn-sōō'ĭng) adj. *(resulting)* resultante, consiguiente; *(following)* siguiente, próximo.

en·sure (ĕn-shŏŏr') tr. **-sured, -sur·ing** *(to insure)* asegurar; *(to guarantee)* garantizar.

en·tail (ĕn-tāl') **I.** tr. *(to bring about)* acarrear, ocasionar; *(to involve)* implicar, suponer; DER. vincular **II.** s. DER. vinculación *f*, vínculo; *(an entailed estate)* mayorazgo, propiedad sujeta a vínculo; *(legacy)* legado.

en·tan·gle (ĕn-tăng'gəl) tr. **-gled, -gling** *(to snarl)* enmarañar, enredar; FIG. *(to confuse)* intrincar, embrollar; *(to involve inextricably)* envolver o implicar de manera inextricable.

en·tente (ŏn-tŏnt') s. *(agreement)* acuerdo, convenio; *(signatories)* aliados.

en·ter (ĕn'tər) tr. *(to go into)* entrar en <*to e. the church* entrar en la iglesia>; *(to penetrate into)* penetrar en, perforar <*the bullet entered the heart* la bala perforó el corazón>; *(to insert)* introducir, insertar <*to e. a key in the lock* insertar una llave en la cerradura>; *(to participate in)* participar en, formar parte de; *(to embark upon)* emprender, empezar <*he entered the toy business* él empezó un negocio de juguetes>; *(to join)* afiliarse, hacerse miembro de; *(to obtain admission to)* ingresar, entrar a; *(to register)* inscribir en <*to e. a horse in the race* inscribir un caballo en la carrera>; *(to take part)* participar, entrar en <*to e. a pri-*

mary entrar en las elecciones preliminares>; *(to take up)* iniciar, abrazar (carrera, profesión); *(to record)* asentar, anotar (orden, pedido); DER. entablar, presentar; COM. declarar, aduanar (cargamento); MIL. alistarse en <*to e. the army* alistarse en el ejército> ♦ **to e. one's head** ocurrírsele a uno, cruzar la mente de uno —intr. *(to go in)* entrar; *(to gain entry)* ingresar; *(to be a part)* participar; *(to register)* inscribirse, matricularse; TEAT. entrar en o salir a escena ♦ **to e. into** *(a contract)* celebrar, concertar; *(to begin)* entablar, iniciar • **not to e. into it** no figurar para nada.

en·ter·i·tis (ĕn'tə-rī'tĭs) s. MED. enteritis *f*.

en·ter·prise (ĕn'tər-prīz') s. *(undertaking, business)* empresa; *(boldness)* arrojo, intrepidez *f*; *(initiative)* iniciativa.

en·ter·pris·ing (ĕn'tər-prī'zĭng) adj. emprendedor *m*.

en·ter·tain (ĕn'tər-tān') tr. *(to amuse)* divertir, entretener; *(to host)* hospedar, agasajar; FIG. *(to consider)* considerar, acariciar (ideas) ♦ **to e. oneself** divertirse —intr. dar fiestas, recibir invitados.

en·ter·tain·er (ĕn'tər-tā'nər) s. *(artist)* artista *mf*; *(host)* anfitrión *m*.

en·ter·tain·ing (ĕn'tər-tā'nĭng) adj. entretenido, divertido.

en·ter·tain·ment (ĕn'tər-tān'mənt) s. *(act)* entretenimiento; *(performance)* espectáculo; *(amusement)* entretenimiento, diversión *f*; *(hospitality)* hospitalidad *f*.

en·thrall (ĕn-thrôl') tr. *(to captivate)* cautivar; *(to enslave)* esclavizar.

en·throne (ĕn-thrōn') tr. **-throned, -thron·ing** entronizar.

en·thuse (ĕn-thōōz') tr. & intr. **-thused, -thus·ing** FAM. entusiasmar(se).

en·thu·si·asm (ĕn-thōō'zē-ăz'əm) s. entusiasmo.

en·thu·si·ast (ĕn-thōō'zē-ăst') s. *(fan)* entusiasta *mf*; *(fanatic)* fanático.

en·thu·si·as·tic (ĕn-thōō'zē-ăs'tĭk) adj. *(glowing)* entusiástico; *(fervent)* fervoroso, caluroso.

en·tice (ĕn-tīs') tr. **-ticed, -tic·ing** *(to attract)* atraer, tentar; *(to seduce)* seducir.

en·tice·ment (ĕn-tīs'mənt) s. *(attraction)* atractivo; *(seduction)* seducción *f*.

en·tire (ĕn-tīr') **I.** adj. *(complete)* entero, total; *(in one piece)* intacto; BOT., ZOOL. entero **II.** s. *(whole)* el todo, totalidad *f*; *(horse)* semental *m*.

en·tire·ty (ĕn-tīr'tē) s. [pl. **-ties**] totalidad *f*.

en·ti·tle (ĕn-tīt'l) tr. **-tled, -tling** *(to bestow a title upon)* titular, intitular; *(to give legal right)* habilitar, dar derecho a ♦ **to be entitled to** tener derecho a.

en·ti·tle·ment (ĕn-tīt'l-mənt) s. *(authorization)* autorización *f*; *(right)* derecho.

en·ti·ty (ĕn'tĭ-tē) s. [pl. **-ties**] *(being)* ser *m*; *(something existing independently)* ente *m*; *(an entirety)* entidad *f*.

en·tomb (ĕn-tōōm') tr. sepultar, enterrar.

en·to·mol·o·gist (ĕn'tə-mŏl'ə-jĭst) s. entomólogo.

en·to·mol·o·gy (ĕn'tə-mŏl'ə-jē) s. entomología.

en·tou·rage (ŏn'tōō-räzh') s. *(retinue)* séquito, acompañamiento; *(environment)* medio ambiente.

en·trails (ĕn'trālz') s.pl. *(guts)* entrañas, tripas; *(viscera)* vísceras.

en·train[1] (ĕn-trān') tr. arrastrar.

en·train[2] (ĕn-trān') tr. despachar por tren —intr. subir al tren.

en·trance[1] (ĕn'trəns) s. *(act)* entrada, ingreso; *(entryway)* entrada, acceso; *(admission)* admisión *f*; MÚS. entrada; TEAT. salida (a escena).

en·trance[2] (ĕn-trăns') tr. **-tranced, -tranc·ing** *(to put in a trance)* poner en trance; *(to fascinate)* fascinar, encantar.

en·trant (ĕn'trənt) s. entrante *mf*, concursante *mf*.

en·trap (ĕn-trăp') tr. **-trapped, -trap·ping** entrampar, hacer caer en una trampa.

en·treat (ĕn-trēt') tr. implorar, suplicar —intr. hacer una súplica, hacer un ruego.

en·treat·y (ĕn-trē'tē) s. [pl. **-ies**] *(request)* pedido; *(petition)* petición *f*; *(plea)* súplica.

en·trée o **en·tree** (ŏn'trā') s. *(admittance)* entrada, admisión *f*; *(main dish)* plato principal.

---

en·trench (ĕn-trĕnch′) tr. atrincherar ♦ **to e. oneself** atrincherarse —intr. atrincherarse.

en·trench·ment (ĕn-trĕnch′mənt) s. atrincheramiento.

en·tre·pre·neur (ŏn′trə-prə-nûr′) s. empresario.

en·tro·py (ĕn′trə-pē) s. FÍS. entropía.

en·trust (ĕn-trŭst′) tr. *(to give over)* entregar; *(to commit)* confiar.

en·try (ĕn′trē) s. [pl. **-tries**] *(act)* entrada; *(place)* entrada, acceso; *(notation)* anotación *f*, registro (en un registro); *(in a dictionary)* entrada, artículo; DEP. *(entrant)* participante *m*, competidor *m*; *(in bookkeeping)* asiento.

en·try·way (ĕn′trē-wā′) s. entrada.

en·twine (ĕn-twīn′) tr. & intr. **-twined, -twin·ing** entrelazar(se), enroscar(se).

e·nu·mer·ate (ĭ-nōō′mə-rāt′, ĭ-nyōō′-) tr. **-at·ed, -at·ing** *(to list)* enumerar; *(to count)* contar.

e·nu·mer·a·tion (ĭ-nōō′mə-rā′shən, -nyōō′-) s. enumeración *f*; *(list)* lista; *(catalogue)* catálogo.

e·nu·mer·a·tive (ĭ-nōō′mə-rā′tĭv, -nyōō′-) adj. enumerativo.

e·nu·mer·a·tor (ĭ-nōō′mə-rā′tər, -nyōō′-) s. enumerador *m*.

e·nun·ci·ate (ĭ-nŭn′sē-āt′) tr. **-at·ed, -at·ing** *(to state precisely)* enunciar; *(to pronounce)* pronunciar, articular; *(to proclaim)* proclamar.

e·nun·ci·a·tion (ĭ-nŭn′sē-ā′shən) s. *(statement)* enunciación *f*; *(pronunciation)* pronunciación *f*, articulación *f*; *(announcement)* declaración *f*.

en·vel·op (ĕn-vĕl′əp) tr. *(to enclose)* envolver; *(to cover)* cubrir; *(to surround)* rodear.

en·ve·lope (ĕn′və-lōp′, ŏn′-) s. *(for letters)* sobre *m*; *(wrapping)* envoltura; *(cover)* cobertura; BIOL. túnica; MAT. envolvente *f*.

en·vel·op·ment (ĕn-vĕl′əp-mənt) s. *(act)* envolvimiento; *(wrapper)* envoltura.

en·vi·a·ble (ĕn′vē-ə-bəl) adj. envidiable.

en·vi·ous (ĕn′vē-əs) adj. envidioso.

en·vi·ron·ment (ĕn-vī′rən-mənt) s. *(surroundings)* medio ambiente, ambiente *m*; *(circumstances)* circunstancias; *(external conditions)* condiciones externas.

en·vi·ron·men·tal (ĕn-vī′rən-mĕn′tl) adj. ambiental.

en·vi·ron·men·tal·ist (ĕn-vī′rən-mĕn′tl-ĭst) s. persona dedicada a proteger el medio ambiente natural.

en·vi·rons (ĕn-vī′rənz) s.pl. *(suburbs)* alrededores *m*, afueras; *(environment)* medio ambiente.

en·vis·age (ĕn-vĭz′ĭj) tr. **-aged, -ag·ing** *(to conceive of)* concebir, proyectar; *(to foresee)* pensar, crear; *(to imagine)* imaginarse, concebir.

en·vi·sion (ĕn-vĭzh′ən) tr. imaginar.

en·voy (ĕn′voi′, ŏn′-) s. *(messenger)* mensajero; POL. *(representative)* representante diplomático.

en·vy (ĕn′vē) I. s. [pl. **-vies**] *(feeling)* envidia; *(envied person)* persona envidiada II. tr. **-vied, -vy·ing** envidiar, tener envidia de <*I e. your good fortune* envidio tu buena suerte> —intr. sentir envidia.

en·wrap (ĕn-răp′) tr. **-wrapped, -wrap·ping** *(to wrap up)* envolver; *(to cover)* cubrir; *(to engross)* absorber.

en·zyme (ĕn′zīm′) s. BIOQUÍM. enzima.

e·on (ē′ŏn′) s. eón *m*.

ep·au·let o **ep·au·lette** (ĕp′ə-lĕt′) s. charretera.

e·phem·er·al (ĭ-fĕm′ər-əl) I. adj. efímero II. s. cosa efímera.

e·phem·er·is (ĭ-fĕm′ər-ĭs) s. [pl. **eph·e·mer·i·des** (ĕf′ə-mĕr′ĭ-dēz′)] efemérides *f*, tablas astronómicas.

E·phe·sians (ĭ-fē′zhənz) s.pl. BÍBL. Efesios.

ep·ic (ĕp′ĭk) I. s. POÉT. épica, poema épico; LIT. epopeya II. adj. épico.

ep·i·cene (ĕp′ĭ-sēn′) I. adj. *(bisexual)* hermafrodita; *(sexless)* asexual, neutro; *(effeminate)* afeminado; GRAM. epiceno II. s. hermafrodita *mf*.

ep·i·cen·ter (ĕp′ĭ-sĕn′tər) s. epicentro.

ep·i·cure (ĕp′ĭ-kyŏŏr′) s. *(gastronome)* gastrónomo; ANT. *(pleasure seeker)* epicúreo.

Ep·i·cu·re·an (ĕp′ĭ-kyŏŏ-rē′ən) adj. & s. epicúreo.

ep·i·cur·ism (ĕp′ĭ-kyŏŏ-rīz′əm) s. epicureísmo.

ep·i·dem·ic (ĕp′ĭ-dĕm′ĭk) I. adj. epidémico, epidemial II. s. MED. epidemia; FIG. *(wave)* ola.

ep·i·de·mi·ol·o·gy (ĕp′ĭ-dē′mē-ŏl′ə-jē) s. MED. epidemiología.

ep·i·der·mis (ĕp′ĭ-dûr′mĭs) s. ANAT., BOT. epidermis *f*.

ep·i·glot·tis (ĕp′ĭ-glŏt′ĭs) s. ANAT., ZOOL. epiglotis *f*.

ep·i·gram (ĕp′ĭ-grăm′) s. epigrama *m*.

ep·i·gram·mat·ic (ĕp′ĭ-grə-măt′ĭk) adj. epigramático.

ep·i·graph (ĕp′ĭ-grăf′) s. epígrafe *m*.

ep·i·lep·sy (ĕp′ə-lĕp′sē) s. MED. epilepsia.

ep·i·lep·tic (ĕp′ə-lĕp′tĭk) adj. & s. MED. epiléptico.

ep·i·logue o **ep·i·log** (ĕp′ə-lôg′) s. epílogo.

e·piph·a·ny (ĭ-pĭf′ə-nē) s. [pl. **-nies**] revelación *f* ♦ **E.** RELIG. Epifanía.

e·pis·co·pal (ĭ-pĭs′kə-pəl) adj. RELIG. episcopal.

E·pis·co·pa·lian (ĭ-pĭs′kə-pāl′yən) adj. & s. RELIG. episcopalista *mf*.

e·pis·co·pate (ĭ-pĭs′kə-pĭt) s. RELIG. episcopado, obispado.

ep·i·sode (ĕp′ĭ-sōd′) s. episodio.

ep·i·sod·ic (ĕp′ĭ-sŏd′ĭk) o **ep·i·sod·i·cal** (-ĭ-kəl) adj. episódico.

e·pis·te·mol·o·gy (ĭ-pĭs′tə-mŏl′ə-jē) s. FILOS. epistemología.

e·pis·tle (ĭ-pĭs′əl) s. epístola ♦ **E.** RELIG. Epístola.

e·pis·to·lar·y (ĭ-pĭs′tə-lĕr′ē) adj. epistolar.

ep·i·taph (ĕp′ĭ-tăf′) s. epitafio.

ep·i·the·li·um (ĕp′ə-thē′lē-əm) s. [pl. **-li·ums** o **-li·a** (-lē-ə)] BIOL. epitelio.

ep·i·thet (ĕp′ə-thĕt′) s. GRAM. *(adjective)* epíteto; *(insult)* insulto.

e·pit·o·me (ĭ-pĭt′ə-mē) s. *(summary)* epítome *m*, resumen *m*; *(embodiment)* personificación *f*.

e·pit·o·mize (ĭ-pĭt′ə-mīz′) tr. **-mized, -miz·ing** *(to sum up)* compendiar, resumir; *(to embody)* personificar.

ep·och (ĕp′ək) s. *(era)* época, era; *(milestone)* acontecimiento importante, hito; ASTRON., GEOL. época.

ep·och·al (ĕp′ə-kəl) adj. *(of an epoch)* perteneciente a o característico de una época; *(epoch-making)* que hace época, memorable.

ep·och-mak·ing (ĕp′ək-mā′kĭng) adj. que hace época, memorable.

ep·onym (ĕp′ə-nĭm′) s. epónimo.

ep·ox·y (ĭ-pŏk′sē) s. [pl. **-ies**] QUÍM. resina epoxídica.

ep·si·lon (ĕp′sə-lŏn′, -lən) s. epsilón *f*.

Ep·som salts (ĕp′səm) s. MED., MIN. sales de Epsom *f*, epsomita.

e·qua·bil·i·ty (ĕk′wə-bĭl′ĭ-tē, ē′kwə-) s. *(uniformity)* uniformidad *f*, igualdad *f*; *(equanimity)* ecuanimidad *f*.

e·qua·ble (ĕk′wə-bəl, ē′kwə-) adj. *(unvarying)* invariable, uniforme; *(even-tempered)* calmo, tranquilo.

e·qual (ē′kwəl) I. adj. *(same)* igual, mismo <*two bundles of e. weight* dos bultos del mismo peso>; *(qualified)* apto <*she is e. to the task* ella es apta para la tarea>; *(adequate)* adecuado; *(evenhanded)* equitativo; *(smooth)* parejo, liso; MAT. igual, equivalente ♦ **all things being e.** si todo sigue igual • **on e. terms** en un plano de igualdad • **to be e.** to ser igual que II. s. igual *mf* ♦ **between equals** de igual a igual • **without e.** sin par III. tr. MAT. *(to be the same as)* ser igual a, ser <*four plus six equals ten* cuatro más seis son diez>; *(to match)* igualar <*to e. an Olympic record* igualar un récord olímpico>.

e·qual·i·ty (ĭ-kwŏl′ĭ-tē) s. [pl. **-ties**] *(state, quality)* igualdad *f*; MAT. ecuación *f*.

e·qual·i·za·tion (ē′kwə-lĭ-zā′shən) s. igualamiento, igualación *f* ♦ **e. fund** fondo de compensación.

e·qual·ize (ē′kwə-līz′) tr. & intr. **-ized, -iz·ing** *(to make equal)* igualar; *(to make uniform)* emparejar, uniformar.

e·qual·iz·er (ē′kwə-lī′zər) s. ELEC., MEC. *(device)* igualador *m*, compensador *m*; JER. *(revolver)* revólver *m*.

e·qual·ly (ē′kwə-lē) adv. igualmente, por igual.

equal sign s. MAT. signo de igualdad o de igual.

e·qua·nim·i·ty (ē′kwə-nĭm′ĭ-tē, ĕk′wə-) s. ecuanimidad *f*.

e·quate (ĭ-kwāt′) tr. **e·quat·ed, e·quat·ing** *(to equal)* igualar; *(to compare)* comparar, equiparar <*trying to e. old age with wisdom* tratando de equiparar la vejez con la sabiduría>; *(to balance)* igualar; MAT. poner en ecuación —intr. ser iguales.

e·qua·tion (ĭ-kwā′zhən) s. *(act)* ecuación *f*; MAT., QUÍM. ecuación *f* ♦ **personal e.** factor o punto de vista personal.

ă rey / ä año / b boca / ch chico / d dar / ĕ el / ē mil / g gato / h joya / hw juez / ī aire / k casa / kw cuan /

e·qua·tor (ĭ-kwā′tər) s. ASTRON., GEOG. ecuador m.
e·qua·to·ri·al (ē′kwə-tôr′ē-əl, ĕk′wə-) I. adj. ecuatorial II. s. ASTRON., GEOG. ecuatorial m.
Equatorial Guinea s. Guinea Ecuatorial.
eq·uer·ry (ĕk′wə-rē) s. [pl. **-ries**] (officer) caballerizo de la casa real; (attendant) ayuda de cámara de la casa real británica.
e·ques·tri·an (ĭ-kwĕs′trē-ən) I. adj. ecuestre II. s. jinete mf.
e·qui·dis·tant (ē′kwə-dĭs′tənt, ĕk′wə-) adj. equidistante.
e·qui·lat·er·al (ē′kwə-lăt′ər-əl, ĕk′wə-) I. adj. equilátero II. s. GEOM. figura equilátera.
e·quil·i·brant (ĭ-kwĭl′ə-brənt) s. FÍS. fuerza equilibrante.
e·quil·i·brate (ĭ-kwĭl′ə-brāt′) tr. **-brat·ed, -brat·ing** equilibrar, poner en equilibrio —intr. equilibrarse, mantenerse en equilibrio.
e·qui·lib·ri·um (ē′kwə-lĭb′rē-əm, ĕk′wə-) s. [pl. **-ri·ums** o **-ri·a** (-rē-ə)] (balance) equilibrio; (poise) equilibrio mental o emocional m.
e·qui·nox (ē′kwə-nŏks′, ĕk′wə-) s. ASTRON. equinoccio.
e·quip (ĭ-kwĭp′) tr. **e·quipped, e·quip·ping** (to furnish) equipar, proveer; FIG. (to prepare) preparar.
e·quip·ment (ĭ-kwĭp′mənt) s. (apparatus) equipo; (tools) herramientas; (furnishings) moblaje m; FIG. (ability) aptitud f, dotes f; AUTO. accesorios; F.C. material móvil m.
eq·ui·ta·ble (ĕk′wĭ-tə-bəl) adj. (exhibiting equity) equitativo; (impartial) imparcial; (just) justo.
eq·ui·ta·bly (ĕk′wĭ-tə-blē) adv. equitativamente.
eq·ui·ta·tion (ĕk′wĭ-tā′shən) s. DEP. equitación f.
eq·ui·ty (ĕk′wĭ-tē) s. [pl. **-ties**] (impartiality) equidad f, imparcialidad f; DER. justicia natural como suplemento a la letra de la ley.
e·quiv·a·lence (ĭ-kwĭv′ə-ləns) o **e·quiv·a·len·cy** (-lən-sē) s. [pl. **-lenc·es** o **-len·cies**] equivalencia.
e·quiv·a·lent (ĭ-kwĭv′ə-lənt) adj. & s. equivalente m.
e·quiv·o·cal (ĭ-kwĭv′ə-kəl) adj. (ambiguous) equívoco, ambiguo; (uncertain) incierto; (doubtful) dudoso.
e·quiv·o·cate (ĭ-kwĭv′ə-kāt′) intr. **-cat·ed, -cat·ing** usar intencionalmente lenguaje equívoco o ambiguo.
e·quiv·o·ca·tion (ĭ-kwĭv′ə-kā′shən) s. (act) uso de lenguaje equívoco; (ambiguity) ambigüedad f.
e·ra (îr′ə, ĕr′ə) s. (period of time) era, época; GEOL., HIST. (period) era, edad f.
e·rad·i·cate (ĭ-răd′ĭ-kāt′) tr. **-cat·ed, -cat·ing** (to wipe out) erradicar, extirpar; (to uproot) desarraigar.
e·rad·i·ca·tion (ĭ-răd′ĭ-kā′shən) s. (removal) erradicación f, extirpación f; (of plants) desarraigo.
e·rase (ĭ-rās′) tr. **e·rased, e·ras·ing** (to expunge) borrar; JER. (to get rid of) matar.
e·ras·er (ĭ-rā′sər) s. goma de borrar, borrador m.
e·ra·sure (ĭ-rā′shər) s. (act) borradura; (mark) raspadura.
er·bi·um (ûr′bē-əm) s. QUÍM. erbio.
ere (âr) I. prep. antes de II. conj. antes que.
e·rect (ĭ-rĕkt′) I. adj. (vertical) erecto, erguido; (stiff) erizado II. tr. (to construct) erigir, construir <this building was erected forty years ago este edificio fue erigido hace cuarenta años>; (to raise upright) levantar; (to establish) establecer <to e. a dynasty establecer una dinastía>; GEOM. trazar, levantar —intr. FISIOL. erguirse.
e·rec·tile (ĭ-rĕk′təl, -tīl′) adj. eréctil.
e·rec·tion (ĭ-rĕk′shən) s. (act) erección f; (of a building) construcción f; FISIOL. erección (del pene).
e·rect·ness (ĭ-rĕkt′nĭs) s. erección f, erguimiento.
e·rec·tor (ĭ-rĕk′tər) s. (one that erects) erector m; FISIOL. músculo erector.
ere·long (âr-lông′) adv. ANT. dentro de poco tiempo.
erg (ûrg) s. FÍS. ergio (unidad de trabajo).
er·go (ûr′gō, âr′-) conj. & adv. (consequently) consiguientemente; (therefore) por tanto, en consecuencia.
er·go·nom·ics (ûr′gə-nŏm′ĭks) s. [ú. con v. sing.] ergonomía.
er·mine (ûr′mĭn) s. ZOOL. armiño (animal y piel).
e·rode (ĭ-rōd′) tr. & intr. **e·rod·ed, e·rod·ing** (to wear away) erosionar(se); (to corrode) corroer(se).
e·rog·e·nous (ĭ-rŏj′ə-nəs) adj. erógeno.
e·ro·sion (ĭ-rō′zhən) s. GEOL. erosión f.
e·ro·sive (ĭ-rō′sĭv) adj. erosivo.

e·rot·ic (ĭ-rŏt′ĭk) I. adj. erótico II. s. poema erótico.
e·rot·i·ca (ĭ-rŏt′ĭ-kə) s.pl. [ú. con v. sing. o pl.] literatura erótica.
e·rot·i·cism (ĭ-rŏt′ĭ-sĭz′əm) o **er·o·tism** (ĕr′ə-tĭz′əm) s. erotismo.
err (ûr, ĕr) intr. (to make an error) errar, equivocarse; (to sin) pecar.
er·rand (ĕr′ənd) s. mandado, recado.
er·rant (ĕr′ənt) adj. (wandering) errante, errabundo; (erring) equivocado.
er·rant·ry (ĕr′ən-trē) s. vida errante.
er·ra·ta (ĭ-rä′tə, ĭ-rä′-) pl. de **erratum**.
er·rat·ic (ĭ-răt′ĭk) adj. (wandering) errático, errante; (irregular) irregular; (eccentric) excéntrico, extravagante.
er·ra·tum (ĭ-rä′təm, ĭ-rä′-) s. [pl. **-ta** (-tə)] errata, error m.
er·ro·ne·ous (ĭ-rō′nē-əs) adj. (mistaken) erróneo, incorrecto; (false) falso.
er·ror (ĕr′ər) s. (mistake) error m, equivocación f; (transgression) transgresión f; (wrongdoing) ofensa, pecado; MAT. error m ♦ **to be in e.** estar en un error • **to commit an e.** cometer un error.
er·satz (ĕr′zäts, ĕr-zäts′) I. adj. (artificial) artificial; (substitute) substituto II. s. substituto.
erst·while (ûrst′hwīl′) I. adj. antiguo, anterior II. adv. ANT. antiguamente.
e·ruct (ĭ-rŭkt′) I. intr. eructar, erutar II. tr. eructar, erutar; GEOL. (to spew out) expeler, arrojar.
e·ruc·ta·tion (ĭ-rŭk-tā′shən, ē′rŭk-) s. eructo.
er·u·dite (ĕr′yə-dīt′) adj. erudito.
er·u·di·tion (ĕr′yə-dĭsh′ən) s. erudición f.
e·rupt (ĭ-rŭpt′) intr. (to spew) brotar o surgir violentamente; (to explode) estallar, explotar; (volcano, geyser) entrar en o hacer erupción; ODONT. salir; MED. hacer erupción —tr. expeler, arrojar.
e·rup·tion (ĭ-rŭp′shən) s. (of a volcano) erupción f; (of a geyser) brote m; (outburst) irrupción f; MED. erupción f.
es·ca·late (ĕs′kə-lāt′) tr. & intr. **-lat·ed, -lat·ing** (war, conflict) extender(se), intensificar(se); (prices, costs) subir.
es·ca·la·tion (ĕs′kə-lā′shən) s. (of war) intensificación f; (of prices) subida.
es·ca·la·tor (ĕs′kə-lā′tər) s. escalera mecánica.
es·ca·pade (ĕs′kə-pād′) s. aventura.
es·cape (ĭ-skāp′) I. intr. **-caped, -cap·ing** (to get free) escaparse, fugarse <se escapó de la cárcel he escaped from jail>; (to leak) escaparse, salirse; (to avoid) escaparse, librarse; BOT. hacerse silvestre, crecer más allá del área cultivada —tr. (to get free of) escapar de, librarse de; (to elude) eludir, escapársele a uno <her last name always escapes me siempre se me escapa su apellido>; (to emit) emitir, salírsele a uno II. s. (breakout) escapatoria, fuga; (a way out) escapatoria, evasión f <his drinking is an e. from reality la bebida es su evasión de la realidad>; (leakage) escape m, salida.
es·cap·ee (ĭ-skā′pē′) s. prófugo, fugitivo.
escape velocity s. ASTRON., FÍS. velocidad de escape o de fuga f.
es·cap·ism (ĭ-skā′pĭz′əm) s. evasión f.
es·cap·ist (ĭ-skā′pĭst) I. adj. de evasión II. s. persona que se evade de la realidad.
es·carp·ment (ĭ-skärp′mənt) s. escarpa, escarpadura.
es·cha·tol·o·gy (ĕs′kə-tŏl′ə-jē) s. TEO. escatología.
es·cheat·age (ĭs-chē′tĭj) s. DER. derecho del estado de adquirir bienes mostrencos.
es·chew (ĭs-chōō′) tr. (to avoid) evitar; (to shun) esquivar, rehuir.
es·cort I. s. (ĕs′kôrt′) (entourage) acompañamiento, séquito; (guards) escolta; (companion) acompañante m; (vehicles) convoy m II. tr. (ĭ-skôrt′) acompañar, escoltar.
es·crow (ĕs′krō′) s. DER. plica ♦ **in e.** DER. en depósito, en custodia de tercera persona.
escrow account s. cuenta en plica, cuenta entregada a terceros en custodia.
es·cu·do (ĭ-skōō′dō) s. [pl. **-dos**] FIN. escudo.
es·cutch·eon (ĭ-skŭch′ən) s. (shield) escudo de armas; (emblem) escudo o placa ornamental; (plate on a door) escu-

dete m; MARÍT. escudo o espejo de popa ♦ **a blot on one's e.** FIG. una mancha en la reputación de uno.

Es·ki·mo (ĕs′kə-mō′) adj. & s. [pl. **Eskimo** o **-mos**] esquimal mf.

Eskimo dog s. perro esquimal.

e·soph·a·gus (ĭ-sŏf′ə-gəs) s. [pl. **-gi** (-jī′)] ANAT., ZOOL. esófago.

es·o·ter·ic (ĕs′ə-tĕr′ĭk) adj. (said of ideas) esotérico; (confidential) confidencial.

es·pe·cial (ĭ-spĕsh′əl) adj. (exceptional) especial, excepcional; (particular) particular.

es·pe·cial·ly (ĭ-spĕsh′ə-lē) adv. especialmente, particularmente.

es·pi·o·nage (ĕs′pē-ə-näzh′, -nĭj) s. espionaje m.

es·pla·nade (ĕs′plə-näd′, -nād′) s. (promenade) explanada; (along a shore) paseo marítimo o costanero.

es·pous·al (ĭ-spou′zəl) s. (adoption) adhesión f, adopción f; (support) apoyo.

es·pouse (ĭ-spouz′) tr. **-poused, -pous·ing** (to marry) casarse con; (to adopt) adoptar <late in life he espoused a new religion en los últimos años de su vida adoptó una nueva religión>.

es·py (ĭ-spī′) tr. **-pied, -py·ing** columbrar, divisar.

es·quire (ĕs′kwīr′, ĭ-skwīr′) s. ANT. escudero; G.B. terrateniente; (title) [ú. en abrev. después del nombre, esp. de abogados] Don, Señor <John Smith, Esq. Señor John Smith>.

es·say I. tr. (ĕ-sā′, ĕs′ā′) (to try) intentar; (to test) probar, ensayar II. s. (ĕs′ā′) (attempt) intento; (test) prueba, ensayo; LIT. ensayo, (composition) composición f, redacción f.

es·say·ist (ĕs′ā′ĭst) s. ensayista mf.

es·sence (ĕs′əns) s. (crucial element) esencia, substancia; (extract) esencia, extracto; (scent) perfume m; (spiritual entity) ente m, fondo ♦ **in e.** esencialmente.

es·sen·tial (ĭ-sĕn′shəl) I. adj. (necessary) esencial; (fundamental) fundamental; (indispensable) indispensable, imprescindible; (intrinsic) intrínseco, inherente II. s. elemento esencial o indispensable ♦ **to get down to the essentials** ir al grano.

essential oil s. aceite esencial m, esencia.

es·tab·lish (ĭ-stăb′lĭsh) tr. (to make firm) establecer; (to install) instalar <to e. a business instalar un negocio>; (to cause recognition) establecer, afirmar; (to found) fundar <to e. a school fundar una escuela>; (to create a state institution of) constituir o reconocer oficialmente (iglesia, religión); (to promulgate) instituir, promulgar <ordinances established by the king ordenanzas promulgadas por el rey>; (to prove) demostrar, probar <he established his innocence from the beginning demostró su inocencia desde el principio> ♦ **to e. oneself** establecerse.

es·tab·lished (ĭ-stăb′lĭsht) adj. (order) establecido; (custom) arraigado; (fact) conocido, sabido; (person, business) de buena fama o reputación; (staff) fijo, de plantilla; (religion) oficial.

established church s. iglesia oficial.

es·tab·lish·ment (ĭ-stăb′lĭsh-mənt) s. (founding) establecimiento <the e. of this business took several years el establecimiento de este negocio llevó varios años>; (place of business) establecimiento, institución f; (organized group) organización f ♦ **E.** (church) iglesia o religión oficial; (ruling class) clase dirigente.

es·tate (ĭ-stāt′) s. (land) hacienda, finca; (property) propiedad f; (fortune) fortuna; (inheritance) herencia <when he died, he left an e. of two million dollars cuando murió él dejó una herencia de dos millones de dólares>; (stage) etapa, edad (de la vida) f; (rank) estado, clase f; DER. testamentaría ♦ **real e.** bienes raíces • **the fourth e.** la prensa.

es·teem (ĭ-stēm′) I. tr. (to prize) estimar, apreciar <we e. courage apreciamos el valor>; (to consider) considerar, estimar II. s. estimación f, aprecio ♦ **to hold someone in high e.** tenerle gran estima a alguien.

es·ter (ĕs′tər) s. QUÍM. éster m.

es·ter·ase (ĕs′tə-rās′) s. BIOQUÍM. esterasa.

Es·ther (ĕs′tər) s. BÍBL. Ester.

es·thete (ĕs′thēt′) s. var. de **aesthete.**

es·thet·ic (ĕs-thĕt′ĭk) adj. var. de **aesthetic.**

es·ti·ma·ble (ĕs′tə-mə-bəl) adj. estimable.

es·ti·mate (ĕs′tə-māt′) I. tr. **-mat·ed, -mat·ing** (to calculate) estimar, calcular aproximadamente; (to evaluate) estimar, juzgar II. s. (-mĭt) (rough calculation) estimación f; (written statement) presupuesto; (opinion) opinión f ♦ **rough e.** cálculo aproximado.

es·ti·ma·tion (ĕs′tə-mā′shən) s. estimación f, valoración f; (opinion) opinión f, juicio <in my e. en mi opinión>; (esteem) estima, aprecio.

es·ti·ma·tor (ĕs′tə-mā′tər) s. tasador m.

es·top·pel (ĕ-stŏp′əl) s. DER. impedimento para que alguien no pueda negar algo previamente afirmado.

es·trange (ĭ-strānj′) tr. **-tranged, -trang·ing** (to alienate) enajenar, alejar <estranged from politics alejado de la política>; (to make hostile) enemistar <a quarrel had estranged him from his family una pelea lo había enemistado con su familia>.

es·trange·ment (ĭ-strānj′mənt) s. (separation) enajenación f, alejamiento; (discord) desavenencia.

es·tro·gen (ĕs′trə-jən) s. BIOQUÍM. estrógeno.

es·trous (ĕs′trəs) adj. VET. en celo, en estro.

es·trus (ĕs′trəs) s. BIOL. estro (período de celo de los mamíferos).

es·tu·ar·y (ĕs′chōō-ĕr′ē) s. [pl. **-ies**] estuario.

e·ta (ā′tə, ē′tə) s. eta.

et cet·er·a o **et·cet·er·a** (ĕt-sĕt′ər-ə) etcétera, y así sucesivamente.

etch (ĕch) tr. & intr. grabar al agua fuerte.

etch·ing (ĕch′ĭng) s. aguafuerte m, grabado.

e·ter·nal (ĭ-tûr′nəl) I. adj. (timeless) eterno, eterno; (interminable) interminable, incesante II. s. ♦ **the E.** RELIG. el Eterno.

e·ter·ni·ty (ĭ-tûr′nĭ-tē) s. [pl. **-ties**] eternidad f.

eth·ane (ĕth′ān′) s. QUÍM. etano.

eth·a·nol (ĕth′ə-nôl′) s. QUÍM. etanol m.

e·ther (ē′thər) s. éter m.

e·the·re·al (ĭ-thîr′ē-əl) adj. (intangible) etéreo; (delicate) tenue.

eth·ic (ĕth′ĭk) s. FILOS. ética ♦ **ethics** FILOS. ética; (discipline) ética profesional.

eth·i·cal (ĕth′ĭ-kəl) adj. ético, moral.

E·thi·o·pi·a (ē′thē-ō′pē-ə) s. Etiopía.

E·thi·o·pi·an (ē′thē-ō′pē-ən) adj. & s. etíope, etiope mf.

eth·nic (ĕth′nĭk) adj. étnico.

eth·no·cen·tric (ĕth′nō-sĕn′trĭk) adj. etnocéntrico.

eth·no·cen·trism (ĕth′nō-sĕn′trĭz′əm) s. etnocentrismo.

eth·nog·ra·phy (ĕth-nŏg′rə-fē) s. etnografía.

eth·nol·o·gy (ĕth-nŏl′ə-jē) s. etnología.

e·thol·o·gy (ĭ-thŏl′ə-jē) s. etología.

e·thos (ē′thŏs′) s. genio, manera de ser distintiva.

eth·yl (ĕth′əl) s. QUÍM. etilo.

ethyl alcohol s. QUÍM. alcohol etílico.

ethyl chloride s. QUÍM. cloruro de etilo.

eth·yl·ene (ĕth′ə-lēn′) s. QUÍM. etileno.

ethylene glycol s. QUÍM. etilenglicol m.

e·ti·ol·o·gy (ē′tē-ol′ə-jē) s. [pl. **-gies**] FILOS., MED. etiología (estudio de las causas).

et·i·quette (ĕt′ĭ-kĕt′) s. (behavior) etiqueta, protocolo; (decorum) buenos modales.

E·trus·can (ĭ-trŭs′kən) adj. & s. HIST. (inhabitant, language) etrusco.

et·y·mol·o·gist (ĕt′ə-mŏl′ə-jĭst) s. etimólogo, etimologista mf.

et·y·mol·o·gy (ĕt′ə-mŏl′ə-jē) s. [pl. **-gies**] etimología.

eu·ca·lyp·tus (yōō′kə-lĭp′təs) s. [pl. **-tus·es** o **-ti** (-tī′)] BOT. eucalipto.

Eu·cha·rist (yōō′kər-ĭst) s. RELIG. Eucaristía.

eu·chre (yōō′kər) I. s. un juego de naipes II. tr. **-chred, -chring** FIG., FAM. burlar.

Eu·clid·e·an o **Eu·clid·i·an** (yōō-klĭd′ē-ən) adj. euclidiano, de o relativo a la geometría euclidiana.

eu·gen·ics (yōō-jĕn′ĭks) s. [ú. con v. sing.] eugenesia (ciencia que estudia el mejoramiento genético de la raza humana).

ā rey / ä año / b boca / ch chico / d dar / ĕ el / ē mil / g gato / h joya / hw juez / ī aire / k casa / kw cuan

eu·lo·gize (yo͞o′lə-jīz′) tr. **-gized, -giz·ing** elogiar, encomiar.
eu·lo·gy (yo͞o′lə-jē) s. [pl. **-gies**] *(oration)* panegírico, oración *f; (praise)* elogio, encomio.
eu·nuch (yo͞o′nək) s. eunuco.
eu·phe·mism (yo͞o′fə-mĭz′əm) s. RET. eufemismo.
eu·pho·ni·ous (yo͞o-fō′nē-əs) adj. eufónico, agradable al oído.
eu·pho·ny (yo͞o′fə-nē) s. [pl. **-nies**] eufonía.
eu·pho·ri·a (yo͞o-fôr′ē-ə) s. euforia.
eu·pho·ri·ant (yo͞o-fôr′ē-ənt) adj. & s. MED., PSIC. estimulante *m.*
eu·phor·ic (yo͞o-fôr′ĭk) adj. eufórico.
Eur·a·sian (yo͞o-rā′zhən) adj. eurasiático.
Eu·rope (yo͝or′əp) s. Europa.
Eu·ro·pe·an (yo͝or′ə-pē′ən) adj. & s. europeo.
European Economic Community s. Mercado Común Europeo.
Eu·ro·pe·an·ize (yo͝or′ə-pē′ə-nīz′) tr. **-ized, -iz·ing** europeizar.
European plan s. plan de alojamiento hotelero sin comidas *m.*
Eu·sta·chian tube (yo͞o-stā′shən, -stā′kē-ən) s. ANAT. tubo *o* trompa de Eustaquio.
eu·tha·na·sia (yo͞o′thə-nā′zhə) s. eutanasia.
e·vac·u·ate (ĭ-văk′yo͞o-āt′) tr. **-at·ed, -at·ing** *(to empty)* desocupar, vaciar; *(to abandon)* evacuar (lugar); *(to withdraw)* retirar, sacar (tropas, civiles) FISIOL. *(to excrete)* evacuar; FÍS. crear *o* dejar un vacío —intr. *(to withdraw)* retirarse; *(to defecate)* defecar.
e·vac·u·a·tion (ĭ-văk′yo͞o-ā′shən) s. *(act)* evacuación *f;* FISIOL. *(excretion)* evacuación, defecación *f; (excrement)* excremento.
e·vac·u·ee (ĭ-văk′yo͞o-ē′) s. evacuado.
e·vade (ĭ-vād′) tr. **e·vad·ed, e·vad·ing** *(to elude)* evitar, eludir; *(to dodge)* evadir; *(to escape)* escaparse de —intr. usar evasivas.
e·vad·er (ĭ-vā′dər) s. evasor *m.*
e·val·u·ate (ĭ-văl′yo͞o-āt′) tr. **-at·ed, -at·ing** *(to examine)* examinar; *(to estimate)* estimar; *(to calculate)* calcular; *(to judge)* juzgar; *(to weigh up)* evaluar.
e·val·u·a·tion (ĭ-văl′yo͞o-ā′shən) s. *(weighing up)* evaluación *f,* valoración *f; (estimation)* cálculo; *(judgment)* opinión *f.*
ev·a·nesce (ĕv′ə-nĕs′) intr. **-nesced, -nesc·ing** desvanecerse, esfumarse.
ev·a·nes·cence (ĕv′ə-nĕs′əns) s. desvanecimiento, disipación *f.*
ev·a·nes·cent (ĕv′ə-nĕs′ənt) adj. evanescente.
e·van·gel (ĭ-văn′jəl) s. RELIG. *(gospel)* evangelio; *(evangelist)* evangelista *mf.*
e·van·gel·i·cal (ē′văn-jĕl′ĭ-kəl, ĕv′ən-) *o* **e·van·gel·ic** (-jĕl′ĭk) adj. evangélico.
e·van·gel·i·cal·ism (ē′văn-jĕl′ĭ-kə-lĭz′əm, ĕv′ən-) s. RELIG. *(preaching)* evangelización *f,* propagación del evangelio *f; (zeal)* celo *o* fervor militante *m.*
e·van·gel·ist (ĭ-văn′jə-lĭst) s. RELIG. evangelista *mf,* evangelizador *m* ♦ **E.** RELIG. Evangelista.
e·van·gel·ize (ĭ-văn′jə-līz′) tr. **-ized, -iz·ing** evangelizar —intr. predicar el evangelio.
e·vap·o·rate (ĭ-văp′ə-rāt′) tr. **-rat·ed, -rat·ing** *(to vaporize)* evaporar; *(to dry)* desecar —intr. *(to vaporize)* evaporarse; FIG. *(to disappear)* evaporarse, desvanecerse.
evaporated milk s. CUL. leche evaporada, leche condensada no azucarada.
e·vap·o·ra·tion (ĭ-văp′ə-rā′shən) s. evaporación *f.*
e·vap·o·ra·tor (ĭ-văp′ə-rā′tər) s. evaporador *m.*
e·va·sion (ĭ-vā′zhən) s. *(act)* evasión *f,* escapatoria; *(flight)* evasión, fuga; *(avoidance)* evasión, evasiva; *(of taxes)* evasión.
e·va·sive (ĭ-vā′sĭv) adj. evasivo.
eve (ēv) s. *(evening before)* víspera; RELIG. *(evening before a feast)* vigilia; POÉT. *(dusk)* crepúsculo; *(night)* noche *f* ♦ **Christmas E.** Nochebuena • **New Year's E.** Noche Vieja • **on the e. of** *(period)* en vísperas de; *(day)* la víspera de.
Eve (ēv) s. BÍBL. Eva.
e·ven (ē′vən) **I.** adj. *(flat)* plano, llano; *(smooth)* liso, parejo; *(level)* a nivel, paralelo; *(uniform)* uniforme, regular;

(equally matched) parejo; *(with equal score)* empatado; *(exact)* exacto, justo; *(equal)* semejante, igual <an e. exchange un canje por otra cosa igual>; *(cool)* sereno, tranquilo; *(fair)* equitativo, justo; MAT. redondo ♦ **e. number** número par • **on an e. keel** FIG. estable, equilibrado • **to be e.** estar mano a mano • **to break e.** ni ganar ni perder • **to get e.** desquitarse • **to make e.** allanar, nivelar • **to stand an e. chance** tener un cincuenta por ciento de probabilidades • **to stay e.** cubrir los gastos **II.** adv. *(yet)* todavía, aun <he is in an e. worse condition than yesterday está en una condición aun peor que la de ayer>; siquiera <he didn't e. cry ni siquiera lloró> ♦ **e. as** precisamente, justo cuando • **e. if** *o* **e. though** aunque, aun cuando • **e. so** aun así, suponiendo que así sea • **e. now** ahora mismo **III.** tr. *(to make even)* emparejar, nivelar; *(to make equal)* igualar ♦ **to e. up** *(to level)* igualar, nivelar; COM. balancear • **to e. up the score** *(to make equal)* igualar; FIG., FAM. *(to get revenge)* ajustar cuentas —intr. emparejarse, nivelarse.
e·ven·hand·ed (ē′vən-hăn′dĭd) adj. *(equitable)* equitativo; *(impartial)* imparcial.
eve·ning (ēv′nĭng) s. *(afternoon)* atardecer *m,* tarde *f; (dusk)* anochecer *m,* noche *f; (entertainment)* noche, velada; FIG. *(decline)* ocaso ♦ **e. class** clase nocturna • **e. performance** función de noche • **e. paper** periódico de la tarde • **good e.!** *(afternoon)* ¡buenas tardes!; *(after sunset)* ¡buenas noches! • **in the e.** por la tarde • **yesterday e.** ayer por la tarde.
evening dress s. *(for men)* traje de etiqueta *m; (for women)* traje de noche *f.*
evening gown s. vestido de noche *o* de cola.
evening star s. lucero de la tarde, estrella vespertina.
e·ven·ness (ē′vən-nĭs) s. *(equality)* igualdad *f; (poise)* ecuanimidad *f,* equilibrio (mental); *(uniformity)* uniformidad *f,* regularidad *f; (smoothness)* lo liso, lo llano; *(impartiality)* imparcialidad *f,* ecuanimidad.
e·ven·song (ē′vən-sông′) s. RELIG. vísperas.
e·vent (ĭ-vĕnt′) s. *(occurrence)* suceso, acontecimiento; *(final result)* consecuencia, resultado; DEP. evento ♦ **in any e.** en todo caso • **in the e. of** en caso de (que).
e·vent·ful (ĭ-vĕnt′fəl) adj. *(full of events)* lleno de acontecimientos; *(momentous)* extraordinario; *(memorable)* memorable.
e·ven·tu·al (ĭ-vĕn′cho͞o-əl) adj. *(possible)* eventual; *(ultimate)* final.
e·ven·tu·al·i·ty (ĭ-vĕn′cho͞o-ăl′ĭ-tē) s. [pl. **-ties**] eventualidad *f.*
e·ven·tu·al·ly (ĭ-vĕn′cho͞o-ə-lē) adv. con el tiempo, a la larga.
e·ven·tu·ate (ĭ-vĕn′cho͞o-āt′) intr. **-at·ed, -at·ing** ♦ **to e. in** resultar en.
ev·er (ĕv′ər) adv. *(always)* siempre <John, e. so thoughtful, sent me flowers today Juan, siempre tan atento, me envió flores hoy>; *(at any time)* alguna vez <have you e. been to Paris? ¿estuviste alguna vez en París?>; *(at all)* nunca, jamás <nobody has e. treated me this way nunca nadie me trató así> ♦ **as e.** como siempre • **better than e.** mejor que nunca • **e. since** *(from the time)* desde que <e. since I came to this country desde que vine a este país>; *(since then)* desde entonces <I saw her last Tuesday, and I have not seen her e. since la vi el martes pasado y no la he vuelto a ver desde entonces> • **did you e.?** FAM. ¿habráse visto?, ¡qué ocurrencia! • **e. so** tan <I am e. so happy me siento tan feliz> • **e. so little** muy poco • **e. so much** mucho, muchísimo • **for e. and a day** *o* **for e. and e.** por siempre jamás, para siempre • **hardly e.** casi nunca • **not e.** nunca.
▲ El adverbio *ever* se usa a menudo en inglés en oraciones interrogativas para enfatizar sorpresa, impaciencia o dificultad. En estos casos su sentido queda traducido por el verbo "poder", o los adverbios "nunca" o "jamás" <how did I e. do that? ¿cómo pude hacerte eso?> <is she e. going to arrive? ¿no va a llegar nunca?>.
ev·er·chang·ing (ĕv′ər-chān′jĭng) adj. cambiadizo, variable.
ev·er·glade (ĕv′ər-glād′) s. terreno pantanoso y bajo cu-

bierto de hierbas altas ♦ **Everglades** región pantanosa en el estado de la Florida, EE. UU.

ev·er·green (ĕv′ər-grēn′) **I.** adj. BOT. *(not deciduous)* de hoja perenne, siempre verde; FIG. *(enduring)* imperecedero **II.** s. BOT. siempreviva, planta de hoja perenne.

ev·er·last·ing (ĕv′ər-lăs′tĭng) **I.** adj. *(eternal)* eterno; *(long-lasting)* perdurable; *(tedious)* interminable, eterno **II.** s. *(eternity)* eternidad *f;* BOT. siempreviva ♦ **The E.** RELIG. el Ser Eterno, el Padre Eterno.

ev·er·more (ĕv′ər-môr′) adv. *(forever)* eternamente, siempre ♦ **for e.** `por *o* para simpre.

eve·ry (ĕv′rē) adj. cada <*e. two hours* cada dos horas>; todo <*e. man* todo hombre>; todos los <*e. child does that* todos los niños hacen eso> ♦ **e. confidence** plena confianza • **e. day** todos los días • **e. now and then** de vez en cuando • **e. once in a while** alguna que otra vez • **e. one** *(each one)* cada uno, cada cual; *(all)* todos, todo el mundo • **e. one of them** todos (sin excepción) • **e. other day** cada dos días, día por medio • **e. so often** alguna que otra vez • **e. time** cada vez, siempre • **e. which way** *(in all directions)* por todas partes; *(in no order)* en total desorden.

eve·ry·bod·y (ĕv′rē-bŏd′ē, -bŭd′ē) pron. *(every person)* cada uno, cada cual; *(all)* todos, todo el mundo.

eve·ry·day (ĕv′rē-dā′) adj. *(daily)* diario, cotidiano <*one's e. routine* la rutina diaria de uno>; *(usual)* común, corriente; *(for ordinary days)* de todos los días <*e. shoes* zapatos de todos los días>.

eve·ry·one (ĕv′rē-wŭn′) pron. *(every person)* cada uno, cada cual; *(all)* todos, todo el mundo ♦ **e. for himself** cada cual por su cuenta.

eve·ry·place (ĕv′rē-plās′) adv. consulte **everywhere.**

eve·ry·thing (ĕv′rē-thĭng′) pron. todo.

eve·ry·where (ĕv′rē-hwâr′) adv. *(in all places)* en todas partes, por todas partes; *(to every place)* a todas partes, por todas partes; *(wherever)* dondequiera que.

e·vict (ĭ-vĭkt′) tr. DER. *(to expel legally)* desalojar; *(to force out)* echar fuera, expulsar; *(to dispossess)* desposeer, privar.

e·vic·tion (ĭ-vĭk′shən) s. desalojamiento.

ev·i·dence (ĕv′ĭ-dəns) **I.** s. *(indication)* indicio, prueba; *(data)* hechos, datos; DER. *(proof)* evidencia, prueba; *(testimony)* testimonio, declaración *f* ♦ **to be in e.** estar a la vista, ser conspicuo • **to give e.** DER. declarar como testigo, prestar declaración • **to show e. of** presentar señales de • **to turn state's e.** DER. dar testimonio en contra de los cómplices **II.** tr. **-denced, -denc·ing** *(to demonstrate)* evidenciar, probar; *(to attest)* atestiguar; *(to declare)* declarar.

ev·i·dent (ĕv′ĭ-dənt) adj. evidente.

ev·i·den·tial (ĕv′ĭ-dĕn′shəl) adj. DER. comprobatorio, probatorio.

ev·i·dent·ly (ĕv′ĭ-dənt-lē, ĕv′ĭ-dĕnt′lē) adv. evidentemente.

e·vil (ē′vəl) **I.** adj. *(wicked)* malo, malvado; *(harmful)* nocivo, perjudicial (consejo); *(baleful)* funesto, pernicioso (influencia, resultados); *(ominous)* nefasto; *(malicious)* maligno, malévolo; *(spiteful)* rencoroso (persona); *(immoral)* malo, perverso **II.** s. *(wickedness)* maldad *f;* *(harm)* mal *m,* perjuicio; *(immorality)* perversidad *f,* mal.

e·vil·do·er (ē′vəl-doo′ər) s. malhechor *m,* malvado.

evil eye s. mal de ojo *m.*

e·vil·mind·ed (ē′vəl-mīn′dĭd) adj. *(malicious)* malicioso; *(evil)* malintencionado; *(salacious)* mal pensado.

e·vince (ĭ-vĭns′) tr. **evinced, evinc·ing** *(to demonstrate)* demostrar; *(to manifest)* manifestar; *(to exhibit)* revelar.

e·vis·cer·ate (ĭ-vĭs′ə-rāt′) tr. **-at·ed, -at·ing** *(the entrails)* destripar; *(an essential part)* quitar la substancia a *o* de.

e·vo·ca·tion (ĕv′ə-kā′shən, ē′və-) s. evocación *f.*

e·voc·a·tive (ĭ-vŏk′ə-tĭv) adj. evocador.

e·voke (ĭ-vōk′) tr. **evoked, evok·ing** evocar.

ev·o·lu·tion (ĕv′ə-loo′shən, ē′və-) s. *(process)* evolución *f;* *(development)* desarrollo; MAT. extracción de raíces *f.*

ev·o·lu·tion·ar·y (ĕv′ə-loo′shə-nĕr′ē, ē′və-) adj. evolutivo.

ev·o·lu·tion·ism (ĕv′ə-loo′shə-nĭz′əm, ē′və-) s. evolucionismo.

ev·o·lu·tion·ist (ĕv′ə-loo′shə-nĭst, ē′və-) s. evolucionista *mf.*

e·volve (ĭ-vŏlv′) tr. **e·volved, e·volv·ing** *(to develop)* desarrollar; *(to formulate)* formular, elaborar; *(to yield)* despedir; BIOL. hacer evolucionar —intr. *(to develop)* desarrollarse; BIOL. evolucionar.

e·volve·ment (ĭ-vŏlv′mənt) s. desarrollo, evolución *f.*

ewe (yoo) s. oveja hembra.

ew·er (yoo′ər) s. aguamanil *m,* jarra.

ex¹ (ĕks) prep. FIN. *(without)* fuera de; *(not including)* sin incluir; *(not participating in)* sin participación en; COM. puesto en.

ex² (ĕks) s. JER. *(former wife)* ex-mujer; *(former husband)* ex-marido.

ex·ac·er·bate (ĭg-zăs′ər-bāt′) tr. **-bat·ed, -bat·ing** exacerbar.

ex·ac·er·ba·tion (ĭg-zăs′ər-bā′shən) s. exacerbación *f.*

ex·act (ĭg-zăkt′) **I.** adj. exacto **II.** tr. quitar por la fuerza ♦ **to e. from** *o* exigir a.

ex·act·ing (ĭg-zăk′tĭng) adj. *(exigent)* exigente; *(severe)* severo; *(rigorous)* riguroso; *(exhausting)* pesado, agotador.

ex·ac·tion (ĭg-zăk′shən) s. exacción *f.*

ex·ac·ti·tude (ĭg-zăk′tĭ-tood′, -tyood′) s. exactitud *f.*

ex·act·ly (ĭg-zăkt′lē) adv. *(accurately)* exactamente; *(precisely)* precisamente <*I am not e. thrilled* no me siento precisamente emocionado>; *(you're right)* tiene usted razón; *(quite true)* es verdad, así es.

ex·act·ness (ĭg-zăkt′nĭs) s. exactitud *f.*

ex·ag·ger·ate (ĭg-zăj′ə-rāt′) tr. & intr. **-at·ed, -at·ing** exagerar.

ex·ag·ger·at·ed (ĭg-zăj′ə-rā′tĭd) adj. exagerado.

ex·ag·ger·a·tion (ĭg-zăj′ə-rā′shən) s. exageración *f.*

ex·alt (ĭg-zôlt′) tr. *(to elevate)* exaltar, elevar; *(to extol)* exaltar, ensalzar; *(to heighten)* aumentar, intensificar.

ex·al·ta·tion (ĕg′zôl-tā′shən) s. *(act, condition)* exaltación *f;* *(exhilaration)* júbilo.

ex·alt·ed (ĭg-zôl′tĭd) adj. *(elevated)* exaltado; *(lofty)* elevado.

ex·am (ĭg-zăm′) s. FAM. examen *m.*

ex·am·i·na·tion (ĭg-zăm′ə-nā′shən) s. *(analysis)* examen *m,* análisis *m;* *(test)* examen, prueba; DER. *(interrogation)* interrogatorio; *(inquiry)* investigación *f.*

ex·am·ine (ĭg-zăm′ĭn) tr. **-ined, -in·ing** *(to inspect)* examinar, revisar; *(to test)* examinar a, someter a un examen (estudiante); *(to scrutinize)* examinar a fondo, escudriñar; MED. examinar a, reconocer a; DER. *(a defendant)* interrogar; *(witness)* hacer declarar.

ex·am·in·er (ĭg-zăm′ə-nər) s. examinador *m.*

ex·am·ple (ĭg-zăm′pəl) s. *(typical instance)* ejemplo; *(specimen)* ejemplo, espécimen *m;* *(model)* ejemplo, modelo; MAT. ejemplo ♦ **to set an e.** dar ejemplo.

ex·as·per·ate (ĭg-zăs′pə-rāt′) tr. **-at·ed, -at·ing** *(to vex)* exasperar; *(to aggravate)* exacerbar.

ex·as·per·a·tion (ĭg-zăs′pə-rā′shən) s. exasperación *f.*

ex·ca·vate (ĕk′skə-vāt′) tr. **-vat·ed, -vat·ing** *(to dig)* excavar; *(to uncover)* desenterrar.

ex·ca·va·tion (ĕk′skə-vā′shən) s. excavación *f.*

ex·ca·va·tor (ĕk′skə-vā′tər) s. *(person)* excavador *m;* *(power shovel)* excavadora.

ex·ceed (ĭk-sēd′) tr. *(to be greater than)* exceder; *(to go beyond)* propasarse en, excederse en.

ex·ceed·ing (ĭk-sē′dĭng) **I.** adj. *(excessive)* excesivo; *(extreme)* extremo; *(extraordinary)* extraordinario **II.** adv. ANT. extremadamente.

ex·ceed·ing·ly (ĭk-sē′dĭng-lē) adv. extremadamente.

ex·cel (ĭk-sĕl′) tr. **-celled, -cel·ling** superar, aventajar —intr. sobresalir, distinguirse.

ex·cel·lence (ĕk′sə-ləns) s. excelencia.

Ex·cel·len·cy (ĕk′sə-lən-sē) s. [pl. **-cies**] Excelencia.

ex·cel·lent (ĕk′sə-lənt) adj. excelente.

ex·cel·si·or (ĭk-sĕl′sē-ər) s. virutas de madera (empleadas para empaquetar).

ex·cept §G1 (ĭk-sĕpt′) **I.** prep. excepto, menos <*everyone e. him* todos menos él> ♦ **e. for** *(were it not for)* si no fuera por, a no ser por <*I would go e. for my headache* iría si no fuera por mi dolor de cabeza>; *(but)* aparte de <*a nice day e. for the rain* un día agradable aparte de la lluvia> **II.** conj. *(only)* sólo que; *(otherwise than)* sino ♦ **e. that**

excepto que, salvo que **III.** tr. exceptuar, excluir —intr. oponerse, objetar.

ex·cept·ing (ĭk-sĕp′tĭng) prep. exceptuando, salvo, con excepción de.

ex·cep·tion (ĭk-sĕp′shən) s. *(exclusion)* excepción *f*, exclusión *f*; *(objection)* reparo, objeción *f* ♦ **the e. proves the rule** la excepción confirma la regla • **to make an e.** hacer una excepción • **to take e. to** estar en desacuerdo con, oponerse a • **with the e. of** a excepción de, excepto.

ex·cep·tion·a·ble (ĭk-sĕp′shə-nə-bəl) adj. DER. *(witness)* impugnable, recusable; *(objectionable)* censurable, reprochable.

ex·cep·tion·al (ĭk-sĕp′shə-nəl) adj. excepcional.

ex·cerpt I. s. (ĕk′sûrpt′) extracto **II.** tr. (ĭk-sûrpt′) extractar, citar ♦ **to e. from** citar de.

ex·cess (ĭk-sĕs′, ĕk′sĕs′) **I.** s. exceso ♦ **in e. of** más que, superior a • **to e.** en *o* con exceso **II.** adj. excesivo.

excess baggage s. exceso de equipaje.

ex·ces·sive (ĭk-sĕs′ĭv) adj. excesivo.

ex·change (ĭks-chānj′) **I.** tr. **-changed, -chang·ing** *(to interchange)* intercambiar; *(to change)* cambiar ♦ **to e. glances** cruzar miradas, cruzarse las miradas • **to e. prisoners** canjear prisioneros • **to e. something for** cambiar algo por • **to e. views** intercambiar opiniones • **to e. words** cruzar palabras **II.** s. *(interchange)* intercambio; *(change)* cambio; *(of prisoners)* canje *m*; COM. *(commodities market)* bolsa, lonja; *(payment system)* documentos cambiarios ♦ **in e. for** a cambio de.

ex·change·a·ble (ĭks-chān′jə-bəl) adj. canjeable ♦ **e. merchandise** artículo canjeable.

exchange rate s. tipo de cambio.

ex·cheq·uer (ĕks′chĕk′ər, ĭks-chĕk′-) s. *(treasury)* tesoro público, fisco; *(funds)* fondos ♦ **E.** G.B. *(ministry)* Ministerio de Hacienda; *(court)* tribunal de hacienda *m*.

ex·cise[1] (ĕk′sīz′) **I.** s. *(indirect tax)* impuesto indirecto; *(license fee)* alcabala **II.** tr. **-cised, -cis·ing** gravar con impuesto indirecto.

ex·cise[2] (ĭk-sīz′) tr. **-cised, -cis·ing** extirpar.

ex·ci·sion (ĭk-sĭzh′ən) s. CIR. excisión *f*, extirpación *f*.

ex·cit·a·ble (ĭk-sī′tə-bəl) adj. excitable.

ex·ci·tant (ĭk-sī′nt) adj. *(exciting)* excitante; *(stimulating)* estimulante.

ex·ci·ta·tion (ĕk′sī-tā′shən) s. excitación *f*.

ex·cite (ĭk-sīt′) tr. **-cit·ed, -cit·ing** *(to thrill)* entusiasmar, emocionar; *(to arouse)* excitar; BIOL., FÍS., FISIOL. excitar.

ex·cit·ed (ĭk-sī′tĭd) adj. *(agitated)* excitado, agitado; *(filled with excitement)* entusiasmado; *(nervous)* nervioso; FÍS. excitado ♦ **to get e.** *(to become agitated)* excitarse, agitarse; *(to become enthusiastic)* entusiasmarse; *(to get nervous)* ponerse nervioso.

ex·cite·ment (ĭk-sīt′mənt) s. *(agitation)* emoción *f*, agitación *f*; *(enthusiasm)* entusiasmo.

ex·cit·er (ĭk-sī′tər) s. *(agitator)* excitador *m*, agitador *m*; ELEC. excitador *m*.

ex·cit·ing (ĭk-sī′tĭng) adj. emocionante.

ex·claim (ĭk-sklām′) intr. exclamar —tr. *(to shout)* gritar; *(to proclaim)* proclamar.

ex·cla·ma·tion (ĕk′sklə-mā′shən) s. exclamación *f*.

exclamation point s. GRAM. signo de admiración.

ex·clam·a·to·ry (ĭk-sklăm′ə-tôr′ē) adj. exclamatorio, exclamativo.

ex·clude (ĭk-sklōōd′) tr. **-clud·ed, -clud·ing** *(to bar)* excluir; *(to disregard)* omitir; *(to expel)* expulsar.

ex·clud·ing (ĭk-sklōō′dĭng) prep. excepto, exceptuando a.

ex·clu·sion (ĭk-sklōō′zhən) s. exclusión *f*.

ex·clu·sive (ĭk-sklōō′sĭv) **I.** adj. *(sole)* exclusivo, único; *(select)* selecto, elegante; *(excluding)* exclusivo, cerrado ♦ **e. interview** entrevista exclusiva • **e. rights** exclusividad • **mutually e.** que se excluyen (principios, cláusulas) **II.** s. noticia de exclusividad.

ex·clu·sive·ness (ĭk-sklōō′sĭv-nĭs) s. exclusividad *f*.

ex·clu·siv·i·ty (ĕk′sklōō-sĭv′ĭ-tē) s. exclusividad *f*.

ex·com·mu·ni·ca·ble (ĕks′kə-myōō′nĭ-kə-bəl) adj. digno de excomunión.

ex·com·mu·ni·cate (ĕks′kə-myōō′nĭ-kāt′) **I.** tr. **-cat·ed,**

-cat·ing excomulgar, anatematizar **II.** s. & adj. (-kĭt) excomulgado.

ex·com·mu·ni·ca·tion (ĕks′kə-myōō′nĭ-kā′shən) s. excomunión *f*.

ex·co·ri·ate (ĭk-skôr′ē-āt′) tr. **-at·ed, -at·ing** *(to abrade)* excoriar; *(to upbraid)* reprochar, recriminar.

ex·co·ri·a·tion (ĭk-skôr′ē-ā′shən) s. excoriación *f*.

ex·cre·ment (ĕk′skrə-mənt) s. excremento.

ex·cres·cence (ĭk-skrĕs′əns) s. MED. excrecencia.

ex·cres·cent (ĭk-skrĕs′ənt) adj. MED. *(protruding)* saliente; *(superfluous)* superfluo.

ex·cre·ta (ĭk-skrē′tə) s.pl. FISIOL. excresiones *f*.

ex·crete (ĭk-skrēt′) tr. **-cret·ed, -cret·ing** FISIOL. excretar.

ex·cre·tion (ĭk-skrē′shən) s. FISIOL. excreción *f*.

ex·cre·to·ry (ĕk′skrĭ-tôr′ē) adj. FISIOL. excretor, excretorio.

ex·cru·ci·ate (ĭk-skrōō′shē-āt′) tr. **-at·ed, -at·ing** *(to torture)* torturar; *(to torment)* atormentar.

ex·cru·ci·at·ing (ĭk-skrōō′shē-ā′tĭng) adj. *(unbearable)* insoportable; *(very painful)* dolorosísimo.

ex·cul·pate (ĕk′skəl-pāt′, ĭk-skŭl′-) tr. **-pat·ed, -pat·ing** exculpar, disculpar.

ex·cul·pa·tion (ĕk′skəl-pā′shən) s. exculpación *f*.

ex·cul·pa·to·ry (ĭk-skŭl′pə-tôr′ē) adj. justificante, que disculpa.

ex·cur·sion (ĭk-skûr′zhən) s. *(outing)* excursión *f*; paseo; *(digression)* digresión *f*; MIL. *(sortie)* salida; *(expedition)* expedición *f*; ASTRON., MED. excursión.

ex·cur·sion·ist (ĭk-skûr′zhə-nĭst) s. excursionista *mf*.

ex·cur·sive (ĭk-skûr′sĭv) adj. *(rambling)* divagador, digresivo; *(desultory)* inconexo.

ex·cus·a·ble (ĭk-skyōō′zə-bəl) adj. perdonable, excusable.

ex·cuse (ĭk-skyōōz′) **I.** tr. **-cused, -cus·ing** *(to forgive)* excusar, disculpar; *(to exempt)* eximir, dispensar ♦ **e. me!** *(I'm sorry!)* ¡discúlpeme!; *(pardon me)* perdone; *(beg your pardon)* con permiso • **to be excused from** estar dispensado de • **to e. oneself for** disculparse de, excusarse de • **to e. someone from** dispensar a alguien de, eximir a alguien de **II.** s. (-skyōōs′) *(explanation)* excusa, disculpa; *(pretext)* excusa, pretexto ♦ **to look for excuses** buscar excusas • **to make excuses (for)** dar excusas (por) • **to make one's excuses to someone** disculparse ante alguien, pedir disculpa a alguien.

ex·e·cra·ble (ĕk′sĭ-krə-bəl) adj. execrable.

ex·e·crate (ĕk′sĭ-krāt′) tr. **-crat·ed, -crat·ing** *(to abhor)* execrar; *(to abominate)* abominar; ANT. *(to curse)* maldecir.

ex·e·cra·tion (ĕk′sĭ-krā′shən) s. *(abomination)* execración *f*; *(curse)* maldición *f*.

ex·e·cute (ĕk′sĭ-kyōōt′) tr. **-cut·ed, -cut·ing** *(to perform)* ejecutar, realizar; *(to do)* hacer; *(to carry out)* ejecutar, llevar a cabo; *(to legalize)* formalizar; *(to fulfill)* ejecutar, cumplir; *(to kill)* ejecutar; MÚS. ejecutar.

ex·e·cut·er (ĕk′sĭ-kyōō′tər) s. *(one who executes)* ejecutor *m*; *(executioner)* verdugo.

ex·e·cu·tion (ĕk′sĭ-kyōō′shən) s. *(act, style)* ejecución *f*; DER. ejecución; *(validation)* legalización *f*.

ex·e·cu·tion·er (ĕk′sĭ-kyōō′shə-nər) s. verdugo.

ex·ec·u·tive (ĭg-zĕk′yə-tĭv) **I.** s. *(administrator)* ejecutivo; POL. *(chief officer)* presidente *m*, jefe de estado *m*; *(branch of government)* poder ejecutivo **II.** adj. ejecutivo.

executive agreement s. acuerdo entre jefes de estado sin ratificación parlamentaria.

executive officer s. MIL. segundo comandante; *(administrator)* director ejecutivo.

executive session s. POL. sesión ejecutiva (a puertas cerradas).

ex·ec·u·tor (ĭg-zĕk′yə-tər) s. DER. ejecutor testamentario, albacea *m*.

ex·ec·u·trix (ĭg-zĕk′yə-trĭks′) s. [pl. **-trix·es** *o* **ex·ec·u·tri·ces** (ĭg-zĕk′yə-trī′sēz′)] DER. testamentaria, albacea *f*.

ex·e·ge·sis (ĕk′sə-jē′sĭs) s. [pl. **-ses** (-sēz′)] exégesis *f*.

ex·em·plar (ĭg-zĕm′plər) s. *(model)* ejemplar *m*, modelo; *(copy)* ejemplar.

ex·em·pla·ry (ĭg-zĕm′plə-rē) adj. ejemplar.

ex·em·pli·fi·ca·tion (ĭg-zĕm′plə-fĭ-kā′shən) s. *(act, example)* ejemplificación *f*; DER. *(certified copy)* copia legalizada.

ex·em·pli·fy (ĭg-zĕm′plə-fī′) tr. **-fied, -fy·ing** *(to serve as an* *example)* ejemplificar; *(to illustrate)* ilustrar; DER. *(to make a certified copy of)* hacer una copia legalizada.

ex·empt (ĭg-zĕmpt′) I. tr. ♦ **to e. from** eximir de II. adj. exento III. s. persona exonerada.

ex·emp·tion (ĭg-zĕmp′shən) s. exención f.

ex·er·cise (ĕk′sər-sīz′) I. s. ejercicio ♦ **exercises** *(workout)* ejercicios; *(ceremony)* ceremonia espiritual o tradicional II. tr. **-cised, -cis·ing** *(to use)* usar de, proceder con <*to e. caution* proceder con cautela>; *(to drill)* ejercitar, entrenar; *(to perform)* ejercer <*to e. one's rights* ejercer uno sus derechos>; *(to preoccupy)* preocupar —intr. ejercitarse.

ex·ert (ĭg-zûrt′) tr. *(strength)* emplear; *(influence)* ejercer ♦ **to e. oneself** esforzarse, afanarse.

ex·er·tion (ĭg-zûr′shən) s. *(of strength)* empleo; *(of influence)* ejercicio; *(effort)* esfuerzo.

ex·fo·li·ate (ĕks-fō′lē-āt′) tr. & intr. **-at·ed, -at·ing** exfoliar(se).

ex·ha·lant (ĕks-hā′lənt) adj. exhalador.

ex·ha·la·tion (ĕks′hə-lā′shən) s. exhalación f.

ex·hale (ĕks-hāl′) intr. & tr. **-haled, -hal·ing** *(to breathe out)* exhalar; *(to emit)* emitir.

ex·haust (ĭg-zôst′) I. tr. *(to use up)* agotar; *(to tire)* cansar; *(to deplete)* empobrecer (tierra); *(to drain)* vaciar, extraer —intr. escaparse II. s. AUTO. escape m, descarga; *(fumes)* gases de escape m; *(device)* tubo de escape.

ex·haust·i·ble (ĭg-zô′stə-bəl) adj. agotable.

ex·haus·tion (ĭg-zôs′chən) s. agotamiento.

ex·haus·tive (ĭg-zô′stĭv) adj. exhaustivo.

ex·hib·it (ĭg-zĭb′ĭt) I. tr. *(to display)* mostrar, exhibir; *(to present)* presentar, exponer; *(to evidence)* demostrar, manifestar; DER. exhibir, presentar (pruebas, documentos) —intr. dar una exhibición, exponer II. s. *(display)* exhibición f, exposición f; *(object)* objeto exhibido, objeto expuesto; DER. prueba instrumental, documento presentado (como evidencia).

ex·hi·bi·tion (ĕk′sə-bĭsh′ən) s. *(act, display)* exhibición f, exposición f; G.B. *(scholarship)* beca.

ex·hi·bi·tion·ism (ĕk′sə-bĭsh′ə-nĭz′əm) s. exhibicionismo.

ex·hi·bi·tion·ist (ĕk′sə-bĭsh′ə-nĭst) s. exhibicionista mf.

ex·hib·i·tor (ĭg-zĭb′ĭ-tər) s. *(of art)* expositor m; CINEM. exhibidor m.

ex·hil·a·rant (ĭg-zĭl′ər-ənt) adj. & s. estimulante m.

ex·hil·a·rate (ĭg-zĭl′ə-rāt′) tr. **-rat·ed, -rat·ing** *(to make cheerful)* alegrar; *(to invigorate)* animar; *(to stimulate)* estimular.

ex·hil·a·rat·ing (ĭg-zĭl′ə-rā′tĭng) adj. *(cheering)* regocijador; *(invigorating)* vigorizante; *(stimulating)* estimulante.

ex·hil·a·ra·tion (ĭg-zĭl′ə-rā′shən) s. entusiasmo, exaltación f.

ex·hort (ĭg-zôrt′) tr. exhortar —intr. urgir, instar.

ex·hor·ta·tion (ĕg′zôr-tā′shən, ĕk′sôr-) s. exhortación f.

ex·hor·ta·tive (ĭg-zôr′tə-tĭv) o **ex·hor·ta·to·ry** (-tôr′ē) adj. exhortativo.

ex·hu·ma·tion (ĕg′zōō-mā′shən, -zyōō′-, ĕk′sōō-, -syōō-) s. exhumación f.

ex·hume (ĭg-zōōm′, -zyōōm′, ĭk-syōōm′, -sōōm′) tr. **-humed, -hum·ing** exhumar, desenterrar.

ex·i·gen·cy (ĕk′sə-jən-sē) s. [pl. **-cies**] *(exigence)* exigencia, necesidad f; *(emergency)* emergencia, caso de urgencia.

ex·i·gent (ĕk′sə-jənt) adj. *(urgent)* urgente; *(demanding)* exigente.

ex·ig·u·ous (ĭg-zĭg′yōō-əs, ĭk-sĭg′-) adj. exiguo.

ex·ile (ĕg′zīl′, ĕk′sīl′) I. s. *(state, removal)* exilio, destierro; *(person)* exiliado, desterrado II. tr. **-iled, -il·ing** exiliar, desterrar.

ex·ist (ĭg-zĭst′) intr. *(to be)* existir, ser; *(to live)* vivir; *(to subsist)* subsistir.

ex·is·tence (ĭg-zĭs′təns) s. *(state)* existencia; *(being)* ser; *(life)* vida; *(entity)* ente m, entidad f ♦ **to come into e.** empezar a existir.

ex·is·tent (ĭg-zĭs′tənt) I. adj. *(having life)* viviente; *(current)* existente, actual II. s. viviente m.

ex·is·ten·tial (ĕg′zĭ-stĕn′shəl, ĕk′sĭ-) adj. existencial.

ex·is·ten·tial·ism (ĕg′zĭ-stĕn′shə-lĭz′əm, ĕk′sĭ-) s. FILOS. existencialismo.

ex·is·ten·tial·ist (ĕg′zĭ-stĕn′shə-lĭst, ĕk′sĭ-) s. & adj. FILOS. existencialista mf.

ex·ist·ing (ĭg-zĭs′tĭng) adj. existente.

ex·it¹ (ĕg′zĭt, ĕk′sĭt) s. TEAT. salida, mutis m.

ex·it² (ĕg′zĭt, ĕk′sĭt) I. s. *(going out)* salida; *(going away)* partida; *(death)* muerte f ♦ **to make one's e.** salir, marcharse II. intr. *(to leave)* salir; *(to die)* morir.

ex·o·bi·ol·o·gy (ĕk′sō-bī-ŏl′ə-jē) s. BIOL. exobiología.

ex·o·dus (ĕk′sə-dəs) s. éxodo, salida ♦ **E.** BÍBL. Éxodo • **the E.** HIST., RELIG. el éxodo de los israelitas de Egipto.

ex·og·a·my (ĕk-sŏg′ə-mē) s. BIOL., SOCIOL. exogamia.

ex·og·e·nous (ĕk-sŏj′ə-nəs) s. BIOL., BOT. exógeno, exogenético.

ex·on·er·ate (ĭg-zŏn′ə-rāt′) tr. **-at·ed, -at·ing** *(from responsibility)* exonerar; *(from blame)* disculpar.

ex·on·er·a·tion (ĭg-zŏn′ə-rā′shən) s. *(freeing)* exoneración f; *(exculpation)* disculpa.

ex·or·bi·tance (ĭg-zôr′bĭ-tns) s. exorbitancia.

ex·or·bi·tant (ĭg-zôr′bĭ-tnt) adj. exorbitante, excesivo.

ex·or·cise (ĕk′sôr-sīz′) tr. **-cised, -cis·ing** exorcizar.

ex·or·cism (ĕk′sôr-sĭz′əm) s. exorcismo.

ex·or·cist (ĕk′sôr-sĭst) s. exorcista mf.

ex·o·skel·e·ton (ĕk′sō-skĕl′ĭ-tn) s. ZOOL. dermatoesqueleto.

ex·o·sphere (ĕk′sō-sfîr′) s. ASTRON. exosfera.

ex·o·ther·mic (ĕk′sō-thûr′mĭk) o **ex·o·ther·mal** (-məl) adj. QUÍM. exotérmico.

ex·ot·ic (ĭg-zŏt′ĭk) I. adj. exótico II. s. *(thing)* cosa exótica; BOT. *(plant)* planta exótica.

ex·pand (ĭk-spănd′) tr. & intr. *(to enlarge)* expandir(se), desarrollar(se); *(to extend)* expandir(se), extender(se); *(metals)* dilatar(se); MAT. desarrollar(se) ♦ **to e. on** extenderse, explayarse.

ex·pand·a·ble (ĭk-spăn′də-bəl) adj. expansible, dilatable.

ex·panse (ĭk-spăns′) s. *(extent)* extensión f; *(expansion)* expansión f.

ex·pan·si·ble (ĭk-spăn′sə-bəl) adj. expansible.

ex·pan·sion (ĭk-spăn′shən) s. *(in volume)* expansión f, dilatación f; *(of a town)* ensanche m; *(of an idea, subject)* ampliación f; COM. *(of trade)* expansión; MAT. desarrollo (de una operación).

ex·pan·sion·ar·y (ĭk-spăn′shə-nĕr′ē) adj. ECON., POL. expancionista, de o en expansión.

expansion bolt s. perno de expansión.

ex·pan·sion·ism (ĭk-spăn′shə-nĭz′əm) s. ECON., POL. expansionismo.

ex·pan·sive (ĭk-spăn′sĭv) adj. *(expanding)* expansivo, extensivo; *(outgoing)* comunicativo; *(broad)* amplio.

ex·pan·sive·ness (ĭk-spăn′sĭv-nĭs) s. *(trait)* expansibilidad f, carácter expansivo; FÍS. expansibilidad, dilatabilidad f.

ex·pa·ti·ate (ĭk-spā′shē-āt′) intr. **-at·ed, -at·ing** extenderse, explayarse.

ex·pa·tri·ate (ĕks-pā′trē-āt′) I. tr. **-at·ed, -at·ing** expatriar, desterrar —intr. expatriarse II. s. (-ĭt, -āt′) exiliado.

ex·pa·tri·a·tion (ĕks-pā′trē-ā′shən) s. expatriación f.

ex·pect (ĭk-spĕkt′) tr. *(to await)* esperar <*I expected you sooner* te esperaba más temprano>; *(to require)* contar con; *(to suppose)* suponer.

ex·pec·tan·cy (ĭk-spĕk′tən-sē) s. [pl. **-cies**] *(state)* expectación f, expectativa; *(prospect)* esperanza.

ex·pec·tant (ĭk-spĕk′tənt) adj. *(having expectations)* expectante; *(pregnant)* embarazada.

ex·pec·ta·tion (ĕk′spĕk-tā′shən) s. *(anticipation)* expectación f, expectativa; *(prospect)* esperanza ♦ **beyond e.** más de lo esperado, superando lo que se esperaba • **contrary to e.** contrariamente a lo esperado • **expectations** expectativas de herencia ♦ **to come up to one's expectations** estar a la altura de las esperanzas de uno.

ex·pec·to·rant (ĭk-spĕk′tər-ənt) adj. & s. MED. expectorante m.

ex·pec·to·rate (ĭk-spĕk′tə-rāt′) tr. & intr. **-rat·ed, -rat·ing** expectorar, escupir.

ex·pe·di·en·cy (ĭk-spē′dē-ən-sē) o **ex·pe·di·ence** (-dē-əns) s. [pl. **-cies** o **-enc·es**] conveniencia.

ex·pe·di·ent (ĭk-spē′dē-ənt) I. adj. conveniente II. s. expediente m, recurso.

ex·pe·dite (ĕk′spĭ-dīt′) I. tr. **-dit·ed, -dit·ing** *(to speed up)* apresurar; *(to facilitate)* dar curso a, facilitar; *(to dispatch)* expedir **II.** adj. *(rapid)* expeditivo; *(unimpeded)* sin impedimento, expedito.

ex·pe·di·tion (ĕk'spĭ-dĭsh'ən) s. expedición f.

ex·pe·di·tion·ar·y (ĕk'spĭ-dĭsh'ə-nĕr'ē) adj. expedicionario.

ex·pe·di·tious (ĕk'spĭ-dĭsh'əs) adj. expeditivo, expedito.

ex·pel (ĭk-spĕl') tr. **-pelled, -pel·ling** *(to force out)* expeler; *(to dismiss)* echar, expulsar.

ex·pend (ĭk-spĕnd') tr. *(to spend)* gastar; *(to consume)* consumir.

ex·pend·a·ble (ĭk-spĕn'də-bəl) **I.** adj. *(that can be used)* gastable, disponible **II.** s. cosa fungible.

ex·pen·di·ture (ĭk-spĕn'dĭ-chər) s. *(outlay)* desembolso; *(expense)* gasto.

ex·pense (ĭk-spĕns') s. gasto ♦ **all expenses paid** con todos los gastos pagados • **at the e. of** a expensas de, a costa de • **expenses** gastos, expensas • **legal expenses** costas • **to meet expenses** hacer frente a los gastos.

ex·pen·sive (ĭk-spĕn'sĭv) adj. costoso, caro.

ex·pe·ri·ence (ĭk-spîr'ē-əns) **I.** s. experiencia ♦ **to have e. in** tener experiencia en **II.** tr. **-enced, -enc·ing** *(to undergo)* experimentar; *(to feel)* sentir ♦ **to e. difficulties** tener dificultades.

ex·pe·ri·enced (ĭk-spîr'ē-ənst) adj. *(skilled)* hábil; *(expert)* experto; *(knowledgeable)* experimentado.

ex·pe·ri·en·tial (ĭk-spîr'ē-ĕn'shəl) adj. experimental, empírico.

ex·per·i·ment (ĭk-spĕr'ə-mənt) **I.** s. experimento **II.** intr. experimentar, hacer experimentos.

ex·per·i·men·tal (ĭk-spĕr'ə-mĕn'tl) adj. experimental.

ex·per·i·men·ta·tion (ĭk-spĕr'ə-mĕn-tā'shən) s. experimentación f.

ex·pert **I.** s. (ĕk'spûrt') experto, perito **II.** adj. (ĕk'spûrt', ĭk-spûrt') experimentado, experto.

ex·per·tise (ĕk'spər-tēz') s. *(skill)* pericia; *(competence)* competencia.

ex·pert·ness (ĕk'spûrt'nĭs) s. pericia, habilidad f.

ex·pi·a·ble (ĕk'spē-ə-bəl) adj. expiable.

ex·pi·ate (ĕk'spē-āt') tr. & intr. **-at·ed, -at·ing** expiar.

ex·pi·a·tion (ĕk'spē-ā'shən) s. expiación f.

ex·pi·ra·tion (ĕk'spə-rā'shən) s. *(termination)* expiración f, caducidad f; *(exhalation)* espiración f; *(death)* expiración; COM. vencimiento.

ex·pire (ĭk-spīr') intr. **-pired, -pir·ing** *(to terminate)* expirar, terminar; *(to lapse)* vencer, caducar <*my passport expired* mi pasaporte caducó>; *(to die)* expirar; *(to exhale)* espirar —tr. espirar.

ex·plain (ĭk-splān') tr. explicar —intr. dar explicaciones ♦ **to e. oneself** explicarse.

ex·plain·a·ble (ĭk-splā'nə-bəl) adj. explicable.

ex·pla·na·tion (ĕk'splə-nā'shən) s. *(explication)* explicación f; *(clarification)* clarificación f.

ex·plan·a·to·ry (ĭk-splăn'ə-tôr'ē) adj. explicativo.

ex·ple·tive (ĕk'splĭ-tĭv) **I.** adj. GRAM. expletivo **II.** s. *(obscenity)* obscenidad f; GRAM. voz expletiva.

ex·pli·ca·ble (ĕk'splĭ-kə-bəl, ĭk-splĭk'ə-) adj. explicable.

ex·pli·cate (ĕk'splĭ-kāt') tr. **-cat·ed, -cat·ing** explicar.

ex·pli·ca·tion (ĕk'splĭ-kā'shən) s. *(explanation)* explicación f; *(exposition)* exposición f.

ex·plic·it (ĭk-splĭs'ĭt) adj. *(clear)* explícito, claro; *(forthright)* franco, directo.

ex·plode (ĭk-splōd') intr. **-plod·ed, -plod·ing** *(to burst violently)* explotar, estallar; *(to break out)* prorrumpir —tr. *(to cause to burst)* hacer explotar; *(to detonate)* detonar; *(to disprove)* desbaratar <*to e. a hypothesis* desbaratar una hipótesis>.

exploded view s. TEC. vista esquemática.

ex·ploit **I.** s. (ĕk'sploit') hazaña, proeza **II.** tr. (ĭk-sploit') explotar.

ex·ploit·a·ble (ĭk-sploi'tə-bəl) adj. explotable.

ex·ploi·ta·tion (ĕk'sploi-tā'shən) s. explotación f.

ex·ploi·ta·tive (ĭk-sploi'tə-tĭv) adj. explotable.

ex·ploit·er (ĭk-sploi'tər) s. explotador m.

ex·plo·ra·tion (ĕk'splə-rā'shən) s. *(exploring)* exploración f; MED. exploración, sondeo.

ex·plor·a·to·ry (ĭk-splôr'ə-tôr'ē) adj. exploratorio.

ex·plore (ĭk-splôr') tr. **-plored, -plor·ing** *(to probe)* explorar <*to e. for gold* explorar en busca de oro>; *(to examine)* examinar; MED. examinar, sondear —intr. hacer una investigación.

ex·plor·er (ĭk-splôr'ər) s. *(person)* explorador m; MED. *(probe)* sonda.

ex·plo·sion (ĭk-splō'zhən) s. explosión f.

ex·plo·sive (ĭk-splō'sĭv) **I.** adj. explosivo **II.** s. ARM. explosivo; FONÉT. explosiva.

ex·plo·sive·ness (ĭk-splō'sĭv-nĭs) s. carácter explosivo.

ex·po·nent (ĭk-spō'nənt, ĕk'spō'-) s. *(interpreter)* expositor m, intérprete mf; *(advocate)* representante mf, exponente mf; MAT. exponente, potencia.

ex·po·nen·tial (ĕk'spə-nĕn'shəl) adj. MAT. exponencial.

ex·port **I.** tr. (ĭk-spôrt') exportar **II.** s. (ĕk'spôrt') exportación f ♦ **e. duty** derecho de exportación.

ex·port·a·ble (ĭk-spôr'tə-bəl) adj. exportable.

ex·por·ta·tion (ĕk'spôr-tā'shən) s. exportación f.

ex·port·er (ĭk-spôr'tər) s. exportador m.

ex·pose (ĭk-spōz') tr. **-posed, -pos·ing** *(to leave unsheltered)* exponer; *(to make visible)* revelar; *(to unmask)* desenmascarar; *(to abandon)* abandonar; FOTOG. exponer ♦ **to be exposed to** estar expuesto a • **to e. oneself** descubrir indecentemente los órganos genitales.

ex·po·sé (ĕk'spō-zā') s. *(of a scandal)* revelación f; *(of facts)* exposición f.

ex·posed (ĭk-spōzd') adj. expuesto, descubierto ♦ **to be e.** estar al descubierto.

ex·po·si·tion (ĕk'spə-zĭsh'ən) s. *(explanation)* exposición f; *(presentation)* presentación f; *(statement)* declaración f; *(exhibition)* exposición.

ex·pos·i·tor (ĭk-spŏz'ĭ-tər) s. expositor m.

ex·pos·tu·late (ĭk-spŏs'chə-lāt') intr. **-lat·ed, -lat·ing** objetar ♦ **to e. with** reconvenir a.

ex·pos·tu·la·tion (ĭk-spŏs'chə-lā'shən) s. *(objection)* objeción f; *(reproach)* reconvención f.

ex·po·sure (ĭk-spō'zhər) s. *(openness)* exposición (a los elementos) f; FIG. *(revelation)* revelación f, descubrimiento; FOTOG. exposición, fotografía; ARQ. orientación f, situación (de una casa) f; PSIC. exhibicionismo ♦ **indecent e.** exhibicionismo • **to make an e.** FOTOG. sacar una fotografía.

exposure meter s. FOTOG. exposímetro, fotómetro.

ex·pound (ĭk-spound') tr. *(to explain)* exponer, explicar; *(to interpret)* interpretar —intr. hacer una exposición detallada.

ex·press (ĭk-sprĕs') **I.** tr. *(to say)* expresar, formular; *(to show)* mostrar, manifestar; *(to make known)* expresar, comunicar; *(to squeeze)* exprimir, sacar; *(to send by rapid transport)* enviar por expreso; MAT. expresar, representar **II.** adj. *(explicit)* expreso, explícito <*it was her e. wish* fue su explícito deseo>; *(rapid)* rápido, expreso; G.B. de entrega inmediata (correo) **III.** adv. por expreso, rápidamente **IV.** s. *(special messenger)* mensajero especial, entrega inmediata; *(rapid transport system)* transporte rápido; *(nonstop transport)* expreso (esp. tren).

ex·pres·sion (ĭk-sprĕsh'ən) s. *(manifestation)* expresión f, señal f <*an e. of gratitude* una señal de agradecimiento>; *(phrase)* expresión, frase f; *(gesture)* gesto; MAT. expresión, representación f.

ex·pres·sion·ism (ĭk-sprĕsh'ə-nĭz'əm) s. ARTE. expresionismo.

ex·pres·sion·ist (ĭk-sprĕsh'ə-nĭst) s. & adj. ARTE. expresionista mf.

ex·pres·sion·less (ĭk-sprĕsh'ən-lĭs) adj. inexpresivo.

ex·pres·sive (ĭk-sprĕs'ĭv) adj. expresivo ♦ **e. of** que expresa, que denota.

ex·press·ly (ĭk-sprĕs'lē) adv. expresamente.

ex·press·way (ĭk-sprĕs'wā') s. autopista.

ex·pro·pri·ate (ĕks-prō'prē-āt') tr. **-at·ed, -at·ing** expropiar, enajenar.

ex·pro·pri·a·tion (ĕks-prō'prē-ā'shən) s. expropiación f.

ex·pul·sion (ĭk-spŭl'shən) s. expulsión f.

ex·punge (ĭk-spŭnj') tr. **-punged, -pung·ing** *(to erase)* borrar <*to e. from the record* borrar del registro>; *(to strike out)* tachar; *(to annihilate)* aniquilar, destruir.

ex·pur·gate (ĕk'spər-gāt') tr. **-gat·ed, -gat·ing** expurgar.

ex·pur·ga·tion (ĕk'spər-gā'shən) s. expurgación f.

ex·qui·site (ĕk'skwĭ-zĭt, ĭk-swĭz'ĭt) **I.** adj. *(beautiful)* exquisito, primoroso; *(fine)* fino, delicado; *(acute)* agudo, vivo **II.** s. petimetre *m*, pisaverde *m*.

ex·tant (ĕk'stənt, ĕk-stănt') adj. existente.

ex·tem·po·ra·ne·ous (ĭk-stĕm'pə-rā'nē-əs) adj. improvisado.

ex·tem·po·rar·y (ĭk-stĕm'pə-rĕr'ē) adj. improvisado.

ex·tem·po·rize (ĭk-stĕm'pə-rīz') tr. & intr. **-rized, -riz·ing** improvisar.

ex·tend (ĭk-stĕnd') tr. *(to spread out)* extender; *(to lengthen)* prolongar <*to e. a road* prolongar un camino>; *(to hold out)* alargar, extender <*to e. the arm* alargar el brazo>; *(to adulterate)* adulterar; *(to enlarge)* agrandar; *(to widen)* ensanchar; *(to expand)* expandir; *(to offer)* ofrecer <*to e. congratulations* ofrecer felicitaciones>; FIN. *(to prolong)* prorrogar; DER. *(to value)* evaluar; *(to seize)* embargar ♦ **to e. an invitation** invitar • **to e. oneself** esforzarse —intr. *(to stretch)* extenderse; *(to reach)* alcanzar.

ex·tend·ed (ĭk-stĕn'dĭd) adj. *(stretched out)* alargado; *(prolonged)* prolongado; *(increased)* aumentado; *(enlarged)* ampliado; IMPR. tipo abierto, extraancho o de ojo extraancho.

ex·ten·si·ble (ĭk-stĕn'sə-bəl) adj. extensible, extensivo.

ex·ten·sion (ĭk-stĕn'shən) s. extensión *f*; *(expansion of a structure)* ampliación *f*; *(annex)* anexo; *(prolongation)* prolongación *f*; COM., DER. *(extra time)* prórroga; *(spatial magnitude)* superficie *f* ♦ **e. ladder** escalera extensible.

ex·ten·sive (ĭk-stĕn'sĭv) adj. extensivo, extenso.

ex·tent (ĭk-stĕnt') s. *(scope)* alcance *m*; *(magnitude)* medida; *(degree)* grado; *(point)* punto; *(space)* extensión *f*; *(area)* área ♦ **to a certain e.** hasta cierto punto • **to a large e.** en gran parte • **to the full e. of** en toda la extensión de.

ex·ten·u·ate (ĭk-stĕn'yōō-āt') tr. **-at·ed, -at·ing** atenuar, mitigar.

ex·ten·u·at·ing (ĭk-stĕn'yōō-ā'tĭng) adj. atenuante.

ex·ten·u·a·tion (ĭk-stĕn'yōō-ā'shən) s. atenuación *f*.

ex·te·ri·or (ĭk-stîr'ē-ər) **I.** adj. *(outer)* exterior; *(external)* externo **II.** s. *(outside)* exterior *m*; *(appearance)* apariencia; *(aspect)* aspecto.

exterior angle s. ángulo externo.

ex·ter·mi·nate (ĭk-stûr'mə-nāt') tr. **-nat·ed, -nat·ing** exterminar.

ex·ter·mi·na·tion (ĭk-stûr'mə-nā'shən) s. exterminio, extirpación *f*.

ex·ter·mi·na·tor (ĭk-stûr'mə-nā'tər) s. exterminador *m*.

ex·ter·nal (ĭk-stûr'nəl) **I.** adj. *(outside)* externo; *(exterior)* exterior; *(superficial)* superficial; *(international)* exterior; FILOS. exterior **II.** s. parte o superficie externa, exterior; *(appearance)* apariencia, aspecto exterior.

external ear s. ANAT. oreja, pabellón de la oreja *m*.

ex·ter·nal·ize (ĭk-stûr'nə-līz') tr. **-ized, -iz·ing** exteriorizar.

ex·tinct (ĭk-stĭngkt') adj. *(no longer existing)* extincto; *(extinguished)* extinguido, apagado; *(inactive)* inactivo; *(void)* suprimido; *(no longer in use)* desaparecido.

ex·tinc·tion (ĭk-stĭngk'shən) s. extinción *f*.

ex·tin·guish (ĭk-stĭng'gwĭsh) tr. *(to snuff)* extinguir, apagar; FIG. *(to destroy)* destruir; *(to eclipse)* eclipsar; DER. *(to settle)* extinguir, amortizar (una deuda); *(to nullify)* anular, derrogar; *(to abolish)* abolir.

ex·tin·guish·a·ble (ĭk-stĭng'gwĭ-shə-bəl) adj. extinguible.

ex·tin·guish·er (ĭk-stĭng'gwĭ-shər) s. *(for fires)* extintor *m*; *(for candles)* apagavelas *m*.

ex·tir·pate (ĕk'stər-pāt') tr. **-pat·ed, -pat·ing** *(to root up)* extirpar; *(to exterminate)* exterminar.

ex·tol o **ex·toll** (ĭk-stōl') tr. **-tolled, -tol·ling** *(to exalt)* exaltar, ensalzar; *(to praise)* alabar.

ex·tort (ĭk-stôrt') tr. *(money)* extorsionar; *(confession, document)* arrancar, sacar por la fuerza.

ex·tor·tion (ĭk-stôr'shən) s. extorsión *f*.

ex·tor·tion·ar·y (ĭk-stôr'shə-nĕr'ē) adj. de extorsión.

ex·tor·tion·ist (ĭk-stôr'shə-nĭst) s. concusionario, autor de extorsiones *m*.

ex·tra (ĕk'strə) **I.** adj. *(extraordinary)* extra, extraordinario; *(additional)* adicional; *(supplementary)* suplementario; *(superior)* superior **II.** s. *(addition)* extra; *(additional charge)* sobreprecio, recargo; *(special edition)* edición especial *f*, extraordinario; *(worker)* supernumerario; CINEM., TEAT. extra *m*, comparsa **III.** adv. excepcionalmente.

ex·tract **I.** tr. (ĭk-străkt') *(to pull out)* extraer, sacar <*to e. a tooth* extraer una muela>; *(to excerpt)* extractar, compendiar; FÍS., QUÍM. extraer, obtener; MAT. extraer, sacar (la raíz de un número) **II.** s. (ĕk'străkt') LIT. extracto, pasaje *m*; *(essence)* esencia, concentrado.

ex·trac·tion (ĭk-străk'shən) s. *(act)* extracción *f*; *(origin)* origen *m*; QUÍM. extracción, extracto.

ex·trac·tive (ĭk-străk'tĭv) **I.** adj. extractivo **II.** s. porción insoluble de un extracto *f*.

ex·trac·tor (ĭk-străk'tər) s. MEC., TEC. extractor *m*; ODONT. tenazas.

ex·tra·cur·ric·u·lar (ĕk'strə-kə-rĭk'yə-lər) adj. extracurricular, fuera del programa de estudios.

ex·tra·dite (ĕk'strə-dīt') tr. **-dit·ed, -dit·ing** *(to surrender)* entregar por extradición; *(to obtain)* obtener la extradición de.

ex·tra·di·tion (ĕk'strə-dĭsh'ən) s. extradición *f*.

ex·tra·mar·i·tal (ĕk'strə-măr'ĭ-tl) adj. adúltero.

ex·tra·mu·ral (ĕk'strə-myoor'əl) adj. de o situado extramuros.

ex·tra·ne·ous (ĭk-strā'nē-əs) adj. *(foreign)* extraño, externo; *(accidental)* accidental; *(irrelevant)* ajeno.

ex·traor·di·nar·y (ĭk-strôr'dn-ĕr'ē, ĕk'strə-ôr'-) adj. extraordinario.

ex·trap·o·late (ĭk-străp'ə-lāt') tr. **-lat·ed, -lat·ing** MAT. extrapolar; *(to project)* proyectar.

ex·trap·o·la·tion (ĭk-străp'ə-lā'shən) s. MAT. extrapolación *f*; *(projection)* proyección *f*.

ex·tra·sen·so·ry (ĕk'strə-sĕn'sə-rē) adj. PSIC. extrasensible.

extrasensory perception s. PSIC. percepción por medios extrasensibles *f*.

ex·tra·ter·res·tri·al (ĕk'strə-tə-rĕs'trē-əl) adj. extraterrestre.

ex·tra·ter·ri·to·ri·al (ĕk'strə-tĕr'ĭ-tôr'ē-əl) adj. extraterritorial.

ex·trav·a·gance (ĭk-străv'ə-gəns) o **ex·trav·a·gan·cy** (-gən-sē) s. [pl. **-ganc·es** o **-gan·cies**] *(quality, thing)* extravagancia; *(of spending)* despilfarro, derroche *m*.

ex·trav·a·gant (ĭk-străv'ə-gənt) **I.** adj. *(lavish)* extravagante; *(wasteful)* gastador, derrochador; *(excessive)* excesivo; *(unrestrained)* desenfrenado; *(exorbitant)* costoso, exorbitante; *(absurd)* estrafalario <*an e. idea* una idea estrafalaria> **II.** s. *(lavish spender)* pródigo; *(wasteful person)* derrochador *m*.

ex·trav·a·gan·za (ĭk-străv'ə-găn'zə) s. MÚS. fantasía; *(entertainment)* entretenimiento espectacular.

ex·tra·ve·hic·u·lar activity (ĕk'strə-vē-hĭk'yə-lər) s. actividad realizada fuera de un vehículo espacial.

ex·tra·vert (ĕk'strə-vûrt') s. var. de **extrovert**.

ex·treme (ĭk-strēm') **I.** adj. *(outermost)* extremo; *(extraordinary)* extraordinario, excepcional; *(greatest)* grande, tremendo <*e. pain* dolor grande>; *(drastic)* drástico, severo <*e. measures* medidas drásticas> **II.** s. extremo ♦ **from one e. to the other** de un extremo al otro • **in the e.** en extremo, en sumo grado • **to carry to extremes** llevar al extremo • **to go to extremes** tomar medidas extremas.

ex·treme·ly (ĭk-strēm'lē) adv. extremadamente.

▲ En muchos casos se expresa empleando el superlativo "-ísimo" con el adjetivo <*extremely interesting* interesantísimo>.

extreme unction s. RELIG. extremaunción *f*.

ex·trem·ism (ĭk-strē'mĭz'əm) s. extremismo.

ex·trem·ist (ĭk-strē'mĭst) s. & s. extremista *mf*; radical *mf*.

ex·trem·i·ty (ĭk-strĕm'ĭ-tē) s. [pl. **-ties**] *(farthest point)* extremidad *f*, extremo; *(utmost degree)* extremo; *(danger)* grave peligro; *(necessity)* necesidad extrema; *(distress)* adversidad *f*; *(end of life)* fin de la vida; *(severe measure)* medida extrema ♦ **extremities** ANAT. extremidades.

ex·tri·cate (ĕk'strĭ-kāt') tr. **-cat·ed, -cat·ing** *(from a difficulty)* librar, sacar; *(to disengage)* desprender.

ex·trin·sic (ĭk-strĭn'sĭk) adj. *(from outside)* extrínseco; *(extraneous)* extraño.

ex·tro·vert (ĕk'strə-vûrt') s. extrovertido.

ex·trude (ĭk-strōōd') tr. **-trud·ed, -trud·ing** *(to push out)* empujar hacia afuera; *(plastic, metal)* extrudir —intr. sobre-salir.

ex·tru·sion (ĭk-strōō'zhən) s. *(of lava)* efusión *f; (of plastic, metal)* extrusión *f.*

ex·u·ber·ance (ĭg-zōō'bər-əns) s. *(act, condition)* exuberancia; *(joy)* alegría; *(effusion)* efusión *f.*

ex·u·ber·ant (ĭg-zōō'bər-ənt) adj. *(full of joy)* exuberante; *(overflowing)* desbordante, efusivo.

ex·ude (ĭg-zōōd', ĭk-sōōd') intr. & tr. **-ud·ed, -ud·ing** exudar, rezumar.

ex·ult (ĭg-zŭlt') intr. exultar, regocijarse.

ex·ul·tant (ĭg-zŭl'tənt) adj. exultante, jubiloso.

ex·ul·ta·tion (ĕk'səl-tā'shən, ĕg'zəl-) s. exultación *f,* júbilo.

eye (ī) **I.** s. ANAT. ojo; *(vision)* visión *f,* vista (sentido) *f. (perspicacity)* ojo *<to have a good e. for paintings>* tener buen ojo para pinturas>; *(glance)* mirada, ojeada; *(attention)* atención *f,* miramiento; *(eye-shaped object)* ojo; *(slipknot)* lazada; FAM. *(detective)* detective *m,* investigador *m;* BOT. botón *m,* yema; METEOR. ojo (de un ciclón); MIL. diana (de un blanco); COST. corchete *m* ♦ **an e. for an e.** ojo por ojo • **before one's very eyes** delante de los propios ojos • **black e.** ojo a la funerala • **e. patch** parche • **glass e.** ojo de cristal • **in a pig's e.!** JER. ¡nunca! • **in the twinkling of an e.** en un abrir y cerrar de ojos • **my e.!** ¡de ningún modo! • **to catch someone's e.** FAM. llamar la atención de alguien • **to give someone the e.** FAM. lanzar una mirada incitante a alguien • **to keep an e. on** vigilar • **to make eyes at** echar miradas a • **to roll one's eyes** poner los ojos en blanco • **to see e. to e.** estar de acuerdo • **to set eyes on** alcanzar a ver • **with an e. to** con miras a • **without batting an e.** sin pestañar • **with the naked e.** a simple vista **II.** tr. **eyed, eye·ing** *o* **ey·ing** *(to see)* ojear, mirar; *(to observe)* observar, contemplar.

eye·ball (ī'bôl') s. ANAT. globo ocular.

eye bank s. MED. banco de ojos.

eye·bolt (ī'bōlt') s. MEC. tornillo *o* perno de ojo.

eye·brow (ī'brou') s. ceja.

eyebrow pencil s. lápiz de cejas *m.*

eye·cup (ī'kŭp') s. lavaojos *m.*

eyed (īd) adj. de *o* con ojos *<blue-e.* de ojos azules>.

eye·drop·per (ī'drŏp'ər) s. cuentagotas *m.*

eye·ful (ī'fōōl') s. vistazo, ojeada.

eye·glass (ī'glăs') s. *(monocle)* monóculo; *(eyecup)* lavaojos *m* ♦ **eyeglasses** anteojos, lentes.

eye·lash (ī'lăsh') s. pestaña.

eye·let (ī'lĭt) s. *(small hole)* ojete *m;* COST. ojalillo.

eye·lid (ī'lĭd') s. ANAT. párpado.

eye opener s. *(revelation)* revelación *f,* sorpresa; FAM. *(drink)* trago.

eye·piece (ī'pēs') s. ocular *m.*

eye shadow s. sombreador *m.*

eye·sight (ī'sīt') s. *(vision)* vista; *(range)* alcance de la vista *m; (view)* vista.

eye·sore (ī'sôr') s. cosa que ofende la vista.

eye·stalk (ī'stôk') s. ZOOL. pedúnculo movible (de los crustáceos).

eye·strain (ī'strān') s. MED. vista fatigada.

eye·tooth (ī'tōōth') s. [pl. **-teeth** (-tēth')] ANAT. colmillo.

eye·wash (ī'wŏsh') s. MED. *(solution)* colirio; FAM. *(nonsense)* tontería.

eye·wit·ness (ī'wĭt'nəs) s. testigo ocular.

ey·rie (âr'ē, îr'ē) s. aguilera.

E·ze·ki·el (ĭ-zē'kē-əl) s. BÍBL. Ezequiel.

Ez·ra (ĕz'rə) s. BÍBL. Esdras.

F

f, F (ĕf) s. [pl. **f's, F's**] sexta letra del alfabeto inglés; MÚS. fa *m* ♦ **F flat, major, minor, sharp** MÚS. fa bemol, mayor, menor, sostenido.

fa (fä) s. MÚS. fa (nota) *m.*

fa·ble (fā'bəl) **I.** s. *(story)* fábula; *(legend)* leyenda; *(lie)* mentira **II.** tr. **-bled, -bling** contar (fábulas).

fa·bled (fā'bəld) adj. *(legendary)* legendario; *(imaginary)* imaginario.

fab·ric (făb'rĭk) s. *(cloth)* tela; *(structure)* estructura.

fab·ri·cate (făb'rĭ-kāt') tr. **-cat·ed, -cat·ing** *(to create)* fabricar, crear; *(to construct)* construir; *(to invent)* inventar.

fab·ri·ca·tion (făb'rĭ-kā'shən) s. *(creation)* fabricación *f; (falsehood)* mentira.

fab·ri·ca·tor (făb'rĭ-kā'tər) s. embustero.

fab·u·list (făb'yə-lĭst) s. *(storyteller)* fabulista *mf; (liar)* embustero.

fab·u·lous (făb'yə-ləs) adj. *(legendary)* fabuloso, legendario; *(barely credible)* increíble, sorprendente; *(wonderful)* estupendo, fabuloso.

fa·çade (fə-säd') s. *(false front)* apariencia; ARQ. fachada.

face (fās) **I.** s. *(of a person)* cara, rostro; *(expression)* semblante *m,* cara *<an angry f.* una cara enojada>; *(grimace)* mueca, gesto; FIG. *(appearance)* apariencia, aspecto; ARQ. *(façade)* fachada, frente *m;* TOP. *(surface)* superficie *f,* faz *f <the f. of the planet* la faz del planeta>; *(of a clock)* esfera; *(of fabric)* derecho (de una tela); GEOM. cara, lado; MIN. *(facet)* faceta; MIL., MIN. frente; IMPR. *(typeface)* ojo ♦ **f. down** boca abajo • **f. to f.** cara a cara, frente a frente • **f. up** boca arriba • **in the f. of** *(in the presence of)* frente a; *(despite)* a pesar de • **on the f. of it** a primera vista, según las apariencias • **to fall flat on one's f.** caerse de bruces • **to look square in the f.** mirar fijamente en los ojos • **to lose f.** perder prestigio, quedar mal • **to one's f.** en la cara de uno • **to save f.** salvar las apariencias • **to show one's f.** dejarse ver, hacer acto de presencia • **to turn red in the f.** ponerse rojo **II.** tr. **faced, fac·ing** *(to turn toward)* ponerse de cara a, mirar hacia *<Jews f. the east when they pray* los judíos miran hacia el este cuando rezan>; *(to look out on)* estar frente a, dar a *<my backyard faces the river* mi traspatio da al río>; *(to confront)* hacer frente a, arrostrar *<to f. the facts* hacer frente a los hechos>; *(to look up a card)* poner boca arriba, mostrar (naipes); TEC. recubrir, revestir; COST. *(to trim)* guarnecer (un borde); TEC. *(to smooth)* alisar, cepillar ♦ **let's f. it** reconozcámoslo • **to be faced with** enfrentarse con • **to f. down** resistir firmemente • **to f. on to** mirar hacia, dar a • **to f. the music** JER. afrontar las consecuencias • **to f. up to** encararse con, enfrentarse a • **to f. with** confrontar con —intr. *(to be situated)* estar orientado hacia, mirar hacia *<our house faces north* nuestra casa mira hacia el norte>; *(to turn)* volverse, voltear la cara ♦ **about f.!** MIL. ¡media vuelta!

face card s. figura (naipe).

face cloth s. paño, toallita.

face·less (fās'lĭs) adj. *(without a face)* sin cara; *(unidentified)* no identificable; FIG. *(anonymous)* anónimo.

face lift·ing (fās'lĭf'tĭng) *o* **face-lift** (-lĭft') s. FIG. *(modernization)* modernización *f,* embellecimiento; *(renewal)* renovación *f,* CIR. rejuvenecimiento de la cara por medio de la cirugía plástica ♦ **to get** *o* **have a face-lift** hacerse la cirugía plástica.

face-off (fās'ôf') s. confrontación *f.*

face-sav·er (fās'sā'vər) s. algo que salva la dignidad.

face-sav·ing (fās'sā'vĭng) adj. que salva la dignidad.

fa·cet (făs'ĭt) s. faceta.

fa·ce·tious (fə-sē'shəs) adj. jocosamente irónico, humorístico.

fa·ce·tious·ness (fə-sē'shəs-nĭs) s. jocosidad *f.*

face value s. *(nominal worth)* valor nominal *m;* FIG. *(apparent value)* valor aparente.

fa·cial (fā'shəl) **I.** adj. facial **II.** s. *(face massage)* masaje *m,* tratamiento facial.

fa·cies (fā'shēz') s. [pl. **facies**] facies *f.*

fac·ile (făs'əl) adj. *(easy)* fácil; *(yielding)* acomodaticio; *(superficial)* superficial ♦ **f. tongue** palabra fácil.

fa·cil·i·tate (fə-sĭl'ĭ-tāt') tr. **-tat·ed, -tat·ing** facilitar.

fa·cil·i·ty (fə-sĭl'ĭ-tē) s. [pl. **-ties**] *(ease)* facilidad *f; (capability)* facilidad, capacidad *f; (pliability)* flexibilidad *f; (building)* edificio, local *m* ♦ **facilities** *(said of credit)* facilidades; *(buildings)* instalaciones *<sports facilities* instalaciones deportivas>; *(public toilet)* servicio, baño.

fac·ing (fā'sĭng) s. *(lining material)* guarnición (de un vestido) f; *(protective covering)* revestimiento.

fac·sim·i·le (făk-sĭm'ə-lē) s. & adj. facsímil m.

fact (făkt) s. hecho <*scientific facts* hechos científicos>; *(reality)* realidad f, verdad <*the f. is that I did not want to come* la verdad es que no quería venir> ♦ **as a matter of f.** en realidad • **facts** datos, información • **in fact** en realidad • **the f. of the matter is** la verdad es • **the facts of life** los hechos de la vida • **the f. remains that** a pesar de todo • **to know for a f.** saber a ciencia cierta • **to stick to the facts** atenerse a los hechos.

fact-find·ing (făkt'fīn'dĭng) adj. de investigación.

fac·tion (făk'shən) s. facción f.

fac·tion·al (făk'shə-nəl) adj. faccioso.

fac·tion·al·ism (făk'shə-nə-lĭz'əm) s. faccionalismo.

fac·ti·tious (făk-tĭsh'əs) adj. facticio.

fac·tor (făk'tər) I. s. factor m II. tr. MAT. dividir en factores.

fac·tored (făk'tərd) adj. MAT. factorializado.

fac·tor·i·za·tion (făk'tər-ĭ-zā'shən) s. MAT. división en factores f.

fac·tor·ize (făk'tə-rīz') tr. **-ized, -iz·ing** dividir en factores.

fac·to·ry (făk'tə-rē) s. [pl. **-ries**] fábrica f.

fac·to·tum (făk-tō'təm) s. factótum m.

fac·tu·al (făk'chōō-əl) adj. *(actual)* basado en hechos; *(real)* verdadero.

fac·tu·al·i·ty (făk'chōō-ăl'ĭ-tē) s. realidad f.

fac·ul·ta·tive (făk'əl-tā'tĭv) adj. facultativo, opcional.

fac·ul·ty (făk'əl-tē) s. [pl. **-ties**] *(ability)* facultad f, don m; *(educators)* cuerpo docente, profesorado; *(university division)* facultad <*the f. of law* la facultad de derecho>; *(professionals)* colegio (de médicos, abogados), *(authorization)* facultad, permiso.

fad (făd) s. manía, novedad f.

fad·dish (făd'ĭsh) adj. que sigue la moda.

fade (făd) intr. **fad·ed, fad·ing** *(brightness)* palidecer; *(sound)* desvanecerse; *(light)* apagarse; *(flower)* marchitarse; *(strength)* debilitarse; *(hope)* desvanecerse; *(color, dye)* desteñirse ♦ **to f. away** *(to waste away)* consumirse; *(to leave gradually)* desvanecerse • **to f. in** CINEM., RAD., TELEV. aparecer o hacer aparecer gradualmente • **to f. out** CINEM., RAD., TELEV. desaparecer o hacer desaparecer gradualmente —tr. desvanecer <*time has faded her beauty* el tiempo desvaneció su belleza>; JER. *(in a dice game)* igualar o aceptar la apuesta II. s. CINEM., RAD., TELEV. *(of image or sound)* desvanecimiento gradual; RAD. *(of a signal)* interrupción de señal f.

fade-in (fād'ĭn') s. CINEM., TELEV. *(image)* fundido, aparición gradual f; CINEM., RAD., TELEV. *(sound)* entrada o crecimiento gradual de volumen.

fade-out (fād'out') s. CINEM., RAD., TELEV. desvanecimiento gradual.

fad·ing (fā'dĭng) s. *(waning)* disminución (de brillo, luz) f; *(decline)* decadencia; RAD. fluctuación f.

fae·ces (fē'sēz) s.pl. var. de **feces**.

fa·er·ie o **fa·er·y** (fâr'ē) I. s. [pl. **-ies**] *(fairy)* hada; *(realm)* reino de las hadas II. adj. encantado.

fag¹ (făg) I. s. *(drudgery)* trabajo, faena; *(drudge)* ganapán m; G.B. *(student)* alumno que sirve a un alumno mayor II. intr. **fagged, fag·ging** trabajar duro ♦ **to be fagged out** estar rendido o molido —tr. ♦ **to f. out** fatigar, cansar.

fag² (făg) s. JER. *(cigarette)* cigarillo.

fag³ (făg) s. JER., DESPEC. *(homosexual)* maricón m.

fag end s. *(frayed end of cloth)* pezolada; *(frayed end of a rope)* punta deshilachada (de una soga); *(inferior remnant)* deshechos m; *(last part)* cabo (de una soga).

fag·got (făg'ət) s. JER., DESPEC. maricón m.

fag·ot o **fag·got** (făg'ət) I. s. *(of sticks)* haz de leña m; *(of iron)* haz de barras de hierro II. tr. formar haces de.

Fahr·en·heit (făr'ən-hīt') adj. Fahrenheit.

fail (fāl) I. intr. *(to be unsuccessful)* fracasar; *(to prove deficient)* fallar; *(to give out)* acabarse; *(to be inadequate)* faltar; *(to weaken)* decaer, debilitarse; *(of a motor)* fallar; *(in school)* no aprobar, aplazarse; COM. *(to go bankrupt)* quebrar; MED. fallar ♦ **to f. as** fallar o fracasar como • **to f. in one's duty** faltar al deber de uno • **to f. to** *(to be unsuccessful in)* no lograr, no alcanzar a <*she failed to satisfy the requirements* no logró satisfacer los requisitos>; *(to neglect to)* dejar de <*she failed to lock the door* dejó de cerrar la puerta con llave> —tr. *(to disappoint)* fallar, frustrar; *(to abandon)* abandonar; *(course, exam)* fallar o salir mal en; *(student)* no aprobar a, suspender a II. s. falta ♦ **without f.** sin falta.

fail·ing (fā'lĭng) I. s. *(failure)* fracaso; *(minor fault)* falla, defecto II. prep. falta de.

fail-safe (fāl'sāf') I. adj. MEC. capaz de compensar errores automáticamente; MIL. que detiene un ataque militar; *(dependable)* que no falla II. s. mecanismo para evitar fallas.

fail·ure (fāl'yər) s. *(unsuccessfulness)* fracaso; *(person)* fracasado; *(weakening)* deterioro, decaimiento; *(nonfulfillment)* incumplimiento; *(malfunctioning)* fallo; *(in school)* suspenso; COM. bancarrota, quiebra ♦ **crop f.** pérdida de la cosecha • **f. to pay** incumplimiento en el pago • **heart f.** ataque al corazón • **power f.** corte de la electricidad.

fain (fān) ANT. I. adv. *(preferably)* preferiblemente; *(happily)* alegremente II. adj. *(ready)* listo, dispuesto; *(pleased)* contento, feliz; *(obliged)* obligado.

faint (fānt) I. adj. **-er, -est** *(indistinct)* borroso, indistinto; *(slight)* vago, ligero; *(pale)* pálido, apagado; *(dizzy)* mareado; *(timid)* tímido; *(weak)* débil ♦ **not to have the faintest idea** no tener la más mínima idea II. s. desmayo ♦ **to fall into a dead f.** desplomarse inconsciente • **to fall into a f.** desmayarse III. intr. desmayarse.

faint-heart·ed (fānt'här'tĭd) adj. *(in convictions)* falto de convicciones; *(in courage)* acobardado, tímido.

faint·ness (fānt'nĭs) s. *(indistinctness)* vaguedad f, falta de claridad; *(paleness)* palidez f; *(dizziness)* desmayo; *(weakness)* debilidad f.

fair¹ (fâr) I. adj. **-er, -est** *(beautiful)* bello, hermoso; *(blond)* rubio; *(light-complected)* blanco; *(impartial)* imparcial; *(just)* justo, equitativo; *(reasonable)* razonable; *(mediocre)* regular; *(permissible)* permisible; *(not cloudy)* despejado; *(unblemished)* limpio; *(readable)* legible; *(specious)* especioso; *(favorable)* favorable, bueno; *(promising)* prometedor, favorable ♦ **as is only f.** como es justo • **f. and square** honrado a carta cabal • **f. enough!** ¡vale!, ¡bien! • **f. game** *(in hunting)* presa o caza lícita; FIG. *(prey)* presa fácil; *(of ridicule)* hazmerreír • **f. skies** cielo despejado • **f. to middling** regular, bastante bueno • **it's not f.!** o **that's no f.!** ¡no hay derecho!, ¡no es justo! • **one's f. share** lo que le corresponde a uno • **to give someone f. warning** prevenir a alguien II. adv. *(justly)* honradamente; *(directly)* directamente, justo <*a blow caught f. in the stomach* un golpe recibido directamente en el estómago> ♦ **to play f.** jugar limpio III. tr. *(to smooth)* alisar; AER., ING. fuselar.

fair² (fâr) s. *(market)* mercado; *(exhibition)* exposición f, feria; *(church bazaar)* tómbola f.

fair·ground (fâr'ground') s. real m, campo para ferias.

fair-haired (fâr'hârd') adj. rubio; FIG. *(favorite)* favorito <*papa's f. boy* el muchacho favorito de papá>.

fair·ly (fâr'lē) adv. *(justly)* justamente, equitativamente; *(actually)* realmente <*the walls f. shook* las paredes realmente temblaron>; *(moderately)* moderadamente, bastante <*he is a f. good painter* es un pintor bastante bueno>; *(suitably)* adecuadamente; *(clearly)* claramente.

fair-mind·ed (fâr'mīn'dĭd) adj. imparcial.

fair·ness (fâr'nĭs) s. *(beauty)* belleza, hermosura; *(impartiality)* imparcialidad f; *(justice)* justicia ♦ **in all f.** para ser justo.

fair play s. juego limpio.

fair shake s. JER. oportunidad f.

fair-spo·ken (fâr'spō'kən) adj. de habla cortés.

fair trade s. COM. intercambio comercial de acuerdo a normas preestablecidas.

fair-trade (fâr'trād') tr. **-trad·ed, -trad·ing** COM. vender bienes de acuerdo a un convenio preestablecido.

fair-trade agreement s. COM. convenio comercial que basa los precios mínimos en normas establecidas por el fabricante.

fair·way (fâr'wā') s. *(open ground)* campo abierto; DEP. *(in golf)* calle f, pista; MARÍT. canal navegable m.

fair-weath·er (fâr'wĕth'ər) adj. *(inconstant)* inconstante, de conveniencia <*a fair-weather friend* amigo de conveniencia>; *(for good weather)* para buen tiempo, para buen clima.

fair·y (fâr′ē) s. [pl. **-ies**] *(magic being)* hada; JER. *(homosexual)* maricón *m*, mariposa.

fair·y·land (fâr′ē-lănd′) s. *(realm)* país de las hadas *m*; FIG. *(enchanting place)* lugar encantador *m*.

fairy tale s. *(story)* cuento de hadas; *(tall tale)* embuste *m*.

fait ac·com·pli (fā′tä-kôN-plē′, fĕt′ä-) s. [pl. **faits ac·complis** (fā′tä-kôN-plē′, fĕt′ä-)] hecho consumado.

faith (fāth) s. *(confidence)* confianza; *(belief)* fe *f*; *(loyalty)* fidelidad *f*, lealtad *f*; RELIG. religión *f* <*people of every f.* personas de todas las religiones>; *(set of beliefs)* doctrina ♦ **in bad f.** de mala fe • **in good f.** de buena fe • **to be of the (Catholic) f.** ser de la religión (católica) • **to break f. with** faltar a la palabra dada a, engañar a • **to have f. in** *o* **put one's f. in someone** tener confianza *o* fe en alguien, fiarse de • **to keep f. with** cumplir la palabra dada a.

faith·ful (fāth′fəl) I. adj. *(true)* fiel; *(loyal)* leal; *(reliable)* digno de confianza <*f. guide* guía digno de confianza>; *(accurate)* fiel, exacto; *(having faith)* creyente II. s.pl. ♦ **the f.** *(members of a faith)* los fieles; *(followers)* los partidarios.

faith·ful·ly (fāth′fə-lē) adv. *(truly)* fielmente; *(loyally)* lealmente; *(accurately)* fielmente, con exactitud; *(piously)* con fe, con devoción ♦ **yours f.** su servidor, suyo atentamente.

faith healer s. persona que cura por medio de la fe.

faith·less (fāth′lĭs) adj. *(disloyal)* infiel, desleal; *(unreliable)* poco digno de confianza; RELIG. descreído, incrédulo.

fake (fāk) I. adj. falso, fraudulento II. s. *(impostor)* impostor *m*; *(fraud)* engaño, timo; *(sham)* falsificación *f* III. tr. **faked, fak·ing** *(to falsify)* falsificar; *(to feign)* fingir; *(to improvise)* improvisar ♦ **to f. someone out** engañar a alguien —intr. engañarse, fingirse.

fak·er (fā′kər) s. *(pretender)* falsificador *m*, fingidor *m*; *(impostor)* impostor *m*; *(swindler)* estafador *m*.

fa·kir (fə-kîr′) s. faquir *m*.

Fa·lan·gism (fə-lăn′jĭz-əm) s. POL. falangismo.

Fa·lan·gist (fə-lăn′jĭst) s. & adj. POL. falangista *mf*.

fal·con (făl′kən, fôl′-) s. ORNIT. halcón *m*; MIL. falcón *m*.

fal·con·er (făl′kə-nər, fôl′-) s. halconero, cetrero.

fal·con·ry (făl′kən-rē, fôl′-) s. halconería, cetrería.

Falk·land Islands (fôk′lənd, fôlk′-) s. Islas Malvinas.

fall (fôl) I. intr. **fell** (fĕl), **fall·en** (fô′lən), **fall·ing** *(to come down)* caer <*the snow was falling silently* la nieve caía silenciosamente>; *(to collapse)* caer, caerse <*she slipped and fell* resbaló y se cayó>; *(to drop wounded or dead)* caer, morir; *(to come to rest)* dar sobre <*the light fell on the book* la luz daba sobre el libro>; *(to hang down)* caer; *(to show consternation)* caerse (la cara); *(to experience defeat)* caer <*the new government fell quickly* el nuevo gobierno cayó en poco tiempo>; *(to slope)* bajar, descender; *(to drop)* bajar (precios, temperatura); *(to diminish)* disminuir (viento, voz); *(to decline in rank)* ser degradado; *(to sin)* caer <*to f. into temptation* caer en la tentación>; *(to become)* quedarse, volverse <*to f. silent* quedarse mudo>; *(to occur)* caer <*Christmas Eve falls on a Tuesday this year* la Nochebuena cae en martes este año>; *(to befall)* corresponder, tocar <*the greatest task fell to him* la labor más ardua le tocó a él>; *(to come under)* estar comprendido, estar incluido <*most languages f. into groups or families* la mayoría de los idiomas están comprendidos en grupos o familias>; *(to be born)* nacer (p. una oveja) ♦ **to f. apart** deshacerse • **to f. asleep** quedarse dormido, dormirse • **to f. away** *(to slope)* inclinarse, descender; *(to come loose)* desprenderse; *(to cave in)* hundirse; *(to disappear)* desaparecer, perderse de vista; *(to decline)* declinar; *(to part company)* alejarse, separarse • **to f. back** *(to fall backwards)* caerse de espaldas; MIL. *(to retreat)* replegarse; *(to lag behind)* quedarse atrás • **to f. behind** *(to lag behind)* quedarse atrás, rezagarse; *(to be late)* atrasarse, retrasarse; *(to be in arrears)* retrasarse (en los pagos) • **to f. down** *(to drop to the ground)* caer, caerse; *(building)* venirse abajo, derrumbarse; FAM. *(to fail)* fallar, fracasar <*to lag in performance)* decaer, fallar • **to f. due** vencer, ser pagadero • **to f. flat** fracasar • **to f. flat on one's face** *(to collapse)* caer de

bruces; *(to fail)* fracasar • **to f. for** FAM. *(person)* enamorarse de, volverse loco por; *(trick)* creerse, tragarse <*he fell for it* se lo tragó> • **to f. from grace** RELIG. perder la gracia; *(to lose favor)* caer en desgracia • **to f. in** *(roof)* hundirse, venirse abajo; MIL. *(soldiers)* formar filas • **to f. in love with** enamorarse de • **to f. into disrepair** deteriorarse • **to f. into the habit of** coger la costumbre de, adquirir el hábito de • **to f. off** *(to come loose)* caerse, desprenderse; *(to decrease)* disminuir, decaer; *(zeal)* enfriarse; *(quality)* empeorar; MARÍT. abatir a sotavento • **to f. on** *o* **upon** *(to land on)* caer de <*he fell on his head* cayó de cabeza>; *(accent)* caer en, recaer en; *(duty)* tocar a, corresponder a; *(to attack)* caer sobre • **to f. out** *(of bed)* caerse; *(of a car)* salirse; *(to quarrel)* reñir, pelear • **to f. over** *(to tip over)* caerse, volcarse; *(to trip over)* tropezar con • **to f. short of** no llegar • **to f. sick** caer enfermo, enfermarse • **to f. through** venirse abajo, fracasar • **to f. to** *(to begin to)* empezar a; *(to befall)* tocar a, corresponder a • **to f. to pieces** *(to break up)* hacerse pedazos, desbaratarse; *(emotionally)* derrumbarse • **to f. within** estar dentro de, estar incluido en II. s. *(act)* caída; *(distance)* caída <*a f. of three stories* una caída desde el segundo piso>; *(autumn)* otoño; *(slope)* caída, declive *m*; *(veil)* velo del sombrero; *(lace)* gorguera, adorno del cuello (del vestido); *(hairpiece)* cola postiza; *(drape)* caída <*the f. of the skirt* la caída de la saya>; MÍL., POL. caída <*the f. of a government* la caída de un gobierno>; *(reduction)* bajada, descenso <*a f. in prices* una bajada de precios>; *(decline)* decadencia, ruina; *(sin)* caída; DEP. *(in wrestling)* caída; ZOOL. *(birth)* nacimiento (esp. de una oveja); *(litter)* camada • **falls** [ú. con v. sing.] *(waterfall)* catarata, cascada; MARÍT. *(hoist)* grúa, aparejo ♦ **the F.** BÍBL. la Caída • **to ride for a f.** ir al fracaso • **to take a bad f.** darse una mala caída, caerse duro.

fal·la·cious (fə-lā′shəs) adj. falaz, engañoso.

fal·la·cy (făl′ə-sē) s. [pl. **-cies**] *(mistaken notion)* idea falsa; *(erroneousness)* error *m*; *(deceptiveness)* falacia; LOG. *(false argument)* falacia, sofisma *m*.

fall·en (fô′lən) part. p. de **fall**.

fall guy s. JER. *(scapegoat)* cabeza de turco, chivo expiatorio; *(dupe)* ingenuo, primo.

fal·li·ble (făl′ə-bəl) adj. falible.

fall·ing-out (fô′lĭng-out′) s. [pl. **fall·ings-out** *o* **fall·ing-outs**] desacuerdo, pelea ♦ **to have a falling-out** pelearse.

falling star s. ASTRON. estrella fugaz.

fall·off (fôl′ôf′) s. baja.

Fal·lo·pi·an tube (fə-lō′pē-ən) s. ANAT. trompa de Falopio, oviducto.

fall·out (fôl′out′) s. *(radiation)* lluvia radioactiva; FIG. *(side effects)* consecuencias.

fal·low (făl′ō) I. adj. FIG. *(inactive)* durmiente, inactivo; AGR. barbechado II. s. AGR. barbecho, rastrojo III. tr. AGR. barbechar.

false (fôls) I. adj. **fals·er, fals·est** *(untrue)* falso; *(unfounded)* infundado <*f. hope* esperanza infundada>; *(erroneous)* erróneo, falso; *(treacherous)* falso, traicionero; *(fake)* postizo <*f. teeth* dientes postizos>; *(provisional)* falso, provisional; MÚS. desafinado ♦ **f. pride** falso orgullo • **f. start** salida mala *o* nula • **f. step** paso en falso, desliz II. adv. *(wrongfully)* falsamente, con falsedad; *(erroneously)* mal.

false alarm s. falsa alarma.

false arrest s. arresto ilegal.

false-heart·ed (fôls′här′tĭd) adj. pérfido, traicionero.

false·hood (fôls′hŏŏd′) s. *(lie)* mentira; *(falsity)* falsedad *f*, falsía.

false·ness (fôls′nĭs) s. falsedad *f*.

false pretense s. DER. estafa, intención fraudulenta.

fal·set·to (fôl-sĕt′ō) I. s. [pl. **-tos**] MÚS. falsete *m* II. adv. en falsete.

fals·ie (fôl′sē) s. FAM. relleno para sostén.

fal·si·fi·ca·tion (fôl′sə-fĭ-kā′shən) s. falsificación *f*.

fal·si·fi·er (fôl′sə-fī′ər) s. falsificador *m*.

fal·si·fy (fôl′sə-fī′) tr. **-fied, -fy·ing** *(to make false)* falsificar; *(to misrepresent)* exponer mal, desvirtuar —intr. mentir.

fal·si·ty (fôl′sĭ-tē) s. [pl. **-ties**] falsía.

fal·ter (fôl'tər) **I.** intr. *(to stumble)* titubear, vacilar; *(to stammer)* balbucear, titubear; *(to hesitate)* vacilar, titubear; *(to fail)* fallar **II.** s. *(unsteady speech, action)* vacilación *f*, titubeo; *(hesitant sound)* balbuceo.

fal·ter·ing (fôl'tər-ĭng) adj. vacilante, titubeante.

fame (fām) **I.** s. *(renown)* fama, renombre *m*; *(reputation)* reputación *f* **II.** tr. **famed, fam·ing** afamar.

famed (fāmd) adj. famoso.

fa·mil·ial (fə-mĭl'yəl) adj. *(pertaining to a family)* familiar; *(hereditary)* de familia.

fa·mil·iar (fə-mĭl'yər) **I.** adj. *(often encountered)* familiar, conocido <*a f. voice* una voz conocida>; *(common)* corriente, común; *(intimate)* de confianza; *(informal)* familiar, llano <*he wrote in a f. style* escribía con un estilo familiar>; *(forward)* confianzudo, fresco ♦ **that does not sound f.** eso no me suena • **to be f. with** estar familiarizado con, conocer • **to be on f. terms with** tener confianza con • **your face looks f.** su cara me parece conocida **II.** s. *(friend)* amigo íntimo; *(spirit)* espíritu protector *m*; *(habitué)* parroquiano.

fa·mil·iar·i·ty (fə-mĭl'yăr'ĭ-tē, -mĭl'ē-ăr'-) s. [pl. **-ties**] *(knowledge)* familiaridad *f*, conocimiento; *(intimacy)* familiaridad, confianza; *(impropriety)* frescura, atrevimiento ♦ **familiarities** libertades.

fa·mil·iar·ize (fə-mĭl'yə-rīz') tr. **-ized, -iz·ing** familiarizar.

fam·i·ly (făm'ə-lē) s. [pl. **-lies**] *(clan)* familia; *(class)* clase *f* <*a f. of insects* una clase de insectos>; CIENT., GRAM. familia ♦ **f. doctor** médico de cabecera • **f. reunion** reunión de familia • **to be one of the f.** ser como de la familia • **to run in the f.** venirle a uno de familia <*his sense of humor runs in the f.* su sentido de humor le viene de familia>.

family man s. *(domestic man)* hombre de familia *m*; *(father)* padre de familia *m*.

family planning s. planeamiento del tamaño de la familia (regulando el número de hijos).

family skeleton s. secreto de familia.

family tree s. *(genealogy)* arbol genealógico; *(ancestry)* antepasados y descendientes.

fam·ine (făm'ĭn) s. *(shortage of food)* hambre *f*; *(drastic shortage)* escasez *f*.

fam·ish (făm'ĭsh) tr. hacer morir de hambre —intr. morirse de hambre.

fam·ished (făm'ĭsht) adj. FIG. muerto de hambre.

fa·mous (fā'məs) adj. *(well-known)* famoso, FAM. *(first-rate)* excelente, ANT. *(notorious)* notorio.

fa·mous·ly (fā'məs-lē) adv. FAM. muy bien <*they got along f.* se llevaban muy bien>.

fan[1] (făn) **I.** s. *(paper)* abanico; *(electric)* ventilador *m*; AGR. aventadora **II.** tr. **fanned, fan·ning** *(to cool)* abanicar; FIG. *(to stir up)* avivar, excitar; AGR. aventar —intr. ♦ **to f. out** abrirse en abanico.

fan[2] (făn) s. FAM. *(enthusiast)* aficionado, hincha *m*.

fa·nat·ic (fə-năt'ĭk) s. & adj. fanático.

fa·nat·i·cal (fə-năt'ĭ-kəl) adj. fanático.

fa·nat·i·cism (fə-năt'ĭ-sĭz'əm) s. fanatismo.

fan belt s. AUTO., MEC. correa del ventilador.

fan·ci·er (făn'sē-ər) s. conocedor, aficionado.

fan·ci·ful (făn'sĭ-fəl) adj. *(imaginative)* imaginativo; *(capricious)* caprichoso.

fan·cy (făn'sē) **I.** s. [pl. **-cies**] *(imagination)* imaginación *f*, fantasía; *(whim)* capricho; *(liking)* afición *f*, gusto; *(notion)* idea, impresión *f* ♦ **to catch o strike one's f.** gustarle o agradarle a uno • **to take a f. to** *(a person)* tomar cariño a; *(an activity)* tomar gusto a **II.** adj. **-ci·er, -ci·est** *(elaborate)* detallado, muy adornado; *(capricious)* caprichoso; *(skillful)* diestro, hábil; *(superior)* fino, selecto; *(exorbitant)* excesivo, exorbitante; *(luxurious)* lujoso <*a f. car* un auto lujoso> **III.** tr. **-cied, -cy·ing** *(to imagine)* imaginar; *(to take a liking to)* cobrar afecto por; *(to like)* gustarle a uno <*I don't f. chocolates* no me gustan los chocolates>; *(to suppose)* suponer ♦ **f. that!** ¡quién lo diría!, ¡imagínese! • **to f. oneself** creerse, imaginarse.

fancy dress s. disfraz *m*.

fan·cy-free (făn'sē-frē') adj. *(carefree)* despreocupado; *(not in love)* sin compromiso amoroso.

fan·cy·work (făn'sē-wûrk') s. COST. labor (ornamental) *f*, bordado.

fan·fare (făn'fâr') s. *(spectacular display)* fanfarria; MÚS. son de trompetas *m*.

fang (făng) s. *(snake's tooth)* diente *m*; *(animal's tooth)* colmillo.

fan mail s. cartas de admiradores.

fan·ny (făn'ē) s. [pl. **-nies**] JER. trasero.

fan·tail (făn'tāl') s. *(tail)* cola en forma de abanico; *(pigeon)* paloma colipava, papamoscas *m*; *(fish)* carpa dorada; MARÍT. bovedilla.

fan·ta·size (făn'tə-sīz') tr. & intr. **-sized, -siz·ing** fantasear.

fan·tas·tic *o* **fan·tas·ti·cal** (făn-tăs'tĭk) (-tĭ-kəl) adj. fantástico.

fan·ta·sy (făn'tə-sē, -zē) s. [pl. **-sies**] fantasía.

far §G22 (fär) **I.** adv. **far·ther** (fär'thər) *o* **fur·ther** (fûr'thər), **far·thest** (fär'thĭst) *o* **fur·thest** (fûr'thĭst) *(distant)* lejos <*do you live very f.?* ¿vive usted muy lejos?>; *(much)* mucho <*f. more* mucho más>; *(very)* muy <*f. different* muy diferente> ♦ **as f. as** *(up to)* hasta <*we drove as f. as Florida* fuimos en auto hasta la Florida>; *(to the extent that)* por lo que <*as f. as I could see* por lo que yo pude observar> • **as f. as I am concerned** por lo que a mí se refiere, por mi parte • **as f. as possible** en lo posible • **by f.** con mucho, con creces • **f. and away** con mucho, con creces • **f. and wide** por todas partes • **f. away** *(at a distance)* lejos; *(in the distance)* a lo lejos • **f. be it from me** no me propongo • **f. from** lejos de • **f. from it** al contrario, ni mucho menos • **f. into** *(very late)* hasta muy avanzado; *(very deep)* hasta muy adentro de • **f. off** *(at a distance)* lejos; *(in the distance)* a lo lejos • **how f.?** *(distance)* ¿a qué distancia? <*how f. is the town?* ¿a qué distancia está el pueblo?>; *(position)* ¿hasta dónde? <*how f. have you read?* ¿hasta dónde has leído?>; *(degree)* ¿hasta qué punto? <*how f. can we trust him?* ¿hasta qué punto podemos confiar en él?> • **in so f. as** *o* **insofar as** en la medida en que • **so f.** *(up to a certain place)* hasta aquí; *(up to now)* hasta ahora; *(to a limited extent)* hasta cierto punto, no muy lejos • **so f. so good** hasta ahora todo va bien • **thus f.** *(up to a certain point)* hasta aquí; *(up to now)* hasta ahora • **to carry something too f.** llevar algo al extremo • **to go f.** *(to achieve much)* llegar lejos, realizar mucho; *(to go a long way)* rendir <*the dollar does not go very f. any more* el dólar ya no rinde mucho> • **to go so f. as** llegar inclusive a • **to go too f.** pasarse de la raya **II.** adj. **farther** *o* **further, farthest** *o* **furthest** *(distant)* otro, opuesto <*on the f. corner* en la otra esquina>; *(lengthy)* largo <*a f. trek* un largo viaje>; POL. *(extreme)* extremo <*the f. right* la extrema derecha> ♦ **a f. cry** *(distance)* una gran distancia; *(difference)* una gran diferencia.

far·ad (făr'əd) s. ELEC. farad *m*, faradio.

far·a·way (făr'ə-wā') adj. *(distant)* lejano, remoto; FIG. *(dreamy)* distraído, soñador.

farce (färs) **I.** s. *(mockery)* farsa; TEAT. farsa, sainete *m* **II.** tr. **farced, farc·ing** *(to fill with jokes)* meter morcillas; CUL. rellenar.

far·ci·cal (fär'sĭ-kəl) adj. *(laughable)* risible, irrisorio; *(absurd)* ridículo, absurdo.

fare (fâr) **I.** intr. **fared, far·ing** *(to turn out)* ir <*the project is faring well* el proyecto va bien>; *(to eat)* alimentarse ♦ **to f. with** arreglárselas **II.** s. *(charge)* tarifa, pasaje *m*; *(passenger)* pasajero; *(food)* comida.

fare-thee-well (fâr'thē-wĕl') s. *(perfection)* perfección *f*; *(extreme)* non plus ultra *m*.

fare·well (fâr-wĕl') **I.** interj. adiós **II.** s. *(good-by)* adiós *m*, despedida; *(parting)* partida.

far-fetched (fär'fĕcht') adj. inverosímil, tirado de los pelos.

far-flung (fär'flŭng') adj. *(wide-ranging)* vasto, extenso; *(remote)* remoto, distante.

fa·ri·na (fə-rē'nə) s. *(flour)* harina; *(starch)* almidón *m*; *(fecula)* fécula.

farm (färm) **I.** s. *(land)* granja, finca; *(farmhouse)* cortijo, alquería; *(water)* criadero; *(baseball club)* club de béisbol subsidiario ♦ **f. machinery** maquinaria agrícola **II.** tr. cultivar ♦ **to f. out** *(to lease out)* ceder por contrato; *(to send* *out work)* encargar un trabajo —intr. labrar la tierra, ser agricultor.

farm·er (fär'mər) s. *(owner)* granjero; *(worker)* agricultor *m*; *(peasant)* labrador *m*, campesino; *(rancher)* hacendado.

farm hand s. peón *m*, mozo de labranza.

farm·house (färm'hous') s. granja.

farm·land (färm'lănd') s. terreno para cultivo, tierra de labrantía.

farm·stead (färm'stĕd') s. granja (tierra e instalaciones).

farm·yard (färm'yärd') s. corral (de una granja) *m*.

far-off (fär'ôf') adj. *(remote)* remoto; *(distant)* distante, lejano.

far-out (fär'out') adj. JER. *(kooky)* alocado, excéntrico; *(fantastic)* fantástico.

far·ra·go (fə-rä'gō, -rä'-) s. [pl. **-goes**] *(medley)* fárrago, mezcolanza; *(conglomeration)* conglomeración *f.*

far-reach·ing (fär'rē'chǐng) adj. de mucho alcance.

far·row (făr'ō) I. s. lechigada de cerdos II. tr. & intr. parir (la marrana).

far-sight·ed (fär'sī'tĭd) adj. hipermétrope; *(foresighted)* prudente, previsor; OFTAL. présbite, hipermétrope.

fart (färt) VULG. I. intr. echarse *o* tirarse un pedo ♦ **to f. around** JER. perder el tiempo en tonterías, malgastar el tiempo II. s. pedo.

far·ther (fär'thər) I. adv. *(in space)* más lejos, a mayor distancia; *(in time)* más adelante; *(moreover)* además; *(to a greater degree)* más ♦ **f. on** más adelante II. adj. *(more distant)* más lejano; *(additional)* ulterior.

far·thest (fär'thĭst) I. adj. *(more remote)* más remoto; *(longest)* más largo II. adv. más lejos.

far·thing (fär'thĭng) s. *(coin)* antiguo cuarto de penique; FIG. *(something of little value)* comino, bledo.

fas·ci·a (făsh'ē-ə) s. [pl. **-ci·ae** (-ē-ē')] *(band)* faja de color; G.B. *(dashboard)* tablero, ANAT. fascia; ARQ. faja, imposta.

fas·ci·nate (făs'ə-nāt') tr. **-nated, -nat·ing** *(to enthrall)* fascinar; *(to charm)* encantar —intr. ejercer fascinación.

fas·ci·nat·ing (făs'ə-nā'tǐng) adj. fascinante, fascinador.

fas·ci·na·tion (făs'ə-nā'shən) s. fascinación *f*, encanto.

fas·cism (făsh'ĭz'əm) s. POL. fascismo.

fas·cist (făsh'ĭst) s. POL. fascista *mf.*

fash·ion (făsh'ən) I. s. *(manner)* manera, modo; *(style)* moda ♦ **after a f.** hasta cierto punto, en cierto modo • **f. magazine** revista de modas • **in f.** de moda • **in one's own f.** al estilo *o* manera personal • **latest f.** *o* **fashions** la última moda • **to be in f.** estar de moda • **to come into f.** ponerse de moda • **to go out of f.** pasar de moda • **to set the f.** dictar la moda II. tr. *(to shape)* formar, moldear; *(to adapt)* amoldar, adaptar ♦ **to f. out of** *o* **from** hacer con <*she fashioned a boat from a piece of wood* hizo una barca con un trozo de madera>.

fash·ion·a·ble (făsh'ə-nə-bəl) adj. *(in style)* de moda; *(elegant)* elegante, de buen tono.

fashion plate s. figurín *m.*

fast¹ (făst) I. adj. **-er, -est** *(quick)* rápido <*a f. lane* un carril rápido>; *(swift)* veloz <*a f. typist* un dactilógrafo veloz>; *(ahead of time)* adelantado (reloj); *(dissipated)* disipado, extravagante <*a f. life* una vida disipada>; *(that will not fade)* inalterable <*f. colors* colores inalterables>; *(secure)* firme (en su lugar); *(stuck)* atascado; *(closed)* firmemente cerrado <*make the shutters f.* asegúrate que los postigos estén firmemente cerrados>; *(loyal)* leal <*f. friend* amigo leal>; *(deep)* profundo (sueño) ♦ **f. money** dinero que se gana rápidamente • **to pull a f. one** hacer una maldad (a alguien) II. adv. **-er, -est** *(securely)* firmemente; *(deeply)* profundamente; *(quickly)* velozmente; *(rapidly)* rápidamente; *(ahead of time)* adelantadamente; *(dissipated)* disipadamente; ANT. *(near by)* cercanamente ♦ **f. and loose** irresponsablemente • **to make f.** *(to tie)* atar; *(to fix)* sujetar • **to stand f.** mantenerse firme.

fast² (făst) I. intr. ayunar II. s. ayuno, abstinencia.

fas·ten (făs'ən) tr. *(to attach)* fijar, asegurar; *(to tie)* atar; *(to join)* ligar; *(to paste)* pegar; *(to close)* cerrar, echar el cerrojo; *(to attribute)* atribuir, echar (la culpa) —intr. *(to*

become fixed) fijarse, afirmarse; *(to cling)* agarrarse, sujetarse.

fas·ten·er (făs'ə-nər) s. sujetador *m.*

fas·ten·ing (făs'ə-nǐng) s. *(affixing)* fijación *f*; *(of a belt, garment)* abrochamiento.

fas·tid·i·ous (fă-stǐd'ē-əs) adj. *(exacting)* exigente; *(finicky)* melindroso; *(meticulous)* meticuloso; *(prudish)* remilgado.

fast·ness (făst'nĭs) s. *(stronghold)* fortaleza; *(firmness)* firmeza; *(rapidity)* rapidez *f*; *(colorfastness)* firmeza, solidez de colores *f.*

fast-track (făst'trăk') adj. extremadamente agresivo.

fat (făt) I. s. *(of people, animals)* grasa; *(used in cooking)* grasa, manteca; *(obesity)* grasa, gordura; *(grease)* grasa, sebo ♦ **the f. of the land** la grosura *o* el meollo de la tierra II. adj. **fat·ter, fat·test** *(plump)* gordo; *(greasy)* grasiento; *(abounding)* repleto <*the cane is f. with sugar* la caña esta repleta de azúcar>; *(lucrative)* lucrativo <*a f. contract* un contrato lucrativo>; *(thick)* grueso; *(large)* grande; *(swollen)* hinchado; *(puffed-up)* inflado ♦ **f. chance** JER. poca *o* ninguna posibilidad • **to get** *o* **grow f.** ponerse gordo, engordar III. tr. & intr. **fat·ted, fat·ting** engordar.

fa·tal (fāt'l) adj. fatal, mortal.

fa·tal·ism (fāt'l-ĭz'əm) s. fatalismo.

fa·tal·ist (fāt'l-ĭst) s. fatalista *mf.*

fa·tal·is·tic (fāt'l-ĭs'tĭk) adj. fatalista.

fa·tal·i·ty (fā-tăl'ĭ-tē) s. [pl. **-ties**] *(death)* fatalidad *f*; *(victim)* muerto, víctima; *(disaster)* fatalidad, calamidad *f*; *(destiny)* fatalismo.

fa·tal·ly (fāt'l-ē) adv. fatalmente, mortalmente.

fat·back (făt'băk') s. tocino.

fat cat s. JER. persona rica *o* influyente.

fate (fāt) s. *(destiny)* destino, sino; *(doom)* fatalidad *f.*

fat·ed (fā'tĭd) adj. *(predetermined)* predestinado; *(doomed)* condenado a la fatalidad.

fate·ful (fāt'fəl) adj. *(predetermined)* predestinado; *(fatal)* fatídico, fatal; *(prophetic)* profético; *(decisive)* fatídico, trascendental.

fat·head (făt'hĕd') s. JER. imbécil *mf*, estúpido.

fat·head·ed (făt'hĕd'ĭd) adj. imbécil.

fa·ther (fä'thər) I. s. *(parent)* padre *m*; *(ancestor)* antepasado; *(founder)* fundador *m* <*he was the f. of modern physics* fue el fundador de la física moderna>; *(old man)* padre ♦ **F.** *(God)* Dios; *(clergyman)* padre • **like f. like son** de tal palo tal astilla II. tr. *(to beget)* engendrar; *(to act as father to)* apadrinar; *(to create)* crear, fundar; *(to be the author of)* ser el autor de; *(to take responsibility for)* aceptar responsabilidad por.

fa·ther·hood (fä'thər-hŏŏd') s. paternidad *f.*

fa·ther-in-law (fä'thər-ĭn-lô') s. [pl. **fa·thers-in-law**] suegro.

fa·ther·land (fä'thər-lănd') s. patria.

fa·ther·less (fä'thər-lĭs) adj. *(without a father)* sin padre; *(orphan)* huérfano de padre.

fa·ther·ly (fä'thər-lē) I. adj. paternal, paterno II. adv. paternalmente.

Father's Day s. día del padre *m.*

fath·om (făth'əm) I. s. MARÍT. braza II. tr. *(to understand)* comprender a fondo; MARÍT. *(to sound)* sondear, sondar.

fath·om·less (făth'əm-lĭs) adj. *(incomprehensible)* incomprensible; MARÍT. insondable.

fa·tigue (fə-tēg') s. *(exhaustion)* fatiga; *(drudgery)* faena ♦ **fatigues** MIL. traje de faena.

fat·ness (făt'nĭs) s. gordura.

fat·so (făt'sō) s. [pl. **-soes**] JER., DESPEC. gordo.

fat·ten (făt'n) tr. *(animals)* engordar, cebar; *(land)* abonar, fertilizar; *(to increase)* aumentar —intr. engordar.

fat·ten·ing (făt'n-ĭng) I. adj. que engorda II. s. ceba, engorde (del ganado) *m.*

fat·ty (făt'ē) I. adj. **-ties** graso, adiposo II. s. [pl. **-ties**] FAM. gordinflón *m.*

fatty acid s. QUÍM. ácido graso.

fat·u·ous (făch'ŏŏ-əs) adj. fatuo.

fau·cet (fô'sĭt) s. grifo, canilla.

fault (fôlt) I. s. *(blame)* culpa; *(shortcoming)* defecto <*in spite of all his faults* a pesar de todos sus defectos>; *(mistake)* error *m*; ELEC., GEOL. falla ♦ **at f.** culpable • **to be at f.** tener la culpa, ser el culpable • **to find f.** criticar, desaprobar **II.** tr. encontrar defectos en <*no one could f. his performance* nadie le encontraba defectos en su actuación> —intr. *(to make a mistake)* equivocarse; GEOL. fracturarse.

fault·find·er (fôlt'fīn'dər) s. criticón m.

fault·find·ing (fôlt'fīn'dĭng) **I.** s. crítica **II.** adj. criticón.

fault·i·ly (fôl'tə-lē) adv. defectuosamente.

fault·less (fôlt'lĭs) adj. perfecto, impecable.

fault·y (fôl'tē) adj. **-i·er, -i·est** defectuoso, imperfecto.

faun (fôn) s. MITOL. fauno.

fau·na (fô'nə) s. [pl. **-nas** *o* **-nae** (-nē')] fauna.

Faust (foust) *o* **Faus·tus** (fou'stəs, fô'-) s. Fausto.

Faust·i·an (fou'stē-ən) adj. faustiano, fáustico.

faux pas (fō pä') s. [pl. **faux pas**] metida *o* metedura de pata.

fa·vor (fā'vər) **I.** s. *(service)* favor m <*he asked me for a f.* me pidió un favor>; *(esteem)* estimación f, aprecio; *(approval)* aprobación f, apoyo; *(favoritism)* favoritismo; *(remembrance)* recordatorio; *(small gift)* obsequio; *(advantage)* favor <*one point in your f.* un punto a favor tuyo> ♦ **favors** favores (de una mujer) • **in f. of** *(to the advantage of)* a favor de; *(made out to)* a nombre de • **to be in f.** ser popular • **to be in f. of** estar a favor de, ser partidario de <*I am not in f. of selling our house* no soy partidario de vender la casa> • **to be out of f.** dejar de ser popular • **to curry f. with someone** tratar de congraciarse con alguien **II.** tr. *(to oblige)* favorecer <*he favored us with a song* nos favoreció con una canción>; *(to be partial to)* preferir <*some fathers f. sons over daughters* algunos padres prefieren los hijos a las hijas>; *(to approve)* favorecer <*I f. his appointment as director* favorezco su nombramiento de director>; *(to aid)* favorecer; *(to be becoming to)* favorecer <*that color favors her* ese color la favorece>; *(to resemble)* parecerse a <*she favors her father* se parece al padre>; *(to treat with care)* tratar con cuidado.

fa·vor·a·ble (fā'vər-ə-bəl) adj. favorable.

fa·vored (fā'vərd) adj. *(special)* favorecido; *(favorite)* preferido, predilecto; *(blessed)* dotado, agraciado ♦ **ill-favored** mal parecido • **well-favored** bien parecido.

fa·vor·ite (fā'vər-ĭt) **I.** s. *(preferred one)* favorito, preferido; *(of royalty)* privado; *(mistress)* querida; DEP. favorito **II.** adj. favorito, preferido.

fa·vor·it·ism (fā'vər-ĭ-tĭz'əm) s. favoritismo.

fa·vour (fā'vər) s. & v. G.B. var. de **favor.**

fawn¹ (fôn) intr. hacer fiestas *(perro)* ♦ **to f. on** *o* **upon** adular, lisonjear.

fawn² (fôn) s. ZOOL. cervato; *(color)* color de gamuza m.

fawn·ing (fôn'ĭng) **I.** adj. adulador, servil **II.** s. adulación f, servilismo.

faze (fāz) tr. **fazed, faz·ing** perturbar, desconcertar.

fe·al·ty (fē'əl-tē) s. [pl. **-ties**] HIST. *(loyalty)* lealtad f; *(faithfulness)* fidelidad f.

fear (fîr) **I.** s. *(fright)* miedo, temor m; *(apprehension)* aprehensión f; *(danger)* peligro ♦ **for f. that** por miedo de que • **to be in f. of** *o* **to have a f. of** tener miedo de • **to put the f. of God into someone** dar un susto mortal a alguien **II.** tr. *(to be afraid)* tener miedo de, temer; *(to suspect)* temer <*I f. that you are wrong* temo que no tengas razón> —intr. tener miedo, temer ♦ **never f.** ¡pierda cuidado!, ¡no hay cuidado!

fear·ful (fîr'fəl) adj. *(frightening)* horrible, espantoso; *(frightened)* temeroso, miedoso; *(anxious)* aprehensivo, inquieto; FAM. *(dreadful)* tremendo, terrible ♦ **to be f. of** temer.

fear·ful·ness (fîr'fəl-nĭs) s. temor m, miedo.

fear·less (fîr'lĭs) adj. intrépido, audaz.

fear·less·ness (fîr'lĭs-nĭs) s. intrepidez m, audacia.

fear·some (fîr'səm) adj. *(frightening)* temible, terrible; *(frightened)* temeroso.

fea·si·bil·i·ty (fē'zə-bĭl'ĭ-tē) s. viabilidad f, posibilidad f.

fea·si·ble (fē'zə-bəl) adj. *(workable)* factible; *(possible)* posible, viable; *(suitable)* servible, conveniente.

feast (fēst) **I.** s. *(banquet)* banquete m, comilona; *(treat)* gozo, deleite m; RELIG. fiesta ♦ **to be a f. for the eyes** ser un regalo para los ojos • **movable f.** fiesta móvil **II.** tr. *(to entertain)* agasajar, banquetear; *(to delight)* deleitar, rega-

lar • **to f. one's eyes on** regalarse la vista con —intr. *(to eat)* banquetear, comer opíparamente; *(to delight in)* gozarse, deleitarse.

feast day s. día festivo.

feat (fēt) s. proeza, hazaña.

feath·er (fĕth'ər) **I.** s. ORNIT. pluma; ZOOL. *(tuft of hair)* moño; *(fringe of hair)* fleco (de pelos); *(triviality)* pequeñez f; *(of an arrow)* plumas; JOY. *(flaw)* nube f, defecto ♦ **a f. in one's cap** un triunfo de uno, un motivo de orgullo • **birds of a f.** gente de la misma calaña • **f. pillow** almohada de plumas • **feathers** *(plumage)* plumas, plumaje; *(clothing)* trapos • **in fine f.** *(in excellent form)* en forma; *(in excellent humor)* de muy buen humor **II.** tr. *(to cover with feathers)* emplumar; *(to thin the edge of)* rebajar el borde de ♦ **to f. one's nest** hacer su agosto (esp. a expensas de los demás) —intr. emplumecer, echar plumas.

feather bed s. *(mattress)* colchón de plumas m; *(bed)* lecho de plumas.

feath·er·bed (fĕth'ər-bĕd') intr. **-bed·ded, -bed·ding** *(to employ extra workers)* contratar más obreros de lo necesario; *(to be employed)* ser contratado como obrero innecesario.

feath·er·bed·ding (fĕth'ər-bĕd'ĭng) s. limitación del rendimiento de obreros por parte de un sindicato f.

feath·er·brain (fĕth'ər-brān') s. FAM. cabeza de chorlito.

feath·ered (fĕth'ərd) adj. *(arrow)* emplumado; *(hat)* con plumas; *(winged)* alado.

feath·er·weight (fĕth'ər-wāt') s. *(lightweight)* peso muy liviano *o* ligero; FIG. *(insignificant person)* persona de escasa importancia; DEP. peso pluma.

feath·er·y (fĕth'ə-rē) adj. *(feathers)* plumoso; *(light)* liviano, ligero como una pluma.

fea·ture (fē'chər) **I.** s. *(characteristic)* característica, rasgo <*rocks were a distinctive f. of the landscape* las piedras eran un rasgo distintivo del paisaje>; *(of a person)* presencia, aspecto; *(of the face)* semblante m, rasgo; CINEM. *(main film)* película principal; PERIOD. *(prominent article)* artículo de primera plana, reportaje especial m ♦ **f. film** película principal • **f. writer** reportero de actualidades, cronista • **features** facciones, fisonomía **II.** tr. **-tured, -turing** *(to showcase)* presentar; *(to be a characteristic of)* tener, incorporar; *(to draw)* representar; *(to describe)* describir; FAM. *(to resemble)* parecerse, tener algo de; *(to imagine)* imaginarse <*f. that!* ¡imagínate eso!>

fea·tured (fē'chərd) adj. CINEM. *(film)* principal; *(role)* estelar; PERIOD. *(article)* de primera plana ♦ **f. actress** actriz estelar, estrella • **sharp-featured** de facciones bien perfiladas.

fea·ture-length (fē'chər-lĕngkth') adj. *(film)* de largo metraje; *(book)* largo, extenso.

feb·rile (fĕb'rəl, fē'brəl) adj. MED. febril.

Feb·ru·ar·y (fĕb'rōō-ĕr'ē, fĕb'yōō-) s. febrero.

fe·cal (fē'kəl) adj. fecal.

fe·ces (fē'sēz) s.pl. excrementos, heces f.

feck·less (fĕk'lĭs) adj. *(lacking purpose)* fútil, inútil; *(ineffective)* ineficaz; *(irresponsible)* irresponsable, irreflexivo.

fe·cund (fē'kənd, fĕk'ənd) adj. fecundo.

fe·cun·date (fē'kən-dāt', fĕk'ən-) tr. **-dat·ed, -dat·ing** *(to fertilize)* fecundar, fertilizar; BIO. fecundar.

fe·cun·di·ty (fĭ-kŭn'dĭ-tē) s. fecundidad f, fertilidad f.

fed (fĕd) pret. y part. p. de **feed.**

fed·er·a·cy (fĕd'ər-ə-sē) s. [pl. **-cies**] ANT. federación f.

fed·er·al (fĕd'ər-əl) **I.** adj. federal **II.** s. ♦ **F.** HIST. soldado federal en la guerra civil de EE. UU.

fed·er·al·ism (fĕd'ər-ə-lĭz'əm) s. federalismo ♦ **F.** la doctrina del partido federalista.

fed·er·al·ist (fĕd'ər-ə-lĭst) s. federalista mf ♦ **F.** miembro del partido federalista (EE. UU.) **II.** adj. federalista.

fed·er·al·ize (fĕd'ər-ə-līz') tr. **-ized, -iz·ing** federalizar, federar; *(to put under federal control)* poner bajo el poder federal.

Federal Reserve System s. FIN. sistema bancario de la reserva federal (en EE. UU.).

fed·er·ate (fĕd'ə-rāt') **I.** tr. & intr. **-at·ed, -at·ing** federar(se), confederar(se) **II.** adj. (fĕd'ə-rĭt) federado.

fed·er·a·tion (fĕd'ə-rā'shən) s. federación f.

fed·er·a·tive (fĕd'ə-rā'tĭv, -ər-ə-) adj. federativo.

fe·do·ra (fĭ-dôr′ə) s. sombrero flexible de fieltro.
fed up adj. harto, disgustado.
fee (fē) **I.** s. *(professional charge)* honorarios, emolumentos; *(tip)* propina; DER. *(estate)* herencia, patrimonio; HIST. feudo ♦ **in f.** DER. en propiedad • **membership f.** cuota de socio • **registration f.** derechos de matrícula **II.** tr. **feed, fee·ing** dar propina a.
fee·ble (fē′bəl) adj. **-bler, -blest** *(weak)* débil; *(inadequate)* inadecuado; *(ineffective)* ineficaz, de poco peso.
fee·ble-mind·ed (fē′bəl-mīn′dĭd) adj. *(mentally deficient)* débil mental; *(stupid)* estúpido, imbécil.
fee·ble·ness (fē′bəl-nĭs) s. debilidad f, endeblez f.
feed (fēd) **I.** tr. **fed** (fēd), **feed·ing** *(to give food to)* dar de comer a; *(to nourish)* alimentar; *(anger, suspicion)* avivar; *(gas, electricity)* suministrar; DEP. pasar, dar pases a; ELEC., MEC. alimentar ♦ **to f. a baby** *(to suckle)* dar de mamar, amamantar; *(to bottle-feed)* dar el biberón a • **to f. a cold** comer bien para curarse de un resfrío • **to f. lines to** dar la réplica a (un actor) • **to f. on** *(to eat)* comer, alimentar <*cows f. on hay* las vacas se alimentan con heno>; FIG. *(to enjoy)* derivar satisfacción de —intr. comer ♦ **to f. oneself** alimentarse **II.** s. AGR. *(fodder)* pienso, forraje m; FAM. *(meal)* comida; MEC. alimentación f. ♦ **to be off one's f.** JER. haber perdido el apetito.
feed·back (fēd′băk′) s. *(information)* información f; ELECTRÓN. realimentación f, retroacción f.
feed·bag (fēd′băg′) s. morral m.
feed·er (fē′dər) s. *(machine)* alimentador m; *(tributary)* afluente m, corriente tributaria; *(branch, road)* ramal m; *(animal)* cebón m, animal de engorde m; ELEC. alimentador; AGR. alimentador, cebador m.
feed·ing (fē′dĭng) s. *(act, meal)* comida; TEC. *(of machine, engine)* alimentación f.
feel (fēl) **I.** tr. **felt** (fĕlt), **feel·ing** *(to experience physically)* sentir; *(to touch)* tocar; *(to examine)* palpar; *(to experience)* experimentar, sentir <*I felt my interest rising* sentí que mi interés crecía>; *(to sense)* percibir <*she felt her father's annoyance* ella percibió el enfado de su padre>; *(to be affected by)* quedar afectado por, sentir <*to f. the loss of someone* sentir la pérdida de alguien> ♦ **it feels cold (hot, warm)** hace frío (calor, calorcito) • **to f. it in one's bones** FIG., FAM. tener el presentimiento que • **to f. one's way** *(to grope)* andar a tientas; *(to be cautious)* actuar con cautela • **to f. out** averiguar, sondear • **to f. the need of** sentir la necesidad de • **to f. up** VULG. sobar, manosear —intr. *(to experience touch)* sentir (por tacto); *(physically)* ser . . . al tacto <*the sheets f. smooth* las sábanas son suaves al tacto>; *(emotionally)* sentirse, estar <*I f. annoyed today* estoy disgustado hoy>; *(to seem)* parecer; *(to grope)* andar a tientas; *(to believe)* creer, pensar <*how do you f. about it?* ¿qué piensas de esto?> ♦ **to f. bad** *(to be ill)* sentirse mal; *(to be sad)* estar triste; *(to feel uncomfortable)* estar incómodo • **to f. bad about** lamentar, sentir • **to f. cold (hot, warm)** tener o sentir frío (calor) • **to f. for** *(to have compassion)* compadecer <*when I heard about his father's death, I really felt for him* cuando me enteré de la muerte de su padre, realmente me compadecí de él>; *(to grope for)* buscar a tientas <*she felt for her keys* buscaba a tientas sus llaves> • **to f. hungry (thirsty, sleepy)** tener hambre (sed, sueño) • **to f. ill** sentirse enfermo • **to f. like** FAM. *(to have a desire for)* tener ganas de <*I f. like dancing* tengo ganas de bailar>; *(to give the impression of)* parecer (como) <*it feels like silk* parece (como) seda al tacto> • **to f. sorry for** compadecer a • **to f. sure that** tener la seguridad de que • **to f. up to** FAM. sentirse con ánimos para **II.** s. *(touch)* tacto; *(perception)* percepción f, sensación f; *(atmosphere)* atmósfera; *(intuition)* intuición f ♦ **to get the f. of** coger el truco de • **to have a f. for** tener sentido o aptitud para.
feel·er (fē′lər) s. *(probe)* tentativa, sondeo; ZOOL. *(antenna)* antena; *(tentacle)* tentáculo ♦ **to put out feelers** FIG. sondear.
feel·ing (fē′lĭng) **I.** s. *(touch)* tacto; *(sensation)* sensación f <*a f. of pain* una sensación de dolor>; *(emotion)* emoción f <*she spoke with great f.* ella habló con gran emoción>; *(impression)* impresión f; *(premonition)* presentimiento <*I*

have a f. that something is wrong* tengo el presentimiento de que algo anda mal>; *(sensibility)* sensibilidad f; *(passion)* pasión f; *(opinion)* opinión f; *(appreciation)* aprecio, sentido <*she has a f. for music* ella tiene aprecio por la música>; *(aptitude)* aptitud f, sentido ♦ **hard feelings** resentimiento • **ill feelings** malos sentimientos • **to have no feelings** no tener sensibilidad, ser insensible • **to hurt one's feelings** herir el amor propio **II.** adj. *(sensitive)* sensible; *(expressing emotion)* conmovedor.
feet (fēt) pl. de **foot.**
feign (fān) tr. & intr. aparentar, fingir.
feint (fānt) s. *(pretense)* finta, amago; MIL. maniobra fingida.
feist·y (fī′stē) adj. **-i·er, -i·est** *(touchy)* irritable, enojadizo; *(spirited)* intrépido, arrojado.
feld·spar (fĕld′spär′) s. MIN. feldespato.
fe·lic·i·ta·tion (fĭ-lĭs′ĭ-tā′shən) s. felicitación f, enhorabuena.
fe·lic·i·tous (fĭ-lĭs′ĭ-təs) adj. *(suitable)* oportuno, apto; *(yielding pleasure)* feliz.
fe·lic·i·ty (fĭ-lĭs′ĭ-tē) s. [pl. **-ties**] *(happiness)* felicidad f; *(phrase)* dicho feliz, ocurrencia.
fe·line (fē′līn′) adj. felino.
fell¹ (fĕl) tr. *(to cut down)* cortar, talar; *(to kill)* acogotar; *(to sew)* sobrecargar.
fell² (fĕl) adj. *(fierce)* cruel, feroz; *(lethal)* siniestro, funesto ♦ **at** o **in one f. swoop** de un solo golpe.
fell³ (fĕl) s. *(hide)* piel f, pellejo.
fell⁴ (fĕl) pret. de **fall.**
fel·la·ti·o (fə-lā′shē-ō′, -lä′tē-ō′) o **fel·la·tion** (-lā′shən) s. felacio, estimulación oral del pene f.
fell·er (fĕl′ər) s. *(one that fells)* talador m, leñador m; *(machine)* máquina taladora; EE. UU., FAM. *(fellow)* tipo, tío; *(youngster)* muchacho.
fel·low (fĕl′ō) **I.** s. *(boy)* muchacho; *(man)* hombre m; *(boyfriend)* compañero; *(guy)* tipo, individuo <*and then this f. came up to me* y entonces este tipo se me acercó>; *(one)* uno <*what is a f. to do?* ¿qué es lo que uno puede hacer?>; *(comrade, associate)* compañero; *(peer)* par m, igual m; *(mate)* pareja; *(of a society)* socio, miembro; *(grant recipient)* becario ♦ **poor f.!** ¡pobre! • **young f.** muchacho, joven **II.** adj. ♦ **f. citizens** ciudadanos, conciudadanos • **f. member** socio, consocio • **f. worker** compañero de trabajo.
fellow man o **fel·low·man** (fĕl′ō-măn′) s. [pl. **men** o **-men** (-mĕn′)] prójimo, semejante m.
fel·low·ship (fĕl′ō-shĭp′) s. *(sharing)* comunidad f (de intereses, ideas) o *(mutual association)* asociación f; *(society)* sociedad f; *(fraternity)* fraternidad f; *(friendship)* compañerismo, camaradería; EDUC. *(grant)* beca; *(foundation)* fundación f ♦ **good f.** espíritu de paz y concordia.
fellow traveler s. POL. simpatizante no afiliado del partido comunista mf.
fel·on (fĕl′ən) **I.** s. ANT. malvado; DER. criminal m, felón m **II.** adj. ANT. malvado, cruel.
fe·lo·ni·ous (fə-lō′nē-əs) adj. ANT. *(wicked)* malvado; DER. criminal, delincuente.
fel·o·ny (fĕl′ə-nē) s. [pl. **-nies**] felonía, delito mayor.
fel·spar (fĕl′spär′) s. var. de **feldspar.**
felt¹ (fĕlt) **I.** s. TEJ. fieltro **II.** adj. de fieltro <*a f. hat* un sombrero de fieltro> **III.** tr. *(to manufacture fabric)* fieltrar; *(a surface)* cubrir de fieltro.
felt² (fĕlt) pret. y part. p. de **feel.**
fe·male (fē′māl′) **I.** adj. *(feminine)* femenino; *(clothes, manners)* de mujer; *(consisting of women)* de mujeres; BIOL. hembra <*a f. giraffe* una jirafa hembra>; MEC. *(screw, receptacle)* hembra; BOT. femenino **II.** s. *(woman)* mujer; *(young woman)* muchacha, chica; BIOL., BOT. hembra.
fem·i·nine (fĕm′ə-nĭn) **I.** adj. *(female)* femenino; *(effeminate)* afeminado, mujeril; GRAM. femenino **II.** s. GRAM. femenino.
fem·i·nin·i·ty (fĕm′ə-nĭn′ĭ-tē) s. feminidad f, feminidad f.
fem·i·nism (fĕm′ə-nĭz′əm) s. feminismo.
fem·i·nist (fĕm′ə-nĭst) s. feminista mf.
fem·i·nize (fĕm′ə-nīz′) tr. & intr. **-nized, -niz·ing** afeminar(se).

---

ng inglés / ŏ la / ō bou / ô corre / oi oigo / ōō uno / ou auto / yōō ciudad / w hueco / y yo / z mismo

fe·mur (fē'mər) s. [pl. **fe·murs** o **fem·o·ra** (fĕm'ər-ə)] ANAT. fémur m.

fen (fĕn) s. ciénaga, pantano.

fence (fĕns) I. s. (barrier) cerca, empalizada <he built a f. around his house levantó una cerca en torno a la casa>; (person) traficante de artículos robados mf; DEP. (for horses) valla; (fencing) esgrima ♦ **to sit on the f.** (to be neutral) nadar entre dos aguas; (to be undecided) ver los toros desde la barrera II. tr. **fenced, fenc·ing** (to surround) cercar, vallar; (to close off) encerrar ♦ **to f. in** (property) cercar; (animals) encerrar ♦ **to f. off** (property) cercar, separar con una cerca; (a road) cerrar • **to f. out** excluir —intr. (to practice fencing) practicar la esgrima; (to hedge) responder con evasivas; (to act as a fence) traficar con artículos robados.

fenc·er (fĕn'sər) s. (builder) cercador m; DEP. esgrimista mf.

fence-sit·ting (fĕns'sĭt'ĭng) s. irresolución f.

fenc·ing (fĕn'sĭng) s. (fences) cerca, empalizada; (material) material de cercas o vallas m; (traffic in stolen goods) tráfico de artículos robados; DEP. esgrima.

fend (fĕnd) tr. ANT. defender ♦ **to f. off** (a blow) parar; (an attack) repeler —intr. G.B. esforzarse ♦ **to f. for oneself** valerse por sí mismo.

fend·er (fĕn'dər) s. (of a car) guardafango, guardabarros; (of a locomotive) quitapiedras m, trompa; (fireplace screen) pantalla; (of a boat) defensa.

fen·es·tra·tion (fĕn'ĭ-strā'shən) s. ARQ. (window distribution) ventanaje m; (opening) abertura, orificio.

fen·nel (fĕn'əl) s. BOT. (plant) hinojo; (seed) semilla de hinojo.

fer·ment I. s. (fûr'mĕnt') (catalyst) fermento; (process) fermentación f; (unrest) agitación f II. tr. (fər-mĕnt') (to catalyze) fermentar; (to excite) agitar —intr. fermentar.

fer·men·ta·tion (fûr'mən-tā'shən) s. (catalysis) fermentación f; (agitation) agitación f.

fer·mi (fûr'mē, fĕr'-) s. FÍS. fermi m.

fer·mi·um (fûr'mē-əm, fĕr'-) s. QUÍM. fermio.

fern (fûrn) s. helecho.

fe·ro·cious (fə-rō'shəs) adj. (fierce) feroz; (intense) violento, brutal.

fe·roc·i·ty (fə-rŏs'ĭ-tē) s. (fierceness) ferocidad f, fiereza; (intensity) violencia, brutalidad f.

fer·ret (fĕr'ĭt) I. s. ZOOL. hurón m II. tr. (to hunt) cazar con hurones; (to expel) sacar, expulsar ♦ **to f. out** descubrir —intr. (to hunt) huronear; (to search) registrar, buscar.

fer·ric (fĕr'ĭk) adj. QUÍM. férrico.

ferric oxide s. QUÍM. óxido férrico, trióxido férrico.

Fer·ris wheel o **fer·ris wheel** (fĕr'ĭs) s. noria, vuelta al mundo.

fer·rite (fĕr'ĭt') s. QUÍM. ferrito; MIN. ferrita.

fer·ro·con·crete (fĕr'ō-kŏn'krēt') s. CONSTR. hormigón armado.

fer·ro·mag·net (fĕr'ō-măg'nĭt) s. FÍS. substancia ferromagnética.

fer·ro·mag·net·ic (fĕr'ō-măg-nĕt'ĭk) adj. FÍS. ferromagnético.

fer·ro·man·ga·nese (fĕr'ō-măng'gə-nēz') s. METAL. ferromanganeso.

fer·rous (fĕr'əs) adj. QUÍM. ferroso.

fer·ru·gi·nous (fə-rōō'jə-nəs) adj. (of iron) ferruginoso; (rust-colored) aherrumbrado.

fer·rule (fĕr'əl) s. (metal cap) virola, contera; (bushing) abrazadera.

fer·ry (fĕr'ē) I. tr. **-ried, -ry·ing** (to transport) transportar en barco o avión a través de río o mar; (to cross) cruzar; (to deliver) entregar II. s. [pl. **-ries**] (ferryboat) transbordador m, ferry m; (pier) embarcadero.

fer·ry·boat (fĕr'ē-bōt') s. transbordador m, ferry m.

fer·ry·man (fĕr'ē-mən) s. [pl. **-men**] barquero.

fer·tile (fûr'tl) adj. (productive) fértil, fecundo; AGR. fértil, feraz; BIOL., BOT. fecundo.

fer·til·i·ty (fər-tĭl'ĭ-tē) s. (richness) fertilidad f; BIOL., BOT. fecundidad f.

fer·til·i·za·tion (fûr'tl-ĭ-zā'shən) s. AGR. fertilización f, abono; BIOL., BOT. fecundación f.

fer·til·ize (fûr'tl-īz') tr. **-ized, -iz·ing** fertilizar, abonar; BIOL., BOT. fecundar.

fer·til·iz·er (fûr'tl-ī'zər) s. AGR. fertilizante m, abono.

fer·vent (fûr'vənt) adj. (ardent) ferviente, fervoroso; (hot) caliente.

fer·vid (fûr'vĭd) adj. (impassioned) fervoroso; (burning) férvido, caliente.

fer·vor (fûr'vər) s. (ardor) fervor m, ardor m; (heat) fervor, calor intenso.

fes·tal (fĕs'tl) adj. festivo.

fes·ter (fĕs'tər) I. intr. (to rot) pudrirse; (to rankle) enconarse; MED. (to suppurate) supurar; (to ulcerate) ulcerarse II. s. MED. úlcera, pústula.

fes·ti·val (fĕs'tə-vəl) I. s. (celebration) fiesta; festival m <an Italian film f. un festival de cine italiano> II. adj. festivo, de fiesta.

fes·tive (fĕs'tĭv) adj. festivo, de fiesta.

fes·tiv·i·ty (fĕ-stĭv'ĭ-tē) s. [pl. **-ties**] (celebration) festividad f, fiesta; (merriment) regocijo ♦ **festivities** diversiones.

fes·toon (fĕ-stōōn') I. s. (garland) festón m, guirnalda; ARQ. festón II. tr. festonear, adornar con guirnaldas.

fe·tal (fēt'l) adj. fetal.

fetch (fĕch) I. tr. (to go after and return with) traer, ir a buscar <shall I f. your bags for you? ¿le busco las maletas?>; (to bring forth) dar <to f. a sigh dar un suspiro>; (to draw) hacer brotar <a blow that fetched blood un golpe que hizo brotar la sangre>; (to bring in as a price) venderse por <it fetched a hundred dollars at auction se vendió por cien dólares en la subasta>; MARÍT. (to arrive at) llegar a ♦ **to f. and carry** llevar y traer • **to f. up** recobrar, recuperar —intr. (to retrieve game) cobrar la presa; MARÍT. (to hold a course) mantener el rumbo; (to turn about) virar, dar vuelta atrás ♦ **fetch!** ¡tráelo! (orden a un perro) • **to f. up** parar, quedarse II. s. (retrieval of game) cobranza; (trick) truco, treta.

fetch·ing (fĕch'ĭng) adj. atractivo, encantador.

fete (fāt, fĕt) I. s. (feast) fiesta; (fair) feria; (elaborate party) festín m II. tr. **fet·ed, fet·ing** festejar.

fet·id (fĕt'ĭd, fē'tĭd) adj. fétido, hediondo.

fet·ish (fĕt'ĭsh, fē'tĭsh) s. fetiche m ♦ **to make a f. of** venerar.

fet·ish·ism (fĕt'ĭ-shĭz'əm, fē'tĭ-) s. fetichismo.

fet·ish·ist (fĕt'ĭ-shĭst, fē'tĭ-) s. fetichista mf.

fet·lock (fĕt'lŏk') s. (spur) espolón m; (tuft of hair) cernejas; (joint) menudillo.

fet·ter (fĕt'ər) I. s. (shackle) grillete m, grillo; (restraint) traba II. tr. (to shackle) poner grilletes o grillos a; (to hamper) poner trabas a.

fet·tle (fĕt'l) s. METAL. brasca ♦ **to be in fine f.** (condition) estar en forma; (spirits) de buen humor.

fe·tus (fē'təs) s. [pl. **-tus·es**] feto.

feud (fyōōd) I. s. enemistad heredada, odio hereditario II. intr. pelear, contender.

feu·dal (fyōōd'l) adj. feudal.

feu·dal·ism (fyōōd'l-ĭz'əm) s. feudalismo.

fe·ver (fē'vər) s. (excitement) agitación f, frenesí m; (craze) fiebre f; MED. (temperature) fiebre, calentura; (disease) fiebre <yellow f. fiebre amarilla> ♦ **to have** o **to be running a high f.** tener mucha fiebre.

fe·ver·ish (fē'vər-ĭsh) adj. febril.

few (fyōō) I. adj. poco <f. cars pocos automóviles> ♦ **a f.** unos • **a f. times** varias veces • **every f. (minutes, miles)** cada dos o tres (minutos, millas) • **the last f. (days, years)** estos últimos (días, años) II. s. pocos ♦ **the f.** la minoría • **the lucky f.** los más afortunados III. pron. pocos <f. of us will come vendremos pocos> ♦ **a f.** unos cuantos • **a f. of** algunos de • **f. and far between** contados, muy espaciados • **quite a f.** muchos.

few·er (fyōō'ər) adj. & pron. menos <the company produced f. products last year la compañía produjo menos productos el año pasado> ♦ **f. than** menos de • **the f. the better** cuantos menos mejor.

few·est (fyōō'ĭst) I. adj. menos II. pron. el menor número <I made fewer mistakes than you, but John made the f. yo hice menos errores que tú, pero Juan hizo el menor número de errores>.

fey (fā) adj. *(doomed)* predestinado a morir; *(dying)* moribundo; *(clairvoyant)* visionario; *(touched)* tocado, fantasioso.

fez (fĕz) s. [pl. **fez·zes**] fez *m*.

fi·an·cé (fē'än-sā') s. novio, prometido.

fi·an·cée (fē'än-sā') s. novia, prometida.

fi·as·co (fē-ăs'kō, -ä'skō) s. [pl. **-coes** o **-cos**] fiasco.

fi·at (fē'ăt', -ät') s. *(order)* orden arbitraria, decreto arbitrario; *(authorization)* fiat *m*, autorización *f*.

fib (fĭb) **I.** s. mentirilla, mentirita **II.** intr. **fibbed, fib·bing** decir mentirillas.

fib·ber (fĭb'ər) s. mentirosillo.

fi·ber (fī'bər) s. *(strand)* fibra; *(strength)* carácter *m*, nervio; ANAT., BOT. fibra.

fi·ber·board (fī'bər-bôrd') s. CONSTR. lámina de fibra, madera de bagazo.

Fi·ber·glas (fī'bər-glăs') s. marca registrada de un tipo de lana de vidrio.

fiber glass s. fibra de vidrio.

fib·ril·la·tion (fĭb'rə-lā'shən, fī'brə-) s. BIOL., MED. fibrilación *f*; MED. arritmia (del corazón).

fi·bro·sis (fī-brō'sĭs) s. MED. fibrosis *m*.

fi·brous (fī'brəs) adj. fibroso.

fib·u·la (fĭb'yə-lə) s. [pl. **-lae** (-lē') o **-las**] ANAT. peroné *m*.

fick·le (fĭk'əl) adj. inconstante, variable.

fic·tion (fĭk'shən) s. *(invented account)* ficción *f*, invención *f*; *(lie)* mentira; LIT. *(work)* obra de imaginación o de ficción; *(genre)* literatura de imaginación, ficción.

fic·tion·al (fĭk'shə-nəl) adj. *(fictitious)* ficticio; LIT. de imaginación, de ficción.

fic·tion·al·ize (fĭk'shə-nə-līz') tr. **-ized, -iz·ing** novelar, novelizar.

fic·ti·tious (fĭk-tĭsh'əs) adj. *(deceitful)* ficticio <*a f. identity* una identidad ficticia>; *(imaginary)* imaginario; *(feigned)* fingido.

fic·tive (fĭk'tĭv) adj. *(fictitious)* ficticio; *(feigned)* fingido; LIT. ficticio, de imaginación.

fid·dle (fĭd'l) **I.** s. FAM. *(trifling)* boberías; MÚS. violín *m* ♦ **fit as a f.** FAM. sano como una manzana • **to play second f.** desempeñar un papel secundario **II.** intr. **-dled, -dling** FAM. tocar el violín ♦ **to f. around** FAM. perder el tiempo • **to f. with** *(a pencil, hat)* juguetear nerviosamente con; *(a radio, car)* jugar con, andar con —tr. FAM. tocar el violín ♦ **to f. the time away** FAM. perder el tiempo.

fid·dler (fĭd'lər) s. FAM. violinista *mf*.

fid·dle·sticks (fĭd'l-stĭks') interj. ¡tonterías!, ¡pamplinas!

fi·del·i·ty (fĭ-dĕl'ĭ-tē, fī-) s. [pl. **-ties**] fidelidad *f* ♦ **high f.** RAD. alta fidelidad.

fidg·et (fĭj'ĭt) **I.** intr. moverse, no estarse quieto ♦ **to f. with** jugar con, manosear —tr. poner nervioso a, inquietar **II.** s. persona que no se está quieta ♦ **fidgets** intranquilidad, nerviosismo • **to have the fidgets** no poder estarse quieto.

fidg·et·y (fĭj'ĭ-tē) adj. nervioso, que no puede estarse quieto.

fi·du·cial (fĭ-dōō'shəl, -dyōō'-) adj. *(fiduciary)* fiduciario; *(standard)* fiducial.

fi·du·ci·ar·y (fĭ-dōō'shē-ĕr'ē, -dyōō'-) adj. & s. [pl. **-ies**] fiduciario.

fie (fī) interj. ¡qué vergüenza!

fief (fēf) s. feudo.

field (fēld) **I.** s. *(area)* campo; AGR. campo, sembrado <*a corn f.* un campo de maíz>; *(area of interest)* campo, esfera; *(area of specialization)* especialidad *f*; *(profession)* profesión *f*; *(business)* ramo; GEOL. yacimiento; HER. campo; DEP. *(playing area)* campo, terreno; *(contestants)* competidores *m*, jugadores *m*; MIL. *(battlefield)* campo de batalla; *(battle)* batalla; FÍS., ÓPT. campo <*f. of view* campo visual> ♦ **f. of activity** campo de actividades • **to take the f.** DEP. ocupar los puestos, salir a jugar; MIL. entrar en campaña **II.** tr. DEP. *(to retrieve)* coger (la pelota) y hacer la jugada; *(to enter in a contest)* poner (un equipo) en el campo; *(to respond to)* responder adecuadamente, manejar <*he fielded the question expertly* manejó la pregunta hábilmente>; *(to put into action)* poner en campaña.

field artillery s. artillería de campaña.

field day s. *(festive day)* día feriado; DEP. *(for athletics)* reunión de atletismo *f*; EDUC. *(for nature study)* día en el campo *m*; MIL. *(for exercises)* día de maniobras ♦ **to have a f.** darse gusto (haciendo algo).

field·er (fēl'dər) s. DEP. jardinero, jugador que juega los jardines (en el béisbol) *m*.

field event s. DEP. competencia atlética (salto, lanzamiento).

field glasses s.pl. prismáticos, gemelos.

field goal s. DEP. *(in football, rugby)* gol de patada; *(basketball)* canasta de dos tantos.

field gun s. ARM., MIL. cañón de campaña *m*.

field hand s. peón *m*, jornalero.

field hospital s. MIL. hospital de campaña *m*.

field magnet s. FÍS. imán inductor *m*.

field marshal s MIL. mariscal de campo *m*.

field mouse s. ratón de campo *m*.

field officer s. MIL. oficial superior *m*.

field of force s. FÍS. campo de fuerza *m*.

field of honor s. *(scene of duel)* campo del honor; *(battlefield)* campo de batalla.

field·test (fēld'tĕst') tr. probar (un aparato) en la práctica.

field trip s. EDUC. excursión *f*.

field·work (fēld'wûrk') s. *(work)* trabajo en el terreno; MIL. *(fortification)* obras de campaña.

fiend (fēnd) s. *(devil)* demonio, diablo; *(wicked person)* demonio, desalmado; FAM. *(addict)* adicto, vicioso; *(enthusiast)* fanático.

fiend·ish (fēn'dĭsh) adj. diabólico.

fiend·ish·ness (fēn'dĭsh-nĭs') s. perversidad *f*, maldad *f*.

fierce (fĭrs) adj. **fierc·er, fierc·est** *(ferocious)* feroz, fiero; *(cruel)* cruel, salvaje; *(mean)* feroz <*he gave me a f. look* me lanzó una mirada feroz>; *(severe)* tremendo, brutal (calor, golpe); *(violent)* violento; *(hard-fought)* reñido; *(bloody)* encarnizado; *(ardent)* ardiente, furioso; *(supporter)* acérrimo; FAM. *(difficult)* terrible <*a f. exam* un examen terrible>.

fierce·ness (fĭrs'nĭs) s. *(ferociousness)* ferocidad *f*; *(cruelty)* crueldad *f*, salvajismo; *(severity)* brutalidad *f*; *(violence)* violencia; *(bloodiness)* encarnizamiento.

fier·y (fĭr'ē) adj. **-i·er, -i·est** *(blazing)* llameante, en llamas <*the f. crater* el cráter llameante>; *(hot)* abrasador; *(feverish)* encendido; *(hair)* rojo; *(flammable)* inflamable; *(glowing)* encendido (crepúsculo, color); *(temper)* fogoso; *(words)* enardecido.

fife (fīf) s. MÚS. pífano, flautín *m*.

fif·teen (fĭf-tēn') s. & adj. quince *m*.

fif·teenth (fĭf-tēnth') **I.** s. *(place)* decimoquinto; *(part)* quinzavo, quinzava parte **II.** adj. *(place)* decimoquinto; *(part)* quinzavo.

fifth (fĭfth) **I.** s. *(place)* quinto; *(part)* quinto, quinta parte; *(capacity)* quinto de galón (medida de capacidad); MÚS. *(interval)* quinta; *(note)* dominante *f* **II.** adj. quinto.

Fifth Amendment s. quinta enmienda a la Constitución de EE. UU.

fifth column s. POL. quinta columna.

fifth wheel s. *(wheel)* rodete *m*; FIG. *(unnecessary person)* persona superflua.

fif·ti·eth (fĭf'tē-ĭth) **I.** s. *(place)* cincuenta; *(part)* quincuagésimo, quincuagésima parte **II.** adj. *(place)* quincuagésimo; *(part)* cincuentavo.

fif·ty (fĭf'tē) adj. & s. [pl. **-ties**] cincuenta *m*.

fif·ty-fif·ty (fĭf'tē-fĭf'tē) adj. FAM. mitad y mitad, a medias ♦ **to go f.** FAM. ir a medias.

fif·ty-one (fĭf'tē-wŭn') s. & adj. cincuenta y uno.

fig (fĭg) s. BOT. *(tree)* higuera; *(fruit)* higo ♦ **not to care a f.** importarle a uno un bledo o un pepino.

fight (fīt) **I.** intr. **fought** (fôt), **fight·ing** *(to struggle)* luchar; MIL. *(to battle)* batallar, luchar; DEP. *(in boxing)* boxear, pelear; *(in wrestling)* combatir, luchar; *(to argue)* reñir ♦ **to f. against odds** luchar con desventaja • **to f. back** defenderse —tr. MIL. *(to battle)* luchar con o contra; DEP. pelear o luchar con; FIG. *(to resist)* combatir <*to f. temptation* combatir la tentación>; *(to try to prevent)* luchar contra, combatir; MIL. *(to engage in)* dar o librar (una batalla) ♦ **to f. a case** DER. litigar o contender judicialmente • **to f.**

it out *(to decide)* decidirlo luchando; *(to resolve)* luchar hasta resolverlo • **to f. off** rechazar, repeler **II.** s. *(struggle)* lucha; MIL. *(combat)* combate *m*, lucha; *(quarrel)* riña, disputa; *(physical conflict)* pelea; DEP. *(boxing match)* pelea; *(wrestling match)* combate, lucha; *(bellicosity)* combatividad *f* ◆ **in a fair f.** en una buena lid • **to have a f.** pelearse • **to pick a f.** FAM. *(physically)* provocar a, armar camorra con; *(verbally)* buscar disputa con.

fight·er (fī′tər) s. *(combatant)* combatiente *mf*; *(boxer)* boxeador *m*, pugilista *m*; *(determined person)* luchador *m*; *(plane)* avión de caza *m*.

fighter plane s. AVIA., MIL. avión de caza *m*.

fig leaf m. BOT. hoja de higuera; *(on a statue)* hoja de parra.

fig·ment (fĭg′mənt) s. invención *f* ◆ **f. of one's imagination** producto de la imaginación.

fig·u·ra·tion (fĭg′yə-rā′shən) s. *(shaping)* figuración *f*; *(shape)* forma; *(outline)* contorno; MÚS. contrapunto figurado.

fig·u·ra·tive (fĭg′yər-ə-tĭv) adj. *(metaphorical)* figurativo, metafórico; *(ornate)* florido.

fig·ure (fĭg′yər) **I.** s. *(number)* número, cifra; *(amount)* precio, valor *m* <*it sold for a large f.* se vendió a un precio muy alto>; *(outline)* figura, perfil *m*; *(body)* figura, cuerpo; *(statuette)* figura, estatua; *(diagram)* diagrama, diseño; *(illustration)* ilustración *f*, dibujo; *(personage)* figura, personaje *m*; *(in dance)* figura, mudanza; LÓG., MÚS. figura; *(object)* forma, silueta <*figures in the distance* siluetas en la distancia> ◆ **figures** cálculos, operaciones aritméticas • **in round figures** en números redondos • **to be good at figures** ser fuerte en aritmética, ser bueno para los números • **to cut a (good, bad, poor) f.** causar una (buena, mala, pobre) impresión • **to keep one's f.** guardar la línea **II.** tr. **-ured, -ur·ing** *(to compute)* computar, calcular; *(to depict)* figurar, representar; *(to adorn)* adornar con un diseño o figuras; FAM. *(to reckon)* imaginar(se), figurar(se) <*I never figured that would happen* nunca me imaginé que pasaría eso>; *(to regard)* considerar; *(to see)* ver <*that's how I f. it* así es cómo lo veo yo> • **to f. out** *(to decipher)* descifrar; *(to solve)* resolver; *(to deduce)* deducir; *(to compute)* computar, calcular; *(to understand)* comprender —intr. *(to compute)* hacer cálculos; *(to appear)* figurar, encontrarse <*her name figured at the top of the list* su nombre figuró a la cabeza de la lista> ◆ **to f. as** pasar por • **to f. on** FAM. contar con <*I had not figured on that* no contaba con eso>.

fig·ured (fĭg′yərd) adj. *(shaped)* formado; *(patterned)* decorado con figuras; *(represented)* representado, figurado.

fig·ure·head (fĭg′yər-hĕd′) s. *(leader)* testaferro; MARÍT. mascarón de proa *m*.

figure of speech s. RET. figura retórica, manera de hablar.

figure skating s. patinaje artístico.

fig·u·rine (fĭg′yə-rēn′) s. estatuilla.

Fiji (fē′jē) s. Fiji.

Fijian (fē′jē-ən) adj. de Fiji.

fil·a·gree (fĭl′ĭ-grē′) s. var. de filigree.

fil·a·ment (fĭl′ə-mənt) s. *(fiber)* filamento; *(thread)* hilaza; BOT., ELEC. filamento.

fil·a·men·tous (fĭl′ə-mĕn′təs) adj. filamentoso.

fil·bert (fĭl′bərt) s. BOT. *(tree)* avellano; *(nut)* avellana.

filch (fĭlch) tr. hurtar, robar.

file¹ (fīl) **I.** s. *(for paper, documents)* archivo; *(for cards)* fichero; *(card)* ficha; *(dossier)* expediente *m*; *(folder)* carpeta; MIL. fila, columna ◆ **in single f.** en fila de a uno, en fila india • **to be on f.** estar archivado, estar registrado **II.** tr. **filed, fil·ing** *(to keep in order)* archivar; *(to put in order)* clasificar, ordenar ◆ **to f. a complaint** sentar una denuncia • **to f. a claim** entablar un reclamo • **to f. a complaint** sentar una denuncia • **to f. an appeal** presentar una apelación • **to f. a petition** presentar una petición o solicitud • **to f. a suit** entablar un juicio —intr. marchar en fila ◆ **to f. by** *(parade, troop)* desfilar; *(in a single line)* pasar uno por uno • **to f. in** entrar en fila • **to f. out** salir en fila.

file² (fīl) **I.** s. *(tool)* lima **II.** tr. **filed, fil·ing** limar.

file clerk s. archivista *mf*.

fi·let¹ (fĭ-lā′, fĭl′ā′) s. encaje de malla cuadrada *m*.

fi·let² (fĭ-lā′, fĭl′ā′) s. filete (de carne, ave, pescado).

fil·i·al (fĭl′ē-əl) adj. filial.

fil·i·bus·ter (fĭl′ə-bŭs′tər) **I.** s. *(adventurer)* filibustero; POL. *(obstructionism)* obstruccionismo; *(tactic)* maniobra obstruccionista **II.** POL. intr. valerse de maniobras obstruccionistas —tr. obstruir (moción, propuesta).

fil·i·gree (fĭl′ĭ-grē′) **I.** s. filigrana **II.** tr. **-greed, -gree·ing** afiligranar.

fil·ing (fī′lĭng) s. *(act)* colocación en un fichero o archivo *f*; *(abrasion)* limadura.

Fil·i·pi·no (fĭl′ə-pē′nō) adj. & s. [pl. **-nos**] filipino.

fill (fĭl) **I.** tr. *(to make full)* llenar; *(to plug up)* rellenar, tapar; ODONT. *(a tooth)* empastar; *(to fulfill)* satisfacer, cumplir con <*to f. the requirements* cumplir con los requisitos>; FARM. preparar (receta); *(to staff)* cubrir, llenar (puesto, vacante); *(to discharge the duties of)* ocupar, desempeñar; *(to pervade)* llenar; FIG. *(to occupy completely)* llenar; CONSTR. terraplenar, rellenar; CUL. rellenar; COM. despachar, ejecutar (pedido, orden); MARÍT. hinchar (velas) ◆ **to f. in** *(a form)* llenar; *(to complete)* completar con (información, detalles); CONSTR. terraplenar, rellenar • **to f. out** *(to enlarge)* ensanchar, redondear; *(a form)* completar; COM. despachar, ejecutar (pedido, orden) • **to f. someone in on** poner a alguien al corriente de • **f. someone's shoes** FIG., FAM. ocupar el puesto de alguien • **to f. up** llenar (hasta el tope) —intr. llenarse ◆ **to f. in for someone** reemplazar a alguien • **to f. out** ensancharse, redondearse (cara, cuerpo) • **to f. up** *(to become full)* llenarse; MARÍT. hincharse (velas) **II.** s. *(enough)* hartura, hartazgo; CONSTR. terraplén *m*, relleno ◆ **to have had one's f. of something** estar harto de algo.

fill·er (fĭl′ər) s. *(added material)* relleno; *(tobacco)* tripa; PERIOD. artículo de relleno; ARQ. plancha, lámina.

fil·let (fĭl′ĭt) **I.** s. *(ribbon)* cinta, banda; CUL. *(of meat, fish)* filete *m*; ARQ., IMPR. filete **II.** tr. *(to decorate)* adornar con cintas; CUL. *(to slice)* cortar en filetes.

fill·ing (fĭl′ĭng) s. *(added material)* relleno; ODONT. empaste *m*; CUL. relleno; TEJ. trama.

filling station s. estación de servicio *f*, gasolinera.

fil·lip (fĭl′əp) s. *(blow)* capirotazo; *(snap)* chasquido; *(stimulus)* estímulo.

fil·ly (fĭl′ē) s. [pl. **-lies**] *(young mare)* potranca, potra; FAM. *(lively girl)* muchacha vivaz.

film (fĭlm) **I.** s. *(coating)* película, capa; MED. *(in eyes)* tela, nube *f*; FOTOG. película; CINEM. *(movie)* película, filme *m*; *(cinema)* cine *m*, cinema *m* ◆ **f. festival** festival de cine • **f. library** cinemateca, filmoteca • **f. studio** estudio cinematográfico **II.** tr. *(to cover)* cubrir con una película o capa; CINEM. *(an event)* filmar; *(a scene)* rodar; *(a play, novel)* hacer una versión fílmica de —intr. CINEM. rodar.

film·mak·er (fĭlm′mā′kər) s. cineasta *mf*.

film pack s. paquete de planchas fotográficas *m*.

film·strip (fĭlm′strĭp′) s. tira de película.

film·y (fĭl′mē) adj. **-i·er, -i·est** *(gauzy)* tenue, diáfano; *(transparent)* transparente; *(hazy)* nubloso.

fil·ter (fĭl′tər) **I.** s. filtro **II.** tr. & intr. filtrar(se) ◆ **to f. in** FIG. entrar poco a poco • **to f. out** saberse, trascender.

filter paper s. papel de filtro *m*.

filth (fĭlth) s. *(dirt)* mugre *f*, suciedad *f*; FIG. *(foulness)* corrupción *f*; *(obscenity)* obscenidad *f*.

filth·i·ness (fĭl′thē-nĭs) s. suciedad *f*, inmundicia.

filth·y (fĭl′thē) adj. **-i·er, -i·est** *(dirty)* sucio, mugriento; FIG. *(obscene)* obsceno; *(vile)* de perros, malo.

fil·trate (fĭl′trāt′) **I.** tr. & intr. **-trat·ed, -trat·ing** filtrar(se) **II.** s. filtrado.

fil·tra·tion (fĭl-trā′shən) s. filtración *f*.

fin (fĭn) **I.** s. *(of fish)* aleta; *(of an aircraft)* plano de deriva; *(of a car, engine)* aleta **II.** tr. **finned, fin·ning** equipar con aletas.

fi·na·gle (fə-nā′gəl) JER. **-gled, -gling** agenciarse, conseguir —intr. *(to deceive)* trampear; *(to plot)* tramar.

fi·nal (fī′nəl) **I.** adj. *(last)* último <*the f. syllable* la última sílaba>; *(concluding)* final <*in the f. stage* en la etapa final>; *(unalterable)* definitivo, terminante ◆ **all sales are f.** no se hacen cambios ni devoluciones **II.** s. DEP. *(competition)* final *f*; EDUC. *(exam)* examen final *m*.

ã rey / ä año / b boca / ch chico / d dar / ĕ el / ē mil / g gato / h joya / hw juez / ī aire / k casa / kw cuan /

fi·nal·e (fə-năl′ē, -nä′lē) s. MÚS. final *m*; TEAT. último acto.

fi·nal·ist (fī′nə-lĭst) s. finalista *mf.*

fi·nal·i·ty (fī-năl′ĭ-tē, fə-) s. [pl. **-ties**] *(of a decision)* irrevocabilidad *f; (decisiveness)* carácter definitivo.

fi·nal·ize (fī′nə-līz′) tr. **-ized, -iz·ing** *(to conclude)* finalizar, concluir; *(to complete)* completar.

fi·nal·ly (fī′nə-lē) adv. finalmente, por último.

fi·nance (fə-năns′, fī-, fī′năns′) I. s. finanzas ♦ **finances** finanzas, fondos II. tr. **-nanced, -nanc·ing** financiar.

finance bill s. POL. ley de presupuestos *f.*

finance company s. sociedad *o* compañía financiera.

fi·nan·cial (fə-năn′shəl, fī-) adj. financiero.

fin·an·cier (fĭn′ən-sîr′, fī′nən-) s. financiero, financista *mf.*

fi·nanc·ing (fə-năn′sĭng, fī′-năn′sĭng) s. financiamiento, financiación *f.*

fin·back (fĭn′băk′) s. ZOOL. rorcual *m*, cachalote *m.*

finch (fĭnch) s. pinzón *m.*

find (fīnd) I. tr. **found** (found), **find·ing** *(to encounter)* encontrar; *(to come across)* topar, dar con; *(to recover)* encontrar, hallar <*I found my keys* encontré mis llaves>; *(to discover)* descubrir; *(to arrive at)* dar en <*the dart found the mark* el dardo dio en el blanco>; *(to regard)* encontrar <*I f. her charm irresistible* encuentro su encanto irresistible>; *(to regain)* recuperar, recobrar; DER. *(verdict)* pronunciar, declarar; *(to supply)* proporcionar, proveer; *(to notice)* observar, hallar; *(to surprise)* sorprender ♦ **to be found** encontrarse, existir <*relics like this one are to be found all over South America* reliquias como ésta se encuentran por toda Sudamérica> • **to f. fault with** *(to criticize)* criticar; *(to disapprove)* desaprobar • **f. favor with** *o* **in the eyes of** caer en gracia a, granjearse la buena voluntad de • **to f. oneself** *(to perceive oneself)* verse, encontrarse; *(to discover oneself)* descubrir uno su verdadera identidad • **to f. one's way to** *(to locate)* encontrar el camino a; FIG. *(to be able to)* darse maña para • **to f. out** *(to investigate)* averiguar; *(to discover)* descubrir; *(to learn about)* enterarse de *o* que; *(to expose)* desenmascarar —intr. ♦ **to f. for** DER. fallar a favor de • **to f. out about** informarse sobre II. s. descubrimiento, hallazgo.

find·er (fīn′dər) s. *(person)* hallador *m*; *(discoverer)* descubridor *m*; FOTOG. visor *m*; ASTRON. buscador *m.*

finder's fee s. COM. comisión de intermediario *f.*

find·ing (fīn′dĭng) s. descubrimiento, hallazgo ♦ **findings** *(of research)* resultados; *(of a report)* conclusiones; DER. *(of a court)* fallo.

fine¹ (fīn) I. adj. **fin·er, fin·est** *(superior)* fino, de buena calidad <*f. china* loza fina>; *(skillful)* excelente <*a f. teacher* un maestro excelente>; *(thin)* fino <*f. thread* hilo fino>; *(very small)* pequeño, chico <*f. print* letras chicas>; *(not coarse)* fino <*f. sand* arena fina>; *(delicate)* fino, delicado <*f. lace* encaje fino>; *(said of weather)* agradable, lindo; *(sharp)* agudo, afilado; *(refined)* refinado, fino; *(healthy)* bien <*I'm f., thank you* me encuentro bien, gracias>; *(subtle)* sutil <*f. differences* diferencias sutiles>; *(sensitive)* bueno <*to have a f. eye for color* tener un buen ojo para los colores>; *(said of gold, silver)* fino, puro; *(said of athletes, horses)* muy bien entrenado ♦ **f. and dandy** FAM. *(agreement)* de acuerdo, estupendo; *(very good)* muy bueno • **(it's) f. with me** FAM. estoy de acuerdo • **one f. day** un buen día • **that's f.!** ¡de acuerdo!, ¡está bien! • **you're a f. one!** FAM. ¡eres increíble!, ¡qué tío! II. adv. *(splendidly)* estupendamente; *(minutely)* finamente; FAM. *(very well)* muy bien ♦ **to cut it too f.** FAM. no darse suficiente tiempo III. tr. & intr. **fined, fin·ing** purificar(se).

fine² (fīn) I. s. multa II. tr. **fined, fin·ing** multar, poner una multa a.

fine art s. arte *m* ♦ **fine arts** bellas artes.

fine·ness (fīn′nĭs) s. *(elegance)* fineza, delicadeza; *(excellence)* perfección *f; (thinness)* finura; *(said of gold, silver)* ley *f.*

fine print s. letra menuda (que aparece frecuentemente en los contratos).

fin·er·y (fī′nə-rē) s. [pl. **-ies**] adornos, galas.

fi·nesse (fə-nĕs′) I. s. *(skill)* finura, delicadeza; *(subtlety)* delicadeza, tacto; *(of judgment)* discernimiento; *(in bridge)* impase *m* II. tr. **-nessed, -ness·ing** ♦ **to f. into** lograr por medio de trucos.

fine-toothed comb (fīn′tōōtht′, -tōōthd′) s. *(for hair)* peine de dientes muy finos y juntos *m*; FIG. *(method of investigation)* método de investigación minuciosa.

fine-tune (fīn′tōōn′, -tyōōn′) tr. **-tuned, -tun·ing** afinar, ajustar sutilmente.

fin·ger (fĭng′gər) I. s. *(of hand, glove)* dedo; *(of land)* lengua; *(measure)* dedo; MEC. uña, trinquete *m* ♦ **index f.** (dedo) índice • **little f.** (dedo) meñique • **middle f.** dedo medio *o* del corazón • **ring f.** (dedo) anular • **to get one's fingers burned** cogerse los dedos • **to keep one's fingers crossed** esperar que todo salga bien • **to lift a f.** mover un dedo • **to put one's f. on** *(to touch)* tocar con el dedo; FIG. *(a sore spot)* poner el dedo en (la llaga); *(to determine)* dar con, decir a ciencia cierta • **to wrap someone around one's little f.** JER. hacer con alguien lo que a uno se le antoje II. tr. *(to handle)* tocar, manosear; MÚS. *(to play)* tocar, digitar; JER. *(to inform on)* denunciar; *(a victim)* marcar.

fin·ger·board (fĭng′gər-bôrd′) s. MÚS. diapasón (de un instrumento de cuerda) *m*; *(keyboard)* teclado.

finger bowl s. aguamanil de mesa *m*, lavafrutas.

fin·ger·ing (fĭng′gər-ĭng) s. MÚS. digitación *f.*

fin·ger·nail s. uña.

fin·ger·print (fĭng′gər-prĭnt′) I. s. huella digital II. tr. tomar las huellas digitales.

finger tip *o* **fin·ger·tip** (fĭng′gər-tĭp′) s. punta *o* yema del dedo.

fin·ick·y (fĭn′ĭ-kē) adj. **-i·er, -i·est** *(fussy)* melindroso; *(fastidious)* quisquilloso.

fin·ish (fĭn′ĭsh) I. tr. *(to complete)* acabar, terminar <*when you f. the exam* cuando terminen el examen>; *(a race, journey)* llegar al final de; *(to use up)* acabar con <*to f. a pie* acabar con un pastel>; *(to perfect)* rematar, dar el toque final a; *(to destroy)* acabar con, liquidar <*the recession finished him* la recesión lo liquidó>; TEC. acabar ♦ **to f. off** *(to complete)* acabar, terminar; *(to perfect)* rematar; *(an opponent)* liquidar • **to f. up** acabar, terminar —intr. acabar, terminar ♦ **to f. (first, second)** llegar *o* quedar (en primer, segundo lugar) • **to f. with someone** romper (relaciones) con alguien II. s. *(end)* final *m*, fin *m* <*a close f.* un final reñido>; *(downfall)* ruina; *(finishing touch)* toque final *m*; *(substance)* pulimento; *(perfection)* perfección *f*; TEC. acabado.

fin·ished (fĭn′ĭsht) adj. *(completed)* acabado, completo; FIG. *(polished)* consumado, excelente; *(ruined)* liquidado, arruinado.

fin·ish·er (fĭn′ĭ-shər) s. TEC. *(person)* acabador *m*; *(machine)* acabadora; DEP. competidor que llega a la meta *m.*

fin·ish·ing (fĭn′ĭsh-ĭng) adj. último ♦ **f. touch** último toque, última mano.

finishing school s. colegio para señoritas.

finish line s. DEP. línea de llegada.

fi·nite (fī′nīt′) adj. *(limited)* finito; GRAM. *(verb)* conjugado.

fink (fĭngk) s. JER. *(strikebreaker)* rompehuelgas *mf*; *(informer)* soplón *m*; *(undesirable person)* persona odiosa.

Fin·land (fĭn′lənd) s. Finlandia.

Finn (fĭn) s. finlandés *m.*

Finn·ish (fĭn′ĭsh) adj. & s. finlandés *m.*

fiord (fyôrd) s. var. de **fjord.**

fir (fûr) s. BOT. abeto.

fire (fīr) I. s. *(blaze)* fuego <*to light the f.* encender el fuego>; *(destructive burning)* incendio <*destroyed by f.* destruido por un incendio>; *(ardor)* fuego, pasión *f*; *(of firearms)* fuego; *(of words)* andanada <*a f. of objections* una andanada de reparos>; JOY. *(of a stone)* aguas, resplandor *m* ♦ **heavy f.** MIL. fuego nutrido • **on a slow f.** CUL. a fuego lento • **to add fuel to the f.** FIG. echar leña al fuego • **to be on f.** estar en llamas *o* ardiendo • **to be** *o* **come under f.** FIG. ser blanco de ataques • **to catch f.** encenderse, coger fuego • **to go through f. and water** ir contra viento y marea • **to have f. in one's belly** FAM. tener mucho entusiasmo • **to open f.** abrir *o* romper fuego • **to set on f** *o* **to set f. to** prenderle *o* pegarle fuego a II. tr. **fired, fir·ing** *(to ignite)* prenderle fuego a, encender; *(to add* *fuel to)* alimentar; *(to arouse)* enardecer, inflamar; *(fire-arm, bullet)* disparar; *(a shot)* tirar; *(a rocket)* lanzar; FAM. *(to hurl)* tirar, arrojar; *(a question, insult)* espetar; *(from a job)* despedir, echar; CERÁM. *(to bake)* cocer ♦ **to f. questions at** bombardear a preguntas • **to f. someone with** avivar (el entusiasmo, la ira) de alguien —intr. *(to flame up)* encenderse; MIL. *(to go off)* disparar; *(to shoot)* disparar, hacer fuego *<to f. on the enemy* disparar contra el enemigo> ♦ **to f. away** disparar sin cesar • **to get fired up** FIG. apasionarse.

fire alarm s. alarma de incendio.

fire·arm (fīr'ärm') s. arma de fuego.

fire·ball (fīr'bôl') s. *(burning sphere)* bola de fuego; ASTRON. bólido, meteoro; ARM., FÍS. bola incandescente.

fire·base (fīr'bās') s. MIL. base de fuego *f.*

fire·boat (fīr'bōt') s. barco bomba (contra incendios).

fire bomb s. bomba incendiaria.

fire·brand (fīr'brănd') s. *(burning wood)* tizón *m*, tea; FIG. *(agitator)* agitador *m*, cizañero; MIL. botafuego.

fire·break (fīr'brāk') s. cortafuego, barrera contra incendios.

fire brigade s. cuerpo de bomberos.

fire·bug (fīr'bŭg') s. FAM. incendiario, pirómano.

fire·crack·er (fīr'krăk'ər) s. cohete *m*, petardo.

fire·damp (fīr'dămp') s. MIN. grisú *m*, mofeta.

fire department s. cuerpo de bomberos (en EE. UU.).

fire drill s. ejercicios contra incendios.

fire·eat·er (fīr'ē'tər) s. *(performer)* pirófago (de un circo); FAM. *(belligerent person)* picapleitos *m*, valentón *m*.

fire engine s. camión de bomberos, bomba de incendios.

fire escape s. salida de urgencia *o* de emergencia.

fire extinguisher s. extintor de incendios *m.*

fire·fight·er (fīr'fī'tər) s. bombero.

fire·fly (fīr'flī') s. [pl. **-flies**] luciérnaga, lampíride *m.*

fire·house (fīr'hous') s. MIL. estación de bomberos *f.*

fire hydrant s. boca de incendios.

fire·light (fīr'līt') s. luz del hogar *f*, lumbre *f.*

fire·man (fīr'mən) s. [pl. **-men**] *(firefighter)* bombero; *(of a locomotive)* fogonero.

fire·place (fīr'plās') s. hogar, chimenea *m*; *(hearth)* hoguera; TEC. solera (de un horno).

fire·plug (fīr'plŭg') s. boca de incendios.

fire·pow·er (fīr'pou'ər) s. MIL. potencia de fuego.

fire·proof (fīr'prōōf') I. adj. *(fire-resistant)* a prueba de fuego, refractario; *(incombustible)* incombustible, ininflamable II. tr. hacer incombustible *o* ininflamable.

fire sale s. COM. liquidación por incendio *f.*

fire screen s. pantalla de chimenea.

fire·side (fīr'sīd') s. *(of a fireplace)* lugar cercano a la chimenea *m*; FIG. *(home)* hogar *m*, casa.

fire station s. estación de bomberos *f.*

fire·trap (fīr'trăp') s. edificio susceptible de incendiarse fácilmente *o* con pocos medios de escape.

fire wall s. *(firebreak)* cortafuego; CONST. muro refractario.

fire·wa·ter (fīr'wô'tər) s. JER. aguardiente *m*, licor fuerte *m.*

fire·wood (fīr'wōōd') s. leña.

fire·work (fīr'wûrk') s. fuego de artificio ♦ **fireworks** fuegos artificiales • **there will be fireworks** FIG. se va a armar la gorda.

fir·ing (fīr'ĭng) s. *(detonation)* disparo, descarga; *(shots)* tiroteo, disparos; *(of a rocket)* lanzamiento; *(fueling)* alimentación *f*; *(fuel)* combustible *m*; FAM. *(from a job)* despido; CERÁM. *(baking)* cocción *f.*

firing line s. FIG. *(vanguard)* vanguardia, puesto delantero; MIL. línea de fuego.

firing pin s. ARM. percusor *m*, aguja de percusión.

firing squad s. *(execution)* pelotón de fusilamiento *m*, piquete de ejecución *m*; *(salute)* piquete de salvas.

firm¹ (fûrm) I. adj. **-er, -est** *(soil, muscle)* firme, duro; *(steady)* firme, sólido *<a f. surface* una superficie sólida>; *(voice, decision)* firme; *(prices, offer)* firme; *(sure)* firme, seguro II. adv. firme ♦ **to stand f.** mantenerse firme.

firm² (fûrm) s. COM. firma, casa.

fir·ma·ment (fûr'mə-mənt) s. firmamento, bóveda celeste.

firm·ness (fûrm'nĭs) s. *(stability)* firmeza, estabilidad *f*; FIG. *(resolution)* resolución *f*, entereza.

first (fûrst) I. adj. *(before all others)* primero *<January is the f. month of the year* enero es el primer mes del año>; *(elementary)* elemental, primario; *(outstanding)* sobresaliente, excelente; *(best)* primero *<f. class* primera clase>; *(principal)* principal; AUTO. primera; MÚS. primero *<f. voice* primera voz> ♦ **at f. hand** de primera mano • **at f. glance** a primera vista • **at f. sight** a primera vista • **f. move** *o* **f. play** salida (en ciertos juegos) • **in the f. place** en primer lugar • **not to know the f. thing about** no saber absolutamente nada de II. adv. *(before all others)* primero *<the trainer dived f.* el entrenador se zambulló primero>; *(before anything else)* primero, antes *<you must finish your dinner f.* tienes que terminar tu cena antes>; *(firstly)* en primer lugar, primero *<f., let me tell you what I think* en primer lugar, déjeme decirle lo que pienso>; *(for the first time)* por primera vez *<when I f. met you, we were in Rome* cuando te conocí por primera vez, estábamos en Roma> ♦ **at f.** en un principio • **f. and foremost** antes que nada, ante todo • **f. of all** ante todo, antes que nada • **to go f.** ser el primero III. s. primero *<he is the f. in his class* él es el primero de la clase>; *(of the month)* primero; *(beginning)* principio; AUTO. primera ♦ **from the very f.** desde el principio • **to be the f. to** ser el primero en.

first aid s. primeros auxilios.

first-born (fûrst'bôrn') adj. & s. primogénito.

first-class (fûrst'klăs') I. adj. *(accommodations, ticket)* de primera clase; *(first-rate)* de primera calidad II. adv. en primera *<to travel f.* viajar en primera>.

first cousin s. primo hermano.

first floor s. *(ground floor)* primer piso, planta baja (en EE. UU.); G.B. el piso encima de la planta baja.

first·hand (fûrst'hănd') adv. & adj. de primera mano.

first lady s. *(foremost woman)* la mujer más destacada; POL. primera dama.

first lieutenant s. MIL. teniente primero.

first·ly (fûrst'lē) adv. en primer lugar, primeramente.

first mate s. MARÍT. segundo oficial.

first name s. *(primer)* nombre *m*, nombre de pila.

first night s. TEAT. noche de estreno *f*, estreno.

first offender s. DER. persona que comete un delito por primera vez.

first papers s.pl. EE. UU. solicitud de nacionalización *f.*

first person s. GRAM., LIT. primera persona.

first-rate (fûrst'rāt') I. adj. de primera clase II. adv. FAM. muy bien.

First World s. DIPL., POL. Primer Mundo (países industrializados no comunistas).

First World War s. HIST. Primera Guerra Mundial.

firth (fûrth) s. *(estuary)* estuario; *(fjord)* fiordo.

fisc (fĭsk) s. COM. fisco, hacienda pública.

fis·cal (fĭs'kəl) s. & adj. fiscal *m.*

fiscal year s. COM. año fiscal, año presupuestario.

fish (fĭsh) s. [pl. **fish** *o* **fish·es**] ICT. *(in the water)* pez *m*; CUL. *(food)* pescado ♦ **a cold f.** FIG., FAM. persona sin sentimientos • **a fine kettle of f.** FIG., FAM. bonito lío • **F.** ASTROL. Piscis • **like a f. out of water** FIG., FAM. como pez fuera del agua • **neither f. nor fowl** FIG. ni chicha ni limonada • **to drink like a f.** FIG., FAM. beber con exceso • **to have other f. to fry** FIG., FAM. tener otras cosas en que ocuparse II. intr. *(to catch)* pescar; FIG. *(to search)* buscar algo ♦ **to f. for** FIG. andar a la pesca de (cumplidos, halagos) • **to f. in troubled waters** FIG. pescar en río revuelto • **to go fishing** ir de pesca —tr. *(to catch)* pescar; FIG. *(to pull)* buscar *o* sacar (algo de un bolsillo, cartera) ♦ **to f. out** agotar los peces en (un lago, río).

fish bait s. cebo para pescar, carnada.

fish·bone (fĭsh'bōn') s. espina de pescado.

fish·bowl *o* **fish bowl** (fĭsh'bōl') s. *(aquarium)* pecera; FIG. *(place)* vidriera.

fish·er (fĭsh'ər) s. *(one that fishes)* pescador *m.*

fish·er·man (fĭsh'ər-mən) s. [pl. **-men**] *(person)* pescador *m*; *(boat)* barco pesquero.

fish·er·y (fĭsh'ə-rē) s. [pl. **-ies**] *(industry)* pesca; *(fishing place)* pesquería, zona pesquera; *(hatchery)* vivero.

fish·eye (fĭsh'ī') adj. FOTOG., ÓPT. de ángulo plano, de 180°.

fish farm s. piscifactoría, vivero.
fish hatchery s. piscifactoría, vivero.
fish hawk s. ORNIT. halieto, pigargo.
fish·hook (fĭsh′hŏŏk′) s. anzuelo.
fish·ing (fĭsh′ĭng) s. *(act)* pesca; *(place)* pesquería, zona de pesca.
fishing ground s. zona de pesca.
fishing rod s. caña de pescar.
fish·mar·ket (fĭsh′mär′kĭt) s. pescadería.
fish·mon·ger (fĭsh′mŭng′gər) s. G.B. pescadero.
fish·net (fĭsh′nĕt′) s. *(fishing net)* red f; *(mesh fabric)* material tejido como una red.
fish·pond (fĭsh′pŏnd′) s. estanque con pesca abundante m.
fish scale s. ICT. escama.
fish story s. FAM. *(implausible tale)* cuento exagerado.
fish·tail (fĭsh′tāl′) I. adj. como cola de pescado II. intr. colear.
fish·wife (fĭsh′wīf′) s. [pl. **-wives** (-wīvz′)] *(woman seller)* pescadera; FAM. *(shrew)* verdulera, mujer gritona.
fish·y (fĭsh′ē) adj. **-i·er, -i·est** *(like a fish)* a pescado; FIG., FAM. *(cold)* frío <a f. stare una mirada fría>; *(suspicious)* sospechoso.
fis·sile (fĭs′əl, -īl′) adj. *(capable of being split)* fisible, escendible; FÍS. fisionable, físil.
fis·sion (fĭsh′ən) s. *(act)* fisión f, escisión f; FÍS. fisión nuclear; BIOL. fisión, segmentación celular f.
fis·sion·a·ble (fĭsh′ə-nə-bəl) adj. FÍS. fisionable.
fission bomb s. FÍS. bomba atómica.
fis·sure (fĭsh′ər) I. s. *(crack)* fisura, grieta; ANAT. fisμra II. tr. & intr. **-sured, -sur·ing** fisurar.
fist (fĭst) s. *(of a hand)* puño; FAM. *(grasp)*· garras, manos; IMPR. manecilla ♦ **to shake one's f. at** amenazar con el puño.
fist·fight (fĭst′fīt′) s. pelea a puñetazos.
fist·ful (fĭst′fŏŏl′) s. [pl. **-fuls**] puñado.
fist·i·cuffs (fĭs′tĭ-kŭfs′) s.pl. *(fistfight)* pelea a puñetazos; *(boxing)* boxeo.
fit¹ (fĭt) I. tr. **fit·ted** *o* **fit, fit·ted, fit·ting** entrar en <this ring does not f. my finger este anillo no me entra en el dedo>; colocar, meter <I can't f. this ring on my finger no puedo meterme este anillo en el dedo>; CARP., CONSTR., MEC. ajustar, encajar en; *(to match)* ajustar, amoldar <let the punishment f. the crime que el castigo se ajuste al crimen>; *(to qualify)* preparar, capacitar; *(to affix)* colocar a *o* en <to f. a handle on a door colocar una manija a una puerta>; COST. *(to alter)* ajustar, entallar; *(to measure)* tomar las medidas; *(to be suitable)* sentar bien <that jacket fits you ese saco te sienta bien> ♦ **to f. in** ver, atender <the doctor can f. you in today el doctor lo puede ver hoy>; tener tiempo para <can you f. in another interview today? ¿tendrás tiempo hoy para otra entrevista?> ♦ **to f. on** COST. probar (vestido, prenda) • **to f. out** *(to equip)* equipar, proveer; MARÍT. *(a ship)* armar • **to have a garment fitted** COST. hacerse arreglar una prenda —intr. caber <this book does not f. in the satchel este libro no cabe en la cartera>; CARP., CONSTR., MEC. ajustar, encajar <the parts f. well las piezas encajan bien>; *(to agree)* concordar <their answers don't f. sus respuestas no concuerdan>; *(to adapt)* ajustar(se), adaptar(se); COST. *(to alter)* entallar, ajustar; *(to be suitable)* sentar bien <this jacket fits well este saco me sienta bien> ♦ **it all fits together now** ahora está todo claro, ahora lo veo todo claro • **to f. in** *o* **into** encajar *o* caber en • **to f. in with** *(said of people)* congeniar con; *(said of things)* cuadrar, estar de acuerdo con • **to f. to a T** FAM. quedar como anillo al dedo II. adj. **fit·ter, fit·test** *(opportune)* oportuno, conveniente; *(healthy)* en buen estado físico, sano; *(competent)* competente, idóneo; *(suitable)* apropiado, digno <a meal f. for a king una comida digna de un rey> ♦ **do as you see f.** haga lo que mejor le parezca oportuno • **f. as a fiddle** FIG., FAM. sano como una manzana • **f. to be tied** FIG., FAM. fuera de sí • **to keep f.** mantenerse en buen estado físico • **to see f.** juzgar conveniente III. s. *(said of things)* ajuste m, encaje m; *(said of clothes)* corte m, entalladura ♦ **tight f.** COST. estrecho.
fit² (fĭt) s. MED. *(sudden attack)* ataque m; *(convulsion)* con-

vulsión f; FIG. *(sudden outburst)* ataque <a f. of jealousy un ataque de celos> ♦ **by fits and starts** a tropezones.
fit·ful (fĭt′fəl) adj. intermitente, irregular.
fit·ness (fĭt′nĭs) s. *(appropriateness)* propiedad f; *(suitability)* conveniencia; *(aptitude)* aptitud f; *(healthiness)* salud f, estado físico.
fit·ted (fĭt′ĭd) adj. *(person)* apto, capacitado; COST. *(clothes)* entallado; *(suit)* hecho a la medida.
fit·ter (fĭt′ər) s. COST. probador m; MEC. ajustador m, montador m.
fit·ting (fĭt′ĭng) I. adj. *(appropriate)* apropiado, oportuno <a f. remark una observación oportuna>; *(proper)* propio, justo <it was f. that he won the contest fue justo que él ganara el concurso> II. s. *(of clothes)* prueba; *(machine part)* parte suelta ♦ **fittings** *(fixtures)* accesorios, guarniciones; *(furnishings)* mobiliario, muebles.
five (fīv) s. & adj. cinco ♦ **f. o'clock** las cinco.
five-and-ten (fīv′ən-tĕn′) *o* **five-and-dime** (-dīm′) s. tienda que vende artículos varios y baratos.
five·fold (fīv′fōld′) adj. *(of five parts)* quíntuple; *(five times as many or much)* quintuplicado.
five hundred s. & adj. quinientos.
fix (fĭks) I. tr. *(to repair)* reparar, componer; *(to fasten)* fijar, asegurar; *(to direct)* fijar, clavar <he fixed his eyes on her clavó sus ojos en ella>; *(to establish)* decidir, fijar <let's f. a time fijemos una hora>; *(to arrange)* arreglar (el cabello); *(to prepare)* preparar <she fixed dinner in ten minutes preparó le cena en diez minutos>; *(to spay)* castrar; FOTOG., QUÍM. fijar; FAM. *(to get even with)* ajustarle las cuentas a; *(to tamper with)* arreglar <to f. a horse race arreglar una carrera de caballos>; *(to solve)* resolver, solucionar ♦ **to f. up** FAM. *(to mend)* reparar, componer; *(to arrange)* organizar; *(to put in order)* arreglar, acomodar —intr. fijarse ♦ **to f. on** *o* **upon** decidir, elegir II. s. *(predicament)* apuro, aprieto; AVIA., MARÍT., RAD. posición f; *(bribery)* soborno; JER. *(dose)* dosis de narcótico f ♦ **to be in a f.** FAM. verse en un aprieto.
fix·ate (fĭk′sāt′) tr. **-at·ed, -at·ing** *(eyes, attention)* fijar; PSIC. obsesionar —intr. *(eyes, attention)* fijarse, concentrarse; PSIC. obsesionarse.
fix·a·tion (fĭk-sā′shən) s. fijación f.
fix·a·tive (fĭk′sə-tĭv) s. fijador m.
fixed (fĭkst) adj. *(unwavering)* fijo <a f. idea una idea fija>; *(stationary)* estacionario; FAM. *(prearranged)* arreglado <the fight was f. la pelea estaba arreglada>; QUÍM. estable.
fixed-point (fĭkst′point′) adj. MAT. de coma decimal fija.
fix·er (fĭk′sər) s. FOTOG., QUÍM. fijador m, fijativo m; FAM. *(briber)* sobornador m; JER. *(pusher)* vendedor ilegal de drogas m.
fix·ings (fĭk′sĭngz) s.pl. FAM. *(accesories)* accesorios, adornos; CUL. guarniciones f.
fix·ture (fĭks′chər) s. *(installation)* instalación fija; *(appliance)* accesorio, artefacto <an electrical f. un artefacto eléctrico>; *(fixing)* arreglo.
fizz (fĭz) I. intr. hacer sonido típico de la efervescencia, burbujear II. s. *(sound)* sonido de efervescencia; *(effervescence)* efervescencia; *(beverage)* bebida efervescente.
fiz·zle (fĭz′əl) I. s. FAM. fracaso, fiasco II. intr. **-zled, -zling** hacer el sonido típico de la efervescencia, burbujear ♦ **to f. out** FAM. quedarse sin energía.
fjord (fyôrd) s. fiordo.
flab (flăb) s. FAM. carne *o* piel fláccida.
flab·ber·gast (flăb′ər-găst′) tr. FAM. asombrar, dejar pasmado *o* atónito.
flab·bi·ness (flăb′ē-nĭs) s. *(limpness)* blandura, flojedad (de músculos) f; *(frailty)* flaqueza, debilidad f.
flab·by (flăb′ē) adj. **-bi·er, -bi·est** *(limp)* fláccido; *(ineffectual)* debilucho.
flac·cid (flăk′sĭd, flăs′ĭd) adj. fláccido.
flack (flăk) I. s. agente de prensa m II. intr. actuar como un agente de prensa.
flag¹ (flăg) I. s. *(banner)* bandera; *(flagship)* buque insignia m; *(masthead)* mástil (de un periódico) m; MÚS. *(cross stroke)* rabo ♦ **f. of surrender** bandera de capitulación *o* rendición • **red f.** bandera roja *o* de peligro • **to keep the f. flying** mantener alto el pabellón • **to pledge allegiance**

to the f. jurar (fidelidad) a la bandera **II.** tr. **flagged, flag·ging** *(to mark)* marcar (con una señal); *(to signal to stop)* hacer parar con señales a (taxi, autobús) ♦ **to f. someone down** detener a alguien haciendo señales.

flag² (flăg) intr. **flagged, flag·ging** *(to hang limply)* colgar fláccidamente; *(to weaken)* debilitarse; *(to falter)* disminuir <*the conversation flagged noticeably* la conversación disminuyó en forma obvia>.

flag³ (flăg) s. *(stone)* lastra, losa.

flag⁴ (flăg) s. BOT. lirio cárdeno.

Flag Day s. EE. UU. día de la bandera (14 de junio) *m.*

flag·el·lant (flăj′ə-lənt, flə-jěl′ənt) s. flagelante *mf.*

flag·el·late (flăj′ə-lāt′) **I.** tr. **-lat·ed, -lat·ing** flagelar **II.** adj. BIOL. flagelado.

flag·el·la·tion (flăj′ə-lā′shən) s. flagelación *f.*

flag·man (flăg′mən) s. [pl. **-men**] *(bearer)* abanderado; *(railway guard)* guardavía *m.*

flag of truce s. bandera blanca de tregua.

flag·on (flăg′ən) s. jarra grande, pichel *m.*

flag·pole (flăg′pōl′) s. mástil *m,* asta *m.*

fla·gran·cy (flā′grən-sē) s. descaro.

fla·grant (flā′grənt) adj. *(glaring)* descarado; *(shocking)* escandaloso; ANT. *(flaming)* ardiente.

flag·ship (flăg′shĭp′) s. COM. casa central; MARÍT., MIL. buque bandera *m,* buque insignia.

flag·staff (flăg′stăf′) s. mástil *m,* asta *m.*

flag·stone (flăg′stōn′) s. lastra; losa.

flag·wav·ing (flăg′wā′vĭng) s. patriotería.

flail (flāl) **I.** s. AGR. mayal *m* **II.** tr. *(to thresh)* desgranar; *(to thrash)* golpear; *(to wave)* agitar —intr. agitarse.

flair (flâr) s. *(natural talent)* don *m,* talento; *(distinctive style)* cachet *m,* elegancia.

flak (flăk) s. MIL. artillería antiaérea; FAM. *(criticism)* crítica excesiva.

flake (flāk) **I.** s. *(scale)* escama; *(chip)* astilla; *(snowflake)* copo de nieve; JER. persona rara **II.** tr. & intr. **flaked, flak·ing** *(to scale)* escamar(se); *(to chip)* astillar(se); *(to cover with flakes)* cubrir(se) (con escamas o astillas) ♦ **to f. out** JER. quedarse dormido, caer rendido.

flak·y (flā′kē) adj. **-i·er, -i·est** *(scaly)* escamoso; JER. *(eccentric)* raro, loco.

flam·boy·an·cy (flăm-boi′ən-sē) s. rimbombancia.

flam·boy·ant (flăm-boi′ənt) **I.** adj. *(extravagant)* rimbombante; *(resplendent)* resplandeciente; *(highly elaborate)* ornamentado; ARQ. flamígero **II.** s. BOT. framboyán *m.*

flame (flām) **I.** s. *(blaze)* llama; *(combustion)* fuego; *(passion)* pasión *f;* FAM. *(sweetheart)* novio, novia **II.** intr. **flamed, flam·ing** *(to burn)* arder, llamear; *(to shine)* brillar ♦ **to f. up** *(a person)* inflamarse; *(a situation)* estallar —tr. MED., CUL. flamear.

flame·proof (flām′prōof′) **I.** adj. ininflamable, incombustible **II.** tr. hacer incombustible.

flame·re·tard·ant (flām′rĭ-tär′dənt) adj. resistente al fuego.

flame·throw·er (flām′thrō′ər) s. MIL. lanzallamas *m.*

flam·ing (flā′mĭng) adj. *(ablaze)* ardiente; FIG. *(like a flame)* llameante (la mirada); *(ardent)* ardiente (una pasión, un abrazo).

fla·min·go (flə-mĭng′gō) s. [pl. **-gos** o **-goes**] *(color)* anaranjado rojizo; ORNIT. flamenco.

flam·ma·ble (flăm′ə-bəl) adj. inflamable.

flan (flăn) s. CUL. flan *m;* NUMIS. cospel *m,* tejo.

Flan·ders (flăn′dərz) s. Flandes.

flange (flănj) **I.** s. *(rim)* pestaña, reborde *m;* *(of a tube)* brida; *(of a wheel)* pestaña, ceja; *(of a rail)* base *f,* patín *m* **II.** tr. **flanged, flang·ing** rebordear, embridar.

flank (flăngk) **I.** s. *(of an animal)* espaldilla, costado; *(of a hill)* lado; *(of a person)* costado; MIL. flanco **II.** tr. flanquear —intr. lindar con, estar contiguo a.

flan·nel (flăn′əl) s. franela ♦ **flannels** *(trousers)* pantalones de franela; *(underclothing)* ropa interior de franela.

flap (flăp) **I.** s. *(of wings)* aleteo; *(of sails)* gualdrapazo; *(of flags)* ondulación *f;* *(of envelopes)* solapa; COST. *(of pockets)* tapa o cartera; *(of garments)* falda, faldón *m;* *(of hats)* ala; *(of shoes)* oreja; AVIA. alerón *m,* flap *m;* CIR. colgajo; JER. *(commotion)* conmoción *f,* jaleo **II.** tr. **flapped, flap·ping** *(wings)* aletear, batir; *(to flail)* agitar (brazos); *(to*

wave) ondear (banderas); *(to sway)* sacudir; *(to slap)* abofetear —intr. *(to flutter)* aletear, batir; *(to flail)* agitar; *(said of sails)* gualdrapear; *(to sway)* sacudir(se), oscilar.

flare (flâr) **I.** intr. **flared, flar·ing** *(to flame up)* llamear; *(to glow)* brillar; *(to spread outward)* acampanarse, ensancharse ♦ **to f. up** *(in flames)* llamear; *(in anger)* encolerizarse; *(to break out)* estallar, declararse (conflicto, epidemia) —tr. *(to cause to flare)* hacer llamear; *(to signal)* señalar (con luces o fuego) **II.** s. *(flame)* llamarada; *(signal)* señal luminosa; *(outburst)* arrebato; *(spreading outward)* ensanchamiento, ensanche *m;* COST. vuelo; ASTRON. erupción *f;* FOTOG. mancha luminosa.

flare-up (flâr′ŭp′) s. *(of flame)* llamarada repentina; *(of light)* explosión de luz *f;* FIG. *(of anger)* estallido.

flash (flăsh) **I.** tr. *(to emit)* lanzar, despedir (luz); *(to reflect)* reflejar; *(to aim)* dirigir <*f. the light over here* dirige la luz hacia aquí>; FAM. *(to flaunt)* enseñar, hacer ostentación de; *(to exhibit quickly)* enseñar, mostrar rápidamente; TEC. *(to coat)* enchapar, laminar ♦ **to f. a smile at** echar una sonrisa a —intr. *(to sparkle)* brillar, destellar; *(to burst into flames)* llamear, arder llamas; FIG. *(to occur suddenly)* pasar o cruzar como un relámpago <*the idea flashed through his mind* la idea le cruzó la mente como un relámpago>; *(to show anger)* relampaguear <*her eyes flashed with hate* sus ojos relampagueaban de odio> ♦ **to f. by** o **past** pasar como un rayo **II.** s. *(of light)* destello, resplandor *m;* FOTOG. flash *m;* *(perception)* rayo de luz; *(instant)* instante *m,* tris *m* <*in a f.* en un instante>; RAD., TELEV. noticia de último momento; FAM. *(flashlight)* linterna; *(showiness)* ostentación *f* ♦ **a f. in the pan** mucho ruido y pocas nueces • **f. of lightning** relámpago, fucilazo • **like a f.** FAM. como un rayo.

flash·back (flăsh′băk′) s. CINEM., TELEV. escena retrospectiva intercalada en la acción presente.

flash bulb s. FOTOG. lámpara de flash.

flash card s. EDUC. tarjeta con números o letras que se usa en la enseñanza.

flash·cube (flăsh′kyōōb′) s. FOTOG. cubo de flash.

flash·er (flăsh′ər) s. ELEC. destellador *m,* emisor de destellos *m.*

flash flood s. inundación repentina, riada.

flash gun s. FOTOG. disparador de lámparas de destello *m.*

flash·i·ness (flăsh′ē-nĭs) s. ostentación *f.*

flash·ing (flăsh′ĭng) **I.** s. CONST. tapajuntas *m,* cubrejuntas *m* **II.** adj. centelleante, intermitente.

flash·light (flăsh′līt′) s. *(portable lamp)* linterna eléctrica; FOTOG. *(flash)* flash *m,* luz relámpago *f.*

flash point s. FÍS., QUÍM. punto de inflamación.

flash unit s. FOTOG. *(system)* sistema de luz de destello electrónico *m;* *(flash gun)* disparador de destellos *m.*

flash·y (flăsh′ē) adj. **-i·er, -i·est** *(bright)* brillante; FIG. *(showy)* llamativo; *(gaudy)* de relumbrón, chillón.

flask (flăsk) s. *(for pocket)* frasco; *(for gunpowder)* polvorín *m;* QUÍM. matraz *m.*

flat¹ (flăt) **I.** adj. **flat·ter, flat·test** *(level)* plano, llano; *(smooth)* raso; *(prone)* tendido, extendido; *(definite)* categórico, terminante <*a f. refusal* una negativa categórica>; *(fixed)* fijo <*a f. rate* una tarifa fija>; *(dull)* aburrido, monótono; *(tasteless)* insípido, soso; *(without bubbles)* sin efervescencia; *(deflated)* desinflado (neumático); FIN. parado, poco activo (mercado); FOTOG., IMPR., PINT. *(uniform)* uniforme, sin contraste; *(matte)* mate, sin brillo; MÚS. bemol <*E f. major* mi bemol mayor>; *(below pitch)* desafinado ♦ **as f. as a pancake** FIG., FAM. liso como la palma de la mano • **f. nose** nariz chata o aplastada **II.** adv. **flat·ter, flat·test** *(horizontally)* horizontalmente, de plano <*he fell f. on the floor* cayó al piso de plano>; FIG. *(completely)* sin más ni más, terminantemente <*he turned the offer down f.* rechazó sin más ni mas la oferta>; *(exactly)* <*he ran the marathon in three hours f.* corrió la maratón en tres horas justas>; MÚS. desafinadamente; FIN. sin intereses ♦ **to be f. broke** FAM. no tener un centavo • **to go f. out** ir a toda velocidad • **to sing** o **play f.** desafinar, desentonar **III.** s. *(expanse)* llanura, llano; *(plane)* plano, superficie *f;* *(seed box)* semillero de cajón; TEAT. bastidor *m*; *(flatcar)* vagón de plataforma *m*; MARÍT. chata; *(tire)* neumático desinflado, pinchazo; *(shoe)* zapato bajo; MÚS. bemol *m* ♦ **the f. of the hand** la palma de la mano **IV.** tr. *(to flatten)* allanar, aplastar; MÚS. bemolar, bajar un semitono —intr. *(to become flattened)* allanar(se), aplastar(se); MÚS. desafinar, desentonar.

flat² (flăt) s. apartamento.

flat·bed (flăt'bĕd') s. camión de carga plano *m*, remolque de plataforma *m*.

flat-bed press s. prensa plana.

flat·boat (flăt'bōt') s. barca chata, chalana.

flat·car (flăt'kär') s. vagón de plataforma *m*, batea.

flat-footed (flăt'fŏŏt'ĭd) adj. *(having flat feet)* de pies planos; *(forthright)* resuelto.

flat·land (flăt'lănd') s. llano, llanura ♦ **flatlands** área formada por llanos, pampa.

flat·ness (flăt'nĭs) s. *(quality)* lo llano; *(expanse)* llanura; *(smoothness)* lisura; *(monotony)* monotonía; *(lack of taste)* insipidez *f*.

flat·ten (flăt'n) **I.** tr. *(to make flat)* achatar; *(to knock down)* derribar, tumbar **II.** intr. achatarse, aplanarse.

flat·ter (flăt'ər) **I.** tr. *(to praise)* adular, halagar; *(to gratify)* halagar; *(to suit)* favorecer <the new hat flatters her el sombrero nuevo la favorece> **II.** intr. emplear lisonjas.

flat·ter·er (flăt'ər-ər) s. adulador *m*, lisonjero.

flat·ter·y (flăt'ə-rē) s. [pl. **-ies**] *(adulation)* adulación *f*, halago; *(excessive praise)* zalamería.

flat·top (flăt'tŏp') s. *(haircut)* corte de pelo cuadrado *m*; MIL. portaaviones *m*.

flat·u·lence (flăch'ə-ləns) s. FIG. *(self-importance)* engreimiento, pomposidad *f*; MED. flatulencia.

flat·u·lent (flăch'ə-lənt) adj. FIG. *(self-important)* engreído, pomposo; MED. flatulento.

flat·ware (flăt'wâr') s. *(tableware)* platos; *(utensils)* cubiertos.

flaunt (flônt) **I.** tr. hacer ostentación de, hacer alarde de <he flaunts his money hace ostentación de su dinero> —intr. *(to show oneself off)* pavonearse; *(to wave)* ondear airosamente **II.** s. ostentación *f*, alarde *m*.

fla·vor (flā'vər) **I.** s. *(taste)* gusto, sabor *m* <mint f. sabor a menta>; *(flavoring)* condimento, aderezo; *(character)* carácter *m*, sabor <exotic f. sabor exótico> **II.** tr. condimentar, aderezar.

fla·vor·ful (flā'vər-fəl) adj. sabroso, gustoso.

fla·vor·ing (flā'vər-ĭng) s. condimento, aderezo.

fla·vor·less (flā'vər-lĭs) adj. insípido, soso.

flaw (flô) **I.** s. *(imperfection)* imperfección *f*, defecto <a f. in his character un defecto en su carácter>; *(error)* falta, error *m* **II.** tr. & intr. poner(se) defectuoso, estropear(se).

flaw·less (flô'lĭs) adj. perfecto, sin defecto.

flax (flăks) s. *(plant)* lino; *(fiber)* fibra de lino; *(color)* color pajizo, amarillo grisáceo.

flax·en (flăk'sən) adj. *(made of flax)* de lino, parecido al lino; *(pale-yellowish)* de color pajizo, amarillo grisáceo; *(blond)* rubio.

flax·seed (flăks'sēd') s. semilla de lino, linaza.

flay (flā) tr. *(to skin)* desollar, despellejar; FIG. *(to strip of money)* despojar; *(to excoriate)* criticar mordazmente.

flea (flē) s. pulga.

flea-bit·ten (flē'bĭt'n) adj. *(covered with fleabites)* picado de pulgas; *(infested with fleas)* infestado de pulgas.

flea market s. mercado de artículos usados.

fleck (flĕk) **I.** s. *(speck)* pinta; *(freckle)* peca **II.** tr. *(to spot)* motear; *(to streak)* vetear.

fled (flĕd) pret. y part. p. de **flee**.

fledge (flĕj) tr. **fledged, fledg·ing** criar (un pájaro hasta que pueda volar) —intr. emplumecer, echar plumas ♦ **to be full-fledged** ser completo, estar hecho y derecho.

fledg·ling *o* **fledge·ling** (flĕj'lĭng) s. *(bird)* pajarito; FIG. *(novice)* novato.

flee (flē) intr. **fled** (flĕd), **flee·ing** *(to run away)* huir, escaparse; *(to vanish)* desvanecerse —tr. *(to run away from)* huir de, escapar de; *(to shun)* evitar.

fleece (flēs) **I.** s. *(wool)* lana; *(sheared wool)* vellón *m*; *(lining material)* muletón *m* **II.** tr. **fleeced, fleec·ing** *(to*

shear) esquilar; *(to cover with fleece)* cubrir con lana; FIG. *(to rob)* desplumar, pelar.

fleec·y (flē'sē) adj. **-i·er, -i·est** lanudo.

fleet¹ (flēt) s. *(of boats)* flota; *(of cars)* escuadra; MIL. armada, fuerza naval.

fleet² (flēt) **I.** adj. **-er, -est** *(rapid)* rápido, ligero; *(ephemeral)* efímero **II.** intr. *(to move swiftly)* apresurarse, pasar *o* moverse velozmente; *(to vanish)* desaparecer —tr. hacer pasar rápidamente.

Fleet Admiral s. Almirante de la Armada Nacional *m*.

fleet·ing (flē'tĭng) adj. *(passing quickly)* fugaz; *(ephemeral)* efímero.

Flem·ing (flĕm'ĭng) s. flamenco.

Flem·ish (flĕm'ĭsh) **I.** adj. flamenco, natural de Flandes **II.** s. *(language)* flamenco.

flesh (flĕsh) **I.** s. *(of people, animals)* carne *f*; *(fat)* gordura, grasa; *(of fruits)* pulpa; *(of vegetables)* parte comestible *m*; *(humanity)* género humano, humanidad *f*; *(kin)* parentesco **II.** tr. *(to feed)* encarnar; *(to fill out)* rellenar; *(to skin)* descarnar —intr. ♦ **to f. out** engordar.

flesh and blood s. *(human nature)* naturaleza humana; *(kin)* parentela, sangre *f*.

flesh·ly (flĕsh'lē) adj. **-li·er, -li·est** *(corporeal)* corpóreo; *(carnal)* carnal, sensual; *(fleshy)* carnudo, carnoso.

flesh wound s. herida superficial.

flesh·y (flĕsh'ē) adj. **-i·er, -i·est** *(of flesh)* de carne, carnoso; *(fat)* gordo, corpulento; *(pulpy)* carnoso, pulposo.

flew (flōō) pret. de **fly¹**.

flex (flĕks) **I.** tr. & intr. doblar(se), encorvar(se) **II.** s. G.B. cable de electricidad *m*.

flex·i·bil·i·ty (flĕk'sə-bĭl'ĭ-tē) *o* **flex·i·ble·ness** (flĕk'sə-bəl-nĭs) s. flexibilidad *f*.

flex·i·ble (flĕk'sə-bəl) adj. *(pliable)* flexible; *(tractable)* dócil; *(adaptable)* adaptable.

flex·or (flĕk'sər) s. ANAT. músculo flexor.

flick¹ (flĭk) **I.** s. *(light blow)* golpecito; *(sound)* chasquido, ruido ligero; *(splash)* salpicadura ligera ♦ **with a f. of the fingers** de un capirotazo **II.** tr. *(to hit)* golpear rápida y ligeramente; *(to snap)* dar un golpecito a <to f. the switch dar un golpecito al interruptor>; *(to remove)* quitar *o* sacar de golpe —intr. moverse bruscamente.

flick² (flĭk) s. FAM. *(film)* película, filme *m*.

flick·er (flĭk'ər) **I.** intr. *(to flutter)* revolotear, aletear; *(to burn unsteadily)* parpadear, titilar —tr. hacer oscilar *o* temblar **II.** s. *(tremor)* temblor, estremecimiento; *(wavering light)* luz oscilante *f*.

fli·er (flī'ər) s. *(pilot)* aviador *m*; *(circular)* volante *m*; *(step)* escalón *m*, peldaño; FAM. *(daring venture)* operación arriesgada.

flight¹ (flīt) **I.** s. *(motion)* vuelo, volada; *(distance)* recorrido; *(plane trip)* viaje aéreo, vuelo; ARM. trayectoria; *(flock)* bandada; *(swift movement)* paso fugaz; *(floor)* piso <we live two flights up vivimos dos pisos más arriba>; AVIA. *(squadron)* escuadrilla ♦ **f. formation** AVIA. formación de vuelo • **f. of fancy** vuelo de la imaginación • **f. of stairs** tramo de escalera • **orbital f.** ASTRONÁUT. vuelo orbital • **reconnaissance f.** AVIA. vuelo de reconocimiento • **to take f.** alzar el vuelo **II.** intr. volar en bandadas (los pájaros).

flight² (flīt) s. *(act of fleeing)* huida, fuga.

flight attendant s. *(stewardess)* aeromoza, azafata; *(steward)* aeromozo.

flight deck s. AVIA. *(of a carrier)* cubierta de aterrizaje; *(of an airplane)* compartimiento de pilotaje.

flight·i·ness (flī'tē-nĭs) s. ligereza.

flight·less (flīt'lĭs) adj. incapaz de volar, que no puede volar.

flight·y (flī'tē) adj. **-i·er, -i·est** *(frivolous)* frívolo, ligero; *(capricious)* caprichoso; *(irresponsible)* casquivano; *(skittish)* alocado.

flim·flam (flĭm'flăm') FAM. **I.** s. *(nonsense)* tontería; *(deception)* engaño **II.** tr. **-flammed, -flam·ming** embaucar.

flim·si·ness (flĭm'zē-nĭs) s. *(weakness)* debilidad *f*, endeblez *f*; *(fragility)* fragilidad *f*, falta de consistencia.

flim·sy (flĭm'zē) **I.** adj. **-si·er, -si·est** *(light)* ligero; *(insub-*

stantial) insubstancial; *(weak)* débil, endeble; *(unconvincing)* flojo **II.** s. [pl. **-sies**] papel cebolla *m*, papel de seda.

flinch (flĭnch) **I.** intr. *(to wince)* sobresaltarse; *(to retreat)* retroceder, recular **II.** s. reculada.

fling (flĭng) **I.** tr. **flung** (flŭng), **fling·ing** *(to throw)* arrojar, tirar; *(to toss aside)* abandonar; *(to toss down)* echar ♦ **to f. about** *o* **around** *(to wave)* agitar (brazos); *(to squander)* despilfarrar (dinero) • **to f. down** echar al suelo, derribar • **to f. out** echar afuera, despedir —intr. precipitarse, lanzarse **II.** s. *(throw)* lanzamiento; FAM. *(spree)* juerga; *(attempt)* tentativa (breve) ♦ **to have a f.** echar una cana al aire, correrse una juerga.

flint (flĭnt) s. *(quartz)* pedernal *m*; *(hard thing)* cosa muy dura.

flint·lock (flĭnt′lŏk′) s. llave *f o* trabuco de chispa.

flint·y (flĭn′tē) adj. **-i·er, -i·est** *(made of flint)* de pedernal; *(unyielding)* inflexible, inexorable.

flip (flĭp) **I.** tr. **flipped, flip·ping** *(to throw)* lanzar, tirar; *(to toss)* echar (algo al aire) <to f. a coin heads or tails echar a cara o cruz> —intr. *(to strike)* dar golpes ligeros *o* rápidos a; *(to move suddenly)* moverse bruscamente *o* a sacudidas; *(to turn a somersault)* hacer un salto mortal *o* una vuelta de carnero; JER. *(to go crazy)* enloquecer; *(to react enthusiastically)* excitarse, alocarse (de entusiasmo) **II.** s. *(tap)* golpe *m*; *(pull)* tirón *m*; *(shake)* sacudida; *(somersault)* salto mortal, vuelta de carnero **III.** adj. FAM. descarado.

flip-flop (flĭp′flŏp′) s. *(bound)* aleteo; *(somersault)* voltereta hacia atrás sobre las manos; FAM. *(reversal)* cambio brusco; ELECTRÓN. basculador monoestable diferido.

flip·pan·cy (flĭp′ən-sē) s. ligereza, falta de seriedad.

flip·pant (flĭp′ənt) adj. *(lacking seriousness)* ligero, sin seriedad; *(frivolous)* frívolo; *(impertinent)* impertinente.

flip·per (flĭp′ər) s. aleta.

flip side s. reverso (de un disco).

flirt (flûrt) **I.** intr. *(to court)* flirtear, coquetear; *(to take chances)* jugar con <to f. with danger jugar con el peligro>; *(to dream of)* soñar con <to f. with an idea soñar con una idea> **II.** s. *(man)* mariposón *m*, galanteador *m*; *(woman)* coqueta.

flir·ta·tion (flûr-tā′shən) s. flirteo, coqueteo.

flir·ta·tious (flûr-tā′shəs) adj. *(woman)* coqueta; *(man)* mariposón, galanteador.

flit (flĭt) **I.** intr. **flit·ted, flit·ting** revolotear **II.** s. *(darting movement)* movimiento rápido; *(flutter)* revoloteo, aleteo.

flit·ter (flĭt′ər) v. var. de **flutter.**

float (flōt) **I.** tr. *(to buoy)* hacer flotar, poner a flote; COM. *(to establish)* fundar; FIN. *(to release)* emitir, poner en circulación; *(a loan)* negociar (un préstamo); *(currency)* dejar fluctuar (la moneda); CONSTR. *(to smooth)* allanar, alisar; *(to flood)* inundar, cubrir con agua —intr. *(to stay suspended)* flotar, sobrenadar; DEP. *(in swimming)* flotar, hacer la plancha; FIN. *(currency)* fluctuar; *(to wander)* vagar, errar **II.** s. *(something that floats)* flotador *m*; MARÍT. *(buoy)* boya; *(life preserver)* salvavidas *m*; *(platform)* balsa, plataforma flotante; *(pontoon)* flotador (de hidroavión) *m*; ICT. *(air sac)* vejiga natatoria.

floa·ta·tion (flō-tā′shən) s. var. de **flotation.**

float·er (flō′tər) s. *(one that floats)* flotador *m*; *(drifter)* persona sin rumbo fijo.

float·ing (flō′tĭng) adj. *(buoyed)* flotante, boyante; *(unattached)* flotante, variante; COM., MEC., MED. flotante.

floating rib s. ANAT. costilla flotante *o* falsa.

flock¹ (flŏk) **I.** s. *(of birds)* bandada; *(of animals)* manada, rebaño; *(of people)* muchedumbre *f*, multitud *f*; RELIG. rebaño, grey *f* **II.** intr. *(to congregate)* congregarse; *(to travel)* moverse en rebaño.

flock² (flŏk) s. *(tuft)* mechón *m*; *(filling)* borra.

floe (flō) s. témpano *o* masa de hielo flotante.

flog (flŏg) tr. **flogged, flog·ging** azotar, flagelar.

flog·ging (flŏg′ĭng) s. *(beating)* paliza; *(flagellation)* flagelación *f*.

flood (flŭd) **I.** s. *(inundation)* inundación *f*; *(high tide)* pleamar *f*; *(torrent)* torrente *m*; *(floodlight)* luz de faro *o* de proyector *m* ♦ **the F.** RELIG. el Diluvio **II.** tr. *(to inundate)* inundar; *(to fill)* inundar, colmar —intr. inundarse.

flood-gate (flŭd′gāt′) s. compuerta de exclusa.

flood·ing (flŭd′ĭng) s. inundación *f*.

flood·light (flŭd′līt′) s. luz de faro *o* de proyector *m*.

flood plain s. terreno aluvial *o* de aluvión.

flood tide s. *(water)* pleamar *f*; FIG. *(climax)* cumbre *f*, cima.

floor (flôr) **I.** s. *(surface)* piso, suelo; *(of a dance hall)* pista; *(story)* piso <we live on the sixth f. vivimos en el sexto piso>; *(bottom)* fondo <the ocean f. el fondo del océano>; ING. *(platform)* tablero (de un puente, estructura); *(assembly members)* delegados, congresistas *mf* <a motion from the f. una moción de los congresistas>; COM. nivel mínimo ♦ **to ask for** *o* **take the f.** pedir *o* tener la palabra • **top f.** piso alto • **to wipe the f. with** FIG., FAM. pegar una paliza a **II.** tr. *(to cover)* solar, poner suelo a; *(to knock down)* echar al suelo, derribar; FIG., FAM. *(the accelerator)* pisar a fondo; *(to stun)* apabullar, dejar confuso.

floor·board (flôr′bôrd′) s. *(board)* tabla de piso; *(of a vehicle)* piso.

floor·ing (flôr′ĭng) s. *(floor)* piso, suelo; *(material)* material para pisos *m*.

floor lamp s. lámpara de pie.

floor leader s. POL. líder de un partido en el congreso *m*.

floor plan s. CONST. plano de piso.

floor show s. espectáculos (de un cabaret) *m*.

floor·walk·er (flôr′wô′kər) s. COM. superintendente de departamento (en un almacén) *m*.

floo·zy *o* **floo·zie** (flōō′zē) s. [pl. **-zies**] JER. prostituta.

flop (flŏp) **I.** s. *(sound)* sonido sordo; FAM. *(failure)* fracaso, fiasco **II.** tr. **flopped, flop·ping** dejar caer (pesadamente) —intr. *(to fall)* desplomarse, dejarse caer (pesadamente); *(to move about)* agitarse; FAM. *(to fail)* fracasar ♦ **to f. into bed** JER. acostarse, dejarse caer en la cama.

flop·house (flŏp′hous′) s. JER. pensión *f o* posada de mala muerte *f*.

flop·py (flŏp′ē) adj. **-pi·er, -pi·est** FAM. flojo, blando.

floppy disk s. COMPUT. disco flexible (de memoria auxiliar).

flo·ra (flôr′ə) s. flora.

flo·ral (flôr′əl) adj. floral.

Flo·rence (flôr′əns) s. Florencia.

Flo·ren·tine (flôr′ən-tēn′, -tīn′) adj. & s. florentino.

flo·res·cence (flô-rĕs′əns) s. *(flourishing)* florecimiento, prosperidad *f*; BOT. florescencia, floración *f*.

flo·rid (flôr′ĭd) adj. *(rosy)* rojo, colorado (díc. de la cara); *(ornate)* florido, ornamentado.

flo·rist (flôr′ĭst) s. florista *mf*.

floss (flôs) **I.** s. *(waste silk fibers)* cadarzo, borra; *(for embroidery)* seda; *(for the teeth)* seda vegetal **II.** tr. limpiarse (los dientes) con seda dental.

flo·tage (flō′tĭj) s. *(flotation)* flotación *f*; *(flotsam)* pecios, materia flotante.

flo·ta·tion (flō-tā′shən) s. *(act)* flotación *f*; COM. *(launching)* lanzamiento (mediante la venta de acciones); MIN. flotación.

flo·til·la (flō-tĭl′ə) s. *(group)* escuadrón *m* <a f. of taxis un escuadrón de taxis>; MARÍT. flotilla.

flot·sam (flŏt′səm) s. *(odds and ends)* fruslerías; *(drifters)* vagabundos; MARÍT. pecios.

flounce¹ (flouns) COST. **I.** s. volante *m*, cairel *m* **II.** tr. **flounced, flounc·ing** adornar con volantes *o* caireles.

flounce² (flouns) **I.** intr. **flounced, flounc·ing** *(to move)* sacudirse, menearse; *(to flounder)* andar con dificultad, andar a tumbos ♦ **to f. out** salir enfadado **II.** s. sacudida.

floun·der¹ (floun′dər) **I.** intr. *(to wallow)* andar con dificultad; *(to grope)* andar a tientas y a ciegas; *(to fumble in speaking)* trastabillar, enredarse (al hablar) **II.** s. tumbo, tropiezo.

floun·der² (floun′dər) s. ICT., CUL. platija, lenguado.

flour (flour) **I.** s. *(powder)* polvo; CUL. harina **II.** tr. *(to coat)* enharinar; *(to mill)* moler, convertir en harina.

flour·ish (flûr′ĭsh) **I.** intr. *(to prosper)* florecer, prosperar; *(to be in one's prime)* brillar, destacarse; *(to make bold movements)* hacer ademanes teatrales —tr. *(to brandish)* blandir (una espada); *(to wave)* agitar, menear **II.** s. *(act of waving)* agitación *f*, meneo; *(in writing)* rasgo, floreo;

(in a signature) rúbrica; *(gesture)* ademán teatral *m*; MÚS. *(elaborate passage)* floreo; *(fanfare)* toque de trompeta *m*.
flout (flout) I. tr. & intr. burlarse (de) II. s. burla, escarnio.
flow (flō) I. intr. *(to course)* fluir, correr; *(to circulate)* circular; ELEC. correr; *(tears)* correr (lágrimas); *(to pour forth)* manar; MARÍT. subir *o* crecer (la marea); *(to abound)* correr <*wine flowed at the party* el vino corría en la fiesta> ♦ **to f. from** FIG. provenir de • **to f. into** desaguar en, desembocar en • **to f. together** MARÍT. confluir (ríos) —tr. *(to flood)* inundar; *(to cause to flow)* hacer fluir II. s. *(of liquids)* flujo; *(of blood)* circulación (de la sangre) *f*; *(stream)* corriente *f*; *(volume)* caudal *m*; *(of tears)* torrente (de lágrimas) *m*; *(course)* curso; *(movement)* movimiento <*the f. of traffic* el movimiento del tráfico>; *(continuity)* fluidez *f*; FISIOL. menstruación *f*; MARÍT. *(rising tide)* flujo, creciente (de la marea) *f*.
flow chart s. COM., INDUS. diagrama de fabricación *m*.
flow diagram s. COM., INDUS. diagrama de operaciones *m*, diagrama de fabricación.
flow·er (flou'ər) I. s. BOT. flor *f*; FIG. *(the best)* flor y nata, crema; *(peak)* flor <*in the f. of youth* en la flor de la juventud> ♦ **flowers** QUÍM. flor • **in f.** BOT. en flor II. intr. BOT. *(to bloom)* florecer, dar flor; FIG. *(to peak)* alcanzar el máximo —tr. adornar con flores, florear.
flower arrangement s. arreglo floral.
flow·er·ing (flou'ər-ĭng) BOT. I. adj. floreciente II. s. florecimiento, floración *f*.
flow·er·pot (flou'ər-pŏt') s. maceta.
flower shop s. florería.
flow·er·y (flou'ə-rē) adj. florido.
flown (flōn) part. p. de **fly**[1].
flu (flō) s. MED. gripe *f*.
flub (flŭb) I. tr. **flubbed**, **flub·bing** chapucear, echar a perder II. s. chapucería.
fluc·tu·ate (flŭk'chōō-āt') intr. **-at·ed, -at·ing** fluctuar —tr. hacer fluctuar.
fluc·tu·a·tion (flŭk'chōō-ā'shən) s. fluctuación *f*.
flue (flō) s. *(of a chimney)* cañón humero; *(boiler pipe)* tubo de caldera; *(duct)* conducto.
flu·en·cy (flō'ən-sē) s. *(eloquence)* dominio <*his f. in French* su dominio del francés>; *(effortlessness)* fluidez *f*, soltura.
flu·ent (flō'ənt) adj. *(eloquent)* perfecto <*he speaks f. French* habla un francés perfecto>; *(fluid)* fluido, fluyente ♦ **to be f. in** hablar perfectamente, dominar (un idioma).
flu·ent·ly (flō'ənt-lē) adv. *(eloquently)* con soltura <*he speaks French f.* habla el francés con soltura>; *(effortlessly)* con fluidez.
flue pipe s. MÚS. caño del órgano.
fluff (flŭf) I. s. *(down)* pelusa; *(trifle)* bobería, nadería; TEAT. pifia, desliz *m* II. tr. *(to make puffy)* mullir <*to f. a pillow* mullir una almohada>; *(to make light)* esponjar, ahuecar; FAM. *(to err)* echar a perder, chapucear; TEAT. pifiar, recitar mal (el libreto) —intr. volverse mullido.
fluff·i·ness (flŭf'ē-nĭs) s. *(frothiness)* esponjosidad *f*; *(softness)* blandura.
fluff·y (flŭf'ē) adj. **-i·er, -i·est** *(downy)* lleno de pelusa; *(like fluff)* lanoso, velloso; *(soft)* mullido; *(frothy)* esponjoso; *(teased)* batido; *(airy)* vaporoso.
flu·id (flō'ĭd) I. s. fluido, líquido II. adj. *(flowing)* fluido, líquido; *(in measurement)* líquido <*two f. ounces* dos onzas líquidas>; *(pliable)* flexible; *(effortless)* fluido, suelto; *(changeable)* variable.
flu·id·i·ty (flō-ĭd'ĭ-tē) s. *(ability to flow)* fluidez *f*; *(changeability)* variabilidad *f*.
fluid ounce s. onza líquida.
fluke[1] (flōk) s. ICT. lenguado, platija.
fluke[2] (flōk) s. *(of anchor)* uña; *(of arrow)* lengüeta; *(of whale)* aleta (de la cola).
fluke[3] (flōk) s. chiripa, tiro de suerte.
fluk·y *o* **fluk·ey** (flō'kē) adj. **-i·er, -i·est** *(lucky)* afortunado, de suerte; *(shifting)* variable <*a f. wind* un viento variable>.
flum·mox (flŭm'əks) tr. JER. desconcertar, despistar.
flung (flŭng) pret. *y* part. p. de **fling**.
flunk (flŭngk) FAM. I. intr. sacar suspenso, fracasar <*ten students flunked* diez alumnos sacaron suspenso> ♦ **to f.**

out ser expulsado (por malas notas) —tr. *(to fail)* sacar suspenso en, fracasar en <*I flunked the chemistry exam* fracasé en el examen de química>; *(to give a failing grade to)* colgar, suspender ♦ **to f. out** expulsar (por malas notas) II. s. suspenso.
flun·ky (flŭng'kē) s. [pl. **-kies**] lacayo.
flu·or (flō'ôr', -ər) s. MIN. fluorita; *(fluorspar)* espato flúor, floruro cálcico (natural).
flu·o·resce (flō'ə-rěs') intr. **-resced, -resc·ing** emitir luz fluorescente.
flu·o·res·cence (flō'ə-rěs'əns) s. fluorescencia.
flu·o·res·cent lamp (flō'ə-rěs'ənt) s. tubo fluorescente, lámpara de luz fría.
fluor·i·da·tion (flōôr'ĭ-dā'shən, flôr'-) s. fluorización *f*.
fluor·ide (flōôr'īd', flôr'-) s. QUÍM. fluoruro.
fluor·ine (flōôr'ēn', flôr'-) s. QUÍM. flúor.
fluor·o·car·bon (flōôr'ō-kär'bən) s. QUÍM. fluorocarburo.
fluor·o·scope (flōôr'ə-skōp', flôr'-) MED. I. s. fluoroscopia, radioscopia II. tr. **-scoped, -scop·ing** hacer una fluoroscopia de.
flu·or·spar (flō'ôr-spär', flōôr'spär') s. MIN. espato flúor, fluorita.
flur·ry (flûr'ē) I. s. [pl. **-ries**] *(gust)* ráfaga, racha; *(snowfall)* nevisca, nevada ligera; *(bustle)* fiebre *f*, frenesí *m*; FIG. *(shower)* lluvia, granizada <*a f. of blows* una lluvia de golpes>; COM. *(active trading)* actividad repentina (de la bolsa) ♦ **snow flurries** nieve ligera II. tr. **-ried, -ry·ing** *(to agitate)* poner nervioso, inquietar; *(to confuse)* aturdir —intr. caer en ráfagas.
flush[1] (flŭsh) I. intr. *(to flow)* fluir abundantemente; *(to blush)* sonrojarse, ruborizarse; *(to glow)* resplandecer; BOT. echar brotes, brotar —tr. *(to redden)* enrojecer <*exercise flushed her face* el ejercicio le enrojeció la cara>; *(to excite)* exaltar <*flushed with victory* exaltado por la victoria>; *(to clean)* limpiar con agua; *(to make even)* nivelar, emparejar ♦ **to f. the toilet** apretar el botón del inodoro, tirar la cadena II. s. *(gush)* flujo rápido *o* abundante; *(blush)* sonrojo, rubor *m*; *(glow)* resplandor *m*; *(exhilaration)* animación *f*, arrebato; BOT. brote *m* III. adj. *(said of a face)* ruboroso, encendido (dic. de la cara); *(vigorous)* vigoroso, lozano; *(plentiful)* copioso, abundante; *(affluent)* adinerado; IMPR. *(not indented)* alineado al margen, sin sangrar (dic. de la tipografía) ♦ **f. against** contra, pegado a • **f. with** parejo, a nivel con <*hang the picture f. with the window* coloca el cuadro a nivel con la ventana> IV. adv. *(even)* al mismo nivel; *(squarely)* de pleno, directo <*the ball hit him f. in the face* la pelota le dio de pleno en la cara>.
flush[2] (flŭsh) I. tr. hacer salir del escondite a —intr. *(to dart out)* salir corriendo; *(to fly from cover)* salir volando II. s. vuelo repentino (de aves).
flush[3] (flŭsh) s. flux *m* ♦ **royal f.** escalera real • **straight f.** escalera de color.
flus·ter (flŭs'tər) I. tr. & intr. poner(se) nervioso II. s. *(agitation)* nerviosismo, agitación *f*; *(confusion)* aturdimiento, turbación *f*.
flute (flōt) I. s. MÚS. *(instrument)* flauta; *(organ stop)* flautado; ARQ. *(groove in a column)* estría; COST. *(groove in cloth)* pliegue *m*, cañón *m* II. tr. **flut·ed, flut·ing** MÚS. tocar en la flauta; ARQ. estriar, acanalar; COST. plegar, encañonar —intr. MÚS. tocar la flauta.
flut·ing (flō'tĭng) s. ARQ. estriado, acanaladura; COST. encañonado, plisado.
flut·ist (flō'tĭst) s. flautista *mf*.
flut·ter (flŭt'ər) I. intr. *(to flap)* revolotear, aletear; *(to wave)* ondear, ondular <*the curtains fluttered in the breeze* las cortinas ondulaban con la brisa>; *(to vibrate)* vibrar, temblar; *(to beat rapidly)* palpitar; *(to flit)* andar inquietamente ♦ **to f. around** dar vueltas intranquilamente —tr. batir, agitar, mover ♦ **to f. one's eyelashes** parpadear, pestañear II. s. *(flap)* revoloteo, aleteo; *(waving)* ondeo, ondulación *f*; *(wink)* parpadeo, pestañeo; *(agitation)* agitación *f*; MED. *(abnormal pulsation)* palpitación *f*; ELECTRÓN. *(sound distortion)* trémolo, oscilación (del sonido) *f* ♦ **to be in a f.** estar nervioso.
flu·vi·al (flō'vē-əl) adj. fluvial.

---

flux (flŭks) I. s. *(flow)* flujo; MARÍT. *(tidal movement)* flujo; *(flood)* torrente *m*; FÍS. *(fluid movement)* flujo; *(flux density)* densidad de flujo *f*; *(lines of force)* flujo magnético; MED. *(discharge)* flujo; *(fluctuation)* fluctuación *f*, cambio; *(movement)* movimiento; METAL. *(deoxidizer)* desoxidante *m*; *(for minerals)* castina II. tr. *(to melt)* fundir, derretir; METAL. añadir un fundente *o* una castina a —intr. *(to become fluid)* fundirse, derretirse; *(to flow)* fluir.

fly¹ I. intr. **flew** (flo͞o), **flown** (flōn), **fly·ing** volar *<in this hemisphere birds f. south in the winter* en este hemisferio los pájaros vuelan hacia el sur en el invierno>; *(to travel)* viajar en avión, volar *<we flew from New York to Rome* volamos de Nueva York a Roma>; AER. volar; *(to flutter)* flotar (cabello, bandera); *(to flee)* huir, escapar; FAM. *(to hurry)* darse prisa *<I must f. now* debo darme prisa>; FIG. *(to rush by)* pasar, irse volando *<time flew by quickly* el tiempo se fue volando>; *(to shatter)* saltar (chispas, astillas) ♦ **to f. around** FIG. ir de un lado a otro • **to f. at** FIG., FAM. arrojarse *o* lanzarse sobre • **to f. in the face of** FIG. ir contra, hacer frente a • **to f. into a rage** FIG. montar en cólera, encolerizarse • **to f. off the handle** FIG., FAM. perder la chaveta, salirse de las casillas • **to f. open** abrirse repentinamente —tr. *(to cause to fly)* hacer volar; *(to pilot)* pilotear; *(to transport)* transportar en avión; *(to cross)* atravesar *o* cruzar en avión *<he flew the Atlantic many times* cruzó el Atlántico en avión muchas veces>; *(to display)* hacer flamear, desplegar (bandera) ♦ **to f. a kite** elevar una cometa, remontar un barrilete II. s. [pl. **flies**] *(flight)* vuelo; *(of trousers)* bragueta; *(flap)* toldo (de carpa); *(of a flag)* ancho *o* envergadura; *(flywheel)* rueda volante; G.B. *(carriage)* coche de punto *m* ♦ **flies** TEAT. telares.

fly² (flī) s. [pl. **flies**] ENTOM. mosca; DEP. mosca, mosquita.
fly·blown (flī'blōn') adj. *(contaminated)* contaminado con cresas; FIG. *(dirty)* sucio, mancillado.
fly·by (flī'bī') s. [pl. **-bys**] ASTRONÁUT. acercamiento, maniobra de exploración.
fly·by-night (flī'bī-nīt') I. adj. ♦ **a f. operation** una operación poco duradera y digna de poca confianza II. s. engañador *m*.
fly·catch·er (flī'kăch'ər, -kĕch'-) s. ORNIT. cazamoscas *m*, moscareta.
fly·er (flī'ər) s. var. de **flier**.
fly·ing (flī'ĭng) I. adj. *(that flies)* volador *<a f. machine* un aparato volador>; *(swiftly moving)* veloz, ligero *<f. fingers* dedos ligeros>; *(brief)* breve, a la carrera *<a f. visit* una visita a la carrera>; AVIA. de aviación ♦ **f. time** duración del vuelo II. s. AVIA. *(flight)* vuelo; *(navigation)* pilotaje *m*, navegación aérea.
flying boat s. hidroavión *m*.
flying buttress s. ARQ. contrafuerte *m*, arco botarete *m*.
flying colors s. éxito rotundo ♦ **to come through** *o* **off with f.** salir muy bien.
flying fish s. ICT. pez volador *m*.
flying saucer s. platillo volador.
flying start s. DEP. *(speedy takeoff)* salida lanzada; *(quick start)* salida a la carrera ♦ **to get off to a f.** empezar muy bien.
fly·leaf (flī'lēf') s. [pl. **-leaves** (-lēvz')] guarda (de un libro).
fly·o·ver (flī'ō'vər) s. G.B. cruce elevado; AVIA. desfile de aviones *m*.
fly·pa·per (flī'pā'pər) s. papel matamoscas *m*.
fly·speck (flī'spĕk') s. *(stain)* mancha de mosca; FIG. *(minute spot)* puntito.
fly swatter s. matamoscas *m*.
fly·trap (flī'trăp') s. *(trap)* mosquero; BOT. atrapamoscas.
fly·weight (flī'wāt') s. DEP. peso mosca.
fly·wheel (flī'hwēl') s. MEC., TEC. volante *m*.
f-number (ĕf'nŭm'bər) s. FOTOG. número indicador de abertura útil.
foal (fōl) I. s. potro II. intr. parir un potro.
foam (fōm) I. s. espuma II. intr. hacer espuma ♦ **to f. at the mouth** espumajear, rabiar —tr. hacer espumoso.
foam rubber s. espuma de caucho.

foam·y (fō'mē) adj. **-i·er**, **-i·est** *(foamlike)* espumoso; *(covered with foam)* lleno de espuma.
fob¹ (fŏb) s. *(pocket)* bolsillo del reloj; *(chain)* leontina, leopoldina; *(ornament)* dije *m*.
fob² (fŏb) tr. **fobbed**, **fob·bing** ♦ **to f. something off on someone** encajarle algo a alguien.
fo·cal (fō'kəl) adj. focal.
focal length s. FOTOG. distancia *o* longitud focal *f*.
focal point s. FÍS., ÓPT. foco, punto focal.
fo·c's·le (fōk'səl) s. var. de **forecastle**.
fo·cus (fō'kəs) I. s. [pl. **-cus·es** *o* **-ci** (-sī')] FÍS., ÓPT., MAT., MED. foco; FIG. *(center)* foco, centro; GEOL. *(of an earthquake)* epicentro ♦ **in f.** enfocado • **out of f.** fuera de foco, desenfocado • **to bring into f.** enfocar II. tr. *(to produce a clear image)* enfocar; *(to adjust a lens)* ajustar (el objetivo); FIG. *(to concentrate)* concentrar, fijar *<he focused all his attention on the problem* fijó toda su atención en el problema> ♦ **to f. on** *(to consider)* enfocar *<they will f. only on the main issues* enfocarán solamente los problemas principales>; *(to concentrate on)* concentrarse en —intr. enfocarse.
fod·der (fŏd'ər) I. s. AGR. forraje *m*, pienso ♦ **cannon f.** carne de cañón II. tr. dar forraje a.
foe (fō) s. *(enemy)* enemigo; *(opponent)* adversario.
foe·tal (fēt'l) adj. var. de **fetal**.
foe·tid (fē'tĭd) adj. var. de **fetid**.
foe·tus (fē'təs) s. var. de **fetus**.
fog (fŏg) I. s. *(haze)* neblina, niebla; *(sea fog)* bruma; *(daze)* confusión *f*, ofuscamiento; FOTOG. velo ♦ **to be in a f.** estar confundido II. tr. **fogged**, **fog·ging** *(to envelop)* envolver en neblina; *(to cover)* empañar; *(to cause to be obscured)* oscurecer, nublar; *(to bewilder)* confundir; FOTOG. velar —intr. ♦ **to f. up** *(to mist up)* empañarse; *(to be obscured)* nublarse; FOTOG. velarse.
fog bank s. nube de bruma *f*.
fog·bound (fŏg'bound') adj. *(immobilized by fog)* detenido por la niebla; *(clouded by fog)* nublado.
fog·gi·ness (fŏ'gē-nĭs) s. nebulosidad *f*.
fog·gy (fŏ'gē) adj. **-gi·er**, **-gi·est** *(fogbound)* lleno de neblina *o* niebla, neblinoso; *(covered by fog)* empañado; *(indistinct)* vago; *(bewildered)* ofuscado, confundido ♦ **not to have the foggiest idea** no tener ni la más mínima idea.
fog·horn (fŏg'hôrn') s. *(voice)* voz ronca; MARÍT. sirena de niebla.
fo·gy (fō'gē) s. [pl. **-gies**] persona chapada a la antigua.
foi·ble (foi'bəl) s. *(weakness)* punto flaco, debilidad *f*; *(blade section)* parte débil de la hoja de la espada *f*.
foil¹ (foil) I. tr. *(to thwart)* frustrar, hacer fracasar; *(to obscure)* hacer engañoso (pista, rastro) II. s. *(repulse)* fracaso; *(trail)* rastro.
foil² (foil) I. s. *(sheet of metal)* lámina fina de metal; *(contrast)* contraste *m*; *(in mirrors)* azogue *m*; JOY. *(of silver, gold)* pan (de oro, plata) *m*; MARÍT. *(hydrofoil)* hidroplano ♦ **to act as a f. to** servir de contraste a, hacer resaltar II. tr. *(to cover)* enchapar; *(to plate)* azogar; *(to set off)* hacer resaltar, realizar.
foil³ (foil) s. ESGR. florete *m* ♦ **foils** esgrima.
foist (foist) tr. *(to palm off)* empujar, encajar; *(to insert fraudulently)* colar, meter *<they foisted unfair provisions into the contract* colaron cláusulas poco equitativas en el contrato>.
fold¹ (fōld) I. tr. *(to double over)* doblar, plegar; *(to draw together)* cruzar *<f. your arms* cruza los brazos>; *(the hands)* enlazar; *(wings)* plegar, recoger; *(to envelop)* envolver, cubrir ♦ **to f. back** doblar (algo que está al revés) • **to f. down** bajar (asiento de silla, mesa plegadiza) • **to f. in** CUL. incorporar (un ingrediente a otros) • **to f. up** *(to wrap up)* envolver; *(to collapse)* plegar (sillas) —intr. *(to become folded)* doblarse, plegarse; *(to fail)* fracasar *<the business folded soon after it was opened* el negocio fracasó poco después de haberse abierto>; FAM. *(to quit, retire)* darse por vencido, retirarse ♦ **to f. under pressure** doblegarse bajo una presión • **to f. up** *(to become folded)* doblarse, plegarse; *(to fail)* fracasar II. s. *(folding)* doblez *m*, pliegue *m*; *(crease)* arruga; GEOL. pliegue, plegamiento; ANAT. pliegue.

fold² (fōld) **I.** s. *(corral)* redil *m*, corral *m*; *(flock)* rebaño; *(church members)* rebaño, grey *m* **II.** tr. meter en el redil.
fold·er (fōl'dər) s. *(person)* plegador *m*; *(machine)* plegadora; *(booklet)* pliego, folleto; *(file)* carpeta.
fol·de·rol (fŏl'də-rŏl') s. *(nonsense)* tontería, disparate *m*; *(trifle)* chuchería, bagatela.
fold·ing (fōl'dĭng) **I.** adj. plegable ♦ **f. camera** cámara de fuelle • **f. knife** navaja • **f. screen** biombo • **f. seat** traspuntín **II.** s. *(of material)* plegadura; GEOL. plegamiento. IMPR. lámina desplegable.
fold-out (fōld'out') s. IMPR. lámina desplegable.
fo·li·age (fō'lē-ĭj) s. follaje *m*.
fo·li·ate (fō'lē-āt') **I.** adj. BOT. foliado, hojoso **II.** tr. **-at·ed**, **-at·ing** *(metals)* batir; *(a mirror)* azogar; *(book pages)* foliar —intr. BOT. hojear.
fo·li·a·tion (fō'lē-ā'shən) s. BOT. foliación *f*; TEC. azogamiento; IMPR. foliación.
fo·li·o (fō'lē-ō') **I.** s. [pl. **-os**] IMPR. *(sheet of paper)* folio; *(book)* infolio, libro en folio **II.** tr. **-oed**, **-o·ing** foliar, paginar.
folk (fōk) **I.** s. [pl. **folk** o **folks**] *(ethnic group)* pueblo, nación *f* ♦ **country f.** campesinos • **folks** *(people)* gente <*folks will talk* la gente va a hacer comentarios>; FAM. *(relatives)* familia <*I am going to see my f.* voy a ver a mi familia> • **the old folks** los viejos, los padres **II.** adj. popular <*a f. hero* un héroe popular>.
folk dance s. *(dance)* baile folklórico; *(music)* música folklórica.
folk·lore (fōk'lôr') s. folklore *m*.
folk·lor·ic (fōk'lôr'ĭk) adj. folklórico.
folk medicine s. medicina popular.
folk music s. música folklórica.
folk singer s. cantante folklórico.
folk song s. canción popular *f*.
folk·sy (fōk'sē) adj. **-si·er**, **-si·est** *(unpretentious)* campechano; *(affable)* afable.
folk·tale (fōk'tāl') s. cuento tradicional.
fol·li·cle (fŏl'ĭ-kəl) s. ANAT., BOT. folículo.
fol·lies (fŏl'ēz) s.pl. [ú. con v. sing.] TEAT. revista.
fol·low (fŏl'ō) **I.** tr. *(to go after)* seguir <*f. the, usher* siga al acomodador>; *(to chase)* perseguir; *(to go along)* proseguir, continuar por <*f. this road to the next light* continúe por este camino hasta el próximo semáforo>; *(to adhere to)* seguir (doctrina, precepto); *(to obey)* seguir, observar <*f. the rules* observe las reglas>; *(to come after)* seguir a <*night follows day* la noche sigue al día>; *(to work at)* dedicarse a, ejercer; *(to listen to)* prestar atención <*I was too tired to f. the lecture* estaba muy cansado como para prestar atención a la conferencia>; *(to watch closely)* seguir (con ojos, mirada); *(to understand)* comprender <*do you f. me?* ¿me comprendes?> ♦ **to f. one's nose** FAM. ir hacia adelante sin mirar ni a un lado ni a otro • **to f. suit** *(in cards)* jugar el mismo palo; FIG. *(to do likewise)* seguir el ejemplo y hacer lo mismo • **to f. the herd** ir con la corriente, dejarse llevar por la corriente • **to follow through** *o* **up** llevar hasta la conclusión, llevar a cabo —intr. seguir <*they lead and we f.* ellos nos guían y nosotros los seguimos>; *(to infer)* inferirse, deducirse <*from his words it follows that* de sus palabras se deduce que> ♦ **as follows** de la siguiente manera <*it will be done as follows* será hecho de la siguiente manera>; lo siguiente <*she replied as follows* ella contestó lo siguiente>; los siguientes <*the objectives are as follows* los objetivos son los siguientes> **II.** s. *(act)* seguimiento, continuación *f*; *(in billiards)* carambola corrida.
fol·low·er (fŏl'ō-ər) s. *(disciple)* discípulo; *(supporter)* partidario; *(admirer)* admirador *m*; *(pursuer)* perseguidor *m*; *(attendant)* ayudante *mf*; *(subordinate)* subalterno; MEC. *(moving part)* pieza movida por otra pieza.
fol·low·ing (fŏl'ō-ĭng) **I.** adj. *(next)* siguiente; *(to be enumerated)* siguientes <*the f. objects* los objetos siguientes> **II.** s. *(adherents)* adherentes *mf*; *(disciples)* discípulos; *(admirers)* admiradores *m*.
fol·low-through (fŏl'ō-thrōō') s. *(completion)* terminación (de una acción, trato) *f*; DEP. aplicación hasta el final (de un movimiento) *f*.
fol·low-up (fŏl'ō-ŭp') **I.** adj. complementario <*a follow-up*

measure medida complementaria> **II.** s. *(complement)* complemento (de un proceso); *(continuation)* resultado, consecuencia <*a follow-up to his latest success* un resultado de su último éxito>.
fol·ly (fŏl'ē) s. [pl. **-lies**] *(foolishness)* tontería; *(silly idea or action)* disparate *m*; ANT. *(evil)* maldad *f* ♦ **follies** [ú. con v. sing.] revista (teatral).
fo·ment (fō-mĕnt') tr. *(to instigate)* fomentar, instigar; MED. aplicar fomentos.
fo·men·ta·tion (fō'mĕn-tā'shən) s. *(instigation)* fomentación *f*, instigacion *f*; MED. *(treatment)* fomentación *(poultice)* cataplasma.
fond (fŏnd) adj. **-er**, **-est** *(affectionate)* cariñoso; *(tender)* tierno; *(doting)* indulgente; *(cherished)* caro <*my fondest wishes* mis más caros deseos>; *(appreciative)* aficionado a <*he is f. of the opera* es aficionado a la ópera>.
fon·dle (fŏn'dl) tr. & intr. **-dled**, **-dling** acariciar.
fond·ness (fŏnd'nĭs) s. *(affection)* afecto, cariño; *(inclination)* inclinación *f*; *(taste)* afición *f*.
font (fŏnt) s. *(source)* fuente *f*; RELIG. pila (de bautismo); IMPR. fundición (de tipos) *f*.
food (fōōd) s. *(edible material)* comida; *(nourishment)* alimento; *(nutritive material)* nutrimento.
food chain s. ECOL. serie sucesiva de organismos en la que cada uno se alimenta del inmediato anterior *f*.
food poisoning s. MED. intoxicación alimenticia.
food processor s. procesador de alimentos *m*.
food stamp s. estampilla gubernamental que sirve como dinero para comprar alimentos.
food·stuff (fōōd'stŭf') s. producto o material alimenticio.
fool (fōōl) **I.** s. *(unwise person)* tonto, necio; *(jester)* bufón *m*; *(dupe)* simplón *m*, ingenuo; *(enthusiastic person)* loco <*he is a f. for horses* es un loco por los caballos>; ANT. *(idiot)* idiota *mf* ♦ **to make a f. of someone** *(to deceive)* poner a alguien en ridículo; *(to pull someone's leg)* tomar el pelo a alguien **II.** tr. *(to trick)* engañar; *(to surprise)* sorprender —intr. *(to toy with)* jugar <*don't f. with the radio* no juegues con la radio> ♦ **to f. around** *(to play)* jugar (sin propósito); JER. *(to have a sexual affair)* encamarse.
fool·har·di·ness (fōōl'här'dē-nĭs) s. imprudencia.
fool·har·dy (fōōl'här'dē) adj. **-di·er**, **-di·est** temerario, imprudente.
fool·ing (fōō'lĭng) s. broma, chacota ♦ **no f.** hablando en serio • **no f.!** ¡no me digas! • **to be just f.** estar sólo bromeando.
fool·ish (fōō'lĭsh) adj. *(silly)* tonto, absurdo; *(embarrassed)* ridículo <*I feel f.* me siento ridículo>.
fool·ish·ness (fōō'lĭsh-nĭs) s. tontería.
fool·proof (fōōl'prōōf') adj. *(impossible to misuse)* a prueba contra mal uso; *(infallible)* infalible.
fools·cap (fōōlz'kăp') s. *(writing paper)* hoja de papel; *(fool's cap)* gorro de bufón.
fool's cap s. *(jester's hat)* gorro de bufón; *(dunce cap)* sombrero de burro.
fool's errand s. empresa inútil.
fool's gold s. MIN. pirita (de cobre o hierro).
fool's paradise s. *(delusive contentment)* falsa felicidad; *(false hope)* falsa esperanza.
foot (fōōt) **I.** s. [pl. **feet** (fēt)] ANAT. pie *m*; ZOOL. pata; *(base)* base *f*; *(of a mountain, bed, page)* pie; *(of furniture)* pata; *(measurement)* pie (doce pulgadas); *(step)* paso <*to walk with a light f.* caminar con paso liviano>; POÉT. pie ♦ **at one's feet** a los pies de uno • **by f.** a pie • **f. soldier** MIL. soldado de infantería • **foots** QUÍM. residuos • **my f.!** JER. ¡tonterías! • **on f.** a pie • **to drag one's feet** *(in walking)* arrastrar los pies; FIG. *(to stall)* roncear, tirarse a la retranca • **to get cold feet** FIG., FAM. coger miedo, asustarse • **to get one's f. in the door** abrir una brecha • **to have one f. in the grave** FIG., FAM. estar con un pie en la sepultura • **to land on one's feet** FIG. caer de pie • **to put one's best f. forward** FIG. adoptar una actitud positiva, hacer lo mejor que uno pueda • **to put one's f. down** FIG. ponerse firme (en actitud, decisión) • **to put one's f. in one's mouth** meter la pata • **to stand on one's own two feet** FIG. ser independiente, valerse por sí mismo **II.** intr.

(to walk) andar, caminar; *(to dance)* bailar —tr. FAM. *(to go by foot)* recorrer, andar; *(to provide with a foot)* hacer o poner el pie a (media, calcetín); FAM. *(to pay)* pagar <*to f. the bill* pagar la cuenta>.

foot·age (fŏŏt'ĭj) s. *(measure)* medida de superficie o longitud (expresada en pies); CINEM. metraje *m.*

foot-and-mouth disease (fŏŏt'n-mouth') s. VET. glosopeda, fiebre aftosa.

foot·ball (fŏŏt'bôl') s. DEP. *(game)* fútbol *m*; *(ball)* pelota de fútbol.

foot brake s. freno de pedal.

foot·bridge (fŏŏt'brĭj') s. puente para peatones *m.*

foot-can·dle (fŏŏt'kăn'dl) s. FÍS. bujía-pie (unidad de luminiscencia) *f.*

foot-drag·ging (fŏŏt'drăg'ĭng) s. morosidad *f.*

foot·fall (fŏŏt'fôl') s. pisada.

foot·gear (fŏŏt'gîr') s. calzado.

foot·hill (fŏŏt'hĭl') s. estribación de una montaña *f.*

foot·hold (fŏŏt'hōld') s. *(support)* lugar de apoyo (para el pie) *m*; FIG. *(starting point)* posición *f* <*to gain a f. to advance a career* tomar posición para avanzar en una profesión>.

foot·ing (fŏŏt'ĭng) s. *(secure foot placement)* pie *m*, equilibrio; *(basis)* base *f* <*the business began on a good f.* el negocio comenzó sobre una buena base>; *(standing)* situación *f*, pie <*we are on equal f.* estamos en pie de igualdad>; ARQ. zarpa; MAT. suma ♦ **to lose one's f.** perder el pie.

foot·lights (fŏŏt'līts') s.pl. TEAT. *(lights)* candilejas; FIG. *(profession)* las tablas.

foot·lock·er (fŏŏt'lŏk'ər) s. baúl pequeño *m.*

foot·loose (fŏŏt'lōōs') adj. *(unattached)* sin obligaciones; *(free)* libre ♦ **f. and fancy free** libre, ligero y contento.

foot·man (fŏŏt'mən) s. [pl. **-men**] *(servant)* lacayo.

foot·note (fŏŏt'nōt') I. s. *(commentary)* nota al pie de la página; *(remark)* anotación II. tr. **-not·ed, -not·ing** anotar.

foot·path (fŏŏt'păth', -päth') s. sendero.

foot-pound (fŏŏt'pound') s. FÍS. pie libra *m.*

foot·print (fŏŏt'prĭnt') s. huella de un pie.

foot·race (fŏŏt'rās') s. DEP. carrera pedestre.

foot·rest (fŏŏt'rĕst') s. apoyo para los pies.

foot soldier s. soldado de infantería.

foot·sore (fŏŏt'sôr') adj. con los pies cansados.

foot·step (fŏŏt'stĕp') s. *(tread)* pisada; *(distance)* paso <*it's a f. away* está a un paso>; *(sound)* pisada; *(track)* huella; *(step)* escalón *m.*

foot·stool (fŏŏt'stōōl') s. taburete *m.*

foot·way (fŏŏt'wā') s. senda para peatones.

foot·wear (fŏŏt'wâr') s. calzado.

foot·work (fŏŏt'wûrk') s. *(legwork)* trabajo que requiere el caminar; DEP. *(agile movement)* juego de piernas.

fop (fŏp) s. petimetre *m.*

fop·per·y (fŏp'ə-rē) s. [pl. **-ies**] afectación *f.*

fop·pish (fŏp'ĭsh) adj. afectado.

for §G41 (fôr, fər) I. prep. □ OBJETIVO para <*he is training f. the Olympics* se está entrenando para las olimpiadas>; en <*John put the house up f. sale* Juan puso la casa en venta>; por <*I did it f. fun* lo hice por gusto> □ DESTINO para <*he left f. Rome* partió para Roma>; hacia <*he headed f. town* se dirigió hacia el centro> □ BENEFICIARIO para <*he is raising money f. the poor* está recaudando dinero para los pobres>; para <*she prepared lunch f. us* ella preparó el almuerzo para nosotros> □ EQUIVALENCIA por <*I paid ten dollars f. the ticket* pagué diez dólares por la entrada>; por <*she repeated the conversation word f. word* repitió la conversación palabra por palabra> □ ALCANCE, DURACIÓN de <*they sent me a bill f. ten dollars* me enviaron una factura de diez dólares>; por <*we talked f. several hours* charlamos por varias horas>; desde hace <*I have been in New York f. six months* estoy en Nueva York desde hace seis meses> □ CONSIDERAR por <*to take f. granted* dar por supuesto>; con <*I mistook you f. the waitress* la confundí a usted con la camarera> □ COMO RESULTADO DE de <*to jump for joy* saltar de alegría>; por <*I did it f. love* lo hice por amor> □ NO OBSTANTE, A PESAR DE a pesar de <*f. all*

his experience he is inefficient a pesar de toda su experiencia él es incompetente>; con <*f. all his money he's an unhappy man* con todo el dinero que tiene, es un hombre infeliz> □ EN CUANTO A, PARA CON para <*he has a gift f. organization* él tiene talento para la organización> □ CONSIDERANDO LA NATURALEZA DE para <*he is backward f. his age* él está atrasado para la edad que tiene>; por <*f. what we paid, we can't complain* por lo que pagamos, no podemos quejarnos> □ EXPRESIONES IDIOMÁTICAS ♦ **as f.** en cuanto a • **f. all that** con todo, a pesar de todo • **f. ever and ever** o **f. ever and a day** por siempre jamás • **f. good** para siempre • **f. the time being** por ahora • **I, for one** yo, personalmente • **to be all f. it** FAM. estar completamente a favor de • **to be f.** estar de parte de • **to be f. someone to** tocarle a alguien <*that's f. me to decide* eso me toca decidirlo a mí>. II. conj. ya que, pues, porque.

for·age (fôr'ĭj) I. s. *(fodder)* forraje *m*; *(search)* búsqueda (de forraje o comida) II. intr. **-aged, -ag·ing** hurgar ♦ **to f. for** buscar hurgando —tr. *(to feed)* dar forraje; *(to plunder)* saquear.

for·ag·er (fôr'ĭ-jər) s. forrajeador *m.*

for·as·much as (fôr'əz-mŭch' əz) conj. puesto que, ya que.

for·ay (fôr'ā') I. s. incursión *f* II. tr. saquear, despojar —intr. hacer incursiones.

for·bad (fər-băd') un pret. de **forbid.**

for·bade (fər-băd', -bād') un pret. de **forbid.**

for·bear¹ (fôr-bâr') tr. **-bore** (-bôr'), **-borne** (-bôrn'), **-bearing** *(to refrain from)* abstenerse de; *(to desist)* desistir de —intr. *(to refrain)* abstenerse; *(to be tolerant)* ser tolerante.

for·bear² (fôr'bâr') s. var. de **forebear.**

for·bear·ance (fôr-bâr'əns) s. *(tolerance)* tolerancia; *(patience)* paciencia; DER. abstención *f.*

for·bid (fər-bĭd') tr. **-bade** (-băd', -bād') o **-bad** (-băd'), **-bidden** (-bĭd'n) o **-bid, -bid·ding** *(to prohibit)* prohibir; *(to preclude)* prevenir <*you must f. him to enter* debes prevenir que entre>.

for·bid·den (fər-bĭd'n) I. un part. p. de **forbid** II. adj. prohibido.

for·bid·ding (fər-bĭd'ĭng) adj. *(prohibitive)* prohibitivo; *(unfriendly)* amenazante, desagradable.

force (fôrs) I. *(potency)* fuerza <*the f. of an explosion* la fuerza de una explosión>; *(personal magnetism)* fuerza, magnetismo; FÍS. fuerza; *(forcefulness)* vigor *m*, fuerza (de declaración, oratoria); *(efficacy)* eficacia, peso <*the f. of logic* el peso de la lógica>; *(power)* poder *m*, fuerza <*the forces of evil* las fuerzas del mal>; *(corps)* cuerpo <*the police f.* cuerpo de policía>; DER. *(effect)* vigencia, validez *f* ♦ **brute f.** fuerza bruta • **by f.** por la fuerza • **by f. of** a fuerza de, por medio de • **f. of habit** la fuerza de la costumbre, hábito • **f. of gravity** FÍS. fuerza de gravedad • **in f.** DER. vigente, en vigor; *(in numbers)* en masa <*the police arrived in f.* la policía se presentó en masa> • **to join forces** unir fuerzas, aliarse • **to put in f.** DER. poner en vigor II. tr. **forced, forc·ing** *(to compel)* compeler, obligar; *(to coerce)* obtener por la fuerza <*to f. a confession* obtener una confesión por la fuerza>; *(to make happen)* forzar; *(to push)* abrirse paso <*he forced his way through the crowd* se abrió paso entre la multitud>; *(to break open)* violentar, forzar <*to f. a lock* forzar una cerradura>; *(to rape)* forzar, violar; *(to impose)* imponer; AGR. *(to grow)* hacer crecer o madurar temprano ♦ **f. back** *(to push back)* rechazar, hacer retroceder; *(to hold back)* contener, reprimir (lágrimas, emoción) • **to f. down** obligar a bajar • **to f. from** sacar a fuerza de • **to f. into a corner** arrinconar • **to f. into bankruptcy** hacer quebrar • **to f. one's hand** obligar a actuar • **to f. open** forzar, abrir por la fuerza • **to f. out** arrancar u obtener por la fuerza • **to f. the issue** forzar la discusión o resolución (de un asunto) • **to f. upon** obligar a tomar o aceptar.

forced (fôrst) adj. *(imposed)* forzado; *(said of a landing)* forzoso; *(not spontaneous)* forzado; *(unnatural)* fingido <*f. smile* una sonrisa fingida>.

force-feed (fôrs'fēd') tr. **-fed** (-fĕd'), **-feed·ing** *(to feed forcibly)* forzar a comer; FIG. *(to oblige to accept)* forzar a aceptar (una política, doctrina).

force field s. ELECTRÓN., FÍS. campo de fuerza.
force·ful (fôrs'fəl) adj. *(strong)* fuerte; *(energetic)* enérgico.
force ma·jeure (fôrs' mä-zhûr') s. fuerza mayor.
for·ceps (fôr'səps) s. [pl. **forceps**] *(pincers)* pinzas; CIR. fórceps *m.*
forc·i·ble (fôr'sə-bəl) adj. *(using force)* forzado; *(forceful)* fuerte.
forc·i·bly (fôr'sə-blē) adv. a la fuerza.
ford (fôrd) I. s. vado II. tr. vadear.
ford·a·ble (fôr'də-bəl) adj. vadeable.
fore (fôr) I. adj. delantero II. s. *(front part)* frente *m*, delantera; MARÍT. proa ♦ **to come to the f.** comenzar a destacarse III. adv. hacia el frente IV. prep. ANT. ante V. interj. *(in golf)* ¡cuidado!
fore·arm¹ (fôr-ärm') tr. prepararse de antemano.
fore·arm² (fôr'ärm') s. ANAT. antebrazo.
fore·bear (fôr'bâr') s. antepasado.
fore·bode (fôr-bōd') tr. **-bod·ed, -bod·ing** *(to portend)* presagiar; *(to have a premonition)* presentir.
fore·bod·ing (fôr-bō'dĭng) I. s. *(premonition)* presentimiento; *(evil omen)* presagio II. adj. ominoso.
fore·cast (fôr'kăst') I. tr. & intr. **-cast** o **-cast·ed, -cast·ing** pronosticar II. s. pronóstico.
fore·cast·er (fôr'kăs'tər) s. pronosticador *m.*
fore·cast·ing (fôr'kăs'tĭng) s. pronosticación *f,* pronóstico.
fore·cas·tle (fōk'səl, fôr'kăs'əl) s. MARÍT. castillo de proa.
fore·close (fôr-klōz') tr. **-closed, -clos·ing** *(to resolve beforehand)* resolver de antemano —intr. DER. ejecutar una hipoteca; DER. privar del derecho de redimir una hipoteca.
fore·clo·sure (fôr-klō'zhər) s. DER. pérdida del derecho a redimir una hipoteca.
fore·deck (fôr'dĕk') s. MARÍT. cubierta de proa.
fore·doom (fôr-doom') tr. *(to doom)* predestinar (negativamente); *(to condemn)* condenar (de antemano).
fore·fa·ther (fôr'fä'thər) s. *(ancestor)* antepasado; *(predecessor)* antecesor *m.*
fore·fin·ger (fôr'fĭng'gər) s. dedo índice.
fore·foot (fôr'foot') s. [pl. **-feet** (-fēt')] ZOOL. pata delantera; MARÍT. pie de la roda *m.*
fore·front (fôr'frŭnt') s. *(foremost part)* parte delantera; *(vanguard)* vanguardia, primera plana.
fore·go¹ (fôr-gō') tr. **-went** (-wĕnt'), **-gone** (-gôn'), **-go·ing** preceder, anteceder.
fore·go² v. var. of **forgo.**
fore·go·ing (fôr'gō'ĭng) s. previo.
fore·gone (fôr'gôn') adj. previo, pasado.
fore·ground (fôr'ground') s. *(forefront)* primera plana; FOTOG., PINT. primer plano.
fore·hand (fôr'hănd') DEP. I. adj. directo, derecho II. s. golpe derecho o directo.
fore·head (fôr'ĭd, -hĕd') s. ANAT. frente *f.*
for·eign (fôr'ĭn) adj. *(from another country)* extranjero; *(exterior)* exterior <*f. trade* comercio exterior>; *(extraneous)* extraño <*he got a f. object in his eye* se le metió un objeto extraño en el ojo>; *(alien)* ajeno <*envy is f. to him* la envidia le es algo ajeno>; *(not appropriate)* impropio; *(irrelevant)* ajeno; DER. sujeto a jurisdicción ajena.
for·eign·er (fôr'ə-nər) s. extranjero, forastero.
foreign exchange s. *(currency)* divisas; COM. cambio exterior.
foreign office s. G.B. Ministerio de Asuntos Exteriores.
foreign service s. servicio diplomático y consular.
fore·knowl·edge (fôr-nŏl'ĭj) s. presciencia.
fore·leg (fôr'lĕg') s. ZOOL. pata delantera, brazo.
fore·lock (fôr'lŏk') s. mechón de pelo *m.*
fore·man (fôr'mən) s. [pl. **-men**] *(supervisor)* capataz; DER. presidente de un jurado *m.*
fore·mast (fôr'məst, -măst') s. MARÍT. palo de trinquete.
fore·men·tioned (fôr'mĕn'shənd) adj. anteriormente mencionado o dicho.
fore·most (fôr'mōst') I. adj. *(first)* primero, delantero; *(paramount)* máximo, supremo II. adv. ante todo, antes de todo.
fore·moth·er (fôr'mŭth'ər) s. antepasada.
fore·name (fôr'nām') s. primer nombre *m*, nombre de pila.
fore·noon (fôr'noon') s. mañana.

fo·ren·sic (fə-rĕn'sĭk) adj. *(rhetorical)* retórico; DER. forense.
fo·ren·sics (fə-rĕn'sĭks) s. [ú. con v. sing.] estudio y práctica de la argumentación.
fore·or·dain (fôr'ôr-dān') tr. predestinar, predeterminar.
fore·part (fôr'pärt') s. *(anterior part)* delantera, la primera parte; *(beginning)* principio.
fore·paw (fôr'pô') s. ZOOL. garra o zarpa de la pata delantera.
fore·play (fôr'plā') s. estimulación erótica previa al acto sexual.
fore·run·ner (fôr'rŭn'ər) s. *(predecessor)* precursor *m*, predecesor *m*; *(ancestor)* antepasado; *(harbinger)* anunciador *m.*
fore·said (fôr'sĕd') adj. antedicho, susodicho.
fore·see (fôr-sē') tr. **-saw** (-sô'), **-seen** (-sēn'), **-see·ing** prever, anticipar.
fore·see·a·ble (fôr-sē'ə-bəl) adj. previsible.
fore·shad·ow (fôr-shăd'ō) tr. presagiar.
fore·shock (fôr'shŏk') s. tremor leve que precede a un terremoto *m.*
fore·shore (fôr'shôr') s. la parte de la playa que cubre la pleamar o la parte comprendida entre el agua y la parte ocupada (cultivada, construida).
fore·short·en (fôr-shôr'tn) tr. *(to curtail)* acortar, abreviar; DIB., PINT. escorzar, degradar en perspectiva.
fore·short·en·ing (fôr-shôr'tn-ĭng) s. DIB., PINT. escorzo.
fore·side (fôr'sīd') s. frente *m*, parte anterior o superior *f.*
fore·sight (fôr'sīt') s. *(vision)* previsión *f,* providencia; *(prudence)* prudencia.
fore·sight·ed (fôr'sī'tĭd) adj. *(astute)* previsor; *(prudent)* prudente, precavido.
fore·skin (fôr'skĭn') s. ANAT. prepucio.
for·est (fôr'ĭst) I. s. *(woods)* bosque *m*, selva <*the Black F.* la Selva Negra>; FIG. *(profusion)* bosque, selva <*a f. of flags* una selva de banderas>; G.B. *(hunting ground)* zona de caza reservada para la corona II. tr. arbolar, poblar de árboles III. adj. forestal, selvático.
fore·stall (fôr-stôl') tr. *(to prevent)* impedir, prevenir; *(to anticipate)* anticipar, adelantar; COM. acaparar, monopolizar.
for·es·ta·tion (fôr'ĭ-stā'shən) s. repoblación forestal *f.*
for·est·er (fôr'ĭ-stər) s. *(expert)* silvicultor *m*; *(ranger)* guardabosque *m*, guarda forestal *m.*
for·est·land (fôr'ĭst-lănd') s. AGR. zona o área boscosa.
forest ranger s. guardabosque *m*, guarda forestal *m.*
for·est·ry (fôr'ĭ-strē) s. *(science)* silvicultura, ciencia forestal; *(forestland)* área boscosa.
fore·swear (fôr-swâr') v. var. de **forswear.**
fore·taste (fôr'tāst') s. *(advance taste)* goce *m* o sabor anticipado; FIG. *(anticipation)* anticipación *f.*
fore·tell (fôr-tĕl') tr. **-told** (-tōld'), **-tell·ing** *(to predict)* predecir, pronosticar; *(to divine)* adivinar, augurar.
fore·tell·er (fôr-tĕl'ər) s. *(fortuneteller)* adivino, nigromante *mf*; *(prophet)* profeta.
fore·tell·ing (fôr-tĕl'ĭng) s. *(prediction)* predicción *f,* presagio; *(prophecy)* profecía.
fore·thought (fôr'thôt') I. s. *(deliberation)* deliberación *f,* premeditación *f*; *(providence)* providencia, previsión *f* II. adj. deliberado, premeditado.
fore·told (fôr-tōld') pret. y part. p. de **foretell.**
fore·top (fôr'tŏp') s. *(forelock)* copete (del caballo) *m*; MARÍT. cofa de trinquete.
for·ev·er (fôr-ĕv'ər, fər-) adv. *(eternally)* por o para siempre, eternamente; *(always)* siempre.
for·ev·er·more (fôr-ĕv'ər-môr', fər-) adv. para siempre jamás, por toda la eternidad.
fore·warn (fôr-wôrn') tr. prevenir, avisar.
fore·went (fôr-wĕnt') pret. de **forgo.**
fore·word (fôr'wərd) s. *(preface)* prólogo, prefacio; *(preamble)* preámbulo.
for·feit (fôr'fĭt) DER. I. s. *(fine)* multa, penalidad *f*; *(loss)* pérdida legal de un derecho; *(forfeiture)* prenda perdida ♦ **forfeits** juego de prendas II. adj. perdido, confiscado III. tr. *(to surrender)* perder cosa o derecho como castigo; *(to seize)* decomisar, confiscar.

for·feit·er (fôr'fĭ-tər) s. DER. el que pierde, el que incurre en una pena (por no cumplir una obligación).

for·fei·ture (fôr'fĭ-chōŏr, -chər) DER. s. *(loss)* pérdida (de título, derecho); *(seizure)* comiso, confiscación *f*; *(fine)* multa; *(forfeited security)* prenda perdida.

for·gave (fər-gāv') pret. de **forgive.**

forge[1] (fôrj) I. s. *(smithy)* forja, hornaza; *(ironworks)* herrería, fundición *f*; TEC. fragua II. tr. **forged, forg·ing** *(to work metal)* fraguar, forjar; FIG. *(to give form to)* forjar, fraguar *<to f. an agreement* fraguar un acuerdo>; *(to counterfeit)* falsificar *<to f. a signature* falsificar una firma> —intr. *(to work at a forge)* trabajar en una fragua; *(to make a forgery)* hacer una falsificación.

forge[2] (fôrj) intr. **forged, forg·ing** avanzar ♦ **to f. ahead** adelantar con esfuerzo.

forg·er (fôr'jər) s. *(counterfeiter)* falsificador *m*; TEC. herrero.

forg·er·y (fôr'jə-rē) s. [pl. **-ies**] *(falsification)* falsificación *f*; *(document)* documento falsificado; *(money)* billete *m* o moneda falsa.

for·get (fər-gĕt') tr. **-got** (-gŏt'), **-got·ten** (-gŏt'n) o **-got, -get·ting** *(to be unable to remember)* olvidar, olvidarse de; *(to leave)* dejar *<I forgot my hat at the restaurant* dejé mi sombrero en el restaurante>; *(to neglect)* descuidar, olvidar *<to f. one's relatives* olvidar a los parientes de uno>; *(to fail to mention)* olvidarse de *<I forgot to thank him* me olvidé de darle las gracias>; *(to banish from one's memory)* olvidarse de *<just f. her and look for somebody else* simplemente olvidate de ella y búscate otra mujer> ♦ **to f. oneself** *(thoughtlessly)* propasarse, extralimitarse; *(unselfishly)* olvidarse de uno mismo —intr. *(to cease remembering)* olvidar *<all I want is to f.* todo lo que quiero es olvidar>; *(to overlook)* olvidarse de *<I forgot about the message* me olvidé de darte el mensaje>.

for·get·ful (fər-gĕt'fəl) adj. *(unable to remember)* olvidadizo, desmemoriado; *(negligent)* negligente, descuidado.

for·get·ful·ness (fər-gĕt'fəl-nĭs) s. *(inability to remember)* falta de memoria, olvido; *(negligence)* negligencia, descuido.

for·get-me-not (fər-gĕt'mē-nŏt') s. BOT. nomeolvides *f*.

for·get·ta·ble (fər-gĕt'ə-bəl) adj. olvidable.

forg·ing (fôr'jĭng) s. TEC. forjadura, forja.

for·giv·a·ble (fər-gĭv'ə-bəl) adj. perdonable.

for·give (fər-gĭv') tr. & intr. **-gave** (-gāv'), **-giv·en** (-gĭv'ən), **-giv·ing** perdonar.'

for·give·ness (fər-gĭv'nĭs) s. *(pardon)* perdón *m*; *(clemency)* indulgencia.

for·giv·ing (fər-gĭv'ĭng) adj. clemente, indulgente.

for·go (fôr-gō') tr. **-went** (-wĕnt'), **-gone** (-gôn'), **-go·ing** renunciar, prescindir de *<I shall f. the pleasure of seeing you* renunciaré el placer de verte>.

for·got (fər-gŏt') pret. y un part. p. de **forget.**

for·got·ten (fər-gŏt'n) un part. p. de **forget.**

fork (fôrk) I. s. *(utensil)* tenedor *m*; AGR. *(implement)* horca, horquilla; *(of a road)* bifurcación *f*; *(of a bicycle)* horquilla; *(of a tree)* horqueta; *(in a river)* horcajo, confluencia; ANAT. horcajadura II. tr. *(to shape)* ahorquillar ♦ **to f. over** FAM. aflojar, desembolsar *<they forked over their entire savings* desembolsaron todos sus ahorros> —intr. bifurcarse.

forked (fôrkt, fôr'kĭd) adj. *(fork-shaped)* ahorquillado; *(river)* dividido; *(road)* bifurcado; *(tail)* hendido; BOT. bífido.

fork lift s. montacargas *m*.

for·lorn (fər-lôrn', fôr-) adj. *(sad)* acongojado, melancólico *<a f. lover* un enamorado acongojado>; *(lonely)* abandonado, desolado; *(wretched in appearance)* calamitoso, de aspecto lamentable; *(hopeless)* sin esperanzas.

form (fôrm) I. s. *(shape)* forma *<a cake in the f. of a guitar* un pastel con forma de guitarra>; *(figure)* figura, cuerpo; *(type)* clase *f*, tipo *<a new f. of animal life* un nuevo tipo de vida animal>; *(convention)* formalismo, convencionalismo; *(manners)* conducta, modales *m*; *(formality)* formalidad *f*; *(document)* formulario *<to fill out a f.* llenar un formulario>; MÚS., RET. *(style)* estilo, forma *<a treatise in the f. of a dialogue* un tratado en forma de diálogo>;

(mold) horma, molde *m*; COST. *(mannequin)* maniquí *m*; IMPR. *(type)* forma; GRAM. forma *<verb f.* forma verbal>; EDUC. *(grade)* año, grado; G.B. *(bench)* banco ♦ **bad f.** algo que no se hace • **for f.'s sake** por pura fórmula, para salvar las apariencias • **to be common f.** ser muy corriente • **to be in good f.** DEP. estar en forma II. tr. *(to shape)* formar; *(to model)* moldear, modelar; *(to instruct)* desarrollar *<to f. the mind* desarrollar la mente>; *(to conceive)* idear, concebir; *(to develop)* contraer, adquirir (hábito); *(to constitute)* formar, constituir *<a group formed by all kinds of people* un grupo constituido por toda clase de gente>; *(to organize)* organizar, formar; GRAM. formar; *(to arrange)* formar, hacer *<f. a circle around the table* formen un círculo alrededor de la mesa> —intr. *(to become formed)* formarse, tomar forma; *(to come into being)* formarse *<ice formed in the pail* se formó hielo en el balde> ♦ **to f. up** MIL. alinearse, formar.

for·mal (fôr'məl) I. adj. *(related to form)* formal *<the f. elements of Greek tragedy* los elementos formales de la tragedia griega>; FILOS. *(essential)* esencial; *(according to conventions)* convencional; *(according to regulation)* formal *<a f. requirement* un requisito formal>; *(official)* oficial *<a f. reprimand* una reprimenda oficial>; *(done in proper form)* en forma, en debida forma *<a f. contract* un contrato en debida forma>; *(protocolar)* protocolario; *(correct)* muy correcto; *(ceremonious)* ceremonioso, circunspecto *<a f. manner* una actitud ceremoniosa>; *(dinner, reception)* de etiqueta *<a f. dance* un baile de etiqueta>; *(done for the sake of form)* de cumplido, formulario *<a purely f. greeting* un saludo estrictamente de cumplido> II. s. *(ceremony)* ceremonia de etiqueta; *(attire)* traje de etiqueta *m*.

for·mal·de·hyde (fôr-măl'də-hīd') s. QUÍM. formaldehido, formol *m*.

for·mal·ism (fôr'mə-lĭz'əm) s. formalismo.

for·mal·ist (fôr'mə-lĭst) s. formalista *mf*.

for·mal·i·ty (fôr-măl'ĭ-tē) s. [pl. **-ties**] *(ceremony)* ceremonia; *(of dress)* etiqueta; *(of style)* corrección *f*; *(of manner)* ceremonia, seriedad *f*; *(requirement)* formalidad *f*, trámite *m*; *(custom)* fórmula ♦ **as a mere f.** para o por cumplir • **formalities** ceremonias, cumplidos.

for·mal·ize (fôr'mə-līz') tr. **-ized, -iz·ing** *(to give shape to)* concretar, definir; *(to make formal)* formalizar.

for·mal·ly (fôr'mə-lē) adv. *(with formality)* formalmente; *(officially)* oficialmente; *(with meticulous formality)* protocolariamente; *(ceremoniously)* ceremoniosamente.

for·mat (fôr'măt') I. s. *(plan)* concepción *f*, plan *m*; *(layout)* formato II. tr. **-mat·ted, -mat·ting** hacer de acuerdo con una forma determinada.

for·ma·tion (fôr-mā'shən) s. *(act)* formación *f*; GEOL., MIL. formación ♦ **in battle f.** MIL. en orden de combate.

for·ma·tive (fôr'mə-tĭv) I. adj. formativo, formante *<a f. influence* una influencia formativa> II. s. GRAM. formante *m*.

form·er[1] (fôr'mər) s. formador *m*.

for·mer[2] (fôr'mər) adj. *(earlier)* antiguo, pasado *<in f. times* en tiempos pasados>; *(of two)* primero, anterior *<her f. plan was better than this one* su primer plan era mejor que éste>; *(said of people)* antiguo, ex *<f. president Carter* el expresidente Carter> ♦ **the f.** el primero, aquél *<John and Paul are good students, but the f. is brighter than the latter* Juan y Pablo son buenos alumnos, pero éste es menos listo que aquél>.

for·mer·ly (fôr'mər-lē) adv. anteriormente, antes.

form-fit·ting (fôrm'fĭt'ĭng) adj. ceñido, ajustado.

for·mic (fôr'mĭk) adj. ENTOM. fórmico, hormigoso; QUÍM. fórmico.

For·mi·ca (fôr-mī'kə) s. marca registrada de un material plástico laminado.

for·mi·da·ble (fôr'mĭ-də-bəl) adj. *(fearful)* formidable; *(awesome)* tremendo, impresionante.

form·less (fôrm'lĭs) adj. *(shapeless)* informe, sin forma; *(lacking order)* desordenado.

form letter s. circular *f*.

for·mu·la (fôr'myə-lə) s. [pl. **-las** o **-lae** (-lē')] fórmula; *(baby food)* mezcla nutritiva preparada; MAT., QUÍM. fórmula.

ã rey / ă año / b boca / ch chico / d dar / ĕ el / ē mil / g gato / h joya / hw juez / ī aire / k casa / kw cuan /

for·mu·late (fôr′myə-lāt′) tr. **-lat·ed, -lat·ing** formular.

for·mu·la·tion (fôr′myə-lā′shən) s. formulación f.

for·ni·cate (fôr′nĭ-kāt′) intr. **-cat·ed, -cat·ing** fornicar.

for·ni·ca·tion (fôr′nĭ-kā′shən) s. fornicación f.

for·ni·ca·tor (fôr′nĭ-kā′tər) s. fornicador m.

for·sake (fər-sāk′) tr. **-sook** (-sŏŏk′), **-sak·en** (-sā′kən), **-sak·ing** (to give up) dejar, renunciar a; (to abandon) abandonar, dejar.

for·sak·en (fər-sā′kən) I. part. p. de **forsake** II. adj. abandonado.

for·sook (fər-sŏŏk′) pret. de **forsake.**

for·sooth (fôr-sŏŏth′) adv. ANT. en verdad, de veras.

for·swear (fôr-swâr′) tr. **-swore** (-swôr′), **-sworn** (-swôrn′), **-swear·ing** (to renounce) abjurar de, renunciar solemnemente a; (to disavow) renegar, repudiar ♦ **to f. oneself** perjurar, jurar en falso —intr. perjurar, jurar en falso.

for·syth·i·a (fôr-sĭth′ē-ə, fər-) s. forsitia.

fort (fôrt) s. MIL. (fortified place) fuerte m; (permanent army post) base militar f ♦ **to hold down the f.** FAM. permanecer en el puesto.

forte (fôrt, fôr′tā′) s. (specialty) fuerte m, punto fuerte; ARM. (of a sword) parte más fuerte de la hoja f.

forth (fôrth) adv. en adelante <from this time f. de ahora en adelante> ♦ **and so f.** (and the like) y cosas así; (et cetera) etcétera, etcétera • **to come f.** (to appear) aparecer, hacer su aparición; (to step forward) adelantarse • **to go f.** ir, irse • **to put f.** (leaves) echar; (argument) adelantar.

forth·com·ing (fôrth-kŭm′ĭng) I. adj. (approaching) próximo, venidero <the f. elections las próximas elecciones>; (available) disponible; (outgoing) afable, amistoso II. s. aparición f.

forth·right (fôrth′rīt′) I. adj. (direct) directo, franco; (straightforward) rotundo, claro II. adv. (frankly) francamente, con franqueza; (directly ahead) derecho.

forth·with (fôrth-wĭth′) adv. en el acto, enseguida.

for·ti·eth (fôr′tē-ĭth) I. s. (place) cuarenta m; (part) cuadragésimo, cuadragésima parte II. adj. (place) cuadragésimo; (part) cuarentavo.

for·ti·fi·ca·tion (fôr′tə-fĭ-kā′shən) s. (reinforcement) refuerzo; (invigoration) fortalecimiento; MIL. fortificación f.

for·ti·fi·er (fôr′tə-fī′ər) s. fortificante m.

for·ti·fy (fôr′tə-fī′) tr. **-fied, -fy·ing** (to reinforce) reforzar; (to invigorate) fortalecer; (food) enriquecer; (wine) encabezar ♦ **to f. oneself with** fortalecerse con —intr. MIL. construir fortificaciones.

for·ti·fy·ing (fôr′tə-fī′ĭng) adj. fortificante.

for·ti·tude (fôr′tĭ-tŏŏd′, -tyŏŏd′) s. fortaleza, fuerza de ánimo.

fort·night (fôrt′nīt′) s. quincena f, quince días m.

fort·night·ly (fôrt′nīt′lē) I. adj. quincenal II. adv. quincenalmente, cada quince días III. s. [pl. **-lies**] publicación quincenal f.

FOR·TRAN (fôr′trăn′) s. COMPUT. nombre de un lenguaje digital.

for·tress (fôr′trĭs) s. fortaleza.

for·tu·i·tous (fôr-tŏŏ′ĭ-təs, -tyŏŏ′-) adj. (accidental) fortuito, casual; (lucky) afortunado.

for·tu·i·ty (fôr-tŏŏ′ĭ-tē, -tyŏŏ′-) s. [pl. **-ties**] (accidental occurrence) casualidad f; (fortuitousness) carácter fortuito, casualidad.

for·tu·nate (fôr′chə-nĭt) adj. afortunado ♦ **to be f.** (person) tener suerte <I was f. to find you tuve la suerte de encontrarte>; (event) ser una suerte <it was f. that you arrived on time fue una suerte que llegaste a tiempo>.

for·tu·nate·ly (fôr′chə-nĭt-lē) adv. afortunadamente, por suerte.

for·tune (fôr′chən) s. (fate) fortuna, destino; (good luck) fortuna, suerte f <I had the good f. to win tuve la suerte de ganar>; (wealth) fortuna, capital m; (large sum of money) fortuna, dineral m ♦ **F.** la Fortuna • **to cost a f.** costar un dineral, costar un ojo de la cara • **to make a f.** hacerse rico.

fortune hunter s. cazador de dotes m.

for·tune·tell·er (fôr′chən-tĕl′ər) s. adivino, adivinador m.

for·tune·tell·ing (fôr′chən-tĕl′ĭng) s. adivinación f, arte de leer el futuro m.

for·ty (fôr′tē) adj. & s. [pl. **-ties**] cuarenta m.

for·ty-five (fôr′tē-fīv′) s. (pistol) pistola de calibre cuarenta y cinco; (record) disco de cuarenta y cinco rpm.

for·ty-nin·er (fôr′tē-nī′nər) s. HIST. buscador de oro de la fiebre de oro de 1849, en California m.

for·ty-one (fôr′tē-wŭn′) s. & adj. cuarenta y uno.

forty winks s. FAM. pestañazo, siestecita.

fo·rum (fôr′əm) s. [pl. **fo·rums** o **fo·ra** (fôr′ə)] (public place) foro; (medium for discussion) tribuna; DER. foro, tribunal m.

for·ward (fôr′wərd) I. adj. (frontal) delantero <the f. section of the bus la parte delantera del autobús>; (eager) ansioso, deseoso; (bold) atrevido, descarado; (progressive) radical, avanzado <a f. concept un concepto avanzado>; (precocious) adelantado, precoz <a f. child un niño precoz>; COM. (future) futuro <f. selling venta futura> II. adv. hacia adelante <a step f. un paso hacia adelante> ♦ **looking f. to seeing you** a la espera de volverle a ver • **to bring f.** (to present) presentar, ofrecer (opinión, idea); TEN. llevar (saldo) • **to come f.** salir hacia afuera, avanzar III. s. DEP. (player) delantero; (position) delantera f IV. tr. (to send on) enviar, reexpedir; (to help advance) promover, fomentar.

for·ward·er (fôr′wər-dər) s. agente expedidor m.

for·ward·ing (fôr′wər-dĭng) s. (sending) envío, expedición f; (service) servicio de transporte.

for·ward·ness (fôr′wərd-nĭs) s. (boldness) atrevimiento, audacia; (progressiveness) progresismo, modernismo; (precocity) precocidad f.

for·wards (fôr′wərdz) adv. adelante, hacia adelante.

fos·sil (fŏs′əl) s. & adj. fósil m.

fossil fuel s. GEOL. combustible fósil m.

fos·sil·ize (fŏs′ə-līz′) tr. & intr. **-ized, -iz·ing** (to become a fossil) fosilizar(se), petrificar(se); FIG. (to become outmoded) volver(se) obsoleto.

fos·ter (fô′stər) I. tr. (to bring up) criar <he fostered two children crió a dos niños>; (to promote) fomentar, promover; (to cherish) abrigar (esperanza, sueño) II. adj. adoptivo <a f. child un hijo adoptivo>.

fought (fôt) pret. y part. p. de **fight.**

foul (foul) I. adj. **-er, -est** (revolting) repugnante, asqueroso; (fetid) fétido, pestilente; (rotten) podrido; (dirty) sucio, puerco; (said of air) viciado; (wicked) perverso; (obscene) obsceno, grosero <f. language lenguaje obsceno>; FAM. (horrible) atroz, horrible <a f. deed una acción horrible>; DEP. sucio o ilegal (golpe, jugada); (obstructed) obstruido, atascado ♦ **by fair means or f.** por las buenas o por las malas • **to fall f. of** enredarse con, ponerse a malas con II. s. DEP. (violation) falta III. adv. sucio, contra las reglas <to play f. jugar sucio> IV. tr. (to make dirty) ensuciar, emporcar; FIG. (to taint) manchar, mancillar; (to obstruct) obstruir, atascar; (to entangle) enredarse en o con; DEP. cometer una falta contra —intr. (to become dirty) ensuciarse; DEP. (to commit a foul) cometer una falta; (to become obstructed) obstruirse, atascarse; (to become entangled) trabarse, enredarse ♦ **to f. up** FAM. hacer una chapuceada.

foul line s. DEP. línea que delimita las zonas prohibidas en los campos de juego.

foul-mouthed (foul′mouthd′, -moutht′) adj. malhablado, desbocado.

foul play s. maniobra o juego sucio.

foul-up (foul′ŭp′) s. FAM. (confusion) confusión f; (mechanical trouble) falla mecánica.

found[1] (found) tr. (to establish) fundar (ciudad, institución); (to base) cimentar, fundamentar (edificio, teoría).

found[2] (found) tr. METAL. fundir.

found[3] (found) pret. y part. p. de **find.**

foun·da·tion (foun-dā′shən) s. (establishment) fundación f; (basis) fundamento, cimiento; (endowment) dotación f, fondos (para fundar una institución); (institution) fundación; (for cosmetics) base f; ARQ. cimientos; CONSTR. asiento, firme (de una carretera) m; COST. forro, refuerzo ♦ **f. stone** CONSTR. primera piedra • **to lay the foundations** sentar las bases.

foun·der[1] (foun′dər) I. intr. (to break down) fracasar, venirse abajo <*the negotiations foundered* las negociaciones fracasaron>; (*to cave in*) desplomarse, hundirse (edificios); —intr. VET. despearse, mancarse; MARÍT. irse a pique, zozobrar; (*to sink*) hundir; VET. mancar, despearse II. s. VET. laminitis *f*, despeadura.

found·er² (foun′dər) s. (*originator*) fundador *m*; METAL. fundidor *m*.

Found·ing Father (foun′dĭng) s. HIST. miembro de la Convención constitucional norteamericana de 1787 ♦ f. fundador.

found·ling (found′lĭng) s. expósito, niño abandonado.

foun·dry (foun′drē) s. [pl. -dries] fundición *f.*

fount (fount) s. (*fountain*) fuente *f*, manantial *m*, FIG. (*source*) fuente, origen *m.*

foun·tain (foun′tən) s. (*spring*) fuente *f*; (*for drinking*) surtidor *m*; (*reservoir*) tanque *m*; FIG. (*source*) fuente, origen *m.*

foun·tain·head (foun′tən-hĕd′) s. (*spring*) manantial *m*, cabecera (de un río); FIG. (*origin*) fuente *f.*

fountain pen s. pluma fuente, estilográfica.

four (fôr) s. & adj. cuatro ♦ f. o'clock las cuatro.

four·di·men·sion·al (fôr′dĭ-mĕn′shə-nəl, -dī-) adj. cuadridimensional, de cuatro dimensiones.

four·fold (fôr′fōld′) I. adj. cuádruple II. adv. cuatro veces.

four·foot·ed (fôr′fŏot′ĭd) adj. cuadrúpedo, de cuatro patas.

four hundred s. & adj. cuatrocientos.

four-leaf clover (fôr′lēf′) s. trébol de cuatro hojas *m.*

four-let·ter word (fôr′lĕt′ər) s. mala palabra, palabrota.

four-post·er (fôr′pō′stər) s. cama con cuatro columnas.

four·score (fôr′skôr′) adj. ochenta.

four·some (fôr′səm) s. (*two couples*) dos parejas; (*game*) partida o partido de cuatro; (*players*) los jugadores de una partida de cuatro, esp. en golf.

four·square (fôr′skwâr′) I. adj. (*square*) cuadrado; (*firmly convinced*) inequívoco; (*forthright*) franco, sincero II. adv. francamente.

four·teen (fôr-tēn′) s. & adj. catorce *m.*

four·teenth (fôr-tēnth′) I. s. (*place*) decimocuarto; (*part*) catorzavo, catorzava parte II. adj. (*place*) decimocuarto; (*part*) catorzavo.

fourth (fôrth) I. s. (*place*) cuarto; (*part*) cuarto, cuarta parte; MÚS. (*interval*) cuarta; (*note*) subdominante *f*; AUTO. cuarta velocidad II. adj. cuarto.

fourth-class (fôrth′klăs′) I. adj. abierto (*correo*) II. adv. por correo abierto.

fourth dimension s. GEOM. cuarta dimensión.

fourth estate s. la prensa.

Fourth of July s. cuatro de julio (día de la independencia de EE. UU.).

Fourth World s. los países menos desarrollados del tercer mundo, especialmente en África y Asia.

four-wheel (fôr′hwēl′) adj. (*having four wheels*) de cuatro ruedas; AUTO. de transmisión o tracción en las cuatro ruedas, de cuatro ruedas motrices.

fowl (foul) I. s. [pl. **fowl** o **fowls**] ORNIT. (*birds*) aves (en general); (*domesticated bird*) ave de corral; CUL. (*meat*) carne de ave *f*, pollo ♦ **neither fish nor f.** ni chicha ni limonada II. intr. cazar aves.

fowl·er (fou′lər) s. cazador de aves *m.*

fox (fŏks) I. s. ZOOL. zorro (animal y piel); (*sly person*) zorro, taimado II. tr. (*to outwit*) embaucar, engañar; (*to baffle*) dejar perplejo, desconcertar; (*to repair*) remendar (zapatos) —intr. fingir, disimular la intención.

fox·hole (fŏks′hōl′) s. MIL. trinchera individual, pozo de tirador.

fox·hound (fŏks′hound′) s. perro raposero.

fox hunt s. caza o cacería de zorros.

fox terrier s. foxterrier (perro) *mf.*

fox·y (fŏk′sē) adj. **-i·er, -i·est** (*cunning*) taimado; (*clever*) astuto; (*color*) rojizo; (*discolored*) descolorido; (*sour*) agrio; FAM. (*sexy*) sensual.

foy·er (foi′ər, foi′ā′) s. (*lobby*) salón de entrada *m*; (*vestibule*) vestíbulo.

fra·cas (frā′kəs, frăk′əs) s. riña, reyerta.

frac·tion (frăk′shən) s. (*fragment*) fragmento, porción *f*; (*part*) parte *f*; MAT. fracción *f*, quebrado.

frac·tion·al (frăk′shə-nəl) adj. (*partial*) fraccionario, fraccionado; (*very small*) minúsculo, insignificante.

frac·tion·ate (frăk′shə-nāt′) tr. **-at·ed, -at·ing** QUÍM. fraccionar.

frac·tion·a·tion (frăk′shə-nā′shən) s. QUÍM. fraccionamiento.

frac·tion·ize (frăk′shə-nīz′) tr. & intr. **-ized, -iz·ing** fraccionar.

frac·tious (frăk′shəs) adj. (*unruly*) indócil, rebelde; (*cranky*) malhumorado, regañón.

frac·ture (frăk′chər) I. s. (*break*) fractura; (*cartilage*) desgarradura; MIN. disyunción *f* ♦ **compound f.** fractura complicada II. tr. **-tured, -tur·ing** (*to break*) fracturar; (*to crack*) agrietar; FIG. (*to disrupt*) quebrantar; (*to violate*) quebrar, violar —intr. fracturarse.

frag·ile (frăj′əl, -īl′) adj. (*brittle*) frágil; (*frail*) endeble; (*flimsy*) insubstancial.

fra·gil·i·ty (frə-jĭl′ĭ-tē) s. (*brittleness*) fragilidad *f*; (*frailness*) endeblez *f*; (*flimsiness*) insubstancialidad *f.*

frag·ment I. s. (frăg′mənt) fragmento II. tr. & intr. (frăg′mĕnt′) fragmentar.

frag·men·tar·y (frăg′mən-tĕr′ē) adj. fragmentario.

frag·men·ta·tion (frăg′mən-tā′shən) s. fragmentación *f.*

fra·grance (frā′grəns) s. fragancia, perfume *m.*

fra·grant (frā′grənt) adj. fragante.

frail (frāl) adj. **-er, -est** (*fragile*) frágil; (*weak*) débil; (*delicate*) delicado; (*easily tempted*) débil.

frail·ness (frāl′nĭs) s. (*fragility*) fragilidad *f*; (*weakness*) debilidad *f.*

frail·ty (frāl′tē) s. [pl. **-ties**] (*fragility*) fragilidad *f*; (*physical weakness*) debilidad *f*; (*moral weakness*) flaqueza.

frame (frām) I. s. (*construction*) construcción *f*; CONSTR. (*structure*) armadura, armazón *f* <*the f. of a house* la armadura de una casa>; (*border*) cerco, marco <*a picture f.* el marco de una foto>; ANAT. (*human body*) constitución *f*, estructura corporal; (*cold frame*) cajonera en frío; (*system*) forma, sistema *m* <*the f. of government* el sistema de gobierno>; DEP. (*round of play*) turno; CINEM. fotograma *m*; JER. (*frame-up*) conspiración *f*; ANT. (*shape*) contorno, figura; MARÍT. cuaderna (de un buque); FIG. (*background*) marco, fondo (de novela, drama); AUTO. chasis *m*, bastidor *m*; MIN. entibación *f*; (*of a bicycle*) cuadro; (*of glasses*) montura, armazón ♦ **f. of mind** estado de ánimo, disposición *f* ♦ **f. saw** sierra bracera, sierra montada o de bastidor II. tr. **framed, fram·ing** (*to construct*) construir, armar; (*to formulate*) formular <*to f. a reply* formular una respuesta>; (*to put a border around*) enmarcar, encuadrar; JER. (*to make seem guilty*) amañar (una acusación para acriminar falsamente) III. adj. de tablas, de madera <*a f. house* una casa de madera>.

frame of reference s. FÍS. sistema de coordenadas *m*; FILOS. punto de referencia; (*context*) contexto.

fram·er (frā′mər) s. (*constructor*) constructor *m*; (*assembler*) armador *m*; (*frame maker*) fabricante de marcos *m.*

frame-up (frām′ŭp′) s. JER. estratagema *m*, maquinación para incriminar a alguien *f.*

frame·work (frām′wûrk′) s. (*form*) forma, estructura; (*system*) sistema *m*; CONSTR. armazón *f*, esqueleto.

fram·ing (frā′mĭng) s. (*framework*) armazón *f*, esqueleto; (*frame*) marco.

franc (frăngk) s. FIN. franco.

France (frăns) s. Francia.

fran·chise (frăn′chīz′) I. s. (*privilege*) derecho, privilegio; POL. (*suffrage*) derecho de voto; COM. concesión *f*, licencia; HIST. franquicia II. tr. **-chised, -chis·ing** otorgar la concesión de, dar una licencia para.

fran·chis·ee (frăn′chī-zē′) s. COM. concesionario (receptor).

fran·chis·er (frăn′chī′zər) s. COM. concesionario (otorgador).

Fran·cis·can (frăn-sĭs′kən) s. RELIG. franciscano.

fran·ci·um (frăn′sē-əm) s. QUÍM. francio.

Fran·co·phile (frăng′kə-fīl′) o **Fran·co·phil** (-fĭl′) s. francófilo.

Fran·co·phobe (frăng′kə-fōb′) s. francófobo.

frank¹ (frăngk) I. adj. **-er, -est** (*candid*) franco, sincero; (*evident*) evidente, claro II. tr. (*to stamp*) franquear; (*to* *mail)* enviar libre de franqueo **III.** s. *(mark)* sello *o* franquicia postal; *(letter)* carta exenta de franqueo.

frank² (frăngk) s. FAM. salchicha, perro caliente.

Frank (frăngk) s. HIST. franco.

frank·furt·er (frăngk′fər-tər) s. CUL. salchicha, perro caliente.

frank·in·cense (frăng′kĭn-sĕns′) s. incienso, olíbano.

frank·ly (frăngk′lē) adv. francamente, sinceramente.

frank·ness (frăngk′nĭs) s. franqueza, sinceridad *f.*

fran·tic (frăn′tĭk) adj. *(desperate)* desesperado; *(nervous)* frenético; ANT. *(insane)* loco.

frat (frăt) s. FAM. club estudiantil masculino.

fra·ter·nal (frə-tûr′nəl) adj. *(brotherly)* fraternal, fraterno; BIOL. fraterno ♦ **f. twins** mellizos.

fra·ter·ni·ty (frə-tûr′nĭ-tē) s. [pl. **-ties**] *(association)* fraternidad *f,* confraternidad *f; (student organization)* asociación estudiantil masculina; *(fellowship)* fraternidad, hermandad *f.*

frat·er·ni·za·tion (frăt′ər-nĭ-zā′shən) s. fraternización *f.*

frat·er·nize (frăt′ər-nīz′) intr. **-nized, -niz·ing** fraternizar.

frat·ri·cide (frăt′rĭ-sīd′) s. *(act)* fratricidio; *(person)* fratricida *mf.*

fraud (frôd) s. *(criminal deception)* fraude *m; (trickery)* engaño; *(person)* impostor *m,* engañador *m.*

fraud·u·lence (frô′jə-ləns) s. fraudulencia.

fraud·u·lent (frô′jə-lənt) adj. fraudulento.

fraught (frôt) **I.** adj. *(charged)* cargado; *(filled)* lleno **II.** s. ANT. *(freight)* carga.

fray¹ (frā) **I.** s. *(brawl)* riña, pelea; *(fight)* combate *m* **II.** tr. *(to alarm)* alarmar, asustar; *(to drive away)* alejar, echar —intr. combatir.

fray² (frā) **I.** tr. *(to wear away)* desgastar, deshilachar; *(to chafe)* rozar —intr. desgastarse, deshilacharse **II.** s. deshiladura.

fraz·zle (frăz′əl) **I.** tr. **-zled, -zling** *(to fray)* desgastar, deshilachar; *(to exhaust)* agotar —intr. *(to wear away)* desgastarse, deshilacharse **II.** s. *(exhaustion)* agotamiento; *(frayed edge)* hilacha ♦ **worn to a f.** *(frayed)* hecho un trapo, FIG. *(exhausted)* completamente agotado.

freak (frēk) **I.** s. *(unusual occurrence)* cosa extraña *o* imprevista; *(monstrosity)* anormalidad *f,* monstruo; *(whim)* capricho, antojo; JER. *(drug user)* narcómano; *(hippie)* hippie *m; (enthusiast)* fanático **II.** intr. & tr. ♦ **to f. out** JER. *(to hallucinate)* alucinar; *(to behave irrationally)* enloquecer; *(to become shocked)* sorprender(se), asustar(se); *(to become excited)* excitar(se).

freak·ish (frē′kĭsh) adj. *(unusual)* extraño, raro; *(abnormal)* anormal; *(unexpected)* inesperado; *(capricious)* caprichoso.

freak-out (frēk′out′) s. JER. estado mental alucinante (producido por drogas).

freak·y (frē′kē) adj. **-i·er, -i·est** *(abnormal)* anormal; *(monstrous)* monstruoso; *(strange)* rare, extraño.

freck·le (frĕk′əl) **I.** s. peca **II.** tr. **-led, -ling** motear, salpicar —intr. cubrirse de pecas.

freck·led (frĕk′əld) adj. pecoso, lleno de pecas.

free (frē) **I.** adj. **fre·er, fre·est** *(at liberty)* libre; *(independent)* libre, independiente; *(not literal)* libre <*a f. translation* una traducción libre>; *(gratis)* gratis, gratuito <*f. admission* entrada gratis>; *(not occupied)* libre, desocupado <*is that seat f.?* ¿está desocupado ese asiento?>; *(unobstructed)* libre, sin obstáculos; *(frank)* franco, sincero; *(forward)* atrevido, impertinente; *(liberal)* liberal, generoso; *(outspoken)* directo, franco; QUÍM. puro; FÍS. libre; *(untied)* suelto, desatado ♦ **for f.** gratis, gratuitamente • **f. advice** consejo gratis • **f. and clear** libre de trabas *o* gravámenes • **f. and easy** *(carefree)* despreocupado; *(informal)* informal; *(unceremonious)* poco ceremonioso • **f. from** *o* **of** s. <*f. from defects* sin defectos> • **f. of charge** gratis • **f. of duty** libre de derechos de aduana • **to be f. from** no tener <*I am f. from debt* no tengo ninguna deuda> • **to be f. to** tener la libertad para, poder <*you are f. to leave any time* puedes irte en cualquier momento> • **to be f. with one's money** no reparar en gastos • **to break f.** soltarse, librarse • **to feel f. to** sentirse con la libertad de • **to give a f. hand** dar plenos poderes, dar carta blanca •

to have a f. hand tener campo libre, tener carta blanca • **to set f.** *(a person)* poner en libertad; *(a slave)* emancipar; *(an animal)* soltar **II.** adv. *(freely)* libremente; *(gratis)* gratis, gratuitamente **III.** tr. **freed, free·ing** *(to liberate)* libertar, poner en libertad; *(to emancipate)* emancipar; *(to let loose)* soltar; *(to rid)* liberar, librar; *(to untangle)* desembarazar, desenredar; *(to exempt)* exentar, eximir <*to f. from taxes* eximir de impuestos>.

free association s. PSIC. asociación libre *f.*

free·base (frē′bās′) intr. **-based, -bas·ing** inhalar cocaína que ha sido purificada con éter.

free·bie *o* **free·bee** (frē′bē) s. JER. dádiva, obsequio de la casa.

free·boot·er (frē′bōō′tər) s. pirata *m.*

free·born (frē′bôrn′) adj. nacido libre.

freed·man (frēd′mən) s. [pl. **-men**] manumiso.

free·dom (frē′dəm) s. *(liberty)* libertad *f; (exemption)* exención *f* <*f. from taxation* exención de impuestos>; *(immunity)* inmunidad *f; (privilege)* privilegio, derecho; *(ease)* facilidad *f,* soltura; *(frankness)* franqueza.

freedom of speech s. libertad de palabra *f.*

freedom of the press s. libertad de prensa *f.*

freed·wom·an (frēd′wŏōm′ən) s. [pl. **-wom·en** (-wĭm′ĭn)] manumisa.

free energy s. FÍS. energía libre.

free enterprise s. COM. libre empresa.

free fall s. FÍS. caída libre.

free-float·ing (frē′flō′tĭng) adj. *(undecided)* indeciso, no comprometido; *(general)* general <*free-floating anxiety* ansiedad general>.

free-for-all (frē′fər-ôl′) s. refriega, pelea.

free·hand (frē′hănd′) adj. a pulso.

free hand s. mano libre *f.*

free·hand·ed (frē′hăn′dĭd) adj. dadivoso, generoso.

free·hold (frē′hōld′) s. *(life tenure)* posición *f* u oficio vitalicio; DER. feudo franco.

free·hold·er (frē′hōl′dər) s. *(estate holder)* persona en posesión de un feudo franco; *(tenured person)* persona con oficio vitalicio.

free lance s. persona que trabaja independientemente sin pertenecer a una empresa.

free-lance (frē′lăns′) **I.** intr. **-lanced, -lanc·ing** trabajar independientemente **II.** adj. independiente.

free-lanc·er (frē′lăn′sər) s. persona que trabaja independientemente sin pertenecer a una empresa.

free-liv·ing (frē′lĭv′ĭng) adj. *(self-indulgent)* libertino; BIOL. independiente.

free·load (frē′lōd′) intr. JER. vivir de arriba *o* a cuesta de otros.

free·load·er (frē′lō′dər) s. JER. parásito.

free love s. amor libre *m.*

free·ly (frē′lē) adv. *(free)* libremente; *(gratis)* gratis, gratuitamente.

free·man (frē′mən) s. [pl. **-men**] *(not a slave)* hombre libre *m; (citizen)* ciudadano.

free·ma·son (frē′mā′sən) s. HIST. albañil *mf* ♦ **F.** francmasón *m,* masón.

free·ma·son·ry (frē′mā′sən-rē) s. camaradería ♦ **F.** francmasonería, masonería.

free on board adj. & adv. COM. franco a bordo.

free port s. puerto libre.

free rein s. rienda libre.

free ride s. FIG. algo obtenido sin esfuerzo *o* sin pagar.

free-spo·ken (frē′spō′kən) adj. franco.

free·stand·ing (frē′stăn′dĭng) adj. estable (sin soportes).

free·style (frē′stīl′) s. DEP. estilo libre (de natación).

free·think·er (frē′thĭng′kər) s. librepensador *m.*

free·think·ing (frē′thĭng′kĭng) **I.** s. librepensamiento **II.** adj. librepensador.

free time s. tiempo libre.

free trade s. COM. librecambio, libre cambio.

free verse s. LIT. verso libre.

free·way (frē′wā′) s. autopista.

free·wheel (frē′hwēl′) intr. vagabundear.

free wheel s. MEC. rueda libre.

---

ng inglés / ŏ la / ō bou / ô corre / oi oigo / ōō uno / ou auto / yŏō ciudad / w hueco / y yo / z mismo

free·wheel·ing (frē'hwē'lĭng) FIG. *(unrestrained)* libre; *(carefree)* despreocupado.
free-will (frē'wĭl') adj. voluntario.
free will s. libre albedrío.
freeze (frēz) I. intr. **froze** (frōz), **fro·zen** (frō'zən), **freez·ing** *(to become frozen)* helarse, congelarse; FIG. *(to be cold)* tener frío, helarse <*I am freezing* me estoy helando>; *(to be stunned)* quedarse helado *o* paralizado ♦ **to f. over** helarse, congelarse (río, lago) • **to f. to death** *(to die)* morirse de frío; FIG., FAM. *(to be cold)* helarse, morirse de frío —intr. *(to congeal)* helar, congelar; *(to chill)* enfriar; *(to preserve)* refrigerar; FIG. *(to treat coolly)* tratar con frialdad; COM., FIN. *(to control)* congelar, bloquear (cuentas, fondos) ♦ **to f. out** *(to exclude)* excluir; *(to get rid of)* deshacerse de II. s. *(freezing)* congelación *f*, congelamiento; *(frost)* helada.
freeze-dry (frēz'drī') tr. **-dried, -dry·ing** secar por congelación.
freez·er (frē'zər) s. congelador *m*.
freez·ing (frē'zĭng) I. adj. glacial ♦ **it's f. cold** hace un frío tremendo II. s. *(of food)* congelación *f*; FIG. *(of prices, armaments)* congelación, bloqueo.
freezing point s. FÍS. punto de congelación.
free zone s. COM. zona libre *o* franca.
freight (frāt) I. s. *(load)* carga; *(train, plane)* flete *m*; *(truck)* mercancías II. tr. *(to transport)* transportar, fletar; *(to load)* cargar.
freight·age (frā'tĭj) s. *(transport)* acarreo; *(charge)* flete *m*; *(cargo)* carga.
freight car s. F.C. vagón de carga *o* de mercancía *m*.
freight·er (frā'tər) s. *(ship)* carguero, buque de carga *m*; *(shipper)* fletador *m*.
freight train s. F.C. tren de carga *o* de mercancía *m*.
french (frĕnch) tr. *(to slice)* lonjear; *(to trim)* recortar.
French (frĕnch) adj. & s. francés *m* ♦ **the F.** los franceses.
French-Ca·na·di·an *o* **French Canadian** (frĕnch'kə-nā'dē-ən) I. s. canadiense de ascendencia francesa *mf* II. adj. franco-canadiense.
french chalk s. jaboncillo de sastre, esteatita.
French door s. puertaventana.
French fries s.pl. patatas *o* papas fritas.
French horn s. MÚS. corno francés.
French leave s. despedida a la francesa ♦ **to take F.** despedirse a la francesa.
French·man (frĕnch'mən) s. [pl. **-men**] francés *m*.
French window s. puertaventana.
French·wom·an (frĕnch'wŏŏm'ən) s. [pl. **-wom·en** (-wĭm'ĭn)] francesa.
fre·net·ic (frə-nĕt'ĭk) adj. frenético.
fre·num (frē'nəm) s. [pl. **-nums** *o* **-na** (-nə)] ANAT. frenillo (de la lengua, glande).
fren·zied (frĕn'zēd) adj. frenético.
fren·zy (frĕn'zē) I. s. [pl. **-zies**] *(excitement)* frenesí *m*; *(delirium)* desvarío; *(craze)* furor *m* II. tr. **-zied, -zy·ing** volver loco.
Fre·on (frē'ŏn') s. QUÍM. freón (marca registrada de un gas usado como refrigerante) *m*.
fre·quence (frē'kwəns) s. frecuencia.
fre·quen·cy (frē'kwən-sē) s. [pl. **-ies**] frecuencia.
frequency distribution s. COMPUT. distribución de frecuencias *f*.
frequency modulation s. RAD. modulación de frecuencia *f*.
fre·quent I. adj. (frē'kwənt) *(common)* frecuente; *(habitual)* habitual II. tr. (frē-kwĕnt') frecuentar.
fre·quent·er (frē-kwĕn'tər) s. frecuentador *m*.
fre·quent·ly (frē'kwənt-lē) adv. frecuentemente.
fres·co (frĕs'kō) I. s. [pl. **-coes** *o* **-cos**] fresco ♦ **al f.** al aire libre II. tr. **-coed, -co·ing** pintar al fresco.
fresh (frĕsh) I. adj. **-er, -est** *(not stale)* fresco <*f. vegetables* verduras frescas>; *(novel)* nuevo <*a f. approach* un nuevo enfoque>; *(not saline)* dulce <*f. water* agua dulce>; *(unused)* nuevo; *(additional)* nuevo <*f. evidence* nuevas pruebas>; *(recent)* reciente; *(inexperienced)* nuevo; *(not tired)* fresco, refrescado; *(pure)* pure <*f. air* aire puro>; ZOOL. recentina; FAM. *(impudent)* fresco, descarado ♦ **f. from** recién llegado de <*f. from Paris* recién llegado de París> • **f.**

from the oven recién sacado del horno • **in the f. air** al aire libre • **to be f. out of** FAM. acabarse de quedar sin <*I am f. out of sugar* me acabo de quedar sin azúcar> II. adv. recientemente, acabado de <*f.-baked bread* pan acabado de hacer> III. s. *(the early part)* fresco, frescor *m* <*the f. of the day* el frescor del día>; *(overflow of a stream)* crecida; *(stream)* corriente de agua dulce *f*.
fresh·en (frĕsh'ən) intr. *(wind)* refrescar; *(to lose saltiness)* desalarse; ZOOL. parir y dar leche como resultado ♦ **to f. up** refrescarse, asearse —tr. *(to refresh)* refrescar; *(to desalinize)* desalarse.
fresh·en·er (frĕsh'ə-nər) s. *(tonic)* fortificante *m*; *(purifier)* purificador *m* <*an air f.* un purificador de aire>.
fresh·et (frĕsh'ĭt) s. *(overflow)* avenida, riada; *(freshwater outlet)* corriente de agua dulce que penetra en el mar *f*.
fresh·ly (frĕsh'lē) adv. recientemente, recién <*f.-baked bread* pan recién horneado>.
fresh·man (frĕsh'mən) s. [pl. **-men**] *(student)* estudiante de primer año *mf*; *(novice)* novato, principiante *mf*.
fresh·ness (frĕsh'nĭs) s. *(newness)* frescura (comestibles, flores); *(coolness)* frescura; *(novelty)* novedad *f*; *(youthfulness)* frescura, lozanía; *(purity)* pureza (aire, agua); FAM. *(impudence)* frescura, descaro.
fresh·wa·ter (frĕsh'wô'tər) adj. de agua dulce.
fret¹ (frĕt) I. intr. **fret·ted, fret·ting** *(to become vexed)* molestarse, irritarse; *(to worry)* preocuparse; *(to complain)* refunfuñar, quejarse; *(to wear away)* desgastarse; *(to become corroded)* carcomerse; *(water)* rizarse, agitarse —tr. *(to annoy)* molestar; *(to erode)* desgastar; *(to corrode)* carcomer; *(to form a passage by erosion)* cavar; *(water)* rizar, agitar II. s. *(erosion)* desgaste *m*; *(worn spot)* parte desgastada *o* carcomida; *(vexation)* molestia, irritación *f*; *(worry)* preocupación *f*.
fret² (frĕt) MÚS. I. s. traste *m* II. tr. **fret·ted, fret·ting** poner trastes a.
fret·ful (frĕt'fəl) adj. *(irritable)* irritable, molesto; *(complaining)* refunfuñón.
fret·work (frĕt'wûrk') s. CARP. calado; ARQ. greca.
Freu·di·an (froi'dē-ən) adj. freudiano.
Freudian slip s. expresión verbal del subconsciente *f*.
fri·ar (frī'ər) s. fraile *m*.
fric·a·tive (frĭk'ə-tĭv) FONÉT. I. s. consonante fricativa II. adj. fricativo.
fric·tion (frĭk'shən) s. *(rubbing)* fricción *f*; *(conflict)* fricción, desacuerdo; FÍS. fricción.
friction match s. fósforo, cerilla.
friction tape s. ELEC. cinta aisladora *o* de fricción.
Fri·day (frī'dē) s. viernes *m*.
fridge (frĭj) s. FAM. refrigerador *m*, nevera.
fried (frīd) pret. y part. p. de **fry¹**.
friend (frĕnd) s. amigo ♦ **a f. in need is a f. indeed** en el peligro se conoce al amigo • **a f. of** un amigo de • **a f. of mine** un amigo mío • **close** *o* **good f.** un amigo íntimo • **dear f.** amigo querido • **F.** cuáquero • **f. of the family** un amigo de la casa • **lifelong f.** amigo de toda la vida *o* de siempre • **man's best f.** el perro • **my best f.** mi mejor amigo • **my honourable f.** G.B., DER. mi honorable amigo • **my learned f.** mi docto amigo, mi eminente colega • **to be (best) friends with** ser muy amigo de • **to be the best of friends** ser muy amigos • **to become good** *o* **fast friends** hacerse buenos amigos • **to have friends in high places** FIG. tener influencia • **to make friends** ganarse amigos, trabar amistad • **to make friends with** hacerse amigo de, trabar amistad con <*we made friends with them right away* nos hicimos amigos de ellos en seguida> • **to part friends** separarse en buenos términos.
friend·less (frĕnd'lĭs) adj. *(without friends)* sin amigos; *(lonely)* solitario.
friend·li·ness (frĕnd'lē-nĭs) s. amigabilidad *f*, amabilidad *f*.
friend·ly (frĕnd'lē) I. adj. **-li·er, -li·est** *(amicable)* amable, simpático; *(warm)* amistoso, acogedor; *(not hostile)* amigo; *(allied)* aliado; *(favorable)* favorable ♦ **f. advice** consejo de amigo • **to be favorable a f. with** ser amigo de • **to be on f. terms with** estar en buenos términos con • **to become f. (with)** hacerse amigo (de) • **to maintain**

ā rey / ă año / b boca / ch chico / d dar / ĕ el / ē mil / g gato / h joya / hw juez / ī aire / k casa / kw cuan /

f. relations with mantener relaciones amistosas con **II.** adv. amigablemente, amistosamente.

friend·ship (frĕnd'shĭp') s. amistad *f.*

fri·er (frī'ər) s. var. de **fryer.**

frieze (frēz) s. *(decorative band)* cenefa; ARQ. friso.

frig·ate (frĭg'ĭt) s. fragata.

fright (frīt) s. *(fear)* miedo, susto; FAM. *(mess)* esperpento.

fright·en (frīt'n) tr. & intr. *(to scare)* asustar(se); *(to alarm)* alarmar(se).

fright·en·ing (frīt'n-ĭng) adj. espantoso.

fright·ful (frīt'fəl) adj. *(dreadful)* espantoso, horrible; *(terrifying)* aterrador, atemorizador; FAM. *(excessive)* tremendo, colosal.

frig·id (frĭj'ĭd) adj. *(cold)* muy frío, helado; *(indifferent)* indiferente, frío; MED. frígido.

Frig·i·daire (frĭj'ĭ-dâr') s. Frigidaire (marca registrada) *m.*

fri·gid·i·ty (fri-jĭd'ĭ-tē) s. *(coldness)* frialdad *f; (indifference)* desapego, indiferencia; MED. frigidez *f.*

frigid zone s. GEOG. zona glacial.

frill (frĭl) **I.** s. COST. *(trim)* encañonado; *(flared edge)* faralá *m,* volante *m;* CUL. guarnición de papel *f;* ZOOL. gola, collarín *m;* FOTOG. arrugamiento ♦ **frills** FAM. adornos **II.** tr. COST. encañonar —intr. FOTOG. arrugarse.

frill·y (frĭl'ē) adj. **-i·er, -i·est** COST. *(trimmed)* con volantes *o* faralás; FIG. *(frivolous)* con muchos adornos.

fringe (frĭnj) **I.** s. COST. *(trim)* franja; *(flounce)* fleco, orla; *(border)* borde *m,* ribete *m;* POL. grupo marginal *o* extremista; OPT. franja ♦ **fringes** margen *<on the fringes of the law* a la margen de la ley*>* • **on the f.** *o* **fringes of** en la periferia de **II.** tr. **fringed, fring·ing** *(to serve as a fringe)* orlar, orillar *<trees fringed the road* los árboles orlaban el camino>; COST. *(to add fringe to)* franjear, ribetear.

fringe benefit s. beneficios suplementarios (como seguro de vida, seguro médico y otros).

frip·per·y (frĭp'ə-rē) s. [pl. **-ies]** *(finery)* perifollos; *(affected elegance)* afectación *f,* cursilería; *(trifle)* baratija, frusleria.

frisk (frĭsk) **I.** intr. retozar, juguetear —tr. *(to shake)* agitar, mover; FAM. *(to search)* cachear, palpar (de armas) **II.** s. *(leap)* brinco, cabriola; *(amusement)* diversión *f; (search)* cacheo, registro (de armas).

frisk·y (frĭs'kē) adj. **-i·er, -i·est** *(playful)* retozón, juguetón; *(lively)* vivo, activo; *(fiery)* fogoso (díc. de caballos).

frit·ter¹ (frĭt'ər) tr. desmenuzar ♦ **to f. away** malgastar.

frit·ter² (frĭt'ər) s. CUL. fritura, fritada.

fri·vol·i·ty (frĭ-vŏl'ĭ-tē) s. frivolidad *f.*

friv·o·lous (frĭv'ə-ləs) adj. *(trivial)* frívolo, baladí; *(useless)* inútil, vano.

frizz (frĭz) **I.** tr. *(to curl)* rizar, encrespar (pelo); TEC. frisar *(tejido)* —intr. rizarse, encresparse **II.** s. rizo, bucle *m.*

friz·zle¹ (frĭz'əl) tr. **-zled, -zling** *(to fry)* achicharrar; *(to scorch)* quemar, retostar —intr. freírse *o* tostarse chirriando.

friz·zle² (frĭz'əl) s. crespo, rizo.

friz·zly (frĭz'lē) adj. **-zli·er, -zli·est** rizado, muy ensortijado.

friz·zy (frĭz'ē) adj. **-zi·er, -zi·est** muy rizado, encrespado.

fro (frō) adv. atrás, hacia atrás ♦ **to and f.** de aquí para allá.

frock (frŏk) s. *(monk's habit)* hábito, vestido talar; *(dress)* vestido (esp. ligero y abierto).

frock coat s. levita.

frog (frŏg) s. ZOOL. rana; FAM. *(in throat)* ronquera, carraspera; DESPEC., JER. *(a Frenchman)* franchute *m.*

frog kick s. DEP. patada de rana (estilo de natación).

frog·man (frŏg'măn') s. [pl. **-men** (-mĕn')] *(diver)* buceador *m,* buzo; MIL. hombre rana.

frol·ic (frŏl'ĭk) **I.** s. *(merriment)* jugueteo, diversión *f; (party)* fiesta, holgorio; *(mischief)* travesura, jugarreta **II.** intr. **-icked, -ick·ing** *(to play merrily)* juguetear, retozar; *(to engage in antics)* hacer travesuras.

frol·ic·some (frŏl'ĭk-səm) adj. juguetón, travieso.

from (frŭm, frŏm) prep. ⎯ DISTANCIA, LUGAR de *<I live twenty miles f. the city* vivo a veinte millas de la ciudad>; desde *<I walked f. my office* vine caminando desde mi oficina>; de *<where are you f.?* ¿de dónde eres?> ⎯ TIEMPO de *<I work f. nine to five* trabajo de nueve a cinco>; desde *<f. that moment* desde aquel momento>; a

partir de *<I'll be available f. Monday on* estaré disponible a partir del lunes> ⎯ ORIGEN, RAZÓN de *<a note f. the teacher* una nota de la maestra>; de parte de *<a message f. him* un mensaje de parte de él>; de parte *<tell him that f. me* dile eso de parte mía>; sacado de, de *<a quotation f. the Bible* una cita de la Biblia>; a causa de, por *<he died f. the heat* murió por el calor> ⎯ SACAR, QUITAR de *<who took this book f. the shelf?* ¿quién sacó este libro del estante?>; de *<liberation f. bondage* la liberación de la esclavitud>; a *<they stole the bicycle f. the child* le robaron la bicicleta al niño> ⎯ DE ACUERDO CON por, según *<f. what he told me, it was your fault* según lo que él me dijo, fue culpa tuya>; por *<he was speaking f. his own experience* él hablaba por experiencia propia> ⎯ DE, ENTRE de *<to protect oneself f. the rain* protegerse de la lluvia>; entre *<she was chosen f. fifty participants* fue elegida entre cincuenta participantes> ⎯ EXPRESIONES IDIOMÁTICAS ♦ **f. above** desde lo alto • **f. afar** desde lejos • **f. bad to worse** de mal en peor • **f. behind** desde atrás, por atrás • **f. day to day** de un día para otro • **f. beginning to end** del principio al fin • **f. birth** de nacimiento • **f. memory** de memoria • **f. now on** de ahora en adelante • **f. time to time** de vez en cuando, ocasionalmente.

frond (frŏnd) s. BOT. fronda.

front (frŭnt) **I.** s. *(forefront)* frente *m,* parte delantera; *(façade)* frente *m,* fachada; *(face)* cara, rostro; *(forehead)* frente *f; (beginning)* principio, comienzo *<it's in the f. of the book* está al principio del libro>; *(demeanor)* postura, posición *f <she maintained a brave f.* ella mantuvo una posición valiente>; *(appearance)* apariencia; MIL. frente *m;* METEOR. frente *m; (coalition)* coalición *f,* frente *m;* FAM. *(cover)* pantalla, fachada; *(field)* campo *<the economic f.* el campo de la economía>; *(of a shirt)* pechera; *(promenade)* malecón *m,* costanera ♦ **from the f.** por delante, de frente • **in f. of** delante de, frente a, en frente de • **out f.** afuera *<the car is parked out f.* el automóvil está estacionado afuera> • **to put on a bold f.** hacer de tripas corazón **II.** adj. *(in the front)* delantero, frontal; FONÉT. anterior, palatal ♦ **f. door** puerta de entrada • **f. organization** organización controlada clandestinamente por un partido político • **f. row** primera fila **III.** tr. *(to face)* dar frente a, dar a *<our house fronts the park* nuestra casa da al parque>; *(to confront)* hacer frente a, afrontar; CONSTR. poner una fachada a —intr. • **to f. on** *o* **onto** mirar (hacia), dar frente (a) • **to f. for** servir de fachada (a).

front·age (frŭn'tĭj) s. CONSTR. anchura de un solar *o* terreno a lo largo de una calle *o* camino; *(direction)* orientación *f; (adjacent land)* terreno frontero ♦ **with f. on** con fachada a.

fron·tal (frŭn'tl) adj. *(at the front)* frontal, de frente; ANAT., METEOR. frontal.

front bench s. G.B. *(in Parliament)* banco azul.

front-end (frŭnt'ĕnd') adj. *(front)* de la parte delantera (de un aparato o vehículo); *(initial)* de la fase inicial (de un proyecto).

fron·tier (frŭn-tîr', frŏn-) **I.** s. *(border)* frontera, límite *m;* FIG. *(unexplored field)* campo **II.** adj. fronterizo *<a f. region* una región fronteriza>.

fron·tiers·man (frŭn-tîrz'mən, frŏn-) s. [pl. **-men]** *(inhabitant)* habitante de la frontera *m;* ANT. *(pioneer)* colonizador *m,* explorador *m* (del oeste de EE. UU.).

fron·tis·piece (frŭn'tĭ-spēs') s. IMPR. frontispicio; ARQ. fachada, frontispicio.

front-line (frŭnt'līn') adj. *(of the vanguard)* de la vanguardia; MIL. de la línea del frente.

front man s. testaferro.

front money s. depósito *o* pago inicial.

front office s. los ejecutivos de una organización.

front-page (frŭnt'pāj') **I.** adj. de primera plana **II.** tr. **-paged, -pag·ing** publicar en primera plana.

front-run·ner (frŭnt'rŭn'ər) s. *(leader)* el que está en ventaja *o* va adelante en una competencia (esp. política); DEP. corredor que se desempeña mejor cuando va adelante.

front·ward (frŭnt'wərd) adj. & adv. al frente, hacia el frente.

front·wards (frŭnt'wərdz) adv. hacia adelante.

frost (frôst) **I.** s. *(ice)* escarcha, helada blanca <*f. on the windows* escarcha en las ventanas>; *(freezing weather)* helada <*an early f.* una helada temprana>; *(freezing process)* congelación *f*; FIG. *(coolness)* frialdad *f*, indiferencia; JER. *(failure)* fracaso **II.** tr. *(to speckle)* empañar (bombilla, vidrio); CUL. escarchar; AGR. quemar —intr. ♦ **to f. over** *o* **up** cubrir con escarcha, empañar.

frost·bite (frôst′bīt′) **I.** s. MED. congelación *f*; AGR. quemadura **II.** tr. **-bit** (-bĭt′), **-bit·ten** (-bĭt′n), **-bit·ing** MED. congelar; AGR. quemar, helar.

frost·bit·ten (frôst′bĭt′n) adj. *(plant)* quemado por el hielo; MED. congelado.

frost·ed (frô′stĭd) adj. *(with ice)* escarchado; *(said of windows, glass)* empañado; *(said of desserts)* escarchado; *(said of foods)* helado, congelado.

frost·ing (frô′stĭng) s. CUL. glaseado; TEC. escarchado, esmerilado.

frost·y (frô′stē) adj. **-i·er, -i·est** *(freezing)* muy frío, de helada <*a f. evening* una noche de helada>; FIG. *(cold)* frío, glacial (sonrisa, recibimiento); *(white)* canoso, cano.

froth (frôth) **I.** s. *(foam)* espuma, espumarajo; FIG. *(triviality)* trivialidad *f*, palabras vanas **II.** tr. cubrir con espuma, hacer espumar —intr. espumar, hacer espuma.

froth·y (frô′thē) adj. **-i·er, -i·est** *(foamy)* espumoso, de espuma; FIG. *(frivolous)* frívolo, insubstancial (carácter).

frown (froun) intr. fruncir el entrecejo ♦ **to f. at** mirar con ceño • **to f. on** *o* **upon** *(to disapprove of)* desaprobar; *(to disdain)* desdeñar, despreciar.

frown·ing (frou′nĭng) adj. ceñudo, ceñoso.

frow·zy *o* **frow·sy** (frou′zē) adj. **-zi·er, -zi·est** *o* **-si·er, -si·est** *(slovenly)* desaseado, desaliñado; *(unkempt)* despeinado; *(smelly)* mal oliente.

froze (frōz) pret. de **freeze.**

fro·zen (frō′zən) adj. *(iced over)* helado, congelado; *(very cold)* gélido, frígido; *(preserved)* congelado; *(numb)* entumecido; FIG. *(paralyzed)* paralizado, inmóvil; *(cold)* frío, insensible; COM. congelado.

frozen food s. alimentos congelados.

fruc·ti·fy (frŭk′tə-fī′, frōōk′-) intr. **-fied, -fy·ing** *(to produce)* producir, fructificar; BOT. fructificar, dar frutos —tr. fertilizar, fecundar.

fruc·tose (frŭk′tōs′, frōōk′-) s. QUÍM. fructosa, azúcar de frutas *m*.

fru·gal (frōō′gəl) adj. *(thrifty)* frugal, parco; *(inexpensive)* económico, barato.

fru·gal·i·ty (frōō-găl′ĭ-tē) s. frugalidad *f*.

fruit (frōōt) **I.** s. [pl. **fruit** *o* **fruits**] *(food)* fruta <*I like f.* me gusta la fruta>; BOT. fruto; *(progeny)* prole *f*, progenie *f*; JER. *(male homosexual)* marica *m* ♦ **candied f.** fruta escarchada • **dried f.** fruta seca • **forbidden f.** FIG. fruta prohibida • **f. compote** compota de fruta • **f. tree** árbol frutal • **fruits** resultados *o* fruto **II.** intr. dar fruto, producir frutas —tr. hacer *o* dar fruto.

fruit·cake (frōōt′kāk′) s. CUL. torta de frutas; JER. *(crazy person)* loco; *(swishy homosexual)* maricón *m*.

fruit cup s. CUL. ensalada de frutas.

fruit·er·er (frōō′tər-ər) s. frutero (vendedor).

fruit fly s. ENTOM. mosca de las frutas, mosca mediterránea.

fruit·ful (frōōt′fəl) adj. *(bearing fruit)* fructífero, fértil; *(prolific)* prolífico, fecundo; *(abounding)* abundante, copioso; *(profitable)* productivo, provechoso.

fruit·ful·ness (frōōt′fəl-nĭs) s. *(capacity)* capacidad fructífera; *(fertility)* fertilidad *f*, fecundidad *f*; *(profitability)* lo fructuoso, carácter provechoso.

fruit·i·ness (frōō′tē-nĭs) s. *(of wine)* olor *o* sabor a fruta *m*; FIG. *(sentimentality)* sentimentalidad *f*; JER. *(homosexuality)* mariconería; *(craziness)* chifladura.

fru·i·tion (frōō-ĭsh′ən) s. *(enjoyment)* fruición *f*, goce *m*; *(fructification)* fructificación *f*; *(accomplishment)* realización *f*, cumplimiento ♦ **to bring to f.** realizar • **to come to f.** realizarse.

fruit·less (frōōt′lĭs) adj. *(unproductive)* improductivo, infructuoso; *(useless)* inútil, vano; BOT. estéril, infecundo.

fruit·y (frōō′tē) adj. **-i·er, -i·est** *(said of wine)* de olor *o* sabor de fruta; *(sentimental)* sentimental.

frump (frŭmp) s. *(plain woman)* mujer desaliñada y gru-

ñona, estantigua; FIG., FAM. *(old-fashioned person)* persona chapada a la antigua.

frump·y (frŭm′pē) adj. **-i·er, -i·est** *(unattractive)* desaliñado, sin atractivo; *(old-fashioned)* chapado a la antigua, anticuado.

frus·trate (frŭs′trāt′) tr. **-trat·ed, -trat·ing** *(to thwart)* frustrar, impedir; *(to disappoint)* frustrar, defraudar.

frus·tra·tion (frŭ-strā′shən) s. frustración *f*.

frus·tum (frŭs′təm) s. [pl. **-tums** *o* **-ta** (-tə)] GEOM. tronco (de cono, pirámide).

fru·tes·cent (frōō-tĕs′ənt) adj. frutescente, arbustivo.

fry¹ (frī) **I.** tr. **fried, fry·ing** *(to cook)* freír; JER. *(to electrocute)* electrocutar —intr. freírse, achicharrarse; JER. *(to be electrocuted)* morir electrocutado **II.** s. [pl. **fries**] fritura, fritada ♦ **fries** patatas *o* papas fritas.

fry² (frī) s. [pl. **fry**] *(young fish)* pececillos ♦ **small f.** gente menuda.

fry·er (frī′ər) s. CUL. *(pan)* freidora, sartén *f*; *(chicken)* pollo para freír.

frying pan s. sartén *f*.

f-stop (ĕf′stŏp′) s. FOTOG. abertura útil del diafragma de una cámara.

fuch·sia (fyōō′shə) s. *(color)* rojo púrpura; BOT. fucsia.

fuck (fŭk) VULG. **I.** tr. & intr. joder, coger ♦ **f. off!** ¡vete a la mierda!, ¡vete al carajo! • **f. you!** ¡vete al carajo! • **to f. up** arruinar, estropear • **to f. around with** joder a, fastidiar a **II.** s. encamada.

fucked-up (fŭkt′ŭp′) adj. VULG. *(screwed-up)* jodido, estropeado; *(confused)* confundido, empelotado.

fuck·ing (fŭk′ĭng) adj. & adv. VULG. *(damn)* maldito, condenado; *(very)* muy, sumamente.

fud·dle (fŭd′l) **I.** tr. *(to intoxicate)* emborrachar; FIG. *(to confuse)* atontar, confundir —intr. empinar el codo, beber **II.** s. *(drunkenness)* embriaguez *f*, borrachera; *(confusion)* confusión *f* ♦ **to be in a f.** *(to be drunk)* estar bebido; *(to be confused)* estar atontado *o* confundido.

fud·dy-dud·dy (fŭd′ē-dŭd′ē) s. [pl. **-dies**] FAM. carcamal *m*.

fudge (fŭj) **I.** s. *(candy)* dulce de chocolate, leche y azúcar *m*; *(nonsense)* tontería, disparate *m* **II.** tr. **fudged, fudging** *(to fake)* fingir, engañar; FIG. *(to dodge)* evadir, eludir —intr. *(to vacillate)* vacilar, fluctuar; *(to cheat)* engañar, estafar ♦ **to f. on** dejar de cumplir con.

fu·el (fyōō′əl) **I.** s. *(combustible)* combustible *m*; FIG. *(stimulant)* pábulo ♦ **to add f. to the fire** FIG. echar leña al fuego • **to be f. for** dar pábulo a **II.** tr. *(furnace)* alimentar; *(auto)* echar gasolina a; *(ship, plane)* abastecer de combustible a; *(to stimulate)* dar pábulo a, animar —intr. abastecerse de combustible.

fuel cell s. QUÍM. celda electroquímica; ELEC. pila seca.

fuel injection s. AUTO., MEC. método de inyección de combustible.

fuel oil s. QUÍM. aceite fuel *m*, aceite combustible.

fuel pump s. surtidor de gasolina *m*, gasolinera.

fu·gi·tive (fyōō′jĭ-tĭv) adj. & s. fugitivo.

fugue (fyōōg) s. MÚS. fuga; MED. amnesia temporal.

füh·rer (fyōōr′ər) s. jefe supremo, caudillo ♦ **F.** título de Adolfo Hitler (en la Alemania nazi).

ful·fill *o* **ful·fil** (fōōl-fĭl′) tr. *(conditions, requirements)* llenar; *(function)* desempeñar; *(contract, promise)* cumplir (con), ejecutar; *(need, wish)* satisfacer; *(project, ambition)* realizar.

ful·fill·ment *o* **ful·fil·ment** (fōōl-fĭl′mənt) s. *(contract, promise)* cumplimiento, ejecución *f*; *(need, wish)* satisfacción *f*; *(project, ambition)* realización *f*.

full (fōōl) **I.** adj. **-er, -est** *(completely filled)* lleno <*a f. pail* un balde lleno>; *(complete)* completo, detallado <*a f. account* un informe completo>; *(maximum)* máximo <*at f. speed* a máxima velocidad>; *(crowded)* repleto, atestado <*a bus f. of people* un ómnibus atestado de gente>; *(occupied to capacity)* completo; *(exact)* exacto <*a f. dozen* una docena exacta>; *(entire)* entero, completo <*he ran a f. mile* corrió una milla entera>; *(total)* total <*he has f. control* él tiene total control>; FIG. *(emotionally charged)* lleno <*she is f. of anxieties* está llena de ansiedades>; pleno <*it happened in f. view of everybody* sucedió a plena vista de todos>; *(plump)* amplio <*a f. figure* un cuerpo amplio>;

COST. *(wide)* ancho, holgado; *(satiated)* saciado, lleno; *(said of meals)* completo <*a f. meal* una comida completa>; *(abundant)* abundante; *(said of flavors)* intenso *(sabor)*; *(of same parents)* carnal <*f. brothers* hermanos carnales> ♦ **f. blast** FIG. a todo vapor, a toda máquina ♦ **f. name** nombre completo, nombre y apellido • **f. powers** plenos poderes • **f. sail** vela llena • **f. speed ahead!** MARÍT. ¡avante a toda máquina! • **f. to the brim** lleno hasta el borde • **to be f.** *(to be satiated)* estar lleno, estar satisfecho; *(to have a full house)* no tener lugar (hotel, teatro) • **to have a f. life** tener una vida plena de actividades • **to the fullest extent** completamente, al máximo II. adv. *(very)* extremadamente, muy <*you did it knowing f. well that I objected* lo hiciste sabiendo muy bien que no te oponía>; *(directly)* directamente, de lleno <*it hit him f. in the face* le dio de lleno en la cara> ♦ **f. grown** crecido, completamente desarrollado • **in f. swing** FIG. en plena operación III. tr. COST. dar amplitud a —intr. llegar al plenilunio IV. s. *(completeness)* máximo; *(totality)* totalidad *f*; *(height)* plenitud *f* ♦ **in f.** completamente, detalladamente • **to pay in f.** pagar íntegramente una deuda.

full-blood·ed (fo͝ol′blŭd′ĭd) adj. *(purebred)* de raza, de casta; *(consanguineous)* de sangre; *(vigorous)* vigoroso, robusto; *(complete)* cabal.

full-blown (fo͝ol′blōn′) adj. BOT. *(having opened)* abierto <*a full-blown tulip* un tulipán abierto>; *(having blossomed)* florecido; *(fully developed)* desarrollado, maduro; *(complete)* completo, consumado.

full-bod·ied (fo͝ol′bŏd′ēd) adj. CUL. aromático y de buen cuerpo.

full dress s. *(male attire)* traje de etiqueta *m*; *(female attire)* traje de noche; MIL. uniforme de gala *m*.

full-dress (fo͝ol′drĕs′) adj. *(complete)* completo, cabal; *(formal)* de etiqueta, de gala <*a full-dress banquet* un banquete de gala>; *(thorough)* minucioso, a fondo.

full·er (fo͝ol′ər) s. TEJ. batanero.

full-fledged (fo͝ol′flĕjd′) adj. *(mature)* desarrollado; *(having full status)* cabal <*a full-fledged lawyer* un abogado cabal>; ORNIT. de plumaje completo.

full-grown (fo͝ol′grōn′) adj. *(plant)* crecido; *(person)* maduro.

full house s. *(of cards)* full *m*, mano completa; *(of people)* sala repleta.

full-length (fo͝ol′lĕngkth′) adj. *(showing the entire length)* de cuerpo entero; *(of a standard length)* de tamaño normal ♦ **film** película de largo metraje.

full moon s. luna llena.

full·ness (fo͝ol′nĭs) s. *(abundance)* abundancia, plenitud *f*; *(satiety)* saciedad *f*, hartura; *(of clothes)* amplitud *f*.

full-scale (fo͝ol′skāl′) adj. *(of actual size)* de tamaño natural; *(employing all resources)* en gran escala, a todo dar <*a f. campaign* una campaña en gran escala>.

full-size (fo͝ol′sīz′) o **full-sized** (-sīzd′) adj. de tamaño natural *o* normal.

full stop s. GRAM. punto ♦ **to come to a f.** FIG. parar en seco.

full swing adv. en plena actividad.

full tilt adv. a toda velocidad, a todo dar.

full-time (fo͝ol′tīm′) adj. de jornada completa.

ful·ly (fo͝ol′ē) adv. *(totally)* completamente, enteramente; *(at least)* por lo menos <*his opinion is f. as important as yours* su opinión es por lo menos tan importante como la tuya>.

ful·mi·nate (fo͝ol′mə-nāt′, fŭl′-) I. intr. **-nat·ed, -nat·ing** *(to denounce)* tronar <*to f. against political chicanery* tronar contra la trapacería política>; *(to explode)* fulminar, estallar —tr. *(to thunder out)* fulminar <*to f. a denunciation* fulminar una denuncia>; *(to cause to explode)* hacer estallar II. s. QUÍM. fulminato.

ful·mi·na·tion (fo͝ol′mə-nā′shən, fŭl′-) s. fulminación *f*.

ful·some (fo͝ol′səm) adj. *(insincere)* empalagoso, hipócrita <*f. praise* elogios empalagosos>; *(offensive)* de mal gusto.

fum·ble (fŭm′bəl) I. intr. **-bled, -bling** *(to handle nervously)* enredarse <*he fumbled with the necktie* se enredó con la corbata>; *(to handle idly)* manosear, jugar; *(to grope awkwardly)* buscar torpemente; *(to proceed awkwardly)* ir a tientas ♦ **to f. for words** buscar las palabras, vacilar —tr.

(to handle clumsily) manejar torpemente; *(to handle idly)* manosear, jugar con; *(to bungle)* estropear; DEP. *(to drop)* dejar caer ♦ **to f. one's way** ir a tientas II. s. torpeza.

fum·bler (fŭm′blər) s. *(clumsy person)* torpe *mf*; DEP. jugador que comete muchos errores (esp. al coger la pelota) *m*.

fum·bling (fŭm′blĭng) adj. torpe.

fume (fyo͞om) I. s. *(smoke)* humo, tufo; *(vapor)* vapor *m*, vaho; *(gas)* gas *m*; FIG. *(anger)* cólera, furia ♦ **fumes** humo II. tr. **fumed, fum·ing** ahumar, echar humo a —intr. *(to smoke)* echar humo, humear; FIG. *(to be angry)* echar humo, enfurecerse <*the crowd was fuming over the delay* la multitud se enfureció por la demora>.

fu·mi·gate (fyo͞o′mĭ-gāt′) tr. & intr. **-gat·ed, -gat·ing** fumigar.

fu·mi·ga·tion (fyo͞o′mĭ-gā′shən) s. fumigación *f*.

fu·mi·ga·tor (fyo͞o′mĭ-gā′tər) s. fumigador *m*.

fun (fŭn) s. *(amusement)* diversión *f*; *(merriment)* alegría ♦ **for f.** *(as a joke)* en broma, bromeando; *(for fun)* para divertirse • **for the f. of it** *(to have fun)* para divertirse; *(for the sake of it)* por gusto • **in f.** en broma, bromeando • **like f.** JER. de eso nada, ni hablar • **to be f.** ser divertido <*clowns are f.* los payasos son divertidos> • **to have f.** divertirse, pasarlo bien • **to make f. of** *o* **to poke f. at** reírse *o* burlarse de • **to spoil the f.** aguar la fiesta • **what f.!** ¡qué divertido!

func·tion (fŭngk′shən) I. s. *(purpose)* función *f*; *(duty)* función, ocupación *f*; *(ceremony)* acto, ceremonia; *(relation)* relación *f* <*growth is a f. of nutrition* el crecimiento está en relación con la nutrición>; ANAT., GRAM., MAT., QUÍM. función ♦ **in one's f. as** en calidad de, en capacidad de II. intr. *(to work properly)* funcionar; *(to serve)* servir, prestar servicio <*to f. as* servir en la capacidad de>.

func·tion·al (fŭngk′shə-nəl) adj. funcional.

functional illiterate s. persona de educación mínima.

func·tion·ar·y (fŭngk′shə-nĕr′ē) s. [pl. **-ies**] funcionario.

func·tion·ing (fŭngk′shə-nĭng) s. funcionamiento.

fund (fŭnd) I. s. *(resource)* fondo; *(source)* fuente *f*; *(organization)* fondo <*monetary f.* fondo monetario> ♦ **funds** fondos, dinero disponible • **the funds** G.B. deuda pública II. tr. COM. *(to furnish)* suministrar fondos para, constituir un fondo para; *(to finance)* financiar, costear; *(to consolidate)* consolidar (una deuda); *(to place in a fund)* colocar en un fondo.

fun·da·ment (fŭn′də-mənt) s. *(principle)* fundamento, base *f*; *(foundation)* cimiento; *(buttocks)* trasero, fondillo; *(anus)* ano.

fun·da·men·tal (fŭn′də-mĕn′tl) I. adj. fundamental II. s. fundamento.

fun·da·men·tal·ism (fŭn′də-mĕn′tl-ĭz′əm) s. adhesión a los fundamentos *f* ♦ **F.** RELIG. movimiento protestante que cree literal e incondicionalmente en la Biblia.

fun·da·men·tal·ist (fŭn′də-mĕn′tl-ĭst) s. RELIG. fundamentalista *mf*.

fundamental particle s. FÍS. partícula elemental *o* fundamental.

fund·ing (fŭn′dĭng) s. financiamiento.

fund raiser s. *(one who raises funds)* recaudador de fondos *m*; *(social function)* acto para la recaudación de fondos.

fund-rais·ing (fŭnd′rā′zĭng) adj. para recaudar fondos, de recaudación de fondos.

fu·ner·al (fyo͞o′nər-əl) s. *(ceremony)* funeral *m*, funerales; *(burial)* entierro; *(procession)* cortejo fúnebre ♦ **f. march** marcha fúnebre • **f. pyre** pira, hoguera • **f. service** misa de cuerpo presente • **f. urn** urna funeraria • **to be one's f.** FAM. ser cosa de uno.

funeral home s. funeraria.

fu·ner·ar·y (fyo͞o′nə-rĕr′ē) adj. funerario, funeral.

fu·ne·re·al (fyo͞o-nîr′ē-əl) adj. fúnebre.

fun·gi (fŭn′jī′) un pl. de **fungus**.

fun·gi·cid·al (fŭn′jĭ-sīd′l, fŭng′gī-) adj. fungicida.

fun·gi·cide (fŭn′jĭ-sīd′, fŭng′gī-) s. fungicida *m*.

fun·gous (fŭng′gəs) adj. BOT. fungal, fungino; MED. fungoso, fungóseo.

fun·gus (fŭng′gəs) s. [pl. **fun·gi** (fŭn′jī′) *o* **fun·gus·es**] BOT. hongo; MED. fungo, hongo.

---

ng inglés / ŏ la / ō bou / ô corre / oi oigo / o͞o uno / ou auto / yo͞o ciudad / w hueco / y yo / z mismo

fun house s. *(haunted house)* casa de brujas; *(house of mirrors)* casa de los espejos.

fu·nic·u·lar (fyoo-nĭk'yə-lər, fə-) adj. & s. funicular *m*.

funk (fŭngk) FAM. I. s. *(panic)* depresión *f*, cobardía; *(person)* cobarde *mf*, gallina *mf* ♦ **to be in a f.** estar desanimado *o* acobardado II. tr. tener miedo a, amilanarse ante —intr. acobardarse, rajarse.

funk·y (fŭng'kē) adj. **-i·er, -i·est** miedoso, nervioso.

fun·nel (fŭn'əl) I. s. *(utensil)* embudo; *(shaft)* túnel *m*; *(stack)* chimenea II. intr. tomar forma de embudo, encañonarse ♦ **to f. through** encauzarse, pasar *<tourists were funneling slowly through customs* los turistas pasaban lentamente a través de la aduana> —tr. *(to pour)* verter por un embudo; *(to channel)* encauzar, dirigir.

fun·ny (fŭn'ē) I. adj. **-ni·er, -ni·est** *(amusing)* divertido, cómico, gracioso *<a very f. story* un cuento muy gracioso>; *(odd)* raro, extraño *<I heard a f. noise* sentí un ruido extraño>; *(fishy)* sospechoso ♦ **that's not f.** eso no es ninguna gracia • **to try to be f.** hacerse el gracioso II. s. [pl. **-nies**] gracia, chiste *m* ♦ **funnies** tiras cómicas, muñequitos.

funny bone FAM. *(sense of humor)* sentido del humor; ANAT. huesito de la alegría.

funny paper s. sección de tiras cómicas *f*, muñequitos.

fur (fûr) I. s. *(garment)* abrigo de piel *o* pieles; *(trimming)* guarnición de piel *f*; *(coating on tongue)* sarro, saburra; ZOOL. *(coat of hair)* pelo, pelaje *m*; *(hide)* piel *f* ♦ **a f. coat** abrigo de piel *o* pieles II. tr. **furred, fur·ring** *(to cover with fur)* cubrir con pieles; *(to line)* forrar con pieles.

fur·bish (fûr'bĭsh) tr. *(to polish)* bruñir, pulir; *(to renovate)* renovar, restaurar.

Fu·ries (fyoor'ēz) s.pl. MITOL. Furias.

fu·ri·ous (fyoor'ē-əs) adj. *(angry, violent)* furioso; *(very fast)* vertiginoso ♦ **at a f. pace** a toda velocidad • **fast and f.** a todo lo que da, a todo meter.

fu·ri·ous·ly (fyoor'ē-əs-lē) adv. *(angrily)* furiosamente; *(violently)* furiosamente, violentamente; *(very fast)* vertiginosamente.

furl (fûrl) I. tr. *(to roll up)* enrollar, plegar; *(wings)* recoger; MARÍT. aferrar —intr. enrollarse, plegarse II. s. *(act)* enrollamiento; *(roll)* rollo.

fur·long (fûr'lông') s. estadio.

fur·lough (fûr'lō) I. s. licencia, permiso ♦ **to be on f.** estar de permiso II. tr. *(to lay off)* suspender temporalmente; MIL. dar licencia *o* permiso a.

fur·nace (fûr'nĭs) s. *(burning chamber)* horno; *(domestic heater)* estufa; FIG. *(hot place)* horno, infierno; *(severe trial)* prueba dura, infierno.

fur·nish (fûr'nĭsh) tr. *(to provide furniture for)* amueblar; *(to supply)* suministrar, proporcionar (dinero, comida); *(to give)* dar (oportunidad); *(proof)* aducir (prueba) ♦ **furnished apartment** apartamento *o* departamento amueblado • **to f. with** suministrar a, proveer de.

fur·nish·ing (fûr'nĭ-shĭng) s. artículo ♦ **furnishings** *(furniture)* mobiliario, moblaje *m*; *(apparel)* ropa, artículos de vestir.

fur·ni·ture (fûr'nĭ-chər) s. *(household articles)* muebles *m*, mobiliario; *(accesories)* accesorios, aditamentos; IMPR. imposiciones *f* ♦ **a piece of f.** un mueble • **f. store** mueblería.

fu·ror (fyoor'ôr') s. *(anger)* furor *m*, arrebato; *(excitement)* frenesí *m*; *(commotion)* conmoción.

fur·ri·er (fûr'ē-ər) s. peletero.

fur·row (fûr'ō) I. s. *(groove)* ranura, estría; *(skin)* surco, arruga; AGR. surco II. tr. *(to wrinkle)* arrugar; AGR. surcar —intr. *(to become wrinkled)* arrugarse; AGR. llenarse de surcos.

fur·ry (fûr'ē) adj. **-ri·er, -ri·est** *(covered with fur)* peludo; *(tongue)* sarroso.

fur·ther (fûr'thər) I. adj. [comp. de **far**] *(more distant)* más lejano, más alejado *<nothing was f. from the truth* no hubo nada más alejado de la verdad>; *(opposite)* otro *<on the f. side of the street* al otro lado de la calle>; *(additional)* otro, más *<I have two f. questions* tengo dos preguntas más>; *(new)* nuevo *<until f. notice* hasta nuevo aviso>; *(higher)* superior *<f. education* educación superior>

II. adv. [comp. de **far**] *(to a greater extent)* más *<we have to study the matter f.* tenemos que estudiar más el asunto>; *(furthermore)* además; *(at or to a more distant point)* más lejos, más allá *<they traveled f. than we did* ellos viajaron más lejos que nosotros> ♦ **f. back** *(in space)* más atrás; *(in time)* antes • **f. on** más adelante III. tr. promover, fomentar.

fur·ther·more (fûr'thər-môr') adv. además.

fur·thest (fûr'thĭst) I. adj. [superl. de **far**] *(more distant)* más lejano; *(remotest)* más remoto *<the f. corner of the earth* el rincón más remoto de la tierra>; *(extreme)* extremo II. adv. [superl. de **far**] *(to the greatest extent)* al extremo; *(at or to the most distant point)* más lejos.

fur·tive (fûr'tĭv) adj. furtivo.

fu·ry (fyoor'ē) s. [pl. **-ries**] *(rage)* furia, ira; *(violent action)* furia, violencia *<the blizzard's f.* la furia de la tormenta>; *(angry woman)* furia ♦ **Furies** MITOL. las (tres) Furias • **to be in a f.** estar furioso.

furze (fûrz) s. BOT. aulaga, árgamo.

fuse¹ (fyooz) s. *(combustible wick)* mecha; ARM. *(device)* espoleta ♦ **to light the f.** encender la mecha.

fuse² (fyooz) I. tr. & intr. **fused, fus·ing** *(to melt)* fundir(se), derretir(se); *(to blend)* fundir(se), combinar(se); *(to merge)* fusionar(se) II. s. ELEC. fusible *m*, tapón *m* ♦ **f. box** caja de fusibles *o* plomos • **to blow a f.** *(to get angry)* enfurecerse, encolerizarse; ELEC. quemar un fusible, fundir(se) un plomo.

fu·se·lage (fyoo'sə-läzh') s. AVIA. fuselaje *m*.

fu·si·ble (fyoo'zə-bəl) adj. fusible.

fu·sil·lade (fyoo'sə-läd', -lād') I. s. *(barrage)* andanada, lluvia *<a f. of insults* una lluvia de insultos>; MIL. descarga repetida, tiroteo II. tr. **-lad·ed, -lad·ing** MIL. *(to attack)* barrer con una descarga; *(to shoot down)* fusilar.

fu·sion (fyoo'zhən) s. *(melting)* fusión *f*, derretimiento; *(smelting)* fundición *f*, colada; FIG. *(mixture)* unión *f*, coalición *f*; FÍS. fusión.

fusion bomb s. FÍS. bomba termonuclear.

fuss (fŭs) I. s. *(commotion)* alboroto, bulla *<can't we give a party without a lot of f.?* ¿no podemos hacer una fiesta sin tanto alboroto?>; *(unwarranted concern)* aspavientos; *(formalities)* cumplidos; *(objection)* quejas; *(quarrel)* lío ♦ **not to be worth the f.** no valer la pena • **to kick up** *o* **to make a f.** armar un lío • **to make a f. over someone** mimar II. intr. *(to get excited)* preocuparse, inquietarse (por boberías); *(to be excessively solicitous)* preocuparse mucho por *<they fussed over their children* se preocupaban mucho por los niños>; *(to be nervously active)* agitarse, andar de acá para allá *<she fussed in the kitchen all afternoon* toda la tarde anduvo de acá para allá en la cocina>; *(to object)* quejarse ♦ **to f. with** jugar con, toquetear —tr. FAM. fastidiar.

fuss·budg·et (fŭs'bŭj'ĭt) s. *(fastidious person)* quisquilloso; *(finicky person)* melindroso.

fuss·i·ness (fŭs'ē-nĭs) s. *(fastidiousness)* carácter quisquilloso; *(finickiness)* escrupulosidad *f*, melindre *m*; *(meticulousness)* meticulosidad *f*; *(ornateness)* recargamiento.

fuss·pot (fŭs'pŏt') s. FAM. *(fastidious person)* quisquilloso; *(finicky person)* melindroso.

fuss·y (fŭs'ē) adj. **-i·er, -i·est** *(easily upset)* susceptible, irritable; *(fastidious)* quisquilloso; *(finicky)* escrupuloso, melindroso; *(meticulous)* meticuloso, concienzudo; *(ornate)* recargado.

fus·ty (fŭs'tē) adj. **-ti·er, -ti·est** *(smelling of mildew)* que huele a viejo, mohoso; *(old-fashioned)* anticuado.

fu·tile (fyoot'l, fyoo'tīl') adj. *(ineffectual)* inútil, vano *<a f. effort* un esfuerzo inútil>; *(useless)* fútil, frívolo.

fu·til·i·ty (fyoo-tĭl'ĭ-tē) s. [pl. **-ties**] *(ineffectuality)* inutilidad *f*; *(uselessness)* frivolidad *f*, futilidad *f*.

fu·ture (fyoo'chər) I. s. futuro, porvenir *m* *<plans for the f.* planes para el futuro>; *(chance of success)* porvenir *<a business with no f.* un negocio sin un porvenir>; GRAM. *(tense)* futuro; *(verb form)* verbo en futuro ♦ **in the f.** en el futuro, en lo sucesivo • **in the near f.** dentro de poco, en fecha próxima • **futures** COM. futuros, bienes de entrega futura II. adj. futuro, venidero *<f. generations* las generaciones venideras>; GRAM. futuro.

ā rey / ä año / b boca / ch chico / d dar / ě el / ē mil / g gato / h joya / hw juez / ī aire / k casa / kw cuan /

future shock s. desadaptación ante el futuro *f*, trauma de cambio *m*.
future tense s. GRAM. tiempo futuro.
fu·tur·ism (fyōō′chə-rĭz′əm) s. futurismo.
fu·tur·ist (fyōō′chər-ĭst) s. futurista *mf*.
fu·tur·ist·ic (fyōō′chə-rĭs′tĭk) adj. futurista.
fu·tu·ri·ty (fyōō-chōōr′ĭ-tē) s. [pl. **-ties**] *(future)* futuro, porvenir *m*; *(condition)* futuridad *f*; *(future event)* acontecimiento futuro.
fuze (fyōōz) s. var. de **fuse**.
fuzz[1] (fŭz) **I.** s. *(light fibers)* pelusa, tamo; *(light hairs)* pelusa, vello **II.** tr. *(to cover with fuzz)* llenar de pelusa; *(to blur)* nublar, empañar.
fuzz[2] (fŭz) s. JER. policía, poli *f*.
fuzz·y (fŭz′ē) adj. **-i·er, -i·est** *(covered with fuzz)* lleno de pelusa; *(downy)* velloso, velludo; *(indistinct)* borroso; *(confused)* confuso, enredado.

G

g, G (jē) s. [pl. **g's, G's**] séptima letra del alfabeto inglés; MÚS. sol *m*; FÍS. signo de la gravedad ♦ **G.** JER. *(one thousand dollars)* mil dólares • **G flat, major, minor, sharp** MÚS. sol bemol, mayor, menor, sostenido.
gab (găb) FAM. **I.** intr. **gabbed, gab·bing** parlotear, picotear **II.** s. parloteo, palique *m* ♦ **to have the gift of g.** FAM. tener mucha labia.
gab·ar·dine (găb′ər-dēn′) s. gabardina.
gab·ble (găb′əl) **I.** intr. **-bled, -bling** *(to babble)* cotorrear; *(to cackle)* graznar —tr. decir atropelladamente **II.** s. *(babble)* cotorreo; *(jumble of noises)* graznido.
gab·by (găb′ē) adj. **-bi·er, -bi·est** FAM. locuaz, hablador.
ga·ble (gā′bəl) s. ARQ. *(of a roof)* hastial *m*, aguilón *m*; *(ornament)* gablete *m*.
gable roof s. ARQ. techo a dos aguas.
Ga·bon (gă-bôn′) s. Gabón *m*.
Ga·bon·ese (găb′ə-nēz′) adj. & s. [pl. **Gabonese**] gabonés *m*.
gad (găd) intr. **gad·ded, gad·ding** deambular, callejear.
gad·a·bout (găd′ə-bout′) s. FAM. trotacalles *mf*, callejero.
gad·fly (găd′flī′) s. [pl. **-flies**] ENTOM. *(fly)* tábano, moscardón *m*; *(person)* persona latosa o pesada.
gadg·et (găj′ĭt) s. FAM. artilugio, dispositivo.
gadg·et·ry (găj′ĭ-trē) s. [pl. **-ries**] *(gadgets)* artilugios, dispositivos; *(construction)* fabricación de artilugios *f*.
gad·o·lin·i·um (găd′l-ĭn′ē-əm) s. QUÍM. gadolinio.
Gael (gāl) s. gaélico.
Gael·ic (gā′lĭk) adj. & s. *(language)* gaélico.
gaff (găf) **I.** s. MARÍT. *(iron hook)* garfio, gancho; MARÍT. *(spar)* pico de cangreja, cangrejo; *(spur)* espolón *m*; *(climbing hook)* pincho; *(hoax)* trampa, truco **II.** tr. *(to harpoon)* enganchar; JER. *(to cheat)* clavar, engañar; *(dice)* cargar (dados).
gaffe (găf) s. *(clumsy error)* metida de pata; *(faux pas)* paso en falso ♦ **to make a g.** meter la pata.
gaf·fer (găf′ər) s. *(old man)* viejo, vejestorio; *(rustic)* patán *m*, rústico.
gag (găg) **I.** s. *(muffling object)* mordaza; *(restraint on free speech)* mordaza, censura; FAM. *(prank)* broma; *(comic remark)* chiste *m* **II.** tr. **gagged, gag·ging** *(to muffle)* amordazar; *(to censor)* amordazar, tapar la boca a; *(to cause to choke)* atorar, ahogar; *(to cause to retch)* hacer arquear, dar náuseas a —intr. *(to choke)* atorarse, ahogarse; *(to retch)* hacer arqueadas; FAM. *(to make jokes)* hacer chistes.
ga·ga (gä′gä) adj. JER. *(giddy)* chocho; *(insane)* chiflado; *(completely infatuated)* loco.
gage[1] (gāj) **I.** s. *(pledge)* prenda, garantía; *(challenge)* reto, desafío.
gage[2] (gāj) s. BOT. ciruela verdal.
gage[3] (gāj) s. & v. var. de **gauge**.
gag·gle (găg′əl) s. *(flock)* manada de gansos; *(group)* grupo.

gai·e·ty (gā′ĭ-tē) s. [pl. **-ties**] *(cheerfulness)* regocijo, alegría; *(finery)* gala.
gai·ly (gā′lē) adv. alegremente, jovialmente.
gain (gān) **I.** tr. *(to win)* ganar; *(to acquire)* adquirir, obtener; *(to earn)* conquistar, granjearse (afecto, respeto); *(to build up)* cobrar <the movement gained strength el movimiento cobró ímpetu>; *(of a timepiece)* adelantarse; COM. *(to increase in value)* subir (acciones); *(to advance)* avanzar, progresar <the player gained ten yards el jugador avanzó diez yardas>; *(to reach)* ganar, alcanzar ♦ **to g. ground** ganar terreno • **to g. weight** engordar, aumentar de peso —intr. *(to become greater)* aumentar; *(to become better)* mejorar; *(to increase in value)* subir (valor) ♦ **to g. on** ganar terreno, acercarse **II.** s. *(profit)* ganancia, beneficio; *(increase)* aumento; ELECTRÓN. *(ratio)* ganancia, amplificación *f* ♦ **a g. in** un aumento en • **gains** *(profits)* ganancias; *(acquisitions)* adquisiciones.
gain·er (gā′nər) s. *(person)* persona beneficiada, ganador *m*; DEP. *(dive)* puntapié a la luna con salto mortal hacia atrás (en natación) *m*.
gain·ful (gān′fəl) adj. ventajoso, lucrativo.
gain·say (gān-sā′) tr. **-said, -say·ing** *(to deny)* negar; *(to oppose)* oponerse a; *(to contradict)* contradecir.
gait (gāt) **I.** s. *(of a person)* andadura, paso; EQUIT. *(of a horse)* paso **II.** tr. EQUIT. adiestrar a un trote.
gai·ter (gā′tər) s. polaina, sobrecalza.
gal (găl) s. FAM. muchacha, chica.
ga·la (gā′lə, găl′ə) **I.** s. gala, fiesta **II.** adj. *(marked by celebration)* de gala; *(merry)* de fiesta.
ga·lac·tic (gə-lăk′tĭk) adj. ASTRON. galáctico; FIG. *(immense)* inmenso, muy grande.
Ga·la·tians (gə-lā′shənz) s. BÍBL. Gálatas *m*.
gal·a·vant (găl′ə-vănt′) v. var. de **gallivant**.
gal·ax·y (găl′ək-sē) s. [pl. **-ies**] ASTRON. galaxia; FIG. *(assemblage)* constelación *f*, pléyade *f* ♦ **the G.** ASTRON. la Galaxia, la Vía Láctea.
gale (gāl) s. *(wind)* vendaval *m*, ventarrón *m*; *(outburst)* explosión (de risa) *f* ♦ **gales of laughter** carcajadas.
Ga·li·cian (gə-lĭsh′ən) adj & s. gallego.
Gal·i·le·an o **Gal·i·lae·an** (găl′ə-lē′ən) **I.** adj. HIST. *(of Galilee)* galileo, de Galilea o *(of Galileo)* de Galileo **II.** s. HIST. *(of Galilee)* galileo; *(Christian)* cristiano, galileo ♦ **the G.** BÍBL. el Galileo, Cristo.
Gal·i·lee (găl′ə-lē′) s. Galilea.
gall[1] (gôl) s. FISIOL. bilis *f*, hiel *f*; ANAT. *(gallbladder)* vesícula biliar, vejiga de hiel; FIG. *(bitterness)* amargura, rencor *m*; *(impudence)* caradura, descaro.
gall[2] (gôl) s. VET. matadura, rozadura; *(exasperation)* exasperación *f*, irritación *f*; BOT. agalla **II.** tr. VET. hacer una matadura o rozadura; *(to chafe)* rozar, excoriar; FIG. *(to exasperate)* molestar, irritar; *(to mortify)* mortificar, vejar —intr. molestarse, irritarse.
gal·lant (găl′ənt) **I.** adj. *(courageous)* gallardo, bizarro; *(dashing)* galano, gallardo; *(stately)* imponente, gallardo; *(chivalrous)* galante; *(flirtatious)* galanteador **II.** s. *(young man)* galán *m*; *(lady's man)* galán, amante *m* **III.** tr. galantear, cortejar —intr. ser galante.
gal·lant·ly (găl′ənt-lē) adv. *(courageously)* gallardamente, con bizarría, valientemente; *(chivalrously)* galantemente; *(flirtatiously)* con galantería, galantemente.
gal·lant·ry (găl′ən-trē) s. [pl. **-ries**] *(courage)* valentía, valor *m*; *(courtliness)* galantería.
gall·blad·der o **gall bladder** (gôl′blăd′ər) s. ANAT. vesícula biliar, vejiga de hiel.
gal·le·on (găl′ē-ən) s. HIST., MARÍT. galeón *m*.
gal·ler·y (găl′ə-rē) s. [pl. **-ies**] *(for spectators)* galería; ARTE., MARÍT., MIL., MIN. galería ♦ **to play to the g.** actuar para la galería, complacer al vulgo.
gal·ley (găl′ē) s. [pl. **-leys**] *(ship)* galera; *(kitchen)* cocina; IMPR. *(tray)* galera; *(galley proof)* galerada.
galley proof s. IMPR. galerada.
galley slave s. HIST., MARÍT. *(slave)* galeote *m*; FIG. *(drudge)* esclavo.
Gal·li·cism (găl′ĭ-sĭz′əm) s. galicismo.
Gal·li·cize (găl′ĭ-sīz′) tr. & intr. **-cized, -ciz·ing** afrancesar(se).

---

ng inglés / ŏ **la** / ō **bou** / ô **corre** / oi **oigo** / ōō **uno** / ou **auto** / yōō **ciudad** / w **hueco** / y **yo** / z **mismo**

gal·li·na·ceous (găl'ə-nā'shəs) adj. ORNIT. gallináceo.
gall·ing (gô'lĭng) adj. irritante, exasperante.
gal·li·um (găl'ē-əm) s. QUÍM. galio.
gal·li·vant (găl'ə-vănt') intr. *(to roam)* callejear; *(to flirt)* flirtear.
gal·lon (găl'ən) s. galón (medida y recipiente) m.
gal·lop (găl'əp) I. s. galope m ♦ **at a g.** al galope • **at full g.** a galope tendido II. tr. *(to cause to gallop)* hacer galopar, hacer ir al galope; *(to transport at a gallop)* llevar (algo) al galope ♦ **to g. through** FIG. hacer de prisa —intr. *(to ride at a gallop)* galopar; FIG. *(to dash)* ir a la carrera.
gal·lop·ing (găl'ə-pĭng) adj. galopante <*g. consumption* tisis galopante>.
gal·lows (găl'ōz) s. [pl. **gallows** o **-lows·es**] *(device for execution)* horca; *(structure for suspending)* armazón m, montante m; *(execution)* ahorcadura.
gallows bird s. FAM. persona que merece ser ahorcada, carne de horca f.
gallows humor s. humor negro.
gall·stone (gôl'stōn') s. MED. cálculo biliar.
gal·op (găl'əp) s. MÚS. galopa (danza y música).
ga·lore (gə-lôr') adj. FAM. en cantidad, a granel.
ga·losh (gə-lŏsh') s. chanclo.
gal·van·ic (găl-văn'ĭk) adj. ELEC., MED. galvánico, del galvanismo; FIG. *(stimulating)* estimulante; *(convulsive)* convulsivo, nervioso.
gal·va·nism (găl'və-nĭz'əm) s. ELEC., MED. galvanismo.
gal·va·nize (găl'və-nīz') tr. **-nized, -niz·ing** ELEC., METAL. galvanizar; FIG. *(to stimulate)* estimular.
galvanized iron s. METAL. hierro galvanizado.
gal·va·nom·e·ter (găl'və-nŏm'ĭ-tər) s. ELEC., FÍS. galvanómetro.
Gam·bi·a (găm'bē-ə) s. Gambia.
Gam·bi·an (găm'bē-ən) adj. & s. gambiano.
gam·bit (găm'bĭt) s. *(chess move)* gambito; FIG. *(remark)* frase para iniciar una conversación f; *(strategy)* estratagema, maniobra.
gam·ble (găm'bəl) I. intr. **-bled, -bling** *(to bet)* jugar (juegos de azar); *(to take a risk)* arriesgarse —tr. *(to bet)* jugar, apostar; *(to risk)* arriesgar ♦ **to g. away** perder en el juego • **to g. on** *(to depend on)* confiar en que, contar con que; *(to bet on)* jugar a, apostar a II. s. *(bet)* jugada; *(risk)* riesgo, empresa arriesgada.
gam·bler (găm'blər) s. jugador m.
gam·bling (găm'blĭng) s. juego ♦ **g. house** casa de juego.
gam·bol (găm'bəl) I. intr. brincar, cabriolar II. s. brinco, cabriola.
gam·brel (găm'brəl) s. ZOOL. *(hock)* corvejón m; *(butcher's hook)* garabato; *(frame for carcasses)* caballete de suspensión (de carnicería) m.
gambrel roof s. ARQ. techo a la holandesa (de ángulo obtuso).
game¹ (gām) I. s. *(diversion)* juego; *(sport)* juego, deporte m; *(single contest in board games)* partida <*we played two games of checkers* jugamos dos partidas de damas>; *(single contest in ball games)* partido; *(in tennis, cards)* juego; *(style of playing)* juego, estilo de jugar <*his tennis g. is brilliant* su estilo de jugar al tenis es brillante>; *(wild animals)* caza; *(fish)* pesca; *(quarry)* presa ♦ **big g.** caza mayor • **board g.** juego de mesa • **fair g.** *(legal game)* caza legal; FIG. *(easy target)* buena presa • **g. of chance** juego de azar • **the g. is up!** FIG. ¡se acabó la jugada! • **to be on to** *o* **to see through someone's g.** conocer el juego a alguien • **to play someone's g.** hacer el juego de alguien • **what's your g.?** FAM. ¿a qué te dedicas? • **to play games** FIG. jugar, andar con trucos II. tr. **gamed, gam·ing** ANT. perder (algo) en el juego —intr. jugar (por dinero) III. adj. **gam·er, gam·est** *(plucky)* valeroso, valiente; FAM. *(willing)* dispuesto, listo.
game² (gām) adj. **gam·er, gam·est** cojo, lisiado.
game·cock (gām'kŏk') s. gallo de pelea.
game·keep·er (gām'kē'pər) s. guardabosque mf; guarda de caza mf.
game plan s. DEP. plan m o estrategia de juego.
game show s. concurso televisivo.
games·man·ship (gāmz'mən-shĭp') s. maestría en juegos.

gam·ete (găm'ēt', gə-mēt') s. BIOL. gameto.
game theory MAT. teoría de juegos (usando la ley de la probabilidad).
ga·me·to·gen·e·sis (gə-mē'tə-jĕn'ĭ-sĭs) *o* **gam·e·tog·e·ny** (găm'ĭ-tŏj'ə-nē) s. BIOL. gametogénesis f, gametogenia (formación de los gametos).
gam·ing (gā'mĭng) s. juego ♦ **g. table** mesa de juego.
gam·ma (găm'ə) s. FILOL. gamma (letra griega); FÍS. rayo gamma.
gamma globulin s. FISIOL., MED. globulina gamma, gamma globulina.
gamma ray s. FÍS. *(radiation)* rayo gamma; *(photon)* fotón de alta energía m.
gam·mon (găm'ən) I. s. *(ham)* jamón ahumado; *(bacon)* tocino salado; *(backgammon victory)* juego doble (en chaquete) II. tr. ganar registrando un juego doble.
gam·o·gen·e·sis (găm'ə-jĕn'ĭ-sĭs) s. BIOL. gamogénesis f, reproducción f.
gam·ut (găm'ət) s. *(range)* gama, serie f; MÚS. *(scale)* gama, escala ♦ **to run the g.** abarcarlo todo, cubrirlo todo.
gam·y (gā'mē) adj. **-i·er, -i·est** *(of meat)* de sabor u olor a carne salvajina; *(spoiled)* maloliente, apestoso; *(plucky)* valeroso, valiente; *(disreputable)* de mala fama; *(scandalous)* escandaloso.
gan·der (găn'dər) s. *(goose)* ganso, ánsar (macho) m; FAM. *(simpleton)* simplón m, tonto; JER. *(glance)* ojeada, mirada ♦ **to take a g. at** echar una ojeada a.
gang (găng) I. s. *(social group)* pandilla, cuadrilla <*the whole g. went to the movies* la cuadrilla entera fue al cine>; *(group of delinquents)* pandilla, banda; *(group of laborers)* cuadrilla, brigada; *(set of tools)* juego <*a g. of chisels* un juego de cinceles>; *(herd)* manada II. intr. ♦ **to g. up** formar una pandilla, agruparse • **to g. up on** atacar en grupo.
gang·bust·er (găng'bŭs'tər) s. JER. funcionario que combate el crimen organizado ♦ **like gangbusters** FAM. con todo, a todo trapo.
gan·gling (găng'glĭng) adj. larguirucho, delgaducho.
gan·gli·on (găng'glē-ən) s. [pl. **-ons** o **gan·gli·a** (-glē-ə)] ANAT. ganglio.
gan·gly (găng'glē) adj. **-glier, -gli·est** larguirucho, delgaducho.
gang·plank (găng'plăngk') s. MARÍT. plancha (de desembarco).
gang·grene (găng'grēn') I. s. MED. gangrena II. tr. & intr. gangrenar(se).
gan·gre·nous (găng'grə-nəs) adj. gangrenoso.
gang·ster (găng'stər) s. gangster m, bandido.
gangue (găng) s. MIN. ganga.
gang·way (găng'wā') s. *(passageway)* pasillo; MARÍT. *(passage)* pasamano, crujía; *(gangplank)* plancha de desembarco; *(opening)* portalón m; MIN. *(main level)* nivel principal m ♦ **gangway!** ¡paso!
gan·net (găn'ĭt) s. ORNIT. alcatraz m, onocrótalo.
gant·let (gônt'lĭt, gănt'-) s. var. de **gauntlet**¹,².
gan·try (găn'trē) s. [pl. **-tries**] *(barrel support)* caballete m; MEC. *(for cranes)* pórtico; FC. *(for signals)* puente transversal de señales m; AER. *(vertical frame)* torre de lanzamiento f.
gaol (jāl) s. & v. G.B. var. de **jail**.
gap (găp) I. s. *(opening)* boquete m, hueco; *(crack)* hendedura; *(between mountains)* desfiladero; *(blank)* espacio; *(lacuna)* laguna (en escrito); *(of time)* intervalo; *(disparity)* diferencia, discrepancia <*a g. between expenses and receipts* una discrepancia entre los gastos y los comprobantes>; ELEC. separación f ♦ **to bridge the g.** salvar las diferencias • **to fill a g.** compensar una deficiencia II. tr. **gapped, gap·ping** hacer un boquete o una brecha en —intr. *(to become open)* abrirse; *(to be open)* estar abierto.
gape (gāp) I. intr. **gaped, gap·ing** *(to yawn)* bostezar; *(to stare)* quedarse boquiabierto; *(to become separated)* abrirse ♦ **to g. at** quedarse mirando con la boca abierta II. s. *(yawn)* bostezo; *(stare)* mirada atónita; *(large opening)* boquete m, brecha ♦ **gapes** [ú. con v. sing.] *(disease)* enfermedad de las aves de corral f, moquillo; *(fit of yawning)* ataque de bostezos m.

gap·er (gā′pər) s. *(one who gapes)* mirón *m*, curioso; ICT. pez cabrilla *m*.

gap·ing (gā′pĭng) adj. *(open)* abierto; *(deep)* profundo.

gar (gär) s. ICT. sollo, pez aguja *m*.

ga·rage (gə-räzh′, -räj′) I. s. garaje *m* II. tr. **-raged, -rag·ing** dejar en un garaje.

garb (gärb) I. s. *(dress)* traje *m*, vestidura; *(guise)* garbo, porte *m* II. tr. vestir.

gar·bage (gär′bĭj) s. *(refuse)* basura, desperdicio; *(worthless thing)* porquería.

gar·ble (gär′bəl) I. tr. **-bled, -bling** *(to distort)* desvirtuar (hechos); *(to scramble)* mezclar; *(to cull)* seleccionar, escoger II. s. *(distortion)* desvirtuación *f*; *(scramble)* mezcla.

gar·den (gär′dn) I. s. *(for flowers)* jardín *m*; *(for vegetables)* huerto, huerta; *(lawn)* jardín; *(fertile region)* vega ♦ **botanical gardens** jardín botánico • **to lead someone down the g. path** engañar a alguien II. tr. *(to cultivate)* cultivar; *(to furnish with a garden)* hacer un jardín a —intr. *(to care for flowers)* trabajar en el jardín; *(to care for vegetables)* cultivar el huerto III. adj. *(of flowers)* de jardín; *(of vegetables)* del huerto, de la huerta ♦ **g. apartments** edificios de apartamentos con jardines • **g. tools** aperos (de jardinería).

gar·den·er (gärd′nər) s. *(of flowers)* jardinero; *(of vegetables)* hortelano.

gar·de·nia (gär-dēn′yə) s. BOT. gardenia.

gar·den·ing (gärd′nĭng) s. *(of flowers)* jardinería; *(of vegetables)* horticultura.

gar·gan·tu·an (gär-găn′chōō-ən) adj. enorme, tremendo.

gar·gle (gär′gəl) I. intr. **-gled, -gling** gargarizar, hacer gárgaras —tr. *(to disinfect)* limpiar haciendo gárgaras; *(to utter)* decir como haciendo gárgaras II. s. *(medication)* gargarismo; *(sound)* gárgara.

gar·goyle (gär′goil′) s. ARQ. gárgola.

gar·ish (gâr′ĭsh) adj. *(gaudy)* chillón, charro; *(flashy)* llamativo.

gar·land (gär′lənd) I. s. *(wreath)* guirnalda; MARÍT. *(rope)* eslinga; *(anthology)* antología II. tr. enguirnaldar.

gar·lic (gär′lĭk) s. BOT., CUL. ajo.

gar·ment (gär′mənt) I. s. vestido, prenda de vestir II. tr. vestir.

gar·ner (gär′nər) I. tr. *(to store)* almacenar, acopiar; *(to accumulate)* acumular II. s. granero.

gar·net (gär′nĭt) s. MIN. granate *m*; *(color)* granate, color rojo oscuro.

gar·nish (gär′nĭsh) I. tr. *(to embellish)* adornar; CUL. *(to decorate)* guarnecer, aderezar (un plato); DER. embargar II. s. *(embellishment)* adorno, ornamento; CUL. guarnición *f*, aderezo.

gar·nish·ee (gär′nĭ-shē′) DER. I. s. embargado II. tr. **-eed, -ee·ing** embargar.

gar·nish·ment (gär′nĭsh-mənt) s. *(ornamentation)* adorno; DER. *(attachment)* embargo; *(injunction)* entredicho.

gar·ni·ture (gär′nĭ-chər) s. *(adornment)* adorno, CUL. *(garnish)* guarnición *f*, aderezo.

gar·ret (gär′ĭt) s. *(room)* buhardilla; *(attic)* ático, desván *m*.

gar·ri·son (gär′ĭ-sən) MIL. I. s. guarnición *f* II. tr. *(to post troops)* poner en guarnición; *(to occupy)* guarnecer.

gar·rote *o* **gar·rotte** (gə-rŏt′) I. s. *(execution method)* garrote *m*; *(strangulation)* estrangulación *f* II. tr. **-rot·ed, -rot·ing** *o* **-rot·ted, -rot·ting** *(to execute)* agarrotar; *(to strangle)* estrangular.

gar·ru·li·ty (gə-rōō′lĭ-tē) s. locuacidad *f*.

gar·ru·lous (gär′ə-ləs) adj. gárrulo, locuaz.

gar·ter (gär′tər) I. s. liga ♦ **G.** *(badge)* Jarretera; *(order)* Orden de la Jarretera II. tr. *(to support)* sostener con una liga; *(to put on)* poner una liga a.

gas (găs) I. s. [pl. **gas·es** *o* **gas·ses**] FÍS., QUÍM. gas *m*; *(gasoline)* gasolina; *(asphyxiant)* gas asfixiante; *(anesthetic)* gas anestésico; MIN. grisú *m*; JER. *(idle talk)* cháchara, palique *m*; *(enjoyable activity)* delicia ♦ **to step on the g.** pisar *o* apretar el acelerador II. tr. **gassed, gas·sing** QUÍM. tratar con gas; *(to poison)* asfixiar *o* envenenar con gas —intr. *(to give off gas)* desprender *o* despedir gas;

JER. *(to talk idly)* chacharear ♦ **to g. up** FAM. llenar el tanque (de un vehículo con gasolina).

gas·bag (găs′băg′) s. AER. bolsa *o* cámara de gas; FIG., FAM. *(chatterbox)* parlanchín *m*, charlatán *m*.

gas chamber s. cámara de gas.

Gas·con (găs′kən) I. s. *(inhabitant, dialect)* gascón *m* II. adj. gascón.

Gas·co·ny (găs′kə-nē) s. Gascuña.

gas·e·ous (găs′ē-əs, găsh′əs) adj. *(of gas)* gaseoso, gaseiforme; FIG. *(tenuous)* insubstancial, tenue.

gash (găsh) I. tr. acuchillar II. s. cuchillada.

gas·i·fi·ca·tion (găs′ə-fĭ-kā′shən) s. gasificación *f*.

gas·i·fy (găs′ə-fī′) tr. & intr. **-fied, -fy·ing** gasificar(se), convertir(se) en gas.

gas jet s. *(gas burner)* mechero *o* quemador de gas *m*; *(flame)* llama.

gas·ket (găs′kĭt) s. MEC. junta, arandella; MARÍT. tomador (de vela) *m*.

gas·light (găs′līt′) s. *(lighting)* luz *f o* alumbrado de gas; *(lamp)* lámpara de gas.

gas main s. cañería principal de gas.

gas mask s. máscara antigás.

gas·o·line *o* **gas·o·lene** (găs′ə-lēn′) s. QUÍM. gasolina, nafta.

gas·om·e·ter (gă-sŏm′ĭ-tər) s. gasómetro.

gasp (găsp) I. intr. *(to take a sudden breath)* quedar boquiabierto; *(to pant)* jadear ♦ **to g. for air** hacer esfuerzos para respirar —tr. decir con el aliento entrecortado II. s. jadeo.

gas station s. estación de servicio para automotores *f*, gasolinera.

gas stove s. cocina a gas.

gas·sy (găs′ē) adj. **-si·er, -si·est** *(of gas)* gaseoso, gaseiforme; JER. *(bombastic)* ampuloso, rimbombante.

gas tank s. tanque de gasolina *f*.

gas·tric (găs′trĭk) adj. ANAT. gástrico.

gas·tri·tis (gă-strī′tĭs) s. MED. gastritis *f*.

gas·tro·en·ter·i·tis (găs′trō-ĕn′tə-rī′tĭs) s. MED. gastroenteritis *f*.

gas·tro·en·ter·ol·o·gy (găs′trō-ĕn′tə-rŏl′ə-jē) s. MED. gastroenterología.

gas·tro·in·tes·ti·nal (găs′trō-ĭn-tĕs′tə-nəl) adj. MED. gastrointestinal.

gas·trol·o·gy (gă-strŏl′ə-jē) s. MED. gastrología.

gas·tro·nome (găs′trə-nŏm′) *o* **gas·tron·o·mer** (gă-strŏn′ə-mər) s. gastrónomo.

gas·tro·nom·ic (găs′trə-nŏm′ĭk) adj. gastronómico.

gas·tron·o·my (gă-strŏn′ə-mē) s. gastronomía.

gas·tro·pod (găs′trə-pŏd′) s. & adj. ZOOL. gasterópodo, gastrópodo.

gas·works (găs′wûrks′) s.pl. [ú. con v. sing.] TEC. fábrica de gas.

gat (găt) s. GEOL. canal *m*.

gate (gāt) s. *(door)* puerta; *(of iron)* verja; F.C. *(barrier)* barrera; *(at an airport)* puerta; *(portal)* pórtico, portal *m*; FIG. *(pathway)* camino; *(floodgate)* compuerta; *(gas valve)* válvula; METAL. *(channel)* taquilla; *(channel)* conducto de colada ♦ **to get the g.** JER. ser puesto de patitas en la calle • **to give someone the g.** JER. poner a uno de patitas en la calle.

gate·crash·er (gāt′krăsh′ər) s. JER. calado, persona que entra sin pagar.

gate·fold (gāt′fōld′) s. IMPR. lámina grande, plegada e insertada en un libro.

gate·house (gāt′hous′) s. *(of a park)* casa del guarda; F.C. *(of railway crossing)* caseta del guardabarrera.

gate·keep·er (gāt′kē′pər) s. portero.

gate·post (gāt′pōst′) s. poste *m*.

gate·way (gāt′wā′) s. *(opening)* pórtico; FIG. *(access)* puerta, entrada; FIG. *(pathway)* camino <*the g. to success* el camino del éxito>.

gath·er (găth′ər) I. tr. *(to collect)* reunir, juntar <*he gathered his books* juntó sus libros>; *(to congregate)* juntar, congregar; *(to infer)* inferir, deducir; *(to pick)* coger <*to g. flowers* coger flores>; *(to harvest)* cosechar, recoger; *(to amass)* acumular; *(to gain gradually)* cobrar, ganar <*to g.*

---

speed ganar velocidad>; COST. *(to pucker)* fruncir; *(to muster)* reunir, cobrar; *(to embrace)* tomar <*to g. a person into one's arms* tomar a una persona en los brazos de uno> ♦ **to g. from** concluir • **to g. one's thoughts** recoger los pensamientos • **to g. together** reunir, juntar • **to g. up** recoger —intr. *(to assemble)* reunirse, congregarse; *(to accumulate)* acumularse, amontonarse; *(to increase gradually)* aumentar; MED. *(to fester)* formarse pus ♦ **g. round!** ¡acérquense! • **to g. together** reunirse, juntarse **II.** s. *(act)* reunión f; *(quantity)* cosecha; COST. *(pucker)* frunce m, pliegue m.

gath·er·ing (găth′ər-ĭng) s. *(collection)* recolección f; *(assembly)* asamblea, reunión f; COST. *(pucker)* frunce m, pliegue m; MED. *(abscess)* absceso.

gauche (gōsh) adj. torpe, sin tacto.

gau·cho (gou′chō) s. gaucho.

gaud·y (gô′dē) adj. **-i·er, -i·est** llamativo, chillón.

gauge (gāj) **I.** s. *(measurement)* medida; *(size)* tamaño, extensión f; *(instrument)* calibrador m, aforador m; FIG. *(indicator)* muestra (de carácter, habilidad); MARÍT. *(position)* barlovento; F.C. entrevía, ancho de vía; ARM. calibre m; TEJ. número de hilos **II.** tr. **gauged, gaug·ing** *(to measure)* medir; FIG. *(to evaluate)* estimar, evaluar (carácter, habilidad); *(to determine)* determinar; *(to graduate)* graduar, calibrar; CONSTR. *(to mix plaster)* mezclar el yeso; *(to cut)* tallar (piedras).

Gaul (gôl) s. HIST. Galia; *(inhabitant)* galo.

Gaul·ish (gô′lĭsh) s. HIST. galo.

gaunt (gônt) adj. *(angular)* enjuto; *(emaciated)* macilento, demacrado; *(desolate)* desolado.

gaunt·let¹ (gônt′lĭt, gänt′-) s. *(medieval glove)* guantelete m; *(glove)* guante m; *(protective glove)* guante de manopla ♦ **to fling** o **throw down the g.** arrojar el guante • **to pick** o **take up the g.** recoger el guante, aceptar el desafío.

gaunt·let² (gônt′lĭt, gänt′-) s. HIST. baqueta ♦ **to run the g.** FIG. sufrir una crítica o desaprobación general.

gauss (gous) s. [pl. **gauss** o **gauss·es**] ELEC. gauss m, gausio (unidad electromagnética).

gauze (gôz) s. *(fabric)* cendal m; *(surgical cloth)* gasa; *(metal mesh)* tela metálica.

ga·vage (gə-väzh′) s. MED. alimentación por sonda f.

gave (gāv) pret. de **give**.

gav·el (găv′əl) **I.** s. *(hammer)* martillo; *(maul)* mazo (de albañil) **II.** tr. golpear (con el martillo).

ga·votte (gə-vŏt′) s. MÚS. gavota.

gawk (gôk) **I.** s. bobo **II.** intr. FAM. papar moscas.

gawk·y (gô′kē) adj. **-i·er, -i·est** torpe, desgarbado.

gay (gā) **I.** adj. **-er, -est** *(merry)* alegre; *(bright)* vistoso; *(dissolute)* disoluto, licencioso; JER. *(homosexual)* homosexual **II.** s. JER. homosexual mf.

gay·e·ty (gā′ĭ-tē) s. var. de **gaiety**.

gay·ly (gā′lē) adv. var. de **gaily**.

gay·ness (gā′nĭs) s. *(merriment)* alegría; *(brightness)* vistosidad f.

gaze (gāz) **I.** intr. **gazed, gaz·ing** ♦ **to g. at** mirar con fijeza, contemplar **II.** s. mirada fija.

ga·ze·bo (gə-zē′bō) s. [pl. **-bos** o **-boes**] *(structure)* mirador m; *(belvedere)* belvedere m.

ga·zelle (gə-zĕl′) s. ZOOL. gacela.

ga·zette (gə-zĕt′) s. *(newspaper)* gaceta, periódico; *(official journal)* gaceta, boletín oficial m.

gaz·et·teer (găz′ĭ-tîr′) s. *(dictionary)* diccionario geográfico; ANT. *(journalist)* gacetero.

gear (gîr) **I.** s. MEC. rueda dentada, engranaje m; AUTO. transmisión f, caja de cambios; *(speed)* velocidad f, marcha <*first g.* primera velocidad>; *(equipment)* equipo; *(personal belongings)* efectos personales; *(paraphernalia)* utensilios, accesorios; EQUIT. *(harness)* aparejos de tiro, arnés m; MARÍT. *(rigging)* aparejo ♦ **in g.** engranado • **to change** o **shift gears** cambiar de velocidad • **to put into g.** engranar **II.** tr. MEC. engranar; *(to outfit)* equipar ♦ **to g. something to** FIG. ajustar o adaptar algo a —intr. MEC. engranar ♦ **to g. (oneself) up** FIG. prepararse.

gear·box (gîr′bŏks′) s. AUTO. caja de cambios o de velocidades; MEC. caja o cárter de engranajes m.

gear·ing (gîr′ĭng) s. MEC. engranaje m, mecanismo de engranajes.

gear·shift (gîr′shĭft′) s. AUTO. mecanismo de cambios, palanca de cambios.

gear·wheel o **gear wheel** (gîr′hwēl′) s. MEC. rueda dentada o de engranaje.

geck·o (gĕk′ō) s. [pl. **-os** o **-oes**] ZOOL. salamanquesa, salamanqueja.

gee (jē) interj. ¡vamos! (a un animal de tiro); FAM. ¡caramba!

geese (gēs) pl. de **goose**.

gee·zer (gē′zər) s. JER. viejo excéntrico, tío.

Gei·ger counter (gī′gər) s. FÍS. contador Geiger m.

gel (jĕl) **I.** s. QUÍM. gel m **II.** intr. **gelled, gell·ing** gelificarse, cuajarse.

gel·a·tin o **gel·a·tine** (jĕl′ə-tn) s. QUÍM. *(protein)* gelatina; *(jelly)* jalea, gelatina.

ge·lat·i·nous (jə-lăt′n-əs) adj. gelatinoso.

ge·la·tion (jĕ-lā′shən) s. QUÍM. gelificación f.

geld (gĕld) tr. **geld·ed** o **gelt** (gĕlt), **geld·ing** castrar, capar.

geld·ing (gĕl′dĭng) s. caballo castrado.

gel·id (jĕl′ĭd) adj. gélido, helado.

gel·ig·nite (jĕl′ĭg-nīt′) s. ARM., QUÍM. gelignita, gelinita.

gelt (gĕlt) un pret. y part. p. de **geld**.

gem (jĕm) **I.** s. *(stone)* piedra preciosa, gema; FIG. *(beloved person or thing)* tesoro, joya; *(muffin)* panecillo **II.** tr. **gemmed, gem·ming** adornar con piedras preciosas.

Gem·i·ni (jĕm′ə-nī′) s. ASTROL. Géminis m.

gem·my (jĕm′ē) adj. *(studded)* lleno de piedras preciosas; *(glittering)* resplandeciente.

gem·ol·o·gy o **gem·mol·o·gy** (jĕ-mŏl′ə-jē) s. estudio de las piedras preciosas.

gem·stone (jĕm′stōn′) s. piedra preciosa.

gen·darme (zhän′därm′) s. gendarme m.

gen·der (jĕn′dər) **I.** s. GRAM. género; *(sex)* sexo **II.** tr. ANT. engendrar.

gene (jēn) s. BIOL. gene m.

ge·ne·a·log·i·cal (jē′nē-ə-lŏj′ĭ-kəl) adj. genealógico.

ge·ne·al·o·gist (jē′nē-ŏl′ə-jĭst, -ăl′-) s. genealogista mf.

ge·ne·al·o·gy (jē′nē-ŏl′ə-jē, -ăl′-) s. [pl. **-gies**] genealogía.

gen·e·ra (jĕn′ər-ə) pl. de **genus**.

gen·er·a·ble (jĕn′ər-ə-bəl) adj. generable, que se puede generar.

gen·er·al (jĕn′ər-əl) **I.** adj. general ♦ **as a g. rule** por regla general, generalmente • **in g.** en general, por lo general **II.** s. MIL. general m.

general assembly s. POL. *(state legislature)* asamblea legislativa (en EE. UU.); RELIG. *(supreme governing body)* presbiterio, asamblea directiva (de los presbiterianos) ♦ **G.A.** Asamblea General (de las Naciones Unidas).

general delivery s. lista de correos.

general election s. elecciones generales f.

gen·er·al·is·si·mo (jĕn′ər-ə-lĭs′ə-mō′) s. MIL. generalísimo.

gen·er·al·ist (jĕn′ər-ə-lĭst) s. persona con conocimientos amplios y hábil en varios campos.

gen·er·al·i·ty (jĕn′ə-răl′ĭ-tē) s. [pl. **-ties**] *(generalization)* generalización f; *(vague statement)* generalidad f, vaguedad f; *(majority)* generalidad, mayoría.

gen·er·al·i·za·tion (jĕn′ər-ə-lĭ-zā′shən) s. generalización f.

gen·er·al·ize (jĕn′ər-ə-līz′) tr. **-ized, -iz·ing** generalizar —intr. *(to form general notions)* hacer generalizaciones; *(to speak vaguely)* hablar en general; MED. *(to spread)* propagarse.

gen·er·al·ly (jĕn′ər-ə-lē) adv. generalmente, por lo general ♦ **g. known** de o por todos conocido • **g. speaking** hablando en términos generales.

general practitioner s. médico general, internista mf.

gen·er·al-pur·pose (jĕn′ər-əl-pûr′pəs) adj. de uso general.

gen·er·al·ship (jĕn′ər-əl-shĭp′) s. MIL. *(rank)* generalato; *(skill)* táctica militar, estrategia; *(leadership)* don de mando m.

general store s. almacén m.

gen·er·ate (jĕn′ə-rāt′) tr. **-at·ed, -at·ing** *(to produce)* producir; *(to engender)* engendrar; ELEC., MAT. generar.

gen·er·a·tion (jĕn′ə-rā′shən) s. generación f ♦ **the younger g.** los jóvenes.

gen·er·a·tor (jĕn′ə-rā′tər) s. generador *m*.

gen·er·a·trix (jĕn′ə-rā′trĭks) s. [pl. **-tri·ces** (-trĭ-sēz′)] GEOM. generatriz *f*.

ge·ner·ic (jə-nĕr′ĭk) adj. genérico.

gen·er·os·i·ty (jĕn′ə-rŏs′ĭ-tē) s. [pl. **-ties**] *(quality)* generosidad *f*; *(act)* acto generoso.

gen·er·ous (jĕn′ər-əs) adj. *(magnanimous)* generoso; *(abundant)* abundante.

gen·e·sis (jĕn′ĭ-sĭs) s. [pl. **-ses** (-sēz′)] génesis *f*, origen *m* ♦ **G.** BÍBL. Génesis *m*.

ge·net·ic (jə-nĕt′ĭk) *o* **ge·net·i·cal** (-ĭ-kəl) adj. genético.

genetic engineering s. BIOL. ingeniería genética.

ge·net·i·cist (jə-nĕt′ĭ-sĭst) s. BIOL. genetista *mf*, geneticista *mf*.

ge·net·ics (jə-nĕt′ĭks) s. BIOL. [ú. con v. sing.] genética.

Ge·ne·va (jə-nē′və) s. Ginebra.

Ge·ne·van (jə-nē′vən) *o* **Gen·e·vese** (jĕn′ə-vēz′) I. adj. *(Geneva)* ginebrino, ginebrés; *(Calvinist)* calvinista II. s. *(inhabitant)* ginebrino, ginebrés *m*; *(Calvinist)* calvinista *mf*.

gen·ial (jēn′yəl) adj. *(friendly)* afable, simpático; *(benign)* benigno, suave.

ge·ni·al·i·ty (jē′nē-ăl′ĭ-tē) s. [pl. **-ties**] *(friendliness)* afabilidad *f*, simpatía; *(pleasantness)* templanza, suavidad *f*.

gen·ial·ly (jēn′yə-lē) adv. *(in a friendly way)* afablemente, simpáticamente; *(pleasantly)* benignamente, suavemente.

ge·nie (jē′nē) s. genio.

gen·i·tal (jĕn′ĭ-tl) I. adj. genital II. s. ♦ **genitals** órganos genitales.

gen·i·ta·li·a (jĕn′ĭ-tā′lē-ə) s.pl. ANAT. órganos genitales.

gen·i·tive (jĕn′ĭ-tĭv) GRAM. I. adj. en caso genitivo, de genitivo II. s. genitivo.

gen·i·to·u·ri·nar·y (jĕn′ĭ-tō-yŏŏr′ə-nĕr′ē) adj. ANAT. genitourinario.

gen·ius (jēn′yəs) s. [pl. **-ius·es**] *(creative power)* genio <*the g. of Leonardo da Vinci* el genio de Leonardo da Vinci>; *(talent)* talento, don *m* <*she has a g. for acting* tiene talento para actuar>; *(ingenuity)* ingenio; *(prevailing spirit)* espíritu *m*, carácter *m*.

Gen·o·a (jĕn′ō-ə) s. Génova.

gen·o·cide (jĕn′ə-sīd′) s. genocidio.

gen·o·type (jĕn′ə-tīp′, jē′nə-) s. BIOL. genotipo.

gen·re (zhän′rə) s. género, clase *f*.

gent (jĕnt) s. FAM. señor *m*, individuo.

gen·teel (jĕn-tēl′) adj. *(refined)* fino; *(polite)* cortés; *(stylish)* gallardo, elegante; *(prudish)* remilgado, cursi.

gen·tian (jĕn′shən) s. BOT. genciana (planta y raíz).

gen·tile (jĕn′tīl′) I. s. *(pagan)* gentil *m*, pagano ♦ **G.** *(non-Jew)* persona no judía; *(non-Mormon)* persona no mormona II. adj. *(not Jewish)* no judío; *(not Mormon)* no mormón.

gen·til·i·ty (jĕn-tĭl′ĭ-tē) s. *(gentry)* nobleza; *(politeness)* gentileza, cortesía; *(obsessive refinement)* remilgo, cursilería.

gen·tle (jĕn′tl) I. adj. **-tler, -tlest** *(kind)* bondadoso, amable; *(tender)* dulce <*a g. mother* una madre dulce>; *(mild)* suave <*a g. breeze* una brisa suave> *(docile)* dócil, apacible; *(tame)* manso <*a g. horse* un caballo manso>; ANT. *(noble)* noble ♦ **of g. birth** bien nacido, de buena familia II. tr. **-tled, -tling** *(to tame)* amansar (esp. un caballo).

gen·tle·folk (jĕn′tl-fōk′) *o* **gen·tle·folks** (-fōks′) s.pl. personas bien nacidas.

gen·tle·man (jĕn′tl-mən) s. *(noble)* gentilhombre *m*, hidalgo; *(well-bred man)* caballero; *(man)* caballero, señor *m*; *(manservant)* criado, sirviente *m* ♦ **gentlemen** *(in letters)* muy señores míos, muy señores nuestros; *(form of address)* caballeros, señores; *(men's room sign)* caballeros.

gentleman's agreement s. pacto de honor, acuerdo entre caballeros.

gen·tle·ness (jĕn′tl-nĭs) s. *(kindness)* bondad *f*, amabilidad *f*; *(tenderness)* dulzura; *(mildness)* suavidad *f*; *(docility)* docilidad *f*; *(tameness)* mansedumbre *f*.

gen·tle·wom·an (jĕn′tl-wŏŏm′ən) s. *(gentry)* dama, señora; *(attendant)* dama de compañía.

gen·tly (jĕnt′lē) adv. *(kindly)* amablemente; *(tenderly)* con dulzura; *(mildly)* suavemente.

gen·try (jĕn′trē) s. *(gentlefolk)* personas bien nacidas; *(people)* gente *f*; G.B. *(upper classes)* alta burguesía.

gen·u·flect (jĕn′yə-flĕkt′) intr. hacer una genuflexión, doblar la rodilla.

gen·u·flec·tion (jĕn′yə-flĕk′shən) s. genuflexión *f*.

gen·u·ine (jĕn′yŏŏ-ĭn) adj. *(real)* verdadero <*g. sorrow* verdadero dolor>; *(authentic)* genuino, auténtico <*g. leather* piel auténtica>; *(sincere)* sincero.

gen·u·ine·ly (jĕn′yŏŏ-ĭn-lē) adv. *(really)* verdaderamente; *(sincerely)* sinceramente, con sinceridad.

gen·u·ine·ness (jĕn′yŏŏ-ĭn-nĭs) s. autenticidad *f*.

ge·nus (jē′nəs) s. [pl. **gen·er·a** (jĕn′ər-ə)] BIOL., LÓG. *(category)* género; *(kind)* clase *f*.

ge·o·cen·tric (jē′ō-sĕn′trĭk) adj. geocéntrico.

ge·o·des·ic (jē′ə-dĕs′ĭk) I. s. GEOM. geodésica II. adj. GEOL. geodésico.

ge·od·e·sy (jē-ŏd′ĭ-sē) s. GEOL. geodesia.

ge·og·ra·pher (jē-ŏg′rə-fər) s. geógrafo.

ge·o·graph·ic (jē′ə-grăf′ĭk) *o* **ge·o·graph·i·cal** (-ĭ-kəl) adj. geográfico.

ge·og·ra·phy (jē-ŏg′rə-fē) s. geografía.

ge·o·log·ic (jē′ə-lŏj′ĭk) *o* **ge·o·log·i·cal** (-ĭ-kəl) adj. geológico.

ge·ol·o·gist (jē-ŏl′ə-jĭst) *o* **ge·ol·o·ger** (-jər) s. geólogo.

ge·ol·o·gy (jē-ŏl′ə-jē) s. [pl. **-gies**] geología.

ge·o·man·cy (jē′ō-măn′sē) s. geomancia (adivinación por medio de líneas y figuras).

ge·om·e·ter (jē-ŏm′ĭ-tər) s. geómetra *m*.

ge·o·met·ric (jē′ə-mĕt′rĭk) *o* **ge·o·met·ri·cal** (-rĭ-kəl) adj. geométrico.

ge·om·e·tri·cian (jē-ŏm′ĭ-trĭsh′ən, jē′ə-mĭ-) *o* **ge·om·e·ter** (jē-ŏm′ĭ-tər) s. geómetra *m*.

geometric progression s. progresión geométrica.

ge·om·e·try (jē-ŏm′ĭ-trē) s. geometría.

ge·o·mor·phic (jē′ə-môr′fĭk) adj. GEOL. geomórfico, parecido a la tierra.

ge·o·mor·phol·o·gy (jē′ō-môr-fŏl′ə-jē) s. GEOL. geomorfología.

ge·o·phys·i·cist (jē′ō-fĭz′ĭ-sĭst) s. GEOL. geofísico.

ge·o·phys·ics (jē′ō-fĭz′ĭks) s.pl. [ú. con v. sing.] GEOL. geofísica.

ge·o·po·lit·i·cal (jē′ō-pə-lĭt′ĭ-kəl) adj. geopolítico.

ge·o·pol·i·tics (jē′ō-pŏl′ĭ-tĭks) s.pl. [ú. con v. sing.] *(study)* geopolítica; HIST. *(doctrine)* doctrina expansionista de los nazis alemanes.

Geor·gian (jôr′jən) adj. & s. georgiano.

geor·gic (jôr′jĭk) *o* **geor·gi·cal** (-jĭ-kəl) I. adj. geórgico, bucólico II. s. POÉT. geórgica.

ge·o·sci·ence (jē′ō-sī′əns) s. ciencia relacionada con la Tierra.

ge·o·ther·mal (jē′ō-thûr′məl) adj. GEOL. geotérmico, de la geotermia.

ge·ot·ro·pism (jē-ŏt′rə-pĭz′əm) s. BIOL., BOT. geotropismo.

ge·ra·ni·um (jə-rā′nē-əm) s. BOT. geranio.

ger·i·at·ric (jĕr′ē-ăt′rĭk) I. adj. MED. geriátrico, de la geriatría II. s. paciente geriátrico.

ger·i·at·rics (jĕr′ē-ăt′rĭks) s.pl. [ú. con v. sing.] MED. geriatría.

germ (jûrm) s. BIOL. germen (embrión) *m*; FIG. *(basis)* germen, origen *m*; MED. *(of a disease)* microbio; *(bacterium)* bacteria; *(bacillus)* bacilo.

Ger·man (jûr′mən) adj. & s. *(inhabitant, language)* alemán *m*.

German Democratic Republic s. República Democrática Alemana.

ger·mane (jər-mān′) adj. pertinente ♦ **g. to** relacionado con, pertinente a.

Ger·man·ic (jər-măn′ĭk) I. adj. germánico II. s. *(language)* germánico.

Ger·man·ism (jûr′mə-nĭz′əm) s. *(custom)* costumbre alemana; *(idiom)* germanismo; *(emulation of German ways)* admiración por lo alemán *f*.

ger·ma·ni·um (jər-mā′nē-əm) s. QUÍM. germanio.

German measles s. MED. rubéola, sarampión alemán *m*.

Ger·man·o·phile (jər-măn′ə-fīl′) s. germanófilo.

Ger·man·o·phobe (jər-măn′ə-fōb′) s. germanófobo.

German shepherd s. pastor alemán *m*, perro policía.

Ger·ma·ny, Federal Republic of (jûr'mə-nē) s. República Federal de Alemania.
germ cell s. BIOL. célula embrionaria.
ger·mi·cide (jûr'mĭ-sīd') s. FARM. germicida *m*, microbicida *m*.
ger·mi·nal (jûr'mə-nəl) adj. germinal, embrionario.
ger·mi·nate (jûr'mə-nāt') intr. **-nat·ed, -nat·ing** germinar, brotar —tr. hacer germinar.
ger·mi·na·tion (jûr'mə-nā'shən) s. germinación *f.*
germ warfare s. MIL. guerra bacteriológica.
ger·on·toc·ra·cy (jĕr'ən-tŏk'rə-sē) s. [pl. **-cies**] gerontocracia, gobierno confiado a los ancianos.
ger·on·tol·o·gy (jĕr'ən-tŏl'ə-jē) s. MED. gerontología (estudio de la vejez).
ger·ry·man·der (jĕr'ē-măn'dər, gĕr'-) tr. dividir (una entidad política) injustamente en distritos electorales para dar ventaja a un partido.
ger·und (jĕr'ənd) s. GRAM. gerundio.
ge·run·dive (jə-rŭn'dĭv) s. GRAM. gerundio adjetivado.
ges·tate (jĕs'tāt') tr. **-tat·ed, -tat·ing** BIOL. *(to carry)* gestar; FIG. *(to conceive)* concebir, gestar (una idea).
ges·ta·tion (jĕ-stā'shən) s. gestación *f.*
ges·tic·u·late (jĕ-stĭk'yə-lāt') intr. **-lat·ed, -lat·ing** gesticular —tr. expresar por gestos.
ges·tic·u·la·tion (jĕ-stĭk'yə-lā'shən) s. gesticulación *f*, gesto.
ges·ture (jĕs'chər) **I.** s. *(body movement)* gesto, ademán *m*; *(courteous act)* detalle *m*; *(token)* muestra **II.** intr. **-tured, -tur·ing** gesticular, hacer ademán —tr. expresar con ademán.
Ge·sund·heit (gə-zŏͦnt'hīt') interj. ¡Jesús!, ¡salud!
get (gĕt) tr. **got** (gŏt), **got** *o* **got·ten** (gŏt'n), **get·ting** *(to obtain)* obtener, conseguir <*did you g. the job?* ¿conseguiste el empleo?>; *(to buy)* comprar <*the apples looked so good that I got two pounds* las manzanas parecían tan buenas que compré dos libras>; *(to receive)* recibir; *(to win)* sacar <*he got a prize* sacó un premio>; *(to attract)* atraer; *(to seize)* agarrar, capturar; *(to catch)* coger, contraer <*to g. the flu* coger la gripe>; *(to cause to become)* causar, hacer que <*the long ride got the children tired* el largo viaje hizo que los niños se cansaran>; *(to prepare)* hacer, preparar <*I'll g. breakfast* prepararé el desayuno>; *(to bring)* traer, alcanzar <*g. my slippers, please* tráeme las pantuflas, por favor>; *(to persuade)* lograr, hacer que <*we couldn't g. her to come with us* no pudimos lograr que ella viniera con nosotros>; FAM. [usado con el verbo *to have*] *(to possess)* poseer, tener <*what have you got in your hand?* ¿qué tienes en la mano?>; *(must)* tener que <*we have got to win* tenemos que ganar>; *(to affect)* conmover, impresionar; *(to annoy)* molestar, irritar; *(to punish)* castigar <*Mom's going to g. you!* ¡mamá te castigará!>; *(to kill)* acabar con; *(to receive as punishment)* recibir <*the thief got three years* el ladrón recibió tres años>; *(to hit)* dar <*the ball got him on the chin* la pelota le dio en la mandíbula>; *(to understand)* entender, comprender <*now I g. what you're saying!* ¡ahora lo comprendo!> *(to hear)* oír bien <*sorry, I didn't g. your name* perdón, no oí bien su nombre>; *(to calculate)* sacar <*g. a total* saca el total>; *(to puzzle)* desconcertar, confundir <*what gets me is that everybody believed him* lo que me desconcierta es que todos le creyeron>; *(to put into contact)* poner con, comunicar con <*can you g. London for me, please?* ¿puede comunicarme con Londres, por favor?>; *(to capture)* coger, captar <*the translator got the spirit of the original work* el traductor captó el espíritu de la obra original>; *(to beget)* engendrar, procrear (los animales); JER. *(to notice)* fijarse <*g. the look on his face* fíjate la expresión de su cara>; *(to ruin)* arruinar <*dope will finally g. him* al final, la droga lo arruinará>; *(to fool)* engañar; *(to arrive)* llegar ♦ **I can't g. over it** no lo puedo creer <*the thief got three... to g. across** *(to make understood)* hacer comprender; *(to cross)* cruzar • **to g. along on** arreglárselas con • **to g. along with** *(someone)* llevarse bien con • **to. g. along without** pasar sin, prescindir de • **to g. around** *(something)* lograr pasar; *(someone)* engatusar • **to g. around to** encontrar tiempo para • **to g. at** averiguar, descubrir (la verdad, un motivo) • **to g. away from** *(place)* escaparse de; *(person)* librarse de • **to g. (some-**

thing) **away from** quitar (algo) a • **to g. away with** *(to succeed in)* conseguir (decir mentiras); *(to steal successfully)* llevarse • **to g. back** recuperar, recobrar • **to g. back at** vengarse de, desquitarse de • **to g. back to** *(to contact)* ponerse de nuevo en contacto con; *(to go back)* volver a • **to g. by** *(something)* lograr pasar; *(someone)* pasar inadvertido (delante de una guardia) • **to g. (something) down** *(to manage to swallow)* pasar (comida); *(to write down)* poner por escrito (algo) • **to g. down to** *(to tackle)* ponerse a; *(a problem)* abordar; *(to begin to consider)* proceder a examinar, pasar a considerar (detalles, datos) • **to g. in with** trabar amistad con • **to g. into** *(clothes)* ponerse (prendas); *(car)* subir a; *(bed, trouble)* meterse en; *(bad habits)* adquirir malas costumbres • **to g. off** apearse de, bajar de (tren) • **to g. (someone) off** *(to send off)* mandar, enviar <*she finally got the kids off to school* finalmente mandó a los chicos a la escuela>; *(to secure release or lesser penalty for)* lograr la absolución *o* una pena leve para • **to g. (something) off** *(letter)* mandar; *(clothing)* quitarse <*I can't g. my boots off* no puedo quitarme las botas>; *(day)* librar, tener libre <*I g. Sundays off* libro los domingos> • **to g. off on** JER. *(drugs)* intoxicarse (con drogas); *(to have a passion for)* apasionarse por • **to g. off with** escapar con <*he got off with a light sentence* escapó con una sentencia poco severa> • **to g. (something) on** ponerse (algo) • **to g. on with** *(to be friendly with)* llevarse bien con; *(to continue with)* seguir con • **to g. on with it** apurarse • **to g. out** *(to make known)* difundir; *(stain)* quitar • **to g. out of** *(bed, chair)* levantarse; *(the city, a country)* alejarse de; *(obligation)* librarse de; *(trouble)* sacar (de); *(the way)* quitarse (de en medio); *(bus, car)* apearse de; *(to exit)* salir de • **to g. (someone) out of** *(obligation)* librar a alguien de; *(trouble)* sacar a alguien de • **to g. (something) out of** *(to pry out of)* sonsacar (información); *(to profit from)* sacar de, obtener de; *(to borrow from a library)* sacar; *(to take out of)* sacar <*g. the car out of the garage* saca el automóvil del garaje> • **to g. over** *(illness)* reponerse de; *(shyness, disappointment)* superar; *(person)* olvidar; *(difficulty)* vencer; *(loss)* sobreponerse de; *(to become accustomed to)* acostumbrarse a • **to g. (something) over** *o* **over with** acabar con • **to g. through** pasar • **to g. through to (someone)** *(to reach by phone)* conseguir comunicación con; *(to be understood)* hacer comprender • **to g. to to** FAM. *(to begin)* comenzar, empezar; *(to manage to)* llegar a • **to g. to** *(to arrive)* llegar a <*when do we g. to New York?* ¿cuándo llegamos a Nueva York?>; *(to tackle)* ocuparse de • **to g. to (someone)** *(to upset)* molestar a alguien; *(to affect)* impresionar, conmover • **to g. (something) up** *(petition, sale)* organizar; *(courage, nerve)* armarse de • **what's gotten into him?** ¿qué le pasa? —intr. *(to become)* ponerse; <*he got well* se puso bien>; *(to turn)* hacerse, hacer <*it's getting cold* empieza a hacer frío> ♦ **to g. ahead** adelantar • **to g. along** *(to leave)* irse, marcharse; *(to grow old)* ponerse viejo; *(in years)* avanzar (en años); *(to progress)* progresar, hacer progresos; *(to manage)* arreglárselas <*we'll g. along one way or another* nos las arreglaremos de una manera u otra>; *(to be friendly)* llevarse bien <*we don't g. along* no nos llevamos bien> • **to g. around** *(to travel)* viajar; *(to move)* desplazarse; *(to go out a lot)* salir mucho, ir a muchos sitios; *(to become known)* difundirse, divulgarse; JER. *(to have a lot of lovers)* tener muchos amantes • **to g. at** *(to suggest)* insinuar; *(to try to express)* explicar • **to g. away** *(to escape)* escaparse; *(to manage to leave)* conseguir irse *o* marcharse; *(to go away)* irse, marcharse; *(to go on vacation)* ir de vacaciones • **to g. back** *(to return)* regresar, volver; *(to return home)* regresar *o* volver a casa • **to g. by** *(something)* lograr pasar; *(someone)* eludir, pasar inadvertido; *(to manage)* arreglárselas • **to g. down** bajar, descender • **to g. in** *(to arrive)* llegar <*what time does his plane g. in?* ¿a qué hora llega su avión?>; *(place)* entrar <*the theater was so crowded we couldn't g. in* el teatro estaba tan lleno que no pudimos entrar>; POL. *(to be elected)* ser elegido; *(to receive)* recibir; *(to return home)* volver *o* regresar a casa • **to g. off** *(bus, train)* apearse; *(punishment, obligation)* librarse <*I g. off at five* salgo del trabajo a las cinco>; *(to come out)* salir <*he got off unharmed* salió ileso>; JER. *(to become high)* intoxicarse (con drogas); *(to have an orgasm)* venirse, acabar • **to g. on** *(bus, train)* montar en; *(to grow old)* ponerse viejo; *(in years)* avanzar (en años); *(to be friendly)* llevarse bien; *(to progress)* hacer progresos, progresar • **to g. out** *(to manage to leave)* lograr salir; *(to become known)* difundirse, divulgarse • **to g. out from under** lograr escapar • **to g. through** *(tax bill, exam)* aprobar; *(the day, crowd)* pasar; *(to reach by phone)* lograr comunicar; *(to manage to arrive)* llegar a su destino (provisiones, mensaje); *(to finish)* terminar • **to g. together** *(to meet)* reunirse, juntarse; *(to agree)* ponerse de acuerdo • **to g. up** *(to stand up)* ponerse de pie, levantarse; *(out of bed)* levantarse (de la cama) • **to g. used to** acostumbrarse a.

get·a·way (gĕt'ə-wā') s. *(escape)* fuga, escape *m*; *(takeoff)* salida.

get-to·geth·er (gĕt'tə-gĕth'ər) s. FAM. fiestecita.

get-up (gĕt'ŭp') s. *(outfit)* atavío, vestimenta; *(style)* diseño (de una publicación); *(spunk)* empuje *m*, energía.

get-up-and-go (gĕt'ŭp-ən-gō') s. ambición *f*, arrojo.

gew·gaw (gyōō'gô') s. baratija, chuchería.

gey·ser (gī'zər) s. géiser *m*.

Gha·na (gä'nə, găn'ə) s. Ghana.

Gha·na·ian (gə-nä'yən) o **Gha·ni·an** (-nī'-) adj. & s. ganés *m*.

ghast·ly (găst'lē) adj. **-li·er, -li·est** *(dreadful)* horrible, horroroso <*a g. accident* un accidente horroroso>; *(ghostly)* cadavérico, espectral; *(terrible)* espantoso <*a g. little book* un librito espantoso>; *(very serious)* atroz, enorme <*a g. error* un error atroz>.

Ghent (gĕnt) s. Gante.

gher·kin (gûr'kĭn) s. BOT. pepinillo.

ghet·to (gĕt'ō) s. [pl. **-tos** o **-toes**] *(slum)* ghetto, barrio pobre segregado; HIST. *(Jewish section)* judería.

ghet·to·ize (gĕt'ō-īz') tr. **-ized, -iz·ing** separar o aislar como en un ghetto.

ghost (gōst) I. s. *(specter)* fantasma *m*, espectro; *(demon)* demonio, espíritu *m*; *(haunting image)* visión *f*; *(vestige)* sombra, asomo <*the g. of a smile* la sombra de una sonrisa>; FOTOG., TELEV. *(secondary image)* sombra; *(ghostwriter)* escritor que escribe para otro, negro; *(nonexistent publication)* publicación fantasma *f* ♦ **not to have a g. of a chance** no tener la más remota posibilidad • **the Holy G.** BÍBL. el Espíritu Santo • **to give up the g.** entregar el alma II. intr. FAM. escribir para otro, hacer de negro —tr. *(to haunt)* rondar por, aparecer en, FAM. *(to write)* escribir (algo) para otro.

ghost·ly (gōst'lē) adj. **-li·er, -li·est** *(spectral)* espectral, fantasmal; RELIG. *(spiritual)* espiritual.

ghost town s. pueblo desierto (después de la conquista del Oeste).

ghost·write (gōst'rīt') intr. & tr. **-wrote** (-rōt'), **-writ·ten** (-rīt'n), **-writ·ing** escribir bajo el nombre de otro.

ghost·writ·er (gōst'rī'tər) s. escritor que escribe para otro *m*, negro.

ghoul (gōōl) s. *(demon)* demonio necrófago; *(grave robber)* profanador de tumbas *m*; FIG. *(fiend)* persona que se deleita con lo repugnante.

ghoul·ish (gōō'lĭsh) adj. diabólico, malvado.

GI (jē'ī') MIL. I. s. [pl. **GIs** o **GI's**] soldado activo o de reserva (de los EE. UU.) II. adj. de soldado.

gi·ant (jī'ənt) I. s. gigante *m* II. adj. gigantesco, gigante.

gi·ant·ism (jī'ən-tĭz'əm) s. gigantismo.

gib·ber (jĭb'ər) I. intr. farfullar II. s. galimatías *m*, jerga.

gib·ber·ish (jĭb'ər-ĭsh) s. galimatías *m*, jerga.

gib·bet (jĭb'ĭt) I. s. *(gallows)* horca, patíbulo; *(structure for public viewing)* picota II. tr. *(to execute)* ahorcar; *(to expose for viewing)* poner en la picota; FIG. *(to defame)* poner en la picota, exponer al desprecio; *(to ridicule)* ridiculizar.

gib·bon (gĭb'ən) s. ZOOL. gibón *m*.

gib·bous (gĭb'əs) adj. *(protuberant)* protuberante, convexo; ASTRON. *(almost full)* casi llena (la luna); *(humpbacked)* jorobado, giboso.

gibe (jīb) I. intr. & tr. **gibed, gib·ing** burlarse, mofarse (de) II. s. burla, mofa.

gib·let (jĭb'lĭt) s. menudos (de ave).

Gib·ral·tar (jĭ-brôl'tər) s. Gibraltar.

gid·di·ness (gĭd'ē-nĭs) s. *(dizziness)* atolondramiento; *(vertigo)* vértigo; *(frivolity)* frivolidad *f*.

gid·dy (gĭd'ē) I. adj. **-di·er, -di·est** *(dizzy)* mareado; *(causing dizziness)* vertiginoso; *(frivolous)* frívolo II. tr. & intr. **-died, -dy·ing** marear(se).

gift (gĭft) I. s. *(present)* regalo, obsequio; *(donation)* donación *f*; *(talent)* talento, aptitud *f*; *(endowment)* don *m*, talento II. tr. *(to give)* regalar, obsequiar; *(to endow with)* dotar.

gift·ed (gĭf'tĭd) adj. *(endowed)* dotado, de muchas dotes; *(talented)* genial, excepcional <*a g. rendition* una interpretación excepcional>.

gig¹ (gĭg) I. s. *(carriage)* calesa; MARÍT. *(boat)* falúa; *(rowboat)* bote de remos *m*, canoa II. intr. **gigged, gig·ging** viajar en calesa.

gig² (gĭg) I. s. *(fishing line)* sedal con varios anzuelos *m*; *(spear)* arpón de pesca *m* II. tr. **gigged, gig·ging** arponear —intr. pescar con varios anzuelos.

gig³ (gĭg) s. JER., MÚS. actuación *f*, presentación *f*.

gi·gan·tic (jī-găn'tĭk) adj. gigantesco.

gi·gan·tism (jī-găn'tĭz'əm) s. MED. *(excessive growth)* gigantismo; *(abnormal size)* gigantez *f*.

gig·gle (gĭg'əl) I. intr. **-gled, -gling** reírse tontamente II. s. risita entrecortada y tonta ♦ **to get** o **have the giggles** estar tentado de risa.

gig·gly (gĭg'lē) adj. de risa fácil.

gig·o·lo (jĭg'ə-lō') s. gigolo.

gild (gĭld) tr. **gild·ed** o **gilt** (gĭlt), **gild·ing** *(to cover with gold)* dorar; FIG. *(to sugar-coat)* dar un falso brillo a.

gild·ing (gĭl'dĭng) s. *(process)* doradura, dorado; *(gold leaf)* pan de oro *m*; *(paint)* pintura dorada; FIG. *(glitter)* oropel *m*.

gill¹ (gĭl) I. s. ICT. agalla, branquia; BOT. laminilla ♦ **gills** ORNIT. *(wattle)* barba; FAM. *(area around the neck)* papada • **to look green about** o **around the gills** tener mala cara II. tr. *(to catch fish)* pescar por las agallas; *(to clean fish)* limpiar (pescado).

gill² (jĭl) s. E.E. U.U. cuatro onzas (líquidas); G.B. cinco onzas (líquidas).

gilt (gĭlt) I. pret. y part. p. de **gild** II. adj. dorado III. s. *(layer of gold)* lámina o chapa de oro; *(glitter)* brillo; *(superficial brilliance)* oropel *m*, falso brillo.

gilt-edged (gĭlt'ĕjd') o **gilt-edge** (-ĕj') adj. *(having gilded edges)* de bordes dorados ♦ **g. securities** FIN. valores de primer orden.

gim·bal (gĭm'bəl, jĭm'-) s. MEC. suspensión de cardán *f*, soporte cardánico ♦ **gimbals** MARÍT. balancines de la brújula.

gim·crack (jĭm'krăk) I. s. baratija, chuchería II. adj. mal hecho.

gim·let (gĭm'lĭt) I. s. MEC. *(tool)* barrena de mano, taladro pequeño; *(cocktail)* cóctel hecho con vodka o ginebra y limón verde II. tr. barrenar III. adj. penetrante.

gim·mick (gĭm'ĭk) s. *(stratagem)* truco <*an advertising g.* un truco publicitario>; *(catch)* trampa, truco; *(gadget)* artefacto.

gim·mick·ry (gĭm'ĭ-krē) s. *(tricks)* trucos; *(catches)* trampas; *(gadgetry)* artefactos innecesarios.

gimp (gĭmp) JER. I. s. *(limp)* renguera, cojera; *(person)* rengo, paticojo II. intr. renguear, cojear.

gimp·y (gĭm'pē) adj. JER. rengo, cojo.

gin¹ (jĭn) s. ginebra.

gin² (jĭn) I. s. MAQ. *(hoisting machine)* cabria; *(pile driver)* martinete *m*; *(trap)* trampa; *(pump)* bomba movida por molino de viento; *(cotton gin)* desmotadora II. tr. **ginned, gin·ning** *(to remove the seeds from)* desmotar (algodón); *(to trap)* atrapar.

gin·ger (jĭn'jər) I. s. BOT., CUL. jengibre *m*; *(color)* color rojizo; FAM. *(liveliness)* garra, chispa II. tr. *(to spice)* echar jengibre a ♦ **to g. up** FAM. avivar, animar <*to g. up the party* animar la fiesta>.

ginger ale s. ginger ale *m*, gaseosa de jengibre.

---

gin·ger·bread (jĭn'jər-brĕd') s. CUL. pan de jengibre *m*; *(decoration)* ornamentación excesiva y elaborada.
gin·ger·ly (jĭn'jər-lē) I. adv. *(carefully)* cuidadosamente; *(cautiously)* cautelosamente II. adj. *(careful)* cuidadoso; *(cautious)* cauteloso.
gin·ger·snap (jĭn'jər-snăp') s. galletita con sabor a jengibre.
gin·ger·y (jĭn'jə-rē) adj. *(said of flavor)* que sabe a jengibre; *(said of remark)* agudo, punzante.
ging·ham (gĭng'əm) s. TEJ. guinga.
gin·gi·vi·tis (jĭn'jə-vī'tĭs) s. ODONT. gingivitis *f*.
gin·seng (jĭn'sĕng') s. BOT. ginsén *m*, ginseng *m*.
gip (jĭp) v. & s. var. de **gyp.**
Gip·sy (jĭp'sē) s. var. de **Gypsy.**
gi·raffe (jə-răf') s. [pl. **-raffes** o **giraffe**] ZOOL. jirafa.
gir·an·dole (jĭr'ən-dōl') s. *(radiating structure)* girándula; *(candleholder)* candelabro (de pared).
gir·a·sol o **gir·o·sol** (jĭr'ə-sôl') s. MIN. ópalo girasol.
gird (gûrd) tr. **gird·ed** o **girt** (gûrt), **gird·ing** *(to secure)* ceñir, atar; *(to surround)* rodear, cercar; FIG. *(to endow)* investir, dotar ♦ **to g. oneself** prepararse.
gird·er (gûr'dər) s. CONSTR. viga.
gir·dle (gûr'dl) I. s. *(sash)* faja; *(belt)* cinturón *m*; *(undergarment)* faja; JOY. arista II. tr. **-dled, -dling** *(to encircle)* rodear <*a moat girdled the castle* un foso rodeaba el castillo>; *(to belt)* ceñir, atar <*she girdled her waist with a red sash* se ciñó la cintura con una faja roja>.
girl (gûrl) s. *(adolescent)* muchacha, niña; *(child)* niña; *(unmarried young woman)* joven *f*, señorita; *(daughter)* hija; *(sweetheart)* novia; DESPEC. *(servant)* muchacha, chica.
girl·friend o **girl friend** (gûrl'frĕnd') s. *(female friend)* amiga; *(of a boy)* novia.
girl·hood (gûrl'hŏod') s. *(childhood)* niñez *f*, infancia; *(adolescence)* juventud *f*.
girl·ish (gûr'lĭsh) adj. de niña.
Girl Scout s. niña exploradora.
girt (gûrt) tr. *(to gird)* ceñir; *(to measure)* medir la circunferencia de —intr. medir de circunferencia.
girth (gûrth) I. s. *(circumference)* circunferencia; *(bulk)* tamaño, dimensiones *f*; *(cinch)* cincha II. tr. *(to measure)* medir la circunferencia de; *(to encircle)* cinchar, ceñir.
gis·mo (gĭz'mō) s. JER. cosa, artefacto.
gist (jĭst) s. *(essence)* esencia, quid *m*; DER. *(of a suit)* motivo principal.
give (gĭv) I. tr. **gave** (gāv), **giv·en** (gĭv'ən), **giv·ing** *(to hand over)* dar <*who gave you this book?* ¿quién te dio este libro?> *(to make a gift of)* regalar <*he gave me flowers for my birthday* me regaló flores para mi cumpleaños>; *(to pay)* dar, pagar <*I'll g. you five dollars an hour* te pagaré cinco dólares la hora>; *(to hand to)* dar, alcanzar <*g. me the scissors, please* dame las tijeras, por favor>; *(to utter)* dar <*he gave a cry of pain* dio un grito de dolor>; *(to bestow)* conferir, otorgar <*to g. authority* conferir autoridad>; *(to donate)* dar, donar <*to g. one's time* donar el tiempo de uno>; *(to cause)* ocasionar, causar <*to g. offense* causar ofensa>; *(to present)* dar <*to g. a recital* dar un recital>; *(to deliver)* pronunciar (discurso); *(to transmit)* transmitir, contagiar <*she gave him the measles* le contagió del sarampión>; *(to supply)* proporcionar, proveer de <*this garden gives us all that we need* esta huerta nos provee de todo lo que necesitamos>; *(to inflict)* imponer (castigo, pena); *(to dispense)* administrar (medicina, sacramentos); *(to yield)* ceder <*to g. ground* ceder terreno>; *(to host)* dar (baile, fiesta); *(to offer)* dar, hacer <*to g. a toast* hacer un brindis>; *(to state)* dar, comunicar (opinión, respuesta); *(to devote)* dedicar, consagrar; FAM. *(to object)* decir, venir con <*don't g. me that* no me vengas con eso> ♦ **to g. a good account of oneself** salir bien, hacerlo bien • **to g. a hand to** ayudar a, darle una mano a • **to g. a lift to** *(to cheer up)* levantar los ánimos; *(to give a ride)* llevar en coche • **to g. a piece of one's mind to** FAM. cantarle las cuarenta a • **to g. away** *(bride)* entregar (la novia) al novio; *(awards)* entregar; *(to divulge)* contar, revelar (secreto, trama); FIG. *(to sell cheaply)* regalar; *(to get rid of)* deshacerse de • **to g. back** devolver • **to g. birth to** *(a child)* dar a luz a; FIG. *(to originate)* originar, producir • **to g. chase** perseguir • **to g. it to someone** FAM. castigar o

reprender a alguien • **to g. notice** *(to resign)* renunciar a (empleo); *(to fire)* despedir (de un empleo); *(to inform)* informar • **to g. off** emitir, despedir (olor, vapor) • **to g. oneself up** entregarse (a las autoridades) • **to g. oneself up to** *(to succumb)* abandonarse a (vicios, desesperación); *(to immerse in)* dedicarse a (estudios, ocupación) • **to g. out** *(to distribute)* distribuir, repartir; *(to proclaim)* proclamar; *(to declare)* declarar, decir • **to g. over** entregar (autoridad, presos) • **to g. rise to** dar lugar a, causar • **to g. someone his due** reconocer a alguien sus méritos • **to g. up** *(to abandon)* abandonar, renunciar a (intento, tarea); *(to hand over)* entregar; *(business)* retirarse de (negocios, actividades); *(to desist)* desistir de, dejar de; *(patient)* desahuciar (enfermo); *(to consider as lost)* dar por perdido • **to g. up the ghost** expirar • **to g. warning** prevenir, advertir —intr. *(to make gifts)* hacer regalos, dar; *(to fail)* fallar; *(to break down)* romperse • **to g. as good as one gets** pagar con la misma moneda • **to g. in** *(to yield)* ceder, aflojarse <*the roof gave in under the weight of the snow* el techo cedió bajo el peso de la nieve>; *(to accede)* acceder <*to g. in to their demands* acceder a sus reclamos>; *(to admit defeat)* darse por vencido, rendirse • **to g. on, upon** o **onto** dar a <*the back windows g. onto the lake* las ventanas de atrás dan al lago> • **to g. out** *(to collapse)* perder las fuerzas; *(to fail)* fallar, pararse; *(to dry up)* terminarse, agotarse • **to g. up** *(to resign oneself)* resignarse; *(to concede defeat)* darse por vencido; *(to lose hope)* perder las esperanzas II. s. elasticidad *f*, flexibilidad *f*.
give-and-take (gĭv'ən-tāk') s. *(compromise)* toma y daca, concesiones mutuas; *(of ideas)* intercambio de ideas.
give·a·way (gĭv'ə-wā') s. FAM. *(something free)* regalo; *(accidental exposure)* revelación involuntaria.
giv·en (gĭv'ən) I. part. p. de **give** II. adj. *(specified)* dado, determinado <*a g. date* una fecha determinada>; *(granted)* dado, teniendo en cuenta <*g. their superiority, we can't expect to win* teniendo en cuenta su superioridad no podemos esperar ganar>; *(inclined)* dado, propenso <*g. to worrying* propenso a preocuparse>; *(presented)* dado, regalado.
given name s. nombre de pila *m*.
giv·ing (gĭv'ĭng) s. don *m* ♦ **g. away** *(of prizes)* reparto; *(of someone)* denuncia • **g. back** devolución • **g. in** entrega • **g. up** abandono.
giz·mo (gĭz'mō) s. var. de **gismo.**
giz·zard (gĭz'ərd) s. ZOOL. molleja.
gla·cé (glă-sā') I. adj. *(glossy)* glaseado; CUL. *(candied)* acaramelado II. tr. **-céed, -cé·ing** *(to glaze)* glasear; CUL. *(to candy)* acaramelar.
gla·cial (glā'shəl) adj. glacial.
gla·ci·a·tion (glā'shē-ā'shən, -sē-) s. helamiento, congelación *f*.
gla·cier (glā'shər) s. GEOL. glaciar *m*, ventisquero.
gla·cis (glā-sē', glăs'ē) s. *(incline)* cuesta, ladera; FORT. *(embankment)* glacis *m*, explanada.
glad (glăd) adj. **glad·der, glad·dest** *(happy)* alegre, contento; *(cheerful)* bueno <*g. tidings* buenas nuevas> ♦ **to be g. to** alegrarse de <*I was g. to hear from him* me alegré de tener noticias suyas> • **to be g. to meet someone** tener mucho gusto en conocer a alguien.
glad·den (glăd'n) tr. alegrar —intr. ANT. alegrarse.
glade (glād) s. claro.
glad hand s. FAM. saludo aspaventoso.
glad·i·a·tor (glăd'ē-ā'tər) s. HIST. gladiador *m*; FIG. *(combatant)* contendiente *mf*.
glad·i·o·lus (glăd'ē-ō'ləs) s. [pl. **-li** (-lī', -lē') o **-lus·es**] gladiolo, gladíolo.
glad·ly (glăd'lē) adv. *(happily)* alegremente; *(willingly)* con mucho gusto, con placer.
glad·ness (glăd'nĭs) s. alegría, júbilo.
glad rags s.pl. FAM. trapitos domingueros.
glad·some (glăd'səm) adj. contento, alegre.
glam·or o **glam·our** (glăm'ər) s. *(charm)* encanto, hechizo; ANT. *(magic)* magia.
glam·or·ize o **glam·our·ize** (glăm'ə-rīz') tr. **-ized, iz·ing** *(to make glamorous)* embellecer; *(to idealize)* idealizar, glorificar.

ă rey / ä año / b boca / ch chico / d dar / ĕ el / ē mil / g gato / h joya / hw juez / ī aire / k casa / kw cuan /

glam·or·ous o **glam·our·ous** (glăm'ər-əs) adj. encantador, hechicero.

glance (glăns) I. intr. **glanced, glanc·ing** *(to glimpse)* echar un vistazo o una mirada <*she didn't even g. at his new outfit* no le echó ni una mirada a su traje nuevo>; *(to eye someone)* lanzar una mirada <*he glanced at her* le lanzó una mirada>; *(to strike)* rozar, rebotar <*a pebble glanced off the windshield* una piedrecita rebotó contra el parabrisas>; *(to glint)* centellear, brillar; *(to make an allusion)* mencionar de paso ♦ **to g. over** o **through** o **at** echar un vistazo, hojear <*he just glanced at the report* nada más que hojeó el informe> —tr. *(to graze)* rozar, rebotar contra; *(to cause to graze)* hacer rebotar contra II. s. *(glimpse)* vistazo, mirada; *(deflection)* rebote m; *(gleam)* centelleo, destello ♦ **at a g.** de un vistazo, con una sola mirada • **at first g.** a primera vista.

gland (glănd) s. ANAT., BOT. glándula; TEC. casquillo (del prensaestopas).

glan·du·lar (glăn'jə-lər) adj. glandular, adenoso.

glans (glănz) s. [pl. **glan·des** (glăn'dēz')] ANAT. *(of the penis)* glande m, bálano; *(of the clitoris)* glande.

glare (glâr) I. intr. **glared, glar·ing** *(to stare angrily)* mirar con rabia; *(to dazzle)* relumbrar, brillar enceguecedoramente; *(to stand out)* saltar a la vista, destacarse —tr. expresar con una mirada furibunda <*he glared his disapproval* expresó su desaprobación con una mirada furibunda> II. s. *(angry stare)* mirada furibunda; *(blinding light)* luz enceguecedora o deslumbrante, resplandor m; *(showy brilliance)* esplendor m, brillo.

glar·ing (glâr'ĭng) adj. *(staring angrily)* airado; *(shining blindingly)* deslumbrador; *(gaudy)* chillón; *(conspicuous)* patente, manifiesto <*g. error* error manifiesto>.

glar·y (glâr'ē) adj. **-i·er, -i·est** deslumbrador, resplandeciente.

glass (glăs) I. s. *(material)* vidrio, cristal m; *(glassware)* cristalería, artículos de cristal; *(glassful)* vaso; *(drinking vessel)* vaso; *(looking glass)* espejo; *(barometer)* barómetro; *(windowpane)* vidrio, cristal; *(spyglass)* catalejo ♦ **cut g.** vidrio tallado • **dark glasses** espejuelos de sol • **glasses** *(spectacles)* espejuelos, anteojos; *(binoculars)* gemelos II. tr. *(to encase in glass)* rodear de cristal(es); *(to make glassy)* poner vidrioso; *(to mirror)* reflejar.

glass blowing s. TEC. soplado del vidrio.

glass·ful (glăs'fool') s. vaso.

glass·mak·ing (glăs'mā'kĭng) s. TEC. vidriería, fabricación de vidrio f.

glass·ware (glăs'wâr') s. cristalería, artículos de cristal.

glass wool s. lana de vidrio.

glass·work (glăs'wûrk') s. *(glassware)* cristalería, artículos de cristal ♦ **glassworks** [ú. con v. sing.] fábrica de vidrio o de cristal.

glass·y (glăs'ē) adj. **-i·er, -i·est** *(resembling glass)* vítreo; *(smooth)* liso; *(expressionless)* vidrioso.

glau·co·ma (glou-kō'mə, glô-) s. MED. glaucoma m.

glaze (glāz) I. s. *(shiny coating)* capa de barniz, barniz m; *(coating of ice)* capa de hielo; *(on pottery)* vidriado, barniz; *(on pastry)* capa de almíbar, garrapiña; ARTE. barniz; *(over the eyes)* nube f II. tr. **glazed, glaz·ing** *(a window)* poner vidrios a; ARTE., CERÁM. barnizar, dar una capa de barniz a; CUL. cubrir con una capa de almíbar, garrapiñar; *(to make lustrous)* glasear, dar brillo a —intr. ponerse vidrioso, nublarse.

gla·zier (glā'zhər) s. vidriero.

glaz·ing (glā'zĭng) s. *(glasswork)* vidriería; *(window glass)* cristales m; *(glaze)* barniz m; *(act)* barnizado.

gleam (glēm) I. s. *(flash of light)* destello; FIG. *(of intelligence)* chispa, pizca; *(of hope)* rayo II. intr. destellar —tr. hacer que (algo) destelle.

glean (glēn) intr. AGR. rastrojar —tr. AGR. *(to gather)* rastrojar; FIG. *(to collect)* recoger, acopiar.

glean·ings (glē'nĭngz) s.pl. cosecha, acopio.

glee (glē) s. *(joy)* regocijo, alegría; MÚS. *(song)* canción coral sin acompañamiento f.

glee club s. MÚS. orfeón m.

glee·ful (glē'fəl) adj. regocijado, alegre.

glee·ful·ness (glē'fəl-nĭs) s. regocijo, alegría.

glen (glĕn) s. valle estrecho, cañada.

glib (glĭb) adj. **glib·ber, glib·best** *(marked by ease)* desenvuelto; *(pat)* fácil; *(insincerely eloquent)* locuaz, de mucha labia <*g. politicians* políticos de mucha labia>.

glib·ness (glĭb'nĭs) s. *(ease)* desenvoltura, soltura; *(unconcern)* prontitud f, irreflexividad f; *(loquacity)* locuacidad f, labia.

glide (glīd) I. intr. **glid·ed, glid·ing** *(to move)* deslizarse; *(to pass imperceptibly)* escurrirse, irse; AVIA. planear; FONÉT. diptongar los sonidos —tr. *(to cause to move)* hacer deslizar; AVIA. hacer planear II. s. *(movement)* deslizamiento; AVIA. planeo; MÚS. ligadura.

glid·er (glī'dər) s. AVIA. *(aircraft)* planeador m; *(swing)* columpio.

glim·mer (glĭm'ər) I. s. *(flicker)* luz trémula; *(trace)* indicio ♦ **a g. of hope** un rayo de esperanza II. intr. *(to shine dimly)* brillar con luz trémula, lucir débilmente.

glimpse (glĭmps) I. s. vistazo, ojeada ♦ **to catch a g. of** vislumbrar, entrever II. tr. & intr. **glimpsed, glimps·ing** vislumbrar ♦ **to g. at** echar un vistazo o una ojeada a.

glint (glĭnt) I. s. *(sparkle)* destello, fulgor m; *(trace)* indicio II. intr. *(to flash)* destellar —tr. hacer destellar.

glis·ten (glĭs'ən) I. intr. resplandecer, brillar II. s. resplandor m, brillo.

glitch (glĭch) s. JER. *(malfunction)* malfuncionamiento; *(minor problem)* pega, dificultad f.

glit·ter (glĭt'ər) I. s. *(brightness)* brillo; COST. *(decoration)* lentejuela, mostacilla II. intr. relucir, brillar.

gloam·ing (glō'mĭng) s. crepúsculo.

gloat (glōt) I. intr. regodearse II. s. regodeo.

glob (glŏb) s. *(drop)* gotita; *(lump)* pelota, masa.

glob·al (glō'bəl) adj. *(spherical)* esférico; *(worldwide)* mundial; *(total)* global.

glob·al·ize (glō'bə-līz') tr. **-ized, -iz·ing** universalizar.

globe (glōb) s. *(of the earth)* globo, esfera (terrestre); *(Earth)* globo terrestre; *(glass sphere)* globo; *(emblem)* orbe m.

globe-trot·ter (glōb'trŏt'ər) s. trotamundos mf.

glob·u·lar (glŏb'yə-lər) adj. *(spherical)* globular; *(worldwide)* mundial.

glob·ule (glŏb'yool) s. glóbulo.

glob·u·lin (glŏb'yə-lĭn) s. BIOQUÍM. globulina.

glock·en·spiel (glŏk'ən-spēl') s. MÚS. carillón de macillo m.

gloom (gloom) I. s. *(partial darkness)* penumbra; *(total darkness)* tinieblas f; *(melancholy)* melancolía, tristeza II. intr. *(to become dark)* entenebrecerse; *(to become overcast)* encapotarse; *(to appear sad)* tener aspecto triste.

gloom·i·ness (gloo'mē-nĭs) s. *(darkness)* penumbra; *(dreariness)* carácter lúgubre m; *(melancholy)* melancolía, tristeza; *(pessimism)* pesimismo.

gloom·y (gloo'mē) adj. **-i·er, -i·est** *(dark)* oscuro; *(dreary)* lúgubre; *(melancholy)* melancólico, triste; *(pessimistic)* pesimista.

glop (glŏp) JER. I. s. amasijo, plasta II. tr. **glopped, glop·ping** llenar de plasta.

Glo·ri·a (glôr'ē-ə) s. RELIG. Gloria m ♦ **g.** nimbo.

glo·ri·fi·ca·tion (glôr'ə-fĭ-kā'shən) s. glorificación f.

glo·ri·fy (glôr'ə-fī') tr. **-fied, -fy·ing** *(to honor)* glorificar; *(to exalt inordinately)* idealizar, poner por las nubes; *(to praise)* alabar.

glo·ri·ous (glôr'ē-əs) adj. *(illustrious)* glorioso <*a g. achievement* una hazaña gloriosa>; *(magnificent)* esplendoroso <*a g. sunset* una puesta de sol esplendorosa>; FAM. *(wonderful)* espléndido, magnífico.

glo·ri·ous·ly (glôr'ē-əs-lē) adv. *(with glory)* gloriosamente; *(magnificently)* magníficamente, espléndidamente.

glo·ry (glôr'ē) I. s. [pl. **-ries**] *(honor)* gloria; *(fame)* fama; *(splendor)* esplendor m; *(bliss of heaven)* gloria, bienaventuranza; *(height of prosperity)* cumbre de la prosperidad f; *(halo)* halo ♦ **to be in one's g.** FIG. estar en la gloria II. intr. **-ried, -ry·ing** ♦ **to g. in** enorgullecerse de, gloriarse de.

gloss¹ (glôs) I. s. *(luster)* lustre m, brillo; *(deceptive attractiveness)* falso brillo, oropel m II. tr. lustrar, pulir ♦ **to g. over** *(to treat superficially)* prestar poca atención a; *(to whitewash)* disimular, encubrir.

gloss² (glôs) I. s. *(explanation)* glosa; *(glossary)* glosario II. tr. glosar.

glos·sa·ry (glô′sə-rē) s. [pl. **-ries**] glosario.

gloss·i·ness (glô′sē-nĭs) s. lustre *m*, brillo.

gloss·y (glô′sē) I. adj. **-i·er, -i·est** *(surface)* lustroso, brillante; *(paper, cloth)* glaseado; *(showy)* vistoso II. s. [pl. **-ies**] fotografía impresa en papel glaseado.

glot·tis (glŏt′ĭs) s. [pl. **-tis·es** *o* **-ti·des** (-ĭ-dēz′)] ANAT. glotis *f.*

glove (glŭv) s. guante *m* ♦ **hand in g.** inseparables • **to fit like a g.** quedar como anillo al dedo • **to handle someone with kid gloves** FIG. tratar a alguien con guantes de seda.

glove compartment s. AUTO. guantera.

glov·er (glŭv′ər) s. guantero.

glow (glō) I. intr. *(to gleam)* resplandecer, brillar; *(to be red-hot)* estar al rojo vivo; *(from passion)* encenderse, abrasarse; *(to be exuberant)* rebosar de orgullo II. s. *(incandescence)* resplandor *m*, brillo; *(of fire)* resplandor, calor *m*; *(warmth of color)* intensidad *f*, luminosidad *f*; *(of sunset)* arrebol *m*, color rojizo; *(blush)* rubor *m*; *(physical warmth)* sensación de bienestar *f*; *(ardor)* ardor *m*, enardecimiento.

glow·er (glou′ər) I. intr. echar chispas por los ojos ♦ **to g. at** echar una mirada furiosa a II. s. mirada furiosa.

glow·ing (glō′ĭng) adj. *(incandescent)* incandescente; *(shining)* resplandeciente; *(face)* radiante; *(color)* vivo; *(light)* brillante; *(enthusiastic)* entusiasta, fervoroso.

glow·worm (glō′wûrm′) s. ENTOM. gusano de luz, luciérnaga.

glu·cose (glōo′kōs′) s. QUÍM. glucosa.

glue (glōo) I. s. *(adhesive)* goma de pegar, pegamento; *(for wood)* cola II. tr. **glued, glu·ing** pegar.

glu·ey (glōo′ē) adj. pegajoso, viscoso.

glum (glŭm) adj. **glum·mer, glum·mest** *(dejected)* abatido, triste; *(gloomy)* taciturno; *(dismal)* lóbrego, sombrío.

glum·ness (glŭm′nĭs) s. *(dejection)* abatimiento, tristeza; *(gloominess)* carácter taciturno; *(dismalness)* lobreguez *f.*

glut (glŭt) I. tr. **glut·ted, glut·ting** hartar, atracar ♦ **to g. the market (with)** COM. inundar *o* abarrotar el mercado (con) —intr. hartarse, atracarse II. s. exceso.

glu·ten (glōot′n) s. QUÍM. gluten *m.*

gluten bread s. CUL. pan de gluten *m.*

glu·te·us (glōo′tē-əs) s. [pl. **-te·i** (-tē-ī′)] ANAT. glúteo.

glu·ti·nous (glōot′n-əs) adj. glutinoso, pegajoso.

glut·ton (glŭt′n) s. *(eater)* glotón *m*; ZOOL. *(wolverine)* glotón ♦ **to be a g. for** FIG. tener resistencia para no cansarse de.

glut·ton·ous (glŭt′n-əs) adj. glotón.

glut·ton·y (glŭt′n-ē) s. glotonería, gula.

glyc·er·ide (glĭs′ə-rīd′) s. QUÍM. glicérido.

glyc·er·in *o* **glyc·er·ine** (glĭs′ər-ĭn) s. QUÍM. glicerina.

glyc·er·ol (glĭs′ə-rôl′) s. QUÍM. glicerol *m.*

gly·co·gen (glī′kə-jĕn′) s. BIOQUÍM. glicógeno.

gly·col (glī′kôl) s. QUÍM. glicol *m*, etilenglicol *m.*

glyph (glĭf) s. ARQ., ESCULT. glifo; *(symbol)* señalización *f.*

G-man (jē′mǎn′) s. agente del F.B.I.

gnarled (närld) adj. *(knotty)* nudoso; *(twisted)* torcido, retorcido; FIG. *(crabby)* malhumorado; *(rugged)* rugoso <*g. hands* manos rugosas>.

gnash (nǎsh) tr. rechinar (los dientes).

gnat (nǎt) s. ENTOM. mosquito, jején *m.*

gnaw (nô) tr. & intr. roer.

gneiss (nīs) s. GEOL. gneis *m.*

gnome (nōm) s. gnomo.

gno·mon (nō′mŏn′) s. gnomon *m.*

gno·sis (nō′sĭs) s. FILOS. gnosis *f.*

gnos·tic (nŏs′tĭk) adj. & s. FILOS. gnóstico, nóstico.

Gnos·ti·cism (nŏs′tĭ-sĭz′əm) s. FILOS. gnosticismo, nosticismo.

gnu (nōo, nyōo) s. ZOOL. ñu *m.*

go §G4 (gō) I. intr. **went** (wĕnt), **gone** (gôn), **go·ing** *(to move along)* ir; *(to proceed)* proseguir, seguir adelante; *(to leave)* irse, marcharse <*go, before I get mad!* ¡vete! antes de que me enoje>; *(to take its course)* andar, marchar <*how is everything going?* ¿cómo anda todo?>; *(to turn out)* salir, resultar <*the rehearsal went well* el ensayo salió bien>; *(to resort to)* acudir, recurrir (ayuda); *(to extend)* ir, llegar <*curtains that go to the floor* cortinas que llegan hasta el piso>; *(to function)* funcionar, andar <*the car won't go* el auto no funciona>; *(to be acceptable)* aceptarse <*anything goes nowadays* todo se acepta hoy en día>; *(to be sold)* venderse <*the painting went to the highest bidder* el cuadro se vendió al postor más alto>; *(to become)* tornarse, volverse <*he went mad* se volvió loco>; *(to belong)* ir, colocarse <*the fork goes to the left of the plate* el tenedor se coloca a la izquierda del plato>; *(to fit)* entrar, caber; *(to pass)* pasar <*the jewelry went to her daughter* las alhajas pasaron a su hija>; *(to be allotted)* destinarse a <*half of my salary goes for rent* la mitad de mi salario se destina a (pagar) mi renta>; *(to say)* decir <*as the saying goes* como lo dice el refrán>; *(to elapse)* transcurrir, pasar (tiempo); *(to be abolished)* ser suprimido; *(to pass away)* desaparecer <*the pain has gone* el dolor desapareció>; *(to be used up)* gastarse; *(to break up)* romperse, averiarse; *(to fail)* fallar <*at eighty, her eyes started to go* a los ochenta años, le empezó a fallar la vista>; *(to die)* morir; *(to be suitable)* hacer juego <*your jacket doesn't go with your trousers* tu saco no hace juego con los pantalones>; *(to have validity)* valer, ser ley <*whatever he says goes* lo que él dice es ley>; FAM. *(to relieve oneself)* ir al baño; *(to act the same as)* hacer <*go like this* hazlo de esta manera>; *(to wait)* esperar <*we still have another hour to go* tenemos que esperar otra hora todavía>; *(to be left)* faltar <*there are ten kilometers to go before we arrive* faltan diez kilómetros para llegar>; *(to endure)* soportar, sufrir ♦ **to go about** *(to undertake)* hacer, emprender • **to go about one's business** ocuparse en los asuntos propios • **to go across** cruzar • **to go after** *(to follow)* seguir a, ir tras de; *(to fetch)* ir por; *(to attack)* caerle a, atacar • **to go against** ir en contra de • **to go all out** FAM. esforzarse al máximo • **to go along** *(to leave)* marcharse, irse; *(to continue)* seguir, continuar • **to go along with** *(to accompany)* acompañar a; *(to agree)* estar de acuerdo • **to go around** circular <*there is a rumor going around the office* hay un rumor que circula por la oficina> • **to go astray** *(to get lost)* extraviarse; FIG. *(to err)* caer en la tentación • **to go away** *(to leave)* irse, marcharse; *(to pass)* pasar (dolor, molestia) • **to go back** *(to return)* volver, regresar; *(to move backward)* volver atrás, retroceder; • **to go back on** *o* **upon one's word** faltar uno a su palabra • **to go before** preceder, ir antes • **to go between** *(to interpose)* interponerse entre; *(to mediate)* mediar entre • **to go by** *(to pass by)* pasar cerca de, pasar por; *(to elapse)* pasar, transcurrir (tiempo); *(to follow)* regirse por, ajustarse a <*to go by the book* ajustarse a las reglas>; *(to be guided by)* guiarse por, juzgar <*I don't go by appearances* yo no juzgo por las apariencias>; *(to be known as)* ser conocido por <*Aurore Dupin went by the name of George Sand* Aurore Dupin era conocida por el nombre de George Sand> • **to go down** *(to descend)* descender, bajar; *(the sun)* ponerse (sol); *(a ship)* hundirse (barco); *(airplane)* venirse abajo, caerse (avión); *(to swallow)* tragar; *(in history)* dejar huella en la historia <*that game will go down in history* ese partido dejará huella en la historia>; COM., FIN. *(to decline)* decaer, bajar; *(to go bankrupt)* quebrar, fracasar • **to go downstairs** bajar (de un piso a otro) • **to go far** *(distance)* ir lejos; FIG. *(to succeed)* hacer carrera <*this man will go far in our company* este hombre hará carrera en nuestra compañía> • **to go for** *(to fetch)* ir por, ir a traer; FAM. *(to delight in)* gustar mucho; *(to attack)* atacar, acometer • **to go forward** adelantar, adelantarse • **to go in** *(to enter)* entrar; *(to fit)* caber, encajar; *(the sun)* ocultarse (sol) • **to go in for** FAM. *(to engage in)* dedicarse a • **to go into** *(to enter)* entrar en; *(to fit)* caber *o* encajar en; *(mourning)* ponerse de (luto); *(to engage in)* dedicarse a; *(to examine)* examinar, investigar; *(to become)* ponerse <*she went into hysterics* se puso histérica> • **to go into effect** entrar en vigencia *o* vigor • **to go off** *(weapon)* dispararse; *(to explode)* hacer explosión; *(to sound)* sonar; *(to leave)* marcharse, irse; *(to turn out)* resultar, salir <*everything went off well* todo salió bien> • **to go on** *(to continue)* continuar, seguir; *(to take place)* suceder, ocurrir; *(to start)* comenzar, empezar; *(to perse-*

vere) perseverar • **to go on strike** declararse en huelga • **to go on the air** empezar a transmitir (por radio *o* televisión) • **to go out** *(to exit)* salir; *(light)* apagarse (luz); *(fire, matches)* extinguirse, apagarse • **to go out of fashion** pasar de moda • **to go over** *(to go across)* cruzar; *(to climb)* pasar por encima de; *(to examine)* examinar; *(to rehearse)* ensayar; *(to review)* repasar • **to go straight** FAM. reformarse • **to go through** *(to traverse)* atravesar; *(to enter)* entrar *o* penetrar por; *(to exit)* salir por; *(to get approval)* aprobarse <*your application went through* su solicitud se aprobó>; *(to experience)* pasar por, sufrir • **to go through hell** FIG., FAM. pasar las de Caín • **to go to** *o* **toward** dirigirse *o* acercarse a • **to go to bed** acostarse • **to go together** *(to harmonize)* armonizar, ser compatible; *(to be sweethearts)* salir *o* ir juntos • **to go to pieces** *(attack of nerves)* sufrir un ataque de nervios; *(despair)* abatirse, darse a la desesperación • **to go to pot** FAM. caer en la degradación • **to go to sleep** dormirse • **to go to show that** demostrar que • **to go under** *(to sink)* hundirse; *(to become bankrupt)* quebrar; *(to fail)* fracasar • **to go up** *(to ascend)* subir; CONSTR. *(to rise)* levantarse (edificios); *(to approach)* acercarse <*he went up to her and asked her to dance* se acercó a ella y la invitó a bailar> • **to go up in smoke** FIG., FAM. esfumarse, malograrse • **to go with** *(to accompany)* acompañar; *(to harmonize)* armonizar, ser compatible • **to go wrong** *(to fail)* fracasar; *(to stray)* ir por mal camino —tr. *(to wager)* apostar <*I'll go another ten dollars on the bet* apuesto otros diez dólares>; *(to tolerate)* tolerar, soportar; *(to follow)* seguir <*to go the same way* seguir el mismo camino> ♦ **to go bail for** DER. salir de fiador por *o* de • **to go halves** *o* **fifty-fifty** FAM. ir a medias *o* por la mitad • **to go it alone** obrar solo y sin ayuda II. s. [pl. **goes**] *(try)* intento; *(turn)* turno; *(energy)* energía ♦ **on the go** en actividad, ocupado • **to have a go at something** intentar algo • **to make a go of something** tener éxito en sacar adelante.

goad (gōd) I. s. *(stick)* aguijada, picana (para ganado); FIG. *(incentive)* aguijón *m* II. tr. ♦ **to g. on** *(to prod an animal)* aguijar, aguijonear; FIG. *(to urge on)* aguijonear, incitar.
go·a·head (gō'ə-hěd') s. FAM. autorización *f,* permiso.
goal (gōl) s. *(objective)* meta, objetivo; DEP. *(area)* meta; *(structure)* portería; *(score)* gol *m,* tanto.
goal·keep·er (gōl'kē'pər) s. DEP. portero, guardameta *m,* arquero.
goal post s. DEP. poste *m.*
goat (gōt) s. ZOOL. *(female)* cabra; ZOOL. *(male)* macho cabrío, cabrón *m; (lecherous man)* hombre lascivo; *(scapegoat)* cabeza de turco ♦ **to get someone's g.** FAM. molestar *o* enojar a alguien.
goat·ee (gō-tē') s. perilla, barbas de chivo.
goat·skin (gōt'skĭn') s. *(skin, leather)* piel de cabra *f; (container)* bota (de piel de cabra).
gob¹ (gŏb) s. pedazo ♦ **gobs** FAM. gran cantidad.
gob² (gŏb) s. JER. marinero.
gob·ble¹ (gŏb'əl) tr. **-bled, -bling** devorar, engullir ♦ **to g. up** FIG., FAM. agotar rápidamente, acabar con —intr. engullirse ávidamente.
gob·ble² (gŏb'əl) I. s. guglú *m,* graznido (del pavo) II. intr. **-bled, -bling** guglutear, graznar (el pavo).
gob·ble·dy·gook *o* **gob·ble·de·gook** (gŏb'əl-dē-gōōk') s. FAM. blablablá.
gob·bler (gŏb'lər) s. ZOOL. pavo (macho).
go-be·tween (gō'bĭ-twēn') s. intermediario.
gob·let (gŏb'lĭt) s. *(glass)* copa; ANT. *(bowl)* tazón *m.*
gob·lin (gŏb'lĭn) s. duende *m,* trasgo.
go-cart (gō'kärt') s. *(wagon)* carrillo; *(frame)* andaderas; *(handcart)* carretilla (de mano); *(stroller)* cochecito (para niños).
god (gŏd) s. *(divine being)* dios; *(idol)* ídolo; *(demigod)* semidiós *m* ♦ **G.** RELIG. Dios.
god·child (gŏd'chīld') s. *(godson)* ahijado, *(goddaughter)* ahijada.
god·daugh·ter (gŏd'dô'tər) s. ahijada.
god·dess (gŏd'ĭs) s. diosa.
god·fa·ther (gŏd'fä'thər) s. padrino.

god·for·sak·en *o* **God·for·sak·en** (gŏd'fər-sā'kən) adj. *(remote)* remoto; *(desolate)* desolado, abandonado.
god·head (gŏd'hěd') s. divinidad *f* ♦ **G.** RELIG. Dios.
god·hood (gŏd'hōōd') s. divinidad *f.*
god·less (gŏd'lĭs) adj. descreído, ateo.
god·like (gŏd'līk') adj. *(resembling a god)* deiforme, como dios; *(divine)* divino.
god·li·ness (gŏd'lē-nĭs) s. *(piousness)* piedad *f; (divinity)* divinidad *f.*
god·ly (gŏd'lē) adj. **-li·er, -li·est** *(pious)* piadoso, pío; *(divine)* divino.
god·moth·er (gŏd'mŭth'ər) s. madrina.
god·par·ent (gŏd'pâr'ənt) s. *(godfather)* padrino; *(godmother)* madrina.
god·send (gŏd'sěnd') s. divina merced, cosa llovida del cielo.
god·son (gŏd'sŭn') s. ahijado.
God·speed (gŏd'spēd') s. bienandanza, buena suerte.
go-get·ter (gō'gět'ər) s. FAM. buscavidas *mf,* persona ambiciosa.
gog·gle (gŏg'əl) I. intr. **-gled, -gling** mirar aturdidamente, mirar con los ojos desorbitados —tr. ♦ **to g. at** mirar con los ojos desorbitados II. s. mirada fija ♦ **goggles** gafas, anteojos.
gog·gle-eyed (gŏg'əl-īd') adj. de ojos saltones.
go·ing (gō'ĭng) I. s. *(departure)* ida, partida <*my g. abroad was sudden* mi ida al extranjero fue repentina>; *(condition underfoot)* piso, superficie (del camino) *f,* FAM. *(progress)* progreso, marcha ♦ **comings and goings** idas y venidas • **good g.!** ¡muy bien! II. adj. *(working)* que funciona; *(flourishing)* que marcha, que funciona <*a g. concern* una empresa que marcha>; *(prevailing)* actual, corriente <*the g. rates* las tasas actuales>; *(available)* que hay, que existe <*the best products* q. los mejores productos que existen>.
go·ing-o·ver (gō'ĭng-ō'vər) s. [pl. **goings-over**] FAM. *(examination)* inspección *f; (beating)* paliza; *(reprimand)* castigo.
go·ings-on (gō'ĭngz-ŏn') s.pl. FAM. actividades *f.*
goi·ter *o* **goi·tre** (goi'tər) s. MED. bocio.
gold (gōld) I. s. *o* oro II. adj. *(made of gold)* de oro; *(golden)* dorado.
gold digger s. JER. mujer vividora, aventurera.
gold·en (gōl'dən) adj. *(made of gold)* de oro <*g. earrings* aretes de oro>; *(color)* áureo, dorado; *(hair)* rubio; *(voice)* de oro; *(precious)* precioso; *(prosperous)* de oro, dorado (época); *(excellent)* excelente <*a g. opportunity* una excelente oportunidad>; *(promising)* prometedor <*a g. boy* un muchacho prometedor>.
golden age s. edad de oro *f.*
golden anniversary s. bodas de oro.
golden calf s. *(image)* becerro de oro; *(money)* oro.
golden eagle s. ORNIT. águila dorada, águila real.
Golden Fleece s. MITOL. vellocino de oro.
golden mean s. justo medio.
golden rule s. regla de oro.
gold-filled (gōld'fĭld') adj. JOY. chapado *o* revestido de oro.
gold-finch (gōld'fĭnch') s. ORNIT. jilguero, cardelina.
gold-fish (gōld'fĭsh') s. [pl. **gold·fish** *o* **gold·fishes**] ICT. pececillo de color.
gold leaf s. JOY. pan de oro *m,* hoja de oro.
gold mine s. FIG., FAM. mina de oro.
gold point s. COM. punto de oro.
gold rush s. fiebre del oro *f.*
gold·smith (gōld'smĭth') s. orfebre *m,* orífice *m.*
gold standard s. COM., FIN. patrón oro *m.*
golf (gŏlf) DEP. I. s. golf *m* II. intr. jugar al golf.
golf·er (gŏl'fər) s. DEP. golfista *mf,* jugador de golf *m.*
gol·ly (gŏl'ē) interj. FAM. ¡Dios mío!, ¡caramba!
go·nad (gō'năd') s. ANAT. gónada.
gon·do·la (gŏn'dl-ə) s. *(barge)* góndola; *(flat-bottomed boat)* barcaza; F.C. *(freight car)* batea; *(of a balloon)* góndola, barquilla.
gon·do·lier (gŏn'dl-îr') s. gondolero.
gone (gŏn) I. part. p. de **go** II. adj. *(past)* pasado, ido; *(dead)* muerto <*he was already g. by the time the ambulance arrived* ya estaba muerto cuando llegó la ambulancia>;

(ruined) arruinado; *(lost)* perdido; *(exhausted)* agotado ♦ **to be far g.** *(to be ill)* estar muy avanzado (en la enfermedad); *(to be drunk)* estar muy bebido • **to be g.** *(to have departed)* haberse ido <*he was g. when we arrived* él se había ido cuando nosotros llegamos>; *(to have disappeared)* haber desaparecido, faltar <*my wallet is g.* me falta la billetera>; *(to be used up)* haberse acabado <*all the chocolates are g.* se han acabado todos los chocolates>; *(to be away)* estar afuera, irse <*how long will you be g.?* ¿por cuánto tiempo te irás?> • **to be g. on** FAM. estar loco por, estar enamorado de.

gon·er (gŏ′nər) s. FAM. *(ill person)* enfermo desahuciado; *(ruined person)* persona arruinada.

gon·fa·lon (gŏn′fə-lŏn′) s. gonfalón *m*, confalón *m*.

gong (gŏng) I. s. MÚS. gong (instrumento de percusión) *m*, batintín *m* II. intr. sonar como un gong.

Gon·gor·ism (gŏng′gə-rĭz′əm) s. LIT. gongorismo.

gon·o·coc·cus (gŏn′ə-kŏk′əs) s. [pl. **-coc·ci** (-kŏk′sī′, -kŏk′-ī)] BACT. gonococo.

gon·or·rhe·a (gŏn′ə-rē′ə) s. MED. gonorrea, blenorragia.

goo (gōō) s. FAM. *(sticky substance)* substancia pegajosa; *(sentimentalism)* sentimentalismo.

goo·ber (gōō′bər) s. cacahuete *m*, maní *m*.

good §G22 (gŏŏd) I. adj. **bet·ter** (bĕt′ər), **best** (bĕst) *(better than average)* bueno; *(suitable)* bueno, adecuado <*a g. outdoor paint* una buena pintura para exteriores>; *(fresh)* bueno, fresco <*the fish is still g.* el pescado todavía está fresco>; *(sound)* bueno, sano <*a g. tooth* un diente sano>; *(satisfactory)* bueno, satisfactorio <*he did a g. job* hizo un buen trabajo>; *(of high quality)* bueno, de gran calidad <*a g. book* un buen libro>; *(discriminating)* bueno, distinguido <*g. taste* buen gusto>; *(beneficial)* bueno, beneficioso <*running is g. exercise for the lungs* correr es un ejercicio beneficioso para los pulmones>; *(competent)* bueno, competente <*a g. professor* un buen profesor>; *(thorough)* bueno, completo <*a g. physical examination* un reconocimiento físico completo>; *(safe)* bueno, seguro <*a g. investment* una buena inversión>; *(valid)* bueno, válido <*a g. reason* una razón válida>; *(genuine)* bueno, auténtico <*a g. dollar bill* un dólar auténtico>; *(ample)* bueno, abundante <*g. resources* recursos abundantes>; *(full)* más de <*I waited a g. hour* esperé más de una hora>; *(pleasant)* bueno, agradable <*a g. life* una vida agradable>; *(favorable)* bueno, favorable <*a g. omen* un augurio favorable>; *(upright)* bueno, justo <*a g. man* un hombre justo>; *(kind)* bueno, amable <*a g. gesture* un gesto amable>; *(loyal)* bueno, leal <*a g. Republican* un republicano leal>; *(obedient)* bueno, obediente <*a g. child* un niño bueno>; *(proper)* correcto, bueno <*g. manners* buenos modales>; *(devout)* bueno, devoto <*a g. Catholic* un católico devoto>; *(reliable)* bueno, digno de confianza <*g. judgment* opinión digna de confianza>; *(fertile)* bueno, fértil <*g. soil* tierra fértil> ♦ **a g. deal** mucho, bastante (tiempo, dinero) • **a g. turn** un favor, una bondad • **all in g. time** todo a su debido tiempo • **as g. as** prácticamente, casi <*as g. as new* casi nuevo> • **g. for a laugh** divertido • **g. for nothing** inútil, no sirve para nada • **g. for you!** *(well done!)* ¡bien hecho!; *(congratulations!)* ¡enhorabuena! • **how g. of you** muy amable de su parte • **in g. standing** de buena reputación, apreciado • **that's a g. one!** JER. ¡un buen chiste! • **to be g. at** tener capacidad para, tener talento para • **to be g. for** *(to be valid)* ser válido por <*my passport is g. for five years* mi pasaporte es válido por cinco años>; *(to last)* durar <*these batteries will be g. for one year* estas pilas durarán un año>; *(to have credit)* tener crédito hasta <*you are g. for two hundred dollars* usted tiene crédito hasta doscientos dólares>; *(to be beneficial)* hacer bien <*this will be g. for you* esto te hará bien>; *(to be appropriate for)* ser bueno para; *(to have the energy for)* sentirse capaz de • **to be g. to (someone)** ser bueno para con alguien, tratar bien a alguien • **to be no g.** ser inútil, ser un perdido • **to be g. enough to** tener la bondad de • **to have a g. mind to** sentirse inclinado a • **to have a g. time** divertirse, pasarlo bien • **to hold g.** valer, tener validez • **to make g.** *(to prosper)* prosperar; *(to cover)* cubrir (un déficit); *(to pay)* pagar; *(to make amends for)* reparar, desagraviar (una injusticia); *(a promise)* cumplir (una promesa) • **to say** *o* **to put in a g. word for** recomendar, hablar en favor de II. s. *(something good)* bien *m*; *(benefit)* beneficio, bien <*for the common g.* por el bien común>; *(goodness)* bondad *f* ♦ **goods** *(wares)* bienes; *(merchandise)* mercancías, géneros; *(effects)* efectos, enseres; *(belongings)* bienes; *(fabric)* tela; JER. *(something incriminating)* pruebas de culpabilidad <*they had the g. on us* tenían pruebas de culpabilidad contra nosotros> • **goods and chattels** muebles y enseres • **to deliver the goods** cumplir lo prometido ♦ **for g.** para siempre, definitivamente • **the g.** lo bueno • **to come to no g.** terminar mal • **to do g.** hacer el bien, ayudar a la gente • **to do someone g.** hacer bien a alguien, sentar bien a alguien III. adv. FAM. bien ♦ **g. and proper** por las buenas • **to feel g.** *(to be satisfied)* estar satisfecho; *(to feel well)* sentirse bien; *(to be pleasurable)* ser agradable, dar gusto • **to give as g. as one gets** devolver golpe por golpe, pagar con la misma moneda IV. interj. ¡bueno!, ¡muy bien!

good-by *o* **good-bye** (gŏŏd-bī′) I. interj. ¡adiós!, ¡hasta luego! II. s. [pl. **good-bys** *o* **good-byes**] adiós, despedida.

good-for-noth·ing (gŏŏd′fər-nŭth′ĭng) I. s. haragán *m*, inútil *m* II. adj. inútil, sin valor.

Good Friday s. RELIG. Viernes Santo.

good·heart·ed (gŏŏd′här′tĭd) adj. bondadoso, de buen corazón.

good-hu·mored (gŏŏd′hyōō′mərd) adj. jovial, alegre.

good-look·ing (gŏŏd′lŏŏk′ĭng) adj. bien parecido, guapo.

good looks s. FAM. buena presencia, apariencia atractiva.

good·ly (gŏŏd′lē) adj. **-li·er**, **-li·est** *(attractive)* atractivo; *(pleasant)* agradable; *(large)* grande, considerable.

good-na·tured (gŏŏd′nā′chərd) adj. bondadoso, de buen corazón.

good·ness (gŏŏd′nĭs) I. s. *(condition)* bondad *f*; *(essence)* substancia, esencia II. interj. ¡Dios mío!, ¡Ave María!

good-sized (gŏŏd′sīzd′) adj. bastante grande.

good-tem·pered (gŏŏd′tĕm′pərd) adj. de buen carácter.

good will *o* **good·will** (gŏŏd′wĭl′) s. buena voluntad.

good·y (gŏŏd′ē) FAM. I. s. [pl. **-ies**] golosina, dulce *m* II. interj. ¡qué bien!

good·y-good·y (gŏŏd′ē-gŏŏd′ē) adj. & s. [pl. **-ies**] santurrón *m*, beato.

goo·ey (gōō′ē) adj. pegajoso, viscoso.

goof (gōōf) JER. I. s. *(fool)* bobo, simplón *m*; *(mistake)* disparate *m*, pifia II. intr. meter la pata ♦ **to g. off** *o* **around** holgazanear.

goof-off (gōōf′ôf′) s. JER. haragán *m*, holgazán *m*.

goof·y (gōō′fē) adj. **-i·er**, **-i·est** JER. tonto, ridículo.

gook (gŏŏk) s. JER. mugre *f*, suciedad *f*.

goon (gōōn) s. FAM. *(thug)* terrorista pagado; JER. *(stupid person)* estúpido, tonto.

goose (gōōs) s. [pl. **geese** (gēs)] ORNIT. ganso, oca; FAM. *(person)* ganso, pavo ♦ **gooses** plancha de sastre • **to cook one's g.** FAM. malograrle los planes a uno.

goose·ber·ry (gōōs′bĕr′ē) s. BOT. *(shrub)* grosellero espinoso; *(fruit)* grosella, uva espina.

goose flesh *o* **goose bumps** s. piel *o* carne de gallina *f*.

goose step s. MIL. paso de ganso.

goose-step (gōōs′stĕp′) intr. **-stepped**, **-step·ping** MIL. ir a paso de ganso.

go·pher (gō′fər) s. ZOOL. *(burrowing animal)* ardillón *m*, ardilla terrestre; *(ground squirrel)* ardilla de tierra; *(tortoise)* tortuga de tierra.

Gor·di·an knot (gôr′dē-ən) s. nudo gordiano.

gore¹ (gôr) tr. **gored**, **gor·ing** cornear.

gore² (gôr) I. s. *(cloth)* sesga, nesga; *(land)* terreno triangular II. tr. **gored**, **gor·ing** cortar en triángulo.

gore³ (gôr) s. sangre coagulada.

gorge (gôrj) I. s. *(ravine)* desfiladero, garganta; FORT. *(entrance)* gola; *(binge)* comilona; *(obstructing mass)* masa que obstruye II. tr. **gorged**, **gorg·ing** *(to stuff)* hartar, atiborrar; *(to devour)* engullir, devorar —intr. ♦ **to g. oneself** hartarse y atiborrarse.

gor·geous (gôr′jəs) adj. *(beautiful)* hermoso, espléndido; FAM. *(delightful)* bonito, encantador <*what a g. day!* ¡qué día tan bonito!>

ă rey / ä año / b boca / ch chico / d dar / ĕ el / ē mil / g gato / h joya / hw juez / ī aire / k casa / kw cuan /

gor·get (gôr′jĭt) s. ARM. *(throat protector)* gorjal *m*; *(collar)* gorguera; TEJ. *(adornment)* toca; ORNIT. collar *m*.

Gor·gon (gôr′gən) s. MITOL. gorgona; *(ugly woman)* mujer muy fea.

go·ril·la (gə-rĭl′ə) s. ZOOL. gorila *m*; FIG. *(brute)* hombre bruto; *(thug)* matón *m*.

gor·mand·ize (gôr′mən-dīz′) intr. **-ized, -iz·ing** glotonear, engullir —tr. devorar.

go·ry (gôr′ē) adj. **-ri·er, -ri·est** *(bloody)* ensangrentado; *(said of a fight)* sangriento.

gosh (gŏsh) interj. ¡cielos!, ¡Dios!

gos·hawk (gŏs′hôk′) s. ORNIT. azor *m*.

gos·ling (gŏz′lĭng) s. ORNIT. ansarino; *(naive person)* simplón *m*, novato.

gos·pel (gŏs′pəl) s. evangelio ♦ **G.** RELIG. Evangelio • **a g. meeting** una reunión evangélica.

gospel music s. música religiosa popular.

gos·sa·mer (gŏs′ə-mər) I. s. *(cobweb)* telaraña fina; *(fabric)* gasa II. adj. muy delgado, muy fino.

gos·sip (gŏs′ĭp) I. s. *(rumor)* chismes *m*; *(gossiper)* chismoso; *(chatter)* charlatanería ♦ **g. column** noticias sociales, crónica social • **piece of g.** chisme II. intr. *(to spread gossip)* chismear, chismorrear; *(to chatter)* charlar.

gos·sip·mon·ger (gŏs′ĭp-mŭng′gər) s. chismoso.

gos·sip·y (gŏs′ĭ-pē) adj. chismoso.

got (gŏt) pret. y un part. p. de **get.**

Goth (gŏth) s. HIST. godo.

Goth·ic (gŏth′ĭk) I. adj. gótico ♦ **g.** cruel, bárbaro II. s. gótico.

GO TO (gō′ tōō′) s. COMPUT. pase a (señal para cambiar de instrucciones) *m*.

got·ten (gŏt′n) un part. p. de **get.**

gouache (gwäsh) s. PINT. aguada (pintura, color y método).

gouge (gouj) I. s. TEC. gubia; FAM. *(amount extorted)* dinero estafado II. tr. **gouged, goug·ing** *(to chisel)* escoplear (con una gubia); FIG. *(to dig out)* excavar; JER. *(to overcharge)* estafar, cobrar un ojo de la cara ♦ **to g. someone's eyes out** arrancarle los ojos a alguien.

gourd (gôrd, gōōrd) s. BOT. *(plant)* calabacera; *(fruit, container)* calabaza.

gourde (gōōrd) s. FIN. gourde (unidad monetaria de Haití).

gour·mand (gōōr-mänd′) s. goloso, glotón *m*.

gour·met (gōōr-mā′, gŏr′mā′) s. gastrónomo.

gout (gout) s. MED. *(disease)* gota; *(clot)* grumo; *(drop)* gota.

gov·ern (gŭv′ərn) tr. *(to rule)* gobernar; *(to control)* controlar, dominar (emociones, personas); *(to determine)* determinar; GRAM. regir —intr. *(to rule)* gobernar; *(to prevail)* prevalecer, predominar.

gov·ern·a·ble (gŭv′ər-nə-bəl) adj. *(that can be ruled)* gobernable; *(manageable)* dócil, que se puede controlar.

gov·er·nance (gŭv′ər-nəns) s. gobernación *f*, gobierno.

gov·ern·ess (gŭv′ər-nĭs) s. institutriz *f*.

gov·ern·ment (gŭv′ərn-mənt) I. s. POL. gobierno; *(administration)* administración *f*, dirección (de un negocio, una organización) *f* II. adj. del gobierno.

gov·ern·men·tal (gŭv′ərn-mĕn′tl) adj. gubernamental, gubernativo.

gov·er·nor (gŭv′ər-nər) s. POL. gobernador *m*; *(manager)* administrador *m*, director *m*; MEC. *(regulator)* regulador automático.

gov·er·nor-gen·er·al (gŭv′ər-nər-jĕn′ər-əl) s. [pl. **governors-general** *o* **governor-generals**] gobernador general *m*.

gov·er·nor·ship (gŭv′ər-nər-shĭp′) s. POL. gobierno.

gown (goun) s. *(formal dress)* vestido largo (de etiqueta); *(ceremonial robe)* toga (de académicos, magistrados).

grab (grăb) I. tr. **grabbed, grab·bing** *(to seize)* agarrar, coger; *(to take suddenly)* echar mano a; *(to arrest)* detener; *(to appropriate unscrupulously)* arrebatar; JER. *(to attract)* interesar, cautivar ♦ **to g. a bite to eat** comer algo a la carrera —intr. ♦ **to g. at** *(to try to seize)* tratar de arrebatar; *(to try to catch)* tratar de agarrar II. s. MEC. cuchara de dos mandíbulas ♦ **g. rail** barra de sostén • **to make a g. at something** tratar de agarrar algo • **up for grabs** disponible.

grab bag s. *(bag)* paquete *m* (con regalos para ser sacados sin mirar); *(item collection)* colección *f* de artículos misceláneos (generalmente de valor).

grab·by (grăb′ē) adj. **-bi·er, -bi·est** *(inclined to grab)* agarrador; *(greedy)* codicioso.

grace (grās) I. s. *(gracefulness)* gracia, elegancia; *(sense of propriety)* cortesía, delicadeza; *(clemency)* gracia, benevolencia; *(favor)* gracia, favor *m*; *(reprieve)* aplazamiento, plazo; TEOL. gracia; *(at table)* bendición de la mesa *f* ♦ **by the g. of** gracias a • **by the g. of God** por la gracia de Dios • **to be in the bad graces of** haber perdido el favor de • **to be in the good graces of** gozar del favor de • **to get into the good graces of** congraciarse con • **to fall from g.** caer en desgracia • **to say g.** bendecir la mesa • **with bad, good g.** de mala, buena gana • **your g.** *(to a duke)* Excelencia; *(to a bishop)* Ilustrísima; *(to a prince)* Alteza II. tr. **graced, grac·ing** ♦ **to g. with one's presence** honrar con la presencia de uno.

grace·ful (grās′fəl) adj. *(showing grace)* agraciado; *(elegant)* elegante; *(polite)* cortés, delicado.

grace·ful·ness (grās′fəl-nĭs) s. gracia, delicadeza.

grace·less (grās′lĭs) adj. *(lacking grace)* sin gracia; *(clumsy)* torpe; *(impolite)* descortés.

Grac·es (grā′sĭz) s.pl. ♦ **the three G.** MITOL. las tres Gracias.

gra·cious (grā′shəs) adj. *(courteous)* amable, cortés *<a g. attitude* una actitud amable>; *(proper)* urbano, delicado; *(compassionate)* compasivo, clemente; *(indulgent)* indulgente; *(graceful)* gracioso, gentil; *(elegant)* elegante ♦ **goodness g.!** *o* **g. me!** ¡válgame Dios!

gra·cious·ness (grā′shəs-nĭs) s. *(courteousness)* amabilidad *f*, cortesía; *(propriety)* delicadeza, urbanidad *f*; *(gracefulness)* gracia.

grad (grăd) s. FAM. graduado.

gra·date (grā′dāt′) intr. **-dat·ed, -dat·ing** graduarse —tr. graduar, ordenar en grados.

gra·da·tion (grā-dā′shən) s. graduación *f*; *(of colors)* degradación *f*.

grade (grād) I. s. *(degree)* grado; *(quality)* calidad *f*, clase *f* *<a poor g. of lumber* una madera de baja calidad>; *(group)* categoría; EDUC. *(class)* año, curso *<he is in third g.* está en tercer año>; *(mark)* nota; *(rank)* grado; *(slope)* pendiente *f* ♦ **g. A eggs** huevos de primera • **to make the g.** FAM. tener éxito II. tr. **grad·ed, grad·ing** *(to classify)* clasificar; *(to mark)* calificar *<to g. the exams* calificar los exámenes>; *(to give a grade to)* dar nota a (un alumno); *(to level)* nivelar; *(to graduate)* graduar; *(to crossbreed)* cruzar (para mejorar la raza) —intr. *(in position)* ocupar un lugar; *(in quality)* ser de calidad *<this wine grades high* este vino es de alta calidad>; *(to change)* convertirse gradualmente.

grade crossing s. *(intersection)* cruce *m*; *(railway crossing)* paso a nivel.

grade school s. escuela primaria.

gra·di·ent (grā′dē-ənt) s. *(inclination rate)* inclinación *f*; *(slope)* cuesta; *(incline)* pendiente *f*; FÍS., MAT. gradiente *m*.

grad·u·al (grăj′ōō-əl) I. adj. gradual, paulatino II. s. RELIG. gradual *m*.

grad·u·al·ism (grăj′ōō-ə-lĭz′əm) s. avance *m* *o* desarrollo gradual.

grad·u·al·ness (grăj′ōō-əl-nĭs) s. carácter gradual *m*.

grad·u·ate (grăj′ōō-āt′) I. intr. **-at·ed, -at·ing** *(to receive a degree)* graduarse; *(to grade)* convertirse gradualmente ♦ **to g. as** graduarse *o* recibirse de —tr. *(to give a degree to)* graduar, diplomar; *(to gradate)* graduar (efecto, termómetro) II. s. (-ĭt) *(person)* graduado, diplomado; *(container)* frasco graduado III. adj. (-ĭt) *(person)* graduado, diplomado; *(studies)* de graduado ♦ **g. school** escuela para graduados.

graduate student s. EDUC. estudiante graduado.

grad·u·a·tion (grăj′ōō-ā′shən) s. EDUC. *(ceremony)* graduación *f*; *(commencement)* entrega de diplomas.

Graec·o-Ro·man (grĕk′ō-rō′mən) adj. var. de **Greco-Roman.**

graf·fi·to (grə-fē′tō) s. [pl. **-ti** (-tē)] inscripción en las paredes *f*.

graft[1] (grăft) AGR., MED. I. tr. injertar —intr. *(to make a* *graft)* hacer un injerto; *(to be grafted)* injertarse II. s. injerto.

graft² (grăft) I. s. *(abuse of position)* concusión f; *(extortion)* extorsión f; *(bribe)* soborno II. tr. & intr. extorsionar.

gra·ham (grā'əm) s. harina de trigo entero.

grail o **Grail** (grāl) s. LIT., RELIG. Grial m; FIG. *(quest)* búsqueda, objetivo.

grain (grān) I. s. *(seed)* grano; *(cereals)* cereales m; *(particle)* grano (de sal, arena); *(bit)* pizca, asomo <*not a g. of truth* ni pizca de verdad>; *(unit of weight)* grano; *(in wood)* grano, fibra; *(in leather)* flor f; *(in stone)* veta, vena; *(in fabrics)* hebra; *(texture)* textura <*coarse g.* textura gruesa> ♦ **to go against one's g.** ir contra el carácter de uno • **to take with a g. of salt** tomar con reservas II. tr. *(to granulate)* granular; *(to make rough)* dar una textura granular a; *(wood, stone)* vetear; *(leather)* granelar —intr. granularse, volverse granuloso.

grain alcohol s. alcohol de grano m.

grain elevator s. AGR. elevador de granos m.

grain·y (grā'nē) adj. **-i·er, -i·est** *(grain-like)* graneado; *(granular)* granular; *(veined)* veteado.

gram (grăm) s. FÍS. gramo (unidad de masa).

gram atom s. FÍS. átomo-gramo.

gra·min·e·ous (grə-mĭn'ē-əs) adj. BOT. gramíneo.

gram·mar (grăm'ər) s. *(study)* gramática; *(basic principles)* elementos.

gram·mar·ian (grə-mâr'ē-ən) s. gramático.

grammar school s. *(grade school)* escuela primaria; G.B. *(high school)* escuela secundaria.

gram·mat·i·cal (grə-măt'ĭ-kəl) adj. gramatical.

gramme (grăm) s. G.B. var. de **gram**.

gram molecule s. FÍS., QUÍM. molécula gramo, mol m.

gram·o·phone (grăm'ə-fōn') s. gramófono, tocadiscos m.

gram·pus (grăm'pəs) s. ZOOL. orca.

gran·a·ry (grăn'ə-rē) s. [pl. **-ries**] granero.

grand (grănd) I. adj. **-er, -est** *(magnificent)* grandioso, magnífico; *(principal)* principal; *(sumptuous)* suntuoso <*g. furnishings* un mobiliario suntuoso>; *(stately)* espléndido; *(dignified)* ilustre, distinguido <*a g. old man* un ilustre anciano>; *(lofty)* elevado (estilo, intención); *(wonderful)* magnífico, fenomenal ♦ **the g. total** la suma total, el total • **to have a g. time** pasarlo fenomenalmente II. s. *(piano)* piano de cola; JER. *(one thousand dollars)* mil dólares.

grand·aunt (grănd'ănt', -änt') s. tía abuela.

grand·child (grănd'chīld') s. *(male)* nieto; *(female)* nieta.

grand·dad (grănd'dăd') o **grand·dad·dy** o **gran·dad·dy** (grăn'dăd'ē) s. *(grandfather)* abuelo, abuelito; FIG. *(archetype)* arquetipo.

grand·daugh·ter (grăn'dô'tər) s. nieta.

gran·dee (grăn-dē') s. *(nobleman)* grande m; *(eminent person)* eminencia.

gran·deur (grăn'jər) s. *(magnificence)* magnificencia; *(nobility)* nobleza; *(greatness)* grandeza.

grand·fa·ther (grănd'fä'thər) s. *(parent's father)* abuelo; *(ancestor)* antepasado.

grandfather clock s. reloj de pie m, reloj de caja.

grandfather file s. cinta o disco magnético que contiene el programa original de una computadora.

gran·dil·o·quence (grăn-dĭl'ə-kwəns) s. grandilocuencia, altisonancia.

gran·dil·o·quent (grăn-dĭl'ə-kwənt) adj. grandilocuente, altisonante.

gran·di·ose (grăn'dē-ōs', grăn'dē-ōs') adj. *(grand)* grandioso, magnífico; *(pompous)* pomposo, ampuloso.

grand jury s. DER. jurado de acusación.

grand larceny s. DER. robo de mayor cuantía.

grand·ma (grăn'mä') s. FAM. abuelita.

grand·moth·er (grănd'mŭth'ər) s. abuela.

grand·neph·ew (grănd'nĕf'yōō) s. sobrino nieto.

grand·ness (grănd'nĭs) s. *(magnificence)* grandiosidad f, magnificencia; *(sumptuousness)* suntuosidad f; *(splendidness)* esplendidez f; *(loftiness)* carácter elevado.

grand·niece (grănd'nēs') s. sobrina nieta.

grand·pa (grăn'pä') s. FAM. abuelo, abuelito.

grand·par·ent (grănd'pâr'ənt) s. *(male)* abuelo; *(female)* abuela.

grand piano s. MÚS. piano de cola.

grand·sire (grănd'sīr') s. ANT. *(grandfather)* abuelo; *(forefather)* antepasado (masculino); *(old man)* viejo.

grand slam s. *(in bridge)* gran slam m; *(in sports)* la conquista de todas las competencias en un circuito profesional.

grand·son (grănd'sŭn') s. nieto.

grand·stand (grănd'stănd') I. s. *(roofed stand)* tribuna; *(spectators)* espectadores m, público II. intr. actuar de manera ostentosa.

grand·un·cle (grănd'ŭng'kəl) s. tío abuelo.

grange (grānj) s. G.B. *(farm)* granja, finca; *(residence)* casa solariega; ANT. *(granary)* granero.

gran·ite (grăn'ĭt) s. granito.

gran·ny o **gran·nie** (grăn'ē) s. [pl. **-nies**] *(grandmother)* abuelita; *(fussy person)* persona minuciosa; *(midwife)* partera.

grant (grănt) I. tr. *(to concede)* conceder <*to g. the right to speak* conceder el derecho a la palabra>; *(to bestow)* otorgar; DER. *(to transfer)* ceder, transferir; *(to acknowledge)* admitir ♦ **granted** o **granting that** suponiendo que • **to take it for granted** dar por sentado • **to take someone for granted** no apreciar suficientemente a alguien II. s. *(act)* concesión f; *(subvention)* subvención f; *(donation)* donación f; *(scholarship)* beca; DER. *(transfer)* cesión f, transferencia.

grant·ee (grăn-tē') s. *(of property)* cesionario; *(of a donation)* donatario; *(of a scholarship)* becario.

grant-in-aid (grănt'ĭn-ād') s. [pl. **grants-in-aid**] subvención f, subsidio.

gran·tor (grăn'tər, -tôr') s. DER. cesionista mf, otorgante mf.

gran·u·lar (grăn'yə-lər) adj. granular.

gran·u·late (grăn'yə-lāt') tr. & intr. granular(se), granear(se).

gran·u·la·tion (grăn'yə-lā'shən) s. granulación f, granulado.

gran·ule (grăn'yōōl) s. *(pellet)* gránulo, granito; ASTRON. gránulo.

grape (grāp) s. BOT. *(vine)* parra, vid f; *(fruit)* uva; *(color)* morado; *(grapeshot)* metralla ♦ **sour grapes** FIG. las uvas están verdes.

grape·fruit (grāp'frōōt') s. BOT. toronja, pomelo (fruto y árbol) ♦ **g. juice** jugo o zumo de pomelo.

grape·shot (grāp'shŏt') s. ARM. metralla.

grape·vine (grāp'vīn') s. BOT. vid f, parra ♦ **to hear something through the g.** FIG. enterarse de algo por medio de chismes.

graph (grăf) I. s. gráfico, diagrama m II. tr. representar mediante un gráfico o diagrama.

graph·ic (grăf'ĭk) I. adj. *(of a graph)* gráfico; *(vivid)* gráfico, vívido II. s. *(work)* obra de artes gráficas, grabado; *(illustration)* ilustración gráfica.

graphic arts s.pl. ARTE. artes gráficas.

graph·ics (grăf'ĭks) s. [ú. con v. sing. o pl.] dibujo lineal.

graph·ite (grăf'īt') s. MIN. grafito.

gra·phol·o·gy (gră-fŏl'ə-jē) s. grafología.

graph paper s. papel cuadriculado.

grap·nel (grăp'nəl) s. MARÍT. rezón m, anclote m.

grap·ple (grăp'əl) I. s. MARÍT. *(iron shaft)* garfio de abordaje; *(grapnel)* rezón m; *(struggle)* lucha cuerpo a cuerpo; *(grip)* apretón m II. tr. *(to grapple)* aferrar (con un garfio); *(to grip)* agarrar —intr. *(to hold firmly)* aferrarse; *(to wrestle)* luchar cuerpo a cuerpo ♦ **to g. with** FIG. afrontar <*to g. with political realities* afrontar las realidades de la política>.

grappling iron o **grappling hook** s. MARÍT. garabato.

grasp (grăsp) I. tr. *(to seize)* agarrar, asir; *(to clasp the hand)* estrechar, apretar; *(to comprehend)* captar, entender —intr. ♦ **to g. at** *(to try to grab)* tratar de agarrar; *(to accept eagerly)* aprovechar II. s. *(grip)* apretón m; *(embrace)* abrazo; *(comprehension)* comprensión f ♦ **beyond one's g.** fuera del alcance de uno • **to have a good g. of** dominar • **within one's g.** al alcance de uno.

grasp·ing (grăs'pĭng) adj. codicioso, avaricioso.

grass (grăs) **I.** s. BOT. *(green herbage)* hierba, yerba; *(lawn)* césped *m*; *(pasture)* pasto; JER. *(marijuana)* yerba, mariguana ♦ **keep off the g.** prohibido pisar el césped • **not to let the g. grow under one's feet** no perder tiempo **II.** tr. *(to seed with grass)* sembrar de hierba; *(to feed livestock)* pastar, apacentar.

grass·hop·per (grăs'hŏp'ər) s. ENTOM. langosta, saltamontes *m*; *(light plane)* avioneta; *(cocktail)* coctel *m* de crema de menta, crema de cacao y nata.

grass·land (grăs'lănd') s. pradera, prado.

grass·roots (grăs'rōōts', -rŏŏts') s.pl. [ú. con v. sing. o pl.] POL. *(local level)* nivel local *m*; *(groundwork)* base *f*; *(source)* fuente *f.*

grass widow s. *(divorced woman)* divorciada; *(temporarily separated)* mujer separada temporariamente de su esposo; *(mistress)* querida abandonada.

grass·y (grăs'ē) adj. **-i·er, -i·est** *(full of grass)* herboso; *(like grass)* de o como pasto.

grate¹ (grāt) **I.** tr. **grat·ed, grat·ing** *(to scrape)* rallar; *(to rub together)* hacer rechinar; *(to irritate)* irritar —intr. *(to rasp)* rechinar (dientes, bisagra) ♦ **to g. on** *(person)* irritar; *(nerves)* irritar; *(ear)* herir, lastimar **II.** s. *(of metal)* chirrido; *(of teeth)* rechinamiento.

grate² (grāt) s. *(grill)* reja, verja; *(for a fireplace)* parrilla; MIN. *(for crushed ore)* tamiz *m*, criba.

grate·ful (grāt'fəl) adj. *(thankful)* agradecido; *(agreeable)* agradable, grato.

grat·er (grā'tər) s. CUL. rallador *m.*

grat·i·fi·ca·tion (grăt'ə-fī-kā'shən) s. gratificación *f.*

grat·i·fy (grăt'ə-fī') tr. **-fied, -fy·ing** *(to please)* gratificar, dar placer; *(to satisfy)* satisfacer; *(to indulge)* complacer; ANT. *(to reward)* gratificar.

grat·ing (grā'tĭng) **I.** s. *(grill)* reja, verja; ÓPT. retícula **II.** adj. *(rasping)* discordante, malsonante; FIG. *(irritating)* molesto.

grat·is (grăt'ĭs) adj. & adv. gratis.

grat·i·tude (grăt'ĭ-tōōd', -tyōōd') s. gratitud *f.*

gra·tu·i·tous (grə-tōō'ĭ-təs, -tyōō'-) adj. *(free)* gratuito; *(unnecessary)* innecesario; *(unjustified)* injustificado.

gra·tu·i·ty (grə-tōō'ĭ-tē, -tyōō'-) s. [pl. **-ties**] *(tip)* propina; *(gift)* dádiva.

gra·va·men (grə-vā'mən) s. [pl. **-va·mens** o **-vam·i·na** (-văm'-ə-nə)] *(grievance)* agravio; DER. *(of an accusation)* fundamento.

grave¹ (grāv) s. *(excavation)* fosa; *(tomb)* tumba, sepultura; FIG. *(death)* muerte *f.*

grave² (grāv) **I.** adj. **grav·er, grav·est** *(important)* muy importante; *(critical)* grave, serio; *(dignified)* grave, solemne; *(somber)* oscuro.

grave³ (grāv) tr. **graved, grav·en** (grā'vən) o **graved, grav·ing** *(to engrave)* grabar, esculpir; FIG. grabar, fijar (en la mente o memoria).

grave·dig·ger (grāv'dĭg'ər) s. sepulturero.

grav·el (grăv'əl) **I.** s. *(rock fragments)* ripio, grava; MED. arenilla **II.** tr. **-eled, -el·ing** *(to surface)* enripiar; FIG. *(to confuse)* confundir, desconcertar; FAM. *(to irritate)* irritar.

grave·ly (grāv'lē) adv. gravemente.

graven image (grā'vən) s. ídolo.

grave robber s. ladrón de tumbas *m.*

grave·stone (grāv'stōn') s. lápida.

grave·yard (grāv'yärd') s. cementerio, camposanto.

grav·id (grăv'ĭd) adj. grávida, embarazada.

grav·i·tate (grăv'ĭ-tāt') intr. **-tat·ed, -tat·ing** FÍS. gravitar; FIG. *(to move towards)* tender hacia, ser atraído por.

grav·i·ta·tion (grăv'ĭ-tā'shən) s. FÍS. gravitación *f*; FIG. *(tendency)* tendencia.

grav·i·ta·tion·al (grăv'ĭ-tā'shə-nəl) adj. FÍS. de gravitación, gravitatorio.

grav·i·ty (grăv'ĭ-tē) s. FÍS. gravedad *f*; *(gravitation)* gravitación *f*; FIG. *(seriousness)* seriedad *f*, gravedad; *(solemnity)* solemnidad *f.*

gra·vure (grə-vyōōr') s. IMPR. *(method)* impresión en hueco *f*; FOTOG. *(photogravure)* fotograbado.

gra·vy (grā'vē) s. [pl. **-vies**] CUL. *(meat juice)* jugo *m*; *(sauce)* salsa; FIG., JER. *(easy gain)* breva.

gravy boat s. salsera.

gray (grā) **I.** s. gris **II.** adj. *(color)* gris; *(gloomy)* gris, triste; *(hoary)* cano ♦ **g. area** zona no definida • **to go o turn g.** encanecer **III.** intr. *(hair)* encanecer; *(to become gray)* volverse gris.

gray·beard (grā'bîrd') s. viejo, anciano.

gray·ish (grā'ĭsh) adj. grisáceo.

gray matter s. ANAT. materia gris.

graze¹ (grāz) intr. **grazed, graz·ing** pacer, pastar —tr. apacentar.

graze² (grāz) **I.** tr. **grazed, graz·ing** *(to brush)* rozar; *(to scrape)* raspar, rasguñar —intr. rozar **II.** s. rozadura.

graz·ing (grā'zĭng) **I.** s. pastoreo, apacentamiento **II.** adj. ♦ **g. land** pasto.

grease (grēs) **I.** s. grasa **II.** tr. **greased, greas·ing** engrasar ♦ **to g. someone's palm** JER. untar la mano de alguien.

grease monkey s. JER. mecánico.

grease paint s. TEAT. maquillaje *m.*

greas·i·ness (grē'sē-nĭs, -zē-) s. untuosidad *f.*

greas·y (grē'sē, -zē) adj. **-i·er, -i·est** *(grease-coated)* engrasado; *(fatty)* grasoso; *(dirty)* grasiento ♦ **g. spoon** JER. fonda, restaurante barato y malo.

great (grāt) **I.** adj. *(large)* grande; *(age)* avanzado; *(important)* grande (novela, pais); *(eminent)* ilustre, grande; FAM. *(very good)* magnífico, bárbaro (fiesta, película) ♦ **a g. while** mucho tiempo • **Alexander the G.** Alejandro Magno • **to be g. at** FAM. ser un hacha en • **to be g. friends** FAM. ser muy amigos • **to have a g. time** pasarlo en grande **II.** s. grande *m* **III.** adv. FAM. muy bien.

great-aunt (grāt'ănt', -änt') s. tía abuela.

Great Britain s. Gran Bretaña.

great·coat (grāt'kōt') s. sobretodo, abrigo.

Great Dane s. gran danés *m.*

great·er o **Great·er** (grā'tər) adj. Gran <*G. Buenos Aires* el Gran Buenos Aires>.

great-grand·child (grāt'grănd'chĭld') s. [pl. **-children** (-chĭl'-drən)] bisnieto.

great-grand·daugh·ter (grāt'grăn'dô'tər) s. bisnieta.

great-grand·fa·ther (grāt'grănd'fä'thər) s. bisabuelo.

great-grand·moth·er (grāt'grănd'mŭth'ər) s. bisabuela.

great-grand·par·ent (grāt'grănd'pâr'ənt) s. bisabuelo.

great-grand·son (grāt'grănd'sŭn') s. bisnieto.

great·heart·ed (grāt'här'tĭd) adj. *(noble)* de alma noble; *(generous)* generoso, magnánimo.

great·ly (grāt'lē) adv. *(very)* muy; *(much)* mucho; *(mainly)* principalmente, en gran parte.

great·ness (grāt'nĭs) s. grandeza.

great-nephew (grāt-nĕf'yōō) s. sobrino nieto.

great-niece (grāt-nēs') s. sobrina nieta.

Great Powers s.pl. DIPL., POL. Grandes Potencias (paises más poderosos).

Great Spirit s. RELIG. Gran Espíritu *m.*

great-uncle (grāt'ŭng'kəl) s. tío abuelo.

Great War s. HIST. Gran Guerra (primera guerra mundial).

greaves (grēvz) s.pl. chicharrones *m.*

Gre·cian (grē'shən) adj. & s. griego.

Grec·o-Ro·man (grĕk'ō-rō'mən) adj. ARTE., HIST. grecorromano.

Greece (grēs) s. Grecia.

greed (grēd) s. *(for wealth)* codicia, avaricia; *(for food)* gula, glotonería.

greed·i·ness (grē'dē-nĭs) s. *(avariciousness)* avaricia, codicia; *(gluttony)* glotonería, gula.

greed·y (grē'dē) adj. **-i·er, -i·est** *(avaricious)* avaricioso, codicioso; *(gluttonous)* goloso, glotón *m*; *(eager)* ávido.

Greek (grēk) **I.** adj. griego **II.** s. *(inhabitant, language)* griego ♦ **it's G. to me** FIG., FAM. para mí eso es griego.

green (grēn) **I.** s. *(color)* verde *m*; *(verdure)* verdor *m*; *(lawn)* césped *m*; DEP. *(for golf)* green (de golf) *m* ♦ **greens** verduras **II.** adj. *(color)* verde; *(unripe)* verde; *(fresh)* fresco; *(sickly)* pálido, lívido; *(inexperienced)* inexperto, novato; *(gullible)* crédulo, simplón ♦ **he is g. with envy** se le come la envidia **III.** intr. verdecer, enverdecer.

green·back (grēn'băk') s. FAM. billete (de cualquier denominación) *m.*

green bean s. BOT., CUL. habichuela verde, judía verde.

---

green·er·y (grē′nə-rē) s. [pl. **-ies**] *(foliage)* follaje *m*, verdor *m*; *(greenhouse)* invernadero.
green·gage (grēn′gāj′) s. ciruela verdal *o* claudia.
green·gro·cer (grēn′grō′sər) s. G.B. verdulero.
green·horn (grēn′hôrn′) s. *(novice)* novato, bisoño; *(dupe)* simplón *m*.
green·house (grēn′hous′) s. invernadero.
green·ish (grē′nĭsh) adj. verdoso.
Green·land (grēn′lənd) s. Groenlandia.
Green·land·er (grēn′lən-dər) s. groenlandés *m*.
green light s. *(traffic signal)* luz verde *f*; FIG. *(permission)* permiso, autorización *f*.
green·ness (grēn′nĭs) s. *(greenery)* verdor *m*; *(inexperience)* inexperiencia.
green·room (grēn′rŏŏm′, -rŏŏm′) s. TEAT., TELEV. sala de espera (para los actores).
green·sward (grēn′swôrd′) s. césped *m*.
green thumb s. FAM. habilidad para la jardinería *f*.
Green·wich time *o* **Green·wich mean time** (grēn′ĭch) s. la hora solar del meridiano de Greenwich.
greet (grēt) tr. *(to welcome)* dar la bienvenida, saludar; *(to receive)* recibir, acoger; *(to be perceived by)* presentarse a (la vista, los ojos).
greet·ing (grē′tĭng) s. *(salutation)* saludo; *(welcome)* recibimiento, bienvenida.
greeting card s. tarjeta.
gre·gar·i·ous (grĭ-gâr′ē-əs) adj. *(group-forming)* gregario; *(sociable)* sociable; BOT. *(in clusters)* arracimado.
gre·gar·i·ous·ness (grĭ-gâr′ē-əs-nĭs) s. gregarismo.
Gre·go·ri·an (grĭ-gôr′ē-ən) adj. gregoriano.
grem·lin (grĕm′lĭn) s. *(imaginary creature)* duende *mf*; FIG. *(mischief-maker)* persona traviesa.
Gre·na·da (grə-nā′də) s. Granada.
gre·nade (grə-nād′) s. ARM., MIL. granada.
Gre·na·di·an (grə-nā′dē-ən) adj. & s. granadino.
gren·a·dier (grĕn′ə-dîr′) s. MIL. *(soldier)* granadero; ICT. *(fish)* granadero.
gren·a·dine (grĕn′ə-dēn′) s. granadina.
grew (grōō) pret. de **grow.**
grey (grā) s., adj. & v. var. de **gray.**
grey·hound (grā′hound′) s. ZOOL. galgo.
grid (grĭd) s. *(grating)* rejilla; CUL. *(rack)* parrilla; *(on a map)* cuadrícula; DEP. *(football field)* campo (de rugby americano); ELEC. *(network)* red *f*.
grid·dle (grĭd′l) CUL. I. s. plancha II. tr. **-dled, -dling** cocinar *o* asar a la plancha.
grid·dle·cake (grĭd′l-kāk′) s. CUL. hojuela, panqueque *m*.
grid·i·ron (grĭd′ī′ərn) s. CUL. *(rack)* parrilla; *(network)* red *f*; *(football field)* campo de rugby americano; TEAT. *(structure)* peine *m*.
grid·lock (grĭd′lŏk′) s. AUTO. embotellamiento de tráfico (en las esquinas).
grief (grēf) s. *(sorrow)* pena, congoja; *(trouble)* desgracia, trastorno ♦ **good g.!** ¡voto al chápiro! • **to come to g.** *(to fail)* fracasar; *(to meet with disaster)* sufrir un desastre.
griev·ance (grē′vəns) s. *(cause for protest)* motivo de queja; *(protest)* queja; *(indignation)* resentimiento; ANT. *(harm)* agravio, injusticia.
grieve (grēv) tr. **grieved, griev·ing** *(to sadden)* dar pena, afligir —intr. apenarse, afligirse; *(to mourn)* lamentarse.
griev·ous (grē′vəs) adj. *(causing grief)* penoso; *(painful)* doloroso; *(serious)* serio, grave.
grif·fin *o* **grif·fon** (grĭf′ən) s. MITOL. grifo (animal mitad águila y mitad león).
grill (grĭl) I. tr. *(to broil)* asar a la parrilla; FAM. *(to cross-examine)* someter a un interrogatorio severo II. s. CUL. *(rack)* parrilla; *(food)* asado a la parrilla; *(restaurant)* restaurante (donde se sirven asados) *m*.
grille *o* **grill** (grĭl) s. *(metal grating)* reja; *(window decor)* verja.
grim (grĭm) adj. **grim·mer, grim·mest** *(unrelenting)* inflexible, inexorable; *(unpleasant)* desagradable; *(forbidding)* imponente, terrible; *(ghastly)* macabro, siniestro; *(gloomy)* tétrico, lúgubre; *(ferocious)* feroz, encarnizado ♦ **the g. truth** la escueta verdad.

grim·ace (grĭm′ĭs, grĭ-mās′) I. s. mueca II. intr. **-aced, -ac·ing** hacer muecas.
grime (grīm) I. s. *(dirt)* mugre *f*; *(soot)* hollín *m* II. tr. **grimed, grim·ing** enmugrecer, ensuciar.
grim·ness (grĭm′nĭs) s. *(relentlessness)* inexorabilidad *f*; *(gloominess)* aspecto tétrico *o* lúgubre; *(ghastliness)* aspecto siniestro.
grim·y (grī′mē) adj. **-i·er, -i·est** *(dirty)* mugriento; *(sooty)* sucio de hollín.
grin (grĭn) I. intr. **grinned, grin·ning** sonreír ♦ **to g. and bear it** soportar estoicamente —tr. expresar con una sonrisa <*he grinned his approval* él expresó su aprobación con una sonrisa> II. s. sonrisa abierta.
grind (grīnd) I. tr. **ground** (ground), **grind·ing** *(to crush)* triturar, pulverizar; *(to sharpen)* amolar; *(a lens)* pulir; *(glass, diamonds)* esmerilar; *(to gnash)* hacer rechinar; *(to mill)* moler (café, trigo); *(to mince)* picar (carne); *(an organ)* tocar ♦ **to g. down** *(to pulverize)* pulverizar; *(to consume gradually)* desgastar; *(to oppress)* agobiar, oprimir • **to g. out** producir rutinariamente • **to g. something into someone's head** meter algo en la cabeza a alguien —intr. *(to mill)* molerse; *(to mince)* picarse; *(to grate)* chirriar, ir dando chirridos; FAM. *(to study hard)* quemarse las pestañas estudiando; *(to work hard)* trabajar mucho; JER. *(to rotate the pelvis)* menear las caderas ♦ **to g. up** triturarse, pulverizarse II. s. FAM. *(student)* empollón *m*; *(task)* trabajo pesado ♦ **a fine g. of coffee** un café de grano fino • **to get back to the g.** *(of a student)* volver a los libros; *(of a worker)* volver al trabajo.
grind·er (grīn′dər) s. *(for knives)* afilador *m*; *(for coffee, pepper)* molinillo; *(for cutlery)* afiladora; *(for meat)* moledora; *(molar)* muela ♦ **grinders** FAM. muelas.
grind·stone (grīnd′stōn′) s. *(stone disk)* amoladera; *(millstone)* muela (de un molino).
grin·go (grĭng′gō) s. [pl. **-gos**] DESPEC. gringo.
grip (grĭp) I. s. *(firm grasp)* asimiento; *(of hands)* apretón *m*; *(mastery)* dominio, conocimiento; *(control)* control *m*, poder *m*; *(handle)* asidero; *(of a racket)* mango; *(of a weapon)* empuñadura; *(valise)* maletín de viaje *m* ♦ **to come to grips with** abordar (un problema) • **to get a good g. on** agarrar bien • **to get a g. on oneself** controlarse, calmarse • **to have a good g. on** tener un buen dominio de II. tr. **gripped, grip·ping** *(to seize firmly)* agarrar; *(a weapon)* empuñar; *(to hold)* apretar (mano, mango); FIG., FAM. *(to enthrall)* cautivar la atención de —intr. agarrarse.
gripe (grīp) FAM. I. tr. **griped, grip·ing** fastidiar, molestar —intr. refunfuñar, quejarse ♦ **to g. about** *o* **at** quejarse de II. s. queja ♦ **gripes** retortijones de estómago.
grippe (grĭp) s. MED. gripe *f*, influenza.
gris·ly (grĭz′lē) adj. **-li·er, -li·est** espantoso, horroroso.
grist (grĭst) s. molienda ♦ **to be g. for the mill** FIG. ser provechoso.
gris·tle (grĭs′əl) s. cartílago.
grit (grĭt) I. s. *(rough granules)* arenilla, granitos de arena; *(texture of stone)* grano; *(sandstone)* asperón *m*; FAM. *(pluck)* agallas, valor *m* II. tr. **grit·ted, grit·ting** llenar de arenilla ♦ **to g. one's teeth** FAM. apretar las dientes.
grits (grĭts) s.pl. maíz a medio moler *m*.
grit·ty (grĭt′ē) adj. **-ti·er, -ti·est** *(coarse)* arenoso, arenisco; *(plucky)* resuelto, animoso.
griz·zly (grĭz′lē) I. adj. **-zli·er, -zli·est** grisáceo, pardusco II. s. [pl. **-zlies**] ZOOL. oso gris.
grizzly bear s. ZOOL. oso gris.
groan (grōn) I. intr. *(to moan)* gemir; *(to creak)* crujir (bajo mucho peso) —tr. decir *o* indicar con gemidos II. s. gemido.
groats (grōts) s.pl. avena mondada y medio molida *m*.
gro·cer (grō′sər) s. tendero, almacenero.
gro·cer·y (grō′sə-rē) s. [pl. **-ies**] tienda de comestibles, almacén *m* ♦ **groceries** comestibles • **g. store** tienda de comestibles, almacén.
grog (grŏg) s. grog (esp. ron con agua) *m*.
grog·gi·ness (grŏg′ē-nĭs) s. *(unsteadiness)* inestabilidad *f*; *(daze)* atontamiento; *(shakiness)* tambaleo.

---

grog·gy (grŏg′ē) adj. **-gi·er, -gi·est** *(unsteady)* inestable; *(dazed)* atontado; *(shaky)* tambaleante.
groin (groin) **I.** s. ANAT. ingle *f*; ARQ. arista (de una bóveda) **II.** tr. ARQ. proveer de aristas a.
grom·met (grŏm′ĭt) s. COST. *(eyelet)* ojal reforzado; *(ring)* arandela de metal *o* plástico; MARÍT. arandela de cabo.
groom (grōōm, grŏŏm) **I.** s. *(horse caretaker)* mozo de cuadra *o* de caballos; *(bridegroom)* novio **II.** tr. cuidar, almohazar (caballos) ♦ **grooming** acicaladura, acicalamiento • **to g. oneself** arreglarse, acicalarse.
grooms·man (grōōmz′mən, grŏŏmz′-) s. padrino de boda.
groove (grōōv) **I.** s. *(channel)* ranura; *(of a record)* surco; FIG., JER. *(niche)* onda; *(routine)* rutina ♦ **in the g.** JER. en plena forma (orador, escritor) • **to get into the g. of things** acostumbrarse **II.** tr. **grooved, groov·ing** hacer ranuras en, acanalar —intr. ♦ **to g.** JER. disfrutar de.
groov·y (grōō′vē) adj. JER. **-i·er, -i·est** *(pleasing)* agradable; *(marvelous)* fenomenal, increíble.
grope (grōp) **I.** intr. **groped, grop·ing** andar a tientas —tr. tentar **II.** s. tiento.
gross (grōs) **I.** adj. *(total)* bruto (ganancias, peso); *(glaring)* craso (mentira, ignorancia); *(vulgar)* grosero, ordinario (chiste, película); *(disgusting)* repugnante; *(unrefined)* ordinario, tosco; *(overweight)* grueso; *(dense)* denso; *(general)* general <*the g. outlines of the plan* las líneas generales del plan>; CIENT. *(macroscopic)* macroscópico ♦ **g. amount** suma total • **g. injustice** injusticia notoria **II.** s. *(total)* total *m*; *(twelve dozen)* gruesa, doce docenas ♦ **by the g.** en gruesas **III.** tr. recaudar dinero en bruto ♦ **to g. someone out** JER. revolver el estómago a alguien, dar asco a alguien.
gross national product s. ECON. producto nacional bruto.
gross·ness (grōs′nĭs) s. *(enormity)* enormidad (de una mentira, una injusticia) *f*; *(vulgarity)* grosería, ordinariez *f*.
gro·tesque (grō-tĕsk′) **I.** adj. grotesco **II.** s. *(style)* grotesco; ARTE. obra grotesca.
gro·tes·que·ry *o* **gro·tes·que·rie** (grō-tĕs′kə-rē) s. [pl. **-ries**] *(condition)* lo grotesco, carácter grotesco; *(thing)* cosa grotesca.
grot·to (grŏt′ō) s. [pl. **-toes** *o* **-tos**] gruta.
grouch (grouch) FAM. **I.** intr. gruñir, refunfuñar **II.** s. *(mood)* mal humor *m*; *(complaint)* gruñido, queja; *(person)* gruñón *m*.
grouch·y (grou′chē) adj. **-i·er, -i·est** FAM. *(growler)* gruñón; *(grumbling)* refunfuñador; *(peevish)* malhumorado.
ground¹ (ground) **I.** s. *(surface)* tierra <*snow covered the g.* la nieve cubría la tierra>; *(soil)* tierra, suelo <*he fell to the g.* cayó al suelo>; FIG. *(area)* terreno, campo (de discusión, estudio); PINT. *(coat)* primera capa; ELEC. *(connection)* toma de tierra; *(device)* objeto al que se ata el alambre de conexión con tierra; DEP. campo, terreno (de juegos) ♦ **from the g. up** desde el principio, completamente • **grounds** *(piece of land)* terreno <*hunting g.* terreno de caza>; *(building ground)* terreno de un edificio; *(basis)* base (de un argumento, creencia); *(cause)* causa, motivo <*grounds for divorce* motivo de divorcio>; *(sediment)* sedimento, poso <*coffee grounds* poso del café> • **to break g.** CONSTR. *(earth)* roturar (tierra); *(to begin construction)* empezar a construir; FIG. *(to begin)* empezar (trabajo, obra) • **to cover the g.** *(distance)* recorrer el trecho; FIG. *(topic)* tratar extensamente un tópico • **to get off the g.** AVIA. despegar; FIG. *(to take off)* levantar vuelo; *(to be carried out)* realizarse • **to hold** *o* **stand one's g.** FIG. mantenerse firme, no ceder • **to run into the g.** FIG. agotar (un tema) **II.** tr. *(to place on the ground)* poner en tierra; *(to base)* basar, fundar (un argumento, teoría); *(to instruct)* enseñar (los rudimentos o los elementos de alguna ciencia); AVIA. impedir volar; FAM. *(to punish)* prohibir salir (como castigo); ELEC. conectar con tierra; MARÍT. hacer varar *o* encallar; PINT. dar fondo; MIL. descansar (armas) ♦ **to be well-grounded in** ser versado en, tener buenos conocimientos de —intr. *(to hit the ground)* dar en tierra; MARÍT. encallar, varar.
ground² (ground) pret. y part. p. de **grind.**
ground crew s. AVIA. personal de tierra *m*.
ground floor s. planta baja, piso bajo.

ground hog s. ZOOL. marmota.
ground·less (ground′lĭs) adj. infundado, sin base.
ground·ling (ground′lĭng) s. *(plant)* planta rastrera; *(animal)* animal terrestre *m*; *(fish)* pez que habita en el fondo del agua *m*; TEAT. *(spectator)* mosquetero.
ground·nut (ground′nŭt′) s. G.B., BOT. *(peanut)* cacahuete *m*, maní *m*; *(vine)* chufa.
ground plan s. ARQ. *(drawing)* plano horizontal, planta; *(strategy)* plan básico, proyecto fundamental.
ground rule s. *(game)* regla de procedimiento (de un juego); *(behavior)* regla *o* norma de comportamiento.
ground sheet s. tela impermeable.
ground speed *o* **ground-speed** (ground′spēd′) s. AVIA. velocidad respecto a tierra *f*.
ground swell s. MARÍT. *(swelling)* mar de fondo *m*, onda marina; FIG. *(opinion)* mar de fondo.
ground water *o* **ground-wa·ter** (ground′wô′tər) s. GEOL. agua subterránea.
ground·work (ground′wûrk′) s. fundamento, base *f*.
ground zero s. MIL. *(target)* blanco de un proyectil; FÍS. *(site)* sitio de una explosión nuclear.
group (grōōp) **I.** s. *(assemblage)* grupo; *(organization)* agrupación *f*; MÚS. *(band)* conjunto **II.** tr. & intr. agrupar(se).
group·ie (grōō′pē) s. JER. *(girl)* admiradora de un grupo de música rock; *(member)* miembro de un grupo que comparte una casa de fin de semana.
group·ing (grōō′pĭng) s. agrupamiento, agrupación *f*.
group therapy s. PSIC. terapia de grupo.
grouse¹ (grous) s. [pl. **grouse** *o* **grous·es**] ORNIT. guaco, urogallo.
grouse² (grous) FAM. **I.** intr. **groused, grous·ing** quejarse, refunfuñar **II.** s. queja, refunfuño.
grout (grout) **I.** s. CONSTR. lechada **II.** tr. rellenar *o* acabar con argamasa, enlechar.
grove (grōv) s. bosquecillo, soto.
grov·el (grŭv′əl, grŏv′-) intr. *(to cringe)* humillarse, rebajarse; *(to creep)* arrastrarse; *(to debase oneself)* envilecerse.
grow (grō) tr. **grew** (grōō), **grown** (grōn), **growing** *(to raise)* cultivar <*to g. flowers* cultivar flores>; *(to let grow)* dejar crecer <*to g. a beard* dejarse crecer la barba> —intr. *(to increase in size)* crecer; *(to expand)* expandirse, agrandarse (comercio, industria); *(to increase)* aumentar <*her anxiety grew* su ansiedad aumentó>; *(to thrive)* crecer <*a plant that grows well in the shade* una planta que crece bien en la sombra>; *(to mature)* madurar (persona) ♦ **to g. accustomed to** acostumbrarse a • **to g. dark** oscurecerse • **to g. from** deberse a, ser el resultado de • **to g. into** llegar a ser, convertirse en • **to g. old** envejecer • **to g. on trees** FIG. encontrarse dondequiera • **to g. on** *o* **upon** *(to become pleasurable to)* llegar a gustar; *(to become acceptable to)* arraigarse (costumbre) • **to g. out of** *(a habit)* perder; *(to result from)* deberse a • **to g. up** *(physically)* crecer; *(mentally)* madurar, hacerse un hombre *o* una mujer; *(to be raised)* criarse <*I grew up in Chicago* me crié en Chicago>.
grow·er (grō′ər) s. AGR. cultivador *m*.
growing pains s.pl. *(of children)* dolores del crecimiento *m*; *(of a business)* dificultades iniciales del desarrollo (de una empresa) *f*.
growl (groul) **I.** s. gruñido **II.** intr. gruñir —tr. expresar con gruñidos.
growl·er (grou′lər) s. *(person)* gruñidor *m*; *(iceberg)* iceberg pequeño; ELEC. probador de inducidos *m*.
grown (grōn) **I.** part. p. de **grow II.** adj. *(mature)* mayor, adulto <*a g. woman* una mujer adulta>; *(covered with)* cubierto de <*a weed-grown area* un área cubierta de maleza.
grown-up (grōn′ŭp′) **I.** adj. *(adult)* adulto; *(grown)* crecido **II.** s. adulto.
growth (grōth) s. *(process of growing)* crecimiento; *(development)* desarrollo <*the g. of commerce* el desarrollo del comercio>; *(increase)* aumento; *(on one's face)* barba; *(of grass)* brote *m*; MED. *(tumor)* tumor *m*; *(production)* producción *f* ♦ **to reach full g.** alcanzar plenitud.

grub (grŭb) I. tr. **grubbed, grub·bing** *(to clear)* limpiar de hierbas, desmalezar; *(to dig up)* desarraigar, arrancar; JER. *(to borrow)* mendigar, pedir —intr. *(to dig)* cavar; *(to rummage)* hurgar; *(to drudge)* afanarse II. s. ZOOL. larva, gusano; *(drudge)* persona afanada; JER. *(food)* comida.

grub·by (grŭb'ē) adj. **-bi·er, -bi·est** *(dirty)* sucio; *(unkempt)* desaliñado, descuidado; *(grub-infested)* agusanado; *(despicable)* despreciable.

grub·stake (grŭb'stāk') s. COM. subvención concedida a un prospector o a una empresa nueva a cambio de parte de las ganancias futuras.

grudge (grŭj) I. tr. **grudged, grudg·ing** *(to begrudge)* escatimar, dar a regañadientes; *(to envy)* envidiar II. s. rencor *m.*

grudg·ing·ly (grŭj'ĭng-lē) adv. a regañadientes, de mala gana.

gru·el (grōo'əl) s. CUL. *(porridge)* gachas *f,* avenate *m;* G.B. *(punishment)* castigo severo.

gru·el·ing o **gru·el·ling** (grōo'ə-lĭng) adj. *(demanding)* abrumador; *(exhausting)* agotador, penoso.

grue·some (grōo'səm) adj. horrible, horrendo.

gruff (grŭf) adj. *(brusque)* brusco; *(hoarse)* ronco.

grum·ble (grŭm'bəl) I. intr. **-bled, -bling** *(to complain)* quejarse; *(to growl)* gruñir —tr. expresar con gruñidos II. s. *(complaint)* queja; *(rumble)* gruñido.

grum·bler (grŭm'blər) s. gruñidor *m,* gruñón *m.*

grum·bling (grŭm'blĭng) adj. gruñón, refunfuñón.

grum·met (grŭm'ĭt) s. var. de **grommet.**

grump (grŭmp) I. s. gruñón *m* ♦ **grumps** mal humor II. intr. *(to complain)* quejarse; *(to mutter)* gruñir, refunfuñar.

grump·y (grŭm'pē) adj. **-i·er, -i·est** malhumorado.

grunt (grŭnt) I. intr. gruñir —tr. expresar con gruñidos II. s. *(sound)* gruñido; JER. *(U.S. soldier)* soldado norteamericano de infantería.

gryph·on (grĭf'ən) s. var. de **griffin.**

G-string (jē'strĭng') s. FAM. taparrabo.

G-suit (jē'sōōt') s. AER., ASTRONÁUT. vestido anti-g (para contrarrestar los efectos de la aceleración en los pilotos y astronautas).

gua·na·co (gwə-nä'kō) s. [pl. **-cos, guanaco**] guanaco.

gua·no (gwä'nō) s. [pl. **-nos**] guano.

gua·ra·ni (gwä'rə-nē') s. [pl. **guarani** o **-nis**] FIN. guaraní (unidad monetaria de Paraguay) *m.*

Gua·ra·ni (gwä'rə-nē') s. [pl. **-nis** o **Guarani**] guaraní *m.*

guar·an·tee (gär'ən-tē') I. s. *(pledge)* garantía (de calidad, de pago); *(promise)* palabra, promesa *<I give you my g.* te doy mi palabra>; *(security)* garantía; *(guarantor)* garante *mf,* fiador *m* ♦ **to be a g. of** asegurar, garantizar II. tr. **-teed, -tee·ing** *(to pledge)* garantizar (producto, deuda); *(to promise)* asegurar, prometer *<he guaranteed to tell the truth* prometió decir la verdad>; *(someone's actions)* responder de; *(to furnish security for)* garantizar, ser fiador de.

guar·an·tor (gär'ən-tôr', gär'ən-tər) s. garante *mf.*

guar·an·ty (gär'ən-tē) I. s. [pl. **-ties**] *(agreement)* garantía; *(guarantor)* garante *mf* II. tr. **-tied, -ty·ing** *(to guarantee)* garantizar; *(to ensure)* asegurar.

guard (gärd) I. tr. *(to defend)* defender, proteger; *(to watch over)* custodiar, guardar; *(to escort)* escoltar *<to g. the President* escoltar al presidente>; *(to keep watch at)* montar guardia en (entrada, salida); TEC. poner un dispositivo protector a —intr. ♦ **to g. against** *(to protect against)* protegerse de; *(to prevent)* evitar, impedir II. s. *(sentinel)* guardia *m,* guardián *m; (body of troops)* guardia *f <the changing of the g.* el relevo de la guardia>; *(escort)* escolta; G.B. *(of a train)* jefe de tren *m;* DEP. *(players)* defensa *m; (defensive position)* guardia (en el boxeo, en esgrima) *<on g.!* ¡en guardia!>; *(act of guarding)* custodia, guardia; *(of a prisoner)* vigilancia; *(safeguard)* protección *f;* TEC. *(on a machine)* dispositivo de protección; *(of a sword)* guarda, guarnición *f* ♦ **off (one's) g.** desprevenido • **on (one's) g.** prevenido, en guardia • **to be on g.** MIL. estar de guardia • **to lower one's g.** bajar la guardia • **under g.** a buen recaudo.

guard·ed (gär'dĭd) adj. *(cautious)* cauto, cauteloso; *(restrained)* mesurado; *(protected)* protegido, custodiado.

guard·house (gärd'hous') s. MIL. *(building)* cuerpo de guardia; *(jail)* cárcel militar *f,* prisión militar *f.*

guard·i·an (gär'dē-ən) s. *(custodian)* guardián *m,* guarda *m;* DER. *(of an orphan)* tutor *m,* curador *m;* RELIG. guardián (de un convento franciscano).

guard·i·an·ship (gär'dē-ən-shĭp') s. *(protection)* protección *f,* amparo; DER. *(responsibility of guardian)* tutela, curaduría; RELIG. guardianía (de la orden de San Francisco).

guard·rail (gärd'rāl') s. *(railing)* baranda, barandilla; F.C. *(of rails)* contrarriel *m,* contracarril *m.*

guard·room (gärd'rōōm', -rōōm') s. MIL. *(building)* cuartel de la guardia *m; (jail)* cárcel o prisión militar *f.*

Gua·te·ma·la (gwä'tə-mä'lə) s. Guatemala.

Gua·te·ma·lan (gwä'tə-mä'lən) adj. & s. guatemalteco.

gua·va (gwä'və) s. BOT. *(tree)* guayabo; *(fruit)* guayaba.

gu·ber·na·to·ri·al (gōō'bər-nə-tôr'ē-əl) adj. *(of a governor)* del gobernador; *(of a government)* gubernativo.

guck (gŭk, gŏok) s. JER. *(messy substance)* substancia barrosa o viscosa; *(filth)* mugre *f.*

guer·ril·la o **gue·ril·la** (gə-rĭl'ə) s. *(person)* guerrillero; ANT. *(warfare)* guerrilla ♦ **g. tactics** táctica guerrillera.

guess (gĕs) I. tr. *(to conjecture)* conjeturar; *(to suppose)* suponer; *(to estimate correctly)* adivinar *<I guessed the truth* adiviné la verdad> ♦ **I g. so** me imagino que sí • **g. who!** ¡adivina! —intr. *(to make a conjecture)* conjeturar, imaginar; *(to estimate correctly)* adivinar ♦ **to g. right** adivinar, acertar • **to keep someone guessing** mantener a alguien en suspenso II. s. conjetura, suposición *f* ♦ **rough g.** cálculo aproximado • **to be one's g. that** imaginarse que • **to take a g.** tratar de adivinar.

guess·work (gĕs'wûrk') s. conjetura.

guest (gĕst) I. s. *(at one's home)* invitado *<to have guests for dinner* tener invitados a cenar>; *(at a hotel)* huésped *m;* BIOL. parásito ♦ **be my g.** FIG., FAM. *(as you wish)* como quieras; *(go ahead)* hazlo si quieres • **g. of honor** invitado de honor • **g. room** cuarto de huéspedes II. tr. *(a person)* hospedar; *(an event)* servir de escenario a.

guff (gŭf) s. JER. disparate *m,* tontería.

guf·faw (gə-fô') I. s. carcajada, risotada II. intr. reírse a carcajadas.

guid·ance (gīd'ns) s. *(act of guiding)* guía; *(direction)* dirección *f,* conducción *f; (leadership)* gobierno; *(counseling)* asesoramiento, consejo ♦ **under the g. of** guiado por.

guide (gīd) I. s. *(leader)* guía *mf; (adviser)* consejero; *(travel guidebook)* guía *f; (instruction manual)* manual *m; (sign)* guía *f,* señal *f; (example)* ejemplo, modelo; *(device)* guía *f* II. tr. *(to lead)* guiar, conducir; *(to steer)* dirigir, encauzar; *(to advise)* aconsejar, orientar; *(to govern)* dirigir, gobernar —intr. servir de guía.

guide·book (gīd'bŏok') s. guía turística, guía del viajero.

guided missile s. ARM. proyectil teledirigido.

guide·line (gīd'līn') s. pauta, línea directiva.

guide·post (gīd'pōst') s. *(post)* poste indicador *m;* FIG. *(sign)* señal *f.*

guild (gĭld) s. *(association)* gremio, asociación *f,* corporación *f;* BOT. *(group)* grupo ecológico de plantas.

guil·der (gĭl'dər) s. FIN. florín *m.*

guild·hall (gĭld'hôl') s. *(meeting hall)* lugar de reunión de un gremio *m; (town hall)* casa de ayuntamiento.

guilds·man (gĭldz'mən) s. [pl. **-men**] *(member)* gremial *m; (politician)* gremialista *mf,* socialista *mf.*

guile (gīl) I. s. *(deceit)* engaño; ANT. *(stratagem)* estratagema *m* II. tr. **guiled, guil·ing** ANT. engañar, burlar.

guile·ful (gīl'fəl) adj. engañoso.

guile·less (gīl'lĭs) adj. *(simple)* simple; *(naive)* inocente, cándido; *(frank)* franco.

guil·lo·tine (gĭl'ə-tēn', gē'ə-) I. s. guillotina II. tr. **-tined, -tin·ing** guillotinar.

guilt (gĭlt) s. *(blame)* culpa; *(remorse)* culpa, culpabilidad *f.*

guilt·less (gĭlt'lĭs) adj. inocente.

guilt·y (gĭl'tē) adj. **-i·er, -i·est** culpable ♦ **not g.** DER. inocente • **to find someone g.** DER. declarar a alguien culpable • **to have a g. conscience** remorderle a uno la conciencia • **to plead g.** DER. declararse culpable.

ă rey / ä año / b boca / ch chico / d dar / ĕ el / ē mil / g gato / h joya / hw juez / ī aire / k casa / kw cuan /

guin·ea (gĭn'ē) s. FIN. guinea (antigua unidad monetaria inglesa).
Guin·ea (gĭn'ē) s. Guinea.
Guin·ea-Bis·sau (gĭ'nē-bĭ-sou') s. Guinea-Bissau.
guinea fowl s. gallina de Guinea.
guinea hen s. ORNIT. gallina de Guinea, gallina pintada.
Guin·e·an (gĭn'ē-ən) adj. & s. guineo.
guinea pig s. ZOOL. cobayo, conejillo de Indias; FIG. (person) conejillo de Indias.
guise (gīz) s. (aspect) apariencia, aspecto; (pretext) pretexto; (dress) vestimenta; ANT. (custom) costumbre f.
gui·tar (gĭ-tär') s. MÚS. guitarra.
gui·tar·ist (gĭ-tär'ĭst) s. guitarrista mf.
gulch (gŭlch) s. barranco, quebrada.
gulf (gŭlf) I. s. (large bay) golfo; (abyss) abismo, sima m; FIG. (gap) abismo; (eddy) remolino II. tr. tragar.
gulf·weed (gŭlf'wēd') s. BOT. sargazo.
gull¹ (gŭl) s. ORNIT. gaviota.
gull² (gŭl) I. s. bobo, crédulo II. tr. engatusar, engañar.
gul·let (gŭl'ĭt) s. (esophagus) esófago; (throat) gaznate m, garganta.
gul·li·bil·i·ty (gŭl'ə-bĭl'ĭ-tē) s. credulidad f.
gul·li·ble (gŭl'ə-bəl) adj. bobo, crédulo.
gul·ly (gŭl'ē) I. s. [pl. **-lies**] badén m, barranco II. tr. & intr. **gul·lied, gul·ly·ing** formar(se) barrancos.
gulp (gŭlp) I. tr. tragar, engullir ♦ **to g. down** tragarse —intr. (to swallow) tragar en seco; FIG. (in fear) tener un nudo en la garganta II. s. (swallow) trago; (mouthful) bocado.
gum¹ (gŭm) I. s. (substance) goma; (resin) gomorresina; (rubber) caucho; (for chewing) chicle m; (glue) pegamento; (tree) gomero II. tr. **gummed, gum·ming** engomar, pegar con goma —intr. exudar goma.
gum² (gŭm) s. ANAT., ODONT. encía.
gum arabic s. goma arábiga.
gum·bo (gŭm'bō) s. [pl. **-bos**] BOT. (okra) quingombó; (soup) sopa de quingombó; (silty soil) gumbo.
gum·drop (gŭm'drŏp') s. caramelito o pastilla de goma.
gum·my (gŭm'ē) adj. **-mi·er, -mi·est** (containing gum) gomoso; (sticky) pegajoso; (viscous) viscoso.
gump·tion (gŭmp'shən) s. FAM. (common sense) cacumen m, sentido común; (initiative) espíritu m, iniciativa.
gum·shoe (gŭm'shōō') JER. I. s. detective m II. intr. **-shoed, -shoe·ing** averiguar furtivamente, fisgar.
gun (gŭn) s. (firearm) arma de fuego; (cannon) cañón m; (handgun) pistola, revólver m; (rifle) rifle m, fusil m; (shotgun) escopeta; (discharge) cañonazo; (hunter) cazador m; (killer) pistolero; (for painting) pistola (para pintar); (for lubricating) inyector m II. tr. **gunned, gun·ning** (to fire upon) disparar; AUTO., FAM. acelerar a fondo (un auto) ♦ **to g. for** andar a la caza de, buscar para matar ♦ **to g. someone down** matar a alguien (a tiros) —intr. (to hunt) cazar; (to shoot) disparar (con un arma de fuego).
gun·boat (gŭn'bōt') s. MARÍT. cañonero, lancha cañonera.
gun carriage m. ARM. cureña.
gun·fight (gŭn'fīt') s. (battle) pelea a tiros; (duel) duelo.
gun·fire (gŭn'fīr') s. (from light weapons) disparos, tiros; (from artillery) cañonazos; (shooting) tiroteo.
gunk (gŭngk) s. FAM. mugre f, porquería.
gun·man (gŭn'mən) s. pistolero.
gun·nel (gŭn'əl) s. var. de **gunwale**.
gun·ner (gŭn'ər) s. MIL. (artilleryman) artillero; (hunter) cazador m.
gun·ner·y (gŭn'ə-rē) s. ARM. artillería (fabricación y manejo de armas).
gun·ny·sack (gŭn'ē-săk') s. saco de arpillera.
gun·pow·der (gŭn'pou'dər) s. ARM. pólvora.
gun·run·ner (gŭn'rŭn'ər) s. traficante de armas mf.
gun·run·ning (gŭn'rŭn'ĭng) s. tráfico o contrabando de armas.
gun·shot (gŭn'shŏt') s. (shot) tiro; (artillery shot) cañonazo; (range) alcance m ♦ **g. wound** balazo, tiro • **within g.** a tiro de fusil.
gun-shy (gŭn'shī') adj. (afraid of noise) asustadizo, espantadizo; (wary) receloso.
gun·sling·er (gŭn'slĭng'ər) s. pistolero.

gun·smith (gŭn'smĭth') s. ARM. armero.
gun·stock (gŭn'stŏk') s. ARM. culata.
gun·wale (gŭn'əl) s. MARÍT. regala, borda.
gur·gle (gûr'gəl) I. intr. **-gled, -gling** (to flow) gorgotear; (to make a sound) gorjear —tr. manifestar gorjeando II. s. (water) gorgoteo; (voice) gorjeo (del niño).
gu·ru (gōōr'ōō) s. (teacher) maestro (leader) líder m; (guide) guía.
gush (gŭsh) I. intr. (to flow) brotar, manar (a borbotones); (to emotionalize) hablar con efusión excesiva —tr. derramar, verter II. s. (outpouring) chorro; (display) efusión excesiva.
gush·er (gŭsh'ər) s. (person) persona efusiva; (oil well) pozo brotante de petróleo.
gush·y (gŭsh'ē) adj. **-i·er, -i·est** efusivo.
gus·set (gŭs'ĭt) s. COST. escudete m.
gus·sy (gŭs'ē) tr. **-sied, -sy·ing** decorar.
gust (gŭst) I. s. (of wind) ventolera, ráfaga; (of smoke) bocanada; FIG. (of anger) acceso, arrebato II. intr. soplar (el viento).
gus·ta·to·ry (gŭs'tə-tôr'ē) adj. gustativo.
gus·to (gŭs'tō) s. [pl. **-toes**] (taste) sabor m, gusto; (zest) deleite m, entusiasmo.
gust·y (gŭs'tē) adj. **-i·er, -i·est** ventoso, borrascoso.
gut (gŭt) I. s. ANAT. intestino, tripa; (string) cuerda de tripa; (channel) estrecho; (fishing tackle) sedal m ♦ **guts** (entrails) tripas, entrañas; JER. (courage) agallas <to have guts tener agallas> II. tr. **gut·ted, gut·ting** (to disembowel) destripar; (fish) limpiar; (to destroy) acabar con el interior de III. adj. JER. (feeling) hondo; (reaction) instintivo; (issue) fundamental; (easy) de jamón, fácil.
gut·less (gŭt'lĭs) adj. JER. sin agallas, cobarde.
guts·y (gŭt'sē) adj. **-i·er, -i·est** JER. con agallas, atrevido.
gut·ta-per·cha (gŭt'ə-pûr'chə) s. QUÍM. gutapercha (látex).
gut·ter (gŭt'ər) I. s. (in a street) cuneta; (on a roof) canalón m, canal m; (furrow) surco; (squalid place) FIG. barrios bajos, calle ♦ **g. language** lenguaje obsceno ♦ **to come from the g.** venir de lo más bajo II. tr. abrir zanjas o surcos en —intr. (to flow) correr; (to melt away) derretirse (una vela) ♦ **to g. out** apagarse (vela).
gut·ter·snipe (gŭt'ər-snīp') s. (boy) golfillo, pilluelo; (idler) vago.
gut·tur·al (gŭt'ər-əl) I. adj. gutural II. s. sonido gutural.
guy¹ (gī) I. s. tirante m, cable de retén m II. tr. atirantar.
guy² (gī) I. s. FAM. tipo, tío ♦ **guys** FAM. (men) muchachos, (women) muchachas.
Guy·a·na (gī-ăn'ə) s. Guayana.
Guy·a·nese (gī'ə-nēz') adj. & s. [pl. **Guyanese**] guyanés m ♦ **the G.** los guyaneses.
guz·zle (gŭz'əl) tr. **-zled, -zling** soplarse, beber mucho —intr. emborracharse.
guz·zler (gŭz'lər) s. (drinker) bebedor m; (drunkard) borracho.
gym (jĭm) s. FAM. (gymnasium) gimnasio; (gymnastics) gimnasia.
gym·kha·na (jĭm-kä'nə) s. G.B. (athletic) competencia atlética; (equestrian) competencia ecuestre.
gym·na·si·um (jĭm-nā'zē-əm) s. [pl. **-si·ums** o **-si·a** (-zē-ə)] (room) gimnasio; (high school) instituto, escuela secundaria superior (en Alemania).
gym·nast (jĭm'năst') s. gimnasta mf.
gym·nas·tic (jĭm-năs'tĭk) adj. gimnástico.
gym·nas·tics (jĭm-năs'tĭks) s. [ú. con v. sing. o pl.] gimnasia.
gym·no·sperm (jĭm'nə-spûrm') s. BOT. gimnosperma, gimnospérmeo.
gy·ne·coc·ra·cy (gī'nĭ-kŏk'rə-sē) s. [pl. **-cies**] ginecocracia.
gy·ne·col·o·gist (gī'nĭ-kŏl'ə-jĭst) s. MED. ginecólogo.
gy·ne·col·o·gy (gī'nĭ-kŏl'ə-jē) s. MED. ginecología.
gyp (jĭp) FAM. I. tr. **gypped, gyp·ping** (to cheat) trampear; (to defraud) estafar II. s. (swindle) estafa; (cheating) trampa; (swindler) estafador m.
gyp·sum (jĭp'səm) s. yeso, sulfato de calcio.
Gyp·sy (jĭp'sē) s. [pl. **-sies**] gitano.
gy·rate (jī'rāt') I. intr. **-rat·ed, -rat·ing** girar, rotar II. adj. BIOL. redondeado.

gy·ra·tion (jĭ-rā'shən) s. giro, rotación *f.*
gyre (jīr) s. *(circle)* círculo; *(spiral)* espiral *m*; POÉT. *(motion)* giro, rotación *f.*
gyr·fal·con (jûr'făl'kən) s. ZOOL. gerifalte *m.*
gy·ro (jī'rō) s. [pl. **-ros**] FÍS. *(gyroscope)* giroscopio, giróscopo; *(gryocompass)* brújula giroscópica.
gy·ro·com·pass (jī'rō-kŭm'pəs) s. MARÍT. brújula giroscópica.
gyro pilot (jī'rō) s. AER., MARÍT. giropiloto, piloto automático.
gy·ro·plane (jī'rə-plān') s. giroavión *m.*
gy·ro·scope (jī'rə-skōp') s. MEC. giroscopio, giróscopo.

H

h, H (āch) s. [pl. **h's, H's**] octava letra del alfabeto inglés.
ha (hä) interj. *(expression of surprise)* ¡ah!; *(expression of triumph)* ¡ja!
Ha·bak·kuk (hăb'ə-kŭk') s. BÍBL. Habacuc *m.*
ha·be·as cor·pus (hā'bē-əs kôr'pəs) s. DER. hábeas corpus *m.*
hab·er·dash·er (hăb'ər-dăsh'ər) s. *(of men's furnishings)* vendedor de artículos para caballeros *m*; G.B. *(of sewing notions)* mercero.
hab·er·dash·er·y (hăb'ər-dăsh'ə-rē) s. [pl. **-ies**] *(men's furnishings)* artículos para caballeros; *(store)* tienda de artículos para caballeros.
hab·it (hăb'ĭt) I. s. *(repeated behavior)* costumbre *f*, hábito; *(character)* carácter *m*, forma de ser; *(addiction)* dependencia <drug *h.* dependencia de la droga>; RELIG. hábito ♦ **bad h.** mala costumbre, mala maña • **out of h.** por costumbre • **riding h.** traje de montar • **to be in the h.** *o* to **make a h. of** tener la costumbre de, acostumbrar • **to get into the h. of** adquirir la costumbre de, darle a uno por • **to kick the h.** FAM. dejar el vicio II. tr. ataviar.
hab·it·a·ble (hăb'ĭ-tə-bəl) adj. habitable.
hab·i·tant (hăb'ĭ-tnt) s. habitante *mf.*
hab·i·tat (hăb'ĭ-tăt') s. hábitat *m.*
hab·i·ta·tion (hăb'ĭ-tā'shən) s. habitación *f.*
hab·it-form·ing (hăb'ĭt-fôr'mĭng) adj. que crea hábito.
ha·bit·u·al (hə-bĭch'ōō-əl) adj. *(chronic)* inveterado, empedernido <a *h.* drinker un bebedor empedernido>; *(usual)* acostumbrado, habitual <his *h.* place su sitio acostumbrado>.
ha·bit·u·al·ly (hə-bĭch'ōō-ə-lē) adv. *(customarily)* habitualmente, normalmente; *(out of habit)* por costumbre.
ha·bit·u·ate (hə-bĭch'ōō-āt') tr. & intr. **-at·ed, -at·ing** habituar(se), acostumbrar(se).
hack¹ (hăk) I. tr. *(to chop)* cortar, tajar; *(to mutilate)* cercenar, recortar (presupuesto, novela); FAM. *(to cope with)* aguantar, resistir —intr. toser ♦ **to h. at** tirar tajos a II. s. *(cut, blow)* tajo, hachazo; *(knife)* machete *m*; *(ax)* hacha; *(hoe)* azadón *m*; *(cough)* tos seca.
hack² (hăk) I. s. *(nag)* jamelgo, penco (de alquiler); *(hireling)* ganapán *m,* asalariado; *(commercial writer)* gacetillero, escritor comercializado; *(carriage)* coche de alquiler *m*; FAM. *(cabby)* taxista *mf* II. tr. *(to hire)* alquilar (un caballo); *(to make banal)* gastar (una palabra, expresión) —intr. FAM. trabajar de taxista III. adj. *(commercial)* comercializado; *(hackneyed)* gastado, trillado.
hack·le (hăk'əl) s. pluma del cuello ♦ **hackles** pelos del cuello • **to get one's hackles up** sacar las garras.
hack·ney (hăk'nē) I. s. *(horse)* trotón *m*, caballo de silla; *(carriage)* coche de alquiler *m* II. tr. gastar, trillar.
hack·neyed (hăk'nēd) adj. gastado, trillado.
hack·saw (hăk'sô') s. sierra para metales.
hack·work (hăk'wûrk') s. trabajo comercializado rutinario.
had (hăd) pret. y part. p. de **have.**
had·dock (hăd'ək) s. [pl. **haddock** *o* **-docks**] ICT. abadejo.
Ha·des (hā'dēz) s. MITOL. *(Pluto)* Plutón *m*; *(kingdom)* Hades *m*; *(hell)* infierno.
had·n't (hăd'nt) contr. de **had not.**
haf·ni·um (hăf'nē-əm) s. QUÍM. hafnio.

haft (hăft) I. s. *(of a tool)* mango; *(of a weapon)* cabo II. tr. poner un mango *o* un cabo a.
hag (hăg) s. *(old woman)* vieja bruja, arpía; *(witch)* bruja.
Hag·ga·i (hăg'ē-ī') s. BÍBL. Ageo.
hag·gard (hăg'ərd) I. adj. *(gaunt)* demacrado; *(wild)* zahareño II. s. halcón zahareño.
hag·gle (hăg'əl) intr. *(to bargain)* regatear; *(to argue)* disputar, discutir ♦ **to h. over** *o* **about** regatear (precio).
hag·gler (hăg'lər) s. regateador *m.*
hag·gling (hăg'lĭng) s. regateo.
hag·i·og·ra·phy (hăg'ē-ŏg'rə-fē) s. [pl. **-ies**] hagiografía.
hag·rid·den (hăg'rĭd'n) adj. atormentado.
Hague, The (hăg) s. La Haya.
hah (hä) interj. var. de **ha.**
ha-ha (hä'hä') interj. ¡ja, ja, ja!
hail¹ (hāl) I. s. *(precipitation)* granizo; *(barrage)* lluvia, andanada <a *h.* of blows una andanada de golpes> II. intr. *(to precipitate)* granizar, caer granizo; FIG. *(to pour down)* llover —tr. lanzar una lluvia *o* una andanada de.
hail² (hāl) I. tr. *(to salute)* saludar; *(to acclaim)* aclamar <they hailed him as king lo aclamaron rey>; *(to call out to)* llamar <to *h.* a cab llamar un taxi> —intr. MARÍT. hacer señales ♦ **to h. from** ser de II. s. *(salute)* saludo; *(shout)* grito III. interj. ¡salve! ♦ **h. to** viva.
hail-fel·low-well-met (hāl'fĕl'ō-wĕl'mĕt') adj. afable, cordial.
Hail Mary s. RELIG. avemaría.
hail·stone (hāl'stōn') s. granizo.
hail·storm (hāl'stôrm') s. granizada.
hair (hâr) s. *(on body, animals)* pelo; *(on a person's head)* pelo, cabello; *(on legs)* vello; *(on horses)* cerda; *(on dogs)* pelusa; FIG. *(narrow margin)* pelo, tris *m* <to escape by a *h.* salvarse por un pelo> ♦ **gray** *o* **white h.** canas • **head of h.** pelo, cabellera • **not to touch a h. on someone's head** no tocarle ni una uña a alguien • **to comb one's h.** peinarse • **to get in someone's h.** tener a alguien hasta la coronilla • **to let one's h. down** soltarse el pelo, echar una cana al aire • **to make one's h. stand on end** ponerle a uno los pelos de punta • **to tear one's h. out** tirarse de los pelos • **to split hairs** hilar demasiado fino.
hair·breadth (hâr'brĕdth') s. var. de **hairsbreadth.**
hair·brush (hâr'brŭsh') s. cepillo (para el cabello).
hair·cut (hâr'kŭt') s. corte de pelo *m* ♦ **to get a h.** cortarse el pelo.
hair·do (hâr'dōō') s. [pl. **-dos**] peinado.
hair·dress·er (hâr'drĕs'ər) s. peluquero.
hair·dress·ing (hâr'drĕs'ĭng) s. *(occupation)* peluquería; *(act)* peinado; *(preparation)* loción *f.*
hair dryer s. secador (para el pelo) *m.*
hair·i·ness (hâr'ē-nĭs) s. vellosidad *f*; JER. *(difficulty)* dificultad *f.*
hair·less (hâr'lĭs) adj. *(having no hair)* sin pelo; *(face)* lampiño, barbilampiño.
hair·line (hâr'līn') s. *(on the forehead)* nacimiento del pelo; *(slender line)* rayita ♦ **to have a receding h.** tener entradas.
hair·net (hâr'nĕt') s. redecilla para el cabello.
hair piece s. *(for a man)* tupé *m*; *(for a woman)* peluquín *m.*
hair·pin (hâr'pĭn') s. *(pin)* horquilla; *(curve)* curva cerrada (de una carretera).
hair-rais·ing (hâr'rā'zĭng) adj. espeluznante.
hairs·breadth *o* **hair's-breadth** (hârz'brĕdth') s. pelo, tris *m* <he won by a *h.* ganó por un pelo>.
hair shirt s. RELIG. cilicio.
hair·split·ting (hâr'splĭt'ĭng) s. argucias, sutilezas.
hair spray s. gomina, laca.
hair style s. peinado.
hair stylist s. peluquero fino.
hair-trig·ger (hâr'trĭg'ər) adj. impulsivo <a *h.* temper un carácter impulsivo>.
hair·y (hâr'ē) adj. **-i·er, -i·est** *(covered with hair)* peludo; *(legs)* lleno de vellos; JER. *(hazardous)* espinoso, duro.
Hai·ti (hā'tē) s. Haití *m.*
Hai·tian (hā'shən) adj. & s. haitiano.
hake (hāk) s. [pl. **hake** *o* **hakes**] ICT. merluza.

ã rey / ä año / b boca / ch chico / d dar / ĕ el / ē mil / g gato / h joya / hw juez / ī aire / k casa / kw cuan /

hal·berd (hăl'bərd, hôl'-) *o* **hal·bert** (-bərt) s. ARM. alabarda.

hal·cy·on (hăl'sē-ən) I. s. ORNIT. alción *m* II. adj. *(tranquil)* apacible; *(prosperous)* venturoso <*h. years* años venturosos>.

hale¹ (hāl) adj. **hal·er, hal·est** robusto, fuerte.

hale² (hāl) tr. **haled, hal·ing** *(to compel to go)* llevar a la fuerza, arrastrar; ANT. *(to pull)* halar.

half (hăf, häf) I. s. [pl. **halves** (hăvz, hävz)] *(equal part)* mitad *f* <*h. the earnings* la mitad de ganancias>; *(part)* parte *f* <*the smaller h.* la parte más pequeña>; DEP. *(playing period)* tiempo <*the second h.* el segundo tiempo>; *(time period)* medio <*four and a h. months* cuatro meses y medio>; G.B. *(school term)* semestre *m* ♦ **better h.** FAM. cara mitad, costilla • **by h.** a la mitad <*a dress reduced by h.* un vestido rebajado a la mitad> • **by halves** a medias • **h. past** y media <*it's h. past three* son las tres y media> • **to go halves** ir a medias II. adj. *(being a half)* medio <*a h. hour* media hora>; *(partial)* a medias <*h. owner* dueño a medias>; *(brother, sister)* medio III. adv. *(partly)* medio, a medias <*h. asleep* medio dormido> ♦ **h. price** a mitad de precio • **not h. bad** FAM. no tan malo.

half-alive (hăf'ə-līv', häf'-) adj. medio muerto.

half-and-half (hăf'ən-hăf', häf'ən-häf') I. adj. mitad y mitad II. adv. a medias III. s. leche con crema *f*.

half·back (hăf'băk') s. DEP. medio.

half-baked (hăf'bākt', häf'-) adj. *(uncooked)* a medio cocer; FAM. *(ill-conceived)* disparatado, precipitado <*a h. plan* un plan disparatado>; *(foolish)* trastornado, tonto.

half blood *o* **half-blood** (hăf'blŭd', häf'-) s. mestizo.

half-blood·ed (hăf'blŭd'ĭd, häf'-) adj. *(family relation)* medio; *(ethnically impure)* mestizo; *(animal)* cruzado.

half boot s. bota corta.

half-breed (hăf'brēd', häf'-) I. s. JER. mestizo II. adj. mestizo, cruzado.

half brother s. medio hermano, hermanastro.

half-caste (hăf'kăst', häf'-) s. & adj. mestizo.

half-cocked (hăf'kŏkt', häf'-) adj. ARM. con el seguro echado; FAM. *(ill-conceived)* descabellado.

half-dead (hăf'dĕd', häf'-) adj. medio muerto.

half dollar s. medio dólar, moneda de cincuenta centavos.

half-full (hăf'fŏŏl', häf'-) adj. medio lleno.

half-heart·ed (hăf'här'tĭd, häf'-) adj. sin entusiasmo, desanimado.

half-hour (hăf'our', häf'-) s. media hora.

half-life (hăf'līf', häf'-) s. FÍS. período de desintegración radioactiva.

half-light (hăf'līt', häf'-) s. media luz.

half-mast (hăf'măst', häf'-) s. ♦ **at h.** a media asta.

half measures s.pl. medidas poco eficaces ♦ **to take h.** FIG. aplicar paños calientes.

half-moon (hăf'mŏŏn', häf'-) s. media luna.

half note s. MÚS. blanca.

half-o·pen (hăf'ō'pən, häf'-) adj. medio abierto, entreabierto.

half pay s. medio sueldo, media paga.

half sister s. media hermana, hermanastra.

half-slip (hăf'slĭp') s. enagua corta.

half step s. MÚS. semitono; MIL. paso corto.

half time s. DEP. descanso (a la mitad del partido).

half·tone (hăf'tōn', häf'-) s. *(tone)* media tinta; IMPR. *(graphic)* grabado reticulado.

half tone s. MÚS. semitono.

half-track (hăf'trăk', häf'-) s. MIL. vehículo de oruga.

half-truth (hăf'trŏŏth', häf'-) s. verdad a medias *f*.

half-way (hăf'wā', häf'-) I. adj. *(midway)* medio, intermedio; *(partial)* parcial, a medias <*h. measures* medidas parciales> II. adv. *(midway)* a la mitad; *(partially)* a medias ♦ **to meet h.** *(on a deal)* partir la diferencia; *(in an argument)* hacer concesiones.

halfway house s. *(stopping place)* paradero a mitad de camino; *(rehabilitation center)* centro de rehabilitación.

half-wit (hăf'wĭt', häf'-) s. *(mentally deficient person)* retrasado mental; *(fool)* tonto, necio.

half-wit·ted (hăf'wĭt'ĭd, häf'-) adj. necio, tonto.

hal·i·but (hăl'ə-bət) s. ICT. halibut *m*.

hal·i·to·sis (hăl'ĭ-tō'sĭs) s. MED. halitosis *f*.

hall (hôl) s. *(corridor)* pasillo, corredor *m*; *(lobby)* vestíbulo, hall *m*; *(large room)* sala <*concert h.* sala de conciertos>; *(classroom building)* facultad *f*; *(dormitory)* residencia estudiantil ♦ **city** *o* **town h.** ayuntamiento.

hal·le·lu·jah (hăl'ə-lŏŏ'yə) interj. & s. aleluya *mf*.

hal·liard (hăl'yərd) s. var. de **halyard**.

hall·mark (hôl'märk') s. *(mark, trait)* sello; *(for metals)* contraste *m*.

hall of fame *o* **Hall of Fame** s. *(building)* museo conmemorativo; *(group of persons)* galería de las estrellas.

hal·loo (hə-lŏŏ') I. interj. *(hey!)* ¡eh!, ¡hola!; *(to urge hounds)* ¡sus! II. s. grito, llamada III. intr. gritar, llamar a gritos.

hal·low (hăl'ō) tr. *(to make holy)* santificar; *(to revere)* venerar.

hal·lowed (hăl'ōd) adj. *(sanctified)* santificado, santo; *(venerated)* venerado.

Hal·low·een *o* **Hal·low·e'en** (hăl'ə-wēn', hŏl'-) s. Víspera de Todos los Santos.

hal·lu·ci·nate (hə-lŏŏ'sə-nāt') tr. & intr. **-nat·ed, -nat·ing** alucinar(se).

hal·lu·ci·na·tion (hə-lŏŏ'sə-nā'shən) s. alucinación *f*.

hal·lu·ci·na·to·ry (hə-lŏŏ'sə-nə-tôr'ē, -tôr'ē) adj. alucinante.

hal·lu·ci·no·gen (hə-lŏŏ'sə-nə-jən) s. alucinógeno (droga que produce alucinaciones).

hal·lu·ci·no·gen·ic (hə-lŏŏ'sə-nə-jěn'ĭk) adj. alucinógeno.

hall·way (hôl'wā') s. *(corridor)* pasillo, corredor *m*; *(entrance hall)* vestíbulo, hall *m*.

ha·lo (hā'lō) I. s. [pl. **-los** *o* **-loes**] *(band of light)* halo; *(aura)* aura; ARTE., RELIG. halo, aureola II. tr. rodear con un halo.

hal·o·gen (hăl'ə-jən) s. QUÍM. halógeno.

halt¹ (hôlt) I. s. *(temporary stop)* alto, parada; *(pause)* interrupción *f* ♦ **to call** *o* **bring a h. to** poner fin a • **to come to a h.** *(to stop moving)* pararse, detenerse; *(pause)* interrumpirse II. tr. & intr. *(movement)* parar(se), detener(se); *(progress)* interrumpir(se) ♦ **halt!** ¡alto!

halt² (hôlt) intr. *(to proceed poorly)* cojear; *(to hobble)* cojear; *(to waver)* titubear, vacilar.

hal·ter (hôl'tər) I. s. *(for a horse)* cabestro, ronzal *m*; *(noose)* dogal *m*, soga; *(bodice)* corpiño sin espalda II. tr. *(a horse)* encabestrar, poner el ronzal a; *(a person)* ahorcar, colgar; *(to restrain)* poner obstáculos a.

halt·ing (hôl'tĭng) adj. *(defective)* cojo, defectuoso; *(wavering)* vacilante, titubeante.

hal·vah *o* **hal·va** (hăl-vä', häl'vä) s. halva, golosina de semillas de sésamo picadas y miel.

halve (hăv, häv) tr. **halved, halv·ing** *(to divide)* partir a la mitad; *(a number)* dividir por dos; *(to reduce)* reducir a la mitad; FAM. *(to share)* compartir, repartirse.

halves (hăvz, hävz) pl. de **half**.

hal·yard (hăl'yərd) s. MARÍT. driza.

ham (hăm) I. s. *(cured meat)* jamón *m*; *(noncured meat)* pernil *m*; *(back of the knee)* corva; FAM. *(performer)* comicastro, mal actor *m*; *(radio operator)* radioaficionado ♦ **hams** nalgas *pl*. II. tr. **hammed, ham·ming** interpretar forzadamente, exagerar.

ham·burg·er (hăm'bûr'gər) *o* **ham·burg** (-bûrg') s. CUL. hamburguesa.

ham·let (hăm'lĭt) s. aldea, caserío.

ham·mer (hăm'ər) I. s. *(tool)* martillo; *(of a gun)* percusor *m*; *(of a piano)* martinete *m*; *(of a clock)* martillo; *(gavel)* mazo, martillo; ANAT., DEP. martillo ♦ **h. and sickle** POL. la hoz y el martillo II. tr. *(to hit)* martillar; *(to defeat)* demoler ♦ **to h. a point home** machacar incansablemente un argumento • **to h. away at** FAM. *(an opponent)* castigar a; *(to repeat)* insistir en, reiterar; *(to work hard at)* trabajar con ahínco en • **to h. out** *(a dent)* sacar a martillazos; *(a contract)* elaborar, llegar a —intr. martillar.

ham·mered (hăm'ərd) adj. repujado.

ham·mer·head (hăm'ər-hěd') s. *(part of tool)* cabeza de martillo; ICT. *(shark)* pez martillo.

hammer lock s. DEP. llave al brazo *f*.

ham·mock (hăm'ək) s. hamaca.

---

ham·per¹ (hăm′pər) I. tr. poner trabas a, estorbar II. s. MA-RÍT. aparejo.

ham·per² (hăm′pər) s. cesto.

ham·ster (hăm′stər) s. ZOOL. hámster *m.*

ham·string (hăm′strĭng′) I. s. tendón de la corva *m* II. tr. **-strung** (-strŭng′), **-string·ing** (to sever) cortar el tendón de la corva a; (to hinder) inutilizar, incapacitar.

hand (hănd) I. s. (of a person) mano *f;* (of clock, gauge) aguja, manecilla; (direction) lado, parte *f* <*at my right h.* a mi lado derecho>; (handwriting) caligrafía, letra; (applause) aplauso, ovación *f* <*the audience gave him a big h.* el público le dio un gran aplauso>; (word) palabra; (manual laborer) obrero; (in a factory) operario; (on a farm) peón *m,* jornalero; (on a ship) tripulante *m;* (expert) experto, perito; (round of cards) mano; EQUIT. (measure) palmo menor; FIG. (influence) influencia; (skill) mano, destreza <*one can see a master's h. in that painting* se puede ver la mano de un maestro en ese cuadro>; (banana cluster) racimo de plátanos; (tobacco bundle) manojo de tabaco ♦ **(at) first h.** (from a reliable source) de primera mano, de buena tinta; (directly) directamente ♦ **at the hands of** en manos de ♦ **by h.** a mano ♦ **by the h.** de·la mano <*take me by the h.* llévame de la mano> ♦ **close at h.** *o* **at h.** muy cerca, a mano ♦ **h. in h.** (holding hands) tomados de la mano; FIG. (jointly) juntos, de acuerdo ♦ **at the gates** ♦ **on the one h.** por una parte ♦ **on the other h.** por otra parte ♦ **out of h.** (out of control) fuera de control; (at once) sin más ni más <*he rejected my proposal out of h.* rechazó mi propuesta sin más ni más> ♦ **out of one's hands** fuera del alcance de uno ♦ **the matter at h.** el asunto que se está estudiando ♦ **to be an old h. at** ser experto *o* perito en, tener mucha experiencia en <*he's an old h. at labor negotiations* es perito en negociaciones laborales> ♦ **to be h. and glove** *o* **h. in glove** ser íntimos ♦ **to be someone's right h.** ser el brazo derecho de alguien ♦ **to bite the h. that feeds you** ser mal agradecido ♦ **to change hands** cambiar de dueño (negocio, empresa) ♦ **to clap one's hands** batir palmas ♦ **to dirty one's hands** ensuciarse las manos ♦ **to force someone's h.** obligar a alguien a hacer algo contra su voluntad ♦ **to get** *o* **have the upper h.** llevar ventaja ♦ **to get** *o* **lay one's hands on** encontrar, localizar ♦ **to give** *o* **lend someone a h. (with)** echar una mano (a) ♦ **to have a free h.** tener carta blanca, tener campo libre ♦ **to have a h. in** tener parte en ♦ **to have one's hands full** tener mucho que hacer, estar muy ocupado ♦ **to have one's hands tied** tener las manos atadas <*I'm sorry, but my hands are tied* lo siento, pero tengo las manos atadas> ♦ **to hold hands** ir cogidos de la mano ♦ **to join hands** combinar esfuerzos, unirse ♦ **to keep one's h. in** no perder la práctica de ♦ **to keep one's hands off** no tocar ♦ **to know something like the back of one's h.** conocer algo como la palma de la mano ♦ **to live from h. to mouth** vivir al día ♦ **to play into someone's hands** hacerle el juego a alguien ♦ **to shake hands** darse la mano <*they shook hands* se dieron la mano> ♦ **to shake hands with someone** *o* **to shake someone's h.** darle la mano a alguien ♦ **to show one's h.** revelar una intención, descubrir su juego ♦ **to take one's life in** *o* **into one's hands** jugarse la vida ♦ **to take someone** *o* **something in h.** hacerse cargo de ♦ **to take something off one's hands** quitarle a alguien algo ♦ **to throw up one's hands** echarse *o* llevarse las manos a la cabeza ♦ **to wait on someone h. and foot** desvivirse por alguien ♦ **to wash one's hands of** lavarse las manos, desentenderse de ♦ **with a firm h.** con mano firme, con firmeza II. tr. (to give) entregar, dar <*h. me the keys* dame las llaves>; (to aid) guiar, ayudar a; MARÍT. aferrar ♦ **to h. down** (to pass

on) transmitir <*traditions handed down from generation to generation* tradiciones transmitidas de generación en generación>; (to adjudge) dictar (fallo, sentencia) ♦ **to h. in** (to turn in) presentar (renuncia); (to give in) entregar (papeles, formularios) ♦ **to h. out** (to administer) dar, aplicar (castigo); (to distribute) repartir, distribuir ♦ **to h. over (to)** (to relinquish) ceder (a); (to give) entregar (a) ♦ **to have to h. it to someone** JER. tener que felicitar a alguien, tener que reconocer los méritos de.

hand·bag (hănd′băg′) s. (woman's bag) cartera, bolso; (hand luggage) maletín *m.*

hand·ball (hănd′bôl′) s. DEP. pelota (vasca).

hand·bill (hănd′bĭl′) s. volante *m,* octavilla.

hand·book (hănd′bŏŏk′) s. (manual) manual *m,* libro de referencias; (guidebook) guía; (of a bookmaker) libreta de apuestas.

hand·car (hănd′kär′) s. F.C. cigüeña, zorrilla.

hand·cart (hănd′kärt′) s. carretilla.

hand·clasp (hănd′klăsp′) s. apretón de manos *m.*

hand·craft (hănd′krăft′) s. var. de **handicraft.**

hand·cuff (hănd′kŭf′) I. s. esposas II. tr. (a prisoner) esposar, poner las esposas; (to render ineffective) maniatar, atar las manos.

hand·ed (hăn′dĭd) adj. ♦ **a four-handed card game** un juego de naipes para cuatro manos.

hand·ful (hănd′fŏŏl′) s. [pl. **-fuls**] puñado <*a h. of passengers* un puñado de pasajeros> ♦ **to be a real h.** ser una verdadera lata ♦ **he's a h. for anybody** hace sudar a cualquiera.

hand grenade s. ARM., MIL. granada de mano.

hand·grip (hănd′grĭp′) s. (handclasp) apretón de manos *m;* (handle) mango; (of bicycle) puño ♦ **handgrips** lucha cuerpo a cuerpo.

hand·gun (hănd′gŭn′) s. ARM. pistola.

hand·hold (hănd′hōld′) s. (grip) apretón *m;* (for supporting oneself) agarradera.

hand·i·cap (hăn′dē-kăp′) I. s. DEP. (race) hándicap *m;* (disadvantage) desventaja; (hindrance) obstáculo; MED. (physical disability) defecto; (mental disability) retraso II. tr. **-capped, -cap·ping** DEP. (a contestant) asignar un hándicap a; (to impede) poner en desventaja, perjudicar.

hand·i·capped (hăn′dē-kăpt′) adj. inválido, impedido.

hand·i·craft (hăn′dē-krăft′) s. (skill) destreza manual; (occupation) artesanía; (product) artículo de artesanía.

hand·i·ly (hăn′dl-ē) adv. (easily) con facilidad; (conveniently) convenientemente.

hand·i·work (hăn′dē-wûrk′) s. (manual labor) trabajo manual; (result of actions) obra <*that must be his h.* eso debe ser obra suya>.

hand·ker·chief (hăng′kər-chĭf) s. pañuelo.

han·dle (hăn′dl) I. tr. **-dled, -dling** (to touch) tocar, andar con; (a tool) andar con; (a boat) dirigir; (a vehicle) manejar, guiar; (animals) llevar; (to deal with) ocuparse de, encargarse de <*my lawyer handles those matters* mi abogado se encarga de esas cosas>; (to represent) representar, ser el agente de; (to manage) tener capacidad para, poder con <*they could not h. so many requests* no pudieron con tantas solicitudes>; (to cope with) poder con, aguantar; (to trade in) tratar en, comerciar en; (to carry) vender, tener <*we don't h. cookbooks* no tenemos libros de cocina> ♦ **h. with care** frágil ♦ **to h. oneself** conducirse, comportarse —intr. (vehicle) manejarse <*a car that handles well* un auto que se maneja bien>; (boat) navegar; (plane) volar II. s. (of a utensil, tool) mango; (of a door) picaporte *m,* manija; (of a door, drawer) manilla, manija; (of a suitcase, cup) asa, asidero; (of a cane, sword) puño; (for cranking or winding) manivela; (means of achievement) pretexto ♦ **to fly off the h.** perder los estribos ♦ **what's your h.?** JER. ¿cómo te llamas?

han·dle·bars (hăn′dl-bärz′) s.pl. manillar *m,* guía.

han·dler (hănd′lər) s. COM. comerciante *m,* tratante *m;* DEP. entrenador *m.*

han·dling (hănd′lĭng) s. (of a tool, car) manejo; (treatment) forma de tratar (un asunto, persona) ♦ **for shipping and h.** para gastos de flete.

hand·made (hănd′mād′) adj. hecho a mano.

hand·maid (hănd′mād′) o **hand·maid·en** (-mād′n) s. *(servant)* doncella; FIG. *(aid)* ayuda.

hand-me-down (hănd′mē-doun′) I. adj. *(used)* de segunda mano; *(shabby)* de mala calidad II. s. prenda de vestir de segunda mano.

hand organ s. MÚS. organillo.

hand·out (hănd′out′) s. *(given to a beggar)* limosna; *(leaflet)* folleto; *(release of information)* comunicado publicitario.

hand·pick (hănd′pĭk′) tr. escoger, seleccionar.

hand·rail (hănd′rāl′) s. pasamano, barandilla.

hand·saw (hănd′sô′) s. serrucho.

hand·set (hănd′sĕt′) s. microteléfono.

hand·shake (hănd′shāk′) s. apretón de manos *m*.

hands-off (hăndz′ôf′) adj. de no intervención.

hand·some (hăn′səm) adj. **-som·er, -som·est** *(woman)* guapa, hermosa; *(man)* bien parecido, guapo; *(animal)* hermoso; *(elegant)* elegante; *(large)* considerable, bueno (recompensa, ganancias); *(in size)* grande.

hand·some·ly (hăn′səm-lē) adv. *(beautifully)* hermosamente, primorosamente; *(elegantly)* elegantemente; *(generously)* generosamente.

hand·some·ness (hăn′səm-nĭs) s. *(beauty)* belleza; *(elegance)* elegancia; *(generosity)* generosidad *f*.

hands-on (hăndz′ŏn′) adj. práctico.

hand·spring (hănd′sprĭng′) s. DEP. voltereta (apoyándose en las manos).

hand·stand (hănd′stănd′) s. pino, parada de cabeza.

hand-to-hand (hănd′tə-hănd′) adj. cuerpo a cuerpo.

hand-to-mouth (hănd′tə-mouth′) adj. precario ♦ **to live h.** vivir al día.

hand·work (hănd′wûrk′) s. trabajo a mano.

hand·write (hănd′rīt′) tr. **-wrote** (-rōt′), **-writ·ten** (-rĭt′ən), **-writ·ing** escribir a mano.

hand·writ·ing (hănd′rī′tĭng) s. *(calligraphy)* escritura; *(characteristic style)* letra *<his h. is very neat* su letra es muy clara>.

hand·y (hăn′dē) adj. **-i·er, -i·est** *(dexterous)* diestro, mañoso; *(accessible)* a mano *<keep the medicine h.* ten la medicina a mano>; *(near)* cercano; *(useful)* conveniente, práctico (manual, herramienta) ♦ **to be h. with** saber manejar ♦ **to come in h.** venir bien.

hand·y·man o **handy man** (hăn′dē-măn′) s. factótum *m*, hombre que hace bricolages *m*.

hang (hăng) I. tr. **hung** (hŭng), **hang·ing** *(to suspend)* suspender, colgar; *(to execute)* ahorcar, colgar *<the murderer was hanged at dawn* el criminal fue ahorcado al amanecer>; *(to fasten)* fijar, ajustar; *(to decorate)* adornar *<to h. a room with curtains* adornar un cuarto con cortinas>; *(one's head)* bajar, inclinar; *(to wallpaper)* empapelar (paredes) ♦ **h. a right** FAM. a la derecha • **to h. out** *(a flag)* enarbolar; *(laundry)* tender (afuera) • **to h. up** FIG. *(to delay)* demorar; *(to put up)* colgar (cuadro) • **to h. up the phone** colgar el teléfono —intr. *(to dangle)* colgar; *(to be executed)* ser ahorcado; *(to hover)* flotar (en el aire); *(to droop)* inclinarse; *(to drape)* caer (tela, prendas); *(to exhibit)* exhibirse (cuadros, pinturas) ♦ **h. in there!** FAM. ¡ánimo! • **to h. around** o **out** FAM. *(to loiter)* haraganear, andar rondando por • **to h. around** o **out with** FAM. juntarse con, asociarse con • **to h. back** quedarse atrás, rezagarse • **to h. by a thread** FIG. pender de un hilo • **to h. in the balance** estar por resolver • **to h. loose** JER. estar tranquilo • **to h. on** *(to wait)* esperar; *(to grasp)* asirse de; FIG. *(to persevere)* persistir; *(to depend on)* depender de *<my whole future hangs on this contract* mi porvenir depende de este contrato> • **to h. on (someone's) every word** FIG. estar pendiente de cada palabra • **to h. onto** guardar, quedarse con • **to h. oneself** ahorcarse • **to h. out** FIG. haraganear • **to h. up** TEL. colgar, cortar la comunicación • **to let it all h. out** JER. *(to be relaxed)* permanecer tranquilo; *(to be candid)* ser franco II. s. *(drape)* caída (de tela, prenda); *(slope)* inclinación *f*, declive *m* ♦ **not to give a h.** FAM. importarle a uno un comino • **to get the h. of something** FAM. *(to get the knack)* cogerle el truco a algo; *(to understand)* lograr entender algo.

han·gar (hăng′ər) s. AVIA. hangar *m*.

hang·dog (hăng′dôg′) I. adj. *(shamefaced)* avergonzado; *(intimidated)* amilanado II. s. zorro, taimado.

hang·er (hăng′ər) s. *(hook)* gancho; *(for clothes)* percha; *(strap)* faja; *(strip of cloth)* colgadura.

hang·er-on (hăng′ər-ŏn′) s. [pl. **hangers-on**] parásito, gorrón *m*.

hang·ing (hăng′ĭng) I. s. *(execution)* ejecución en la horca *f*; *(method of execution)* horca *<condemned to death by h.* condenado a morir en la horca> II. adj. *(projecting downward)* colgante, pendiente; *(severe)* implacable (juez, jurado).

hang·man (hăng′mən) s. verdugo.

hang·out (hăng′out′) s. guarida, punto de reunión.

hang·o·ver (hăng′ō′vər) s. *(after drinking)* resaca; *(holdover)* vestigio.

hang-up (hăng′ŭp′) s. FAM. *(emotional problem)* complejo, problema *m*; *(obstacle)* traba.

hank (hăngk) s. *(coil)* madeja; MARÍT. anillo de una vela.

han·ker (hăng′kər) intr. tener ganas de, anhelar.

han·ker·ing (hăng′kər-ĭng) s. *(desire)* deseo, ganas; *(nostalgia)* añoranza.

han·kie o **han·ky** (hăng′kē) s. [pl. **-kies**] FAM. pañuelo.

han·ky-pan·ky (hăng′kē-păng′kē) s. JER. *(mischievous activity)* truquitos, jueguitos; *(foolish talk or action)* boberías ♦ **there's some h. going on** hay algo que no huele bien.

han·som (hăn′səm) s. cabriolé *m*.

hap·haz·ard (hăp-hăz′ərd) I. adj. fortuito II. s. accidente *m*, casualidad *f* III. adv. sin ton ni son, a la buena de Dios.

hap·less (hăp′lĭs) adj. desventurado.

hap·pen (hăp′ən) intr. *(to come to pass)* pasar, suceder *<what happened?* ¿qué pasó?>; *(to take place)* producirse, ocurrir *<it all happened yesterday* todo ocurrió ayer> ♦ **how does it h. that . . .?** ¿cómo es posible que . . .? • **if you h. to talk to him** si por casualidad hablaras con él • **it (so) happens that** o **as it happens** da la casualidad de que • **no matter what happens** o **whatever happens** pase lo que pase • **to h. on** dar con • **to h. to be** dar la casualidad de ser o estar.

hap·pen·ing (hăp′ə-nĭng) s. *(event)* acontecimiento, suceso; ARTE. *(spectacle)* happening *m*.

hap·pen·stance (hăp′ən-stăns′) s. casualidad *f* ♦ **by h.** de casualidad.

hap·pi·ly (hăp′ə-lē) adv. *(pleasurably)* felizmente; *(fortunately)* por suerte, afortunadamente; *(merrily)* alegremente; *(appropriately)* acertadamente ♦ **to be h. married** ser feliz en el matrimonio • **to live h.** vivir feliz.

hap·pi·ness (hăp′ē-nĭs) s. *(joy)* felicidad *f*, dicha; *(merriment)* alegría; *(appropriateness)* acierto, propiedad *f*.

hap·py (hăp′ē) adj. **-pi·er, -pi·est** *(enjoying pleasure)* feliz, dichoso *<a h. marriage* un matrimonio feliz>; *(fortunate)* afortunado, dichoso *<a h. outcome* un desenlace dichoso>; *(fulfilled)* contento *<I'm not h. in my job* no estoy contento con mi trabajo>; *(merry)* alegre *<a h. song* una canción alegre>; *(appropriate)* acertado, feliz; *(overly involved with)* obsesionado *<money-happy* obsesionado por el dinero> ♦ **h. birthday!** ¡feliz cumpleaños!, ¡felicidades! • **to be as h. as a lark** estar más alegre que una pascua • **to be h. to hear that** alegrarse de saber que • **to be very h. for someone** alegrarse mucho por alguien.

hap·py-go-luck·y (hăp′ē-gō-lŭk′ē) adj. despreocupado.

Haps·burg (hăps′bûrg′) s. HIST. Habsburgo.

ha·ra-ki·ri (hä′rə-kîr′ē) s. haraquiri *m*.

ha·rangue (hə-răng′) I. s. arenga II. tr. & intr. **-rangued, -rangu·ing** arengar.

ha·rass (hə-răs′, hăr′əs) tr. *(to besiege)* acosar, hostigar *<to h. with threats* acosar con amenazas>; *(to annoy)* molestar; *(to wear out)* agobiar; MIL. acosar, hostilizar.

ha·rass·ment (hə-răs′mənt, hăr′əs-) s. *(besiegement)* acoso, hostigamiento; *(plaguing)* tormento continuo.

har·bin·ger (här′bĭn-jər) I. s. *(herald)* heraldo; *(omen)* presagio; *(forerunner)* precursor *m* II. tr. anunciar, presagiar.

har·bor (här′bər) I. s. *(for ships)* puerto, bahía; *(refuge)* puerto, refugio II. tr. *(to protect)* proteger; *(to conceal)* encubrir (criminal); (to lodge) albergar; (hopes) abrigar, tener; (resentment) guardar.

har·bor·age (här'bər-ĭj) s. (for a ship) fondeadero; (refuge) refugio, asilo.

har·bor·mas·ter (här'bər-măs'tər) s. capitán del puerto m.

hard (härd) **I.** adj. **-er, -est** (solid) duro, sólido; (firm) firme; (resistant) resistente; (difficult) difícil, arduo; (rugged) fuerte, robusto; FIG. (strong-minded) decidido, resuelto; (diligent) diligente; (vigorous) fuerte <a h. blow un golpe fuerte>; (inclement) duro, inclemente <a long, h. winter un invierno largo e inclemente>; (stern) rígido, severo <a h. taskmaster un supervisor severo>; (trying) duro, difícil <a h. life una vida dura>; (callous) cruel, de piedra; (damaging) perjudicial, dañino <snow and ice are h. on a car's finish la nieve y el hielo son dañinos para el acabado de un automóvil>; (bad) malo, adverso <h. luck mala suerte>; (undeniable) innegable, incontestable (evidencia); (penetrating) penetrante (mirada); (said of liquor) de alto contenido alcohólico, fuerte <h. liquor licor fuerte>; (said of water) dura (agua); FONÉT. fuerte ♦ **h. and fast** riguroso, invariable <h. and fast rules of behavior reglas invariables de comportamiento> • **h. drugs** drogas adictivas • **h. to deal with** de trato difícil, intratable • **no h. feelings** sin resentimiento • **to be h. on** (someone) ser muy duro con alguien; (to criticize) criticar severamente **II.** adv. (intensely) duramente, mucho <to work h. trabajar mucho>; (vigorously) vigorosamente, con fuerza; (badly) malamente, gravemente; (with great distress) penosamente, con gran dificultad; (firmly) firmemente, fuertemente; (close) cerca, próximo ♦ **h. on the heels of** pisándole los talones a • **to be h. at it** trabajar con ahínco • **to be h. hit by** estar severamente afectado por • **to be h. up** encontrarse sin dinero, no tener un centavo.

hard·back (härd'băk') **I.** adj. encuadernado **II.** s. libro encuadernado.

hard·bit·ten (härd'bĭt'n) adj. curtido por la experiencia.

hard·boiled (härd'boild') adj. (egg) duro; FAM. (callous) duro; (unsentimental) práctico.

hard·bound (härd'bound') **I.** adj. encuadernado **II.** s. libro encuadernado.

hard cash s. FAM. metálico, dinero contante y sonante.

hard core s. núcleo, médula.

hard-core o **hard·core** (härd'kôr') adj. (inveterate) empedernido, endurecido <a h. criminal un malhechor empedernido>; (persisting) arraigado; (pornography) explícito, crudo.

hard·cov·er (härd'kŭv'ər) **I.** adj. encuadernado **II.** s. libro encuadernado.

hard·en (här'dn) tr. (to make hard) endurecer; (to inure) curtir, acostumbrar; (to make callous) endurecer; (in outline) perfilar, dar mayor nitidez a —intr. (to become hard) endurecerse; COM. (to rise) subir (precios); (to become stable) estabilizarse; (to become inured) acostumbrarse.

hard·en·ing (här'dn-ĭng) s. endurecimiento.

hard·hat (härd'hăt') adj. FAM. (conservative) muy conservador, reaccionario; JER. (chauvinist) patriotero ♦ **a h. job** un trabajo en la construcción.

hard hat s. (helmet) casco protector; FAM. (worker) trabajador de construcción m; JER. (chauvinistic person) chauvinista mf; FAM. (ultraconservative) ultraconservador m.

hard·head·ed (härd'hĕd'ĭd) adj. (stubborn) testarudo, porfiado; (realistic) práctico, realista.

hard·heart·ed (härd'här'tĭd) adj. duro de corazón, sin sentimientos.

har·di·hood (här'dē-hŏŏd') s. (boldness) temeridad f, osadía; (impudence) atrevimiento, descaro.

har·di·ness (här'dē-nĭs) s. (ruggedness) robustez f; (intrepidness) temeridad f, atrevimiento; (endurance) resistencia.

hard labor s. DER. trabajos forzados.

hard landing s. ASTRONÁUT. aterrizaje por impacto m.

hard line s. (firm position) postura firme; (uncompromising attitude) actitud intransigente f.

hard-line o **hard·line** (härd'lĭn') adj. (firm) firme; (uncompromising) intransigente.

hard·lin·er (härd'lĭ'nər) s. intransigente mf.

hard·ly (härd'lē) adv. (just) apenas <I had h. closed my eyes

when they woke me up apenas había cerrado los ojos cuando me despertaron>; (almost not) escasamente, casi no <it is so dark I can h. see anything está tan oscuro que casi no veo nada>; (probably not) difícilmente <they will h. come in this storm difícilmente vendrán con esta tormenta>; (harshly) duramente, severamente; (painfully) a duras penas, con dificultad.

hard·ness (härd'nĭs) s. (quality) dureza; (severity) severidad f, rigor m <the h. of winter el rigor del invierno>; (insensitivity) insensibilidad f.

hard-nosed (härd'nōzd') adj. cabezón, obstinado.

hard palate s. ANAT. paladar duro u óseo.

hard sell s. FAM. táctica de ventas agresiva.

hard·ship (härd'shĭp') s. (privation) penuria; (difficulty) dificultad f; (trial) prueba.

hard·top (härd'tŏp') s. automóvil de techo duro parecido al de un convertible m.

hard·ware (härd'wâr') s. (utensils) ferretería, artículos de ferretería; COMPUT. (equipment) equipo, maquinaria; TEC. (machines) maquinaria; FAM. (weapons) hierros, armas (esp. militares) ♦ **h. store** ferretería.

hard-won (härd'wŭn') adj. ganado con mucha dificultad.

hard·wood (härd'wŏŏd') s. (wood) madera dura; (tree) árbol de madera dura m.

har·dy¹ (här'dē) adj. **-di·er, -di·est** (rugged) robusto; (intrepid) temerario, atrevido; (enduring) resistente (planta, persona).

har·dy² (här'dē) s. cortafrío.

hare (hâr) s. ZOOL. liebre f ♦ **mad as a March h.** más loco que una cabra.

hare-brained (hâr'brānd') adj. atolondrado, desatinado.

hare·lip (hâr'lĭp') s. labio leporino o hendido.

har·em (hâr'əm) s. harén m.

hark (härk) intr. escuchar, prestar atención ♦ **to h. back to** remontarse a.

har·le·quin (här'lĭ-kwĭn) **I.** s. arlequín m ♦ **H.** Arlequín **II.** adj. de losanges.

har·lot (här'lət) s. ramera.

harm (härm) **I.** s. (injury) daño, perjuicio; (evil) mal m <the h. is done el mal está hecho> ♦ **out of h.'s way** a salvo • **to do more h. than good** hacer más daño que bien **II.** tr. (to hurt) hacer daño; (to damage) dañar, estropear; (to wrong) perjudicar.

harm·ful (härm'fəl) adj. (having ill effects) perjudicial; (damaging) dañino <a h. insect un insecto dañino>; (causing injury) nocivo.

harm·less (härm'lĭs) adj. inocuo.

har·mon·ic (här-mŏn'ĭk) **I.** adj. armónico **II.** s. MÚS. armónico; FÍS. frecuencia armónica.

har·mon·i·ca (här-mŏn'ĭ-kə) s. MÚS. armónica.

har·mon·ics (här-mŏn'ĭks) s. [ú. con v. sing.] MÚS. armonía.

har·mo·ni·ous (här-mō'nē-əs) adj. armonioso.

har·mo·ni·um (här-mō'nē-əm) s. MÚS. armonio.

har·mo·ni·za·tion (här'mə-nĭ-zā'shən) s. MÚS. armonización f.

har·mo·nize (här'mə-nīz') tr. & intr. **-nized, -niz·ing** armonizar.

har·mo·niz·er (här'mə-nī'zər) s. armonizador m.

har·mo·ny (här'mə-nē) s. [pl. **-ies**] armonía.

har·ness (här'nĭs) **I.** s. (for animals) arnés m, arreos; (straps) correas; ANT. (armor) arnés, armadura **II.** tr. (a horse) poner las guarniciones a, enjaezar; (to hitch) enganchar; FIG. (an energy source) aprovechar, utilizar.

harp (härp) MÚS. **I.** s. arpa **II.** intr. tocar el arpa ♦ **to h. on** machacar, insistir en.

harp·ist (här'pĭst) s. MÚS. arpista mf.

har·poon (här-pŏŏn') MARÍT. **I.** s. arpón m **II.** tr. arponear.

har·poon·er (här-pŏŏ'nər) s. MARÍT. arponero.

harp·si·chord (härp'sĭ-kôrd') s. MÚS. clavicordio, clavicémbalo.

harp·si·chord·ist (härp'sĭ-kôr'dĭst) s. MÚS. clavicembalista mf.

har·py (här'pē) s. [pl. **-ies**] arpía ♦ **H.** MITOL. arpía.

har·que·bus (här'kwə-bəs) s. ARM. arcabuz m.

har·ri·dan (här'ĭ-dn) s. tarasca, regañona.

har·ri·er¹ (här'ē-ər) s. ORNIT. especie de halcón.

ā rey / ä año / b boca / ch chico / d dar / ĕ el / ē mil / g gato / h joya / hw juez / ī aire / k casa / kw cuan /

har·ri·er² (hăr′ē-ər) s. ZOOL. *(dog)* lebrel *o* sabueso pequeño; DEP. *(runner)* corredor a campo traviesa *m.*
har·row (hăr′ō) I. s. AGR. grada II. tr. AGR. *(soil)* gradar; *(to distress)* atormentar.
har·row·ing (hăr′ō-ĭng) adj. espantoso, desgarrador <*a h. experience* una experiencia espantosa>.
har·ry (hăr′ē) tr. **-ried, -ry·ing** *(to raid)* arrasar, merodear; *(to harass)* atormentar, acosar.
harsh (härsh) adj. **-er, -est** *(voice)* áspero; *(smell, sound)* penetrante; *(words)* áspero, duro; *(punishment)* fuerte; *(weather)* malo, inclemente; *(person)* cruel, severo.
harsh·ness (härsh′nĭs) s. *(unpleasantness)* aspereza; *(severity)* dureza; *(of the weather)* inclemencia; *(sternness)* crueldad *f.*
hart (härt) s. [pl. **harts** *o* **hart**] ZOOL. venado, ciervo.
har·um-scar·um (hâr′əm-skâr′əm) I. adj. alocado II. adv. a la buena de Dios.
har·vest (här′vĭst) I. s. *(gathering)* cosecha, recolección *f*; *(of sugar cane)* zafra; *(of grapes)* vendimia; FIG. *(result of an action)* fruto ♦ **h. festival** fiesta de la cosecha II. tr. *(to gather)* cosechar, recolectar; FIG. *(to reap)* segar (mieses) —intr. cosechar, hacer la cosecha.
har·vest·er (här′vĭ-stər) s. *(of fruit)* recolector *m*; *(of grains)* segador *m*; *(of sugar cane)* cortador *m*; *(machine)* segadora.
has (hăz) tercera persona sing. del pres. indic. de **have.**
has-been (hăz′bĭn′) s. FAM. persona acabada, vieja gloria.
hash¹ (hăsh) I. s. CUL. *(dish)* picadillo; *(jumble)* mescolanza, revoltillo; FIG. *(reworking of material)* refrito ♦ **to settle someone's h.** acallar a alguien II. tr. CUL. *(to mince)* picar; FAM. *(to mangle)* enredar, armarse un lío con ♦ **to h. out** *o* **over** repasar, discutir a fondo.
hash² (hăsh) s. JER. hachís *m.*
hash·ish (hăsh′ēsh′, -ĭsh) *o* **hash·eesh** (-ēsh′) s. hachís *m.*
has·n't (hăz′ənt) contr. de **has not.**
hasp (hăsp) s. cierre engoznado, aldaba de candado.
has·sle (hăs′əl) FAM. I. s. *(argument)* reyerta, jaleo; *(trouble)* lío, enredo II. tr. **-sled, -sling** fastidiar, molestar.
has·sock (hăs′ək) s. *(cushion)* cojín *m*, almohadón *m*; *(grass)* mata de hierba.
haste (hāst) s. *(swiftness)* celeridad *f*, prisa; *(precipitateness)* precipitación *f* ♦ **in h.** de prisa, precipitadamente • **to make h.** darse prisa.
has·ten (hā′sən) intr. darse prisa, apresurarse —tr. apresurar.
hast·i·ly (hā′stə-lē) adv. *(quickly)* apresuradamente, rápidamente; *(rashly)* precipitadamente.
hast·y (hā′stē) adj. **-i·er, -i·est** *(quick)* apresurado, rápido; *(rash)* precipitado <*a h. decision* una decisión precipitada> ♦ **to be h.** precipitarse.
hat (hăt) I. s. sombrero ♦ **at the drop of a h.** al menor pretexto, sin pretexto alguno • **h. in hand** humildemente • **my h.!** ¡naranjas!, ¡a otro con ese cuento! • **to keep under one's h.** no decir nada de, mantener secreto • **to pass the h.** pasar la gorra • **to take one's h. off to** reconocer el mérito de • **to talk through one's h.** *(to talk nonsense)* decir disparates; *(to bluff)* fanfarronear • **to throw** *o* **toss one's h. into the ring** POL. postularse como candidato II. tr. poner un sombrero a.
hat·box (hăt′bŏks′) s. sombrerera.
hatch¹ (hăch) s. *(on the floor)* trampa; *(on the roof)* claraboya; *(on the wall)* ventanilla; MARÍT. *(on the deck)* escotilla; *(floodgate)* compuerta.
hatch² (hăch) I. intr. salir del cascarón —tr. *(to produce young)* sacar pollos (del cascarón); *(an egg)* empollar; FIG. *(to contrive)* urdir, tramar (plan) II. s. *(incubation)* incubación *f*; *(breaking out)* salida del cascarón; *(brood)* cría, pollada.
hatch³ (hăch) I. tr. sombrear con rayas II. s. raya fina.
hatch·er·y (hăch′ə-rē) s. [pl. **-ies**] criadero (de peces, aves).
hatch·et (hăch′ĭt) s. hacha, hachuela ♦ **to bury the h.** envainar la espada, hacer las paces.
hatchet man s. JER. *(murderer)* matón *m*, asesino profesional; *(henchman)* esbirro.
hatch·ing (hăch′ĭng) s. *(incubation)* incubación *f*; *(from the egg)* salida del cascarón; ARTE. sombreado.

hatch·way (hăch′wā′) s. MARÍT. *(hatch)* escotilla; *(stairway)* escalera.
hate (hāt) I. tr. **hat·ed, hat·ing** *(to despise)* odiar, aborrecer <*I hate him* lo odio>; *(to dislike)* detestar, odiar <*he hates washing dishes* detesta lavar los platos> —intr. sentir odio II. s. odio.
hate·ful (hāt′fəl) adj. *(detestable)* odioso; *(full of hatred)* rencoroso.
hath (hăth) ANT. tercera persona sing., tiempo presente, de **have.**
ha·tred (hā′trĭd) s. odio, aborrecimiento.
hat·ter (hăt′ər) s. sombrerero ♦ **mad as a h.** FAM. más loco que una cabra.
haugh·ti·ness (hô′tē-nĭs) s. altivez *f*, altanería.
haugh·ty (hô′tē) adj. **-ti·er, -ti·est** altivo, altanero.
haul (hôl) I. tr. *(to tug)* halar, tirar de; *(to drag)* arrastrar; *(to transport)* transportar; MARÍT. torcer a barlovento —intr. *(to pull)* tirar; MARÍT. *(to change course)* tirar, virar ♦ **to h. off** coger impulso II. s. *(strong pull)* tirón *m*; *(pulling)* tirada; *(transport)* transporte *m*; *(distance)* tirada, tramo; *(load)* carga; *(of fish)* redada ♦ **over the long h.** a la larga.
haul·age (hô′lĭj) s. *(act)* transporte *m*; *(cost)* flete *m.*
haunch (hônch) s. *(hindquarter)* cuarto trasero; *(hip)* cadera; *(for food)* pernil *m*; ARQ. riñón de una bóveda *m.*
haunt (hônt) I. tr. *(to appear)* aparecer a (fantasmas); FIG. *(to frequent)* rondar, frecuentar; *(to obsess)* perseguir, obsesionar ♦ **to be haunted** estar embrujado *o* encantado (una casa) —intr. rondar II. s. *(for beasts, criminals)* antro, guarida; *(for habitués)* lugar predilecto.
haunt·ing (hôn′tĭng) adj. obsesionante, inolvidable.
haut·boy *o* **haut·bois** (hō′boi′, ō′boi′) s. MÚS. oboe *m.*
Ha·van·a (hə-văn′ə) s. La Habana.
Ha·van·an (hə-văn′ən) adj. & s. habanero.
have §G11, 13 (hăv) I. tr. **had** (hăd), **hav·ing** *(to own)* tener <*I h. two cars* tengo dos automóviles>; *(to possess)* tener, poseer <*he has great tact in negotiations* posee gran tacto en las negociaciones>; *(to keep in the mind)* retener, conservar (en la memoria); *(to acquire)* obtener, conseguir; *(to receive)* recibir <*I had a letter from my aunt* recibí una carta de mi tía>; *(to suffer from)* tener, sufrir de <*I h. rheumatic fever* sufro de fiebre reumática>; *(to experience)* pasar <*to h. a good time* pasarlo bien>; *(to find)* tener, encontrar <*I h. no words to express my gratitude* no encuentro palabras para expresar mi gratitud>; *(to assert)* decir <*as the Bible has it* según lo dice la Biblia>; *(to cause to be done)* hacer <*h. your clothes cleaned* haga que le limpien su ropa>; *(to cause to)* mandar <*I had him run an errand for me* lo mandé a que me hiciera una diligencia>; *(to permit)* permitir, tolerar <*I will not h. that language in my house* no toleraré ese vocabulario en mi casa>; FAM. *(to outwit)* tener agarrado <*she has you on every point of the argument* te tiene agarrado en cada punto de la discusión>; FAM. *(to cheat)* engañar <*we were had in that business deal* nos engañaron en esa transacción>; *(to give birth to)* dar a luz, alumbrar; *(to be obligated to)* deber <*I h. to get there on time* debo llegar a tiempo>; FAM. *(to engage in sexual intercourse with)* tener relaciones sexuales con ♦ **to h. a drink** tomar un trago • **to h. a grudge against** tenerle inquina a • **to h. a mind to** tener ganas de, querer • **to h. a word with** discutir brevemente, hablar unas palabras • **to h. breakfast** desayunar • **to h. dinner** cenar • **to h. had it** estar hasta la coronilla • **to h. it in for** FAM. tenérsela jurada a • **to h. it out with** *(to argue with)* habérselas con; *(to settle differences)* resolver un problema *o* diferencias • **to h. lunch** almorzar • **to h. on** llevar puesto (ropa, sombrero) • **to h. one's eye on** *(to watch)* vigilar, no perder de vista; *(to desire)* haberle echado el ojo a • **to h. to do with** tener que ver con —aux. haber <*he regretted that he had lost his temper* él lamentó que se había enojado>; hacer <*it has been snowing for a week* hace una semana que está nevando> ♦ **had better** *o* **best** más vale que <*I had better leave* más vale que me vaya> • **had rather** *o* **had sooner** preferir <*I had rather die than surrender* preferiría morir a entregarme> II. s. el que tiene ♦ **the haves and the have-nots** los ricos y los pobres.

ha·ven (hā′vən) s. *(port)* abra, puerto; *(shelter)* refugio; *(for tourists, lovers)* paraíso.

have-not (hăv′nŏt′) s. pobre *mf*; <*the haves and the have-nots* los ricos y los pobres>.

have·n't (hăv′ənt) contr. de **have not.**

hav·er·sack (hăv′ər-săk′) s. morral *m*, mochila.

hav·oc (hăv′ək) s. *(devastation)* devastación *f*, estragos; *(chaos)* caos *m*, desorden *m* ♦ **to wreak h.** crear un caos, causar estragos.

haw¹ I. s. balbuceo, muletilla II. intr. balbucear.

haw² (hô) s. BOT. *(fruit)* baya del espino; *(hawthorn)* espino.

Ha·wai·i (hə-wä′ē) s. Hawai.

Ha·wai·ian (hə-wä′yən) adj. & s. hawaiano.

hawk¹ (hôk) I. s. ORNIT. halcón *m*; FIG. *(shark)* tiburón *(persona) m*; FAM. *(warmonger)* partidario de la guerra, militarista *mf*; *(aggressive speaker)* águila, león *m* II. intr. *(to hunt)* cazar con halcones; *(to strike)* caer como un halcón.

hawk² (hôk) intr. & tr. pregonar, vender por las calles.

hawk³ (hôk) intr. carraspear —tr. ♦ **to h. up** arrojar tosiendo.

hawk·er (hô′kər) s. pregonero, vendedor ambulante *m*.

hawk·ish (hô′kĭsh) adj. *(aggressive)* agresivo; *(favoring force)* militarista.

haw·ser (hô′zər) s. MARÍT. estacha, guindaleza.

haw·thorn (hô′thôrn′) s. BOT. espino.

hay (hā) I. s. *(dried grass)* heno; JER. *(pittance)* miseria, paja ♦ **to hit the h.** FIG., FAM. acostarse, irse a roncar II. tr. *(to dry)* secar (heno); *(to feed)* dar forraje a.

hay·cock (hā′kŏk′) s. G.B. almiar *m*, montón de heno *m*.

hay fever s. MED. fiebre del heno *f*.

hay·loft (hā′lôft′) s. AGR. henil *m*.

hay·mow (hā′mou′) s. AGR. henil *m*.

hay·rick (hā′rĭk′) s. almiar *m*.

hay·seed (hā′sēd′) s. *(seed)* semilla de heno; *(straw)* tamo; JER. *(yokel)* paleto, patán *m*.

hay·stack (hā′stăk′) s. AGR. almiar *m*.

hay·wire (hā′wīr′) adj. FAM. *(person)* loco <*to go h.* volverse loco>; *(device)* descontrolado; *(scheme)* desorganizado.

haz·ard (hăz′ərd) I. s. *(danger)* riesgo, peligro; *(chance)* azar *m*; *(in golf)* obstáculo II. tr. *(to endanger)* poner en peligro, arriesgar; *(to venture)* aventurar <*to h. a guess* aventurar una conjetura>.

haz·ard·ous (hăz′ər-dəs) adj. *(dangerous)* peligroso; *(chancy)* azaroso, arriesgado; *(harmful)* perjudicial <*h. to your health* perjudicial para la salud>.

haze¹ (hāz) I. s. *(atmospheric condition)* neblina, niebla ligera; *(mental state)* confusión *f*, ofuscación II. intr. nublarse, anublarse.

haze² (hāz) tr. MARÍT. abrumar con faenas; *(to initiate)* someter a ritos de iniciación.

ha·zel (hā′zəl) I. s. BOT. *(shrub)* avellano; *(color)* color de avellana II. adj. de avellano; *(eyes, hair)* de color de avellana.

ha·zel·nut (hā′zəl-nŭt′) s. BOT. avellana.

haz·i·ness (hā′zē-nĭs) s. nebulosidad *f*.

haz·y (hā′zē) adj. **-i·er, -i·est** *(misty)* nebuloso, brumoso; *(unclear)* nebuloso, confuso.

H-bomb (āch′bŏm′) s. bomba H., bomba de hidrógeno.

he §G29 (hē) I. pron. él <*he is my good friend, John* él es mi buen amigo, Juan> ♦ **he who** el que, quien II. s. *(male)* varón *m* <*is the baby a he?* ¿es varón el bebé?>; *(animal)* macho <*is the cat a he?* ¿es macho el gato?>.

head (hĕd) I. s. ANAT., ZOOL. cabeza; *(intelligence)* cabeza, inteligencia <*you have to use your h. to do this work* tienes que usar la cabeza para hacer este trabajo>; *(ability)* cabeza, habilidad *f* <*a good h. for mathematics* gran habilidad para las matemáticas>; FIG. *(composure)* aplomo <*he kept his h.* mantuvo su aplomo>; *(person)* cabeza, persona <*lunch cost us five dollars a h.* el almuerzo nos costó cinco dólares por persona>; *(leader)* cabeza, líder *m* <*the Pope is the h. of the Catholic Church* el papa es la cabeza de la Iglesia Católica>; *(director)* director *m*; *(chief)* jefe *m*; *(foremost position)* cabeza, frente *m* <*I marched at the h. of*

the parade marché a la cabeza del desfile>; *(extremity)* cabeza, punta <*the h. of a pin* la cabeza de un alfiler>; *(top)* tope *m*, parte superior *f*; *(place)* cabeza, cabecera <*the h. of the table* la cabecera de la mesa>; *(of fluids)* carga, presión *f* <*h. of steam* presión de vapor>; *(foam)* espuma (de cerveza); *(cream)* nata (de leche); MED. punta de un furúnculo *o* absceso (en donde se forma el pus; *(of a cane)* puño (de bastón); *(of a hammer)* cabeza (de martillo); *(of an arrow)* punta (de flecha); *(of a tape recorder)* cabeza (grabadora, sonora); *(of a drum)* parche (de tambor) *m*; *(of a page)* principio (de página, libro); *(headline)* título, titular *m* (de libro, periódico); MIN. galería, socavón *m*; GEOG. cabo, promontorio; BOT. repollo, cabeza (de lechuga, coliflor); MARÍT. *(bow)* proa; *(toilet)* letrina; ZOOL. *(antlers)* astas (de venado); AUTO. culata (de cilindro) ♦ **from h. to foot** de arriba abajo, completamente • **h. of hair** cabellera abundante • **h. over heels** locamente, perdidamente <*to be h. over heels in love with someone* estar locamente enamorado de alguien> • **heads** [ú. con v. sing. o ú. con pl.] cara (de moneda) • **heads or tails** cara o cruz • **not to make heads or tails of** FAM. no encontrar ni pies ni cabeza a, no entender (algo) • **off the top of one's h.** sin pensar mucho en ello • **to be over one's h.** FIG. estar (algo) fuera de la capacidad de uno • **to be soft** *o* **weak in the h.** FAM. estar tocado de la cabeza • **to bring to a h.** forzar el desenlace (de un asunto) • **to get it into one's h. (to do something)** FAM. metérsele a uno la idea de (hacer algo) • **to get (something) through one's** *o* **someone's h.** comprender algo *o* hacerle comprender algo a alguien • **to go to one's h.** subírsele a la cabeza • **to keep one's h. above water** FIG. mantenerse a flote, ir tirando • **to laugh one's h. off** FIG., FAM. reír a mandíbula batiente • **to stand on one's h.** FIG. hacer lo imposible (para satisfacer a alguien) • **to talk one's h. off** FAM. hablar hasta por los codos II. tr. *(to lead)* encabezar, dirigir <*the mayor headed the committee* el alcalde encabezó la comisión>; *(to be first)* ir *o* estar a la cabeza de <*unemployment should h. the list of priorities of the new government* el desempleo debería estar a la cabeza de las prioridades del nuevo gobierno>; *(to cause to go)* enfilar *o* llevar hacia <*let's h. the horses home* enfilemos los caballos hacia la casa>; DEP. *(in soccer)* cabecear (la pelota); *(to put a heading on)* poner título a ♦ **to h. off** *(to prevent)* prevenir; *(to block)* desviar —intr. *(to proceed)* dirigirse, ir; BOT. repollar; *(to originate)* originarse, nacer (río, manantial) ♦ **to h. back** regresar, volver • **to h. for** *o* **toward** dirigirse hacia, ir con rumbo a III. adj. *(principal)* principal, central <*h. office* oficina central>; *(at the head)* delantero, a la cabeza; MARÍT. de proa ♦ **h. cook** primer cocinero.

head·ache (hĕd′āk′) s. MED. *(pain)* dolor de cabeza *m*; FAM. *(annoyance)* quebradero de cabeza.

head·band (hĕd′bănd′) s. *(band for the head)* cinta; IMPR. *(of a page)* cabecera *(of a book)* cabezada.

head·board (hĕd′bôrd′) s. cabecera (de la cama).

head·dress (hĕd′drĕs′) s. tocado.

head·ed (hĕd′ĭd) adj. *(nail)* de cabeza; *(page)* con encabezamiento; *(stationery)* con membrete ♦ **two-headed** de dos cabezas, bicéfalo.

head·er (hĕd′ər) s. MEC. descabecedor *m*; AGR. cosechadora; CONSTR., MEC. colector *m*; *(brick)* ladrillo puesto a tizón (de canto); ARQ. brochal *m*; FAM. *(headlong dive)* salto *o* caída de cabeza.

head·first (hĕd′fûrst′) adv. *(headlong)* de cabeza; *(impetuously)* precipitadamente, sin pensar.

head·gear (hĕd′gîr′) s. *(headdress)* tocado; *(hat)* sombrero; *(helmet)* casco; *(of a horse)* cabezada.

head·hunt·er (hĕd′hŭn′tər) s. *(tribesman)* cazador de cabezas *m*; JER. *(recruiter)* reclutador (de empleados) *m*.

head·ing (hĕd′ĭng) s. *(title)* encabezamiento, título; *(introduction)* introducción *f*; *(of a letter)* membrete *m*; *(section)* apartado *m*; AVIA., MARÍT. rumbo, derrotero.

head·lamp (hĕd′lămp′) s. AUTO. faro, luz delantera.

head·land (hĕd′lənd, -lănd′) s. GEOG. *(point)* punta; *(cape)* cabo; *(promontory)* promontorio.

head·less (hĕd′lĭs) adj. *(without a head)* sin cabeza, acéfalo;

(decapitated) decapitado, degollado; FIG. *(without a leader)* sin cabeza, sin jefe; *(foolish)* tonto.
head·light (hĕd′līt′) s. AUTO. faro, luz delantera.
head·line (hĕd′līn′) I. s. *(in a newspaper)* titular m; *(in a book)* titulillo ♦ **headlines** sumario de noticias • **to make the headlines** aparecer en primera plana II. tr. **-lined, -lin·ing** poner titulillo a.
head·lin·er (hĕd′lī′nər) s. TEAT. actor de cartelera m.
head·lock (hĕd′lŏk′) s. DEP. llave de cabeza f.
head·long (hĕd′lông′) I. adv. *(headfirst)* de cabeza; *(impetuously)* precipitadamente, sin pensar II. adj. *(headfirst)* de cabeza; *(impetuous)* precipitado.
head·man (hĕd′măn′) s. jefe m.
head·mas·ter o **head master** (hĕd′măs′tər) s. director (de un colegio) m.
head·mis·tress o **head mistress** (hĕd′mĭs′trĭs) s. directora (de un colegio).
head·most (hĕd′mōst′) adj. principal, más eminente.
head·on (hĕd′ŏn′) adj. & adv. de frente.
head·phone (hĕd′fōn′) s. RAD. audífono, auricular m.
head·piece (hĕd′pēs′) s. *(covering)* casco, yelmo; *(headset)* juego de audífonos o auriculares.
head pin s. DEP. bolo delantero.
head·quar·ter (hĕd′kwôr′tər) tr. & intr. MIL. acuartelar(se); *(to locate)* establecer(se) provisionalmente.
head·quar·ters (hĕd′kwôr′tərz) s.pl. [ú. con v. sing. o pl.] MIL. cuartel general m; *(police precinct)* jefatura; *(of a corporation)* oficina central; *(of an organization)* sede f; *(center of operations)* centro de operaciones.
head·rest (hĕd′rĕst′) s. *(of a chair)* cabecera; AUTO. *(of a seat)* apoyo para la cabeza.
head·set (hĕd′sĕt′) s. auriculares m, audífonos.
heads·man (hĕdz′mən) s. verdugo.
head start s. *(advantage)* ventaja; *(beginning)* comienzo antes de los demás.
head·stone (hĕd′stōn′) s. piedra o lápida sepulcral.
head·strong (hĕd′strông′) adj. voluntarioso, terco.
head-trip (hĕd′trĭp′) s. JER. *(experience)* viaje (alucinatorio) m; *(self-examination)* introspección f.
head·wait·er (hĕd′wā′tər) s. jefe de comedor m.
head·wa·ter (hĕd′wô′tər) s. cabecera, fuentes (de un río) f.
head·way (hĕd′wā′) s. *(advance)* avance m; *(progress)* progreso; *(clearance)* altura libre, espacio sobrante ♦ **to make h.** avanzar, progresar.
head wind s. viento en contra o de frente.
head·work (hĕd′wûrk′) s. trabajo mental.
head·y (hĕd′ē) adj. **-i·er, -i·est** *(intoxicating)* embriagante, embriagador; *(wine)* fuerte.
heal (hēl) tr. *(to cure)* curar; *(to remedy)* remediar, resolver —intr. *(a person)* curarse; *(a wound)* sanar, cicatrizarse.
heal·er (hē′lər) s. curandero.
heal·ing (hē′lĭng) I. adj. curativo II. s. curación f.
health (hĕlth) s. *(of a person)* salud f <to be in good h. estar bien de salud>; *(of a community)* sanidad f ♦ **to be in bad h.** estar mal de salud • **to your h.!** ¡salud!
health food s. alimentos naturales o macrobióticos.
health·ful (hĕlth′fəl) adj. sano, saludable.
health·i·ness (hĕl′thē-nĭs) s. buena salud.
health insurance s. seguro médico.
health spa s. centro de ejercicios.
health·y (hĕl′thē) adj. **-i·er, -i·est** *(possessing good health)* sano, saludable; *(air, place)* salubre; *(attitude)* sano; *(appetite)* bueno; *(sizable)* generoso, considerable ♦ **to feel h.** sentirse bien de salud.
heap (hēp) I. s. *(pile)* montón m; FAM. *(a lot)* montón; JER. *(jalopy)* cacharro, cafetera II. tr. *(to pile up)* amontonar, apilar; *(to overfill)* llenar hasta los topes.
hear (hîr) tr. **heard** (hûrd), **hear·ing** *(to perceive)* oír <have you heard her sing? ¿la ha oído cantar?>; *(to listen to)* escuchar <we heard the entire speech escuchamos todo el discurso>; *(to attend)* asistir a, oír (misa, conferencia); *(a faint sound)* sentir <did you h. footsteps on the stairs? ¿sentiste pasos en la escalera?>; *(to know)* enterarse de, saber <we have already heard what happened ya nos enteramos de lo que pasó>; DER. *(a witness)* oír; *(a case)* ver ♦ **to have never heard of** no conocer • **to h. about** o **of** ente-

rarse de, oír hablar de • **to h. out** escuchar hasta el final • **to make oneself heard** *(to speak loud)* hablar alto; *(to speak one's mind)* decir lo que uno piensa —intr. oír ♦ **I won't h. of it!** ¡ni hablar! • **to h. from** tener noticias de, saber algo.
hear·er (hîr′ər) s. oyente mf.
hear·ing (hîr′ĭng) s. *(sense)* oído; *(earshot)* alcance del oído m <out of h. fuera del alcance del oído>; DER. audiencia ♦ **hard of h.** duro de oído • **to give someone a fair h.** escuchar a alguien sin prejuicios.
hearing aid s. MED. audífono, aparato para sordos.
hear·ken (här′kən) intr. *(to listen)* escuchar, atender; *(to give heed)* prestar atención.
hear·say (hîr′sā′) s. rumores m.
hearse (hûrs) s. carroza fúnebre, coche fúnebre m.
heart (härt) s. ANAT. corazón m; *(center of sensibilities)* alma, corazón <he has a kind h. tiene buen corazón>; *(of a place)* corazón, centro; *(courage)* corazón, ánimo; *(of lettuce, cabbage)* cogollo ♦ **after one's own h.** como le gusta a uno • **at h.** en el fondo • **by h.** de memoria • **from one's h.** de todo corazón • **h. and soul** en cuerpo y alma, con toda el alma • **hearts** *(card suit)* corazón, copas • **in one's h. of hearts** en lo más hondo del corazón de uno • **in the h. of winter** en pleno invierno • **my h. sank** se me cayó el alma a los pies • **not to have one's h. in something** hacer algo sin entusiasmo • **the h. of the matter** el quid, el meollo • **to be near** o **close** o **dear to one's h.** ser muy querido para uno, tocarle a uno en el alma • **to break someone's h.** *(to disappoint)* decepcionar, defraudar; *(to hurt profoundly)* partirle el alma a alguien, herir a uno en el alma • **to eat one's h. out** consumirse (esp. de envidia) • **to get to the h. of** llegar al fondo de • **to have a change of h.** cambiar de parecer • **to have h. trouble** no andar bien del corazón • **to have one's h. in the right place** tener buenas intenciones • **to have one's h. set on** encapricharse en • **to have the h. to** tener valor para • **to lose h.** descorazonarse • **to one's heart's content** hasta saciarse • **to take h.** cobrar ánimo • **to take to h.** tomar a pecho • **to wear one's h. on one's sleeve** mostrar fácilmente los sentimientos • **with all one's h.** de todo corazón.
heart·ache (härt′āk′) s. tristeza, pena.
heart attack s. MED. ataque cardiaco o al corazón, infarto.
heart·beat (härt′bēt′) s. latido (del corazón).
heart·break (härt′brāk′) s. *(sorrow)* angustia, pena; *(disappointment)* decepción f.
heart·break·ing (härt′brā′kĭng) adj. que parte el corazón.
heart·bro·ken (härt′brō′kən) adj. *(sorrowful)* angustiado, apenado; *(disappointed)* decepcionado ♦ **to be h.** tener partido el corazón.
heart·burn (härt′bûrn′) s. MED. acidez f, acedía.
heart disease s. problemas del corazón m.
heart·en (här′tn) tr. animar, alentar.
heart failure s. MED. colapso (cardiaco).
heart·felt (härt′fĕlt′) adj. *(sincere)* sincero (alegría, agradecimiento); *(grief, sympathy)* más sentido.
hearth (härth) s. *(of a fireplace)* hogar m; FIG. *(home)* hogar.
heart·land (härt′lănd′) s. MIL., POL. *(region)* zona de importancia estratégica; *(center)* centro.
heart·less (härt′lĭs) adj. *(person)* sin corazón; *(action, words)* despiadado, cruel.
heart-rend·ing (härt′rĕn′dĭng) adj. desgarrador.
heart·sick (härt′sĭk′) adj. desconsolado.
heart-strick·en (härt′strĭk′ən) adj. angustiado, afligido.
heart·strings (härt′strĭngz′) s.pl. fibras del corazón, sentimientos.
heart-struck (härt′strŭk′) adj. var. de **heart-stricken.**
heart·throb (härt′thrŏb′) s. *(heartbeat)* latido del corazón; *(sweetheart)* enamorado.
heart-to-heart (härt′tə-härt′) adj. cándido, franco.
heart·wood (härt′wōōd′) s. BOT. duramen m.
heart·y (här′tē) adj. **-i·er, -i·est** *(warm)* cordial, sincero <a h. welcome una cordial bienvenida>; *(unequivocal)* sincero, franco <h. congratulations sinceras felicitaciones>; *(robust)* robusto; *(appetite)* bueno; *(satisfying)* abundante

<a h. meal una comida abundante> ♦ **to be a h. eater** ser de buen comer.

heat (hēt) **I.** s. *(intense warmth)* calor m <*the sun's h.* el calor del sol>; *(sensation)* calor; *(for a building)* calefacción f <*he turned off the h.* apagó la calefacción>; *(intense action)* calor <*in the h. of battle* en el calor de la batalla>; *(estrus)* estro, celo (de los animales); DEP. *(in a race)* carrera, serie (eliminatoria) f; JER. *(police)* jara, poli f ♦ **h. energy** energía térmica • **in h.** ZOOL. en celo • **in the h. of the day** en lo más caluroso del día **II.** tr. *(to make hot)* calentar; *(to excite)* acalorar ♦ **to h. up** calentar —intr. *(to become hot)* calentarse; *(to become excited)* acalorarse ♦ **to h. up** recalentarse.

heat capacity s. FÍS. calor específico.

heat·ed (hē'tǐd) adj. *(air, water)* caliente; FIG. *(debate)* acalorado.

heat·er (hē'tər) s. *(radiator)* radiador calorífero; *(stove)* estufa, calentador m; JER. *(pistol)* pistola, revólver m.

heat exchanger s. FÍS. cambiador de calor m.

heat exhaustion s. MED. postración causada por el calor excesivo.

heath (hēth) s. BOT. *(plant)* brezo; *(land)* breñal m.

hea·then (hē'thən) s. [pl. **-thens** o **-then**] & adj. *(unconverted)* pagano; *(savage)* salvaje m.

hea·then·ish (hē'thə-nǐsh) adj. *(unconverted)* pagano; *(savage)* salvaje.

heath·er (hěth'ər) s. BOT. brezo.

heat·ing (hē'tǐng) **I.** adj. *(warming)* calentador; FÍS. calorífico **II.** s. *(act)* calentamiento; *(system)* calefacción f <*central h.* calefacción central>.

heat lightning s. METEOR. relámpago de calor.

heat prostration s. MED. abatimiento causado por el calor excesivo.

heat rash s. MED. miliaria.

heat shield s. protector contra el calor m.

heat stroke s. MED. insolación f.

heat treatment s. METAL., TEC. tratamiento térmico.

heat wave s. METEOR. ola de calor.

heave (hēv) **I.** tr. **heaved, hove** (hōv), **heav·ing** *(to hoist)* alzar, levantar (con mucho esfuerzo); *(to hurl)* arrojar, tirar; *(to utter painfully)* exhalar, emitir; GEOL. desplazar (horizontalmente) —intr. *(to bulge)* levantarse, elevarse; FAM. *(to retch)* basquear, nausear; MARÍT. *(to move)* virar, moverse (un barco); *(to raise)* izar ♦ **to h. to** ponerse al pairo o en facha **II.** s. *(throw)* tiro; GEOL. desplazamiento (horizontal); *(upward movement)* elevación f, levantamiento ♦ **heaves** [ú. con v. sing. o pl.] *(act of retching)* náuseas, arcadas; VET. huélfago.

heav·en (hěv'ən) s. RELIG. cielo <*to go to h.* ir al cielo>; *(paradise)* paraíso <*the lake was h.* el lago era un paraíso> ♦ **for Heaven's sake!** ¡por Dios!, ¡por amor de Dios! • **good heavens!** ¡Dios mío!, ¡cielos! • **H. forbid!** ¡Dios no lo quiera! • **H. forbid that** Dios nos libre de • **h. knows** Dios es testigo • **heavens** cielo, firmamento • **in seventh h.** en el séptimo cielo • **thank H.!** ¡gracias a Dios! • **to move h. and earth** mover cielo y tierra.

heav·en·ly (hěv'ən-lē) adj. *(celestial)* celestial; ASTRON. celeste (cuerpo); FIG. *(delightful)* divino, sublime.

heav·en·ward (hěv'ən-wərd) adv. hacia el cielo.

heav·i·ly (hěv'ə-lē) adj. *(weightily)* pesadamente; *(intensely)* profundamente; *(excessively)* mucho <*to be h. in debt* deber mucho>; *(with difficulty)* penosamente, con dificultad.

heav·i·ness (hěv'ē-nǐs) s. *(weight)* peso, pesantez f; *(discomfort)* pesadez f; *(slowness)* lentitud f; *(clumsiness)* torpeza; *(lack of vitality)* languidez f, decaimiento.

heav·y (hěv'ē) **I.** adj. **-i·er, -i·est** *(weighty)* pesado <*this piano is h.* este piano es pesado>; *(dense)* denso, pesado <*a h. oil* un aceite pesado>; *(thick)* espeso <*h. syrup* almíbar espeso>; *(abundant)* fuerte <*h. rainfall* lluvia fuerte>; *(profound)* profundo <*h. silence* silencio profundo>; *(violent)* bravo, borrascoso <*h. sea* mar borrascoso>; *(clumsy)* torpe; *(slow)* lento, tardo; *(stout)* corpulento; *(excessive)* fuerte <*h. drinker* bebedor fuerte>; *(grave)* grave, serio (situación, asunto); *(arduous)* arduo, dificultoso (tarea, trabajo); *(large-scale)* en gran escala (inversionista, comprador); *(onerous)* gravoso, oneroso (impuestos, responsa-

bilidades); *(not readily digested)* pesado, indigesto (comida); *(coarse)* grueso <*h. paper* papel grueso>; *(weighed down)* abatido, oprimido <*h. heart* corazón oprimido>; *(tired)* cansado; *(stern)* duro <*to treat someone with a h. hand* tratar a alguien con mano dura>; *(foul)* cargado <*air h. with smoke* aire cargado de humo>; *(pungent)* fuerte <*a h. scent* un olor fuerte>; *(weary)* amodorrado, soñoliento (ojos, cuerpo); *(said of industries)* pesado (industria); *(pregnant)* encinta, embarazada; TEAT. *(said of a role)* serio (papel); FÍS. pesado; MIL. *(artillery)* pesado; *(said of fire)* intenso **II.** adv. *(heavily)* pesadamente; *(slowly)* lentamente **III.** s. [pl. **-ies**] TEAT. villano.

heav·y-du·ty (hěv'ē-dōō'tē, -dyōō'-) adj. *(designed for hard work)* de servicio pesado (máquina, equipo); *(to withstand wear)* resistente, de poco desgaste (tela, cable).

heav·y-hand·ed (hěv'ē-hăn'dǐd) adj. *(clumsy)* torpe; *(oppressive)* de mano dura, despótico.

heav·y-heart·ed (hěv'ē-här'tǐd) adj. abatido, afligido.

heav·y-set (hěv'ē-sět') adj. corpulento.

heavy water s. QUÍM. agua pesada.

heav·y·weight (hěv'ē-wāt') s. *(boxer)* peso pesado; FAM. *(big shot)* persona importante.

He·bra·ic (hǐ-brā'ǐk) o **He·bra·i·cal** (-ǐ-kəl) adj. hebraico.

He·bra·ism (hē'brā-ǐz'əm) s. hebraísmo.

He·brew (hē'brōō) **I.** adj. hebreo **II.** s. *(inhabitant, language)* hebreo ♦ **Hebrews** BÍBL. Epístola a los Hebreos.

hec·a·tomb (hěk'ə-tōm') s. hecatombe f.

heck (hěk) **I.** interj. ¡diablos! **II.** s. infierno ♦ **a h. of a** del diablo • **for the h. of it** por gusto, porque sí • **what the h.!** ¡qué diablos!

heck·le (hěk'əl) tr. **-led, -ling** interrumpir (a un orador).

heck·ler (hěk'lər) s. persona que interrumpe a un orador.

hec·tare (hěk'târ') s. hectárea.

hec·tic (hěk'tǐk) adj. ajetreado, agitado <*a h. week* una semana agitada>.

hec·to·gram o **hec·to·gramme** (hěk'tə-grăm') s. hectogramo.

hec·to·li·ter o **hec·to·li·tre** (hěk'tə-lē'tər) s. hectolitro.

hec·to·me·ter o **hec·to·me·tre** (hěk'tə-mē'tər) s. hectómetro.

hec·tor (hěk'tər) **I.** s. matón m, fanfarrón m **II.** tr. intimidar con bravatas.

he'd (hēd) contr. de **he had, he would.**

hedge (hěj) **I.** s. *(row of shrubs)* seto vivo, seto; FIN. *(means of protection)* seguro, inversión defensiva (esp. contra pérdidas); *(in gambling)* apuesta compensatoria; *(excuse)* evasiva **II.** tr. **hedged, hedg·ing** *(to enclose)* cercar (con un seto); *(to hem in)* encerrar; *(to hinder)* restringir, obstruir; FIN. *(to protect)* compensar —intr. *(to plant hedges)* plantar setos; FIN. hacer operaciones compensatorias; *(in gambling)* hacer apuestas compensatorias; *(to skirt)* andarse con rodeos, irse por la tangente.

hedge·hog (hěj'hôg') s. ZOOL. erizo.

hedge·hop (hěj'hōp') intr. **-hopped, -hop·ping** AVIA. volar a ras de tierra.

hedge·row (hěj'rō') s. seto, seto vivo.

he·don·ism (hēd'n-ĭz'əm) s. hedonismo.

he·don·ist (hēd'n-ĭst) s. hedonista mf.

hee·bie-jee·bies (hē'bē-jē'bēz) s.pl. JER. desasosiego, nervios ♦ **to have the h.** estar hecho un manojo de nervios.

heed (hēd) **I.** intr. & tr. hacer caso (a, de), prestar atención a **II.** s. *(attention)* atención f; *(care)* cuidado ♦ **to pay** o **take h. to** prestar atención a.

heed·ful (hēd'fəl) adj. *(attentive)* atento; *(careful)* cuidadoso ♦ **to be h. of** prestar atención a.

heed·less (hēd'lĭs) adj. descuidado, incauto ♦ **to be h. of** no hacer caso a.

hee-haw (hē'hô') s. *(bray)* rebuzno; *(guffaw)* risotada, carcajada.

heel¹ (hēl) **I.** s. ANAT. *(of the foot)* talón m, calcañar m; *(of the hand)* talón; *(of a shoe, a sock)* talón; *(of a shoe sole)* tacón m; *(of bread)* punta; MARÍT. *(of a mast)* pie m; *(of the keel)* talón; JER. *(cad)* canalla m ♦ **Achilles' h.** talón de Aquiles • **head over heels** patas arriba, al revés • **high heels** zapatos de tacones altos • **to be at** o **on someone's heels** andar pisándole los talones a alguien • **to be head**

over heels in love estar locamente enamorado • **to kick up one's heels** echar una cana al aire, divertirse • **to take to one's heels** poner pies en polvorosa • **to turn on one's h.** dar media vuelta, volverse rápidamente **II.** tr. poner el talón *o* tacón a (media, zapato) —intr. seguir de cerca.

heel² (hēl) MARÍT. **I.** tr. & intr. escorar, inclinar(se) **II.** s. escora, inclinación *f*.

heft (hĕft) **I.** s. *(weight)* peso; *(heaviness)* pesadez *f* **II.** tr. *(to test the weight of)* sopesar; *(to lift)* levantar, alzar —intr. pesar, tener peso.

heft·y (hĕf'tē) adj. **-i·er, -i·est** *(weighty)* pesado; *(strong)* robusto, vigoroso, fuerte; *(amount)* fuerte, cuantioso.

he·gem·o·ny (hĭ-jĕm'ə-nē) s. [pl. **-nies**] hegemonía.

he·gi·ra (hĭ-jī'rə) s. huida, éxodo ♦ **H.** RELIG. hégira, héjira.

heif·er (hĕf'ər) s. novilla.

height (hīt) s. *(altitude)* altura, alto <*h. above sea level* altura sobre el nivel del mar>; *(summit)* cima, cumbre *f* <*the heights of the Andes* las cumbres de los Andes>; *(zenith)* punto culminante, cumbre <*at the h. of her career* en la cumbre de su carrera>; *(of madness, stupidity)* colmo; *(of a person)* estatura <*of average h.* de mediana estatura>; GEOG. *(elevation)* altura, elevación *f*; *(hill)* colina; *(mountain)* montaña.

height·en (hīt'n) tr. & intr. *(to increase)* aumentar(se); *(to enhance)* intensificar(se), realzar(se); *(to make higher)* hacer(se) más alto, elevar(se).

hei·nous (hā'nəs) adj. atroz, nefando.

heir (âr) s. heredero ♦ **universal h.** DER. heredero único.

heir apparent s. [pl. **heirs apparent**] DER. heredero forzoso.

heir·ess (âr'ĭs) s. heredera (de una fortuna).

heir·loom (âr'lōom') s. reliquia de familia.

heir presumptive s. [pl. **heirs presumptive**] DER. presunto heredero.

heist (hīst) JER. **I.** tr. robar, hurtar **II.** s. robo, hurto.

held (hĕld) pret. y part. p. de **hold¹**.

he·li·a·cal (hĭ-lī'ə-kəl) adj. ASTRON. helíaco, del sol.

hel·i·cal (hĕl'ĭ-kəl, hē'lĭ-) adj. helicoidal.

hel·i·cop·ter (hĕl'ĭ-kŏp'tər, hē'lĭ-) s. AVIA. helicóptero.

he·li·o·cen·tric (hē'lē-ō-sĕn'trĭk) adj. ASTRON. heliocéntrico.

he·li·o·graph (hē'lē-ə-grăf') **I.** s. ASTRON. heliógrafo; FÍS. heliógrafo, heliógrafo **II.** tr. comunicar por heliógrafo.

he·li·o·trope (hē'lē-ə-trōp') s. BOT. heliotropo (planta, flor *o* color); *(valerian)* valeriana; MIN. heliotropo, sanguinaria; FÍS. heliotropo.

he·li·ot·ro·pism (hē'lē-ŏt'rə-pĭz'əm) s. BIOL. heliotropismo.

hel·i·port (hĕl'ə-pôrt', hē'lə-) s. AER. helipuerto.

he·li·um (hē'lē-əm) s. QUÍM. helio.

he·lix (hē'lĭks) s. [pl. **-lix·es** *o* **hel·i·ces** (hĕl'ĭ-sēz', hē'l-)] ANAT., GEOM. hélice *f*; ARQ. espiral *f*, voluta.

hell (hĕl) **1.** s. MITOL., RELIG. infierno ♦ **a h. of a** FAM. *(extremely bad)* del diablo, más malo que el diablo <*it was a h. of a job* fue un trabajo más malo que el diablo>; *(extremely good)* tremendo, buenísimo <*it was a h. of a party* fue una fiesta buenísima> • **a h. of a lot** FAM. un montón, muchísimo • **come h. or high water** FIG., FAM. pase lo que pase, contra viento y marea • **go to h.!** FAM. ¡vete al diablo! ¡vete al infierno! • **h. to pay** FAM. un lío del diablo • **just for the h. of it** FAM. por puro gusto • **like h.** FAM. *(a lot)* muchísimo; *(to rain)* a chorros; *(to work)* como un negro; *(to laugh)* a carcajadas • **to be h.** ser insoportable • **to give someone h.** encenderle los pelos a alguien, poner a alguien como un trapo • **to go through h.** pasarlas negras • **to go to h.** echarse a perder • **to h. with it!** FAM. ¡al diablo!, ¡qué diablos! • **to raise h.** FAM. armar una de todos los diablos • **what the h. . . .** qué diablos . . . • **who the h. . . .?** ¿quién diablos . . .? **II.** intr. ♦ **to h. around** correrse una juerga, jaranearse **III.** interj. JER. ¡demonio!, ¡caramba!

he'll (hĕl) contr. de **he shall, he will.**

hell-bent (hĕl'bĕnt') adj. ♦ **to be h. on** FAM. estar empeñado en.

hell·cat (hĕl'kăt') s. *(shrew)* arpía, bruja; *(tormentor)* torturador *m*.

Hel·len·ic (hĕ-lĕn'ĭk) adj. helénico, helenístico.

Hel·le·nism (hĕl'ə-nĭz'əm) s. helenismo.

Hel·le·nis·tic (hĕl'ə-nĭs'tĭk) *o* **Hel·len·is·ti·cal** (-tĭ-kəl) adj. helenístico.

hell·fire (hĕl'fīr') s. fuego del infierno.

hell·hole (hĕl'hōl') s. ratonera, lugar de mala muerte *m*.

hell·ion (hĕl'yən) s. FAM. bribón *m*, diablo.

hell·ish (hĕl'ĭsh) adj. infernal.

hel·lo (hĕ-lō', hə-) **I.** interj. ¡hola! **II.** s. ♦ **to say h.** saludar.

helm (hĕlm) s. MARÍT. timón *m*; *(leadership)* timón, mando.

hel·met (hĕl'mĭt) s. ARM. *(piece of armor)* yelmo; *(head covering)* casco; *(of a diver)* escafandra.

helms·man (hĕlmz'mən) s. MARÍT. timonel *m*.

help (hĕlp) **I.** tr. *(to aid)* ayudar <*h. me find the book* ayúdame a encontrar el libro>; *(to relieve)* aliviar, mitigar <*medicine to h. your cold* medicamento para aliviar tu resfriado>; *(to save)* socorrer, auxiliar <*to h. someone in danger* auxiliar a alguien en peligro>; *(to prevent, avoid)* evitar <*I cannot h. his laziness* no puedo evitar su holgazanería>; *(to wait on)* trabajar (de camarero *o* en una tienda); *(to serve)* servir <*may I h. you?* ¿puedo servirle en algo?> ♦ **to h. oneself to** *(to take)* tomar *o* mangar (algo); *(to serve oneself)* servirse (alimento) • **to h. someone out** darle una mano a alguien —intr. *(to be of service)* ser útil; *(to give assistance)* prestar asistencia **II.** s. *(aid)* ayuda; *(assistance)* asistencia; *(succor)* socorro, auxilio; *(relief)* alivio; *(remedy)* remedio; *(person)* ayudante *mf*; *(employee)* empleado; *(servant)* sirviente *m*; *(employees)* empleados; *(servants)* sirvientes ♦ **to ask for h.** pedir ayuda • **to be beyond h.** no tener remedio.

help·er (hĕl'pər) s. *(assistant)* ayudante *mf*, asistente *m*; *(contributor)* colaborador *m*.

help·ful (hĕlp'fəl) adj. *(useful)* útil; *(beneficial)* provechoso; *(accommodating)* servicial; *(kind)* amable.

help·ing (hĕl'pĭng) s. ración *f* ♦ **to have another h.** servirse más, repetir.

help·less (hĕlp'lĭs) adj. *(defenseless)* desamparado, indefenso <*h. as a baby* indefenso como un niño>; *(powerless)* impotente, incapaz; *(disabled)* inválido, desvalido; *(without remedy)* sin remedio.

help·less·ness (hĕlp'lĭs-nĭs) s. *(defenselessness)* desamparo, desvalidez *f*; *(powerlessness)* impotencia; *(incapability)* incapacidad *f*.

help·mate (hĕlp'māt') s. *(companion)* compañero; *(spouse)* esposo.

hel·ter-skel·ter (hĕl'tər-skĕl'tər) **I.** adj. *(hurried)* atropellado; *(haphazard)* sin pies ni cabeza, desordenado **II.** s. *(turmoil)* alboroto, barullo; *(confusion)* confusión *f*, desorden *m* **III.** adv. FAM. a troche y moche, sin orden ni concierto.

helve (hĕlv) s. mango (de una herramienta).

Hel·ve·tian (hĕl-vē'shən) adj. & s. helvecio.

hem¹ (hĕm) **I.** s. *(edge)* borde *m*, orilla; COST. dobladillo, bastilla **II.** tr. **hemmed, hem·ming** COST. dobladillar, bastillar; FIG. *(to enclose)* encerrar, rodear.

hem² (hĕm) **I.** interj. ¡ejem! **II.** s. tos simulada **III.** intr. **hemmed, hem·ming** *(to utter)* decir ¡ejem!; *(to hesitate)* carraspear, vacilar al hablar ♦ **to h. and haw** titubear, vacilar al hablar.

he-man (hē'măn') s. FAM. macho.

he·mat·ic (hĭ-măt'ĭk) **I.** adj. hemático, de la sangre **II.** s. hemático.

he·ma·tol·o·gist (hē'mə-tŏl'ə-jĭst) s. MED. hematólogo.

he·ma·tol·o·gy (hē'mə-tŏl'ə-jē) s. MED. hematología.

he·ma·to·ma (hē'mə-tō'mə) s. [pl. **-mas** *o* **-ma·ta** (-mə-tə)] MED. hematoma *m*.

hem·i·cy·cle (hĕm'ĭ-sī'kəl) s. ARQ. hemiciclo, anfiteatro; GEOM. semicírculo.

hem·i·ple·gia (hĕm'ĭ-plē'jə) s. MED. hemiplejia, hemiplejía.

hem·i·ple·gic (hĕm'ĭ-plē'jĭk) adj. MED. hemipléjico.

hem·i·sphere (hĕm'ĭ-sfîr') s. ANAT., GEOM. hemisferio, semisfera; FIG. *(field)* campo, sector *m*; ASTRON., GEOG. hemisferio.

hem·i·spher·ic (hĕm'ĭ-sfîr'ĭk, -sfĕr'-) *o* **hem·i·spher·i·cal** (-ĭ-kəl) adj. hemisférico.

hem·i·stich (hĕm'ĭ-stĭk') s. POÉT. hemistiquio.

hem·line (hĕm'līn') s. COST. bastilla, ruedo (de un vestido, falda).

---

hem·lock (hĕm'lŏk') s. BOT. *(evergreen)* abeto, pinabete (árbol o madera) *m; (poisonous plant)* cicuta.

he·mo·di·al·y·sis (hē'mō-dī-ăl'ĭ-sĭs) s. MED. diálisis de la sangre *f.*

he·mo·glo·bin (hē'mə-glō'bĭn) s. BIOQUÍM. hemoglobina.

he·mo·phil·i·a (hē'mə-fĭl'ē-ə) s. MED. hemofilia.

he·mo·phil·i·ac (hē'mə-fĭl'ē-ăk') s. MED. hemofílico.

hem·or·rhage (hĕm'ər-ĭj) I. s. MED. hemorragia, flujo de sangre II. intr. **-rhaged, -rhag·ing** sufrir una hemorragia, sangrar.

hem·or·rhag·ic (hĕm'ə-răj'ĭk) adj. MED. hemorrágico.

hem·or·rhoid (hĕm'ə-roid') s. MED. hemorroide *f,* almorrana ♦ **hemorrhoids** hemorroides, almorranas.

hem·or·rhoid·al (hĕm'ə-roid'l) adj. MED. hemorroidal.

hemp (hĕmp) s. *(plant fiber)* cáñamo; *(hashish)* hachís *m; (marijuana)* marihuana.

hem·stitch (hĕm'stĭch') s. COST. vainica.

hen (hĕn) s. *(domestic fowl)* gallina; *(female bird)* hembra ♦ **old h.** JER. vieja.

hen·bane (hĕn'bān') s. BOT. beleño negro.

hence (hĕns) adv. *(therefore)* en consecuencia, por lo tanto; *(from now)* de aquí a <*a year h.* de aquí a un año>; *(from this source)* de aquí <*she loves art, h.* her interest in colors ella ama el arte, de aquí su afición a los colores>.

hence·forth (hĕns'fôrth') adv. de ahora en adelante.

hench·man (hĕnch'mən) s. [pl. **-men**] *(trusted follower)* hombre de confianza *m; (bodyguard)* guardaespaldas *m; (supporter)* secuaz *m,* partidario; *(gangster)* gángster *m.*

hen·house (hĕn'hous') s. gallinero.

hen·na (hĕn'ə) I. s. BOT. alcana, alheña (planta, tinte o color) II. tr. **-naed, -na·ing** teñir con alheña.

hen·peck (hĕn'pĕk') tr. FAM. dominar (al marido).

hep (hĕp) adj. var. de **hip²**.

he·pat·ic (hĭ-păt'ĭk) I. adj. hepático II. s. FAM. *(drug)* droga (hepática); BOT. hepática (planta).

hep·a·ti·tis (hĕp'ə-tī'tĭs) s. MED. hepatitis *f.*

hep·ta·gon (hĕp'tə-gŏn') s. GEOM. heptágono.

hep·tam·e·ter (hĕp-tăm'ĭ-tər) s. LIT. heptámetro.

her §G23, 29 (hər, hûr) I. pron. pers. la <*I saw h. last night* la vi anoche>; le <*and I told h.* y le dije>; ella <*that the present was for h.* que el regalo era para ella> II. adj. pos. su <*h. mother asked* su madre preguntó>; de ella <*was the present h. idea or his?* ¿fue el regalo idea de ella o de él?>.

her·ald (hĕr'əld) I. s. *(messenger)* heraldo, anunciador *m; (harbinger)* precursor *m* II. tr. proclamar.

he·ral·dic (hə-răl'dĭk) adj. heráldico.

her·al·dry (hĕr'əl-drē) s. [pl. **-ries**] *(study)* heráldica; *(coat of arms)* blasón *m,* escudo de armas; *(book)* armorial *m,* libro de armas; *(pageantry)* pompa heráldica.

herb (ûrb, hûrb) s. hierba ♦ **herbs** CUL. finas hierbas.

her·ba·ceous (hûr-bā'shəs, ûr-) adj. herbáceo.

herb·age (ûr'bĭj, hûr'-) s. herbaje *m,* pasto.

herb·al (hûr'bəl, ûr'-) adj. herbario.

herb·al·ist (hûr'bə-lĭst, ûr'-) s. herbolario.

her·bar·i·um (hûr-bâr'ē-əm, ûr-) s. [pl. **-i·ums** o **-i·a** (-ē-ə)] herbario.

her·bi·cide (hûr'bĭ-sīd', ûr'-) s. herbicida.

her·bi·vore (hûr'bə-vôr', ûr'-) s. ZOOL. herbívoro.

her·biv·o·rous (hûr-bĭv'ər-əs, ûr-) adj. ZOOL. herbívoro.

her·cu·le·an (hûr'kyə-lē'ən, hûr-kyoo'lē-) adj. hercúleo, enorme.

Her·cu·les (hûr'kyə-lēz') s. ASTRON., MITOL. Hércules.

herd (hûrd) I. s. *(of domestic animals)* hato, rebaño; *(of wild animals)* manada; *(crowd)* muchedumbre *f,* multitud *f; (common people)* plebe *f,* turba II. intr. *(to come together)* reunirse en manada; *(to associate)* asociarse —tr. *(to round up)* reunir en manada (animales); *(to watch)* guardar, pastorear (ganado); *(to drive)* conducir (en manada); *(to gather people)* agrupar, apiñar.

herd·er (hûr'dər) s. *(of cattle)* vaquero; *(of sheep)* pastor *m; (livestock owner)* ganadero.

herds·man (hûrdz'mən) s. ganadero.

here (hîr) I. adv. *(in this place)* aquí <*I live h.* yo vivo aquí>; *(to this place)* aquí, acá <*come h.* ven acá>; *(now)* en este momento, ahora <*we'll adjourn the meeting h.* levantaremos la sesión ahora>; *(on this point)* aquí, en este

punto <*h. I must disagree with you* en este punto debo discrepar con usted>; *(in this life)* en esta vida; *(in this condition)* en el estado presente ♦ **h. and there** aquí y allá • **h. we are** *(on arrival)* ya llegamos; *(on completion)* ya está • **that's neither h. nor there** eso no tiene nada que ver, eso no viene al caso II. adj. [ú. como énfasis, sin traducirse] <*my friend h. will pay you* este amigo mío le pagará> III. interj. *(at roll call)* ¡presente! (al pasar lista); *(offering something)* ¡toma! (al ofrecer algo) ♦ **look h.!** ¡mire!, ¡oiga!

here·a·bout (hîr'ə-bout') o **here·a·bouts** (-bouts') adv. por aquí.

here·af·ter (hîr-ăf'tər) I. adv. *(after this)* de ahora en adelante, en lo sucesivo; *(at a future time)* en un futuro II. s. la otra vida, el más allá.

here·by (hîr-bī') adv. *(by this means)* por este medio; *(by this document)* por la presente.

he·red·i·tar·y (hə-rĕd'ĭ-tĕr'ē) adj. hereditario.

he·red·i·ty (hə-rĕd'ĭ-tē) s. [pl. **-ies**] BIOL. herencia.

here·in (hîr-ĭn') adv. *(in this matter)* en esto; *(inside)* aquí, dentro; *(in this document)* en la presente, en ésta.

here·in·af·ter (hîr'ĭn-ăf'tər) adv. más adelante, a continuación.

here·of (hîr-ŭv', -ŏv') adv. de esto, acerca de esto.

here·on (hîr-ŏn') adv. sobre esto, acerca de esto.

her·e·sy (hĕr'ĭ-sē) s. [pl. **-sies**] herejía.

her·e·tic (hĕr'ĭ-tĭk) s. hereje *mf.*

he·ret·i·cal (hə-rĕt'ĭ-kəl) adj. herético.

here·to·fore (hîr'tə-fôr') adv. hasta ahora.

here·up·on (hîr'ə-pŏn') adv. *(at this)* en esto; *(at this moment)* en este punto, sobre esto; *(immediately after this)* a continuación.

here·with (hîr-wĭth') adv. adjunto ♦ **enclosed h.** remito adjunto.

her·i·ta·ble (hĕr'ĭ-tə-bəl) adj. BIOL. hereditario; DER. heredable.

her·i·tage (hĕr'ĭ-tĭj) s. DER. *(inheritance)* herencia; *(legacy)* patrimonio.

her·maph·ro·dite (hər-măf'rə-dīt') s. hermafrodita *mf.*

her·met·ic (hər-mĕt'ĭk) o **her·met·i·cal** (-ĭ-kəl) adj. hermético.

her·mit (hûr'mĭt) s. ermitaño.

her·mit·age (hûr'mĭ-tĭj) s. RELIG. ermita.

her·ni·a (hûr'nē-ə) s. [pl. **-as** o **-ae** (-ē)] MED. hernia.

he·ro (hîr'ō) s. [pl. **-roes**] héroe *m; (protagonist)* protagonista *mf,* héroe; JER. *(sandwich)* emparedado grande.

he·ro·ic (hĭ-rō'ĭk) I. adj. heroico II. s. POÉT. verso heroico ♦ **heroics** rimbombancia.

her·o·in (hĕr'ō-ĭn) s. FARM., QUÍM. heroína (narcótico).

her·o·ine (hĕr'ō-ĭn) s. *(brave woman)* heroína; LIT. *(protagonist)* heroína, protagonista.

her·o·ism (hĕr'ō-ĭz'əm) s. heroísmo.

her·on (hĕr'ən) s. ORNIT. garza.

her·pes (hûr'pēz) s. MED. herpes *m.*

her·ring (hĕr'ĭng) s. [pl. **herring** o **-rings**] ICT. arenque *m.*

her·ring·bone (hĕr'ĭng-bōn') s. *(pattern)* espinapez *f,* espina de pescado (en pisos, paredes); COST. punto de espina, espiga (en telas).

hers §G32 (hûrz) pron. pos. suyo <*this car is h.* este auto es suyo>; el suyo < *I have my own car, I don't need h.* tengo mi propio auto, no necesito el suyo>; de ella <*it is h., not her husband's* es de ella, no de su esposo>; el de ella <*this car is h., not his* este auto es el de ella, no el de él>.

her·self §G37 (hûr-sĕlf') pron. pers. *(reflexively)* se <*she hurt h.* se lastimó>; *(emphatically)* ella misma <*she h. wasn't certain* ella misma no estaba segura>; sí, sí misma <*she did it to h.* se lo hizo a sí misma>; en persona, personalmente <*she was here, h.* ella estuvo aquí, en persona> ♦ **by h.** sola.

hertz (hûrts) s. FÍS. hertzio, hercio.

he's (hēz) contr. de **he is, he has.**

hes·i·tan·cy (hĕz'ĭ-tn-sē) s. [pl. **-cies**] vacilación *f,* indecisión *f.*

hes·i·tant (hĕz'ĭ-tnt) adj. *(undecided)* vacilante, indeciso; *(speech, step)* vacilante.

hes·i·tate (hĕz'ĭ-tāt') intr. **-tat·ed, -tat·ing** *(to pause in uncer-*

tainty) vacilar; *(to be reluctant)* no decidirse <*he hesitated to ask for help* no se decidía a pedir ayuda>; *(not to dare)* temer, no atreverse <*she hesitated to tell them* no se atrevía a decírselo>; *(to falter)* vacilar, titubear (al hablar).

hes·i·ta·tion (hĕz'ĭ-tā'shən) s. *(indecision)* vacilación *f,* indecisión *f; (vacillation)* vacilación, titubeo.

het·er·o·dox (hĕt'ər-ə-dŏks') adj. heterodoxo; *(heretic)* herético.

het·er·o·dox·y (hĕt'ər-ə-dŏk'sē) s. [pl. **-dox·ies**] heterodoxia.

het·er·o·dyne (hĕt'ər-ə-dīn') **I.** adj. ELEC., RAD. heterodino **II.** tr. heterodinar (frecuencia).

het·er·o·ge·ne·i·ty (hĕt'ə-rō'jə-nē'ĭ-tē) s. heterogeneidad *f.*

het·er·o·ge·ne·ous (hĕt'ər-ə-jē'nē-əs) adj. heterogéneo; *(incongruous)* incongruente, diferente.

het·er·o·nym (hĕt'ər-ə-nĭm') s. GRAM. heterónimo.

het·er·o·sex·u·al (hĕt'ə-rō-sĕk'shōō-əl) adj. & s. heterosexual.

het·er·o·sex·u·al·i·ty (hĕt'ə-rō-sĕk'shōō-ăl'ĭ-tē) s. heterosexualidad *f.*

heu·ris·tic (hyōō-rĭs'tĭk) **I.** adj. heurístico **II.** s. heurística.

hew (hyōō) tr. **hewed, hewed** *o* **hewn** (hyōōn), **hew·ing** *(to shape)* labrar, tallar; *(to cut)* cortar, talar (árboles); *(to cleave)* hendir, partir —intr. hachear, dar golpes; FIG. *(to conform)* conformarse, ajustarse.

hex (hĕks) **I.** s. *(evil spell)* embrujo, maleficio; *(jinx)* aojo, mal de ojo **II.** tr. maleficiar, embrujar.

hex·a·gon (hĕk'sə-gŏn') s. GEOM. hexágono.

hex·ag·o·nal (hĕk-săg'ə-nəl) adj. hexagonal.

hex·a·gram (hĕk'sə-grăm') s. GEOM. hexagrama.

hex·a·he·dron (hĕk'sə-hē'drən) s. [pl. **-drons** *o* **-dra** (-drə)] GEOM. hexaedro.

hex·am·e·ter (hĕk-săm'ĭ-tər) s. LIT. hexámetro.

hey (hā) interj. ¡eh!, ¡oiga!

hey·day (hā'dā') s. *(height)* apogeo, auge (de un período) *m; (prime)* flor *f,* lo mejor (de la vida).

hi (hī) interj. ¡oye!, ¡hola!

hi·a·tus (hī-ā'təs) s. [pl. **-tus** *o* **-tus·es**] *(crack)* grieta, abertura; FIG. *(gap)* vacío, laguna; ANAT., FONÉT. hiato.

hi·ber·nal (hī-bûr'nəl) adj. hibernal, invernal; POÉT. hiemal.

hi·ber·nate (hī'bər-nāt') intr. ZOOL. hibernar; *(to winter)* invernar (personas).

hi·ber·na·tion (hī'bər-nā'shən) s. BIOL. hibernación *f,* invernación *f.*

hi·bis·cus (hī-bĭs'kəs) s. BOT. hibisco.

hic·cup *o* **hic·cough** (hĭk'əp) **I.** s. hipo ♦ **to have the hiccups** tener hipo **II.** intr. **-cupped, -cup·ping** *o* **-coughed, -cough·ing** tener hipo, hipar.

hick (hĭk) FAM. **I.** s. patán *m,* aldeano **II.** adj. rústico, de campo.

hick·o·ry (hĭk'ə-rē) s. [pl. **-ries**] BOT. nogal americano.

hid (hĭd) pret. y part. p. de **hide**[1].

hid·den (hĭd'n) un part. p. de **hide**[1].

hide[1] (hĭd) tr. **hid** (hĭd), **hid·den** (hĭd'n) *o* **hid, hid·ing** *(to put out of sight)* ocultar, esconder; *(to conceal)* ocultar, disimular; *(to cover up)* ocultar, tapar; *(to turn away)* volver (la vista por vergüenza o pena) —intr. *(to keep oneself out of sight)* esconderse, ocultarse; *(to seek refuge)* refugiarse ♦ **to h. out** esconderse.

hide[2] (hĭd) **I.** s. cuero, piel *f* **II.** tr. **hid·ed, hid·ing** dar latigazos ♦ **to tan someone's h.** darle una paliza a • **not to see h. nor hair of** no ver el pelo de.

hide-and-seek (hĭd'n-sēk') s. escondidas, escondite *m* <*to play h.* jugar a las escondidas>.

hide·a·way (hĭd'ə-wā') s. *(hide-out)* escondite *m; (secluded place)* retiro.

hide·bound (hĭd'bound') adj. *(cattle)* con la piel pegada a los huesos; *(narrow-minded)* de miras estrechas, cerrado.

hid·e·ous (hĭd'ē-əs) adj. *(ugly)* espantoso, horrible; *(atrocious)* atroz.

hide-out (hĭd'out') s. *(hideaway)* escondite *m; (for animals, criminals)* madriguera, guarida.

hid·ing (hī'dĭng) s. *(concealment)* ocultación *f; (place)* escondite *m;* FAM. *(beating)* paliza ♦ **h. place** escondite • **in h.** escondido <*to remain in h.* quedarse escondido> • **to**

come out of h. salir de su escondite • **to go into h.** esconderse.

hi·er·arch (hī'ə-rärk') s. jerarca *m.*

hi·er·ar·chic (hī'ə-rär'kĭk) *o* **hi·er·ar·chi·cal** (-kĭ-kəl) adj. jerárquico.

hi·er·ar·chy (hī'ə-rär'kē) s. [pl. **-chies**] jerarquía.

hi·er·at·ic (hī'ə-răt'ĭk) adj. hierático.

hi·er·o·glyph (hī'ər-ə-glĭf') s. jeroglífico.

hi·er·o·glyph·ic (hī'ər-ə-glĭf'ĭk) adj. & s. jeroglífico ♦ **hieroglyphics** jeroglíficos.

hi·fa·lu·tin (hī'fə-lōōt'n) adj. var. de **highfalutin.**

hi-fi (hī'fī') s. *(high fidelity)* alta fidelidad; *(system)* aparato de alta fidelidad.

hig·gle·dy-pig·gle·dy (hĭg'əl-dē-pĭg'əl-dē) **I.** adv. *(in disarray)* desordenadamente; *(confusedly)* sin pies ni cabeza **II.** adj. desordenado, patas arriba.

high (hī) **I.** adj. **-er, -est** *(having height)* alto (montaña, techo); *(tall)* de alto, de altura <*a cabinet ten feet h.* un armario de diez pies de altura>; *(in quantity, quality)* alto, elevado; caro; *(peaking)* culminante <*the h. point* el punto culminante>; *(important)* importante, alto <*a h. official* un alto funcionario>; *(lofty)* elevado, grande <*he has a h. opinion of himself* tiene un gran concepto de sí mismo>; *(wind, fever)* fuerte; *(Mass, street)* mayor; MÚS. *(voice)* agudo; *(note)* alto; GRAM. alto <*H. German* alto alemán>; FONÉT. *(vowel)* cerrado; *(advanced)* avanzado (forma de vida, tecnología); *(of rivers, tides)* alto, crecido; *(serious)* grave (delito); *(treason)* alto; FAM. *(drunk)* borracho; *(drugged)* drogado ♦ **h. and dry** *(person)* plantado, desamparado; *(ship)* en seco • **h. and mighty** FAM. arrogante • **h. priority** primera importancia • **h. society** alta sociedad • **to be h. in** tener un alto contenido de (vitaminas, grasa) • **to be h. time** ya ser hora • **to be in h. spirits** estar de excelente humor • **to get h.** FAM. *(drunk)* emborracharse; *(drugged)* endrogarse • **to live the h. life** vivir por todo lo alto • **to the highest degree** hasta el máximo **II.** adv. **-er, -est** en lo alto, alto ♦ **h. above** *o* **over** muy por encima de • **h. priced** caro, de lujo • **h. up** en lo alto • **to fly h.** FIG. picar muy alto • **to go as h. as** llegar hasta • **to look h. and low** buscar por todas partes • **to run h.** *(spirits)* estar exaltado (ánimos, pasiones) • **to sing h.** cantar en un tono alto *o* agudo **III.** s. *(height)* altura, AUTO. *(gear)* directa; METEOR. zona de alta presión ♦ **on h.** en las alturas • **to be on a h.** JER. *(happy)* estar de excelente humor; *(intoxicated)* estar ahumado • **to reach a h.** *(in intensity)* llegar al punto culminante; *(in quantity)* batir el récord.

high·ball (hī'bôl') s. whisky con agua *o* gaseosa y hielo *m.*

high·born (hī'bôrn') adj. de noble cuna, de alta alcurnia.

high·boy (hī'boi') s. cómoda alta.

high·brow (hī'brou') FAM. **I.** s. *(intellectual)* intelectual *mf; (pedant)* pedante *mf* **II.** adj. culto.

high·chair (hī'châr') s. silla alta para niños.

high-class (hī'klăs') adj. de alta categoría, de primera clase.

high court s. DER. tribunal superior *m.*

high·er (hī'ər) adj. [comp. de **high**] *(more elevated)* más alto; *(greater)* mayor; *(advanced)* superior <*h. mathematics* matemáticas superiores>.

higher education s. enseñanza superior.

high·er-up (hī'ər-ŭp') s. FAM. superior (en rango, clase) *m.*

high explosive s. explosivo de gran potencia.

high·fa·lu·tin (hī'fə-lōōt'n) adj. FAM. pomposo, pretencioso.

high fidelity s. RAD. alta fidelidad.

high-flown (hī'flōn') adj. *(lofty)* sublime, exaltado; *(pretentious)* pomposo, altisonante.

high frequency s. RAD. alta frecuencia.

high-grade (hī'grād') adj. de calidad superior.

high-hand·ed (hī'hăn'dĭd) adj. *(arrogant)* arrogante; *(dictatorial)* tiránico, despótico.

high-hat (hī'hăt') **I.** tr. **-hat·ted, -hat·ting** tratar desdeñosamente (a alguien) **II.** adj. desdeñoso, engreído **III.** s. *(snob)* esnob *mf; (vain person)* vanidoso, presumido.

high·jack (hī'jăk') v. var. de **hijack.**

high jinks s.pl. jarana, jolgorio.

high jump s. DEP. salto de altura.

high·land (hī'lənd) **I.** s. terreno montañoso ♦ **highlands** región montañosa, tierras altas **II.** adj. montañoso ♦ **H.** GEOG. de las regiones montañosas de Escocia.

high·land·er (hī'lən-dər) s. montañés *m* ♦ **H.** habitante de las regiones montañosas de Escocia.

high·lev·el (hī'lĕv'əl) adj. de alto nivel (negociaciones, funcionario).

high·light (hī'līt') **I.** s. ARTE. *(light area)* toque de luz *m*; *(outstanding event)* suceso principal; *(best part)* momento culminante, mejor parte *f* <the h. of the trip la mejor parte del viaje>; *(entertainment)* atracción principal *f* **II.** tr. *(to lighten)* iluminar; *(to emphasize)* hacer resaltar, destacar.

high·ly (hī'lē) adv. *(greatly)* altamente <h. visible altamente visible>; *(extremely)* extremadamente <h. unlikely extremadamente improbable>; *(very)* muy <h. appreciative muy agradecido>; *(very well)* muy bien <a h. paid job un empleo muy bien pagado> ♦ **to speak h. of someone** hablar muy bien de alguien.

High Mass s. RELIG. misa mayor.

high·mind·ed (hī'mīn'dĭd) adj. *(idealistic)* idealista, noble; ANT. *(haughty)* orgulloso, arrogante.

high·ness (hī'nĭs) s. altura ♦ **H.** Alteza.

high noon s. *(noon)* pleno mediodía; *(stage)* cenit *m*, punto culminante.

high·per·for·mance (hī'pər-fôr'məns) adj. AUTO. de alto rendimiento (coche, motor).

high·pitched (hī'pĭcht') adj. MÚS. *(note)* agudo; *(voice)* chillón; *(roof)* empinado; *(activity)* frenético.

high·pow·ered (hī'pou'ərd) o **high·pow·er** (-pou'ər) adj. de alta potencia, de gran fuerza o energía; FIG. *(energetic)* activo, dinámico (persona).

high·pres·sure (hī'prĕsh'ər) adj. de alta presión; FIG., FAM. *(tenacious)* tenaz, insistente (persona).

high relief s. ARTE. alto relieve.

high·rise (hī'rīz') s. edificio de muchos pisos.

high·road (hī'rōd') s. G.B. *(highway)* carretera; *(direct path)* camino real <the h. to happiness el camino real de la felicidad>.

high school s. EDUC. escuela de segunda enseñanza, escuela secundaria ♦ **h. diploma** bachillerato • **h. teacher** maestro de escuela secundaria.

high seas s. alta mar.

high·spir·it·ed (hī'spĭr'ĭ-tĭd) adj. *(daring)* animoso, valiente; *(energetic)* vivo, activo; *(merry)* alegre; *(horse)* brioso.

high·strung (hī'strŭng') adj. muy nervioso.

high·tail (hī'tāl') intr. JER. salir corriendo.

high·tech (hī'tĕk') adj. de tecnología avanzada.

high technology s. tecnología avanzada.

high·ten·sion (hī'tĕn'shən) adj. ELEC. de alta tensión o voltaje.

high·test (hī'tĕst') adj. de alta volatilidad u octanaje (díc. de gasolina).

high tide s. MARÍT. marea alta, pleamar *f*; FIG. *(climax)* culminación *f*, punto culminante.

high·toned (hī'tōnd') adj. *(superior)* de alta categoría; FAM. *(pretentious)* de mucho copete, pretencioso.

high·wa·ter mark (hī'wô'tər) s. MARÍT. marea alta, pleamar *f*; *(of a river)* avenida, crecida (de un río).

high·way (hī'wā') s. carretera, autopista.

high·way·man (hī'wā'mən) s. salteador de caminos *m*.

hi·jack (hī'jăk') tr. FAM. *(to stop and rob)* asaltar (tren, persona); *(goods)* robarse; *(to commandeer)* tomar posesión por fuerza (de un vehículo).

hi·jack·er (hī'jăk'ər) s. *(robber)* asaltante *mf*; *(of airplanes)* secuestrador *m*, pirata aéreo.

hi·jack·ing (hī'jăk'ĭng) s. *(robbery)* asalto; *(takeover)* secuestro.

hike (hīk) **I.** intr. hiked, hik·ing *(for pleasure)* caminar, ir de excursión; *(to travel on foot)* caminar, ir a pie ♦ **to h. up** subirse, arremangarse <this dress hikes up in the back este vestido se sube por detrás> —tr. aumentar (precios, alquileres) ♦ **to h. up** subir **II.** s. *(long walk)* excursión *f*, caminata; *(rise)* aumento, subida ♦ **take a h.!** JER. ¡váyase a paseo o a bañar! • **to go on o to take a h.** ir de excursión.

hik·er (hī'kər) s. excursionista *mf*.

hik·ing (hī'kĭng) s. caminata, excursión a pie *f*.

hi·lar·i·ous (hĭ-lâr'ē-əs) adj. *(situation, joke)* para morirse de risa; *(merry)* muy divertido.

hi·lar·i·ty (hĭ-lâr'ĭ-tē) s. hilaridad *f*.

hill (hĭl) s. *(elevation)* colina, cerro; *(heap)* montón *m*; *(slope)* cuesta ♦ **to be over the h.** FAM. ir cuesta abajo, estar entrado en años.

hill·bil·ly (hĭl'bĭl'ē) s. [pl. **-lies**] FAM. campesino, patán *m*.

hill·ock (hĭl'ək) s. montecillo.

hill·side (hĭl'sīd') s. ladera (de un cerro o colina).

hill·top (hĭl'tŏp') s. cima, cumbre (de un cerro o colina) *f*.

hill·y (hĭl'ē) adj. **-i·er, -i·est** cerril, montuoso.

hilt (hĭlt) s. puño, mango ♦ **to the h.** *(to the limit)* hasta las cachas o cuello; *(thoroughly)* totalmente.

him §G29 (hĭm) pron. pers. le, lo <they accepted h. lo aceptaron>; le <they sent h. a letter le mandaron una carta>; él <the letter was addressed to h. la carta iba dirigida a él>.

him·self §G37 (hĭm-sĕlf') pron. pers. *(reflexively)* se <he hit h. se golpeó>; *(emphatically)* él mismo <he h. couldn't believe it él mismo no podía creerlo>; *(after a preposition)* sí, sí mismo <he talked about h. habló de sí mismo>; *(in person)* en persona, personalmente <he will go h. irá él personalmente ♦ **by h.** solo.

hind¹ (hīnd) adj. trasero, posterior.

hind² (hīnd) s. ZOOL. cierva; ICT. mero.

hin·der (hĭn'dər) tr. *(progress)* dificultar; *(movement)* retardar, obstaculizar; *(person)* entorpecer, incapacitar; *(solution)* impedir; *(negotiations)* obstruir, poner trabas a ♦ **to h. someone from** impedirle a alguien (hacer algo).

hind·er·most (hĭn'dər-mōst') adj. var. de **hindmost.**

Hin·di (hĭn'dē) s. hindi *m*.

hind·most (hīnd'mōst') adj. *(rear)* trasero, posterior; *(last)* último.

hin·drance (hĭn'drəns) s. impedimento, obstáculo.

hind·sight (hīnd'sīt') s. retrospección *f*, visión retrospectiva.

Hin·du (hĭn'dōō) s. & adj. hindú *m*.

Hin·du·ism (hĭn'dōō-ĭz'əm) s. RELIG. hinduismo.

Hin·du·stan (hĭn'dōō-stän') s. Indostán.

Hin·du·sta·ni (hĭn'dōō-stä'nē) **I.** adj. indostánico, indostanés **II.** s. *(inhabitant, language)* indostaní *m*.

hinge (hĭnj) **I.** s. *(device)* bisagra, gozne *m*; ZOOL. *(of mollusks)* charnela; *(of a matter)* eje *m*, punto esencial **II.** tr. hinged, hing·ing poner bisagras a —intr. ♦ **to h. on** depender de.

hin·ny (hĭn'ē) s. [pl. **-nies**] burdégano.

hint (hĭnt) **I.** s. *(intimation)* indicación *f*, insinuación *f*; *(tip)* sugerencia, consejo <hints on buying a car sugerencias para la compra de un automóvil>; *(clue)* idea, pista <just to give you a h. para darle una idea>; *(trace)* pizca ♦ **not a h. of** ni rastro de • **to drop someone a** tirar una indirecta a alguien • **to take a o the h.** darse por aludido **II.** tr. insinuar, dar a entender —intr. ♦ **to h. at** *(to intimate)* insinuar, dar a entender; *(to allude to)* aludir a, hacer alusión.

hin·ter·land (hĭn'tər-länd') s. interior (de un país) *m*.

hip¹ (hĭp) s. ANAT. cadera; ARQ. caballete *m* ♦ **h. joint** ANAT. articulación de la cadera.

hip² (hĭp) adj. JER. **hip·per, hip·pest** *(aware)* al tanto (de la moda, acontecimientos); *(fashionable)* de moda, excéntrico.

hip³ (hĭp) interj. ♦ **h., h., hurrah!** ¡hurra!, ¡viva!, ¡olé!

hip·bone (hĭp'bōn') s. ANAT. cía, hueso de la cadera.

hip·pie (hĭp'ē) s. [pl. **-pies**] hippie *mf*.

hip·po (hĭp'ō) s. [pl. **-pos**] FAM. hipopótamo.

Hip·po·crat·ic oath (hĭp'ə-krăt'ĭk) s. juramento hipocrático.

hip·po·drome (hĭp'ə-drōm') s. HIST. *(stadium)* hipódromo; *(for horse shows)* pista de concursos hípicos.

hip·po·pot·a·mus (hĭp'ə-pŏt'ə-məs) s. [pl. **-mus·es** o **-mi** (-mī')] ZOOL. hipopótamo.

hip·py (hĭp'ē) s. [pl. **-pies**] var. de **hippie.**

hip·ster (hĭp'stər) s. JER. persona al tanto de la moda.

hire (hīr) **I.** tr. hired, hir·ing *(to employ)* contratar, emplear; *(to rent)* alquilar ♦ **now hiring** se necesitan empleados • **to h. out** alquilar —intr. ♦ **to h. out as** aceptar trabajo de (fotógrafo, traductor) **II.** s. *(wages)* sueldo; *(rent)* alquiler *m* ♦ **for h.** se alquila (casa, barco).

hire·ling (hīr′lĭng) s. *(for menial tasks)* asalariado; *(mercenary)* mercenario.

hir·ing (hīr′ĭng) s. *(employment)* contratación *f*, empleo; *(renting)* alquiler *m*.

hir·sute (hûr′sōōt′) adj. hirsuto.

his §G23, 32 (hĭz) **I.** adj. pos. su <*h. wallet* su billetera>; de él <*is that h. towel or hers?* ésa es la toalla de él o la de ella?> **II.** pron. pos. suyo <*these keys are h.* estas llaves son suyas>; el suyo <*I'll drive my car, not h.* manejaré mi automóvil, no el suyo>; de él <*it is h.*, *not his wife's* es de él, no de su esposa>; el de él <*this book is h.* este libro es el de él>.

His·pan·ic (hĭ-spăn′ĭk) **I.** adj. hispánico, hispano **II.** s. norteamericano de ascendencia hispana.

His·pan·i·cism (hĭ-spăn′ĭ-sĭz′əm) s. hispanismo.

His·pan·i·cist (hĭ-spăn′ĭ-sĭst) s. hispanista *mf*.

His·pan·o·phile (hĭ-spăn′ə-fīl′) s. hispanófilo.

His·pan·o·phobe (hĭ-spăn′ə-fōb′) s. hispanófobo.

hiss (hĭs) **I.** s. *(for attention)* siseo (para llamar la atención); *(catcall)* abucheo, silbido (de desagrado o desaprobación); *(whistling)* silbido (de serpiente, aire, vapor) **II.** tr. *(to whistle)* silbar, sisear; *(to boo)* abuchear, silbar —intr. silbar.

his·ta·mine (hĭs′tə-mēn′, -mĭn) s. BIOQUÍM. histamina.

his·tol·o·gist (hĭ-stŏl′ə-jĭst) s. MED. histólogo.

his·tol·o·gy (hĭ-stŏl′ə-jē) s. histología.

his·to·ri·an (hĭ-stôr′ē-ən) s. historiador *m*.

his·to·ric (hĭ-stôr′ĭk) *o* **his·to·ri·cal** (hĭ-stôr′ĭ-kəl) adj. histórico.

his·to·ri·og·ra·pher (hĭ-stôr′ē-ŏg′rə-fər) s. *(specialist)* historiógrafo; *(historian)* historiador oficial *m*.

his·to·ri·og·ra·phy (hĭ-stôr′ē-ŏg′rə-fē) s. historiografía.

his·to·ry (hĭs′tə-rē) s. [pl. **-ries**] *(account, events)* historia; *(background)* historial *m* <*a h. of heart disease* un historial de problemas cardiacos> ♦ **to go down in h.** pasar a la historia • **to make h.** dejar huella en la historia, crear un precedente.

his·tri·on·ic (hĭs′trē-ŏn′ĭk) *o* **his·tri·on·i·cal** (-ĭ-kəl) adj. histriónico, teatral.

his·tri·on·ics (hĭs′trē-ŏn′ĭks) s. [ú. con v. sing.] TEAT. histrionismo; FIG. *(emotional behavior)* [ú. con v. pl.] teatro, comedia.

hit (hĭt) **I.** tr. **hit, hit·ting** *(to strike)* pegar a, golpear; *(to collide with)* chocar contra *o* con <*the train hit a car* el tren chocó contra un auto>; *(to strike with a projectile)* dar en <*he fired and hit the target* disparó y dio en el blanco>; *(to batter)* azotar <*the hurricane hit many cities* el huracán azotó muchas ciudades>; *(to reach)* llegar a, alcanzar; *(to suit)* ajustarse a; FIG., FAM. *(to occur)* ocurrir <*the idea h. me all of a sudden* la idea se me ocurrió de repente> ♦ **to h. home** FIG. tocar un punto vulnerable • **h. it off (with)** FIG., FAM. llevarse bien con, hacer buenas migas con • **to h. on** FIG., FAM. encontrar, dar con (respuesta, solución) • **to h. the ceiling** *o* **roof** FIG., FAM. encolerizarse • **to h. the hay** *o* **the sack** FIG., JER. irse a la cama • **to h. the jackpot** JER. sacarse el premio gordo • **to h. the nail on the head** FIG. dar en el clavo • **to h. the road** FIG., JER. irse, partir • **to h. the spot** FIG., FAM. ser exactamente lo que hace falta —intr. FIG. *(to occur)* desatarse, atacar ♦ **to h. below the belt** FIG., FAM. dar un golpe bajo **II.** s. *(blow)* golpe *m*; *(collision)* choque *m*; *(shot)* tiro; *(success)* éxito ♦ **h. or miss** al azar • **to be a h. with someone** caerle simpático a alguien.

hit-and-run (hĭt′n-rŭn′) adj. que atropella y huye (díc. del conductor de un vehículo).

hitch (hĭch) **I.** tr. *(to hook up)* enganchar; *(oxen)* uncir ♦ **to h. a ride** FAM. hacerse llevar en automóvil • **to h. to** enganchar a <*he hitched the trailer to the car* enganchó el remolque al coche> • **to h. up** *(oxen)* uncir; *(pants, socks)* subirse —intr. FAM. *(to hitchhike)* hacer autostop, viajar a dedo; *(to move haltingly)* andar con vacilación, cojear; *(to get entangled)* enredarse; *(to get fastened)* engancharse a ♦ **to get hitched** FAM. casarse **II.** s. FAM. *(problem)* dificultad *f*, problema *m*; *(impediment)* obstáculo, tropiezo; MIL. *(term of service)* período de servicio militar; MARÍT. *(knot)* vuelta de cabo; *(tug)* tirón *m*; *(limp)* cojera; *(de-*

vice) enganche *m* ♦ **to go off without a h.** salir sin dificultad.

hitch·hike (hĭch′hīk′) intr. hacer autostop —tr. solicitar (un viaje) por autostop.

hitch·hik·er (hĭch′hī′kər) s. autostopista *mf*, el que hace autostop.

hith·er (hĭth′ər) **I.** adv. acá, hacia acá **II.** adj. citerior, más cercano.

hith·er·to (hĭth′ər-tōō′) adv. hasta ahora, hasta aquí.

hive (hīv) **I.** s. *(container)* colmena; *(colony)* enjambre *m*; FIG. *(busy place)* colmena **II.** tr. **hived, hiv·ing** *(bees)* meter en la colmena; *(honey)* guardar; FIG. *(to store up)* acumular, almacenar —intr. FIG. vivir apiñados.

hives (hīvz) s.pl. MED. urticaria.

ho (hō) interj. *(to attract attention)* ¡eh!, ¡oiga!; *(whoa!)* ¡so!, ¡alto!

hoa·gie (hō′gē) s. FAM. sandwich *m o* emparedado grande.

hoar (hôr, hōr) **I.** adj. *(hair)* cano, gris; *(frost)* blanco, blanquizco; *(very old)* vetusto, antiguo **II.** s. escarcha.

hoard (hôrd) **I.** s. *(cache)* tesoro escondido, provisión acumulada (para uso futuro) **II.** intr. acumular, acaparar —intr. atesorar *o* guardar algo (escondiéndolo).

hoard·er (hôr′dər) s. *(amasser)* acumulador (de dinero, fortuna) *m*; *(monopolizer)* acaparador (de artículos, productos) *m*.

hoard·ing (hôr′dĭng) s. G.B. *(fence)* valla *o* cerca provisional (alrededor de una construcción); *(billboard)* valla publicitaria, cartelera.

hoar·frost (hôr′frôst′) s. escarcha, helada blanca.

hoarse (hôrs) adj. **hoars·er, hoars·est** *(voice)* ronco, enronquecido; *(harsh)* discordante, chirriante (sonido).

hoarse·ness (hôrs′nĭs) s. ronquedad *f*, aspereza (sonido); MED. ronquera, carraspera (voz).

hoar·y (hôr′ē) adj. **-i·er, -i·est** *(hair)* cano, blanquecino; BOT., ZOOL. canescente; FIG. *(very old)* vetusto, antiguo.

hoax (hōks) **I.** s. *(practical joke)* broma pesada; *(lie)* engaño, trampa; *(trick)* mistificación *f* **II.** tr. *(to deceive)* engañar, burlar; *(to play a trick on)* gastar una broma pesada.

hob¹ (hŏb) s. *(fireplace shelf)* repisa interior (de la chimenea); MEC. *(tool)* fresa.

hob² (hŏb) s. *(elf)* duende *m*.

hob·ble (hŏb′əl) **I.** intr. **-bled, -bling** cojear, renguear —tr. *(an animal)* trabar, manear; *(to cripple)* hacer cojear; FIG. *(to hamper)* obstaculizar, impedir **II.** s. *(awkward walk)* cojera; *(device)* traba, maniota.

hob·by (hŏb′ē) s. [pl. **-bies**] pasatiempo, afición *f*.

hob·by·horse (hŏb′ē-hôrs′) s. *(toy)* caballito de madera; *(rocking horse)* caballo mecedor; *(topic)* tema favorito; *(obsession)* obsesión *f*.

hob·gob·lin (hŏb′gŏb′lĭn) s. *(elf)* duende *m*; FIG. *(bugbear)* espantajo.

hob·nail (hŏb′nāl′) s. tachuela, clavo (para suelas de botas).

hob·nob (hŏb′nŏb′) intr. **-nobbed, -nob·bing** codearse, tratarse con familiaridad.

ho·bo (hō′bō) [pl. **-boes** *o* **-bos**] *(vagrant)* vago, vagabundo; *(migratory worker)* temporero, trabajador errante *m*.

Hob·son's choice (hŏb′sənz) s. callejón sin salida, elección forzosa.

hock¹ (hŏk) **I.** s. ZOOL. jarrete *m*, corvejón (articulación) *m*; ORNIT. tarso (articulación) **II.** tr. desjarretar.

hock² (hŏk) s. G.B. vino blanco del Rin.

hock³ (hŏk) FAM. **I.** tr. empeñar **II.** s. empeño, prenda.

hock·ey (hŏk′ē) s. DEP. hockey *m* ♦ **ice h.** hockey sobre hielo.

hock·shop (hŏk′shŏp′) s. FAM. casa de empeños.

ho·cus (hō′kəs) tr. *(to deceive)* engañar, trampear; *(to infuse)* echar una droga en (comida o bebida).

ho·cus-po·cus (hō′kəs-pō′kəs) **I.** s. *(magic trick)* pasapasa *m*, truco; *(trickery)* engaño, trampa **II.** tr. engañar, trampear **III.** interj. abracadabra.

hod (hŏd) s. *(trough)* cuezo, capecho (de albañil); *(coal scuttle)* cubo para carbón.

hodge-podge (hŏj′pŏj′) s. mezcolanza, almodrote *m*.

hoe (hō) **I.** s. azada, azadón *m* **II.** tr. & intr. **hoed, hoe·ing** azadonar.

hoe-down (hō'doun') s. contradanza norteamericana.
hog I. s. ZOOL. cerdo, puerco; FIG., FAM. *(pig)* cerdo, cochino ♦ **to go whole h.** FIG., FAM. ir hasta el final • **to live high on the h.** FIG., FAM. vivir en la abundancia II. tr. **hogged, hog·ging** acaparar.
ho·gan (hō'gän') s. choza típica de los indios navajos.
hog·gish (hō'gĭsh, hŏg'ĭsh) adj. *(greedy)* voraz, egoísta; *(gluttonous)* glotón; *(filthy)* puerco, guarro.
hogs·head (hôgz'hĕd') s. *(unit)* medida equivalente aproximadamente a 239 litros; *(barrel)* barril *m*, tonel *m*.
hog-tie *o* **hog·tie** (hôg'tī') tr. **-tied, -ty·ing** *o* **-tie·ing** *(to tie)* atar juntas las patas de; FIG. *(to impede)* poner trabas, inmovilizar.
hog·wash (hôg'wŏsh') s. *(swill)* bazofia, desperdicios (para alimentar a los cerdos); FIG. *(nonsense)* disparates *m*, tonterías.
ho-hum (hō'hŭm') interj. expresa aburrimiento.
hoi pol·loi (hoi' pǝ-loi') s. populacho, masas.
hoist (hoist) I. tr. *(to lift up)* alzar, levantar; *(to raise)* enarbolar, izar (banderas, velas) II. s. *(crane)* grúa; *(derrick)* cabria; *(lift)* montacargas *m*.
hoi·ty-toi·ty (hoi'tē-toi'tē) adj. presumido ♦ **to be** *o* **act h.** darse pote.
hok·ey (hō'kē) adj. **-i·er, i·est** JER. *(corny)* cursi; *(trite)* banal; *(artificial)* artificial; *(phony)* falso.
ho·kum (hō'kǝm) s. *(nonsense)* faramalla, farfolla, *(artifice)* artificio (para atraer al público).
hold¹ (hōld) I. tr. **held, hold·ing** *(to grasp)* asir, agarrar <*h. the racket firmly* agarra la raqueta con fuerza>; *(to take)* sostener, tener; *(to support)* sujetar, sostener <*the nail was too small to h. the mirror* el clavo era muy pequeño para sostener el espejo>; *(to keep in place)* mantener, sujetar <*I will h. the ladder while you change the light bulb* yo sujetaré la escalera mientras tú cambias la bombilla>; *(to own)* ser dueño de, poseer <*this organization holds a lot of property* esta organización es dueña de muchas propiedades>; *(to keep in custody)* tener bajo custodia <*they are holding him for questioning* le tienen bajo custodia para interrogarle>; *(to keep)* retener <*h. him until I get there* reténganle hasta que yo llegue>; *(to accommodate)* tener capacidad para, caber <*the car holds six people* en este automóvil caben seis personas>; *(to control)* detener, contener <*the dam held the flood waters* la presa contuvo las aguas de la inundación>; MIL. *(to occupy)* ocupar, retener <*the soldiers held the village for three days* los soldados ocuparon el pueblo durante tres días>; *(to defend)* defender <*to h. the fort* defender el fuerte>; *(to maintain)* continuar, seguir <*an airplane holding course* un avión que mantiene su rumbo>; *(to sustain)* mantener (interés, atención); *(to reserve)* reservar; *(to consider)* creer <*I h. his statement to be true* creo que su declaración es verdadera>; *(to occupy)* desempeñar, ocupar (puesto, cargo); *(to convene)* celebrar <*the board held its first meeting yesterday* la junta celebró su primera reunión ayer>; *(to possess)* poseer, tener (título); MÚS. sostener; *(to reserve)* guardar, reservar <*we are holding a room for you* reservamos un cuarto para usted> ♦ **h. everything!** *(just a moment)* ¡un momento!; *(stop)* ¡paren! • **h. it!** *(don't move)* ¡no se muevan!; *(wait)* ¡esperen! • **h. the phone!** FIG. ¡un momento! • **h. your horses!** FIG., FAM. ¡espérate un momento! • **not to h. a candle to** FIG., FAM. no poder compararse con • **to be left holding the bag** FIG., FAM. *(to be stuck)* cargar con el muerto; *(to be empty-handed)* quedarse con las manos vacías • **to h. a conversation (with)** tener una conversación (con) • **to h. a grudge** guardar rencor • **to h. a gun on** apuntar con una pistola a • **to h. an inquest** *o* **inquiry** hacer una encuesta • **to h. at bay** mantener *o* tener a raya • **to h. back** *(to retain)* reprimir, contener; *(to impede)* impedir • **to h. captive** mantener cautivo • **to h. court** presidir el tribunal • **to h. dear** estimar, apreciar • **to h. down** *(to oppress)* oprimir; *(to pin down)* sujetar, mantener sujeto (persona); *(to contain)* contener, moderar (precios) • **to h. down a job** *(to have a job)* tener un trabajo; *(to keep a job)* conservar el puesto de trabajo • **to h. hands** ir cogidos de la mano • **to h. in** *(emotions)* contener, reprimir; *(one's stomach)* contraer • **to h. it against someone** guardar rencor a alguien

• **to h. it in** JER. aguantarse • **to h. off** *(to put off)* aplazar, demorar (decisión); *(to keep away)* alejar, apartar (enemigo) • **to h. one's breath** *(not to breathe)* contener la respiración; *(to wait)* FIG., FAM. esperar • **to h. one's ground** mantenerse firme • **to h. one's head high** llevar la cabeza muy alta • **to h. one's liquor** beber sin embriagarse, aguantar la bebida • **to h. one's own** defenderse • **to h. one's tongue** callar, guardar silencio • **to h. on tight** agarrar fuertemente • **to h. on to** *(to grip)* asirse de, agarrarse a <*h. on to the banister* agárrate al pasamanos>; *(to keep)* seguir con • **to h. out** *(hope)* dar (esperanza); *(one's tongue)* alargar, tender • **to h. (something) over** *(to threaten)* amenazar con (algo); *(to extend)* continuar; *(to assert)* afirmar, sostener que • **to h. the fort** FIG. quedarse vigilando • **to h. the line on** FIG. mantenerse firme • **to h. to** hacer cumplir <*he held her to her promise* le hizo cumplir su promesa> • **to h. together** mantener unido • **to h. up** FAM. *(to delay)* demorar, atrasar <*the traffic held us up* el tráfico nos atrasó>; *(to rob)* asaltar, atracar (persona, banco); *(to lift)* levantar, alzar; *(to keep up)* sujetar; *(to stop)* detener, parar <*what's holding up traffic?* ¿qué es lo que detiene el tráfico?> • **to h. water** FIG. ser lógico *o* válido (razón, argumento) —intr. *(to grip)* asirse, agarrarse <*h. tight!* ¡agárrate fuerte!>; *(to be firm)* mantenerse, sostenerse; *(to be valid)* valer, seguir en vigor <*my offer still holds* mi oferta sigue en vigor> ♦ **h. on, please** un momento por favor, no cuelgue (el auricular del teléfono) • **to h. back** *(to vacillate)* vacilar; *(to refrain from acting)* contenerse • **to h. forth on** hablar de • **to h. off** *(to maintain a distance)* mantenerse a distancia; *(to delay)* tardar, demorarse • **to h. on** *(to grip)* agarrarse bien; *(to continue)* seguir, proseguir; *(to wait)* aguardar, esperar • **to h. out** *(to last)* durar <*these tires should h. out another year* estos neumáticos durarán otro año>; *(to resist)* aguantar, resistir <*the troops held out bravely without food* las tropas resistieron valientemente sin comida>; *(not to yield)* no ceder • **to h. out on (someone)** FAM. tener secretos con • **to h. over** aplazar, diferir • **to h. to** continuar *o* seguir firme en • **to h. up** *(of weather)* seguir bueno <*I hope the weather holds up* espero que el tiempo siga bueno>; *(of good weather)* seguir funcionando, aguantar II. s. *(grip)* asidero; *(influence)* influencia <*a writer with a strong h. on the public* un escritor de gran influencia en el público>; *(control)* control *m*, dominio; *(prison cell)* celda (de prisión); MÚS. calderón *m* ♦ **to gain a firm h. over someone** llegar a dominar a alguien • **to get a h. of** *(to grasp)* agarrar, coger; *(to obtain)* procurar, conseguir; *(to find)* encontrar • **to get a h. on** *o* **of oneself** controlarse, dominarse • **to have a h. on** *o* **over** tener gran influencia sobre • **to lose one's h. (on)** perder el control de.
hold² (hōld) s. MARÍT. bodega; AER. cabina de carga.
hold·er (hōl'dǝr) s. *(person)* poseedor *m*; *(owner)* propietario; *(tenant)* arrendatario; *(handle)* agarradera, asidero; FIN. *(of bonds, shares)* poseedor, tenedor *m*; *(of passport, title)* titular *mf*; *(of cigarettes)* boquilla.
hold·ing (hōl'dĭng) s. arrendamiento, inquilinato ♦ **holdings** FIN. *(property)* propiedades; *(capital)* valores en cartera; *(land)* posesión *o* pertenencia (de tierras).
holding company s. FIN. compañía tenedora *o* matriz.
hold·out (hōld'out') s. persona que obstaculiza un acuerdo.
hold·o·ver (hōld'ō'vǝr) s. remanente (esp. una persona que permanece en su puesto después de haber concluido su período normal) *m*.
hold·up (hōld'ŭp') s. *(delay)* demora; *(robbery)* asalto, atraco (a mano armada).
hole (hōl) I. s. *(hollow)* hueco; *(in the ground)* hoyo; *(in a road)* bache *m*; *(small opening)* agujero <*a h. in the radiator* un agujero en el radiador>; *(large opening)* boquete *m*; *(in the clouds)* claro, abertura; *(burrow)* madriguera, cueva; *(squalid dwelling)* ratonera; *(town)* pueblo de mala muerte; *(dungeon)* cueva, mazmorra; *(flaw)* falla; *(predicament)* apuro, aprieto <*I got him out of the h.* le saqué del apuro>; *(in golf)* hoyo ♦ **h. in one** FIG. hoyo en uno • **h. in the wall** FIG. ratonera • **in the h.** FAM. endeudado • **to make a h. in** FIG. llevarse una buena tajada de II. tr. **holed, hol·ing** agujerear —intr. ♦ **to h. up** esconderse.

ā rey / ä año / b boca / ch chico / d dar / ĕ el / ē mil / g gato / h joya / hw juez / ī aire / k casa / kw cuan /

hol·i·day (hŏl′ĭ-dā′) **I.** s. día feriado <*the 4th of July is a h.* el 4 de julio es un día feriado>; RELIG. *(holy day)* fiesta de guardar, día de fiesta; *(day off)* día libre, asueto ♦ **holidays** G.B. vacaciones **II.** intr. G.B. veranear, pasar las vacaciones.

ho·li·er-than-thou (hō′lē-ər-*thən-thou*′) adj. santurrón.

ho·li·ness (hō′lē-nĭs) s. santidad *f* ♦ **His H.** RELIG. Su Santidad.

ho·lism (hō′lĭz′əm) s. FILOS. holismo.

hol·land (hŏl′ənd) s. TEJ. holanda, holán *m.*

Hol·land (hŏl′ənd) s. Holanda.

Hol·land·er (hŏl′ən-dər) s. holandés *m.*

hol·ler (hŏl′ər) **I.** intr. & tr. gritar **II.** s. grito.

hol·low (hŏl′ō) **I.** adj. *(not solid)* hueco, ahuecado; *(concave)* cóncavo; *(sunken)* hundido; *(reverberating)* retumbante, resonante (sonido); FIG. *(insincere)* falso; *(deceptive)* engañoso; *(empty)* vano <*a h. triumph* un triunfo vano> **II.** s. *(hole)* cavidad *f*, hueco; *(concavity)* concavidad *f*; *(depression)* depresión *f*; FIG. *(emptiness)* vacío <*a h. in one's life* un vacío en la vida de uno>; *(where people live)* hondonada **III.** tr. ♦ **to h. out** ahuecar —intr. ahuecarse.

hol·low·ness (hŏl′ō-nĭs) s. *(hole)* cavidad *f*, hueco, FIG. *(falseness)* falsedad *f*, falsía.

hol·ly (hŏl′ē) s. [pl. **-lies**] BOT. acebo.

hol·ly·hock (hŏl′ē-hŏk′) s. BOT. malva loca, malvarrosa.

Hol·ly·wood (hŏl′ē-wŏŏd′) s. Hollywood.

hol·mi·um (hŏl′mē-əm) s. QUÍM. holmio.

holm oak s. BOT. encina.

ho·lo·caust (hŏ′lə-kôst′, hŏl′ə-) s. *(destruction)* destrucción completa (por el fuego); *(sacrifice)* holocausto, sacrificio ♦ **the H.** HIST. exterminio en masa de los judíos europeos por los nazis.

ho·lo·gram (hŏ′lə-grăm′, hŏl′ə-) s. FOTOG. holograma *m.*

ho·lo·graph (hŏ′lə-grăf′, hŏl′ə-) s. DER. hológrafo, ológrafo; *(hologram)* holograma *m.*

ho·lo·graph·ic (hŏ′lə-grăf′ĭk, hŏl′ə-) o **ho·lo·graph·i·cal** (-ĭ-kəl) adj. hológrafo.

ho·log·ra·phy (hŏ-lŏg′rə-fē) s. FOTOG. holografía, fotografía en tres dimensiones.

hol·ster (hōl′stər) s. pistolera, funda de pistola.

ho·ly (hō′lē) adj. RELIG. **-li·er, li·est** *(sacred)* santo, sacro; *(consecrated)* consagrado, bendito; *(revered)* venerable; *(saintly)* santo, pío.

Holy Ark s. RELIG. Arca Sagrada (en el judaísmo).

Holy Communion s. RELIG. Sagrada Comunión.

holy day o **ho·ly·day** (hō′lē-dā′) s. RELIG. fiesta de guardar, día de fiesta *m.*

Holy Father s. RELIG. Santo Padre.

Holy Ghost s. RELIG. Espíritu Santo.

Holy Grail s. RELIG. Santo Grial.

Holy Land s. Tierra Santa.

Holy Office s. RELIG. Santo Oficio.

holy orders s. RELIG. órdenes sagradas ♦ **to take h.** RELIG. ordenarse.

Holy See s. Santa Sede.

Holy Spirit s. RELIG. Espíritu Santo.

holy water s. RELIG. agua bendita.

hom·age (hŏm′ĭj, ŏm′-) s. DER., HIST. ceremonia de sumisión del vasallo al señor feudal; *(honor)* homenaje *m.*

home (hōm) s. *(house)* casa <*they did not search his h.* no registraron su casa>; *(residence)* domicilio <*we mailed the letter to your h.* le enviamos la carta a su domicilio>; *(household)* hogar *m* <*divorce ruins many homes* el divorcio destruye muchos hogares>; *(headquarters)* sede *f* <*h. of the dance company* la sede de la compañía de baile>; *(institution)* asilo <*a h. for the elderly* un asilo de ancianos> ♦ **a h. away from h.** lugar donde uno está como en su propia casa • **at h. and abroad** dentro y fuera del país • **make yourself at h.** está usted en su casa • **rest h.** sanatorio, casa de reposo • **to be away from h.** estar de viaje, estar fuera • **to be** o **feel at h.** *(in a place)* sentirse como en la casa de uno; *(in a situation)* sentirse a gusto • **to make oneself at h.** ponerse cómodo • **to make one's h.** establecerse **II.** adj. *(pertaining to a home)* casero, doméstico <*h. cooking* cocina casera>; *(pertaining to a family)* de familia

<*h. life* vida de familia>; *(national)* nacional, del país <*h. front* frente nacional>; *(native)* natal, nativo; *(internal)* interior (mercado, política); *(team)* local, de casa; *(game)* en casa ♦ **h. address** dirección (particular) • **h. port** puerto de origen **III.** adv. ♦ **at h.** en casa <*we'll be at h. tonight* estaremos en casa esta noche> • **nothing to write h. about** nada del otro mundo • **to be h.** *(not out)* estar, estar en casa <*is your father h.?* ¿está tu padre?>; *(after a trip)* estar de vuelta, llegar • **to come h.** volver, regresar a casa • **to go h.** irse a casa <*she went h.* se fue a casa> • **to see** o **take someone h.** acompañar a alguien hasta casa • **to strike** o **hit h.** dar en el blanco (flecha, palabras) • **to stay h.** quedarse en casa **IV.** intr. **homed, hom·ing** *(pigeons)* volver a casa; *(missile, aircraft)* autodirigirse ♦ **h. in on** acercarse <*they were homing in on the truth* se estaban acercando a la verdad>.

home base s. DEP. base meta *f* ♦ **to get to h.** FIG. alcanzar una meta.

home·bod·y (hōm′bŏd′ē) s. [pl. **-ies**] persona hogareña, persona casera.

home-brew (hōm′brōō′) s. bebida alcohólica hecha en casa (esp. cerveza).

home·com·ing (hōm′kŭm′ĭng) s. regreso al hogar.

home economics s. economía doméstica.

home economist s. ecónomo.

home front s. frente civil (en una guerra) *m.*

home-grown (hōm′grōn′) adj. de cosecha propia.

home·land (hōm′lănd′) s. patria.

home·less (hōm′lĭs) adj. sin hogar.

home·li·ness (hōm′lē-nĭs) s. *(lack of beauty)* falta de atractivo, fealdad *f*; *(simplicity)* simplicidad *f*, sencillez *f.*

home·ly (hōm′lē) adj. **-li·er, -li·est** *(not attractive)* sin atractivo, feúcho; *(domestic)* doméstico, casero; *(plain)* sencillo, llano; *(unsophisticated)* rústico, tosco.

home·made (hōm′mād′) adj. hecho en casa, casero.

home·mak·er (hōm′mā′kər) s. ama de casa.

ho·me·op·a·thy (hō′mē-ŏp′ə-thē) s. MED. homeopatía (método).

ho·me·o·path·ic (hō′mē-ō-păth′ĭk) adj. homeopático, homeópta.

ho·me·o·sta·sis (hō′mē-ō-stā′sĭs) s. BIOL. homeóstasis *f.*

hom·er (hō′mər) s. *(in baseball)* jonrón *m*; *(pigeon)* paloma mensajera.

home rule s. POL. autonomía.

home run s. DEP. jonrón *m.*

home·sick (hōm′sĭk′) adj. nostálgico.

home·spun (hōm′spŭn′) **I.** adj. *(woven in the home)* tejido en casa; *(homemade)* casero; *(simple)* sencillo **II.** s. tela tejida en casa.

home·stead (hōm′stĕd′) **I.** s. *(farm)* granja; FAM. *(home)* casa, hogar *m* **II.** intr. & tr. tomar posesión legalmente (de tierras).

home·stretch (hōm′strĕch′) s. etapa final.

home·town (hōm′toun′) s. *(birthplace)* ciudad *f* o pueblo de origen; *(town of residence)* ciudad o pueblo de residencia.

home·ward (hōm′wərd) **I.** adj. de vuelta, de regreso (a casa) **II.** adv. hacia casa ♦ **homewards** (-wərdz) hacia casa.

home·work (hōm′wûrk′) s. *(schoolwork)* deberes *m*, tareas escolares; FIG. *(preparation)* trabajo preliminar.

hom·ey (hō′mē) adj. **-i·er, -i·est** FAM. *(homelike)* hogareño; *(intimate)* íntimo.

hom·i·cid·al (hŏm′ĭ-sīd′l, hŏ′mĭ-) adj. homicida.

hom·i·cide (hŏm′ĭ-sīd′, hŏ′mĭ-) s. *(murder)* homicidio; *(murderer)* homicida *mf.*

hom·i·ly (hŏm′ə-lē) s. [pl. **-lies**] *(sermon)* homilía, sermón *m*; FIG. *(lecture)* sermón, rapapolvo.

homing pigeon s. paloma mensajera.

hom·i·nid (hŏm′ə-nĭd′) s. & adj. homínido.

hom·i·noid (hŏm′ə-noid′) adj. & s. ANTROP., ZOOL. hominoideo.

hom·i·ny (hŏm′ə-nē) s. CUL. maíz pelado y seco ♦ **h. grits** CUL. maíz molido grueso.

ho·mo¹ (hō′mō) s. ANTROP. homo (individuo, género).

ho·mo² (hō′mō) s. [pl. **ho·mos**] JER. homosexual *mf.*

ho·mo·e·rot·i·cism (hō′mō-ĭ-rŏt′ĭ-sīz′əm) o **ho·mo·er·o·tism** (-ĕr′ə-tīz′əm) s. homoerotismo, homosexualidad *f.*

ho·mo·ge·ne·i·ty (hō'mə-jə-nē'ĭ-tē, hŏm'ə-) s. homogeneidad f.

ho·mo·ge·ne·ous (hō'mə-jē'nē-əs) adj. homogéneo.

ho·mog·e·ni·za·tion (hō-mŏj'ə-nĭ-zā'shən) s. homogeneización f.

ho·mog·e·nize (hō-mŏj'ə-nīz') tr. hacer homogéneo, homogeneizar.

hom·o·graph (hŏm'ə-grăf') s. GRAM. homógrafo.

ho·mol·o·gous (hō-mŏl'ə-gəs) adj. BIOL., MAT., QUÍM. homólogo (órganos, términos, compuestos).

hom·o·logue o **hom·o·log** (hŏm'ə-lôg', hō'mə-) s. BIOL., MAT., QUÍM. órgano, elemento o compuesto homólogo.

ho·mol·o·gy (hō-mŏl'ə-jē) s. [pl. **-gies**] BIOL., LÓG., MAT. homología.

hom·o·nym (hŏm'ə-nĭm', hō'mə-) s. BIOL., GRAM. homónimo.

ho·mo·phile (hō'mə-fīl') adj. & s. homosexual mf; (advocate) defensor de los homosexuales m.

hom·o·phone (hŏm'ə-fōn', hō'mə-) s. GRAM. homófono.

hom·o·phon·ic (hŏm'ə-fŏn'ĭk) adj. GRAM. homófono; MÚS. unísono.

ho·moph·o·ny (hō-mŏf'ə-nē) s. GRAM., MÚS. homofonía.

ho·mo·sex·u·al (hō'mō-sĕk'shōō-əl) adj. & s. homosexual mf.

ho·mo·sex·u·al·i·ty (hō'mō-sĕk'shōō-ăl'ĭ-tē) s. homosexualidad f.

ho·mun·cu·lus (hō-mŭng'kyə-ləs) s. [pl. **-li** (-lī')] (small man) homúnculo, duendecillo; (manikin) hombrecillo, enano.

hom·y (hō'mē) adj. var. de **homey**.

hon·cho (hŏn'chō) JER. I. s. jefe m, caudillo II. tr. ser jefe de.

Hon·du·ran (hŏn-dŏŏr'ən, -dyŏŏr'-) adj. & s. hondureño.

Hon·du·ras (hŏn-dŏŏr'əs, -dyŏŏr'-) s. Honduras f.

hone (hōn) I. s. (whetstone) piedra de afilar; (tool) muela de esmerilar II. tr. **honed, hon·ing** (to sharpen) afilar; FIG. (to perfect) perfeccionar, pulir <you must h. your writing style debes pulir tu estilo>.

hon·est (ŏn'ĭst) I. adj. (decent) honesto; (honorable) honrado, recto; (truthful) veraz; (sincere) sincero, franco; (genuine) genuino, legítimo; (fair) justo, equitativo; (virtuous) decente II. interj. te lo juro, te lo prometo <I didn't do it, h. no lo he hecho yo, te lo aseguro>.

hon·est·ly (ŏn'ĭst-lē) adv. (decently) honestamente; (frankly) sinceramente, francamente.

hon·es·ty (ŏn'ĭ-stē) s. honestidad f; (integrity) integridad f, honradez f; (truthfulness) veracidad f; (sincerity) sinceridad f, franqueza f.

hon·ey (hŭn'ē) I. s. (of bees) miel f; FIG. (sweetness) dulzura; (term of endearment) tesoro, encanto ♦ **a h. of a** una maravilla de II. tr. **-eyed** o **-ied, -ey·ing** (to sweeten) endulzar; FIG. (to flatter) engatusar, halagar.

hon·ey·bee (hŭn'ē-bē') s. ENTOM. abeja (melera).

hon·ey·comb (hŭn'ē-kōm') I. s. panal m; FIG., CONSTR. panales; METAL. sopladura II. tr. (to perforate) acribillar, agujerear; (to riddle) permear.

hon·ey·dew (hŭn'ē-dōō') s. (secretion) ligamaza, secreción dulce de algunos insectos y plantas; (melon) variedad de melón dulce.

honeydew melon s. una variedad de melón dulce.

hon·eyed (hŭn'ēd) adj. (with honey) con miel, endulzado con miel; FIG. (sweet) meloso.

hon·ey·moon (hŭn'ē-mōōn') I. s. luna de miel II. intr. pasar la luna de miel.

hon·ey·moon·er (hŭn'ē-mōō'nər) s. recién casado.

hon·ey·suck·le (hŭn'ē-sŭk'əl) s. BOT. madreselva.

Hong Kong (hŏng'kŏng') s. Hong Kong.

hon·ied (hŭn'ēd) adj. var. de **honeyed**.

honk (hŏngk) I. s. (goose cry) graznido (del ganso); (horn sound) bocinazo (de un automóvil) II. tr. & intr. tocar la bocina.

hon·ky o **hon·kie** (hŏng'kē) s. [pl. **-kies**] DESPEC., JER. blanquito (palabra despectiva para personas de la raza blanca).

hon·ky-tonk (hŏng'kē-tŏngk') I. s. JER. tabernucho II. adj. MÚS. de ritmo sincopado y clásico del jazz III. intr. JER. andar por tabernuchos.

hon·or (ŏn'ər) I. s. (virtue) honor m, honra f; (decoration) condecoración f; (probity) probidad f ♦ **on my h.!** ¡palabra de honor! • **to be on one's h.** estar obligado por el honor • **to consider it an h. to** tener la honra • **to do the honors** rendir honores • **to graduate with honors** obtener un título con la máxima calificación • **word of h.** palabra de honor • **your H.** Su Señoría II. tr. (to esteem) honrar; COM. aceptar (un cheque) ♦ **to h. a contract** cumplir un contrato • **to h. one's word** cumplir la palabra.

hon·or·a·ble (ŏn'ər-ə-bəl) adj. (decent) honorable; (praiseworthy) honroso; (honest) honrado; (illustrious) excelentísimo (gobernador, alcalde); (honorific) honorífico.

honorable mention s. accésit m, mención honorífica.

hon·or·a·bly (ŏn'ər-ə-blē) adv. honorablemente.

hon·o·rar·i·um (ŏn'ə-râr'ē-əm) s. [pl. **-i·ums** o **-i·a** (-ē-ə)] honorarios.

hon·or·ar·y (ŏn'ə-rĕr'ē) adj. honorario.

hon·or·ee (ŏn'ə-rē') s. homenajeado.

hon·or·if·ic (ŏn'ə-rĭf'ĭk) I. adj. honorífico II. s. tratamiento honorífico.

hon·our (ŏn'ər) s. & v. G.B. var. de **honor**.

hood (hōod) s. (of a garment) capucha, caperuza; (of an academic robe) muceta; (of a falcon) capirote m; (of a fireplace) campana; (of a carriage) capota; (of a car) capó; (of a bird) cresta.

hood·ed (hōod'ĭd) adj. (with hood) encapuchado, con capucha; (hood-shaped) con forma de capucha; ZOOL. encapirotado.

hood·lum (hōod'ləm, hōod'-) s. (gangster) maleante m, matón m; (ruffian) rufián m.

hoo·doo (hōo'dōo) I. s. [pl. **-doos**] (voodoo) vudú m; (bad luck) yeta II. tr. ojar, embrujar.

hood·wink (hōod'wĭngk') tr. (to deceive) engañar; (to trick) embaucar; ANT. (to blindfold) vendar (los ojos); ANT. (to conceal) esconder.

hoo·ey (hōo'ē) s. JER. (nonsense) tonterías.

hoof (hōof, hōof) I. s. [pl. **hoofs** o **hooves** (hōovz, hōovz)] (of an animal) pezuña; JER. (of a person) pata, pie m II. tr. ♦ **to h. it** FAM. ir andando —intr. JER. (to dance) bailar; (to walk) caminar.

hoofed (hōoft, hōoft) adj. (having hoofs) con cascos; (ungulate) ungulado.

hoof·er (hōof'ər) s. bailarín (esp. de zapateado) m.

hook (hōok) I. s. (for catching, suspending) gancho, garfio <a picture h. un gancho para colgar cuadros>; (for fishing) anzuelo; (dress fastener) corchete m; (in a road) curva, recodo; (for clothes) percha; (sickle) hoz f; DEP. (in baseball) curva; (in boxing) gancho ♦ **by h. or by crook** por las buenas o por las malas • **h., line, and sinker** JER. del todo • **hooks** FAM. garras • **off the h.** descolgado (teléfono) • **to get one's hooks into** FAM. echarle mano a, agarrar • **to let someone off the h.** JER. dejar que alguien se escape II. tr. (to fasten) enganchar <to h. a trailer to a car enganchar un remolque a un coche>; FIG., FAM. (to snare) pescar <she couldn't h. him no le pudo pescar>; JER. (to steal) robar; (to bend) encorvar, doblar (en forma de gancho); (to pierce) enganchar; DEP. (in boxing) dar un gancho a ♦ **to get hooked on** JER. (to become addicted to) enviciarse con; (to get caught on) engancharse en • **to h. up** (to attach) enganchar; ELEC. (to couple) acoplar; (to wire) poner los cables a; (to connect) conectar; (to assemble) armar; (to fasten clothes) abrocharse —intr. (to bend) encorvarse; (to turn) doblar, torcer; (to be fastened) engancharse ♦ **to h. up** abrocharse.

hook·ah (hōok'ə) s. (pipe) narguile (pipa turca) m.

hook-and-lad·der truck (hōok'ən-lăd'ər) s. camión de bomberos (que acarrea las escalerillas) m.

hooked (hōokt) adj. (bent) ganchudo; (with a hook) con gancho; FIG. (addicted) adicto a las drogas; (trapped) enviciado ♦ **h. rug** alfombra de nudo.

hook·er (hōok'ər) s. (one that hooks) enganchador m; JER. (prostitute) prostituta.

hook-nosed (hōok'nōzd') adj. de nariz aguileña.

hook·up (hōok'ŭp') s. ELEC., RAD., TELEV. (circuits) red de circuitos f; (system) sistema de conexión m; (transmission) transmisión en circuito f; FIG., FAM. (connection) conexión f.

ā rey / ä año / b boca / ch chico / d dar / ĕ el / ē mil / g gato / h joya / hw juez / ī aire / k casa / kw cuan /

hook·worm (hŏŏk'wûrm') s. ZOOL. anquilostoma *m*, lombriz intestinal *m*.

hook·y (hŏŏk'ē) s. FAM. ausencia injustificada ♦ **to play h.** hacer novillos.

hoo·li·gan (hŏŏ'lĭ-gən) s. FAM. rufián *m*, maleante *m*.

hoop (hŏŏp, hōōp) I. s. *(circle)* aro; *(circular band)* fleje (de tonel) *m*, zuncho II. tr. *(to hold together)* enzunchar; *(to circle)* cercar, ceñir.

hoop·la (hŏŏp'lä', hōōp'-) s. *(commotion)* alboroto; *(misleading talk)* galimatías.

hoop skirt s. miriñaque *m*.

hoo·ray (hŏŏ-rā') interj., s., & v. var. de **hurrah.**

hoot (hŏŏt) I. intr. *(owl)* ulular; *(to boo)* abuchear ♦ **to h. with laughter** carcajearse —tr. *(to boo)* abuchear; *(to express)* manifestar a gritos II. s. *(of an owl)* ululato; *(of a car)* bocinazo; *(shout)* grito; *(cry of derision)* risotada ♦ **it was a h.** JER. era para morirse de risa • **not to give a h.** no importarle a uno un comino.

hoot·en·an·ny (hŏŏt'n-ăn'ē) s. reunión en que se toca música folklórica *f*.

hooves (hŏŏvz, hōōvz) un pl. de **hoof.**

hop[1] (hŏp) I. intr. **hopped, hop·ping** *(to jump)* saltar, brincar <*to h. out of bed* saltar de la cama>; *(to skip)* saltar con un pie, saltar a la pata coja ♦ **to h. to it** echar manos a la obra —tr. *(to jump)* saltar, brincar; *(to jump aboard)* subirse, coger (un vehículo) II. *(jump)* brinco, salto; *(rebound)* rebote *m*; FAM. *(dance)* baile *m*; *(short trip)* vuelo corto ♦ **h., skip, and a jump** distancia corta.

hop[2] (hŏp) I. s. BOT. *(vine)* lúpulo; JER. *(narcotic)* narcótico, estupefaciente *m* II. tr. **hopped, hop·ping** sazonar con lúpulo ♦ **hops** frutos desecados del lúpulo.

hope (hŏp) I. intr. **hoped, hop·ing** *(to wish)* esperar; ANT. *(to trust)* tener fe ♦ **I should h. so!** ¡eso espero! • **to h. against h.** aferrarse a la esperanza • **to h. for** tener esperanzas de —tr. esperar II. s. esperanza ♦ **to be beyond h.** ser un caso desesperado • **to build up** *o* **raise one's hopes** hacerse ilusiones • **to have high hopes** tener muchas esperanzas.

hope·ful (hŏp'fəl) I. adj. *(having hope)* esperanzado; *(hope-inspiring)* que inspira esperanza; *(promising)* prometedor II. s. *(aspirant)* aspirante *m*; *(candidate)* candidato (político).

hope·ful·ly (hŏp'fə-lē) adv. *(in a hopeful manner)* esperanzadamente; *(it is to be hoped)* se espera, es de esperarse.

hope·ful·ness (hŏp'fəl-nĭs) s. *(hope)* esperanza; *(promise)* promesa (de un futuro mejor).

hope·less (hŏp'lĭs) adj. *(despairing)* desesperado; *(bleak)* desolado; *(incurable)* incurable; *(impossible)* imposible ♦ **h. case** caso perdido.

hope·less·ly (hŏp'lĭs-lē) adv. desesperadamente, irremediablemente.

hop·per (hŏp'ər) s. *(jumper)* saltador *m*, brincador *m*; *(container)* tolva; *(freight car)* vagón tolva *m*.

hop·scotch (hŏp'skŏch') s. rayuela.

horde (hôrd) s. horda, multitud *f*.

ho·ri·zon (hə-rī'zən) s. horizonte *m*.

hor·i·zon·tal (hôr'ĭ-zŏn'tl) adj. & s. horizontal *f*.

hor·mo·nal (hôr-mō'nəl) adj. BIOL., BIOQUÍM. hormonal.

hor·mone (hôr'mōn') s. BIOL., BIOQUÍM. hormona.

horn (hôrn) I. s. *(of animals)* cuerno, asta; *(of a new moon)* cuerno; *(of an anvil)* punta de un yunque; *(foghorn)* bocina; AUTO., ELEC., RAD. bocina; MÚS. *(French horn)* trompa; FAM. *(telephone)* trompeta; JER. *(telephone)* teléfono ♦ **to blow one's own h.** echarse flores II. intr. ♦ **to h. in** JER. entremeterse, inmiscuirse en III. adj. de cuerno, hecho de cuerno.

horn·bill (hôrn'bĭl') s. ORNIT. cálao.

horned (hôrnd) adj. encornado, cornudo.

hor·net (hôr'nĭt) s. ENTOM. avispón *m*.

horn of plenty s. cornucopia.

horn·y (hôr'nē) adj. **-i·er, -i·est** *(with horns)* cornudo; *(made of horn)* córneo; *(calloused)* calloso; JER., VULG. *(sexually aroused)* caliente, cachondo.

ho·rol·o·gy (hô-rŏl'ə-jē) s. relojería.

hor·o·scope (hôr'ə-skōp') s. horóscopo.

hor·ren·dous (hô-rĕn'dəs) adj. *(hideous)* horrendo; *(dreadful)* terrible.

hor·ri·ble (hôr'ə-bəl) adj. *(dreadful)* horrible, espantoso; *(disagreeable)* desagradable.

hor·ri·bly (hôr'ə-blē) adv. *(dreadfully)* horriblemente; *(terribly)* terriblemente <*a h. humid climate* un clima terriblemente húmedo>.

hor·rid (hôr'ĭd) adj. *(dreadful)* hórrido, espantoso; *(disagreeable)* desagradable; *(offensive)* repulsivo.

hor·rif·ic (hô-rĭf'ĭk) adj. *(horrible)* horrible; *(terrifying)* aterrorizador.

hor·ri·fy (hôr'ə-fī') tr. **-fied, -fy·ing** *(to cause horror)* horrorizar; *(to shock)* pasmar, escandalizar.

hor·ror (hôr'ər) s. *(fear)* horror *m*, pavor *m*; *(abhorrence)* aversión *f*; FIG., FAM. *(ugly thing)* espanto ♦ **h. film** película de miedo.

hors d'oeuvre (ôr dûrv') s. [pl. **hors d'oeuvres** *o* **hors d'oeuvre**] entremés *m*.

horse (hôrs) I. s. ZOOL. caballo; MIL. *(cavalry)* caballería; CARP., CONSTR. *(four-legged frame)* caballete *m*, burro; DEP. *(in gymnastics)* potro; JER. *(heroin)* heroína (droga) ♦ **a h. of another** *o* **a different color** eso es otro cantar • **from the horse's mouth** de buena tinta • **gift h.** caballo regalado • **to get on one's high h.** tener muchos humos • **to hold one's horses** contenerse II. tr. **horsed, hors·ing** proveer de caballos; *(to haul)* tirar con fuerza —intr. estar en celo, estar salida (la yegua) ♦ **to h. around** jugar alborotosamente III. adj. *(of a horse)* hípico; *(mounted)* a caballo, montado a caballo; *(drawn)* tirado por caballos; FIG. *(large)* grande; *(crude)* ordinario.

horse·back (hôrs'băk') s. *(back)* lomo del caballo; *(hogback)* arista (de una montaña) ♦ **to ride h.** montar a caballo.

horse chestnut s. BOT. *(tree)* castaño de Indias; *(fruit)* castaña de Indias.

horse-drawn (hôrs'drôn') adj. tirado por caballos (vehículo).

horse·flesh (hôrs'flĕsh') s. *(flesh)* carne de caballo *f*; *(horses)* caballos (en general).

horse·fly *o* **horse fly** (hôrs'flī') s. ENTOM. tábano.

horse·hair (hôrs'hâr') s. *(hair)* pelo de caballo; *(cloth)* tela de crin.

horse·hide (hôrs'hīd') s. cuero de caballo.

horse·man (hôrs'mən) s. [pl. **-men**] *(rider)* jinete *m*; *(breeder)* criador (de caballos) *m*; *(horse lover)* caballista *m*.

horse·man·ship (hôrs'mən-shĭp') s. equitación *f*.

horse opera s. FAM. obra que trata de vaqueros.

horse·play (hôrs'plā') s. FAM. juego rudo, juego de manos.

horse·pow·er (hôrs'pou'ər) s. FÍS. caballo de fuerza *o* de vapor; *(power)* potencia, caballo.

horse racing s. carreras de caballos.

horse·rad·ish (hôrs'răd'ĭsh) s. BOT., CUL. rábano picante.

horse sense s. FAM. sentido común.

horse·shoe (hôrs'shōō') I. s. herradura ♦ **horseshoes** juego en que se tira a un hito con herraduras II. tr. **-shoed, -shoe·ing** herrar (a un caballo).

horse thief s. cuatrero.

horse trade s. negociación *f* (astuta y enérgica).

horse·whip (hôrs'hwĭp') I. s. *(whip)* fuste *m*, látigo (para caballos) II. tr. **-whipped, -whip·ping** azotar, dar latigazos a.

horse·wom·an (hôrs'wŏŏm'ən) s. [pl. **-wom·en** (-wĭm'ĭn)] *(rider)* jinete *f*; *(breeder)* criadora (de caballos); *(horse lover)* caballista *f*.

hors·y *o* **hors·ey** (hôr'sē) adj. **-i·er, -i·est** *(horse-like)* caballuno; *(horse-loving)* aficionado (a los caballos).

hor·ta·tive (hôr'tə-tĭv) adj. hortatorio.

hor·ta·to·ry (hôr'tə-tôr'ē) adj. hortatorio.

hor·ti·cul·ture (hôr'tĭ-kŭl'chər) s. horticultura.

hor·ti·cul·tur·ist (hôr'tĭ-kŭl'chər-ĭst) s. horticultor *m*.

hose (hōz) I. s. [pl. **hose**] *(stockings)* medias; *(socks)* calcetines *m*; *(flexible tube)* [pl. **hos·es**] manguera II. tr. **hosed, hos·ing** *(to water)* regar (con manguera); *(to wash)* lavar (con manguera).

Ho·se·a (hō-zē'ə, -zā'ə) s. BÍBL. Oseas *m*.

ho·sier·y (hō′zhə-rē) s. *(stockings and socks)* medias; G.B. *(hose and underclothing)* ropa interior (incluyendo las medias); *(business)* calcetería.

hos·pice (hŏs′pĭs) s. hospicio.

hos·pi·ta·ble (hŏs′pĭ-tə-bəl, hŏ-spĭt′ə-) adj. *(welcoming)* hospitalario; *(receptive)* receptivo; *(favorable)* favorable <*h. environment* ambiente favorable>.

hos·pi·tal (hŏs′pĭt′l) s. *(clinic)* hospital *m*; *(home)* hogar *m* (para ancianos o maltrechos); *(repair shop)* taller *m*.

hos·pi·tal·i·ty (hŏs′pĭ-tăl′ĭ-tē) s. [pl. **-ties**] hospitalidad *f*.

hos·pi·tal·i·za·tion (hŏs′pĭt′l-ĭ-zā′shən) s. hospitalización *f*.

hos·pi·tal·ize (hŏs′pĭt′l-īz′) tr. **-ized, -iz·ing** hospitalizar.

host¹ (hōst) **I.** s. *(at a meal)* anfitrión *m*; *(of an inn)* posadero, mesonero; TEAT., TELEV., RAD. presentador *m*, animador *m*; BIOL. huésped *m* **II.** tr. FAM. ser el anfitrión de.

host² (hōst) s. *(multitude)* multitud *f*, muchedumbre *f*; *(army)* hueste *f*.

host³ *o* **Host** (hōst) s. RELIG. hostia.

hos·tage (hŏs′tĭj) s. rehén *mf* ◆ **to hold h.** tener como rehén.

hos·tel (hŏs′təl) **I.** s. *(youth lodging)* albergue (para jóvenes) *m*; *(inn)* hostería **II.** intr. *(to stay at hostels)* viajar hospedándose en albergues.

hos·tel·ry (hŏs′təl-rē) s. [pl. **-ries**] *(inn)* hostería *f*; *(hotel)* hotel *m*.

host·ess (hō′stĭs) s. *(host)* anfitriona; *(waitress)* camarera; *(airline stewardess)* azafata.

hos·tile (hŏs′təl, -tīl′) **I.** adj. *(unfriendly)* hostil; *(antagonistic)* antagónico **II.** s. enemigo.

hos·til·i·ty (hŏ-stĭl′ĭ-tē) s. [pl. **-ties**] *(enmity)* hostilidad *f*; *(antagonism)* antagonismo; *(hostile act)* acto hostil ◆ **hostilities** hostilidades, actos de guerra.

hot (hŏt) adj. **hot·ter hot·test** *(very warm)* caliente; *(climate)* caluroso, cálido; *(sun)* abrasador; *(spicy)* picante; ELEC. que lleva corriente; *(radioactive)* radioactivo; *(temper)* vivo; *(controversial)* muy discutido <*h. issue* problema muy discutido>; *(heated)* acalorado; FAM. *(sexually excited)* caliente; *(stolen)* robado; *(fugitive)* fugitivo; *(popular)* de gran popularidad <*h. new singer* un nuevo cantante de gran popularidad>; *(excellent)* excelente, estupendo; *(skillful)* competente; *(lucky)* con mucha suerte; MÚS. muy rítmico ◆ **h. off the press** de última hora • **h. on the trail** *(of someone)* sobre la pista (de alguien) • **in h. pursuit** tras los talones • **in h. water** FAM. en un lío • **to be h.** *(person)* FAM. tener calor; *(weather)* hacer calor; *(things)* estar caliente • **to have the hots for** JER. estar caliente con.

hot air s. JER. palabrería.

hot·bed (hŏt′bĕd′) s. *(soil bed)* almajara; FIG. *(growth environment)* semillero <*a h. of new ideas* un semillero de ideas nuevas>.

hot-blood·ed (hŏt′blŭd′ĭd) adj. fogoso.

hot cake s. CUL. panqueque *m* ◆ **to sell like hot cakes** FIG. venderse rápidamente.

hotch·potch (hŏch′pŏch′) s. *(hodgepodge)* mescolanza; DER. colación de bienes *f*.

hot dog **I.** s. *(sandwich)* perro caliente (con salchicha); *(frankfurter)* salchicha **II.** interj. FAM. exclamación de entusiasmo *f*.

hot-dog (hŏt′dôg′) intr. **-dogged, -dog·ging** JER. hacer acrobacios (al esquiar).

ho·tel (hō-tĕl′) s. hotel *m*.

hot·foot (hŏt′fŏŏt′) **I.** intr. ir de prisa <*h. it to the bank* vaya de prisa al banco> **II.** adv. rápidamente.

hot·head (hŏt′hĕd′) s. persona impulsiva y precipitada.

hot·head·ed (hŏt′hĕd′ĭd) adj. *(quick to anger)* arrebatado; *(impetuous)* impetuoso, precipitado.

hot·house (hŏt′hous′) **I.** s. invernadero **II.** adj. *(greenhouse-like)* de invernadero; FIG. *(delicate)* delicado.

hot line s. línea de emergencia (telefónica).

hot·ly (hŏt′lē) adv. *(warmly)* acaloradamente; *(passionately)* apasionadamente; *(violently)* violentamente.

hot pepper s. BOT. ají *m*.

hot plate s. *(cooking device)* plancha, calentador (eléctrico) *m*; *(portable cooker)* hornillo (portátil), infiernillo.

hot rod *o* **hot-rod** *o* **hot-rod** (hŏt′rŏd′) s. automóvil modificado para mayor velocidad.

hot seat s. JER. *(electric chair)* silla eléctrica; FAM. *(position of stress)* situación crítica.

hot-shot (hŏt′shŏt′) s. JER. *(ace)* as (persona brillante) *mf*; *(express train)* tren de carga expreso.

hot springs s. agua termal, fuente de agua termal *f*.

hot-wa·ter bottle (hŏt-wô′tər) s. bolsa de agua caliente.

hound (hound) **I.** s. *(hunting dog)* podenco; FAM. *(dog)* perro; *(scoundrel)* canalla *m*; *(enthusiast)* aficionado **II.** tr. *(to harass)* acosar, perseguir; *(to nag)* importunar.

hour (our) s. hora ◆ **hours** *(schedule)* horario; RELIG. horas.

hour·glass (our′glăs′) s. reloj de arena *m*.

hour hand s. horario, manecilla de las horas.

hour·ly (our′lē) **I.** adj. *(every hour)* horario; *(frequent)* frecuente; *(by the hour)* por hora **II.** adv. *(at every hour)* a cada hora; *(frequently)* frecuentemente; *(by the hour)* por horas <*I get paid h.* me pagan por horas>.

house (hous) **I.** s. casa; *(home)* hogar *m*, vivienda; *(animal shelter)* cobertura (para un animal); *(auditorium)* teatro, sala; *(audience)* público; *(dwelling for students)* pensión *f*, internado; *(dwelling for religious persons)* convento; *(commercial firm)* casa, firma; *(legislative body)* cámara (del parlamento); ASTROL. casa (división del zodiaco) ◆ **a good h.** *(a big audience)* mucho público; *(a good audience)* buen público • **full h.** lleno (teatro) • **H.** casa (de una familia noble) • **to bring the h. down** ser un exitazo **II.** tr. (houz) **housed,** *(to lodge)* alojar, albergar; *(to shelter)* proteger; *(to keep)* guardar; *(to store)* almacenar; *(to contain)* contener —intr. alojarse, albergarse.

house arrest s. arresto domiciliario.

house·boat (hous′bōt′) s. casa flotante.

house·break·ing (hous′brā′kĭng) s. allanamiento (robo casero).

house·bro·ken (hous′brō′kən) adj. *(trained)* enseñado en limpieza (dic. de un animal casero); FIG. *(tame)* amansado, dócil.

house·clean·ing (hous′klē′nĭng) s. *(of a house)* limpieza de la casa; *(of bad conditions)* limpieza.

house·coat (hous′kōt′) s. bata (de casa).

house·fly (hous′flī′) s. ENTOM. mosca común.

house·hold (hous′hōld′) s. casa (establecimiento doméstico).

house·hold·er (hous′hōl′dər) s. *(owner)* dueño de casa; *(head of house)* cabeza de familia.

house·keep·er (hous′kē′pər) s. ama de llaves.

house·keep·ing (hous′kē′pĭng) s. manejo de una casa.

house·maid (hous′mād′) s. empleada doméstica, criada.

house·moth·er (hous′mŭth′ər) s. supervisora *o* directora de una residencia para jóvenes.

House of Commons s. G.B., HIST., POL. Cámara de los Comunes (en Inglaterra y Canadá).

House of Lords s. G.B. Cámara de los Lores.

House of Representatives s. POL. Cámara de Representantes (en EE. UU.).

house organ s. boletín para empleados *o* clientes de una organización *m*.

house·top (hous′tŏp′) s. tejado (de una casa).

house·warm·ing (hous′wôr′mĭng) s. fiesta para el estreno de una casa.

house·wife (hous′wīf′) s. [pl. **-wives** (wīvz′)] ama de casa.

house·work (hous′wûrk′) s. quehaceres domésticos.

hous·ing (hou′zĭng) s. *(houses)* casas *f*; *(place to live)* vivienda; *(storage)* almacenaje *m*; MEC. bastidor *m*, caja; AUTO. cárter *m*; ARQ. empotramiento.

housing development s. unidad vecinal *f*.

hove (hōv) un part. p. de **heave.**

hov·el (hŭv′əl, hŏv′-) s. *(miserable dwelling)* cuchitril *m*; *(shed)* cobertizo.

hov·er (hŭv′ər, hŏv′-) **I.** intr. *(eagle, helicopter)* cernerse; *(bird, insect)* revolotear ◆ **to h. around** rondar • **to h. between** vacilar • **to h. over** cernerse sobre **II.** s. revoloteo.

how §G40 **I.** adv. *(in what manner)* cómo <*h. does this machine work?* ¿cómo funciona esta máquina?>; *(in what condition)* qué tal, cómo <*h. do I look in this jacket?* ¿qué tal luzco con esta chaqueta?>; *(to what extent)* cuánto, qué

<h. tall are you? ¿qué altura tienes?>; *(why)* cómo, por qué *<h. is it you're late?* ¿por qué llegas tarde?>; *(with what meaning)* cómo *<h. should I interpret this?* ¿cómo debo interpretar esto?>; *(by what name)* cómo *<h. is it called?* ¿cómo se llama?>; *(what)* cómo *<how is that again?* ¿cómo dijo?> ♦ **and h.!** ¡y cómo! • **h. about . . .?** ¿qué te parece si . . .? *<h. about dinner tonight?* ¿qué te parece si cenamos juntos esta noche?> • **h. about it?** FAM. *(what do you think?)* ¿qué te parece? *<it would be nice to go to the movies tonight—h. about it?* sería lindo ir al cine esta noche ¿qué te parece?>; *(how about doing it?)* ¿qué te parece si lo haces? *<you promised you would clean the attic— h. about it?* prometiste que limpiarías el ático ¿qué te parece si lo haces?> • **h. about me?** ¿y yo, qué? • **how are you?** ¿cómo está usted? • **h. big is it?** ¿cómo es de grande?, ¿de qué tamaño es? • **h. come?** FAM. *(why?)* ¿cómo es qué?, ¿cómo es posible que? *<h. come every time I call you are never home?* ¿cómo es posible que cada vez que te llamo tú no estás en casa?>; *(for what reason?)* ¿debido a qué?, ¿cómo es eso? *<you were fired? h. come?* ¿te despidieron? ¿cómo es eso?> • **h. could you!** ¡no te da vergüenza? • **h. do you do?** *(how are you?)* ¿cómo está usted? • **h. far?** *(how far away?)* ¿a qué distancia? *<how far is the station from here?* ¿a qué distancia de aquí está la estación?>; *(to what point?)* ¿hasta dónde? *<h. far does this train go?* ¿hasta dónde va este tren?> • **h. fast?** *(at what speed?)* ¿a qué velocidad? *<h. fast can this car go?* ¿a qué velocidad puede andar este automóvil?>; *(how quickly)* ¿con qué rapidez? *<h. fast can you fix me an omelet?* ¿con qué rapidez me puedes preparar una tortilla?> • **h. is that again?** ¿cómo? • **h. long?** *(length)* ¿cómo . . . de largo? *<h. long is the rope?* ¿cómo es de largo la soga?>; *(time)* ¿cuánto tiempo? *<how long will you be?* ¿cuánto tiempo tardarás?> • **h. many?** ¿cuántos? (en número, cantidad) • **h. much?** ¿cuánto? (en precio, costo) • **h. old are you?** ¿cuántos años tienes?, ¿qué edad tienes? • **h. so?** ¿cómo? **II.** conj. *(in what manner)* cómo *<he forgot h. he did it* se olvidó cómo lo hizo>; *(that)* que *<he told them h. he had a family to support* les dijo que tenía una familia que mantener> **III.** s. ♦ **the h.** el cómo.

how·dy (hou′dē) interj. REG. ¡hola!

how·ev·er (hou-ĕv′ər) **I.** adv. *(by whatever manner)* de cualquier modo que, como quiera que *<h. you do it, the result will be the same* de cualquier modo que lo hagas, el resultado será el mismo>; *(by whatever means)* cómo *<h. did you get it?* ¿cómo lo conseguiste?>; *(to whatever degree)* por . . . que *<she always finished the job, h. tired she was* ella siempre terminaba su tarea, por cansada que estuviera> ♦ **h. it may be** sea lo que sea • **h. much** por más que, por mucho que **II.** conj. no obstante, sin embargo *<the tickets are expensive; h., we will go* las entradas son caras; no obstante, iremos>.

how·itz·er (hou′ĭt-sər) s. ARM., MIL. obús m.

howl (houl) **I.** intr. *(dogs, wolves)* aullar; *(with pain)* gritar, dar alaridos; *(wind)* bramar, rugir; JER. *(to laugh)* reír a carcajadas —tr. gritar, decir a gritos **II.** s. *(of dogs, wolves)* aullido; *(of pain)* alarido; *(of wind)* bramido, rugido; JER. *(something funny)* cosa extremadamente graciosa.

howl·er (hou′lər) s. aullador m; *(one that shouts)* gritador m; ZOOL. *(monkey)* mono aullador; FAM. *(mistake)* plancha, gazapo.

how·so·ev·er (hou′sō-ĕv′ər) adv. *(by whatever manner)* de cualquier modo; *(to whatever degree)* por muy.

hub (hŭb) s. *(wheel center)* cubo (de una rueda, hélice); FIG. *(center)* centro, foco.

hub·bub (hŭb′ŭb′) s. *(babble)* vocerío; *(uproar)* bullicio; *(confusion)* confusión f, tumulto.

huck·le·ber·ry (hŭk′əl-bĕr′ē) s. [pl. **-ries**] BOT. arándano.

huck·ster (hŭk′stər) **I.** s. *(peddler)* vendedor ambulante m, buhonero; JER. *(advertising agent)* agente de publicidad mf **II.** tr. *(to peddle)* vender; *(to promote)* promover —intr. regatear.

hud·dle (hŭd′l) **I.** s. *(crowd)* grupo, turba; *(conference)* conferencia, reunión (pequeña o privada) **II.** intr. **-dled, -dling** apiñarse, amontonarse ♦ **to h. up** agazaparse, acu-

rrucarse —tr. *(to bunch)* apiñar, amontonar; *(to hunch)* encorvar (la espalda).

hue (hyōō) s. *(color)* color m, tinte m; *(shade)* matiz m, intensidad de color f; *(appearance)* apariencia.

hue and cry s. *(shout)* grito de alarma; *(public protest)* protesta pública.

huff (hŭf) **I.** s. *(fit of anger)* arranque de furia m; *(pique)* malhumor m **II.** intr. *(to puff)* resoplar; *(to threaten emptily)* fanfarronear; *(to take offense)* indignarse, ofenderse —tr. *(to inflate)* inflar; *(to anger)* enojar, irritar.

huff·y (hŭf′ē) adj. **-i·er, -i·est** *(touchy)* quisquilloso; *(irritated)* irritado, molesto; *(indignant)* indignado; *(arrogant)* arrogante, altivo.

hug (hŭg) **I.** tr. **hugged, hug·ging** *(to embrace)* abrazar; *(to cling to)* ceñirse a; FIG. *(to cherish)* aferrarse a (ideas) —intr. *(to embrace)* abrazarse **II.** s. abrazo.

huge (hyōōj) adj. **hug·er, hug·est** enorme, tremendo.

huge·ly (hyōōj′lē) adv. enormemente, tremendamente.

huge·ness (hyōōj′nĭs) s. enormidad f.

hug·ger·mug·ger (hŭg′ər-mŭg′ər) **I.** s. *(muddle)* confusión f; *(secrecy)* secreto **II.** adj. *(jumbled)* confuso; *(secret)* secreto **III.** tr. ocultar, mantener en secreto —intr. actuar subrepticiamente.

Hu·gue·not (hyōō′gə-nŏt′) s. HIST., RELIG. hugonote m.

huh (hŭ) interj. usado para expresar interrogación, sorpresa o indiferencia.

hulk (hŭlk) **I.** s. *(ship)* carraca; *(hull)* casco; *(large person, thing)* armatoste m **II.** intr. *(to loom)* surgir amenazadoramente; *(to move clumsily)* moverse pesadamente.

hulk·ing (hŭl′kĭng) adj. *(unwieldy)* de manejo difícil; *(massive)* pesado.

hull (hŭl) **I.** s. BOT. *(pod)* vaina; *(husk)* hollejo; *(shell)* cáscara; AVIA., MARÍT. casco **II.** tr. desvainar, descascarillar.

hul·la·ba·loo o **hul·la·bal·loo** (hŭl′ə-bə-lōō′) s. [pl. **-loos**] FAM. *(noise)* bullicio; *(uproar)* alboroto.

hul·lo (hə-lō′) interj. & s. var. de **hello.**

hum (hŭm) **I.** intr. **hummed, hum·ming** *(a song)* tararear, canturrear; *(bees, engines)* zumbar; FAM. *(to be active)* hervir, estar muy activo —tr. tararear, canturrear **II.** s. zumbido **III.** interj. ¡ejem!

hu·man (hyōō′mən) **I.** adj. humano **II.** s. humano, ser humano.

human being s. ser humano.

hu·mane (hyōō-mān′) adj. *(kind)* bondadoso, compasivo; *(humanistic)* humanístico.

hu·man·ism (hyōō′mə-nĭz′əm) s. humanismo.

hu·man·ist (hyōō′mə-nĭst) s. humanista mf.

hu·man·i·tar·i·an (hyōō-măn′ĭ-târ′ē-ən) **I.** adj. humanitario **II.** s. filántropo, persona humanitaria.

hu·man·i·tar·i·an·ism (hyōō-măn′ĭ-târ′ē-ə-nĭz′əm) s. humanitarismo.

hu·man·i·ty (hyōō-măn′ĭ-tē) s. [pl. **-ties**] *(human race)* humanidad f; *(humanness)* naturaleza humana; *(benevolence)* humanidad ♦ **the humanities** las humanidades.

hu·man·ize (hyōō′mə-nīz′) tr. **-ized, -iz·ing** humanizar.

hu·man·kind (hyōō′mən-kīnd′) s. raza humana, humanidad f.

hu·man·ly (hyōō′mən-lē) adv. humanamente.

hu·man·oid (hyōō′mə-noid′) **I.** adj. humanoide, de apariencia humana **II.** s. androide mf.

hum·ble (hŭm′bəl) **I.** adj. **-bler, -blest** *(meek)* humilde *<in my h. opinion* a mi humilde parecer>; *(submissive)* sumiso; *(unpretentious)* simple (sin pretensiones) **II.** tr. **-bled, -bling** humillar ♦ **to h. oneself** humillarse.

hum·ble·bee (hŭm′bəl-bē′) s. ENTOM. abejón m.

hum·ble·ness (hŭm′bəl-nĭs) s. humildad f.

humble pie s. CUL. pastel m de menudos de venado o cerdo ♦ **to eat h.** FIG. disculparse de manera humillante.

hum·bly (hŭm′blē) adv. humildemente.

hum·bug (hŭm′bŭg′) **I.** s. *(hoax)* patraña; *(trickster)* embaucador m; *(nonsense)* tontería **II.** tr. & intr. **-bugged, -bug·ging** engañar, embaucar.

hum·ding·er (hŭm′dĭng′ər) s. JER. maravilla.

hum·drum (hŭm′drŭm′) **I.** adj. aburrido, monótono **II.** s. plomo (persona pesada y aburrida).

hu·mec·tant (hyōō-mĕk′tənt) s. & adj. humectante m.

hu·mer·us (hyōō'mər-əs) s. ANAT. húmero.
hu·mid (hyōō'mĭd) adj. húmedo.
hu·mid·i·fi·ca·tion (hyōō-mĭd'ə-fĭ-kā'shən) s. humedecimiento, humectación f.
hu·mid·i·fi·er (hyōō-mĭd'ə-fī'ər) s. humedecedor m, humectador m.
hu·mid·i·fy (hyōō-mĭd'ə-fī') tr. **-fied, -fy·ing** humedecer.
hu·mid·i·ty (hyōō-mĭd'ĭ-tē) s. humedad f.
hu·mi·dor (hyōō'mĭ-dôr') s. bote que mantiene húmedo el tabaco m.
hu·mil·i·ate (hyōō-mĭl'ē-āt') tr. **-at·ed, -at·ing** humillar.
hu·mil·i·a·tion (hyōō-mĭl'ē-ā'shən) s. humillación f; (degradation) degradación f; (disgrace) vergüenza.
hu·mil·i·ty (hyōō-mĭl'ĭ-tē) s. [pl. **-ties**] humildad f.
hum·ming·bird (hŭm'ĭng-bûrd') s. ORNIT. colibrí m, picaflor m.
hum·mock (hŭm'ək) s. (mound) montecillo; (knoll) otero; (ice ridge) montículo de hielo.
hu·mor (hyōō'mər) s. (comicality) humor m; (mood) humor <to be in no h. for no tener humor para>; FISIOL. humor ♦ **to have a good sense of h.** tener buen sentido del humor.
hu·mor·ist (hyōō'mər-ĭst) s. humorista mf; (performer) cómico.
hu·mor·less (hyōō'mər-lĭs) adj. (without humor) sin humor, solemne; (not funny) sin gracia.
hu·mor·ous (hyōō'mər-əs) adj. (funny) cómico; (employing humor) humorista.
hu·mour (hyōō'mər) s. G.B. var. de **humor.**
hump (hŭmp) I. s. (of a person, camel) joroba, giba; (in the ground) montecillo ♦ **to be over the h.** haber vencido la mayor dificultad II. tr. JER., VULG. joder —intr. JER. (to exert oneself) matarse, esforzarse ♦ **to h. over** encorvarse.
hump·back (hŭmp'băk') s. (hunchback) jorobado; MED. cifosis f; (whale) ballena jorobada.
hump·backed (hŭmp'băkt') adj. jorobado.
humph (hŭmf) interj. ¡puf!, ¡uh! (expresión de desagrado o desdén).
hu·mus (hyōō'məs) s. AGR. humus m, mantillo m.
Hun (hŭn) s. HIST. huno; DESPEC. (German) alemán m ♦ **hun** vándalo.
hunch (hŭnch) I. s. (intuitive feeling) corazonada; (hump) giba; (lump) protuberancia II. tr. (to bend over) doblar (la espalda); (to push) empujar —intr. (to crouch) agacharse <the girl hunched in a corner la muchacha se agachó en un rincón>; (to thrust forward) adelantarse ♦ **to h. up** estar con el cuerpo encorvado.
hunch·back (hŭnch'băk') s. (humpback) jorobado; MED. cifosis f; (hunched back) joroba.
hun·dred (hŭn'drĭd) I. s. [pl. **hundred** o **-dreds**] (cardinal number) ciento; FAM. (bill) billete de cien dólares m; (in the third position) centena; (administrative division) división administrativa del condado ♦ **a h. per cent** cien por cien • **a h. times** cien veces • **by the h.** o **by the hundreds** por centenares • **one h.** cien, ciento II. adj. cien, ciento.
hun·dred·fold (hŭn'drĭd-fōld') I. adj. céntuplo II. s. céntuplo ♦ **to repay a h.** devolver ciento por uno.
hun·dredth (hŭn'drĭdth) I. adj. centésimo, centavo II. s. (in a series) centésimo, centavo; (part) centésima parte.
hun·dred·weight (hŭn'drĭd-wāt') s. [pl. **-weight** o **-weights**] quintal m.
hung (hŭng) un pret. y part. p. de **hang** ♦ **h. jury** DER. jurado que no llega a un fallo unánime.
Hun·gar·i·an (hŭng-gâr'ē-ən) adj. & s. (inhabitant, language) húngaro.
Hun·ga·ry (hŭng'gə-rē) s. Hungría.
hun·ger (hŭng'gər) I. s. (for food) hambre f; FIG. (desire) sed f, deseo <h. for adventure sed de aventuras> II. intr. tener hambre —tr. hacer pasar hambre, hambrear ♦ **to h. for** o **after** tener sed o hambre de.
hunger strike s. huelga de hambre.
hung jury s. DER. jurado en desacuerdo.
hung over adj. que sufre una resaca.
hun·gry (hŭng'grē) adj. **-gri·er, gri·est** (for food) hambriento; FIG. (avid) ávido, sediento; (craving) de hambre <h. look cara de hambre>.
hung up adj. FAM. ♦ **to be h. about** estar preocupado por

<he is h. about his job está preocupado por su empleo> • **to be h. on** estar obsesionado con <he is h. on his looks está obsesionado con su aspecto> • **to get h.** demorarse <he got h. in traffic se demoró por el tráfico>.
hunk (hŭngk) s. FAM. (chunk) trozo (grande); (male) hombre varonil m.
hun·ker (hŭng'kər) I. intr. agacharse, ponerse en cuclillas II. s. ♦ **hunkers** caderas.
hun·ky-do·ry (hŭng'kē-dôr'ē) adj. JER. muy bien, estupendo.
hunt (hŭnt) I. tr. (for sport) cazar; (to pursue) perseguir, acosar; (to search for) buscar ♦ **to h. down** (to capture) capturar; (to search for) buscar • **to h. for** buscar —intr. cazar, ir de caza o de cacería; (to search) buscar ♦ **to go hunting** ir de caza II. s. caza, cacería; (pursuit) persecución f, acoso; (search) búsqueda.
hunt·er (hŭn'tər) s. (person) cazador m; (searcher) buscador m; (dog) podenco, perro de caza; (horse) caballo de caza.
hunt·ing (hŭn'tĭng) I. s. (game) caza, cacería; (search) búsqueda II. adj. de caza.
hunting lodge s. pabellón de caza m.
hunt·ress (hŭn'trĭs) s. cazadora.
hunts·man (hŭnts'mən) s. [pl. **-men**] (hunter) cazador m; (hounds' manager) montero mayor.
hur·dle (hûr'dl) I. s. (barrier) valla; FIG. (obstacle) barrera, obstáculo II. tr. **-dled, -dling** (to jump) saltar; (to overcome) vencer, salvar (un obstáculo) —intr. saltar vallas ♦ **hurdles** DEP. carrera de vallas <to compete in the hurdles participar en la carrera de vallas>.
hur·dler (hûrd'lər) s. DEP. corredor de vallas m.
hur·dy-gur·dy (hûr'dē-gûr'dē) s. [pl. **-dies**] MÚS. zanfonía.
hurl (hûrl) I. tr. arrojar, lanzar —intr. abalanzarse II. s. lanzamiento.
hur·ly-bur·ly (hûr'lē-bûr'lē) s. [pl. **-lies**] tumulto, batahola.
hur·rah (hōō-rä', -rô') o **hur·ray** (-rā') I. interj. & s. ¡hurra!, ¡ole! II. tr. & intr. vitorear.
hur·ri·cane (hûr'ĭ-kān') s. METEOR. huracán m.
hur·ried (hûr'ēd) adj. (rapid) apresurado; (rushed) apurado, apremiado.
hur·ry (hûr'ē) I. intr. **-ried, -ry·ing** darse prisa, apurarse ♦ **to h. along** ir de prisa • **to h. away** marcharse de prisa • **to h. back** volver de prisa • **to h. off** irse de prisa • **to h. on** irse corriendo • **to h. up** apresurarse —tr. (to hasten) apurar; (to rush) dar prisa a, apurar; (to speed progress) llevar a toda prisa ♦ **to h. after** seguir a • **to h. along** (something) acelerar; (someone) llevar o llevarse rápidamente II. s. (haste) prisa; (urgent condition) apuro ♦ **in a h.** de prisa • **to be in a h.** tener prisa • **to be in a h. to** tener prisa por.
hur·ry-scur·ry (hûr'ē-skûr'ē) I. intr. **-ried, -ry·ing** actuar precipitada y confusamente II. s. precipitación f, confusión f.
hurt (hûrt) I. tr. (to injure) hacer daño, herir; (to distress) hacer sufrir, angustiar; (to damage) dañar, perjudicar <high prices will h. sales los precios altos perjudicarán las ventas> ♦ **to h. someone's feelings** ofenderle a alguien —intr. doler <my head hurts me duele la cabeza>; (to suffer) sufrir ♦ **to get h.** lastimarse, hacerse daño • **to h. oneself** lastimarse II. s. (harm) daño; (pain) dolor m; (injury) herida; (anguish) angustia; (wrong) mal m.
hurt·ful (hûrt'fəl) adj. (causing injury) hiriente, lesivo; (causing health hazard) nocivo; (detrimental) perjudicial; (harmful) dañoso.
hur·tle (hûr'tl) intr. **-tled, -tling** abalanzarse —tr. arrojar, lanzar (con fuerza).
hus·band (hŭz'bənd) I. s. marido, esposo II. tr. economizar, ahorrar.
hus·band·man (hŭz'bənd-mən) s. [pl. **-men**] labrador m, agricultor m.
hus·band·ry (hŭz'bən-drē) s. AGR. (crops) agricultura, labranza; (livestock) cría de ganado; (economy) economía, ahorro.
hush (hŭsh) I. tr. (to silence) callar, hacer callar; (to calm) calmar, aquietar ♦ **to h. up** (scandal) silenciar, encubrir; (person) hacer callar —intr. (to be still) aquietarse; (to be

quiet) callarse **II.** s. *(silence)* silencio; *(stillness)* quietud *f*
III. interj. ¡silencio! ♦ **h. up!** ¡cállate!
hush-hush (hŭsh′hŭsh′) adj. FAM. *(secret)* secreto; *(confidential)* confidencial.
hush money s. FAM. soborno (para que no se divulgue algo).
husk (hŭsk) **I.** s. *(hull of a vegetable)* vaina; *(shell)* cáscara; *(framework)* armazón *f* **II.** tr. descascarar, desvainar.
husk·i·ness (hŭs′kē-nĭs) s. *(hoarseness)* ronquera; *(ruggedness)* robusteza.
husk·y¹ (hŭs′kē) adj. **-i·er, -i·est** *(hoarse)* ronco; *(husk-like)* como cáscara; *(with a husk)* cascarudo.
husk·y² (hŭs′kē) **I.** adj. **-i·er, -i·est** FAM. *(rugged)* robusto; *(burly)* fornido **II.** s. [pl. **-ies**] persona fornida.
hus·ky³ (hŭs′kē) s. [pl. **-kies**] perro esquimal.
hus·sar (hə-zär′) s. HIST., MIL. húsar *m*.
hus·sy (hŭz′ē, hŭs′ē) s. [pl. **-sies**] *(saucy girl)* pícara; *(immoral woman)* mujer libertina.
hust·ings (hŭs′tĭngz) s.pl. [ú. con v. sing. o pl.] G.B. *(electoral process)* proceso electoral; *(court)* tribunal de autoridades municipales *m*; *(platform)* tribuna pública.
hus·tle (hŭs′əl) **I.** tr. **-tled, -tling** *(to shove)* empujar; FAM. *(to hurry)* apurar; *(to swindle)* estafar —intr. *(to push)* abrirse paso a codazos <*the police hustled through the crowd* la policía se abrió paso a codazos entre la muchedumbre>; FAM. *(to hurry)* apresurarse; *(to bustle)* ajetrearse; *(to obtain deceitfully)* estafar; *(to work as a prostitute)* trabajar de prostituta **II.** s. FAM. *(hurry)* prisa; *(bustle)* ajetreo; *(swindle)* estafa.
hus·tler (hŭs′lər) s. *(busy person)* persona enérgica, buscavidas *mf*; FAM. *(swindler)* estafador *m*; *(prostitute)* prostituta, puta.
hut (hŭt) **I.** s. *(dwelling)* choza; MIL. *(barracks)* barraca **II.** tr. & intr. **hut·ted, hut·ting** refugiar(se) en una choza.
hutch (hŭch) s. *(rabbit cage)* jaula (para conejos); *(cupboard)* alacena; *(chest)* arca, cajón *m*; *(hut)* choza.
hy·a·cinth (hī′ə-sĭnth) s. BOT. jacinto; *(color)* azul purpúreo; MIN. jacinto.
hy·ae·na (hī-ē′nə) s. ZOOL. hiena.
hy·brid (hī′brĭd) s. BIOL. híbrido; *(half-breed)* mestizo; FILOL. híbrido.
hy·brid·i·za·tion (hī′brĭ-dĭ-zā′shən) s. hibridación *f*.
Hy·dra (hī′drə) s. ASTRON., MITOL. Hidra; ZOOL. [pl. **-dras** o **-drae** (-drē)] hidra.
hy·dran·gea (hī-drān′jə, -drăn′-) s. BOT. hortensia.
hy·drant (hī′drănt) s. boca de agua (esp. para incendios).
hy·drate (hī′drāt) **I.** s. QUÍM. hidrato **II.** tr. & intr. **-drat·ed, -drat·ing** hidratar(se).
hy·dra·tion (hī-drā′shən) s. QUÍM. hidratación *f*.
hy·drau·lic (hī-drô′lĭk) adj. hidráulico, de la hidráulica.
hy·drau·lics (hī-drô′lĭks) s.pl. [ú. con v. sing.] FÍS. hidráulica.
hy·dro·car·bon (hī′drə-kär′bən) s. QUÍM. hidrocarburo.
hy·dro·ceph·a·lous (hī′drō-sĕf′ə-ləs) adj. hidrocéfalo, hidrocefálico.
hy·dro·ceph·a·lus (hī′drō-sĕf′ə-ləs) o **hy·dro·ceph·a·ly** (-lē) s. MED. hidrocefalia.
hy·dro·chlo·ric acid (hī′drə-klôr′ĭk) s. QUÍM. ácido clorhídrico.
hy·dro·chlo·ride (hī′drə-klôr′īd′) s. QUÍM. clorhidrato.
hy·dro·dy·nam·ics (hī′drō-dī-năm′ĭks) s.pl. [ú. con v. sing.] FÍS. hidrodinámica.
hy·dro·e·lec·tric (hī′drō-ĭ-lĕk′trĭk) adj. hidroeléctrico.
hy·dro·flu·or·ic acid (hī′drō-flōō-ôr′ĭk) s. QUÍM. ácido fluorhídrico.
hy·dro·gen (hī′drə-jən) s. QUÍM. hidrógeno.
hy·dro·gen·ate (hī′drə-jə-nāt′, hī-drŏj′ə-) tr. **-at·ed, -at·ing** QUÍM. hidrogenar.
hydrogen bomb s. ARM., MIL. bomba de hidrógeno.
hydrogen peroxide s. QUÍM. peróxido de hidrógeno, agua oxigenada.
hy·drol·o·gy (hī-drŏl′ə-jē) s. hidrología.
hy·drol·y·sis (hī-drŏl′ĭ-sĭs) s. QUÍM. hidrólisis *f*.
hy·dro·lyze (hī′drə-līz′) tr. & intr. **-lyzed, -liz·ing** hidrolizar(se).

hy·drom·e·ter (hī-drŏm′ĭ-tər) s. HIDRÁUL. hidrómetro; *(densimeter)* densímetro (de flotación).
hy·dro·pho·bi·a (hī′drə-fō′bē-ə) s. MED., PSIC. hidrofobia.
hy·dro·pho·bic (hī′drə-fō′bĭk) s. MED., PSIC. hidrofóbico; QUÍM. hidrófobo.
hy·dro·phone (hī′drə-fōn′) s. HIDRÁUL., MARÍT. hidrófono.
hy·dro·plane (hī′drə-plān′) **I.** s. AVIA. hidroavión *m*; MARÍT. hidroplano **II.** intr. **-planed, -plan·ing** *(to skim along)* deslizarse o posarse como un hidroavión; *(to travel)* viajar en un hidroavión.
hy·dro·pon·ics (hī′drə-pŏn′ĭks) s.pl. [ú. con v. sing.] AGR. hidroponía, hidropónica (acuicultura).
hy·dro·sphere (hī′drə-sfîr′) s. hidrosfera.
hy·dro·stat·ics (hī′drə-stăt′ĭks) s.pl. [ú. con v. sing.] HIDRÁUL. hidrostática.
hy·dro·ther·a·py (hī′drə-thĕr′ə-pē) s. MED. hidroterapia.
hy·drot·ro·pism (hī-drŏt′rə-pĭz′əm) s. BIOL. hidrotropismo.
hy·drous (hī′drəs) adj. *(watery)* acuoso, aguado; QUÍM. hidratado.
hy·drox·ide (hī-drŏk′sīd′) s. QUÍM. hidróxido.
hy·e·na (hī-ē′nə) s. ZOOL. hiena.
hy·giene (hī′jēn′) s. higiene (ciencia, práctica, estado) *f*.
hy·gi·en·ic (hī′jē-ĕn′ĭk, hī-jēn′-) adj. *(healthful)* higiénico, de la higiene; *(sanitary)* sanitario.
hy·gi·en·ics (hī′jē-ĕn′ĭks, hī-jēn′-) s.pl. [ú. con v. sing.] higiene *f*.
hy·gien·ist (hī-jēn′ĭst) s. higienista *mf*.
hy·grom·e·ter (hī-grŏm′ĭ-tər) s. FÍS., METEOR. higrómetro, higroscopio.
hy·gro·scop·ic (hī′grə-skŏp′ĭk) adj. higroscópico.
hy·men (hī′mən) s. ANAT. himen *m*; ANT. himeneo, casamiento.
hy·me·nop·ter·an (hī′mə-nŏp′tə-rŏn′) s. & adj. ENTOM. himenóptero.
hymn (hĭm) **I.** s. himno **II.** tr. alabar o glorificar con himnos —intr. cantar himnos.
hym·nal (hĭm′nəl) s. libro de himnos, himnario.
hymn·book (hĭm′bŏŏk′) s. libro de himnos.
hype (hīp) **I.** s. JER. *(deception)* engaño, superchería; *(exaggerated promotion)* publicidad exagerada; *(hypodermic)* jeringa hipodérmica; *(drug addict)* narcómano **II.** tr. **hyped, hyp·ing** *(to promote)* promocionar (con exageraciones); *(to stimulate)* excitar (por medio de drogas estimulantes).
hyped-up (hīpt′ŭp′) adj. JER. excitado, entusiasmado.
hy·per·a·cid·i·ty (hī′pər-ə-sĭd′ĭ-tē) s. MED. hiperacidez *f*.
hy·per·ac·tive (hī′pər-ăk′tĭv) adj. hiperactivo.
hy·per·bo·la (hī-pûr′bə-lə) s. [pl. **-las** o **-lae** (-lē)] GEOM. hipérbola.
hy·per·bo·le (hī-pûr′bə-lē) s. RET. hipérbole *f*.
hy·per·bol·ic (hī′pər-bŏl′ĭk) o **hy·per·bol·i·cal** (-ĭ-kəl) adj. hiperbólico.
hy·per·crit·i·cal (hī′pər-krĭt′ĭ-kəl) adj. hipercrítico.
hy·per·gly·ce·mi·a (hī′pər-glī-sē′mē-ə) s. MED. hiperglicemia, hiperglucemia.
hy·per·sen·si·tive (hī′pər-sĕn′sĭ-tĭv) adj. hipersensible.
hy·per·sen·si·tiv·i·ty (hī′pər-sĕn′sĭ-tĭv′ĭ-tē) s. hipersensibilidad *f*.
hy·per·ten·sion (hī′pər-tĕn′shən) s. MED. hipertensión *f*.
hy·per·ten·sive (hī′pər-tĕn′sĭv) adj. & s. MED. hipertenso.
hy·per·ther·mi·a (hī′pər-thûr′mē-ə) s. MED. hipertermia.
hy·per·thy·roid·ism (hī′pər-thī′roi-dĭz′əm) s. MED. hipertiroidismo.
hy·per·tro·phy (hī-pûr′trə-fē) **I.** s. BIOL., MED. hipertrofia **II.** tr. & intr. **-phied, -phy·ing** hipertrofiar(se).
hy·per·ven·ti·la·tion (hī′pər-vĕn′tl-ā′shən) s. MED. hiperventilación *f*.
hy·phen (hī′fən) **I.** s. guión *m* **II.** tr. unir o separar con guión.
hy·phen·ate (hī′fə-nāt′) tr. **-at·ed, -at·ing** GRAM. unir con guión *(palabras)*; *(to divide)* separar con guión *(sílabas)*.
hy·phen·a·tion (hī′fə-nā′shən) s. GRAM. *(connection)* unión con guión *f*; *(division)* separación con guión *f*.
hyp·no·sis (hĭp-nō′sĭs) s. [pl. **-ses** (-sēz′)] MED., PSIC. hipnosis *f*.

hyp·no·ther·a·py (hĭp′nō-thĕr′ə-pē) s. MED., PSIC. hipnoterapia.
hyp·not·ic (hĭp-nŏt′ĭk) I. adj. hipnótico, de la hipnosis II. s. hipnótico (medicamento); *(hypnotized person)* persona hipnotizada.
hyp·no·tism (hĭp′nə-tĭz′əm) s. MED., PSIC. hipnotismo, hipnosis f.
hyp·no·tist (hĭp′nə-tĭst) s. hipnotizador m, hipnotista mf.
hyp·no·tize (hĭp′nə-tīz′) tr. **-tized, -tiz·ing** MED., PSIC. hipnotizar; FIG. *(to fascinate)* magnetizar.
hy·po·cen·ter (hī′pə-sĕn′tər) s. FÍS. superficie inmediatamente debajo de una explosión nuclear f; GEOF. hipocentro (sísmico).
hy·po·chon·dri·a (hī′pə-kŏn′drē-ə) s. MED. hipocondría; ANAT. hipocondrios.
hy·po·chon·dri·ac (hī′pə-kŏn′drē-ăk′) I. s. MED. hipocondríaco (paciente) II. adj. MED. hipocondríaco, de la hipocondría; ANAT. hipocondríaco, del hipocondrio.
hy·poc·ri·sy (hĭ-pŏk′rĭ-sē) s. [pl. **-sies**] hipocresía.
hyp·o·crite (hĭp′ə-krĭt′) s. hipócrita mf.
hyp·o·crit·i·cal (hĭp′ə-krĭt′ĭ-kəl) adj. hipócrita.
hy·po·derm (hī′pə-dûrm′) s. var. de **hypodermis.**
hy·po·der·mic (hī′pə-dûr′mĭk) I. adj. ANAT., MED. hipodérmico, subcutáneo II. s. MED. injección f, aguja o jeringa hipodérmica.
hypodermic needle s. MED. aguja hipodérmica.
hypodermic syringe s. MED. jeringa hipodérmica.
hy·po·der·mis (hī′pə-dûr′mĭs) s. ANAT., BOT., ZOOL. hipodermis f.
hy·po·gly·ce·mi·a (hī′pō-glī-sē′mē-ə) s. MED. hipoglicemia.
hy·pos·ta·sis (hī-pŏs′tə-sĭs) s. [pl. **-ses** (-sēz′)] FILOS., TEOL. hipóstasis f, fundamento (esencia); MED. hipóstasis, sedimento.
hy·po·sul·fite (hī′pō-sŭl′fīt′) s. QUÍM. hiposulfito; *(sodium thiosulfate)* tiosulfato de sodio (comúnmente).
hy·po·ten·sion (hī′pō-tĕn′shən) s. MED. hipotensión f.
hy·pot·e·nuse (hī-pŏt′n-ōōs′) s. GEOM. hipotenusa.
hy·po·thal·a·mus (hī′pō-thăl′ə-məs) s. ANAT. hipotálamo.
hy·poth·e·cate (hī-pŏth′ĭ-kāt′) tr. **-cat·ed, -cat·ing** COM., DER. hipotecar, empeñar.
hy·poth·e·nuse (hī-pŏth′ə-nōōs′) s. var. de **hypotenuse.**
hy·po·ther·mi·a (hī′pō-thûr′mē-ə) s. MED. hipotermia.
hy·poth·e·sis (hī-pŏth′ĭ-sĭs) s. [pl. **-ses** (-sēz′)] hipótesis f, suposición f.
hy·poth·e·size (hī-pŏth′ĭ-sīz′) intr. **-sized, -siz·ing** formar una hipótesis.
hy·po·thet·i·cal (hī′pə-thĕt′ĭ-kəl) o **hy·po·thet·ic** (-ĭk) adj. *(conjectural)* hipotético, supuesto; *(contingent)* contingente, dependiente.
hy·po·thy·roid·ism (hī′pō-thī′roi-dĭz′əm) s. MED. hipotiroidismo.
hys·sop (hĭs′əp) s. BOT. hisopo; RELIG. hisopo, aspersorio (de agua bendita).
hys·ter·ec·to·my (hĭs′tə-rĕk′tə-mē) s. [pl. **-mies**] CIR. histerectomía.
hys·ter·i·a (hĭ-stĕr′ē-ə, -stîr′-) s. MED. histeria, histerismo; FAM. *(fit)* acceso, ataque de nervios m.
hys·ter·ic (hĭ-stĕr′ĭk) I. s. MED. histérico (persona) ♦ **hysterics** [ú. con v. sing. o pl.] *(fit)* paroxismo, exaltación (nerviosa) f; *(attack of hysteria)* ataque de histeria m II. adj. histérico.
hys·ter·i·cal (hĭ-stĕr′ĭ-kəl) adj. MED. histérico; *(emotional)* emocional (persona).
hys·ter·ics (hĭ-stĕr′ĭks) s. [ú. con v. sing. o pl.] histerismo, crisis de histeria f.

I

i, I (ī) s. [pl. **i's, I's**] novena letra del alfabeto inglés.
I §G29 (ī) I. pron. yo *<I did it myself* lo hice yo mismo> II. s. [pl. **I's**] FILOS. yo, ego.
i·am·bic (ī-ăm′bĭk) POÉT. I. adj. yámbico II. s. yambo ♦ **iambics** verso o poema escrito con pie yámbico.

I·be·ri·a (ī-bîr′ē-ə) s. Iberia.
I·be·ri·an (ī-bîr′ē-ən) I. adj. ibérico, ibero *<I. peninsula* península ibérica> II. s. *(inhabitant)* ibero (habitante); *(language)* lengua ibera.
i·bi·dem (ĭb′ĭ-dĕm′) adv. ibidem, alli mismo.
i·bis (ī′bĭs) s. ORNIT. ibis m.
Ic·a·rus (ĭk′ər-əs) s. MITOL. Ícaro.
ice (īs) I. s. *(frozen water)* hielo *<she slipped on the i.* resbaló en el hielo>; *(dessert)* helado escarchado; FAM. *(unfriendliness)* hielo, frialdad f; *(diamonds)* diamantes m ♦ **i. cube** cubito de hielo • **to break the i.** *(to relax)* romper el hielo; *(to begin)* dar el primer paso • **to cut no i.** FAM. *(a person)* ser un cero a la izquierda; *(an argument)* no convencer, no surtir efecto • **to keep on i.** *(food)* conservar en hielo; FAM. *(to keep in reserve)* tener en reserva; *(to hold incommunicado)* tener incomunicado • **to put on i.** FAM. dejar para más adelante • **to tread on thin i.** pisar terreno peligroso II. tr. **iced, ic·ing** *(cake)* alcorzar, escarchar; *(to freeze)* helar, congelar; *(to chill)* congelar; *(to cover with ice)* cubrir de hielo —intr. helarse.
ice age s. GEOL. período glaciar ♦ **I.** la época glaciar.
ice ax s. DEP. pico de alpinista, piqueta.
ice bag s. MED. bolsa de hielo.
ice·berg (īs′bûrg′) s. *(floating mass)* iceberg m, montaña de hielo flotante; FIG., FAM. *(cold person)* témpano.
ice·boat (īs′bōt′) s. DEP. bote con patines y velas m; *(ice-breaker)* rompehielos m.
ice·bound (īs′bound′) adj. rodeado o bloqueado por el hielo.
ice·box (īs′bŏks′) s. nevera, refrigerador m.
ice·break·er (īs′brā′kər) s. MARÍT. *(ship)* rompehielos m; *(pier apron)* espolón m, tajamar m.
ice cap s. GEOG., METEOR. casquete polar m.
ice-cold (īs′kōld′) adj. helado.
ice cream s. CUL. helado.
ice-cream cone (īs′krēm′) s. CUL. *(wafer)* barquillo, cucurucho; *(ice cream)* helado en barquillo o cucurucho.
iced (īst) adj. *(frozen)* congelado, helado; *(cooled)* enfriado, refrigerado; CUL. *(coated)* escarchado, garapiñado.
ice hockey s. DEP. hockey sobre hielo m.
Ice·land (īs′lənd) s. Islandia.
Ice·land·er (īs′lən-dər) s. islandés m.
Ice·land·ic (īs-lăn′dĭk) adj. & s. *(inhabitant, language)* islandés m.
ice·man (īs′măn′) s. [pl. **-men** (-mĕn′)] *(seller)* vendedor de hielo m; *(deliverer)* repartidor de hielo m.
ice pack s. *(floating mass)* banco de témpanos flotantes; MED. compresa de hielo.
ice pick s. *(awl)* punzón para romper hielo m; *(climber's tool)* piqueta.
ice skate s. *(blade)* cuchilla (de patín); *(skate)* patín de hielo m.
ice-skate (īs′skāt′) intr. **-skat·ed, -skat·ing** patinar sobre hielo.
ich·thy·ol·o·gy (ĭk′thē-ŏl′ə-jē) s. ictiología (estudio de los peces).
i·ci·cle (ī′sĭ-kəl) s. *(spike)* carámbano; FIG., FAM. *(cold person)* témpano.
ic·i·ly (ī′sə-lē) adv. fríamente, con frialdad.
ic·ing (ī′sĭng) s. CUL. *(sugar coating)* alcorza, escarchado; DEP. *(in ice hockey)* jugada antirreglamentaria.
i·con (ī′kŏn′) s. RELIG. icono.
i·con·o·clasm (ī-kŏn′ə-klăz′əm) s. iconoclasia.
i·con·o·clast (ī-kŏn′ə-klăst′) s. iconoclasta mf.
i·con·o·clas·tic (ī-kŏn′ə-klăs′tĭk) adj. iconoclasta.
i·co·nog·ra·phy (ī′kə-nŏg′rə-fē) s. [pl. **-phies**] iconografía.
ic·tus (ĭk′təs) [pl. **-tus·es** o ictus] MED. paroxismo, ataque repentino.
ic·y (ī′sē) adj. **-i·er, -i·est** *(resembling ice)* helado *<i. fingers* dedos helados>; *(ice-covered)* cubierto de hielo; *(freezing)* helado, glacial; *(person, look)* glacial.
id (ĭd) s. PSIC. id m.
I'd (īd) contr. de **I had, I would,** y **I should.**
ID card (ī′dē′) s. carnet m, tarjeta de identificación.
i·de·a (ī-dē′ə) s. *(concept)* idea; *(intention)* intención f; *(plan)* proyecto, plan m ♦ **bright i.** idea genial • **not to**

have the faintest o **the slightest i.** no tener la menor idea • **that's the i.!** ¡eso es! • **to get an i.** *(to get a notion of)* hacerse una idea; *(to think of)* ocurrírsele a uno una idea • **to get an i. into one's head** metérsele a uno una idea en la cabeza • **to get ideas** hacerse ilusiones • **to get the i.** darse cuenta • **what's the big i.?** FAM. ¿a qué viene eso?

i·de·al (ī-dē'əl) **I.** s. *(perfection)* ideal m; *(model)* modelo **II.** adj. ideal <*an i. day for the beach* un día ideal para la playa>.

i·de·al·ism (ī-dē'ə-līz'əm) s. idealismo.

i·de·al·ist (ī-dē'ə-līst) s. idealista mf.

i·de·al·is·tic (ī-dē'ə-līs'tīk) adj. idealista.

i·de·al·i·za·tion (ī-dē'ə-lī-zā'shən) s. idealización f.

i·de·al·ize (ī-dē'ə-līz') tr. **-ized, -iz·ing** idealizar —intr. crearse un ideal.

i·de·al·ly (ī-dē'ə-lē) adv. *(perfectly)* perfectamente; *(theoretically)* idealmente, en el mejor de los casos.

i·den·ti·cal (ī-dĕn'tī-kəl) adj. *(alike)* idéntico <*i. parts* piezas idénticas>; *(same)* mismo <*the i. words* las mismas palabras>; *(twins)* idéntico.

identical twin s. gemelo idéntico.

i·den·ti·fi·a·ble (ī-dĕn'tə-fī'ə-bəl) adj. identificable ♦ **easily i.** de fácil identificación.

i·den·ti·fi·ca·tion (ī-dĕn'tə-fī-kā'shən) s. identificación f ♦ **i. papers** documentos de identidad.

identification card s. carnet m, tarjeta de identificación.

i·den·ti·fi·er (ī-dĕn'tə-fī'ər) s. *(person)* identificador m; *(sign)* signo de identificación.

i·den·ti·fy (ī-dĕn'tə-fī') tr. **-fied, -fy·ing** identificar —intr. identificarse.

i·den·ti·ty (ī-dĕn'tī-tē) s. [pl. **-ties**] identidad f ♦ **i. papers** documentos de identidad.

identity card s. tarjeta o documento de identidad.

id·e·o·gram (īd'ē-ə-grăm') o **id·e·o·graph** (-grăf') s. ideograma m.

i·de·o·log·i·cal (ī'dē-ə-lŏj'ī-kəl, īd'ē-) o **i·de·o·log·ic** (-lŏj'īk) adj. ideológico.

i·de·o·logue (ī'dē-ə-lŏg', īd'ē-) s. ideólogo.

i·de·ol·o·gy (ī'dē-ŏl'ə-jē, īd'ē-) s. [pl. **-gies**] ideología.

ides (īdz) s. [ú. con v. sing.] HIST. idus m, idos.

id est (īd' ĕst') LAT. es decir.

id·i·o·cy (īd'ē-ə-sē) s. [pl. **-cies**] *(subnormal development)* idiotez f; *(stupidity)* estupidez f; *(foolish deed)* necedad f.

id·i·om (īd'ē-əm) s. *(idiomatic expression)* modismo, locución f; *(jargon)* jerga, idioma m <*legal i.* jerga jurídica>; *(style)* estilo.

id·i·o·mat·ic (īd'ē-ə-măt'īk) adj. idiomático ♦ **i. expression** modismo.

id·i·o·syn·cra·sy (īd'ē-ō-sīng'krə-sē) s. [pl. **-sies**] *(behavioral characteristic)* idiosincrasia; MED. hipersensibilidad (a una droga) f.

id·i·o·syn·crat·ic (īd'ē-ō-sīn-krăt'īk) adj. idiosincrásico.

id·i·ot (īd'ē-ət) s. *(deficient individual)* idiota mf; *(fool)* tonto.

id·i·ot·ic (īd'ē-ŏt'īk) adj. idiota, tonto.

i·dle (īd'l) **I.** adj. **i·dler, i·dlest** *(inactive)* ocioso; *(unemployed)* parado, desempleado; *(machinery)* parado; *(lazy)* vago, haragán; *(not founded in fact)* vano (temor, amenaza) ♦ **i. gossip** cuentos de viejas • **i. talk** palabras vacías **II.** intr. **i·dled, i·dling** *(to loaf)* haraganear; *(to move lazily)* vagar; *(machinery)* funcionar en vacío —tr. *(a worker)* dejar parado o desempleado; *(a motor)* hacer funcionar en vacío.

idle character s. COMPUT. carácter que indica que el canal de transmisión está disponible.

i·dle·ness (īd'l-nīs) s. *(inaction)* ociosidad f; *(unemployment)* paro, desempleo; *(laziness)* vagancia, haraganería.

i·dler (īd'lər) s. *(person)* ocioso, vago; MEC. *(pulley)* polea muerta o loca.

i·dly (īd'lē) adv. *(inactively)* ociosamente; *(lazily)* haraganamente.

i·dol (īd'l) s. ídolo.

i·dol·a·ter (ī-dŏl'ə-tər) s. idólatra mf.

i·dol·a·trous (ī-dŏl'ə-trəs) adj. *(person)* idólatra; *(constituting idolatry)* idolátrico.

i·dol·a·try (ī-dŏl'ə-trē) s. idolatría.

i·dol·ize (īd'l-īz') tr. **-ized, -iz·ing** *(to worship)* idolatrar; *(to admire blindly)* admirar ciegamente.

i·dyll o **i·dyl** (īd'l) s. idilio.

i·dyl·lic (ī-dīl'īk) adj. idílico.

if (īf) **I.** conj. *(whether)* si <*ask if he will come* pregunta si él vendrá>; *(granting that)* si, en caso que <*if that's true, what should we do?* en caso que eso sea cierto, ¿qué hemos de hacer?>; *(even though)* si bien, aunque <*a cute if useless trinket* una chuchería simpática, si bien inservible> ♦ **if and when** si es que, siempre y cuando • **if at all** si es que <*I'll study later, if at all* estudiaré más tarde, si es que lo hago> • **if I were you** yo en tu lugar, yo que tú **II.** s. ♦ **no ifs, ands, or buts** no hay pero que valga.

ig·loo (ĭg'lōō) s. [pl. **-loos**] iglú m.

ig·ne·ous (ĭg'nē-əs) adj. ígneo.

ig·nite (ĭg-nīt') tr. **-nit·ed, -nit·ing** *(to set fire to)* encender, prender o pegar fuego; FIG. *(to excite)* excitar, estimular —intr. encenderse.

ig·ni·tion (ĭg-nĭsh'ən) s. *(action)* ignición f; AUTO. encendido.

ig·no·ble (ĭg-nō'bəl) adj. *(dishonorable)* innoble, bajo; *(plebeian)* plebeyo; *(common)* común.

ig·no·min·i·ous (ĭg'nə-mĭn'ē-əs) adj. *(shameful)* ignominioso, vergonzoso; *(degrading)* degradante.

ig·no·min·y (ĭg'nə-mĭn'ē) s. [pl. **-ies**] ignominia.

ig·no·ra·mus (ĭg'nə-rā'məs) s. ignorante mf.

ig·no·rance (ĭg'nər-əns) s. ignorancia.

ig·no·rant (ĭg'nər-ənt) adj. *(uneducated)* ignorante; *(primitive)* primitivo; *(unaware)* desconocedor, ignorante.

ig·nore (ĭg-nôr') tr. **-nored, -nor·ing** *(to disregard)* no prestar atención a, no hacer caso de; *(to leave out)* pasar por alto.

i·gua·na (ĭ-gwä'nə) s. ZOOL. iguana.

i·kon (ī'kŏn') s. var. de **icon.**

il·e·um (ĭl'ē-əm) s. [pl. **-e·a** (-ē-ə)] ANAT. íleon m.

ilk (ĭlk) s. clase f, índole f.

I'll (īl) contr. de **I shall** y **I will.**

ill (īl) **I.** adj. **worse** (wûrs), **worst** (wûrst) *(sick)* enfermo, malo; *(hostile)* malo <*i. intentions* malas intenciones> ♦ **i. effects** *(of an action)* consecuencias f; *(of a medication)* efectos, malestar • **to be in i. health** estar mal de salud • **to fall** o **be taken i.** enfermarse, caer enfermo • **to feel i.** sentirse mal **II.** adv. **worse, worst** *(not well)* mal <*i. paid for her work* mal remunerada por su trabajo>; *(scarcely)* mal, poco <*i. prepared* poco preparado> ♦ **I can i. afford to** no puedo darme el lujo de • **i. at ease** incómodo **III.** s. *(evil)* mal m; *(disaster)* mal, desgracia; *(ailment)* mal <*social ills* males sociales>.

ill-ad·vised (ĭl'əd-vīzd') adj. *(person)* imprudente; *(action)* poco atinado, imprudente.

ill-bred (ĭl'brĕd') adj. *(impolite)* mal educado; *(not thoroughbred)* impuro, mezclado (díc. de raza).

ill-con·sid·ered (ĭl'kən-sĭd'ərd) adj. *(not properly considered)* poco estudiado; *(unwise)* imprudente.

il·le·gal (ĭ-lē'gəl) **I.** adj. ilegal, ilícito **II.** s. inmigrante ilegal mf.

illegal alien s. inmigrante ilegal mf.

il·le·gal·i·ty (ĭl'ē-găl'ĭ-tē) s. [pl. **-ties**] *(quality)* ilegalidad f; *(unlawful act)* acto ilegal.

il·leg·i·bil·i·ty (ĭ-lĕj'ə-bĭl'ĭ-tē) s. ilegibilidad f.

il·leg·i·ble (ĭ-lĕj'ə-bəl) adj. ilegible.

il·le·git·i·ma·cy (ĭl'ə-jĭt'ə-mə-sē) s. ilegitimidad f.

il·le·git·i·mate (ĭl'ə-jĭt'ə-mĭt) adj. *(illegal)* ilegal; *(bastard)* ilegítimo, bastardo; *(illogical)* ilógico.

ill-fat·ed (ĭl'fā'tĭd) adj. *(unfortunate)* desdichado, malaventurado; *(doomed)* condenado al fracaso; *(unlucky)* desafortunado.

ill-got·ten (ĭl'gŏt'n) adj. mal obtenido, mal habido.

ill-hu·mored (ĭl'hyōō'mərd) adj. malhumorado.

il·lib·er·al (ĭ-lĭb'ər-əl) adj. conservador, intolerante.

il·lic·it (ĭ-lĭs'ĭt) adj. *(unlawful)* ilícito; *(illegal)* ilegal.

il·lit·er·a·cy (ĭ-lĭt'ər-ə-sē) s. [pl. **-cies**] analfabetismo.

il·lit·er·ate (ĭ-lĭt'ər-ĭt) s. & adj. *(unable to read or write)* analfabeto; *(culturally ignorant)* inculto, ignorante mf.

ill-man·nered (ĭl'măn'ərd) adj. *(rude)* mal educado, descortés; *(bad-mannered)* de malos modales.

---

ill·na·tured (ĭl′nā′chərd) adj. *(sullen)* de mal genio, malhumorado; *(surly)* hosco; *(spiteful)* malicioso; *(nasty)* avieso.

ill·ness (ĭl′nĭs) s. enfermedad *f.*

il·log·i·cal (ĭ-lŏj′ĭ-kəl) adj. *(contradicting logic)* ilógico; *(senseless)* sin sentido.

ill-pre·pared (ĭl′prī-pârd′) adj. mal preparado.

ill-starred (ĭl′stärd′) adj. *(ill-fated)* malaventurado, desafortunado; *(unlucky)* de mala suerte, de mal agüero.

ill-suit·ed (ĭl′sōō′tĭd) adj. impropio.

ill-tem·pered (ĭl′tĕm′pərd) adj. *(having a bad temper)* de mal genio, de mal carácter; *(irritable)* enojadizo.

ill-treat (ĭl′trēt′) tr. maltratar, tratar cruelmente.

ill-treat·ment (ĭl′trēt′mənt) s. maltrato.

il·lu·mi·nate (ĭ-lōō′mə-nāt′) tr. **-nat·ed, -nat·ing** *(to provide light)* iluminar, alumbrar; *(building)* iluminar, adornar con luces; *(a page, book)* miniar, iluminar.

il·lu·mi·nat·ing (ĭ-lōō′mə-nā′tĭng) adj. *(oil, gas)* de alumbrado; *(book)* instructivo; *(solution, remark)* revelador.

il·lu·mi·na·tion (ĭ-lōō′mə-nā′shən) s. *(act, source)* iluminación *f,* alumbrado; *(of a person, problem, page)* iluminación, miniatura; Fís. iluminancia.

ill-use I. tr. (ĭl′yōōz′) **-used, -us·ing** maltratar II. s. (-yōōs′) maltrato.

il·lu·sion (ĭ-lōō′zhən) s. *(perception, concept)* ilusión *f; (performed by a magician)* truco; TEJ. cendal *m* ♦ **to be under an i.** engañarse.

il·lu·sion·al (ĭ-lōō′zhən-əl) adj. ilusorio.

il·lu·sion·ist (ĭ-lōō′zhə-nĭst) s. ilusionista *mf.*

il·lu·sive (ĭ-lōō′sĭv) adj. ilusivo, ilusorio.

il·lu·so·ry (ĭ-lōō′sə-rē) adj. *(illusive)* ilusorio; *(deceptive)* engañoso.

il·lus·trate (ĭl′ə-strāt′, ĭ-lŭs′trāt′) tr. & intr. **-trat·ed, -trat·ing** ilustrar.

il·lus·tra·tion (ĭl′ə-strā′shən) s. *(act, state)* ilustración *f; (example)* ilustración, ejemplo.

il·lus·tra·tive (ĭ-lŭs′trə-tĭv, ĭl′ə-strā′tĭv) adj. ilustrativo ♦ **to be i. of** ilustrar, ejemplificar.

il·lus·tra·tor (ĭl′ə-strā′tər, ĭ-lŭs′trā′-) s. ilustrador *m.*

il·lus·tri·ous (ĭ-lŭs′trē-əs) adj. ilustre.

ill will s. mala voluntad, enemistad *f.*

I'm (ĭm) contr. de **I am.**

im·age (ĭm′ĭj) I. s. ARTE., FÍS., LIT. imagen *f <a very clear i.* una imagen muy clara>; *(reputation)* reputación *f <public i.* reputación pública> ♦ **in one's own i.** a imagen de uno • **mirror i.** reflejo exacto, espejo II. tr. **-aged, -ag·ing** representar, retratar.

im·age·ry (ĭm′ĭj-rē) s. [pl. **-ries**] LIT., PSIC. imágenes *f;* ARTE. imaginería.

i·mag·i·na·ble (ĭ-măj′ə-nə-bəl) adj. imaginable.

i·mag·i·nar·y (ĭ-măj′ə-nĕr′ē) adj. imaginario.

imaginary number s. MAT. imaginaria, número imaginario.

i·mag·i·na·tion (ĭ-măj′ə-nā′shən) s. *(power of the mind)* imaginación *f; (resourcefulness)* imaginación, inventiva ♦ **to have no i.** ser una persona sin imaginación.

i·mag·i·na·tive (ĭ-măj′ə-nə-tĭv, -nā′tĭv) adj. *(of a creative imagination)* imaginativo; *(make-believe)* fantasioso; *(false)* imaginario.

i·mag·ine (ĭ-măj′ĭn) tr. **-ined, -in·ing** *(to envision)* imaginar, concebir; *(to suppose)* imaginarse, suponer —intr. imaginarse ♦ **just i.!** ¡imagínate!

i·mam (ĭ-mäm′) s. RELIG. imán *m.*

im·bal·ance (ĭm-băl′əns) s. desequilibrio, falta de equilibrio.

im·be·cile (ĭm′bə-sĭl) I. s. imbécil *mf* II. adj. *(deficient)* imbécil; *(stupid)* estúpido.

im·be·cil·i·ty (ĭm′bə-sĭl′ĭ-tē) s. [pl. **-ties**] *(quality, condition)* imbecilidad *f; (foolish act)* disparate *m.*

im·bed (ĭm-bĕd′) v. var. de **embed.**

im·bibe (ĭm-bīb′) tr. **-bibed, -bib·ing** *(to drink)* beber; FIG. *(to absorb)* absorber, empaparse de o en —intr. beber.

im·bri·cate (ĭm′brĭ-kāt′) adj. imbricado.

im·bro·glio (ĭm-brōl′yō) s. [pl. **-glios**] *(entanglement)* embrollo, enredo; *(disagreement)* embrollo, lío; *(tangle)* maraña.

im·bue (ĭm-byōō′) tr. **-bued, -bu·ing** *(to inspire)* imbuir; *(to saturate)* empapar, saturar.

im·i·ta·ble (ĭm′ĭ-tə-bəl) adj. imitable.

im·i·tate (ĭm′ĭ-tāt′) tr. **-tat·ed, -tat·ing** *(to model after)* imitar; *(to reproduce)* reproducir, copiar.

im·i·ta·tion (ĭm′ĭ-tā′shən) s. imitación *f* ♦ **i. fur** piel de imitación • **i. leather** cuero artificial • **in i. of** a imitación de.

im·i·ta·tive (ĭm′ĭ-tā′tĭv) adj. *(involving imitation)* imitativo, imitador; *(not original)* imitado ♦ **i. of** que imita a.

im·i·ta·tor (ĭm′ĭ-tā′tər) s. imitador *m.*

im·mac·u·late (ĭ-măk′yə-lĭt) adj. *(stainless)* inmaculado; *(pure)* puro; *(fault-free)* perfecto; *(clean)* limpio; RELIG. inmaculado, purísimo.

Immaculate Conception s. RELIG. Inmaculada Concepción, la Purísima (Concepción).

im·ma·nence (ĭm′ə-nəns) *o* **im·ma·nen·cy** (-nən-sē) s. inmanencia.

im·ma·nent (ĭm′ə-nənt) adj. *(existing within)* inmanente; *(inherent)* inherente; *(subjective)* subjetivo.

im·ma·te·ri·al (ĭm′ə-tîr′ē-əl) adj. *(formless)* incorpóreo; *(unimportant)* sin importancia; *(inconsequential)* sin trascendencia ♦ **to be i.** ser ajeno al asunto.

im·ma·ture (ĭm′ə-chŏŏr′) adj. *(not fully grown)* inmaduro; *(unripe)* verde; *(person)* inmaduro.

im·ma·tur·i·ty (ĭm′ə-chŏŏr′ĭ-tē) s. falta de madurez.

im·meas·ur·a·ble (ĭ-mĕzh′ər-ə-bəl) adj. *(incapable of being measured)* inmensurable; *(vast)* inconmensurable, ilimitado.

im·me·di·a·cy (ĭ-mē′dē-ə-sē) s. [pl. **-cies**] *(condition, quality)* inmediatez *f; (proximity)* inmediación *f,* proximidad *f; (of a problem)* urgencia; *(of danger)* inminencia.

im·me·di·ate (ĭ-mē′dē-ĭt) adj. *(occurring at once)* inmediato *<i. medical care* atención médica inmediata>; *(direct)* inmediato, directo; *(very soon)* próximo *<the i. future* el futuro próximo>; *(danger)* inminente; *(problem)* urgente; FILOS. *(directly apprehended)* intuitivo ♦ **i. vicinity** inmediaciones.

im·me·di·ate·ly (ĭ-mē′dē-ĭt-lē) I. adv. *(at once)* inmediatamente, en seguida; *(directly)* directamente II. conj. en cuanto.

im·me·mo·ri·al (ĭm′ə-môr′ē-əl) adj. inmemorial.

im·mense (ĭ-mĕns′) adj. *(large)* inmenso, enorme; *(vast)* inconmensurable, sin límites; JER. *(excellent)* excelente, estupendo.

im·men·si·ty (ĭ-mĕn′sĭ-tē) s. [pl. **-ties**] inmensidad *f.*

im·merge (ĭ-mûrj′) intr. **-merged, -merg·ing** sumergirse.

im·merse (ĭ-mûrs′) tr. **-mersed, -mers·ing** *(to submerge)* sumergir; *(to baptize)* bautizar por inmersión; FIG. *(to absorb)* enfrascar, absorber.

im·mer·sion (ĭ-mûr′zhən) s. *(act)* inmersión *f; (baptism)* bautismo por inmersión; ASTRON. inmersión.

im·mi·grant (ĭm′ĭ-grənt) s. inmigrante *mf.*

im·mi·grate (ĭm′ĭ-grāt′) intr. **-grat·ed, -grat·ing** inmigrar.

im·mi·gra·tion (ĭm′ĭ-grā′shən) s. inmigración *f.*

im·mi·nence (ĭm′ə-nəns) *o* **im·mi·nen·cy** (-nən-sē) s. inminencia.

im·mi·nent (ĭm′ə-nənt) adj. inminente.

im·mo·bile (ĭ-mō′bəl, -bīl′) adj. *(not moving)* inmóvil; *(not movable)* inmovible; *(fixed)* fijo; *(not changing)* inmutable.

im·mo·bil·i·ty (ĭm′ō-bĭl′ĭ-tē) s. inmovilidad *f.*

im·mo·bi·lize (ĭ-mō′bə-līz′) tr. **-lized, -liz·ing** inmovilizar.

im·mod·er·ate (ĭ-mŏd′ər-ĭt) adj. *(exceeding bounds)* inmoderado; *(extreme)* extremado, excesivo.

im·mod·est (ĭ-mŏd′ĭst) adj. *(not humble)* inmodesto; *(indecent)* indecente; *(arrogant)* arrogante.

im·mod·es·ty (ĭ-mŏd′ĭ-stē) s. *(lack of modesty)* inmodestia; *(indecency)* indecencia; *(arrogance)* arrogancia.

im·mo·late (ĭm′ə-lāt′) tr. **-lat·ed, -lat·ing** *(to sacrifice)* inmolar; *(to destroy)* destruir.

im·mo·la·tion (ĭm′ə-lā′shən) s. inmolación *f.*

im·mor·al (ĭ-môr′əl) adj. inmoral.

im·mor·al·ist (ĭ-môr′ə-lĭst) s. persona que preconiza la inmoralidad.

im·mo·ral·i·ty (ĭm′ô-răl′ĭ-tē) s. [pl. **-ties**] inmoralidad *f.*

im·mor·tal (ĭ-môr′tl) I. adj. *(not mortal)* inmortal; *(imper-*

ishable) imperecedero **II.** s. inmortal *mf* ♦ **the Immortals**
MITOL. los dioses.
im·mor·tal·i·ty (ĭm'ôr-tăl'ĭ-tē) s. inmortalidad *f.*
im·mor·tal·ize (ĭ-môr'tl-īz') tr. **-ized, -iz·ing** inmortalizar.
im·mov·a·ble (ĭ-mōō'və-bəl) adj. *(not movable)* inamovible;
(immobile) inmóvil; *(unalterable)* inalterable; *(unyielding)*
inflexible; *(unemotional)* inconmovible, inmutable.
im·mune (ĭ-myōōn') adj. MED. inmune; FIG. *(exempt)*
exento ♦ **i. from** exento de.
im·mu·ni·ty (ĭ-myōō'nĭ-tē) s. [pl. **-ties**] *(quality, condition)*
inmunidad *f; (exemption)* exención *f* ♦ **i. from** exención
de.
im·mu·ni·za·tion (ĭm'yə-nĭ-zā'shən) s. MED. inmunización *f.*
im·mu·nize (ĭm'yə-nīz') tr. **-nized, -niz·ing** inmunizar.
im·mu·no·ge·net·ics (ĭm'yə-nō-jə-nĕt'ĭks) s. [ú. con v.
sing.] MED. inmunogenética (relación entre la inmunidad y
la herencia genética).
im·mu·no·gen·ic (ĭm'yə-nō-jĕn'ĭk) adj. inmunógeno, inmu-
nizador.
im·mu·nol·o·gist (ĭm'yə-nŏl'ə-jĭst) adj. & s. MED. especialista en inmunología *mf.*
im·mu·nol·o·gy (ĭm'yə-nŏl'ə-jē) s. MED. inmunología.
im·mu·no·ther·a·py (ĭm'yə-nō-thĕr'ə-pē) s. MED. inmunote-
rapia.
im·mure (ĭ-myōōr') tr. **-mured, -mur·ing** *(to wall)* emparedar, murar; FIG. *(to imprison)* encarcelar, confinar; *(to
build in)* empotrar; *(to entomb in a wall)* sepultar entre
paredes.
im·mu·ta·ble (ĭ-myōō'tə-bəl) adj. inmutable.
imp (ĭmp) s. diablillo, niño travieso.
im·pact **I.** s. (ĭm'păkt') *(force)* impacto, choque *m; (colli-
sion)* choque, golpe *m; (impression)* impresión *f, (influence)* efecto, consecuencias <*the i. of automation on
labor* las consecuencias de la automatización para los tra-
bajadores> **II.** tr. (ĭm-păkt') *(to strike)* chocar contra;
FAM. *(to affect)* afectar.
im·pair (ĭm-pâr') tr. deteriorar, dañar.
im·pair·ment (ĭm-pâr'mənt) s. deterioro, daño.
im·pale (ĭm-pāl') tr. **-paled, -pal·ing** *(to pierce)* empalar;
FIG. *(to transfix)* atravesar <*impaled by grief* atravesado
por la pena>.
im·pal·pa·ble (ĭm-păl'pə-bəl) adj. *(not perceptible to touch)*
impalpable; *(intangible)* intangible; *(imperceptible)* imperceptible.
im·pan·el (ĭm-păn'əl) tr. DER. elegir (un jurado).
im·part (ĭm-pärt') tr. *(to bestow)* impartir; *(to disclose)* dar a
conocer.
im·par·tial (ĭm-pär'shəl) adj. imparcial.
im·par·ti·al·i·ty (ĭm-pär'shē-ăl'ĭ-tē) s. imparcialidad *f.*
im·pass·a·ble (ĭm-păs'ə-bəl) adj. *(not traversable)* intransitable; *(insurmountable)* infranqueable.
im·passe (ĭm'păs') s. *(dead-end street)* callejón sin salida *m;*
FIG. *(stalemate)* atolladero, estancamiento.
im·pas·si·ble (ĭm-păs'ə-bəl) adj. *(insensitive)* insensible;
(impassive) impasible.
im·pas·sion (ĭm-păsh'ən) tr. apasionar.
im·pas·sioned (ĭm-păsh'ənd) adj. apasionado.
im·pas·sive (ĭm-păs'ĭv) adj. *(unemotional)* impasible; *(indifferent)* indiferente.
im·pas·siv·i·ty (ĭm'pă-sĭv'ĭ-tē) s. *(impassiveness)* impasibili-
dad *f; (indifference)* indiferencia.
im·pa·tience (ĭm-pā'shəns) s. impaciencia.
im·pa·tient (ĭm-pā'shənt) adj. impaciente ♦ **to be i. with** no
tener paciencia con • **to get i.** perder la paciencia • **to
make i.** impacientar.
im·peach (ĭm-pēch') tr. DER., POL. *(to charge)* acusar, denunciar; *(to prosecute)* enjuiciar; *(to bring into question)*
poner en tela de juicio; *(to discredit)* desacreditar; *(to censure)* censurar.
im·peach·a·ble (ĭm-pē'chə-bəl) adj. DER., POL. *(chargeable)*
acusable; *(questionable)* controvertible, discutible; *(open
to attack)* censurable.
im·peach·ment (ĭm-pēch'mənt) s. DER., POL. *(charging)*
acusación *f; (prosecution)* enjuiciamiento; *(of someone's
truthfulness)* puesta en tela de juicia; *(attack)* censura.
im·pec·ca·ble (ĭm-pĕk'ə-bəl) adj. *(faultless)* impecable;

(flawless) sin fallas; *(perfect)* perfecto; *(incapable of
wrongdoing)* incapaz de hacer mal.
im·pe·cu·ni·ous (ĭm'pĭ-kyōō'nē-əs) adj. falto de dinero,
pobre, indigente.
im·pe·dance (ĭm-pēd'ns) s. ELEC. impedancia (cociente
entre la tensión y la corriente).
im·pede (ĭm-pēd') tr. **-ped·ed, -ped·ing** *(to bar)* impedir; *(to
delay)* retardar; *(to obstruct)* obstruir.
im·ped·i·ment (ĭm-pĕd'ə-mənt) s. *(hindrance)* impedimento; *(obstacle)* obstáculo; *(defect)* defecto; DER. impedimento.
im·ped·i·men·ta (ĭm-pĕd'ə-mĕn'tə) s.pl. *(objects)* efectos
(que retardan u obstruyen); MIL. *(supplies, equipment)* im-
pedimenta.
im·pel (ĭm-pĕl') tr. **-pelled, -pel·ling** *(to compel)* compeler,
obligar; *(to drive)* incitar, inducir; *(to propel)* propulsar,
empujar; *(to drive forward)* impeler, impulsar.
im·pend (ĭm-pĕnd') intr. *(to hover menacingly)* cernerse, cer-
nirse; *(to be imminent)* ser inminente.
im·pen·e·tra·bil·i·ty (ĭm-pĕn'ĭ-trə-bĭl'ĭ-tē) s. impenetrabili-
dad *f.*
im·pen·e·tra·ble (ĭm-pĕn'ĭ-trə-bəl) adj. impenetrable.
im·pen·i·tent (ĭm-pĕn'ĭ-tnt) adj. impenitente.
im·per·a·tive (ĭm-pĕr'ə-tĭv) **I.** adj. *(commanding)* imperioso; *(mandatory)* indispensable **II.** s. *(command)* orden
f; GRAM. imperativo.
im·per·cep·ti·ble (ĭm'pər-sĕp'tə-bəl) adj. imperceptible.
im·per·fect (ĭm-pûr'fĭkt) **I.** adj. *(flawed)* imperfecto; *(defective)* defectuoso; GRAM. imperfecto **II.** s. GRAM. imperfecto.
im·per·fec·tion (ĭm'pər-fĕk'shən) s. *(lack of perfection)* imperfección *f; (defect)* defecto, desperfecto.
im·pe·ri·al (ĭm-pîr'ē-əl) **I.** adj. imperial <*i. Rome* la Roma
imperial>; *(majestic)* augusto, señorial; *(outstanding)* soberbio; *(weights and measures)* sistema inglés de medidas
m **II.** s. emperador *m.*
im·pe·ri·al·ism (ĭm-pîr'ē-ə-lĭz'əm) s. imperialismo.
im·pe·ri·al·ist (ĭm-pîr'ē-ə-lĭst) s. imperialista *mf.*
im·pe·ri·al·is·tic (ĭm-pîr'ē-ə-lĭs'tĭk) adj. imperialista.
im·per·il (ĭm-pĕr'əl) tr. *(to put in peril)* poner en peligro; *(to
risk)* arriesgar.
im·pe·ri·ous (ĭm-pîr'ē-əs) adj. *(domineering)* altanero, imperioso; *(urgent)* urgente, imperativo; ANT. *(regal)* real, majestuoso.
im·per·ish·a·ble (ĭm-pĕr'ĭ-shə-bəl) adj. imperecedero.
im·pe·ri·um (ĭm-pîr'ē-əm) s. [pl. **-ri·a** (ē-ə)] *(power)* imperio,
poder absoluto; DER. soberanía, potestad *f.*
im·per·ma·nence (ĭm-pûr'mə-nəns) s. temporalidad *f.*
im·per·ma·nent (ĭm-pûr'mə-nənt) adj. no permanente,
temporal.
im·per·me·a·bil·i·ty (ĭm-pûr'mē-ə-bĭl'ĭ-tē) s. impermeabili-
dad *f.*
im·per·me·a·ble (ĭm-pûr'mē-ə-bəl) adj. impermeable.
im·per·mis·si·ble (ĭm'pər-mĭs'ə-bəl) adj. no permisible,
inadmisible.
im·per·son·al (ĭm-pûr'sə-nəl) adj. impersonal <*an i. remark*
un comentario impersonal>; *(showing no warmth)* frío;
GRAM. *(verb)* impersonal; *(pronoun)* indefinido.
im·per·son·ate (ĭm-pûr'sə-nāt') tr. **-at·ed, -at·ing** *(to pose as)*
hacerse pasar por; TEAT. *(to play the part of)* hacer el papel
de.
im·per·son·a·tion (ĭm-pûr'sə-nā'shən) s. *(imitation)* imitación *f;* TEAT. *(role interpretation)* interpretación *f.*
im·per·son·a·tor (ĭm-pûr'sə-nā'tər) s. *(imitator)* imitador
m; TEAT. *(actor)* intérprete *mf.*
im·per·ti·nence (ĭm-pûr'tn-əns) s. *(act, word)* impertinencia; *(insolence)* insolencia.
im·per·ti·nent (ĭm-pûr'tn-ənt) adj. *(rude)* impertinente; *(insolent)* insolente; *(irrelevant)* impertinente.
im·per·turb·a·ble (ĭm'pər-tûr'bə-bəl) adj. imperturbable.
im·per·vi·ous (ĭm-pûr'vē-əs) adj. *(unaffected by)* insensible
<*i. to criticism* insensible a la crítica> ♦ **i. to water** imper-
meable.
im·pe·ti·go (ĭm'pĭ-tī'gō) s. MED. impétigo.
im·pet·u·os·i·ty (ĭm-pĕch'ōō-ŏs'ĭ-tē) s. [pl. **-ties**] impetuosidad *f.*

im·pet·u·ous (ĭm-pĕch'ŏŏ-əs) adj. *(rash)* impetuoso; *(impulsive)* impulsivo; *(forceful)* vigoroso.

im·pe·tus (ĭm'pĭ-təs) s. [pl. **-tus·es**] Fís. *(force)* ímpetu *m*; FIG. *(impulse)* impulso; *(stimulus)* ímpetu, brío.

im·pi·e·ty (ĭm-pī'ĭ-tē) s. [pl. **-ties**] *(quality, state)* impiedad *f*; *(act)* acto impío.

im·pinge (ĭm-pĭnj') intr. **-pinged, -ping·ing ♦ to i. against** chocar con *o* contra • **to i. on** *o* **upon** *(to invade)* invadir, violar, usurpar; *(to have an effect on)* impresionar, hacer impacto en.

im·pi·ous (ĭm'pē-əs, ĭm-pī'-) adj. *(not pious)* impío; *(irreverent)* irreverente; *(lacking respect)* irrespetuoso.

imp·ish (ĭm'pĭsh) adj. pícaro.

im·plac·a·ble (ĭm-plăk'ə-bəl, -plā'kə-) adj. *(relentless)* implacable; *(inexorable)* inexorable.

im·plant I. tr. (ĭm-plănt') *(to entrench firmly)* implantar, arraigar; FIG. *(to instill)* inculcar; MED. *(to insert)* injertar, implantar II. s. (ĭm'plănt') MED. injerto.

im·plan·ta·tion (ĭm'plăn-tā'shən) s. *(inculcation)* implantación *f*, inculcación *f*; MED. implantación.

im·plau·si·ble (ĭm-plô'zə-bəl) adj. *(unbelievable)* inverosímil; *(improbable)* improbable.

im·ple·ment I. s. (ĭm'plə-mənt) *(utensil)* utensilio, instrumento; *(equipment)* enser *m*, aparejo; *(means)* instrumento II. tr. (-mĕnt') *(to carry out)* poner en práctica; *(a law)* hacer efectivo, aplicar; *(to supply)* equipar.

im·ple·men·ta·tion (ĭm'plə-mən-tā'shən) s. *(of a plan)* puesta en práctica; *(of a law)* aplicación *f*; *(execution)* ejecución *f*, realización *f*.

im·pli·cate (ĭm'plĭ-kāt') tr. **-cat·ed, -cat·ing** *(to involve)* comprometer, implicar; *(to imply)* implicar.

im·pli·ca·tion (ĭm'plĭ-kā'shən) s. *(act, condition)* implicación *f*; *(indication)* indicación indirecta; *(inference)* inferencia; *(consequence)* consecuencia, repercusión *f*; *(complicity)* complicidad *f*.

im·plic·it (ĭm-plĭs'ĭt) adj. *(understood)* implícito; *(unquestioning)* absoluto <i. trust confianza absoluta>.

im·plied (ĭm-plīd') adj. implícito.

im·plode (ĭm-plōd') intr. **-plod·ed, -plod·ing** implosionar —tr. FONÉT. implosionar.

im·plore (ĭm-plôr') tr. **-plored, -plor·ing** *(to beseech)* implorar; *(to plead)* rogar, suplicar.

im·plo·sion (ĭm-plō'zhən) s. *(inward collapse)* implosión *f*; FONÉT. *(of a stop consonant)* implosión.

im·ply (ĭm-plī') tr. **-plied, -ply·ing** *(to entail)* implicar, significar <that implies a good deal of work eso significa mucho trabajo>; *(to hint)* dar a entender, insinuar <what are you implying? ¿qué insinúa usted?>.

im·po·lite (ĭm'pə-līt') adj. descortés.

im·po·lite·ly (ĭm'pə-līt'lē) adv. descortésmente, con descortesía.

im·po·lite·ness (ĭm'pə-līt'nĭs) s. descortesía.

im·pol·i·tic (ĭm-pŏl'ĭ-tĭk) adj. impolítico, imprudente.

im·pon·der·a·ble (ĭm-pŏn'dər-ə-bəl) adj. imponderable.

im·port I. tr. (ĭm-pôrt') *(goods)* importar; *(to signify)* significar, querer decir —intr. tener importancia <it imports little tiene poca importancia> II. s. (ĭm'pôrt') *(something imported)* artículo importado; COM. *(importation)* importación *f*; *(significance)* importancia <of little i. de poca importancia> ♦ **i. duties** COM. derechos de importación *o* de aduana.

im·port·a·ble (ĭm-pôr'tə-bəl) adj. importable.

im·por·tance (ĭm-pôr'tns) s. importancia ♦ **of the greatest i.** de gran importancia, primordial • **to be of i.** ser importante, tener importancia.

im·por·tant (ĭm-pôr'tnt) adj. *(consequential)* importante; *(prominent)* importante, de importancia <i. people personas de importancia> ♦ **it's not i.** no tiene importancia, no importa.

im·por·ta·tion (ĭm'pôr-tā'shən) s. COM. importación *f*.

im·port·er (ĭm-pôr'tər) s. COM. importador *m*.

im·por·tu·nate (ĭm-pôr'chə-nĭt) adj. importuno, fastidioso.

im·por·tune (ĭm'pôr-tōōn', ĭm-pôr'chən) tr. **-tuned, -tun·ing** importunar, fastidiar.

im·por·tu·ni·ty (ĭm'pôr-tōō'nĭ-tē, -tyōō'-) s. [pl. **-ties**] importunidad *f*.

im·pose (ĭm-pōz') tr. **-posed, -pos·ing** *(to establish)* imponer <to i. a settlement imponer un arreglo>; IMPR. imponer; *(to pass off)* engañar con ♦ **to i. oneself** imponerse —intr. ♦ **to i. on** *o* **upon** abusar de <he imposed upon her generosity abusó de su generosidad>.

im·pos·ing (ĭm-pō'zĭng) adj. imponente.

im·po·si·tion (ĭm'pə-zĭsh'ən) s. *(act)* imposición *f*; *(unfair demand)* abuso; *(burden)* gravamen *m*; IMPR. imposición.

im·pos·si·bil·i·ty (ĭm-pŏs'ə-bĭl'ĭ-tē) s. [pl. **-ties**] *(condition, quality)* imposibilidad *f*; *(something impossible)* imposible *m*, algo imposible.

im·pos·si·ble (ĭm-pŏs'ə-bəl) adj. *(unworkable)* imposible <an i. plan un proyecto imposible>; *(unbearable)* imposible, insoportable <an i. child un niño insoportable>; *(unacceptable)* inaceptable ♦ **to do the i.** hacer lo imposible • **to make it i. for someone to** impedirle a alguien.

im·pos·tor (ĭm-pŏs'tər) s. impostor *m*.

im·po·tence (ĭm'pə-tns) *o* **im·po·ten·cy** (-tn-sē) s. impotencia.

im·po·tent (ĭm'pə-tnt) adj. *(powerless)* impotente; *(weak)* débil; MED. *(sexually incapable)* impotente.

im·pound (ĭm-pound') tr. *(to confine)* encerrar; *(cars)* poner en un depósito; *(dogs)* meter en la perrera; DER. *(to seize)* embargar, confiscar; *(water)* embalsar.

im·pov·er·ish (ĭm-pŏv'ər-ĭsh) tr. *(people)* empobrecer; *(resources)* agotar.

im·pov·er·ish·ment (ĭm-pŏv'ər-ĭsh-mənt) s. *(of people)* empobrecimiento; *(of resources)* agotamiento.

im·prac·ti·ca·ble (ĭm-prăk'tĭ-kə-bəl) adj. *(unworkable)* impracticable, irrealizable; *(said of a road)* impracticable, intransitable.

im·prac·ti·cal (ĭm-prăk'tĭ-kəl) adj. *(not practical)* que no es práctico; *(theoretical)* teórico; *(impracticable)* impracticable.

im·prac·ti·cal·i·ty (ĭm-prăk'tĭ-kăl'ĭ-tē) s. [pl. **-ties**] impracticabilidad *f*.

im·pre·cise (ĭm'prĭ-sīs') adj. impreciso.

im·pre·ci·sion (ĭm'prĭ-sĭzh'ən) s. imprecisión *f*.

im·preg·na·ble (ĭm-prĕg'nə-bəl) adj. *(castle, fort)* inexpugnable; FIG. *(firm)* inquebrantable, invulnerable.

im·preg·nate (ĭm-prĕg'nāt') I. tr. **-nat·ed, -nat·ing** BIOL. *(to make pregnant)* dejar preñada; *(an ovum)* fecundar; *(to permeate)* impregnar, empapar; *(with ideas)* saturar, llenar II. adj. impregnado.

im·preg·na·tion (ĭm'prĕg-nā'shən) s. BIOL. *(insemination)* inseminación *f*; *(fertilization)* fecundación *f*; *(permeation)* impregnación *f*.

im·pre·sa·ri·o (ĭm'prĭ-sär'ē-ō') s. [pl. **-os**] TEAT. empresario.

im·press¹ I. tr. (ĭm-prĕs') *(to produce with pressure)* imprimir; *(to stamp)* estampar, marcar; *(to affect)* impresionar, causar impresión <his sincerity impressed me su sinceridad me impresionó>; *(to implant)* inculcar ♦ **I was not impressed** no me pareció gran cosa • **not to be easily impressed** no dejarse impresionar fácilmente II. s. (ĭm'prĕs') *(act)* impresión *f*; *(mark)* marca, señal *f*; *(seal)* sello.

im·press² (ĭm-prĕs') I. tr. *(people)* reclutar a la fuerza; *(property)* requisar II. s. *(of people)* reclutamiento obligatorio; *(of property)* requisa.

im·pres·sion (ĭm-prĕsh'ən) s. *(act)* impresión *f*; *(mark)* marca, señal *f*; *(feeling)* impresión <we discussed our impressions cambiamos impresiones>; *(effect)* efecto <his words made a strong i. sus palabras tuvieron mucho efecto>; *(memory)* recuerdo, idea; IMPR. *(printing)* tirada, edición *f*; *(single copy)* ejemplar *m* ♦ **to be under** *o* **have the i. that** tener la impresión de que, creer que • **to make a good i.** causar buena impresión.

im·pres·sion·a·ble (ĭm-prĕsh'ə-nə-bəl) adj. impresionable.

im·pres·sion·ism (ĭm-prĕsh'ə-nĭz'əm) s. ARTE. impresionismo.

im·pres·sion·ist (ĭm-prĕsh'ə-nĭst) s. ARTE. impresionista *mf*; TEAT. *(impersonator)* imitador *m*.

im·pres·sion·is·tic (ĭm-prĕsh'ə-nĭs'tĭk) adj. ARTE. impresionista; *(subjective)* subjetivo, personal; *(impressionable)* impresionable.

im·pres·sive (ĭm-prĕs'ĭv) adj. impresionante.

ā rey / ä año / b boca / ch chico / d dar / ĕ el / ē mil / g gato / h joya / hw juez / ī aire / k casa / kw cuan /

im·press·ment (ĭm-prĕs′mənt) s. requisa, requisición *f.*

im·pri·ma·tur (ĭm′prə-mä′tŏor′) s. *(license to print)* imprimátur *m; (official sanction)* aprobación *f,* permiso oficial (esp. eclesiástico).

im·print I. tr. (ĭm-prĭnt′) *(to engrave)* imprimir, estampar; *(to mark)* marcar; *(to impress on)* grabar II. s. (ĭm′prĭnt′) *(impression)* impresión *f,* marca; *(on cloth)* diseño; *(influence)* impronta, sello; IMPR. *(on a page)* pie de imprenta *m.*

im·pris·on (ĭm-prĭz′ən) tr. aprisionar, encarcelar.

im·pris·on·ment (ĭm-prĭz′ən-mənt) s. aprisionamiento, encarcelamiento.

im·prob·a·bil·i·ty (ĭm-prŏb′ə-bĭl′ĭ-tē) s. [pl. **-ties**] improbabilidad *f.*

im·prob·a·ble (ĭm-prŏb′ə-bəl) adj. improbable.

im·promp·tu (ĭm-prŏmp′tōō, -tyōō) I. adj. improvisado II. adv. *(spontaneously)* improvisadamente; *(unexpectedly)* de repente III. s. improvisación *f;* MUS. impromptu *m.*

im·prop·er (ĭm-prŏp′ər) adj. *(inappropriate)* impropio; *(inadequate)* inadecuado <*i. care* atención inadecuada>; *(indecorous)* incorrecto, indebido; *(incorrect)* impropio, inexacto.

im·pro·pri·e·ty (ĭm′prə-prī′ĭ-tē) s. [pl. **-ties**] *(inappropriateness)* falta de propiedad, carácter inadecuado; *(improper act)* falta de corrección; *(in using language)* impropiedad *f.*

im·prove (ĭm-prōōv′) tr. **-proved, -prov·ing** *(to make better)* mejorar; *(to upgrade)* hacer mejoras en; *(a text)* corregir, retocar; *(in quality)* mejorar la calidad de; *(productivity)* aumentar, incrementar; *(a skill, product)* perfeccionar <*she improved her tennis serve* perfeccionó su saque de tenis>; *(one's attitude)* reformar, cambiar; *(one's intellect)* superar, desarrollar; COM. *(to make more valuable)* aumentar el valor de, valorar ♦ **to i. one's appearance** hacerse más presentable —intr. *(to become better)* mejorar; *(patient)* mejorar(se); *(skill)* perfeccionarse; *(in one's studies)* adelantar, progresar; *(product)* aumentar de calidad; *(price)* aumentar ♦ **to i. on** o **upon** mejorar.

im·prove·ment (ĭm-prōōv′mənt) s. *(betterment)* mejora, mejoramiento; *(in quality)* aumento de calidad; *(in productivity)* aumento; *(of a skill)* perfeccionamiento; *(in attitude)* reforma, cambio; *(in intellectual capacity)* superación *f,* desarrollo; *(in one's studies)* adelanto, progreso; *(in health)* mejoría; *(in value)* valoración *f; (in a building)* reforma, arreglo; *(in a facility)* ampliación *f* ♦ **to make improvements in** *(a product)* perfeccionar; *(a house)* hacer reformas.

im·prov·i·dent (ĭm-prŏv′ĭ-dənt) adj. *(unthrifty)* gastador; *(unwise)* imprévido, imprevisor.

im·pro·vi·sa·tion (ĭm-prŏv′ĭ-zā′shən, ĭm′prə-vĭ-) s. improvisación *f.*

im·prov·i·sa·to·ry (ĭm-prŏv′ĭ-zə-tôr′ē) adj. improvisador, improvisado.

im·pro·vise (ĭm′prə-vīz′) tr. & intr. **-vised, -vis·ing** improvisar.

im·pru·dence (ĭm-prōōd′ns) s. imprudencia.

im·pru·dent (ĭm-prōōd′nt) adj. imprudente.

im·pu·dence (ĭm′pyə-dns) o **im·pu·den·cy** (-dn-sē) s. impudencia, descaro.

im·pu·dent (ĭm′pyə-dnt) adj. *(brash)* impudente, descarado.

im·pugn (ĭm-pyōōn′) tr. impugnar.

im·pulse (ĭm′pŭls′) s. *(force)* impulso; *(urge)* impulso <*my first i. was to tell him off* mi primer impulso fue reprenderle>; ELEC., FÍS., FISIOL. impulso ♦ **on i.** sin reflexionar.

im·pul·sion (ĭm-pŭl′shən) s. impulsión *f,* impulso.

im·pul·sive (ĭm-pŭl′sĭv) adj. *(person)* impulsivo, impetuoso; *(act)* impetuoso, irreflexivo.

im·pu·ni·ty (ĭm-pyōō′nĭ-tē) s. [pl. **-ties**] impunidad *f.*

im·pure (ĭm-pyŏor′) adj. *(not pure)* impuro; *(adulterated)* mezclado; *(air)* contaminado.

im·pu·ri·ty (ĭm-pyŏor′ĭ-tē) s. [pl. **-ties**] *(quality, condition)* impureza; *(adulteration)* mezcla; *(of the air)* contaminación *f; (contaminant)* impureza, suciedad *f.*

im·pute (ĭm-pyōōt′) tr. **-put·ed, -put·ing** imputar, atribuir.

in (ĭn) I. prep. □ DENTRO, EN en <*she's in the garden* está en el jardín> <*she lives in a villa in France* ella vive en una

villa en Francia>; dentro de <*put it in the garbage can* ponlo dentro del cubo de la basura>; de <*the curtains in my room are dusty* las cortinas de mi cuarto están llenas de polvo> <*the best hotel in New York* el mejor hotel de Nueva York>; a <*to arrive in Rio* llegar a Río>; con <*you shouldn't go out in this weather* no deberías salir con este tiempo>; por <*we walked in the castle gardens* paseamos por los jardines del castillo> □ ESTILO, FORMA en <*it is written in verse* está escrito en verso>; a, con <*do it in ink* hágalo a tinta>; por <*in writing* por escrito> <*in order of appearance* por orden de aparición> <*cut in half* cortado por el medio>; de <*she was dressed in red* estaba vestida de rojo> <*she's no longer in mourning* ya no está de luto> <*he's deaf in one ear* es sordo de un oído> <*covered in glory* cubierto de gloria> <*one in ten* uno de cada diez> □ HORA, TIEMPO a <*in time* a tiempo>; por <*in the morning* por la mañana>; durante <*in the daytime* durante el día>; de <*at nine o'clock in the morning* a las nueve de la mañana>; en <*in 1920* en 1920, en el año 1920> <*he fixed the watch in ten minutes* reparó el reloj en diez minutos> <*in March* en marzo>; durante, bajo <*in the reign of* durante el reinado de>; dentro de <*I'll be back in an hour* volveré dentro de una hora> □ TIEMPO ATMOSFÉRICO a <*we sat in the sun* nos sentamos al sol>; bajo <*in the rain* bajo la lluvia> <*we walked in a scorching sun* caminamos bajo un sol abrasador> □ CON VERBOS al, mientras <*in running after the bus* mientras corría para tomar el autobús> □ DESPUÉS DE UN SUPERLATIVO de <*the biggest in the world* el más grande del mundo> □ EXPRESIONES IDIOMÁTICAS ♦ **in a big way** a lo grande • **in anger** con enojo • **in cash** en efectivo • **in chains** encadenado • **in despair** desesperado • **in fashion** de moda • **in good health** bien de salud • **in itself** por sí mismo • **in love** enamorado • **in the distance** a lo lejos • **in tears** llorando • **in this way** de este modo • **in that** ya que, porque • **those in . . .** los que se dedican a . . . <*those in politics* los que se dedican a la política> II. adv. *(inside)* dentro, adentro <*bring it in here* tráelo aquí adentro>; *(in power)* en el poder; *(in fashion)* de moda <*miniskirts are in again* las minifaldas están de moda nuevamente>; *(in season)* en su tiempo o estación ♦ **In and out** yendo y viniendo, entrando y saliendo • **to be in** *(home, office)* estar <*is the doctor in?* ¿está el doctor?>; POL. *(in power)* estar en el poder • **to be in for** FAM. *(punishment)* estar condenado a (castigo en prisión); *(hospital)* estar internado para (operación, observación) • **to be in for a hard time** FAM. ir a pasar un mal rato • **to be in for it** FAM. ir a recibir un castigo (por algo hecho) • **to be in on** *(to participate)* participar en, tomar parte en; *(to know)* estar enterado de, estar al tanto de • **to be in with someone** FAM. gozar del favor de alguien, estar en buenas relaciones con alguien • **to be o feel all in** FAM. estar agotado, no poder más • **to have it in for someone** FAM. tenerle antipatía a alguien III. adj. *(fashionable)* de moda <*the in thing to wear* lo que está de moda llevar>; *(entering)* de entrada <*the in door* la puerta de entrada> ♦ **the in party** FAM. el partido en el poder IV. s. influencia ♦ **the ins and outs** los pormenores, los detalles • **to have an in somewhere** tener influencia en algún sitio.

in·a·bil·i·ty (ĭn′ə-bĭl′ĭ-tē) s. inhabilidad *f,* incapacidad *f.*

in·ac·ces·si·bil·i·ty (ĭn′ăk-sĕs′ə-bĭl′ĭ-tē) s. inaccesibilidad *f.*

in·ac·ces·si·ble (ĭn′ăk-sĕs′ə-bəl) adj. inaccesible.

in·ac·cu·ra·cy (ĭn-ăk′yər-ə-sē) s. [pl. **-cies**] *(lack of accuracy)* inexactitud *f; (error)* error *m,* equivocación *f.*

in·ac·cu·rate (ĭn-ăk′yər-ĭt) adj. *(not accurate)* inexacto; *(incorrect)* erróneo, incorrecto.

in·ac·tion (ĭn-ăk′shən) s. inacción *f.*

in·ac·tive (ĭn-ăk′tĭv) adj. *(not active)* inactivo; MIL. en reserva, de reserva.

in·ac·tiv·i·ty (ĭn′ăk-tĭv′ĭ-tē) s. inactividad *f,* falta de actividad.

in·ad·e·qua·cy (ĭn-ăd′ĭ-kwə-sē) s. [pl. **-cies**] *(unsuitability)* falta de adecuación, inadecuación *f; (insufficiency)* insuficiencia.

in·ad·e·quate (ĭn-ăd′ĭ-kwĭt) adj. *(unsuitable)* inadecuado; *(insufficient)* insuficiente.

in·ad·mis·si·bil·i·ty (ĭn′əd-mĭs′ə-bĭl′ĭ-tē) s. inadmisibilidad *f.*

in·ad·mis·si·ble (ĭn′əd-mĭs′ə-bəl) adj. inadmisible.

in·ad·ver·tence (ĭn′əd-vûr′tns) s. *(quality)* falta de atención; *(mistake)* falta, error *(por descuido) m.*

in·ad·ver·tent (ĭn′əd-vûr′tnt) adj. *(inattentive)* inadvertido, descuidado; *(unintentional)* involuntario, accidental.

in·ad·vis·a·bil·i·ty (ĭn′əd-vī′zə-bĭl′ĭ-tē) s. inconveniencia.

in·ad·vis·a·ble (ĭn′əd-vī′zə-bəl) adj. *(not recommended)* desaconsejable; *(unwise)* imprudente.

in·al·ien·a·ble (ĭn-āl′yə-nə-bəl) adj. inalienable, inenajenable.

in·al·ter·a·ble (ĭn-ôl′tər-ə-bəl) adj. inalterable.

in·ane (ĭn-ān′) adj. **-an·er, -an·est** *(futile)* inane, fútil; *(empty)* vacío; *(silly)* tonto, necio.

in·an·i·mate (ĭn-ăn′ə-mĭt) adj. *(not living)* falto de vida; *(dull)* desanimado, apagado.

in·a·ni·tion (ĭn′ə-nĭsh′ən) s. MED. inanición *f.*

in·an·i·ty (ĭn-ăn′ĭ-tē) s. [pl. **-ties**] *(futility)* inanidad *f,* futilidad *f; (absurdity)* necedad *f,* insensatez *f.*

in·ap·pli·ca·ble (ĭn-ăp′lĭ-kə-bəl, ĭn′ə-plĭk′ə-) adj. que no viene al caso.

in·ap·pre·cia·ble (ĭn′ə-prē′shə-bəl) adj. inapreciable, insignificante.

in·ap·pro·pri·ate (ĭn′ə-prō′prē-ĭt) adj. impropio, inadecuado.

in·ap·pro·pri·ate·ness (ĭn′ə-prō′prē-ĭt-nĭs) s. impropiedad *f.*

in·apt (ĭn-ăpt′) adj. *(inappropriate)* impropio, inadecuado; *(inept)* inepto, inhábil.

in·ap·ti·tude (ĭn-ăp′tĭ-tōōd′, -tyōōd′) s. *(inappropriateness)* impropiedad *f; (ineptitude)* ineptitud *f,* inhabilidad *f.*

in·ar·tic·u·late (ĭn′är-tĭk′yə-lĭt) adj. *(not clear)* falto de articulación; *(lacking clear speech)* incapaz de expresarse; *(unexpressed)* mudo; BIOL. inarticulado.

in·as·much as (ĭn′əz-mŭch′əz) conj. *(since)* ya que, puesto que; *(insofar as)* en la medida en que.

in·at·ten·tion (ĭn′ə-tĕn′shən) s. *(lack of attention)* inatención *f,* falta de atención; *(neglect)* desatención *f,* distracción *f.*

in·at·ten·tive (ĭn′ə-tĕn′tĭv) adj. desatento, distraído.

in·au·di·ble (ĭn-ô′də-bəl) adj. inaudible.

in·au·gu·ral (ĭn-ô′gyər-əl) I. adj. inaugural II. s. *(speech)* discurso inaugural *f,* inauguración *f.*

in·au·gu·rate (ĭn-ô′gyə-rāt′) tr. **-rat·ed, -rat·ing** *(to begin)* inaugurar <*to i. a new service* inaugurar un nuevo servicio>; POL. *(to induct into office)* investir del cargo a.

in·au·gu·ra·tion (ĭn-ô′gyə-rā′shən) s. *(beginning)* inauguración *f;* POL. investidura, toma de posesión.

in·aus·pi·cious (ĭn′ô-spĭsh′əs) adj. desfavorable, poco propicio.

in between prep. entre.

in-be·tween (ĭn′bĭ-twēn′) I. adj. intermedio II. s. término medio.

in·board (ĭn′bôrd′) adj. MARÍT. dentro del casco.

in·born (ĭn′bôrn′) adj. congénito, innato.

in·bound (ĭn′bound′) adj. que viene, de venida.

in·bred (ĭn′brĕd′) adj. *(consanguineous)* consanguíneo; *(innate)* innato.

in·breed (ĭn′brēd′) tr. **-bred** (-brĕd′), **-breed·ing** *(animals)* procrear en consanguinidad; *(people)* engendrar por endogamia.

in·breed·ing (ĭn′brē′dĭng) s. *(people)* endogamia; *(animals)* procreación en consanguinidad *f.*

In·ca (ĭng′kə) s. [pl. **Inca** *o* **-cas**] *(inhabitant)* inca *mf; (ruler)* inca *m.*

in·cal·cu·la·ble (ĭn-kăl′kyə-lə-bəl) adj. *(indeterminate)* incalculable; *(unpredictable)* imprevisible.

in cam·e·ra (ĭn kăm′ər-ə) adv. DER. a puerta cerrada.

In·can (ĭng′kən) I. s. *(inhabitant)* inca *mf; (language)* quechua *m* II. adj. incaico, incásico.

in·can·des·cence (ĭn′kən-dĕs′əns) s. incandescencia.

in·can·des·cent (ĭn′kən-dĕs′ənt) adj. incandescente.

in·can·ta·tion (ĭn′kăn-tā′shən) s. *(invocation)* invocación *f; (spell)* sortilegio, conjuro.

in·can·ta·to·ry (ĭn-kăn′tə-tôr′ē) adj. mágico.

in·ca·pa·bil·i·ty (ĭn-kā′pə-bĭl′ĭ-tē) s. incapacidad *f.*

in·ca·pa·ble (ĭn-kā′pə-bəl) adj. *(not capable)* incapaz; *(incompetent)* incompetente; *(handicapped)* imposibilitado; DER. *(ineligible)* incapaz ♦ **to be i. of love** no poder amar.

in·ca·pac·i·tate (ĭn′kə-păs′ĭ-tāt′) tr. **-tat·ed, -tat·ing** *(to disable)* incapacitar; *(to disqualify)* descalificar; DER. *(to make ineligible)* incapacitar.

in·ca·pac·i·ta·tion (ĭn′kə-păs′ĭ-tā′shən) s. *(disability)* inhabilitación *f;* DER. privación de la capacidad *f.*

in·ca·pac·i·ty (ĭn′kə-păs′ĭ-tē) s. [pl. **-ties**] *(lack of capacity)* incapacidad *f,* inhabilidad *f;* DER. *(disqualification)* incapacidad *f.*

in·car·cer·ate (ĭn-kär′sə-rāt′) tr. **-at·ed, -at·ing** encarcelar.

in·car·cer·a·tion (ĭn-kär′sə-rā′shən) s. encarcelamiento.

in·car·nate I. adj. (ĭn-kär′nĭt) encarnado II. tr. (-nāt′) **-nat·ed, -nat·ing** encarnar.

in·car·na·tion (ĭn′kär-nā′shən) s. encarnación *f* ♦ **the I.** TEO. la Encarnación.

in·cen·di·ar·y (ĭn-sĕn′dē-ĕr′ē) I. adj. incendiario II. s. [pl. **-ies**] *(arsonist)* incendiario, pirómano *m; (bomb)* bomba incendiaria; *(agitator)* sedicioso, agitador *m.*

incendiary bomb s. MIL. bomba incendiaria.

in·cense¹ (ĭn-sĕns′) tr. **-censed, -cens·ing** encolerizar, enfurecer.

in·cense² (ĭn′sĕns′) I. s. *(sticks, smoke)* incienso; *(pleasant smell)* perfume *m; (flattery)* incienso, adulación *f* II. tr. **-censed, -cens·ing** incensar.

in·cen·tive (ĭn-sĕn′tĭv) I. s. *(inducement)* incentivo, aliciente *m; (motive)* motivación *f* II. adj. motivador.

in·cep·tion (ĭn-sĕp′shən) s. *(beginning)* principio, comienzo; BIOL., MED. ingestión *f.*

in·cer·ti·tude (ĭn-sûr′tĭ-tōōd′, -tyōōd′) s. *(uncertainty)* incertidumbre *f; (doubt)* duda; *(insecurity)* inseguridad *f.*

in·ces·sant (ĭn-sĕs′ənt) adj. incesante.

in·cest (ĭn′sĕst′) s. incesto.

in·ces·tu·ous (ĭn-sĕs′chōō-əs) adj. incestuoso.

inch (ĭnch) I. s. *(measure)* pulgada; FIG. *(small amount)* pizca, poquito ♦ **every i. of the way** todo el camino • **give him an i. and he'll take a mile** dale la mano y te cogerá el brazo • **i. by i.** *(by small amounts)* palmo a palmo; *(by small degrees)* poco a poco • **to know every i. of** conocer como la palma de la mano • **within an i. of** a punto de II. intr. avanzar poco a poco —tr. mover poco a poco.

in·cho·ate (ĭn-kō′ĭt) adj. *(incipient)* incipiente; *(rudimentary)* rudimentario; DER. incoado.

in·ci·dence (ĭn′sĭ-dəns) s. *(occurrence)* incidencia; *(extent)* extensión *f; (frequency)* frecuencia, índice *m* <*a high i. of crime* un elevado índice de crímenes>.

in·ci·dent (ĭn′sĭ-dənt) I. s. *(occurrence)* incidente *m* <*an international i.* un incidente internacional>; *(event)* suceso, acontecimiento <*a terrible i.* un suceso horrible> ♦ **full of i.** lleno de incidentes • **without i.** sin novedad II. adj. incidente ♦ **i. to** que acompaña a, propio de.

in·ci·den·tal (ĭn′sĭ-dĕn′tl) I. adj. *(related)* incidente; *(minor)* accesorio <*i. expenses* gastos accesorios>; *(of minor importance)* secundario ♦ **i. clause** inciso • **i. to** que acompaña a, propio de II. s. ♦ **incidentals** imprevistos.

in·ci·den·tal·ly (ĭn′sĭ-dĕn′tl-ē) adv. *(casually)* incidentalmente, casualmente; *(by the way)* a propósito, entre paréntesis.

in·cin·er·ate (ĭn-sĭn′ə-rāt′) tr. & intr. **-at·ed, -at·ing** incinerar(se), quemar(se).

in·cin·er·a·tion (ĭn-sĭn′ə-rā′shən) s. incineración *f.*

in·cin·er·a·tor (ĭn-sĭn′ə-rā′tər) s. incinerador *m.*

in·cip·i·ent (ĭn-sĭp′ē-ənt) adj. incipiente.

in·cise (ĭn-sīz′) tr. **-cised, -cis·ing** *(to cut)* cortar, hacer una incisión en; *(to engrave)* tallar, grabar.

in·ci·sion (ĭn-sĭzh′ən) s. *(act, cut)* incisión *f,* corte *m; (scar)* cicatriz *f.*

in·ci·sive (ĭn-sī′sĭv) adj. *(mentally sharp)* penetrante, agudo; *(biting)* incisivo, mordaz.

in·ci·sor (ĭn-sī′zər) s. ANAT., ZOOL. incisivo, diente incisivo.

in·cite (ĭn-sīt′) tr. **-cit·ed, -cit·ing** incitar.

in·cite·ment (ĭn-sīt′mənt) s. *(act)* incitación *f; (incentive)* estímulo, incentivo.

in·clem·en·cy (ĭn-klĕm′ən-sē) s. inclemencia.

in·clem·ent (ĭn-klĕm′ənt) adj. inclemente.

ã rey / ä año / b boca / ch chico / d dar / ĕ el / ē mil / g gato / h joya / hw juez / ī aire / k casa / kw cuan /

in·clin·a·ble (ĭn-klī'nə-bəl) adj. inclinable.

in·cli·na·tion (ĭn'klə-nā'shən) s. *(tendency)* inclinación *f*, tendencia <*an i. toward dictatorship* una tendencia a la dictadura>; *(preference)* preferencia, gusto <*to follow one's inclinations* dejarse llevar por los gustos de uno>; *(nod)* saludo; *(tilt)* inclinación, declive *m* ♦ **to have an i. to** tener tendencia a.

in·cline **I.** intr. (ĭn-klīn') **-clined, -clin·ing** *(to slant)* inclinarse; *(to tend)* tender <*she inclines to exaggerate* tiende a exagerar>; *(bow)* saludar —tr. inclinar ♦ **if you feel so inclined** si usted desea • **to be inclined to** *(to prefer)* estar dispuesto a; *(to tend to)* tener tendencia a; *(an illness)* ser propenso a **II.** s. (ĭn'klīn') inclinación *f*, pendiente *f*.

in·clined (ĭn-klīnd') adj. *(disposed to)* dispuesto <*to be i. to* estar dispuesto a>; *(sloping)* inclinado ♦ **musically i.** que le atrae la música.

inclined plane s. GEOM., MEC. plano inclinado.

in·clo·sure (ĭn-klō'zhər) s. var. de **enclosure.**

in·clude (ĭn-klōōd') tr. **-clud·ed, -clud·ing** incluir, abarcar.

in·clud·ed (ĭn-klōō'dĭd) adj. incluido, incluso <*they lost everything they owned, their house i.* perdieron todo lo que poseían, incluso la casa>.

in·clu·sion (ĭn-klōō'zhən) s. inclusión *f*.

in·clu·sive (ĭn-klōō'sĭv) adj. inclusive <*chapters one to ten, i.* del capítulo uno al diez inclusive>; *(comprehensive)* inclusivo.

in·cog·ni·to (ĭn-kŏg'nĭ-tō', ĭn'kŏg-nē'tō) **I.** adj. incógnito **II.** adv. de incógnito **III.** s. [pl. **-tos**] incógnito.

in·co·her·ence (ĭn'kō-hîr'əns) o **in·co·her·en·cy** (-ən-sē) s. incoherencia.

in·co·her·ent (ĭn'kō-hîr'ənt) adj. incoherente.

in·com·bus·ti·ble (ĭn'kəm-bŭs'tə-bəl) **I.** adj. incombustible, no inflamable **II.** s. substancia incombustible.

in·come (ĭn'kŭm') s. *(receipts)* ingresos *m*, entrada; *(on investments)* renta; *(interest)* rédito; *(profit)* utilidades *f* ♦ **gross i.** TEN. entrada bruta • **net i.** TEN. entrada neta.

income tax s. impuesto sobre los ingresos o utilidades.

in·com·ing (ĭn'kŭm'ĭng) **I.** adj. *(entering)* entrante, que entra; *(new)* nuevo **II.** s. *(entrance)* entrada; *(arrival)* llegada.

in·com·men·su·ra·ble (ĭn'kə-měn'sər-ə-bəl, -shər-) adj. inconmensurable.

in·com·men·su·rate (ĭn'kə-měn'sər-ĭt, -shər-) adj. *(disproportionate)* desproporcionado; *(inadequate)* inadecuado, insuficiente; *(incommensurable)* inconmensurable.

in·com·mu·ni·ca·bil·i·ty (ĭn'kə-myōō'nĭ-kə-bĭl'ĭ-tē) s. incomunicabilidad *f*.

in·com·mu·ni·ca·ble (ĭn'kə-myōō'nĭ-kə-bəl) adj. incomunicable.

in·com·mu·ni·ca·do (ĭn'kə-myōō'nĭ-kä'dō) adj. incomunicado.

in·com·pa·ra·ble (ĭn-kŏm'pər-ə-bəl) adj. incomparable.

in·com·pat·i·bil·i·ty (ĭn'kəm-păt'ə-bĭl'ĭ-tē) s. [pl. **-ties**] incompatibilidad *f*, falta de compatibilidad.

in·com·pat·i·ble (ĭn'kəm-păt'ə-bəl) adj. incompatible.

in·com·pe·tence (ĭn-kŏm'pĭ-tns) o **in·com·pe·ten·cy** (-tn-sē) s. incompetencia, incapacidad *f*.

in·com·pe·tent (ĭn-kŏm'pĭ-tnt) **I.** adj. incompetente, incapaz **II.** s. persona incompetente.

in·com·plete (ĭn'kəm-plēt') adj. incompleto.

in·com·plete·ness (ĭn'kəm-plēt'nĭs) s. estado incompleto, calidad de incompleto *f*.

in·com·pli·ant (ĭn'kəm-plī'ənt) adj. *(inflexible)* inflexible; *(disobedient)* desobediente.

in·com·pre·hen·si·ble (ĭn-kŏm'prĭ-hěn'sə-bəl) adj. incomprensible.

in·com·pre·hen·sion (ĭn-kŏm'prĭ-hěn'shən) s. incomprensión *f*.

in·com·press·i·ble (ĭn'kəm-prěs'ə-bəl) adj. incompresible, incomprimible.

in·con·ceiv·a·ble (ĭn'kən-sē'və-bəl) adj. *(not comprehendible)* inconcebible; *(incredible)* increíble.

in·con·clu·sive (ĭn'kən-klōō'sĭv) adj. *(not conclusive)* no concluyente, inconcluyente; *(not convincing)* poco concluyente, poco convincente.

in·con·gru·ent (ĭn-kŏng'grōō-ənt, ĭn'kŏn-grōō'ənt) adj. incongruente.

in·con·gru·i·ty (ĭn'kŏn-grōō'ĭ-tē) s. [pl. **-ties**] incongruencia.

in·con·gru·ous (ĭn-kŏng'grōō-əs) adj. incongruo, incongruente ♦ **i. with** incompatible con, que no concuerda con.

in·con·se·quence (ĭn-kŏn'sĭ-kwəns) s. inconsecuencia.

in·con·se·quent (ĭn-kŏn'sĭ-kwənt) adj. *(not in line with)* inconsecuente; *(haphazard)* inconexo, ilógico; *(insignificant)* insignificante, sin trascendencia.

in·con·se·quen·tial (ĭn-kŏn'sĭ-kwěn'shəl) adj. *(lacking importance)* insignificante, sin trascendencia; *(inconsequent)* inconsecuente.

in·con·sid·er·a·ble (ĭn'kən-sĭd'ər-ə-bəl) adj. insignificante, trivial.

in·con·sid·er·ate (ĭn'kən-sĭd'ər-ĭt) adj. *(thoughtless)* falto de consideración; *(without consideration for others)* desconsiderado.

in·con·sid·er·a·tion (ĭn'kən-sĭd'ə-rā'shən) s. *(thoughtlessness)* inconsideración *f*; *(toward others)* desconsideración *f*.

in·con·sis·ten·cy (ĭn'kən-sĭs'tən-sē) s. [pl. **-cies**] *(state, quality)* inconsecuencia, falta de lógica; *(irregularity)* irregularidad *f*; *(contradiction)* contradicción *f*.

in·con·sis·tent (ĭn'kən-sĭs'tənt) adj. *(erratic)* inconsecuente; *(irregular)* irregular; *(contradictory)* contradictorio ♦ **i. with** que no concuerda con, en contradicción con.

in·con·sol·a·ble (ĭn'kən-sō'lə-bəl) adj. inconsolable, desconsolado.

in·con·spic·u·ous (ĭn'kən-spĭk'yōō-əs) adj. no conspicuo, discreto.

in·con·stan·cy (ĭn-kŏn'stən-sē) s. [pl. **-cies**] inconstancia.

in·con·stant (ĭn-kŏn'stənt) adj. inconstante.

in·con·test·a·ble (ĭn'kən-těs'tə-bəl) adj. incontestable.

in·con·ti·nence (ĭn-kŏn'tə-nəns) s. incontinencia.

in·con·ti·nent (ĭn-kŏn'tə-nənt) adj. incontinente.

in·con·tro·vert·i·ble (ĭn-kŏn'trə-vûr'tə-bəl) adj. incontrovertible, indiscutible.

in·con·ven·ience (ĭn'kən-vēn'yəns) **I.** s. *(state, quality)* inconveniencia; *(bother)* inconveniente *m*, molestia **II.** tr. **-ienced, -ienc·ing** incomodar, molestar.

in·con·ven·ient (ĭn'kən-vēn'yənt) adj. *(not convenient)* inconveniente; *(bothersome)* molesto; *(inopportune)* inoportuno.

in·con·vert·i·ble (ĭn'kən-vûr'tə-bəl) adj. inconvertible.

in·cor·po·rate **I.** tr. (ĭn-kôr'pə-rāt') **-rat·ed, -rat·ing** *(to include)* incorporar, incluir; *(a business)* constituir en sociedad; *(to embody)* plasmar —intr. *(to merge)* unirse; *(business)* constituirse en sociedad **II.** adj. (-pər-ĭt) *(merged)* incorporado; *(business)* constituido en sociedad.

in·cor·po·rat·ed (ĭn-kôr'pə-rā'tĭd) adj. *(included)* incorporado; *(business)* constituido en sociedad.

in·cor·po·rat·ing (ĭn-kôr'pə-rā'tĭng) adj. FILOL. polisintético.

in·cor·po·ra·tion (ĭn-kôr'pə-rā'shən) s. *(act)* incorporación *f*; *(merging)* unión *f*; *(of a business)* constitución en sociedad anónima *f*.

in·cor·po·ra·tive (ĭn-kôr'pə-rā'tĭv) adj. de incorporación.

in·cor·po·re·al (ĭn'kôr-pôr'ē-əl) adj. incorpóreo.

in·cor·rect (ĭn'kə-rěkt') adj. *(erroneous)* incorrecto; *(inaccurate)* inexacto; *(inappropriate)* inadecuado.

in·cor·rect·ness (ĭn'kə-rěkt'nĭs) s. *(of answer, behavior)* incorrección *f*, falta de corrección; *(inaccuracy)* inexactitud *f*; *(of an allegation)* falsedad *f*.

in·cor·ri·gi·ble (ĭn-kôr'ĭ-jə-bəl) **I.** adj. *(not corrigible)* incorregible; *(not controllable)* indócil **II.** s. persona incorregible.

in·cor·rupt·i·ble (ĭn'kə-rŭp'tə-bəl) adj. incorruptible.

in·crease **I.** intr. (ĭn-krēs') **-creased, -creas·ing** *(to become greater)* aumentar; *(prices)* subir —tr. *(to make greater)* aumentar; *(prices)* aumentar, subir; *(production)* incrementar **II.** s. (ĭn'krēs') *(rise)* aumento; *(in prices)* subida, alza; *(in production)* incremento ♦ **to be on the i.** ir en aumento, aumentar.

in·creas·ing (ĭn-krē'sĭng) adj. creciente.

in·creas·ing·ly (ĭn-krē'sĭng-lē) adv. cada vez más.

in·cred·i·ble (ĭn-krěd'ə-bəl) adj. increíble.

---

in·cre·du·li·ty (ĭn'krĭ-dōō'lĭ-tē, -dyōō'-) s. incredulidad f.

in·cred·u·lous (ĭn-krĕj'ə-ləs) adj. incrédulo.

in·cre·ment (ĭng'krə-mənt) s. (increase) incremento, aumento; MAT. incremento ♦ **unearned i.** ECON. plusvalía.

in·cre·men·tal (ĭn'krə-mĕn'tl) adj. de incremento, de aumento.

in·cre·tion (ĭn-krē'shən) s. FISIOL. increción f, secreción interna.

in·crim·i·nate (ĭn-krĭm'ə-nāt') tr. -nat·ed, -nat·ing incriminar.

in·crim·i·na·tion (ĭn-krĭm'ə-nā'shən) s. incriminación f.

in·crim·i·na·to·ry (ĭn-krĭm'ə-nə-tôr'ē) adj. incriminador.

in·cu·bate (ĭng'kyə-bāt') tr. -bat·ed, -bat·ing (by bodily heat) incubar, empollar; (artificially) incubar; (to foment) fomentar —intr. incubar.

in·cu·ba·tion (ĭng'kyə-bā'shən) s. incubación f ♦ **i. period** MED. período de incubación o de latencia.

in·cu·ba·tor (ĭng'kyə-bā'tər) s. incubadora.

in·cu·bus (ĭng'kyə-bəs) s. [pl. -bus·es o -bi (-bī')] (evil spirit) íncubo, demonio íncubo; (nightmare) pesadilla; (burden) carga.

in·cul·cate (ĭn-kŭl'kāt') tr. -cat·ed, -cat·ing inculcar.

in·cul·pa·tion (ĭn'kŭl-pā'shən) s. inculpación f.

in·cum·ben·cy (ĭn-kŭm'bən-sē) s. [pl. -cies] (obligation) incumbencia; POL. (of an office) mandato, ejercicio del cargo; (term) mandato.

in·cum·bent (ĭn-kŭm'bənt) I. adj. (resting) apoyado; POL. (of an office) actual ♦ **to be i. on** o **upon someone** incumbirle o corresponderle a alguien II. s. POL. titular m; RELIG. beneficiado.

in·cur (ĭn-kûr') tr. -curred, -cur·ring incurrir.

in·cur·a·ble (ĭn-kyŏŏr'ə-bəl) adj. (not curable) incurable; (stubborn) incurable, irremediable.

in·cur·sion (ĭn-kûr'zhən) s. incursión f.

in·da·mine (ĭn'də-mēn') s. QUÍM. indamina.

in·debt·ed (ĭn-dĕt'ĭd) adj. (in debt) endeudado; (owing gratitude) agradecido <to be i. to someone estarle agradecido a alguien>.

in·debt·ed·ness (ĭn-dĕt'ĭd-nĭs) s. (debts) deudas f, obligaciones f; (gratitude) agradecimiento.

in·de·cen·cy (ĭn-dē'sən-sē) s. [pl. -cies] indecencia.

in·de·cent (ĭn-dē'sənt) adj. indecente ♦ **i. exposure** DER. exhibicionismo.

in·de·ci·pher·a·ble (ĭn'dĭ-sī'fər-ə-bəl) adj. indescifrable.

in·de·ci·sion (ĭn'dĭ-sĭzh'ən) s. indecisión f, irresolución f.

in·de·ci·sive (ĭn'dĭ-sī'sĭv) adj. (inconclusive) incierto, dudoso; (irresolute) indeciso, irresoluto; (indefinite) indefinido, vago.

in·de·ci·sive·ness (ĭn'dĭ-sī'sĭv-nĭs) s. (inconclusiveness) incertidumbre f; (irresoluteness) indecisión f, falta de decisión; (vagueness) falta de definición, vaguedad f.

in·dec·o·rous (ĭn-dĕk'ər-əs) adj. indecoroso.

in·deed (ĭn-dēd') I. adv. (truly) verdad, verdaderamente <it is i. a surprise to see you es verdaderamente una sorpresa verte>; (in fact) en efecto <it was i. a good movie fue, en efecto, una buena película>; (of course) claro <you may i. sit down claro que puede sentarse> ♦ **indeed?** ¿de veras?, ¿de verdad? • **that is i. a luxury** eso sí que es lujo • **yes i.!** ¡claro que sí! II. interj. de veras, verdad, sí.

in·de·fat·i·ga·ble (ĭn'dĭ-făt'ĭ-gə-bəl) adj. infatigable, incansable.

in·de·fen·si·ble (ĭn'dĭ-fĕn'sə-bəl) adj. (inexcusable) imperdonable, carente de toda justificación; (untenable) insostenible; (vulnerable to attack) indefensible, indefendible.

in·de·fin·a·ble (ĭn'dĭ-fī'nə-bəl) adj. indefinible, indescriptible.

in·def·i·nite (ĭn-dĕf'ə-nĭt) adj. (indeterminate) indefinido <for an i. period por un período indefinido>; (uncertain) incierto, impreciso; (vague) vago; GRAM. indefinido, indeterminado.

indefinite article s. GRAM. artículo indefinido.

in·def·i·nite·ly (ĭn-dĕf'ə-nĭt-lē) adv. indefinidamente.

in·del·i·bil·i·ty (ĭn-dĕl'ə-bĭl'ĭ-tē) s. indelebilidad f.

in·del·i·ble (ĭn-dĕl'ə-bəl) adj. indeleble, imborrable.

in·del·i·ca·cy (ĭn-dĕl'ĭ-kə-sē) s. [pl. -cies] indelicadeza, falta de delicadeza.

in·del·i·cate (ĭn-dĕl'ĭ-kĭt) adj. (offensive) indelicado, poco delicado; (coarse) indecoroso; (tactless) falto de tacto.

in·dem·ni·fi·ca·tion (ĭn-dĕm'nə-fĭ-kā'shən) s. indemnización f.

in·dem·ni·fy (ĭn-dĕm'nə-fī') tr. -fied, -fy·ing (to insure) asegurar; (to compensate) indemnizar, compensar.

in·dem·ni·ty (ĭn-dĕm'nĭ-tē) s. [pl. -ties] (security, exemption) indemnidad f; (compensation) indemnización f.

in·dent I. tr. (ĭn-dĕnt') IMPR. (to set in from the margin) sangrar; (to cut) cortar (un documento) en forma aserrada; (to serrate) dentar, hacer hendiduras en; CARP. (to notch) hacer muescas en; (to join) machihembrar —intr. formar una hendidura II. s. (ĭn-dĕnt', ĭn'dĕnt') (on the coastline) hendidura de la costa; (notch) muesca.

in·den·ta·tion (ĭn'dĕn-tā'shən) s. (notch) muesca; (of a border, coastline) hendidura, quebradura; IMPR. sangría.

in·den·tion (ĭn-dĕn'shən) s. IMPR. sangría; ANT. (indentation) muesca, abolladura.

in·den·ture (ĭn-dĕn'chər) I. s. DER. (document) documento cortado en dos partes; (contract) contrato que obliga a un joven a servir a amo colonial durante cierto plazo II. tr. -tured, -tur·ing DER. ligar por contrato.

in·de·pend·ence (ĭn'dĭ-pĕn'dəns) s. (state, quality) independencia; ANT. suficiencia económica.

Independence Day s. EE. UU. día de la independencia (4 de julio) m.

in·de·pend·ent (ĭn'dĭ-pĕn'dənt) I. adj. (free) independiente; (not contingent) autónomo, por cuenta propia ♦ **of i. means** con recursos propios, adinerado • **to be i. of** no depender de II. s. independiente mf.

in·de·pend·ent·ly (ĭn'dĭ-pĕn'dənt-lē) adv. independientemente ♦ **i. of what he may say** no obstante lo que diga • **to work i.** trabajar por cuenta propia.

in-depth (ĭn'dĕpth') adj. en profundidad, profundo.

in·de·scrib·a·ble (ĭn'dĭ-skrī'bə-bəl) adj. (not describable) indescriptible; (ineffable) inefable, indescriptible.

in·de·struc·ti·ble (ĭn'dĭ-strŭk'tə-bəl) adj. indestructible.

in·de·ter·min·a·ble (ĭn'dĭ-tûr'mə-nə-bəl) adj. indeterminable.

in·de·ter·mi·na·cy (ĭn'dĭ-tûr'mə-nə-sē) s. indeterminación f.

in·de·ter·mi·nate (ĭn'dĭ-tûr'mə-nĭt) adj. (uncertain) indeterminado, incierto <of i. age de edad incierta>; (vague) vago; (indeterminable) indeterminable; BOT. racimoso.

in·dex (ĭn'dĕks') I. s. [pl. -dex·es o -di·ces (-dĭ-sēz')] (alphabetical list) índice m; (sign) índice, indicio; IMPR. (fist) manecilla; (of an instrument) indicador m; MAT. índice ♦ **cost-of-living i.** índice del costo de vida • I. RELIG. índice • **i. card** ficha, tarjeta II. tr. (to list) poner un índice a; (to indicate) indicar, señalar; (to regulate) regular (precios).

index finger s. dedo índice.

index number s. COM. número índice o indicador.

In·di·a (ĭn'dē-ə) s. (la) India.

India ink s. tinta china.

In·di·an (ĭn'dē-ən) adj. & s. (American Indian) indio; (from India) indio, hindú mf.

Indian corn s. BOT. maíz m.

Indian file s. fila india.

Indian Ocean s. océano Índico.

Indian summer s. FAM. veranillo de San Martín.

India rubber s. jebe m, caucho.

In·dic (ĭn'dĭk) I. adj. índico, indio II. s. (language) indio.

in·di·cate (ĭn'dĭ-kāt') tr. -cat·ed, -cat·ing indicar.

in·di·ca·tion (ĭn'dĭ-kā'shən) s. (sign) indicación f; (symptom) síntoma m; (statement) manifestación f; (measurement) medida.

in·dic·a·tive (ĭn-dĭk'ə-tĭv) I. adj. indicativo ♦ **to be i. of** indicar, ser un indicio de II. s. GRAM. indicativo.

in·di·ca·tor (ĭn'dĭ-kā'tər) s. (gauge, needle) indicador m; ECON. (index) índice m.

in·di·ces (ĭn'dĭ-sēz') un pl. de **index.**

in·dict (ĭn-dīt') tr. (to accuse) acusar.

in·dict·a·ble (ĭn-dī'tə-bəl) adj. DER. que merece acusación legal.

in·dict·ment (ĭn-dīt'mənt) s. (accusation) acusación f; DER. (written statement) acto de acusación por gran jurado.

ã rey / ä año / b boca / ch chico / d dar / ĕ el / ē mil / g gato / h joya / hw juez / ī aire / k casa / kw cuan /

In·dies (ĭn′dēz) s.pl. Indias ♦ **East I.** Indias Orientales • **West I.** Indias Occidentales.

in·dif·fer·ence (ĭn-dĭf′ər-əns) s. indiferencia ♦ **to be of supreme i. to someone** no importarle a alguien en lo absoluto.

in·dif·fer·ent (ĭn-dĭf′ər-ənt) adj. *(apathetic)* indiferente; *(impartial)* desinteresado; *(unimportant)* indiferente, insignificante; *(mediocre)* regular; BIOL. sin diferenciación.

in·dif·fer·ent·ly (ĭn-dĭf′ər-ənt-lē) adv. *(apathetically)* indiferentemente; *(impartially)* desinteresadamente; *(neither well nor badly)* de modo regular.

in·di·gence (ĭn′dĭ-jəns) s. indigencia.

in·dig·e·nous (ĭn-dĭj′ə-nəs) adj. *(native)* indígena, nativo; *(innate)* innato, ingénito.

in·di·gent (ĭn′dĭ-jənt) **I.** adj. *(impoverished)* indigente, pobre; ANT. *(lacking)* falto **II.** s. indigente *mf*, pobre *mf*.

in·di·gest·i·ble (ĭn′dĭ-jĕs′tə-bəl, -dĭ-) adj. indigestible.

in·di·ges·tion (ĭn′dĭ-jĕs′chən, -dĭ-) s. indigestión *f*.

in·dig·nant (ĭn-dĭg′nənt) adj. indignado.

in·dig·na·tion (ĭn′dĭg-nā′shən) s. indignación *f*.

in·dig·ni·ty (ĭn-dĭg′nĭ-tē) s. [pl. **-ties**] *(lack of dignity)* indignidad *f*; *(affront)* ultraje *m*, afrenta.

in·di·go (ĭn′dĭ-gō′) s. [pl. **-gos** o **-goes**] BOT., QUÍM. índigo, añil *m*.

in·di·rect (ĭn′dĭ-rĕkt′, -dĭ-) adj. *(not direct)* indirecto; *(roundabout)* que anda con rodeos; *(secondary)* indirecto, derivado.

in·di·rec·tion (ĭn′dĭ-rĕk′shən, -dĭ-) s. *(quality, state)* carácter indirecto; *(aimlessness)* falta de dirección; *(deviousness)* rodeos, tortuosidad *f*.

indirect object s. GRAM. complemento indirecto.

in·dis·cern·i·ble (ĭn′dĭ-sûr′nə-bəl, -zûr′-) **I.** adj. indiscernible, imperceptible **II.** s. cosa indiscernible o imperceptible.

in·dis·creet (ĭn′dĭ-skrēt′) adj. indiscreto.

in·dis·cre·tion (ĭn′dĭ-skrĕsh′ən) s. indiscreción *f*, imprudencia.

in·dis·crim·i·nate (ĭn′dĭ-skrĭm′ə-nĭt) adj. *(undiscriminating)* sin criterio <*an i. reader* un lector sin criterio>; *(random)* al azar; *(jumbled)* indistinto; *(unrestrained)* ciego (admiración, alabanza).

in·dis·crim·i·na·tive (ĭn′dĭ-skrĭm′ə-nə-tĭv) adj. que no discrimina o discierne.

in·dis·pens·a·ble (ĭn′dĭ-spĕn′sə-bəl) adj. indispensable, imprescindible.

in·dis·pose (ĭn′dĭ-spōz′) tr. **-posed, -pos·ing** *(to disincline)* quitar las ganas; *(to disqualify)* inhabilitar; *(to sicken)* indisponer.

in·dis·posed (ĭn′dĭ-spōzd′) adj. *(slightly ill)* indispuesto; *(disinclined)* adverso, maldispuesto.

in·dis·po·si·tion (ĭn·dĭs′pə-zĭsh′ən) s. *(disinclination)* aversión *f*; *(slight ailment)* indisposición *f*.

in·dis·put·a·ble (ĭn′dĭ-spyōō′tə-bəl) adj. indisputable, incuestionable.

in·dis·sol·u·ble (ĭn′dĭ-sŏl′yə-bəl) adj. indisoluble.

in·dis·tinct (ĭn′dĭ-stĭngkt′) adj. indistinto.

in·dis·tinc·tive (ĭn′dĭ-stĭngk′tĭv) adj. corriente, sin distinción.

in·dis·tin·guish·a·ble (ĭn′dĭ-stĭng′gwĭ-shə-bəl) adj. indistinguible.

in·di·um (ĭn′dē-əm) s. QUÍM. indio.

in·di·vid·u·al (ĭn′də-vĭj′ōō-əl) **I.** adj. *(for or by a single person)* individual; *(distinctive)* particular, propio (estilo, manera) **II.** s. individuo ♦ **private i.** particular.

in·di·vid·u·al·ism (ĭn′də-vĭj′ōō-ə-lĭz′əm) s. individualismo.

in·di·vid·u·al·ist (ĭn′də-vĭj′ōō-ə-lĭst) s. individualista *mf*.

in·di·vid·u·al·is·tic (ĭn′də-vĭj′ōō-ə-lĭs′tĭk) adj. individualista.

in·di·vid·u·al·i·ty (ĭn′də-vĭj′ōō-ăl′ĭ-tē) s. [pl. **-ties**] *(distinctness)* individualidad *f*, particularidad *f*; *(distinctive identity)* personalidad *f* <*expressing one's i.* que expresa la personalidad de uno>.

in·di·vid·u·al·ize (ĭn′də-vĭj′ōō-ə-līz′) tr. **-ized, -iz·ing** *(to make individual)* individualizar; *(to particularize)* particularizar.

in·di·vid·u·al·ly (ĭn′də-vĭj′ōō-ə-lē) adv. *(one by one)* individualmente, uno por uno; *(separately)* por separado.

in·di·vis·i·bil·i·ty (ĭn′də-vĭz′ə-bĭl′ĭ-tē) s. indivisibilidad *f*.

in·di·vis·i·ble (ĭn′də-vĭz′ə-bəl) adj. indivisible.

In·do·chi·na (ĭn′dō-chī′nə) s. GEOG. Indochina.

in·doc·tri·nate (ĭn-dŏk′trə-nāt′) tr. **-nat·ed, -nat·ing** adoctrinar.

in·doc·tri·na·tion (ĭn-dŏk′trə-nā′shən) s. adoctrinamiento.

In·do-Eu·ro·pe·an (ĭn′dō-yoŏr′ə-pē′ən) s. & adj. indoeuropeo.

in·do·lence (ĭn′də-ləns) s. indolencia.

in·do·lent (ĭn′də-lənt) adj. *(lazy)* indolente; MED. *(causing no pain)* indolente, indoloro.

in·dom·i·ta·ble (ĭn-dŏm′ĭ-tə-bəl) adj. indomable, indómito.

In·do·ne·sia (ĭn′də-nē′zhə) s. Indonesia.

In·do·ne·sian (ĭn′də-nē′zhən) adj. & s. *(inhabitant, language)* indonesio.

in·door (ĭn′dôr′) adj. *(interior)* interior, interno; *(within doors)* de puertas adentro.

in·doors (ĭn-dôrz′) adv. dentro, bajo techo.

in·du·bi·ta·ble (ĭn-dōō′bĭ-tə-bəl, -dyōō′-) adj. indudable, indubitable.

in·duce (ĭn-dōōs′, -dyōōs′) tr. **-duced, -duc·ing** *(to cause)* ocasionar, causar; *(childbirth)* provocar; *(to infer)* inducir; FÍS. inducir ♦ **to i. to** inducir a que, lograr convencer de que.

in·duce·ment (ĭn-dōōs′mənt, -dyōōs′-) s. *(act, process)* inducción *f*; *(of childbirth)* provocación *f*; *(incentive)* incentivo, aliciente *m*; *(lure)* atractivo.

in·duct (ĭn-dŭkt′) tr. *(into office)* instalar, instaurar; *(into a society)* admitir; *(to initiate)* iniciar; *(into military service)* reclutar; FÍS. inducir.

in·duc·tance (ĭn-dŭk′təns) s. ELEC. inductancia.

in·duc·tee (ĭn-dŭk-tē′) s. *(new member)* nuevo miembro; *(recruit)* recluta *m*.

in·duc·tion (ĭn-dŭk′shən) s. ELEC., LÓG., MAT. inducción *f*; *(into office, position)* instalación *f*; *(into a society)* admisión *f*; MIL. incorporación a filas *f*.

induction coil s. ELEC. bobina o carrete *m* de inducción.

in·duc·tive (ĭn-dŭk′tĭv) adj. *(logic)* inductivo, de la inducción; ELEC. inductivo, inductor; *(inducing)* inductor, instigador.

in·duc·tor (ĭn-dŭk′tər) s. *(one that induces)* inductor *m*; ELEC., QUÍM. inductor.

in·dulge (ĭn-dŭlj′) tr. **-dulged, -dulg·ing** *(to pamper)* consentir, mimar; *(to gratify)* satisfacer; RELIG. conceder indulgencia a ♦ **to i. oneself** darse gusto —intr. entregarse a, darse a ♦ **to i. in** *(pleasure)* permitirse o darse el lujo de; *(to engage in)* complacerse en.

in·dul·gence (ĭn-dŭl′jəns) **I.** s. *(humoring)* complacencia; *(pampering)* consentimiento; *(in pleasures)* gratificación *f*, satisfacción *f*; *(in vices)* abandono, desenfreno; *(luxury)* lujo, capricho <*cigarettes are his only i.* los cigarrillos son su único capricho>; *(favor)* favor *m*; RELIG. indulgencia **II.** tr. **-genced, -genc·ing** RELIG. indulgenciar.

in·dul·gent (ĭn-dŭl′jənt) adj. indulgente.

in·dus·tri·al (ĭn-dŭs′trē-əl) **I.** adj. industrial ♦ **i. accident** accidente de trabajo • **i. relations** relaciones laborales • **i. revolution** revolución industrial **II.** s. empresa industrial, industria ♦ **industrials** COM. valores industriales.

in·dus·tri·al·ism (ĭn-dŭs′trē-ə-lĭz′əm) s. industrialismo.

in·dus·tri·al·ist (ĭn-dŭs′trē-ə-lĭst) s. industrial *m*, industrialista *mf*.

in·dus·tri·al·i·za·tion (ĭn-dŭs′trē-ə-lĭ-zā′shən) s. industrialización *f*.

in·dus·tri·al·ize (ĭn-dŭs′trē-ə-līz′) tr. & intr. **-ized, -iz·ing** industrializar(se).

industrial park s. zona industrial.

in·dus·tri·ous (ĭn-dŭs′trē-əs) adj. *(diligent)* industrioso, diligente; ANT. *(skillful)* industrioso.

in·dus·tri·ous·ness (ĭn-dŭs′trē-əs-nĭs) s. *(in a job)* diligencia; *(in school)* aplicación *f*.

in·dus·try (ĭn′də-strē) s. [pl. **-tries**] industria <*the textile i.* la industria textil>; *(management)* empresariado; *(diligence)* diligencia; *(in school)* aplicación *f* ♦ **tourist i.** turismo.

---

in·e·bri·ate I. tr. (ĭn-ē′brē-āt′) **-at·ed, -at·ing** *(to intoxicate)* embriagar, emborrachar; FIG. *(to exhilarate)* embriagar II. adj. & s. (-ĭt) borracho, ebrio.

in·e·bri·at·ed (ĭn-ē′brē-ā′tĭd) adj. embriagado.

in·e·bri·a·tion (ĭn-ē′brē-ā′shən) s. embriaguez *f*, borrachera.

in·ed·i·ble (ĭn-ĕd′ə-bəl) adj. incomible, incomestible.

in·ef·fa·ble (ĭn-ĕf′ə-bəl) adj. inefable.

in·ef·fec·tive (ĭn′ĭ-fĕk′tĭv) adj. ineficaz.

in·ef·fec·tu·al (ĭn′ĭ-fĕk′chŏŏ-əl) adj. *(vain)* vano, inútil; *(ineffective)* ineficaz.

in·ef·fi·cien·cy (ĭn′ĭ-fĭsh′ən-sē) s. [pl. **-cies**] ineficiencia, ineficacia.

in·ef·fi·cient (ĭn′ĭ-fĭsh′ənt) adj. *(not efficient)* ineficiente; *(inefficacious)* ineficaz; *(incompetent)* incompetente; *(wasteful)* ineficiente; *(useless)* inútil; *(incapable)* incapaz.

in·e·las·tic (ĭn′ĭ-lăs′tĭk) adj. *(not elastic)* no elástico, rígido; *(unyielding)* inflexible; FÍS. inelástico.

in·e·las·tic·i·ty (ĭn′ĭ-lă-stĭs′ĭ-tē) s. FÍS., MEC. falta de elasticidad; *(inflexibility)* inflexibilidad *f.*

in·el·e·gant (ĭn-ĕl′ĭ-gənt) adj. inelegante, poco elegante.

in·el·i·gi·bil·i·ty (ĭn-ĕl′ĭ-jə-bĭl′ĭ-tē) s. inelegibilidad *f.*

in·el·i·gi·ble (ĭn-ĕl′ĭ-jə-bəl) I. adj. *(not qualified)* no apto; *(unsuited)* inadecuado; *(not eligible)* inelegible II. s. persona inelegible.

in·e·luc·ta·ble (ĭn′ĭ-lŭk′tə-bəl) adj. ineluctable, inevitable.

in·ept (ĭn-ĕpt′) adj. *(incompetent)* inepto, incapaz; *(inappropriate)* inapropiado, inadecuado; *(senseless)* absurdo, tonto.

in·ep·ti·tude (ĭn-ĕp′tĭ-tōōd′, -tyōōd′) s. ineptitud *f*, incapacidad *f.*

in·ept·ness (ĭn-ĕpt′nĭs) s. ineptitud *f*, incapacidad *f.*

in·e·qual·i·ty (ĭn′ĭ-kwŏl′ĭ-tē) s. [pl. **-ties**] *(lack of equality, unevenness)* desigualdad *f*; *(injustice)* injusticia.

in·eq·ui·ta·ble (ĭn-ĕk′wĭ-tə-bəl) adj. injusto.

in·eq·ui·ty (ĭn-ĕk′wĭ-tē) s. [pl. **-ties**] injusticia.

in·ert (ĭn-ûrt′) adj. inerte.

in·er·tia (ĭn-ûr′shə) s. FÍS. inercia; FIG. *(inaction)* inercia, desidia.

in·er·tial (ĭn-ûr′shəl) adj. FÍS. inercial, de inercia.

in·ert·ness (ĭn-ûrt′nĭs) s. inercia.

in·es·cap·a·ble (ĭn′ĭ-skă′pə-bəl) adj. ineludible, inevitable.

in·es·ti·ma·ble (ĭn-ĕs′tə-mə-bəl) adj. ˙inestimable.

in·ev·i·ta·bil·i·ty (ĭn-ĕv′ĭ-tə-bĭl′ĭ-tē) s. inevitabilidad *f.*

in·ev·i·ta·ble (ĭn-ĕv′ĭ-tə-bəl) adj. inevitable, ineludible.

in·ex·act (ĭn′ĭg-zăkt′) adj. inexacto.

in·ex·act·i·tude (ĭn′ĭg-zăk′tĭ-tōōd′, -tyōōd′) s. inexactitud *f.*

in·ex·cus·a·ble (ĭn′ĭk-skyōō′zə-bəl) adj. inexcusable, imperdonable.

in·ex·haust·i·ble (ĭn′ĭg-zô′stə-bəl) adj. inagotable.

in·ex·o·ra·ble (ĭn-ĕk′sər-ə-bəl) adj. inexorable.

in·ex·pen·sive (ĭn′ĭk-spĕn′sĭv) adj. barato, poco costoso.

in·ex·pe·ri·ence (ĭn′ĭk-spîr′ē-əns) s. inexperiencia, falta de experiencia.

in·ex·pe·ri·enced (ĭn′ĭk-spîr′ē-ənst) adj. *(lacking experience)* sin experiencia; *(lacking knowledge)* inexperto.

in·ex·pert (ĭn-ĕk′spûrt′) adj. inexperto.

in·ex·pli·ca·ble (ĭn-ĕk′splĭ-kə-bəl, ĭn′ĭk-splĭk′ə-) adj. inexplicable.

in·ex·plic·it (ĭn′ĭk-splĭs′ĭt) adj. no explícito, vago.

in·ex·press·i·ble (ĭn′ĭk-sprĕs′ə-bəl) adj. inexpresable, indecible.

in·ex·pres·sive (ĭn′ĭk-sprĕs′ĭv) adj. inexpresivo.

in·ex·tin·guish·a·ble (ĭn′ĭk-stĭng′gwĭsh-ə-bəl) adj. inextinguible, inapagable.

in ex·tre·mis (ĭn ĕk-strē′mĭs) adv. LAT. in extremis, en los últimos instantes de vida.

in·ex·tri·ca·ble (ĭn-ĕk′strĭ-kə-bəl) adj. inextricable.

in·fal·li·bil·i·ty (ĭn-făl′ə-bĭl′ĭ-tē) s. infalibilidad *f.*

in·fal·li·ble (ĭn-făl′ə-bəl) adj. infalible.

in·fa·mous (ĭn′fə-məs) adj. *(notorious)* infame, de mala fama; *(odious)* odioso; *(causing horror)* infame, infamatorio; DER. *(convicted)* infame.

in·fa·my (ĭn′fə-mē) s. [pl. **-mies**] infamia.

in·fan·cy (ĭn′fən-sē) s. [pl. **-cies**] *(period)* infancia; *(beginning)* infancia, principio; DER. *(state)* minoría de edad.

in·fant (ĭn′fənt) s. *(child)* infante *mf*, niño; DER. *(minor)* menor de edad *mf.*

in·fan·ti·cide (ĭn-făn′tĭ-sīd′) s. *(killing)* infanticidio; *(killer)* infanticida *mf.*

in·fan·tile (ĭn′fən-tīl′) adj. infantil ♦ **i. paralysis** MED. parálisis infantil.

in·fan·til·ism (ĭn′fən-tə-lĭz′əm) s. MED. infantilismo.

in·fan·try (ĭn′fən-trē) s. [pl. **-tries**] MIL. infantería.

in·fan·try·man (ĭn′fən-trē-mən) s. [pl. **-men**] MIL. soldado de infantería.

in·farct (ĭn′färkt, ĭn-färkt′) s. MED. infarto.

in·fat·u·ate (ĭn-făch′ōō-āt′) I. tr. **-at·ed, -at·ing** *(to make foolish)* infatuar, atontar; *(to inspire with foolish love)* enamorar locamente II. adj. (-ĭt) locamente enamorado.

in·fat·u·at·ed (ĭn-făch′ōō-ā′tĭd) adj. *(in love)* locamente enamorado; *(foolish)* encaprichado ♦ **to be i. with** estar locamente enamorado de.

in·fat·u·a·tion (ĭn-făch′ōō-ā′shən) s. enamoramiento, encaprichamiento.

in·fea·si·ble (ĭn-fē′zə-bəl) adj. no factible, impracticable.

in·fect (ĭn-fĕkt′) tr. *(to contaminate)* infectar, contaminar; *(to give a disease to)* infectar, contagiar; FIG. *(to affect)* contagiar (entusiasmo).

in·fec·tion (ĭn-fĕk′shən) s. MED. infección *f*; FIG. *(contagion)* contagio.

in·fec·tious (ĭn-fĕk′shəs) adj. MED. *(containing infection)* infeccioso; *(transmitted by infection)* contagioso <an i. disease una enfermedad contagiosa>; FIG. *(easily communicated)* contagioso.

in·fe·lic·i·tous (ĭn′fĭ-lĭs′ĭ-təs) adj. *(unhappy)* infeliz, desgraciado; *(inappropriate)* inapropiado, desacertado; *(inopportune)* inoportuno.

in·fe·lic·i·ty (ĭn′fĭ-lĭs′ĭ-tē) s. [pl. **-ties**] *(unhappiness)* infelicidad *f*; *(misfortune)* infortunio; *(blunder)* desacierto; *(unsuitability)* inoportunidad *f.*

in·fer (ĭn-fûr′) tr. **-ferred, -fer·ring** *(to deduce)* inferir, deducir; *(to conclude)* concluir —intr. hacer inferencias.

in·fer·a·ble (ĭn-fûr′ə-bəl) adj. que puede inferirse, deducible.

in·fer·ence (ĭn′fər-əns) s. *(act)* inferencia; *(deduction)* inferencia, deducción *f.*

in·fer·en·tial (ĭn′fə-rĕn′shəl) adj. que se infiere, que se deduce.

in·fe·ri·or (ĭn-fîr′ē-ər) adj. & s. inferior *m.*

in·fe·ri·or·i·ty (ĭn-fîr′ē-ôr′ĭ-tē) s. inferioridad *f.*

inferiority complex s. PSIC. complejo de inferioridad.

in·fer·nal (ĭn-fûr′nəl) adj. *(relating to hell)* infernal; FAM. *(devilish)* infernal, endemoniado; *(abominable)* abominable, detestable.

in·fer·no (ĭn-fûr′nō) s. [pl. **-nos**] infierno.

in·fer·tile (ĭn-fûr′tl) adj. infértil, estéril.

in·fer·til·i·ty (ĭn′fər-tĭl′ĭ-tē) s. infertilidad *f*, esterilidad *f.*

in·fest (ĭn-fĕst′) tr. infestar, plagar.

in·fes·ta·tion (ĭn′fĕ-stā′shən) s. infestación *f*, plaga.

in·fi·del (ĭn′fĭ-dəl) s. RELIG. infiel *mf*, incrédulo.

in·fi·del·i·ty (ĭn′fĭ-dĕl′ĭ-tē) s. [pl. **-ties**] *(disloyalty)* deslealtad *f*; *(marital unfaithfulness)* infidelidad conyugal *f*; RELIG. infidelidad.

in·field (ĭn′fēld′) s. *(farmland)* tierras cercanas a las casas de una granja; DEP. *(baseball)* cuadro *o* diamante *m* interior (de una cancha de béisbol); *(race track)* campo interior (de una pista de carreras).

in·fight·ing (ĭn′fī′tĭng) s. *(fighting)* lucha *o* boxeo cuerpo a cuerpo; *(contention)* lucha interna (en una organización *o* grupo).

in·fil·trate (ĭn-fĭl′trāt′) I. tr. **-trat·ed, -trat·ing** *(to permeate)* infiltrar; *(to enter secretly)* infiltrarse en —intr. infiltrarse II. s. MED. infiltración *f.*

in·fil·tra·tion (ĭn′fĭl-trā′shən) s. infiltración *f.*

in·fi·nite (ĭn′fə-nĭt) I. adj. infinito ♦ **with i. care** con muchísimo cuidado II. s. infinito.

in·fin·i·tes·i·mal (ĭn-fĭn′ĭ-tĕs′ə-məl) I. adj. infinitesimal, pequeñísimo II. s. MAT. cantidad infinitesimal *f.*

in·fin·i·tive (ĭn-fĭn′ĭ-tĭv) s. GRAM. infinitivo.

in·fin·i·tude (ĭn-fĭn′ĭ-tōōd′, -tyōōd′) s. infinitud *f*, infinidad *f.*

ã rey / ä año / b boca / ch chico / d dar / ĕ el / ē mil / g gato / h joya / hw juez / ī aire / k casa / kw cuan /

in·fin·i·ty (ĭn-fĭn′ĭ-tē) s. [pl. **-ties**] *(quality, condition)* infinidad *f*; MAT. infinito.

in·firm (ĭn-fûrm′) adj. *(feeble)* débil, enfermizo; *(irresolute)* débil, irresoluto; *(insecure)* inseguro.

in·fir·ma·ry (ĭn-fûr′mə-rē) s. [pl. **-ries**] enfermería, dispensario.

in·fir·mi·ty (ĭn-fûr′mĭ-tē) s. [pl. **-ties**] *(weakness)* debilidad *f*; *(illness)* enfermedad *f*, achaque *m*; FIG. *(moral weakness)* debilidad *f*, flaqueza; *(defect)* defecto (de carácter).

in·flame (ĭn-flām′) tr. **-flamed, -flam·ing** *(to ignite)* prender fuego, encender; *(to arouse)* inflamar, avivar; MED. *(to swell)* inflamar —intr. *(to catch fire)* inflamarse, encenderse; *(to become excited)* acalorarse; MED. *(to become swollen)* inflamarse.

in·flam·ma·ble (ĭn-flăm′ə-bəl) adj. *(flammable)* inflamable; *(irascible)* irascible, irritable.

in·flam·ma·tion (ĭn′flə-mā′shən) s. inflamación *f*.

in·flam·ma·to·ry (ĭn-flăm′ə-tôr′ē) adj. *(inciting)* incitante; *(tending to inflame)* incendiario; MED. *(swollen)* inflamatorio.

in·flate (ĭn-flāt′) tr. **-flat·ed, -flat·ing** *(to distend with a gas)* inflar, hinchar; ECON. causar la inflación de (la moneda) —intr. inflarse, hincharse.

in·flat·ed (ĭn-flā′tĭd) adj. *(distended)* inflado, hinchado; FIG. *(of the ego)* henchido; *(bombastic)* pomposo, rimbombante; ECON. *(of wages, prices)* excesivo.

in·fla·tion (ĭn-flā′shən) s. inflación *f* ♦ **runaway i.** ECON. inflación incontrolable.

in·fla·tion·ar·y (ĭn-flā′shə-nĕr′ē) adj. ECON. inflacionario, inflacionista.

in·flect (ĭn-flĕkt′) tr. *(to bend)* doblar, torcer; *(voice)* dar una inflexión a; GRAM. *(a verb)* conjugar; *(noun, pronoun)* declinar.

in·flec·tion (ĭn-flĕk′shən) s. inflexión *f*.

in·flec·tion·al (ĭn-flĕk′shən-əl) adj. inflexional.

in·flex·i·bil·i·ty (ĭn-flĕk′sə-bĭl′ĭ-tē) s. inflexibilidad *f*.

in·flex·i·ble (ĭn-flĕk′sə-bəl) adj. *(rigid)* inflexible, rígido; *(unyielding)* inflexible, indoblegable.

in·flex·ion (ĭn-flĕk′shən) s. G.B. var. de **inflection**.

in·flict (ĭn-flĭkt′) tr. infligir, causar (derrota, pena) ♦ **to i. on** *o* **upon** imponer (algo) a alguien

in·flic·tion (ĭn-flĭk′shən) s. *(act)* imposición *f*; *(punishment)* castigo.

in·flight (ĭn′flīt′) adj. AVIA. en *o* durante el vuelo.

in·flow (ĭn′flō′) s. *(act, process)* afluencia; *(of people, capital)* afluencia, flujo.

in·flu·ence (ĭn′flōō-əns) I. s. influencia, influjo ♦ **a man of i.** un hombre influyente • **to be an important i. on** tener mucha influencia sobre • **to be easily influenced** dejarse influenciar fácilmente • **to drive under the i.** conducir embriagado • **to have i.** ser influyente II. tr. **-enced, -enc·ing** *(to have power over)* influir en, ejercer influencia sobre; *(to affect)* influir en.

in·flu·en·tial (ĭn′flōō-ĕn′shəl) adj. influyente.

in·flu·en·za (ĭn′flōō-ĕn′zə) s. MED. influenza, gripe *f*.

in·flux (ĭn′flŭks′) s. afluencia, entrada.

in·form (ĭn-fôrm′) tr. *(to notify)* informar, comunicar; *(to warn)* avisar <*I was not informed in time* no me avisaron a tiempo> ♦ **to be happy to i. someone that** tener el placer de comunicarle a alguien que —intr. ♦ **to i. on** delatar, denunciar.

in·for·mal (ĭn-fôr′məl) adj. *(casual)* informal; *(unofficial)* extraoficial; *(agreement)* no legalizado; *(easygoing)* sencillo, familiar; *(unceremonious)* sin ceremonia, sin etiqueta; *(dress)* de diario, de calle; *(language)* familiar.

in·for·mal·i·ty (ĭn′fôr-măl′ĭ-tē) s. [pl. **-ties**] *(quality)* falta de formalización; *(of a person)* sencillez *f*; *(of an occasion)* ausencia de ceremonia; *(of language)* familiaridad *f*, llaneza.

in·form·ant (ĭn-fôr′mənt) s. *(informer)* delator *m*; *(source)* informante *mf*, informador *m*.

in·for·ma·tion (ĭn′fər-mā′shən) s. *(data)* información *f*, datos <*i. for a biography* datos para una biografía>; *(knowledge)* conocimientos <*the current i. about evolution* los conocimientos actuales acerca de la evolución>; *(news)* información, informes *m*; DER. *(accusation)* acusación fiscal

f; COMPUT. información, datos ♦ **for your i.** para su conocimiento.

information theory s. COMPUT. teoría de probabilidades de información.

in·form·a·tive (ĭn-fôr′mə-tĭv) adj. informativo.

in·formed (ĭn-fôrmd′) adj. *(having information)* informado, enterado; *(educated)* educado, culto ♦ **an i. appraisal** una evaluación bien fundada • **to keep someone i.** tener a alguien al corriente.

in·form·er (ĭn-fôr′mər) s. delator *m*, soplón *m*.

in·frac·tion (ĭn-frăk′shən) s. infracción *f*, violación *f*.

in·fran·gi·ble (ĭn-frăn′jə-bəl) adj. infrangible, inviolable.

in·fra·red (ĭn′frə-rĕd′) adj. FÍS. infrarrojo.

in·fra·struc·ture (ĭn′frə-strŭk′chər) s. infraestructura.

in·fre·quen·cy (ĭn-frē′kwən-sē) *o* **in·fre·quence** (-kwəns) s. poca frecuencia.

in·fre·quent (ĭn-frē′kwənt) adj. *(rare)* infrecuente, raro; *(occasional)* infrecuente, ocasional.

in·fringe (ĭn-frĭnj′) tr. **-fringed, -fring·ing** infringir, violar —intr. ♦ **to i. on** *o* **upon** usurpar, abusar de.

in·fringe·ment (ĭn-frĭnj′mənt) s. *(violation)* infracción *f*, violación (de una ley) *f*; *(encroachment)* usurpación (de derechos) *f*.

in·fu·ri·ate (ĭn-fyŏŏr′ē-āt′) tr. **-at·ed, -at·ing** enfurecer.

in·fuse (ĭn-fyŏōz′) tr. **-fused, -fus·ing** *(to introduce)* infundir; *(to soak)* hacer una infusión.

in·fu·sion (ĭn-fyŏō′zhən) s. infusión *f*.

in·gen·ious (ĭn-jēn′yəs) adj. *(imaginative)* ingenioso; ANT. *(brilliant)* genial.

in·gé·nue (ăn′zhə-nōō′) s. joven ingenua; TEAT. ingenua.

in·ge·nu·i·ty (ĭn′jə-nōō′ĭ-tē, -nyōō′-) s. [pl. **-ties**] *(cleverness)* ingeniosidad *f*, ingenio; *(device)* aparato ingenioso.

in·gen·u·ous (ĭn-jĕn′yŏō-əs) adj. *(naive)* ingenuo; *(frank)* cándido.

in·gest (ĭn-jĕst′) tr. *(to swallow)* ingerir; FIG. *(to absorb)* absorber.

in·ges·tion (ĭn-jĕs′chən) s. ingestión *f*.

in·glo·ri·ous (ĭn-glôr′ē-əs) adj. *(not famous)* desconocido, obscuro; *(ignominious)* ignominioso; *(shameful)* vergonzoso.

in·got (ĭng′gət) s. *(mass of metal)* lingote *m*, barra; *(mold)* lingotera, molde de fundición *m*.

in·grain (ĭn-grān′) I. tr. *(to dye)* teñir penetrando al grano; *(to inculcate)* inculcar II. adj. *(deeply rooted)* arraigado; TEJ. *(color)* teñido en el hilo III. s. TEJ. hilo teñido.

in·grained (ĭn-grānd′) adj. arraigado.

in·grate (ĭn′grāt′) s. persona ingrata.

in·gra·ti·ate (ĭn-grā′shē-āt′) tr. **-at·ed, -at·ing** congraciarse.

in·grat·i·tude (ĭn-grăt′ĭ-tōōd′, -tyōōd′) s. ingratitud *f*.

in·gre·di·ent (ĭn-grē′dē-ənt) s. ingrediente *m*.

in·group (ĭn′grōōp′) s. FAM. grupo excluyente (de gente con intereses y creencias comunes).

in·grown (ĭn′grōn′) adj. *(grown inward)* crecido hacia adentro; *(innate)* innato, congénito ♦ **i. toenail** uña encarnada.

in·growth (ĭn′grōth′) s. *(act)* crecimiento hacia adentro; *(thing)* cosa que crece hacia adentro.

in·hab·it (ĭn-hăb′ĭt) tr. *(to reside in)* residir en, vivir en; *(to occupy)* habitar.

in·hab·it·a·ble (ĭn-hăb′ĭ-tə-bəl) adj. habitable.

in·hab·i·tant (ĭn-hăb′ĭ-tnt) s. habitante *mf*.

in·hab·i·ta·tion (ĭn-hăb′ĭ-tā′shən) s. habitación *f*, acto de habitar.

in·hab·it·ed (ĭn-hăb′ĭ-tĭd) adj. *(occupied)* habitado; *(populated)* poblado.

in·ha·lant (ĭn-hā′lənt) I. adj. inhalante II. s. medicamento para inhalación.

in·ha·la·tion (ĭn′hə-lā′shən) s. inhalación *f*.

in·ha·la·tor (ĭn′hə-lā′tər) s. inhalador *m*.

in·hale (ĭn-hāl′) tr. **-haled, -hal·ing** *(to draw in)* aspirar, inspirar; MED. inhalar —intr. aspirar aire.

in·hal·er (ĭn-hā′lər) s. *(person)* persona que hace inhalaciones; *(device)* inhalador *m*.

in·har·mon·ic (ĭn′här-mŏn′ĭk) adj. MÚS. inarmónico.

in·har·mo·ni·ous (ĭn′här-mō′nē-əs) adj. MÚS. *(not harmonic)* inharmónico; *(discordant)* discordante; *(discrepant)* discrepante.

in·here (ĭn-hîr′) intr. **-hered, -her·ing** ser inherente.
in·her·ence (ĭn-hîr′əns) *o* **in·her·en·cy** (-ən-sē) s. inherencia.
in·her·ent (ĭn-hîr′ənt) adj. inherente, intrínseco.
in·her·it (ĭn-hĕr′ĭt) tr. heredar —intr. recibir herencia.
in·her·it·a·ble (ĭn-hĕr′ĭ-tə-bəl) adj. *(capable of inheriting)* que puede heredar; *(capable of being inherited)* heredable, transmisible.
in·her·i·tance (ĭn-hĕr′ĭ-tns) s. *(act)* sucesión *f; (thing)* herencia; *(heritage)* patrimonio; BIOL. herencia.
inheritance tax s. impuesto sobre sucesiones, impuesto a la herencia.
in·her·i·tor (ĭn-hĕr′ĭ-tər) s. heredero.
in·hib·it (ĭn-hĭb′ĭt) tr. *(to restrain)* inhibir, reprimir; *(to prevent)* impedir, detener; *(to prohibit)* prohibir.
in·hi·bi·tion (ĭn′hə-bĭsh′ən) s. inhibición *f.*
in·hib·i·tive (ĭn-hĭb′ĭ-tĭv) adj. inhibitorio.
in·hib·i·tor (ĭn-hĭb′ĭ-tər) s. FÍS., QUÍM. inhibidor *m.*
in·hos·pi·ta·ble (ĭn-hŏs′pĭ-tə-bəl, ĭn′hŏ-spĭt′ə-) adj. *(unfriendly)* inhospitalario; *(barren)* inhóspito.
in·house (ĭn′hous′) adj. interno, de la casa (de una organización, compañía).
in·hu·man (ĭn-hyōō′mən) adj. *(brutal)* inhumano, cruel; *(insensitive)* insensible; *(cold)* frío; *(monstrous)* no humano.
in·hu·mane (ĭn′hyōō-mān′) adj. inhumano.
in·hu·man·i·ty (ĭn′hyōō-măn′ĭ-tē) s. [pl. **-ties**] *(lack of pity)* inhumanidad *f; (cruelty)* crueldad *f.*
in·im·i·cal (ĭn-ĭm′ĭ-kəl) adj. *(contrary)* contrario, adverso <*habits i. to good health* hábitos adversos a la buena salud>; *(hostile)* hostil.
in·im·i·ta·ble (ĭn-ĭm′ĭ-tə-bəl) adj. inimitable.
in·iq·ui·ty (ĭ-nĭk′wĭ-tē) s. [pl. **-ties**] *(wickedness)* iniquidad *f; (act)* maldad *f; (sin)* pecado.
in·i·tial (ĭ-nĭsh′əl) **I.** adj. *(first)* inicial, primero <*my i. impression* mi primera impresión>; *(letter)* inicial **II.** s. *(first letter)* inicial *f; (decorated letter)* letra florida ♦ **initials** *(of a person)* iniciales; *(of an organization)* siglas **III.** tr. firmar con las iniciales.
in·i·tial·ly (ĭ-nĭsh′ə-lē) adv. *(firstly)* inicialmente, originalmente; *(at first)* al principio.
in·i·ti·ate (ĭ-nĭsh′ē-āt′) **I.** tr. **-at·ed, -at·ing** iniciar, comenzar; *(proceedings)* entablar; *(to admit)* iniciar, admitir **II.** adj. & s. (-ĭt) iniciado.
in·i·ti·a·tion (ĭ-nĭsh′ē-ā′shən) s. *(beginning)* iniciación *f;* comienzo; *(ceremony)* iniciación.
in·i·ti·a·tive (ĭ-nĭsh′ə-tĭv) **I.** s. iniciativa <*to take the i.* tomar la iniciativa> ♦ **on one's own i.** por iniciativa propia **II.** adj. preliminar.
in·ject (ĭn-jĕkt′) tr. *(to force into)* inyectar; MED. inyectar; *(a patient)* poner una inyección a; FIG. *(into a conversation)* introducir.
in·jec·tion (ĭn-jĕk′shən) s. MED., TEC. inyección *f.*
in·ju·di·cious (ĭn′jōō-dĭsh′əs) adj. poco juicioso, imprudente.
in·junc·tion (ĭn-jŭngk′shən) s. *(command)* orden *f,* mandato; DER. *(summons)* requerimiento judicial, intimación *f; (prohibition)* entredicho, interdicto.
in·jure (ĭn′jər) tr. **-jured, -jur·ing** *(to hurt)* lastimar, herir; *(to impair)* dañar, averiar; FIG. *(to wound)* herir; *(to slander)* difamar; DER. *(to damage)* perjudicar, agraviar.
in·ju·ri·ous (ĭn-jōōr′ē-əs) adj. *(harmful)* dañino, perjudicial; *(offensive)* injurioso, ofensivo; *(slanderous)* difamatorio, calumnioso.
in·ju·ry (ĭn′jə-rē) s. [pl. **-ries**] *(damage)* daño, perjuicio; *(wound)* herida; DER. *(wrong)* daño, perjuicio; ANT. *(insult)* insulto.
in·jus·tice (ĭn-jŭs′tĭs) s. injusticia.
ink (ĭngk) **I.** s. *(pigment)* tinta; ICT. *(secretion)* tinta **II.** tr. entintar ♦ **to i. in** marcar con tinta • **to i. over** cubrir con tinta.
ink·blot (ĭngk′blŏt′) s. *(stain)* mancha de tinta; PSIC. *(pattern)* manchas de tinta usadas en la prueba Rorschach.
ink·ling (ĭng′klĭng) s. *(hint)* indicio; *(suspicion)* sospecha; *(vague idea)* vaga idea, ligera idea.
ink·well (ĭngk′wĕl′) s. tintero.

in·laid (ĭn′lād′) adj. *(set into a surface)* incrustado; *(decorated)* con obra de incrustación, taraceado.
in·land (ĭn′lănd′, -lənd) **I.** adj. *(of a country, region)* interior, del interior; *(domestic)* interno, nacional **II.** adv. tierra adentro, hacia el interior **III.** s. GEOL. interior (de un país) *m.*
in·land·er (ĭn′lənd-ər) s. habitante del interior *mf.*
in·law (ĭn′lô) s. pariente político.
in·lay (ĭn-lā′) **I.** tr. (ĭn-lā′) **-laid** (-lād′), **-lay·ing** incrustar, taracear **II.** s. (ĭn′lā′) incrustación *f,* taracea; ODONT. empaste *m.*
in·let (ĭn′lĕt′) s. *(bay)* cala, ensenada; *(estuary)* estuario, estero; *(passage of water)* brazo (de mar, río); TEC. *(opening)* entrada, admisión *f.*
in·line (ĭn′lĭn′) adj. & adv. TEC. en línea, en serie.
in·mate (ĭn′māt′) s. *(resident)* residente *mf,* inquilino; *(of a hospital)* paciente *mf,* enfermo; *(prisoner)* presidiario, preso.
in·most (ĭn′mōst′) adj. *(farthest within)* más interno, más adentro; *(most intimate)* más profundo, más íntimo.
inn (ĭn) s. *(lodging house)* posada, hostería; *(tavern)* taverna.
in·nards (ĭn′ərdz) s.pl. FAM. *(viscera)* vísceras, entrañas; *(inside)* interior (de una máquina, equipo) *m.*
in·nate (ĭ-nāt′) adj. innato.
in·ner (ĭn′ər) adj. *(interior)* interior, interno <*an i. room* una habitación interior>; FIG. *(profound)* profundo, recóndito <*i. meaning* significado profundo>; *(of the spirit)* íntimo ♦ **i. circle** esfera de mayor influencia.
inner city s. distrito pobre del centro de una ciudad.
inner ear s. ANAT. oído interno.
in·ner·most (ĭn′ər-mōst′) adj. *(farthest within)* más interno, más adentro; *(most intimate)* más profundo, más íntimo.
inner tube s. AUTO. cámara de un neumático.
in·ning (ĭn′ĭng) s. DEP. inning *m.*
inn·keep·er (ĭn′kē′pər) s. posadero, mesonero.
in·no·cence (ĭn′ə-səns) s. *(state, virtue)* inocencia; BOT. azulejo, aciano.
in·no·cent (ĭn′ə-sənt) **I.** adj. inocente ♦ **i. of** carente de, desprovisto de **II.** s. inocente *mf.*
in·noc·u·ous (ĭ-nŏk′yōō-əs) adj. *(harmless)* inocuo, inofensivo; *(insipid)* insípido, poco interesante.
in·no·vate (ĭn′ə-vāt′) tr. & intr. **-vat·ed, -vat·ing** innovar.
in·no·va·tion (ĭn′ə-vā′shən) s. innovación *f.*
in·no·va·tive (ĭn′ə-vā′tĭv) adj. innovador.
in·no·va·tor (ĭn′ə-vā′tər) s. innovador *m.*
in·nu·en·do (ĭn′yōō-ĕn′dō) s. [pl. **-does**] *(insinuation)* insinuación *f,* indirecta; DER. *(interpretation)* insinuación; *(explanation)* explicación *f,* paréntesis *m.*
in·nu·mer·a·ble (ĭ-nōō′mər-ə-bəl, ĭ-nyōō′-) adj. innumerable.
in·ob·ser·vance (ĭn′əb-zûr′vəns) s. *(inattention)* inatención *f,* falta de atención; *(nonobservance)* inobservancia (de una ley, costumbre).
in·ob·ser·vant (ĭn′əb-zûr′vənt) adj. *(inattentive)* desatento, distraído; *(of a law, custom)* inobservante.
in·ob·tru·sive (ĭn′əb-trōō′sĭv) adj. discreto.
in·oc·u·lant (ĭ-nŏk′yə-lənt) s. MED. inóculo.
in·oc·u·late (ĭ-nŏk′yə-lāt′) tr. **-lat·ed, -lat·ing** MED. inocular, vacunar ♦ **to i. against** inocular contra.
in·oc·u·la·tion (ĭ-nŏk′yə-lā′shən) MED. *(act, process)* s. inoculación *f,* vacunación *f; (inoculant)* inóculo, vacuna.
in·o·dor·ous (ĭn-ō′dər-əs) adj. inodoro.
in·of·fen·sive (ĭn′ə-fĕn′sĭv) adj. inofensivo.
in·op·er·a·ble (ĭn-ŏp′ər-ə-bəl) adj. *(not practicable)* impracticable; CIR. *(not operable)* inoperable.
in·op·er·a·tive (ĭn-ŏp′ər-ə-tĭv) adj. *(inefficacious)* inoperante, ineficaz; *(not functioning)* que no funciona; DER. *(without effect)* inaplicable, inválido.
in·op·por·tune (ĭn-ŏp′ər-tōōn′, -tyōōn′) adj. inoportuno.
in·or·di·nate (ĭn-ôr′dn-ĭt) adj. *(excessive)* inmoderado, excesivo; *(disorderly)* desordenado.
in·or·gan·ic (ĭn′ôr-găn′ĭk) adj. QUÍM. inorgánico.
in·pa·tient (ĭn′pā′shənt) s. paciente internado en un hospital *mf.*
in·phase (ĭn-fāz′) adj. ELEC. de la misma fase, en fase.
in·put (ĭn′pōōt′) s. *(participation)* participación *f;* COMPUT.

(terminal) entrada (de corriente o potencia); *(information)* ingreso de información, entrada; MEC., TEC. energía *o* potencia consumida para efectuar un trabajo.

in·quest (ĭn′kwĕst′) DER. s. *(inquiry)* indagatoria, encuesta; *(jury)* jurado indagatorio; *(investigation)* investigación *f*, averiguación *f.*

in·quire (ĭn-kwīr′) intr. **-quired, -quir·ing** *(to ask a question)* hacer una pregunta, inquirir; *(to investigate)* hacer una examinación *o* examen ♦ **to i. about** *o* **after** preguntar por • **to i. into** *(something)* investigar sobre (algo) —tr. preguntar por, averiguar.

in·quir·er (ĭn-kwīr′ər) s. *(one who asks)* inquiridor *m*; *(researcher)* investigador *m.*

in·quir·y (ĭn′quĭr′ē, ĭng′kwə-rē) s. [pl. **-ies**] *(act, question)* pregunta; *(investigation)* investigación *f*, inquisición *f.*

in·qui·si·tion (ĭng′kwĭ-zĭsh′ən) s. *(act, investigation)* inquisición *f*, investigación *f*; DER. *(inquest)* investigación ♦ **the I.** la Inquisición, el Santo Oficio.

in·quis·i·tive (ĭn-kwĭz′ĭ-tĭv) adj. *(prying)* preguntón, inquisitivo; *(curious)* curioso.

in·quis·i·tive·ness (ĭn-kwĭz′ĭ-tĭv-nĭs) s. curiosidad *f.*

in·quis·i·tor (ĭn-kwĭz′ĭ-tər) s. RELIG. inquisidor *m*; DER. investigador *m*; *(inquirer)* inquiridor *m*, investigador.

in·road (ĭn′rōd′) s. *(invasion)* invasión *f*; *(raid)* incursión *f*, correría; FIG. *(intrusion)* intrusión *f* ♦ **inroads into** usurpación de.

in·rush (ĭn′rŭsh′) s. *(influx)* irrupción *f*, flujo; *(inflow)* entrada repentina.

in·sane (ĭn-sān′) adj. *(mad)* loco, demente; FIG. *(absurd)* insensato, disparatado <*an i. scheme* un proyecto disparatado> ♦ **i. asylum** manicomio.

in·san·i·ty (ĭn-săn′ĭ-tē) s. [pl. **-ties**] *(madness)* locura, demencia; DER. *(unsoundness of mind)* enajenación mental *f*; FIG. *(folly)* insensatez *f*, locura.

in·sa·tia·ble (ĭn-sā′shə-bəl) adj. insaciable.

in·scribe (ĭn-skrīb′) tr. **-scribed, -scrib·ing** *(in a register)* inscribir; *(on a plaque)* grabar; *(to dedicate)* dedicar, firmar; GEOM. inscribir.

in·scrip·tion (ĭn-skrĭp′shən) s. *(engraving)* inscripción *f*; *(enrollment)* inscripción; *(dedication)* dedicatoria.

in·scru·ta·bil·i·ty (ĭn-skrōō′tə-bĭl′ĭ-tē) s. inescrutabilidad *f.*

in·scru·ta·ble (ĭn-skrōō′tə-bəl) adj. inescrutable.

in·sect (ĭn′sĕkt′) s. ENTOM. insecto; FIG. *(contemptible person)* insecto, bicho.

in·sec·ti·cide (ĭn-sĕk′tĭ-sīd′) s. insecticida *m.*

in·sec·tiv·o·rous (ĭn′sĕk-tĭv′ər-əs) adj. BOT., ZOOL. insectívoro.

in·se·cure (ĭn′sĭ-kyŏŏr′) adj. inseguro.

in·se·cu·ri·ty (ĭn′sĭ-kyŏŏr′ĭ-tē) s. [pl. **-ties**] inseguridad *f.*

in·sem·i·nate (ĭn-sĕm′ə-nāt′) tr. **-nat·ed, -nat·ing** *(to sow)* sembrar, plantar; *(to introduce semen)* inseminar.

in·sem·i·na·tion (ĭn-sĕm′ə-nā′shən) s. inseminación *f.*

in·sem·i·na·tor (ĭn-sĕm′ə-nā′tər) s. inseminador *m.*

in·sen·sate (ĭn-sĕn′sāt′) adj. *(inanimate)* inanimado; *(unconscious)* inconsciente; *(unfeeling)* insensible; *(foolish)* insensato, tonto.

in·sen·si·bil·i·ty (ĭn-sĕn′sə-bĭl′ĭ-tē) s. *(lack of feelings)* insensibilidad *f*; *(unconsciousness)* inconsciencia.

in·sen·si·ble (ĭn-sĕn′sə-bəl) adj. *(imperceptible)* insensible, imperceptible; *(unconscious)* inconsciente; *(callous)* insensible; *(unaffected)* insensible <*i. to the cold* insensible al frío>; *(irrational)* irrazonable.

in·sen·si·tive (ĭn-sĕn′sĭ-tĭv) adj. insensible.

in·sen·si·tiv·i·ty (ĭn-sĕn′sĭ-tĭv′ĭ-tē) *o* **in·sen·si·tive·ness** (ĭn-sĕn′sĭ-tĭv-nĭs) s. insensibilidad *f.*

in·sen·tient (ĭn-sĕn′shənt) adj. inconsciente.

in·sep·a·ra·bil·i·ty (ĭn-sĕp′ər-ə-bĭl′ĭ-tē) s. inseparabilidad *f.*

in·sep·a·ra·ble (ĭn-sĕp′ər-ə-bəl) adj. inseparable.

in·sert I. tr. (ĭn-sûrt′) *(to introduce)* insertar, introducir; *(interpolate)* interpolar, intercalar II. s. (ĭn′sûrt′) inserción *f.*

in·ser·tion (ĭn-sûr′shən) s. *(act)* inserción *f*; COST. entredós *m*; *(page)* encarte *m*; *(advertisement)* anuncio; ANAT., BOT. inserción.

in·set I. tr. (ĭn-sĕt′) **-set, -set·ting** insertar II. s. (ĭn′sĕt′) *(a page)* recuadro; *(in a publication)* encarte *m*, página inter-

calada; *(in a dress)* entredós *m*; *(inflow)* influjo, entrada (de agua).

in·shore (ĭn′shôr′) adj. *(close to a shore)* cercano a la orilla; *(toward a shore)* hacia la orilla.

in·side (ĭn-sīd′, ĭn′sīd′) I. s. *(inner part)* interior *m*, parte de adentro *f* <*the i. of my washing machine is rusting* la parte de adentro de mi lavadora se está oxidando> ♦ **insides** FAM. entrañas, tripas • **to be on the i.** *(position of confidence)* ocupar un puesto de confianza; *(to have access to information)* tener acceso a información confidencial • **to know something** *o* **someone i. out** conocer algo *o* a alguien a fondo • **to turn something i. out** poner algo al revés (prenda, bolsa) II. adj. *(inner)* interior, interno <*an i. room* una habitación interior>; *(confidential)* confidencial, secreto <*i. information* información confidencial> ♦ **an i. job** delito cometido por alguien que trabaja en el lugar de un crimen III. adv. *(within)* dentro, adentro <*it's raining, come i.* está lloviendo, ven adentro>; *(on the other side)* por dentro <*blue outside and yellow i.* azul por fuera y amarillo por dentro> IV. prep. dentro de ♦ **i. of** FAM. en menos de, dentro de <*the car will be ready i. of a week* el automóvil estará listo dentro de una semana>.

inside out adv. al revés ♦ **to know something i.** conocer algo a fondo o en todos sus detalles • **to turn i.** *(blouse, coat)* volver al revés; FIG. *(room, drawer)* registrar de arriba abajo.

in·sid·er (ĭn-sī′dər) s. *(member)* miembro de un grupo; *(well-informed person)* persona enterada *o* informada.

inside track s. DEP. *(path)* pista interior; FIG. *(advantageous position)* ventaja.

in·sid·i·ous (ĭn-sĭd′ē-əs) adj. insidioso.

in·sid·i·ous·ness (ĭn-sĭd′ē-əs-nĭs) s. insidia.

in·sight (ĭn′sīt′) s. *(penetration)* penetración *f*, perspicacia; *(glimpse)* idea ♦ **to have an i.** darse cuenta, descubrir.

in·sight·ful (ĭn′sīt′fəl) adj. perspicaz.

in·sig·ni·a (ĭn-sĭg′nē-ə) *o* **in·sig·ne** (-nē) s. [pl. **insignia** *o* **-ni·as**] *(badge)* insignia; *(emblem)* emblema *m*; *(sign)* marca, distintivo.

in·sig·nif·i·cance (ĭn′sĭg-nĭf′ĭ-kəns) s. insignificancia.

in·sig·nif·i·cant (ĭn′sĭg-nĭf′ĭ-kənt) adj. insignificante.

in·sin·cere (ĭn-sĭn-sîr′) adj. *(not sincere)* insincero; *(hypocritical)* hipócrita.

in·sin·cer·i·ty (ĭn′sĭn-sĕr′ĭ-tē) s. insinceridad *f.*

in·sin·u·ate (ĭn-sĭn′yŏŏ-āt′) tr. **-at·ed, -at·ing** insinuar ♦ **to i. oneself into** insinuarse en —intr. hacer insinuaciones, insinuarse.

in·sin·u·at·ing (ĭn-sĭn′yŏŏ-ā′tĭng) adj. insinuante, insinuador.

in·sin·u·a·tion (ĭn-sĭn′yŏŏ-ā′shən) s. insinuación *f.*

in·sip·id (ĭn-sĭp′ĭd) adj. *(tasteless)* insípido, soso; FIG. *(dull)* insípido, insulso.

in·sist (ĭn-sĭst′) intr. insistir ♦ **to i. on** *o* **upon** *(doing)* empeñarse en, insistir en; *(something)* exigir, insistir en —tr. ♦ **to i. that** insistir en que.

in·sis·tence (ĭn-sĭs′təns) *o* **in·sis·ten·cy** (-tən-sē) s. insistencia.

in·sis·tent (ĭn-sĭs′tənt) adj. insistente.

in·so·far as (ĭn′sō-fär′) conj. en cuanto a, en la medida en que, hasta donde.

in·sole (ĭn′sōl′) s. plantilla del zapato.

in·so·lence (ĭn′sə-ləns) s. insolencia, descaro.

in·so·lent (ĭn′sə-lənt) adj. insolente, descarado.

in·sol·u·bil·i·ty (ĭn-sŏl′yə-bĭl′ĭ-tē) s. insolubilidad *f.*

in·sol·u·ble (ĭn-sŏl′yə-bəl) adj. *(not soluble)* insoluble, que no se disuelve; *(insolvable)* que no se puede resolver.

in·solv·a·ble (ĭn-sŏl′və-bəl) adj. que no se puede resolver.

in·sol·ven·cy (ĭn-sŏl′vən-sē) s. COM. insolvencia.

in·sol·vent (ĭn-sŏl′vənt) adj. & s. COM. insolvente *mf.*

in·som·ni·a (ĭn-sŏm′nē-ə) s. insomnio.

in·som·ni·ac (ĭn-sŏm′nē-ăk′) I. adj. insomne II. s. persona insomne.

in·so·much as (ĭn′sō-mŭch′) conj. puesto que, ya que.

in·sou·ci·ance (ĭn-sōō′sē-əns) s. despreocupación *f.*

in·sou·ci·ant (ĭn-sōō′sē-ənt) adj. despreocupado.

in·spect (ĭn-spĕkt′) tr. *(to examine)* inspeccionar; MIL. *(to review)* pasar revista.

in·spec·tion (ĭn-spĕk'shən) s. *(examination)* inspección *f*; MIL. *(review)* revista.

in·spec·tor (ĭn-spĕk'tər) s. *(official)* inspector *m*; *(police officer)* inspector de policía *m*.

in·spi·ra·tion (ĭn'spə-rā'shən) s. *(encouragement)* inspiración *f*; *(inhalation)* inspiración, aspiración *f* ♦ **to be an i. to somebody** servir de inspiración *o* de ejemplo a alguien.

in·spi·ra·tion·al (ĭn'spə-rā'shə-nəl) adj. inspirador, inspirante.

in·spire (ĭn-spīr') tr. **-spired, -spir·ing** *(to stimulate)* inspirar, motivar; *(to arouse)* suscitar <*to i. devotion in a man* suscitar la devoción de un hombre>; *(to create)* infundir <*his courage inspired our confidence* su valentía nos infundió confianza>; MED. *(to inhale)* inhalar ♦ **to be inspired by** estar motivado *o* inspirado por ● **to i. with** infundir, llenar de —intr. comunicar inspiración; BIOL. *(to inhale)* inspirar, inhalar.

in·spired (ĭn-spīrd') adj. inspirado, de inspiración.

in·spir·ing (ĭn-spīr'ĭng) adj. *(that inspires)* inspirador; *(encouraging)* alentador.

in·sta·bil·i·ty (ĭn'stə-bĭl'ĭ-tē) s. [pl. **-ties**] inestabilidad *f*.

in·stall *o* **in·stal** (ĭn-stôl') tr. **-stalled, -stall·ing** instalar ♦ **to i. oneself** instalarse.

in·stal·la·tion (ĭn'stə-lā'shən) s. *(act, system)* instalación *f*; MIL. base *f*.

in·stall·ment¹ *o* **in·stal·ment** (ĭn-stôl'mənt) s. *(payment)* plazo, pago <*to pay in installments* pagar a plazos>; *(of a publication)* entrega *f* ♦ **i. plan** pago a plazos ● **monthly i.** mensualidad ● **on the i. plan** a plazos, con facilidades de pago.

in·stall·ment² *o* **in·stal·ment** (ĭn-stôl'mənt) s. instalación *f*.

in·stance (ĭn'stəns) I. s. *(example)* ejemplo, muestra; *(case)* caso; DER. *(suit)* juicio, proceso ♦ **at the i. of** a instancias de, a petición de <*at the i. of his wife* a instancias de su esposa> ● **for i.** por ejemplo ● **in many instances** en muchos casos II. tr. **-stanced, -stanc·ing** *(to cite)* poner por caso; *(to exemplify)* ilustrar.

in·stant (ĭn'stənt) I. s. *(example)* instante *m*, momento ♦ **in an i.** en un instante ● **the i.** en cuanto <*the i. something happens* en cuanto suceda algo> ● **this i.** al instante, en seguida II. adj. *(immediate)* inmediato <*i. attention* atención inmediata>; *(urgent)* urgente, apremiante <*an i. need for workers* una falta apremiante de trabajadores>; *(food)* instantáneo.

in·stan·ta·ne·ous (ĭn'stən-tā'nē-əs) adj. instantáneo.

in·stant·ly (ĭn'stənt-lē) I. adv. *(immediately)* instantáneamente, inmediatamente; ANT. *(urgently)* urgentemente II. conj. tan pronto como.

instant replay s. reproducción *o* repetición inmediata de un evento por video-cinta *f*.

in·state (ĭn-stāt') tr. **-stat·ed, -stat·ing** instalar, establecer (en un cargo).

in·stead (ĭn-stĕd') adv. *(in place of)* en su lugar <*I couldn't go; she went i.* no pude ir; ella fue en mi lugar>; *(rather than)* en cambio <*to feel like crying and laugh i.* tener ganas de llorar y, en cambio, reír>.

instead of prep. en lugar de, en vez de.

in·step (ĭn'stĕp') s. empeine *m*.

in·sti·gate (ĭn'stĭ-gāt') tr. **-gat·ed, -gat·ing** *(to goad)* instigar; *(to foment)* fomentar.

in·sti·ga·tion (ĭn'stĭ-gā'shən) s. instigación *f*.

in·sti·ga·tor (ĭn'stĭ-gā'tər) s. instigador *m*.

in·still *o* **in·stil** (ĭn-stĭl') tr. **-stilled, -still·ing** instilar, verter gota a gota ♦ **to i. in** *o* **into** instilar, impartir (ideas, principios).

in·stinct I. s. (ĭn'stĭngkt') instinto <*my i. warned me* mi instinto me avisó> ♦ **by i.** por instinto, instintivamente II. adj. (ĭn-stĭngkt') ♦ **i. with** lleno de.

in·stinc·tive (ĭn-stĭngk'tĭv) adj. instintivo.

in·sti·tute (ĭn'stĭ-tōōt', -tyōōt') I. tr. **-tut·ed, -tut·ing** *(to establish)* instituir, establecer; *(to initiate)* iniciar; DER. *(proceedings)* entablar; *(to invest)* investir, instaurar II. s. *(rule)* instituto; *(organization)* instituto, institución *f* <*an i. for the deaf* una institución para los sordos>; EDUC. *(institution)* instituto; *(workshop)* seminario ♦ **institutes** DER. instituciones.

in·sti·tu·tion (ĭn'stĭ-tōō'shən, -tyōō'-) s. *(establishment)* institución *f*, establecimiento; *(practice)* institución, tradición *f*; *(organization)* sociedad *f*, institución; *(for old people)* asilo; *(for the mentally ill)* manicomio; *(for orphans)* hospicio; FAM. *(fixture)* institución ♦ **correctional i.** correccional *m*.

in·sti·tu·tion·al (ĭn'stĭ-tōō'shə-nəl, -tyōō'-) adj. *(of an institution)* institucional; *(said of a church)* provista de beneficencias ♦ **i. care** atención médica (en un asilo, manicomio).

in·sti·tu·tion·al·ism (ĭn'stĭ-tōō'shə-nə-lĭz'əm) s. *(adherence to established forms)* institucionalismo, apoyo de las instituciones (esp. de la iglesia); *(use of charitable institutions)* beneficencia.

in·sti·tu·tion·al·ize (ĭn'stĭ-tōō'shə-nə-lĭz', -tyōō'-) tr. **-ized, -iz·ing** *(to give the character of)* institucionalizar; *(an old person)* meter en un asilo; *(a convicted person)* meter en la cárcel.

in·struct (ĭn-strŭkt') tr. *(to teach)* instruir, enseñar; *(to direct)* dar instrucciones; *(to give orders to)* mandar, ordenar.

in·struc·tion (ĭn-strŭk'shən) s. *(teaching)* instrucción *f*, enseñanza; *(lesson)* lección *f*; *(order)* instrucción, orden *f* ♦ **instructions** *(directions)* instrucciones; *(orders)* órdenes.

in·struc·tion·al (ĭn-strŭk'shə-nəl) adj. de instrucción.

in·struc·tive (ĭn-strŭk'tĭv) adj. instructivo.

in·struc·tor (ĭn-strŭk'tər) s. instructor *m*.

in·stru·ment I. s. (ĭn'strə-mənt) *(device)* instrumento, aparato; MÚS. instrumento <*wind i.* instrumento de viento>; FIG. *(means)* instrumento, medio; DER. instrumento, escritura *f*. (-měnt') *(to equip)* equipar con instrumentos; DER. dirigir un instrumento a.

in·stru·men·tal (ĭn'strə-měn'tl) I. adj. instrumental ♦ **to be i. in** *o* **to** ayudar a, contribuir a II. s. GRAM. instrumental *m*.

in·stru·men·tal·ist (ĭn'strə-měn'tl-ĭst) s. FILOS., MÚS. instrumentista *mf*.

in·stru·men·tal·i·ty (ĭn'strə-měn-tăl'ĭ-tē) s. [pl. **-ties**] *(quality)* carácter instrumental *m*; *(means)* mediación *f* ♦ **by** *o* **through the i. of** por medio de.

in·stru·men·ta·tion (ĭn'strə-měn-tā'shən) MÚS. s. *(arrangement)* instrumentación *f*; *(use of instruments)* uso de instrumentos.

instrument panel s. AER., AUTO. tablero de instrumentos.

in·sub·or·di·nate (ĭn'sə-bôr'dn-ĭt) adj. insubordinado.

in·sub·or·di·na·tion (ĭn'sə-bôr'dn-ā'shən) s. insubordinación *f*.

in·sub·stan·tial (ĭn'səb-stăn'shəl) adj. *(imaginary)* infundado; *(flimsy)* flojo; *(insignificant)* insubstancial, insignificante.

in·suf·fer·a·ble (ĭn-sŭf'ər-ə-bəl) adj. *(not sufferable)* inaguantable; *(intolerable)* intolerable.

in·suf·fi·cien·cy (ĭn'sə-fĭsh'ən-sē) s. [pl. **-cies**] insuficiencia.

in·suf·fi·cient (ĭn'sə-fĭsh'ənt) adj. insuficiente.

in·su·lar (ĭn'sə-lər, ĭns'yə-) adj. *(of an island)* insular; *(narrow-minded)* estrecho de miras.

in·su·lar·i·ty (ĭn'sə-lăr'ĭ-tē, ĭns'yə-) s. *(character)* insularidad *f*; *(narrow-mindedness)* estrechez de miras *f*.

in·su·late (ĭn'sə-lāt') tr. **-lat·ed, -lat·ing** *(to isolate)* aislar, apartar; CONSTR., ELEC., FÍS. aislar.

in·su·la·tion (ĭn'sə-lā'shən) s. ELEC., FÍS. *(act)* aislamiento; CONSTR., ELEC. *(insulator)* aislador *m*, material aislante *m*.

in·su·la·tor (ĭn'sə-lā'tər) s. ELEC., FÍS. aislador *m*, aislante *m*.

in·su·lin (ĭn'sə-lĭn) s. BIOQUÍM. insulina.

in·sult I. tr. (ĭn-sŭlt') insultar, ofender II. s. (ĭn'sŭlt') *(offense)* insulto, ofensa; MED. *(trauma)* trauma *m*.

in·sult·ing (ĭn-sŭl'tĭng) adj. *(offensive)* insultante, ofensivo; *(shameful)* vergonzoso <*an i. performance* una actuación vergonzosa>.

in·su·per·a·ble (ĭn-sōō'pər-ə-bəl) adj. insuperable.

in·sup·port·a·ble (ĭn'sə-pôr'tə-bəl) adj. *(intolerable)* insoportable; *(unjustifiable)* injustificable, indefendible <*an i. claim* un reclamo injustificable>.

in·sur·a·ble (ĭn-shōōr'ə-bəl) adj. asegurable.

in·sur·ance (ĭn-shōōr'əns) s. COM. seguro <*it is illegal to drive without i.* conducir sin seguro es ilegal>; FIG. *(protec-*

tive measure) seguridad *f*, protección *f* ♦ **i. broker** corredor de seguros • **comprehensive i.** seguro a todo riesgo • **i. premium** prima de seguro • **to take out i.** sacar(se) un seguro.

in·sure (ĭn-shŏŏr′) tr. **-sured, -sur·ing** asegurar —intr. *(to cover oneself)* asegurarse; *(to sell insurance)* vender seguros.

in·sured (ĭn-shŏŏrd′) s. asegurado.

in·sur·er (ĭn-shŏŏr′ər) s. asegurador *m.*

in·sur·gence (ĭn-sûr′jəns) s. insurrección *f*, levantamiento.

in·sur·gen·cy (ĭn-sûr′jən-sē) s. [pl. **-cies**] *(rebellion)* rebelión *f*; *(insurgence)* insurrección *f*, levantamiento.

in·sur·gent (ĭn-sûr′jənt) adj. & s. insurgente *mf*, insurrecto.

in·sur·mount·a·ble (ĭn′sər-moun′tə-bəl) adj. insuperable, insalvable.

in·sur·rec·tion (ĭn′sə-rĕk′shən) s. insurrección *f.*

in·sur·rec·tion·al (ĭn′sə-rĕk′shən-əl) adj. insurreccional.

in·sur·rec·tion·ist (ĭn′sə-rĕk′shə-nĭst) s. insurrecto, insurgente *mf.*

in·tact (ĭn-tăkt′) adj. *(not impaired)* intacto, ileso; *(whole)* entero, íntegro.

in·ta·glio (ĭn-tăl′yō, -täl′-) s. [pl. **-glios**] *(design)* talla; *(process)* talladura; *(gemstone)* piedra preciosa grabada; *(printing, die)* grabado en hueco.

in·take ((ĭn′tăk′) s. *(act, opening)* entrada, toma; *(entrance)* entrada, admisión *f*; MAQ., MEC. admisión, aspiración *f*; HIDRÁUL. toma; *(thing taken in)* consumo (esp. de energía).

in·tan·gi·bil·i·ty (ĭn-tăn′jə-bĭl′ĭ-tē) s. intangibilidad *f.*

in·tan·gi·ble (ĭn-tăn′jə-bəl) I. adj. intangible II. s. cosa intangible.

in·te·ger (ĭn′tĭ-jər) s. MAT. *(whole number)* entero, número entero; *(whole)* totalidad *f.*

in·te·gral (ĭn′tĭ-grəl, ĭn-tĕg′rəl) I. adj. *(constituent)* constituyente, integrante *<an i. part of his work* una parte integrante de su trabajo>; *(complete)* entero, íntegro; MAT. integral II. s. *(totality)* totalidad *f*, integridad *f*; MAT. (ĭn′tĭ-grəl) integral *f.*

integral calculus s. MAT. cálculo integral.

in·te·grate (ĭn′tĭ-grāt′) tr. **-grat·ed, -grat·ing** *(to unify)* integrar; *(to desegregate)* eliminar la segregación racial en, integrar racialmente; MAT. integrar —intr. integrarse.

in·te·grat·ed (ĭn′tĭ-grā′tĭd) adj. integrado.

integrated circuit s. ELECTRÓN. circuito integrado.

in·te·gra·tion (ĭn′tĭ-grā′shən) s. integración *f* ♦ **racial i.** integración racial.

in·te·gra·tion·ist (ĭn′tĭ-grā′shə-nĭst) s. integracionista *mf*, partidario de la integración.

in·teg·ri·ty (ĭn-tĕg′rĭ-tē) s. integridad *f.*

in·tel·lect (ĭn′tl-ĕkt′) s. *(intelligence)* intelecto, inteligencia; *(intellectual)* intelectual *mf*, persona inteligente.

in·tel·lec·tu·al (ĭn′tl-ĕk′chōō-əl) adj. & s. intelectual *mf.*

in·tel·lec·tu·al·ism (ĭn′tl-ĕk′chōō-ə-lĭz′əm) s. intelectualismo.

in·tel·lec·tu·al·ize (ĭn′tl-ĕk′chōō-ə-līz′) tr. **-ized, -iz·ing** intelectualizar.

in·tel·li·gence (ĭn-tĕl′ĭ-jəns) s. *(mental capacity)* inteligencia; *(news)* informes *m*, noticias; MIL. *(information)* información secreta ♦ **Central I. Agency** Agencia Central de Inteligencia (de EE. UU.).

intelligence quotient s. cociente intelectual *o* de inteligencia *m.*

in·tel·li·gent (ĭn-tĕl′ĭ-jənt) adj. *(mentally acute)* inteligente; *(knowing)* sensato; *(smart)* astuto ♦ **i. being** ser dotado de inteligencia.

in·tel·li·gent·si·a (ĭn-tĕl′ĭ-jĕnt′sē-ə, -gĕnt′-) s. intelectualidad *f*, clase intelectual *f.*

in·tel·li·gi·bil·i·ty (ĭn-tĕl′ĭ-jə-bĭl′ĭ-tē) s. inteligibilidad *f.*

in·tel·li·gi·ble (ĭn-tĕl′ĭ-jə-bəl) adj. inteligible.

in·tem·per·ance (ĭn-tĕm′pər-əns) s. intemperancia, falta de moderación.

in·tem·per·ate (ĭn-tĕm′pər-ĭt) adj. *(not temperate)* intemperante, descomedido; *(said of a climate)* inclemente; *(excessive)* excesivo.

in·tend (ĭn-tĕnd′) tr. *(to plan)* proponerse, tener la intención *<I i. seeing her* tengo la intención de verla>; *(to contem-*

plate) pensar *<what do you i. to do now?* ¿qué piensas hacer ahora?>; *(to mean)* querer decir ♦ **to be intended for** *(to be meant for)* estar destinado a, ser para; *(to be directed at)* ir dirigido • **to fully i. to** tener la firme intención de.

in·ten·dance (ĭn-tĕn′dəns) s. *(management)* gerencia; *(intendancy)* intendencia.

in·ten·dant (ĭn-tĕn′dənt) s. intendente *mf.*

in·tend·ed (ĭn-tĕn′dĭd) I. adj. *(planned)* proyectado, previsto; *(intentional)* intencional, deliberado; *(future)* futuro II. s. FAM. *(engaged man)* prometido; *(engaged woman)* prometida.

in·tense (ĭn-tĕns′) adj. *(forceful)* intenso, fuerte; *(extreme)* sumo, enorme (concentración, cuidado); *(deep)* intenso, profundo (cariño, mirada); *(said of a person)* vehemente, ardiente.

in·ten·si·fi·ca·tion (ĭn-tĕn′sə-fĭ-kā′shən) s. intensificación *f.*

in·ten·si·fy (ĭn-tĕn′sə-fī′) tr. **-fied, -fy·ing** intensificar, aumentar; FOTOG. reforzar —intr. intensificarse, aumentar.

in·ten·si·ty (ĭn-tĕn′sĭ-tē) s. [pl. **-ties**] *(concentration)* intensidad *f <i. of color>* intensidad de color>; *(of a person)* vehemencia; FÍS. intensidad.

in·ten·sive (ĭn-tĕn′sĭv) I. adj. *(concentrated)* intensivo *<i. training* entrenamiento intensivo>; *(in-depth)* profundo; AGR., FÍS., GRAM. intensivo II. s. GRAM. elemento intensivo.

intensive care s. MED. cuidado intensivo en una clínica.

in·tent (ĭn-tĕnt′) I. s. *(purpose)* intención *f*, propósito; *(meaning)* sentido, significado ♦ **malicious i.** malas intenciones, fines delictivos • **to** *o* **for all intents and purposes** al fin y al cabo, prácticamente II. adj. *(fixed)* fijo *<his eyes were i. on the horizon>* tenía los ojos fijos en el horizonte> ♦ **i. on** *o* **upon** *(determined to)* resuelto a, determinado a *<he was i. on securing their freedom* él estaba resuelto a obtener su libertad>; *(engrossed in)* atento *o* absorto a *<she was i. on her work* ella estaba absorta en su trabajo>.

in·ten·tion (ĭn-tĕn′shən) s. intención *f*, propósito ♦ **to be one's i. to** proponerse, tener la intención de • **honorable intentions** intención de matrimonio • **with the best (of) intentions** de buena fe.

in·ten·tion·al (ĭn-tĕn′shə-nəl) adj. intencional, deliberado.

in·ten·tion·al·ly (ĭn-tĕn′shə-nə-lē) adv. intencionalmente, deliberadamente.

in·ter (ĭn-tûr′) tr. **-terred, -ter·ring** enterrar.

in·ter·act (ĭn′tər-ăkt′) intr. actuar recíprocamente, influenciar uno a otro.

in·ter·ac·tion (ĭn′tər-ăk′shən) s. interacción *f*, acción recíproca.

in·ter·ac·tive (ĭn′tər-ăk′tĭv) adj. recíproco.

interactive terminal s. ELECTRÓN. terminal interactivo.

in·ter·A·mer·i·can (ĭn′tər-ə-mĕr′ĭ-kən) adj. interamericano.

in·ter·breed (ĭn′tər-brēd′) tr. & intr. **-bred** (-brĕd′), **-breed·ing** cruzar(se) animales de especie diferente.

in·ter·ca·late (ĭn′tûr′kə-lāt′) tr. **-lat·ed, -lat·ing** intercalar.

in·ter·cede (ĭn′tər-sēd′) intr. **-ced·ed, -ced·ing** interceder.

in·ter·cept I. tr. (ĭn′tər-sĕpt′) *(letter, messenger)* interceptar; MAT. cortar II. s. (ĭn′tər-sĕpt′) MAT. intersección *f.*

in·ter·cep·tion (ĭn′tər-sĕp′shən) s. *(act, state)* interceptación *f*; MAT. intersección *f.*

in·ter·cep·tor *o* **in·ter·cep·ter** (ĭn′tər-sĕp′tər) s. *(one that intercepts)* interceptor *m*; MIL. *(plane)* avión interceptador *o* de caza *m.*

in·ter·ces·sion (ĭn′tər-sĕsh′ən) s. intercesión *f*, mediación *f.*

in·ter·ces·sor (ĭn′tər-sĕs′ər) s. intercesor *m*, mediador *m.*

in·ter·change I. tr. (ĭn′tər-chānj′) **-changed, -chang·ing** *(to exchange)* intercambiar; *(to switch)* alternar, cambiar —intr. alternarse, cambiarse II. s. (ĭn′tər-chānj′) *(exchange)* intercambio; *(switch)* alternación *f*, cambio; *(highway junction)* empalme de carreteras *m.*

in·ter·change·a·ble (ĭn′tər-chān′jə-bəl) adj. intercambiable.

in·ter·col·le·giate (ĭn′tər-kə-lē′jĭt) adj. interuniversitario.

in·ter·com (ĭn′tər-kŏm′) s. sistema de intercomunicación *m*, intercomunicador *m.*

in·ter·com·mu·ni·cate (ĭn′tər-kə-myōō′nĭ-kāt′) intr. **-cat·ed, -cat·ing** intercomunicarse, comunicarse.

---

ng inglés / ŏ la / ō bou / ô corre / oi oigo / ōō uno / ou auto / yōō ciudad / w hueco / y yo / z mismo

in·ter·com·mu·ni·ca·tion (ĭn′tər-kə-myōō′nĭ-kā′shən) s. intercomunicación f.

in·ter·con·nect (ĭn′tər-kə-nĕkt′) intr. & tr. conectar.

in·ter·con·nect·ed (ĭn′tər-kə-nĕk′tĭd) adj. TEC. conectado; FIG. *(facts)* ligado, relacionado.

in·ter·con·nec·tion (ĭn′tər-kə-nĕk′shən) s. conexión f, interconexión f.

in·ter·con·ti·nen·tal (ĭn′tər-kŏn′tə-nĕn′tl) adj. intercontinental.

in·ter·cos·tal (ĭn′tər-kŏs′təl) adj. ANAT., BOT. intercostal.

in·ter·course (ĭn′tər-kôrs′) s. *(exchange)* intercambio, relaciones sociales f; *(trade)* comercio, tráfico; *(coitus)* coito, cópula.

in·ter·de·nom·i·na·tion·al (ĭn′tər-dĭ-nŏm′ə-nā′shə-nəl) adj. RELIG. entre varias sectas religiosas.

in·ter·de·pend·ence (ĭn′tər-dĭ-pĕn′dəns) s. interdependencia.

in·ter·de·pend·ent (ĭn′tər-dĭ-pĕn′dənt) adj. interdependiente.

in·ter·dict I. tr. (ĭn′tər-dĭkt′) *(to prohibit)* interdecir, vedar, prohibir; MIL. *(to cut)* cortar (la línea de comunicación del enemigo). II. s. (ĭn′tər-dĭkt′) DER., RELIG. interdicto.

in·ter·dic·tion (ĭn′tər-dĭk′shən) s. *(prohibition)* interdicción f, prohibición f; DER., RELIG. interdicto.

in·ter·est (ĭn′trĭst, -tər-ĭst) I. s. *(curiosity, concern)* interés m ‹it aroused the reader's i. despertó el interés del lector›; *(benefit)* provecho, beneficio ‹a decision that is not in the public i. una decisión que no redunda en beneficio público›; COM. *(share)* acción f, participación f; COM. *(on money)* interés, rédito (en un préstamo); *(in an industry)* sociedad f, industria ‹the textile i. la industria textil› • compound i. COM. interés compuesto • in the i. of peace en aras de la paz • simple i. interés simple • i. rate COM. tipo de interés • to act in one's own interests obrar en beneficio propio • to be in one's best i. to ser mejor para uno que • to be of i. ser interesante • to have a controlling i. in a company tener la mayoría de las acciones de una empresa • to have an i. in interesarse por, estar interesado en • to pay back with i. FIG. pagar con creces • to take an i. in interesarse por o en • vested interests intereses creados II. tr. interesar ♦ to i. someone in hacer que alguien se interese en o por.

in·ter·est·ed (ĭn′trĭ-stĭd, -tər-ĭ-) adj. interesado ‹the i. parties las partes interesadas› ♦ to be i. in tener interés en o por, interesarle a uno.

in·ter·est·ing (ĭn′trĭ-stĭng, -tər-ĭ-) adj. interesante.

in·ter·face (ĭn′tər-fās′) I. s. FÍS., QUÍM. entrecara, superficie de contacto o separación f; COMPUT. conector entre unidades (sistema) II. tr. & intr. -faced, -fac·ing unir(se) por medio de una entrecara.

in·ter·fere (ĭn′tər-fîr′) intr. -fered, -fer·ing *(to impede)* obstruir, obstaculizar; DEP. *(to obstruct a pass)* obstruir ilegalmente una jugada; *(to meddle)* intervenir, entrometerse (en asuntos de otros); *(horse)* trastrabillar; FÍS., RAD. interferir ♦ to i. with *(movement)* estorbar, impedir; *(a plan)* echar a perder; *(someone's business)* interferir, entrometerse o meterse en.

in·ter·fer·ence (ĭn′tər-fîr′əns) s. *(act, process)* interferencia; *(meddling)* intervención f, intromisión f; DEP. obstrucción f; FÍS., RAD. interferencia.

in·ter·fer·on (ĭn′tər-fîr′ŏn′) s. BIOQUÍM. interferona.

in·ter·ga·lac·tic (ĭn′tər-gə-lăk′tĭk) adj. ASTRON. intergaláctico, que ocurre entre galaxias.

in·ter·gov·ern·men·tal (ĭn′tər-gŭv′ərn-mĕn′tl) adj. intergubernamental.

in·ter·im (ĭn′tər-ĭm) I. s. interín m II. adj. interino, provisional.

in·te·ri·or (ĭn-tîr′ē-ər) I. adj. *(internal)* interior, interno; FIG. *(deeper)* interior, profundo; *(inland)* interior, de tierra adentro II. s. *(inner part)* el interior, la parte de adentro; FIG. *(soul)* interior m, alma; *(inland region)* tierra adentro, interior (de un país, región).

interior decoration s. decoración de interiores f.

interior monologue s. LIT., TEAT. monólogo interior.

in·ter·ject (ĭn′tər-jĕkt′) tr. interponer.

in·ter·jec·tion (ĭn′tər-jĕk′shən) s. *(interposition)* interposición f; GRAM. interjección f.

in·ter·lace (ĭn′tər-lās′) tr. & intr. -laced, -lac·ing entrelazar(se).

in·ter·lard (ĭn′tər-lärd′) tr. entreverar, salpicar.

in·ter·line (ĭn′tər-līn′) tr. -lined, -lin·ing interlinear.

in·ter·lin·e·ar (ĭn′tər-lĭn′ē-ər) adj. interlineal.

in·ter·lin·ing (ĭn′tər-lī′nĭng) s. COST. entretela.

in·ter·lock (ĭn′tər-lŏk′) intr. entrelazarse, trabarse.

in·ter·loc·u·tor (ĭn′tər-lŏk′yə-tər) s. interlocutor m.

in·ter·loc·u·to·ry (ĭn′tər-lŏk′yə-tôr′ē) adj. interlocutorio.

in·ter·lope (ĭn′tər-lōp′) intr. -loped, -lop·ing *(trading rights)* traficar sin licencia; *(to meddle)* entrometerse.

in·ter·lop·er (ĭn′tər-lō′pər) s. *(trafficker)* traficante sin licencia mf; *(meddler)* entrometido.

in·ter·lude (ĭn′tər-lōōd′) s. *(period of time)* intermedio, intervalo; *(episode)* episodio; TEAT. entremés m; MÚS. interludio.

in·ter·mar·riage (ĭn′tər-măr′ĭj) s. *(into another group)* matrimonio mixto (entre miembros de distintas razas, religiones); *(within one's family)* matrimonio entre parientes consanguíneos.

in·ter·mar·ry (ĭn′tər-măr′ē) intr. -ried, -ry·ing *(into another group)* casarse personas de distintos grupos (raza, religión); *(within one's family)* casarse entre sí o entre parientes consanguíneos.

in·ter·me·di·ar·y (ĭn′tər-mē′dē-ĕr′ē) I. s. [pl. -ies] *(mediator)* intermediario; *(stage)* fase intermedia II. adj. *(acting as a mediator)* intermediario; *(intermediate)* intermedio, medianero.

in·ter·me·di·ate (ĭn′tər-mē′dē-ĭt) I. adj. intermedio II. s. intermediario III. intr. (-āt′) -at·ed, -at·ing *(to mediate)* intermediar; *(to intervene)* intervenir.

in·ter·me·di·a·tion (ĭn′tər-mē′dē-ā′shən) s. *(mediation)* mediación f; *(intervention)* intervención f.

in·ter·me·di·a·tor (ĭn′tər-mē′dē-ā′tər) s. intermediario, mediador m.

in·ter·ment (ĭn-tûr′mənt) s. entierro.

in·ter·mi·na·ble (ĭn-tûr′mə-nə-bəl) adj. interminable.

in·ter·min·gle (ĭn′tər-mĭng′gəl) tr. & intr. -gled, -gling entremezclar(se).

in·ter·mis·sion (ĭn′tər-mĭsh′ən) s. *(act)* intermisión f, interrupción f; *(interval)* intervalo; *(recess)* pausa; TEAT. intermedio, entreacto.

in·ter·mit·tent (ĭn′tər-mĭt′nt) adj. intermitente.

in·ter·mix (ĭn′tər-mĭks′) tr. & intr. entremezclar(se).

in·tern I. s. (ĭn′tûrn′) *(student)* médico residente; *(internee)* persona internada II. intr. (ĭn-tûrn′) trabajar como interno —tr. internar, recluir (esp. en tiempo de guerra).

in·ter·nal (ĭn-tûr′nəl) adj. *(inner)* interno; *(intrinsic)* intrínseco, inherente; *(within the body)* interno ‹i. injuries lesiones internas›; *(domestic)* interior, nacional ♦ i. conflicts conflictos internos, luchas intestinas • i. trade comercio interior.

in·ter·nal-com·bus·tion engine (ĭn-tûr′nəl-kəm-bŭs′chən) s. MEC. motor de combustión interna m.

in·ter·nal·ize (ĭn-tûr′nə-līz′) tr. -ized, -iz·ing *(to make internal)* hacer interno o suyo; *(to adopt)* adoptar ideas o conceptos (como actitud o creencia).

in·ter·nal·ly (ĭn-tûr′nə-lē) adv. internamente, interiormente.

internal medicine s. medicina interna.

internal revenue s. ECON. rentas públicas (en EE. UU.).

in·ter·na·tion·al (ĭn′tər-năsh′ə-nəl) I. adj. internacional II. s. ♦ I. Internacional (organización socialista o comunista) f.

in·ter·na·tion·al·ism (ĭn′tər-năsh′ə-nə-lĭz′əm) s. internacionalismo.

in·ter·na·tion·al·ist (ĭn′tər-năsh′ə-nə-lĭst) s. internacionalista mf.

in·ter·na·tion·al·ize (ĭn′tər-năsh′ə-nə-līz′) tr. -ized, -iz·ing internacionalizar.

in·terne (ĭn′tûrn′) s. & v. var. de **intern**.

in·ter·nec·ine (ĭn′tər-nĕs′ēn′, -nē′sīn′) adj. *(mutually destructive)* de aniquilación mutua; *(bloody)* sangriento; *(internal)* interno, faccioso.

in·tern·ee (ĭn′tûr-nē′) s. persona internada.

in·ter·nist (ĭn′tûr′nĭst) s. MED. internista *mf.*

in·tern·ment (ĭn-tûrn′mənt) s. internamiento, reclusión *f.*

in·ter·of·fice (ĭn′tər-ô′fĭs) adj. interno, (de) dentro de la misma empresa.

in·ter·pen·e·trate (ĭn′tər-pĕn′ĭ-trāt′) tr. **-trat·ed, -trat·ing** penetrar —intr. compenetrarse.

in·ter·per·son·al (ĭn′tər-pûr′sə-nəl) adj. personal, de intercambio personal.

in·ter·plan·e·tar·y (ĭn′tər-plăn′ĭ-tĕr′ē) adj. interplanetario.

in·ter·play (ĭn′tər-plā′) I. s. interacción *f* II. intr. obrar recíprocamente.

in·ter·po·late (ĭn-tûr′pə-lāt′) tr. **-lat·ed, -lat·ing** interpolar —intr. hacer interpolaciones.

in·ter·po·la·tion (ĭn-tûr′pə-lā′shən) s. interpolación *f.*

in·ter·pose (ĭn′tər-pōz′) tr. **-posed, -pos·ing** *(to place between)* interponer; *(to interject)* intervenir con (un comentario) —intr. *(to come between)* interponerse; *(to intervene)* intervenir; *(to interrupt)* interrumpir.

in·ter·pos·er (ĭn′tər-pōz′ər) s. mediador *m.*

in·ter·po·si·tion (ĭn′tər-pə-zĭsh′ən) s. interposición *f.*

in·ter·pret (ĭn-tûr′prĭt) tr. *(to elucidate)* interpretar <*to i. a dream* interpretar un sueño>; *(to understand)* entender; TEAT. *(to represent)* interpretar —intr. *(to explain)* proporcionar una explicación; *(to translate)* servir de intérprete.

in·ter·pret·a·ble (ĭn-tûr′prĭ-tə-bəl) adj. interpretable.

in·ter·pre·ta·tion (ĭn-tûr′prĭ-tā′shən) s. interpretación *f* ♦ **to bear a different i.** poder entenderse de otro modo.

in·ter·pre·ta·tive (ĭn-tûr′prĭ-tā′tĭv) adj. interpretativo, aclaratorio.

in·ter·pret·er (ĭn-tûr′prĭ-tər) s. intérprete *mf.*

in·ter·pre·tive (ĭn-tûr′prĭ-tĭv) adj. interpretativo, aclaratorio.

in·ter·ra·cial (ĭn′tər-rā′shəl) adj. entre las razas.

in·ter·reg·num (ĭn′tər-rĕg′nəm) s. [pl. **-nums** o **-na** (-nə)] *(interim)* interregno; *(gap)* intervalo.

in·ter·re·late (ĭn′tər-rĭ-lāt′) tr. & intr. **-lat·ed, -lat·ing** correlacionar(se).

in·ter·re·lat·ed (ĭn′tər-rĭ-lā′tĭd) adj. correlativo, mutuamente relacionado.

in·ter·re·la·tion·ship (ĭn′tər-rĭ-lā′shən-shĭp′) s. relación *f,* correlación *f.*

in·ter·ro·gate (ĭn-tĕr′ə-gāt′) tr. **-gat·ed, -gat·ing** interrogar.

in·ter·ro·ga·tion (ĭn-tĕr′ə-gā′shən) s. *(formal questioning)* interrogación *f; (close questioning)* interrogatorio.

interrogation point s. GRAM. signo de interrogación.

in·ter·rog·a·tive (ĭn′tə-rŏg′ə-tĭv) I. adj. GRAM. interrogativo; *(questioning)* interrogativo <*an i. attitude* una actitud interrogativa> II. s. GRAM. interrogativo.

in·ter·rog·a·tor (ĭn-tĕr′ə-gā′tər) s. interrogador *m.*

in·ter·rog·a·to·ry (ĭn′tə-rŏg′ə-tôr′ē) I. adj. interrogativo II. s. [pl. **-ries**] pregunta escrita contestada bajo juramento.

in·ter·rupt (ĭn′tə-rŭpt′) tr. interrumpir.

in·ter·rupt·er (ĭn′tə-rŭp′tər) s. interruptor *m.*

in·ter·rup·tion (ĭn′tə-rŭp′shən) s. *(break)* interrupción *f; (pause)* pausa.

in·ter·scho·las·tic (ĭn′tər-skə-lăs′tĭk) adj. escolar, interescolar.

in·ter·sect (ĭn′tər-sĕkt′) tr. *(to cut across)* cruzar, cortar; *(to form an intersection with)* cruzarse con; GEOM. cortar —intr. cruzarse.

in·ter·sec·tion (ĭn′tər-sĕk′shən) s. *(act, process)* intersección *f; (of streets)* bocacalle *f; (of roads)* cruce *m.*

in·ter·ses·sion (ĭn′tər-sĕsh′ən) s. EDUC. vacaciones de finales de semestre *f.*

in·ter·space I. tr. (ĭn′tər-spās′) **-spaced, -spac·ing** espaciar II. s. (ĭn′tər-spās′) espacio intermedio.

in·ter·sperse (ĭn′tər-spûrs′) tr. **-spersed, -spers·ing** *(to distribute)* entreverar, entremezclar; *(to give variety to)* salpicar <*to i. a story with funny remarks* salpicar un cuento con comentarios graciosos>.

in·ter·sper·sion (ĭn′tər-spûr′zhən) s. entrevero, mezcla.

in·ter·state I. adj. (ĭn′tər-stāt′) adj. interestatal, entre provincias ♦ **i. highway system** red de carreteras nacionales II. s. (ĭn′tər-stāt′) carretera nacional.

in·ter·stel·lar (ĭn′tər-stĕl′ər) adj. interestelar, intersideral.

in·ter·stice (ĭn-tûr′stĭs) s. [pl. **-sti·ces** (-stĭ-sēz′)] intersticio.

in·ter·sti·tial (ĭn′tər-stĭsh′əl) adj. intersticial.

in·ter·twine (ĭn′tər-twīn′) tr. & intr. **-twined, -twin·ing** entrelazar(se), entretejer(se).

in·ter·ur·ban (ĭn′tər-ûr′bən) adj. interurbano.

in·ter·val (ĭn′tər-vəl) s. *(space)* intervalo, espacio <*at two-inch intervals* a intervalos de dos pulgadas>; *(time)* intervalo, pausa; MÚS. intervalo ♦ **at intervals** a intervalos, a ratos • **at regular intervals** con regularidad.

in·ter·vene (ĭn′tər-vēn′) intr. **-vened, -ven·ing** *(to come between)* intervenir <*he intervened to prevent a fight* intervino para evitar una pelea>; *(to occur)* ocurrir, sobrevenir; *(to intercede)* mediar, interceder; POL. interferir, intervenir (en asuntos de otra nación); DER. interponer tercería.

in·ter·ven·tion (ĭn′tər-vĕn′shən) s. intervención *f.*

in·ter·ven·tion·ist (ĭn′tər-vĕn′shə-nĭst) s. POL. intervencionista *mf.*

in·ter·view (ĭn′tər-vyōō′) I. s. entrevista II. tr. & intr. entrevistar(se).

in·ter·view·er (ĭn′tər-vyōō′ər) s. *(one who interviews)* entrevistador *m; (newsman)* reportero.

in·ter·weave (ĭn′tər-wēv′) tr. & intr. **-wove** (-wōv′), **-wo·ven** (-wō′vən), **-weav·ing** *(to weave together)* entretejer(se); *(to intertwine)* entremezclar(se).

in·tes·ta·cy (ĭn-tĕs′tə-sē) s. DER. falta de testamento.

in·tes·tate (ĭn-tĕs′tāt′) adj. & s. DER. intestado.

in·tes·ti·nal (ĭn-tĕs′tə-nəl) adj. intestinal.

in·tes·tine (ĭn-tĕs′tĭn) s. ANAT. intestino ♦ **large i.** intestino grueso • **small i.** intestino delgado.

in·ti·ma·cy (ĭn′tə-mə-sē) s. [pl. **-cies**] *(condition)* intimidad *f; (sexual relations)* relaciones íntimas.

in·ti·mate¹ (ĭn′tə-mĭt) I. adj. *(close)* íntimo, entrañable <*i. friends* amigos íntimos>; *(profound)* profundo <*an i. understanding* un profundo conocimiento>; *(innermost)* íntimo, secreto <*i. thoughts* pensamientos íntimos>; *(private)* íntimo, privado ♦ **to become i.** intimar • **to be i. with someone** EUFEM. tener relaciones sexuales con alguien II. s. íntimo.

in·ti·mate² (ĭn′tə-māt′) tr. **-mat·ed, -mat·ing** *(to imply)* dar a entender, insinuar; *(to announce)* anunciar, notificar.

in·tim·i·date (ĭn-tĭm′ĭ-dāt′) tr. **-dat·ed, -dat·ing** intimidar.

in·tim·i·da·tion (ĭn-tĭm′ĭ-dā′shən) s. intimidación *f.*

in·ti·ma·tion (ĭn′tə-mā′shən) s. *(hint)* insinuación *f; (insight)* indicio; *(intuition)* intuición *f; (notice)* noticia.

in·to (ĭn′tōō) prep. *(to the inside of)* a <*come i. my office* pase a mi oficina>; *(to the interior of)* dentro de <*to put something i. a box* poner algo dentro de una caja>; *(to the occupation of)* a <*to go i. medicine* dedicarse a la medicina>; *(to the condition of)* en <*break it i. pieces* rómpelo en pedazos>; *(to be included in)* en <*to enter i. an agreement* participar en o tomar parte en un acuerdo>; *(against)* contra <*to ram i. a tree* chocar contra un árbol>; *(to)* a <*look i. the distance* mira a la distancia>; *(towards)* hacia <*a journey i. the future* un viaje hacia el futuro> ♦ **i. the bargain** por añadidura • **well i.** bien entrado, bien avanzado <*the construction will last well i. next year* la construcción durará hasta bien entrado el año próximo>.

in·tol·er·a·ble (ĭn-tŏl′ər-ə-bəl) adj. intolerable.

in·tol·er·ance (ĭn-tŏl′ər-əns) s. intolerancia.

in·tol·er·ant (ĭn-tŏl′ər-ənt) adj. intolerante ♦ **to be i. of** no poder tolerar.

in·to·na·tion (ĭn′tə-nā′shən) s. entonación *f.*

in·tone (ĭn-tōn′) tr. **-toned, -ton·ing** *(to chant)* recitar melódicamente; *(to pray)* salmodiar —intr. decir.

in·tox·i·cant (ĭn-tŏk′sĭ-kənt) I. s. *(drink)* bebida alcohólica; *(drug)* estupefaciente *m* II. adj. embriagador.

in·tox·i·cate (ĭn-tŏk′sĭ-kāt′) tr. **-cat·ed, -cat·ing** *(to make drunk)* embriagar, emborrachar; FIG. *(to excite)* embriagar, excitar; MED. *(to poison)* intoxicar.

in·tox·i·ca·tion (ĭn-tŏk′sĭ-kā′shən) s. *(state)* embriaguez *f;* MED. *(poisoning)* intoxicación *f.*

in·trac·ta·ble (ĭn-trăk′tə-bəl) adj. *(unruly)* ingobernable, indisciplinado; *(sullen)* huraño, intratable; *(insoluble)* insoluble; MED. incurable.

in·tra·mu·ral (ĭn'trə-myŏor'əl) adj. situado intramuros ♦ **i. sports** actividades deportivas en una escuela u otra institución.

in·tran·si·gence (ĭn-trăn'sə-jəns) s. intransigencia.

in·tran·si·gent (ĭn-trăn'sə-jənt) adj. intransigente, intolerante.

in·tran·si·tive (ĭn-trăn'sĭ-tĭv) GRAM. **I.** adj. intransitivo **II.** s. verbo intransitivo.

in·tra·state (ĭn'trə-stāt') adj. que existe dentro de los límites de un estado.

in·tra·u·ter·ine (ĭn'trə-yōō'tər-ĭn) adj. MED. intrauterino.

intrauterine device s. MED. artefacto anticonceptivo intrauterino.

in·tra·ve·nous (ĭn'trə-vē'nəs) adj. MED. intravenoso.

in·trep·id (ĭn-trĕp'ĭd) adj. intrépido.

in·tre·pid·i·ty (ĭn'trĕ-pĭd'ĭ-tē) o **in·trep·id·ness** (ĭn-trĕp'ĭd-nĭs) s. intrepidez *f.*

in·tri·ca·cy (ĭn'trĭ-kə-sē) s. [pl. **-cies**] *(elaborateness)* complejidad *f; (complexity)* carácter intrincado.

in·tri·cate (ĭn'trĭ-kĭt) adj. *(elaborate)* complejo; *(complex)* intrincado.

in·trigue I. s. (ĭn'trēg) *(plot)* intriga; *(love affair)* amorío secreto **II.** intr. & tr. (ĭn-trēg') **-trigued, -trigu·ing** intrigar.

in·trigu·er (ĭn-trē'gər) s. intrigante *mf.*

in·trin·sic (ĭn-trĭn'sĭk) adj. intrínseco.

in·tro·duce (ĭn'trə-dōōs', -dyōōs') tr. **-duced, -duc·ing** *(to present)* presentar <*to i. a friend* presentar a un amigo>; *(to bring into use)* introducir <*they introduced a new fashion* introdujeron una nueva moda>; *(to market)* lanzar al mercado; POL. *(bill)* presentar; *(to broach)* sacar a colación; *(to make known)* dar a conocer; *(to initiate)* iniciar, familiarizar <*this class will i. you to tennis* esta clase los familiarizará con el tenis>; *(to add)* introducir, añadir; *(into a new surrounding)* traer <*dandelions were introduced from Europe* el diente de león fue traído de Europa>; *(to insert)* introducir, insertar (llave); *(to preface)* presentar, prologar (libro).

in·tro·duc·tion (ĭn'trə-dŭk'shən) s. *(act)* introducción *f* <*the i. of new ideas* la introducción de nuevas ideas>; *(presentation)* presentación *f* <*when the introductions were over* cuando se terminaron las presentaciones>; *(of a product)* lanzamiento; *(preface)* introducción, prólogo; MÚS. preludio.

in·tro·duc·to·ry (ĭn'trə-dŭk'tə-rē) adj. *(that introduces)* introductorio, preliminar; *(said of a course)* de introducción ♦ **i. to** que sirve de introducción a.

in·tro·mis·sion (ĭn'trə-mĭsh'ən) s. *(introduction)* inserción *f,* introducción *f; (admission)* admisión *f.*

in·tro·spect (ĭn'trə-spĕkt') intr. hacer examen de introspección.

in·tro·spec·tion (ĭn'trə-spĕk'shən) s. introspección *f.*

in·tro·spec·tive (ĭn'trə-spĕk'tĭv) adj. introspectivo.

in·tro·ver·sion (ĭn'trə-vûr'zhən) s. introversión *f.*

in·tro·vert (ĭn'trə-vûrt') **I.** tr. & intr. PSIC. centrar(se) en sí mismo; MED. invaginar(se) **II.** s. *(person)* introvertido; MED. invaginación *f.*

in·tro·vert·ed (ĭn'trə-vûr'tĭd) adj. introvertido.

in·trude (ĭn-trōōd') tr. **-trud·ed, -trud·ing** meter por fuerza (en) ♦ **to i. on** o **upon** imponer —intr. *(to interlope)* inmiscuirse, entrometerse <*to i. into a person's privacy* inmiscuirse en la vida privada de una persona>; *(to interrupt)* molestar, interrumpir <*are we intruding?* ¿molestamos?> ♦ **to i. upon a conversation** interrumpir una conversación.

in·trud·er (ĭn-trōō'dər) s. intruso.

in·tru·sion (ĭn-trōō'zhən) s. *(meddling)* intrusión *f; (imposition)* molestia; *(interruption)* interrupción *f.*

in·tru·sive (ĭn-trōō'sĭv) adj. intruso.

in·tu·it (ĭn-tōō'ĭt, -tyōō'-) tr. intuir.

in·tu·i·tion (ĭn'tōō-ĭsh'ən, -tyōō-) s. intuición *f.*

in·tu·i·tive (ĭn-tōō'ĭ-tĭv, -tyōō'-) adj. intuitivo.

in·tu·i·tive·ly (ĭn-tōō'ĭ-tĭv-lē, -tyōō'-) adv. intuitivamente, por intuición.

in·un·date (ĭn'ŭn-dāt') tr. **-dat·ed, -dat·ing** *(to overflow)* inundar, anegar; FIG. *(to swamp)* abrumar.

in·un·da·tion (ĭn'ŭn-dā'shən) s. inundación *f.*

in·ure (ĭn-yŏor') tr. **-ured, -ur·ing** *(to accustom)* acostumbrar, habituar; *(to harden)* curtir, endurecer.

in·vade (ĭn-vād') tr. **-vad·ed, -vad·ing** *(to raid)* invadir; *(someone's privacy)* no respetar, meterse en; *(someone's rights)* infringir, violar —intr. hacer una invasión.

in·vad·er (ĭn-vā'dər) s. invasor *m.*

in·vag·i·nate (ĭn-văj'ə-nāt') tr. & intr. **-nat·ed, -nat·ing** MED. invaginar(se).

in·va·lid[1] (ĭn'və-lĭd) **I.** s. inválido **II.** adj. *(disabled)* inválido; *(ill)* enfermo **III.** tr. *(to disable)* dejar inválido; *(to make ill)* enfermar.

in·val·id[2] (ĭn-văl'ĭd) adj. *(null)* nulo, inválido; *(faulty)* defectuoso, imperfecto (razonamiento, afirmación).

in·val·i·date (ĭn-văl'ĭ-dāt') tr. **-dat·ed, -dat·ing** invalidar, anular.

in·val·i·da·tion (ĭn-văl'ĭ-dā'shən) s. invalidación *f,* anulación *f.*

in·va·lid·i·ty (ĭn'və-lĭd'ĭ-tē) s. [pl. **-ties**] *(nullity)* falta de validez, nulidad *f; (faultiness)* carácter inadmisible *m;* MED. *(infirmity)* invalidez *f.*

in·val·u·a·ble (ĭn-văl'yōō-ə-bəl) adj. *(priceless)* invalorable, de incalculable valor <*i. paintings* pinturas de incalculable valor>; *(indispensable)* inapreciable, inestimable.

in·var·i·a·bil·i·ty (ĭn-vâr'ē-ə-bĭl'ĭ-tē) s. invariabilidad *f.*

in·var·i·a·ble (ĭn-vâr'ē-ə-bəl) adj. invariable.

in·var·i·a·bly (ĭn-vâr'ē-ə-blē) adv. invariablemente.

in·var·i·ant (ĭn-vâr'ē-ənt) **I.** adj. invariable, constante **II.** s. MAT. invariante *m.*

in·va·sion (ĭn-vā'zhən) s. *(raid)* invasión *f; (of privacy)* entrometimiento *m; (of rights)* transgresión *f.*

in·vec·tive (ĭn-vĕk'tĭv) **I.** s. invectiva, vituperio **II.** adj. insultante, vituperador.

in·veigh (ĭn-vā') intr. lanzar invectivas ♦ **to i. against** vituperar.

in·vei·gle (ĭn-vā'gəl, -vē'-) tr. **-gled, -gling** *(to lure)* embaucar, engatusar; *(to wheedle)* sonsacar, obtener arteramente.

in·vent (ĭn-vĕnt') tr. inventar.

in·ven·tion (ĭn-vĕn'shən) s. *(act)* invención *f* <*the i. of the printing press* la invención de la imprenta>; *(new device)* invención, invento; *(falsehood)* invención, patraña; *(skill)* inventiva.

in·ven·tive (ĭn-vĕn'tĭv) adj. *(of invention)* de invención; *(creative)* inventivo, creador.

in·ven·tor (ĭn-vĕn'tər) s. inventor *m.*

in·ven·to·ry (ĭn'vən-tôr'ē) **I.** s. [pl. **-ries**] *(detailed list)* inventario; COM. *(stock)* existencias; *(evaluation)* descripción *f* **II.** tr. **-ried, -ry·ing** inventariar.

in·verse (ĭn'vûrs') **I.** adj. *(reversed)* inverso; *(inverted)* al revés **II.** s. MAT. inverso ♦ **the i. of** lo inverso de, lo contrario de.

in·ver·sion (ĭn-vûr'zhən) s. inversión *f.*

in·vert I. tr. (ĭn-vûrt') *(to reverse)* invertir; QUÍM. someter a inversión (azúcar) **II.** s. (ĭn'vûrt') PSIC. invertido, homosexual *mf.*

in·ver·te·brate (ĭn-vûr'tə-brĭt, -brāt') adj. & s. ZOOL. invertebrado.

inverted commas s.pl. G.B. comillas.

in·vest (ĭn-vĕst') tr. *(money)* invertir <*to i. in real estate* invertir en bienes raíces>; *(effort)* dedicar (tiempo, energía); *(to endow)* conferir; *(to install in office)* investir, instalar (en un cargo); *(to envelop)* cubrir, envolver <*to i. with a mantle of mystery* cubrir con un manto de misterio>; *(to adorn)* revestir —intr. COM. invertir dinero, hacer una inversión.

in·ves·ti·gate (ĭn-vĕs'tĭ-gāt') tr. **-gat·ed, -gat·ing** *(to explore)* investigar; *(to analyze)* analizar, examinar —intr. hacer investigaciones.

in·ves·ti·ga·tion (ĭn-vĕs'tĭ-gā'shən) s. investigación *f.*

in·ves·ti·ga·tive (ĭn-vĕs'tĭ-gā'tĭv) adj. de investigación.

in·ves·ti·ga·tor (ĭn-vĕs'tĭ-gā'tər) s. investigador *m.*

in·ves·ti·ture (ĭn-vĕs'tĭ-chōor', -chər) s. *(ceremony)* investidura; *(vesture)* vestidura.

in·vest·ment (ĭn-vĕst'mənt) s. COM. *(act)* inversión (de dinero) *f; (investiture)* investidura, instalación *f* ♦ **i. fund** FIN. fondo de inversiones.

in·ves·tor (ĭn-vĕs′tər) s. inversionista *mf.*

in·vet·er·ate (ĭn-vĕt′ər-ĭt) adj. *(deep-rooted)* inveterado, arraigado; *(confirmed)* empedernido, incorregible.

in·vid·i·ous (ĭn-vĭd′ē-əs) adj. *(offensive)* provocador, que causa mala voluntad; *(discriminatory)* denigrante.

in·vig·o·rate (ĭn-vĭg′ə-rāt′) tr. **-rat·ed, -rat·ing** dar vigor a.

in·vig·o·ra·tion (ĭn-vĭg′ə-rā′shən) s. *(strengthening)* fortalecimiento; *(livening up)* animación *f.*

in·vin·ci·bil·i·ty (ĭn-vĭn′sə-bĭl′ĭ-tē) *o* **in·vin·ci·ble·ness** (ĭn-vĭn′sə-bəl-nĭs) s. invencibilidad *f.*

in·vin·ci·ble (ĭn-vĭn′sə-bəl) adj. invencible.

in·vi·o·la·ble (ĭn-vī′ə-lə-bəl) adj. inviolable.

in·vi·o·late (ĭn-vī′ə-lĭt) adj. inviolado.

in·vis·i·bil·i·ty (ĭn-vĭz′ə-bĭl′ĭ-tē) s. invisibilidad *f.*

in·vis·i·ble (ĭn-vĭz′ə-bəl) I. adj. invisible II. s. lo invisible.

invisible ink s. tinta simpática.

in·vi·ta·tion (ĭn′vĭ-tā′shən) s. *(request)* invitación *f; (treat)* convite *m.*

in·vite I. tr. (ĭn-vīt′) **-vit·ed, -vit·ing** *(to ask)* invitar <*to i. someone to a wedding* invitar a alguien a una boda>; *(to treat)* convidar; *(to encourage)* alentar, solicitar <*to i. questions* solicitar preguntas>; *(to bring on)* provocar, buscar <*to i. disaster* buscar el desastre> II. s. (ĭn′vīt′) FAM. invitación *f.*

in·vit·ing (ĭn-vī′tĭng) adj. *(attractive)* atrayente; *(tempting)* tentador; *(seductive)* provocativo, incitante; *(appetizing)* apetitoso.

in·vo·ca·tion (ĭn′və-kā′shən) s. invocación *f.*

in·voice (ĭn′vois′) COM. I. factura ♦ **as per i.** según factura II. tr. **-voiced, -voic·ing** facturar, extender factura.

in·voke (ĭn-vōk′) tr. **-voked, -vok·ing** *(to enforce)* invocar; *(to resort to)* invocar, apelar a.

in·vol·un·tar·i·ly (ĭn-vŏl′ən-tăr′ə-lē) adv. *(not willingly)* involuntariamente; *(unintentionally)* sin querer.

in·vol·un·tar·y (ĭn-vŏl′ən-tĕr′ē) adj. involuntario.

in·vo·lute (ĭn′və-lōōt′) I. adj. *(involved)* complicado, intrincado; BOT. involuto II. s. GEOM. involuta.

in·vo·lu·tion (ĭn′və-lōō′shən) s. *(intricacy)* complicación *f,* enredo; MAT. elevación (a una potencia) *f;* BIOL. involución *f.*

in·volve (ĭn-vŏlv′) tr. **-volved, -volv·ing** *(to contain)* comprender, incluir <*the problem involves many different factors* el problema comprende muchos factores distintos>; *(to deal with)* concernir a; *(to entail)* implicar, entrañar <*the project will i. a lot of work* el proyecto entraña mucho trabajo>; *(to implicate)* comprometer, involucrar <*to be involved in a scandal* estar involucrado en un escándalo>; *(to engross)* abstraer, absorber; *(to complicate)* complicar, enredar; MAT. elevar (a una potencia) ♦ **those involved** los interesados • **to be emotionally involved** tener relaciones serias.

in·volved (ĭn-vŏlvd′) adj. complicado, enredado.

in·volve·ment (ĭn-vŏlv′mənt) s. *(entanglement)* envolvimiento, comprometimiento; *(implication)* implicación *f,* participación *f* <*his i. in the murder* su participación en el asesinato>; *(engrossment)* abstraimiento; *(intricateness)* intrincación *f.*

in·vul·ner·a·bil·i·ty (ĭn-vŭl′nər-ə-bĭl′ĭ-tē) s. invulnerabilidad *f.*

in·vul·ner·a·ble (ĭn-vŭl′nər-ə-bəl) adj. invulnerable.

in·ward (ĭn′wərd) I. adj. *(inner)* interior, interno; *(familiar)* íntimo, familiar II. adv. hacia adentro.

in·ward·ly (ĭn′wərd-lē) adv. *(within)* interiormente; *(to oneself)* para los adentros de uno.

in·ward·ness (ĭn′wərd-nĭs) s. *(familiarity)* familiaridad *f; (spirituality)* espiritualidad *f; (essential nature)* carácter intrínseco.

in·wards (ĭn′wərdz) adv. hacia dentro, hacia el interior.

i·o·dide (ī′ə-dīd′) s. QUÍM. yoduro.

i·o·dine (ī′ə-dīn′, -dēn′) s. QUÍM. yodo.

i·o·dize (ī′ə-dīz′) tr. **-dized, -diz·ing** QUÍM. yodar.

i·on (ī′ən, ī′ŏn′) s. FÍS., QUÍM. ion *m.*

I·o·ni·an Sea (ī-ō′nē-ən) s. mar Jónico.

i·on·ic (ī-ŏn′ĭk) adj. FÍS., QUÍM. iónico, de los iones.

Ionic order s. ARQ. orden jónico.

i·on·i·za·tion (ī′ə-nĭ-zā′shən) s. FÍS., QUÍM. ionización (acción, estado) *f.*

ionization chamber s. FÍS. cámara de ionización.

i·on·ize (ī′ə-nīz′) tr. & intr. **-ized, -iz·ing** FÍS., QUÍM. ionizar(se).

i·on·o·sphere (ī-ŏn′ə-sfîr′) s. METEOR. ionosfera.

i·o·ta (ī-ō′tə) s. *(letter)* iota; *(bit)* ápice *m,* pizca <*not one i. of truth* ni pizca de verdad>.

IOU (ī′ō-yōō′) s. [pl. **IOU's** *o* **IOUs**] pagaré *m,* vale *m* *(abreviatura fonética de I owe you* yo le debo).

IQ *o* **I.Q.** (ī′kyōō′) s. cociente intelectual *m.*

I·ran (ī-răn′, ī-rän′) s. Irán *m.*

I·ra·ni·an (ī-rā′nē-ən, ī-rä′-) I. adj. iraní II. s. *(inhabitant)* iraní, iranio; *(language)* iranio.

I·raq (ī-răk′, ī-räk′) s. Iraq *m.*

I·raq·i (ī-răk′ē, ī-räk′ē) adj. & s. [pl. **Iraqi** *o* **-is**] iraquí *mf* ♦ **the I.** los iraquíes.

i·ras·ci·ble (ī-răs′ə-bəl) adj. irascible, iracundo.

i·rate (ī-rāt′) adj. colérico, airado.

ire (īr) s. ira.

ire·ful (īr′fəl) adj. iracundo.

Ire·land (īr′lənd) s. Irlanda ♦ **Northern I.** Irlanda del Norte.

ir·i·des·cence (ĭr′ĭ-dĕs′əns) s. iridiscencia, irisación *f.*

ir·i·des·cent (ĭr′ĭ-dĕs′ənt) adj. iridiscente, irisado.

ir·id·i·um (ī-rĭd′ē-əm) s. QUÍM. iridio.

i·ris (ī′rĭs) s. [pl. **i·ris·es** *o* **i·ri·des** (ī′rĭ-dēz′, îr′ĭ-)] OFTAL. iris *m;* BOT. lirio, lis *f;* METEOR. arco iris.

I·rish (ī′rĭsh) I. adj. irlandés II. s. *(language)* irlandés *m* ♦ **the I.** los irlandeses.

I·rish·man (ī′rĭsh-mən) s. [pl. **-men**] irlandés *m.*

Irish moss s. BOT. musgo de Irlanda.

Irish setter s. perro perdiguero de raza irlandesa.

I·rish·wom·an (ī′rĭsh-wōōm′ən) s. [pl. **-wom·en** (-wĭm′ĭn)] irlandesa.

irk (ûrk) tr. irritar, sacar de quicio.

irk·some (ûrk′səm) adj. irritante.

i·ron (ī′ərn) I. s. *(metal)* hierro; FIG. *(firmness)* hierro <*a will of i.* una voluntad de hierro>; *(for branding)* hierro candente; *(golf club)* palo de golf; *(for pressing clothes)* plancha; *(harpoon)* arpón *m;* MED. *(preparation)* vitamina que contiene hierro ♦ **in irons** encadenado • **irons** grilletes II. tr. *(to press)* planchar; *(to fetter)* encadenar, engrillar; *(to clad with iron)* herrar ♦ **to i. out** allanar, resolver —intr. planchar.

Iron Age s. ARQUEOL. Edad de Hierro *f.*

i·ron·clad (ī′ərn-klăd′) I. adj. *(sheathed)* acorazado, blindado; *(strict)* estricto, riguroso II. s. MARÍT. acorazado.

Iron Curtain s. POL. cortina de hierro.

iron horse s. FAM. locomotora, ferrocarril *m.*

i·ron·ic (ī-rŏn′ĭk) *o* **i·ron·i·cal** (-ĭ-kəl) adj. irónico, mordaz.

i·ron·ing (ī′ər-nĭng) s. planchado.

ironing board s. tabla de planchar.

i·ro·nist (ī′rə-nĭst) s. LIT. ironista *mf.*

iron lung s. MED. pulmón de acero *m.*

iron ore s. MIN. mineral de hierro *m.*

i·ron·ware (ī′ərn-wâr′) s. quincalla, ferretería.

i·ron·works (ī′ərn-wûrks′) s.pl. [ú. con v. sing. o pl.] fundición de hierro *f.*

i·ro·ny (ī′rə-nē) s. [pl. **-nies**] ironía.

Ir·o·quoi·an (ĭr′ə-kwoi′ən) adj. & s. iroqués *m.*

ir·ra·di·ate (ī-rā′dē-āt′) tr. **-at·ed, -at·ing** *(to emit)* irradiar; FIG. *(to enlighten)* iluminar —intr. *(to emit rays)* brillar; *(to become radiant)* iluminarse.

ir·ra·di·a·tion (ī-rā′dē-ā′shən) s. *(act, condition)* irradiación *f;* MED. *(therapy)* irradiación.

ir·ra·tion·al (ī-răsh′ə-nəl) adj. *(not rational)* irracional; *(illogical)* ilógico; *(absurd)* absurdo.

ir·ra·tion·al·i·ty (ī-răsh′ə-năl′ĭ-tē) s. [pl. **-ties**] *(state, quality)* irracionalidad *f; (idea)* disparate *m; (act)* absurdo.

ir·rec·on·cil·a·ble (ī-rĕk′ən-sī′lə-bəl) adj. *(beyond reconciliation)* irreconciliable; *(differences)* insuperable, insalvable; *(ideas)* incompatible, inconciliable.

ir·re·cov·er·a·ble (ĭr′ĭ-kŭv′ər-ə-bəl) adj. *(not recoverable)* irrecuperable; *(irreparable)* irreparable, irremediable.

ir·re·deem·a·ble (ĭr′ĭ-dē′mə-bəl) adj. COM. *(annuity, loan)* irredimible, no amortizable; *(paper currency)* inconvertible, no convertible en moneda; FIG. *(without remedy)* irremediable; *(incorrigible)* incorregible.

ir·re·duc·i·ble (ĭr′ĭ-dōō′sə-bəl, -dyōō′-) adj. irreducible, irreductible.

ir·ref·u·ta·ble (ĭ-rĕf′yə-tə-bəl, ĭr′ĭ-fyōō′tə-) adj. irrefutable, irrebatible.

ir·reg·u·lar (ĭ-rĕg′yə-lər) I. adj. *(not regular)* irregular (forma, orden, práctica); *(uneven)* desigual (superficie, ritmo); *(merchandise)* imperfecto II. s. *(merchandise)* mercancía imperfecta; *(militiaman)* soldado irregular, miliciano.

ir·reg·u·lar·i·ty (ĭ-rĕg′yə-lăr′ĭ-tē) s. [pl. -ties] *(quality)* irregularidad *f; (of a surface)* desigualdad *f; (constipation)* estreñimiento.

ir·rel·e·vance (ĭ-rĕl′ə-vəns) s. *(quality, state)* improcedencia, falta de pertinencia; *(remark)* comentario fuera de lugar.

ir·rel·e·van·cy (ĭ-rĕl′ə-vən-sē) s. [pl. -cies] *(quality, state)* improcedencia, falta de pertinencia; *(remark)* comentario fuera de lugar.

ir·rel·e·vant (ĭ-rĕl′ə-vənt) adj. inaplicable, improcedente ♦ **to be i.** no venir al caso, estar fuera de lugar ♦ **to be i. to** no tener nada que ver con.

ir·re·lig·ious (ĭr′ĭ-lĭj′əs) adj. irreligioso.

ir·re·me·di·a·ble (ĭr′ĭ-mē′dē-ə-bəl) adj. irremediable.

ir·re·mis·si·ble (ĭr′ĭ-mĭs′ə-bəl) adj. irremisible.

ir·rep·a·ra·ble (ĭ-rĕp′ər-ə-bəl) adj. irreparable.

ir·re·place·a·ble (ĭr′ĭ-plā′sə-bəl) adj. irreemplazable, irremplazable.

ir·re·pres·si·ble (ĭr′ĭ-prĕs′ə-bəl) adj. incontrolable, incontenible.

ir·re·proach·a·ble (ĭr′ĭ-prō′chə-bəl) adj. irreprochable, intachable.

ir·re·sist·i·ble (ĭr′ĭ-zĭs′tə-bəl) adj. irresistible.

ir·res·o·lute (ĭ-rĕz′ə-lōōt′) adj. irresoluto, indeciso.

ir·res·o·lute·ness (ĭ-rĕz′ə-lōōt′nĭs) s. irresolución *f,* indecisión *f.*

ir·res·o·lu·tion (ĭ-rĕz′ə-lōō′shən) s. irresolución *f,* indecisión *f.*

ir·re·solv·a·ble (ĭr′ĭ-zŏl′və-bəl) adj. *(not resolvable)* irresoluble, sin solución; *(irreducible)* irreductible, irreducible.

ir·re·spec·tive (ĭr′ĭ-spĕk′tĭv) adj. ANT. inatento, descuidado ♦ **i. of** sin tener en cuenta, no obstante.

ir·re·spon·si·bil·i·ty (ĭr′ĭ-spŏn′sə-bĭl′ĭ-tē) s. *(quality, state)* irresponsabilidad *f;* FIN. insolvencia.

ir·re·spon·si·ble (ĭr′ĭ-spŏn′sə-bəl) I. adj. *(lacking responsibility)* irresponsable; FIN. *(not financially fit)* insolvente II. s. irresponsable *mf.*

ir·re·triev·a·ble (ĭr′ĭ-trē′və-bəl) adj. *(not recoverable)* irrecuperable; *(mistake)* irreparable.

ir·rev·er·ence (ĭ-rĕv′ər-əns) s. irreverencia, falta de respeto.

ir·rev·er·ent (ĭ-rĕv′ər-ənt) adj. irreverente, irrespetuoso.

ir·re·vers·i·ble (ĭr′ĭ-vûr′sə-bəl) adj. *(not reversible)* irreversible; *(damage)* irreparable, irremediable; *(decision)* irrevocable.

ir·rev·o·ca·ble (ĭ-rĕv′ə-kə-bəl) adj. irrevocable.

ir·ri·gate (ĭr′ĭ-gāt′) tr. **-gat·ed, -gat·ing** AGR. irrigar, regar; MED. irrigar.

ir·ri·ga·tion (ĭr′ĭ-gā′shən) s. *(of lands)* irrigación *f,* riego; *(of a wound)* irrigación *f.*

ir·ri·ta·bil·i·ty (ĭr′ĭ-tə-bĭl′ĭ-tē) s. irritabilidad *f.*

ir·ri·ta·ble (ĭr′ĭ-tə-bəl) adj. irritable.

ir·ri·ta·ble·ness (ĭr′ĭ-tə-bəl-nĭs) s. irritabilidad *f.*

ir·ri·tant (ĭr′ĭ-tnt) I. adj. irritante II. s. substancia irritante.

ir·ri·tate (ĭr′ĭ-tāt′) tr. **-tat·ed, -tat·ing** irritar.

ir·ri·tat·ing (ĭr′ĭ-tā′tĭng) adj. irritante, molesto.

ir·ri·tat·ing·ly (ĭr′ĭ-tā′tĭng-lē) adv. do modo irritante, fastidiosamente.

ir·ri·ta·tion (ĭr′ĭ-tā′shən) s. irritación *f.*

ir·rupt (ĭ-rŭpt′) tr. *(to burst in)* irrumpir; *(to increase abruptly)* reproducirse súbitamente.

ir·rup·tion (ĭ-rŭp′shən) s. *(bursting in)* irrupción *f; (of a population)* reproducción súbita.

is (ĭz) tercera persona sing. del pres. indic. de **be.**

I·sa·iah (ī-zā′ə, ī-zī′ə) s. BÍBL. Isaías.

i·sin·glass (ī′zĭng-glăs′) s. CUL. cola de pescado, colapez *f;* MIN. mica.

Is·lam (ĭs′ləm, ĭz′-, ĭs-läm′) s. RELIG. islam *m; (people)* islam, pueblo musulmán.

Is·lam·ic (ĭs-läm′ĭk, ĭz-, -lä′mĭk) adj. islámico.

Is·lam·ite (ĭs′lə-mīt′, ĭz′-) s. RELIG. islamita *mf.*

is·land (ī′lənd) I. s. GEOG. isla; *(in a street)* isleta, zona de seguridad II. tr. aislar.

is·land·er (ī′lən-dər) s. isleño, habitante de una isla *mf.*

isle (īl) s. *(island)* isla; *(islet)* isleta, islote *m* ♦ **the British Isles** las Islas Británicas.

is·let (ī′lĭt) s. isleta, islote *m.*

ism (ĭz′əm) s. FAM. ismo.

is·n't (ĭz′ənt) contr. de **is not.**

i·so·bar (ī′sə-bär′) s. METEOR. isobara; FÍS., QUÍM. isóbaro.

i·so·cline (ī′sə-klīn′) s. GEOL. pliegue isoclinal *m.*

i·so·gon·ic (ī′sə-gŏn′ĭk) adj. isógono.

i·so·late (ī′sə-lāt′) I. tr. **-lat·ed, -lat·ing** *(to separate)* aislar; *(a prisoner)* incomunicar II. adj. (-lĭt, -lāt′) *(solitary)* aislado; *(prisoner)* incomunicado.

i·so·la·tion (ī′sə-lā′shən) s. aislamiento ♦ **i. ward** MED. pabellón de cuarentena.

i·so·la·tion·ism (ī′sə-lā′shə-nĭz′əm) s. POL. aislacionismo.

i·so·la·tion·ist (ī′sə-lā′shə-nĭst) s. POL. aislacionista *mf.*

i·so·mer (ī′sə-mər) s. FÍS., QUÍM. isómero.

i·som·er·ism (ī-sŏm′ə-rĭz′əm) s. FÍS., QUÍM. isomería.

i·so·met·ric (ī′sə-mĕt′rĭk) o **i·so·met·ri·cal** (-rĭ-kəl) I. adj. isométrico II. s. línea isométrica ♦ **isometrics** [ú. con v. sing.] ejercicio isométrico.

i·som·e·try (ī-sŏm′ĭ-trē) s. *(of measure)* igualdad de medidas *f;* GEOG. *(of elevation)* igualdad de altura.

i·so·mor·phic (ī′sə-môr′fĭk) adj. isomorfo.

i·so·mor·phism (ī′sə-môr′fĭz′əm) s. BIOL., MAT., MIN., QUÍM. isomorfismo.

i·sos·ce·les (ī-sŏs′ə-lēz′) adj. GEOM. isósceles.

i·so·therm (ī′sə-thûrm′) s. FÍS., METEOR. isoterma, línea isoterma.

i·so·tope (ī′sə-tōp′) s. FÍS., QUÍM. isótopo.

Is·ra·el (ĭz′rē-əl) s. Israel *m.*

Is·rae·li (ĭz-rā′lē) I. adj. israelí, israelita II. s. [pl. **Israeli** o **-lis**] israelí *mf,* israelita *mf.*

Is·ra·el·ite (ĭz′rē-ə-līt′) adj. & s. israelita *mf.*

is·su·ance (ĭsh′ōō-əns) s. COM. emisión.

is·sue (ĭsh′ōō) I. s. *(money, stamps, shares)* emisión *f; (distribution)* distribución *f,* reparto; *(edition)* edición *f,* tirada; *(publication)* publicación *f; (copy)* número; *(result)* resultado, consecuencia; *(proceeds)* rédito, beneficio; *(offspring)* descendencia, progenie *f; (point under discussion)* punto, cuestión *f; (problem)* problema *m; (crux)* quid *m,* punto crucial; *(decisive point)* punto decisivo; *(outlet)* salida; MED. *(discharge)* derrame *m; (suppuration)* exutorio; ANT. *(termination)* hecho ♦ **at i.** en discusión, en desacuerdo • **to force the i.** forzar una decisión • **to raise the i. of** plantear el problema de • **to take i. with** estar en desacuerdo con II. intr. **-sued, -su·ing** *(to come out)* salir; *(to emanate)* emanar de, surgir de; *(to be descended)* descender de; *(to be circulated)* ser emitido; *(to be published)* ser publicado; *(to result from)* resultar de; *(to result in)* resultar en — tr. *(to emit)* emitir; *(to distribute)* repartir, distribuir; *(to publish)* publicar.

is·su·er (ĭsh′ōō-ər) s. *(of a document, note)* otorgante *mf,* expedidor *m; (of supplies)* distribuidor *m.*

isth·mus (ĭs′məs) s. [pl. **-mus·es** o **-mi** (-mī′)] ANAT., GEOG. istmo.

it §G12, 29 (ĭt) I. pron. [no traducido] él, ella, ello *<has the mail come? yes, it just arrived* ¿ha llegado el correo? sí, acaba de llegar>; lo, la *<do you know this song? yes, I know it well* ¿conoces esta canción? sí, la conozco bien>; le *<give it a good push* dale un empujón fuerte>; ello, eso *<we were thinking about it just yesterday* justamente ayer estábamos pensando en eso>; [no se traduce en oraciones impersonales] *<it is snowing* está nevando> II. s. *(in a children's game)* el que la lleva (en el juego de la pega o mancha).

I·tal·ian (ĭ-tăl′yən) adj. & s. *(inhabitant, language)* italiano.

I·tal·ian·ism (ĭ-tăl′yə-nĭz′əm) s. italianismo.

ã rey / ä año / b boca / ch chico / d dar / ĕ el / ē mil / g gato / h joya / hw juez / ī aire / k casa / kw cuan /

i·tal·ic (ĭ-tăl′ĭk, ī-tăl′-) s. & adj. IMPR., TIP. bastardilla, cursiva (letra).

i·tal·i·cize (ĭ-tăl′ĭ-sīz′, ī-tăl′-) tr. **-cized, -ciz·ing** *(to print)* escribir *o* imprimir en cursiva *o* bastardilla; *(to underscore)* subrayar.

It·a·ly (ĭt′l-ē) s. Italia.

itch (ĭch) I. s. *(skin sensation)* picazón *f*, comezón *f*; MED. *(rash)* sarna, salpullido; FIG. *(desire)* comezón, prurito ♦ **to have an i.** *o* **the i. to** estar desesperado por, estar loco por II. intr. *(to feel an itch)* picar, sentir picazón <*my ear itches* me pica el oído>; FIG. *(to have a craving for)* desear con avidez, anhelar; *(to desire)* estar desesperado por <*I am itching to go* estoy desesperado por ir> —tr. *(to cause to itch)* dar picazón; *(to scratch)* rascarse.

itch·i·ness (ĭch′ē-nĭs) s. *(skin sensation)* picazón *f*, comezón *f*; *(desire)* comezón, ganas.

itch·y (ĭch′ē) adj. **-i·er, -i·est** *(causing an itch)* que da picazón; FIG. *(restless)* impaciente.

i·tem (ī′təm) I. s. *(unit)* artículo <*how many items did you purchase?* ¿cuántos artículos compró usted?>; *(on an agenda)* asunto, punto; *(in a performance)* número; *(of a document)* ítem *m*, apartado; *(of a form)* artículo, casilla; TEN. *(entry)* partida; *(of information)* detalle *m*; *(in a newspaper)* suelto, artículo II. adv. ítem.

i·tem·i·za·tion (ī′tə-mĭ-zā′shən) s. enumeración *f*.

i·tem·ize (ī′tə-mīz′) tr. **-ized, -iz·ing** enumerar, detallar.

i·tem·iz·er (ī′tə-mī′zər) s. persona que detalla *o* especifica.

it·er·ate (ĭt′ə-rāt′) tr. **-at·ed, -at·ing** iterar, repetir.

it·er·a·tion (ĭt′ə-rā′shən) s. iteración *f*, repetición *f*.

i·tin·er·ant (ī-tĭn′ər-ənt) I. adj. ambulante II. s. persona ambulante.

i·tin·er·ar·y (ī-tĭn′ə-rĕr′ē) s. [pl. **-ies**] *(route)* itinerario, ruta; *(account)* relación de un viaje *f*; *(guide)* itinerario, guía.

it'll (ĭt′l) contr. de **it will** y **it shall.**

its §G23 (ĭts) adj. pos. su <*the dog was looking for its bone* el perro buscaba su hueso>.

it's (ĭts) contr. de **it is** y **it has.**

it·self §G37 (ĭt-sĕlf′) pron. se <*this record player turns i. off automatically* este tocadiscos se apaga automáticamente>; sí mismo <*the cat saw i. in the mirror* el gato se vio a sí mismo en el espejo>; sólo <*the yarn is. is more expensive than the sweater* la lana sóla es más cara que el suéter>; mismo <*the trouble is in the motor i.* el problema es el motor mismo>; mismo <*the bird picked up all the twigs i.* el pájaro juntó todas las ramitas él mismo>; de sí, por sí mismo <*of i.* de sí *o* por sí mismo> ♦ **(all) by i.** solo.

I've (īv) contr. de **I have.**

i·vo·ry (ī′və-rē) I. s. [pl. **-ries**] *(substance in tusks)* marfil *m*; *(tusk)* colmillo (esp. de elefante); *(ivory-like substance)* marfilina; *(color)* color marfil *m*; *(article)* artículo de marfil ♦ **ivories** FAM. *(piano keys)* teclas; *(dice)* dados; *(teeth)* colmillos, dientes II. adj. de color marfil.

Ivory Coast, the s. la Costa de Marfil.

ivory tower s. FIG. torre de marfil *f*.

i·vy (ī′vē) s. [pl. **-vies**] hiedra, yedra.

Ivy League s. asociación de universidades prestigiosas del este de EE. UU. *f*.

J

J, J (jā) s. [pl. **J's, J's**] décima letra del alfabeto inglés.

jab (jăb) I. tr. **jabbed, jab·bing** *(to poke)* hurgonear; *(to prick)* pinchar, punzar; *(to stab)* clavar; *(to punch)* dar un golpe corto, golpear; *(with the elbow)* dar un codazo a —intr. *(to prick)* pinchar; *(to deliver a quick punch)* asestar un golpe rápido ♦ **to j. into** clavar en II. s. *(prick)* pinchazo; *(with the elbow)* codazo; *(in boxing)* golpe corto.

jab·ber (jăb′ər) I. intr. *(to chatter)* parlotear, cotorrear; *(to babble)* farfullar, barbullar —tr. farfullar, barbullar II. s. *(chatter)* parloteo; *(jabbering)* barbulla.

jab·ber·er (jăb′ər-ər) s. charlatán *m*.

jac·a·ran·da (jăk′ə-răn′də) s. BOT. jacarandá (árbol y madera) *m*.

ja·cinth (jā′sĭnth) s. MIN. jacinto.

jack (jăk) I. s. *(sailor)* marinero; *(in cards)* valet *m*; *(in Spanish cards)* sota; *(jackass)* asno, burro; *(bootjack)* sacabotas *m*; *(flag)* pabellón *m*, bandera de proa; FAM. *(fellow)* tipo, tío; *(money)* dinero, mosca; ELEC. enchufe hembra *m*, toma de corriente; MEC. gato, cric *m* ♦ **jacks** tabas II. tr. ♦ **to j. up** *(to lift)* alzar con el gato; FAM. *(to raise)* aumentar (precios, sueldos) —intr. ♦ **to j. off** VULG. hacerse la paja.

jack·al (jăk′əl) s. ZOOL. chacal *m*; FIG. *(lackey)* paniaguado.

jack·a·napes (jăk′ə-nāps′) s. *(conceited person)* mequetrefe *m*; *(mischievous child)* diablillo.

jack·ass (jăk′ăs′) s. ZOOL. asno, burro; FIG. *(person)* burro, tonto.

jack·boot (jăk′boot′) s. MIL. bota alta *o* de montar; FIG. *(bully)* mandón *m*; POL. *(regime)* régimen totalitario *o* tiránico (esp. militar).

jack·daw (jăk′dô′) s. ORNIT. chova.

jack·et (jăk′ĭt) I. s. *(coat)* saco, chaqueta; *(of a book)* sobrecubierta, forro; *(of a record)* envoltura, cubierta; *(of a file)* carpeta; *(of potatoes)* piel *f*; *(of pipes, tubes)* camisa; *(of a bullet)* casquillo II. tr. poner una cubierta a.

jack·ham·mer (jăk′hăm′ər) s. MEC. perforadora neumática.

jack-in-the-box (jăk′ĭn-thə-bŏks′) s. [pl. **jack-in-the-boxes** *o* **jacks-in-the-box**] caja de sorpresa (con muñeco de resorte).

jack·knife (jăk′nīf′) I. s. [pl. **-knives**] *(pocketknife)* navaja, cortaplumas *m*; DEP. *(dive)* salto de carpa II. tr. **-knifed, -knif·ing** *(to cut)* cortar con una navaja; *(to stab)* dar un navajazo a; *(to fold)* doblar como una najava —intr. doblarse *o* plegarse como una navaja.

jack-of-all-trades (jăk′əv-ôl′trādz′) s. [pl. **jacks-of-all-trades**] persona de muchos oficios, factótum *m*.

jack-o'-lantern (jăk′ə-lăn′tərn) s. *(lantern)* lámpara hecha con una calabaza *o* zapallo; *(ignis fatuus)* fuego fatuo.

jack·pot (jăk′pŏt′) s. premio gordo ♦ **to hit the j.** *(prize)* sacarse el premio gordo; FIG. *(success)* tener gran éxito *o* suerte.

jack rabbit s. ZOOL. liebre norteamericana.

jack·screw (jăk′skroo′) s. MEC. gato *o* cric de tornillo *m*.

jack·straw (jăk′strô′) s. pajita ♦ **jackstraws** juego de las pajitas.

jack-tar *o* **Jack-tar** (jăk′tär′) s. marinero.

Jac·o·be·an (jăk′ə-bē′ən) HIST. I. adj. jacobino, de la época de Jacobo I (de Inglaterra) II. s. personaje de la época de Jacobo I *m*.

Jac·o·bin (jăk′ə-bĭn) s. HIST. jacobino; POL. *(radical)* jacobino, extremista *mf*.

Jac·o·bite (jăk′ə-bīt′) s. HIST. jacobita (partidario de Jacobo II *o* de los Estuardos) *mf*.

jade¹ (jād) s. MIN. jade *m*; *(color)* verde jade *m*.

jade² (jād) I. s. *(horse)* jamelgo, rocín *m*; *(disreputable woman)* mujerzuela II. tr. **jad·ed, jad·ing** agotar, extenuar —intr. cansarse, fatigarse.

jad·ed (jā′dĭd) adj. *(wearied)* cansado, agotado; *(sated)* harto, saciado; *(bitter)* amargado.

jag¹ (jăg) I. s. *(sharp point)* punta saliente; *(barb)* púa II. tr. **jag·ged, jag·ging** *(to notch)* dentar, mellar; *(to cut unevenly)* cortar desigualmente.

jag² (jăg) s. FAM. juerga ♦ **to go on a j.** ir de juerga • **to have a j. on** estar borracho.

jag·ged (jăg′ĭd) adj. *(notched)* dentado, mellado; *(uneven)* cortado irregularmente.

jag·ged·ness (jăg′ĭd-nĭs) s. melladura.

jag·uar (jăg′wär′) s. ZOOL. jaguar *m*.

jai a·lai (hī′ lī′, hī′ ə-lī′) s. DEP. jai alai *m*, pelota vasca.

jail (jāl) I. s. cárcel *f*, prisión *f* II. tr. encarcelar.

jail·bird (jāl′bûrd′) s. FAM. presidiario, preso.

jail·break (jāl′brāk′) s. escape *o* fuga de una prisión.

jail·er *o* **jail·lor** (jā′lər) s. carcelero.

jal·ap (jăl′əp) s. BOT., FARM. jalapa.

ja·lop·y (jə-lŏp′ē) s. [pl. **-ies**] FAM. cacharro, armatoste (vehículo destartalado) *m*.

ja·lou·sie (jăl′ə-sē) s. ARQ. celosía.

---

jam¹ (jăm) I. tr. **jammed, jam·ming** *(to cause to lock)* trabar, atascar; *(to fill to excess)* atestar, llenar por completo <people jammed the theater la gente llenó por completo el teatro>; *(to clog)* atorar, atascar; RAD. causar interferencias en ♦ **to be jammed with** estar atestado *o* atiborrado de • **to j. (something) in** apretar, forzar <he jammed the cork in the bottle forzó el corcho en la botella> • **to j. on the brakes** frenar en seco • **to j. one's finger in a door** pillarse el dedo en una puerta —intr. *(to become locked)* atascarse, trabarse; *(a firearm)* encasquillarse; *(brakes)* agarrotarse; MÚS. improvisar II. s. *(blockage)* atasco, atoramiento; *(congestion)* apiñamiento ♦ **to be in a j.** FAM. estar en un apuro *o* un aprieto • **traffic j.** embotellamiento del tráfico.

jam² (jăm) s. CUL. mermelada.

Ja·mai·ca s. Jamaica.

Ja·mai·can s. & adj. jamaiquino, jamaicano.

jamb (jăm) s. ARQ. jamba.

jam·bo·ree (jăm′bə-rē′) s. *(of Boy Scouts)* reunión internacional de niños exploradores *f*; FAM. *(good time)* francachela, juerga.

James (jāmz) s. BÍBL. Jaime, Jacobo.

jam·ming s. *(blockage)* atascamiento, atasco; RAD. interferencia.

jam ses·sion s. MÚS. sesión de jazz improvisado *f*.

jan·gle (jăng′gəl) I. intr. **jan·gled, jan·gling** *(to sound harshly)* sonar de modo discordante; *(said of bells)* cencerrear —tr. hacer sonar de modo discordante ♦ **to j. one's nerves** irritar *o* exacerbar a uno II. s. *(harsh metallic sound)* sonido discordante; *(of bells)* cencerreo.

jan·is·sar·y (jăn′ĭ-sĕr′ē) s. [pl. **-ies**] HIST. jenízaro (soldado turco).

jan·i·tor (jăn′ĭ-tər) s. *(cleaning man)* empleado de limpieza; *(doorman)* portero.

Jan·sen·ism (jăn′sə-nĭz′əm) s. TEO. jansenismo.

Jan·u·ar·y (jăn′yōō-ĕr′ē) s. [pl. **-ies**] enero.

Jap (jăp) s. JER., DESPEC. japonés *m*.

ja·pan (jə-păn′) s. laca *o* charol japonés *m*.

Ja·pan (jə-păn′) s. Japón *m*.

Jap·a·nese (jăp′ə-nēz′) adj. & s. [pl. **Japanese**] *(inhabitant, language)* japonés *m* ♦ **the J.** los japoneses.

jape (jāp) I. tr. **japed, jap·ing** burlarse de, mofarse de —intr. burlarse, bromear II. s. burla, broma.

Ja·pon·i·ca (jə-pŏn′ĭ-kə) s. BOT. *(fruit)* membrillo japonés; *(camellia)* camelia japonesa.

jar¹ (jär) s. *(jug)* jarra (recipiente y contenido); *(jam pot)* tarro, pote *m*.

jar² (jär) I. intr. **jarred, jar·ring** *(to make a harsh sound)* chirriar <the brakes jarred as the car stopped los frenos chi­rriaron al parar el carro>; *(to shake)* vibrar, sacudirse ♦ **to j. on one's nerves** ponerle a uno los nervios de punta • **to j. with** divergir, no concordar con —tr. *(to shake)* sacudir <the blast jarred the whole house la explosión sacudió la casa entera>; *(to startle)* estremecer <the news jarred him la noticia le estremeció> ♦ **to j. one's nerves** irritar II. s. *(jolt)* choque *m*, sacudida; *(shock)* choque; *(harsh sound)* estridor *m*, sonido estridente.

jar·di·niere (jär′dn-îr′, zhär′də-nyâr′) s. *(stand)* jardinera; *(pot)* jarrón *m*.

jar·ful s. jarra, pote (el contenido) *m*.

jar·gon (jär′gən) s. *(gibberish)* jerigonza, galimatías *m*; *(specialized language)* jerga.

jas·mine (jăz′mĭn) s. BOT. jazmín *m*; *(color)* amarillo (de claro a brillante).

jas·per (jăs′pər) s. MIN. jaspe *m*.

ja·to (jā′tō) s. AER. despegue con ayuda de cohetes *m*.

jaun·dice (jôn′dĭs) s. MED. ictericia.

jaun·diced (jôn′dĭst, jän′-) adj. MED. ictérico; *(yellowish)* amarillo, cetrino; FIG. *(envious)* envidioso; *(bitter)* amargado, rencoroso.

jaunt (jônt) I. s. paseo, excursión *f* II. intr. ir de paseo *o* de excursión.

jaun·ti·ness s. *(confidence)* desenvoltura; *(elegance)* elegancia, garbo.

jaunt·y (jôn′tē) adj. **-ti·er, -ti·est** *(self-confident)* desenvuelto, confiado; *(stylish)* elegante, apuesto.

Ja·va (jăv′ə, jä′və) s. Java.

Jav·a·nese (jăv′ə-nēz′) adj. & s. [pl. **Javanese**] *(inhabitant, language)* javanés *m* ♦ **the J.** los javaneses.

jave·lin (jăv′lən) s. jabalina ♦ **j. throw** lanzamiento de la jabalina.

jaw (jô) I. s. ANAT. mandíbula, quijada; JER. *(back talk)* réplica insolente; *(chatter)* cháchara; MEC. *(of a wrench, pliers)* mandíbula, mordaza ♦ **jaws** fauces • **the jaws of death** las garras de la muerte II. intr. JER. hablar por los codos, parlotear.

jaw·bone (jô′bōn′) s. ANAT., ZOOL. mandíbula.

jaw·break·er (jô′brā′kər) s. *(hard candy)* caramelo duro; JER. *(tongue twister)* trabalenguas *m*.

jay (jā) s. ORNIT. arrendajo; FIG. *(chatterbox)* cotorra, parlanchín *m*; JER. *(fool)* tonto, necio.

jay·walk (jā′wôk′) intr. cruzar la calle sin prudencia.

jay·walk·er s. peatón imprudente *m*.

jazz (jăz) I. s. MÚS. jazz *m*; JER. palabrería, cuentos ♦ **all that j.** FAM. la mar de cosas II. tr. *(to play)* tocar al estilo del jazz; JER. *(to exaggerate)* camelear, engañar ♦ **to j. up** FAM. avivar, animar.

jaz·zy (jăz′ē) adj. **-i·er, -i·est** MÚS. de jazz, sincopado; JER. *(showy)* chillón, llamativo.

jea·lous (jĕl′əs) adj. celoso <a j. wife una esposa celosa>; *(envious)* envidioso; *(vigilant)* celoso, escrupuloso; *(apprehensive)* receloso, aprensivo ♦ **to be j. of** tener celos de, estar celoso de.

jeal·ous·y (jĕl′ə-sē) s. [pl. **-ies**] *(fear of loss)* celos *m*; *(envy)* envidia; *(apprehension)* aprensión *f*, recelo.

jeans (jēns) s. pantalones vaqueros *m*.

Jeep (jēp) s. jeep (marca registrada) *m*.

jeer (jîr) I. intr. *(to mock)* mofarse, burlarse; *(to boo)* abuchear —tr. *(to abuse)* insultar; *(to taunt)* provocar ♦ **to j. at** burlarse *o* mofarse de II. s. *(mockery)* mofa, burla; *(boo)* rechifla, abucheo.

jeer·ing I. adj. burlón, sarcástico II. s. *(booing)* abucheo; *(taunt)* mofa, burla.

Je·ho·vah (jĭ-hō′və) s. Jehová *m*.

Jehovah's Witnesses s. RELIG. Testigos de Jehová.

je·june (jĭ-jōōn′) adj. *(insubstantial)* poco alimenticio; *(uninteresting)* aburrido, insípido; *(immature)* inmaduro, pueril.

je·ju·num (jĭ-jōō′nəm) s. [pl. **-na**] ANAT. yeyuno.

jell (jĕl) I. intr. & tr. *(to congeal)* coagular(se), cuajar(se); FAM. *(to crystallize)* cristalizar(se), formar(se) (idea, opinión).

jel·ly (jĕl′ē) I. s. [pl. **-ies**] jalea II. tr. **-lied, -ly·ing** convertir en jalea —intr. convertirse en jalea, cuajarse.

jelly bean s. caramelo de gelatina azucarada, confite de goma *m*.

jel·ly·fish (jĕl′ē-fĭsh′) s. [pl. **-fish** *o* **-fish·es**] ICT. medusa, aguamar *f*.

jen·net (jĕn′ĭt) s. jaca, jumenta.

jen·ny (jĕn′ē) s. [pl. **-nies**] *(female donkey)* asna, burra; *(female wren)* hembra del reyezuelo; *(spinning machine)* máquina de hilar.

jeop·ard·ize (jĕp′ər-dīz′) tr. **-ized, -iz·ing** arriesgar, poner en peligro.

jeop·ard·y (jĕp′ər-dē) s. riesgo, peligro.

jer·e·mi·ad (jĕr′ə-mī′əd) s. jeremíada, lamentación *f*.

Jer·e·mi·ah (jĕr′ə-mī′ə) s. BÍBL. Jeremías *m*.

Jer·i·cho s. Jericó.

jerk¹ (jûrk) I. tr. *(to yank)* dar un tirón a, tironear de; *(to throw)* tirar bruscamente ♦ **to j. something out** decir a trompicones —intr. *(to jolt)* moverse a sacudones; *(to twitch)* moverse espasmódicamente <his legs jerked from fatigue sus piernas se movían espasmódicamente de can­sancio> ♦ **to j. off** VULG. hacerse la paja II. s. *(yank)* tirón *m*, sacudida; *(spasmodic movement)* espasmo; FAM. *(idiot)* idiota *mf*, estúpido.

jerk² (jûrk) tr. CUL. tasajear, charquear.

jer·kin (jûr′kĭn) s. justillo, jubón *m*.

jerk·water (jûrk′wô′tər) adj. FAM. *(remote)* remoto e insignificante (dic. de pueblo); *(trivial)* trivial.

jerk·y¹ (jûr′kē) adj. **-ier, -iest** *(spasmodic)* espasmódico; *(uneven)* desigual; *(said of a vehicle)* que traquetea.

jerk·y² (jûr′kē) s. CUL. tasajo, charqui *m*.

ā rey / ä año / b boca / ch chico / d dar / ĕ el / ē mil / g gato / h joya / hw juez / ī aire / k casa / kw cuan /

jer·ry·build (jĕr'ē-bĭld') tr. **-built, -build·ing** construir o fabricar rápidamente y con mala calidad.

jer·sey (jûr'zē) s. [pl. **-eys**] *(fabric)* tejido de jersey, tejido elástico; *(garment)* chaqueta de punto (de jersey) ♦ **J.** Jersey (raza de ganado).

Je·ru·sa·lem (jə-rōō'sə-ləm) s. Jerusalén.

Jerusalem artichoke raíz comestible de girasol f.

jess (jĕs) **I.** s. pihuela (que se ajusta a la pata del halcón) **II.** tr. colocar pihuelas a.

jes·sa·mine (jĕs'ə-mĭn) s. var. de **jasmine.**

jest (jĕst) **I.** s. *(joke)* chiste m, broma; *(mockery)* burla, mofa; *(laughingstock)* hazmerreír m ♦ **in j.** en broma **II.** intr. *(to joke)* bromear, chancear; *(to scoff)* mofarse, burlarse —tr. ridiculizar a, burlarse de.

jes·ter (jĕs'tər) s. bufón m, bromista mf.

Jes·u·it (jĕzh'ōō-ĭt) s. jesuita m.

Je·sus (jē'zəs) s. Jesús.

Je·sus Christ (jē'zəs krĭst) s. Jesucristo.

jet¹ (jĕt) **I.** s. MIN. azabache m; *(color)* color azabache m, negro lustroso **II.** adj. de color azabache, azabachado.

jet² (jĕt) **I.** s. *(stream of liquid)* chorro; *(nozzle)* boca, boquilla; *(airplane)* jet m, avión a reacción m; *(engine)* reactor m, motor de reacción m **II.** intr. **jet·ted, jet·ting** *(to fly)* volar en jet; *(to spurt)* salir a chorro —tr. lanzar o arrojar en chorro.

jet en·gine (jĕt ĕn'jĭn) s. motor de reacción m, motor a chorro m.

jet fight·er (jĕt fī'tər) s. avión de caza a reacción m.

jet lag s. AER. cansancio causado por la diferencia de horario entre diferentes zonas.

jet·lin·er (jĕt lī'nər) s. avión de pasajeros a reacción m.

jet plane (jĕt plān) s. avión de propulsión a chorro o reacción m.

jet-pro·pelled (jĕt'prə-pĕld') adj. propulsado por motor a chorro o a reacción.

jet pro·pul·sion (jĕt prə-pŭl'shən) s. propulsión a chorro f, propulsión a reacción.

jet·sam (jĕt'səm) s. MARÍT. echazón f; FIG. *(odds and ends)* cosa desechada por inútil.

jet·ti·son (jĕt'ĭ-sən) **I.** tr. MARÍT. *(to cast off)* echar al mar; FIG. *(to discard)* descartar, desechar **II.** s. echazón f.

jet·ty (jĕt'ē) s. [pl. **-ties**] *(breakwater)* escollera, malecón m; *(wharf)* muelle m.

Jew (jōō) s. judío.

jew·el (jōō'əl) **I.** s. *(gem)* gema, piedra preciosa; *(ornament)* joya, alhaja; *(in watches)* rubí m; FIG. *(treasure)* joya (persona, cosa) **II.** tr. enjoyar, alhajar <*jeweled comb* peine alhajado>.

jew·el·er o **jew·el·ler** (jōō'ə-lər) s. joyero ♦ **jeweler's** joyería.

jew·el·ry (jōō'əl-rē) s. joyas, alhajas.

Jew·ess (jōō'ĭs) s. judía.

jew·fish (jōō'fĭsh') s. [pl. **jewfish** o **-fish·es**] ICT. cherna, mero.

Jew·ish (jōō'ĭsh) adj. judío.

Jew·ry (jōō'rē) s. *(people)* pueblo judío; HIST. *(district)* judería.

jew's-harp o **jews-harp** (jōōz'härp') s. MÚS. birimbao.

Jez·e·bel (jĕz'ə-bĕl') s. BÍBL. Jezabel ♦ **j.** mujer intrigante f.

jib¹ (jĭb) s. MARÍT. foque m; MEC. aguilón m, pescante (de grúa) m.

jib² (jĭb) intr. **jibbed, jib·bing** *(horse)* plantarse o resistirse; *(person)* resistirse.

jib boom (jĭb bōōm) s. MARÍT. botalón de foque m.

jibe¹ (jĭb) intr. **jibed, jib·ing** FAM. concordar, estar de acuerdo.

jibe² (jĭb) v. & s. var. de **gibe.**

jif·fy (jĭf'ē) o **jiff** (jĭf) s. FAM. instante m, santiamén m <*in a j.* en un santiamén>.

jig (jĭg) **I.** s. *(dance, music)* giga; *(hook)* anzuelo de cuchara; MEC. patrón m, guía; MIN. criba ♦ **the j. is up** JER. se acabó la fiesta **II.** intr. **jigged, jig·ging** *(to dance)* bailar la giga; *(to bob)* andar a saltitos; MEC. trabajar con una guía o patrón.

jig·ger¹ (jĭg'ər) s. *(dancer)* bailador de giga m; *(measure)* medida para licores; *(gadget)* chuchería, chisme m; MEC. taladro; MARÍT. aparejuelo.

jig·ger² (jĭg'ər) s. ENTOM. nigua.

jig·gle (jĭg'əl) **I.** tr. & intr. **-gled, -gling** zangolotear(se), menear(se) **II.** s. zangoloteo, meneo.

jig·saw (jĭg'sô') s. TEC. sierra caladora, sierra de vaivén.

jig·saw puz·zle (jĭg'sô' pŭz'əl) s. rompecabezas m.

jilt (jĭlt) **I.** tr. dejar plantado, dar calabazas **II.** s. mujer que rechaza a un pretendiente f.

Jim Crow o **jim crow** (jĭm' krō') s. EE. UU., HIST. práctica sistemática de segregación racial.

jim-jams (jĭm'jămz') s.pl. JER. *(jitters)* nerviosismo, agitación f; *(delirium tremens)* delirium tremens m.

jim·my (jĭm'ē) **I.** s. [pl. **-mies**] ganzúa, palanca **II.** tr. **-mied, -my·ing** forzar con una ganzúa o palanca.

jin·gle (jĭng'gəl) **I.** intr. **-gled, -gling** *(ringing sound)* cascabelear, tintinear; *(rhyming sound)* rimar —tr. hacer tintinear **II.** s. *(ringing sound)* cascabeleo, tintineo; RAD., TELEV. anuncio rimado y cantado.

jin·go (jĭng'gō) s. [pl. **-goes**] jingoísta mf, patriotero ♦ **by j.** ¡caramba! **II.** adj. jingoísta, patriotero.

jin·go·ism (jĭng'gō-ĭz'əm) s. jingoísmo, patriotería.

jin·go·istic adj. jingoísta.

jinks (jĭngks) s.pl. ♦ **high j.** *(rambunctious play)* jolgorio, juerga; *(mischief)* jugarreta, travesura.

jinx (jĭngks) FAM. **I.** s. *(person, object)* gafe m, cenizo (que trae mala suerte); *(condition)* mal de ojo m, mala suerte **II.** tr. traer mala suerte a.

jit·ney (jĭt'nē) s. [pl. **-neys**] FAM. colectivo, ómnibus m.

jit·ter (jĭt'ər) **I.** intr. temblar (de miedo, nervios) **II.** s. ♦ **jitters** *(nerves)* nerviosismo; *(agitation)* agitación f ♦ **to give someone the jitters** poner nervioso a alguien • **to have the jitters** estar nervioso.

jit·ter·bug (jĭt'ər-bŭg') s. baile popular de los años cuarenta m.

jit·ter·y (jĭt'ə-rē) adj. **-i·er, -i·est** FAM. *(nervous)* nervioso, agitado; *(trembling)* tembloroso, trémulo.

jive (jīv) JER. **I.** s. MÚS. ritmo sincopado, jazz m; *(jazz jargon)* jerga de los músicos de jazz; *(empty talk)* cháchara **II.** intr. **jived, jiv·ing** MÚS. tocar o bailar música de jazz; *(to kid)* bromear —tr. engatusar, embaucar.

job (jŏb) **I.** s. *(task)* tarea, quehacer m; *(work)* obra, trabajo; *(employment)* trabajo, empleo <*to look for a j.* buscar un empleo>; *(responsibility)* deber m, responsabilidad f <*it's her j. to wash the car* su responsabilidad es lavar el coche>; JER. *(robbery)* atraco, golpe m ♦ **bad j.** FAM. cosa inútil, fracaso <*their marriage turned out to be a bad j.* su matrimonio resultó un fracaso> • **odd jobs** chapuzas, trabajos de poca monta • **on the j.** FAM. en su puesto <*the police are always on the j.* la policía siempre está en su puesto> • **to be out of a j.** estar sin trabajo • **to do a j. on** FAM. dañar, arruinar <*he really did a j. on my hair!* ¡él realmente me arruinó el pelo!> **II.** intr. **jobbed, job·bing** *(to work at odd jobs)* trabajar en chapuzas; *(to do piecework)* trabajar a destajo; *(to work as a middleman)* trabajar como corredor o intermediario —tr. *(to buy, sell)* comprar y vender como intermediario; *(to subcontract)* dar trabajo a destajo.

Job (jŏb) BÍBL. Job m.

job action s. huelga o paro laboral.

job·ber (jŏb'ər) s. COM. *(middleman)* intermediario; *(pieceworker)* trabajador a destajo m.

job·hold·er (jŏb'hōl'dər) s. persona que tiene un trabajo fijo, empleado.

job·less (jŏb'lĭs) adj. sin trabajo.

job lot (jŏb lŏt) s. COM. *(miscellaneous goods)* mercancías variadas que se venden por lote; *(cheap goods)* lote de mercancías baratas.

job print·er (jŏb prĭn'tər) s. IMPR. impresor (de circulares, tarjetas) m.

jock·ey (jŏk'ē) **I.** s. [pl. **-eys**] jockey mf, jinete (de carreras) mf **II.** tr. **-eyed, -ey·ing** *(to ride)* montar (un caballo); *(to maneuver)* maniobrar <*he jockeyed the car into a tight space* maniobró el coche en un pequeño espacio>; *(to trick)* embaucar, engañar —intr. *(to race)* montar caballos (en carreras); *(to manipulate)* manipular.

jock·strap *o* **jock strap** (jŏk străp) s. DEP. suspensorio, suspensor *m*.

jo·cose (jō-kōs′) adj. jocoso, divertido.

joc·u·lar (jŏk′yə-lər) adj. jocoso, humorístico.

joc·u·lar·i·ty (jŏk′yə-lăr′ĭ-tē) s. jocosidad *f*, humor *m*.

joc·und (jŏk′ənd) adj. jocundo, jovial.

joc·und·i·ty (jō-kŭn′dĭ-tē) s. jocundidad *f*, jovialidad *f*.

jodh·purs (jŏd′pərz) s.pl. pantalones de montar *m*.

jog (jŏg) I. tr. **jogged, jog·ging** (*to push lightly*) empujar levemente; (*to nudge*) dar un codazo a; (*the memory*) refrescar, estimular —intr. (*to trot slowly*) cabalgar a trote corto; (*to run*) correr despacio; (*to proceed leisurely*) avanzar pausadamente II. s. (*slight push*) empujoncito, sacudida ligera; (*nudge*) codazo; (*slow pace*) paso lento.

jog·ger (jŏg′ər) s. persona que corre despacio para hacer ejercicio.

jog·gle (jŏg′əl) I. tr. **-gled, -gling** mover *o* sacudir ligeramente, traquetear —intr. moverse con sacudidas II. s. sacudida, traqueteo.

john (jŏn) s. JER. (*toilet*) retrete *m*, excusado; (*customer*) cliente (de una prostituta) *m*.

John (jŏn) s. BÍBL. Juan.

John Bull (jŏn bool′) s. FIG. (*England*) Inglaterra; (*the English*) los ingleses; (*an Englishman*) el inglés típico.

John Doe (jŏn dō′) s. DER. (*unidentified person*) Fulano de Tal, Juan Pérez; FAM. (*average man*) la persona típica *o* corriente.

John Han·cock (jŏn hăn′kok′) s. FAM. firma (de una persona).

join (join) I. tr. (*to unite*) juntar, unir; (*forces*) aunar; (*in marriage*) unir <*to j. two persons in marriage* unir a dos personas en matrimonio>; (*parcels of land*) lindar con; (*a cause*) abrazar; (*political party*) afiliarse a; (*church, club*) hacerse socio de; (*business firm*) entrar en, ingresar en; (*road, river*) dar *o* empalmar con; (*people*) encontrarse *o* reunirse con <*we'll j. you after lunch* nos encontraremos con ustedes después del almuerzo>; MIL. alistarse en; MAT. unir ♦ **to j. forces with** aliarse con ♦ **to j. hands** FIG. darse las manos, ayudarse mutuamente ♦ **to j. together** juntar —intr. (*to become united*) juntarse, unirse; (*in marriage*) unirse; (*roads*) empalmar, unirse; (*rivers*) confluir; (*lines*) empalmar ♦ **to j. in** tomar parte en, participar en ♦ **to j. up** MIL. alistarse ♦ **to j. up with** encontrarse *o* reunirse con II. s. juntura, unión *f*.

join·er (joi′nər) s. (*participant*) persona que se une a grupos *o* causas; G.B. (*carpenter*) ebanista *m*.

joint (joint) I. s. (*joining*) junta, unión *f*; (*brace*) abrazadera; (*hinge*) bisagra; ANAT. coyuntura, articulación *f*; BOT. nudo; GEOL. grieta de roca; CUL. corte para asar *m*; JER. (*marijuana*) cigarrillo de marihuana; (*sleazy place*) tugurio ♦ **out of j.** (*bone*) dislocado; (*disordered*) en desorden; (*out of sorts*) de mal humor II. adj. (*shared*) común, en común <*j. ownership* propiedad en común>; (*collective*) colectivo, mutuo <*a j. effort* un esfuerzo mutuo> III. tr. juntar, ensamblar.

joint·ed adj. (*articulated*) articulado; BOT. (*knotted*) nudoso.

joint·ly (joint′lē) adv. (*together*) conjuntamente, en conjunto; (*in common*) en común.

joint-stock company (joint′stŏk′) s. COM. sociedad anónima.

joist (joist) ARQ. I. s. vigueta, viga II. tr. proveer de viguetas *o* vigas a.

joke (jōk) I. s. (*funny story*) chiste *m*; (*amusing remark*) gracia <*not to get the j.* no verle la gracia>; (*prank*) broma, chanza <*he can't take a j.* él no sabe tomar una broma>; (*laughingstock*) hazmerreír *m* ♦ **as a j.** en broma • **off-color** *o* **dirty j.** chiste verde • **practical j.** broma pesada • **to crack a j.** decir un chiste • **to make a j. of everything** tomar todo en broma • **to play a j. on someone** hacerle una broma a alguien II. intr. **joked, jok·ing** contar chistes, bromear ♦ **joking apart** hablando en serio, fuera de bromas • **to j. around** estar de broma, bromear • **you must be joking** tú estás bromeando —tr. embromar, gastar bromas.

jok·er (jō′kər) s. (*funny person*) bromista *mf*; (*cards*) como-

dín *m*; FAM. (*clause*) cláusula (astutamente incluida en un documento); (*wise guy*) tío, sujeto.

jok·ing·ly adv. en broma.

jol·li·ty (jŏl′ĭ-tē) s. regocijo, alegría.

jol·ly (jŏl′ē) I. adj. **-lier, -li·est** (*fun-loving*) alegre, jovial; (*enjoyable*) agradable, placentero; G.B. (*very*) muy <*she is a j. good cook* ella es una muy buena cocinera> II. intr. **-lied, -ly·ing** burlarse, hacer burla —tr. mantener el humor III. s. [pl. **-lies**] G.B. jarana, fiesta.

jol·ly-boat (jŏl′ē-bōt′) s. MARÍT. bote auxiliar *m*, esquife *m*.

Jolly Rog·er (rŏj′ər) s. MARÍT. bandera pirata.

jolt (jōlt) I. tr. (*to bump into*) dar un empujón *o* sacudida a; (*to shake*) sacudir; FIG. (*to shock*) sobresaltar, alarmar <*the news jolted us* la noticia nos sobresaltó> —intr. sacudirse, traquetear II. s. (*jerk*) sacudida, empujón *m*; FIG. (*shock*) choque *m*, susto.

jolt·ing s. AUTO. traqueteo.

Jonah (jō′nə) s. BÍBL. Jonás.

jon·quil (jŏng′kwĭl) s. BOT. junquillo.

Jor·dan (jôr′dn) s. (*country*) Jordania; (*river*) Jordán *m*.

jordan almond s. (*nut*) almendra española (usada en pastelería); (*candy*) almendra confitada.

Jor·da·ni·an adj. & s. jordano.

josh (jŏsh) tr. bromear, dar broma —intr. estar de broma, bromear.

Josh·u·a (jŏsh′ōō-ə) s. BÍBL. Josué.

joss (jŏs) s. RELIG. (*idol*) ídolo chino; (*image*) imagen china.

jos·tle (jŏs′əl) I. intr. & tr. **-tled, -tling** (*to shove*) empujar, dar empellones; (*to elbow*) codear, dar codazos II. s. empujón *m*, empellón *m*.

jot (jŏt) I. s. pizca, ápice *m* II. tr. **jot·ted, jot·ting** ♦ **to j. down** anotar, apuntar.

joule (jōōl, joul) s. FÍS. julio (unidad).

jounce (jouns) I. intr. **jounced, jounc·ing** dar tumbos (al viajar en un vehículo), sacudirse —tr. sacudir, traquetear II. s. tumbo, sacudimiento.

jour·nal (jûr′nəl) s. (*diary*) diario (personal); (*official record*) acta, diario de debates; (*in bookkeeping*) diario, libro diario; (*newspaper*) diario, periódico; (*periodical*) revista, boletín <*New England J. of Medicine* el Boletín Médico de New England>; MEC. muñón *m*.

jour·nal·ese (jûr′nə-lēz′) s. estilo periodístico.

jour·nal·ism (jûr′nə-liz′əm) s. periodismo.

jour·nal·ist (jûr′nə-lĭst) s. periodista *mf*, cronista *mf*.

jour·nal·istic (jûr′nə-lĭs′tĭk) adj. periodístico.

jour·nal·ize (jûr′nə-līz′) tr. **-ized, -iz·ing** (*in bookkeeping*) pasar al diario (en contabilidad) —intr. escribir *o* anotar en un diario.

jour·ney (jûr′nē) I. s. [pl. **-neys**] (*travel*) viaje *m*; (*distance*) jornada, día de viaje *m* II. intr. viajar —tr. recorrer.

jour·ney·man (jûr′nē-mən) s. [pl. **-men**] oficial *m*, obrero competente.

joust (joust, jŭst, jōōst) I. s. (*combat*) justa; DEP. (*tournament*) torneo; FIG. (*competition*) combate *m* II. intr. justar, tornear.

Jove (jōv) s. MITOL. Júpiter *m* ♦ **by J.** ¡por Júpiter!, ¡por Dios!

jo·vi·al (jō′vē-əl) adj. jovial, alegre.

jo·vi·al·i·ty s. jovialidad *f*, alegría.

jowl (joul) s. (*jaw*) quijada, mandíbula; (*cheek*) mejilla; (*double chin*) papada.

joy (joi) I. s. (*cheerfulness*) alegría, júbilo; (*delight*) regocijo, motivo de alegría <*the child is a great j. to his parents* el niño es un motivo de gran alegría para sus padres> ♦ **to jump for j.** saltar de alegría II. intr. alegrarse, regocijarse.

joy·ful (joi′fəl) adj. (*full of joy*) jubiloso, gozoso; (*expressing joy*) alegre, contento.

joy·less (joi′lĭs) adj. sin alegría.

joy·less·ness s. tristeza, abatimiento.

joy·ous (joi′əs) adj. alegre, gozoso.

joy·ous·ness s. alegría, regocijo.

joy·ride (joi′rīd′) s. FAM. paseo alocado en coche (esp. sin permiso del dueño).

joy·stick *o* **joy stick** (joi′stĭk′) s. JER. palanca de mando (esp. de un avión).

---

ju·bi·lance s. júbilo, alborozo.
ju·bi·lant (jōo′bə-lənt) adj. jubiloso, alborozado.
ju·bi·la·tion (jōo′bə-lā′shən) s. *(feeling)* júbilo, exultación *f*; *(manifestation)* regocijo, alborozo.
ju·bi·lee (jōo′bə-lē′) s. *(fiftieth anniversary)* quincuagésimo aniversario; *(celebration)* celebración *f*; *(jubilation)* júbilo, gozo; RELIG. jubileo ♦ **J.** BÍBL. jubileo.
Ju·dae·a (jōo-dē′ə, -dā′ə) s. var. de **Judea.**
Ju·da·ic (jōo-dā′ĭk) o **Ju·da·i·cal** (-ĭ-kəl) adj. judaico.
Ju·da·ism (jōo′dē-ĭz′əm) s. judaísmo.
Ju·da·ize (jōo′dē-īz′) tr. **-ized, iz·ing** judaizar, convertir al judaísmo —intr. adoptar el judaísmo.
Ju·das (jōo′dəs) s. BÍBL. Judas; FIG. *(traitor)* traidor *m*.
Judas tree (jōo′dəs trē) s. BOT. ciclamor *m*, algarrobo loco.
Jude (jōod) s. BÍBL. Judas.
Ju·de·a (jōo-dē′ə, -dā′ə) s. GEOG., HIST. Judea.
Ju·de·o-Chris·tian (jōo-dā′ō-krĭs′chən) adj. & s. judeocristiano.
judge (jŭj) I. tr. **judged, judg·ing** *(to try)* juzgar; *(to determine)* determinar, evaluar; *(to declare)* declarar <*they judged her innocent* la declararon inocente>; FAM. *(to assess)* juzgar, evaluar; *(to regard)* considerar <*I j. him a fool* lo considero un tonto> —intr. *(to decide)* juzgar, decidir (como un juez); *(to form an opinion)* juzgar, estimar ♦ **judging from** *o* **by** a juzgar por **II.** s. *(in a court of law)* juez *m*; *(in a contest)* juez, árbitro; *(expert)* experto ♦ **Judges** BÍBL. Jueces.
judge·ment s. var. de **judgment.**
judge·ship (jŭj′shĭp′) s. magistratura, juzgado.
judg·ment (jŭj′mənt) s. *(good sense)* juicio, discernimiento; *(opinion)* juicio, opinión *f*; *(ruling)* opinión, dictamen *m*; *(estimate)* cálculo aproximado <*make a j. of the distance* haga un cálculo aproximado de la distancia>; DER. *(judicial decisión)* decisión *f*, fallo; *(court act)* resolución *f*, disposición *f*; *(writ)* orden judicial *f*, mandato jurídico ♦ **the J.** TEO. el juicio final.
Judgment Day s. RELIG. día del juicio final *m*.
ju·di·ca·ture (jōo′dĭ-kə-chōor′) s. DER. judicatura.
ju·di·cial (jōo-dĭsh′əl) adj. DER. judicial; *(critical)* crítico.
ju·di·cial·ly adv. judicialmente.
ju·di·ci·ar·y (jōo-dĭsh′ē-ĕr′ē) I. adj. judicial, judiciario II. s. [pl. **-aries**] *(the judicial branch)* el poder judicial *m*; *(judicature)* judicatura, los jueces.
ju·di·cious (jōo-dĭsh′əs) adj. sensato, juicioso.
Judith (jōo′dĭth) s. BÍBL. Judit.
ju·do (jōo′dō) s. DEP. judo.
jug (jŭg) I. s. *(jar)* jarra, cántaro (recipiente y contenido); JER. cárcel *f*, chirona II. tr. **jug·ged, jug·ging** *(to stew)* estofar en un recipiente de barro; JER. *(to jail)* encarcelar, meter en chirona.
jug·ger·naut (jŭg′ər-nôt′) s. fuerza irresistible.
jug·gle (jŭg′əl) I. tr. **-gled, -gling** *(to do tricks with)* hacer malabares con; *(to manipulate)* hacer trampas con —intr. *(to do tricks)* hacer juego de manos; *(to use trickery)* hacer trampas II. s. *(act)* juegos malabares; *(trick)* truco, ardid *m*.
jug·gler (jŭg′lər) s. *(performer)* malabarista *mf*; *(deceiver)* maquinador *m*.
Ju·go·sla·vi·a (yōo′gō-slä′vē-ə) var. de **Yugoslavia.**
jug·u·lar (jŭg′yə-lər) adj. & s. ANAT. yugular *f* ♦ **j. vein** vena yugular.
juice (jōos) I. s. *(fluid)* jugo; *(of fruits, vegetables)* zumo, jugo; *(of meat)* jugo; FISIOL. jugo <*gastric juices* jugos gástricos>; JER. *(energy)* poder *m* <*I have to get my creative juices going* tengo que poner a trabajar mis poderes creativos>; *(electricity)* electricidad *f*; *(fuel)* gasolina II. tr. **juiced, juic·ing** exprimir ♦ **to j. up** FAM. animar, vigorizar.
juic·i·ness s. jugosidad *f*.
juic·y (jōo′sē) adj. **-i·er, -i·est** *(full of juice)* zumoso, jugoso; *(racy)* picante, sabroso (historia, chisme); *(lucrative)* lucrativo.
ju·jit·su (jōo-jĭt′sōo) s. DEP. jiu-jitsu *m*, lucha japonesa.
ju·jube (jōo′jōob′) s. *(tree)* azufaifo, jinjolero; *(fruit)* azufaifa, jinjol *m*.

juke box (jōok bŏks) s. tocadiscos automático de moneda *m*.
ju·lep (jōo′ləp) s. julepe (medicinal) *m* ♦ **mint j.** julepe de menta (bebida alcohólica).
Ju·lian (jōol′yən) HIST. I. adj. juliano (ref. al período de Julio César) II. s. Juliano (emperador romano).
Ju·ly (jōo-lī′) s. julio.
jum·ble (jŭm′bəl) I. intr. **-bled, -bling** mezclarse —tr. *(to mix)* mezclar; *(to muddle)* embarullar, confundir <*I always j. up their names* yo siempre confundo sus nombres> II. s. *(mess)* revoltijo, embrollo; *(state)* mescolanza, confusión *f*.
jum·bo (jŭm′bō) I. s. [pl. **-bos**] coloso (persona, animal, cosa) II. adj. muy grande, enorme.
jump (jŭmp) I. intr. *(to leap up)* saltar; *(to be startled)* sobresaltarse <*the noise made me j.* el ruido me sobresaltó>; *(to respond quickly)* apresurarse, moverse <*when I give an order I expect you to j.!* ¡cuando te doy una orden espero que te muevas!>; *(to rise)* subir repentinamente, dar un salto (precios, temperatura); *(to skip)* pasar por alto, saltear <*we jumped ten pages* nos saltamos diez páginas>; FAM. *(to get lively)* animarse <*this nightclub jumps after midnight* este club nocturno se anima después de las doce> ♦ **go j. in the lake!** ¡vaya usted a freír espárragos! • **to j. at** *o* **on someone for** echarse encima de alguien por • **to j. at** *(a chance)* aprovechar; *(offer, invitation)* apresurarse a aceptar • **to j. down someone's throat** estallar, ponerse furioso con alguien • **to j. for joy** saltar de alegría • **to j. in** *o* **into** *(a car)* saltar a, subir de un salto; *(water)* saltar a, tirarse a; *(new project)* emprender • **to j. on** subir de un salto a (autobús, tren) • **to j. out of** *(window)* saltar de; *(bed)* saltar *o* salir de; *(bus)* salir de, bajar de un salto • **to j. over** saltar, pasar algo de un salto • **to j. to conclusions** sacar conclusiones precipitadamente • **to j. up** levantarse de un salto —tr. *(to leap over)* saltar, saltar por encima de <*to j. a fence* saltar una cerca>; *(to attack)* agredir, atacar <*muggers jumped him in the park* unos asaltantes lo atacaron en el parque>; *(to increase suddenly)* elevar, aumentar (precios); *(in checkers)* comer; *(in bridge)* elevar ♦ **to j. a horse** saltar con un caballo • **to j. bail** fugarse estando bajo fianza • **to j. ship** FIG. irse, abandonar • **to j. the gun** apresurarse, adelantarse en hacer *o* decir algo • **to j. the tracks** salirse de las vías, descarrilarse II. s. *(leap)* salto, brinco; *(major change)* cambio, salto; *(sudden movement)* sobresalto; *(rise)* aumento, salto (precios, temperatura); *(short trip)* viaje corto; *(checkers)* captura; DEP. valla, obstáculo ♦ **high j.** DEP. salto de altura • **long j.** DEP. salto de longitud • **to get** *o* **have a j. on** llevar *o* tener una ventaja sobre.
jump·er¹ (jŭm′pər) s. *(one that jumps)* saltador *m*, brincador *m*; ELEC. alambre de cierre *m*, cable de empalme *m*.
jump·er² (jŭm′pər) s. *(dress)* vestido sin mangas; *(smock)* jubón suelto.
jump·i·ness s. nerviosismo, nerviosidad *f*.
jumping bean s. frijol brincador *m*.
jumping jack s. *(toy)* títere *m*; *(exercise)* salto en el lugar (con las piernas separadas y las manos tocándose sobre la cabeza, retornando a la posición inicial de piernas juntas y brazos a los costados).
jump·ing-off place (jŭm′pĭng-ôf′, -ŏf′) s. FAM. *(remote spot)* lugar muy remoto; FIG. *(starting point)* punto de partida (de negocio).
jump seat s. AUTO., AVIA. asiento portátil plegadizo, traspuntín *m*; *(in a sports car)* asiento trasero.
jump-start (jŭmp′stärt′) tr. AUTO. hacer arrancar a (un motor) conectándolo con un cable de empalme a la batería de otro motor.
jump suit (jŭmp′sōot′) s. uniforme de paracaidistas *m* ♦ **jumpsuit** mono, traje de faena.
jump·y (jŭm′pē) adj. **-i·er, -i·est** *(jerky)* espasmódico, saltón; *(nervous)* nervioso.
junc·tion (jŭngk′shən) s. *(joint)* juntura, conexión *f*; *(of rivers)* confluencia *f*; *(of railroads)* empalme *m*.
junc·ture (jŭngk′chər) s. juntura, unión *f* ♦ **at this j.** en este momento, en estas circunstancias.
June (jōon) s. junio.

---

jun·gle (jŭng'gəl) s. *(tropical forest)* selva; *(tangle)* maraña; *(maze)* laberinto ♦ **the asphalt j.** FIG. la jungla de asfalto.
jun·ior (jōon'yər) **I.** adj. *(younger)* más joven <*she is two years my j.* ella es dos años más joven que yo>; *(son of)* hijo <*William Jones, Jr.* William Jones, hijo>; *(for young people)* juvenil, para gente joven <*j. dresses* vestidos para gente joven>; *(in rank)* subalterno, nombrado recientemente; *(said of a school)* de penúltimo año; *(lesser)* secundario, inferior **II.** s. *(youngster)* joven *mf*, menor (en edad) *mf*; *(rank)* subordinado; *(student)* estudiante de penúltimo año *mf.*
junior college s. EE. UU., EDUC. colegio universitario (para los dos primeros años de estudios).
ju·ni·per (jōo'nə-pər) s. BOT. enebro común, junípero.
junk¹ (jŭngk) **I.** s. *(scrap)* chatarra, hierro viejo; FAM. *(useless objects)* trastos viejos, cachivaches *m*; JER. *(drug)* heroína; MARÍT. *(dried beef)* cecina; *(rope)* cuerda gastada ♦ **j. mail** FAM. propaganda no solicitada que se recibe por correo **II.** tr. *(to discard)* echar a la basura, desechar; *(to scrap)* reducir a chatarra.
junk² (jŭngk) s. MARÍT. junco (embarcación china).
junk·et (jŭng'kĭt) **I.** s. CUL. crema de leche y cuajo; *(feast)* festín *m*, banquete *m*; *(paid-for trip)* jira, viaje (pagado con fondos públicos) *m* **II.** intr. *(to celebrate)* festejar, agasajar; *(to travel)* ir de jira *o* viaje (pagado con fondos públicos).
junk·ie (jŭng'kē) s. [pl. **-ies**] JER. *(narcotics user)* drogadicto, toxicómano; *(devotee)* adicto <*a sports j.* un adicto a los deportes>.
junk·man (jŭngk'măn') s. [pl. **-men** (-mən)] trapero, chatarrero.
junk·y (jŭng'kē) s. var. de **junkie.**
junk·yard (jŭngk'yärd') s. depósito de chatarra *o* carros viejos.
Ju·no (jōo'nō) s. MITOL. Juno *f.*
jun·ta (hōon'tə) s. POL. junta militar; *(council)* junta, asamblea.
Ju·pi·ter (jōo'pĭ-tər) s. ASTRON., MITOL. Júpiter *m.*
Ju·ras·sic (jōo-răs'ĭk) adj. & s. GEOL. jurásico.
ju·rid·i·cal (jōo-rĭd'ĭ-kəl) *o* **ju·rid·ic** adj. DER. jurídico.
ju·ris·dic·tion (jōor-ĭs-dĭk'shən) s. jurisdicción *f.*
ju·ris·dic·tion·al adj. jurisdiccional.
ju·ris·pru·dence (jōor'ĭs-prōod'ns) s. DER. jurisprudencia.
ju·rist (jōor'ĭst) s. DER. jurista *mf.*
ju·ror (jōor'ər) s. jurado (persona) *mf.*
ju·ry (jōor'ē) s. [pl. **-ries**] jurado, tribunal *m.*
jury box s. DER. tribuna del jurado.
jury duty s. deber cívico de formar parte de un jurado.
jury·man (jōor'ē-măn') s. [pl. **-men** (-mən)] DER. miembro de un jurado.
just (jŭst) **I.** adj. *(fair)* justo; *(equitable)* recto, imparcial; *(righteous)* justo, honrado <*a j. cause* una cause justa>; *(legitimate)* legítimo, justificado <*j. grounds for complaint* motivo justificado de quejas>; *(accurate)* exacto, preciso **II.** adv. *(exactly)* justo, justamente <*it is j. the right amount* es justamente la cantidad correcta>; *(recently)* recién, recientemente <*a book j. published* un libro recién publicado>; *(a moment ago)* recién, hace poco <*I j. saw her* recién la ví>; *(nearby)* no más que, apenas <*they live j. a few bocks from here* viven apenas a unas cuadras de aquí>; *(barely)* por muy poco <*you j. missed the bus* perdiste el ómnibus por muy poco>; *(merely)* simplemente, solamente <*he went j. because his friends were going* fue sólo porque sus amigos iban>; *(really)* verdaderamente, simplemente <*it is j. beautiful* es verdaderamente hermoso>; *(possibly)* posiblemente, quizás <*it j. might work* posiblemente funcione> ♦ **it's j. as well** es igual, da lo mismo • **j. a second!** ¡un momento! • **j. about** *(not quite)* casi <*dinner is j. about ready* la comida está casi lista>; *(positively)* ya <*I'm j. about fed up* ya estoy harto>; *(soon)* pronto <*it's j. about dinnertime* pronto será la hora de cenar> • **j. about to** a punto de <*I was j. about to say it* estaba a punto de decirlo> • **j. as** *(precisely)* lo mismo que, al igual que <*as I told you* lo mismo que yo te dije>; *(in every way)* tal como, tal y como <*j. as I thought!* ¡tal como pensaba!>; *(when)* cuando, al momento que <*he came j. as

I was leaving llegó justo cuando me iba> • **j. as if** *o* **though** lo mismo que si <*it's j. as if he were still alive* es lo mismo que si él estuviera vivo> • **j. in case** por si acaso • **j. in time to** *o* **for** justo a tiempo para • **j. like** *(same as)* como, igual que <*she's talented, j. like her mother* es talentosa, igual que su madre>; *(typical of)* propio de, muy de <*that's j. like him!* ¡eso es muy de él!> • **j. my luck!** ¡qué suerte la mía! • **j. now** en este momento • **j. so** a su gusto, ni más ni menos • **j. the same** sin embargo <*I don't have the time, but I'll go j. the same* no tengo el tiempo pero sin embargo iré> • **j. think** *o* **imagine!** ¡fíjate!, ¡imagínate! • **not j. yet** todavía no • **to have j.** acabar de <*I've j. gotten here* acabo de llegar>.
jus·tice (jŭs'tĭs) s. *(equity)* justicia; *(righteousness)* rectitud *f*; DER. *(administration of law)* justicia; *(judge)* juez *mf* ♦ **to do j. to** *(to enjoy fully)* apreciar debidamente; *(to show fully)* tratar debidamente • **to bring someone to j.** aprehender y enjuiciar • **j. of the peace** DER. juez de paz *mf.*
jus·ti·fi·a·ble (jŭs'tə-fī'ə-bəl) adj. justificable.
jus·ti·fi·ca·tion (jŭs'tə-fĭ-kā'shən) s. justificación *f.*
jus·ti·fy (jŭs'tə-fī') tr. **-fied, -fy·ing** justificar; IMPR. justificar.
just·ly adv. justamente, con justicia.
just·ness s. *(equity)* justicia; *(righteousness)* rectitud *f*; *(fairness)* imparcialidad *f*; *(accurateness)* exactitud *f.*
jut (jŭt) **I.** intr. **jut·ted, jut·ting** ♦ **to j. out** resaltar, sobresalir, proyectarse **II.** s. saliente *f*, resalto.
jute (jōot) s. FAM. yute (planta, fibra, tejido) *m.*
ju·ve·nes·cent (jōo'və-nĕs'ənt) adj. rejuveneciente.
ju·ve·nile (jōo'və-nəl, -nīl') **I.** adj. *(youthful)* joven, juvenil; *(immature)* infantil; *(of minors)* de menores **II.** s. *(young person)* joven *mf*; *(child)* niño; *(book)* libro para niños; TEAT. galán joven *m*, actor juvenil *m* ♦ **j. court** tribunal de menores • **j. delinquency** delincuencia juvenil • **j. delinquent** delincuente juvenil.
ju·ve·nil·i·ty (jōo'və-nĭl'ĭ-tē) s. [pl. **-ties**] juventud *f.*
jux·ta·pose (jŭk'stə-pōz') tr. yuxtaponer.
jux·ta·po·si·tion (jŭk'stə-pə-zĭsh'ən) s. yuxtaposición *f.*

K

k, K (kā) s. [pl. **k's, K's**] undécima letra del alfabeto inglés; FAM. *(thousand)* mil *m* <*a salary of $24k* un sueldo de $24,000 dólares (al año)>; COMPUT. mil bitios <*a computer with a 256K memory* una computadora con una memoria de 256.000 bitios de capacidad>.
kaf·fir (kăf'ər) s. BOT. especie de sorgo *f* ♦ **K.** cafre, kafir.
Kaf·ka·esque (käf'kə-ĕsk', käf'-) adj. kafkaiano, kafkiano.
Kai·ser (kī'zər) s. HIST. káiser *m.*
Kai·ser·in (kī'zər-ĭn) s. HIST. esposa del káiser.
kale (kāl) s. BOT., CUL. col rizada, berza común.
ka·lei·do·scope (kə-lī'də-skōp') s. caleidoscopio, calidoscopio.
ka·lei·do·scop·ic (kə-lī'də-skŏp'ĭk) s. caleidoscópico, calidoscópico.
kame (kām) s. GEOL. morena.
ka·mi·ka·ze (kä'mĭ-kä'zē) s. MIL. kamikaze *m.*
Kam·pu·che·a (kăm'pə-chē'ə) consulte **Democratic Kampuchea.**
Kam·pu·che·an (kăm'pə-chē'ən) s. & adj. kampucheano.
kan·ga·roo (kăng'gə-rōo') s. ZOOL. canguro *m.*
kangaroo court s. FOR., JER. tribunal desautorizado *o* incompetente.
Kan·ti·an (kăn'tē-ən, kän'-) adj. FILOS. kantiano.
ka·o·lin *o* **ka·o·line** (kā'ə-lĭn) s. MIN. caolín *m*, arcilla blanca.
Ka·pell·meis·ter (kə-pĕl'mī'stər) s. director de una orquesta *o* coro *m.*
ka·pok (kā'pŏk') s. TEJ. kapoc *m*, capoc *m.*
kap·pa (kăp'ə) s. kappa (letra griega).
ka·put *o* **ka·putt** (kä-pōot', -pōot') adj. FAM. *(destroyed)* acabado; *(out of order)* descompuesto.

kar·a·kul (kăr′ə-kəl) s. ZOOL. *(sheep)* caracul *m*; *(fur)* astrakán *m*.

kar·at (kăr′ət) s. JOY. quilate *m*.

ka·ra·te (kə-rä′tē) s. DEP. karate.

kar·ma (kär′mə) s. RELIG. *(reaction)* karma *m*; *(destiny)* destino; FAM. *(atmosphere)* ambiente *m*.

kart (kärt) s. AUTO. kart (pequeño coche deportivo o de carrera) *m*.

kart·ing (kär′tĭng) s. karting *m*, carrera de karts.

Kash·mir (kăsh′mîr′, kăzh′-) s. Cachemira.

ka·ty·did (kā′tē-dĭd′) s. ENTOM. saltamontes *m*.

kay·ak (kī′ăk′) s. kayac *m*, kayak (canoa de los esquimales) *m*.

kay·o (kā-ō′) DEP., JER. **I.** s. [pl. **-os**] golpe que pone fuera de combate (en boxeo) *m* **II.** tr. **-oed, -o·ing** poner fuera de combate (en boxeo).

ka·zoo (kə-zōō′) s. chicharra (instrumento).

ke·bab o **ke·bob** (kə-bŏb′) s. carne sasonada y asada en espetones.

kedge (kĕj) **I.** s. MARÍT. ancla pequeña **II.** tr. **kedged, kedg·ing** espiar (una embarcación) con un ancla pequeña.

keel (kēl) **I.** s. AVIA., BOT., MARÍT., ZOOL. quilla; POÉT. *(ship)* navío ♦ **to be on an even k.** *(ship)* no tener diferencia de calado; *(calm)* estar tranquilo **II.** tr. MARÍT. echar a pique, hacer zozobrar —intr. irse a pique, zozobrar ♦ **to k. over** *(to collapse)* desplomarse; *(to topple over)* volcarse.

keel·boat (kēl′bōt′) s. MARÍT. chalana fluvial (con quilla, sin velas).

keel·haul (kēl′hôl′) tr. HIST., MARÍT. hacer pasar por debajo de la quilla (como castigo); *(to rebuke)* refutar.

keel·son (kēl′sən, kĕl′-) s. MARÍT. sobrequilla.

keen[1] (kēn) adj. **-er, -est** *(blade)* afilado; *(intellect)* agudo, penetrante; *(sense)* agudo, fino <*k. eyesight* vista aguda>; *(interest)* vivo, profundo; *(pain)* agudo, punzante; *(appetite)* bueno; *(question)* incisivo; *(competition)* reñido, fuerte; *(enthusiastic)* entusiasta; JER. *(great)* fantástico ♦ **to be k. on** *(to like)* gustarle a uno <*he was k. on her* ella le gustaba>; *(to wish to)* estar desesperado por, tener muchas ganas de <*he is k. on going* tiene muchas ganas de ir>.

keen[2] (kēn) **I.** s. lamento fúnebre **II.** intr. gemir, lamentarse.

keen·ly (kēn′lē) adv. *(acutely)* agudamente, detenidamente; *(intensely)* vivamente, profundamente; *(to feel)* agudamente; *(to look at)* de modo penetrante, fijamente; *(enthusiastically)* con entusiasmo ♦ **to be k. aware of** darse perfecta cuenta de.

keen·ness (kēn′nĭs) s. *(of a blade)* filo; *(of the intellect)* agudeza, penetración *f*; *(of a sense)* agudeza, finura; *(of emotions)* intensidad *f*, profundidad *f*; *(of pain)* agudeza ♦ **k. for** entusiasmo o interés por <*his k. for sports* su interés por los deportes>.

keep (kēp) **I.** tr. **kept** (kĕpt), **keep·ing** *(to retain)* quedarse con <*are you going to k. the money you found?* ¿vas a quedarte con el dinero que encontraste?>; *(to put aside)* guardar <*k. some for later* guarda algo para más tarde>; *(to support)* sostener, mantener <*I k. a wife and two children on my small salary* mantengo a una esposa y dos hijos con mi pequeño sueldo>; *(to store)* guardar <*where do you k. your saw?* ¿en dónde guardas la sierra?>; *(to tend)* dar hospedaje a, alojar <*to k. boarders* dar hospedaje a huéspedes>; *(to raise)* criar (gallinas, abejas); *(to preserve)* mantener, conservar <*refrigerators k. food fresh* los refrigeradores conservan la comida fresca>; *(to continue)* mantener; *(to make entries in)* llevar (diario, cuentas); *(to detain)* detener, demorar <*what is keeping you?* ¿que es lo que te detiene?>; *(to fulfill)* cumplir, respetar <*to k. one's word* cumplir la palabra de uno>; *(to celebrate)* celebrar, observar (fiesta, conmemoración); *(to protect)* proteger, guardar <*banks k. money for people* los bancos guardan el dinero de la gente> ♦ **k. your chin up!** ¡ánimo! • **k. the change** quédese con la vuelta • **to k. an appointment** acudir a una cita • **to k. an eye on** vigilar • **to k. a secret** guardar un secreto • **to k. away** mantener alejado • **to k. back** *(tears)* contener, detener (lágrimas); *(not to divulge)* ocultar (información); *(to withhold)* quedarse con • **to k.**

(someone) company acompañar, hacer compañía • **to k. down** *(to oppress)* oprimir, sojuzgar; *(costs, temperature)* mantener bajo (costos, temperatura); *(to restrict)* restringir, limitar • **to k. faith with** tener confianza en • **to k. from** *(to prevent)* impedir <*they kept me from speaking out* me impidieron expresar mi opinión>; *(to conceal)* ocultar <*the information they kept from me was crucial* la información que me ocultaron era crítica> • **to k. house** manejar una casa • **to k. in** no dejar salir, mantener dentro • **to k. on** *(clothing)* no quitarse, dejarse puesto <*k. your shoes on* no te quites los zapatos>; *(an employee)* no despedir, retener • **to k. one's cool** JER. conservar la calma • **to k. one's distance** mantener distancia • **to k. one's eyes open** *(to stay awake)* no dormirse; FIG. *(to be alert)* mantenerse alerta • **to k. one's hands off** no tocar • **to k. one's head** no perder la cabeza • **to k. one's nose clean** FIG. no meterse en líos • **to k. out** no dejar entrar • **to k. out of** FIG. no meterse <*k. out of my affairs* no te metas en mis asuntos> • **to k. pace with** ir al mismo paso que • **to k. (someone) posted** tener (a alguien) al corriente • **to k. (someone) quiet** hacer callar (a alguien) • **to k. someone waiting** hacer esperar a alguien • **to k. score** llevar la cuenta • **to k. tabs on** vigilar, tener bajo observación • **to k. the peace** mantener la paz • **to k. time** *(watch)* marcar la hora (el reloj); MÚS. llevar el compás • **to k. track of** seguir de cerca, controlar • **to k. under lock and key** guardar con siete llaves o bajo llave • **to k. up** *(to continue)* continuar, proseguir <*k. up the good work* continúe haciendo tan buen trabajo>; *(to prevent from sleeping)* tener en vela <*the storm kept me up all night* la tormenta me tuvo en vela toda la noche>; *(to maintain)* mantener <*to k. up a property* mantener una propiedad> • **to k. up appearances** guardar las apariencias • **to k. up with** *(work)* tener al día; *(the neighbors)* achantar a (los vecinos) • **to k. up with the times** ser muy de su época —intr. *(to stay)* permanecer, quedarse; *(to remain fresh)* conservarse <*the fish won't k. until tomorrow* el pescado no se conservará hasta mañana>; *(to continue)* seguir, continuar; *(to refuse to stop)* no dejar de <*he kept shouting* no dejó de gritar> ♦ **k. off** prohibido pisar • **k. out** prohibida la entrada • **to k. at it** FAM. perseverar, persistir • **to k. away** mantenerse a distancia • **to k. away from** *(troubles, problems)* no meterse en (líos, problemas); *(liquor, food)* abstenerse de (bebida, comida); *(people)* evitar el encuentro con • **to k. cool** JER. conservar la calma • **to k. going** *(to proceed)* seguir; *(to manage)* ir tirando • **to k. in touch** mantenerse en contacto • **to k. on** seguir, continuar <*k. on talking* continúa hablando> • **to k. out** no entrar, permanecer fuera • **to k. quiet** quedarse callado • **to k. to** *(promise, word)* cumplir (promesa, palabra); *(right, left)* mantenerse a (derecha, izquierda) • **to k. up** ir al paso de, alcanzar **II.** s. *(care)* custodia, protección *f*; *(of a castle)* torreón *m* ♦ **for keeps** para siempre • **to earn one's k.** ganarse la vida o el sustento.

keep·er (kē′pər) s. *(guard)* guarda *m*, guardián *m*; *(prison guard)* carcelero; *(gamekeeper)* guardabosque *m*; *(curator)* conservador *m*; MEC. *(latch)* seguro; ELEC. *(of a magnet)* armadura.

keep·ing (kē′pĭng) s. *(guarding)* guardia, custodia; *(upkeep)* conservación *f*, mantenimiento; *(observance)* cumplimiento; *(custody)* cuidado, cargo <*in his k.* a cargo suyo> ♦ **in safe k.** a buen recaudo, en lugar seguro • **to be in k. with** estar de acuerdo con • **to be out of k. with** no estar de acuerdo con.

keep·sake (kēp′sāk′) s. *(memento)* recuerdo; *(present)* regalo.

keg (kĕg) s. barril *m*.

kelp (kĕlp) s. BOT. kelp *m*, varec (alga marina) *m*.

Kelt (kĕlt) s. var. de **Celt**.

Kelt·ic (kĕl′tĭk) s. & adj. var. de **Celtic**.

kel·vin (kĕl′vĭn) s. FÍS. kelvin (unidad de temperatura) *m*.

kempt (kĕmpt) adj. limpio, arreglado.

ken (kĕn) s. vista ♦ **beyond one's k.** fuera de comprensión o alcance.

ken·nel (kĕn′əl) **I.** s. *(dog shelter)* perrera; *(pack of dogs)* jauría; *(lair)* guarida **II**. tr. & intr. meter(se) en la perrera.

Ken·ya (kĕn'yə, kĕn'-) s. Kenya.

Ken·yan (kĕn'yən, kĕn'-) adj. & s. keniano.

Ke·ogh plan (kē'ō) s. plan de retiro *o* de jubilación *m*.

ke·pi (kā'pē, kĕp'ē) s. MIL. quepis *m*, kepis *m*.

kept (kĕpt) pret. y part. p. de **keep.**

ker·a·tin (kĕr'ə-tĭn) s. BIOL. queratina.

kerb (kûrb) s. G.B. var. de **curb.**

ker·chief (kûr'chĭf) s. *(scarf)* pañuelo (de cabeza); *(handkerchief)* pañuelo.

kerf (kûrf) s. CARP. tajo, corte *m*.

ker·mes (kûr'mēz) s. ENTOM. quermes *m*, carmes *m*.

ker·mis *o* **ker·mess** (kûr'mĭs) s. quermés *f*, kermés *f*.

kern *o* **kerne** (kûrn) s. HIST. *(foot soldier)* soldado de infantería medieval de Irlanda *o* de Escocia; *(boor)* patán *m*, palurdo.

ker·nel (kûr'nəl) s. *(of cereals)* grano; *(of a nut)* masa (de la semilla); FIG. *(core)* meollo, médula ♦ **a k. of truth** un fondo de verdad.

ker·o·sene *o* **ker·o·sine** (kĕr'ə-sēn', kăr'-) s. QUÍM. queroseno, querosén *m*.

kes·trel (kĕs'trəl) s. ORNIT. cernícalo.

ketch (kĕch) s. MARÍT. queche *m*.

ketch·up (kĕch'əp, kăch'-) s. CUL. salsa de tomate (condimento).

ke·tone (kē'tōn') s. QUÍM. quetona, cetona.

ket·tle (kĕt'l) s. *(metal pot)* marmita, hervidor *m*; *(teakettle)* tetera ♦ **a nice** *o* **fine k. of fish** FIG. un berenjenal • **that's another k. of fish** FIG. eso es otro cantar.

ket·tle·drum (kĕt'l-drŭm') s. MÚS. timbal *m*.

kew·pie (kyōō'pē) s. muñequita de mejillas encarnadas y ojos grandes (marca registrada).

key¹ (kē) **I**. s. [pl. **keys**] *(of a lock, clock)* llave (de cerradura, reloj) *f*; *(wedge)* chaveta, cuña; ARQ. *(keystone)* clave *f*, dovela; *(of a piano, typewriter)* tecla (del piano, máquina de escribir); MÚS. *(of wind instruments)* llave, pistón *m*; *(tonality)* tonalidad *f*, tono; ELEC. llave, interruptor *m*; TELEG. manipulador *m*; *(pitch)* tono <*she spoke in a high k.* habló en un tono alto>; *(style)* estilo (de un escrito, discurso); *(solution)* solución *f*, explicación *f*; *(set of answers)* tabla, cuadro ♦ **in k.** MÚS. afinado; FIG. *(in harmony)* en armonía, de acuerdo • **master k.** llave maestra • **off k.** MÚS. desafinado **II**. adj. *(fundamental)* fundamental, importante <*a k. decision* una decisión fundamental>; *(strategic)* estratégico <*to hold a k. position* mantener una posición estratégica>; *(important)* clave <*a k. word* una palabra clave> **III**. tr. *(to lock)* cerrar con llave; *(to encode)* codificar; ARQ. colocar la clave en (un arco); MÚS. afinar ♦ **to be keyed to** *(to be appropriate for)* ser apropiado para; *(to provide explanations for)* dar la explicación de • **to be keyed up about** *(to be excited)* estar entusiasmado a causa de; *(to be nervous)* estar nervioso a causa de.

key² (kē) s. GEOG. cayo, isleta.

key·board (kē'bôrd') **I**. s. teclado **II**. tr. IMPR. componer (mediante teclado).

key·board·er (kē'bôr'dər) s. IMPR. operador del teclado *m*.

key·card (kē'kärd') s. COMPUT. tarjeta (codificada, que se usa para accionar un mecanismo).

key club s. club privado (cuyos miembros obtienen una llave de identificación).

keyed (kēd) adj. TEC. que tiene llaves *o* teclas; MÚS. templado.

key·hole (kē'hōl') s. MEC. ojo de la cerradura, bocallave *f*.

key money s. gratificación pecuniaria hecha a un arrendador (para asegurar un arriendo) *f*.

Keynes·i·an (kān'zē-ən) adj. ECON., POL. keynesiano.

key·note (kē'nōt') s. MÚS. nota tónica, tónica (de llave, escala); FIG. *(keystone)* piedra angular, idea fundamental.

keynote address s. discurso inaugural *o* de apertura.

key·punch (kē'pŭnch') COMPUT. **I**. s. perforadora de tarjetas **II**. tr. & intr. procesar en una perforadora de teclado.

key·punch·er (kē'pŭn'chər) s. COMPUT. perforador de tarjetas *m*.

key·punch·ing (kē'pŭn'chĭng) s. COMPUT. perforación (de tarjetas, cintas) *f*.

key signature s. MÚS. armadura.

key·stone (kē'stōn') s. ARQ. *(stone)* clave *f*, dovela; FIG. *(main principle)* piedra angular, fundamento.

key·stroke (kē'strōk') s. COMPUT. golpe de la tecla *m*.

kha·ki (kăk'ē, kä'kē) **I**. s. *(color)* color caqui *m*; *(cloth)* caqui *m* ♦ **khakis** uniforme de color caqui *m* **II**. adj. de color caqui.

khan (kän, kăn) s. kan *m*.

khan·ate (kä'nāt', kăn'āt') s. kanato, jurisdicción de un kan *f*.

khe·dive (kə-dēv') s. HIST. jedive (virrey de turquía) *m*.

khi (kī) s. var. de **chi.**

Khmer (kə-mâr') s. [pl. **Khmer** *o* **Khmers**] *(inhabitant, language)* kmer *mf* ♦ **the K.** *o* **Khmers** los kmer.

kib·butz (kĭ-bŏŏts', -bōōts') s. [pl. **kib·but·zim** (kĭb'ŏŏtsēm')] kibbutz *m*.

kib·itz (kĭb'ĭts) intr. FAM. *(to meddle)* dar consejos no solicitados; *(to chat)* charlar.

ki·bosh (kī'bŏsh') s. ♦ **to put the k. on something** FAM. ponerle fin *o* término a algo.

kick (kĭk) **I**. intr. *(people)* patear, dar puntapiés; *(animals)* cocear, dar coces; *(firearm)* dar un culatazo (un arma); DEP. patear; FAM. *(to complain)* quejarse <*what is he kicking about?* ¿de qué se está quejando?> ♦ **to be alive and kicking** FIG. estar vivito y coleando • **to k. around** FAM. andar rodando • **to k. off** DEP. dar el puntapié inicial; FIG. *(to die)* estirar la pata • **to k. oneself** reprocharse —tr. *(people)* patear, dar un puntapié a; *(animals)* dar coces a; *(firearm)* dar un culatazo en; DEP. *(to punt, pass)* patear; *(to score)* marcar, meter (un gol) ♦ **to k. around** FAM. *(to abuse)* maltratar; *(to consider)* considerar *o* discurrir (idea, problema) • **to k. in** *(one's share)* aportar (dinero); *(a door)* derribar a patadas • **to k. off** poner en marcha, empezar • **to k. out** echar a patadas • **to k. the bucket** FIG., FAM. estirar la pata • **to k. the habit** librarse de un vicio • **to k. up a fuss** FAM. armar un bochinche • **to k. up one's heels** FIG., FAM. jaranear, echar una cana al aire **II**. s. *(of a person)* patada, puntapié *m*; *(of an animal)* patada, coz *f*; DEP. *(in swimming, soccer)* patada (en natación, fútbol); *(of a firearm)* culatazo; JER. *(complaint)* queja, protesta; *(of a motor)* fuerza, vigor *m*; *(of a drink, drug)* fuerza, efecto estimulante ♦ **for kicks** FAM. por gusto, por diversión • **kicks** sensación, emoción • **to be on a k.** estar obsesionado • **to get a k. out of** FAM. encontrar placer en.

kick·back (kĭk'băk') s. *(reaction)* reacción *f*; JER. *(payment)* tajada, coima.

kick·er (kĭk'ər) s. *(in football)* chutador *m*; FAM. *(turn of events)* sorpresa; *(pitfall)* trampa.

kick·off (kĭk'ôf') s. DEP. saque inicial *m*; FIG. *(beginning)* comienzo.

kick plate s. resguardo metálico (de la parte inferior de la puerta).

kick·stand (kĭk'stănd') s. soporte (de bicicleta, motocicleta) *m*.

kick·y (kĭk'ē) adj. **-i·er, -i·est** JER. excitante.

kid (kĭd) **I**. s. ZOOL. *(goat)* cabrito; *(other animals)* cría; *(meat)* cabrito, carne de cabrito *f*; *(leather)* cabritilla <*k. gloves* guantes de cabritilla>; FAM. *(child)* niño, muchacho; JER. *(pal)* muchachón *m* ♦ **a k. brother** un hermano menor • **that's k. stuff** *(fit for a child)* eso es cosa de niños; *(easily accomplished)* eso lo hace cualquiera **II**. tr. **kid·ded, kid·ding** FAM. *(to tease)* bromear con; *(to fool)* tomar el pelo a —intr. FAM. *(to tease)* bromear, jugar; ZOOL. parir ♦ **are you kidding?** *(really?)* ¿de verdad?; *(of course not)* ¡de eso nada!, ¡ni en broma! • **no kidding!** ¡mentira!, ¡no me digas! • **to k. oneself** engañarse, hacerse ilusiones.

kid·der (kĭd'ər) s. bromista *mf*.

kid·dy *o* **kid·die** (kĭd'ē) s. [pl. **-dies**] FAM. niñito, crío.

kid glove s. guante de cabritilla *m* ♦ **to handle with kid gloves** FIG. tratar con guante blanco.

kid·nap (kĭd'năp') tr. secuestrar, raptar.

ă rey / ä año / b boca / ch chico / d dar / ĕ el / ē mil / g gato / h joya / hw juez / ī aire / k casa / kw cuan /

kid·nap·er o **kid·nap·per** (kĭd′năp′ər) s. secuestrador *m*, raptor *m*.

kid·nap·ing o **kid·nap·ping** (kĭd′năp′ĭng) s. secuestro, rapto.

kid·ney (kĭd′nē) s. [pl. **-neys**] ANAT., ZOOL. *(organ)* riñón *m*; FAM. *(kind)* clase *f*, índole *f*.

kidney bean s. BOT., CUL. frijol colorado, habichuela rosada.

kidney stone s. MED. piedra (nefrítica), cálculo renal.

kid·skin (kĭd′skĭn′) s. cabritilla.

Kil·i·man·ja·ro (kĭl′ə-mən-jär′ō) s. Kilimanjaro.

kill (kĭl) **I.** tr. *(to put to death)* matar; *(to slaughter)* sacrificar, matar (animales); *(to destroy)* destruir, aniquilar; FIG. *(to overpower)* arruinar <*garlic killed the taste of the meat* el ajo arruinó el sabor de la carne>; *(to turn off)* apagar (motor, luz); JER. *(to finish off)* agotar, terminar (botella de bebida); *(to hurt)* matar <*these shoes are killing me* estos zapatos me están matando>; *(to delete)* suprimir; *(to make laugh)* hacer morir de risa <*his jokes killed me* sus chistes me hicieron morir de risa> ◆ **to k. off** exterminar ◆ **to k. time** *(to wait)* hacer tiempo; *(to idle)* matar el tiempo ◆ **to k. two birds with one stone** FIG., FAM. matar dos pájaros de un tiro —intr. *(to cause death)* matar <*DDT kills quickly* D.D.T. mata rápidamente>; *(to commit murder)* cometer homicidio ◆ **to be dressed to k.** ir vestido con mucha elegancia **II.** s. *(acto)* matanza; *(animal)* caza, cacería; *(brook)* arroyo, riachuelo.

kill·deer (kĭl′dîr′) s. [pl. **killdeer** o **-deers**] ORNIT. frailecillo norteamericano.

kill·er (kĭl′ər) s. *(person)* asesino; *(animal)* carnicero ◆ **cancer is a k.** el cáncer es mortal.

killer whale s. ZOOL. orca.

kill·ing (kĭl′ĭng) **I.** s. *(murder)* asesinato; *(slaughter)* matanza ◆ **to make a k.** FIG., FAM. ganar gran cantidad de dinero (esp. en operaciones financieras) **II.** adj. *(deadly)* que mata, mortal; *(exhausting)* agotador, abrumador; FIG. *(funny)* graciosísimo.

kill·joy (kĭl′joi′) s. aguafiestas *mf*.

kiln (kĭln, kĭl) TEC. **I.** s. horno **II.** tr. secar o cocer en el horno.

ki·lo (kē′lō) s. [pl. **-los**] kilo, kilogramo.

kil·o·baud (kĭl′ə-bôd′) s. COMPUT. kilobaudio.

kil·o·bit (kĭl′ə-bĭt′) s. COMPUT. kilobitio.

kil·o·cal·o·rie (kĭl′ə-kăl′ə-rē) s. FÍS. kilocaloría.

kil·o·cy·cle (kĭl′ə-sī′kəl) s. RAD. kilociclo.

kil·o·gram (kĭl′ə-grăm′) s. kilogramo.

kilogram calorie s. FÍS. kilocaloría.

kil·o·gram-me·ter (kĭl′ə-grăm′-mē′tər) s. FÍS. kilográmetro.

kil·o·li·ter (kĭl′ə-lē′tər) s. kilolitro.

kil·o·me·ter (kĭl′ə-mē′tər, kĭ-lŏm′ĭ-tər) s. kilómetro.

kil·o·met·ric (kĭl′ə-mět′rĭk) adj. kilométrico.

kil·o·rad (kĭl′ə-răd′) s. FÍS. kilorad *m*.

kil·o·ton (kĭl′ə-tŭn′) s. FÍS. kilotonelada corta, mil toneladas; ARM. kilotón (fuerza explosiva) *m*.

kil·o·watt (kĭl′ə-wŏt′) s. ELEC. kilovatio.

kil·o·watt-hour (kĭl′ə-wŏt-our′) s. ELEC. kilovatio-hora.

kilt (kĭlt) **I.** s. falda escocesa, kilt *m* **II.** tr. plegar (alrededor del cuerpo).

kil·ter (kĭl′tər) s. FAM. buena condición ◆ **to be out of k.** estar descompuesto, no funcionar bien.

ki·mo·no (kĭ-mō′nō) s. [pl. **-nos**] kimono, quimono.

kin (kĭn) s. *(relative)* pariente *m*; *(family)* familia; *(kinsfolk)* parientes, parentela ◆ **next of k.** pariente más cercano.

kind¹ (kīnd) adj. **-er**, **-est** *(warmhearted)* bueno; *(friendly)* amistoso; *(generous)* generoso; *(benevolent)* bondadoso, benévolo; *(understanding)* comprensivo; *(courteous)* cortés, amable <*it is very k. of you* es muy amable de su parte> ◆ **would you be so k. as to?** ¿tendrá usted la bondad de?

kind² (kīnd) s. *(class)* género, especie *f*; *(type)* tipo, clase *f* <*what k. of airplane is that?* ¿qué tipo de avión es ése?> ◆ **a k. of** un cierto <*we all felt a k. of emptiness when she left* todos sentimos un cierto vacío cuando ella partió> ◆ **all kinds of** FAM. *(plenty of)* de sobra <*we have all kinds of time to finish the job* tenemos tiempo de sobra para termi-

nar el trabajo>; *(many)* de todas clases, toda clase de ◆ **In k.** *(in the same manner)* del mismo modo, de igual manera; *(not with money)* en especie (no en dinero) ◆ **k. of** FAM. un poco <*it's k. of cold today* hace un poco de frío hoy> ◆ **of the k.** semejante, por el estilo <*I said nothing of the k.* yo no dije nada por el estilo> ◆ **to repay in k.** FIG. pagar con la misma moneda ◆ **two of a k.** un par.

kin·der·gar·ten (kĭn′dər-gär′tn) s. jardín de infantes *m*, kindergarten *m*.

kin·der·gart·ner (kĭn′dər-gärt′nər) s. *(child)* alumno de un jardín de infantes; *(teacher)* maestro de un jardín de infantes.

kind·heart·ed (kīnd′här′tĭd) adj. bondadoso, de buen corazón.

kind·heart·ed·ness (kīnd′här′tĭd-nĭs) s. bondad *f*, buen corazón.

kin·dle (kĭn′dl) tr. **-dled**, **-dling** *(to ignite)* encender; FIG. *(to arouse)* encender, provocar —intr. encenderse.

kind·li·ness (kīnd′lē-nĭs) s. *(benevolence)* benignidad *f*, benevolencia; *(amiability)* amabilidad *f*, afabilidad *f*.

kin·dling (kĭnd′lĭng) s. leña, astillas.

kind·ly (kīnd′lē) **I.** adj. **-li·er**, **-li·est** *(benevolent)* bondadoso; *(friendly)* amable; *(pleasant)* agradable; *(climate)* benigno **II.** adv. *(out of kindness)* bondadosamente; *(in a kind manner)* amablemente; *(pleasantly)* agradablemente ◆ **k. take a seat** tenga la bondad de sentarse ◆ **to take k. to** aceptar de buena gana ◆ **to take something k.** apreciar algo.

kind·ness (kīnd′nĭs) s. bondad *f*, amabilidad *f* ◆ **have the k. to** por favor, tenga la bondad de ◆ **to do someone a k.** hacer un favor a alguien.

kin·dred (kĭn′drĭd) **I.** s. *(clan)* clan *m*, tribu *f*; *(kinfolk)* parentela, parientes *m* **II.** adj. *(of the same ancestry)* emparentado; FIG. *(related)* afín, similar <*k. emotions* emociones afines> ◆ **k. spirits** almas gemelas.

kin·e·mat·ic (kĭn′ə-măt′ĭk) adj. FÍS. cinemático.

kin·e·mat·ics (kĭn′ə-măt′ĭks) s. [ú. con v. sing.] FÍS. cinemática.

kin·e·scope (kĭn′ĭ-skōp′) s. TELEV. cinescopio.

ki·ne·si·ol·o·gist (kə-nē′sē-ŏl′ə-jĭst) s. MED. kinesiólogo, quinesiólogo.

ki·ne·si·ol·o·gy (kə-nē′sē-ŏl′ə-jē) s. MED. kinesiología, quinesiología.

kin·es·the·sia (kĭn′ĭs-thē′zhə) s. FISIOL. quinestesia, kinestesia.

ki·net·ic (kĭ-nět′ĭk, kī-) adj. FÍS. cinético.

kinetic art s. ARTE. arte cinético.

kinetic energy s. FÍS. energía cinética.

ki·net·ics (kĭ-nět′ĭks, kī-) s. [ú. con v. sing.] FÍS. cinética.

kin·folk (kĭn′fōk′) o **kin·folks** (-fōks′) s.pl. parentela, parientes *m*.

king (kĭng) s. *(monarch)* rey *m*; *(in cards, chess)* rey; *(in checkers)* dama ◆ **to live like a k.** vivir a cuerpo de rey ◆ **Book of Kings** BÍBL. libro de los Reyes ◆ **the Three Kings** BÍBL. los Reyes Magos.

king·bird (kĭng′bûrd′) s. ORNIT. tirano.

king·bolt (kĭng′bōlt′) s. F.C. perno pinzote; TEC. pivote *m*.

king crab s. ZOOL. centolla.

king·dom (kĭng′dəm) s. reino ◆ **the plant k.** el reino vegetal ◆ **the wild k.** el reino de la selva.

kingdom come s. ◆ **till k.** hasta el Día del Juicio Final ◆ **to blow someone to k.** mandar a alguien de cabeza al otro mundo.

king·fish·er (kĭng′fĭsh′ər) s. ORNIT. martín pescador *m*.

King James Bible (jāmz) s. BÍBL. Biblia autorizada por el rey Jacobo I.

king·li·ness (kĭng′lē-nĭs) s. majestuosidad *f*.

king·ly (kĭng′lē) **I.** adj. **-li·er**, **-li·est** *(royal)* real; *(majestic)* majestuoso **II.** adv. majestuosamente.

king·pin (kĭng′pĭn′) s. *(in bowling)* bolo central; FAM. *(essential person)* persona principal, persona clave; *(essential thing)* piedra angular.

king post s. ARQ. pendolón *m*, nabo.

King's English s. inglés correcto.

king·ship (kĭng′shĭp′) s. *(throne)* trono; *(reign)* reino, reinado; *(majesty)* majestad *f*, realeza; *(monarchy)* monarquía.

king-size (kĭng'sīz') *o* **king-sized** (-sīzd') adj. *(huge)* enorme, gigante; *(big)* de tamaño grande, grande; *(long)* largo.

kink (kĭngk) I. s. *(in a wire)* rosca, vuelta; *(tight curl)* rizo; *(muscle spasm)* punzada, calambre *m*; *(flaw)* falla; *(mental quirk)* manía, extravagancia; *(clever idea)* ocurrencia II. tr. & intr. *(a wire)* enroscar(se); *(hair)* rizar(se).

kink·y (kĭng'kē) adj. **-i·er, -i·est** *(wire)* enroscado, retorcido; *(hair)* rizado; FAM. *(perverted)* pervertido.

kins·folk (kĭnz'fōk') s.pl. var. de **kinfolk.**

kin·ship (kĭn'shĭp') s. parentesco.

kins·man (kĭnz'mən) s. [pl. **-men**] *(relative)* pariente *m*; *(compatriot)* compatriota *m*.

kins·wom·an (kĭnz'wŏŏm'ən) s. [pl. **-wom·en** (-wĭm'ən)] *(relative)* parienta; *(compatriot)* compatriota *f*.

ki·osk (kē'ŏsk') s. quiosco, kiosco.

kip (kĭp) s. piel de cordero *o* de becerro *f*.

kip·per (kĭp'ər) ICT., CUL. I. s. *(salmon)* salmón zancado; *(smoked herring)* arenque ahumado II. tr. ahumar (pescado).

Ki·ri·ba·ti (kĭr'ĭ-bä'tē) s. Kiribati.

kirk (kûrk) s. iglesia ♦ **The K.** RELIG. la Iglesia de Escocia.

kir·mess (kûr'mĭs) s. var. de **kermis.**

kirsch (kĭrsh) s. kirsch (licor de cerezas) *m*.

kis·met (kĭz'mĕt') s. destino.

kiss (kĭs) I. tr. besar, dar un beso a *<did she kiss you?* ¿te dio un beso?>; *(to brush against)* rozar ♦ **to k. away** consolar a besos • **to k. off** FAM. despachar, despedir • **to k. something goodbye** FAM. decir adiós a algo, despedirse de algo —intr. besarse II. s. *(with the lips)* beso; *(slight touch)* roce *m*; *(candy)* bombón *m*; *(meringue)* merengue ♦ **good-bye k.** beso de despedida • **goodnight k.** beso de despedida por la noche • **to blow someone a k.** tirar un beso a alguien.

kiss·er (kĭs'ər) s. *(person)* besucón *m*; JER. *(mouth, face)* hocico, trompa.

kiss of death s. JER. beso de Judas.

kiss-off (kĭs'ôf') s. FAM. despido.

kit¹ (kĭt) s. *(set of implements)* equipo, conjunto de utensilios; *(collection of items)* juego de artículos *<a travel k.* un juego de artículos de viaje>; *(container)* estuche *m*, caja ♦ **first-aid k.** botiquín *m* • **the whole k. and caboodle** FAM. la colección entera.

kit² s. *(kitten)* gatito; *(furry animal)* animalito.

kitch·en (kĭch'ən) s. cocina ♦ **k. sink** fregadero • **k. utensils** utensilios de cocina.

kitchen cabinet s. *(cupboard)* armario de cocina; POL. *(advisers)* camarilla.

kitch·en·er (kĭch'ə-nər) s. *(person)* ranchero, cocinero; G.B. *(stove)* fogón *m*.

kitch·en·ette (kĭch'ə-nĕt') s. cocina pequeña, kitchenette *f*.

kitchen garden s. huerto.

kitchen police s. MIL. servicio de cocina.

kitch·en·ware (kĭch'ən-wâr') s. batería de cocina, utensilios de cocina.

kite (kīt) I. s. *(toy)* cometa; MARÍT. *(sail)* sobrejuanete *m*; ORNIT. milano; COM. *(false paper)* cheque *m o* documento falso ♦ **go fly a k.!** FAM. ¡piérdete! II. intr. **kit·ed, kit·ing** volar como una cometa.

kith and kin (kĭth'ən kĭn') s.pl. parientes y amigos.

kitsch (kĭch) s. *(bad taste)* mal gusto pretensioso (esp. en arte); *(thing)* obra artística pretensiosa de mal gusto.

kit·ten (kĭt'n) I. s. gatito II. intr. parir (gatitos).

kit·ten·ish (kĭt'n-ĭsh) adj. *(playful)* juguetón; *(coy)* coquetón.

kit·ty¹ (kĭt'ē) s. [pl. **-ties**] *(in cards)* puesta del ganador (para costear el juego); *(pool of money)* banca, pozo.

kit·ty² (kĭt'ē) s. [pl. **-ties**] *(cat)* gato; *(kitten)* gatito.

kit·ty-cor·nered (kĭt'ē-kôr'nərd) adj. esquinado.

kitty litter s. material absorbente que se coloca dentro de la caja para excrementos de animales domésticos (esp. gatos) *m*.

ki·wi (kē'wē) s. ORNIT. kiwi *m*.

Klax·on (klăk'sən) s. AUTO. claxon *m*, klaxon *m* (marca registrada).

Kleen·ex (klē'nĕks') s. marca registrada de unos pañuelitos de papel.

klep·to·ma·ni·a (klĕp'tə-mā'nē-ə) s. cleptomanía.

klep·to·ma·ni·ac (klĕp'tə-mā'nē-ăk') s. cleptómano.

klutz (klŭts) s. JER. *(fool)* tonto; *(bungler)* zarramplín *m*, chambón *m*.

knack (năk) s. *(skill)* maña, facilidad *f* *<a k. for taking pictures* facilidad para sacar fotos>; *(natural talent)* don *m* *<she has a k. for saying the right thing* tiene el don de decir lo correcto>.

knap·sack (năp'săk') s. mochila.

knave (nāv) s. *(unprincipled person)* bribón *m*, bellaco; ANT. *(servant)* sirviente *m*; *(jack)* sota (de la baraja), jota (de las cartas internacionales).

knav·er·y (nā'və-rē) s. bribonada, bellaquería.

knav·ish (nā'vĭsh) adj. bribón, bellaco.

knead (nēd) tr. *(to mix)* amasar, heñir; *(to massage)* dar masaje; FIG. *(to shape)* moldear, formar.

knead·er (nēd'ər) s. amasador *m*.

knee (nē) I. s. *(of a person)* rodilla; *(of a quadruped)* codillo; *(of a garment)* rodillera; MEC. codo ♦ **to bend one's k.** doblar la rodilla • **to bring someone to his knees** FIG. poner a alguien de rodillas • **to go down on one's knees** caer de hinojos II. tr. **kneed, knee·ing** dar *o* golpear con la rodilla.

knee breeches s.pl. calzón corto, pantalones cortos.

knee·cap (nē'kăp') s. ANAT. rótula; *(covering)* rodillera.

knee-deep (nē'dēp') adj. *(knee-high)* que llega hasta las rodillas; *(submerged to the knees)* metido hasta las rodillas *<k. in mud* metido hasta las rodillas en el fango>; FIG. *(deeply occupied)* sumido.

knee-high (nē'hī') I. adj. que llega hasta las rodillas II. s. media a la altura de las rodillas.

kneel (nēl) intr. **knelt** (nĕlt) *o* **kneeled, kneel·ing** arrodillarse.

knee·pad (nē'păd') s. rodillera.

knell (nĕl) I. intr. & tr. sonar lúgubremente (campana) II. s. *(toll)* toque a muerto *o* de difuntos *m*; FIG. *(bad omen)* mal presagio ♦ **to sound the k. of** presagiar el fin de.

knelt (nĕlt) un pret. y part. p. de **kneel.**

knew (nōō, nyōō) pret. de **know.**

Knick·er·bock·er (nĭk'ər-bŏk'ər) s. HIST. neoyorquino.

knick·er·bock·ers (nĭk'ər-bŏk'ərz) s.pl. bombachos, pantalones bombachos (ceñidos bajo las rodillas).

knick·ers (nĭk'ərz) s.pl. *(bloomers)* bragas *f*; *(knickerbockers)* bombachos, pantalones bombachos (ceñidos bajo las rodillas).

knick·knack (nĭk'năk') s. chuchería.

knife (nīf) I. s. [pl. **knives** (nīvz)] *(cutting instrument)* cuchillo *<kitchen k.* cuchillo de cocina>; *(blade)* cuchilla; *(weapon)* cuchillo, puñal *m*; MED. *(scalpel)* cuchilla, bisturí *m* ♦ **to go under the k.** someterse a una operación quirúrgica, operarse II. tr. **knifed, knif·ing** *(to cut)* cortar (con un cuchillo); *(to stab)* dar una puñalada a, apuñalar; FAM. *(to betray)* apuñalar por la espalda, traicionar.

knife-edge (nīf'ĕj') s. filo.

knight (nīt) I. s. *(soldier)* caballero; FIG. *(defender)* paladín *m*, campeón *m*; *(in chess)* caballo II. tr. HIST. armar caballero; G.B. *(to honor)* conceder el título de *Sir* a.

knight er·rant (ĕr'ənt) s. [pl. **knights errant**] HIST. *(knight)* caballero andante; FIG. *(quixotic person)* Don Quijote *m*.

knight·hood (nīt'hŏŏd') s. *(rank)* rango *o* título de caballero; *(chivalry)* caballerosidad *f*; *(knights)* caballería, cuerpo de caballeros.

knight·ly (nīt'lē) adj. caballeresco.

Knight Templar s. [pl. **Knights Templars**] HIST. templario, caballero del Temple.

knit (nĭt) I. tr. **knit** *o* **knit·ted, knit·ting** *(a garment)* tejer; *(to unite)* trabar, unir; *(brows)* fruncir —intr. *(to sew)* tejer, hacer punto; *(to unite)* trabarse, unirse; *(brows)* fruncirse; MED. *(bone)* soldarse II. s. *(garment)* prenda de punto; *(cloth)* género de punto.

knit·ting (nĭt'ĭng) s. tejido, labor de punto *f*.

ã rey / ä año / b boca / ch chico / d dar / ĕ el / ē mil / g gato / h joya / hw juez / ī aire / k casa / kw cuan /

knitting needle s. aguja de tejer *o* de hacer punto.
knit·wear (nĭt'wâr') s. artículos de punto.
knives (nīvz) pl. de **knife.**
knob (nŏb) s. *(of a door)* perilla; *(dial)* botón *m*; *(protuberance)* protuberancia, prominencia; *(hill)* loma, cerro (prominente).
knock (nŏk) I. tr. *(to hit)* golpear, pegar <*someone just knocked me on the head* alguien me acaba de golpear en la cabeza>; *(to break through)* hacer <*they knocked a hole in the wall* hicieron un agujero en la pared>; JER. *(to criticize)* poner por el piso, poner por los suelos ♦ **k. it off!** ¡basta ya! • **to k. around** FAM. *(to consider)* considerar (idea); *(to abuse)* maltratar • **to k. against** chocar contra • **to k. down** *(to strike down)* derribar, tumbar; *(to disassemble)* desmontar, desarmar; FAM. *(to reduce)* rebajar (precio, costo) • **to k. for a loop** JER. dejar pasmado • **to k. off** *(to cause to fall)* hacer caer, tirar <*he knocked the lamp off the table* hizo caer la lámpara de la mesa>; FAM. *(to stop)* parar, suspender (tarea, trabajo); *(to do quickly)* despachar, terminar con; *(to deduct)* rebajar en; JER. *(to kill)* liquidar; *(to rob)* birlar, limpiar • **to k. out** *(to render unconscious)* dejar sin sentido, hacer perder el conocimiento; *(in boxing)* poner fuera de combate (en boxeo); *(to render inoperative)* estropear • **to k. over** tirar (vasa, lámpara) • **to k. up** JER. *(to make pregnant)* preñar, dejar preñada; G.B., FAM. *(to awaken)* despertar; *(to wear out)* fatigar, agotar —intr. *(to strike)* golpear, llamar <*someone is knocking at the door* alguien está llamando a la puerta>; *(to clash)* golpear; AUTO., MEC. pistonear *o* detonar (un motor) ♦ **to k. around** FAM. vagar, merodear • **to k. off** FAM. *(to pause)* parar (tarea, trabajo); *(to leave work)* terminar, salir del trabajo <*we knocked off early* salimos del trabajo temprano> • **to k. oneself out** FAM. matarse II. s. *(blow)* golpe *m*; *(rap)* toque *m*, llamada; AUTO., MEC. pistoneo, golpeteo; FIG., FAM. *(criticism)* crítica.
knock·a·bout (nŏk'ə-bout') I. s. MARÍT. chalupa II. adj. *(rowdy)* alborotador; *(rough)* violento; *(clothes)* de andar, de diario; *(sturdy)* resistente.
knock·down (nŏk'doun') I. adj. *(overwhelming)* demoledor; *(furniture)* desmontable; *(punch)* que derriba II. s. *(in boxing)* caída; *(blow, shock)* golpe demoledor *m*.
knock·er (nŏk'ər) s. *(on door)* aldaba; FAM. *(petty critic)* criticón *m*.
knock·ing (nŏk'ĭng) s. *(at the door)* aldabonazo, llamada a la puerta; *(blow)* golpe *m*.
knock·knee (nŏk'nē') s. piernas zambas.
knock·kneed (nŏk'nēd') adj. patizambo.
knock·out (nŏk'out') s. *(in boxing)* knock-out *m*; JER. *(attractive person or thing)* maravilla; *(success)* exitazo ♦ **a k. punch** un golpe que derriba.
knoll (nōl) s. loma, montículo.
knot (nŏt) I. s. nudo <*there are knots in my shoelaces* hay nudos en los cordones de mis zapatos>; MIL. *(braid)* galón *m*; *(group)* grupo <*a k. of fans* un grupo de admiradores>; *(bond)* lazo *o* vínculo (matrimonial); *(difficulty)* dificultad *f*, problema *m* <*there are several knots in our plan* hay algunos problemas en nuestros planes>; *(in wood)* nudo; MED. *(lump)* nudosidad *f*; MARÍT. nudo ♦ **to get tied up in knots** FAM. enredarse, crearse dificultades • **to tie the k.** FIG., FAM. casarse II. tr. **knot·ted, knot·ting** *(to tie)* atar con un nudo, anudar; *(to entangle)* enredar, enmarañar —intr. *(to become entangled)* enredarse; *(to form knots)* anudarse.
knot·hole (nŏt'hōl') s. hueco (que deja un nudo en la madera).
knot·ted (nŏt'ĭd) adj. *(tied)* anudado; *(intricate)* enredado, enmarañado; *(gnarled)* nudoso; *(military jacket)* adornado con galones.
knot·ty (nŏt'ē) adj. **-ti·er, -ti·est** *(tied in knots)* lleno de nudos; *(gnarled)* nudoso; FIG. *(puzzling)* enredado, enmarañado.
know (nō) tr. **knew** (nōō, nyōō), **known** (nōn), **know·ing** *(to comprehend)* saber <*I know arithmetic* sé aritmética>; *(to be acquainted with)* conocer <*I do not know that country* no conozco ese país>; *(to perceive)* entender, comprender <*I know how you are feeling* comprendo cómo te sientes>;

(to recognize) reconocer <*you would not have known me in my new outfit* no me hubieras reconocido con mi ropa nueva>; *(to distinguish)* distinguir <*to k. right from wrong* distinguir el bien del mal>; ANT. conocer (carnalmente) ♦ **to get to k. someone** llegar a conocer a alguien • **to let someone k.** hacer saber a alguien • **to make known** hacer saber *o* conocer • **to k. about** saber de • **to k. all about something** estar enterado de algo • **to k. by heart** saber de memoria • **to k. how to** saber <*I know how to swim* yo sé nadar> • **to k. one's own mind** saber lo que uno quiere • **to k. the score** *o* **what's what** saber lo que pasa —intr. saber ♦ **as far as I k.** que yo sepa • **how should I k.!** ¡yo qué sé! • **I k.** yo sé • **I ought to k.!** ¡lo sabré yo! • **to k. best** saber mejor que nadie • **to k. better** saber lo que debe hacerse <*after years of experience she should k. better* con tantos años de experiencia ella debería saber lo que debe hacerse> • **to k. better than to** saber que no se debe • **to k. each other** conocerse • **to k. for sure** estar seguro • **to k. only too well that** saber perfectamente que II. s. ♦ **to be in the k.** FAM. estar en la onda, estar al tanto.
know·a·ble (nō'ə-bəl) adj. conocible.
know-how (nō'hou') s. *(ability)* habilidad *f*; *(experience)* experiencia; *(knowledge)* preparación *f*, conocimientos.
know·ing (nō'ĭng) adj. *(intelligent)* instruido, preparado; *(aware)* de complicidad <*a k. glance* una mirada de complicidad>; *(shrewd)* astuto, hábil; *(deliberate)* deliberado.
know·ing·ly (nō'ĭng-lē) adv. *(intelligently)* de modo instruido, con preparación; *(shrewdly)* astutamente, hábilmente; *(deliberately)* deliberadamente, a sabiendas ♦ **to glance k. at** dirigir una mirada de complicidad a.
know-it-all (nō'ĭt-ôl') s. FAM. sabelotodo *mf*.
knowl·edge (nŏl'ĭj) s. *(understanding)* conocimiento <*k. of a language* el conocimiento de un idioma>; *(information)* conocimientos, saber *m* <*k. about outer space* conocimientos sobre el espacio extraterrestre>; *(erudition)* erudición; ♦ **carnal k.** conocimiento carnal • **it is common k. that** todo el mundo sabe que, es del dominio público que • **it has come to my k. that** me enteré de que • **not to my k.** no que yo sepa • **to have a working k. of** tener conocimientos prácticos de, dominar los principios de • **to have a thorough k. of** conocer a fondo • **to have no k. of** no saber nada de • **to my k.** que yo sepa • **to the best of my k.** según mi entender • **with full k. of the facts** DER. con conocimiento de causa • **without my k.** sin saberlo yo.
knowl·edge·a·ble (nŏl'ĭ-jə-bəl) adj. instruido, informado ♦ **to be k. about** conocer bien, saber mucho de.
known (nōn) I. part. p. de **know** II. adj. conocido <*a k. criminal* un criminal conocido>.
know-noth·ing (nō'nŭth'ĭng) s. *(ignoramus)* ignorante *mf*; *(agnostic)* agnóstico.
knuck·le (nŭk'əl) I. s. ANAT. *(of finger)* nudillo; CUL. *(cut of meat)* codo, codillo <*pig's knuckles* codos de cerdo>; *(of a hinge)* ojo (de una bisagra) ♦ **brass knuckles** manopla • **to rap someone's knuckles** dar en los nudillos II. intr. **-led, -ling** ♦ **to k. down** aplicarse duro • **to k. under** ceder, rendirse.
knuck·le-dust·ers (nŭk'əl-dŭs'tərz) s.pl. JER. manopla.
knuck·le·head (nŭk'əl-hĕd') s. persona estúpida, cabeza de alcornoque.
knur (nûr) s. BOT. nudo.
knurl (nûrl) s. *(knot)* nudo; *(on a coin)* gráfila, grafila.
KO DEP., JER. I. tr. (kā'ō') **KO'd, KO'ing** dar un knock-out, noquear II. s. (kā-ō') [pl. **KO's**] knock-out *m*.
ko·a·la (kō-ä'lə) s. ZOOL. koala *m*.
kohl (kōl) s. sombra (de ojos).
ko·la (kō'lə) s. BOT. cola.
kola nut s. BOT. nuez de cola *f*.
kook (kōōk) s. JER. persona alocada, excéntrico.
kook·y (kōō'kē) adj. **-i·er, -i·est** JER. alocado, excéntrico.
ko·peck (kō'pěk') s. FIN. copec (centésima parte de un rublo) *m*.
Ko·ran (kə-răn', -rän') s. RELIG. Corán *m*, Alcorán *m*.
Ko·re·a, Democratic People's Republic of (kə-rē'ə) República Popular Democrática de Corea.
Ko·re·an (kə-rē'ən) adj. & s. *(inhabitant, language)* coreano.
Korea, Republic of s. República de Corea.

ko·sher (kō'shər) adj. RELIG. *(conforming to dietary laws)* conforme al régimen alimenticio judío; *(specializing in kosher food)* de alimentos aptos para judíos; JER. *(proper)* conforme a las reglas, correcto; *(genuine)* legítimo.

kow·tow (kou-tou') intr. *(to salute)* hacer una reverencia china; FIG. *(to fawn)* humillarse, postrarse.

kraft (kräft) s. kraft *m*, papel de empaquetar *m*.

K ration s. MIL. ración militar *f*, ración de alimentos concentrados.

Krem·lin (krĕm'lĭn) s. POL. Kremlin *m*.

Krem·lin·ol·o·gy (krĕm'lə-nŏl'ə-jē) s. POL. análisis de la política del Kremlin *m*.

Krish·na (krĭsh'nə) s. RELIG. Krisna (avatar principal de Visnú) *m*.

kro·na (krō'nə) s. [pl. **-nor** (-nôr')] FIN. corona sueca.

kro·ne (krō'nə) s. [pl. **-ner** (-nər)] FIN. corona noruega.

kro·ner (krō'nər) s. FIN. corona danesa.

kro·nor (krō'nôr) pl. de **krona**.

Kru·ger·rand (krōō'gə-ränd', -ränd') s. FIN. moneda de oro de Sud Africa.

kryp·ton (krĭp'tŏn') s. QUÍM. criptón *m*.

ku·dos (kyōō'dŏz', kōō'-) s. prestigio, fama.

Ku Klux Klan (kōō' klŭks klän', kyōō') s. Ku Klux Klan (secta racista de EE. UU.) *m*.

küm·mel (kĭm'əl) s. kummel *m*, cúmel *m*.

kum·quat (kŭm'kwŏt') s. BOT. quinoto, naranjita china (arbusto *y* fruta).

Kurd (kûrd) s. curdo, kurdo (oriundo de Kurdistán).

Kurd·ish (kûr'dĭsh) s. curdo, kurdo (idioma).

Ku·wait (kə-wāt') s. Kuwait *m*.

Ku·wai·ti (kə-wā'tē) adj. & s. kuwaití *mf*.

ky·mo·graph (kī'mə-grăf') s. FÍS. quimógrafo.

ky·pho·sis (kī-fō'sĭs) s. MED. cifosis *f*.

Kyr·i·e (kîr'ē-ā') s. RELIG. kirie *m*.

L

l, L (ĕl) s. [pl. **l's, L's**] duodécima letra del alfabeto inglés.

la (lä) s. MÚS. la (nota *y* tono) *m*.

lab (lăb) s. laboratorio.

la·bel (lā'bəl) I. s. *(tag)* rótulo, etiqueta; *(brand name)* marca de fábrica; FIG. *(epithet)* etiqueta <*she doesn't deserve her l. as a cheat* ella no se merece su etiqueta de tramposa>; COMPUT. rótulo II. tr. *(to mark)* rotular, marcar; FIG. *(to describe)* describir, calificar.

la·bi·a (lā'bē-ə) pl. de **labium**.

la·bi·al (lā'bē-əl) I. adj. ANAT. labial, de los labios; FONÉT. labial II. s. FONÉT., GRAM. consonante labial *f*.

la·bi·ate (lā'bē-āt') I. adj. *(lipped)* labiado, con labios; BOT. labiado (flor, planta) II. s. planta labiada.

la·bi·um (lā'bē-əm) s. [pl. **-bi·a** (-bē-ə)] ANAT. labio (genital); BOT., ZOOL. labio.

la·bor (lā'bər) I. s. *(work)* trabajo, labor *f* <*manual l.* trabajo manual>; *(task)* tarea, faena; *(effort)* esfuerzo; *(workers)* mano de obra *f*, obreros; *(union)* sindicato; *(childbirth)* parto <*to be in l.* estar de parto> ♦ **hard l.** trabajos forzosos • **L.** G.B. laborismo • **l. of love** FIG. trabajo emprendido sin pensar en recompensa II. intr. *(to work)* trabajar <*to l. in vain* trabajar de balde>; *(to toil)* afanarse; *(to strive)* esforzarse; *(to plod)* moverse con dificultad, avanzar penosamente <*to l. up a hill* moverse con dificultad cuesta arriba>; MED. estar de parto; MARÍT. balancear, cabecear ♦ **to l. over** tomarse trabajo en, esmerarse en • **to l. under a delusion** tener una falsa impresión —tr. *(to belabor)* insistir en <*I will not l. the point* no insistiré en el punto> III. adj. laboral <*a l. dispute* un conflicto laboral> ♦ **L.** G.B. laborista • **l. camp** campo de trabajo • **l. force** mano de obra • **l. pains** dolores de parto • **l. relations** relaciones laborales.

lab·o·ra·to·ry (lăb'rə-tôr'ē) s. [pl. **-ries**] laboratorio.

Labor Day s. día del trabajador (primer lunes de septiembre en EE. UU.).

la·bored (lā'bərd) adj. *(difficult)* trabajoso, dificultoso; *(strained)* forzado, pesado.

la·bor·er (lā'bər-ər) s. *(worker)* trabajador *m*, obrero; *(unskilled worker)* peón *m*; *(day worker)* jornalero.

la·bo·ri·ous (lə-bôr'ē-əs) adj. *(labored)* laborioso; *(industrious)* industrioso, trabajador.

la·bo·ri·ous·ness (lə-bôr'ē-əs-nĭs) s. laboriosidad *f*.

la·bor·ite (lā'bə-rīt') s. laborista *mf* ♦ **L.** POL. miembro del partido laborista.

labor market s. mercado de trabajo.

la·bor·sav·ing (lā'bər-sā'vĭng) adj. que conserva *o* que economiza mano de obra.

labor shortage s. escasez de mano de obra *f*.

labor supply s. disponibilidad de mano de obra *f*.

labor union s. sindicato, gremio de trabajadores.

la·bour (lā'bər) s. G.B. var. de **labor.**

lab·y·rinth (lăb'ə-rĭnth') s. *(maze)* laberinto; *(confusion)* confusión *f*, enredo; *(inner ear)* cavidad interior del oído *f*.

lab·y·rin·thine (lăb'ə-rĭn'thĭn, -thēn') *o* **lab·y·rin·thi·an** (-thē-ən) adj. laberíntico.

lac (lăk) s. laca.

lace (lās) I. s. *(fabric)* encaje *m*; *(trim)* puntilla; *(shoelace)* cordón de zapato *m*; *(ribbon)* cinta; MIL. galón *m* II. tr. **laced, lac·ing** *(to tie)* encordonar; *(to thrash)* dar una paliza a; *(to spike)* echar licor a ♦ **to l. into someone** reprochar a alguien —intr. atarse.

lace-cur·tain (lās'kûr'tn) adj. que aspira a pertenecer a la clase media.

lac·er·ate (lăs'ə-rāt') I. tr. **-at·ed, -at·ing** *(to rip)* lacerar; FIG. *(to distress)* angustiar, herir (sentimientos) II. adj. *(torn)* lacerado; *(wounded)* herido, lastimado; BOT. lacerado, dentado.

lac·er·a·tion (lăs'ə-rā'shən) s. *(act)* laceración *f*; *(wound)* rasgón *m*, desgarradura.

lach·ry·mal (lăk'rə-məl) I. adj. lacrimal, lagrimal II. s.pl. **lachrymals** glándulas lacrimales *o* lagrimales.

lach·ry·mose (lăk'rə-mōs') adj. lacrimoso, lloroso.

lac·ing (lā'sĭng) s. *(lace)* cordón *m*; *(braid)* galón *m*; *(beating)* paliza; *(touch of liquor)* gota de licor.

lack (lăk) I. s. *(deficiency)* falta, carencia <*l. of money* falta de dinero>; *(need)* escasez *f* <*there is a l. of water in this area* hay escasez de agua en este sector> ♦ **for l. of** por falta de • **there is no l. of** no hay escasez de, hay suficiente II. tr. *(to be without)* carecer de, faltar <*he lacks courage* le falta valor>; *(to need)* necesitar <*what is it that you l.?* ¿qué es lo que necesitas?>; *(to require)* hacer falta, requerir(se) <*we are lacking five votes* nos hacen falta cinco votos>; *(to have no)* no tener <*some rabbits l. tails* algunos conejos no tienen rabo> —intr. *(to be needed)* hacer falta <*money is lacking for the campaign* hace falta dinero para la campaña> ♦ **to l. in** no tener, carecer de.

lack·a·dai·si·cal (lăk'ə-dā'zĭ-kəl) adj. *(indifferent)* indiferente; *(apathetic)* apático.

lack·a·day (lăk'ə-dā') interj. ANT. ¡ay de mi!, ¡mal haya!

lack·ey (lăk'ē) I. s. [pl. **-eys**] *(servant)* lacayo; *(toady)* adulador II. tr. **-eyed, -ey·ing** servir (obsequiosamente).

lack·ing (lăk'ĭng) I. adj. *(deficient)* deficiente, falto de <*a weak person is l. in strength* una persona débil está falta de energía> ♦ **to be l.** faltar II. prep. sin <*l. contacts you'll never find a good job* sin contactos nunca conseguirás un buen trabajo>.

lack·lus·ter (lăk'lŭs'tər) adj. apagado, deslucido.

la·con·ic (lə-kŏn'ĭk) adj. lacónico, breve.

lac·o·nism (lăk'ə-nĭz'əm) s. laconismo, brevedad *f*.

lac·quer (lăk'ər) I. s. *(synthetic coating)* pintura al duco, laca; *(varnish)* barniz *m* II. tr. *(to coat)* pintar al duco, laquear; *(to varnish)* barnizar.

lac·ri·mal (lăk'rə-məl) adj. & s.pl. var. de **lachrymal.**

lac·ri·ma·tion (lăk'rə-mā'shən) s. MED. lagrimeo.

la·crosse (lə-krôs') s. DEP. juego de pelota similar a la vilorta.

lac·tase (lăk'tās') s. BIOQUÍM. lactasa.

lac·tate (lăk'tāt') I. intr. **-tat·ed, -tat·ing** lactar, secretar leche II. s. lactato.

lac·ta·tion (lăk-tā'shən) s. lactación *f*, secreción de leche *f*; *(suckling)* lactancia.

lac·tic (lăk'tĭk) adj. láctico.
lactic acid s. QUÍM. ácido láctico.
lac·tose (lăk'tōs') s. QUÍM. lactosa.
la·cu·na (lə-kōō'nə, -kyōō'-) s. [pl. **-nae** (-nē) o **-nas**] *(blank)* laguna, claro; *(cavity)* laguna, hueco (abertura).
lac·y (lā'sē) adj. **-i·er, -i·est** de encaje.
lad (lăd) s. *(youth)* joven m, chico; *(fellow)* amigo.
lad·der (lăd'ər) s. *(device)* escalera, escala; FIG. *(status)* escala, jerarquía *<he is high on the executive l.* él figura en lo alto de la jerarquía ejecutiva>; G.B. *(in a stocking)* carrera ♦ **at the top of the l.** FIG. en la cumbre.
lad·die (lăd'ē) s. joven m, chico.
lade (lād) tr. **lad·ed, lad·en** (lād'n) o **lad·ed, lad·ing** *(to load)* cargar; FIG. *(to burden)* agobiar; *(to bale out)* achicar —intr. *(to load)* tomar carga; *(to ladle)* servir con cucharón.
lad·en (lād'n) **I.** un part. p. de **lade II.** adj. *(loaded)* cargado; FIG. *(burdened)* agobiado, abrumado.
la·di·da o **la·de·da** (lä'dē-dä') adj. FAM. repipi, afectado.
la·dies (lā'dēz') pl. de **lady.**
ladies' man s. var. de **lady's man.**
lad·ing (lā'dĭng) s. *(cargo)* carga, flete m ♦ **bill of l.** COM., MARÍT. conocimiento de embarque.
la·dle (lād'l) **I.** s. cucharón m **II.** tr. **-dled, -dling** servir con cucharón.
la·dy (lā'dē) s. [pl. **-dies**] *(woman)* dama; *(married woman)* señora; *(wife)* esposa ♦ **first l.** primera dama • **Lady** G.B. título que se antepone al nombre de la hija o esposa de un noble • **l. doctor** doctora • **l. lawyer** abogada • **l. of the evening** prostituta • **l. of the house** ama o señora de la casa • **lady's maid** doncella • **leading l.** primera actriz • **Our Lady** RELIG. Nuestra Señora, la Virgen María • **young l.** señorita.
lady beetle s. ENTOM. mariquita.
la·dy·bird (lā'dē-bûrd') s. ENTOM. mariquita.
la·dy·bug (lā'dē-bŭg') s. ENTOM. mariquita.
la·dy·fin·ger (lā'dē-fĭng'gər) s. lengua de gato, plantilla.
lady in waiting s. [pl. **ladies in waiting**] dama de honor.
la·dy·kill·er (lā'dē-kĭl'ər) s. JER. tenorio.
la·dy·like (lā'dē-līk') adj. *(well-bred)* bien educada; *(sensitive)* delicada.
la·dy·love (lā'dē-lŭv') s. amada.
la·dys·fin·ger (lā'dēz-fĭng'ər) s. var. de **ladyfinger.**
la·dy·ship (lā'dē-shĭp') s. excelencia, señoría (tratamiento de nobleza) ♦ **your l.** vuestra excelencia o señoría.
lady's man s. hombre galanteador m.
lag¹ (lăg) **I.** intr. **lagged, lag·ging** *(to straggle)* rezagarse, retrasarse; *(to flag)* aflojar(se) ♦ **to l. behind** estar retrasado, retrasarse **II.** s. *(laggard)* remolón m; *(delay)* dilación f, retraso *<a month's l.* un mes de retraso>; *(interval)* intervalo.
lag² (lăg) **I.** s. *(stave)* duela de un barril; *(lath)* listón (de madera) m **II.** tr. **lagged, lag·ging** revestir, cubrir (con listones).
lag³ (lăg) JER. **I.** tr. **lagged, lag·ging** *(to arrest)* arrestar; *(to jail)* encarcelar **II.** s. convicto.
la·ger (lä'gər) s. tipo de cerveza originado en Alemania.
lag·gard (lăg'ərd) adj. & s. rezagado, remolón m.
lag·ging (lăg'ĭng) s. TEC. camisa aisladora, revestimiento calorífugo; CONSTR. encostilado de excavaciones; entablado de moldes.
la·goon (lə-gōōn') s. laguna.
la·ic (lā'ĭk) o **la·i·cal** (-ĭ-kəl) **I.** adj. laico, secular **II.** s. seglar mf.
la·i·cize (lā'ĭ-sīz') tr. **-cized, -ciz·ing** laicizar.
laid (lād) pret. y part. p. de **lay¹.**
laid-back (lād'băk') adj. FAM. *(relaxed)* despreocupado, tranquilo; *(easygoing)* de trato fácil.
lain (lān) part. p. de **lie¹.**
lair (lâr) s. guarida, madriguera.
lais·sez faire o **lais·ser faire** (lĕs'ā fâr') s. ECON., POL. doctrina de no intervención.
la·i·ty (lā'ĭ-tē) s. [pl. **-ties**] *(laymen)* laicos; *(nonprofessionals)* profanos.
lake¹ (lāk) s. lago.
lake² (lāk) s. *(dye)* laca (pigmento); *(color)* rojo obscuro.

lam¹ (lăm) tr. & intr. **lammed, lam·ming** JER. zurrar, dar una paliza.
lam² (lăm) JER. **I.** intr. **lammed, lam·ming** fugarse, huir **II.** s. fuga, escape m ♦ **to take it on the l.** largarse.
la·ma (lä'mə) s. RELIG. lama m.
La·marck·i·an (lə-mär'kē-ən) adj. & s. BIOL. lamarquiano, lamarquista f.
la·ma·ser·y (lä'mə-sĕr'ē) s. [pl. **-ies**] RELIG. lamasería, convento de lamas.
La·maze (lə-mäz') adj. MED. según el método Lamaze (dic. del parto).
lamb (lăm) s. *(sheep)* cordero; *(meat)* carne de cordero f; *(lambskin)* piel de cordero f, corderina; FIG. *(dear)* cielo, amor m; *(dupe)* manso, inocente mf ♦ **l. chop** CUL. chuleta de cordero • **L. of God** RELIG. Cordero de Dios.
lam·baste (lăm-bāst') o **lam·bast** (-băst') tr. **-bast·ed, -bast·ing** FAM. *(to thrash)* dar una paliza; *(to scold)* poner como trapo, regañar duramente.
lamb·da (lăm'də) s. lambda (letra griega).
lam·bent (lăm'bənt) adj. *(flickering)* vacilante; *(glowing)* de suave brillo o luminosidad; FIG. *(bright)* vivo, brillante.
lamb·skin (lăm'skĭn') s. corderina, piel de cordero f.
lamb's wool s. lana de cordero, añinos.
lame (lām) **I.** adj. **lam·er, lam·est** *(disabled)* cojo, renco; *(stiff)* tullido; FIG. *(weak)* débil *<a l. excuse* una excusa débil>** II.** tr. **lamed, lam·ing** *(to cause to limp)* dejar cojo; *(to cripple)* lisiar, baldar.
la·mé (lă-mā') s. TEJ. lamé m.
lame·brain (lām'brān') s. tonto.
lame duck s. *(officeholder)* funcionario no reelegido y a punto de terminar su plazo; *(ineffective person)* incapaz mf.
la·mel·la (lə-mĕl'ə) s. [pl. **-mel·lae** (-mĕl'ē') o **-mel·las**] ZOOL. lámina, BOT. laminilla, membrana.
lame·ness (lām'nĭs) s. *(disability)* cojera; *(rigidity)* tullidez f; FIG. *(weakness)* debilidad f.
la·ment (lə-mĕnt') **I.** tr. *(to mourn)* lamentar, llorar; *(to regret)* deplorar —intr. lamentarse **II.** s. *(lamentation)* lamento; *(elegy)* elegía.
la·men·ta·ble (lə-mĕn'tə-bəl, lăm'ən-) adj. *(sad)* lamentable; *(deplorable)* deplorable.
lam·en·ta·tion (lăm'ən-tā'shən) s. lamentación f, lamento.
Lam·en·ta·tions (lăm'ən-tā'shənz) s. [ú. con v. sing.] BÍBL. Lamentaciones.
la·ment·ed (lə-mĕn'tĭd) adj. lamentado, llorado.
lam·i·na (lăm'ə-nə) s. [pl. **-nae** (-nē') o **-nas**] *(plate)* lámina, hoja; BOT., ZOOL. lámina.
laminar flow (lăm'ə-nər) s. FÍS. flujo o régimen laminar m.
lam·i·nate (lăm'ə-nāt') **I.** tr. **-nat·ed, -nat·ing** laminar —intr. dividirse o partirse en láminas **II.** adj. & s. (-nĭt, -nāt') laminado.
lam·i·nat·ed (lăm'ə-nā'tĭd) adj. laminado.
lam·i·na·tion (lăm'ə-nā'shən) s. *(process)* laminación f, laminado; *(lamina)* lámina.
lamp (lămp) s. *(device)* lámpara; FIG. *(beacon)* antorcha.
lamp·black (lămp'blăk') s. negro de humo.
lamp·light (lămp'līt') s. luz de la lámpara f.
lamp·light·er (lămp'lī'tər) s. farolero.
lam·poon (lăm-pōōn') **I.** s. *(spoof)* pasquín m, libelo; *(satire)* sátira **II.** tr. pasquinar, satirizar.
lam·poon·er (lăm-pōō'nər) s. satirista mf.
lamp·post (lămp'pōst') s. poste de farol m.
lam·prey (lăm'prē) s. [pl. **-preys**] ICT. lamprea.
lamp·shade (lămp'shād') s. pantalla de lámpara.
lance (lăns) **I.** s. *(weapon)* lanza; *(harpoon)* harpón m; *(soldier)* lancero; CIR. *(knife)* lanceta **II.** tr. **lanced, lanc·ing** *(with a weapon)* lancear; CIR. *(with a knife)* abrir con una lanceta.
lance corporal s. MIL. cabo interino.
lanc·er (lăn'sər) s. MIL. lancero ♦ **lancers** lanceros (baile y música).
lan·cet (lăn'sĭt) s. *(knife)* lanceta; *(arch)* ojiva.
land (lănd) **I.** s. *(solid ground)* tierra, tierra firme *<the sailors sighted l.* los marineros avistaron tierra firme>; *(soil)* suelo, tierra *<this l. is fertile* esta tierra es fértil>; *(tract)* campo, terreno *<desert l.* terreno desértico>; *(country)*

tierra, país m <*known throughout the l.* conocido en todo el país>; *(people)* pueblo, población f <*all the l. mourned the death of the king* toda la población lamentó la muerte del rey>; *(real estate)* bienes raíces m; FIG. *(realm)* reino; *(landed estate)* finca, hacienda ♦ **by l.** por tierra • **dry l.** tierra firme • **l. agent** corredor de fincas rurales • **l.-based** AER., MIL. de tierra • **l. of milk and honey** FIG. tierra de Jauja, paraíso terrenal • **l. of plenty** tierra de abundancia • **lands** tierras, posesiones • **native l.** patria, tierra o país natal • **no man's l.** tierra de nadie • **on l.** en tierra • **to get the lay of the l.** FIG. examinar el terreno • **to see how the l. lies** FIG. tantear el terreno **II.** tr. *(to unload)* desembarcar, descargar <*they landed the cargo* desembarcaron el cargamento>; *(to bring to earth)* aterrizar <*the pilot landed the airplane* el piloto aterrizó el avión>; FAM. *(to catch)* coger, atrapar (un pez); *(to win)* lograr, conseguir <*to l. a good contract* conseguir un buen contrato>; *(to deliver)* dar, asestar <*to l. a blow on the head* asestar un golpe en la cabeza> ♦ **to l. (someone) in** llevar (a alguien) a <*that kind of behavior will l. you in jail* ese comportamiento te llevará a la cárcel> —intr. *(to arrive)* arribar, atracar <*the ship landed at the port* el barco atracó en el puerto>; *(to disembark)* desembarcar <*all the passengers landed safely* todos los pasajeros desembarcaron sin accidente>; *(to alight)* posarse; *(to come to rest)* caer <*the man landed on his back* el hombre cayó de espaldas>; AER. *(on the earth)* aterrizar; *(on the moon)* alunizar ♦ **to l. on one's feet** *(from a fall)* caer de pie; FIG. *(to emerge safely)* salir adelante (de una situación) • **to l. on one's head** caer de cabeza • **to l. up** ir a parar <*he landed up in jail* fue a parar en la cárcel>.

lan·dau (lăn′dô′) s. *(carriage)* landó (coche tirado por caballos); *(car)* automóvil descapotable m.
land bank s. banco hipotecario.
land·ed (lăn′dĭd) adj. hacendado ♦ **l. gentry** terratenientes • **l. property** bienes raíces.
land·fall (lănd′fôl′) s. AVIA. aterrizaje m; MARÍT. recalada.
land·fill (lănd′fĭl′) s. CONSTR. método de rehabilitación de tierras o la tierra rehabilitada.
land grant s. concesión de tierras por parte del gobierno.
land·hold·er (lănd′hōl′dər) s. terrateniente mf.
land·hold·ing (lănd′hōl′dĭng) s. tenencia de tierras.
land·ing (lăn′dĭng) s. *(on land)* aterrizaje m; *(on the sea)* amerizaje m, amaraje m; *(on the moon)* alunizaje m; *(of passengers)* desembarco; *(of cargo)* desembarque m; *(site)* desembarcadero; *(of a staircase)* descanso, rellano ♦ **crash** o **emergency l.** aterrizaje de emergencia.
landing craft s. MIL. lancha de desembarco.
landing deck s. AVIA. cubierta de aterrizaje.
landing field s. AVIA. campo de aterrizaje.
landing force s. MIL. cuerpo expedicionario.
landing gear s. AVIA. tren de aterrizaje m.
landing net s. salabardo, redeña.
landing stage s. desembarcadero.
landing strip s. AVIA. pista de aterrizaje.
land·la·dy (lănd′lā′dē) s. [pl. **-dies**] *(owner)* propietaria, dueña; *(innkeeper)* patrona.
land·locked (lănd′lŏkt′) adj. *(of land)* sin salida al mar; *(of inland waters)* de agua dulce.
land·lord (lănd′lôrd′) s. *(owner)* propietario, arrendador m; *(innkeeper)* mesonero.
land·lub·ber (lănd′lŭb′ər) s. FAM. marinero de agua dulce.
land·mark (lănd′märk′) s. *(marker)* marca, señal f; *(boundary marker)* mojón m; *(event)* acontecimiento histórico, fecha memorable; *(site, building)* monumento histórico.
land·mass (lănd′măs′) s. área de terreno grande.
land mine s. MIL. mina terrestre.
land office s. oficina del catastro (tierras).
land·of·fice business s. negocio de gran movimiento.
land·own·er (lănd′ō′nər) s. terrateniente mf, propietario.
land·poor (lănd′pŏŏr′) adj. que no puede trabajar las tierras (por carecer de recursos).
land reform s. reforma agraria.
land·scape (lănd′skāp′) **I.** s. *(view)* paisaje m, panorama; ARTE. paisaje **II.** tr. **-scaped, -scap·ing** ornamentar (un terreno) —intr. dedicarse a la jardinería ornamental.
landscape architect s. arquitecto que diseña jardines.
landscape gardener s. experto en jardinería ornamental.
land·scap·ing (lănd′skā′pĭng) s. jardinería ornamental.
land·scap·ist (lănd′skā′pĭst) s. ARTE. paisajista mf.
land·slide (lănd′slīd′) s. *(dislodging)* desprendimiento de tierra, derrumbamiento; *(avalanche)* avalancha; POL. *(great victory)* triunfo electoral aplastante.
lands·man (lăndz′mən) s. [pl. **-men**] hombre que vive en la tierra m.
land·ward (lănd′wərd) **I.** adj. más cerca de la tierra **II.** adv. hacia la tierra.
lane (lān) s. *(path)* senda, vereda; *(alley)* callejón m, callejuela; *(country road)* camino; *(for ships, aircraft)* ruta; *(of a highway)* vía, carril m <*a four-lane highway* una carretera de cuatro carriles>; DEP. *(in a racecourse, pool)* calle f; *(in bowling)* pista.
lan·guage (lăng′gwĭj) s. *(speech)* lenguaje m <*l. is the essence of civilization* el lenguaje es la esencia de la civilización>; *(dialect)* lengua, idioma m <*the Spanish l.* el idioma español>; *(style, vocabulary)* lenguaje <*concise l.* lenguaje conciso>; *(linguistics)* lingüística; *(wording)* términos (de un contrato, una ley); COMPUT. lenguaje ♦ **bad** o **foul l.** lenguaje obsceno, palabrotas • **dead l.** lengua muerta • **living l.** lengua viva • **native l.** lengua materna • **strong l.** palabras mayores o fuertes • **to use bad l.** ser mal hablado.
lan·guid (lăng′gwĭd) adj. lánguido.
lan·guish (lăng′gwĭsh) intr. *(to become weak)* languidecer; *(to dwindle)* decaer; *(to stagnate)* estancarse; *(to waste away)* pudrirse <*to l. in prison* pudrirse en la cárcel> ♦ **to l. for** consumirse por, penar por (cariño, nostalgia).
lan·guish·ing (lăng′gwĭsh′ĭng) adj. *(weak)* lánguido, decaído; *(longing)* enamorado; *(lingering)* prolongado, dilatado; *(slow)* lento.
lan·guor (lăng′gər) s. languidez f.
lan·guor·ous (lăng′gər-əs) adj. lánguido.
lan·iard (lăn′yərd) s. var. de **lanyard**.
lank (lăngk) adj. **-er, -est** *(gaunt)* delgado; *(limp)* lacio <*l. hair* cabello lacio>.
lank·y (lăng′kē) adj. **-i·er, -i·est** larguirucho.
lan·o·lin (lăn′ə-lĭn) s. lanolina.
lan·tern (lăn′tərn) s. *(portable light)* linterna, farol de mano m; *(in a lighthouse)* fanal m; *(slide projector)* proyector de diapositivas m; ARQ. linterna, cupulino.
lantern jaw s. quijada larga y prominente.
lan·tha·nide (lăn′thə-nīd′) s. QUÍM. lantánido (tierra rara).
lan·tha·num (lăn′thə-nəm) s. QUÍM. lantano.
lan·yard (lăn′yərd) s. MARÍT. acollador m, cuerda; MIL. cuerda y gancho de disparo.
Lao (lou) **I.** adj. laosiano, lao **II.** s. [pl. **Lao** o **Laos**] *(inhabitant, language)* laosiano, lao ♦ **the L.** los laosianos.
Lao People's Democratic Republic s. República Democrática Popular Lao.
La·os (lä′ōs′, lous) s. Laos m.
La·o·tian (lā-ō′shən) adj. & s. laosiano.
lap¹ (lăp) s. *(of a person)* falda, regazo <*she put the baby on her l.* puso al niño en su regazo>; *(of a garment)* falda ♦ **in the l. of luxury** FIG. rodeado de lujo • **to drop** o **fall into one's l.** FIG. caerle a uno del cielo.
lap² (lăp) **I.** tr. **lapped, lap·ping** *(to fold)* doblar, plegar; *(to wrap)* envolver; *(to overlap)* cubrir parcialmente, traslapar; *(in a race)* sacar una vuelta (o vueltas) de ventaja; *(to polish)* pulir, esmerilar; CARP. ensamblar —intr. cubrirse, envolverse ♦ **to l. over** *(to overlap)* imbricarse, traslaparse; *(to extend out)* sobresalir **II.** s. *(overlap)* traslapo, solapa; *(of a race)* vuelta a la pista <*the second l. of the race* la segunda vuelta de la carrera>; *(of a swimming pool)* largo (de piscina); *(segment)* etapa <*the last l. of the hike* la última etapa del paseo>; *(layer)* recubrimiento; *(polishing disk)* rueda de pulir, bruñidor m.
lap³ (lăp) **I.** tr. **lapped, lap·ping** *(to drink)* beber a lengüetadas; *(to wash)* bañar, besar <*the waves l. the shore* las olas besan la orilla> ♦ **to l. up** *(to drink)* lamer, beber a lengüetadas; FIG. *(to accept eagerly)* aceptar con entu-

siasmo —intr. *(to drink)* lengüetear, sorber; *(to wash)* chapotear **II.** s. *(act)* lametón *m*, lengüetada; *(sound)* chapoteo.
lap dog s. perro faldero.
la·pel (lə-pĕl′) s. solapa (de una vestimenta).
lap·i·dar·y (lăp′ĭ-dĕr′ē) s. [pl. **-ies**] & adj. lapidario.
lap·is laz·u·li (lăp′ĭs lăz′yə-lē) s. MIN. lapislázuli *m*, lazulita.
lap joint s. TEC. junta de solapa *o* recubrimiento.
Lap·land (lăp′lănd′) s. Laponia.
Lapp (lăp) adj. & s. *(inhabitant, language)* lapón *m*.
lapse (lăps) **I.** intr. **lapsed, laps·ing** *(to drift)* caer, deslizarse <*l.* into a coma caer en coma>; *(to fail)* faltar <*to l.* from one's duty faltar al deber de uno>; *(to subside)* decaer, desvanecerse <*my enthusiasm lapsed* mi entusiasmo se desvaneció>; *(to elapse)* pasar, transcurrir <*several years had lapsed* habían transcurrido varios años>; DER. *(to expire)* caducar ♦ **to l. into one's old habits** volver a las mismas costumbres • **to l. into silence** dejar de hablar, quedarse callado **II.** s. *(slip)* desliz *m*, fallo <*a l. of memory* un fallo de la memoria>; *(error)* lapso, equivocación *f*; *(moral error)* desliz, falta; *(passage of time)* transcurso; *(interval)* lapso, período; DER. *(expiration)* caducidad *f*; *(slip of the tongue or pen)* lapsus *m*.
lapsed (lăpst) adj. *(elapsed)* transcurrido <*l.* time tiempo transcurrido>; *(expired)* caduco.
lap·wing (lăp′wĭng′) s. ORNIT. avefría, quincineta.
lar·board (lär′bərd) MARÍT. **I.** s. babor *m* **II.** adj. de babor **III.** adv. a babor.
lar·ce·nist (lär′sə-nĭst) s. ladrón *m*, ratero.
lar·ce·nous (lär′sə-nəs) adj. culpable de robo.
lar·ce·ny (lär′sə-nē) s. [pl. **-nies**] hurto, robo.
larch (lärch) s. BOT. alerce *m*, lárice (árbol y madera) *m*.
lard (lärd) **I.** s. lardo, manteca de cerdo **II.** tr. lardar, mechar con manteca de cerdo ♦ **to l. with** FIG. sazonar *o* adornar (informe, discurso).
lar·der (lär′dər) s. despensa.
large (lärj) **I.** adj. **larg·er, larg·est** *(big)* grande; *(comprehensive)* extenso, amplio; *(tolerant)* liberal <*a l.* and generous spirit un espíritu liberal y generoso>; MARÍT. *(fair)* bueno, favorable (viento) ♦ **l. as life** de tamaño natural **II.** adv. **larg·er, larg·est** grande <*to write l.* escribir con letra grande> ♦ **at l.** *(at liberty)* libre, en libertad <*the convict is still at l.* el presidiario está aún en libertad>; *(at length)* extensamente <*we talked at l.* hablamos extensamente>; *(in general)* en general <*the country at l.* el país en general>; POL. que representa todo un estado *o* distrito • **by and l.** en general, por lo general • **l. order** FAM. tarea peliaguda.
large-heart·ed (lärj′här′tĭd) adj. magnánimo.
large intestine s. ANAT. intestino grueso.
large·ly (lärj′lē) adv. *(mainly)* mayormente, en gran parte; *(amply)* considerablemente, ampliamente.
large-mind·ed (lärj′mīn′dĭd) adj. de amplias miras.
large·ness (lärj′nĭs) s. *(bulk)* grandor *m*, gran tamaño; *(vastness)* amplitud *f*, extensión *f*.
large-scale (lärj′skāl′) adj. *(extensive)* en gran escala; *(made large)* a gran escala (modelo, mapa).
lar·gess *o* **lar·gesse** (lär-zhĕs′, -jĕs′) s. *(generosity)* largueza, generosidad *f*; *(gift)* diva, donativo.
larg·ish (lär′jĭsh) adj. más bien grande, bastante grande.
lar·i·at (lăr′ē-ət) s. *(lasso)* lazo (para ganado); *(for picketing)* cabestro.
lark[1] (lärk) s. ORNIT. alondra.
lark[2] (lärk) **I.** s. *(carefree adventure)* parranda, calaverada; *(binge)* juerga <*to go on a l.* ir de juerga>; *(prank)* broma ♦ **to do something for a l.** hacer algo para divertirse **II.** intr. bromear, juguetear.
lark·spur (lärk′spûr′) s. BOT. espuela de caballero, consuelda.
lar·va (lär′və) s. [pl. **-vae** (-vē)] ENTOM. larva.
lar·val (lär′vəl) adj. larval.
la·ryn·ge·al (lə-rĭn′jē-əl, lăr′ən-jē′əl) adj. laríngeo.
la·ryn·ges (lə-rĭn′jēz) un pl. de **larynx**.
lar·yn·gi·tis (lăr′ən-jī′tĭs) s. MED. laringitis *f*.
lar·yn·gol·o·gy (lăr′ən-gŏl′ə-jē) s. MED. laringología.

lar·ynx (lăr′ĭngks) s. [pl. **la·ryn·ges** (lə-rĭn′jēz) *o* **lar·ynx·es**] ANAT. laringe *f*.
las·civ·i·ous (lə-sĭv′ē-əs) adj. lascivo.
lase (lāz) intr. **lased, las·ing** FÍS. funcionar como láser.
la·ser (lā′zər) s. FÍS. láser *m*.
lash[1] (lăsh) **I.** s. *(blow)* azote *m*, latigazo; *(of the elements)* azote, embate *m*; *(of a tail)* coletazo; *(whip)* azote, látigo; *(reprimand)* increpación *f*, regaño; *(dig)* sarcasmo; *(eyelash)* pestaña **II.** tr. *(to strike)* azotar, dar latigazos a; *(elements)* azotar, golpear <*sleet was lashing the roof* el granizo azotaba el techo>; *(to wag)* agitar con fuerza; *(to criticize)* fustigar, increpar; *(to goad)* incitar, impulsar ♦ **to l. out at** fulminar contra, fustigar —intr. *(to dash)* moverse con rapidez; *(to strike)* dar latigazos, restallar <*the brambles lashed across his body* las zarzas restallaban contra su cuerpo> ♦ **to l. out** encolerizarse, estallar de ira.
lash[2] (lăsh) tr. atar.
lash·ing (lăsh′ĭng) s. *(whipping)* azotaina, tunda de azotes; *m*; *(criticism)* fustigación *f*, regaño; *(for binding)* atadura, amarradura.
lass (lăs) s. *(girl)* muchacha, joven *f*; *(sweetheart)* novia.
las·sie (lăs′ē) s. muchacha, joven *f*.
las·si·tude (lăs′ĭ-tōōd′, -tyōōd′) s. lasitud *f*, cansancio.
las·so (lăs′ō, lă-sōō′) **I.** s. [pl. **-sos** *o* **-soes**] lazo **II.** tr. coger con un lazo.
last[1] (lăst) **I.** adj. *(final)* último <*the l.* game of the season el último partido de la temporada>; *(past)* pasado <*he spoke with her l. year* habló con ella el año pasado>; *(newest)* último <*the l.* thing in evening dresses el último grito en trajes de noche>; *(authoritative)* definitivo, final; *(least likely)* último <*the l. person whom we would have suspected* la última persona de quien hubiéramos sospechado>; *(latest possible)* último <*the l. minute* el último momento>; *(lowest)* inferior, menor <*l. prize* el premio menor>; *(terminal)* último <*her l. days* sus últimos días> ♦ **l. but not least** el último en orden pero no en importancia • **l. night** anoche • **that's the l. straw** ¡eso es el colmo! • **the night before l.** anteanoche, antes de anoche **II.** adv. *(at the end)* el último, en último lugar <*he came in l.* llegó en último lugar>; *(most recently)* la última vez <*we l. saw him in Paris* le vimos la última vez en París>; *(finally)* por último, finalmente <*and l., add the butter* y finalmente, añada la mantequilla> **III.** s. *(one that is last)* el último; *(the end)* final *m* <*he held out until the l.* resistió hasta el final> ♦ **at long l.!** ¡por fin!, ¡al fin! • **this is the l. of it** éste es el último de todos, con éste terminamos • **to the l.** hasta el fin, hasta lo último.
last[2] (lăst) intr. *(to go on)* durar <*the war lasted four years* la guerra duró cuatro años>; *(to survive)* sobrevivir <*he was not expected to l.* no se esperaba que sobreviviera>; *(to wear well)* durar <*these shoes lasted a long time* estos zapatos me duraron mucho tiempo>; *(to be enough)* bastar, alcanzar <*will our water l.?* ¿nos alcanzará el agua?>; FIG. *(to endure)* perdurar <*diamonds l. forever* los diamantes perduran para siempre> ♦ **to l. out** alcanzar, ser suficiente —tr. bastar, alcanzar <*this amount of money won't last us a year* esta cantidad de dinero no nos alcanzará para un año> • **to l. out** resistir, aguantar <*he will not l. out the voyage* no resistirá el viaje>.
last[3] (lăst) s. horma (de zapato).
last-ditch (lăst′dĭch′) adj. desesperado, último <*a l.* effort un último esfuerzo>.
last·ing (lăs′tĭng) **I.** adj. *(enduring)* duradero, perdurable; *(profound)* profundo; *(tough)* fuerte, resistente **II.** s. tela fuerte.
Last Judgment s. BÍBL. Juicio Final.
last·ly (lăst′lē) adv. *(finally)* por último, finalmente; *(in conclusion)* en conclusión.
last-min·ute (lăst′mĭn′ĭt) adj. de última hora.
last name s. apellido.
last straw s. colmo, acabóse *m*.
Last Supper s. BÍBL. Última Cena (de Jesucristo).
last word s. *(authority)* última palabra; *(latest thing)* última palabra, último grito.
latch (lăch) **I.** s. pestillo, aldabilla **II.** tr. cerrar con pestillo *o* aldabilla.

latch·key (lăch′kē′) s. [pl. **-keys**] llave (de picaporte) f.

latch·string (lăch′strĭng′) s. cordón del picaporte m.

late §G22 (lāt) **I.** adj. **lat·er, lat·est** (behind schedule) retrasado, atrasado <the bus is l. el autobús está atrasado>; (at an advanced hour) a una hora avanzada o tardía <a l. supper una cena a una hora avanzada>; (at the end) a fines de <in the l. 19th century a fines del siglo XIX>; (recent) reciente <a l. discovery un descubrimiento reciente>; (former) antiguo, anterior <the company's l. president el anterior presidente de la empresa>; (dead) fallecido, difunto <his l. father was a good writer su difunto padre era un buen escritor> ♦ **l. arrival** recién llegado • **to get l.** hacerse tarde • **to make someone l.** retrasar a alguien **II.** adv. **lat·er, lat·est** (tardy) tarde <a train that arrived l. un tren que llegó tarde>; (at the end) tardíamente, recientemente <it was a project undertaken l. in his career fue un proyecto emprendido tardíamente en su carrera>; (recently) hasta <she was in mourning as l. as last month estuvo de luto hasta el mes pasado> ♦ **better l. than never** más vale tarde que nunca • **l. in life** a una edad avanzada • **l. in the day** tarde • **later on** luego, más tarde • **of l.** recientemente, últimamente • **too l.** to o **for** demasiado tarde para • **to stay up l.** quedarse levantado hasta muy tarde.

late·com·er (lāt′kŭm′ər) s. (tardy person) retrasado; (newcomer) recién llegado, nuevo.

la·teen sail (lə-tēn′) s. MARÍT. vela latina.

late·ly (lāt′lē) adv. recientemente, últimamente ♦ **until l.** hasta hace poco.

la·ten·cy (lāt′n-sē) s. estado latente, latencia.

late·ness (lāt′nĭs) s. (tardiness) tardanza, llegada tardía <l. will affect your wages las tardanzas afectarán su salario>; (delay) demora, retraso.

la·tent (lāt′nt) adj. latente.

lat·er (lāt′ər) **I.** adj. comp. (last) último, posterior <his l. achievements sus logros posteriores>; (more recent) más reciente **II.** adv. comp. más tarde, después <six weeks l. seis semanas más tarde> ♦ **l. on** luego, después • **no l. than** no más tarde que • **(I'll) see you l.** hasta luego.

lat·er·al (lăt′ər-əl) **I.** adj. lateral **II.** s. (part) parte lateral f; (projection) aleta; FONÉT. sonido lateral.

lat·est (lā′tĭst) **I.** adj. (most recent) último <the l. news las últimas noticias>; (newest) más reciente <his l. novel su novela más reciente> **II.** adv. el último <he came l. vino el último> **III.** s. lo último, lo más reciente ♦ **at the l.** a más tardar • **the very l.** el último grito, la última moda.

la·tex (lā′tĕks′) s. BOT. látex (savia del árbol) m; (paint) pintura látex.

lath (lăth) **I.** s. [pl. **laths** (lăthz, lăths)] (wood) listón m; (metal) lata; (lathing) listonería, enlistonado **II.** tr. (with wood) listonar; (with metal) enlatar.

lathe (lāth) **I.** s. MEC. torno **II.** tr. **lathed, lath·ing** tornear.

lath·er (lăth′ər) **I.** s. (foam) espuma (de jabón); (froth) espumarajo (de la boca); FIG., FAM. (agitation) agitación f, nerviosidad f ♦ **to get oneself into a l.** agitarse, ponerse histérico **II.** tr. enjabonar, cubrir con espuma —intr. espumar, hacer espuma (jabón).

lat·i·fun·di·um (lăt′ə-fŭn′dē-əm) s. [pl. **-di·a** (-dē-ə)] latifundio.

Lat·in (lăt′n) **I.** adj. latino **II.** s. (language) latín m; (people) latino (esp. de América Latina).

Latin America s. América Latina, Latinoamérica.

Lat·in·A·mer·i·can (lăt′n-ə-mĕr′ĭ-kən) adj. latinoamericano.

Latin American s. latinoamericano.

Lat·in·ate (lăt′n-āt′) adj. latino, del latín.

Lat·in·ism (lăt′n-ĭz′əm) s. latinismo.

Lat·in·ist (lăt′n-ĭst) s. latinista mf.

Lat·in·ize (lăt′n-īz′) tr. & intr. **-ized, -iz·ing** latinizar.

La·ti·no (lə-tē′nō) s. [pl. **-nos**] FAM. latinoamericano.

lat·ish (lā′tĭsh) **I.** adj. un poco tardío **II.** adv. un poco tarde.

lat·i·tude (lăt′ĭ-tōōd′, -tyōōd′) s. (extent) amplitud f; (freedom) libertad f, margen de libertad m; ASTRON., GEOG. latitud f.

lat·i·tu·di·nal (lăt′ĭ-tōōd′n-əl, -tyōōd′-) adj. latitudinal.

lat·i·tu·di·nar·i·an (lăt′ĭ-tōōd′n-âr′ē-ən, -tyōōd′-) adj. & s. latitudinario.

la·trine (lə-trēn′) s. letrina, retrete m.

lat·ter (lăt′ər) adj. (second) éste <Peter and John are good players, but the l. is smarter than the former Pedro y Juan son buenos jugadores, pero éste es más inteligente que aquél>; (nearer the end) último <the l. part of the book la última parte del libro>; (later) más reciente, último <in l. times en los tiempos más recientes>.

lat·ter-day (lăt′ər-dā′) adj. reciente, de nuestros días.

Latter-day Saint s. Santo del último día.

lat·tice (lăt′ĭs) **I.** s. (framework) enrejado, celosía; (window) ventana con celosía; FÍS. red cristalina **II.** tr. **-ticed, -tic·ing** enrejar, poner celosía a un enrejado.

lat·tice·work (lăt′ĭs-wûrk′) s. enrejado, celosía.

Lat·vi·a (lăt′vē-ə) s. Latvia.

Lat·vi·an (lăt′vē-ən) adj. & s. (inhabitant, language) latvio, letón m.

laud (lôd) **I.** tr. (to glorify) loar, alabar; (to give praise to) elogiar, encomiar **II.** s. (glorification) loa, alabanza; (praise) elogio, encomio; (song) canto de alabanza ♦ **lauds** RELIG. [ú. con v. sing. o pl.] laudes.

laud·a·ble (lô′də-bəl) adj. loable, laudable.

lau·da·num (lôd′n-əm) s. FARM. láudano.

laud·a·to·ry (lô′də-tôr′ē) adj. laudatorio.

laugh (lăf, läf) **I.** intr. reír, reírse <to l. at a joke reírse de un chiste> ♦ **to be nothing to l. about** no ser cosa de risa • **to burst out laughing** soltar la carcajada, echarse a reír a carcajadas • **to l. at** (to show amusement) reírse con; (to ridicule) reírse de, burlarse de • **to l. in someone's face** echarse a reír en la cara de alguien • **to l. in the face of death** reírse de la muerte, desafiar la muerte • **to l. it up** divertirse • **to l. out loud** reírse a carcajadas • **to l. up one's sleeve** reírse para los adentros • **to make (someone) l.** dar risa, hacer reír —tr. expresar riendo <he laughed his appreciation expresó su aprecio riendo> ♦ **to l. away** o **off** tomar a risa • **to l. one's head off** reírse a más no poder • **to l. an actor off the stage** burlarse de un actor hasta sacarlo del escenario **II.** s. (act, sound) risa; FAM. (cause for laughing) chiste m, cosa de risa ♦ **for laughs** para hacer reír • **good for a l.** divertido • **loud l.** carcajada • **to have a good l.** reírse mucho • **to have the last l.** ser el último que ríe.

laugh·a·ble (lăf′ə-bəl, läf′ə-) adj. (funny) cómico; (ludicrous) ridículo, absurdo.

laugh·ing (lăf′ĭng, läf′ĭng) **I.** adj. risueño <l. face cara risueña> ♦ **it's no l. matter** no es cosa de risa **II.** s. risa.

laughing gas s. QUÍM. gas hilarante m, óxido nitroso.

laugh·ing·stock (lăf′ĭng-stŏk′, läf′ĭng-) s. hazmerreír m.

laugh·ter (lăf′tər, läf′-) s. (soft, medium) risa, risas; (loud) carcajadas ♦ **to burst into l.** echarse a reír a carcajadas • **uncontrollable l.** risa nerviosa.

launch[1] (lônch) **I.** tr. (to propel) lanzar <to l. a missile lanzar un cohete>; (to put into the water) botar; (to initiate) iniciar, emprender; (to give a start) lanzar; (to found) fundar; (to debut) estrenar —intr. lanzarse **II.** s. (act) lanzamiento; (into the sea) botadura ♦ **to l. forth** o **out on** emprender • **to l. into** lanzarse en **II.** s. (act) lanzamiento; (into the sea) botadura.

launch[2] (lônch) s. MARÍT. lancha.

launch·er (lôn′chər) s. (one that launches) lanzador m; MIL. (grenades) lanzagranadas m; (rockets) lanzacohetes m.

launch·ing (lôn′chĭng) s. (of a missile) lanzamiento; (of a ship) botadura; FIG. (of a product, campaign) lanzamiento, inauguración f ♦ **l. ramp** rampa de lanzamiento.

launch pad o **launching pad** s. plataforma de lanzamiento.

launch vehicle s. AER., ASTRONÁUT. sección propulsadora de proyectiles guiados.

laun·der (lôn′dər) **I.** tr. (to wash) lavar; (clothes) lavar y planchar; FIG. (money) lavar o pasar por intermediario (dinero) —intr. (to undergo washing) lavarse, resistir el lavado; (to wash and iron) lavar y planchar ropa **II.** s. MIN. lavadero, batea.

laun·dered (lôn′dərd) adj. (clothes) lavado y planchado; (money) que ha pasado por otras manos.

laun·der·er (lôn′dər-ər) s. lavandero.

ā rey / ä año / b boca / ch chico / d dar / ĕ el / ē mil / g gato / h joya / hw juez / ī aire / k casa / kw cuan /

laun·der·ette (lôn′də-rĕt′) s. lavandería automática.
laun·dress (lôn′drĭs) s. lavandera.
Laun·dro·mat (lôn′drə-măt′) s. marca registrada de una cadena de lavanderías automáticas.
laun·dry (lôn′drē) s. [pl. **-dries**] *(soiled clothes)* ropa, ropa sucia; *(clean clothes)* ropa, ropa limpia; *(place)* lavandería ♦ **to do the l.** lavar la ropa.
lau·re·ate (lôr′ē-ĭt) adj. & s. laureado.
lau·rel (lôr′əl) s. BOT. laurel *m*, lauro ♦ **laurels** FIG. laureles, distinción • **to rest on one's laurels** dormirse en los laureles.
la·va (lä′və, lăv′ə) s. GEOL. lava.
la·va·bo (lə-vā′bō) s. [pl. **-boes**] RELIG. lavatorio; *(washbowl)* lavabo.
lav·age (lăv′ĭj, lä-väzh′) s. MED. lavado (de un órgano).
lav·a·to·ry (lăv′ə-tôr′ē) s. [pl. **-ries**] *(room)* servicios; *(washbasin)* lavamanos *m*, lavabo; *(toilet)* inodoro, retrete *m*.
lav·en·der (lăv′ən-dər) **I.** s. BOT. *(plant)* lavanda, alhucema; *(color)* color lavanda *m* **II.** adj. de color lavanda.
lav·ish (lăv′ĭsh) **I.** adj. *(generous)* generoso; *(prodigal)* pródigo, manirroto; *(extravagant)* lujoso, espléndido **II.** tr. prodigar, derrochar ♦ **to l. (something) on someone** colmar a alguien de (algo).
lav·ish·ness (lăv′ĭsh-nĭs) s. *(generosity)* generosidad *f*; *(prodigality)* prodigalidad *f*, derroche *m*; *(extravagance)* lujo, esplendor *m*.
law (lô) s. DER. *(rule)* ley *f* <*the l. applies equally to all citizens* la ley se aplica a todos los ciudadanos por igual>; *(code)* fuero, código; *(jurisprudence)* jurisprudencia, derecho <*to study l.* estudiar derecho>; *(principle)* ley, principio <*the laws of physics* las leyes de la física>; FAM. *(police)* policía; LÓG., MAT. regla ♦ **by l.** según la ley • **common l.** derecho consuetudinario • **l. and order** orden público • **l. school** facultad de derecho • **officer of the l.** policía • **to break the l.** quebrantar la ley • **to lay down the l.** dictar la ley • **to practice l.** ejercer la abogacía • **to take the l. into one's own hands** tomarse la ley por la propia mano.
law·a·bid·ing (lô′ə-bī′dĭng) adj. respetuoso de la ley ♦ **l. citizen** ciudadano responsable.
law·break·er (lô′brā′kər) s. infractor de la ley *m*.
law·ful (lô′fəl) adj. *(allowed by law)* legal, lícito; *(recognized by law)* legítimo; *(law-abiding)* respetuoso de la ley.
law·ful·ly (lô′fə-lē) adv. legalmente, conforme a la ley.
law·ful·ness (lô′fəl-nĭs) s. *(legality)* legalidad *f*; *(of an heir)* legitimidad *f*.
law·giv·er (lô′gĭv′ər) s. legislador *m*.
law·less (lô′lĭs) adj. *(unruly)* desordenado, rebelde; *(unlawful)* ilegal, ilícito; *(anarchistic)* sin ley, anárquico.
law·less·ness (lô′lĭs-nĭs) s. *(unruliness)* desorden *m*, rebeldía; *(unlawfulness)* ilegalidad *f*; *(anarchy)* anarquía.
law·mak·er (lô′mā′kər) s. legislador *m*.
law·mak·ing (lô′mā′kĭng) s. legislación *f*.
law merchant s. [pl. **laws merchant**] derecho comercial, código de comercio.
lawn¹ (lôn) s. césped *m*.
lawn² (lôn) s. TEJ. linón *m*.
lawn mower s. cortacéspedes *m*, cortadora de césped.
lawn tennis s. DEP. tenis sobre hierba *m*.
law·ren·ci·um (lô-rĕn′sē-əm) s. QUÍM. laurencio.
law·suit (lô′sōōt′) s. DER. pleito, juicio.
law·yer (lô′yər) s. abogado, jurista *mf*.
lax (lăks) adj. **-er**, **-est** *(morals)* laxo; *(discipline)* flojo; *(remiss)* descuidado; *(slack)* flojo; *(bowels)* flojo; FONÉT. relajado.
lax·a·tive (lăk′sə-tĭv) s. & adj. MED. laxante *m*.
lax·i·ty (lăk′sĭ-tē) s. *(looseness)* laxitud *f*; *(slackness)* flojedad *f*; *(relaxation)* relajación *f*, relajamiento; *(negligence)* negligencia, descuido.
lax·ness (lăks′nĭs) s. *(of morals)* laxitud *f*; *(of discipline)* flojedad *f*; *(remissness)* descuido; *(of a rope)* flojedad; *(of bowels)* flojedad.
lay¹ (lā) **I.** tr. **laid** (lād), **lay·ing** *(to place)* poner <*l. your hand on your heart* póngase la mano en el corazón>; *(to cause to lie)* acostar <*she laid the child in the cradle* acostó al niño en la cuna>; *(to put)* colocar, poner <*he laid the book on the desk* puso el libro encima del escritorio>; *(to*

impute) achacar, atribuir <*she laid the blame on him* le atribuyó la culpa a él>; *(to set)* poner <*l. the table for five* pon la mesa para cinco>; *(to devise)* trazar *o* hacer (planes); *(to ascribe)* dar, poner <*to l. stress on clarity of expression* dar énfasis a la claridad de la expresión>; *(to submit)* presentar, someter <*he laid the case before the committee* sometió el caso ante la comisión>; *(to spread)* extender (barniz, pintura); *(to wager)* apostar; *(to impose)* imponer (multa, impuesto); ZOOL. *(eggs)* poner; JER., VULG. *(to have sexual intercourse with)* acostarse con ♦ **to be laid up** guardar cama • **to l. an egg** *(animals)* poner un huevo; JER. *(to fail)* fracasar • **to l. aside** *(to give up)* abandonar <*to l. aside all hope of rescue* abandonar toda esperanza de salvación>; *(to put aside)* guardar, dejar a un lado • **to l. away** *(to save)* guardar para el futuro; *(to stock)* guardar, reservar • **to l. bare** *o* **open** FIG. revelar, poner al descubierto • **to l. by** *o* **in** guardar, almacenar • **to l. claim to** reclamar los derechos a • **to l. down** *(to put to bed)* acostar; *(to establish)* dictar, establecer <*he laid down the conditions for settling the dispute* estableció las condiciones para resolver la disputa> • **to l. down one's arms** MIL. rendirse, darse por vencido • **to l. down one's life for** ofrendar *o* sacrificar la vida por • **to l. down the law** FIG. asentar un principio • **to l. eyes on** poner los ojos en, echar la vista encima a • **to l. hands on** FAM. *(to catch)* coger, atrapar; *(to hit)* poner la mano encima <*if I ever l. my hands on him, I'll kill him* si alguna vez le pongo la mano encima, lo mato>; RELIG. dar imposición de manos a • **to l. into** JER. *(to beat)* apalear; *(to scold)* regañar, reñir • **to l. it on (thick)** JER. exagerar • **to l. low** derribar <*he laid his opponent low* derribó a su contrincante> • **to l. off** *(to dismiss)* despedir (esp. temporalmente); JER. *(to stop)* dejar, abandonar (costumbre, vicio); *(to refrain from)* dejar de • **to l. one's cards on the table** poner las cartas sobre la mesa • **to l. out** *(to plan)* planear, proyectar; *(to spread out)* preparar; *(to prepare for burial)* amortajar; FAM. *(to spend)* gastar <*he laid out twenty dollars for the gift* gastó veinte dólares en el regalo> • **to l. siege to** asediar, sitiar • **to l. to** MARÍT. hacer poner en facha (el barco) • **to l. to rest** *(to bury)* enterrar; *(to refute)* refutar <*he laid to rest the rumor that he had resigned* refutó el rumor de que había renunciado> • **to l. up** *(to confine to bed)* obligar a guardar cama; *(to dock)* atracar • **to l. waste to** asolar, arrasar —intr. *(to produce eggs)* poner huevos, aovar; *(to bet)* apostar, hacer una apuesta ♦ **to l. over** pararse, detenerse • **to l. to** MARÍT. situarse, colocarse • **to l. to** MARÍT. pairar el barco **II.** s. *(of a rope)* dirección *f o* sesgo (del hilo de una cuerda *o* cable); *(share)* participación (en ganancia) *f*; JER., VULG. *(sexual intercourse)* coito ♦ **l. of the land** FIG. configuración *o* disposición de los elementos en una situación.
lay² (lā) adj. *(secular)* secular, laico; *(not professional)* lego.
lay³ (lā) s. *(song)* cantar *m*.
lay⁴ (lā) pret. de **lie¹**.
lay·er (lā′ər) **I.** s. *(coating)* capa; *(hen)* gallina ponedora; GEOL. estrato; AGR. acodo **II.** tr. AGR. acodar —intr. *(to separate)* separarse en capas; AGR. arraigar.
lay·er·ing (lā′ər-ĭng) *o* **lay·er·age** (-ĭj) s. AGR. acodadura.
lay·ette (lā-ĕt′) s. ajuar de niño *m*, canastilla para bebé.
lay·man (lā′mən) s. [pl. **-men**] *(laic)* laico, seglar *m*; FIG. *(nonprofessional)* lego, profano.
lay·off (lā′ôf′) s. *(suspension)* suspensión de empleados *f*; *(dismissal)* despido; *(unemployment)* cesación de trabajo *f*.
lay·out (lā′out′) s. *(plan)* disposición *f*, distribución *f* <*the l. of an apartment* la distribución de un apartamento>; *(sketch)* trazado; IMPR. *(design)* diseño, composición *f*; *(dummy)* maqueta.
lay·o·ver (lā′ō′vər) s. *(by train, boat)* escala; *(by car, train)* parada.
laz·a·ret·to (lăz′ə-rĕt′ō) *o* **laz·a·ret** (-rĕt′) s. [pl. **-ret·tos** *o* **-rets**] lazareto.
laze (lāz) intr. **lazed, laz·ing** holgazanear, gandulear —tr. ♦ **to l. away** perder, desperdiciar el tiempo.
la·zi·ness (lā′zē-nĭs) s. *(idleness)* pereza, haraganería; *(sluggishness)* lentitud *f*.

laz·u·lite (lăz′ə-līt′, lăzh′ə-) s. MIN. lazulita, lazurita.
la·zy (lā′zē) adj. **-zi·er, -zi·est** *(idle)* perezoso, haragán; *(sluggish)* lento ♦ **l. afternoon** tarde de flojera *o* pereza.
la·zy·bones (lā′zē-bōnz′) s.pl. [ú. con v. sing. o pl.] JER. remolón *m,* vago.
lazy Susan s. bandeja giratoria.
LCD (ĕl′sē-dē′) s. COMPUT. presentación numérica por intermedio de un cristal líquido y un impulso eléctrico.
lea (lē, lā) s. POÉT. prado, pradera.
leach (lēch) QUÍM. **I.** tr. & intr. lixiviar(se) **II.** s. lixiviación *f.*
lead¹ (lēd) **I.** tr. **led** (lĕd), **lead·ing** *(to guide)* guiar, conducir; *(to command)* dirigir, mandar *<generals l. armies* los generales mandan ejércitos>; *(to induce)* inducir *<fear of cancer leads many people to give up smoking* el miedo al cáncer induce a mucha gente a dejar de fumar>; *(to direct)* dirigir; *(to head)* ser el primero de, encabezar *<his name leads the list* su nombre encabeza la lista>; *(to be ahead of)* llevar una ventaja de *<he led the runner-up by three minutes* le llevaba una ventaja de tres minutos al subcampeón>; *(to live)* llevar *<to l. a life of crime* llevar una vida entregada al crimen>; *(in cards)* salir con; *(to aim a gun)* apuntar delante de ♦ **to l. astray** descarriar, llevar por mal camino • **to l. (someone) by the nose** FAM. llevar de las narices • **to l. in** *o* **into** hacer entrar en, llevar a • **to l. off** *(to begin)* iniciar, empezar • **to l. on** *(to entice)* seducir, tentar; *(to deceive)* engañar, embaucar • **to l. the field** ser el primero, ir a la cabeza • **to l. the way** enseñar el camino a, dar el ejemplo —intr. *(to be first)* ser primero, estar a la cabeza; *(to go first)* guiar, enseñar el camino; *(to command)* mandar; *(to go)* llevar, conducir *<this discussion is leading nowhere* esta discusión no conduce a nada>; *(in cards)* ser mano, salir ♦ **to l. off** empezar, dar comienzo • **to l. on** guiar, enseñar el camino **II.** s. *(position)* primer lugar *m,* delantera; *(margin)* ventaja *<he has a four-yard l. in the race* lleva una ventaja de cuatro yardas en la carrera>; *(clue)* indicación *f,* pista; CINEM., TEAT. *(principal role)* papel principal *m; (actor)* protagonista *mf;* PERIOD. *(introduction)* párrafo introductor; *(news story)* artículo *o* noticia principal; *(in card playing)* mano *<it's your l.* tú eres mano>; *(leash)* traílla, correa *(para animales);* MIN. filón *m,* vena; ELEC. conductor *m;* MÚS. tema principal *m;* DEP. golpe inicial *(en el boxeo)* ♦ **to be in the l.** ir a la cabeza, ir primero • **to follow the l. of** seguir el ejemplo de • **to take the l. (in a race)** tomar la delantera, adelantarse; *(to command)* tomar el mando **III.** adj. principal *<the l. violin* el violinista principal>.
lead² (lĕd) **I.** s. QUÍM. plomo; *(of a pencil)* mina; MARÍT. sonda; IMPR. regleta ♦ **leads** plomo, tiras de plomo • **to fill someone full of l.** acribillar a alguien a balazos **II.** tr. *(to cover)* cubrir con plomo; *(to line)* forrar con plomo; *(to secure)* emplomar *(una ventana);* IMPR. espaciar, regletear.
lead·ed gasoline (lĕd′əd) s. nafta que contiene plomo.
lead·en (lĕd′n) adj. *(of lead)* plúmbeo, de plomo; *(dark grey)* plomizo, de color plomo; FIG. *(heavy)* pesado; *(sluggish)* tardo, lento; *(depressed)* deprimido, desanimado.
lead·er (lē′dər) s. *(guide)* guía *mf,* conductor *m; (chief)* jefe *m,* líder *m <the l. of the expedition* el jefe de la expedición>; *(politician)* caudillo; *(first)* primero; *(horse)* caballo delantero; *(pipe)* canalón *m,* conducto; *(on a fishing line)* sotileza; MÚS. *(conductor)* director *m; (main instrumentalist)* instrumentista principal *mf;* COM. artículo de reclamo, oferta *(para atraer clientes);* BOT. yema terminal; G.B. *(editorial)* editorial principal *m* ♦ **to be the l. in** ser el primero en.
lead·er·ship (lē′dər-shĭp′) s. *(position)* dirección *f,* mando; *(capacity)* dotes de mando *f* ♦ **party l.** POL. jefatura, liderato.
lead-in (lēd′ĭn′) **I.** s. *(introduction)* introducción *f;* RAD. bajada de antena, entrada **II.** adj. de entrada.
lead·ing¹ (lē′dĭng) adj. *(foremost)* primero, que va a la cabeza *<l. candidate* el candidato que va a la cabeza>; *(main)* principal *<the l. story* la noticia principal>; TEAT. primero *<l. lady* primera actriz> ♦ **l. question** pregunta capciosa.

lead·ing² (lĕd′ĭng) s. *(rim)* emplomado; IMPR. interlineación *f.*
leading edge (lē′dĭng) s. AER., MARÍT. borde anterior *m,* borde de ataque.
lead line (lēd) s. MARÍT. sonda.
lead·off (lēd′ôf′) s. *(opening move)* comienzo, principio; *(person)* iniciador *m,* persona que comienza.
lead pencil (lĕd) s. lápiz de mina *o* de grafito *m.*
lead poisoning s. MED. saturnismo.
lead-time (lĕd′tīm′) s. *(completion time)* tiempo requerido para completar un proyecto; COM. *(for a delivery)* tiempo desde la orden de pedido hasta la entrega.
leaf (lēf) **I.** s. [pl. **leaves** (lēvz)] BOT. hoja; *(foliage)* follaje *m,* hojas; *(sheet of paper)* hoja; *(page)* página; *(folio)* folio; *(sheet of metal)* lámina; *(of table, door, shutter)* hoja; AUTO. hoja ♦ **gold l.** pan de oro • **in l.** con hojas • **l. tobacco** tabaco en rama • **to shake like a l.** temblar como un azogado • **to turn over a new l.** empezar una nueva vida, hacer borrón y cuenta nueva **II.** intr. BOT. echar hojas —tr. hojear ♦ **to l. through** hojear.
leaf·less (lēf′lĭs) adj. BOT. áfilo, que no tiene hojas.
leaf·let (lēf′lĭt) s. *(pamphlet)* folleto, panfleto; *(advertisement)* prospecto; *(flier)* volante *m,* octavilla; BOT. hojuela, folíolo.
leaf mold s. BOT. moho *o* añublo del follaje.
leaf spring s. AUTO. ballesta, muelle de hojas *m.*
leaf·stalk (lēf′stôk′) s. BOT. pecíolo.
leaf·y (lē′fē) adj. **-i·er, -i·est** *(covered with leaves)* frondoso, hojoso; *(consisting of leaves)* compuesto de hojas, laminado; *(leaflike)* en forma de hoja.
league¹ (lēg) **I.** s. *(alliance)* liga, alianza; *(organization)* asociación *f,* sociedad *f;* DEP. liga ♦ **to be out of one's l.** FIG. estar en competencia desigual **II.** intr. & tr. **leagued, leagu·ing** aliar(se), unir(se).
League of Nations s. Sociedad *f o* Liga de las Naciones.
lea·guer (lē′gər) s. MIL. sitio, cerco.
leagu·er (lē′gər) s. miembro de una liga *o* de una asociación.
leak (lēk) **I.** intr. *(container)* salirse, tener un agujero *<the radiator leaks* el radiador se sale>; *(pipe)* tener fugas; *(faucet)* salirse, gotear; *(roof)* gotear; *(boat)* hacer agua; *(shoes)* mojarse ♦ **to l. in** filtrarse, colarse • **to l. out** *(to escape)* salirse, escaparse; *(to become known)* divulgarse, saberse —tr. divulgar *<he leaked the secret to the enemy* divulgó el secreto al enemigo> **II.** s. *(in a container)* agujero; *(in a pipe)* fuga, escape *m; (in a faucet, roof)* gotera; *(in a boat)* vía de agua; *(escape)* salida, escape *<he couldn't stop the oil l.* no pudo detener la salida del aceite>; *(disclosure)* divulgación *f* ♦ **security l.** divulgación de información secreta • **to spring a l.** *(container)* empezar a salirse, hacérsele un agujero a; *(boat)* empezar a hacer agua • **to take a l.** JER. hacer aguas, orinar.
leak·age (lē′kĭj) s. *(escaping)* salida, escape *m; (entering)* filtración *f,* penetración *f; (amount lost)* pérdida.
leak·y (lē′kē) adj. **-i·er, -i·est** *(container)* que se sale, que tiene agujeros; *(pipe, valve)* que tiene fugas; *(faucet)* que se sale, que gotea; *(roof)* que tiene goteras; *(boat)* que hace agua.
lean¹ (lēn) **I.** intr. **leaned** *o* **leant** (lĕnt), **lean·ing** *(to incline)* inclinarse, estar inclinado *<that wall leans badly* esa pared se inclina peligrosamente>; *(to rest on)* apoyarse, reclinarse *<he leaned against the railing* se reclinó contra la baranda>; *(to rely)* depender de, contar con *<you can l. on me for help* puedes contar con mi ayuda>; *(to tend)* inclinarse *<they l. toward new methods* se inclinan hacia métodos modernos>; FAM. *(to exert pressure)* hacer presión ♦ **to l. back** *(against the wall)* recostarse; *(in a chair)* reclinarse • **to l. forward** inclinarse, echarse hacia adelante • **to l. over** inclinarse • **to l. over backwards to** FAM. esforzarse al máximo para, hacer todo lo posible para —tr. *(to rest)* apoyar, recostar *<he leaned his head on her shoulder* recostó la cabeza en el hombro de ella>; *(to cause to incline)* inclinar, ladear **II.** s. inclinación *f.*
lean² (lēn) **I.** adj. **-er, -est** *(thin)* delgado, flaco; *(meat)* ma-

gro, sin grasa; *(fuel, ore)* pobre ♦ **l. years** años de las vacas flacas, años de escasez **II.** s. CUL. carne sin grasa *f.*

lean·ing (lē'nĭng) s. *(tendency)* tendencia; *(proclivity)* proclividad *f,* inclinación *f.*

leant (lĕnt) un pret. y part. p. de **lean¹**.

lean-to (lēn'tōō') s. cobertizo.

leap (lēp) **I.** intr. **leaped** *o* **leapt** (lĕpt, lēpt), **leap·ing** saltar ♦ **to l. at the chance** no dejar escapar la oportunidad —tr. *(to jump over)* saltar por encima de; *(a horse)* hacer saltar **II.** s. *(act)* salto, brinco; FIG. *(step)* paso *<a great l. for mankind* un gran paso para la humanidad> ♦ **by leaps and bounds** a grandes pasos, a pasos agigantados.

leap·frog (lēp'frŏg') **I.** s. pídola **II.** tr. **-frogged, -frog·ging** saltar por encima de —intr. jugar a la pídola.

leapt (lĕpt, lēpt) un pret. y part. p. de **leap**.

leap year s. año bisiesto.

learn (lûrn) tr. **learned** *o* **learnt** (lûrnt), **learn·ing** *(to master)* aprender; *(to memorize)* aprender, aprenderse; *(to find out)* saber, enterarse de *<he finally learned the truth* por fin supo la verdad> ♦ **to l. by heart** *o* **by rote** aprender de memoria • **to l. from experience** aprender por experiencia • **to l. one's lesson** FIG. escarmentar —intr. *(to gain mastery)* aprender; *(from one's misfortunes)* escarmentar *<when will you finally l.?* ¿cuándo escarmentarás?> ♦ **to l. how** aprender *<I never learned how to swim* nunca aprendí nadar>.

learn·ed (lûr'nĭd) adj. *(person)* docto, erudito *<my l. colleague* mi docto colega>; *(publication)* erudito, especializado ♦ **to be l. in** saber mucho de.

learn·er (lûr'nər) s. principiante *mf* ♦ **to be a fast l.** aprender rápidamente • **to be a slow l.** aprender con trabajo.

learn·ing (lûr'nĭng) s. *(instruction)* aprendizaje *m,* estudio; *(knowledge)* saber *m,* erudición *f* ♦ **a hunger for l.** una sed de aprender • **men of l.** eruditos.

learning disability s. dificultad de aprendizaje *f.*

learn·ing-dis·a·bled (lûr'nĭng-dĭs-ā'bəld) adj. incapacitado para aprender.

learnt (lûrnt) un pret. y part. p. de **learn**.

lease (lēs) **I.** s. *(contract)* contrato de arrendamiento, arrendamiento; *(duration)* alquiler *m* *<a two-year l.* alquiler por dos años> ♦ **to get a new l. on life** FIG. empezar una nueva vida **II.** tr. **leased, leas·ing** *(to grant use)* arrendar, dar en arriendo; *(to rent)* alquilar, tomar en arriendo.

lease·hold (lēs'hōld') s. inquilinato, arrendamiento; *(property)* propiedad arrendada.

lease·hold·er (lēs'hōl'dər) s. inquilino, arrendatario.

leash (lēsh) **I.** s. correa, traílla **II.** tr. *(animals)* atraillar; *(to control)* controlar, dominar.

leas·ing (lē'sĭng) s. *(lease)* alquiler *m,* arrendamiento; ANT. *(lie)* mentira.

least §G22, 28 (lēst) **I.** adj. *(in importance)* menor, (más) mínimo *<I haven't got the l. idea* no tengo ni la más mínima idea>; *(in magnitude)* mínimo, más pequeño *<the l. effort wears thin* con el más pequeño esfuerzo lo agota> ♦ **not the l. bit** en lo más mínimo, ni un poquito • **that's the l. of my worries** eso es lo de menos **II.** adv. menos **III.** s. lo menos *<the l. I could do* lo menos que podría hacer> ♦ **at l.** *(not less than)* por lo menos; *(in any event)* al menos • **at the very l.** como mínimo • **not in the l.** en absoluto, en lo más mínimo • **to say the l.** *(in a positive sense)* sin exagerar; *(in a pejorative sense)* por no decir otra cosa.

least common denominator s. MAT. mínimo común denominador.

least common multiple s. MAT. mínimo común múltiple.

least·wise (lēst'wīz') adv. FAM. *(anyway)* de todas maneras; *(at least)* por lo menos, al menos.

leath·er (lĕth'ər) **I.** s. cuero, piel *f* ♦ **l. belt** cinturón de cuero **II.** tr. *(to cover)* cubrir con cuero; FAM. *(to beat)* zurrar, azotar.

leath·er·ette (lĕth'ə-rĕt') s. tela vinílica que imita el cuero.

leath·er·neck (lĕth'ər-nĕk') s. JER. soldado de infantería de marina en EE. UU.).

leath·er·y (lĕth'ə-rē) adj. *(like leather)* parecido al cuero; *(weathered)* curtido *<a l. face* una cara curtida>; *(said of cooked meat)* correoso, duro.

leave¹ (lēv) tr. **left** (lĕft), **leav·ing** *(to go away from)* salir de, marcharse de *<they left their house early* salieron de su casa temprano>; *(to forget)* olvidar, dejar *<I left my wallet at home* dejé mi billetera en casa>; *(to let stay)* dejar *<l. all the lights on* deja todas las luces encendidas>; *(to result in)* dejar *<the fire left them homeless* el incendio los dejó sin hogar>; *(to have remaining)* dejar *<the mother died leaving three sons* la madre murió dejando tres hijos>; *(to bequeath)* dejar, legar; *(to entrust)* encomendar, dejar *<l. the matter to him* deja el asunto en manos de él>; *(to abandon)* dejar, abandonar *<he left his family a year ago* abandonó a su familia hace un año>; *(to remove oneself from)* dejar (de pertenecer a), separarse de (ocupación, carrera); *(to deposit)* dejar *<I left my luggage at the station* dejé mi equipaje en la estación> ♦ **l. alone** dejar tranquilo, dejar en paz *<l. me alone!* ¡déjame tranquilo!> • **to l. behind** *(to outdistance)* dejar atrás; *(to depart without)* irse *o* partir sin • **to l. in the dark** FIG. dejar a oscuras, dejar sin entender • **to l. it at that** dejarlo así, dejar las cosas como están • **to l. much to be desired** dejar mucho que desear • **to l. no stone unturned** FIG., FAM. no escamotear esfuerzos • **to l. out** omitir, excluir • **to l. word** dejar dicho —intr. *(to go)* irse, marcharse; *(to depart)* salir, partir ♦ **to be left** quedar *<there's some food left* queda algo de comida> • **to be left in the lurch** FIG. quedarse colgado *o* plantado • **to be left over** quedar, sobrar • **to l. off** *(to stop)* dejar, parar *<let's resume the reading where we left off yesterday* continuemos la lectura donde paramos ayer>.

leave² (lēv) s. *(permission)* permiso; MIL. permiso, licencia *<to be on l.* estar de licencia> ♦ **l. of absence** permiso, licencia • **to take (one's) l. of someone** despedirse de alguien.

leave³ (lēv) intr. **leaved, leav·ing** BOT. echar hojas.

leaved (lēvd) adj. *(with leaves)* hojoso, cubierto de hojas; *(table, door)* de hojas.

leav·en (lĕv'ən) **I.** s. *(yeast)* levadura; FIG. *(catalyst)* estímulo, fermento **II.** tr. *(to add leavening to)* leudar; *(to ferment)* fermentar ♦ **to l. with** FIG. imbuir, impregnar.

leav·en·ing (lĕv'ə-nĭng) s. *(leaven)* levadura; *(fermentation)* fermentación *f.*

leaves (lēvz) pl. de **leaf**.

leave-tak·ing (lēv'tā'kĭng) s. despedida.

leav·ing (lē'vĭng) s. partida, salida.

leav·ings (lē'vĭngz) s.pl. residuos, sobras.

Leb·a·nese (lĕb'ə-nēz') **I.** adj. libanés **II.** s. [pl. **Lebanese**] libanés *m* ♦ **the L.** los libaneses.

Leb·a·non (lĕb'ə-nən) s. Líbano.

lech·er (lĕch'ər) s. libertino, lujurioso.

lech·er·ous (lĕch'ər-əs) adj. libertino, lujurioso.

lech·er·y (lĕch'ə-rē) s. libertinaje *m,* lujuria.

lec·i·thin (lĕs'ə-thĭn) s. lecitina.

lec·tern (lĕk'tərn) s. atril *m,* facistol *m.*

lec·tor (lĕk'tər) s. RELIG. lector *m.*

lec·ture (lĕk'chər) **I.** s. *(discourse)* conferencia; *(course)* curso, clase *f* *<a series of lectures on art* una serie de clases en arte>; *(reprimand)* reprimenda, sermón *m* *<the children got a l. when they came home late* los niños recibieron una reprimenda por llegar tarde a casa> **II.** intr. **-tured, -tur·ing** *(to give a discourse)* dictar conferencia; *(in a university)* dar *o* dictar un curso —tr. dar una conferencia a ♦ **to l. on** dar una conferencia sobre • **to l. (someone) on** *o* **about** reprender (a alguien) sobre, sermonear (a alguien) sobre.

lec·tur·er (lĕk'chər-ər) s. *(lecture giver)* conferenciante *mf,* conferencista *mf*; *(professor)* profesor *m.*

led (lĕd) pret. y part. p. de **lead¹**.

LED (ĕl'ē-dē', lĕd) s. COMPUT. LED (diodo emisor de luz).

ledge (lĕj) s. *(of a wall)* repisa, anaquel *m*; *(of a window)* antepecho; *(on a cliff)* reborde *m,* saliente *m*; *(in the ocean)* banco de arrecifes; MIN. vena, veta.

ledg·er (lĕj'ər) s. *(book)* libro mayor; *(tombstone)* lápida sepulcral; *(wooden support)* travesaño de andamio.

lee (lē) MARIT. **I.** s. *(side)* sotavento, socaire *m*; *(shelter)* abrigo, protección *f* **II.** adj. de sotavento, a sotavento.

leech (lēch) **I.** s. ZOOL. sanguijuela; FIG. *(parasite)* parásito,

vividor *m* **II.** tr. sangrar ♦ **to l. off someone** pegarse a alguien como parásito.
leek (lēk) s. puerro.
leer (lîr) **I.** intr. mirar de reojo *o* de soslayo **II.** s. mirada de reojo *o* de soslayo.
leer·y (lîr′ē) adj. **-i·er, -i·est** *(suspicious)* suspicaz; *(distrustful)* desconfiado; *(wary)* cauteloso.
lees (lēz) s.pl. sedimento de un líquido.
lee·ward (lē′wərd, lōō′ərd) MARÍT. **I.** adj. de sotavento, a sotavento **II.** s. sotavento, banda de sotavento.
lee·way (lē′wā′) s. AVIA., MARÍT. *(drift)* FIG. *(margin)* margen (de dinero, tiempo) *m*; *(latitude)* campo, libertad *f.*
left[1] (lĕft) **I.** adj. izquierdo <*my l. foot hurts* me duele el pie izquierdo> ♦ **I.** *o* **L.** POL. izquierdista, de izquierda • **l. hook** gancho de izquierda **II.** s. *(location)* izquierda, lado izquierdo; *(left hand)* mano izquierda, izquierda; *(in boxing)* directo *o* golpe de izquierda *m* ♦ **on** *o* **to the l.** a *o* por la izquierda ♦ **I.** *o* **L.** POL. izquierda **III.** adv. a la izquierda, hacia la izquierda.
left[2] (lĕft) pret. & part. p. de **leave**[1].
left-hand (lĕft′hănd′) adj. *(on the left)* de la izquierda; *(for left-handed people)* para zurdos ♦ **on the l. side** a la izquierda, a mano izquierda • **to make a l. turn** doblar a la izquierda.
left-hand·ed (lĕft′hăn′dĭd) **I.** adj. *(person)* zurdo; *(utensil)* para zurdos <*l. scissors* tijeras para zurdos>; *(awkward)* torpe ♦ **l. compliment** piropo de doble filo **II.** adv. con la mano izquierda.
left-hand·er (lĕft′hăn′dər) s. zurdo.
left·ism *o* **Left·ism** (lĕf′tīz′əm) s. POL. izquierdismo.
left·ist *o* **Left·ist** (lĕf′tĭst) s. & adj. POL. izquierdista *mf.*
left·o·ver (lĕft′ō′vər) **I.** adj. sobrante, restante **II.** s. ♦ **leftovers** *(remnants)* sobras, restos; CUL. plato hecho de restos de comida.
left wing s. POL. izquierda, ala izquierda (de un grupo).
left-wing (lĕft′wĭng′) adj. POL. izquierdista, de izquierdas.
left-wing·er (lĕft′wĭng′ər) s. POL. izquierdista *mf.*
left·y (lĕf′tē) s. [pl. **-ies**] JER. *(left-handed person)* zurdo; POL. *(leftist)* izquierdista *mf.*
leg (lĕg) **I.** s. *(of a person)* pierna; *(of an animal)* pata; *(of furniture)* pata, pie *m*; *(of a tripod)* soporte *m*, pie *m*; *(of trousers)* pierna, pernera; FIG. *(in a journey)* etapa; GEOM. cateto; CUL. *(of poultry)* muslo; *(of lamb)* pierna; DEP. *(in sailing)* bordada; *(in relay races)* tramo, trecho ♦ **not to have a l. to stand on** FAM. carecer de una razón válida, no tener en que basar un argumento • **on its last legs** FIG., FAM. sin recursos, en las últimas • **to pull someone's l.** FIG., FAM. tomarle el pelo a alguien • **to shake a l.** FIG., FAM. apresurarse, darse prisa • **to stretch one's legs** *(to stretch)* estirar las piernas; FIG. *(to take a walk)* dar un paseo **II.** intr. **legged, leg·ging** ♦ **to l. it** FAM. ir a pie, ir caminando.
leg·a·cy (lĕg′ə-sē) s. [pl. **-cies**] DER. *(inheritance)* herencia, legado; FIG. *(heritage)* patrimonio, herencia.
le·gal (lē′gəl) adj. *(relating to the law)* jurídico <*l. files* expedientes jurídicos>; *(lawful)* legal, lícito; *(statutory)* legítimo <*l. owner* propietario legítimo> ♦ **l. adviser** asesor jurídico • **l. fees** honorarios de abogado • **l. profession** abogacía • **l. right** derecho civil • **to take l. action** poner una demanda, entablar pleito.
legal age s. DER. mayoría de edad ♦ **of l. age** mayor de edad.
le·gal·ese (lē′gə-lēz′) s. vocabulario legal especializado.
legal holiday s. día de fiesta legal *m*, feriado oficial.
le·gal·ism (lē′gə-lĭz′əm) s. legalismo.
le·gal·ist (lē′gə-lĭst) s. legalista *mf.*
le·gal·is·tic (lē′gə-lĭs′tĭk) adj. legalista.
le·gal·i·ty (lē-găl′ĭ-tē) s. [pl. **-ties**] legalidad *f* ♦ **legalities** trámites legales *o* jurídicos.
le·gal·i·za·tion (lē′gə-lĭ-zā′shən) s. legalización *f.*
le·gal·ize (lē′gə-līz′) tr. **-ized, -iz·ing** *(to make legal)* legalizar; *(to authorize)* legitimar, autorizar; *(to approve)* legitimar, aprobar.
le·gal·ly (lē′gə-lē) adv. legalmente.
legal pad s. bloc de papel rayado de 8½ por 14 pulgadas.

legal tender s. moneda de curso legal.
leg·ate (lĕg′ĭt) s. legado (enviado papal).
leg·a·tee (lĕg′ə-tē′) s. DER. legatario.
le·ga·tion (lĭ-gā′shən) s. *(legate)* legado (enviado papal); *(diplomatic mission)* legación *f.*
leg·end (lĕj′ənd) s. *(myth)* leyenda; *(person)* mito; *(inscription)* leyenda, inscripción *f*; *(explanatory note)* pie *m* ♦ **a l. in one's own time** un mito vivo.
leg·en·dar·y (lĕj′ən-dĕr′ē) adj. legendario.
leg·er·de·main (lĕj′ər-də-mān′) s. *(sleight of hand)* juego de manos, prestidigitación *f*; *(trickery)* truco.
leg·ged (lĕg′ĭd, lĕgd) adj. *(people)* de piernas <*a long-legged woman* una mujer de piernas largas>; *(animals, furniture)* de patas <*four-legged* de cuatro patas>.
leg·gings (lĕg′ĭngz) s.pl. polainas.
leg·gy (lĕg′ē) adj. **-gi·er, -gi·est** *(having long legs)* de piernas largas, zanquilargo; *(having attractive legs)* de piernas atractivas.
leg·i·bil·i·ty (lĕj′ə-bĭl′ĭ-tē) s. legibilidad *f.*
leg·i·ble (lĕj′ə-bəl) adj. legible.
le·gion (lē′jən) s. legión *f* ♦ **L.** organización nacional de excombatientes (en EE. UU.).
le·gion·ar·y (lē′jə-nĕr′ē) **I.** adj. legionario, de la legión **II.** s. [pl. **-ies**] legionario, miembro de la legión.
le·gion·naire (lē′jə-nâr′) s. legionario.
leg·is·late (lĕj′ĭ-slāt′) intr. **-lat·ed, -lat·ing** legislar, promulgar leyes —tr. disponer *o* establecer por ley.
leg·is·la·tion (lĕj′ĭ-slā′shən) s. legislación *f.*
leg·is·la·tive (lĕj′ĭ-slā′tĭv) **I.** adj. legislativo **II.** s. cuerpo *o* poder legislativo.
leg·is·la·tor (lĕj′ĭ-slā′tər) s. legislador *m.*
leg·is·la·ture (lĕj′ĭ-slā′chər) s. legislatura, cuerpo *o* poder legislativo *m.*
le·git (lə-jĭt′) adj. JER. legítimo.
le·git·i·ma·cy (lə-jĭt′ə-mə-sē) s. legitimidad *f.*
le·git·i·mate (lə-jĭt′ə-mĭt) **I.** adj. *(lawful)* lícito; *(reasonable)* válido <*a l. complaint* una queja válida>; *(authentic)* legítimo, auténtico; *(child)* legítimo; *(theater)* serio, auténtico **II.** tr. (-māt′) **-mat·ed, -mat·ing** *(to justify)* validar, justificar; *(to declare legitimate)* legitimar.
le·git·i·ma·tize (lə-jĭt′ə-mə-tīz′) tr. **-tized, -tiz·ing** legitimar.
le·git·i·mi·za·tion (lə-jĭt′ə-mĭ-zā′shən) s. legitimación *f.*
le·git·i·mize (lə-jĭt′ə-mīz′) tr. **-mized, -miz·ing** legitimar.
leg·ume (lĕg′yōōm′, lə-gyōōm′) s. legumbre *f.*
le·gu·mi·nous (lə-gyōō′mə-nəs) adj. leguminoso.
leg·work (lĕg′wûrk′) s. FAM. trabajo que requiere caminar *o* viajar mucho.
lei (lā) s. guirnalda hawaiana de flores.
lei·sure (lē′zhər, lĕzh′ər) s. ocio ♦ **at l.** *(comfortably)* cómodamente; *(not employed)* desocupado • **at one's l.** en los ratos libres de uno • **l. time** tiempo libre.
lei·sure·ly (lē′zhər-lē, lĕzh′ər-) **I.** adj. sin prisa, pausado **II.** adv. sin prisa, pausadamente.
leit·mo·tif *o* **leit·mo·tiv** (līt′mō-tēf′) s. leitmotiv *m*, tema central *m.*
lem·ma (lĕm′ə) s. [pl. **-mas** *o* **-ma·ta** (-mə-tə)] LÓG., MAT. lema *m.*
lem·ming (lĕm′ĭng) s. ZOOL. lemming *m*, ratón de Noruega *o* campestre *m.*
lem·on (lĕm′ən) **I.** s. BOT. *(tree)* limonero; *(fruit)* limón *m*; *(color)* limonado, limón, amarillo; FAM. *(person)* melón *m*; *(car)* cacharro, maula ♦ **l. grove** limonar **II.** adj. limonado, limón, amarillo.
lem·on·ade (lĕm′ə-nād′) s. limonada.
lem·pi·ra (lĕm-pîr′ə) s. FIN. lempira (unidad monetaria de Honduras) *m.*
le·mur (lē′mər) s. ZOOL. lémur *m.*
lend (lĕnd) tr. **lent** (lĕnt), **lend·ing** *(to loan)* prestar <*will you l. me five dollars?* ¿me prestas cinco dólares?>; *(to impart)* dar, impartir <*to l. a feeling of warmth* impartir una sensación de bienestar> ♦ **to l. itself to** prestarse a • **to l. someone a hand** ayudar, dar una mano a alguien —intr. prestar dinero, hacer préstamos.
lend·er (lĕn′dər) s. *(one who lends)* prestador *m*; COM. *(business person)* prestamista *mf.*
lending library s. biblioteca de préstamo.

lend-lease (lĕnd′lēs′) s. préstamo y arriendo.
length (lĕngkth) s. *(measurement)* largo, longitud *f* <*the l. of the room* la longitud de la habitación>; *(quality)* largura, extensión *f*; *(piece)* pedazo, tramo <*a l. of rope* un tramo de soga>; *(of cloth)* corte *m*; *(in a race)* cuerpo <*the horse won by two lengths* el caballo sacó dos cuerpos de ventaja>; *(extent)* longitud, extensión <*the l. of the novel* la extensión de la novela>; *(distance)* distancia <*focal l.* distancia focal>; *(of a journey)* recorrido; *(of clothing)* largo; *(duration)* duración *f* <*the l. of the meeting* la duración de la reunión>; *(period)* período, espacio; FONÉT. cantidad *f*
♦ **along the l. of** a lo largo de • **at great l.** por extenso, con lujo de detalles • **at l.** *(eventually)* al cabo, por fin; *(fully)* por extenso, detenidamente • **to go to great lengths** hacer todo lo posible • **to keep somebody at arm's l.** mantener a alguien a distancia • **to travel the l. of** recorrer todo.
length·en (lĕngk′thən) tr. & intr. *(an object)* alargar(se), estirar(se); *(time)* prolongar(se).
length·en·ing (lĕngk′thə-nĭng) s. *(object)* alargamiento; *(time)* prolongación *f*.
length·wise (lĕngkth′wīz′) **I.** adv. longitudinalmente **II.** adj. longitudinal.
length·y (lĕngk′thē) adj. **-i·er, -i·est** *(prolonged)* prolongado; *(long)* largo.
le·nien·cy (lēn′yən-sē) o **le·nience** (-yəns) indulgencia, poca severidad.
le·nient (lēn′yənt) adj. indulgente, poco severo.
Len·in·grad (lĕn′ĭn-grăd′) s. Leningrado.
Len·in·ism (lĕn′ə-nĭz′əm) s. POL. leninismo.
Len·in·ist (lĕn′ə-nĭst) s. leninista *mf*.
lens (lĕnz) s. FÍS., ÓPT. lente *mf* <*contact lenses* lentes de contacto>; *(magnifying glass)* lupa, lente de aumento; FOTOG. lente, objetivo.
lent (lĕnt) pret. y part. p. de **lend.**
Lent (lĕnt) s. RELIG. cuaresma.
Lent·en (lĕn′tən) adj. *(relative to Lent)* cuaresmal, de cuaresma; FIG. *(meager)* magro, escaso.
len·ti·cel (lĕn′tĭ-sĕl′) s. BOT. lenticela, lentejuela.
len·til (lĕn′təl) s. lenteja.
len·to (lĕn′tō) MÚS. **I.** adv. lentamente **II.** adj. & s. [pl. **-tos**] lento.
Le·o (lē′ō) s. ASTROL., ASTRON. Leo, León *m*.
le·o·nine (lē′ə-nīn′) adj. leonino.
leop·ard (lĕp′ərd) s. ZOOL. leopardo (animal y piel).
le·o·tard (lē′ə-tärd′) s. malla de acróbatas y bailarines.
lep·er (lĕp′ər) s. leproso.
lep·i·dop·ter·an (lĕp′ĭ-dŏp′tər-ən) s. ENTOM. lepidóptero.
lep·i·dop·ter·ist (lĕp′ĭ-dŏp′tər-ĭst) s. entomólogo que se ocupa del estudio de los lepidópteros.
lep·i·dop·ter·ous (lĕp′ĭ-dŏp′tər-əs) adj. ENTOM. lepidóptero.
lep·re·chaun (lĕp′rĭ-kŏn′, -kôn′) s. MITOL. duende *m*, gnomo (irlandés).
lep·ro·sy (lĕp′rə-sē) s. MED. lepra.
lep·rous (lĕp′rəs) adj. leproso.
lep·ton (lĕp′tŏn′) s. FÍS. leptón *m*.
Les·bi·an (lĕz′bē-ən) s. *(person from Lesbos)* lesbiano, lesbio
♦ **l.** lesbiana (mujer homosexual).
Les·bos (lĕz′bŏs) s. Lesbos.
lese maj·es·ty (lēz′ măj′ĭ-stē) s. DER. crimen de lesa majestad *m*.
le·sion (lē′zhən) s. MED. lesión *f*.
Le·so·tho (lē-sō′tō) s. Lesotho.
less §G22, 28 (lĕs) **I.** adj. *(not as much)* menos <*to have l. time* tener menos tiempo>; *(not as great)* inferior, menor <*a matter of l. importance* un asunto de menor importancia> • **in l. than no time** en un abrir y cerrar de ojos, en el acto • **l. than** menos de lo que <*they drank l. than I expected* ellos bebieron menos de lo que yo esperaba>; menos que <*some people have l. drive than others* algunas personas tienen menos motivación que otras>; menos de <*l. than ten dollars* menos de diez dólares> • **no l. than** *(as much as)* nada menos que; *(at least)* por lo menos • **nothing l. than** nada menos que **II.** prep. *(minus)* menos <*five l. two is three* cinco menos dos son tres> **III.** adv. menos <*it costs l.* cuesta menos> ♦ **l. and l.** cada vez menos • **l.**

than *(not at all)* no ser nada <*you are being l. than honest* no estás siendo nada honesto; *(far from)* ni mucho menos • **more or l.** más o menos • **much l.** mucho menos, menos aún <*I'm not blaming anyone, much l. you* no culpo a nadie, mucho menos a ti> • **none the l.** sin embargo, a pesar de todo • **so much the l.** tanto menos • **the l. . . . the l. . . .** cuanto menos . . . menos . . . **IV.** s. menos *m* <*the l. you study the l. you learn* cuanto menos estudias menos aprendes> ♦ **l. than** menos de lo que **V.** pron. no tantos <*many things begin badly, l. end well* muchas cosas empiezan mal, no tantas terminan bien>.
les·see (lĕ-sē′) s. DER. locatario, arrendatario.
less·en (lĕs′ən) tr. & intr. disminuir, reducir(se).
less·er (lĕs′ər) adj. *(less important)* menor; *(smaller)* más pequeño.
Les·ser An·til·les (lĕs′ər ăn-tĭl′ēz) s.pl. Antillas Menores.
les·son (lĕs′ən) **I.** s. *(class)* lección *f*, clase *f* <*to give Russian lessons* dar clases de ruso>; *(in a text)* lección; RELIG. lección, lectura ♦ **to learn one's l.** FIG. escarmentar • **to take lessons** tomar clases, aprender • **to teach someone a l.** FIG. dar una lección a alguien **II.** tr. aleccionar.
les·sor (lĕs′ôr′) s. DER. locador *m*, arrendador *m*.
lest (lĕst) conj. *(for fear that)* por temor a que, por miedo de que <*he did not move l. the guard should hear him* no se movió por temor a que el guardia lo sintiera>; *(so as to prevent that)* para (que) no <*call us l. we forget* llámanos para que no se nos olvide>.
let¹ §G1, 6 (lĕt) **I.** tr. **let, let·ting** *(to permit)* permitir <*please, l. me finish* por favor, permítame terminar o permítame continuar>; *(to allow)* dejar <*l. the baby cry all he wants* deja llorar al niño todo lo que quiera>; *(to rent)* alquilar; *(to lease)* arrendar ♦ **to l. by** o **through** dejar pasar • **to l. down** *(to lower)* bajar; *(to lengthen)* alargar; *(hair)* dejar caer o soltar; FIG. *(to disappoint)* fallar, decepcionar • **to l. go** *(to fire)* despedir; *(to set free)* dejar en libertad; *(to release)* soltar • **to l. in** *(cold, animal)* dejar entrar; *(visitor)* hacer pasar • **to l. it all hang out** JER. hablar o actuar abiertamente • **to l. it go at that** dejarlo así, no hacer o decir más • **to l. know** avisar, dar a conocer • **to l. off** *(to release)* dejar salir o escapar (fluido); *(to exempt)* eximir, dispensar de; *(to forgive)* perdonar; *(firearm)* disparar; *(to explode)* hacer estallar o explotar • **to l. oneself go** *(to enjoy)* soltarse, desatarse; *(to neglect)* descuidarse, abandonarse • **to l. out** *(to permit to go out)* dejar salir; *(to set free)* poner en libertad; *(garments)* ensanchar, extender; *(to divulge)* divulgar; *(scream)* pegar, despedir; *(to rent)* alquilar • **to l. slip** dejar escapar —intr. *(to become rented)* alquilarse; *(to become leased)* arrendarse ♦ **to l. on** *(to divulge)* admitir, revelar el secreto; *(to pretend)* fingir • **to l. up** FAM. *(to cease)* cesar; *(to slacken)* aflojarse; *(wind, rain)* disminuirse —aux. [ú. con sugerencias, avisos, u órdenes] <*let's see* veamos> <*l. x equal y* supongamos que x es igual a y> **II.** conj. ♦ **l. alone** y mucho menos, ni siquiera <*she can't crawl, l. alone walk* ella no puede gatear y mucho menos andar>.
let² (lĕt) s. *(obstacle)* obstáculo, impedimento; *(tennis stroke)* let *m*.
let·down (lĕt′doun′) s. *(decrease)* disminución *f*, aminoramiento; *(disappointment)* decepción *f*, desilusión *f*; AVIA. *(descent)* descenso.
le·thal (lē′thəl) adj. letal, mortífero.
le·thar·gic (lə-thär′jĭk) adj. letárgico.
leth·ar·gy (lĕth′ər-jē) s. letargo.
le·the (lē′thē) s. olvido ♦ **L.** MITOL. Lete, Leteo.
let's (lĕts) contr. de **let us.**
Lett (lĕt) s. *(inhabitant, language)* latvio, letón *m*.
let·ter (lĕt′ər) **I.** s. *(symbol)* letra (de un alfabeto); *(note)* carta; COM., DER. carta; IMPR. tipo, carácter *m* ♦ **capital l.** mayúscula • **cover l.** carta adjunta • **dead l.** letra muerta • **l. of introduction** carta de presentación • **letters** letras, erudición <*a man of letters* un hombre de letras> • **open l.** carta abierta • **small l.** minúscula • **to the l.** a la letra, al pie de la letra **II.** tr. *(to inscribe)* rotular o inscribir letras en; IMPR. imprimir o estampar con letras —intr. escribir cartas.

---

letter bomb s. carta explosiva.
let·ter·box (lĕt′ər-bŏks′) s. apartado, buzón m.
letter carrier s. cartero, repartidor de cartas.
let·tered (lĕt′ərd) adj. *(literate)* literato, letrado; *(erudite)* erudito, culto; *(marked with letters)* rotulado, estampado con letras.
letter file s. carpeta.
let·ter·head (lĕt′ər-hĕd′) s. *(heading)* membrete m; *(stationery)* papel membreteado.
let·ter·ing (lĕt′ər-ĭng) s. *(labeling)* rotulado, rotulación f; *(label)* rótulo, letrero.
letter of credit s. COM. carta de crédito.
letter opener s. abrecartas m.
let·ter-per·fect (lĕt′ər-pûr′fĭkt) adj. preciso, exacto.
let·ter·press (lĕt′ər-prĕs′) s. *(process)* impresión tipográfica; *(printed text)* texto impreso.
letters patent s.pl. DER. título o patente de privilegio.
let·tuce (lĕt′əs) s. BOT. lechuga; JER. *(money)* dinero, lana.
let·up (lĕt′ŭp′) s. *(slowdown)* disminución f; *(pause)* pausa, interrupción f.
leu·ke·mi·a (lōō-kē′mē-ə) s. MED. leucemia.
leu·ko·cyte o **leu·co·cyte** (lōō′kə-sīt′) s. ANAT. leucocito.
leu·ko·ma o **leu·co·ma** (lōō-kō′mə) s. MED. leucoma.
le·vant (lə-vănt′) s. marroquín m, tafilete m.
Le·vant (lə-vănt′) s. GEOG. Levante m.
le·vant·er (lə-văn′tər) s. viento de Levante ♦ **L.** levantino.
le·va·tor (lə-vā′tər) s. [pl. **le·va·to·res** (lĕv′ə-tôr′ēz)] *(muscle)* músculo elevador; *(instrument)* levantador m.
lev·ee¹ (lĕv′ē) s. *(on a river)* ribero, dique m; *(on a field)* bordo; *(pier)* muelle fluvial m.
lev·ee² (lĕv′ē, lə-vē′) s. HIST. *(on arising from bed)* recepción dada por un rey al levantarse de la cama f; *(formal reception)* recepción, besamanos m.
lev·el (lĕv′əl) **I.** s. *(position)* nivel m <sea l. nivel del mar>; *(height)* altura <at knee l. a la altura de la rodilla>; *(instrument)* nivel o spirit l. nivel de aire>; *(flat land)* llano, llanura; *(floor of a building)* piso, FIG. *(index)* índice m; *(rank)* posición f, categoría ♦ **at ground l.** a ras de tierra • **on the l.** FIG. honesto, limpio • **to be on a l. with** estar a la misma altura con, ser comparable con **II.** adj. *(flat)* plano, llano; *(horizontal)* horizontal, a nivel; *(even)* parejo, igual; *(equal)* igual, uniforme; *(steady)* uniforme <she spoke in a l. tone habló en un tono uniforme>; *(rational)* juicioso, equilibrado; CUL. *(not heaping)* al ras, raso <a l. tablespoon una cucharada rasa> ♦ **to do one's l. best** FAM. hacer uno todo lo posible **III.** tr. *(to make level)* nivelar; *(to make flat)* allanar, aplanar; *(to raze)* arrasar, echar por tierra <the tornado leveled the houses el tornado arrasó las casas>; *(to knock down)* derribar <he leveled his opponent él derribó a su oponente>; *(to aim)* apuntar (arma); FIG. *(to make uniform)* emparejar, igualar; *(to direct)* dirigir (crítica, acusaciones) ♦ **to l. off** nivelar —intr. nivelarse, igualarse ♦ **to l. off** *(to stabilize)* estabilizarse; AVIA. enderezarse.
lev·el·er (lĕv′ə-lər) s. nivelador m.
lev·el·head·ed (lĕv′əl-hĕd′ĭd) adj. equilibrado, juicioso.
leveling rod s. TOP. jalón de mira m, mira de nivelar.
lev·el·ler (lĕv′ə-lər) s. var. de leveler.
lev·el·ness (lĕv′əl-nĭs) s. *(evenness)* nivel m; *(uniformity)* uniformidad f.
lev·er (lĕv′ər, lē′vər) **I.** s. *(machine)* palanca, alzaprima; *(crank)* palanca, manubrio; FIG. *(means)* influencia, palanca **II.** tr. apalancar, levantar con una palanca.
lev·er·age (lĕv′ər-ĭj, lē′vər-) **I.** s. *(action)* apalancamiento; *(power)* fuerza de una palanca; FIG. *(influence)* poder m, influencia **II.** tr. **-aged, -ag·ing** FIG. *(to support)* proveer o suplir poder; *(to affect)* afectar poderosamente.
lev·er·et (lĕv′ər-ĭt) s. lebrato (liebre joven).
lev·i·a·ble (lĕv′ē-ə-bəl) adj. imponible, recaudable.
le·vi·a·than (lə-vī′ə-thən) s. BÍBL. leviatán m; *(animal)* animal gigantesco; *(something very large)* gigante m.
lev·i·gate (lĕv′ĭ-gāt′) tr. **-gat·ed, -gat·ing** *(to pulverize)* pulverizar; *(to suspend in liquid)* levigar; *(to polish)* pulir.
lev·i·tate (lĕv′ĭ-tāt′) tr. & intr. **-tat·ed, -tat·ing** mantener(se) en el aire por levitación, elevar(se) con el solo poder de la mente.

lev·i·ta·tion (lĕv′ĭ-tā′shən) s. levitación f.
Le·vit·i·cus (lə-vĭt′ĭ-kəs) s. BÍBL. Levítico.
lev·i·ty (lĕv′ĭ-tē) s. *(buoyancy)* ligereza; *(frivolity)* frivolidad f, ligereza; *(inconstancy)* inconstancia.
lev·y (lĕv′ē) **I.** tr. **-ied, -y·ing** *(to impose)* exigir, imponer; *(to collect)* recaudar; *(to confiscate)* embargar; *(to draft)* levar, reclutar ♦ **to l. a war on** hacer la guerra a —intr. embargar propiedades **II.** s. [pl. **-ies**] *(imposition)* exacción f, imposición f; *(collection)* recaudación f; *(confiscation)* embargo; *(draft)* leva, reclutamiento; *(tax)* impuesto; *(surcharge)* sobretasa.
lewd (lōōd) adj. **-er, -est** *(lustful)* lujurioso, lascivo; *(obscene)* obsceno, indecente.
lewd·ness (lōōd′nĭs) s. lujuria, lascivia.
lex·i·cal (lĕk′sĭ-kəl) adj. *(relating to vocabulary)* léxico; *(lexicographical)* lexicográfico, lexicológico.
lex·i·cog·ra·pher (lĕk′sĭ-kŏg′rə-fər) s. lexicógrafo.
lex·i·cog·ra·phy (lĕk′sĭ-kŏg′rə-fē) s. lexicografía.
lex·i·con (lĕk′sĭ-kŏn′) s. *(dictionary)* lexicón m, diccionario; *(vocabulary)* léxico, vocabulario.
ley (lā, lē) s. var. de lea.
li·a·bil·i·ty (lī′ə-bĭl′ĭ-tē) s. [pl. **-ties**] *(responsibility)* responsabilidad f, obligación f; *(subjection)* sujeción f <l. to prosecution sujeción a juicio>; *(debt)* deuda, obligación; *(hindrance)* desventaja, inconveniente m; *(proneness)* susceptibilidad f, propensidad f ♦ **l. insurance** seguro de responsabilidad civil • **assets and liabilities** COM. el activo y el pasivo.
li·a·ble (lī′ə-bəl) adj. *(responsible)* responsable <l. for damages responsable por daños y perjuicios>; *(obligated)* obligado <l. for military service obligado al servicio militar>; *(subject)* sujeto <l. to criminal charges sujeto a cargos criminales>; *(prone)* susceptible, propenso <l. to sunburn propenso a quemarse>; *(likely)* probable <it is l. to rain today es probable que llueva hoy>.
li·ai·son (lē′ā-zŏn′, lē-ā′zŏn) s. *(means of communication)* enlace m <press l. enlace de prensa>; *(love affair)* romance m, relaciones amorosas; FONÉT. enlace ♦ **l. officer** MIL. oficial de enlace.
li·a·na (lē-ä′nə, -ăn′ə) o **li·ane** (-än′, -ăn′) s. BOT. bejuco, liana.
li·ar (lī′ər) s. mentiroso.
li·ba·tion (lī-bā′shən) s. *(ritual)* libación f; FAM. *(beverage)* bebida.
lib·ber (lĭb′ər) s. FAM. proponente de la liberación mf, persona que milita por la liberación.
li·bel (lī′bəl) **I.** s. *(published statement)* libelo, escrito difamatorio; *(act)* difamación f <to sue for l. plantear pleito por difamación>; *(lie)* calumnia ♦ **l. suit** pleito por difamación> **II.** tr. *(to defame)* difamar; *(to malign)* calumniar.
li·bel·er (lī′bə-lər) o **li·bel·ist** (-lĭst) s. *(defamer)* libelista mf, difamador m; *(maligner)* calumniador m.
li·bel·ous o **li·bel·lous** (lī′bə-ləs) adj. *(defamatory)* difamatorio; *(maligning)* calumniador.
lib·er·al (lĭb′ər-əl) **I.** adj. POL. liberal; *(tolerant)* tolerante; *(generous)* generoso; *(abundant)* abundante, amplio; *(not literal)* libre ♦ **L.** POL. liberal **II.** s. liberal mf ♦ **L.** POL. liberal.
liberal arts s. artes liberales f, humanidades f.
lib·er·al·ism (lĭb′ər-ə-lĭz′əm) s. liberalismo.
lib·er·al·i·ty (lĭb′ə-răl′ĭ-tē) s. [pl. **-ties**] *(broad-mindedness)* liberalidad f, amplitud de miras f; *(generosity)* liberalidad, generosidad f; *(donation)* donación f.
lib·er·al·i·za·tion (lĭb′ər-ə-lĭ-zā′shən) s. liberalización f.
lib·er·al·ize (lĭb′ər-ə-līz′) tr. & intr. **-ized, -iz·ing** liberalizar(se).
lib·er·al·ly (lĭb′ər-ə-lē) adv. *(generously)* liberalmente, generosamente; *(not literally)* libremente.
lib·er·ate (lĭb′ə-rāt′) tr. **-at·ed, -at·ing** *(to free)* liberar, libertar; QUÍM. liberar, separar; JER. *(to steal)* pillar, apropiarse de.
lib·er·a·tion (lĭb′ə-rā′shən) s. liberación f.
lib·er·a·tion·ist (lĭb′ə-rā′shə-nĭst) s. proponente de la liberación mf, persona que milita por la liberación.
lib·er·a·tor (lĭb′ə-rā′tər) s. liberador m, libertador m.

Li·be·ri·a (lī-bîr′ē-ə) s. Liberia.
Li·be·ri·an (lī-bîr′ē-ən) adj. & s. liberiano.
lib·er·tar·i·an (lĭb′ər-târ′ē-ən) s. libertario, partidario de la libertad o del libre albedrío.
lib·er·tar·i·an·ism (lĭb′ər-târ′ē-ə-nĭz′əm) s. doctrina liberal o del libre albedrío.
lib·er·tine (lĭb′ər-tēn′) s. & adj. libertino.
lib·er·ty (lĭb′ər-tē) s. [pl. **-ties**] *(freedom)* libertad *f;* MARÍT. permiso, licencia ♦ **at l.** *(free)* libre, en libertad; *(idle)* desocupado, ocioso • **to be at l.** to estar en libertad de, tener permiso para <*I am not at l. to discuss these matters* no tengo permiso para discutir estos asuntos> • **to take liberties with (someone)** tomarse libertades con o permitirse confianzas con (alguien) • **to take the l. to** o of tomarse la libertad de.
li·bid·i·nous (lī-bĭd′n-əs) adj. libidinoso.
li·bi·do (lī-bē′dō, -bī′-) s. [pl. **-dos**] libido *f.*
Li·bra (lī′brə, lē′-) s. ASTROL., ASTRON. Libra ♦ **l.** HIST. libra (antigua medida).
li·brar·i·an (lī-brâr′ē-ən) s. bibliotecario.
li·brar·y (lī′brĕr′ē) s. [pl. **-ies**] biblioteca <*the public l.* la biblioteca pública> ♦ **lending l.** biblioteca de préstamo • **reference l.** biblioteca de consulta.
li·bra·tion (lī-brā′shən) s. ASTRON. libración *f.*
li·bret·tist (lī-brĕt′ĭst) s. MÚS. libretista *mf.*
li·bret·to (lī-brĕt′ō) s. [pl. **-bret·tos** o **-bret·ti** (-brĕt′ē)] MÚS. libreto.
Lib·y·a (lĭb′ē-ə) s. Libia ♦ **Libyan Arab Jamahiriya** Jamahiriya Árabe Libia.
Lib·y·an (lĭb′ē-ən) adj. & s. libio.
lice (līs) un pl. de **louse**.
li·cence (lī′səns) s. G.B. var. de **license**.
li·cense (lī′səns) I. s. *(permission)* licencia, permiso; *(card)* carnet *m* <*driver's l.* carnet de manejar>; *(latitude, freedom)* libertad *f;* *(licentiousness)* libertinaje *m* II. tr. **-censed, -cens·ing** *(to authorize)* licenciar, autorizar; *(to accredit)* acreditar ♦ **to be licensed to** estar autorizado para, tener licencia para.
li·cens·ee (lī′sən-sē′) s. *(license holder)* titular de una licencia *mf;* *(authorized dealer)* concesionario.
license plate s. patente *f,* placa (de matrícula).
li·cens·er (lī′sən-sər) s. expedidor de una licencia o permiso *m.*
li·cen·ti·ate (lī-sĕn′shē-ĭt) s. *(person)* licenciado; *(degree)* licenciatura.
li·cen·tious (lī-sĕn′shəs) adj. licencioso.
li·chen (lī′kən) s. BOT., MED. liquen *m.*
lic·it (lĭs′ĭt) adj. lícito.
lick (lĭk) I. tr. *(with the tongue)* lamer <*the child licked the ice cream quickly* el niño lamió el helado rápidamente>; FIG. *(to touch lightly)* lamer <*the waves licked the rocks* las olas lamían las rocas>; JER. *(to beat)* cascar, zurrar; *(to defeat)* vencer <*he licked his opponent* venció a su contrincante> • **to l. clean** limpiar a lametazos • **to l. one's chops** esperar con entusiasmo • **to l. someone's boots** adular servilmente a alguien, hacer la pelotilla a alguien ♦ **intr.** lamer II. s. *(licking)* lametazo, lengüetada; *(small quantity)* pizca, ápice *m;* *(salt)* salegar *m;* JER. *(blow)* golpe *m* ♦ **to give a l. and a promise** FIG., FAM. hacer rápida y superficialmente.
lick·e·ty-split (lĭk′ĭ-tē-splĭt′) adv. FAM. rapidísimamente, a gran velocidad.
lick·ing (lĭk′ĭng) s. JER. *(beating)* paliza; *(defeat)* derrota.
lick·spit·tle (lĭk′spĭt′l) s. parásito, adulón *m.*
lic·o·rice (lĭk′ər-ĭs, -ĭsh) s. regaliz *m.*
lid (lĭd) I. s. *(cover)* tapa; *(eyelid)* pestaña; BOT. opérculo; JER. *(hat)* bombín *m,* techo ♦ **to flip one's l.** JER. descubrir, revelar • **to flip one's l.** JER. pegar el grito en el cielo • **to flip one's l. over** perder el seso por, volverse loco por • **to put the l. on** FAM. poner frenos a II. tr. **lid·ded, lid·ding** poner la tapa a.
lid·less (lĭd′lĭs) adj. *(without a lid)* sin tapa; ANT. *(sleepless)* despierto; *(watchful)* vigilante.
lie¹ (lī) I. intr. **lay** (lā), **lain** (lān), **ly·ing** *(to recline)* acostarse <*he lay under a tree* él se acostó bajo un árbol>; *(to be stretched out)* estar tendido, yacer <*I was lying on*

the grass when the storm broke out estaba acostado sobre la hierba cuando se desató la tormenta>; *(to remain)* quedarse <*he lay motionless* se quedó sin mover>; *(to be situated)* encontrarse, estar situado <*the lake lies beyond the hill* el lago está situado más allá de la colina>; *(to be buried)* estar enterrado, yacer; *(to be admissible)* ser admisible; FIG. *(to consist)* radicar, residir <*the solution to illiteracy lies in education* la solución para el analfabetismo reside en la educación> ♦ **to l. back** inclinarse hacia atrás • **to l. down** tenderse, acostarse • **to l. in** estar de parto • **to l. low** FAM. *(to keep out of sight)* esconderse temporalmente, ocultarse; *(to hide one's intentions)* ocultar las intenciones • **to l. with** depender <*the decision lies with him* la decisión depende de él> • **to take (it) lying down** FAM. aceptar (algo) sin protestar II. s. *(position)* posición *f,* postura; *(direction)* dirección *f,* orientación *f;* *(lair)* cubil *m,* guarida.
lie² (lī) I. s. mentira, embuste *m* ♦ **pack of lies** sarta de mentiras • **to give the l. to** desmentir • **to tell a l.** decir una mentira, mentir • **white l.** mentira piadosa II. intr. **lied, ly·ing** mentir.
Liech·ten·stein (lĭk′tən-stīn′) s. Liechtenstein.
lie detector s. aparato detector de mentiras.
liege (lēj) I. s. HIST. *(lord)* señor feudal *m;* *(vassal)* vasallo; *(subject)* súbdito II. adj. *(feudal)* feudal; *(loyal)* leal, fiel.
lien (lēn, lē′ən) s. DER. derecho de retención.
lieu (lōō) s. ♦ **in l. of** en lugar de, en vez de.
lieu·ten·an·cy (lōō-tĕn′ən-sē) s. MIL. tenientazgo; *(deputation)* lugartenencia.
lieu·ten·ant (lōō-tĕn′ənt) s. MIL. teniente *m;* MARÍT. alférez de navío *m;* *(deputy)* lugarteniente *m.*
lieutenant colonel s. MIL. teniente coronel *m.*
lieutenant commander s. MARÍT. capitán de corbeta *m.*
lieutenant general s. MIL. teniente general *m.*
lieutenant governor s. vice gobernador *m.*
life (līf) s. [pl. **lives** (līvz)] *(existence)* vida, existencia; *(organisms)* vida <*marine l.* vida marina>; *(human being)* gente *f,* vida <*so many lives were lost in that war* tantas vidas se perdieron en esa guerra>; *(lifetime)* vida <*I have lived in this house all my l.* he vivido en esta casa toda mi vida>; *(usefulness)* duración *f;* *(biography)* biografía, vida; *(activity)* animación *f* <*there is not much l. in the streets* no hay mucha animación en las calles>; *(animating force)* alma <*the l. of the party* el alma de la fiesta>; *(vivacity)* vivacidad *f,* vida <*full of l.* lleno de vida>; *(imprisonment)* cadena perpetua ♦ **a matter of l. and death** una cuestión de vida o muerte • **as large** o **as big as l.** *(life-size)* de tamaño natural; *(in person)* en persona • **for l.** por toda la vida • **for dear l.** o **for one's l.** como para salvar la propia vida • **in early l.** en la juventud • **in later l.** en los últimos años • **not on your l.!** JER. ¡ni en sueños!, ¡de ninguna manera! • **that's l.!** ¡así es la vida! • **to bring back to l.** reanimar, resucitar • **to come to l.** *(to revive)* volver en sí, recobrar los sentidos; FIG. *(to become lively)* reanimarse o cobrar vida • **to have the time of one's l.** divertirse mucho, pasarlo muy bien • **to take one's own l.** quitarse la vida, suicidarse • **true to l.** verosímil.
life belt s. cinturón salvavidas *m.*
life·blood (līf′blŭd′) s. *(blood)* sangre *f;* *(indispensable part)* alma, parte vital *f.*
life·boat (līf′bōt′) s. bote salvavidas *m,* lancha de salvamento.
life buoy s. salvavidas *m.*
life cycle s. BIOL. ciclo vital.
life expectancy s. esperanza o promedio de vida, índice de longevidad *m.*
life·guard (līf′gärd′) s. bañero, guarda de playa *mf.*
life history s. ciclo biológico, historia del ciclo vital.
life imprisonment s. DER. prisión a cadena perpetua *f.*
life insurance s. seguro de vida.
life jacket s. chaleco salvavidas.
life·less (līf′lĭs) adj. *(inanimate)* inanimado; *(uninhabited)* deshabitado; *(dead)* muerto, difunto; FIG. *(dull)* sin vida, sin animación.
life·like (līf′līk′) adj. *(appearing alive)* que parece vivo; *(natural)* natural; *(accurate)* fiel.

---

life line s. MARÍT. *(for rescue)* cuerda de salvamento; *(of divers)* cordel de señales (de buzos) *m*; *(supply line)* línea vital de transporte; *(in palmistry)* línea de la vida.

life·long (līf'lông') adj. de toda la vida.

life preserver s. *(buoy, vest)* salvavidas *m*; G.B. *(weapon)* vergajo, cachiporra flexible.

lif·er (lī'fər) s. JER. presidiario condenado a prisión perpetua.

life raft s. balsa salvavidas.

life·sav·er (līf'sā'vər) s. *(lifeguard)* bañero, guarda de playa *mf*; FIG. *(salvation)* salvación *f*.

life·sav·ing (līf'sā'vĭng) I. s. salvamento, socorrismo II. adj. de salvamento ♦ l. jacket chaleco salvavidas.

life sentence s. DER. cadena perpetua.

life-size (līf'sīz') o **life-sized** (-sīzd') adj. de tamaño natural.

life span s. duración de vida *f*, vida.

life·style o **life-style** o **life style** (līf'stīl') s. estilo de vida.

life·sup·port system (līf'sə-pôrt') s. MED. sistema de mantenimiento de vida *m*.

life·time (līf'tīm') s. vida *<in one's l.* en la vida de uno>.

life·work (līf'wûrk') s. *(chief work)* obra principal de la vida (de alguien); *(entire work)* trabajo de toda la vida.

lift (lĭft) I. tr. *(to raise)* alzar, levantar *<l. the piano very carefully* levanten el piano con mucho cuidado>; *(to hoist)* elevar, izar; *(to revoke)* levantar, revocar *<to l. a ban* revocar una prohibición>; *(blockade, siege)* levantar, alzar; *(to elate)* exaltar, elevar; *(to transport)* transportar (por avión); FAM. *(to steal)* escamotear, birlar *<someone lifted my wallet* alguien me birló la billetera>; *(to plagiarize)* plagiar ♦ **not to l. a finger for** o **to** no hacer nada por • **to l. up** alzar, levantar —intr. *(to rise)* levantarse; *(to ascend)* ascender, subir; *(to soar)* elevarse; *(to disperse)* disiparse ♦ **to l. off** AER. despegar II. s. *(act)* alzamiento, levantamiento; *(load)* carga; *(elevation)* elevación *f*, altura; *(rise of ground)* elevación; *(elation)* exaltación *f*, elevación; *(of a shoe)* tapa; *(help)* ayuda; MIN. juego de bombas; AER. fuerza ascensional; MEC. gato; G.B. *(elevator)* ascensor ♦ **to give someone a l.** *(to transport)* llevar a alguien en un vehículo; *(to cheer up)* levantarle a alguien el ánimo.

lift·er (līf'tər) s. alzador *m*, levantador *m*.

lift·ing (līf'tĭng) I. s. *(act)* alzamiento, levantamiento II. adj. que alza o levanta.

lift·off (līft'ôf') s. ASTRONÁUT. despegue *m*.

lig·a·ment (līg'ə-mənt) s. *(connecting tissue)* ligamento; *(bond)* ligazón *f*, ligadura.

li·gate (lī'gāt') tr. **-gat·ed, -gat·ing** ligar.

li·ga·tion (lī-gā'shən) s. ligadura.

lig·a·ture (līg'ə-chŏor', -chər) I. s. *(binding)* ligadura; MED., MÚS. ligadura; TIP. ligado II. tr. **-tured, -tur·ing** ligar.

light¹ (līt) I. s. *(lamp)* luz *f <turn the lights on* enciende las luces>; *(radiation)* luz *<ultraviolet l.* luz ultravioleta>; *(illumination)* luz, iluminación *f*; *(daylight)* luz *<the l. of the day* la luz del día>; *(streetlamp)* luz, farol *m*; *(traffic light)* luz, semáforo; *(window)* ventana; *(skylight)* claraboya; *(headlight)* luz, faro; *(lighthouse)* faro, fanal *m*; *(flame)* fuego *<have you got a l.?* ¿me puedes dar fuego?>; FIG. *(spiritual awareness)* luz, iluminación; *(viewpoint)* aspecto, punto de vista *<I never saw the matter in that light* nunca vi el asunto desde ese punto de vista>; *(luminary)* lumbrera, eminencia *<he is one of the leading lights of science* él es una de las destacadas lumbreras de la ciencia>; *(gleam)* brillo *<the l. in her eyes* el brillo en sus ojos>; PINT. luz *<l. and shade* luz y sombra> ♦ **at first l.** al rayar la luz del día • **in l. of** en vista de, considerando • **in the cold l. of day** FIG. fríamente, desapasionadamente • **lights** FIG. *(opinions)* luces, conocimientos • **to bring to l.** FIG. sacar a luz, revelar • **to shed** o **throw l. on** FIG. arrojar luz sobre, aclarar • **to come to l.** salir a la luz, ser revelado • **to give the green l.** FIG. aprobar la realización (de un proyecto) • **to see in a different l.** FIG. mirar con otros ojos, mirar desde otro punto de vista • **to see the l.** FIG., RELIG. iluminarse; *(to understand)* comprender, darse cuenta • **to see the l. of day** salir a luz, nacer II. tr. **light·ed** o **lit** (līt), **light·ing** *(to ignite)* encender; *(to turn on)* encender, prender *<who lit this lamp?* ¿quién encendió esta lámpara?>; *(to illuminate)* alumbrar, iluminar *<fireworks lit the sky* los fuegos artificiales iluminaron el cielo> ♦ **to l. up** iluminar —intr. encenderse ♦ **to l. up (sky)** alumbrarse, iluminarse; *(face)* iluminarse; *(cigarette)* encender III. adj. **-er, -est** *(said of colors)* claro *<a light-brown coat* un abrigo color marrón claro>; *(not dark)* blanco *<a l. complexion* una tez blanca>; *(of hair)* rubio; *(bright)* bien iluminado *<a l. room* un cuarto bien iluminado> ♦ **to grow l.** clarear, hacerse de día>.

light² (līt) I. adj. **-er, -est** *(lightweight)* ligero, liviano; FIG. *(easily digested)* ligero, liviano; *(not forceful)* suave, leve; *(slight)* fino *<a l. rain* una lluvia fina>; *(faint)* débil; *(easy)* ligero, liviano *<l. work* trabajo liviano>; *(frivolous)* superficial, de poca importancia *<a l. chat* una charla de poca importancia>; *(blithe)* alegre, contento *<a l. heart* un corazón alegre>; *(low in alcohol)* de bajo contenido alcohólico ♦ **as l. as air** liviano como el aire • **l. in the head** mareado • **to be l. on one's feet** ser ligero de pies, moverse con agilidad • **to make l. of** no tomar en serio, restar importancia a II. adv. **-er, -est** ligeramente ♦ **to travel l.** viajar con poco equipaje III. intr. **light·ed** o **lit** (līt), **light·ing** *(to descend)* bajar; *(to dismount)* apearse, desmontar; *(to alight)* posarse ♦ **to l. out** FAM. largarse —tr. ♦ **to l. into someone** atacar o embestir a alguien • **to l. on** o **upon** *(to land on)* posarse; *(to come across)* tropezar con.

light bulb s. bombilla.

light·en¹ (līt'n) tr. *(to illuminate)* alumbrar, iluminar; *(to brighten)* aclarar —intr. *(to become lighter)* aclararse; *(to shine)* brillar; *(to flash)* relampaguear.

light·en² (līt'n) tr. *(to make less heavy)* aligerar, quitar peso a; *(to unload)* descargar; *(to relieve)* aliviar *<his presence lightened our work* su presencia nos alivió el trabajo>; *(to gladden)* alegrar —intr. *(to become lighter)* aligerarse, volverse menos pesado; *(to be relieved)* aliviarse; *(to gladden)* alegrarse.

light·er¹ (līt'tər) s. encendedor *m*.

light·er² (līt'tər) MARÍT. I. s. *(barge)* barcaza, gabarra II. tr. transportar en barcaza o en gabarra.

light·er-than-air (lī'tər-thən-âr') adj. AER. más liviano que el aire.

light·face (līt'fās') s. IMPR. letra fina.

light-fin·gered (līt'fĭng'gərd) adj. *(dextrous)* diestro de manos; FIG. *(thieving)* listo de manos, ligero de dedos.

light-foot·ed (līt'fŏot'ĭd) adj. ligero de pies.

light·head·ed (līt'hĕd'ĭd) adj. *(delirious)* delirante; *(dizzy)* mareado; *(frivolous)* frívolo; *(silly)* casquivano, ligero de cascos.

light·heart·ed (līt'här'tĭd) adj. *(carefree)* despreocupado; *(cheerful)* alegre, contento.

light heavyweight s. DEP. peso semipesado (en boxeo).

light·house (līt'hous') s. faro.

light·ing (lī'tĭng) s. *(illumination)* iluminación *f*; *(artificial illumination)* alumbrado, luz (artificial) *f*; *(ignition)* ignición *f*, encendido.

light·ly (līt'lē) adv. *(gently)* ligeramente, suavemente; *(sparingly)* ligeramente; *(superficially)* levemente *<l. wounded* levemente herido>; *(nimbly)* ágilmente, con gracia; *(blithely)* despreocupadamente; *(indifferently)* a la ligera *<don't treat this work l.* no tomes este trabajo a la ligera> ♦ **to dress l.** no ponerse mucha ropa • **to let off l.** dar un castigo leve a • **to speak l. of** no hablar muy bien de • **to take l.** no dar importancia a • **to walk l.** caminar con paso ligero.

light meter s. FOTOG. fotómetro.

light·ness¹ (līt'nĭs) s. *(brightness)* luminosidad *f*, claridad *f*; *(of a color)* claridad *f*.

light·ness² (līt'nĭs) s. *(of weight)* ligereza, poco peso; *(of force)* ligereza, suavidad *f*; *(agility)* agilidad *f*, gracia; *(blitheness)* despreocupación *f*; *(levity)* levedad *f*; *(delicacy)* delicadeza.

light·ning (līt'nĭng) I. s. METEOR. rayo, relámpago; FIG., FAM. *(sudden stroke of fortune)* golpe de fortuna *m* II. intr. descargar un rayo o relámpago III. adj. FIG. relámpago *<a l. visit* una visita relámpago>.

ã rey / ä año / b boca / ch chico / d dar / ĕ el / ē mil / g gato / h joya / hw juez / ī aire / k casa / kw cuan /

light·ning arrester s. pararrayos *m.*
light·ning bug s. luciérnaga.
light·ning rod s. pararrayos *m.*
light pen s. COMPUT. lápiz luminoso, lápiz óptico.
light·ship (līt'shǐp') s. MARÍT. buque faro.
light·some (līt'səm) adj. *(graceful)* garboso; *(nimble)* ágil, ligero; *(cheerful)* animado; *(silly)* frívolo.
lights out s. MIL. retreta (toque militar para recogerse); *(bedtime)* hora de acostarse.
light·struck (līt'strŭk') adj. FOTOG. velado.
light wave s. FÍS., ÓPT. onda luminosa.
light·weight (līt'wāt') s. *(light person)* persona de poco peso; *(in boxing)* peso ligero *o* liviano; FIG., FAM. *(nobody)* pelele *m*, pelagatos *m.*
light-year *o* **light year** (līt'yîr') s. ASTRON. año luz.
lig·ne·ous (lǐg'nē-əs) adj. leñoso, lignario.
lig·nin (lǐg'nǐn) s. BOT., QUÍM. lignina.
lig·nite (lǐg'nīt') s. MIN. lignita, lignito.
lig·num vi·tae (lǐg'nəm vī'tē) s. [pl. **lignum vi·taes**] BOT. guayaco, palo santo (árbol y madera).
lik·a·ble (lī'kə-bəl) adj. agradable, grato.
like¹ (līk) I. tr. **liked, lik·ing** *(to enjoy)* gustar <*he likes going to the movies* le gusta ir al cine>; *(to want)* desear, querer <*I would l. a cup of coffee* quisiera una taza de café> ♦ **how do you like . . . ?** *(to regard)* parecer <*how do you l. New York?* ¿qué le parece Nueva York?> —intr. desear, querer <*if you l., we can meet you there* si quiere, podemos encontrarnos allí> ♦ **as you l.** como usted quiera II. s. ♦ **likes and dislikes** simpatías y antipatías, gustos y aversiones.
like² (līk) I. prep. *(similar to)* semejante, como <*he has a camera l. mine* él tiene una cámara fotográfica como la mía>; *(in a similar manner)* igual que, como <*he can swim l. a fish* él nada como un pez>; *(typical of)* típico, propio <*it is not l. you to get angry so easily* no es propio de ti el enojarte tan fácilmente>; *(such as)* (tal) como <*I enjoy sports l. swimming and skiing* me gustan los deportes tales como la natación y el esquí> ♦ **l. it** como eso <*they had never done anything l. it* ellos nunca habían hecho algo como eso> • **l. this** *(in this way)* así <*write it l. this* escríbalo así>; *(such as this one)* como éste <*I bought a car l. this* compré un auto como éste> • **l. that** *(in that way)* así; *(such as that one)* como aquél • **something l.** algo así como • **that's more l. it!** ¡eso es mucho mejor! II. adj. *(similar)* similar, parecido <*on this and l. occasions* en ésta y en ocasiones similares>; *(equal)* igual, equivalente <*a glass of wine and a l. amount of seltzer* un vaso de vino y una cantidad igual de soda> ♦ **l. father like son** de tal palo tal astilla III. adv. ♦ **l. hell** JER. *(a lot)* muchísimo, como locos <*we worked l. hell to finish on time* trabajamos como locos para terminar a tiempo>; *(no way)* de ninguna manera, ni muerto <*l. hell am I going out in this weather!* ¡ni muerto salgo con este tiempo!> IV. s. semejante *mf*, igual *mf* ♦ **and the l.** FAM. y cosas por el estilo • **the likes of** personas como V. conj. como <*to dance l. she does requires practice* bailar como lo hace ella requiere práctica> ♦ **to look l.** parecer que <*it looks l. we'll finish on time* parece que vamos a terminar a tiempo>.
like·a·ble (lī'kə-bəl) adj. var. de **likable.**
like·li·hood (līk'lē-hŏŏd') s. probabilidad *f.*
like·ly (līk'lē) I. adj. **-li·er, -li·est** *(probable)* probable; *(plausible)* creíble, verosímil; *(suitable)* apropiado, adecuado; *(promising)* prometedor ♦ **that's a l. story!** ¡vaya cuento! • **to be l. to** ser probable que <*they are l. to become angry with him* es probable que ellos se enfaden con él> II. adv. probablemente <*he will very l. arrive on Friday* muy probablemente él llegará el viernes> • **as l. as not** *o* **l. as not** probablemente, a lo mejor.
like-mind·ed (līk'mīn'dǐd) adj. del mismo parecer, de la misma opinión.
lik·en (lī'kən) tr. *(to equate)* equiparar; *(to compare)* comparar.
like·ness (līk'nǐs) s. *(resemblance)* semejanza, parecido; *(appearance)* forma, apariencia; *(representation)* retrato, imagen *f.*
like·wise (līk'wīz') adv. *(similarly)* del mismo modo, igual-

mente; *(in the same way)* lo mismo <*to feel l.* pensar lo mismo>; *(moreover)* además <*he sings and l. plays the guitar* canta y además toca la guitarra>.
lik·ing (lī'kǐng) s. *(fondness)* afición *f* <*a l. for cars* afición a los automóviles>; *(taste)* gusto <*this food is not to my l.* esta comida no es de mi gusto> ♦ **to have a l. for** *(something)* ser aficionado a; *(someone)* tener simpatía a *o* por • **to take a l. to** *(something)* aficionarse a; *(someone)* prenderse de.
li·lac (lī'lək, -lŏk') I. s. BOT. lila (arbusto y flor); *(color)* lila, morado II. adj. de color lila, morado.
Lil·li·pu·tian *o* **lil·li·pu·tian** (lǐl'ə-pyōō'shən) I. s. liliputiense *mf* II. adj. *(diminutive)* liliputiense; *(trivial)* trivial.
lilt (lǐlt) I. s. *(tune)* canción alegre *f*; *(cadence)* ritmo; *(accent)* deje *m* II. tr. & intr. cantar *o* hablar alegremente.
lil·y (lǐl'ē) s. [pl. **-ies**] BOT. lirio.
lil·y-liv·ered (lǐl'ē-lǐv'ərd) adj. *(cowardly)* cobarde; *(timid)* tímido.
lily of the valley s. [pl. **lilies of the valley**] muguete *m*, lirio de los valles.
lily pad s. BOT. hoja de nenúfar.
lil·y-white (lǐl'ē-hwīt') adj. *(white)* blanco como la nieve; FIG. *(irreproachable)* intachable; *(innocent)* inocente; FIG., FAM. *(all white)* para blancos.
Li·ma (lē'mə) s. GEOG. Lima.
li·ma bean (lī'mə) s. frijol *m*, haba.
limb¹ (lǐm) I. s. BOT. rama; ANAT. miembro, extremidad *f*; *(representative)* representante *m* ♦ **loss of a l.** mutilación • **out on a l.** FAM. en un aprieto • **to tear l. from l.** despedazar II. tr. desmembrar.
limb² (lǐm) s. ASTRON., BOT., TEC. limbo.
lim·ber (lǐm'bər) I. adj. *(flexible)* flexible; *(agile)* ágil II. tr. volver ágil —intr. ♦ **to l. up** prepararse haciendo ejercicios.
lim·ber·ness (lǐm'bər-nǐs) s. *(flexibility)* flexibilidad *f*; *(agility)* agilidad *f.*
lim·bo (lǐm'bō) s. [pl. **-bos**] *(oblivion)* nada; *(jail)* prisión *f* ♦ **L.** TEOL. limbo • **to keep something in l.** dejar algo en veremos.
lime¹ (līm) s. BOT. *(tree)* limero, lima; *(fruit)* lima.
lime² (līm) s. QUÍM. cal *f*; *(birdlime)* liga II. tr. **limed, lim·ing** *(wall, surface)* encalar; *(soil)* abonar con cal; *(to smear)* untar con liga; *(to catch)* coger con liga (pájaros).
lime³ (līm) s. *(linden tree)* tilo.
lime·kiln (līm'kǐl', -kǐln') s. TEC. calera, horno de cal.
lime·light (līm'līt') s. *(stage light)* luz de calcio *f*; FIG. *(focus)* centro de atención.
lim·er·ick (lǐm'ər-ǐk) s. POÉT. poema de cinco versos (generalmente jocoso) *m.*
lime·stone (līm'stōn') s. piedra caliza, caliza.
lime·wa·ter (līm'wô'tər) s. agua de cal *f.*
lim·ey (lī'mē) s. [pl. **-eys**] JER. *(sailor)* marinero (inglés); *(Englishman)* inglés *m.*
lim·it (lǐm'ǐt) I. s. *(boundary)* límite *m*; *(maximum)* máximo; MAT. límite ♦ **limits** límites, confines <*within the city limits* dentro de los confines de la ciudad> • **speed l.** velocidad máxima • **that's the l.!** ¡eso es el colmo! • **the sky's the l.** FAM. todo es posible • **weight l.** limitación de peso • **within limits** hasta cierto punto II. tr. limitar ♦ **to be limited to** *(to be found only in)* encontrarse solamente en; *(in quantity)* no poder exceder • **to l. oneself to** limitarse a, determinarse solamente.
lim·it·a·ble (lǐm'ǐ-tə-bəl) adj. limitable.
lim·i·ta·tion (lǐm'ǐ-tā'shən) s. *(restriction)* limitación *f*, restricción *f*; DER. prescripción *f* ♦ **limitations** *(restrictions)* restricciones; *(shortcomings)* deficiencias.
lim·it·ed (lǐm'ǐ-tǐd) adj. *(restricted)* limitado; *(reduced)* reducido <*a l. number* un número reducido>; *(qualified)* módico <*l. success* éxito módico>; POL. constitucional ♦ **for a l. time only** por corto plazo solamente • **of l. means** corto de recursos II. s. (tren) expreso.
limited company s. COM. sociedad de responsabilidad limitada *f*, sociedad anónima.
limited edition s. tirada de un número reducido de ejemplares.
limited liability s. COM. responsabilidad limitada.

limited partnership s. COM. sociedad en comandita f.

limited war s. guerra táctica, guerra de objetivos específicos.

lim·it·ing (lĭm'ĭ-tĭng) adj. *(that limits)* limitativo, restrictivo; GRAM. determinativo.

lim·it·less (lĭm'ĭt-lĭs) adj. ilimitado, sin límites.

limn (lĭm) tr. *(to describe)* describir; *(to paint, draw)* pintar, dibujar.

lim·o (lĭm'ō) s. [pl. **-os**] limosina.

lim·ou·sine (lĭm'ə-zēn') s. limosina.

limp (lĭmp) I. intr. *(to walk lamely)* cojear; FIG. *(to move haltingly)* arrastrarse, ir dando tumbos II. s. cojera ♦ **to walk with a l.** cojear III. adj. **-er, -est** *(flaccid)* fláccido; *(hanging)* caído; *(hair)* lacio; *(weak)* débil ♦ **to feel l.** sentirse desfallecer • **to let one's muscles go l.** aflojar los músculos.

lim·pet (lĭm'pĭt) s. *(mollusk)* lapa; FIG. *(person)* persona pegajosa; MIL. mina magnética.

lim·pid (lĭm'pĭd) adj. límpido, claro.

limp·ness (lĭmp'nĭs) s. *(flaccidity)* flaccidez f; *(weakness)* debilidad f.

lim·y (lī'mē) adj. **lim·i·er, -i·est** *(sticky)* pegajoso; *(said of lime)* calizo.

lin·age (lī'nĭj) s. *(number of lines)* número de líneas; *(payment)* pago por líneas.

linch·pin (lĭnch'pĭn') s. *(locking pin)* pezonera; FIG. *(essential item)* parte esencial f.

lin·den (lĭn'dən) s. BOT. tilo.

line¹ (lĭn) I. s. *(mark)* línea, raya; *(wrinkle)* arruga; *(boundary)* frontera, límite m; *(contour)* contorno, línea; *(wire)* cable m; *(rope)* cabo; *(cord)* cordón m, cordel m; *(fishing line)* sedal m; *(clothesline)* cuerda para tender la ropa, tendedero; *(pipes)* tubería, cañería; *(transportation)* línea <*a bus l.* una línea de autobuses>; *(company)* compañía <*shipping l.* compañía naviera>; *(railroad track)* vía; *(trajectory)* trayecto, trayectoria; *(method)* línea, curso <*a l. of action* curso de acción>; *(plan)* plan m; *(posture)* postura; *(occupation)* ocupación f; *(specialty)* especialidad f, rama <*that is out of my l.* eso no es de mi especialidad>; *(merchandise)* surtido <*a l. of shoes* un surtido de zapatos>; *(row)* hilera, fila <*a l. of trees* una hilera de árboles>; *(queue)* cola <*to stand in l.* hacer cola>; *(series)* serie f, sucesión f; *(ancestry)* ascendencia, familia; *(verse)* verso; *(brief letter)* letras, líneas; ELEC., MÚS., TEL. línea; MIL. *(formation)* línea; *(trench)* trinchera ♦ **along these lines** en estos términos • **along the lines of** algo como • **in l. with** en conformidad con, de acuerdo con • **lines** TEAT. diálogo; MIL. líneas • **down the l.** en el futuro • **l. of work** ocupación • **on the l.** *(on the telephone)* en el teléfono; *(in jeopardy)* en peligro <*to put one's life on the l.* poner la vida en peligro> • **the end of the l.** FIG. el final, el fin • **to be in l. for** ser candidato para (promoción, aumento) • **to be out of l.** comportarse incorrectamente • **to bring into l.** traer al orden • **to draw the l.** fijar límites • **to drop someone a l.** ponerle a alguien unas letras • **to feed, give o hand someone a l.** embaucar a alguien • **to get a l. on someone** FAM. obtener información sobre alguien • **to hold the l. on** restringir • **to lay it on the l.** hablar con franqueza, ser franco • **to read between the lines** leer entre líneas • **to step out of l.** salirse de lo que está establecido • **to toe the l.** conformarse II. tr. **lined, lin·ing** *(to mark)* rayar, trazar líneas en; *(to border)* bordear ♦ **to l. up** alinear, poner en fila —intr. ♦ **to l. up** *(people)* alinearse, ponerse en fila; *(to queue up)* hacer cola, ponerse en fila; MIL. formarse.

line² (lĭn) tr. **lined, lin·ing** *(to put lining in)* forrar; *(to cover)* cubrir <*moisture lined the cave's walls* la humedad cubría las paredes de la cueva>; TEC. *(to coat)* revestir; *(brakes)* guarnecer ♦ **to l. one's pockets** forrarse de dinero, enriquecerse.

lin·e·age¹ (lĭn'ē-ĭj) s. linaje m, estirpe m.

line·age² (lī'nĭj) s. var. de **linage**.

lin·e·al (lĭn'ē-əl) adj. *(in direct line)* en línea directa (de sucesión); *(hereditary)* hereditario; *(linear)* lineal.

lin·e·a·ment (lĭn'ē-ə-mənt) s. lineamiento ♦ **lineaments** facciones f.

lin·e·ar (lĭn'ē-ər) adj. GEOM. linear, lineal <*l. perspective* perspectiva lineal>; MAT., TEC. lineal <*l. accelerator* acelerador lineal de partículas>; BOT. lineal *(hoja)*.

linear equation s. MAT. ecuación lineal o de primer grado f.

linear measure s. medida de longitud.

lined (līnd) adj. *(ruled)* rayado <*l. paper* papel rayado>; *(with inside lining)* forrado.

line drawing s. dibujo lineal (esp. el usado para un clisé).

line·man (līn'mən) s. [pl. **-men**] ELEC. instalador o reparador de líneas m; F.C. guardavía m.

lin·en (lĭn'ən) I. s. *(material)* lino, hilo; *(linen goods)* lencería ♦ **l. closet** lencería • **linens** ropa de cama • **table l.** mantelería • **to wash one's dirty l. in public** sacar a relucir los trapos sucios II. adj. de lino, de hilo.

line of credit s. COM. crédito máximo que se puede extender a un cliente.

line of sight s. FÍS., ÓPT. línea visual, línea de mira; ELECTRÓN. vía óptica, horizonte óptico.

line printer s. COMPUT. impresora de línea, impresora de alta velocidad.

lin·er¹ (lī'nər) s. *(in drawing)* delineador m; *(ship)* trasatlántico, barco de travesía; AVIA. avión de línea o travesía.

lin·er² (lī'nər) s. TEC. *(person)* revestidor m; *(lining)* forro, revestimiento.

lines·man (līnz'mən) s. [pl. **-men**] ELEC. guardalínea m, instalador o reparador de líneas m; DEP. juez de línea m.

line-up o **line·up** (līn'ŭp') s. CRIMIN. fila (de personas); DEP. alineación f, formación de un equipo f; *(group)* grupo de personas o cosas.

ling (lĭng) s. [pl. **ling** o **lings**] ICT. abadejo, molva.

lin·ger (lĭng'gər) intr. *(to tarry)* quedarse <*they lingered a while at the table* se quedaron un rato en la mesa>; *(to lag behind)* quedarse atrás; *(before dying)* durar; *(to persist)* persistir, subsistir <*the memory still lingers* aún subsiste el recuerdo> ♦ **to l. over** demorarse en • **to l. over a meal** comer sin darse prisa —tr. ♦ **to l. away** desperdiciar, perder.

lin·ge·rie (län'zhə-rē', -rā') s. lencería, ropa interior (de mujer).

lin·ger·ing (lĭng'gər-ĭng) adj. *(persistent)* persistente; *(prolonged)* prolongado.

lin·go (lĭng'gō) s. [pl. **-goes**] FAM. *(obscure language)* jerigonza; *(foreign language)* idioma m; *(jargon)* jerga <*medical l.* jerga médica>.

lin·gua fran·ca (lĭng'gwə frăng'kə) s. [pl. **lingua fran·cas** o **lin·guae fran·cae** (lĭng'gwē frăng'kē)] lengua franca.

lin·gual (lĭng'gwəl) I. adj. *(tonguelike)* lingual; *(linguistic)* lingüístico II. s. FONÉT. sonido lingual.

lin·guist (lĭng'gwĭst) s. *(polyglot)* políglota; *(specialist)* lingüista mf.

lin·guis·tic (lĭng-gwĭs'tĭk) adj. lingüístico.

lin·guis·tics (lĭng-gwĭs'tĭks) s. [ú. con v. sing.] lingüística.

lin·i·ment (lĭn'ə-mənt) s. linimento, untura.

lin·ing (lī'nĭng) s. *(of clothes)* forro; TEC. forro, revestimiento.

link (lĭngk) I. s. *(of a chain)* eslabón m; *(element)* enlace m; *(connection)* unión f, conexión f; *(unit of length)* eslabón de agrimensor (que equivale a 20 cm.); MED. vástago de unión o transmisión; ELEC. fusible m, plomo; QUÍM. enlace; FIG. *(bond)* vínculo, lazo; *(tie)* eslabón ♦ **weak l.** punto flaco o débil II. tr. & intr. *(to unite)* unir(se), enlazar(se); *(to connect)* eslabonar(se), conectar(se); *(to associate)* vincular(se); *(to combine)* ligar(se); *(to couple)* acoplar(se) ♦ **to l. up with** unir(se) a • **to l. together** unir(se).

link·age (lĭng'kĭj) s. *(linking)* eslabonamiento, encadenamiento; *(bond)* unión f, enlace m; MEC. *(coupling)* acoplamiento; *(joint)* articulación f; ELEC. medida de flujo magnético; BIOL., QUÍM. enlace; DIPL., POL. relación f.

linked (lĭngkt) adj. *(connected)* conectado, enlazado; *(united)* vinculado; *(combined)* ligado; BIOL. asociado, unido.

link·ing (lĭng'kĭng) s. *(linkage)* eslabonamiento, encadenamiento; *(connection)* unión f, conexión f; *(coupling)* acoplamiento; *(joint)* articulación f; FIG. *(bond)* vínculo, lazo.

links (lĭngks) s.pl. *(golf course)* campo de golf; *(dunes)* médanos (en Escocia).

link·up (lĭngk'ŭp') s. AER. acoplamiento; *(meeting)* reunión *f*, encuentro; *(by telephone)* conexión *f*.

li·no·le·um (lĭ-nō'lē-əm) s. linóleo.

Li·no·type (lī'nə-tīp') s. IMPR. marca registrada de una máquina de linotipia.

lin·seed oil (lĭn'sēd') s. aceite de linaza *m*.

lint (lĭnt) s. *(fuzz)* pelusa, tamo; *(wound dressing)* hilas (para vendajes).

lin·tel (lĭn'tl) s. ARQ. dintel *m*, lintel (de puertas, ventanas) *m*.

lint·er (lĭn'tər) s. máquina desfibradora (de algodón, lino) ♦ **linters** tamo, pelusa.

li·on (lī'ən) s. ZOOL. león *m*; FIG. *(ferocious person)* león; *(celebrity)* celebridad *f* ♦ **L.** ASTROL. León, Leo • **the lion's share** la parte del león, la mejor parte.

li·on·ess (lī'ə-nĭs) s. ZOOL. leona.

li·on·heart·ed (lī'ən-här'tĭd) adj. muy valiente.

li·on·ize (lī'ə-nīz') tr. **-ized, -iz·ing** agasajar, celebrar.

lip (lĭp) **I.** s. ANAT. labio; *(edge)* reborde *m*; *(rim)* pico (de jarra); JER. insolencia, impertinencia; ZOOL. belfo; BOT. labelo; MED. labio, borde *m* ♦ **to keep a stiff upper l.** poner a mal tiempo buena cara • **to lick one's lips** FIG. relamerse • **to smack one's lips** hacer un chasquido con los labios **II.** tr. **lipped, lipping** *(to touch)* tocar con los labios; *(to utter)* murmurar, susurrar; *(to lap)* bañar **III.** adj. FONÉT. labial <*l. consonant* consonante labial>.

lip·id (lĭp'ĭd) *o* **lip·ide** (-īd') s. BIOQUÍM. lípido.

li·po·ma (lĭ-pō'mə) s. MED. lipoma *m*.

lip-read (lĭp'rēd') tr. & intr. **-read** (-rĕd'), **read·ing** leer los labios.

lip reading s. lectura de los labios.

lip service s. *(insincere words)* jarabe de pico *m*; *(false praise)* alabanza falsa ♦ **to pay** *o* **give l. to** fingir estar de acuerdo con.

lip·stick (lĭp'stĭk') s. lápiz labial *m*.

liq·ue·fac·tion (lĭk'wə-făk'shən) s. FÍS. licuefacción *f*.

liq·ue·fi·er (lĭk'wə-fī'ər) s. aparato de licuefacción.

liq·ue·fy *o* **liq·ui·fy** (lĭk'wə-fī') tr. & intr. **-fied, -fy·ing** licuefacer(se), derretir(se).

li·queur (lĭ-kûr', -kyŏor') s. licor *m*.

liq·uid (lĭk'wĭd) **I.** s. *(fluid)* líquido; FONÉT. consonante líquida **II.** adj. *(fluid)* líquido; *(clear)* claro, transparente <*l. brown eyes* ojos pardos transparentes>; *(flowing)* límpido; FONÉT. líquida.

liquid assets s. COM., FIN. activo (líquido).

liq·ui·date (lĭk'wĭ-dāt') tr. **-dat·ed, -dat·ing** COM. *(a debt, business)* liquidar; *(assets)* convertir en efectivo; *(to abolish, kill)* liquidar; FAM. *(to murder)* matar, asesinar.

liq·ui·da·tion (lĭk'wĭ-dā'shən) s. liquidación *f*.

liquid crystal s. ELECTRÓN. cristal líquido.

liq·uid·i·ty (lĭ-kwĭd'ĭ-tē) s. *(fluidity)* liquidez *f*, fluidez *f*; COM., FIN. liquidez.

liquid measure s. medida para líquidos (unidad o sistema).

liq·ui·fy (lĭk'wə-fī') v. var. de **liquefy**.

liq·uor (lĭk'ər) **I.** s. *(alcohol)* licor *m*, bebida alcohólica; *(broth)* jugo; *(solution)* licor **II.** tr. *(leather)* engrasar ♦ **to be liquored up** JER. estar borracho.

liq·uo·rice (lĭk'ər-ĭs, -ĭsh) s. G.B. var. de **licorice**.

li·ra (lîr'ə) s. [pl. **li·re** (lîr'ā) *o* **li·ras**] FIN. lira.

Lis·bon (lĭz'bən) s. Lisboa.

lisp (lĭsp) **I.** s. ceceo **II.** intr. cecear —tr. decir ceceando.

lis·some *o* **lis·som** (lĭs'əm) adj. *(flexible)* flexible; *(willowy)* elástico; *(nimble)* ágil.

list¹ (lĭst) **I.** s. lista <*a shopping l.* una lista de compras> ♦ **wine l.** carta de vinos **II.** tr. *(to itemize)* hacer una lista de, enumerar; *(to register)* poner en una lista, inscribir ♦ **to l. oneself as** presentarse como • **to be listed** figurar, constar.

list² (lĭst) **I.** s. *(stripe)* lista, raya; ARQ., CARP., TEJ. listón *m* ♦ **lists** liza, palestra • **to enter the lists** salir a la palestra **II.** tr. *(to edge)* sacar un listón a; ARQ., CARP., TEJ. poner un listón a; AGR. arar.

list³ (lĭst) MARÍT. **I.** s. escora **II.** intr. escorar —tr. hacer escorar.

lis·ten (lĭs'ən) intr. *(to hear)* oír, escuchar; *(to heed advice)* prestar atención ♦ **to l. for** estar atento a • **to l. in on** escuchar a hurtadillas • **to l. to reason** atender a razones • **to l. up** escuchar bien.

lis·ten·er (lĭs'ə-nər) s. oyente *mf*; RAD. radioyente *mf*, radioescucha *mf*.

list·ing (lĭs'tĭng) s. *(act)* alistamiento; *(insertion)* inscripción en una lista *f*; *(list entry)* listado; *(list)* lista.

list·less (lĭst'lĭs) adj. *(spiritless)* desganado; *(apathetic)* apático.

list price s. COM. precio de lista.

lit¹ (lĭt) un pret. y part. p. de **light¹**.

lit² (lĭt) un pret. y part. p. de **light²**.

lit·a·ny (lĭt'n-ē) s. [pl. **-nies**] letanía.

li·ter (lē'tər) s. litro.

lit·er·a·cy (lĭt'ər-ə-sē) s. alfabetismo.

lit·er·al (lĭt'ər-əl) adj. *(not figurative)* literal <*l. sense* sentido literal>; *(verbatim)* literal <*a l. translation* una traducción literal>; *(true)* escueto, llano; *(by letters)* alfabético ♦ **l. minded** sin imaginación, prosáico.

lit·er·al·ly (lĭt'ər-ə-lē) adv. *(strictly)* literalmente, al pie de la letra; *(actually)* de veras; FAM. *(in a manner of speaking)* por así decirlo ♦ **l. impossible** materialmente imposible.

lit·er·ar·y (lĭt'ə-rĕr'ē) adj. literario.

lit·er·ate (lĭt'ər-ĭt) **I.** adj. *(able to read and write)* que sabe leer y escribir; *(educated)* letrado, instruido; *(literary)* literato; *(well-written)* culto, pulido **II.** s. persona letrada *o* instruida.

lit·er·a·ti (lĭt'ə-rä'tē) s.pl. literatos.

lit·er·a·ture (lĭt'ər-ə-chŏor', -chər) s. *(belles-lettres)* literatura <*to study French l.* estudiar literatura francesa>; *(research)* bibliografía, documentación *f* <*to know the l.* conocer la bibliografía>; *(printed material)* folletos, impresos.

lithe (līth) adj. *(supple)* flexible, elástico; *(graceful)* grácil.

lith·i·um (lĭth'ē-əm) s. QUÍM. litio.

lith·o·graph (lĭth'ə-grăf') **I.** s. litografía **II.** tr. litografiar.

li·thog·ra·pher (lĭ-thŏg'rə-fər) s. litógrafo.

li·thog·ra·phy (lĭ-thŏg'rə-fē) s. litografía.

lith·o·sphere (lĭth'ə-sfîr') s. GEOG. litosfera.

Lith·u·a·ni·a (lĭth'ōō-ā'nē-ə) s. Lituania.

Lith·u·a·ni·an (lĭth'ōō-ā'nē-ən) adj. & s. *(inhabitant, language)* lituano.

lit·i·gant (lĭt'ĭ-gənt) s. & adj. litigante *mf*.

lit·i·gate (lĭt'ĭ-gāt') tr. & intr. **-gat·ed, -gat·ing** litigar, pleitear.

lit·i·ga·tion (lĭt'ĭ-gā'shən) s. litigio, pleito.

lit·i·ga·tor (lĭt'ĭ-gā'tər) s. litigante *mf*.

li·ti·gious (lĭ-tĭj'əs) adj. litigioso.

lit·mus (lĭt'məs) s. QUÍM. tornasol *m* ♦ **l. paper** papel de tornasol *m*.

litmus test s. *(scientific test)* prueba de acidez (usando papel de tornasol); FIG. *(test)* prueba determinante.

li·tre (lē'tər) s. G.B. var. de **liter**.

lit·ter (lĭt'ər) **I.** s. *(conveyance)* litera; *(stretcher)* camilla; *(bedding)* lecho de paja (para los animales); *(animal's young)* camada, cría; *(trash)* basura; *(scraps of paper)* papeles *m* **II.** tr. *(to give birth to)* parir (dic. de los animales); *(to make untidy)* ensuciar, tirar basura en; *(to cover)* estar esparcido por <*the pieces from the ceiling littered the floor* los pedazos del techo estaban esparcidos por el piso>; *(to scatter)* esparcir, regar —intr. *(to give birth)* parir; *(to scatter litter)* tirar basura.

lit·ter·bag (lĭt'ər-băg') s. bolsa de basura.

lit·ter·bug (lĭt'ər-bŭg') s. FAM. persona que arroja basura en lugares públicos.

lit·ter·ing (lĭt'ər-ĭng) s. ♦ **no l.** prohibido tirar basura.

lit·tle §G28 (lĭt'l) **I.** adj. **lit·tler** *o* **less** (lĕs), **lit·tlest** *o* **least** (lēst) *(small)* pequeño; *(short)* bajo; *(brief)* breve; *(not much)* poco <*l. money* poco dinero>; *(trivial)* trivial, sin importancia; *(petty)* estrecho <*l. mind* mente estrecha>; *(mean)* despreciable, miserable ♦ **l. finger** dedo meñique • **l. ones** los niños, la gente menuda • **l. toe** dedo pequeño del pie • **the l. people** *(dwarfs)* los enanos; *(general populace)* la gente humilde • **the l. woman** FAM. la esposa, la mujer **II.** adv. **less, least** *(not much)* poco <*he sleeps l.* él

duerme poco>; *(not at all)* no <*l. did I know that* no me
imaginé que>; *(somewhat)* un poco, algo <*she's a l. better*
está algo mejor> ♦ **as l. as possible** lo menos possible • **l.
by l.** poco a poco • **not a l.** bastante <*not a l. surprised*
bastante sorprendido> • **to be l. better than** FIG. ser igual
que III. s. *(small amount)* poco <*give me a l.* dame un
poco>; *(short distance)* poco <*a l. down the road* un poco
más abajo>; *(short time)* instante *m,* momento ♦ **from
what l.** por lo poco que • **l. or nothing** casi nada • **to think
l. of** tener mala opinión de.

Little Bear s. ASTRON. Osa Menor.

Little Dipper s. ASTRON. Carro Menor, Osa Menor.

lit·to·ral (lĭt′ər-əl) adj. & s. litoral *m.*

li·tur·gi·cal (lĭ-tûr′jĭ-kəl) o **li·tur·gic** (-jĭk) adj. litúrgico.

li·tur·gics (lĭ-tûr′jĭks) s. [ú. con v. sing.] RELIG. liturgia.

lit·ur·gist (lĭt′ər-jĭst) s. liturgista *mf.*

lit·ur·gy (lĭt′ər-jē) s. [pl. **-gies**] RELIG. liturgia.

liv·a·ble o **live·a·ble** (lĭv′ə-bəl) adj. *(habitable)* habitable;
(bearable) soportable, tolerable.

live¹ (lĭv) intr. **lived, liv·ing** *(to exist)* existir, vivir <*everyone
has a right to l.* todos tienen derecho a vivir>; *(to remain
alive)* vivir, durar <*she does not think he is going to l. long*
ella no cree que él dure mucho>; *(to subsist)* vivir, mantenerse; *(to reside)* residir, vivir; *(to conduct oneself)* vivir,
llevar una vida; *(to enjoy life)* vivir, disfrutar de la vida
<*he knows how to l.* sabe disfrutar de la vida>; FIG. *(to
last)* vivir, perdurar <*his name will l. in the minds of us all*
su nombre perdurará en el recuerdo de todos nosotros> ♦
to l. and learn vivir para ver • **to l. in** vivir donde se
trabaja • **to l. on** vivir, perdurar —tr. *(to lead)* vivir,
llevar <*rich people l. a life of ease* los ricos llevan una vida
fácil>; *(to experience)* tener <*I lived a happy childhood*
tuve una infancia feliz>; *(to practice)* practicar, poner en
práctica <*they truly lived their religion* practicaban verdaderamente su religión> • **to l. down** lograr borrar de la
memoria (falta, cargo) • **to l. it up** FAM. correr las grandes
juergas, vivir la vida • **to l. off** *(someone)* vivir a expensas
de; *(the land)* vivir de • **to l. through** sobrevivir • **to l. up
to** *(to conform with)* actuar en conformidad con; *(to fulfill)*
cumplir • **to l. with** *(to reside with)* vivir con; *(to tolerate)*
tolerar, aceptar <*they have to l. with the situation* tienen
que aceptar la situación>.

live² (līv) I. adj. *(living)* vivo <*a l. cat* un gato vivo>; *(of
current interest)* actual <*a l. topic* un tema actual>; *(burning)* encendido <*a l. cigarette* un cigarrillo encendido>;
ARM. sin estallar <*a l. bomb* una bomba sin estallar>;
ELEC. con corriente <*a l. wire* un alambre con corriente>;
MIN. no extraído; RAD., TELEV. en directo <*a l. television
program* un programa de televisión en directo>; DEP. en
juego II. adv. en directo <*the debate will be telecast l.* el
debate será televisado en directo>.

live·a·ble (lĭv′ə-bəl) adj. var. de **livable.**

live-in (lĭv′ĭn′) adj. residente, con cama <*l. maid* sirvienta
con cama>.

live·li·hood (lĭv′lē-hŏŏd′) s. *(means of support)* medios de
ganarse la vida <*singing is his l.* el canto es su medio de
ganarse la vida>; *(subsistence)* sustento.

live·li·ness (lĭv′lē-nĭs) s. *(activity)* vida, animación *f;* *(vividness)* vivacidad *f,* viveza.

live load (līv) s. carga móvil, carga variable.

live·long (lĭv′lông′) adj. entero, completo ♦ **all the l. day**
todo el santo día.

live·ly (līv′lē) I. adj. **-li·er, -li·est** *(full of life)* lleno de vida,
vivaz; *(spirited)* alegre; *(animated)* animado; *(keen)* vivo,
grande; *(sharp)* agudo; *(vivid)* vivo; *(quick)* rápido;
(brisk) vigoroso II. adv. *(energetically)* con fuerza; *(in a
spirited manner)* vivamente; *(quickly)* rápido.

li·ven (lī′vən) tr. & intr. animar(se) ♦ **to l. up** animar(se).

live oak (līv) s. BOT. encina o roble perenne *m.*

liv·er (lĭv′ər) s. ANAT., CUL. hígado.

liv·er² (lĭv′ər) s. ♦ **fast l.** calavera *m,* juerguista *mf.*

liv·er·ied (lĭv′ə-rēd) adj. de librea.

liv·er·ish (lĭv′ər-ĭsh) s. *(bilious)* que padece del hígado; *(irritable)* enojadizo.

Liv·er·pud·li·an (lĭv′ər-pŭd′lē-ən) I. adj. de Liverpool II. s.
habitante de Liverpool *mf.*

liv·er·wurst (lĭv′ər-wûrst′) s. salchicha o embutido de hígado.

liv·er·y (lĭv′ə-rē) s. [pl. **-ies**] *(uniform)* librea; *(stable)* caballeriza de alquiler; DER. entrega (esp. de tierras).

livery stable s. caballeriza, cuadra de caballos de alquiler.

lives (līvz) pl. de **life.**

live·stock (līv′stŏk′) s. ganado.

live wire (līv) s. ELEC. cable con corriente *m;* *(vivacious person)* persona vivaz y activa.

liv·id (lĭv′ĭd) adj. *(black-and-blue)* lívido; *(pallid)* pálido;
(furious) furioso.

liv·ing (lĭv′ĭng) I. adj. *(alive)* vivo <*is he l. or dead?* ¿está
vivo o muerto?>; *(extant)* viviente, contemporáneo <*famous l. painters* pintores famosos contemporáneos>;
(vivid) lleno de vida, vívido; FAM. *(absolute)* verdadero <*a
l. doll* una verdadera muñeca> ♦ **l. conditions** condiciones de vida • **l. death** muerte en vida • **l. expenses** gastos
de manutención • **l. language** lengua viva • **the l.** los
vivos II. s. *(subsistence)* vida <*the cost of l.* el costo de la
vida>; *(lifestyle)* modo de vivir ♦ **to earn** o **to make a l.**
ganarse la vida.

living allowance s. dietas.

living quarters s.pl. vivienda, alojamiento.

living room s. sala de estar.

living wage s. salario suficiente para vivir, salario vital.

living will s. DER. última voluntad de morir, en lugar de ser
mantenido vivo por medios artificiales (en caso de enfermedad).

liz·ard (lĭz′ərd) s. ZOOL. lagarto.

lla·ma (lä′mə) s. ZOOL. llama.

lo (lō) interj. ¡he aquí!

load (lōd) I. s. *(weight)* peso; *(cargo)* carga, cargamento;
(workload) trabajo, tareas; *(capacity)* cabida, capacidad *f;*
(of a firearm) carga; *(of an engine)* rendimiento; FIG.
(stress) peso, presión *f;* MEC. resistencia; ELEC. carga; FIN.
recargo ♦ **get a l. of this!** JER. ¡fíjate!, ¡mira esto! • **loads**
FAM. montón, muchísimo • **to take a l. off one's feet** FIG.
sentarse • **to take a l. off one's mind** FIG. sacarse un peso
de encima II. tr. *(to fill)* cargar <*to l. a ship* cargar un
barco>; llenar <*the waiters loaded the table with food* los
mozos llenaron la mesa de comida>; *(to burden)* agobiar,
abrumar <*loaded with worries* agobiado por las preocupa-
ciones>; *(gun, camera, dice)* cargar; *(to adulterate)* adulterar; *(to add a fee)* recargar ♦ **to l. down** o **up** cargar
—intr. cargar(se).

load·ed (lō′dĭd) adj. *(full)* cargado; FIG. *(tricky)* intencionado <*a l. question* una pregunta intencionada>; JER.
(drunk) borracho, embriagado; *(rich)* rico, forrado de dinero.

load·er (lō′dər) s. COMPUT. realizador *m.*

load·ing (lō′dĭng) s. *(act)* carga; *(filler)* relleno; COM. sobre-
prima; ELEC. carga.

load·star (lōd′stär′) s. var. de **lodestar.**

load·stone (lōd′stōn′) s. var. de **lodestone.**

loaf¹ (lōf) s. [pl. **loaves** (lōvz)] *(bread)* pan *m;* *(shaped mass)*
hogaza, barra.

loaf² (lōf) intr. haraganear, holgazanear.

loaf·er (lō′fər) s. *(idle person)* holgazán *m;* *(shoe)* mocasín
m.

loam (lōm) s. GEOL. marga; AGR. mantillo, tierra labrantía;
CONSTR. adobe *m.*

loan (lōn) I. s. COM. préstamo, empréstito; *(something lent)*
préstamo ♦ **on l.** prestado II. tr. prestar.

loan shark s. FAM. usurero.

loan-word o **loan·word** (lōn′wûrd′) s. palabra tomada de
otro idioma.

loath (lōth) adj. *(reluctant)* poco dispuesto, renuente; *(disinclined)* reacio ♦ **to be l. to** estar poco dispuesto a.

loathe (lōth) tr. **loathed, loath·ing** *(to hate)* odiar; *(to abhor)*
aborrecer.

loath·ing (lō′thĭng) s. odio, aborrecimiento.

loath·some (lōth′səm) adj. odioso, repugnante.

loaves (lōvz) pl. de **loaf.**

lob (lŏb) I. tr. **lobbed, lob·bing** volear —intr. *(to plod)*
moverse pesadamente; *(in tennis)* lanzar la pelota voleada
II. s. volea alta.

---

lob·by (lŏb′ē) **I.** s. [pl. **-bies**] *(foyer)* vestíbulo; *(waiting room)* sala de espera; *(special interest group)* grupo de presión **II.** intr. **-bied, -by·ing** POL. ejercer presiones —tr. *(a bill)* persuadir para que se apruebe; *(an official)* tratar de persuadir a.

lob·by·ing (lŏb′ē-ĭng) s. POL. campaña de persuasión legislativa.

lob·by·ist (lŏb′ē-ĭst) s. POL. procurador de influencia legislativa *m.*

lobe (lŏb) s. ANAT. lóbulo.

lobed (lŏbd) adj. lobulado.

lo·bot·o·my (lō-bŏt′ə-mē) s. [pl. **-mies**] MED. lobotomía.

lob·ster (lŏb′stər) s. ZOOL. langosta, bogavante (animal y su carne) *m.*

lob·ule (lŏb′yo͞ol) s. lóbulo.

lo·cal (lō′kəl) **I.** adj. *(regional)* local; *(localized)* de la localidad, del lugar; *(road)* vecinal; *(not express)* local <*l. train* tren local>; *(restricted)* restringido; *(provincial)* provinciano, limitado; MED. *(anesthesia, infection)* local; *(remedy)* externo ♦ **l. call** TEL. llamada urbana • **l. government** gobierno municipal • **l. news** noticias de la ciudad **II.** s. *(train)* tren local; *(bus)* ómnibus local; *(chapter)* sección local *f* ♦ **she's a l.** ella es de aquí • **the locals** la gente de la localidad *o* del lugar.

local anesthetic s. anestésico local.

local color s. LIT. color local *m.*

lo·cale (lō-kăl′) s. *(locality)* sitio, lugar *m*; *(scene)* escena (de un acontecimiento).

lo·cal·ism (lō′kə-lĭz′əm) s. *(idiom)* localismo; *(custom)* regionalismo; *(local interests)* localismo.

lo·cal·i·ty (lō-kăl′ĭ-tē) s. [pl. **-ties**] *(district)* localidad *f*; *(place)* sitio; *(region)* región *f.*

lo·cal·ize (lō′kə-līz′) tr. & intr. **-ized, -iz·ing** localizar(se).

lo·cal·ly (lō′kə-lē) adv. *(regionally)* en la localidad, en la región; MED. externamente.

lo·cate (lō′kāt′) tr. **-cat·ed, -cat·ing** *(to find)* localizar, encontrar; *(to place)* ubicar, colocar —intr. establecerse, asentarse.

lo·ca·tion (lō-kā′shən) s. *(position)* localización *f*; *(place)* lugar *m*, sitio; CINEM. exteriores <*to film on l.* rodar los exteriores>.

lo·ca·tive (lŏk′ə-tĭv) s. & adj. GRAM. locativo.

loch (lŏKH, lŏk) s. lago.

lo·chi·a (lō′kē-ə, lŏk′ē-ə) s.pl. MED. loquios.

lo·ci (lō′sī′, -kī′) pl. de **locus**.

lock¹ (lŏk) **I.** s. *(device)* cerradura; *(of a canal)* esclusa; *(gunlock)* llave (de un arma) *f*; *(entanglement)* enredo; *(interlocking)* entrelazamiento; *(wrestling hold)* llave ♦ **l., stock, and barrel** FAM. por completo, completamente • **under l. and key** bajo llave **II.** tr. *(to fasten)* cerrar con llave <*to l. a door* cerrar una puerta con llave>; *(to interlock)* trabar; *(to clasp)* coger(se), tomar(se) <*the girls locked arms and walked away* las muchachas se tomaron del brazo y se alejaron>; *(to invest)* inmovilizar (capital) ♦ **to be locked in combat** estar luchando cuerpo a cuerpo • **to l. horns with** reñir con • **to l. in** encerrar • **to l. out** *(to shut out)* cerrar la puerta a; *(to withhold work from)* dejar sin trabajo (a empleados hasta aceptar convenio laboral) • **to l. up** *(to confine)* encerrar; *(to fasten)* cerrar con llave; *(to store)* guardar en lugar cerrado; *(to put in jail)* encarcelar; *(to make certain)* asegurar resultados de —intr. *(to close)* cerrarse <*the door won't l. with this key* la puerta no se cierra con esta llave>; *(to interlock)* trabarse; *(to jam)* agarrotarse; *(a firearm)* encasquillarse ♦ **to be locked in** estar encerrado • **to be locked out** estar fuera sin llave • **l. together** unirse, enlazarse • **to l. up** echar la llave, cerrar.

lock² (lŏk) s. *(of hair)* mecha; *(of wool, cotton)* vedija ♦ **locks** POÉT. cabello.

lock·age (lŏk′ĭj) s. *(of a ship)* paso por una esclusa; *(toll)* portazgo de esclusa; *(system)* sistema de esclusas *m.*

lock·er (lŏk′ər) s. *(closet)* ropero, armario; *(trunk)* baúl *m*; *(refrigerator)* cámara frigorífica; *(one who locks)* cerrador *m.*

locker room s. vestuario (de un gimnasio, club).

lock·et (lŏk′ĭt) s. guardapelo, relicario.

lock·ing (lŏk′ĭng) **I.** s. *(shutting)* cierre *m*; *(fixing)* fijación *f* **II.** adj. *(shutting)* de cierre; *(fixing)* fijador, de fijación.

lock·jaw (lŏk′jô′) s. MED. *(tetanus symptom)* trismo; *(tetanus)* tétano.

lock·nut *o* **lock nut** (lŏk′nŭt′) s. TEC. contratuerca, tuerca de seguridad.

lock·out (lŏk′out′) s. cierre patronal de un lugar de trabajo *m.*

lock·smith (lŏk′smĭth′) s. cerrajero.

lock step s. *(march)* marcha cerrada; *(standardized procedure)* proceder automático.

lock·up (lŏk′ŭp′) s. FAM. *(jail cell)* calabozo; *(closing)* cierre *m.*

lo·co (lō′kō) **I.** s. [pl. **-cos**] BOT. loco **II.** tr. **-coed, -co·ing** *(to poison)* envenenar con loco; FAM. *(to craze)* enloquecer, volver loco **III.** adj. FAM. loco, chiflado.

lo·co·mo·tion (lō′kə-mō′shən) s. locomoción *f*, fuerza motriz.

lo·co·mo·tive (lō′kə-mō′tĭv) **I.** s. locomotora **II.** adj. *(railway)* locomotor, locomotivo; *(of an engine)* locomotriz, locomóvil.

lo·co·mo·tor (lō′kə-mō′tər) adj. locomotor, locomotriz.

lo·co·weed (lō′kō-wēd′) s. BOT. loco.

lo·cus (lō′kəs) s. [pl. **lo·ci** (-sī′, -kī′)] *(place)* lugar *m*, localidad *f*; GEOM. lugar geométrico; BIOL. posición de un gene *f.*

lo·cust (lō′kəst) s. ENTOM. langosta, saltamontes *m*; *(cicada)* cigarra; BOT. acacia blanca, algarrobo (árbol y madera).

lo·cu·tion (lō-kyo͞o′shən) s. *(word, phrase)* locución *f*; *(phraseology)* fraseología.

lode (lŏd) s. MIN. veta, filón *m.*

lode·star (lŏd′stär′) s. ASTRON. estrella polar; FIG. *(north)* norte *m*, guía *m.*

lode·stone (lŏd′stōn′) s. MIN. piedra imán, magnetita.

lodge (lŏj) **I.** s. *(cabin)* casa de campo; *(inn)* posada; *(organization, meeting hall)* logia (masónica); *(den)* madriguera **II.** tr. **lodged, lodg·ing** *(to house)* alojar, hospedar; *(to deposit)* depositar; *(to place)* colocar; *(to embed)* alojar, incrustar; *(to register)* presentar, sentar <*to l. a complaint* sentar una queja>; *(to vest)* conferir, otorgar —intr. *(to be housed)* alojarse, hospedarse; *(to become embedded)* alojarse, incrustarse.

lodge·ment (lŏj′mənt) s. var. de **lodgment**.

lodg·er (lŏj′ər) s. inquilino.

lodg·ing (lŏj′ĭng) s. alojamiento ♦ **lodgings** *(sleeping accommodations)* alojamiento; *(rooms)* habitaciones.

lodg·ment (lŏj′mənt) s. *(lodging)* alojamiento; *(deposit)* depósito; MIL. *(foothold)* posición firme *f*; *(beachhead)* cabeza de playa.

loft (lôft) **I.** s. *(upper floor)* piso sin dividir (sobre un local comercial); *(attic)* desván *m*; *(gallery)* galería; *(hayloft)* pajar *m*; *(pigeon coop)* palomar *m* **II.** tr. *(to store)* almacenar; *(to propel)* lanzar (la pelota en alto).

loft·i·ness (lôf′tē-nĭs) s. *(height)* altura, elevación *f*; FIG. *(nobility)* nobleza; *(arrogance)* arrogancia, altanería.

loft·y (lôf′tē) adj. **-i·er, -i·est** *(high)* alto, elevado; FIG. *(elevated)* elevado, *(noble)* noble; *(arrogant)* arrogante, altanero.

log¹ (lôg) **I.** s. *(tree trunk)* tronco; *(length of wood)* leño *m*; MARÍT. *(measuring device)* corredera; *(logbook)* cuaderno de bitácora, diario de a bordo; AVIA. diario de vuelo; *(travel journal)* diario; *(register)* registro; *(data book)* cuaderno de notas ♦ **like a bump on a l.** FIG. a la bartola • **to sleep like a l.** dormir como un tronco **II.** tr. **logged, log·ging** *(a section of land)* talar los árboles de; *(trees)* aserrar; MARÍT. consignar en el cuaderno de bitácora; AVIA. consignar en el diario de vuelo ♦ **to l. hours** AVIA. tener horas de vuelo • **to l. miles** recorrer una distancia de millas • **to l. years with a company** trabajar años en una empresa —intr. cortar y transportar árboles.

log² (lôg) s. MAT. logaritmo.

lo·gan·ber·ry (lō′gən-bĕr′ē) s. BOT. frambuesa americana.

log·a·rithm (lôg′gə-rĭth′əm) s. MAT. logaritmo.

log·book (lôg′bo͝ok′) s. AER., MARÍT. diario de navegación *o* de vuelo.

log cabin s. cabaña de troncos.

loge (lōzh) s. TEAT. *(box)* palco; *(mezzanine)* primer balcón de butacas m.

log·ger (lô'gər) s. *(lumberjack)* leñero; *(tractor)* cargadora de troncos.

log·ger·head (lô'gər-hĕd') s. *(turtle)* tortuga de mar; *(tool)* hierro candente para derretir brea; FAM. *(dolt)* alcornoque m; *(large head)* cabeza grande, cabezota ♦ **to be at loggerheads with** estar en desacuerdo con.

log·gi·a (lô'jē-ə) s. ARQ. logia; TEAT. *(open balcony)* palco abierto.

log·ging (lô'gĭng) s. explotación forestal f.

log·ic (lôj'ĭk) s. *(rationality)* lógica, dialéctica; COMPUT. sistema de circuitos (lógicos) m.

log·i·cal (lôj'ĭ-kəl) adj. lógico.

logical circuit s. COMPUT. circuito lógico.

log·i·cal·ly (lôj'ĭ-kə-lē) adv. lógicamente.

lo·gi·cian (lō-jĭsh'ən) s. lógico, dialéctico.

lo·gis·tic (lō-jĭs'tĭk) o **lo·gis·ti·cal** (-tĭ-kəl) adj. logístico.

lo·gis·tics (lō-jĭs'tĭks) s. [ú. con v. sing. o pl.] logística.

log·jam (lôg'jăm') s. *(floating logs)* atasco de troncos flotantes inmovilizados; FIG. *(deadlock)* punto muerto, atolladero.

log·nor·mal (lôg-nôr'məl) adj. de la función logarítmica de distribución normal.

lo·go·gram (lô'gə-grăm') s. signo taquigráfico.

lo·go·type (lô'gə-tīp') s. logotipo.

log·roll (lôg'rōl') tr. POL. conseguir la aprobación de —intr. darse ayuda recíproca.

log·roll·ing (lôg'rō'lĭng) s. *(birling)* juego que consiste en pararse sobre troncos que están en el agua y hacerlos girar; POL. *(favor exchange)* intercambio de favores políticos.

lo·gy (lô'gē) adj. **-gi·er, -gi·est** pesado, torpe.

loin (loin) s. ANAT. lomo; *(flank)* ijada, ijar (de un animal) m; CUL. *(of beef)* solomillo; *(of pork)* lomo ♦ **loins** ANAT. *(between the thighs and groin)* ingle f; *(reproductive organs)* órganos genitales.

loin·cloth (loin'klôth') s. taparrabo.

loi·ter (loi'tər) intr. *(to stand idly)* holgazanear; *(to delay)* retrasarse; *(to dawdle)* perder el tiempo.

loi·ter·er (loi'tər-ər) s. azotacalles mf, vagabundo.

loll (lôl) intr. *(to slouch)* repantigarse; *(to droop)* pender ♦ **to l. around** no dar golpe —tr. dejar pender.

lol·li·pop o **lol·ly·pop** (lôl'ē-pŏp') s. chupetín m, pirulí m.

Lom·bard (lŏm'bärd') s. *(Germanic tribe)* lombardo, longobardo; *(native of Lombardy)* lombardo.

Lom·bar·dy (lŏm'bär'dē) s. Lombardía.

Lon·don (lŭn'dən) s. Londres.

Lon·don·er (lŭn'də-nər) s. londinense mf.

lone (lōn) adj. *(solitary)* solo, solitario; *(sole)* único <*the l. doctor in the village* el único médico de la aldea>; *(isolated)* solitario.

lone·li·ness (lōn'lē-nĭs) s. soledad f.

lone·ly (lōn'lē) adj. **-li·er, -li·est** *(alone)* solo <*I felt l.* me sentí solo>; *(companionless)* solitario, solo; *(isolated)* solitario <*a l. village* un pueblo solitario>.

lon·er (lō'nər) s. FAM. solitario ♦ **to be a l.** gustarle a uno estar solo.

lone·some (lōn'səm) adj. *(lonely)* solo; *(companionless)* solitario; *(lone)* solitario.

long¹ (lông) I. adj. **-er, -est** *(not short)* largo <*a l. list* una lista larga>; *(lengthy)* largo <*a l. journey* un viaje largo>; *(in distance)* de largo, de longitud <*a foot l.* un pie de largo>; *(drawn-out)* largo, prolongado <*it was a l. game* fue un partido largo>; FONÉT. largo ♦ **in the l. run** a la larga • **to be l. on** COM., FIN. acumular (mercaderías o valores) a la espera de una subida de precios; *(to have much of)* tener mucho • **to take a l. time** tardar mucho II. adv. mucho tiempo <*have you known her l.?* ¿hace mucho tiempo que la conoces?> ♦ **all morning l.** (durante) toda la mañana, la mañana entera • **as l. as** *(while)* mientras <*I will love you as l. as I live* te amaré mientras viva>; *(if)* si, siempre y cuando <*I will pay for our dinner now as l. as you pay me back later* yo pagaré por la cena ahora siempre y cuando tú me pagues luego> • **how l.?** *(time)* ¿cuánto tiempo?; *(length)* ¿qué largo? • **l. ago** o **since** hace mucho tiempo • **l. before** mucho antes • **l. into the**

night hasta altas horas de la noche • **l. live the King¡** ¡viva el Rey! • **no longer** ya no, no más • **so l.!** FAM. ¡hasta luego!, ¡adiós! • **so l. as** con tal que, siempre que III. s. mucho tiempo ♦ **before l.** dentro de poco • **for l.** mucho tiempo • **the l. and the short of (something)** la esencia de (algo).

long² (lông) intr. ♦ **to l. for** añorar, desear con ansia • **to l. to** anhelar, desear ardientemente.

long·boat (lông'bōt') s. MARÍT. chalupa, lancha.

long·bow (lông'bō') s. arco.

long distance s. TEL. *(system)* sistema telefónico interurbano; *(call)* llamada interurbana.

long-dis·tance (lông'dĭs'təns) adj. & adv. de larga distancia.

lon·gev·i·ty (lŏn-jĕv'ĭ-tē) s. longevidad f.

long face s. FIG. cara larga.

long·hair (lông'hâr') s. FAM. *(intellectual)* bohemio; *(music lover)* melómano; *(hippie)* hippie mf.

long·haired (lông'hârd') adj. pelilargo, de pelo largo.

long·hand (lông'hănd') s. letra cursiva, escritura cursiva.

long·horn (lông'hôrn') s. ZOOL. ganado de cuernos largos.

long·ing (lông'ĭng) s. anhelo, deseo.

long·ish (lông'ĭsh) adj. bastante largo.

lon·gi·tude (lŏn'jĭ-tōōd', -tyōōd') s. ASTRON., GEOG. longitud f.

lon·gi·tu·di·nal (lŏn'jĭ-tōōd'n-əl, -tyōōd'-) adj. longitudinal.

long johns s.pl. FAM. calzón interior largo.

long jump s. DEP. salto de longitud.

long-lived (lông'līvd', -lĭvd') adj. *(people)* de larga vida, longevo; *(things)* duradero; FIG. *(persistent)* persistente.

long-play·ing (lông'plā'ĭng) adj. de larga duración (disco).

long-range (lông'rānj') adj. de largo alcance, de gran alcance.

long·shore·man (lông'shôr'mən) s. [pl. **-men**] MARÍT. estibador m, cargador o descargador de muelle m.

long shot s. *(entry)* competidor con poca probabilidad de ganar m; *(bet)* apuesta arriesgada; *(venture)* empresa aventurada ♦ **not by a l.** ni mucho menos.

long-sight·ed (lông'sī'tĭd) adj. MED. présbita, présbite; FIG. previsor, perspicaz.

long-stand·ing (lông'stăn'dĭng) adj. duradero.

long-suf·fer·ing (lông'sŭf'ər-ĭng) adj. sufrido, resignado.

long suit s. *(cards)* palo fuerte (de naipes); FIG. *(strength)* punto fuerte (de uno).

long-term (lông'tûrm') adj. a largo plazo.

long-time (lông'tīm') adj. antiguo, viejo.

long ton s. tonelada larga, tonelada inglesa.

long-wind·ed (lông'wĭn'dĭd) adj. *(talkative)* verboso, prolijo; *(endless)* sin fin.

long·wise (lông'wīz') adv. a lo largo, longitudinalmente.

loo¹ (lōō) s. [pl. **loos**] un juego de naipes.

loo² (lōō) s. [pl. **loos**] G.B., FAM. excusado, retrete m.

look (lōōk) I. intr. *(to see)* mirar <*l. this way* mira para este lado>; *(to turn one's attention)* mirar, fijarse <*l. over here!* ¡mira! ¡fíjate!>; *(to search)* buscar <*he looked everywhere* buscó por todas partes>; *(to seem)* parecer, tener aspecto de <*he looks sick* tiene aspecto de enfermo>; *(to appear)* estar <*he looks pale* está pálido>; *(to face)* estar orientado hacia, dar a <*the window looks north* la ventana da al norte> ♦ **l. alive!** ¡apresúrate! • **l. here!** ¡un momento! • **l. out!** ¡cuidado! • **l. who's talking!** FIG. ¡mira quien habla! • **not much to l. at** FAM. feo • **not to l. good** ser de mal agüero (situación) • **not to l. oneself** tener mala cara • **to l. ahead** mirar al futuro • **to l. alike** parecerse • **to l. away** apartar la mirada • **to l. back** *(to turn around)* mirar hacia atrás; *(to remember)* recordar el pasado • **to l. down** bajar la mirada, bajar los ojos • **to l. good** *(healthy)* tener buena cara; *(attractive)* tener buen aspecto • **to l. on** mirar • **to l. up** *(to raise the eyes)* levantar la mirada; *(to get better)* ir mejorando, ponerse mejor —tr. *(to turn one's eyes on)* mirar <*he looked her in the face* la miró a la cara>; *(to express)* expresar con la mirada o con los ojos ♦ **it depends on how you l. at it** depende de cómo se mire • **to l. after** *(someone)* cuidar a, ocuparse de; *(something)* ocuparse de, encargarse de • **to l. after** o **out for oneself** cuidarse • **to l. around for** estar en busca de, buscar • **to l. at** *(to go over)* mirar, echar un vistazo a; *(to see)* mirar, fijarse; *(to face)* encarrar con; *(examine)* repasar, examinar; FIG. *(to be interested in)* mirar, fijarse en • **to l. back on** FIG. to **l. daggers at** FIG. mirar echando chispas • **to l. down on** despreciar • **to l. down one's nose at** FAM. menospreciar • **to l. for** *(to search for)* buscar; *(to expect)* esperar • **to l. forward to** anticipar • **to l. good on** quedar bien <*that dress looks good on you* este vestido te queda bien> • **to l. in on (someone)** pasar por casa de (alguien), hacer una breve visita (a alguien) • **to l. into** *(to investigate)* investigar; *(to gaze into)* mirar • **to l. like** *(to resemble)* parecerse a <*do I l. like my father?* ¿me parezco a mi padre?>; *(in a general way)* parecer <*you l. like a doctor with the white jacket or* pareces un médico con esa chaqueta blanca>; *(likely to)* parecer que <*it looks like rain* parece que va a llover>; *(likely to be)* parecer <*it looks like a bad year for farmers* parece un año malo para los labradores> • **to l. on** *o* **upon** *(to face)* dar a; *(to consider)* estimar, considerar • **to l. one's age** aparentar la edad • **to l. out** *o* **out of** asomarse a, mirar por • **to l. out for** *(to watch for)* estar al acecho de; *(to be wary about)* estar atento *o* preparado para; *(to expect)* esperar; *(to take care of)* cuidar a • **to l. out on** dar a • **to l. over** *(to go over)* mirar, echar un vistazo a; *(to examine)* examinar, repasar • **to l. (someone) up** *(to go to see)* ir a ver *o* visitar (a alguien); *(to come to see)* venir a ver *o* visitar (a alguien) • **to l. someone up and down** mirar a alguien de arriba abajo • **to l. (something) up** buscar (algo en libro, diccionario) • **to l. through** *(to peer)* mirar por; *(to search)* buscar por, registrar • **to l. to** *(to glance)* mirar hacia; *(to turn to)* acudir a, recurrir a; *(to be careful about)* cuidar a, atender a • **to l. up to (someone)** respetar, tener en estima **II.** s. *(quick glance)* ojeada, vistazo; *(gaze)* mirada; *(aspect)* aspecto, apariencia; *(in fashion)* moda, estilo • **by the l. of it** según las apariencias • **by the l. of things** según parece • **looks** *(appearance)* aspecto, apariencia <*good looks* buena apariencia>; *(beauty)* belleza • **not to like the l. of** FAM. no gustarle a uno el aspecto de • **to give (someone) a l.** FAM. lanzar una mirada de desaprobación (a alguien) • **to have (someone's) looks** parecerse a • **to have the l. of** parecer, tener aspecto de • **to lose one's looks** envejecer, ponerse feo • **to take** *o* **have a l. at** mirar, echar un vistazo a • **to take a good l. at** mirar bien.

look·a·like (lo͝ok′ə-līk′) s. persona que se parece a otra, doble *mf.*

look·er (lo͝ok′ər) s. *(spectator)* espectador *m*; JER. *(attractive person)* guapo.

look·er-on (lo͝ok′ər-ŏn′) s. [pl. **look·ers-on**] espectador *m.*

look-in (lo͝ok′ĭn′) s. *(visit)* visita corta; *(glance)* ojeada.

looking glass s. espejo.

look·out (lo͝ok′out′) s. *(watch)* vigilancia; *(watchtower)* atalaya; *(vantage point)* mirador *m*; *(outlook)* perspectiva, panorama *m*; *(problem)* asunto <*his health is his own l.* su salud es asunto suyo>; MARÍT. vigía *m* • **to be on the l. for** estar al acecho de.

loom¹ (lo͞om) **I.** intr. *(to appear)* aparecer, surgir; *(to arise)* aparecerse; *(to impend)* amenazar, ser inminente • **to l. large** ser de mucha importancia **II.** s. aparición *f.*

loom² (lo͞om) s. telar *m.*

loon¹ (lo͞on) s. ORNIT. somorgujo.

loon² (lo͞on) s. *(simpleton)* bobo; *(idler)* perezoso.

loon·y (lo͞o′nē) FAM. **I.** adj. **-i·er, -i·est** *(silly)* bobo; *(crazy)* chalado • **l. bin** manicomio **II.** s. [pl. **-ies**] loco, lunático.

loop (lo͞op) **I.** s. *(length of line)* lazo; *(coil)* vuelta; *(bend)* curva; *(circular path)* vuelta, círculo; *(fastener)* presilla; ELEC. circuito cerrado; AVIA. rizo • **to knock** *o* **throw for a l.** *(to bewilder)* desconcertar; *(to upset)* trastornar, descomponer **II.** tr. *(length of line)* hacer un lazo en; *(to coil)* dar una vuelta a; *(to tie)* enlazar; *(to fasten)* atar con un lazo; AVIA. rizar; ELEC. conectar cerrando el circuito • **to l. the l.** AVIA. rizar el rizo —intr. *(length of line)* hacer un lazo; *(to coil)* tener vueltas; *(to bend)* hacer una curva; *(to move)* serpentear; AVIA. hacer un rizo.

loop·hole (lo͞op′hōl′) s. MIL. tronera, aspillera; FIG. *(a way out)* escapatoria, pretexto.

loose (lo͞os) **I.** adj. **loos·er, loos·est** *(unfastened)* suelto;

(slack) flojo; *(untied)* desatado, suelto; *(not tight)* holgado <*l. clothing* ropa holgada>; *(not compact)* poco compacto; *(vague)* vago, indefinido <*l. plans* planes indefinidos>; *(not fast)* desvaído <*a l. dye* un color desvaído>; *(idle)* irresponsable <*l. talk* charla irresponsable>; *(lewd)* relajado, disoluto; *(promiscuous)* ligero, liviano; *(not literal)* libre <*a l. translation* una traducción libre>; *(not packaged)* a granel; QUÍM. libre **II.** adv. • **to break l.** *(to become detached)* romperse; *(to run away)* escaparse • **to come** *o* **get l.** aflojarse, desatarse • **to hang l.** JER. quedarse calmo • **to set** *o* **turn l.** soltar, libertar **III.** tr. **loosed, loos·ing** *(to release)* soltar, poner en libertad; *(to shoot)* disparar —intr. *(to become loose)* soltarse; *(to fire)* disparar **IV.** s. • **on the l.** FAM. *(free)* suelto; *(on a spree)* de parranda.

loose end s. *(free extremity)* cabo suelto; FIG. *(matter, problem)* asunto pendiente, problema sin resolver *m* • **to be at loose ends** FIG. no saber qué hacer • **to tie up the loose ends** FIG. atar cabos.

loose-leaf (lo͞os′lēf′) adj. de hojas sueltas <*a l. notebook* un cuaderno de hojas sueltas>.

loose·ly (lo͞os′lē) adv. *(not tightly)* sueltamente; *(vaguely)* vagamente; *(not tautly)* flojamente; *(freely)* libremente; *(amply)* holgadamente; *(immorally)* disolutamente; *(irresponsibly)* irresponsablemente.

loos·en (lo͞o′sən) tr. *(to make less tight)* aflojar; *(to untie)* desatar; *(to ease)* aflojar, relajar; *(bowels)* aliviar, descargar • **to l. one's grip over** dar más libertad a • **to l. someone's tongue** hacer soltar la lengua a alguien • **to l. up on someone** ser menos riguroso con alguien —intr. *(to become less tight)* aflojarse; *(to become less severe)* aflojarse, relajarse • **to l. up** entrar en calor.

loose·ness (lo͞os′nĭs) s. *(slackening)* aflojamiento; *(fullness)* holgura; *(degradation)* degradación *f*, licencia; *(vagueness)* vaguedad *f.*

loos·en·ing (lo͞o′sə-nĭng) s. *(slackening)* aflojamiento; *(of the bowels)* alivio; *(of muscles)* calentamiento.

loot (lo͞ot) **I.** s. *(booty)* botín *m*, presa; JER. *(money)* dinero **II.** tr. *(to pillage)* pillar, saquear; *(to take as booty)* llevar como botín —intr. entregarse al saqueo.

loot·er (lo͞o′tər) s. saqueador *m.*

loot·ing (lo͞o′tĭng) s. saqueo.

lop (lŏp) tr. **lopped, lop·ping** *(to trim)* podar; *(to eliminate)* eliminar.

lope (lōp) **I.** intr. **loped, lop·ing** correr a paso largo **II.** s. paso largo.

lop-eared (lŏp′îrd′) adj. de orejas gachas *o* caídas.

lop·sid·ed (lŏp′sī′dĭd) adj. *(unsymmetrical)* desproporcionado; *(leaning)* inclinado, ladeado; *(table, stool)* cojo; FIG. *(unbalanced)* desequilibrado.

lo·qua·cious (lō-kwā′shəs) adj. locuaz.

lo·quac·i·ty (lō-kwăs′ĭ-tē) s. locuacidad *f.*

lo·ran (lôr′ăn′) s. AVIA., MARÍT., RAD. lorán (sistema electrónico de navegación) *m.*

lord (lôrd) **I.** s. *(feudal)* señor *m*; *(noble)* noble *m*; FIG. *(man of power)* magnate *m* <*the lords of industry* los magnates de la industria> *(expert)* campeón *o* dear • **good** *o* **dear L.!** ¡Dios mío! • **L.** G.B. *(title)* lord; RELIG. Señor • **l. and master** dueño y señor • **l. of the manor** señor feudal • **my l.** G.B. *(noble)* señor; *(a bishop)* Ilustrísima; *(a judge)* señor juez • **the House of Lords** *o* **the Lords** G.B., POL. la Cámara de los Lores **II.** intr. • **to l. it over someone** dominar a alguien.

Lord Chancellor s. [pl. **Lords Chancellor**] G.B. presidente de la Cámara de los Lores *m.*

lord·ly (lôrd′lē) adj. **-li·er, -li·est** *(of a lord)* señorial; *(dignified)* noble; *(arrogant)* altivo, arrogante.

lor·do·sis (lôr-dō′sĭs) s. MED. lordosis *f.*

Lord's Day *o* **Lord's day** s. RELIG. día del señor *m*, domingo.

lord·ship (lôrd′shĭp′) s. *(title)* señoría; *(lands)* señorío; *(authority)* señorío.

Lord's Prayer s. RELIG. padrenuestro.

lore (lôr) s. *(tradition)* tradición *f*; *(belief)* creencia popular; *(knowledge)* ciencia, saber *m.*

---

ng inglés / ŏ la / ō bou / ô corre / oi oigo / o͞o uno / ou auto / yo͞o ciudad / w hueco / y yo / z mismo

lor·gnette (lôrn-yĕt′) s. *(eyeglasses)* impertinentes m; *(opera glasses)* gemelos de teatro con mango.

lorn (lôrn) adj. *(bereft)* despejado; *(forlorn)* abandonado, desamparado.

Lor·raine (lô-rān′) s. Lorena.

lor·ry (lôr′ē) s. [pl. **-ries**] *(horse-drawn wagon)* carro de plataforma de cuatro ruedas; F.C. *(railway carriage)* batea, vagoneta; G.B. *(truck)* camión m.

lose (lōōz) tr. **lost** (lôst), **los·ing** *(to mislay)* perder; *(to fail to win)* perder; *(to cost)* costar, hacer perder <*his arrogance lost him his job* su arrogancia le costó el empleo>; *(to run slow)* atrasar ♦ **get lost!** JER. ¡vete al demonio! • **to be lost** estar perdido • **to be lost in thought** estar absorto en los pensamientos • **to get lost** perderse • **to give up for lost** dar por perdido • **to l. face** desprestigiarse • **to l. ground** perder terreno • **to l. heart** desanimarse • **to l. one's heart to** enamorarse de • **to l. one's mind** enloquecer, perder la razón o el juicio • **to l. one's temper** perder los estribos, encolerizarse • **to l. oneself in** perderse en • **to l. one's way** perderse • **to l. out on** perder • **to l. sight of** *(not to see)* perder de vista; *(objectivity)* perder la objetividad • **to l. sleep over** preocuparse de • **to l. track of** *(people, things)* perder la pista de; *(time)* perder la noción de • **to l. weight** perder peso, adelgazar —intr. perder ♦ **to l. out** perder, salir perdiendo.

los·er (lōō′zər) s. *(one that loses)* perdedor m; *(one that fails)* fracasado; *(lost cause)* causa perdida ♦ **to be a good l.** saber perder.

loss (lôs) s. *(act of losing)* pérdida; *(defeat)* derrota; *(lost game)* juego perdido; *(destruction)* estrago, daño ♦ **losses** MIL. bajas; COM. pérdidas • **l. of life** muertos, víctimas • **l. of movement** parálisis • **to be at a l.** *(to be puzzled)* no saber qué hacer; *(for words)* no encontrar palabras con que expresarse • **to be one's l.** salir perdiendo • **to cut one's losses** cortar por lo sano • **to sell at a l.** vender con pérdida.

loss leader s. COM. artículo de lanzamiento.

loss ratio s. COM. relación entre las primas y los reclamos pagados (por una compañía de seguros en un tiempo determinado) f.

lost (lôst) I. pret. y part. p. de **lose** II. adj. *(person)* perdido; *(misplaced)* perdido, extraviado; *(confused)* perdido, desorientado; *(condemned)* perdido, condenado <*a l. soul* un alma perdida>; *(engrossed)* absorto <*l. in thought* absorto en los pensamientos> ♦ **l. and found** oficina de objetos perdidos • **l. art** arte olvidado • **l. cause** causa perdida.

lot (lôt) I. s. *(drawing)* sorteo; *(share)* parte f, porción f; *(fate)* suerte f, sino; *(people)* grupo de personas; *(kind)* tipo <*he is a bad l.* es un tipo de mala calaña>; *(articles for sale)* lote m, partida; *(large amount)* gran cantidad, mucho <*a l. of people* gran cantidad de gente>; *(land)* solar m, lote m; CINEM. estudio ♦ **by l.** por sorteo • **lots of** cantidades de, mucho • **to draw lots** echar suertes • **to improve one's l.** mejorar la suerte • **to throw in one's l. with** compartir la suerte de II. tr. **lot·ted, lot·ting** *(to allot)* asignar, repartir; *(to divide)* dividir (en lotes o terrenos).

loth (lôth) adj. var. de **loath**.

Lo·thar·i·o (lō-thâr′ē-ō′) s. [pl. **-os**] tenorio.

lo·tion (lō′shən) s. loción f.

lot·ter·y (lôt′ə-rē) s. [pl. **-ies**] *(contest)* lotería; FIG. *(chance)* lance m, lotería.

lot·to (lôt′ō) s. lotería (juego casero).

lo·tus (lō′təs) s. BOT. loto.

lo·tus-eat·er (lō′təs-ē′tər) s. LIT. lotófago; FIG. *(sybarite)* soñador m, persona indolente.

loud (loud) I. adj. **-er, -est** *(high in volume)* alto; *(voice)* fuerte <*a l. yell* un grito fuerte>; *(noisy)* ruidoso, bullicioso <*a l. party* una fiesta bulliciosa>; *(applause)* fuerte, caluroso; *(insistent)* insistente; *(gaudy)* chillón, llamativo <*a l. necktie* una corbata llamativa>; *(loudmouthed)* gritón ♦ **in a l. voice** en voz alta, a gritos II. adv. **-er, -est** *(loudly)* alto <*don't speak so l.* no hables tan alto>; *(to sound, yell, sing)* fuerte; *(insistently)* insistentemente ♦ **to say something out l.** decir algo en voz alta.

loud·en (loud′n) tr. & intr. intensificar(se), volver(se) más fuerte.

loud·mouth (loud′mouth′) FAM. s. *(shouter)* gritón m; *(boaster)* fanfarrón m.

loud·ness (loud′nĭs) s. volumen m, fuerza.

loud·speak·er (loud′spē′kər) s. altavoz m, altoparlante m.

Lou·i·si·an·a (lōō-ē′zē-ă′nə) s. Luisiana.

lounge (lounj) I. intr. **lounged, loung·ing** *(to loll)* repantigarse; *(to idle)* gandulear —tr. gastar ociosamente, malgastar (el tiempo) II. s. *(waiting room)* sala de espera; *(lobby)* vestíbulo; *(snack bar)* cantina; *(sitting room)* sala de estar; *(couch)* sofá m.

lounge car s. F.C. coche salón m.

lounge chair s. tumbona.

lour (lou′ər) v. & s. var. de **lower¹**.

louse (lous) I. s. [pl. **lice** (līs)] ENTOM. piojo; JER. [pl. **lous·es**] canalla mf, sinvergüenza mf II. tr. **loused, lous·ing** ♦ **to l. up** o **up on** estropear, echar a perder —intr. ♦ **to l. up** hacer una pifia.

lous·y (lou′zē) adj. **-i·er, -i·est** *(infested with lice)* piojoso, lleno de piojos; *(unpleasant)* vil, malísimo <*a l. headache* un dolor de cabeza malísimo>; *(worthless)* pésimo ♦ **a l. trick** una cochinada • **l. with money** JER. forrado de dinero.

lout (lout) s. patán m, bruto.

lou·ver o **lou·vre** (lōō′vər) s. *(blind)* persiana; *(slat)* tablilla; ARQ. lumbrera; AUTO. rejilla de ventilación.

lov·a·ble (lŭv′ə-bəl) adj. *(adorable)* adorable, encantador; *(endearing)* cautivador, atractivo.

lov·age (lŭv′ĭj) s. BOT. ligustro, alheña.

love (lŭv) I. s. *(feeling)* amor m, cariño; *(lover)* amor <*my first l.* mi primer amor>; DEP. cero (en tenis y otros juegos) ♦ **for the l. of** por el amor de • **l. o with l.** *(affectionately)* un cariñoso saludo; *(cordially)* un cordial saludo (al terminar una carta) • **my l.** amor mío, mi amor • **not for l. or money** por nada del mundo • **to be in l.** estar enamorado • **to fall in l.** enamorarse • **to give** o **to send one's l. to** dar o mandar recuerdos a • **to make l.** hacer el amor II. tr. **loved, lov·ing** *(to adore)* amar, querer; *(to have sex with)* hacer el amor con, tener relaciones sexuales con; *(to enjoy)* gustarle a uno, encantar <*he loves to swim* le gusta nadar>; *(to need)* necesitar ♦ **I'd l. to!** ¡con mucho gusto!, ¡me encantaría! —intr. amar, querer.

love·a·ble (lŭv′ə-bəl) adj. var. de **lovable**.

love affair s. *(relationship)* amorío; *(enthusiasm)* gran entusiasmo.

love apple s. ANT. tomate m.

love·bird (lŭv′bûrd′) s. ORNIT. periquito.

love child s. hijo natural.

love feast s. RELIG. ágape m.

love knot s. lazo de amor.

love·less (lŭv′lĭs) adj. sin amor.

love·li·ness (lŭv′lē-nĭs) s. belleza, hermosura.

love·lorn (lŭv′lôrn′) adj. *(forsaken)* abandonado por el amado; *(languishing)* herido de amor, suspirando de amor.

love·ly (lŭv′lē) I. adj. **-li·er, -li·est** *(loving)* amable, cariñoso; *(nice)* encantador; *(beautiful)* hermoso, bello ♦ **to have a l. time** pasarlo muy bien II. s. [pl. **-lies**] FAM. belleza, beldad f III. adv. hermosamente.

love·mak·ing (lŭv′mā′kĭng) s. *(sexual intercourse)* relaciones sexuales f; *(courtship)* galanteo.

love potion s. filtro amoroso.

lov·er (lŭv′ər) s. *(paramour)* amante mf, querido; *(devotee)* aficionado.

love seat s. confidente m, sofá de dos asientos m.

love·sick (lŭv′sĭk′) adj. enfermo de amor, herido de amor.

love·sick·ness (lŭv′sĭk′nĭs) s. mal de amores m.

lov·ing (lŭv′ĭng) adj. *(feeling love)* amoroso; *(affectionate)* cariñoso; *(exhibiting love)* tierno.

loving cup s. *(wine vessel)* copa de la amistad; *(award)* trofeo, copa.

lov·ing-kind·ness (lŭv′ĭng-kīnd′nĭs) s. *(affection)* cariño afectuoso; *(compassion)* compasión f; *(kindness)* bondad f.

low¹ (lō) I. adj. **-er, -est** *(in height, intensity)* bajo; *(in qual-*

ity) inferior; *(décolleté)* escotado; *(shallow)* bajo, poco profundo; *(humble)* plebeyo, humilde *<a person of l. origin* una persona de origen humilde>; *(mean)* (mean) malo *<to pull a l. stunt* hacer una mala jugada>; *(unfavorable)* desfavorable, malo *<to have a l. opinion of someone* tener una mala opinión de alguien>; *(coarse)* vulgar, grosero; *(low-priced)* bajo, pequeño *<a l. wage* un salario bajo>; *(cheap)* barato, bajo; MÚS. bajo, grave; ASTRON., GEOG. bajo; FONÉT. abierta ♦ **l. front** METEOR. depresión • **l. gear** AUTO. primera • **in l. spirits** abatido, deprimido • **to be l. on** estar escaso de • **to lay l.** derribar *<he laid his opponent l.* derribó a su contrincante> • **to lie l.** FAM. *(to keep out of sight)* esconderse temporalmente; *(to hide one's intentions)* ocultar las intenciones **II.** adv. **-er, -est** *(of position, level)* bajo; *(poorly)* pobremente *<you value yourself too l.* te valorizas muy pobremente>; *(softly)* bajo, en voz baja *<speak l.* habla en voz baja>; *(cheaply)* barato, a bajo precio **III.** s. *(level)* punto más bajo; METEOR. depresión *f*; AUTO. primera.

low² (lō) **I.** s. mugido **II.** intr. mugir.
low beam s. AUTO. luz baja *o* de crucero.
low·born (lō′bôrn′) adj. de humilde cuna, plebeyo.
low·boy (lō′boi′) s. cómoda baja.
low·bred (lō′brĕd′) adj. grosero, vulgar.
low·brow (lō′brou′) **I.** s. ignorante *mf*, persona inculta **II.** adj. *(uncultured)* ignorante, inculto; *(vulgar)* grosero, vulgar.
low comedy s. TEAT. farsa, sainete *m*.
low-cost (lō′kôst′) adj. barato, de bajo costo.
Low Countries s. Países Bajos.
low-cut (lō′kŭt′) adj. muy escotado (vestido).
low·down (lō′doun′) s. JER. la pura verdad.
low-down (lō′doun′) adj. FAM. *(despicable)* vil, bajo; *(depressed)* deprimido.
low·er¹ *o* **lour** (lou′ər) **I.** intr. *(to scowl)* fruncir el ceño; *(to cloud over)* nublarse, encapotarse **II.** s. *(scowl)* ceño; *(cloudiness)* encapotamiento.
low·er² (lō′ər) **I.** adj. más bajo, inferior ♦ **l. case** IMPR. caja baja **II.** tr. *(to take down)* bajar; *(to reduce)* disminuir, reducir *<to l. the price* reducir el precio>; *(to weaken)* debilitar; *(to downgrade)* rebajar —intr. *(to move down)* bajar; *(to diminish)* disminuir, reducir ♦ **to l. oneself** rebajarse, humillarse.
low·er-case (lō′ər-kās′) **I.** adj. IMPR. de caja baja, minúscula **II.** tr. **-cased, -cas·ing** *(to set)* componer con minúsculas.
lower class s. clase baja, clase obrera.
low·er·class·man (lō′ər-klăs′mən) s. [pl. **-men**] EDUC. estudiante de primero *o* segundo año (de un colegio *o* universidad) *mf*.
Lower House s. POL. Cámara Baja.
low·er·ing (lou′ər-ĭng) adj. *(frowning)* ceñudo, con el entrecejo fruncido; FIG. *(overcast)* encapotado, amenazador.
low·er·most (lō′ər-mōst′) adj. más bajo que todo, ínfimo.
lower world s. *(abode of the dead)* mundo subterráneo; *(earth)* (la) tierra.
low·er·y (lou′ə-rē) adj. encapotado, amenazador.
lowest common denominator s. MAT. mínimo común denominador.
low frequency s. ELEC., RAD. baja frecuencia.
low gear s. AUTO. primera (velocidad).
low-grade (lō′grād′) adj. de calidad inferior.
low·ing (lō′ĭng) s. mugido.
low-key (lō′kē′) *o* **low-keyed** (-kēd′) adj. *(subdued)* de baja intensidad, suave; *(color)* de tono obscuro.
low·land (lō′lənd) s. tierra baja.
low·land·er (lō′lən-dər) s. habitante de las tierras bajas *mf* ♦ **L.** habitante de la Baja Escocia.
low-lev·el (lō′lĕv′əl) adj. *(rank)* de grado inferior, subalterno; *(level)* de bajo nivel; ELEC. de baja intensidad.
low·life (lō′līf′) s. *(plebeian)* plebeyo, *(despicable person)* persona ruin, perverso.
low·li·ness (lō′lē-nĭs) s. *(humility)* humildad *f*; *(poverty)* pobreza.
low·ly (lō′lē) **I.** adj. **-li·er, -li·est** *(plebeian)* bajo, inferior;

(humble) humilde; *(prosaic)* prosaico, ordinario **II.** adv. *(humbly)* humildemente; *(softly)* bajo.
Low Mass s. RELIG. misa rezada.
low-mind·ed (lō′mīn′dĭd) adj. *(coarse)* grosero, vulgar; *(mean)* malvado, ruin.
low-necked (lō′nĕkt′) *o* **low-neck** (-nĕk′) adj. de escote bajo, escotado.
low·ness (lō′nĭs) s. *(shortness)* falta de altura; *(meanness)* bajeza, vileza; *(humility)* humildad *f*; MÚS. gravedad (de sonido, voz) *f*.
low-pitched (lō′pĭcht′) adj. MÚS. *(voice)* grave, bajo; ARQ. *(roof)* poco inclinado; *(room)* de techo bajo.
low-pres·sure (lō′prĕsh′ər) adj. *(atmosphere)* de baja presión; *(person)* relajado.
low-priced (lō′prīst′) adj. barato, de bajo precio.
low profile s. conducta *o* acción personal deliberadamente reservada ♦ **to keep a l.** comportarse reservadamente.
low relief s. ARTE. bajo relieve, bajorrelieve *m*.
low-rise (lō′rīz′) adj. CONSTR. de uno *o* dos pisos (sin elevadores).
low-spir·it·ed (lō′spĭr′ĭ-tĭd) adj. abatido, desalentado.
low-ten·sion (lō′tĕn′shən) adj. ELEC. de baja tensión *o* voltaje.
low tide s. MARÍT. marea baja, bajamar *f*.
low water s. *(in a river, lake)* nivel mínimo; *(low tide)* marea baja, bajamar *f*.
lox¹ (lōks) s. CUL. salmón ahumado.
lox² (lōks) s. FÍS. oxígeno líquido.
loy·al (loi′əl) adj. leal, fiel.
loy·al·ist (loi′ə-lĭst) s. legitimista *mf*, gubernamental *mf* ♦ **L.** *(Tory)* conservador *m*; *(in Spain)* republicano.
loy·al·ty (loi′əl-tē) s. [pl. **-ties**] lealtad *f*, fidelidad *f*.
loz·enge (lŏz′ənj) s. GEOM. rombo; *(cough drop)* pastilla, tableta.
LP (ĕl′pē′) s. disco de larga duración.
LSD (ĕl′ĕs-dē′) s. QUÍM. ácido lisérgico, LSD (droga).
lub·ber (lŭb′ər) s. *(clumsy fellow)* palurdo; *(sailor)* marinero de agua dulce.
lube (lōōb) s. *(aceite)* lubricante *m*.
lu·bri·cant (lōō′brĭ-kənt) s. & adj. lubricante *m*, lubrificante *m*.
lu·bri·cate (lōō′brĭ-kāt′) tr. **-cat·ed, -cat·ing** lubricar, lubrificar; FIG. *(to smooth out)* suavizar, alisar.
lu·bri·ca·tion (lōō′brĭ-kā′shən) s. lubricación *f*, lubrificación *f*.
lu·bri·ca·tor (lōō′brĭ-kā′tər) s. lubricante *m*, lubrificante *m*.
lu·bri·cious (lōō-brĭsh′əs) adj. *(slippery)* lúbrico, resbaladizo; *(lewd)* lascivo, lujurioso; *(salacious)* salaz, licencioso; *(tricky)* mañoso, tramposo.
lu·bric·i·ty (lōō-brĭs′ĭ-tē) s. *(slipperiness)* lubricidad *f*, lisura; *(lewdness)* lascivia, lujuria; *(trickiness)* maña, trampa.
lu·cent (lōō′sənt) adj. *(luminous)* luminoso, brillante; *(clear)* claro, transparente.
lu·cid (lōō′sĭd) adj. *(intelligible)* lúcido, claro; *(sane)* cuerdo, de claro entendimiento; *(translucent)* translúcido, diáfano.
lu·cid·i·ty (lōō-sĭd′ĭ-tē) s. *(clarity)* lucidez *f*, claridad *f*; *(brilliance)* brillantez *f*, transparencia.
Lu·ci·fer (lōō′sə-fər) s. RELIG. Lucifer *m*, Satanás *m*; ASTRON. Lucífero ♦ **l.** fósforo de fricción.
Lu·cite (lōō′sīt′) s. lucita (marca registrada de un plástico).
luck (lŭk) **I.** s. fortuna, suerte *f* ♦ **as l. would have it** la suerte quiso que • **for l.** para que traiga buena suerte • **good l.!** ¡buena suerte! • **hard** *o* **bad l.** mala suerte • **no such l.!** ¡ojalá! • **stroke of l.** golpe de suerte • **to be in l.** estar de suerte • **to be out of l.** no tener suerte • **to push one's l.** FAM. arriesgarse innecesariamente • **to try one's l.** probar suerte **II.** intr. ♦ **to l. out** FAM. tener suerte.
luck·i·ly (lŭk′ə-lē) adv. afortunadamente, por suerte.
luck·less (lŭk′lĭs) adj. desafortunado.
luck·y (lŭk′ē) adj. **-i·er, -i·est** *(fortunate)* afortunado; *(fortuitous)* fortuito, oportuno; *(bringing good luck)* que trae suerte *<l. number* número que trae suerte> ♦ **it was l. that** menos mal que • **l. break** coyuntura favorable • **thank your l. stars!** ¡bendice tu buena estrella!
lu·cra·tive (lōō′krə-tĭv) adj. lucrativo, provechoso.

lu·cre (lōō'kər) s. lucro, ganancia.

lu·di·crous (lōō'dĭ-krəs) adj. absurdo, ridículo.

luff (lŭf) MARÍT. I. s. orza II. intr. orzar.

lug¹ (lŭg) s. MEC. *(handle)* agarradera, asa; *(nut)* orejera; *(of a harness)* correa de las varas; JER. *(blockhead)* mentecato; ELEC. lengüeta de conexión (para soldaduras).

lug² (lŭg) tr. & intr. **lugged, lug·ging** arrastrar, halar.

lug·gage (lŭg'ĭj) s. equipaje *m*.

luggage rack s. AUTO. portaequipajes *m*; F.C. redecilla.

lug·sail (lŭg'səl) s. MARÍT. vela al tercio.

lu·gu·bri·ous (lōō-gōō'brē-əs) adj. lúgubre, triste.

Luke (lōōk) s. BÍBL. Lucas.

luke·warm (lōōk'wôrm') adj. *(mildly warm)* tibio, templado; FIG. *(indifferent)* indiferente.

lull (lŭl) I. tr. *(to soothe)* calmar, sosegar; FIG. *(to deceive)* embaucar —intr. calmarse, sosegarse II. s. *(calm interval)* momento de calma, cese temporal *m*; *(pause)* pausa <*a l. in the conversation* una pausa en la conversación>.

lull·a·by (lŭl'ə-bī') I. s. [pl. **-bies**] canción de cuna *f*, nana II. tr. **-bied, -by·ing** arrullar, acunar.

lum·ba·go (lŭm-bā'gō) s. MED. lumbago.

lum·bar (lŭm'bər) I. adj. ANAT. lumbar, de la región lumbar II. s. parte lumbar *f*.

lum·ber¹ (lŭm'bər) I. s. *(timber)* maderos; *(plank)* tabla; G.B. *(junk)* trastos viejos II. tr. *(to fell timber)* talar; *(to cut wood)* cortar madera; G.B. *(to clutter)* abarrotar, atestar —intr. cortar madera.

lum·ber² (lŭm'bər) intr. *(to move clumsily)* avanzar pesadamente; *(to rumble by)* avanzar con estruendo.

lum·ber·er (lŭm'bər-ər) s. *(woodcutter)* leñador *m*; *(wood dealer)* maderero.

lum·ber·ing (lŭm'bər-ĭng) I. adj. *(movement)* pesado, torpe; *(person)* que anda pesadamente *o* ruidosamente II. s. explotación forestal *f*, industria maderera.

lum·ber·jack (lŭm'bər-jăk') s. leñador *m*.

lum·ber·man (lŭm'bər-măn) s. [pl. **-men** (-měn')] leñador *m*, maderero.

lumber mill s. aserradero.

lumber room s. cuarto de trastos, cuarto trastero.

lum·ber·yard (lŭm'bər-yärd') s. almacén *m o* depósito de madera.

lu·men (lōō'mən) s. [pl. **-mens** *o* **-mi·na** (-mə-nə)] ANAT. lumen *m*, abertura; FÍS. lumen.

lu·mi·nance (lōō'mə-nəns) s. FÍS. luminancia.

lu·mi·nar·y (lōō'mə-něr'ē) s. [pl. **-ies**] ASTRON. luminar *m*, cuerpo luminoso; FIG. *(dignitary)* luminar, lumbrera.

lu·mi·nes·cence (lōō'mə-něs'əns) s. FÍS. luminiscencia.

lu·mi·nes·cent (lōō'mə-něs'ənt) adj. FÍS. luminiscente.

lu·mi·nos·i·ty (lōō'mə-nŏs'ĭ-tē) s. luminosidad *f*.

lu·mi·nous (lōō'mə-nəs) adj. *(emitting light)* luminoso, luciente; *(illuminated)* iluminado; *(lucid)* lúcido, claro; *(enlightened)* ilustrado, culto.

lum·mox (lŭm'əks) s. FAM. porro, necio.

lump¹ (lŭmp) I. s. *(mass)* montón *m*, masa; *(of soil, sugar)* terrón *m*; *(glob)* grumo; *(piece)* pedazo, trozo <*a l. of coal* un trozo de carbón>; *(totality)* conjunto; *(dolt)* alcornoque *m*; MED. *(swelling)* bulto; *(on the head)* chichón *m* ♦ **to have a l. in one's throat** FIG. tener un nudo en la garganta • **to take one's lumps** aguantar II. tr. *(to amass)* amontonar; *(to make into a mass)* apelotonar ♦ **to l. together** juntar —intr. *(to become lumpy)* hacerse grumos; *(to lumber)* andar dando tumbos.

lump² (lŭmp) tr. FAM. soportar, tolerar.

lump·ish (lŭm'pĭsh) adj. *(cumbersome)* torpe, pesado; *(dull)* tedioso; *(stupid)* estúpido.

lump sum s. suma total *o* global.

lump·y (lŭm'pē) adj. **-i·er, -i·est** *(filled with lumps)* aterronado; *(a liquid)* grumoso; *(cumbersome)* pesado, torpe; MARÍT. agitado, picado (mar).

lu·na·cy (lōō'nə-sē) s. [pl. **-cies**] *(mental derangement)* locura, demencia; *(insanity)* insania, locura; FIG. *(foolishness)* locura, insensatez *f*; *(foolish act)* desatino, tontería.

lu·nar (lōō'nər) adj. ASTRON. lunar, de la luna.

lunar excursion module *o* **lunar module** s. ASTRONÁUT. astronave diseñada especialmente para alunizaje.

lunar landing s. ASTRONÁUT. alunizaje *m*.

lunar month s. ASTRON. mes lunar *m*.

lunar year s. ASTRON. año lunar.

lu·na·tic (lōō'nə-tĭk) I. adj. MED. *(insane)* loco, demente; *(for the insane)* de locos, para locos; FIG. *(giddily foolish)* disparatado, descabellado <*a l. decision* una decisión descabellada> II. s. lunático, demente *mf*.

lunatic fringe s. minoría fanática extremista.

lu·na·tion (lōō-nā'shən) s. ASTRON. lunación *f*.

lunch (lŭnch) I. s. almuerzo II. intr. almorzar ♦ **out to l.** FAM. chiflado • **to have** *o* **eat l.** almorzar, comer.

lunch·eon (lŭn'chən) s. almuerzo.

lunch·eon·ette (lŭn'chə-nět') s. restaurante pequeño, cafetería.

lunch·room (lŭnch'rōōm', -rŏōm') s. restaurante pequeño.

lunch·time (lŭnch'tīm') s. hora de comer.

lung (lŭng) s. ANAT. pulmón *m*.

lunge (lŭnj) I. s. *(in fencing)* estocada; *(sudden movement)* arremetida, embestida II. intr. **lunged, lung·ing** dar una estocada ♦ **to l. at** arremeter contra —tr. lanzar.

lung·er¹ (lŭng'jər) s. arremetedor *m*.

lung·er² (lŭng'ər) s. FAM. tísico.

lu·ni·so·lar (lōō'nĭ-sō'lər) adj. ASTRON. lunisolar.

lun·y (lōō'nē) adj. & s. var. de **loony**.

lu·pine¹ *o* **lu·pin** (lōō'pĭn) s. BOT. altramuz *m*, lupino.

lu·pine² (lōō'pīn') adj. *(wolf-like)* lupino, lobuno; FIG. *(ravenous)* rapaz, voraz.

lu·pus (lōō'pəs) s. MED. lupus *m*.

lurch¹ (lûrch) I. intr. *(to stagger)* tambalearse, hacer eses; *(of a ship)* guiñar, dar guiñadas II. s. *(movement)* tambaleo, bamboleo; *(of a ship)* guiñada, bandazo.

lurch² (lûrch) s. **to leave someone in the l.** dejar a alguien plantado *o* en la estacada.

lure (lōōr) I. s. *(temptation)* tentación *f*; *(appeal)* atracción *f*; *(bait)* cebo, carnada II. tr. **lured, lur·ing** *(to entice)* tentar, seducir.

lu·rid (lōōr'ĭd) adj. *(gruesome)* horrible, espeluznante; *(sensational)* sensacional, chocante; *(glowing)* resplandeciente; *(sallow)* pálido, cetrino.

lurk (lûrk) intr. *(to lie in wait)* estar al acecho; *(to sneak)* andar a hurtadillas, moverse furtivamente; FIG. *(to exist unobserved)* rondar, estar latente.

lus·cious (lŭsh'əs) adj. *(delicious)* suculento, exquisito; *(sensual)* voluptuoso <*a l. woman* una mujer voluptuosa>.

lush¹ (lŭsh) adj. **-er, -est** *(thick)* lujuriante, exuberante; *(plentiful)* pródigo, abundante; *(luxurious)* suntuoso <*l. carpets* alfombras suntuosas>; *(delicious)* suculento, exquisito.

lush² (lŭsh) JER. I. s. *(drunkard)* borrachín *m*, borracho; *(liquor)* licor *m* II. intr. emborracharse.

lush·ness (lŭsh'nĭs) s. *(thickness)* exuberancia; *(plentifulness)* prodigalidad *f*, abundancia; *(luxuriance)* suntuosidad *f*; *(deliciousness)* suculencia, exquisitez *f*.

lust (lŭst) I. s. *(sexual craving)* lujuria, lascivia; *(overwhelming desire)* ansia, anhelo II. intr. anhelar, codiciar ♦ **to l. after** *(someone)* codiciar; *(something)* desear.

lus·ter (lŭs'tər) I. s. *(sheen)* lustre *m*, brillo; *(splendor)* lustre, esplendor *m*; *(pendant)* gota de cristal, colgante *m*; *(chandelier)* araña; *(polishing substance)* pulimento; *(fabric)* lustrina; *(of precious stones)* aguas, brillo II. tr. lustrar, dar brillo a —intr. brillar, resplandecer.

lus·ter·less (lŭs'tər-lĭs) adj. deslustrado, sin brillo.

lust·ful (lŭst'fəl) adj. lujurioso, lascivo.

lus·tre (lŭs'tər) s. & v. G.B. var. de **luster**.

lus·trous (lŭs'trəs) adj. *(glowing)* lustroso, brillante; *(eyes)* brillante.

lus·trum (lŭs'trəm) s. lustro, quinquenio.

lust·y (lŭs'tē) adj. **-i·er, -i·est** *(robust)* fuerte; *(lustful)* lascivo.

lute¹ (lōōt) s. MÚS. laúd *m*.

lute² (lōōt) s. TEC. zulaque *m*, luten *m*.

lu·te·ti·um *o* **lu·te·ci·um** (lōō-tē'shē-əm) s. QUÍM. lutecio.

Lu·ther·an (lōō'thər-ən) adj. & s. luterano.

lut·ist (lōō'tĭst) s. *(maker)* fabricante de laúdes *mf*; *(player)* tañedor de laúd *m*.

lux (lŭks) s. [pl. **lux·es** *o* **lu·ces** (lōō'sēz')] FÍS. lux (unidad de iluminación) *m*.

ã rey / ä año / b boca / ch chico / d dar / ĕ el / ē mil / g gato / h joya / hw juez / ī aire / k casa / kw cuan /

luxe (lŏŏks, lŭks) s. lujo.
Lux·em·bourg o **Lux·em·burg** (lŭk′səm-bûrg′, lŏŏk′-səm-bŏŏrg′) s. Luxemburgo.
Lux·em·bourg·i·an o **Lux·em·burg·i·an** (lŭk′səm-bûr′gē-ən, lŏŏk′səm-bŏŏr′-) adj. & s. luxemburgués m.
lux·u·ri·ance (lŭg-zhŏŏr′ē-əns, lŭk-shŏŏr′-) s. (thickness) exuberancia; (lushness) suntuosidad f.
lux·u·ri·ant (lŭg-zhŏŏr′ē-ənt, lŭk-shŏŏr′-) adj. (thick) lujuriante, exuberante; (luxurious) suntuoso.
lux·u·ri·ate (lŭg-zhŏŏr′ē-āt′, lŭk-shŏŏr′-) intr. **-at·ed, -at·ing** crecer con exuberancia ♦ **to l. in** deleitarse con.
lux·u·ri·ous (lŭg-zhŏŏr′ē-əs, lŭk-shŏŏr′-) adj. (sumptuous) lujoso; (lush) suntuoso <l. silks sedas suntuosas>.
lux·u·ry (lŭg′zhə-rē, lŭk′shə-) s. [pl. **-ries**] (frill) cosa superflua; (extravagance) lujo ♦ **to live in l.** vivir espléndidamente.
ly·ce·um (lī-sē′əm) s. (hall) auditorio, sala de conferencias; (organization) ateneo.
Ly·ci·an (lĭsh′ē-ən) s. & adj. licio (de una antigua región de Asia Menor).
lyd·dite (lĭd′īt′) s. ARM. lidita (explosivo).
lye (lī) s. lejía; QUÍM. hidróxido de sodio o potasio.
ly·ing¹ (lī′ĭng) I. part. pres. de **lie¹** II. adj. (reclining) tendido, acostado; (located) situado III. s. reposo, descanso.
ly·ing² (lī′ĭng) I. part. pres. de **lie²** II. adj. (untruthful) mentiroso; (not true) falso III. s. (fibbing) mentira; (lies) mentiras.
ly·ing-in (lī′ĭng-ĭn′) s. [pl. **ly·ings-in** o **ly·ing-ins**] parto.
lymph (lĭmf) s. ANAT., FISIOL. linfa.
lym·phat·ic (lĭm-făt′ĭk) I. adj. (of the lymph) linfático; FIG. (sluggish) indolente, apático II. s. ANAT., FISIOL. vaso linfático.
lymph node s. ANAT. ganglio linfático.
lym·pho·cyte (lĭm′fə-sīt′) s. ANAT. linfocito (glóbulo blanco).
lym·pho·ma (lĭm-fō′mə) s. [pl. **-mas** o **-ma·ta** (-mə-tə)] MED. linfoma m.
lynch (lĭnch) tr. linchar.
lynch·ing (lĭn′chĭng) s. linchamiento.
lynch law s. condena de un sospechoso sin someterle a un proceso legal.
lynx (lĭngks) s. ZOOL. lince m.
lynx-eyed (lĭngks′īd′) adj. de vista muy aguda.
lyre (līr) s. MÚS. lira.
lyre-bird (līr′bûrd′) s. ORNIT. ave lira f.
lyr·ic (lĭr′ĭk) I. adj. lírico II. s. LIT. (poem) poema lírico; (genre) lírica; (poet) lírico ♦ **lyrics** MÚS. letra (de una canción).
lyr·i·cal (lĭr′ĭ-kəl) adj. lírico.
lyr·i·cism (lĭr′ĭ-sĭz′əm) s. lirismo.
lyr·i·cist (lĭr′ĭ-sĭst) s. autor de la letra de una canción m.
lyr·ist (līr′ĭst) s. (lyricist) autor de la letra de una canción m; (player) tañedor de lira m.
ly·ser·gic acid di·eth·yl·am·ide (lī-sûr′jĭk, dī′ĕth-əl-ăm′īd) s. QUÍM. dietilamida del ácido lisérgico, LSD.

M

m, M (ĕm) s. [pl. **m's, M's**] decimotercera letra del alfabeto inglés.
ma (mä) s. FAM. mamá.
Ma'am (măm) s. FAM. contr. de **Madam.**
ma·ca·bre (mə-kä′brə) adj. horripilante, espantoso, macabro.
mac·ad·am (mə-kăd′əm) s. macadán m, macadam m.
mac·ad·am·ize (mə-kăd′ə-mīz′) tr. **-ized, -iz·ing** macadamizar, pavimentar con macadán.
ma·caque (mə-kăk′, -käk′) s. ZOOL. macaco.
mac·a·ro·ni (măk′ə-rō′nē) s.pl. CUL. macarrones m.
mac·a·roon (măk′ə-rŏŏn′) s. CUL. macarrón m, mostachón m.
ma·caw (mə-kô′) s. ORNIT. guacamayo, ara m.

mace¹ (mās) s. (weapon) maza, clava; (staff) maza ceremonial; (macebearer) macero.
mace² (mās) s. (spice) macia, macís f.
Mace (mās) s. QUÍM. aerosol irritante (marca registrada) m.
Mac·e·do·ni·an (măs′ĭ-dō′nē-ən) I. adj. macedonio, macedónico II. s. (inhabitant, language) macedón m, macedonio.
mac·er·ate (măs′ə-rāt′) tr. **-at·ed, -at·ing** macerar, ablandar —intr. macerarse.
mac·er·a·tion (măs′ə-rā′shən) s. maceración f.
Mach o **mach** (mäk) s. AER. número de Mach.
ma·chet·e (mə-shĕt′ē) s. machete m.
Mach·i·a·vel·li·an (măk′ē-ə-vĕl′ē-ən) I. adj. maquiavélico II. s. maquiavelista mf.
ma·chin·a·ble (mə-shē′nə-bəl) adj. labrable, trabajable.
mach·i·nate (măk′ə-nāt′, măsh′-) tr. & intr. **-nat·ed, -nat·ing** maquinar, complotar.
mach·i·na·tion (măk′ə-nā′shən, măsh′-) s. maquinación f, complot m.
ma·chine (mə-shēn′) I. s. máquina <a sewing m. una máquina de coser>; (device) mecanismo; (aircraft) avión m, aparato; FIG. (person) máquina, autómata m; (group of persons) maquinaria <political m. maquinaria política>; TEAT. tramoya ♦ **copying m.** copiadora ♦ **slot m.** tragaperras • **washing m.** lavadora II. tr. & intr. **-chined, -chin·ing** trabajar a máquina.
machine gun s. ametralladora.
ma·chine-gun (mə-shēn′gŭn′) tr. **-gunned, -gun·ning** ametrallar.
machine language s. COMPUT. lenguaje de la máquina m, código en lenguaje de la máquina.
ma·chin·er·y (mə-shē′nə-rē) s. [pl. **-ies**] (machines) maquinaria <industrial m. maquinaria industrial>; (working parts) mecanismo; FIG. (system) maquinaria, mecanismo <diplomatic m. la maquinaria diplomática>; TEAT. tramoya; LIT. recurso.
machine shop s. taller de maquinaria m.
machine tool s. máquina herramienta.
ma·chin·ist (mə-shē′nĭst) s. (machine operator) maquinista mf; (mechanic) mecánico; MARÍT. ayudante de máquinas m; ANT., TEAT. tramoyista m.
ma·chis·mo (mä-chēz′mō) s. machismo.
mac·in·tosh (măk′ĭn-tŏsh′) s. var. de **mackintosh.**
mack·er·el (măk′ər-əl) s. [pl. **mackerel** o **-els**] ICT. caballa, escombro.
mackerel sky s. cielo aborregado.
mack·i·naw (măk′ə-nô′) s. (coat) chamarra de lana gruesa; (boat) chalana que se utilizaba en los Grandes Lagos.
mack·in·tosh o **mac·in·tosh** (măk′ĭn-tŏsh′) s. G.B. (raincoat) impermeable m; ANT. (fabric) gabardina.
mac·ra·mé (măk′rə-mā′) s. COST. macramé m.
mac·ro (măk′rō′) s. [pl. **-ros**] COMPUT. macroinstrucción f.
mac·ro·bi·ot·ics (măk′rō-bī-ŏt′ĭks) s. [ú. con v. sing.] MED. macrobiótica.
mac·ro·code (măk′rə-kōd′) s. COMPUT. macrocodificación f, macrocódigo (sistema).
mac·ro·cosm (măk′rə-kŏz′əm) s. (universe) macrocosmo, el mundo entero (universo); FIG. (system) sistema descriptivo (en gran escala) m.
mac·ro·cos·mic (măk′rə-kŏz′mĭk) adj. macrocósmico, del universo.
mac·ro·ec·o·nom·ics (măk′rō-ĕk′ə-nŏm′ĭks, -ē′kə-) s. [ú. con v. sing.] ECON. POL. macroeconomía.
mac·ro·mol·e·cule (măk′rō-mŏl′ĭ-kyŏŏl′) s. FÍS., QUÍM. macromolécula.
mac·ro·scop·ic (măk′rə-skŏp′ĭk) o **mac·ro·scop·i·cal** (-ĭ-kəl) adj. macroscópico.
mad (măd) adj. **mad·der, mad·dest** (insane) loco; FAM. (angry) enojado, airado; (foolish) loco <he'd have to be m. to go back tendría que estar loco para volver>; (senseless) descabellado, insensato; (frantic) arrebatado, frenético; (dog) rabioso ♦ **like m.** como un loco <to run like m. correr como un loco> • **m. as a hatter** o **as a March hare** más loco que una cabra, loco de remate • **raving m.** loco de atar • **to be mad about** (something) encantarle algo a uno; (someone) estar loco por; (to be angry about) estar

enojado o enfadado por • **to be m. at** estar enojado o enfadado con • **to drive someone m.** volver loco a alguien • **to get m.** enojarse, enfadarse • **to make someone m.** hacer que alguien se enoje.

Mad·a·gas·car (măd'ə-găs'kər) s. Madagascar m.

Mad·am (măd'əm) s. [pl. **Mes·dames** (mā-däm', -däm')] señora <*M. Ambassador* señora embajadora> ♦ s. [pl. **mad·ams** (măd'əmz)] *(in a household)* señora; *(in a brothel)* patrona (de un prostíbulo).

mad·cap (măd'kăp') I. s. calavera m, tarambana mf II. adj. *(wild)* alocado, atolondrado.

mad·den (măd'n) tr. *(to drive insane)* enloquecer; *(to make angry)* enfurecer —intr. enfurecerse.

mad·den·ing (măd'n-ĭng) adj. *(tending to drive mad)* enloquecedor; *(irritating)* irritante, exasperante.

made (măd) I. pret. y part. p. de **make** II. adj. *(constructed)* hecho, construido <*a well-made suit* un traje bien hecho>; *(invented)* inventado ♦ **to have got it m.** *(success)* tener el éxito asegurado; *(lifestyle)* darse buena vida.

Ma·dei·ra (mə-dîr'ə, -děr'ə) s. GEOG. Madera; *(wine)* vino de Madera.

made-to-or·der (măd'tōō-ôr'dər) adj. hecho a la medida.

made-up (măd'ŭp') adj. *(invented)* inventado, ficticio <*a m. story* una historia inventada>; *(with make-up)* maquillado, pintado.

mad·house (măd'hous') s. *(asylum)* manicomio; FIG. *(place of disorder)* casa de locos.

mad·ly (măd'lē) adv. *(insanely)* locamente <*she's m. in love* está locamente enamorada>; *(wildly)* como un loco.

mad·man (măd'măn', -mən) s. [pl. **-men** (-měn')] loco, demente mf.

mad·ness (măd'nĭs) s. *(insanity)* locura, demencia; *(fury)* furia, rabia; *(enthusiasm)* entusiasmo.

Ma·don·na (mə-dŏn'ə) s. RELIG. Madona, Nuestra Señora (dic. de la Virgen María); ANT. *(madam)* señora.

mad·ras (măd'rəs) s. TEJ. *(fabric)* madrás m; *(handkerchief)* pañuelo grande de colores brillantes.

Ma·drid (mə-drĭd') s. Madrid.

mad·ri·gal (măd'rĭ-gəl) s. LIT., MÚS. madrigal m.

mad·wom·an (măd'wŏŏm'ən) s. [pl. **-wom·en** (-wĭm'ĭn)] loca, mujer demente f.

mael·strom (māl'strəm) s. *(whirlpool)* remolino; FIG. *(situation)* torbellino (de pasiones).

maes·tro (mī'strō) s. [pl. **-tros** o **-tri** (-strē)] maestro.

Ma·fi·a (mä'fē-ə) s. mafia.

Ma·fi·o·so (mä'fē-ō'sō) s. [pl. **-si** (-sē)] mafioso.

mag (măg) s. JER. revista.

mag·a·zine (măg'ə-zēn') s. *(periodical)* revista; *(ammunition storehouse)* polvorín m; *(in a ship)* santabárbara, pañol de municiones m; *(for a gun)* peine (de municiones) m; *(in a camera)* depósito (de la película); *(compartment)* cargador (de un mecanismo) m.

Ma·gel·lan, Strait of (mə-jěl'ən) s. GEOG. Estrecho de Magallanes.

ma·gen·ta (mə-jěn'tə) s. QUÍM. fucsina; *(color)* rojo purpúreo.

mag·got (măg'ət) s. ENTOM. larva, gusano; *(whim)* capricho, antojo.

ma·gi (mā'jī') pl. de **magus** ♦ **the M.** BÍBL. los Reyes Magos.

mag·ic (măj'ĭk) I. s. *(sorcery)* magia; FIG. *(mysterious quality)* magia, encanto <*the m. of the woods* el encanto del bosque> ♦ **as if by m.** como por arte de magia, como por encanto II. adj. mágico <*m. wand* varita mágica>.

mag·i·cal (măj'ĭ-kəl) adj. mágico.

mag·i·cal·ly (măj'ĭ-kə-lē) adv. *(by magic)* por arte de magia, mágicamente; *(enchantingly)* embrujadoramente, hechiceramente.

ma·gi·cian (mə-jĭsh'ən) s. *(wizard)* mago, hechicero; *(entertainer)* mago, prestidigitador m.

magic lantern s. linterna mágica.

mag·is·te·ri·al (măj'ĭ-stîr'ē-əl) adj. *(authoritative)* magistral <*in a m. tone* con tono magistral>; *(authoritarian)* dominante, autoritario; *(of a magistrate)* de magistrado.

mag·is·tra·cy (măj'ĭ-strə-sē) s. [pl. **-cies**] *(position)* magistratura; *(district)* jurisdicción de magistrado f.

mag·is·trate (măj'ĭ-strāt') s. *(civil officer)* magistrado; *(judge)* juez municipal m.

mag·ma (măg'mə) s. [pl. **-mas** o **-ma·ta** (-mə-tə)] GEOL. magma m.

Mag·na Char·ta o **Mag·na Car·ta** (măg'nə kär'tə) s. HIST. Carta Magna; *(law)* leyes que garantizan los derechos civiles y políticos f.

mag·na cum lau·de (măg'nə kōōm lou'də) adv. EDUC. con honores.

mag·na·nim·i·ty (măg'nə-nĭm'ĭ-tē) s. [pl. **-ties**] *(quality)* magnanimidad f; *(act)* acto magnánimo.

mag·nan·i·mous (măg-năn'ə-məs) adj. magnánimo.

mag·nate (măg'nāt', -nĭt) s. magnate m, potentado.

mag·ne·sia (măg-nē'zhə) s. QUÍM. magnesia, óxido de magnesio.

mag·ne·si·um (măg-nē'zē-əm) s. QUÍM. magnesio.

mag·net (măg'nĭt) s. FÍS. imán m, piedra imán; *(electromagnet)* electroimán m; *(something attractive)* persona o cosa atractiva.

mag·net·ic (măg-nět'ĭk) adj. FÍS., GEOF. magnético, imantado; FIG. *(attractive)* atractivo, magnético.

magnetic compass s. MARÍT. brújula, brújula magnética.

magnetic field s. FÍS. campo magnético.

magnetic flux s. FÍS. flujo magnético.

magnetic north s. GEOF., MARÍT. norte magnético.

magnetic pole s. FÍS. polo del imán; GEOF. polo magnético.

magnetic recording s. ACÚS., ELECTRÓN. grabación magnética, registro magnético.

magnetic tape s. ACÚS., ELECTRÓN. cinta magnética o magnetofónica.

mag·net·ism (măg'nĭ-tĭz'əm) s. FÍS. magnetismo.

mag·net·i·za·tion (măg'nĭ-tĭ-zā'shən) s. FÍS. magnetización f, imantación f.

mag·net·ize (măg'nĭ-tīz') tr. **-ized, -iz·ing** FÍS. magnetizar, imantar; FIG. *(to attract)* magnetizar, fascinar.

mag·ne·to (măg-nē'tō) s. [pl. **-tos**] AUTO., ELEC. magneto, generador eléctrico.

mag·ne·to·mo·tive force (măg-nē'tō-mō'tĭv) s. FÍS. fuerza magnetomotriz.

mag·ne·to·sphere (măg-nē'tə-sfîr') s. ASTRON., GEOF. magnetoesfera, esfera magnética.

mag·nif·ic (măg-nĭf'ĭk) adj. *(exalted)* exaltado, sublime; *(large)* enorme; *(pompous)* pomposo, grandilocuente.

mag·ni·fi·ca·tion (măg'nə-fĭ-kā'shən) s. *(enlargement)* ampliación f, agrandamiento; ÓPT. amplificación, aumento; FIG. *(glorification)* glorificación f.

mag·nif·i·cence (măg-nĭf'ĭ-səns) s. magnificencia.

mag·nif·i·cent (măg-nĭf'ĭ-sənt) adj. magnificente, magnífico.

mag·ni·fi·er (măg'nə-fī'ər) s. *(magnifying glass)* lente de aumento f, lupa; ÓPT. sistema amplificador m.

mag·ni·fy (măg'nə-fī') tr. **-fied, -fy·ing** *(to enlarge)* aumentar <*success magnified his influence* el éxito aumentó su influencia>; *(to exaggerate)* exagerar; ÓPT. *(image)* aumentar; ACÚS. *(sound)* amplificar.

magnifying glass s. lente de aumento f, lupa.

mag·ni·tude (măg'nĭ-tōōd', -tyōōd') s. *(size)* magnitud f, grandeza; *(amplitude)* volumen (de un sonido) m; *(importance)* magnitud, envergadura; ASTRON., MAT. magnitud.

mag·no·lia (măg-nōl'yə) s. BOT. magnolia.

mag·num (măg'nəm) s. magnum m, botella de 1.5 litros (de capacidad).

magnum opus s. obra maestra.

mag·pie (măg'pī') s. ORNIT. urraca; FIG. *(chatterbox)* cotorra, urraca.

ma·gus (mā'gəs) s. [pl. **ma·gi** (mā'jī')] RELIG. mago (sacerdote zoroástrico); *(sorcerer)* mago, nigromante m ♦ **M.** BÍBL. Rey Mago.

Mag·yar (măg'yär, măg'-) adj. & s. *(inhabitant, language)* magiar, húngaro.

ma·hog·a·ny (mə-hŏg'ə-nē) I. s. [pl. **-nies**] BOT. caoba (árbol y madera); *(color)* color caoba m II. adj. *(made of wood)* de caoba <*a m. desk* un escritorio de caoba>; *(reddish brown)* de color caoba.

maid (mād) s. *(servant)* sirvienta, criada; *(unmarried* *woman)* soltera; *(girl)* muchacha; *(virgin)* virgen *f*, doncella.

maid·en (mād'n) **I.** s. doncella **II.** adj. *(befitting a young girl)* virginal <*a m. blush* un rubor virginal>; *(unmarried)* soltera; *(inexperienced)* novato; *(virgin)* virgen, intacto <*m. territory* territorio virgen>; *(first)* primero <*m. voyage* primera travesía>.

maid·en·head (mād'n-hĕd') s. *(virginity)* virginidad *f*; ANAT. himen *m*.

maid·en·hood (mād'n-hŏod') s. *(celibacy)* soltería; *(virginity)* virginidad *f*, doncellez *f*.

maiden name s. apellido de soltera.

maid·in·wait·ing (mād'n-wā'tĭng) s. [pl. **maids-in-wait·ing**] dama de compañía, dama (de una reina o princesa).

maid of honor s. [pl. **maids of honor**] dama de honor.

maid·ser·vant (mād'sûr'vənt) s. criada, sirvienta.

mail¹ (māl) **I.** s. correo ♦ **air m.** via aérea • **by return m.** a vuelta de correo • **the mails** el correo • **to do the m.** *(to write)* escribir la correspondencia; *(to sort)* clasificar la correspondencia **II.** tr. *(to send by mail)* enviar o mandar por correo; *(to post)* echar al correo **III.** adj. postal ♦ **m. truck** camión de correo.

mail² (māl) s. *(armor)* malla, cota de malla; ZOOL. *(shell)* concha, caparazón *m*.

mail·box (māl'bŏks') s. buzón *m*.

mail carrier s. cartero.

mail·ing (mā'lĭng) s. correo, envío.

mail·man (māl'măn') s. [pl. **-men** (-mĕn')] cartero.

mail order s. pedido postal, pedido hecho por correo.

mail-or·der house (māl'ôr'dər) s. empresa que vende por correo.

maim (mām) tr. *(to disable)* mutilar, lisiar; FIG. *(to impair)* dañar, estropear.

main (mān) **I.** adj. *(most important)* principal <*the m. entrance* la entrada principal>; *(office)* central; *(floor)* principal; *(street)* principal, mayor; *(valve)* maestro; MARÍT. *(sail, mast)* mayor; *(beam)* maestro ♦ **by m. strength** a viva fuerza • **the m. body of** el grueso de • **the m. point** el punto principal, lo fundamental • **the m. thing** lo principal o esencial **II.** s. *(for water, gas)* tubería principal; *(for electricity)* cable principal *m*; ANT. *(mainland)* tierra firme; POÉT. *(ocean)* alta mar; MARÍT. *(mainsail)* vela mayor; *(mainmast)* palo mayor ♦ **in the m.** principalmente • **with might and m.** con todas las fuerzas de uno.

main·frame (mān'frām') s. COMPUT. elaborador central *m*.

main·land (mān'lănd') s. tierra firme, continente *m*.

main·line (mān'līn') intr. **-lined, -lin·ing** JER. inyectar(se) estupefacientes directamente en una vena.

main·ly (mān'lē) adv. principalmente, especialmente.

main roy·al·mast (roi'əl-məst, -măst') s. MARÍT. palo mayor.

main·sail (mān'səl, -sāl') s. MARÍT. vela mayor.

main·spring (mān'sprĭng') s. MEC. muelle real *m*; FIG. *(motivating force)* causa principal, fuerza motriz.

main·stay (mān'stā') s. MARÍT. estay mayor *m*; FIG. *(support)* soporte principal *m*, pilar *m*.

main·stream (mān'strēm') s. corriente principal *f*.

main street s. calle mayor *f*, calle principal.

main·tain (mān-tān') tr. *(to carry on)* mantener <*to m. good relations* mantener buenas relaciones>; *(speed)* mantener; *(silence)* guardar; *(to preserve)* mantener, conservar <*to m. a custom* conservar una costumbre>; *(to keep in good repair)* cuidar, conservar <*they m. the streets very well* cuidan mucho las calles>; *(to provide for)* mantener, sostener; MIL. *(a position)* mantener; *(to affirm)* mantener, sostener ♦ **to m. composure** mantenerse sereno, no inmutarse • **to m. one's ground** mantenerse firme.

main·te·nance (mān'tə-nəns) s. *(act)* mantenimiento *m*; *(upkeep)* cuidado, conservación *f* ♦ **m. staff** personal de servicio.

maize (māz) s. BOT. maíz *m*; *(color)* amarillo.

ma·jes·tic (mə-jĕs'tĭk) o **ma·jes·ti·cal** (-tĭ-kəl) adj. majestuoso.

maj·es·ty (măj'ĭ-stē) s. [pl. **-ties**] *(dignity)* majestad *f*; *(splendor)* majestuosidad *f*, esplendor *m* <*in all its m.* en todo

su esplendor> ♦ **Her** o **His** o **Your M.** Su Majestad, Majestad.

ma·jor (mā'jər) **I.** adj. *(greater)* mayor; *(principal)* principal; *(important)* importante; *(extensive)* extenso; *(serious)* grave <*a m. illness* una enfermedad grave>; DER. *(of legal age)* mayor de edad; MÚS. mayor **II.** s. MIL. comandante *m*; DER. mayor de edad *mf*; EDUC. *(specialization)* especialidad *f* (en EE. UU.) **III.** intr. ♦ **to m. in** EDUC. especializarse en.

Ma·jor·ca (mə-jôr'kə, -yôr'-) s. Mallorca.

ma·jor-do·mo (mā'jər-dō'mō) s. [pl. **-mos**] mayordomo.

ma·jor·ette (mā'jə-rĕt') s. bastonera, guaripolera.

major general s. MIL. general de división *m*.

ma·jor·i·ty (mə-jôr'ĭ-tē) s. [pl. **-ties**] *(greater number)* mayoría, mayor parte *f* <*the m. of the workers* la mayoría de los trabajadores>; *(of votes)* mayoría <*her m. was five votes* sacó cinco votos de mayoría>; DER. *(legal age)* mayoría (de edad); MIL. comandancia ♦ **the great** o **the vast m.** la inmensa mayoría • **to be in a m.** constituir la mayoría, predominar.

majority leader s. POL. dirigente de la mayoría parlamentaria *mf*.

majority rule s. POL. gobierno de la mayoría.

major league s. DEP. liga principal.

ma·jor-league (mā'jər-lēg') adj. FAM. importante, principal.

make §G1 (māk) **I.** tr. **made** (mād), **mak·ing** *(to cause)* hacer <*to m. something happen* hacer que ocurra algo>; *(to create)* hacer, crear; *(to fashion)* hacer, confeccionar; *(to build)* construir; *(to form)* formar; *(to manufacture)* elaborar, fabricar; *(a decision)* tomar; *(payment)* efectuar; *(a speech)* pronunciar, hacer; *(an agreement)* celebrar, concertar; *(excuses)* presentar; DEP. *(a goal)* marcar; FAM. *(train)* alcanzar <*did you m. the train?* ¿alcanzaste el tren?>; *(to appoint)* hacer, nombrar <*they made him treasurer* le nombraron tesorero>; *(to be the cause of)* causar, ocasionar <*he made problems for all of us* nos causó problemas a todos nosotros>; *(to compose)* componer (música, versos); *(to prepare)* hacer, preparar (comida); *(bed)* hacer (la cama); *(to establish)* establecer como <*to m. a rule* establecer como norma>; *(to traverse)* recorrer; *(to attain)* llegar a <*he made lieutenant* llegó a teniente>; *(to be accepted into)* entrar en <*he made the basketball team* entró en el equipo de baloncesto>; *(to earn)* ganar; *(to yield)* dar, producir (dinero, utilidad); *(friends)* hacer (amigos); *(to compel)* obligar a, forzar a <*they made him leave the room* le obligaron a salir del cuarto>; *(to be good for)* servir para hacer; *(to become)* ser <*he will m. a fine physician* será un buen médico>; *(to think of as)* pensar, deducir <*I don't know what to m. of his decision* no sé qué pensar de su decisión>; *(to add up to)* ser, equivaler a <*a hundred cents m. a dollar* cien centavos equivalen a un dólar>; *(to count as)* ser <*this makes my second play* ésta es mi segunda obra de teatro>; JER. *(to seduce)* seducir; MARÍT. *(to reach)* llegar a, arribar a ♦ **to m. a face** hacer una mueca • **to m. a fool of** *(to ridicule)* poner en ridículo; *(to cheat)* engañar, embaucar • **to m. a fuss** armar un escándalo • **to m. a go of something** tener éxito en sacar adelante (algo) • **to m. a hit** FAM. causar buena impresión • **to m. a living** ganarse la vida • **to m. a long face** poner una cara larga • **to m. a mistake** cometer un error, equivocarse • **to m. a move** *(in games)* hacer una jugada; *(to act)* obrar • **to m. an appointment** citar • **to m. a point** hacer una observación • **to m. a point of** dar mucha importancia a • **to m. a practice of** acostumbrar, tener por costumbre • **to m. a record of** asentar • **to m. a stop** *(to halt)* detenerse; *(to pause)* hacer una pausa • **to m. available to** poner a la disposición de • **to m. clear** poner en claro, aclarar • **to m. difficult** dificultar • **to m. easy** facilitar • **to m. ends meet** llegar a fin de mes (con lo que se gana) • **to m. eyes at** hacerle ojos a • **to m. for** *(to head toward)* ir hacia, dirigirse a; *(to create)* crear (dificultades, problemas) • **to m. friends** hacer amistades • **to m. fun of** burlarse de • **to m. headway** avanzar, progresar • **to m. into** convertir en, transformar en • **to m. it** *(to succeed)* tener éxito, conseguir lo deseado; FAM. *(have sex)* tener relaciones sexuales • **to m. it right** *(to rectify)* rectificar,

enmendar; *(to compensate)* compensar • **to m. known** hacer saber, dar a conocer • **to m. light of** *o* **little of** dar poca importancia a, hacer poco caso de • **to m. love** hacer el amor • **to m. much of** dar mucha importancia a • **to m. no difference** no importar, ser indiferente • **to m. off with** irse con, llevarse • **to m. oneself known** darse a conocer • **to m. out** *(to fill out)* hacer (factura, cheque); *(to comprehend)* entender; *(to prove)* hacer pasar por <*he tried to m. me out to be a liar* intentó hacerme pasar por mentiroso>; *(to perceive)* distinguir, divisar • **to m. peace** hacer las paces • **to m. progress** hacer progresos, progresar • **to m. public** hacer público, publicar • **to m. ready** preparar • **to m. sail** MARÍT. zarpar • **to m. sense** tener sentido • **to m. the best of** sacar el mejor partido de • **to m. time** ganar tiempo • **to m. up** *(to prepare)* preparar (comida); *(to assemble)* hacer, confeccionar (vestidos, ropa); *(to fabricate)* inventar (cuento, historia); *(to compensate)* recobrar, recuperar (tiempo perdido); *(to constitute)* integrar (comité, directorio); *(to apply make-up to)* maquillar(se); IMPR. compaginar, armar • **to m. use of** hacer uso de • **to m. war** hacer la guerra • **to m. way** avanzar, progresar • **to m. worse** empeorar —intr. formarse ♦ **to m. believe** fingir • **to m. do** arreglárselas • **to m. for** *o* contribuir a, servir para • **to m. good** salir bien • **to m. haste** darse prisa, apresurarse • **to m. love** hacer el amor • **to m. merry** divertirse • **to m. off** largarse, huir • **to m. out** *(to get along)* salir (bien, mal); *(to embrace)* abrazar • **to m. sure** asegurarse • **to m. up** hacer las paces II. s. *(manufacture)* manufactura, fabricación *f*; *(in clothes)* hechura, confección *f*; *(style)* corte *m*; *(brand)* marca, nombre de fábrica *m*; *(type)* tipo, modelo; FIG. *(stature)* estatura ♦ **to be on the m.** *(ambition)* buscar su propio provecho; JER. *(seduction)* tener intención de seducir.
make·be·lieve (māk′bǐ-lēv′) I. s. fingimiento, simulación *f* II. adj. fingido, simulado.
mak·er (mā′kər) s. *(manufacturer)* constructor *m,* fabricante *m*; DER. *(signer)* firmante de un pagaré *m*; ANT. *(poet)* poeta *m* ♦ **M.** RELIG. Hacedor *m,* Creador *m.*
make·read·y (māk′rĕd′ē) s. IMPR. ajuste que se hace a las formas, planchas, tintas y papel en el proceso de impresión *m.*
make·shift (māk′shǐft′) I. s. reemplazo provisional, improvisación *f* II. adj. improvisado, temporal.
make·up *o* **make-up** (māk′ŭp′) s. *(arrangement)* construcción *f*, composición *f*; *(temperament)* temperamento, carácter *m*; *(cosmetics)* cosméticos *f*; *(of an actor)* maquillaje *m*; IMPR. compaginación *f,* ajuste *m.*
make·work (māk′wûrk′) s. trabajo ocioso *o* inútil.
mak·ing (mā′kǐng) s. *(creation)* creación *f* <*the m. of new jobs* la creación de nuevos puestos de trabajo>; *(manufacture)* fabricación *f*; *(production)* producción *f*; *(of a dress)* confección *f*; *(of a meal)* preparación *f*; *(of statements, plans)* formulación *f*; *(of a will)* redacción *f* ♦ **in the m.** *(plans)* en preparación; *(war)* en potencia; *(country)* en desarrollo; *(history)* en marcha • **to be of one's own m.** ser obra propia • **to be the m. of someone** hacer que alguien triunfe • **to have the makings of** tener los elementos necesarios para llegar a ser.
Mal·a·chi (māl′ə-kī′) s. BÍBL. Malaquías.
mal·a·chite (māl′ə-kīt′) s. MIN. malaquita.
mal·ad·just·ed (māl′ə-jŭs′tǐd) adj. MEC. desajustado; FIG. *(person)* inadaptado.
mal·ad·just·ment (māl′ə-jŭst′mənt) s. *(faulty adjustment)* adjuste defectuoso, mal ajuste *m*; PSIC. inadaptación *f.*
mal·ad·min·is·ter (māl′əd-mǐn′ǐ-stər) tr. administrar mal, manejar ineficazmente.
mal·a·droit (māl′ə-droit′) adj. *(clumsy)* desmañado, torpe; *(tactless)* sin tacto.
mal·a·dy (māl′ə-dē) s. [pl. **-dies**] *(disease)* enfermedad *f,* mal *m*; *(ailment)* dolencia; *(disturbance)* trastorno.
Mal·a·ga (māl′ə-gə) s. málaga (vino de Málaga).
Mal·a·gas·y (māl′ə-gās′ē) I. adj. malgache II. s. [pl. **Malagasy** *o* **-gas·ies**] *(inhabitant, language)* malgache *mf.*
mal·aise (mă-lāz′) s. malestar *m,* indisposición *f.*
mal·a·prop·ism (māl′ə-prŏp′ĭz′əm) s. uso cómicamente incorrecto *o* inapropiado de una palabra.

ma·lar·i·a (mə-lâr′ē-ə) f. MED. malaria, paludismo.
ma·lar·key *o* **ma·lar·ky** (mə-lär′kē) s. JER. charlatanería, faramalla.
Mal·a·thi·on (măl′ə-thī′ŏn′) s. QUÍM. Malatión (marca registrada de un insecticida) *m.*
Ma·la·wi (mə-lä′wē) s. Malawi.
Ma·la·wi·an (mə-lä′wē-ən) adj. & s. *(inhabitant, language)* malawiano.
Ma·lay (mə-lā′, mā′lā′) I. adj. malayo II. s. *(inhabitant, language)* malayo; ZOOL. malayo (ave de corral).
Ma·lay·an (mə-lā′ən, mā′lā′-) adj. & s. malayo.
Ma·lay·sia (mə-lā′zhə) s. Malasia.
Ma·lay·sian (mə-lā′zhən) adj. & s. malasio.
mal·con·tent (māl′kən-tĕnt′) I. adj. malcontento, revoltoso II. s. persona descontenta *o* revoltosa.
Mal·dives (môl′dīvz′, māl′-) s. Maldivas *f.*
Mal·div·i·an (môl-dīv′ē-ən, māl-) adj. & s. *(inhabitant, language)* maldivo.
male (māl) I. adj. *(person)* varón *m* <*a m. child* un hijo varón>; *(masculine)* masculino <*m. sex* sexo masculino>; *(manly)* varonil, viril; *(clothes, choir)* de hombres; *(school)* de varones; BIOL. macho; MEC. macho II. s. *(person)* varón *m,* hombre *m*; BIOL. macho.
mal·e·dic·tion (māl′ǐ-dĭk′shən) s. *(curse)* maldición *f*; *(slander)* calumnia.
mal·e·fac·tor (māl′ə-făk′tər) s. *(criminal)* criminal *m,* malhechor *m*; *(evildoer)* malvado, perverso.
ma·lef·ic (mə-lĕf′ĭk) adj. maléfico.
ma·lev·o·lence (mə-lĕv′ə-ləns) s. malevolencia, malicia.
ma·lev·o·lent (mə-lĕv′ə-lənt) adj. malévolo, maligno.
mal·fea·sance (māl-fē′zəns) s. DER. mala conducta, incorrección (esp. de un empleado público) *f.*
mal·for·ma·tion (māl′fôr-mā′shən) s. malformación *f,* deformación *f.*
mal·formed (māl-fôrmd′) adj. mal formado, malhecho.
mal·func·tion (māl-fŭngk′shən) I. intr. funcionar mal II. s. funcionamiento defectuoso.
Ma·li (mä′lē) s. Mali *m.*
Ma·li·an (mä′lē-ən) adj. & s. maliense *mf.*
mal·ice (māl′ĭs) s. *(ill will)* malicia, malignidad *f*; DER. premeditación *f,* intención maliciosa.
ma·li·cious (mə-lĭsh′əs) adj. *(ill-willed)* malicioso, maligno; DER. premeditado, delictuoso.
ma·lign (mə-līn′) I. tr. *(to speak evil of)* difamar, calumniar II. adj. maligno, malévolo.
ma·lig·nan·cy (mə-lĭg′nən-sē) *o* **ma·lig·nance** (-nəns) s. [pl. **-cies** *o* **-nanc·es**] *(quality)* malignidad *f,* malevolencia; MED. *(tumor)* malignidad *f.*
ma·lig·nant (mə-lĭg′nənt) adj. *(evil)* maligno, malévolo; *(harmful)* nocivo, pernicioso; MED. maligno.
ma·lig·ni·ty (mə-lĭg′nĭ-tē) s. [pl. **-ties**] *(ill will)* malignidad *f,* malevolencia; *(act)* acto maligno.
ma·lin·ger (mə-lĭng′gər) intr. fingirse enfermo (para no trabajar).
ma·lin·ger·er (mə-lĭng′gər-ər) s. enfermo fingido.
mall (môl) s. *(promenade)* paseo, alameda; *(shopping center)* galería.
mal·lard (māl′ərd) s. [pl. **mallard** *o* **-lards**] ORNIT. pato silvestre.
mal·le·a·bil·i·ty (māl′ē-ə-bǐl′ĭ-tē) s. maleabilidad *f.*
mal·le·a·ble (māl′ē-ə-bəl) adj. maleable.
mal·let (māl′ĭt) s. *(hammer)* mazo, mallo; DEP. mazo, mallete *m*; MÚS. palillo.
Ma·llor·ca (mä-yôr′kä) s. GEOG. Mallorca.
mal·low (māl′ō) s. BOT. malva.
malm·sey (mäm′zē) s. [pl. **-seys**] malvasía (vino).
mal·nour·ished (māl-nûr′ĭsht) adj. desnutrido.
mal·nu·tri·tion (māl′nōō-trĭsh′ən, -nyōō-) s. desnutrición *f,* nutrición defectuosa.
mal·o·dor·ous (māl-ō′dər-əs) adj. maloliente, hediondo.
mal·prac·tice (māl-prăk′tĭs) s. MED. *(improper treatment)* tratamiento erróneo; *(negligence)* negligencia; *(unethical conduct)* conducta inmoral.
malt (môlt) I. s. *(grain)* malta; *(beer)* cerveza de malta; *(malted milk)* leche malteada II. tr. maltear.
Mal·ta (môl′tə) s. Malta.

ã rey / ä año / b boca / ch chico / d dar / ĕ el / ē mil / g gato / h joya / hw juez / ī aire / k casa / kw cuan /

Mal·tese (môl-tēz′) **I.** adj. maltés **II.** s. [pl. **Maltese**] maltés *m* ♦ **the M.** los malteses.

malted milk s. CUL. leche malteada.

Mal·thu·sian (măl-thōō′zhən, môl-) adj. & s. maltusiano.

mal·tose (môl′tōs′) s. QUÍM. maltosa.

mal·treat (măl-trēt′) tr. maltratar.

mal·treat·ment (măl-trēt′mənt) s. maltrato, maltratamiento.

ma·ma *o* **mam·ma** (mä′mə) s. mamá, mama.

mam·mal (măm′əl) s. ZOOL. mamífero.

Mam·ma·li·a (mə-mā′lē-ə) s.pl. ZOOL. mamíferos.

mam·ma·li·an (mə-mā′lē-ən) s. & adj. ZOOL. mamífero.

mam·ma·ry (măm′ə-rē) adj. mamario.

mammary gland s. ANAT. glándula mamaria.

mam·mog·ra·phy (mə-mŏg′rə-fē) s. MED. mamografía.

Mam·mon (măm′ən) s. BÍBL. Mammón ♦ **m.** riqueza, oro.

mam·moth (măm′əth) **I.** s. *(elephant)* mamut *m*; *(something large)* cosa enorme *o* gigantesca **II.** adj. enorme, gigantesco.

mam·my (măm′ē) s. [pl. **-mies**] *(mother)* mamá, mamita; DESPEC. *(black nanny)* niñera negra (en EE. UU.).

man (măn) **I.** s. [pl. **men** (mĕn)] *(male)* hombre *m*, varón *m*; *(person)* hombre, persona <*all men are created equal* todos los hombres han sido creados iguales>; *(mankind)* el hombre, la humanidad <*the accomplishments of m.* los logros del hombre>; ZOOL. hombre; *(manly person)* hombre, persona viril; TEO. hombre; FAM. *(husband)* hombre, marido; *(lover)* hombre, amante *m*; *(fellow)* hombre, amigo <*look, m.* mira, hombre>; *(servant)* criado, sirviente *m*; HIST. *(vassal)* vasallo, siervo; *(in a game)* pieza (de ajedrez, damas); *(player)* jugador *m*; MARÍT. *(ship)* barco ♦ **m. and wife** marido y mujer • **m. of his word** hombre de palabra • **men** *(workers)* trabajadores, obreros; *(servicemen)* soldados <*officers and men* oficiales y soldados> • **men's room** servicio *o* baño para caballeros • **no man's land** tierra de nadie • **the M.** JER. *(the police)* la policía; *(the white man)* el hombre blanco • **to a m.** hasta el último, todos <*they objected, to a m.* todos pusieron reparos> • **to be one's own m.** ser un hombre independiente **II.** tr. **manned, man·ning** *(airplane, ship)* tripular (avión, barco); *(to staff)* dotar *o* proveer de personal; MIL. *(to furnish with troops)* proveer de efectivos; *(to operate)* manejar (cañones) **III.** interj. ¡hombre!

man about town s. hombre de mundo *m*.

man·a·cle (măn′ə-kəl) **I.** s. *(handcuff)* esposas *f*; FIG. *(restraint)* restricción *f*, freno **II.** tr. **-cled, -cling** *(to fetter)* poner esposas, esposar; FIG. *(to restrain)* restringir.

man·age (măn′ĭj) tr. **-aged, -ag·ing** *(to control)* controlar, dominar; *(a business)* dirigir; *(property)* administrar; *(affairs)* dirigir, llevar <*to m. foreign policy* dirigir la política extranjera>; *(to supervise)* dirigir <*to m. new personnel* dirigir a los empleados nuevos>; *(to arrange)* arreglárselas <*I'll m. to come on Friday* me las arreglaré para venir el viernes>; *(food, drink)* poder con <*can you m. another beer?* ¿puedes con otra cerveza?>; *(to operate)* manejar ♦ **not to be able to m. someone** no poder con alguien —intr. *(to direct)* dirigir los negocios; *(to get along)* arreglárselas.

man·age·a·ble (măn′ĭ-jə-bəl) adj. *(controllable)* manejable, manuable; *(person)* dócil; *(business)* manejable; *(task)* factible, realizable ♦ **of m. size** manuable.

man·age·ment (măn′ĭj-mənt) s. *(control)* manejo, dirección *f*; *(supervision)* gerencia, dirección; *(skill)* habilidad *f* o capacidad directiva.

man·ag·er (măn′ĭ-jər) s. *(administrator)* gerente *m*, director *m*; *(entertainer's agent)* empresario, apoderado; DEP. *(trainer)* entrenador *m*.

man·a·ge·ri·al (măn′ə-jîr′ē-əl) adj. directivo, ejecutivo.

man-at-arms (măn′ət-ärmz′) s. [pl. **men-at-arms**] MIL. soldado (esp. de caballería).

man·a·tee (măn′ə-tē′) s. ZOOL. manatí *m*, vaca marina.

man·chi·neel (măn′chĭ-nēl′) s. BOT. manzanillo.

Man·chu (măn′chōō, măn-chōō′) **I.** adj. manchú, manchuriano **II.** s. [pl. **Man·chu** *o* **Man·chus**] *(inhabitant, language)* manchú *m*, manchuriano.

man·da·mus (măn-dā′məs) s. DER. mandamiento, orden judicial *f*.

man·da·rin (măn′də-rĭn) **I.** s. mandarín *m* ♦ **M.** mandarina (lenguaje) **II.** adj. ♦ **m. orange** mandarina.

man·date (măn′dāt′) **I.** s. *(command)* mandato, orden *f*; DER., POL. mandato; *(territory)* territorio bajo mandato **II.** tr. **-dat·ed, -dat·ing** *(a territory)* colocar bajo mandato; *(to require)* ordenar, decretar.

man·da·to·ry (măn′də-tôr′ē) adj. *(obligatory)* forzoso, obligatorio; *(holding a mandate)* mandante.

man-day (măn′dā′) s. día-hombre *m*.

man·di·ble (măn′də-bəl) s. ANAT. mandíbula.

man·do·lin (măn′dl-ĭn′) s. MÚS. mandolina.

man·drake (măn′drāk′) s. BOT. mandrágora (planta, raíz).

man·drill (măn′drəl) s. ZOOL. mandril *m*.

mane (mān) s. ZOOL. *(horse's hair)* crin (del caballo) *m*; *(lion's hair)* melena (del león); *(human hair)* melena.

man-eat·er (măn′ē′tər) s. *(animal)* animal que come carne humana; *(cannibal)* caníbal *m*, antropófago.

ma·neu·ver (mə-nōō′vər, -nyōō′-) **I.** s. maniobra **II.** intr. maniobrar; *(to manipulate)* manipular.

ma·neu·ver·a·bil·i·ty (mə-nōō′vər-ə-bĭl′ĭ-tē, -nyōō′-) s. *(ease of handling)* maniobrabilidad *f*, facilidad de maniobrarse *f*; *(of a person)* disposición a dejarse manipular *f*.

ma·neu·ver·a·ble (mə-nōō′vər-ə-bəl, -nyōō′-) s. maniobrable, manejable.

man Friday s. FIG. *(servant)* criado fiel; *(employee)* mano derecha, hombre de confianza *m*.

man·ful (măn′fəl) adj. *(virile)* varonil, viril; *(masculine)* masculino, de hombres.

man·ga·nate (măng′gə-nāt′) s. QUÍM. manganato.

man·ga·nese (măng′gə-nēz′) s. QUÍM. manganeso.

mange (mānj) s. MED. sarna; VET. roña, sarna perruna.

man·ger (măn′jər) s. pesebre *m*, comedero.

man·gle[1] (măng′gəl) tr. **-gled, -gling** *(to mutilate)* mutilar; *(to destroy)* destrozar, destruir; FIG. *(to spoil)* mutilar <*to m. a speech* mutilar un discurso>.

man·gle[2] s. *(pressing device)* planchadora a rodillo.

man·go (măng′gō) s. [pl. **-goes** *o* **-gos**] BOT. mango (árbol y fruta).

man·grove (măng′grōv′) s. BOT. mangle *m*.

man·gy (măn′jē) adj. **-i·er, -i·est** MED., VET. sarnoso, roñoso; FIG., FAM. *(shabby)* asqueroso, sucio.

man·han·dle (măn′hăn′dl) tr. **-dled, -dling** *(to abuse)* maltratar, tratar duramente; *(to handle roughly)* mover a brazo *o* a mano.

Man·hat·tan (măn-hăt′n) s. manhattan (cóctel de vermut con whisky) *m*.

man·hole (măn′hōl′) s. registro, boca de acceso.

man·hood (măn′hŏŏd′) s. *(adulthood)* madurez *f*; *(sexual adulthood)* edad viril *f*; *(manliness)* hombría; *(men)* hombres *m* ♦ **to grow to m.** hacerse hombre.

man-hour (măn′our′) s. hora-hombre *f*.

man·hunt (măn′hŭnt′) s. búsqueda de una persona (esp. un criminal).

ma·ni·a (mā′nē-ə) s. *(craze)* manía, obsesión *f*; MED. *(illness)* manía, locura ♦ **to have a m. for** estar obsesionado por.

ma·ni·ac (mā′nē-ăk′) s. MED. *(insane)* maníaco; FIG. *(crackpot)* loco <*to drive like a m.* manejar como un loco>.

ma·ni·a·cal (mə-nī′ə-kəl) *o* **ma·ni·ac** (mā′nē-ăk′) adj. MED. *(insane)* maníaco, maniaco; FIG. *(mad)* loco.

man·ic (măn′ĭk) adj. MED. maníaco, maniaco.

man·ic-de·pres·sive (măn′ĭk-dĭ-prĕs′ĭv) s. MED. maníacodepresivo, maniacodepresivo.

man·i·cure (măn′ĭ-kyŏŏr′) **I.** s. manicura **II.** tr. **-cured, -cur·ing** *(fingernails)* hacer la manicura a; *(to trim)* recortar.

man·i·cur·ist (măn′ĭ-kyŏŏr′ĭst) s. manicuro, manicura.

man·i·fest (măn′ə-fĕst′) **I.** adj. manifiesto, patente ♦ **to make m.** poner de manifiesto; *(to reveal)* manifestar; *(to prove)* demostrar **II.** tr. *(to reveal)* manifestar; *(to prove)* demostrar **III.** s. *(list)* manifiesto (de carga); *(list of passengers)* relación de pasajeros *f*.

man·i·fes·ta·tion (măn′ə-fĕ-stā′shən) s. *(act)* manifestación *f*, declaración *f*; *(public demonstration)* manifestación, demostración *f*.

man·i·fes·to (măn'ə-fĕs'tō) **I.** s. [pl. **-toes** o **-tos**] manifiesto, proclama **II.** intr. **-toed, -to·ing** publicar un manifiesto.

man·i·fold (măn'ə-fōld') **I.** adj. *(multiple)* diverso, múltiple; *(having many features)* variado **II.** s. *(complex whole)* diversidad *f*, multiplicidad *f*; *(a copy)* copia; AUTO. colector de escape *m* **III.** tr. *(to make copies)* multicopiar; *(to multiply)* diversificar, multiplicar.

man·i·kin o **man·ni·kin** (măn'ĭ-kĭn) s. *(dwarf)* enano, pigmeo; *(model)* maniquí *m*, modelo.

ma·nil·a o **ma·nil·la** o **Ma·nil·la** (mə-nĭl'ə) s. *(cigar)* manila; *(hemp)* manila, abacá *m*; *(paper)* papel amarillo (de empaquetar), papel de estraza; *(color)* carmelita claro.

Manila hemp s. BOT. abacá, cáñamo de Manila.

Manila paper s. papel de Manila *m*, papel amarillo (de empaquetar).

man in the street s. hombre de la calle *m*, hombre común.

man·i·oc (măn'ē-ŏk') o **man·i·o·ca** (măn'ē-ō'kə) s. BOT. mandioca, yuca.

ma·nip·u·late (mə-nĭp'yə-lāt') tr. **-lat·ed, -lat·ing** *(to handle)* manipular, manejar; *(to falsify)* alterar, falsificar.

ma·nip·u·la·tion (mə-nĭp'yə-lā'shən) s. *(handling)* manipulación *f*; *(falsification)* alteración *f*, falsificación *f*.

ma·nip·u·la·tive (mə-nĭp'yə-lā'tĭv, -lə-) o **ma·nip·u·la·to·ry** (-lə-tôr'ē) adj. de manipuleo.

ma·nip·u·la·tor (mə-nĭp'yə-lā'tər) s. *(operator)* manipulador *m*; *(falsifier)* alterador *m*, falsificador *m*.

man·kind (măn'kīnd') s. *(human race)* humanidad *f*, género humano; *(men)* los hombres *m*, el sexo masculino.

man·like (măn'līk') adj. *(befitting a man)* varonil, masculino; *(resembling a man)* parecido al hombre, hombruno.

man·li·ness (măn'lē-nĭs) s. *(manfulness)* carácter varonil *m*, hombría; *(masculinity)* masculinidad *f*.

man·ly (măn'lē) **I.** adj. **-li·er, -li·est** *(manful)* varonil; *(masculine)* masculino; *(activity)* de hombres **II.** adv. como un hombre, varonilmente.

man·made (măn'mād') adj. artificial, hecho por el hombre.

man·na (măn'ə) s. BÍBL., BOT. maná ♦ **like m. from heaven** como maná llovido del cielo.

manned (mănd) adj. tripulado.

man·ne·quin (măn'ĭ-kĭn) s. *(dummy)* maniquí *m*, armazón *m*; *(model)* maniquí, modelo.

man·ner (măn'ər) s. *(way)* manera, modo *<in a threatening m.* de modo amenazador>; *(way of acting)* comportamiento, conducta *<a m. beyond reproach* una conducta irreprochable>; *(air)* aire *m*, porte *m* *<an aristocratic m.* un aire aristocrático>; *(attitude)* actitud *f* *<an intolerant m.* una actitud intolerante>; ARTE. *(style)* manera, estilo; *(kind)* clase *f*, tipo *<we saw all m. of people* vimos todo tipo de gente> ♦ **after the m.** o **in the m. of** a la manera de, al estilo de • **in a m. of speaking** *(figuratively)* por así decirlo; *(to a certain extent)* en cierto modo • **in such a m. that** de tal forma que • **in the usual m.** como siempre • **manners** *(breeding)* modales *<good manners* buenos modales>; *(politeness)* educación *<it is bad manners to remain seated* quedarse sentado es de mala educación> • **to have manners** tener buenos modales.

man·nered (măn'ərd) adj. amanerado, afectado ♦ **well-m.** de buenos modales • **ill-m.** de malos modales.

man·ner·ism (măn'ə-rĭz'əm) s. *(affected style)* amaneramiento, afectación *f*; *(peculiarity)* maña, peculiaridad *f*; ARTE. *(style)* manierismo.

man·ner·ly (măn'ər-lē) **I.** adj. de buenos modales, bien educado **II.** adv. educadamente.

man·nish (măn'ĭsh) adj. *(befitting a man)* varonil, masculino; *(resembling a man)* hombruno.

ma·noeu·vre (mə-nōō'vər, -nyōō'-) s. G.B. var. de **maneuver.**

man of God s. hombre de iglesia *m*, cura *m*.

man of letters s. hombre de letras *m*, literato.

man of the cloth s. religioso, clérigo.

man of the house s. hombre de la casa *m*.

man of the world s. hombre de mundo *m*.

man-of-war (măn'ə-wôr') s. [pl. **men-of-war** (mĕn'-)] buque de guerra *m*.

man·or (măn'ər) s. *(landed estate)* finca; *(mansion)* casa solariega; HIST. *(fief)* señorío, feudo.

man·pow·er (măn'pou'ər) s. *(physical strength)* fuerza humana; *(labor)* mano de obra disponible.

man·sard (măn'särd') s. ARQ. *(roof)* techo mansarda; *(upper story)* mansarda, desván *m*.

manse (măns) s. RELIG. *(rectory)* rectoría; ANT. *(mansion)* mansión *f*.

man·ser·vant (măn'sûr'vənt) s. [pl. **men·ser·vants** (mĕn'sûr'vənts)] sirviente *m*, criado.

man·sion (măn'shən) s. *(stately house)* casa grande; *(manor house)* casa solariega; ASTROL. casa del cielo.

man-sized (măn'sīzd') o **man-size** (-sīz') adj. FAM. de gran tamaño, muy grande.

man·slaugh·ter (măn'slô'tər) s. DER. homicidio impremeditado o involuntario.

man·ta (măn'tə) s. chal *m*, capa de algodón rústica ♦ **m. ray** ICT. manta.

man·tel (măn'tl) s. *(ornamental facing)* manto (de la chimenea); *(shelf)* repisa de la chimenea.

man·tel·piece (măn'tl-pēs') s. repisa de la chimenea.

man·tis·sa (măn-tĭs'ə) s. MAT. mantisa.

man·tle (măn'tl) **I.** s. *(cloak)* manto; FIG. *(cover)* manto, capa; *(mantel)* manto, repisa (de la chimenea); ANAT. corteza cerebral; GEOL. *(layer of earth)* manto; *(casing)* camisa exterior (de alto horno); ORNIT., ZOOL. manto **II.** tr. **-tled, -tling** cubrir, tapar —intr. *(to spread over a surface)* extenderse, desparramarse; *(to blush)* ruborizarse.

man·tle·piece (măn'tl-pēs') s. var. de **mantelpiece.**

man-to-man (măn'tə-măn') adj. de hombre a hombre.

man·u·al (măn'yōō-əl) **I.** adj. *(by hand)* manual; AUTO. manual, mecánico **II.** s. *(book)* manual *m*; MÚS. teclado (de un órgano); MIL. ejercicio de armas.

manual alphabet s. alfabeto dactilológico.

manual training s. enseñanza de trabajo manual o de artes y oficios.

man·u·fac·to·ry (măn'yə-făk'tə-rē) s. [pl. **-ries**] fábrica, manufactura.

man·u·fac·ture (măn'yə-făk'chər) **I.** tr. **-tured, -tur·ing** *(to make)* manufacturar, fabricar *<to m. tires* fabricar gomas>; *(clothing)* confeccionar; FIG. *(to produce mechanically)* fabricar; *(to concoct)* fabricar, inventar **II.** s. *(process)* manufactura, fabricación *f*; *(product)* producto manufacturado.

man·u·fac·tured (măn'yə-făk'chərd) adj. fabricado, manufacturado.

man·u·fac·tur·er (măn'yə-făk'chər-ər) s. fabricante *m*.

man·u·fac·tur·ing (măn'yə-făk'chər-ĭng) **I.** adj. manufacturero **II.** s. fabricación *f*, manufactura.

man·u·mis·sion (măn'yə-mĭsh'ən) s. manumisión *f*.

man·u·mit (măn'yə-mĭt') tr. **-mit·ted, -mit·ting** manumitir, emancipar.

ma·nure (mə-nōōr', -nyōōr') **I.** s. estiércol *m*, abono **II.** tr. **-nured, -nur·ing** estercolar, abonar.

man·u·script (măn'yə-skrĭpt') **I.** s. *(handwritten document)* manuscrito; *(author's copy)* original *m* ♦ **to be in m.** estar escrito a mano **II.** adj. manuscrito.

Manx (măngks) **I.** adj. de la Isla de Man **II.** s. [pl. **Manx**] habitante o lenguaje de Man; *(tailless cat)* gato sin cola.

man·y §22 (mĕn'ē) **I.** adj. *more* (môr), *most* (mōst) muchos *<m. friends* muchos amigos> ♦ **as m.** igual número *<we read eleven scripts in as m. days* leímos once guiones en igual número de días> • **as m. . . . as** más . . . que *<there were twice as m. children as adults* había dos veces más niños que adultos> • **how m.?** ¿cuántos? *<how m. years?* ¿cuántos años?> • **m. a** muchos *<m. a man* muchos hombres> • **m. people** mucha gente • **too m.** demasiado **II.** s. [ú. con v. pl.] muchos *<m. of us have children* muchos de nosotros tenemos hijos> ♦ **a great m.** muchos, muchísimos *<a great m. gathered at the dance* muchísimos se reunieron en el baile> • **as m. as** *(the same number)* tantos como *<she has as m. as he* ella tiene tantos como él>; *(up to)* hasta *<as m. as 50 people will come* vendrán hasta 50 personas> • **not m.** no muchos • **the m.** *(most people)* la mayoría; *(the masses)* la muchedumbre, las masas **III.** pron. [ú. con v. pl.] muchos *<m. are called but few*

are chosen muchos son los llamados, pero pocos los escogidos>.

man·y·fold (měn'ē-fōld') *adv.* múltiples veces.

Mao·ism (mou'ĭz'əm) *s.* POL. maoísmo.

map (măp) **I.** *s.* mapa *m* <*relief m.* mapa en relieve>; *(chart)* carta; *(of a city)* plano; JER. *(face)* hocico ♦ **outline** *o* **skeleton m.** mapa mudo • **to be off the m.** no estar ni en el mapa, estar en un sitio perdido • **to put on the m.** dar fama • **to wipe off the m.** borrar del mapa **II.** *tr.* **mapped, mapping** *(to make a map of)* trazar un mapa de; *(a city)* trazar un plano de; *(to explore)* hacer una exploración cartográfica de; *(to plan)* planear, proyectar <*to m. out an advertising campaign* planear una campaña publicitaria>.

ma·ple (mā'pəl) *s.* BOT. arce *m*, ácere *m*.

maple sugar *s.* azúcar de arce *m*.

maple syrup *s.* jarabe de arce *m*.

map·mak·er (măp'mā'kər) *s.* cartógrafo.

map·mak·ing (măp'mā'kĭng) *s.* cartografía.

map·ping (măp'ĭng) *s.* *(mapmaking)* cartografía; MAT. correlación *f.*

mar (mär) **I.** *tr.* **marred, marring** *(to damage)* dañar, estropear; *(to disfigure)* desfigurar **II.** *s.* mancha, marca (que desfigura).

mar·a·bou *o* **mar·a·bout** (măr'ə-boō') *s.* ORNIT. marabú *m.*

mar·a·thon (măr'ə-thŏn') *s.* DEP. *(race)* maratón *m*; *(contest)* competencia de resistencia <*dance m.* competencia de resistencia de baile>.

ma·raud (mə-rôd') *intr.* pecorear, merodear —*tr.* pillar, saquear.

ma·raud·er (mə-rô'dər) *s.* merodeador *m.*

mar·ble (mär'bəl) **I.** *s.* *(rock, sculpture)* mármol *m*; *(for children)* bola, canica • **to lose one's marbles** JER. aflojársele a uno un tornillo • **to play marbles** jugar a las bolas **II.** *tr.* **-bled, -bling** jaspear, vetear **III.** *adj.* *(streaked)* jaspeado, veteado; *(white and smooth)* marmóreo; FIG. *(unfeeling)* de mármol.

mar·bled (mär'bəld) *adj.* jaspeado, veteado.

mar·bling (mär'blĭng) *s.* *(surface decoration)* marmoración *f*; *(imitation marble)* jaspeadura.

marc (märk) *s.* *(pulpy residue)* orujo; *(brandy)* aguardiente (hecho de orujo) *m.*

march¹ (märch) **I.** *intr.* MIL. marchar; *(to parade)* desfilar; *(to walk)* ir a pie; FIG. *(to advance)* avanzar, pasar <*the days marched on* los días pasaban> ♦ **forward m.!** ¡de frente! • **to m. on** seguir la marcha, no detenerse • **to m. up to** acercarse a —*tr.* MIL. *(to cause to march)* hacer marchar; *(to traverse)* recorrer (marchando) ♦ **to m. someone off** llevarse a alguien **II.** *s.* MIL. marcha; *(parade)* desfile *m*; *(demonstration)* marcha <*protest m.* marcha de protesta>; *(pace)* paso; *(progression)* marcha, progreso; *(of time)* transcurso; *(distance)* caminata <*a week's m.* caminata de una semana>; MÚS. marcha <*funeral m.* marcha fúnebre> ♦ **forced m.** marcha forzada • **on the m.** en marcha.

march² (märch) **I.** *s.* marca, frontera **II.** *intr.* lindar, colindar.

March (märch) *s.* marzo.

march·er (mär'chər) *s.* *(demonstrator)* manifestante *mf.*

marching orders *s.pl.* MIL. órdenes de movilización *m.*

mar·chio·ness (mär'shə-nĭs) *s.* marquesa.

Mar·di gras (mär'dē grä') *s.* martes de carnaval *m*, martes antes de cuaresma.

mare (mâr) *s.* ZOOL. yegua.

mare's nest *s.* [pl. **mare's nests** *o* **mares' nests**] *(hoax)* bola, engaño; *(complicated situation)* olla de grillos, maraña.

mar·ga·rine *o* **mar·ga·rin** (mär'jər-ĭn) *s.* QUÍM. margarina, oleomargarina.

mar·ga·ri·ta (mär'gə-rē'tə) *s.* margarita (cóctel mexicano hecho con tequila).

mar·gin (mär'jĭn) **I.** *s.* *(edge)* margen *f*, orilla; *(of a page)* margen *m* <*to note in the m.* anotar al margen>; *(limit)* límite *m*; *(advantage)* margen *m*, excedente *m* <*a m. of 500 votes* un margen de 500 votos>; *(extra amount)* margen *m* <*m. of safety* margen de seguridad>; COM. *(mini-*

mum return) margen *m* <*m. of profit* margen de ganancias>; FIN. *(collateral)* garantía **II.** *tr.* *(a page)* marginar, dejar un margen en; *(to border)* lindar con; *(to enter in the margin)* escribir al margen; FIN. *(a transaction)* depositar una garantía para.

mar·gin·al (mär'jə-nəl) *adj.* *(beside)* marginal; GEOG. colindante; *(barely acceptable)* mínimo, reducido <*m. ability* capacidad mínima>.

mar·gi·na·li·a (mär'jə-nā'lē-ə) *s.pl.* notas marginales, apostillas.

mar·grave (mär'grāv') *s.* HIST. margrave (título de ciertos príncipes alemanes) *m.*

mar·gue·rite (mär'gə-rēt', -gyə-) *s.* BOT. margarita (planta o flor).

Mar·i·an (mâr'ē-ən) RELIG. **I.** *s.* devoto de la Virgen María **II.** *adj.* mariano, marista.

mar·i·cul·ture (măr'ĭ-kŭl'chər) *s.* el cultivo *o* crianza de organismos marinos (en su propio medio).

mar·i·gold (măr'ĭ-gōld') *s.* BOT. caléndula, maravilla.

mar·i·jua·na *or* **mar·i·hua·na** (măr'ə-wä'nə) *s.* *(drug)* mariguana; *(hemp)* cáñamo índico.

ma·ri·na (mə-rē'nə) *s.* marina.

mar·i·nade (măr'ə-nād') **I.** *s.* CUL. escabeche *m* **II.** *tr.* **-naded, -nading** escabechar, marinar.

mar·i·nate (măr'ə-nāt') *tr.* **-nated, -nating** escabechar, marinar.

ma·rine (mə-rēn') **I.** *adj.* MARÍT. marítimo <*m. exploration* exploración marítima>; *(formed in the sea)* marino <*m. life* vida marina>; *(nautical)* náutico <*m. engineer* ingeniero naval **II.** *s.* *(fleet)* marina <*merchant m.* marina mercante>; *(painting)* marina; *(soldier)* soldado de marina ♦ **marines** infantería de marina.

Marine Corps *s.* MIL. Infantería de Marina (de EE. UU.).

mar·i·ner (măr'ə-nər) *s.* marinero, marino.

mar·i·o·nette (măr'ē-ə-nět') *s.* títere *m*, marioneta.

mar·i·tal (măr'ĭ-tl) *adj.* *(of marriage)* matrimonial; *(of a husband)* marital.

mar·i·time (măr'ĭ-tīm') *adj.* marítimo.

mar·jo·ram (mär'jər-əm) *s.* BOT. mejorana, amáraco.

mark¹ (märk) **I.** *s.* *(sign)* marca; *(scratch)* marca, raya; *(spot)* marca, mancha; *(dot)* marca, punto; *(trace)* marca, huella; *(cross)* cruz (en lugar de firma) *f*; GRAM. *(punctuation mark)* signo de puntuación; *(grade)* nota, calificación *f*; *(stamp)* marca (de fábrica); *(notch)* muesca (en el ganado); MARÍT. *(device)* señal *f*, indicador de nivel *m*; *(indication)* signo, indicio; FIG. *(standard)* altura, nivel *m* <*schoolwork that is not up to the m.* tarea escolar que no está a la altura>; *(attention)* atención *f* <*a matter unworthy of m.* un asunto que no es digno de atención>; *(target)* blanco; FIG., FAM. *(dupe)* primo, incauto; *(goal)* fin *m*, objetivo; *(reference point)* punto de referencia, señal; *(impression)* huella, sello (personal); DEP. *(starting line)* línea de salida; *(record)* récord *m*, marca <*to set a new m.* establecer un nuevo récord>; ANT. *(boundary)* límite *m*, frontera ♦ **a m. of distinction** un sello de distinción • **M.** marca (de un producto) • **marks** *(appraisal)* evaluación; *(rating)* calificación • **to be off** *o* **beside the m.** FIG. *(off the target)* no alcanzar el fin deseado; *(off the subject)* fuera del tema; *(inaccurate)* incorrecto, erróneo • **to hit the m.** FIG. *(to succeed)* tener éxito; *(to be right)* acertar, dar en el clavo • **to make one's m.** FIG. *(to succeed)* tener éxito; *(to achieve fame)* distinguirse • **to miss the m.** *(to fail)* no tener éxito; *(to be inaccurate)* no dar en el clavo • **to toe the m.** obrar como se debe **II.** *tr.* *(to make a m. on)* marcar; *(to scratch)* marcar, rayar; *(to draw)* dibujar <*he marked a square on the board* dibujó un cuadrado en el encerado>; *(to incise)* grabar; *(to indicate)* marcar, señalar <*to m. a spot* señalar un lugar>; FIG. *(to characterize)* caracterizar <*the exuberance that marks her writings* la exuberancia que caracteriza sus escritos>; COM. *(to tag)* poner (precios); *(to grade)* calificar, poner notas a <*the professor marked the examination papers* el profesor calificó los exámenes>; *(to notice)* advertir, observar <*m. her expression* observa su expresión>; *(to consider)* prestar atención <*m. my words* presta atención a lo que digo>; DEP. *(to keep score)* marcar, anotar (tantos) ♦ **to m. down**

(to write down) apuntar, anotar; COM. *(to reduce)* rebajar (precios) • **to m. off** *(to demarcate)* demarcar, marcar; *(to note)* apuntar, marcar; COM. *(to reduce)* rebajar (precios); FIG. *(to differentiate)* diferenciar • **to m. out** tachar • **to m. time** MIL. marcar el paso; FIG. *(to wait)* hacer tiempo • **to m. up** *(to deface)* estropear; *(to scratch)* rayar; COM. *(to increase)* aumentar (precios) —intr. *(to make a m.)* marcar; *(to spot)* mancharse <*the floor marks easily* el piso se mancha con facilidad>; *(to scratch)* rayarse; *(to notice)* fijarse, prestar atención; DEP. *(to keep score)* marcar (tantos); *(to grade)* calificar, poner notas <*his teacher marks strictly* su profesor califica con mucho rigor>.
mark² (märk) s. FIN. marco.
Mark (märk) s. BÍBL. Marcos.
mark·down (märk′doun′) s. rebaja, reducción de precio *f.*
marked (märkt) adj. *(having a mark)* marcado <*a m. book* un libro marcado>; *(noticeable)* notable, manifiesto <*a m. difference* una diferencia notable> ♦ **a m. man** un hombre señalado *o* fichado.
mark·ed·ly (märʹkĭd-lē) adv. *(in a marked manner)* marcadamente; *(noticeably)* notablemente, manifiestamente.
mark·er (märʹkər) s. *(one that marks)* marcador *m;* *(grader)* calificador *m;* JER. *(promissory note)* pagaré *m.*
mar·ket (märʹkĭt) I. s. *(place)* mercado; *(for a commodity)* mercado <*the coffee m.* el mercado del café>; *(demand)* mercado, salida <*is there a m. for this product?* ¿este producto tiene salida?>; *(stock market)* bolsa ♦ **black m.** estraperlo, mercado negro • **buyer's m.** mercado que favorece al comprador • **Common M.** Mercado Común • **foreign** *o* **overseas m.** mercado exterior • **foreign exchange m.** mercado de cambios • **free m.** mercado libre • **m. price** precio corriente *o* de mercado • **m. research** análisis de mercados • **seller's m.** mercado que favorece al vendedor • **to be in the m. for** querer comprar • **to be on the m.** estar en venta • **to corner the m. in** acaparar el mercado de • **to find a ready m.** tener fácil salida • **to play the m.** jugar a la bolsa • **to put on the m.** poner en venta II. tr. *(to sell)* poner a la venta, vender; *(to introduce into the market)* comercializar —intr. *(to deal)* mercadear, comerciar; *(to go shopping)* hacer las compras.
mar·ket·a·ble (märʹkĭ-tə-bəl) adj. *(fit to be sold)* comercial; *(salable)* vendible, de fácil venta.
mar·ket·er (märʹkĭ-tər) s. *(seller)* vendedor *m;* *(of new products)* mercantilizador *m,* lanzador *m.*
mar·ket·ing (märʹkĭ-tĭng) s. *(buying and selling)* comercio; *(of new products)* mercadeo, comercialización *f.*
mar·ket·place *o* **market place** (märʹkĭt-plās′) s. *(market)* mercado, plaza del mercado; *(world of business)* mundo mercantil; FIG. *(center)* centro de intercambio (de ideas, opiniones).
market value s. ECON. valor comercial *m.*
mark·ing (märʹkĭng) s. *(mark)* marca, señal *f;* *(act)* marcación *f;* ZOOL. pinta.
marks·man (märks′mən) s. [pl. **-men**] tirador (al blanco) *m.*
marks·man·ship (märks′mən-shĭp′) s. puntería, buena puntería.
mark·up (märk′ŭp′) s. COM. *(rise)* aumento, subida (de precios); *(profit margin)* margen de beneficio *o* de ganancia bruta *m.*
marl (märl) I. s. AGR., GEOL. marga II. tr. margar, abonar con marga.
mar·lin (märʹlĭn) s. ICT. pez vela, aguja.
mar·ma·lade (märʹmə-lād′) s. mermelada.
mar·mo·re·al (märmôrʹē-əl) *o* **mar·mo·re·an** (-ē-ən) adj. marmóreo, parecido al mármol.
mar·mo·set (märʹmə-sĕt′) s. ZOOL. tití (mono) *m.*
mar·mot (märʹmət) s. ZOOL. marmota.
ma·roon¹ (mə-rōōn′) I. tr. *(to put ashore)* abandonar; *(to isolate)* aislar II. s. persona abandonada.
ma·roon² (mə-rōōn′) s. & adj. marrón *m,* castaño.
mar·quee (mär-kē′) s. *(tent)* tienda de campaña (grande); *(of a theater, hotel)* marquesina.
mar·quess (märʹkwĭs) s. G.B. var. de **marquis.**
mar·quis (märʹkwĭs, mär-kē′) s. marqués *m.*
mar·quise (mär-kēz′) s. *(marchioness)* marquesa *f;* JOY. talla elíptica.

mar·riage (märʹĭj) s. *(wedlock)* matrimonio; *(wedding)* boda, casamiento; FIG. *(close union)* unión *f;* *(in cards)* tute *m* ♦ **m. articles** contrato matrimonial • **m. by proxy** matrimonio por poderes • **m. certificate** partida de matrimonio • **to be related by m.** tener parentesco político • **to take someone in m.** contraer matrimonio con alguien.
mar·riage·a·ble (märʹĭ-jə-bəl) adj. casadero, núbil, que está en edad de casarse.
marriage of convenience s. matrimonio de conveniencia *o* de interés.
mar·ried (märʹēd) I. adj. *(having a spouse)* casado; *(conjugal)* matrimonial, conyugal <*m. bliss* dicha conyugal> ♦ **m. couple** matrimonio • **m. name** apellido de casada • **to be a m. man** ser casado, estar casado • **to get m.** casarse II. s. casado.
mar·row (märʹō) s. ANAT. médula, tuétano; *(spinal cord)* médula espinal; FIG. *(innermost part)* meollo, médula; *(vitality)* vitalidad, *f,* vigor *m.*
mar·row·bone (märʹō-bōn′) s. CUL. hueso medular (para sazonar sopa).
mar·ry (märʹē) tr. **-ried, -ry·ing** *(to join in marriage)* casar <*the priest married them* el sacerdote los casó>; *(to take in marriage)* casarse con <*he married an older woman* se casó con una mujer mayor>; *(to give in marriage)* dar en casamiento; MARÍT. *(ropes)* trenzar; FIG. *(to unite)* unir ♦ **to m. into** emparentar con • **to m. off** casar <*he married off all his daughters* casó a todas sus hijas> • **to m. wealth** casarse con alguien de buena familia —intr. *(to wed)* casarse; FIG. *(to unite)* unirse ♦ **to m. beneath oneself** casarse con alguien de clase inferior.
Mars (märz) s. ASTRON., MITOL. Marte *m.*
Mar·seilles *o* **Mar·seille** (mär-sā′) s. Marsella.
marsh (märsh) s. pantano, marisma.
mar·shal (märʹshəl) I. s. MIL. mariscal *m* <*field m.* mariscal de campo>; *(high-ranking officer)* comandante en jefe *m;* *(police chief)* jefe de policía *m;* *(fire chief)* jefe de bomberos; *(of a ceremony)* maestro de ceremonias; *(of a parade)* jefe, director *m* II. tr. *(troops, procession)* formar; *(to organize)* organizar, poner en orden; *(to usher)* acompañar ceremoniosamente ♦ **to m. (forces) against** movilizar (fuerzas) en contra de.
marsh gas s. QUÍM. gas de los pantanos *m,* metano.
marsh·land (märsh′lănd′) s. terreno pantanoso.
marsh·mal·low (märsh′mĕl′ō, -măl′ō) s. BOT. malvavisco; *(candy)* bombón de merengue blando *m.*
marsh·y (märʹshē) adj. **-i·er, -i·est** pantanoso.
mar·su·pi·al (mär-sōō′pē-əl) adj. & s. ZOOL. marsupial *m.*
mar·su·pi·um (mär-sōō′pē-əm) s. [pl. **-pi·a** (-pē-ə)] bolsa (marsupial).
mart (märt) s. *(market)* mercado; ANT. *(fair)* feria, exposición regional *f.*
mar·ten (märʹtn) s. [pl. **marten** *o* **-tens**] ZOOL. marta (animal y piel).
mar·tial (märʹshəl) adj. *(warlike)* marcial; *(military)* militar; *(bellicose)* bélico, belicoso.
martial art s. arte marcial *o* de defensa personal *m.*
martial law s. ley marcial *f.*
Mar·tian (märʹshən) adj. & s. marciano (del planeta Marte).
mar·tin (märʹtn) s. ORNIT. avión *m,* vencejo.
mar·ti·net (mär′tn-ĕt′) s. MIL. ordenancista *mf;* *(dogmatist)* persona autoritaria.
mar·tin·gale (märʹtn-gāl′) s. EQUIT. gamarra, amarra; MARÍT. moco de bauprés.
Mar·ti·nique (mär′tn-ēk′) s. Martinica.
mar·tyr (märʹtər) I. s. mártir *mf* II. tr. martirizar.
mar·tyr·dom (märʹtər-dəm) s. martirio.
mar·tyr·ize (märʹtə-rīz′) tr. **-ized, -iz·ing** martirizar.
mar·vel (märʹvəl) I. s. *(wonder)* maravilla; *(astonishment)* asombro, admiración *f* II. intr. maravillarse —tr. admirarse de.
mar·vel·ous *o* **mar·vel·lous** (märʹvə-ləs) adj. *(wonderful)* maravilloso; *(miraculous)* milagroso.
Marx·i·an (märk′sē-ən) s. & adj. marxista *mf.*
Marx·ism (märk′sĭz′əm) s. marxismo.
Marx·ism-Len·in·ism (märk′sĭz′əm-lĕn′ĭ-nĭz′əm) s. marxismo-leninismo.

Marx·ist (märk'sĭst) s. & adj. marxista *mf.*
mar·zi·pan (mär'zə-păn', märt'sə-păn') s. CUL. mazapán *m.*
mas·car·a (mă-skăr'ə) s. rimel *m.*
mas·cot (măs'kŏt') s. mascota.
mas·cu·line (măs'kyə-lĭn) adj. & s. masculino.
mas·cu·lin·i·ty (măs'kyə-lĭn'ĭ-tē) s. masculinidad *f.*
mash (măsh) **I.** s. *(for brewing)* malta remojada, malta empastada; *(for animals)* afrecho remojado, mezcla de granos molidos; *(mixture)* mezcla, mezcolanza; CUL. *(purée)* puré *m* **II.** tr. *(to crush)* machacar, majar; *(to grind)* moler, triturar; CUL. hacer puré de.
mash·er (măsh'ər) s. *(utensil)* moledor *m*, majador *m*; JER. *(man)* seductor *m*, galanteador *m.*
mask (măsk) **I.** s. *(covering)* máscara <*the surgeon wears a m.* el cirujano lleva una máscara>; *(face covering)* antifaz *m*, careta; *(gas mask)* máscara antigás; *(mold)* mascarilla, máscara (mortuoria); FIG. *(disguise)* máscara, apariencia; MIL. camuflaje *m*; FOTOG. ocultador *m*; *(costume)* disfraz (para baile) *m*; *(masque)* baile de disfraces *m* **II.** tr. *(to cover)* enmascarar, cubrir (el rostro); *(to disguise)* disimular <*the spice masks the meat's strong flavor* la especia disimula el sabor fuerte de la carne>; *(to cover up)* encubrir, ocultar; FOTOG. ocultar, poner ocultador a; MIL. camuflar —intr. ponerse una máscara.
masked (măskt) adj. *(wearing a mask)* enmascarado; FIG. *(disguised)* disfrazado, oculto; *(latent)* latente (enfermedad, virus).
masked ball s. baile de máscaras *o* de disfraces *m.*
mask·ing (măs'kĭng) s. PSIC. enmascaramiento.
masking tape s. cinta adhesiva.
mas·o·chism (măs'ə-kĭz'əm) s. masoquismo.
mas·o·chist (măs'ə-kĭst) s. masoquista *mf.*
mas·o·chis·tic (măs'ə-kĭs'tĭk) adj. masoquista.
ma·son (mā'sən) s. *(bricklayer)* albañil *m*; *(stonecutter)* cantero ♦ **M.** mason, francmasón.
Ma·son-Dix·on Line (mā'sən-dĭk'sən) s. EE. UU., HIST. línea entre los estados del norte y los del sur en la Guerra Civil.
Ma·son jar (mā'sən) s. pote de Mason *m.*
ma·son·ry (mā'sən-rē) s. [pl. -ries] *(trade)* albañilería; *(brickwork)* obra de albañilería, mampostería; *(stonework)* cantería ♦ **M.** masonería, francmasonería.
masque (măsk) s. HIST., TEAT. *(entertainment)* espectáculo alegórico; *(masked ball)* baile de disfraces *m.*
mas·quer·ade (măs'kə-rād') **I.** s. *(party)* mascarada, fiesta de disfraces; *(costume)* disfraz *m*; FIG. *(pretense)* farsa **II.** intr. **-ad·ed, -ad·ing** ♦ **to m. as** *(to disguise oneself as)* disfrazarse de; FIG. *(to pose as)* hacerse pasar por.
mas·quer·ad·er (măs'kə-rā'dər) s. *(disguised person)* persona disfrazada, máscara; FIG. *(pretender)* farsante *mf*, impostor *m.*
mass (măs) **I.** s. *(lump)* masa <*a m. of clay* una masa de arcilla>; *(shapeless form)* bulto; *(of people)* grupo, muchedumbre *f* <*a m. of students* una muchedumbre de estudiantes>; *(large amount)* montón *m*; *(majority)* mayoría, mayor parte *f*; *(physical bulk)* volumen *m*; FÍS. masa ♦ **the masses** las masas **II.** tr. *(to gather)* agrupar, amontonar; *(to form)* hacer una masa con —intr. agruparse, congregarse en masa **III.** adj. de las masas ♦ **m. hysteria** histeria colectiva • **m. evacuation** evacuación en masa • **m. media** medios de comunicación de masas.
Mass *o* **mass** (măs) s. RELIG. misa ♦ **High M.** misa mayor • **Low M.** misa rezada • **Midnight M.** misa del gallo • **to go to M.** ir a misa • **to hear M.** oír misa • **to say M.** decir misa.
mas·sa·cre (măs'ə-kər) **I.** s. masacre *f*, matanza **II.** tr. **-cred, -cring** matar en masa, masacrar.
mas·sage (mə-säzh', -säj') **I.** s. masaje *m* **II.** tr. **-saged, -sag·ing** dar masajes a, masajear.
mass·cult (măs'kŭlt') s. cultura de las masas.
mas·seur (mă-sûr') s. masajista *m.*
mas·seuse (mă-soez') s. masajista *f.*
mas·sive (măs'ĭv) adj. *(huge)* monumental, colosal <*a m. undertaking* una empresa monumental>; *(bulky)* enorme, masivo; *(solid)* macizo.
mass number s. FÍS., QUÍM. número de masa.

mass-pro·duce (măs'prə-dōōs', -dyōōs') tr. **-duced, -duc·ing** fabricar en gran escala, producir en serie.
mass production s. producción en masa *f*, fabricación en serie *f.*
mast (măst) s. MARÍT. mástil *m*, palo (de embarcación); *(pole)* poste *m*; TEC. torre *f.*
mas·tec·to·my (mă-stĕk'tə-mē) s. [pl. -mies] CIR. mastectomía.
mas·ter (măs'tər) **I.** s. *(expert)* maestro, perito; *(scholar)* erudito, sabio; *(leader)* maestro; EDUC. *(teacher)* maestro, profesor *m*; *(degree)* maestría (título académico entre la licenciatura y el doctorado); *(employer)* patrón *m*; *(owner)* amo (de esclavos, animales); *(of a household)* señor (de la casa) *m*; *(proprietor)* dueño, propietario <*the m. of a large tea plantation* el dueño de una gran plantación de té>; MARÍT. *(captain)* capitán (de barco mercante) *m*; *(craftsman)* maestro (de un oficio); ARTE. *(artist)* gran maestro; *(old master)* maestro (título clásico); *(painting)* obra de pintor clásico; TEC. *(original)* original *m*; *(victor)* triunfador *m*, vencedor *m* ♦ **M.** *(Christ)* Maestro; *(youth)* señorito • **m. of ceremonies** maestro de ceremonias **II.** adj. *(of a master)* maestro, magistral; *(main)* principal <*the m. bedroom* el dormitorio principal>; *(original)* original <*a m. tape* una cinta magnetofónica original> **III.** tr. *(to rule)* gobernar, mandar; *(to become expert in)* lograr dominar *o* a conocer a fondo <*she mastered the language in a year* logró dominar el idioma en un año>; *(to overcome)* vencer, superar <*to m. the addiction to drugs* superar la dependencia de las drogas>; *(to tame)* domesticar (persona, animal).
mas·ter-at-arms (măs'tər-ət-ärmz') s. [pl. **mas·ters-at-arms**] MARÍT. sargento de marina.
mas·ter·ful (măs'tər-fəl) adj. *(imperious)* dominante, imperioso; *(fit to command)* capaz, diestro; *(revealing mastery)* magistral; *(skillful)* hábil, experto.
master key s. llave maestra.
mas·ter·ly (măs'tər-lē) **I.** adj. magistral, genial **II.** adv. magistralmente, genialmente.
mas·ter·mind (măs'tər-mīnd') **I.** s. cerebro, genio creador y director **II.** tr. ser el cerebro de, dirigir.
master of arts s. EDUC. *(degree)* título universitario posterior al de la licenciatura en humanidades *o* letras; *(person)* persona que posee este título.
master of ceremonies s. *(presiding person)* maestro de ceremonias; *(entertainer)* animador *o* presentador de un espectáculo *m.*
master of science s. EDUC. *(degree)* título universitario posterior al de la licenciatura en ciencias; *(person)* persona que posee este título.
mas·ter·piece (măs'tər-pēs') s. obra maestra.
master plan s. plan maestro.
master race s. raza superior.
mas·ter·ship (măs'tər-shĭp') s. *(occupation of a master)* magisterio (ocupación de un maestro); *(skill)* maestría, destreza.
mas·ter·stroke (măs'tər-strōk') s. golpe maestro.
mas·ter·work (măs'tər-wûrk') s. obra maestra.
mas·ter·y (măs'tə-rē) s. [pl. -ies] *(skill)* maestría, habilidad *f*; *(rule)* gobierno, poder *m.*
mast·head (măst'hĕd') s. *(of a mast)* tope *m*; IMPR. cabecera.
mas·tic (măs'tĭk) s. BOT. *(tree)* almácigo; *(resin)* almáciga; *(cement)* mástique *m*, pegamento.
mas·ti·cate (măs'tĭ-kāt') tr. **-cat·ed, -cat·ing** *(to chew)* masticar, mascar; *(to grind)* moler.
mas·ti·ca·tion (măs'tĭ-kā'shən) s. masticación *f.*
mas·tiff (măs'tĭf) s. ZOOL. mastín (perro) *m.*
mas·ti·tis (mă-stī'tĭs) s. MED., VET. mastitis *f.*
mas·to·don (măs'tə-dŏn') s. PALEON. mastodonte *m.*
mas·toid (măs'toid') **I.** s. ANAT. mastoides *f*, apófisis mastoidea; MED. mastoiditis *f* **II.** adj. mastoideo, mastoidal.
mas·tur·bate (măs'tər-bāt') tr. & intr. **-bat·ed, -bat·ing** masturbar(se).
mas·tur·ba·tion (măs'tər-bā'shən) s. masturbación *f*, onanismo.
mat¹ (măt) **I.** s. *(floor covering)* estera; *(doormat)* esterilla; *(under a lamp)* tapete *m*; *(placemat)* salvamanteles *m*;

DEP. *(floor pad)* colchoneta; *(tangled mass)* maraña, greña <*a m. of hair* una greña de pelo> **II.** tr. **mat·ted, mat·ting** *(a floor)* esterar; *(to tangle)* enmarañar; *(to interweave over)* entretejerse sobre —intr. enmarañarse.

mat² (măt) **I.** s. *(cardboard border)* orla, marco de cartón; *(dull finish)* acabado mate **II.** tr. **mat·ted, mat·ting** *(a picture)* poner un marco de cartón a; *(glass, metal)* dar un acabado mate a **III.** adj. mate.

match¹ (măch) **I.** s. *(peer)* par *m*, igual *m* <*in her profession she is without m.* en su profesión ella no tiene par>; *(pair)* juego, conjunto <*the purse and the shoes are a good m.* el bolso y los zapatos hacen juego>; *(marriage)* matrimonio <*a royal m.* un matrimonio real>; DEP. *(game)* partido <*a soccer m.* un partido de fútbol>; *(in boxing)* combate *m* <*a boxing m.* un combate de boxeo> ♦ **to be a good m.** *(mate)* ser un buen partido; *(to harmonize)* hacer juego • **to be a m. for** poder competir con, ser digno rival para • **to make a m.** arreglar una boda • **to meet one's m.** encontrar la horma de su zapato, hallar un rival digno de uno **II.** tr. *(to equal)* ser igual a, corresponder a; *(to go with)* hacer juego con <*the coat matches the dress* el abrigo hace juego con el vestido>; *(to pit against)* oponer <*he matched his strength against his friend's* opuso su fuerza a la de su amigo>; *(to equal)* igualar; *(to compare)* comparar, equiparar; *(to provide equal funds)* dar una cantidad igual a <*the government will m. all private donations* el gobierno dará una cantidad igual a la de todos los donativos particulares>; ELEC. *(to couple)* conectar (dos circuitos eléctricos) —intr. hacer juego <*the coat and the dress m.* el abrigo y el vestido hacen juego>.

match² (măch) s. *(stick)* fósforo, cerilla; *(wick)* mecha (detonante).

match·book (măch′bŏŏk′) s. talonario *o* sobre de fósforos *m*.

match·box (măch′bŏks′) s. caja de fósforos *o* de cerillas, fosforera.

match·less (măch′lĭs) adj. sin igual, sin par.

match·mak·er (măch′mā′kər) s. *(for marriages)* casamentero; *(for sporting events)* organizador (de eventos deportivos) *m*.

mate¹ (māt) **I.** s. *(one of a pair)* compañero <*the m. to this glove* el compañero de este guante>; *(spouse)* compañero, cónyuge *mf*; *(male)* macho; *(female)* hembra; *(companion)* compañero, socio, MARÍT. piloto; *(assistant)* ayudante *m* **II.** tr. **mat·ed, mat·ing** *(to join)* hermanar; *(to marry)* casar; ZOOL. aparear, acoplar —intr. *(to marry)* casarse; ZOOL. *(to breed)* aparearse, juntarse.

mate² (māt) **I.** s. mate *m*, jaque mate (en ajedrez) *m* **II.** intr. & tr. **mat·ed, mat·ing** dar mate (a), dar jaque mate (a).

ma·té (mä′tā′) s. mate *m*.

ma·te·ri·al (mə-tîr′ē-əl) **I.** s. *(substance)* material *m*; *(idea)* material <*m. for a comedy* material para una comedia>; *(cloth)* tejido, tela ♦ **materials** materiales **II.** adj. *(physical)* material; *(noticeable)* notable <*a m. improvement* una mejora notable>; *(relevant)* pertinente, FILOS. material.

ma·te·ri·al·ism (mə-tîr′ē-ə-lĭz′əm) s. materialismo.

ma·te·ri·al·ist (mə-tîr′ē-ə-lĭst) s. materialista *mf*.

ma·te·ri·al·is·tic (mə-tîr′ē-ə-lĭs′tĭk) adj. materialista.

ma·te·ri·al·i·ty (mə-tîr′ē-ăl′ĭ-tē) s. [pl. **-ties**] *(condition)* materialidad *f*; DER. *(importance)* importancia, pertinencia.

ma·te·ri·al·ize (mə-tîr′ē-ə-līz′) tr. **-ized, -iz·ing** materializar, hacer realidad —intr. *(to become effective)* realizarse, concretarse; *(to take physical form)* concretizarse; *(to appear)* materializarse.

ma·te·ri·al·ly (mə-tîr′ē-ə-lē) adv. *(concretely)* materialmente; *(substancially)* substancialmente.

ma·te·ri·el *o* **ma·té·ri·el** (mə-tîr′ē-ĕl′) s. MIL. material *m*, suministros y pertrechos.

ma·ter·nal (mə-tûr′nəl) adj. *(motherly)* maternal; *(of one's mother)* materno.

ma·ter·ni·ty (mə-tûr′nĭ-tē) s. *(motherhood)* maternidad *f*; *(motherliness)* cuidado *o* cariño maternal.

math (măth) s. matemática, matemáticas.

math·e·mat·i·cal (măth′ə-măt′ĭ-kəl) *o* **math·e·mat·ic** (-măt′ĭk) adj. matemático.

math·e·ma·ti·cian (măth′ə-mə-tĭsh′ən) s. matemático.

math·e·mat·ics (măth′ə-măt′ĭks) s. [ú. con v. sing.] matemática, matemáticas.

maths (măths) s. G.B. matemática, matemáticas.

mat·i·nee *o* **mat·i·née** (măt′n-ā′) s. TEAT. matiné *m*, función de la tarde.

mat·ing (mā′tĭng) s. *(of persons)* unión *f*; *(of animals)* apareamiento, acoplamiento.

mat·ins (măt′nz) s. [ú. con v. sing. *o* pl.] maitines *m*.

ma·tri·arch (mā′trē-ärk′) s. matriarca.

ma·tri·ar·chal (mā′trē-är′kəl) *o* **ma·tri·ar·chic** (-är′kĭk) adj. matriarcal.

ma·tri·ar·chate (mā′trē-är′kĭt) s. matriarcado.

ma·tri·ar·chy (mā′trē-är′kē) s. [pl. **-chies**] matriarcado.

ma·tri·ces (mā′trĭ-sēz′) un pl. de **matrix**.

mat·ri·cide (măt′rĭ-sīd′) s. *(act)* matricidio; *(person)* matricida *mf*.

ma·tric·u·late (mə-trĭk′yə-lāt′) **I.** tr. & intr. **-lat·ed, -lat·ing** matricular(se) **II.** s. matriculado.

ma·tric·u·la·tion (mə-trĭk′yə-lā′shən) s. matriculación *f*, matrícula.

mat·ri·lin·e·al (măt′rə-lĭn′ē-əl) adj. materno, por línea materna.

mat·ri·mo·ni·al (măt′rə-mō′nē-əl) adj. matrimonial.

mat·ri·mo·ny (măt′rə-mō′nē) s. [pl. **-nies**] matrimonio.

ma·trix (mā′trĭks) s. [pl. **-tri·ces** (-trĭ-sēz′) *o* **-trix·es**] matriz *f*.

ma·tron (mā′trən) s. *(mother)* matrona; *(supervisor)* directora (de una residencia); *(head nurse)* enfermera jefe; *(prison guard)* matrona.

ma·tron·ly (mā′trən-lē) **I.** adj. matronal, de matrona **II.** adv. como una matrona.

matron of honor s. [pl. **matrons of honor**] madrina de boda.

matte¹ (măt) s. acabado mate.

matte² (măt) s. METAL. mata (sulfuro múltiple).

mat·ted (măt′ĭd) adj. *(with mats)* esterado, cubierto con esteras; *(tangled)* enmarañado, enredado (pelo, maleza).

mat·ter (măt′ər) **I.** s. *(material)* materia; *(substance)* materia, sustancia <*inorganic m.* materia inorgánica>; *(subject)* materia, asunto; *(concern)* cuestión *f*, cosa <*a personal m.* una cuestión personal>; *(approximate quantity)* cosa, cuestión <*it was only a m. of a few cents* era cosa de unos centavos nada más>; IMPR. *(composed type)* plomo ♦ **as a m. of course** normalmente, por costumbre • **as a m. of fact** de hecho • **as if nothing were the m.** como si tal cosa, como si nada hubiera sucedido • **as matters stand** tal y como están las cosas • **for that m.** en cuanto a eso • **gray m.** materia gris • **in the m. of** en lo tocante a • **no m.** no importa • **no m. how** sea como sea • **no m. what happens** pase lo que pase • **no m. when** sea cuando sea • **nothing's the m.** no pasa nada • **on the m. of** respecto a • **printed m.** impresos • **small m.** asunto sin importancia • **to be a m. of form** ser una formalidad • **to be a m. of great concern to them** ser algo que les preocupa mucho • **to be a m. of taste** ser cuestión de gusto • **to be another m.** ser cosa aparte • **to be no laughing m.** no ser cosa de risa • **make matters worse** para colmo de males • **what's the m.?** ¿qué sucede? **II.** intr. importar <*it doesn't matter to me* no me importa>.

matter of course s. cosa *o* resultado natural, acontecimiento esperado.

mat·ter-of-fact (măt′ər-əv-făkt′) adj. *(practical)* práctico; *(factual)* realista; *(prosaic)* prosaico.

Mat·thew (măth′yōō) s. BÍBL. Mateo.

mat·ting (măt′ĭng) s. *(floor covering)* estera, esterilla *f*; *(frame)* orla, marco de cartón.

mat·tock (măt′ək) s. piqueta, azadón *m*.

mat·tress (măt′rĭs) s. colchón *m*.

mat·u·rate (măch′ə-rāt′) intr. & tr. **-rat·ed, -rat·ing** *(to mature)* madurar; *(to suppurate)* supurar.

mat·u·ra·tion (măch′ə-rā′shən) s. *(growing process)* maduración *f*; *(suppuration)* supuración *f*.

ma·ture (mə-chŏŏr′, -tŏŏr′) **I.** adj. **-tur·er, -tur·est** *(devel-*

oped) maduro; (*considered*) madurado, meditado <*a m. plan of action* un plan de acción meditado>; FIN. (*due*) pagadero, vencido II. tr. **-tured, -tur·ing** madurar —intr. (*to develop*) madurar; FIN. ser pagadero, vencer.

ma·tur·i·ty (mə-chŏŏr′ĭ-tē, -tŏŏr′-) s. [pl. **-ties**] (*development*) madurez *f*; FIN. vencimiento ♦ **to reach m.** (*to develop*) llegar a la madurez; FIN. ser pagadero, vencer.

maud·lin (môd′lĭn) adj. sensiblero.

maul (môl) I. s. mazo, almádana II. tr. (*to split*) partir con un mazo; (*to handle roughly*) maltratar; (*to beat*) apalear, aporrear; (*to injure*) herir gravemente, lacerar.

Maun·dy Thursday (môn′dē) s. RELIG. Jueves Santo.

Mau·ri·ta·ni·a (môr′ĭ-tā′nē-ə) s. Mauritania.

Mau·ri·ta·ni·an (môr′ĭ-tā′nē-ən) adj. & s. mauritano.

Mau·ri·tian (mô-rĭsh′ən) adj. & s. mauriciano.

Mau·ri·tius (mô-rĭsh′əs) s. Mauricio.

mau·so·le·um (mô′sə-lē′əm) s. [pl. **-le·ums** *o* **-le·a** (-lē′ə)] mausoleo.

mauve (mōv) s. & adj. malva *m*.

mav·er·ick (măv′ər-ĭk) s. (*unbranded animal*) res sin marcar *f*; (*runaway animal*) res *o* caballo escapado de la manada; FIG. (*dissenter*) disidente *mf*.

maw (mô) s. (*of a ruminant*) cuajar *m*; (*of a lion*) fauces *f*; FIG. (*opening*) estómago.

mawk·ish (mô′kĭsh) adj. (*sentimental*) sensiblero; (*sickening*) repugnante, nauseabundo.

max·il·la (măk-sĭl′ə) s. [pl. **max·il·las** *o* **max·il·lae** (măk-sĭl′ē)] ANAT. maxilar superior *m*; ZOOL. maxilar (de los artrópodos).

max·im (măk′sĭm) s. máxima, axioma.

max·i·ma (măk′sə-mə) un pl. de **maximum**.

max·i·mal (măk′sə-məl) adj. máximo.

max·i·mal·ist (măk′sə-mə-lĭst) s. POL. maximalista *mf*, bolchevique *mf*.

max·i·mize (măk′sə-mīz′) tr. **-mized, -miz·ing** (*to increase*) aumentar *o* llevar al máximo; (*to assign great importance to*) dar máxima importancia a; MAT. maximizar.

max·i·mi·za·tion (măk′sə-mĭ-zā′shən) s. MAT. maximización *f*.

max·i·mum (măk′sə-məm) I. s. [pl. **-mums** *o* **-ma** (-mə)] máximo ♦ **a m. of** como máximo II. adj. máximo.

max·well (măks′wěl′) s. FÍS. maxwel (unidad de medida de flujo magnético) *m*.

may §G11 (mā) aux. [pret. **might** (mīt)] ☐ INDICANDO PERMISO poder <*m. I go?* ¿puedo irme? *yes, you m.* sí puedes> ☐ EXPRESANDO CORTESÍA permitir <*m. I use your telephone, please?* ¿me permite usar el teléfono, por favor?> ☐ PARA INDICAR PROBABILIDAD poder (que), ser posible (que) <*it m. rain tomorrow* es posible que llueva mañana> ☐ EXPRESANDO UN DESEO ojalá que <*m. all your wishes come true!* ¡ojalá que se cumplan todos sus deseos!> ☐ NO SE TRADUCE <*they wrote so that we might know their plans* nos escribieron para que supiéramos sus planes> ♦ **. . . as one m.** por mucho que . . . <*talk as she m., she will never convince me* por mucho que ella hable, no me convencerá> • **be that as it m.** sea como fuere • **come what m.** pase lo que pase • **if I m.** si me lo permite • **long m. he live!** ¡que viva muchos años! • **m. as well** más vale que, mejor que.

May (mā) s. (*month*) mayo; FIG. (*youth*) primavera.

Ma·ya (mä′yə) s. [pl. **Maya** *o* **-yas**] HIST. maya *mf*; (*language*) maya *m*.

Ma·yan (mä′yən) I. adj. maya, de los mayas II. s. (*inhabitant, language*) maya *mf*.

may·be (mā′bē) adj. (*perhaps*) quizá, quizás; (*possibly*) tal vez.

may·day (mā′dā′) s. señal de socorro (en radiotelegrafía) *f*.

May Day s. (*May first*) (fiesta del) primero de mayo; (*labor day*) día del obrero *m*.

may·flow·er (mā′flou′ər) s. BOT. espino.

may·fly (mā′flī′) s. [pl. **-flies**] ENTOM. mosca de mayo, mosca efímera *f*.

may·hap (mā′hăp′) adv. quizás, tal vez.

may·hem (mā′hěm′) s. DER. mutilación criminal *f*; (*havoc*) estrago; (*destruction*) destrucción *f*.

may·on·naise (mā′ə-nāz′) s. CUL. mayonesa.

may·or (mā′ər) s. alcalde *m*.

may·or·al·ty (mā′ər-əl-tē) s. [pl. **-ties**] alcaldía.

may·pole *o* **May·pole** (mā′pōl′) s. mayo (palo adornado).

maze (māz) s. laberinto ♦ **to be in a m.** FIG. estar confundido.

me §G29 (mē) pron. ☐ COMO COMPLEMENTO DIRECTO DE UN VERBO me <*she helped me* ella me ayudó> ☐ COMO COMPLEMENTO INDIRECTO DE UN VERBO me <*the school offered me the job* la escuela me ofreció el puesto> ☐ COMO COMPLEMENTO DE UNA PREPOSICIÓN mí <*this letter is addressed to me* esta carta está dirigida a mí> ♦ **it's me** FAM. soy yo • **with me** conmigo.

mead (mēd) s. aguamiel *f*, hidromel *m*.

mead·ow (měd′ō) s. prado, pradera.

mead·ow·lark (měd′ō-lärk′) s. ORNIT. sabanero, triguero.

mea·ger (mē′gər) adj. (*lean*) flaco, magro; (*scanty*) escaso, exiguo; (*feeble*) pobre.

mea·ger·ness (mē′gər-nĭs) s. (*leanness*) flaqueza; (*scantiness*) escasez *f*; (*feebleness*) pobreza.

mea·gre (mē′gər) adj. var. de **meager**.

meal¹ (mēl) s. (*ground edible grain*) harina; (*ground grain*) grano molido.

meal² (mēl) s. comida.

meal·ie (mē′lē) s. mazorca de maíz ♦ **mealies** maíz.

meal ticket s. (*card*) tarjeta *o* boleta que da derecho a una comida; JER. (*financial supporter*) sustento, fuente de ingresos *f*.

meal·time (mēl′tīm′) s. hora de comer.

meal·y (mē′lē) adj. **-i·er, -i·est** (*granular*) harinoso; (*made of meal*) de harina; (*sprinkled with meal*) enharinado; (*pale*) pálido.

meal·y-mouthed (mē′lē-mou*th*d′, -mouth′) adj. meloso, camandulero.

mean¹ (mēn) tr. **meant** (měnt), **mean·ing** (*to signify*) significar, querer decir <*what does that word m.?* ¿qué quiere decir esa palabra?> (*to intend*) tener la intención de <*I meant to return early* tenía la intención de volver temprano>; (*to address*) dirigir <*the dig was not meant for you* la pulla no iba dirigida a ti>; (*to allude to*) referirse a <*do you m. me?* ¿se refiere usted a mí?>; (*to entail*) comportar, implicar <*to type it means a lot of work* pasarlo a máquina implica mucho trabajo>; (*for a specific purpose*) destinar <*the building is meant for storage* el edificio está destinado al almacenamiento> ♦ **not to m. to do something** hacer algo sin querer • **to m. business** no estar jugando • **to m. it** hablar en serio • **to m. nothing to someone** (*to be meaningless*) ser incomprensible para uno; (*to be unfamiliar*) no decirle nada a uno, no sonarle a uno —intr. (*to matter*) significar, importar <*their opinion meant little to him* su opinión le importaba poco> ♦ **to m. well** tener buenas intenciones.

mean² (mēn) adj. **-er, -est** (*inferior*) malo, inferior; (*lowly*) pobre, humilde <*a m. hut* una humilde choza>; (*base*) ruin, bajo; (*stingy*) miserable, tacaño; (*malevolent*) malo, vil <*the m. wolf* el lobo malo>; (*malicious*) mal intencionado <*a m. remark* un comentario mal intencionado>; FAM. (*ill-tempered*) de malas pulgas; JER. (*difficult*) malo, difícil <*a m. street to cross* una calle mala de cruzar> ♦ **to be m. to someone** ser malo con alguien, tratar mal a alguien • **to play a m. game of** JER. ser un bárbaro en.

mean³ (mēn) I. s. (*middle point*) punto medio; (*moderation*) término medio; MAT. (*average*) promedio; (*arithmetic mean*) media; LÓG. medio ♦ **a man of means** un hombre de dinero • **by all means** (*certainly*) sin duda, absolutamente; (*of course*) por supuesto; (*please*) por favor <*by all means sit down* siéntese por favor> • **by any means** del modo que sea, como sea • **by means of** por medio de, mediante • **by no means** (*in no way*) de ningún modo; (*in no sense*) nada <*it was by no means simple* no fue nada sencillo> • **golden m.** justo medio • **means** (*procedures*) medios <*the end did not justify the means* el fin no justificaba los medios>; (*method*) forma, manera <*the best means to achieve it* la forma mejor de hacerlo>; (*instrument*) medios <*means of transportation* medios de transporte>; (*wealth*) medios, recursos • **to live beyond one's means** gastar más de lo que uno tiene II. adj. (*occupying*

me·an·der (mē-ăn'dər) I. intr. *(stream)* serpentear; *(to wander)* andar sin rumbo fijo, vagar II. s. *(of a stream, path)* meandro ♦ **meanders** FIG. vueltas.

mean·ing (mē'nĭng) I. s. *(sense)* significado, sentido <*in the fullest m.* of the word en el pleno sentido de la palabra>; *(intent)* significado, propósito; *(significance)* significación *f*, sentido <*customs now empty of all m.* costumbres ya carentes de todo sentido> ♦ **full of m.** cargado de sentido, expresivo • **what's the m. of?** *(a word)* ¿qué significa?, ¿qué quiere decir?; *(a look)* ¿a qué viene? II. adj. significativo, expresivo ♦ **well-m.** bien intencionado.

mean·ing·ful (mē'nĭng-fəl) adj. significativo.

mean·ing·less (mē'nĭng-lĭs) adj. *(insignificant)* insignificante, sin importancia; *(senseless)* sin sentido.

mean·ness (mēn'nĭs) s. *(of quality, position)* inferioridad *f*; *(of birth)* humildad *f*; *(baseness)* ruindad *f*, bajeza; *(stinginess)* tacañería; *(malevolence)* maldad *f*; *(malicious act)* maldad, canallada.

meant (mĕnt) pret. y part. p. de **mean¹**.

mean·time (mēn'tīm') I. s. ínterin *m* II. adv. entretanto, mientras tanto.

mean time s. ASTRON. tiempo medio.

mean·while (mēn'hwīl') I. s. ínterin *m* II. adv. entretanto, mientras tanto.

mea·sles (mē'zəlz) s. [ú. con v. sing.] MED. sarampión *m*; *(German measles)* rubéola.

mea·sly (mēz'lē) adj. **-sli·er, -sli·est** MED. que tiene sarampión; JER. *(meager)* exiguo, ínfimo.

meas·ur·a·ble (mĕzh'ər-ə-bəl) adj. mensurable, medible.

meas·ure (mĕzh'ər) I. s. *(measurement)* medida <*length, area, volume, and mass are basic measures* la longitud, el área, el volumen y la masa son medidas básicas>; *(unit)* unidad de medida *f*; *(system)* sistema (de medidas) *m*; *(device)* medida (instrumento); *(measuring)* medida, medición *f*; *(limited amount)* medida <*a m.* of recognition cierto reconocimiento>; *(bounds)* límite *m* <*a generosity knowing no m.* una generosidad que no tiene límite>; *(moderation)* moderación *f*; *(bill)* proyecto de ley; *(law)* ley *f*; POÉT. *(meter)* medida, metro; MÚS. *(bar)* compás *m*; *(rhythm)* ritmo; *(movement)* paso (de baile); MAT. *(factor)* factor, *m*, submúltiplo ♦ **beyond m.** *(in excess)* excesivamente; *(without limit)* sin límite; FIG. *(beyond expectations)* más de lo esperado • **for good m.** por añadidura • **in great m.** en gran parte • **in a** o **some m.** hasta cierto punto • **made to m.** hecho a la medida • **measures** medidas <*to take drastic measures* tomar medidas drásticas> • **to take the m. of** FIG. calibrar II. tr. **-ured, -ur·ing** *(to gauge)* medir <*to m. a room* medir una habitación>; *(to estimate)* estimar, juzgar; *(to be a measure of)* medir <*a clock measures time* un reloj mide el tiempo>; FIG. *(to weigh)* medir, ponderar (palabras) ♦ **to m. off** medir • **to m. out** *(to dole out)* repartir, distribuir (midiendo); *(to mete out)* impartir (justicia, castigo) —intr. ♦ **to m. up to** FIG. estar a la altura de, tener capacidad para (puesto, empleo).

meas·ured (mĕzh'ərd) adj. *(regular in rhythm)* acompasado, regular; *(restrained)* mesurado, comedido <*m. words* palabras mesuradas>; *(slow and stately)* acompasado, LIT. *(poem)* métrico.

meas·ure·less (mĕzh'ər-lĭs) adj. inmensurable, inconmensurable.

meas·ure·ment (mĕzh'ər-mənt) s. *(measuring)* medición *f*, medida <*the m. of length* la medida de la longitud>; *(system)* sistema (de medidas) *m*; *(dimension)* dimensión *f*, medida.

meas·ur·er (mĕzh'ər-ər) s. medidor *m*.

meat (mēt) s. *(edible flesh)* carne *f*; *(fleshy part)* parte interior de algo comestible *f*; *(essence)* meollo, substancia; JER. *(forte)* fuerte *m*.

meat·ball (mēt'bôl') s. CUL. albóndiga; JER. *(stupid person)* estúpido.

meat·less (mēt'lĭs) adj. *(without meat)* sin carne; RELIG. de vigilia.

meat loaf s. CUL. carne mechada.

meat market s. carnicería.

meat·y (mē'tē) adj. **-i·er, -i·est** *(fleshy)* carnoso, carnudo; FIG. *(substantial)* substancioso.

mec·ca (mĕk'ə) s. meca ♦ **M.** GEOG., RELIG. Meca.

me·chan·ic (mĭ-kăn'ĭk) s. mecánico (persona).

me·chan·i·cal (mĭ-kăn'ĭ-kəl) I. adj. MEC. mecánico, de máquinas; FIG. *(like a machine)* maquinal, automático <*his reaction was quick and m.* su reacción fue rápida y maquinal> II. s. IMPR. composición *f*.

mechanical drawing s. DIB., MEC. dibujo mecánico *o* industrial.

mechanical engineering s. ingeniería mecánica.

me·chan·ics (mĭ-kăn'ĭks) s.pl. [ú. con v. sing. o pl.] FÍS. mecánica; TEC. mecanismo; FIG. técnica (de un arte, ciencia, sistema).

mech·a·nism (mĕk'ə-nĭz'əm) s. mecanismo.

mech·a·nist (mĕk'ə-nĭst) s. CIENT., FILOS. mecanicista *mf*; *(mechanician)* mecánico.

mech·a·nis·tic (mĕk'ə-nĭs'tĭk) adj. BIOL., FILOS. mecanicista; *(mechanical)* mecánico.

mech·a·ni·za·tion (mĕk'ə-nĭ-zā'shən) s. mecanización *f*.

mech·a·nize (mĕk'ə-nīz') tr. **-nized, -niz·ing** mecanizar.

med·al (mĕd'l) s. medalla.

med·al·ist (mĕd'l-ĭst) s. *(engraver)* medallista *mf*; *(recipient)* persona galardonada *o* premiada (con una medalla); *(champion)* campeón *m*.

me·dal·lion (mĭ-dăl'yən) s. medallón *m*.

med·dle (mĕd'l) intr. **-dled, -dling** entrometerse, entremeterse ♦ **to m. with** *(to tamper)* manosear.

med·dler (mĕd'lər) s. entrometido, entremetido.

med·dle·some (mĕd'l-səm) adj. entrometido.

me·di·a (mē'dē-ə) [pl. de **medium**] s. medios publicitarios (prensa, radio, televisión) ♦ **advertising m.** medios de publicidad • **broadcast m.** medios de difusión *o* de radiodifusión.

me·di·a·cy (mē'dē-ə-sē) s. mediación *f*.

me·di·ae·val (mē'dē-ē'vəl, mĕd'ē-) adj. var. de **medieval**.

media event s. acontecimiento organizado en forma llamativa para alcanzar amplia publicidad (por los órganos de difusión).

me·di·an (mē'dē-ən) I. adj. *(middle)* mediano, intermedio; *(value)* medio II. s. *(median point)* punto medio; *(middle value)* valor medio; GEOM. *(line)* mediana.

me·di·ate (mē'dē-āt') tr. **-at·ed, -at·ing** *(to reconcile)* ser mediador en; *(to negotiate)* negociar como mediador (acuerdo, convenio); *(to transmit)* transmitir, comunicar —intr. mediar.

me·di·a·tion (mē'dē-ā'shən) s. *(intervention)* intervención *f*, interposición *f*; DER. *(arbitration)* mediación *f*.

me·di·a·tor (mē'dē-ā'tər) s. mediador *m*.

med·ic (mĕd'ĭk) s. *(doctor)* médico; *(surgeon)* cirujano; *(student)* estudiante de medicina *mf*; MIL. auxiliar médico.

Med·i·caid o **med·i·caid** (mĕd'ĭ-kād') s. programa de ayuda médica para los pobres (en EE. UU.) *m*.

med·i·cal (mĕd'ĭ-kəl) adj. médico <*m. treatment* tratamiento médico> II. s. FAM. reconocimiento médico.

medical examiner s. DER. médico forense.

me·dic·a·ment (mĭ-dĭk'ə-mənt, mĕd'ĭ-kə-) s. medicamento, medicina.

Med·i·care o **med·i·care** (mĕd'ĭ-kâr') s. programa de asistencia médica para ancianos (en EE. UU.) *m*.

med·i·cate (mĕd'ĭ-kāt') tr. **-cat·ed, -cat·ing** *(to treat)* medicinar; *(to permeate)* impregnar de (sustancia medicinal).

med·i·ca·tion (mĕd'ĭ-kā'shən) s. *(medicine)* medicamento; *(treatment)* tratamiento médico.

med·i·cine (mĕd'ĭ-sĭn) s. *(profession)* medicina; *(medication)* medicina, medicamento; *(charm)* amuleto; *(rite)* cura ♦ **forensic m.** medicina forense • **to give someone a taste of his own m.** pagarle a uno con la misma moneda • **to take one's m.** FIG. atenerse a las consecuencias.

medicine man s. *(of a tribe)* hechicero; *(of a medicine show)* curandero.

me·di·e·val (mē'dē-ē'vəl, mĕd'ē-) adj. HIST. medieval.

me·di·e·val·ism (mē'dē-ē'və-lĭz'əm, mĕd'ē-) s. *(customs)* medievalismo; *(study)* estudio (de la Edad Media).

me·di·e·val·ist (mē'dē-ē'və-lĭst, mĕd'ē-) s. HIST. medievalista *mf*.

me·di·o·cre (mē′dē-ō′kər) adj. mediocre.
me·di·oc·ri·ty (mē′dē-ŏk′rĭ-tē) s. [pl. **-ties**] mediocridad f.
med·i·tate (mĕd′ĭ-tāt′) tr. **-tat·ed, -tat·ing** *(to ponder)* meditar; *(to plan)* tramar. —intr. meditar, reflexionar.
med·i·ta·tion (mĕd′ĭ-tā′shən) s. meditación f.
med·i·ta·tive (mĕd′ĭ-tā′tĭv) adj. meditabundo, contemplativo.
med·i·ter·ra·ne·an (mĕd′ĭ-tə-rā′nē-ən) adj. mediterráneo ♦ **M.** del Mar Mediterráneo, mediterráneo (país).
Mediterranean fever s. MED. fiebre de Malta f, fiebre del Mediterráneo.
me·di·um (mē′dē-əm) **I.** s. [pl. **-di·a** (-dē-ə) *o* **-di·ums**] *(mean)* medio, término medio <*happy m.* justo medio>; *(means)* medio <*through the m. of* por medio de>; *(press)* medio (de comunicación) <*the mass media* los medios de comunicación de masas>; *(spiritualist)* médium mf; BIOL., FÍS. *(environment, substance)* medio <*culture m.* medio de cultivo>; *(art form)* arte m **II.** adj. mediano, regular <*at m. speed* a mediana velocidad>.
medium of exchange s. FIN. medio de cambio.
med·ley (mĕd′lē) s. [pl. **-leys**] *(jumble)* mescolanza, revoltijo; *(mixture)* mezcla; MÚS. popurrí m.
me·dul·la (mə-dŭl′ə) s. [pl. **-dul·las** *o* **-dul·lae** (-dŭl′ē)] ANAT., BOT. médula.
medulla ob·lon·ga·ta (ŏb′lông-gä′tə) s. [pl. **-ga·tas** *o* **-ga·tae** (-gä′tē)] ANAT. médula oblonga.
meek (mēk) adj. **-er, -est** *(patient)* paciente; *(humble)* humilde; *(submissive)* manso.
meer·schaum (mîr′shəm, -shôm′) s. MIN. espuma de mar; *(pipe)* pipa hecha de espuma de mar.
meet (mēt) **I.** tr. **met** (mĕt), **meet·ing** *(to come upon)* encontrar, encontrarse con <*to m. a friend at the beach* encontrarse con un amigo en la playa>; *(to be present at arrival)* recibir <*I met her at the station* la recibí en la estación>; *(to be introduced)* conocer <*very pleased to m. you* encantado de conocerle>; *(to come into the presence of)* entrevistarse con <*the Pope met the President yesterday* el Papa se entrevistó con el Presidente ayer>; *(to join)* unirse con <*route 9 meets route 20* la carretera 9 se une con la carretera 20>; *(to perceive)* percibir, ver <*there is more here than meets the eye* aquí hay más de lo que se ve>; *(to undergo)* pasar por, experimentar; *(to confront)* hacer frente a <*to m. an enemy* hacer frente a un enemigo>; *(to conform with)* salir adelante; *(to conform with)* acceder <*they met our demands* accedieron a nuestras demandas>; *(to satisfy)* satisfacer <*he meets all requirements* él satisface todos los requisitos>; *(to pay)* pagar <*we have enough money to m. our debts* tenemos suficiente dinero para pagar nuestras deudas> —intr. *(to come together)* encontrarse, verse <*we have met before* nos hemos visto antes>; *(to be joined)* empalmarse, unirse <*the roads m. one mile from here* las carreteras se unen a una milla de aquí>; *(to contend)* enfrentarse a <*the two teams m. next Sunday* los dos equipos se enfrentan el domingo próximo>; *(to make acquaintance)* conocerse <*they met by chance* se conocieron casualmente>; *(to assemble)* reunirse <*the board meets tonight* la junta se reúne esta noche>; *(to converge)* confluir ♦ **to m. someone halfway** hacer concesiones mutuas **II.** s. DEP. encuentro.
meet·ing (mē′tĭng) s. *(gathering)* reunión f; *(encounter)* encuentro; POL. mitin m; *(assembly)* asamblea, junta; RELIG. congregación f.
meet·ing·house (mē′tĭng-hous′) s. RELIG. templo.
meg·a·cy·cle (mĕg′ə-sī′kəl) s. FÍS., RAD. megaciclo; *(megahertz)* megahertzio (megaciclo por segundo).
meg·a·lith (mĕg′ə-lĭth′) s. ARQUEOL. megalito.
meg·a·lo·ma·ni·a (mĕg′ə-lō-mā′nē-ə) s. PSIC. megalomanía.
meg·a·lop·o·lis (mĕg′ə-lŏp′ə-lĭs) s. megalópolis f.
meg·a·phone (mĕg′ə-fōn′) s. ACÚS. megáfono, portavoz m.
me·gap·o·lis (mə-găp′ə-lĭs) s. var. de **megalopolis**.
meg·a·ton (mĕg′ə-tŭn′) s. FÍS. megatón (unidad de fuerza explosiva) m.
meg·a·watt (mĕg′ə-wŏt′) s. FÍS. megavatio.
me·grim (mē′grĭm) s. MED. migraña, jaqueca; ANT. *(whim)* capricho, antojo ♦ **megrims** depresión, melancolía.

mei·o·sis (mī-ō′sĭs) s. [pl. **-ses** (-sēz′)] BIOL. meiosis f, meyosis f; RET. litote f.
mel·an·cho·li·a (mĕl′ən-kō′lē-ə) s. PSIC. melancolía.
mel·an·chol·ic (mĕl′ən-kŏl′ĭk) adj. melancólico.
mel·an·chol·y (mĕl′ən-kŏl′ē) **I.** s. melancolía, tristeza **II.** adj. *(melancholic)* melancólico; *(depressing)* triste; *(pensive)* meditabundo.
mel·a·nin (mĕl′ə-nĭn) s. BIOQUÍM. melanina (pigmento).
mel·a·nism (mĕl′ə-nĭz′əm) s. BIOL., MED. melanismo, melanosis f.
mel·a·no·ma (mĕl′ə-nō′mə) s. [pl. **-mas** *o* **-ma·ta** (-mə-tə)] MED. melanoma m.
Mel·ba toast (mĕl′bə) s. CUL. tostada (de pan).
meld (mĕld) tr. & intr. unir(se), fusionar(se).
me·lee *o* **mê·lée** (mā′lā′) s. *(fighting)* pelea confusa; *(free-for-all)* pelotera, refriega; *(tumult)* tumulto.
mel·io·rate (mĕl′yə-rāt′) tr. **-rat·ed, -rat·ing** mejorar —intr. mejorarse, progresar.
mel·io·ra·tion (mĕl′yə-rā′shən) s. *(amelioration)* mejoramiento; *(improvement)* mejora, adelanto.
mel·lif·lu·ous (mə-lĭf′lōō-əs) adj. melifluo, dulce.
mel·low (mĕl′ō) **I.** adj. **-er, -est** *(full-flavored)* sazonado, maduro; *(wine)* añejo; *(resonant)* dulce; *(mature)* maduro; *(relaxed)* reposado, tranquilo; *(intoxicated)* achispado; AGR. mollar **II.** tr. & intr. *(fruit, person)* madurar; *(wine)* añejar(se); FIG. *(to soften)* suavizar(se).
me·lo·de·on (mə-lō′dē-ən) s. MÚS. melodión m, melodina.
me·lod·ic (mə-lŏd′ĭk) adj. melódico.
me·lo·di·ous (mə-lō′dē-əs) adj. melodioso, canoro.
mel·o·dra·ma (mĕl′ə-drä′mə, -drăm′ə) s. melodrama m.
mel·o·dra·mat·ic (mĕl′ə-drə-măt′ĭk) adj. *(emotional)* melodramático; *(histrionic)* histriónico.
mel·o·dra·mat·ics (mĕl′ə-drə-măt′ĭks) s. [ú. con v. sing. o pl.] *(theatrics)* teatralidad f; *(conduct)* conducta melodramática.
mel·o·dy (mĕl′ə-dē) s. [pl. **-dies**] MÚS. *(harmony)* melodía; *(musical quality)* aire melódico.
mel·on (mĕl′ən) s. BOT. melón m; *(watermelon)* sandía.
melt (mĕlt) **I.** intr. *(to liquefy)* derretirse (nieve, helado); *(to dissolve)* disolverse, diluirse (azúcar, gelatina); METAL. fundirse; *(to vanish)* desvanecerse (niebla, noche); FIG. *(to merge)* fusionarse, fundirse (colores); *(to soften)* ablandarse, suavizarse (sentimientos) —tr. *(to liquefy)* licuar, derretir; *(to dissolve)* disolver; *(to smelt)* fundir; FIG. *(to blend)* mezclar, combinar; *(to soften)* ablandar, suavizar **II.** s. *(melting)* derretimiento; METAL. *(smelting)* fundición f; *(amount smelted)* hornada, colada.
melt·down (mĕlt′doun′) s. FÍS. fusión del núcleo del reactor nuclear f.
melting point s. FÍS. punto de fusión.
melting pot s. FÍS., QUÍM. crisol m, fusor m; FIG. crisol de razas (díc. de EE. UU.).
mem·ber (mĕm′bər) s. *(part of a group)* socio, miembro; BOT., GRAM., MAT. miembro; ANAT. *(limb)* extremidad f, miembro; *(penis)* pene m.
mem·ber·ship (mĕm′bər-shĭp′) s. *(in a group)* calidad de miembro f; *(number)* número total de socios o miembros (en un grupo).
mem·brane (mĕm′brān′) s. BIOL., QUÍM. membrana.
mem·bra·nous (mĕm′brə-nəs) adj. membranoso.
me·men·to (mə-mĕn′tō) s. [pl. **-tos** *o* **-toes**] recuerdo, recordatorio.
mem·o (mĕm′ō) s. [pl. **-os**] memorándum m.
mem·oir (mĕm′wär′) s. *(biography)* biografía; *(autobiography)* autobiografía ♦ **to write one's memoirs** escribir uno sus memorias.
mem·o·ra·bil·i·a (mĕm′ər-ə-bĭl′ē-ə) s.pl. *(events)* acontecimientos o eventos memorables; *(mementos)* recuerdos.
mem·o·ra·ble (mĕm′ər-ə-bəl) adj. memorable, notable.
mem·o·ran·dum (mĕm′ə-răn′dəm) s. [pl. **-dums** *o* **-da** (-də)] *(short note)* nota, apunte m; COM., DER., DIPL. memorándum m.
me·mo·ri·al (mə-môr′ē-əl) **I.** s. *(monument)* monumento conmemorativo; *(petition)* petición f; memorial m **II.** adj. conmemorativo.

Memorial Day s. día conmemorativo de los caídos (en EE. UU.).

me·mo·ri·al·ize (mə-môr′ē-ə-līz′) tr. **-ized, -iz·ing** *(to commemorate)* conmemorar; *(to petition)* dirigir (una petición) a.

mem·o·rize (mĕm′ə-rīz′) tr. **-rized, -riz·ing** memorizar, aprender de memoria.

mem·o·ry (mĕm′ə-rē) s. [pl. **-ries**] *(recall)* memoria <*to have an excellent m.* tener una memoria excelente>; *(recollection)* recuerdo <*childhood memories* recuerdos de niñez>; COMPUT. memoria ♦ **from m.** de memoria • **if my m. serves me well** si no me falla la memoria • **in m. of** en memoria o en conmemoración de • **to call to m.** traer a la memoria • **to commit something to m.** aprenderse algo de memoria • **within my m.** que yo recuerde.

men (mĕn) pl. de **man.**

men·ace (mĕn′ĭs) **I.** s. *(threat)* amenaza; *(annoying person)* pesado **II.** tr. & intr. **-aced, -ac·ing** amenazar.

me·nag·er·ie (mə-năj′ə-rē) s. ZOOL. *(collection)* colección de animales salvajes *f*; *(place)* casa de fieras.

mend (mĕnd) **I.** tr. *(to repair)* reparar, arreglar; TEJ. remendar, zurcir; FIG. *(to reform)* reformar, mejorar; *(rectify)* remediar ♦ **to one's ways** enmendarse —intr. *(to heal)* curar, sanar; FIG. *(to correct)* enmendarse, reformarse **II.** s. *(improvement)* mejoría; *(repair)* reparación *f*; *(patch)* remiendo; *(darn)* zurcido ♦ **to be on the m.** ir mejorando.

men·da·cious (mĕn-dā′shəs) adj. mentiroso, mendaz.

men·dac·i·ty (mĕn-dăs′ĭ-tē) s. mendacidad *f*, mentira.

men·de·le·vi·um (mĕn′dl-ē′vē-əm) s. QUÍM. mendelevio.

Men·de·li·an (mĕn-dē′lē-ən) adj. BIOL. mendeliano.

men·di·cant (mĕn′dĭ-kənt) **I.** adj. mendicante **II.** s. *(beggar)* mendigo; RELIG. mendicante *mf*.

men·folk (mĕn′fōk′) o **men·folks** (-fōks′) s.pl. *(men)* hombres *m*; *(male members)* varones, miembros masculinos (de una comunidad).

me·ni·al (mē′nē-əl) **I.** adj. *(domestic)* doméstico; *(servile)* servil **II.** s. criado, sirviente *m*.

me·nin·ges (mə-nĭn′jēz) s. MED. meninges *f*.

men·in·gi·tis (mĕn′ĭn-jī′tĭs) s. MED. meningitis *f*.

Men·non·ite (mĕn′ə-nīt′) s. RELIG. menonita.

men·o·pause (mĕn′ə-pôz′) s. FISIOL. menopausia.

Me·no·rah (mə-nôr′ə) s. RELIG. menora.

Me·nor·ca (mē-nôr′kä) s. GEOG. Minorca.

men·or·rha·gi·a (mĕn′ə-rā′jē-ə) s. MED. menorragia.

men·ses (mĕn′sēz′) s.pl. [ú. con v. sing. o pl.] FISIOL. menstruo, menstruación *f*.

men's room s. servicio para hombres.

men·stru·al (mĕn′strōō-əl) adj. FISIOL. menstrual; *(monthly)* mensual.

men·stru·ate (mĕn′strōō-āt′) intr. **-at·ed, -at·ing** FISIOL. menstruar.

men·stru·a·tion (mĕn′strōō-ā′shən) s. FISIOL. menstruación *f*.

men·stru·ous (mĕn′strōō-əs) adj. var. de **menstrual.**

men·su·ra·ble (mĕn′sər-ə-bəl, -shər-) adj. mensurable.

men·su·ral (mĕn′sər-əl, -shər-) adj. *(measurable)* mensurable; MÚS. que tiene notas musicales de un valor fijo.

men·su·ra·tion (mĕn′sə-rā′shən, -shə-) s. *(act)* medición *f*, mensura; MAT. cálculo de magnitudes geométricas.

mens·wear (mĕnz′wâr′) s. COST. ropa para hombres.

men·tal (mĕn′tl) adj. *(intellectual)* mental; *(performed in the mind)* mental <*m. arithmetic* cálculo mental>; *(insane)* mental, alienado <*a m. patient* un enfermo mental>; *(psychiatric)* psiquiátrico <*m. hospital* hospital psiquiátrico> ♦ **m. derangement** MED. alienación mental.

mental age s. edad mental *f*.

men·tal·i·ty (mĕn-tăl′ĭ-tē) s. [pl. **-ties**] *(intellectual capabilities)* mentalidad *f*; *(turn of mind)* modo de pensar.

mental retardation s. retardación mental *f*.

men·thol (mĕn′thôl′) s. FARM., QUÍM. mentol *m*.

men·tho·lat·ed (mĕn′thə-lā′tĭd) adj. mentolado.

men·tion (mĕn′shən) **I.** tr. mencionar, aludir a **II.** s. *(allusion)* mención *f*, alusión *f* ♦ **honorable m.** mención honorífica, accésit (en un concurso) • **not worthy of m.** sin importancia • **to make m. of** hacer mención de.

Men·tor (mĕn′tôr′) s. MITOL. Mentor ♦ **m.** mentor *m*, tutor *m*.

men·u (mĕn′yōō, mā′nyōō) s. menú *m*, carta.

me·ow (mē-ou′) **I.** s. maullido **II.** intr. maullar.

Meph·i·stoph·e·les (mĕf′ĭ-stŏf′ə-lēz′) s. Mefistófeles.

me·phi·tis (mə-fī′tĭs) s. *(stench)* hedor *m*, emanación mefítica (de la tierra).

mer·can·tile (mûr′kən-tēl′, -tīl′) adj. COM. mercantil, comercial.

mer·can·til·ism (mûr′kən-tē′-līz′əm, -tĭ′-) ECON. POL. s. *(theory)* mercantilismo; *(commercialism)* comercialismo.

mer·can·til·ist (mûr′kən-tē′lĭst, -tĭ′-) s. mercantilista *mf*.

mer·ce·nar·y (mûr′sə-nĕr′ē) **I.** adj. *(selfish)* interesado; MIL. mercenario **II.** s. [pl. **-ies**] mercenario.

mer·cer (mûr′sər) s. G.B., TEJ. mercero.

mer·chan·dise (mûr′chən-dīs′) **I.** s. mercancía, mercadería **II.** tr. (-dīz′) **-dised, -dis·ing** *(to buy and sell)* comerciar; *(to promote)* promover (la venta de) —intr. negociar.

mer·chan·dis·er (mûr′chən-dī′zər) s. COM. promotor de ventas *m*.

mer·chant (mûr′chənt) **I.** s. *(tradesman)* mercader *m*, comerciante *mf*; *(shopkeeper)* tendero, vendedor *m* **II.** adj. *(of commercial trade)* comercial, mercantil; MARÍT. mercante.

mer·chant·man (mûr′chənt-mən) s. [pl. **-men**] MARÍT. buque mercante *m*; ANT. *(merchant)* mercader *m*.

merchant marine s. MARÍT. marina mercante (flota y personal).

mer·ci·ful (mûr′sĭ-fəl) adj. misericordioso, compasivo.

mer·ci·ful·ly (mûr′sĭ-fə-lē) adv. misericordiosamente, compasivamente.

mer·ci·less (mûr′sĭ-lĭs) adj. despiadado, cruel.

mer·cu·rate (mûr′kyə-rāt′) tr. **-rat·ed, -rat·ing** QUÍM. tratar o combinar con mercurio.

mer·cu·ri·al (mər-kyŏŏr′ē-əl) adj. volátil; QUÍM. mercurial, mercúrico ♦ **M.** ASTRON., MITOL. mercurial.

mer·cu·ric (mər-kyŏŏr′ĭk) adj. QUÍM. mercúrico.

mer·cu·ro·chrome (mər-kyŏŏr′ə-krōm′) s. FARM. mercurocromo.

mer·cu·ry (mûr′kyə-rē) s. QUÍM. mercurio; FIG. *(temperature)* temperatura <*the m. is falling* la temperatura está bajando> ♦ **M.** ASTRON., MITOL. Mercurio.

mer·cy (mûr′sē) s. [pl. **-cies**] *(clemency)* clemencia, piedad *f*; *(compassion)* compasión *f*, misericordia; *(relief)* alivio ♦ **to be at the m. of** estar a (la) merced de • **to have m. on** tener piedad de, tener misericordia de • **to show m. to** demostrar compasión hacia.

mercy killing s. eutanasia.

mere[1] (mîr) adj. *(simple)* mero, puro <*it was m. nonsense* fueron puros disparates>; *(no more than)* tan sólo, no más que <*he is a m. employee* no es más que un empleado>.

mere[2] (mîr) s. *(small lake)* laguna; *(marsh)* pantano.

mere·ly (mîr′lē) adv. *(simply)* meramente, simplemente <*not m. a lie, but perjury* no simplemente una mentira, sino falso testimonio>; *(no more than)* tan sólo, no más que <*she's m. an assistant* no es más que una ayudanta>; *(just)* sólo, solamente <*I m. told him the truth* sólo le dije la verdad>.

mer·e·tri·cious (mĕr′ĭ-trĭsh′əs) adj. *(gaudy)* llamativo, chillón; *(insincere)* engañoso.

mer·gan·ser (mər-găn′sər) s. ORNIT. mergo.

merge (mûrj) tr. & intr. **merged, merg·ing** *(to unite)* unir(se), combinar(se); COM. fusionar(se), unir(se).

merg·er (mûr′jər) s. COM. fusión *f*, unión *f*.

me·rid·i·an (mə-rĭd′ē-ən) **I.** s. ASTRON., GEOG. meridiano **II.** adj. ASTRON., GEOG. meridiano; FIG. *(maximal)* máximo.

me·rid·i·o·nal (mə-rĭd′ē-ə-nəl) adj. ASTRON., GEOG. meridiano, meridional.

me·ringue (mə-răng′) s. CUL. merengue *m*.

me·ri·no (mə-rē′nō) s. [pl. **-nos**] ZOOL. merino (oveja y lana).

mer·it (mĕr′ĭt) **I.** s. *(quality)* mérito <*a book of m.* un libro de mérito>; *(virtue)* mérito; *(praiseworthy feature)* ventaja <*the merits of country life* las ventajas de la vida rural> ♦ **m. raise** aumento (de sueldo) por excelencia • **merits**

DER. fondo • **on one's merits** según las cualidades de uno **II.** tr. & intr. merecer.

mer·i·toc·ra·cy (mĕr′ĭ-tŏk′rə-sē) s. [pl. **-cies**] *(class)* élite intelectual *o* académica; POL. gobierno por dicha élite.

mer·i·to·ri·ous (mĕr′ĭ-tôr′ē-əs) adj. meritorio.

mer·lin (mûr′lĭn) s. ORNIT. esmerejón *m.*

Mer·lin (mûr′lĭn) s. Merlín *m.*

mer·maid (mûr′mād′) s. MITOL. sirena.

mer·man (mûr′măn′) s. [pl. **-men** (-mĕn′)] MITOL. tritón *m.*

mer·ri·ly (mĕr′ĭ-lē) adv. *(in a jolly manner)* alegremente; *(festively)* alborozadamente.

mer·ri·ment (mĕr′ĭ-mənt) s. *(gaiety)* alegría, alborozo; *(amusement)* diversión *f; (laughter)* risas.

mer·ry (mĕr′ē) adj. **-ri·er, -ri·est** *(jolly)* alegre <*a m. tune* una melodía alegre>; *(entertaining)* divertido; *(brisk)* ligero ♦ **the more the merrier** mientras más, mejor • **M. Christmas** Felices Pascuas, Feliz Navidad • **to make m.** divertirse.

mer·ry-go-round (mĕr′ē-gō-round′) s. *(platform)* tiovivo, carrusel *m;* FIG. *(whirl)* giro rápido, remolino.

mer·ry·mak·ing (mĕr′ē-mā′kĭng) s. fiesta, juerga.

mes·cal (mĕ-skăl′) s. BOT. mezcal *m; (liquor)* aguardiente de mezcal *m; (agave)* pita (planta).

mes·ca·line (mĕs′kə-lēn′) s. QUÍM. mescalina (droga alucinógena).

mesh (mĕsh) **I.** s. *(in a network)* malla <*a fishnet of fine m.* una red de malla fina>; MEC. *(of gear teeth)* engranaje *m* ♦ **meshes** *(cords, wires)* malla; FIG. *(webs)* redes <*the meshes of politics* las redes de la política> • **to be out of m.** estar desengranado **II.** tr. *(to entangle)* enredar; MEC. engranar ♦ **to m. together** FIG. enlazar —intr. *(to become entangled)* enredarse; MEC. engranar; FIG. *(to harmonize)* encajar.

mesh·work (mĕsh′wûrk′) s. retículo, red *f.*

mes·mer·ism (mĕz′mə-rĭz′əm) s. mesmerismo.

mes·mer·ize (mĕz′mə-rīz′) tr. **-ized, -iz·ing** *(to hypnotize)* hipnotizar; *(to enthrall)* cautivar, encantar.

mes·o·derm (mĕz′ə-dûrm′) s. BIOL. mesodermo.

mes·o·morph (mĕz′ə-môrf′) s. ANTROP. mesomorfo.

mes·on (mĕz′ŏn′, mē′zŏn′) s. FÍS., QUÍM. mesón (partícula subatómica) *m.*

mes·o·sphere (mĕz′ə-sfîr′) s. METEOR. mesosfera.

mes·quite (mĕ-skēt′) s. BOT. mezquite *m.*

mess (mĕs) **I.** s. *(disorder)* caos *m,* desorden *m* <*this house is a m.* esta casa es un desorden>; *(dirty condition)* asquerosidad *f* <*this sink is a m.!* ¡este lavabo es una asquerosidad!> *(difficulty)* embrollo, lío <*to get oneself into a m.* meterse en un lío>; FAM. *(person)* persona de aspecto sucio *o* desaliñado; *(serving)* ración *f,* plato (de comida); MIL. *(dining hall)* comedor *m; (meal)* rancho, comida ♦ **to make a m. of** *(to soil)* ensuciar; *(to disarrange)* desordenar; *(to spoil)* estropear, echar a perder **II.** tr. ♦ **to m. up** *(to soil)* ensuciar <*he messed up the wall with grafitti* ensució la pared con garabatos>; *(to disarrange)* desordenar, desarreglar; *(to spoil)* estropear, echar a perder <*to m. up a test* echar a perder un examen>; JER. *(to manhandle)* maltratar <*the thief messed up his victim* el ladrón maltrató a su víctima> —intr. *(to disarrange)* desordenar; *(to meddle in)* entrometerse en, meterse en ♦ **to m. around with** FAM. *(to putter)* pasar el tiempo, entretenerse con <*on his vacation, he messed around with his books* en las vacaciones se entretuvo con sus libros>; *(to associate with)* tener trato *o* tratarse con; *(to have sex with)* tener relaciones sexuales con • **to m. with** FAM. molestar <*don't m. with me* no me molestes>.

mes·sage (mĕs′ĭj) s. mensaje *m.*

mes·sen·ger (mĕs′ən-jər) s. *(courier)* mensajero; ANT. *(forerunner)* heraldo, precursor *m;* MARÍT. virador *m.*

mess hall s. comedor *m.*

Mes·si·ah (mə-sī′ə) s. RELIG. Mesías *m,* redentor futuro de Israel (para los judíos) *m; (among Christians)* Mesías, Jesucristo ♦ **m.** mesías, redentor.

mes·si·an·ic *o* **Mes·si·an·ic** (mĕs′ē-ăn′ĭk) adj. *(of a messiah)* mesiánico; RELIG. Mesiánico, del Mesías.

mes·si·a·nism (mĕs′ē-ə-nĭz′əm, mə-sī′ə-) s. RELIG. mesianismo, creencia en un mesías; FIG. *(strong belief)* confianza en un mesías.

mess kit s. juego portátil de efectos de cocina y de mesa.

mess·mate (mĕs′māt′) s. MIL. compañero de rancho.

Messrs. (mĕs′ərz) s.pl. Sres. (abreviatura).

mess·y (mĕs′ē) adj. **-i·er, -i·est** *(disorderly)* revuelto, desordenado; *(filthy)* asqueroso, sucio; *(slovenly)* desaseado; *(imprecise)* caótico, confuso <*a m. essay* un ensayo caótico>; *(complicated)* complicado <*a m. divorce* un divorcio complicado>.

met (mĕt) pret. y part. p. de **meet.**

met·a·bol·ic (mĕt′ə-bŏl′ĭk) adj. BIOL., FISIOL. metabólico, del metabolismo; ENTOM. metabólico, metamórfico.

me·tab·o·lism (mə-tăb′ə-lĭz′əm) s. BIOL., FISIOL. metabolismo; ENTOM. metamorfosis *f.*

me·tab·o·lize (mə-tăb′ə-līz′) tr. & intr. **-lized, -liz·ing** FISIOL. metabolizar(se), transformar(se) mediante el metabolismo.

met·a·eth·ics (mĕt′ə-ĕth′ĭks) s. [ú. con v. sing.] metaética.

met·a·gen·e·sis (mĕt′ə-jĕn′ĭ-sĭs) s. BIOL. metagénesis *f.*

met·al (mĕt′l) **I.** s. *(substance)* metal *m; (metallic object)* objeto de metal; FIG. *(mettle)* temple *m,* carácter *m* **II.** tr. *(roads)* cubrir con grava, macadamizar (un camino); *(to cover with metal)* cubrir con metal (un objeto).

met·a·lin·guis·tics (mĕt′ə-lĭng-gwĭs′tĭks) s. [ú. con v. sing.] metalingüística.

met·al·lic (mə-tăl′ĭk) adj. metálico.

met·al·log·ra·phy (mĕt′l-ŏg′rə-fē) s. METAL. metalografía.

met·al·loid (mĕt′l-oid′) QUÍM. **I.** s. metaloide *m* **II.** adj. metalóidico, metaloideo.

met·al·lur·gy (mĕt′l-ûr′jē) s. metalurgia.

met·al·work (mĕt′l-wûrk′) s. *(craft)* metalistería, trabajo del metal; *(things)* objetos de metal.

met·a·mor·phic (mĕt′ə-môr′fĭk) adj. metamórfico.

met·a·mor·phism (mĕt′ə-môr′fĭz′əm) s. GEOL. *(alteration)* metamorfismo; *(metamorphosis)* metamorfosis *f.*

met·a·mor·phose (mĕt′ə-môr′fōz′, -fōs′) tr. & intr. metamorfosear(se), transformar(se) ♦ **to m. into** metamorfosearse en.

met·a·mor·pho·sis (mĕt′ə-môr′fə-sĭs) s. [pl. **-ses** (-sēz′)] metamorfosis *f,* transformación *f.*

met·a·mor·phous (mĕt′ə-môr′fəs) adj. var. de **metamorphic.**

met·a·phor (mĕt′ə-fôr′) s. RET. metáfora.

met·a·phor·ic (mĕt′ə-fôr′ĭk) *o* **met·a·phor·i·cal** (-ĭ-kəl) adj. metafórico.

met·a·phrase (mĕt′ə-frāz′) LIT. **I.** s. metafrasis *f,* traducción literal *f* **II.** tr. manipular una traducción para alterar sutilmente su sentido.

met·a·phys·i·cal (mĕt′ə-fĭz′ĭ-kəl) adj. metafísico.

met·a·phys·ics (mĕt′ə-fĭz′ĭks) s. [ú. con v. sing.] FILOS. metafísica.

me·tas·ta·sis (mə-tăs′tə-sĭs) s. [pl. **-ses** (-sēz′)] MED. metástasis *f.*

met·a·tar·sal (mĕt′ə-tär′səl) ANAT. **I.** adj. metatarsiano, del metatarso **II.** s. hueso metatarsiano.

met·a·tar·sus (mĕt′ə-tär′səs) s. [pl. **-si** (-sī′)] ANAT. metatarso.

mete¹ (mĕt) tr. **met·ed, met·ing** *(to distribute)* repartir, distribuir; *(to deal out)* imponer, dar <*to m. out punishment* dar un castigo>.

mete² (mĕt) s. confín *m,* límite *m.*

me·tem·psy·cho·sis (mə-tĕm′sī-kō′sĭs) s. [pl. **-ses** (-sēz′)] metempsicosis *f,* transmigración *f.*

me·te·or (mē′tē-ər) s. ASTRON. estrella fugaz, bólido; *(meteoroid)* meteorito; METEOR. meteoro, meteoro (fenómeno atmosférico).

me·te·or·ic (mē′tē-ôr′ĭk) adj. ASTRON., METEOR. meteórico; FIG. *(like a meteor)* meteórico <*a m. political career* una carrera política meteórica>; METEOR. atmosférico, de la atmósfera.

me·te·or·ite (mē′tē-ə-rīt′) s. ASTRON. meteorito, piedra meteórica.

me·te·or·oid (mē′tē-ə-roid′) s. ASTRON. meteorito, aerolito.

me·te·or·o·log·i·cal (mē′tē-ə-rə-lŏj′ĭ-kəl) adj. meteorológico.

me·te·or·ol·o·gist (mē'tē-ə-rŏl'ə-jĭst) s. meteorólogo, meteorologista *mf.*

me·te·or·ol·o·gy (mē'tē-ə-rŏl'ə-jē) s. meteorología.

meteor shower s. METEOR. lluvia de estrellas fugaces.

me·ter¹ (mē'tər) s. POÉT. metro; MÚS. tiempo, compás *m.*

me·ter² (mē'tər) s. FÍS. metro (unidad de longitud).

me·ter³ (mē'tər) s. *(device)* contador *m.*

meth·a·done hydrochloride (mĕth'ə-dōn') s. FARM. hidrocloruro de metadona.

meth·am·phet·a·mine (mĕth'ăm-fĕt'ə-mēn', -mĭn) s. FARM. metanfetamina.

meth·ane (mĕth'ān') s. QUÍM. metano.

meth·od (mĕth'əd) s. *(plan)* método; *(procedure)* método, procedimiento <*practical methods* procedimientos prácticos>; *(of payment)* modo (de pagar).

me·thod·i·cal (mə-thŏd'ĭ-kəl) *o* **me·thod·ic** (-ĭk) metódico.

Meth·od·ism (mĕth'ə-dĭz'əm) s. RELIG. metodismo, doctrina protestante ◆ **m.** adherencia tenaz al procedimiento sistemático.

Meth·od·ist (mĕth'ə-dĭst) s. RELIG. metodista *mf* ◆ **m.** persona metódica.

meth·od·ize (mĕth'ə-dīz') tr. **-ized, -iz·ing** metodizar, sistematizar.

meth·od·o·log·i·cal (mĕth'ə-də-lŏj'ĭ-kəl) adj. metodológico.

meth·od·ol·o·gy (mĕth'ə-dŏl'ə-jē) s. [pl. **-gies**] metodología.

meth·yl (mĕth'əl) s. QUÍM. metilo.

meth·yl·ate (mĕth'ə-lāt') QUÍM. I. s. metilato II. tr. mezclar con alcohol metílico, desnaturalizar <*methylated spirit* alcohol desnaturalizado>; *(to combine with the methyl radical)* combinar con metilo.

methyl chloride s. QUÍM. cloruro de metilo.

me·tic·u·lous (mə-tĭk'yə-ləs) adj. *(careful)* meticuloso; *(overscrupulous)* minucioso.

me·tic·u·lous·ness (mə-tĭk'yə-ləs-nĭs) s. meticulosidad *f.*

mé·tier (mā-tyā') s. *(occupation)* oficio, profesión *f; (specialty)* especialidad *f.*

me·ton·y·my (mə-tŏn'ə-mē) s. [pl. **-mies**] RET. metonimia.

me·tre (mē'tər) s. G.B. var. de **meter¹** y **meter²**.

met·ric¹ (mĕt'rĭk) adj. métrico, del sistema métrico.

met·ric² (mĕt'rĭk) s. *(standard)* patrón de medida *m;* MAT. métrica (función geométrica).

met·ri·cal (mĕt'rĭ-kəl) adj. GRAM. métrico, de la métrica; *(of measurement)* métrico, del metro.

met·rics (mĕt'rĭks) s. [ú. con v. sing.] GRAM. métrica.

metric system s. FÍS. sistema métrico (de pesas y medidas).

metric ton s. tonelada métrica.

met·ro (mĕt'rō) s. [pl. **-ros**] metro, ferrocarril subterráneo.

met·ro·nome (mĕt'rə-nōm') s. MÚS. metrónomo.

me·trop·o·lis (mə-trŏp'ə-lĭs) s. metrópoli *f.*

met·ro·pol·i·tan (mĕt'rə-pŏl'ĭ-tn) I. adj. metropolitano II. s. RELIG. metropolitano; *(resident)* habitante de una metrópoli *m.*

met·tle (mĕt'l) s. *(character)* entereza; *(courage)* temple *m,* valor *m* <*to show one's m. in combat* mostrar el valor de uno en el combate> ◆ **on one's m.** puesto a prueba • **to prove one's m.** dar pruebas del valor de uno.

met·tle·some (mĕt'l-səm) adj. valiente, animoso.

mew¹ (myōō) s. *(cage)* jaula para halcones; *(hideaway)* escondite *m; (small street)* callejón *m,* callejuela.

mew² (myōō) I. intr. maullar, mayar II. s. maullido.

mewl (myōōl) intr. lloriquear, gimotear.

Mex·i·can (mĕk'sĭ-kən) adj. & s. mexicano, mejicano.

Mex·i·co (mĕk'sĭ-kō') s. México, Méjico.

mez·za·nine (mĕz'ə-nēn') s. entresuelo.

mez·zo·tint (mĕt'sō-tĭnt') s. ARTE. *(method of engraving)* mediatinta; *(print)* grabado a buril.

mi (mē) s. MÚS. mi *m.*

mi·as·ma (mī-ăz'mə, mē-) s. [pl. **-mas** *o* **-ma·ta** (-mə-tə)] miasma *m.*

mi·ca (mī'kə) s. MIN. mica.

Mi·cah (mī'kə) s. BÍBL. Miqueas.

mice (mīs) pl. de **mouse**.

Mich·ael·mas (mĭk'əl-məs) s. día de San Miguel *m.*

Mick·ey Finn (mĭk'ē fĭn') s. JER. bebida alcohólica con alguna droga.

mi·cro (mī'krō) s. FAM., COMPUT. microordenador *m,* microcomputadora.

mi·cro·a·nal·y·sis (mī'krō-ə-năl'ĭ-sĭs) s. QUÍM. microanálisis *m.*

mi·crobe (mī'krōb') s. BACT. microbio, germen *m.*

mi·cro·bi·cide (mī-krō'bĭ-sīd') s. microbicida, bactericida.

mi·cro·bi·ol·o·gy (mī'krō-bī-ŏl'ə-jē) s. microbiología.

mi·cro·bus (mī'krō-bŭs') s. AUTO. microbús *m.*

mi·cro·ceph·a·ly (mī'krō-sĕf'ə-lē) s. MED. microcefalia.

mi·cro·chem·is·try (mī'krō-kĕm'ĭ-strē) s. QUÍM. microquímica.

mi·cro·chip (mī'krō-chĭp') s. COMPUT. microchip *m,* microplaqueta.

mi·cro·cir·cuit (mī'krō-sûr'kĭt) s. ELECTRÓN. microcircuito.

mi·cro·com·put·er (mī'krō-kəm-pyōō'tər) s. COMPUT. microordenador *m,* microcomputadora.

mi·cro·cosm (mī'krə-kŏz'əm) s. microcosmo.

mi·cro·ec·o·nom·ics (mī'krō-ĕk'ə-nŏm'ĭks, -ē'kə-) s. [ú. con v. sing.] microeconomía.

mi·cro·e·lec·tron·ics (mī'krō-ĭ-lĕk-trŏn'ĭks) s. [ú. con v. sing.] ELECTRÓN. microelectrónica.

mi·cro·fiche (mī'krō-fēsh') s. [pl. **microfiche** *o* **-fich·es**] COMPUT. microficha.

mi·cro·film (mī'krə-fĭlm') I. s. FOTOG. micropelícula, microfilm *m* II. tr. reproducir en microfilm.

mi·crog·ra·phy (mī-krŏg'rə-fē) s. FÍS. micrografía.

mi·crom·e·ter (mī-krŏm'ĭ-tər) s. FÍS. micrómetro.

mi·crom·e·try (mī-krŏm'ĭ-trē) s. FÍS. micrometría.

mi·cron (mī'krŏn') s. [pl. **-crons** *o* **-cra** (-krə)] FÍS. micrón *m,* micra (unidad de longitud).

mi·cro·or·gan·ism (mī'krō-ôr'gə-nĭz'əm) s. BIOL. microorganismo.

mi·cro·phone (mī'krə-fōn') s. ACÚS., RAD. micrófono.

mi·cro·proc·es·sor (mī'krō-prŏs'ĕs-ər) s. COMPUT. microprocesador *m.*

mi·cro·scope (mī'krə-skōp') s. FÍS. microscopio.

mi·cro·scop·ic (mī'krə-skŏp'ĭk) *o* **mi·cro·scop·i·cal** (-ĭ-kəl) adj. microscópico.

mi·cros·co·py (mī-krŏs'kə-pē) s. FÍS. microscopia, microscopía.

mi·cro·sec·ond (mī'krō-sĕk'ənd) s. microsegundo.

mi·cro·sur·ger·y (mī'krō-sûr'jə-rē) s. CIR. microcirugía.

mi·cro·wave (mī'krə-wāv') s. ELECTRÓN., RAD. microonda, onda ultracorta.

microwave oven s. horno de microondas.

mic·tu·rate (mĭk'chə-rāt') intr. **-rat·ed, -rat·ing** orinar, mear.

mid¹ (mĭd) adj. *(middle)* medio <*midafternoon* media tarde>; FONÉT. intermedio ◆ **in mid-April** a mediados de abril • **in m. course** a media carrera • **in m. ocean** en medio del océano.

mid² (mĭd) prep. POÉT. entre, en medio de.

mid·air (mĭd'âr') s. el aire, punto en medio del aire <*floating in m.* flotando en el aire> ◆ **m. collision** AVIA. choque en pleno vuelo.

Mi·das (mī'dəs) s. MITOL. Midas.

mid·brain (mĭd'brān') s. ANAT. mesencéfalo.

mid·day (mĭd'dā') I. s. mediodía *m* II. adj. del mediodía.

mid·den (mĭd'n) s. muladar *m,* estercolero.

mid·dle (mĭd'l) I. adj. *(halfway)* medio <*the m. point* el punto medio>; *(intermediate)* intermedio; *(medium)* mediano <*a man of m. age* un hombre de edad mediana>; *(in the center)* (de) en medio; LÓG. medio; GRAM. medio ◆ **m. man** intermediario • **M. West** GEOG. estados centrales del norte de EE. UU. II. s. *(center)* centro <*the m. of a circle* el centro de un círculo>; *(inside)* medio, mitad *f* <*in the m. of the book* en la mitad del libro>; *(mean)* medio, punto medio; *(waist)* cintura; LÓG. término medio; GRAM. voz media ◆ **in the m. of** en medio de III. tr. **-dled, -dling** *(to center)* centrar, colocar en el centro; MARÍT. *(to fold)* doblar por la mitad, doblar en dos.

middle age s. edad mediana, edad madura.

mid·dle-aged (mĭd'l-ājd') adj. de mediana edad, de edad madura.

Middle Ages s.pl. Edad Media.
Middle America s. *(U.S. middle class)* clase media estadounidense, considerada conservadora; *(American heartland)* región central de EE. UU. que se considera compuesta de pequeñas ciudades y pueblos.
mid·dle·brow (mĭd'l-brou') I. s. FAM. persona de cultura mediana II. adj. de cultura mediana.
middle class s. clase media.
mid·dle-class (mĭd'l-klăs') adj. de la clase media.
middle distance s. ARTE. segundo plano, segundo término; DEP. medio fondo, semifondo.
middle ear s. ANAT. oído medio.
Middle East s. GEOG. Oriente Medio.
Middle Eastern adj. del Oriente Medio.
middle ground s. ARTE. segundo término, segundo plano; *(point of view)* punto de vista intermedio.
mid·dle·man (mĭd'l-măn') s. [pl. **-men** (-měn')] intermediario.
middle management s. grupo de personas que ocupan puestos directivos intermedios.
mid·dle·most (mĭd'l-mōst') adj. central.
mid·dle-of-the-road (mĭd'l-əv-thə-rōd') adj. *(moderate)* moderado; POL. centrista.
middle school s. EDUC. escuela en la que se estudia desde el grado quinto al octavo, escuela intermedia.
mid·dle·weight (mĭd'l-wāt') s. DEP. peso medio (en el boxeo).
mid·dling (mĭd'lĭng) adj. *(medium)* mediano; *(mediocre)* ordinario, mediocre.
mid·dy (mĭd'ē) s. [pl. **-dies**] FAM. *(midshipman)* guardiamarina m; *(blouse)* marinera.
Mid·east (mĭd'ēst') s. GEOG. Oriente Medio.
midge (mĭj) s. ENTOM. mosca, mosquito; *(small person)* persona pequeña.
midg·et (mĭj'ĭt) I. s. *(small person)* enano; *(small object)* objeto pequeño II. adj. *(miniature)* en miniatura *<a m. automobile* un automóvil en miniatura>.
mid·i (mĭd'ē) s. falda que cae hasta media pierna.
mid·land (mĭd'lənd) I. s. parte central (de un país o región) f II. adj. del interior, del centro.
mid·most (mĭd'mōst') I. adj. central II. adv. en el centro, en el medio.
mid·night (mĭd'nīt') s. *(time)* medianoche f; *(intense darkness)* obscuridad intensa ♦ **to burn the m. oil** FIG. quemarse las pestañas o las cejas.
midnight sun s. sol de medianoche m.
mid·point (mĭd'point') s. punto céntrico.
mid·riff (mĭd'rĭf') s. ANAT. diafragma m, abdomen superior m.
mid·sec·tion (mĭd'sĕk'shən) s. sección media (esp. la parte abdominal del cuerpo).
mid·ship (mĭd'shĭp') adj. MARÍT. del medio del barco, en el medio del barco.
mid·ship·man (mĭd'shĭp'mən) s. [pl. **-men**] guardiamarina m.
mid·ships (mĭd'shĭps') adv. MARÍT. en medio del barco.
midst (mĭdst) I. s. medio ♦ **in our m.** entre nosotros • **in the m. of** *(in the center of)* en medio de; *(in mid progress)* en pleno *<in the m. of war* en plena guerra> II. prep. entre, en medio de.
mid·stream (mĭd'strēm') s. medio de la corriente o del río.
mid·sum·mer (mĭd'sŭm'ər) s. *(middle of the summer)* pleno verano; *(summer solstice)* solsticio de verano.
Midsummer Day s. día de San Juan (24 de junio) m.
mid·term (mĭd'tûrm') s. EDUC. mitad del semestre o del curso f; POL. mitad del mandato (de un político) ♦ **mid-terms** serie de exámenes parciales.
mid·town (mĭd'toun') s. centro de una ciudad.
mid·way (mĭd'wā') I. s. avenida central (de una feria o exposición) II. adv. a mitad del camino, a medio camino III. adj. ♦ **the m. point** *(intermediate point)* el punto intermedio; *(halfway)* la mitad del camino.
mid·week (mĭd'wēk') s. medio de la semana, mitad de la semana f.
Mid·west (mĭd'wĕst') s. GEOG. los estados centrales de EE. UU.

mid·wife (mĭd'wīf') [pl. **-wives** (-wīvz')] I. s. comadrona, partera II. tr. **-wifed** o **-wived** (-wīvd'), **-wif·ing** o **-wiv·ing** (-wī'vĭng) partear.
mid·wife·ry (mĭd'wīf'rē, -wĭf'-) s. obstetricia, partería.
mid·win·ter (mĭd'wĭn'tər) s. *(middle of the winter)* pleno invierno; *(winter solstice)* solsticio de invierno.
mid·year (mĭd'yîr') s. *(time)* mitad del año f ♦ **midyears** EDUC. serie de exámenes parciales de mitad del año.
mien (mēn) s. *(bearing)* porte m *<a person of noble m.* una persona de porte noble>; *(aspect)* aspecto.
miff (mĭf) I. s. *(huff)* enfado, malhumor m; *(tiff)* riña, altercado II. tr. ofender, disgustar.
might¹ (mīt) s. poder m, fuerzas *<she tried with all her m.* trató con todas sus fuerzas>.
might² §G11 (mīt) aux. [pret. de **may**] □ INDICANDO UNA CONDICIÓN CONTRARIA A LA REALIDAD poder *<she m. help if she knew the truth* ella podría ayudar si supiera la verdad> □ INDICANDO POSIBILIDAD O PROBABILIDAD ser posible que *<it m. rain* es posible que llueva> □ MANIFESTANDO EXTREMA CORTESÍA poder *<m. I go?* ¿podría retirarme?> □ EXPRESANDO OBLIGACIÓN deber *<you m. try to come* debe procurar venir>.
might·i·ly (mī'tl-ē) adv. *(powerfully)* poderosamente, con fuerza; *(greatly)* grandemente, extremadamente.
might·y (mī'tē) I. adj. **-i·er, -i·est** *(powerful)* poderoso; *(imposing)* imponente, grandioso II. adv. FAM. extremadamente.
mi·graine (mī'grān') s. MED. jaqueca, migraña.
mi·grant (mī'grənt) I. s. *(emigrant)* emigrante mf; *(itinerant worker)* trabajador ambulante m II. adj. migratorio.
mi·grate (mī'grāt') intr. **-grat·ed, -grat·ing** emigrar.
mi·gra·tion (mī-grā'shən) s. *(act)* emigración f; *(group)* grupo de emigrantes.
mi·gra·to·ry (mī'grə-tôr'ē) adj. *(mobile)* migratorio *<m. birds* aves migratorias>; *(roving)* ambulante, nómada.
mike (mīk) s. FAM. micrófono.
mi·kron (mī'krŏn') s. var. de **micron**.
mil (mĭl) *(unit of length)* milipulgada, milésima de pulgada; ARM. mil (unidad angular) m.
mi·la·dy (mĭ-lā'dē) s. *(English noblewoman)* miladi f; *(chic woman)* mujer elegante f.
mil·age (mī'lĭj) s. var. de **mileage**.
Mi·lan (mī-lăn', -län') s. Milán.
mild (mīld) adj. **-er, -est** *(in character)* apacible; *(manners)* suave, moderado; *(in taste, in effect)* suave *<m. cigarettes* cigarrillos suaves>; *(in alcohol content)* flojo; *(in force)* suave, ligero *<a m. push* un empujón suave>; *(temperate)* benigno, templado; *(slope)* suave; *(lenient)* poco severo; MED. *(cold)* leve.
mildew (mĭl'dōō', -dyōō') I. s. *(fungus)* moho; AGR. *(on wheat)* añublo, tizón m; *(on vine)* mildiu (de la vid) m II. tr. & intr. *(to become mildewed)* enmohecer(se); AGR. *(on wheat)* añublar(se), atizonar(se).
mild·ly (mīld'lē) adv. *(kindly)* apaciblemente; *(moderately)* suavemente; *(leniently)* ligeramente; MED. ligeramente ♦ **to put it m.** sin ir más allá.
mild·ness (mīld'nĭs) s. *(of character)* apacibilidad f; *(moderation)* suavidad f; *(temperateness)* benignidad f; *(leniency)* poca severidad; MED. benignidad.
mile (mīl) s. *(distance)* milla; *(race)* carrera de una milla ♦ **to be off by a m.** FIG. estar lejos de la cuenta.
mile·age (mī'lĭj) s. *(total length)* distancia en millas; *(miles traveled)* recorrido en millas; *(allowance)* gastos de viaje (pagados por millas); FAM. *(usefulness)* rendimiento, utilidad f.
mile·post (mīl'pōst') s. poste miliario, mojón m.
mil·er (mī'lər) s. DEP. *(runner)* corredor de la milla m; *(horse)* caballo entrenado para correr una milla.
mile·stone (mīl'stōn') s. *(stone marker)* piedra miliaria; FIG. *(important event)* jalón m, hito *<to be a m.* marcar un hito>.
mi·lieu (mēl-yœ') s. medio, ambiente m.
mil·i·tan·cy (mĭl'ĭ-tn-sē) s. *(combativeness)* militancia, combatividad f; *(aggressiveness)* belicosidad f.
mil·i·tant (mĭl'ĭ-tnt) I. adj. *(combative)* militante, comba-

tivo <*a communist m.* un comunista militante>; *(aggressive)* belicoso **II.** s. militante *mf.*

mil·i·ta·rism (mĭl′ĭ-tə-rĭz′əm) s. militarismo.

mil·i·ta·rist (mĭl′ĭ-tər-ĭst) s. militarista *mf.*

mil·i·ta·ris·tic (mĭl′ĭ-tə-rĭs′tĭk) adj. militarista.

mil·i·ta·rize (mĭl′ĭ-tə-rīz′) tr. **-rized, -riz·ing** militarizar.

mil·i·tar·y (mĭl′ĭ-tĕr′ē) **I.** adj. militar **II.** s. los militares, las fuerzas armadas.

military attaché s. DIPL. agregado militar.

military intelligence s. *(information)* información importante por su valor militar *f; (military branch)* servicio de inteligencia militar.

military police s. policía militar.

mil·i·tate (mĭl′ĭ-tāt′) intr. **-tat·ed, -tat·ing** militar <*the facts m. against this interpretation* los hechos militan en contra de esta interpretación>.

mi·li·tia (mə-lĭsh′ə) s. milicia.

mi·li·tia·man (mə-lĭsh′ə-mən) s. [pl. **-men**] miliciano.

milk (mĭlk) **I.** s. leche *f* ♦ **chocolate m.** leche con chocolate • **m. products** productos lácteos • **not to cry over spilled m.** a lo hecho, pecho • **powdered m.** leche en polvo • **skim m.** leche desnatada • **the m. of human kindness** la flor de la bondad • **whole m.** leche sin desnatar **II.** tr. *(animals)* ordeñar; *(to drain off)* sacar <*to m. a snake of its venom* sacar el veneno a una serpiente>; *(to draw out)* sacar; *(information)* sonsacar; *(money)* chupar ♦ **to m. someone dry** exprimir a alguien como una naranja —intr. dar leche.

milk chocolate s. chocolate con leche *m.*

milk fever s. MED. fiebre láctea; VET. fiebre de leche *o* del parto.

milk·maid (mĭlk′mād′) s. *(woman who milks cows)* ordeñadora; *(woman who sells milk)* lechera.

milk·man (mĭlk′măn′) s. [pl. **-men** (-mĕn′)] lechero.

milk of magnesia s. FARM. leche de magnesia *f.*

milk run s. JER. misión militar aérea de poca duración *o* poco peligrosa.

milk shake s. CUL. batido de leche.

milk·sop (mĭlk′sŏp′) s. gallina *m.*

milk sugar s. QUÍM. lactosa.

milk tooth s. diente de leche *m.*

milk·weed (mĭlk′wĕd′) s. BOT. algodoncillo.

milk·y (mĭl′kē) adj. **-i·er, -i·est** *(like milk)* lechoso; *(cloudy)* turbio, nublado.

Milky Way s. ASTRON. Vía Láctea.

mill[1] (mĭl) **I.** s. *(for grains)* molino; *(for spices, coffee)* molinillo; CUL. *(press)* prensa (de frutas); *(grinder)* trituradora; METAL. *(stamping machine)* prensa; *(lathe)* torno; *(for cutting)* fresa; *(polisher)* pulidor *m; (roller)* laminadora; *(factory)* fábrica <*a steel m.* una fábrica de acero>; FIG. *(laborious process)* engranajes *m* <*the legislative m.* los engranajes legislativos> ♦ **run of the m.** corriente y moliente • **sugar m.** ingenio • **textile m.** fábrica de tejidos • **to go through the m.** FIG. *(to suffer)* pasarlas negras; *(to learn)* aprender a golpes **II.** tr. *(to grind)* moler; *(minerals)* triturar; *(cloth)* abatanar; *(to process)* tratar; *(to lathe)* tornear; *(to cut)* fresar; *(to polish)* pulir; *(to roll)* laminar; *(a coin)* acanalar; *(to whip)* batir —intr. arremolinarse <*the people milling around in the square* la gente que se arremolina por la plaza>.

mill[2] (mĭl) s. FIN. milésimo de dólar.

mill·dam (mĭl′dăm′) s. presa de molino.

mil·le·nar·i·an (mĭl′ə-nâr′ē-ən) **I.** adj. milenario **II.** s. RELIG. milenario.

mil·le·nar·y (mĭl′ə-nĕr′ē) adj. & s. [pl. **-ies**] milenario.

mil·len·ni·um (mə-lĕn′ē-əm) s. [pl. **-ni·ums** *o* **-ni·a** (-ē-ə)] *(one thousand years)* milenio; RELIG. reinado de los mil años; FIG. *(period of joy)* época de paz y prosperidad, edad de oro *f.*

mil·le·pede (mĭl′ə-pēd′) s. var. de **millipede.**

mill·er (mĭl′ər) s. *(operator)* molinero, molendero; MEC. fresadora (máquina); ENTOM. mariposa.

mil·les·i·mal (mə-lĕs′ə-məl) adj. & s. milésimo.

mil·let (mĭl′ĭt) s. BOT. millo, mijo (planta y semilla).

mil·liard (mĭl′yərd) s. G.B. mil millones *m.*

mil·li·bar (mĭl′ə-bär) s. FÍS., METEOR. milibar *m.*

mil·li·gram (mĭl′ə-grăm′) s. miligramo.

mil·li·li·ter (mĭl′ə-lē′tər) s. mililitro.

mil·li·me·ter (mĭl′ə-mē′tər) s. milímetro.

mil·li·ner (mĭl′ə-nər) s. sombrerero.

mil·li·ner·y (mĭl′ə-nĕr′ē) s. sombrerería de señoras.

mill·ing (mĭl′ĭng) s. *(grinding)* molienda, moledura (esp. de granos); MED. fresado; MIN. trituración (de minerales) *f; (of coins)* cordoncillo.

mil·lion (mĭl′yən) s. [pl. **million** *o* **-lions**] millón *m* ♦ **millions** millones, gran cantidad.

mil·lion·aire (mĭl′yə-nâr′) s. millonario.

mil·lionth (mĭl′yənth) s. millonésimo.

mil·li·pede (mĭl′ə-pēd′) s. ENTOM. milpiés *m.*

mil·li·sec·ond (mĭl′ĭ-sĕk′ənd) s. milisegundo.

mill·pond (mĭl′pŏnd′) s. represa de molino.

mill·race (mĭl′rās′) s. *(stream)* corriente de agua del saetín *f; (channel)* saetín *m,* canal de molino *m.*

mill·stone (mĭl′stōn′) s. *(stone)* muela, piedra de molino; FIG. *(burden)* peso agobiador.

mill·stream (mĭl′strēm′) s. corriente de agua del saetín *f.*

mi·lo (mī′lō) s. [pl. **-los**] BOT. especie de sorgo *f.*

mi·lord (mĭ-lôrd′) s. milord *m.*

milque·toast (mĭlk′tōst′) s. persona de carácter tímido y reservado.

milt (mĭlt) ZOOL. **I.** s. lecha **II.** tr. impregnar las huevas de los peces.

mime (mīm) **I.** s. HIST. mimo; TEAT. *(pantomime)* pantomima; *(mimic performer)* pantomimo **II.** tr. **mimed, mim·ing** *(to mimic)* remedar, imitar; *(to pantomime)* imitar los gestos de, hacer una pantomima de —intr. actuar de pantomima.

mim·e·o·graph (mĭm′ē-ə-grăf′) **I.** s. *(machine)* mimeógrafo; *(copy)* copia hecha con el mimeógrafo **II.** tr. & intr. mimeografiar, sacar copias con el mimeógrafo.

mi·me·sis (mĭ-mē′sĭs, mī-) s. LIT., RET. mimesis *f;* BIOL. mimetismo; MED. mimética (sintomatología imitativa)

mi·met·ic (mĭ-mĕt′ĭk, mī-) adj. BIOL. mimético, mímico; FIG. *(pretended)* simulado, fingido.

mim·ic (mĭm′ĭk) **I.** tr. **-icked, -ick·ing** *(to ape)* remedar, imitar; BIOL. simular **II.** s. TEAT. *(mime)* pantomimo; *(impersonator)* imitador *m; (copy)* imitación *f* **III.** adj. *(imitative)* mímico, imitativo; *(make-believe)* simulado, fingido.

mim·ic·ry (mĭm′ĭ-krē) s. [pl. **-ries**] TEAT. mímica; *(aping)* imitación *f;* BIOL. mimetismo.

mi·mo·sa (mĭ-mō′sə) s. BOT. mimosa.

min·a·ret (mĭn′ə-rĕt′) s. ARQ. alminar *m.*

min·a·to·ry (mĭn′ə-tôr′ē) *o* **min·a·to·ri·al** (mĭn′ə-tôr′ē-əl) adj. amenazador, amenazante.

mince (mĭns) **I.** tr. **minced, minc·ing** *(to cut)* desmenuzar, picar (carne); *(in talking)* decir remilgadamente —intr. *(to walk)* andar con pasos menudos; *(to speak)* hablar remilgadamente **II.** s. carne picada.

mince·meat (mĭns′mēt′) s. *(chopped meat)* carne picada; *(mixture)* mezcla de fruta picada y especias ♦ **to make m. of** JER. hacer pedazos.

minc·ing (mĭn′sĭng) adj. remilgado.

mind (mīnd) **I.** s. *(consciousness)* mente *f* <*the powers of the m.* los poderes de la mente>; *(spirit)* espíritu *m* <*m. and matter* el espíritu y la materia>; *(intelligence)* inteligencia, cabeza <*to learn mathematics one must have a good m.* para aprender matemáticas uno ha de tener una buena inteligencia>; *(intellect)* cerebro <*the greatest minds of the century* los mayores cerebros del siglo>; *(memory)* memoria <*to slip one's m.* irse de la memoria>; *(mentality)* mentalidad *f* <*the public m.* la mentalidad del público>; *(psychology)* psicología <*the criminal m.* la psicología del criminal>; *(opinion)* opinión *f,* parecer *m* <*I may change my m.* quizá cambie de opinión>; *(attention)* atención *f* <*he gives his m. to his work* pone atención en su trabajo> ♦ **to bear in m.** tener presente, recordar • **to be in one's right m.** *o* **to be of sound m.** estar uno en sus cabales, estar uno en su sano juicio • **to be of a m. to** estar dispuesto a • **to be out of one's m.** haber perdido el juicio • **to change one's m.** cambiar de idea • **to give someone a piece of one's m.** decir a alguien cuatro verdades • **to**

have a m. to estar dispuesto a • **to have in m.** *(to remember)* recordar <*they still have him in m.* ellos todavía le recuerdan>; *(to think of)* tener presente <*we have in m. the difficulties of the task* tenemos presente las dificultades de la tarea>; *(to plan)* planear • **to know one's m.** saber lo que uno quiere • **to lose one's m.** enloquecer, perder la razón *o* el juicio • **to make up one's m.** decidirse • **to one's m.** *(in one's opinion)* en opinión de uno, al modo de ver de uno • **to set one's m. on** proponerse, estar resuelto a • **to speak one's m.** hablar sin rodeos, hablar con franqueza II. tr. *(to heed)* escuchar, prestar atención a <*m. my words!* ¡preste atención a lo que digo!>; *(to obey)* obedecer <*the children m. their mother* los niños obedecen a su madre>; *(to watch out for)* tener cuidado con <*m. the step* tenga cuidado con el escalón>; *(to dislike)* molestar <*they do not m. the cold* no les molesta el frío>; *(to look after)* atender a, cuidar <*to m. babies* cuidar niños>; *(to worry about)* preocuparse por <*don't m. me* no te preocupes por mí> ♦ **m. your manners!** ¡preste atención a sus modales! • **¡m. your own business!** ¡no te entrometas! • **not to m.** *(not to object)* no tener inconveniente, no tener nada en contra <*I don't m. if you smoke* no tengo inconveniente en que fumes>; *(not to care)* no importar, dar igual <*I don't m. if you stay or go* no me importa si te quedas o te vas> —intr. *(to give heed)* prestar atención; *(to be obedient)* obedecer; *(to care)* preocuparse <*to m. about one's health* preocuparse por la salud de uno>; *(to be careful)* tener cuidado <*if you don't m., you will fall* si no tienes cuidado te caerás> ♦ **never m.** *(don't worry)* no se preocupe; *(it doesn't matter)* no importa, da igual.

mind-blow·ing (mīnd'blō'ĭng) adj. FAM. para maravillarse.

mind·ed (mīn'dĭd) adj. *(capable at)* de mente, de mentalidad <*commercially m.* de mentalidad mercantil>; *(disposed toward)* dispuesto.

mind·ful (mīnd'fəl) adj. atento, cuidadoso.

mind·less (mīnd'lĭs) adj. *(stupid)* estúpido; *(without purpose)* sin sentido <*m. violence* violencia sin sentido>; *(careless)* descuidado, negligente.

mind reading s. *(guessing)* lectura del pensamiento, adivinación del pensamiento *f*; *(telepathy)* telepatía mental.

mind·set (mīnd'sĕt') s. disposición mental que predetermina la reacción de una persona en una situación *f*.

mind's eye s. imaginación *f*.

mine¹ (mīn) I. s. MIN. mina <*a silver m.* una mina de plata>; FIG. *(abundant supply)* mina, caudal *m* <*a m. of knowledge* una mina de conocimientos>; MIL. *(tunnel, device)* mina ♦ **land m.** MIL. mina terrestre • **to lay mines** MIL. poner minas II. tr. **mined, min·ing** *(to extract)* extraer <*to m. coal* extraer carbón>; *(to dig a mine)* minar, cavar una mina; *(to destroy)* volar (con minas) ♦ **to m. for** MIN. *(a terrain)* cavar en busca de; FIG. *(to delve into)* investigar (algo) en busca de —intr. *(to extract minerals)* extraer minerales; *(to work in a mine)* trabajar en una mina.

mine² §G32 (mīn) pron. [ú. con v. sing. *o* pl.] (el) mío <*those boots are m.* esas botas son mías> <*if you can't find your hat, take m.* si no encuentras tu sombrero, toma el mío>.

mine detector s. MIL. detector de minas *m*.

mine·field (mīn'fēld') s. MIL. campo de minas, campo minado.

mine·lay·er (mīn'lā'ər) s. MARÍT. minador (barco) *m*.

min·er (mī'nər) s. MIN. minero; *(machine)* minero continuo; MIL. minador *m*, zapador *m*.

min·er·al (mĭn'ər-əl) s. & adj. mineral *m*.

min·er·al·ize (mĭn'ər-ə-līz') tr. **ized, -iz·ing** *(petrify)* petrificar, fosilizar; *(to impregnate with minerals)* mineralizar —intr. petrificarse, fosilizarse.

min·er·al·o·gist (mĭn'ə-rŏl'ə-jĭst, -răl'-) s. mineralogista *mf*.

min·er·al·o·gy (mĭn'ə-rŏl'ə-jē, -răl'-) s. mineralogía *f*.

mineral oil s. FARM., QUÍM. aceite mineral *m*.

mineral water s. agua mineral.

Mi·ner·va (mĭ-nûr'və) s. MITOL. Minerva.

mine sweeper s. MARÍT. dragaminas *m*.

min·gle (mĭng'gəl) tr. **-gled, -gling** mezclar —intr. mezclarse <*he mingled with the crowd* se mezcló con la multitud>.

min·i (mĭn'ē) s. [pl. **-is** (-ēz)] *(something small)* algo más pequeño de lo normal; *(miniskirt)* minifalda.

min·i·a·ture (mĭn'ē-ə-choor', -chər) I. s. *(small replica)* miniatura; *(art of painting)* arte de pintar miniaturas *m* II. adj. en miniatura.

min·i·a·tur·ize (mĭn'ē-ə-chə-rīz') tr. **-ized, -iz·ing** miniaturizar.

min·i·bike (mĭn'ē-bīk') s. pequeña motocicleta.

min·i·bus (mĭn'ē-bŭs') s. microbús *m*.

min·i·com·put·er (mĭn'ē-kəm-pyoo'tər) s. COMPUT. computadora pequeña mayor que una microcomputadora.

min·im (mĭn'ĭm) s. *(fluid measure)* gota; MÚS. mínima, blanca; FIG. *(jot)* pizca.

min·i·mal (mĭn'ə-məl) I. adj. mínimo II. s. MAT. mínimo.

min·i·mize (mĭn'ə-mīz') tr. **-mized, -miz·ing** *(to reduce)* empequeñecer; FIG. minimizar <*he minimized the magnitude of the crisis* minimizó la magnitud de la crisis>.

min·i·mum (mĭn'ə-məm) s. & adj. [pl. **-mums** *o* **-ma** (-mə)] mínimo.

minimum wage s. *(lowest wage)* salario mínimo; *(living wage)* mínimo vital, salario vital.

min·ing (mī'nĭng) s. minería (industria); MIL. minado, siembra de minas (explosivos).

min·ion (mĭn'yən) s. *(favorite)* favorito, predilecto; *(sycophant)* adulador *m*, servil *m*; *(subordinate official)* funcionario subordinado.

min·i·skirt (mĭn'ē-skûrt') s. minifalda.

min·is·ter (mĭn'ĭ-stər) I. s. DIPL., POL. ministro; RELIG. pastor *m*, ministro; *(agent)* ministro ♦ **Prime M.** POL. primer ministro, presidente del gobierno *m* II. intr. *(to tend)* atender, asistir <*to m. to the homeless* asistir a las personas sin hogar>; RELIG. oficiar de pastor *o* ministro —tr. *(to dispense)* suministrar; RELIG. administrar.

min·is·te·ri·al (mĭn'ĭ-stîr'ē-əl) adj. POL. ministerial; RELIG. pastoral.

minister plenipotentiary s. DIPL. ministro plenipotenciario.

min·is·trant (mĭn'ĭ-strənt) I. s. ministrador *m* II. adj. ministrante.

min·is·tra·tion (mĭn'ĭ-strā'shən) s. *(aid)* ayuda, servicio; RELIG. ministerio.

min·is·try (mĭn'ĭ-strē) s. [pl. **-tries**] POL. ministerio; RELIG. *(calling)* sacerdocio, vocación sacerdotal *f*; *(clergy)* clero ♦ **to enter the m.** RELIG. hacerse clérigo.

Ministry s. POL. Consejo de Ministros, Gabinete *m*.

min·i·um (mĭn'ē-əm) s. MIN., QUÍM. minio.

mink (mĭngk) s. [pl. **mink** *o* **minks**] ZOOL. visón (animal y piel) *m*.

min·now (mĭn'ō) s. [pl. **minnow** *o* **-nows**] ICT. pez pequeño.

Mi·no·an (mĭ-nō'ən) adj. HIST. minoico.

mi·nor (mī'nər) I. adj. *(in amount, size, extent)* menor, pequeño <*m. repairs* pequeños arreglos>; *(in importance)* secundario, de poca importancia <*m. issues* cuestiones de poca importancia>; *(in rank)* inferior; *(in stature)* menor, secundario <*a m. poet* un poeta menor>; *(in seriousness)* pequeño <*m. problems* pequeños problemas>; MED. *(injury, operation)* leve; *(interest)* escaso, poco; *(in age)* menor de edad; LÓG. menor; MÚS. menor <*C minor* do menor> II. s. *(underage person)* menor de edad *mf*; EDUC. *(area of study)* especialización secundaria; LÓG. menor *f*; MÚS. *(key)* tono menor III. intr. ♦ **to m. in** EDUC. estudiar (una asignatura) como especialización secundaria.

Mi·nor·ca (mĭ-nôr'kə) s. Menorca.

Mi·nor·ite (mī'nə-rīt') s. RELIG. menor *m*, fraile franciscano.

mi·nor·i·ty (mə-nôr'ĭ-tē, mī-) s. [pl. **-ties**] *(group)* minoría; *(member)* miembro de un grupo minoritario; *(age)* menoría, minoría.

minority leader s. POL. dirigente de la minoría parlamentaria *mf*.

mi·nor-league (mī'nər-lēg') adj. FAM. de posición *o* importancia secundaria <*a m. politician* un político de importancia secundaria>.

minor orders s.pl. RELIG. órdenes menores *f*.

minor premise s. LÓG. premisa menor.

min·ster (mĭn'stər) s. G.B. *(church)* iglesia de un monasterio; *(cathedral)* catedral *f*.

---

min·strel (mĭn′strəl) s. MÚS., TEAT. trovador *m*; POÉT. poeta lírico; *(performer)* cantor y actor cómico.
minstrel show s. EE. UU. representación de obra corta y cómica con cante y baile (esp. parodiando a los negros) *f.*
mint¹ (mĭnt) I. s. *(place)* casa de la moneda, ceca; FIG. *(fortune)* cantidad grande (esp. de dinero) *f*; *(source)* fuente *f*, mina <*a m. of useful ideas* una mina de ideas útiles> II. tr. *(to coin)* acuñar <*to m. money* acuñar dinero>; FIG. *(to invent)* inventar, idear <*to m. a phrase* idear una frase> III. adj. nuevo, sin usar ♦ **in m. condition** como nuevo.
mint² (mĭnt) s. BOT. menta, hierbabuena; *(candy)* pastilla de menta, menta.
mint·age (mĭn′tĭj) s. *(act of minting)* acuñación *f*; *(coins)* moneda acuñada; *(fee)* derechos de cuño, monedaje *m*; *(stamp on a coin)* cuño, sello.
mint julep s. whisky helado y sazonado con menta.
min·u·end (mĭn′yŏŏ-ĕnd′) s. MAT. minuendo.
min·u·et (mĭn′yŏŏ-ĕt′) s. minué (baile y música) *m.*
mi·nus (mī′nəs) I. prep. MAT. menos <*the total m. one* el total menos uno>; FAM. *(without)* sin <*I got my wallet back m. the money* me devolvieron la cartera sin el dinero> II. adj. MAT. negativo <*m. quantity* cantidad negativa> III. s. MAT. signo menos, menos *m*; FIG. *(deficiency)* deficiencia, defecto.
min·us·cule (mĭn′ə-skyŏŏl′, mĭ-nŭs′kyŏŏl′) I. s. minúscula II. adj. minúsculo.
minus sign s. MAT. signo menos.
min·ute¹ (mĭn′ĭt) I. s. *(60 seconds)* minuto; *(moment)* minuto, momento <*he'll come back in a m.* volverá dentro de un minuto> ♦ **any m.** de un momento a otro • **at the last m.** a última hora • **just a m.!** ¡un momento! • **the m. something happens** en cuanto algo seceda • **this very m.** ahora mismo • **to take a m.** detenerse un momento a • **until the last m.** hasta el último momento • **wait a m.!** ¡un momento! • **minutes** acta, actas II. tr. **-ut·ed, -ut·ing** *(to draft notes)* minutar, tomar notas de; *(to take minutes)* levantar acta de.
mi·nute² (mī-nŏŏt′, -nyŏŏt′, mĭ-) adj. *(tiny)* diminuto, minúsculo; *(insignificant)* insignificante <*m. errors* equivocaciones insignificantes>; *(thorough)* minucioso <*a m. inspection* una inspección minuciosa>.
min·ute hand (mĭn′ĭt) s. minutero.
min·ute·man (mĭn′ĭt-măn′) s. [pl. **-men** (-mĕn′)] miliciano (en la Guerra de Independencia de EE. UU.).
minute steak s. CUL. bistec al minuto *m*, filete al minuto *m.*
mi·nu·ti·a (mĭ-nŏŏ′shē-ə, -nyŏŏ′-) s. [pl. **-ti·ae** (-shē-ē′)] minucias, pequeños detalles <*the m. of daily life* los pequeños detalles de la vida cotidiana>.
minx (mĭngks) s. *(pert girl)* joven coqueta *o* descarada; ANT. *(promiscuous woman)* mujer lasciva.
mir·a·cle (mĭr′ə-kəl) s. *(event)* milagro; *(wonder)* maravilla, prodigio; TEAT. *(play)* auto sacramental *m.*
miracle play s. TEAT. auto sacramental.
mi·rac·u·lous (mĭ-răk′yə-ləs) adj. milagroso.
mi·rage (mĭ-räzh′) s. *(optical phenomenon)* espejismo; FIG. *(illusion)* ilusión *f*, espejismo.
mire (mīr) I. s. *(muddy place)* lodazal *m*, ciénaga; *(mud)* lodo, fango II. tr. **mired, mir·ing** *(to cover with mud)* enlodar, encenagar; *(to bog down)* atascar, empantanar —intr. atascarse, empantanarse.
mirk (mûrk) s. var. de **murk.**
mirk·y (mûr′kē) adj. var. de **murky.**
mir·ror (mĭr′ər) I. s. *(reflecting surface)* espejo; FIG. *(representation)* espejo, reflejo <*the play is a m. of society* la obra es un reflejo de la sociedad> II. tr. reflejar.
mirth (mûrth) s. *(glee)* alegría, regocijo; *(hilarity)* hilaridad *f*, risas.
mirth·ful (mûrth′fəl) adj. alegre, jovial.
mirth·less (mûrth′lĭs) adj. triste, sin alegría.
mir·y (mī′rē) adj. **-i·er, -i·est** cenagoso, fangoso.
mis·ad·ven·ture (mĭs′əd-vĕn′chər) s. desastre *m*, calamidad *f.*
mis·ad·vise (mĭs′əd-vīz′) tr. **-vised, -vis·ing** aconsejar mal, dar malos consejos.
mis·a·ligned (mĭs′ə-līnd′) adj. mal alineado, desalineado.
mis·a·lign·ment (mĭs′ə-līn′mənt) s. desalineación *f.*

mis·al·li·ance (mĭs′ə-lī′əns) s. *(unsuitable alliance)* mal casamiento; *(marriage)* matrimonio con persona de clase inferior.
mis·an·thrope (mĭs′ən-thrōp′) s. misántropo.
mis·an·throp·ic (mĭs′ən-thrŏp′ĭk) adj. misantrópico.
mis·an·thro·pist (mĭs-ăn′thrə-pĭst) s. misántropo.
mis·an·thro·py (mĭs-ăn′thrə-pē) s. misantropía.
mis·ap·pli·ca·tion (mĭs-ăp′lĭ-kā′shən) s. mala aplicación, uso indebido.
mis·ap·ply (mĭs′ə-plī′) tr. **-plied, -ply·ing** aplicar mal.
mis·ap·pre·hend (mĭs-ăp′rĭ-hĕnd′) tr. comprender mal.
mis·ap·pre·hen·sion (mĭs-ăp′rĭ-hĕn′shən) s. mala interpretación, malentendido.
mis·ap·pro·pri·ate (mĭs′ə-prō′prē-āt′) tr. **-at·ed, -at·ing** *(to misuse)* apropiar erróneamente; *(to embezzle)* malversar (fondos); *(to use illegally)* utilizar ilegalmente.
mis·ap·pro·pri·a·tion (mĭs′ə-prō′prē-ā′shən) s. *(embezzlement)* malversación *f*, desfalco; *(misuse)* mal uso, uso ilegal.
mis·be·got·ten (mĭs′bĭ-gŏt′n) adj. *(illegitimate)* ilegítimo, bastardo; *(ill-conceived)* mal concebido, mal calculado <*another m. plan* otro plan mal concebido>.
mis·be·have (mĭs′bĭ-hāv′) tr. & intr. **-haved, -hav·ing** portarse mal, conducirse mal.
mis·be·hav·ior (mĭs′bĭ-hāv′yər) s. mala conducta, mal comportamiento.
mis·be·lief (mĭs′bĭ-lēf′) s. *(wrong belief)* creencia errónea *o* falsa; RELIG. herejía.
mis·cal·cu·late (mĭs-kăl′kyə-lāt′) tr. & intr. **-lat·ed, -lat·ing** calcular mal.
mis·cal·cu·la·tion (mĭs-kăl′kyə-lā′shən) s. cálculo erróneo, error *m.*
mis·call (mĭs-kôl′) tr. llamar equivocadamente, llamar erróneamente <*he was miscalled Samuel* le llamaban erróneamente Samuel>.
mis·car·riage (mĭs-kăr′ĭj) s. *(mismanagement)* mala administración; *(failure)* fracaso <*the m. of a plan* el fracaso de un plan>; MED. aborto.
mis·car·ry (mĭs-kăr′ē) intr. **-ried, -ry·ing** *(to go astray)* perderse, extraviarse; *(to fail)* malograrse, frustrarse; MED. abortar.
mis·cast (mĭs-kăst′) tr. **-cast, -cast·ing** TEAT. *(an actor)* dar un papel poco apropiado a un actor; *(a play)* hacer mal el reparto de una obra.
mis·ceg·e·na·tion (mĭ-sĕj′ə-nā′shən, mĭs′ī-jə-) s. cruce de razas *m*, mestizaje *m.*
mis·cel·la·ne·ous (mĭs′ə-lā′nē-əs) adj. *(mixed)* misceláneo, diverso <*m. items* artículos diversos>; *(diversified)* variado <*a m. student body* un estudiantado variado> ♦ **m. assortment** surtido variado.
mis·cel·la·ny (mĭs′ə-lā′nē) s. [pl. **-nies**] miscelánea.
mis·chance (mĭs-chăns′) s. *(unfortunate occurrence)* infortunio, desgracia; *(bad luck)* mala suerte.
mis·chief (mĭs′chĭf) s. *(offense)* injuria, agravio; *(damage)* daño, destrucción *f*; *(prank)* travesura; *(perverseness)* perversidad *f*, malicia <*full of m.* lleno de malicia>.
mis·chie·vous (mĭs′chə-vəs) adj. *(causing mischief)* malicioso, malévolo; *(playful)* travieso <*a m. child* un niño travieso>; *(troublesome)* molesto, importuno <*a m. prank* una travesura molesta>; *(harmful)* dañino.
mis·ci·ble (mĭs′ə-bəl) adj. QUÍM. miscible, mezclable.
mis·clas·si·fi·ca·tion (mĭs-klăs′ə-fĭ-kā′shən) s. clasificación incorrecta.
mis·clas·si·fy (mĭs-klăs′ə-fī′) tr. **-fied, -fy·ing** clasificar incorrectamente.
mis·con·ceive (mĭs′kən-sēv′) tr. **-ceived, -ceiv·ing** interpretar incorrectamente, comprender mal.
mis·con·cep·tion (mĭs′kən-sĕp′shən) s. concepto erróneo, malentendido.
mis·con·duct I. s. (mĭs-kŏn′dŭkt) *(misbehavior)* mala conducta; *(adultery)* adulterio; *(bad management)* mala administración; *(malfeasance)* malversación *f* II. tr. (mĭs′kən-dŭkt′) administrar mal.
mis·con·struc·tion (mĭs′kən-strŭk′shən) s. *(misunderstanding)* mala interpretación; GRAM. mala construcción (de una oración).

ã rey / ä año / b boca / ch chico / d dar / ĕ el / ē mil / g gato / h joya / hw juez / ī aire / k casa / kw cuan /

mis·con·strue (mĭs'kən-strōō') tr. -strued, -stru·ing interpretar mal.

mis·count I. tr. & intr. (mĭs-kount') contar mal II. s. (mĭs'kount') recuento erróneo.

mis·cre·ant (mĭs'krē-ənt) I. s. (evildoer) malhechor m, persona malvada; RELIG. (infidel) infiel mf, hereje mf II. adj. (villainous) bellaco; RELIG. infiel, hereje.

mis·cue (mĭs-kyōō') I. s. (in billiards) pifia; FIG. (mistake) error m, desacierto II. intr. -cued, -cu·ing (in billiards) pifiar; FIG., TEAT. equivocarse de texto.

mis·deal I. tr. & intr. (mĭs-dēl') -dealt (-dĕlt'), -deal·ing repartir mal (los naipes) II. s. (mĭs'dēl') reparto erróneo (de naipes).

mis·deed (mĭs-dēd') s. delito, fechoría.

mis·de·mean·or (mĭs'dĭ-mē'nər) s. (misdeed) fechoría; DER. falta leve, delito menor.

mis·de·mean·our (mĭs'dĭ-mē'nər) s. G.B. var. de **misdemeanor.**

mis·di·ag·nose (mĭs-dī'əg-nōs') tr. -nosed, -nos·ing diagnosticar incorrectamente.

mis·di·ag·no·sis (mĭs-dī'əg-nō'sĭs) s. [pl. -ses (-sēz')] diagnóstico incorrecto.

mis·di·rect (mĭs'dĭ-rĕkt', -dī-) tr. (to instruct incorrectly) dirigir erradamente; (to put a wrong address) poner mal las señas.

mis·di·rec·tion (mĭs'dĭ-rĕk'shən, -dī-) s. (wrong instruction) mala dirección, información errónea; DER. (from a judge) instrucciones erróneas (al jurado).

mis·do (mĭs'dōō') tr. -did (-dĭd'), -done (-dŭn'), -do·ing hacer mal.

mis·do·ing (mĭs-dōō'ĭng) s. (villainy) mala acción; (fault) falta.

mis·doubt (mĭs-dout') tr. sospechar.

mis·em·ploy (mĭs'ĕm-ploi') tr. emplear o utilizar mal.

mi·ser (mī'zər) s. avaro, avariento.

mis·er·a·ble (mĭz'ər-ə-bəl) adj. (very unhappy) desgraciado, desdichado; (disagreeable) desagradable; (contemptible) despreciable, vil; (deplorable) lamentable, deplorable; (mean) miserable, abyecto; (inadequate) miserable, mísero; (inferior) sin valor, de mala calidad.

mis·er·a·bly (mĭz'ər-ə-blē) adv. miserablemente.

mi·ser·li·ness (mī'zər-lē-nĭs) s. mezquindad f, avaricia.

mi·ser·ly (mī'zər-lē) adj. mezquino, avariento.

mis·er·y (mĭz'ə-rē) s. [pl. -ies] (poverty) miseria, pobreza; (unhappiness) infelicidad f, desdicha; (misfortune) desgracia; FAM. (pain) dolor (prolongado) m.

mis·es·ti·mate (mĭs-ĕs'tə-māt') tr. -mat·ed, -mat·ing estimar erróneamente, calcular mal.

mis·fea·sance (mĭs-fē'zəns) s. DER. ejecución ilegal de un procedimiento lícito f.

mis·file (mĭs-fīl') tr. -filed, -fil·ing archivar mal.

mis·fire (mĭs-fīr') I. intr. -fired, -fir·ing (motor, gun) fallar; FIG. (to fail) fallar, no tener éxito II. s. (ignition) fallo de encendido; (detonation) fallo de tiro; FIG. (failure) fracaso.

mis·fit (mĭs'fĭt') s. (object, clothing) cosa o prenda que encaja o cae mal; (person) persona inadaptada.

mis·for·tune (mĭs-fôr'chən) s. (bad luck) infortunio, desgracia; (calamity) calamidad f, desastre m; (mishap) percance m, revés m.

mis·giv·ing (mĭs-gĭv'ĭng) s. duda, aprensión f.

mis·gov·ern (mĭs-gŭv'ərn) tr. desgobernar, gobernar mal.

mis·guide (mĭs-gīd') tr. -guid·ed, -guid·ing (to guide badly) orientar o dirigir mal; (to advise badly) aconsejar mal; (to lead astray) descaminar.

mis·guid·ed (mĭs-gī'dĭd) adj. descaminado.

mis·han·dle (mĭs-hăn'dl) tr. -dled, -dling (to botch) manejar mal; (to maltreat) maltratar.

mis·hap (mĭs'hăp') s. accidente m, desgracia.

mis·hear (mĭs-hîr') tr. -heard (-hûrd'), -hear·ing oír mal, entender mal o imperfectamente.

mish·mash (mĭsh'măsh') s. revoltijo, mezcolanza.

mis·i·den·ti·fy (mĭs'ī-dĕn'tə-fī') tr. -fied, -fy·ing identificar mal o erróneamente.

mis·im·pres·sion (mĭs'ĭm-prĕsh'ən) s. impresión errónea o imperfecta.

mis·in·form (mĭs'ĭn-fôrm') tr. informar mal, dar informes erróneos.

mis·in·for·ma·tion (mĭs-ĭn'fər-mā'shən) s. información errónea.

mis·in·ter·pret (mĭs'ĭn-tûr'prĭt) tr. interpretar mal.

mis·in·ter·pre·ta·tion (mĭs'ĭn-tûr'prĭ-tā'shən) s. mala interpretación.

mis·judge (mĭs-jŭj') tr. & intr. -judged, -judg·ing juzgar mal.

mis·judg·ment (mĭs-jŭj'mənt) s. juicio equivocado, estimación errónea.

mis·la·bel (mĭs-lā'bəl) tr. clasificar o calificar mal.

mis·lay (mĭs-lā') tr. -laid (-lād'), -lay·ing (to misplace) extraviar, perder; (to place incorrectly) colocar mal.

mis·lead (mĭs-lēd') tr. -led (-lĕd'), -lead·ing (to lead incorrectly) descaminar; (to deceive) engañar.

mis·lead·ing (mĭs-lē'dĭng) adj. engañoso.

mis·led (mĭs-lĕd') pret. y part. p. de **mislead.**

mis·like (mĭs-līk') I. tr. -liked, -lik·ing no gustar de II. s. aversión f, antipatía.

mis·man·age (mĭs-măn'ĭj) tr. -aged, -ag·ing manejar o administrar mal.

mis·man·age·ment (mĭs-măn'ĭj-mənt) s. mala dirección o administración.

mis·mar·riage (mĭs-măr'ĭj) s. matrimonio desacertado.

mis·match (mĭs-măch') I. tr. emparejar mal II. s. emparejamiento mal hecho o desacertado.

mis·mate (mĭs-māt') tr. -mat·ed, -mat·ing emparejar mal.

mis·name (mĭs-nām') tr. -named, -nam·ing dar nombre que no corresponde a la realidad.

mis·no·mer (mĭs-nō'mər) s. nombre poco apto; (wrong name) nombre equivocado, nombre inadecuado.

mi·sog·a·my (mĭ-sŏg'ə-mē) s. misogamia, odio al matrimonio.

mi·sog·y·ny (mĭ-sŏj'ə-nē) s. misoginia, odio a las mujeres.

mis·o·ri·ent (mĭs-ôr'ē-ĕnt') tr. orientar mal.

mis·per·ceive (mĭs'pər-sēv') tr. -ceived, -ceiv·ing percibir o comprender mal.

mis·place (mĭs-plās') tr. -placed, -plac·ing (to mislay) colocar fuera de su lugar; (to lose) extraviar, perder; (to bestow mistakenly) otorgar o dar indebidamente (confianza).

mis·play (mĭs-plā') I. s. mala jugada II. tr. jugar mal.

mis·print I. tr. (mĭs-prĭnt') imprimir mal II. s. (mĭs'prĭnt') error de imprenta m, errata.

mis·pri·sion (mĭs-prĭzh'ən) s. DER. (maladministration) mala administración (de una oficina pública); (neglect) ocultación f o encubrimiento de un crimen.

mis·pro·nounce (mĭs'prə-nouns') tr. & intr. -nounced, -nounc·ing pronunciar mal o incorrectamente.

mis·quo·ta·tion (mĭs'kwō-tā'shən) s. cita errónea o equivocada.

mis·quote (mĭs-kwōt') tr. -quot·ed, -quot·ing citar incorrectamente.

mis·read (mĭs-rēd') tr. -read (-rĕd'), -read·ing (to read inaccurately) leer mal; (to misinterpret) entender o interpretar mal.

mis·rep·re·sent (mĭs-rĕp'rĭ-zĕnt') tr. (to distort) tergiversar; (to represent dishonestly) representar mal (a alguien).

mis·rep·re·sen·ta·tion (mĭs-rĕp'rĭ-zĕn-tā'shən) s. (distortion) tergiversación f; (fraud) representación fraudulenta.

mis·rule (mĭs-rōōl') I. tr. -ruled, -rul·ing desgobernar, gobernar mal II. s. (misgovernment) desgobierno, mal gobierno; (disorder) desorden m, caos m.

miss¹ (mĭs') I. tr. (a shot) errar, fallar; (a target) no dar en (el blanco); (train, bus) perder <we missed the plane perdimos el avión>; (not to catch) escapársele a uno, írsele a uno <he missed the ball se le fue la pelota>; (not to meet) no encontrar <they missed him at the theater no le encontraron en el cine>; (not to see) no ver <she missed you at the party no te vio en la fiesta>; (not to obtain) no obtener <they missed the prize no obtuvieron el premio>; (not to perceive) no darse cuenta de, no captar; (not to achieve) no lograr, no conseguir <he missed winning the race no logró ganar la carrera>; (not to attend) faltar <she missed two classes faltó a dos clases>; (not to perform) perder <to m. a day of work perder un día de trabajo>; (to leave out) saltarse <*he missed a name in typing the list* se saltó un nombre al pasar la lista a máquina>; *(a chance)* perder, desperdiciar (una oportunidad); *(to fail to enjoy)* perderse <*you missed a great movie* te perdiste una gran película>; *(to avoid)* lograr evitar, librarse de <*we missed the traffic* logramos evitar el tráfico>; *(to discover the absence of)* notar que a uno le falta <*he missed his wallet today* hoy notó que le faltaba la billetera>; *(to regret the absence of)* echar de menos, extrañar <*he misses his wife* extraña a su esposa>; *(to get wrong)* no acertar <*to m. five questions on a test* no acertar cinco preguntas de un examen> ♦ **to m. one's turn** perder el turno • **to m. out on** perderse • **to m. the boat** FAM., FIG. írsele a uno el tren • **to m. the mark** FIG. equivocarse • **to m. the point** no comprender • **you can't miss it** *(a place)* no tiene pérdida; *(an object)* salta a la vista, en seguida se ve —intr. *(to fail to hit)* fallar; *(engine)* fallar; *(to be absent)* faltar <*two rings are missing* faltan dos sortijas>; *(to fail)* fracasar ♦ **it never misses** FAM. nunca falla • **you can't m.** FAM. no hay forma de perder II. s. *(failure to hit)* fallo, tiro errado; *(failure to succeed)* fracaso, fallo.

miss² (mĭs) s. señorita ♦ **M. Brown** la señorita Brown.

mis·sal (mĭs′əl) s. RELIG. misal *m.*

mis·shape (mĭs-shāp′) tr. **-shaped** o **-shap·en** (-shā′pən), **-shap·ing** desfigurar, deformar.

mis·shap·en (mĭs-shā′pən) adj. deformado.

mis·sile (mĭs′əl, -īl′) s. *(weapon)* arma arrojadiza; *(projectile)* proyectil *m*; *(guided missile)* cohete o misil teledirigido; *(ballistic missile)* proyectil balístico.

mis·sile·ry o **mis·sil·ry** (mĭs′əl-rē) s. *(science)* ciencia de la construcción y utilización de cohetes teledirigidos; *(missiles)* cohetes teledirigidos *m.*

miss·ing (mĭs′ĭng) adj. *(lost)* perdido; *(disappeared)* desaparecido; *(absent)* ausente; *(lacking)* que falta; *(less)* menos.

missing link s. ANTROP. eslabón perdido; FIG. *(something lacking)* eslabón perdido.

mis·sion (mĭsh′ən) s. RELIG. misión *f*; DIPL. *(embassy)* delegación, embajada; *(task)* misión <*a secret m.* una misión secreta>; *(welfare organization)* beneficencia; *(calling)* misión *f*, cometido.

mis·sion·ar·y (mĭsh′ə-nĕr′ē) I. s. [pl. **-ies**] misionero II. adj. misionero, misional.

mis·sis (mĭs′ĭz) s. FAM. señora, esposa, mujer *f.*

Mis·sis·sip·pi (mĭs′ĭ-sĭp′ē) s. Misisipí.

mis·sive (mĭs′ĭv) s. misiva.

Mis·sou·ri (mĭ-zŏŏr′ē) s. Misuri.

mis·spell (mĭs-spĕl′) tr. **-spelled** o **-spelt** (-spĕlt′), **-spel·ling** ortografiar o deletrear mal.

mis·spell·ing (mĭs-spĕl′ĭng) s. falta de ortografía.

mis·spend (mĭs-spĕnd′) tr. **-spent** (-spĕnt′), **-spend·ing** malgastar.

mis·state (mĭs-stāt′) tr. **-stat·ed, -stat·ing** exponer o relatar mal.

mis·step (mĭs-stĕp′) s. *(misplaced step)* paso en falso, tropezón *m*; FIG. *(blunder)* desacierto, patochada.

mis·sus (mĭs′ĭz) s. var. de **missis**.

miss·y (mĭs′ē) s. [pl. **-ies**] FAM. señorita.

mist (mĭst) I. s. *(fog)* niebla, neblina; *(at sea)* bruma; *(haze)* calina; *(vapor)* vapor *m*; FIG. oscuridad *f* II. intr. *(to fog up)* cubrirse de niebla; *(to blur)* empañarse; *(to become obscured)* oscurecer —tr. velar.

mis·tak·a·ble (mĭ-stā′kə-bəl) adj. equívoco, confundible.

mis·take (mĭ-stāk′) I. s. *(error)* error *m*, equivocación *f* <*to make a m.* cometer un error> II. tr. **-took** (-stŏŏk′), **-tak·en** (-stā′kən), **-tak·ing** *(to misinterpret)* interpretar o entender mal; *(to identify incorrectly)* confundir <*he mistook her for her sister* le confundió con su hermana> —intr. errar, equivocarse.

mis·tak·en (mĭ-stā′kən) adj. *(wrong)* equivocado, errado; *(inexact)* erróneo.

Mis·ter (mĭs′tər) s. señor <*come in, Mr. Smith* pase, señor Smith> ♦ **hey, m.!** FAM. ¡oiga! • **watch out, m.** FAM. cuidado, socio.

Mister Char·lie (chär′lē) s. JER. nombre peyorativo que los negros dan al hombre blanco.

mis·tle·toe (mĭs′əl-tō′) s. BOT. muérdago.

mis·took (mĭ-stŏŏk′) pret. de **mistake**.

mis·tral (mĭs′trəl) s. METEOR. mistral *m.*

mis·treat (mĭs-trēt′) tr. *(to handle roughly)* maltratar; *(to abuse)* abusar de.

mis·treat·ment (mĭs-trēt′mənt) s. maltrato, trato malo.

mis·tress (mĭs′trĭs) s. *(head of a household)* señora <*is the m. in?* ¿está la señora?>; *(lover)* querida, amante *f*; *(owner, controller)* dueña <*she's the m. of his heart* es dueña de su corazón>; *(expert)* experta <*a m. of cooking* una experta en cocina>; G.B. *(schoolteacher)* maestra.

mis·tri·al (mĭs-trī′əl) s. DER. juicio nulo (por error de procedimiento o desacuerdo del jurado).

mis·trust (mĭs-trŭst′) I. s. desconfianza, recelo II. tr. & intr. *(to lack confidence)* desconfiar (de); *(to be doubtful)* dudar (de).

mis·trust·ful (mĭs-trŭst′fəl) adj. desconfiado, receloso.

mist·y (mĭs′tē) adj. **-i·er, -i·est** *(clouded)* nebuloso, brumoso; *(obscured)* empañado; FIG. *(vague)* vago, confuso.

mis·un·der·stand (mĭs-ŭn′dər-stănd′) tr. **-stood** (-stŏŏd′), **-stand·ing** entender o interpretar mal.

mis·un·der·stand·ing (mĭs-ŭn′dər-stăn′dĭng) s. *(failure to understand)* malentendido; *(mistake)* equivocación *f*, error *m*; *(disagreement)* desacuerdo, disputa.

mis·un·der·stood (mĭs-ŭn′dər-stŏŏd′) pret. y part. p. de **misunderstand**.

mis·us·age (mĭs-yŏŏ′sĭj) s. *(ill treatment)* maltrato, abuso; *(improper application)* mal uso.

mis·use I. s. (mĭs-yŏŏs′) *(improper use)* mal empleo; *(mistreatment)* maltrato II. tr. (mĭs-yŏŏz′) **-used, -us·ing** *(to use incorrectly)* emplear mal; *(to mistreat)* maltratar, abusar de.

mis·ven·ture (mĭs-vĕn′chər) s. var. de **misadventure**.

mis·word (mĭs-wûrd′) tr. *(to express incorrectly)* expresar mal; *(to word improperly)* decir o redactar mal.

mite¹ (mīt) s. ENTOM. arador *m*, acárido.

mite² (mīt) s. *(amount of money)* suma ínfima; *(coin)* ardite *m*, moneda pequeña; *(small object)* pizca.

mi·ter (mī′tər) I. s. RELIG. mitra; CARP. *(joint, edge)* inglete *m* II. tr. unir a inglete.

miter box CARP. caja de ingletes.

miter square s. CARP. escuadra de inglete, falsa escuadra.

mit·i·gate (mĭt′ĭ-gāt′) tr. & intr. **-gat·ed, -gat·ing** *(to moderate)* mitigar(se); *(to calm)* calmar(se).

mit·i·ga·tion (mĭt′ĭ-gā′shən) s. *(relief)* mitigación *f*; *(moderation)* moderación *f.*

mi·to·sis (mī-tō′sĭs) s. [pl. **-ses** (-sēz′)] BIOL. mitosis *f.*

mi·tre (mī′tər) G.B. var. de **miter**.

mitt (mĭt) s. *(woman's glove)* mitón *m*; *(baseball glove)* guante de béisbol *m*; JER. *(hand)* mano *f*; *(fist)* puño.

mit·ten (mĭt′n) s. manopla.

mix (mĭks) I. tr. *(to blend)* mezclar; *(a drink)* preparar; *(to combine)* mezclar, combinar; *(people)* mezclar, juntar; BIOL. *(to crossbreed)* cruzar ♦ **to get mixed up in** meterse en • **to m. in** agregar a, añadir a • **to m. it up** JER. llegar a las manos, venir a los puños • **to m. up** *(to confuse)* confundir; *(to jumble)* mezclar; *(to involve)* meter, comprometer —intr. *(to become blended)* mezclarse; *(to be able to blend)* ligar; *(to go well together)* pegar <*these colors don't m.* estos colores no pegan>; *(to associate)* juntarse, andar <*to m. with rich people* andar con los ricos>; *(to get along)* llevarse bien (con la gente); BIOL. *(to be crossbred)* cruzarse II. s. *(mixture)* mezcla; *(for a cake)* masa.

mixed (mĭkst) adj. *(blended)* mezclado; *(conflicting)* contradictorio <*m. emotions* sentimientos contradictorios>; *(results)* no del todo satisfactorio; *(having various ingredients)* mixto; *(assorted)* surtido ♦ **to have m. feelings about** tener dudas acerca de.

mixed bag s. FAM. colección variada, surtido (de diferentes cosas).

mixed drink s. cóctel *m*, trago combinado.

mixed grill s. CUL. plato combinado, asado completo.

mixed marriage s. matrimonio mixto (entre personas de distintas razas o religiones).

mixed-up (mĭkst′ŭp′) adj. FAM. confundido, que no sabe lo que quiere.

ā rey / ä año / b boca / ch chico / d dar / ĕ el / ē mil / g gato / h joya / hw juez / ī aire / k casa / kw cuan /

mix·er (mǐk'sər) s. *(sociable person)* persona sociable; *(blending machine)* mezcladora; *(blending appliance)* batidora; *(beverage)* bebida (para mezclar); *(gathering)* fiesta informal para que la gente se conozca.

mix·ture (mǐks'chər) s. *(mix)* mezcla, mixtura; TEJ. tela de mezclilla, mezclilla; QUÍM. mixtura, mezcla.

mix-up (mǐks'ŭp') s. *(confusion)* confusión f, lío; FAM. *(fight)* pelea, pelotera.

miz·zen·mast (mǐz'ən-məst, -măst') s. MARÍT. *(sail)* mesana; *(mast)* palo de mesana.

mne·mon·ic (nǐ-mǒn'ǐk) I. adj. mnemotécnico, nemónico II. s. fórmula *o* rima nemónica.

mne·mon·ics (nǐ-mǒn'ǐks) s. [u. con v. sing.] mnemotécnica, nemónica.

moan (mōn) I. s. *(sound)* gemido, quejido; *(complaint)* queja; *(lamentation)* lamentación f II. intr. *(to groan)* gemir; *(to complain)* quejarse; *(to lament)* lamentarse —tr. lamentar, quejarse de.

moat (mōt) s. foso (de un castillo).

mob (mǒb) I. s. *(crowd)* multitud f, muchedumbre f; *(disorderly crowd)* turba, tropel m; *(masses)* populacho, plebe f; FAM. *(gang)* pandilla II. tr. **mobbed, mob·bing** *(to crowd in)* atestar; *(to attack in a crowd)* atacar, atropellar (en masa); *(to throng around)* rodear <*fans mobbed the movie star* los aficionados rodearon a la estrella de cine>.

mob·cap (mǒb'kăp') s. HIST. cofia.

mo·bile (mō'bəl, -bǐl') I. adj. *(movable)* móvil, movible; *(character)* cambiadizo, inconstante; *(society)* sin divisiones rígidas (de clase) II. s. (mō'bēl') ARTE. móvil m.

mobile home s. casa móvil *o* rodante.

mo·bil·i·ty (mō-bǐl'ǐ-tē) s. *(quality)* movilidad f; *(of character)* inconstancia, volubilidad f.

mo·bi·li·za·tion (mō'bə-lǐ-zā'shən) s. movilización f.

mo·bi·lize (mō'bə-līz') tr. & intr. **-lized, -liz·ing** movilizar(se).

mob·ster (mǒb'stər) s. JER. gángster m, pandillero.

moc·ca·sin (mǒk'ə-sǐn) s. *(shoe)* mocasín (calzado) m; ZOOL. mocasín (serpiente).

mo·cha (mō'kə) s. moca m.

mock (mǒk) I. tr. *(to deride)* despreciar, desdeñar; *(to ridicule)* mofarse de, ridiculizar; *(to imitate)* imitar, copiar; *(to deceive)* defraudar —intr. mofarse de, burlarse de II. s. *(act)* mofa, burla; *(laughingstock)* hazmerreír m, objeto de burla; *(imitation)* imitación f, mímica III. adv. fingidamente IV. adj. *(simulated)* simulado; *(false)* falso, fingido.

mock·er·y (mǒk'ə-rē) s. [pl. **-ies**] *(derision)* mofa, burla; *(object of ridicule)* objeto de burla; *(imitation)* imitación f, remedo; *(parody)* parodia ♦ **to make a m. of** *(to ridicule)* ridiculizar; *(to make a sham of)* parodiar.

mock-he·ro·ic (mǒk'hǐ-rō'ǐk) s. TEAT. épico-burlesco.

mock·ing·bird (mǒk'ǐng-bûrd') s. ORNIT. sinsonte m.

mock orange s. BOT. jeringuilla, celinda.

mock-up *o* **mock-up** (mǒk'ŭp') s. maqueta, modelo a escala.

mod (mǒd) I. s. COST. moda (estilo) II. adj. de moda, al día.

mo·dal (mōd'l) adj. modal.

mo·dal·i·ty (mō-dăl'ǐ-tē) s. [pl. **-ties**] modalidad f.

mode (mōd) s. *(manner)* modo, manera; *(modality)* modalidad f; *(fashion)* moda; FILOS., GRAM., MAT., MÚS. modo.

mod·el (mōd'l) I. s. *(miniature)* modelo, maqueta <*a m. of a building* la maqueta de un edificio>; *(pattern)* modelo, patrón m; *(description)* modelo <*a mathematical m.* un modelo matemático>; *(prototype)* muestra, prototipo; *(style)* modelo <*what m. is your car?* ¿cuál es el modelo de su automóvil?>; FIG. *(example)* modelo, ejemplo <*a m. of decorum* un modelo de decoro>; *(subject)* modelo mf <*the painter's m.* el modelo de un pintor>; *(mannequin)* modelo mf, maniquí m II. tr. *(to construct)* hacer un modelo de; *(to shape)* modelar <*she modeled a figure in clay* modeló una figura de arcilla>; FIG. *(to follow)* seguir el modelo de, tomar como modelo <*a daughter models her manners on her mother's* las hijas toman como modelo los modales de su madre>; *(to display)* presentar <*the mannequins modeled the spring fashion* los maniquíes presentaron la moda de primavera>; DIB., PINT. modelar ♦ **to m. after** *o* **on** construir según (modelo, diseño) —intr. *(to design)* modelar, hacer figuras <*they like to m. in clay* les gusta hacer figuras de arcilla>; *(to pose)* servir de modelo, posar <*she models for a painter* posa para un pintor> III. adj. *(typical)* modelo <*a m. house* una casa modelo>; *(exemplary)* modelo, ejemplar <*a m. child* un niño modelo>.

mod·el·ing (mōd'l-ǐng) s. *(profession)* profesión de modelo f; *(production of designs)* creación de modelos f; *(representation)* modelado.

mo·dem (mō'dĕm') s. COMPUT., RAD. modem m.

mod·er·ate (mōd'ər-ǐt) I. adj. *(not excessive)* moderado; *(reasonable)* módico <*a m. price* un precio módico>; *(mild)* moderado <*a m. climate* un clima moderado>; *(medium)* mediano, regular II. s. moderado III. tr. (-ə-rāt') **-at·ed, -at·ing** *(to temper)* moderar; *(to preside over)* presidir —intr. *(to abate)* moderarse; *(to act as a moderator)* servir de moderador.

mod·er·ate·ly (mōd'ər-ǐt-lē) adv. moderadamente.

mod·er·a·tion (mōd'ə-rā'shən) s. moderación f.

mod·er·a·tor (mōd'ə-rā'tər) s. moderador m; *(mediator)* mediador m, árbitro.

mod·ern (mōd'ərn) I. adj. moderno II. s. persona moderna, moderno.

mod·ern·ism (mōd'ər-nǐz'əm) s. modernismo.

mod·ern·ist (mōd'ər-nǐst) s. modernista mf.

mo·dern·i·ty (mə-dûr'nǐ-tē) s. modernidad f, carácter moderno.

mod·ern·i·za·tion (mōd'ər-nǐ-zā'shən) s. modernización f.

mod·ern·ize (mōd'ər-nīz') tr. & intr. **-ized, -iz·ing** modernizar(se).

mod·est (mōd'ǐst) adj. *(unpretentious)* modesto; *(reserved)* discreto, recatado <*a m. woman* una mujer recatada>; *(in dress)* pudoroso; *(in quantity)* módico <*a m. income* ingresos módicos>; *(in force)* moderado.

mod·es·ty (mōd'ǐ-stē) s. *(demureness)* modestia; *(decency)* pudor m; *(in quantity)* modicidad f; *(moderation)* moderación f.

mod·i·cum (mōd'ǐ-kəm) s. [pl. **-cums** *o* **-ca** (-kə)] pizca, ápice m.

mod·i·fi·ca·tion (mōd'ə-fǐ-kā'shən) s. modificación f.

mod·i·fi·er (mōd'ə-fī'ər) s. *(person)* modificador m; GRAM. modificativo, calificativo.

mod·i·fy (mōd'ə-fī') tr. **-fied, -fy·ing** *(to alter)* modificar, cambiar; *(to moderate)* moderar, atenuar; GRAM. modificar, calificar —intr. modificarse.

mod·ish (mō'dǐsh) adj. de moda.

mo·diste (mō-dēst') s. COST. modista mf.

mod·u·lar (mōj'ə-lər) adj. FÍS., MAT. modular, del módulo; *(furniture)* de módulos.

mod·u·late (mōj'ə-lāt') tr. & intr. **-lat·ed, -lat·ing** modular.

mod·u·la·tion (mōj'ə-lā'shən) s. modulación f.

mod·u·la·tor (mōj'ə-lā'tər) s. modulador m.

mod·ule (mōj'ōol) s. ARQ., FÍS. módulo; ELECTRÓN. *(component)* componente m; ASTRONÁUT. módulo, cápsula.

mod·u·lus (mōj'ə-ləs) s. [pl. **-li** (-lī')] FÍS., MAT. módulo, coeficiente m.

Mo·ghul (mō'gəl) s. var. de **Mogul.**

mo·gul (mō'gəl) s. pequeño montículo en una pista de esquiar.

Mo·gul (mō'gəl) s. HIST. mogol (uno de los seguidores de Baber) m; *(mongol)* mogol m, mongol m ♦ **m.** FIG. *(important person)* persona importante, magnate m.

mo·hair (mō'hâr') s. *(hair)* mohair m; *(fabric)* tela de mohair.

Mo·ham·med·an (mō-hăm'ǐ-dn) adj. & s. RELIG. mahometano, musulmán m.

Mo·ham·med·an·ism (mō-hăm'ǐ-dn-ǐz'əm) s. RELIG. mahometismo, islam m.

moi·ré (mwä-rā') *o* **moire** (mwär, mwä-rā') s. TEJ. moaré m, muaré m.

moist (moist) adj. **-er, -est** *(wet)* mojado; *(damp)* húmedo; *(rainy)* lluvioso; *(tearful)* lloroso (ojos).

mois·ten (moi'sən) tr. & intr. humedecer(se), mojar(se).

moist·ness (moist'nǐs) s. humedad f.

mois·ture (mois'chər) s. humedad f.

mois·tur·ize (mois'chə-rīz') tr. **-ized, -iz·ing** humedecer.

mois·tur·iz·er (mois'chə-rī'zər) s. cosa que humedece, humectador *m*.

mo·lar (mō'lər) I. s. ANAT. molar *m*, muela II. adj. ANAT. molar, del diente molar; FÍS., QUÍM. molar.

mo·las·ses (mə-lăs'ĭz) s. melaza.

mold¹ (mōld) I. s. *(hollow form)* molde *m*; *(model)* modelo, patrón *m*; *(molded item)* vaciado; *(shape)* forma, corte *m* <*the oval m. of her face* la forma ovalada de su cara>; *(character)* carácter *m*, temple *m* <*of heroic m.* de temple heroico>; ARQ. moldura ♦ **to be cast in the m. of** estar cortado por el patrón de II. tr. *(to shape)* moldear; *(to influence)* formar, moldear <*to m. young minds* moldear espíritus jóvenes>; *(clothes)* ceñir; *(to make a mold of)* hacer un molde de ♦ **to m. oneself on** tomar como modelo a.

mold² (mōld) BIOL. I. s. moho II. intr. enmohecerse.

mold³ (mōld) s. AGR. *(soil)* mantillo, tierra vegetal; G.B. *(earth)* tierra; *(grave)* sepulcro, tumba.

mold·er (mōl'dər) tr. & intr. desmoronar(se).

mold·ing (mōl'dĭng) s. *(molded thing)* pieza moldeada; ARQ. moldura.

mold·y (mōl'dē) adj. **-i·er, -i·est** *(containing mold)* mohoso; *(musty)* enmohecido.

mole¹ (mōl) s. ANAT. lunar *m*.

mole² (mōl) s. ZOOL. *(animal)* topo; *(skin)* piel de topo *f*; FIG. *(spy)* espía *mf*.

mole³ (mōl) s. *(breakwater)* malecón *m*, rompeolas *m*; *(harbor)* muelle *m*.

mole⁴ (mōl) s. QUÍM. mol *m*, molécula gramo.

mo·lec·u·lar (mə-lĕk'yə-lər) adj. FÍS., QUÍM. molecular.

molecular weight s. FÍS., QUÍM. peso molecular.

mol·e·cule (mŏl'ĭ-kyōōl') s. FÍS., QUÍM. molécula; FIG. *(bit)* pedacito, trocito.

mole·hill (mōl'hĭl') s. topera.

mole·skin (mōl'skĭn') s. peil de topo *f*.

mo·lest (mə-lĕst') tr. *(to annoy)* molestar; *(to harass sexually)* abusar *o* atacar sexualmente.

mo·lest·er (mə-lĕs'tər) s. *(person who disturbs)* molestador *m*; *(person who harasses sexually)* persona que comete abusos sexuales.

moll (mŏl) s. JER. *(companion)* querida de un gángster, pandillera; *(prostitute)* golfa.

mol·li·fy (mŏl'ə-fī') tr. **-fied, -fy·ing** *(to placate)* apaciguar, aplacar; *(to soften)* ablandar, molificar.

mol·lusk *o* **mol·lusc** (mŏl'əsk) s. ZOOL. molusco.

mol·ly·cod·dle (mŏl'ē-kŏd'l) I. s. FAM. niño mimado, alfeñique *mf*; *(effeminate man)* marica *m* II. tr. **-dled, -dling** mimar.

Mo·lo·tov cocktail (mŏl'ə-tôf') s. cóctel Molotov *m*.

molt (mōlt) I. tr. & intr. mudar (las plumas o la piel) II. s. muda (de las plumas o la piel).

mol·ten (mōl'tən) adj. *(melted)* derretido; *(made by melting)* fundido; *(glowing)* brillante.

mo·lyb·de·num (mə-lĭb'də-nəm) s. QUÍM. molibdeno.

mom (mŏm) s. FAM. mamá.

mom-and-pop (mŏm'ən-pŏp') adj. FAM. pequeño <*a mom-and-pop business* un negocio pequeño>.

mo·ment (mō'mənt) s. *(instant)* momento; *(period of importance)* momento <*the most important m.* el momento más importante>; *(importance)* importancia <*of great m.* de mucha importancia>; FÍS. momento ♦ **any m.** de un momento a otro • **at the last m.** en el último momento, a última hora • **at the** *o* **this m.** este momento • **for the m.** por el momento • **from that m. on** a partir de ese momento • **in a m.** *(all of a sudden)* en un momento; *(in a little while)* dentro de unos momentos; *(right away)* en seguida • **just a m.!** *o* **one m.!** *o* **wait a m.!** ¡un momento! • **not for a m.!** ¡ni muerto! • **the man of the m.** el hombre del momento • **the m. something happens** en cuanto algo suceda • **this very m.** ahora mismo • **to be all over in a m.** suceder en un instante, pasar en un abrir y cerrar de ojos • **until the last m.** hasta el último momento • **to have one's moments** tener uno sus momentos.

mo·men·tar·i·ly (mō'mən-târ'ə-lē) adv. *(for a moment)* momentáneamente; *(at any moment)* de un momento a otro; *(at every moment)* a cada momento.

mo·men·tar·y (mō'mən-tĕr'ē) adj. momentáneo.

moment of truth s. TAUR. *(final kill)* última suerte, hora de matar; *(crucial time)* hora de la verdad.

mo·men·tous (mō-mĕn'təs) adj. trascendental, de gran importancia.

mo·men·tum (mō-mĕn'təm) s. [pl. **-ta** (-tə) *o* **-tums**] FÍS. momento; FIG. *(impulse)* ímpetu *m*, impulso (personal); FILOS. importancia, momento.

Mon·a·can (mŏn'ə-kən, mə-nä'kən) adj. & s. monegasco.

Mon·a·co (mŏn'ə-ko', mə-nä'kō) s. Mónaco.

mo·nad (mō'năd') s. BIOL., FILOS., QUÍM. mónada.

mon·arch (mŏn'ərk) s. *(ruler)* monarca *m*; ENTOM. mariposa grande de color anaranjado y negro.

mo·nar·chi·cal (mə-när'kĭ-kəl) *o* **mo·nar·chic** (-kĭk) adj. monárquico.

mon·ar·chism (mŏn'ər-kĭz'əm) s. POL. monarquismo.

mon·ar·chist (mŏn'ər-kĭst) s. & adj. monárquico.

mon·ar·chy (mŏn'ər-kē) s. [pl. **-chies**] monarquía.

mon·as·ter·y (mŏn'ə-stĕr'ē) s. [pl. **-ies**] monasterio.

mo·nas·tic (mə-năs'tĭk) *o* **mo·nas·ti·cal** (-tĭ-kəl) I. adj. monástico, monacal II. s. monje *m*.

mo·nas·ti·cism (mə-năs'tĭ-sĭz'əm) s. monaquismo, monacato.

mon·a·tom·ic (mŏn'ə-tŏm'ĭk) adj. QUÍM. monatómico, monoatómico; *(univalent)* monovalente, univalente.

mon·au·ral (mŏ-nôr'əl) adj. ACÚS., RAD. monaural, monoaural (audición, sistema).

Mon·day (mŭn'dē) s. lunes *m*.

Mo·né·gasque (mŏn'ĭ-găsk') adj. & s. monegasco.

mon·e·tar·ism (mŏn'ĭ-tər-ĭzm') s. ECON. monetarismo.

mon·e·tar·y (mŏn'ĭ-tĕr'ē) adj. monetario.

mon·e·tize (mŏn'ĭ-tīz') tr. **-tized, -tiz·ing** *(to establish as legal tender)* monetizar, dar curso legal; *(to coin)* monetizar, amonedar.

mon·ey (mŭn'ē) s. [pl. **mon·eys** *o* **mon·ies**] *(in general)* dinero; *(currency)* moneda ♦ **m. doesn't grow on trees** el dinero no cae del cielo • **m. in hand** dinero contante • **m. talks** el dinero todo lo puede • **not for all the m. in the world** ni por todo el oro del mundo • **not for love or m.** por nada del mundo • **paper m.** papel moneda • **ready m.** dinero disponible • **time is m.** el tiempo es oro • **to be in the m.** estar entre los ganadores • **to be made of m.** ser millonario • **to be rolling in m.** estar nadando en dinero, ser millonario • **to coin m.** FIG. forrarse de dinero • **to come into m.** heredar dinero • **to get one's m.'s worth out of** sacar provecho de • **to give someone a run for his m.** hacer sudar a alguien, hacer pasar un mal rato a alguien • **to make m.** *(to earn)* ganar dinero; *(to produce money)* dar dinero • **to put m. into** invertir dinero en • **to put m. on** apostar a • **your m. or your life!** ¡la bolsa o la vida!

mon·ey·bag (mŭn'ē-băg') s. monedero, cartera ♦ **moneybags** FAM. *(wealth)* fortuna; *(rich person)* ricachón *m*.

mon·ey·chang·er (mŭn'ē-chān'jər) s. *(person)* cambista *mf*; *(machine)* máquina que cambia monedas *o* billetes.

mon·eyed (mŭn'ēd) adj. rico, adinerado.

mon·ey·lend·er (mŭn'ē-lĕn'dər) s. prestamista *mf*.

mon·ey·mak·er (mŭn'ē-mā'kər) s. *(person)* amasador de dinero *m*, experto en ganar dinero; *(thing)* mina *o* fuente de dinero *f*.

mon·ey·mak·ing (mŭn'ē-mā'kĭng) I. s. enriquecimiento II. adj. *(person)* que hace dinero, que gana mucho dinero; *(business)* lucrativo, productivo.

money market s. FIN. mercado monetario.

money of account s. moneda imaginaria.

money order s. giro postal.

Mon·gol (mŏng'gəl, -gōl') I. s. *(inhabitant, language)* mongol *m* II. adj. mongol, de Mongolia.

Mon·go·li·a (mŏng-gō'lē-ə) s. Mongolia.

Mon·go·li·an (mŏng-gō'lē-ən) adj. & s. *(inhabitant, language)* mongol *m*.

mon·gol·ism (mŏng'gə-lĭz'əm) s. MED. mongolismo.

Mon·gol·oid (mŏng'gə-loid') adj. & s. mongólico ♦ **m.** MED. mongoloide, mongólico.

mon·goose (mŏng'gōōs') s. ZOOL. mangosta.

mon·grel (mŭng'grəl, mŏng'-) s. & adj. híbrido, mestizo (esp. perro cruzado).

ã rey / ä año / b boca / ch chico / d dar / ĕ el / ē mil / g gato / h joya / hw juez / ī aire / k casa / kw cuan /

mon·grel·ize (mŭng′grə-līz′, mŏng′-) tr. **-ized, -iz·ing** hibridar, mestizar.

mon·ick·er (mŏn′ĭ-kər) s. var. de **moniker.**

mon·ied (mŭn′ēd) adj. var. de **moneyed.**

mon·ies (mŭn′ēz′) un pl. de **money.**

mon·i·ker (mŏn′ĭ-kər) s. JER. *(name)* nombre *m*; *(nickname)* apodo.

mo·nil·i·form (mə-nĭl′ə-fôrm′) adj. BOT., ZOOL. moniliforme.

mo·nism (mō′nĭz′əm, mŏn′ĭz′-) s. FILOS. monismo.

mo·ni·tion (mə-nĭsh′ən) s. *(admonition)* admonición *f*; *(counsel)* consejo; RELIG. monitorio.

mon·i·tor (mŏn′ĭ-tər) **I.** s. *(person)* monitor *m*; ELEC., MARÍT. *(device)* monitor; ZOOL. varano **II.** tr. RAD., TELEV. *(signal quality)* comprobar, verificar; *(for radiation)* determinar (la contaminación radioactiva de); *(to keep track of)* vigilar (electrónicamente); *(by listening)* escuchar; *(to supervise)* vigilar —intr. servir de monitor.

mon·i·to·ry (mŏn′ĭ-tôr′ē) **I.** adj. admonitorio, amonestador **II.** s. [pl. **-ries**] RELIG. monitorio.

monk (mŭngk) s. RELIG. monje *m.*

mon·key (mŭng′kē) **I.** s. [pl. **-keys**] ZOOL. *(ape)* mono; FIG., FAM. *(mischievous person)* mono, mico; TEC. maza (de martinete); JER. *(duped person)* persona engañada *o* ridiculizada; JER. *(drug addiction)* toxicomanía **II.** intr. **-keyed, -key·ing ♦ to m. around** hacer travesuras *o* payasadas • **to m. with** *o* **around with** manosear *o* jugar con algo —tr. remedar, imitar **♦ to make a m. out of someone** tomar el pelo a alguien.

monkey business s. JER. *(silly act)* tontería; *(trickery)* trampería, trucos; *(mischief)* diablura.

mon·key·shines (mŭng′kē-shīnz′) s.pl. JER. payasadas, diabluras.

monkey wrench s. MEC. llave inglesa, llave de cremallera *o* ajustable.

monk·hood (mŭngk′hŏŏd′) s. *(monasticism)* monacato; *(monks)* frailería, monjes *m.*

monk·ish (mŭng′kĭsh) adj. *(of monks)* monástico, monacal; *(of frairs)* frailuno, frailesco; *(of self-denial)* abnegado.

mon·o¹ (mŏn′ō) s. MED. mononucleosis *f.*

mon·o² (mŏn′ō) adj. ACÚS., RAD. monoaural.

mon·o·chro·mat·ic (mŏn′ə-krō-măt′ĭk) adj. monocromático, monocromo.

mon·o·chrome (mŏn′ə-krōm′) s. monocromo.

mon·o·cle (mŏn′ə-kəl) s. OPT. monóculo.

mon·o·cot·y·le·don (mŏn′ə-kŏt′l-ēd′n) *o* **mon·o·cot** (mŏn′ə-kŏt′) s. BOT. monocotiledón *m*, monocotiledoneo.

mo·noc·ra·cy (mə-nŏk′rə-sē) s. POL. autocracia.

mo·noc·u·lar (mə-nŏk′yə-lər) adj. monocular.

mon·o·cyte (mŏn′ə-sīt′) s. BIOL., FISIOL. monocito.

mon·o·dy (mŏn′ə-dē) s. [pl. **-dies**] *(elegiac verse)* elegía; MÚS. monodia.

mo·nog·a·mist (mə-nŏg′ə-mĭst) s. monógamo.

mo·nog·a·mous (mə-nŏg′ə-məs) adj. monógamo.

mo·nog·a·my (mə-nŏg′ə-mē) s. monogamia.

mon·o·gram (mŏn′ə-grăm′) **I.** s. monograma *m* **II.** tr. marcar con un monograma.

mon·o·graph (mŏn′ə-grăf′) s. monografía.

mon·o·lin·gual (mŏn′ə-lĭng′gwəl) adj. monolingüe.

mon·o·lith (mŏn′ə-lĭth′) s. monolito.

mon·o·lith·ic (mŏn′ə-lĭth′ĭk) adj. monolítico.

mo·nol·o·gue (mŏn′ə-lôg′) *o* **mon·o·log** (mŏn′ə-lôg′) s. monólogo.

mon·o·ma·ni·a (mŏn′ə-mā′nē-ə) s. monomanía.

mon·o·mor·phic (mŏn′ō-môr′fĭk) adj. QUÍM. monomórfico; ZOOL. monomorfo.

mon·o·nu·cle·o·sis (mŏn′ō-nōō′klē-ō′sĭs, -nyōō′-) s. MED. mononucleosis *f.*

mon·o·pho·bi·a (mŏn′ə-fō′bē-ə) s. PSIC. monofobia.

mon·o·plane (mŏn′ə-plān′) s. AVIA. monoplano.

mo·nop·o·list (mə-nŏp′ə-lĭst) s. monopolizador *m.*

mo·nop·o·lis·tic (mə-nŏp′ə-lĭs′tĭk) adj. monopolizador.

mo·nop·o·lize (mə-nŏp′ə-līz′) tr. **-lized, -liz·ing** *(to acquire a monopoly of)* monopolizar; *(a conversation)* dominar, adueñarse de.

mo·nop·o·liz·er (mə-nŏp′ə-lī′zər) s. monopolizador *m.*

mo·nop·o·ly (mə-nŏp′ə-lē) s. [pl. **-lies**] monopolio.

mon·o·rail (mŏn′ə-rāl′) s. F.C. monocarril *m*, monorriel *m.*

mon·o·syl·lab·ic (mŏn′ə-sĭ-lăb′ĭk) adj. *(word)* monosílabo *(palabra)*; *(language)* monosilábico (idioma).

mon·o·syl·la·ble (mŏn′ə-sĭl′ə-bəl) s. monosílabo.

mon·o·the·ism (mŏn′ə-thē′ĭz′əm) s. RELIG. monoteísmo.

mon·o·tone (mŏn′ə-tōn′) **I.** s. monotonía **♦ to speak in a m.** hablar con voz monótona **II.** adj. monótono.

mo·not·o·nous (mə-nŏt′n-əs) adj. monótono.

mo·not·o·ny (mə-nŏt′n-ē) s. monotonía.

mon·o·type (mŏn′ə-tīp′) s. BIOL. monotipo.

Mon·o·type (mŏn′ə-tīp′) s. IMPR. marca registrada de una máquina de monotipia.

mon·o·va·lent (mŏn′ə-vā′lənt) adj. QUÍM. monovalente, univalente; MED. monovalente.

mon·ox·ide (mə-nŏk′sīd′) s. QUÍM. monóxido.

mon·soon (mŏn-sōōn′) s. METEOR. monzón *m.*

mon·ster (mŏn′stər) s. monstruo.

mon·strance (mŏn′strəns) s. RELIG. custodia.

mon·stros·i·ty (mŏn-strŏs′ĭ-tē) s. [pl. **-ties**] monstruosidad *f.*

mon·strous (mŏn′strəs) adj. monstruoso.

mon·tage (mŏn-täzh′, môN-) s. ARTE., CINEM., FOTOG. montaje *m.*

mon·tane (mŏn-tān′) adj. montano.

month (mŭnth) s. mes *m* **♦ it will take him a m. of Sundays** tardará siglos en hacerlo • **never in a m. of Sundays** nunca.

month·ly (mŭnth′lē) **I.** adj. mensual **♦ m. installment** *o* m. **payment** mensualidad **II.** adv. mensualmente, una vez al mes **III.** s. [pl. **-lies**] revista mensual, mensuario **♦ monthlies** MED., FAM. mes, reglas.

mon·u·ment (mŏn′yə-mənt) s. *(memorial)* monumento; *(boundary marker)* mojón *m.*

mon·u·men·tal (mŏn′yə-mĕn′tl) adj. monumental.

moo (mōō) **I.** intr. mugir **II.** s. mugido.

mooch (mōōch) tr. JER. *(to sponge)* conseguir gratis; *(to steal)* robar, birlar —intr. *(to sponge)* gorronear; *(to idle)* haraganear.

mooch·er (mōō′chər) s. JER. *(sponger)* gorrero, sablista *mf*; *(idler)* vago; *(robber)* ratero.

mood (mōōd) s. *(temporary feeling)* humor *m*, estado de ánimo; *(disposition)* disposición (de ánimo) *f*; GRAM. modo; *(whim)* capricho **♦ to be in a bad (good) m.** estar de mal (buen) humor • **to be in the m. for** tener ganas de.

mood·i·ness (mōō′dē-nĭs) s. *(bad mood)* malhumor *m*; *(sadness)* tristeza, melancolía; *(unstable mood)* humor cambiadizo.

mood·y (mōō′dē) adj. **-i·er, -i·est** *(in a bad mood)* malhumorado; *(sad)* triste; *(whimsical)* caprichoso.

moon (mōōn) **I.** s. *(satellite)* luna; *(month)* mes *m*; *(moonlight)* claro de luna **♦ crescent m.** media luna • **many moons ago** hace muchas lunas • **once in a blue m.** de Pascuas a Ramos • **waning m.** luna menguante • **waxing m.** luna creciente **II.** intr. *(to wander about)* estar en la luna, mirar a las musarañas; *(to exhibit infatuation)* mirar lánguidamente —tr. **♦ to m. one's time away** pasarse el tiempo mirando a las musarañas.

moon·beam (mōōn′bēm′) s. rayo de luna.

moon·calf (mōōn′kăf′, -käf′) s. [pl. **-calves** (-kăvz′, -kävz′)] *(fool)* bobalicón *m*, idiota *mf*; *(freak)* monstruo.

moon·faced (mōōn′fāst′) adj. de cara redonda, carirredondo.

moon·light (mōōn′līt′) **I.** s. luz de la luna *f*, claro de luna **II.** intr. **-light·ed, -light·ing** FAM. tener otro empleo además del principal (esp. de noche).

moon·light·er (mōōn′lī′tər) s. JER. persona que tiene otro empleo además del principal.

moon·scape (mōōn′skāp′) s. *(view of the moon)* paisaje lunar *m*; *(desolate landscape)* paisaje desolado.

moon·shine (mōōn′shīn′) s. *(moonlight)* luz de la luna *f*, claro de luna; FAM. *(something foolish)* pamplinas *f*; JER. *(whiskey)* alcohol destilado ilegalmente *m.*

moon·shin·er (mōōn′shī′nər) s. JER. persona que destila licor ilegalmente.

moon·stone (mōōn′stōn′) s. MIN. piedra de la luna, adularia.

moon·struck (mōōn'strŭk') adj. *(insane)* lunático, chiflado; *(dazed)* atontado, distraído.

moon·walk (mōōn'wôk') s. ASTRONÁUT. caminata exploratoria sobre la superficie lunar.

moon·y (mōō'nē) adj. **-i·er, -i·est** *(moonlike)* parecido a la luna; *(dreamy)* soñador; *(absent-minded)* distraído.

moor¹ (mōōr) tr. MARÍT. *(by cable)* amarrar; *(by anchor)* anclar; *(to secure)* amarrar, sujetar —intr. *(with cables)* echar las amarras; *(with anchors)* echar el ancla; *(to be secured)* estar amarrado.

moor² (mōōr) s. GEOG. terreno pantanoso *o* yermo.

Moor (mōōr) s. moro.

moor·age (mōōr'ĭj) s. *(place)* amarradero; *(act)* amarradura, amarre *m; (charge)* amarraje *m.*

moor·ing (mōōr'ĭng) s. AER., MARÍT. *(cable)* amarra; *(act)* amarradura, amarre *m; (place)* amarradero ♦ **moorings** FIG. amarras.

moose (mōōs) s. [pl. **moose**] ZOOL. anta, alce *m.*

moot (mōōt) adj. ♦ **a m. point** un punto debatible.

mop (mŏp) **I.** s. *(household implement)* estropajo; *(of hair)* greña **II.** tr. **mopped, mop·ping** *(to wash)* fregar; *(to wipe)* limpiar, secar —intr. ♦ **to m. up** limpiar, secar.

mope (mōp) **I.** intr. **moped, mop·ing** abatirse, estar abatido **II.** s. persona abatida *o* apática ♦ **mopes** abatimiento, apatía.

mo·ped (mō'pĕd') s. ciclomotor *m.*

mop·pet (mŏp'ĭt) s. niño.

mop-up (mŏp'ŭp') s. MIL. limpieza.

mo·raine (mə-rān') s. GEOL. morrena, morena.

mor·al (môr'əl) **I.** adj. *(ethical)* moral; *(person)* recto; *(decision)* honrado **II.** s. *(lesson)* moraleja <*the m. of the story* la moraleja del cuento>; *(maxim)* máxima ♦ **morals** *(ethics)* principios morales <*a person with no morals* una persona sin principios morales>; *(conduct)* moral • **loose morals** costumbres relajadas • **to draw a m. from** sacar una moraleja de.

mo·rale (mə-răl') s. moral *f,* estado de ánimo.

mor·al·ism (môr'ə-lĭz'əm) s. *(maxim)* máxima, precepto moral; *(moralization)* moralización *f; (concern)* moralismo.

mor·al·ist (môr'ə-lĭst) s. *(student, teacher)* moralista *mf; (person who moralizes)* moralizador *m; (person who leads a moral life)* persona honrada.

mor·al·is·tic (môr'ə-lĭs'tĭk) adj. moralizador.

mo·ral·i·ty (mə-răl'ĭ-tē) s. [pl. **-ties**] *(quality)* moralidad *f; (morals)* moral *f; (lesson)* moralidad *f,* moraleja.

mor·al·ize (môr'ə-līz') tr. **-ized, -iz·ing** *(to interpret)* interpretar según la moral; *(to point out the lesson of)* sacar la moraleja de; *(to reform)* moralizar —intr. moralizar.

mo·rass (mə-răs') s. *(bog)* ciénaga, pantano; FIG. *(mess)* embrollo, lío.

mor·a·to·ri·um (môr'ə-tôr'ē-əm) s. [pl. **-ri·ums** *o* **-ri·a** (-ē-ə)] DER. moratoria.

mo·ray (môr'ā) s. ICT. morena.

mor·bid (môr'bĭd) adj. morboso.

mor·bid·i·ty (môr-bĭd'ĭ-tē) s. morbosidad *f.*

mor·dant (môr'dnt) **I.** adj. *(sarcastic)* mordaz; *(acute)* agudo (dolor); *(in dyeing)* mordiente **II.** s. mordiente *m* **III.** tr. tratar con un mordiente a.

more §G22, 28 (môr) **I.** adj. *(greater in number)* más <*I am carrying m. packages than you* llevo más paquetes que tú>; *(greater in quantity)* mayor, superior <*my current salary is m. than last year's* mi sueldo actual es superior al del año pasado>; *(additional)* más <*they need m. food* necesitan más comida> **II.** s. *(a greater number)* más <*two rooms are not enough, we need m.* dos cuartos no son suficientes, necesitamos más>; *(a greater quantity)* más <*this food will not be sufficient; we will need m.* esta comida no será suficiente; necesitaremos más>; *(additional amount)* más <*they told me m. about their trip* me contaron más sobre su viaje> ♦ **and what is m.** y lo que es más, y además • **the m. . . . the m. . . .** cuanto más . . . más . . . <*the m. you work, the m. you earn* cuanto más trabaja uno, más gana> • **the m. the merrier** cuanto más, mejor **III.** pron. *(something greater)* más <*m. was expected of him* se esperaba más de él>; *(greater number)* más <*they opened only two bottles,* but there were m. in the refrigerator abrieron sólo dos botellas, pero había más en la nevera> **IV.** adv. *(in a greater extent)* más <*this task is m. difficult than the other one* esta tarea es más difícil que la otra>; *(in addition)* más <*say it once m.* dígalo una vez más> ♦ **any m.** más <*they will not come back any m.* no vendrán más> • **m. and m.** cada vez más • **m. or less** más *o* menos • **m. than** *(with adjectives)* más que <*this model is m. recent than the other* este modelo es más reciente que el otro>; *(with numbers)* más de <*they paid m. than one hundred dollars* pagaron más de cien dólares> • **much m.** mucho más • **no m.** ya no • **one m.** uno más, otro • **to be no m.** *(to exist no longer)* ya no existir; *(to be dead)* haber fallecido.

mo·rel (mə-rĕl') s. BOT. morilla, cagarria.

more·o·ver (môr-ō'vər) adv. además, por otra parte.

mo·res (môr'āz') s.pl. *(customs)* costumbres *f,* usos; *(traditions)* tradiciones *f.*

mor·ga·nat·ic (môr'gə-năt'ĭk) adj. morganático.

morgue (môrg) s. *(place)* depósito de cadáveres; *(file)* archivo (de un periódico).

mor·i·bund (môr'ə-bənd) adj. moribundo.

mo·ri·on (môr'ē-ŏn') s. HIST. morrión (casco metálico antiguo) *m.*

Mor·mon (môr'mən) s. RELIG. mormón *m.*

morn (môrn) s. POÉT. *(morning)* mañana; *(dawn)* alborada, alba.

morn·ing (môr'nĭng) s. *(part of day)* mañana; FIG. *(beginning)* comienzo, principio.

morn·ing-glo·ry (môr'nĭng-glôr'ē) s. BOT. dondiego de día, campanilla.

morning sickness s. MED. naúseas del embarazo.

morning star s. lucero del alba.

Mo·roc·can (mə-rŏk'ən) adj. & s. marroquí *mf.*

mo·roc·co (mə-rŏk'ō) s. marroquí *m,* tafilete *m.*

Mo·roc·co (mə-rŏk'ō) s. Marruecos *m.*

mo·ron (môr'ŏn') s. MED. morón *m,* retardado mental; FAM. *(stupid person)* imbécil *m.*

mo·ron·ic (mə-rŏn'ĭk) adj. MED. morónico; FAM. *(stupid)* imbécil.

mo·rose (mə-rōs') adj. malhumorado.

mor·pheme (môr'fēm') s. GRAM. morfema *m.*

mor·phine (môr'fēn') s. QUÍM. morfina.

mor·phol·o·gy (môr-fŏl'ə-jē) s. BIOL., GRAM. morfología.

mor·ris (môr'ĭs) s. ANT. danza morisca inglesa.

mor·row (môr'ō) s. *(tomorrow)* día siguiente *m;* FIG. *(future)* futuro, porvenir *m.*

Morse code (môrs) s. TELEG. código Morse.

mor·sel (môr'səl) s. *(bite)* bocado; *(piece)* pedazo; *(delicacy)* manjar *m.*

mor·tal (môr'tl) **I.** adj. *(subject to death)* mortal; *(human)* humano; *(fatal)* mortal; *(terrible)* terrible <*m. fear* miedo terrible>; RELIG. *(sin)* mortal **II.** s. *(human being)* mortal *m; (individual)* tipo.

mor·tal·i·ty (môr-tăl'ĭ-tē) s. [pl. **-ties**] *(condition)* mortalidad *f; (deaths)* mortandad *f; (death rate)* mortalidad.

mor·tal·ly (môr'tl-ē) adv. *(fatally)* mortalmente; *(terribly)* terriblemente.

mortal sin s. RELIG. pecado mortal.

mor·tar (môr'tər) **I.** s. *(vessel)* mortero, almirez *m;* MEC. trituradora; ARM. mortero; CONSTR. *(cement)* mortero, argamasa **II.** tr. CONSTR. argamasar; MIL. bombardear con morteros.

mor·tar·board (môr'tər-bôrd') s. *(mortar holder)* esparavel *m; (hat)* birrete *m.*

mort·gage (môr'gĭj) **I.** s. *(pledge, claim)* hipoteca; *(contract)* contrato de hipoteca **II.** tr. **-gaged, -gag·ing** hipotecar.

mort·ga·gee (môr'gĭ-jē') s. acreedor hipotecario.

mort·ga·gor (môr'gĭ-jôr', môr'gĭ-jər) s. deudor hipotecario.

mor·tice (môr'tĭs) s. var. de **mortise**.

mor·ti·cian (môr-tĭsh'ən) s. empresario de pompas fúnebres.

mor·ti·fi·ca·tion (môr'tə-fĭ-kā'shən) s. *(humiliation)* mortificación *f; (torment)* tormento; MED. necrosis *f;* gangrena.

mor·ti·fy (môr'tə-fī') tr. **-fied, -fy·ing** *(to humiliate)* mortificar; *(to deny oneself)* mortificar, macerar (apetitos) —intr. *(to deny oneself)* mortificarse; MED. gangrenarse.

mor·ti·fy·ing (môr'tə-fī'ĭng) adj. mortificador, mortificante.

ä rey / ä año / b boca / ch chico / d dar / ĕ el / ē mil / g gato / h joya / hw juez / ī aire / k casa / kw cuan /

mor·tise (môr′tĭs) s. CARP. mortaja, muesca.
mort·main (môrt′mān′) s. DER. manos muertas.
mor·tu·ar·y (môr′chōō-ĕr′ē) s. [pl. -ies] mortuorio.
mo·sa·ic (mō-zā′ĭk) s. mosaico.
Mo·sa·ic (mō-zā′ĭk) adj. RELIG. mosaico.
Mos·cow (mŏs′kou′) s. Moscú.
mo·sey (mō′zē) intr. -seyed, -sey·ing FAM. (to stroll) deambular; (to move along) irse, largarse.
Mos·lem (mŏz′ləm) RELIG. I. adj. (of Islam) islámico, musulmán II. s. musulmán m, islamita mf.
mosque (mŏsk) s. mezquita.
mos·qui·to (mə-skē′tō) s. [pl. -toes o -tos] mosquito.
mosquito net s. mosquitero.
moss (môs) s. BOT. musgo; (bog) pantano.
moss·back (môs′băk′) s. FIG., FAM. retrógrado, anticuado.
moss·y (mô′sē) adj. -i·er, -i·est (covered with moss) musgoso; (resembling moss) parecido al musgo; (antiquated) anticuado.
most §G22, 28 (mōst) I. adj. (greatest in quantity) más . . . que todos los demás <she makes the m. money ella gana más dinero que todos los demás>; (greatest in measure) mayor, máximo <it aroused the m. interest suscitó el mayor interés>; (almost all) la mayoría de, la mayor parte de <m. people like television a la mayoría de las personas les gusta la televisión> ♦ for the m. part en su mayor parte, en su mayoría II. s. (the greatest amount) la mayor parte <they put up m. of the money pusieron la mayor parte del dinero>; (the majority) la mayoría <those customers have much better taste than m. esos clientes tienen mucho mejor gusto que la mayoría> ♦ at (the) m. como máximo, a lo sumo • the m. lo más, lo máximo • to make the m. of aprovechar al máximo, sacar el mayor partido de III. pron. la mayoría, la mayor parte <m. of the children were absent la mayoría de los niños estaban ausentes> IV. adv. (in the highest degree) más . . . que todos los demás <this house costs m. esta casa cuesta más que todas las demás>; [como superlativo] más <she is the m. intelligent woman I have ever met es la mujer más inteligente que he conocido>; (very) muy, sumamente <a m. unusual circumstance una circunstancia muy rara>; FAM. (almost) casi <m. everyone agrees casi todos están de acuerdo> ♦ m. certainly con toda seguridad • m. likely muy probablemente • m. of all sobre todo.
most·ly (mōst′lē) adv. (for the most part) en su mayor parte <the task is m. done la tarea está hecha en su mayor parte>; (principally) principalmente; (usually) generalmente.
mote (mōt) s. (particle) partícula; (speck) mota.
mo·tel (mō-tĕl′) s. motel m.
mo·tet (mō-tĕt′) s. MÚS. motete m.
moth (môth) s. [pl. moths (môthz, môths)] ENTOM. mariposa nocturna; (clothes moth) polilla.
moth·ball (môth′bôl′) s. bola de naftalina ♦ in o into moth-balls en condición de almacenamiento prolongado.
moth·ball (môth′bôl′) tr. almacenar, guardar (por largo tiempo).
moth·eat·en (môth′ēt′n) adj. (eaten away) apolillado; (old) viejo.
moth·er (mŭth′ər) I. s. (parent) madre f; (origin) madre; (cause) causa <poverty is the m. of many ills la pobreza es la causa de muchos males>; (mother superior) superiora II. adj. (motherly) materno <m. love amor materno>; (tongue) materno; (country) madre III. tr. (to give birth to) dar a luz a; (to produce) ser la fuente de, dar lugar a; (to protect) cuidar como una madre.
mother cell s. BIOL. célula madre.
Mother Goose s. LIT. La Oca Cuentista (supuesta autora de versos infantiles).
moth·er·hood (mŭth′ər-hŏŏd′) s. maternidad f.
moth·er-in-law (mŭth′ər-ĭn-lô′) s. [pl. moth·ers-in-law] suegra.
moth·er·land (mŭth′ər-lănd′) s. (country of birth) patria, suelo natal; (country of ancestors) madre patria.
moth·er·ly (mŭth′ər-lē) adj. materno, maternal.
moth·er-of-pearl (mŭth′ər-əv-pûrl′) s. madreperla, nácar m.

Mother's Day s. Día de la Madre m.
mother superior s. RELIG. madre superiora.
mother tongue s. (one's native language) lengua materna; (root language) lengua madre (latín, griego).
moth·proof (môth′prŏŏf′) I. adj. a prueba de polillas II. tr. hacer a prueba de polillas.
moth·y (mô′thē) adj. -i·er, -i·est apolillado, lleno de polillas.
mo·tif (mō-tēf′) s. ARQ., ARTE., MÚS. motivo.
mo·tile (mōt′l, mō′tīl′) adj. BIOL. móvil, movible.
mo·tion (mō′shən) I. s. (movement) movimiento m; (gesture) ademán m, gesto; MÚS. cambio de tono; DER. (petition, claim) pedimento; (proposal) moción f ♦ to set in m. poner en marcha II. tr. indicar con la mano —intr. hacer señas o una señal.
mo·tion·less (mō′shən-lĭs) adj. inmóvil.
motion picture s. filme m, película cinematográfica.
motion sickness s. mareo, náuseas (producidas por el movimiento).
mo·ti·vate (mō′tə-vāt′) tr. -vat·ed, -vat·ing motivar.
mo·ti·va·tion (mō′tə-vā′shən) s. motivación f.
mo·ti·va·tion·al (mō′tə-vā′shə-nəl) adj. que motiva, que impulsa.
mo·tive (mō′tĭv) I. s. (reason) motivo; (cause) causa; (impulse for a crime) móvil m II. adj. (causing action) motor, motriz; (impelling) impulsor, incitador.
mot·ley (mŏt′lē) adj. (heterogeneous) variado, diverso; (multicolored) multicolor, abigarrado.
mo·to·cross (mō′tō-krôs′) s. DEP. motocross m.
mo·to·neu·ron (mō′tə-nŏŏr′ŏn′, -nyŏŏr′-) s. FISIOL. motoneurona, neurona motora.
mo·tor (mō′tər) I. s. (device) motor m; (automobile) automóvil m II. adj. motor, motriz <m. power fuerza motriz>; (driven by a motor) de motor; FISIOL. motor III. intr. ir en automóvil.
mo·tor·bike (mō′tər-bīk′) s. (motorcycle) motocicleta liviana; (motorized bicycle) velomotor m, bicicleta a motor.
mo·tor·boat (mō′tər-bōt′) s. bote a motor m, lancha motora.
mo·tor·cade (mō′tər-kād′) s. caravana o desfile m de automóviles.
mo·tor·car (mō′tər-kär′) s. automóvil m, coche m.
motor court s. motel m, posada para motoristas.
mo·tor·cy·cle (mō′tər-sī′kəl) I. s. motocicleta, moto f II. intr. -cled, -cling ir o viajar en motocicleta.
mo·tor·cy·clist (mō′tər-sī′klĭst) s. motociclista mf.
motor home s. tipo de casa a remolque con motor.
motor inn s. motel m, hotel con estacionamiento m.
mo·tor·ist (mō′tər-ĭst) s. automovilista mf, motorista mf.
mo·tor·ize (mō′tə-rīz′) tr. -ized, -iz·ing motorizar.
motor lodge s. motel m.
mo·tor·man (mō′tər-mən) s. [pl. -men] conductor m, maquinista (de tranvía o tren eléctrico) mf.
motor pool s. MIL. servicio común de vehículos motorizados.
motor scooter s. scooter m.
motor vehicle s. vehículo automotor, vehículo motorizado.
mo·tor·way (mō′tər-wā′) s. G.B. autopista.
mot·tle (mŏt′l) I. tr. -tled, -tling motear, jaspear II. s. (spot) mancha o veta de color; (pattern) diseño o apariencia veteada.
mot·tled (mŏt′ld) adj. moteado, veteado.
mot·to (mŏt′ō) s. [pl. -toes o -tos] lema m, divisa f.
mould (mōld) s. & v. G.B. var. de mold.
moult (mōlt) s. & v. G.B. var. de molt.
mound (mound) I. s. montículo II. tr. (to fortify) terraplenar; (to heap) amontonar.
mount¹ (mount) I. tr. (to climb) subir <she mounted the stairs subió la escalera>; (to get up on) subir a <to m. the rostrum subir a la tribuna>; (a horse) montar, montarse en; (to provide with a horse) proporcionar un caballo a; (to copulate with) montar, cubrir; (to fix in place) pegar, fijar; (to carry out) emprender, lanzar <to m. an advertising campaign emprender una campaña publicitaria>; MEC., TEAT. montar; MIL. (guns) montar; (sentries) apostar (a un centinela); (an attack) lanzar (un ataque) —intr. (to move upward) ascender, subir; (to ride) montar; (to increase)

aumentar **II.** s. *(animal)* montura, cabalgadura; *(for a device)* base *f*, soporte *m*; *(for a jewel)* montura, engaste *m*; *(for a photograph)* borde *m*; *(for microscopy)* portaobjeto; *(for a gun)* cureña.

mount² (mount) s. monte *m*, montaña.

moun·tain (moun'tən) s. *(mount)* montaña; FIG. *(large heap)* montón *m*, pila; *(large quantity)* montón, sinnúmero.

mountain ash s. BOT. serbal *m*.

mountain dew s. FAM. whisky (destilado ilegalmente).

moun·tain·eer (moun'tə-nîr') **I.** s. *(inhabitant)* montañés *m*; *(mountain climber)* alpinista *mf*, montañero **II.** intr. hacer alpinismo, escalar montañas.

mountain goat s. ZOOL. cabra de las Montañas Rocosas.

mountain laurel s. calmia.

mountain lion s. ZOOL. puma *m*, león americano.

moun·tain·ous (moun'tə-nəs) adj. *(hilly)* montañoso; *(immense)* inmenso, gigantesco.

mountain range s. cordillera, sierra.

mountain sheep s. ZOOL. musmón *m*.

mountain sickness s. MED. mal de montaña *m*, soroche *m*.

moun·tain·side (moun'tən-sīd') s. ladera *o* falda de una montaña.

moun·tain·top (moun'tən-tŏp') s. cima *o* cumbre de una montaña *f*.

moun·te·bank (moun'tə-băngk') s. *(hawker)* saltabanco.

mount·ed (moun'tĭd) adj. montado.

Mount·ie *o* **Mount·y** (moun'tē) s. [pl. **-ies**] FAM. miembro de la policía montada canadiense.

mount·ing (moun'tĭng) s. *(of a horse)* montura, montadura; *(of a jewel)* engaste *m*, montura; TEAT., TEC. montaje *m*.

mourn (môrn) intr. *(to express sorrow)* llorar; *(to express grief for a death)* lamentarse; *(to be in mourning)* estar de luto —tr. llorar, lamentar (la muerte de).

mourn·er (môr'nər) s. *(person)* persona que está de luto; *(at a funeral)* doliente *mf*.

mourn·ful (môrn'fəl) adj. *(feeling grief)* dolorido, triste; *(arousing grief)* penoso.

mourn·ful·ness (môrn'fəl-nĭs) s. tristeza, pesar *m*.

mourn·ing (môr'nĭng) s. *(sadness)* duelo, dolor *m*, pena; *(period)* luto, duelo ♦ **to be in m.** estar de luto.

mourning dove s. ORNIT. especie de paloma torcaza *f*.

mouse (mous) **I.** s. [pl. **mice** (mīs)] ZOOL. ratón *m*; FAM. *(coward)* cobarde *m*; *(black eye)* ojo a la funerala **II.** intr. (mouz) **moused, mous·ing** *(to hunt mice)* cazar ratones; *(to prowl)* andar al acecho.

mous·er (mou'zər) s. ratonero, gato *o* animal que caza ratones *m*.

mouse·trap (mous'trăp') s. ratonera.

mous·ey (mou'sē) adj. var. de **mousy.**

mousse (mōos) s. CUL. postre frío espumoso a base de crema batida y gelatina.

mous·tache (mŭs'tăsh', mə-stăsh') s. var. de **mustache.**

mous·y (mou'sē) adj. **-i·er, -i·est** *(like a mouse)* ratonesco, ratonil; FAM. *(dull gray)* pardusco; *(timid)* tímido.

mouth (mouth) **I.** s. [pl. **mouths** (mouthz)] ANAT. boca <*open your m.!* ¡abra la boca!>; *(dependent)* boca <*she has nine mouths to feed* tiene nueve bocas que alimentar>; *(grimace)* mueca, gesto; *(spokesman)* portavoz *m*, vocero; *(natural opening)* boca (de volcán, mina); *(of a river)* boca, desembocadura; *(of a container)* boca (de jarra); MEC., ARM. boca ♦ **by word of m.** contado por una persona a otra • **from the horse's m.** de buena tinta • **not to open one's m.** no decir esta boca es mía • **to be down in the m.** estar deprimido • **to foam at the m.** echar espuma por la boca • **to have a big m.** ser un bocazas • **to keep one's m. shut** callar(se) • **to live from hand to m.** vivir al día • **to make one's m. water** hacérsele a uno la boca agua • **to put words into someone's m.** poner palabras en boca de alguien • **to shoot one's m. off** JER. hablar más de la cuenta • **watch your m.!** FAM. ¡ten cuidado con lo que dices! **II.** tr. (mouth) *(to pronounce)* pronunciar; *(to utter)* decir (de forma afectada); *(to form words soundlessly)* articular en silencio; *(to take into the mouth)* meter en la boca —intr. *(to declaim)* hablar con rimbombancia; *(to grimace)* hacer muecas ♦ **to m. off** hablar con descaro.

mouth·ful (mouth'fōol') s. *(of food)* bocado; *(of smoke)* bocanada ♦ **you said a m.!** FAM. ¡muy bien dicho!

mouth organ s. MÚS. *(harmonica)* armónica; *(panpipe)* siringa.

mouth·piece (mouth'pēs') s. *(of a musical instrument)* boquilla; *(of a telephone)* micrófono, bocina; FAM. *(spokesman)* vocero, portavoz *m*; JER. *(lawyer)* penalista *mf*, abogado (defensor).

mouth-to-mouth (mouth'tə-mouth') adj. de boca a boca.

mouth·wash (mouth'wŏsh') s. enjuague *m*.

mouth·y (mou'thē, -thē) adj. **-i·er, -i·est** bombástico, ampuloso.

mov·a·bil·i·ty (mōo'və-bĭl'ĭ-tē) s. movilidad *f*.

mov·a·ble (mōo'və-bəl) **I.** adj. *(mobile)* movible, móvil; *(varying in date)* móvil <*a m. feast* una fiesta móvil>; DER. *(effects)* mobiliario; *(property)* mueble **II.** s. ♦ **movables** *(furniture)* muebles; DER. *(property)* bienes muebles.

move (mōov) **I.** intr. **moved, mov·ing** *(to change place)* moverse <*don't m.!* ¡no se mueva!>; *(to change position)* cambiar de postura <*she moved in her sleep* cambió de postura mientras dormía>; *(to advance)* avanzar, progresar; *(to follow a course)* moverse <*the earth moves in orbit around the sun* la tierra se mueve en órbita alrededor del sol>; *(to relocate)* mudarse; COM. *(to sell)* venderse <*furs m. slowly in summer* los abrigos de piel se venden mal en verano>; *(to be stirred)* moverse <*leaves moving in the breeze* hojas que se mueven con la brisa>; MEC. *(to operate)* ponerse en marcha, funcionar; *(to act)* actuar, entrar en acción; *(to be active)* moverse <*to m. in diplomatic circles* moverse en los medios diplomáticos>; *(to make a motion)* presentar una moción, proponer; FAM. *(to depart)* irse <*it's time to get moving* es hora de irse>; *(the bowels)* evacuarse (el vientre); *(in a game)* jugar, hacer una jugada ♦ **to m. about** *o* **around** *(to change position)* cambiar de sitio; *(to be in motion)* moverse; *(to come and go)* ir y venir, circular • **to m. along** *o* **forward** avanzar, seguir adelante • **to m. away** alejarse • **to m. in** *(to settle)* instalarse; *(to enter)* entrar • **to m. in** *o* **on** *(to advance)* avanzar; *(to control)* intentar apoderarse de; *(to change residence)* mudarse • **to m. out** irse • **to m. up** *(to go up)* subir; *(to be promoted)* ascender —tr. *(to change the place of)* trasladar, cambiar de lugar <*I moved my office* trasladé mi oficina>; *(to change the position of)* mover <*she moved her fingers* movió los dedos de la mano>; *(in games)* mover <*to m. a pawn in chess* mover un peón en el ajedrez>; *(to prompt)* impulsar; *(to rouse)* mover a, inducir a <*disgust moved him to speak up* la repugnancia le indujo a hablar>; MEC. *(to set in motion)* poner en marcha *o* en funcionamiento; *(to cause to function)* hacer funcionar; *(to cause to progress)* hacer progresar; *(to shake)* mover, sacudir <*the wind moved the flowers* el viento movía las flores>; *(to stir)* conmover <*her sad story moved him deeply* su relato triste le conmovió profundamente>; *(to propose)* proponer <*the judge moved adjournment* el juez propuso la suspensión de la sesión>; COM. *(to sell)* vender <*this dealer can m. a lot of goods* este comerciante puede vender muchas mercancías>; *(the bowels)* mover, evacuar (el vientre) ♦ **to m. up** *(to make go up)* subir; *(to advance)* adelantar (una fecha); *(to promote)* ascender **II.** s. *(movement)* movimiento; *(change of residence)* mudanza, traslado; *(moving of a piece)* jugada <*it is a good m.* es una buena jugada>; *(player's turn)* turno <*it's my m.* es mi turno>; *(step)* paso, gestión *f* <*my next m. is to buy a car* mi próximo paso es comprar un automóvil> ♦ **on the m.** *(moving around)* andando de acá para allá; *(active)* activo <*they are on the m. again* están activos de nuevo> • **to get a m. on** FAM. empezar a moverse.

move·a·ble (mōo'və-bəl) adj. & s. var. de **movable.**

move·ment (mōov'mənt) s. *(motion)* movimiento <*the Earth's m.* el movimiento de la Tierra>; *(of vehicles)* tránsito, circulación *f*; MIL. *(maneuver)* desplazamiento; *(transportation)* transporte *m*; *(transfer)* traslado; *(gesture)* gesto; POL. movimiento <*the peace m.* el movimiento en pro de la paz>; *(tendency)* tendencia <*m. toward conservatism* una tendencia al conservatismo>; COM. *(in stocks)* actividad *f*; *(in price)* fluctuación *f*; *(of* *sales)* venta; FISIOL. *(of bowels)* evacuación (del vientre) *f*; LIT. *(of a plot)* desarrollo (de la trama); *(of a poem)* cadencia (de un poema); MÚS. movimiento; *(mechanism)* mecanismo (de un reloj); *(operation)* funcionamiento.

mov·er (mōō′vər) s. *(promoter)* promotor *m*; *(instigator)* fomentador *m*; *(proposer of a motion)* autor *m*; *(transporter)* persona que hace mudanzas. ♦ **movers** agencia de mudanzas.

mov·ie (mōō′vē) s. *(film)* película; *(theater)* cine *m*, sala de cine ♦ **movies** cine.

movie camera s. CINEM. cámara.

mov·ie·go·er (mōō′vē-gō′ər) s. aficionado al cine.

mov·ie·mak·er (mōō′ve-mā′kər) s. cineasta *mf*.

movie star s. estrella de cine.

movie theater s. cine *m*.

mov·ing (mōō′vĭng) adj. *(changing position)* móvil; *(changing residence)* de mudanza; *(in motion)* en movimiento, en marcha; *(driving)* motor, motriz; *(touching)* conmovedor, patético.

moving picture s. película (cinematográfica).

mow[1] (mou) s. *(barn)* granero, henil *m*; *(stored feed)* montón de heno *o* de gavillas *m*, hacina.

mow[2] (mō) tr. mowed *o* mown (mōn), mow·ing *(to cut down)* segar; *(to cut growth from)* cortar, segar.

mow·er (mō′ər) s. *(person)* segador *m*; *(machine)* segadora; *(for a lawn)* cortacéspedes *m*.

mow·ing (mō′ĭng) s. AGR. *(reaping)* siega; *(the lawn)* corte *m* ♦ **m. machine** AGR. *(for crops)* segadora; *(for a lawn)* cortacéspedes *m*.

mown (mōn) un part. p. de **mow**[2].

mox·ie (mŏk′sē) s. *(pluck)* coraje *m*; *(pep)* energía, brío.

Mo·zam·bic·an (mō′zəm-bē′kən) adj. & s. mozambiqueño.

Mo·zam·bique (mō′zəm-bēk′) s. Mozambique *m*.

Moz·a·rab (mō-zăr′əb) s. HIST. mozárabe *mf*.

mo·zet·ta (mō-zĕt′ə) s. RELIG. muceta.

Mr. (mĭs′tər) s. [abr. de **Mister**; pl. **Messrs.** (mĕs′ərz)] Sr.

Mrs. (mĭs′ĭz) s. [abr. de **Mistress**; pl. **Mmes.** (mā-däm′, -däm′)] Sra.

Ms. *o* **Ms** (mĭz) s. abr. que se usa en vez de **Mrs.** *o* de **Miss.**

mu (myōō, mōō) s. my (letra griega) *f*.

much §G28 (mŭch) I. adj. **more** (môr), **most** (mōst) mucho <*m. rain* mucha lluvia> ♦ **as m. . . . as** tanta . . . como • **as m. . . . as you need** todo . . . que le haga falta • **how m.?** ¿cuánto? • **three times as m.** tres veces más • **too m.** demasiado II. s. *(a lot)* mucho <*is there m. to read?* ¿hay mucho que leer?>; *(large part)* gran parte *f* <*m. of the crop was lost* se perdió gran parte de la cosecha> ♦ **as m. again** otro tanto • **as m. as** tanto como • **as m. as to say** como si dijera • **at so m. a yard** a tanto la yarda • **I thought as m.** ya me lo figuraba • **it's as m. as anybody can do** es todo lo que se puede hacer • **not so m. as** ni siquiera • **not to be m.** no ser gran cosa • **not to be m. of** *(a singer)* no ser gran cosa como (cantante); *(a party)* poderse llamar a duras penas (una fiesta) • **not to think m. of** *(something)* no creer que (algo) valga gran cosa; *(someone)* no tener un gran concepto de (alguien) • **so m.** tanto • **so m. for that** ahí quedó la cosa, borrón y cuenta nueva • **so m. so that** tanto que • **so m. the better** tanto mejor, mejor así • **there's not m. to it** no es muy complicado • **this** *o* **that m.** un tanto así • **to be too m. of a good thing** ser demasiado • **to do as m.** hacer otro tanto, hacer lo mismo • **to make m. of** dar mucha importancia a • **to say this m. for someone** decir esto en defensa de alguien • **too m.** demasiado • **twice as m.** el doble III. adv. *(a lot)* mucho; *(very)* muy <*m. obliged* muy agradecido>; *(just about)* casi, poco más *o* menos <*m. the same color* poco más *o* menos el mismo color> ♦ **ever so m.** muchísimo • **however m.** por mucho que • **how m.?** ¿cuánto? • **how m. is it?** ¿cuánto es? • **m. to my amazement** con gran sorpresa mía • **to m. rather** preferir • **very m.** mucho, muy.

mu·ci·lage (myōō′sə-lĭj) s. BOT. mucílago; *(adhesive)* goma de pegar *(esp. de origen vegetal)*.

muck (mŭk) I. s. *(mud)* lodo; *(dirt)* suciedad *f*; *(manure)* estiércol *m*; *(fertile soil)* mantillo, humus *m*; *(refuse)* desperdicio, basura II. tr. *(to fertilize)* estercolar, abonar; FAM. *(to dirty)* ensuciar; *(to remove the refuse)* retirar los

desperdicios (de una mina) ♦ **to m. up** *(to dirty)* ensuciar; *(to spoil)* echar a perder; *(to bungle)* chapucear.

muck·a·muck (mŭk′ə-mŭk′) s. JER. persona importante.

muck·rake (mŭk′rāk′) intr. **-raked, -rak·ing** descubrir *o* revelar escándalos.

muck·rak·er (mŭk′rā′kər) s. revelador de escándalos públicos *m*.

muck·y (mŭk′ē) adj. **-i·er, -i·est** sucio, asqueroso.

mu·cous (myōō′kəs) adj. mucoso.

mucous membrane s. ANAT. membrana mucosa.

mu·cus (myōō′kəs) s. mucosidad *f*, moco.

mud (mŭd) s. *(dirt)* barro, lodo; FIG. *(slanderous charges)* difamación *f*, calumnia; *(degradation)* vilipendio ♦ **to throw** *o* **sling m. at someone** calumniar a alguien, arrastrar a alguien por los suelos.

mud·dle (mŭd′l) tr. **-dled, -dling** *(to muddy)* enturbiar; *(to jumble)* embrollar; *(to befuddle)* atontar; *(to bungle)* chapucear; *(to stir)* revolver, mezclar —intr. obrar *o* pensar confusamente ♦ **to m. through** salir bien a pesar de torpezas.

mud·dle-head·ed (mŭd′l-hĕd′ĭd) adj. *(confused)* confuso, confundido; *(stupid)* estúpido, despistado.

mud·dy (mŭd′ē) I. adj. **-di·er, -di·est** *(full of mud)* fangoso, lleno de lodo; *(soiled)* lleno de fango; *(cloudy)* turbio; *(complexion)* terroso; *(confused)* turbio II. tr. **-died, -dy·ing** *(to soil)* enfangar, llenar de fango; *(a river)* llenar de fango; *(to make cloudy)* enturbiar; *(to make confused)* enturbiar ♦ **to m. the waters** FIG. complicar una situación.

mud flat s. marisma.

mud·guard (mŭd′gärd′) s. guardabarros *m*, guardafango.

mud·sling·er (mŭd′slĭng′ər) s. calumniador *m*, infamador *m*.

mud·sling·ing (mŭd′slĭng′ĭng) s. calumnia, vilipendio.

mu·ez·zin (myōō-ĕz′ĭn) s. RELIG. almuecín *m*, almuédano.

muff[1] (mŭf) I. tr. & intr. *(to bungle)* hacer mal (algo); *(to spoil)* perder, desperdiciar (una ocasión); DEP. dejar caer, dejar escapar (la pelota) II. s. chapucería, torpeza.

muff[2] (mŭf) s. manguito (para las manos).

muf·fin (mŭf′ĭn) s. CUL. mollete *m*, panecillo.

muf·fle[1] (mŭf′əl) I. tr. **-fled, -fling** *(to wrap up one's face)* embozar; *(to cover)* tapar; *(to deaden a sound)* amortiguar; *(to make vague)* confundir II. s. amortiguador *m*.

muf·fle[2] (mŭf′əl) s. ANAT., ZOOL. hocico, morro.

muf·fler (mŭf′lər) s. *(scarf)* bufanda; AUTO. silenciador *m*.

muf·ti (mŭf′tē) s. traje de paisano *m*, traje de civil.

mug[1] (mŭg) s. jarra (recipiente y contenido).

mug[2] (mŭg) I. s. JER. *(face)* jeta, hocico; FAM. *(hoodlum)* rufián *m* II. tr. **mugged, mug·ging** *(to take a mugshot)* fotografiar; *(to assault)* asaltar, atracar —intr. JER. exagerar los gestos.

mug·ger (mŭg′ər) s. asaltante *mf*.

mug·ging (mŭg′ĭng) s. asalto, ataque (con intento de robo) *m*.

mug·gy (mŭg′ē) adj. **-gi·er, -gi·est** bochornoso, caluroso y húmedo.

Mu·ham·mad·an *o* **Mu·ham·med·an** (mōō-hăm′ĭ-dn) s. var. de **Mohammedan**.

mu·lat·to (mə-lăt′ō, -lä′tō) s. [pl. **-tos** *o* **-toes**] mulato.

mul·ber·ry (mŭl′bĕr′ē) s. [pl. **-ries**] BOT. *(tree)* morera, moral *m*; *(berry)* mora; *(color)* color morado.

mulch (mŭlch) I. s. AGR. pajote *m* II. tr. cubrir con pajote.

mule[1] (myōōl) s. *(animal)* mulo; BIOL. híbrido estéril; FAM. *(stubborn person)* mula, testarudo; TEC. máquina de hilar; *(hauling vehicle)* tractor *m*.

mule[2] (myōōl) s. *(slipper)* chinela, pantufla.

mule-skin·ner (myōōl′skĭn′ər) s. FAM. mulero, arriero.

mu·le·ta (mōō-lā′tə) s. TAUR. muleta.

mule·teer (myōō′lə-tîr′) s. mulero, arriero.

mul·ish (myōō′lĭsh) adj. terco, testarudo.

mull[1] (mŭl) tr. CUL. calentar con especias.

mull[2] (mŭl) tr. & intr. *(to ponder)* meditar, ponderar (sobre).

mul·lein (mŭl′ən) s. BOT. gordolobo, barbasco.

mul·let (mŭl′ĭt) s. [pl. **mullet** *o* **-lets**] ICT. mújol *m*, lisa ♦ **red m.** salmonete *m*.

mul·lion (mŭl′yən) s. ARQ. parteluz *m*, mainel *m*.

mul·ti·ad·dress (mŭl′tē-ăd′rĕs′) adj. COMPUT. de dirección múltiple.

mul·ti·cel·lu·lar (mŭl′tē-sĕl′yə-lər) adj. BIOL. multicelular, pluricelular.

mul·ti·col·ored (mŭl′tĭ-kŭl′ərd) adj. multicolor.

mul·ti·di·men·sion·al (mŭl′tē-dĭ-mĕn′shə-nəl) adj. multidimensional.

mul·ti·far·i·ous (mŭl′tə-fâr′ē-əs) adj. múltiple, variado.

mul·ti·fold (mŭl′tə-fōld′) adj. (manifold) doblado varias veces; (multiple) múltiple.

mul·ti·form (mŭl′tə-fôrm′) adj. multiforme.

mul·ti·lat·er·al (mŭl′tē-lăt′ər-əl) adj. GEOM. multilátero; (involving more than two countries) multilateral.

mul·ti·lev·el (mŭl′tē-lĕv′əl) o **mul·ti·lev·eled** (-əld) adj. de varios niveles.

mul·ti·lin·gual (mŭl′tē-lĭng′gwəl) adj. (written in several languages) multilingüe, políglota; (using several languages) políglota.

mul·ti·me·di·a (mŭl′tē-mē′dē-ə) adj. que incluye el uso de various medios de comunicación en masa.

mul·ti·mil·lion·aire (mŭl′tē-mĭl′yə-nâr′) s. multimillonario.

mul·ti·na·tion·al (mŭl′tē-năsh′ə-nəl) adj. & s. multinacional f.

mul·ti·ple (mŭl′tə-pəl) I. adj. (manifold) múltiple; MAT. múltiplo II. s. MAT. múltiplo.

mul·ti·ple-choice (mŭl′tə-pəl-chois′) adj. que ofrece varias respuestas con sólo una correcta (dic. de un exámen).

multiple sclerosis s. MED. esclerosis múltiple f, esclerosis en placas.

mul·ti·plex (mŭl′tə-plĕks′) adj. (multiple) múltiple; ELECTRÓN. múltiplex.

mul·ti·pli·cand (mŭl′tə-plĭ-kănd′) s. MAT. multiplicando.

mul·ti·pli·ca·tion (mŭl′tə-plĭ-kā′shən) s. multiplicación f.

multiplication sign s. signo de multiplicar.

multiplication table s. tabla de multiplicar.

mul·ti·plic·i·ty (mŭl′tə-plĭs′ĭ-tē) s. [pl. -ties] multiplicidad f.

mul·ti·pli·er (mŭl′tə-plī′ər) s. multiplicador m.

mul·ti·ply (mŭl′tə-plī′) tr. & intr. -plied, -ply·ing multiplicar(se).

mul·ti·pur·pose (mŭl′tē-pûr′pəs) adj. multiuso.

mul·ti·ra·cial (mŭl′tē-rā′shəl) adj. de diversas razas.

mul·ti·stage (mŭl′tĭ-stāj′) adj. de varias etapas.

mul·ti·tude (mŭl′tĭ-tōōd′, -tyōōd′) s. multitud f.

mul·ti·tu·di·nous (mŭl′tĭ-tōōd′n-əs, -tyōōd′-) adj. multitudinario.

mul·ti·va·lent (mŭl′tə-vā′lənt) adj. QUÍM. polivalente; BIOL. multivalente, polivalente.

mum¹ (mŭm) adj. silencioso ♦ **to keep m.** guardar silencio.

mum² (mŭm) s. G.B., FAM. mamá.

mum³ (mŭm) s. BOT., FAM. crisantemo.

mum·ble (mŭm′bəl) I. tr. -bled, -bling mascullar —intr. balbucir, barbullar II. s. refunfuño.

mum·bo jum·bo (mŭm′bō jŭm′bō) s. (fetish) fetiche m, espantajo; (ritual) ritual m, conjuro; (gibberish) galimatías m, jerigonza.

mum·mer (mŭm′ər) s. (actor) mimo; (masked person) máscara mf, enmascarado.

mum·mer·y (mŭm′ə-rē) s. [pl. -ies] (pantomime) pantomima; (mascarade) mascarada; (farse) farsa.

mum·mi·fi·ca·tion (mŭm′ə-fĭ-kā′shən) s. momificación f.

mum·mi·fy (mŭm′ə-fī′) tr. & intr. -fied, -fy·ing momificar(se).

mum·my¹ (mŭm′ē) s. [pl. -mies] (corpse) momia.

mum·my² (mŭm′ē) s. [pl. -mies] FAM. (mommy) mamá.

mumps (mŭmps) s.pl. MED. paperas f.

munch (mŭnch) tr. ronzar.

mun·dane (mŭn′dān′) adj. mundano.

mu·nic·i·pal (myōō-nĭs′ə-pəl) adj. municipal.

mu·nic·i·pal·i·ty (myōō-nĭs′ə-păl′ĭ-tē) s. [pl. -ties] (political unit) municipalidad f, municipio; (body of officials) ayuntamiento, consejo municipal.

mu·nic·i·pal·ize (myōō-nĭs′ə-pə-līz′) tr. -ized, -iz·ing municipalizar.

mu·ni·fi·cence (myōō-nĭf′ĭ-səns) s. munificencia f.

mu·nif·i·cent (myōō-nĭf′ĭ-sənt) adj. munificente, munífico.

mu·ni·tion (myōō-nĭsh′ən) MIL. I. s. (ammunition) municiones f; (materiel) pertrechos II. tr. amunicionar.

mu·on (myōō′ŏn′) s. FÍS. muón (partícula subatómica) m.

mu·ral (myōŏr′əl) I. s. ARTE. pintura mural, fresco II. adj. mural.

mur·der (mûr′dər) I. s. (killing) asesinato; DER. (homicide) homicidio; (massacre) matanza <the m. of innocent children la matanza de niños inocentes>; JER. (something uncomfortable or difficult) cosa espantosa ♦ **first-degree m.** o **m. in the first degree** DER. homicidio premeditado • **second-degree m.** o **m. in the second degree** DER. asesinato impremeditado • **to cry m.** poner el grito en el cielo • **to get away with m.** FAM. salirse siempre con la suya • **to go through m.** pasarlas moradas II. tr. (to kill) asesinar, matar; (to destroy) destrozar; (to defeat) hacer polvo, aplastar.

mur·der·er (mûr′dər-ər) s. asesino, homicida mf.

mur·der·ess (mûr′dər-ĭs) s. asesina, homicida.

mur·der·ous (mûr′dər-əs) adj. (capable of murder) asesino; DER. (homicidal) homicida; FAM. (severe) terrible.

murk (mûrk) s. (darkness) obscuridad f; (gloom) lobreguez f.

murk·y (mûr′kē) adj. -i·er, -i·est (dark) obscuro; (somber) sombrío; (gloomy) lóbrego.

mur·mur (mûr′mər) I. s. (sound) murmullo; MED. soplo cardíaco II. tr. & intr. murmurar.

mur·rain (mûr′ĭn) s. VET. morriña, epizootia; (pestilence) plaga o peste de los animales f.

mus·cat (mŭs′kăt′) s. BOT. uva o vid moscatel f; (wine) vino moscatel.

mus·ca·tel (mŭs′kə-tĕl′) s. (wine) vino moscatel; (grape) uva o pasa moscatel.

mus·cle (mŭs′əl) I. s. ANAT. músculo; (power) fuerza II. intr. -cled, -cling abrirse paso a la fuerza.

mus·cle-bound (mŭs′əl-bound′) adj. con los músculos abarrotados o endurecidos.

Mus·co·vite (mŭs′kə-vīt′) adj. & s. moscovita mf.

mus·cu·lar (mŭs′kyə-lər) adj. (pertaining to muscle) muscular; (having strong muscles) musculoso.

muscular dystrophy s. MED. distrofia muscular.

mus·cu·la·ture (mŭs′kyə-lə-chōŏr′, -chər) s. musculatura.

muse (myōōz) I. intr. mused, mus·ing meditar —tr. decir meditativamente II. s. meditación profunda.

Muse (myōōz) s. MITOL. musa ♦ **m.** (source of inspiration) musa.

mu·se·um (myōō-zē′əm) s. museo.

mush¹ (mŭsh) s. CUL. gachas de harina de maíz; (soft thing) masa muy blanda; FAM. (sentimentality) sentimentalismo, sensiblería.

mush² (mŭsh) I. intr. viajar en trineo tirado por perros II. s. viaje en trineo tirado por perros m.

mush·room (mŭsh′rōōm′, -rōōm′) I. s. BOT. hongo, seta; CUL. champiñón m; (shape) hongo II. intr. (to grow) crecer rápidamente; (to spread out) esparcirse; (to resemble a mushroom) tomar la forma de un hongo.

mush·y (mŭsh′ē) adj. -i·er, -i·est (soft) blando, suave; FAM. (sentimental) sensiblero, sentimentaloide; (amorous) enamoradizo.

mu·sic (myōō′zĭk) s. música; (score) partitura; (pleasing sound) melodía ♦ **to be m. to one's ears** ser lo que uno quiere escuchar, complacer muchísimo • **to face the m.** FAM. afrontar las consecuencias • **to set to m.** poner música a.

mu·si·cal (myōō′zĭ-kəl) I. adj. (of music) de música; (like music) musical; (fond of music) aficionado a la música II. s. comedia musical.

musical chairs s.pl. (game) juego de las sillas vacías; FAM. (rearrangement) cambio.

musical comedy s. CINEM., TEAT. comedia musical.

mu·si·cal·i·ty (myōō′zĭ-kăl′ĭ-tē) s. musicalidad f.

music box s. caja de música.

music hall s. (auditorium) sala de conciertos; G.B. (vaudeville theater) teatro de variedades.

mu·si·cian (myōō-zĭsh′ən) s. músico.

mu·si·col·o·gist (myōō′zĭ-kŏl′ə-jĭst) s. musicólogo.

mu·si·col·o·gy (myōō′zĭ-kŏl′ə-jē) s. musicología.

ă rey / ä año / b boca / ch chico / d dar / ĕ el / ē mil / g gato / h joya / hw juez / ī aire / k casa / kw cuan /

mus·ing (myōō'zĭng) **I.** adj. meditativo, contemplativo **II.** s. meditación f, contemplación f.

musk (mŭsk) s. *(secretion)* almizcle m; *(smell)* olor almizcleño ♦ **m. deer** ZOOL. almizclero.

mus·kel·lunge (mŭs'kə-lŭnj') s. [pl. **muskellunge** o **-lunges**] ICT. lucio, sollo americano.

mus·ket (mŭs'kĭt) s. ARM. mosquete m.

mus·ket·eer (mŭs'kĭ-tîr') s. mosquetero.

mus·ket·ry (mŭs'kĭ-trē) s. *(muskets)* mosquetes m; *(firing)* mosquetazos m; *(technique)* mosquetería.

musk·mel·on (mŭsk'mĕl'ən) s. BOT. melón m.

musk·rat (mŭsk'răt') s. [pl. **muskrat** o **-rats**] ZOOL. rata almizclera, rata almizclada; *(fur)* piel de rata almizclera f.

musk rose s. BOT. rosa almizcleña.

musk·y (mŭsk'ē) adj. **-i·er, -i·est** almizcleño.

Mus·lim (mŭz'lĭm, mŏŏz'-) s. & adj. musulmán m.

mus·lin (mŭz'lĭn) s. TEJ. muselina.

muss (mŭs) **I.** tr. *(to untidy)* desordenar; *(to rumple)* arrugar **II.** s. *(mess)* desorden m; *(squabble)* riña.

mus·sel (mŭs'əl) s. ZOOL. mejillón m.

muss·y (mŭs'ē) adj. **-i·er, -i·est** FAM. desordenado.

must¹ §G11 (mŭst) **I.** aux. *(indicating an obligation)* deber, tener que *<citizens m. register in order to vote* los ciudadanos deben inscribirse para poder votar>; *(indicating a necessity)* deber, tener que *<plants m. have oxygen in order to live* las plantas deben tener oxígeno para poder vivir>; *(indicating a probability)* deber de *<it m. be his friend* debe de ser su amigo>; *(indicating an admonition)* deber *<he m. not go alone* no debe ir solo> ♦ **it m. not be** eso no debe permitirse **II.** s. FAM. cosa indispensable, necesidad f ♦ **that exhibit is a m.** esa exposición es para no perdérsela, no deje de ver esa exposición.

must² (mŭst) s. *(staleness)* ranciedad f, rancidez f; *(mold)* moho.

must³ (mŭst) s. mosto (de la uva).

mus·tache (mŭs'tăsh', mə-stăsh') s. bigote m, bigotes.

mus·tang (mŭs'tăng') s. ZOOL. mustang m, mustango (potro salvaje).

mus·tard (mŭs'tərd) s. mostaza.

mustard gas s. QUÍM. gas mostaza m.

mustard plaster s. MED. sinapismo, cataplasma de mostaza.

mus·ter (mŭs'tər) **I.** tr. MIL. *(to summon)* enrolar, alistar; *(to convene)* reunir, congregar ♦ **to m. up courage** armarse de valor — intr. reunirse, juntarse **II.** s. MIL. revista; *(roll)* lista, rol m; *(meeting)* reunión f, asamblea ♦ **to pass m.** ser aceptable.

muster roll s. MIL. lista de revista; MARÍT. rol m, lista de dotación; *(inventory)* inventario, lista.

must·n't (mŭs'ənt) contr. de **must not.**

must·y (mŭs'tē) adj. **-i·er, -i·est** *(moldy)* mohoso; *(smelly)* que huele a cerrado; *(antiquated)* anticuado; *(dull)* flojo.

mu·ta·ble (myōō'tə-bəl) adj. *(variable)* variable, mudable; *(inconstant)* inconstante.

mu·tant (myōōt'nt) s. BIOL. mutante m.

mu·tate (myōō'tāt') tr. & intr. **-tat·ed, -tat·ing** mudar(se), cambiar(se); BIOL. transformar(se) (por mutación).

mu·ta·tion (myōō-tā'shən) s. *(change)* cambio, alteración f; BIOL. mutación f.

mute (myōōt) **I.** adj. **mut·er, mut·est** *(unable to speak)* mudo; *(silent)* callado, sin decir palabra *<he remained m.* se quedó callado> ♦ **to stand m.** DER. negarse a declararse culpable o inocente **II.** s. *(person)* mudo; MÚS. sordina; FONÉT. *(letter)* letra muda; *(plosive)* oclusiva **III.** tr. **mut·ed, mut·ing** *(a sound)* amortiguar; MÚS. *(an instrument)* poner sordina a; *(a color)* apagar.

mut·ed (myōō'tĭd) adj. sordo.

mu·ti·late (myōōt'l-āt') tr. **-lat·ed, -lat·ing** mutilar.

mu·ti·la·tion (myōōt'l-ā'shən) s. mutilación f.

mu·ti·neer (myōōt'n-îr') s. amotinado, amotinador m.

mu·ti·nous (myōōt'n-əs) adj. *(rebellious)* amotinador, rebelde; *(uncontrollable)* indócil, ingobernable.

mu·ti·ny (myōōt'n-ē) **I.** s. [pl. **-nies**] motín m, sedición f **II.** intr. **-nied, -ny·ing** amotinarse.

mutt (mŭt) s. JER. *(dog)* perro cruzado; FAM. *(fool)* tonto, bobo.

mut·ter (mŭt'ər) **I.** intr. & tr. *(to murmur)* murmurar; *(to grumble)* refunfuñar **II.** s. *(murmur)* murmullo; *(grumbling)* refunfuño.

mut·ton (mŭt'n) s. carne de carnero f, carnero.

mutton chop s. chuleta de carnero.

mut·ton·head (mŭt'n-hĕd') s. JER. persona estúpida.

mu·tu·al (myōō'chōō-əl) adj. *(reciprocal)* mutuo *<m. aid* ayuda mutua>; *(common)* mutuo, común ♦ **by m. agreement** de común acuerdo • **m. company** COM. compañía de seguros mutuos.

mutual fund s. COM. *(fund)* fondo mutualista (de inversión).

mutual insurance s. COM. seguro mutuo.

mu·tu·al·ism (myōō'chōō-ə-lĭz'əm) s. BIOL. mutualismo.

mu·tu·al·ize (myōō'chōō-ə-līz') tr. **-ized, -iz·ing** volver mutuo, convertir en mutualidad.

muz·zle (mŭz'əl) **I.** s. ZOOL. *(snout)* hocico, morro; *(leather restraint)* bozal m; FIG. *(restraint)* mordaza; *(gun)* boca (de un arma de fuego) **II.** tr. **-zled, -zling** *(to put a leather restraint on)* poner bozal a; FIG. *(to restrain)* amordazar.

my §G23 (mī) **I.** adj. pos. mi *<my home* mi hogar>; mío *<my dear sir* muy señor mío> **II.** interj. ¡caramba!, ¡Dios mío!

my·col·o·gy (mī-kŏl'ə-jē) s. BOT. micología.

my·co·sis (mī-kō'sĭs) s. [pl. **-ses** (-sēz')] MED. micosis f.

my·o·pi·a (mī-ō'pē-ə) s. OFTAL. miopía; FIG. *(shortsightedness)* miopía, imprevisión f.

my·op·ic (mī-ŏp'ĭk, -ō'pĭk) adj. OFTAL. miope.

myr·i·ad (mîr'ē-əd) **I.** adj. innumerable **II.** s. miríada.

myrrh (mûr) s. BOT. *(resin)* mirra; *(sweet cicely)* perifollo oloroso.

myr·tle (mûr'tl) s. BOT. mirto, arrayán m.

my·self §G37 (mī-sĕlf') pron. yo mismo *<I did it m.* lo hice yo mismo>; me *<I hurt m.* me hice daño>; mí (mismo) *<I did it for m.* lo hice para mí> ♦ **as for m.** en cuanto a mí • **(all) by m.** completamente solo.

mys·te·ri·ous (mī-stîr'ē-əs) adj. misterioso.

mys·ter·y (mĭs'tə-rē) s. [pl. **-ies**] *(enigma)* misterio; CINEM. película policíaca; LIT. novela policíaca.

mystery play s. TEAT. drama o auto sacramental.

mys·tic (mĭs'tĭk) adj. & s. místico.

mys·ti·cal (mĭs'tĭ-kəl) adj. místico.

mys·ti·cism (mĭs'tĭ-sĭz'əm) s. misticismo.

mys·ti·fi·ca·tion (mĭs'tə-fĭ-kā'shən) s. *(act)* mistificación f; *(confusion)* confusión f, perplejidad f.

mys·ti·fy (mĭs'tə-fī') tr. **-fied, -fy·ing** *(to perplex)* mistificar, enredar; *(to confuse)* confundir, desorientar.

mys·tique (mī-stēk') s. misterio secreto, mística.

myth (mĭth) s. mito.

myth·i·cal (mĭth'ĭ-kəl) adj. mítico.

myth·o·log·i·cal (mĭth'ə-lŏj'ĭ-kəl) adj. mitológico.

my·thol·o·gist (mī-thŏl'ə-jĭst) s. mitologista mf.

my·thol·o·gize (mī-thŏl'ə-jīz') tr. **-gized, -giz·ing** convertir en mito — intr. *(to relate a myth)* relatar un mito; *(to construct a myth)* crear un mito; *(to study myths)* analizar mitos.

my·thol·o·gy (mī-thŏl'ə-jē) s. [pl. **-gies**] mitología.

my·thos (mī'thŏs', mĭth'ŏs') s. [pl. **my·thoi** (mī'thoi', mĭth'oi')] *(myth)* mito; *(mythology)* mitología; *(cult)* culto.

N

n, N (ĕn) s. [pl. **n's, N's**] decimocuarta letra del alfabeto inglés.

nab (năb) tr. **nabbed, nab·bing** JER. *(to arrest)* arrestar, detener; *(to grab)* coger, agarrar.

na·bob (nā'bŏb') s. *(Moslem prince)* nabab m; FIG. *(wealthy man)* hombre muy rico.

na·celle (nə-sĕl') s. AER. barquilla.

na·cre (nā'kər) s. nácar m.

na·cre·ous (nā'krē-əs) adj. nacáreo.

na·dir (nā'dər) s. ASTRON. nadir m; FIG. *(lowest point)* punto más bajo.

---

nag¹ (năg) **I.** tr. **nagged, nag·ging** (to scold) regañar, reñir; (to pester) fastidiar, importunar —intr. (to find fault) criticar; (to scold) regañar; (to complain) quejarse, poner reparos a todo **II.** s. (scolder) regañón m; (complainer) queja.

nag² (năg) s. (old horse) jamelgo; JER. (racehorse) caballo de carreras.

Na·hum (nā'həm, nā'əm) s. BÍBL. Nahum.

nai·ad (nā'əd, nī'-) s. náyade f.

nail (nāl) **I.** s. (metal spike) clavo; (finger, toe) uña; (of animals) garra ♦ **to be as hard as nails** FIG. tener corazón de piedra • **to bite one's nails** morderse o comerse las uñas • **to hit the n. on the head** FIG. dar en el clavo, acertar **II.** tr. (to fasten) clavar, asegurar con clavos; FIG. (to hold) dejar clavado <fear nailed him to his seat el miedo le dejó clavado en su asiento>; FAM. (to catch) coger, atrapar <I nailed him on his way out le atrapé a la salida>; (to detect) descubrir; (to bring down) derribar ♦ **to n. down** (to fasten) clavar, sujetar con clavos; FIG. (to find out) descubrir; (to get) obtener <to n. down a contract obtener un contrato>; (to establish) establecer firmemente • **to n. up** cerrar con clavos, clavar.

nail·brush (nāl'brŭsh') s. cepillo para las uñas, cepillo de uñas.

nail clippers s. cortaúñas m.

nail file s. lima para las uñas, lima de uñas.

nail polish s. esmalte de uñas m.

nail scissors s.pl. (ú. con v. sing. o pl.) tijeras para las uñas, tijeras de uñas.

nain·sook (nān'sŏok') s. TEJ. nansú m.

na·ive o **na·ïve** (nä-ēv') adj. cándido, ingenuo.

na·ive·té o **na·ïve·té** (nä'ēv-tā') s. candor m, ingenuidad f.

naked (nā'kĭd) adj. desnudo ♦ **to go n.** ir desnudo • **the n. truth** la pura verdad, la verdad escueta • **to go n.** ir desnudo.

naked eye s. simple vista <to the n. a simple vista>.

na·ked·ness (nā'kĭd-nĭs) s. desnudez f.

nam·by-pam·by (năm'bē-păm'bē) **I.** adj. soso, insípido **II.** s. [pl. **-bies**] persona insípida.

name (nām) **I.** s. (first name) nombre m; (last name) apellido; (reputation) fama, reputación f <a bad n. una mala reputación>; FAM. (celebrity) celebridad f, personalidad f <a big n. in politics una celebridad en el mundo de la política> ♦ **full n.** nombre, nombre y apellido • **in n. only** de nombre solamente • **in the n. of** en nombre de • **my n. is** me llamo • **n. brand** FAM. marca conocida • **to be on a first-name basis with** tratarse de tú, tutearse • **to call someone names** insultar a alguien • **to go by the n. of** (real name) llamarse; (fictitious name) ser conocido por el nombre de • **to know by n.** conocer de nombre • **to make a n. for oneself** hacerse un nombre • **what's your n.?** ¿cómo se llama Ud.? o ¿cómo te llamas? **II.** tr. **named, nam·ing** (to call) llamar <we named her Mary la llamamos María>; (to identify) dar el nombre de <she named her assailant dio el nombre del agresor>; (to mention) nombrar, mencionar <just to n. a few por mencionar algunos>; (to specify) dar, fijar (hora, precio); (to appoint) nombrar <she was named president la nombraron presidenta>.

name day s. santo, día onomástico.

name·less (nām'lĭs) adj. sin nombre, anónimo.

name·ly (nām'lē) adv. es decir, a saber.

name·plate (nām'plāt') s. (plaque) placa o letrero con el nombre; (brand) marca.

name·sake (nām'sāk') s. tocayo, homónimo.

Na·mib·i·a (nə-mĭb'ē-ə) s. Namibia.

Na·mib·i·an (nə-mĭb'ē-ən) adj. & s. namibio.

nan·a (năn'ə) s. (nurse) nodriza, niñera; (grandmother) abuela.

nan·keen (năn-kēn') s. TEJ. nanquín m, mahón m.

nan·ny o **nan·nie** (năn'ē) s. [pl. **-nies**] niñera.

nanny goat s. ZOOL. cabra.

nan·o·sec·ond (năn'ə-sĕk'ənd) s. FÍS. nanosegundo.

nap¹ (năp) **I.** s. siesta ♦ **to take a n.** dormir la siesta **II.** intr. **napped, nap·ping** echar o dormir la siesta ♦ **to catch someone napping** FIG. coger a alguien desprevenido.

nap² (năp) s. lanilla, peluza ♦ **against the n.** a contrapelo.

na·palm (nā'päm') MIL. **I.** s. napalm m, materia inflamable **II.** tr. quemar o abrasar con napalm.

nape (nāp, năp) s. ANAT. nuca.

na·per·y (nā'pə-rē) s. mantelería.

naph·tha (năf'thə, năp'-) s. QUÍM. nafta.

naph·tha·lene (năf'thə-lēn', năp'-) s. QUÍM. naftalina.

naph·thol (năf'thôl', năp'-) s. QUÍM. naftol m.

nap·kin (năp'kĭn) s. (at table) servilleta; (towel) toalla ♦ **sanitary n.** toalla higiénica.

Na·ples (nā'pəlz) s. Nápoles.

na·po·le·on (nə-pō'lē-ən) s. CUL. milhojas m; NUMIS. napoleón m.

narc (närk) s. JER. agente de policía que se ocupa de detener a los traficantes de estupefacientes.

nar·cis·sism (när'sĭ-sĭz'əm) s. PSIC. narcisismo.

nar·cis·sus (när-sĭs'əs) s. [pl. **-cis·sus·es** o **-cis·si** (-sĭs'ī')] BOT. narciso ♦ **N.** MITOL. Narciso.

nar·co·lep·sy (när'kə-lĕp'sē) s. MED. narcolepsia.

nar·co·sis (när-kō'sĭs) s. MED. narcosis f.

nar·cot·ic (när-kŏt'ĭk) s. & adj. narcótico, estupefaciente m.

nar·co·tism (när'kə-tĭz'əm) s. MED. narcotismo, narcosis f.

nar·co·tize (när'kə-tīz') tr. **-tized, -tiz·ing** MED. narcotizar.

nard (närd) s. BOT. nardo.

nar·is (nâr'ĭs) s. [pl. **-es** (-ēz)] orificio o ventana de la nariz.

nark (närk) s. var. de **narc**.

nar·rate (năr'āt') tr. **-rat·ed, -rat·ing** narrar, relatar.

nar·ra·tion (nă-rā'shən) s. narración f, relato.

nar·ra·tive (năr'ə-tĭv) **I.** s. (mode) narrativa; (account) relato **II.** adj. narrativo.

nar·ra·tor (năr'āt'ər) s. narrador m.

nar·row (năr'ō) **I.** adj. **-er, -est** (not wide) angosto, estrecho; (rigid) estrecho, rígido; (restricted) restringido, limitado (intereses, interpretación); (barely sufficient) escaso, pequeño; (strict) estricto <in the narrowest sense of the word en el sentido más estricto de la palabra>; (intolerant) intolerante, de miras estrechas ♦ **to have a n. escape** librarse por los pelos, escaparse por un pelo **II.** tr. (to make narrow) estrechar; (to limit) limitar, reducir ♦ **to n. down** limitar, reducir • **to n. it down to** reducirse a —intr. estrecharse **III.** s. pasaje estrecho ♦ **narrows** estrecho.

narrow gauge s. F.C. vía estrecha; (train) tren de vía estrecha.

nar·row·ing (năr'ō-ĭng) s. (tightening) estrechamiento; FIG. (limitation) limitación f.

nar·row·ly (năr'ō-lē) adv. (with little width) estrechamente; (strictly) estrictamente; (with close scrutiny) de cerca, minuciosamente; (barely) por poco.

nar·row-mind·ed (năr'ō-mīn'dĭd) adj. de miras estrechas, de mentalidad estrecha.

nar·row-mind·ed·ness (năr'ō-mīn'dĭd-nĭs) s. estrechez de miras f.

nar·row·ness (năr'ō-nĭs) s. (of ideas, width) estrechez f; (of an examination) minuciosidad f; (of a definition) lo limitado; (interpretation) rigidez f.

nar·thex (när'thĕks') s. ARQ. nártex m.

nar·whal (när'wəl) s. ZOOL. narval m.

nar·y (nâr'ē) adj. REG. ninguno.

na·sal (nā'zəl) s. & adj. nasal.

na·sal·i·ty (nā-zăl'ĭ-tē) s. nasalidad f.

na·sal·ly (nā'zə-lē) adv. con voz gangosa.

nas·cent (năs'ənt, nā'sənt) adj. naciente.

nas·ti·ness (năs'tē-nĭs) s. (odor) peste f; (taste) sabor horrible m; (dirtiness) suciedad f; (obscenity) obscenidad f; (vileness) maldad f.

nas·tur·tium (nə-stûr'shəm) s. BOT. capuchina.

nas·ty (năs'tē) adj. **-ti·er, -ti·est** (filthy) sucio, asqueroso; (unpleasant) espantoso, asqueroso; (cruel) antipático; (malicious) malicioso, malintencionado; (morally offensive) obsceno, repugnante; (uncomfortable) molesto (tos, catarro); (painful) lamentable; (serious) grave, de gravedad (accidente, caída); (troublesome) difícil (asunto, problema) ♦ **to be n. to (someone)** portarse mal con alguien, tratar mal a alguien • **to have a n. mind** ser un mal pensado.

na·tal (nāt'l) adj. natal.

na·tal·i·ty (nā-tăl'ĭ-tē) s. [pl. **-ties**] natalidad f.

na·ta·to·ri·al (nā'tə-tôr'ē-əl, năt'ə-) adj. natatorio.
na·ta·to·ri·um (nā'tə-tôr'ē-əm, năt'ə-) s. [pl. **-ri·ums** o **-ri·a** (-ē-ə)] piscina cubierta.
na·tion (nā'shən) s. *(country)* nación *f; (people)* pueblo.
na·tion·al (năsh'ə-nəl) adj. & s. nacional.
national debt s. ECON. POL. deuda pública.
National Guard s. guardia nacional (en EE. UU.).
national in·come s. ECON. POL. renta nacional.
na·tion·al·ism (năsh'ə-nə-lĭz'əm) s. nacionalismo.
na·tion·al·ist (năsh'ə-nə-lĭst) s. nacionalista *mf.*
na·tion·al·is·tic (năsh'ə-nə-lĭs'tĭk) adj. nacionalista.
na·tion·al·i·ty (năsh'ə-năl'ĭ-tē) s. [pl. **-ties**] nacionalidad *f,* ciudadanía.
na·tion·al·i·za·tion (năsh'ə-nə-lĭ-zā'shən) s. nacionalización *f.*
na·tion·al·ize (năsh'ə-nə-līz') tr. **-ized, -iz·ing** nacionalizar.
national monument s. monumento nacional.
national park s. parque nacional *m.*
National Socialism s. POL. nacionalsocialismo.
na·tion·hood (nā'shən-hōŏd') s. la condición de ser una nación, independencia.
na·tion·wide (nā'shən-wīd') adj. por toda la nación.
na·tive (nā'tĭv) **I.** adj. *(inborn)* natural, innato; *(inhabitant)* nativo <*n. Spaniard* español nativo>; *(country, town)* natal; *(language)* materno; *(customs)* originario; *(product)* del país <*n. corn* maíz del país>; MIN. nativo <*n. gold* oro nativo> ♦ **to be n. to** ser originario de (díc. de costumbres, plantas, animales) **II.** s. nativo, indígena *mf* ♦ **to be a n. of** *(by birth)* ser nativo o natural de; *(original inhabitant)* ser nativo o indígena de; BOT., ZOOL. ser originario de.
na·tive-born (nā'tĭv-bôrn') adj. de nacimiento.
na·tiv·ism (nā'tĭ-vĭz'əm) s. POL. nacionalismo; FILOS. nativismo.
na·tiv·i·ty (nə-tĭv'ĭ-tē) s. [pl. **-ties**] nacimiento ♦ **N.** natividad (de Cristo).
nat·ty (năt'ē) adj. **-ti·er, -ti·est** FAM. elegante.
nat·u·ral (năch'ər-əl) **I.** adj. *(by nature)* natural; *(inherent)* nato, inherente; MÚS. natural ♦ **to be n. for** ser natural o lógico que <*it is n. for you to feel that way* es lógico que te sientas así> • **to be n. to** ser propio de **II.** s. FAM. *(person)* persona particularmente dotado; MÚS. *(note)* nota natural; *(sign)* becuadro ♦ **to be a n.** tener talento.
natural food s. alimentos sin conservantes.
natural gas s. QUÍM. gas natural *m.*
natural history s. historia natural.
nat·u·ral·ism (năch'ər-ə-lĭz'əm) s. naturalismo.
nat·u·ral·ist (năch'ər-ə-lĭst) s. naturalista *mf.*
nat·u·ral·is·tic (năch'ər-ə-lĭs'tĭk) adj. naturalista.
nat·u·ral·ize (năch'ər-ə-līz') tr. **-ized, -iz·ing** *(an alien)* naturalizar; *(to adapt)* adaptar —intr. *(an alien)* naturalizarse; *(to become adapted)* adaptarse.
nat·u·ral·ly (năch'ər-ə-lē) adv. *(of course)* naturalmente, por supuesto; *(by nature)* por naturaleza; *(without pretense)* con naturalidad, naturalmente.
nat·u·ral·ness (năch'ər-əl-nĭs) s. naturalidad *f.*
natural resource s. recurso natural.
natural science s. ciencias naturales.
natural selection s. BIOL. selección natural *f.*
na·ture (nā'chər) s. *(universe)* naturaleza, natura <*the beauty of n.* la belleza de la naturaleza>; *(character)* tipo, índole *f* <*of a confidential n.* de índole confidencial>; *(essence)* naturaleza <*the n. of the problem* la naturaleza del problema>; *(temperament)* natural *m,* temperamento <*sweet n.* buen temperamento> ♦ **against God and n.** contra la naturaleza, contra natura • **by n.** por naturaleza • **second n. to** fácil para • **something in the n. of** una especie de, algo así como • **to be in one's n.** ser propio de (alguien) • **to be in the n. of things (that)** ser natural (que).
naught (nôt) **I.** s. POÉT. nada; MAT. cero **II.** adj. insignificante, inútil.
naugh·ti·ness (nô'tē-nĭs) s. *(mischievousness)* picardía; *(disobedience)* desobediencia; *(bad behavior)* mala conducta.
naugh·ty (nô'tē) adj. **-ti·er, -ti·est** *(mischievous)* travieso, pícaro; *(disobedient)* desobediente; *(bad)* malo.
Na·u·ru (nä-ōō'rōō) s. Nauru.
Na·u·ru·an (nä-ōō'rōō-ən) adj. & s. nauruano.

nau·sea (nô'zhə) s. *(sickness)* náusea; FIG. *(disgust)* asco, repugnancia.
nau·se·ate (nô'zē-āt') tr. **-at·ed, -at·ing** *(to cause to feel nausea)* dar náuseas a; FIG. *(to disgust)* dar asco o repugnancia a —intr. *(to feel sick)* tener náuseas; FIG. *(to be disgusted)* asquearse.
nau·se·at·ing (nô'zē-ā'tĭng) adj. nauseabundo, asqueroso.
nau·seous (nô'shəs) adj. nauseabundo.
nau·ti·cal (nô'tĭ-kəl) adj. náutico.
nautical mile s. milla marina.
nau·ti·lus (nôt'l-əs) s. [pl. **-lus·es** o **-li** (-l-ī')] ZOOL. nautilo.
na·val (nā'vəl) adj. naval.
Nav·ar·rese (năv'ə-rēz') adj. & s. navarro ♦ **the N.** los navarros.
nave[1] (nāv) s. ARQ. nave *f.*
nave[2] (nāv) s. *(hub)* cubo (de rueda).
na·vel (nā'vəl) s. ANAT. ombligo; FIG. *(middle)* punto medio, centro.
nav·i·ga·ble (năv'ĭ-gə-bəl) adj. navegable.
nav·i·gate (năv'ĭ-gāt') intr. & tr. **-gat·ed, -gat·ing** navegar.
nav·i·ga·tion (năv'ĭ-gā'shən) s. navegación *f.*
nav·i·ga·tion·al (năv'ĭ-gā'shə-nəl) adj. de navegación.
nav·i·ga·tor (năv'ĭ-gā'tər) s. navegante *m.*
nav·vy (năv'ē) s. [pl. **-vies**] G.B. peón *m,* bracero.
na·vy (nā'vē) s. [pl. **-vies**] *(warships)* marina de guerra, flota; *(color)* azul marino o oscuro ♦ **the N.** la marina, la armada.
navy bean s. BOT. judía blanca.
navy blue s. & adj. azul marino.
navy yard s. astillero.
nay (nā) **I.** adv. *(no)* no; *(and moreover)* mejor dicho, más bien **II.** s. *(vote)* voto en contra; *(refusal)* negativa.
Naz·a·rene (năz'ə-rēn') **I.** adj. nazareno **II.** s. *(inhabitant)* nazareno; RELIG. *(Christian)* cristiano, nazareno ♦ **the N.** RELIG. el Nazareno.
Naz·a·reth (năz'ə-rĭth) s. Nazaret.
Na·zi (nät'sē, năt'-) adj. & s. [pl. **-zis**] nazi *mf.*
Na·zism (nät'sĭz'əm, năt'-) o **Na·zi·ism** (-sē-ĭz'əm) s. POL. nazismo.
Ne·an·der·thal (nē-ăn'dər-thôl') s. & adj. PALEON. neandertal *m;* FIG. *(crude person)* grosero.
Neanderthal man s. ANTROP. hombre de neandertal *m.*
neap tide s. marea muerta.
Ne·a·pol·i·tan (nē'ə-pŏl'ĭ-tn) adj. & s. napolitano.
near (nîr) **I.** adv. **-er, -est** *(close)* cerca, próximo; *(almost)* casi <*n. exhausted* casi agotado>; *(closely related)* íntimo, cercano ♦ **n. and far** por todas partes • **to be o draw n.** acercarse **II.** adj. **-er, -est** *(close)* inmediato, próximo <*in the n. future* en un futuro próximo>; *(closely related)* cercano, allegado; *(direct)* directo, corto <*the nearest route to town* la ruta más directa al pueblo>; *(stingy)* tacaño ♦ **n. and dear** íntimo • **to be a n. miss** fallar por poco • **nowhere n.** muy lejos de **III.** prep. *(close to)* cerca de, junto a; *(almost)* casi; *(toward)* hacia <*n. the end of the week* hacia fines de semana> **IV.** tr. acercarse a, aproximarse a —intr. acercarse, aproximarse.
near·by (nîr'-bī') **I.** adj. cercano, próximo **II.** adv. cerca.
Near East s. Cercano Oriente.
Near Eastern adj. del Cercano Oriente.
near·ly (nîr'lē) adv. casi.
near·ness (nîr'nĭs) s. proximidad *f,* cercanía.
near·sight·ed (nîr'sī'tĭd) adj. OFTAL. miope, corto de vista.
neat (nēt) **I.** adj. **-er, -est** *(tidy)* limpio, pulcro; *(orderly)* ordenado; *(well-done)* esmerado, bien hecho *(trabajo); (clear)* claro (letra); *(clever)* acertado, ingenioso; *(skillful)* elegante, pulcro; COM. *(net)* neto; *(undiluted, as liquor)* solo; JER. *(terrific)* fantástico **II.** adv. solo <*I take my whiskey n.* tomo el whisky solo>.
neat·en (nēt'n) tr. ordenar.
neath o **'neath** (nēth) contr. de **beneath.**
neat·ly (nēt'lē) adv. *(to dress)* con esmero; *(to work)* con cuidado.
neat·ness (nēt'nĭs) s. *(tidiness)* pulcritud *f,* limpieza; *(orderliness)* orden *m; (care)* esmero; *(clarity)* claridad (de letra) *f; (skillfulness)* elegancia, pulcritud.
neat's-foot oil (nēts'fōŏt') s. aceite de pata de vaca *m.*

neb (nĕb) s. *(beak)* pico; *(snout)* hocico, morro; *(tip)* punta.

neb·u·la (nĕb'yə-lə) s. [pl. **-lae** (-lē') o **-las**] ASTRON. nebulosa.

neb·u·lar (nĕb'yə-lər) adj. nebuloso.

neb·u·lize (nĕb'yə-līz') tr. atomizar.

neb·u·los·i·ty (nĕb'yə-lŏs'ĭ-tē) s. [pl. **-ties**] nebulosidad *f*; ASTRON. nebulosa.

neb·u·lous (nĕb'yə-ləs) adj. *(vague)* nebuloso, vago; ASTRON. nebuloso.

nec·es·sar·i·ly (nĕs'ĭ-sâr'ə-lē) adv. necesariamente.

nec·es·sar·y (nĕs'ĭ-sĕr'ē) I. adj. *(essential)* necesario, indispensable; *(inevitable)* inevitable II. s. [pl. **-ies**] cosa necesaria.

ne·ces·si·tate (nə-sĕs'ĭ-tāt') tr. **-tat·ed, -tat·ing** necesitar, requerir.

ne·ces·si·tous (nə-sĕs'ĭ-təs) adj. *(poor)* necesitado, indigente; *(pressing)* urgente, apremiante.

ne·ces·si·ty (nə-sĕs'ĭ-tē) s. [pl. **-ties**] necesidad *f* ♦ **out of n.** por necesidad.

neck (nĕk) I. s. *(of people)* cuello; *(of animals)* pescuezo, cogote *m*; *(of garments)* cuello; *(of bottles)* gollete *m*; MÚS. mástil *m*; GEOG. *(isthmus)* istmo; *(strait)* estrecho ♦ **by a n.** DEP. por una cabeza • **n. and n.** parejos • **n. of the woods** FIG. parajes • **stiff n.** MED. tortícolis • **'o be a pain in the n.** FIG. *(someone)* ser un pesado; *(something)* ser una lata • **to break one's n.** MED. romperse el cuello; FIG. *(to work hard)* deslomarse, matarse trabajando • **to break one's n. for** o **to** FIG. hacer todo lo posible para • **to risk** o **stick out one's n.** FIG. arriesgarse • **to save (someone's) n.** FIG. salvarle el pellejo a alguien • **to wring (someone's) n.** FIG. retorcerle a uno el pescuezo • **up to one's n.** metido hasta el cuello II. intr. *(to kiss)* besuquearse; *(to hug)* abrazarse.

neck·er·chief (nĕk'ər-chĭf) s. pañuelo para el cuello.

neck·ing (nĕk'ĭng) s. ARQ. collarino; FAM. *(hugs)* caricias; *(kissing)* besuqueo.

neck·lace (nĕk'lĭs) s. collar *m*.

neck·line (nĕk'līn') s. escote (de un vestido) *m*.

neck·tie (nĕk'tī') s. corbata *f*.

neck·wear (nĕk'wâr') s. prendas de vestir que se llevan en el cuello.

nec·ro·log·ic (nĕk'rə-lŏj'ĭk) o **nec·ro·log·i·cal** (-ĭ-kəl) adj. necrológico.

ne·crol·o·gy (nə-krŏl'ə-jē) s. [pl. **-gies**] necrología.

nec·ro·man·cy (nĕk'rə-măn'sē) s. necromancia, nigromancia.

nec·rop·o·lis (nə-krŏp'ə-lĭs) s. [pl. **-lis·es** o **-leis** (-lās')] necrópolis *f*.

ne·cro·sis (nə-krō'sĭs) s. MED. necrosis *f*, gangrena.

nec·tar (nĕk'tər) s. BOT., MITOL. néctar *m*.

nec·tar·ine (nĕk'tə-rēn') s. griñón *m*, pelón *m*.

née o **nee** (nā) adj. Úsase después del apellido de casada de una mujer <*Mrs. Jane Doe, née Smith* la sra. Jane Smith de Doe>.

need (nēd) I. s. *(necessity)* necesidad *f* <*the n. for love* la necesidad de cariño>; *(trouble)* necesidad, apuro <*in his hour of n.* en su momento de apuro> ♦ **if n. be** si fuera necesario, en caso de necesidad • **needs** necesidades <*to understand her needs* comprender sus necesidades> • **there's no n. to** no es necesario, no hace falta • **to be in n.** estar necesitado • **to be in n. of** necesitar • **to feel the n. to** verse en la necesidad de II. tr. necesitar —intr. estar necesitado ♦ **to n. to** *(to have to)* deber, tener que <*I n. to sit down* tengo que sentarme>; *(to be necessary to)* ser necesario o preciso <*she needs to be told* es necesario decírselo> —aux. *(to be necessary to)* tener que, deber <*you n. not come* no tienes que venir>; *(must)* ser necesario, hacer falta <*n. it be done now?* ¿hace falta hacerlo ahora?>.

need·ful (nēd'fəl) adj. necesario, requerido.

need·i·ness (nē'dē-nĭs) s. necesidad *f*, indigencia.

nee·dle (nēd'l) I. s. aguja II. tr. **-dled, -dling** coser; FAM. *(to torment)* hacer rabiar, pinchar.

nee·dle·fish (nēd'l-fĭsh') s. [pl. **needlefish** o **-fish·es**] ICT. aguja *m*.

nee·dle·point (nēd'l-point') s. *(of a compass)* punta seca; *(lace)* encaje de aguja *m*.

need·less (nēd'lĭs) adj. innecesario, superfluo ♦ **n. to say** huelga decir que, ni que decir tiene.

need·less·ly (nēd'lĭs-lē) adv. innecesariamente.

needle valve s. MEC. válvula de aguja.

nee·dle·wom·an (nēd'l-woom'ən) s. [pl. **-wom·en** (-wĭm'ĭn)] costurera.

nee·dle·work (nēd'l-wûrk') s. costura, labor *f*.

need·n't (nēd'nt) contr. de **need not**.

needs (nēdz) adv. ANT., POÉT. necesariamente ♦ **he must n. go** no tiene más remedio que ir.

need·y (nē'dē) adj. **-i·er, -i·est** necesitado, indigente ♦ **the n.** los pobres.

ne'er (nâr) adv. POÉT. nunca, jamás.

ne'er-do-well (nâr'doo-wĕl') adj. & s. inútil *mf*.

ne·far·i·ous (nə-fâr'ē-əs) adj. infame, nefario.

ne·far·i·ous·ness (nə-fâr'ē-əs-nĭs) s. infamia.

ne·gate (nĭ-gāt') tr. **-gat·ed, -gat·ing** *(to deny)* negar; *(to nullify)* anular.

ne·ga·tion (nĭ-gā'shən) s. negación *f*.

neg·a·tive (nĕg'ə-tĭv) I. adj. negativo II. s. *(act)* negativa <*to answer in the n.* contestar con una negativa>; GRAM. negación *f*; FOTOG. negativo; MAT. término negativo, cantidad negativa.

negative feedback s. ELECTRÓN., RAD. realimentación negativa.

neg·a·tive·ly (nĕg'ə-tĭv-lē) adv. negativamente.

neg·a·tive·ness (nĕg'ə-tĭv-nĭs) s. negación *f*.

neg·a·tiv·ism (nĕg'ə-tĭ-vĭz'əm) o **neg·a·tiv·i·ty** (nĕg'ə-tĭv'ə-tē) s. negativismo.

ne·glect (nĭ-glĕkt') I. tr. descuidar ♦ **to n. one's duty** faltar al deber de uno, no cumplir con el deber • **to n. to** olvidarse de <*she neglected to thank him* se olvidó de darle las gracias> II. s. descuido, negligencia ♦ **out of** o **through n.** por negligencia.

ne·glect·ful (nĭ-glĕkt'fəl) adj. descuidado, negligente.

neg·li·gee o **neg·li·gée** o **neg·li·gé** (nĕg'lĭ-zhā') s. negligé *m*, salto de cama.

neg·li·gence (nĕg'lĭ-jəns) s. negligencia.

neg·li·gent (nĕg'lĭ-jənt) adj. negligente, descuidado.

neg·li·gi·ble (nĕg'lĭ-jə-bəl) adj. insignificante.

ne·go·tia·bil·i·ty (nĭ-gō'shə-bĭl'ĭ-tē) s. negociabilidad *f*.

ne·go·tia·ble (nĭ-gō'shə-bəl) adj. negociable.

ne·go·ti·ate (nĭ-gō'shē-āt') intr. **-at·ed, -at·ing** negociar —tr. *(to arrange)* negociar; FIG. *(obstacle)* franquear; *(curves)* tornar.

ne·go·ti·a·tion (nĭ-gō'shē-ā'shən) s. negociación *f*.

ne·go·ti·a·tor (nĭ-gō'shē-ā'tər) s. negociador *m*.

ne·gri·tude (nē'grĭ-tōod', -tyōod') s. negritud *f*.

Ne·gro (nē'grō) I. s. [pl. **-groes**] negro II. adj. negro <*the N. race* la raza negra>.

Ne·groid (nē'groid') adj. negroide.

Ne·he·mi·ah (nē'hə-mī'ə, nē'ə-) s. BÍBL. Nehemías.

neigh (nā) I. s. relincho II. intr. relinchar.

neigh·bor (nā'bər) I. s. *(person who lives nearby)* vecino; *(fellow human)* prójimo II. tr. ser vecino de —intr. estar contiguo.

neigh·bor·hood (nā'bər-hood') s. *(district)* barrio; *(people)* vecindad *f*, vecindario ♦ **in the n. of** FAM. cerca de, casi.

neigh·bor·li·ness (nā'bər-lē-nĭs) s. buena vecindad.

neigh·bor·ly (nā'bər-lē) adj. *(relations)* de buena vecindad; *(person, action)* amable.

neigh·bour (nā'bər) s. & v. G.B. var. de **neighbor**.

nei·ther §G36, 39 (nē'thər, nī'-) I. adj. ninguno de los dos <*n. shoe fits* ninguno de los zapatos me está bien> II. pron. ninguno (de dos), ni uno ni otro <*n. of them fits* ni uno ni otro me está bien> III. conj. & adv. tampoco <*she doesn't like winter and n. do I* a ella no le gusta el invierno y a mí tampoco> ♦ **n . . . nor** ni . . . ni <*n. you nor I will go* no iremos ni tú ni yo>.

nem·a·tode (nĕm'ə-tōd') s. ZOOL. nematodo.

nem·e·sis (nĕm'ĭ-sĭs) s. [pl. **-ses** (-sēz')] *(avenger)* vengador *m*; *(punishment)* justo castigo; *(rival)* rival *mf*.

ne·o·clas·sic (nē'ō-klăs'ĭk) o **ne·o·clas·si·cal** (-ĭ-kəl) adj. neoclásico.

ã rey / ä año / b boca / ch chico / d dar / ĕ el / ē mil / g gato / h joya / hw juez / ī aire / k casa / kw cuan

ne·o·clas·si·cism (nē'ō-klăs'ĭ-sīz'əm) s. neoclasicismo.
ne·o·co·lo·ni·al·ism (nē'ō-kə-lō'nē-ə-līz'əm) s. POL. neocolonialismo.
ne·o·dym·i·um (nē'ō-dĭm'ē-əm) s. QUÍM. neodimio.
ne·o·gen·e·sis (nē'ō-jĕn'ĭ-sĭs) s. BIOL. neogénesis f.
ne·o·lith (nē'ə-lĭth') s. herramienta o objeto del período neolítico.
Ne·o·lith·ic (nē'ə-lĭth'ĭk) adj. GEOL. neolítico.
ne·ol·o·gism (nē-ŏl'ə-jĭz'əm) s. neologismo.
ne·ol·o·gist (nē-ŏl'ə-jĭst) s. neólogo.
ne·on (nē'ŏn') s. QUÍM. neón m.
ne·o·phyte (nē'ə-fīt') s. neófito.
ne·o·plasm (nē'ə-plăz'əm) s. neoplasma m, neoplasia f.
ne·o·prene (nē'ə-prēn') s. QUÍM. neopreno.
Ne·pal (nə-pôl', -păl') s. Nepal m.
Nep·al·ese (nĕp'ə-lēz') I. adj. nepalés II. s. [pl. **Nepalese**] (inhabitant, language) nepalés m ♦ the N. los nepaleses.
ne·pen·the (nĭ-pĕn'thē) s. MITOL. nepente (bebida mágica) m.
neph·ew (nĕf'yōō) s. sobrino.
ne·phrit·ic (nə-frĭt'ĭk) adj. MED. nefrítico.
ne·phri·tis (nə-frī'tĭs) s. MED. nefritis f.
ne plus ultra (nā' plōōs ōōl'trä) s. LAT. no más allá.
nep·o·tism (nĕp'ə-tĭz'əm) s. nepotismo.
Nep·tune (nĕp'tōōn', -tyōōn') s. ASTRON., MITOL. Neptuno.
nep·tu·ni·um (nĕp-tōō'nē-əm, -tyōō'-) s. QUÍM. neptunio.
Ne·ro (nîr'ō) s. HIST. Nerón.
nerve (nûrv) I. s. ANAT., BOT. nervio; FIG., FAM. (boldness) descaro, tupé m <the n. of him! ¡qué descaro!> ♦ **nerves of steel** nervios de acero ♦ **to be a bundle of nerves** FIG. estar hecho un manojo de nervios ♦ **to get on one's nerves** FIG. ponerle nervioso a uno ♦ **to lose one's n.** FIG. ponerse nervioso ♦ **to set one's nerves on edge** FIG. ponerle a uno los nervios de punta ♦ **to strain every n.** FIG. esforzarse al máximo II. tr. animar, dar ánimos a.
nerve cell s. ANAT. célula nerviosa, neurona.
nerve center s. ANAT., FISIOL. centro nervioso.
nerve fiber s. ANAT. fibra nerviosa.
nerve gas s. MIL. gas neurotóxico.
nerve·less (nûrv'lĭs) adj. sin nervios.
nerve-rack·ing (nûrv'răk'ĭng) adj. que crispa los nervios, exasperante.
nerv·ous (nûr'vəs) adj. MED. nervioso; (uneasy) nervioso, aprensivo; (high-strung) irritable, excitable ♦ **n. breakdown** depresión nerviosa ♦ **to be n. about** tener miedo a.
nerv·ous·ly (nûr'və-slē) adv. nerviosamente.
nerv·ous·ness (nûr'vəs-nĭs) s. (fearfulness) nerviosidad f, nerviosismo; (anxiety) ansiedad f.
nervous system s. ANAT. sistema nervioso.
nerv·y (nûr'vē) adj. -i·er, -i·est (brazen) descarado; (vigorous) fuerte, vigoroso; G.B. (nervous) nervioso.
ne·science (nĕsh'əns) s. nesciencia, ignorancia.
nest (nĕst) I. s. (of birds) nido; (of hens) nidal m; (of animals) madriguera; (of wasps) avispero; (cozy place) morada; (nestful) nidada; (of boxes, drawers) juego; FIG. (hotbed) semillero ♦ **empty n.** FIG. casa vacía ♦ **to leave the n.** FIG. irse a vivir por su cuenta II. intr. (to occupy) anidar; (to build) hacer su nido —tr. (to fit into) encajar; (to hunt) buscar nidos.
nest egg s. (of a hen) nidal m; FIG. (savings) ahorros, economías.
nest·ing (nĕs'tĭng) s. cloquera.
nes·tle (nĕs'əl) tr. -tled, -tling ♦ **to be nestled among** estar situado en ♦ **to be nestled in** (a place) estar al abrigo o al amparo de; (someone's arms) acurrucarse en (los brazos de alguien) ♦ **to n.** (something) poner con mimo (algo) ♦ **to n. up into** arrimarse a, apretarse contra —intr. acurrucarse.
nest·ling (nĕst'lĭng) s. polluelo.
net¹ (nĕt) I. s. DEP. red f; (fabric) tul m; (trap) red, trampa; (snare) cebo, lazo II. tr. **net·ted, net·ting** coger o atrapar con una red.
net² (nĕt) I. adj. (after deductions) neto <n. benefit beneficio neto>; (final) final <the n. result el resultado final> II. s. (profit) ganancia neta; (price) precio neto; (weight)

peso neto III. tr. **net·ted, net·ting** COM. (to yield) producir; (to clear) ganar neto.
neth·er (nĕth'ər) adj. inferior.
Neth·er·land·er (nĕth'ər-lăn'dər) s. neerlandés m.
Neth·er·land·ish (nĕth'ər-lăn'dĭsh) adj. neerlandés.
Neth·er·lands (nĕth'ər-ləndz) s. Países Bajos.
neth·er·most (nĕth'ər-mōst') adj. más bajo, más profundo.
neth·er·world (nĕth'ər-wûrld') s. (Hades) reino de los muertos; (hell) infierno.
net·ting (nĕt'ĭng) s. (net) red f; (fishing) pesca con red.
net·tle (nĕt'l) I. s. BOT. ortiga II. tr. **-tled, -tling** (to sting) picar; (to irritate) irritar.
net·tle·some (nĕt'l-səm) adj. irritante, molesto.
net·work (nĕt'wûrk') s. red f.
neu·ral (nŏor'əl) adj. ANAT. neural, de los nervios.
neu·ral·gia (nŏo-răl'jə, nyŏo-) s. MED. neuralgia.
neu·ral·gic (nŏo-răl'jĭk, nyŏo-) adj. MED. neurálgico.
neu·ras·the·ni·a (nŏor'əs-thē'nē-ə, nyŏor'-) s. MED. neurastenia.
neu·ri·tis (nŏo-rī'tĭs, nyŏo-) s. MED. neuritis f.
neu·rol·o·gist (nŏo-rŏl'ə-jĭst, nyŏo-) s. MED. neurólogo.
neu·rol·o·gy (nŏo-rŏl'ə-jē, nyŏo-) s. MED. neurología.
neu·ron (nŏor'ŏn', nyŏor'-) o **neu·rone** (-ōn') s. ANAT. neurona.
neu·rop·a·thy (nŏo-rŏp'ə-thē, nyŏo-) s. MED. neuropatía.
neu·ro·sis (nŏo-rō'sĭs, nyŏo-) s. [pl. **-ses** (-sēz')] MED. neurosis f.
neu·ro·sur·ger·y (nŏor'ō-sûr'jə-rē, nyŏor'-) s. CIR. neurocirujía.
neu·rot·ic (nŏo-rŏt'ĭk, nyŏo-) adj. & s. neurótico.
neu·ter (nŏo'tər, nyŏo'-) I. adj. neutro II. s. GRAM. neutro; VET. animal castrado III. tr. castrar, capar.
neu·tral (nŏo'trəl, nyŏo'-) I. adj. (impartial) neutral; (achromatic) neutro; FÍS., QUÍM. neutro II. s. neutral mf; AUTO. punto muerto.
neu·tral·ism (nŏo'trə-lĭz'əm, nyŏo'-) s. neutralismo.
neu·tral·i·ty (nŏo-trăl'ĭ-tē, nyŏo-) s. neutralidad f.
neu·tral·i·za·tion (nŏo'trə-lĭ-zā'shən, nyŏo'-) s. neutralización f.
neu·tral·ize (nŏo'trə-līz', nyŏo'-) tr. **-ized, -iz·ing** neutralizar.
neu·tral·iz·er (nŏo'trə-lī'zər, nyŏo'-) s. neutralizador m.
neutral spirits s. QUÍM. [ú. con v. sing. o pl.] alcohol etílico.
neu·tron (nŏo'trŏn', nyŏo'-) s. FÍS. neutrón m.
nev·er (nĕv'ər) adv. nunca, jamás ♦ **n. again** nunca más ♦ **n. ever** nunca jamás ♦ **n. fear** no tema ♦ **n. mind** no importa.
nev·er·more (nĕv'ər-môr') adv. nunca más.
nev·er-nev·er land (nĕv'ər-nĕv'ər) s. país de ensueños m.
nev·er·the·less (nĕv'ər-thə-lĕs') adv. sin embargo, no obstante <the plan may fail, but we must try it n. el plan puede fracasar pero no obstante, debemos intentarlo>.
new (nŏo, nyŏo) I. adj. **-er, -est** (original) nuevo; (recent) reciente; (modern) moderno; (additional) distinto ♦ **there is nothing n. under the sun** no hay nada nuevo bajo el sol ♦ **what's n.?** ¿qué hay de nuevo? II. adv. recién, recientemente <new-mown grass pasto recién cortado>.
new·born (nŏo'bôrn', nyŏo'-) I. adj. (just born) recién nacido; FIG. (born anew) vuelto a nacer, renacido II. s. niño recién nacido.
New Cal·e·do·ni·a (kăl'ĭ-dō'nē-ə, -dōn'yə) s. Nueva Caledonia.
new·com·er (nŏo'kŭm'ər, nyŏo'-) s. recién llegado.
new·el (nŏo'əl, nyŏo'-) s. (circular staircase) nabo, eje (de una escalera de caracol) m ♦ **n. post** poste de una escalera m.
New England s. Nueva Inglaterra.
New Eng·land·er (ĭng'glən-dər) s. habitante de Nueva Inglaterra mf.
new-fan·gled (nŏo'făng'gəld, nyŏo'-) adj. (novel) nuevo, novedoso; (modern) moderno.
new·found (nŏo'found', nyŏo'-) adj. nuevo.
New·found·land (nŏo'fənd-lənd, nyŏo'-) s. Terranova.
New Guin·ea (gĭn'ē) s. Nueva Guinea.
New Guinea, Papua s. Papua Nueva Guinea.

New Heb·ri·des (hĕb'rĭ-dēz') s.pl. Nuevas Hébridas.
new·ly (nōō'lē, nyōō'-) adv. *(anew)* nuevamente; *(recently)* recientemente.
new·ly-wed (nōō'lē-wĕd', nyōō'-) s. recién casado.
new moon s. luna nueva.
new·ness (nōō'nĭs, nyōō'-) s. novedad *f.*
New Or·leans (ôr'lənz, ôr-lēnz') s. Nueva Orleáns.
news (nōōz, nyōōz) s.pl. [u. con v. sing.] *(information)* noticia <*that's good n.* es una buena noticia>; *(newsworthy material)* actualidad *f*; *(recent events)* noticias; *(broadcast)* noticias, noticiario ♦ **that's n. to me!** ¡eso es para mí una novedad! • **to break the n.** dar una noticia a.
news agency s. agencia de noticias.
news·boy (nōōz'boi', nyōōz'-) s. *(seller)* muchacho vendedor de periódicos; *(deliverer)* muchacho que reparte periódicos.
news·break (nōōz'brāk', nyōōz'-) s. noticia o suceso de interés.
news·cast (nōōz'kăst', nyōōz'-) s. noticiario.
news·cast·er (nōōz'kăs'tər, nyōōz'-) s. RAD., TELEV. presentador de noticias *m,* locutor *m.*
news·let·ter (nōōz'lĕt'ər, nyōōz'-) s. hoja informativa, boletín *m.*
news·man (nōōz'măn', nyōōz'-) s. [pl. **-men** (-mĕn')] PERIOD. reportero, periodista *m.*
news·pa·per (nōōz'pā'pər, nyōōz'-) s. periódico, diario.
news·pa·per·man (nōōz'pā'pər-măn', nyōōz'-) s. [pl. **-men** (-mĕn')] PERIOD. *(reporter)* periodista *m*; *(owner)* dueño de un periódico.
news·pa·per·wom·an (nōōz'pā'pər-wōōm'ən, nyōōz'-) s. [pl. **-wom·en** (-wĭm'ĭn)] PERIOD. *(reporter)* periodista *f*; *(owner)* dueña de un periódico.
news·print (nōōz'prĭnt', nyōōz'-) s. papel de periódico *m.*
news·reel (nōōz'rēl', nyōōz'-) s. noticiario cinematográfico.
news release s. PERIOD. comunicado de prensa.
news·room (nōōz'rōōm', -rŏŏm', nyōōz'-) s. sala de redacción.
news·stand (nōōz'stănd', nyōōz'-) s. quiosco (de periódicos).
news·wor·thy (nōōz'wûr*th*ē, nyōōz'-) adj. de interés periodístico.
news·y (nōō'zē, nyōō'-) adj. **-i·er, -i·est** FAM. lleno de noticias, informativo.
newt (nōōt, nyōōt) s. ZOOL. tritón *m.*
New Testament s. BÍBL. Nuevo Testamento.
new·ton (nōōt'n, nyōōt'n) s. FÍS. newton *m,* neutonio (unidad de fuerza).
New·to·ni·an (nōō-tō'nē-ən, nyōō-) adj. FÍS. newtoniano, neutoniano.
New World s. Nuevo Mundo (América).
New Year s. año nuevo.
New Year's Day s. primer día del año *m.*
New Year's Eve s. Nochevieja.
New York (yôrk) s. Nueva York.
New York·er (yôr'kər) s. neoyorquino.
New Zea·land (zē'lənd) s. Nueva Zelandia.
New Zea·land·er (zē'lən-dər) s. neozelandés *m.*
next (nĕkst) I. adj. *(in time)* que viene, próximo <*n. Monday* el lunes que viene>; *(adjacent)* de al lado <*the n. room* la habitación de al lado>; *(following)* siguiente <*the n. day* el día siguiente> ♦ **to be n.** ser el siguiente ▪ **what n.!** ¡y ahora, qué! • **who's n.?** ¿quién es el siguiente? II. adv. después, luego <*what will you do n.?* ¿qué vas a hacer después?> ♦ **n. to** *(beside)* junto a, al lado de <*sit n. to me* siéntate junto a mí>; *(almost)* casi <*n. to nothing* casi nada>; *(after)* después de • **to come n.** seguir, venir después • **when n.** cuando . . . la próxima vez <*when n. you come* cuando vengas la próxima vez>.
next door adv. al lado <*she lives n.* vive al lado>.
next-door (nĕkst'dôr') adj. de al lado <*the n. neighbor* el vecino de al lado>.
next of kin s. *(relative)* pariente más cercano; DER. *(heirs)* parientes con derecho a una herencia.
nex·us (nĕk'səs) s. [pl. **nexus** o **-us·es**] nexo, vínculo.
ni·a·cin (nī'ə-sĭn) s. QUÍM. ácido nicotínico.
Ni·ag·a·ra Falls (nī-ăg'rə, -ər-ə) s. Cataratas del Niágara.

nib (nĭb) s. *(of a pen)* punta (de una pluma de escribir); ORNIT. pico.
nib·ble (nĭb'əl) I. tr. **-bled, -bling** *(to eat)* mordiscar, comer a bocaditos; *(to gnaw)* roer —intr. *(to bite)* morder, picar <*the fish nibbled at the bait* el pez mordía la carnada>; *(to eat)* comisquear II. s. *(eating)* mordisco, mordisqueo; *(morsel)* bocadito, pedacito; FIG. *(offer)* oferta.
Nic·a·ra·gua (nĭk'ə-rä'gwə) s. Nicaragua.
Nic·a·ra·guan (nĭk'ə-rä'gwən) adj. & s. nicaragüense *mf.*
nice (nīs) I. adj. **nic·er, nic·est** *(friendly)* amable, bueno <*a n. person* una buena persona>; *(pleasant)* agradable; *(attractive)* bonito, lindo; *(refined)* refinado; *(well-done)* bien hecho <*n. job* trabajo bien hecho>; *(virtuous)* decente <*she is a n. girl* ella es una chica decente>; *(considerate)* delicado ♦ **n. and** FAM. muy, bien <*n. and warm* bien calentito> • **to be n. to** ser amable con <*be n. to your sister* sé amable con tu hermana> • **to have a n. time** pasarlo bien, divertirse II. adv. **nic·er, nic·est** bien <*that smells n.* eso huele bien>.
Nice (nēs) s. Niza.
nice·ly (nīs'lē) adv. *(kindly)* amablemente; *(well)* bien.
nice·ness (nīs'nĭs) s. amabilidad *f.*
ni·ce·ty (nī'sĭ-tē) s. [pl. **-ties**] *(exactness)* precisión *f,* exactitud *f*; *(subtle distinction)* sutileza; *(refinement)* finura, delicadeza.
niche (nĭch, nēsh) I. s. ARQ. hornacina, nicho; FIG. *(place)* colocación *f,* lugar *m* <*to find one's niche in life* encontrar el lugar de uno en la vida> II. tr. **niched, nich·ing** poner en un nicho.
nick (nĭk) I. s. *(notch)* muesca; *(cut)* rasguño, corte *m*; *(on a blade)* mella ♦ **in the n. of time** en el momento crucial II. tr. *(to notch)* hacer muescas en; *(to cut)* cortar, rasguñar.
nick·el (nĭk'əl) I. s. QUÍM. níquel *m*; *(U.S. coin)* moneda de cinco centavos II. tr. niquelar.
nick·el-and-dime (nĭk'əl-ən-dīm') I. adj. FAM. *(of little worth)* de poco dinero; *(small-time)* de poca monta II. intr. **-dimed, -dim·ing** economizar.
nick·el·o·de·on (nĭk'ə-lō'dē-ən) s. *(movie house)* cine (en el que se pagaban cinco centavos por la entrada); *(juke box)* máquina de discos.
nick·nack (nĭk'năk') s. var. de **knickknack.**
nick·name (nĭk'nām') I. s. apodo II. tr. **-named, -nam·ing** apodar.
nic·o·tine (nĭk'ə-tēn') s. nicotina.
niece (nēs) s. sobrina.
nif·ty (nĭf'tē) adj. **-ti·er, -ti·est** JER. formidable, estupendo.
Ni·ger (nī'jər) s. Níger *m.*
Ni·ge·ri·a (nī-jîr'ē-ə) s. Nigeria.
Ni·ge·ri·an (nī-jîr'ē-ən) adj. & s. nigeriano.
nig·gard (nĭg'ərd) s. & adj. tacaño, avaro.
nig·gard·li·ness (nĭg'ərd-lē-nĭs) s. tacañería, avaricia.
nig·gard·ly (nĭg'ərd-lē) adj. *(stingy)* tacaño, avaro; *(meager)* escaso.
nig·ger (nĭg'ər) s. DESPEC., JER. negro, persona de color.
nig·gle (nĭg'əl) intr. **-gled, -gling** pararse en pequeñeces, reparar en minucias.
nig·gling (nĭg'lĭng) adj. demasiado meticuloso o cuidadoso.
nigh (nī) I. adv. cerca II. adj. próximo III. prep. cerca de.
night (nīt) I. s. *(hours of darkness)* noche *f*; *(nightfall)* anochecer *m*; FIG. *(darkness)* ocaso, oscuridad *f* ♦ **all n. long** toda la noche • **at** *o* **by n.** de noche • **day and n.** día *y* noche <*to work day and n.* trabajar día *y* noche> • **far into the n.** hasta altas horas de la noche • **good n.!** ¡buenas noches! • **last n.** anoche, ayer por la noche • **nights** de noche <*to work nights* trabajar de noche> • **opening n.** TEAT. noche de estreno • **the n. before** la noche anterior • **the n. before last** antes de anoche, anteanoche • **to have a bad n.** pasar una mala noche, dormir mal • **to have a sleepless n.** pasar la noche en blanco *o* en vela • **to make a n. of it** FAM. pasarse la noche de juerga • **to say good n. (to someone)** dar las buenas noches (a alguien) • **to stay out all n.** trasnochar • **to stay** *o* **spend the n.** pasar la noche, pernoctar II. adj. nocturno, de la noche.
night blindness s. MED. ceguera nocturna.

ã rey / ä año / b boca / ch chico / d dar / ĕ el / ē mil / g gato / h joya / hw juez / ī aire / k casa / kw cuan

night·cap (nīt′kăp′) s. *(worn in bed)* gorro de dormir; FAM. *(drink)* bebida tomada antes de acostarse.
night·clothes (nīt′klōthz′) s.pl. ropa de dormir.
night·club (nīt′klŭb′) s. club nocturno.
night·dress (nīt′drĕs′) s. camisón *m*, camisa de dormir.
night·fall (nīt′fôl′) s. anochecer *m*, caída de la noche.
night·gown (nīt′goun′) s. camisa de dormir, camisón *m*.
night·hawk (nīt′hôk′) s. ORNIT. chotacabras *m*; FIG., FAM. *(night owl)* pájaro nocturno, noctámbulo (persona).
night·ie (nīt′tē) s. [pl. **-ies**] FAM. camisón *m*.
night·in·gale (nīt′n-gāl′) s. ORNIT. ruiseñor *m*.
night·jar (nīt′jär′) s. ORNIT. chotacabras *m*.
night letter s. TELEG. telegrama de noche *m*.
night·life (nīt′līf′) s. vida nocturna.
night·light (nīt′līt′) s. lamparilla.
night·long (nīt′lông′) I. adj. que dura toda la noche II. adv. durante toda la noche.
night·ly (nīt′lē) I. adj. *(nocturnal)* nocturno, de noche; *(every night)* de todas las noches II. adv. *(every night)* todas las noches, cada noche <*performances are given n.* se dan funciones todas las noches>; *(at night)* por la noche <*n. rounds* visitas por la noche>.
night·mare (nīt′mâr′) s. pesadilla.
night owl s. ZOOL. lechuza, búho; FIG. *(person)* trasnochador *m*, noctámbulo.
night school s. escuela nocturna.
night·shade (nīt′shăd′) s. BOT. hierba mora.
night shift s. turno de noche.
night·shirt (nīt′shûrt′) s. camisa de dormir.
night·stick (nīt′stĭk′) s. porra de policía.
night·time (nīt′tīm′) s. noche *f* ♦ **in the n.** de noche.
night·y (nī′tē) s. var. de **nightie**.
ni·hil·ism (nī′ə-lĭz′əm, nē′-) s. nihilismo.
ni·hil·ist (nī′ə-lĭst, nē′-) s. nihilista *mf*.
ni·hil·is·tic (nī′ə-lĭs′tĭk, nē′-) adj. nihilista.
nil (nĭl) s. *(nothing)* nada; *(zero)* cero.
Nile (nīl) s. Nilo.
nim·ble (nĭm′bəl) adj. **-bler, -blest** ágil.
nim·bo·stra·tus (nĭm′bō-strā′təs, -străt′əs) s. METEOR. nimboestrato.
nim·bus (nĭm′bəs) s. [pl. **-bi** (-bī′) *o* **-bus·es**] METEOR. nimbo; *(halo)* nimbo, aureola.
nin·com·poop (nĭn′kəm-pōōp′) s. bobo, necio.
nine (nīn) s. & adj. nueve *m*.
nine hundred s. & adj. novecientos.
nine·pins (nīn′pĭnz′) s. bolos (juego).
nine·teen (nīn-tēn′) s. & adj. diecinueve *m*.
nine·teenth (nīn-tēnth′) s. & adj. *(ordinal)* decimonoveno, decimonono; *(fraction)* diecinueveavo, diecinueveava parte.
nine·ti·eth (nīn′tē-ĭth) s. & adj. nonagésimo, noventavo.
nine·ty (nīn′tē) s. & adj. noventa.
nine·ty-one (nīn′tē-wŭn′) s. & adj. noventa y uno.
nin·ny (nĭn′ē) s. [pl. **-nies**] simplón *m*, tonto.
ninth (nīnth′) s. & adj. noveno.
ni·o·bi·um (nī-ō′bē-əm) s. QUÍM. niobio.
nip (nĭp) I. tr. **nipped, nip·ping** *(to pinch)* pellizcar; *(to bite)* morder; *(to chill)* helar; JER. *(to snatch)* asir, coger; *(to steal)* birlar ♦ **to n. in the bud** cortar de raíz **—** **to n. off** cortar —intr. beber (licor) a traguitos II. s. *(pinch)* pellizco; *(bite)* mordedura; *(sip)* trago, traguito; *(bit)* pedacito; *(remark)* pulla; *(tang)* sabor picante *m* ♦ **n. and tuck** reñida • **there's a n. in the air** hace fresco.
nip·per (nĭp′ər) s. ZOOL. *(of a crustacean)* pinza; G.B., FAM. *(boy)* chaval *m*, chiquillo ♦ **nippers** *(forceps)* pinzas; *(pincers)* tenazas; *(pliers)* alicates.
nip·ping (nĭp′ĭng) adj. *(sharp)* cortante; FIG. *(biting)* mordiente, mordaz.
nip·ple (nĭp′əl) s. ANAT. pezón *m*; *(on a bottle)* tetilla del biberón.
Nip·pon·ese (nĭp′ə-nēz′) adj. & s. japonés *m*, nipón *m*.
nip·py (nĭp′ē) adj. **-pi·er, -pi·est** *(flavor)* picante; *(cold)* frío.
nit (nĭt) s. liendre *f*.
ni·ter (nī′tər) s. QUÍM. nitro, nitrato potásico.
nit-pick (nĭt′pĭk′) intr. FAM. pararse en pequeñeces.

ni·trate (nī′trāt′) I. s. QUÍM. nitrato; *(fertilizer)* nitrato de potasio, nitrato de sodio II. tr. **-trat·ed, -trat·ing** nitratar.
ni·tre (nī′tər) s. G.B. var. de **niter**.
ni·tric (nī′trĭk) adj. nítrico.
nitric acid s. QUÍM. ácido nítrico.
ni·tri·fi·ca·tion (nī′trə-fĭ-kā′shən) s. QUÍM. nitrificación *f*.
ni·trite (nī′trīt′) s. QUÍM. nitrito.
ni·tro·cel·lu·lose (nī′trō-sĕl′yə-lōs′) s. QUÍM. nitrocelulosa.
ni·tro·gen (nī′trə-jən) s. QUÍM. nitrógeno.
ni·tro·glyc·er·in *o* **ni·tro·glyc·er·ine** (nī′trō-glĭs′ər-ĭn) s. QUÍM. nitroglicerina.
ni·trous (nī′trəs) adj. QUÍM. nitroso.
nit·ty-grit·ty (nĭt′ē-grĭt′ē) s. JER. esencia *o* meollo (de algo).
nit·wit (nĭt′wĭt′) s. FAM. bobalicón *m*, papanatas *m*.
nix (nĭks) FAM. I. s. nada II. adv. no III. tr. prohibir ♦ **n. it!** ¡no lo hagas!
no §G39 (nō) I. adv. no <*no, I'm not going* no, no voy> ♦ **no longer** ya no • **no more** *(nothing else)* ya no . . . más <*I want no more* ya no quiero más>; *(not any)* no más <*there's no more wine* no queda más vino> • **to be no better than** FIG. no ser más que, ser igual *o* lo mismo que • **to be no good** *(useless)* no servir de nada; *(person, thing)* no ser nada bueno • **to say no** decir que no II. adj. *(not any)* no <*he has no money* no tiene dinero>; *(not one)* no . . . ninguno <*she has no hope* no tiene ninguna esperanza>; *(not at all)* ninguno <*she is no actress* no es ninguna actriz> • **by no means** de ninguna manera • **in no time** en un abrir y cerrar de ojos • **no admittance** prohibida la entrada • **no matter!** ¡no importa! • **no more, no less** ni más, ni menos • **no other** más <*I see no other way out* no veo más solución> • **no smoking** prohibido fumar • **no such thing** no . . . tal cosa, eso <*I said no such thing* no dije tal cosa> • **no way!** ¡nunca!, ¡jamás! • **of little or no** de casi ningún *(interés, valor)* • **with no** sin <*with no chance of* sin la oportunidad de> III. s. [pl. **noes**] no <*he wouldn't take no for an answer* no estaba dispuesto a aceptar un no como respuesta> ♦ **noes** votos en contra <*the noes have it* hay mayoría de votos en contra>.
no-ac·count (nō′ə-kount′) adj. FAM. inútil.
No·ah (nō′ə) s. BÍBL. Noé.
nob[1] (nŏb) s. JER. *(head)* cabeza, coco.
nob[2] (nŏb) s. JER. *(person)* pez gordo.
no·bel·i·um (nō-bĕl′ē-əm) s. QUÍM. nobelio.
No·bel Prize (nō-bĕl′) s. premio Nobel.
no·bil·i·ty (nō-bĭl′ĭ-tē) s. [pl. **-ties**] nobleza.
no·ble (nō′bəl) I. adj. **-bler, -blest** *(aristocratic)* noble; *(majestic)* grandioso; QUÍM. inerte (gas) II. s. noble *mf*.
no·ble·man (nō′bəl-mən) s. [pl. **-men**] noble *m*.
no·ble·ness (nō′bəl-nĭs) s. nobleza.
no·ble·wom·an (nō′bəl-wōōm′ən) s. [pl. **-wom·en** (-wĭm′ĭn)] noble *f*.
no·bly (nō′blē) adv. noblemente.
no·bod·y §G39 (nō′bŏd′ē) I. pron. nadie ♦ **n. else** nadie más • **to be nobody's fool** no ser tomado por tonto II. s. [pl. **-ies**] don nadie *m*, nadie *m*.
noc·tam·bu·lism (nŏk-tăm′byə-lĭz′əm) s. *(night walking)* noctambulismo; *(sleepwalking)* sonambulismo.
noc·tur·nal (nŏk-tûr′nəl) adj. nocturno.
noc·turne (nŏk′tûrn′) s. PINT. escena nocturna; MÚS. nocturno.
nod (nŏd) I. intr. **nod·ded, nod·ding** *(flowers, trees)* balancearse, inclinarse; *(from sleepiness)* dar cabezadas; *(in agreement)* asentir con la cabeza; *(in greeting)* saludar con la cabeza ♦ **to n. off** echar una cabezada, dormirse —tr. inclinar (la cabeza) ♦ **to n. hello** *o* **a greeting** saludar con una inclinación de cabeza • **to n. one's agreement** asentir con la cabeza II. s. inclinación de cabeza *f* ♦ **to get the n.** obtener la aprobación • **to give someone a n.** saludar a alguien con una inclinación de cabeza • **to give the n.** asentir, aprobar.
nod·al (nōd′l) adj. nodal.
node (nōd) s. *(protuberance)* protuberancia, bulto; BOT. nudo; ANAT., FÍS., MED. nodo.
nod·u·lar (nŏj′ə-lər) adj. nodular.
nod·ule (nŏj′ōol) s. nódulo.

---

ng inglés / ŏ la / ō bou / ô corre / oi oigo / ōō uno / ou auto / yōō ciudad / w hueco / y yo / z mismo

No·ël o **No·el** (nō-ĕl′) s. Navidad *f* ♦ **n.** villancico de Navidad.

no-fault (nō′fôlt′) adj. DER. sin responsabilidad.

nog (nŏg) s. CUL. ponche de huevo *m*, rompopo.

nog·gin (nŏg′ĭn) s. *(cup)* tacita; *(measure)* media taza; JER. *(head)* cabeza, coco.

no-go (nō′gō′) adj. JER. que no está listo.

no-good (nō′gŏŏd′) **I.** adj. *(useless)* inútil; *(very bad)* malísimo; *(vile)* vil **II.** s. inútil *mf.*

no·how (nō′hou′) adv. de ninguna manera, de ningún modo.

noise (noiz) s. *(sound)* ruido; ELECTRÓN., FÍS. ruido parásito, interferencia ♦ **to make n.** o **a n.** hacer ruido • **to make a lot of n. about** FIG. *(to talk)* hablar mucho de; *(to complain)* quejarse de.

noise·less (noiz′lĭs) adj. silencioso, sin ruido.

noise·mak·er (noiz′mā′kər) s. *(person)* persona que hace ruido; *(device)* matraca.

nois·i·ness (noi′zē-nĭs) s. ruido.

noi·some (noi′səm) adj. *(foul)* fétido; *(harmful)* nocivo.

noi·some·ness (noi′səm-nĭs) s. *(stench)* fetidez *f*; *(harmfulness)* nocividad *f.*

nois·y (noi′zē) adj. **-i·er, -i·est** ruidoso.

no-load (nō′lōd′) adj. FIN. sin comisión de ventas.

no·mad (nō′măd′) s. nómada *mf.*

no·mad·ic (nō-măd′ĭk) adj. nómada.

no man's land s. tierra de nadie.

nom de plume (nŏm′ də plōōm′) s. seudónimo.

no·men·cla·ture (nō′mən-klā′chər) s. nomenclatura.

nom·i·nal (nŏm′ə-nəl) adj. *(in name)* nominal; *(of shares)* nominativo; *(trifling)* insignificante.

nom·i·nal·ly (nŏm′ə-nə-lē) adv. nominalmente.

nom·i·nate (nŏm′ə-nāt′) tr. **-nat·ed, -nat·ing** *(to appoint)* nombrar; *(to propose as a candidate)* proponer como candidato.

nom·i·na·tion (nŏm′ə-nā′shən) s. nombramiento.

nom·i·na·tive (nŏm′ə-nə-tĭv) adj. & s. COM., GRAM. nominativo.

nom·i·nee (nŏm′ə-nē′) s. candidato.

non·ac·cep·tance (nŏn′ăk-sĕp′təns) s. falta de aceptación, rechazo.

non·age (nŏn′ĭj, nō′nĭj) s. *(minority)* minoría de edad; *(immaturity)* inmadurez *f.*

non·ag·gres·sion (nŏn′ə-grĕsh′ən) s. no agresión *f.*

non·a·ligned (nŏn′ə-līnd′) adj. POL. no alineado.

non·at·ten·dance (nŏn′ə-tĕn′dəns) s. falta de asistencia, ausencia.

non·break·a·ble (nŏn-brā′kə-bəl) adj. irrompible.

nonce (nŏns) s. momento <for the n. por el momento>.

nonce word s. palabra inventada.

non·cha·lance (nŏn′shə-läns′) s. imperturbabilidad *f.*

non·cha·lant (nŏn′shə-länt′) adj. imperturbable, impasible.

non·com·bat·ant (nŏn′kəm-băt′nt, -kŏm′bə-tnt) s. & adj. MIL. no combatiente *mf.*

non·com·bus·ti·ble (nŏn′kəm-bŭs′tə-bəl) adj. incombustible.

non·com·mis·sioned officer (nŏn′kə-mĭsh′ənd) s. MIL. suboficial *m.*

non·com·mit·tal (nŏn′kə-mĭt′l) adj. evasivo.

non·com·pli·ance (nŏn′kəm-plī′əns) s. incumplimiento.

non·con·duc·tor (nŏn′kən-dŭk′tər) s. ELEC. aislante *m.*

non·con·form·ist (nŏn′kən-fôr′mĭst) adj. & s. no conformista *mf*, disidente *mf.*

non·con·form·i·ty (nŏn′kən-fôr′mĭ-tē) s. no conformidad *f*, disidencia.

non·de·nom·i·na·tion·al (nŏn′dĭ-nŏm′ə-nā′shə-nəl) adj. RELIG. no sectario, no afiliado con una secta religiosa.

non·de·script (nŏn′dĭ-skrĭpt′) **I.** adj. de poco o ningún carácter **II.** s. persona o cosa sin carácter distintivo.

non·de·struc·tive (nŏn′dĭ-strŭk′tĭv) adj. no destructivo.

non·dis·crim·i·na·tion (nŏn′dĭ-skrĭm′ə-nā′shən) s. ausencia de discriminación.

non·drink·er (nŏn-drĭng′kər) s. no bebedor *m.*

none §G36 (nŭn) **I.** pron. *(nobody)* nadie, ninguno <n. dares to do it nadie se atreve a hacerlo>; *(not one)* ninguno <n. of them went ninguno de ellos fue>; *(not any)*

nada <we have n. of that paper no nos queda nada de ese papel> ♦ **to be n. of one's business** no ser asunto de uno • **n. but** solamente • **n. other than** nadie o nada menos que **II.** adv. no <he is n. too happy él no está muy contento>.

non·en·ti·ty (nŏn-ĕn′tĭ-tē) s. [pl. **-ties**] *(nonexistence)* nada; *(person)* nulidad *f*, don nadie *m.*

non·es·sen·tial (nŏn′ĭ-sĕn′shəl) adj. no esencial.

none·such (nŭn′sŭch′) s. *(person)* persona sin igual; *(thing)* cosa sin par.

none·the·less (nŭn′thə-lĕs′) adv. sin embargo, no obstante.

non·ex·ist·ence (nŏn′ĭg-zĭs′təns) s. inexistencia.

non·ex·ist·ent (nŏn′ĭg-zĭs′tənt) adj. inexistente.

non·fat (nŏn′făt′) adj. sin grasa.

non·fea·sance (nŏn-fē′zəns) s. DER. incumplimiento.

non·fic·tion (nŏn-fĭk′shən) s. literatura no novelesca.

non·flam·ma·ble (nŏn-flăm′ə-bəl) adj. no inflamable.

non·hu·man (nŏn-hyōō′mən) adj. no humano.

non·in·ter·ven·tion (nŏn-ĭn′tər-vĕn′shən) s. POL. no intervención *f.*

non·in·volve·ment (nŏn′ĭn-vŏlv′mənt) s. *(lack of involvement)* no implicación *f*; *(nonintervention)* no intervención *f.*

non·met·al (nŏn-mĕt′l) s. QUÍM. metaloide *m.*

non·ne·go·tia·ble (nŏn′nĭ-gō′shə-bəl) adj. COM. no negociable.

no-no (nō′nō′) s. [pl. **-no's** o **-nos**] FAM. *(something forbidden)* algo prohibido o inadmisible; *(faux pas)* metida de pata.

non·non·sense (nŏ′nŏn′sĕns′) adj. práctico.

non·pa·reil (nŏn′pə-rĕl′) **I.** adj. sin igual, sin par **II.** s. *(person)* persona sin igual; *(thing)* cosa sin par.

non·par·ti·san (nŏn-pär′tĭ-zən) adj. independiente.

non·pay·ment (nŏn-pā′mənt) s. falta de pago.

non·per·for·mance (nŏn′pər-fôr′məns) s. incumplimiento.

non·per·son (nŏn-pûr′sən) s. persona cuya existencia no se reconoce.

non·plus (nŏn-plŭs′) **I.** s. perplejidad *f* **II.** tr. dejar perplejo, desconcertar.

non·pro·duc·tive (nŏn′prə-dŭk′tĭv) adj. improductivo.

non·pro·fes·sion·al (nŏn′prə-fĕsh′ə-nəl) adj. & s. no profesional *mf.*

non·prof·it (nŏn-prŏf′ĭt) adj. sin fin lucrativo.

non·prof·it·mak·ing (nŏn-prŏf′ĭt-mā′kĭng) adj. no lucrativo.

non·res·i·dent (nŏn-rĕz′ĭ-dənt) adj. & s. no residente *mf*, transeúnte *mf.*

non·re·sis·tance (nŏn′rĭ-zĭs′təns) s. falta de resistencia, pasividad *f.*

non·re·stric·tive (nŏn′rĭ-strĭk′tĭv) adj. sin restricción.

non·re·turn·a·ble (nŏn′rĭ-tûr′nə-bəl) adj. sin devolución.

non·sched·uled (nŏn-skĕj′ōōld) adj. no regular.

non·sec·tar·i·an (nŏn′sĕk-târ′ē-ən) adj. no sectario.

non·sense (nŏn′sĕns′) s. disparate *m*, desatino ♦ **n.!** ¡tonterías!

non·sen·si·cal (nŏn-sĕn′sĭ-kəl) adj. disparatado, desatinado.

non·skid (nŏn′skĭd′) adj. antideslizante.

non·stan·dard (nŏn-stăn′dərd) adj. no reglamentario.

non·stop (nŏn′stŏp′) **I.** adv. sin parar **II.** adj. *(train)* directo; *(plane)* sin escalas.

non·sup·port (nŏn′sə-pôrt′) s. DER. falta de pago de la pensión alimenticia.

non·tax·a·ble (nŏn-tăk′sə-bəl) adj. no imponible, exento de impuestos.

non·trans·fer·a·ble (nŏn′trăns-fûr′ə-bəl) adj. intransferible.

non·un·ion (nŏn-yōōn′yən) adj. *(not belonging to a union)* no sindicado; *(not dealing with unions)* que no emplea miembros de un sindicato.

non·use (nŏn′yōōs′) s. falta de uso.

non·vi·a·ble (nŏn-vī′ə-bəl) adj. no viable.

non·vi·o·lence (nŏn-vī′ə-ləns) s. FILOS., POL. no violencia.

noo·dle (nōōd′l) s. CUL. tallarín *m*, fideo; JER. *(head)* coco; *(fool)* tonto.

nook (nŏŏk) s. *(corner)* rincón *m*; *(hidden spot)* escondrijo.

ã rey / ä año / b boca / ch chico / d dar / ĕ el / ē mil / g gato / h joya / hw juez / ī aire / k casa / kw cuan /

noon (nōon) I. s. mediodía *m* ♦ **at high n.** a mediodía II. adj. de mediodía.
noon·day (nōon'dā') I. s. mediodía *m* II. adj. de mediodía.
no one *o* **no-one** (nō'wŭn') pron. nadie, ninguno.
noon·time (nōon'tīm') s. mediodía *m*.
noose (nōos) I. s. *(knot)* nudo corredizo; *(of a rope)* dogal *m*; *(trap)* trampa II. tr. **noosed, noos·ing** coger con un lazo.
nor §G41 (nôr) conj. ni *<he was neither willing n. able* ni quería ni podía>; ni tampoco *<I have never gone there, n. do I want to* yo nunca fui allí ni tampoco quiero ir>.
Nor·dic (nôr'dĭk) adj. & s. nórdico.
norm (nôrm) s. norma.
nor·mal (nôr'məl) I. adj. *(common)* normal; GEOM. perpendicular, normal; QUÍM. neutro, normal II. s. *(usual)* normalidad *f*, nivel normal *m*; GEOM. perpendicular *f*, normal *f* ♦ **to return to n.** volver a la normalidad.
nor·mal·i·ty (nôr-măl'ĭ-tē) s. normalidad *f*.
nor·mal·ize (nôr'mə-līz') tr. **-ized, -iz·ing** normalizar.
normal school s. EDUC. escuela normal.
Nor·man (nôr'mən) adj. & s. normando.
Nor·man·dy (nôr'mən-dē) s. Normandía.
nor·ma·tive (nôr'mə-tĭv) adj. normativo.
Norse (nôrs) adj. & s. escandinavo.
Norse·man (nôrs'mən) s. [pl. **-men**] escandinavo.
north (nôrth) I. s. norte *m* ♦ **N.** región nórdica *o* septentrional II. adj. del norte *<n. wind* viento del norte> III. adv. hacia el norte.
North Africa s. Africa del Norte.
North African adj. & s. norteafricano.
North America s. América del Norte, Norteamérica.
North American adj. & s. norteamericano.
north·bound (nôrth'bound') adj. con rumbo al norte.
north·east (nôrth-ēst') I. s. noreste *m*, nordeste *m* II. adj. del noreste, nordeste III. adv. hacia el nordeste.
north·east·er (nôrth-ē'stər) s. viento del nordeste, nordeste *m*.
north·east·er·ly (nôrth-ē'stər-lē) I. adj. del nordeste II. adv. hacia el nordeste.
north·east·ern (nôrth-ē'stərn) adj. del nordeste.
north·east·ward (nôrth-ēst'wərd) I. adv. & adj. hacia el nordeste II. s. dirección *o* región nordeste *f*.
north·er (nôr'thər) s. norte *m*, cierzo (viento del norte).
north·er·ly (nôr'thər-lē) I. adj. norte, del norte II. s. [pl. **-lies**] norte *m*, viento del norte III. adv. hacia el norte.
north·ern (nôr'thərn) adj. septentrional, del norte ♦ **N.** de la región norte ♦ **n. lights** METEOR. aurora boreal.
north·ern·er (nôr'thər-nər) s. norteño.
Northern Hemisphere s. GEOG. hemisferio norte.
Northern Ireland s. Irlanda del Norte.
north·ern·most (nôr'thərn-mōst') adj. más septentrional.
North Korea s. Corea del Norte.
north·land (nôrth'lănd') s. región *o* tierra del norte *f*.
North·man (nôrth'mən) s. [pl. **-men**] escandinavo.
north·north·east (nôrth'nôrth-ēst') I. s. nornordeste *m* II. adj. nornordeste, del nornordeste III. adv. hacia el nornordeste.
north·north·west (nôrth'nôrth-wĕst') I. s. nornoroeste *m* II. adj. nornoroeste, del nornoroeste III. adv. hacia el nornoroeste.
North Pole s. GEOG. Polo Norte.
North Sea s. Mar del Norte *m*.
North Star s. ASTRON. estrella polar.
north·ward (nôrth'wərd) I. adv. & adj. hacia el norte II. s. norte (punto, dirección, región) *m*.
north·west (nôrth-wĕst') I. s. noroeste *m* II. adj. del noroeste III. adv. hacia el noroeste.
north·west·er (nôrth-wĕs'tər) s. viento del noroeste.
north·west·er·ly (nôrth-wĕs'tər-lē) I. adj. del noroeste II. adv. hacia el noroeste.
north·west·ern (nôrth-wĕs'tərn) adj. del noroeste.
north·west·ward (nôrth-wĕst'wərd) I. adv. & adj. hacia el noroeste II. s. dirección *o* región noroeste *f*.
Nor·way (nôr'wā') s. Noruega.
Nor·we·gian (nôr-wē'jən) adj. & s. *(inhabitant, language)* noruego.

nose (nōz) I. s. *(of people, dogs)* nariz *f*; *(of other animals)* hocico; *(of wine)* boca, aroma *m*; *(sense of smell)* olfato; *(knack)* olfato ♦ *n. for news* olfato para las noticias>; *(of a boat)* proa, nariz; *(of a plane)* morro, nariz ♦ **as plain as the n. on one's face** más claro que el agua • **not to be able to see past the n. on one's face** no ver más allá de las narices • **on the n.** exacto • **right under one's n.** en las mismas narices, delante de las narices • **to blow one's n.** sonarse, sonarse la nariz • **to follow one's n.** seguir recto • **to keep one's n. out of another's business** no meter la nariz *o* las narices en asuntos ajenos • **to lead by the n.** manejar al antojo de uno • **to look down one's n. at** FAM. *(someone)* mirar por encima del hombro a; *(something)* mirar con desprecio • **to pay through the n.** FAM. pagar un dineral • **to poke** *o* **stick one's n. into** FAM. meter la nariz *o* las narices en • **to turn up one's n. at** FAM. despreciar, desdeñar • **to win by a n.** DEP., FAM. ganar por un pelo II. tr. **nosed, nos·ing** *(to smell)* olfatear; *(to nuzzle)* empujar con el hocico —intr. husmear ♦ **to n. along** *o* **forward** avanzar con cuidado • **to n. around** husmear.
nose·bleed (nōz'blēd') s. hemorragia nasal.
nose cone s. ARM., ASTRONÁUT. morro.
nosedive (nōz'dīv') s. AER. picado.
nose·gay (nōz'gā') s. ramillete de flores *m*.
nose·piece (nōz'pēs') s. *(of eyeglasses)* puente *m*; *(noseband)* muserola.
no·sey (nō'zē) adj. var. de **nosy**.
nosh (nŏsh) s. FAM. bocado, tentempié *m*.
no-show (nō-shō') s. JER. pasajero que no utiliza su reservación sin cancelarla ♦ **no-shows** los que no asisten a un espectáculo para el cual tienen entradas.
nos·tal·gia (nə-stăl'jə) s. nostalgia.
nos·tal·gic (nə-stăl'jĭk) adj. nostálgico.
nos·tril (nŏs'trəl) s. ventana de la nariz.
nos·trum (nŏs'trəm) s. panacea.
nos·y (nō'zē) adj. **-i·er, -i·est** entrometido.
not §G13, 39 (nŏt) adv. no *<I will n. go* no iré> ♦ **are you coming or n.?** ¿vienes o no? • **certainly n.** ¡de ninguna manera! • **fear n.!** ¡no temas! • **if n.** en caso contrario • **I'm afraid n.** temo que no • **n. a chance!** ¡de ninguna manera! • **n. at all!** ¡de ningún modo!, ¡en absoluto! • **n. even** ni siquiera • **n. likely!** ¡ni hablar! • **n. me!** FAM. ¡yo no! • **n. to mention** por no mencionar • **n. yet** ya no, todavía no • **of course n.!** ¡claro que no!
no·ta·bil·i·ty (nō'tə-bĭl'ĭ-tē) s. [pl. **-ties**] *(quality)* notabilidad *f*; *(person)* notabilidad, personaje *m*.
no·ta·ble (nō'tə-bəl) I. adj. notable, memorable II. s. notable *m*, personaje *m*.
no·ta·bly (nō'tə-blē) adv. notablemente.
no·ta·rize (nō'tə-rīz') tr. **-rized, -riz·ing** DER. hacer certificar por notario.
no·ta·ry (nō'tə-rē) s. [pl. **-ries**] notario, escribano.
notary public s. [pl. **notaries public**] notario.
no·ta·tion (nō-tā'shən) s. MAT., MÚS. notación *f*; *(brief note)* nota, anotación *f*.
notch (nŏch) I. s. *(cut)* muesca, corte *m*; *(mountain pass)* desfiladero; FAM. *(level)* grado, nivel *m* ♦ **to take someone down a n.** FAM. bajar los humos a alguien II. tr. *(to cut)* hacer una muesca en, cortar; *(to record)* marcar.
note (nōt) I. s. *(letter)* nota *<send me a n.* envíame una nota>; *(in a text)* nota, comentario; DIPL., POL. *(formal letter)* nota *<n. of protest* nota de protesta>; FIN. *(money)* billete *m* *<bank n.* billete de banco>; *(animal call)* trino; *(element)* nota, tono *<a n. of despair* una nota de desesperación>; *(renown)* renombre *m* *<a writer of n.* un escritor de renombre>; *(mention)* mención *f*; *(importance)* importancia *<nothing of n.* nada de importancia>; COM. *(I.O.U.)* pagaré *m*; MÚS. *(tone, symbol)* nota; *(in a keyboard)* tecla ♦ **notes** notas, apuntes *<to take notes* tomar notas *o* apuntes> • **to compare notes** FIG. cambiar impresiones • **to make a n. of** *o* **to take n. of** tomar nota de • **to strike a false n.** FIG. desentonar II. tr. **not·ed, not·ing** *(to notice)* notar, advertir *<to n. a change* notar un cambio>; *(to mention)* señalar; *(to observe)* fijarse en, observar *<n. what happens next* fíjense en lo que ocurre después>.
note·book (nōt'book') s. cuaderno, libro de apuntes.

not·ed (nō′tĭd) adj. notable, eminente.
note of hand s. COM. pagaré *m*, vale *m*.
note·pa·per (nōt′pā′pər) s. papel de cartas *m*, papel de escribir.
note·wor·thy (nōt′wûr′thē) adj. notable, digno de mención.
noth·ing §G39 (nŭth′ĭng) I. pron. *(not anything)* no . . . nada *<she believes in n.* no cree en nada>; *(obscurity)* la nada *<to rise from n.* surgir de la nada> ♦ **for n.** *(for free)* por nada *<he gave it to me for n.* me lo dió por nada>; *(in vain)* para nada *<she did all that work for n.* hizo todo ese trabajo para nada>; *(for no reason)* sin motivo *<he yelled at me for n.* me gritó sin motivo> • **n. at all** nada de nada • **n. but** sólo *<to buy n. but the best* comprar sólo lo mejor> • **n. doing!** FAM. ¡ni hablar! • **n. else** nada más • **there's n. . . . about it** no es nada *<there's n. funny about it* no es nada gracioso> • **there's n. like** no hay nada como *<there's n. like home-baked bread* no hay nada como el pan hecho en casa> • **there's n. to it** es sencillísimo • **to be n.** no ser nada • **to be n. to write home about** FAM. no ser nada del otro mundo • **to come to n.** quedar en nada • **to have n. to do with** no tener nada que ver con • **to make n. of** no dar importancia a • **to say n. of . . .** por no hablar de . . . • **to stop at n.** no reparar en nada • **to think n. of** no suponer nada (para uno) *<he thinks n. of swimming a mile* para él no supone nada nadar una milla> II. s. nada, nadería ♦ **to be a big** *o* **a real n.** *(person)* ser un cero a la izquierda; *(thing)* no valer nada III. adv. ♦ **n. less than** nada menos que • **n. like** no . . . nada *<she is n. like her mother* no se parece nada a su madre> IV. adj. JER. de nada *<he has a n. part in the play* tiene un papel de nada en la obra>.
noth·ing·ness (nŭth′ĭng-nĭs) s. *(void)* nada; *(trifle)* insignificancia.
no·tice (nō′tĭs) I. s. *(attention)* atención *f <it caught my n.* me llamó la atención>; *(warning)* aviso, notificación *f <she arrived without prior n.* llegó sin previo aviso>; PERIOD. *(announcement)* anuncio *<the n. of their marriage* el anuncio de su matrimonio>; ARTE., TEAT. *(review)* crítica, reseña; COM. *(to an employee)* despido, aviso de despido; *(to an employer)* dimisión *f*; *(to a tenant, landlord)* aviso; *(sign)* letrero ♦ **at a moment's n.** sin previo aviso • **on (such) short n.** en tan poco tiempo *<I can't make dinner for ten on such short n.* no puedo hacer cena para diez en tan poco tiempo> • **to be on n.** estar avisado • **to escape one's n.** escapársele a uno • **to put on** *o* **serve n.** *(to inform)* hacer saber, notificar; *(to warn)* advertir, avisar • **to take n.** *(of someone)* hacer caso (a alguien); *(of something)* hacer caso (de algo), prestar atención (a algo) • **until further n.** hasta nuevo aviso II. tr. **noticed, no·tic·ing** *(to note)* observar; *(to see)* fijarse en, reparar en *<she hadn't noticed the color before* no se había fijado antes en el color>; *(to realize)* darse cuenta de, advertir.
no·tice·a·ble (nō′tĭ-sə-bəl) adj. *(perceptible)* notable, sensible; *(obvious)* evidente, obvio ♦ **it is barely n.** casi no se nota.
no·ti·fi·ca·tion (nō′tə-fĭ-kā′shən) s. notificación *f*, aviso.
no·ti·fy (nō′tə-fī′) tr. **-fied, -fy·ing** notificar, avisar.
no·tion (nō′shən) s. *(idea)* noción *f*, idea; *(opinion)* opinión *f*, creencia; *(whim)* capricho ♦ **notions** artículos de mercería • **to have no n.** *o* **not to have the slightest n.** no tener la más mínima idea.
no·to·ri·e·ty (nō′tə-rī′ĭ-tē) s. notoriedad *f*, mala fama.
no·to·ri·ous (nō-tôr′ē-əs) adj. notorio.
no·to·ri·ous·ness (nō-tôr′ē-əs-nĭs) s. mala fama.
not·with·stand·ing (nŏt′wĭth-stăn′dĭng) I. prep. a pesar de *<the motion passed, our objections n.* la moción se aprobó a pesar de nuestras objeciones> II. adv. no obstante, sin embargo III. conj. a pesar de que.
nou·gat (nōō′gət) s. CUL. turrón de almendras *m*.
nought (nôt) s. & adj. var. de **naught.**
noun (noun) s. GRAM. sustantivo, nombre *m*.
nour·ish (nûr′ĭsh) tr. *(to feed)* nutrir, alimentar; *(to promote)* fomentar, alentar; *(to maintain)* abrigar, sostener (esperanzas).
nour·ish·ment (nûr′ĭsh-mənt) s. alimento.
no·va (nō′və) s. [pl. **-vae** (-vē) *o* **-vas**] ASTRON. nova.

No·va Sco·tia (nō′və skō′shə) s. Nueva Escocia.
no·va·tion (nō-vā′shən) s. DER. novación *f*.
nov·el (nŏv′əl) I. s. novela II. adj. nuevo, original.
nov·el·ette (nŏv′ə-lĕt′) s. novela corta.
nov·el·ist (nŏv′ə-lĭst) s. novelista *mf*.
nov·el·is·tic (nŏv′ə-lĭs′tĭk) adj. novelístico.
no·vel·la (nō-vĕl′ə) s. [pl. **-vel·las** *o* **-vel·le** (-vĕl′ē)] cuento, novela corta.
nov·el·ty (nŏv′əl-tē) s. [pl. **-ties**] novedad *f*, innovación *f* ♦ **novelties** chucherías, baratijas.
No·vem·ber (nō-vĕm′bər) s. noviembre *m*.
nov·ice (nŏv′ĭs) s. *(beginner)* novato, principiante *mf*; RELIG. novicio.
no·vi·ti·ate (nō-vĭsh′ē-ĭt, -āt′) s. *(period)* período de aprendizaje; RELIG. noviciado.
No·vo·cain (nō′və-kān′) s. FARM. novocaína (marca registrada de un anestésico local).
now (nou) I. adv. *(at present)* ahora *<I can't leave n.* no puedo irme ahora>; *(immediately)* ahora mismo *<do it n.!* ¡hazlo ahora mismo!>; *(as things are)* ahora ya *<n. we won't be able to stay* ahora ya no podemos quedarnos>; *(then)* entonces *<n. the trouble began* entonces empezaron los problemas> ♦ **just n.** *(at present)* ahora mismo, en este momento; *(recently)* ahora mismo, hace un momento *<he left just n.* se fue hace un momento> • **n. . . . n.** ora . . . ora, ya . . . ya • **n., n.** vamos, vamos *<n., n., don't cry* vamos, vamos, no llores> • **n. and again** *o* **n. and then** de vez en cuando • **n. or never** ahora o nunca • **n. then** ahora bien • **right n.!** ¡ahora mismo! II. conj. ya que, ahora que *<n. that you mention it* ahora que lo mencionas> III. s. ♦ **by n.** ya *<you should have finished by n.* ya tenías que haber terminado> • **for n.** por ahora • **from n. on** de ahora en adelante • **not n.** ahora no • **until** *o* **up to n.** hasta ahora IV. adj. FAM. *(current)* actual *<the n. generation* la generación actual>; JER. *(trendy)* moderno.
now·a·days (nou′ə-dāz′) adv. hoy día, hoy en día.
no·way (nō′wā′) *o* **no·ways** (nō′wāz′) adv. de ningún modo, de ninguna manera.
no way interj. FAM. de ninguna manera.
no·where §G39 (nō′hwâr′) I. adv. *(not anywhere)* por ninguna parte *<he is n. to be found* no se le encuentra por ninguna parte>; *(no place)* a ninguna parte *<where are you going?* ¿adónde vas? a ninguna parte>; *(not in any place)* en ninguna parte *<n. in the world* en ninguna parte del mundo> ♦ **n. else** en ninguna otra parte • **n. near as good** ni mucho menos tan bueno • **to get n.** FIG. no conseguir nada II. s. nada *<to appear out of n.* salir de la nada> ♦ **in the middle of n.** en el quinto pino.
no-win (nō′wĭn′) adj. que no puede ganar.
nox·ious (nŏk′shəs) adj. nocivo, dañino.
noz·zle (nŏz′əl) s. boquilla.
nth (ĕnth) adj. MAT. enésimo *<ten to the n. power* diez elevado a la enésima potencia>; FIG. *(highest)* al máximo, al extremo.
nu (nōō, nyōō) s. ny (letra griega) *f*.
nu·ance (nōō-äns′, nyōō-) s. matiz *m*.
nub (nŭb) s. *(lump)* protuberancia; *(core)* esencia.
Nu·bi·a (nōō′bē-ə) s. GEOG. Nubia.
Nu·bi·an (nōō′bē-ən) adj. & s. nubiense *mf* ♦ **N. Desert** Desierto de Nubia.
nu·bile (nōō′bəl, -bīl′, nyōō′-) adj. núbil, en edad de casarse.
nuclear (nōō′klē-ər, nyōō′-) adj. nuclear.
nuclear energy s. FÍS. energía nuclear.
nuclear fission s. FÍS. fisión nuclear *f*.
nuclear fusion s. FÍS. fusión nuclear *f*.
nuclear reaction s. FÍS. reacción nuclear *f*.
nuclear reactor s. FÍS. reactor nuclear *m*.
nu·cle·on (nōō′klē-ŏn′, nyōō′-) s. FÍS. nucleón *m*.
nu·cle·on·ics (nōō′klē-ŏn′ĭks, nyōō′-) s. [ú. con v. sing.] FÍS. nucleónica.
nu·cle·us (nōō′klē-əs, nyōō′-) [pl. **-cle·i** (-klē-ī′) *o* **-cle·us·es**] s. *(core)* núcleo; CIENT. núcleo.
nude (nōōd, nyōōd) s. & adj. **nud·er, nud·est** desnudo ♦ **in the n.** al desnudo.

ā rey / ä año / b boca / ch chico / d dar / ĕ el / ē mil / g gato / h joya / hw juez / ī aire / k casa / kw cuan /

nudge (nŭj) **I.** tr. **nudged, nudg·ing** dar un codazo a **II.** s. codazo.

nud·ism (nōō′dĭz′əm, nyōō′-) s. nudismo.

nud·ist (nōō′dĭst, nyōō′-) s. & adj. nudista mf.

nu·di·ty (nōō′dĭ-tē, nyōō′-) s. desnudez f.

nu·ga·to·ry (nōō′gə-tôr′ē, nyōō′-) adj. (trifling) insignificante, trivial; (ineffective) ineficaz.

nug·get (nŭg′ĭt) s. MIN. pepita <gold n. pepita de oro>.

nui·sance (nōō′səns, nyōō′-) s. (person) pesado, latoso; (thing) fastidio, molestia; DER. (conduct) perjuicio, daño ♦ to make a n. of oneself molestar, dar la lata.

null (nŭl) **I.** adj. (invalid) nulo; (insignificant) insignificante; (nonexistent) inexistente ♦ n. and void DER. nulo y sin valor **II.** s. cero.

nul·li·fi·ca·tion (nŭl′ə-fĭ-kā′shən) s. anulación f.

nul·li·fy (nŭl′ə-fī′) tr. **-fied, -fy·ing** anular.

nul·li·ty (nŭl′ĭ-tē) s. [pl. **-ties**] DER. nulidad f.

numb (nŭm) **I.** adj. **-er, -est** (deadened) entumecido, aterido <n. with cold entumecido de frío>; (paralyzed) petrificado, paralizado <n. with fear petrificado de miedo>. **II.** tr. (to deaden) entumecer; (to paralyze) paralizar, dejar helado.

num·ber (nŭm′bər) **I.** s. (numeral) número; (total) número, total m <the n. of students in a class el número de estudiantes en una clase>; FAM. (clothing) modelo; JER. (person) tipo; GRAM., MÚS., PERIOD. número ♦ a n. of (several) varios <on a n. of occasions en varias ocasiones>; (a lot) muchos <a n. of students didn't show up muchos estudiantes no se presentaron> • any n. of muchos <any n. of possibilities muchas posibilidades> • beyond n. innumerable • by the numbers (mechanically) mecánicamente; (strictly) de uno en uno • few o small in n. pocos • phone n. número de teléfono • numbers (many) muchos; MAT. (calculating) números <she is good at numbers se le dan bien los números>; LIT. (verse) versos; (meter) metro(s) • Numbers BÍBL. Números • to do a n. on FAM. dañar, arruinar • to have someone's n. tener a alguien calado <I've got your n. te tengo calado> • without n. sin número • your n. is up FAM. te llegó la hora **II.** tr. (to mark) numerar, poner número a; (to limit) contar <his days are numbered tiene los días contados>; (to have) tener <the collection numbers ten thousand volumes la colección tiene diez mil volúmenes> ♦ to be numbered among contar —intr. ser <we numbered twenty éramos veinte> ♦ to n. in contarse <the visitors numbered in the thousands los visitantes se contaban por miles>.

num·ber·ing (nŭm′bər-ĭng) s. (counting) recuento, enumeración f; (of pages) numeración f ♦ n. machine TEC. numerador.

num·ber·less (nŭm′bər-lĭs) adj. innumerable, sin número.

number plate s. placa de matrícula.

numbers game s. lotería ilegal o clandestina.

numb·ness (nŭm′nĭs) s. entumecimiento.

numb·skull (nŭm′skŭl′) s. var. de numskull.

nu·men (nōō′mən, nyōō′-) s. [pl. **-mi·na** (-mə-nə)] (spirit) numen f; FIG. (genius) genio.

nu·mer·a·ble (nōō′mər-ə-bəl, nyōō′-) adj. numerable.

nu·mer·al (nōō′mər-əl, nyōō′-) **I.** s. número ♦ Arabic n. número arábigo • Roman n. número romano **II.** adj. numeral.

nu·mer·ate (nōō′mə-rāt′, nyōō′-) tr. **-at·ed, -at·ing** enumerar, contar.

nu·mer·a·tion (nōō′mə-rā′shən, nyōō′-) s. numeración f.

nu·mer·a·tor (nōō′mə-rā′tər, nyōō′-) s. MAT. numerador m.

nu·mer·i·cal (nōō-mĕr′ĭ-kəl, nyōō-) o **nu·mer·ic** (-mĕr′ĭk) adj. numérico.

nu·mer·ol·o·gy (nōō′mə-rŏl′ə-jē, nyōō′-) s. numerología.

nu·mer·ous (nōō′mər-əs, nyōō′-) adj. numeroso.

nu·mis·mat·ic (nōō′mĭz-măt′ĭk, nyōō′-) adj. numismático.

nu·mis·mat·ics (nōō′mĭz-măt′ĭks, nyōō′-) s. [ú. con v. sing.] numismática.

num·skull (nŭm′skŭl′) s. tonto, mentecato.

nun (nŭn) s. monja, religiosa.

nun·ci·a·ture (nŭn′sē-ə-chōōr′, -chər) s. RELIG. nunciatura.

nun·ci·o (nŭn′sē-ō′) s. [pl. **-os**] RELIG. nuncio (apostólico).

nun·ner·y (nŭn′ə-rē) s [pl. **-ies**] convento de monjas.

nup·tial (nŭp′shəl) **I.** adj. nupcial **II.** s.pl. **nuptials** nupcias, boda.

nurse (nûrs) **I.** s. (of patients) enfermero; (wet nurse) nodriza, ama de leche; (of children) niñera **II.** tr. **nursed, nur·sing** (infant) criar, amamantar; (patient) cuidar, asistir; (cold) tratar; (grudge) guardar; (drink) beber lentamente —intr. (mother) dar de mamar; (infant) mamar; (to be a nurse) ser enfermero; (to be a nursemaid) ser niñera.

nurse·maid (nûrs′mād′) o **nurs·er·y·maid** (nûr′sə-rē-mād′) s. niñera.

nurs·er·y (nûr′sə-rē) s. [pl. **-ies**] (room) cuarto de los niños; (school) guardería infantil; AGR. vivero.

nurs·er·y·man (nûr′sə-rē-mən) s. [pl. **-men**] AGR. encargado de un vivero.

nursery rhyme s. poesía infantil.

nursery school s. EDUC. escuela de párvulos.

nurs·ing (nûr′sĭng) s. (profession) profesión de enfermero f; (of patient) cuidado, asistencia; (suckling) lactancia.

nursing home s. MED. hogar de ancianos m.

nurs·ling (nûrs′lĭng) s. niño de pecho.

nur·ture (nûr′chər) **I.** s. (sustenance) alimentación f, nutrición f; (food) alimento; (rearing) crianza, educación f **II.** tr. **-tured, -tur·ing** (to nourish) alimentar, nutrir; (children) criar, educar; (business) fomentar; (plants) cultivar.

nut (nŭt) s. (fruit) fruto seco, nuez f; JER. (odd person) estrafalario; (crazy person) chiflado, chalado; (fan) entusiasta mf, fanático <a sports n. un entusiasta de los deportes>; (head) melón m, coco; MEC. (for bolts) tuerca; MÚS. (of stringed instruments) ceja; (of a bow) nuez ♦ a hard o tough n. to crack FIG. un hueso duro de roer • nuts JER., VULG. huevos, cojones.

nut·crack·er (nŭt′krăk′ər) s. (implement) cascanueces m; ORNIT. cascanueces.

nut·meg (nŭt′mĕg′) s. BOT., CUL. nuez moscada.

nu·tri·a (nōō′trē-ə, nyōō′-) s. ZOOL. nutria (animal y piel).

nu·tri·ent (nōō′trē-ənt, nyōō′-) **I.** adj. nutritivo **II.** s. alimento nutritivo.

nu·tri·ment (nōō′trə-mənt, nyōō′-) s. alimento nutritivo.

nu·tri·tion (nōō-trĭsh′ən, nyōō-) s. nutrición f, alimentación f.

nu·tri·tion·al (nōō-trĭsh′ə-nəl, nyōō-) adj. nutritivo.

nu·tri·tion·ist (nōō-trĭsh′ə-nĭst, nyōō-) s. especialista en problemas de nutrición mf.

nu·tri·tious (nōō-trĭsh′əs, nyōō-) adj. nutritivo.

nu·tri·tive (nōō′trĭ-tĭv, nyōō′-) adj. nutritivo, alimenticio.

nuts (nŭts) FAM. **I.** adj. chalado, chiflado ♦ n. about (someone, something) chiflado o chalado por <n. about opera chiflado por la ópera> • to drive someone n. volver loco a alguien • to go n. volverse loco • to go n. over o about (someone, something) volverse loco por **II.** interj. ¡naranjas de la China!

nut·shell (nŭt′shĕl′) s. cáscara de nuez ♦ in a n. en pocas palabras.

nut·ty (nŭt′ē) adj. **-ti·er, -ti·est** (containing nuts) con muchas nueces; (flavor) con sabor a nuez; JER. (crazy) loco, chiflado.

nuz·zle (nŭz′əl) tr. **-zled, -zling** hocicar —intr. (with the nose) hocicar; (to nestle) acurrucarse, arroparse.

ny·lon (nī′lŏn′) s. nylon m, nilón m (marca registrada de fibra sintética) ♦ nylons medias de nilón.

nymph (nĭmf) s. MITOL. ninfa; ENTOM. ninfa.

nym·pho·ma·ni·a (nĭm′fə-mā′nē-ə) s. MED. ninfomanía.

nym·pho·ma·ni·ac (nĭm′fə-mā′nē-ăk′) adj. & s. MED. ninfómana, ninfomaníaca.

O

o, O (ō) s. [pl. **o's, O's**] (letter) decimoquinta letra del alfabeto inglés; (zero) cero.

O (ō) interj. ¡oh!

oaf (ōf) s. (stupid person) tonto, simplón m; (uncouth person) zoquete m, patán m.

oaf·ish (ō'físh) adj. tonto, idiota.
oak (ōk) s. BOT. roble (árbol y madera) *m.*
oak apple s. BOT. agalla *f.*
oak·en (ō'kən) adj. de roble.
oa·kum (ō'kəm) s. MARÍT. estopa, malacuenda.
oar (ôr) I. s. *(wooden pole)* remo; *(oarsman)* remero II. tr. hacer avanzar con el remo —intr. remar, mover el remo.
oar·lock (ôr'lŏk') s. MARÍT. horquilla, chumacera.
oars·man (ôrz'mən) s. [pl. **-men**] remero, remador *m.*
o·a·sis (ō-ā'sĭs) s. [pl. **-ses** (-sēz')] oasis *m.*
oat (ōt) s. BOT. avena (planta y grano) ♦ **to feel one's oats** FIG., FAM. estar lleno de vigor.
oath (ōth) s. *(declaration)* juramento <*under o.* bajo juramento>; *(blasphemy)* blasfemia; *(imprecation)* imprecación *f*, maldición *f.*
oat·meal (ōt'mēl') s. CUL. *(uncooked)* copas de avena; *(porridge)* gachas de avena.
O·ba·di·ah (ō'bə-dī'ə) s. BÍBL. Abdías.
ob·bli·ga·to (ŏb'lĭ-gä'tō) s. [pl. **-tos** o **-ti** (-tē)] MÚS. obligado.
ob·du·ra·cy (ŏb'dŏŏ-rə-sē, -dyŏŏ-) s. *(hardness)* endurecimiento; *(hardheartedness)* insensibilidad *f*; *(obstinateness)* obstinación *f*; *(unyieldingness)* inflexibilidad *f.*
ob·du·rate (ŏb'dŏŏ-rĭt, -dyŏŏ-) adj. *(hardened)* endurecido; *(hardhearted)* insensible; *(obstinate)* obstinado; *(unyielding)* inflexible.
o·be·di·ence (ō-bē'dē-əns) s. obediencia.
o·be·di·ent (ō-bē'dē-ənt) adj. obediente.
o·bei·sance (ō-bā'səns, ō-bē'-) s. *(gesture)* cortesía, reverencia; *(attitude)* deferencia, homenaje *m* ♦ **to pay o.** to rendir homenaje a.
ob·e·lisk (ŏb'ə-lĭsk) s. obelisco.
o·bese (ō-bēs') adj. obeso, gordo.
o·be·si·ty (ō-bē'sĭ-tē) s. obesidad *f*, gordura.
o·bey (ō-bā') tr. *(people)* obedecer; *(the law)* respetar; *(orders)* cumplir, acatar —intr. ser obediente, obedecer.
ob·fus·cate (ŏb'fə-skāt', ŏb-fŭs'kāt') tr. **-cat·ed, -cat·ing** *(to darken)* ofuscar, oscurecer; *(to confuse)* ofuscar, confundir.
ob·fus·ca·tion (ŏb'fə-skā'shən) s. ofuscación *f*, ofuscamiento.
o·bit (ō'bĭt) s. FAM. obituario, necrología.
o·bit·u·ar·y (ō-bĭch'ōŏ-ĕr'ē) s. [pl. **-ies**] obituario, necrología.
ob·ject¹ (əb-jĕkt') intr. *(to raise objections)* hacer objeciones; *(to disapprove)* desaprobar, oponerse —tr. objetar.
ob·ject² (ŏb'jĭkt) s. *(thing)* objeto <*a large o.* un objeto grande>; *(focus)* objeto, centro <*to be the o. of an investigation* ser el objeto de una investigación>; *(purpose)* objeto, propósito <*the o. of this meeting* el propósito de esta reunión>; *(goal)* objeto, meta; GRAM. complemento ♦ **an o. of ridicule** un blanco de burlas • **price is no o.** no importa el precio.
ob·jec·ti·fi·ca·tion (əb-jĕk'tə-fĭ-kā'shən) s. objetivación *f.*
ob·jec·ti·fy (əb-jĕk'tə-fī') tr. **-fied, -fy·ing** objetivar.
ob·jec·tion (əb-jĕk'shən) s. *(challenge)* objeción *f*, reparo <*please state your objections* haga el favor de decir qué reparos tiene usted>; *(before a judge)* protesta; *(disapproval)* inconveniente *m* <*there's no o. to her doing the job* no hay inconveniente en que ella haga el trabajo> ♦ **have you any o.?** ¿le molesta? • **if there are no objections** si no hay nada que objetar • **o. overruled** DER. no se admite la protesta • **to make** *o* **raise an o.** hacer una objeción, poner un reparo.
ob·jec·tion·a·ble (əb-jĕk'shə-nə-bəl) adj. *(behavior)* reprobable, digno de censura; *(language)* ofensivo; *(person, idea)* intolerable.
ob·jec·tive (əb-jĕk'tĭv) I. adj. *(real)* objetivo; GRAM. complementario ♦ **to be o. about** considerar objetivamente II. s. *(reality)* objetivo; *(aim)* objetivo, fin *m*; *(lens)* objetivo.
ob·jec·tive·ly (əb-jĕk'tĭv-lē) adv. objetivamente.
ob·jec·tiv·ism (əb-jĕk'tĭ-vĭz'əm) s. FILOS. objetivismo.
ob·jec·tiv·i·ty (ŏb'jĕk-tĭv'ĭ-tē) s. objetividad *f.*
object lens s. FOTOG., ÓPT. objetivo.
object lesson s. lección práctica, demostración *f.*

ob·jec·tor (əb-jĕk'tər) s. objetor *m* <*conscientious o.* objetor de conciencia>.
ob·jur·gate (ŏb'jər-gāt', ŏb-jûr'gāt') tr. **-gat·ed, -gat·ing** reprender, increpar.
ob·late¹ (ō-blāt') adj. con forma de esfera achatada por los polos.
ob·late² (ŏb'lāt') s. RELIG. oblato.
ob·la·tion (ə-blā'shən) s. RELIG. *(offering)* oblación *f*; *(Eucharist)* oblata.
ob·li·gate (ŏb'lĭ-gāt') tr. **-gat·ed, -gat·ing** obligar ♦ **to be obligated to** tener la obligación de.
ob·li·ga·tion (ŏb'lĭ-gā'shən) s. *(a binding tie)* obligación *f*; *(duty)* deber *m*; *(commitment)* compromiso; COM. obligación, compromiso <*he met his obligations* cumplió sus obligaciones> ♦ **of o.** RELIG. de precepto • **to be under an o. to** tener la obligación o el deber de • **to be under an o. to someone** estarle reconocido a alguien, tenerle mucho que agradecer a alguien • **to feel an o. to** sentirse obligado a • **without o.** sin compromiso.
ob·lig·a·to·ry (ə-blĭg'ə-tôr'ē, ŏb'lĭ-gə-) adj. obligatorio.
o·blige (ə-blīj') tr. **o·bliged, o·blig·ing** *(to constrain)* obligar <*she is not obliged to do it* nada le obliga a hacerlo>; *(to do a favor for)* hacer un favor a <*he obliged us by arriving early* nos hizo el favor de llegar temprano>; *(to humor)* complacer <*he said it to o. us* lo dijo por complacernos> ♦ **much obliged** muy agradecido • **to be obliged to** verse obligado a • **to be obliged to someone** estarle muy reconocido *o* agradecido a alguien.
ob·li·gee (ŏb'lə-jē') s. DER. acreedor *m.*
o·blig·ing (ə-blī'jĭng) adj. *(eager to please)* complaciente; *(eager to help)* servicial.
ob·li·gor (ŏb'lĭ-gôr', -jôr') s. DER. deudor *m.*
o·blique (ə-blēk') I. adj. *(inclined)* oblicuo; *(evasive)* indirecto; *(in family descent)* colateral ♦ **o. angle** GEOM. ángulo oblicuo II. s. GEOM. línea oblicua.
o·blique·ness (ə-blēk'nĭs) s. *(sloping angle)* oblicuidad *f*; *(evasiveness)* carácter indirecto.
o·blit·er·ate (ə-blĭt'ə-rāt') tr. **-at·ed, -at·ing** *(to erase)* borrar; *(to annihilate)* arrasar, aniquilar.
o·blit·er·a·tion (ə-blĭt'ə-rā'shən) s. *(erasure)* borradura; *(annihilation)* arrasamiento, aniquilación *f.*
o·bliv·i·on (ə-blĭv'ē-ən) s. *(forgetting)* olvido <*to lapse into o.* sumirse en el olvido>; *(unmindfulness)* falta de conciencia; *(pardon)* amnistía ♦ **to cast into o.** echar al olvido.
o·bliv·i·ous (ə-blĭv'ē-əs) adj. *(forgetful)* olvidadizo; *(unmindful)* inconsciente.
ob·long (ŏb'lông') I. adj. oblongo, rectangular II. s. rectángulo.
ob·lo·quy (ŏb'lə-kwē) s. [pl. **-quies**] *(abusive language)* injurias, vituperios; *(ill repute)* ignominia, deshonra.
ob·nox·ious (ŏb-nŏk'shəs) adj. *(disagreeable)* desagradable; *(odious)* odioso; *(person)* insoportable.
o·boe (ō'bō) s. MÚS. oboe *m.*
ob·scene (əb-sēn') adj. *(lewd)* obsceno; *(indecent)* indecente; *(gesture)* grosero; *(loathsome)* repugnante, soez <*an o. lie* una mentira soez> ♦ **o. joke** chiste verde • **o. language** groserías, malas palabras.
ob·scen·i·ty (əb-sēn'ĭ-tē) s. [pl. **-ties**] *(lewdness)* obscenidad *f*; *(indecency)* indecencia; *(word, act)* grosería, indecencia.
ob·scu·rant·ism (ŏb-skyŏŏr'ən-tĭz'əm, ŏb'skyŏŏ-răn'-) s. oscurantismo.
ob·scure (əb-skyŏŏr') I. adj. **-scur·er, -scur·est** *(dim)* oscuro; *(faintly perceptible)* indistinto, vago; *(sound)* apagado; *(remote)* perdido, retirado <*an o. village* una aldea retirada>; *(inconspicuous)* imperceptible, intangible <*an o. flaw* un defecto imperceptible>; *(not well-known)* oscuro, desconocido; *(ambiguous)* oscuro, confuso <*o. reasoning* razonamiento oscuro>; *(meaning)* oculto, recóndito II. tr. **-scured, -scur·ing** *(to make dim)* oscurecer; *(to hide)* ocultar <*snow obscured the road* la nieve ocultaba la carretera>; *(to complicate)* enredar, complicar ♦ **to o. someone's view** tapar la vista de alguien.
ob·scu·ri·ty (əb-skyŏŏr'ĭ-tē) s. oscuridad *f.*
ob·se·quies (ŏb'sĭ-kwēz) s.pl. exequias, funerales *m.*
ob·se·qui·ous (əb-sē'kwē-əs) adj. servil, adulador.
ob·serv·a·ble (əb-zûr'və-bəl) adj. observable, perceptible.

---

ob·ser·vance (əb-zûr′vəns) s. *(obedience)* observancia, cumplimiento; *(of a holiday)* celebración *f*, conmemoración *f*; *(of a religious feast)* costumbre de guardar *f*; *(observation)* observación *f*.

ob·ser·vant (əb-zûr′vənt) adj. *(alert)* observador, que se fija en todo; *(of the law)* respetuoso; *(of one's duty)* cumplidor ♦ **to be o. of** *(the law)* respetar; *(one's duty)* cumplir con.

ob·ser·va·tion (ŏb′zər-vā′shən) s. observación *f* ♦ **o. deck** mirador • **to be under o.** MED. estar en observación • **to escape o.** pasar desapercibido.

ob·ser·va·to·ry (əb-zûr′və-tôr′ē) s. [pl. **-ries**] ASTRON. observatorio; *(overlook)* mirador *m*.

ob·serve (əb-zûrv′) tr. **-served, -serv·ing** *(to perceive)* observar, notar; *(to watch closely)* observar <*to o. a child's behavior* observar el comportamiento de un niño>; *(to remark)* observar, decir <*as he has just observed* como acaba de decir>; *(a contract, duty)* cumplir con; *(law)* acatar; *(silence, a feast)* guardar; *(a holiday)* celebrar; *(to exercise)* proceder con <*to o. all precautions* proceder con todas las precauciones>; ASTRON., MED. observar —intr. darse cuenta, percatarse ♦ **to o. on** *o* **upon** hacer una observación sobre.

ob·serv·er (əb-zûr′vər) s. observador *m*.

ob·serv·ing (əb-zûr′vĭng) adj. *(alert)* observador, que se fija en todo; *(of precepts)* observante.

ob·sess (əb-sĕs′) tr. obsesionar ♦ **to be obsessed by** *o* **with** estar obsesionado por.

ob·ses·sion (əb-sĕsh′ən) s. obsesión *f* ♦ **to have an o. for** tener obsesión por.

ob·ses·sive (əb-sĕs′ĭv) adj. obsesivo.

ob·sid·i·an (əb-sĭd′ē-ən) s. MIN. obsidiana.

ob·so·lesce (ŏb′sə-lĕs′) intr. **-lesced, -lesc·ing** *(word)* volverse obsoleto, caer en desuso; *(fashion)* caer en desuso; *(equipment, method)* anticuarse, volverse anticuado.

ob·so·les·cence (ŏb′sə-lĕs′əns) s. caída en desuso.

ob·so·les·cent (ŏb′sə-lĕs′ənt) adj. *(word, fashion)* que cae en desuso; *(equipment, method)* que se vuelve anticuado.

ob·so·lete (ŏb′sə-lēt′) adj. *(no longer in use)* obsoleto, caído en desuso; *(no longer useful)* anticuado, fuera de uso; *(method)* rudimentario; *(fashion)* anticuado ♦ **to make o.** volver anticuado, volver inservible en la actualidad.

ob·sta·cle (ŏb′stə-kəl) s. *(impediment)* obstáculo; *(to negotiations)* traba.

ob·ste·tri·cian (ŏb′stĭ-trĭsh′ən) s. MED. obstetra *mf*, tocólogo.

ob·stet·ric (əb-stĕt′rĭk) *o* **ob·stet·ri·cal** (-rĭ-kəl) adj. MED. obstétrico.

ob·stet·rics (əb-stĕt′rĭks) s. [ú. con v. sing. o pl.] MED. obstetricia, tocología.

ob·sti·na·cy (ŏb′stə-nə-sē) s. [pl. **-cies**] obstinación *f*, terquedad *f*.

ob·sti·nate (ŏb′stə-nĭt) adj. *(stubborn)* obstinado, terco; *(unmanageable)* indócil, intratable; MED. rebelde.

ob·strep·er·ous (əb-strĕp′ər-əs) adj. *(noisy)* estrepitoso, ruidoso; *(rebellious)* revoltoso; *(turbulent)* turbulento.

ob·struct (əb-strŭkt′) tr. *(to dam)* obstruir, atorar; *(to hinder)* estorbar, dificultar; *(to cut off from sight)* tapar.

ob·struc·tion (əb-strŭk′shən) s. *(obstacle)* obstrucción *f*, obstáculo; *(impediment)* impedimento; *(act)* obstrucción; MED. obstrucción, oclusión *f*.

ob·struc·tion·ism (əb-strŭk′shə-nĭz′əm) s. obstruccionismo.

ob·struc·tion·ist (əb-strŭk′shə-nĭst) s. obstruccionista *mf*.

ob·struc·tive (əb-strŭk′tĭv) adj. obstructivo, que obstruye.

ob·tain (əb-tān′) tr. *(to procure)* obtener, lograr; *(to acquire)* adquirir —intr. *(to prevail)* prevalecer; *(to exist)* existir.

ob·tain·a·ble (əb-tā′nə-bəl) adj. obtenible, asequible.

ob·trude (əb-trōōd′) tr. **-trud·ed, -trud·ing** *(to impose)* imponer, introducir a la fuerza; *(to thrust out)* sacar —intr. manifestarse.

ob·tru·sion (əb-trōō′zhən) s. *(intrusion)* intrusión *f*; *(meddling)* entrometimiento.

ob·tru·sive (əb-trōō′sĭv) adj. *(projecting)* saliente, protuberante; *(brash)* atrevido, impertinente; *(noticeable)* llamativo, que se nota.

ob·tuse (əb-tōōs′, -tyōōs′) adj. *(blunt)* obtuso, romo; FIG. *(dimwitted)* obtuso, torpe; GEOM. obtuso.

ob·verse (ŏb′vûrs′) I. adj. del anverso II. s. anverso ♦ **the o. is also true** también se puede decir lo contrario.

ob·vi·ate (ŏb′vē-āt′) tr. **-at·ed, -at·ing** obviar, evitar.

ob·vi·ous (ŏb′vē-əs) adj. *(apparent)* obvio, patente <*an o. lie* una mentira patente>; *(transparent)* evidente <*an o. scheme* una estratagema evidente> ♦ **the o. solution** la solución más indicada • **to be very o.** ser muy obvio, saltar a la vista.

ob·vi·ous·ly (ŏb′vē-əs-lē) adv. *(clearly)* evidentemente <*they o. didn't do it* evidentemente no lo hicieron>; *(of course)* por supuesto; sin duda ♦ **he was o. upset** se veía que estaba disgustado.

ob·vi·ous·ness (ŏb′vē-əs-nĭs) s. evidencia.

oc·a·ri·na (ŏk′ə-rē′nə) s. MÚS. ocarina.

oc·ca·sion (ə-kā′zhən) I. s. *(time)* ocasión *f* <*we met on several occasions* nos encontramos en varias ocasiones>; *(event)* acontecimiento <*an important o.* un acontecimiento importante>; *(opportunity)* ocasión, oportunidad *f* <*a propitious o.* una ocasión favorable>; *(cause)* ocasión <*to give o. to* dar ocasión a>; *(reason)* motivo <*his odd behavior was the o. for laughter* su extraño comportamiento fue motivo de risa>; *(need)* ocasión, caso <*done for the o.* hecho para el caso>; *(gathering)* acontecimiento ♦ **as the o. requires** según el caso, según se necesite • **on o.** ocasionalmente, de vez en cuando • **on one o.** en cierta ocasión, una vez • **on the o. of** con ocasión de, con motivo de • **should the o. arise** *(in case of need)* llegado el momento, de ser el caso; *(if there is opportunity)* si se presenta la ocasión • **to be equal to** *o* **to rise to the o.** estar a la altura de las circunstancias II. tr. ocasionar, provocar.

oc·ca·sion·al (ə-kā′zhə-nəl) adj. *(infrequent)* aislado, algún que otro <*an o. call* una llamada aislada>; *(for the occasion)* de circunstancia; *(for auxiliary use)* para casos de necesidad ♦ **o. showers** lluvia intermitente • **to have an o. cigarette** fumarse un cigarrillo de vez en cuando • **to receive an o. letter** recibir alguna que otra carta.

oc·ca·sion·al·ly (ə-kā′zhə-nə-lē) adv. de vez en cuando, una *o* alguna que otra vez.

Oc·ci·dent (ŏk′sĭ-dənt) s. Occidente *m*.

oc·ci·den·tal *o* **Oc·ci·den·tal** (ŏk′sĭ-dĕn′tl) adj. & s. occidental *mf*.

Oc·ci·den·tal·ism (ŏk′sĭ-dĕn′tl-ĭz′əm) s. occidentalismo.

oc·cip·i·tal (ŏk-sĭp′ĭ-tl) adj. & s. ANAT. occipital *m*.

oc·ci·put (ŏk′sə-pət) s. [pl. **oc·cip·i·ta** (ŏk-sĭp′ĭ-tə) *o* **oc·ci·puts**] ANAT. occipucio.

oc·clude (ə-klōōd′) tr. **-clud·ed, -clud·ing** MED. ocluir; *(to obstruct)* obstruir, tapar.

oc·clu·sion (ə-klōō′zhən) s. MED. oclusión *f*; *(obstruction)* obstrucción *f*.

oc·cult (ə-kŭlt′, ŏk′ŭlt′) I. adj. *(supernatural)* oculto, sobrenatural; *(hidden)* oculto II. s. ciencias ocultas, magia III. tr. & intr. ocultar(se).

oc·cul·ta·tion (ŏk′ŭl-tā′shən) s. ASTRON. ocultación *f*.

oc·cult·ism (ə-kŭl′tĭz′əm) s. ocultismo.

oc·cu·pan·cy (ŏk′yə-pən-sē) s. [pl. **-cies**] *(act)* ocupación *f*; *(of a house)* residencia; *(of a hotel room)* estancia.

oc·cu·pant (ŏk′yə-pənt) s. *(tenant)* inquilino; *(guest)* huésped *m*; *(passenger)* pasajero.

oc·cu·pa·tion (ŏk′yə-pā′shən) s. *(employment)* ocupación *f*, profesión *f*; *(job)* trabajo <*it's a very dangerous o.* es un trabajo muy arriesgado>; *(pastime)* tarea, pasatiempo; *(of a dwelling)* ocupación, residencia; MIL., POL. ocupación ♦ **o. forces** MIL. fuerzas de ocupación.

oc·cu·pa·tion·al (ŏk′yə-pā′shə-nəl) adj. ocupacional, de trabajo.

occupational therapy s. terapia ocupacional.

oc·cu·pied (ŏk′yə-pīd′) adj. *(busy)* ocupado; *(apartment)* alquilado; *(in use)* ocupado.

oc·cu·py (ŏk′yə-pī′) tr. **-pied, -py·ing** *(space)* ocupar; *(time)* emplear ♦ **to o. oneself with** *(to engage in)* ponerse a; *(to busy oneself in)* entretenerse con, ocuparse en.

oc·cur (ə-kûr′) intr. **-curred, -cur·ring** *(to take place)* ocurrir, suceder <*when did it o.?* ¿cuándo ocurrió?>; *(to come about)* producirse, haber <*heavy rains o. during the summer* se producen fuertes lluvias en el verano>; *(to be peculiar to)* darse <*it only occurs in females* sólo se da en las hembras>; *(to be found)* encontrarse <*this species only occurs in Africa* esta especie sólo se encuentra en Africa> ♦ **it occurs to me that** se me ocurre que • **the idea never occurred to me** nunca se me ocurrió, nunca me pasó por la mente.

oc·cur·rence (ə-kûr′əns) s. *(incident)* suceso <*an unexpected o.* un suceso inesperado>; *(event)* acontecimiento; *(instance)* caso; *(presence)* presencia ♦ **such cases are an unusual o.** esos casos no se dan a menudo • **to be an everyday o.** suceder todos los días.

o·cean (ō′shən) s. océano ♦ **oceans of** FIG. la mar de.

o·cean·ar·i·um (ō′shə-nâr′ē-əm) s. [pl. **-i·ums** *o* **-i·a** (-ē-ə)] acuario grande con agua de mar.

O·ce·an·i·a (ō′shē-ăn′ē-ə) s. Oceanía.

o·ce·an·ic (ō′shē-ăn′ĭk) adj. oceánico.

ocean liner s. transatlántico.

o·cean·og·ra·phy (ō′shə-nŏg′rə-fē) s. oceanografía.

oc·e·lot (ŏs′ə-lŏt′, ō′sə-) s. ZOOL. ocelote *m.*

o·cher *o* **o·chre** (ō′kər) s. MIN. ocre *m; (color)* ocre.

och·loc·ra·cy (ŏk-lŏk′rə-sē) s. [pl. **-cies**] oclocracia (gobierno de la multitud).

o'clock (ə-klŏk′) adv. ♦ **one o.** la una • **it's ten o.** son las diez.

oc·ta·gon (ŏk′tə-gŏn′) s. GEOM. octágono, octógono.

oc·tag·o·nal (ŏk-tăg′ə-nəl) adj. octagonal, octogonal.

oc·ta·he·dron (ŏk′tə-hē′drən) s. [pl. **-drons** *o* **-dra** (-drə)] GEOM. octaedro.

oc·tane (ŏk′tān′) s. QUÍM. octano.

octane number s. AUTO. índice de octano *m*, graduación octánica.

oc·tant (ŏk′tənt) s. ASTRON., GEOM., MARÍT. octante *m.*

oc·tave (ŏk′tĭv, -tāv′) s. MÚS., POÉT., RELIG. octava.

oc·ta·vo (ŏk-tā′vō, -tä′-) IMPR. **I.** s. [pl. **-vos**] libro en octavo **II.** adj. en octavo.

oc·tet (ŏk-tĕt′) s. MÚS., POÉT. octeto.

Oc·to·ber (ŏk-tō′bər) s. octubre *m.*

oc·to·dec·i·mo (ŏk′tə-dĕs′ə-mō′) IMPR. **I.** s. [pl. **-mos**] libro de tamaño decimoctavo **II.** adj. de tamaño decimoctavo.

oc·to·ge·nar·i·an (ŏk′tə-jə-nâr′ē-ən) adj. & s. octogenario.

oc·to·pus (ŏk′tə-pəs) s. [pl. **-pus·es** *o* **-pi** (-pī′)] ZOOL. óctopo, pulpo.

oc·to·roon (ŏk′tə-rōōn′) s. ochavón *m*, mestizo.

oc·tu·ple (ŏk′tə-pəl, ŏk-tōō′pəl, -tyōō′-) **I.** adj. óctuplo, óctuple **II.** tr. **-pled, -pling** octuplicar, multiplicar por ocho.

oc·u·lar (ŏk′yə-lər) adj. *(of the eye)* ocular; *(visual)* ocular, visual.

oc·u·list (ŏk′yə-lĭst) s. oculista *mf.*

OD (ō-dē′) **I.** s. JER. dosis excesiva de drogas **II.** intr. **OD'd, OD'ing** darse una dosis excesiva.

o·da·lisque *o* **o·da·lisk** (ō′də-lĭsk′) s. odalisca.

odd (ŏd) adj. **-er, -est** *(unusual)* raro, extraño <*an o. person* una persona rara>; *(in excess of)* pico <*thirty-odd guests* treinta y pico invitados>; *(remaining)* de sobra, de más; *(being one of a set)* suelto <*an o. shoe* un zapato suelto>; *(isolated)* aislado; *(irregular)* irregular, esporádico; *(said of a size)* irregular, poco corriente; *(remote)* perdido, retirado; MAT. impar, non ♦ **at o. intervals** de rato en rato • **how very o.!** ¡qué cosa más rara o curiosa! • **in one's o. moments** en los ratos libres de uno • **o. change** cambio suelto • **o. or even?** ¿pares o nones? • **the o. man out** la excepción • **to do o. jobs** trabajar en lo que se le presente a uno.

odd·ball (ŏd′bôl′) s. FAM. tipo raro, persona excéntrica.

odd·i·ty (ŏd′ĭ-tē) s. [pl. **-ties**] *(persona)* excéntrico; *(strangeness)* rareza, singularidad *f.*

odd lot s. cantidad *f* que difiere de la unidad normal de intercambio (esp. una cantidad de menos de cien acciones).

odd·ly (ŏd′lē) adv. extrañamente ♦ **o. enough** por extraño que parezca, aunque parezca mentira.

odd·ment (ŏd′mənt) s. saldo, retal *m* ♦ **oddments** cosillas, retazos.

odds (ŏdz) s.pl. *(advantage)* ventaja, superioridad *f* <*to give*

o. to dar ventaja a>; *(chances)* probabilidades *f*, posibilidades *f; (difference)* ventaja, diferencia <*she won by considerable o.* ganó con una ventaja considerable> ♦ **by all o.** sin duda, indiscutiblemente • **the o. are against it** no es muy probable • **the o. are in their favor** tienen todas las probabilidades a favor suyo • **the o. are that** lo más probable es que • **to be at o. with** *(something)* no concordar con, contradecir; *(someone)* estar de punta con; *(someone on an issue)* no estar de acuerdo con • **to even up the o.** eliminar las desventajas • **to fight against the o.** luchar contra las probabilidades • **to set two people at o.** enemistar a dos personas.

odds and ends s.pl. cachivaches *m*, retazos.

ode (ōd) s. POÉT. oda.

o·di·ous (ō′dē-əs) adj. odioso.

o·di·um (ō′dē-əm) s. *(hate)* odio, rencor *m; (strong dislike)* aversión *f*, antipatía; *(disgrace)* deshonra, oprobio.

o·dom·e·ter (ō-dŏm′ĭ-tər) s. AUTO. odómetro.

o·don·tol·o·gy (ō′dŏn-tŏl′ə-jē) s. odontología.

o·dor (ō′dər) s. *(smell)* olor *m; (repute)* reputación *f*, fama.

o·dor·if·er·ous (ō′də-rĭf′ər-əs) adj. odorífero, odorífico.

o·dor·less (ō′dər-lĭs) adj. inodoro.

o·dor·ous (ō′dər-əs) adj. *(odoriferous)* oloroso; *(fragrant)* fragante, perfumado; *(malodorous)* maloliente, pestilente.

o·dour (ō′dər) s. G.B. var. de **odor.**

O·dys·seus (ō-dĭs′yōōs′, ō-dĭs′ē-əs) s. MITOL. Odiseo, Ulises.

od·ys·sey (ŏd′ĭ-sē) s. [pl. **-seys**] odisea ♦ **The O.** LIT. la Odisea.

Oed·i·pus (ĕd′ə-pəs, ē′də-) s. MITOL. Edipo.

Oedipus complex s. PSIC. complejo de Edipo.

oe·nol·o·gy (ē-nŏl′ə-jē) s. enología.

o'er (ôr) contr. de **over.**

oe·soph·a·gus (ĭ-sŏf′ə-gəs) s. var. de **esophagus.**

of §G32 (ŏv, ŭv, əv) prep. *(general meaning)* de <*the best years of my life* los mejores años de mi vida> <*I am proud of you* estoy orgulloso de ti> <*a cup of tea* una taza de té>; *(indicating time)* menos, para <*it is ten minutes of four* son las cuatro menos diez, faltan diez minutos para las cuatro>; *(indicating source)* de . . . parte <*it is very kind of you* es muy gentil de su parte> ♦ **a friend of mine** un amigo mío • **all of them** todos ellos • **lots of** mucho • **of age** mayor de edad • **of course** naturalmente, por supuesto • **of late** recientemente, últimamente • **sort of** *o* **kind of** algo, un poco.

off (ôf) **I.** adv. *(distant)* lejos, a distancia <*the next town is some way o.* el próximo pueblo está a cierta distancia>; *(away)* a <*a place five miles o.* un lugar a cinco millas (de distancia)>; *(indicating time)* faltar para <*the picnic is three days o.* faltan tres días para el picnic>; *(indicating discount)* de menos, de descuento <*ten per cent o.* diez por ciento de descuento>; *(off stage)* fuera de escena, entre bastidores ♦ **o. and on** de vez en cuando • **o. with you!** ¡lárgate! **II.** adj. *(said of lights, appliances)* apagado; *(not operating)* desconectado, fuera de servicio; *(canceled)* cancelado <*the meeting is o.* la reunión se ha cancelado>; *(slim)* remoto, lejano <*an o. chance* una posibilidad remota>; *(farther)* más distante, opuesto; *(slack)* menor, más bajo <*production was o. this year* la producción fue más baja este año>; *(said of quality, performance)* inferior, peor; *(incorrect)* equivocado, erróneo; *(eccentric)* raro; *(free)* libre <*I am o. Saturday* estoy libre el sábado> ♦ **an off-color remark** un comentario de mal gusto • **in the o. position** en posición de cerrado • **o. season** fuera de temporada • **to be better o.** *(money)* andar mejor de dinero; *(situation)* estar mejor; *(alternative)* ser mejor para uno • **to be well-off** estar muy bien económicamente • **to have an o. day** tener un día malo **III.** prep. *(from)* de <*take your feet o. my desk* quita los pies de mi escritorio>; *(branching from)* que sale de, que arranca de <*an artery o. the heart* una arteria que sale del corazón>; *(near)* frente a, a la altura de <*the submarine was o. the coast* el submarino estaba frente a la costa>; *(away from)* fuera, lejos de <*o. the beaten track* fuera del camino trillado>; *(down from)* desde, por <*to fall o. a cliff* caer por un precipicio>; *(by means of)* gracias a, de <*he lives o. his pension* vive de su pensión> ✦ **to be o. base** estar incorrecto • **to be o. key** estar fuera de tono • **to be o. the mark** estar fuera de foco • **to be o. the record** decir algo en forma no oficial • **to live o. someone** vivir a costa de alguien **IV.** intr. irse —tr. JER. finiquitar.

of·fal (ô′fal) s. *(entrails)* menudos, asaduras; *(refuse)* desperdicios, desecho.

off·beat (ôf′bēt′) **I.** s. MÚS. tiempo débil **II.** adj. JER. excéntrico, raro.

off-Broad·way (ôf′brôd′wā′) adj. TEAT. que se presenta fuera de Broadway (distrito de salas de teatro de Nueva York).

off-col·or (ôf′kŭl′ər) adj. *(discolored)* desteñido; *(improper)* subido de tono, de mal gusto; G.B. *(in bad spirits)* malo, indispuesto.

of·fence (ə-fĕns′) s. G.B. var. de **offense.**

of·fend (ə-fĕnd′) tr. *(to insult)* ofender <*I'm sorry if I offended you* le pido disculpas si le ofendí>; *(to displease)* ofender; *(to violate)* violar, infringir ✦ **please don't be offended** por favor, no se vaya a ofender • **to be offended at** *o* **by** ofenderse por, tomar a mal • **to o. common sense** ir en contra del sentido común • **to o. one's sensibilities** herir los sentimientos de uno —intr. ser ofensivo.

of·fend·er (ə-fĕn′dər) s. *(one who offends)* ofensor m; *(criminal)* infractor m; *(sinner)* pecador m ✦ **first o.** DER. infractor sin antecedentes penales • **second o.** DER. reincidente.

of·fense (ə-fĕns′) s. *(act)* ofensa; *(crime)* delito; *(sin)* ofensa, pecado; *(outrage)* afrenta, insulto <*an o. to all human beings* una afrenta a todos los seres humanos>; *(attack)* ofensiva, ataque m; DEP. *(team)* equipo con la pelota; *(scoring ability)* ofensiva ✦ **minor o.** DER. delito leve • **no o.** *o* **no o. meant** sin intención de ofender • **second o.** DER. reincidencia • **to give o.** ofender • **to take o. at** ofenderse por, tomar a mal.

of·fen·sive (ə-fĕn′sĭv) **I.** adj. *(insulting)* ofensivo, insultante <*an o. remark* un comentario ofensivo>; *(obscene)* grosero; *(unpleasant)* desagradable <*an o. smell* un olor desagradable>; DEP., MIL. ofensivo ✦ **to be o. to the ear** resultar desagradable al oído • **to be o. to someone** ofender a alguien **II.** s. ofensiva ✦ **on the o.** a la ofensiva • **to take the o.** tomar la ofensiva.

of·fer (ô′fər) **I.** tr. *(to proffer)* ofrecer <*to o. a gift* ofrecer un donativo>; *(to propose)* presentar, proponer <*she offered other plans* propuso otros planes>; *(to present for sale)* vender <*to o. books at reduced prices* vender libros a precio reducido>; *(to bid)* ofrecer, hacer una oferta <*my friend offered forty dollars for the table* mi amigo ofreció cuarenta dólares por la mesa>; *(to volunteer)* ofrecerse a <*the gentleman offered to accompany her* el caballero se ofreció a acompañarla>; *(to put up)* oponer <*to o. resistance* oponer resistencia>; *(to provide)* proporcionar <*a hotel that offers conference facilities* un hotel que proporciona un lugar para conferencias>; *(to present)* presentar ✦ **to o. an apology** pedir disculpas —intr. *(to volunteer)* ofrecerse; *(to present itself)* presentarse <*if the opportunity offers itself* si se presenta la oportunidad>; RELIG. hacer una ofrenda **II.** s. *(act)* oferta, ofrecimiento <*an o. of money* una oferta de dinero>; *(suggestion)* sugerencia; *(proposal)* oferta ✦ **a bona fide o.** una oferta en firme • **on o.** en venta.

of·fer·er *o* **of·fer·or** (ô′fər-ər) s. *(one who offers)* oferente mf; *(bidder)* licitador m.

of·fer·ing (ô′fər-ĭng) s. *(act)* oferta, ofrecimiento; *(donation)* donativo; RELIG. oblación f, ofrenda.

of·fer·to·ry (ô′fər-tôr′ē) s. [pl. **-ries**] RELIG. colecta ✦ **O.** RELIG. ofertorio.

off·hand (ôf′hănd′) *o* **off-hand·ed** (ôf′hăn′dəd) **I.** adv. de improviso, sin pensarlo ✦ **do you know it o.?** ¿lo recuerda usted?, ¿lo sabe usted de memoria? • **I can't recall o.** no recuerdo en este momento • **I couldn't say o.** no le sé decir así de pronto **II.** adj. *(extemporaneous)* improvisado <*an o. comment* un comentario improvisado>; *(informal)* desenvuelto ✦ **to be very o. about it** no tomarlo en serio • **to treat in an o. manner** no concederle mucha importancia a.

off-hour (ôf′our′) s. hora de poco tráfico.

of·fice (ô′fĭs) s. *(place of business)* oficina <*main o.* oficina central>; *(room)* oficina, despacho <*come by my o. at three o'clock* pase por mi despacho a las tres>; *(of a doctor)* consultorio, consulta; *(of a lawyer)* bufete m; *(department)* sección f, departamento <*she works in the accounting o.* trabaja en la sección de contaduría>; *(task)* oficio, deber m; POL. *(in government)* cargo, funciones f <*the o. of vice president* el cargo de vicepresidente>; *(Department)* ministerio <*the British Home O.* el Ministerio del Interior del Reino Unido>; *(public position)* cargo público; RELIG. oficio ✦ **o. building** edificio de oficinas • **o. clerk** *o* **worker** oficinista • **o. hours** *(in an office)* horario de oficina; *(in a professional's office)* horario de consulta • **o. supplies** artículos de oficina • **o. work** trabajo de oficina • **through the good offices of** gracias a los buenos oficios de • **to be in o.** POL. *(an official)* ocupar un cargo; *(an administration)* estar en el poder • **to hold o.** ocupar un cargo • **to leave o.** renunciar a un cargo • **to take o.** asumir un cargo.

of·fice·hold·er (ô′fĭs-hōl′dər) s. POL. funcionario.

of·fi·cer (ô′fĭ-sər) s. *(in the government)* oficial m, funcionario; *(in a company)* dirigente m, director m; MARÍT., MIL. oficial; *(policeman)* agente de policía m, vigilante m ✦ **commanding o.** MIL. comandante • **customs o.** agente de aduana • **law-enforcement o.** agente de policía • **naval o.** oficial de marina.

of·fi·cial (ə-fĭsh′əl) **I.** adj. oficial **II.** s. *(in the government)* oficial, funcionario <*a minor o.* un funcionario subalterno>; *(in a company)* dirigente m, director m; *(referee)* árbitro.

of·fi·cial·ese (ə-fĭsh′ə-lēz′) s. lenguaje burocrático.

of·fi·cial·ly (ə-fĭsh′ə-lē) adv. oficialmente.

of·fi·ci·ant (ə-fĭsh′ē-ənt) s. RELIG. oficiante m.

of·fi·ci·ate (ə-fĭsh′ē-āt′) intr. **-at·ed, -at·ing** RELIG. oficiar; *(to serve as)* hacer las veces de; *(to referee)* arbitrar.

of·fi·cious (ə-fĭsh′əs) adj. *(meddling)* oficioso, entrometido; *(unofficial)* oficioso.

of·fi·cious·ness (ə-fĭsh′əs-nĭs) s. oficiosidad f.

off·ing (ô′fĭng) s. ✦ **in the o.** a la vista, en perspectiva.

off·ish (ô′fĭsh) adj. esquivo, reservado.

off-key (ôf′kē′) adj. MÚS. *(out of tune)* desentonado, desafinado; *(inappropriate)* fuera de tono.

off-lim·its (ôf′lĭm′ĭts) adj. prohibida la entrada (a un cierto grupo).

off-line (ôf′lĭn′) adj. que no se encuentra bajo el control de una computadora central.

off-load (ôf′lōd′) tr. ASTRONÁUT. *(to launch)* lanzar; AVIA. *(to unload)* descargar, desembarcar.

off-print (ôf′prĭnt′) s. IMPR. separata, tirada aparte (de un artículo, extracto).

off-put·ting (ôf′pŏŏt′ĭng) adj. *(disconcerting)* desconcertante; *(repellent)* repelente.

off-screen (ôf′skrēn′) adj. & adv. CINEM., TELEV. *(out of sight)* que no es visible para el espectador; FIG. *(in private)* en privado.

off-sea·son (ôf′sē′zən) s. baja estación.

off·set I. tr. (ôf-sĕt′) **-set, -set·ting** *(to compensate)* compensar <*strengths that o. their weaknesses* cualidades que compensan sus deficiencias>; *(to counteract)* contrarrestar; IMPR. *(to print)* imprimir en offset; *(to blot)* manchar (de tinta) **II.** s. (ôf′sĕt′) *(compensation)* compensación f; *(consequence)* resultado indirecto, ramificación f; ARQ. resalto, acodo; BOT. acodo, retallo; IMPR. *(printing)* offset m; *(blot)* calco ✦ **o. press** offset, prensa rotativa.

offset printing s. IMPR. offset m.

off·shoot (ôf′shōōt′) s. *(branch)* ramal m; *(descendant)* descendiente mf, vástago; BOT. retoño, vástago.

off·shore (ôf′shôr′) **I.** adj. *(on the sea)* de costa afuera, de mar adentro <*an o. oil platform* una torre de perforación de mar adentro>; *(near the coast)* cercano a la costa; *(wind)* que sopla de la costa; *(foreign)* en el extranjero <*an o. bank account* una cuenta bancaria en el extranjero> **II.** adv. mar adentro.

off·side *o* **off side** (ôf′sĭd′) adj. DEP. fuera de juego, en off-side.

---

off·spring (ôf'sprĭng') s. [pl. **offspring**] *(progeny)* progenie *f*, prole *f*; *(result)* resultado; *(product)* producto.
off-the-rack (ôf'thə-răk') adj. de confección.
off-the-wall (ôf'thə-wôl') adj. FAM. extraño, raro.
off-white (ôf'hwīt') **I.** s. color crudo **II.** adj. de color crudo, blancuzco.
oft (ôft) adv. frecuentemente, a menudo.
of·ten (ô'fən) adv. frecuentemente, a menudo ♦ **as o. as** siempre que, cada vez que • **as o. as not** la mitad de las veces, no pocas veces • **every so o.** alguna que otra vez • **how o.?** *(frequency)* ¿cuántas veces?; *(interval)* ¿cada cuánto? • **more o. than not** la mayoría de las veces • **not very o.** pocas veces • **too o.** con demasiada frecuencia.
of·ten·times (ô'fən-tīmz') adv. frecuentemente, a menudo.
off-the-rec·ord (ôf'thə-rĕk'ərd) adj. *(unofficial)* extraoficial, oficioso; *(confidential)* confidencial.
oft·times (ôf'tīmz') adv. var. de oftentimes.
o·gee (ō'jē') s. ARQ. cimacio, gola.
o·give (ō'jīv') s. ARQ. ojiva; MAT. distribución de frecuencia *f*.
o·gle (ō'gəl) **I.** tr. **-gled, -gling** mirar con avidez —intr. mirar ávidamente **II.** s. mirada codiciosa *o* insinuante.
o·gre (ō'gər) s. *(monster)* ogro; FIG., FAM. *(fiend)* ogro, malvado.
oh (ō) interj. *(expressing surprise)* ¡oh!; *(expressing pain)* ¡ay!; *(used in direct address)* ¡eh! *‹oh, waiter!* ¡eh, camarero!›; *(expressing understanding)* ¡ah! *‹oh, I see* ¡ah, ya veo!›.
ohm (ōm) s. ELEC. ohm *m*, ohmio.
oil (oil) **I.** s. *(greasy substance)* aceite *m*; *(fuel)* petróleo; *(lubricant)* aceite lubricante; CUL. aceite; RELIG. aceite, óleo *‹Holy Oil* los Santos Óleos›; ARTE. óleo; FIG., FAM. *(flattery)* coba, adulación *f* **II.** tr. *(to lubricate)* lubricar, aceitar; CUL. aceitar, echar aceite a ♦ **to o. someone's hand** *o* **palm** FAM. sobornar, aceitarle la mano a alguien —intr. aceitarse, llenarse de aceite **III.** adj. de aceite, aceitero *‹o. production* producción aceitera›; MIN. petrolero, del petróleo; ARTE., RELIG. de óleo, al óleo *‹o. painting* pintura al óleo›.
oil burner s. *(heating unit)* caldera a petróleo; *(heating device)* quemador de petróleo *m*.
oil·can (oil'kăn') s. aceitera, alcuza.
oil·cloth (oil'klôth') s. hule *m*, encerado.
oil drum s. TEC. tambor *m o* tanque para petróleo *m*.
oiled (oild) adj. *(lubricated)* lubricado, aceitado; FIG., FAM. *(bribed)* sobornado; JER. *(drunk)* borracho.
oil·er (oi'lər) s. *(oilman)* lubricador *m*, engrasador *m*; *(oilcan)* aceitera, alcuza; *(oil well)* pozo petrolífero; FAM. *(raincoat)* impermeable (esp. hecho de hule) *m*.
oil field s. MIN. yacimiento petrolífero.
oil gauge s. AUTO., TEC. indicador del nivel de aceite *o* petróleo *m*.
oil heating s. TEC. sistema de calefacción a petróleo *m*.
oil industry s. industria petrolífera.
oil paint s. PINT. pintura al óleo.
oil painting s. pintura (cuadro) al óleo.
oil pan s. AUTO., MEC. cárter *m*, colector de aceite *m*.
oil shale s. MIN. pizarra *o* esquisto bituminoso.
oil·skin (oil'skĭn') s. *(fabric)* tela impermeable, hule *m*; *(garment)* traje de hule *m*, impermeable *m*.
oil slick s. capa de petróleo en la superficie del agua.
oil·stone (oil'stōn') s. TEC. piedra de asentar, afiladera.
oil well s. MIN. pozo petrolífero.
oil·y (oi'lē) adj. **-i·er, -i·est** *(greasy)* aceitoso, grasoso; FIG., FAM. *(unctuous)* untuoso, zalamero.
oink (oingk) s. onomatopeya del gruñido del cerdo.
oint·ment (oint'mənt) s. ungüento, pomada.
O.K. *o* **OK** *o* **o·kay** (ō-kā') **I.** s. [pl. **O.K.'s** *o* **OK's** *o* **o·kays**] aprobación *f*, autorización *f ‹I got the O.K. from the boss* conseguí la autorización del jefe› **II.** tr. **O.K.'d, O.K.'ing** *o* **OK'd, OK'ing** *o* **o·kayed, o·kay·ing** aprobar, autorizar **III.** interj. ¡muy bien!, ¡de acuerdo!
O·kie (ō'kē) s. JER. trabajador agrícola migratorio de Oklahoma (en EE. UU.).
o·kra (ō'krə) s. *(plant, fruit)* quimbombó, quingombó; *(gumbo)* sopa de quingombó.

old §G22 (ōld) **I.** adj. **-er, -est** *(aged)* viejo, anciano *‹an o. man* un hombre viejo›; *(elderly)* mayor; *(not new)* viejo, antiguo *‹an o. book* un libro viejo›; *(looking old)* envejecido *‹a prematurely o. face* un rostro envejecido prematuramente›; *(mature)* maduro, mayor; *(of age)* de edad *‹she was twelve years o.* ella tenía doce años de edad›; *(ancient)* antiguo *‹an o. civilization* una civilización antigua›; *(former)* antiguo *‹my o. classmate* mi antiguo compañero de clase›; *(worn out)* viejo, usado *‹an o. coat* un abrigo viejo›; *(familiar)* viejo *‹an o. friend* un viejo amigo›; *(experienced)* experimentado ♦ **a ripe o. age** una edad avanzada • **any o. thing** cualquier cosa • **any o. time** en cualquier momento • **any o. way** de cualquier manera • **as o. as the hills** más viejo que Matusalén *o* que andar a pie **II.** s. antigüedad *f ‹stories about the heroes of o.* relatos sobre los héroes de la antigüedad› ♦ **the o.** *(something)* lo viejo; *(people)* los viejos, los ancianos *‹the care of the o.* el cuidado de los ancianos›.
old boy s. G.B. ex alumno, antiguo alumno.
old country s. madre patria, terruño.
old·en (ōl'dən) adj. viejo, antiguo *‹o. times* tiempos antiguos *o* pasados›.
old-fash·ioned (ōld'făsh'ənd) adj. *(outdated)* pasado de moda, anticuado; *(person)* chapado a la antigua.
Old Glory s. FAM. la bandera nacional de EE. UU.
old guard s. guardia vieja.
old hand s. *(experienced person)* experto; *(veteran)* veterano.
old hat adj. FAM. *(old-fashioned)* anticuado, pasado de moda; *(trite)* trillado.
old lady s. JER. vieja (madre, esposa).
old-line (ōld'līn') adj. *(conservative)* conservador, chapado a la antigua; *(traditional)* tradicional.
old maid s. FAM. *(spinster)* solterona; *(fastidious person)* melindroso.
old man s. JER. *(father, husband)* viejo; *(man in authority)* jefe *m*, patrón *m*.
old master s. ARTE. *(artist)* gran maestro; *(work of art)* obra de un gran maestro.
Old Nick s. FAM. Pedro Botero (diablo).
old school s. vieja escuela.
old·ster (ōld'stər) s. FAM. viejo, anciano.
Old Testament s. BÍBL. Antiguo Testamento.
old-time (ōld'tīm') adj. de tiempos pasados, de antaño.
old-tim·er (ōld'tī'mər) s. FAM. *(veteran)* veterano; *(oldster)* viejo, anciano; *(old-fashioned person)* persona chapada a la antigua.
old wives' tale s. cuento de viejas.
Old World s. viejo mundo.
old-world (ōld'wûrld') adj. *(quaint)* pintoresco; *(pertaining to the Old World)* de los tiempos antiguos, del viejo mundo.
o·le·ag·i·nous (ō'lē-ăj'ə-nəs) adj. oleaginoso, aceitoso.
o·le·an·der (ō'lē-ăn'dər) s. BOT. adelfa, baladre *m*.
o·le·in (ō'lē-ĭn) s. QUÍM. oleína.
o·le·o (ō'lē-ō') s. margarina.
o·le·o·mar·ga·rine (ō'lē-ō-mär'jə-rĭn) s. oleomargarina.
ol·fac·to·ry (ŏl-făk'tə-rē) adj. olfativo, olfatorio *‹o. nerve* nervio olfatorio›.
ol·i·garch (ŏl'ĭ-gärk') s. oligarca *mf*.
ol·i·gar·chic (ŏl'ĭ-gär'kĭk) *o* **ol·i·gar·chi·cal** (-kĭ-kəl) adj. oligárquico.
ol·i·gar·chy (ŏl'ĭ-gär'kē) s. [pl. **-chies**] oligarquía.
ol·i·gop·o·ly (ŏl'ĭ-gŏp'ə-lē) s. [pl. **-lies**] ECON. oligopolio.
ol·ive (ŏl'ĭv) s. BOT. *(tree)* olivo; *(fruit)* oliva, aceituna; *(color)* verde oliva *m* ♦ **Mount of Olives** Monte de los Olivos.
olive branch s. rama de olivo.
olive drab s. *(cloth)* tela kaki (para uniformes militares); *(color)* kaki *m*, verde oliva *m*.
olive oil s. aceite de oliva *m*.
O·lym·pi·ad (ə-lĭm'pē-ăd') s. olimpiada.
O·lym·pi·an (ə-lĭm'pē-ən) **I.** adj. olímpico **II.** s. MITOL. *(god)* dios del Olimpo *m*; *(contestant)* participante en los juegos olímpicos *mf*.

O·lym·pic (ə-lǐm′pǐk) adj. olímpico ♦ **O. games** juegos olímpicos • **Olympics** juegos olímpicos.

O·lym·pus (ə-lǐm′pəs) s. GEOG., MITOL. Olimpo.

O·man (ō-män′) s. Omán *m*.

O·man·i (ō-mä′nē) adj. & s. omaní *mf*.

om·buds·man (ŏm′bŭdz′mən) s. [pl. **-men**] mediador en asuntos de interés público *m*.

o·me·ga (ō-měg′ə, ō-mē′gə, ō-mä′-) s. *(Greek letter)* omega; FIG. *(end)* fin *m*; FÍS. *(particle)* omega.

om·e·let o **om·e·lette** (ŏm′ə-lǐt) s. CUL. tortilla.

o·men (ō′mən) **I.** s. presagio, agüero **II.** tr. presagiar, augurar.

om·i·cron (ŏm′ĭ-krŏn, ō′mĭ-) s. ómicron (letra griega) *f*.

om·i·nous (ŏm′ə-nəs) adj. ominoso, de mal agüero.

o·mis·si·ble (ō-mǐs′ə-bəl) adj. que se puede omitir.

o·mis·sion (ō-mǐsh′ən) s. *(act, state)* omisión *f*; *(slip)* olvido, descuido.

o·mit (ō-mǐt′) tr. **o·mit·ted, o·mit·ting** *(to leave out)* omitir, excluir; *(to pass over)* omitir, pasar por alto ♦ **to o. to** *(to forget)* olvidar; *(to fail to do)* dejar de.

om·ni·bus (ŏm′nǐ-bŭs′) **I.** s. *(bus)* ómnibus *m*, autobús *m*; *(book)* antología **II.** adj. que incluye varias cosas.

om·ni·di·rec·tion·al (ŏm′nǐ-dǐ-rěk′shə-nəl, -dǐ-) adj. RAD. omnidireccional (antena).

om·nip·o·tence (ŏm-nǐp′ə-tns) s. omnipotencia.

om·nip·o·tent (ŏm-nǐp′ə-tnt) adj. omnipotente.

om·ni·pres·ence (ŏm′nǐ-prěz′əns) s. omnipresencia.

om·ni·pres·ent (ŏm′nǐ-prěz′ənt) adj. omnipresente.

om·ni·range (ŏm′nǐ-rānj′) s. AVIA., RAD. radiofaro omnidireccional.

om·ni·scient (ŏm-nǐsh′ənt) adj. omnisciente, omniscio.

om·ni·vore (ŏm′nə-vôr′) s. ZOOL. omnívoro.

om·niv·o·rous (ŏm-nǐv′ər-əs) adj. omnívoro.

on (ŏn) **I.** prep. *(on top of)* en, encima de, sobre *<put it on the table* ponlo sobre la mesa>; en *<a picture on the wall* un cuadro en la pared>; en *<sit on that chair* siéntate en esa silla>; a, sobre *<he threw the books on the floor* tiró los libros al piso>; *(upon)* al *<on entering the room* al entrar al cuarto>; bajo *<on my responsibility* bajo mi responsabilidad>; por *<on all sides* por todos (los) lados>; *(against)* contra *<an attack on freedom of speech* un ataque contra la libertad de palabra>; *(according to)* según *<it was done on my instructions* se hizo según mis instrucciones>; el *<on July third* el tres de julio>; *<to live on bread and water* vivir de pan y agua>; *(for)* por *<to travel on business* viajar por negocios>; *(about)* en, sobre *<we agree on everything* estamos de acuerdo en todo>; *(dealing with)* relacionado con, sobre *<a book on astronomy* un libro sobre astronomía>; con *<I live on fifty dollars a week* vivo con cincuenta dólares por semana> ♦ **on account** a cuenta • **on account of** debido a, a causa de • **on an average** por término medio • **on duty** en servicio • **on fire** ardiendo, en llamas • **on hand** a mano, disponible • **on pain of death** bajo pena de muerte • **on purpose** a propósito, adrede • **on sale** en venta • **on time** puntualmente • **on vacation** de vacaciones **II.** adv. puesto *<the pan has the lid on* la cacerola tiene la tapa puesta> ♦ **and so on** y así sucesivamente, etcétera • **farther on** más allá • **from now on** de ahora en adelante • **further on** más adelante • **later on** más tarde • **on and off** de vez en cuando • **on and on** sin parar, continuamente **III.** adj. *(in operation)* prendido, encendido *<the television is on* el televisor está encendido>; *(said of gas, electricity)* encendido *<the stove is on* la hornilla está encendida>; *(said of a tap)* abierto; *(said of brakes, alarms)* puesto; *(planned)* planeado *<I have nothing on for this weekend* no tengo nada planeado para este fin de semana>; *(in progress)* empezado, comenzado *<the program is on* el programa ha comenzado>.
▲ El adverbio *on* no se traduce literalmente cuando acompaña ciertos verbos, como *to come, to put, to go*, etc. Para su traducción consúltense esos verbos directamente.

o·nan·ism (ō′nə-nǐz′əm) s. onanismo, masturbación *f*.

on·board (ŏn-bôrd′) adv. a bordo.

once (wŭns) **I.** adv. *(one time)* una vez *<I eat o. a day* yo como una vez al día>; *(formerly)* en otro tiempo, otrora *<a o. powerful man* un hombre en otro tiempo poderoso>;

(at any time) alguna vez *<if o. I had been given the chance* si alguna vez se me hubiese dado la oportunidad> ♦ **a cousin o. removed** *(one's cousin's child)* sobrino segundo; *(one's parent's cousin)* tío segundo • **all at o.** *(all together)* todos al mismo tiempo; *(suddenly)* de repente • **at o.** *(immediately)* inmediatamente, en seguida *<he has to leave at o.* tiene que partir inmediatamente>; *(at the same time)* al mismo tiempo *<all of them sang at o.* todos ellos cantaron al mismo tiempo> • **o. again** otra vez • **o. and for all** de una vez para siempre, de una vez por todas • **o. in a while** de vez en cuando • **o. more** una vez más, otra vez • **o. too often** una vez más de lo prudente • **o. upon a time** *(long ago)* en un principio, hace mucho tiempo *<o. upon a time there were gods only* en un principio sólo había dioses>; *(in stories)* érase una vez, había una vez **II.** s. una vez, una ocasión *<o. is enough* una vez es suficiente> ♦ **for o.** una vez siquiera, por una vez **III.** conj. una vez que, tan pronto como *<o. he goes, we can clean up* tan pronto como él se vaya podremos limpiar> **IV.** adj. antiguo *<the o. capital of the nation* la antigua capital de la nación>.

once-o·ver (wŭns′ō′vər) s. JER. *(look)* ojeada, vistazo; *(check)* revisada a la ligera.

on·col·o·gy (ŏn-kŏl′ə-jē) s. MED. oncología.

on·com·ing (ŏn′kŭm′ǐng) **I.** adj. que viene, próximo **II.** s. llegada.

one §G29, 36 (wŭn) **I.** adj. *(one entity)* un, uno *<o. tree* un árbol>; *(unique)* solo, único *<the o. thing we have in common* la única cosa que tenemos en común>; *(indefinite)* uno, un cierto *<they will come o. day* vendrán un día>; *(the same)* mismo *<we all ran in o. direction* todos corrimos en la misma dirección>; *(a certain)* un tal, cierto *<o. Mr. Smith* un tal Sr. Smith>; *(unified)* mismo, idéntico *<we are of o. mind* somos de un mismo pensar> ♦ **o. and the same** el mismo • **o. or two people** poca gente • **the o. and only** el incomparable • **to become** o **make o.** casarse **II.** s. *(number)* uno; *(unit)* unidad *f*; *(one-dollar bill)* billete de un dólar *m*; *(time)* la una *<it's o. o'clock* es la una (en punto)> ♦ **all in o.** de una sola pieza • **o. of two things** una de dos • **to be at o.** estar de común acuerdo • **to be o. up** tener la ventaja • **to have o. for the road** beber otro trago antes de partir **III.** pron. dem. ♦ **that o.** aquél • **this o.** éste • **which o.?** ¿cuál? **IV.** pron. indef. uno *<o. of my children* uno de mis hijos>; uno *<o. is not perfect* uno no es perfecto>; se *<one doesn't do such things* esas cosas no se hacen> ♦ **all in o.** a la vez, todos juntos • **I, for o.** yo, por lo menos • **o. and all** todo el mundo, todos • **o. another** el uno al otro, se *<they love o. another* se quieren> • **o. never knows** nunca se sabe • **one's** de uno, su.

one-di·men·sion·al (wŭn′dǐ-měn′shə-nəl, -dǐ-) adj. unidimensional.

one-hand·ed (wŭn′hăn′dǐd) adj. *(having one hand)* manco; *(performed with one hand)* con una sola mano.

one-horse (wŭn′hôrs′) adj. *(drawn by one horse)* tirado por un solo caballo; FIG. *(insignificant)* insignificante.

one hundred s. & adj. cien *m* ♦ **o. per cent** cien por ciento, cien por cien.

one-man (wŭn′măn′) adj. *(team, committee)* que consiste de un solo miembro; *(for one person)* para una sola persona; *(by one person)* de una sola persona; *(for one individual)* individual.

one·ness (wŭn′nǐs) s. *(singleness)* unidad *f*; *(uniqueness)* calidad de único *f*; *(wholeness)* integridad *f*; *(unison)* igualdad *f*.

one-night stand (wŭn′nīt′) s. *(performance)* función de una sola noche *f*; *(sexual encounter)* relación sexual de una sola noche *f*.

on·er·ous (ŏn′ər-əs, ō′nər-) adj. oneroso.

one·self §G37 (wŭn-sělf′) o **one's self** (wŭn sělf′, wŭnz) pron. *(one's own self)* sí, sí mismo, uno mismo *<to have faith in o.* tener fe en uno mismo>; *(reflexively)* se *<to brace o. for something* prepararse para algo>; *(emphatically)* uno mismo ♦ **by o.** solo • **to be o.** comportarse con naturalidad • **to come to o.** volver en sí.

one-shot (wŭn′shŏt′) adj. único, que no se repite.

---

ng inglés / ŏ la / ō bou / ô corre / oi oigo / ŏŏ uno / ou auto / yŏŏ ciudad / w hueco / y yo / z mismo

one·sid·ed (wŭn′sī′dĭd) adj. *(partial)* parcial; *(unequal)* desigual; *(existing only on one side)* de un solo lado; *(asymmetrical)* asimétrico.

one·time (wŭn′tīm′) adj. antiguo, de otro tiempo.

one·time (wŭn′tīm′) adj. de una sola vez.

one-to-one (wŭn′tə-wŭn′) adj. *(allowing the pairing of)* en proporción de una a uno; MAT. exacto.

one-track (wŭn′trăk′) adj. F.C. de una sola vía, de un solo carril ♦ **to have a o. mind** no poder pensar más que en una sola cosa.

one-up (wŭn′ŭp′) tr. **-upped, -up·ping** FAM. practicar el arte de superar a competidores.

one-up·man·ship (wŭn-ŭp′mən-shĭp′) s. FAM. arte de superar a competidores *m*.

one-way (wŭn′wā′) adj. *(street)* de sentido único, de una sola dirección; *(ticket)* de ida solamente.

on·go·ing (ŏn′gō′ĭng) adj. *(current)* en curso, actual; *(in progress)* en marcha, que va hacia adelante.

on·ion (ŭn′yən) s. cebolla.

on·ion·skin (ŭn′yən-skĭn′) s. papel cebolla *m*, papel delgado.

on-line (ŏn′līn′) adj. *(under computer control)* bajo el control de una computadora central; *(ongoing)* en marcha, que va hacia adelante.

on·look·er (ŏn′lŏŏk′ər) s. espectador *m*.

on·ly (ŏn′lē) I. adj. *(sole)* único, solo <an *o.* son un hijo único>; *(best)* mejor II. adv. *(merely)* sólo, solamente <*o.* three survived sólo sobrevivieron tres>; *(simply)* solamente, simplemente <I *o.* work here simplemente trabajo aquí>; *(solely)* únicamente <facts known *o.* to us hechos que únicamente nosotros conocíamos>; *(with the final result)* para <they received a raise *o.* to be laid off recibieron un aumento para ser despedidos>; *(as recently as)* no hace más de <she called me *o.* last month no hace más de un mes que me llamó>; *(in the immediate past)* apenas <I *o.* just saw her apenas acabo de verla> ♦ **if o.** ojalá • **not o. . . . but also** no sólo . . . sino también • **o. too** muy, de veras III. conj. *(except)* sólo que <we would have gone, *o.* it rained hubiéramos ido, sólo que llovió>; *(but)* pero <you may go, *o.* be careful puedes ir, pero ten cuidado>.

on·o·mat·o·poe·ia (ŏn′ə-măt′ə-pē′ə) s. onomatopeya.

on·rush (ŏn′rŭsh′) s. *(forward movement)* arremetida, embestida; *(assault)* ataque *m*, carga.

on·shore (ŏn′shôr′) I. adj. que se dirige hacia la orilla o la costa; *(on land)* en tierra II. adv. hacia la orilla o la costa.

on·slaught (ŏn′slôt′) s. ataque violento *m*.

on-stage (ŏn′stāj′) I. adj. CINEM., TEAT. situado o que ocurre en un escenario II. adv. en un escenario.

on·to (ŏn′tŏŏ) prep. *(upon)* sobre, encima de; FAM. *(aware of)* al tanto de, al corriente de.

on·tog·e·ny (ŏn-tŏj′ə-nē) s. [pl. **-nies**] BIOL. ontogenia, ontogénesis *f*.

on·tol·o·gy (ŏn-tŏl′ə-jē) s. FILOS. ontología.

o·nus (ō′nəs) s. *(burden)* carga; *(obligation)* obligación *f*.

on·ward (ŏn′wərd) adj. & adv. hacia adelante.

on·wards (ŏn′wərdz) adv. hacia adelante.

on·yx (ŏn′ĭks) s. MIN. ónix *m*, ónice *m*.

o·o·cyte (ō′ə-sīt′) s. BIOL. ovocito, oocito.

oo·dles (ōŏd′lz) s.pl. FAM. montones *m*.

o·o·gen·e·sis (ō′ə-jĕn′ə-sĭs) s. BIOL. oogénesis *f*.

oomph (ŏŏmf) s. JER. *(enthusiasm)* vitalidad *f*, energía; *(sex appeal)* atractivo sexual.

oops (ōŏps, wŏŏps) interj. usado para expresar sorpresa o consternación.

ooze[1] (ōŏz) I. tr. **oozed, ooz·ing** *(to give off)* rezumar, supurar; FIG. *(to radiate)* rebozar de <she oozes confidence rebosa de confianza> —intr. *(to seep)* rezumarse, fluir; *(to sweat)* sudar, exudar ♦ **to o. away** FIG. acabarse, agotarse II. s. *(act)* exudación *f*; *(used in tanning)* zumaque *m*.

ooze[2] (ōŏz) s. *(soft mud)* cieno, fango; *(bog)* pantano, ciénaga.

ooz·y[1] (ōŏ′zē) adj. **-i·er, -i·est** *(dripping)* húmedo, que gotea.

ooz·y[2] (ōŏ′zē) adj. **-i·er, -i·est** *(slimy)* cenagoso, legamoso.

o·pac·i·ty (ō-păs′ĭ-tē) s. [pl. **-ties**] *(quality, state)* opacidad *f*; *(of meaning)* obscuridad *f*, falta de claridad.

o·pal (ō′pəl) s. MIN. ópalo.

o·pal·esce (ō′pə-lĕs′) intr. **-esced, -esc·ing** emitir reflejos opalescentes.

o·pal·es·cence (ō′pə-lĕs′əns) s. opalescencia.

o·paque (ō-pāk′) I. adj. *(not transparent)* opaco; *(without luster)* mate, sin brillo; FIG. *(obtuse)* obtuso II. s. FOTOG. pintura opaca.

op art (ŏp) s. arte óptico, arte op.

o·pen (ō′pən) I. adj. *(not shut)* abierto <o. doors puertas abiertas>; *(said of fields)* descampado; *(said of view)* libre, despejado; *(without covering)* descubierto; *(without top)* destapado; *(extended)* abierto, extendido <o. arms brazos abiertos>; *(having gaps)* abierto <o. ranks filas abiertas>; *(said of fabric)* poco tupido; *(distributed sparsely)* extendido; <o. population población extendida>; *(public)* público <an o. meeting una reunión pública>; *(unrestricted)* sin restricción; *(vulnerable)* expuesto <o. to attack expuesto al ataque>; *(not occupied)* vacante, libre <the job is still o. el puesto está aún vacante>; *(accessible)* accesible, disponible; *(undecided)* pendiente <an o. question una cuestión pendiente>; *(frank)* franco, sincero <I will be o. with you te seré franco>; *(unprejudiced)* sin prejuicios; IMPR. espaciado; MÚS. *(of a wind instrument)* sin sordina; *(of a stringed instrument)* no pisado <an open string una cuerda no pisada>; FONÉT. abierta; POL. abierto a todos; ELEC. abierto <an o. electric circuit un circuito eléctrico abierto>; COM. libre, franco <o. port puerto franco>; *(unconventional)* no convencional <o. education educación no convencional>; *(generous)* generoso <an o. hand una mano generosa> ♦ **half o.** entreabierto • **in o. court** en audiencia pública • **o. car** automóvil descapotable o convertible • **o. for business** abierto al público • **to be o. to** *(to be ready to take)* estar dispuesto a recibir (ideas, crítica); *(to be exposed to)* estar expuesto a; *(to be available to)* ser abierto a <this university is o. to all esta universidad es para todos> • **to lay o.** *(to unclose)* abrir; *(to expose)* exponer • **wide o.** abierto de par en par • **with an o. hand** con mano generosa, con generosidad II. tr. *(to unclose)* abrir <to o. a door abrir una puerta>; *(to unfasten)* desatar; *(to clear)* despejar <to o. a path despejar un camino>; *(to unblock)* desatascar <to o. a drain desatascar una tubería>; *(to cut into)* abrir <to o. an old wound abrir una vieja herida>; *(to make spaces)* abrir <to o. ranks abrir filas>; *(to uncover)* destapar; *(to unwrap)* desempaquetar, desenvolver; *(to unfold)* desplegar; *(to begin)* iniciar, empezar <to o. a meeting empezar una reunión>; *(to set up)* abrir, establecer <to o. a new business establecer un nuevo negocio>; *(in cards)* abrir; *(to make available)* hacer accesible; *(to reveal)* descubrir, revelar; DER. *(to recall)* volver a poner en debate ♦ **to o. court** abrir la sesión o audiencia • **to o. fire** abrir fuego, romper el fuego • **to o. out** ensanchar • **to o. someone's eyes** abrirle los ojos a alguien • **to o. up** *(to make available)* hacer accesible; CIR. *(a patient)* abrir; *(to explore)* explorar • **to o. up to someone** abrirse a alguien —intr. *(to become open)* abrirse; *(to become unfastened)* desatarse; *(to separate)* entreabrirse; *(to unfold)* desplegarse; *(to become revealed)* descubrirse; *(to become understanding)* hacerse comprensible; *(to start a business)* inaugurar, iniciar; *(to begin)* empezar, comenzar <we opened with a list of complaints comenzamos con una lista de quejas>; *(to bet)* abrir el juego (en póker); TEAT. *(a season)* empezar la temporada <they opened in New York empezaron la temporada en Nueva York>; *(performances)* estrenarse <the play opened in Boston la obra se estrenó en Boston> ♦ **to o. into** dar a, comunicar con • **to o. on** dar a • **to o. onto** dar a • **to o. out** *(to unfold)* desplegar; *(to extend)* extenderse; *(to become open)* abrirse; *(to develop)* desarrollarse • **to o. up** *(to spread out)* extenderse; *(to begin)* empezar; FAM. *(to start firing)* romper el fuego, abrir el fuego; *(to speak freely)* abrirse III. s. *(clear space)* lugar abierto; DEP. *(contest)* torneo o campeonato abierto ♦ **in the o.** *(in the open air)* al aire libre; *(in the country)* en el campo; *(on the sea)* en mar abierto; *(in a clear space)* a campo abierto • **to bring into the o.** revelar, sacar a la luz • **to come into the o.** *(to appear)* salir a la luz; *(to speak freely)* decir lo que uno piensa.

o·pen-air (ō′pən-âr′) adj. al aire libre.

o·pen-and-shut (ō'pən-ən-shŭt') adj. *(not difficult)* simple; *(obvious)* evidente, obvio.

open door s. *(free access)* libre acceso; *(equal right)* igualdad de derecho *f*; COM. puertas abiertas.

o·pen-end (ō'pən-ĕnd') adj. sin límite fijo, abierto *<an o. contract* un contrato abierto>.

o·pen-end·ed (ō'pən-ĕn'dĭd) adj. abierto, ilimitado.

o·pen-end investment company s. COM. fondo mutualista.

open enrollment s. política universitaria de inscripción que no se basa en calificaciones académicas.

o·pen·er (ō'pə-nər) s. *(can opener)* abridor *m*, abrelatas *m*; TEAT. *(act)* primer acto (de un espectáculo de variedades); DEP. *(game)* primer partido (de un campeonato) ♦ **for openers** para comenzar.

o·pen-eyed (ō'pən-īd') adj. *(surprised)* con los ojos abiertos; *(alert)* alerta, vigilante.

o·pen-faced (ō'pən-fāst') adj. *(said of a face)* de cara franca, sincero; *(said of a sandwich)* sin tapa.

o·pen-hand·ed (ō'pən-hăn'dĭd) adj. generoso, maniabierto.

o·pen-heart (ō'pən-härt') adj. CIR. de corazón abierto.

o·pen-heart·ed (ō'pən-här'tĭd) adj. *(frank)* franco, sincero; *(kindly)* generoso.

open house s. recepción general *f*.

o·pen·ing (ō'pə-nĭng) s. *(aperture)* abertura, orificio; *(hole)* hueco; *(breach)* grieta; *(clearing)* claro *<there was an o. in the clouds* se abrió un claro en las nubes>; *(first stage)* principio, comienzo; *(of a movie, play)* estreno; *(of an exhibition)* inauguración *f*; *(of a store)* apertura, inauguración; *(in chess)* apertura; *(chance)* oportunidad *f*; *(job)* puesto, vacante *f*; *(act)* apertura; FOTOG. abertura ♦ **o. ceremonies** actos de inauguración • **o. day** *(beginning)* primer día; *(inauguration)* inauguración • **o. night** noche de estreno • **o. play** DEP. salida • **o. price** FIN. cotización inicial.

open letter s. carta abierta.

o·pen·ly (ō'pən-lē) adj. *(candidly)* francamente; *(without prejudice, shame)* abiertamente; *(publicly)* públicamente.

o·pen-mind·ed (ō'pən-mīn'dĭd) adj. *(receptive)* receptivo; *(liberal)* liberal; *(impartial)* imparcial.

o·pen-mouthed (ō'pən-mou*th*d', -mou*th*t') adj. *(amazed)* boquiabierto; *(vociferous)* vociferante.

o·pen·ness (ō'pən-nĭs) s. *(condition)* abertura; *(frankness)* franqueza; *(open-mindedness)* liberalidad *f*.

open season s. DEP. temporada de caza.

open secret s. secreto a voces.

open ses·a·me (sĕs'ə-mē) s. ¡ábrete sésamo!, palabras mágicas.

open shop s. fábrica que emplea a trabajadores sindicales y a los que no lo son.

open stock s. existencias reponibles.

op·er·a¹ (ŏp'ər-ə) s. MÚS. ópera ♦ **light o.** MÚS. opereta.

op·er·a² (ŏ'pər-ə, ŏ'prə) pl. de **opus.**

op·er·a·ble (ŏp'ər-ə-bəl) s. *(functional)* que funciona, *(practicable)* operable, factible; CIR. operable.

opera glasses s.pl. gemelos de teatro, prismáticos.

opera house s. ópera, teatro de la ópera.

op·er·ant (ŏp'ər-ənt) I. adj. operante II. s. operario.

op·er·ate (ŏp'ə-rāt') intr. **-at·ed, -at·ing** *(to work)* funcionar, trabajar *<the radio is not operating properly* la radio no funciona bien>; *(to have an effect)* actuar, surtir efecto *<medicines that o. quickly* medicinas que actúan rápidamente>; *(to perform surgery)* operar *<to o. on someone for* operar a alguien de>; COM. *(to deal)* efectuar operaciones *<the company operates in the European market* la compañía efectúa operaciones en el mercado europeo>; MIL. operar, maniobrar —tr. *(to drive)* manejar; *(tool)* usar; *(machines)* trabajar en, ocuparse de *<he operates the furnaces* trabaja en los hornos>; *(to control)* hacer funcionar, accionar *<the first button operates the turntable* el primer botón hace funcionar el tocadiscos>; *(to manage)* manejar, administrar *<she operates a beauty salon* maneja una peluquería>; *(to bring about)* efectuar, producir *<to o. changes* producir cambios> ♦ **operated by** TEC. que funciona con.

op·er·at·ic (ŏp'ə-răt'ĭk) adj. MÚS. operístico, de opera; *(histrionic)* teatral, melodramático.

op·er·at·ics (ŏp'ə-răt'ĭks) s. [ú. con v. sing. o pl.] teatralidad *f*, melodrama *m*.

op·er·at·ing (ŏp'ə-rā'tĭng) adj. *(operational)* que funciona, en condiciones de servicio; COM. *(profit, expenses)* de explotación; *(costs)* de mantenimiento; MED. *(surgeon)* que opera; *(surgical)* quirúrgico ♦ **o. instructions** instrucciones • **o. range** radio de acción • **o. room** CIR. sala de operaciones, quirófano.

operating system s. COMPUT. sistema de programación *m*.

op·er·a·tion (ŏp'ə-rā'shən) s. *(act, condition)* funcionamiento; *(of the intellect)* operación *f*; *(of vehicles, tools)* manejo; *(management)* administración *f*; *(transaction)* operación; *(of a mine)* explotación *f*; *(effect)* acción *f*; efecto *<the o. of the drug* el efecto del medicamento>; *(process)* operación, procedimiento, trabajo *<the o. of preparing a plan* el procedimiento de preparar un plan>; *(undertaking)* maniobra *<it was a difficult o.* fue una maniobra difícil>; CIR., MAT., MIL. operación ♦ **method of o.** forma de actuar, procedimiento • **to be in o.** *(to be functioning)* estar funcionando; *(law)* estar en efecto *o* en vigor • **to come** *o* **go into o.** DER. entrar en efecto *o* en vigor; MEC. *(machine)* empezar a funcionar • **to perform an o. on someone** operar a alguien • **to undergo an o. for** ser operado de • **operations** COM. actividades; *(work)* obras.

op·er·a·tion·al (ŏp'ə-rā'shə-nəl) adj. *(pertaining to operation)* de operación, de operaciones; *(ready to function)* en condiciones de servicio; *(functioning)* en funcionamiento; MIL. *(ready to fight)* operacional; *(fighting)* de combate.

op·er·a·tive (ŏp'ər-ə-tĭv, -ə-rā'tĭv) I. adj. *(effective)* operativo, operante; *(functioning)* en condiciones de servicio; *(in effect)* en efecto, en vigor; CIR. operatorio, quirúrgico II. s. *(worker)* operario; *(agent)* agente secreto; *(detective)* detective privado.

op·er·a·tor (ŏp'ə-rā'tər) s. *(of a machine)* operario; TEL. operadora, telefonista *mf*; *(of a vehicle)* conductor *m*; *(of an elevator)* ascensorista *mf*; *(owner)* propietario; *(manager)* administrador *m*, empresario; *(dealer)* agente *m*; *(speculator)* especulador *m*; FAM. *(clever person)* maquinador *m*, tramoyista *mf*; MAT. *(symbol)* operador *m* ♦ **tour o.** agente de viajes.

op·er·et·ta (ŏp'ə-rĕt'ə) s. MÚS. opereta.

o·phid·i·an (ō-fĭd'ē-ən) adj. & s. ZOOL. ofidio.

oph·thal·mi·a (ŏf-thăl'mē-ə, ŏp-) s. oftalmía.

oph·thal·mic (ŏf-thăl'mĭk, ŏp-) adj. oftálmico.

oph·thal·mol·o·gist (ŏf'thăl-mŏl'ə-jĭst, ŏp'-) s. oftalmólogo.

oph·thal·mol·o·gy (ŏf'thăl-mŏl'ə-jē, ŏp'-) s. oftalmología.

o·pi·ate (ō'pē-ĭt, -āt') I. s. *(opium drug)* opiato; *(narcotic drug)* narcótico; FIG. *(sedative)* sedativo, calmante *m* II. adj. *(containing opium)* opiado; *(narcotic)* narcótico.

o·pine (ō-pīn') tr. **o·pined, o·pin·ing** opinar.

o·pin·ion (ō-pĭn'yən) s. opinión *f* ♦ **an expert o.** una opinión entendida, un juicio pericial • **in my o.** a mi juicio, a mi modo de ver • **in the o. of the experts** según los entendidos • **it's a matter of o.** es cuestión de opinión • **public o.** opinión pública • **to be of somone's o.** opinar lo mismo que alguien, estar de acuerdo con alguien *<I am of your o.* estoy de acuerdo contigo> • **to be of the o. that** opinar que, ser de la opinión de que • **to get a second o.** consultar a otra persona • **to have a high (low) o. of someone** tener buena (mala) opinión de alguien • **to stick to one's o.** aferrarse a la opinión de uno.

o·pin·ion·at·ed (ə-pĭn'yə-nā'tĭd) adj. obstinado, porfiado.

o·pin·ion·a·tive (ə-pĭn'yə-nā'tĭv) adj. *(of an opinion)* doctrinal; *(opinionated)* obstinado, porfiado.

o·pi·um (ō'pē-əm) s. FARM. opio.

opium poppy s. BOT. amapola, adormidera.

o·pos·sum (ə-pŏs'əm, pŏs'əm) s. [pl. **opossum** *o* **-sums**] ZOOL. zarigüeya, oposum *m*.

op·po·nent (ə-pō'nənt) I. s. *(adversary)* adversario, oponente *mf*; *(antagonist)* antagonista *mf* II. adj. *(opposing)* opuesto, contrario; *(antagonistic)* antagónico.

op·por·tune (ŏp'ər-tōōn', -tyōōn') adj. oportuno.

op·por·tun·ism (ŏp'ər-tōō'nĭz'əm, -tyōō'-) s. oportunismo.

op·por·tun·ist (ŏp′ər-tōō′nĭst, -tyōō′-) s. oportunista *mf.*

op·por·tu·ni·ty (ŏp′ər-tōō′nĭ-tē, -tyōō′-) s. [pl. **-ties**] oportunidad *f*, ocasión *f.*

op·pos·a·ble (ə-pō′zə-bəl) adj. oponible.

op·pose (ə-pōz′) tr. **-posed, -pos·ing** *(to be against)* oponerse <*he opposed the idea* se opuso a la idea>; *(to combat)* resistir, hacer frente a; *(to set against)* oponer, contraponer —intr. oponerse.

op·po·site (ŏp′ə-zĭt) **I.** adj. *(in movement)* opuesto, contrario <*he walked in the o. direction* caminó en dirección contraria>; *(in location)* de enfrente <*the o. house* la casa de enfrente>; *(side)* otro <*on the o. side of the street* del otro lado de la calle>; *(riverbank)* opuesto; *(contrary)* opuesto, contrario <*they have o. views* sostienen opiniones contrarias>; BOT., GEOM. opuesto ♦ **the o. sex** el otro sexo • **to be on o. sides of the fence** ver las cosas de modo opuesto **II.** s. contrario ♦ **it is just the o.** es todo lo contrario • **the o. is also true** se puede decir lo contrario **III.** adv. enfrente ♦ **to be directly o.** estar frente por frente • **to sit o. at the table** sentarse uno frente al otro en la mesa **IV.** prep. enfrente de, frente a <*he parked o. the bank* se estacionó frente al banco>.

op·po·si·tion (ŏp′ə-zĭsh′ən) s. *(act, condition)* oposición *f*; *(resistance)* oposición, resistencia <*he met strong o.* encontró gran resistencia>; *(obstacle)* obstáculo; POL. oposición, partido de la oposición; ASTRON. oposición ♦ **to act in o. to** obrar en contra de • **to be in o. to** *(to disagree with)* estar en desacuerdo con; *(to be against)* estar en contra de; *(placement)* estar frente a.

op·press (ə-prĕs′) tr. *(to subjugate)* oprimir; *(to depress)* deprimir (mente, espíritu); *(to weigh upon)* agobiar.

op·pres·sion (ə-prĕsh′ən) s. *(act, state)* opresión *f*; *(feeling)* opresión, ahogo.

op·pres·sive (ə-prĕs′ĭv) adj. *(hard to bear)* opresivo; *(harsh)* severo; *(tyrannical)* tiránico; *(said of a feeling)* agobiador.

op·pres·sor (ə-prĕs′ər) s. opresor *m.*

op·pro·bri·ous (ə-prō′brē-əs) adj. *(disgraceful)* oprobioso; *(shameful)* vergonzoso; *(infamous)* infame.

op·pro·bri·um (ə-prō′brē-əm) s. *(disgrace)* oprobio; *(ignominy)* ignominia; *(contempt)* desdén *m.*

opt (ŏpt) intr. optar ♦ **to o. for** *o* **to o.** optar por.

op·tic (ŏp′tĭk) **I.** adj. óptico <*o. nerve* nervio óptico> **II.** s. ojo, óptica.

op·ti·cal (ŏp′tĭ-kəl) adj. óptico.

optical illusion s. ilusión óptica.

op·ti·cian (ŏp-tĭsh′ən) s. *(maker)* óptico; *(seller)* dueño de una óptica.

op·tics (ŏp′tĭks) s. [ú. con v. sing.] FÍS. óptica.

op·ti·ma (ŏp′tə-mə) un pl. de **optimum**.

op·ti·mal (ŏp′tə-məl) adj. óptimo, mejor <*for o. results* para mejores resultados>.

op·ti·mism (ŏp′tə-mĭz′əm) s. optimismo.

op·ti·mist (ŏp′tə-mĭst) s. optimista *mf.*

op·ti·mis·tic (ŏp′tə-mĭs′tĭk) adj. optimista ♦ **to feel o.** tener optimismo.

op·ti·mize (ŏp′tə-mīz′) tr. **-mized, -miz·ing** *(to make most effective)* mejorar en todo lo posible; *(to make the most of)* hacer rendir lo más posible.

op·ti·mum (ŏp′tə-məm) **I.** s. [pl. **-ma** (-mə) *o* **-mums**] ♦ **the o.** lo óptimo **II.** adj. *(best)* óptimo, mejor; *(most favorable)* más favorable.

op·tion (ŏp′shən) s. *(choice)* opción *f*, alternativa <*what are our options?* ¿qué alternativas tenemos?>; COM. *(right)* opción <*without the o. to buy* sin opción a comprar> ♦ **at the o. of** a discreción de, a petición de • **it is a viable o.** está dentro de lo posible • **to have no o.** *o* **not to have any options** no quedarle a uno otra alternativa *o* más remedio.

op·tion·al (ŏp′shə-nəl) adj. opcional, facultativo <*the exam is o.* el examen es facultativo>.

op·tom·e·trist (ŏp-tŏm′ĭ-trĭst) s. optómetra *mf.*

op·tom·e·try (ŏp-tŏm′ĭ-trē) s. optometría.

op·u·lence (ŏp′yə-ləns) s. opulencia.

op·u·lent (ŏp′yə-lənt) adj. opulento.

o·pus (ō′pəs) s. [pl. **o·per·a** (ō′pər-ə, ŏp′ər-ə) *o* **o·pus·es**] MÚS. opus *m*; LIT. obra.

or §G41 (ôr) conj. o <*hot or cold* caliente o frío>; *(after a negative)* ni <*he will not go with you or anybody else* no irá contigo ni con nadie> ♦ **hurry up or they'll leave** apúrate que se van, apúrate o si no se van • **or else** si no • **or so** unos, más o menos <*thirty or so* treinta más o menos>.

o·ra (ôr′ə) pl. de **os¹**.

or·a·cle (ôr′ə-kəl) s. oráculo.

o·rac·u·lar (ô-răk′yə-lər) adj. *(of an oracle)* del oráculo; *(prophetic)* profético.

o·ral (ôr′əl) **I.** adj. *(spoken)* oral, verbal; MED. oral <*o. vaccine* vacuna oral> ♦ **o. hygiene** higiene bucal **II.** s. examen oral *m.*

oral contraceptive s. MED. anticonceptivo oral, píldora anticonceptiva.

o·ral·ly (ôr′ə-lē) adv. *(spoken)* oralmente; MED. *(through the mouth)* por vía oral.

or·ange (ôr′ĭnj) **I.** s. BOT. *(tree)* naranjo; *(fruit)* naranja; *(color)* naranja *m*, anaranjado ♦ **o. blossom** BOT. azahar • **o. grove** naranjal • **o. grower** productor de naranjas • **o. juice** jugo *o* zumo de naranja **II.** adj. de color naranja, anaranjado.

or·ange·ade (ôr′ĭn-jād′) s. naranjada.

o·rang·u·tan (ə-răng′ə-tăn′) *o* **o·rang·ou·tang** (-tăng′) s. ZOOL. orangután *m.*

o·rate (ô-rāt′) intr. **o·rat·ed, o·rat·ing** declamar.

o·ra·tion (ô-rā′shən) s. oración *f*, discurso.

or·a·tor (ôr′ə-tər) s. orador *m.*

or·a·tor·i·cal (ôr′ə-tôr′ĭ-kəl) adj. oratorio.

or·a·to·ry¹ (ôr′ə-tôr′ē) s. *(declamation)* oratoria; *(skill)* elocuencia; *(bombastic speaking)* declamación *f.*

or·a·to·ry² (ôr′ə-tôr′ē) s. [pl. **-ries**] RELIG. oratorio.

orb (ôrb) s. orbe *m* **II.** tr. ANT. circundar.

or·bit (ôr′bĭt) **I.** s. ASTRON., ASTRONÁUT. órbita; *(range)* órbita, influencia ♦ **to go into o.** ASTRONÁUT. entrar en órbita **II.** tr. *(to revolve around)* girar alrededor de, dar vueltas alrededor de; ASTRONÁUT. *(a satellite)* poner en órbita —intr. *(to revolve)* girar, dar vueltas; ASTRONÁUT. *(to be in orbit)* estar en órbita.

or·bit·al (ôr′bĭ-tl) adj. orbital.

or·chard (ôr′chərd) s. huerto.

or·ches·tra (ôr′kĭ-strə) s. MÚS. orquesta ♦ **o. pit** orquesta, foso de la orquesta • **o. seats** butacas de platea.

or·ches·tral (ôr-kĕs′trəl) adj. orquestal.

or·ches·trate (ôr′kĭ-strāt′) tr. **-trat·ed, -trat·ing** MÚS. orquestar, instrumentar; *(to organize)* organizar, preparar.

or·ches·tra·tion (ôr′kĭ-strā′shən) s. MÚS. orquestación *f.*

or·chid (ôr′kĭd) **I.** s. BOT. *(plant, flower)* orquídea; *(color)* malva *m* **II.** adj. malva.

or·dain (ôr-dān′) tr. RELIG. ordenar <*to be ordained as a priest* ser ordenado de sacerdote>; *(to order)* ordenar, decretar; *(to predestine)* disponer, predestinar.

or·deal (ôr-dēl′) s. *(trial)* prueba dura; *(torment)* sufrimiento, suplicio.

or·der (ôr′dər) **I.** s. *(succession)* orden *m* <*in alphabetical o.* por orden alfabético>; *(arrangement)* orden *m*, disposición *f* <*the o. of ships in the harbor* la disposición de los barcos en el puerto>; *(social structure)* orden *m*, orden social <*the evils of the old o.* los males del viejo orden>; *(rule of law)* orden *m* <*o. was restored after the riot* se restableció el orden después del motín>; *(procedure)* regla, orden *m*; *(decree)* orden *f*, decreto; MIL. *(command)* orden *f*; COM. *(request)* pedido, encargo <*to place an o. for ten books* hacer un pedido de diez libros>; *(goods)* pedido, mercancía <*they delivered the o.* entregaron la mercancía>; *(portion of food)* porción *f*, ración *f* <*an o. of rice* una porción de arroz>; *(organization)* orden *f*, sociedad *f* <*the O. of Masons* la sociedad de los masones>; *(distinguished persons)* orden *f* <*the O. of the Garter* la Orden de la Jarretera>; *(insignia)* condecoración *f*; *(quality)* calidad *f* <*poetry of a high o.* poesía de una gran calidad>; *(kind)* tipo, índole *f*; *(rank)* categoría; DER. *(direction)* mandamiento, orden del juez *f*; RELIG. orden *f* <*the Franciscan O.* la orden franciscana>; ARQ. orden *m* <*the Doric o.* el orden dórico>; BIOL. orden *m*; MAT. grado ♦ **a tall o.** FAM. una encomienda difícil • **by o. of** por orden de • **in bad o.** *(mechanism)* descompuesto; *(situation)* desordenado • **in good o.** en buen estado, en buenas condiciones • **in o.** *(in*

place) en orden; *(in good condition)* en buenas condiciones; *(working)* funcionando; *(within the rules)* en regla; *(in a meeting)* aceptable, admisible *‹the motion is in o.* la moción es aceptable›; *(appropriate)* pertinente; *(natural)* natural, lógico • **in o. that** a fin de que, para que • **in o. to** a fin de, para • **in short o.** pronto, en seguida • **orders** *(social class)* orden, clase; MIL. orden *f;* RELIG. *(ecclesiastical rank)* orden *mf;* *(holy orders)* órdenes sagradas • **out of o.** *(out of place)* en desorden; *(not in good condition)* en malas condiciones; *(not working)* no funcionando, descompuesto *‹the machine is out of o.* la máquina está descompuesta›; *(against the rules)* (que) no está en regla; *(in a meeting)* inaceptable; *(inappropriate)* impertinente; *(sick)* enfermo • **pay to the o. of** páguese a la orden de • **to take Holy Orders** ordenarse, recibir las órdenes sagradas **II.** tr. *(to command)* ordenar, mandar *‹they ordered him to leave* le ordenaron que se fuera›; *(to request)* encargar, pedir *‹to o. merchandise* pedir mercancía›; *(to decree)* mandar, disponer *‹the judge ordered a recount of ballots* el juez mandó un recuento de los votos›; *(to arrange)* arreglar, ordenar; RELIG. ordenar; MED. mandar, recetar ♦ **to o. in** mandar (entrar, traer) —intr. *(to give a command)* dar una orden; *(to make a request)* hacer un pedido *o* encargo.
order blank s. orden de pedido *f.*
or·der·er (ôr′dər-ər) s. ordenador *m.*
or·der·ly (ôr′dər-lē) **I.** adj. *(neat)* ordenado, en orden; *(methodical)* metódico, ordenado; *(peaceful)* pacífico **II.** s. [pl. **-lies**] *(hospital attendant)* ayudante *m,* ordenanza *mf;* MIL. *(soldier)* ordenanza *m* **III.** adv. *(systematically)* sistemáticamente; *(regularly)* regularmente.
order of the day s. *(prescribed activities)* orden del día *f;* programa de actividades *m;* FAM. *(norm)* norma, costumbre *f.*
or·di·nal (ôr′dn-əl) **I.** adj. ordinal **II.** s. MAT. número ordinal, ordinal *m.*
ordinal number s. MAT. número ordinal.
or·di·nance (ôr′dn-əns) s. *(order)* ordenanza, decreto; *(custom)* costumbre *f;* *(statute)* estatuto; RELIG. Eucaristía.
or·di·nar·i·ly (ôr′dn-âr′ə-lē) adv. ordinariamente, por regla general.
or·di·nar·y (ôr′dn-ĕr′ē) **I.** adj. *(usual)* ordinario, corriente *‹it was an o. day* fue un día corriente›; *(plain)* corriente, cualquiera *‹this is not just an o. typewriter* ésta no es una máquina de escribir cualquiera›; *(average)* medio *‹the o. Englishman* el inglés medio›; *(mediocre)* ordinario, mediocre **II.** s. [pl. **-ies**] DER., RELIG. ordinario, obispo diocesano; *(part of the Mass)* ordinario (de la misa) ♦ **above the o.** excepcional, destacado • **out of the o.** fuera de lo común, extraordinario.
ordinary seaman s. MARÍT. marinero.
or·di·nate (ôr′dn-ĭt) **I.** adj. dispuesto en hileras **II.** s. MAT. ordenada.
or·di·na·tion (ôr′dn-ā′shən) s. *(arrangement)* ordenación *f,* arreglo; RELIG. ordenación.
ord·nance (ôrd′nəns) s. MIL. *(weapons)* armamentos, equipos de guerra; *(branch)* división de armamentos *f;* *(artillery)* artillería.
or·dure (ôr′jər) s. *(excrement)* heces *f,* excrementos; FIG. *(filth)* inmundicia.
ore (ôr) s. MIN. mineral *m,* mena.
o·reg·a·no (ə-rĕg′ə-nō′) s. orégano.
or·gan (ôr′gən) s. BIOL., MÚS. órgano; *(agency)* organismo; *(publication)* órgano ♦ **o. music** música de órgano.
or·gan·dy *o* **or·gan·die** (ôr′gən-dē) s. [pl. **-dies**] organdí *m.*
organ grinder s. MÚS. organillero.
or·gan·ic (ôr-găn′ĭk) adj. ANAT., BIOL., QUÍM., orgánico; *(natural)* orgánico, natural *‹o. food* alimento natural›.
or·gan·ism (ôr′gə-nĭz′əm) s. BIOL., BOT., ZOOL. organismo; FIG. *(system)* organismo.
or·gan·ist (ôr′gə-nĭst) s. MÚS. organista *mf.*
or·gan·i·za·tion (ôr′gə-nĭ-zā′shən) s. *(act, process)* organización *f;* *(system)* organización, organismo.
or·gan·i·za·tion·al (ôr′gə-nĭ-zā′shə-nəl) adj. de una organización.
or·gan·ize (ôr′gə-nīz′) tr. **-ized, -iz·ing** *(to put in order)* orga-

nizar, ordenar; *(to arrange)* arreglar, sistematizar; *(to unite for action)* organizar; *(to form)* formar, organizar —intr. *(to develop)* organizarse; *(to be formed)* constituirse.
organized labor s. ECON., POL. obreros sindicalizados, unión de trabajadores *f.*
or·gan·iz·er (ôr′gə-nī′zər) s. organizador *m.*
or·gan·za (ôr-găn′zə) s. TEJ. organdí *m.*
or·gasm (ôr′găz′əm) s. orgasmo.
or·gi·as·tic (ôr′jē-ăs′tĭk) adj. orgiástico.
or·gy (ôr′jē) s. [pl. **-gies**] *(sexual)* orgía; *(indulgence)* orgía, festín *m.*
o·ri·ent (ôr′ē-ənt, -ĕnt′) **I.** s. *(east)* oriente *m;* *(luster)* oriente; *(pearl)* perla de mucho oriente ♦ **O.** Oriente, Levante **II.** adj. POÉT. *(eastern)* levantino, oriental; *(lustrous)* de mucho oriente, brillante; ANT. *(sun)* naciente **III.** tr. (-ĕnt′) orientar ♦ **to o. oneself** orientarse.
o·ri·en·tal (ôr′ē-ĕn′tl) adj. & s. oriental *mf* ♦ **O.** oriental, asiático.
o·ri·en·tal·ism (ôr′ē-ĕn′tl-ĭz′əm) s. orientalismo.
Oriental rug s. alfombra oriental.
o·ri·en·tate (ôr′ē-ĕn-tāt′) tr. & intr. **-tat·ed, -tat·ing** orientar(se).
o·ri·en·ta·tion (ôr′ē-ĕn-tā′shən) s. orientación *f.*
or·i·fice (ôr′ə-fĭs) s. orificio.
or·i·gin (ôr′ə-jĭn) s. *(source)* origen *m;* *(of a flight, object)* origen, procedencia; *(ancestry)* origen, cuna ♦ **to be of humble origins** ser de origen humilde • **to have its origins in** originarse en.
o·rig·i·nal (ə-rĭj′ə-nəl) **I.** adj. *(novel)* original *‹an o. play, not an adaptation* una obra de teatro original, no una adaptación›; *(first)* original, primero *‹the o. settlers* los primeros pobladores›; *(authentic)* legítimo *‹the painting was o.* el cuadro era legítimo›; *(own)* propio *‹he sang one of his o. songs* cantó una de sus propias canciones›; *(innovative)* original; *(inventive)* de mucha imaginación, creativo **II.** s. *(first form)* modelo original *‹they later modified the o.* después modificaron el modelo original›; ARTE. *(work, model)* original *m;* *(unique person)* persona original.
o·rig·i·nal·i·ty (ə-rĭj′ə-năl′ĭ-tē) s. *(quality)* originalidad *f;* *(inventiveness)* imaginación *f,* inventiva.
o·rig·i·nal·ly (ə-rĭj′ə-nə-lē) adv. *(initially)* en un principio, primeramente; *(in a distinctive manner)* originalmente, con originalidad.
original sin s. TEO. pecado original.
o·rig·i·nate (ə-rĭj′ə-nāt′) tr. **-nat·ed, -nat·ing** *(to introduce)* originar, producir *‹the solution originated other problems* la solución originó otros problemas›; *(to invent)* crear —intr. *(to start)* originarse, surgir; *(to have its origins)* ser originario *o* oriundo de *‹his family originated in Africa* su familia es oriunda de Africa› ♦ **to o. with someone** *(project, action)* ser obra de alguien; *(idea)* ser de alguien, ocurrírsele a alguien.
o·rig·i·na·tion (ə-rĭj′ə-nā′shən) s. *(origin)* origen *m;* *(invention)* creación *f.*
o·rig·i·na·tor (ə-rĭj′ə-nā′tər) s. autor *m,* creador *m.*
o·ri·ole (ôr′ē-ōl′) s. ORNIT. oropéndola, oriol *m.*
Or·lon (ôr′lŏn′) s. TEJ. orlón (marca registrada) *m.*
or·i·son (ôr′ĭ-sən) s. oración *f,* plegaria.
or·na·ment (ôr′nə-mənt) **I.** s. *(decoration)* ornamento, adorno; FIG. *(source of pride)* honra **II.** tr. (-mĕnt′) adornar, ornamentar.
or·na·men·tal (ôr′nə-mĕn′tl) **I.** adj. ornamental, decorativo **II.** s. algo ornamental.
or·na·men·ta·tion (ôr′nə-mĕn-tā′shən) s. *(act)* ornamentación *f,* decoración *f;* *(decoration)* ornamento, adorno.
or·nate (ôr-nāt′) adj. *(heavily ornamented)* recargado; FIG. *(flowery)* florido, galano.
or·ner·y (ôr′nə-rē) adj. **-i·er, -i·est** FAM. *(stubborn)* terco, testarudo.
or·ni·thol·o·gist (ôr′nə-thŏl′ə-jĭst) s. ornitólogo.
or·ni·thol·o·gy (ôr′nə-thŏl′ə-jē) s. ornitología.
o·ro·tund (ôr′ə-tŭnd′) adj. *(sonorous)* sonoro; *(pompous)* pomposo, bombástico.
or·phan (ôr′fən) **I.** s. & adj. huérfano **II.** tr. dejar huérfano.

---

ng inglés / ŏ la / ō bou / ô corre / oi oigo / ōō uno / ou auto / yōō ciudad / w hueco / y yo / z mismo

or·phan·age (ôr′fə-nĭj) s. *(institution)* orfanato, orfelinato; *(condition)* orfandad f.

Or·phe·us (ôr′fē-əs, -fyōōs′) s. MITOL. Orfeo.

Or·phic (ôr′fĭk) adj. LIT. órfico, de Orfeo.

or·tho·don·tics (ôr′thə-dŏn′tĭks) s. [ú. con v. sing.] ODONT. ortodoncia.

or·tho·dox (ôr′thə-dŏks′) adj. ortodoxo, tradicional.

Orthodox Church s. RELIG. iglesia ortodoxa.

Orthodox Judaism s. RELIG. judaísmo ortodoxo.

or·tho·dox·y (ôr′thə-dŏk′sē) s. RELIG. ortodoxia, creencia ortodoxa.

or·tho·gen·e·sis (ôr′thō-jĕn′ĭ-sĭs) s. ortogénesis f.

or·thog·o·nal (ôr-thŏg′ə-nəl) adj. GEOM. ortogonal.

or·tho·graph·ic (ôr′thə-grăf′ĭk) o **or·tho·graph·i·cal** (-ĭ-kəl) adj. GEOM., GRAM. ortográfico.

or·thog·ra·phy (ôr-thŏg′rə-fē) s. GRAM. ortografía.

or·tho·pe·dic o **or·tho·pae·dic** (ôr′thə-pē′dĭk) adj. MED. ortopédico.

or·tho·pe·dics o **or·tho·pae·dics** (ôr′thə-pē′dĭks) s. [ú. con v. sing.] MED. ortopedia.

os¹ (ŏs) s. [pl. **o·ra** (ôr′ə)] *(mouth)* boca; *(opening)* orificio.

os² (ŏs) s. [pl. **os·sa** (ŏs′ə)] ANAT. hueso.

Os·car (ŏs′kər) s. CINEM. Oscar (premio) m.

os·cil·late (ŏs′ə-lāt′) intr. **-lat·ed, -lat·ing** *(to swing)* oscilar; *(vacillate)* vacilar; ELECTRÓN., FÍS. oscilar.

os·cil·la·tion (ŏs′ə-lā′shən) s. FÍS. *(act)* oscilación f; *(fluctuation)* fluctuación f, variación f.

os·cil·la·tor (ŏs′ə-lā′tər) s. ELEC., RAD. oscilador m.

os·cil·lo·scope (ŏ-sĭl′ə-skōp′) s. FÍS. oscilógrafo.

os·cu·late (ŏs′kyə-lāt′) tr. & intr. **-lat·ed, -lat·ing** besar(se).

os·cu·la·tion (ŏs′kyə-lā′shən) s. *(kiss)* beso, ósculo; GEOM. osculación f.

o·sier (ō′zhər) s. *(tree)* mimbrera, mimbre m; *(twig)* mimbre.

os·mi·um (ŏz′mē-əm) s. QUÍM. osmio.

os·mose (ŏz′mōs′, ŏs′-) tr. **-mosed, -mos·ing** FÍS., FISIOL., QUÍM. someter a ósmosis —intr. difundirse por ósmosis.

os·mo·sis (ŏz-mō′sĭs) s. ósmosis f.

os·prey (ŏs′prē) s. [pl. **-preys**] ORNIT. pigargo.

os·sa (ŏs′ə) pl. de **os²**.

os·se·ous (ŏs′ē-əs) adj. óseo, de hueso.

os·si·fy (ŏs′ə-fī′) tr. & intr. **-fied, -fy·ing** *(to become bony)* osificar(se), convertir(se) en hueso; *(to become hard)* endurecer(se).

os·su·ar·y (ŏsh′ōō-ĕr′ē) s. [pl. **-ies**] osario, osar m.

os·te·i·tis (ŏs′tē-ī′tĭs) s. MED. osteítis f.

os·ten·si·ble (ŏ-stĕn′sə-bəl) adj. *(seeming)* supuesto, aparente; *(professed)* ostensible, manifiesto.

os·ten·sive (ŏ-stĕn′sĭv) adj. *(ostensible)* ostensible; *(demonstrative)* ostensivo, demostrativo.

os·ten·ta·tion (ŏs′tĕn-tā′shən) s. *(showiness)* ostentación f, alarde m; ANAT. *(exhibition)* espectáculo, exhibición f.

os·ten·ta·tious (ŏs′tĕn-tā′shəs) s. ostentoso.

os·te·o·my·e·li·tis (ŏs′tē-ō-mī′ə-lī′tĭs) s. MED. osteomielitis f.

os·te·o·path (ŏs′tē-ə-păth′) o **os·te·op·a·thist** (ŏs′tē-ŏp′ə-thĭst) s. MED. osteópata mf.

os·te·op·a·thy (ŏs′tē-ŏp′ə-thē) s. MED. osteopatía.

os·tra·cism (ŏs′trə-sĭz′əm) s. ostracismo.

os·tra·cize (ŏs′trə-sīz′) tr. **-cized, -ciz·ing** excluir, condenar al ostracismo.

os·trich (ŏs′trĭch) s. [pl. **-trich·es** o **ostrich**] ORNIT. *(African bird)* avestruz m; *(rhea)* ñandú m.

oth·er (ŭth′ər) I. adj. *(remaining)* otro *<the o. hand* la otra mano>; *(additional)* otro, demás *<John and the o. boys* Juan y los demás niños>; *(different)* diferente, distinto *<it is o. than you think* es distinto a lo que usted piensa> ♦ **every o. day** cada dos días, un día sí y otro no • **on the o. hand** por otra parte • **o. people** otros • **the o. one** el otro • **o. ones** otros II. s. otro *<one took a taxi, and the o. walked* uno tomó un taxi y el otro se fue caminando> ♦ **a few others** otros pocos • **each o.** uno a otro • **no o.** ningún otro • **no o. than** nadie más que • **others** otros III. pron. otro *<something or o.* una cosa u otra> ♦ **others** los otros, los demás • **sometime or o.** cualquier día IV. adv. ♦ **o. than** *(differently)* de otro modo, de otra

forma *<I could not do o. than I did* no pude hacerlo de otro modo>; *(anything but)* otra cosa que.

oth·er·di·rect·ed (ŭth′ər-dĭ-rĕk′tĭd, -dī-) adj. dictado por otro, ajeno.

oth·er·wise (ŭth′ər-wīz′) I. adv. *(differently)* de otro modo, de otra forma *<it happened o.* sucedió de otro modo>; *(under other circumstances)* de lo contrario, si no *<o. I might have helped them* de lo contrario les habría podido ayudar>; *(in other respects)* por lo demás, a no ser por eso *<an o. reasonable man* a no ser por eso, una persona razonable> II. adj. diferente, otro *<the evidence is o.* la evidencia es otra>.

oth·er·world·ly (ŭth′ər-wûrld′lē) adj. *(spiritual)* espiritual; *(dreamy)* que está en las nubes.

o·ti·ose (ō′shē-ōs′, ō′tē-) adj. *(indolent)* ocioso; *(useless)* ocioso, inútil.

ot·ter (ŏt′ər) s. [pl. **otter** o **-ters**] ZOOL. nutria (animal y piel).

ot·to·man (ŏt′ə-mən) s. [pl. **-mans**] *(sofa)* otomana; *(footstool)* banqueta (para los pies); TEJ. *(fabric)* otomán m.

Ot·to·man (ŏt′ə-mən) adj. & s. [pl. **-mans**] otomano.

ouch¹ (ouch) interj. ¡ay!

ouch² (ouch) s. JOY. *(setting)* montura, engaste m; *(brooch)* broche m; *(buckle)* hebilla con piedras preciosas.

ought §G11 (ôt) I. aux. *(to be obliged)* deber *<you o. to work harder than that* deberías trabajar mucho más>; *(to be wise)* convenir, ser conveniente *<you o. to wear a raincoat* conviene que lleves una gabardina>; *(to be desirable)* tener que *<you o. to have been there; it was great fun* tendrías que haber estado allí; fue muy divertido>; *(to be likely)* deber de *<she o. to finish by next week* debe de terminar para la semana próxima> II. s. deber m, obligación f.

ounce¹ (ouns) s. *(unit of weight)* onza (28,35 gramos); *(unit of capacity)* onza (29,57 mililitros); *(bit)* pizca, poquito.

ounce² (ouns) s. ZOOL. onza, jaguar m.

our §G23 (our) adj. pos. nuestro *<our car* nuestro automóvil>.

Our Father s. RELIG. padrenuestro.

Our Lady s. RELIG. Nuestra Señora, la Virgen.

ours §G32 (ourz) pron. pos. [ú. con v. sing. o pl.] (el) nuestro *<that car is o.* ese automóvil es (el) nuestro> *<o. were the only suggestions adopted* las nuestras fueron las únicas sugerencias adoptadas>.

our·self (our-sĕlf′) pron. nos, a nosotros [ú. en estilo oficial o real].

our·selves §G37 (our-sĕlvz′) pron. *(used reflexively)* nos *<we should wash o.* debemos lavarnos>; nosotros, nosotros mismos *<we did it o.* lo hicimos nosotros mismos>.

oust (oust) tr. *(to force out)* expulsar, echar; *(to dispossess)* desposeer.

oust·er (ou′stər) s. *(ejection)* expulsión f; DER. *(eviction)* desalojo; *(dispossession)* despojo ilegal.

out (out) I. adv. *(away from)* fuera *<o. of the office* fuera de la oficina>; *(outside)* afuera *<come o. and play* ven a jugar afuera>; *(to a finish)* hasta el final *<to argue it o.* discutirlo hasta el final>; *(on strike)* en huelga ♦ **a way o.** una escapatoria • **all o.** con tesón • **inside o.** al revés • **on the voyage o.** en el viaje de ida • **o. and o.** completamente • **o. for** empeñado en • **o. here** *(around here)* por aquí; *(outside)* aquí fuera • **o. loud** en voz alta • **o. there** *(around there)* por allí; *(outside)* allá fuera • **o. of joint** MED. dislocado • **on the outs with** FAM. estar reñido con • **to be o.** *(not at home)* no estar en casa; *(a prisoner)* estar libre; *(a book, article)* haberse publicado; *(sun, moon)* haber salido; *(flowers)* estar abiertas; *(fire)* estar apagado; *(fads)* haber pasado de moda; *(chance)* quedar descartado; *(to be eliminated)* quedar excluido; *(not in power)* estar fuera del poder; *(money)* faltar *<I am o. ten dollars* me faltan diez dólares> • **to be o. cold** haber perdido el sentido o el conocimiento • **to be o. of commission** estar fuera de servicio, no funcionar • **to be o. of it** FAM. *(to be left out)* no estar metido en un asunto; *(to be unaware)* no estar en el ojo • **to be o. of order** *(disordered)* estar en desorden; *(not in good condition)* estar en malas condiciones; *(not working)* no funcionar; *(against the rules)* no

estar en regla; *(in a meeting)* ser inaceptable, ser inadmisible <*the motion is o. of order* la moción es inaceptable>; *(to be inappropriate)* ser impertinente **II.** adj. *(exterior)* exterior, extremo; *(absent)* ausente <*she was o. when I called* estaba ausente cuando llamé>; *(outgoing)* saliente; *(exhausted)* agotado <*the oil supply is o.* el aceite está agotado>; *(extinguished)* apagado <*the fire is o.* el fuego está apagado>; *(impossible)* imposible <*a taxi is o., because we do not have the money* un taxi es imposible porque no tenemos dinero>; *(not in fashion)* fuera de moda; *(threadbare)* raído <*a jacket o. at the elbow* una chaqueta raída en el codo **III.** prep. *(through)* por <*he fell o. the window* cayó por la ventana>; *(beyond)* fuera de, al lado de <*o. this door is the garage* al otro lado de esta puerta está el garaje> **IV.** s. *(person)* político que está fuera del poder; FAM. *(way out)* salida <*the window was my only o.* la ventana era mi única salida>; *(excuse)* excusa <*to have an o.* tener una excusa>; *(solution)* solución *f*; IMPR. *(omission)* bordón *m*, omisión (de palabra) *f* ♦ **on the outs** FAM. enemistado • **the ins and outs** los pormenores, los detalles **V.** intr. descubrirse, hacer público <*the truth will o.* la verdad se descubrirá> —tr. *(to expel)* echar, expulsar; G.B. *(to knock unconscious)* poner fuera de combate en boxeo **VI.** interj. ¡fuera!
▲ Para obtener información adicional sobre el uso de *out* como preposición, consulte **out of**.

out·age (ou'tĭj) s. *(missing piece)* parte faltante *f*; *(power cut)* corte de electricidad temporal *m*.

out-and-out (out'n-out') adj. completo, total <*he was an o. idiot* era un idiota total>.

out·back (out'băk') s. GEOG. interior de Australia y Nueva Zelandia *m*.

out·bid (out-bĭd') tr. **-bid, -bid·den** (-bĭd'n) *o* **-bid, -bid·ding** superar a, ofrecer más que.

out·board (out'bôrd') adj. MARÍT. fuera de borda; AVIA. más alejado del fuselaje.

outboard motor s. MARÍT. motor fuera de borda *m*, motor exterior.

out·bound (out'bound') adj. de salida, que sale.

out·break (out'brāk') s. *(sudden appearance)* brote *m* <*an o. of the flu* un brote de la gripe>; *(eruption)* erupción *f*; *(outburst)* estallido.

out·build·ing (out'bĭl'dĭng) s. dependencia, anexo.

out·burst (out'bûrst') s. arranque (de emoción, actividad) *m*.

out·cast (out'kăst') s. paria *mf*.

out·class (out-klăs') tr. ser muy superior a, superar.

out·come (out'kŭm') s. *(result)* resultado; *(consequence)* consecuencia.

out·crop GEOL. **I.** s. (out'krŏp') afloramiento **II.** intr. (out-krŏp') **-cropped, -crop·ping** aflorar.

out·cry (out'krī') s. [pl. **-cries**] *(protest)* protesta; *(cry)* grito; *(clamor)* alboroto.

out·dat·ed (out-dā'tĭd) adj. *(obsolete)* obsoleto, caído en desuso; *(antiquated)* anticuado.

out·dis·tance (out-dĭs'təns) tr. **-tanced, -tanc·ing** *(to outrun)* dejar atrás; *(to surpass)* sobrepasar.

out·do (out-dōō') tr. **-did** (-dĭd), **-done** (-dŭn'), **-do·ing** *(to surpass)* superar, aventajar; *(to defeat)* vencer.

out·door (out'dôr') adj. al aire libre.

out·doors (out-dôrz') **I.** adv. *(in the open)* al aire libre; *(outside)* (a)fuera **II.** s. el aire libre.

out·doors·man (out-dôrz'mən) s. [pl. **-men**] hombre que gusta del aire libre, la pesca *o* la caza *m*.

out·er (ou'tər) adj. *(outside)* exterior; *(external)* externo.

outer ear s. ANAT. oído externo.

out·er·most (ou'tər-mōst') adj. más alejado, más exterior.

outer space s. ASTRON., ASTRONÁUT. espacio exterior (interplanetario, interestelar).

out·face (out-fās') tr. **-faced, -fac·ing** *(to stare down)* hacer bajar la vista; *(to defy)* desafiar.

out·field (out'fēld') s. DEP. *(area)* campo externo; *(players)* jugadores externos.

out·fit (out'fĭt') **I.** s. *(equipment)* equipo; *(equipping)* equipamiento; *(tools)* juego de herramientas; *(clothing)* traje

m, conjunto; FAM. *(military unit)* unidad *f*; *(business)* empresa **II.** tr. **-fit·ted, -fit·ting** equipar.

out·flank (out-flăngk') tr. *(to go round)* desbordar el flanco de (un opositor); *(to outwit)* aventajar tácticamente.

out·flow (out'flō') s. flujo.

out·fox (out-fŏks') tr. FAM. ganar en astucia, burlar.

out·go I. tr. (out-gō') **-went** (-wĕnt), **-gone** (-gôn'), **-go·ing** *(to exceed)* exceder; *(to surpass)* sobrepasar, aventajar **II.** s. (out'gō') [pl. **-goes**] *(expenditure)* gasto; *(outflow)* salida.

out·go·ing (out'gō'ĭng) adj. *(departing)* de salida, que sale; *(retiring)* saliente (de un cargo o posición); *(friendly)* amistoso, sociable.

out·grow (out-grō') tr. **-grew** (-grōō'), **-grown** (-grōn'), **-grow·ing** *(to surpass)* crecer más que; *(to lose)* perder <*with time he outgrew his prejudices* con el tiempo perdió sus prejuicios> ♦ **to o. one's clothes** quedarle la ropa chica a uno.

out·growth (out'grōth') s. *(offshoot)* brote *m*; *(result)* resultado, consecuencia.

out·guess (out-gĕs') tr. *(to anticipate)* anticipar; *(to outwit)* ser más astuto que.

out·house (out'hous') s. excusado, retrete *m*.

out·ing (ou'tĭng) s. *(pleasure trip)* excursión *f*; *(walk)* paseo.

out·land (out'lănd') s. país extranjero, extranjero ♦ **outlands** regiones más apartadas del país.

out·land·ish (out-lăn'dĭsh) adj. *(strange)* raro, extraño; *(remote)* apartado, remoto; *(unconventional)* extravagante; *(absurd)* absurdo.

out·last (out-lăst') tr. *(to last longer than)* durar más que <*these shoes will o. all others* estos zapatos durarán más que todos los demás>; *(to live longer than)* vivir más que; *(to survive)* sobrevivir.

out·law (out'lô') **I.** s. *(criminal)* malhechor *m*, criminal *m*; *(fugitive)* forajido; DER. persona sin derechos civiles **II.** tr. prohibir, declarar fuera de la ley.

out·lay I. s. (out'lā') desembolso, gastos **II.** tr. (out-lā') **-laid** (-lād'), **-lay·ing** desembolsar, gastar.

out·let (out'lĕt') s. *(vent)* salida; *(hole)* abertura; *(socket)* tomacorriente *m*; *(drain)* desagüe *m*; FIG. *(for feelings)* desahogo, forma de desahogar <*an o. for his resentment* una forma de desahogar su resentimiento>; *(for energies)* forma de descargar, forma de dar rienda suelta a; COM. *(market)* salida, mercado; *(store)* distribuidor *m*.

out·line (out'līn') **I.** s. *(contour)* contorno <*a clean o.* un contorno nítido>; *(profile)* perfil *m*; *(shape)* silueta; *(general description)* idea general; *(summary)* resumen *m*, compendio; *(draft)* guión *m*, esquema *m*; ARTE. bosquejo, esbozo; TEC. trazado ♦ **in broad o.** en líneas generales, a grandes rasgos • **o. map** mapa mudo **II.** tr. **-lined, -lin·ing** *(to draw the lines of)* trazar las líneas o los contornos de; *(to profile)* perfilar; *(to give a description of)* dar una idea general de, trazar a grandes rasgos; *(to summarize)* resumir; *(to sketch)* bosquejar, esbozar; TEC. hacer el trazado de ♦ **to be outlined against** dibujarse contra, perfilarse sobre.

out·live (out-lĭv') tr. **-lived, -liv·ing** *(a person)* sobrevivir; *(to endure longer than)* aguantar más que ♦ **to o. its useful·ness** volverse inútil, perdurar inútilmente.

out·look (out'lŏōk') s. *(vantage point)* mirador *m*; *(view)* panorama *m*, vista; *(point of view)* punto de vista; *(attitude)* actitud *f*; *(chance of success)* perspectivas, porvenir *m* <*there is a bad o. for the textile industry* las perspectivas de la industria textil son malas>; *(chance)* posibilidades *f* <*a bad o. for new jobs* pocas posibilidades de más empleos>.

out loud adv. en voz alta.

out·ly·ing (out'lī'ĭng) adj. alejado del centro ♦ **the o. sub·urbs** las afueras de la ciudad.

out·ma·neu·ver (out'mə-nōō'vər, -nyōō'-) tr. *(to outdo)* ser más hábil que, superar; AUTO. moverse mejor que.

out·mod·ed (out-mō'dĭd) adj. *(old-fashioned)* anticuado, pasado de moda; *(obsolete)* anticuado, inútil.

out·most (out'mōst') adj. más alejado, más remoto.

out·num·ber (out-nŭm'bər) tr. superar en número, ser más numeroso que ♦ **we were outnumbered three to one** eran tres veces más que nosotros.

out of prep. *(from inside of)* de <*she took a dress o. of the closet* sacó un vestido del armario>; *(from a source)* de <*a house made o. of stone* una casa de piedra>; *(away from)* distante de <*thirty miles o. of Boston* treinta millas distante de Boston>; *(without)* sin <*o. of money* sin dinero>; *(because of)* por <*I read it o. of curiosity* lo leí por curiosidad>; *(from among)* de cada <*five o. of six votes* cinco votos de cada seis> ♦ **o. of sight** *(beyond view)* fuera de la vista; JER. *(interjection)* ¡increíble!, ¡fantástico! • **to work o. of** depender de <*he works o. of the Philadelphia branch* él depende de la sucursal de Filadelfia>.

out-of-date (out'əv-dāt') adj. *(outmoded)* anticuado, pasado de moda; *(obsolete)* anticuado.

out-of-door (out'əv-dôr') adj. var. de **outdoor**.

out-of-doors (out'əv-dôrz') adv. & s. var. de **outdoors**.

out-of-pock·et (out'əv-pŏk'ĭt) adj. ♦ **o. expenses** gastos o desembolsos ocasionales.

out-of-the-way (out'əv-thə-wā') adj. *(remote)* retirado, apartado; *(secluded)* aislado, solitario; *(unusual)* fuera de lo común, insólito.

out·pa·tient (out'pā'shənt) s. MED. paciente que no está hospitalizado *mf.*

out·post (out'pōst') s. MIL. *(detachment)* avanzada; *(station)* puesto avanzado; *(settlement)* puesto fronterizo.

out·pour·ing (out'pôr'ĭng) s. *(of feelings)* efusión *f*; *(of opinions)* manifestación efusiva; *(of people)* torrente *m*, avalancha.

out·put (out'pŏŏt') I. s. *(production)* producción *f*; *(energy)* potencia, energía; *(yield)* rendimiento; ELEC. potencia de salida; COMPUT. salida II. tr. **-put·ted** *o* **-put, -put·ting** producir, generar.

out·rage (out'rāj') I. s. *(atrocity)* ultraje *m*, atrocidad *f*; *(lawless act)* desafuero; *(destructive act)* atropello; *(insult)* insulto, afrenta; *(anger)* indignación *f* <*public o.* indignación pública> ♦ **an o. against** un atentado contra, un atropello a II. tr. **-raged, -rag·ing** *(to make angry)* indignar; *(to shock)* escandalizar; *(to commit an outrage upon)* ultrajar, atropellar; *(to rape)* violar.

out·ra·geous (out-rā'jəs) adj. *(atrocious)* ultrajante, atroz; *(flagrant)* flagrante; *(infuriating)* intolerable, indignante <*it's o. that they should talk that way* es indignante que hablen de esa manera>; *(exorbitant)* exorbitante, excesivo.

out·rank (out-răngk') tr. *(to rank higher than)* tener un rango superior a; *(to surpass)* tener más categoría que, ser superior a.

out·reach I. tr. (out-rēch') *(to surpass)* superar; *(to extend outward)* alargar, extender ♦ **to o. oneself** ir más allá de los límites de uno, extralimitarse II. s. (out'rēch') *(reach)* alcance *m*; *(to a community)* servicio especial de asistencia pública.

out·rid·er (out'rī'dər) s. *(attendant)* acompañante montado; *(escort)* escolta *m.*

out·rig·ger (out'rĭg'ər) s. MARÍT. *(float)* flotador lateral *m*, batanga; *(vessel)* embarcación equipada con un flotador lateral.

out·right (out'rīt') I. adv. *(frankly)* sin reservas, francamente; *(obviously)* patentemente, descaradamente; *(entirely)* totalmente; *(utterly)* absolutamente <*it was o. silly* fue absolutamente absurdo>; *(categorically)* rotundamente; *(straightway)* en el acto <*they shot him o.* lo balearon en el acto> II. adj. *(unqualified)* sin reservas; *(frank)* franco; *(obvious)* patente, descarado; *(complete)* total, completo <*the o. cost* el costo total>; *(out-and-out)* absoluto <*o. viciousness* maldad absoluta>; *(categorical)* rotundo <*an o. no* un no rotundo>.

out·run (out-rŭn') tr. **-ran** (-răn'), **-run, -run·ning** *(to run faster than)* correr más rápido que, dejar rezagado; *(to escape from)* librarse de; *(to exceed)* sobrepasar, superar.

out·sell (out-sĕl') tr. **-sold** (-sōld'), **-sell·ing** *(in quantity)* vender más que; *(in salesmanship)* vender mejor que; *(a product)* venderse mejor que.

out·set (out'sĕt') s. *(beginning)* principio, comienzo; *(initial stage)* inicio.

out·shine (out-shīn') tr. **-shone** (-shōn'), **-shin·ing** *(to glow*

out·shoot I. tr. (out-shŏŏt') **-shot** (-shŏt'), **-shoot·ing** disparar mejor que —intr. *(to extend)* extenderse; *(to protrude)* sobresalir II. s. (out'shŏŏt') *(outgrowth)* brote *m*; *(projection)* saliente *f.*

out·side (out-sīd') I. s. *(exterior)* exterior *m* <*the o. of a house* el exterior de una casa>; *(appearance)* apariencia, superficie *f* ♦ **at the o.** como mucho, como máximo <*we will be leaving in ten days at the o.* saldremos dentro de diez días, como mucho> • **from the o.** desde fuera • **on the o.** por fuera • **o. in** al revés II. adj. *(external)* exterior <*o. assistance* ayuda exterior>; *(maximum)* más elevado, máximo <*the cost exceeded even my o. estimate* el costo superó incluso mis cálculos más elevados>; *(slight)* remoto <*an o. possibility* una posibilidad remota> ♦ **o. influence** influencia de afuera III. adv. *(on the outside)* fuera, afuera <*to step o.* ir afuera>; *(outdoors)* en la calle, a la calle; *(beyond)* más allá de ciertos límites ♦ **come o.!** ¡salga afuera! IV. prep. *(on the outer side of)* fuera de; *(beyond the limits of)* fuera de <*o. our plans* fuera de nuestros planes>; FAM. *(except)* excepto, fuera de <*no information o. the figures given* no hay datos, fuera de las cifras dadas>.

outside of prep. *(beyond)* fuera de; *(except)* excepto.

out·sid·er (out-sī'dər) s. *(stranger)* forastero; *(nonparticipant)* persona no participante; *(long shot)* concursante de pocas posibilidades de triunfo *mf*; *(aloof person)* apartado.

out·size (out'sīz') I. s. *(large)* tamaño descomunal; *(garment)* prenda de talle muy grande II. adj. descomunal.

out·skirts (out'skŭrts') s.pl. afueras (de ciudad, campamento).

out·smart (out-smärt') tr. ser más astuto *o* vivo que.

out·spend (out-spĕnd') tr. **-spent** (-spĕnt'), **-spend·ing** gastar más que.

out·spo·ken (out-spō'kən) adj. abierto, franco ♦ **to be o.** no tener pelos en la lengua.

out·spo·ken·ness (out-spō'kən-nĭs) s. franqueza.

out·spread (out-sprĕd') I. tr. & intr. **-spread, -spread·ing** extender(se), desplegar(se) II. adj. extendido, desplegado III. s. (out'sprĕd') extensión *f*, despliegue *m.*

out·stand·ing (out-stăn'dĭng) adj. *(projecting)* sobresaliente, saliente; *(prominent)* sobresaliente, destacado <*an o. athlete* un atleta destacado>; *(exceptional)* sobresaliente, excepcional <*an o. achievement* un logro excepcional>; *(superior)* notable, excelente <*an o. product* un producto excelente>; *(not resolved)* pendiente.

out·stare (out-stâr') tr. **-stared, -star·ing** hacer bajar la vista.

out·stay (out-stā') tr. *(to remain longer than)* quedarse más tiempo que; *(to endure)* aguantar más que.

out·stretch (out-strĕch') tr. *(to extend)* extender; *(to lengthen)* alargar.

out·strip (out-strĭp') tr. **-stripped, -strip·ping** *(to leave behind)* dejar atrás; *(to exceed)* exceder, sobrepasar.

out·take (out'tāk') s. *(vent)* respiradero; CINEM. toma de película no utilizada; MÚS., RAD. grabación no utilizada.

out·talk (out-tôk') tr. *(to outdo)* ganar hablando; *(to talk more than)* hablar más que; *(to outwit)* vencer con la palabra.

out·ward (out'wərd) I. adj. *(outer)* exterior, externo; *(toward the outside)* hacia afuera; *(physical)* material; *(superficial)* superficial, aparente ♦ **outward-bound flight** vuelo de salida • **o. signs** señales II. adv. *(toward the outside)* hacia afuera; *(externally)* exteriormente III. s. *(exterior)* exterior *m*; *(the external world)* mundo material.

out·wards (out'wərdz) adv. var. de **outward**.

out·wear (out-wâr') tr. **-wore** (-wôr'), **-worn** (-wôrn'), **-wear·ing** *(to wear out)* gastar, desgastar con uso; *(to outlast)* durar más que; *(to outgrow)* dejar atrás.

out·weigh (out-wā') tr. *(to weigh more than)* pesar más que; *(to mean more than)* importar más que.

out·wit (out-wĭt') tr. **-wit·ted, -wit·ting** *(cleverness)* ser más astuto *o* vivo que; *(in intelligence)* ser más inteligente que.

out·work[1] (out-wûrk') tr. *(to work more than)* trabajar más *o* mejor que.

out·work² (out'wûrk') s. MIL. defensa externa a la fortificación principal.

o·va (ō'və) pl. de ovum.

o·val (ō'vəl) I. adj. ovalado, oval II. s. óvalo.

o·va·ry (ō'və-rē) s. [pl. -ries] ovario.

o·vate (ō'vāt') adj. (egg-shaped) aovado, ovalado; BOT. aovado.

o·va·tion (ō-vā'shən) s. ovación f.

ov·en (ŭv'ən) s. horno.

ov·en·proof (ŭv'ən-prŏof') adj. de horno, utilizable en el horno.

o·ver (ō'vər) I. prep. (above) sobre, encima de <*a sign o. the door* un letrero encima de la puerta>; (across) por encima de <*a jump o. the fence* un salto por encima de la valla>; (on the other side of) al otro lado de <*a village o. the border* un pueblo al otro lado de la frontera>; (on) encima de, encima de <*he put his coat o. his shoulders* se puso el abrigo por encima de los hombros>; (throughout) por todo, a través de <*to travel o. the country* viajar por todo el país>; (so as to cover or close) para tapar o cerrar <*to put rocks o. a cave entrance* poner piedras para tapar o cerrar la entrada de una cueva>; (up to) hasta; (higher than) por encima de; (during) durante <*o. the past two years* du­rante los dos últimos años>; (until the end of) hasta el final de <*to stay o. the holidays* quedarse hasta el final de las fiestas>; (more than, in quantity) más de <*o. ten miles* más de diez millas>; (more than, in degree) más que <*they like tennis o. all other sports* les gusta el tenis más que todos los demás deportes>; (in preference to) antes que <*she chose the yellow o. the green* escogió el amarillo antes que el verde>; (upon) sobre <*his influence o. children* su influen­cia sobre los niños>; (while) mientras <*let's discuss it o. dinner* hablemos de ello mientras cenamos>; (concerning) sobre, acerca de <*an argument o. methods* una discusión sobre los métodos>; (by means of) por <*o. the telephone* por teléfono> (by reason of) por <*to fight o. the dinner check* pelear por pagar la cena>; (against) con <*to stum­ble o. a difficulty* tropezar con una dificultad> ♦ **o. a barrel** a merced de los demás • **o. all** total, de extremo a extremo • **o. one's head** (above) por encima de la cabeza de uno; (beyond one's abilities) por encima de la comprensión o capacidad de uno II. adv. (above) encima, por encima; (across) al otro lado, enfrente; (at some distance) allá <*o. in Europe* allá en Europa>; (throughout) por todas partes <*to wander all o.* pasear por todas partes>; (from beginning to end) del principio al fin, de arriba abajo <*to read a book o.* leer un libro del principio al fin>; (again) otra vez, de nuevo <*count your cards o.* cuente sus cartas otra vez>; (more) más <*ten times o.* diez veces más> ♦ **all o.** (everywhere) por todas partes; (completely) completamente • **o. again** otra vez, de nuevo • **o. and above** además de • **o. and o.** una y otra vez • **o. here** aquí, acá • **o. there** (there) allí, allá; FAM. (Europe) en el frente, en Europa • **o. with** FAM. (done) hecho; (finished) acabado • **to be all o.** (to be everywhere) estar por todas partes; (to be finished) haberse acabado • **to be all o. with (someone)** haberse terminado todo para (alguien), ser el fin para (alguien) III. adj. (upper) superior; (outer) exterior, externo; (in excess) demasiado, excesivo; (finished) acabado, terminado <*the work is o.* el trabajo está terminado> IV. s. COM. excedente m, superávit m; MIL. (shot) tiro largo V. tr. pasar por encima o a través de.

o·ver·a·bun·dance (ō'vər-ə-bŭn'dəns) s. (abundance) superabundancia, sobreabundancia; (excess) exceso.

o·ver·a·bun·dant (ō'vər-ə-bŭn'dənt) adj. superabundante, sobreabundante.

o·ver·a·chieve (ō'vər-ə-chēv') intr. -chieved, -chiev·ing lograr resultados mejores que los esperados.

o·ver·a·chiev·er (ō'vər-ə-chē'vər) s. persona que logra resultados superiores a lo esperado.

o·ver·act (ō'vər-ăkt') tr. & intr. exagerar.

o·ver·ac·tive (ō'vər-ăk'tĭv) adj. demasiado activo.

o·ver·age¹ (ō'vər-ĭj) s. COM. (excess) excedente (mercancía, dinero) m.

o·ver·age² (ō'vər-āj') adj. pasado de la edad requerida.

o·ver·all o **o·ver·all** (ō'vər-ôl') I. adj. (from one end to an

other) de punta a punta; (comprehensive) comprensivo, total II. adv. en general, generalmente III. s. (ō'vər-ôl') guardapolvo.

o·ver·alls (ō'vər-ôlz') s.pl. mono, overol m.

o·ver·arch (ō'vər-ärch') tr. arquearse sobre.

o·ver·awe (ō'vər-ô') tr. -awed, -aw·ing intimidar, impresionar.

o·ver·bear (ō'vər-bâr') tr. -bore (-bôr'), -borne (-bôrn'), -bear·ing (to crush down) oprimir; (to dominate) dominar (con fuerza o autoridad) —intr. dar demasiados frutos o hijos.

o·ver·bear·ing (ō'vər-bâr'ĭng) adj. (overwhelming) avasallador; (predominant) predominante; (domineering) autoritario; (arrogant) arrogante.

o·ver·bid I. tr. (ō'vər-bĭd') -bid, -bid·den (-bĭd'n) o -bid, -bid·ding hacer una mejor oferta que (alguien) —intr. ofrecer más que otro II. s. (ō'vər-bĭd') oferta mayor.

o·ver·bite (ō'vər-bīt') s. oclusión defectuosa de los dientes superiores.

o·ver·blown (ō'vər-blōn') adj. (blown down) derribado de un soplido; FIG. (conceited) inflado, pomposo.

o·ver·board (ō'vər-bôrd') adv. por la borda ♦ **man o.!** ¡hombre al agua! • **to go o.** FIG., FAM. írsele la mano, pasarse de la raya.

o·ver·book (ō'vər-bŏok') tr. & intr. vender o reservar más localidades de las que hay disponibles (en).

o·ver·build (ō'vər-bĭld') tr. & intr. -built (-bĭlt'), -build·ing sobreedificar.

o·ver·bur·den (ō'vər-bûr'dn) tr. (to overload) sobrecargar; (to overwhelm) agobiar.

o·ver·cap·i·tal·ize (ō'vər-kăp'ĭ-tl-īz') tr. -ized, -iz·ing COM., FIN. sobrecapitalizar, capitalizar con exceso.

o·ver·cast (ō'vər-kăst') I. adj. nublado, encapotado II. s. (covering) capa, cubierta; (of clouds) cubierta de nubes, nublado III. tr. (ō'vər-kăst') anublar, encapotar, cubrir.

o·ver·cau·tious (ō'vər-kô'shəs) adj. demasiado cauteloso.

o·ver·charge I. tr. & intr. (ō'vər-chärj') -charged, -charging (to charge too much) cobrar demasiado; (to overload) cargar demasiado II. s. (ō'vər-chärj') (price) precio excesivo; (load) carga excesiva.

o·ver·coat (ō'vər-kōt') s. sobretodo, abrigo.

o·ver·come (ō'vər-kŭm') tr. -came (-kām'), -come, -com·ing (to defeat) derrotar; (to conquer) conquistar; (to surmount) superar; (to affect deeply) afectar profundamente <*to be o. by grief* estar afectado profundamente por un dolor> —intr. (to surmount) superar; (to be victorious) salir victorioso.

o·ver·com·pen·sate (ō'vər-kŏm'pən-sāt') tr. & intr. -sat·ed, -sat·ing sobrecompensar.

o·ver·com·pen·sa·tion (ō'vər-kŏm'pən-sā'shən) s. sobrecompensación f.

o·ver·con·fi·dent (ō'vər-kŏn'fĭ-dnt) adj. demasiado confiado.

o·ver·crowd (ō'vər-kroud') tr. atestar, sobrellenar.

o·ver·de·vel·op (ō'vər-dĭ-vĕl'əp) tr. (to overdo) desarrollar con exceso; FOTOG. revelar en exceso.

o·ver·do (ō'vər-dōo') tr. -did (-dĭd'), -done (-dŭn'), -do·ing (to do too much) hacer demasiado; (to carry too far) exagerar (dieta, ejercicio); (to exhaust) desgastar, agotar; (to cook too much) cocinar demasiado —intr. hacer demasiado.

o·ver·dose I. s. (ō'vər-dōs') dosis excesiva II. tr. & intr. (ō'vər-dōs') -dosed, -dos·ing dar(se) una dosis excesiva.

o·ver·draft (ō'vər-drăft') s. COM., FIN. giro en descubierto, sobregiro.

o·ver·draw (ō'vər-drô') tr. -drew (-drōo'), -drawn (-drôn'), -draw·ing COM., FIN. (funds) girar en descubierto; (to stretch) estirar demasiado; (to exaggerate) exagerar.

o·ver·drawn (ō'vər-drôn') adj. COM., FIN. al descubierto.

o·ver·dress I. intr. (ō'vər-drĕs') vestirse con más lujo de lo necesario II. s. (ō'vər-drĕs') delantal m.

o·ver·drive (ō'vər-drīv') s. AUTO. sobremarcha.

o·ver·due (ō'vər-dōo', -dyōo') adj. (unpaid) vencido (en el pago); (delayed) retrasado; (long in coming) esperado desde hace tiempo.

o·ver·eat (ō'vər-ēt') intr. **-ate** (-āt'), **-eat·en** (-ēt'n), **-eat·ing** comer demasiado.

o·ver·em·pha·sis (ō'vər-ĕm'fə-sĭs) s. énfasis exagerado.

o·ver·em·pha·size (ō'vər-ĕm'fə-sīz') tr. & intr. **-sized, -siz·ing** dar mucho énfasis (a), enfatizar demasiado.

o·ver·es·ti·mate (ō'vər-ĕs'tə-māt') tr. **-mat·ed, -mat·ing** sobreestimar, avaluar exageradamente.

o·ver·es·ti·ma·tion (ō'vər-ĕs'tə-mā'shən) s. estimación exagerada, avalúo exagerado.

o·ver·ex·ert (ō'vər-ĭg-zûrt') tr. esforzar demasiado ♦ **to o. oneself** esforzarse demasiado.

o·ver·ex·pose (ō'vər-ĭk-spōz') tr. **-posed, -pos·ing** (to expose too much) exponer demasiado; FOTOG. sobreexponer.

o·ver·ex·po·sure (ō'vər-ĭk-spō'zhər) s. (excessive exposure) exposición excesiva; (excessive advertisement) publicidad excesiva; FOTOG. sobreexposición f.

o·ver·ex·tend (ō'vər-ĭk-stĕnd') tr. (to expand too much) extender demasiado; (to widen too much) ampliar demasiado.

o·ver·flow I. intr. (ō'vər-flō') (to flow over) desbordarse; (container, waterway) desbordarse, rebosar ♦ **to o. with** FIG. rebosar de —tr. (to spill over) desbordar, salirse de <the waters overflowed the dam las aguas desbordaron el dique>; (to flood) inundar; (to cause to fill) llenar hasta los topes II. s. (ō'vər-flō') (act) desbordamiento; (flood) inundación f; (excess) excedente m, exceso; (outlet) desagüe m.

o·ver·graze (ō'vər-grāz') tr. **-grazed, -graz·ing** apacentar excesivamente.

o·ver·grow (ō'vər-grō') tr. **-grew** (-grōō'), **-grown** (-grōn'), **-grow·ing** cubrir —intr. crecer demasiado.

o·ver·grown (ō'vər-grōn') adj. (covered with growth) cubierto <a garden o. with weeds un jardín cubierto de hierba mala>.

o·ver·growth (ō'vər-grōth') s. BOT. tapiz de vegetación m; (excessive size) desarrollo o crecimiento excesivo.

o·ver·hand (ō'vər-hănd') I. adj. DEP. por arriba, por lo alto <an o. tennis serve un saque de tenis por arriba> II. s. DEP. (throw) tirada por arriba o por lo alto; (stroke) golpe por arriba o por lo alto m; COST. costura montada.

o·ver·hang I. tr. (ō'vər-hăng') **-hung** (-hŭng'), **-hang·ing** (to project beyond) sobresalir por encima de; (to hang over) colgar por encima de; (to threaten) pender sobre, amenazar; (to ornament) adornar con colgaduras —intr. (to project) sobresalir; (to hang) colgar II. s. (ō'vər-hăng') saliente m.

o·ver·haul I. tr. (ō'vər-hôl') (to examine for repairs) revisar, inspeccionar; (to dismantle) desmontar, desarmar; (to repair) reparar, hacer una reparación general de; (to renovate) renovar, rehacer; (to catch up with) alcanzar, dar alcance a II. s. (ō'vər-hôl') (examination) revisión f, inspección f; (repair job) reparación general f; (renovation) renovación f.

o·ver·head (ō'vər-hĕd') I. adj. (located above) de arriba; (light) en el techo, del techo; (railway) elevado; (wire) aéreo; COM. general II. s. COM. gastos generales III. adv. (above) arriba, por sobre la cabeza; (up) para o hacia arriba <look o. mira para arriba>.

o·ver·hear (ō'vər-hîr') tr. **-heard** (-hûrd'), **-hear·ing** oír por casualidad, alcanzar a oír.

o·ver·heat (ō'vər-hēt') tr. (to heat too much) recalentar, calentar demasiado; (to excite) acalorar, exaltar —intr. recalentarse, calentarse demasiado.

o·ver·in·dulge (ō'vər-ĭn-dŭlj') tr. **-dulged, -dulg·ing** (to please excessively) ser indulgente con; (to spoil) mimar demasiado —intr. darse todo lo que uno quiere, no saberse controlar ♦ **to o. in** no saberse controlar con.

o·ver·in·dul·gence (ō'vər-ĭn-dŭl'jəns) s. (permissiveness) exceso de indulgencia, consentimiento excesivo; (excessive gratification) exceso, falta de control <o. in food becomes a habit el exceso de comida se vuelve un vicio>.

o·ver·in·dul·gent (ō'vər-ĭn-dŭl'jənt) adj. (permissive) demasiado indulgente; (said of parent) que mima demasiado a sus hijos.

o·ver·joyed (ō'vər-joid') adj. loco de contento ♦ **to be o. at** estar loco de contento con.

o·ver·kill I. s. (ō'vər-kĭl') MIL. capacidad excesiva de represalia nuclear; (excessive killing) destrucción innecesaria, matanza excesiva; FIG. (excessive action) medidas excesivas II. tr. (ō'vər-kĭl') MIL. descargar una fuerza nuclear excesiva contra.

o·ver·land (ō'vər-lănd') I. adj. (journey, road) terrestre; (transportation) que va por tierra II. adv. por tierra, por vía terrestre.

o·ver·lap I. tr. (ō'vər-lăp') **-lapped, -lap·ping** (to lie over) superponer(se) a, recubrir <this edge should not o. the other one este borde no debería superponerse al otro>; (to coincide partly with) coincidir en parte con —intr. (to lie over something) superponerse, recubrirse; (to coincide partly) coincidir en parte <their duties o. sus funciones coinciden en parte> II. s. (ō'vər-lăp') (part) parte superpuesta; (act) superposición f, recubrimiento.

o·ver·lay I. tr. (ō'vər-lā') **-laid** (-lād'), **-lay·ing** (to cover) cubrir, extender sobre; (with wood, metal) revestir, enchapar II. s. (ō'vər-lā') (cover) cubierta; (coat) capa; (of wood, metal) chapa, revestimiento; TIP. alza, calzo.

o·ver·leap (ō'vər-lēp') tr. **-leaped** o **-leapt** (-lĕpt') **-leap·ing** (to jump) saltar sobre, saltar por encima; (to ignore) pasar por alto; (to defeat oneself) hacer fracasar.

o·ver·lie (ō'vər-lī') tr. **-lay** (-lā'), **-lain** (-lān'), **-ly·ing** (to lie) yacer sobre; (to kill) sofocar, asfixiar (yaciendo sobre alguien).

o·ver·load I. tr. (ō'vər-lōd') sobrecargar II. s. (ō'vər-lōd') sobrecarga.

o·ver·look (ō'vər-lōōk') I. tr. (from a higher place) mirar desde lo alto; (to rise above) dominar <the lighthouse overlooks the sea el faro domina el mar>; (view, window) dar a, tener vista a <my window overlooks the street mi ventana da a la calle>; (to disregard) dejar pasar, pasar por alto; (to supervise) supervisar, controlar II. s. mirador m.

o·ver·long (ō'vər-lông') adj. & adv. demasiado largo.

o·ver·lord (ō'vər-lôrd') s. (lord) señor m, amo; (chief) jefe supremo.

o·ver·ly (ō'vər-lē) adv. demasiado.

o·ver·man (ō'vər-măn') s. [pl. **-men** (-mĕn')] capataz m.

o·ver·much (ō'vər-mŭch') I. adj. (too much) demasiado; (excessive) excesivo II. adv. excesivamente III. s. exceso.

o·ver·night (ō'vər-nīt') I. adj. (for a night) por la noche, por una noche <o. guests huéspedes por una noche>; (sudden) repentino, inesperado <an o. success un éxito inesperado> II. adv. (during the night) durante o por la noche; (suddenly) bruscamente, de la noche a la mañana ♦ **to stay o.** pasar la noche.

overnight bag s. neceser m, maletín de viaje m.

o·ver·op·ti·mis·tic (ō'vər-ŏp'tə-mĭs'tĭk) adj. demasiado optimista.

o·ver·pass I. s. (ō'vər-păs') paso superior, puente m II. tr. (ō'vər-păs') (to pass across) atravesar; (to surpass) superar; (to disregard) sobrepasar (los límites).

o·ver·pay (ō'vər-pā') tr. **-paid** (-pād') **-pay·ing** (to overcompensate) pagar demasiado (sueldo, jornal); (to pay too much) pagar demasiado por (objeto, servicio) —intr. pagar demasiado.

o·ver·play (ō'vər-plā') tr. exagerar.

o·ver·pop·u·la·tion (ō'vər-pŏp'yə-lā'shən) s. superpoblación f.

o·ver·pow·er (ō'vər-pou'ər) tr. (to vanquish) vencer, subyugar; (to overwhelm) abrumar.

o·ver·pow·er·ing (ō'vər-pou'ər-ĭng) adj. (overwhelming) abrumador; (irresistible) irresistible.

o·ver·praise (ō'vər-prāz') tr. **-praised, -prais·ing** alabar demasiado.

o·ver·price (ō'vər-prīs') tr. **-priced, -pric·ing** poner un precio demasiado alto a ♦ **to be overpriced** tener un precio muy alto, costar más de lo que vale.

o·ver·pro·duce (ō'vər-prə-dōōs', -dyōōs') tr. **-duced, -duc·ing** producir en exceso, sobrepasarse en la producción de.

o·ver·pro·duc·tion (ō'vər-prə-dŭk'shən) s. superproducción f, sobreproducción f.

o·ver·pro·tect (ō'vər-prə-tĕkt') tr. proteger excesivamente.

o·ver·qual·i·fied (ō'vər-kwŏl'ə-fīd') adj. excesivamente preparado o capacitado.

---

o·ver·rate (ō'vər-rāt') tr. **-rat·ed, -rat·ing** sobrestimar, supervalorar ♦ **to be overrated** tener demasiada fama.

o·ver·reach (ō'vər-rēch') tr. *(to reach beyond)* ir más allá de; *(to exceed)* extralimitarse en ♦ **to o. oneself** extralimitarse —intr. *(to go too far)* ir demasiado lejos, pasarse de la raya; *(horses)* alcanzarse.

o·ver·re·act (ō'vər-rē-ăkt') intr. reaccionar de modo exagerado.

o·ver·ride I. tr. (ō'vər-rīd') **-rode** (-rōd'), **-rid·den** (-rĭd'n), **-rid·ing** *(to ride across)* atravesar; *(to trample upon)* pisotear, pasar por encima de; *(a horse)* reventar; *(to prevail over)* imponerse a, hacer a un lado a <*budgetary concerns overrode all other considerations* las inquietudes presupuestarias se impusieron a todas las demás consideraciones>; *(to nullify)* anular II. s. (ō'vər-rīd') COM. comisión *f.*

o·ver·ripe (ō'vər-rīp') adj. *(too ripe)* pasado; *(decadent)* decadente.

o·ver·rule (ō'vər-rool') tr. **-ruled, -rul·ing** *(a person)* declarar improcedentes las acciones o alegatos de; *(to rule against)* decidir en contra de, no aceptar; *(to declare null)* anular, rescindir.

o·ver·run I. tr. (ō'vər-rŭn') **-ran** (-răn'), **-run, -run·ning** *(to defeat)* destruir, aplastar; *(to invade)* invadir <*locusts overran the prairie* las langostas invadieron la pradera>; *(time limit)* pasarse de, durar más de —intr. *(to overflow)* desbordarse; *(to exceed)* excederse; *(in time)* durar más de lo previsto II. s. (ō'vər-rŭn') IMPR. *(extra copies)* recorrido; *(of estimated costs)* costo por sobre el presupuesto.

o·ver·seas (ō'vər-sēz') o **o·ver·sea** (-sē') I. adv. en el extranjero, al extranjero II. adj. *(foreign)* extranjero; *(flight, shipment)* al exterior, al extranjero; *(trade)* exterior.

o·ver·see (ō'vər-sē') tr. **-saw** (-sô'), **-seen** (-sēn'), **-see·ing** *(to supervise)* supervisar, estar a cargo de; *(to examine)* examinar, inspeccionar.

o·ver·se·er (ō'vər-sē'ər) s. *(foreman)* capataz *m;* *(supervisor)* supervisor *m.*

o·ver·sell (ō'vər-sĕl') tr. **-sold** (-sōld'), **-sell·ing** *(to sell too much)* vender por sobre la capacidad de producción; *(to try to persuade)* empujar a comprar.

o·ver·sen·si·tive (ō'vər-sĕn'sĭ-tĭv) adj. hipersensible.

o·ver·sexed (ō'vər-sĕkst') adj. sexualmente insaciable.

o·ver·shad·ow (ō'vər-shăd'ō) tr. *(to cast a shadow over)* hacer sombra a, oscurecer; *(to eclipse)* eclipsar.

o·ver·shoe (ō'vər-shoo') s. chanclo, bota de agua.

o·ver·shoot (ō'vər-shoot') tr. **-shot** (-shŏt'), **-shoot·ing** *(to miss)* irse por encima de <*the arrow overshot the mark* la flecha se fue por encima del blanco>; *(a runway, goal)* pasarse de —intr. *(to miss)* pasarse; *(to go too far)* pasarse de la raya.

o·ver·shot (ō'vər-shŏt') adj. *(projecting)* saliente.

o·ver·sight (ō'vər-sīt') s. *(omission)* descuido, omisión *f;* *(watchful care)* vigilancia, supervisión *f.*

o·ver·sim·pli·fy (ō'vər-sĭm'plə-fī') tr. **-fied, -fy·ing** simplificar demasiado.

o·ver·size (ō'vər-sīz') o **o·ver·sized** (-sīzd') adj. *(too large)* demasiado grande; *(said of clothes)* de talla especial, de las tallas más grandes.

o·ver·skirt (ō'vər-skûrt') s. sobrefalda.

o·ver·sleep (ō'vər-slēp') intr. **-slept** (-slĕpt'), **-sleep·ing** dormir demasiado, quedarse dormido <*I was late because I overslept* llegué tarde porque me quedé dormido> —tr. quedarse dormido para <*I overslept my appointment* me quedé dormido para la cita>.

o·ver·spend (ō'vər-spĕnd') intr. **-spent** (-spĕnt'), **-spend·ing** gastar más de lo debido, pasarse del presupuesto —tr. gastar más de <*we overspent our income* gastamos más de los ingresos que tenemos>.

o·ver·state (ō'vər-stāt') tr. **-stat·ed, -stat·ing** *(to exaggerate)* exagerar; *(to emphasize)* insistir demasiado en.

o·ver·state·ment (ō'vər-stāt'mənt) s. *(exaggeration)* exageración *f;* *(emphatic statement)* afirmación que se cae de su peso *f.*

o·ver·stay (ō'vər-stā') tr. quedarse más tiempo del permitido por ♦ **to o. one's welcome** quedarse más de lo conveniente, prolongar demasiado la visita.

o·ver·step (ō'vər-stĕp') tr. **-stepped, -step·ping** traspasar, pasar de ♦ **to o. one's limits** extralimitarse.

o·ver·stock I. tr. (ō'vər-stŏk') tener existencias excesivas de, almacenar en exceso II. s. (ō'vər-stŏk') existencias excesivas.

o·ver·stuff (ō'vər-stŭf') tr. rellenar abundantemente ♦ **to o. oneself** FIG., FAM. hartarse hasta reventar.

o·ver·sub·scribe (ō'vər-səb-skrīb') tr. **-scribed, -scrib·ing** suscribir en exceso de la oferta ♦ **to be oversubscribed** tener un exceso de suscriptores.

o·ver·sup·ply I. s. (ō'vər-sə-plī') [pl. **-plies**] suministro excesivo ♦ **an o. of** un exceso de II. tr. (ō'vər-sə-plī') **-plied, -ply·ing** suministrar en exceso ♦ **to be oversupplied with** tener un exceso de.

o·vert (ō-vûrt') adj. *(observable)* ostensible, patente <*o. lies* mentiras patentes>; *(professed)* declarado <*o. hostility* hostilidad declarada>.

o·ver·take (ō'vər-tāk') tr. **-took** (-took'), **-tak·en** (-tā'kən), **-tak·ing** *(to catch up with)* alcanzar; *(to pass)* pasar, adelantar <*the car overtook us on the hill* el auto nos pasó en la loma>; *(to take by surprise)* sorprender; *(to possess)* adueñarse de, apoderarse de <*fear overtook the soldiers* el miedo se apoderó de los soldados> ♦ **to be overtaken by grief** sucumbir al dolor • **to be overtaken by sleep** ser vencido por el sueño.

o·ver·tax (ō'vər-tăks') tr. *(to tax excessively)* oprimir con impuestos, imponer impuestos excesivos a; *(to exhaust)* agotar <*it overtaxed our strength* agotó nuestras fuerzas> ♦ **to o. oneself** esforzarse demasiado.

o·ver-the-count·er (ō'vər-thə-koun'tər) adj. *(stock)* que se vende fuera de la bolsa; *(drug)* que se despacha sin receta médica.

o·ver·throw I. tr. (ō'vər-thrō') **-threw** (-throo'), **-thrown** (-thrōn'), **-throw·ing** *(to overturn)* volcar, tumbar; *(to oust)* derrocar; *(to dethrone)* destronar II. s. (ō'vər-thrō') *(of an object)* derribamiento; *(ouster)* derrocamiento; *(dethronement)* destronamiento; *(downfall)* caída; *(of a ball)* tiro largo.

o·ver·time (ō'vər-tīm') I. s. *(hours, payment)* horas extras; DEP. *(extra playing time)* tiempo suplementario, prórroga II. adv. más de lo normal ♦ **to work o.** trabajar horas extras.

o·ver·tone (ō'vər-tōn') s. *(hint)* insinuación *f*, sugestión *f*; MÚS. armónico ♦ **an o. o overtones of** una nota de.

o·ver·ture (ō'vər-choor', -chər) s. *(proposal)* oferta, propuesta; MÚS. obertura.

o·ver·turn I. tr. (ō'vər-tûrn') *(to turn over)* volcar, voltear; *(to capsize)* hacer zozobrar; *(to oust)* derrocar; *(to revoke)* revocar; *(to upset)* trastornar —intr. *(to turn over)* volcarse, voltearse; *(a vehicle)* dar una vuelta; *(to capsize)* zozobrar II. s. (ō'vər-tûrn') *(of a vehicle)* vuelco; *(ouster)* derrocamiento.

o·ver·use I. tr. (ō'vər-yooz') **-used, -us·ing** usar o emplear excesivamente, abusar de II. s. (-yoos') uso o empleo excesivo, abuso.

o·ver·val·ue (ō'vər-văl'yoo) tr. **-ued, -u·ing** sobrestimar, encarecer excesivamente.

o·ver·view (ō'vər-vyoo') s. *(survey)* panorama *m*, visión general *f*; *(summary)* repaso, resumen *m.*

o·ver·ween·ing (ō'vər-wē'nĭng) adj. *(overbearing)* altanero, arrogante; *(excessive)* desmesurado.

o·ver·weight (ō'vər-wāt') I. adj. *(weighing too much)* excesivamente pesado, pasado de peso; *(obese)* obeso, gordo II. tr. *(to overload)* sobrecargar; *(to overemphasize)* exagerar III. s. (ō'vər-wāt') sobrepeso, exceso de peso.

o·ver·whelm (ō'vər-hwĕlm') tr. *(to overcome)* sumergir, tragarse; *(to defeat)* arrollar, aplastar; *(to weigh down)* abrumar <*she was overwhelmed by grief* estaba abrumada de dolor>; *(to lavish)* abrumar, colmar <*they overwhelmed him with compliments* lo abrumaron de elogios>; *(with requests)* acosar ♦ **to be overwhelmed with joy** rebosar de contento • **we were overwhelmed by letters** las cartas nos llegaban a montones.

o·ver·whelm·ing (ō'vər-hwĕl'mĭng) adj. *(staggering)* abrumador; *(victory, success)* arrollador; *(majority)* inmenso; *(irresistible)* incontenible, irresistible.

o·ver·work **I.** tr. (ō′vər-wûrk′) *(to work too hard)* hacer trabajar demasiado, abusar de; *(to repeat excessively)* valerse excesivamente de, abusar de —intr. trabajar demasiado **II.** s. (ō′vər-wûrk′) exceso de trabajo.

o·ver·write (ō′vər-rīt′) tr. & intr. **-wrote** (-rōt′), **-writ·ten** (-rĭt′n), **-writ·ing** escribir demasiado, elaborar excesivamente.

o·ver·wrought (ō′vər-rôt′) adj. *(agitated)* muy alterado, sobrexcitado; *(extremely ornate)* recargado.

o·vi·duct (ō′vĭ-dŭkt′) s. ANAT. oviducto.

o·vip·a·rous (ō-vĭp′ər-əs) adj. BIOL. ovíparo.

o·void (ō′void′) o **o·voi·dal** (ō-voi′dl) adj. ovoide.

o·vu·late (ō′vyə-lāt′, ŏv′yə-) intr. **-lat·ed, -lat·ing** BIOL. ovular.

o·vule (ō′vyōōl, ŏv′yōōl) s. BOT., ZOOL. óvulo.

o·vum (ō′vəm) s. [pl. **o·va** (ō′və)] BIOL. óvulo.

owe (ō) tr. **owed, ow·ing** *(financially, morally)* deber <*I o. him an apology* le debo disculpas>; *(to be indebted for)* deber <*he owes his success to his father* le debe su éxito al padre> ♦ **to o. it to oneself** merecérselo • **to o. someone for** deber a alguien • **to o. someone thanks for** estarle agradecido a alguien por —intr. deber, tener deudas.

ow·ing (ō′ĭng) adj. por saldar, por pagarse.

owing to prep. debido a, por (causa de).

owl (oul) s. ORNIT. lechuza, búho.

owl·ish (ou′lĭsh) adj. semejante a una lechuza.

own (ōn) **I.** adj. propio <*in my o. house* en mi propia casa> ♦ **by their o. admission** según ellos mismos lo reconocieron • **he buys his o. cigarettes** él mismo se compra los cigarrillos • **it's my o. money** es mi dinero • **of her o. accord** por su propia voluntad • **to be one's o. man** *(to be independent)* no depender de nadie; *(to think independently)* ser una persona con gran libertad de criterio **II.** s. lo mío, lo tuyo, lo suyo, lo nuestro, lo vuestro ♦ **all of one's o.** muy de uno • **of one's o.** *(belonging to oneself)* propio <*they have a business of their o.* tienen su propio negocio>; *(peculiar to oneself)* de uno; *(for use by oneself)* para uno <*they gave me a card of my o.* me dieron una tarjeta para mí> • **to be on one's o.** *(to be independent)* no depender de nadie, arreglárselas por cuenta propia; *(to be alone)* estar solo • **to call something one's o.** decir que algo le pertenece a uno • **to come into one's o.** lograr el éxito merecido • **to do something on one's o.** *(unaided)* hacer algo sin ayuda de nadie; *(independently)* hacer algo por cuenta propia; *(without authorization)* hacer algo sin contar con nadie • **to get one's o. back** tomar revancha, desquitarse • **to hold one's o.** *(to maintain one's place)* mantenerse firme, saberse defender; *(with somebody)* mantenerse al nivel de (alguien); *(in a skill)* defenderse **III.** tr. *(to have)* ser dueño de, tener <*he owns a business* tiene un negocio>; *(to admit)* reconocer; *(to confess)* confesar ♦ **to o. up to** confesar • **who owns this scarf?** ¿de quién es esta bufanda? —intr. ♦ **to o. up** confesar.

own·er (ō′nər) s. dueño, propietario.

own·er·ship (ō′nər-shĭp′) s. *(state)* posesión f; *(legal right)* propiedad f.

ox (ŏks) s. [pl. **ox·en** (ŏk′sən)] ZOOL. buey m.

ox·bow (ŏks′bō′) s. *(of an ox)* collera de yugo; *(of a river)* recodo, meandro.

ox·en (ŏk′sən) pl. de **ox.**

ox·eye (ŏks′ī′) s. BOT. ojo de buey, albihar m; ARQ. ojo de buey.

ox·ford (ŏks′fərd) s. *(shoe)* zapato bajo con cordones; TEJ. *(cloth)* tela de algodón.

ox·i·dant (ŏk′sĭ-dnt) s. QUÍM. oxidante m.

ox·i·da·tion (ŏk′sĭ-dā′shən) s. QUÍM. oxidación f.

ox·ide (ŏk′sīd′) s. QUÍM. óxido.

ox·i·dize (ŏk′sĭ-dīz′) tr. & intr. **-dized, -diz·ing** QUÍM. oxidar(se).

Ox·o·ni·an (ŏk-sō′nē-ən) adj. & s. oxoniense (de la ciudad o universidad de Oxford) mf.

ox·tail (ŏks′tāl′) s. rabo de buey.

ox·y·a·cet·y·lene (ŏk′sē-ə-sĕt′l-ĭn) adj. QUÍM. oxiacetilénico.

ox·y·gen (ŏk′sĭ-jən) s. QUÍM. oxígeno.

ox·y·gen·ate (ŏk′sĭ-jə-nāt′) o **ox·y·gen·ize** (-nīz′) tr. **-at·ed, -at·ing** o **-ized, -iz·ing** QUÍM. oxigenar.

ox·y·gen·a·tion (ŏk′sĭ-jə-nā′shən) s. QUÍM. oxigenación f.

oxygen mask s. MED. máscara de oxígeno.

oxygen tent s. MED. tienda de oxígeno.

ox·y·mo·ron (ŏk′sē-môr′ŏn′) s. RET. oxímoron m.

o·yez (ō′yĕs′, ō′yĕz′) interj. DER. ¡oíd!, ¡atención!

oys·ter (oi′stər) s. ZOOL. ostra.

oys·ter·man (oi′stər-mən) s. [pl. **-men**] *(person)* ostricultor m, ostrero; *(ship)* barco ostrero.

o·zone (ō′zōn′) s. QUÍM. ozono; FIG., FAM. *(fresh air)* aire puro o fresco.

ozone layer s. METEOR. ozonosfera.

o·zo·no·sphere (ō-zō′nə-sfîr′) s. METEOR. ozonosfera.

P

p, P (pē) s. [pl. **p's, P's**] decimosexta letra del alfabeto inglés ♦ **to mind one's p's and q's** tener cuidado con lo que uno hace.

pa (pä) s. FAM. papá m.

pab·u·lum (păb′yə-ləm) s. pábulo, alimento.

pace (pās) **I.** s. *(step)* paso; *(walking speed)* paso <*she quickened her p.* apresuró el paso>; *(speed of an activity)* ritmo, tren m <*the fast p. of modern life* el ritmo acelerado de la vida moderna>; *(manner of walking)* paso, modo de andar; *(of a horse)* paso ♦ **at a snail's p.** a paso de tortuga • **to keep p. with** *(to match the speed of)* avanzar al mismo paso que, no quedarse atrás con relación a; *(to keep abreast of)* mantenerse al corriente de • **to set the p.** *(to set the speed)* fijar el paso, establecer el ritmo; *(to set an example)* dar la pauta • **to put someone through his paces** poner a alguien a prueba **II.** tr. **paced, pac·ing** *(to stride across)* ir y venir por, pasearse por; *(to measure)* medir a pasos; *(to set the speed)* establecer el paso de ♦ **to p. off** medir a pasos • **to p. oneself** coger el ritmo de uno —intr. *(to walk)* pasear; *(horse)* andar al paso.

pace·mak·er (pās′mā′kər) s. *(person)* corredor que toma la delantera m; MED. marcapasos, marcapaso.

pac·er (pā′sər) s. *(horse)* caballo de paso de andadura; *(person)* el que marca el paso.

pace·set·ter (pās′sĕt′ər) s. *(pacer)* el que marca el paso; *(leader)* el que da la pauta.

pach·y·derm (păk′ĭ-dûrm′) s. ZOOL. paquidermo.

pa·cif·ic (pə-sĭf′ĭk) o **pa·cif·i·cal** (-ĭ-kəl) adj. pacífico.

Pacific Ocean s. océano Pacífico.

pac·i·fi·ca·tion (păs′ə-fĭ-kā′shən) s. pacificación f.

pac·i·fi·er (păs′ə-fī′ər) s. *(one that pacifies)* pacificador m; *(for a baby)* chupete m.

pac·i·fism (păs′ə-fĭz′əm) s. pacifismo.

pac·i·fist (păs′ə-fĭst) s. pacifista mf.

pac·i·fy (păs′ə-fī′) tr. **-fied, -fy·ing** pacificar, apaciguar.

pack (păk) **I.** s. *(bundle)* paquete m, fardo; *(knapsack)* mochila; *(batch)* lote m; *(small package)* paquete, caja; *(of cigarettes)* cajetilla; *(of matches)* cajita; *(of cards)* baraja; *(of dogs)* jauría; *(of wolves)* manada; *(of people)* pandilla, banda; *(cosmetic paste)* máscara; MED. *(gauze)* compresa; *(ice pack)* compresa de hielo ♦ **a p. of lies** una sarta de mentiras **II.** tr. *(to wrap up)* envolver; *(to fill up)* llenar; *(for traveling)* hacer, preparar <*to p. a suitcase* hacer una maleta>; *(for shipping)* embalar; *(to place into)* poner <*p. everything into that box* pon todo en esa caja>; *(to package)* empacar, empaquetar; *(to crowd together)* apiñar, apretar <*they packed everybody into the same room* apiñaron a todo el mundo en la misma habitación>; *(to compact)* prensar; *(a voting panel)* llenar de partidarios; MED. envolver en paños ♦ **to p. a hard punch** FAM. tener un puño de hierro, pegar duro • **to p. a pistol** FAM. llevar una pistola • **to p. down** prensar, comprimir • **to p. it in** ponerle punto final • **to p. someone off to** despachar a alguien para, mandar a alguien para • **to be packed in like sardines** estar como sardinas en lata • **to send someone packing** mandar a alguien con la mú-

---

sica a otra parte, mandar a alguien a paseo —intr. *(for traveling)* hacer las maletas; *(to become compacted)* prensarse, endurecerse; *(dirt)* formar terrones; *(people)* apiñarse, apretarse ♦ **to p. up** *(for traveling)* hacer las maletas; *(to leave)* liar el petate, recoger los bártulos.

pack·age (păk′ĭj) I. s. *(parcel)* paquete *m*; *(container)* envase *m*; *(bundle)* bulto II. tr. **-aged, -ag·ing** empaquetar, envasar.

package deal s. COM. propuesto *o* transacción *f* global; POL. convenio global.

package store s. tienda de vinos y licores.

package tour s. viaje de turismo con todo incluido *m*.

pack·ag·ing (păk′ĭ-jĭng) s. embalaje *m*, envase *m*.

pack animal s. animal de carga *m*.

packed (păkt) adj. *(crowded)* lleno, atestado <*a p. auditorium* un auditorio atestado>; *(compressed)* apiñado; FAM. *(filled with)* lleno de <*a thrill-p. television program* un programa de televisión lleno de emoción>.

pack·er (păk′ər) s. embalador *m*, envasador *m*.

pack·et (păk′ĭt) s. *(small package)* paquete pequeño; *(boat)* paquebote *m*; JER. *(sum of money)* dineral *m*.

pack·horse (păk′hôrs′) s. caballo de carga.

pack·ing (păk′ĭng) s. *(process, material)* embalaje *m*, envase *m*; *(filling)* relleno; MED. paño caliente.

pack rat s. ZOOL. animal roedor de América del Norte *m*.

pack·sad·dle (păk′săd′l) s. albarda.

pack train s. reata de animales de carga.

pact (păkt) s. pacto, convenio.

pad¹ (păd) I. s. *(cushion)* almohadilla, cojín *m*; *(stuffing)* relleno; *(on the floor)* colchoneta; *(on the shoulders)* hombrera; *(on the chest)* peto; *(on the knees)* rodillera; *(saddle)* albardilla; *(for inking)* tampón *m*, almohadilla; *(of paper)* bloc *m*; *(leaf)* hoja grande; *(of animals)* pulpejo; *(paw)* pata; *(launch pad)* pista de lanzamiento; JER. *(apartment)* nido, guarida II. tr. **pad·ded, pad·ding** *(to place a cushion on)* poner una almohadilla *o* un cojín a; *(to upholster)* rellenar; *(clothes)* forrar, enguatar; *(an armrest, crib)* forrar, acolchonar; *(the shoulders)* poner hombreras en; FAM. *(to lengthen)* rellenar (informe); *(an account)* hinchar, aumentar.

pad² (păd) I. intr. **pad·ded, pad·ding** *(to go about)* andar, caminar; *(to walk inaudibly)* pisar suavemente, avanzar silenciosamente —tr. recorrer (camino) a pie II. s. paso quedo, pisada silenciosa.

pad·ded (păd′ĭd) adj. *(provided with a cushion)* con una almohadilla *o* un cojín; *(upholstered)* rellenar; *(clothes)* forrado, enguatado; *(armrest, crib)* acolchonado; *(shoulders)* con hombreras; *(speech, report)* rellenado; *(account)* hinchado, aumentado ♦ **p. cell** celda acolchonada.

pad·ding (păd′ĭng) s. *(act)* acolchado, enguatado; *(material)* relleno; FIG. *(in speech, writing)* relleno.

pad·dle¹ (păd′l) I. s. *(oar)* pagaya, canalete *m*; *(of waterwheel)* paleta, álabe *m*; *(for mixing, for beating clothes)* paleta; ZOOL. *(flipper)* aleta II. intr. **-dled, -dling** *(to row)* remar con pagaya; *(to move)* chapotear —tr. *(to propel)* hacer avanzar con pagaya; *(to stir)* mover con una paleta; *(to spank)* azotar.

pad·dle² (păd′l) intr. **-dled, -dling** *(splash)* chapotear; *(to toddle)* hacer pinitos, andar a gatas.

paddle boat s. MARÍT. vapor de ruedas *m*, hidropedal *m*.

paddle wheel s. MARÍT. rueda de paletas *o* de álabes.

pad·dock (păd′ək) I. s. *(large enclosure)* potrero, dehesa; *(corral)* paddock *m*, corral de exhibición *m* II. tr. encerrar en un potrero.

pad·dy (păd′ē) s. [pl. **-dies**] *(rice)* arroz con cáscara *m*; *(rice field)* arrozal *m*.

paddy wagon s. JER. coche celular *m*.

pad·lock (păd′lŏk′) I. s. candado II. tr. cerrar con candado.

pa·dre (pä′drā, -drē) s. padre *m*.

pae·an (pē′ən, -ŏn′) s. peán *m*.

pa·gan (pā′gən) I. s. RELIG. pagano; *(hedonist)* hedonista *mf* II. adj. pagano.

pa·gan·ism (pā′gə-nĭz′əm) s. paganismo.

page¹ (pāj) I. s. HIST. *(in chivalry, at court)* paje *m*, escudero; *(at wedding)* paje; *(in hotel)* botones *m*; *(in theater)* acomodador *m*; DER. *(in court)* paje II. tr. **paged, pag·ing** *(to summon)* llamar; *(to attend)* servir como paje.

page² (pāj) I. s. *(of paper)* página; *(type set)* plana, molde *m*; *(memorable event)* página <*an exciting p. in American history* una página emocionante de la historia americana>; COMPUT. página, segmento de programas *o* datos (de longitud fija) II. tr. **paged, pag·ing** *(to number)* paginar (las páginas); *(to order)* compaginar (libro, revista) —intr. hojear, pasar las páginas (de un libro).

pag·eant (păj′ənt) s. *(show)* espectáculo, celebración *f*; *(procession)* desfile histórico, cabalgata histórica; *(pageantry)* pompa, boato.

pag·eant·ry (păj′ən-trē) s. [pl. **-ries**] *(spectacle)* espectáculo; *(pomp)* pompa; *(flashy display)* exhibición llamativa.

page boy s. *(at court, wedding)* paje *m*; *(at a hotel)* botones *m*, mensajero.

pag·i·nate (păj′ə-nāt′) tr. **-nat·ed, -nat·ing** paginar.

pag·i·na·tion (păj′ə-nā′shən) s. paginación *f*.

pa·go·da (pə-gō′də) s. pagoda.

paid (pād) pret. y part. p. de **pay**.

pail (pāl) s. cubo, balde (recipiente y contenido) *m*.

pain (pān) I. s. *(physical sensation)* dolor *m*; *(distress)* pena, sufrimiento ♦ **on** *o* **under p. of** so pena de, bajo pena de • **pains** MED. dolores del parto; *(efforts)* esfuerzos; *(care)* cuidado • **to be a p. in the neck** FIG., FAM. *o* **to be a p. in the ass** JER., VULG. *(somebody)* ser un pesado; *(something)* ser una lata, dar lata • **to be in p.** tener dolores, sufrir • **to take pains** *(efforts)* hacer esfuerzos, empeñarse; *(care)* esmerarse II. tr. *(physically)* doler <*my arm pains me* me duele el brazo>; *(mentally)* dar pena, dar lástima —intr. doler.

pain·ful (pān′fəl) adj. *(hurtful)* doloroso; FIG. *(difficult)* difícil, penoso; *(pitiful)* lastimoso, lamentable.

pain·kill·er (pān′kĭl′ər) s. calmante *m*.

pain·less (pān′lĭs) adj. indoloro, sin dolor.

pains·tak·ing (pānz′tā′kĭng) I. adj. esmerado, cuidadoso II. s. esmero, cuidado.

paint (pānt) I. s. *(coating)* pintura; *(coloring matter)* colorante *m*; FAM. *(make-up)* pintura, afeite *m*; *(pinto)* caballo pinto II. tr. *(picture, house)* pintar; FAM. *(to make up)* pintar, maquillar; FIG. *(to depict)* pintar, describir; MED. dar toques (de tintura) a —intr. *(as a hobby)* pintar <*I love to p.* me encanta pintar>; *(as a profession)* pintar, ser pintor <*I didn't know you p.* no sabía que eras pintor> ♦ **to p. the town red** JER. irse de juerga, tirar una cana al aire.

paint·brush (pānt′brŭsh′) s. *(for house painters)* brocha; ARTE. pincel *m*.

paint·er (pān′tər) s. pintor (obrero y artista) *m*.

paint·ing (pān′tĭng) s. *(process)* pintura; *(picture)* pintura, cuadro.

pair (pâr) I. s. [pl. **pair** *o* **pairs**] *(two of a kind)* par *m* <*a p. of shoes* un par de zapatos>; *(persons, mated animals)* pareja <*a p. of hunters* una pareja de cazadores>; *(of horses)* tronco; *(of oxen)* yunta; *(in cards)* par, pareja ♦ **p. of pants** par de pantalones, pantalones • **p. of pliers** alicates • **in pairs** de dos en dos II. tr. *(to match up)* parear, casar; *(to group)* juntar, emparejar; *(to mate)* aparear —intr. hacer pareja, hacer juego ♦ **to p. off** *o* **up** formar parejas.

pa·ja·mas (pə-jä′məz, -jăm′əz) s.pl. pijama *m*, piyama *m*.

Pak·i·stan (păk′ĭ-stăn′, pä′kĭ-stän′) s. Pakistán *m*.

Pak·i·stan·i (păk′ĭ-stăn′ē, pä′kĭ-stän′ē) adj. & s. pakistaní *mf*, paquistano.

pal (păl) I. s. FAM. amigote *m*, compinche *m* II. intr. **palled, pal·ling** ♦ **to p. around with** ser amigo de • **to p. up with** hacerse amigo de.

pal·ace (păl′ĭs) s. palacio.

pal·a·din (păl′ə-dĭn) s. paladín *m*.

pal·an·quin *o* **pal·an·keen** (păl′ən-kēn′) s. palanquín *m*; litera.

pal·at·a·ble (păl′ə-tə-bəl) adj. *(to the taste)* sabroso, apetitoso; FIG. *(agreeable)* aceptable.

pal·a·tal (păl′ə-tl) I. adj. ANAT. del paladar; FONÉT. palatal II. s. sonido palatal.

pal·ate (păl′ĭt) s. paladar *m*.

pa·la·tial (pə-lā′shəl) adj. *(of a palace)* palaciego; *(splendid)* espléndido, magnífico.

pa·lat·i·nate (pə-lăt′n-āt′) s. palatinado.

pal·a·tine (păl′ə-tīn′) I. s. *(soldier)* soldado palatino; *(official)* funcionario palatino; *(feudal lord)* señor feudal *m* II. adj. palatino.

pa·lav·er (pə-lăv′ər, -lä′vər) I. s. *(idle chatter)* palabrería; *(cajolery)* engatusamiento II. tr. engatusar —intr. palabrear, paliquear.

pale¹ (pāl) s. *(stake)* estaca; *(wooden fence)* empalizada; FIG. *(boundary)* límite *m*, margen *f* ♦ **to be beyond the p.** FIG. no ser aceptable.

pale² (pāl) I. adj. **pal·er, pal·est** *(complexion)* pálido; *(color)* claro <*p. blue* azul claro>; *(dim light)* tenue, sin brillo II. tr. **paled, pal·ing** poner pálido, hacer palidecer —intr. palidecer.

pa·le·og·ra·phy (pā′lē-ŏg′rə-fē) s. *(study)* paleografía; *(documents)* documentos estudiados en paleografía.

Pa·le·o·lith·ic (pā′lē-ə-lĭth′ĭk) adj. & s. GEOL. paleolítico.

pa·le·on·tol·o·gy (pā′lē-ŏn-tŏl′ə-jē) s. paleontología.

Pal·es·tine (păl′ĭ-stīn′) s. Palestina.

Pal·es·tin·i·an (păl′ĭ-stīn′ē-ən) adj. & s. palestino.

pal·ette (păl′ĭt) s. PINT. *(board)* paleta; *(range of colors)* gama de colores.

palette knife s. PINT. espátula.

pal·frey (pôl′frē) s. [pl. **-freys**] ANT. palafrén (caballo manso) *m*.

pal·i·mo·ny (păl′ə-mō′nē) s. FAM. asignación que, por mandato judicial, da un hombre a su antigua amante *o* compañera.

pal·imp·sest (păl′ĭmp-sĕst′) s. palimpsesto.

pal·in·drome (păl′ĭn-drōm′) s. palíndromo.

pal·i·sade (păl′ĭ-sād′) I. s. *(fence)* estacada, cerca; *(stake)* estaca ♦ **palisades** acantilado, risco II. tr. **-sad·ed, -sad·ing** empalizar, cercar.

pall¹ (pôl) s. *(of a coffin)* paño mortuorio; *(coffin)* ataúd *m*, féretro; FIG. *(covering)* capa, cortina <*a p. of smoke* una cortina de humo>; RELIG. *(of a chalice)* palia; *(pallium)* palio ♦ **to cast a p. over** producir un efecto deprimente en.

pall² (pôl) intr. *(to become boring)* perder su sabor <*his sense of humor began to p. on us* su sentido de humor empezaba a perder su sabor para nosotros>; *(to become dull)* volverse aburrido; *(to become satiated)* saciarse, cansarse —tr. hartar, empalagar.

pal·la·di·um¹ (pə-lā′dē-əm) s. QUÍM. paladio.

pal·la·di·um² (pə-lā′dē-əm) s. [pl. **-di·a** (-dē-ə) *o* **-di·ums**] *(sacred object)* paladión *m*; FIG. *(safeguard)* salvaguardia, garantía.

pall·bear·er (pôl′bâr′ər) s. portador del féretro *m*.

pal·let¹ (păl′ĭt) s. PINT., TEC. paleta.

pal·let² (păl′ĭt) s. *(pad)* jergón *m*.

pal·li·ate (păl′ē-āt′) tr. **-at·ed, -at·ing** *(to extenuate)* paliar, mitigar; *(to mitigate)* reducir, disminuir.

pal·li·a·tive (păl′ē-ā′tĭv, păl′yə-) adj. & s. paliativo.

pal·lid (păl′ĭd) adj. pálido.

pall-mall (pĕl′mĕl′, păl′măl′, pôl′môl′) s. DEP., HIST. mallo (juego de bolas y mazos).

pal·lor (păl′ər) s. palidez *f*.

palm¹ (päm) I. s. *(of a hand, glove)* palma; *(measure)* palmo; *(of an oar)* pala ♦ **to grease someone's p.** *o* **to cross someone's p.** untar la mano a alguien • **to have an itching p.** ser codicioso • **to know like the p. of one's hand** conocer como la palma de la mano II. tr. *(to conceal)* escamotear; *(to pick up)* escamotear, echar mano a ♦ **to p. something off on someone** encajarle *o* clavarle algo a alguien.

palm² (päm) s. *(tree)* palma, palmera; FIG. *(emblem)* palma (de victoria) ♦ **to bear** *o* **to carry off the p.** llevarse la palma • **to yield the p.** conceder la victoria.

pal·mate (păl′māt′) *o* **pal·mat·ed** (-mā′tĭd) adj. palmeado.

pal·met·to (păl-mĕt′ō) s. [pl. **-tos** *o* **-toes**] BOT. palmito.

palm·ist (pä′mĭst) s. quiromántico.

palm·is·try (pä′mĭ-strē) s. quiromancia.

palm oil s. aceite de palma *m*.

Palm Sunday s. RELIG. Domingo de Ramos.

palm·y (pä′mē) adj. *(full of palms)* lleno de palmas; *(prosperous)* próspero <*p. days* días prósperos>.

pal·o·mi·no (păl′ə-mē′nō) s. [pl. **-nos**] ZOOL. caballo pardusco con la crin y el rabo blancos.

palp (pălp) s. ZOOL. palpo (pieza bucal articulada).

pal·pa·ble (păl′pə-bəl) adj. *(tangible)* palpable; *(obvious)* evidente.

pal·pate (păl′pāt′) tr. **-pat·ed, -pat·ing** palpar.

pal·pi·tate (păl′pĭ-tāt′) intr. **-tat·ed, -tat·ing** palpitar.

pal·pi·ta·tion (păl′pĭ-tā′shən) s. palpitación *f*.

pal·sied (pôl′zēd) adj. MED. paralítico; *(trembling)* temblante.

pal·sy (pôl′zē) I. s. [pl. **-sies**] MED. *(paralysis)* parálisis *f*; *(nervous disorder)* perlesía II. tr. **-sied, -sy·ing** paralizar.

pal·sy-wal·sy (păl′zē-wăl′zē) adj. JER. íntimo.

pal·try (pôl′trē) adj. **-tri·er, -tri·est** *(petty)* miserable; *(insignificant)* insignificante; *(worthless)* despreciable.

pam·pa (păm′pə) s. pampa.

pam·per (păm′pər) tr. *(to coddle)* mimar, consentir; ANT. *(to glut)* saciar, hartar.

pam·phlet (păm′flĭt) s. *(brochure)* folleto; *(lampoon)* panfleto, libelo.

pam·phlet·eer (păm′flĭ-tîr′) I. s. folletista *mf* II. intr. escribir y publicar folletos.

pan¹ (păn) I. s. *(for cooking)* cazuela, cacerola; *(frying pan)* sartén *f*; *(on a scale)* plato, platillo; JER. *(face)* morro, jeta; MIN. batea; GEOL. depresión *f*; ARM. cazoleta II. tr. **panned, pan·ning** MIN. lavar en una batea; FAM. *(to review harshly)* poner por los suelos —intr. ♦ **to p. out** FAM. salir bien, dar buen resultado.

pan² (păn) s. BOT. hoja del betel.

pan³ (păn) intr. & tr. **panned, pan·ning** CINEM. girar la cámara para hacer una toma panorámica (de).

Pan (păn) s. MITOL. Pan *m*.

pan·a·ce·a (păn′ə-sē′ə) s. panacea.

pa·nache (pə-năsh′, -näsh′) s. *(plume)* penacho; *(dash)* brío, garbo.

Pan·a·ma (păn′ə-mä′, -mô′) s. Panamá.

Panama, Isthmus of s. Istmo de Panamá.

Panama Canal s. Canal de Panamá *m*.

Panama hat s. jipijapa *m*, panamá *m*.

Pan·a·ma·ni·an (păn′ə-mā′nē-ən) adj. & s. panameño.

Pan-A·mer·i·can (păn′ə-mĕr′ĭ-kən) adj. panamericano.

pan·cake (păn′kāk′) I. s. hojuela, panqueque *m* II. intr. **-caked, -cak·ing** AVIA. aterrizar casi verticalmente —tr. AVIA. hacer aterrizar un avión casi verticalmente.

pan·chro·mat·ic (păn′krō-măt′ĭk) adj. FOTOG. pancromático.

pan·cre·as (păng′krē-əs) s. ANAT. páncreas *m*.

pan·da (păn′də) s. ZOOL. panda *m*.

pan·dem·ic (păn-dĕm′ĭk) I. adj. *(general)* general; MED. *(epidemic)* pandémico II. s. MED. pandemia.

pan·de·mo·ni·um (păn′də-mō′nē-əm) s. *(uproar)* pandemónium *m*; *(noise)* ruido, alboroto.

pan·der (păn′dər) I. s. alcahuete *m*, proxeneta *mf* II. intr. alcahuetear ♦ **to p. to** satisfacer, agradar.

Pan·do·ra (păn-dôr′ə) s. MITOL. Pandora.

Pandora's box s. caja de Pandora.

pane (pān) s. *(of window, door)* hoja de vidrio; *(glass)* vidrio, cristal *m*; *(panel)* panel *m*.

pan·e·gyr·ic (păn′ə-jîr′ĭk) s. panegírico.

pan·el (păn′əl) I. s. *(of a door, window)* panel *m*; *(of a ceiling)* artesón *m*; *(of a wall)* entrepaño *m*; *(of a fence)* tramo; *(of a dress)* tabla, paño; *(for oil painting)* panel, tabla; *(jury)* jurado; *(group)* grupo <*p. of experts* grupo de expertos>; ELEC. tablero, cuadro de distribución; AER., AUTO. panel, tablero de instrumentos II. tr. *(a door, wall)* poner paneles en; *(a dress)* hacer tablas *o* paños a; *(a jury)* elegir.

panel discussion s. discusión de un tema de interés general por un grupo de personas *f*.

pan·el·ing (păn′ə-lĭng) s. ARQ., CARP. revestimiento de madera.

pan·el·ist (păn′ə-lĭst) s. miembro de un grupo de discusión.

panel truck s. camioneta de reparto.

pang (păng) s. *(of pain)* punzada, dolor agudo; FIG. *(of con-*

science) remordimiento; *(emotional distress)* tormento, angustia.

pan·han·dle¹ (păn′hăn′dl) tr. & intr. **-dled, -dling** FAM. mendigar, pedir.

pan·han·dle² (păn′hăn′dl) s. mango de sartén *o* caldero.

pan·han·dler (păn′hăn′dlər) s. FAM. mendigo, pordiosero.

Pan-Hel·len·ic *o* **Pan·hel·len·ic** (păn′hə-lĕn′ĭk) adj. panhelénico.

pan·ic (păn′ĭk) I. s. *(terror)* pánico; JER. *(funny person)* persona extremadamente chistosa II. adj. pánico ♦ **P.** MITOL. relativo al dios Pan III. tr. & intr. **-icked, -ick·ing** aterrar(se), asustar(se).

panic button s. FIG. botón que se aprieta demostrando pánico *m;* *(response)* respuesta apresurada.

pan·ick·y (păn′ĭ-kē) adj. lleno de pánico, aterrorizado ♦ **to get p.** entrarle pánico a uno.

pan·ic-strick·en (păn′ĭk-strĭk′ən) adj. lleno de pánico, sobrecogido de terror.

pan·nier (păn′yər, păn′ē-ər) s. *(basket)* cesto, canasta; *(on a pack animal)* serón *m;* *(of a skirt)* miriñaque *m.*

pan·o·ply (păn′ə-plē) s. [pl. **-plies**] panoplia.

pan·o·ram·a (păn′ə-răm′ə, -rä′mə) s. *(view)* panorama *m;* CINEM. panorámica.

pan·o·ram·ic (păn′ə-răm′ĭk) adj. panorámico.

pan·pipe (păn′pīp′) s. MÚS. zampoña, siringa.

pan·sy (păn′zē) s. [pl. **-sies**] BOT. pensamiento, trinitaria; JER. *(homosexual)* marica *m.*

pant (pănt) I. intr. *(to breathe)* jadear; *(to throb)* palpitar, latir ♦ **to p. for** *o* **after** suspirar por, anhelar —tr. pronunciar con palabras entrecortadas II. s. *(gasp)* jadeo; *(of an engine)* resoplido; *(throb)* latido, palpitación *f.*

pan·ta·loon (păn′tə-lōōn′) s. ♦ **pantaloons** pantalones *m.*

pant·dress (pănt′drĕs′) s. falda pantalón *f.*

pan·the·ism (păn′thē-ĭz′əm) s. panteísmo.

pan·the·on (păn′thē-ŏn′) s. panteón *m.*

pan·ther (păn′thər) s. ZOOL. pantera.

pant·ies (păn′tēz) s.pl. bragas, bombachas.

pan·ting (păn′tĭng) I. s. jadeo II. adj. jadeante.

pan·to·graph (păn′tə-grăf′) s. pantógrafo.

pan·to·mime (păn′tə-mīm′) I. s. TEAT. *(performance)* pantomima; *(actor)* pantomimo, mimo II. tr. **-mimed, -miming** representar por gestos —intr. expresarse por medio de gestos.

pan·try (păn′trē) s. [pl. **-tries**] despensa.

pants (pănts) s.pl. *(trousers)* pantalones *m;* *(underpants)* calzoncillos *m* ♦ **to be caught with one's p. down** ser sorprendido en una posición embarazosa • **to wear the p. in the family** mandar en la familia.

pant·suit *o* **pants suit** (pănt′sōōt′) s. traje de mujer con pantalones *m.*

pant·y·hose (păn′tē-hōz′) s. media pantalón (prenda interior).

pant·y·waist (păn′tē-wāst′) s. JER. hombre afeminado.

pap (păp) s. *(food)* papilla; *(something insubstantial)* tonterías; JER. *(favors)* patrocinio político.

pa·pa (pä′pə, pə-pä′) s. papá *m.*

pa·pa·cy (pā′pə-sē) s. [pl. **-cies**] papado, pontificado.

pa·pal (pā′pəl) adj. papal, pontificio.

pa·pa·ya (pə-pī′ə) s. BOT. *(tree)* papayo; *(fruit)* papaya.

pa·per (pā′pər) I. s. *(material)* papel *m;* *(document)* documento; *(essay)* ensayo, informe *m;* *(composition)* trabajo escrito, composición *f;* *(in a symposium)* ponencia, disertación *f* ‹*to give a p.* dar una disertación›; *(newspaper)* periódico, diario; JER. *(free pass)* entrada de favor; COM. papel, letra ♦ **blotting p.** papel secante • **brown p.** papel de estraza, papel de empaquetar • **drawing p.** papel de dibujo • **filter p.** papel de filtro • **glossy p.** papel cuché • **music p.** papel pautado *o* de música • **on p.** *(in writing)* por escrito; *(in theory)* sobre el papel ‹*it looks good on p.* sobre el papel, parece bueno› • **papers** *(personal writings)* papeles *(privados)*; *(identity papers)* papeles, documentación *(personales)*; *(ship's papers)* patente de navegación, papeles de a bordo • **ruled p.** papel de rayas • **tissue p.** papel de seda • **to get down on p.** apuntar • **to put pen to p.** empezar a escribir • **tracing p.** papel de calcar • **wax p.** waxed p.** papel encerado • **weekly p.** semanario • **wrap-**

ping p. papel de envolver II. tr. *(to wrap)* envolver; *(to wallpaper)* empapelar; JER. *(a theater)* repartir entradas de favor para ♦ **to p. over** *(to conceal)* tapar, esconder; *(to play down)* restar importancia a III. adj. *(made of paper)* de papel ‹*a p. doll* una muñeca de papel›; *(theoretical)* teórico, por realizar ♦ **p. cup** vaso de cartón • **p. industry** industria papelera • **p. mill** fábrica de papel, papelera • **p. plate** plato de cartón.

pa·per·back (pā′pər-băk′) s. libro en rústica, libro de bolsillo.

pa·per·board (pā′pər-bôrd′) s. cartón *m.*

pa·per·bound (pā′pər-bound′) adj. en rústica.

paper bag s. saco *o* bolsa de papel.

paper boy s. vendedor de periódicos *m,* repartidor de periódicos *m.*

paper clip s. sujetapapeles *m,* presilla.

paper cutter s. guillotina, cortapapeles *m.*

pa·per·hang·er (pā′pər-hăng′ər) s. *(paperer)* empapelador *m;* JER. *(one who passes bad checks)* el que gira cheques sin fondos.

pa·per·knife (pā′pər-nīf′) s. [pl. **-knives** (-nīvz′)] cortapapeles *m.*

paper money s. papel moneda *m,* billete de banco *m.*

pa·per·weight (pā′pər-wāt′) s. pisapapeles *m.*

pap·er·work *o* **paper work** (pā′pər-wûrk′) s. papeleo *m.*

pa·pier-mâ·ché (pā′pyā-mä-shā′) s. cartón piedra *m,* papel maché *m.*

pa·pil·la (pə-pĭl′ə) s. [pl. **-pil·lae** (-pĭl′lē)] ANAT. papila.

pa·pist (pā′pĭst) s. DESPEC. papista *mf.*

pa·poose *o* **pap·poose** (pă-pōōs′) s. niño indio norteamericano.

pap·py¹ (păp′ē) adj. **-pi·er, -pi·est** *(doughy)* pastoso; *(mushy)* blando.

pap·py² (păp′ē) s. [pl. **-pies**] papá *m,* papi *m.*

pa·pri·ka (pə-prē′kə, păp′rĭ-) s. *(spice)* paprika, pimentón *m;* *(color)* pimiento rojo vivo.

Pap test (păp) s. MED. examen Pap *o* Papanicolaou (del cuello del útero *o* la vagina para detectar el cáncer) *m.*

Pap·u·an (păp′yōō-ən) adj. & s. papú *mf.*

Pap·u·a New Guin·ea (păp′yōō-ə nōō′ gĭn′ē) s. Papua Nueva Guinea.

pa·py·rus (pə-pī′rəs) s. [pl. **-rus·es** *o* **-ri** (-rī′)] papiro.

par (pär) I. s. *(average)* promedio; *(equivalence)* igualdad *f,* paridad *f;* *(in golf)* par *m;* COM. *(face value)* valor nominal *m;* *(parity)* par, paridad ♦ **to be on a p. with** ser igual a, estar en un pie de igualdad con • **to buy at p.** COM. comprar a la par • **to place something on a p. with** equiparar algo con II. tr. **parred, par·ring** hacer par III. adj. *(normal)* normal, regular; COM. *(nominal)* nominal; *(at parity)* a la par ♦ **that's p. for the course** FIG., FAM. eso es normal *o* regular.

par·a·ble (păr′ə-bəl) s. RELIG. parábola.

pa·rab·o·la (pə-răb′ə-lə) s. GEOM. parábola (línea curva).

par·a·bol·ic (păr′ə-bŏl′ĭk) *o* **par·a·bol·i·cal** (-ĭ-kəl) adj. GEOM., RELIG. parabólico.

par·a·chute (păr′ə-shōōt′) I. s. AER. paracaídas *m;* ZOOL. patagio, membrana alar II. tr. **-chut·ed, -chut·ing** lanzar *o* dejar caer en paracaídas —intr. saltar en paracaídas.

par·a·chut·ist (păr′ə-shōō′tĭst) s. paracaidista *mf.*

pa·rade (pə-rād′) I. s. *(procession)* procesión *f,* desfile *m;* *(succession)* desfile, presentación *f* ‹*a p. of fads and styles* desfile de modas y estilos›; *(pompous display)* ostentación *f,* alarde *m* ‹*a p. of wealth* un alarde de riqueza›; *(bandwagon)* causa triunfante; *(promenade)* paseo público; MIL. *(of troops)* revista *o* desfile de tropas, parada II. tr. **-raded, -rad·ing** *(to march)* hacer desfilar; *(to flaunt)* exhibir, hacer alarde de ♦ **to p. down** *o* **up** pasearse por • **to p. the troops** MIL. hacer desfilar las tropas —intr. *(to take part)* desfilar; MIL. formar en parada ♦ **to p. around** FAM. pasearse, caminar ‹*to p. around the house in one's underwear* caminar por la casa en ropa interior›.

par·a·digm (păr′ə-dīm′, -dĭm′) s. GRAM. paradigma *m;* *(example)* modelo, paradigma.

par·a·dise (păr′ə-dīs′, -dīz′) s. *(heaven)* cielo, gloria; *(delight)* paraíso ♦ **P.** Edén.

par·a·dox (păr′ə-dŏks′) s. paradoja.

---

ng inglés / ŏ la / ō bou / ô corre / oi oigo / ōō uno / ou auto / yōō ciudad / w hueco / y yo / z mismo

par·a·dox·i·cal (păr'ə-dŏk'sĭ-kəl) adj. paradójico.

par·af·fin (păr'ə-fĭn) I. s. *(wax)* parafina; G.B. *(fuel)* petróleo, queroseno II. tr. parafinar.

par·a·gon (păr'ə-gŏn') s. *(perfection)* dechado, modelo; *(diamond)* diamante perfecto; IMPR. paragona.

par·a·graph (păr'ə-grăf') I. s. *(section)* párrafo, parágrafo; *(mark)* párrafo ♦ **new p.** punto y aparte II. tr. dividir en párrafos.

Par·a·guay (păr'ə-gwī', -gwā') s. Paraguay m.

Par·a·guay·an (păr'ə-gwī'ən, -gwā'-) adj. & s. paraguayo.

par·a·keet (păr'ə-kēt') s. ORNIT. perico, periquito.

par·al·lax (păr'ə-lăks') s. OPT. paralaje (cambio aparente de la posición de un objeto al cambiar el punto de observación) f.

par·al·lel (păr'ə-lĕl') I. adj. paralelo <*p. curves* curvas paralelas>; *(like)* paralelo, análogo <*p. arguments* razonamientos análogos>; *(corresponding)* correspondiente; ELEC., GRAM., MÚS. paralelo II. adv. en línea paralela III. s. GEOM. paralela; *(match)* igual m <*an action without p.* una acción sin igual>; *(comparison)* paralelo, analogía; GEOG. paralelo <*the 25th p.* el paralelo 25>; IMPR. barras ♦ **to draw a p. between** establecer un paralelo entre, comparar IV. tr. *(to place parallel to)* colocar en paralela con; *(to be parallel to)* extenderse en línea paralela a; *(to match)* ser igual a, correr parejo con; *(to compare with)* comparar con, ser análogo a <*her story parallels mine* su historia es análoga a la mía>.

parallel bars s.pl. DEP. barras paralelas.

par·al·lel·e·pi·ped (păr'ə-lĕl'ə-pī'pĭd) s. GEOM. paralelepípedo.

par·al·lel·ism (păr'ə-lĕl-ĭz'əm) s. paralelismo.

par·al·lel·o·gram (păr'ə-lĕl'ə-grăm') s. GEOM. paralelogramo.

pa·ral·y·sis (pə-răl'ĭ-sĭs) s. [pl. **-ses** (-sēz')] MED. parálisis f; *(stoppage)* paralización f, estancamiento.

par·a·lyt·ic (păr'ə-lĭt'ĭk) adj. & s. paralítico.

par·a·ly·za·tion (păr'ə-lĭ-zā'shən) s. paralización f.

par·a·lyze (păr'ə-līz') tr. **-lyzed, -lyz·ing** MED. paralizar; *(to make helpless)* paralizar <*paralyzed by fear* paralizado de miedo>; *(to obstruct)* entorpecer, paralizar.

par·a·lyz·er (păr'ə-lī'zər) s. paralizador m.

par·a·me·cium (păr'ə-mē'shəm) s. [pl. **-cia** (-shə) o **-ciums**] ZOOL. paramecio.

par·a·med·ic (păr'ə-mĕd'ĭk) s. integrante de la profesión paramédica mf.

pa·ram·e·ter (pə-răm'ĭ-tər) s. MAT. parámetro; FIG. *(boundary)* límite m.

par·a·mil·i·tar·y (păr'ə-mĭl'ĭ-tĕr'ē) adj. paramilitar.

par·a·mount (păr'ə-mount') I. adj. *(foremost)* principal; *(supreme)* superior, supremo II. s. soberano.

par·a·mour (păr'ə-mŏŏr') s. amante mf.

par·a·noi·a (păr'ə-noi'ə) s. PSIC. paranoia.

par·a·noi·ac (păr'ə-noi'ăk') s. & adj. PSIC. paranoico.

par·a·noid (păr'ə-noid') adj. & s. PSIC. paranoico.

par·a·pet (păr'ə-pĭt, -pĕt') s. *(railing)* baranda, antepecho; MIL. parapeto.

par·a·pher·na·lia (păr'ə-fər-nāl'yə, -fə-nāl'-) s.pl. [ú. con v. sing. o pl.] *(belongings)* avíos; *(equipment)* conjunto de aparatos, accesorios; DER. *(property)* bienes parafernales m.

par·a·phrase (păr'ə-frāz') I. s. paráfrasis f II. tr. & intr. **-phrased, -phras·ing** parafrasear.

par·a·ple·gi·a (păr'ə-plē'jē-ə) s. MED. paraplejía, parálisis f.

par·a·ple·gic (păr'ə-plē'jĭk) adj. & s. MED. parapléjico.

par·a·pro·fes·sion·al (păr'ə-prə-fĕsh'ə-nəl) s. ayudante o auxiliar de un profesional mf.

par·a·psy·chol·o·gy (păr'ə-sī-kŏl'ə-jē) s. parapsicología (estudio de fenómenos psicológicos aún no comprendidos).

par·a·site (păr'ə-sīt') s. BIOL. *(organism)* parásito; FIG. *(hanger-on)* parásito, vividor m.

par·a·sit·ic (păr'ə-sĭt'ĭk) o **par·a·sit·i·cal** (-ĭ-kəl) adj. parasítico, parasitario.

par·a·sit·ism (păr'ə-sī-tĭz'əm) s. MED. parasitismo.

par·a·si·tol·o·gy (păr'ə-sī-tŏl'ə-jē) s. BIOL. parasitología.

par·a·sol (păr'ə-sôl') s. parasol m, sombrilla.

par·a·troop·er (păr'ə-trōō'pər) s. MIL. soldado paracaidista.

par·a·troops (păr'ə-trōōps') s.pl. MIL. tropas paracaidistas.

par·boil (pär'boil') tr. CUL. *(to boil)* sancochar; *(to heat up)* calentar bien.

par·cel (pär'səl) I. s. *(package)* paquete m, fardo; *(of land)* parcela; *(consignment)* partida, lote m; *(party)* grupo, partida II. tr. *(to package)* empaquetar ♦ **to p. out** repartir en lotes o porciones, parcelar (terreno).

parcel post s. servicio de paquete o encomienda postal.

parch (pärch) tr. *(to dry out)* resecar; *(to roast)* tostar; *(thirst)* resecar; *(sun)* agostar —intr. resecarse.

parch·ment (pärch'mənt) s. pergamino.

par·don (pär'dn) I. tr. *(to forgive)* perdonar; *(an offense)* remitir, disculpar; *(to excuse)* excusar, dejar pasar ♦ **p. me** perdóneme, dispénseme II. s. *(forgiveness)* perdón m; *(exemption)* indulto (acto y documento); RELIG. indulgencia ♦ **I beg your p.?** ¿cómo?, ¿cómo dijo?

par·don·a·ble (pär'dn-ə-bəl) adj. perdonable, excusable.

par·don·er (pär'dn-ər) s. HIST. buldero.

pare (pâr) tr. **pared, par·ing** *(to peel)* mondar, pelar; *(to clip)* recortar; *(to whittle away)* cortar ♦ **to p. down** disminuir, reducir.

par·e·gor·ic (păr'ə-gôr'ĭk) s. FARM., MED. elíxir paregórico.

par·ent (pâr'ənt) s. *(father)* padre m; *(mother)* madre f; *(forefather)* antepasado, antecesor m; *(cause)* causa, origen m; BIOL. padre (organismo) ♦ **p. company** COM. casa matriz ● **parents** padres.

par·ent·age (pâr'ən-tĭj) s. *(lineage)* linaje m; *(origin)* origen m; *(father)* paternidad f; *(mother)* maternidad f.

pa·ren·tal (pə-rĕn'tl) adj. *(of father)* paternal; *(of mother)* maternal; *(of both parents)* de los padres.

pa·ren·the·sis (pə-rĕn'thĭ-sĭs) s. [pl. **-ses** (-sēz')] GRAM., IMPR., MAT. paréntesis m; FIG. *(interval)* paréntesis, intervalo ♦ **in parentheses** entre paréntesis.

par·en·thet·i·cal (păr'ən-thĕt'ĭ-kəl) o **par·en·thet·ic** (-ĭk) adj. *(explanatory)* explicativo; *(within parentheses)* entre paréntesis.

par·ent·hood (pâr'ənt-hŏŏd') s. *(father)* paternidad f; *(mother)* maternidad f.

pa·re·sis (pə-rē'sĭs, păr'ĭ-) s. MED. paresia.

par·fait (pär-fā') s. postre congelado a base de crema o mantecado.

par·he·lion (pär-hēl'yən) s. [pl. **-he·lia** (-hēl'yə)] METEOR. parhelio.

pa·ri·ah (pə-rī'ə) s. paria mf.

pa·ri·e·tal (pə-rī'ĭ-tl) adj. & s. parietal m ♦ **parietals** reglas de conducta en residencias universitarias.

par·i·mu·tu·el (păr'ĭ-myŏŏ'chŏŏ-əl) s. *(system)* sistema de apuestas mutuas m; *(machine)* totalizador m.

par·ing (pâr'ĭng) s. *(skin)* cáscara; *(peeling)* peladura, mondadura; *(trimming)* recorte m.

paring knife s. cuchillo para mondar.

Par·is¹ (păr'ĭs) s. MITOL. Paris (príncipe de Troya).

Par·is² (păr'ĭs) s. *(city)* París.

par·ish (păr'ĭsh) s. RELIG. parroquia; G.B. subdivisión de un condado f ♦ **p. church** iglesia parroquial ● **p. priest** párroco.

pa·rish·ion·er (pə-rĭsh'ə-nər) s. RELIG. feligrés m.

Pa·ri·sian (pə-rē'zhən, -rĭzh'ən) adj. & s. parisiense mf, parisino.

par·i·ty (păr'ĭ-tē) s. [pl. **-ties**] *(equality)* paridad f, igualdad f <*nuclear p.* igualdad nuclear>; COM. *(value)* paridad.

park (pärk) I. s. *(land)* parque m <*national p.* parque nacional>; DEP. *(stadium)* estadio; *(preserve)* coto; MIL. parque ♦ **car p.** G.B. aparcamiento, playa de estacionamiento II. tr. *(a vehicle)* estacionar, aparcar; FAM. *(to place)* plantar, depositar <*he parked himself on the sofa* se plantó en el sofá>; MIL. agrupar en orden —intr. estacionarse, parquearse ♦ **no parking** prohibido estacionar.

par·ka (pär'kə) s. abrigo de piel con capucha.

parking lot s. aparcamiento, playa de estacionamiento.

parking meter s. parquímetro.

parking place o **parking space** s. plaza o lugar m de estacionamiento.

Par·kin·son's disease (pär'kĭn-sənz) s. MED. enfermedad de Parkinson f.

park·way (pärk'wā') s. avenida, bulevar m.

ã rey / ä año / b boca / ch chico / d dar / ĕ el / ē mil / g gato / h joya / hw juez / ī aire / k casa / kw cuan /

par·lance (pär′ləns) s. *(idiom)* lenguaje *m,* habla *m* <*legal p.* lenguaje legal> ♦ **in common p.** en lenguaje corriente.
par·lay (pär′lā′, -lē) **I.** tr. *(to bet)* apostar un pároli; *(to exploit)* explotar **II.** s. pároli *m.*
par·ley (pär′lē) MIL. **I.** s. [pl. **-leys**] parlamento, negociaciones *f* **II.** intr. parlamentar.
par·lia·ment (pär′lə-mənt) s. POL. parlamento ♦ **P.** G.B. Parlamento.
par·lia·men·tar·i·an (pär′lə-měn-târ′ē-ən) s. parlamentario ♦ **P.** G.B. HIST. partidario del Parlamento Largo.
par·lia·men·ta·ry (pär′lə-měn′tə-rē) adj. parlamentario.
parliamentary law s. DER. reglamento parlamentario.
par·lor (pär′lər) s. *(in a house)* sala de recibo; *(at an inn, tavern)* salita de estar; *(for business)* salón *m* <*beauty p.* salón de belleza> ♦ **funeral p.** funeraria • **ice-cream p.** heladería.
parlor car s. F.C. coche salón *m.*
par·lour (pär′lər) s. G.B. var. de **parlor.**
par·lous (pär′ləs) adj. peligroso.
Par·nas·sus (pär-năs′əs) s. MITOL. Parnaso.
pa·ro·chi·al (pə-rō′kē-əl) adj. RELIG. parroquial; FIG. *(provincial)* provincial.
pa·ro·chi·al·ism (pə-rō′kē-ə-lĭz′əm) s. mentalidad pueblerina.
parochial school s. escuela parroquial.
par·o·dy (pär′ə-dē) **I.** s. [pl. **-dies**] parodia **II.** tr. **-died, -dy·ing** parodiar.
pa·role (pə-rōl′) **I.** s. DER. *(release)* libertad bajo palabra *f*; MIL. *(password)* santo y seña; FIG. *(word of honor)* palabra de honor ♦ **p. officer** policía encargado de vigilar (a un liberado) • **p. violation** DER. violación de la palabra empeñada • **to be out on p.** estar libre bajo palabra **II.** tr. **-roled, -rol·ing** poner en libertad bajo palabra.
pa·rol·ee (pə-rō′lē′) s. convicto en libertad condicional.
pa·rot·id (pə-rŏt′ĭd) s. ANAT. parótida ♦ **p. gland** glándula parótida.
par·ox·ysm (pär′ək-sĭz′əm) s. FIG. *(outburst)* paroxismo; PATOL. *(crisis)* crisis *f*; *(convulsion)* paroxismo.
par·quet (pär-kā′) **I.** s. TEAT. *(main floor)* patio de butacas; *(orchestra)* platea; *(floor of parquetry)* parqué *m,* entarimado **II.** tr. poner parqué, entarimar un piso.
par·quet·ry (pär′kĭ-trē) s. [pl. **-ries**] CARP. entarimado, mosaico de madera.
par·ri·cide (pär′ĭ-sīd′) s. *(person)* parricida *mf*; *(act)* parricidio.
par·rot (pär′ət) **I.** s. *(bird)* papagayo, loro; *(person)* cotorra, loro **II.** tr. repetir como un loro.
par·ry (pär′ē) **I.** tr. **-ried, -ry·ing** ESGR. *(to deflect)* parar, esquivar (un ataque); FIG. *(to evade)* evadir, eludir —intr. ESGR. hacer una parada o un quite **II.** s. [pl. **-ries**] ESGR. *(act)* parada, quite *m*; FIG. *(evasion)* evasión *f,* escape *m.*
parse (pärs) tr. **parsed, pars·ing** GRAM. analizar gramaticalmente —intr. ser analizable gramaticalmente.
par·si·mo·ni·ous (pär′sə-mō′nē-əs) adj. *(stingy)* parsimonioso, avaro; *(sparing)* parco.
par·si·mo·ny (pär′sə-mō′nē) s. *(avarice)* parsimonia, avaricia; *(frugality)* frugalidad *f,* parquedad *f.*
pars·ley (pär′slē) s. perejil *m.*
pars·nip (pär′snĭp′) s. chirivía, pastinaca.
par·son (pär′sən) s. RELIG. *(clergyman)* párroco *m*; *(Protestant clergyman)* pastor protestante *m.*
par·son·age (pär′sə-nĭj) s. RELIG. rectoría, casa parroquial.
part (pärt) **I.** s. *(segment)* parte *f*; *(portion)* parte, porción *f*; *(piece in a machine)* pieza <*spare parts* piezas de repuesto>; *(role)* papel *m*; *(of the hair)* raya del pelo; MÚS. parte; GRAM. parte <*parts of speech* partes de la oración> ♦ **aliquot p.** MAT. parte alícuota • **for my p.** por mi parte, por lo que a mí se refiere • **for the better p. of a week** durante la mayor parte de la semana, casi toda la semana • **for the most p.** generalmente, por lo general • **in p.** en parte • **on the p. of** de parte de • **p. and parcel** parte integrante, parte esencial • **the best p.** lo mejor • **the greater p.** la mayor parte • **to be p. of** formar parte de • **to do one's p.** hacer lo que le corresponde a uno • **to have no p. in** no tener nada que ver con • **to look the p.** parecerlo, venirle bien el papel a uno • **to play a p. in** jugar o

desempeñar un papel en, contribuir a • **to take someone's p.** ponerse de parte de alguien • **to take something in good p.** tomar algo en buena parte • **to take p. in** tomar parte en, participar en • **in these parts** en estas regiones, por estos rumbos • **private parts** ANAT. partes pudendas **II.** tr. *(to divide)* dividir; *(to break)* partir, romper; *(to come between)* apartar <*he parted the boxers* apartó a los boxeadores>; *(to push aside)* abrirse paso entre <*the detective parted the onlookers* el detective se abrió paso entre los curiosos> ♦ **to p. company with** separarse de, romper relaciones con • **to p. one's hair** hacerse la raya • **to p. with** *(to get rid of)* deshacerse de; *(to spend)* soltar, gastar —intr. *(to come apart)* separarse, apartarse; *(to separate)* separarse <*they pledged that they would never p.* juraron que nunca habrían de separarse>; *(to leave)* irse <*she parted without saying goodbye* se fue sin despedirse> **III.** adv. en parte, parcialmente ♦ **it was p. dry** estaba medio seco • **p. yellow, p. green** mitad amarillo y mitad verde **IV.** adj. parcial ♦ **p. owner** copropietario.
par·take (pär-tāk′) intr. **-took** (-tōōk′), **-tak·en** (-tā′kən), **-tak·ing** *(to participate)* participar, tomar parte; *(to have a quality)* tener algo de (una cualidad) —tr. ♦ **to p. in** participar de, tomar parte en • **to p. of** *(to share)* compartir <*will you p. of this delicious meal?* ¿desea compartir esta deliciosa comida?>.
part·ed (pär′tĭd) adj. *(divided)* dividido; *(separated)* separado; BOT. partido; ANT. fallecido, muerto.
par·the·no·gen·e·sis (pär′thə-nō-jěn′ĭ-sĭs) s. ZOOL. partenogénesis *f.*
Par·the·non (pär′thə-nŏn′) s. HIST. Partenón *m.*
par·tial (pär′shəl) adj. *(not total)* parcial, incompleto; *(biased)* parcial; MAT. parcial ♦ **p. to** *(fond of)* partidario, aficionado <*p. to horror movies* aficionado a películas de horror>.
partial fraction s. MAT. fracción parcial *f.*
par·ti·al·i·ty (pär′shē-ăl′ĭ-tē) s. [pl. **-ties**] parcialidad *f* ♦ **p. for** afición a o para.
par·tial·ly (pär′shə-lē) adv. parcialmente, en parte.
par·tic·i·pant (pär-tĭs′ə-pənt) s. & adj. participante *mf,* partícipe *mf.*
par·tic·i·pate (pär-tĭs′ə-pāt′) intr. **-pat·ed, -pat·ing** participar —tr. compartir.
par·tic·i·pa·tion (pär-tĭs′ə-pā′shən) s. participación *f.*
par·tic·i·pa·tor (pär-tĭs′ə-pā′tər) s. participante *mf.*
par·ti·ci·ple (pär′tĭ-sĭp′əl) s. GRAM. participio.
par·ti·cle (pär′tĭ-kəl) s. *(small part)* partícula; FIG. *(trace)* pizca, traza; FÍS., GRAM., RELIG. partícula.
par·ti-col·ored (pär′tē-kŭl′ərd) adj. multicolor.
par·tic·u·lar (pər-tĭk′yə-lər) **I.** adj. *(specific)* particular, en particular <*any p. day?* ¿un día en particular?>; *(special)* particular, especial <*of p. interest* de interés especial>; *(fussy)* exigente, minucioso <*p. housekeeper* ama de llaves minuciosa>; LÓG. privativo, restringido ♦ **in p.** especialmente, en particular • **to be p. about** ser exigente con **II.** s. particularidad *f,* detalle *m* <*in every p.* en cada detalle> ♦ **particulars** pormenores <*to go into particulars* entrar en pormenores>.
par·tic·u·lar·i·ty (pər-tĭk′yə-lăr′ĭ-tē) s. [pl. **-ties**] *(individuality)* particularidad *f*; *(exactitude)* precisión *f,* minuciosidad *f.*
par·tic·u·lar·ize (pər-tĭk′yə-lə-rīz′) tr. **-ized, -iz·ing** *(to itemize)* detallar; *(to specify)* especificar —intr. entrar en detalles, especificar.
par·tic·u·lar·ly (pər-tĭk′yə-lər-lē) adv. *(especially)* especialmente, máxime; *(specifically)* específicamente, en particular; *(individually)* particularmente <*that moment belonged p. to him* ese momento le perteneció particularmente a él>.
part·ing (pär′tĭng) **I.** s. *(separation)* separación *f,* división *f*; *(departure)* partida, despedida ♦ **p. of the ways** punto o momento de separación **II.** adj. de partida, de despedida <*a p. gift* un regalo de despedida>.
par·ti·san¹ (pär′tĭ-zən) **I.** s. *(supporter)* partidario, prosélito; MIL. guerrillero **II.** adj. POL. *(of a party)* partidista <*p. loyalty* lealtad partidista>; *(of a supporter)* partidario

<p. view opinión de partidario>; *(biased)* parcial; MIL. de guerrilleros.
par·ti·san² (pär'tĭ-zən) s. MIL., HIST. alabarda.
par·tite (pär'tīt') adj. partido, dividido (en partes).
par·ti·tion (pär-tĭsh'ən) I. s. *(of a territory, estate)* partición *f*; *(wall)* tabique *m*, mampara; LÓG., MAT. división II. tr. dividir, repartir ♦ **to p. off** separar con un tabique.
part·ly (pärt'lē) adv. en parte.
part·ner (pärt'nər) s. *(in a business)* socio, asociado; *(in an organization)* socio, miembro asociado; *(in a marriage)* cónyuge *mf*, consorte *mf*; *(in a dance)* pareja; *(in cards, tennis)* pareja, compañero; *(on the police force)* pareja; *(in crime)* cómplice *m*.
part·ner·ship (pärt'nər-shĭp') s. asociación *f*, sociedad *f* ♦ **to form a p. with** *o* **to go into p. with** asociarse con.
part of speech s. GRAM. parte de la oración *f*.
par·took (pär-tŏŏk') pret. de **partake**.
par·tridge (pär'trĭj) s. [pl. **partridge** *o* **-tridg·es**] ORNIT. perdiz *f*.
part-time (pärt'tīm') adj. & adv. por horas.
part-tim·er (pärt'tī'mər) s. trabajador por horas.
par·tu·ri·ent (pär-tyŏŏr'ē-ənt, -tŏŏr'-) adj. MED. parturienta.
par·tu·ri·tion (pär'tyŏŏ-rĭsh'ən, pär'chə-) s. parto.
part·way (pärt'wā') adv. FAM. hasta cierto punto, en parte.
par·ty (pär'tē) I. s. [pl. **-ties**] *(gathering)* fiesta <*birthday p.* fiesta de cumpleaños>; POL. partido <*the Democratic Party's candidate* el candidato del partido democrático>; *(group)* grupo <*a p. of six for dinner* un grupo de seis para cenar>; *(team)* equipo <*search p.* equipo de búsqueda>; FAM. *(person)* tipo, individuo; MIL. partida, destacamento; DER. parte <*the injured p.* la parte ofendida> ♦ **cocktail p.** cóctel de recepción, cóctel • **dinner p.** cena, banquete • **p. dress** vestido de fiesta • **p. loyalties** POL. lealtades partidistas • **p. politics** política del partido *o* partidos • **to be a p. to** *(accessory)* ser cómplice en; *(participant)* participar en, tener algo que ver con • **to have, give** *o* **throw a p.** dar una fiesta II. intr. **-tied, -ty·ing** FAM. *(to attend a party)* participar en una fiesta; *(to carouse)* parrandear, jaranearse <*we partied all night* nos jaraneamos toda la noche>.
party line s. *(telephone)* línea colectiva; POL. *(principles)* línea política.
par value s. COM., ECON. valor a la par *m*.
par·ve·nu (pär'və-nōō', -nyōō') s. advenedizo, nuevo rico.
pas·chal (pǎs'kəl) adj. RELIG. pascual ≺*p. lamb* cordero pascual>.
pa·sha (pä'shə, pǎsh'ə) s. bajá (título honorífico en Turquía) *m*.
pass (pǎs) I. intr. *(to proceed)* pasar; *(to extend)* pasar, atravesar; *(to overtake)* pasar, rebasar (en un automóvil); *(to elapse)* pasar, transcurrir <*as the days passed* a medida que pasaban los días>; *(to cross)* cruzarse <*the ships passed in the night* los barcos se cruzaron en la noche>; *(to be transferred)* ser traspasado, pasar a nombre *o* a manos de; *(to cease)* pasar, pasarse; *(to die)* morir; *(to happen)* acontecer, tener lugar; *(in an examination, course)* aprobar; *(to be adopted)* pasar, ser adoptado (moción, proyecto de ley); *(to be acceptable)* pasar, admitirse; *(currency)* pasar, tener curso legal; DEP. *(to a teammate)* pasar, hacer un pase; *(in a table game)* pasar (en el dominó, naipes) ♦ **in passing** de paso • **to be passing through** estar de paso • **to let (something) p.** dejar pasar algo, no hacer caso de algo • **to p. away** *(to die)* fallecer, pasar a mejor vida • **to p. by** *(to go by)* pasar; *(to go right past)* pasar de largo • **to p. on** *(to go on)* pasar <*to p. on to the next question* pasar a la próxima pregunta>; *(to die)* fallecer, pasar a mejor vida • **to p. out** desmayarse • **to p. over** *(to extend above)* pasar por encima de; *(rain, storm)* pasar (lluvia, tormenta); *(to join)* pasarse <*to p. over to the opposition* pasarse al bando de la oposición> —tr. *(to leave behind)* pasar <*we have already passed the church* ya pasamos la iglesia>; *(to go past)* pasar por delante de <*you will p. my house on the way* en el camino pasarás por delante de mi casa>; *(to come across)* cruzarse con <*I passed him when he came in* me crucé con él cuando entraba>; *(to go across)* pasar, cruzar <*to p. enemy lines* cruzar las líneas del enemigo>; *(to cause to move)* pasar <*to p. a cable through the hole* pasar un

cable por el hueco>; *(to exceed)* sobrepasar, superar; *(to spend)* pasar, pasarse <*she passed the winter in Vermont* se pasó el invierno en el estado de Vermont>; *(to circulate)* pasar, transmitir; *(deceitfully)* pasar, colar; *(to hand over)* pasar <*please p. the bread* ¿me pasa el pan, por favor?>; *(to issue from)* salir <*no secrets p. her lips* no hay secreto que salga de su boca>; *(an examination, student)* pasar, aprobar; *(to adopt)* adoptar (moción); *(to approve)* aprobar <*Congress passed the bill* el Congreso aprobó la ley>; *(to be approved)* ser aprobado *o* aceptado por <*the bill passed the Senate* la ley fue aprobada por el Senado>; DER. *(sentence)* dictar; DEP. *(a ball)* pasar; FISIOL. desocupar, evacuar ♦ **to p. along** *o* **around** pasar • **to p. by** *(to stop by)* pasar por; *(to go by)* pasar cerca de; *(to overlook)* pasar por alto (error, delito) • **to p. comprehension** *o* **belief** ser incomprensible • **to p. down** pasar <*the customs were passed down from one generation to the next* las costumbres pasaron de generación en generación> • **to p. for** pasar por <*to p. for a doctor* pasar por doctor> • **to p. in** entregar • **to p. judgment on** *(person)* juzgar a; *(issue)* juzgar sobre • **to p. muster** pasar, recibir el visto bueno • **to p. off** *(to palm off)* pasar, colar; *(to present)* hacer pasar <*to p. it off as a joke* hacer pasar por un chiste> • **to p. oneself off as** hacerse pasar por • **to p. on** pasar, transmitir • **to p. out** repartir, distribuir • **to p. over** pasar por alto • **to p. the buck** echar a otro el muerto, lavarse las manos • **to p. the hat** pasar el cepillo • **to p. the time of day** pasar el rato charlando • **to p. up** *(opportunity)* dejar pasar, desperdiciar; *(offer)* rechazar (oferta) II. s. *(passage)* paso, pasaje *m*; *(transfer)* paso, traspaso; *(gap)* paso, desfiladero; *(strait)* paso, estrecho; *(written permit)* pase *m*; *(authorization)* permiso, licencia; *(safe-conduct)* salvoconducto; *(free ticket)* pase (gratis); *(by an aircraft)* pasada; *(predicament)* paso, situación (difícil) *f* <*what has brought things to this p.?* ¿qué ha ocasionado esta situación?>; *(with one's hands)* pase (de hipnotizador, mago); *(in a table game)* pase; DEP., TAUR. pase ♦ **pretty p.** mal paso, lío • **to bring to p.** lograr, realizar • **to come to p.** ocurrir, acontecer • **to make a p. at** tratar de conquistar, hacer insinuaciones (amorosas) a.
pass·a·ble (pǎs'ə-bəl) adj. *(traversable)* transitable; *(acceptable)* aceptable; *(satisfactory)* pasable.
pas·sage (pǎs'ĭj) s. *(transit)* paso <*birds of p.* aves de paso>; *(of time)* paso, transcurso <*with the p. of time* con el paso del tiempo>; *(transition)* paso, transición *f*; POL. *(of a bill)* aprobación *f*, promulgación *f*; *(journey)* pasaje *m*, travesía; *(ticket)* pasaje <*to book a p.* sacar pasaje>; *(authorization)* paso, permiso <*free p.* paso franco>; *(path)* paso, pasadizo; *(corridor)* corredor *m*, pasillo; LIT., MÚS. pasaje; MED. evacuación (del vientre) *f* ♦ **nasal passages** ANAT. fosas nasales • **p. at arms** MIL. encuentro armado, combate • **selected passages** LIT. selecciones.
pas·sage·way (pǎs'ĭj-wā') s. *(alley)* callejón *m*; *(corridor)* corredor *m*.
pass·book (pǎs'bŏŏk') s. *(bankbook)* libreta de banco *o* de depósitos; COM. libro de cuenta y razón.
pas·sé (pǎ-sā') adj. *(out-of-date)* anticuado, pasado de moda; *(aged)* avejentado, en decadencia.
pas·sel (pǎs'əl) s. FAM. montón *m*.
pas·sen·ger (pǎs'ən-jər) s. pasajero, viajero.
pas·ser-by *o* **pas·ser·by** (pǎs'ər-bī') s. [pl. **pas·sers-by** *o* **pas·sers·by**] transeúnte *mf*.
pass·ing (pǎs'ĭng) I. adj. *(going by)* pasante, que pasa; *(transitory)* pasajero, transitorio; *(casual)* casual, de pasada ♦ **p. grade** EDUC. calificación aprobatoria II. adv. ♦ **p. fair** sumamente bella III. s. *(act)* pasada, transcurso; *(death)* fallecimiento; *(of a car)* adelantamiento.
pas·sion (pǎsh'ən) s. pasión *f* ♦ **P.** RELIG. pasión • **to have a p. for** adorar.
pas·sion·ate (pǎsh'ə-nĭt) adj. *(impassioned)* apasionado; *(choleric)* colérico, irascible; *(amorous)* amoroso, apasionado; *(ardent)* ardiente, fervoroso.
pas·sion·flow·er (pǎsh'ən-flou'ər) s. BOT. pasionaria.
pas·sion·less (pǎsh'ən-lĭs) adj. desapasionado.
Passion play s. RELIG., TEAT. auto de la Pasión.
Passion Week s. RELIG. Semana de (la) Pasión.

ā rey / ä año / b boca / ch chico / d dar / ĕ el / ē mil / g gato / h joya / hw juez / ī aire / k casa / kw cuan /

pas·sive (păs′ĭv) **I.** adj. *(not active)* pasivo; *(compliant)* pasivo, sumiso; *(inert)* inerte; inactivo; COM. que no devenga intereses; ELECTRÓN., GRAM., QUÍM. pasivo **II.** s. GRAM. voz pasiva.
pas·sive·ness (păs′ĭv-nĭs) s. pasividad *f.*
passive resistance s. POL. resistencia pasiva.
pas·siv·i·ty (pă-sĭv′ĭ-tē) s. pasividad *f.*
pass·key (păs′kē′) s. [pl. **-keys**] llave maestra.
Pass·o·ver (păs′ō′vər) s. RELIG. Pascua (de los judíos).
pass·port (păs′pôrt′) s. *(document)* pasaporte *m*; *(means)* pasaporte, salvoconducto.
pass·word (păs′wûrd′) s. contraseña, santo y seña.
past (păst) **I.** adj. *(over)* pasado, acabado <*our troubles are p.* nuestros problemas están acabados>; *(previous)* pasado <*the p. month* el mes pasado>; *(former)* anterior, último <*the p. president* el presidente anterior>; GRAM. pretérito, pasado ♦ **in times p.** en tiempos pasados • **the p. few** estos últimos <*in the p. few days* en estos últimos días> **II.** s. *(time)* pasado <*to live in the p.* vivir en el pasado>; *(background)* pasado, antecedentes *m* <*an actor with a colorful p.* un actor con unos antecedentes pintorescos>; *(background)* historia <*a man with a p.* un hombre con historia>; GRAM. pretérito, pasado **III.** adv. al pasar (por el lado) <*she waved as she walked p.* ella saludó al pasar> **IV.** prep. *(by)* por delante de <*he walked p. the bank* pasó por delante del banco>; *(on the far side of)* más allá de <*it's just p. the school* está un poco más allá de la escuela>; *(older than)* más de <*he's p. sixty* él tiene más de sesenta años>; *(beyond)* ya no <*I'm p. caring* ya no me importa>; *(plus)* y <*it's ten p. two* son las dos y diez> ♦ **it's p.** (someone) no extrañarse de parte de (alguien) <*I wouldn't put it p. him* no me extrañaría de su parte>.
pas·ta (pä′stə) s. CUL. *(dough)* masa de harina de trigo (para hacer tallarines); *(dish)* plato de pastas.
paste¹ (pāst) s. *(adhesive)* engrudo; *(dough)* pasta, masa <*tomato p.* pasta de tomate>; *(clay)* barro; JOY. *(glass)* estrás *m*; *(artificial gem)* imitación *f* **II.** tr. **past·ed, past·ing** *(to stick)* pegar; *(to cover)* engrudar ♦ **to p. up** IMPR. preparar una maqueta de.
paste² (pāst) JER. **I.** tr. **past·ed, past·ing** pegar, dar un puñetazo **II.** s. puñetazo.
paste·board (pāst′bôrd′) s. *(paperboard)* cartón *m*; *(ticket)* billete *m*, boleto; *(playing card)* naipe *m*, carta; *(visiting card)* tarjeta de visita.
pas·tel (pă-stĕl′) s. pastel *m* ♦ **p. blue** azul pastel.
paste-up (pāst′ŭp′) s. *(collage)* montaje *m*, collage *m*; IMPR. maqueta.
pas·teur·i·za·tion (păs′chər-ĭ-zā′shən, păs′tər-) s. pasteurización *f*, pasterización *f.*
pas·teur·ize (păs′chə-rīz′, păs′tə-) tr. **-ized, -iz·ing** pasteurizar, pasterizar.
pas·tiche (pă-stēsh′, pä-) s. LIT., MÚS., TEAT. pastiche *m.*
pas·time (păs′tīm′) s. pasatiempo.
past master s. experto, perito.
pas·tor (păs′tər) s. RELIG. *(minister)* pastor *m*; *(shepherd)* pastor.
pas·tor·al (păs′tər-əl) **I.** adj. *(of shepherds)* pastoril; *(rural)* pastoral, bucólico; RELIG. pastoral <*p. letter* carta pastoral> **II.** s. pastoral *f.*
pas·tor·ate (păs′tər-ĭt) s. *(office)* parroquia, curato; *(body of pastors)* pastores *m.*
past participle s. GRAM. participio pasado.
past perfect s. GRAM. pluscuamperfecto.
pas·try (pā′strē) s. [pl. **-tries**] *(paste)* pasta; *(cakes)* pasteles *m.*
past tense s. GRAM. tiempo pasado, pretérito.
pas·tur·age (păs′chər-ĭj) s. *(vegetation)* pastura, pasto; *(land)* pastura, apacentadero; DER. pasturaje *m*; *(business)* apacentamiento, adehesamiento.
pas·ture (păs′chər) **I.** s. *(vegetation)* pastura, pasto; *(land)* pastura, apacentadero; *(action)* apacentamiento, pastoreo ♦ **to put out to p.** *(to graze)* apacentar, pastorear; FIG. *(to retire)* jubilar, retirar **II.** tr. **-tured, -tur·ing** pastorear, apacentar —intr. pastar, pacer.
past·y¹ (pā′stē) **I.** adj. **-i·er, -i·est** *(like paste)* pastoso; *(pale)* pálido **II.** s. [pl. **-ies**] TEAT. cubrepezón decorativo.

pas·ty² (păs′tē) s. [pl. **-ties**] pastel *m*, empanada (de carne o pescado).
PA system (pē′ā′) s. (sistema de) altavoces *m*, altoparlantes *m.*
pat (păt) **I.** tr. **pat·ted, pat·ting** *(to tap)* dar palmaditas o golpecitos a; *(to stroke affectionately)* pasar la mano a, acariciar; *(to mold)* moldear a palmaditas o golpecitos ♦ **to p. oneself on the back** FIG. congratularse • **to p. someone on the back** FIG. felicitar a alguien —intr. andar con ruido de pasos ligeros **II.** s. *(with the hand)* palmadita, *(with an object)* golpecito; *(caress)* caricia; *(sound)* ruido ligero; *(small mass)* porción *f*, pelotita <*a p. of butter* una pelotita de mantequilla> ♦ **to give someone a p. on the back** FIG. felicitar a alguien **III.** adj. *(timely)* oportuno; *(exactly right)* preciso; *(contrived)* preparado, pronto <*a p. answer* una respuesta preparada> **IV.** adv. ♦ **to have something down p.** FAM. saberse algo al dedillo • **to stand p.** mantenerse firme.
patch (păch) **I.** s. *(on clothes)* parche *m*, remiendo; *(on a tire)* parche; *(in patchwork)* retazo; *(over a wound, eye)* parche; *(field)* siembra, bancal *m* <*a cabbage p.* un bancal de coles>; *(of road)* tramo; *(of color)* mancha ♦ **to have o to go through a bad p.** pasar por momentos difíciles, atravesar una mala racha **II.** tr. *(to put a patch on)* poner un parche a; *(to repair poorly)* remendar o arreglar mal ♦ **to p. a quilt** confeccionar una colcha de retazos • **to p. together** confeccionar • **to p. up** *(clothes)* poner parches a, remendar; *(to repair)* remendar, arreglar; *(to settle)* arreglar • **to p. up a quarrel** hacer las paces.
patch·work (păch′wûrk′) s. *(needlework)* labor hecha con retazos; *(jumble)* mezcolanza.
patch·y (păch′ē) adj. **-i·er, -i·est** *(marked by patches)* de remiendos, remendado; *(uneven)* desigual, irregular.
pate (pāt) s. FAM. *(head)* cabeza, coronilla; *(brains)* sesos, mollera.
pâte (pät) s. barro para hacer cerámica.
pâ·té (pä-tā′, pă-) s. CUL. *(meat paste)* pasta de carne (esp. de hígado); *(pastry)* pastel *m*, empanada de carne o de pescado.
pa·tel·la (pə-tĕl′ə) s. [pl. **-tel·lae** (-tĕl′ē)] ANAT. rótula; ZOOL. patela.
pa·ten·cy (păt′n-sē, pāt′n-) s. evidencia.
pat·ent (păt′nt) **I.** s. patente *f* ♦ **p. pending** patente pendiente • **to get a p.** patentar **II.** adj. *(obvious)* patente, evidente <*p. insincerity* insinceridad patente>; *(of patents)* de patentes; BOT., BIOL. abierto, extendido ♦ **p. flour** harina de primera **III.** tr. patentar.
pat·ent·ee (păt′n-tē′) s. poseedor de una patente *m.*
patent leather s. charol *m.*
pat·ent·ly (păt′nt-lē, pāt′nt-) adv. patentemente, evidentemente ♦ **to be p. obvious** saltar a la vista.
patent medicine s. medicamento patentado, específico.
patent office s. oficina de patentes.
patent right s. derecho de patente.
pa·ter (pā′tər) s. G.B. padre *m.*
pa·ter·fa·mil·i·as (pä′tər-fə-mĭl′ē-əs) s. [pl. **pa·tres·fa·mil·i·as** (pä′trēz-fə-mĭl′ē-əs)] HIST. paterfamilias *m*; *(father)* padre.
pa·ter·nal (pə-tûr′nəl) adj. *(fatherly)* paternal; *(of the father's side)* paterno.
pa·ter·nal·ism (pə-tûr′nə-lĭz′əm) s. paternalismo.
pa·ter·nal·is·tic (pə-tûr′nə-lĭs′tĭk) adj. paternalista.
pa·ter·ni·ty (pə-tûr′nĭ-tē) s. *(fatherhood)* paternidad *f*; *(paternal descent)* linaje *m*, filiación paterna; FIG. *(authorship)* paternidad.
pa·ter·nos·ter (pä′tər-nŏs′tər, pä′tər-) s. RELIG. paternóster *m*, padrenuestro.
path (păth, päth) s. *(trail)* sendero, senda; *(track)* camino, pista <*bicycle p.* pista para bicicletas>; *(course)* curso, trayectoria; FIG. *(way)* camino, senda; *(of a planet)* órbita.
pa·thet·ic (pə-thĕt′ĭk) adj. patético.
pathetic fallacy s. RET. prosopopeya.
path·find·er (păth′fīn′dər, päth′-) s. *(explorer)* explorador *m*; *(pioneer)* pionero.

---

path·less (păth'lĭs, päth'-) adj. *(unmarked by paths)* sin sendero *o* camino, virgen; *(unexplored)* inexplorado.
path·o·gen (păth'ə-jən) *o* **path·o·gene** (-ə-jēn') s. MED. agente *m o* microbio patógeno.
path·o·gen·e·sis (păth'ə-jĕn'ĭ-sĭs) s. MED. patogénesis *f,* patogenia.
path·o·gen·ic (păth'ə-jĕn'ĭk) *o* **path·o·ge·net·ic** (-jə-nĕt'ĭk) adj. MED. patógeno.
path·o·log·i·cal (păth'ə-lŏj'ĭ-kəl) *o* **path·o·log·ic** (-ĭk) adj. MED. patológico.
pa·thol·o·gist (pă-thŏl'ə-jĭst) s. MED. patólogo.
pa·thol·o·gy (pă-thŏl'ə-jē) s. [pl. **-gies**] MED. patología.
pa·thos (pā'thŏs') s. pathos *m,* patetismo.
path·way (păth'wā', päth'-) s. *(trail)* sendero, senda; *(track)* camino pista.
pa·tience (pā'shəns) s. *(forbearance)* paciencia; G.B. *(game)* solitario (juego de naipes) ♦ **to be out of p.** habérsele agotado a uno la paciencia.
pa·tient (pā'shənt) adj. & s. paciente *mf.*
pa·tient·ly (pā'shənt-lē) adv. pacientemente.
pat·i·na (păt'n-ə, pə-tē'nə) s. pátina.
pat·i·o (păt'ē-ō', pä'tē-ō') s. [pl. **-os**] patio, terraza.
pat·ois (păt'wä') s. [pl. **pat·ois** (-wäz')] dialecto regional.
pa·tri·arch (pā'trē-ärk') s. patriarca *m.*
pa·tri·ar·chal (pā'trē-är'kəl) *o* **pa·tri·ar·chic** (-kĭk) adj. patriarcal.
pa·tri·ar·chy (pā'trē-är'kē) s. [pl. **-chies**] patriarcado.
pa·tri·cian (pə-trĭsh'ən) s. HIST. *(of a Roman family)* patricio; *(aristocrat)* patricio, aristócrata *mf.*
pat·ri·cide (păt'rĭ-sīd') s. *(act)* parricidio; *(person)* parricida *mf.*
pat·ri·mo·ny (păt'rə-mō'nē) s. [pl. **-nies**] patrimonio.
pa·tri·ot (pā'trē-ət) s. patriota *mf.*
pa·tri·ot·ic (pā'trē-ŏt'ĭk) adj. patriótico.
pa·tri·ot·ism (pā'trē-ə-tĭz'əm) s. patriotismo.
pa·trol (pə-trōl') I. s. *(action)* ronda, patrulla; *(group)* patrulla II. tr. **-trolled, -trol·ling** rondar, vigilar —intr. rondar, patrullar.
patrol car s. coche patrullero, coche patrulla *m.*
pa·trol·man (pə-trōl'mən) s. [pl. **-men**] policía *mf,* guardia *mf.*
patrol wagon s. coche celular *m.*
pa·tron (pā'trən) s. *(sponsor)* benefactor *m,* patrocinador *m; (customer)* cliente *m; (protector)* protector *m,* defensor *m.*
pa·tron·age (pā'trə-nĭj, păt'rə-) s. *(support)* patrocinio, auspicio; *(manner)* condescendencia, aire protector *m; (clientele)* clientela; POL. *(power)* influencia política; *(appointments)* favores políticos.
pa·tron·ize (pā'trə-nīz', păt'rə-) tr. *(to support)* patrocinar, auspiciar; *(a business)* ser cliente de, frecuentar; *(to condescend to)* tratar con condescendencia, tratar con aire protector.
patron saint s. RELIG. patrono, santo patrón.
pat·ro·nym·ic (păt'rə-nĭm'ĭk) s. & adj. patronímico.
pat·sy (păt'sē) s. [pl. **-sies**] JER. pelele *mf,* simplón *m.*
pat·ter¹ (păt'ər) I. intr. *(to tap)* golpetear, tamborilear; *(to walk)* andar *o* corretear con pisadas ligeras II. s. golpeteo, tamborileo.
pat·ter² (păt'ər) I. intr. charlar, parlotear —tr. farfullar, balbucir II. s. *(cant)* jerga; *(mumble)* barboteo; *(chatter)* parloteo, palique *m.*
pat·tern (păt'ərn) I. s. *(model)* modelo, ejemplo; *(for cutting garments)* patrón *m,* molde *m; (decorative design)* diseño, dibujo; *(on fabrics)* estampado; *(combination of actions)* patrón, norma <behavioral patterns normas de conducta>; *(regularity)* regularidad *f;* ARM. dispersión (de tiro) *f;* TELEV. imagen *f,* patrón ♦ **to set a p. for** dar la pauta para II. tr. *(to ornament)* adornar con diseños; *(fabrics)* estampar ♦ **to p. after** *o* **on** imitar el ejemplo de.
pat·ty (păt'ē) s. [pl. **-ties**] CUL. *(cake)* empanada, pastelillo; croqueta de carne picada *o* pescado; *(candy)* caramelo (chato y ovalado).
pau·ci·ty (pô'sĭ-tē) s. *(fewness)* número pequeño; *(scarcity)* escasez *f.*

paunch (pônch) s. *(potbelly)* barriga, vientre *m; (rumen)* panza de los rumiantes.
paunch·y (pôn'chē) adj. **-i·er, -i·est** panzón, barrigón.
pau·per (pô'pər) I. s. *(poor person)* pobre *mf,* indigente *mf; (beggar)* mendigo II. tr. empobrecer.
pau·per·ism (pô'pə-rĭz'əm) s. pauperismo.
pau·per·ize (pô'pə-rīz') tr. **-ized, -iz·ing** empobrecer, depauperar.
pause (pôz) I. intr. **paused, paus·ing** *(mentally)* hacer una pausa; *(physically)* pararse, detenerse; *(to hesitate)* vacilar II. s. *(brief stop)* pausa; *(rest)* descanso; MÚS., POÉT. pausa ♦ **to give (someone) p.** hacer preocuparse (a alguien).
pa·vane *o* **pa·van** (pə-vän', -văn') s. pavana.
pave (pāv) tr. **paved, pav·ing** *(with blocks)* adoquinar; *(with asphalt, concrete)* pavimentar; *(with bricks)* enladrillar; *(with cobblestones)* empedrar ♦ **to p. the way for** preparar el terreno *o* el camino para.
pave·ment (pāv'mənt) s. *(surface, material)* pavimento; G.B. *(sidewalk)* acera.
pa·vil·ion (pə-vĭl'yən) s. *(at a fair, hospital)* pabellón *m;* JOY. *(surface)* pabellón.
pav·ing (pā'vĭng) s. *(act)* pavimentación *f; (material)* pavimento.
paw (pô) I. s. *(of animals)* pata; FAM. *(human hand)* manaza, manota II. tr. *(to strike)* dar zarpazos a; *(to scratch)* escarbar (la tierra); *(to handle)* manosear, toquetear ♦ **to p. at** manosear —intr. piafar, escarbar la tierra.
pawl (pôl) s. MEC. trinquete *m.*
pawn¹ (pôn) I. s. *(object)* prenda; *(condition, act)* empeño, pignoración *f; (hostage)* rehén *mf* II. tr. *(to leave as security)* empeñar, pignorar; *(to risk)* arriesgar, aventurar.
pawn² (pôn) s. *(chessman)* peón *m;* FIG. *(person)* pelele *m,* juguete *m.*
pawn·bro·ker (pôn'brō'kər) s. prestamista *mf.*
pawn·shop (pôn'shŏp') s. casa de empeños.
pay (pā) I. tr. **paid** (pād), **pay·ing** *(to give)* pagar; *(to yield as a return)* dar, producir; FIG. *(to profit)* compensar; *(visit, compliment)* hacer; *(respects)* presentar; *(attention)* prestar ♦ **to p. away** *(a rope)* soltar; *(money)* pagar • **to p. back** *(money)* devolver, reembolsar; *(someone)* pagar; *(an insult)* devolver; *(to take revenge on)* vengarse de • **to p. cash** pagar al contado • **to p. down** *(cash)* pagar al contado; *(as a first payment)* dejar una señal de • **to p. expenses** cubrir gastos • **to p. in cash** pagar en efectivo • **to p. money into an account** ingresar dinero en una cuenta • **to p. off** *(debts)* saldar, liquidar; *(creditor)* reembolsar; *(mortgage)* redimir; *(troops)* licenciar; *(employee)* despedir; FAM. *(to bribe)* sobornar; *(to get even with)* vengarse de; MARÍT. *(rope)* arriar; *(crew)* despedir • **to p. on account** pagar a cuenta • **to p. one's dues** merecérselo • **to p. one's way** pagar uno su parte • **to p. out** *(someone)* pagar; *(money)* desembolsar; MARÍT. *(line)* arriar, soltar • **to p. over** pagar • **to p. the piper** pagar las consecuencias • **to p. through the nose** pagar un dineral • **to p. up** pagar —intr. *(to give money)* pagar; *(debt)* saldar una deuda; *(to be profitable)* ser rentable; *(to be worthwhile)* compensar ♦ **it pays** vale la pena • **to p. in full** pagarlo todo • **to p. for it** pagarlas • **to p. in advance** pagar por adelantado • **to p. off** *(of a ship)* inclinarse a sotavento; *(to be advantageous)* dar resultado; *(to be profitable)* merecer la pena • **to p. up** pagar una deuda II. s. *(act of paying)* paga, pago; *(of employee)* paga, sueldo; *(of day worker)* jornal *m; (of workman)* salario; *(recompense)* pago; *(person)* pagador (bueno, malo) *m* ♦ **in the p. of** a sueldo de, pagado por • **retirement p.** jubilación, pensión • **to be in the p. of** estar al servicio de • **to draw one's p.** cobrar • **to stop something out of someone's p.** descontar algo del sueldo de alguien III. adj. de paga ♦ **p. telephone** teléfono público.
pay·a·ble (pā'ə-bəl) adj. *(due)* pagadero <p. in three installments pagadero en tres cuotas>; *(profitable)* lucrativo, ganancioso ♦ **accounts p.** TEN. cuentas a pagar • **p. to** a favor de.
pay·check (pā'chĕk') s. cheque de pago de sueldo *m.*
pay·day (pā'dā') s. día de pago *m.*
pay dirt s. MIN. tierra, mineral *m o* grava de alto contenido

metálico; FIG., JER. *(profitable discovery)* filón *m,* hallazgo.

pay·ee (pā-ē′) s. *(of a check)* beneficiario; *(of a draft)* tenedor de una letra *m.*

pay·er (pā′ər) s. pagador *m.*

pay·ing (pā′ĭng) I. adj. *(who pays)* que paga <*a p. visitor* un visitante que paga>; *(profitable)* provechoso, rentable II. s. pago.

pay·load (pā′lōd′) s. *(profitable cargo)* carga útil, carga de pago; MIL. carga explosiva; ASTRONÁUT. peso de la tripulación y el equipo de un cohete espacial; AER. peso total del pasaje y carga.

pay·mas·ter (pā′măs′tər) s. pagador *m,* cajero.

pay·ment (pā′mənt) s. *(action, amount)* pago; *(reward)* recompensa, pago ♦ **advance p.** anticipo • **cash p.** pago al contado • **deferred p.** pago a plazos *o* postergado • **down p.** desembolso inicial • **p. on account** pago a cuenta • **to stop p.** suspender el pago.

pay·off (pā′ôf′) s. *(payment)* pago; *(payday)* día de pago *m;* FAM. *(end result)* resultado final; *(retribution)* retribución *f,* venganza; *(bribe)* soborno, coima.

pay·o·la (pā-ō′lə) s. JER. soborno, coima.

pay·roll *o* **pay roll** (pā′rōl′) s. *(list)* nómina de pagos, planilla de pagos; *(total)* suma de dinero para pago de sueldos.

pay station s. teléfono público.

pay-TV (pā′tē-vē′) s. sistema de pago de televisión por cable *m.*

pea (pē) s. BOT. guisante *m,* arveja ♦ **like two peas in a pod** parecidos como dos gotas de agua.

peace (pēs) s. *(absence of hostility)* paz *f; (harmony)* armonía <*conjugal p.* armonía matrimonial>; *(law and order)* orden público; *(serenity)* paz, tranquilidad *f* ♦ **at p.** *(serene)* en calma, tranquilo <*my mind is at p.* tengo la conciencia tranquila>; *(free from strife)* en paz • **p. be with you** la paz sea con vosotros • **p. of mind** tranquilidad de espíritu • **p. treaty** tratado de paz • **rest in p.** en paz descanse • **to be at p. with oneself** tener la conciencia tranquila • **to hold** *o* **to keep one's p.** guardar silencio • **to keep the p.** mantener el orden • **to make p.** hacer las paces.

peace·a·ble (pē′sə-bəl) adj. pacífico.

peace·a·bly (pē′sə-blē) adv. *(peacefully)* pacíficamente, de modo pacífico; *(serenely)* en paz, apaciblemente.

peace·ful (pēs′fəl) adj. *(peaceable)* pacífico <*a p. nation* un país pacífico>; *(tranquil)* apacible, tranquilo <*a very p. spot* un lugar muy tranquilo>.

peace keeping *o* **peace-keep·ing** (pēs′kē′pĭng) adj. de pacificación.

peace-lov·ing (pēs′lŭv′ĭng) adj. pacífico, amante de la paz.

peace-mak·er (pēs′mā′kər) s. *(one who makes peace)* pacificador *m; (mediator)* árbitro.

peace offering s. *(propitiation)* regalo que expresa el deseo de hacer las paces; *(to a deity)* ofrenda propiciatoria.

peace officer s. agente del orden público *mf.*

peace pipe s. pipa de la paz.

peace·time (pēs′tīm′) s. época de paz.

peach¹ (pēch) s. *(tree)* melocotonero, duraznero; *(fruit)* melocotón *m,* durazno; *(color)* color melocotón *m;* FAM. *(gem)* monada, bombón *m* <*she's a p.* es un bombón>.

peach² (pēch) intr. & tr. JER. delatar <*he peached me to the cops* me delató a la poli>.

peach·y (pē′chē) adj. **-i·er, -i·est** *(surface)* aterciopelado, velloso; FAM. *(great)* precioso, perfecto.

pea·cock (pē′kŏk′) I. s. ORNIT. pavo real II. intr. FIG. pavonearse.

pea·fowl (pē′foul′) s. [pl. **peafowl** *o* **-fowls**] ORNIT. pavo real.

pea·hen (pē′hĕn′) s. ORNIT. pava real.

peak¹ (pēk) I. s. *(of a roof)* punta; *(of a mountain)* punta, cima, cumbre *f; (mountain)* pico; *(of a cap)* visera; *(climax)* punto culminante <*it was written at the p. of his career* fue escrito en el punto culminante de su carrera>; *(maximum)* tope *m,* máximo <*earnings reached their p.* las ganancias llegaron al máximo>; MARÍT. *(of sail)* puño (de la cangreja); *(of a gaff)* punta (de la botavara) II. tr. *(to bring to a climax)* hacer culminar; *(to bring to a maximum)*

traer al máximo —intr. *(to be formed into a peak)* formar un pico; *(to climax)* culminar, llegar al punto culminante; *(to achieve a maximum)* llegar al tope *o* al máximo III. adj. máximo <*p. load* carga máxima> ♦ **p. hours** *(of traffic)* horas punta, horas de mayor tránsito; *(of consumption)* horas de mayor consumo • **p. season** plena temporada, temporada alta.

peak² (pēk) intr. demacrarse, consumirse.

peaked¹ (pēkt, pē′kĭd) adj. puntiagudo.

peak·ed² (pē′kĭd) adj. demacrado, consumido.

peal (pēl) I. s. *(ringing)* repiqueteo, repique *m; (chime)* carillón *m* ♦ **peals of laughter** carcajadas II. intr. *(to ring)* repiquetear, repicar —tr. hacer resonar, tañer.

pe·an (pē′ən) s. var. de **paean.**

pea·nut (pē′nət) I. s. BOT. cacahuate *m,* maní *m* ♦ **peanuts** FIG., JER. (casi) nada <*to work for peanuts* trabajar por nada> II. adj. de maní <*p. oil* aceite de maní>.

peanut butter s. manteca de maní *o* cacahuate.

pear (pâr) s. BOT. *(tree)* peral *m; (fruit)* pera.

pearl (pûrl) I. s. *(gem)* perla, aljófar *m; (mother-of-pearl)* madreperla, nácar *m;* FIG. *(treasure)* perla, joya; IMPR. perla II. tr. adornar *o* cubrir con perlas —intr. *(to fish)* pescar perlas; *(to form beads)* formarse en perlas III. adj. perlado, de perlas.

pearl diver s. pescador de perlas *m.*

pearl·y (pûr′lē) adj. **-i·er, -i·est** *(in color)* perlino <*p. teeth* dientes perlinos>; *(with pearls)* perlado, perlificado; *(with mother-of-pearl)* nacarado, nacarino ♦ **p. whites** FAM. los dientes.

peas·ant (pĕz′ənt) s. *(laborer)* campesino; *(rustic)* campesino, rústico; *(boor)* patán *m,* palurdo.

peas·ant·ry (pĕz′ən-trē) s. campesinado, los campesinos.

pea·shoot·er (pē′shōō′tər) s. bodoquera, cerbatana.

pea soup s. *(soup)* sopa de arvejas *o* de guisantes; FAM. *(fog)* niebla espesa.

peat (pēt) s. AGR. turba.

peat bog s. AGR. turbera.

peat moss s. BOT. musgo de pantano; AGR. turba.

peb·ble (pĕb′əl) I. s. guijarro, canto rodado II. tr. **-bled, -bling** pavimentar con guijas.

peb·bly (pĕb′lē) adj. **-bli·er, -bli·est** guijarroso.

pe·can (pĭ-kän′, -kăn′) BOT. s. *(tree)* pacana, nogal pacanero; *(nut)* pacana, nuez lisa.

pec·ca·dil·lo (pĕk′ə-dĭl′ō) s. [pl. **-loes** *o* **-los**] pecadillo, falta leve.

pec·cant (pĕk′ənt) adj. *(guilty)* pecador, culpable; *(erring)* corrompido.

pec·ca·ry (pĕk′ə-rē) s. [pl. **-ries**] ZOOL. pecarí *m,* saíno.

peck¹ (pĕk) I. tr. *(bird)* picotear; *(a hole)* punzar; *(to pick up)* recoger con el pico (granos, insectos); FAM. *(to kiss)* besar —intr. picotear ♦ **to p. at** *(bird)* picotear; *(food)* picar; *(to criticize)* regañar, rezongar II. s. *(of a bird)* picotazo, picotada; *(of people)* beso.

peck² (pĕk) s. *(measuring unit)* celemín *m;* FAM. *(large quantity)* montón *m,* sinnúmero.

peck·er (pĕk′ər) s. *(one that pecks)* picoteador *m;* VULG. *(penis)* pene *m;* G.B. *(courage)* coraje *m,* ánimo.

pecking order s. ORNIT. ley del más fuerte *f;* FIG. *(hierarchy)* jerarquía.

pec·tin (pĕk′tĭn) s. BIOQUÍM. pectina.

pec·to·ral (pĕk′tər-əl) I. adj. pectoral II. s. *(muscle)* músculo pectoral; *(fin)* aleta pectoral; FARM., RELIG. pectoral *m;* ARM. peto.

pec·u·late (pĕk′yə-lāt′) tr. & intr. **-lat·ed, -lat·ing** malversar, desfalcar.

pe·cu·liar (pĭ-kyōōl′yər) I. adj. *(unusual)* peculiar, particular; *(odd)* raro, extraño; *(special)* especial, singular; *(distinctive)* peculiar, característico ♦ **p. to** peculiar a, característico de II. s. privilegio *o* propiedad particular *f.*

pe·cu·li·ar·i·ty (pĭ-kyōō′lē-ăr′ĭ-tē) s. *(particularity)* peculiaridad *f,* particularidad *f; (odd way)* rareza; *(distinctive feature)* rasgo característico, característica; *(eccentricity)* excentricidad *f,* idiosincracia.

pe·cu·ni·ar·y (pĭ-kyōō′nē-ĕr′ē) adj. pecuniario.

ped·a·gog·ic (pĕd′ə-gŏj′ĭk, -gŏj′ĭk) *o* **ped·a·gog·i·cal** (-gŏj′ĭ-kəl, -gŏj′ĭ-kəl) adj. pedagógico.

---

ng inglés / ŏ la / ō bou / ô corre / oi oigo / ōō uno / ou auto / yōō ciudad / w hueco / y yo / z mismo

ped·a·gog·ics (pĕd'ə-gŏj'ĭks, -gŏj'ĭks) s. pedagogía.
ped·a·gogue (pĕd'ə-gŏg') s. pedagogo.
ped·a·go·gy (pĕd'ə-gŏ'jē, -gŏj'ē) s. pedagogía.
ped·al (pĕd'l) **I.** s. pedal *m* **II.** adj. del pie, del pedal **III.** intr. pedalear —tr. dar a los pedales de.
ped·ant (pĕd'nt) s. pedante *mf*, ANT. *(schoolmaster)* maestro.
pe·dan·tic (pə-dăn'tĭk) adj. pedante, pedantesco.
ped·ant·ry (pĕd'n-trē) s. [pl. **-ries**] pedantería.
ped·dle (pĕd'l) tr. **-dled, -dling** *(to sell)* ir vendiendo de puerta en puerta; FIG. *(to disseminate)* difundir, diseminar —intr. *(to travel about selling)* vender de puerta en puerta, ser buhonero; *(to waste time)* emplearse en bagatelas *o* fruslerías.
ped·dler (pĕd'lər) s. buhonero, vendedor ambulante *m*.
ped·er·ast (pĕd'ə-răst') s. pederasta *m*.
ped·er·as·ty (pĕd'ə-răs'tē) s. pederastia.
ped·es·tal (pĕd'ĭ-stəl) **I.** s. pedestal *m* **II.** tr. poner *o* colocar en un pedestal.
pe·des·tri·an (pə-dĕs'trē-ən) **I.** s. peatón *m*, caminante *mf* **II.** adj. *(walking)* pedestre; FIG. *(ordinary)* pedestre, ordinario.
pe·di·at·ric (pē'dē-ăt'rĭk) adj. MED. pediátrico.
pe·di·a·tri·cian (pē'dē-ə-trĭsh'ən) s. MED. pediatra *mf*.
pe·di·at·rics (pē'dē-ăt'rĭks) s. MED. pediatría.
pe·di·at·rist (pē'dē-ăt'rĭst) s. MED. pediatra *mf*.
ped·i·cure (pĕd'ĭ-kyōōr') **I.** s. *(treatment)* pedicura <*to get a p.* hacerse una pedicura>; *(specialist)* pedicuro, callista *mf* **II.** tr. **-cured, -curing** hacer la pedicura a.
ped·i·gree (pĕd'ĭ-grē') s. *(lineage)* linaje *m*, ascendencia; *(family tree)* árbol genealógico, genealogía; *(animal's ancestry)* pedigrí *m*.
ped·i·ment (pĕd'ə-mənt) s. ARQ. frontón *m*.
pe·dol·o·gy¹ (pē-dŏl'ə-jē) s. pedología (estudio del desarrollo de los niños).
pe·dol·o·gy² (pē-dŏl'ə-jē) s. pedología, edafología (estudio de la tierra apta para cultivos).
pe·dom·e·ter (pĭ-dŏm'ĭ-tər) s. pedómetro.
pe·dun·cle (pē'dŭng'kəl, pĭ-dŭng'-) s. ANAT., BOT., ZOOL. pedúnculo.
pee (pē) VULG. **I.** intr. **peed, peeing** mear, orinar **II.** s. meada, orinada.
peek (pēk) **I.** intr. *(to glance)* echar una ojeada; *(to look furtively)* atisbar, mirar a hurtadillas; *(to become visible)* mostrarse, asomar **II.** s. atisbo, ojeada <*to take a p. at* echar una ojeada> ♦ **to get a p. at** alcanzar a ver un poco (de algo).
peek·a·boo (pē'kə-bōō') **I.** s. escondite *m*, cucú *m* **II.** adj. *(sheer)* transparente.
peel¹ (pēl) **I.** s. cáscara, mondadura **II.** tr. *(to pare)* pelar, mondar; *(to unpaste)* despegar; *(to strip away)* quitar —intr. *(to lose the covering)* pelarse; *(to shed skin)* despellejarse; *(to lose bark)* descortezarse; *(to become unpasted)* despegarse; *(to undress)* desvestirse, desnudarse ♦ **to p. off** AER. salirse de la formación (para aterrizar o atacar); *(to leave)* irse, partir.
peel² (pēl) s. *(baking tool)* pala de horno; IMPR. colgador *m*, espito.
peel·er (pē'lər) s. *(kitchen implement)* pelador *m*; JER. *(stripteaser)* mujer que se desnuda en espectáculos de cabaret *f*.
peel·ing (pē'lĭng) s. peladura, mondadura.
peep¹ (pēp) **I.** intr. pipiar, piar **II.** s. pío, piada ♦ **I don't want to hear a p. out of you!** FAM. ¡no digas ni pío!
peep² (pēp) **I.** intr. *(to glance)* echar una ojeada; *(to peer from behind)* atisbar, mirar a hurtadillas; *(to become visible)* mostrarse, asomarse **II.** s. *(glance)* ojeada; *(furtive look)* atisbo, atisbadura; *(first appearance)* asomo.
peep·er¹ (pē'pər) s. ZOOL. *(frog)* rubeta, rana; *(bird)* pollito.
peep·er² (pē'pər) s. *(person)* mirón *m*; JER. *(eye)* ojo.
peep·hole (pēp'hōl') s. mirilla.
peep·ing Tom (pē'pĭng tŏm') s. FIG., FAM. mirón *m*.
peep·show *o* **peep show** (pēp'shō') s. exhibición erótica (a través de una mirilla).
peep sight s. ARM. alza de mirilla.

peer¹ (pîr) intr. *(to look)* mirar curiosamente, mirar con atención; *(to peep out)* aparecer, asomar.
peer² (pîr) s. *(equal)* semejante *mf*; *(nobleman)* par *m*; *(member of British peerage)* noble inglés *m*.
peer·age (pîr'ĭj) s. *(title)* rango *o* dignidad de par *f*; *(peers)* pares *m*, cuerpo de pares; *(listing of peers)* libro nobiliario, guía de la nobleza *o* de los pares.
peer·ess (pîr'ĭs) s. paresa.
peer·less (pîr'lĭs) adj. sin par, sin igual.
peeve (pēv) **I.** tr. **peeved, peeving** irritar, poner de malhumor *o* furioso **II.** s. *(vexation)* queja, quejumbre *f*; *(bad mood)* malhumor *m*, enojo ♦ **pet p.** motivo de enojo.
pee·vish (pē'vĭsh) adj. *(querulous)* irritable, picajoso; *(ill-tempered)* malhumorado; *(contrary)* testarudo, terco.
pee·vish·ness (pē'vĭsh-nĭs) s. *(querulousness)* irritabilidad *f*, quisquillosidad *f*; *(ill-temper)* malhumor *m*; *(contrariness)* testarudez *f*, terquedad *f*.
pee·wee (pē'wē) s. FAM. cosa *o* persona pequeña.
peg (pĕg) **I.** s. *(plug, spike)* clavija; *(wooden stake)* estaca; *(clothes hook)* percha, gancho; *(claw)* garfio; *(degree)* grado, escalón *m*; *(pretext)* pretexto; FAM. *(wooden leg)* pata de palo; MÚS. clavija ♦ **to be a square p. in a round hole** estar como pez fuera del agua, no encajar ♦ **to take someone down a p.** bajar los humos a alguien ♦ **to p. down** sujetar con estacas —intr. ♦ **to p. away** trabajar con ahínco ♦ **to p. away at** machacar, afanarse por.
pegged, peg·ging *(to fasten)* sujetar con una clavija; *(to plug)* tapar con una clavija; *(to mark)* marcar con clavijas ♦ **to have someone pegged** FAM. conocer el juego de alguien ♦ **to p. down** sujetar con estacas —intr. ♦ **to p. away** trabajar con ahínco ♦ **to p. away at** machacar, afanarse por.
peg·board (pĕg'bôrd') s. *(for the kitchen, garage)* tabla de madera prensada perforada (para colgar herramientas, ollas, ordenadamente); *(for scoring)* tablero perforado (para anotar puntos).
peg leg s. FAM. pata de palo.
pe·jo·ra·tive (pĭ-jôr'ə-tĭv, pĕj'ə-rā'tĭv) **I.** adj. peyorativo, despectivo **II.** s. palabra despectiva.
Pe·kin·ese (pē'kə-nēz') s. & adj. var. de **Pekingese.**
Pe·king (pē'kĭng') s. Pekín, Pequín.
Pe·king·ese (pē'kĭng-ēz') **I.** s. [pl. **Pekingese**] *(inhabitant, language)* pequinés *m*, pekinés *m*; *(dog)* pequinés **II.** adj. pequinés, pekinés.
pe·lag·ic (pə-lăj'ĭk) adj. pelágico.
pel·i·can (pĕl'ĭ-kən) s. ORNIT. pelícano, pelicano.
pel·la·gra (pə-lăg'rə, -lā'grə) s. MED. pelagra.
pel·let (pĕl'ĭt) **I.** s. *(small ball)* bolita, pelotilla; *(pill)* píldora; *(bullet)* bala; *(shot)* perdigón *m*; *(stone)* proyectil (de piedra) *m* **II.** tr. tirar bolitas a.
pel·li·cle (pĕl'ĭ-kəl) s. película.
pell-mell *o* **pell·mell** (pĕl'mĕl') adv. *(helter-skelter)* desordenadamente, confusamente; *(headlong)* atropelladamente, vehementemente.
pel·lu·cid (pə-lōō'sĭd) adj. *(transparent)* translúcido, transparente; FIG. *(clear)* lúcido, claro.
Pel·o·pon·ne·sian (pĕl'ə-pə-nē'zhən) HIST. adj. & s. peloponense *mf*.
Pel·o·pon·ne·sus *o* **Pel·o·pon·ne·sos** (pĕl'ə-pə-nē'səs) s. Peloponeso.
pelt¹ (pĕlt) s. piel *f*, pellejo.
pelt² (pĕlt) **I.** tr. *(to bombard)* lanzar, arrojar; *(to strike)* apedrear; *(to beat down)* granizar *o* llover sobre —intr. *(to strike repeatedly)* golpear con fuerza repetidamente; *(to run)* correr ♦ **to p. down** llover a cántaros **II.** s. *(whack)* golpe *m*; *(speed)* velocidad *f* ♦ **at full p.** a toda velocidad.
pel·ves (pĕl'vēz') un pl. de **pelvis.**
pel·vic (pĕl'vĭk) adj. pélvico, pelviano.
pel·vis (pĕl'vĭs) s. [pl. **-vis·es** *o* **-ves** (-vēz')] ANAT., ZOOL. pelvis *f*.
pem·mi·can *o* **pem·i·can** (pĕm'ĭ-kən) s. *(American Indian food)* pemicán *m*; *(emergency ration)* conserva de carne seca.
pen¹ (pĕn) **I.** s. *(instrument)* pluma; *(ball-point)* bolígrafo; *(fountain pen)* pluma estilográfica; FIG. *(writer)* pluma ♦ **pens** ORNIT. plumas **II.** tr. **penned, pen·ning** escribir, redactar <*I penned a brief note* redacté una breve nota>.
pen² (pĕn) **I.** s. *(corral)* corral *m*; *(coop)* gallinero; *(sty)*

pocilga; *(dock)* muelle para submarinos *m* **II. tr. penned** *o* **pent** (pĕnt)**, pen·ning** acorralar, encerrar.
pen³ (pĕn) s. JER. *(jail)* chirona, prisión *f.*
pe·nal (pē′nəl) adj. penal <*p. code* código penal>.
pe·nal·ize (pē′nə-līz′, pĕn′ə-) tr. **-ized, -iz·ing** penalizar, castigar.
pen·al·ty (pĕn′əl-tē) s. [pl. **-ties**] *(punishment)* pena <*the death p.* la pena de muerte>; *(fine)* multa; *(consequences)* consecuencias <*he neglected his health and paid the p.* no se preocupó por su salud y sufrió las consecuencias>; FIN. *(for early withdrawal)* descuento; DEP. *(for an infraction)* castigo, penalty *m; (in soccer)* tiro penal *m,* pena máxima ♦ **on** *o* **under p. of** so pena de, bajo pena de.
pen·ance (pĕn′əns) **I.** s. penitencia <*to do p.* hacer penitencia> **II. tr. -anced, -anc·ing** imponer penitencia a.
Pe·na·tes (pə-nā′tēz) s.pl. HIST. penates.
pence (pĕns) s. G.B. peniques *m.*
pen·chant (pĕn′chənt) s. inclinación *f,* propensión *f* <*to have a p. for* tener inclinación por>.
pen·cil (pĕn′səl) **I.** s. *(implement)* lápiz *m* <*colored pencils* lápices de colores>; *(artist's style)* pincel *m; (ray)* haz de luz *m* ♦ **p. sharpener** sacapuntas **II. tr.** *(to write)* escribir con un lápiz; *(to sketch)* esbozar a lápiz ♦ **to p. someone in** FAM. hacer planes tentativos con alguien.
pencil pusher s. FAM. chupatintas *m.*
pen·dant *o* **pen·dent** (pĕn′dənt) **I.** s. *(of a necklace, bracelet)* colgante *m,* dije *m; (earring)* pendiente *m; (of a chandelier)* colgante; pinjante *m; (of a pair)* complemento, pareja **II. adj.** *(suspended)* pendiente, colgante; *(projecting)* sobresaliente; FIG. *(pending)* pendiente.
pend·ing (pĕn′dĭng) **I. adj.** *(not settled)* pendiente; *(imminent)* inminente **II. prep.** *(during)* durante; *(until)* hasta <*p. his arrival* hasta su llegada>.
pen·du·lar (pĕn′jə-lər) adj. pendular.
pen·du·lous (pĕn′jə-ləs) adj. *(hanging loosely)* colgante, pendiente; *(wavering)* oscilante.
pen·du·lum (pĕn′jə-ləm) s. péndulo.
pe·nes (pē′nēz) un pl. de **penis.**
pen·e·tra·bil·i·ty (pĕn′ĭ-trə-bĭl′ĭ-tē) s. penetrabilidad *f.*
pen·e·tra·ble (pĕn′ĭ-trə-bəl) adj. penetrable.
pen·e·trant (pĕn′ĭ-trənt) **I. adj.** penetrante **II. s.** cosa que penetra.
pen·e·trate (pĕn′ĭ-trāt′) tr. **-trat·ed, -trat·ing** *(pierce)* penetrar; *(to imbue)* penetrar, extenderse por <*the odor penetrated the whole house* el olor se extendió por toda la casa>; *(to understand)* entender, descubrir <*to p. the mysteries of nature* descubrir los misterios de la naturaleza>; *(to affect deeply)* conmover —intr. penetrar.
pen·e·trat·ing (pĕn′ĭ-trā′tĭng) adj. *(that penetrates)* penetrante; *(perspicacious)* penetrante, perspicaz.
pen·e·tra·tion (pĕn′ĭ-trā′shən) s. *(act, process)* penetración *f; (perspicacity)* penetración *f,* perspicacia.
pen·e·tra·tive (pĕn′ĭ-trā′tĭv) adj. penetrante.
pen·guin (pĕng′gwĭn) s. ORNIT. pingüino.
pen·hold·er (pĕn′hōl′dər) s. portaplumas *m,* mango de pluma.
pen·i·cil·lin (pĕn′ĭ-sĭl′ĭn) s. penicilina.
pen·i·cil·li·um (pĕn′ĭ-sĭl′ē-əm) s. [pl. **-i·ums** *o* **-i·a** (-ē-ə)] BOT. penicillium *m.*
pen·in·su·la (pə-nĭn′syə-lə, -sə-lə) s. península.
pe·nis (pē′nĭs) s. [pl. **-nis·es** *o* **-nes** (-nēz)] pene *m.*
pen·i·tence (pĕn′ĭ-təns) s. penitencia.
pen·i·tent (pĕn′ĭ-tənt) **I. adj.** penitente, arrepentido **II. s.** penitente *mf,* persona que expresa arrepentimiento.
pen·i·ten·tial (pĕn′ĭ-tĕn′shəl) adj. penitencial.
pen·i·ten·tia·ry (pĕn′ĭ-tĕn′shə-rē) s. [pl. **-ries**] *(prison)* penitenciaría, penal *f;* RELIG. *(tribunal)* penitenciaría; *(canon)* penitenciario.
pen·knife (pĕn′nīf′) s. [pl. **-knives** (-nīvz′)] navaja, cortaplumas *m.*
pen·light (pĕn′līt′) s. linterna pequeña con forma de estilográfica.
pen·man (pĕn′mən) s. [pl. **-men**] *(scribe)* calígrafo; *(expert in penmanship)* maestro de escritura; *(writer)* escritor *m.*
pen·man·ship (pĕn′mən-shĭp′) s. caligrafía.
pen name *o* **pen·name** (pĕn′nām′) s. seudónimo de autor.

pen·nant (pĕn′ənt) s. *(flag)* pendón *m,* gallardete *m; (emblem)* insignia; DEP. *(small flag)* banderín *m.*
pen·ni·less (pĕn′ə-lĭs) adj. *(without a penny)* sin dinero, sin un real *o* peso; *(very poor)* indigente, en la miseria.
pen·non (pĕn′ən) s. *(banner on a lance)* pendón *m,* grímpola; *(flag)* estandarte *m,* bandera; POÉT. *(wing)* ala.
pen·ny (pĕn′ē) s. [pl. **-nies**] G.B., FIN. penique *m; (cent)* centavo ♦ **a p. for your thoughts** ¿en qué estás pensando? • **not to have a p. to one's name** no tener un céntimo • **to cost a pretty p.** costar el ojo de la cara.
penny pincher s. FAM. tacaño, mezquino.
pen·ny·weight (pĕn′ē-wāt′) s. peso equivalente a 24 granos *o* a un gramo y medio.
pen·ny·wise (pĕn′ē-wīz′) adj. ♦ **to be p. and pound-foolish** hacer economías de chicha y nabo.
pen·ny·worth (pĕn′ē-wûrth′) s. *(what a penny will buy)* valor de un penique *m; (modicum)* pizca; *(bargain)* ganga.
pe·nol·o·gy (pē-nŏl′ə-jē) s. penología.
pen pal s. amigo epistolar *o* por correspondencia.
pen·sion¹ (pĕn′shən) **I.** s. pensión *f,* jubilación *f* **II. tr.** pensionar ♦ **to p. off** jubilar.
pen·sion² (päŋ-syôŋ′) s. pensión *f,* casa de huéspedes.
pen·sion·er (pĕn′shə-nər) s. pensionado, jubilado.
pen·sive (pĕn′sĭv) adj. *(thoughtful)* pensativo, meditabundo; *(withdrawn)* abstraído; *(melancholic)* melancólico.
pen·sive·ness (pĕn′sĭv-nĭs) s. *(thoughtfulness)* aire meditabundo; *(melancholy)* melancolía.
pent (pĕnt) **I.** un pret. y part. p. de **pen²** **II. adj.** acorralado, encerrado.
pen·ta·cle (pĕn′tə-kəl) s. pentáculo.
pen·tad (pĕn′tăd′) s. grupo de cinco.
pen·ta·gon (pĕn′tə-gŏn′) s. GEOM. pentágono ♦ **P.** el Pentágono.
pen·ta·he·dron (pĕn′tə-hē′drən) s. [pl. **-drons** *o* **-dra** (-drə)] GEOM. pentaedro.
pen·tam·e·ter (pĕn-tăm′ĭ-tər) s. POÉT. pentámetro.
pen·tane (pĕn′tān′) s. QUÍM. pentano.
Pen·ta·teuch (pĕn′tə-tōōk′, -tyōōk′) s. BÍBL. Pentateuco.
pen·tath·lon (pĕn-tăth′lən) s. DEP. pentatlón *m.*
Pen·te·cost (pĕn′tĭ-kôst′) s. RELIG. Pentecostés *m.*
Pen·te·cos·tal (pĕn′tĭ-kŏs′təl) adj. de Pentecostés.
pent·house (pĕnt′hous′) s. *(rooftop apartment)* ático; *(rooftop shelter)* cobertizo de máquinas; *(shed)* alero.
pent-up (pĕnt′ŭp′) adj. reprimido, contenido.
pe·nult (pē′nŭlt′, pĭ-nŭlt′) *o* **pe·nul·ti·ma** (pĭ-nŭl′tə-mə) s. GRAM. penúltima sílaba.
pe·nul·ti·mate (pĭ-nŭl′tə-mĭt) adj. & s. penúltimo.
pe·num·bra (pĭ-nŭm′brə) s. [pl. **-brae** (-brē) *o* **-bras**] penumbra.
pe·nu·ri·ous (pə-nōŏr′ē-əs, -nyōŏr′-) adj. *(stingy)* tacaño, avaro; *(barren)* estéril, pobre; *(needy)* pobre; indigente.
pen·u·ry (pĕn′yə-rē) s. penuria.
pe·on (pē′ŏn′) s. *(laborer)* peón *m,* bracero; *(servant)* criado; *(menial worker)* obrero sin categoría.
pe·on·age (pē′ə-nĭj) *o* **pe·on·ism** (-nĭz′əm) s. *(condition)* condición de peón *f; (system)* sistema de dependencia por endeudamiento que padecen los peones.
pe·o·ny (pē′ə-nē) s. [pl. **-nies**] BOT. peonía.
peo·ple (pē′pəl) **I. s. [pl. people]** *(nation)* pueblo <*the American p.* el pueblo norteamericano>; *(persons)* gente *m* <*country p.* gente del campo>; *(in definite numbers)* personas <*only about ten p. came* sólo vinieron unas diez personas>; *(citizens)* ciudadanos; *(subordinates)* gente, empleados; *(inhabitants)* gente, personas, habitantes *m* <*a city with several million p.* una ciudad de varios millones de habitantes>; *(family)* familia; *(ancestors)* antepasados; *(human beings)* personas, seres humanos <*they're p., not animals* son personas, no bestias>; *(beings)* seres *m* <*the furry little p. of the woods* los pequeños seres peludos del bosque> ♦ **many p.** mucha gente, muchas personas • **most p.** la mayoría de la gente • **peoples** pueblos • **people's republic** república popular • **old p.** los viejos • **poor p.** los pobres • **the common p.** *o* **the p.** el pueblo, la gente común y corriente • **young p.** los jóvenes **II. tr. -pled, -pling** poblar.

pep (pĕp) FAM. I. s. ánimo, empuje *m* II. tr. **pepped, pep·ping ◊ to p. up** animar, vigorizar.
pep·lum (pĕp'lŭm) s. peplo.
pep·per (pĕp'ər) I. s. *(plant)* pimentero; *(condiment)* pimienta; *(fruit)* pimiento II. tr. *(to season)* sazonar con pimienta; *(to pelt)* acribillar; *(to enliven)* salpicar.
pep·per-and-salt (pĕp'ər-ən-sôlt') adj. entrecano.
pep·per·corn (pĕp'ər-kôrn') s. BOT. *(berry)* grano de pimienta; *(insignificant thing)* bagatela, bicoca.
pepper mill s. molinillo de pimienta.
pep·per·mint (pĕp'ər-mĭnt') s. *(plant)* hierbabuena, menta; *(candy)* pastilla de menta.
pep·per·y (pĕp'ə-rē) adj. *(containing pepper)* picante; *(hot-tempered)* irascible, de mal humor; *(stinging)* mordaz, picante.
pep pill s. JER. píldora de anfetamina, estimulante *m.*
pep·py (pĕp'ē) adj. **-pi·er, -pi·est** FAM. lleno de vida, vivaz.
pep·sin (pĕp'sĭn) s. BIOQUÍM. pepsina.
pep talk s. exhortación *f*, palabras destinadas a levantar el ánimo ◊ **to give someone a p.** animar a alguien.
pep·tic (pĕp'tĭk) I. adj. péptico II. s. substancia péptica, agente digestivo.
per (pûr) prep. *(for every)* por <*two tickets p. person* dos entradas por persona>; *(expressing rate)* por, a <*$45 p. day* $45 al día>; *(by means of)* por, por medio de; *(according to)* según <*as p. instructions* según las instrucciones> ◊ **as p. usual** como de costumbre • **miles p. hour** millas por hora • **99 cents p. gallon** 99 centavos el galón • **p. day** por día.
per·am·bu·late (pə-răm'byə-lāt') tr. **-lat·ed, -lat·ing** recorrer —intr. deambular, pasearse.
per·am·bu·la·tor (pə-răm'byə-lā'tər) s. G.B. cochecito de niño.
per an·num (pər ăn'əm) adv. por año, al año.
per·cale (pər-kāl') s. percal *m.*
per cap·i·ta (pər kăp'ĭ-tə) adv. & adj. per cápita, por cabeza.
per·ceive (pər-sēv') tr. **-ceived, -ceiv·ing** *(with the senses)* percibir; *(to notice)* notar, percatarse de <*he immediately perceived their hostility* en seguida notó su hostilidad>; *(to understand)* comprender.
per cent *o* **per·cent** (pər-sĕnt') I. adv. por ciento ◊ **to be a hundred p. right** tener toda la razón • **to be a hundred p. satisfied** estar cien por ciento satisfecho, estar completamente satisfecho II. s. [pl. **per cent** *o* **percent**] por ciento <*sixty p. of the members* el sesenta por ciento de los socios>; *(percentage)* tanto por ciento, porcentaje *m* <*a large p. of her salary* un tanto por ciento elevado de su sueldo> III. adj. ◊ **a seven p. sales tax** un impuesto sobre las ventas del siete por ciento • **at 5.4 p. interest** con un interés del 5,4 por ciento.
per·cent·age (pər-sĕn'tĭj) s. *(percent)* porcentaje *m*, tanto por ciento <*a p. of the profits* un tanto por ciento de las ganancias>; *(part)* porcentaje, parte *f* <*a large p. of the crop* gran parte de la cosecha>; FAM. *(gain)* provecho, ventaja.
per·cen·tile (pər-sĕn'tīl') s. percentil *m.*
per·cept (pûr'sĕpt') s. percepción *f.*
per·cep·ti·ble (pər-sĕp'tə-bəl) adj. perceptible.
per·cep·tion (pər-sĕp'shən) s. *(action)* percepción *f*; *(insight)* percepción, comprensión *f.*
per·cep·tive (pər-sĕp'tĭv) adj. perceptivo.
per·cep·tiv·i·ty (pûr'sĕp-tĭv'ĭ-tē) s. perceptividad *f.*
per·cep·tu·al (pər-sĕp'chōo-əl) adj. de percepción.
perch¹ (pûrch) I. s. *(for birds)* percha; *(high place)* posición *f*, sitio II. intr. *(to roost)* posarse; *(to balance)* balancearse en un sitio elevado —tr. colocar, situar en un sitio elevado.
perch² (pûrch) s. [pl. **perch** *o* **perch·es**] ICT. perca.
per·chance (pər-chăns') adv. *(perhaps)* quizás, acaso; *(by chance)* por casualidad.
per·cip·i·ent (pər-sĭp'ē-ənt) adj. & s. perceptor *m.*
per·co·late (pûr'kə-lāt') tr. **-lat·ed, -lat·ing** *(to filter)* colar, filtrar; *(coffee)* filtrar —intr. *(to filter)* colarse, filtrarse; *(coffee)* filtrarse; *(to ooze)* infiltrarse; FAM. *(to get lively)* animarse, avivarse.

per·co·la·tion (pûr'kə-lā'shən) s. *(filtering)* filtración *f*, filtrado; FIG. *(infiltration)* infiltración *f.*
per·co·la·tor (pûr'kə-lā'tər) s. percolador *m*, cafetera de filtro.
per·cuss (pər-kŭs') tr. MED. percutir.
per·cus·sion (pər-kŭsh'ən) s. percusión *f.*
percussion cap s. ARM. pistón *m*, cápsula fulminante.
percussion instrument s. MÚS. instrumento de percusión.
per·cus·sion·ist (pər-kŭsh'ə-nĭst) s. músico que toca instrumentos de percusión.
per·cus·sive (pər-kŭs'ĭv) adj. percutiente, de percusión.
per di·em (pər dē'əm, dī'əm) I. adv. diariamente II. s. dieta *(retribución)* III. adj. diario.
per·di·tion (pər-dĭsh'ən) s. perdición *f.*
per·du·ra·ble (pər-dŏor'ə-bəl, -dyŏor'-) adj. perdurable.
per·e·gri·nate (pĕr'ĭ-grə-nāt') intr. **-nat·ed, -nat·ing** peregrinar —tr. recorrer.
per·e·grine falcon (pĕr'ə-grĭn) s. ORNIT. halcón peregrino.
per·emp·to·ry (pə-rĕmp'tə-rē) adj. *(imperative)* perentorio; *(dictatorial)* autoritario, dictatorial.
per·en·ni·al (pə-rĕn'ē-əl) I. adj. perenne II. s. BOT. planta perenne.
per·fect (pûr'fĭkt) I. adj. *(flawless)* perfecto <*a p. circle* un círculo perfecto>; *(consummate)* perfecto, consumado <*a p. artist* un artista consumado>; *(true)* perfecto, verdadero <*a p. lady* una verdadera señora>; *(complete)* perfecto, completo; *(ideal)* ideal <*the p. husband* el esposo ideal>; BOT. completo; GRAM., MÚS. perfecto ◊ **just p.!** ¡perfecto! II. s. GRAM. pretérito perfecto III. (pər-fĕkt') tr. perfeccionar.
per·fect·i·bil·i·ty (pər-fĕk'tə-bĭl'ĭ-tē) s. perfectibilidad *f.*
per·fect·i·ble (pər-fĕk'tə-bəl) adj. perfectible.
per·fec·tion (pər-fĕk'shən) s. *(state, quality)* perfección *f*; *(perfecting)* perfeccionamiento ◊ **to do something to p.** hacer algo a la perfección.
per·fec·tion·ism (pər-fĕk'shə-nĭz'əm) s. perfeccionismo.
per·fec·tion·ist (pər-fĕk'shə-nĭst) s. perfeccionista *mf.*
per·fect·ly (pûr'fĭkt-lē) adv. *(in a perfect way)* perfectamente, a la perfección; *(completely)* completamente <*p. content* completamente satisfecho>; *(utterly)* absolutamente <*p. dreadful* absolutamente espantoso> ◊ **to know p. well that** FIG. saber de sobra que.
per·fid·i·ous (pər-fĭd'ē-əs) adj. pérfido.
per·fi·dy (pûr'fĭ-dē) s. [pl. **-dies**] perfidia.
per·fo·rate (pûr'fə-rāt') I. tr. **-rat·ed, -rat·ing** perforar, agujerear II. adj. perforado, agujereado.
per·fo·rat·ed (pûr'fə-rā'tĭd) adj. perforado.
per·fo·ra·tion (pûr'fə-rā'shən) s. perforación *f.*
per·fo·ra·tor (pûr'fə-rā'tər) s. *(person)* perforador *m*; *(machine)* perforadora.
per·force (pər-fôrs') adv. forzosamente, por fuerza.
per·form (pər-fôrm') tr. *(to do)* ejecutar, hacer; *(a function)* desempeñar; TEAT. *(a role)* hacer, interpretar; *(a play)* representar; MÚS. ejecutar, tocar ◊ **to p. surgery** operar • **to p. wonders** obrar maravillas —intr. *(to function)* funcionar, trabajar; *(to fulfill an obligation)* cumplir; TEAT. *(to act)* actuar; *(to do tricks)* hacer trucos; *(to sing)* cantar.
per·form·ance (pər-fôr'məns) s. *(doing)* ejecución *f*, realización *f*; *(of a function)* ejecución, desempeño; *(of a play)* representación *f*; *(of a role, musical composition)* interpretación *f*; *(in a competition)* actuación *f*; *(functioning)* funcionamiento <*the p. of the car has improved* el funcionamiento del auto ha mejorado>; *(of an engine)* rendimiento; *(show)* función *f* <*benefit p.* función benéfica> ◊ **in the p. of** en el ejercicio de.
per·form·er (pər-fôr'mər) s. *(actor)* artista *m*, actor *m*; *(actress)* artista, actriz *f*; *(musician)* intérprete *mf*, músico; *(dancer)* bailarín *m.*
per·fume I. s. (pûr'fyōom', pər-fyōom') *(liquid)* perfume *m*; *(scent)* aroma *m*, perfume II. tr. (pər-fyōom') **-fumed, -fum·ing** perfumar.
per·fum·er·y (pər-fyōo'mə-rē) s. [pl. **-ies**] perfumería.
per·func·to·ry (pər-fŭngk'tə-rē) adj. *(routine)* rutinario; *(indifferent)* indiferente; *(superficial)* superficial, somero.
per·fuse (pər-fyōoz') tr. **-fused, -fus·ing** *(to suffuse)* inundar, bañar; *(to diffuse)* introducir, hacer penetrar.

---

per·fu·sion (pər-fyoō'zhən) s. MED. perfusión *f.*
per·go·la (pûr'gə-lə) s. pérgola.
per·haps (pər-hăps') adv. quizá, quizás.
per·i·car·di·um (pĕr'ĭ-kär'dē-əm) s. [pl. **-di·a** (-dē-ə)] ANAT. pericardio.
per·i·cra·ni·um (pĕr'ĭ-krā'nē-əm) s. [pl. **-ni·a** (-nē-ə)] ANAT. pericráneo.
per·i·do·tite (pĕr'ĭ-dō'tīt', pə-rīd'ə-tīt') s. MIN. peridotita.
per·i·gee (pĕr'ə-jē) s. ASTRON. perigeo.
per·i·he·li·on (pĕr'ə-hē'lē-ən) s. [pl. **-li·a** (-lē-ə)] ASTRON. perihelio.
per·il (pĕr'əl) I. s. *(danger)* peligro; *(risk)* peligro, riesgo ♦ **at one's p.** por propia cuenta y riesgo • **in p. (of)** en peligro (de) II. tr. poner en peligro, arriesgar.
per·il·ous (pĕr'ə-ləs) adj. peligroso, arriesgado.
per·il·ous·ly (pĕr'ə-ləs-lē) adv. peligrosamente, arriesgadamente.
pe·rim·e·ter (pə-rĭm'ĭ-tər) s. MAT., MIL. perímetro; *(limits)* perímetro, límite *m.*
pe·ri·od (pîr'ē-əd) s. *(time)* período, periodo *<a p. of six months* un período de seis meses>; *(term)* plazo *<within a three-week p.* dentro de un plazo de tres semanas>; *(age)* época *<the pre-Columbian p.* la época precolombina>; *(stage)* etapa, época; *(class)* hora, clase *f <first p.* la primera clase>; *(playing time)* tiempo; *(menstruation)* período, regla; *(punctuation mark)* punto; ASTRON., FÍS., GEOL. período ♦ **during that p.** por aquella época, por aquel entonces • **p. costumes** trajes de época • **postwar p.** posguerra.
pe·ri·od·ic (pîr'ē-ŏd'ĭk) adj. periódico.
pe·ri·od·i·cal (pîr'ē-ŏd'ĭ-kəl) I. adj. *(periodic)* periódico; *(of a journal)* de publicaciones periódicas, de revistas II. s. publicación periódica, revista.
pe·ri·o·dic·i·ty (pîr'ē-ə-dĭs'ĭ-tē) s. periodicidad *f.*
periodic law s. QUÍM. ley periódica.
periodic table s. QUÍM. tabla periódica.
per·i·o·don·tal (pĕr'ē-ō-dŏn'tl) adj. periodontal.
per·i·os·te·um (pĕr'ē-ŏs'tē-əm) s. [pl. **-te·a** (-tē-ə)] ANAT. periostio.
per·i·pa·tet·ic (pĕr'ə-pə-tĕt'ĭk) I. adj. ambulante, peripatético II. s. caminante *mf.*
pe·riph·er·al (pə-rĭf'ər-əl) I. adj. *(of the periphery)* periférico; *(auxiliary)* auxiliar II. s. COMPUT. equipo periférico.
pe·riph·er·y (pə-rĭf'ə-rē) s. [pl. **-ies**] periferia.
pe·riph·ra·sis (pə-rĭf'rə-sĭs) s. [pl. **-ses** (-sēz')] perífrasis *f.*
per·i·phras·tic (pĕr'ə-frăs'tĭk) adj. GRAM., RET. perifrástico.
per·i·scope (pĕr'ĭ-skōp') s. ÓPT. periscopio.
per·ish (pĕr'ĭsh) intr. *(to die)* perecer, morir; *(to spoil)* estropearse, echarse a perder; *(to disappear)* desaparecer.
per·ish·a·ble (pĕr'ĭ-shə-bəl) I. adj. *(said of goods)* perecedero; *(ephemeral)* efímero, pasajero II. s. ♦ **perishables** artículos de fácil deterioro.
per·i·stal·sis (pĕr'ĭ-stôl'sĭs, -stăl'-) s. [pl. **-ses** (-sēz')] FISIOL. peristalsis *f.*
per·i·style (pĕr'ĭ-stīl') s. ARQ. peristilo.
per·i·to·ne·um (pĕr'ĭ-tə-nē'əm) s. [pl. **-ne·a** (-nē'ə) *o* **-ne·ums**] ANAT. peritoneo.
per·i·to·ni·tis (pĕr'ĭ-tə-nī'tĭs) s. MED. peritonitis *f.*
per·i·wig (pĕr'ĭ-wĭg') s. peluca.
per·i·win·kle[1] (pĕr'ĭ-wĭng'kəl) s. ZOOL. bígaro, caracol de mar *m.*
per·i·win·kle[2] (pĕr'ĭ-wĭng'kəl) s. BOT. vincapervinca.
per·jure (pûr'jər) tr. *(to lie)* perjurar, jurar en falso ♦ **to p. oneself** perjurarse.
per·ju·ri·ous (pər-joŏr'ē-əs) adj. perjurador, perjuro.
per·ju·ry (pûr'jə-rē) s. [pl. **-ries**] perjurio ♦ **to commit p.** *(to swear)* jurar en falso; *(to testify)* prestar falso testimonio.
perk[1] (pûrk) intr. proyectarse, sobresalir ♦ **to p. up** animarse, reanimarse —tr. alzar, levantar ♦ **to p. up** *(to cheer up)* animarse, reanimarse; *(to spruce up)* adornar, engalanar; *(to improve)* ir mejor, ir mejorando • **to p. up one's ears** aguzar las orejas.
perk[2] (pûrk) s. FAM. *(bonus)* ganancia extra, obvención *f*; *(tip)* propina, gratificación *f*; *(privilege)* privilegio que corresponde a ciertos puestos.

perk·y (pûr'kē) adj. **-i·er, -i·est** *(cheerful)* airoso; *(animated)* animado, vivaz.
perm (pûrm) I. s. ondulación permanente *f* II. tr. & intr. hacer(se) un permanente.
per·ma·frost (pûr'mə-frôst') s. GEOL. permafrost *m*, permagel *m.*
per·ma·nence (pûr'mə-nəns) s. *(quality)* permanencia; *(of a law)* estabilidad *f*; *(of a conquest)* duración *f.*
per·ma·nen·cy (pûr'mə-nən-sē) s. [pl. **-cies**] *(quality)* permanencia; *(something permanent)* cosa permanente.
per·ma·nent (pûr'mə-nənt) I. adj. permanente ♦ **p. address** domicilio II. s. permanente *f*, ondulación permanente *f <to get a p.* hacerse un permanente>.
permanent press s. planchado permanente.
permanent tooth s. diente permanente *m.*
permanent wave s. ondulación permanente *f*, ondulado permanente del pelo.
per·man·ga·nate (pər-măn'gə-nāt') s. QUÍM. permanganato.
per·me·a·bil·i·ty (pûr'mē-ə-bĭl'ĭ-tē) s. permeabilidad *f.*
per·me·a·ble (pûr'mē-ə-bəl) adj. permeable.
per·me·ate (pûr'mē-āt') tr. & intr. **-at·ed, -at·ing** penetrar, infiltrar(se).
per·mis·si·ble (pər-mĭs'ə-bəl) adj. permisible, lícito.
per·mis·sion (pər-mĭsh'ən) s. permiso, autorización *f.*
per·mis·sive (pər-mĭs'ĭv) adj. *(permitted)* permisivo; *(tolerant)* tolerante, indulgente; *(optional)* facultativo.
per·mit I. tr. (pər-mĭt') **-mit·ted, -mit·ting** *(to allow)* permitir, dejar; *(to give consent to)* dar permiso a, dejar; *(to afford)* permitir ♦ **permit me!** ¡permítame! • **to be permitted** *(action)* permitirse *<swimming is not permitted here* aquí no se permite nadar>; *(person)* poder *<students are permitted to smoke* los estudiantes pueden fumar> —intr. ♦ **if circumstances p.** si las circunstancias lo permiten • **if time permits** *o* **time permitting** si hay tiempo II. s. (pûr'mĭt) permiso, licencia.
per·mu·ta·tion (pûr'myoō-tā'shən) s. *(transformation)* permuta, permutación *f*; *(alteration)* cambio, alteración *f*; MAT. permutación.
per·mute (pər-myoōt') tr. **-mut·ed, -mut·ing** permutar.
per·ni·cious (pər-nĭsh'əs) adj. *(deadly)* pernicioso, fatal; *(harmful)* dañino, perjudicial.
pernicious anemia s. MED. anemia perniciosa.
per·nick·e·ty (pər-nĭk'ĭ-tē) adj. var. de **persnickety.**
per·o·rate (pĕr'ə-rāt') intr. **-rat·ed, -rat·ing** perorar.
per·o·ra·tion (pĕr'ə-rā'shən) s. peroración *f.*
per·ox·ide (pə-rŏk'sīd') I. s. QUÍM. peróxido; *(hydrogen peroxide)* peróxido de hidrógeno, agua oxigenada II. tr. **-id·ed, -id·ing** QUÍM. *(to treat)* tratar con peróxido; *(to bleach)* descolorar, aclarar con agua oxigenada.
per·pen·dic·u·lar (pûr'pən-dĭk'yə-lər) I. adj. GEOM. perpendicular; *(vertical)* vertical *<p. drop* caída vertical> ♦ **p. to** perpendicular a *o* con II. s. GEOM. perpendicular *f*; *(plumb line)* plomada; *(vertical line)* vertical *f.*
per·pen·dic·u·lar·i·ty (pûr'pən-dĭk'yə-lăr'ĭ-tē) s. perpendicularidad *f.*
per·pe·trate (pûr'pĭ-trāt') tr. **-trat·ed, -trat·ing** DER. *(to commit)* perpetrar, cometer; *(to perform)* hacer *<to p. a practical joke* hacer una broma pesada>.
per·pe·tra·tion (pûr'pĭ-trā'shən) s. DER. perpetración *f.*
per·pe·tra·tor (pûr'pĭ-trā'tər) s. DER. *(one who perpetrates)* perpetrador *m*, responsable *mf*; *(originator)* responsable, autor *m.*
per·pet·u·al (pər-pĕch'oō-əl) adj. *(endless)* perpetuo *<p. friendship* amistad perpetua>; *(constant)* constante, continuo *<p. nagging* críticas continuas>; *(eternal)* eterno.
perpetual motion s. movimiento perpetuo.
per·pet·u·ate (pər-pĕch'oō-āt') tr. **-at·ed, -at·ing** perpetuar.
per·pet·u·a·tion (pər-pĕch'oō-ā'shən) s. perpetuación *f.*
per·pe·tu·i·ty (pûr'pĭ-toō'ĭ-tē, -tyoō'-) s. [pl. **-ties**] *(quality, state)* perpetuidad *f*; *(annuity)* renta perpetua ♦ **in p.** para siempre.
per·plex (pər-plĕks') tr. *(to confuse)* confundir, desconcertar; *(to make intricate)* complicar, embrollar.
per·plexed (pər-plĕkst') adj. *(confused)* perplejo, confuso; *(intricate)* intrincado, embrollado.

per·plex·i·ty (pər-plĕk′sĭ-tē) s. [pl. **-ties**] *(state, condition)* perplejidad *f*; *(confusion)* confusión *f*.

per·qui·site (pûr′kwĭ-zĭt) s. *(bonus)* obvención *f*, ganancia extra; *(tip)* propina, gratificación *f*; *(privilege)* privilegio que corresponde a un puesto.

per se (pər sā′, sē) adv. por sí mismo, propiamente dicho.

per·se·cute (pûr′sĭ-kyōōt′) tr. **-cut·ed, -cut·ing** *(to oppress)* perseguir; *(to harass)* acosar, atormentar; *(to bother)* molestar.

per·se·cu·tion (pûr′sĭ-kyōō′shən) s. persecución *f*.

per·se·cu·tor (pûr′sĭ-kyōō′tər) s. perseguidor *m*.

per·se·ver·ance (pûr′sə-vîr′əns) s. perseverancia.

per·se·vere (pûr′sə-vîr′) intr. **-vered, -ver·ing** perseverar.

Per·sia (pûr′zhə) s. Persia.

Per·sian (pûr′zhən) **I.** adj. persa, pérsico **II.** s. *(inhabitant, language)* persa *mf*.

Persian cat s. gato persa.

Persian Gulf s. GEOG. Golfo Pérsico.

per·sim·mon (pər-sĭm′ən) s. BOT. caqui *m*.

per·sist (pər-sĭst′, -zĭst′) intr. persistir, empeñarse ♦ **to p. in** persistir en.

per·sist·ence (pər-sĭs′təns, -zĭs′-) o **per·sist·en·cy** (-tən-sē) s. *(insistence)* persistencia, empeño; *(tenacity)* tenacidad *f*, perseverancia; *(continuance)* persistencia.

per·sist·ent (pər-sĭs′tənt, -zĭs′-) adj. *(persevering)* persistente; *(continuous)* continuo, constante; *(enduring)* persistente; BOT., ZOOL. persistente.

per·snick·e·ty (pər-snĭk′ĭ-tē) adj. FAM. *(said of a person)* puntilloso, quisquilloso; *(said of work)* delicado, minucioso; *(demanding)* exigente.

per·son (pûr′sən) s. *(human being)* persona; FAM. *(guy)* tipo; DER., GRAM., TEOL. persona ♦ **in p.** en persona • **in the first p.** en primera persona • **in the p. of** en la persona de • **no p.** nadie • **some p.** alguien.

per·son·a·ble (pûr′sə-nə-bəl) adj. *(attractive)* bien parecido, atractivo; *(pleasing)* agradable.

per·son·age (pûr′sə-nĭj) s. personaje *m*.

per·son·al (pûr′sə-nəl) **I.** adj. *(individual)* personal; *(private)* particular; *(in person)* en persona; *(for one's use)* de uso personal <p. articles artículos de uso personal>; *(intimate)* personal, de carácter personal <something p. to tell you algo de carácter personal que decirte>; *(bodily)* corporal; GRAM. personal ♦ **to get p.** hacer comentarios de carácter personal • **to make a p. appearance** presentarse en persona **II.** s. mensaje personal *m*.

personal effects s.pl. efectos personales.

per·son·al·i·ty (pûr′sə-năl′ĭ-tē) s. [pl. **-ties**] *(of a person, place)* personalidad *f*; FAM. *(celebrity)* personaje *m*, figura.

per·son·al·ize (pûr′sə-nə-līz′) tr. **-ized, -iz·ing** personalizar, personificar.

per·son·al·ly (pûr′sə-nə-lē) adv. *(in person)* personalmente; *(in a personal manner)* de modo personal <don't take it p. no lo tomes de modo personal>.

personal pronoun s. GRAM. pronombre personal *m*.

personal property s. DER. bienes muebles *m*.

per·son·al·ty (pûr′sə-nəl-tē) [pl. **-ties**] DER. bienes muebles *m*.

per·so·na non gra·ta (pər-sō′nə nŏn grä′tə, grăt′ə) adj. persona no grata, persona non grata.

per·son·ate (pûr′sə-nāt′) tr. **-at·ed, -at·ing** *(to portray)* hacer el papel de; *(to impersonate)* hacerse pasar por.

per·son·i·fi·ca·tion (pər-sŏn′ə-fĭ-kā′shən) s. personificación *f* ♦ **to be the p. of evil** ser el mal personificado.

per·son·i·fy (pər-sŏn′ə-fī′) tr. **-fied, -fy·ing** personificar.

per·son·nel (pûr′sə-nĕl′) s. personal *m*.

per·spec·tive (pər-spĕk′tĭv) **I.** s. perspectiva ♦ **to put things in their p.** apreciar las cosas en su justo valor **II.** adj. en perspectiva.

per·spi·ca·cious (pûr′spĭ-kā′shəs) adj. perspicaz.

per·spi·cac·i·ty (pûr′spĭ-kăs′ĭ-tē) s. perspicacia.

per·spi·cu·i·ty (pûr′spĭ-kyōō′ĭ-tē) s. perspicuidad *f*, claridad *f*.

per·spic·u·ous (pər-spĭk′yōō-əs) adj. perspicuo, claro.

per·spi·ra·tion (pûr′spə-rā′shən) s. sudor *m*, transpiración *f*.

per·spire (pər-spīr′) tr. & intr. **-spired, -spir·ing** sudar, transpirar.

per·suad·a·ble (pər-swā′də-bəl) adj. fácil de persuadir.

per·suade (pər-swād′) tr. **-suad·ed, -suad·ing** *(to win over)* persuadir; *(to convince)* convencer.

per·sua·sion (pər-swā′zhən) s. *(act, condition)* persuasión *f*; *(persuasiveness)* persuasiva; *(conviction)* convicción *f*, creencia; *(religion)* credo, religión *f*; *(sect)* secta.

per·sua·sive (pər-swā′sĭv) adj. persuasivo.

per·sua·sive·ness (pər-swā′sĭv-nĭs) s. persuasión *f*.

pert (pûrt) adj. **-er, -est** *(saucy)* impertinente, atrevido; *(vivacious)* animado, vivaz; *(jaunty)* alegre, gracioso.

per·tain (pər-tān′) intr. *(to relate to)* concernir; *(to belong)* pertenecer; *(to be suitable)* ser apropiado.

per·ti·na·cious (pûr′tn-ā′shəs) adj. *(tenacious)* pertinaz, tenaz; *(obstinate)* porfiado, obstinado.

per·ti·nence (pûr′tn-əns) o **per·ti·nen·cy** (-ən-sē) s. pertinencia.

per·ti·nent (pûr′tn-ənt) adj. pertinente.

per·turb (pər-tûrb′) tr. *(to disturb)* perturbar; *(to worry)* preocupar, inquietar; *(to unsettle)* descomponer; ASTRON., FÍS. perturbar.

per·tur·ba·tion (pûr′tər-bā′shən) s. *(act)* perturbación *f*; *(agitation)* agitación *f*; *(worry)* preocupación *f*, inquietud *f*; ASTRON., FÍS. perturbación.

per·tus·sis (pər-tŭs′ĭs) s. MED. tos ferina, tos convulsiva.

Pe·ru (pə-rōō′) s. Perú *m*.

pe·ruke (pə-rōōk′) s. peluquín *m*, peluca.

pe·rus·al (pə-rōō′zəl) s. *(reading)* lectura atenta, lectura cuidadosa; *(examination)* examen *m*.

pe·ruse (pə-rōōz′) tr. **-rused, -rus·ing** *(to read)* leer atentamente, leer cuidadosamente; *(to examine)* examinar, escudriñar.

Pe·ru·vi·an (pə-rōō′vē-ən) adj. & s. peruano.

per·vade (pər-vād′) tr. **-vad·ed, -vad·ing** *(to spread through)* invadir, extenderse por; *(to permeate)* penetrar, impregnar.

per·va·sive (pər-vā′sĭv) adj. penetrante.

per·va·sive·ness (pər-vā′sĭv-nĭs) s. capacidad de penetración *f*.

per·verse (pər-vûrs′) adj. *(perverted)* perverso, depravado <p. behavior conducta depravada>; *(willful)* empecinado, terco.

per·ver·sion (pər-vûr′zhən) s. *(corruption)* perversión *f*; *(distortion)* desnaturalización *f*, tergiversación *f*; *(sexual act)* acto pervertido o contra natura.

per·ver·si·ty (pər-vûr′sĭ-tē) s. [pl. **-ties**] *(perversion)* perversión *f*; *(willfulness)* empecinamiento, terquedad *f*.

per·vert I. tr. (pər-vûrt′) *(to corrupt)* pervertir; *(to misuse)* abusar de; *(one's talent)* prostituir (talento); *(to distort)* desnaturalizar, tergiversar **II.** s. (pûr′vûrt′) pervertido *(sexual)*.

per·vert·ed (pər-vûr′tĭd) adj. *(corrupt)* pervertido; *(distorted)* tergiversado.

per·vi·ous (pûr′vē-əs) adj. *(permeable)* permeable; *(open)* penetrable.

pe·se·ta (pə-sā′tə) s. FIN. peseta.

pes·ky (pĕs′kē) adj. **-ki·er, -ki·est** FAM. molesto, maldito.

pe·so (pā′sō) s. [pl. **-sos**] FIN. peso.

pes·sa·ry (pĕs′ə-rē) s. [pl. **-ries**] MED. pesario.

pes·si·mism (pĕs′ə-mĭz′əm) s. pesimismo.

pes·si·mist (pĕs′ə-mĭst) s. pesimista *mf*.

pes·si·mis·tic (pĕs′ə-mĭs′tĭk) adj. pesimista.

pest (pĕst) s. *(insect)* insecto; *(person)* pelmazo, persona molesta; *(plant, animal)* plaga, peste *f*; *(pestilence)* peste, pestilencia.

pes·ter (pĕs′tər) tr. molestar, fastidiar ♦ **to p. someone (for something)** importunar a alguien sin parar (para obtener algo).

pes·ti·cide (pĕs′tĭ-sīd′) s. pesticida, insecticida.

pes·tif·er·ous (pĕ-stĭf′ər-əs) adj. *(bringing disease)* pestífero, pestilente; *(contaminated)* nocivo, malsano; *(morally evil)* pernicioso; FAM. *(bothersome)* molesto.

pes·ti·lence (pĕs′tə-ləns) s. pestilencia, peste *f*.

pes·ti·lent (pĕs′tə-lənt) o **pes·ti·len·tial** (pĕs′tə-lĕn′shəl) adj. *(deadly)* mortífero; *(causing epidemic)* pestífero, pesti-

---

ă rey / ä año / b boca / ch chico / d dar / ě el / ē mil / g gato / h joya / hw juez / ī aire / k casa / kw cuan /

lente; *(contaminated)* nocivo, malsano; *(pernicious)* pernicioso; *(annoying)* molesto.

pes·tle (pĕs'əl, pĕs'təl) I. mano (de mortero) *f* II. tr. & intr. **-tled, -tling** majar.

pet[1] (pĕt) I. s. *(animal)* animal domesticado; *(person)* favorito, preferido II. adj. *(domestic)* domesticado; *(favorite)* favorito ♦ **p. name** nombre cariñoso III. tr. **pet·ted, pet· ting** *(to caress)* acariciar; *(to pamper)* mimar —intr. FAM. acariciarse.

pet[2] (pĕt) I. s. enojo, mal humor *m* II. intr. **pet·ted, pet·ting** enojarse.

pet·al (pĕt'l) s. BOT. pétalo.

pe·tard (pĭ-tärd') s. petardo.

pe·ter (pē'tər) intr. ♦ **to p. out** *(to disappear slowly)* desaparecer lentamente; *(diminish)* disminuir; *(to become exhausted)* agotarse, acabarse.

Pe·ter (pē'tər) s. BÍBL. Pedro ♦ **to rob P. to pay Paul** FAM. desnudar a un santo para vestir a otro.

pet·i·ole (pĕt'ē-ōl') s. BOT., ZOOL. pecíolo, peciolo.

pe·tite (pə-tēt') I. adj. pequeña, chiquita II. s. tamaño pequeño.

petite bour·geoi·sie (bŏŏr'zhwä-zē') s. pequeña burguesía.

pe·ti·tion (pə-tĭsh'ən) I. s. *(document)* petición *f*, solicitud *f*; DER. petición, demanda II. tr. ♦ **to p. for** DER. presentar demanda a • **to p. (someone)** pedir a (alguien).

pe·ti·tion·er (pə-tĭsh'ə-nər) s. *(one who petitions)* peticionario, solicitante *mf*; DER. *(one who enters a plea)* demandante *mf*.

pet·it jury (pĕt'ē) s. jurado de juicio (compuesto de doce personas).

Pe·tri dish (pē'trē) s. BIOL. platillo *o* cápsula de Petri (para cultivos microbiológicos).

pet·ri·fac·tion (pĕt'rə-făk'shən) *o* **pet·ri·fi·ca·tion** (-fĭ-kā'shən) s. petrificación *f*, fosilización *f*.

pet·ri·fy (pĕt'rə-fī') tr. & intr. **-fied, -fy·ing** petrificar(se).

pet·ro·chem·i·cal (pĕt'rō-kĕm'ĭ-kəl) s. producto petroquímico.

pet·ro·dol·lar (pĕt'rō-dŏl'ər) s. ECON., FIN. petrodólar *m*.

pet·rol (pĕt'rəl) s. G.B. gasolina.

pe·tro·le·um (pə-trō'lē-əm) s. petróleo.

petroleum jelly s. FARM. petrolato.

pe·trol·o·gy (pə-trŏl'ə-jē) s. GEOL., MIN. petrología.

pet·ro·pol·i·tics (pĕt'rō-pŏl'ĭ-tĭks) s. [ú. con v. sing. o pl.] manipulación de la producción y venta del petróleo con ciertas finalidades económicas y políticas.

pet·rous (pĕt'rəs) adj. *(stony)* pétreo, rocoso; ANAT. petrosal, petroso.

pet·ti·coat (pĕt'ē-kōt') I. s. *(skirt)* enaguas *f*; JER. *(woman)* mujer *f*; *(girl)* muchacha II. adj. *(feminine)* femenino; *(by women)* de mujeres <**p. government** gobierno de mujeres>.

pet·ti·fog·ger (pĕt'ē-fŏg'ər) s. picapleitos *m*.

pet·ti·ness (pĕt'ē-nĭs) s. *(smallness)* pequeñez *f*; *(petty behavior)* mezquindad *f*.

pet·ting (pĕt'ĭng) s. FAM. besuqueo.

pet·tish (pĕt'ĭsh) adj. malhumorado, displicente.

pet·ty (pĕt'ē) adj. **-ti·er, -ti·est** *(insignificant)* insignificante, trivial; *(narrow-minded)* mezquino; FAM. *(spiteful)* rencoroso.

petty cash s. caja chica, fondo para gastos menores.

petty larceny s. DER. hurto menor, ratería.

petty officer s. MARÍT. contramaestre *m*, cabo de mar.

pet·u·lance (pĕch'ə-ləns) *o* **pet·u·lan·cy** (-lən-sē) s. *(bad humor)* malhumor *m*; *(irritability)* susceptibilidad *f*.

pet·u·lant (pĕch'ə-lənt) adj. *(peevish)* malhumorado, irritable; *(contemptuous)* petulante.

pe·tu·nia (pĭ-tōōn'yə, -tyōōn'-) s. BOT. petunia; *(color)* color púrpura violáceo *m*.

pew (pyōō) s. banco de iglesia ♦ **pews** congregación.

pew·ter (pyōō'tər) I. s. *(alloy)* peltre *m*; *(utensils)* utensilios de peltre II. adj. de peltre.

pe·yo·te (pā-ō'tē) *o* **pe·yo·tl** (pā-ōt'l) s. peyote *m*.

pfen·nig (fĕn'ĭg) s. [pl. **pfen·nigs** *o* **pfen·ni·ge** (fĕn'ĭ-gə)] FIN. pfennig (centavo alemán) *m*.

pha·e·ton (fā'ĭ-tn) s. faetón *m*.

phage (fāj) s. bacteriófago.

phag·o·cyte (făg'ə-sīt') s. fagocito.

pha·lanx (fā'lăngks') s. [pl. **pha·lanx·es** *o* **pha·lan·ges** (fə-lăn'jēz)] falange *f*.

phal·li (făl'ī) un pl. de **phallus**.

phal·lic (făl'ĭk) adj. fálico.

phal·lus (făl'əs) s. [pl. **phal·li** (făl'ī') *o* **phal·lus·es**] falo.

phan·tasm (făn'tăz'əm) s. *(phantom)* fantasma *m*; *(image)* ilusión *f*.

phan·tas·ma·go·ri·a (făn-tăz'mə-gôr'ē-ə) adj. fantasmagoría.

phan·tom (făn'təm) I. s. *(phantasm)* fantasma *m*; *(image)* ilusión *f* II. adj. *(ghostlike)* fantasmal; *(unreal)* ilusorio, ficticio.

Phar·aoh *o* **phar·aoh** (fâr'ō) s. faraón *m*.

phar·i·sa·ic (făr'ĭ-sā'ĭk) *o* **phar·i·sa·i·cal** (-ĭ-kəl) adj. farisaico.

phar·i·see (fâr'ĭ-sē) s. fariseo, hipócrita *mf*.

phar·ma·ceu·ti·cal (fär'mə-sōō'tĭ-kəl) *o* **phar·ma·ceu·tic** (-tĭk) adj. & s. farmacéutico.

phar·ma·ceu·tics (fär'mə-sōō'tĭks) s. [ú. con v. sing.] farmacia (ciencia).

phar·ma·cist (fär'mə-sĭst) s. farmacéutico.

phar·ma·col·o·gy (fär'mə-kŏl'ə-jē) s. FARM. farmacología.

phar·ma·co·poe·ia (fär'mə-kə-pē'ə) s. FARM. farmacopea.

phar·ma·cy (fär'mə-sē) s. [pl. **-cies**] farmacia (práctica o tienda).

pha·ryn·ge·al (fə-rĭn'jē-əl) *o* **pha·ryn·gal** (-rĭng'əl) adj. faríngeo.

phar·yn·ges (fə-rĭn'jēz) un pl. de **pharynx**.

phar·yn·gi·tis (făr'ĭn-jī'tĭs) s. MED. faringitis *f*.

phar·ynx (făr'ĭngks) s. [pl. **pha·ryn·ges** (fə-rĭn'jēz) *o* **phar·ynx·es**] ANAT. faringe *f*.

phase (fāz) I. s. *(stage)* fase *f*; ASTRON., BIOL., FÍS. fase ♦ **in p.** ELEC., FÍS. en fase, sincronizado • **out of p.** ELEC., FÍS. desfasado II. tr. **phased, phas·ing** *(to plan)* planear por fases, escalonar; ELEC., FÍS. poner en fase ♦ **to p. in** introducir progresivamente • **to p. out** eliminar *o* reducir progresivamente.

phase-out (fāz'out') s. TEC. eliminación gradual *f*.

pheas·ant (fĕz'ənt) s. [pl. **pheas·ants** *o* **pheasant**] ORNIT. faisán *m*.

phe·nix (fē'nĭks) s. var. de **phoenix**.

Phe·no·bar·bi·tal (fē'nō-bär'bĭ-tôl') s. FARM. marca registrada de un sedativo.

phe·nol (fē'nôl') s. QUÍM. fenol *m*, ácido fénico.

phe·nom·e·na (fĭ-nŏm'ə-nə) un pl. de **phenomenon**.

phe·nom·e·nal (fĭ-nŏm'ə-nəl) adj. fenomenal.

phe·nom·e·nal·ism (fĭ-nŏm'ə-nə-lĭz'əm) s. FILOS. fenomenalismo, fenomenismo.

phe·nom·e·nol·o·gy (fĭ-nŏm'ə-nŏl'ə-jē) s. FILOS., FÍS. fenomenología.

phe·nom·e·non (fĭ-nŏm'ə-nŏn') s. [pl. **-na** (-nə) *o* **-nons**] fenómeno.

phe·no·type (fē'nə-tīp') s. BIOL. fenotipo (caracteres hereditarios comunes).

phen·yl (fĕn'əl, fē'nəl) s. QUÍM. fenilo.

phew (fyōō) interj. ¡uy!, ¡puf!

phi (fī) s. phi *f*, fi *f*.

phi·al (fī'əl) s. *(bottle)* frasco pequeño; *(ampule)* ampolla *f*.

Phi Be·ta Kap·pa (fī' bā'tə kăp'ə) s. EDUC. sociedad de estudiantes universitarios de grandes méritos académicos *f*.

Phil·a·del·phi·a (fĭl'ə-dĕl'fē-ə) s. Filadelfia ♦ **P. lawyer** FAM. abogado muy astuto.

phi·lan·der (fĭ-lăn'dər) intr. galantear, ser mujeriego.

phi·lan·der·er (fĭ-lăn'dər-ər) s. galanteador *m*, tenorio.

phil·an·throp·ic (fĭl'ən-thrŏp'ĭk) *o* **phil·an·throp·i·cal** (-ĭ-kəl) adj. filantrópico.

phi·lan·thro·pist (fĭ-lăn'thrə-pĭst) s. filántropo.

phi·lan·thro·py (fĭ-lăn'thrə-pē) s. [pl. **-pies**] *(benevolence)* filantropía; *(institution)* institución filantrópica.

phi·lat·e·ly (fĭ-lăt'l-ē) s. filatelia.

phil·har·mon·ic (fĭl'här-mŏn'ĭk, fĭl'ər-) I. adj. filarmónico II. s. *(orchestra)* orquesta filarmónica; *(supporting group)* sociedad filarmónica.

Phi·lip·pi·ans (fĭ-lĭp'ē-ənz) s. BÍBL. filipenses.

Phi·lip·pic (fĭ-lĭp′ĭk) s. HIST. Filípica (de Demóstenes o de Cicerón) ♦ **p.** filípica.
Phil·ip·pine (fĭl′ə-pēn′) adj. filipino.
Phil·ip·pines (fĭl′ə-pēnz′) I. s. HIST. Filipinas.
Phil·is·tine (fĭl′ĭ-stēn′) I. s. HIST. *(inhabitant)* filisteo; *(boor)* persona inculta *o* ignorante II. adj. inculto.
Phil·is·tin·ism *o* **phil·is·tin·ism** (fĭl′ĭ-stē′nĭz′əm) s. prosaísmo.
phil·o·den·dron (fĭl′ə-dĕn′drən) s. [pl. **-drons** *o* **-dra** (-drə)] BOT. filodendro.
phi·lol·o·gy (fĭ-lŏl′ə-jē) s. filología.
phi·los·o·pher (fĭ-lŏs′ə-fər) s. filósofo.
philosophers' stone *o* **philosopher's stone** s. piedra filosofal.
phil·o·soph·i·cal (fĭl′ə-sŏf′ĭ-kəl) *o* **phil·o·soph·ic** (-ĭk) adj. filosófico.
phil·o·soph·i·cal·ly (fĭl′ə-sŏf′ĭ-klē) adv. filosóficamente.
phi·los·o·phize (fĭ-lŏs′ə-fīz′) intr. **-phized, -phiz·ing** filosofar.
phi·los·o·phiz·er (fĭ-lŏs′ə-fī′zər) s. filosofador *m*.
phi·los·o·phy (fĭ-lŏs′ə-fē) s. [pl. **-phies**] filosofía ♦ **Doctor of P.** doctor en filosofía y letras • **one's p. of** el concepto que uno tiene de.
phil·ter *o* **phil·tre** (fĭl′tər) I. s. poción *f*, filtro II. tr. encantar.
phle·bi·tis (flĭ-bī′tĭs) s. MED. flebitis *f*.
phle·bot·o·my (flĭ-bŏt′ə-mē) s. [pl. **-mies**] flebotomía.
phlegm (flĕm) s. *(mucus)* flema, moco; *(sluggishness)* lentitud *f*, cachaza; *(equanimity)* flema, ecuanimidad *f*.
phleg·mat·ic (flĕg-măt′ĭk) *o* **phleg·mat·i·cal** (-ĭ-kəl) adj. FISIOL. flemático; *(calm)* flemático, cachazudo.
phlo·em (flō′ĕm′) s. BOT. floema, líber (tejido de conducción) *m*.
phlox (flŏks) s. [pl. **phlox** *o* **phlox·es**] BOT. flox *m*.
pho·bi·a (fō′bē-ə) s. fobia.
Phoe·bus (fē′bəs) s. MITOL. Febo.
Phoe·ni·cia (fĭ-nĭsh′ə, -nē′shə) s. Fenicia.
Phoe·ni·cian (fĭ-nĭsh′ən, -nē′shən) HIST. I. adj. fenicio II. s. *(inhabitant, language)* fenicio.
phoe·nix (fē′nĭks) s. MITOL. fénix *m*; *(paragon)* fénix ♦ **p.** ASTRON. ave fénix *f*.
phone[1] (fōn) s. FONÉT. fonema *m*.
phone[2] (fōn) s. FAM. I. s. *(telephone)* teléfono; *(earphone)* audífono, auricular *m* II. tr. & intr. **phoned, phon·ing** telefonear, llamar por teléfono.
phone call s. llamada telefónica.
pho·neme (fō′nēm′) s. FONÉT. fonema *m*.
pho·net·ic (fə-nĕt′ĭk) adj. fonético.
phonetic alphabet s. alfabeto fonético.
pho·ne·ti·cian (fō′nĭ-tĭsh′ən) *o* **pho·net·i·cist** (fə-nĕt′ĭ-sĭst) s. fonetista *mf*.
pho·net·ics (fə-nĕt′ĭks) s. [ú. con v. sing.] fonética.
pho·ney (fō′nē) adj. & s. var. de **phony**.
phon·ic (fŏn′ĭk) adj. fónico.
phon·ics (fŏn′ĭks) s. [ú. con v. sing.] *(science)* acústica; *(phonetics)* fonética.
pho·no·gram (fō′nə-grăm′) s. GRAM. fonograma *m*.
pho·no·graph (fō′nə-grăf′) s. fonógrafo, gramófono ♦ **p. record** disco fonográfico.
pho·nog·ra·phy (fə-nŏg′rə-fē) s. fonografía.
pho·nol·o·gy (fə-nŏl′ə-jē) s. GRAM. fonología.
pho·ny (fō′nē) FAM. I. adj. **-ni·er, -ni·est** *(fraudulent)* falso; *(fake)* postizo II. s. [pl. **-nies**] *(object)* camelo; *(person)* farsante *mf*, camelista *mf*.
phoo·ey (fōō′ē) interj. ¡puf!
phos·phate (fŏs′fāt′) s. fosfato.
phos·phine (fŏs′fēn′) s. QUÍM. fosfina.
phos·phor (fŏs′fər, -fôr′) s. FÍS. substancia fosforescente *o* luminiscente.
phos·pho·resce (fŏs′fə-rĕs′) intr. **-resced, -resc·ing** FÍS. fosforecer.
phos·pho·res·cence (fŏs′fə-rĕs′əns) s. FÍS. *(light emission)* fosforescencia; *(bioluminescence)* bioluminiscencia.
phos·pho·res·cent (fŏs′fə-rĕs′ənt) adj. fosforescente.
phos·phor·ic (fŏs-fôr′ĭk) adj. QUÍM. fosfórico.
phos·pho·rism (fŏs′fə-rĭz′əm) s. MED. fosforismo.

phos·pho·rus (fŏs′fər-əs, fŏs-fôr′əs) s. QUÍM. fósforo.
pho·to (fō′tō) s. [pl. **-tos**] foto, fotografía.
pho·to·cell (fō′tō-sĕl′) s. ELECTRÓN. fotocélula, célula *o* pila fotoeléctrica.
pho·to·chem·is·try (fō′tō-kĕm′ĭ-strē) s. FÍS., QUÍM. fotoquímica.
pho·to·com·po·si·tion (fō′tō-kŏm′pə-zĭsh′ən) s. FOTOG., TIP. fotocomposición *f*.
pho·to·cop·i·er (fō′tə-kŏp′ē-ər) s. FOTOG. fotocopiadora.
pho·to·cop·y (fō′tə-kŏp′ē) I. tr. **-ied, -y·ing** fotocopiar II. s. [pl. **-ies**] fotocopia.
pho·to·dra·ma (fō′tə-drä′mə, -drăm′ə) s. CINE. drama cinematográfico.
pho·to·e·lec·tric (fō′tō-ĭ-lĕk′trĭk) *o* **pho·to·e·lec·tri·cal** (-trĭ-kəl) adj. ELECTRÓN., FÍS. fotoeléctrico.
photoelectric cell s. ELECTRÓN. célula fotoeléctrica.
pho·to·e·lec·tron (fō′tō-ĭ-lĕk′trŏn′) s. FÍS. fotoelectrón *m*.
pho·to·en·grave (fō′tō-ĕn-grāv′) tr. **-graved, -grav·ing** IMPR. fotograbar.
pho·to·en·grav·ing (fō′tō-ĕn-grā′vĭng) s. FOTOG., TIP. fotograbado.
photo finish s. DEP. final de carrera decidido por foto *m*; FIG. *(close contest)* competencia muy reñida.
pho·to·flash (fō′tō-flăsh′) s. FOTOG. flash *m*, luz relámpago *f*.
pho·to·gen·ic (fō′tə-jĕn′ĭk) adj. fotogénico; BIOL. fosforescente.
pho·to·graph (fō′tə-grăf′) I. s. fotografía, foto *f* II. tr. fotografiar, sacar una fotografía —intr. ♦ **to p. well** salir bien en las fotografías.
pho·tog·ra·pher (fə-tŏg′rə-phər) s. fotógrafo.
pho·to·graph·ic (fō′tə-grăf′ĭk) *o* **pho·to·graph·i·cal** (-ĭ-kəl) adj. fotográfico.
pho·tog·ra·phy (fə-tŏg′rə-fē) s. fotografía.
pho·to·gra·vure (fō′tə-grə-vyōōr′) s. IMPR. fotograbado.
pho·to·ki·ne·sis (fō′tō-kĭ-nē′sĭs) s. BIOL. fotocinesis *f*.
pho·tol·y·sis (fō-tŏl′ĭ-sĭs) s. BOT., FÍS., QUÍM. fotólisis *f*.
pho·tom·e·ter (fō-tŏm′ĭ-tər) s. FÍS. fotómetro.
pho·tom·e·try (fō-tŏm′ĭ-trē) s. FÍS. fotometría.
pho·to·mon·tage (fō′tō-mŏn-täzh′) s. fotomontaje *m*, montaje fotográfico.
pho·ton (fō′tŏn′) s. FÍS. fotón *m*.
pho·to·off·set (fō′tō-ôf′sĕt′) s. IMPR. offset *m*.
pho·to·play (fō′tō-plā′) s. CINE. drama cinematográfico.
pho·to·re·al·ism (fō′tō-rē′ə-lĭz′əm) s. PINT. fotorealismo (estilo).
pho·to·sen·si·tive (fō′tō-sĕn′sĭ-tĭv) adj. FÍS. fotosensible.
pho·to·sphere (fō′tə-sfîr′) s. ASTRON. fotosfera.
pho·to·stat (fō′tə-stăt′) s. FOTOG. fotostato, copia fotostática ♦ **P.** marca registrada de un procedimiento de reproducción fotográfica.
pho·to·syn·the·sis (fō′tō-sĭn′thĭ-sĭs) s. BOT., QUÍM. fotosíntesis *f*.
pho·to·tel·e·graph (fō′tō-tĕl′ĭ-grăf′) tr. fototelegrafiar.
pho·tot·ro·pism (fō-tŏt′rə-pĭz′əm) s. BOT. fototropismo; QUÍM. fototropía.
pho·to·type·set·ting (fō′tō-tīp′sĕt′ĭng) s. IMPR. fotocomposición *f*.
pho·to·vol·ta·ic (fō′tō-vŏl-tā′ĭk) adj. FÍS. fotovoltaico.
phrase (frāz) I. s. frase *f*; *(expression)* frase, locución *f*; MÚS. frase ♦ **set p.** frase hecha II. tr. **phrased, phras·ing** *(in speaking)* formular, expresar; *(in writing)* redactar; MÚS. frasear.
phrase book s. diccionario de expresiones.
phra·se·ol·o·gy (frā′zē-ŏl′ə-jē) s. [pl. **-gies**] fraseología.
phras·ing (frā′zĭng) s. *(wording)* estilo, lenguaje *m* <*the p. of the paragraph* el lenguaje del párrafo>; *(phraseology)* fraseología; MÚS. fraseo.
phre·net·ic (frə-nĕt′ĭk) *o* **phre·net·i·cal** (-ĭ-kəl) var. de **frenetic**.
phre·nol·o·gy (frĭ-nŏl′ə-jē) s. ANAT. frenología.
Phryg·i·a (frĭj′ē-ə) s. Frigia.
Phryg·i·an (frĭj′ē-ən) adj. & s. frigio.
phthi·sis (thī′sĭs) *o* **phthis·ic** (tĭz′ĭk) s. MED. tisis *f*.
phy·la (fī′lə) pl. de **phylum**.

phy·lac·ter·y (fĭ-lăk'tə-rē) s. [pl. **-ies**] RELIG. filacteria; *(amulet)* amuleto, talismán *m*.
phyl·lox·e·ra (fĭl'ŏk-sîr'ə, fĭ-lŏk'sər-ə) s. ENTOM. filoxera.
phy·log·e·ny (fī-lŏj'ə-nē) s. [pl. **-nies**] BIOL. filogenia.
phy·lum (fī'ləm) s. [pl. **-la** (-lə)] BIOL. filum *m*, filo; FILOL. filo.
phys·i·at·ry (fĭz'ē-ăt'rē) s. MED. fisioterapia, fisiatría.
phys·ic (fĭz'ĭk) s. *(medicine)* medicamento; *(cathartic)* catártico.
phys·i·cal (fĭz'ĭ-kəl) **I.** adj. *(bodily)* físico <*p.* strength fuerza física>; FIG. *(material)* material, físico <*p.* impossibility imposibilidad física>; FÍS. físico **II.** s. reconocimiento médico <*to get a p.* hacerse un reconocimiento médico>.
physical education s. educación física.
physical examination s. reconocimiento médico.
physical geography s. geografía física.
physical medicine s. medicina física.
physical science s. ciencia física.
phy·si·cian (fĭ-zĭsh'ən) s. MED. médico, facultativo.
phys·i·cist (fĭz'ĭ-sĭst) s. FÍS. físico.
phys·ics (fĭz'ĭks) s. [ú. con v. sing.] física.
phys·i·og·no·my (fĭz'ē-ŏg'nə-mē) s. [pl. **-mies**] fisonomía.
phys·i·o·log·i·cal (fĭz'ē-ə-lŏj'ĭ-kəl) *o* **phys·i·o·log·ic** (-ĭk) adj. fisiológico.
phys·i·ol·o·gist (fĭz'ē-ŏl'ə-jĭst) s. fisiólogo.
phys·i·ol·o·gy (fĭz'ē-ŏl'ə-jē) s. fisiología.
phys·i·o·ther·a·py (fĭz'ē-ō-thĕr'ə-pē) s. MED. fisioterapia.
phy·sique (fĭ-zēk') s. físico, constitución del cuerpo *f*.
phy·tol·o·gy (fī-tŏl'ə-jē) s. CIENT. fitología, botánica.
pi (pī) s. [pl. **pis**] pi (letra griega) *f*; MAT. pi (número).
pi·an·ism (pē'ə-nĭz'əm, pē-ăn'ĭz'əm) s. MÚS. arte de tocar el piano *m*.
pi·an·ist (pē-ăn'ĭst, pē'ə-nĭst) s. pianista *mf*.
pi·a·nis·tic (pē'ə-nĭs'tĭk) adj. pianístico.
pi·an·o¹ (pē-ăn'ō, -ä'nō) s. [pl. **-os**] MÚS. piano.
pi·a·no² (pē-ä'nō) MÚS. **I.** adv. *(softly)* piano **II.** s. [pl. **-nos**] pasaje a ejecutarse piano *m*.
piano bar s. bar que presenta a un pianista como entretenimiento.
pi·an·o·for·te (pē-ăn'ō-fôr'tē, -fôrt', -ä'nō-) s. MÚS. pianoforte *m*, piano.
pi·as·ter *o* **pi·as·tre** (pē-ăs'tər, -ä'stər) s. FIN. piastra.
pi·az·za (pē-ăz'ə, -ä'zə) s. [pl. **pi·az·zas** *o* **pi·az·ze** (pē-ăt'sä, -ät'-)] *(square)* plaza; *(colonnade)* columnata, peristilo; *(verandah)* galería, terraza.
pi·ca¹ (pī'kə) s. IMPR. pica (unidad de anchura tipográfica).
pi·ca² (pī'kə) s. MED., VET. pica, malacia.
Pic·ar·dy (pĭk'ər-dē) s. Picardía.
pic·a·resque (pĭk'ə-rĕsk') **I.** adj. picaresco **II.** s. persona picaresca, pícaro.
pic·a·yune (pĭk'ē-yōōn') **I.** adj. *(paltry)* insignificante; *(petty)* mezquino **II.** s. ♦ **it's not worth a p.** no vale un pepino.
pic·co·lo¹ (pĭk'ə-lō) s. [pl. **-los**] MÚS. flautín *m*.
pic·co·lo² (pĭk'ə-lō) adj. pequeño <*a p.* trumpet una trompeta pequeña>.
pick¹ (pĭk) **I.** tr. *(to choose)* escoger, elegir; *(to decide on)* seleccionar; *(to gather)* coger, recoger <*to p.* flowers coger flores>; *(to strip clean)* limpiar, mondar <*to p.* the bones limpiar los huesos>; *(to pluck)* desplumar; *(to tear off)* sacar, arrancar; *(to probe)* escarbar (con los dedos, utensilio); *(to break up)* cavar (tierra); *(a hole)* abrir (agujero); *(to peck)* picar, picotear; MÚS. puntear, pulsar ♦ **to have a bone to p. with** FIG., FAM. tener que pedir cuenta a ● **to p. a fight** buscar bronca ● **to p. a lock** abrir un candado con una ganzúa ● **to p. apart** *(to tear)* destrozar, despedazar; *(to refute)* echar por tierra (argumento, testimonio) ● **to p. holes in** buscar las fallas de (argumento) ● **to p. off** *(to kill)* matar de un solo tiro; DEP. *(in football)* cortar, interceptar (pase) ● **to p. oneself up** levantarse ● **to p. one's nose** hurgarse la nariz ● **to p. one's teeth** mondarse los dientes ● **to p. one's way** abrirse paso con cuidado ● **to p. out** *(to choose)* escoger, seleccionar; *(to distinguish)* distinguir (persona, edificio); MÚS. *(a tune)* teclear de oído ● **to p. over** inspeccionar ● **to p. someone's brains** FIG. explotar

los conocimientos de alguien ● **to p. someone's pocket** robar algo del bolsillo de alguien ● **to p. up** *(to lift)* coger <*to p.* up the phone coger el teléfono>; *(fallen object)* recoger (del piso); *(to tidy)* recoger (habitación); *(to stop for)* recoger (a un amigo); FAM. *(to buy)* comprar; *(to learn)* aprender; *(to notice)* encontrar; *(a habit)* coger, adquirir; pagar (cuenta); *(a disease)* coger, pescar (enfermedad); RAD., TELEV. *(to receive)* coger, captar (estación); *(speed)* coger, cobrar (velocidad); JER. *(to arrest)* pescar, coger; *(to meet casually)* ligar con (persona); *(a scent, trail)* descubrir, encontrar; *(to continue)* reanudar, proseguir ● **to p. up on** darse cuenta de —intr. *(with a tool)* picar; *(to decide)* decidir cuidadosamente ♦ **to p. and choose** andar con miramientos al escoger ● **to p. at** *(a scab)* escarbarse; *(food)* picar, picotear; FAM. *(to nag)* cogerla con ● **to p. on** *(to tease)* atormentar <*they are always picking on him* siempre lo atormentan>; *(to bully)* abusar de (una persona) ● **to p. up** *(to resume)* continuar; FAM. *(to improve)* mejorar; *(to pack)* recoger los bártulos <*to just p.* up and leave recoger los bártulos e irse> **II.** s. *(comb)* peineta; *(choice)* elección *f*, selección *f*; *(of produce)* recogida, cosecha ♦ **the p. of the crop** *o* **of the litter** la flor y nata ● **to have the p. of** poder escoger entre ● **to take one's p.** elegir lo que uno quiera.
pick² (pĭk) s. *(tool)* piqueta, pico; *(picklock)* ganzúa; MÚS. plectro, púa.
pick³ (pĭk) TEJ. **I.** s. *(thread)* hilo del tejido; *(passage)* golpe de lanzadera *m* **II.** tr. lanzar (la lanzadera).
pick·a·back (pĭk'ə-băk') **I.** adv. a cuestas, sobre los hombros **II.** s. paseo a cuestas.
pick·a·nin·ny (pĭk'ə-nĭn'ē) s. [pl. **-nies**] DESPEC. negrito.
pick·ax *o* **pick·axe** (pĭk'ăks') **I.** s. piqueta, zapapico **II.** intr. **-axed, -ax·ing** trabajar con piqueta *o* zapapico —tr. demoler con piqueta *o* zapapico.
picked (pĭkt) adj. escogido, selecto.
pick·er (pĭk'ər) s. *(person, tool)* recogedor *m*; *(of cotton)* desmontadora.
pick·er·el (pĭk'ər-əl) s. [pl. **pickerel** *o* **-rels**] ICT. pez norteamericano parecido al lucio.
pick·et (pĭk'ĭt) **I.** s. *(stake)* estaca; MIL. piquete *m*; *(strikers)* piquete (de huelga); *(demonstrators)* manifestantes *m* **II.** tr. *(to enclose)* cercar con estacas; *(a factory, military post)* guardar *o* vigilar con piquetes —intr. vigilar, estar de guardia.
picket fence s. cerca de estacas puntiagudas.
picket line s. piquetes (de huelguistas, manifestantes) *m*.
pick·ing (pĭk'ĭng) s. *(harvest)* cosecha, recolección *f*; *(choice)* selección *f* ♦ **pickings** sobras, restos.
pick·le (pĭk'əl) **I.** s. CUL. *(food)* encurtido; *(solution)* salmuera, escabeche *m*; FAM. *(plight)* lío <*to be in a p.* estar metido en un lío> **II.** tr. **-led, -ling** encurtir, conservar en vinagre.
pick·led (pĭk'əld) adj. CUL. *(food)* en salmuera *o* escabeche; FAM. *(person)* borracho, bebido.
pick·ling (pĭk'lĭng) s. encurtido.
pick·lock (pĭk'lŏk') s. *(person)* ladrón de ganzúa *m*, ratero; *(instrument)* ganzúa.
pick·pock·et (pĭk'pŏk'ĭt) s. carterista *mf*, ratero.
pick·proof (pĭk'prōōf') adj. a prueba de robos.
pick·up (pĭk'ŭp') s. *(collection)* recogida, *(ability to accelerate)* arrancada, poder de aceleración *m*; *(truck)* camioneta; *(phonograph)* fonocaptor *m*; *(reception)* recepción (de sonido, luz) *f*; *(receiver)* receptor *m*; *(broadcast)* transmisión *f*; FAM. *(increase)* aumento <*a p.* in sales un aumento de las ventas>; *(improvement)* mejora; JER. *(arrest)* arresto, detención *f*; *(casual acquaintance)* ligue *m*.
pickup truck s. camioneta de reparto.
pick·y (pĭk'ē) adj. **-i·er, -i·est** FAM. difícil, quisquilloso.
pic·nic (pĭk'nĭk) **I.** s. *(meal)* merienda *o* comida campestre; FAM. *(easy task)* cosa *o* tarea fácil *o* tirada; *(pleasant experience)* experiencia *o* rato placentero, placer *m* ♦ **to be no p.** FAM. no ser fácil ● **to go on a p.** ir de merienda **II.** intr. **-nicked, -nick·ing** merendar *o* comer al aire libre.
pic·ric acid (pĭk'rĭk) s. QUÍM. ácido pícrico.
Pict (pĭkt) s. HIST. *(inhabitant)* picto.
pic·to·gram (pĭk'tə-grăm') s. pictograma *m*.

---

ng inglés / ŏ la / ō bou / ô corre / oi oigo / ōō uno / ou auto / yōō ciudad / w hueco / y yo / z mismo

pic·to·graph (pĭk′tə-grăf′) s. pictografía.
pic·to·ri·al (pĭk-tôr′ē-əl) adj. *(of, with pictures)* pictórico; *(descriptive)* descriptivo, gráfico; *(illustrated)* ilustrado.
pic·ture (pĭk′chər) I. s. *(painting)* cuadro, pintura; *(illustration)* ilustración *f* <*children like books with pictures* a los niños les gustan los libros con ilustraciones>; *(photograph)* fotografía <*to take a p.* sacar una fotografía>; *(portrait)* retrato; *(mental image)* imagen *f*, idea <*I don't have a clear p. of the situation* no tengo una imagen clara de la situación>; *(description)* descripción *f*, cuadro; *(physical image)* retrato, imagen <*she's the p. of her mother* es el retrato de la madre>; *(embodiment)* imagen viva; *(film)* película, filme *m*; *(on a television screen)* imagen <*the p. was blurry* la imagen estaba borrosa> ♦ **p. postcard** tarjeta postal con cuadro • **p. tube** TELEV. tubo de pantalla • **pretty as a p.** una monada • **to be out of the p.** quedar fuera del juego • **to come into the p.** aparecer • **to give somebody the general p.** dar a alguien una idea general • **to paint a rosy p. of** pintar un cuadro muy optimista de • **to change the whole p.** cambiarlo todo II. tr. **-tured, -tur·ing** *(to paint)* pintar (un cuadro); *(to draw)* dibujar; *(to visualize)* imaginarse <*I can't p. him as a salesman* no me lo imagino de vendedor>; *(to describe)* pintar, representar.
picture book s. libro ilustrado.
picture frame s. marco (de cuadro).
pic·tur·esque (pĭk′chə-rĕsk′) adj. *(quaint)* pintoresco; *(typical)* típico <*a p. French café* un café francés típico>; *(language)* descriptivo, gráfico.
picture window s. ventanal *m*.
picture writing s. pictografía.
pid·dle (pĭd′l) tr. **-dled, -dling** emplear en tonterías <*to p. away one's time* emplear el tiempo en tonterías> —intr. *(to diddle)* malgastar el tiempo; FAM. *(to urinate)* orinar, hacer pipí.
pid·dling (pĭd′lĭng) adj. insignificante, trivial.
pidg·in (pĭj′ĭn) s. lengua franca, lengua macarrónica.
Pidgin English s. lengua franca basada en el inglés utilizada en intercambios comerciales en el Asia oriental.
pie (pī) s. CUL. *(with meat)* empanada; *(with fruit)* pastel *m*; *(cake)* tarta ♦ **as American as apple p.** FIG., FAM. muy americano, típicamente americano • **as easy as p.** FIG., FAM. muy fácil • **p. in the sky** FIG. ilusiones • **to have a finger in the p.** FIG. estar metido *o* pringado en el asunto.
pie·bald (pī′bôld′) I. adj. *(horse)* pío; *(cat, dog)* moteado II. s. caballo pío.
piece (pēs) I. s. *(portion)* pedazo, trozo <*a p. of cake* un trozo de tarta>; *(in a set)* pieza; *(specimen)* muestra <*he brought a p. of his work with him* trajo una muestra de su trabajo>; *(coin)* moneda <*a ten-cent p.* una moneda de diez centavos>; *(in a board game)* pieza; *(firearm)* arma; *(rifle)* escopeta; *(distance)* tramo, trecho <*it's down the road a p.* está un trecho más abajo en esta misma carretera>; LIT., MÚS. obra ♦ **a p. of advice** un consejo • **a p. of clothing** una prenda de ropa • **a p. of furniture** un mueble • **a p. of (good) luck** una suerte • **a p. of jewelry** una prenda • **a p. of land** un terreno, una parcela • **a p. of luggage** una maleta, un bulto • **a p. of news** una noticia • **a p. of nonsense** un disparate • **a p. of paper** *(sheet)* un papel; *(scrap)* un pedazo de papel • **p. by p.** *(bit by bit)* pedazo por pedazo; *(part by part)* pieza por pieza • **to be a p. of cake** FIG., FAM. ser facilísimo • **to get a p. of the action** FAM. *(of an activity)* no quedarse fuera de la fiesta; *(of the profits)* sacar la tajada de uno • **to get there in one p.** *(object)* llegar en buen estado; *(person)* llegar sano y salvo • **to give someone a p. of one's mind** FAM. cantar a alguien las cuarenta, decir a alguien cuatro verdades • **to say one's p.** decir lo que uno piensa • **to be in pieces** *(to be unassembled)* estar desarmado *o* desmontado; *(to be shattered)* estar hecho pedazos *o* añicos • **to break something to pieces** *o* **in pieces** hacer algo pedazos *o* trizas • **to go to pieces** FIG., FAM. no poderse dominar • **to tear to pieces** *(to rend)* desgarrar, despedazar; *(to criticize)* criticar; *(to refute)* desbaratar II. tr. **pieced, piec·ing** ♦ **to p. together** *(to put together)* armar pedazo por pedazo; *(a puzzle)* armar; *(to rearrange)* rehacer; *(to figure out)* atar los cabos de.

piece goods s.pl. géneros, telas que se venden por yardas.
piece·meal (pēs′mēl′) I. adv. *(bit by bit)* a trozos; *(gradually)* poco a poco; *(into pieces)* por partes II. adj. hecho poco a poco.
piece of eight s. FIN. peso (antigua moneda española).
piece·work (pēs′wûrk′) s. trabajo a destajo ♦ **to do p.** trabajar a destajo.
pie chart s. gráfico circular.
pied·mont (pēd′mŏnt′) I. adj. al pie de las montañas II. s. región al pie de las montañas *f.*
pied piper s. *(enticer)* engañador *m*, seductor *m*; *(leader)* persona que crea ilusiones falsas a sus seguidores.
pier (pîr) s. MARÍT. *(for ships)* muelle *m*, embarcadero; ARQ. *(of a bridge)* pila; *(of an arch)* pilar *m*; *(between windows)* entreventana; *(buttress)* contrafuerte *m*.
pierce (pîrs) tr. **pierced, pierc·ing** *(to puncture)* traspasar, atravesar <*the knife pierced his arm* el cuchillo le traspasó el brazo>; *(to perforate)* perforar; *(to penetrate)* atravesar, abrirse paso por; FIG. *(to move deeply)* conmover; *(to shatter)* romper <*to p. the silence* romper el silencio> ♦ **to p. a hole in** hacer un agujero en • **to p. one's heart** FIG. traspasar el corazón de uno • **to p. someone's ears** FIG. traspasar los oídos de alguien • **to p. the air** herir el aire • **to have** *o* **get one's ears pierced** abrirse las orejas, hacerse agujeros en las orejas.
pierc·ing (pîr′sĭng) adj. *(sharp)* agudo; *(look)* penetrante; *(wind)* cortante.
pie·tà *o* **Pie·tà** (pyā-tä′) s. ARTE. piedad (pintura *o* escultura) *f.*
pi·e·tism (pī′ĭ-tĭz′əm) s. *(piety)* piedad *f*; *(exaggerated piety)* mojigatería, beatería ♦ **P.** RELIG. pietismo.
pi·e·ty (pī′ĭ-tē) s. [pl. **-ties**] piedad *f.*
pi·e·zo·e·lec·tric·i·ty (pī-ē′zō-ə-lĕk-trĭs′ĭ-tē) s. piezoelectricidad *f.*
pif·fle (pĭf′əl) s. tontería, disparate *m.*
pig (pĭg) I. s. *(hog)* cerdo, puerco; *(young hog)* lechón *m*, cochinillo; *(pork)* lechón <*roast p.* lechón asado>; FAM. *(glutton)* tragón *m*, glotón *m*; *(slob)* cochino, puerco; METAL. *(lead)* lingote *m*; *(mold)* lingotera; *(iron)* lingote de arrabio; JER., DESPEC. *(police officer)* policía *m* ♦ **a p. in a poke** algo (comprado) sin saber exactamente qué es • **to make a p. of oneself** hartarse como un puerco II. intr. **pigged, pig·ging** parir (lechones) ♦ **to p. out** comer como un puerco.
pi·geon (pĭj′ən) s. ORNIT. paloma; JER. *(dupe)* tonto, bobalicón *m.*
pi·geon·hole (pĭj′ən-hōl′) I. s. *(for birds)* casillero; *(cubbyhole)* casilla; *(category)* categorización *f*, clasificación *f* II. tr. **-holed, -hol·ing** *(to file)* archivar; *(to categorize)* encasillar, clasificar; *(to shelve)* dar carpetazo a.
pi·geon-toed (pĭj′ən-tōd′) adj. de pies que apuntan hacia adentro.
pig·ger·y (pĭg′ə-rē) s. [pl. **-ies**] porqueriza, chiquero.
pig·gish (pĭg′ĭsh) adj. *(greedy)* glotón; *(pigheaded)* testarudo.
pig·gy (pĭg′ē) s. [pl. **-gies**] cerdito.
pig·gy·back (pĭg′ē-băk′) I. adv. *(on the back)* a cuestas, sobre los hombros; *(in transportation)* en vagón plataforma II. tr. llevar III. adj. ♦ **p. ride** paseo a cuestas • **p. shipment** transporte en vagón plataforma.
piggy bank s. alcancía, hucha.
pig·head·ed (pĭg′hĕd′ĭd) adj. testarudo, terco.
pig iron s. arrabio, hierro en lingotes.
pig Latin s. jerigonza, jerga (de niños).
pig·let (pĭg′lĭt) s. cochinillo, lechón *m.*
pig·ment (pĭg′mənt) I. s. *(coloring matter)* pigmento, colorante *m*; BIOL. pigmento II. tr. pigmentar.
pig·men·ta·tion (pĭg′mən-tā′shən) s. BIOL. pigmentación *f.*
Pig·my (pĭg′mē) s. & adj. var. de **Pygmy.**
pig·pen (pĭg′pĕn′) s. pocilga.
pig·skin (pĭg′skĭn′) s. *(skin)* piel de cerdo *f*; *(leather)* cuero de cerdo; *(football)* pelota (de fútbol americano); *(saddle)* silla de montar.
pig·sty (pĭg′stī′) s. [pl. **-sties**] pocilga.
pig·tail (pĭg′tāl′) s. *(hair)* coleta, trenza; *(tobacco)* andullo de tabaco.

ã rey / ä año / b boca / ch chico / d dar / ĕ el / ē mil / g gato / h joya / hw juez / ī aire / k casa / kw cuan /

pike¹ (pīk) **I.** s. *(spear)* pica **II.** tr. **piked, pik·ing** picar, herir con la pica.

pike² (pīk) s. [pl. **pike** o **pikes**] *(fish)* lucio.

pike³ (pīk) **I.** s. *(turnpike)* carretera de peaje; *(tollgate)* barrera de peaje; *(toll)* peaje *m* **II.** intr. **piked, pik·ing** moverse o ir rápidamente.

pike⁴ (pīk) s. G.B. *(hill)* pico, cumbre de montaña *f.*

pike⁵ (pīk) s. *(sharp point)* punta.

pik·er (pī'kər) s. JER. tacaño (esp. uno que juega o especula en muy pequeña escala).

pi·las·ter (pī-lăs'tər) s. ARQ. pilastra.

pil·chard (pĭl'chərd) s. ICT. sardina.

pile¹ (pīl) **I.** s. *(heap)* pila, montón *m;* FAM. *(large quantity)* pila, montón; *(funeral pyre)* pira funeraria; JER. *(fortune)* fortuna <*to make a p.* hacer fortuna>; FÍS. pila atómica, reactor atómico; ELEC. pila, batería **II.** tr. **piled, pil·ing** *(to heap)* apilar, amontar; *(to fill)* llenar ♦ **to p. it on** exagerar • **to p. up** apilar, amontonar —intr. amontonarse ♦ **to p. in** entrar en tropel • **to p. up** acumularse.

pile² (pīl) **I.** s. *(footing)* pilote *m;* HER. pila; HIST. *(javelin)* pilo **II.** tr. **piled, pil·ing** clavar pilotes en, empilonar.

pile³ (pīl) s. *(furry surface)* pelo.

pile driver s. *(machine)* martinete *m;* *(person)* malacatero de martinete.

piles (pīlz) s.pl. hemorroides *f,* almorranas.

pile·up (pīl'ŭp') s. accidente entre varios vehículos *m.*

pil·fer (pĭl'fər) tr. & intr. robar, hurtar.

pil·fer·age (pĭl'fər-ĭj) s. robo, sisa.

pil·grim (pĭl'grĭm) s. *(devotee)* peregrino; *(traveler)* viajante *mf* ♦ **P.** HIST. peregrino (uno de los ingleses puritanos que fundaron la colonia de Plymouth en Norteamérica).

pil·grim·age (pĭl'grə-mĭj) **I.** s. peregrinación *f,* peregrinaje *m* ♦ **to make a p.** ir en peregrinación **II.** intr. **-aged, -ag·ing** peregrinar.

pil·ing (pī'lĭng) s. ARQ. *(foundation)* cimentación con pilotes *f;* *(piles)* conjunto de pilotes, pilotaje *m.*

pill (pĭl) **I.** s. *(tablet)* píldora; *(oral contraceptive)* píldora anticonceptiva; JER. *(person)* pelmazo ♦ **a bitter p.** FIG. una píldora difícil **II.** tr. JER. rechazar —intr. formar (una tela) pelotillas o bolitas.

pil·lage (pĭl'ĭj) **I.** tr. & intr. **-laged, -lag·ing** pillar, saquear **II.** s. pillaje *m,* saqueo.

pil·lag·er (pĭl'ĭ-jər) s. pillador *m,* saqueador *m.*

pil·lar (pĭl'ər) **I.** s. *(column)* pilar *m,* columna; FIG. *(main support)* pilar, soporte *m* ♦ **from p. to post** de la Ceca a la Meca **II.** tr. sostener con pilares.

pill·box (pĭl'bŏks') s. *(for tablets)* cajita para píldoras o pastillas; *(hat)* pequeño sombrero sin ala (de mujer); MIL. fortín *m.*

pil·lion (pĭl'yən) s. *(pad)* grupera; *(motorcycle cushion)* asiento trasero (en motocicletas); *(saddle)* silla ligera de montar.

pil·lo·ry (pĭl'ə-rē) **I.** s. [pl. **-ries**] picota, cepo **II.** tr. **-ried, -ry·ing** poner en la picota.

pil·low (pĭl'ō) **I.** s. *(for sleeping)* almohada; *(for decoration)* almohadón *m;* *(in making lace)* almohadilla **II.** tr. *(to rest)* hacer descansar sobre una almohada; *(to support)* servir de almohada.

pil·low·case (pĭl'ō-kās') s. funda de almohada.

pi·lot (pī'lət) **I.** s. AVIA. piloto; MARÍT. *(in a port)* práctico del puerto; *(helmsman)* piloto, timonel *m;* MEC. guía; *(leader)* guía *mf,* director *m;* *(of a locomotive)* quitapiedras *m;* *(of a stove)* piloto; TELEV. programa de introducción de una serie *m* ♦ **automatic p.** AVIA. piloto automático **II.** tr. pilotear **III.** adj. *(trial)* piloto, experimental <*a p. project* un proyecto experimental>; *(guiding)* modelo.

pi·lot·age (pī'lə-tĭj) s. AVIA., MARÍT. pilotaje *m.*

pilot burner s. mechero piloto, mechero encendedor.

pilot fish s. ICT. pez piloto *m.*

pi·lot·house (pī'lət-hous') s. MARÍT. timonera, cabina del piloto.

pi·lot·ing (pī'lə-tĭng) s. AVIA., MARÍT. *(occupation)* pilotaje *m;* MARÍT. *(coastal navigation)* navegación por señales o sondeo *f.*

pilot light s. *(igniter)* llama piloto, mechero encendedor; *(pilot lamp)* lámpara indicadora, piloto.

pi·men·to (pĭ-měn'tō) s. [pl. **-tos**] BOT. pimiento, ají *m,* pimienta de Jamaica.

pi·mien·to (pĭ-měn'tō, -myěn'-) s. [pl. **-tos**] BOT. pimiento morrón.

pimp (pĭmp) **I.** s. proxeneta *mf,* alcahuete *m* **II.** intr. alcahuetear.

pim·per·nel (pĭm'pər-něl') s. BOT. murajes *m;* pimpinela.

pim·ple (pĭm'pəl) s. grano.

pim·ply (pĭm'plē) adj. granujiento, espinilloso.

pin (pĭn) **I.** s. *(for fabrics)* alfiler *m;* *(badge)* insignia; *(brooch)* broche *m;* *(bit)* pizca; *(cotter)* pasador *m,* chaveta; *(bolt)* perno; *(peg)* clavija; MARÍT. *(belaying pin)* cabilla; *(thole pin)* escálamo; MÚS. clavija; *(in bowling)* bolo; *(in gold)* asta (del banderín) ♦ **to hear a p. drop** FIG. oír el vuelo de una mosca • **to be on pins and needles** estar como en brasas • **to be steady on one's pins** FAM. tener las patas o las piernas duras **II.** tr. **pinned, pin·ning** *(to fasten)* prender con un alfiler o con alfileres; *(in wrestling)* sujetar a (un contrincante) contra la lona (en la lucha libre) ♦ **to p. against** acorralar, sujetar contra (una pared) • **to p. down** *(to fasten on)* sujetar, asegurar; *(to immobilize)* inmovilizar; *(to establish)* determinar, precisar <*we could not p. down the cause* no pudimos precisar el motivo>; *(to force to be specific)* hacer que (alguien) sea más preciso • **to p. on** *(to fasten on)* prender en; *(hopes)* cifrar o depositar en; *(to blame)* echar la culpa a (alguien) de • **to p. up** *(hair)* sujetar(se) (el pelo) con horquillas; *(a notice)* clavar con chinchetas.

pin·a·fore (pĭn'ə-fôr') s. delantal *m.*

pin·ball (pĭn'bôl') s. billar romano.

pince-nez (păns'nā', pĭns'-) s. [pl. **pince-nez**] quevedos *m.*

pin·cer (pĭn'sər) s. pinza.

pin·cers (pĭn'sərz) s.pl. [ú. con v. sing.] *(tool, claws)* pinzas, tenazas *f;* MIL. movimiento de pinzas, movimiento de tenazas.

pinch (pĭnch) **I.** tr. *(using one's fingers)* pellizcar; *(to catch)* cogerse, pillarse <*she pinched her finger in the drawer* se cogió el dedo con la gaveta>; *(to squeeze)* apretar <*these shoes pinch my toes* estos zapatos me aprietan en los dedos>; *(to cause hardship)* hacer pasar privaciones, poner en aprietos a; JER. *(to steal)* ratear, mangar; *(to arrest)* pescar, prender ♦ **to p. off** quitar con los dedos • **to p. pennies** andar con tacañerías, escatimar gastos • **to be pinched for money** estar escaso de dinero • **to be pinched with** estar transido de (dolor, frío) —intr. *(garment)* apretar (a uno); *(to economize)* escatimar gastos ♦ **to p. and scrape** escatimar gastos **II.** s. *(using one's fingers)* pellizco; *(of seasoning)* pizca <*a p. of pepper* una pizca de pimienta>; *(of snuff)* pulgarada o polvo; JER. *(theft)* robo; *(arrest)* detención *f* ♦ **in a p.** en caso de apuro o de necesidad • **to feel the p.** pasar apuros, verse apretado.

pinch·ers (pĭn'chərz) s.pl. var. de **pincers.**

pinch-hit (pĭnch'hĭt') intr. **-hit, -hit·ting** *(in baseball)* sustituir a otro bateador; FIG. sustituir a otro en una emergencia.

pin curl s. rizo sujetado con horquillas.

pin·cush·ion (pĭn'kōosh'ən) s. acerico, alfiletero.

pine¹ (pīn) s. BOT. pino (árbol y madera).

pine² (pīn) intr. **pined, pin·ing** ♦ **to p. away** consumirse, languidecer • **to p. for** suspirar por, anhelar.

pin·e·al (pĭn'ē-əl) adj. en forma de piña; ANAT. pineal.

pine·ap·ple (pīn'ăp'əl) s. BOT. piña, ananás *m;* JER. *(hand grenade)* pequeña granada de mano.

pine cone s. piña (del pino).

pine needle s. aguja de pino, piniche *m.*

pine nut s. BOT. piñón *m.*

pine tar s. brea de pino.

pin·ey (pī'nē) adj. var. de **piny.**

pin·feath·er (pĭn'fěth'ər) s. ORNIT. cañón (pluma naciente) *m.*

ping (pĭng) **I.** s. sonido metálico **II.** intr. producir un sonido metálico.

Ping-Pong (pĭng'pông') s. ping pong *m,* pimpón (marca registrada) *m.*

---

ng inglés / ŏ la / ō bou / ô corre / oi oigo / ōō uno / ou auto / yōō ciudad / w hueco / y yo / z mismo

pin·head (pǐn′hěd′) s. *(head of a pin)* cabeza de alfiler; FIG. *(trifle)* cosa pequeña e insignificante; JER. *(stupid person)* tonto, bobo.

pin·hole (pǐn′hōl′) s. agujero de alfiler.

pin·ion¹ (pǐn′yən) I. s. ORNIT. ala II. tr. *(a bird)* cortar las alas a; *(a person)* maniatar.

pin·ion² (pǐn′yən) s. TEC. piñón *m*.

pink¹ (pǐngk) I. s. BOT. clavel (flor y planta) *m*; *(color)* rosado, rosa; POL., JER. *(leftist)* rojillo ♦ **in the p.** rebosante de salud • **in the p. of** en perfecto estado de II. adj. **-er, -est** *(in color)* rosado, rosa; JER. *(leftist)* rojillo.

pink² (pǐngk) tr. *(to prick)* herir levemente; *(to decorate)* festonear; *(to perforate)* picar, perforar (tela, papel).

pink³ (pǐngk) s. MARÍT. pingue *m*.

pink·eye o **pink eye** (pǐngk′ī′) s. MED., VET. conjuntivitis aguda.

pink·ie (pǐng′kē) s. FAM. dedo meñique.

pinking shears s. COST. tijeras dentadas.

pink·ish (pǐng′kǐsh) adj. *(in color)* rosáceo; JER. *(in doctrine)* comunistoide, rojillo.

pink·o (pǐng′kō) s. [pl. **-os**] POL., JER. rojillo.

pink·y (pǐng′kē) s. [pl. **-ies**] FAM. dedo meñique.

pin money s. dinero para imprevistos, dinero para pequeños gastos.

pin·nace (pǐn′ǐs) s. MARÍT. *(sailing boat)* pinaza; *(small ship)* chalupa o bote de motor *m*.

pin·na·cle (pǐn′ə-kəl) I. s. ARQ. pináculo; *(peak)* pico, cima; *(summit)* cumbre *f* II. tr. **-cled, -cling** *(to crown)* coronar o rematar (con un pináculo); *(to elevate)* poner en un pedestal, elevar a la fama.

pin·nate (pǐn′āt′) adj. *(pennate)* alado; BOT. pinada.

pi·noch·le o **pi·noc·le** (pē′nŭk′əl, -nōk′-) s. juego de naipes.

pin·point (pǐn′point′) I. s. punta de alfiler II. tr. *(to point out)* señalar; *(to locate)* localizar o identificar con precisión; *(to aim)* apuntar con precisión III. adj. *(precise)* preciso, exacto; *(minuscule)* minúsculo; ARM. de precisión.

pin·prick (pǐn′prǐk′) I. s. *(pin's puncture)* alfilerazo; *(minor wound)* pinchazo; *(minor annoyance)* molestia II. tr. & intr. dar alfilerazos.

pins and needles s. hormigueo (por falta de circulación sanguínea) ♦ **on p.** ansioso, en ascuas.

pin·stripe (pǐn′strīp′) I. s. raya fina II. adj. de rayas finas.

pint (pǐnt) s. pinta (recipiente y contenido).

pin·to (pǐn′tō) I. s. [pl. **-tos** o **-toes**] caballo pinto II. adj. pintado, de varios colores.

pinto bean s. frijol moteado, judía pinta.

pint-size (pǐnt′sīz′) o **pint-sized** (-sīzd′) adj. FAM. pequeño, diminuto.

pin-up (pǐn′ŭp′) I. s. *(picture)* fotografía de una mujer atractiva; *(woman)* mujer atractiva II. adj. atractivo.

pin·wheel (pǐn′hwēl′) s. *(toy)* molinillo; *(fireworks)* rueda de fuegos artificiales, girándula.

pin·y (pǐ′nē) adj. **-i·er, -i·est** de pinos ♦ **a p. odor** un olor a pino.

pi·on (pǐ′ŏn′) s. FÍS. pión *m*.

pi·o·neer (pǐ′ə-nîr′) I. s. *(settler)* pionero, colonizador *m*; *(innovator)* pionero, precursor *m* <a p. in aviation un pionero de la aviación>; MIL. zapador *m* II. adj. *(innovating)* innovador; *(of settlers)* de pionero o colonizador III. tr. *(to explore)* explorar, iniciar la exploración de; *(to open up)* marcar nuevos rumbos en; *(to settle)* colonizar; *(a science)* sentar las bases de —intr. ♦ **to p. in** marcar nuevos rumbos en.

pi·ous (pǐ′əs) adj. *(devout)* piadoso; *(hypocritical)* beato; *(commendable)* digno de alabanza.

pip¹ (pǐp) s. *(seed)* pepita, semilla pequeña de fruta; FIG., FAM. *(remarkable thing)* joya, perla.

pip² (pǐp) I. tr. **pipped, pip·ping** romper el cascarón —intr. piar II. s. RAD. señal (silbido corto) *f*.

pip³ (pǐp) s. *(on dice, dominoes)* punto; *(spot)* punto, mancha; *(rootstock)* rizoma *m*; *(radar signal)* señal *f*; G.B., MIL. estrella.

pip⁴ (pǐp) *(of birds)* moquillo; JER. *(minor ailment)* malestar *m*.

pipe (pīp) I. s. *(for liquids, gas)* tubería, cañería; *(piece of pipe)* tubo; *(for tobacco)* pipa; *(in an organ)* tubo, cañón *m*; *(birdcall)* canto, silbido; *(whistle)* pito, silbato; JER. *(easy task)* tarea fácil; MIN. veta vertical; GEOL. chimenea; ANAT. tubo ♦ **exhaust p.** tubo de escape • **put that in your p. and smoke it!** FAM. ¡chúpate ésa! • **pipes** *(tubes)* tubería, cañería; *(bagpipe)* gaita II. tr. **piped, pip·ing** *(liquids, gas)* conducir por tuberías; *(to provide with pipes)* instalar tuberías o cañerías en; MÚS. tocar (una pieza) en la flauta; *(to furnish with piping)* poner ribetes a ♦ **to p. into** traer por medio de tuberías o cañerías • **to p. someone aboard** MARÍT. tocar el pito o el silbato para recibir a alguien a bordo —intr. MÚS. tocar; *(to screech)* chillar; *(bird)* cantar ♦ **to p. down** JER. cerrar el pico, callarse la boca • **to p. up** prorrumpir chillando.

pipe cleaner s. limpiapipas *m*.

pipe dream s. ilusión *f*, castillos en el aire *m*.

pipe·fit·ting (pīp′fǐt′ǐng) s. *(act)* instalación de tuberías *f*; *(section of pipe)* acoplamiento o accesorio de tuberías.

pipe·line (pīp′līn′) s. *(gas)* gasoducto; *(oil)* oleoducto; *(information)* conducto; *(supply)* línea, conducto.

pipe organ s. MÚS. órgano.

pip·er (pī′pər) s. MÚS. *(flutist)* flautista *mf*; *(bagpiper)* gaitero; TEC. *(installer)* montador de tuberías *m*; COST. persona que pone ribetes.

pi·pette o **pi·pet** (pī-pět′) s. pipeta, probeta.

pipe wrench s. llave para tubos *f*.

pip·ing (pī′pǐng) I. s. *(of a building)* tubería, cañería; *(shrill sound)* pitido; *(on clothing)* ribete *m* II. adj. ♦ **p. voice** voz aguda III. adv. ♦ **p. hot** CUL. muy caliente.

pip·pin (pǐp′ǐn) s. *(apple)* reineta; *(pip)* pepita, semilla de una fruta; JER. *(admired thing)* joya, maravilla.

pip-squeak (pǐp′skwēk′) s. *(contemptible person)* mequetrefe *m*; *(insignificant person)* cero a la izquierda, poca cosa.

pi·quant (pē′kənt, -känt′) adj. *(spicy)* picante; *(provocative)* provocativo; *(stinging)* mordaz, punzante.

pique (pēk) I. s. pique *m*, resentimiento ♦ **in a fit of p.** por resentimiento II. tr. **piqued, piqu·ing** *(to vex)* picar, molestar; *(to arouse)* despertar (curiosidad, interés).

pi·ra·cy (pī′rə-sē) s. [pl. **-cies**] *(at sea)* piratería, *(of books)* edición pirata, edición no autorizada.

pi·rate (pī′rǐt) I. s. *(at sea)* pirata *m*; FIG. *(thief)* persona que comete fraudes II. tr. **-rat·ed, -rat·ing** *(to rob)* robar, pillar; *(to reproduce illicitly)* hacer una edición pirata de —intr. piratear.

pi·rogue (pī-rōg′) s. piragua.

pir·ou·ette (pír′ōō-ět′) I. s. pirueta, cabriola II. intr. **-et·ted, -et·ting** piruetear, hacer cabriolas.

pis·ca·to·ri·al (pǐs′kə-tôr′ē-əl) o **pis·ca·to·ry** (pǐs′kə-tôr′ē) adj. piscatorio.

Pi·sces (pī′sēz) s. ASTROL. Piscis *m*.

pi·scine (pī′sēn′, pǐs′īn′) adj. *(of fish)* de peces; *(like a fish)* pisciforme.

piss (pǐs) VULG. I. intr. mear, orinar —tr. ♦ **to p. in** o **on** mear en • **to p. someone off** enojar a alguien II. s. *(urine)* meada, orina; *(action)* meada.

pis·ta·chi·o (pǐ-stăsh′ē-ō′, -stä′shē-ō′) s. [pl. **-os**] BOT. *(tree)* pistachero, alfóncigo; *(nut)* pistacho, alfóncigo.

pis·til (pǐs′təl) s. BOT. pistilo.

pis·tol (pǐs′təl) I. s. pistola II. tr. tirar con pistola.

pis·tol-whip (pǐs′təl-hwǐp′) tr. **-whipped, -whip·ping** golpear con una pistola.

pis·ton (pǐs′tən) s. MEC. pistón *m*, émbolo; MÚS. pistón, llave *f*.

piston ring s. MEC. anillo del pistón, aro del émbolo.

piston rod s. MEC. varilla del pistón, vástago del émbolo.

pit¹ (pǐt) I. s. *(hole)* hoyo, pozo; *(mine)* mina; *(quarry)* cantera; *(trap)* trampa; *(hovel)* cuchitril *m*; *(for cockfights)* reñidero; *(cockpit)* gallera; *(armpit)* sobaco; *(pockmark)* picadura o marca de viruela; *(of a stock exchange)* sección de la bolsa dedicada a una sola mercancía; *(for a mechanic)* foso; *(at a racecourse)* puesto ♦ **in the p. of one's stomach** en la boca del estómago • **orchestra p.** foso de la orquesta • **the pits** JER. lo peor de lo peor II. tr. **pit·ted, pit·ting** *(to make holes in)* llenar de hoyos; *(by a disease)* llenar de picaduras o de marcas ♦ **to p. against** oponer <a civil war that pitted brother against brother una guerra civil

que opuso a un hermano contra otro> —intr. *(surface)* llenarse de hoyos; *(skin)* llenarse de picaduras o de marcas.

pit² (pĭt) **I.** s. hueso (de frutas) **II.** tr. **pit·ted, pit·ting** deshuesar (frutas).

pi·ta¹ (pē′tə) s. pan griego de poca levadura, en forma de bolsa para relleno.

pi·ta² (pē′tə) s. BOT. pita, agave *m*, maguey *m*.

pit·a·pat (pĭt′ə-păt′) **I.** intr. **-patted, -pat·ting** *(to move)* moverse con paso ligero; *(to beat)* latir rápidamente **II.** s. *(of steps)* paso ligero; *(of beats)* latido, palpitación *f* **III.** adv. ♦ **to go p.** latir rápidamente (el corazón).

pitch¹ (pĭch) **I.** s. *(sticky substance)* pez *f*; *(bitumen)* alquitrán *m*, brea; *(resin)* resina **II.** tr. embrear, embetunar.

pitch² (pĭch) **I.** tr. *(to throw)* lanzar, tirar; *(hay)* echar; *(a tent)* montar, armar; *(a stake)* plantar o clavar; *(to adjust)* ajustar <he pitched his speech to the party line ajustó el discurso a la línea política del partido>; *(to incline)* inclinar; MÚS. *(a tune)* entonar (melodía); *(an instrument)* ajustar el tono de; COM. *(a product)* pregonar las virtudes de ♦ **to p. camp** acampar —intr. *(to fall)* caerse, caer; *(to lurch)* tambalearse, dar tumbos; *(horse)* corcovear; *(spacecraft)* dar sacudidas; *(plane, ship)* cabecear; *(to slope)* inclinarse; DEP. *(in baseball)* lanzar ♦ **to be in there pitching** FAM. estar bregando ♦ **to be pitched off** ser arrojado o caerse de ♦ **to p. in** FAM. *(to set to work)* meter manos a la obra; *(to help)* dar una mano ♦ **to p. into** *(to fall into)* caer a; *(to assault)* arremeter contra **II.** s. *(throw)* lanzamiento, tiro; *(intensity)* grado; *(of a ship)* cabeceo; *(slope)* inclinación *f*; JER. *(talk)* charlatanería <sales p. charlatanería de vendedor>; *(of a roof)* pendiente (del tejado) *f*; *(of an arch)* elevación *f*; ACÚS. tono o altura; MÚS. tono; MEC. diapasón *m* <standard p. diapasón normal>; *(of screw, propeller)* paso ♦ **to reach a feverish p.** llegar a un punto culminante • **to work at a feverish p.** trabajar a todo dar.

pitch-black (pĭch′blăk′) adj. *(dark)* oscuro como boca de lobo; *(black)* negro como el carbón o como la noche.

pitch·blende (pĭch′blĕnd′) s. MIN. pechblenda, pecblenda.

pitch-dark (pĭch′därk′) adj. oscuro como boca de lobo.

pitched battle s. batalla campal.

pitch·er¹ (pĭch′ər) s. DEP. lanzador *m*.

pitch·er² (pĭch′ər) s. *(vessel)* jarra, cántaro (contenido y recipiente); BOT. ascidia, hoja utricular.

pitch·fork (pĭch′fôrk′) **I.** s. horquilla, horca **II.** tr. *(to lift)* amontonar con horquilla; *(to toss)* echar con horquilla.

pitch pipe s. MÚS. diapasón *m*.

pit·e·ous (pĭt′ē-əs) adj. *(exciting pity)* lastimoso, lastimero; *(pathetic)* patético; *(compassionate)* compasivo.

pit·fall (pĭt′fôl′) s. *(trap)* trampa; *(danger)* peligro, escollo; *(difficulty)* dificultad *f.*

pith (pĭth) **I.** s. BOT. médula; *(essence)* meollo **II.** tr. *(plants)* quitar la médula a; *(animals)* matar cortando la médula.

pith·e·can·thro·pus (pĭth′ĭ-kăn′thrə-pəs) s. ANTROP., ETNOL. pitecántropo.

pith helmet s. casco hecho de fibras vegetales.

pith·y (pĭth′ē) adj. **-i·er, -i·est** *(resembling pith)* meduloso; *(of pith)* medular; *(concise)* conciso; *(substantial)* substancial; *(expressive)* expresivo.

pit·i·a·ble (pĭt′ē-ə-bəl) adj. *(lamentable)* lamentable, deplorable; *(arousing pity)* lastimoso, digno de compasión; *(despicable)* despreciable, miserable.

pit·i·ful (pĭt′ĭ-fəl) adj. *(arousing pity)* lastimoso, digno de compasión; *(lamentable)* lamentable; *(contemptible)* despreciable, miserable.

pit·i·less (pĭt′ĭ-lĭs) adj. *(without pity)* despiadado, desalmado; *(unmitigated)* implacable, duro.

pit stop s. DEP. parada en un puesto (en una carrera automovilística); FAM. *(stop during trip)* parada durante un viaje para descansar y comer.

pit·tance (pĭt′ns) s. *(salary)* miseria, sueldo de hambre; *(amount)* miseria, cantidad miserable *f.*

pit·ted (pĭt′ĭd) adj. *(pockmarked)* picado de viruelas; *(with holes)* hoyoso; *(fruit)* deshuesado.

pit·ter-pat·ter (pĭt′ər-păt′ər) **I.** s. *(tapping)* serie de golpeci-

tos *f*, golpeteo; *(of the rain)* tamborileo **II.** intr. *(to tap)* golpetear; *(to rain)* tamborilear.

pi·tu·i·tar·y (pĭ-tōō′ĭ-tĕr′ē, -tyōō′-) **I.** s. [pl. **-ies**] ANAT., ZOOL. glándula pituitaria; MED. *(extract)* extracto pituitario **II.** adj. pituitario.

pituitary gland s. ANAT., ZOOL. glándula pituitaria.

pit viper s. ZOOL. crótalo.

pit·y (pĭt′ē) **I.** s. [pl. **-ies**] *(compassion)* compasión *f*, piedad *f*; *(regrettable fact)* ¡lástima!, ¡qué pena! **II.** intr. & tr. **-ied, -y·ing** compadecerse de.

piv·ot (pĭv′ət) **I.** s. MEC. *(shaft)* pivote *m*, gorrón *m*; FIG. *(center)* eje *m*; DEP. *(turn)* pivote **II.** tr. *(to mount)* montar sobre un pivote; *(to turn)* hacer girar ♦ **to p. on** *(to turn)* girar sobre; *(to depend on)* depender de, basarse en —intr. girar sobre un eje.

piv·o·tal (pĭv′ə-tl) adj. *(turning)* giratorio, de giro; *(essential)* fundamental, cardinal.

pix (pĭks) s. var. de **pyx.**

pix·ie (pĭk′sē) s. & adj. var. de **pixy.**

pix·i·lat·ed (pĭk′sə-lā′tĭd) adj. FAM. chiflado.

pix·y (pĭk′sē) **I.** s. [pl. **-ies**] duendecillo, hada traviesa **II.** adj. travieso.

piz·za (pēt′sə) s. pizza.

piz·ze·ri·a (pēt′sə-rē′ə) s. pizzería.

PL/1 (pē′ĕl-wŭn′) s. COMPUT. lenguaje de programación de alto nivel (para la ciencia y el comercio) *m.*

plac·a·ble (plăk′ə-bəl, plā′kə-) adj. placable, aplacable.

plac·ard (plăk′ärd′) **I.** s. *(poster)* cartel *m*; *(notice)* letrero; *(nameplate)* rótulo, placa **II.** tr. *(to announce)* anunciar por medio de carteles; *(to post)* poner o fijar carteles.

pla·cate (plā′kāt′, plăk′āt′) tr. **-cat·ed, -cat·ing** aplacar, apaciguar.

place (plās) **I.** s. *(area)* lugar *m*, sitio; *(locale)* local *m*; *(house)* casa <they own a summer p. tienen una casa de veraneo>; *(home)* apartamento, casa; *(spot)* lugar, puesto; *(seat)* asiento; *(place setting)* cubierto <please set another p. ponga otro cubierto, por favor>; *(position)* lugar <I would rather not be in your p. preferiría no estar en tu lugar>; *(in a book)* página por donde iba <I lost my p. perdí la página por donde iba>; *(function)* función *f* <the p. of art in society la función del arte en la sociedad>; *(proper location)* lugar, sitio <everything was in its p. todo estaba en su lugar>; *(rank)* posición (social) *f*; *(standing)* lugar, puesto <fourth p. cuarto lugar>; *(in a line)* puesto ♦ **all over the p.** por todas partes • **any p.** en o a dondequiera • **from p. to p.** de un lugar a otro • **if I were in your p.** yo que tú • **in high places** en las altas esferas • **in p.** en orden • **in p. of** en lugar de, en vez de • **in the first p.** en primer lugar • **not to be one's p.** no corresponderle a uno, no ser uno quien para <it is not my p. to tell them no me corresponde a mí decírselo> • **out of p.** fuera de lugar • **p. of business** *(office)* despacho; *(shop)* comercio • **p. of residence** domicilio • **to change places** cambiar de puesto • **to find a p.** encontrar donde • **to go places** FAM. llegar lejos, triunfar • **to keep someone in his p.** tener a raya a alguien • **to know one's p.** saber guardar las distancias • **to put someone in his p.** poner a alguien en su lugar • **to take p.** *(to happen)* tener lugar; *(to be held)* celebrarse • **to take the p. of** sustituir **II.** tr. **placed, plac·ing** *(to put)* colocar, poner; *(to situate)* situar, ubicar <the house is poorly placed la casa no está bien situada>; *(to arrange)* poner (en orden, fila); *(in a school, home)* poner, internar (en escuela, asilo); *(in a job)* colocar; *(for adoption)* poner (en casa, familia); *(to appoint)* poner, colocar; *(to rank)* poner (en primero, segundo lugar); *(estimate)* calcular (valor, cantidad); *(to date)* situar cronológicamente; *(a bet)* hacer; *(a call)* pedir ♦ **to be able to p. (a person, face)** saber dónde uno ha visto (a una persona, una cara) • **to p. an order** hacer un pedido • **to p. before** plantear a • **to p. emphasis on** hacer hincapié en, subrayar • **to p. one's confidence in** confiar o depositar la confianza de uno en —intr. clasificarse entre los tres primeros.

pla·ce·bo (plə-sē′bō) s. [pl. **-bos** o **-boes**] MED. placebo.

place mat s. mantelito individual.

place·ment (plās′mənt) s. colocación *f.*

pla·cen·ta (plə-sĕn′tə) s. [pl. **-tas** o **-tae** (-tē)] ANAT., BOT. placenta.

plac·er (plăs′ər) s. MIN. *(bank)* placer *m*, banco de arena; *(deposit)* yacimiento aurífero.

placer mining s. MIN. explotación de placeres *f*.

place setting s. cubierto, servicio de mesa para una persona.

plac·id (plăs′ĭd) adj. *(calm)* tranquilo, apacible; *(satisfied)* complacido, satisfecho.

pla·cid·i·ty (plə-sĭd′ĭ-tē) s. placidez *f*, apacibilidad *f*.

pla·gia·rism (plā′jə-rĭz′əm) s. plagio.

pla·gia·rist (plā′jər-ĭst) s. plagiario.

pla·gia·rize (plā′jə-rīz′) tr. & intr. **-rized, -riz·ing** plagiar.

plague (plāg) **I.** s. *(disease)* peste *f*; *(of insects)* plaga; *(nuisance)* molestia, fastidio; FIG. *(outbreak)* plaga **II.** tr. **plagued, plagu·ing** *(to annoy)* molestar, fastidiar; *(to distress)* atormentar; *(to worry)* preocupar; *(with questions)* asar (con preguntas) ♦ **to avoid like the p.** huir de (algo) como de la peste.

plague·some (plăg′səm) adj. *(of a plague)* pestilente; FIG. *(annoying)* fastidioso, pesado.

plaice (plās) s. [pl. **plaice** o **plaic·es**] ICT. platija, acedia.

plaid (plăd) s. TEJ. *(scarf)* manta escocesa; *(cloth)* tela o género a cuadros; *(pattern)* diseño a la escocesa o a cuadros.

plain (plān) **I.** adj. **-er, -est** *(obvious)* claro, evidente; *(simple)* llano, sencillo; *(honest)* honrado; *(straightforward)* claro, sin rodeos; *(unmixed)* puro, solo <p. vanilla ice cream helado de vainilla solo>; *(unaffected)* llano, corriente; *(unpatterned)* sencillo o sin adornos; *(unattractive)* nada atractivo, nada llamativo <she is a very p. girl no es nada atractiva>; *(utter)* puro, absoluto <p. terror puro terror> ♦ **in p. sight** a la vista de todos ♦ **the p. truth** la pura verdad ♦ **to make it p. that** manifestar claramente que, poner de manifiesto que **II.** s. GEOL. llanura, llano ♦ **plains** praderas **III.** adv. *(bluntly)* claro, sin rodeos <he spoke p. to me me habló claro>; *(utterly)* absolutamente, totalmente <it was just p. silly era algo totalmente estúpido>.

plain·clothes·man (plān′klōz′mən) s. [pl. **-men**] *(policeman)* policía *m*; *(detective)* detective *m*.

plain·ly (plān′lē) adv. *(obviously)* claramente, evidentemente; *(simply)* sencillamente; *(frankly)* francamente; *(straightforwardly)* claro, sin rodeos <to put it p. hablando claro>.

plain·ness (plān′nĭs) s. *(obviousness)* claridad *f*, evidencia; *(simplicity)* sencillez *f*; *(frankness)* franqueza; *(of appearance)* falta de atractivo.

plain sailing s. FIG. asunto o cosa fácil.

plains·man (plānz′mən) s. [pl. **-men**] llanero.

plain·song (plān′sông′) s. MÚS. canto llano, canto gregoriano.

plain·spo·ken (plān′spō′kən) adj. franco.

plaint (plānt) s. *(complaint)* queja; *(lamentation)* lamento, quejido; DER. *(grievance)* querella, demanda.

plain·tiff (plān′tĭf) s. DER. demandante *mf*, querellante *mf*.

plain·tive (plān′tĭv) adj. quejumbroso.

plait (plăt, plāt) **I.** s. *(hair)* trenza; *(pleat)* pliegue *m* **II.** tr. *(to braid)* trenzar (el pelo); *(to pleat)* plisar; *(to intertwine)* entrelazar.

plan (plăn) **I.** s. *(method)* plan *m* <p. of attack plan de ataque>; *(program)* plan, programa *m* <an exercise p. un programa de ejercicios>; *(schedule)* programa <payment p. programa de pagos>; *(intention)* intención *f* <our p. is to wait tenemos la intención de esperar>; *(project)* plan, proyecto <an ambitious p. un proyecto ambicioso>; *(outline)* esquema *m*; *(diagram)* plano ♦ **on the installment p.** a plazos • **to change one's plans** cambiar de idea o intención • **to go according to p.** marchar bien o según lo previsto • **to have plans for** *(to be busy)* tener planes para; *(someone)* pensar hacer con (alguien) • **to make plans** hacer planes, planear **II.** tr. **planned, plan·ning** *(to think out)* planear, proyectar; *(to project)* planificar; *(to draw)* hacer el plano de; *(to design)* diseñar ♦ **to p. for** esperar —intr. hacer planes ♦ **to p. on** *(to count on)* con-

tar con, hacerse la idea de; *(to intend to)* pensar; *(to expect)* esperar.

pla·nar (plā′nər) adj. *(of a plane)* plano; *(flat)* aplanado.

plane¹ (plān) **I.** s. MAT. *(surface)* superficie plana o lisa; *(level)* nivel *m*; *(airplane)* avión *m*; *(wing)* ala; CARP. cepillo **II.** adj. MAT. plano; *(level)* plano, nivelado ♦ **p. angle** ángulo plano o rectilíneo **III.** tr. **planed, plan·ing** CARP. acepillar.

plane² (plān) intr. **planed, plan·ing** *(to glide)* planear; *(to travel)* viajar o volar en avión.

plane geometry s. geometría plana.

plan·er (plā′nər) s. *(wood)* cepilladora; *(metal)* alisadora.

plan·et (plăn′ĭt) s. ASTROL., ASTRON. planeta *m*.

plan·e·tar·i·um (plăn′ĭ-târ′ē-əm) s. [pl. **-i·ums** o **-i·a** (-ē-ə)] planetario.

plan·e·tar·y (plăn′ĭ-tĕr′ē) adj. ASTRON. planetario; *(earthly)* terrestre; *(erratic)* errante; MEC. planetario.

plan·e·toid (plăn′ĭ-toid′) s. ASTRON. asteroide *m*.

plane tree s. BOT. plátano.

planet wheel s. MEC. rueda planetaria.

plan·gent (plăn′jənt) adj. *(reverberating)* reverberante; *(resounding)* resonante; *(plaintive)* plañidero.

plank (plăngk) **I.** s. *(board)* tablón *m*; POL. punto **II.** tr. *(to cover)* entablar; *(to broil)* cocinar a la plancha ♦ **to p. down** FAM. *(to lay down)* tirar con violencia; *(to pay out)* desembolsar.

plank·ing (plăng′kĭng) s. *(platform)* entarimado, tablado; *(planks)* entablado.

plank·ton (plăngk′tən) s. BIOL. plancton *m*.

planned economy s. economía planificada.

plan·ner (plăn′ər) s. planificador *m*.

plan·ning (plăn′ĭng) **I.** s. planificación *f* <family p. planificación familiar> **II.** adj. planificador <p. board comisión planificadora>.

pla·no·con·cave (plā′nō-kŏn-kāv′) adj. plano-cóncavo.

pla·no·con·vex (plā′nō-kŏn-vĕks′) adj. plano-convexo.

plant (plănt) **I.** s. BOT. planta; *(factory)* fábrica; *(buildings and equipment)* planta, instalación *f*; JER. *(false evidence)* prueba falsa (que se deja a propósito); *(spy)* espía *m* ♦ **p. life** BOT. la vida vegetal, la flora • **the p. kingdom** BIOL. el reino vegetal **II.** tr. AGR. *(to seed)* plantar; *(to sow)* sembrar; *(to stock)* echar (peces) en (un lago, río); *(to fix)* plantar <he planted his feet plantó los pies>; *(to found)* establecer, fundar; FIG. *(to implant)* infundir, inculcar; JER. *(spies)* apostar; *(evidence)* sembrar, colocar; *(a blow)* asestar ♦ **to p. something on someone** comprometer a alguien escondiendo algo robado en su ropa o casa.

plan·tain¹ (plăn′tən) s. BOT. *(weed)* plantaina, llantén *m*.

plan·tain² (plăn′tən) s. BOT. *(tropical plant)* plátano; *(fruit)* banano.

plan·ta·tion (plăn-tā′shən) s. *(agricultural area)* plantación *f*; *(field)* plantío; *(estate)* hacienda.

plant·er (plăn′tər) s. *(pot)* tiesto; AGR. *(machine)* sembradora.

plaque (plăk) s. *(plate)* placa; *(medal)* medalla; *(badge)* insignia; BIOL. plaqueta; ODONT. placa.

plash (plăsh) **I.** s. *(splash)* salpicadura; *(sound)* chapoteo **II.** tr. salpicar —intr. chapotear.

plas·ma (plăz′mə) o **plasm** (plăz′əm) s. BIOL. plasma *m*; *(whey)* suero.

plas·ter (plăs′tər) **I.** s. ARTE., CONSTR. yeso; MED. *(of a cast)* escayola; *(of a pack)* emplasto, cataplasma **II.** tr. *(a wall, ceiling)* enyesar, enlucir; *(to repair)* tapar con yeso <to p. over the holes tapar los huecos con yeso>; FIG. *(to cover)* llenar, cubrir <he plastered the walls with pinups llenó las paredes de fotos de mujeres>; *(a limb)* escayolar; *(to smear)* untar; FAM. *(to inflict damage on)* hacer daño a.

plas·ter·board (plăs′tər-bôrd′) s. cartón-yeso, cartón de yeso *m*.

plaster cast s. ESCULT. vaciado en yeso; MED. enyesado.

plas·tered (plăs′tərd) s. JER. borracho.

plas·ter·er (plăs′tər-ər) s. enlucidor *m*.

plas·ter·ing (plăs′tər-ĭng) s. *(act)* enyesado; *(coating)* enlucido, enyesado; FIG. *(licking)* tunda, paliza.

plaster of Paris s. ESCULT. sulfato de cal, yeso mate.

plas·tic (plăs′tĭk) **I.** adj. *(pliable)* plástico; *(well-formed)* escultórico; *(of plastic)* de plástico; *(artificial)* artificial **II.** s. *(compound)* plástico; JER. *(credit card)* tarjeta de crédito.

plas·tic·i·ty (plă-stĭs′ĭ-tē) s. plasticidad *f.*

plas·ti·cize (plăs′tĭ-sīz′) tr. & intr. **-cized, -ciz·ing** plastificar.

plas·ti·ciz·er (plăs′tĭ-sī′zər) s. plastificante *m.*

plastic surgery s. cirugía plástica o estética.

plas·tron (plăs′trən) s. *(breastplate)* peto; ESGR. plastrón *m*; *(dicky)* pecherín *m*; *(of a man's shirt)* plastrón, pechera; ZOOL. peto, concha interior.

plat (plăt) **I.** tr. **plat·ted, plat·ting** entrelazar **II.** s. trenza.

plate (plăt) **I.** s. *(plaque)* placa; *(of metal)* plancha, lámina; TEC. *(coating)* revestimiento; IMPR. *(illustration)* grabado, lámina; *(stereotype)* estereotipo, plancha; ARM. plancha de blindaje; FOTOG. placa; MED. *(of teeth)* (placa de) la dentadura postiza; ARQ. *(of a roof)* viga horizontal; DEP. *(cup)* copa de oro o de plata; *(in baseball)* base del bateador *f*; *(dish)* plato (recipiente y contenido); *(service and food)* cubierto; *(tableware)* vajilla; RELIG. *(for collection)* platillo, bandeja; *(of beef)* falda; ANAT., ZOOL. lámina; ELEC. *(anode)* ánodo, placa; *(electrode)* electrodo **II.** tr. **plat·ed, plat·ing** *(with metal)* chapar; *(with gold)* dorar; *(with silver)* platear; *(with nickel)* niquelar; *(to armor)* blindar; IMPR. *(to make a stereotype from)* hacer un estereotipo de; *(paper)* satinar, glasear.

pla·teau (plă-tō′) s. [pl. **-teaus** o **-teaux** (-tōz′)] GEOG. meseta, altiplanicie *f*, altiplano.

plat·ed (plā′tĭd) adj. *(coated)* enchapado <*silver-p.* enchapado en plata>; *(armored)* blindado.

plate·ful (plāt′fōol) s. [pl. **-fuls**] *(plate)* plato (lleno de); *(portion)* porción *f.*

plate glass s. vidrio cilindrado, luna.

plate·let (plāt′lĭt) s. BIOL. plaqueta.

plat·en (plăt′n) s. IMPR. *(moving part)* platina; *(of a typewriter)* rodillo.

plat·er (plā′tər) s. *(person)* chapista *mf*, plateador *m*; JER. *(horse)* penco, jamelgo.

plat·form (plăt′fôrm′) s. *(for speakers)* plataforma; *(railroad)* andén *m*; POL. programa político.

platform car s. batea, vagón de plataforma *m.*

platform scale s. báscula, romana de plataforma.

plat·ing (plā′tĭng) s. *(coating of metal)* capa metálica, enchapado; *(of gold)* dorado; *(of silver)* plateado; *(of nickel)* niquelado; *(armor plate)* blindaje *m.*

plat·i·num (plăt′n-əm) s. QUÍM. platino.

platinum blond s. rubio platinado.

plat·ter (plăt′ər) s. *(serving dish)* fuente *f*; *(course)* plato; JER. *(record)* disco fonográfico.

plat·y·pus (plăt′ə-pəs) s. ZOOL. ornitorrinco.

plau·dits (plô′dĭts) s.pl. aplausos.

plau·si·bil·i·ty (plô′zə-bĭl′ĭ-tē) s. plausibilidad *f.*

plau·si·ble (plô′zə-bəl) adj. *(acceptable)* plausible, verosímil; *(specious)* especioso, engañoso.

play (plā) **I.** intr. *(to amuse oneself)* jugar; *(to take part)* jugar, participar en el juego <*he is not playing because of an injury* no juega a causa de una lesión>; *(to gamble)* jugar; *(to jest)* bromear; *(to pretend to be)* hacerse <*to p. dumb* hacerse el tonto>; *(to feign)* fingirse <*to p. sick* fingirse enfermo>; *(to act)* actuar, trabajar <*to p. in a comedy* actuar en una comedia>; *(to be performed)* poner, dar <*a good movie is playing next week* la semana próxima dan una buena película>; MÚS. *(to perform)* tocar <*the band was playing* la orquesta estaba tocando>; *(to stream)* chorrear, correr <*the fountains played in the courtyard* las fuentes chorreaban en el patio>; *(to flicker)* bailar <*the light played on the water* la luz bailaba en el agua> ♦ **to p. along** cooperar • **to p. around** *(to joke)* bromear, tomar el pelo; *(to flirt)* flirtear, coquetear; *(to have fun)* retozar, juguetear • **to p. at** *(a game)* jugar a; *(to feign)* fingirse • **to p. by ear** tocar de oído • **to p. fair** o **by the rules** jugar limpio • **to p. for** *(money)* jugar por; *(a team)* jugar con • **to p. in Peoria** FIG. ser aceptable al pueblo • **to p. into someone's hands** hacer a alguien el juego • **to p. on** aprovecharse de • **to p. up to** FAM. adular, halagar • **to p. with** *(to fiddle with)* jugar con; *(to consider)* darle vueltas

en la cabeza • **to p. with fire** FIG. jugar con fuego —tr. TEAT. *(to act)* desempeñar (un papel); *(to act as)* hacer de <*to p. the villain* hacer de malo>; *(to give performances in)* representar obras en, actuar en <*they played Detroit last week* actuaron en Detroit la semana pasada>; *(to pretend to be)* jugar a <*the boys played cowboy* los muchachos jugaban a los vaqueros>; *(to participate in)* jugar, jugar a; *(to compete against)* jugar contra <*this team played the Boston team* este equipo jugó contra el equipo de Boston>; *(to use a card)* jugar <*to p. the queen of hearts* jugar la reina de copas>; *(to move a piece)* mover (una pieza de ajedrez, damas); *(to bet)* jugarse, apostar; *(to discharge)* enfocar, dirigir <*to p. a hose on a fire* dirigir una manguera hacia el fuego>; MÚS. *(to perform on)* tocar <*to p. the guitar* tocar la guitarra>; *(to perform)* tocar, interpretar <*the orchestra played a symphony* la orquesta interpretó una sinfonía>; *(to put on)* poner <*to p. a record* poner un disco> ♦ **to p. a joke on** gastar una broma a • **to p. a trick on** hacer una jugarreta a • **to p. back** poner (algo grabado) • **to p. ball** FIG. cooperar • **to p. both ends against the middle** meter discordia entre los rivales • **to p. down** quitar importancia a • **to p. games** FIG. andar con rodeos • **to p. hardball** FIG. jugar duro • **to p. havoc with** causar estragos • **to p. it by ear** FIG. improvisar sobre la marcha • **to p. it cool** tomarlo con calma • **to p. off** DEP. jugar un partido de desempate • **to p. one against the other** manipular a dos personas una contra la otra • **p. one's cards right** FIG. maniobrar bien • **to p. out** *(to exhaust)* agotar; *(to finish)* acabar • **to p. possum** o **dead** hacerse el dormido o el muerto • **to p. the field** FIG. salir o andar con más de una persona • **to p. the fool** hacerse el tonto • **to p. the game** FIG. jugar limpio • **to p. up** resaltar **II.** s. *(drama)* obra, pieza; *(performance)* teatro, representación *f* <*to go to a p.* ir al teatro>; *(activity)* juego; *(move)* jugada; *(gambling)* juego; *(looseness)* juego, holgura; *(turn)* turno; *(operation)* juego <*to come into p.* entrar en juego>; *(dealings)* jugada <*foul p.* jugada sucia> ♦ **in p.** *(in jest)* en broma; DEP. en juego • **out of p.** DEP. fuera de juego • **p. on words** juego de palabras • **to make a p. for** FAM. *(to scheme)* intrigar; *(to proposition)* hacer proposiciones a.

play·a·ble (plā′ə-bəl) adj. MÚS. interpretable, que se puede interpretar; TEAT. representable.

play-act (plā′ăkt′) intr. *(to act)* desempeñar un papel, actuar; *(to pretend)* fingir; *(to overreact)* hacer la comedia.

play·back (plā′băk′) s. *(of a tape)* reproducción *f*; *(sound)* sonido pregrabado.

play·bill (plā′bĭl′) s. *(poster)* cartel *m*; *(program)* programa *m.*

play·boy (plā′boi′) s. hombre de mundo *m.*

play·er (plā′ər) s. *(of games)* jugador *m*; *(actor)* actor *m*; *(actress)* actriz *f*; *(musician)* ejecutante *mf*, músico.

player piano s. MÚS. pianola, piano mecánico.

play·ful (plā′fəl) adj. *(frolicsome)* juguetón; *(humorous)* humorístico; *(jesting)* retozón; *(happy)* alegre.

play·ful·ness (plā′fəl-nĭs) s. *(character)* carácter juguetón *m*; *(happiness)* alegría.

play·go·er (plā′gō′ər) s. aficionado al teatro.

play·ground (plā′ground′) s. jardín *m* o terreno para jugar.

play·house (plā′hous′) s. *(theater)* teatro; *(for children)* casita para juego de niños.

playing card s. naipe *m*, carta.

playing field s. campo de juego.

play·mate (plā′māt′) s. compañero (de juego).

play-off (plā′ôf′) s. DEP. partido de desempate.

play·pen (plā′pĕn′) s. corral *m*, corralito para niños.

play·room (plā′rōom′, -rŏŏm′) s. cuarto de jugar.

play·thing (plā′thĭng′) s. juguete *m.*

play·time (plā′tīm′) s. recreo.

play·wright (plā′rīt′) s. dramaturgo, autor de teatro *m.*

pla·za (plä′zə, plăz′ə) s. *(square)* plaza; *(parking area)* área de estacionamiento.

plea (plē) s. *(entreaty)* súplica, imploración *f*; *(excuse)* pretexto; DER. *(allegation)* alegato ♦ **to make a p. for leniency** suplicar o implorar clemencia.

pleached (plēcht) adj. protegido por ramas entrelazadas.

---

plead (plēd) intr. **plead·ed** o **pled** (plĕd), **plead·ing** *(to beg)* suplicar, implorar <*to p. for leniency* implorar clemencia>; *(to argue for)* abogar, interceder; DER. *(to enter a plea)* contestar a los cargos; *(to address a court)* hacer un alegato ♦ **to p. guilty** DER. declararse culpable • **to p. not guilty** DER. declararse inocente —tr. *(as a plea)* alegar <*to p. self-defense* alegar legítima defensa>; *(as an excuse)* alegar, pretextar <*to p. illness* pretextar una enfermedad>; *(a case)* defender; FIG. *(a cause)* defender, salir en defensa de.

plead·ing (plē'dĭng) s. *(begging)* súplicas, imploraciones f; DER. *(defense)* defensa; *(presentation)* alegato; *(response)* contestación f.

pleas·ant (plĕz'ənt) adj. *(pleasing)* agradable; *(welcome)* grato (sorpresa, cambio); *(enjoyable)* ameno.

pleas·ant·ly (plĕz'ənt-lē) adv. *(pleasingly)* agradablemente; *(amiably)* amablemente ♦ **to be p. surprised** sentirse gratamente sorprendido.

pleas·ant·ness (plĕz'ənt-nĭs) s. *(pleasingness)* carácter agradable m; *(amiability)* amabilidad f.

pleas·ant·ry (plĕz'ən-trē) s. [pl. **-ries**] gracia, chiste m ♦ **pleasantries** conversación amena.

please (plēz) tr. **pleased, pleas·ing** *(to be agreeable to)* agradar, gustar <*this job pleases me* este trabajo me agrada>; *(to satisfy)* contentar, satisfacer <*it is impossible to p. everyone* es imposible contentar a todo el mundo>; *(to make happy)* complacer <*it pleases us to see that he remembers* nos complace ver que él se acuerda>; *(the senses)* agradar; *(to be the will of)* querer <*it pleased them to wait* quisieron esperar> ♦ **easy to p.** fácil de agradar • **hard to p.** muy exigente • **p. God** quiera Dios • **p.** *(polite request)* por favor <*p. close the door* cierre la puerta, por favor>; *(formal request)* se ruega <*p. do not touch* se ruega no tocar>; *(polite affirmation)* por supuesto • **to be pleased that** alegrarse de que • **to be pleased to** tener el placer de, tener mucho gusto en • **to be pleased with** estar satisfecho o contento con • **to p. oneself** hacer uno lo que quiere o lo que le parece —intr. *(to be agreeable)* agradar, gustar; *(to wish)* parecer, querer <*do whatever you p.* haz lo que quieras> • **if you p.** *(if you will)* por favor, haga el favor de <*follow me, if you p.* haga el favor de seguirme>; *(if you can imagine)* ¡figúrate!, ¡figúrese!

pleas·ing (plē'zĭng) adj. *(enjoyable)* agradable; *(welcome)* grato; *(amiable)* amable, placentero.

pleas·ur·a·ble (plĕzh'ər-ə-bəl) adj. agradable, grato.

pleas·ure (plĕzh'ər) I. s. *(delight)* placer m, gusto; *(amusement)* placer <*the pleasures of a large city* los placeres de una gran ciudad>; *(sensual gratification)* placer (sensual); *(wish)* voluntad f <*at p.* a voluntad> ♦ **p. cruise** crucero de excursión • **to be a p. to** *(to gratify)* ser un placer, dar gusto; *(to be glad to)* tener mucho gusto en <*it's a p. to meet you* (tengo) mucho gusto en conocerle> • **to be one's p. to** tener el placer de, complacerle a uno <*it's my p. to introduce you to you ...*> • **to take p. in** gustarle a uno • **with p.** con gusto II. tr. & intr. **-ured, -ur·ing** complacer(se).

pleat (plēt) I. s. pliegue m II. tr. *(a skirt)* plisar; *(a piece of paper)* plegar, doblar.

pleb (plĕb) s. *(plebeian)* plebeyo; *(freshman)* estudiante de primer año mf.

ple·be·ian (plĭ-bē'ən) I. adj. HIST. *(in Rome)* plebeyo; *(common)* ordinario, bajo II. s. HIST. plebeyo.

pleb·i·scite (plĕb'ĭ-sīt') s. POL. plebiscito.

plec·trum (plĕk'trəm) s. [pl. **-trums** o **-tra** (-trə)] MÚS. plectro, púa.

pled (plĕd) un pret. y part. p. de **plead**.

pledge (plĕj) I. s. *(promise)* promesa; *(obligation)* compromiso, obligación f <*this administration will honor its pledges* este gobierno hará honor a sus compromisos>; *(pawn)* prenda; *(as security)* entrega de prenda; *(token)* prueba <*as a p. of devotion* como prueba de devoción> ♦ **p. of allegiance** voto de lealtad • **to put** o **leave in p.** empeñar, dejar en prenda • **to take** o **make a p. (to)** FAM. comprometerse a • **to take the p.** FAM. jurar abstenerse de la bebida II. tr. **pledged, pledg·ing** *(to promise)* prometer; *(to vow)* hacer voto de <*he pledged allegiance to his country*

hizo voto de lealtad a la patria>; *(to bind)* exigir <*the president pledged me to secrecy* el presidente me exigió guardar el secreto>; *(to pawn)* dar en prenda, empeñar; *(a fraternity)* comprometerse a hacerse socio de (un club estudiantil) ♦ **to be pledged to** haber prometido • **to p. one's word** dar la palabra de uno —intr. hacer una promesa.

pledg·or o **pledge·or** (plĕj'ər, plĕ-jôr') s. DER. prendador m.

ple·na·ry (plē'nə-rē, plĕn'ə-) adj. plenario, completo.

plen·i·po·ten·ti·ar·y (plĕn'ə-pə-tĕn'shē-ĕr'ē) adj. & s. [pl. **-ies**] POL. plenipotenciario.

plen·i·tude (plĕn'ĭ-tōōd', -tyōōd') s. *(abundance)* abundancia; *(fullness)* plenitud f.

plen·te·ous (plĕn'tē-əs) adj. *(abundant)* abundante, copioso; *(productive)* productivo, fructífero.

plen·ti·ful (plĕn'tĭ-fəl) adj. copioso, abundante.

plen·ty (plĕn'tē) I. s. *(abundance)* abundancia; *(affluence)* afluencia II. adj. *(abundant)* abundante; *(sufficient)* suficiente, bastante <*six will be p.* seis será suficiente> ♦ **p. of** *(a lot of)* bastante <*you have p. of money* tienes bastante dinero>; *(more than enough)* de sobra <*we have p. of time* tenemos tiempo de sobra> III. adv. FAM. muy <*it's p. cold* está muy frío>.

ple·o·nasm (plē'ə-năz'əm) s. pleonasmo.

pleth·o·ra (plĕth'ər-ə) s. plétora.

ple·thor·ic (plĕ-thôr'ĭk) adj. MED. pletórico; FIG. pletórico, ampuloso.

pleu·ri·sy (plŏŏr'ĭ-sē) s. MED. pleuresía.

Plex·i·glas (plĕk'sĭ-glăs') s. TEC. plexiglas (marca registrada de un termoplástico transparente) m.

plex·us (plĕk'səs) s. [pl. **plexus** o **plex·us·es**] ANAT. plexo; *(network)* red f, entrelazamiento.

pli·a·ble (plī'ə-bəl) adj. *(easily bent)* maleable, flexible; FIG. *(docile)* dócil, flexible.

pli·an·cy (plī'ən-sē) s. flexibilidad f.

pli·ant (plī'ənt) adj. *(malleable)* maleable, flexible; FIG. *(docile)* dócil, flexible.

pli·cate (plī'kāt') adj. BOT., ZOOL. plegado, plisado.

pli·ers (plī'ərz) s. MEC. alicates m, tenazas f.

plight¹ (plīt) s. apuro, situación difícil f.

plight² (plīt) tr. *(one's word, oath)* empeñar o dar uno su palabra; *(loyalty)* prometer ♦ **to p. one's troth** dar palabra de matrimonio.

plinth (plĭnth) s. ARQ. *(of a column)* plinto, orlo; *(base block)* zócalo; *(stand)* pedestal m.

plod (plŏd) intr. **plod·ded, plod·ding** ♦ **to p.** o **p. along** *(to walk)* andar trabajosamente; *(to work)* trabajar lentamente —tr. ♦ **to p. away at** perseverar en • **to p. through** *(to walk)* andar trabajosamente.

plonk (plŏngk, plŭngk) v., s. & adv. var. de **plunk**.

plop (plŏp) I. intr. **plopped, plop·ping** ♦ **to p. down** caerse de golpe, desplomarse —tr. dejar caer con ruido apagado II. s. ruido apagado.

plot (plŏt) I. s. *(of land)* parcela, terreno; *(for burial)* cuadro; *(patch)* cuadro <*a vegetable p.* un cuadro de verduras>; *(ground plan)* plano; *(story line)* trama, argumento; *(conspiracy)* complot m, conspiración f ♦ **garden p.** jardín II. tr. **plot·ted, plot·ting** *(to chart)* trazar <*to p. a ship's course* trazar la trayectoria de un barco>; *(to scheme)* tramar <*to p. an assassination* tramar un asesinato>; *(a story)* idear el argumento de; MAT. *(points)* marcar; *(a curve)* trazar; *(an equation)* representar gráficamente —intr. conspirar.

plot·ter (plŏt'ər) s. *(schemer)* intrigante mf; *(conspirator)* conspirador m.

plot·ting (plŏt'ĭng) s. *(scheming)* intriga; *(conspiracy)* conspiración f; *(graphical representation)* representación gráfica.

plough (plou) s. & v. G.B. var. de **plow**.

plov·er (plŭv'ər, plō'vər) s. ZOOL. chorlito.

plow (plou) I. s. *(implement)* arado; *(snowplow)* quitanieves m II. tr. *(a field)* arar; *(to furrow)* surcar, hacer surcos (con el arado); *(to clear)* abrir; *(through water)* surcar <*to p. the high seas* surcar los mares> ♦ **to p. back** FIN. reinvertir (ganancias) • **to p. through** *(a crowd)* abrirse paso a través de; *(a novel, report)* leer con dificultad • **to p. under** *(to overwhelm)* agobiar, abrumar; *(to bury)* enterrar • **to p. up** arar, roturar —intr. *(a field)* arar la tierra; *(to allow plowing)* ararse <this soil plows well esta tierra se ara bien> ◆ **to p. into** FAM. *(to strike)* arremeter *o* precipitarse contra; *(to undertake)* acometer • **to p. through** *(a crowd)* abrirse paso a través de; *(to plod)* leer con dificultad (novela, informe).

plow·a·ble (plou′ə-bəl) adj. AGR. arable.

plow·boy (plou′boi′) s. *(worker)* yuguero, yuntero; *(country boy)* joven campesino.

plow·ing (plou′ĭng) s. arada.

plow·land (plou′lănd′) s. tierra de labranza.

plow·man (plou′mən) s. [pl. **-men**] *(worker)* labrador *m*; *(farmer)* campesino.

plow·share (plou′shâr′) s. reja del arado.

ploy (ploi) s. truco, estratagema.

pluck (plŭk) **I.** tr. *(to pick)* coger <p. a rose coge una rosa>; *(eyebrows)* pelar; *(a chicken)* desplumar; *(to pull out)* arrancar; JER. *(to steal)* robar, estafar; MÚS. pulsar, puntear ◆ **to p. up one's courage** armarse de valor —intr. dar un tirón ◆ **to p. up** animarse **II.** s. *(tug)* tirón *m*; *(courage)* valor *m*, arrojo.

pluck·y (plŭk′ē) adj. **-i·er, -i·est** resuelto, valeroso.

plug (plŭg) **I.** s. *(for a drain, hole)* tapón *m*; ELEC. enchufe *m*; *(spark plug)* bujía; *(fireplug)* boca de incendio; *(of tobacco)* mascada, andullo; FAM. *(publicity)* propaganda, publicidad *f*; JER. *(horse)* penco; *(gunshot)* balazo **II.** tr. **plugged, plug·ging** *(to stop up)* poner un tapón a, tapar; *(to fill)* tapar; *(to insert)* poner <to p. a cork in a bottle poner un corcho a una botella>; JER. *(to shoot)* pegar un tiro a, meter un plomo a; *(to punch)* dar un puñetazo a; FAM. *(to publicize)* hacer propaganda de ◆ **to p. in** enchufar • **to p. up** tapar —intr. ◆ **to p. away** FAM. trabajar obstinadamente • **to p. away at** perseverar en • **to p. for** matarse *o* afanarse por.

plug-in (plŭg′ĭn′) adj. con enchufe.

plum (plŭm) **I.** s. BOT. *(tree)* ciruelo; *(fruit)* ciruela; CUL. *(raisin)* pasa; *(color)* color ciruela; FIG. breva, chollo **II.** adj. de color ciruela.

plum·age (plōō′mĭj) s. plumaje *m*.

plumb (plŭm) **I.** s. plomada ◆ **to be out of** *o* **off p.** no estar a plomo **II.** adj. *(vertical)* a plomo, vertical; FAM. *(utter)* completo <a p. fool un completo idiota> **III.** adv. *(vertically)* a plomo, verticalmente; FAM. *(utterly)* completamente <p. exhausted completamente agotado> **IV.** tr. MARÍT. sondar; *(to probe into)* sondear (intenciones); *(to seal)* emplomar ◆ **to p. up** CONSTR. aplomar.

plumb bob s. CONSTR. plomada, plomo.

plumb·er (plŭm′ər) s. plomero, fontanero.

plumb·ing (plŭm′ĭng) s. *(pipes)* cañería, tubería; *(trade)* plomería.

plumb line s. plomada, tranquil *m*.

plumb rule s. nivel *m*.

plume (plōōm) **I.** s. *(feather)* pluma; *(on a helmet)* penacho, plumero; FIG. *(column)* penacho <a p. of smoke un penacho de humo> **II.** tr. **plumed, plum·ing** *(to adorn)* emplumar; *(to preen)* arreglarse las plumas ◆ **to p. oneself on** vanagloriarse de.

plum·met (plŭm′ĭt) **I.** s. *(of a plumb line)* plomo; FIG. *(weight)* lastre *m*, peso **II.** intr. *(object)* caer a plomo; *(plane)* caer en picado.

plum·my (plŭm′ē) adj. **-mi·er, -mi·est** *(fruit)* lleno de ciruelas; *(desirable)* escogido, envidiable; *(voice)* pastosa.

plump¹ (plŭmp) **I.** adj. **-er, -est** *(chubby)* rechoncho, regordete; *(ample)* abundante **II.** tr. engordar —intr. ponerse regordete; *(sails)* hincharse.

plump² (plŭmp) **I.** intr. caer *o* dejarse caer pesadamente <to p. into a chair dejarse caer pesadamente en una butaca> ◆ **to p. for** declararse a favor de —tr. dejar caer pesadamente **II.** s. *(heavy fall)* caída pesada; *(sound of fall)* ruido sordo **III.** adj. rotundo, sin rodeos **IV.** adv. *(with an impact)* con un ruido sordo; *(straight down)* a plomo; *(directly)* rotundamente, sin rodeos.

plump·ness (plŭmp′nĭs) s. *(fatness)* gordura; *(of an impact)*

pesadez (de un golpe, caída) *f*; *(of a statement)* carácter rotundo.

plum pudding s. CUL. budín de ciruelas *m*.

plun·der (plŭn′dər) **I.** tr. *(to pillage)* saquear; *(to steal)* robar —intr. robar **II.** s. *(booty)* botín *m*; *(plundering)* saqueo.

plun·der·er (plŭn′dər-ər) s. saqueador *m*.

plunge (plŭnj) **I.** tr. **plunged, plung·ing** *(to thrust)* hundir, meter; *(a knife)* hundir, clavar; *(to cast)* hundir, sumir <the news plunged us into despondency la noticia nos sumió en la desesperación> —intr. *(to submerge)* sumergirse; *(to dive)* zambullirse, tirarse de cabeza; *(to sink)* hundirse; *(into a condition)* hundirse, sumirse; *(into an activity)* meterse de cabeza en; *(to rush)* precipitarse; *(to fall)* caer; *(to dash downward)* precipitarse, descender a pico; *(to descend)* precipitarse hacia abajo, bajar vertiginosamente; FAM. *(to take a chance)* jugarse el todo por el todo ◆ **to p. ahead** *o* **forward** precipitarse a **II.** s. *(dive)* zambullidura, clavado; *(fall)* caída; *(in prices)* baja vertiginosa; *(swim)* chapuzón *m*, baño ◆ **to take a p.** bajar vertiginosamente • **to take the p.** dar el paso decisivo.

plung·er (plŭn′jər) s. MEC. *(piston)* émbolo; *(for pipes, drains)* desatascador *m*.

plunk (plŭngk) **I.** tr. MÚS. puntear ◆ **to p.** *o* **p. down** dejar caer pesadamente —intr. hacer un ruido sordo ◆ **to p. down in** *o* **on** caer *o* dejarse caer pesadamente **II.** s. *(twang)* rasgueo, punteo; *(hollow sound)* ruido sordo; *(blow)* golpe seco **II.** adv. *(with a thud)* con ruido sordo; *(exactly)* exactamente <p. in the middle exactamente en el medio>.

plu·per·fect (plōō-pûr′fĭkt) GRAM. **I.** adj. pluscuamperfecto **II.** s. pretérito pluscuamperfecto.

plu·ral (plŏŏr′əl) **I.** adj. plural **II.** s. *(number)* plural *m*; *(word)* palabra en plural.

plu·ral·ism (plŏŏr′ə-lĭz′əm) s. pluralismo.

plu·ral·is·tic (plŏŏr′ə-lĭs′tĭk) adj. pluralista.

plu·ral·i·ty (plŏŏ-răl′ĭ-tē) s. [pl. **-ties**] *(state)* pluralidad *f*; *(large part)* mayor parte ◆ **by a p. of votes** POL. por mayoría de votos.

plu·ral·ize (plŏŏr′ə-līz′) tr. **-ized, -iz·ing** GRAM. pluralizar —intr. pasar al plural, convertirse en plural.

plus (plŭs) **I.** prep. MAT. *(added to)* más <two p. three dos más tres>; *(increased by)* más, y además <wages p. dividends sueldo más dividendos>; *(besides)* además de <p. the information already existing además de la información ya existente> **II.** adj. *(positive)* positivo; *(extra)* adicional, extra <a p. benefit una ventaja adicional>; FAM. *(and more)* extraordinario <she has personality p. tiene una personalidad extraordinaria>; *(credit)* de entradas, de ingresos **III.** s. [pl. **plus·es** *o* **plus·ses**] ventaja **IV.** conj. FAM. y además <she's got talent, p. she works hard tiene talento y además trabaja mucho>.

plus fours s.pl. DEP. *(pantalones)* bombachos.

plush (plŭsh) **I.** s. TEJ. felpa **II.** adj. TEJ. afelpado, de felpa; FAM. *(luxurious)* lujoso.

plush·y (plŭsh′ē) adj. **-i·er, -i·est** TEJ. afelpado, de felpa; FAM. *(luxurious)* lujoso.

plus sign s. MAT. símbolo de sumar, signo de más.

Plu·to (plōō′tō) s. ASTRON., MITOL. Plutón *m*.

plu·toc·ra·cy (plōō-tŏk′rə-sē) s. [pl. **-cies**] POL. plutocracia.

plu·to·crat (plōō′tə-krăt′) s. plutócrata *mf*.

plu·to·crat·ic (plōō′tə-krăt′ĭk) *o* **plu·to·crat·i·cal** (-ĭ-kəl) adj. plutocrático.

Plu·to·ni·an (plōō-tō′nē-ən) *o* **Plu·ton·ic** (-tŏn′ĭk) adj. ASTRON., MITOL. plutoniano.

plu·to·ni·um (plōō-tō′nē-əm) s. QUÍM. plutonio.

plu·vi·al (plōō′vē-əl) *o* **plu·vi·an** (-ən) adj. METEOR. pluvial.

ply¹ (plī) **I.** tr. **plied, ply·ing** *(to twist)* enrollar; *(to fold)* doblar **II.** s. [pl. **plies**] *(of cloth)* capa; *(of wool)* cabo; *(of wood)* chapa; *(of paper)* pliego.

ply² (plī) tr. **plied, ply·ing** *(to wield)* manejar; *(to practice)* ejercer; *(to traverse)* hacer el trayecto de ◆ **to p. with** *(questions)* acosar con; *(food)* ofrecer —intr. ◆ **to p. at a trade** ejercer una profesión • **to p. between** hacer el servicio entre, ir y venir entre.

ply·wood (plī′wŏŏd′) s. madera terciada *o* contrachapada.

---

p.m. (pē-ĕm′) adj. [abr. de **post meridiem**] *(of the afternoon)* de la tarde *<at 3 p.m.* a las tres de la tarde>; *(of the night)* de la noche *<at 11 p.m.* a las once de la noche>.

pneu·mat·ic (nōō-măt′ĭk, nyōō-) adj. FÍS., ZOOL. neumático; FILOS. *(spiritual)* espiritual.

pneu·mat·ics (nōō-măt′ĭks, nyōō-) s. [ú. con v. sing.] FÍS. neumática.

pneu·mo·coc·cus (nōō′mə-kŏk′əs, nyōō′-) s. [pl. **-coc·ci** (-kŏk′sī′, -kŏk′ī′)] BIOL., MED. neumococo.

pneu·mo·nia (nōō-mōn′yə, nyōō-) s. MED. pulmonía.

pneu·mon·ic (nōō-mŏn′ĭk) adj. MED. neumónico.

poach¹ (pōch) tr. CUL. cocer a fuego lento, escalfar.

poach² (pōch) intr. *(to hunt illegally)* cazar en vedado; *(to fish illegally)* pescar en vedado; *(to become muddy)* enfangarse; *(to sink)* mecerse en un fangal —tr. *(to muddy)* pisotear; *(game)* cazar en vedado; *(fish)* pescar en vedado.

poach·er (pō′chər) s. *(hunter)* cazador furtivo; *(fisherman)* pescador furtivo.

pock (pŏk) MED. I. s. *(pustule)* pústula; *(pockmark)* cicatriz de viruela *f*, cacaraña II. tr. picar de viruelas.

pock·et (pŏk′ĭt) I. s. *(of a garment)* bolsillo *m*; *(pouch)* bolsa pequeña; *(cavity)* cavidad *f*, hueco; *(of a pool table)* tronera, hueco; *(area, group)* foco *<pockets of civilization* focos de civilización>; *(of air)* bolsa de aire, bache *m*; ZOOL. bolsa; MIN. *(of gas, oil)* bolsa; *(of ore)* filón *m* ♦ **to dip into one's p.** sacar (dinero) del bolsillo de uno, echar mano al bolsillo de uno • **to have (someone) in one's p.** FIG. tener (a alguien) en el bolsillo • **to line one's pockets** forrarse (de dinero) II. adj. de bolsillo *<p. calculator* calculadora de bolsillo> III. tr. *(to place in one's pocket)* meterse *o* guardarse en el bolsillo; *(to take dishonestly)* echarse en el bolsillo, llevarse; *(to tolerate)* tragarse; *(in billiards)* meter en la tronera.

pocket billiards s.pl. billar americano, billar de casino.

pock·et·book (pŏk′ĭt-bōōk′) s. *(billfold)* billetera; *(purse)* cartera de mano, monedero; *(financial resources)* recursos; *(book)* libro de bolsillo.

pocket edition s. edición de bolsillo *f*.

pock·et·ful (pŏk′ĭt-fōōl′) s. [pl. **pock·et·fuls** *o* **pock·ets·ful**] bolsillo (lleno de).

pock·et·knife (pŏk′ĭt-nīf′) s. [pl. **-knives** (-nīvz′)] navaja, cortaplumas *m*.

pocket money s. dinero para gastos personales.

pock·et·sized (pŏk′ĭt-sīzd′) *o* **pock·et·size** (-sīz′) adj. de bolsillo.

pocket veto s. POL. veto indirecto (por parte del presidente o gobernador en EE. UU.).

pock·mark (pŏk′märk′) I. s. cacaraña, cicatriz de viruela *f* II. tr. picar de viruelas.

pod¹ (pŏd) I. s. *(of peas)* vaina; FIG. *(covering)* cubierta II. tr. desvainar —intr. producir vainas.

pod² (pŏd) s. ICT. cardumen *m*.

pod³ (pŏd) s. MEC. *(groove)* ranura; *(socket)* mandril *m*.

po·di·a·trist (pə-dī′ə-trĭst) s. MED. podiatra *m*.

po·di·a·try (pə-dī′ə-trē) s. MED. podiatría.

po·di·um (pō′dē-əm) s. [pl. **-di·a** (-dē-ə) *o* **-di·ums**] *(platform)* podio, estrado; ARQ. *(pedestal)* pedestal *m*.

Po·dunk (pō′dŭngk′) s. FAM. ciudad pequeña.

po·em (pō′əm, -ĭm) s. LIT. *(verse composition)* poema *m*, poesía; *(poetic composition)* poema, composición poética.

po·et (pō′ĭt) s. LIT. poeta *mf*.

po·et·as·ter (pō′ĭ-tăs′tər) s. poetastro.

po·et·ess (pō′ĭ-tĭs) s. LIT. poetisa.

po·et·ic (pō-ĕt′ĭk) adj. poético.

po·et·i·cal (pō-ĕt′ĭ-kəl) adj. LIT. *(of a poem)* poético; *(idealized)* idealizado.

poetic justice s. justicia poética.

poetic license s. LIT. licencia poética.

po·et·ics (pō-ĕt′ĭks) s. [ú. con v. sing.] LIT. *(criticism)* poética; *(treatise)* arte poética.

poet laureate s. [pl. **poets laureate** *o* **poet laureates**] LIT. poeta laureado.

po·et·ry (pō′ĭ-trē) s. poesía.

po·grom (pə-grŏm′, pō′grəm) s. HIST. pogromo.

poign·ance (poin′yəns) *o* **poign·an·cy** (-yən-sē) s. *(sadness)*

patetismo; *(intensity)* intensidad *f*; *(sarcasm)* mordacidad *f*.

poign·ant (poin′yənt) adj. *(painful)* agudo, intenso; *(sad)* patético; *(touching)* conmovedor; *(cutting)* mordaz; *(pungent)* punzante.

poin·set·ti·a (poin-sĕt′ē-ə, -sĕt′ə) s. BOT. flor de Pascua *f*.

point (point) I. s. *(tip)* punta *<there's no p. on my pencil* mi lápiz no tiene punta>; GEOG. *(cape)* punta; *(dot)* punto; *(of number)* coma *<one p. five* uno coma cinco>; *(degree)* punto *<boiling p.* punto de ebullición>; *(subject)* tema *m* *<stick to the p.* no te salgas del tema>; *(item)* punto; *(spot)* punto, lugar *m*; *(moment)* punto, momento; *(detail)* punto *<they explained it p. by p.* lo explicaron punto por punto>; *(trait)* punto *<it's not one of my strong points* no es mi punto fuerte>; *(reason)* motivo, razón *f* *<there's no p. in going on* no hay ningún motivo para continuar>; DEP. punto, tanto; FIN. entero *<the stock market was up two points* la bolsa subió dos enteros>; *(of dog)* punta, parada; IMPR., MAT. punto; ELEC. contacto ♦ **at the p. of** a punto de • **at this p.** a estas alturas *<at this p. in time* en este momento> • **beside the p.** fuera de propósito, que no viene al caso • **in p. of fact** en realidad • **on points** DEP. por puntos • **that's just the p.!** ¡eso es!, ¡ahí está el detalle! • **that's not the p.** eso no tiene nada que ver, no es eso • **to come to the p.** ir al grano • **to make one's p.** salirse con la suya • **to make a p. of** creerse en la obligación de • **to miss the p.** no comprender • **to reach the p. of no return** no poder volver atrás • **to stretch the p.** ir más allá del límite • **to the point** a propósito, pertinente • **what's the p.?** ¿para qué? II. tr. *(to aim)* apuntar; *(to show)* indicar *<to p. the way* indicar el camino>; *(to sharpen)* sacar punta a, afilar; *(a dog)* parar; CONSTR. *(to fill)* unir con mortero, rellenar ♦ **to p. at** apuntar con *<don't p. your finger at me* no me apuntes con el dedo> • **to p. out** *(to show)* apuntar, señalar; *(to note)* señalar *<I'd like to p. out that* quisiera señalar que> • **to p. up** poner de relieve —intr. *(with the finger)* apuntar; *(to aim)* apuntar a *<to p. north* apuntar al norte>; *(dogs)* pararse; *(ships)* navegar de bolina ♦ **to p. at** señalar (con el dedo) • **to p. to** *(to show)* señalar; *(to suggest)* indicar que *<everything points to his guilt* todo indica que es culpable>.

point·blank (point′blăngk′) I. adj. *(straight)* directo; *(at a close range)* a quemarropa; *(blunt)* categórico II. adv. *(directly)* directamente, a quemarropa; *(without hesitation)* sin rodeos, categóricamente.

point·ed (poin′tĭd) adj. *(sharp)* puntiagudo, afilado; *(critical)* mordaz; *(intended)* intencional; *(conspicuous)* evidente, obvio; ARQ. ojival, apuntado.

point·er (poin′tər) s. *(indicator)* indicador *m*; *(of a scale)* fiel *m*; *(of a watch)* manecilla; *(stick)* puntero; *(dog)* perro de muestra; *(tip)* consejo útil.

poin·til·lism (pwăn′tē-ĭz′əm) s. ARTE. puntillismo.

point·less (point′lĭs) adj. *(meaningless)* sin sentido; *(useless)* inútil; *(irrelevant)* que no viene al caso.

point of honor s. punto de honor.

point of no return s. AER. punto del cual no se puede regresar.

point of order s. cuestión de orden *f*.

point of view s. *(standpoint)* punto de vista; *(attitude)* actitud *f*.

point·y (poin′tē) adj. **-i·er, -i·est** puntiagudo.

poise¹ (poiz) I. tr. **poised, pois·ing** poner en equilibrio —intr. *(balanced)* estar en equilibrio; *(suspended)* estar suspendido II. s. *(equilibrium)* equilibrio; *(composure)* aplomo, serenidad *f*; *(bearing)* porte *m*.

poise² (poiz) s. FÍS. poise (unidad de viscosidad) *m*.

poi·son (poi′zən) I. s. *(toxin)* veneno, ponzoña; *(insecticide)* insecticida II. tr. *(to kill)* envenenar; *(to pollute)* contaminar; *(one's mind, a friendship)* envenenar III. adj. venenoso, envenenado.

poi·son·er (poi′zə-nər) s. envenenador *m*.

poison gas s. gas tóxico *o* venenoso.

poi·son·ing (poi′zə-nĭng) s. envenenamiento.

poison ivy s. BOT. zumaque venenoso.

poison oak s. BOT. zumaque venenoso.

ã rey / ä año / b boca / ch chico / d dar / ě el / ē mil / g gato / h joya / hw juez / ī aire / k casa / kw cuan /

poi·son·ous (poi′zə-nəs) adj. *(venomous)* venenoso; *(toxic)* tóxico.

poison sumac s. BOT. zumaque venenoso.

poke¹ (pōk) **I.** tr. **poked, pok·ing** *(to jab)* pinchar, aguijonear; *(with one's elbow)* dar codazo <*she poked him in the ribs* le dio un codazo en las costillas>; *(with one's finger)* dar con la punta del dedo; *(to thrust)* meter <*he poked his head through the opening* metió la cabeza en la abertura> • **to p. a hole** hacer hueco • **to p. fun at** burlarse de • **to p. one's nose into** meter las narices en • **to p. out** *(to gouge)* sacar; *(to stick out)* sacar o asomar (cabeza, brazo) —intr. *(to meddle)* meterse ♦ **to p. along** caminar lentamente • **to p. around** *(to search)* fisgonear, hurgar; *(to look around)* curiosear • **to p. at** *(an animal)* pinchar, aguijonear; *(a fire)* atizar • **to p. out** asomar **II.** s. *(jab)* pinchazo; *(with one's elbow)* codazo; *(dawdler)* pachorrudo, vago.

poke² (pōk) s. *(bonnet)* papalina.

pok·er¹ (pō′kər) s. atizador m, hurgón m.

pok·er² (pō′kər) s. póker, póquer (juego de naipes) m.

poker face s. cara inmutable.

po·key (pō′kē) s. [pl. **-keys**] JER. prisión f, cárcel f.

pok·y o **pok·ey** (pō′kē) FAM. adj. **pok·i·er, pok·i·est** *(slow)* lerdo; *(shabby)* desgarbado; *(small)* diminuto, pequeño.

Po·land (pō′lənd) s. Polonia.

po·lar (pō′lər) adj. *(of a pole)* polar; *(frigid)* frígido; *(opposite)* opuesto.

polar bear s. ZOOL. oso polar.

polar cap s. casquete polar m.

polar circle s. GEOG. círculo polar.

polar coordinate s. GEOG. coordenada polar.

Po·lar·is (pə-lăr′ĭs, -lär′-) s. ASTRON. estrella polar, polar f; ARM. proyectil atómico teledirigido (de EE. UU.).

po·lar·i·ty (pō-lăr′ĭ-tē) s. [pl. **-ties**] polaridad f.

po·lar·i·za·tion (pō′lər-ĭ-zā′shən) s. polarización f.

po·lar·ize (pō′lə-rīz′) tr. **-ized, -iz·ing** polarizar.

Po·lar·oid (pō′lə-roid′) s. polaroid (marca registrada).

pole¹ (pōl) s. *(axis)* polo.

pole² (pōl) **I.** s. *(post)* poste m, palo; *(of a carriage)* lanza; *(measure)* medida de longitud; *(spar)* mástil m ♦ **ski p.** bastón de esquiar • **telephone p.** poste de teléfono **II.** tr. **poled, pol·ing** *(to propel)* empujar con una pértiga; *(to support)* sostener con un palo.

Pole (pōl) s. polaco.

pole·ax o **pole·axe** (pōl′ăks′) s. MIL. alabarda, hacha de mango largo.

pole bean s. BOT. fríjol trepador m; judía trepadora.

pole·cat (pōl′kăt′) ZOOL. s. *(feline)* turón m; *(skunk)* mofeta, zorrillo.

po·lem·ic (pə-lĕm′ĭk) **I.** s. *(controversy)* polémica, controversia; *(polemicist)* polemista mf ♦ **polemics** [ú. con v. sing.] RET., TEOL. polémica **II.** adj. polémico.

po·lem·i·cal (pə-lĕm′ĭ-kəl) adj. polémico.

po·lem·i·cist (pə-lĕm′ĭ-sĭst) o **po·lem·ist** (pə-lĕm′ĭst, pōl′ə-mĭst) s. polemista mf.

pole·star (pōl′stär′) s. ASTRON. estrella polar; FIG. *(principle)* principio orientador.

pole·vault (pōl′vôlt′) **I.** s. DEP. salto con garrocha, salto con pértiga **II.** intr. saltar con garrocha.

po·lice (pə-lēs′) **I.** s. [pl. **police**] [ú. con v. pl.] *(governmental department)* policía; *(officers)* policía <*the p. were waiting for him* la policía le estaba esperando>; *(private group)* policía, patrulla; MIL. *(cleaning)* limpieza (del campamento, cuartel) **II.** tr. **-liced, -lic·ing** *(to patrol)* patrullar, vigilar; *(to keep in order)* mantener el orden en; *(to oversee)* vigilar, supervisar; MIL. *(to clean)* limpiar.

police action s. MIL. intervención f, operación militar sin declaración de guerra f.

police dog s. perro policía.

police force s. policía, fuerza pública.

po·lice·man (pə-lēs′mən) s. [pl. **-men**] policía m.

police officer s. agente de policía mf, policía mf.

police power s. fuerza pública.

police record s. antecedentes penales m.

police state s. POL. estado policial o policíaco.

police station s. jefatura de policía, comisaría.

po·lice·wom·an (pə-lēs′woŏm′ən) s. [pl. **-wom·en** (-wĭm′ĭn)] mujer policía f.

pol·i·cy¹ (pŏl′ĭ-sē) s. [pl. **-cies**] *(of a government)* política <*foreign p.* política exterior>; *(of a business)* norma <*it is not our p. to accept checks* tenemos por norma no aceptar cheques>; *(course of action)* sistema m, táctica.

pol·i·cy² (pŏl′ĭ-sē) s. [pl. **-cies**] *(written contract)* póliza <*insurance p.* póliza de seguros>; *(numbers game)* lotería ilegal.

pol·i·cy·hold·er (pŏl′ĭ-sē-hōl′dər) s. asegurado.

po·li·o (pō′lē-ō′) s. MED. polio f, poliomielitis f.

po·li·o·my·e·li·tis (pō′lē-ō-mī′ə-lī′tĭs) s. poliomielitis f.

pol·ish (pŏl′ĭsh) **I.** tr. *(to wax)* encerar; *(to shine)* limpiar; *(metals)* bruñir; *(nails)* esmaltar o pintar; *(to refine)* pulir ♦ **to p. off** FAM. despachar —intr. *(to become shiny)* pulirse; *(to become refined)* pulirse **II.** s. *(shininess)* brillo, lustre m; *(wax)* cera; *(for metals)* líquido de bruñir; *(for nails)* esmalte m, pintura; *(act)* pulimento; *(refinement)* finura o refinamiento ♦ **shoe p.** betún.

Po·lish (pō′lĭsh) adj. & s. polaco.

pol·ished (pŏl′ĭsht) adj. *(shiny)* pulido; *(shoes)* brilloso, lustroso; *(metals)* bruñido; *(nails)* esmaltado o pulido; *(refined)* refinado, fino; *(style)* pulido.

pol·ish·er (pŏl′ĭ-shər) s. *(person, instrument)* pulidor m; *(floor-polishing machine)* enceradora f.

pol·it·bu·ro (pŏl′ĭt-byoŏr′ō, pə-lĭt′-) s. POL. politburó.

po·lite (pə-līt′) adj. **-lit·er, -lit·est** *(courteous)* cortés, atento; *(proper)* correcto, de buena educación <*it is not p. to leave so early* no es de buena educación irse tan temprano>; *(refined)* educado, fino <*in p. society* entre personas educadas>.

po·lite·ness (pə-līt′nĭs) s. *(courteousness)* cortesía; *(refinement)* educación f, finura.

pol·i·tic (pŏl′ĭ-tĭk) adj. *(artful)* diplomático; *(clever)* astuto; *(judicious)* prudente; *(cunning)* taimado.

po·lit·i·cal (pə-lĭt′ĭ-kəl) adj. político.

political science s. ciencias políticas.

pol·i·ti·cian (pŏl′ĭ-tĭsh′ən) s. POL. político; *(politico)* politiquero.

po·lit·i·cize (pə-lĭt′ĭ-sīz′) intr. **-cized, -ciz·ing** hacer política —tr. politizar.

pol·i·tick (pŏl′ĭ-tĭk′) intr. politiquear.

pol·i·ti·co (pə-lĭt′ĭ-kō′) s. politiquero.

pol·i·tics (pŏl′ĭ-tĭks) s. [ú. con v. sing. o pl.] política ♦ **to talk p.** hablar de política.

pol·i·ty (pŏl′ĭ-tē) s. [pl. **-ties**] *(form of government)* gobierno, forma de gobierno; *(nation)* estado.

pol·ka (pōl′kə, pō′kə) **I.** s. polca **II.** intr. bailar la polca.

pol·ka dot (pō′kə) s. TEJ. *(dots)* puntos, lunares m; *(fabric)* tela de puntos o lunares; *(pattern)* diseño de puntos o lunares.

poll (pōl) **I.** s. POL. *(casting of votes)* votación f; *(number of votes)* votos, votación; *(survey)* encuesta; *(of the head)* coronilla ♦ **polls** POL. urnas, centro electoral • **to go to the polls** ir a las urnas, votar **II.** tr. *(to garner)* obtener, recibir <*he polled 35 percent of the votes* obtuvo el 35 por ciento de los votos>; *(to register)* registrar los votos de; *(to cast)* dar (un voto); *(to question)* hacer una encuesta de; *(hair, horns)* cortar; *(to shear)* esquilar; *(to prune)* podar —intr. POL. ir a las urnas, votar.

pol·len (pŏl′ən) s. BOT. polen m.

pollen count s. medida de la concentración de polen en el aire.

pol·li·nate (pŏl′ə-nāt′) tr. **-nat·ed, -nat·ing** BOT. polinizar.

pol·li·na·tion (pŏl′ə-nā′shən) s. BOT. polinización f.

poll·ing (pō′lĭng) s. POL. votación f.

polling place s. lugar de votación m.

pol·li·wog (pŏl′ē-wŏg′) s. ZOOL. renacuajo.

poll·ster (pōl′stər) s. entrevistador m, encuestador m.

poll tax s. capitación f.

pol·lut·ant (pə-loŏt′nt) s. agente contaminador m.

pol·lute (pə-loŏt′) tr. **-lut·ed, -lut·ing** *(to corrupt)* corromper; *(to contaminate)* contaminar.

pol·lu·tion (pə-loŏ′shən) s. contaminación f.

Pol·ly·an·na (pŏl′ē-ăn′ə) s. persona de un optimismo extremo.

pol·ly·wog (pŏl′ē-wŏg′) s. var. de **polliwog**.
po·lo (pō′lō) s. DEP. *(on horseback)* polo; *(water polo)* polo acuático.
pol·o·naise (pŏl′ə-nāz′, pō′lə-) s. MÚS. polonesa.
po·lo·ni·um (pə-lō′nē-əm) s. QUÍM. polonio.
polo shirt s. polo.
pol·ter·geist (pōl′tər-gīst′) s. espíritu burlón *m*, duende *m*.
pol·troon (pŏl-trōōn′) s. ANT. cobarde *m*.
pol·y·an·drous (pŏl′ē-ăn′drəs) adj. poliandro.
pol·y·an·dry (pŏl′ē-ăn′drē) s. poliandria.
pol·y·chro·mat·ic (pŏl′ē-krō-măt′ĭk) adj. policromo.
pol·y·chrome (pŏl′ē-krōm′) I. adj. policromado II. s. policromo.
pol·y·clin·ic (pŏl′ē-klĭn′ĭk) s. policlínica, policlínico.
pol·y·es·ter (pŏl′ē-ĕs′tər) s. QUÍM., TEJ. poliéster *m*.
pol·y·eth·yl·ene (pŏl′ē-ĕth′ə-lēn′) s. QUÍM. polietileno.
po·lyg·a·mist (pə-lĭg′ə-mĭst) s. polígamo.
po·lyg·a·mous (pə-lĭg′ə-məs) adj. polígamo.
po·lyg·a·my (pə-lĭg′ə-mē) s. poligamia.
pol·y·glot (pŏl′ē-glŏt′) I. adj. políglota II. s. *(person)* polígloto; *(bible)* biblia políglota; *(mixture)* poliglotía.
pol·y·gon (pŏl′ē-gŏn′) s. GEOM. polígono.
pol·y·graph (pŏl′ē-grăf′) s. polígrafo.
pol·y·he·dron (pŏl′ē-hē′drən) s. [pl. **-drons** o **-dra** (-drə)] GEOM. poliedro.
pol·y·math (pŏl′ē-măth′) s. & adj. erudito.
pol·y·mer (pŏl′ē-mər) s. QUÍM. polímero.
po·lym·er·i·za·tion (pə-lĭm′ər-ĭ-zā′shən, pŏl′ə-mər-) s. QUÍM. polimerización *f*.
pol·y·mer·ize (pŏl′ə-mə-rīz′) tr. & intr. polimerizar.
pol·y·mor·phic (pŏl′ē-môr′fĭk) adj. polimórfico.
pol·y·mor·phism (pŏl′ē-môr′fĭz′əm) s. BIOL., QUÍM. polimorfismo.
pol·y·mor·phous (pŏl′ē-môr′fəs) adj. polimorfo.
Pol·y·ne·sia (pŏl′ə-nē′zhə) s. GEOG. Polinesia.
Pol·y·ne·sian (pŏl′ə-nē′zhən) adj. & s. polinesio.
pol·y·no·mi·al (pŏl′ē-nō′mē-əl) MAT. I. adj. polinómico II. s. polinomio.
pol·yp (pŏl′ĭp) s. MED., ZOOL. pólipo.
pol·y·phon·ic (pŏl′ē-fŏn′ĭk) adj. MÚS. polifónico.
po·lyph·o·ny (pə-lĭf′ə-nē) s. [pl. **-nies**] MÚS. polifonía.
pol·y·syl·lab·ic (pŏl′ē-sĭ-lăb′ĭk) adj. polisílabo, polisilábico.
pol·y·syl·la·ble (pŏl′ē-sĭl′ə-bəl) s. GRAM. polisílabo.
pol·y·tech·nic (pŏl′ē-tĕk′nĭk) I. adj. politécnico II. s. instituto politécnico, escuela politécnica.
pol·y·the·ism (pŏl′ē-thē-ĭz′əm) s. RELIG. politeísmo (pluralidad de dioses).
pol·y·un·sat·u·rat·ed (pŏl′ē-ŭn-săch′ə-rā′tĭd) adj. QUÍM. que contiene muchos enlaces no saturados (dic. de grasas y aceites).
pol·y·u·re·thane (pŏl′ē-yōōr′ə-thān′) s. QUÍM. poliuretano.
pol·y·va·lent (pŏl′ē-vā′lənt) adj. BACT., QUÍM. polivalente.
pol·y·vi·nyl (pŏl′ē-vī′nəl) s. QUÍM. polivinilo.
polyvinyl chloride s. QUÍM. cloruro de polivinilo.
pom·ace (pŭm′ĭs, pŏm′-) s. *(pulp)* pulpa de manzana; *(residue)* bagazo.
po·made (pō-mād′, -măd′) I. s. pomada II. tr. **-mad·ed, -mad·ing** untar con pomada.
po·man·der (pō′măn′dər) s. *(bag)* almohadilla perfumada; *(box)* cajita de perfumes.
pome·gran·ate (pŏm′grăn′ĭt, pŭm′-) BOT. s. *(tree)* granado; *(fruit)* granada.
pom·mel (pŭm′əl, pŏm′-) I. s. *(of a weapon)* pomo; *(of a saddle)* perilla II. tr. aporrear, dar puñetazos.
pomp (pŏmp) s. *(splendor)* pompa; *(ostentation)* ostentación *f*.
pom·pa·dour (pŏm′pə-dôr′) s. copete (peinado) *m*.
Pom·pe·ii (pŏm-pā′, -pā′ē) s. Pompeya.
pom·pom (pŏm′pŏm′) o **pom·pon** (-pŏn′) s. borla, madroño.
pom·pos·i·ty (pŏm-pŏs′ĭ-tē) s. pomposidad *f*.
pom·pous (pŏm′pəs) adj. *(exaggerated)* pomposo; *(pretentious)* presumido, pagado de sí mismo; *(ceremonious)* ceremonioso.
pond (pŏnd) s. charca, estanque *m*.

pon·der (pŏn′dər) tr. examinar, sopesar —intr. meditar, reflexionar.
pon·der·a·ble (pŏn′dər-ə-bəl) adj. ponderable.
pon·der·ous (pŏn′dər-əs) adj. *(massive)* voluminoso; *(heavy)* pesado; *(labored)* laborioso.
pond lily s. BOT. nenúfar *m*.
pone (pōn) s. pan de maíz *m*, arepa.
pon·iard (pŏn′yərd) I. s. puñal *m*, daga II. tr. atravesar con un puñal, apuñalar.
pon·tiff (pŏn′tĭf) RELIG. s. *(bishop)* pontífice *m*, obispo; *(Pope)* Sumo Pontífice, papa *m*.
pon·tif·i·cal (pŏn-tĭf′ĭ-kəl) RELIG. I. adj. *(of a bishop)* pontifical; *(authoritative)* autoritario; FIG. *(pretentious)* pretencioso II. s. *(book)* pontifical *m* ♦ **pontificals** pontifical.
pon·tif·i·cate I. s. (pŏn-tĭf′ĭ-kĭt, -kāt′) pontificado II. intr. (-kāt′) **-cat·ed, -cat·ing** RELIG. pontificar; *(to behave pompously)* pontificar, hablar con suficiencia.
pon·toon (pŏn-tōōn′) s. *(bridge)* pontón flotante *m*; *(structure)* pontón; *(float)* flotador *m*.
pontoon bridge s. puente de pontones *m*.
po·ny (pō′nē) s. [pl. **-nies**] *(horse)* poney *m*, jaca; FAM. *(racehorse)* caballo de carreras; *(liquor glass)* copa de licor.
pony express s. HIST. sistema postal por medio de hombres a caballos (en EE. UU.) *m*.
po·ny·tail (pō′nē-tāl′) s. cola de caballo (peinado).
pooch (pōōch) s. JER. perro.
poo·dle (pōōd′l) s. perro de lanas, caniche *m*.
pooh (pōō) interj. ¡bah!
pooh-pooh (pōō′pōō′) tr. FAM. desdeñar, despreciar.
pool¹ (pōōl) s. *(small pond)* charca; *(puddle)* charco <*a p. of blood* un charco de sangre>; *(in a stream)* pozo; *(for swimming)* piscina, alberca.
pool² (pōōl) I. s. *(betting fund)* banco, bolsa (de apuestas); *(team)* equipo, agrupación *f* <*typing p.* equipo de mecanógrafas>; *(of vehicles)* parque móvil *m*; *(common fund)* fondos comunes, capital común *m*; *(agreement)* consorcio; *(billiards)* billar americano II. tr. & intr. reunir(se), juntar(se).
pool hall s. salón de billar *m*.
pool table s. mesa de billar.
poop¹ (pōōp) MARÍT. s. *(stern)* popa; *(poop deck)* toldilla.
poop² (pōōp) tr. dejar sin resuello ♦ **to be pooped out** FAM. estar exhausto.
poop³ (pōōp) s. JER. información *f* ♦ **to get the p. on** informarse de.
poop deck s. MARÍT. toldilla.
poor (pōōr) adj. **-er, -est** *(impoverished)* pobre <*too p. to eat well* muy pobre para comer bien>; *(depleted)* pobre, escaso <*p. in proteins* pobre en proteínas>; *(mediocre)* malo, mediocre <*he is a p. student* es mal estudiante>; *(inadequate)* malo <*a p. choice* una mala elección>; *(soil)* pobre o poco fértil; *(scarce)* escaso; *(judgment)* escaso, poco; *(humble)* modesto <*in my p. opinion* en mi modesta opinión>; *(pitiable)* pobre <*the p. fellow* el pobre hombre> ♦ **p. thing!** ¡pobrecito!, ¡el pobre! • **p. you!** ¡pobre de ti! • **the p.** los pobres • **to be in p. health** no estar bien de salud • **to be p. at** no ser bueno en.
poor box s. RELIG. cepillo de los pobres.
poor farm s. granja para alojar a los indigentes.
poor·house (pōōr′hous′) s. casa de beneficencia, asilo para los pobres.
poor law s. DER. ley de asistencia pública *f*.
poor·ly (pōōr′lē) adv. pobremente ♦ **to be feeling p.** FAM. sentirse mal, estar indispuesto.
poor white s. blanco pobre (persona de raza blanca y de baja condición económica).
pop¹ (pŏp) I. intr. **popped, pop·ping** *(to make an explosive sound)* estallar, chasquear; *(cork)* saltar; *(to burst)* estallar, explotar; *(to open wide)* abrirse; *(to shoot)* disparar ♦ **to p. over** pasar a ver • **to p. in** *(to enter)* entrar de sopetón; *(to visit)* pasar o caer (por un lugar) • **to p. into view** aparecer o presentarse a la vista de repente • **to p. off** FAM. *(to leave)* salir disparado; *(to die)* morirse de un día para otro; *(to speak)* vociferar • **to p. out** *(cork, eyes)* saltar; *(to step out)* salir un momento; *(to spring)* salir de sopetón •

ã rey / ä año / b boca / ch chico / d dar / ĕ el / ē mil / g gato / h joya / hw juez / ī aire / k casa / kw cuan /

to p. up *(to appear)* aparecer de repente; *(to come up)* surgir, suscitarse —tr. *(to uncork)* hacer saltar; *(corn)* hacer (rosetas de maíz); *(to explode)* hacer estallar *o* explotar; *(to put)* meter <*she popped the grape into her mouth* se metió la uva en la boca>; *(a firearm)* disparar; *(to hit)* pegar (un golpe) ♦ **to p. open** abrir (botella) haciendo sonar • **to p. out** asomar • **to p. pills** zamparse píldoras • **to p. the question** FAM. proponer casarse, pedir la mano II. s. *(explosive sound)* estallido, chasquido; *(of a cork)* taponazo; *(of a firearm)* tiro, disparo; *(soda pop)* gaseosa III. adv. *(with a popping sound)* con un estallido; *(abruptly)* de súbito, de repente ♦ **to go p.** explotar.
pop² (pŏp) s. FAM. papi *m*, papá *m*.
pop³ (pŏp) adj. FAM. *(music)* popular, moderno; *(of pop music)* de música moderna.
pop art s. pop art *m*.
pop·corn (pŏp′kôrn′) s. CUL. palomitas *o* rosetas de maíz.
pope (pōp) s. RELIG. papa *m*; *(authority)* máxima autoridad ♦ **Pope** Papa, Sumo Pontífice.
pope·dom (pōp′dəm) s. RELIG. papado.
pop·er·y (pō′pə-rē) s. RELIG. papismo.
pop·eyed (pŏp′īd′) adj. *(having bulging eyes)* de ojos saltones; *(amazed)* sorprendido, asombrado.
pop·gun (pŏp′gŭn′) s. pistola de aire comprimido (de juguete).
pop·in·jay (pŏp′ĭn-jā′) s. pedante *mf.*
pop·ish (pō′pĭsh) adj. DESPEC. papista.
pop·lar (pŏp′lər) s. BOT. *(deciduous tree)* álamo (árbol y madera); *(tulip tree)* tulipero.
pop·lin (pŏp′lĭn) s. TEJ. popelín *m*, popelina.
pop·pa (pä′pə) s. papá *m*.
pop·per (pŏp′ər) s. CUL. utensilio para tostar maíz; JER. *(ampule)* nitrato de amilo (usado ilícitamente como estimulante).
pop·pet (pŏp′ĭt) s. MEC. cabezal *m*.
pop·py (pŏp′ē) s. [pl. **-pies**] *(flower)* amapola; *(narcotic)* adormidera.
pop·py·cock (pŏp′ē-kŏk′) s. tonterías.
pop·u·lace (pŏp′yə-lĭs) s. *(the masses)* vulgo, populacho; *(population)* población *f*, habitantes *m*.
pop·u·lar (pŏp′yə-lər) adj. *(well-liked)* popular; *(respected)* estimado; *(of the people)* popular <*the p. vote* el voto popular>; *(election)* democrático; *(in vogue)* de moda; *(prevalent)* generalizado, común <*a p. misunderstanding* un error generalizado>.
popular front s. POL. frente popular *m*.
pop·u·lar·i·ty (pŏp′yə-lăr′ĭ-tē) s. popularidad *f.*
pop·u·lar·i·za·tion (pŏp′yə-lər-ĭ-zā′shən) s. popularización *f*, propagación *f.*
pop·u·lar·ize (pŏp′yə-lə-rīz′) tr. **-ized, -iz·ing** popularizar, propagar.
pop·u·late (pŏp′yə-lāt′) tr. **-lat·ed, -lat·ing** *(to people)* poblar; *(to inhabit)* habitar.
pop·u·la·tion (pŏp′yə-lā′shən) s. *(neighborhood)* vecindario; *(inhabitants)* población *f*; *(populating)* población; ECOL. colonia.
population explosion s. explosión demográfica.
pop·u·lism (pŏp′yə-lĭz′əm) s. POL. populismo.
pop·u·list (pŏp′yə-lĭst) s. & adj. POL. populista *mf.*
pop·u·lous (pŏp′yə-ləs) adj. *(full of people)* populoso, muy poblado; *(numerous)* numeroso; *(manifold)* múltiple.
por·ce·lain (pôr′sə-lĭn) s. porcelana.
porch (pôrch) s. *(house entrance)* porche *m*; *(verandah)* veranda.
por·cine (pôr′sīn′) adj. porcino.
por·cu·pine (pôr′kyə-pīn′) s. ZOOL. puercoespín *m.*
pore¹ (pôr) intr. **pored, por·ing** ♦ **to p. over** *(to gaze)* mirar fijamente; *(to examine)* examinar, estudiar detenidamente; *(to ponder)* meditar sobre, reflexionar sobre.
pore² (pôr) s. ANAT., BOT. poro.
pork (pôrk) s. *(meat)* cerdo, carne de cerdo *f*; FIG., JER. *(favors)* favores políticos.
pork barrel s. JER. proyecto gubernamental que beneficia a los electores de un legislador.
pork·er (pôr′kər) s. cebón (puerco) *m.*

pork·pie *o* **pork pie** (pôrk′pī′) s. CUL. empanada de carne de cerdo; *(hat)* sombrero de copa baja.
por·no (pôr′nō) *o* **porn** (pôrn) s. JER. pornografía ♦ **a p. flick** JER. una película pornográfica.
por·nog·ra·pher (pôr-nŏg′rə-fər) s. pornógrafo.
por·no·graph·ic (pôr′nə-grăf′ĭk) adj. pornográfico.
por·nog·ra·phy (pôr-nŏg′rə-fē) s. pornografía.
po·ros·i·ty (pə-rŏs′ĭ-tē) s. [pl. **-ties**] porosidad *f.*
po·rous (pôr′əs) adj. poroso.
por·phy·ry (pôr′fə-rē) s. [pl. **-ries**] MIN. pórfiro.
por·poise (pôr′pəs) s. [pl. **porpoise** *o* **-pois·es**] ZOOL. marsopa.
por·ridge (pôr′ĭj) s. gachas de avena.
por·rin·ger (pôr′ĭn-jər) s. plato hondo con asa.
port¹ (pôrt) I. s. *(harbor)* puerto; *(haven)* puerto, refugio; COMPUT. puerta, portilla (de conexión para transferencia de datos) II. adj. portuario <*p. authority* autoridad portuaria>.
port² (pôrt) I. s. MARÍT. babor *m* II. adj. a babor, de babor III. tr. girar a babor.
port³ (pôrt) s. MARÍT. *(porthole)* portilla; MEC. *(opening)* orificio; *(weapon hole)* tronera, cañonera; G.B. *(gateway)* puerta (en Escocia).
port⁴ (pôrt) s. *(wine)* oporto.
port⁵ (pôrt) I. tr. MIL. *(to carry)* terciar (el arma) II. s. MIL. *(position)* posición terciada del arma; *(bearing)* porte *m*, conducta.
por·ta·ble (pôr′tə-bəl) I. adj. portátil II. s. máquina portátil.
por·tage (pôr′tĭj) I. s. *(carrying)* porteo, transporte *m*; *(route)* ruta de porteo II. tr. **-taged, -tag·ing** transportar.
por·tal (pôr′tl) I. s. *(entrance)* portal *m*; ANAT. vena porta II. adj. porta.
por·tal-to-por·tal (pôr′tl-tə-pôr′tl) adj. COM. de puerta a puerta.
portal vein s. ANAT. vena porta.
Port-au-Prince (pôrt′ō-prĭns′, -prăns′) s. Puerto Príncipe.
port·cul·lis (pôrt-kŭl′ĭs) s. FORT. rastrillo (de la puerta de un castillo).
por·tend (pôr-tĕnd′) tr. *(to presage)* presagiar, *(to indicate)* indicar; *(to suggest)* sugerir.
por·tent (pôr′tĕnt′) s. *(omen)* augurio; *(significance)* significado; *(prodigy)* portento, prodigio.
por·ten·tous (pôr-tĕn′təs) adj. *(foreboding)* de mal agüero; *(prodigious)* portentoso, prodigioso; *(awe-inspiring)* portentoso.
por·ter¹ (pôr′tər) s. *(luggage carrier)* changador *m*, mozo; *(train attendant)* camarero, mozo (de tren).
por·ter² (pôr′tər) s. G.B. *(doorman)* portero.
por·ter³ (pôr′tər) s. *(beer)* cerveza negra.
por·ter·house (pôr′tər-hous′) s. *(steak)* bistec de filete *m*; ANT. *(alehouse)* bodegón *m*, mesón *m.*
port·fo·li·o (pôrt-fō′lē-ō′) s. [pl. **-os**] *(briefcase)* cartera; *(folder)* carpeta; *(collection)* obra; POL. cartera; FIN. cartera ♦ **minister without p.** ministro sin cartera.
port·hole (pôrt′hōl′) s. MARÍT. ojo de buey, portilla; MIL. tronera.
por·ti·co (pôr′tĭ-kō′) s. [pl. **-coes** *o* **-cos**] pórtico.
por·tion (pôr′shən) I. s. *(part)* porción *f*, parte *f*; *(share)* parte, lote *m*; *(serving)* porción, ración *f*; *(of an inheritance)* parte; *(dowry)* dote *f*; *(fate)* suerte *f*, destino II. tr. dividir ♦ **to p. out** repartir, distribuir.
Port·land cement (pôrt′lənd) s. cemento portland.
port·ly (pôrt′lē) adj. **-li·er, -li·est** *(stout)* grueso; *(corpulent)* corpulento.
port·man·teau (pôrt-măn′tō) s. [pl. **-teaus** *o* **-teaux** (-tōz)] G.B. portamanteo, maleta.
port of call s. MARÍT. puerto de escala.
port of entry s. lugar de entrada *m.*
por·trait (pôr′trĭt) s. retrato.
por·trait·ist (pôr′trĭ-tĭst) s. retratista *mf.*
por·trai·ture (pôr′trĭ-chŏŏr′, -chər) s. *(art)* pintura de retratos; *(portrait)* retrato; *(portraits)* retratos.
por·tray (pôr-trā′) tr. *(to represent)* retratar; *(to depict)* describir; TEAT. representar.

por·tray·al (pôr-trā'əl) s. *(portrait)* retrato; *(description)* descripción *f;* TEAT. representación *f.*

por·tray·er (pôr-trā'ər) s. retratista *mf.*

Por·tu·gal (pôr'chə-gəl) s. Portugal *m.*

Por·tu·guese (pôr'chə-gēz') I. adj. portugués II. s. [pl. **Por·tuguese**] *(inhabitant, language)* portugués *m* ♦ **the P.** los portugueses.

pose¹ (pōz) I. intr. **posed, pos·ing** *(for a portrait)* posar; *(to affect an attitude)* asumir una pose ♦ **to p. as** hacerse pasar por —tr. *(to place)* posar, colocar; *(to model)* hacer posar, colocar; *(to present)* plantear <*to p. a question* plantear una cuestión>; *(a threat)* representar II. s. *(for a portrait)* pose *f,* postura; *(attitude)* pose, afectación *f* ♦ **to be just a p.** ser puro teatro.

pose² (pōz) tr. **posed, pos·ing** *(to puzzle)* desconcertar, dejar perplejo.

Po·sei·don (pō-sīd'n) s. MITOL. Poseidón.

posh (pŏsh) adj. FAM. *(fashionable)* elegante <*a p. suburb* un elegante barrio de las afueras>; *(luxurious)* de lujo <*a p. apartment* un apartamento de lujo>; *(exclusive)* selecto.

pos·it (pŏz'ĭt) tr. *(to place)* situar, colocar; *(to postulate)* proponer, postular.

po·si·tion (pə-zĭsh'ən) I. s. *(location)* posición *f,* situación *f;* *(place)* lugar *m,* sitio; *(post)* puesto; *(posture)* posición, postura <*an uncomfortable p.* una postura incómoda>; *(advantageous place)* posición favorable; *(situation)* posición, situación <*in an awkward p.* en una posición difícil>; *(point of view)* postura, actitud *f* <*our p. on the issue* nuestra postura con respecto a la cuestión>; *(status)* posición social; *(job)* puesto <*a p. with a bank* un puesto en un banco>; MARÍT., MIL. posición ♦ **in a sitting p.** sentado • **in a standing p.** de pie, parado • **to be in a p. to** estar en situación *o* en condiciones de II. tr. *(to place)* colocar, poner; MIL. *(guns)* emplazar ♦ **to p. oneself** ponerse en un lugar favorable.

pos·i·tive (pŏz'ĭ-tĭv) I. adj. *(affirmative)* positivo; *(emphatic)* tajante <*she gave me a p. "no"* me dió un "no" tajante>; *(express)* explícito, expreso <*a p. demand* una demanda explícita>; *(irrefutable)* categórico, rotundo <*p. proof* una prueba rotunda>; *(sure)* seguro, cierto <*are you p.?* ¿estás seguro?>; FAM. *(absolute)* absoluto, verdadero <*a p. disgrace* una verdadera vergüenza>; *(constructive)* positivo; FÍS., FOTOG., GRAM. positivo II. s. *(plus)* positivo; ELEC. polo positivo; GRAM. positivo; FOTOG. positiva.

pos·i·tive·ly (pŏz'ĭ-tĭv-lē) adv. *(in a positive way)* positivamente; *(truly)* verdaderamente <*he was p. furious* estaba verdaderamente furioso>.

pos·i·tive·ness (pŏz'ĭ-tĭv-nĭs) s. *(certainty)* certeza, seguridad *f;* *(dogmatism)* dogmatismo, porfía; *(reality)* realidad *f,* verdad *f.*

pos·i·tiv·ism (pŏz'ĭ-tĭ-vĭz'əm) s. FILOS. positivismo.

pos·i·tron (pŏz'ĭ-trŏn') s. ELECTRÓN., FÍS. positrón *m,* positón *m.*

pos·se (pŏs'ē) s. grupo de civiles armados que ayudan a la policía.

pos·sess (pə-zĕs') tr. *(to have)* poseer; *(an attribute)* poseer, tener; *(to dominate)* poseer, dominar <*to be possessed by the devil* estar poseído por el demonio>; *(to control)* dominar <*he possessed his temper* dominó su cólera>; *(to obsess)* obsesionar; *(to drive)* impulsar, llevar <*what possessed him to do it?* ¿qué lo impulsó a hacerlo?> ♦ **to p. oneself of** apoderarse de.

pos·sessed (pə-zĕst') adj. *(by a spirit)* poseído, poseso; *(by an idea)* obsesionado; *(crazed)* fuera de sí, demente; *(calm)* dueño de sí mismo ♦ **to be p. of** *(to own)* poseer, tener; *(to be blessed with)* estar dotado de.

pos·ses·sion (pə-zĕsh'ən) s. *(ownership)* posesión *f;* *(domination)* posesión, dominación *f;* *(property)* posesión, propiedad *f;* *(holding)* tenencia <*legal p. of the apartment* tenencia legal del apartamento>; *(territory)* posesión; *(self-control)* dominio de sí mismo; *(by a spirit)* posesión; *(obsession)* obsesión *f* ♦ **in one's p.** en poder *o* en manos de uno • **possessions** posesiones, bienes • **to be in full p. of one's faculties** tener uno pleno dominio de sus facultades • **to be in p. of** poseer, tener • **to come into p. of** hacerse de, adquirir • **to get** *o* **take p. of** apoderarse de.

pos·ses·sive (pə-zĕs'ĭv) I. adj. *(of ownership)* posesivo; *(domineering)* dominante; *(jealous)* celoso; GRAM. posesivo II. s. GRAM. posesivo.

possessive adjective s. GRAM. adjetivo posesivo.

pos·ses·sive·ness (pə-zĕs'ĭv-nĭs) s. *(domineering quality)* carácter dominante *m;* *(jealousy)* celos.

possessive pronoun s. GRAM. pronombre posesivo.

pos·ses·sor (pə-zĕs'ər) s. poseedor *m,* dueño.

pos·si·bil·i·ty (pŏs'ə-bĭl'ĭ-tē) s. [pl. **-ties**] posibilidad *f* ♦ **to be a p.** ser posible • **to have possibilities** ser prometedor • **within the realm of p.** dentro de lo posible.

pos·si·ble (pŏs'ə-bəl) adj. *(feasible)* posible, factible <*a p. solution* una solución posible>; *(potential)* posible <*a p. source of oil* una posible fuente de petróleo> ♦ **as far as p.** en *o* dentro de lo posible • **as much as p.** todo lo posible • **as soon as p.** lo antes posible • **if p.** de ser posible, si es posible • **to be p. (that)** ser posible (que), poder ser (que).

pos·sum (pŏs'əm) s. var. de **opossum**.

post¹ (pōst) I. s. *(pole)* poste *m;* *(stake)* palo, estaca; DEP. *(goal post)* poste; *(line)* línea de salida II. tr. *(to fasten up)* pegar, fijar (carteles); *(to cover)* fijar en <*to p. a wall with posters* fijar carteles en una pared>; *(to announce)* anunciar; *(to denounce)* denunciar públicamente; *(to publish)* publicar (un nombre) ♦ **to p. up** pegar, fijar (carteles).

post² (pōst) I. s. MIL. *(base)* base *f;* *(position)* puesto <*stay at your posts* permanezcan en sus puestos>; *(office)* puesto, cargo <*a government p.* un cargo en el gobierno> II. tr. MIL. *(a guard)* apostar; *(an officer)* enviar, destinar (a un lugar); *(bail)* dar (fianza).

post³ (pōst) I. s. G.B. *(mail)* correo <*by p.* por correo>; *(delivery)* reparto <*this morning's p.* el reparto de esta mañana>; *(collection)* recogida; HIST. *(station, courier)* posta II. intr. *(to hasten)* viajar de prisa; *(to ride)* trotar —tr. *(to mail)* echar (al correo); *(to inform)* poner al corriente; *(to transfer)* pasar (partida); COMPUT. almacenar ♦ **to keep someone posted about** tener a alguien al corriente de III. adv. por correo ♦ **p. haste** a toda prisa.

post·age (pō'stĭj) s. *(charge)* franqueo; *(expense)* gastos de franqueo.

postage meter s. máquina de franqueo.

postage stamp s. sello (postal), estampilla.

post·al (pō'stəl) adj. & s. postal *f.*

postal card s. tarjeta postal.

postal order s. G.B. giro postal.

postal service s. servicio de correos.

post·bel·lum (pōst-bĕl'əm) adj. de la posguerra.

post·box *o* **post box** (pōst'bŏks') s. buzón *m.*

post card *o* **post·card** (pōst'kärd') s. tarjeta postal.

post·co·lo·ni·al (pōst'kə-lō'nē-əl) adj. de después de la época colonial.

post·date (pōst-dāt') tr. **-dat·ed, -dat·ing** posfechar, poner fecha posterior a.

post·er (pō'stər) s. *(announcement)* cartel *m,* afiche *m;* *(person)* cartelero.

pos·te·ri·or (pō-stîr'ē-ər) I. adj. posterior II. s. FAM. trasero.

pos·te·ri·or·i·ty (pō-stîr'ē-ôr'ĭ-tē) s. posterioridad *f.*

pos·ter·i·ty (pō-stĕr'ĭ-tē) s. posteridad *f.*

Post Exchange s. MIL. tienda reservada para militares en una base (marca registrada).

post-free (pōst'frē') adj. G.B. con franqueo pagado.

post·grad·u·ate (pōst-grăj'ōō-ĭt) adj. & s. postgraduado.

post·haste (pōst'hāst') adv. a toda prisa.

post·hole (pōst'hōl') s. agujero para poste.

post·hu·mous (pŏs'chə-məs) adj. póstumo.

post·hyp·not·ic suggestion (pōst'hĭp-nŏt'ĭk) s. sugestión posthipnótica.

pos·til·ion *o* **pos·til·lion** (pō-stĭl'yən) s. postillón *m.*

post·im·pres·sion·ism (pōst'ĭm-prĕsh'ə-nĭz'əm) s. ARTE. postimpresionismo.

post·man (pōst'mən) s. [pl. **-men**] cartero.

post·mark (pōst'märk') I. s. matasellos II. tr. sellar (una estampilla), matasellar.

post·mas·ter (pōst'măs'tər) s. administrador de correos *m.*

postmaster general s. [pl. **postmasters general**] EE. UU. director general de correos *m*.

post·me·rid·i·an (pōst'mə-rĭd'ē-ən) adj. postmeridiano.

post me·rid·i·em (pōst' mə-rĭd'ē-əm) adj. postmeridiano, de la tarde.

post·mis·tress (pōst'mĭs'trĭs) s. administradora de correos.

post·mor·tem (pōst-môr'təm) I. adj. postmórtem, que sucede después de la muerte II. s. autopsia.

postmortem examination s. autopsia.

post·na·sal (pōst-nā'zəl) adj. postnasal.

post·na·tal (pōst-nāt'l) adj. postnatal.

post office s. correo, casa de correos.

post·op·er·a·tive (pōst-ŏp'ər-ə-tĭv) adj. postoperatorio.

post·paid (pōst'pād') adj. con franqueo pagado.

post·par·tum (pōst-pär'təm) adj. MED. de después del parto.

post·pone (pōst-pōn') tr. **-poned, -pon·ing** (*to delay*) posponer, postergar; (*to put off*) diferir, aplazar.

post·pone·ment (pōst-pōn'mənt) s. (*delay*) postergación *f*; (*putting off*) aplazamiento.

post·script (pōst'skrĭpt') s. (*of a letter*) posdata; (*in a book*) nota final.

post time s. DEP. período de tiempo previo a la lanzada de una carrera de caballos después del cual ya no se aceptan más apuestas.

pos·tu·late (pŏs'chə-lāt') I. tr. **-lat·ed, -lat·ing** (*to demand*) postular, solicitar; (*to assume the truth of*) considerar como un postulado, postular; (*to take for granted*) dar por sentado II. s. postulado.

pos·tu·la·tion (pŏs'chə-lā'shən) s. (*demand*) postulación *f*; (*assumption*) postulación, suposición *f*.

pos·ture (pŏs'chər) I. s. (*stance*) postura; (*attitude*) postura, actitud *f* II. intr. **-tured, -tur·ing** (*to pose*) posar, asumir una pose ♦ **to p. as** presumir, darse tono de —tr. colocar en una postura, hacer posar.

post·tur·er (pŏs'chər-ər) s. actor *m*, impostor *m*.

post·war (pōst'wôr') adj. de la postguerra.

po·sy (pō'zē) s. [pl. **-sies**] (*flower*) flor *f*; (*bunch*) ramillete de flores *m*.

pot (pŏt) I. s. (*for cooking*) cazuela, olla; (*for preserving*) tarro, envase *m*; (*tankard*) jarra; (*earthenware*) jarrón (de adorno) *m*; (*flowerpot*) maceta, tiesto; (*in cards*) platillo, puesta; FAM. (*common fund*) fondo común; (*pot shot*) tiro a mansalva; FAM. (*potbelly*) barrigón *m*, panza; JER. (*marijuana*) yerba ♦ **pots and pans** batería (de cocina) • **to go to p.** FAM. echarse a perder II. tr. **pot·ted, pot·ting** (*a plant*) plantar en una maceta; (*to preserve*) conservar en tarros; FAM. (*to shoot*) matar a tiros; (*to win*) pescar, coger —intr. FAM. disparar, tirar.

po·ta·ble (pō'tə-bəl) adj. potable ♦ **potables** s. bebidas, bebestibles.

pot·ash (pŏt'ăsh') s. QUÍM. potasa.

po·tas·sic (pə-tăs'ĭk) adj. QUÍM. potásico.

po·tas·si·um (pə-tăs'ē-əm) s. QUÍM. potasio.

po·ta·to (pə-tā'tō) s. [pl. **-toes**] patata, papa (planta y tubérculo).

potato chips s.pl. CUL. hojuelas de patatas fritas, papas fritas.

pot·bel·ly (pŏt'bĕl'ē) s. [pl. **-lies**] (*stomach*) panza, barriga; (*stove*) salamandra.

pot·boil·er (pŏt'boi'lər) s. obra artística de calidad mediocre hecha con fin de lucro.

po·ten·cy (pōt'n-sē) s. [pl. **-cies**] (*power*) potencia; (*potential*) potencialidad *f*.

po·tent (pōt'nt) adj. (*powerful*) potente; (*cogent*) poderoso; (*strong*) fuerte; (*virile*) viril.

po·ten·tate (pōt'n-tāt') s. (*powerful person*) potentado; (*monarch*) monarca.

po·ten·tial (pə-tĕn'shəl) I. adj. potencial, posible II. s. (*possibility*) posibilidad *f*; FÍS., GRAM., MAT. potencial; ELEC. voltaje *m*.

potential energy s. FÍS. energía potencial.

po·ten·ti·al·i·ty (pə-tĕn'shē-ăl'ĭ-tē) s. [pl. **-ties**] potencialidad *f*.

pot·ful (pŏt'fool') s. [pl. **-fuls**] (*amount*) olla <*a p. of rice* una olla de arroz>; FIG., FAM. (*large amount*) montón *m* <*a p. of money* un montón de dinero>.

pot·head (pŏt'hĕd') s. JER. fumador de marihuana *m*.

poth·er (pŏth'ər) I. s. (*commotion*) confusión *f*, lío; (*cloud*) nube (de polvo, vapor) *f* II. tr. confundir —intr. preocuparse por pequeñeces.

pot·hold·er (pŏt'hōl'dər) s. agarrador para utensilios calientes *m*.

pot·hole (pŏt'hōl') s. (*road pit*) bache *m*; (*hole*) hueco (en una roca); (*mud hole*) hueco.

pot·hook (pŏt'hook') s. (*bent iron*) garabato (para utensilios); FIG. (*scrawl*) garabato ♦ **pothooks** (*scrawl*) garabatos; (*shorthand*) taquigrafía.

po·tion (pō'shən) s. poción *f* ♦ **love p.** filtro de amor.

pot·latch (pŏt'lăch') s. fiesta entre los indios del noroeste norteamericano en la que el anfitrión ofrece y recibe regalos.

pot·luck (pŏt'lŭk') s. lo que venga, lo que haya <*we'll have p. for dinner* comeremos lo que haya para la cena>.

pot·pour·ri (pō'poo-rē') s. [pl. **-ris**] (*mixture*) popurrí *m*; (*sachet*) pebete *m*.

pot·sherd (pŏt'shûrd') s. fragmentos de cerámica en las excavaciones arqueológicas.

pot shot s. (*shot*) tiro al azar; FIG. (*criticism*) crítica gratuita y oportunista ♦ **to take a p. at someone** (*to shoot*) tirar al azar a alguien; (*to criticize*) criticar a alguien gratuitamente.

pot·tage (pŏt'ĭj) s. CUL. sopa, potaje *m*.

pot·ted (pŏt'ĭd) adj. (*plant*) en maceta; (*food*) en conserva; JER. (*drunk*) borracho; (*stoned*) drogado.

pot·ter (pŏt'ər) s. alfarero.

potter's field s. hoyanca, fosa común.

potter's wheel s. rueda *o* torno de alfarero.

pot·ter·y (pŏt'ə-rē) s. [pl. **-ies**] alfarería.

pot·ty¹ (pŏt'ē) G.B. adj. **-ti·er, -tiest** (*trivial*) trivial; (*intoxicated*) levemente borracho; (*silly*) chiflado.

pot·ty² (pŏt'ē) s. [pl. **-ties**] FAM. orinal para niños *m*.

pouch (pouch) I. s. (*small bag*) bolsa pequeña; (*for game*) morral *m*, zurrón *m*; (*for ammunition*) cartuchera; (*under the eyes*) bolsa; ZOOL. bolsa ♦ **diplomatic p.** valija diplomática • **mail p.** valija de correos • **tobacco p.** petaca II. tr. (*to insert*) meter en una bolsa; (*to pocket*) echarse al bolsillo, llevarse; (*to form*) formar bolsas en.

poul·tice (pōl'tĭs) MED. I. s. cataplasma II. tr. **-ticed, -tic·ing** aplicar una cataplasma.

poul·try (pōl'trē) s. aves de corral *f*.

pounce¹ (pouns) I. intr. **pounced, pounc·ing** (*to spring*) saltar sobre; (*to attack*) abalanzarse sobre —tr. ♦ **to p. on** (*to attack*) saltar sobre; (*to seize*) abalanzarse sobre; (*an opportunity*) no perder II. s. (*attack*) ataque repentino; (*jump*) salto repentino; (*claw*) garra.

pounce² (pouns) I. s. (*powder*) arenilla; (*charcoal*) cisquero II. tr. **pounced, pounc·ing** (*to powder*) polvorear (con arenilla); (*to transfer*) estarcir.

pounce³ (pouns) tr. **pounced, pounc·ing** (*to emboss*) repujar.

pound¹ (pound) s. [pl. **pound** *o* **pounds**] FIN., FÍS. libra ♦ **p. troy** libra de doce onzas • **p. weight** peso de una libra.

pound² (pound) I. tr. (*to strike*) golpear; (*to hammer*) martillear; (*waves*) azotar, batir; (*to grind*) moler; (*to crush*) machacar; FIG. (*to instill*) inculcar —intr. (*to strike*) dar golpes <*he pounded on the table* dio golpes en la mesa>; (*to move heavily*) andar con paso pesado; (*the heart*) palpitar, latir violentamente; (*waves*) batir II. s. (*blow*) golpe *m*; (*sound*) ruido de golpes.

pound³ (pound) s. (*for dogs*) perrera; (*for cats, property*) depósito; (*jail*) cárcel *f*.

pound·age¹ (poun'dĭj) s. (*weight*) peso; (*rate*) tasa; (*tax*) impuesto.

pound·age² (poun'dĭj) s. (*confinement*) retención de animales *f*; (*cost*) costo de rescate.

pound·al (poun'dl) s. FÍS. poundal (unidad de fuerza) *m*.

pound-fool·ish (pound'foo'lĭsh) adj. ♦ **to be penny-wise and p.** hacer economías de chicha y nabo.

pound of flesh s. FIG. deuda cobrada sin escrúpulos.

pound sterling s. FIN. libra esterlina.

pour (pôr) **I.** tr. *(a liquid)* echar <*to p. water into a glass* echar agua en un vaso>; *(to serve)* servir <*she poured coffee for us* nos sirvió café>; *(to spill)* verter, derramar ♦ **to p. cold water on** FIG. echar un jarro de agua fría a • **to p. money into** invertir mucho dinero en • **to p. out** *(a liquid)* verter, echar; *(one's feelings)* dar rienda suelta a (emociones) • **to p. one's heart out to someone** descubrir el pecho a alguien, abrirse con alguien —intr. *(to flow)* manar, correr; *(to gush)* salir a chorros; *(to rain)* llover a cántaros, diluviar; *(to serve)* servir bebidas ♦ **to p. in** *(people)* entrar en tropel; *(letters)* llegar en abundancia • **to p. into** FIG. inundar • **to p. out** *(liquid)* salir a chorros; *(people)* salir en tropel **II.** s. diluvio.

pout¹ (pout) **I.** intr. *(with the lips)* hacer pucheros; *(to sulk)* poner mala cara —tr. *(to say)* decir haciendo pucheros; *(the lips)* hacer pucheros **II.** s. *(of the lips)* puchero; *(sulk)* mala cara.

pout² (pout) s. [pl. **pout** o **pouts**] ICT. abadejo, mustela.

pov·er·ty (pŏv'ər-tē) s. pobreza, miseria; *(deficiency)* carencia, escasez f; AGR., RELIG. pobreza.

poverty level s. ECON. pobreza, miseria.

pov·er·ty-strick·en (pŏv'ər-tē-strĭk'ən) adj. indigente, muy pobre ♦ **to be p.** estar en la miseria.

pow·der (pou'dər) **I.** s. *(dust)* polvo; *(cosmetic, medicinal)* polvos <*talcum p.* polvos de talco>; *(gunpowder)* pólvora; *(snow)* nieve seca ♦ **to take a p.** JER. poner pies en polvorosa **II.** tr. *(to pulverize)* hacer polvo, pulverizar; *(to sprinkle)* espolvorear; JER. *(to defeat)* hacer polvo a, dar una paliza a ♦ **to p. one's face** ponerse polvos (en la cara) —intr. hacerse polvo, pulverizarse.

powder flask s. polvorín m.

powder horn s. chifle m, cuerno para la pólvora.

powder keg s. *(cask)* tonel m, cuñete de pólvora m; FIG. *(situation)* polvorín m.

powder puff s. mota, borla (de empolvarse).

pow·der-puff (pou'dər-pŭf') adj. de mujeres <*p. football* fútbol de mujeres>.

powder room s. tocador m, servicios (de las damas).

pow·der·y (pou'də-rē) adj. *(composed of powder)* en polvo; *(fine)* fino; *(dusty)* polvoriento, lleno de polvo.

pow·er (pou'ər) **I.** s. *(capacity)* poder m; *(faculty)* facultad f, capacidad f <*the p. of speech* la facultad del habla>; *(physical strength)* fuerza, vigor m; *(authority)* poder <*to be in p.* estar en el poder>; DER. *(right)* potestad f; *(person)* fuerza, influencia; *(nation)* potencia <*the Western powers* las potencias occidentales>; *(might)* poder, potencia <*the p. of this nation* el poder de esta nación>; *(forcefulness)* impacto <*a novel of unusual p.* una novela de un impacto excepcional>; FÍS. *(workrate)* potencia; *(force)* fuerza; *(energy)* energía <*nuclear p.* energía nuclear>; *(electricity)* electricidad f, corriente f <*the p. failed* falló la corriente>; MAT. potencia <*to the nth p.* a la enésima potencia>; ÓPT. potencia ♦ **powers** *(faculty)* poder, capacidad <*his powers of concentration* su capacidad de concentración>; TEO. *(angels)* potestades • **the powers that be** las autoridades ♦ **to come to p.** subir al poder • **to exceed one's p.** extralimitarse **II.** tr. TEC. suministrar energía a ♦ **to be powered by** funcionar con.

pow·er·boat (pou'ər-bōt') s. bote a motor m, autobote m.

power brake s. AUTO. servofreno.

power broker s. político de gran influencia por sus contactos.

power dive s. AVIA. picado con motor.

pow·er-dive (pou'ər-dīv') tr. & intr. **-dived** o **-dove** (-dōv'), **-div·ing** AVIA. picar con motor a toda marcha.

power drill s. TEC. *(portable drill)* taladro eléctrico; *(large drill)* perforadora mecánica.

ow·er·ful (pou'ər-fəl) adj. *(mighty)* poderoso; *(potent)* potente; *(strong)* fuerte; *(convincing)* convincente; FIG., FAM. *(a lot)* muchísimo <*it did a p. lot of good* hizo muchísimo bien>.

pow·er·house (pou'ər-hous') s. *(station)* central de energía eléctrica; *(person)* persona de mucha energía.

pow·er·less (pou'ər-lĭs) adj. *(lacking power)* impotente; *(helpless)* indefenso; *(ineffectual)* inútil; *(lacking authority)* sin autoridad ♦ **to be p. to** no poder.

power line s. línea de transmisión eléctrica, línea de fuerza eléctrica.

power of attorney s. DER. poder (legal) m.

power pack s. ELEC. transformador portátil m.

power plant s. *(power source)* grupo motor o electrógeno; *(generator)* central de energía f.

power politics s. política de fuerza.

power shovel s. pala mecánica, excavadora.

power station s. central de energía f.

power steering s. AUTO. servodirección f, dirección asistida.

power structure s. FIG. círculo gobernante (de sociedad o institución).

power tool s. MAQ. herramienta eléctrica.

power unit s. *(for measurement)* unidad de potencia f; ELEC. grupo electrógeno.

pow·wow (pou'wou') **I.** s. FIG. conferencia **II.** intr. conferenciar.

pox (pŏks) MED. s. *(smallpox)* viruela; *(chicken pox)* varicela; *(syphilis)* sífilis f.

prac·ti·ca·bil·i·ty (prăk'tĭ-kə-bĭl'ĭ-tē) s. carácter practicable m, viabilidad f.

prac·ti·ca·ble (prăk'tĭ-kə-bəl) adj. *(feasible)* practicable, viable <*a p. solution* una solución viable>; *(usable)* utilizable.

prac·ti·cal (prăk'tĭ-kəl) adj. *(useful)* práctico; *(pragmatic)* pragmático, práctico ♦ **for all p. purposes** prácticamente, a fin de cuentas.

prac·ti·cal·i·ty (prăk'tĭ-kăl'ĭ-tē) s. *(usefulness)* carácter práctico; *(pragmatism)* espíritu práctico.

practical joke s. broma pesada.

prac·ti·cal·ly (prăk'tĭk-lē) adv. *(in a practical way)* de modo práctico; *(almost)* prácticamente, casi <*p. everyone was there* estaba casi todo el mundo>.

practical nurse s. enfermera sin título (pero autorizada para ejercer).

prac·tice (prăk'tĭs) **I.** tr. **-ticed, -tic·ing** *(to perform repeatedly)* practicar <*to p. a dance step* ensayar un paso de baile>; *(to train in)* ejercitarse o entrenarse en <*to p. martial arts* ejercitarse en las artes marciales>; MÚS. estudiar; *(to rehearse)* ensayar; *(to use)* ejercer, proceder con <*to p. restraint* proceder con moderación>; *(a profession)* ejercer; *(to observe)* practicar, profesar <*to p. one's religion* practicar la religión de uno> ♦ **to p. what one preaches** actuar según la doctrina de uno —intr. *(to drill)* hacer prácticas o ejercicios; *(to train)* ejercitarse, entrenarse; MÚS. estudiar; *(as a professional)* ejercer **II.** s. *(repeated performance)* práctica <*to learn with p.* aprender con la práctica>; *(training)* ejercicios; MÚS. estudio, ejercicios; *(rehearsal)* ensayo; *(custom)* costumbre f <*it was his p. to get up late* tenía la costumbre de levantarse tarde>; *(use)* práctica <*to put into p.* poner en práctica>; *(of a profession)* ejercicio <*the p. of medicine* el ejercicio de la medicina>; *(of a doctor)* clientela <*a physician with a large p.* un médico con una clientela numerosa>; *(of a lawyer)* bufete m; DER. *(procedure)* procedimiento ♦ **practices** procedimientos <*dubious business practices* procedimientos comerciales dudosos> • **to be out of p.** no estar en forma • **to make a p. of** tener por costumbre, acostumbrar • **to set up a p.** *(as a doctor)* poner un consultorio; *(as a lawyer)* abrir un bufete.

prac·ticed (prăk'tĭst) adj. *(skilled)* experimentado, experto; *(learned by practice)* adquirido con la práctica.

prac·tic·er (prăk'tĭ-sər) s. practicador m.

prac·tic·ing (prăk'tĭ-sĭng) adj. *(professional)* que ejerce <*a p. dentist* un dentista que ejerce>; RELIG. practicante, devoto.

prac·tise (prăk'tĭs) v. G.B. var. de **practice**.

prac·ti·tion·er (prăk-tĭsh'ə-nər) s. *(professional)* profesional mf; RELIG. persona que cura (en la iglesia de la Ciencia Cristiana) ♦ **general p.** MED. médico general.

prae·di·al (prē'dē-əl) adj. predial.

prae·to·ri·an (prē-tôr'ē-ən) HIST. **I.** adj. pretoriano **II.** s. pretor m.

prag·mat·ic (prăg-măt'ĭk) o **prag·mat·i·cal** (-ĭ-kəl) **I.** adj.

pragmático, práctico **II.** s. *(sanction)* sanción pragmática; *(meddler)* entrometido.

prag·ma·tism (prăg′mə-tĭz′əm) s. pragmatismo.

prag·ma·tist (prăg′mə-tĭst) s. pragmatista *mf.*

Prague (präg) s. Praga.

prai·rie (prâr′ē) s. GEOG. llanura, planicie *f.*

prairie dog s. ZOOL. marmota de las praderas.

prairie schooner s. HIST. carromato de los pioneros de Norteamérica.

praise (prāz) **I.** s. *(commendation)* alabanza, elogio; *(laudation)* alabanza (de Dios) ♦ **p. be to God!** ¡alabado sea Dios! • **to sing the praises of** cantar las alabanzas de **II.** tr. **praised, prais·ing** *(to commend)* alabar, elogiar; *(to worship)* alabar ♦ **to p. to the skies** poner por las nubes.

prais·er (prā′zər) s. alabador *m.*

praise·wor·thy (prāz′wûr′thē) adj. elogiable, loable.

pram (prăm) s. G.B. cochecito de niño.

prance (prăns) **I.** intr. **pranced, pranc·ing** EQUIT. *(to spring)* cabriolar; FIG. *(to strut)* pavonearse —tr. EQUIT. hacer cabriolar a **II.** s. cabriola.

prank[1] (prăngk) s. *(trick)* jugarreta, travesura; *(joke)* broma ♦ **to play a p. on someone** gastar una broma a.

prank[2] (prăngk) tr. *(to dress up)* engalanar; *(to adorn)* adornar —intr. pavonearse, jactarse.

prank·ish (prăng′kĭsh) adj. travieso, pícaro.

prank·ster (prăngk′stər) s. bromista *mf.*

pra·se·o·dym·i·um (prā′zē-ō-dĭm′ē-əm) s. QUÍM. praseodimio.

prate (prāt) **I.** tr. **prat·ed, prat·ing** decir sin sentido —intr. parlotear **II.** s. parloteo.

prat·fall (prăt′fôl′) s. FAM. caída de nalgas.

prat·tle (prăt′l) **I.** tr. **-tled, -tling** balbucear —intr. parlotear **II.** s. parloteo.

prawn (prôn) **I.** s. camarón *m,* gamba **II.** intr. pescar camarones.

prax·is (prăk′sĭs) s. [pl. **-es** (-sēz′)] *(practice)* práctica; *(custom)* costumbre *f.*

pray (prā) intr. *(to say a prayer)* rezar, orar <*let us p.* oremos>; *(to plead)* rogar, suplicar —tr. *(to appeal to)* rogar, pedir (a Dios); *(to beg)* rogar, suplicar ♦ **p. God** por Dios • **p. tell!** ¡te ruego que me lo digas!

pray·er[1] (prā′ər) s. rezador *m,* orador *m.*

prayer[2] (prâr) s. RELIG. *(to a deity)* rezo, oración *f; (request)* ruego, súplica ♦ **Lord's P.** RELIG. padrenuestro • **to say one's prayers** rezar.

prayer beads s.pl. RELIG. rosario.

prayer book s. RELIG. devocionario, libro de oraciones.

prayer·ful (prâr′fəl) adj. devoto.

prayer meeting s. RELIG. reunión de fieles (en la Iglesia Evangélica) *f.*

praying mantis s. ENTOM. mantis religiosa, predicador *m.*

preach (prēch) tr. *(religious instruction)* predicar; *(to exhort)* exhortar, *(to deliver)* dar, pronunciar un sermón —intr. *(to deliver)* predicar ♦ **to p. at** sermonear a.

preach·er (prē′chər) s. RELIG. *(minister)* pastor *m; (one who preaches)* predicador *m.*

preach·ment (prēch′mənt) s. *(act)* prédica, sermón *m; (sermonizing)* sermón.

preach·y (prē′chē) adj. **-i·er, -i·est** sermoneador.

pre·ad·o·les·cence (prē′ăd′l-ĕs′əns) s. preadolescencia.

pre·am·ble (prē′ăm′bəl) s. preámbulo.

pre·am·pli·fi·er (prē-ăm′plə-fī′ər) s. ELECTRÓN., RAD. preamplificador *m.*

pre·ar·range (prē′ə-rānj′) tr. **-ranged, -rang·ing** preparar de antemano.

pre·as·signed (prē′ə-sīnd′) adj. asignado de antemano.

preb·end (prĕb′ənd) s. RELIG. prebenda.

Pre·cam·bri·an (prē-kăm′brē-ən) **I.** adj. precámbrico, precambriano **II.** s. GEOL. era precámbrica.

pre·car·i·ous (prĭ-kâr′ē-əs) adj. precario.

pre·cau·tion (prĭ-kô′shən) s. *(safeguard)* precaución *f; (caution)* cautela ♦ **as a p.** por precaución • **to take precautions** tomar precauciones.

pre·cau·tion·ar·y (prĭ-kô′shə-nĕr′ē) adj. preventivo.

pre·cau·tious (prĭ-kô′shəs) adj. cauteloso, precavido.

pre·cede (prĭ-sēd′) tr. **-ced·ed, -ced·ing** *(to come before)*

preceder, anteceder; *(to preface)* comenzar, empezar <*to p. a speech with an anecdote* comenzar un discurso con una anécdota> —intr. preceder, anteceder.

prec·e·dence (prĕs′ĭ-dns, prĭ-sēd′ns) o **prec·e·den·cy** (prĕs′ĭ-dn-sē, prĭ-sēd′n-sē) s. *(antecedence)* precedencia; *(priority)* prioridad *f* ♦ **to take p. over** tener prioridad sobre.

prec·e·dent I. s. (prĕs′ĭ-dnt) precedente *m* ♦ **no p. for** no tener precedente • **to set a p.** sentar un precedente **II.** adj. (prĭ-sēd′nt, prĕs′ĭ-dnt) **pre·ced·ent** precedente.

pre·ced·ing (prĭ-sē′dĭng) adj. *(antecedent)* precedente; *(previous)* previo.

pre·cen·tor (prĭ-sĕn′tər) s. RELIG. chantre *m.*

pre·cept (prē′sĕpt′) s. *(principle)* precepto; DER. *(writ)* mandato judicial.

pre·cep·tor (prĭ-sĕp′tər, prē′sĕp′-) s. preceptor *m.*

pre·ces·sion (prē-sĕsh′ən) s. *(precedence)* precedencia; ASTRON., FÍS. *(motion)* precesión *f.*

pre·cinct (prē′sĭngkt′) s. *(police district)* zona de patrulla; *(police station)* jefatura de policía, comisaría; *(election district)* distrito electoral; *(area)* recinto <*church p.* el recinto de la iglesia> ♦ **precincts** *(area)* recinto <*school precincts* el recinto de la escuela>; *(boundary)* límites <*within the precincts of* dentro de los límites de>; *(neighborhood)* alrededores; FIG. *(province)* campo, esfera.

pre·ci·os·i·ty (prĕsh′ē-ŏs′ĭ-tē, prĕs′ē-) s. [pl. **-ties**] preciosismo (esp. de lenguaje).

pre·cious (prĕsh′əs) **I.** adj. *(valuable)* precioso; *(cherished)* valioso, preciado; *(beloved)* querido; *(overrefined)* amanerado; FAM. *(arrant)* consumado, cabal **II.** adv. *(very)* muy <*he has p. little talent* tiene muy poco talento>.

precious stone s. piedra preciosa.

prec·i·pice (prĕs′ə-pĭs) s. precipicio.

pre·cip·i·tance (prĭ-sĭp′ĭ-tns) o **pre·cip·i·tan·cy** (-tn-sē) s. precipitación *f.*

pre·cip·i·tant (prĭ-sĭp′ĭ-tnt) **I.** adj. *(rushing headlong)* que se precipita o despeña; *(rash)* precipitado, atropellado; *(sudden)* repentino, imprevisto **II.** s. QUÍM. precipitado.

pre·cip·i·tate I. tr. (prĭ-sĭp′ĭ-tāt′) **-tat·ed, -tat·ing** *(to bring on)* desencadenar, provocar; *(to hurl downward)* precipitar, arrojar; METEOR. condensar; QUÍM. precipitar —intr. METEOR. condensarse; *(to fall)* precipitarse, despeñarse **II.** adj. (-tĭt) precipitado **III.** s. (-tāt′, -tĭt) QUÍM. precipitado.

pre·cip·i·ta·tion (prĭ-sĭp′ĭ-tā′shən) s. *(fall)* precipitación *f,* despeñamiento; *(haste)* precipitación, atropello; METEOR., QUÍM. precipitación.

pre·cip·i·tous (prĭ-sĭp′ĭ-təs) adj. *(steep)* escarpado; *(hasty)* precipitado; *(rash)* atropellado.

pré·cis (prā-sē′) **I.** s. [pl. **pré·cis** (prā-sēz′)] resumen *m* **II.** tr. resumir.

pre·cise (prĭ-sīs′) adj. *(clear)* preciso, claro; *(exact)* preciso, exacto; *(very)* preciso, mismo <*at that p. moment* en ese preciso momento>; *(scrupulous)* meticuloso, cuidadoso ♦ **to be p.** para ser precisos o exacto.

pre·cise·ly (prĭ-sīs′lē) adv. *(clearly)* con precisión, con claridad; *(exactly)* precisamente, justamente <*that is p. what we need* es precisamente lo que nos hace falta>; *(on the dot)* en punto <*p. twelve o'clock* las doce en punto> ♦ **precisely!** ¡eso es!, ¡exactamente!

pre·cise·ness (prĭ-sīs′nĭs) s. precisión *f.*

pre·ci·sion (prĭ-sĭzh′ən) **I.** s. precisión *f,* exactitud *f* **II.** adj. TEC. de precisión.

pre·clude (prĭ-klo̅o̅d′) tr. **-clud·ed, -clud·ing** *(to exclude)* excluir; *(to avoid)* evitar; *(to prevent)* impedir, prevenir.

pre·clu·sion (prĭ-klo̅o̅′zhən) s. *(exclusion)* exclusión *f; (prevention)* prevención *f.*

pre·co·cious (prĭ-kō′shəs) adj. precoz.

pre·coc·i·ty (prĭ-kŏs′ĭ-tē) s. precocidad *f.*

pre·cog·ni·tion (prē′kŏg-nĭsh′ən) s. precognición *f.*

pre·co·lo·ni·al (prē′kə-lō′nē-əl) adj. precolonial.

pre·Co·lum·bi·an (prē′kə-lŭm′bē-ən) adj. precolombino.

pre·con·ceive (prē′kən-sēv′) tr. **-ceived, -ceiv·ing** preconcebir.

pre·con·cep·tion (prē′kən-sĕp′shən) s. *(conception)* preconcepción *f; (prejudice)* prejuicio.

---

pre·con·di·tion (prē′kən-dĭsh′ən) **I.** s. *(condition)* condición previa; *(requisite)* requisito previo **II.** tr. preparar de antemano.

pre·cook (prē-kŏŏk′) tr. *(in advance)* cocinar con anticipación, precocer; *(partially)* cocer parcialmente.

pre·cur·sor (prī-kûr′sər) s. precursor *m.*

pre·cur·so·ry (prī-kûr′sə-rē) adj. *(preceding)* precursor; *(preliminary)* preliminar; *(premonitory)* premonitorio.

pre·da·cious o **pre·da·ceous** (prī-dā′shəs) adj. predatorio, de rapiña.

pre·date (prē-dāt′) tr. **-dated, -dat·ing** *(to precede)* preceder; *(to give prior date to)* poner una fecha anterior a.

pre·da·tion (prī-dā′shən) s. *(plundering)* depradación *f;* *(hunting)* caza predatoria.

pred·a·tor (prĕd′ə-tər) s. *(hunter)* predator *m;* *(pillager)* depradador *m.*

pred·a·to·ry (prĕd′ə-tôr′ē) adj. *(predacious)* de rapiña; *(plundering)* depradador.

pre·de·cease (prē′dī-sēs′) tr. **-ceased, -ceas·ing** morir antes que.

pred·e·ces·sor (prĕd′ĭ-sĕs′ər, prē′dĭ-) s. *(forerunner)* predecesor *m;* *(ancestor)* antepasado.

pre·des·ti·nate (prē-dĕs′tə-nāt′) **I.** tr. **-nat·ed, -nat·ing** predestinar **II.** adj. predestinado.

pre·des·ti·na·tion (prē-dĕs′tə-nā′shən) s. *(act, condition)* predestinación *f;* *(destiny)* destino, sino.

pre·des·tine (prē-dĕs′tĭn) tr. **-tined, -tin·ing** predestinar.

pre·de·ter·mi·na·tion (prē′dī-tûr′mə-nā′shən) s. predeterminación *f.*

pre·de·ter·mine (prē′dĭ-tûr′mĭn) tr. **-mined, -min·ing** *(to fix in advance)* predeterminar; *(to predispose)* predisponer.

pred·i·ca·ble (prĕd′ĭ-kə-bəl) adj. predicable.

pre·dic·a·ment (prī-dĭk′ə-mənt) s. *(difficult situation)* apuro, situación difícil *f;* LÓG. *(category)* predicamento.

pred·i·cate **I.** tr. (prĕd′ĭ-kāt′) **-cat·ed, -cat·ing** *(to base)* fundar, basar <*predicated on assumptions* fundado en suposiciones; *(to affirm)* aseverar, afirmar; LÓG. predicar **II.** s. (-kĭt) GRAM., LÓG. predicado **III.** adj. (-kĭt) GRAM. predicativo.

pred·i·ca·tion (prĕd′ĭ-kā′shən) s. *(assertion)* aseveración *f,* afirmación *f;* LÓG. predicación *f.*

pre·dict (prī-dĭkt′) tr. *(to foretell)* predecir, vaticinar; *(to forecast)* pronosticar.

pre·dict·a·bil·i·ty (prī-dĭk′tə-bĭl′ĭ-tē) s. carácter previsible *m.*

pre·dict·a·ble (prī-dĭk′tə-bəl) adj. *(event)* previsible; *(behavior)* invariable, constante; *(person)* de reacciones previsibles.

pre·dic·tion (prī-dĭk′shən) s. *(foretelling)* predicción *f;* *(prophecy)* profecía *f;* *(forecast)* pronóstico.

pre·dic·tive (prī-dĭk′tĭv) adj. profético.

pre·dic·tor (prī-dĭk′tər) s. vaticinador *m,* pronosticador *m.*

pred·i·lec·tion (prĕd′l-ĕk′shən, prēd′-) s. predilección *f,* preferencia.

pre·dis·pose (prē′dī-spōz′) tr. **-posed, -pos·ing** predisponer.

pre·dis·po·si·tion (prē′dĭs′pə-zĭsh′ən) s. *(inclination)* predisposición *f;* *(tendency)* tendencia; *(propensity)* propensión *f.*

pre·dom·i·nance (prī-dŏm′ə-nəns) o **pre·dom·i·nan·cy** (-nən-sē) s. *(ascendancy)* predominio; *(preponderance)* preponderancia.

pre·dom·i·nant (prī-dŏm′ə-nənt) adj. predominante, prevalente.

pre·dom·i·nate (prī-dŏm′ə-nāt′) intr. **-nat·ed, -nat·ing** *(to dominate)* predominar; *(to prevail)* prevalecer —tr. *(to dominate over)* predominar sobre; *(to prevail over)* prevalecer sobre.

pre·em·i·nence o **pre·em·i·nence** (prē-ĕm′ə-nəns) s. preeminencia, superioridad *f.*

pre·em·i·nent o **pre·em·i·nent** (prē-ĕm′ə-nənt) adj. preeminente, superior.

pre·empt (prē-ĕmpt′) tr. *(to displace)* supeditar; *(to appropriate)* apropiarse de; TELEV. substituir, sustituir.

pre·emp·tion o **pre·emp·tion** (prē-ĕmp′shən) s. *(right)* derecho preferente de compra; *(purchase)* adquisición por

derecho preferente de compra *f;* *(appropriation)* apropiación *f;* TELEV. substitución *f.*

pre·emp·tive o **pre·emp·tive** (prē-ĕmp′tĭv) adj. DER. de o con privilegio de compra; MIL. preventivo (ataque).

preen (prēn) tr. arreglar, limpiar ◆ **to p. oneself** *(to dress showily)* emperejilarse; *(to primp)* pavonearse • **to p. oneself on** actuar vanidosamente —intr. pavonearse.

pre·es·tab·lish o **pre·es·tab·lish** (prē′ĭ-stăb′lĭsh) tr. preestablecer.

pre·ex·ist o **pre·ex·ist** (prē′ĭg-zĭst′) tr. existir antes que —intr. preexistir.

pre·ex·is·tence o **pre·ex·is·tence** (prē′ĭg-zĭs′təns) s. preexistencia.

pre·fab (prē′făb′) s. CONSTR. estructura prefabricada.

pre·fab·ri·cate (prē-făb′rĭ-kāt′) tr. **-cat·ed, -cat·ing** prefabricar.

pref·ace (prĕf′ĭs) **I.** s. *(prologue)* prefacio, prólogo; *(introduction)* prólogo, preludio ◆ **P.** RELIG. prefacio **II.** tr. **-aced, -ac·ing** *(to introduce)* prologar, poner un prólogo a; *(to serve as an introduction to)* servir de prólogo a; *(to begin)* dar comienzo a ◆ **to be prefaced by** *(book)* tener a modo de prólogo; *(situation)* estar precedido de.

pref·a·to·ry (prĕf′ə-tôr′ē) adj. *(introductory)* introductorio; *(preliminary)* preliminar.

pre·fect (prē′fĕkt′) s. prefecto.

pre·fec·ture (prē′fĕk′chər) s. prefectura.

pre·fer (prī-fûr′) tr. **-ferred, -fer·ring** *(to like better)* preferir; DER. *(a creditor)* dar preferencia a; *(charges)* presentar, formular.

pref·er·a·bil·i·ty (prĕf′ər-ə-bĭl′ĭ-tē) s. carácter preferible o preferente *m.*

pref·er·a·ble (prĕf′ər-ə-bəl) adj. preferible.

pref·er·a·bly (prĕf′ər-ə-blē) adv. preferiblemente, preferentemente.

pref·er·ence (prĕf′ər-əns) s. preferencia <*in p. to* con preferencia a> ◆ **to be one's p.** preferir • **to have no p.** serle igual o darle lo mismo (a uno).

pref·er·en·tial (prĕf′ə-rĕn′shəl) adj. preferente, preferencial <*p. treatment* trato preferente>.

pre·fer·ment (prī-fûr′mənt) s. *(advancement)* adelanto; *(promotion)* ascenso.

preferred stock s. FIN. acciones preferidas.

pre·fig·u·ra·tion (prē-fĭg′yə-rā′shən) s. prefiguración *f.*

pre·fig·ure (prē-fĭg′yər) tr. **-ured, -ur·ing** *(to presage)* prefigurar; *(to imagine)* figurarse de antemano.

pre·fix (prē-fĭks′, prē′fĭks′) **I.** tr. GRAM. poner un prefijo a; *(to put before)* anteponer **II.** s. (prē′fĭks′) GRAM. *(affix)* prefijo; *(title)* título.

preg·na·ble (prĕg′nə-bəl) adj. *(vulnerable)* vulnerable; MIL. *(conquerable)* expugnable.

preg·nan·cy (prĕg′nən-sē) s. [pl. **-cies**] MED. embarazo, gravidez *f.*

preg·nant (prĕg′nənt) adj. *(woman)* encinta, embarazada; *(female animal)* preñada; FIG. *(creative)* fecundo, prolífico; *(filled)* lleno <*p. with hope* lleno de esperanzas>; *(meaningful)* significativo <*a p. pause* una pausa significativa>; *(profuse)* abundante.

pre·heat (prē-hēt′) tr. precalentar.

pre·hen·sile (prē-hĕn′səl, -sīl′) adj. prensil.

pre·his·tor·ic (prē′hĭ-stôr′ĭk) o **pre·his·tor·i·cal** (-ĭ-kəl) adj. prehistórico.

pre·his·to·ry (prē-hĭs′tə-rē) s. prehistoria.

pre·ig·ni·tion (prē′ĭg-nĭsh′ən) s. AUTO., MEC. preignición *f,* preencendido.

pre·in·dus·tri·al (prē′ĭn-dŭs′trē-əl) adj. preindustrial.

pre·judge (prē-jŭj′) tr. **-judged, -judg·ing** prejuzgar, juzgar de antemano.

prej·u·dice (prĕj′ə-dĭs) **I.** s. *(bias)* prejuicio, prejuicios <*religious p.* prejuicios de religión>; *(injury)* perjuicio, menoscabo <*without p. to* sin perjuicio de> ◆ **to be prejudiced against** tener prejuicios contra **II.** tr. **-diced, -dic·ing** *(to bias)* crear prejuicios a, predisponer; *(to injure)* perjudicar; *(rights)* menoscabar.

prej·u·di·cial (prĕj′ə-dĭsh′əl) adj. perjudicial.

prej·u·di·cious (prĕj′ə-dĭsh′əs) adj. perjudicial.

prel·a·cy (prĕl′ə-sē) s. [pl. **-cies**] RELIG. *(office)* prelacía;

(prelates) prelados; *(administration)* administración de prelados *f.*
prel·ate (prĕl'ĭt) s. RELIG. prelado.
pre·lim·i·nar·y (prĭ-lĭm'ə-nĕr'ē) I. adj. preliminar ♦ **p. investigation** DER. instrucción II. s. [pl. **-ies**] *(something preparatory)* preliminar *m*; EDUC. *(examination)* examen preliminar *m* ♦ **preliminaries** preliminares, preparativos.
pre·lit·er·ate (prē-lĭt'ər-ĭt) adj. perteneciente a una cultura sin lenguaje escrito.
prel·ude (prĕl'yōōd', prā'lōōd') I. s. preludio II. tr. & intr. **-ud·ed, -ud·ing** preludiar.
pre·mar·i·tal (prē-mār'ĭ-tl) adj. premarital, prenupcial.
pre·ma·ture (prē'mə-chōōr') adj. prematuro.
pre·med (prē'mĕd') FAM. I. adj. preparatorio para el ingreso en la facultad de medicina II. s. estudiante que se prepara para el ingreso en la facultad de medicina *mf.*
pre·med·i·cal (prē-mĕd'ĭ-kəl) adj. previo a estudios de medicina.
pre·med·i·tate (prē-mĕd'ĭ-tāt') tr. & intr. **-tat·ed, -tat·ing** premeditar.
pre·med·i·tat·ed (prē-mĕd'ĭ-tā'tĭd) adj. premeditado.
pre·med·i·ta·tion (prē-mĕd'ĭ-tā'shən) s. premeditación *f.*
pre·men·stru·al (prē-mĕn'strōō-əl) adj. premenstrual.
pre·mi·er (prē'mē-ər, prĕm'ē-, prĭ-mîr') I. adj. *(first)* primero; *(chief)* principal II. s. *(minister)* primer ministro; *(of a Canadian province)* presidente *m.*
pre·mière (prĭ-mîr', prĭm-yâr') TEAT. I. s. *(opening)* estreno; *(leading lady)* actriz principal *f* II. tr. & intr. **-mièred, -mièr·ing** estrenar III. adj. primero, principal.
prem·ise (prĕm'ĭs) I. s. premisa ♦ **premises** DER. *(of a document)* artículos preliminares (de escritura); *(site)* local; *(building)* edificio II. tr. **-ised, -is·ing** *(to introduce)* dar comienzo a; *(in an argument)* sentar como premisa —intr. formular una premisa.
pre·mi·um (prē'mē-əm) s. *(prize)* premio, recompensa; *(fee)* prima; *(installment)* prima (de un seguro) ♦ **to be at a p.** COM. estar por sobre la par; FIG. *(to be in demand)* ser muy solicitado, tener mucha demanda • **to put a p. on** FIG. valorar mucho, dar gran importancia a.
pre·mo·lar (prē-mō'lər) adj. & s. premolar *m.*
pre·mo·ni·tion (prē'mə-nĭsh'ən, prĕm'ə-) s. *(foreboding)* premonición *f*; *(presentiment)* presentimiento; *(forewarning)* advertencia.
pre·na·tal (prē-nāt'l) adj. prenatal.
pre·oc·cu·pa·tion (prē-ŏk'yə-pā'shən) s. preocupación *f.*
pre·oc·cu·pied (prē-ŏk'yə-pīd') adj. *(worried)* preocupado <p. about preocupado por>; *(absorbed)* absorto <p. with absorto en>; *(occupied)* ocupado previamente.
pre·oc·cu·py (prē-ŏk'yə-pī') tr. **-pied, -py·ing** *(to worry)* preocupar; *(to engross)* absorber; *(to occupy before another)* ocupar anticipadamente.
pre·or·dain (prē'ôr-dān') tr. preordinar.
prep (prĕp) FAM. I. adj. preparatorio, preliminar ♦ **p. school** escuela secundaria privada II. s. *(school)* escuela preparatoria; G.B. *(homework)* deber *m*, tarea escolar.
pre·pack·age (prē-păk'ĭj) tr. **-aged, -ag·ing** preempaquetar.
pre·paid (prē-pād') adj. *(paid beforehand)* pagado por adelantado; *(letter)* franqueado; *(carriage paid)* con el porte pagado.
prep·a·ra·tion (prĕp'ə-rā'shən) s. *(readiness)* preparación *f*; *(medicine)* preparado ♦ **preparations** preparativos.
pre·par·a·tive (prĭ-păr'ə-tĭv) I. adj. preparatorio II. s. preparativo.
pre·par·a·to·ry (prĭ-păr'ə-tôr'ē) adj. preparatorio, preliminar ♦ **p. to** antes de.
preparatory school s. escuela preparatoria.
pre·pare (prĭ-pâr') tr. **-pared, -par·ing** *(to ready)* preparar, disponer; *(to arrange)* hacer, preparar ♦ **to be prepared for** estar preparado para • **to be prepared to** estar dispuesto a • **to p. oneself for** prepararse para —intr. prepararse.
pre·par·ed·ness (prĭ-pâr'ĭd-nĭs) s. *(readiness)* preparación *f*; MIL. estado de preparación.
pre·pay (prē-pā') tr. **-paid** (-pād'), **-pay·ing** pagar por adelantado *o* anticipado.

pre·pay·ment (prē-pā'mənt) s. pago adelantado *o* anticipado.
pre·pon·der·ance (prĭ-pŏn'dər-əns) *o* **pre·pon·der·an·cy** (-ən-sē) s. preponderancia.
pre·pon·der·ant (prĭ-pŏn'dər-ənt) adj. *(superior)* preponderante; *(dominant)* predominante.
prep·o·si·tion (prĕp'ə-zĭsh'ən) s. GRAM. preposición *f.*
pre·pos·sess (prē'pə-zĕs') tr. *(to obsess)* obsesionar, preocupar; *(to influence)* predisponer (a favor); *(to impress)* impresionar *(favorablemente).*
pre·pos·sess·ing (prē'pə-zĕs'ĭng) adj. *(pleasing)* agradable; *(attractive)* atractivo.
pre·pos·ter·ous (prĭ-pŏs'tər-əs) adj. absurdo, ridículo.
prep·pie *o* **prep·py** (prĕp'ē) s. [pl. **-pies**] FAM. *(student)* alumno de una escuela preparatoria; *(youth)* joven de modales tradicionales *mf.*
pre·pu·bes·cence (prē'pyōō-bĕs'əns) s. prepubescencia.
pre·pu·bes·cent (prē'pyōō-bĕs'ənt) adj. FISIOL. anterior a la pubertad.
pre·puce (prē'pyōōs') s. ANAT. prepucio.
pre·req·ui·site (prē-rĕk'wĭ-zĭt) I. s. condición previa, requisito previo II. adj. *(necessary)* necesario *o* requerido de antemano.
pre·rog·a·tive (prĭ-rŏg'ə-tĭv) s. prerrogativo.
pres·age (prĕs'ĭj, prĭ-sāj') I. s. *(indication)* presagio; *(presentiment)* presentimiento II. tr. **-aged, -ag·ing** *(to portend)* presagiar; *(a presentiment of)* presentir.
pres·by·ter (prĕz'bĭ-tər) s. RELIG. presbítero.
pres·by·te·ri·an (prĕz'bĭ-tîr'ē-ən) I. adj. presbiteriano II. s. ♦ **P.** RELIG. presbiteriano.
Presbyterian Church s. RELIG. iglesia presbiteriana.
pres·by·ter·y (prĕz'bĭ-tĕr'ē) s. [pl. **-ies**] RELIG. *(in a church)* presbiterio; *(presbyterian court)* tribunal eclesiástico presbiteriano; *(priest's residence)* casa parroquial.
pre·school (prē'skōōl') I. adj. preescolar II. s. jardín de infantes *m.*
pre·science (prē'shəns, prĕsh'əns) s. presciencia, conocimiento de las cosas futuras.
pre·scient (prē'shənt, prĕsh'ənt) adj. presciente.
pre·scribe (prĭ-skrīb') tr. **-scribed, -scrib·ing** *(to order)* prescribir; MED. *(a drug)* recetar; *(treatment)* mandar, ordenar —intr. *(to establish)* establecer, dictar; MED. *(a drug)* hacer recetas; DER. *(to assert, invalidate)* prescribir.
pre·script (prē'skrĭpt') I. s. norma, regla II. adj. prescripto, establecido.
pre·scrip·tion (prĭ-skrĭp'shən) s. *(prescribing)* prescripción *f*; MED. *(written order)* receta; *(medicine)* remedio; DER. prescripción.
prescription drug s. FARM. remedio vendido solamente bajo receta médica.
pre·scrip·tive (prĭ-skrĭp'tĭv) adj. *(sanctioned)* establecido; *(establishing rules)* preceptivo.
pres·ence (prĕz'əns) s. *(being present)* presencia; *(bearing)* porte *m*, talle *m*; *(confidence)* seguridad *f* ♦ **in the p. of** en presencia de.
presence of mind s. presencia de ánimo, presteza mental.
pres·ent¹ (prĕz'ənt) I. s. *(now)* presente *m*, actualidad *f*; GRAM. presente ♦ **at p.** en el presente, en la actualidad • **by these presents** DER. por la presente • **for the p.** por el momento, por ahora • **up to the p.** hasta el presente, hasta ahora II. adj. *(current)* presente, actual <their p. difficulties sus dificultades actuales>; *(month)* corriente; *(year)* en curso; *(at hand)* presente <the people p. las personas presentes>; GRAM. presente ♦ **at the p. time** en este momento • **those p.** los presentes • **to be p.** asistir • **to be p. at** *(to be)* haber en <how many people were p. at the demonstration? ¿cuántas personas había en la manifestación?>; *(to witness)* presenciar.
pre·sent² I. tr. (prĭ-zĕnt') *(to introduce)* presentar <may I p. Miss Jones? le presento a la señorita Jones>; *(to put on)* presentar, poner <to p. a play poner una comedia>; *(to give)* regalar, obsequiar; *(to confer)* entregar, dar; *(to display)* presentar, mostrar <to p. one's credentials presentar las credenciales>; *(a case)* exponer; *(a problem)* plantear; *(an invoice)* pasar; *(arms)* presentar; *(charges)* formular ♦ **presenting . . .** CINEM., TEAT. con . . . • **to p. itself** presen-

tarse • **to p. oneself** presentarse **II.** s. (prĕz'ənt) **pres·ent** *(gift)* presente *m*, regalo.

pre·sent·a·ble (prī-zĕn'tə-bəl) adj. presentable ♦ **to be p.** tener buena presencia.

pres·en·ta·tion (prĕz'ən-tā'shən, prē'zən-) s. *(act)* presentación *f*; *(of a play)* representación *f*; *(introduction)* presentación; *(conferral)* entrega; *(of a report)* presentación; *(of a case, argument)* exposición *f*; *(of an invoice)* paso, extensión *f*; MED., POL., RELIG. presentación ♦ **on p. of** al presentar.

pres·ent-day (prĕz'ənt-dā') adj. actual, de hoy en día.

pre·sen·ti·ment (prī-zĕn'tə-mənt) s. presentimiento.

pres·ent·ly (prĕz'ənt-lē) adv. *(soon)* dentro de poco; *(now)* en este momento, actualmente.

pre·sent·ment (prī-zĕnt'mənt) s. *(presentation)* presentación *f*; TEAT. representación *f*; *(exhibition)* exposición *f*; DER. declaración del jurado *f*; COM. extensión *f*.

present participle s. GRAM. participio presente, gerundio.

present perfect s. GRAM. pretérito perfecto.

present tense s. GRAM. tiempo presente, presente *m*.

pre·serv·a·ble (prī-zûr'və-bəl) adj. conservable.

pres·er·va·tion (prĕz'ər-vā'shən) s. *(protection)* preservación *f*, protección *f*; *(of customs, foodstuffs)* conservación *f*.

pres·er·va·tion·ist (prĕz'ər-vā'shə-nĭst) s. persona dedicada a la conservación de monumentos históricos.

pre·ser·va·tive (prī-zûr'və-tĭv) **I.** adj. preservativo **II.** s. QUÍM. conservante *m*, preservador (de alimentos) *m*.

pre·serve (prī-zûrv') **I.** tr. **-served, -serv·ing** *(to protect)* preservar, proteger; *(to maintain unchanged)* conservar; *(to keep intact)* conservar, mantener <*to p. one's dignity* mantener la dignidad>; *(food)* conservar, poner en conserva; *(game)* proteger (para cacería) **II.** s. *(area)* coto, vedado; FIG. *(province)* terreno ♦ **preserves** CUL. confitura, compota.

pre·serv·er (prī-zûr'vər) s. preservador *m*.

pre·side (prī-zīd') intr. **-sid·ed, -sid·ing** presidir ♦ **to p. at** o **over** presidir.

pres·i·den·cy (prĕz'ĭ-dən-sē) s. [pl. **-cies**] *(office, term)* presidencia; *(of a corporation)* dirección *f*; *(of a university)* rectoría ♦ **P.** POL. presidencia.

pres·i·dent (prĕz'ĭ-dənt) s. *(of a body of people)* presidente *m*; *(of a corporation)* director *m*; *(of a university)* rector *m* ♦ **P.** POL. presidente.

pres·i·dent-e·lect (prĕz'ĭ-dənt-ĭ-lĕkt') s. presidente electo.

pres·i·den·tial (prĕz'ĭ-dĕn'shəl) adj. presidencial.

pre·sid·i·um (prī-sĭd'ē-əm) s. [pl. **-i·a** (-ē-ə) o **-i·ums**] POL. presidium *m*.

pre·sort (prē-sôrt') tr. clasificar (correspondencia) en zonas postales antes de llevarla al correo.

press¹ (prĕs) **I.** tr. *(to bear down on)* apretar; *(to squeeze)* prensar; *(to compress)* comprimir <*they p. cotton into bales* comprimen el algodón en balas>; *(to iron)* planchar; *(to embrace)* abrazar dando un apretón; *(to entreat)* instar <*I pressed him to stay* le insté a que se quedara>; *(to harass)* hostigar, acosar; *(to hurry)* apremiar, acuciar; *(to insist on)* presentar con insistencia, insistir en ♦ **to be pressed for money** o **time** estar con apuros de dinero o de tiempo • **to p. one's luck** forzar la suerte —intr. *(to use force)* apretar, ejercer presión; *(to trouble)* pesar, abrumar; *(to be urgent)* urgir, apremiar <*the hour presses* el tiempo apremia>; *(to crowd)* apiñarse, apretujarse <*the crowd pressed into the room* la multitud se apiñaba en el cuarto>; *(to ask insistently)* importunar, incomodar ♦ **to p. ahead** o **forward** avanzar con determinación • **to p. for** pedir con insistencia • **to p. on** seguir adelante **II.** s. *(machine)* prensa; *(for printing)* imprenta; *(journalists)* prensa; *(crowding)* apiñamiento; *(crowd)* multitud *f*, muchedumbre *f* <*they were lost in the p.* estaban perdidos en la multitud>; *(urgency)* prisa, urgencia; *(closet)* armario, ropero ♦ **to get good (bad) p.** tener buena (mala) prensa • **to go to p.** dar a la imprenta.

press² (prĕs) tr. MIL. levar, reclutar por la fuerza; *(to commandeer)* requisar.

press agent s. agente de prensa *mf*.

press association s. agencia de prensa.

press box s. tribuna de la prensa.

press conference s. conferencia de prensa.

press·ing (prĕs'ĭng) **I.** adj. *(urgent)* urgente; *(need)* apremiante; *(insistent)* insistente **II.** s. *(of olives, records)* prensado; *(ironing)* planchado; *(of metals)* estampado.

press·man (prĕs'mən) s. [pl. **-men**] IMPR. *(press operator)* prensista *m*; G.B. *(newspaperman)* periodista *m*.

press release s. comunicado de prensa.

press·room (prĕs'rōōm', -rŏŏm') s. taller de imprenta *m*.

press·run (prĕs'rŭn') s. IMPR. tirada.

press secretary s. secretario de prensa, encargado de relaciones periodísticas.

pres·sure (prĕsh'ər) **I.** s. *(weight)* presión *f*; *(compression)* compresión *f*; *(force)* fuerza, presión; FIG. *(urgency)* apremio, presión <*he acted under financial p.* actuó bajo presión económica> ♦ **blood p.** tensión o presión arterial • **to be under a lot of p.** estar en una situación tensa • **to bring p. to bear on** o **to put p. on** FIG. ejercer presión sobre **II.** tr. **-sured, -sur·ing** ejercer presión o influencia sobre.

pressure cooker s. CUL. olla de presión; FIG. *(crisis atmosphere)* situación en atmósfera de apremio y urgencia.

pressure gauge s. FÍS. manómetro, indicador de presión *m*.

pressure group s. POL. grupo de presión.

pressure suit s. AERONÁUT. traje presurizado.

pres·sur·ize (prĕsh'ə-rīz') tr. **-ized, -iz·ing** AER., FÍS. presurizar.

pres·ti·dig·i·ta·tion (prĕs'tĭ-dĭj'ĭ-tā'shən) s. prestidigitación *f*.

pres·tige (prĕ-stēzh', -stēj') s. prestigio.

pres·ti·gious (prĕ-stē'jəs, -stĭj'əs) adj. prestigioso.

pre·sum·a·ble (prī-zōō'mə-bəl) adj. presumible.

pre·sum·a·bly (prī-zōō'mə-blē) adv. según es de presumir o suponer.

pre·sume (prī-zōōm') tr. **-sumed, -sum·ing** *(to suppose)* suponer <*I p. the bus will be on time* supongo que el autobús llegará a la hora>; *(to dare)* tener el atrevimiento de; *(to pretend)* pretender, creerse <*he presumes to know everything* se cree que lo sabe todo> ♦ **to be presumed** suponerse, creerse —intr. presumir ♦ **to p. on** abusar de.

pre·sum·ing (prī-zōō'mĭng) adj. presumido, presuntuoso.

pre·sump·tion (prī-zŭmp'shən) s. *(supposition)* presunción *f*, suposición *f*; *(effrontery)* osadía, atrevimiento; DER. presunción.

pre·sump·tive (prī-zŭmp'tĭv) adj. *(providing evidence)* presuntivo; *(presumed)* presunto, supuesto <*an heir p.* un heredero presunto>.

pre·sump·tu·ous (prī-zŭmp'chōō-əs) adj. *(arrogant)* presuntuoso, pretencioso <*it would be p. to say that* decir eso sería pretencioso>; *(rash)* atrevido, osado.

pre·sup·pose (prē'sə-pōz') tr. **-posed, -pos·ing** presuponer.

pre·tence (prē'tĕns', prī-tĕns') s. G.B. var. de **pretense**.

pre·tend (prī-tĕnd') tr. *(to feign)* fingir, simular <*he pretended that he was insane* fingió que estaba loco>; *(illness, deafness)* hacerse; *(ignorance)* alegar, pretextar; *(to oneself)* imaginarse <*she pretended that she was the queen* se imaginó que era la reina>; *(to claim)* pretender <*I do not p. to know* no pretendo saberlo> ♦ **let's p. that** supongamos que —intr. *(to feign)* fingir; *(to dissemble)* disimular ♦ **to be just pretending** estar jugando • **to p. to the throne** pretender al trono.

pre·tend·ed (prī-tĕn'dĭd) adj. *(reputed)* presunto, supuesto; *(feigned)* falso, fingido.

pre·tend·er (prī-tĕn'dər) s. *(one who feigns)* fingidor *m*, simulador *m*; *(hypocrite)* hipócrita *mf*; *(claimant)* pretendiente (al trono) *mf*.

pre·tense (prē'tĕns', prī-tĕns') s. *(feigning)* fingimiento, simulación *f*; *(pretext)* pretexto; *(claim)* pretensión *f*; *(affectation)* ostentación *f*; *(pretentiousness)* presunción *f* ♦ **to make no p. to** no pretender • **under false pretenses** por fraude • **under the p. of** con el pretexto de.

pre·ten·sion (prī-tĕn'shən) s. *(pretext)* pretexto; *(claim)* pretensión *f*; *(pretentiousness)* presunción *f*; *(ostentation)* ostentación *f*.

pre·ten·tious (prī-tĕn'shəs) adj. *(presumptuous)* pretencioso, presuntuoso; *(ostentatious)* ostentoso.

pret·er·it o **pret·er·ite** (prĕt'ər-ĭt) s. & adj. GRAM. pretérito.

ã rey / ä año / b boca / ch chico / d dar / ĕ el / ē mil / g gato / h joya / hw juez / ī aire / k casa / kw cuan /

pre·ter·nat·u·ral (prē′tər-năch′ər-əl) adj. *(unusual)* preternatural; *(supernatural)* sobrenatural.
pre·test I. s. (prē′tĕst′) prueba, examen (preliminar) m II. tr. & intr. (prē-tĕst′) hacer una prueba preliminar.
pre·text (prē′tĕkst′) I. s. pretexto, excusa II. tr. alegar dando excusas, pretextar.
pret·ti·fy (prĭt′ĭ-fī′) tr. **-fied, -fy·ing** embellecer, emperifollar.
pret·ty (prĭt′ē) I. adj. **-ti·er, -ti·est** *(person)* guapo, lindo <*a p. girl* una chica guapa>; *(thing)* bonito, lindo <*what a p. dress!* ¡qué vestido más bonito!>; FAM. *(considerable)* considerable <*a p. sum* una suma considerable> ♦ **a p. boy** chico guapo, guapito • **a p. mess** IRON. un buen lío • **a p. penny** mucho dinero II. adv. bastante <*p. good* bastante bueno> ♦ **p. much** más o menos • **to be sitting p.** FAM. tener una buena posición III. tr. **-tied, -ty·ing** ♦ **to p. up** FAM. acicalar.
pret·zel (prĕt′səl) s. galleta salada en forma de lazo.
pre·vail (prĭ-vāl′) intr. *(to persist)* prevalecer; *(to win)* triunfar, vencer; *(to predominate)* predominar, regir ♦ **to p. on** o **upon** persuadir o convencer a • **to p. over** o **against** vencer.
pre·vail·ing (prĭ-vā′lĭng) adj. *(frequent)* prevaleciente; *(predominant)* predominante; *(current)* corriente; *(widespread)* común.
prev·a·lence (prĕv′ə-ləns) s. predominio.
prev·a·lent (prĕv′ə-lənt) adj. *(common)* común; *(general)* generalizado.
pre·var·i·cate (prĭ-văr′ĭ-kāt′) intr. **-cat·ed, -cat·ing** *(to twist)* tergiversar; *(to lie)* mentir; DER. prevaricar.
pre·vent (prĭ-vĕnt′) tr. *(to avoid)* evitar; *(to impede)* impedir <*to p. from doing something* impedir que se haga algo>.
pre·vent·a·ble (prĭ-vĕn′tə-bəl) adj. evitable.
pre·ven·ta·tive (prĭ-vĕn′tə-tĭv) adj. & s. var. de **preventive.**
pre·ven·tion (prĭ-vĕn′shən) s. *(act)* prevención f; *(hindrance)* impedimento; *(obstacle)* obstáculo.
pre·ven·tive (prĭ-vĕn′tĭv) I. adj. preventivo II. s. *(measure)* medida preventiva; MED. remedio preventivo.
pre·view (prē′vyōō′) I. s. *(advance showing)* exhibición preliminar f; CINEM. *(trailer)* trailer m, avance m; *(introductory experience)* muestra parcial II. tr. *(to view)* ver antes que otros; *(to show)* exhibir previamente.
pre·vi·ous (prē′vē-əs) adj. *(prior)* previo, anterior; FAM. *(premature)* prematuro.
pre·vi·ous·ly (prē′vē-əs-lē) adv. antes, previamente.
previous to prep. antes de.
pre·vi·sion (prē-vĭzh′ən) s. previsión f.
pre·war (prē′wôr′) adj. antes de la guerra, de preguerra.
prey (prā) I. s. *(animal)* presa; FIG. *(victim)* víctima II. intr. ♦ **to p. on** *(to hunt)* cazar; *(to exploit)* explotar; *(to victimize)* hacer víctima de; *(to plunder)* pillar; FIG. *(to weigh)* abrumar <*doubts preyed on his mind* las dudas abrumaban a su mente>.
price (prīs) I. s. *(cost)* precio; FIN. cotización f <*the p. of gold* la cotización del oro>; *(worth)* precio, valor m; FIG. *(toll)* precio, costo <*the p. of independence* el precio de la independencia ♦ **asking p.** precio inicial • **at any p.** a cualquier precio, cueste lo que cueste • **beyond p.** que no tiene precio, inestimable • **ceiling p.** precio tope • **closing p.** FIN. cotización al cierre • **discount p.** precio de descuento • **full p.** precio fuerte • **list p.** precio de lista o de tasa • **market p.** precio de mercado o corriente • **not at any p.** *(in no way)* de ningún modo; *(not even as a gift)* ni regalado; *(regardless of price)* ni a precio de oro • **opening p.** FIN. cotización inicial • **sale p.** precio de saldo, precio reducido • **to pay a high** o **heavy p.** FIG. pagar caro • **to put a p. on** poner precio a • **to rise in p.** *(to cost more)* subir de precio; *(to be worth more)* aumentar de valor • **unit p.** precio por unidad • **what is the p. of . . .?** ¿cuánto cuesta . . .? II. tr. **priced, pric·ing** *(to establish)* poner precio a; *(to find out)* averiguar el precio de <*they spent the day pricing cars* pasaron el día averiguando el precio de los automóviles> ♦ **to be priced at** tener un precio de, costar • **to be priced out of the market** tener un precio excesivo, costar demasiado.
price index s. FIN. índice de precios m.

price·less (prīs′lĭs) adj. *(valuable)* sin precio, de gran valor; *(amusing)* muy divertido.
price tag s. *(label)* etiqueta de precio; FIG. *(price)* precio.
pric·ey (prī′sē) adj. **-i·er, -i·est** FAM. caro.
prick (prĭk) I. s. *(act)* pinchazo; *(of an insect)* picadura; *(sting)* pinchazo; *(of jealousy, curiosity)* punzada, aguijón m; *(pointed object)* aguijón, pincho; *(thorn)* espina; *(goad, bee sting)* aguijón; JER., VULG. *(penis)* pinga, polla; *(person)* hijo de puta II. tr. *(to pierce)* pinchar <*to p. with a pin* pinchar con un alfiler>; *(conscience)* remorder; *(jealousy, curiosity)* picar ♦ **to p. up its** o **one's ears** *(a dog)* erguir las orejas; FIG. *(to listen)* aguzar el oído —intr. *(to hurt)* picar; *(to gallop)* galopar, ir al galope; *(ears)* erguirse.
prick·er (prĭk′ər) s. punzón m, púa.
prick·le (prĭk′əl) I. s. *(point)* púa; *(thorn)* espina; *(spine)* pincho; *(sensation)* picazón f II. tr. **-led, -ling** *(to prick)* pinchar; *(to tingle)* picar —intr. *(to tingle)* sentir picazón; *(to rise up)* salpullir.
prick·ly (prĭk′lē) adj. **-li·er, -li·est** *(with prickles)* espinoso; *(stinging)* que causa picazón; *(vexatious)* erizado; *(irritable)* quisquilloso.
prickly heat s. MED. salpullido causado por el calor.
prickly pear s. BOT. *(cactus plant)* nopal m, chumbera; *(fruit)* nopal, higo chumbo o de tuna.
pride (prīd) I. s. *(in others)* orgullo <*motherly p.* orgullo materno>; *(self-respect)* amor propio, dignidad f <*to rob a man of his p.* despojar a un hombre de su dignidad>; *(conceit)* orgullo; *(source)* orgullo <*the p. of their country* el orgullo de su país>; *(best)* flor f; *(prime)* flor <*the p. of youth* la flor de la edad>; *(of lions)* manada de leones ♦ **the p. and joy of** el orgullo de • **to swallow one's p.** tragarse el orgullo • **to take p. in** *(achievements)* estar orgulloso de; *(work)* esmerarse en II. tr. **prid·ed, prid·ing** ♦ **to p. oneself on** estar orgulloso de, enorgullecerse de.
prie-dieu (prē-dyœ′) s. [pl. **-dieus** o **-dieux** (-dyœz′)] reclinatorio.
priest (prēst) s. RELIG. *(Catholic minister)* sacerdote m, cura; *(minister)* presbítero, pastor m.
priest·ess (prē′stĭs) s. sacerdotisa.
priest·hood (prēst′hŏŏd) s. *(office)* sacerdocio; *(clergy)* clerecía, clero.
priest·ly (prēst′lē) adj. sacerdotal.
prig (prĭg) s. *(prude)* mojigato; *(snob)* pedante mf.
prim (prĭm) I. adj. **prim·mer, prim·mest** *(too proper)* estirado, remilgado; *(affected)* forzado; *(neat)* arreglado II. tr. **primmed, prim·ming** ♦ **to p. oneself** acicalarse, arreglarse.
pri·ma·cy (prī′mə-sē) s. [pl. **-cies**] primacía.
pri·ma fa·cie (prī′mə fā′shē) adv. a primera vista ♦ **p. evidence** DER. prueba suficiente a primera vista.
pri·mal (prī′məl) adj. *(first)* original; *(fundamental)* primordial, fundamental; *(primary)* primario.
pri·mar·i·ly (prī-mâr′ə-lē) adv. *(originally)* originalmente, primitivamente; *(principally)* principalmente, primordialmente.
pri·mar·y (prī′mĕr′ē, -mə-rē) I. adj. *(first)* primario; *(primitive)* primitivo <*a p. instinct* un instinto primitivo>; *(foremost)* primordial, fundamental <*her p. purpose* su objetivo primordial>; *(basic)* primario, básico <*a p. element* un elemento básico>; *(direct)* directo, primario <*a p. effect* un efecto primario>; ELEC., GEOL., ORNIT., QUÍM. primario II. s. [pl. **-ies**] *(first in order)* lo primero; *(first in importance)* lo principal; POL. *(caucus)* reunión electoral f; *(election)* elección primaria o preliminar; *(color)* color primario.
primary accent s. acento primario.
primary color s. color primario.
primary election s. POL. elección primaria o preliminar.
primary school s. escuela primaria.
pri·mate (prī′māt′) s. RELIG. primado; ZOOL. primate m.
prime (prīm) I. adj. *(primary)* primero, primordial <*the p. reason* el motivo primordial>; *(main)* fundamental; *(first)* primero; *(choice)* de primera (calidad) <*p. cut* corte de primera>; MAT. primo ♦ **of p. importance** de la mayor importancia II. s. *(dawn)* alba, amanecer m; *(spring)* pri-

mavera; *(age)* flor de la vida *f*, plenitud *f* <*to be in one's p.* estar en la flor de la vida>; *(pick)* flor y nata, lo mejor; *(in fencing)* primera posición; IMPR. virgulilla, comilla; RELIG. prima; MAT. número primo ♦ **to be past one's p.** haber pasado la plenitud **III.** tr. *primed, prim·ing (to prepare)* preparar, alistar; *(gun, motor)* cebar, cargar; *(with primer)* dar una primera mano de pintura a; *(to coach)* preparar, aleccionar <*he primed the defendant* aleccionó al acusado> ♦ **to p. the pump** FAM. estimular (díc. de economía, participación).

prime meridian s. primer meridiano.

prime minister s. POL. primer ministro.

prime mover s. ELEC., FÍS., MEC. fuerza motriz; FIG. *(force)* promotor *m*; FILOS. primera causa.

prime number s. MAT. número primo.

prim·er¹ (prĭm'ər) s. *(textbook)* texto elemental; *(manual)* manual *m*.

prim·er² (prī'mər) s. *(one that primes)* cebador *m*; *(detonator)* detonador *m*; PINT. primera mano.

prime rate s. COM., FIN. tasa preferida.

pri·me·val (prī-mē'vəl) adj. *(earliest)* primordial, primitivo; *(original)* prístino.

prim·ing (prī'mĭng) s. *(explosive)* detonador *m*; *(size)* imprimación *f*.

prim·i·tive (prĭm'ĭ-tĭv) **I.** adj. *(primeval)* primitivo, primigenio; *(unsophisticated)* primitivo, rudimentario; ARTE. BIOL., GRAM. primitivo; GEOL. primario **II.** s. *(man)* primitivo, hombre primitivo; *(artist)* primitivo.

prim·i·tiv·ism (prĭm'ĭ-tĭ-vĭz'əm) s. primitivismo.

pri·mo·gen·i·tor (prī'mō-jĕn'ĭ-tər) s. primogenitor *m*.

pri·mo·gen·i·ture (prī'mō-jĕn'ĭ-chōŏr', -chər) s. primogenitura.

pri·mor·di·al (prī-môr'dē-əl) adj. primordial.

primp (prĭmp) tr. & intr. acicalar(se), emperejilar(se).

prim·rose (prĭm'rōz') s. BOT. primavera, prímula.

primrose path s. FIG. vida placentera, camino de rosas.

prince (prĭns) s. príncipe *m* ♦ **crown p.** príncipe heredero.

prince charming s. el príncipe azul.

prince consort s. príncipe consorte *m*.

prince·dom (prĭns'dəm) s. principado.

prince·ly (prĭns'lē) adj. **-li·er, -li·est** *(of a prince)* principesco; *(royal)* real; *(munificent)* magnífico, suntuoso.

Prince of Wales s. Príncipe de Gales.

prin·cess (prĭn'sĭs) **I.** s. princesa **II.** adj. *(dress cut)* de corte princesa.

prin·ci·pal (prĭn'sə-pəl) **I.** adj. principal **II.** s. *(of a school)* director *m*; *(performer)* primera figura; COM., FIN. principal *m*; *(of a crime)* autor *m*.

prin·ci·pal·i·ty (prĭn'sə-păl'ĭ-tē) s. [pl. **-ties**] principado ♦ **principalities** TEO. principado (orden de ángeles).

prin·ci·pal·ly (prĭn'sə-pə-lē) adv. principalmente.

prin·ci·ple (prĭn'sə-pəl) s. *(law)* principio; *(policy)* principio, norma <*she makes it a p. to help others* tiene por principio ayudar a los demás> ♦ **a man of p.** un hombre de principios • **a matter of p.** una cuestión de principios • **in p.** en principio • **on p.** por principio.

prin·ci·pled (prĭn'sə-pəld) adj. de principios.

print (prĭnt) **I.** s. *(impression)* impresión *f*, huella; *(stamp, seal)* estampa, cuño; *(letters)* letra, tipo <*large p.* letra de imprenta>; FOTOG. copia; *(engraving)* grabado, estampa; *(fabric)* estampado ♦ **in p.** impreso, publicado • **out of p.** agotado **II.** tr. *(to make an impression)* imprimir, marcar; *(book)* imprimir; *(edition)* tirar, hacer una tirada; *(to publish)* publicar; FOTOG. copiar, sacar, tirar; *(to write plainly)* escribir con letras de imprenta *o* de molde; FIG. *(to impress)* imprimir, grabar —intr. *(to be a printer)* trabajar como impresor; *(to write plainly)* escribir con letras de imprenta *o* de molde; *(book, publication)* imprimirse.

print·a·ble (prĭn'tə-bəl) adj. *(that can be printed)* imprimible; *(publishable)* publicable.

printed circuit s. ELEC., ELECTRÓN. circuito impreso.

printed matter s. impresos.

print·er (prĭn'tər) s. *(person)* impresor *m*; *(machine)* impresora.

print·ing (prĭn'tĭng) s. IMPR. *(art, business)* imprenta; *(act,*

quality of run) impresión *f*; *(run)* tiraje *m*; *(written characters)* letra de imprenta; *(layout)* tipografía.

printing press s. IMPR. prensa.

print·mak·ing (prĭnt'mā'kĭng) s. ARTE. grabado, estampado.

print-out (prĭnt'out') s. COMPUT. salida impresa, impresión de una computadora *f*.

pri·or¹ (prī'ər) adj. previo ♦ **p. to** antes de.

pri·or² (prī'ər) s. RELIG. prior *m*.

pri·or·ess (prī'ər-ĭs) s. RELIG. priora.

pri·or·i·ty (prī-ôr'ĭ-tē) s. [pl. **-ties**] *(order precedence)* prioridad *f*; *(time precedence)* anterioridad *f*.

pri·o·ry (prī'ə-rē) s. [pl. **-ies**] RELIG. priorato.

prise (prīz) v. & s. var. de **prize³**.

prism (prĭz'əm) s. FÍS., MAT. prisma *m*.

pris·mat·ic (prĭz-măt'ĭk) *o* **pris·mat·i·cal** (-ĭ-kəl) adj. prismático.

pris·on (prĭz'ən) **I.** s. *(jail)* cárcel *f*, prisión *f*; FIG. *(confinement)* prisión, cárcel ♦ **to put in** *o* **send to p.** encarcelar **II.** tr. encarcelar, poner en prisión.

prison camp s. MIL. campamento para prisioneros; *(penitentiary)* prisión *f*.

pris·on·er (prĭz'ə-nər) s. MIL. prisionero; *(in a prison)* preso; *(under arrest)* detenido; *(accused)* acusado.

prisoner of war s. prisionero de guerra.

pris·sy (prĭs'ē) adj. **-si·er, -si·est** remilgado.

pris·tine (prĭs'tēn') adj. *(earliest)* prístino, original; *(primitive)* primitivo; *(pure)* puro; FIG. *(uncorrupted)* virgen.

prith·ee (prĭ*th*'ē) interj. ANT. ¡te lo ruego!, por favor.

pri·va·cy (prī'və-sē) s. [pl. **-cies**] *(seclusion)* intimidad *f*; *(isolation)* aislamiento, soledad *f*; *(secrecy)* secreto ♦ **not to have any p.** no tener vida privada.

pri·vate (prī'vĭt) **I.** adj. *(personal)* privado; *(not public)* particular; *(secluded)* solitario ♦ **in p.** *(not publicly)* en privado; *(confidentially)* confidencialmente; *(closed-door)* a puerta cerrada • **p. citizen** particular **II.** s. soldado raso ♦ **privates** partes pudendas.

private detective s. detective privado.

private enterprise s. COM., FIN. *(private sector)* sector privado; *(business)* empresa particular.

pri·va·teer (prī'və-tîr') s. corsario.

private house s. casa particular.

pri·vate·ly (prī'vĭt-lē) adv. *(in private)* en privado, privadamente; *(secretly)* secretamente; *(one on one)* personalmente; *(confidentially)* confidencialmente.

pri·va·tion (prī-vā'shən) s. privación *f*.

priv·et (prĭv'ĭt) s. BOT. alheña.

priv·i·lege (prĭv'ə-lĭj) **I.** s. *(prerogative)* privilegio; COM. preferencia, prerrogativa ♦ **to have the p. of** tener el honor de **II.** tr. **-leged, -leg·ing** privilegiar ♦ **to be privileged to** *(lucky)* tener el privilegio de; *(honored to)* tener el honor de.

priv·i·leged (prĭv'ə-lĭjd) adj. privilegiado ♦ **p. communication** comunicación confidencial • **to be p. to** tener el privilegio de.

priv·y (prĭv'ē) **I.** adj. privado ♦ **p. seal** G.B. sello real • **to be p. to** estar enterado de, tener conocimiento privilegiado de **II.** s. [pl. **-ies**] *(latrine)* excusado, retrete rústico; DER. interesado.

Privy Council s. G.B. consejo del rey.

prize¹ (prīz) **I.** s. *(award)* premio; FIG. *(treasure)* premio, recompensa ♦ **cash p.** premio en metálico **II.** adj. *(given as a prize)* de premio; *(given a prize)* premiado <*a p. cow* una vaca premiada>; *(outstanding)* de primera categoría ♦ **p. idiot** tonto de remate **III.** tr. *prized, priz·ing* valorar, apreciar.

prize² (prīz) s. MARÍT. *(ship)* presa; *(capture)* presa, captura.

prize³ (prīz) **I.** tr. *prized, priz·ing* ♦ **to p. open** *o* **up** abrir *o* levantar con una palanca **II.** s. *(leverage)* apalancamiento; *(lever)* palanca.

prize·fight (prīz'fīt') s. DEP. pelea *o* combate profesional de boxeo *m*.

prize·fight·er (prīz'fī'tər) s. boxeador profesional *m*.

prize winner s. ganador de un premio *m*.

pro¹ (prō) **I.** s. [pl. **pros**] ♦ **the pros and cons** el pro y el contra **II.** adv. a favor **III.** prep. a favor de **IV.** adj. partidario.

pro² (prō) FAM. **I.** s. [pl. **pros**] *(professional)* profesional *mf,* experto; *(in sports)* profesional **II.** adj. DEP. profesional <*p. football* fútbol profesional>.

prob·a·bil·i·ty (prŏb'ə-bĭl'ĭ-tē) s. [pl. **-ties**] probabilidad *f.*

prob·a·ble (prŏb'ə-bəl) adj. *(likely)* probable; *(plausible)* verosímil.

probable cause s. DER. motivo presunto.

prob·a·bly (prŏb'ə-blē) adv. *(most likely)* probablemente; *(presumably)* presuntamente.

pro·bate (prō'bāt') DER. **I.** s. validación legal *f,* legalización (de un testamento) *f* **II.** tr. **-bat·ed, -bat·ing** validar legalmente, legalizar.

probate court s. DER. tribunal sucesorio.

pro·ba·tion (prō-bā'shən) s. *(period)* período de prueba; DER. *(freedom)* libertad condicional *f* ♦ **p. officer** DER. encargado de la vigilancia de los que están en libertad condicional • **to be on p.** *(on trial)* estar a prueba; DER. *(free)* estar en libertad condicional.

pro·ba·tion·er (prō-bā'shə-nər) s. *(person on probation)* persona a prueba; DER. *(delinquent)* delincuente en libertad condicional *mf.*

pro·ba·tive (prō'bə-tĭv) *o* **pro·ba·to·ry** (-tôr'ē) adj. probatorio.

probe (prōb) **I.** s. ASTRON., MED. *(device)* sonda; *(exploration)* sondeo; *(investigation)* investigación *f* **II.** tr. **probed, prob·ing** *(to explore)* sondar; *(to investigate)* investigar, indagar —intr. indagar ♦ **to p. for** sondear, sondar • **to p. into** *(to explore)* explorar; *(to investigate)* investigar.

pro·bi·ty (prō'bĭ-tē) s. probidad *f.*

prob·lem (prŏb'ləm) **I.** s. problema *m* **II.** adj. difícil <*a p. child* un niño difícil>.

prob·lem·at·i·cal (prŏb'lə-măt'ĭ-kəl) *o* **prob·lem·at·ic** (-ĭk) adj. *(difficult)* problemático; *(doubtful)* dudoso.

pro·bos·cis (prō-bŏs'ĭs) s. [pl. **-cis·es** *o* **-ci·des** (-ĭ-dēz')] ZOOL. trompa; ENTOM. probóscide *f*; *(human nose)* trompa, nariz *f.*

pro·ce·dur·al (prə-sē'jər-əl) adj. DER. de procedimiento.

pro·ce·dure (prə-sē'jər) s. procedimiento.

pro·ceed (prə-sēd') intr. *(to act)* proceder, actuar <*how should I p.?* ¿cómo he de actuar?>; *(to continue)* proseguir, continuar <*please p.* continúe, por favor>; *(to go forward)* avanzar <*p. with caution* avancen con cuidado>; *(to move along)* ir, desarrollar <*a project that is proceeding well* un proyecto que va bien>; *(to carry on)* proceder <*to p. to eat one's breakfast* proceder a tomar el desayuno> ♦ **to p. against** DER. proceder contra • **to p. from** proceder de, provenir de • **to p. with** seguir con, proseguir.

pro·ceed·ing (prə-sē'dĭng) s. procedimiento, acción *f* ♦ **proceedings** *(sequence of events)* curso de la acción, acontecimientos; *(minutes)* actas; DER. proceso.

pro·ceeds (prō'sēdz') s.pl. ganancias, beneficios.

proc·ess (prŏs'ĕs', prō'sĕs') **I.** s. *(treatment)* procedimiento <*the manufacturing p.* el procedimiento de fabricación>; *(method)* proceso <*the learning p.* el proceso de aprender>; DER. *(summons)* citación *f*; *(of writs, proceedings)* proceso; BIOL. apéndice *m,* protuberancia; IMPR. fotograbado ♦ **in p.** en marcha, en curso • **in the p.** al hacerlo, en el curso de ello • **to be in (the) p. of** estar en vías de, estar <*the lake is in the p. of drying up* el lago se está secando> **II.** tr. *(an application)* tramitar; *(to treat)* tratar; *(to convert)* transformar <*to p. crude oil into plastic* transformar petróleo crudo en plástico>; FOTOG. revelar; COMPUT. procesar; DER. procesar.

proc·ess·ing (prŏs'ĕs'ĭng, prō'sĕs'-) s. *(of food)* tratamiento; *(of raw materials)* transformación *f*; FOTOG. revelado; COMPUT. procesamiento ♦ **data p.** COMPUT. procesamiento de datos; *(science)* informática.

pro·ces·sion (prə-sĕsh'ən) **I.** s. *(parade)* procesión *f,* desfile *m*; *(orderly course)* progresión *f,* sucesión *f* **II.** intr. ir en procesión, desfilar.

pro·ces·sion·al (prə-sĕsh'ə-nəl) **I.** adj. procesional **II.** s. *(book)* procesionario; *(hymn)* himno procesionario.

pro·claim (prō-klām') tr. *(to declare)* proclamar; *(to extol)* elogiar, alabar.

proc·la·ma·tion (prŏk'lə-mā'shən) s. *(act)* proclamación *f*; *(announcement)* proclama, bando.

pro·cliv·i·ty (prō-klĭv'ĭ-tē) s. [pl. **-ties**] propensión *f,* inclinación *f.*

pro·con·sul (prō-kŏn'səl) s. HIST. *(Roman governor)* procónsul *m*; *(of colonial empires)* gobernador *m.*

pro·cras·ti·nate (prō-krăs'tə-nāt') **-nat·ed, -nat·ing** no decidirse, aplazar una decisión —tr. aplazar, postergar.

pro·cras·ti·na·tion (prō-krăs'tə-nā'shən) s. dilación *f,* retraso.

pro·cras·ti·na·tor (prō-krăs'tə-nā'tər) s. persona dada a la postergación.

pro·cre·ate (prō'krē-āt') tr. & intr. **-at·ed, -at·ing** procrear.

pro·cre·a·tion (prō'krē-ā'shən) s. procreación *f.*

pro·cre·a·tive (prō'krē-ā'tĭv) adj. procreador.

proc·tol·o·gy (prŏk-tŏl'ə-jē) s. MED. proctología.

proc·tor (prŏk'tər) **I.** s. vigilante *mf* **II.** tr. vigilar.

pro·cum·bent (prō-kŭm'bənt) adj. BOT. procumbente; *(prone)* boca abajo.

proc·u·ra·tor (prŏk'yə-rā'tər) s. DER. procurador *m.*

pro·cure (prō-kyoor') tr. **-cured, -cur·ing** *(to obtain)* obtener, lograr adquirir; *(a woman)* alcahuetear —intr. dedicarse al proxenetismo.

pro·cure·ment (prō-kyoor'mənt) s. obtención *f,* logro.

pro·cur·er (prō-kyoor'ər) s. alcahuete *m.*

prod (prŏd) **I.** tr. **prod·ded, prod·ding** *(to jab)* pinchar, punzar; *(to goad)* estimular, avivar **II.** s. *(goad)* aguijón *m*; *(stimulus)* estímulo, acicate *m.*

prod·i·gal (prŏd'ĭ-gəl) adj. & s. pródigo.

pro·di·gious (prə-dĭj'əs) adj. *(enormous)* enorme; *(marvelous)* maravilloso, prodigioso; *(portentous)* portentoso.

prod·i·gy (prŏd'ə-jē) s. [pl. **-gies**] prodigio.

pro·duce **I.** tr. (prə-dōōs', -dyōōs') **-duced, -duc·ing** *(to yield)* producir; *(to manufacture)* fabricar, hacer; *(to give rise to)* causar, ocasionar; *(to show)* exhibir, mostrar; *(to remove)* sacar; TEAT. presentar al público, poner en escena; CINEM., TELEV. producir; MAT. *(area, volume)* ampliar; *(line)* prolongar —intr. producir **II.** s. (prŏd'ōōs, prō'dōōs) producto.

pro·duc·er (prə-dōō'sər, -dyōō'-) s. *(manufacturer)* productor *m,* fabricante *m*; TEAT. director de escena *m*; CINEM. productor; *(furnace)* horno gasógeno.

producer goods s.pl. ECON. elementos de producción.

pro·duc·i·ble (prə-dōō'sə-bəl, -dyōō'-) adj. producible.

prod·uct (prŏd'əkt) s. *(something produced)* producto; *(result)* producto, resultado; MAT., QUÍM. producto ♦ **gross national p.** producto nacional bruto.

pro·duc·tion (prə-dŭk'shən) s. *(act)* producción *f*; *(product)* producto; *(output)* rendimiento; TEAT. *(performance)* representación *f*; CINEM. producción.

pro·duc·tive (prə-dŭk'tĭv) adj. *(producing)* productivo; *(fertile)* fértil; *(constructive)* constructivo.

pro·duc·tiv·i·ty (prō'dŭk-tĭv'ĭ-tē, prŏd'ək-) s. productividad *f.*

pro·em (prō'ĕm') s. proemio.

prof (prŏf) s. FAM. profe *m,* profesor *m.*

prof·a·na·tion (prŏf'ə-nā'shən) s. profanación *f.*

pro·fane (prə-fān') **I.** adj. *(blasphemous)* blasfemo, profano; *(secular)* secular, profano <*sacred and p. music* música religiosa y profana>; *(not initiated)* profano; *(vulgar)* vulgar, soez **II.** tr. **-faned, -fan·ing** profanar.

pro·fan·i·ty (prə-făn'ĭ-tē) s. [pl. **-ties**] *(condition)* profanidad *f*; *(vulgar language)* lenguaje obsceno *o* blasfemo.

pro·fess (prə-fĕs') tr. *(to affirm)* declarar, proclamar; *(to pretend)* pretender <*he professes to be an expert* pretende ser un experto>; RELIG. profesar ♦ **to p. one's innocence** declararse inocente —intr. RELIG. profesar.

pro·fessed (prə-fĕst') adj. *(declared)* declarado <*a p. enemy* un enemigo declarado>; *(pretended)* supuesto, fingido; RELIG. profeso.

pro·fes·sion (prə-fĕsh'ən) s. *(occupation)* profesión *f*; *(body of professionals)* profesión; *(avowal)* profesión, declaración *f* ♦ **by p.** de profesión <*a writer by p.* escritor de profesión>.

pro·fes·sion·al (prə-fĕsh'ə-nəl) I. adj. *(of a profession)* profesional; *(expert)* perito, experto II. s. *(doctor, athlete)* profesional *mf*; *(expert)* perito, experto.

pro·fes·sion·al·ism (prə-fĕsh'ə-nə-lĭz'əm) s. profesionalismo.

pro·fes·sion·al·ly (prə-fĕsh'ə-nə-lē) adv. *(in a professional manner)* de modo profesional; *(expertly)* con pericia, expertamente ♦ **to play p.** DEP. ser un jugador profesional.

pro·fes·sor (prə-fĕs'ər) s. *(teacher)* profesor *m*; *(university professor)* catedrático.

pro·fes·so·ri·al (prō'fĭ-sôr'ē-əl, prŏf'ĭ-) adj. profesoral.

pro·fes·sor·ship (prə-fĕs'ər-shĭp') s. profesorado, cátedra.

prof·fer (prŏf'ər) I. tr. ofrecer, proponer II. s. oferta, propuesta.

pro·fi·cien·cy (prə-fĭsh'ən-sē) s. [pl. **-cies**] competencia, capacidad *f*.

pro·fi·cient (prə-fĭsh'ənt) I. adj. capaz, competente II. s. experto.

pro·file (prō'fīl') I. s. *(facial)* perfil *m*; *(outline)* perfil, silueta; *(biography)* retrato, reseña biográfica; *(description)* descripción *f* ♦ **in p.** de perfil • **to keep a low p.** no llamar la atención, hacerse pasar desapercibido II. tr. **-filed, -fil·ing** perfilar.

prof·it (prŏf'ĭt) I. s. *(benefit)* beneficio, provecho; COM. beneficio, ganancia ♦ **net p.** COM. beneficio neto, ganancia neta • **profits** COM. *(from investments)* rentas; *(gains)* ganancias, utilidades • **to make a p.** COM. *(person)* sacar *o* ganar dinero; *(business)* rendir ganancias, dar dinero • **to sell at a p.** COM. vender con ganancia • **to show a p.** COM. ganar dinero • **to turn something to p.** sacar provecho de algo II. intr. servir <*it profits little to complain* de poco sirve quejarse> • **to p. by** *o* **from** COM. sacar dinero de; *(to enefit from)* sacar provecho de.

prof·it·a·bil·i·ty (prŏf'ĭ-tə-bĭl'ĭ-tē) s. COM. carácter lucrativo, rentabilidad *f*.

prof·it·a·ble (prŏf'ĭ-tə-bəl) adj. *(beneficial)* beneficioso, provechoso <*a p. meeting* una reunión provechosa>; COM. lucrativo, rentable.

prof·it·a·bly (prŏf'ĭ-tə-blē) adv. *(beneficially)* provechosamente, con provecho; COM. lucrativamente, productivamente.

profit and loss s. ganancias y pérdidas.

prof·i·teer (prŏf'ĭ-tîr') I. s. logrero, aprovechón *m* II. intr. aprovecharse.

prof·it·less (prŏf'ĭt-lĭs) adj. *(without benefit)* sin provecho, inútil; COM. que no rinde utilidades, improductivo.

profit sharing s. participación en los beneficios *f*.

prof·li·ga·cy (prŏf'lĭ-gə-sē) s. *(dissoluteness)* libertinaje *m*; *(lavishness)* prodigalidad *f*.

prof·li·gate (prŏf'lĭ-gĭt) I. adj. *(dissolute)* libertino, disoluto; *(wasteful)* derrochador, despilfarrador II. s. manirroto, pródigo.

pro for·ma (prō fôr'mə) adj. pro forma, por la forma.

pro·found (prə-found') adj. **-er, -est** profundo.

pro·fun·di·ty (prə-fŭn'dĭ-tē) s. [pl. **-ties**] profundidad *f*.

pro·fuse (prə-fyōōs') adj. *(copious)* profuso, copioso; *(extravagant)* pródigo <*p. in his compliments* pródigo en sus cumplidos>.

pro·fu·sion (prə-fyōō'zhən) s. *(abundance)* profusión *f*, abundancia; *(extravagance)* prodigalidad *f*, liberalidad *f*.

pro·gen·i·tor (prō-jĕn'ĭ-tər) s. *(ancestor)* antepasado; *(parent)* progenitor *m*.

prog·e·ny (prŏj'ə-nē) s. [pl. **-nies**] *(offspring)* progenie *m*, prole *f*; *(product)* producto, resultado.

pro·ges·ter·one (prō-jĕs'tə-rōn') s. BIOQUÍM. progesterona.

prog·no·sis (prŏg-nō'sĭs) s. [pl. **-ses** (-sēz')] pronóstico.

prog·nos·tic (prŏg-nŏs'tĭk) I. adj. *(of a prognosis)* pronosticador; *(foretelling)* adivinatorio II. s. *(omen)* augurio, presagio; MED. pronóstico.

prog·nos·ti·cate (prŏg-nŏs'tĭ-kāt') tr. **-cat·ed, -cat·ing** *(to predict)* predecir, profetizar; *(to portend)* pronosticar.

prog·nos·ti·ca·tion (prŏg-nŏs'tĭ-kā'shən) s. *(act)* pronosticación *f*; *(forecast)* pronóstico; *(omen)* augurio, presagio; *(foreboding)* presentimiento.

pro·gram (prō'grăm', -grəm) I. s. programa *m* II. tr. programar.

pro·gramme (prō'grăm', -grəm) s. & v. G.B. var. de **program**.

pro·gram·mer *o* **pro·gram·er** (prō'grăm'ər, -grə-mər) s. COMPUT., EDUC. programador *m*.

pro·gram·ming *o* **pro·gram·ing** (prō'grăm'ĭng, -grə-mĭng) s. programación *f*.

prog·ress I. s. (prŏg'rĕs, prō'grĕs') *(advance)* progreso, avance *m*; *(development)* desarrollo; *(of events)* marcha, curso; *(improvement)* progreso, adelanto <*a supporter of p.* un partidario del progreso> ♦ **p. report** *(of a task)* informe sobre el estado del trabajo; *(on a patient)* informe sobre el estado del paciente • **to be in p.** estar en curso • **to make p.** *(to advance)* progresar, hacer progresos <*he made no p.* no progresó nada>; *(to improve)* mejorar II. intr. (prə-grĕs') **pro·gress** *(to advance)* progresar, avanzar; *(to improve)* mejorar.

pro·gres·sion (prə-grĕsh'ən) s. *(movement)* progreso, avance *m*; *(improvement)* progreso, adelanto; MAT., MÚS. progresión *f*.

pro·gres·sive (prə-grĕs'ĭv) I. adj. *(advancing)* progresivo <*a p. decline* una decadencia progresiva>; POL. progresista; GRAM., MED. progresivo II. s. POL. progresista *mf*.

pro·gres·sive·ly (prə-grĕs'ĭv-lē) adv. *(gradually)* progresivamente, cada vez más <*to get p. worse* empeorar cada vez más>; POL. de modo progresista.

pro·hib·it (prō-hĭb'ĭt) tr. *(to forbid)* prohibir; *(to prevent)* impedir.

pro·hi·bi·tion (prō'ə-bĭsh'ən) s. prohibición *f* ♦ **P.** EE. UU. el período durante el cual estaban prohibidas las bebidas alcohólicas.

pro·hi·bi·tion·ist (prō'ə-bĭsh'ə-nĭst) s. prohibicionista *mf* ♦ **P.** miembro del partido prohibicionista.

pro·hib·i·tive (prō-hĭb'ĭ-tĭv) *o* **pro·hib·i·to·ry** (-tôr'ē) adj. prohibitivo.

proj·ect I. s. (prŏj'ĕkt') proyecto II. tr. (prə-jĕkt') **pro·ject** *(to protrude)* hacer sobresalir, sacar; *(missile, image)* proyectar; *(to convey)* sugerir <*to p. a romantic mood* sugerir un ambiente romántico>; *(feelings)* atribuir; *(to plan)* proyectar, planear; *(to predict)* hacer un cálculo *o* pronóstico de; MAT. proyectar ♦ **to p. oneself** into imaginarse en —intr. *(to protrude)* sobresalir, salir; *(to speak)* hablar claramente.

pro·jec·tile (prə-jĕk'təl, -tĭl') I. s. proyectil *m* II. adj. arrojadizo <*p. weapons* armas arrojadizas>; *(impelling)* proyectante, impelente.

pro·jec·tion (prə-jĕk'shən) s. *(of missile, image)* proyección *f*; *(of a mood)* sugestión *f*; *(protuberance)* saliente *m*, punta; *(plan)* proyecto, plan *m*; *(estimate)* cálculo, pronóstico <*a sales p.* un pronóstico de las ventas>; *(of feelings)* atribución *f*; CART., GEOM. proyección.

pro·jec·tion·ist (prə-jĕk'shə-nĭst) s. operador de cine que proyecta las películas *m*.

pro·jec·tor (prə-jĕk'tər) s. CINEM., ÓPT. proyector *m*; *(planner)* proyectista *mf*.

pro·le·tar·i·an (prō'lĭ-târ'ē-ən) adj. & s. proletario.

pro·le·tar·i·at (prō'lĭ-târ'ē-ĭt) s. proletariado.

pro·lif·er·ate (prə-lĭf'ə-rāt') intr. **-at·ed, -at·ing** proliferar, multiplicarse —tr. hacer crecer *o* aumentar.

pro·lif·er·a·tion (prə-lĭf'ə-rā'shən) s. proliferación *f*.

pro·lif·ic (prə-lĭf'ĭk) adj. prolífico.

pro·lix (prō-lĭks') adj. prolijo, verboso.

pro·logue *o* **pro·log** (prō'lôg') s. prólogo, introducción *f*.

pro·long (prə-lông') tr. prolongar, extender.

pro·lon·gate (prə-lông'gāt') tr. **-gat·ed, -gat·ing** prolongar.

pro·lon·ga·tion (prō'lông-gā'shən) s. prolongación *f*.

prom (prŏm) s. baile de gala organizado por los estudiantes de un colegio *o* universidad (en EE. UU.).

prom·e·nade (prŏm'ə-nād', -näd') I. s. *(stroll)* paseo, vuelta; *(path)* paseo, alameda; *(dance step)* paseo; *(ball)* baile de etiqueta *m* ♦ **p. deck** MARÍT. cubierta de paseo II. intr. **-nad·ed, -nad·ing** pasearse —tr. pasear.

pro·me·thi·um (prə-mē'thē-əm) s. QUÍM. prometio.

prom·i·nence (prŏm'ə-nəns) *o* **prom·i·nen·cy** (-nən-sē) s. *(condition, quality)* prominencia; *(importance)* importancia; ASTRON. protuberancia (solar).

prom·i·nent (prŏm'ə-nənt) adj. *(protuberant)* prominente; *(conspicuous)* conspicuo; *(eminent)* eminente, notable.

prom·is·cu·i·ty (prŏm'ĭ-skyōō'ĭ-tē, prō'mĭ-) s. [pl. **-ties**] promiscuidad *f.*

pro·mis·cu·ous (prə-mĭs'kyōō-əs) adj. *(indiscriminate)* promiscuo, mezclado; *(in sexual relations)* libertino, licencioso; *(casual)* casual, fortuito.

prom·ise (prŏm'ĭs) I. s. promesa ♦ **to break one's p.** faltar a su palabra • **to keep one's p.** cumplir su promesa • **to show p.** ser prometedor II. tr. **-ised, -is·ing** prometer —intr. hacer una promesa.

Promised Land s. BÍBL. Tierra de Promisión ♦ **p. l.** FIG. tierra de promisión.

prom·is·ing (prŏm'ĭ-sĭng) adj. prometedor, que promete.

prom·i·sor (prŏm'ĭ-sôr') s. DER. prometedor *m.*

prom·is·so·ry (prŏm'ĭ-sôr'ē) adj. promisorio.

promissory note s. pagaré *m.*

prom·on·to·ry (prŏm'ən-tôr'ē) s. [pl. **-ties**] GEOG. promontorio; ANAT. protuberancia, promontorio.

pro·mot·a·ble (prə-mō'tə-bəl) adj. digno de promoción.

pro·mote (prə-mōt') tr. **-mot·ed, -mot·ing** *(employee, officer)* ascender; *(student)* adelantar o pasar de año; *(to further)* promover, fomentar; *(to advocate)* apoyar, defender; *(to advertise)* promocionar (un producto); *(to finance)* financiar.

pro·mot·er (prə-mō'tər) s. promotor *m.*

pro·mo·tion (prə-mō'shən) s. *(act, advancement)* ascenso; *(furtherance)* fomento.

prompt (prŏmpt) I. adj. **-er, -est** *(punctual)* puntual; *(without delay)* pronto, rápido II. tr. *(to incite)* incitar, impulsar; *(to inspire)* inspirar, sugerir; TEAT. apuntar III. s. *(reminder)* aviso; *(cue)* apunte *m;* COM. plazo límite.

prompt·er (prŏmp'tər) s. *(one who prompts)* incitador *m,* instigador *m;* TEAT. apuntador *m.*

prompt·ly (prŏmpt'lē) adv. *(without delay)* prontamente; *(on time)* puntualmente.

prompt·ness (prŏmpt'nĭs) s. prontitud *f.*

prom·ul·gate (prŏm'əl-gāt', prō'məl-) tr. **-gat·ed, -gat·ing** DER. *(a law)* promulgar; *(to make known)* difundir.

prom·ul·ga·tion (prŏm'əl-gā'shən, prō'məl-) s. promulgación *f.*

prom·ul·ga·tor (prŏm'əl-gā'tər, prō'məl-) s. promulgador *m.*

prone (prōn) adj. & adv. prono, boca abajo ♦ **to be p.** to ser propenso a.

prong (prông) I. s. *(pointed part)* púa, punta; *(of a fork)* diente *m;* *(in mechanics)* uña, diente II. tr. pinchar.

pronged (prôngd) adj. dentado, provisto de púas.

prong·horn (prông'hôrn') s. [pl. **pronghorn** o **-horns**] ZOOL. ciervo norteamericano.

pro·nom·i·nal (prō-nŏm'ə-nəl) adj. GRAM. pronominal.

pro·noun (prō'noun') s. GRAM. pronombre *m.*

pro·nounce (prə-nouns') tr. **-nounced, -nounc·ing** *(to articulate)* pronunciar; *(to say)* pronunciarse <how do you p. your name? ¿cómo se pronuncia su nombre?>; *(to declare)* declarar; DER. pronunciar (sentencia) ♦ **to p. oneself** pronunciarse —intr. pronunciarse.

pro·nounced (prə-nounst') adj. pronunciado, marcado.

pro·nounce·ment (prə-nouns'mənt) s. declaración *f.*

pro·nounc·ing (prə-noun'sĭng) adj. fonético <a p. dictionary diccionario fonético>.

pro·nun·ci·a·tion (prə-nŭn'sē-ā'shən) s. *(act)* pronunciación *f;* FONÉT. transcripción fonética (de una palabra).

proof (prōōf) I. s. *(evidence)* prueba, pruebas; *(test)* prueba <to put one's beliefs to the p. poner a prueba las convicciones de uno>; *(alcoholic content)* grado; DER. prueba; FOTOG., IMPR., MAT. prueba ♦ **in p. of** en prueba de • **p. positive** prueba concluyente • **to show** o **to give p. of** dar prueba de II. tr. *(to run off)* tirar una prueba; *(to proofread)* corregir las pruebas de; *(to make resistant to)* hacer resistente a; *(to request proof of age)* pedir que alguien dé prueba de mayoría de edad —intr. IMPR. corregir pruebas.

proof·read (prōōf'rēd') tr. **-read** (-rĕd'), **-read·ing** IMPR. corregir —intr. corregir pruebas.

proof·read·er (prōōf'rē'dər) s. IMPR. corrector de pruebas o galeradas *m.*

prop¹ (prŏp) I. s. *(rigid support)* puntal *m;* FIG. *(support)* apoyo, sostén *m;* AGR. horca, rodrigón *m;* MIN. entibo; MARÍT. escora II. tr. **propped, prop·ping** ♦ **to p. up** *(to support)* apuntalar, entibar; FIG. *(prices)* mantener • **to p. open** mantener abierto.

prop² (prŏp) s. TEAT. accesorio.

prop³ (prŏp) s. FAM. hélice *f.*

prop·a·gan·da (prŏp'ə-găn'də) s. propaganda.

prop·a·gan·dist (prŏp'ə-găn'dĭst) s. propagandista *mf.*

prop·a·gan·dis·tic (prŏp'ə-găn-dĭs'tĭk) adj. propagandístico.

prop·a·gan·dize (prŏp'ə-găn'dīz') tr. **-dized, -diz·ing** *(to promote)* hacer propaganda de; *(to indoctrinate)* exponer a la propaganda. —intr. hacer propaganda.

prop·a·gate (prŏp'ə-gāt') tr. & intr. **-gat·ed, -gat·ing** propagar(se).

prop·a·ga·tion (prŏp'ə-gā'shən) s. propagación *f.*

pro·pane (prō'pān') s. QUÍM. propano.

pro·pel (prə-pĕl') tr. **-pelled, -pel·ling** propulsar, impeler.

pro·pel·lant o **pro·pel·lent** (prə-pĕl'ənt) I. s. ARM. carga de proyección; AER. propulsante *m* II. adj. propulsor, impelente.

pro·pel·ler o **pro·pel·lor** (prə-pĕl'ər) s. hélice *f.*

pro·pen·si·ty (prə-pĕn'sĭ-tē) s. [pl. **-ties**] propensión *f.*

prop·er (prŏp'ər) I. adj. *(appropriate)* apropiado; *(right)* debido, oportuno <at the p. time a su debido tiempo>; *(itself)* propio, mismo <in the city p. en la ciudad misma>; *(exact)* exacto <the p. term el término exacto>; *(correct)* correcto, indicado <the p. procedure el procedimiento correcto>; *(characteristic)* propio, característico <an effect p. to fluids un efecto propio de los fluidos>; *(seemly)* correcto; GRAM., MAT. propio ♦ **to be p. for someone to** corresponderle a alguien (hacer algo) • **to do the p. thing** o **what is p.** hacer lo que es debido o correcto • **to say the p. thing** decir lo más correcto o indicado II. adv. ♦ **good and p.** FAM. como es debido.

prop·er·ly (prŏp'ər-lē) adv. *(appropriately)* apropiadamente; *(strictly)* propiamente <p. speaking propiamente dicho>; *(correctly)* correctamente, bien <you should use it p. debes usarlo correctamente>; *(in a seemly way)* correctamente, como es debido <p. dressed correctamente vestido>.

prop·er noun s. nombre propio.

prop·er·ty (prŏp'ər-tē) s. [pl. **-ties**] propiedad *f;* *(possessions)* bienes *m;* TEAT. *(article)* accesorio ♦ **man of p.** hombre rico • **personal p.** bienes muebles • **that's our p.** eso es de nuestra propiedad, eso es nuestro • **to be common p.** ser del dominio público.

property tax s. impuesto sobre la propiedad, contribución territorial *f.*

proph·e·cy (prŏf'ĭ-sē) s. [pl. **-cies**] profecía.

proph·e·sy (prŏf'ĭ-sī') tr. & intr. **-sied, -sy·ing** *(to predict)* predecir; *(divinely)* profetizar.

proph·et (prŏf'ĭt) s. profeta *m.*

proph·et·ess (prŏf'ĭ-tĭs) s. profetisa.

pro·phet·ic (prə-fĕt'ĭk) o **pro·phet·i·cal** (-ĭ-kəl) adj. profético.

pro·phy·lac·tic (prō'fə-lăk'tĭk, prŏf'ə-) adj. & s. profiláctico.

pro·phy·lax·is (prō'fə-lăk'sĭs, prŏf'ə-) s. [pl. **-lax·es** (-lăk'sēz')] MED. profilaxis *f.*

pro·pin·qui·ty (prə-pĭng'kwĭ-tē) s. *(proximity)* proximidad *f,* cercanía; *(kinship)* parentesco; *(similarity)* semejanza.

pro·pi·ti·ate (prə-pĭsh'ē-āt') tr. **-at·ed, -at·ing** aplacar, propiciar.

pro·pi·ti·a·tion (prə-pĭsh'ē-ā'shən) s. *(act)* apaciguamiento, aplacamiento; RELIG. sacrificio propiciatorio.

pro·pi·ti·a·to·ry (prə-pĭsh'ē-ə-tôr'ē) adj. propiciatorio.

pro·pi·tious (prə-pĭsh'əs) adj. *(auspicious)* propicio, favorable; *(kindly)* bueno, bondadoso.

pro·po·nent (prə-pō'nənt) s. proponente *mf.*

pro·por·tion (prə-pôr'shən) I. s. *(relation)* proporción *f;* *(part)* parte *f,* porción *f* <a large p. of the profits una gran parte de las ganancias>; *(balance)* proporción, armonía; MAT. proporción ♦ **proportions** dimensiones, tamaño • **in**

p. proporcionado • **out of p.** desproporcionado **II.** tr. proporcionar.

pro·por·tion·al (prə-pôr′shə-nəl) adj. *(relative)* proporcional; MAT. proporcional ♦ **p. to** proporcional a, en proporción con.

proportional representation s. POL. representación proporcional *f.*

pro·por·tion·ate I. adj. (prə-pôr′shə-nĭt) proporcional, en proporción *<to be p. to* ser proporcional a> **II.** tr. (-nāt′) **-at·ed, -at·ing** proporcionar.

pro·pos·al (prə-pō′zəl) s. *(act)* propuesta, proposición *f*; *(of marriage)* propuesta de matrimonio o matrimonial.

pro·pose (prə-pōz′) tr. **-posed, -pos·ing** *(to suggest)* sugerir, proponer; *(to nominate)* nombrar, proponer; *(a toast)* brindar, proponer un brindis; *(to intend)* tener intención de, tener el propósito de —intr. *(to make a proposal)* proponerse; *(marriage)* ofrecer matrimonio.

prop·o·si·tion (prŏp′ə-zĭsh′ən) **I.** s. *(plan)* proposición *f*, plan *m*; FAM. *(matter)* asunto, problema *m <that is a tough p.* ése es un problema difícil de resolver>; *(immoral proposal)* proposición deshonesta; LÓG. proposición **II.** tr. FAM. hacer una propuesta deshonesta (a una mujer).

pro·pound (prə-pound′) tr. proponer, plantear.

pro·pri·e·tar·y (prə-prī′ĭ-tĕr′ē) **I.** adj. *(of an owner)* propietario; *(patented)* patentado **II.** s. [pl. **-ies**] *(owner)* propietario, dueño; *(ownership)* propiedad *f*; *(medicine)* remedio patentado.

pro·pri·e·tor (prə-prī′ĭ-tər) s. propietario, dueño.

pro·pri·e·tor·ship (prə-prī′ĭ-tər-shĭp′) s. propiedad *f*, derecho de propiedad.

pro·pri·e·tress (prə-prī′ĭ-trĭs) s. propietaria, dueña.

pro·pri·e·ty (prə-prī′ĭ-tē) s. [pl. **-ties**] *(appropriateness)* conveniencia; *(decency)* decencia ♦ **proprieties** convenciones.

pro·pul·sion (prə-pŭl′shən) s. propulsión *f.*

pro·pyl (prō′pĭl) s. QUÍM. propilo.

pro·pyl·ene (prō′pə-lēn′) s. QUÍM. propileno.

pro ra·ta (prō rā′tə, rät′ə) adv. a prorrata, en proporción.

pro·rate (prō-rāt′) tr. **-rat·ed, -rat·ing** prorratear.

pro·sa·ic (prō-zā′ĭk) adj. prosaico.

pro·sce·ni·um (prō-sē′nē-əm) s. TEAT. proscenio.

pro·scribe (prō-skrīb′) tr. **-scribed, -scrib·ing** proscribir.

pro·scrib·er (prō-skrī′bər) s. proscriptor *m.*

pro·scrip·tion (prō-skrĭp′shən) s. proscripción *f.*

prose (prōz) **I.** s. prosa **II.** adj. en prosa′ *<p. works* obras en prosa>.

pros·e·cute (prŏs′ĭ-kyōōt′) tr. **-cut·ed, -cut·ing** *(to wage)* proseguir, continuar; DER. *(a person)* procesar; *(claim, case)* entablar —intr. entablar una acción judicial.

prosecuting attorney s. DER. acusador público, fiscal *mf.*

pros·e·cu·tion (prŏs′ĭ-kyōō′shən) s. DER. *(act)* procesamiento, enjuiciamiento; *(trial)* proceso, juicio; *(prosecuting attorney)* acusador público, fiscal *mf.*

pros·e·cu·tor (prŏs′ĭ-kyōō′tər) s. DER. *(plaintiff)* demandante *mf*, querellante *mf*; *(lawyer)* acusador *m*; *(prosecuting attorney)* acusador público, fiscal *mf.*

pros·e·lyte (prŏs′ə-līt′) **I.** s. prosélito **II.** tr. **-lyt·ed, -lyt·ing** convertir —intr. ganar prosélitos.

pros·e·ly·tism (prŏs′ə-lĭ-tĭz′əm) s. proselitismo.

pros·e·ly·tize (prŏs′ə-lĭ-tīz′) intr. **-tized, -tiz·ing** ganar prosélitos —tr. convertir.

pros·o·dy (prŏs′ə-dē) s. *(study)* métrica; *(system)* prosodia.

pros·pect (prŏs′pĕkt′) **I.** s. *(outlook)* perspectiva; *(expectation)* esperanza, expectativa; COM. *(customer)* cliente probable *m*; *(candidate)* candidato probable; *(exposure)* orientación *f*; *(view)* vista ♦ **prospects** perspectivas, probabilidades • **to have prospects** tener porvenir **II.** tr. prospectar —intr. hacer una prospección ♦ **to p. for** buscar.

pro·spec·tive (prə-spĕk′tĭv) adj. *(expected)* esperado, futuro; *(likely to be)* presunto, probable *<a p. client* un cliente presunto>.

pros·pec·tor (prŏs′pĕk′tər) s. explorador *m*, buscador *m.*

pro·spec·tus (prə-spĕk′təs) s. prospecto, folleto.

pros·per (prŏs′pər) intr. prosperar, medrar —tr. favorecer, fomentar.

pros·per·i·ty (prō-spĕr′ĭ-tē) s. prosperidad *f.*

pros·per·ous (prŏs′pər-əs) adj. *(flourishing)* próspero; *(well-off)* acomodado, adinerado; *(favorable)* favorable, propicio.

pros·tate (prŏs′tāt′) s. ANAT. próstata.

pros·the·sis (prŏs-thē′sĭs) s. [pl. **-ses** (-sēz′)] MED. prótesis *f.*

pros·ti·tute (prŏs′tĭ-tōōt′, -tyōōt′) **I.** s. prostituta **II.** tr. **-tut·ed, -tut·ing** ♦ **to p. oneself** prostituirse.

pros·ti·tu·tion (prŏs′tĭ-tōō′shən, -tyōō′-) s. prostitución *f.*

pros·trate (prŏs′trāt′) **I.** tr. **-trat·ed, -trat·ing** postrar **II.** adj. *(lying down)* postrado; BOT. procumbente.

pros·tra·tion (prŏs-strā′shən) s. postración *f.*

pro·style (prō′stīl′) adj. ARQ. próstilo.

pros·y (prō′zē) adj. **-i·er, -i·est** *(everyday)* prosaico; *(dull)* aburrido.

pro·tac·tin·i·um (prō′tăk-tĭn′ē-əm) s. QUÍM. protactinio.

pro·tag·o·nist (prō-tăg′ə-nĭst) s. protagonista *mf.*

pro·te·an (prō′tē-ən, prō-tē′-) adj. proteico, versátil.

pro·tect (prə-tĕkt′) tr. *(to guard)* proteger; ECON. *(industry)* proteger, fomentar; FIN. *(to assure payment)* respaldar.

pro·tect·er (prə-tĕk′tər) s. protector *m.*

pro·tec·tion (prə-tĕk′shən) s. *(act, condition)* protección *f*; *(pass)* salvoconducto; ECON. protección; JER. *(money)* dinero pagado a o por una organización criminal.

pro·tec·tion·ism (prə-tĕk′shə-nĭz′əm) s. ECON. proteccionismo.

pro·tec·tion·ist (prə-tĕk′shə-nĭst) s. ECON. proteccionista *mf.*

pro·tec·tive (prə-tĕk′tĭv) adj. & s. protector *m.*

pro·tec·tor (prə-tĕk′tər) s. protector *m.*

pro·tec·tor·ate (prə-tĕk′tər-ĭt) s. protectorado *f.*

pro·té·gé (prō′tə-zhā′) s. protegido.

pro·tein (prō′tēn′) s. BIOQUÍM. proteína.

pro·test I. tr. (prə-tĕst′) *(to object to)* protestar contra; *(to affirm)* protestar de *<he protested his innocence* protestó de su inocencia>; COM., DER. protestar (una letra) —intr. protestar **II.** s. (prō′tĕst′) *(action)* protesta; *(statement)* protesto; *(objection)* protesta ♦ **under p.** contra su voluntad.

Prot·es·tant (prŏt′ĭ-stənt) s. & adj. RELIG. protestante *mf.*

Prot·es·tant·ism (prŏt′ĭ-stən-tĭz′əm) s. RELIG. protestantismo.

prot·es·ta·tion (prŏt′ĭ-stā′shən, prō′tĭ-) s. protesta.

pro·test·er (prə-tĕs′tər) s. persona que protesta.

pro·to·col (prō′tə-kôl′) **I.** s. protocolo **II.** intr. hacer un protocolo.

pro·to·mor·phic (prō′tə-môr′fĭk) adj. protomórfico.

pro·ton (prō′tŏn′) s. FÍS. protón *m.*

pro·to·plasm (prō′tə-plăz′əm) s. BIOL. protoplasma *m.*

pro·to·type (prō′tə-tīp′) s. prototipo.

pro·to·zo·an (prō′tə-zō′ən) s. ZOOL. protozoario, protozoo.

pro·tract (prō-trăkt′) tr. *(to prolong)* prolongar; *(to plot)* levantar, trazar (un plano); ANAT. empujar, sacar fuera.

pro·trac·tile (prō-trăk′təl, -tīl′) adj. protráctil.

pro·trac·tion (prō-trăk′shən) s. *(prolongation)* prolongación *f*; TOP. *(drawing)* trazado de plano.

pro·trac·tor (prō-trăk′tər) s. DIB., TOP. transportador *m*; ANAT. músculo extensor o tensor.

pro·trude (prō-trōōd′) tr. **-trud·ed, -trud·ing** sacar —intr. sobresalir, resaltar.

pro·tru·sion (prō-trōō′zhən) s. *(act)* acción de sacar *f*; *(state)* condición prominente *f*, prominencia; *(projection)* saliente *m.*

pro·tru·sive (prō-trōō′sĭv) adj. *(protruding)* sobresaliente, saliente; *(obtrusive)* intruso, entremetido.

pro·tu·ber·ance (prō-tōō′bər-əns, -tyōō′-) s. protuberancia, prominencia.

pro·tu·ber·ant (prō-tōō′bər-ənt, -tyōō′-) adj. protuberante, saliente.

proud (proud) **-er, -est** adj. *(of others)* orgulloso *<he is very p. of her success* está muy orgulloso de su éxito>; *(of oneself)* satisfecho, muy contento; *(dignified)* orgulloso *<too p. to beg* demasiado orgulloso para pedir limosna>; *(memorable)* memorable *<a p. moment* un momento memorable>; *(arrogant)* soberbio, altanero; *(honorable)* honorable, notable *<a p. name* un nombre honorable>;

ã **rey** / ä **año** / b **boca** / ch **chico** / d **dar** / ĕ **el** / ē **mil** / g **gato** / h **joya** / hw **juez** / ī **aire** / k **casa** / kw **cuan** /

(*magnificent*) grandioso, imponente; (*spirited*) animoso, brioso ♦ **to be p. to** tener el honor de.
proud·ly (proud'lē) adv. orgullosamente.
prove (prōōv) tr. **proved, proved** *o* **prov·en** (prōō'vən), **prov·ing** (*to establish*) probar, demostrar <*I proved him wrong* demostré que estaba equivocado>; (*to test*) poner a prueba; MAT. hacer la prueba, comprobar; DER. comprobar, verificar (un testamento); IMPR. sacar prueba de; ANT. (*to undergo*) experimentar —intr. salir, resultar <*it proved difficult* resultó difícil> ♦ **to p. out** FAM. tener éxito, conseguir su propósito.
prov·en (prōō'vən) I. adj. probado, comprobado II. un part. p. de **prove.**
prov·e·nance (prŏv'ə-nəns) s. origen *m*, procedencia.
Pro·ven·çal (prō'vən-säl', prŏv'ən-) adj. & s. provenzal *m*.
Pro·vence (prə-väNs') s. Provenza.
prov·en·der (prŏv'ən-dər) s. (*fodder*) forraje *m*; (*food*) comida.
prov·erb (prŏv'ûrb') s. refrán *m*, proverbio.
pro·ver·bi·al (prə-vûr'bē-əl) adj. proverbial.
Prov·erbs (prŏv'ûrbz') s. [ú. con v. sing.] BÍBL. Proverbios.
pro·vide (prə-vīd') tr. **-vid·ed, -vid·ing** (*to supply*) suministrar <*to p. with food* suministrar alimentos>; (*to make available*) proveer, proporcionar; (*to stipulate*) estipular, disponer —intr. proveer ♦ **to p. for** (*one's family*) mantener; (*something to come*) prever.
pro·vid·ed (that) (prə-vī'dĭd) conj. con tal que, a condición de que.
prov·i·dence (prŏv'ĭ-dəns) s. providencia ♦ **divine P.** la Providencia Divina, Dios.
prov·i·dent (prŏv'ĭ-dənt) adj. (*providing*) providente; (*economical*) económico.
prov·i·den·tial (prŏv'ĭ-dĕn'shəl) adj. providencial.
pro·vid·er (prə-vī'dər) s. proveedor *m*.
pro·vid·ing (prə-vī'dĭng) conj. ♦ **p. that** con tal que, a condición que.
prov·ince (prŏv'ĭns) s. (*territory*) provincia; (*field*) esfera, campo <*within the p. of history* en el campo de la historia>; (*jurisdiction*) competencia, incumbencia, RELIG. provincia ♦ **provinces** provincias.
pro·vin·cial (prə-vĭn'shəl) I. adj. (*of a province*) provincial; (*unsophisticated*) provinciano, rústico; (*narrow*) de miras estrechas II. s. provinciano.
pro·vin·cial·ism (prə-vĭn'shə-lĭz'əm) s. provincialismo.
proving ground s. campo de pruebas, campo de ensayos.
pro·vi·sion (prə-vĭzh'ən) I. s. (*act*) provisión *f*; (*supply*) provisión, suministro; (*stipulation*) estipulación *f*, cláusula ♦ **provisions** provisiones • **to make provisions for** (*the future*) prever; (*one's family*) mantener II. tr. proveer, abastecer.
pro·vi·sion·al (prə-vĭzh'ə-nəl) *o* **pro·vi·sion·ar·y** (-vĭzh'ə-nĕr'ē) adj. provisional.
pro·vi·so (prə-vī'zō) s. [pl. **-sos** *o* **-soes**] cláusula, condición *f*.
pro·vi·so·ry (prə-vī'zə-rē) adj. condicional.
pro·vo·ca·teur (prə-vŏk'ə-tûr') s. agente provocador *m*.
prov·o·ca·tion (prŏv'ə-kā'shən) s. provocación *f*.
pro·voc·a·tive (prə-vŏk'ə-tĭv) I. adj. provocativo II. s. (*stimulant*) estimulante *m*; (*incentive*) incentivo.
pro·voke (prə-vōk') tr. **-voked, -vok·ing** provocar.
pro·vok·ing (prə-vō'kĭng) adj. (*that provokes*) provocativo; (*annoying*) fastidioso, irritante.
pro·vost (prō'vōst', prŏv'əst) s. (*Scottish mayor*) alcalde *m*; (*keeper*) guardián de prisión *m*; EDUC., RELIG. prepósito, preboste *m*.
prow (prou) s. MARÍT. proa.
prow·ess (prou'ĭs) s. (*skill*) habilidad *f*, destreza; (*courage*) valor *m*, bravura.
prowl (proul) I. tr. & intr. merodear, rondar II. s. ronda, merodeo ♦ **on the p.** buscando algo.
prowl car s. coche patrulla *m*.
prox·i·mate (prŏk'sə-mĭt) adj. (*very near*) próximo; (*approximate*) aproximado.
prox·im·i·ty (prŏk-sĭm'ĭ-tē) s. proximidad *f*.
prox·y (prŏk'sē) s. [pl. **-ies**] (*person*) apoderado, represen-

tante *mf*; (*authority*) procuración *f*, poder *m*; (*authorization*) poder ♦ **by p.** por poderes, por poder.
prude (prōōd) s. mojigato, gazmoño.
pru·dence (prōōd'ns) s. prudencia.
pru·dent (prōōd'nt) adj. prudente.
pru·den·tial (prōō-dĕn'shəl) adj. prudencial.
prud·er·y (prōō'də-rē) s. [pl. **-ies**] mojigatería, gazmoñería.
prud·ish (prōō'dĭsh) adj. mojigato, gazmoño.
prune[1] (prōōn) s. (*fruit*) ciruela pasa; JER. (*ill-tempered person*) persona de mal genio.
prune[2] (prōōn) tr. & intr. **pruned, prun·ing** (*to trim*) podar; FIG. (*to remove*) cortar, cercenar; (*to reduce*) reducir, disminuir <*to p. the budget* reducir el presupuesto>.
pruning hook s. podadera.
pru·ri·ent (prōōr'ē-ənt) adj. lascivo, libidinoso.
Prus·sia (prŭsh'ə) s. Prusia.
Prus·sian (prŭsh'ən) adj. & s. HIST. prusiano.
prus·sic acid (prŭs'ĭk) s. QUÍM. ácido prúsico.
pry[1] (prī) I. intr. **pried, pry·ing** fisgar, curiosear II. s. [pl. **pries**] (*act*) fisgoneo, curioseo; (*snoop*) fisgón *m*, entremetido.
pry[2] (prī) I. tr. **pried, pry·ing** ♦ **to p. off** palancar • **to p. open** abrir con una palanca • **to p. out of** FIG. arrancar (secreto, información) II. s. [pl. **pries**] MEC. (*device*) palanca; (*leverage*) apalancamiento.
pry·ing (prī'ĭng) I. adj. fisgón, entremetido II. s. fisgoneo, curioseo.
psalm (säm) I. s. salmo, cántico ♦ **Psalms** BIBL. libro de los Salmos II. tr. cantar *o* ensalzar en salmos.
psalm·book (säm'bŏŏk') s. salterio.
psalm·ist (sä'mĭst) s. salmista *mf*.
psalm·o·dy (sä'mə-dē, säl'mə-) s. [pl. **-dies**] salmodia.
Psal·ter *o* **psal·ter** (sôl'tər) s. RELIG. salterio.
pseu·do (sōō'dō) adj. seudo, supuesto.
pseu·do·nym (sōōd'n-ĭm') s. seudónimo.
pseu·do·sci·ence (sōō'dō-sī'əns) s. seudociencia.
psi (sī) s. psi *f*.
psil·o·cy·bin (sĭl'ə-sī'bĭn, sī'lə-) s. QUÍM. silocibina (halucinógeno).
pso·ri·a·sis (sə-rī'ə-sĭs) s. MED. psoriasis, soriasis *f*.
psy·che (sī'kē) s. (*soul*) alma, espíritu *m*; (*mind*) psique *f*, psiquis *f* ♦ **P.** MITOL. Psique, Psiquis.
psy·che·de·li·a (sī'kĭ-dē'lē-ə) s. psicodelia, sicodelia.
psy·che·del·ic (sī'kĭ-dĕl'ĭk) adj. & s. psicodélico, sicodélico.
psy·chi·at·ric (sī'kē-ăt'rĭk) adj. psiquiátrico, siquiátrico.
psy·chi·a·trist (sĭ-kī'ə-trĭst, sī-) s. MED. psiquiatra *mf*, siquiatra *mf*.
psy·chi·a·try (sĭ-kī'ə-trē, sī-) s. MED. psiquiatría, siquiatría.
psy·chic (sī'kĭk) *o* **psy·chi·cal** (-kĭ-kəl) I. adj. psíquico, síquico II. s. medium *m*.
psy·cho·a·nal·y·sis (sī'kō-ə-năl'ĭ-sĭs) s. psicoanálisis *m*, sicoanálisis.
psy·cho·an·a·lyze (sī'kō-ăn'ə-līz') tr. **-lyzed, -lyz·ing** psicoanalizar, sicoanalizar.
psy·cho·dra·ma (sī'kə-drä'mə, -drăm'ə) s. MED. psicodrama *m*, sicodrama *m*.
psy·cho·log·i·cal (sī'kə-lŏj'ĭ-kəl) adj. psicológico, sicológico.
psy·chol·o·gist (sī-kŏl'ə-jĭst) s. psicólogo, sicólogo.
psy·chol·o·gy (sī-kŏl'ə-jē) s. [pl. **-gies**] psicología, sicología.
psy·cho·met·rics (sī'kə-mĕt'rĭks) s. [ú. con v. sing.] psicometría, sicometría.
psy·cho·path (sī'kə-păth') s. MED. psicópata *mf*, sicópata *mf*.
psy·chop·a·thy (sī-kŏp'ə-thē) s. MED. psicopatía, sicopatía.
psy·cho·sis (sī-kō'sĭs) s. [pl. **-ses** (-sēz')] MED. psicosis *f*, sicosis *f*.
psy·cho·so·mat·ic (sī'kə-sō-măt'ĭk) adj. & s. MED. psicosomático, sicosomático.
psy·cho·ther·a·py (sī'kō-thĕr'ə-pē) s. MED. psicoterapia, sicoterapia.
psy·chot·ic (sī-kŏt'ĭk) I. s. MED. psicópata *mf*, sicópata *mf* II. adj. psicopático, sicopático.
ptar·mi·gan (tär'mĭ-gən) s. [pl. **ptarmigan** *o* **-gans**] ORNIT. perdiz blanca, lagópodo.

PT boat (pē'tē') s. lancha torpedera (en la Armada de EE. UU.).

pter·o·dac·tyl (tĕr'ə-dăk'təl) s. ZOOL. pterodáctilo.

Ptol·e·ma·ic (tŏl'ə-mā'ĭk) adj. ASTRON., HIST. ptolemaico, tolemaico.

pto·maine poisoning (tō'mān') s. MED. envenenamiento por tomaínas.

pub (pŭb) s. taberna, cantina.

pu·ber·ty (pyoo'bər-tē) s. pubertad f.

pu·bes (pyoo'bēz) I. pl. de **pubis** II. s. [pl. **pubes**] ANAT. (region) pubis m; (hair) vello púbico.

pu·bes·cence (pyoo-bĕs'əns) s. pubescencia.

pu·bes·cent (pyoo-bĕs'ənt) adj. pubescente.

pu·bic (pyoo'bĭk) adj. ANAT. pubiano, púbico.

pu·bis (pyoo'bĭs) s. [pl. **-bes** (-bēz')] ANAT. pubis m.

pub·lic (pŭb'lĭk) adj. & s. público ♦ **in p.** en público • **to make p.** publicar.

pub·lic-ad·dress system (pŭb'lĭk-ə-drĕs') s. sistema de altavoces m.

pub·li·can (pŭb'lĭ-kən) s. G.B. tabernero, cantinero.

public assistance s. beneficencia pública.

pub·li·ca·tion (pŭb'lĭ-kā'shən) s. publicación f.

public defender s. defensor de oficio m.

public domain s. propiedad pública, dominio público.

public house s. G.B. taberna, cantina.

pub·li·cist (pŭb'lĭ-sĭst) s. publicista mf.

pub·lic·i·ty (pŭ-blĭs'ĭ-tē) s. publicidad f.

pub·li·cize (pŭb'lĭ-sīz') tr. **-cized, -ciz·ing** publicar, divulgar.

public prosecutor s. DER. fiscal mf.

public relations s.pl. relaciones públicas.

public school s. (in the United States) escuela pública; (in Great Britain) colegio particular.

public servant s. funcionario.

pub·lic-spir·it·ed (pŭb'lĭk-spĭr'ĭ-tĭd) adj. de espíritu cívico.

public television s. televisión no comercial f.

public utility s. empresa de servicio público ♦ **public utilities** FIN. acciones de empresas de servicio público.

public works s.pl. obras públicas.

pub·lish (pŭb'lĭsh) tr. & intr. publicar ♦ **published by** editado por.

pub·lish·a·ble (pŭb'lĭ-shə-bəl) adj. publicable.

pub·lish·er (pŭb'lĭ-shər) s. editor m.

puck (pŭk) s. DEP. disco (en hockey sobre hielo).

Puck (pŭk) s. duende m, Puck (personaje literario).

puck·er (pŭk'ər) I. tr. fruncir —intr. ♦ **to p. up** arrugarse II. s. arruga, fruncido.

puck·ish (pŭk'ĭsh) adj. travieso, juguetón.

pud·ding (pood'ĭng) s. CUL. (dessert) budín m; (sausage) embutido ♦ **black o blood p.** morcilla.

pud·dle (pŭd'l) I. s. (pool) charco; (paste) argamasa, mezcla de arcilla y grava II. tr. **-dled, -dling** (into pools) enturbiar; (into paste) mezclar; (metal) pudelar —intr. chapotear en el barro.

pud·dling (pŭd'lĭng) s. METAL. pudelado; HIDRÁUL. cimiento hidráulico.

pu·den·dum (pyoo-dĕn'dəm) s. [pl. **-da** (-də)] ANAT. vulva ♦ **pudenda** partes pudendas, genitales.

pudg·y (pŭj'ē) adj. **-i·er, -i·est** regordete, rechoncho.

pu·er·ile (pyoo'ər-əl, -ə-rīl') adj. pueril, infantil.

pu·er·per·al (pyoo-ûr'pər-əl) adj. MED. puerperal.

Puer·to Ri·can (pôr'tə rē'kən, pwĕr'tō) adj. & s. puertorriqueño, borinqueño.

Puer·to Ri·co (pôr'tə rē'kō, pwĕr'tō) s. Puerto Rico.

puff (pŭf) I. s. (of breath) resoplido; (of air) soplo; (of wind) soplido; (of smoke, steam) bocanada; (of a cigarette) chupada, fumada; (swelling) hinchazón f; (pastry) buñuelo; (for powder) borla; (of hair) mechón m; (of fabric) pliegue m; (flattery) bombo II. intr. (to blow) soplar; (to breathe) resoplar, resollar; (to emit smoke) echar bocanadas; (to smoke) fumar, pitar ♦ **to p. up** (to swell) hincharse, inflarse; FIG. (to become vain) engreírse, envanecerse —tr. (to blow) soplar; (to smoke) fumar; (to praise) ensalzar, dar bombo a ♦ **to p. up** (to swell) hinchar; FIG. (to make vain) engreír, envanecer.

puffed-up (pŭft'ŭp') adj. engreído.

puff·er (pŭf'ər) s. FAM. (smoker) fumador m; ICT. pez globo.

puff·er·y (pŭf'ə-rē) s. bombo, publicidad exagerada.

puf·fin (pŭf'ĭn) s. ORNIT. frailecillo.

puff pastry s. CUL. hojaldre m.

puff·y (pŭf'ē) adj. **-i·er, -i·est** (swollen) hinchado; (panting) jadeante.

pug[1] (pŭg) s. (dog) doguillo; (nose) nariz respingona.

pug[2] (pŭg) I. s. (clay) arcilla amasada; (machine) amasadera II. tr. **pugged, pug·ging** (to knead) amasar, mezclar; (to fill) rellenar con arcilla o con argamasa.

pug[3] (pŭg) s. huella, rastro (de un animal).

pug[4] (pŭg) s. JER. boxeador m.

pu·gi·lism (pyoo'jə-lĭz'əm) s. pugilismo.

pu·gi·list (pyoo'jə-lĭst) s. pugilista m, púgil m.

pug·na·cious (pŭg-nā'shəs) adj. belicoso, batallador.

pug·nac·i·ty (pŭg-năs'ĭ-tē) s. belicosidad f, espíritu batallador m.

pug nose s. nariz respingona.

puis·sance (pwĭs'əns) s. poder m, poderío.

puke (pyook) I. intr. & tr. **puked, puk·ing** vomitar II. s. vómito.

pul·chri·tude (pŭl'krĭ-tood', -tyood') s. belleza.

pule (pyool) intr. **puled, pul·ing** gimotear, quejarse.

pull (pool) I. tr. (to move) tirar de <to p. the door open tirar de la puerta para abrirla>; (to extract) sacar, extraer <to p. teeth sacar muelas>; (to tug at) tirar de, halar <they pulled the rope tiraron de la cuerda>; (to squeeze) apretar <to p. the trigger apretar el gatillo>; (to stretch) estirar; (to strain) torcerse <to p. a muscle torcerse un músculo>; FAM. (to attract) traer; (to do) hacer <don't p. any funny business no hagas tonterías>; JER. (to draw out) sacar (un arma); MARÍT. (to operate) mover (los remos); (to propel) hacer avanzar remando (una embarcación); (to carry) llevar, tener (remos); IMPR. sacar, tirar (una prueba) ♦ **to p. apart** (to rend) desgarrar, rasgar; FIG. (to criticize) criticar, censurar • **to p. a fast one** jugarle una mala pasada a • **to p. down** (to demolish) echar abajo, derribar; (to lower) bajar; (to reduce) rebajar; FAM. (to get) cobrar, sacar <to p. down a good salary sacar un buen sueldo> • **to p. for** (to cheer) animar; (to support) apoyar • **to p. in** (to restrain) contener; FAM. (to arrest) detener; (to attract) atraer • **to p. off** (to take off) quitar; (to carry out) llevar a cabo • **to p. on** (to dress) ponerse (ropa); (to tug at) tirar de • **to p. one's punches** (boxer) no pegar a fondo; FIG. (to hold back) andarse con rodeos • **to p. oneself together** componerse, dominarse • **to p. one's weight** FIG. hacer la parte que le corresponde a uno • **to p. someone's leg** FIG. tomarle el pelo a alguien • **to p. strings** FIG. conseguir algo por influencias • **to p. the rug out from under someone** FIG. dejar a alguien en la estacada • **to p. the wool over someone's eyes** FIG. engañar a alguien • **to p. up** (socks) subirse; (a chair) acercar —intr. (to tug) tirar; (to row) remar ♦ **to p. ahead** destacarse • **to p. at** (to tug on) tirar de; (a pipe) dar chupadas a; (a bottle) beber de • **to p. away** dejar atrás • **to p. in** (to enter) entrar en la estación (tren); (to arrive) llegar <we pulled in at midnight llegamos a medianoche>; (to depart) retirarse • **to p. out** (to depart) salir <the train has just pulled out el tren acaba de salir>; (to withdraw) retirarse • **to p. over** AUTO. ceñirse • **to p. through** (to survive danger) salir de un apuro; (to survive an illness) salir de una enfermedad • **to p. together** aunar sus esfuerzos • **to p. up** (to stop) pararse, detenerse; (to move ahead) adelantarse II. s. (tug) tirón m; (effort) esfuerzo, trabajo <a hard p. un gran esfuerzo>; (knob, cord) tirador m; (inhalation) chupada; JER. (influence) enchufe m, palanca <he has p. with the boss tiene enchufe con el jefe>; FAM. (appeal) atracción f; FÍS. atracción, fuerza de atracción <magnetic p. fuerza de atracción magnética>.

pull·back (pool'băk') s. retirada (de tropas).

pul·let (pool'ĭt) s. ZOOL. pollo, polla.

pul·ley (pool'ē) s. [pl. **-leys**] MEC. polea, roldana.

Pull·man (pool'mən) s. F.C. pullman m.

pull·out (pool'out') s. (of troops) retirada; (of a plane) restablecimiento.

ã rey / ä año / b boca / ch chico / d dar / ĕ el / ē mil / g gato / h joya / hw juez / ī aire / k casa / kw cuan /

pull·o·ver (pŏŏl'ō'vər) s. jersey *m*, suéter *m*.
pul·lu·late (pŭl'yə-lāt') intr. **-lat·ed, -lat·ing** pulular.
pul·mo·nar·y (pŏŏl'mə-nĕr'ē, pŭl'-) adj. pulmonar <*p. vein* vena pulmonar>.
pulp (pŭlp) **I.** s. BOT. médula; *(for paper)* pulpa, pasta; BOT., ODONT. pulpa; JER. *(publication)* revista *o* libro sensacionalista **II.** tr. reducir a pulpa *o* pasta —intr. ponerse como pulpa.
pul·pit (pŏŏl'pĭt, pŭl'-) s. RELIG. *(platform)* púlpito; *(clergyman)* clero; *(preaching)* predicación *f*.
pulp·wood (pŭlp'wŏŏd') s. madera para pasta de papel.
pul·sar (pŭl'sär') s. ASTRON. púlsar *m*.
pul·sate (pŭl'sāt') intr. **-sat·ed, -sat·ing** *(to throb)* pulsar, latir; *(to quiver)* temblar.
pul·sa·tion (pŭl-sā'shən) s. pulsación *f*, latido.
pulse¹ (pŭls) **I.** s. *(heart rate)* pulso, latido <*she took my p.* me tomó el pulso>; *(amplification)* pulsación *f*, vibración *f*; FIG. *(opinion)* opinión *f*; RAD. impulso **II.** intr. **pulsed, puls·ing** *(to beat)* pulsar, latir; *(to vibrate)* vibrar.
pulse² (pŭls) s. BOT. *(seed)* legumbre *f*; *(leguminous plant)* planta leguminosa.
pulse·jet (pŭls'jĕt') s. AER. pulsorreactor *m*.
pul·ver·ize (pŭl'və-rīz') **-ized, -iz·ing** *(to crush)* pulverizar, reducir a polvo; FIG. *(to destroy)* pulverizar —intr. pulverizarse, reducirse a polvo.
pul·ver·iz·er (pŭl'və-rī'zər) s. TEC. pulverizador *m*; *(crusher)* machacadora, trituradora.
pu·ma (pyōō'mə, pŏō'-) s. ZOOL. puma *m*.
pum·ice (pŭm'ĭs) **I.** s. piedra pómez **II.** tr. **-iced, -ic·ing** apomazar, pulir con piedra pómez.
pum·mel (pŭm'əl) tr. aporrear, apuñear.
pump¹ (pŭmp) **I.** s. MEC. bomba <*suction p.* bomba aspirante>; AUTO. surtidor *m* **II.** tr. *(to operate)* bombear; *(blood)* impulsar; *(to move up and down)* mover de arriba abajo ♦ **to p. someone for information** FIG. sonsacarle información (a alguien) • **to p. (something) into** *(air)* inyectar en; FIG. *(money)* invertir *o* meter en • **to p. out** achicar • **to p. up** inflar.
pump² (pŭmp) s. zapato bajo y liso, escarpín *m*.
pum·per·nick·el (pŭm'pər-nĭk'əl) s. pan integral de centeno *m*.
pump·ing (pŭm'pĭng) **I.** adj. de bombeo <*p. system* sistema de bombeo> **II.** s. TEC. bombeo.
pump·kin (pŭmp'kĭn, pŭng'-) s. BOT. calabaza, zapallo (planta y fruto); *(color)* anaranjado intenso.
pun (pŭn) **I.** s. retruécano, juego de palabras **II.** intr. **punned, pun·ning** hacer retruécanos *o* juegos de palabras.
punch¹ (pŭnch) **I.** s. *(for piercing)* punzón *m*; *(for nails)* botador *m*; *(for paper)* perforadora; *(for tickets)* máquina de picar billetes; *(countersink)* avellanador *m*, broca de avellanar **II.** tr. *(tickets)* picar; *(metal, leather)* taladrar; *(holes)* hacer —intr. utilizar un punzón.
punch² (pŭnch) **I.** tr. *(to hit)* dar un puñetazo; *(to poke)* golpear ♦ **p. in** marcar la hora de llegada al trabajo • **p. out** marcar la hora de salida del trabajo **II.** s. *(blow)* puñetazo; *(in boxing)* pegada; *(vigor)* vigor *m*, fuerza.
punch³ (pŭnch) s. *(beverage)* ponche *m*.
Punch (pŭnch) s. Polichinela *m*.
Punch and Ju·dy (jŏō'dē) s. FIG. teatro de títeres.
punch bowl s. ponchera.
punch card s. tarjeta perforada.
punch-drunk (pŭnch'drŭngk') adj. FAM. *(confused)* aturdido, atontado; DEP. *(in boxing)* groggy, aturdido por los golpes.
pun·cheon (pŭn'chən) s. *(structural framing)* puntal de madera *m*, pie derecho; *(tool)* punzón *m*; *(measurement)* medida de líquidos igual a 84 galones *o* 318 litros.
punch·er (pŭn'chər) s. *(tool)* punzón *m*; *(machine)* perforadora; *(cowboy)* vaquero.
Pun·chi·nel·lo (pŭn'chə-nĕl'ō) s. Polichinela *m*.
punching bag s. DEP. saco de arena (para el entrenamiento de los boxeadores).
punch line s. gracia (de un cuento, chiste).
punch press s. MEC. prensa cortadora.
punch tape s. cinta perforada.
punch·y (pŭn'chē) adj. **-i·er, -i·est** aturdido (a puñetazos).

punc·til·i·ous (pŭngk-tĭl'ē-əs) adj. puntilloso.
punc·tu·al (pŭngk'chŏō-əl) adj. *(prompt)* puntual; *(exact)* exacto.
punc·tu·al·i·ty (pŭngk'chŏō-ăl'ĭ-tē) s. puntualidad *f*.
punc·tu·ate (pŭngk'chŏō-āt') tr. **-at·ed, -at·ing** GRAM. puntuar; *(to interrupt)* interrumpir; *(to stress)* acentuar, recalcar.
punc·tu·a·tion (pŭngk'chŏō-ā'shən) s. GRAM. puntuación *f*.
punctuation mark s. GRAM. signo de puntuación.
punc·ture (pŭngk'chər) **I.** tr. **-tured, -tur·ing** *(to perforate)* perforar; *(a tire)* pinchar; *(the skin)* puncionar, pinchar; FIG. *(to deflate)* rebajar —intr. agujerearse **II.** s. *(perforation)* perforación *f*; *(in a tire)* pinchazo ♦ **p. wound** MED. punción.
pun·dit (pŭn'dĭt) s. *(in India)* pandit *m*; *(learned person)* erudito, sabio; *(authority)* autoridad *f*, experto <*a political p.* un experto en política>.
pun·gen·cy (pŭn'jən-sē) s. *(piquancy)* picante *m*; *(mordacity)* mordacidad *f*.
pun·gent (pŭn'jənt) adj. *(acrid)* acre; *(piquant)* picante; *(penetrating)* penetrante; FIG. *(caustic)* mordaz, cáustico.
Pu·nic (pyōō'nĭk) adj. & s. púnico.
pun·ish (pŭn'ĭsh) tr. *(to correct)* castigar; *(to injure)* maltratar —intr. imponer castigo.
pun·ish·a·ble (pŭn'ĭ-shə-bəl) adj. punible, castigable.
pun·ish·ment (pŭn'ĭsh-mənt) s. *(act, condition)* castigo; *(penalty)* pena, FAM. *(mistreatment)* maltrato.
pu·ni·tive (pyōō'nĭ-tĭv) adj. punitivo.
punitive damages s.pl. DER. daños punitivos.
Punjab s. Pendjab.
Pun·ja·bi (pŭn-jä'bē, -jäb'ē) s. *(inhabitant)* penjabo; *(language)* penjabi *m*.
punk¹ (pŭngk) s. *(tinder)* yesca; *(Chinese incense)* incienso chino.
punk² (pŭngk) JER. **I.** s. joven sin experiencia *mf* **II.** adj. sin mérito.
pun·ster (pŭn'stər) s. aficionado a los retruécanos *o* juegos de palabras.
punt¹ (pŭnt) **I.** s. batea, barquichuelo de fondo plano **II.** tr. *(to propel)* impeler una batea; *(to carry)* llevar en batea —intr. ir en batea.
punt² (pŭnt) DEP. **I.** s. patada **II.** tr. dar una patada a, patear (la pelota) —intr. dar una patada *o* patear la pelota.
pun·ty (pŭn'tē) s. [pl. **-ties**] TEC. puntel.
pu·ny (pyōō'nē) adj. **-ni·er, -ni·est** débil, enclenque.
pup (pŭp) **I.** s. ZOOL. *(puppy)* cachorro, cría de perro; *(young animal)* cría; FAM. *(conceited youth)* mocoso **II.** intr. **pupped, pup·ping** parir cachorros.
pu·pa (pyōō'pə) s. [pl. **-pae** (-pē) *o* **-pas**] ENTOM. crisálida.
pu·pil¹ (pyōō'pəl) s. *(student)* alumno; DER. *(minor)* pupilo.
pu·pil² (pyōō'pəl) s. ANAT. pupila.
pup·pet (pŭp'ĭt) s. TEAT. marioneta, títere *m*; *(doll)* muñeca; FIG. *(person)* títere, pelele *m* ♦ **p. show** función de títeres, teatro de títeres.
pup·pet·eer (pŭp'ĭ-tîr') s. TEAT. titiritero.
pup·pet·ry (pŭp'ĭ-trē) s. TEAT. [pl. **-ries**] *(art)* arte del titiritero *m*; *(actions)* movimientos de los títeres; FIG. *(performance)* representación dramática afectada.
pup·py (pŭp'ē) s. [pl. **-pies**] *(pup)* cachorro; *(conceited youth)* mocoso; *(inexperienced youth)* joven inexperto.
pup tent s. pequeña tienda de campaña.
pur·blind (pûr'blīnd') adj. *(partly blind)* cegato; *(dull)* ciego, falto de comprensión.
pur·chase (pûr'chĭs) **I.** tr. **-chased, -chas·ing** *(to buy)* comprar <*to p. machinery* comprar maquinaria>; *(to acquire)* adquirir; *(to earn)* ganar, conseguir; MEC. *(to hold)* sujetar con aparejo; *(to move)* apalancar **II.** s. *(buy)* compra; *(grip)* asidero, agarre *m*; MEC. *(lever)* palanca; *(position)* apoyo, punto de apoyo ♦ **p. order** COM. pedido.
pur·chas·er (pûr'chĭ-sər) s. comprador *m*.
purchasing power s. COM., FIN. poder adquisitivo.
pure (pyŏŏr) adj. **pur·er, pur·est** *(unadulterated)* puro; *(clean)* limpio; *(chaste)* casto, virgen.
pure·blood (pyŏŏr'blŭd') *o* **pure·blood·ed** (-blŭd'ĭd) adj. de pura sangre, de pura raza.

pure·bred (pyŏor'brĕd') I. adj. de pura sangre, de pura raza II. s. animal de pura raza o de pura sangre m.
pu·rée (pyŏo-rā') I. tr. **-réed, -rée·ing** hacer un puré de II. s. puré m.
pure·ly (pyŏor'lē) adv. puramente.
pure·ness (pyŏor'nĭs) s. pureza.
pur·ga·tion (pûr-gā'shən) s. MED., RELIG. purgación f.
pur·ga·tive (pûr'gə-tĭv') I. adj. purgativo, purgante II. s. purgante m, purga.
pur·ga·to·ry (pûr'gə-tôr'ē) I. s. [pl. **-ries**] purgatorio II. adj. purgatorio, purgativo.
purge (pûrj) I. tr. **purged, purg·ing** purgar II. s. (act) purgamiento, purgación f; POL. purga; MED. purga, purgante m.
pu·ri·fi·ca·tion (pyŏor'ə-fĭ-kā'shən) s. purificación f.
pu·ri·fi·er (pyŏor'ə-fī'ər) s. (person) purificador m; TEC. depurador m.
pu·ri·fy (pyŏor'ə-fī') tr. **-fied, -fy·ing** RELIG. purificar; (to refine) refinar —intr. purificarse.
pur·ism (pyŏor'ĭz'əm) s. purismo.
pur·ist (pyŏor'ĭst) s. purista mf.
Pu·ri·tan (pyŏor'ĭ-tn) s. & adj. HIST., RELIG. puritano.
pu·ri·tan·i·cal (pyŏor'ĭ-tăn'ĭ-kəl) adj. puritano.
Pu·ri·tan·ism (pyŏor'ĭ-tn-ĭz'əm) s. RELIG. puritanismo.
pu·ri·ty (pyŏor'ĭ-tē) s. pureza.
purl¹ (pûrl) I. intr. susurrar, murmurar II. s. susurro, murmullo.
purl² (pûrl) I. tr. (in knitting) hacer punto al revés; (to edge) ribetear —intr. (in knitting) hacer con puntos al revés; (to edge) poner ribetes, poner orlas II. s. (edging) puntilla; (metal thread) ribete de hilo de oro o de plata m ♦ **p. o p. stitch** punto al revés.
pur·loin (pər-loin') tr. hurtar, robar.
pur·ple (pûr'pəl) I. s. (color) violeta, morado; (cloth) púrpura II. adj. (color) purpúreo, morado; (royal) imperial, regio; (rhetorical) recargado.
Purple Heart s. EE. UU. condecoración concedida a los soldados heridos en el campo de batalla.
pur·port I. tr. (pər-pôrt') (to claim) pretender; (to seem) parecer; (to mean) significar, implicar II. s. (pûr'pôrt') (meaning) significado, significación f; (apparent meaning) lo que parece significar.
pur·port·ed (pər-pôr'tĭd) adj. supuesto <a p. crime un supuesto crimen>.
pur·pose (pûr'pəs) I. s. (goal) finalidad f, objetivo; (intention) propósito, intención f ♦ **for all intents and purposes** para todos los efectos • **for the p. of** con el objeto de • **on p.** a propósito, adrede • **to good p.** de una manera muy eficaz • **to little p.** para poco • **to no p.** para nada • **to serve the p.** servir para el caso II. tr. **-posed, -pos·ing** proponerse, tener intención de.
pur·pose·ful (pûr'pəs-fəl) adj. (person) determinado, resuelto; (activity) útil.
pur·pose·less (pûr'pəs-lĭs) adj. (without purpose) sin propósito, sin objetivo; (pointless) inútil; (aimless) vago.
pur·pose·ly (pûr'pəs-lē) adv. adrede, a propósito.
pur·po·sive (pûr'pə-sĭv) adj. (useful) útil; (intentional) intencional, deliberado.
purr (pûr) I. s. (of a cat) ronroneo; (of an engine) zumbido II. intr. (a cat) ronronear; (an engine) zumbar —tr. expresar con ronroneos.
purse (pûrs) I. s. (moneybag) monedero, portamonedas m; (handbag) bolso; (money) bolsa; (prize) premio II. tr. **pursed, purs·ing** apretar (labios).
purs·er (pûr'sər) s. MARÍT. contador m.
purse strings s.pl. cordones de la bolsa m ♦ **to loosen the p.** FAM. aflojar o soltar la mosca.
pur·su·ance (pər-sōo'əns) s. cumplimiento, ejecución f.
pur·su·ant (pər-sōo'ənt) adj. ♦ **p. to** según, de acuerdo con.
pur·sue (pər-sōo') tr. **-sued, -su·ing** (to chase) perseguir; (to strive for) aspirar a, buscar <to p. happiness buscar la felicidad>; (to follow) seguir, continuar (plan, acción); (to devote oneself to) dedicarse a; (to annoy) atormentar.
pur·su·er (pər-sōo'ər) s. perseguidor m.
pur·suit (pər-sōot') s. (chase) persecución f; (striving)

busca, búsqueda <the p. of happiness la búsqueda de la felicidad>; (activity) pasatiempo ♦ **in p. of** en pos de o en búsqueda de.
pu·ru·lence (pyŏor'ə-ləns, pyŏor'yə-) s. MED. (condition) purulencia; (pus) pus m.
pu·ru·lent (pyŏor'ə-lənt, pyŏor'yə-) adj. purulento.
pur·vey (pər-vā') tr. proveer, abastecer.
pur·vey·or (pər-vā'ər) s. (furnisher) proveedor m, abastecedor m; (distributor) distribuidor m.
pur·view (pûr'vyōo) s. (scope) alcance m, esfera; (outlook) perspectiva; DER. alcance de un estatuto o ley.
pus (pŭs) s. MED. pus m.
push (pŏosh) I. tr. (to press against) empujar <to p. the door empujar la puerta>; (to thrust) empujar; (to urge forward) hacer adelantar; (to press) presionar, ejercer presión; (to extend) extender; JER. (to sell) vender (un producto); (to promote) promover; (to recommend) enchufar, recomendar ♦ **he is pushed for time** tiene poco tiempo • **to be pushed for money** andar escaso de dinero • **to p. around** FAM. intimidar • **to p. aside** (people) apartar a empujones; (things) apartar con la mano • **to p. away** apartar • **to p. back** (to press against) empujar; (to repel) hacer retroceder, rechazar; (hair) echar hacia atrás • **to p. down** (to press down) apretar; (a house) derribar, tirar abajo; (someone) hacer caer • **to p. in** (to press against) empujar; (a pole) hincar • **to p. off** quitar • **to p. on** (work) apresurar, activar; (a pupil) hacer adelantar • **to p. out** (of a place) echar; (a boat) echar al agua; (competitors) eliminar; (claws) sacar; (roots, blossoms) hacer salir • **to p. one's luck** forzar la suerte • **to p. one's way** abrirse paso a empujones • **to p. over** (something) volcar; (someone) hacer caer • **to p. someone on to do something** empujar a alguien a hacer algo • **to p. someone out of the way** apartar a alguien a empujones • **to p. something open** abrir algo empujándolo • **to p. through** (to pass through) pasar por, sacar por; (to carry out) llevar a cabo; (a bill) hacer aceptar • **to p. up** empujar • **to p. up** (to lift) levantar; (prices) hacer subir; (someone) ayudar a subir (empujándole) —intr. (to press hard) empujar <to p. with all one's strength empujar uno con todas sus fuerzas>; (to put pressure on) ejercer presión, presionar; (to advance) abrirse paso a empujones; (to expend great effort) esforzarse ♦ **to p. ahead** avanzar, seguir adelante • **to p. back** retroceder • **to p. forward** avanzar • **to p. in** (to get in) meterse a empujones; (in a line) colarse • **to p. off** FAM. largarse, irse • **to p. on** seguir adelante, continuar II. s. (thrust) empujón m; (drive) empuje m <to have plenty of p. tener mucho empuje>; (stimulus) empuje, impulso; (effort) empujón; (of a bull) embestida; MIL. ofensiva ♦ **at a p.** en un apuro, en caso de necesidad • **to get the p.** ser despedido • **to give a p. on the bell** tocar el timbre • **to give someone a p.** FAM. enchufar a alguien, recomendar a alguien • **when it comes to the p.** cuando llega el momento decisivo.
push button s. ELEC., RAD. pulsador m, botón de contacto m.
push·cart (pŏosh'kärt') s. carretilla de mano.
push·er (pŏosh'ər) s. (one that pushes) empujador m, impulsador m; FAM. (ambitious person) ambicioso, arribista mf; JER. (narcotics seller) vendedor de estupefacientes m.
push·ing (pŏosh'ĭng) adj. (energetic) emprendedor, enérgico; (enterprising) ambicioso; (forward) atrevido.
push·o·ver (pŏosh'ō'vər) s. (easy thing) cosa muy fácil de hacer, ganga; (dupe) pelele m.
push·pin (pŏosh'pĭn') s. (pin) chincheta, alfiler de cabeza grande m; (game) crucillo, juego de alfileres.
push·rod o **push rod** (pŏosh'rŏd') s. AUTO. varilla o palanca de válvula (en un motor de explosión).
push·up (pŏosh'ŭp') s. (exercise) plancha; COMPUT. sección de información que se utiliza de abajo hacia arriba.
push·y (pŏosh'ē) adj. **-i·er, -i·est** FAM. insistente, molestoso.
pu·sil·la·nim·i·ty (pyŏo'sə-lə-nĭm'ĭ-tē) s. pusilanimidad f.
pu·sil·lan·i·mous (pyŏo'sə-lăn'ə-məs) adj. pusilánime.
puss¹ (pŏos) s. FAM. (cat) minino, gatito; (girl) chica, moza.
puss² (pŏos) s. JER. (mouth) hocico; (face) cara, jeta.

ã rey / a año / b boca / ch chico / d dar / ĕ el / ē mil / g gato / h joya / hw juez / ī aire / k casa / kw cuan /

puss·y¹ (pŏŏs′ē) s. [pl. **-ies**] FAM. *(kitten)* gatito, minino; BOT. *(catkin)* amento.

puss·y² (pŏŏs′ē) s. [pl. **-ies**] JER., VULG. concha, chucha.

puss·y·cat (pŏŏs′ē-kăt′) *(cat)* gato; FAM. *(amiable person)* persona afable.

puss·y·foot (pŏŏs′ē-fŏŏt′) intr. *(to move cautiously)* andar cautelosamente; JER. *(to act cautiously)* andarse con tiento, no decidirse.

pussy willow s. BOT. sauce común *m.*

pus·tu·lant (pŭs′chə-lənt) adj. MED. pustuloso.

pus·tu·lar (pŭs′chə-lər) adj. MED. pustuloso.

pus·tu·la·tion (pŭs′chə-lā′shən) s. MED. *(formation)* pustulación *f; (pustule)* pústula.

pus·tule (pŭs′chŏŏl) s. MED. pústula.

put (pŏŏt) **I.** tr. put, put·ting *(to place)* poner, colocar; *(to insert)* meter <*she p. her hand in her pocket* metió la mano en el bolsillo>; *(to add)* echar <*he p. sugar in his coffee* le echó azúcar al café>; *(to expose to)* poner <*you p. me in an awkward situation* me pusiste en una situación difícil>; *(to submit)* formular, hacer <*I p. a question to the judge* le hice una pregunta al juez>; *(to subject)* someter <*to p. a prisoner to torture* someter a un preso a tortura>; *(to attribute)* dar <*to p. a false interpretation on events* dar una interpretación falsa a los acontecimientos>; *(to impute)* echar <*don't p. the blame on me* no me eches la culpa>; *(to estimate)* calcular; *(to attach)* dar <*to p. a high value on friendship* dar gran valor a la amistad>; *(to impose)* gravar con <*to p. a tax on cigarettes* gravar con un impuesto sobre los cigarrillos>; *(to bet)* poner, jugar <*to p. ten dollars on a horse* jugar diez dólares en un caballo>; *(to invest)* poner, invertir <*to p. money in stocks* poner dinero en acciones>; *(to translate)* traducir; *(to say)* decir <*I don't know how to p. it* no sé como decírtelo>; *(to render)* poner <*p. it into verse* póngalo en verso>; *(to hurl)* lanzar, tirar (pesa) ♦ **to p. across** hacer comprender *o* entender • **to p. aside** *(to move)* poner *o* dejar a un lado; *(to save)* guardar; FAM. *(to imprison)* enjaular, aprisionar; *(to institutionalize)* meter en un manicomio; *(to consume)* zamparse, echarse entre pecho y espalda (comida) • **to p. back** volver a poner en su sitio • **to p. before** *(to submit)* someter a; *(to place before)* anteponer • **to p. by** guardar • **to p. down** *(to let go of)* soltar <*p. me down!* ¡suéltame!>; *(to suppress)* sofocar, reprimir; *(to write down)* apuntar; *(to include)* poner en la lista; *(to criticize)* poner por los suelos; *(to attribute)* achacar, atribuir <*p. it down to my inexperience* achácalo a mi falta de experiencia>; *(as a down payment)* hacer un desembolso inicial de • **to p. forth** *(to sprout)* brotar; *(to offer)* presentar, proponer • **to p. in** *(to insert)* meter; *(to spend)* pasar; *(to install)* poner <*to p. in central heating* poner calefacción central>; *(to present)* presentar; *(to plant)* plantar • **to p. in a good word for** hablar por *o* en favor de • **to p. into words** expresar • **to p. it mildly** sin exagerar • **to p. off** *(to postpone)* aplazar, diferir; *(to offend)* dar asco, asquear; *(to make wait)* hacer esperar • **to p. on** TEAT. montar, poner en escena; *(clothes)* ponerse; *(to affect)* afectar; *(to turn on)* encender • **to p. on the brakes** echar el freno • **to p. on weight** engordar • **to p. one over on** engañar • **to p. one's finger on** FIG. acertar • **to p. one's foot down** FIG. dar prueba de autoridad • **to p. one's foot in one's mouth** FIG. meter la pata • **to p. one's house in order** arreglar uno sus asuntos • **to p. out** *(to extinguish)* apagar; *(to inconvenience)* molestar; *(to publish)* publicar; *(to display)* sacar, mostrar • **to p. the bite on him** FAM. dar un sablazo, pedir dinero a • **to p. the finger on** FAM. denunciar a, delatar a • **to p. the screws to** apretar las clavijas *o* los tornillos • **to p. through** *(to accomplish)* llevar a cabo; *(to enact)* hacer aprobar; *(to cause)* hacer pasar <*you p. me through a lot of trouble* me hiciste pasar muchos apuros>; TEL. poner con • **to p. to bed** *(a child)* echar en la cama, acostar; *(newspaper)* preparar para la impresión • **to p. to death** matar, ejecutar • **to p. together** atar cabos • **to p. up** *(to build)* levantar, construir; *(to can)* envasar, poner en tarro; *(to nominate)* proponer; *(to provide)* poner, adelantar; *(to offer)* poner <*to p. up for sale* poner en venta>; *(to lodge)* hospedar, alojar; *(to hang up)* colgar, poner • **to p. up to** incitar a • **to p.**

upon abusar de —intr. ♦ **to p. about** MARÍT. cambiar de rumbo • **to p. down roots** instalarse • **to p. in** MARÍT. hacer escala en un puerto • **to p. out** *o* **out to sea** hacerse a la mar, zarpar • **to p. up or shut up** FAM. soportar sin quejarse, aguantar • **to p. up with** aguantar, soportar **II.** s. tiro, lanzamiento **III.** adj. ♦ **to be hard p. to** serle a uno difícil • **to stay p.** quedarse en su sitio.

pu·ta·tive (pyōō′tə-tĭv) adj. putativo.

put-down (pŏŏt′doun′) s. JER. desdén *m*, injuria (esp. en la forma de una oración tajante).

put·off (pŏŏt′ôf′) s. pretexto, excusa.

put·on (pŏŏt′ŏn′) **I.** adj. simulado, fingido **II.** s. JER. *(act)* engaño; *(book)* farsa literaria hecha como broma.

pu·tre·fac·tion (pyōō′trə-făk′shən) s. *(of matter)* putrefacción *f*, descomposición *f; (condition)* podredumbre *f*, corrupción *f.*

pu·tre·fy (pyōō′trə-fī′) tr. & intr. **-fied, -fy·ing** pudrir(se), descomponer(se).

pu·tres·cent (pyōō-trĕs′ənt) adj. putrescente.

pu·trid (pyōō′trĭd) adj. *(decomposed)* descompuesto, pútrido; *(rotten)* putrefacto, podrido; MED. gangrenoso; FIG. *(corrupt)* corrompido; *(vile)* asqueroso, repugnante.

putt (pŭt) DEP. **I.** s. *(golf stroke)* golpe corto, tiro al hoyo **II.** tr. & intr. dar un golpe corto a, tirar al hoyo.

putt·er (pŭt′ər) **I.** intr. no hacer nada de particular —tr. ♦ **to p. away** perder (horas, tiempo). **II.** s. palo de golf.

put·ty (pŭt′ē) s. [pl. **-ties**] masilla.

put-up (pŏŏt′ŭp′) adj. FAM. amañado, arreglado de antemano.

puz·zle (pŭz′əl) **I.** tr. **-zled, -zling** desconcertar, dejar perplejo ♦ **to p. out** resolver, descifrar —intr. ♦ **to be puzzled** estar perplejo *o* desconcertado • **to p. over** reflexionar, meditar **II.** s. *(problem)* enigma *m*, misterio; *(riddle)* acertijo; *(bewilderment)* perplejidad *f* ♦ **crossword p.** crucigrama • **jigsaw p.** rompecabezas.

puz·zle·ment (pŭz′əl-mənt) s. perplejidad *f*, desconcierto.

puz·zler (pŭz′lər) s. enigma *m*, misterio.

Pyg·ma·lion (pĭg-māl′yən) s. MITOL. Pigmalión.

Pyg·my (pĭg′mē) **I.** s. [pl. **-mies**] pigmeo ♦ **p.** pigmeo, enano **II.** adj. pigmeo ♦ **p.** *(small)* pigmeo, pequeño; *(trivial)* trivial, banal.

py·ja·mas (pə-jä′məz, -jăm′əz) s. G.B. var. de **pajamas.**

py·lon (pī′lŏn′) s. HIST. *(gateway)* pilón *m*; AVIA. torre marcadora del curso del vuelo; ELEC. poste *m*, torre metálica; *(temporary leg)* poste provisional *m.*

py·or·rhe·a (pī′ə-rē′ə) s. ODONT. piorrea.

pyr·a·mid (pĭr′ə-mĭd′) **I.** s. pirámide *f* **II.** tr. construir (una tesis *o* argumento) progresivamente (a base de una premisa general) —intr. aumentar rápidamente ♦ **to p. in stocks** especular con acciones.

py·ram·i·dal (pĭ-răm′ĭ-dl) adj. piramidal.

pyre (pīr) s. pira, hoguera.

Pyr·e·nees (pĭr′ə-nēz′) s. Pirineos.

py·re·thrin (pī-rē′thrĭn) s. QUÍM. piretrina.

py·ret·ic (pī-rĕt′ĭk) adj. MED. pirético.

Py·rex (pī′rĕks′) s. pirex (marca registrada de un vidrio resistente al calor) *m.*

py·rite (pī′rīt′) s. MIN. pirita, pirita de hierro.

py·ri·tes (pī-rī′tēz, pī′rīts′) s. [pl. **pyrites**] MIN. pirita.

py·rog·ra·phy (pī-rŏg′rə-fē) s. pirograbado, grabado al fuego (proceso, producto).

py·rol·y·sis (pī-rŏl′ĭ-sĭs) s. QUÍM. pirólisis *f.*

py·ro·man·cy (pī′rə-măn′sē) s. piromancia, adivinación por medio del fuego *f.*

py·ro·ma·ni·a (pī′rō-mā′nē-ə) s. piromanía.

py·ro·ma·ni·ac (pī′rō-mā′nē-ăk′) s. & adj. pirómano.

py·ro·tech·nic (pī′rə-tĕk′nĭk) adj. pirotécnico.

py·ro·tech·nics (pī′rə-tĕk′nĭks) s.pl. [ú. con v. sing.] pirotecnia.

Pyr·rhic victory (pĭr′ĭk) s. HIST. victoria pírrica; FIG. *(costly victory)* triunfo excesivamente costoso.

Py·thag·o·re·an (pĭ-thăg′ə-rē′ən) s. & adj. FILOS. pitagórico.

Pyth·i·an (pĭth′ē-ən) adj. HIST. pítico.

---

py·thon (pī′thŏn′) s. ZOOL. pitón *m*; *(spirit)* espíritu adivino; *(person)* adivino ♦ **P.** MITOL. Pitón.
py·tho·ness (pī′thə-nĭs, pĭth′ə-) s. MITOL. pitonisa.
pyx (pĭks) s. RELIG. píxide *f*; *(coin chest)* urna.
pyx·is (pĭk′sĭs) s. [pl. **-i·des** (-sī-dēz′)] BOT. pizidio (cápsula).

Q

q, Q (kyōō) s. [pl. **q's, Q's**] decimoséptima letra del alfabeto inglés.
Qa·tar (kä′tär′, -tər) s. Qatar.
q.t. (kyōō′tē′) s. ♦ **on the q.t.** JER. calladamente.
quack¹ (kwăk) **I.** s. graznido (del pato) **II.** intr. graznar.
quack² (kwăk) s. *(doctor)* curandero, matasanos *m*; *(charlatan)* charlatán *m*, impostor *m*.
quack·er·y (kwăk′ə-rē) s. *(medicine)* curandería; *(charlatanism)* charlatanería.
quad¹ (kwŏd) s. patio cuadrangular.
quad² (kwŏd) s. IMPR. cuadratín *m*.
quad³ (kwŏd) s. cuatrillizo.
quad·ran·gle (kwŏd′răng′gəl) s. GEOM. cuadrángulo; ARQ. plaza, patio (de una universidad).
quad·rant (kwŏd′rənt) s. cuadrante *m*.
quad·ra·phon·ic (kwŏd′rə-fŏn′ĭk) adj. ACÚS., RAD. cuadrifónico.
quad·rate (kwŏd′rāt′) **I.** s. *(square)* cuadrado; *(cube)* cubo **II.** adj. cuadrado.
quad·rat·ic (kwŏ-drăt′ĭk) adj. MAT. cuadrático.
quadratic equation s. MAT. ecuación cuadrática.
quad·ra·ture (kwŏd′rə-chōōr′, -chər) s. cuadratura.
quad·ren·ni·al (kwŏ-drĕn′ē-əl) adj. cuadrienal.
quad·ri·ceps (kwŏd′rĭ-sĕps′) s. ANAT. cuadriceps *m*.
quad·ri·lat·er·al (kwŏd′rə-lăt′ər-əl) s. & adj. cuadrilátero.
qua·drille¹ (kwə-drĭl′, kə-) s. cuadrilla (baile).
qua·drille² (kwə-drĭl′, kə-) s. cuatrillo, cascarela.
quad·ril·lion (kwŏ-drĭl′yən) s. mil billones *m*; G.B. cuatrillón *m*.
quad·ri·par·tite (kwŏd′rə-pär′tīt′) adj. cuadripartito.
quad·ri·ple·gi·a (kwŏd′rə-plē′jē-ə) s. MED. cuadriplejía.
quad·ri·ple·gic (kwŏd′rə-plē′jĭk) adj. & s. cuadripléjico.
quad·ri·va·lent (kwŏd′rə-vā′lənt) adj. QUÍM. tetravalente.
quad·roon (kwŏ-drōōn′) s. cuarterón *m*.
quad·ru·ped (kwŏd′rə-pĕd′) s. ZOOL. cuadrúpedo.
quad·ru·ple (kwŏ-drōō′pəl, kwŏd′rōō-pəl) **I.** adj. cuádruple **II.** s. cuádruplo **III.** tr. & intr. **-pled, -pling** cuadruplicar(se).
quad·ru·plet (kwŏ-drōō′plĭt, kwŏd′rə-) s. *(group of four)* cuádruplo; *(offspring)* cuatrillizo.
quad·ru·pli·cate (kwŏ-drōō′plĭ-kĭt) **I.** adj. & s. cuádruplo ♦ **in q.** por cuadruplicado **II.** tr. & intr. (-kāt′) **-cat·ed, -cat·ing** cuadruplicar(se).
quaff (kwŏf, kwăf) tr. & intr. beber a grandes tragos.
quag·gy (kwăg′ē, kwŏg′ē) adj. **-gi·er, -gi·est** *(muddy)* pantanoso, cenagoso; *(flabby)* fofo, blando.
quag·mire (kwăg′mīr′, kwŏg′-) s. *(land)* pantano, tremedal *m*; *(predicament)* pantano, atolladero.
quail¹ (kwāl) s. [pl. **quail** o **quails**] ORNIT. codorniz *f*.
quail² (kwāl) intr. amilanarse, acobardarse.
quaint (kwānt) adj. **-er, -est** *(picturesque)* pintoresco, de sabor anticuado; *(charming)* encantador; *(strange)* raro, singular.
quaint·ness (kwānt′nĭs) s. *(picturesqueness)* carácter pintoresco, sabor anticuado; *(charm)* encanto; *(strangeness)* rareza, singularidad *f*.
quake (kwāk) **I.** intr. **quaked, quak·ing** *(physically)* temblar; *(emotionally)* estremecerse **II.** s. temblor *m*.
Quak·er (kwā′kər) s. RELIG. cuáquero.
qual·i·fi·ca·tion (kwŏl′ə-fĭ-kā′shən) s. *(act)* calificación *m*, caracterización *f*; *(requirement)* requisito, condición *f* <*a q. for membership* uno de los requisitos para ser socio>; *(restriction)* restricción *f*, reserva <*without q.* sin reserva> ♦ **qualifications** *(competence)* capacidad, aptitud; *(certification)* credenciales.

qual·i·fied (kwŏl′ə-fīd′) adj. *(competent)* capacitado, competente <*we need q. individuals* necesitamos personas capacitadas>; *(certified)* acreditado, titulado <*a q. technician* un técnico acreditado>; *(voter)* capacitado; *(restricted)* restringido, limitado; *(approval)* con reservas.
qual·i·fi·er (kwŏl′ə-fī′ər) s. GRAM. calificativo.
qual·i·fy (kwŏl′ə-fī′) tr. **-fied, -fy·ing** *(to characterize)* calificar, caracterizar; *(to make competent)* capacitar, habilitar; *(to entitle)* dar derecho a <*that does not q. him to be rude to us* eso no le da derecho a tratarnos mal>; *(to certify)* acreditar, titular; *(to moderate)* atenuar; GRAM. modificar ♦ **to q. one's statements** hacer declaraciones menos tajantes —intr. *(for a position)* tener las capacidades necesarias; DEP. clasificarse ♦ **to q. as** *(a professional)* sacar el título de; FIG. *(a father, poet)* merecer el título de.
qual·i·fy·ing (kwŏl′ə-fī′ĭng) adj. *(exam)* eliminatorio; GRAM. calificativo.
qual·i·ta·tive (kwŏl′ĭ-tā′tĭv) adj. cualitativo.
qualitative analysis s. QUÍM. análisis cualitativo.
qual·i·ty (kwŏl′ĭ-tē) s. [pl. **-ties**] *(nature)* calidad *f*; *(property)* característica; *(attribute)* cualidad *f* <*to possess many fine qualities* poseer muchas buenas cualidades>; *(grade)* calidad <*service of the highest q.* servicio de la más alta calidad>; *(high status)* categoría; MÚS. timbre *m*.
quality control s. control de la calidad *m*.
qualm (kwäm, kwôm) s. *(nausea)* náusea; *(doubt)* duda, incertidumbre *m*; *(scruple)* remordimiento ♦ **to have no qualms about** no vacilar en • **to have qualms about** no estar seguro si uno debe (hacer algo).
quan·da·ry (kwŏn′də-rē) s. [pl. **-ries**] *(dilemma)* dilema *m*; *(difficulty)* apuro, aprieto.
quan·ta (kwŏn′tə) pl. de **quantum**.
quan·ti·fi·a·ble (kwŏn′tə-fī′ə-bəl) adj. que se puede expresar cuantitativamente.
quan·ti·fi·ca·tion (kwŏn′tə-fĭ-kā′shən) s. cuantificación *f*.
quan·ti·fi·er (kwŏn′tə-fī′ər) s. COMPUT., FÍS. cuantificador *m*.
quan·ti·fy (kwŏn′tə-fī′) tr. **-fied, -fy·ing** determinar la cantidad de.
quan·ti·ta·tive (kwŏn′tĭ-tā′tĭv) adj. cuantitativo.
quantitative analysis s. QUÍM. análisis cuantitativo.
quan·ti·ty (kwŏn′tĭ-tē) s. [pl. **-ties**] cantidad *f* ♦ **in q.** en grandes cantidades • **unknown q.** incógnita.
quan·tum (kwŏn′təm) s. [pl. **-ta** (-tə)] *(quantity)* cantidad *f*; *(portion)* parte *f*; FÍS. cuanto, quantum *m*.
quantum jump s. FÍS. transición cuántica; FIG. *(abrupt change)* desviación repentina.
quantum mechanics s. FÍS. mecánica cuántica.
quantum theory s. FÍS. teoría cuántica.
quar·an·tine (kwôr′ən-tēn′) **I.** s. cuarentena **II.** tr. **-tined, -tin·ing** poner en cuarentena.
quark (kwôrk) s. FÍS. quark (partícula subatómica hipotética) *m*.
quar·rel¹ (kwôr′əl) **I.** s. pelea, discusión *f* ♦ **to have no q. with** no tener nada en contra de **II.** intr. *(to argue)* pelear, discutir <*he never quarrels with his superiors* nunca discute con sus superiores>; *(to disagree)* estar en desacuerdo <*to q. with the law* estar en desacuerdo con la ley>; *(to complain)* quejarse ♦ **to q. over** discutir.
quar·rel² (kwôr′əl) s. *(bolt)* lance de ballesta *m*; *(pane)* cuadrado de vidrio.
quar·rel·er (kwôr′ə-lər) s. pendenciero.
quar·rel·ing (kwôr′ə-lĭng) **I.** s. disputas *f* **II.** adj. pendenciero, peleón.
quar·rel·some (kwôr′əl-səm) adj. pendenciero.
quar·ry¹ (kwôr′ē) s. [pl. **-ries**] presa.
quar·ry² (kwôr′ē) **I.** s. [pl. **-ries**] MIN. *(pit)* cantera; FIG. *(source)* fuente (de información) *f* **II.** tr. **-ried, -ry·ing** MIN. *(stone)* sacar (piedra de una cantera); *(land)* excavar —intr. ♦ **to q. for** FIG. buscar (datos).
quart (kwôrt) s. cuarto (de galón).
quar·ter (kwôr′tər) **I.** s. *(fourth part)* cuarto, cuarta parte <*a q. of the students* la cuarta parte de los alumnos>; *(of a dollar)* veinticinco centavos; *(of an hour, mile)* cuarto de hora, milla); *(of a year)* trimestre *m*; *(direction)* dirección

f; (neighborhood) barrio; *(of the horizon)* cuadrante *m;* *(mercy)* cuartel *m <to give q. to the enemy* dar cuartel al enemigo>; GEOM. cuadrante; HER. cuartel; ZOOL. cuarto *<hindquarters* cuartos traseros>; DEP. *(period)* tiempo ♦ **(a) q. after** *o* **past** y cuarto *<a q. after six* las seis y cuarto> • **(a) q. to** *o* **of** menos cuarto *<a q. to four* las cuatro menos cuarto> • **at close quarters** *(at close range)* de cerca; *(to fight)* cuerpo a cuerpo • **from all quarters** de todas partes *o* lados • **living quarters** residencia, vivienda • **quarters** MIL. *(station)* puesto; *(barracks)* cuartel; *(group)* medios, esferas *<from the highest quarters* de las altas esferas> II. tr. *(into quarters)* dividir en cuartos, cuartear; *(to separate)* dividir; *(to lodge)* alojar; *(to crisscross)* recorrer (en busca de una presa); HER. cuartelar; MEC. colocar en ángulo recto; MIL. acuartelar ♦ **to draw and q.** descuartizar —intr. MIL. *(troops)* acuartelarse; *(to lodge)* alojarse, hospedarse; *(to crisscross)* recorrer el terreno III. adj. cuarto de *<a q. inch* un cuarto de pulgada>.

quar·ter·back (kwôr′tər-băk′) I. s. jugador que dirige la jugada *m* II. tr. dirigir.

quarter day s. día de pagos trimestrales *m.*

quar·ter·deck (kwôr′tər-děk′) s. MARÍT. alcázar *m.*

quar·ter·fi·nal (kwôr′tər-fī′nəl) s. DEP. cuarto de final ♦ **quarterfinals** cuartos de final.

quarter horse s. caballo cuarto de milla.

quar·ter-hour *o* **quarter hour** (kwôr′tər-our′) s. cuarto de hora.

quar·ter·ly (kwôr′tər-lē) I. adj. trimestral II. s. [pl. **-lies**] publicación trimestral *f* III. adv. trimestralmente, cada tres meses.

quar·ter·mas·ter (kwôr′tər-măs′tər) s. MIL. oficial de intendencia *m;* MARÍT. cabo de mar.

quar·tern (kwôr′tərn) s. cuarto, cuarta parte.

quarter note s. MÚS. negra.

quarter section s. cuarto de una milla cuadrada.

quar·ter·staff (kwôr′tər-stăf′) s. [pl. **-staves** (-stāvz′)] ARM. vara, garrocha.

quar·ter·tone (kwôr′tər-tōn′) s. MÚS. cuarto de tono.

quar·tet *o* **quar·tette** (kwôr-tět′) s. cuarteto.

quar·tile (kwôr′tīl′, -tīl) s. MAT. cuartila, cuartil *m.*

quar·to (kwôr′tō) s. [pl. **-tos**] libro en cuarto.

quartz (kwôrts) s. MIN. cuarzo.

quartz·ite (kwôrt′sīt′) s. MIN. cuarcita.

quartz lamp s. lámpara de cuarzo.

qua·sar (kwā′zär′, -sär′) s. ASTRON. cuásar *m.*

quash (kwŏsh) tr. DER. *(to annul)* anular, derogar; *(to suppress)* sofocar (levantamiento, emoción).

qua·si (kwā′zī′, kwä′zē) adj. cuasi, aparente *<a q. success* un éxito aparente>.

quas·sia (kwŏsh′ə) s. BOT. cuasia.

qua·ter·nar·y (kwŏt′ər-nĕr′ē) I. adj. cuaternario ♦ **Q.** GEOL. cuaternario II. s. grupo de cuatro ♦ **the Q.** GEOL. el período cuaternario.

quat·rain (kwŏt′rān′) s. LIT. cuarteto.

quat·re·foil (kăt′ər-foil′, kăt′rə-) s. BOT. flor cuadrifoliada; ARQ. cuatrifolio.

qua·ver (kwā′vər) I. intr. *(to tremble)* temblar; *(to trill)* trinar —tr. decir con voz trémula II. s. *(sound)* temblor (de la voz) *m;* MÚS. *(trill)* trino.

quay (kē, kā) s. muelle *m,* embarcadero.

quay·age (kē′ĭj, kā′-) s. *(charge)* derechos de muelle; *(quays)* muelles *m.*

quea·si·ness (kwē′zē-nĭs) s. *(nausea)* náusea; *(disgust)* asco; *(uneasiness)* inquietud *f;* *(squeamishness)* delicadeza.

quea·sy *o* **quea·zy** (kwē′zē) adj. **-si·er, -si·est** *o* **-zi·er, -zi·est** *(nauseated)* bascoso, con náuseas; *(easily upset)* delicado, débil (estómago); *(sickening)* nauseabundo, repugnante; *(uneasy)* inquieto, intranquilo; *(difficult)* complicado, difícil; *(squeamish)* fastidioso, remilgado.

Que·bec (kwĭ-běk′) s. Quebec.

Quech·ua (kěch′wə) s. [pl. **Quechua** *o* **-uas**] quechua, quichua.

queen (kwēn) I. s. *(monarch)* reina; *(woman)* reina *<beauty q.* reina de belleza>; *(in cards, chess)* reina; ENTOM. reina;

JER. *(homosexual)* marica *m,* maricón *m* II. tr. *(a woman)* coronar reina; *(a pawn)* coronar —intr. reinar ♦ **to q. it over** FAM. darse aires de.

Queen Anne's lace (ănz) s. BOT. zanahoria silvestre, dauco.

queen consort s. [pl. **queens consort**] reina consorte.

queen·ly (kwēn′lē) adj. **-li·er, -li·est** de reina, majestuoso.

queen mother s. reina madre.

queen-size (kwēn′sīz′) adj. muy grande.

queer (kwîr) I. adj. **-er, -est** *(strange)* raro, extraño; *(odd)* curioso; *(eccentric)* excéntrico, estrafalario; *(suspicious)* sospechoso; JER. *(counterfeit)* falso ♦ **to feel q.** no sentirse bien II. s. JER., DESPEC. maricón *m,* marica *m* III. tr. JER. fastidiar, arruinar.

queer·ness (kwîr′nĭs) s. rareza, extrañeza.

quell (kwěl) tr. *(a riot)* sofocar; *(emotions)* controlar, dominar.

quench (kwěnch) tr. *(flames, fire)* apagar; *(enthusiasm)* enfriar, matar; *(an uprising)* sofocar; *(thirst)* matar; *(metals)* templar.

quench·a·ble (kwěn′chə-bəl) adj. apagable.

quern (kwûrn) s. molinillo de mano.

quer·u·lous (kwěr′ə-ləs, kwěr′yə-) adj. quejumbroso.

que·ry (kwîr′ē) I. s. [pl. **-ries**] *(question)* pregunta; *(inquiry)* averiguación *f;* *(doubt)* duda; *(mark)* signo de interrogación II. tr. **-ried, -ry·ing** *(to put in doubt)* poner en duda; *(to question)* preguntar; *(to interrogate)* interrogar.

quest (kwěst) I. s. *(search)* búsqueda; *(by a knight)* demanda ♦ **in q. of** en busca de II. intr. & tr. buscar.

ques·tion (kwěs′chən) I. s. *(inquiry)* pregunta *<did you hear the question?* ¿oyó usted la pregunta?>; *(issue)* cuestión *f,* asunto; *(problem)* problema *m;* *(proposition)* moción *f;* *(doubt)* duda *<there is no q. about its validity* no hay duda alguna de su validez>; GRAM. oración interrogativa ♦ **beyond q.** fuera de duda, indiscutible • **burning q.** cuestión candente • **in q.** en cuestión • **to ask someone a q.** *o* **to put a q. to someone** hacer una pregunta a alguien • **to be beside the q.** no venir al caso • **to beg the q.** hacer una petición de principio • **to be out of the q.** ser imposible • **to call into q.** cuestionar, poner en tela de juicio • **to come into q.** plantearse • **to raise the q. of** plantear la cuestión de • **without q.** sin duda II. tr. *(to ask)* hacer una pregunta a; DER. *(to interrogate)* interrogar; *(to dispute)* poner en tela de juicio —intr. preguntar.

ques·tion·a·ble (kwěs′chə-nə-bəl) adj. *(problematic)* cuestionable, discutible; *(uncertain)* dudoso; *(shady)* dudoso, sospechoso.

ques·tion·a·bly (kwěs′chə-nə-blē) adv. cuestionablemente.

ques·tion·er (kwěs′chə-nər) s. interrogador *m.*

ques·tion·ing (kwěs′chə-nĭng) I. s. preguntas *f* II. adj. *(that questions)* interrogativo; *(inquisitive)* inquisitivo.

question mark s. *(symbol)* signo de interrogación; *(doubt)* interrogante *m.*

ques·tion·naire (kwěs′chə-nâr′) s. cuestionario.

quet·zal (kět-säl′) s. [pl. **-zals** *o* **-za·les** (-sä′lās)] ORNIT. quetzal *m;* FIN. quetzal (unidad monetaria guatemalteca).

queue (kyōō) I. s. *(line)* cola, fila (de vehículos, personas); *(pigtail)* coleta, trenza II. intr. **queued, queu·ing** ♦ **to q. up** hacer cola.

quib·ble (kwĭb′əl) I. intr. **-bled, -bling** andar con sutilezas II. s. sutileza.

quib·bler (kwĭb′lər) s. sutilizador *m,* sofista *mf.*

quiche (kēsh) s. CUL. pastel de queso y huevos *m.*

quick (kwĭk) I. adj. **-er, -est** *(fast)* rápido; *(bright)* listo; *(alert)* vivo, despierto *<a q. mind* una mente despierta>; *(keen)* vivo, ágil; *(reply)* pronto; *(excitable)* irascible *<a q. temper* un temperamento irascible ♦ **to be q. about something** hacer algo rápidamente • **to be q. to act** obrar sin perder tiempo • **to be q. to take offense** ofenderse por nada II. s. médula *<the q. of the matter* la médula del asunto> ♦ **the q. and the dead** los vivos y los muertos • **to cut someone to the q.** herir a alguien en lo más vivo III. adv. rápido, rápidamente *<to get rich q.* hacerse rico rápidamente>.

quick-and-dirt·y (kwĭk′ən-dûr′tē) adj. de mala calidad.

quick assets s.pl. COM. activo disponible.

quick·en (kwĭk′ən) tr. *(to accelerate)* apresurar, acelerar <*q. your pace* apresura el paso>; *(pulse)* acelerarse; *(to revive)* resucitar; *(to stimulate)* reavivar (apetito, imaginación) —intr. *(to accelerate)* apresurarse, acelerarse; *(to revive)* resucitar; *(fetus)* empezar a moverse.

quick-freeze (kwĭk′frēz′) tr. **-froze** (-frōz′), **-fro·zen** (-frō′zən), **-freez·ing** congelar rápidamente (los alimentos).

quick·ie (kwĭk′ē) s. FAM. cosa hecha rápidamente.

quick·lime (kwĭk′līm′) s. cal viva.

quick·ly (kwĭk′lē) adv. rápidamente.

quick·ness (kwĭk′nĭs) s. *(speed, promptness)* rapidez *f*; *(alertness)* viveza; *(nimbleness)* agilidad *f*.

quick·sand (kwĭk′sănd′) s. arena movediza.

quick·sil·ver (kwĭk′sĭl′vər) I. s. QUÍM. mercurio, azogue *m* II. adj. variable, caprichoso.

quick·step (kwĭk′stĕp′) s. MIL., MÚS. pasodoble *m*.

quick-tem·pered (kwĭk′tĕm′pərd) adj. de mucho genio, irascible.

quick time s. MIL. paso ligero.

quick-wit·ted (kwĭk′wĭt′ĭd) adj. listo, agudo.

quid[1] (kwĭd) s. mascada (de tabaco).

quid[2] (kwĭd) s. [pl. **quid** o **quids**] JER., G.B. libra esterlina.

quid·di·ty (kwĭd′ĭ-tē) s. [pl. **-ties**] *(essence)* quid *m*, esencia; *(quibble)* sutileza, equívoco.

quid pro quo (kwĭd′ prō kwō′) s. *(exchange)* compensación *f*.

qui·es·cent (kwī-ĕs′ənt) adj. *(not moving)* quieto, tranquilo; *(dormant)* inactivo.

qui·et (kwī′ĭt) I. adj. **-er, -est** *(silent)* callado, silencioso; *(calm)* tranquilo <*a q. evening* una noche tranquila>; *(not showy)* discreto <*a q. color* un color discreto>; COM. inactivo ♦ **be q.!** *(silent)* ¡cállate!; *(still)* ¡estate quieto! • **to be q.** *(not noisy)* no hacer ruido; *(to stop talking)* callarse II. s. *(calm)* calma, quietud *f*; *(silence)* silencio; *(rest)* descanso, reposo III. tr. *(to silence)* hacer callar; *(to calm)* tranquilizar, calmar —intr. ♦ **to q. down** calmarse, tranquilizarse.

qui·et·ly (kwī′ĭt-lē) adv. *(silently)* calladamente, silenciosamente; *(calmly)* tranquilamente.

qui·et·ness (kwī′ĭt-nĭs) s. *(silence)* silencio; *(calmness)* tranquilidad *f*, quietud *f*; *(rest)* descanso, reposo.

qui·e·tude (kwī′ĭ-tōōd′, -tyōōd′) s. quietud *f*.

qui·e·tus (kwī-ē′təs) s. *(end)* punto final; *(death)* muerte *f*; *(of a debt)* finiquito ♦ **to put the q. on** acabar con.

quill (kwĭl) I. s. *(feather, pen)* pluma; *(stem)* cañón (de una pluma) *m*; *(of a porcupine)* púa; TEJ. canilla II. tr. encañonar (hilo, tela).

quilt (kwĭlt) I. s. edredón *m*, colcha II. tr. acolchar.

quilt·ing (kwĭl′tĭng) s. acolchado.

quince (kwĭns) s. BOT. membrillo (árbol y fruto).

qui·nine (kwī′nīn′) s. FARM. quinina.

quinine water s. agua de quina.

quin·quen·nial (kwĭn-kwĕn′ē-əl) I. adj. quinquenal II. s. quinquenio.

quin·sy (kwĭn′zē) s. MED. angina, amigdalitis *f*.

quint (kwĭnt) s. quíntuplo, quintillizo.

quin·tal (kwĭn′tl) s. quintal *m*.

quin·tes·sence (kwĭn-tĕs′əns) s. quintaesencia.

quin·tet o **quin·tette** (kwĭn-tĕt′) s. quinteto.

quin·tile (kwĭn′tīl′, kwĭn′tĭl) s. ASTROL. aspecto quintal.

quin·til·lion (kwĭn-tĭl′yən) s. trillón *m*; G.B. quintillón *m*.

quin·tu·ple (kwĭn-tŭp′əl, kwĭn′tə-pəl) I. adj. & s. quíntuple *m* II. tr. & intr. **-pled, -pling** quintuplicar(se).

quin·tu·plet (kwĭn-tŭp′lĭt, kwĭn′tə-plĭt) s. *(group of five)* quíntuplo; *(offspring)* quintillizo.

quin·tu·pli·cate (kwĭn-tōō′plĭ-kĭt) I. adj. & s. quíntuplo ♦ **in q.** por quintuplicado II. tr. (-kāt′) **-cat·ed, -cat·ing** sacar cinco copias de.

quip (kwĭp) I. s. *(witticism)* ocurrencia; *(gibe)* pulla II. intr. **quipped, quip·ping** *(to jest)* decir sarcásticamente; *(to gibe)* tirar pullas.

quip·ster (kwĭp′stər) s. *(wit)* persona ocurrente; *(giber)* pullista *mf*.

quire (kwīr) s. mano (de papel) *f*.

quirk (kwûrk) s. *(twist)* vuelta; *(flourish)* rasgo; *(idiosyncracy)* peculiaridad *f*, singularidad *f*; *(vagary)* capricho

<*a q. of fortune* un capricho de la suerte>; *(equivocation)* evasiva; ARQ. *(groove)* avivador *m*.

quirk·y (kwûr′kē) adj. **-i·er, -i·est** *(peculiar)* peculiar, singular; *(capricious)* caprichoso.

quirt (kwûrt) s. EQUIT. cuarta, fusta.

quis·ling (kwĭz′lĭng) s. colaboracionista *mf*, traidor *m*.

quit (kwĭt) I. tr. **quit** o **quit·ted** (kwĭt′ĭd), **quit·ting** *(to leave)* salir de, irse de <*I normally q. work at five* normalmente salgo de mi empleo a las cinco>; *(to give up)* abandonar, dejar (un trabajo, la universidad); *(to stop)* dejar de <*she finally quit smoking* finalmente ella dejó de fumar> —intr. *(to stop)* parar <*I q. at five* paro a las cinco>; *(to give up)* desistir, abandonar; *(to resign)* renunciar, dimitir II. adj. ♦ **to be q. of** estar libre de.

quit·claim (kwĭt′klām′) DER. I. s. renuncia II. tr. renunciar.

quite (kwīt) adv. *(completely)* totalmente, completamente <*we are q. satisfied* estamos totalmente satisfechos>; *(altogether)* del todo <*it is not q. finished* no está del todo terminado>; *(absolutely)* completamente, absolutamente <*q. true* absolutamente cierto>; *(exactly)* exactamente <*it is not q. what I need* no es exactamente lo que necesito>; *(rather)* bastante <*q. long* bastante largo>; FAM. *(very)* muy <*the novel is q. good* la novela es muy buena> ♦ **a bit** o **q. a few** bastante • **q. a while** un buen rato • **q. so!** ¡así es! • **to be q. a** ser un gran • **to be q. enough** bastar • **to be q. the thing** estar muy de moda.

quits (kwĭts) adj. ♦ **to be q.** estar iguales o en paz • **to call it q.** *(to break off)* dejarlo así; *(to give up)* darse por vencido.

quit·tance (kwĭt′ns) s. *(release)* quitanza; *(repayment)* compensación *f*.

quit·ter (kwĭt′ər) s. ♦ **to be a q.** darse por vencido fácilmente.

quiv·er[1] (kwĭv′ər) I. intr. *(to tremble)* temblar; *(to vibrate)* estremecerse II. s. *(tremor)* temblor *m*; *(vibration)* estremecimiento.

quiv·er[2] (kwĭv′ər) s. carcaj *m*, aljaba.

quix·ot·ic (kwĭk-sŏt′ĭk) adj. quijotesco.

quiz (kwĭz) I. tr. **quizzed, quiz·zing** *(to question)* interrogar; *(to test)* examinar II. s. *(questioning)* interrogatorio; *(test)* prueba, examen.

quiz show s. concurso de televisión.

quiz·zi·cal (kwĭz′ĭ-kəl) adj. *(questioning)* curioso, perplejo; *(teasing)* burlón; *(odd)* curioso, raro.

quiz·zi·cal·ly (kwĭz′ĭ-kə-lē) adv. *(questioningly)* con curiosidad, con perplejidad; *(teasingly)* burlonamente; *(oddly)* curiosamente.

quoin (koin, kwoin) s. ARQ. *(angle)* esquina; *(cornerstone)* piedra angular; IMPR. cuña.

quoit (kwoit, koit) s. herrón *m* ♦ **quoits** hito (juego).

quo·rum (kwôr′əm) s. quórum *m*.

quo·ta (kwō′tə) s. cuota.

quot·a·ble (kwō′tə-bəl) adj. *(words)* digno de citarse; *(prices)* cotizable.

quo·ta·tion (kwō-tā′shən) s. *(act, passage)* cita; *(of prices)* cotización ♦ **end of q.** hasta aquí la cita.

quotation mark s. IMPR. comillas.

quote (kwōt) I. tr. **quot·ed, quot·ing** *(words, source)* citar; *(example, price)* dar; FIN. cotizar —intr. citar, hacer una cita ♦ **and I q.** y cito sus palabras II. s. FAM. *(quotation)* cita; *(mark)* comilla <*in quotes* entre comillas> ♦ **q. unquote** entre comillas.

quoth (kwōth) tr. ANT., POÉT. [ú. sólo en primera y tercera persona del pretérito con sujeto postpuesto] dije, dijo.

quo·tid·i·an (kwō-tĭd′ē-ən) adj. *(daily)* diario, cotidiano; *(commonplace)* común.

quo·tient (kwō′shənt) s. MAT. cociente *m*.

R

r, R (är) s. [pl. **r's, R's**] decimoctava letra del alfabeto inglés ♦ **the three R's** EDUC., FAM. lectura, escritura y aritmética.

rab·bi (răb′ī) o **rab·bin** (răb′ĭn) s. [pl. **-bis** o **-bins**] RELIG. rabino.

rab·bin·i·cal (rə-bĭn′ĭ-kəl) o **rab·bin·ic** (-ĭk) adj. rabínico.

rab·bit (răb′ĭt) s. [pl. **rabbit** o **-bits**] ZOOL. conejo; *(fur)* piel de conejo *f.*

rabbit ears s.pl. FAM. antena de televisión.

rabbit punch s. golpe en la nuca *m.*

rabbit warren s. madriguera de conejos, conejera.

rab·ble¹ (răb′əl) s. *(mob)* gentío, multitud ruidosa ♦ **the r.** el populacho, la chusma.

rab·ble² (răb′əl) METAL. I. s. hurgón *m* II. tr. **-bled, -bling** agitar.

rab·ble-rous·er (răb′əl-rou′zər) s. demagogo.

rab·id (răb′ĭd) adj. *(with rabies)* rabioso; FIG. *(fanatic)* fanático; *(raging)* feroz.

ra·bies (rā′bēz) s. MED., VET. rabia.

rac·coon (ră-kōōn′) s. [pl. **-coons** o **raccoon**] *(animal)* mapache *m*; *(fur)* piel de mapache *f.*

race¹ (rās) s. *(people)* raza <*the white r.* la raza blanca>; *(group)* estirpe *f*; BOT. subespecie *f*; ZOOL. raza ♦ **the human r.** la raza humana.

race² (rās) I. s. *(contest)* carrera <*a bicycle r.* una carrera ciclista>; *(escalation)* carrera <*the arms r.* la carrera de armamentos>; *(course)* curso (del tiempo); *(of water)* corriente *f*; TEC. saetín *m*; MEC. anillo de rodadura; AER. estela ♦ **r. against time** o **the clock** carrera contra reloj • **r. car** coche de carreras • **r. car driver** corredor • **the races** las carreras II. intr. **raced, rac·ing** *(to compete)* correr, competir; *(to run)* correr; *(as a driver)* ser corredor; *(engine)* embalarse ♦ **to r. around** ajetrearse —tr. *(to compete against)* competir con, correr contra; *(horse)* hacer correr; *(engine)* acelerar al máximo ♦ **I'll r. you (home, to the corner)** te echo una carrera (a casa, a la esquina) • **to r. after** o **for** perseguir, ir detrás de • **to r. against time** o **the clock** correr contra reloj.

race³ (rās) s. BOT. raíz *f.*

race·course (rās′kôrs′) s. DEP. *(horse racetrack)* hipódromo; *(auto racetrack)* autódromo.

race·horse (rās′hôrs′) s. caballo de carreras.

ra·ceme (rā-sēm′) s. BOT. racimo.

rac·er (rā′sər) s. *(person)* corredor *m*; *(snake)* culebra.

race riot s. disturbio racial.

race·track (rās′trăk′) s. *(course)* pista; *(horse racetrack)* hipódromo.

race·way (rās′wā′) s. *(artificial channel)* saetín *m*; *(car racetrack)* autódromo; ELEC. conducto (para cables).

ra·chis (rā′kĭs) s. [pl. **-chis·es** o **-chi·des** (-kə-dēz′)] BIOL. raquis *m.*

ra·chi·tis (rə-kī′tĭs) s. raquitismo.

ra·cial (rā′shəl) adj. racial.

ra·cial·ism (rā′shə-lĭz′əm) s. G.B. var. de **racism.**

ra·cial·ly (rā′shə-lē) adv. racialmente.

rac·ing (rā′sĭng) s. carreras de caballo.

rac·ism (rā′sĭz′əm) s. racismo.

rac·ist (rā′sĭst) adj. & s. racista *mf.*

rack¹ (răk) I. s. *(in a train, car)* portaequipajes *m*; *(for hats, coats)* percha; *(in billiards)* taquera; *(for feed)* pesebre *m*, comedero; *(of a pinion)* cremallera; *(torture instrument)* potro; *(of pain)* tormento <*the r. of a severe toothache* el tormento de un agudo dolor de muelas>; *(of antlers)* cornamenta; IMPR. chibalete *m* ♦ **r. and pinion steering** AUTO. engranaje de cremallera y piñón • **to be on the r.** FAM. estar atormentado • **to go to r. and ruin** venirse abajo II. tr. *(in billiards)* poner en una taquera; *(to hurt)* hacer sufrir; *(to torture)* torturar en el potro ♦ **to be racked by** o **with** *(guilt, remorse)* estar atormentado por (una culpa, remordimientos) • **to r. one's brains** devanarse los sesos • **to r. up** FAM. acumular.

rack² (răk) I. s. pasitrote *m*, entrepaso (del caballo) II. intr. andar a pasitrote.

rack³ (răk) I. s. nubes arrastradas por el viento II. intr. ser llevado por el viento (nubes, niebla).

rack⁴ (răk) s. destrucción *f.*

rack·et¹ (răk′ĭt) s. raqueta <*tennis r.* raqueta de tenis>.

rack·et² (răk′ĭt) I. s. *(uproar)* alboroto <*what's all the r. about?* ¿qué alboroto es éste?>; *(fraud)* timo, estafa; *(extortion)* extorsión *f*; JER. *(business)* negocio, ocupación *f* II. intr. llevar una vida alegre.

rack·et·eer (răk′ĭ-tîr′) I. s. persona que hace negocios deshonestos II. intr. hacer negocios deshonestos.

rack·et·eer·ing (răk′ĭ-tîr′ĭng) s. *(bribery)* soborno; *(blackmail)* chantaje *m*; *(business)* negocio ilegal.

rack·et·y (răk′ĭ-tē) adj. ruidoso.

rac·on·teur (răk′ŏn-tûr′) s. *(story teller)* cuentista *mf*; *(anecdote teller)* anecdotista *mf.*

rac·quet (răk′ĭt) s. var. de **racket**¹.

rac·y (rā′sē) adj. **-i·er, -i·est** *(distinctive)* característico; *(risqué)* picante (chiste); *(lively)* animado.

rad (răd) s. FÍS. rad *m.*

ra·dar (rā′där) s. ELECTRÓN. radar *m.*

ra·dar·scope (rā′där-skōp′) s. pantalla de radar.

ra·di·al (rā′dē-əl) I. adj. radial II. s. *(radius)* radio; *(tire)* neumático radial.

radial engine s. motor en estrella *m.*

radial symmetry s. simetría radial.

radial tire o **radial ply tire** s. neumático radial.

ra·di·an (rā′dē-ən) s. MAT. radián *m.*

ra·di·ance (rā′dē-əns) o **ra·di·an·cy** (-ən-sē) s. *(shine)* resplandor *m*; FÍS. radiación *f.*

ra·di·ant (rā′dē-ənt) adj. FIG., FÍS. radiante.

radiant energy s. FÍS. energía radiante.

ra·di·ate (rā′dē-āt′) I. intr. **-at·ed, -at·ing** *(to shine)* brillar; *(to spread out)* radiar; *(to branch out)* salir; FÍS. irradiar, emitir —tr. radiar, irradiar II. adj. (rā′dē-ĭt) radiado.

ra·di·a·tion (rā′dē-ā′shən) s. radiación *f.*

radiation sickness s. MED. enfermedad provocada por la radiación.

ra·di·a·tor (rā′dē-ā′tər) s. radiador *m.*

rad·i·cal (răd′ĭ-kəl) adj. & s. radical *m.*

rad·i·cal·ism (răd′ĭ-kə-lĭz′əm) s. radicalismo.

rad·i·cal·ize (răd′ĭ-kə-līz′) tr. **-ized, -iz·ing** radicalizar.

rad·i·cal·ly (răd′ĭ-kə-lē) adv. radicalmente.

radical sign s. MAT. radical *m.*

rad·i·ces (răd′ĭ-sēz′) un pl. de **radix.**

rad·i·cle (răd′ĭ-kəl) s. ANAT., BOT. radícula.

ra·di·i (rā′dē-ī′) un pl. de **radius.**

ra·di·o (rā′dē-ō′) I. s. radio *f* II. tr. **-oed, -o·ing** radiar, transmitir por radio —intr. mandar un mensaje por radio.

ra·di·o·ac·tive (rā′dē-ō-ăk′tĭv) adj. radiactivo, radioactivo.

ra·di·o·ac·tiv·i·ty (rā′dē-ō-ăk-tĭv′ĭ-tē) s. FÍS. radiactividad *f*, radioactividad *f.*

radio astronomy s. radioastronomía.

radio beacon s. radiofaro.

ra·di·o·broad·cast (rā′dē-ō-brôd′kăst′) tr. & intr. **-cast** o **-cast·ed, -cast·ing** radiar.

ra·di·o·broad·cast·er (rā′dē-ō-brôd′kăs′tər) s. locutor de radio *m.*

ra·di·o·car·bon (rā′dē-ō-kär′bən) s. QUÍM. radiocarbono.

radiocarbon dating s. FÍS. método del carbono 14 para determinar la edad de vestigios orgánicos.

ra·di·o·cast (rā′dē-ō-kăst′) tr. **-cast** o **-cast·ed, -cast·ing** —intr. radiar.

radio compass s. radiocompás *m.*

ra·di·o·el·e·ment (rā′dē-ō-ĕl′ə-mənt) s. radioelemento.

radio frequency s. radiofrecuencia *f.*

ra·di·o·gram (rā′dē-ō-grăm′) s. TELEG. radiograma *m*; FÍS., MED. radiografía.

ra·di·o·graph (rā′dē-ō-grăf′) I. s. MED. radiografía II. tr. radiografiar.

ra·di·og·ra·phy (rā′dē-ŏg′rə-fē) s. FÍS., MED. radiografía.

ra·di·o·i·so·tope (rā′dē-ō-ī′sə-tōp′) s. FÍS., MED. radioisótopo.

ra·di·o·lo·ca·tion (rā′dē-ō-lō-kā′shən) s. FÍS., RAD. radiolocalización *f.*

ra·di·ol·o·gist (rā′dē-ŏl′ə-jĭst) s. MED. radiólogo.

ra·di·ol·o·gy (rā′dē-ŏl′ə-jē) s. MED. radiología; FÍS. radioscopía.

ra·di·o·man (rā′dē-ō-măn′) s. [pl. **-men** (-mĕn′)] RAD. operador de radio *m*; TELEG. radiotelegrafista *mf.*

ra·di·om·e·ter (rā′dē-ŏm′ĭ-tər) s. FÍS. radiómetro *m.*

ra·di·om·e·try (rā′dē-ŏm′ĭ-trē) s. radiometría *f.*

radio navigation s. AVIA., MARÍT. radionavegación *f.*

---

ng **inglés** / ŏ **la** / ō **bou** / ô **corre** / oi **oigo** / ōō **uno** / ou **auto** / yōō **ciudad** / w **hueco** / y **yo** / z **mismo**

radio network s. red de emisoras f.
ra·di·o·phone (rā'dē-ō-fōn') s. radiófono.
radio receiver s. radiorreceptor m.
ra·di·os·co·py (rā'dē-ŏs'kə-pē) s. radioscopia.
radio set s. aparato de radio.
ra·di·o·sonde (rā'dē-ō-sŏnd') s. METEOR. radiosonda.
radio spectrum s. RAD. radioespectro.
radio station s. emisora.
ra·di·o·tel·e·phone (rā'dē-ō-tĕl'ə-fōn') s. radioteléfono.
radio telescope s. radiotelescopio.
ra·di·o·ther·a·py (rā'dē-ō-thĕr'ə-pē) s. radioterapia.
radio transmission s. radiotransmisión f.
radio transmitter s. radiotransmisor m.
radio wave s. onda radioeléctrica o hertziana.
rad·ish (răd'ĭsh) s. rábano (planta y raíz).
ra·di·um (rā'dē-əm) s. QUÍM. radio.
radium therapy s. MED. radioterapia.
ra·di·us (rā'dē-əs) s. [pl. **-di·i** (-dē-ī') o **-di·us·es**] ANAT., MAT., MEC. radio.
ra·dix (rā'dĭks) s. [pl. **rad·i·ces** (răd'ĭ-sēz', rā'dĭ-) o **-dix·es**] BIOL., BOT. raíz f; MAT. raíz, base f.
ra·don (rā'dŏn') s. QUÍM. radón m.
raf·fi·a (răf'ē-ə) s. rafia (planta y fibra).
raff·ish (răf'ĭsh) adj. (vulgar) vulgar; (showy) ostentoso; (rakish) libertino.
raf·fle¹ (răf'əl) I. s. rifa II. tr. & intr. **-fled, -fling** rifar.
raf·fle² (răf'əl) s. (rubbish) basura; (debris) escombros m.
raft¹ (răft) I. s. balsa II. tr. transportar en balsa —intr. ♦ **to r.** o **go rafting** ir en balsa.
raft² (răft) s. FAM. (great number) montón m, sinnúmero.
raft·er (răf'tər) s. par (de un techo) m.
rag¹ (răg) s. (cloth) trapo; JER. (newspaper) periodicucho; BOT. membrana ♦ **rags** harapos.
rag² (răg) tr. **ragged, rag·ging** (to scold) regañar; JER. (to tease) tomar el pelo a.
rag³ (răg) s. (slate) pizarra.
rag⁴ (răg) s. música de jazz de ritmo sincopado.
rag·a·muf·fin (răg'ə-mŭf'ĭn) s. golfo.
rag·bag (răg'băg') s. (bag) bolsa para retazos; FIG. (mixture) mezcolanza.
rag doll s. muñeca de trapo.
rage (rāj) I. s. (of storm, sea) furia; (of person) rabia, furia ♦ **to be all the r.** estar en boga, hacer furor ♦ **to fly into a r.** enfurecerse II. intr. **raged, rag·ing** (storm) bramar; (plague, fire) propagarse.
rag·ged (răg'ĭd) adj. (beggar) andrajoso; (sleeve) raído; (garden) descuidado; (edge) mellado; (cliff, rocks) recortado; (performance) desigual; (cry) discordante.
rag·lan (răg'lən) s. COST. raglán m ♦ **r. sleeve** manga raglán.
rag·man (răg'măn') s. [pl. **-men** (-mĕn')] trapero.
ra·gout (ră-gōō') s. CUL. guiso, ragú m.
rag·tag (răg'tăg') adj. (ragged) andrajoso; (falling apart) destartalado.
rag·time (răg'tīm') s. MÚS. música de jazz de ritmo sincopado.
rag·weed (răg'wēd') s. BOT. (ambrosia) ambrosía; G.B. (ragwort) zuzón m.
rah (rä) interj. ¡hurra!
raid (rād) I. s. (by military) incursión f, ataque sorpresivo; (by police) redada, batida; (by thieves) asalto; (by speculators) maniobra II. tr. (by military) atacar por sorpresa; (by police) hacer una redada en; (by criminals) asaltar —intr. hacer una incursión.
raid·er (rā'dər) s. (attacker) invasor m; (thief) ladrón m.
rail¹ (rāl) I. s. (for protection) barandilla; (of a racetrack) cerca, barrera; (for a train) riel m ♦ **by r.** por ferrocarril • **rails** FIN. ferrocarriles II. tr. ♦ **to r. off** cercar con barras.
rail² (rāl) s. ORNIT. rascón m.
rail³ (rāl) intr. ♦ **to r. against** denostar contra.
rail fence s. cerco de postes.
rail·head (rāl'hĕd') s. F.C. cabeza de línea; MIL. cabeza de etapa ferroviaria.
rail·ing (rā'lĭng) s. (of balcony) baranda; (of stairs) pasamanos m.
rail·ler·y (rā'lə-rē) s. [pl. **-ies**] burla.

rail·road (rāl'rōd') I. s. F.C. (track) vía férrea; (system) ferrocarril m II. tr. (to transport) transportar por ferrocarril; FIG., FAM. (bill, law) hacer votar apresuradamente; (person) encarcelar bajo acusación falsa.
railroad car s. coche de ferrocarril m, vagón m.
railroad crossing s. cruce de ferrocarril m, paso a nivel.
railroad station s. estación ferroviaria.
railroad flat s. apartamento con habitaciones unas detrás de otras.
rail·road·ing (rāl'rō'dĭng) s. F.C. (operation) funcionamiento; (construction) construcción de ferrocarriles f.
rail-split·ter (rāl'splĭt'ər) s. aserrador f.
rail·way (rāl'wā) s. (railroad) ferrocarril m; (track) vía.
railway carriage s. coche m, vagón m.
rai·ment (rā'mənt) s. BÍBL. vestido, vestimenta.
rain (rān) I. s. lluvia ♦ **(come) r. or shine** FIG. pase lo que pase • **in the r.** bajo la lluvia • **the rains** la época de las lluvias II. intr. llover ♦ **to r. down** FIG. llover • **to r. on** llover • **it never rains but it pours** las desgracias nunca vienen solas, llueve sobre mojado —tr. ♦ **to r. cats and dogs** llover a cántaros.
rain·bow (rān'bō') s. arco iris.
rain check s. (ticket) entrada, contraseña (para asistir más tarde a un evento cancelado a causa de la lluvia) ♦ **to take a r.** FIG. comprometerse a hacer algo más adelante, dejar para otro momento.
rain·coat (rān'kōt') s. impermeable m.
rain date s. segunda fecha establecida para un espectáculo al aire libre, por si llueve.
rain·drop (rān'drŏp') s. gota de lluvia.
rain·fall (rān'fôl') s. (shower) aguacero; (precipitation) precipitación f.
rain forest s. selva tropical.
rain gauge o **rain gage** s. METEOR. pluviómetro.
rain·mak·er (rān'mā'kər) s. persona que puede atraer la lluvia por poderes mágicos.
rain·mak·ing (rān'mā'kĭng) s. ritual mágico para atraer la lluvia.
rain·storm (rān'stôrm') s. tempestad de lluvia f, temporal m.
rain·wa·ter (rān'wô'tər) s. agua de lluvia.
rain·wear (rān'wâr') s. ropa impermeable.
rain·y (rā'nē) adj. **-i·er, -i·est** lluvioso.
rainy day s. tiempos difíciles.
raise (rāz) I. tr. **raised, rais·ing** (a hand, head) levantar, alzar <the student raised his hand el alumno levantó la mano>; (window, gate) subir; (land) divisar; (flag) izar; (dust) levantar; (a ship) sacar a flote; (to set upright) levantar; (building, monument) levantar; (welt, blister) producir, levantar; (the dead) evocar, llamar; (prices, wages) subir, aumentar; (production) incrementar; (voice) levantar, alzar; (the spirit) levantar; (rank, level) ascender; (animals) criar; (crop) cultivar; (children) criar, educar; (question, issue) plantear; (objection, point) hacer, formular; (a lawsuit) plantear; (a shout) dar; (a laugh, commotion) causar, provocar; (phlegm) sacar; (doubts, expectations) crear, suscitar; (on a radio) comunicar con; (to arouse) sublevar <to r. the people sublevar al pueblo>; (funds, money) recaudar, juntar; (an army) reclutar; (siege) levantar; MARÍT. levantar, levar; CUL. hacer subir; MAT. elevar a una potencia; COM. obtener ♦ **to be raised** criarse, educarse • **to r. cain** o **hell** FAM. armar una de todos los diablos II. s. aumento (de precios, sueldos).
raised (rāzd) adj. (in relief) en relieve; (embossed) repujado.
rai·sin (rā'zĭn) s. pasa, pasa de uva.
ra·jah o **ra·ja** (rä'jə) s. rajá m.
rake¹ (rāk) I. s. (for the garden) rastrillo; (for the fireplace) hurgón m; (for gambling) rastrillo II. tr. **raked, rak·ing** (lawn, soil) rastrillar; (leaves) recoger con el rastrillo; (to scratch) rascar; FIG. (to sweep) rastrear; MIL. (with gunfire) ametrallar, barrer; (with the eye) abarcar ♦ **to r. for** buscar en • **to r. in** ganar en abundancia • **to r. over the coals** censurar duramente • **to r. up** sacar a relucir <to r. up old gossip sacar a relucir chismes del pasado> • **to r. up** o **together** reunir —intr. hurgar, revolver.

ā rey / ä año / b boca / ch chico / d dar / ĕ el / ē mil / g gato / h joya / hw juez / ī aire / k casa / kw cuan /

rake² (rāk) s. *(libertine)* libertino, Don Juan.
rake³ (rāk) I. tr. & intr. **raked, rak·ing** inclinar(se) II. s. inclinación.
rake-off (rāk'ôf') s. JER. comisión *f.*
rak·er (rā'kər) s. *(person)* rastrillador *m*; *(machine)* rastrilladora.
rak·ish¹ (rā'kĭsh) adj. *(jaunty)* desenvuelto; MARÍT. aerodinámico.
rak·ish² (rā'kĭsh) adj. *(libertine)* libertino, donjuanesco.
ral·ly¹ (rāl'ē) I. tr. **-lied, -ly·ing** *(to assemble)* reunir; *(to revive)* reanimar; *(to pull together)* recobrar (ánimo, fuerzas) —intr. *(to meet)* reunirse; *(to join)* organizarse; *(to recover)* recuperarse ♦ **to r. round someone** tomar el partido de alguien • **to r. to** adherirse a (partido, doctrina) II. s. [pl. **-lies**] *(assembly)* reunión *f*, mitin *m* <*a political r.* un mitin político>; *(reassembling)* reunión; COM., MED. *(recovery)* recuperación *f*; AUTO. rally *m.*
ral·ly² (rāl'ē) tr. & intr. **-lied, -ly·ing** burlar(se de).
ram (rām) I. s. ZOOL. carnero; MAQ., MEC. *(weight)* pisón *m*; *(of pump)* émbolo; *(hydraulic)* ariete *m*; HIST., MIL. ariete; MARÍT. espolón *m* ♦ **R.** ASTRON. Aries II. tr. **rammed, ram·ming** *(to pound)* apisonar; *(to stuff)* apretar, meter a la fuerza; *(to crash into)* chocar con.
Ram·a·dan (rām'ə-dän') s. RELIG. ramadán *m.*
ram·ble (rām'bəl) I. intr. **-bled, -bling** *(to walk)* pasear; *(to wind)* serpentear; *(to digress)* divagar II. s. paseo.
ram·bler (rām'blər) s. *(walker)* caminante *mf*; *(digressor)* divagador *m*; BOT. rosal trepador *m.*
ram·bling (rām'blĭng) adj. *(wandering)* vagabundo; *(aimless)* sin orden ni concierto.
ram·bunc·tious (rām-bŭngk'shəs) adj. alborotador.
ram·i·fi·ca·tion (rām'ə-fĭ-kā'shən) s. ramificación *f.*
ram·jet (rām'jĕt') s. AER. estatorreactor *m.*
ra·mose (rā'mōs') adj. ramoso.
ramp (rămp) s. *(slope)* rampa; *(staircase)* escalerilla movible (para aviones).
ram·page I. s. (rām'pāj') ♦ **to be on the r.** alborotar • **to go on a r.** andar destrozándolo todo II. intr. (rām-pāj') **-paged, -pag·ing** ♦ **to r. through** andar destrozándolo todo.
ram·pant (rām'pənt) adj. *(corruption, inflation)* desenfrenado; *(growth)* abundante; HER. rampante; ARQ. por tranquil.
ram·part (rām'pärt', -pərt) I. s. *(fortification)* muralla; *(defense)* defensa II. tr. amurallar.
ram·rod (rām'rŏd') s. *(loading rod)* taco; *(cleaning rod)* baqueta.
ram·shack·le (rām'shăk'əl) adj. desvencijado.
ran (răn) pret. de **run.**
ranch (rănch) I. s. hacienda, rancho II. intr. llevar una hacienda.
ranch·er (răn'chər) s. *(person)* estanciero, hacendado; *(house)* casa de una sola planta.
ranch house s. *(on a ranch)* hacienda, estancia; *(house)* casa de campo.
ranch·ing (răn'chĭng) s. trabajo en una hacienda.
ranch·man (rănch'mən) s. [pl. **-men**] estanciero, ranchero.
ran·cid (răn'sĭd) adj. *(rank)* rancio; FIG. *(offensive)* ofensivo.
ran·cor (răng'kər) s. rencor *m.*
ran·cor·ous (răng'kər-əs) adj. rencoroso.
ran·dom (răn'dəm) adj. *(haphazard)* hecho al azar, fortuito <*a r. selection* una selección hecha al azar>; *(aleatory)* aleatorio ♦ **at a r. guess** a ojo de buen cubero • **at r.** al azar.
ran·dom-ac·cess (răn'dəm-ăk'sĕs') adj. COMPUT. acceso directo *o* fortuito.
ran·dom·ize (răn'də-mīz') tr. **-ized, -iz·ing** CIENT. experimentar de manera aleatoria.
random variable s. COMPUT. variable casual *o* aleatoria.
ran·dy (răn'dē) adj. **-di·er, -di·est** cachondo.
rang (răng) pret. de **ring².**
range (rānj) I. s. *(reach)* alcance *m* <*within viewing r.* al alcance de la vista>; *(scope)* extensión *f*, amplitud *f* <*the r. of his knowledge* la extensión de sus conocimientos>; *(ability)* capacidad *f* <*a limited intellectual r.* una capaci-

dad intelectual limitada>; *(sphere)* campo, esfera; *(gamut)* gama, escala; *(variety)* variedad *f*, gama; *(stove)* cocina; *(of merchandise)* variedad, surtido; *(of a bullet, signal)* alcance; *(of a ship, aircraft)* radio de acción; *(outdoor firing range)* campo de tiro; *(shooting gallery)* galería de tiro; *(testing area)* campo de pruebas; *(for livestock)* terreno de pasto; *(habitat)* habitat *m*; *(class)* esfera, nivel *m*; *(row)* hilera, fila; GEOG. cordillera, cadena; MÚS. registro (de instrumento, voz); MIL. distancia (del blanco) ♦ **at close r.** *(closely)* de cerca; *(pointblank)* a quemarropa • **r. of vision** campo visual • **within firing r.** a tiro II. tr. **ranged, rang·ing** *(in rows)* alinear, poner en fila; *(to classify)* ordenar, clasificar; *(a telescope)* enfocar; *(a gun)* apuntar; *(a target)* calcular la distancia; *(to traverse)* recorrer <*when wolves ranged these regions* cuando los lobos recorrían estas comarcas>; *(livestock)* apacentar ♦ **to r. oneself against** ponerse en contra de • **to r. oneself with** ponerse de parte de —intr. *(to extend)* extenderse; *(in exploration)* recorrer; *(to wander)* rondar; *(to live)* habitar; *(to grow)* darse (en una región) ♦ **to r. from . . . to . . .** ir de . . . a . . . , oscilar entre . . . y . . . .
range finder s. telémetro.
range·land (rānj'lănd') s. praderas.
rang·er (rān'jər) s. *(of a forest)* guardabosques *m*; *(of a region)* policía *m*; *(wanderer)* trotamundos *m* ♦ **R.** MIL. soldado de un comando.
rang·y (rān'jē) adj. **-i·er, -i·est** *(tall and slender)* alto y delgado; *(spacious)* espacioso; *(roving)* vagabundo.
rank¹ (răngk) I. *(row, line)* fila; *(in society)* clase *f* <*people of all ranks* gente de todas clases>; *(high status)* rango; *(quality)* clase, categoría <*a writer of the first r.* un escritor de primera categoría>; MIL. grado ♦ **ranks** MIL. *(soldiers)* tropa, soldados rasos; *(numbers)* filas <*in the party ranks* en las filas del partido> • **to break ranks** romper filas • **to close (the) ranks** MIL. cerrar las filas • **to join the ranks of** unirse con, llegar a ser uno de • **to r. above** ser superior a • **to r. among** *o* **with** figurar entre II. tr. *(in rows)* poner en fila, alinear; *(in order)* clasificar, poner en orden; *(to outrank)* superar, ser superior —intr. clasificarse <*she ranked first* se clasificó la primera> ♦ **to r. high** ocupar una alta posición.
rank² (răngk) adj. *(plant growth)* tupido; *(soil)* fértil; *(food)* rancio; *(smell)* maloliente; *(absolute)* completo, total.
rank and file s. *(soldiers)* soldados rasos; *(ordinary people)* masa, gente común *f*; *(of trade unions)* base *f*, miembros.
rank·ing (răng'kĭng) adj. superior.
ran·kle (răng'kəl) intr. **-kled, -kling** doler (insulto) —tr. irritar.
ran·sack (răn'săk) tr. *(to search)* registrar; *(to plunder)* saquear.
ran·som (răn'səm) I. s. *(release)* rescate *m*; *(price)* rescate; RELIG. redención *f* II. tr. *(to obtain the release)* rescatar; *(to free)* liberar; RELIG. redimir.
rant (rănt) I. tr. & intr. vociferar II. s. discurso rimbombante.
rant·er (răn'tər) s. orador rimbombante *m.*
rap¹ (răp) I. s. golpecito, golpe seco ♦ **to beat the r.** JER. librarse de una condena • **to take the r.** JER. pagar el pato, cargar con la culpa de algo II. tr. **rapped, rap·ping** *(to strike)* golpear, dar un golpe en; *(to criticize)* criticar ♦ **to r. out** espetar, soltar —intr. ♦ **to r. on** *(door)* llamar a; *(table)* golpear.
rap² (răp) s. FAM. bledo, comino <*I don't give a r.* no me importa un comino>.
rap³ (răp) JER. intr. **rapped, rap·ping** *(to discuss)* discutir; *(to talk)* conversar II. s. *(discussion)* discusión *f*; *(conversation)* conversación *f.*
ra·pa·cious (rə-pā'shəs) adj. *(ravenous)* rapaz; *(voracious)* voraz; *(plundering)* saqueador; *(bird, animal)* de rapiña, rapaz.
ra·pac·i·ty (rə-păs'ĭ-tē) s. rapacidad *f.*
rape¹ (rāp) s. *(forced intercourse)* violación *f*; *(abduction)* rapto; FIG. *(violation)* violación *f*; *(plunder)* saqueo II. tr. **raped, rap·ing** *(to force sexually)* violar; FIG. *(to plunder)* saquear.
rape² (rāp) s. BOT. colza.

---

rap·id (răp′ĭd) **I.** adj. **-er, -est** rápido, veloz **II.** s. ◆ **rapids** rápidos, rabión *m.*

rap·id-fire (răp′ĭd-fīr′) adj. *(continuous)* seguido; ARM. de tiro rápido.

ra·pid·i·ty (rə-pĭd′ĭ-tē) s. rapidez *f.*

rap·id·ly (răp′ĭd-lē) adv. rápidamente.

rapid transit s. sistema de transporte urbano *m.*

ra·pi·er (rā′pē-ər) s. espadín *m,* estoque *m.*

rap·ine (răp′ĭn) s. rapiña, saqueo.

rap·ist (rā′pĭst) s. *(sexual molester)* violador *m;* *(kidnapper)* raptor *m.*

rap·port (ră-pôr′) s. relación *f.*

rap·proche·ment (ră′prōsh-mäN′) s. acercamiento.

rap·scal·lion (răp-skăl′yən) s. pillo, golfo.

rapt (răpt) adj. *(enraptured)* embelesado, extasiado; *(engrossed)* ensimismado, absorto *<she was r. in thought* estaba absorta en sus pensamientos>.

rap·tor (răp′tər) s. ave de rapiña *f.*

rap·ture (răp′chər) **I.** s. éxtasis *m* **II.** tr. **-tured, -tur·ing** embelesar, extasiar.

rap·tur·ous (răp′chər-əs) adj. extasiado.

rare[1] (râr) adj. **rar·er, rar·est** *(uncommon)* raro; *(infrequent)* poco frecuente; *(special)* poco común; *(gas, air)* enrarecido.

rare[2] (râr) adj. **rar·er, rar·est** CUL. jugoso, poco hecho.

rare·bit (râr′bĭt) s. CUL. tostadas con queso derretido.

rare earth s. QUÍM. elemento raro.

rar·e·fac·tion (râr′ə-făk′shən) s. rarefacción *f,* enrarecimiento.

rar·e·fied (râr′ə-fīd′) adj. *(esoteric)* esotérico; *(elevated)* refinado.

rar·e·fy (râr′ə-fī′) tr. **-fied, -fy·ing** *(to thin)* enrarecer; *(to purify)* purificar; *(to refine)* refinar —intr. enrarecerse, rarificarse (gases).

rare·ly (râr′lē) adv. *(not often)* raras veces, raramente; *(exceptionally)* excepcionalmente; *(wonderfully)* maravillosamente.

rar·ing (râr′ĭng) adj. FAM. impaciente *<he's r. to get started* está impaciente por empezar>.

rar·i·ty (râr′ĭ-tē) s. [pl. **-ties**] rareza.

ras·cal (răs′kəl) s. tunante *m,* bribón *m.*

rase (rāz) v. var. de **raze.**

rash[1] (răsh) adj. *(act)* precipitado; *(person)* impetuoso.

rash[2] (răsh) s. *(skin eruption)* sarpullido; FIG. *(outbreak)* ola.

rash·er (răsh′ər) s. lonja de jamón, tocino.

rash·ly (răsh′lē) adv. *(hastily)* precipitadamente; *(impetuously)* impetuosamente; *(without thought)* irreflexivamente.

rash·ness (răsh′nĭs) s. *(haste)* precipitación *f;* *(lack of prudence)* imprudencia; *(impetuosity)* impetuosidad *f;* *(lack of thought)* irreflexión *f.*

rasp (răsp) **I.** tr. *(to scrape)* raspar; *(to file)* escofinar ◆ **to r. one's nerves** crispar los nervios ◆ **to r. out** decir con voz áspera —intr. *(person)* hablar con voz áspera; *(sound)* chirriar **II.** s. *(file)* escofina; *(act)* raspado; *(sound)* chirrido.

rasp·ber·ry (răz′bĕr′ē) s. [pl. **-ries**] *(plant)* frambueso; *(fruit)* frambuesa; *(color)* color frambuesa *m;* JER. *(jeering sound)* abucheo.

rasp·y (răs′pē) adj. **-i·er, -i·est** áspero.

rat (răt) **I.** s. *(rodent)* rata; FIG., JER. *(low person)* canalla *m;* *(betrayer)* traidor *m;* *(informer)* soplón *f;* FAM. *(hair)* postizo ◆ **to smell a r.** FAM. sospechar algo **II.** intr. **rat·ted, rat·ting** *(to hunt)* cazar ratas; JER. *(to inform)* delatar *<to r. on a friend* delatar a un amigo>.

rat·a·ble (rā′tə-bəl) adj. *(appraisable)* valorable; *(proportional)* proporcional; G.B. *(taxable)* imponible.

ratch·et (răch′ĭt) s. MEC. *(tool)* trinquete *m;* *(pawl)* uña; *(wheel)* rueda de trinquete.

rate[1] (rāt) **I.** s. *(index)* índice *m <death r.* índice de mortalidad>; *(speed)* velocidad *f <a r.* a una velocidad de>; *(coefficient)* coeficiente *m <r. of increase* coeficiente de incremento>; *(percentage)* porcentaje *m,* tanto por ciento; *(rhythm)* ritmo; *(cost per unit)* precio, tarifa *<postal r.* tarifa postal>; *(level)* nivel *m,* tipo *<pay r.* tipo

de sueldo>; FIN. *(charge)* interés *m;* *(payment)* tipo (de interés, cambio) ◆ **at any r.** de todos modos, de todas formas • **at this r.** a este paso, así *<we'll never get there at this r.* a este paso nunca llegaremos> • **first-r.** de primera clase **II.** tr. **rat·ed, rat·ing** *(to estimate)* estimar; *(to value)* valorar; *(to classify)* clasificar; *(for taxation)* tasar, valorar; *(to deserve)* merecer, ser digno de *<she rates a special treatment* merece un tratamiento especial>; CINEM. clasificar —intr. ◆ **to be rated (as)** ser considerado como • **to r. high** ocupar una alta posición • **to r. with somebody** FAM. gozar de la estima de alguien.

rate[2] (rāt) tr. & intr. **rat·ed, rat·ing** regañar.

rate of exchange s. FIN. cambio, tipo de cambio.

rate-pay·er (rāt′pā′ər) s. G.B. contribuyente *mf.*

rath·er (răth′ər, rä′thər) adv. *(more exactly)* mejor dicho, más bien *<he is my friend, or r., he was my friend* es mi amigo, o mejor dicho, era mi amigo>; *(quite)* bastante *<she is r. nice* es bastante agradable>; *(somewhat)* un poco, algo *<he is r. tired* está un poco cansado>; *(to some degree)* hasta cierto punto *<he r. felt that this was wrong* le parecía que hasta cierto punto no era correcto>; *(on the contrary)* al contrario, sino que *<the plane is not arriving; r., it is leaving* el avión no llega sino que se va> ◆ **anything r. than** cualquier cosa menos (que) • **but r.** sino (que) *<I did not mean you but r. your sister* no me refería a ti sino a tu hermana> • **I would r. (go, come)** prefiero o preferiría (ir, venir) • **I would r. not** no tengo deseos, mejor no • **r. than** en vez de *<I would r. do it tomorrow than today* prefiero o preferiría hacerlo mañana en vez de hoy>.

rat·i·fi·ca·tion (răt′ə-fĭ-kā′shən) s. ratificación *f.*

rat·i·fy (răt′ə-fī′) tr. **-fied, -fy·ing** ratificar.

rat·ing[1] (rā′tĭng) s. *(standing)* clasificación *f;* *(rank)* rango; *(credit rating)* solvencia; RAD., TELEV. popularidad (de un programa) *f;* G.B., MARÍT. marinero ◆ **power r.** TEC. potencia.

rat·ing[2] (rā′tĭng) s. *(scolding)* bronca *<she gave him a r.* le echó una bronca>.

ra·tio (rā′shō) s. [pl. **-tios**] proporción *f,* relación *f;* MAT. razón *f.*

ra·ti·oc·i·nate (răsh′ē-ŏs′ə-nāt′) tr. **-nat·ed, -nat·ing** raciocinar.

ra·tion (răsh′ən, rā′shən) **I.** s. ración *f,* porción *f* ◆ **rations** MIL. provisiones, víveres • **to put on r.** racionar **II.** tr. racionar ◆ **to r. out** racionar.

ra·tion·al (răsh′ə-nəl) adj. *(of the reason)* racional; *(sensible)* razonable, sensato; *(logical)* lógico; MAT. racional.

ra·tion·ale (răsh′ə-năl′) s. *(reason)* razón fundamental *f,* fundamento; *(explanation)* exposición razonada, explicación *f.*

ra·tion·al·ism (răsh′ə-nə-lĭz′əm) s. FILOS. racionalismo.

ra·tion·al·i·ty (răsh′ə-năl′ĭ-tē) s. [pl. **-ties**] racionalidad *f.*

ra·tion·al·i·za·tion (răsh′ə-nə-lĭ-zā′shən) s. racionalización *f.*

ra·tion·al·ize (răsh′ə-nə-līz′) tr. **-ized, -iz·ing** racionalizar.

rational number s. MAT. número racional.

ra·tion·ing (răsh′ə-nĭng, rā′shə-) s. racionamiento.

rat·line (răt′lĭn) s. MARÍT. flechaste *m.*

rat race s. JER. ajetreo, lucha incesante.

rats·bane (răts′bān′) s. raticida *m,* matarratas *m.*

rat·tan (ră-tăn′) s. BOT. rota, junco de Indias.

rat·tle (răt′l) **I.** intr. **-tled, -tling** *(vehicle)* traquetear; *(machine gun)* repiquetear; *(hail, rain)* tamborilear; *(window, door)* golpetear (con el viento); *(teeth)* castañetear; FAM. *(to talk)* parlotear ◆ **to r. along** o **by** ir o pasar traqueteando • **to r. on** seguir parloteando —tr. *(to shake)* sacudir, agitar; FAM. *(to unnerve)* poner nervioso; *(to disconcert)* desconcertar ◆ **to r. off** despachar, decir rápidamente **II.** s. *(of vehicle)* traqueteo; *(of hail, rain)* tamborileo, repiqueteo; *(of gun)* repiqueteo, tableteo; *(of door, window)* golpe *m;* *(of teeth)* castañeteo; *(of baby)* sonajero; FAM. *(loud talk)* jaleo, alboroto; ZOOL. cascabel *m;* MED. estertor *m.*

rat·tle-brained (răt′l-brānd′) adj. casquivano, ligero de cascos.

rat·tler (răt′lər) s. *(snake)* serpiente de cascabel *f,* crótalo; *(train)* tren de carga *m.*

ā rey / ä año / b boca / ch chico / d dar / ĕ el / ē mil / g gato / h joya / hw juez / ī aire / k casa / kw cuan /

rat·tle·snake (răt′l-snāk′) s. ZOOL. serpiente de cascabel *f*, crótalo.

rat·tle·trap (răt′l-trăp′) s. cacharro (vehículo).

rat·tling (răt′lĭng) I. adj. FAM. *(animated)* animado; *(excellent)* excelente II. adv. muy <*a r. good party* una fiesta muy buena>.

rat·trap (răt′trăp′) s. *(device)* ratonera; FIG. *(dwelling)* pocilga.

rat·ty (răt′ē) adj. -ti·er, -ti·est *(of rats)* ratonil; *(infested)* infestado de ratas; JER. *(dilapidated)* destartalado; *(shabby)* andrajoso; G.B. *(annoyed)* enojado; *(irritable)* irritable.

rau·cous (rô′kəs) adj. *(harsh)* ronco; *(boisterous)* estridente.

raun·chy (rôn′chē) adj. -chi·er, -chi·est JER. *(grimy)* sucio; *(vulgar)* vulgar; *(sexually explicit)* pornográfico; *(lustful)* lascivo.

rav·age (răv′ĭj) I. tr. -aged, -ag·ing *(by fire, tornado)* destruir totalmente, destrozar; *(by army)* pillar, saquear II. s. *(by fire, tornado)* destrucción *f*, destrozo; *(by army)* pillaje *m* ♦ **ravages** estragos.

rave (rāv) I. intr. raved, rav·ing *(to speak irrationally)* delirar, desvariar; *(to rage)* bramar, estar desencadenado (viento, mar) ♦ **to r. about** hablar con entusiasmo de, estar loco por II. s. ♦ **to get raves** o **r. reviews** FAM. recibir críticas entusiastas.

rav·el (răv′əl) I. tr. *(cloth)* deshilar, deshilachar; FIG. *(to clarify)* aclarar; *(to tangle)* enredar, enmarañar —intr. deshilarse, deshilacharse II. s. *(thread)* hilacha; *(tangle)* enmarañamiento.

ra·ven[1] (rā′vən) I. s. cuervo II. adj. negro y brillante.

rav·en[2] (răv′ən) I. tr. & intr. *(to devour)* devorar; *(to seek prey)* buscar una presa II. s. *(voracity)* voracidad *f*; *(booty)* botín *m*.

rav·en·ous (răv′ə-nəs) adj. *(hungry)* hambriento; *(voracious)* voraz; *(predatory)* rapaz ♦ **to be r. for** tener muchas ganas de.

ra·vine (rə-vēn′) s. barranco.

rav·ing (rā′vĭng) I. adj. FAM. extraordinario <*a r. beauty* una belleza extraordinaria> ♦ **to be a r. maniac** o **lunatic** estar loco de atar II. s. ♦ **ravings** desvaríos, divagaciones.

ra·vi·o·li (răv′ē-ō′lē) s. CUL. ravioles *m*.

rav·ish (răv′ĭsh) tr. *(to seize)* raptar; *(to rape)* violar; FIG. *(to enrapture)* embelesar.

rav·ish·ing (răv′ĭ-shĭng) adj. encantador, cautivador.

raw (rô) adj. *(uncooked)* crudo <*r. meat* carne cruda>; *(not refined)* sin refinar, bruto; *(fresh)* fresco <*r. plaster* yeso fresco>; *(pure)* puro, sin mezcla <*r. spirit* alcohol puro>; *(weather)* frío y húmedo; *(unfair)* injusto <*a r. punishment* un castigo injusto>; *(crude)* crudo; *(wood)* verde; FIG. *(inexperienced)* novato; *(socially coarse)* tosco, grosero; MED. *(throat)* inflamado; *(wound)* en carne viva ♦ **in the r.** *(in the original state)* en estado original; FAM. *(naked)* desnudo • **to get a r. deal** JER. recibir un tratamiento injusto.

raw·boned (rô′bōnd′) adj. enjuto.

raw data s. COMPUT. datos sin procesar *m*.

raw deal s. JER. tratamiento injusto.

raw·hide (rô′hīd′) s. cuero sin curtir.

raw material s. materia prima.

ray[1] (rā) s. FÍS. rayo; MAT. radio; BOT. radio; FIG. *(trace)* rayo, resquicio <*there is a r. of hope* hay un rayo de esperanza>.

ray[2] (rā) s. ICT. raya.

ray·less (rā′lĭs) adj. *(dark)* oscuro; BOT. sin radios.

ray·on (rā′ŏn′) s. rayón *m*.

raze (rāz) tr. razed, raz·ing *(to level)* arrasar, demoler; *(to scrape)* raspar; *(to shave off)* cortar; ANT. *(to erase)* borrar.

ra·zor (rā′zər) s. navaja de afeitar.

ra·zor·back (rā′zər-băk′) s. *(hill)* cerro abrupto; ZOOL. *(wild hog)* cerdo salvaje; *(rorqual)* rorcual *m*.

razor blade s. cuchilla *u* hoja de afeitar.

razor-edge s. filo.

razz (răz) tr. JER. tomar el pelo a, burlarse de.

raz·zle-daz·zle (răz′əl-dăz′əl) s. FAM. deslumbramiento, colorido.

re[1] (rā) s. MÚS. re *m*.

re[2] (rē) prep. respecto a, referente a.

reach (rēch) I. tr. *(to stretch out)* alargar, extender <*she reached out her arms* extendió los brazos>; *(to touch)* alcanzar, llegar a o hasta <*the rope did not r. the bottom* la soga no llegó hasta el fondo>; *(to get to)* alcanzar, coger <*I could not r. the book* no pude alcanzar el libro>; *(to arrive at)* llegar a; *(to attain)* alcanzar <*to r. the speed of sound* alcanzar la velocidad del sonido>; *(to arrive at)* llegar a manos de <*the letter reached me yesterday* la carta llegó a mis manos ayer>; *(on the phone)* ponerse en contacto con, comunicarse con; *(to get through to)* impresionar; *(in length)* llegar o extenderse hasta <*the property reaches the shore* la finca se extiende hasta la costa>; *(in height)* llegar a; *(in amount)* alcanzar, ascender a <*sales reached the thousands* las ventas ascendieron a miles de dólares>; *(in age)* llegar a, cumplir (años); FAM. *(to pass)* alcanzar, pasar (la sal, un objeto); *(to hit)* alcanzar, pegar en ♦ **to r. someone's heart** llegar al corazón de alguien —intr. *(to touch)* llegar <*I can barely r.* apenas llego>; *(with the hand)* alargar la mano <*the usher reached over the seats* el acomodador alargó la mano por encima de las butacas>; *(to try to grasp)* tratar de coger o agarrar <*the policeman reached for his gun* el policía trató de agarrar la pistola> ♦ **as far as the eye can r.** hasta donde alcanza la vista • **to r. as far as** o **(up) to** *(in height)* llegar a <*the mud reached up to my knees* el fango me llegaba a las rodillas>; *(in length)* llegar o extenderse hasta • **to r. down** inclinarse, agacharse • **to r. for the stars** o **moon** FIG. aspirar a lo inalcanzable • **to r. in** meter la mano • **to r. into** *(a place)* meter la mano en; *(amount)* alcanzar, ascender a • **to r. out** extender la mano, asistir a los necesitados • **to r. up** alzar la mano II. s. *(extent)* alcance *m* <*keep out of the r. of children* manténgase fuera del alcance de los niños>; *(comprehension)* comprensión *f*; *(of river, canal)* tramo recto; *(of cord, arm)* extensión *f* ♦ **within r.** *(of the hand)* al alcance de la mano; *(by transportation)* cerca <*within easy r.* muy cerca>.

re·act (rē-ăkt′) intr. reaccionar.

re·ac·tance (rē-ăk′təns) s. ELEC. reactancia.

re·ac·tant (rē-ăk′tənt) s. QUÍM. agente reactor *m*.

re·ac·tion (rē-ăk′shən) s. reacción *f*.

reaction time s. CIENT. tiempo de reacción.

re·ac·ti·vate (rē-ăk′tə-vāt′) tr. -vat·ed, -vat·ing reactivar.

re·ac·tive (rē-ăk′tĭv) adj. reactivo.

re·ac·tor (rē-ăk′tər) s. QUÍM. reactivo; ELEC. bobina, reactor *m*; FÍS. reactor.

read (rēd) I. tr. read (rĕd), read·ing *(a book, music)* leer; *(a language)* saber leer <*he reads Latin* sabe leer latín>; *(thoughts)* leer, adivinar <*one could r. disappointment in her eyes* se adivinaba la decepción en su mirada>; *(to interpret)* leer, interpretar; *(the future)* leer, adivinar; *(to learn from)* leer <*he r. that crime would decrease* leyó que la criminalidad disminuiría>; *(to substitute)* leer, sustituir; G.B. *(to study)* cursar, estudiar; RAD. captar, oír <*I r. you fine* te oigo bien>; IMPR. leer, corregir; TEC. *(to register)* marcar <*the dial reads 32°* la esfera marca 32°>; *(an instrument)* leer, ver cuánto marca ♦ **to r. about** leer acerca de • **to r. into** *(to attribute)* atribuir (a) <*he r. a different meaning into it* le atribuyó un sentido distinto>; COMPUT. transferir a • **to r. off** leer en voz alta • **to r. out** *(to read aloud)* leer en voz alta; *(to expel)* expulsar (de una agrupación) • **to r. over** *(to go over)* leer, repasar; *(to reread)* leer, releer • **to r. someone like a book** saber lo que alguien está pensando • **to r. someone's palm** leerle la mano a alguien • **to r. up on** informarse acerca de —intr. *(to read characters)* leer; *(to be worded)* rezar, decir <*the letter reads as follows* la carta dice lo siguiente>; *(to indicate)* rezar, indicar ♦ **to r. between the lines** leer entre líneas • **to r. (well, poorly)** leerse (bien, mal) II. s. lectura ♦ **to be a good r.** ofrecer un rato de lectura agradable III. adj. ♦ **well-read** muy leído.

read·a·ble (rē′də-bəl) adj. *(legible)* legible; *(interesting)* interesante (libro, revista).

read·er (rē′dər) s. *(for pleasure)* lector *m*; *(for a professor)* corrector de exámenes *m; (for a publisher)* lector de manuscritos; *(schoolbook)* libro de lecturas; *(anthology)* antología ♦ **I'm not much of a r.** no me gusta mucho la lectura.

read·er·ship (rĕ'dər-shĭp') s. *(readers)* lectores en conjunto (de una publicación) *m;* G.B. *(office)* lectoría.

read·i·ly (rĕd'l-ē) adv. *(promptly)* prontamente; *(willingly)* de buena gana; *(easily)* con facilidad <*the money is r. available* el dinero se consigue con facilidad>.

read·i·ness (rĕd'ē-nĭs) s. buena disposición <*his r. to cooperate* su buena disposición para cooperar>.

read·ing (rĕ'dĭng) s. *(act)* lectura <*r. and writing* la lectura y la escritura>; *(material)* lectura <*the list of readings for the course* la lista de lecturas del curso>; *(recitation)* lectura <*the r. of the will* la lectura del testamento>; *(recital)* lectura, recital *m; (interpretation)* interpretación *f,* modo de ver (problema, situación); *(version)* versión *f,* variante (de un texto) *f;* TEC. indicación *f,* medida; COMPUT. transferencia ♦ **r. room** sala de lectura • **the r. public** el público lector, los lectores • **to take a r.** TEC. medir.

re·ad·just (rē'ə-jŭst') tr. reajustar, readaptar.

re·ad·just·ment (rē'ə-jŭst'mənt) s. reajuste *m.*

read-out (rēd'out') s. COMPUT. información impresa.

read·y (rĕd'ē) I. adj. **-i·er, -i·est** *(prepared)* listo, preparado <*dinner is r.* la cena está lista>; *(willing)* dispuesto <*he was r. to believe them* estaba dispuesto a creerles>; *(liable)* listo <*r. to quit the job* listo para irse del trabajo>; *(about to)* a punto de <*the shed looked r. to collapse* el cobertizo parecía estar a punto de derrumbarse>; *(clever)* agudo, vivo <*a r. wit* un ingenio agudo>; *(answer)* rápido; *(nimble)* suelto (movimientos); *(available)* disponible ♦ **r. cash** *o* **money** dinero contante • **r.!, set!, go!** ¡preparados!, ¡listos!, ¡fuera! • **to get r.** *(to prepare)* preparar(se); *(to fix up)* arreglar(se) • **to make r.** preparar(se) II. tr. **-ied, -y·ing** preparar III. s. ♦ **at the r.** MIL. en posición de disparar.

read·y-made (rĕd'ē-mād') adj. *(made)* hecho; *(preconceived)* preconcebido.

read·y-to-wear (rĕd'ē-tə-wâr') COST. I. adj. hecho, confeccionado II. s. ropa hecha.

re·af·firm (rē'ə-fûrm') tr. reafirmar.

re·af·fir·ma·tion (rē'ăf'ər-mā'shən) s. reafirmación *f.*

re·a·gent (rē-ā'jənt) s. QUÍM. reactivo.

re·al¹ (rē'əl) I. adj. *(actual)* real <*it happened in r. life* sucedió en la vida real>; *(true)* verdadero <*his r. reason* sus verdaderos motivos>; *(objective)* cierto <*can such things be r.?* ¿es que esas cosas pueden ser ciertas?>; *(genuine)* verdadero, fundamental <*the r. problem is poverty* el verdadero problema es la pobreza>; *(worthy of the name)* verdadero, de verdad; *(serious)* de verdad <*in r. trouble* en un lío de verdad>; DER., FÍS., MAT. real ♦ **for r.** FAM. *(authentic)* de verdad; *(really)* de veras II. adv. FAM. muy, mucho <*r. fast* muy rápido>.

re·al² (rā-äl') s. HIST. real (moneda española) *m.*

real estate s. bienes inmuebles *m,* bienes raíces *m.*

re·a·lign (rē'ə-līn') tr. *(tires)* realinear; *(people)* reagrupar.

re·a·lign·ment (rē'ə-līn'mənt) s. *(of tires)* realineación *f; (of people)* reagrupación *f.*

re·al·ism (rē'ə-lĭz'əm) s. realismo.

re·al·ist (rē'ə-lĭst) s. realista *mf.*

re·al·is·tic (rē'ə-lĭs'tĭk) adj. realista.

re·al·is·ti·cal·ly (rē'ə-lĭs'tĭ-kə-lē) adv. de manera realista, con realismo.

re·al·i·ty (rē-ăl'ĭ-tē) s. [pl. **-ties**] *(actuality)* realidad *f; (fact)* hecho; *(artistic accuracy)* realismo.

re·al·i·za·tion (rē'ə-lĭ-zā'shən) s. *(understanding)* comprensión *f; (fulfillment)* realización *f,* logro.

re·al·ize (rē'ə-līz') tr. **-ized, -iz·ing** *(to comprehend)* comprender, darse cuenta de; *(to attain)* realizar, hacer realidad <*to r. a dream* hacer realidad un sueño>; COM. *(to profit)* obtener, sacar <*to r. large profits* obtener grandes beneficios>; *(to convert into money)* realizar, convertir en dinero.

re·al·ly (rē'ə-lē) adv. *(in reality)* en realidad; *(truly)* verdaderamente, realmente <*that was a r. enjoyable evening* fue una noche verdaderamente agradable>; *(very)* muy ♦ **r.!** ¡hay que ver! • **r.?** ¿de veras?, ¿de verdad?

realm (rĕlm) s. *(kingdom)* reino; *(field)* esfera, terreno.

real number s. MAT. cantidad real *f.*

re·al·tor (rē'əl-tər, -tôr') s. corredor de fincas *m.*

re·al·ty (rē'əl-tē) s. [pl. **-ties**] bienes raíces *m.*

ream¹ (rēm) s. *(paper)* resma ♦ **reams** FIG. montones.

ream² (rēm) tr. *(to enlarge)* abocardar, escariar; *(to squeeze)* exprimir.

ream·er (rē'mər) s. *(tool)* escariador *m; (juice extractor)* exprimidor (de naranjas, limones) *m.*

re·an·i·mate (rē-ăn'ə-māt') tr. **-mat·ed, -mat·ing** reanimar.

re·an·i·ma·tion (rē-ăn'ə-mā'shən) s. reanimación *f.*

reap (rēp) tr. & intr. FIG. *(to collect rewards)* cosechar (elogios, riquezas), AGR. *(to cut)* segar; *(to harvest)* cosechar.

reap·er (rē'pər) s. AGR. *(person)* segador *m; (machine)* segadora.

re·ap·pear (rē'ə-pîr') intr. reaparecer, resurgir.

re·ap·pear·ance (rē'ə-pîr'əns) s. reaparición *f.*

re·ap·point (rē'ə-point') tr. nombrar de nuevo.

re·ap·point·ment (rē'ə-point'mənt) s. nuevo nombramiento.

re·ap·por·tion (rē'ə-pôr'shən) tr. repartir de nuevo.

re·ap·por·tion·ment (rē'ə-pôr'shən-mənt) s. *(redistribution)* nueva distribución *f,* POL. nueva distribución de la representación en el congreso.

re·ap·prais·al (rē'ə-prā'zəl) s. revaluación *f.*

rear¹ (rîr) I. s. *(back part)* parte trasera; *(of a house, bus)* fondo; *(of army, fleet)* retaguardia; FAM. *(buttocks)* nalgas ♦ **at the r. of** detrás de • **to bring up the r.** MIL. cerrar la marcha II. adj. trasero, de atrás.

rear² (rîr) tr. *(animals)* criar; *(plants)* cultivar, cuidar; *(children)* cuidar, educar; *(head)* alzar, erguir; *(building)* erigir, levantar —intr. *(horse)* encabritarse; *(building, mountain)* elevarse.

rear admiral s. MARÍT. contraalmirante *m.*

rear guard s. retaguardia.

rear-guard (rîr'gärd') adj. de retaguardia.

rear·ing (rîr'ĭng) s. *(of children)* crianza; *(of the head)* erguimiento; *(of a monument)* erección *f; (of animals)* cría; *(of plants)* cultivo.

re·arm (rē-ärm') tr. & intr. rearmar(se).

re·ar·ma·ment (rē-är'mə-mənt) s. MIL. rearme *m.*

rear·most (rîr'mōst') adj. último.

re·ar·range (rē'ə-rānj') tr. **-ranged, -rang·ing** *(to arrange again)* volver a arreglar; *(change order)* disponer de otro modo.

re·ar·range·ment (rē'ə-rānj'mənt) s. nuevo arreglo, nueva disposición *f.*

rear·view mirror (rîr'vyoo') s. espejo retrovisor.

rear·ward¹ (rîr'wərd) I. adj. último II. adv. hacia atrás III. s. fondo.

rear·ward² (rîr'wôrd') s. retaguardia.

rea·son (rē'zən) I. s. *(basis)* razón *f,* motivo <*I have my reasons for doing it this way* tengo mis motivos para hacerlo así>; *(intelligence)* razón, intelecto; *(sanity)* razón, juicio <*to loose one's r.* perder el juicio> ♦ **all the more r. (to)** razón de más (para) • **by r. of** en virtud de • **for no r.** sin ningún motivo • **the r. why** el porqué, la razón por la cual • **there is no (good) r. for** no hay razón que valga para • **there is no r. to** no hay razón para • **to be within r.** ser razonable • **to have no r.** no tener por qué • **to have r. to** tener motivos para • **to listen to r.** avenirse a razones • **to stand to r.** ser evidente • **with (good) r.** con razón II. intr. *(to think)* razonar; *(to discuss)* discutir —tr. razonar ♦ **r. out** concluir, resolver.

rea·son·a·ble (rē'zə-nə-bəl) adj. razonable.

rea·son·a·bly (rē'zə-nə-blē) adv. razonablemente.

rea·son·er (rē'zə-nər) s. *(thinker)* razonador *m; (arguer)* discutidor *m.*

rea·son·ing (rē'zə-nĭng) s. razonamiento.

re·as·sess (rē'ə-sĕs') tr. *(a tax)* fijar de nuevo; *(to revalue)* valorar de nuevo.

re·as·sur·ance (rē'ə-shoor'əns) s. *(confidence)* confianza, seguridad *f; (tranquillity)* tranquilidad *f; (promise)* promesa; COM. reaseguro.

re·as·sure (rē'ə-shoor') tr. **-sured, -sur·ing** *(to restore confi-*

dence to) dar confianza, tranquilizar; *(to assure again)* asegurar nuevamente; COM. reasegurar.

re·bate (rē′bāt′) COM. **I.** s. descuento, rebaja <*ten-dollar r.* una rebaja de diez dólares>; *(repayment)* reembolso **II.** tr. **-bat·ed, -bat·ing** *(to discount)* rebajar, descontar; *(to repay)* reembolsar.

re·bel I. intr. (rĭ-bĕl′) **-belled, -bel·ling** rebelarse, sublevarse ♦ **to r. against** *(to defy)* desafiar a; *(to revolt)* rebelarse contra **II.** s. **reb·el** (rĕb′əl) rebelde *mf* ♦ **r. soldiers** soldados rebeldes.

re·bel·lion (rĭ-bĕl′yən) s. rebelión *f.*

re·bel·lious (rĭ-bĕl′yəs) adj. rebelde.

re·bel·lious·ness (rĭ-bĕl′yəs-nĭs) s. rebeldía.

re·birth (rē-bûrth′) s. renacimiento.

re·born (rē-bôrn′) adj. renacido ♦ **to be r.** volver a nacer.

re·bound I. intr. (rē-bound′) *(ball)* rebotar; FIG. *(person)* recuperarse —tr. hacer rebotar **II.** s. (rē′bound′) rebote *m* ♦ **to marry on the r.** casarse después del divorcio.

re·broad·cast (rē-brôd′kăst′) **I.** tr. **-cast** *o* **-cast·ed, -cast·ing** retransmitir **II.** s. retransmisión *f.*

re·buff (rĭ-bŭf′) **I.** s. *(refusal)* rechazo; *(repulse)* repulsa; *(snub)* desaire *m*; *(setback)* revés *m* **II.** tr. *(to refuse)* rechazar; *(to snub)* desairar.

re·build (rē-bĭld′) tr. & intr. **-built** (-bĭlt′), **-build·ing** reconstruir.

re·build·ing (rē-bĭl′dĭng) s. reconstrucción *f.*

re·buke (rĭ-byōōk′) **I.** tr. **-buked, -buk·ing** reprender, regañar **II.** s. reprimenda.

re·bus (rē′bəs) s. [pl. **-bus·es**] jeroglífico.

re·but (rĭ-bŭt′) tr. & intr. **-but·ted, -but·ting** refutar.

re·but·tal (rĭ-bŭt′l) s. refutación *f.*

re·but·ter (rĭ-bŭt′ər) s. *(person)* persona que refuta algo; DER. contrarréplica.

re·cal·ci·trant (rĭ-kăl′sĭ-trənt) **I.** adj. recalcitrante **II.** s. persona recalcitrante.

re·call I. tr. (rĭ-kôl′) *(workers, officials)* hacer volver, llamar; *(diplomat)* retirar; *(product)* retirar del mercado; *(to remind)* recordar, traer a la memoria <*this movie recalls my visit to Rome* esta película me trae a la memoria mi visita a Roma>; *(to remember)* recordar, acordarse de; *(to revoke)* revocar, anular; *(to bring back)* restituir, devolver **II.** s. (rē′kôl′) *(of diplomat)* retiro; *(of a product)* retiro del mercado; *(recollection)* recuerdo; *(revocation)* revocación *f*, anulación *f*; *(of a public official)* destitución *f*; MIL. toque de llamada *m.*

re·cant (rĭ-kănt′) tr. & intr. retractar(se).

re·can·ta·tion (rē′kăn-tā′shən) s. retractación *f.*

re·cap¹ I. tr. (rē-kăp′) **-capped, -cap·ping** *(bottle)* volver a tapar; *(tire)* recauchutar **II.** s. (rē′kăp′) neumático recauchutado.

re·cap² (rē′kăp′) FAM. **I.** tr. **-capped, -cap·ping** recapitular **II.** s. recapitulación *f.*

re·cap·i·tal·ize (rē-kăp′ĭ-tl-īz′) tr. **-ized, -iz·ing** COM. volver a capitalizar.

re·ca·pit·u·late (rē′kə-pĭch′ə-lāt′) tr. **-lat·ed, -lat·ing** recapitular —intr. resumir.

re·ca·pit·u·la·tion (rē′kə-pĭch′ə-lā′shən) s. recapitulación *f.*

re·cap·ture (rē-kăp′chər) **I.** s. MIL. reconquista; DER. recobro **II.** tr. **-tured, -tur·ing** *(one's youth, past)* hacer revivir; *(prisoner)* volver a capturar; MIL. reconquistar; DER. *(goods)* recobrar.

re·cast (rē-kăst′) tr. **-cast, -cast·ing** *(bell, medal)* refundir; *(ideas)* expresar de otra manera, reconstruir; *(play, opera)* cambiar el reparto de.

re·cede (rĭ-sēd′) intr. **-ced·ed, -ced·ing** *(to move back)* retroceder; *(to slope)* inclinarse; *(to become distant)* alejarse.

re·cede (rē-sēd′) tr. **-ced·ed, -ced·ing** volver a ceder.

re·ceipt (rĭ-sēt′) **I.** s. *(reception)* recepción *f*; *(slip)* recibo ♦ **on r. of** al recibo de, al recibir • **receipts** ingresos, entradas **II.** tr. *(to acknowledge)* acusar recibo; *(to issue)* dar un recibo —intr. dar un recibo.

re·ceiv·a·ble (rĭ-sē′və-bəl) COM. **I.** adj. *(acceptable)* aceptable, admisible (condición *o* como pago); *(due)* a cobrar <*accounts r.* cuentas a cobrar> **II.** s. ♦ **receivables** cuentas a cobrar.

re·ceive (rĭ-sēv′) tr. **-ceived, -ceiv·ing** *(present, letter)* recibir; *(salary)* percibir, cobrar; *(honor, title)* recibir; *(blow, punishment)* recibir; *(to support)* recibir, aguantar <*this beam receives the whole weight* esta viga recibe todo el peso>; *(to take in)* recoger <*a tank receiving rainwater* un tanque que recoge la lluvia>; *(to admit)* recibir, aceptar <*to r. new members* aceptar socios nuevos>; *(into a church)* recibir; *(to greet)* recibir, dar la bienvenida a; *(to shelter)* acoger, dejar entrar; *(stolen property)* ocultar; *(an impression)* recibir; *(a theory, opinion)* recibir, acoger (teoría, opinión); *(confession)* oír, escuchar —intr. recibir; RELIG. comulgar ♦ **to be well received** recibir una buena acogida.

re·ceiv·er (rĭ-sē′vər) s. *(one who receives)* recibidor *m*, receptor *m*; DER. *(of stolen goods)* ocultador *m*; administrador judicial *m*; QUÍM. recipiente *m*; ELECTRÓN., RAD. receptor; TEL. auricular *m.*

re·ceiv·er·ship (rĭ-sē′vər-shĭp′) s. DER. receptoría.

receiving line s. fila de recepción.

re·cent (rē′sənt) adj. reciente ♦ **R.** GEOL. holoceno.

re·cent·ly (rē′sənt-lē) adv. recientemente.

re·cep·ta·cle (rĭ-sĕp′tə-kəl) s. *(container)* receptáculo; *(floral support)* receptáculo; *(outlet)* enchufe hembra *m.*

re·cep·tion (rĭ-sĕp′shən) s. recepción *f.*

re·cep·tion·ist (rĭ-sĕp′shə-nĭst) s. recepcionista *mf.*

re·cep·tive (rĭ-sĕp′tĭv) adj. receptivo.

re·cep·tiv·i·ty (rē′sĕp-tĭv′ĭ-tē) s. receptividad *f.*

re·cep·tor (rĭ-sĕp′tər) s. receptor *m.*

re·cer·ti·fi·ca·tion (rē-sûr′tə-fĭ-kā′shən) s. renovación de certificación *f.*

re·cess (rē′sĕs′, rĭ-sĕs′) **I.** s. *(in school)* recreo <*one-hour r.* recreo de una hora>; *(in meeting)* interrupción *f*; *(in wall)* hueco; *(for statue)* nicho ♦ **recesses** *(of mind)* partes recónditas • **to be in r.** *(Congress)* estar clausurado; *(school)* estar cerrada por vacaciones **II.** tr. *(to place in a recess)* poner en un hueco; *(to create a recess in)* hacer un hueco en —intr. *(Congress)* suspender la sesión; *(school)* cerrar por vacaciones.

re·ces·sion (rĭ-sĕsh′ən) s. *(withdrawl)* retirada; RELIG. procesión del clero hacia la sacristía *f*; COM., FIN. recesión *f.*

re·ces·sion·al (rĭ-sĕsh′ə-nəl) **I.** adj. de retirada **II.** s. RELIG. *(hymn)* himno de fin de oficio; *(recession)* procesión del clero hacia la sacristía *f.*

re·ces·sive (rĭ-sĕs′ĭv) **I.** adj. *(receding)* que tiende a retroceder; BIOL. recesivo **II.** s. BIOL. *(trait)* rasgo recesivo; *(organism)* organismo de carácter recesivo.

re·charge (rē-chärj′) tr. **-charged, -charg·ing** recargar.

re·cid·i·vism (rĭ-sĭd′ə-vĭz′əm) s. reincidencia.

rec·i·pe (rĕs′ə-pē) s. receta.

re·cip·i·ent (rĭ-sĭp′ē-ənt) adj. & s. receptor *m.*

re·cip·ro·cal (rĭ-sĭp′rə-kəl) **I.** adj. recíproco, mutuo; GRAM., MAT. recíproco **II.** s. MAT. número recíproco.

re·cip·ro·cate (rĭ-sĭp′rə-kāt′) tr. **-cat·ed, -cat·ing** *(to return)* corresponder a <*to r. someone's love* corresponder al amor de alguien>; *(to exchange)* intercambiar, cambiar —intr. *(to respond)* corresponder; TECH. tener movimiento alternativo.

reciprocating engine s. MEC. motor alternativo.

re·cip·ro·ca·tion (rĭ-sĭp′rə-kā′shən) s. reciprocidad *f.*

rec·i·proc·i·ty (rĕs′ə-prŏs′ĭ-tē) s. [pl. **-ties**] reciprocidad *f.*

re·ci·sion (rĭ-sĭzh′ən) s. rescisión *f*, anulación *f.*

re·cit·al (rĭ-sīt′l) s. *(recitation)* recitación *f*; *(performance)* recital *m*; *(narration)* narración *f*, relato.

rec·i·ta·tion (rĕs′ĭ-tā′shən) s. *(recital)* recitación *f*; *(narration)* narración *f*, relato.

rec·i·ta·tive (rĕs′ĭ-tā′tĭv, rĭ-sī′tə-tĭv) adj. recitativo.

re·cite (rĭ-sīt′) tr. & intr. **-cit·ed, -cit·ing** *(poem, lesson)* recitar; *(story)* narrar, relatar; *(list)* enumerar.

re·cit·er (rĭ-sī′tər) s. recitador *m.*

reck·less (rĕk′lĭs) adj. *(careless)* imprudente; *(rash)* precipitado; *(wild)* temerario.

reck·on (rĕk′ən) tr. *(to count)* contar (días, horas); *(to compute)* calcular; *(to regard as)* considerar como; FAM. *(to assume)* creer, suponer ♦ **to r. on** contar con —intr. calcular ♦ **to r. with** tener en cuenta.

reck·on·er (rĕk′ə-nər) s. calculador *m*; MAT. tabla.

---

reck·on·ing (rĕk′ə-nĭng) s. *(calculation)* cálculo, cómputo; *(bill)* cuenta, factura; AVIA., MARÍT. cálculo de posición, estima ♦ **day of r.** Día del Juicio Final.

re-claim (rĭ-klām′) tr. *(from desert, sea)* ganar, recobrar; *(from a swamp)* sanear; *(waste products)* recuperar; *(person)* reformar, enmendar.

re-claim (rē-klām′) tr. reclamar.

rec·la·ma·tion (rĕk′lə-mā′shən) s. *(of possession)* reclamación *f*, reclamo; *(of land)* recuperación *f*, aprovechamiento; *(of swamp)* saneamiento; *(of waste)* recuperación; *(of a person)* enmienda.

re-cline (rĭ-klīn′) tr. & intr. **-clined, -clin·ing** reclinar(se), recostar(se).

re·cluse (rĕk′lŏŏs′, rĭ-klŏŏs′) **I.** s. solitario, ermitaño **II.** adj. solitario, retirado.

re·clu·sive (rĭ-klŏŏ′sĭv, -zĭv) adj. solitario, retirado.

rec·og·ni·tion (rĕk′əg-nĭsh′ən) s. reconocimiento.

rec·og·niz·a·ble (rĕk′əg-nī′zə-bəl) adj. reconocible.

re·cog·ni·zance (rĭ-kŏg′nĭ-zəns, -kŏn′ĭ-) s. *(guarantee)* fianza; *(recognition)* reconocimiento; DER. *(obligation)* compromiso, obligación *f*.

rec·og·nize (rĕk′əg-nīz′) tr. **-nized, -niz·ing** *(to know from before)* reconocer; *(parliamentary procedure)* dar la palabra a.

re·coil I. intr. (rĭ-koil′) *(a spring)* aflojarse; ARM. *(firearm)* dar un culatazo; *(a canon)* retroceder ♦ **to r. at** *(in fear)* tener horror a; *(in disgust)* tener asco a, sentir repugnancia por • **to r. on** recaer sobre **II.** s. (rē′koil′, rĭ-koil′) *(of spring)* aflojamiento; *(in fear)* horror *m*, espanto; *(in disgust)* asco, repugnancia; ARM. *(of firearm)* culatazo; *(of cannon)* retroceso.

rec·ol·lect (rĕk′ə-lĕkt′) tr. recordar, acordarse de —intr. acordarse.

re-col·lect (rē′kə-lĕkt′) tr. *(to collect again)* volver a recoger.

rec·ol·lec·tion (rĕk′ə-lĕk′shən) s. *(memory)* recuerdo, memoria; *(contemplation)* recogimiento.

re·com·bi·nant (rē-kŏm′bə-nənt) s. BIOL. organismo en el que se ha realizado una combinación genética.

recombinant DNA s. BIOL. ADN preparado en el laboratorio.

re·com·bi·na·tion (rē-kŏm′bə-nā′shən) s. BIOL. formación en la descendencia de combinaciones genéticas inexistentes en los padres *f*.

rec·om·mend (rĕk′ə-mĕnd′) tr. *(to endorse)* recomendar <to r. someone for a job recomendar a alguien para un trabajo>; *(to advise)* recomendar, aconsejar; *(to entrust)* encargar, encomendar.

rec·om·mend·a·ble (rĕk′ə-mĕn′də-bəl) adj. *(worth recommending)* recomendable; *(advisable)* aconsejable.

rec·om·men·da·tion (rĕk′ə-mĕn-dā′shən) s. *(act)* recomendación *f*; FAM. *(letter)* carta de recomendación.

rec·om·pense (rĕk′əm-pĕns′) · **I.** tr. **-pensed, -pens·ing** *(to compensate)* compensar, indemnizar; *(to reward)* recompensar **II.** s. *(compensation)* compensación *f*, indemnización *f*; *(reward)* recompensa.

rec·on·cil·a·ble (rĕk′ən-sī′lə-bəl) adj. *(that can be reconciled)* reconciliable; *(that can be settled)* conciliable; *(compatible)* compatible.

rec·on·cile (rĕk′ən-sīl′) tr. **-ciled, -cil·ing** *(people)* reconciliar; *(differences)* conciliar; *(to dispute)* arreglar ♦ **to be reconciled to** o **to r. oneself to** resignarse a • **r. with** hacer compatible con.

rec·on·cil·i·a·tion (rĕk′ən-sīl′ē-ā′shən) s. *(of a relationship)* reconciliación *f*; *(settlement)* conciliación *f*; *(adjustment)* arreglo, ajuste *m*.

rec·on·dite (rĕk′ən-dīt′, rĭ-kŏn′dīt′) adj. *(abstruse)* abstruso; *(obscure)* recóndito, oculto.

re·con·di·tion (rē′kən-dĭsh′ən) tr. arreglar, poner como nuevo.

re·con·firm (rē′kən-fûrm′) tr. reconfirmar.

re·con·nais·sance o **re·con·nois·sance** (rĭ-kŏn′ə-səns) s. reconocimiento.

re·con·noi·ter (rē′kə-noi′tər, rĕk′ə-) tr. reconocer —intr. hacer un reconocimiento.

re·con·sid·er (rē′kən-sĭd′ər) tr. & intr. *(decision)* reconsiderar, volver a considerar; DER. examinar nuevamente.

re·con·sid·er·a·tion (rē′kən-sĭd′ə-rā′shən) s. reconsideración *f*.

re·con·sti·tute (rē-kŏn′stĭ-tōōt′, -tyōōt′) tr. **-tut·ed, -tut·ing** *(to reorganize)* reconstituir, reorganizar; CUL. hidratar.

re·con·struct (rē′kən-strŭkt′) tr. reconstruir.

re·con·struc·tion (rē′kən-strŭk′shən) s. reconstrucción *f* ♦ **R.** EE. UU., HIST. período durante el cual el gobierno federal tenía el control de los estados secesionistas.

re·con·vene (rē′kən-vēn′) tr. **-vened, -ven·ing** convocar de nuevo —intr. reunirse de nuevo.

re·cord I. tr. (rĭ-kôrd′) *(to set down)* consignar, registrar <to r. the main events consignar los acontecimientos principales>; *(to note down)* apuntar, anotar; *(to tally)* consignar, llevar cuenta de; *(to register)* marcar, indicar (termómetro, barómetro); *(to indicate)* dejar constancia de; TEC. grabar —intr. TEC. grabar; *(to register)* registrar **II.** s. **rec·ord** (rĕk′ərd) *(evidence)* constancia <we have no r. of it no tenemos constancia de ello>; *(account)* relación *f*; *(tally)* cuenta; *(testimony)* testimonio <her letters are a r. of her suffering sus cartas son testimonio de su sufrimiento>; *(document)* documento; *(register)* registro; *(of conduct)* historial *m* <his political r. su historial político>; *(dossier)* expediente *m*; *(clinical history)* historial médico; *(of a soldier, employee)* hoja de servicios; *(of a criminal)* antecedentes *m*; *(best performance)* récord *m*, plusmarca <to hold the speed r. tener el récord de velocidad>; *(proceedings)* acta; *(for a phonograph)* disco; *(recording)* grabación *f* ♦ **for the r.** para que así conste • **in r. time** en un tiempo récord • **in r. numbers** en cantidades sin precedentes • **matter of r.** hecho documentado • **off-the-record** oficioso • **police r.** antecedentes policiales o penales • **r. breaker** DEP. batidor de récords, plusmarquista • **r. changer** tocadiscos automático • **r. player** tocadiscos • **records** archivos • **to be off the r.** ser oficioso o extraoficial • **to be on r.** *(data)* haberse registrado <it was the coldest day on r. fue el día más frío que se hubiera registrado>; *(fact)* constar • **to break the r.** batir el récord • **to go on r.** hacer constar, declararse públicamente • **to have a clean r.** no tener antecedentes penales • **to say something off the r.** declarar algo de modo confidencial.

re·cord·er (rĭ-kôr′dər) s. *(device)* grabadora; *(judge)* magistrado municipal, juez municipal *m*; MÚS. flauta dulce.

re·cord·ing (rĭ-kôr′dĭng) s. *(sound)* grabación *f*; *(narration)* narración *f*, relación *f*; *(census)* censo; *(register)* registro.

re·count (rĭ-kount′) tr. *(to narrate)* relatar; *(to enumerate)* enumerar.

re-count I. tr. (rē-kount′) volver a contar, hacer el recuento de **II.** s. (rē′kount′) recuento.

re·coup (rĭ-kōōp′) tr. *(to recover)* recuperar; DER. deducir, descontar ♦ **to r. for** indemnizar por —intr. recuperarse.

re-course (rē′kôrs′, rĭ-kôrs′) s. recurso ♦ **to have r. to** recurrir a, valerse de.

re·cov·er (rĭ-kŭv′ər) tr. *(to regain)* recuperar; *(for losses)* cobrar ♦ **to r. oneself** recuperarse —intr. *(to get better)* recuperarse, reponerse <to r. from an illness recuperarse de una enfermedad>; *(country, economy)* recuperarse; *(in lawsuit)* ganar un pleito.

re-cov·er (rē-kŭv′ər) tr. recubrir, cubrir de nuevo.

re·cov·er·a·ble (rĭ-kŭv′ər-ə-bəl) adj. recuperable.

re·cov·er·y (rĭ-kŭv′ə-rē) s. [pl. **-ies**] recuperación *f*.

recovery room s. MED. sala de recuperación.

rec·re·ant (rĕk′rē-ənt) adj. & s. *(disloyal)* desleal *mf*; *(coward)* cobarde *mf*.

rec·re·ate (rĕk′rē-āt′) tr. & intr. **-at·ed, -at·ing** divertir(se).

re-cre·ate (rē′krē-āt′) tr. **-at·ed, -at·ing** recrear, crear de nuevo.

rec·re·a·tion (rĕk′rē-ā′shən) s. recreo.

rec·re·a·tion·al (rĕk′rē-ā′shə-nəl) adj. recreativo.

re·crim·i·nate (rĭ-krĭm′ə-nāt′) tr. & intr. **-nat·ed, -nat·ing** recriminar.

re·crim·i·na·tion (rĭ-krĭm′ə-nā′shən) s. recriminación *f*.

re·crim·i·na·tive (rĭ-krĭm′ə-nā′tĭv) o **re·crim·i·na·to·ry** (-tôr′ē) adj. recriminador, recriminatorio.

re·cru·des·cence (rē′krōō-dĕs′əns) s. recrudecimiento.

re·cruit (rĭ-krōōt′) **I.** tr. *(employees)* contratar; *(students)* matricular, registrar; MIL. reclutar, alistar —intr. MIL. reclutar **II.** s. MIL. recluta *m*, quinto; *(new member)* socio nuevo.

re·cruit·er (rĭ-krōō'tər) s. reclutador *m*.

re·cruit·ment (rĭ-krōōt'mənt) s. reclutamiento.

rec·tal (rĕk'təl) adj. ANAT. rectal, del recto.

rec·tan·gle (rĕk'tăng'gəl) s. rectángulo.

rec·tan·gu·lar (rĕk-tăng'gyə-lər) adj. rectangular.

rec·ti·fi·a·ble (rĕk'tə-fī'ə-bəl) adj. rectificable.

rec·ti·fi·ca·tion (rĕk'tə-fĭ-kā'shən) s. rectificación *f*.

rec·ti·fi·er (rĕk'tə-fī'ər) s. ELEC., MEC. rectificador *m*.

rec·ti·fy (rĕk'tə-fī') tr. **-fied, -fy·ing** *(to correct)* rectificar, corregir; ELEC., QUÍM. rectificar.

rec·ti·lin·e·ar (rĕk'tə-lĭn'ē-ər) adj. rectilíneo.

rec·ti·tude (rĕk'tĭ-tōōd', -tyōōd') s. rectitud *f*.

rec·to (rĕk'tō) s. [pl. **-tos**] IMPR. recto.

rec·tor (rĕk'tər) s. *(of a parish)* cura párroco; *(of an order)* superior *m*; *(of a school)* director *m*; *(of a college, university)* rector *m*.

rec·to·ry (rĕk'tə-rē) s. [pl. **-ries**] RELIG. *(house)* casa del cura; *(office)* rectoría.

rec·tum (rĕk'təm) s. [pl. **-tums** o **-ta** (-tə)] ANAT. recto.

re·cum·bent (rĭ-kŭm'bənt) adj. *(reclining)* recostado; *(resting)* reposado ♦ **r. statue** estatura yacente.

re·cu·per·ate (rĭ-kōō'pə-rāt', -kyōō'-) tr. & intr. **-at·ed, -at·ing** recuperar(se).

re·cu·per·a·tion (rĭ-kōō'pə-rā'shən, -kyōō'-) s. recuperación *f*.

re·cu·per·a·tive (rĭ-kōō'pə-rā'tĭv, -kyōō'-) adj. recuperativo.

re·cur (rĭ-kûr') intr. **-curred, -cur·ring** *(to happen again)* repetirse, volver a ocurrir; MAT., MED. reproducirse ♦ **to r. to** *(to resort to)* recurrir a; *(to return)* volver a.

re·cur·rence (rĭ-kûr'əns) s. *(repetition)* repetición *f*, reaparición *f*; *(return)* vuelta; MED. reproducción *f*, reaparición.

re·cur·rent (rĭ-kûr'ənt) adj. *(appearing again)* que se repite; *(periodic)* periódico, cíclico; ANAT., MAT. recurrente.

re·cur·ring (rĭ-kûr'ĭng) adj. periódico.

re·curve (rē-kûrv') tr. & intr. **-curved, -curv·ing** doblar(se) hacia atrás.

re·cy·cle (rē-sī'kəl) tr. **-cled, -cling** *(to use again)* utilizar de nuevo; *(to recondition)* convertir.

red (rĕd) **I.** s. *(color)* rojo, colorado; *(dye)* colorante rojo ♦ **R.** POL. rojo, comunista • **r. propaganda** propaganda comunista • **to be in the r.** *(business)* tener pérdidas; *(person)* estar endeudado • **to see r.** ponerse furioso • **to wear r.** vestirse de rojo **II.** adj. **red·der, red·dest** *(in color)* rojo, colorado; *(wine)* tinto; *(steak)* poco hecho; *(animal)* de pelo rojo; *(skin)* rojo, colorado <*r. cheeks* mejillas coloradas>; *(embarrassed)* rojo, colorado; *(angry)* rojo ♦ **red-haired** pelirrojo • **r. tape** trámites, papeleo.

re·dact (rĭ-dăkt') tr. redactar.

red·bait (rĕd'bāt') tr. acusar de comunista a.

red·bird (rĕd'bûrd') s. ORNIT. cardenal de cresta roja *m*.

red blood cell s. glóbulo rojo.

red-blood·ed (rĕd'blŭd'ĭd) adj. vigoroso.

red·breast (rĕd'brĕst') s. ORNIT. petirrojo; ICT. pez luna *m*.

red·cap (rĕd'kăp') s. maletero, mozo de equipajes.

red cent s. FAM. céntimo, centavo (cosa de valor insignificante).

red·coat (rĕd'kōt') s. HIST. soldado inglés (durante la guerra de independencia de EE. UU. y la Guerra de 1812).

Red Cross s. Cruz Roja.

red·den (rĕd'n) tr. teñir o pintar de rojo —intr. *(a thing)* enrojecer; *(a person)* ruborizarse.

red·dish (rĕd'ĭsh) adj. rojizo.

re·dec·o·rate (rē-dĕk'ə-rāt') intr. & tr. **-rat·ed, -rat·ing** cambiar la decoración (de).

re·dec·o·ra·tion (rē-dĕk'ə-rā'shən) s. cambio de decorado.

re·deem (rĭ-dēm') tr. *(to recover ownership of)* redimir, cancelar; *(to pay)* pagar; *(to fulfill)* cumplir; *(to convert into cash)* vender, hacer efectivo; *(to rescue)* rescatar; *(to recover)* recobrar, recuperar; FIG. *(to save from sin)* redimir, salvar; *(to make up for)* compensar.

re·deem·a·ble (rĭ-dē'mə-bəl) adj. redimible.

re·deem·er (rĭ-dē'mər) s. redentor *m* ♦ **R.** RELIG. Redentor.

re·demp·tion (rĭ-dĕmp'shən) s. *(of a mortgage)* cancelación *f*, extinción *f*; *(from pawn)* desempeño, liberación *f*; *(of an*

obligation) pago de una obligación; FIG. *(rescue)* rescate *m*; *(salvation)* redención *f*.

re·de·ploy (rē'dĭ-ploi') tr. MIL. cambiar de frente.

re·de·ploy·ment (rē'dĭ-ploi'mənt) s. MIL. cambio de frente.

re·de·vel·op (rē'dĭ-vĕl'əp) tr. *(to develop again)* perfeccionar; *(an area)* reurbanizar.

re·de·vel·op·ment (rē'dĭ-vĕl'əp-mənt) s. *(perfecting)* perfeccionamiento; *(of an area)* reurbanización *f*.

red fox s. zorro rojo.

red giant s. ASTRON. estrella gigante.

red-hand·ed (rĕd'hăn'dĭd) adj. & adv. con las manos en la masa, en flagrante delito.

red·head (rĕd'hĕd') s. *(person)* pelirrojo; ORNIT. pato americano.

red herring s. *(fish)* arenque ahumado; *(false issue)* tema introducido en una discusión sólo para desvirtuarla.

red-hot (rĕd'hŏt') **I.** adj. *(very hot)* candente; *(excited)* animado; *(ardent)* ardiente; *(dangerous)* peligroso; *(new)* muy reciente; *(sensational)* sensacional **II.** s. *(hot dog)* perro caliente, salchicha; *(candy)* caramelo.

red ink s. COM. pérdida, déficit *m*.

re·di·rect (rē'dĭ-rĕkt', -dī'-) tr. *(to change the direction of)* cambiar la dirección de; *(to send again)* reexpedir; *(to reroute)* mostrar o señalar otro camino.

re·dis·count (rē-dĭs'kount') COM. **I.** tr. volver a descontar **II.** s. redescuento.

re·dis·cov·er (rē'dĭ-skŭv'ər) tr. descubrir de nuevo, volver a descubrir.

re·dis·cov·er·y (rē'dĭ-skŭv'ə-rē) s. [pl. **-ies**] nuevo descubrimiento.

re·dis·trib·ute (rē'dĭ-strĭb'yōōt) tr. **-ut·ed, -ut·ing** distribuir de nuevo, redistribuir.

re·dis·trict (rē-dĭs'trĭkt) POL. tr. volver a dividir en distritos.

red-let·ter (rĕd'lĕt'ər) adj. *(holiday)* feriado, de fiesta; *(memorable)* memorable (día).

red light s. *(traffic light)* semáforo, luz roja; *(deterrent)* señal de peligro *f*.

red-light district (rĕd'līt') s. barrio de burdeles.

red·line (rĕd'līn') tr. & intr. **-lined, -lin·ing** no conceder préstamo para vivienda o seguro a barrios considerados como gran riesgo financiero.

red·neck (rĕd'nĕk') s. JER. *(white laborer)* campesino blanco del sur de EE. UU.; DESPEC. *(conservative person)* partidario de un orden sociopolítico conservador y racista.

red·ness (rĕd'nĭs) s. color rojo.

re·do (rē-dōō') tr. **-did** (-dĭd'), **-done** (-dŭn'), **-do·ing** *(to do over again)* volver a hacer, rehacer; *(to redecorate)* decorar de nuevo.

red·o·lent (rĕd'l-ənt) adj. *(aromatic)* fragante, oloroso; *(suggestive)* sugestivo, evocador; *(saturated)* impregnado.

re·dou·ble (rē-dŭb'əl) tr. & intr. **-bled, -bling** redoblar.

re·doubt (rĭ-dout') s. FORT. reducto.

re·doubt·a·ble (rĭ-dou'tə-bəl) adj. *(arousing fear)* temible; *(formidable)* formidable; *(worthy of respect)* respetable.

re·dound (rĭ-dound') intr. ♦ **to r. to** o **upon** *(to reflect)* recaer sobre; *(to contribute)* contribuir a; *(to accrue)* redundar en.

red-pen·cil (rĕd'pĕn'səl) tr. *(to mark in red)* marcar con rojo; FIG. *(to cross out)* tachar.

red pepper s. BOT. pimiento; CUL. pimiento rojo picante en polvo.

re·dress (rĭ-drĕs') **I.** tr. *(to remedy)* remediar, reparar; *(to rectify)* rectificar, enmendar; *(to compensate)* compensar, resarcir; *(to adjust)* reajustar **II.** s. *(reparation)* reparación *f*; *(rectification)* rectificación *f*, enmienda; *(compensation)* compensación *f*; *(adjustment)* reajuste *m*.

Red Sea s. Mar Rojo.

red·skin (rĕd'skĭn') s. DESPEC. piel roja (indio de EE. UU.) *m*.

red snapper s. ICT. guachinango, pagro.

red tape s. papeleo, burocracia.

re·duce (rĭ-dōōs', -dyōōs') tr. **-duced, -duc·ing** *(to lessen)* reducir, disminuir <*to r. speed* reducir la velocidad>; COM. rebajar; MIL. *(to conquer)* conquistar, tomar (ciudad, posición); *(in rank)* degradar (un oficial); *(a revolt)* reducir, sofocar; *(to bring to a state)* convertir, reducir <*enemy* *bombers reduced the city to ashes* los bombardeos enemigos redujeron la ciudad a cenizas>; MAT., MED., QUÍM. reducir ♦ **at reduced prices** a precios reducidos • **to r. someone to** reducir *o* llevar a alguien a —intr. *(to become diminished)* disminuir, reducirse; *(to lose weight)* adelgazar.

re·duc·i·ble (rǐ-dōō′sə-bəl, -dyōō′-) adj. reducible.

reducing agent s. QUÍM. agente reductor *m.*

re·duc·tion (rǐ-dŭk′shən) s. *(act)* reducción *f*; *(diminution)* rebaja, disminución *f*; *(in length)* acortamiento; *(in width)* estrechamiento; *(in weight)* adelgazamiento; *(discount)* descuento, rebaja; MIL. degradación *f.*

re·dun·dan·cy (rǐ-dŭn′dən-sē) s. [pl. **-cies**] redundancia.

re·dun·dant (rǐ-dŭn′dənt) s. *(superfluous)* superfluo; *(excessive)* excesivo; GRAM. reduntante.

re·du·pli·cate (rǐ-dōō′plǐ-kāt′, -dyōō′-) tr. & intr. **-cat·ed, -cat·ing** *(to repeat)* reiterar, repetir; *(to redouble)* reduplicar(se), repetir(se).

re·du·pli·ca·tion (rǐ-dōō′plǐ-kā′shən, -dyōō′-) s. *(repetition)* reiteración *f*, repetición *f*; *(doubling)* reduplicación *f.*

red·wood (rĕd′wŏŏd′) s. BOT. *(tree)* secoya; *(wood)* madera de secoya.

re·ech·o (rē-ĕk′ō) intr. **-oed, -o·ing** resonar, repercutir —tr. hacer resonar.

reed (rēd) s. BOT. *(plant)* caña; *(stalk)* tallo de caña; MÚS. *(primitive wind instrument)* caramillo; *(flexible strip)* lengüeta; *(instrument)* instrumento de lengüeta; TEJ. peine de telar *m.*

reed organ s. MÚS. armonio.

re·ed·u·cate *o* **re·ed·u·cate** (rē-ĕj′ə-kāt′) tr. **-cat·ed, -cat·ing** *(to instruct again)* reeducar; *(to rehabilitate)* rehabilitar.

reed·y (rē′dē) adj. **-i·er, -i·est** *(full of reeds)* lleno de cañas; *(made of reeds)* hecho de caña; *(thin)* como la caña, delgado; *(sound)* agudo.

reef¹ (rēf) s. GEOL. arrecife *m*, escollo; MIN. vena, filón *m.*

reef² (rēf) MARÍT. **I.** s. rizo (de vela) **II.** tr. arrizar.

reef·er¹ (rē′fər) s. *(person)* guardiamarina *m*; *(jacket)* chaquetón *m.*

reef·er² (rē′fər) s. JER. *(joint)* cigarrillo de marihuana, porro.

reek (rēk) **I.** intr. *(to smoke)* humear, echar humo; *(to stink)* apestar; FIG. *(to smell)* oler —tr. *(to exude)* despedir (olor, humo); *(to smoke)* ahumar **II.** s. *(stench)* olor *m*; *(smoke)* humo; *(vapor)* vapor *m*, vaho.

reel¹ (rēl) **I.** s. *(device for winding)* carrete *m*, bobina; *(fishing rod)* carrete de caña de pescar; CINEM. rollo; FOTOG. rollo; *(spool)* devanadera; *(Scottish dance)* baile escocés *m*; *(Virginia reel)* baile de figuras en EE. UU. **II.** tr. enrollar en un carrete ♦ **to r. in** *o* **up** *(rope, cord)* cobrar; *(fish)* tirar *o* sacar del agua enrollando el cordel en el carrete • **to r. off** *(thread)* desenrollar, devanar; *(to recite fluently)* recitar de un tirón.

reel² (rēl) **I.** intr. *(to stagger)* tambalear(se); *(to go round)* dar vueltas; *(to feel dizzy)* tener vértigo —tr. hacer girar **II.** s. *(movement)* tambaleo.

re·e·lect *o* **re·e·lect** (rē′ĭ-lĕkt′) tr. reelegir.

re·e·lec·tion *o* **re·e·lec·tion** (rē′ĭ-lĕk′shən) s. POL. reelección *f.*

re·en·act *o* **re·en·act** (rē′ĕn-ăkt′) tr. *(to enact again)* aprobar de nuevo (ley); *(to perform again)* volver a representar; *(to recreate)* recrear.

re·en·force *o* **re·en·force** (rē′ĕn-fôrs′) v. var. de **reinforce.**

re·en·list *o* **re·en·list** (rē′ĕn-lĭst′) tr. & intr. MIL. rèenganchar(se).

re·en·ter *o* **re·en·ter** (rē-ĕn′tər) intr. volver a entrar —tr. volver a apuntar.

re·en·try *o* **re·en·try** (rē-ĕn′trē) s. [pl. **-tries**] *(act)* reingreso, nueva entrada; DER. recuperación de una posesión *f.*

re·es·tab·lish *o* **re·es·tab·lish** (rē′ĭ-stăb′lĭsh) tr. restablecer.

reeve (rēv) s. *(in Canada)* presidente del concejo *m*; G.B., HIST. *(officer)* alto funcionario local.

re·ex·am·i·na·tion *o* **re·ex·am·i·na·tion** (rē′ĭg-zăm′ə-nā′shən) s. *(review)* nuevo examen *f*; DER. nuevo interrogatorio.

re·ex·am·ine *o* **re·ex·am·ine** (rē′ĭg-zăm′ĭn) tr. **-ined, -in·ing** *(to review)* reexaminar; DER. volver a interrogar.

re·fec·to·ry (rĭ-fĕk′tə-rē) s. [pl. **-ries**] refectorio, comedor *m.*

re·fer (rĭ-fûr′) tr. **-ferred, -fer·ring** *(to direct to)* remitir; *(to send to)* enviar <*my dentist referred me to an orthodontist* mi dentista me envió a un ortodontista>; *(to attribute to)* atribuir <*he refers that verse to Shakespeare* atribuye ese verso a Shakespeare>; *(to situate)* situar; *(to submit to)* someter a (juicio, investigación) —intr. *(to pertain)* referirse; *(to allude)* aludirse; *(to turn to)* referirse, consultar <*she referred to the dictionary* consultó el diccionario>; *(to apply)* aplicar <*the ruling refers to all the cases* la decisión se aplica a todos los casos>.

ref·er·ee (rĕf′ə-rē′) **I.** s. *(arbiter)* árbitro; DEP. juez árbitro, árbitro **II.** tr. & intr. **-reed, -ree·ing** arbitrar.

ref·er·ence (rĕf′ər-əns) s. *(act)* referencia; *(allusion)* alusión *f*, mención *f*; *(footnote)* referencia, nota; *(text referred to)* texto de referencia; *(source)* fuente de referencia *f*; *(mark)* llamada (en un texto); *(person)* fiador *m*, garante *m*; *(recommendation)* referencia, recomendación *f*; DER. arbitraje *m* ♦ **r. mark** llamada • **with r. to** *(a letter)* con relación a, con referencia a; *(as regards)* en cuanto a.

reference book s. libro de consulta.

ref·er·en·dum (rĕf′ə-rĕn′dəm) s. [pl. **-dums** *o* **-da** (-də)] POL. referéndum *m*, plebiscito.

ref·er·ent (rĕf′ər-ənt) s. *(referring item)* término que sirve para encontrar un significado; *(thing referred to)* cosa a la que se refiere.

re·fer·ral (rĭ-fûr′əl) s. referencia.

re·fill **I.** tr. (rē-fĭl′) rellenar, llenar de nuevo **II.** s. (rē′fĭl′) *(new filling)* recambio; *(subsequent filling)* carga.

re·fill·a·ble (rē-fĭl′ə-bəl) adj. recambiable, recargable.

re·fine (rĭ-fīn′) tr. & intr. **-fined, -fin·ing** refinar(se), purificar(se).

re·fined (rĭ-fīnd′) adj. *(pure)* refinado, puro; *(elegant)* fino, cortés; *(precise)* sutil.

re·fine·ment (rĭ-fīn′mənt) s. *(oil, sugar)* refinación *f*, refinado; *(of metals)* purificación *f*; *(of a person)* refinamiento; *(improvement)* mejoramiento.

re·fin·er·y (rĭ-fī′nə-rē) s. [pl. **-ies**] *(oil)* refinería *f*; *(sugar)* ingenio de azúcar.

re·fin·ish (rē-fĭn′ĭsh) tr. *(to put a new finish on)* dar un acabado nuevo a; *(to varnish)* barnizar.

re·fin·ish·er (rē-fĭn′ĭ-shər) s. lustrador de muebles *m.*

re·fit **I.** tr. & intr. (rē-fĭt′) **-fit·ted, -fit·ting** reparar(se) **II.** s. (rē′fĭt′) reparación *f.*

re·flect (rĭ-flĕkt′) tr. *(to send back)* reflejar; *(to manifest)* revelar, manifestar <*her eyes r. her sorrow* sus ojos revelan su tristeza> ♦ **to r. on** *o* **upon** pensar (sobre) <*I'll r. on it* lo pensaré> • **to r. well on** ayudar, redundar en beneficio de —intr. *(to be sent back)* reflejarse; *(to think)* reflexionar; meditar.

reflecting telescope s. ÓPT. telescopio reflector.

re·flec·tion (rĭ-flĕk′shən) s. *(image)* reflejo <*the r. of clouds in the lake* el reflejo de nubes en el lago>; *(of sound)* eco; *(contemplation)* reflexión *f*, meditación *f*; *(criticism)* crítica; ANAT. repliegue *m* ♦ **on r.** después de pensarlo, pensándolo bien.

re·flec·tive (rĭ-flĕk′tĭv) adj. *(of reflection)* que refleja, reflector; *(meditative)* pensativo.

re·flec·tiv·i·ty (rē′flĕk-tĭv′ĭ-tē) s. [pl. **-ties**] capacidad reflectora.

re·flec·tor (rĭ-flĕk′tər) s. *(object)* reflector *m*; *(surface)* superficie reflectora; *(telescope)* telescopio reflector; AUTO. catafaro.

re·flex (rē′flĕks′) adj. *(reflected)* reflejado; *(involuntary)* reflejo <*r. action* acción refleja>.

reflex camera s. FOTOG. cámara reflex.

re·flex·ion (rĭ-flĕk′shən) s. G.B. var. de **reflection.**

re·flex·ive (rĭ-flĕk′sĭv) **I.** adj. *(verb, pronoun)* reflexivo; *(movement)* reflejo **II.** s. GRAM. *(verb)* verbo reflexivo; *(pronoun)* pronombre reflexivo.

re·flux (rē′flŭks′) s. reflujo.

re·for·est (rē-fôr′ĭst) tr. repoblar con árboles.

re·for·es·ta·tion (rē-fôr′ĭ-stā′shən) s. repoblación forestal *f.*

---

re·form (rǐ-fôrm′) I. tr. & intr. reformar(se) II. s. reforma ♦ **land r.** reforma agraria.
re-form (rē-fôrm′) tr. & intr. formar(se) de nuevo.
ref·or·ma·tion (rěf′ər-mā′shən) s. reforma ♦ **R.** RELIG. la Reforma.
re·for·ma·to·ry (rǐ-fôr′mə-tôr′ē) s. [pl. **-ries**] I. reformatorio, casa de corrección II. adj. reformatorio.
re·formed (rǐ-fôrmd′) adj. reformado.
re·form·er (rǐ-fôr′mər) s. reformador m.
re·form·ism (rǐ-fôr′mǐz′əm) s. reformismo.
re·form·ist (rǐ-fôr′mǐst) s. reformista mf.
reform school s. reformatorio.
re·fract (rǐ-frǎkt′) tr. Fís., ÓPT. refractar (luz, rayos).
refracting telescope s. telescopio refractor.
re·frac·tion (rǐ-frǎk′shən) s. Fís. refracción f.
re·frac·tive index (rǐ-frǎk′tǐv) s. Fís. índice de refracción m.
re·frac·tor (rǐ-frǎk′tər) s. refractor m.
re·frac·to·ry (rǐ-frǎk′tə-rē) I. adj. (person, animal) obstinado, indócil; Fís., MIN. refractario; MED. intratable II. s. [pl. **-ries**] Fís., MIN. material refractario.
re·frain¹ (rǐ-frān′) intr. ♦ **to r. from** abstenerse de.
re·frain² (rǐ-frān′) s. MÚS., POÉT. estribillo.
re·fresh (rǐ-frěsh′) tr. & intr. refrescar(se).
re·fresh·er (rǐ-frěsh′ər) adj. ♦ **r. course** curso de repaso.
re·fresh·ing (rǐ-frěsh′ǐng) adj. (that refreshes) refrescante; (restorative) reparador; (encouraging) alentador; (pleasant) placentero.
re·fresh·ment (rǐ-frěsh′mənt) s. refresco ♦ **refreshments** refrigerio, colación f.
re·frig·er·ant (rǐ-frǐj′ər-ənt) adj. & s. refrigerante m.
re·frig·er·ate (rǐ-frǐj′ə-rāt′) tr. **-at·ed, -at·ing** refrigerar.
re·frig·er·a·tion (rǐ-frǐj′ə-rā′shən) s. refrigeración f.
re·frig·er·a·tor (rǐ-frǐj′ə-rā′tər) s. nevera, frigorífico.
re·fu·el (rē-fyōō′əl) tr. echar gasolina a o en —intr. repostar(se).
ref·uge (rěf′yōōj) I. s. refugio ♦ **to take r. in** refugiarse en II. intr. **-uged, -ug·ing** ANT. refugiar(se).
ref·u·gee (rěf′yōō-jē′) s. refugiado.
re·ful·gent (rǐ-fōol′jənt, -fŭl′-) adj. refulgente.
re·fund I. tr. (rǐ-fŭnd′) reembolsar, devolver —intr. hacer un reembolso II. s. (rē′fŭnd′) reembolso.
re·fund (rē-fŭnd′) tr. consolidar (una deuda).
re·fund·a·ble (rǐ-fŭn′də-bəl) adj. reembolsable.
re·fur·bish (rē-fûr′bĭsh) tr. restaurar (mueble, casa).
re·fur·nish (rē-fûr′nĭsh) tr. amueblar de nuevo.
re·fus·al (rǐ-fyōō′zəl) s. (act) negativa; COM. opción f.
re·fuse¹ (rǐ-fyōōz′) tr. **-fused, -fus·ing** (offer, food) no aceptar; (admittance, permission) negar, denegar; DEP. (horse) rehusar saltar (un obstáculo) ♦ **to r. to** (help, go) negarse a, rehusar a; (get old, start) resistirse a —intr. (to say no) negarse; (horse) pararse.
ref·use² (rěf′yōos) s. desperdicios, basura.
ref·u·ta·tion (rěf′yōō-tā′shən) s. refutación f, rebatimiento.
re·fute (rǐ-fyōot′) tr. **-fut·ed, -fut·ing** refutar, rebatir.
re·gain (rē-gān′) tr. recuperar, recobrar.
re·gal (rē′gəl) adj. (royal) real, regio; (splendid) magnífico, majestuoso.
re·gale (rǐ-gāl′) tr. **-galed, -gal·ing** (to entertain) agasajar; (to amuse) entretener ♦ **to r. on** deleitarse con —intr. deleitarse.
re·ga·lia (rǐ-gāl′yə) s.pl. (of royalty) insignias reales; (office, membership) atributos; (finery) adornos.
re·gard (rǐ-gärd′) I. tr. (to watch) observar, mirar <he regarded us suspiciously nos observó con desconfianza>; (to consider) considerar <I r. him as a fool le considero un imbécil o considero que es un imbécil>; (to esteem) respetar, apreciar; (to concern) referirse a, concernir <this item regards your question este artículo se refiere a su pregunta>; (to heed) tener en cuenta, prestar atención a <no one regarded his words nadie tuvo en cuenta sus palabras> ♦ **as regards** o **regarding** con respecto a, en cuanto a —intr. (to gaze) observar, mirar; (to heed) prestar atención II. s. (gaze) mirada; (attention) consideración f, atención f <due r. was not given to the problem no se dio la debida consideración al problema>; (care) consideración; (esteem) respeto, aprecio ♦ **in** o **with r. to** con respecto o con referencia a • **in (this, that) r.** por lo que a (esto, eso) se refiere • **of small r.** de poca monta • **to give (little, much) r.** preocuparse (mucho, poco) por • **to give** o **to send one's regards to someone** saludar o dar recuerdos a alguien • **to have r. for** (to respect) respetar; (to care for) tomar en consideración • **with best regards** o **regards** saludos cordiales de • **without r. to** sin tomar en consideración.

re·gard·ing (rǐ-gär′dǐng) prep. (concerning) con respecto a, en cuanto a <all letters r. this matter toda la correspondencia con respecto a este asunto>; (relating to) referente o relativo a <issues r. moral values cuestiones relativas a los valores morales>.
re·gard·less (rǐ-gärd′lǐs) adv. (anyway) a pesar de todo, de todos modos; (come what may) pase lo que pase.
regardless of prep. (without regard to) sin tener en cuenta, sin reparar en <r. of the consequences sin reparar en las consecuencias>; (in spite of) a pesar de <I jumped, r. of their warnings salté, a pesar de sus advertencias> ♦ **r. of what they do** hagan lo que hagan • **r. of what they say** digan lo que digan.
re·gat·ta (rǐ-gä′tə, -gät′ə) s. DEP. regata.
re·gen·cy (rē′jən-sē) I. s. [pl. **-cies**] regencia II. adj. ♦ **R.** de estilo regencia.
re·gen·er·ate I. tr. & intr. (rǐ-jěn′ə-rāt′) **-at·ed, -at·ing** regenerar(se) II. s. (-ər-ĭt) regenerado III. adj. (-ər-ĭt) (renewed) renovado.
re·gen·er·a·tion (rǐ-jěn′ə-rā′shən) s. regeneración f.
re·gen·er·a·tive (rǐ-jěn′ə-rā′tǐv, -ər-ə-) adj. regenerador.
re·gent (rē′jənt) s. (sovereign) regente mf; EDUC. miembro de la junta directiva ♦ **board of regents** EDUC. junta directiva.
reg·i·cide (rěj′ǐ-sīd′) s. (act) regicidio; (killer) regicida mf.
re·gime o **ré·gime** (rā-zhēm′) s. régimen m.
reg·i·men (rěj′ə-mən) s. MED. régimen m.
reg·i·ment (rěj′ə-mənt) I. s. MIL. regimiento II. tr. regimentar.
reg·i·men·ta·tion (rěj′ə-měn-tā′shən) s. reglamentación estricta.
re·gion (rē′jən) s. (area) región f; (zone) zona; (territory) territorio; (sphere) esfera; ANAT., ZOOL. región.
re·gion·al (rē′jə-nəl) adj. regional.
reg·is·ter (rěj′ǐ-stər) I. s. (book) registro <to sign the hotel r. firmar el registro del hotel>; (entry) registro, inscripción f; (of a ship, students) matrícula; TEC. (recorder) registrador m; (meter) contador m; (for heat) regulador (de calefacción) m; MEC. correspondencia exacta (de piezas); IMPR. registro; MÚS. (of voice, instrument) registro <lower r. registro bajo>; (organ stop) registro II. tr. (to record) registrar; (a birth, death) declarar; (a ship, students) matricular; (vehicle) sacar la matrícula de; (a trademark) registrar; (complaint) presentar; (to indicate) marcar <the thermometer registers 85 degrees el termómetro marca 85 grados>; (to detect) registrar; (gain, loss) experimentar; (emotion) manifestar, expresar; (mail) certificar —intr. (at the polls, hotel) inscribirse; (at school) matricularse; FIG. (name, face) quedarse grabado en la memoria de uno; MIL. alistarse; MEC. corresponder exactamente (partes); IMPR. estar en registro.
reg·is·tered (rěj′ǐ-stərd) adj. (trademark) registrado; (student, vehicle) matriculado; (certified) titulado <a r. pharmacist un farmacéutico titulado>.
registered mail s. correo certificado.
registered nurse s. enfermera diplomada.
reg·is·trant (rěj′ǐ-strənt) s. persona que se inscribe o se matricula.
reg·is·trar (rěj′ǐ-strär′) s. (of the register office) jefe de registros civiles m; (university) secretario general, matriculador m; (of a hospital) encargado de admisiones.
reg·is·tra·tion (rěj′ǐ-strā′shən) s. (of voters) inscripción f; (of students) matrícula; (for the draft) alistamiento ♦ **r.** o **car r.** AUTO. matrícula.
reg·is·try (rěj′ǐ-strē) s. [pl. **-tries**] (office, book) registro; MARÍT. matrícula.
reg·nant (rěg′nənt) adj. (reigning) reinante; (predominant) predominante.

re·gress I. intr. (rĭ-grĕs′) retroceder —tr. hacer retroceder II. s. (rē′grĕs′) retroceso.
re·gres·sion (rĭ-grĕsh′ən) s. *(reversion)* regresión f, retroceso.
re·gres·sive (rĭ-grĕs′ĭv) adj. regresivo.
re·gret (rĭ-grĕt′) I. tr. **-gret·ted, -gret·ting** *(to be sorry for)* arrepentirse de; *(to be sorry about)* sentir, lamentar <*I r. not going* lamento no ir> II. s. *(sorrow)* pena, pesar m; *(remorse)* arrepentimiento ♦ **regrets** excusas <*to send regrets* enviar excusas> • **to have no regrets** no arrepentirse de nada.
re·gret·ful (rĭ-grĕt′fəl) adj. *(sorrowful)* pesaroso; *(remorseful)* arrepentido.
re·gret·ful·ly (rĭ-grĕt′fə-lē) adv. *(sorrowfully)* con pesar, sentidamente; *(unfortunately)* desafortunadamente; *(against one's will)* con disgusto.
re·gret·ta·ble (rĭ-grĕt′ə-bəl) adj. *(lamentable)* lamentable; *(deplorable)* deplorable.
re·group (rē-grōōp′) tr. & intr. reagruparse.
reg·u·lar (rĕg′yə-lər) I. adj. *(normal)* normal <*during r. office hours* durante las horas normales de oficina>; *(customary)* habitual, de costumbre <*we did not sit in our r. places* no nos sentamos en los puestos de costumbre>; *(product)* normal <*the r., not the special oil filter* el filtro de aceite normal, no el especial>; *(even)* regular, uniforme <*r. features* facciones regulares>; *(conventional)* normal, acostumbrado <*the r. way of closing a deal* la forma acostumbrada de cerrar un trato>; *(periodic)* regular; MED. *(pulse)* normal; *(work)* fijo; *(customer)* habitual, fijo; *(proper)* correcto, apropiado; FAM. *(nice)* decente, bueno <*a r. guy* un tipo decente>; RELIG. regular; GEOM., GRAM. regular ♦ **to make r. use of** emplear con regularidad II. s. *(clothing size)* normal, mediano; FAM. *(customer)* cliente fijo, parroquiano; MIL., RELIG. regular m.
regular army s. ejército regular.
reg·u·lar·i·ty (rĕg′yə-lăr′ĭ-tē) s. [pl. **-ties**] regularidad f.
reg·u·lar·ize (rĕg′yə-lə-rīz′) tr. **-ized, -iz·ing** regularizar.
reg·u·lar·ly (rĕg′yə-lər-lē) adv. *(normally)* normalmente; *(customarily)* por lo regular; *(methodically)* regularmente.
reg·u·late (rĕg′yə-lāt′) tr. **-lat·ed, -lat·ing** *(to control)* reglamentar; *(to adjust)* regular.
reg·u·la·tion (rĕg′yə-lā′shən) s. *(act)* regulación f, reglamentación f; *(rule)* regla, principio; *(set of rules)* reglamento.
reg·u·la·tive (rĕg′yə-lā′tĭv) adj. regulativo.
reg·u·la·tor (rĕg′yə-lā′tər) s. ELEC., TEC. *(device)* regulador m; *(in a watch)* registro; *(clock)* cronómetro regulador.
reg·u·la·to·ry (rĕg′yə-lə-tôr′ē) adj. regulativo, regulador.
re·gur·gi·tate (rē-gûr′jĭ-tāt′) intr. **-tat·ed, -tat·ing** regurgitar —tr. vomitar.
re·gur·gi·ta·tion (rē-gûr′jĭ-tā′shən) s. regurgitación f.
re·ha·bil·i·tate (rē′hə-bĭl′ĭ-tāt′) tr. **-tat·ed, -tat·ing** *(criminal, addict)* reeducar, rehabilitar; *(building, neighborhood)* restaurar.
re·ha·bil·i·ta·tion (rē′hə-bĭl′ĭ-tā′shən) s. *(to a former condition)* rehabilitación f; *(restoration)* restauracion f; MED. reeducación f.
re·hash I. tr. (rē-hăsh′) volver a repetir, machacar II. s. (rē′hăsh′) repetición (de viejos temas, argumentos) f.
re·hear·ing (rē-hîr′ĭng) s. DER. revisión f.
re·hears·al (rĭ-hûr′səl) s. *(drill)* prueba, simulacro; TEAT. ensayo.
re·hearse (rĭ-hûrs′) tr. **-hearsed, -hears·ing** *(story)* recitar; TEAT., TELEV. ensayar —intr. ensayar.
reign (rān) I. s. *(sovereign's tenure)* reinado; *(kingdom)* reino; *(dominance)* régimen m, dominio II. intr. reinar.
re·im·burs·a·ble (rē′ĭm-bûr′sə-bəl) adj. reembolsable.
re·im·burse (rē′ĭm-bûrs′) tr. **-bursed, -burs·ing** *(to repay)* reembolsar; *(to compensate)* indemnizar.
re·im·burse·ment (rē′ĭm-bûrs′mənt) s. *(repayment)* reembolso; *(compensation)* indemnización f.
re·im·port I. tr. (rē′ĭm-pôrt′) reimportar II. s. (rē-ĭm′pôrt′) reimportación f.
rein (rān) I. s. rienda ♦ **reins** riendas <*to take the reins of government* tomar las riendas del gobierno> • **to draw in the reins** *(of animal)* tirar de las riendas; *(to slow down)*

detenerse • **to give free r. to** dar rienda suelta a • **to keep a tight r. on** atar corto a II. tr. poner riendas a ♦ **to r. in** refrenar —intr. ♦ **to r. in** detenerse.
re·in·car·nate (rē′ĭn-kär′nāt′) tr. **-nat·ed, -nat·ing** reencarnar.
re·in·car·na·tion (rē-ĭn′kär-nā′shən) s. reencarnación f.
rein·deer (rān′dîr′) s. [pl. **-deer** o **-deers**] ZOOL. reno.
re·in·fec·tion (rē′ĭn-fĕk′shən) s. MED. reinfección f.
re·in·force (rē′ĭn-fôrs′) tr. **-forced, -forc·ing** *(to strengthen)* reforzar, fortalecer; CONSTR. reforzar, armar; PSIC. afirmar.
reinforced concrete s. hormigón o cemento armado.
re·in·force·ment (rē′ĭn-fôrs′mənt) s. *(strengthening)* refuerzo; CONSTR. armazón m; PSIC. refuerzo ♦ **reinforcements** MIL. refuerzos.
reins (rānz) s.pl. FIG. *(seat of passions)* entrañas; ANAT. riñones m.
re·in·state (rē′ĭn-stāt′) tr. **-stat·ed, -stat·ing** *(to restore to office)* restituir, reintegrar; *(to reestablish)* restablecer; *(to rehabilitate)* rehabilitar.
re·in·state·ment (rē′ĭn-stāt′mənt) s. *(restoration)* restauración f, reintegración f; *(rehabilitation)* rehabilitación f.
re·in·sur·ance (rē′ĭn-shōōr′əns) s. COM. reaseguro.
re·in·sure (rē′-ĭn-shōōr′) tr. **-sured, -sur·ing** COM. reasegurar.
re·in·te·grate (rē-ĭn′tĭ-grāt′) tr. **-grat·ed, -grat·ing** reintegrar.
re·in·vest (rē′ĭn-vĕst′) tr. COM. reinvertir, volver a invertir.
re·in·vest·ment (rē′ĭn-vĕst′mənt) s. COM. reinversión f.
re·is·sue (rē-ĭsh′ōō) I. tr. **-sued, -su·ing** reeditar —intr. volver a editarse II. s. reedición f.
re·it·er·ate (rē-ĭt′ə-rāt′) tr. **-at·ed, -at·ing** reiterar.
re·it·er·a·tion (rē-ĭt′ə-rā′shən) s. reiteración f.
re·ject I. tr. (rĭ-jĕkt′) *(to refuse)* rechazar, rehusar; *(to discard)* desechar; *(vomit)* vomitar, arrojar II. s. (rē′jĕkt′) *(thing)* desecho; *(person)* persona rechazada.
re·jec·tion (rĭ-jĕk′shən) s. *(action)* rechazo, rechazamiento; *(reject)* cosa rechazada, desecho.
re·joice (rĭ-jois′) tr. & intr. **-joiced, -joic·ing** regocijar(se), alegrar(se) ♦ **to r. in** tener el honor de.
re·joic·ing (rĭ-joi′sĭng) s. *(feeling, expression)* regocijo; *(celebration)* fiesta.
re·join (rĭ-join′) tr. responder, replicar —intr. *(to respond)* responder, replicar; DER. contestar.
re·join (rē-join′) tr. *(to come together with)* volver a juntarse con; *(to reunite)* juntar de nuevo —intr. volver a juntarse.
re·join·der (rĭ-join′dər) s. respuesta, réplica; DER. contrarréplica, contestación f.
re·ju·ve·nate (rĭ-jōō′və-nāt′) tr. **-nat·ed, -nat·ing** rejuvenecer.
re·ju·ve·na·tion (rĭ-jōō′və-nā′shən) s. rejuvenecimiento.
re·kin·dle (rē-kĭn′dl) tr. & intr. **-dled, -dling** volver a encender.
re·lapse I. intr. (rĭ-lăps′) **-lapsed, -laps·ing** *(into silence, thought)* hundirse, sumirse; *(into paganism, bad health)* recaer; *(into crime, error)* reincidir II. s. (rē′lăps′) *(into silence, thought)* hundimiento; *(into paganism, bad health)* recaída; *(into crime, error)* reincidencia.
re·late (rĭ-lāt′) tr. **-lat·ed, -lat·ing** *(to tell)* relatar, contar; *(to associate)* relacionar, asociar <*to r. one thing to another* asociar una cosa con otra> —intr. *(to have connection)* estar relacionado con, tener que ver con; *(to interact)* relacionarse; *(to identify with)* identificarse ♦ **to r. to** estar relacionado con, tener que ver con • **to r. (well, poorly) with** relacionarse (bien, mal) con.
re·lat·ed (rĭ-lā′tĭd) adj. *(connected)* relacionado; *(by blood, marriage)* emparentado ♦ **to be r. to** ser pariente de.
re·la·tion (rĭ-lā′shən) s. *(connection, account)* relación f, conexión f; *(kinship)* parentesco; *(relative)* pariente mf <*he's no r. of mine* no es pariente mío> ♦ **in r. to** en relación a • **relations** *(dealings)* relaciones <*labor relations* relaciones laborales>; *(sexual)* relaciones sexuales • **to bear no r. to** no tener ninguna relación con.
re·la·tion·al (rĭ-lā′shə-nəl) adj. *(of kinship)* de parentesco; *(related)* que expresa relación.

---

re·la·tion·ship (rĭ-lā'shən-shĭp') s. *(relation)* relación *f; (kinship)* parentesco; *(tie)* vínculo.

rel·a·tive (rĕl'ə-tĭv) **I.** adj. relativo **II.** s. *(kin)* pariente *mf; (term)* relativo.

relative clause s. GRAM. oración de relativo *f.*

relative humidity s. humedad relativa.

rel·a·tive·ly (rĕl'ə-tĭv-lē) adv. relativamente.

relative pronoun s. GRAM. pronombre relativo.

relative to prep. relativo a.

rel·a·tiv·ism (rĕl'ə-tĭ-vĭz'əm) s. FILOS. relativismo.

rel·a·tiv·i·ty (rĕl'ə-tĭv'ĭ-tē) s. relatividad *f.*

re·lax (rĭ-lăks') tr. *(to loosen)* aflojar; *(to ease)* relajar —intr. *(to ease)* relajarse; *(to become less tense)* relajarse ♦ **r.!** ¡cálmate!

re·lax·ant (rĭ-lăk'sənt) s. & adj. relajante *m.*

re·lax·a·tion (rĕ'lăk-sā'shən) s. *(of muscles)* relajación *f; (of tension)* relajación, aflojamiento; *(of discipline)* relajación, relajamiento; *(of efforts)* disminución *f; (state)* descanso, reposo; *(recreation)* distracción *f <she collects stamps for r.* ella colecciona estampillas como distracción>; FISIOL. distensión *f.*

re·laxed (rĭ-lăkst') adj. *(not strict)* relajado; *(loose)* relajado; *(calm)* tranquilo.

re·lay (rē'lā') **I.** s. *(of animals)* posta; *(of workers)* relevo; *(of messages)* transmisión *f; (of news)* difusión *f;* DEP. carrera de relevos; ELEC. relevador *m,* relé *m;* ELECTRÓN., RAD., TELEV. repetidor *m* **II.** tr. *(messages)* transmitir; *(news)* difundir; ELEC. regular con relé; ELECTRÓN., RAD., TELEV. retransmitir —intr. retransmitir.

re·lay (rē-lā') tr. **-laid** (-lād'), **-lay·ing** *(to place again)* volver a colocar; *(track)* volver a tender (vías).

relay race s. DEP. carrera de relevos.

re·lease (rĭ-lēs') **I.** tr. **-leased, -leas·ing** *(prisoners, animals)* poner en libertad; *(from one's grip)* soltar; *(from debt, promise)* descargar; *(for sale)* poner en venta; *(a book)* publicar *<the publisher finally released the dictionary* la editorial finalmente publicó el diccionario>; *(right, claim)* renunciar a; *(smoke, flames)* emitir, echar; *(clutch)* desembragar; *(brakes)* soltar; *(film)* estrenar; *(record)* sacar **II.** s. *(of prisoners, animals)* liberación *f,* puesta en libertad; *(of film)* estreno; *(of book)* publicación *f; (permission)* autorización para publicar *f; (record)* disco, grabación *f <the pianist has a new r.* el pianista tiene una nueva grabación>; *(communiqué)* anuncio; *(of right, claim)* cesión *f; (of smoke, flames)* escape *m;* MEC. disparador *m.*

re·lease (rē-lēs') tr. **-leased, -leas·ing** alquilar de nuevo, volver a arrendar.

rel·e·gate (rĕl'ĭ-gāt') tr. **-gat·ed, -gat·ing** relegar.

rel·e·ga·tion (rĕl'ĭ-gā'shən) s. relegación *f.*

re·lent (rĭ-lĕnt') intr. *(to become milder)* ablandarse, aplacarse; *(to give in)* ceder.

re·lent·less (rĭ-lĕnt'lĭs) adj. *(without pity)* implacable; *(increasing)* incesante.

rel·e·vance (rĕl'ə-vəns) o **rel·e·van·cy** (-vən-sē) s. pertinencia.

rel·e·vant (rĕl'ə-vənt) adj. *(pertinent)* pertinente; *(related)* relacionado.

re·li·a·bil·i·ty (rĭ-lī'ə-bĭl'ĭ-tē) s. seriedad *f.*

re·li·a·ble (rĭ-lī'ə-bəl) adj. *(person)* de confianza; *(company)* serio; *(machine)* seguro, fiable; *(data, source)* fidedigno.

re·li·ance (rĭ-lī'əns) s. confianza.

re·li·ant (rĭ-lī'ənt) adj. *(having reliance)* confiado; *(demonstrating reliance)* confiable.

rel·ic (rĕl'ĭk) s. reliquia ♦ **relics** restos mortales.

re·lief (rĭ-lēf') s. *(alleviation)* alivio; *(assistance)* ayuda, socorro; *(replacement)* relevo *<the nurse's r. arrived early* el relevo de la enfermera llegó temprano>; ARTE., GEOG. relieve *m;* DER. compensación *f* ♦ **in r.** en relieve • **to be on r.** vivir de la beneficencia • **what a r.!** ¡qué alivio!

relief map s. mapa en relieve *m.*

re·lieve (rĭ-lēv') tr. **-lieved, -liev·ing** *(to alleviate)* aliviar, mitigar *<this medication will r. the pain* esta medicina le aliviará el dolor>; *(to set free)* liberar *<your long letter relieves me of my worries* su larga carta me libera de mis preocupaciones>; *(to give aid)* auxiliar, socorrer *<this money will r. the refugees* este dinero socorrerá a los refu-

giados>; *(to release from a job)* destituir; *(to replace)* relevar, reemplazar; *(boredom)* disipar; *(drabness)* alegrar; *(to set off)* poner de relieve, realzar ♦ **to r. oneself** EUFEM. hacer las necesidades.

re·li·gion (rĭ-lĭj'ən) s. religión *f.*

re·li·gious (rĭ-lĭj'əs) **I.** adj. *(of a religion)* religioso *<r. order* orden religiosa>; *(pious)* piadoso, devoto; *(conscientious)* concienzudo **II.** s. [pl. **religious**] religioso.

re·li·gious·ly (rĭ-lĭj'əs-lē) adv. religiosamente.

re·lin·quish (rĭ-lĭng'kwĭsh) tr. *(to abandon)* abandonar; *(to desist from)* desistir de; *(to renounce)* renunciar a; *(to release)* soltar.

rel·i·quar·y (rĕl'ĭ-kwĕr'ē) s. [pl. **-ies**] relicario.

rel·ish (rĕl'ĭsh) **I.** s. *(liking)* gusto, afición *f <a r. for luxury* afición por el lujo>; *(pleasure)* placer *m;* deleite *m <to eat with r.* comer con deleite>; *(excitement)* emoción *f; (trace)* toque *m <a r. of malice in her words* un toque de malicia en sus palabras>; CUL. *(condiment)* condimento, salsa; *(flavor)* gusto, sazón *f* **II.** tr. encantar ♦ **I don't r. (the idea, the prospect)** no me gusta o no me hace ninguna gracia (la idea, posibilidad).

re·live (rē-lĭv') tr. **-lived, -liv·ing** volver a vivir, recordar —intr. volver a vivir.

re·load (rē-lōd') tr. & intr. recargar.

re·lo·cate (rē-lō'kāt') tr. & intr. **-cat·ed, -cat·ing** volver a establecer(se).

re·lo·ca·tion (rē'lō-kā'shən) s. situación o ubicación nueva.

re·luc·tance (rĭ-lŭk'təns) o **re·luc·tan·cy** (-tən-sē) s. *(disinclination)* disgusto, desgana; ELEC. reluctancia.

re·luc·tant (rĭ-lŭk'tənt) adj. *(reticent)* reacio; *(unwilling)* poco dispuesto; *(opposing)* contrario.

re·ly (rĭ-lī') intr. **-lied, -ly·ing** ♦ **to r. on** o **upon** *(to depend)* depender de; *(to trust)* confiar en, contar con.

rem (rĕm) s. FÍS. rem *m.*

re·main (rĭ-mān') intr. *(to keep being)* continuar, seguir; *(to stay)* permanecer, quedarse *<I remained in New York* me quedé en Nueva York>; *(to be left)* quedar, sobrar *<nothing remains of his fortune* no queda nada de su fortuna> ♦ **there remains** queda • **to r. to be (seen, done)** quedar por (ver, hacer).

re·main·der (rĭ-mān'dər) **I.** s. *(rest)* resto *<the r. of the day* el resto del día>; *(others)* los demás, los otros *<ten came in and the r. stayed outside* diez entraron y los demás se quedaron fuera>; MAT. resto **II.** tr. vender como saldo de edición sin salida.

re·main·ing (rĭ-mā'nĭng) adj. restante, sobrante.

re·mains (rĭ-mānz') s.pl. *(parts left)* restos; *(corpse)* restos mortales; *(unpublished writing)* escritos inéditos de un escritor fallecido; *(ruins)* vestigios.

re·make (rē-māk') **I.** tr. **-made** (-mād'), **-mak·ing** rehacer, hacer de nuevo **II.** s. nueva versión.

re·mand (rĭ-mănd') DER. **I.** tr. *(to prison)* volver a mantener bajo custodia; *(into someone's custody)* encarcelar o poner bajo custodia; *(to a lower court)* remitir al tribunal inferior **II.** s. *(prisoner)* reenvío a prisión; *(of a case)* remisión *f.*

re·mark (rĭ-märk') **I.** tr. *(to comment)* comentar; *(to notice)* observar, advertir ♦ **to r. on** hacer un comentario u observación sobre —intr. hacer un comentario u observación **II.** s. comentario, observación *f <to make a r. about* hacer un comentario sobre> ♦ **worthy of r.** notable.

re·mark·a·ble (rĭ-mär'kə-bəl) adj. *(notable)* notable; *(extraordinary)* extraordinario; *(uncommon)* no común; *(considerable)* considerable; *(admirable)* admirable.

re·mar·riage (rē-măr'ĭj) s. segundo matrimonio, segundas nupcias.

re·mar·ry (rē-măr'ē) intr. **-ried, -ry·ing** volver a casarse.

re·match (rē'măch') s. desquite *m.*

re·me·di·a·ble (rĭ-mē'dē-ə-bəl) adj. remediable.

re·me·di·al (rĭ-mē'dē-əl) adj. *(surgery)* reparador; *(treatment)* curativo; *(exercise)* correctivo; *(student)* atrasado; *(course)* de estudiantes atrasados.

rem·e·dy (rĕm'ĭ-dē) s. [pl. **-dies**] *(medicine)* remedio, medicamento; *(solution)* remedio; DER. recurso **II.** tr. **-died, -dy·ing** remediar.

re·mem·ber (rĭ-mĕm'bər) tr. *(to recall)* acordarse de, recordar; *(to keep in memory)* retener, conservar en la memoria; *(to bear in mind)* tener presente, tener en cuenta; *(to reward)* recompensar; *(to give greetings from)* dar recuerdos *o* saludos de <*r. me to your mother* da mis recuerdos a tu mamá> —intr. *(to bear in mind)* acordarse; *(to have memory)* hacer memoria ♦ **as far as I can r.** si mal no recuerdo.

re·mem·brance (rĭ-mĕm′brəns) s. recuerdo ♦ **in r. of** en conmemoración de • **to have no r. of** no recordar, no acordarse de.

re·mil·i·ta·rize (rē-mĭl′ĭ-tə-rīz′) tr. -**rized, -riz·ing** remilitarizar.

re·mind (rĭ-mīnd′) tr. recordar ♦ **that reminds me!** ¡a propósito!

re·mind·er (rĭ-mīn′dər) s. *(of a date)* recordatorio; *(of a due bill)* aviso, notificación *f; (warning)* advertencia, señal *f.*

rem·i·nisce (rĕm′ə-nĭs′) intr. -**nisced, -nisc·ing** recordar el pasado.

rem·i·nis·cence (rĕm′ə-nĭs′əns) s. recuerdo ♦ **reminiscences** memorias.

rem·i·nis·cent (rĕm′ə-nĭs′ənt) adj. evocador.

re·miss (rĭ-mĭs′) adj. negligente, descuidado.

re·mis·sion (rĭ-mĭsh′ən) s. *(pardon)* remisión *f,* perdón *m; (lessening)* disminución *f; (from debt, obligation)* exoneración *f;* MED. remisión.

re·mit (rĭ-mĭt′) tr. -**mit·ted, -mit·ting** *(money, sins)* remitir; *(obligation)* rescindir, revocar; *(efforts)* disminuir; DER. devolver a un tribunal inferior —intr. *(money)* enviar dinero, girar; *(pain, fever)* disminuir.

re·mit·tal (rĭ-mĭt′l) s. *(forgiveness)* remisión *f,* perdón *m; (exoneration)* exoneración *f;* DER. remisión.

re·mit·tance (rĭ-mĭt′ns) s. remesa, envío.

re·mit·tent (rĭ-mĭt′nt) adj. MED. remitente.

rem·nant (rĕm′nənt) s. *(remainder)* remanente *m,* resto; *(of fabric)* retal *m,* retazo; *(trace)* vestigio, indicio.

re·mod·el (rē-mŏd′l) tr. reconstruir, reformar.

re·mon·strance (rĭ-mŏn′strəns) s. protesta.

re·mon·strant (rĭ-mŏn′strənt) I. adj. que protesta II. s. protestador *m.*

re·mon·strate (rĭ-mŏn′strāt′) tr. -**strat·ed, -strat·ing** decir en señal de protesta —intr. protestar.

re·morse (rĭ-môrs′) s. *(regret)* remordimiento; ANT. *(compassion)* compasión *f.*

re·morse·less (rĭ-môrs′lĭs) adj. *(without remorse)* sin remordimiento; *(merciless)* despiadado.

re·mote (rĭ-mōt′) adj. -**mot·er, -mot·est** *(far away)* remoto, lejano; *(distantly related)* lejano; *(aloof)* distante.

remote control s. telemando, control remoto.

re·mote·ly (rĭ-mōt′lē) adv. remotamente ♦ **not to be r. to blame** no tener ni la más mínima culpa.

re·mote·ness (rĭ-mōt′nĭs) s. *(distance)* lejanía; *(improbability)* improbabilidad *f.*

re·mount I. tr. (rē-mount′) *(horse)* volver a montarse en; *(photo)* volver a enmarcar; *(gem)* volver a engarzar II. s. (rē′mount′) remonta.

re·mov·a·ble (rĭ-mōō′və-bəl) adj. *(movable)* movible, móvil; *(transportable)* transportable; *(said of an employee)* amovible.

re·mov·al (rĭ-mōō′vəl) s. *(elimination)* eliminación *f; (transfer)* traslado; *(relocation)* mudanza; *(from a job)* despido; *(from office)* destitución *f;* MED. extirpación *f.*

re·move (rĭ-mōōv′) I. tr. -**moved, -mov·ing** *(to take away)* quitar; *(to transfer)* trasladar; *(to take off)* quitarse <*she asked him to r. his hat* le pidió que se quitara el sombrero>; *(to eliminate)* eliminar; *(doubt, fear)* disipar; *(from a job)* despedir; *(from office)* destituir; CIR. *(to take out)* extirpar, quitar —intr. mudarse, trasladarse II. s. *(distance)* distancia. ·

re·moved (rĭ-mōōvd′) adj. *(distant)* distante <*a house far r. from the town* una casa muy distante del pueblo> ♦ **first cousin once r.** primo segundo.

re·mu·ner·ate (rĭ-myōō′nə-rāt′) tr. -**at·ed, -at·ing** *(to pay)* remunerar; *(to compensate)* recompensar.

re·mu·ner·a·tion (rĭ-myōō′nə-rā′shən) s. remuneración *f.*

re·mu·ner·a·tive (rĭ-myōō′nər-ə-tĭv, -nə-rā′tĭv) adj. remunerativo.

ren·ais·sance (rĕn′ə-säns′, -zäns′, rĭ-nā′səns) I. s. renacimiento ♦ **the R.** HIST. el Renacimiento II. adj. ♦ **R.** renacentista, del Renacimiento.

re·nal (rē′nəl) adj. ANAT. renal.

re·nas·cent (rĭ-năs′ənt, -nā′sənt) adj. renaciente.

rend (rĕnd) tr. **rent** (rĕnt) *o* **rend·ed, rend·ing** *(to tear)* desgarrar, rasgar; *(power)* arrancar, arrebatar; *(to distress)* destrozar ♦ **to r. to pieces** desgarrar.

ren·der (rĕn′dər) tr. *(report, statement)* presentar, someter; *(help)* dar; *(homage)* rendir; *(to yield)* entregar, rendir; *(to depict)* representar, describir; *(to perform)* interpretar (papel, obra); *(to translate)* traducir; *(to pronounce)* pronunciar (sentencia, veredicto); *(to make)* hacer (inútil, superfluo); *(to cause to become)* dejar, quedar <*the accident rendered them helpless* el accidente les dejó incapacitados>; CUL. derretir; CONSTR. enlucir, dar una capa de enlucido ♦ **for services rendered** por servicios prestados.

ren·dez·vous (rän′dā-vōō′) I. s. [pl. -**vous** (-vōōz′)] *(place)* lugar de reunión *m; (meeting)* cita; AER., MIL. punto de reunión II. tr. & intr. -**voused** (-vōōd′), -**vous·ing** (-vōō′ĭng) reunir(se).

ren·di·tion (rĕn-dĭsh′ən) s. *(presentation)* presentación *f,* entrega; *(translation)* versión *f,* traducción *f;* MÚS., TEAT. interpretación *f.*

ren·e·gade (rĕn′ĭ-gād′) I. s. renegado II. intr. -**gad·ed, -gad·ing** renegar.

re·nege (rĭ-nĭg′, -nĕg′) intr. -**neged, -neg·ing** *(to back out)* no cumplir una promesa; *(in cards)* renunciar ♦ **to r. on (an agreement, deal)** volverse atrás.

re·ne·go·ti·ate (rē′nĭ-gō′shē-āt′) tr. -**at·ed, -at·ing** negociar de nuevo.

re·new (rĭ-nōō′, -nyōō′) tr. *(subscription, contract)* renovar; *(to resume)* reanudar; *(to revive)* reavivar; *(to replenish)* llenar de nuevo, volver a llenar; *(to replace)* renovar —intr. renovarse.

re·new·a·ble (rĭ-nōō′ə-bəl, -nyōō′-) adj. renovable.

re·new·al (rĭ-nōō′əl, -nyōō′-) s. *(of a contract)* renovación *f; (of negotiations)* reanudación *f; (reestablishment)* restablecimiento.

ren·in (rĕn′ĭn) s. BIOL. renina.

re·nom·i·nate (rē-nŏm′ə-nāt′) tr. -**nat·ed, -nat·ing** volver a nominar *o* nombrar (candidato).

re·nom·i·na·tion (rē-nŏm′ə-nā′shən) s. nueva nominación.

re·nounce (rĭ-nouns′) I. tr. & intr. -**nounced, -nounc·ing** renunciar (a) II. s. renuncio (en naipes).

ren·o·vate (rĕn′ə-vāt′) tr. -**vat·ed, -vat·ing** *(to restore)* restaurar; *(to renew)* renovar.

ren·o·va·tion (rĕn′ə-vā′shən) s. *(restoration)* restauración *f,* reforma; *(renewal)* renovación *f.*

re·nown (rĭ-noun′) s. renombre *m,* fama; ANT. *(report)* noticia; *(rumor)* rumor *m.*

re·nowned (rĭ-nound′) adj. renombrado.

rent¹ (rĕnt) I. s. *(payment)* alquiler *m,* renta <*one month's r.* un mes de alquiler>; *(income)* renta, ingresos ♦ **for r.** se alquila • **to pay the r.** pagar el alquiler de la casa II. tr. *(house, car)* alquilar; *(land)* arrendar ♦ **to r. out** alquilar —intr. alquilarse.

rent² (rĕnt) I. un pret. & part. p. de **rend** II. s. *(rip)* rasgón *m,* rasgadura; *(split)* raja, hendidura; *(schism)* escisión *f,* división *f.*

rent·al (rĕn′tl) I. s. *(amount)* alquiler *m; (property)* propiedad alquilada ♦ **(truck, movie) rentals** COM. se alquilan (camiones, películas) II. adj. de alquiler.

rent control s. control de alquileres (por parte del gobierno) *m.*

rent·er (rĕn′tər) s. *(of a house)* inquilino; *(of land)* arrendatario.

re·num·ber (rē-nŭm′bər) tr. volver a numerar.

re·nun·ci·a·tion (rĭ-nŭn′sē-ā′shən) s. renunciación *f,* renuncia.

re·oc·cu·py (rē-ŏk′yə-pī′) tr. -**pied, -py·ing** volver a ocupar.

re·o·pen (rē-ō′pən) tr. & intr. *(to open again)* reabrir(se); *(to take up again)* reanudar(se).

re·or·der (rē-ôr′dər) I. tr. *(to order again)* volver a hacer un pedido de, hacer un nuevo pedido de; *(to straighten out)*

ã rey / ä año / b boca / ch chico / d dar / ĕ el / ē mil / g gato / h joya / hw juez / ī aire / k casa / kw cuan /

volver a ordenar; *(to rearrange)* reorganizar —intr. hacer un nuevo pedido **II.** s. nuevo pedido, nueva orden.

re·or·gan·i·za·tion (rē-ôr′gə-nĭ-zā′shən) s. reorganización *f.*

re·or·gan·ize (rē-ôr′gə-nīz′) tr. & intr. **-ized, -iz·ing** reorganizar(se).

re·o·ri·en·ta·tion (rē-ôr′ē-ĕn-tā′shən) s. nueva orientación.

rep (rĕp) s. FAM. representante *mf.*

re·paid (rē-pād′) part. p. y pret. de repay.

re·pair¹ (rĭ-pâr′) **I.** tr. *(car)* reparar; *(shoes, clothes)* remendar **II.** s. reparación *f* ♦ **closed for repairs** cerrado por reformas • **in bad r.** *o* **in a bad state of r.** en mal estado • **to be beyond r.** no tener arreglo.

re·pair² (rĭ-pâr′) **I.** intr. ir, acudir **II.** s. lugar de reunión habitual *m.*

re·pair·man (rĭ-pâr′măn) s. [pl. **-men** (-mĕn′)] reparador *m*, técnico.

rep·a·ra·ble (rĕp′ər-ə-bəl) adj. reparable.

rep·a·ra·tion (rĕp′ə-rā′shən) s. reparación *f* ♦ **reparations** COM. indemnización.

re·par·a·tive (rĭ-păr′ə-tĭv) *o* **re·par·a·to·ry** (-tôr′ē) adj. reparador.

rep·ar·tee (rĕp′ər-tē′) s. *(reply)* réplica; *(conversation)* conversación con rápida sucesión de réplicas *f.*

re·past (rĭ-păst′) s. comida.

re·pa·tri·ate (rē-pā′trē-āt′) **I.** tr. **-at·ed, -at·ing** repatriar **II.** s. (-ĭt, -āt′) repatriado.

re·pa·tri·a·tion (rē-pā′trē-ā′shən) s. repatriación *f.*

re·pay (rē-pā′) tr. **-paid** (-pād′), **-pay·ing** *(to pay back)* pagar; *(to return)* devolver; *(to compensate)* compensar, pagar ♦ **to r. someone in kind** pagar a alguien con la misma moneda —intr. pagar, hacer un pago.

re·pay·a·ble (rē-pā′ə-bəl) adj. reembolsable, reintegrable.

re·pay·ment (rē-pā′mənt) s. *(of a debt)* pago, liquidación *f*; *(of money)* devolución *f*, reembolso; *(reward)* recompensa.

re·peal (rĭ-pēl′) **I.** tr. *(to revoke)* revocar; *(to annul)* anular **II.** s. *(revocation)* revocación *f*; *(annulment)* anulación *f.*

re·peat (rĭ-pēt′) **I.** tr. *(to say again)* repetir, decir de nuevo <to r. a word repetir una palabra>; *(to recite)* recitar; *(to tell)* contar <to r. a secret contar un secreto>; *(to do again)* repetir (experimento, curso) ♦ **to r. after** repetir a continuación • **to r. oneself** repetirse —intr. *(to say again)* repetir; *(to do again)* repetir; *(to vote)* votar más de una vez **II.** s. *(repetition)* repetición *f*; RAD., TELEV. segunda difusión; MÚS. repetición.

re·peat·a·ble (rĭ-pē′tə-bəl) adj. repetible.

re·peat·ed (rĭ-pē′tĭd) adj. repetido.

re·peat·er (rĭ-pē′tər) s. *(watch)* reloj de repetición *m*; *(firearm)* arma de repetición; *(student)* estudiante repetidor *mf*; *(voter)* elector que vota más de una vez *m*; *(criminal)* criminal reincidente *mf.*

re·peat·ing (rĭ-pē′tĭng) adj. de repetición.

repeating decimal s. MAT. fracción decimal periódica.

re·pel (rĭ-pĕl′) tr. **-pelled, -pel·ling** *(to drive back)* repeler, rechazar; *(to reject)* rechazar; *(to disgust)* repeler, repugnar; *(to be resistant to)* repeler ♦ **to r. each other** repelerse.

re·pel·lent (rĭ-pĕl′ənt) **I.** adj. *(repelling)* repelente; *(repulsive)* repelente, repugnante ♦ **water-repellent** impermeable **II.** s. ♦ **insect r.** producto contra los insectos.

re·pent (rĭ-pĕnt′) intr. & tr. arrepentirse (de).

re·pen·tance (rĭ-pĕn′təns) s. arrepentimiento.

re·pen·tant (rĭ-pĕn′tənt) adj. arrepentido.

re·per·cus·sion (rē′pər-kŭsh′ən, rĕp′ər-) s. *(influence)* repercusión *f*; *(sound)* repercusión, reverberación *f.*

rep·er·toire (rĕp′ər-twär′) s. repertorio.

rep·er·to·ry (rĕp′ər-tôr′ē) s. [pl. **-ries**] *(repertoire)* repertorio; *(theater)* teatro de repertorio; *(repository)* depósito, almacén *m.*

rep·e·ti·tion (rĕp′ĭ-tĭsh′ən) s. *(act)* repetición *f*; *(recitation)* recitación *f*; *(copy)* copia.

rep·e·ti·tious (rĕp′ĭ-tĭsh′əs) adj. repetitivo, reiterativo.

re·pet·i·tive (rĭ-pĕt′ĭ-tĭv) adj. repetitivo, reiterativo.

re·phrase (rē-frāz′) tr. **-phrased, -phras·ing** decir *o* expresar de otra manera.

re·place (rĭ-plās′) tr. **-placed, -plac·ing** *(to put back)* repo-

ner, poner de nuevo en su lugar; *(to supplant)* suplantar, suplir; *(to get another)* reemplazar, sustituir.

re·place·a·ble (rĭ-plā′sə-bəl) adj. reemplazable.

re·place·ment (rĭ-plās′mənt) s. *(putting back)* reposición *f*; *(substitution)* reemplazo, substitución *f*; *(person)* substituto, relevo; DEP. suplente *mf*; MIL. reemplazo, relevo ♦ **r.** *o* **r. part** repuesto.

re·plant (rē-plănt′) tr. replantar, plantar de nuevo.

re·play I. tr. (rē-plā′) *(game)* volver a jugar; *(videotape)* volver a poner; *(music)* volver a tocar; *(play)* volver a representar **II.** s. (rē′plā′) TELEV. repetición *f.*

re·plen·ish (rĭ-plĕn′ĭsh) tr. *(to fill again)* volver a llenar, llenar de nuevo; FIG. *(to restore)* llenar, restaurar —intr. volver a llenarse, llenarse de nuevo.

re·plen·ish·ment (rĭ-plĕn′ĭsh-mənt) s. reabastecimiento.

re·plete (rĭ-plēt′) adj. repleto.

rep·li·ca (rĕp′lĭ-kə) s. réplica, copia.

rep·li·cate (rĕp′lĭ-kāt′) tr. & intr. **-cat·ed, -cat·ing** duplicar(se), repetir(se).

rep·li·ca·tion (rĕp′lĭ-kā′shən) s. *(reply)* DER. réplica; *(echo)* reverberación *f*, eco; *(reproduction)* reproducción *f.*

re·ply (rĭ-plī′) **I.** intr. & tr. **-plied, -ply·ing** contestar, responder <to r. to the question responder a la pregunta> **II.** s. [pl. **-plies**] respuesta, contestación *f* <to get no r. no recibir respuesta>.

re·port (rĭ-pôrt′) **I.** s. *(account)* información *f*, relato; *(official account)* informe *m*; *(of news)* reportaje *m*; *(of pupils)* boletín *m*; *(rumor)* rumor *m* <according to reports según los rumores>; *(reputation)* reputación *f*, fama; *(noise)* estampido, detonación *f* <the r. of a rifle el estampido de un rifle>; DER. recopilación de decisiones *f* ♦ **annual r.** COM. informe anual • **weather r.** boletín meteorológico **II.** tr. *(to give an account of)* presentar un informe sobre; *(to recount)* relatar; *(to tell of)* informar, comunicar; *(to denounce)* denunciar <she reported him to the police le denunció a la policía> ♦ **it is reported that** se dice que • **to r. for** *(professionally)* ser reportero de, hacer reportajes para <he reports for the Times es reportero del Times>; *(military duty)* incorporarse; *(work)* presentarse a *o* para • **to r. on** *(event)* hacer un informe sobre; *(news)* escribir una crónica de —intr. *(to present a report)* presentar un informe; *(to show up)* presentarse.

re·port·age (rĭ-pôr′tĭj, rĕp′ər-täzh′) s. reportaje *m.*

report card s. boletín de notas *o* de calificaciones *m.*

re·port·ed·ly (rĭ-pôr′tĭd-lē) adv. según se informa *o* se dice.

re·port·er (rĭ-pôr′tər) s. *(journalist)* reportero, periodista *mf*; FOR. relator (en tribunales) *m.*

re·pose¹ (rĭ-pōz′) **I.** s. *(rest)* reposo, descanso; *(sleep)* sueño; *(composure)* compostura, serenidad *f*; *(calm)* tranquilidad *f*, calma **II.** tr. **-posed, -pos·ing** ♦ **to r. oneself** descansar —intr. ♦ **to r. on** descansar sobre.

re·pose² (rĭ-pōz′) tr. **-posed, -pos·ing** poner, depositar (confianza, esperanzas).

re·pos·i·to·ry (rĭ-pŏz′ĭ-tôr′ē) s. [pl. **-ries**] *(place)* almacén *m*, depósito; *(tomb)* panteón *m*; *(person)* depositario.

re·pos·sess (rē′pə-zĕs′) tr. *(to regain possession of)* recuperar, volver a tomar posesión de; *(to give back)* devolver.

rep·re·hend (rĕp′rĭ-hĕnd′) tr. reprender.

rep·re·hen·si·ble (rĕp′rĭ-hĕn′sə-bəl) adj. reprensible.

rep·re·hen·sion (rĕp′rĭ-hĕn′shən) s. reprensión *f.*

rep·re·sent (rĕp′rĭ-zĕnt′) tr. *(to symbolize, portray)* representar; *(to describe)* describir; *(act, speak for)* representar; *(to exemplify)* ser un ejemplo de; *(to equal)* equivaler ARTE., TEAT. representar.

rep·re·sen·ta·tion (rĕp′rĭ-zĕn-tā′shən) s. ARTE., TEAT. representación *f*; DER. declaración *f*; POL. delegación *f.*

rep·re·sen·ta·tive (rĕp′rĭ-zĕn′tə-tĭv) **I.** s. representante *mf* ♦ **R.** POL. representante, diputado **II.** adj. *(representing)* representativo; *(typical)* típico, característico.

re·press (rĭ-prĕs′) tr. & intr. reprimir.

re·pres·sion (rĭ-prĕsh′ən) s. represión *f.*

re·pres·sive (rĭ-prĕs′ĭv) adj. represivo.

re·pres·sor (rĭ-prĕs′ər) s. represor *m.*

re·prieve (rĭ-prēv′) **I.** tr. **-prieved, -priev·ing** *(pain)* aliviar temporalmente; DER. *(execution)* suspender la ejecución de; *(sentence)* conmutar la pena de **II.** s. *(from pain)* alivio temporal; DER. *(of an execution)* suspensión de la ejecución *f*; *(of a sentence)* conmutación *f*.

rep·ri·mand (rĕp′rə-mănd′) I. tr. reprender, regañar II. s. reprimenda.

re·print s. I. (rē′prĭnt′) *(of book, stamp)* reimpresión *f*; *(of article)* tirada aparte, separata II. tr. (rē-prĭnt′) *(book, stamp)* reimprimir; *(article, chapter)* tirar aparte.

re·pri·sal (rĭ-prī′zəl) s. represalia.

re·prise (rĭ-prēz′) s. *(resumption)* reanudación *f*; MÚS. repetición *f*.

re·proach (rĭ-prōch′) I. tr. reprochar II. s. *(blame)* crítica; *(rebuke)* reproche *m* ♦ **to be above** o **beyond r.** ser intachable.

re·proach·ful (rĭ-prōch′fəl) adj. reprobador.

rep·ro·bate (rĕp′rə-bāt′) I. s. *(unprincipled person)* malvado; TEO. réprobo II. adj. *(unprincipled)* malvado; TEO. réprobo III. tr. **-bat·ed, -bat·ing** *(to condemn)* reprobar; TEO. condenar.

re·proc·ess (rē-prŏs′ĕs′, -prō′sĕs′) tr. someter de nuevo a algún procedimiento.

re·pro·duce (rē′prə-dōōs′, -dyōōs′) tr. & intr. **-duced, -duc·ing** reproducir(se).

re·pro·duc·tion (rē′prə-dŭk′shən) s. reproducción *f*.

re·pro·duc·tive (rē′prə-dŭk′tĭv) adj. reproductivo.

re·proof (rĭ-prōōf′) s. reprobación *f*, reprimenda.

re·prove (rĭ-prōōv′) tr. **-proved, -prov·ing** *(to scold)* reprobar, reprender; *(to disappprove)* desaprobar, criticar.

rep·tile (rĕp′təl, -tīl′) s. ZOOL. reptil *m*; FIG. *(person)* rastrero.

rep·til·i·an (rĕp-tĭl′ē-ən) adj. & s. reptil *m*.

re·pub·lic (rĭ-pŭb′lĭk) s. república.

re·pub·li·can (rĭ-pŭb′lĭ-kən) adj. & s. republicano ♦ **R.** POL. republicano.

Republican Party s. POL. Partido Republicano.

re·pu·di·ate (rĭ-pyōō′dē-āt′) tr. **-at·ed, -at·ing** *(to reject)* repudiar; DER. negarse a reconocer.

re·pu·di·a·tion (rĭ-pyōō′dē-ā′shən) s. *(act)* repudiación *f*, repudio; DER. desconocimiento.

re·pug·nance (rĭ-pŭg′nəns) o **re·pug·nan·cy** (-nən-sē) s. repugnancia.

re·pug·nant (rĭ-pŭg′nənt) adj. *(repulsive)* repugnante, repulsivo; *(repellent)* repelente; LOG. contradictorio.

re·pulse (rĭ-pŭls′) I. tr. **-pulsed, -puls·ing** repeler, rechazar II. s. *(act)* repulsión *f*, repulsa; *(rejection)* rechazo.

re·pul·sion (rĭ-pŭl′shən) s. *(act)* repulsión *f*; *(aversion)* repugnancia, aversión *f*; FÍS. repulsión.

re·pul·sive (rĭ-pŭl′sĭv) adj. *(disgusting)* repulsivo, repugnante; *(repellent)* repelente.

rep·u·ta·ble (rĕp′yə-tə-bəl) adj. *(honorable)* honorable, respetable; *(in correct usage)* castizo, puro.

rep·u·ta·tion (rĕp′yə-tā′shən) s. reputación *f*, fama.

re·pute (rĭ-pyōōt′) I. tr. **-put·ed, -put·ing** ♦ **to be reputed to be** tener fama de II. s. reputación *f*, fama.

re·put·ed (rĭ-pyōō′tĭd) adj. *(generally considered)* reputado; *(supposed)* supuesto.

re·quest (rĭ-kwĕst′) I. tr. *(to ask for)* pedir, rogar; *(to ask someone)* solicitar, demandar II. s. ruego, solicitud *f* ♦ **available on r.** disponible a petición • **by popular r.** a petición del público • **to r. the pleasure of your company at** o **for** tener el placer de invitarle a.

req·ui·em (rĕk′wē-əm, rē′kwē-) s. LIT., MÚS. réquiem *m*; *(mass)* misa de réquiem.

re·quire (rĭ-kwīr′) tr. **-quired, -quir·ing** *(to need)* requerir, necesitar; *(to demand)* requerir, exigir; *(to oblige)* obligar ♦ **to be required** *(needed)* necesitarse, requerirse; *(necessary)* exigirse • **to have all that one requires** tener todo lo que hace falta • **what is required of me?** ¿qué se exige que yo haga?

re·quire·ment (rĭ-kwīr′mənt) s. *(prerequisite)* requisito; *(need)* necesidad *f*.

req·ui·site (rĕk′wĭ-zĭt) I. adj. necesario, indispensable II. s. requisito.

req·ui·si·tion (rĕk′wĭ-zĭsh′ən) I. s. *(request)* solicitud *f*; MIL. requisición *f*, requisa; DIPL. petición *f* II. tr. requisar.

re·quit·al (rĭ-kwīt′l) s. *(act)* desquite *m*; *(return)* compensación *f*.

re·quite (rĭ-kwīt′) tr. **-quit·ed, -quit·ing** *(to make return for)* corresponder a; *(to avenge)* vengarse de, desquitarse de.

re·route (rē-rōōt′, -rout′) tr. **-rout·ed, -rout·ing** cambiar el itinerario o la trayectoria de, desviar.

re·run CINEM., TELEV. I. s. (rē′rŭn′) reestreno II. tr. (rē-rŭn′) **-ran** (-răn), **-run·ning** reestrenar.

re·sale (rē′sāl′) s. reventa.

re·sched·ule (rē-skĕj′ōōl, -əl) tr. **-uled, -ul·ing** *(event)* volver a programar; *(debt)* reestructurar.

re·scind (rĭ-sĭnd′) tr. *(to make void)* rescindir; *(to annul)* anular, cancelar; *(to repeal)* abrogar.

re·scis·sion (rĭ-sĭzh′ən) s. *(act)* rescisión *f*; *(annulment)* anulación *f*, cancelación *f*; *(abrogation)* abrogación *f*.

res·cue (rĕs′kyōō) I. tr. **-cued, -cu·ing** *(to save)* rescatar, salvar; MAR. recobrar II. s. *(action)* rescate *m*, salvamento; DER. recuperación *f* ♦ **to come to one's r.** acudir en auxilio de alguien.

res·cu·er (rĕs′kyōō-ər) s. salvador *m*.

re·search (rĭ-sûrch′, rē′sûrch′) I. s. *(study)* investigación *f*; *(search)* búsqueda, busca II. intr. hacer una investigación —tr. ♦ **to r. into** hacer una investigación sobre.

re·search·er (rĭ-sûr′chər, rē′sûr′chər) s. investigador *m*.

re·sell (rē-sĕl′) tr. **-sold** (-sōld′), **-sell·ing** revender.

re·sem·blance (rĭ-zĕm′bləns) s. parecido, semejanza.

re·sem·ble (rĭ-zĕm′bəl) tr. **-bled, -bling** parecerse a.

re·sent (rĭ-zĕnt′) tr. resentirse por, ofenderse por.

re·sent·ful (rĭ-zĕnt′fəl) adj. resentido.

re·sent·ment (rĭ-zĕnt′mənt) s. resentimiento.

res·er·va·tion (rĕz′ər-vā′shən) s. *(of room, table)* reservación *f*; *(condition)* reserva <they accepted the plan with reservations aceptaron el plan con reservas>; *(land)* reserva, coto ♦ **Indian r.** reserva de indios.

re·serve (rĭ-zûrv′) I. tr. **-served, -serv·ing** reservar ♦ **to r. one's judgment on** reservarse el juicio acerca de II. s. reserva ♦ **cash reserves** reservas en metálico • **game r.** coto de caza • **in r.** de reserva • **reserves** MIL. reservas III. adj. de reserva <r. supplies provisiones de reserva>.

reserve bank s. FIN. banco de reserva.

re·served (rĭ-zûrvd′) adj. *(held in reserve)* reservado, guardado; *(marked by self-restraint)* reservado, discreto.

re·serv·ist (rĭ-zûr′vĭst) s. MIL. reservista *mf*.

res·er·voir (rĕz′ər-vwär′, -vwôr′) s. *(body of water)* embalse *m*; *(for ink)* depósito.

re·set (rē-sĕt′) tr. **-set, -set·ting** *(bone)* encajar; *(clock)* poner en hora; *(gem)* volver a engastar; IMPR. recomponer.

re·shape (rē-shāp′) tr. **-shaped, -shap·ing** rehacer, reformar.

re·side (rĭ-zīd′) intr. **-sid·ed, -sid·ing** *(to live somewhere)* residir, vivir; FIG. *(to exist)* residir, radicar.

res·i·dence (rĕz′ĭ-dəns) s. residencia ♦ **in r.** residente.

res·i·den·cy (rĕz′ĭ-dən-sē) s. [pl. **-cies**] residencia.

res·i·dent (rĕz′ĭ-dənt) I. s. *(inhabitant)* residente *mf*; MED. interno II. adj. *(residing)* residente; *(permanent)* fijo <r. population población fija>; ZOOL. no migratorio ♦ **r. alien** extranjero residente.

res·i·den·tial (rĕz′ĭ-dĕn′shəl) adj. residencial.

re·sid·u·al (rĭ-zĭj′ōō-əl) I. adj. residual II. s. residuo.

re·sid·ue (rĕz′ĭ-dōō′, -dyōō′) s. *(remainder)* residuo, resto; CIENT. residuo; DER. bienes residuales *m*.

re·sid·u·um (rĭ-zĭj′ōō-əm) s. [pl. **-u·a** (-ōō-ə)] *(residue)* residuo; DER. bienes residuales *m*.

re·sign (rĭ-zīn′) tr. *(to quit)* renunciar, dimitir; *(to relinquish)* ceder ♦ **to r. oneself to** resignarse a —intr. dimitir.

res·ig·na·tion (rĕz′ĭg-nā′shən) s. *(act)* renuncia; *(statement)* renuncia, dimisión *f*; *(unresisting acceptance)* resignación *f*.

re·signed (rĭ-zīnd′) adj. resignado.

re·sil·ience (rĭ-zĭl′yəns) o **re·sil·ien·cy** (-yən-sē) s. *(elasticity)* elasticidad *f*; *(buoyancy)* rebote *m*; MEC. resiliencia.

re·sil·ient (rĭ-zĭl′yənt) adj. *(flexible)* elástico, flexible; MEC. resiliente.

res·in (rĕz′ĭn) I. s. BOT. resina; QUÍM. resina sintética o artificial II. tr. untar con resina.

res·in·ous (rĕz′ə-nəs) adj. resinoso.

re·sist (rĭ-zĭst′) tr. & intr. resistir ♦ **I couldn't r. laughing**

no pude aguantar la risa • **not to be able to r.** no poder resistir.
re·sis·tance (rǐ-zǐs′təns) s. resistencia.
re·sis·tant (rǐ-zǐs′tənt) adj. resistente.
re·sist·i·ble (rǐ-zǐs′tə-bəl) adj. resistible.
re·sis·tor (rǐ-zǐs′tər) s. ELEC. resistor *m*, resistencia.
res·o·lute (rĕz′ə-lōōt′) adj. *(determined)* determinado, resuelto; *(unwavering)* firme.
res·o·lu·tion (rĕz′ə-lōō′shən) s. *(determination, statement)* resolución *f*; ÓPT. análisis *m*; DER. resolución, fallo; MÚS. resolución ♦ **to make a r.** tomar una resolución • **to show r.** mostrarse resuelto.
re·solv·a·ble (rǐ-zŏl′və-bəl) adj. resoluble, soluble.
re·solve (rǐ-zŏlv′) I. tr. **-solved, -solv·ing** resolver ♦ **to r. (itself) into** convertirse en <*his resentment resolved itself into resignation* su resentimiento se convirtió en resignación> —intr. resolver, decidir <*he resolved to study* decidió estudiar> II. s. resolución *f*.
re·solved (rǐ-zŏlvd′) adj. resuelto.
re·sol·vent (rǐ-zŏl′vənt) I. adj. QUÍM. solvente, disolvente; MED. resolutivo II. s. MED. resolutivo.
res·o·nance (rĕz′ə-nəns) s. resonancia.
res·o·nant (rĕz′ə-nənt) adj. resonante.
res·o·nate (rĕz′ə-nāt′) intr. **-nat·ed, -nat·ing** resonar —tr. hacer resonar.
res·o·na·tor (rĕz′ə-nā′tər) s. FÍS. resonador *m*.
re·sorp·tion (rē-sôrp′shən, -zôrp′-) s. resorción *f*.
re·sort (rǐ-zôrt′) I. intr. ♦ **to r. to** *(censorship, violence)* recurrir a; *(the beach, movies)* frecuentar II. s. *(place)* lugar de temporada *m* <*winter r.* lugar de temporada invernal>; *(gathering)* reunión *f*; *(recourse)* recurso <*only as a last r.* sólo como último recurso>.
re·sound (rǐ-zound′) intr. *(sound)* resonar; *(fame, glory)* tener resonancia <*her fame resounded far and wide* su fama tenía resonancia en el mundo entero> —tr. cantar, celebrar.
re·sound·ing (rǐ-zoun′dǐng) adj. resonante.
re·source (rē′sôrs, rǐ-sôrs′) s. recurso, medio ♦ **natural resources** recursos naturales • **resources** *(means)* recursos, medios; *(assets)* bienes, riquezas.
re·source·ful (rǐ-sôrs′fəl) adj. listo, ingenioso.
re·source·ful·ness (rǐ-sôrs′fəl-nǐs) s. ingenio, habilidad *f*.
re·spect (rǐ-spĕkt′) I. tr. *(to esteem)* respetar, estimar <*they r. you* le respetan a Ud.>; *(the law, elders)* respetar; *(to concern)* concernir, referirse a II. s. *(esteem)* respeto, estima <*they have a great deal of r. for you* le tienen mucho respeto>; *(consideration)* consideración *f* <*to have no r. for others* no tener ningún respeto a los demás>; *(aspect)* aspecto <*in every r.* en todos los aspectos>; *(reference)* referencia, relación *f* <*with r. to this problem* con relación a este problema> ♦ **in other respects** por lo demás, por otra parte • **in that r.** en cuanto a eso • **in this r.** a este respecto • **out of r. for** en consideración a, por respeto a • **to command r.** hacerse respetar • **to pay one's respects** presentar los respetos.
re·spect·a·bil·i·ty (rǐ-spĕk′tə-bǐl′ĭ-tē) s. respetabilidad *f*.
re·spect·a·ble (rǐ-spĕk′tə-bəl) adj. *(person)* respetable; *(sum)* considerable, respetable; *(clothes)* decoroso; *(job, effort)* bastante bueno.
re·spect·ful (rǐ-spĕkt′fəl) adj. respetuoso.
re·spect·ing (rǐ-spĕk′tǐng) prep. respecto a, en cuanto a.
re·spec·tive (rǐ-spĕk′tǐv) adj. respectivo <*their r. fields* sus campos respectivos>.
re·spec·tive·ly (rǐ-spĕk′tǐv-lē) adv. respectivamente.
res·pi·ra·tion (rĕs′pə-rā′shən) s. respiración *f*.
res·pi·ra·tor (rĕs′pə-rā′tər) s. MED. respirador *m*; *(face mask)* mascarilla, careta.
res·pi·ra·to·ry (rĕs′pər-ə-tôr′ē, rǐ-spīr′ə-) adj. respiratorio, de la respiración.
respiratory system s. FISIOL. sistema respiratorio.
re·spire (rǐ-spīr′) I. tr. & intr. **-spired, -spir·ing** respirar.
res·pite (rĕs′pĭt) I. s. *(pause)* respiro, tregua; DER. suspensión temporal *f* II. tr. **-pit·ed, -pit·ing** *(to delay)* posponer, aplazar; DER. suspender.
re·splen·dent (rǐ-splĕn′dənt) adj. *(filled with splendor)* resplandeciente, reluciente; *(brilliant)* lustroso, brillante.

re·spond (rǐ-spŏnd′) intr. *(to answer)* responder, contestar; *(to react)* responder, reaccionar ♦ **to r. to** responder a *(una carta, tratamiento)*.
re·spon·dent (rǐ-spŏn′dənt) I. adj. respondedor II. s. *(person who responds)* persona que responde; DER. demandado.
re·sponse (rǐ-spŏns′) s. *(to a question)* respuesta, contestación *f*; *(to a solicitation, proposal)* acogida; *(to a stimulus, treatment)* reacción *f*; RELIG. *(to a priest)* contestación; *(responsory)* responsorio.
re·spon·si·bil·i·ty (rǐ-spŏn′sə-bǐl′ĭ-tē) s. [pl. **-ties**] responsabilidad *f* ♦ **on one's own r.** bajo su propia responsabilidad • **that is not my r.** eso no es asunto mío • **to assume** *o* **take r. for** asumir la responsabilidad de.
re·spon·si·ble (rǐ-spŏn′sə-bəl) adj. *(accountable)* responsable; *(position)* de responsabilidad; *(person)* digno de confianza ♦ **to be r. for** ser responsable de • **to be r. to** ser responsable ante <*he is r. to the people* es responsable ante el pueblo>.
re·spon·si·bly (rǐ-spŏn′sə-blē) adv. con seriedad, con formalidad.
re·spon·sive (rǐ-spŏn′sĭv) adj. sensible ♦ **not to be very r.** no demostrar mucho interés • **r. to** sensible a.
re·spon·sive·ly (rǐ-spŏn′sĭv-lē) adv. con sensibilidad.
re·spon·sive·ness (rǐ-spŏn′sĭv-nǐs) s. *(sensitivity)* sensibilidad *f*; *(comprehension)* comprensión *f*; *(interest)* interés *m*.
rest¹ (rĕst) I. s. *(repose)* reposo, descanso; *(peace)* sosiego, tranquilidad *f*; *(sleep)* sueño; *(death)* paz (de los muertos) *f*; *(respite)* respiro; *(caesura)* cesura; *(support)* soporte *m*, base *m*; MÚS. pausa ♦ **after a good night's r.** después de haber pasado una buena noche • **at r.** *(asleep)* dormido; *(dead)* muerto; *(quiet)* tranquilo; *(motionless)* quieto; *(free)* en paz • **to come to r.** pararse • **to give it a r.** JER. dejar descansar • **to lay to r.** enterrar • **to put to r.** olvidarse de, dejar de pensar en • **to take a r.** descansar un rato II. intr. *(to stop)* pararse; *(to lie down)* descansar, reposar; *(to be relaxed)* quedarse tranquilo, descansar; *(to be supported)* apoyarse en; *(to be placed)* pesar sobre; *(to depend)* depender de; *(to remain)* quedarse, permanecer; *(to be leased)* basarse, radicar; *(to be fixed)* fijarse; DER. terminar el alegato ♦ **let it r.** déjalo estar • **may he r. in peace** que en paz descanse • **to r. up** descansar bien —tr. *(to give rest to)* dejar descansar <*I stopped and rested my horse* me detuve y dejé descansar a mi caballo>; *(to place)* apoyar <*to r. one's head* apoyar la cabeza>; *(hopes)* poner; *(defense)* basar; *(to halt)* parar, detener; DER. concluir (presentación de alegatos) ♦ **God r. his soul** que Dios le tenga en su gloria • **to r. on** *o* **against** recaer sobre • **to r. one's case** DER. terminar el alegato • **to r. one's eyes on** fijar la mirada en • **to r. with** recaer sobre.
rest² (rĕst) I. s. ♦ **the r.** *(remainder)* el resto; *(others)* los demás II. intr. quedarse <*you can r. assured* puedes quedarte tranquilo>.
re·start (rē-stärt′) tr. *(a car, machine)* volver a poner en marcha; *(to begin again)* volver a empezar.
re·state (rē-stāt′) tr. **-stat·ed, -stat·ing** volver a exponer, plantear de nuevo.
res·tau·rant (rĕs′tər-ənt, -tə-ränt′) s. restaurante *m*.
res·tau·ra·teur (rĕs′tər-ə-tûr′) *o* **res·tau·ran·teur** (-tə-rän-tûr′) s. dueño de un restaurante.
rest·ful (rĕst′fəl) adj. *(tranquil)* reposado, tranquilo; *(quiet)* quieto, sosegado.
rest home s. *(for sick people)* sanatorio; *(for old people)* asilo de ancianos.
rest·ing (rĕs′tǐng) adj. BOT. latente.
res·ti·tute (rĕs′tǐ-tōōt′, -tyōōt′) tr. **-tut·ed, -tut·ing** restituir.
res·ti·tu·tion (rĕs′tǐ-tōō′shən, -tyōō′-) s. *(restoring)* restitución *f*; *(restoration)* restauración *f*; *(indemnification)* indemnización *f*.
res·tive (rĕs′tǐv) adj. *(uneasy)* inquieto, intranquilo; *(refractory)* indócil; *(horse)* repropio.
rest·less (rĕst′lǐs) adj. inquieto, agitado.
re·stock (rē-stŏk′) tr. reabastecer.
res·to·ra·tion (rĕs′tə-rā′shən) s. *(of painting, monarch)* res-

tauración f; *(of employee, officer)* reintegración f; *(of order, relations)* reintegro ♦ **R.** HIST. Restauración.

re·stor·a·tive (rĭ-stôr′ə-tĭv) adj. & s. reconstituyente m, fortificante m.

re·store (rĭ-stôr′) tr. **-stored, -stor·ing** *(order, relations)* restablecer; *(painting, monarch)* restaurar; *(employee, officer)* reintegrar.

re·strain (rĭ-strān′) tr. *(to repress)* reprimir, refrenar; *(to limit)* restringir, limitar; *(to confine)* recluir, encerrar.

re·strained (rĭ-strānd′) adj. *(restricted)* restringido, limitado; *(reserved)* reservado, discreto.

re·straint (rĭ-strānt′) s. *(constraint)* represión f; *(limitation)* restricción f; *(moderation)* moderación f, reserva; *(self-control)* dominio (de uno mismo) ♦ **to keep under r.** mantener encerrado.

re·strict (rĭ-strĭkt′) tr. restringir, limitar.

re·strict·ed (rĭ-strĭk′tĭd) adj. *(limited)* restringido, limitado; *(excluding)* prohibido.

re·stric·tion (rĭ-strĭk′shən) s. restricción f, limitación f.

re·stric·tive (rĭ-strĭk′tĭv) adj. restrictivo.

rest room s. baño, servicios m.

re·struc·ture (rē-strŭk′chər) tr. **-tured, -tur·ing** reestructurar.

re·sult (rĭ-zŭlt′) I. intr. ♦ **to r. from** resultar de • **to r. in** tener como resultado, resultar en II. s. resultado ♦ **as a r. of** a causa de.

re·sul·tant (rĭ-zŭl′tənt) adj. & s. resultante f.

re·sume (rĭ-zōōm′) tr. **-sumed, -sum·ing** *(talking, negotiations)* reanudar; *(working)* reasumir ♦ **to r. one's seat** volver a sentarse —intr. *(working)* reanudar; *(talking, negotiations)* proseguir.

rés·u·mé (rĕz′ə-mā′) s. *(curriculum vitae)* curriculum vitae m; G.B. *(summary)* resumen m.

re·sump·tion (rĭ-zŭmp′shən) s. *(beginning again)* reanudación f; *(taking on again)* continuación f.

re·sur·face (rē-sûr′fəs) tr. **-faced, -fac·ing** revestir (una superficie) —intr. salir de nuevo a la superficie.

re·surge (rĭ-sûrj′) intr. **-surged, -surg·ing** resurgir.

re·sur·gence (rĭ-sûr′jəns) s. resurgimiento.

re·sur·gent (rĭ-sûr′jənt) adj. renaciente.

res·ur·rect (rĕz′ə-rĕkt′) tr. & intr. resucitar.

res·ur·rec·tion (rĕz′ə-rĕk′shən) s. *(revival)* restablecimiento; RELIG. resurrección f ♦ **R.** RELIG. Resurrección.

re·sus·ci·tate (rĭ-sŭs′ĭ-tāt′) tr. **-tat·ed, -tat·ing** MED. resucitar, reanimar.

re·sus·ci·ta·tion (rĭ-sŭs′ĭ-tā′shən) s. *(revival)* renacimiento; MED. resucitación f, reanimación f.

re·sus·ci·ta·tive (rĭ-sŭs′ĭ-tā′tĭv) adj. resucitador.

re·sus·ci·ta·tor (rĭ-sŭs′ĭ-tā′tər) s. resucitador m.

re·tail (rē′tāl′) COM. I. s. venta al por menor o al detalle II. adj. *(store)* minorista; *(price, trade)* al por menor, al detalle III. tr. vender al por menor. ♦ **to r. for** venderse al por menor por IV. adv. ♦ **to sell r.** vender al por menor.

re·tail·er (rē′tā′lər) s. minorista mf, detallista mf.

re·tail·ing (rē′tā′lĭng) s. venta al por menor.

re·tain (rĭ-tān′) tr. *(to keep, hold)* retener; *(lawyer)* contratar; *(one's sense of humor)* conservar.

re·tain·a·ble (rĭ-tā′nə-bəl) adj. conservable.

re·tain·er¹ (rĭ-tā′nər) s. *(servant)* criado; *(employee)* empleado; *(device)* dispositivo de retención.

re·tain·er² (rĭ-tā′nər) s. *(fee)* anticipo.

re·tain·ment (rĭ-tān′mənt) s. retención f.

re·take (rē-tāk′) I. tr. **-took** (-tōōk′), **-tak·en** (-tā′kən), **-tak·ing** volver a tomar, recuperar; CINEM. volver a rodar II. s. (rē′tāk′) recuperación f, recobro; CINEM. nueva toma.

re·tal·i·ate (rĭ-tăl′ē-āt′) intr. **-at·ed, -at·ing** tomar represalias, desquitarse —tr. devolver (golpe, insulto).

re·tal·i·a·tion (rĭ-tăl′ē-ā′shən) s. venganza, represalias.

re·tal·i·a·tive (rĭ-tăl′ē-ā′tĭv) o **re·tal·i·a·to·ry** (-ə-tôr′ē) adj. vengativo.

re·tard (rĭ-tärd′) I. tr. & intr. retardar(se), retrasar(se) II. s. retardo, retraso.

re·tar·dant (rĭ-tär′dənt) adj. que retarda.

re·tar·date (rĭ-tär′dāt′) s. atrasado mental.

re·tar·da·tion (rē′tär-dā′shən) s. *(act)* atraso, retraso; MED. atraso mental.

re·tard·ed (rĭ-tär′dĭd) adj. atrasado (mentalmente).

retch (rĕch) intr. tener náuseas —tr. vomitar, devolver.

re·tell (rē-tĕl′) tr. **-told** (-tōld′), **-tell·ing** volver a contar, contar de nuevo (historia, cuento).

re·tell·ing (rē-tĕl′ĭng) s. nueva narración.

re·ten·tion (rĭ-tĕn′shən) s. *(retainment)* retención f; *(memory)* memoria; MED. retención f.

re·ten·tive (rĭ-tĕn′tĭv) adj. retentivo ♦ **r. memory** memoria retentiva.

re·think (rē-thĭngk′) tr. & intr. **-thought** (-thôt′), **-think·ing** volver a pensar.

ret·i·cence (rĕt′ĭ-səns) s. reserva, reticencia.

ret·i·cent (rĕt′ĭ-sənt) adj. reservado, reticente.

ret·i·cle (rĕt′ĭ-kəl) s. retículo, retícula.

re·tic·u·lar (rĭ-tĭk′yə-lər) adj. *(netlike)* reticular; *(intricate)* intrincado.

ret·i·cule (rĕt′ĭ-kyōōl′) s. *(handbag)* bolso; *(reticle)* retículo, retícula.

re·tic·u·lum (rĭ-tĭk′yə-ləm) s. [pl. **-la** (-lə)] BIOL., ZOOL. retículo; ASTRON. Retícula (constelación).

ret·i·na (rĕt′n-ə) s. [pl. **ret·i·nas** o **ret·i·nae** (rĕt′n-ē′)] ANAT. retina.

ret·i·ni·tis (rĕt′n-ī′tĭs) s. OFTAL. retinitis f.

ret·i·nue (rĕt′n-ōō′, rĕt′n-yōō′) s. séquito, comitiva.

re·tire (rĭ-tīr′) intr. **-tired, -tir·ing** *(to go to bed)* acostarse, irse a dormir <*in the country we r. early* en el campo nos vamos a dormir temprano>; *(to stop working)* jubilarse <*my doctor retired last year* mi médico se jubiló el año pasado>; *(to retreat)* retirarse —tr. *(employee)* jubilar; COM., DEP., MIL. retirar.

re·tired (rĭ-tīrd′) adj. *(secluded)* retirado, apartado <*they lived in a r. spot* vivían en un lugar apartado>; *(not working)* jubilado <*a r. doctor* un médico jubilado>.

re·tir·ee (rĭ-tīr′ē′) s. jubilado.

re·tire·ment (rĭ-tīr′mənt) s. *(withdrawal)* retiro; *(from business)* jubilación f ♦ **r. age** edad de jubilación • **to go into r.** *(worker)* jubilarse; *(artist)* retirarse.

re·tir·ing (rĭ-tīr′ĭng) adj. *(shy)* tímido; *(reserved)* reservado, retraído; *(modest)* modesto, recatado.

re·tool (rē-tōōl′) tr. *(with tools)* equipar de nuevo; *(to reorganize)* reorganizar.

re·tort¹ (rĭ-tôrt′) I. tr. *(to return)* devolver (insulto, ofensa); *(to reply)* replicar II. s. réplica.

re·tort² (rĭ-tôrt′) s. QUÍM. retorta.

re·touch I. tr. (rē-tŭch′) retocar —intr. hacer retoques II. s. (rē′tŭch′) retoque m.

re·trace (rē-trās′) tr. **-traced, -trac·ing** *(to trace again)* trazar de nuevo; *(one's ancestry)* remontarse a; *(past)* reconstruir ♦ **to r. one's steps** desandar lo andado, volver sobre los pasos.

re·tract (rĭ-trăkt′) tr. & intr. *(to disavow)* retractar(se); *(to draw back)* retraer(se).

re·tract·a·ble o **re·tract·i·ble** (rĭ-trăk′tə-bəl) adj. *(capable of recanting)* retractable; *(that draws back)* retráctil.

re·trac·tile (rĭ-trăk′tĭl, -tīl′) adj. retráctil.

re·trac·tion (rĭ-trăk′shən) s. *(disavowal)* retractación f; *(drawing back)* retracción f.

re·trac·tor (rĭ-trăk′tər) s. ANAT. músculo retractor; MED. retractor m.

re·train (rē-trān′) intr. entrenar de nuevo.

re·tread I. tr. (rē-trĕd′) recauchutar II. s. (rē′trĕd′) neumático recauchutado.

re·treat (rĭ-trēt′) I. s. *(going back)* retirada; *(refuge)* refugio <*a mountain r.* un refugio en la montaña>; *(seclusion)* retiro <*spiritual r.* retiro espiritual>; MIL. *(withdrawal)* retirada <*the army's r.* la retirada del ejército>; *(signal)* retreta <*to sound r.* tocar retreta> ♦ **to beat a hasty r.** FAM. batirse en retirada II. intr. retirarse —tr. mover hacia atrás.

re·trench (rĭ-trĕnch′) tr. *(to reduce)* reducir, disminuir; *(to remove)* suprimir —intr. ahorrar, hacer economías.

re·trench·ment (rĭ-trĕnch′mənt) s. *(reduction)* reducción f, disminución f; *(removal)* supresión f, omisión f; *(saving)* ahorro, economías.

---

re·tri·al (rē-trī′əl) s. DER. nuevo juicio.

ret·ri·bu·tion (rĕt′rə-byōō′shən) s. castigo.

re·triev·a·ble (rĭ-trē′və-bəl) adj. recuperable.

re·triev·al (rĭ-trē′vəl) s. *(act)* recuperación *f; (in hunting)* cobranza ♦ **beyond** o **past r.** irreparable.

re·trieve (rĭ-trēv′) tr. **-trieved, -triev·ing** *(to get back)* recuperar; *(to restore)* rehabilitar, restaurar; *(to rectify)* subsanar, reparar; *(to remember)* recordar; *(in hunting)* cobrar, recobrar; COM. resarcirse de —intr. cobrar (la caza).

re·triev·er (rĭ-trē′vər) s. perro cobrador.

ret·ro·ac·tive (rĕt′rō-ăk′tĭv) adj. retroactivo.

ret·ro·cede (rĕt′rō-sēd′) intr. retroceder —tr. devolver.

ret·ro·grade (rĕt′rə-grād′) I. adj. retrógrado II. intr. **-grad·ed, -grad·ing** *(to retreat)* retroceder; *(to regress)* degenerar, deteriorarse.

ret·ro·gress (rĕt′rə-grĕs′) intr. *(to regress)* degenerar, deteriorarse; *(to move backwards)* retroceder.

ret·ro·gres·sion (rĕt′rə-grĕsh′ən) s. regresión *f,* retroceso.

ret·ro·rock·et (rĕt′rō-rŏk′ĭt) s. AER. retrocohete *m.*

ret·ro·spect (rĕt′rə-spĕkt′) s. ♦ **in r.** retrospectivamente.

ret·ro·spec·tion (rĕt′rə-spĕk′shən) s. retrospección *f.*

ret·ro·spec·tive (rĕt′rə-spĕk′tĭv) adj. retrospectivo.

re·try (rē-trī′) tr. **-tried, -try·ing** DER. *(case)* rever; *(person)* volver a juzgar.

re·turn (rĭ-tûrn′) I. intr. *(to come back)* volver, regresar *<to r. in a moment* volver dentro de un momento>; *(to respond)* responder, replicar; *(to revert)* retornar, revertir ♦ **to r. from the dead** resucitar de entre los muertos —tr. *(to give back)* devolver *<she returned the book to the library* devolvió el libro a la biblioteca>; *(to put back)* poner de nuevo, volver a colocar; *(sound)* repercutir; *(profits, interest)* producir, proporcionar; *(light)* reflejar; *(report)* presentar; *(judgment)* dictar, dar; *(ball, serve)* devolver; *(legislator)* reelegir; *(in cards)* jugar, seguir (el mismo palo); *(phone call)* devolver (llamada); *(love, kindness)* corresponder; *(lost, stolen property)* restituir ♦ **to r. like for like** pagar con la misma moneda II. s. *(coming back)* vuelta, regreso *<his r. to the country* su regreso al campo>; *(giving back)* devolución *f; (exchange)* cambio; *(repayment)* pago; *(response)* respuesta; *(profits)* ganancia; *(of a typewriter)* retroceso; *(act, ball)* devolución *f; (of a building)* ala; *(ticket)* billete de ida y vuelta *m; (of a document)* retorno; *(statement)* declaración (de impuestos) *f* ♦ **by r. mail** a vuelta de correo • **in r.** *(for) (as a reward)* en recompensa, en pago; *(in exchange)* a cambio • **many happy returns (of the day)** que cumpla usted muchos años más • **r. address** remite, remitente • **r. ticket** billete de vuelta o de regreso • **r. trip** viaje de regreso • **returns** *(income)* ingresos; *(in an election)* resultados.

re·turn·a·ble (rĭ-tûr′nə-bəl) adj. *(that can be returned)* restituible, reintegrable; DER. devolutivo.

re·turn·ee (rĭ-tûr′nē′) s. persona que ha vuelto o regresado (de un viaje).

re·u·ni·fi·ca·tion (rē-yōō′nə-fĭ-kā′shən) s. reunificación *f.*

re·u·ni·fy (rē-yōō′nə-fī′) tr. **-fied, -fy·ing** reunificar.

re·un·ion (rē-yōōn′yən) s. reunión *f.*

re·u·nite (rē′yōō-nīt′) tr. & intr. **-nit·ed, -nit·ing** reunir(se).

re·us·a·ble (rē-yōō′zə-bəl) adj. que puede volverse a usar.

re·use I. tr. (rē-yōōz′) **-used, -us·ing** volver a usar II. s. (rē-yōōs′) nuevo empleo.

rev (rĕv) FAM. I. s. revolución (de un motor) *f* II. tr. **revved, rev·ving** ♦ **to r. up** *(car)* acelerar —intr. ♦ **to r. up** *(engine)* embalarse.

re·val·i·date (rē-văl′ĭ-dāt′) tr. **-dat·ed, -dat·ing** revalidar.

re·val·u·ate (rē-văl′yōō-āt′) tr. **-at·ed, -at·ing** valorar de nuevo, revalorizar.

re·val·u·a·tion (rē-văl′yōō-ā′shən) s. revaluación *f,* revalorización *f.*

re·val·ue (rē-văl′yōō) tr. **-ued, -u·ing** FIN. revalorizar.

re·vamp (rē-vămp′) tr. *(to renovate)* renovar, modernizar; *(to fix)* arreglar.

re·veal (rĭ-vēl′) tr. revelar.

rev·eil·le (rĕv′ə-lē) s. MIL. diana.

rev·el (rĕv′əl) I. intr. jaranear, juerguearse ♦ **to r. in** deleitarse en, gozar de II. s. jarana, juerga.

rev·e·la·tion (rĕv′ə-lā′shən) s. revelación *f* ♦ **R.** BÍBL. Apocalipsis de San Juan.

rev·el·er (rĕv′ə-lər) s. juerguista *mf.*

rev·el·ry (rĕv′əl-rē) s. [pl. **-ries**] jarana, juerga.

re·venge (rĭ-vĕnj′) I. tr. **-venged, -veng·ing** vengar, vengarse de II. s. venganza ♦ **to take r. on someone** vengarse de alguien.

re·venge·ful (rĭ-vĕnj′fəl) adj. vengativo.

rev·e·nue (rĕv′ə-nōō′, -nyōō′) s. *(from property, investments)* ingreso, renta; *(income source)* fuente de ingresos *f; (of a government)* rentas públicas.

re·ver·ber·ate (rĭ-vûr′bə-rāt′) intr. & tr. **-at·ed, -at·ing** reverberar(se).

re·ver·ber·a·tion (rĭ-vûr′bə-rā′shən) s. reverberación *f.*

re·vere (rĭ-vîr′) tr. **-vered, -ver·ing** reverenciar, venerar.

rev·er·ence (rĕv′ər-əns) I. s. reverencia ♦ **(His, Your) R.** RELIG. (Su, Vuestra) Reverencia • **to hold in r.** reverenciar II. tr. **-enced, -enc·ing** reverenciar.

rev·er·end (rĕv′ər-ənd) I. adj. reverendo II. s. RELIG., FAM. reverendo.

rev·er·ent (rĕv′ər-ənt) adj. reverente.

rev·er·en·tial (rĕv′ə-rĕn′shəl) adj. reverencial.

rev·er·ie (rĕv′ə-rē) s. ensueño.

re·ver·sal (rĭ-vûr′səl) s. *(of direction, opinion)* cambio; DER. revocación *f.*

re·verse (rĭ-vûrs′) I. adj. *(opposite)* opuesto, contrario *<r. direction* dirección contraria>; *(inverse)* inverso *<in r. order* en orden inverso> ♦ **the r. side** *(of cloth)* revés, vuelta; *(of a form)* dorso; *(of a page, medal)* reverso; *(of a coin)* cruz, reverso II. s. *(opposite)* lo opuesto, lo contrario *<he did the r. of what she said* hizo lo contrario de lo que ella dijo>; *(of cloth)* revés *m,* vuelta; *(of a page, medal)* reverso; *(of a coin)* cruz *f,* reverso; *(setback)* revés, infortunio; AUTO. marcha atrás ♦ **just the r.** todo lo contrario • **to put in** o **into r.** AUTO. poner en marcha atrás III. tr. **-versed, -vers·ing** *(to invert)* invertir; *(to turn inside out)* volver al revés; *(to transpose)* transponer; *(to change)* cambiar (política, situación); DER. revocar, anular ♦ **to r. oneself** cambiar de opinión, contradecirse • **to r. the charges** TEL. llamar a cobro revertido —intr. *(to turn around)* voltearse; AUTO. dar marcha atrás.

reverse gear s. AUTO. marcha atrás.

re·vers·i·bil·i·ty (rĭ-vûr′sə-bĭl′ĭ-tē) s. reversibilidad *f.*

re·vers·i·ble (rĭ-vûr′sə-bəl) adj. reversible.

re·ver·sion (rĭ-vûr′zhən) s. reversión *f.*

re·ver·sion·ar·y (rĭ-vûr′zhə-nĕr′ē) o **re·ver·sion·al** (-zhə-nəl) adj. DER. reversionario.

re·ver·sion·er (rĭ-vûr′zhə-nər) s. DER. persona que tiene derecho de reversión.

re·vert (rĭ-vûrt′) intr. ♦ **to r. to** *(to return to)* volver a revertir; DER. revertir.

re·vest (rē-vĕst′) tr. reinstalar, restablecer.

re·vet·ment (rĭ-vĕt′mənt) s. *(facing)* revestimiento; *(barricade)* muro de contención.

re·view (rĭ-vyōō′) I. tr. *(to re-examine)* volver a examinar; *(to go over)* repasar; *(to examine)* examinar, analizar; *(to criticize)* reseñar, criticar (libro, película); DER. revisar; MIL. pasar revista a —intr. *(to study)* repasar *<to r. for an exam* repasar para un examen>; *(to write reviews)* escribir reseñas o críticas II. s. *(examination)* examen *m; (restudying)* repaso; *(critique)* crítica; *(report)* análisis *m; (publication)* publicación *f,* revista; MIL. revista; DER. revisión *f;* TEAT. *(revue)* revista.

re·view·er (rĭ-vyōō′ər) s. *(inspector)* revisor *m,* inspector *m; (critic)* crítico.

re·vile (rĭ-vīl′) tr. **-viled, -vil·ing** injuriar, insultar —intr. proferir injurias.

re·vise (rĭ-vīz′) tr. **-vised, -vis·ing** *(to correct)* revisar, corregir; *(to modify)* modificar.

Revised Version s. versión revisada de la Biblia inglesa protestante.

re·vis·er o **re·vi·sor** (rĭ-vī′zər) s. *(person who re-examines)* revisor *m;* IMPR. corrector *m.*

re·vi·sion (rĭ-vĭzh′ən) s. *(correction)* corrección *f; (modification)* modificación *f; (re-examination)* revisión *f;* IMPR. corrección.

re·vi·sion·ism (rĭ-vĭzh′ə-nĭz′əm) s. revisionismo.
re·vi·sion·ist (rĭ-vĭzh′ə-nĭst) s. revisionista *mf.*
re·vis·it (rē-vĭz′ĭt) I. tr. visitar de nuevo, volver a visitar II. s. nueva visita.
re·vi·so·ry (rĭ-vī′zə-rē) adj. revisor.
re·vi·tal·i·za·tion (rē-vīt′l-ĭ-zā′shən) s. revitalización *f.*
re·vi·tal·ize (rē-vīt′l-īz′) tr. -ized, -iz·ing revitalizar.
re·viv·al (rĭ-vī′vəl) s. *(of a patient)* reanimación *f; (of economy, trade)* reactivación *f; (of interest, style)* renacimiento; *(of custom)* restablecimiento; *(of a play, film)* reposición *f,* reestreno ♦ **r.** *o* **religious r.** despertar religioso • **r.** *o* **r. meeting** asamblea evangelista.
re·viv·al·ism (rĭ-vī′və-lĭz′əm) s. RELIG. evangelismo.
re·viv·al·ist (rĭ-vī′və-lĭst) s. RELIG. evangelista *m.*
re·vive (rĭ-vīv′) tr. -vived, -viv·ing *(patient)* resucitar, revivir; *(person)* reanimar; *(plan)* restaurar; *(custom)* restablecer; *(interest)* renovar; *(memories)* resucitar; *(economy, trade)* reactivar; *(hopes)* despertar; *(play, film)* reponer, reestrenar —intr. *(to resuscitate)* resucitar; *(to reanimate)* reanimarse, volver en sí; *(to grow anew)* renacer; *(to reactivate)* reactivarse, recuperarse.
re·viv·i·fy (rē-vĭv′ə-fī′) tr. -fied, -fy·ing revivificar.
rev·o·ca·ble (rĕv′ə-kə-bəl) adj. revocable.
rev·o·ca·tion (rĕv′ə-kā′shən) s. revocación *f.*
re·vok·a·ble (rĭ-vō′kə-bəl) adj. var. de **revocable.**
re·voke (rĭ-vōk′) I. tr. -voked, -vok·ing revocar —intr. renunciar (en juegos de naipes). II. s. renuncio (en naipes).
re·volt (rĭ-vōlt′) I. intr. rebelarse, sublevarse —tr. repugnar, repeler II. s. *(rebellion)* rebelión *f,* sublevación *f; (dissent)* rebeldía *<in r.* en rebeldía>.
re·volt·ing (rĭ-vōl′tĭng) adj. repugnante, asqueroso.
rev·o·lu·tion (rĕv′ə-lōō′shən) s. POL., SOCIOL. revolución *f;* ASTRON. *(around sun, planet)* revolución; ASTRON., TEC. *(around axis)* rotación *f.*
rev·o·lu·tion·ar·y (rĕv′ə-lōō′shə-nĕr′ē) adj. & s. [pl. -ies] revolucionario.
Revolutionary War s. HIST. guerra de la independencia de los EE. UU.
rev·o·lu·tion·ist (rĕv′ə-lōō′shə-nĭst) s. revolucionario.
rev·o·lu·tion·ize (rĕv′ə-lōō′shə-nīz′) tr. -ized, -iz·ing revolucionar.
re·volve (rĭ-vŏlv′) intr. -volved, -volv·ing girar —tr. *(to turn)* hacer girar; *(to ponder)* considerar (idea, plan) ♦ **to r. around** girar alrededor de • **to r. on** girar sobre.
re·volv·er (rĭ-vŏl′vər) s. revólver *m.*
re·vue (rĭ-vyōō′) s. TEAT. revista.
re·vul·sion (rĭ-vŭl′shən) s. *(disgust)* repugnancia, asco; *(reaction)* reacción *f,* cambio brusco.
re·ward (rĭ-wôrd′) I. s. recompensa, premio II. tr. recompensar, premiar.
re·ward·ing (rĭ-wôr′dĭng) adj. *(remunerative)* remunerador; *(useful)* provechoso, útil.
re·wind (rē-wīnd′) tr. -wound (-wound′), -wind·ing *(watch)* dar cuerda a; *(film)* rebobinar.
re·wire (rē-wīr′) tr. -wired, -wir·ing cambiar el alambre de.
re·word (rē-wûrd′) tr. *(to express differently)* expresar con otras palabras; *(to repeat)* repetir.
re·work (rē-wûrk′) tr. revisar (discurso, obra).
re·write I. tr. (rē-rīt′) -wrote (-rōt′), -writ·ten (-rĭt′n), -writ·ing *(to write again)* escribir de nuevo; *(to rework)* redactar de nuevo II. s. (rē′rīt′) ♦ **to do a r.** escribir de nuevo.
re·zone (rē-zōn′) tr. -zoned, -zon·ing dividir en nuevas zonas.
rhap·sod·ic (răp-sŏd′ĭk) *o* **rhap·sod·i·cal** (-ĭ-kəl) adj. rapsódico.
rhap·so·dize (răp′sə-dīz′) intr. -dized, -diz·ing ♦ **to r. about** *u on* poner por las nubes.
rhap·so·dy (răp′sə-dē) s. [pl. -dies] MÚS., POÉT. rapsodia ♦ **to go into rhapsodies over** *o* **about** poner por las nubes.
rhe·a (rē′ə) s. ORNIT. ñandú *m.*
rhe·ni·um (rē′nē-əm) s. QUÍM. renio.
rhe·o·stat (rē′ə-stăt′) s. ELEC. reóstato.
Rhesus factor s. BIOQUÍM. factor Rh (de la sangre) *m.*
rhe·sus monkey (rē′səs) s. macaco de la India.
rhet·o·ric (rĕt′ər-ĭk) s. retórica.
rhe·tor·i·cal (rĭ-tôr′ĭ-kəl) adj. retórico.

rhetorical question s. pregunta retórica.
rhet·o·ri·cian (rĕt′ə-rĭsh′ən) s. retórico.
rheum (rōōm) s. *(in the eyes)* legaña, lagaña; *(in the nose)* mucosidad *f.*
rheu·mat·ic (rōō-măt′ĭk) I. adj. reumático II. s. reumático ♦ **rheumatics** FAM. dolores del reumatismo.
rheumatic fever s. MED. fiebre reumática.
rheu·ma·tism (rōō′mə-tĭz′əm) s. MED. reumatismo.
rheu·ma·toid (rōō′mə-toid′) *o* **rheu·ma·toi·dal** (rōō′mə-toi′dl) adj. MED. reumatoideo.
rheumatoid arthritis s. MED. reúma articular *m,* artritis reumatoidea.
Rh factor s. BIOQUÍM. factor Rh (de la sangre) *m.*
Rhine (rīn) s. Rin.
rhine·stone (rīn′stōn′) s. diamante falso.
rhi·ni·tis (rī-nī′tĭs) s. MED. rinitis *f.*
rhi·no (rī′nō) s. [pl. -nos] FAM. rinoceronte *m.*
rhi·noc·er·os (rī-nŏs′ər-əs) s. [pl. **rhinoceros** *o* -os·es] rinoceronte *m.*
rhi·nol·o·gy (rī-nŏl′ə-jē) s. MED. rinología.
rhi·zome (rī′zōm′) s. BOT. rizoma *m.*
Rh-neg·a·tive (är′ăch-nĕg′ə-tĭv) s. BIOQUÍM. Rh negativo.
rho (rō) s. rho (letra griega) *f.*
rho·di·um (rō′dē-əm) s. QUÍM. rodio.
rho·do·den·dron (rō′də-dĕn′drən) s. rododendro.
rhom·bic (rŏm′bĭk) adj. GEOM. rómbico, rombal; GEOL., QUÍM. ortorrómbico.
rhom·boid (rŏm′boid′) GEOM. I. s. romboide *m* II. adj. romboidal.
rhom·bus (rŏm′bəs) s. [pl. -bus·es *o* -bi (-bī′)] GEOM. rombo.
Rhone *o* **Rhône** (rōn) s. Ródano.
Rh-pos·i·tive (är′ăch-pŏs′ĭ-tĭv) s. BIOQUÍM. Rh positivo.
rhu·barb (rōō′bärb′) s. BOT. ruibarbo; JER. *(discussion)* riña.
rhum·ba (rŭm′bə, rōōm′-) s. var. de **rumba.**
rhyme (rīm) I. s. rima ♦ **without r. or reason** a tontas y a locas, sin ton ni son II. intr. & tr. rhymed, rhym·ing rimar.
rhyme·ster (rīm′stər) s. rimador *m.*
rhythm (rĭth′əm) s. ritmo.
rhyth·mi·cal (rĭth′mĭ-kəl) *o* **rhyth·mic** (-mĭk) adj. rítmico.
rhythm method s. MED. método de Ogino (anticonceptivo).
ri·al·to (rē-ăl′tō) s. [pl. -tos] *(theatrical district)* distrito teatral; *(marketplace)* mercado.
rib (rĭb) I. s. ANAT. costilla; *(of an umbrella)* varilla; *(of a vault)* arista; *(of an arch)* nervio, nervadura; *(in knitting)* cordoncillo, bordón *m; (of a feather)* cañón *m; (of a leaf)* nervio; JER. *(joke)* broma; AVIA., CUL. costilla II. tr. ribbed, rib·bing *(a ship)* reforzar con cuadernas *o* costillas; *(a garment)* acanalar; JER. *(to tease)* tomar el pelo a.
rib·ald (rĭb′əld) I. adj. verde, obsceno II. s. persona atrevida *o* procaz.
rib·bing (rĭb′ĭng) s. *(of an umbrella)* varillas; *(of a wing)* costillas; *(of a leaf)* nervadura; *(of a hull)* costillas, cuadernas; *(of a vault)* aristas; *(of an arch)* nervios; *(of a garment)* cordoncillos, bordones *m; (of a feather)* cañones *m;* JER. *(teasing)* broma, tomadura de pelo.
rib·bon (rĭb′ən) s. *(of fabric)* cinta *<a yellow r.* una cinta amarilla>; *(of an order)* cordón *m; (of a decoration)* galón *m* ♦ **r.** *o* **typewriter r.** cinta de máquina de escribir • **ribbons** FAM. *(reins)* riendas • **to tear to ribbons** hacer jirones II. tr. encintar.
rib cage s. caja torácica.
ri·bo·fla·vin (rī′bə-flā′vĭn) s. QUÍM. riboflavina.
ri·bo·nu·cle·ic acid (rī′bō-nōō-klē′ĭk, -nyōō-) s. BIOQUÍM. ácido ribonucleico.
ri·bo·some (rī′bə-sōm′) s. BIOL. ribosoma *m.*
rice (rīs) I. s. arroz *m* ♦ **r. field** *o* **paddy** arrozal • **r. pudding** budín de arroz II. tr. riced, ric·ing pasar por un cedazo, colar.
rice paper s. papel de arroz *m.*
ric·er (rī′sər) s. CUL. pasapuré *m.*
rich (rĭch) I. adj. -er, -est *(person, food)* rico; *(magnificent)* magnífico; *(soil, meadow)* fértil, rico; *(productive)* productivo; *(dessert)* con mucha (materia) grasa; *(voice)* potente;

ā rey / ä año / b boca / ch chico / d dar / ĕ el / ē mil / g gato / h joya / hw juez / ī aire / k casa / kw cuan /

(color) vivo, intenso; FAM. *(amusing)* gracioso, divertido ♦ **to be r. in** abundar en • **to get r.** hacerse rico **II.** s. ♦ **the r.** los ricos.

rich·es (rĭch′ĭz) s.pl. *(wealth)* riqueza; *(possessions)* riquezas.

rich·ly (rĭch′lē) adv. *(in a rich manner)* ricamente; *(fully)* bien <a r. deserved punishment un castigo bien merecido>.

rich·ness (rĭch′nĭs) s. riqueza.

rick (rĭk) s. *(of hay)* almiar m; *(twist)* esguince m.

rick·ets (rĭk′ĭts) s.pl. [ú. con v. sing.] MED. raquitismo.

rick·et·y (rĭk′ĭ-tē) adj. **-i·er, -i·est** *(shaky)* destartalado, desvencijado; MED. raquítico.

rick·sha o **rick·shaw** (rĭk′shô′) s. cochecillo tirado por una o dos personas.

ric·o·chet (rĭk′ə-shā′, -shĕt′) **I.** intr. rebotar **II.** s. rebote m.

ric·tus (rĭk′təs) s. rictus m, mueca.

rid (rĭd) tr. **rid** o **rid·ded, rid·ding** librar ♦ **to be r. of** estar libre de • **to r. oneself of** librarse de.

rid·dance (rĭd′ns) s. liberación f ♦ **good r.!** ¡al fin me lo quité de encima!

rid·den (rĭd′n) **I.** part. p. de **ride II.** adj. acosado, agobiado.

rid·dle¹ (rĭd′l) **I.** tr. **-dled, -dling** *(to perforate)* acribillar <riddled with bullets acribillado a balazos>; *(to sieve)* cribar; *(to permeate)* llenar **II.** s. *(sieve)* criba.

rid·dle² (rĭd′l) **I.** s. *(puzzle)* acertijo; *(person, situation)* enigma m, misterio ♦ **to talk** o **speak in riddles** hablar en clave **II.** tr. **-dled, -dling** adivinar.

ride (rīd) **I.** intr. **rode** (rōd), **rid·den** (rĭd′n), **rid·ing** *(a horse)* montar, cabalgar; *(a car, bicycle)* montar; *(to move)* andar; *(to travel)* ir; *(to piggyback)* ser llevado a cuestas; *(to depend)* depender; *(to continue)* seguir su curso; MARÍT. *(to float)* navegar <to r. into port navegar hasta el puerto>; *(to lie)* estar anclado ♦ **to be riding high** estar en plena forma • **to let r.** dejar tranquilo • **to r. astride** montar a horcajadas • **to r. up** *(clothing)* subirse —tr. *(a horse)* montar a; *(a camel, bicycle)* montar en; *(a car)* conducir, guiar; *(to piggyback)* ir sobre; *(to float along)* surcar <to r. the waves surcar las olas>; *(to travel over)* recorrer; *(to overlie)* cubrir; *(to take part in)* correr, participar en (carrera); *(to control)* dominar, tiranizar; *(to cause to ride)* llevar; *(to tease)* burlarse de, ridiculizar; *(to rag)* regañar, reñir; *(the mind)* acosar, agobiar <ridden with guilt acosado por la culpa>; MARÍT. quedar anclado ♦ **to r. a horse up the hill** subir la colina a caballo • **to r. down** *(to run over)* atropellar; *(to overtake)* adelantar; *(to exhaust)* agotar; *(to overcome)* vencer • **to r. on** depender de • **to r. out** aguantar, soportar • **to r. out the storm** capear el temporal • **to r. to death** *(a horse)* causar la muerte por agotamiento; *(to exhaust)* agotar; *(to repeat)* repetir hasta la saciedad **II.** s. *(trip)* viaje m; *(tour)* vuelta f; *(path)* camino de herradura; *(device)* vehículo; *(means for transportation)* medio de transporte ♦ **to give someone a r.** llevar a alguien • **to go for a r.** dar un paseo (a caballo, en coche) • **to take for a r.** JER. *(to murder)* dar el paseo, asesinar; *(to cheat)* dar gato por liebre.

rid·er (rī′dər) s. *(on a horse)* jinete m; *(on a bicycle)* ciclista mf; *(on a motorcycle)* motorista mf; DER. cláusula añadida.

ridge (rĭj) **I.** s. *(of spine)* lomo, grupa; *(of a wave)* cresta; *(of hills)* cordillera, cadena; *(rocks)* estría, arista; *(on ocean floor)* escollo; *(of nose)* caballete; *(in cloth)* cordoncillo **II.** tr. **ridged, ridg·ing** AGR. surcar —intr. rizarse.

ridge·pole (rĭj′pōl′) s. ARQ. cumbrera, parhilera.

rid·i·cule (rĭd′ĭ-kyōōl′) **I.** s. ridículo **II.** tr. **-culed, -cul·ing** ridiculizar, poner en ridículo.

ri·dic·u·lous (rĭ-dĭk′yə-ləs) adj. ridículo.

rid·ing (rī′dĭng) s. *(of a vehicle)* marcha; *(of a horse)* equitación f.

riding habit s. traje de montar m.

rife (rīf) adj. **rif·er, rif·est** *(widespread)* corriente; *(abounding)* abundante ♦ **r. with** repleto de, lleno de.

riff (rĭf) s. MÚS. frase musical repetida.

rif·fle (rĭf′əl) **I.** s. *(shoal)* banco de arena; *(ripple)* onda, rizo **II.** tr. **-fled, -fling** peinar (naipes) ♦ **to r. through** *(papers, files)* pasar rápidamente; *(book)* hojear.

riff·raff (rĭf′răf′) s. *(persona)* gentuza, chusma; *(rubbish)* basura.

ri·fle¹ (rī′fəl) **I.** s. *(for hunting)* rifle m; MIL. fusil m ♦ **r. range** campo de tiro • **rifles** MIL. fusileros **II.** tr. **-fled, -fling** *(to notch)* rayar.

ri·fle² (rī′fəl) tr. **-fled, -fling** *(to pillage)* saquear; *(to rob)* robar.

ri·fle·man (rī′fəl-mən) s. [pl. **-men**] fusilero.

ri·fle·ry (rī′fəl-rē) s. tiro al blanco (con rifle).

ri·fling (rī′flĭng) s. ARM. rayado.

rift¹ (rĭft) **I.** s. FIG. *(in a friendship)* ruptura; *(in a political party)* escisión f; GEOL. *(fault)* falla; *(fissure)* grieta, fisura **II.** tr. & intr. agrietar(se).

rift² (rĭft) s. *(shallow)* vado; *(backwash)* contracorriente f.

rig (rĭg) **I.** tr. **rigged, rig·ging** *(to equip)* equipar; *(an election)* amañar; MARÍT. *(a boat)* aparejar; *(a mast)* enjarciar ♦ **the fight was rigged** DEP. hubo tongo en el combate • **to be rigged out as** vestirse de • **to be rigged out in** vestirse con • **to r. out as** vestirse de • **to r. out in** o **to r. oneself out in** vestir(se) en • **to r. out with** equipar de o con • **to r. up** *(a tent, shelter)* preparar rápidamente; *(a boat)* aparejar; *(a mast)* enjarciar **II.** s. FAM. *(truck)* camión m; *(outfit)* traje m, vestimenta; MARÍT. aparejo; HIST. *(carriage)* carruaje m, coche de caballos m ♦ **r.** o **fishing r.** aparejo de pesca • **drilling r.** o **oil r.** torre de perforación.

rig·a·doon (rĭg′ə-dōōn′) s. MÚS. rigodón m.

rig·a·ma·role (rĭg′ə-mə-rōl′) s. var. de **rigmarole.**

rig·ger (rĭg′ər) s. MARÍT. aparejador m; AER. montador m.

rig·ging (rĭg′ĭng) s. *(equipment)* equipo; MARÍT. aparejo, jarcia; CONSTR. andamio protector.

right (rīt) **I.** adj. *(just)* justo <it is not r. to treat them like that no es justo tratarlos así>; *(upright)* bueno, correcto <it is not right to lie no es bueno mentir>; *(correct)* correcto <the r. answer la respuesta correcta>; *(exact)* exacto (palabra, hora); *(grounded)* acertado, fundado (temor, sospecha); *(appropriate)* más indicado, adecuado <the r. approach el planteamiento más indicado>; *(ideal)* ideal; *(proper)* debido <in its r. place en su debido sitio>; *(opportune)* oportuno, conveniente <the r. time to act el momento oportuno de actuar>; *(conditions)* bueno, favorable <if the tide is r. si la marea es favorable>; *(in order)* en orden; *(healthy)* bien <she was not feeling r. no se sentía bien>; *(opposite the left)* derecho <my r. eye el ojo derecho>; *(in boxing)* de derecha; *(straight)* recto; POL. de derecha, derechista; GEOM. recto ♦ **all r.** *(fine)* bastante bien; *(reliable)* de confianza; bien <are you all r.? ¿te encuentras bien?> • **all r.?** ¿está bien?, ¿de acuerdo? • **all r.!** *(enough)* ¡está bien!, ¡basta!; *(great)* ¡perfecto!, ¡fantástico! • **is that r.?** ¿de verdad? • **isn't that r.?** o **r.?** ¿verdad? • **it's all r. by** o **with me** estoy de acuerdo • **it's just not r.!** ¡no hay derecho! • **r.!** *(exactly)* ¡así mismo!, ¡eso es!; *(correct)* ¡de acuerdo! • **r. you are!** ¡tienes razón! • **that's r.** así mismo, eso es • **to be all r. for someone to** poder <is it all r. for me to come in? ¿puedo pasar?> • **to be in one's r. mind** estar bien de la cabeza • **to be just r. for** hacer falta <that chair is just r. for the bedroom esa silla es exactamente lo que hace falta para el dormitorio> • **to be r.** tener razón • **to be r. there** o **r. back** volver enseguida • **to prove someone r.** demostrar que alguien tiene razón • **to put r.** arreglar • **to turn out all r.** salir bien **II.** s. *(justice)* justicia <r. will prevail la justicia se impondrá>; *(good)* bien m <to reward r., not wrong premiar el bien, no el mal>; *(side, hand)* derecha <to turn to the r. doblar a la derecha>; *(in boxing)* derechazo; *(claim)* derecho <the r. to vote el derecho al voto>; POL. derecha ♦ **all rights reserved** reservados todos los derechos • **by rights** de derecho • **by what r. . . . ?** ¿con qué derecho . . . ? • **in its own r.** de por sí • **in one's own r.** por derecho propio • **to be in the r.** tener razón • **to be within one's rights** estar uno en su derecho • **to exercise one's rights** hacer valer los derechos • **to have a r. to** tener derecho a • **to know r. from wrong** saber distinguir lo bueno de lo malo • **to make a r.** doblar a la derecha • **to set** o **put to rights** enderezar • **who gave you the r. o what gives you the r. . . . ?** ¿con qué derecho . . . ? **III.** adv. *(directly)* directo, directamente <they came r. home vinieron derecho a casa>; *(well)* bien <it doesn't work r. no funciona bien>; *(exactly)* exactamente, justo <r. at the end justo al final>; *(immediately)*

inmediatamente; *(squarely)* en pleno <*r. in the middle of the street* en pleno centro de la calle>; *(justly, correctly)* bien <*he did it r.* lo hizo bien>; *(to the right)* a la derecha; FAM. *(very)* muy ♦ **go r. ahead** siga, continúe • **if I remember r.** si mal no recuerdo • **not to be able to do anything r.** no lograr hacer nada bien • **r. and left** a diestro y siniestro • **r. around the corner** a la vuelta de la esquina • **r. behind** justo detrás • **r. face!** MIL. ¡derecha! • **R. Honorable** G.B. ilustrísimo • **r. now** *o* **this instant** ahora mismo, en este momento • **r. (over) here** aquí mismo • **r. (over) there** ahí mismo • **R. Reverend** reverendísimo • **r. then and there** en el acto • **r. through** *(continuously)* sin parar; *(from side to side)* de lado a lado • **to come r.** in pasar, entrar • **to go r. by someone** portarse bien con alguien • **to get r.** *(to do)* hacer bien; *(to understand)* entender bien; *(to answer)* contestar bien • **to go** *o* **keep r. on doing something** seguir haciendo algo como si nada • **to guess r.** acertar • **to serve one r.** habérselo buscado, tenérselo bien merecido IV. tr. & intr. enderezar(se).
right angle s. ángulo recto.
right away adv. inmediatamente.
right·eous (rī′chəs) I. adj. *(morally right)* recto; *(honest)* honrado; *(just)* justo II. s. gente honrada.
right field s. DEP. jardín derecho.
right·ful (rīt′fəl) adj. *(just)* justo, equitativo; *(true)* legítimo.
right-hand (rīt′hănd′) adj. a la derecha <*a r. turn* una vuelta a la derecha> ♦ **on the r. side** a la derecha, al lado derecho • **r. man** brazo derecho.
right-hand·ed (rīt′hăn′dĭd) adj. *(person)* que usa la mano derecha; *(pitch)* con la mano derecha; *(tool, desk)* para la mano derecha; TEC. *(screw)* de izquierda a derecha.
right·ism *o* **Right·ism** (rī′tĭz′əm) s. POL. derechismo.
right·ist (rī′tĭst) s. POL. derechista mf.
right·ly (rīt′lē) adv. *(correctly)* correctamente; *(properly)* con razón, con derecho; *(justly)* justamente; FAM. *(really)* realmente, en realidad ♦ **r. so** con razón • **r. or wrongly** con razón o sin ella, mal que bien.
right-mind·ed (rīt′mīn′dĭd) adj. *(morally right)* recto; *(honest)* honrado; *(just)* justo.
right·ness (rīt′nĭs) s. *(fairness)* justicia; *(accuracy)* precisión f, exactitud f.
right off adv. inmediatamente.
right of search s. DER., MARÍT. derecho de inspección, derecho de visita.
right of way *o* **right-of-way** (rīt′əv-wā′) s. [pl. **rights-of-way** *o* **right-of-ways**] DER. *(right)* derecho de paso o de vía; *(path)* pasaje autorizado, pista con derecho de paso; *(public land)* servidumbre de vía f; AUTO. preferencia de paso, prioridad f.
right on interj. ¡adelante!, ¡así se (habla, hace, dice)!
right-on (rīt′ŏn′) adj. JER. *(trendy)* de moda; *(absolutely right)* absolutamente correcto o exacto.
right-think·ing (rīt′thĭng′kĭng) adj. honrado, recto.
right-to-life (rīt′tə-līf′) adj. en contra del aborto.
right-to-work law (rīt′tə-wûrk′) s. ley estatal que permite que el obrero no pertenezca al sindicato en una empresa.
right triangle s. triángulo rectángulo.
right whale s. ballena del sur.
right wing s. POL. derecha.
right winger s. POL. derechista mf.
rig·id (rĭj′ĭd) adj. rígido.
ri·gid·i·ty (rĭ-jĭd′ĭ-tē) s. [pl. -ties] rigidez f.
rig·id·ly (rĭj′ĭd-lē) adv. rígidamente.
rig·ma·role (rĭg′mə-rōl′) s. galimatías m.
rig·or (rĭg′ər) s. *(strictness, accuracy)* rigor m; MED. escalofríos m; METEOR. rigor.
rigor mor·tis (môr′tĭs) s. MED. rigidez cadavérica.
rig·or·ous (rĭg′ər-əs) adj. riguroso.
rig·or·ous·ness (rĭg′ər-əs-nĭs) s. rigurosidad f.
rig·our (rĭg′ər) s. G.B. var. de **rigor**.
rile (rīl) tr. **riled, ril·ing** *(to vex)* irritar; *(to roil)* enturbiar.
rill *o* **rille** (rĭl) s. riachuelo.
rim (rĭm) I. s. *(of cup, bowl)* borde m; *(of coin, brick)* canto; *(of barrel)* aro; *(of wheel)* llanta II. tr. **rimmed, rim·ming** bordear.

rime¹ (rīm) I. s. escarcha II. tr. **rimed, rim·ing** cubrir de escarcha.
rime² (rīm) s. & v. var. de **rhyme**.
rime·ster (rīm′stər) s. var. de **rhymester**.
rind (rīnd) s. *(of fruits)* cáscara; *(of cheese)* corteza.
ring¹ (rĭng) I. s. *(circular object)* aro, argolla; *(formation)* anillo; *(circle)* círculo; *(of people)* círculo <*they formed a r. around us* formaron un círculo en torno nuestro>; *(on finger)* anillo, sortija <*engagement r.* anillo de compromiso>; *(for curtains)* anilla; *(for keys)* llavero; *(for exhibitions)* pista <*a circus r.* una pista de circo>; *(for bullfights)* ruedo; *(in boxing)* ring m, cuadrilátero; *(of criminals)* cadena, organización f; *(of spies)* red f; *(of traders)* cartel m; *(in a tree trunk)* anillo; MEC. aro; QUÍM. cadena; ASTRON. anillo II. tr. *(to encircle)* rodear; *(to form into a ring)* anillar; *(a tree)* cortar en redondo la corteza de; *(animal's nose)* anillar ♦ **to r. in** rodear (el ganado) —intr. *(to form circles)* formar círculos; *(to move)* moverse en círculo.
ring² (rĭng) I. intr. **rang** (răng), **rung** (rŭng), **ring·ing** *(bells)* sonar, repicar; *(telephone, doorbell)* sonar; *(at a door)* tocar el timbre; *(to resound)* resonar; *(ears)* zumbar, sonar; *(to buzz)* estremecerse ♦ **r. (false, true)** sonar a (falso, cierto) • **to r. for someone** llamar a alguien • **to r. out** oírse —tr. *(a bell, buzzer)* tocar; *(a coin)* hacer sonar; *(to telephone)* llamar, telefonear ♦ **to r. a bell** FIG. sonarle a uno <*it does not r. a bell* no me suena> • **to r. down the curtain on** poner fin a, acabar con • **to r. in** anunciar • **to r. out** despedir • **to r. the hour** dar la hora • **to r. up** G.B. llamar, telefonear II. s. *(sound)* sonido (metálico); *(of telephone, buzzer)* timbre m; *(of bell)* repique m, tañido; *(tinkle)* tintineo; *(resonance)* resonancia; *(of one's voice)* timbre, tono; *(telephone call)* telefonazo <*I'll give you a r. tomorrow* mañana te doy un telefonazo>; *(quality)* tono <*the offer has a suspicious r.* la oferta tiene un tono sospechoso>; *(set)* juego de campanas; *(act)* toque (de una campana, timbre) m ♦ **r. has a familiar r.** me suena • **to have a r. of truth** tener trazas de ser verdad.
ring·bolt (rĭng′bōlt′) s. TEC. armella, cáncamo.
ringed (rĭngd) adj. *(wearing a ring)* que lleva anillo (esp. de matrimonio); *(bird)* anillado; *(planet)* rodeado por un anillo.
ring·er¹ (rĭng′ər) s. DEP. aro que da en el blanco.
ring·er² (rĭng′ər) s. *(of a bell)* campanero; DEP., JER. *(in a race)* intruso ♦ **to be a r. for** ser la viva imagen de.
ring finger s. anular m.
ring·ing (rĭng′ĭng) I. adj. sonoro, resonante II. s. *(of bells)* tañido; *(of buzzer, alarm)* toque m; *(of phone)* timbre m; *(in the ears)* zumbido.
ring·lead·er (rĭng′lē′dər) s. cabecilla m.
ring·let (rĭng′lĭt) s. *(hair)* bucle m, rizo; *(small circle)* arillo.
ring·mas·ter (rĭng′măs′tər) s. maestro de ceremonias.
ring·side (rĭng′sīd′) s. DEP. cercanías del cuadrilátero ♦ **to sit at r.** sentarse en primera fila.
ring·worm (rĭng′wûrm′) s. MED., VET. tiña.
rink (rĭngk) s. pista ♦ **ice-skating r.** pista de hielo • **roller-skating r.** pista de patinaje.
rin·ky-dink (rĭng′kē-dĭngk′) JER. I. adj. anticuado II. s. persona anticuada.
rinse (rĭns) I. tr. **rinsed, rins·ing** enjuagar II. s. enjuague m.
rins·er (rĭn′sər) s. recipiente para enjuagar m.
ri·ot (rī′ət) I. s. *(tumult)* disturbio, tumulto <*the riots in the prison* los disturbios de la prisión>; *(disturbance)* motín m, sedición f; FIG. *(profusion)* exuberancia (de colores) m; *(display)* exuberancia (de plantas) ♦ **r. act** DER. ley de orden público • **r. police** guardia de asalto • **to be a r.** ser divertidísimo (persona, cuento) II. intr. alborotarse, amotinarse —tr. ♦ **to r. away** *(time)* perder tiempo en frivolidades; *(money)* derrochar, despilfarrar.
ri·ot·er (rī′ə-tər) s. alborotador m.
ri·ot·ous (rī′ə-təs) adj. *(living)* desenfrenado; *(crowd)* alborotado; *(glee)* bullicioso; *(growth)* exuberante.
rip¹ (rĭp) I. tr. **ripped, rip·ping** rasgar, desgarrar ♦ **to r. apart** desgarrar • **r. off** *(to remove)* arrancar, quitar; JER. *(to rob)* robar <*he ripped off a store* robó una tienda>;

ã rey / ä año / b boca / ch chico / d dar / ĕ el / ē mil / g gato / h joya / hw juez / ī aire / k casa / kw cuan /

(to steal) hurtar, limpiar; *(to charge too much)* aprovecharse de • **to r. open** abrir de un tirón *o* desgarrando • **to r. out** *(tear out)* arrancar; *(a seam)* descoser; FAM. *(to utter)* soltar <*to r. out an oath* soltar un juramento> • **to r. up** desgarrar, destrozar • **to r. wood** *(along the grain)* serrar leña al hilo *o* a lo largo —intr. rasgarse, desgarrarse ♦ **to r. by** *o* **past** ir volando, ir a todo gas • **to r. into** abalanzarse sobre, acometer II. s. *(tear)* rasgón *m*, desgarrón *m*; *(split, seam)* descosido; *(ripsaw)* sierra de cortar al hilo.

rip² (rĭp) s. *(water)* aguas revueltas.

rip³ (rĭp) s. *(dissolute person)* calavera; *(horse)* rocín *m*, matalón *m*.

ri·par·i·an (rĭ-pâr′ē-ən) adj. ribereño.

rip·cord (rĭp′kôrd′) s. *(of parachute)* cuerda de apertura; *(of balloon)* cuerda de desgarre.

ripe (rīp) adj. **rip·er, rip·est** *(fruit)* maduro; *(cheese)* hecho; *(wine)* añejo; *(judgment)* sensato, maduro; *(advanced)* avanzado <*at the r. old age of ninety years* a la avanzada edad de noventa años>; *(ready)* listo, preparado <*r. for marriage* listo para el matrimonio>; *(opportune)* oportuno <*the time is r.* el momento es oportuno> ♦ **it's not r.** está verde, no está maduro • **the time is r. for** ha llegado el momento de.

rip·en (rī′pən) tr. & intr. madurar.

ripe·ness (rīp′nĭs) s. madurez *f*.

rip·off (rĭp′ôf′) s. FAM. *(swindle)* timo; *(imitation)* imitación *f*, plagio ♦ **r. artist** FAM. engañador.

ri·poste (rĭ-pōst′) I. s. *(retort)* réplica; ESGR. respuesta II. intr. **-post·ed, -post·ing** replicar.

rip·per (rĭp′ər) s. *(person who saws)* serrador *m*; *(ripsaw)* sierra de cortar al hilo; CONSTR. rompedor de caminos *m*.

rip·ping (rĭp′ĭng) adj. FIG., FAM. estupendo, excelente.

rip·ple¹ (rĭp′əl) I. tr. & intr. **-pled, -pling** *(water)* rizarse; *(wheat)* ondular; *(stream)* murmurar II. s. *(on water)* rizo, onda; *(in sand, fabric)* onda; *(of laughter)* carcajada general; *(of stream, water)* murmullo.

rip·ple² (rĭp′əl) s. TEC., TEJ. desgranadora.

rip-roar·ing (rĭp′rôr′ĭng) *o* **rip-roar·i·ous** (rĭp′rôr′rē-əs) adj. FAM. alegre, animado.

rip·saw (rĭp′sô′) s. sierra de hender.

rip tide s. corriente turbulenta, revuelta *f*.

rise (rīz) I. intr. **rose** (rōz), **ris·en** (rĭz′ən), **ris·ing** *(to stand up)* levantarse, ponerse de pie; *(to get up)* levantarse <*I usually r. at six o'clock in the morning* suelo levantarme a las seis de la mañana>; *(balloon, spirits)* elevarse; *(temperature, prices)* subir; *(in rank, position)* ascender, subir; *(water level)* crecer; *(a river)* nacer; *(voice)* alzarse, levantarse; *(tide)* subir; *(sun)* salir; *(wind)* levantarse; *(pressure)* aumentar; *(stock market)* estar en alza; *(dough)* levantarse; *(buildings)* levantarse, elevarse; *(road, ground)* subir; *(bubbles)* levantarse; *(hills, mountains)* elevarse, alzarse; TEAT. subir ♦ **to r. above** *(to overcome)* sobreponerse a; *(to loom over)* surgir • **to r. against** levantarse *o* sublevarse contra • **to r. early** madrugar, levantarse temprano • **to r. from nothing** surgir de la nada • **to r. from the dead** resucitar de entre los muertos • **to r. in rebellion** sublevarse • **to r. to one's feet** ponerse de pie, levantarse • **to r. to power** subir al poder • **to r. to the occasion** ponerse a la altura de las circunstancias • **to r. to the surface** salir a la superficie • **to r. up (against)** levantarse *o* sublevarse contra • **to r. up in arms** alzarse en armas II. s. *(ascension)* subida, ascensión *f*; *(elevation)* elevación *f*, altura; *(of road, ground)* cuesta, subida; *(of prices, temperature)* subida; *(in water level)* crecida; *(of value, salary)* aumento; *(in rank)* ascenso; *(in pressure, rate)* aumento, elevación; *(of sun, moon)* salida; *(of river)* nacimiento; *(in the voice)* elevación; *(to power)* subida, ascensión; *(revolt)* levantamiento; *(development)* crecimiento, desarrollo; COM. alza ♦ **r. and fall** MARÍT. flujo y reflujo; HIST. grandeza y decadencia • **to give r. to** ocasionar, dar lugar a.

ris·en (rĭz′ən) part. p. de **rise.**

ris·er (rī′zər) s. ♦ **early r.** madrugador • **late r.** dormilón.

ris·i·ble (rĭz′ə-bəl) adj. *(laughing)* risueño; *(ludicrous)* risible.

ris·ing (rī′zĭng) I. adj. *(balloon)* ascendente; *(tide, anger)*

creciente; *(promising)* prometedor; *(sun, moon)* naciente; *(prices, temperature)* que sube II. s. *(of a balloon)* ascenso; *(uprising)* levantamiento, alzamiento; *(resurrection)* resurrección *f*; *(of sun, moon)* salida; *(of prices, temperature)* subida.

risk (rĭsk) I. s. riesgo, peligro II. tr. arriesgarse a, exponerse a.

risk·i·ness (rĭs′kē-nĭs) s. riesgo, peligro.

risk·y (rĭs′kē) adj. **-i·er, -i·est** arriesgado, peligroso.

ris·qué (rĭ-skā′) adj. escabroso, de color subido.

rite (rīt) s. rito ♦ **R.** RELIG. rito, iglesia • **funeral rites** exequias • **last rites** extremaunción.

rit·u·al (rĭch′ōō-əl) s. ritual *m*.

rit·u·al·is·tic (rĭch′ōō-ə-lĭs′tĭk) adj. ritualista.

rit·u·al·ize (rĭch′ōō-ə-līz′) intr. **-ized, -iz·ing** participar en rituales —tr. someter a un ritual.

ritz·y (rĭt′sē) adj. **-i·er, -i·est** JER. lujoso.

ri·val (rī′vəl) I. s. *(competitor)* rival *m*; ANT. *(associate)* socio, compañero II. intr. & tr. rivalizar (con).

ri·val·ry (rī′vəl-rē) s. [pl. **-ries**] rivalidad *f*.

rive (rīv) tr. & intr. **rived, rived** *o* **riv·en** (rĭv′ən), **riv·ing** hender(se), rajar(se).

riv·er (rĭv′ər) s. río.

riv·er·bank (rĭv′ər-băngk′) s. ribera, orilla.

riv·er·bed (rĭv′ər-bĕd′) s. cauce *m*.

riv·er·boat (rĭv′ər-bōt′) s. barco, embarcación de río *f*.

riv·er·ine (rĭv′ə-rīn′, -rēn′) adj. *(of a river)* fluvial; *(on a riverbank)* ribereño.

riv·er·side (rĭv′ər-sīd′) s. ribera, orilla.

riv·et (rĭv′ĭt) I. s. MAQ. remache *m*, roblón *m* II. tr. *(the attention)* cautivar, captar; *(the eyes)* fijar; MAQ. remachar, roblonar.

riv·et·er (rĭv′ĭ-tər) s. *(person)* remachador *m*; *(machine)* remachadora.

Riv·i·er·a (rĭv′ē-âr′ə) s. *(in Italy)* Riviera; *(in France)* Costa Azul.

riv·u·let (rĭv′yə-lĭt) s. arroyo, riachuelo.

roach¹ (rōch) s. [pl. **roach** *o* **roach·es**] ICT. *(European fish)* gobio; *(North American sunfishes)* especie de carpa pequeña *f*.

roach² (rōch) s. ENTOM. cucaracha.

roach³ (rōch) s. JER. colilla de cigarrillo de marihuana).

road (rōd) s. *(highway)* carretera; *(street)* calle *f*; *(route, path)* camino; *(way, track)* vía; *(railroad)* vía férrea ♦ **r. company** TEAT. compañía ambulante • **r. map** mapa de carreteras • **r. narrows** estrechamiento de carretera • **roads** MARÍT. rada, fondeadero • **the r. to** el camino de *o* a • **to be on the r.** TEAT. estar de gira • **to hit the r.** FAM. largarse, irse • **to hold the r.** AUTO. agarrarse.

road agent s. HIST. salteador de caminos *m*, bandolero.

road·bed (rōd′bĕd′) s. *(foundation)* infraestructura (de carretera); *(surface)* firme (de carretera) *m*; F.C. terraplén *m*.

road·block (rōd′blŏk′) s. *(by police, military)* barricada; FIG. *(obstacle)* obstáculo, impedimento.

road hog s. conductor imprudente *m*.

road·house (rōd′hous′) s. taberna *o* sala de baile en un camino rural.

road·run·ner (rōd′rŭn′ər) s. ORNIT. correcaminos.

road show s. TEAT. espectáculo presentado por una compañía ambulante.

road·side (rōd′sīd′) s. borde de la carretera *m*.

road sign s. señal de tráfico *f*.

road·stead (rōd′stĕd′) s. MARÍT. rada, fondeadero.

road·ster (rōd′stər) s. AUTO. coche de dos plazas *m*.

road·way (rōd′wā′) s. carretera.

road·work (rōd′wûrk′) s. DEP. carrera al aire libre.

roam (rōm) I. intr. & tr. vagar (por) II. s. vagabundeo.

roan (rōn) I. adj. ruano (caballo) II. s. *(color)* marrón rojizo; *(horse)* caballo ruano.

roar (rôr) I. intr. *(people)* vociferar, berrear; *(lion)* rugir; *(sea, wind)* bramar; *(audience)* reírse estrepitosamente; *(thunder)* retumbar; *(horse)* respirar difícilmente, padecer huélfago ♦ **to r. by** *o* **past** pasar zumbando • **to r. with anger** rugir de cólera • **to r. with laughter** reírse a carcajadas —tr. ♦ **to r. o. r. out** decir a gritos, vociferar II. s. *(of a person)* rugido, berrido; *(of a lion)* rugido; *(of a cow)* mugido; *(of a bull)* bramido; *(of wind, sea)* bramido; *(of traffic)* estruendo; *(of thunder)* fragor *m*; *(of the crowd)* clamor *m* ♦ **roars of laughter** carcajadas.

roar·ing (rôr'ĭng) **I.** adj. *(lively)* ruidoso, estrepitoso; *(thriving)* próspero <*a r. trade* un negocio próspero> **II.** adv. extremamente, muy <*r. drunk* muy borracho>.

roast (rōst) **I.** tr. *(to cook)* asar <*to r. meat* asar carne>; *(to brown)* tostar (café, maní); FAM. *(to ridicule)* burlarse de; *(to criticize)* poner por los suelos, poner verde; METAL. tostar, calcinar —intr. *(to cook)* asarse; *(to brown)* tostarse; FIG. *(to feel hot)* achicharrarse, asarse ♦ **to be roasting** FIG. achicharrarse, asarse **II.** s. CUL. *(roasted)* asado; *(cut of meat)* carne para asar *f* **III.** adj. asado <*r. chicken* pollo asado> ♦ **r. beef** CUL. rosbif.

roast·er (rō'stər) s. *(pan)* asador *m*, tostador *m*; *(animal)* animal para asar *m*.

roast·ing (rō'stĭng) **I.** adj. achicharrante **II.** s. *(of meat)* asado; *(of coffee)* tostado; FAM. *(criticism)* sermón *m*, rapapolvo.

rob (rŏb) tr. **robbed, rob·bing** robar ♦ **I was robbed** FIG. me han estafado ♦ **to r. of** FIG. *(unjustly)* quitar, robar <*they robbed him of his reputation* le quitaron la reputación>; *(injuriously)* quitar, dejar sin <*the disease robbed him of his voice* la enfermedad le dejó sin voz> —intr. robar.

rob·ber (rŏb'ər) s. *(thief)* ladrón *m*; *(highwayman)* salteador *m*; *(brigand)* bandido.

rob·ber·y (rŏb'ə-rē) s. [pl. **-ies**] robo.

robe (rōb) **I.** s. *(of a judge)* toga; *(of a priest)* sotana; *(of a monk)* hábito; *(for lounging)* bata ♦ **robes** vestiduras, ropaje **II.** tr. & intr. **robed, rob·ing** vestir(se).

rob·in (rŏb'ĭn) s. ORNIT. *(North American songbird)* tordo norteamericano; *(small Old World bird)* petirrojo.

ro·bot (rō'bət, -bŏt') s. robot *m*, autómata *m*.

ro·bot·ics (rō-bŏt'ĭks) s. [ú. con v. sing.] estudio y aplicación de la tecnología de los robots.

ro·bust (rō-bŭst') adj. *(vigorous)* robusto; *(labor)* duro; *(plant)* resistente; *(said of flavor, taste)* aromático, rico.

rock¹ (rŏk) s. GEOL. *(stone)* roca; *(cliff, crag)* peñasco, peña; FIG. *(foundation)* base *f*, soporte *m*; JER. *(diamond)* diamante *m* ♦ **as solid as a r.** FIG. firme como una roca • **like a r.** *o* **as hard as a r.** FIG. duro como una piedra • **on the rocks** FAM. con hielo <*rum on the rocks* ron con hielo> • **to be on the rocks** FAM. *(a marriage)* andar mal; *(business)* ir a la ruina • **to be the R. of Gibraltar** FIG. ser fuerte.

rock² (rŏk) **I.** intr. *(to sway)* balancearse <*the chair is rocking* la silla se balancea>; *(to shake)* estremecerse —tr. *(a chair)* balancear; *(baby, cradle)* mecer; *(houses)* sacudir, hacer temblar; FIG. *(to upset)* dejar estupefacto; *(boat)* zarandear; *(ore)* lavar ♦ **don't r. the boat** JER. deja las cosas como están • **to r. to sleep** mecer **II.** s. *(swaying)* balanceo; MÚS. rock 'n' roll *m*.

rock-and-roll (rŏk'ən-rōl') s. var. de **rock 'n' roll.**

rock bottom I. s. fondo **II.** adj. bajísimo <*r. prices* precios bajísimos>.

rock crystal s. MIN. cristal de roca *m*.

rock dove s. ZOOL. paloma, zorita.

rock·er (rŏk'ər) s. *(chair)* mecedora; *(chair, cradle leg)* arco; MIN. criba; MÚS. *(musician)* rockero ♦ **to be off one's r.** JER. estar chalado • **to go off one's r.** JER. perder la cabeza, volverse loco.

rocker arm s. AUTO. balancín *m*.

rock·et (rŏk'ĭt) **I.** s. *(engine)* cohete *m*; *(weapon)* cohete, proyectil *m*; *(firework)* cohete, petardo **II.** intr. *(to skyrocket)* subir rápidamente; *(birds)* levantar el vuelo.

rocket engine s. AER. motor de cohete *o* de reacción *m*.

rock·et·ry (rŏk'ĭ-trē) s. AER., FÍS. estudio y técnica de los cohetes.

rock·ing (rŏk'ĭng) **I.** adj. oscilante **II.** s. balanceo.

rocking chair s. mecedora.

rocking horse s. caballito de balancín.

rock 'n' roll (rŏk'ən-rōl') s. MÚS. rock and roll *m*.

rock-ribbed (rŏk'rĭbd') adj. *(land)* rocoso; FIG. *(stern)* severo, austero.

rock salt s. sal gema *f*.

rock wool s. lana mineral.

rock·y¹ (rŏk'ē) adj. **-i·er, -i·est** *(stony)* rocoso; FIG. *(firm)* duro; *(difficult)* difícil.

rock·y² (rŏk'ē) adj. **-i·er, -i·est** *(shaky)* bamboleante; *(weak)* débil.

Rocky Mountains s.pl. GEOG. Montañas Rocosas.

ro·co·co (rə-kō'kō, rō'kə-kō') adj. & s. ARTE. rococó *m*.

rod (rŏd) s. *(bar, pole)* barra; *(punishing stick)* vara; *(staff)* bastón (de mando) *m*; *(measure)* medida de longitud equivalente a 5,03m; JER. *(pistol)* pistolón *m*; ANAT. bastoncillo; BACT. bastoncito; F.C. barra de tracción ♦ **curtain r.** barra • **divining r.** varita divinatoria • **leveling r.** TOP. jalón • **lightning r.** pararrayos • **measuring r.** vara de medir • **piston r.** AUTO. biela • **square r.** medida de superficie equivalente a 25,3m² • **rod-shaped** FIG. de forma de bastoncillo • **rod-shaped bacteria** BACT. bastoncillos.

rode (rōd) pret. de **ride.**

ro·dent (rōd'nt) adj. & s. ZOOL. roedor *m*.

ro·de·o (rō'dē-ō', rō-dā'ō) s. [pl. **-os**] rodeo.

roe¹ (rō) s. ICT. *(fish eggs)* hueva; *(spawn)* freza.

roe² (rō) s. ZOOL. corzo.

roe deer s. ZOOL. corzo.

roent·gen (rĕnt'gən) s. FÍS. roentgen (unidad de radiación) *m*.

ro·ga·to·ry (rō'gə-tôr'ē) adj. rogatorio.

rog·er (rŏj'ər) interj. RAD. ¡recibido!

rogue (rōg) s. *(scoundrel)* pícaro; *(elephant)* elefante *m*.

rogues' gallery s. archivo fotográfico de delincuentes.

rogu·ish (rō'gĭsh) adj. *(dishonest)* deshonesto; *(mischievous)* pícaron, bribón.

roil (roil) tr. *(to muddy)* enturbiar; FIG. *(to vex)* irritar —intr. estar irritado.

rois·ter·ous (roi'stər-əs) adj. de jarana.

role *o* **rôle** (rōl) s. TEAT., FIG. papel *m*.

roll (rōl) **I.** intr. *(to wallow)* revolcarse <*the puppy rolled in the mud* el perrito se revolcaba en el barro>; *(prairie, hills)* ondular; *(thunder)* retumbar; *(cannons)* tronar; *(drum)* redoblar; *(yarn, cloth)* enrollarse; *(to proceed)* ponerse en marcha; AVIA., MARÍT. balancearse ♦ **to be rolling in money** *o* **in it** estar nadando en plata • **to get rolling** FAM. ponerse en marcha • **to r. around** *(in the mud)* revolcarse; *(to arrive)* llegar <*when summer rolls around* cuando llegue el verano> • **to r. away (from)** alejarse de • **to r. by** pasar (los días, un coche) • **to r. down** correr por <*tears rolled down his face* las lágrimas le corrían por la cara> • **to r. down** *o* **to go rolling down** rodar por, bajar *o* caerse rodando por • **to r. in** *o* **to come rolling in** llegar en abundancia • **to r. off** *o* **to go rolling off** caerse rodando • **to r. on** pasar (los días, años) • **to r. out** desenrollar • **to r. out of bed** salir de la cama • **to r. over** dar una vuelta • **to r. to a stop** seguir rodando hasta pararse • **to r. up** *(map, blinds)* enrollarse; *(in a vehicle)* presentarse, aparecer —tr. *(to cause to roll)* hacer rodar; *(to wheel)* empujar; *(a cigarette)* liar; *(dough)* pasar el rodillo por; *(drums)* redoblar; JER. *(to rob)* desplumar; CINEM. rodar; AVIA., MARÍT. mover ♦ **to r. back** COM., FIN. bajar, reducir (inflación, precios) • **to r. down** *(wheeled, round object)* empujar por; *(car windows)* bajar • **to r. in** envolver en • **to r. on** tender con el rodillo • **to r. one's eyes (up)** poner los ojos en blanco • **to r. oneself (up) in a blanket** envolverse en una manta • **to r. oneself (up) into a ball** hacerse un ovillo • **to r. out** *(a map, scroll)* desenrollar; *(wheeled, round object)* rodar; *(dough)* extender con el rodillo • **to r. over** derribar • **to r. up** *(wheeled, round object)* rodar; *(paper, rug)* enrollar; *(one's sleeves)* arremangar **II.** s. *(of paper, film)* rollo; *(of plane, boat)* balanceo; *(of the ocean)* oleaje *m*; *(of money)* fajo; *(trill)* gorjeo; *(bread)* bollo, panecillo ♦ **r.** *o* **drum r.** redoble • **r. of thunder** retumbo • **r. of tobacco** rollo • **rolls** *(records)* archivos; *(register)* listas • **to call the r.** pasar lista.

roll·a·way (rō'lə-wā') adj. ♦ **r. bed** cama con ruedas.

roll·back (rōl'băk') s. ECON. reducción (de precios, sueldos) hacia un nivel anterior *f*.

roll call s. acto de pasar lista.

roll·er (rō'lər) s. *(cylinder)* rodillo; *(small wheel)* ruedecilla;

(for road) apisonadora; *(for the hair)* rulo; *(wave)* ola, ola grande; ORNIT. pichón volteador *m.*
roller bearing s. TEC. cojinete de rodillos *m.*
roller coaster s. montaña rusa.
roller skate s. patín de ruedas *m.*
rol·lick·ing (rŏl′ĭ-kĭng) adj. *(carefree)* jovial; *(high-spirited)* animado; *(boisterous)* bullicioso.
rolling mill s. *(factory)* taller de laminación *m;* *(machine)* tren de laminación *m.*
rolling pin s. CUL. rodillo.
rolling stock s. F.C. material rodante *m.*
roll·o·ver (rōl′ō′vər) s. AUTO. vuelta de campana.
ro·ly-po·ly (rō′lē-pō′lē) I. adj. rechoncho, regordete II. s. [pl. **-lies**] *(person)* persona rechoncha; G.B., CUL. brazo gitano.
Ro·man (rō′mən) I. adj. HIST., IMPR., RELIG. romano ♦ **R. Catholic Church** RELIG. Iglesia Católica Romana II. s. romano ♦ **r.** IMPR. letra romano.
Roman candle s. vela romana.
Roman Catholic adj. & s. RELIG. católico romano.
Roman Catholicism s. RELIG. catolicismo.
ro·mance (rō-măns′) I. s. *(tale of heroes)* libro; *(novel)* novela romántica; *(romantic character)* lo romántico; *(love, affair)* aventura amorosa, amores *m* <*in search of r.* en busca de amores>; *(adventure, excitement)* aventura; MÚS. romanza ♦ **R.** lenguas romances *o* románicas II. adj. ♦ **R.** romance III. intr. **-manced, -manc·ing** *(to fantasize)* fantasear; FAM. *(to woo)* galantear —tr. FAM. galantear.
Romance language s. lengua romance *o* románica.
Ro·man·esque (rō′mə-něsk′) ARTE. I. adj. románico II. s. arte románico, románico.
Roman holiday s. *(enjoyment)* orgía romana; *(riot)* motín *m.*
Ro·ma·ni·a (rō-mā′nē-ə) s. var. de **Rumania.**
Ro·ma·ni·an (rō-mā′nē-ən) s. & adj. var. de **Rumanian.**
Roman nose s. nariz aguileña.
Roman numeral s. número romano.
ro·man·tic (rō-măn′tĭk) adj. & s. romántico.
ro·man·ti·cism (rō-măn′tĭ-sĭz′əm) s. romanticismo.
ro·man·ti·cize (rō-măn′tĭ-sīz′) tr. **-cized, -ciz·ing** hacer romántico —intr. tener ideas románticas.
Rom·a·ny (rŏm′ə-nē, rō′mə-) s. [pl. **Romany** *o* **-nies**] *(gypsy)* gitano; *(language)* lengua de los gitanos, caló *m.*
Rome (rōm) s. Roma.
romp (rŏmp) I. intr. juguetear, retozar ♦ **to r. home** *o* **through something** JER. ganar con facilidad II. s. *(play)* juguetear, retozo; *(girl)* muchacha retozona.
romp·er (rŏm′pər) s. persona retozona ♦ **rompers** pelele.
ron·deau (rŏn′dō) s. [pl. **-deaux** (-dōz)] LIT. letrilla (poema lírico de origen francés); MÚS. rondó *m.*
rönt·gen (rĕnt′gən) s. var. de **roentgen.**
rood (rōōd) s. *(crucifix)* crucifijo; *(measure)* cuarta parte de un acre.
roof (rōōf, rōōf) I. s. *(of a building)* techo, tejado; *(of the mouth)* paladar *m;* FIG. *(home)* techo <*to live under the same r.* vivir bajo el mismo techo> ♦ **convertible r.** AUTO. capota • **to hit** *o* **raise the r.** poner el grito en el cielo II. tr. techar.
roof·er (rōō′fər, rōōf′ər) s. techador *m.*
roof·ing (rōō′fĭng, rōōf′ĭng) s. techumbre *f.*
roof·less (rōōf′lĭs, rōōf′-) adj. *(house)* sin techo; FIG. *(homeless person)* sin hogar.
roof·top (rōōf′tŏp′, rōōf′-) s. tejado.
roof·tree (rōōf′trē′, rōōf′-) s. ARQ. cumbrera.
rook¹ (rōōk) I. s. ORNIT. grajo II. tr. JER. timar.
rook² (rōōk) s. torre *f* (en ajedrez).
rook·er·y (rōōk′ə-rē) s. [pl. **-ies**] FAM. *(tenement)* casa de vecindad destartalada; ZOOL. colonia (esp. de grajos).
rook·ie (rōōk′ē) s. JER. *(recruit)* recluta *mf;* *(in sports, police)* novato ♦ **r. cop** policía novato.
room (rōōm, rōōm) I. s. *(in house, hotel)* habitación *f,* cuarto; *(for meetings)* sala <*conference r.* sala de conferencias>; *(a spot)* sitio <*is there r. for me?* ¿hay sitio para mí?>; *(space)* espacio, sitio <*the children have r. to play* los niños tienen sitio para jugar>; *(people)* sala <*the whole r. laughed* toda la sala se rió> ♦ **rooms** alojamiento •

there is always r. for one more donde comen seis comen siete • **there is r. for improvement** podría mejorarse • **to make r. for** hacer sitio para • **to take up r.** ocupar sitio II. intr. alojarse ♦ **to r. together** *o* **with** compartir la habitación (con).
room and board s. pensión completa.
room·er (rōō′mər, rōōm′ər) s. huésped *m.*
room·ful (rōōm′fōōl′, rōōm′-) s. [pl. **-fuls**] habitación llena, cuarto lleno <*a r. of people* un cuarto lleno de gente>.
rooming house s. pensión *f,* casa de huéspedes.
room·mate (rōōm′māt′, rōōm′-) s. compañero de cuarto.
room service s. servicio en las habitaciones (en hoteles).
room·y (rōō′mē, rōōm′ē) adj. **-i·er, -i·est** espacioso, amplio.
roost (rōōst) I. s. *(perch)* percha, palo; *(coop)* gallinero; FIG. *(shelter)* lugar de descanso *m* II. intr. *(birds)* posarse para dormir; *(to sleep)* pasar la noche ♦ **to rule the r.** FIG. mandar, llevar la voz cantante.
roost·er (rōō′stər) s. gallo.
root¹ (rōōt, rōōt) I. s. FIG. *(origin)* origen *m;* *(base)* fundamento, base *f; (basic core)* centro, núcleo <*the r. of a problem* el centro de un problema>; ANAT., BOT., MAT. raíz *f* ♦ **to be at the r. of** FIG. ser la raíz de *(mal, problema)* • **to get to the r. of** FIG. ir a la raíz de • **to pull up by the roots** extirpar, arrancar de raíz • **to put down roots** FIG. radicarse, establecerse (en un país) • **to take r.** BOT. echar raíces II. intr. echar raíces —tr. arraigar ♦ **to r. out** extirpar.
root² (rōōt, rōōt) tr. *(to dig)* hocicar —intr. *(to rummage)* rebuscar.
root³ (rōōt, rōōt) intr. ♦ **to r. for** animar <*to r. for a team* animar a un equipo>.
root beer s. bebida no alcohólica hecha de raíces.
root canal s. ODONT. empaste de la raíz (de un diente) *m.*
root cellar s. AGR. bodega en la que se guardan legumbres.
root hair s. BOT. pelos absorbentes.
root·less (rōōt′lĭs, rōōt′-) adj. FIG. *(without roots)* desarraigado; BOT. carente de raíces.
root·stock (rōōt′stŏk′, rōōt′-) s. FIG. *(source)* fuente *f,* origen *m;* BOT. rizoma.
rope (rōp) I. s. *(cord)* soga, cuerda; *(lasso)* lazo; *(of onions, garlic)* ristra; *(of pearls)* sarta, hilo; DEP. cuerda; MARÍT. maroma ♦ **at the end of one's r.** FIG. en un aprieto • **to know the ropes** FIG. *(procedures)* estar al tanto (de las cosas); *(tricks)* conocer todos los trucos • **to learn the ropes** ponerse al tanto • **to show the ropes** poner al tanto II. tr. **roped, rop·ing** *(to tie)* amarrar, atar; *(to lasso)* coger con lazo ♦ **to r. in** embaucar, enredar • **to r. off** acordonar —intr. ahilarse.
rope·walk (rōp′wôk′) s. cordelería.
rop·y (rō′pē) adj. **-i·er, -i·est** *(resembling a rope)* fibroso; *(viscous)* viscoso.
ror·qual (rôr′kwəl) s. ZOOL. rorcual *m.*
ro·sa·ry (rō′zə-rē) s. [pl. **-ries**] RELIG. rosario.
rose¹ (rōz) I. s. *(color)* rosa, color de rosa; *(ornament)* rosa; *(nozzle)* roseta (de regadera, ducha); BOT. *(plant)* rosal *m; (flower)* rosa; JOY. rosa, diamante rosa *m;* ARQ. rosetón *m;* MARÍT. rosa náutica, rosa de los vientos ♦ **life is not a bed of roses** la vida no es un camino de rosas • **to come up roses** salir bien II. adj. rosa, de color rosa.
rose² (rōz) pret. de **rise.**
ro·sé (rō-zā′) s. rosado, clarete *m.*
ro·se·ate (rō′zē-ĭt) adj. *(color)* rosado; FIG. *(optimistic)* optimista.
rose·bud (rōz′bŭd′) s. BOT. capullo.
rose·bush (rōz′bōōsh′) s. BOT. rosal *m.*
rose-col·ored (rōz′kŭl′ərd) adj. *(color)* rosa, rosado; FIG. *(optimist)* optimista ♦ **to look at the world through r. glasses** FIG. verlo todo color de rosa.
rose fever s. FIG. fiebre de primavera *f.*
rose garden s. rosaleda.
rose·mar·y (rōz′mĕr′ē) s. [pl. **-ies**] BOT., CUL. romero.
rose of Shar·on (shăr′ən) s. rosa de Siria.
rose quartz s. MIN. diamante rosa *m.*
ro·sette (rō-zĕt′) s. *(ornament)* escarapela; *(marking)* rosetón *m;* ARQ. florón *m;* BOT. roseta.
rose water s. agua de rosas.

---

ng inglés / ŏ la / ō bou / ô corre / oi oigo / ōō uno / ou auto / yōō ciudad / w hueco / y yo / z mismo

rose window s. rosetón m.

rose·wood (rōz′wo͝od′) s. BOT. (tree) palo de rosa; (wood) palisandro.

Ro·si·cru·cian (rō′zĭ-kro͞o′shən, rōz′ĭ-) s. & adj. rosacruz.

ros·in (rŏz′ĭn) I. s. colofonia II. tr. frotar con colofonia.

ros·ter (rŏs′tər) s. lista, registro.

ros·trum (rŏs′trəm) s. [pl. **-trums** o **-tra** (-trə)] (dais) plataforma, estrado; BIOL., HIST. espolón m.

ros·y (rō′zē) adj. **-i·er, -i·est** (pink) rosado, de color de rosa; (complexion) sonrosado; FIG. (future) prometedor; (view) optimista.

rot (rŏt) I. intr. **rot·ted, rot·ting** pudrirse, descomponerse ♦ **to r. away** pudrirse, descomponerse —tr. pudrir, descomponer II. s. (process) putrefacción f, descomposición f; (substance) podredumbre f; (nonsense) tontería, sandez f III. interj. ¡tonterías!, ¡sandeces!

ro·ta (rō′tə) s. G.B. (roster) nómina; (rotation) lista ♦ **R.** RELIG. rota.

Ro·tar·i·an (rō-târ′ē-ən) s. rotario.

ro·ta·ry (rō′tə-rē) I. adj. rotatorio II. s. [pl. **-ries**] (device) rotativa; (traffic circle) glorieta, plaza circular.

Rotary Club s. Club Rotario (organización internacional).

rotary engine s. MEC. rotativa.

rotary plow s. arado rotatorio.

ro·tate (rō′tāt′) intr. **-tat·ed, -tat·ing** (to spin) girar; (crops) alternar; (workers, officials) turnarse —tr. (crops, wheels) alternar; (workers) turnarse.

ro·ta·tion (rō-tā′shən) s. (turning) giro, rotación f; (turn) revolución f.

ro·ta·tive (rō′tā′tĭv) adj. (rotatory) rotatorio, giratorio; (alternative) rotativo.

ro·ta·tor (rō′tā′tər) s. MEC. parte o pieza rotatoria; MARÍT. hélice f; ANAT. músculo rotatorio.

rote (rōt) s. rutina ♦ **to learn by r.** aprender por repetición.

rot·gut (rŏt′gŭt′) s. JER. licor de mala calidad m, matarratas m.

ro·tis·ser·ie (rō-tĭs′ə-rē) s. CUL. asador m.

ro·to·gra·vure (rō′tə-grə-vyo͝or′) s. IMPR. rotograbado.

ro·tor s. AER., ELEC., MEC. rotor m.

rot·ten (rŏt′n) adj. **-er, -est** (meat, fruit) estropeado; (wood) carcomido; (smell) podrido; (egg) podrido; (person, trick) malo; (weather) malísimo, pésimo ♦ **to feel r.** encontrarse fatal • **to smell r.** oler a podrido.

ro·tund (rō-tŭnd′) adj. (rounded) redondo; (plump) regordete; (sonorous) rotundo, sonoro.

ro·tun·da (rō-tŭn′də) s. rotonda.

rou·ble (ro͞o′bəl) s. FIN. rublo.

rou·é (ro͞o-ā′) s. libertino, Don Juan.

rouge (ro͞ozh) I. s. (for cheeks) colorete m; (lipstick) lápiz de labios m, carmín m; (for polishing) colcótar m II. tr. rouged, roug·ing poner colorete a, pintar.

rough (rŭf) I. adj. **-er, -est** (not smooth) áspero <r. hands manos ásperas>; (uneven) accidentado, desigual <r. ground terreno accidentado>; (coarse) basto, burdo; (turbulent) borrascoso, agitado <r. seas mar agitado>; (inclement) inclemente; (stormy) tempestuoso, (trying) difícil, malo <to have a r. day tener un día malo>; (rowdy) alborotador; (rude) tosco, grosero; (requiring strength) difícil, duro <r. work trabajo duro>; (voice) bronco; (uncouth) inculto, tosco; (approximate) aproximado <a r. estimate un cálculo aproximado>; (incomplete) preliminar <a r. sketch un boceto preliminar>; JOY. en bruto ♦ **as a r. guess** a ojo de buen cubero • **r. draft** borrador • **r. sketch** boceto • **to be r. on someone** (person) tratar a alguien con dureza; (situation) ser una mala suerte para alguien • **to give someone a r. idea** dar a alguien una idea aproximada • **to give someone a r. time** hacer pasar un mal rato a alguien • **to have a r. time** (season) pasar una temporada muy mala; (moment) pasar un mal rato II. s. (ground) terreno accidentado o desigual; (in golf) hierba alta, maleza; (ruffian) matón m, rufián m ♦ **in the r.** JOY. en bruto III. tr. poner áspero ♦ **to r. it** FIG. vivir sin comodidades, pasar apuros • **to r. out** bosquejar • **to r. up** (hair, feathers) erizar, levantar; (someone) darle una paliza a IV. adv. (uncouthly) rudamente; (unskillfully) toscamente ♦ **to play r.** jugar duro.

rough·age (rŭf′ĭj) s. alimento difícil de digerir que contribuye al movimiento peristáltico.

rough-and-read·y (rŭf′ən-rĕd′ē) adj. tosco pero eficaz.

rough-and-tum·ble (rŭf′ən-tŭm′bəl) adj. desordenado, agitado.

rough·cast (rŭf′kăst′) s. (plaster) mezcla gruesa; (model) modelo tosco.

rough·en (rŭf′ən) tr. & intr. poner áspero.

rough·hewn (rŭf′hyo͞on′) adj. (without finishing) desbastado; (sketched) esbozado, bosquejado.

rough·house (rŭf′hous′) I. s. jaleo, trifulca II. intr. **-housed, -hous·ing** armar jaleo, armar una trifulca.

rough·ly (rŭf′lē) adv. (crudely) toscamente; (about) más o menos, aproximadamente ♦ **to treat r.** maltratar.

rough·neck (rŭf′nĕk′) s. (uncouth person) grosero; (rowdy) matón m; (worker) obrero en un pozo de petroleo.

rough·ness (rŭf′nĭs) s. (of a surface, the skin) aspereza, rugosidad f; (of a road) desigualdad f; (of sea) encrespamiento; (of character) brusquedad f; (of language) grosería; (of labor) dureza.

rough·rid·er (rŭf′rī′dər) s. domador de caballos m ♦ **R.** EE. UU., HIST. soldado de caballería.

rough·shod (rŭf′shŏd′) adj. herrado con ramplones ♦ **to ride r. over** tratar sin miramientos.

rou·lette (ro͞o-lĕt′) s. ruleta.

round (round) I. adj. (spherical, curved) redondo; (labialized) labial; (complete) completo, bueno <a r. dozen una docena completa>; (whole) redondo <in r. numbers en números redondos>; aproximado <a r. estimate un cálculo aproximado>; (large) considerable, cuantioso <a r. sum una suma cuantiosa>; (finished) acabado, perfecto <a r. style un estilo perfecto>; (sonorous) sonoro <a r. voice una voz sonora>; (fast) bueno <to go at a r. pace ir a buen paso>; (blunt) franco; (forceful) fuerte (castigo, golpe); (plump) regordete, relleno ♦ **r. trip** viaje de ida y vuelta II. s. (circle) círculo; (sphere) esfera; (curve) curva; (of a ladder) escalón m, peldaño; (of a chair) travesaño, listón m; (of beef) rueda, tajada; (of bread) rebanada, tajada; (group) grupo, círculo (social); (movement) vuelta; (of earth) revolución f; (dance) baile (en corro) m; (series) serie f <a r. of parties una serie de fiestas>; (of talks) ronda; (range) alcance m <the r. of human knowledge el alcance del conocimiento humano>; (of drinks) ronda; (of applause) salva; ARM. descarga; DEP. (stage) ronda, vuelta; (of golf) partido; (in boxing) asalto; MÚS. canon m ♦ **to make one's rounds** (police, patrol) hacer la ronda; (salesperson) hacer el recorrido; (doctor) hacer las visitas III. tr. (to make round) redondear; (to go around) doblar, dar la vuelta a; FONÉT. labializar ♦ **to r. off** (to make round) redondear (objeto, número); (to finish off) acabar, rematar • **to r. out** (to make round) redondear; (to complete) terminar, completar • **to r. up** (animals) acorralar, rodear; (people) reunir —intr. ♦ **to r. into** dar vueltas, rondar • **to r. off** acabar, rematar • **to r. out** ponerse relleno IV. adv. (around) alrededor; (everywhere) por todas partes; (here and there) aquí y allá ♦ **all r.** para todos • **all year r.** durante todo el año • **is there enough to go r.?** ¡hay bastante para todos? • **r. about** a eso de • **r. and r.** dando vueltas a la redonda • **to gather r.** apiñarse V. prep. (around) alrededor de <r. the world alrededor del mundo>; (throughout) durante todo <r. the year durante todo el año>; (on the other side of) a la vuelta de <r. the corner a la vuelta de la esquina>.

round·a·bout (round′ə-bout′) adj. indirecto, con rodeos ♦ **to take a r. route** dar un rodeo • **to talk in a r. way** andar con rodeos.

round·ed (round′dĭd) adj. redondo, esférico.

roun·de·lay (round′də-lā′) s. MÚS., POÉT. rondó.

round·er (round′ər) s. (tool) herramienta para redondear; FAM. (libertine) libertino, calavera m.

round·house (round′hous′) s. JER. (punch) gancho; F.C. depósito de locomotoras; MARÍT. chupeta.

round·ish (round′dĭsh) adj. regordete.

round·ly (round′lē) adv. (circular) redondamente; (thoroughly) rotundamente.

round·ness (round′nĭs) s. redondez f.

---

round robin s. *(tournament)* torneo; *(petition)* memorial firmado en círculo; *(letter)* carta enviada en cadena.
round-shoul·dered (round'shōl'dərd) adj. cargado de hombros.
Round Table s. HIST. Tabla Redonda (del rey Arturo y sus caballeros) ♦ **r.** mesa redonda.
round-the-clock (round'thə-klŏk') adj. que dura veinticuatro horas, continuo.
round trip s. viaje de ida y vuelta *m.*
round·up (round'ŭp') s. *(of cattle)* rodeo; *(by the police)* redada; *(summary)* resumen *m* <a news *r.* un resumen de las noticias>.
rouse (rouz) tr. **roused, rous·ing** despertar ♦ **to r. from** *(sleep)* despertar; *(apathy)* sacudir —intr. despertarse.
rous·ing (rou'zĭng) adj. *(stirring)* conmovedor; *(lively)* animado; FAM. *(lie)* enorme.
roust (roust) tr. despertar, suscitar.
roust·a·bout (roust'tə-bout') s. *(wharf laborer)* estibador *m*; *(laborer)* peón *m.*
rout¹ (rout) I. s. *(retreat)* desbandada; *(defeat)* derrota completa; *(mob)* tumulto; *(rabble)* chusma; *(riot)* disturbio II. tr. *(to cause to retreat)* poner en fuga; *(to defeat)* derrotar.
rout² (rout) I. intr. *(to dig)* hocicar; *(to rummage)* hurgar II. tr. ♦ **to r. out** hacer salir, echar fuera • **to r. out** *o* **up** *(to dig up)* hocicar; *(to uncover)* descubrir.
route (rōōt, rout) I. s. *(road)* carretera; *(for public vehicles)* recorrido; *(for delivery)* recorrido; FIG. *(means)* camino II. tr. **rout·ed, rout·ing** mandar, encaminar.
rou·tine (rōō-tēn') I. s. *(procedure, performance)* rutina; *(habit)* hábito; JER. *(act)* manía II. adj. *(standard)* rutinario; *(habitual)* habitual; *(ordinary)* común y corriente.
rou·tine·ly (rōō-tēn'lē) adv. habitualmente.
rove (rōv) I. intr. **roved, rov·ing** vagar, errar —tr. vagar por II. s. vagabundeo.
rov·er (rō'vər) s. *(wanderer)* vagabundo; *(pirate)* pirata *mf*, corsario; *(vessel)* barco pirata.
row¹ (rō) s. línea, fila ♦ **in a r.** *(in succession)* seguidos <he lost three fights in a r. perdió tres encuentros seguidos>; *(in a line)* en fila • **in rows** en filas.
row² (rō) I. intr. remar ♦ **to go rowing** dar un paseo en bote • **to r. across the river** cruzar el río a remo *o* remando —tr. *(a boat)* hacer avanzar con el remo; *(passengers)* llevar en un bote a remo; *(oars, rowers)* ser movido por; DEP. competir con II. s. ♦ **to go for a r.** pasear en bote.
row³ (rou) I. s. *(quarrel)* pelea; *(noise)* jaleo II. intr. pelearse, reñir.
row·boat (rō'bōt') s. bote de remos *m.*
row·dy (rou'dē) I. s. [pl. **-dies**] camorrista *mf*, pendenciero II. adj. **-di·er, -di·est** pendenciero, camorrista.
row·el (rou'əl) I. s. rodaja (de la espuela) II. tr. espolear.
row·er (rō'ər) s. remador *m*, remero.
row house s. casa en hilera.
row·ing (rō'ĭng) s. remo.
row·lock (rō'lŏk') s. MARÍT. tolete *m*, escálamo.
roy·al (roi'əl) I. adj. real II. s. FAM. *(person)* miembro de una familia real; MARÍT. sobrejuanete *m.*
roy·al·ist (roi'ə-lĭst) s. HIST., POL. monárquico, realista *mf* ♦ **R.** realista.
royal jelly s. jalea real.
roy·al·ly (roi'ə-lē) adv. regiamente, magníficamente.`
royal palm s. BOT. palma real, palmiche *m.*
roy·al·ty (roi'əl-tē) s. [pl. **-ties**] *(royals)* familia real; *(rank, power)* realeza; *(payment)* derechos de autor ♦ **to be r.** ser miembro de una familia real.
RPG (är'pē-jē') s. COMPUT. lenguaje de programación RPG (diseñado para generar información comercial) *m.*
rub (rŭb) I. tr. **rubbed, rub·bing** *(someone else)* friccionar, dar friegas <the nurse rubbed his back la enfermera le friccionó la espalda>; *(one's hands)* frotarse; *(to irritate)* irritar <his laziness was beginning to r. me su pereza estaba empezando a irritarme>; *(to chafe)* rozar; *(to polish)* limpiar frotando <to r. a table limpiar una mesa frotándola> ♦ **to r. against** frotar contra • **to r. down** *(the body)* friccionar; *(a horse)* almohazar • **to r. elbows** *o* **shoulders with** codearse con • **to r. in** *o* **into** *u* **on** frotar con • **to r. it**

in FAM. machacar • **to r. off** quitar frotando • **to r. off on** *(good qualities)* transmitírsele a uno; *(bad qualities)* pegársele a uno • **to r. out** *(to erase)* borrar; JER. *(to kill)* liquidar, matar • **to r. the wrong way** irritar, molestar • **to r. together** *(one's hands)* frotarse; *(two objects)* frotar —intr. *(object)* rozar; *(person)* friccionarse (el cuerpo) ♦ **to r. off** quitarse frotando • **to r. (up) against** rozar contra II. s. *(rubbing)* frotamiento; *(massage)* fricción *f* <a back *r.* una fricción de la espalda>; *(unevenness)* aspereza; *(act, remark)* desaire *m*, insulto; *(difficulty)* dificultad *f.*
rub·ber (rŭb'ər) s. BOT. *(natural)* caucho; *(synthetic)* goma, caucho; *(eraser)* goma de borrar; JER. *(condom)* condón *m*, preservativo ♦ **r. ball** pelota de goma • **rubbers** chanclos.
rubber band s. goma.
rub·ber·ize (rŭb'ə-rīz') tr. **-ized, -iz·ing** cauchutar.
rub·ber·neck (rŭb'ər-nĕk') JER. I. s. mirón *m*, fisgón *m* II. intr. curiosear.
rubber plant s. BOT. árbol del caucho.
rubber stamp s. *(stamp)* sello de goma; *(person)* persona que aprueba automáticamente; *(approval)* aprobación automática.
rub·ber-stamp (rŭb'ər-stămp') tr. *(to mark)* marcar con un sello de goma; *(to approve)* aprobar automáticamente.
rubber tree s. gomero, árbol del caucho *m.*
rub·ber·y (rŭb'ə-rē) adj. elástico.
rub·bing (rŭb'ĭng) s. *(polishing)* frotamiento; *(representation)* calco.
rub·bish (rŭb'ĭsh) s. *(garbage)* basura; *(waste)* desperdicio, desecho; *(nonsense)* tontería, disparate *m.*
rub·ble (rŭb'əl) s. *(fragments)* escombros; *(rock pieces)* cascote *m*, grava; *(masonry)* morrillo.
rub·down (rŭb'doun') s. masaje.
rube (rōōb) s. JER. patán *m*, palurdo.
ru·bel·la (rōō-bĕl'ə) s. MED. rubéola.
ru·be·o·la (rōō-bē'ə-lə, rōō'bē-ō'la) s. MED. sarampión *m*; rubéola.
ru·bid·i·um (rōō-bĭd'ē-əm) s. QUÍM. rubidio.
ru·ble (rōō'bəl) s. var. de **rouble**.
ru·bric (rōō'brĭk) s. rúbrica.
ru·by (rōō'bē) I. s. [pl. **-bies**] *(color)* color de rubí *m*; MIN. rubí *m*; IMPR. tipo de 5,5 puntos II. adj. de color de rubí.
ruck¹ (rŭk) s. *(of things)* montón *m*; *(of people)* vulgo.
ruck² (rŭk) I. tr. & intr. plegar(se), arrugar(se) II. s. arruga.
ruck·sack (rŭk'săk', rōōk'-) s. mochila.
ruck·us (rŭk'əs) s. FAM. trifulca, jaleo.
rud·der (rŭd'ər) s. FIG. *(direction)* dirección *f*; AVIA., MARÍT. timón *m.*
rud·dy (rŭd'ē) adj. **-di·er, -di·est** *(healthy)* rubicundo; *(reddish)* rojizo; G.B., JER. *(bloody)* maldito, condenado.
rude (rōōd) adj. **rud·er, rud·est** *(primitive)* primitivo, rudo; *(humble)* humilde; *(unlearned)* rústico, inculto; *(discourteous)* grosero, descortés; *(crude)* crudo; *(sudden)* brusco, repentino ♦ **to make r. remarks** decir groserías.
rude·ly (rōōd'lē) adv. descortésmente, groseramente.
rude·ness (rōōd'nĭs) s. *(roughness)* rudeza; *(impoliteness)* descortesía; *(coarseness)* tosquedad *f.*
ru·di·ment (rōō'də-mənt) s. rudimento ♦ **rudiments** *(beginning)* rudimentos; BIOL. embrión, germen.
ru·di·men·ta·ry (rōō'də-mĕn'tə-rē) adj. rudimentario.
rue¹ (rōō) tr. **rued, ru·ing** arrepentirse de, lamentar.
rue² (rōō) s. BOT. ruda.
rue·ful (rōō'fəl) adj. *(inspiring compassion)* lastimoso; *(sorrowful)* pesaroso; *(repentant)* arrepentido.
ruff (rŭf) s. *(collar)* gorguera, gola; *(on animals, birds)* collarín *m.*
ruffed grouse (rŭft) s. ORNIT. bonasa americana.
ruf·fi·an (rŭf'ē-ən) s. *(rowdy fellow)* rufián *m*; *(gangster)* matón *m.*
ruf·fle¹ (rŭf'əl) I. s. *(on a garment)* volante plegado *o* fruncido; *(on a bird)* collarín *m*; *(commotion)* jaleo, conmoción *f*; *(annoyance)* molestia, fastidio; *(vexation)* enojo, enfado; *(on the water)* escarceo, rizo II. tr. **-fled, -fling** *(water)* agitar, rizar; *(cloth)* plegar; *(feathers)* erizar; *(one's hair)* desgreñar; *(a person)* aturdir; *(pages)* pasar

rápidamente; *(cards)* barajar ♦ **to r. one's composure** *o* **calm** agitarse —intr. agitarse ♦ **to r.** *o* **get ruffled** enojarse.
ruf·fle² (rŭf′əl) I. s. *(beating)* redoble *m* II. intr. **-fled, -fling** *(to beat)* redoblar.
ru·fous (rōō′fəs) adj. rufo, bermejo.
rug (rŭg) s. *(floor covering)* alfombra; *(animal skin)* piel *f*; G.B. *(coverlet)* manta.
Rug·by (rŭg′bē) s. DEP. rugby *m*.
rug·ged (rŭg′ĭd) adj. *(terrain, road)* desigual, escabroso; *(mountains)* escarpado; *(features, face)* duro; *(climate)* riguroso; *(pioneer)* vigoroso, robusto.
rug·ged·ness (rŭg′ĭd-nĭs) s. *(of terrain, road)* desigualdad *f*; *(of mountains, rocks)* escabrosidad *f*; *(of features, face)* dureza; *(of climate)* rigurosidad *f*; *(of pioneers)* robustez *f*, fuerza.
rug·ger (rŭg′ər) s. G.B., DEP. rugby *m*.
ru·in (rōō′ĭn) I. s. ruina ♦ **ruins** ruinas • **to be one's r.** ser la propia ruina • **to go to** *o* **to fall into r.** caer en ruinas • **to lie** *o* **to be in ruins** estar en ruinas II. tr. *(financially)* arruinar; *(one's health, reputation)* arruinar; *(crops, party)* estropear; *(plans)* echar abajo; *(morally)* deshonrar.
ru·in·a·tion (rōō′ə-nā′shən) s. ruina.
ru·in·ous (rōō′ə-nəs) adj. ruinoso.
rule (rōōl) I. s. *(control)* dominio, mando <*under foreign r.* bajo dominio extranjero>; *(power)* poder *m*, mando <*the people have the r.* el pueblo tiene el poder>; *(reign)* reinado <*the r. of Philip II* el reinado de Felipe II>; *(law)* regla <*the rules of the game* las reglas del juego>; MAT. regla <*slide r.* regla de cálculo>; DER. fallo; IMPR. filete *m*; RELIG. regla <*the r. of St. Benedict* la regla de San Benito> ♦ **as a r.** por lo regular • **as a general r.** por regla general, por lo general • **as a r. of thumb** de forma práctica • **hard and fast r.** regla inflexible • **rules** reglamento • **rules and regulations** reglamento • **rules of the road** reglamento del tráfico • **the exception proves the r.** la excepción confirma la regla • **to be the r.** *(to be the law)* ser la regla; *(to be normal)* ser normal <*violence is the r. in that area* la violencia es normal en esa zona> • **to make it a r. to** ser un deber para uno • **to play by the rules** obrar como es debido II. tr. **ruled, rul·ing** *(to govern)* gobernar, dirigir <*to r. a country* gobernar un país>; *(to control)* dominar; *(to decree)* decretar; *(to decide)* decidir; *(to declare)* declarar; *(with lines)* rayar ♦ **to r. off** trazar una línea • **to r. out** *(to exclude)* excluir, descartar; *(to make impossible)* hacer imposible, impedir <*the snowstorm ruled out their meeting* la tormenta de nieve hizo imposible su reunión> • **to r. over** dominar, regir —intr. *(to govern)* gobernar, mandar <*the majority rules* manda la mayoría>; *(to decide)* decidir; DER. *(to issue a decision)* fallar ♦ **to r. against** *(to decide against)* prohibir <*they ruled against television* prohibieron la televisión>; DER. fallar en contra.
rul·er (rōō′lər) s. *(sovereign)* gobernante *m*; *(measuring strip)* regla.
rul·ing (rōō′lĭng) I. adj. *(class, party)* gobernante, dirigente; *(passion, sentiment)* dominante, predominante II. s. *(act)* gobierno; DER. decisión *f*, fallo.
rum¹ (rŭm) s. *(liquor)* ron *m*; *(beverage)* bebida alcohólica.
rum² (rŭm) adj. **rum·mer, rum·mest** G.B. raro, extraño.
Ru·ma·ni·a (rōō-mā′nē-ə) s. Rumania.
Ru·ma·ni·an (rōō-mā′nē-ən) adj. & s. *(inhabitant, language)* rumano.
rum·ba (rŭm′bə, rōōm′-) s. MÚS. rumba.
rum·ble (rŭm′bəl) I. intr. **-bled, -bling** *(vehicle, traffic)* rodar con estrépito; *(gunfire, thunder)* retumbar; JER. *(gang)* meterse en una pelea callejera —tr. *(to utter)* decir con voz cavernosa; *(to polish)* pulir con tambor de limpieza II. s. *(of gunfire, thunder)* fragor *m*, estruendo; *(tumbling box)* tambor de limpieza *m*; JER. *(fight)* pelea callejera.
rumble seat s. AUTO. asiento trasero descubierto.
ru·men (rōō′mən) s. [pl. **-mi·na** (-mə-nə) *o* **-mens**] ZOOL. herbario.
ru·mi·nant (rōō′mə-nənt) I. s. ZOOL. rumiante *m* II. adj. ZOOL. rumiante; FIG. *(meditative)* pensativo.

ru·mi·nate (rōō′mə-nāt′) intr. **-nat·ed, -nat·ing** ZOOL. rumiar; FIG. *(to consider)* considerar —tr. reflexionar.
ru·mi·na·tion (rōō′mə-nā′shən) s. ZOOL. rumia; FIG. *(meditation)* reflexión *f*.
rum·mage (rŭm′ĭj) I. tr. **-maged, -mag·ing** revolver, hurgar —intr. revolver, hurgar desordenadamente II. s. *(search)* búsqueda desordenada; *(jumble)* objetos diversos.
rummage sale s. *(charity sale)* venta benéfica; COM. liquidación *f* ♦ **to have a r.** *(for charity)* vender artículos con fines benéficos; *(for business)* hacer una liquidación.
rum·my¹ (rŭm′ē) s. *(game)* rami *m*.
rum·my² (rŭm′ē) s. [pl. **-mies**] JER. *(drunkard)* borracho.
ru·mor (rōō′mər) I. s. rumor *m* II. tr. rumorear.
ru·mor·mon·ger (rōō′mər-mŭng′gər) s. chismoso.
ru·mour (rōō′mər) s. & v. G.B. var. de **rumor.**
rump (rŭmp) s. *(of an animal)* ancas, grupa; *(of beef)* cuarto trasero; *(of a person)* nalgas.
rum·ple (rŭm′pəl) I. tr. **-pled, -pling** arrugar —intr. arrugarse II. s. arruga.
rum·pus (rŭm′pəs) s. jaleo.
rumpus room s. cuarto de juegos.
rum·run·ner (rŭm′rŭn′ər) s. *(person)* contrabandista de licores *m*; *(boat)* barco de contrabando de licores.
run (rŭn) I. intr. **ran** (răn), **run, run·ning** *(to go fast)* correr <*they like running in the morning* les gusta correr por la mañana>; *(to flee)* echar a correr, huir <*the thief grabbed the money and ran* el ladrón cogió el dinero y echó a correr>; *(to keep company)* andar, ir <*he ran with a wild crowd* andaba con un grupo de gente extraña>; *(to migrate)* emigrar <*the salmon are already running* los salmones ya están emigrando>; *(to call)* acudir <*he is always running to his lawyer* siempre acude a su abogado>; *(to race)* correr, participar (en carrera); *(to finish)* llegar <*this horse ran last* este caballo llegó el último>; *(to be in operation)* estar en marcha, andar; *(to be in service)* circular, estar en servicio; *(to ply)* circular, ir y venir <*the ferry runs every hour* el transbordador va y viene cada hora>; *(to sail)* navegar <*to r. before the wind* navegar con el viento en popa>; *(to supperate)* supurar; *(to discharge mucus)* moquear; *(to water)* llorar (los ojos); *(to melt)* derretirse; *(to spread)* correrse (color, tinta); *(to reach)* ir, llegar <*this road runs to the next town* esta carretera va hasta la próxima ciudad>; *(to climb)* subir <*ivy is running up the wall* la hiedra sube por la pared>; *(to accompany)* ir <*fishing rights r. with ownership of the land* el derecho a la pesca va con la propiedad del terreno>; *(to unravel)* soltarse, correrse (los puntos en mallas, medias); *(to continue)* ser válido <*a lease with one year to r.* un contrato de alquiler que es válido por un año>; *(to accumulate)* acumularse (interés); *(to be worded)* decir, rezar <*how does the second verse r.?* ¿cómo dice el segundo verso?>; *(to stretch)* estar colocado <*shelves ran along the walls* los estantes estaban colocados a lo largo de las paredes>; *(to be a candidate)* presentarse como candidato; *(to flow)* correr; *(to function)* andar, marchar <*this car runs well* este coche marcha bien>; *(to depart)* salir <*the bus runs every hour* el autobús sale cada hora>; *(to get going)* irse <*it's late, we've got to r.* es tarde, debemos irnos>; *(to extend)* extenderse; *(to tend)* inclinarse, tender; *(to range)* oscilar; *(to travel)* correr <*the road runs parallel to the coast* la carretera corre paralela a la costa>; *(to cost)* costar <*what do these watches r.?* ¿cuánto cuestan estos relojes?> ♦ **cheap to r.** económico • **r. for your life** *o* **lives!** ¡sálvese quien pueda! • **the thought keeps running through my head** no puedo sacarme esta idea de la cabeza • **to come running** acudir <*don't come running to me* no acudas a mí> • **to r. across** dar con • **to r. aground** MARÍT. encallar, varar • **to r. along** ir <*r. along!* ¡vete!> • **to r. around** *(to roam)* andar, deambular; *(to be unfaithful)* andar con otras mujeres u otros hombres • **to r. around (shouting, singing)** ir (gritando, cantando) • **to r. away** *(to flee)* fugarse; *(to elope)* fugarse con un amante; *(to stampede)* salir en desbandada • **to r. away** *o* **to r. away from home** irse de casa, abandonar el hogar • **to r. back** volver corriendo • **to r. cold** helarse • **to r. high** exaltarse (ánimos) • **to r. in** entrar un momento • **to r. in**

the family venir de familia • **to r. loose** andar suelto • **to r. low** o **short** (to be scarce) ser escaso, escasear; (not to have enough) quedar poco • **to r. off** (to flee) escaparse, fugarse; (to leave) irse; (to overflow) salirse (líquido) • **to r. off at the mouth** hablar más de la cuenta • **to r. on** (to chatter) hablar sin cesar; (to elapse) pasar (el tiempo) • **to r. out** (to be exhausted) acabarse, agotarse <my patience has run out se me ha acabado la paciencia>; (to expire) expirar; (to overflow) salirse (líquido); (to leave) salir corriendo • **to r. over** (to overflow) rebosar; (to go beyond) durar más de lo previsto <the meeting ran over by ten minutes la reunión duró diez minutos más de lo previsto>; (to come) acudir; (to go) ir <to r. over to the store ir a la tienda> • **to r. smoothly** ir sobre ruedas, ir bien • **to r. to** (to last) durar; (to hurry) correr a <he ran to meet them corrió a su encuentro> • **to r. up** dejar que se acumulen —tr. (to cover) recorrer, cubrir (distancia); (to cause to run) correr, hacer correr (un animal); (to do by running) hacer <to r. an errand hacer un recado>; (to chase) acosar, correr <to r. a fox correr un zorro>; (to cause to compete) correr <he ran two horses in the Derby corrió dos caballos en el Derby>; (to present) presentar de candidato <they ran him for mayor le presentaron de candidato para alcalde>; (to operate) hacer funcionar <to r. a machine hacer funcionar una máquina>; (to transport) llevar <to r. me into town llévame a la ciudad>; (to smuggle) pasar de contrabando <to r. guns pasar armas de contrabando>; (to get past) romper, traspasar <to r. a roadblock romper una barricada>; (to cause to flow) dejar correr o salir; (to smelt) fundir (metal); (to mold) vaciar, moldear; (to draw) trazar <to r. a line between two points trazar una línea entre dos puntos>; (to sew) bastear, hilvanar; (to present) dar, poner (película, obra); (to publish) publicar <to r. an advertisement publicar un anuncio>; (to be subjected to) correr <to r. a risk correr un riesgo>; (to perform) hacer, llevar a cabo <to r. an experiment llevar a cabo un experimento>; (to direct) dirigir <she ran the campaign by herself dirigió la campaña ella misma>; (to manage) llevar (casa, negocio); (to cost) costar <this room will r. you fifty dollars esta habitación le costará cincuenta dólares>; (to follow) seguir <to r. its course seguir su curso>; (to extend) hacer correr; (to add) poner ♦ **to r. a red light** pasar con la luz roja • **to r. a temperature** o **fever** tener fiebre • **to r. across** tropezar con • **to r. after** perseguir, ir detrás de • **to r. against** ir en contra de • **to r. around** rodear • **to r. around with** andar con • **to r. away from** huir de • **to r. away with** (to make off with) llevarse; (to win) ganar con facilidad • **to r. by again** decir de nuevo • **to r. down** (to knock down) atropellar, pillar; (to capture) dar con, encontrar; (to disparage) hablar mal de, poner por los suelos; (to exhaust) agotar; (to review) repasar; (to race down) bajar corriendo <she ran down the street bajó la calle corriendo>; (to stream down) correr por • **to r. for** (to go get) ir corriendo a buscar <r. for the doctor ve corriendo a buscar al médico>; (to last) durar <the film runs for two hours la película dura dos horas>; (to compete for) presentar la candidatura a o para, presentarse a o para • **to r. in** (to insert) insertar; JER. (to arrest) meter en la cárcel, detener; IMPR. poner seguido • **to r. into** (to prick) clavarse en <she ran the needle into her finger se clavó la aguja en el dedo>; (to meet by chance) encontrarse con, tropezar con; (to collide with) chocar contra; (to encounter) tropezar con (dificultades); (to amount to) llegar a, alcanzar (suma); (to go into) entrar corriendo en; (to lead into) desembocar en • **to r. into debt** contraer deudas • **to r. into port** MARÍT. entrar en el puerto • **to r. low on** o **to r. short of** andar escaso de • **to r. off** (to print) tirar; (to drive off) echar de <he ran us off the road nos echó de la carretera>; (to write) redactar rápidamente (carta, artículo) • **to r. off with** (to steal) llevarse; (to elope) fugarse con • **to r. on** funcionar con <cars r. on gas los coches funcionan con gasolina>; IMPR. enlazar • **to r. one's eye down (the page)** echar un vistazo a (la página) • **to r. one's fingers through** pasarse la mano por • **to r. out** echar • **to r. out of** (to overflow) salirse de (líquido); (to leave) salir corriendo de; (to use up) acabársele a uno, quedarse uno sin <we ran out of milk

se nos acabó la leche> • **to r. out on** abandonar, dejar • **to r. over** (to drive over) pasar por encima de; (to go over) recorrer, repasar • **to r. the length of** correr de un extremo a otro de • **to r. the show** FAM. llevar la voz cantante • **to r. through** (to stab) traspasar (con arma blanca); (to squander) despilfarrar; (to rehearse) ensayar; (to cut through) pasar por <the highway runs through town la carretera pasa por la ciudad> • **to r. to** ascender a, alcanzar • **to r. up** (to go up) subir corriendo <to r. up the steps subir las escaleras corriendo>; (prices) hacer subir; (flag) izar • **to r. up** o **over to someone** acercarse a alguien corriendo • **to r. up against** tropezar con (persona, dificultad) **II.** s. (trip) recorrido, trayecto <this train makes the r. from Boston to New York in five hours este tren hace el trayecto de Boston a Nueva York en cinco horas>; (race) carrera <to win the ten-mile r. ganar en la carrera de las diez millas>; (visit) visita <a r. into town una visita a la ciudad>; (track) pista <a ski r. una pista de esquí>; (printing) tirada <a r. of a thousand copies una tirada de mil ejemplares>; (period) período <a r. of five hours un período de cinco horas>; (flow) flujo; (duration) duración f; (stream) arroyo; (length) tramo; (direction) dirección f <the r. of the grain la dirección de la fibra>; (enclosure) corral m <a chicken r. un corral de gallinas>; (in stockings) carrera; (blemish) mancha; (series) serie f <a r. of dry summers una serie de veranos sin lluvia>; (in cards) escalera; (trend) dirección, curso <the r. of events el curso de los acontecimientos>; MÚS. carrerilla; MIN. veta, filón m; ICT. migración f ♦ **a r. of (good, bad) luck** una (buena, mala) racha • **at a r.** corriendo • **average** o **common r.** mayoría • **in the long r.** a la larga • **in the short r.** por el momento • **on the r.** (hurrying) corriendo <on the r. all day corriendo todo el día>; (fleeing) huyendo; (while running) a la carrera <to eat on the r. comer a la carrera> • **there was a r. on the bank** los cuentacorrentistas se agruparon en el banco para retirar el dinero • **to break into a r.** echar a correr • **to give someone the r. of the house** poner la casa a disposición de alguien • **to give someone a r. for his money** (competition) hacer competencia a alguien; (satisfaction) dar satisfacción a alguien • **to go for a r.** ir a correr • **to have a long r.** (play, film) permanecer mucho tiempo en el cartel; (factory, mill) estar mucho tiempo en funcionamiento • **to have the r. of a place** tener libre acceso a un lugar • **to have the runs** FAM. tener diarrea • **to make a r. for it** correr (para alcanzar o evitar algo).

run·a·bout (rŭn′ə-bout′) s. (car) coche pequeño; (motorboat) lancha pequeña; (tramp) vagabundo.

run·a·round (rŭn′ə-round′) s. evasiva ♦ **to give someone the r.** FAM. dar excusas, eludir una respuesta en firme.

run·a·way (rŭn′ə-wā′) **I.** s. (slave) esclavo fugitivo; (child) niño desertor; (horse) caballo desbocado; FAM. (victory) victoria abrumadora **II.** adj. (slave) fugitivo; (horse) desbocado; (child) desertor; (victory, success) fácil, abrumador; (inflation) galopante, incontrolable.

run-down (rŭn′doun′) **I.** s. informe detallado **II.** adj. (building, neighborhood) en estado de deterioro; (person) agotado; (watch) parado.

rune (rōōn) s. (magic) magia; (letter) runa.

rung[1] (rŭng) s. (step) peldaño, escalón m; (crosspiece) barrote m, travesaño.

rung[2] (rŭng) pret. y part. p. de **ring**[2].

run-in (rŭn′ĭn′) **I.** s. (quarrel) riña; IMPR. inserción f **II.** adj. insertado.

run·nel (rŭn′əl) s. (brook) arroyo; (narrow channel) canaleja.

run·ner (rŭn′ər) s. (racer) corredor m; (messenger) mensajero, recadero; (collector) cobrador m; (solicitor) viajante m; (smuggler) contrabandista mf; (vessel) barco contrabandista; (of a skate) cuchilla; (of a sled) patín m; (of drawer, sliding door) guía, cursor m; (for table, dresser) tapete m; (for stairs) alfombra; (for hall) alfombra de pasillo; BOT. (creeper, vine) planta trepadora; METAL. orificio de colada.

run·ner-up (rŭn′ər-ŭp′) s. segundo (en una competencia).

run·ning (rŭn′ĭng) **I.** s. (of a business) dirección f, administración f; (of a machine, household) manejo; (of water) chorro; *(smuggling)* contrabando; *(of an article, ad)* publicación *f*; *(jogging)* footing *m* ♦ **to be in the r.** FIG. tener posibilidades de ganar • **to be out of the r.** FIG. no tener ninguna posibilidad de ganar **II.** adj. *(flowing)* corriente *<r. water* agua corriente*>*; *(knot)* corredizo; *(sore)* que supura ♦ **r. horse** DEP. caballo de carretera • **r. track** DEP. pista **III.** adv. seguido *<four years r.* cuatro años seguidos*>*.

running board s. AUTO. estribo.

running gear s. mecanismo de locomotora.

running light s. AVIA., MARÍT. luz de posición *f*.

running mate s. DEP. pareja; POL. candidato a la vice presidencia.

running start s. salida lanzada.

run·ny (rŭn'ē) adj. **-ni·er, -ni·est** *(liquid)* líquido; *(terrain)* corredizo, movedizo; *(nose)* que gotea.

run-off (rŭn'ôf') s. *(overflow)* derrame *m*; *(competition)* carrera de desempate.

run-of-the-mill (rŭn'ɔv-thə-mĭl') adj. corriente y moliente.

run-on (rŭn'ŏn', -ôn') s. IMPR. texto seguido.

runt (rŭnt) s. *(animal)* animal pequeño; DESPEC. *(person)* enano, persona de poca estatura.

run-through (rŭn'thrōō') s. *(review)* repaso, lectura rápida; *(rehearsal)* ensayo.

run·way (rŭn'wā') s. *(of a stream)* cauce *m*; *(ramp)* rampa; AVIA. pista de despegue y aterrizaje.

ru·pee (rōō-pē', rōō'pē) s. FIN. rupia.

rup·ture (rŭp'chər) **I.** s. DIPL. ruptura; MED. *(of muscle, tissue)* desgarre *m*; *(of an organ)* ruptura, rotura; *(hernia)* hernia **II.** tr. **-tured, -tur·ing** DIPL. romper; MED. *(an organ)* reventar; *(muscle, tissue)* desgarrarse —intr. DIPL. romper; MED. *(an organ)* reventarse; *(muscle, tissue)* desgarrarse.

ru·ral (rōōr'əl) adj. rural.

rural free delivery s. distribución gratuita del correo en las regiones rurales.

ru·ral·ize (rōōr'ə-līz') intr. & tr. **-ized, -iz·ing** volver(se) rústico.

rural route s. zona rural de correos.

ruse (rōōs, rōōz) s. artimaña, treta.

rush¹ (rŭsh) **I.** intr. *(to run)* ir de prisa *<he rushed to the bank* fue de prisa al banco*>*; *(to hurry)* apresurarse, darse prisa; *(to flow)* correr ♦ **blood rushed to her face** se puso colorada, se sonrojó • **to r. around** correr por todas partes • **to r. back** regresar corriendo • **to r. by** o **past** pasar corriendo • **to r. in** entrar corriendo • **to r. off** marcharse • **to r. out** salir corriendo o de prisa *<he rushed out of the room* salió de la habitación corriendo*>* • **to r. (right) over** acudir, ir corriendo • **to r. through** hacer de prisa, despachar rápidamente —tr. *(a person)* dar prisa, apurar *<if you r. me I'll never get done* si me apuras no acabaré nunca*>*; *(a job)* hacer precipitadamente; *(an order)* ejecutar urgentemente; *(to take)* llevar de prisa o con urgencia *<they rushed her to the hospital* la llevaron con urgencia al hospital*>* ♦ **to r. at** abalanzarse sobre • **to r. by** o **past** pasar corriendo por el lado de • **to r. for** precipitarse hacia • **to r. into** FIG. meterse en • **to r. things** precipitar las cosas • **to r. to conclusions** sacar conclusiones apresuradas **II.** s. *(of activity)* gran demanda; *(haste)* prisa; *(migration)* afluencia; *(onslaught)* fiebre *f <the gold r.* la fiebre del oro*>*; *(bustle)* bullicio, ajetreo; *(crush)* aglomeración de gente *f*; *(of wind)* ráfaga; *(of water)* torrente *m*; *(of emotion)* arrebato; *(narcotic high)* sensación eufórica (después de drogarse) ♦ **in a mad r.** precipitadamente • **rushes** CINEM. copión • **there's no r.** no corre prisa • **there was a (mad) r. to** la gente se apresuró a (hacer algo) • **to be in a r.** andar con prisa • **to be in no r.** no tener prisa **III.** adj. urgente *<a r. order* un pedido urgente*>*.

rush² (rŭsh) s. BOT. junco.

rush hour s. hora punta, hora de mayor congestión.

rush·ing (rŭsh'ĭng) **I.** s. precipitación *f* **II.** adj. impetuoso.

rusk (rŭsk) s. *(biscuit)* galleta; *(cake)* bizcocho tostado.

rus·set (rŭs'ĭt) **I.** s. color rojizo **II.** adj. rojizo, marrón.

Rus·sia (rŭsh'ə) s. Rusia.

Rus·sian (rŭsh'ən) adj. & s. *(inhabitant, language)* ruso.

Russian roulette s. ruleta rusa.

rust (rŭst) **I.** s. *(on metal)* herrumbre *f*; *(on plants)* roya, tizón *m* **II.** intr. *(metal)* oxidarse, enmohecerse; *(the mind)* entumecerse; *(leaves)* volverse rojizo —tr. *(metal)* oxidar, enmohecer; *(the mind)* entumecer; *(leaves)* volver rojizo.

rus·tic (rŭs'tĭk) adj. & s. rústico.

rus·ti·cate (rŭs'tĭ-kāt') intr. **-cat·ed, -cat·ing** (ir a) vivir en el campo —tr. CONSTR. construir al estilo rústico.

rus·tic·i·ty (rŭ-stĭs'ĭ-tē) s. [pl. **-ties**] rusticidad *f*.

rust·i·ness (rŭs'tē-nĭs) s. oxidación *f*, moho.

rus·tle (rŭs'əl) **I.** intr. **-tled, -tling** *(leaves)* susurrar; *(paper, fabric)* crujir; *(to move fast)* moverse con rapidez, agitarse; *(cattle)* robar ganado —tr. *(leaves)* hacer susurrar; *(paper, fabric)* hacer crujir; *(cattle)* robar. **II.** s. susurro.

rus·tler (rŭs'lər) s. *(thief)* ladrón de ganado *m*, cuatrero; *(diligent person)* persona emprendedora.

rust-proof (rŭst'prōōf') adj. inoxidable.

rust·y (rŭs'tē) adj. **-i·er, -i·est** *(corroded)* oxidado, mohoso; *(brownish)* rojizo ♦ **to be r.** *(object)* estar oxidado; *(person)* estar falto de práctica.

rut¹ (rŭt) **I.** s. *(by vehicles)* carril *m*; *(routine)* rutina *<to be in a r.* ser esclavo de la rutina*>* **II.** tr. **rut·ted, rut·ting** surcar.

rut² (rŭt) ZOOL. **I.** s. celo **II.** intr. **rut·ted, rut·ting** estar en celo.

ru·ta·ba·ga (rōō'tə-bā'gə, rōōt'ə-) s. BOT. colinabo, nabo sueco.

ru·the·ni·um (rōō-thē'nē-əm) s. QUÍM. rutenio.

ruth·less (rōōth'lĭs) adj. despiadado, cruel.

rut·ty (rŭt'ē) adj. **-ti·er, -ti·est** lleno de surcos.

Rwan·da (rōō-än'də) s. Rwanda.

Rwan·dan (rōō-än'dən) adj. & s. rwandés *m*.

Rx (är'ĕks') s. MED. *(prescription)* receta médica; *(remedy)* remedio medicinal.

rye¹ (rī) s. BOT., CUL. centeno; *(whiskey)* whisky de centeno.

rye² (rī) s. gitano.

rye grass s. BOT. ballico.

S

s, S (ĕs) s. [pl. **s's, S's**] decimonovena letra del alfabeto inglés.

Sab·bath (săb'əth) s. RELIG. *(Sunday)* domingo; *(Saturday)* sábado.

sab·bat·i·cal (sə-băt'ĭ-kəl) o **sab·bat·ic** (-ĭk) **I.** adj. sabático **II.** s. licencia sabática.

sa·ber (sā'bər) **I.** s. sable *m* **II.** tr. herir o matar con un sable.

saber rattling s. demostración amenazante de fuerza militar *f*.

sa·ble (sā'bəl) **I.** s. ZOOL. marta cebellina (animal y piel) ♦ **sables** trajes de luto *m* **II.** adj. negro.

sa·bot (să-bō') s. zueco.

sab·o·tage (săb'ə-täzh') **I.** s. sabotaje *m* **II.** tr. **-taged, -tag·ing** sabotear.

sab·o·teur (săb'ə-tûr') s. saboteador *m*.

sac (săk) s. ANAT., BOT. saco.

sac·cha·rin (săk'ər-ĭn) s. QUÍM. sacarina.

sac·cha·rine (săk'ər-ĭn, -ə-rēn') adj. *(sweet)* empalagoso; QUÍM. sacarino.

sac·er·do·tal (săs'ər-dōt'l) adj. sacerdotal.

sa·chem (sā'chəm) s. cacique indio norteamericano.

sa·chet (să-shā') s. almohadilla perfumada.

sack¹ (săk) **I.** s. *(bag, bagful)* saco (bolsa y contenido); JER. *(bed)* catre *m*, cama *<to hit the s.* echarse en la cama*>* ♦ **s. race** DEP. carrera de sacos • **to get the s.** JER. ser despedido **II.** tr. *(to bag)* ensacar; JER. *(to fire)* despedir, echar *<to get sacked* ser despedido*>* ♦ **to s. out** FAM. acostarse, echarse.

sack² (săk) **I.** tr. *(to rob)* saquear **II.** s. *(looting)* saqueo.

sack³ (săk) s. HIST. vino blanco seco.

sack·cloth (săk'klôth') s. *(cloth)* tela de saco arpillera; HIST. sayal *m*.
sack·ing (săk'ĭng) s. *(of a city)* saqueo; FAM. *(dismissal)* despido.
sa·cra (sā'krə) pl. de **sacrum**.
sa·cral¹ (sā'krəl) adj. ANAT. sacro.
sa·cral² (sā'krəl) adj. RELIG. sacro, sagrado.
sac·ra·ment (săk'rə-mənt) s. RELIG. sacramento ♦ **the Holy S.** el Santísimo Sacramento.
sac·ra·men·tal (săk'rə-měn'tl) adj. & s. sacramental *m*.
sa·crar·i·um (sə-krâr'ē-əm) s. [pl. -i·a (-ē-ə)] RELIG. *(sacristy)* sacristía; *(piscina)* piscina.
sa·cred (sā'krĭd) adj. RELIG. *(worthy of worship)* sacro, sagrado; *(venerable)* venerable; *(holy)* consagrado (pan, vino) ♦ **nothing is s. anymore** no se respeta nada • **s. to** consagrado *o* dedicado a.
Sacred College RELIG. Sacro Colegio.
sacred cow s. FIG. vaca sagrada.
sa·cred·ness (sā'krĭd-nĭs) s. santidad *f*.
sac·ri·fice (săk'rə-fīs') I. s. sacrificio ♦ **at a s.** COM. con pérdida • **to make a s.** to ofrecer un sacrificio a • **to make sacrifices for** hacer sacrificios por II. tr. **-ficed, -fic·ing** *(to offer, give up)* sacrificar; COM. vender con pérdida ♦ **to s. oneself** sacrificarse —intr. *(to offer)* ofrecer un sacrificio; *(to give up)* hacer sacrificios.
sac·ri·fi·cial (săk'rə-fĭsh'əl) adj. sacrificatorio, de sacrificio.
sac·ri·lege (săk'rə-lĭj) s. sacrilegio.
sac·ri·le·gious (săk'rə-lĕ'jəs, -lĭj'əs) adj. sacrílego.
sac·ris·tan (săk'rĭ-stən) s. sacristán *m*.
sac·ris·ty (săk'rĭ-stē) s. [pl. **-ties**] RELIG. sacristía.
sac·ro·il·i·ac (săk'rō-ĭl'ē-ăk', sā'krō-) ANAT. I. adj. sacroilíaco II. s. región sacroilíaca.
sac·ro·sanct (săk'rō-săngkt') adj. sacrosanto.
sa·crum (sā'krəm) s. [pl. **-cra** (-krə)] ANAT. sacro.
sad (săd) adj. **sad·der, sad·dest** *(unhappy, depressing)* triste; *(regrettable)* lamentable ♦ **s. to say that** la triste verdad es que, desgraciadamente • **to be s. about** entristecerse por • **to make s.** entristecer.
sad·den (săd'n) tr. & intr. entristecer(se).
sad·dle (săd'l) I. s. *(of a horse)* silla de montar; *(of a bicycle)* sillín *m*; *(cut of meat)* cuarto trasero; GEOG. *(depression)* depresión *f*, garganta; *(ridge)* puerto, paso II. tr. **-dled, -dling** ensillar ♦ **to s. with** cargar con (responsabilidades) —intr. ♦ **to s. up** *(a horse)* ensillar; *(to mount)* montar en la silla (de un caballo).
sad·dle·bag (săd'l-băg') s. alforja.
saddle blanket s. sudadero.
saddle horse s. caballo de silla.
sad·dler (săd'lər) s. talabartero, guarnicionero.
saddle roof s. tejado de dos hastiales *o* de dos aguas.
sad·dler·y (săd'lə-rē) s. [pl. **-ries**] talabartería, guarnicionería.
saddle soap s. producto para limpiar y suavizar el cuero.
saddle stitch s. COST. punto; IMPR. puntada en el pliegue de las hojas (para encuadernar un libro).
Sad·du·cee (săj'ə-sē') s. RELIG. saduceo.
sa·dism (sā'dĭz'əm, săd'ĭz'-) s. sadismo.
sa·dist (sā'dĭst, săd'ĭst) s. sádico.
sa·dis·tic (sə-dĭs'tĭk) adj. sádico.
sa·dis·ti·cal·ly (sə-dĭs'tĭ-kə-lē) adv. sádicamente.
sad·ly (săd'lē) adv. *(sorrowfully)* tristemente; *(lamentably)* lamentablemente.
sad·ness (săd'nĭs) s. tristeza.
sa·do·mas·o·chism (sā'dō-măs'ə-kĭz'əm, săd'ō-) s. sadomasoquismo.
sad sack s. FIG., FAM. desgraciado.
sa·fa·ri (sə-fä'rē) s. safari *m*.
safe (sāf) I. adj. **saf·er, saf·est** *(secure)* seguro <*s. place* lugar seguro>; *(cautious)* prudente, seguro ♦ **have a s. trip!** *(if driving)* ¡conduce con cuidado!; *(if travelling)* ¡ten cuidado!, ¡cuídate! • **is it s. for small children?** ¿no es peligroso para niños? • **is it s. to (take, do)?** ¿no es peligroso (tomar, hacer)? • **it is s. to say that** se puede decir con seguridad que • **s. and sound** sano y salvo • **s. from** a salvo de • **to be on the s. side** para mayor seguridad • **to be s.** estar a salvo • **to play it s.** actuar con precaución

II. s. *(for money, papers)* caja de caudales, caja fuerte; JER. *(condom)* preservativo.
safe-con·duct (sāf'kŏn'dŭkt) s. salvoconducto.
safe-crack·er (sāf'krăk'ər) s. ladrón de cajas fuertes *m*.
safe-de·pos·it box (sāf'dĭ-pŏz'ĭt) s. caja de seguridad.
safe·guard (sāf'gärd') I. s. *(protection)* salvaguardia, salvaguarda; *(guarantee)* garantía; *(safety device)* dispositivo de seguridad ♦ **to be a s. against** evitar, proteger contra II. tr. salvaguardar, proteger.
safe·keep·ing (sāf'kē'pĭng) s. depósito, protección *f*.
safe·ly (sāf'lē) adv. *(when travelling)* sano y salvo, sin accidente; *(when driving)* con cuidado; *(when speaking)* sin temor a equivocarse, con toda seguridad.
safe·ness (sāf'nĭs) s. seguridad *f*.
safe·ty (sāf'tē) s. [pl. **-ties**] seguridad *f* <*to endanger the s. of pedestrians* poner en peligro la seguridad de los peatones> ♦ **s. belt** AUTO., AVIA. cinturón de seguridad • **s.** *o* **s. catch** ARM. seguro <*is the s. on?* ¿está puesto el seguro?> • **s. catch** cadena de seguridad • **s. measures** medidas de seguridad • **to get to s.** ponerse a salvo • **to put on the s.** ARM. poner el seguro.
safety circuit s. ELECTRÓN. circuito de seguridad.
safety net s. *(net)* red (en un circo) *f*; *(guarantee)* garantía.
safety pin s. imperdible *m*.
safety razor s. maquinilla de afeitar.
safety valve s. válvula de seguridad.
saf·flow·er (săf'lou'ər) s. BOT. alazor *m*, cártamo.
saf·fron (săf'rən) s. *(color)* color de azafrán *m*; BOT. azafrán *m*.
sag (săg) I. intr. **sagged, sag·ging** *(skin, clothes)* colgar; *(board, door)* combarse; *(clothesline)* aflojarse; *(production, sales)* decaer; *(prices)* bajar II. s. *(decline)* caída; *(in board, door)* comba.
sa·ga (sä'gə) s. *(prose narrative)* saga; *(epic)* epopeya; *(report)* informe detallado.
sa·ga·cious (sə-gā'shəs) adj. sagaz.
sa·gac·i·ty (sə-găs'ĭ-tē) s. sagacidad *f*.
sage¹ (sāj) I. s. sabio II. adj. **sag·er, sag·est** *(wise)* sabio; *(prudent)* prudente; ANT. *(serious)* solemne, grave.
sage² (sāj) s. BOT. salvia.
sage·brush (sāj'brŭsh') s. BOT. artemisia, artemisia.
sag·ging (săg'ĭng) I. s. *(sinking)* hundimiento; *(decline)* baja II. adj. *(sunken)* hundido; *(declining)* decreciente.
Sag·it·tar·i·us (săj'ĭ-târ'ē-əs) s. ASTROL. Sagitario.
Sa·ha·ra (sə-hâr'ə) s. Sahara *m*.
sa·hib (sä'ĭb) s. señor *m*.
said (sĕd) I. pret. y part. p. de **say** II. adj. DER. dicho, antedicho.
sail (sāl) I. s. *(trip)* viaje *o* paseo en barco; *(of windmill)* brazo, aspa; MARÍT. vela ♦ **s.** *o* **sails** HIST. velero, barco de vela • **to make s.** desplegar las velas • **to set s.** hacerse a la vela • **under full s.** a toda vela • **under s.** con las velas alzadas II. intr. MARÍT. *(to navigate)* navegar; *(to travel)* ir *o* viajar en barco <*we sailed to France* fuimos a Francia en barco>; *(to set out)* zarpar, partir; *(to operate a sailboat)* navegar (a la vela); *(to soar)* volar, planear ♦ **to s. away** MARÍT. irse • **to s. by** pasar volando —tr. MARÍT. *(an ocean)* cruzar, atravesar; *(one's boat)* botar ♦ **to s. around** *(a cape)* doblar; *(the world)* dar la vuelta a • **to s. into** *(one's work)* emprender, acometer; *(person)* regañar, criticar • **to s. the seas** surcar los mares • **to s. through** *(the air)* volar; *(one's exams, work)* despachar *o* hacer fácilmente; *(customs)* pasar rápidamente por.
sail·boat (sāl'bōt') s. velero, barco de vela.
sail·cloth (sāl'klôth') s. lona para velas, toldos, etc.
sail·er (sā'lər) s. MARÍT. velero muy manejable.
sail·fish (sāl'fĭsh') s. [pl. **sailfish** *o* **-fish·es**] pez vela *m*.
sail·ing (sā'lĭng) s. *(navigation)* navegación *f*; *(sport)* deporte de la vela *m*; *(departure)* salida ♦ **to be smooth s.** FIG. *(to be easy)* ser pan comido.
sail·or (sā'lər) s. marinero, marino.
sail·plane (sāl'plān') s. planeador *m*.
saint (sānt) I. s. santo II. tr. canonizar.
saint·ed (sān'tĭd) adj. *(canonized)* santo, canonizado; *(holy)* santo, sagrado.

saint·hood (sānt'hŏŏd') s. *(status)* santidad *f; (saints)* santos (en conjunto).

Saint Lu·cia (lōō'shə) s. Santa Lucía.

Saint Lu·cian (lōō'shən) adj. & s. santalucense *mf.*

saint·ly (sānt'lē) adj. **-li·er, -li·est** santo.

Saint Nich·o·las (nĭk'ə-ləs) *o* **Saint Nick** (nĭk) s. San Nicolás *m,* Papá Noel *m.*

Saint Pat·rick's Day (păt'rĭks) s. día de San Patricio (17 de marzo) *m.*

saint's day s. RELIG. *(of a place)* día del santo patrón *m; (of a person)* santo, día onomástico.

Saint Va·len·tine's Day (văl'ən-tīnz') s. día de San Valentín *m,* día de los enamorados.

Saint Vin·cent and the Gren·a·dines (vĭn'sənt; grĕn'ə-dēnz') s. San Vicente y las Granadas.

saith (sĕth) ANT. tercera persona sing. del pres. de **say.**

sake¹ (sāk) ♦ **for God's** *o* **goodness'** *o* **heaven's s.!** ¡por dios!, ¡por el amor de Dios! • **for one's own s.** por el proprio bien de uno • **for the s. of (one's children, health)** por (los hijos, la salud) • **to fight for the s. of fighting** luchar por luchar.

sa·ke² *o* **sa·ki** (sä'kĕ, -kē) s. sake (bebida) *m.*

sal (săl) s. sal *f.*

sa·laam (sə-läm') I. s. zalema II. tr. & intr. saludar con una zalema.

sal·a·bil·i·ty (săl'lə-bĭl'ĭ-tē) s. posibilidad de venta *f.*

sal·a·ble (să'lə-bəl) adj. vendible, que se vende fácilmente.

sa·la·cious (sə-lā'shəs) adj. salaz.

sal·ad (săl'əd) s. *(dish)* ensalada; *(vegetable)* verdura; *(lettuce)* lechuga.

salad days s. días de juventud *m.*

salad dressing s. aderezo, aliño para ensalada.

salad oil s. aceite para ensalada *m.*

sal·a·man·der (săl'ə-măn'dər) s. ZOOL. salamandra ♦ **s.** *o* **s. stove** salamandra.

sa·la·mi (sə-lä'mē) s. salame *m.*

sal·a·ried (săl'ə-rēd) adj. *(person)* salariado; *(work)* a sueldo.

sal·a·ry (săl'ə-rē) s. [pl. **-ries**] salario, sueldo.

sale (sāl) s. venta ♦ **clearance s.** liquidación • **for s.** *(available)* en venta; *(sign)* se vende • **on s.** *(available)* en venta; *(at a reduced price)* en liquidación • **s.** liquidación • **s. price** precio de saldo • **sales** venta • **to have a s.** *(store)* estar de liquidación; *(individual)* ofrecer a la venta • **to put up for s.** poner en venta.

sale·a·ble (sā'lə-bəl) adj. var. de **salable.**

sales check s. factura.

sales·clerk (sālz'klûrk') s. vendedor *m,* dependiente *m.*

sales·girl (sālz'gûrl') s. vendedora, dependienta.

sales·man (sālz'mən) s. [pl. **-men**] *(in a store)* vendedor *m,* dependiente *m; (representative)* representante *m,* agente comercial *m; (on the road)* viajante de comercio *m.*

sales·man·ship (sālz'mən-shĭp') s. arte de vender *m.*

sales·per·son (sālz'pûr'sən) s. *(man)* vendedor *m; (woman)* vendedora.

sales tax s. impuesto a las ventas.

sales·wom·an (sālz'wŏŏm'ən) s. [pl. **-wom·en** (-wĭm'ĭn)] *(in a store)* vendedora, dependienta; *(representative)* representante *f,* agente comercial *f; (on the road)* viajante de comercio *f.*

sal·ic (săl'ĭk) adj. MIN., GEOL. sálico.

sal·ic·y·late (sə-lĭs'ə-lāt', săl'ə-sĭl'ĭt) s. QUÍM. salicilato.

sa·li·ence (sā'lē-əns) *o* **sa·li·en·cy** (-ən-sē) s. *(prominence)* prominencia; *(highlight)* rasgo sobresaliente.

sa·li·ent (sā'lē-ənt) I. adj. *(projecting)* saliente; *(prominent)* sobresaliente, dominante II. s. MIL. saliente *m.*

sa·lif·er·ous (sə-lĭf'ər-əs) adj. GEOL. salífero.

sa·line (sā'lēn', -lĭn') I. adj. *(taste)* salado, salobre; MED., MIN. salino II. s. ♦ **s. cathartic** FARM. sal hepática • **s. solution** MED. solución salina.

sal·i·nize (săl'ə-nīz') tr. **-nized, -niz·ing** QUÍM. salinizar, tratar con sal.

sa·li·va (sə-lī'və) s. saliva.

sal·i·var·y (săl'ə-vĕr'ē) s. salival, salivar.

salivary gland s. ANAT. glándula salival.

sal·i·vate (săl'ə-vāt') intr. **-vat·ed, -vat·ing** salivar —tr. hacer salivar.

sal·low¹ (săl'ō) I. adj. **-er, -est** cetrino II. tr. poner cetrino.

sal·low² (săl'ō) s. BOT. sauce *m.*

sal·ly (săl'ē) I. intr. **-lied, -ly·ing** *(to go forth)* salir; MIL. hacer una salida ♦ **to s. forth** salir II. s. [pl. **-lies**] *(outburst)* arranque; *(quip)* salida, ocurrencia; *(jaunt)* paseo, vuelta; *(adventure)* salida, MIL. salida.

salm·on (săm'ən, sä'mən) s. [pl. **salmon** *o* **-ons**] *(color)* color salmón *m;* ICT. salmón *m.*

sal·mo·nel·la (săl'mə-nĕl'ə) s. [pl. **-nel·lae** (-nĕl'ē) *o* **-nel·las** *o* **-nel·la**] BACT. salmonela.

sa·lon (sə-lŏn') s. salón *m.*

sa·loon (sə-lōōn') s. *(tavern)* taberna, bar *m; (hall, lounge)* salón *m,* sala.

sa·loon·keep·er (sə-lōōn'kē'pər) s. tabernero, cantinero.

sal·si·fy (săl'sə-fē) s. BOT. salsifí *m.*

salt (sôlt) I. s. *(seasoning)* sal *f,* FIG. *(flavor)* salero, sal; QUÍM. sal ♦ **not to be worth one's s.** no valer gran cosa • **old s.** FIG., FAM. viejo lobo de mar • **s. water** agua salada • **salts** *(for bath)* sales de baño; *(for catharsis)* sales minerales; *(of Epsom)* sale de la Higuera; *(for reviving)* sales aromáticas • **the s. of the earth** FIG. la sal de la tierra • **to take with a grain of s.** FIG. acoger con reservas II. tr. *(to season)* echar sal a; *(to preserve)* salar, curar con sal; FIG. *(a speech, writing)* salpicar; *(a mine)* colocar mineral en ♦ **to s. away** FAM. guardar, ahorrar.

salt·box (sôlt'bŏks') s. casa de dos departamentos al frente y uno en el contrafrente, con un techo gran declive en la parte de atrás.

salt·cel·lar (sôlt'sĕl'ər) s. salero.

sal·tine (sôl-tēn') s. galleta salada.

salt lick s. salegar *m.*

salt marsh s. salina.

salt·pe·ter (sôlt'pē'tər) s. *(caliche)* caliche *m,* nitrato de Chile; QUÍM. nitrato de sodio *o* potasio.

salt·shak·er (sôlt'shā'kər) s. salero.

salt·wa·ter (sôlt'wô'tər) adj. de agua salada.

salt·works (sôlt'wûrks') s.pl. [ú. con v. sing. o pl.] salinas, refinería de sal.

salt·y (sôl'tē) adj. **-i·er, -i·est** *(saline)* salino; *(with salt)* salado; FIG. *(witty)* agudo, ingenioso; *(lively)* picante.

sa·lu·bri·ous (sə-lōō'brē-əs) adj. salubre, saludable.

sal·u·tar·y (săl'yə-tĕr'ē) adj. *(healthy)* saludable; *(beneficial)* benéfico.

sal·u·ta·tion (săl'yə-tā'shən) s. *(greeting)* saludo; *(bow)* reverencia; *(in a letter)* saludo.

sa·lu·ta·to·ri·an (sə-lōō'tə-tôr'ē-ən) s. estudiante que pronuncia el discurso de salutación en la ceremonia de entrega de diplomas.

sa·lu·ta·to·ry (sə-lōō'tə-tôr'ē) I. s. [pl. **-ries**] discurso de apertura II. adj. de saludo.

sa·lute (sə-lōōt') I. tr. **-lut·ed, -lut·ing** saludar —intr. hacer un saludo II. s. *(greeting)* saludo; MIL. saludo, salva.

Sal·va·do·ri·an (săl'və-dôr'ē-ən) *o* **Sal·va·do·ran** (-dôr'ən) adj. & s. salvadoreño.

sal·vage (săl'vĭj) I. s. MARÍT. *(rescue)* salvamento; *(things)* objetos salvados; *(compensation)* prima de salvamento II. tr. **-vaged, -vag·ing** salvar.

sal·vage·a·ble (săl'vĭ-jə-bəl) adj. salvable.

sal·vag·er (săl'vĭ-jər) s. MARÍT. salvador *m.*

sal·va·tion (săl-vā'shən) s. salvación *f.*

Salvation Army Ejército de Salvación.

salve (săv, sāv) I. s. *(ointment)* ungüento, pomada; FIG. *(comfort)* bálsamo II. tr. **salved, salv·ing** FIG. apaciguar, tranquilizar.

sal·ver (săl'vər) s. bandeja.

sal·vi·a (săl'vē-ə) s. salvia.

sal·vo (săl'vō) s. [pl. **-vos** *o* **-voes**] salva (de cañonazos, aplausos).

Sa·mar·i·tan (sə-măr'ĭ-tn) s. samaritano.

sa·mar·i·um (sə-mâr'ē-əm) s. QUÍM. samario.

sam·ba (săm'bə) I. s. samba II. intr. bailar samba.

same (sām) I. adj. *(selfsame)* mismo <*we still live in the s. house* todavía vivimos en la misma casa>; *(corresponding)*

mismo; *(identical)* igual <*I have the s. dress* tengo un vestido igual> ♦ **at the s. time** *(however)* sin embargo; *(simultaneously)* al mismo tiempo • **s. difference** *o* **thing** FAM. lo mismo • **the s. old story** la historia de siempre • **to be of the s. mind** pensar igual **II.** adv. del mismo modo, igual <*I feel the s. as before* pienso igual que antes> **III.** pron. *(person)* el mismo <*I'm not the same anymore* ya no soy el mismo>; *(thing)* lo mismo ♦ **all** *o* **just the s.** sin embargo, a pesar de todo • **everything is the s.** todo sigue igual • **it's all the s. to me** me da igual *o* lo mismo • **the s. to you!** *(in friendship)* ¡igualmente!; *(in anger)* ¡te deseo lo mismo!
same·ness (sām′nĭs) s. *(identity)* igualdad *f*, identidad *f*; *(monotony)* monotonía, uniformidad *f*.
Sa·mo·a (sə-mō′ə) s. Samoa.
Sa·mo·an (sə-mō′ən) adj. & s. samoano.
sam·ple (săm′pəl) **I.** s. *(piece)* muestra; CIENT. espécimen *m* **II.** tr. **-pled, -pling** CIENT. tomar una muestra de; CUL. probar.
sam·pler (săm′plər) s. *(person)* catador *m*; COST. dechado.
sam·pling (săm′plĭng) s. *(sample)* muestra; *(sample-taking)* toma de muestras; CUL. catadura.
Sam·u·el (săm′yōo-əl) s. BÍBL. Samuel.
Sam·u·rai (săm′ə-rī′) s. [pl. **samurai** *o* **-rais**] samurai *m*.
san·a·tive (săn′ə-tĭv) adj. sanativo, curativo.
san·a·to·ri·um (săn′ə-tôr′ē-əm) *o* **san·a·tar·i·um** (-târ′-əm) s. [pl. **-to·ri·ums** *o* **-to·ri·a** (-tôr′ē-ə) *o* **-tar·i·ums** *o* **-tar·i·a** (-târ′ē-ə)] sanatorio.
sanc·ti·fi·ca·tion (săngk′tə-fĭ-kā′shən) s. santificación *f*.
sanc·ti·fi·er (săngk′tə-fī′ər) s. santificador *m*.
sanc·ti·fy (săngk′tə-fī′) tr. **-fied, -fy·ing** *(to consecrate, purify)* santificar; *(to sanction)* sancionar.
sanc·ti·mo·ni·ous (săngk′tə-mō′nē-əs) adj. beato, mojigato.
sanc·ti·mo·ny (săngk′tə-mō′nē) s. santurronería, mojigatería.
sanc·tion (săngk′shən) **I.** s. sanción *f* **II.** tr. sancionar.
sanc·ti·ty (săngk′tĭ-tē) s. *(holiness)* santidad *f*; *(inviolability)* inviolabilidad *f*.
sanc·tu·ar·y (săngk′chōo-ĕr′ē) s. [pl. **-ies**] FIG. *(refuge)* refugio, asilo; *(game preserve)* coto; RELIG. santuario.
sanc·tum (săngk′təm) s. [pl. **-tums** *o* **-ta** (-tə)] *(holy place)* santuario; *(private place)* sanctasanctórum *m*.
sand (sănd) **I.** s. arena ♦ **sands** *(land)* arenales; *(beach)* playa • **the sands are running out** queda poco tiempo **II.** tr. *(icy road)* enarenar; *(wood)* lijar.
san·dal (săn′dl) s. sandalia.
san·dal·wood (săn′dl-wood′) s. sándalo.
sand·bag (sănd′băg′) **I.** s. saco de arena **II.** tr. **-bagged, -bag·ging** *(to protect)* proteger con sacos de arena; *(to hit)* golpear como con un saco de arena; FIG. *(to coerce)* forzar, obligar.
sand·bank (sănd′băngk′) s. banco de arena.
sand·bar (sănd′bär′) s. banco *o* arrecife *m* de arena.
sand·blast (sănd′blăst′) **I.** s. *(blast)* chorro de arena; *(machine)* limpiadora de chorro de arena **II.** tr. limpiar con chorro de arena.
sand·box (sănd′bŏks′) s. *(for children)* cajón de arena (para juego de niños) *m*; *(ink drier)* salvadera; F.C. arenero.
sand dune s. duna, médano.
sand·er (săn′dər) s. *(distributor)* persona *o* aparato que esparce arena; *(sanding machine)* lijadora, F.C. arenero.
sand·lot (sănd′lŏt′) s. solar, baldío.
sand·man (sănd′măn′) s. personaje de cuento que adormece a los niños *m*.
sand·pa·per (sănd′pā′pər) **I.** s. papel de lija *m* **II.** tr. lijar.
sand·pi·per (sănd′pī′pər) s. ORNIT. aguzanieves *f*.
sand·stone (sănd′stōn′) s. MIN. arenisca.
sand·storm (sănd′stôrm′) s. tempestad de arena *f*.
sand·wich (sănd′wĭch) s. emparedado, bocadillo, sandwich *m*.
sandwich board s. carteles que lleva el hombre anuncio *m*.
sand·y (săn′dē) adj. **-i·er, -i·est** *(full of sand, like sand)* arenoso; *(color)* rubio rojizo.
sane (sān) adj. **san·er, san·est** *(mentally healthy)* cuerdo, sano; *(reasonable)* razonable, sensato.

San·for·ized (săn′fə-rīzd′) s. marca registrada de una tela sanforizada.
sang (săng) pret. de **sing.**
san·gui·nar·y (săng′gwə-nĕr′ē) adj. *(bloodthirsty)* sanguinario; *(with much blood)* sangriento.
san·guine (săng′gwĭn) adj. *(having blood)* sanguíneo; *(optimistic)* optimista.
san·i·tar·i·um (săn′ĭ-târ′ē-əm) s. [pl. **-i·ums** *o* **-i·a** (-ē-ə)] sanatorio.
san·i·tar·y (săn′ĭ-tĕr′ē) adj. sanitario.
sanitary engineer s. ingeniero de sanidad.
sanitary napkin s. paño higiénico, toalla higiénica.
san·i·ta·tion (săn′ĭ-tā′shən) s. saneamiento, higiene *f*.
san·i·tize (săn′ĭ-tīz′) tr. **-tized, -tiz·ing** sanear.
san·i·ty (săn′ĭ-tē) s. *(mental soundness)* cordura, juicio; *(sensibleness)* sensatez *f*.
sank (săngk) un pret. de **sink.**
San·skrit (săn′skrĭt′) s. sánscrito.
San·ta Claus (săn′tə klôz′) s. Papá Noel *m*.
São To·me and Prin·ci·pe (soun tə-mā′; prĭn′sə-pə) s. Santo Tomé y Príncipe.
sap[1] (săp) s. FIG. *(fluid)* savia; *(vitality)* vitalidad *f*, JER. *(dupe)* bobo, pelele *m*; *(blackjack)* cachiporra; BOT. savia.
sap[2] (săp) **I.** s. MIL. zapa **II.** tr. **sapped, sap·ping** FIG. *(to deplete)* agotar; MIL. zapar, socavar.
sa·pi·ent (sā′pē-ənt) adj. sapiente.
sap·less (săp′lĭs) adj. *(dry)* sin savia; FIG. *(weak)* débil.
sap·ling (săp′lĭng) s. *(tree)* árbol joven *m*; FIG. *(youth)* jovenzuelo, mozalbete *m*.
sap·o·dil·la (săp′ə-dĭl′ə, -dē′yə) s. BOT. zapote (árbol y fruto) *m*.
sap·o·na·ceous (săp′ə-nā′shəs) adj. saponáceo.
sa·pon·i·fi·ca·tion (sə-pŏn′ə-fĭ-kā′shən) s. QUÍM. saponificación *f*.
sap·per (săp′ər) s. MIL. zapador *m*.
sap·phire (săf′īr′) **I.** s. *(gem)* zafiro; *(color)* color de zafiro *m* **II.** adj. zafirino.
sap·py (săp′ē) adj. **-pi·er, -pi·est** *(full of sap)* lleno de savia; JER. *(mawkish)* sensiblero; *(foolish)* tontuelo.
sap·ro·phyte (săp′rə-fīt′) s. BIOL., BOT. saprófito.
sap·wood (săp′wood′) s. BOT. albura.
sar·a·band *o* **sar·a·bande** (săr′ə-bănd′) s. MÚS. zarabanda.
Sar·a·cen (săr′ə-sən) s. HIST. sarraceno.
Sa·ran (sə-răn′) s. marca registrada de un material plástico usado para empaquetar.
sa·ra·pe (sə-rä′pē) s. var. de **serape.**
sar·casm (sär′kăz′əm) s. sarcasmo.
sar·cas·tic (sär-kăs′tĭk) adj. sarcástico.
sar·co·ma (sär-kō′mə) s. [pl. **-ma·ta** (-mə-tə) *o* **-mas**] MED. sarcoma *m*.
sar·coph·a·gus (sär-kŏf′ə-gəs) s. [pl. **-gi** (-jī′) *o* **-gus·es**] sarcófago.
sar·dine (sär-dēn′) s. sardina.
Sar·din·i·a (sär-dĭn′ē-ə) s. Cerdeña.
Sar·din·i·an (sär-dĭn′ē-ən) adj. & s. sardo.
sar·don·ic (sär-dŏn′ĭk) adj. sardónico.
sar·gas·so (sär-găs′ō) s. BOT. sargazo.
sar·sa·pa·ril·la (săs′pə-rĭl′ə, särs′-) s. BOT. zarzaparrilla.
sar·to·ri·al (sär-tôr′ē-əl) adj. de sastre, de sastrería.
sash[1] (săsh) s. *(bank)* faja, fajín *m*.
sash[2] (săsh) **I.** s. *(frame)* marco *m* **II.** tr. poner un marco a.
sa·shay (să-shā′) intr. FAM. pavonearse.
sass (săs) FAM. **I.** s. impertinencia **II.** tr. hablar con insolencia a.
sas·sa·fras (săs′ə-frăs′) s. sasafrás *m*.
sas·sy (săs′ē) adj. **-si·er, -si·est** descarado, fresco.
sat (săt) pret. y part. p. de **sit.**
Sa·tan (sāt′n) s. Satanás *m*, Satán *m*.
sa·tan·ic (sə-tăn′ĭk) *o* **sa·tan·i·cal** (-ĭ-kəl) adj. satánico.
satch·el (săch′əl) s. cartapacio, cartera.
sate (sāt) tr. **sat·ed, sat·ing** *(to satisfy fully)* saciar; *(to glut)* hartar.
sa·teen (să-tēn′) s. satén *m*.
sat·el·lite (săt′l-īt′) s. satélite *m*.
sa·tia·ble (sā′shə-bəl) adj. saciable.

sa·ti·ate (sā′shē-āt′) I. tr. -at·ed, -at·ing *(to satisfy fully)* saciar; *(to glut)* hartar II. adj. (-ĭt) saciado.
sa·ti·a·tion (sā′shē-ā′shən) s. saciedad *f*, hartura.
sa·ti·e·ty (sə-tī′ĭ-tē) s. saciedad *f*, hartura.
sat·in (săt′n) s. raso, satén *m*.
sat·in·y (săt′n-ē) adj. satinado.
sat·ire (săt′īr′) s. sátira.
sa·tir·i·cal (sə-tĭr′ĭ-kəl) *o* **sa·tir·ic** (-ĭk) adj. satírico.
sat·i·rist (săt′ər-ĭst) s. satírico, escritor satírico.
sat·i·rize (săt′ə-rīz′) tr. -rized, -riz·ing satirizar.
sat·is·fac·tion (săt′ĭs-făk′shən) s. *(gratification)* satisfacción *f*; *(compensation)* compensación *f*.
sat·is·fac·to·ry (săt′ĭs-făk′tə-rē) adj. satisfactorio.
sat·is·fi·a·ble (săt′ĭs-fī′ə-bəl) adj. que puede satisfacerse.
sat·is·fy (săt′ĭs-fī′) tr. -fied, -fy·ing *(need, desire)* satisfacer; *(obligation)* cumplir con; *(requirements)* cumplir con, satisfacer; *(creditor)* pagar una deuda a, reembolsar; *(to please)* contentarse *<she'll have to be satisfied with half* tendrá que contentarse con la mitad>; *(to assure)* convencer *<I'm still not satisfied* todavía no estoy convencida> —intr. dar satisfacción.
sat·is·fy·ing (săt′ĭs-fī′ĭng) adj. *(gratifying)* satisfactorio; *(experience)* agradable; *(food)* sustancioso; *(argument)* convincente.
sa·trap (sā′trăp′) s. HIST. sátrapa.
sat·u·rant (săch′ər-ənt) QUÍM. I. adj. saturante, saturativo II. s. substancia saturativa.
sat·u·rate (săch′ə-rāt′) tr. -rat·ed, -rat·ing *(to soak)* empapar; *(to imbue thoroughly)* saturar; QUÍM. saturar.
sat·u·rat·ed (săch′ə-rā′tĭd) adj. *(soaked)* empapado; *(full)* saturado; GEOL., QUÍM. saturado.
sat·u·ra·tion (săch′ə-rā′shən) s. saturación *f*.
Sat·ur·day (săt′ər-dē) s. sábado.
Sat·urn (săt′ərn) s. ASTRON., MITOL. Saturno.
sat·ur·na·li·a (săt′ər-nā′lē-ə) s.pl. [ú. con v. sing.] bacanales *f* ♦ **S.** HIST. saturnales *f*.
sat·ur·nine (săt′ər-nīn′) adj. saturnino.
sa·tyr (sā′tər, săt′ər) s. *(person)* sátiro; ENTOM. sátiro ♦ **s.** *o* **S.** MITOL. sátiro.
sa·ty·ri·a·sis (sā′tə-rī′ə-sĭs, săt′ə-) s. MED. satiriasis (exacerbación sexual masculina) *f*.
sauce (sôs) I. s. CUL. *(gravy)* salsa; *(compote)* compota; *(zest)* aderezo, aliño; *(impudence)* descaro, frescura; JER. *(liquor)* trago II. tr. **sauced, sauc·ing** *(to season)* echar salsa a; FAM. *(to be rude to)* insolentarse con ♦ **to s. up** aderezar, aliñar.
sauce·pan (sôs′păn′) s. cacerola, cazo.
sau·cer (sô′sər) s. platillo.
sauc·y (sô′sē) adj. -i·er, -i·est *(impertinent)* descarado, insolente; *(piquant)* pícaro.
Sau·di (sou′dē, sô′-) adj. & s. árabe saudita *mf*.
Saudi A·ra·bi·a (ə-rā′bē-ə) s. Arabia Saudita.
Saudi A·ra·bi·an (ə-rā′bē-ən) adj. & s. árabe saudita *mf*.
sau·na (sô′nə) s. sauna.
saun·ter (sôn′tər) I. intr. pasearse, deambular II. s. paseo.
sau·ri·an (sôr′ē-ən) ZOOL. s. & adj. saurio.
sau·sage (sô′sĭj) s. salchicha, embutido.
sau·té (sō-tā′, sô-) CUL. I. tr. -téed *o* -téd, -té·ing saltear II. s. comida salteada.
sav·a·ble (sā′və-bəl) s. salvable.
sav·age (săv′ĭj) I. adj. salvaje; *(ferocious)* feroz, violento; *(cruel)* cruel II. s. salvaje *mf* III. tr. -aged, -ag·ing atacar violentamente.
sav·age·ness (săv′ĭj-nĭs) s. *(savagery)* salvajismo; *(savage act)* salvajada; *(ferociousness)* ferocidad *f*; *(violence)* violencia; *(cruelty)* crueldad *f*.
sav·age·ry (săv′ĭj-rē) s. [pl. -ries] *(quality)* salvajismo; *(act)* salvajada.
sa·van·na *o* **sa·van·nah** (sə-văn′ə) s. sabana.
sa·vant (să-vänt′) s. sabio.
save¹ (sāv) I. tr. **saved, sav·ing** *(to rescue)* salvar *<the fireman saved the girl's life* el bombero le salvó la vida a la muchacha>; *(to keep)* guardar *<s. that for later* guarda eso para más tarde>; *(to obviate)* evitar *<that saved me an extra trip* eso me evitó un viaje extra>; *(money)* ahorrar; *(time)* ganar, ahorrarse; *(one's strength)* ahorrar, escati-

mar; DEP. parar; TEO. salvar ♦ **God s. the Queen!** ¡Dios guarde a la Reina! • **s. it!** JER. ¡basta!, ¡déjalo! • **to s. face** salvar las apariencias • **to s. one's breath** ahorrar saliva, no gastar saliva • **to s. oneself the trouble** ahorrarse la molestia • **to s. the day** salvar la situación —intr. ahorrar ♦ **to s. up** ahorrar II. s. DEP. parada.
save² (sāv) I. prep. salvo, excepto II. conj. a no ser que ♦ **s. for** excepto por, salvo por • **s. that** a menos que, si no fuera porque.
save·a·ble (sā′və-bəl) adj. var. de **savable.**
save·all (sāv′ôl′) s. apuracabos *m*.
sav·er (sā′vər) s. *(of lives)* salvador *m*; *(of money)* ahorrador *m*.
sav·ing (sā′vĭng) I. s. *(rescue)* salvamento; *(economy)* economía, ahorro *<a ten-dollar s.* un ahorro de diez dólares>; DER. salvedad *f* ♦ **savings** ahorros II. prep. & conj. salvo, exepto.
savings account s. cuenta de ahorros.
savings bank s. caja de ahorros.
sav·ior (sāv′yər) s. salvador ♦ **the S.** RELIG. el Salvador, el Redentor.
sa·vor (sā′vər) I. s. *(taste)* sabor *m*, gusto; *(smell)* olor *m*, aroma *m*; FIG. *(element)* sabor II. intr. saber, oler.
sa·vor·y¹ (sā′və-rē) adj. *(appetizing)* sabroso; *(piquant)* picante; *(inoffensive)* inofensivo.
sa·vor·y² (sā′və-rē) s. [pl. -ies] BOT. ajedrea.
sa·vour (sā′vər) s. & v. G.B. var. de **savor.**
sav·vy (săv′ē) JER. I. intr. -vied, -vy·ing JER. comprender, entender II. s. *(good sense)* entendimiento, sentido común; *(know-how)* saber cómo se hace algo *m* III. adj. -vi·er, -vi·est con sentido común, práctico.
saw¹ (sô) I. s. *(handsaw)* serrucho; *(machine)* sierra II. tr. **sawed, sawed** *o* **sawn** (sôn), **saw·ing** aserrar, serrar.
saw² (sô) s. *(saying)* dicho; *(proverb)* proverbio, refrán *m* ♦ **old s.** viejo dicho.
saw³ (sô) pret. de **see¹.**
saw·buck (sô′bŭk′) s. JER. *(bill)* billete de diez dólares *m*; CARP. burro.
saw·dust (sô′dŭst′) s. aserrín *m*, serrín *m*.
sawed-off (sôd′ôf′) adj. *(shortened)* cortado; JER. *(short)* pequeño, diminuto ♦ **s. shotgun** ARM. escopeta de cañones cortados.
saw·fish (sô′fĭsh′) s. [pl. sawfish *o* -fish·es] pez sierra *m*.
saw·horse (sô′hôrs′) s. CARP. burro.
saw·mill (sô′mĭl′) s. aserradero, serrería.
sawn (sôn) part. p. de **saw¹.**
saw-toothed (sô′tŏŏtht′) adj. serrado.
saw·yer (sô′yər) s. *(person)* aserrador *m*; ENTOM. termes *m*, comején *m*.
sax (săks) s. FAM. saxófono.
sax·horn (săks′hôrn′) s. MÚS. bombardino.
Sax·on (săk′sən) s. & adj. HIST. *(Germanic people)* sajón *m*; *(Anglo-Saxon)* anglosajón *m*.
sax·o·phone (săk′sə-fōn′) s. saxofón *m*, saxófono.
say (sā) I. tr. **said** (sĕd), **say·ing** *(to utter aloud)* decir *<what did you s.?* ¿qué dijiste?>; *(to state)* decir, afirmar; *(to communicate)* decir; *(mass)* decir; *(prayer)* rezar; *(to indicate)* indicar, marcar *<the clock says it's 5:00* el reloj marca las cinco>; *(to suppose)* suponer, asumir *<let's s. that you are right* supongamos que tienes razón> ♦ **as they s.** como dicen • **enough said!** ¡basta! • **I'll s.!** ¡ya lo creo! • **it goes without saying** huelga decir, es obvio • **it is easier said than done** es más fácil decirlo que hacerlo • **it is said** se dice, se rumorea • **let's s.** digamos • **no sooner said than done** dicho y hecho • **not to s.** por no decir *<it is difficult, not to s. impossible* es difícil, por no decir imposible> • **s.!** ¡oiga! • **saying and doing** decir y hacer • **s. no more!** ¡no me digas más!, ¡ni una palabra más! • **so to s.** por así decirlo • **that is to s.** o sea, es decir • **there is no saying** es imposible decir • **they s. that . . .** dicen que . . . • **to s. good-bye to someone** despedirse de alguien • **to s. good morning to someone** darle los buenos días a alguien • **to s. nothing of** por no hablar de, por no mencionar • **to s. (over) again** volver a decir, repetir • **to s. the least** por lo menos, si no hay algo peor • **to s. the word** dar la orden • **to s. to oneself** decir para sí • **what do you s.?** ¿qué te

parece? • **when all is said and done** al fin y al cabo • **you can s. that again!** ¡ya lo creo! • **you don't s.!** ¡no me digas! • **you said it!** ¡dímelo a mí!, ¡tú lo has dicho! —intr. hablar **II.** s. *(opinion)* voz f, opinión f <*he had no s. in the matter* él no tuvo ninguna voz en el asunto>; *(turn to speak)* uso de la palabra **III.** adv. *(approximately)* aproximadamente <*there were, s., five hundred people present* había, aproximadamente, quinientas personas presentes>; *(for instance)* por ejemplo <*a woodwind, s. an oboe* un instrumento de viento, un oboe por ejemplo>.

say·ing (sā′ĭng) s. dicho, refrán m.

say-so (sā′sō′) s. [pl. **-sos**] FAM. *(assertion)* afirmación f; *(judgment)* opinión f; *(power)* poder m; *(authority)* autoridad f; *(word)* palabra.

scab (skăb) **I.** s. *(worker)* obrero que se niega a sindicarse; *(strikebreaker)* esquirol m, rompehuelgas m; *(scoundrel)* canalla m, sinvergüenza mf; MED. costra, postilla; BOT., VET. roña, escabro **II.** intr. **scabbed, scab·bing** FAM. *(to take a job)* sustituir a un huelguista; MED. formar costra.

scab·bard (skăb′ərd) **I.** s. vaina, funda **II.** tr. envainar, enfundar.

scab·by (skăb′ē) adj. **-bi·er, -bi·est** *(with scabs)* costroso; FAM. *(vile)* vil, despreciable; VET. roñoso.

sca·bies (skā′bēz′) s. [pl. **scabies**] MED., VET. sarna.

scab·rous (skăb′rəs, skā′brəs) adj. escabroso.

scads (skădz) s.pl. FAM. montones m <*s. of money* montones de dinero>.

scaf·fold (skăf′əld) **I.** s. *(for workers)* andamio; *(for executions)* cadalso, patíbulo **II.** tr. poner un andamio a.

scaf·fold·ing (skăf′əl-dĭng) s. andamiaje m.

sca·lar (skā′lər) **I.** s. número escalar **II.** adj. escalar.

scal·a·wag (skăl′ə-wăg′) s. FAM. pícaro, bribón m.

scald (skôld) **I.** tr. *(to scorch)* escaldar; CUL. *(vegetables)* escaldar; *(milk)* calentar casi hasta el hervor —intr. escaldarse **II.** s. BOT., MED. escaldadura.

scald·ing (skôl′dĭng) adj. hirviente, hirviendo.

scale¹ (skāl) **I.** s. *(flake)* escama <*s. of rust* escama de moho>; *(of oxide)* capa de óxido; *(of kettle, pipe)* incrustaciones f; BOT., MED., ZOOL. escama **II.** tr. **scaled, scal·ing** *(fish)* quitar las escamas a, escamar; *(over water)* hacer rebotar —intr. ♦ **to s. off** *(skin)* pelarse; *(paint)* descascararse ♦ **to s. up** cubrirse de incrustaciones.

scale² (skāl) **I.** s. *(proportion)* escala, proporción f; *(level)* escala <*on a grand s.* en gran escala>; *(classification)* escala <*sliding s.* escala móvil>; MAT., MÚS. escala ♦ **to pay s.** COM. pagar el sueldo establecido por el sindicato **II.** tr. **scaled, scal·ing** *(wall, mountain)* escalar; *(to adjust)* adaptar, ajustar; *(logs, trees)* medir; *(to proportion)* hacer a escala ♦ **to s. down** reducir a escala • **to s. up** aumentar a escala.

scale³ (skāl) **I.** s. *(balance)* balanza, báscula; *(tray of a balance)* platillo (de balanza) **II.** tr. & intr. **scaled, scal·ing** pesar.

scaled (skāld) adj. escamoso.

sca·lene (skā′lēn′, skā-lēn′) s. GEOM. escaleno.

scal·ing (skā′lĭng) s. *(climbing)* escalada; *(adjustment)* ajuste m.

scal·lion (skăl′yən) s. *(young onion)* cebollino; *(shallot)* escalonia, chalote m.

scal·lop (skŏl′əp, skăl′-) **I.** s. *(mollusk)* venera, vieira; *(of meat)* escalope m; *(frill)* festón m; onda m **II.** tr. COST. festonear, ondular; CUL. *(to bake)* guisar al gratén; *(to cut)* cortar (carne) en escalopes.

scal·ly·wag (skăl′ē-wăg′) s. var. de **scalawag.**

scalp (skălp) **I.** s. HIST. *(trophy)* escalpe m, escalpo; ANAT. cuero cabelludo ♦ **to be out for someone's s.** pedir la cabeza de alguien **II.** tr. HIST. *(to cut)* escalpar, quitar el cuero cabelludo; FAM. *(tickets)* revender; *(stocks, bonds)* especular con o en —intr. FAM. dedicarse a la reventa.

scal·pel (skăl′pəl) s. CIR. escalpelo, bisturí m.

scalp·er (skăl′pər) s. *(of bonds)* especulador m; *(of tickets)* revendedor m.

scal·y (skā′lē) adj. **-i·er, -i·est** *(with scales)* escamoso; JER. *(mean)* mezquino; *(despicable)* despreciable.

scam (skăm) s. JER. estafa, trampa.

scamp¹ (skămp) s. pícaro.

scamp² (skămp) tr. ejecutar descuidadamente, chapucear.

scam·per (skăm′pər) **I.** intr. corretear **II.** s. correteo.

scan (skăn) **I.** tr. **scanned, scan·ning** *(to examine)* escudriñar, explorar; *(to look around)* recorrer con la mirada; *(to glance at)* ojear, echar un vistazo a; *(to measure verse)* escandir; ELECTRÓN. registrar, explorar —intr. ELECTRÓN. registrar, explorar; POÉT. escandir ♦ **to s. o s. well** estar bien medido (verso) **II.** s. *(examination)* escudriñamiento; *(field of vision)* radio de visión.

scan·dal (skăn′dl) s. *(disgrace)* escándalo; *(gossip)* chismorreo, habladurías.

scan·dal·ize (skăn′dl-īz′) tr. **-ized, -iz·ing** escandalizar.

scan·dal·mon·ger (skăn′dl-mŭng′gər, -mŏng′-) s. murmurador m, propagador de escándalos m.

scan·dal·ous (skăn′dl-əs) adj. *(shocking)* escandaloso; *(defamatory)* difamatorio, injuriante.

Scan·di·na·vi·a (skăn′də-nā′vē-ə) s. Escandinavia.

Scan·di·na·vi·an (skăn′də-nā′vē-ən) adj. & s. escandinavo.

scan·di·um (skăn′dē-əm) s. QUÍM. escandio.

scan·ner (skăn′ər) s. TELEV. dispositivo explorador; ELECTRÓN. antena giratoria; MED. tomógrafo.

scan·ning (skăn′ĭng) s. exploración f.

scan·sion (skăn′shən) s. POÉT. escansión (medición del verso) f.

scant (skănt) **I.** adj. **-er, -est** escaso ♦ **to be s. of** tener poco **II.** tr. escatimar.

scant·i·ly (skăn′tl-ē) adv. escasamente.

scant·i·ness (skăn′tē-nĭs) s. escasez f.

scant·y (skăn′tē) adj. **-i·er, -i·est** *(barely sufficient)* escaso; *(small)* pequeño.

scape·goat (skāp′gōt′) s. *(person)* cabeza de turco, víctima propiciatoria; BÍBL. chivo expiatorio.

scap·u·la (skăp′yə-lə) s. [pl. **-las** o **-lae** (-lē′)] ANAT. escápula, omóplato.

scap·u·lar (skăp′yə-lər) **I.** s. RELIG. escapulario; ORNIT. pluma escapular **II.** adj. ANAT. escapular.

scar¹ (skär) **I.** s. *(mark)* cicatriz f **II.** tr. **scarred, scar·ring** *(a surface)* señalar; *(the skin)* dejar una cicatriz en —intr. cicatrizar(se).

scar² (skär) s. *(rock)* farallón m, peñón m.

scar·ab (skăr′əb) s. escarabajo.

scarce (skârs) adj. **scarc·er, scarc·est** *(rare)* raro; *(insufficient)* escaso ♦ **to become s.** escasear.

scarce·ly (skârs′lē) adv. *(barely)* apenas <*we can s. see the other shore* apenas podemos ver la otra orilla>; *(hardly)* casi no; *(surely not)* seguramente no ♦ **s. ever** casi nunca.

scar·ci·ty (skâr′sĭ-tē) s. [pl. **-ties**] *(shortage)* escasez f; *(rarity)* rareza.

scare (skâr) **I.** tr. **scared, scar·ing** asustar, espantar ♦ **I was scared by the thunder** me asustó el trueno • **to be scared of** asustarse de, tener miedo de • **to be scared stiff** o **to death** estar muerto de miedo, tener un miedo espantoso • **to s. away** o **off** espantar, ahuyentar • **to s. to death** dar un miedo espantoso —intr. asustarse **II.** s. *(fear)* miedo; *(panic)* pánico; *(alarm)* alarma ♦ **you gave me quite a s.!** ¡qué susto me has dado!

scare·crow (skâr′krō′) s. *(figure)* espantapájaros m, espantajo; FIG. *(scary thing)* espantajo; *(haggard person)* espantajo, esperpento.

scare·mon·ger (skâr′mŭng′gər) s. alarmista mf.

scarf¹ (skärf) s. [pl. **scarfs** o **scarves** (skärvz)] *(muffler)* bufanda; *(kerchief)* pañuelo <*silk s.* pañuelo de seda>; *(runner)* tapete m; MIL. banda.

scarf² (skärf) CARP. **I.** s. [pl. **scarfs**] ♦ **s. o s. joint** empalme **II.** tr. empalmar.

scarf·skin (skärf′skĭn′) s. ANAT. epidermis f.

scar·i·fi·ca·tion (skăr′ə-fĭ-kā′shən) s. escarificación f.

scar·i·fy¹ (skăr′ə-fī′) tr. **-fied, -fy·ing** *(the skin, topsoil)* escarificar; *(to criticize)* criticar severamente.

scar·i·fy² (skăr′ə-fī′) tr. **-fied, -fy·ing** asustar, espantar.

scar·la·ti·na (skär′lə-tē′nə) s. MED. escarlatina.

scar·let (skär′lĭt) s. & adj. escarlata ♦ **s. woman** HIST., HUM. mujer de mala vida.

scarlet fever s. MED. escarlatina.

scarp (skärp) s. escarpa.

scarves (skärvz) un pl. de **scarf¹.**

scar·y (skâr′ē) adj. -i·er, -i·est *(frightening)* espantoso, pavoroso; *(alarming)* alarmante; *(easily scared)* asustadizo.

scat¹ (skăt) intr. **scat·ted, scat·ting** FAM. largarse ♦ **scat!** ¡lárgate!, ¡vete!

scat² (skăt) s. MÚS. improvisación vocal en jazz *f.*

scathe (skā*th*) tr. **scathed, scath·ing** *(to scorch)* abrasar; FIG. *(to criticize)* vituperar, fustigar.

scath·ing (skā′*th*ĭng) adj. severísimo.

sca·tol·o·gy (skă-tŏl′ə-jē) s. escatología.

scat·ter (skăt′ər) I. tr. *(to disperse)* dispersar; *(to strew)* esparcir, desparramar; FÍS. dispersar —intr. dispersarse II. s. *(dispersion)* dispersión *f*; *(handful)* puñado.

scat·ter·brain (skăt′ər-brān′) s. FAM. cabeza de chorlito.

scat·ter·brained (skăt′ər-brānd′) adj. ligero de cascos, atolondrado.

scat·ter·ing (skăt′ər-ĭng) I. s. *(of people, things)* dispersión *f*, esparcimiento; FÍS. dispersión ♦ **a s. of** unos pocos, unos cuantos II. adj. disperso.

scav·enge (skăv′ənj) tr. **-enged, -eng·ing** *(to salvage)* recoger (basura); *(to pick over)* buscar entre (desechos); *(to find)* encontrar entre la basura; MAQ. expulsar (gases); METAL. limpiar —intr. buscar en la basura.

scav·en·ger (skăv′ən-jər) s. *(person)* trapero; ZOOL. animal que se alimenta de carroña *m*; QUÍM. eliminador *m*.

sce·nar·i·o (sĭ-nâr′ē-ō′) s. [pl. -os] TEAT. argumento; CINEM. guión *m.*

sce·nar·ist (sĭ-nâr′ĭst) s. CINEM. guionista *mf.*

scene (sēn) s. *(place)* lugar, escenario <*the s. of an accident* el lugar de un accidente>; *(view, setting)* escena; CINEM., TEAT. escena; *(display)* escena <*he made a s. in public* hizo una escena en público>; JER. *(sphere)* mundo, medio; *(situation)* situación *f* <*a bad s.* una mala situación> ♦ **behind the scenes** *(backstage)* entre bastidores; *(in private)* en privado • **to come on the s.** aparecer.

scen·er·y (sē′nə-rē) s. [pl. -ies] *(landscape)* paisaje *m*, vista; TEAT. decorado.

sce·nic (sē′nĭk) adj. *(of a landscape)* del paisaje; *(picturesque)* pintoresco; TEAT. escénico; *(dramatic)* dramático.

scent (sĕnt) I. s. *(smell)* olor *m*; *(trail)* rastro, pista; *(sense of smell)* olfato; *(inkling)* indicio ♦ **to pick up the s.** encontrar la pista, hallar el rastro • **to throw off the s.** despistar II. tr. *(to smell)* oler, olfatear; FIG. *(to sense)* olfatear, presentir <*to s. danger* olfatear un peligro>; *(to perfume)* perfumar —intr. olfatear.

scep·ter (sĕp′tər) I. s. cetro II. tr. investir de autoridad real.

scep·tic (skĕp′tĭk) s. var. de **skeptic.**

scep·ti·cal (skĕp′tĭ-kəl) adj. var. de **skeptical.**

sched·ule (skĕj′ōōl) I. s. *(program)* programa *m*; *(timetable)* horario <*train s.* horario de trenes>; *(over a period of time)* calendario, agenda; *(plan)* plan *m* <*production s.* plan de producción>; *(list)* lista, inventario; *(appendix)* apéndice *m* ♦ **to arrive on s.** llegar a la hora • **to be behind s.** *(train, plane)* llevar retraso; *(work, project)* estar atrasado • **to go according to s.** desarrollarse como estaba previsto, no tener retraso II. tr. **-uled, -ul·ing** *(train, plane)* fijar el horario de; *(meeting, production)* programar ♦ **to be scheduled** estar programado, estar previsto.

sche·ma (skē′mə) s. [pl. -ma·ta (-mə-tə)] *(outline)* esquema *m*; *(plan)* plan *m*, proyecto.

sche·mat·ic (skē-măt′ĭk) I. adj. esquemático II. s. esquema *m.*

scheme (skēm) I. s. *(plan)* plan *m*, proyecto; *(system)* sistema *m*, procedimiento; *(plot)* estratagema *f*, ardid *m*; *(outline)* esquema *m*; *(arrangement)* combinación *f* <*color s.* combinación de colores> II. tr. **schemed, schem·ing** *(to plan)* planear; *(to plot)* tramar —intr. conspirar.

schem·er (skē′mər) s. intrigante *mf.*

schil·ling (shĭl′ĭng) s. FIN. chelín *m.*

schism (sĭz′əm, skĭz′-) s. POL. escisión *f*; RELIG. cisma *m.*

schis·mat·ic (sĭz-măt′ĭk, skĭz-) adj. cismático.

schist (shĭst) s. MIN. esquisto.

schis·to·so·mi·a·sis (shĭs′tə-sō-mī′ə-sĭs) s. MED. esquistosomiasis *f.*

schiz·o (skĭt′sō) s. [pl. -os] JER. esquizofrénico.

schiz·oid (skĭt′soid′) adj. & s. PSIC. esquizofrénico.

schiz·o·phre·ni·a (skĭt′sə-frē′nē-ə) s. PSIC. esquizofrenia.

schiz·y (skĭt′sē) adj. -i·er, -i·est JER. chiflado, loco.

schmaltz *o* **schmalz** (shmälts) s. JER. *(music)* música sentimental; *(sentimentality)* sensiblería.

schnapps (shnäps, shnăps) s. aguardiente *m.*

schol·ar (skŏl′ər) s. *(erudite person)* erudito, sabio; *(specialist)* especialista *mf*; *(student)* alumno, estudiante *mf*; *(scholarship holder)* becario.

schol·ar·ly (skŏl′ər-lē) adj. erudito.

schol·ar·ship (skŏl′ər-shĭp′) s. *(learning, knowledge)* erudición *f*; *(financial aid)* beca.

scho·las·tic (skə-lăs′tĭk) I. adj. *(of schools)* escolar; *(academic)* académico; *(pedantic)* pedante ♦ **S.** FILOS. escolástico II. s. pedante *mf* ♦ **S.** FILOS. escolástico.

scho·las·ti·cism (skə-lăs′tĭ-sĭz′əm) s. escolatiscismo ♦ **S.** FILOS., TEO. escolasticismo, escolástica.

school¹ (skōōl) I. s. *(for children)* escuela; *(for teens)* instituto, colegio; *(college, university)* universidad *f*; *(division of university)* facultad *f* <*law s.* facultad de derecho>; *(class)* clase *f* <*to miss s.* faltar a clase>; *(students)* alumnado, estudiantado; *(style)* escuela <*s. of painting* escuela de pintura>; *(conventions)* escuela <*to be of the old s.* ser de la vieja escuela>; *(learning place)* escuela <*the s. of hard knocks* la escuela del infortunio>; MIL. reglamento ♦ **business s.** *(commercial)* escuela de comercio; *(in university)* facultad de ciencias económicas • **driving s.** escuela para aprender a conducir • **military s.** academia militar • **night s.** escuela nocturna • **s. of thought** escuela filosófica, pensamiento • **s. year** año escolar • **secretarial s.** escuela de secretariado • **summer s.** curso(s) de verano • **Sunday s.** RELIG. escuela dominical • **to teach s.** ser profesor *o* maestro • **too young for s.** demasiado joven para ir a la escuela II. tr. *(to educate)* educar; *(to train)* disciplinar ♦ **to s. oneself** disciplinarse • **to s. oneself in (patience)** aprender a ser (paciente).

school² (skōōl) I. s. *(of fish)* cardumen *m*, banco II. intr. *(to swim)* nadar en cardúmenes (los peces).

school age s. edad escolar *f.*

school·book (skōōl′bŏŏk′) s. libro de texto.

school·boy (skōōl′boi′) s. alumno, colegial *m.*

schooled (skōōld) adj. educado.

school·girl (skōōl′gûrl′) s. alumna, colegiala.

school·house (skōōl′hous′) s. colegio, escuela.

school·ing (skōō′lĭng) s. *(instruction)* instrucción *f*, educación *f*; *(training)* entrenamiento.

school·marm (skōōl′märm′) *o* **school·ma'am** (-mäm′, -măm′) s. FAM. maestra anticuada.

school·mas·ter (skōōl′măs′tər) s. *(teacher)* maestro; ICT. pargo.

school·mate (skōōl′māt′) s. compañero de escuela.

school·mis·tress (skōōl′mĭs′trĭs) s. maestra.

school·room (skōōl′rōōm′, -rŏŏm′) s. aula, sala de clase.

school·teach·er (skōōl′tē′chər) s. maestro, maestra.

schoo·ner (skōō′nər) s. *(glass)* jarra, tarro (de cerveza); MARÍT. goleta.

schwa (shwä) s. FONÉT. símbolo de vocal inacentuada.

sci·at·ic (sī-ăt′ĭk) adj. ANAT., MED. ciático.

sci·at·i·ca (sī-ăt′ĭ-kə) s. MED. ciática.

sci·ence (sī′əns) s. ciencia.

science fiction s. ciencia ficción.

sci·en·tif·ic (sī′ən-tĭf′ĭk) adj. científico.

sci·en·tif·i·cal·ly (sī′ən-tĭf′ĭ-kə-lē) adv. científicamente.

scientific method s. método *o* procedimiento científico.

sci·en·tist (sī′ən-tĭst) s. científico.

sci-fi (sī′fī′) s. FAM. ciencia ficción.

scim·i·tar (sĭm′ĭ-tər) s. cimitarra.

scin·til·la (sĭn-tĭl′ə) s. vestigio, huella.

scin·til·late (sĭn′tl-āt′) intr. **-lat·ed, -lat·ing** *(to sparkle)* chispear; *(to twinkle)* centellear —tr. echar (chispazos, centellas).

scin·til·la·tion (sĭn′tl-ā′shən) s. *(action)* centelleo; ASTRON. titilación *f*; FÍS. centelleo.

sci·on (sī′ən) s. *(descendant)* descendiente *mf*, vástago; BOT. *(shoot)* púa.

scis·sion (sĭzh′ən, sĭsh′-) s. escisión *f.*

scis·sor (sĭz′ər) tr. cortar con tijeras.

ã rey / ä año / b boca / ch chico / d dar / ĕ el / ē mil / g gato / h joya / hw juez / ī aire / k casa / kw cuan /

scis·sors (sĭz′ərz) s.pl. tijeras *f* ♦ **a pair of s.** (unas) tijeras • **s. hold** DEP. tijera, tijereta • **s. jump** DEP. salto de tijera.
scissors kick s. DEP. tijereta.
scle·ro·ma (sklə-rō′mə) s. [pl. **-ma·ta**] MED. escleroma.
scle·ro·sis (sklə-rō′sĭs) s. ˙MED. esclerosis *f.*
scle·rot·ic (sklə-rŏt′ĭk) I. adj. esclerótico II. s. esclerótica.
scoff (skŏf) I. intr. & tr. mofarse (de), burlarse (de) II. s. mofa, burla.
scoff·er (skŏf′ər) s. mofador *m*, burlón *m.*
scoff·law (skŏf′lô′) s. persona que burla la ley.
scold (skōld) I. intr. & tr. regañar, reprender II. s. regañón *m.*
scold·ing (skōl′dĭng) s. regaño ♦ **to give a s.** regañar.
scol·lop (skŏl′əp) s. & v. var. de **scallop.**
sconce¹ (skŏns) s. MIL. fortín *m.*
sconce² (skŏns) s. candelabro de pared.
scone (skōn, skŏn) s. bizcocho, galleta.
scoop (sko͞op) I. s. *(ladle)* cucharón *m*; *(for ice cream)* pinzas *f*; *(amount)* cucharadas; PERIOD., JER. noticia sensacional; CIR. legra; MAQ. *(of shovel)* cuchara; *(of dredge)* cangilón *m* II. tr. ♦ **to s. into** meter en • **to s. out** MARÍT. *(with a bucket)* achicar; *(with the hands, paws)* cavar; *(with a spoon)* excavar, cavar, sacar • **to s. up** *(with the hands)* coger; *(with a spoon)* sacar.
scoop·er (sko͞o′pər) s. *(tool)* gubia; ORNIT. avoceta.
scoot (sko͞ot) intr. andar rápidamente.
scoot·er (sko͞o′tər) s. *(child's vehicle)* patineta; *(motor vehicle)* motoneta.
scope (skōp) s. *(area)* esfera, ámbito <*not within the s. of our investigations* fuera del ámbito de nuestras investigaciones>; *(extent)* amplitud *f*; *(reach)* alcance *m*; *(freedom)* libertad *f* <*they give me plenty of s. in my work* me dan mucha libertad en mi trabajo>; FAM. *(instrument)* instrumento de observación (esp. microscopio).
scorch (skôrch) I. tr. *(to burn)* quemar; *(to censure)* censurar, criticar *(to burn)* quemarse II. s. quemadura.
scorch·er (skôr′chər) s. FAM. día abrasador *m*, día excesivamente caluroso.
score (skôr) I. s. *(notch)* muesca; *(line)* raya; *(scratch)* arañazo; *(twenty)* veintena; DEP. tanteo, tantos; EDUC. calificación *f*, nota; MÚS. *(composition)* partitura; *(music)* música ♦ **final s.** DEP. resultado • **on that s.** en cuanto a eso, a ese respecto • **scores of** muchos, montones de • **to keep s.** apuntar los tantos • **to know the score** FIG., FAM. *(the facts)* conocer el percal; *(the tricks)* sabérselas todas • **to settle the s.** ajustar cuentas II. tr. **scored, scor·ing** *(to notch)* hacer una muesca en; *(to mark off)* apuntar (mediante rayas) en; *(to scratch)* rayar; *(to cross out)* tachar; DEP. *(to gain)* marcar <*to s. two points* marcar dos tantos>; *(to count as)* valer <*a touchdown scores six points* un tanto vale seis puntos>; *(to win)* lograr, conseguir (éxito victoria); *(to berate)* regañar, reprender; FAM. *(to get)* lograr, conseguir (drogas, billetes); EDUC. *(to get)* sacar (nota); *(to grade)* calificar; MÚS. *(to orchestrate)* orquestar; *(to arrange)* arreglar —intr. FAM. *(to win)* tener éxito; *(to seduce sexually)* lograr tener relaciones sexuales; DEP. *(to make a point)* marcar un tanto; *(to keep score)* tantear.
score·board (skôr′bôrd′) s. DEP. marcador *m*, tanteador *m.*
score·card (skôr′kärd′) s. DEP. tanteador *m.*
score·keep·er (skôr′kē′pər) s. DEP. tanteador *m.*
score·less (skôr′lĭs) adj. DEP. sin tantos.
scor·er (skôr′ər) s. *(scorekeeper)* tanteador *m*; *(player)* jugador que marca tantos; *(in soccer)* goleador *m*; *(thing that notches)* marcador *m.*
sco·ri·a (skôr′ē-ə) s. [pl. **-ri·ae** (-rē-ē′)] escoria.
scor·ing (skôr′ĭng) s. *(in sports)* tanteo; *(scratching)* rayado; *(incision)* incisión *f*; EDUC. nota, calificación *f*; MÚS. orquestación *f.*
scorn (skôrn) I. s. desprecio, menosprecio ♦ **he's the s. of the team** el equipo le desprecia II. tr. despreciar ♦ **to s. to do** no dignarse hacer —intr. mofarse, burlarse.
scorn·ful (skôrn′fəl) adj. desdeñoso.
Scor·pi·o (skôr′pē-ō′) s. ASTROL. Escorpión *m.*
scor·pi·on (skôr′pē-ən) s. escorpión *m.*
Scor·pi·us (skôr′pē-əs) s. ASTROL. Escorpión *m.*

Scot (skŏt) s. escocés *m.*
scotch¹ (skŏch) I. tr. *(to injure)* herir (ligeramente); *(to thwart)* frustrar; *(to suppress)* suprimir II. s. *(wound)* herida; *(line)* raya, muesca.
scotch² (skŏch) I. tr. *(a wheel)* calzar II. s. calza, cuña (para ruedas).
Scotch (skŏch) I. adj. *(of Scotland)* escocés; *(frugal)* frugal II. s. whisky escocés *m* ♦ **the S.** los escoceses.
scot-free (skŏt′frē′) adj. *(from obligation)* sin pagar; *(from punishment)* sin castigo.
Scot·land (skŏt′lənd) s. Escocia.
Scots (skŏts) I. adj. *(Scottish)* escocés II. s. *(dialect)* escocés *m.*
Scots·man (skŏts′mən) s. [pl. **-men**] escocés *m.*
Scots·wom·an (skŏts′wo͝om′ən) s. [pl. **-wom·en** (-wĭm′ĭn)] escocesa.
Scot·tish (skŏt′ĭsh) I. adj. escocés II. s. [pl. **Scottish**] escocés *m* ♦ **the S.** los escoceses.
scoun·drel (skoun′drəl) s. bribón *m*, canalla *m.*
scour¹ (skour) I. tr. *(pots, sink)* fregar, restregar; *(wool)* limpiar; *(wheat)* cribar; *(land)* desbrozar; *(pipe)* baldear; GEOL. derrubiar —intr. VET. tener diarrea II. s. *(scrubbing)* restregón *m*, fregado; *(of land)* desbrozo; *(for wool)* detergente *m*; GEOL. lugar derrubiado ♦ **scours** VET. diarrea.
scour² (skour) tr. *(to search)* batir; *(to range over)* recorrer —intr. *(to run)* correr • **to s. after** correr en busca de>.
scourge (skûrj) I. s. azote *m* II. tr. **scourged, scourg·ing** azotar, flagelar.
scour·ings (skou′rĭngz) s.pl. *(refuse)* basura; FIG. *(scum)* heces *f*, escoria.
scout¹ (skout) I. tr. *(to reconnoiter)* reconocer, explorar; *(to evaluate)* evaluar (talento de persona) ♦ **to s. for** buscar personas de talento para —intr. buscar ♦ **to s. around for** hacer una batida por II. s. *(act)* reconocimiento, exploración *f*; *(talent scout)* descubridor de personas de talento *m*; FAM. *(fellow)* sujeto, tipo; MIL. explorador *m* ♦ **s. o boy s.** niño explorador • **s. plane** MIL. avión de reconocimiento.
scout² (skout) tr. rechazar con desprecio, desdeñar —intr. burlarse.
scout·ing (skou′tĭng) s. actividades de los niños exploradores *f.*
scout·mas·ter (skout′măs′tər) s. jefe de niños exploradores *m.*
scow (skou) s. MARÍT. chalana.
scowl (skoul) I. intr. fruncir el ceño —tr. decir frunciendo el ceño II. s. ceño.
scrab·ble (skrăb′əl) I. intr. & tr. **-bled, -bling** garrapatear II. s. garrapato.
scrag (skrăg) I. s. *(person)* persona esquelética; *(animal)* animal esquelético; *(meat)* pescuezo; JER. *(neck)* pescuezo II. tr. **scragged, scrag·ging** FAM. torcer el pescuezo a.
scrag·gly (skrăg′lē) adj. **-gli·er, -gli·est** *(unkempt)* desaseado; *(sparse)* ralo.
scrag·gy (skrăg′ē) adj. **-gi·er, -gi·est** *(rough)* áspero; *(lean)* flaco.
scram (skrăm) intr. **scrammed, scram·ming** FAM. largarse.
scram·ble (skrăm′bəl) I. intr. **-bled, -bling** *(on hands and knees)* gatear; *(to climb)* trepar; AVIA., MIL. despegar ♦ **to s. out** salir a gatas • **to s. up** trepar —tr. *(to mix)* mezclar; *(to jumble)* revolver; *(to gather)* recoger; CUL. revolver; ELECTRÓN. perturbar ♦ **to s. for** pelearse por o para • **to s. into one's clothes** vestirse rápidamente • **to s. over** o **through** gatear por • **s. together** mezclar II. s. *(walk)* camino difícil; *(struggle)* pelea, lucha <*a s. for power* una lucha por el poder>; AVIA., MIL. despegue *m.*
scrambled eggs s.pl. huevos revueltos *m.*
scram·bler (skrăm′blər) s. RAD. aparato para perturbar las emisiones radiofónicas.
scrap¹ (skrăp) I. s. *(of food, paper)* pedazo, trozo; *(of truth)* ápice *m*; *(of evidence)* pizca, chispa; *(waste)* desperdicios; *(of fabric)* retal *m* ♦ **s. o s. iron** o **s. metal** INDUS. chatarra • **scraps** *(of food)* sobras, restos; *(of fried fat)* chicharrones; *(waste)* desechos II. tr. **scrapped, scrap·ping** *(to dis-*

card) desechar; INDUS. *(ships)* desguazar; *(machines)* desmontar.
scrap² (skrăp) JER. **I.** intr. **scrapped, scrap·ping** pelearse **II. s.** pelea.
scrap·book (skrăp'book') s. albúm de recortes *m.*
scrape (skrāp) **I.** tr. **scraped, scrap·ing** *(a fender, knee)* raspar, arañar; *(shoes, boots)* limpiar; CUL. rallar ♦ **to s. off** *o* **out** quitar (raspando) • **to s. together** *o* **up** lograr reunir —intr. *(to graze)* rozar; *(to scrimp)* ahorrar, hacer economías ♦ **to s. by** ir tirando, arreglárselas • **to s. through** aprobar a duras penas (examen) **II. s.** *(act)* raspado; *(sound)* chirrido; *(on skin)* rasguño; *(scuffle)* riña, pelea.
scrap·er (skrā'pər) s. rascador *m*, raspador *m.*
scrap heap s. *(heap)* montón de chatarra *m*; *(place)* basurero.
scrap·py¹ (skrăp'ē) adj. **-pi·er, -pi·est** fragmentario, incompleto.
scrap·py² (skrăp'ē) adj. **-pi·er, -pi·est** peleador *m.*
scratch (skrăch) **I.** tr. *(to mark)* rayar; *(to claw)* arañar <*the cat scratched me* el gato me arañó>; *(to rub)* rascarse <*she scratched her head* se rascó la cabeza>; *(to inscribe)* grabar <*he scratched his name on the table* grabó su nombre en la mesa>; *(to scrawl)* garabatear; *(chicken)* escarbar; DEP. *(horse, athlete)* retirar; *(game, race)* cancelar ♦ **to s. one's head** FIG. rascarse la cabeza • **to s. out** *(to cross out)* tachar; *(to poke out)* sacar • **to s. the surface** FIG. *(to consider superficially)* no profundizar mucho; *(to have just started)* haber recién empezado (a hacer, investigar) —intr. *(to claw)* arañar; *(to rub)* rascarse; *(to mark)* rayarse; *(pen)* chirriar; DEP. retirarse **II. s.** *(on surface)* raya; *(on skin)* arañazo; *(scrawl)* garabato; *(sound)* chirrido; JER. *(money)* cuartos, plata; DEP. participante retirado ♦ **from s.** *(from nothing)* de la nada; *(from the beginning)* desde el principio • **to come up to s.** estar a la altura de las circunstancias, satisfacer los requisitos • **to feel up to s.** sentirse en forma **III.** adj. *(done hastily)* improvisado; *(haphazard)* al azar ♦ **s. feed** comida de aves de corral • **s. paper** papel (de) borrador • **s. team** DEP. equipo improvisado.
scratch·pad (skrăch'păd') s. *(paper)* bloc para apuntes *m*; COMPUT. memoria auxiliar.
scratch·y (skrăch'ē) adj. **-i·er, -i·est** *(surface, record)* rayado; *(fabric, undergrowth)* que pica; *(sound)* chirriante; *(handwriting)* garabatoso; *(pen)* que raspea.
scrawl (skrôl) tr. & intr. garabatear.
scraw·ny (skrô'nē) adj. **-ni·er, -ni·est** flacucho.
scream (skrēm) **I.** intr. *(person)* chillar, gritar; *(headlines, color)* ser llamativo ♦ **it's enough to make you s.** es para pegarse un tiro • **to s. out in pain** gritar de dolor • **to s. with laughter** matarse de risa, reír a carcajadas —tr. gritar, vociferar **II. s.** *(of a person)* grito, chillido; *(of laughter)* carcajadas ♦ **to be a s.** ser divertidísimo.
scream·er (skrē'mər) s. *(person)* gritón *m*, chillón *m*; *(bird)* ave chillona; JER. *(headline)* titular sensacionalista *m* ♦ **to be a s.** JER. ser graciosísimo, ser divertidísimo.
scream·ing (skrē'mĭng) **I.** s. grito **II.** adj. *(color, clothes)* chillón, llamativo; *(sound)* estridente; FIG. *(very funny)* divertidísimo, graciosísimo.
screech (skrēch) **I.** intr. *(to scream)* chillar; *(to make a shrill noise)* chirriar **II.** s. chillido.
screech owl s. ORNIT. lechuza.
screen (skrēn) **I.** s. *(for privacy)* biombo, mampara; *(for windows)* alambrera; *(for fireplace)* pantalla; *(for sifting)* criba, tamiz *m*; FIG. *(curtain)* cortina; *(cover)* pantalla; TEC. pantalla; IMPR. trama; MIL. *(of troops)* cobertura; *(of planes, ships)* protección *f* ♦ **s. door** puerta de tela metálica **II.** tr. *(to hide)* ocultar; *(to protect)* proteger, resguardar; *(to sift)* cribar, tamizar; *(a porch)* poner una alambrera a; *(one's eyes, face)* protegerse, resguardarse; *(applicants, candidates)* pasar por el tamiz; CINEM. proyectar ♦ **to s. out** descartar.
screen·ing (skrē'nĭng) s. *(wire mesh)* tela metálica; CINEM. proyección *f* ♦ **screenings** cribaduras, cerniduras.
screen·play (skrēn'plā') s. CINEM. guión *m.*
screen test s. CINEM. prueba cinematográfica.
screen·writ·er (skrēn'rī'tər) s. CINEM. guionista *mf.*

screw (skroo) **I.** s. *(turn)* vuelta; JER., VULG. *(intercourse)* polvo; CARP. tornillo ♦ **to have a loose s.** faltarle un tornillo a uno, tener flojos los tornillos • **to put the screws on someone** apretarle las clavijas a alguien **II.** tr. ♦ **s. it!** JER., VULG. ¡que se joda! • **s. you!** JER., VULG. ¡jódete! • **to have one's head screwed on right** FAM. tener la cabeza bien puesta *o* en su sitio • **to s. in** *o* **into** CARP. atornillar, enroscar • **to s. on** tapar • **to s. on** *o* **to** CARP. atornillar • **to s. open** *o* **off** destapar • **to s. out of** FAM. estafar • **to s. over** JER. estafar • **to s. someone** JER. *(to harm)* perjudicar a alguien; *(to cheat)* estafar; JER., VULG. *(to sleep with)* coger *o* joder a alguien • **to s. up** *(to botch)* arruinar, fastidiar; *(one's face)* apretar; *(one's courage)* cobrar (ánimos), armarse de (valentía) —intr. JER., VULG. coger, joder; CARP. *(to turn)* enroscarse; *(to attach)* fijarse atornillando.
screw·ball (skroo'bôl') adj. & s. JER. excéntrico, estrafalario.
screw·driv·er (skroo'drī'vər) s. destornillador *m.*
screwed-up (skrood'ŭp') adj. JER. fastidiado, desbaratado.
screw thread s. rosca de tornillo.
screw-up (skroo'ŭp') s. JER. metedura de pata.
screw·y (skroo'ē) adj. **-i·er, -i·est** JER. *(crazy)* chiflado, descabellado; *(amiss)* impropio, errado.
scrib·ble (skrĭb'əl) **I.** tr. & intr. **-bled, -bling** garabatear **II.** s. garabato.
scrib·bler (skrĭb'lər) s. *(scrawler)* emborronador *m*; *(author)* escritorzuelo.
scribe (skrīb) **I.** s. *(of Jewish law)* escriba *m*; FAM. *(writer)* escritorzuelo; HIST. *(clerk, copyist)* escribiente *m* **II.** tr. **scribed, scrib·ing** escribir con punzón en madera *o* metal.
scrib·er (skrī'bər) s. punzón *m.*
scrim (skrĭm) s. lienzo legero de algodón *o* lino.
scrim·mage (skrĭm'ĭj) **I.** s. *(skirmish)* escaramuza; DEP. entrenamiento **II.** intr. **-maged, -mag·ing** DEP. entrenarse.
scrimp (skrĭmp) intr. hacer economías ♦ **to s. and save** apretarse el cinturón —tr. escatimar.
scrim·shaw (skrĭm'shô') s. talla hecha en una barba de ballena.
scrip¹ (skrĭp) s. *(of paper)* trozo *o* pedazo de papel; *(money)* vale *m.*
scrip² (skrĭp) s. *(certificate)* título provisional de propiedad.
script (skrĭpt) **I.** s. *(handwriting)* caligrafía, letra cursiva; IMPR. letra cursiva; DER. original *m*; CINEM., TELEV. guión *m* **II.** tr. CINEM. hacer un guión de.
scrip·tur·al (skrĭp'chər-əl) adj. escrito ♦ **S.** bíblico.
Scrip·ture (skrĭp'chər) s. *(sacred book)* Sagrada Escritura, Bíblia; *(passage)* pasaje de la Biblia *m* ♦ **Scriptures** Sagradas Escrituras.
script·writ·er (skrĭpt'rī'tər) s. guionista *mf.*
scrod (skrŏd) s. ICT. bacalao.
scrof·u·la (skrŏf'yə-lə) s. MED. escrófula.
scroll (skrōl) s. HIST. rollo de pergamino; ARTE. voluta.
scroll·work (skrōl'wûrk') s. volutas.
Scrooge (skrooj) s. JER. tacaño, avaro.
scro·tum (skrō'təm) s. [pl. **-ta** (-tə) *o* **-tums**] ANAT. escroto.
scrounge (skrounj) tr. **scrounged, scroung·ing** JER. sacar hurgando ♦ **to s. up** conseguir de gorra —intr. gorronear ♦ **to s. around** tr. buscar hurgando.
scrub¹ (skrŭb) **I.** tr. **scrubbed, scrub·bing** *(floor, pans)* fregar; *(clothes)* restregar; *(gases)* depurar; JER. *(to cancel)* anular, cancelar —intr. fregar **II.** s. fregado ♦ **s. brush** cepillo.
scrub² (skrŭb) s. *(shrub)* árbol achaparrado; *(thicket)* matorral *m*; FAM. *(animal)* animal pequeño; *(nobody)* don nadie *m*; DEP. jugador suplente *m* ♦ **s. team** DEP. equipo de reservas.
scrub·ber (skrŭb'ər) s. *(person)* fregón *m*; *(of gases)* depurador *m.*
scrub·bing (skrŭb'ĭng) s. fregado.
scrub·by (skrŭb'ē) adj. **-bi·er, -bi·est** *(covered with scrub)* cubierto de maleza; *(stunted)* achaparrado; *(wretched)* miserable, despreciable.
scrub pine s. BOT. pino.
scrub·wom·an (skrŭb'woom'ən) s. [pl. **-wom·en** (-wĭm'ĭn)] fregona.
scruff (skrŭf) s. nuca, cogote *m.*

ã rey / ä año / b boca / ch chico / d dar / ĕ el / ē mil / g gato / h joya / hw juez / ī aire / k casa / kw cuan /

scruf·fy (skrŭf'ē) adj. **-fi·er, -fi·est** *(shabby)* desaliñado; G.B. *(scaly)* escamoso.

scrump·tious (skrŭmp'shəs) adj. FAM. de rechupete.

scrunch (skrŭnch) I. tr. ♦ **to s. up** *(paper, hat)* aplastar; *(one's shoulders)* encorvarse; *(one's face)* torcer —intr. encorvarse II. s. crujido.

scru·ple (skrōō'pəl) s. *(ethical objection)* escrúpulo; *(bit)* pizca; FARM. escrúpulo ♦ **scruples** escrúpulos <*to have no scruples* no tener escrúpulos>.

scru·pu·lous (skrōō'pyə-ləs) adj. escrupuloso.

scru·ta·ble (skrōō'tə-bəl) adj. comprensible.

scru·ti·nize (skrōōt'n-īz') tr. **-nized, -niz·ing** escudriñar.

scru·ti·ny (skrōōt'n-ē) s. [pl. **-nies**] escrutinio.

scu·ba (skōō'bə) s. DEP. escafandra autónoma.

scud (skŭd) I. intr. **scud·ded, scud·ding** *(to skim along)* correr, deslizarse; MARÍT. correr viento en popa II. *(scudding)* carrera; *(clouds)* nubes livianas impulsadas por el viento; *(gust)* ráfaga de viento; *(shower)* chaparrón m.

scuff (skŭf) I. intr. estropear (los zapatos) ♦ **to s. along** caminar arrastrando los pies —tr. *(one's feet)* arrastrar; *(one's shoes)* estropear II. s. *(act)* arrastre de los pies m; *(slipper)* chancleta.

scuf·fle¹ (skŭf'əl) I. intr. **-fled, -fling** *(to fight)* pelearse, reñir; *(to scuff)* arrastrar los pies II. s. pelea, refriega.

scuf·fle² (skŭf'əl) s. *(hoe)* azada de arrastre.

scull (skŭl) I. s. *(long oar)* espadilla; DEP. *(oar)* remo; *(boat)* bote de remo m II. tr. impulsar con remo o espadilla —intr. remar.

scul·ler·y (skŭl'ə-rē) s. [pl. **-ies**] trascocina.

scul·lion (skŭl'yən) s. ANT. marmitón m, pinche de cocina m.

sculpt (skŭlpt) tr. esculpir.

sculp·tor (skŭlp'tər) s. escultor m.

sculp·tress (skŭlp'trĭs) s. escultora.

sculp·tur·al (skŭlp'chər-əl) adj. escultural.

sculp·ture (skŭlp'chər) I. s. escultura II. tr. **-tured, -tur·ing** esculpir.

scum (skŭm) I. s. *(on a pond)* verdín m; *(on liquids)* telilla; *(on milk)* nata; *(on metal)* escoria; FIG. *(people)* hez f, escoria II. tr. **scummed, scum·ming** *(milk)* espumar, desnatar; *(metals)* quitar la escoria de.

scup·per (skŭp'ər) s. MARÍT. imbornal m, émbornal m.

scurf (skûrf) s. *(dandruff)* caspa; *(scab)* costra; *(skin)* escamillas.

scur·ri·lous (skûr'ə-ləs) adj. *(foul-mouthed)* grosero; *(insulting)* difamatorio.

scur·ry (skûr'ē) I. intr. **-ried, -ry·ing** *(to scamper)* correr; *(to swirl about)* escabullirse II. s. [pl. **-ries**] huida.

scur·vy (skûr'vē) I. s. MED. escorbuto II. adj. **-vi·er, -vi·est** *(mean)* ruin, vil; ANT. *(scaly)* costroso.

scut·ter (skŭt'ər) intr. G.B. correr.

scut·tle¹ (skŭt'l) I. s. *(in a building)* trampilla; MARÍT. escotilla II. tr. **-tled, -tling** FAM. *(to discard)* desechar, abandonar; MARÍT. barrenar, dar barreno a.

scut·tle² (skŭt'l) s. *(for coal)* cubo, balde m; *(for vegetables, flowers)* cesta, canasta.

scut·tle³ (skŭt'l) I. intr. **-tled, -tling** ♦ **to s. away** o **off** escabullirse • **to s. down** bajar corriendo II. s. huida.

scythe (sīth) I. s. AGR. guadaña II. tr. **scythed, scyth·ing** guadañar, segar.

sea (sē) I. s. mar mf ♦ **at s.** en el mar • **by the s.** a (la) orilla del mar • **heavy s.** marejada • **on the high seas** en alta mar • **S.** *(large)* Mar <*Caspian S.* Mar Caspio>; *(small)* Lago <*S. of Tiberias* Lago de Tiberíades> • **to be at s. about** estar en un mar de dudas o confuso sobre • **to go to s.** hacerse marinero • **to put to s.** hacerse a la mar II. adj. *(marine)* marino <*a s. animal* un animal marino>; *(saltwater)* de mar; *(navigational)* de marear <*s. chart* carta de marear>; *(naval)* naval <*s. battle* batalla naval>; *(maritime)* marítimo.

sea anchor s. MARÍT. ancla flotante.

sea anemone s. ZOOL. anémona de mar.

sea·bed (sē'bĕd) s. fondo del mar.

sea bird s. ave marina.

sea·board (sē'bôrd') s. *(seacoast)* playa; *(land near sea)* litoral m, costa.

sea·borne (sē'bôrn') adj. por mar, marítimo.

sea captain s. capitán de marina mercante m.

sea·coast (sē'kōst') s. litoral m, costa.

sea cow s. ZOOL. manatí m, vaca marina.

sea·dog (sē'dôg') s. *(seal)* foca; FAM. *(sailor)* lobo de mar.

sea·far·er (sē'fâr'ər) s. marinero.

sea·far·ing (sē'fâr'ĭng) I. s. marinería II. adj. marinero.

sea·food (sē'fōōd') s. *(shellfish)* mariscos; *(fish)* pescado.

sea·fowl (sē'foul') s. ave marina.

sea·go·ing (sē'gō'ĭng) adj. *(ocean voyages)* de alta mar; *(people)* marinero; *(trade)* marítimo.

sea gull s. ORNIT. gaviota.

sea horse s. ICT. caballo de mar, hipocampo.

seal¹ (sēl) I. s. *(emblem, stamp)* sello; *(pledge)* garantía <*s. of approval* garantía de aprobación>; *(sticker)* precinto; *(closure)* cierre m <*airtight s.* cierre hermético> ♦ **wax s.** sello de lacre II. tr. *(document, treaty)* sellar, poner el sello a; *(with wax)* lacrar, sellar con lacre; *(envelope)* cerrar; *(one's fate)* determinar, decidir irrevocablemente; *(against leakage)* cerrar herméticamente; DER. precintar ♦ **to s. in** encerrar • **to s. off** *(street, area)* acordonar; *(pipe)* cerrar herméticamente • **to s. up** CARP. *(crevice, hole)* tapar; *(envelope)* cerrar.

seal² (sēl) I. s. ZOOL. foca; *(pelt)* piel de foca f II. intr. cazar focas.

sea-lane (sē'lān') s. ruta o vía marítima.

seal·ant (sē'lənt) s. sellador m.

sea legs s.pl. FAM. equilibrio a bordo de un barco.

seal·er¹ (sē'lər) s. pintura o barniz utilizado para sellar una superficie.

seal·er² (sē'lər) s. cazador de focas m.

sea level s. nivel del mar m.

sealing wax s. lacre m.

sea lion s. ZOOL. león marino, otaria.

seal ring s. sello.

seal·skin (sēl'skĭn') s. piel de foca f.

seam (sēm) I. s. *(of coat, stocking)* costura; *(scar)* cicatriz f; *(mark)* marca; *(crease)* arruga; GEOL. veta, filón m; CARP. junta, juntura ♦ **to be bursting at the seams** *(to be too large for a garment)* estallar por las costuras; FIG. *(to overflow with people)* rebosar de gente II. tr. *(to stitch)* unir con una costura; *(to line)* marcar; CARP. juntar.

sea·man (sē'mən) s. [pl. **-men**] marinero.

sea·man·ship (sē'mən-shĭp') s. pericia náutica.

sea mile s. milla marina.

seam·less (sēm'lĭs) adj. sin costura.

seam·stress (sēm'strĭs) s. costurera.

seam·y (sē'mē) adj. **-i·er, -i·est** *(with seams)* con costuras; *(sordid)* sórdido.

sé·ance (sā'äns') s. *(meeting)* sesión f; *(spiritualistic session)* sesión de espiritismo.

sea otter s. ZOOL. nutria de mar.

sea·plane (sē'plān') s. hidroavión m.

sea·port (sē'pôrt') s. puerto marítimo.

sea power s. *(country)* potencia naval; *(naval strength)* fuerza o poderío naval.

sear¹ (sîr) I. tr. & intr. marchitar(se) II. s. quemadura.

sear² (sîr) s. ARM. muelle real m.

sear³ (sîr) adj. var. de **sere**.

search (sûrch) I. tr. *(to go over)* registrar, buscar en; *(by police)* registrar; *(one's conscience)* examinar ♦ **s. me!** FAM. ¡yo qué sé! • **to s. for** buscar • **to s. in** o **through** registrar, buscar en • **to s. one's memory** intentar recordar • **to s. out** descubrir —intr. buscar II. s. *(act)* búsqueda; *(of a house, car)* registro; *(of a person)* cacheo; *(of a ship)* visita ♦ **in s. of** en busca de.

search·er (sûr'chər) s. buscador m.

search·ing (sûr'chĭng) adj. *(examining closely)* minucioso <*a s. investigation* una investigación minuciosa>; *(observant)* penetrante.

search·light (sûrch'līt') s. reflector m, proyector m.

search party s. partida de buscadores.

search warrant s. DER. mandamiento de registro, orden de registro m.

sea·scape (sē'skāp') s. *(view)* vista marina; PINT. marina.

sea serpent s. MITOL. serpiente de mar f.

sea·shell (sē'shĕl') s. concha marina.
sea·shore (sē'shôr') s. *(beach)* playa, orilla del mar; *(coast)* costa, litoral *m.*
sea·sick (sē'sĭk') adj. mareado ♦ **to get s.** marearse.
sea·sick·ness (sē'sĭk'nĭs) s. mareo.
sea·side (sē'sīd') s. *(beach)* playa; *(coast)* costa, litoral *m* ♦ **s. resort** estación balnearia.
sea·son (sē'zən) **I.** s. *(of the year)* estación *f* <*the four seasons* las cuatro estaciones>; *(of crops, hunting)* temporada <*harvest s.* temporada de la cosecha>; *(of animals)* época <*mating s.* época del celo>; *(of festivities)* temporada ♦ **in s.** *(of produce)* en sazón; *(of animals)* en celo • **off s.** COM., DEP. temporada baja • **off-season rates** tarifas de fuera de temporada • **out of s.** fuera de temporada **II.** tr. *(food)* sazonar, condimentar <*highly seasoned* bien sazonado>; *(lecture, speech)* amenizar; *(wood)* secar; *(to accustom)* acostumbrar, habituar; *(discipline, rules)* moderar —intr. *(wood)* secarse; *(to temper)* moderarse; *(to get accustomed to)* acostumbrarse.
sea·son·a·ble (sē'zə-nə-bəl) adj. *(weather, clothing)* propio de la estación; *(timely)* a su tiempo, oportuno.
sea·son·al (sē'zə-nəl) adj. *(rains)* estacional; *(unemployment)* temporal; *(worker)* temporero ♦ **s. worker** temporero.
sea·son·ing (sē'zə-nĭng) s. *(spice)* condimento, aderezo; *(of wood)* secado; *(of wine)* maduramiento.
season ticket s. abono.
seat (sēt) **I.** s. *(in a room, vehicle)* asiento <*take a s., please* tome asiento, por favor>; *(of a chair)* asiento; *(for an event)* localidad *f,* entrada <*we have seats for the game* tenemos localidades para el partido>; *(of trousers)* fondillos *m; (of a bicycle)* sillín *m; (of government)* sede *f; (of learning)* centro; *(of a country)* capital *f; (in legislature)* escaño, banco; *(buttocks)* trasero *f* ♦ **by the s. of one's pants** FAM. por los pelos • **take your seats** siéntense • **to have a good s.** EQUIT. montar bien (a caballo) **II.** tr. *(to place)* sentar <*s. her next to me* siéntela a mi lado>; *(to provide)* tener cabida o sitio para <*the theater seats three hundred* el teatro tiene sitio para trescientas personas>; *(to install)* instalar ♦ **please be seated** siéntense por favor.
seat belt s. cinturón de seguridad *m.*
seat·ing (sē'tĭng) s. *(places)* asientos; *(placement)* colocación *f;* MEC. asiento ♦ **s. arrangement** distribución de los asientos.
sea urchin s. ZOOL. erizo de mar.
sea wall s. rompeolas *m,* dique *m.*
sea·ward (sē'wərd) **I.** adj. que da al mar **II.** adv. hacia el mar.
sea·wa·ter (sē'wô'tər) s. agua de mar.
sea·way (sē'wā') s. *(sea route)* ruta o vía marítima; *(of ship)* estela; *(rough sea)* mar gruesa.
sea·weed (sē'wēd') s. alga.
sea·wor·thy (sē'wûr'*th*ē) adj. **-thi·er, -thi·est** en condiciones de navegar.
se·ba·ceous (sĭ-bā'shəs) s. sebáceo.
seb·or·rhe·a o **seb·or·rhoe·a** (sĕb'ə-rē'ə) s. seborrea.
se·bum (sē'bəm) s. BIOL. sebo.
se·cant (sē'kănt) s. & adj. GEOM., TRIG. secante *f.*
se·cede (sĭ-sēd') intr. **-ced·ed, -ced·ing** separarse.
se·ces·sion (sĭ-sĕsh'ən) s. secesión *f,* separación *f* ♦ **The War of S.** EE. UU., HIST. la Guerra de Secesión.
se·ces·sion·ist (sĭ-sĕsh'ə-nĭst) s. secesionista *mf,* separatista *mf.*
se·clude (sĭ-kloōd') tr. **-clud·ed, -clud·ing** *(to keep apart)* recluir; *(to isolate)* aislar ♦ **to s. oneself from** apartarse de, retirarse de.
se·clud·ed (sĭ-kloō'dĭd) adj. *(person)* solitario; *(place)* aislado, apartado.
se·clu·sion (sĭ-kloō'zhən) s. reclusión *f,* aislamiento ♦ **in s.** apartado.
sec·ond¹ (sĕk'ənd) s. *(unit of time)* segundo; FAM. *(moment)* momento <*wait a s.* espera un momento>.
sec·ond² (sĕk'ənd) **I.** adj. *(in order, time)* segundo <*s. in line* segundo en la cola>; *(another)* otro <*a s. chance* otra oportunidad>; MEC. segundo ♦ **every s.** *(student, book)*

uno de cada dos (estudiantes, libros); *(day, year)* cada dos (días, años) • **s. cousin** primo segundo • **s. floor** primer piso (en países hispánicos) • **the s. one** el segundo • **to be s. banana** desempeñar un papel secundario • **to be s. to none** no tener igual • **who wants a s. helping?** ¿quién quiere repetir? **II.** s. *(in order, time)* segundo <*to come in s.* llegar segundo>; *(in boxing)* cuidador *m,* segundo; *(in a duel)* padrino; MÚS. segunda; MEC. segunda ♦ **seconds** *(food)* una porción más; COM. artículos con pequeños desperfectos • **the s. of May** el dos de mayo **III.** tr. *(to attend)* secundar, ayudar; *(motion, idea)* apoyar **IV.** adv. en segundo lugar <*to finish s.* terminar en segundo lugar>.
sec·ond·ar·y (sĕk'ən-dĕr'ē) **I.** adj. secundario **II.** s. [pl. **-ies**] *(subordinate)* subalterno; ORNIT. rémige secundaria; ELEC. circuito secundario; ASTRON. satélite *m.*
secondary education s. enseñanza media, segunda enseñanza.
secondary school s. instituto de segunda enseñanza, escuela secundaria.
second best s. lo mejor después del primero, segundo ♦ **to be s.** ser de segunda clase.
sec·ond-best (sĕk'ənd-bĕst') adj. segundo.
second childhood s. FIG. segunda infancia.
second class s. segunda clase.
sec·ond-class (sĕk'ənd-klăs') **I.** adj. de segunda clase ♦ **s. citizen** FIG. persona inferior **II.** adv. en segunda (clase).
Second Coming s. BÍBL. la segunda venida de Cristo.
second fiddle s. MÚS. segundo violín ♦ **to play s.** FIG. desempeñar un papel secundario.
second generation s. COMPUT. segunda generación.
sec·ond-gen·er·a·tion (sĕk'ənd-jĕn'ə-rā'shən) adj. de segunda generación.
second growth s. bosque renacido.
sec·ond-guess (sĕk'ənd-gĕs') tr. *(to criticize)* criticar; *(to anticipate)* anticiparse a.
sec·ond-hand (sĕk'ənd-hănd') **I.** adj. *(furniture, books)* de segunda mano, de ocasión; *(clothes)* usado, viejo; *(information)* de segunda mano **II.** adv. de segunda mano.
second hand s. segundero (de reloj).
second lieutenant s. alférez *m,* subteniente *m.*
sec·ond·ly (sĕk'ənd-lē) adv. en segundo lugar.
second nature s. hábito, costumbre arraigada.
second person s. GRAM. segunda persona.
sec·ond-rate (sĕk'ənd-rāt') adj. de segunda categoría.
second sight s. clarividencia.
second thought s. ♦ **on s.** pensándolo bien • **to have second thoughts** tener dudas.
second wind s. ♦ **to get one's s.** FIG. recobrar el aliento o las fuerzas.
Second World War s. Segunda Guerra Mundial.
se·cre·cy (sē'krĭ-sē) s. [pl. **-cies**] *(concealment)* secreto <*in strict s.* en el mayor secreto>; *(discretion)* discreción *f,* reserva.
se·cret (sē'krĭt) **I.** adj. *(kept hidden)* secreto; *(secluded)* oculto, escondido **II.** s. secreto ♦ **as a s.** confidencialmente • **s.** RELIG. secreta • **to keep a s.** guardar un secreto.
sec·re·tar·i·al (sĕk'rĭ-târ'ē-əl) adj. de secretario.
sec·re·tar·i·at (sĕk'rĭ-târ'ē-ĭt) s. secretariado, secretaría.
sec·re·tar·y (sĕk'rĭ-tĕr'ē) s. [pl. **-ies**] *(person)* secretario; *(desk)* secreter *m; (government minister)* ministro <*S. of Education* ministro de Educación>.
sec·re·tar·y-gen·er·al (sĕk'rĭ-tĕr'ē-jĕn'ər-əl) s. [pl. **sec·re·tar·ies-gen·er·al**] secretario general.
Secretary of State s. ministro de Relaciones Exteriores (en EE. UU.); G.B. ministro con cartera.
se·crete¹ (sĭ-krēt') tr. **-cret·ed, -cret·ing** FISIOL. *(to generate a substance)* secretar, segregar.
se·crete² (sĭ-krēt') tr. **-cret·ed, -cret·ing** *(to hide)* esconder, ocultar.
se·cre·tion (sĭ-krē'shən) s. FISIOL. secreción *f.*
se·cre·tive (sē'krĭ-tĭv) adj. *(disposed to secrecy)* sigiloso; *(silent)* callado.
se·cret·ly (sē'krĭt-lē) adv. secretamente.
se·cre·to·ry (sĭ-krē'tə-rē) adj. FISIOL. secretor, secretorio.
secret service s. servicio secreto.

ã **rey** / ä **año** / b **boca** / ch **chico** / d **dar** / ĕ **el** / ē **mil** / g **gato** / h **joya** / hw **juez** / ī **aire** / k **casa** / kw **cuan** /

sect (sĕkt) s. secta.

sec·tar·i·an (sĕk-târ'ē-ən) s. & adj. sectario.

sec·tion (sĕk'shən) **I.** s. *(for assembly)* sección *f*, parte *f*; *(of a cake)* trozo; *(of an orange)* gajo; *(of a document)* párrafo, aparte *m*; *(of a newspaper)* sección, página <*the sports s.* la página de deportes>; *(of track, tubing)* tramo; *(of a town)* barrio, parte *f*; *(of a country)* parte *f*, región *f*; DER. artículo; *(of the population)* sector *m*, clase *f*; CIR. sección; DIB., GEOM. sección, corte *m*; MIL. sección **II.** tr. *(to divide)* dividir en secciones; CIR. seccionar.

sec·tion·al (sĕk'shə-nəl) **I.** adj. *(local)* local, regional; *(furniture)* desmontable **II.** pieza desmontable.

sec·tion·al·ism (sĕk'shə-nə-lĭz'əm) s. regionalismo, localismo.

sec·tion·al·ize (sĕk'shə-nə-līz') tr. **-ized, -iz·ing** dividir en regiones.

sec·tor (sĕk'tər) **I.** s. sector *m* **II.** tr. dividir en sectores.

sec·u·lar (sĕk'yə-lər) **I.** adj. *(life)* mundano; *(music)* profano; *(school)* laico; *(clergy, court)* secular **II.** s. *(clergy)* secular *m*; *(layman)* seglar *m*.

sec·u·lar·ism (sĕk'yə-lə-rĭz'əm) s. laicismo.

sec·u·lar·ize (sĕk'yə-lə-rīz') tr. **-ized, -iz·ing** secularizar.

se·cure (sĭ-kyŏor') **I.** adj. **-cur·er, -cur·est** *(safe, certain)* seguro; *(well-fastened)* asegurado ◆ **s. from** protegido contra **II.** tr. **-cured, -cur·ing** *(door, fort)* asegurar; *(a loan, rights)* asegurar, garantizar; *(aid, job)* obtener, conseguir; *(boat)* amarrar ◆ **to s. from** proteger contra.

se·cu·ri·ty (sĭ-kyŏor'ĭ-tē) s. [pl. **-ties**] *(of a country, people)* seguridad *f* <*national s.* seguridad nacional>; *(of a loan)* garantía *f* ◆ **securities** FIN. valores.

Security Council s. Consejo de Seguridad (de la O.N.U.).

security guard s. guardia *m*.

se·dan (sĭ-dăn') s. *(automobile)* sedán *m*; *(portable chair)* silla de manos.

se·date¹ (sĭ-dāt') adj. sosegado, sereno.

se·date² (sĭ-dāt') tr. **-dat·ed, -dat·ing** MED. administrar calmantes.

se·da·tion (sĭ-dā'shən) s. MED. sedación *f*.

sed·a·tive (sĕd'ə-tĭv) s. & adj. sedante *m*, calmante *m*.

sed·en·tar·y (sĕd'n-tĕr'ē) adj. sedentario.

sedge (sĕj) s. BOT. juncia.

sed·i·ment (sĕd'ə-mənt) s. sedimento, poso.

sed·i·men·ta·ry (sĕd'ə-mĕn'tə-rē) o **sed·i·men·tal** (-mĕn'tl) adj. sedimentario.

sed·i·men·ta·tion (sĕd'ə-mən-tā'shən) s. sedimentación *f*.

se·di·tion (sĭ-dĭsh'ən) s. sedición *f*.

se·di·tious (sĭ-dĭsh'əs) adj. sedicioso.

se·duce (sĭ-dōōs', -dyōōs') tr. **-duced, -duc·ing** seducir.

se·duc·er (sĭ-dōō'sər, -dyōō'-) s. seductor *m*.

se·duc·tion (sĭ-dŭk'shən) s. seducción *f*.

se·duc·tive (sĭ-dŭk'tĭv) adj. seductivo, seductor.

se·duc·tress (sĭ-dŭk'trĭs) s. seductora.

sed·u·lous (sĕj'ə-ləs) adj. diligente, asiduo.

sed·u·lous·ness (sĕj'ə-ləs-nĭs) s. asiduidad *f*, diligencia.

see¹ (sē) tr. saw (sô), seen (sĕn), see·ing *(to observe)* ver <*I saw you do it* te vi hacerlo>; *(to make out)* ver, divisar <*can you s. the coast?* ¿ves la costa?>; *(to picture)* ver, percibir *(to visualize)* ver, imaginarse; *(to understand)* comprender, entender <*I don't s. how they did it* no entiendo cómo lo hicieron>; *(to recognize)* ver, reconocer <*I s. now that I was wrong* ahora reconozco que estaba equivocado>; *(to regard)* ver, considerar <*I saw it was my duty* consideré que era mi obligación>; *(to make sure)* asegurarse de, encargarse de <*s. that they take all they need* asegúrate de que se llevan todo lo que necesiten>; *(to visit with)* encontrarse con <*I saw some friends yesterday* ayer me encontré con algunos amigos>; *(to date)* salir con <*I'm not seeing him anymore* ya no salgo con él>; *(to socialize with)* verse <*we hardly ever s. them* no nos vemos casi nunca>; *(to consult)* ir a ver, consultar <*you must s. a doctor* debes consultar a un médico>; *(to attend)* atender, recibir <*the doctor will s. you in a moment* el doctor le recibirá dentro de un momento>; *(to escort)* acompañar <*I'll s. you home* la acompañaré hasta su casa>; *(a bet)* aceptar; *(to know)* conocer <*this car has seen better days* este coche ha conocido mejores tiempos>; *(to observe)* ver <*I want to s. how it's done* quiero ver cómo se hace>; *(to notice)* ver, notar ◆ **as I s. it** por lo que veo • **I could s. it coming** FIG. lo veía venir • **I saw it in his eyes** se lo vi en la cara • **I saw it with my own (two) eyes** lo vi con mis propios ojos • **it is worth seeing** merece la pena verse • **seeing is believing** ver para creer • **s. what I mean?** ¿ves? • **s. you!** ¡hasta luego! • **s. you later** o **soon!** ¡hasta luego!, ¡hasta pronto! • **s. you (on) Saturday!** ¡hasta el sábado! • **that remains to be seen** eso está por verse • **there's nothing to s.** no hay nada que merezca la pena verse • **to go s.** o **to go and s.** ir a ver • **to s. eye to eye** ver las cosas de la misma manera • **to s. into (past, future)** ver (el pasado, futuro) • **to s. off** ir a despedirse de • **to s. one's way clear to** ver claramente el modo de • **to s. oneself** verse • **to s. out** acompañar hasta la puerta • **to s. red** FIG. echar chispas, ponerse furioso • **to s. stars** FIG. ver las estrellas • **to s. the light** comprender, darse cuenta • **to s. the point** comprender, ver el sentido de lo dicho • **to s. (someone) through** ayudar a pasar a (alguien) por • **to s. (something) through** llevar (una cosa) a cabo • **to s. things** ver visiones • **to s. to** atender a, ocuparse de • **you have to s. it to believe it** hay que verlo para creerlo —intr. *(to perceive)* ver; *(to understand)* comprender <*I s.* comprendo>; *(to consider)* ver, pensar <*let me s.* déjame pensar> ◆ **as far as the eye can s.** hasta donde alcanza la vista • **let's s.** a ver, veamos • **s.?** ¿ves?, ¿te enteras? • **s. for yourself!** ¡vea usted mismo! • **s. here!** ¡mire!, ¡oiga! • **s. if I care!** ¡a mí no me importa! • **seeing that . . .** ya que . . . • **to s. fit** creer conveniente • **to s. through someone** calar a alguien, conocer el juego de alguien • **to wait and s.** ver • **you s. . . .** es que . . . • **you'll s.!** ¡ya verás! • **we'll s.** veremos • **we'll s. about that!** ¡ya (lo) veremos!

see² (sē) s. RELIG. sede *f* ◆ **Holy S.** Santa Sede.

seed (sēd) s. [pl. **seeds** o **seed**] *(of a plant)* semilla; *(for planting)* semilla, simiente *f*; *(germ)* germen *m*, semilla <*the s. of revolt* el germen de la rebelión>; *(in fruits, vegetables)* pepita; BIBL. *(progeny)* descendencia; *(sperm)* semen *m* ◆ **in s.** BOT. germinado • **s. corn** AGR. maíz de siembra • **to go to s.** *(plants)* granar; *(a place)* echarse a perder, deteriorarse • **to sow the seeds of** FIG. sembrar **II.** tr. *(field, lawn)* sembrar; *(fruit)* despepitar; *(clouds)* sembrar las nubes con yoduro potásico; DEP. preseleccionar —intr. BOT. granar; AGR. sembrar.

seed·bed (sēd'bĕd') s. semillero.

seed·er (sē'dər) s. sembradora.

seed·ling (sēd'lĭng) s. AGR., BOT. plantón *m*.

seed money s. presupuesto inicial.

seed pearl s. aljófar *m*.

seed·pod (sēd'pŏd') s. BOT. vaina, cápsula.

seed·y (sē'dē) adj. **-i·er, -i·est** *(clothing)* raído, desgastado; *(person)* pachucho, enfermizo; *(place)* sórdido; BOT. granado.

see·ing (sē'ĭng) conj. visto, puesto ◆ **s. that** visto que, puesto que.

seek (sēk) tr. **sought** (sôt), **seek·ing** *(employment, shelter)* buscar; *(fame, wealth)* aspirar a, anhelar; *(aid, advice)* solicitar, pedir ◆ **to be (highly) sought after** *(person)* ser (muy) solicitado; *(things)* ser (muy) cotizado • **to s. out** buscar, ir o andar en busca de • **to s. to** tratar de (hacer algo) —intr. ◆ **to s.** o **to s. after** buscar, ir buscando • **to s. for** buscar, ir o andar en busca de.

seek·er (sē'kər) s. buscador *m*.

seem (sēm) intr. parecer <*he seems honest* parece honrado> ◆ **incredible as it may s.** aunque parezca increíble • **it hardly seems possible that** parece mentira que • **it seems that** parece que • **so it seems** o **would s.** así parece, parece que es así • **what seems to be the trouble?** ¿pasa algo?, ¿qué pasa?

seem·ing (sē'mĭng) **I.** adj. aparente, supuesto **II.** s. apariencia.

seem·ing·ly (sē'mĭng-lē) adv. aparentemente, por lo visto.

seem·ly (sēm'lē) **I.** adj. **-li·er, -li·est** *(decorous)* decente, decoroso; *(handsome)* bien parecido, atractivo **II.** adv. correctamente.

seen (sēn) part. p. de **see¹**.

seep (sēp) intr. rezumarse, filtrarse.

seep·age (sē′pĭj) s. filtración f.
seer (sîr, sē′ər) s. vidente mf, adivino.
seer·suck·er (sîr′sŭk′ər) s. tejido rayado en relieve.
see·saw (sē′sô′) I. s. (for children) subibaja m, columpio; (movement) vaivén m II. intr. (children) columpiarse; (to oscillate) oscilar.
seethe (sēth) intr. **seethed, seeth·ing** (liquid) hervir, borbotar; FIG. (inferno) agitarse; (person) estar agitado ♦ **to be seething with anger** estar ardiendo de cólera —tr. empapar, remojar.
see-through (sē′thrōō′) adj. transparente.
seg·ment (sĕg′mənt) I. s. (part) segmento, sección f; BIOL., GEOM. segmento II. tr. & intr. (sĕg-mĕnt′) segmentar(se), dividir(se) en segmentos.
seg·men·tar·y (sĕg′mən-tĕr′ē) adj. segmentario.
seg·men·ta·tion (sĕg′mən-tā′shən) s. segmentación f.
seg·ment·ed (sĕg′mĕn′tĭd) adj. dividido en segmentos.
seg·re·gate (sĕg′rĭ-gāt′) I. tr. & intr. **-gat·ed, -gat·ing** segregar(se), separar(se) II. adj. (-gĭt, -gāt′) aislado, separado.
seg·re·ga·tion (sĕg′rĭ-gā′shən) s. segregación f.
seg·re·ga·tion·ist (sĕg′rĭ-gā′shə-nĭst) s. segregacionista mf.
seine (sān) I. s. jábega II. tr. & intr. **seined, sein·ing** pescar con jábega.
Seine (sān, sĕn) s. Sena.
seism (sī′zəm) s. seismo, sismo.
seis·mic (sīz′mĭk) adj. sísmico.
seis·mo·graph (sīz′mə-grăf′) s. sismógrafo.
seis·mol·o·gy (sīz-mŏl′ə-jē) s. sismología.
seis·mom·e·ter (sīz-mŏm′ĭ-tər) s. sismómetro.
seiz·a·ble (sē′zə-bəl) adj. (that can be seized) asible; DER. embargable.
seize (sēz) tr. **seized, seiz·ing** (to grab) agarrar, asir; (power, a city) tomar, apoderarse de; (to arrest) detener; (to confiscate) incautarse de; FIG. (the imagination) captar; (opportunity, idea) aprovechar, no dejar pasar; (fear, panic) apoderarse de; MARÍT. amarrar ♦ **to be seized by** o **with** (panic, fear) estar sobrecogido por; (a desire) entrarle a uno; (illness) darle a uno un ataque de • **to s. on** o **upon** aprovecharse de —intr. ♦ **to s.** o **s. up** MEC. (engine) agarrotarse; (to become clogged) atascarse.
seiz·ing (sē′zĭng) s. MARÍT. trinca, ligadura.
sei·zure (sē′zhər) s. (of a person) detención f; (of goods) embargo; (of a town, power) toma; MED. ataque m.
sel·dom (sĕl′dəm) adv. raramente, rara vez.
se·lect (sĭ-lĕkt′) I. tr. & intr. (to choose) escoger, elegir; DEP. seleccionar II. adj. (chosen) selecto, escogido; (club) exclusivo; (merchandise) de primera calidad.
se·lect·ee (sĭ-lĕk′tē′) s. (selected person) elegido; MIL. recluta m.
se·lec·tion (sĭ-lĕk′shən) s. (choice) selección f, elección f; (collection) surtido; LIT., MÚS. trozo escogido, selección ♦ **natural s.** BIOL. selección natural.
se·lec·tive (sĭ-lĕk′tĭv) adj. selectivo.
se·lec·tive·ly (sĭ-lĕk′tĭv-lē) adv. selectivamente.
se·lec·tiv·i·ty (sĭ-lĕk′tĭv′ĭ-tē) s. selectividad f.
se·lect·man (sĭ-lĕkt′măn′) s. [pl. **-men** (-mĕn′)] concejal m.
se·lec·tor (sĭ-lĕk′tər) s. (person) seleccionador m; TEC. selector m.
se·le·ni·um (sĭ-lē′nē-əm) s. QUÍM. selenio.
self (sĕlf) I. s. [pl. **selves** (sĕlvz)] (oneself) sí mismo, uno mismo <to think of others before s. pensar en los demás antes que en sí mismo>; (personality) personalidad f <her true s. was revealed se manifestó su verdadera personalidad>; (side) lado <my better s. mi lado bueno>; (ego) yo <his other s. su otro yo>; COM. al portador m <payable to s. pagadero al portador> ♦ **to be back to one's old** o **former s.** volver a ser el mismo de siempre II. pron. uno mismo, sí mismo III. adj. mismo, idéntico, igual.
self-ab·sorbed (sĕlf′əb-sôrbd′, -zôrbd′) adj. ensimismado.
self-a·buse (sĕlf′ə-byōōs′) s. (self-reproach) autocrítica; (masturbation) masturbación f.
self-act·ing (sĕlf′ăk′tĭng) adj. automático.
self-ad·dressed (sĕlf′ə-drĕst′) adj. con la dirección del remitente <a s. envelope un sobre con la dirección del remitente>.

self-ag·gran·dize·ment (sĕlf′ə-grăn′dĭz-mənt) s. exaltación de sí mismo f.
self-ap·point·ed (sĕlf′ə-poin′tĭd) adj. nombrado por sí mismo.
self-as·ser·tion (sĕlf′ə-sûr′shən) s. (presumption) presunción f; (aggressiveness) agresividad f.
self-as·ser·tive (sĕlf′ə-sûr′tĭv) adj. (conceited) presumido; (aggressive) agresivo.
self-as·sur·ance (sĕlf′ə-shōōr′əns) s. confianza en sí mismo.
self-as·sured (sĕlf′ə-shōōrd′) adj. seguro de sí mismo.
self-a·ware (sĕlf′ə-wâr′) adj. consciente de su propia personalidad.
self-cen·tered (sĕlf′sĕn′tərd) adj. egocéntrico.
self-clos·ing (sĕlf′klōz′ĭng) adj. de cierre automático.
self-com·mand (sĕlf′kə-mănd′) s. dominio de sí mismo.
self-com·pla·cent (sĕlf′kəm-plā′sənt) adj. engreído.
self-com·posed (sĕlf′kəm-pōzd′) adj. dueño de sí mismo.
self-con·fessed (sĕlf′kən-fĕst′) adj. reconocido por uno mismo.
self-con·fi·dence (sĕlf′kŏn′fĭ-dəns) s. confianza en sí mismo.
self-con·scious (sĕlf′kŏn′shəs) adj. cohibido, tímido.
self-con·tained (sĕlf′kən-tānd′) adj. (self-sufficient) autónomo, independiente; (reserved) reservado, poco comunicativo.
self-con·tempt (sĕlf′kən-tĕmpt′) s. desprecio de sí mismo.
self-con·tent (sĕlf′kən-tĕnt′) adj. satisfecho de sí mismo.
self-con·tra·dic·to·ry (sĕlf′kŏn′trə-dĭk′tə-rē) adj. que se contradice a sí mismo, contradictorio.
self-con·trol (sĕlf′kən-trōl′) s. dominio de sí mismo ♦ **to lose one's s.** perder la calma, ponerse nervioso.
self-cor·rect·ing (sĕlf′kə-rĕk′tĭng) adj. con corrector.
self-de·cep·tion (sĕlf′dĭ-sĕp′shən) s. engaño de sí mismo.
self-de·feat·ing (sĕlf′dĭ-fē′tĭng) adj. contraproducente.
self-de·fense (sĕlf′dĭ-fĕns′) s. (defense) autodefensa; DER. legítima defensa ♦ **in s.** en defensa propia.
self-de·ni·al (sĕlf′dĭ-nī′əl) s. abnegación f.
self-de·struct (sĕlf′dĭ-strŭkt′) intr. autodestruirse.
self-de·struc·tion (sĕlf′dĭ-strŭk′shən) s. autodestrucción f.
self-de·ter·mi·na·tion (sĕlf′dĭ-tûr′mə-nā′shən) s. autodeterminación f.
self-dis·ci·pline (sĕlf′dĭs′ə-plĭn) s. autodisciplina.
self-doubt (sĕlf′dout′) s. desconfianza en sí mismo.
self-ed·u·cat·ed (sĕlf′ĕj′ə-kā′tĭd) adj. autodidacta.
self-ef·fac·ing (sĕlf′ĭ-fā′sĭng) adj. humilde, modesto.
self-em·ployed (sĕlf′ĕm-ploid′) adj. que trabaja por cuenta propia.
self-es·teem (sĕlf′ĭ-stēm′) s. amor propio.
self-ev·i·dent (sĕlf′ĕv′ĭ-dənt) adj. evidente, patente.
self-ex·plan·a·to·ry (sĕlf′ĭk-splăn′ə-tôr′ē) adj. obvio, evidente.
self-ex·pres·sion (sĕlf′ĭk-sprĕsh′ən) s. expresión de la propia personalidad f.
self-ful·fill·ing (sĕlf′fōōl-fĭl′ĭng) adj. que llega a cumplirse.
self-gov·ern·ment (sĕlf′gŭv′ərn-mənt) s. (autonomy) autonomía; (self-control) dominio de sí mismo.
self-grat·i·fi·ca·tion (sĕlf′grăt′ə-fĭ-kā′shən) s. satisfacción de los deseos propios f.
self-help (sĕlf′hĕlp′) s. esfuerzo propio.
self-im·age (sĕlf′ĭm′ĭj) s. representación de sí mismo f.
self-im·por·tance (sĕlf′ĭm-pôr′tns) s. presunción f.
self-im·posed (sĕlf′ĭm-pōzd′) adj. que uno se impone a sí mismo.
self-im·prove·ment (sĕlf′ĭm-prōōv′mənt) s. superación propia.
self-in·crim·i·na·tion (sĕlf′ĭn-krĭm′ə-nā′shən) s. DER. autoincriminación f.
self-in·duced (sĕlf′ĭn-dōōst′, -dyōōst′) adj. (wound, criticism) que uno se hace a sí mismo; ELEC. autoinducido.
self-in·dul·gence (sĕlf′ĭn-dŭl′jəns) s. desenfreno.
self-in·flict·ed (sĕlf′ĭn-flĭk′tĭd) adj. que uno se inflige a sí mismo.
self-in·ter·est (sĕlf′ĭn′trĭst, -ĭn′tər-ĭst) s. (one's own interest) interés propio; (selfishness) egoísmo.

ā rey / ä año / b boca / ch chico / d dar / ĕ el / ē mil / g gato / h joya / hw juez / ī aire / k casa / kw cuan /

self·in·volved (sĕlf′ĭn-vŏlvd′) adj. que piensa en su propio interés.
self·ish (sĕl′fĭsh) adj. egoísta, interesado.
self·ish·ness (sĕl′fĭsh-nĭs) s. egoísmo.
self·jus·ti·fy·ing (sĕlf′jŭs′tə-fī′ĭng) adj. que se justifica a sí mismo.
self·knowl·edge (sĕlf′nŏl′ĭj) s. conocimiento de sí mismo.
self·less (sĕlf′lĭs) adj. desinteresado.
self·load·ing (sĕlf′lō′dĭng) adj. ARM. autocargador, de autocarga.
self·love (sĕlf′lŭv′) s. *(selfishness)* egoísmo; PSIC. narcisismo.
self·made (sĕlf′mād′) adj. logrado por propio esfuerzo ♦ **s. man** hombre que ha triunfado por su propio esfuerzo.
self·per·pet·u·at·ing (sĕlf′pər-pĕch′ōō-ā′tĭng) adj. que se mantiene indefinidamente.
self·pit·y (sĕlf′pĭt′ē) s. compasión de sí mismo *f.*
self·por·trait (sĕlf′pôr′trĭt) s. autorretrato.
self·pos·ses·sion (sĕlf′pə-zĕsh′ən) s. aplomo, sangre fría.
self·pres·er·va·tion (sĕlf′prĕz′ər-vā′shən) s. instinto de la propia conservación.
self·pro·claimed (sĕlf′prō-klāmd′) adj. supuesto.
self·pro·pelled (sĕlf′prə-pĕld′) adj. autopropulsado.
self·re·al·i·za·tion (sĕlf′rē′ə-lĭ-zā′shən) s. realización propia.
self·re·gard (sĕlf′rĭ-gärd′) s. *(selfishness)* amor propio; *(self-respect)* dignidad *f.*
self·reg·u·lat·ing (sĕlf′rĕg′yə-lā′tĭng) adj. TEC. autorregulador.
self·re·li·ance (sĕlf′rĭ-lī′əns) s. confianza en sí mismo.
self·re·proach (sĕlf′rĭ-prōch′) s. remordimiento.
self·re·spect (sĕlf′rĭ-spĕkt′) s. dignidad *f.*
self·re·straint (sĕlf′rĭ-strānt′) s. control *m,* dominio de sí mismo.
self·righ·teous (sĕlf′rī′chəs) adj. santurrón.
self·ris·ing (sĕlf′rī′zĭng) adj. CUL. que no necesita levadura.
self·rule (sĕlf′rōōl′) s. *(autonomy)* autonomía; *(democracy)* democracia.
self·sac·ri·fice (sĕlf′săk′rə-fīs′) s. sacrificio de sí mismo.
self·same (sĕlf′sām′) adj. mismo, mismísimo.
self·sat·is·fac·tion (sĕlf′săt′ĭs-făk′shən) s. satisfacción propia.
self·sat·is·fied (sĕlf′săt′ĭs-fīd′) adj. satisfecho de sí mismo.
self·seek·ing (sĕlf′sē′kĭng) I. adj. egoísta II. s. egoísmo.
self·serv·ice (sĕlf′sûr′vĭs) adj. de autoservicio (tienda, restaurante).
self·serv·ing (sĕlf′sûr′vĭng) adj. egoísta.
self·styled (sĕlf′stīld′) adj. supuesto.
self·suf·fi·cient (sĕlf′sə-fĭsh′ənt) *o* **self·suf·fic·ing** (-fī′sĭng) adj. *(not dependent)* independiente, autosuficiente; *(self-confident)* seguro de sí mismo.
self·sup·port (sĕlf′sə-pôrt′) s. independencia económica.
self·sus·tain·ing (sĕlf′sə-stā′nĭng) adj. que se mantiene por sus propios medios.
self·taught (sĕlf′tôt′) adj. autodidacta.
self·will (sĕlf′wĭl′) s. obstinación *f.*
self·wind·ing (sĕlf′wīn′dĭng) adj. de cuerda automática (reloj).
sell (sĕl) I. tr. **sold** (sōld), **sell·ing** *(to vend)* vender <*to s. real estate* vender propiedades>; *(to deal in)* vender <*he sells shoes* vende zapatos>; *(to promote)* hacer vender; FIG. *(one's soul)* vender (la propia alma) ♦ **to be sold on** estar convencido de, entusiasmarse por *o* con • **to s. a bill of goods** FIG. engañar, timar • **to s. down the river** FIG. traicionar • **to s. for** venderse por • **to s. off** COM. liquidar • **to s. on** FIG. hacer aceptar, convencer de • **to s. oneself** venderse • **to s. short** *(to underestimate)* subestimar; FIN. vender al descubierto —intr. *(to vend)* venderse <*to s. well* venderse bien>; FIG. *(to be accepted)* ser aceptado ♦ **to be sold out** estar agotados • **to s. like hot cakes** FIG. venderse como rosquillas *o* pan caliente • **to s. out** *(to liquidate)* liquidar todas las existencias; *(to betray one's cause)* venderse <*he sold out to the enemy* se vendió al enemigo> II. s. *(hoax)* camelo, engaño; *(selling)* venta ♦ **hard s.** publicidad agresiva • **soft s.** publicidad discreta.
sell·a·ble (sĕl′ə-bəl) adj. vendible.

sell·er (sĕl′ər) s. *(vender)* vendedor *m;* *(dealer)* comerciante *mf* ♦ **best s.** éxito de librería, best seller *m* • **quick s.** artículo que se vende fácilmente • **seller's market** COM. mercado favorable al vendedor.
sell·ing (sĕl′ĭng) adj. de venta (artículo, precio).
sell·out (sĕl′out′) s. FAM. *(traitor)* traidor *m;* COM. liquidación total *f;* DEP., TEAT. lleno, éxito de taquilla.
selt·zer (sĕlt′sər) s. agua de seltz.
sel·vage *o* **sel·vedge** (sĕl′vĭj) TEJ. orillo.
selves (sĕlvz) pl. de **self.**
se·man·tic (sĭ-măn′tĭk) adj. semántico.
se·man·tics (sĭ-măn′tĭks) s. [ú. con v. sing.] semántica.
sem·a·phore (sĕm′ə-fôr′) F.C., MARÍT. I. s. semáforo II. tr. **-phored, -phor·ing** transmitor por semáforo —intr. hacer señales con semáforo.
sem·blance (sĕm′bləns) s. *(appearance)* apariencia; *(copy)* copia; *(trace)* huella.
se·mei·ol·o·gy (sē′mī-ŏl′ə-jē) s. var. de **semiology.**
se·men (sē′mən) s. semen *m,* esperma.
se·mes·ter (sə-mĕs′tər) s. semestre *m.*
sem·i·an·nu·al (sĕm′ē-ăn′yōō-əl) adj. semestral.
sem·i·ar·id (sĕm′ē-ăr′ĭd) adj. semiárido (clima, terreno).
sem·i·au·to·mat·ic (sĕm′ē-ô′tə-măt′ĭk) adj. semiautomático.
sem·i·cir·cle (sĕm′ī-sûr′kəl) s. semicírculo.
sem·i·cir·cu·lar (sĕm′ī-sûr′kyə-lər) adj. semicircular.
sem·i·co·lon (sĕm′ī-kō′lən) s. punto y coma.
sem·i·con·duc·tor (sĕm′ē-kən-dŭk′tər) s. ELEC. semiconductor *m.*
sem·i·con·scious (sĕm′ē-kŏn′shəs) adj. semiconsciente.
sem·i·fi·nal DEP. I. s. (sĕm′ē-fī′nəl) semifinal *f* II. adj. (sĕm′ē-fī′nəl) semifinalista.
sem·i·fi·nal·ist (sĕm′ē-fī′nəl-ĭst) s. semifinalista *mf.*
sem·i·lit·er·ate (sĕm′ē-lĭt′ər-ĭt) adj. medio analfabeto.
sem·i·month·ly (sĕm′ē-mŭnth′lē) I. adj. bimensual, quincenal II. adv. dos veces al mes III. s. [pl. **-lies**] publicación bimensual *f.*
sem·i·nal (sĕm′ə-nəl) adj. FIG. *(creative)* creativo; FISIOL. seminal.
sem·i·nar (sĕm′ə-när′) s. *(conference)* reunión *f;* EDUC. seminario.
sem·i·nar·i·an (sĕm′ə-nâr′ē-ən) s. *(in a college)* estudiante que asiste a un seminario *mf;* RELIG. seminarista *m.*
sem·i·nar·y (sĕm′ə-nĕr′ē) s. [pl. **-ies**] EDUC., TEO. seminario.
se·mi·ol·o·gy (sē′mē-ŏl′ə-jē) s. semiología.
sem·i·pre·cious (sĕm′ē-prĕsh′əs) adj. semiprecioso ♦ **s. stone** piedra fina.
sem·i·pri·vate (sĕm′ē-prī′vĭt) adj. para dos o tres personas.
sem·i·skilled (sĕm′ē-skĭld′) adj. no especializado, poco entrenado.
Sem·ite (sĕm′īt′) s. semita *mf.*
Se·mit·ic (sə-mĭt′ĭk) adj. semítico, semita.
Sem·i·tism (sĕm′ī-tĭz′əm) s. semitismo.
sem·i·tone (sĕm′ē-tōn′) s. MÚS. semitono.
sem·i·trail·er (sĕm′ē-trā′lər) s. semirremolque *m.*
sem·i·trans·par·ent (sĕm′ē-trăns-pâr′ənt) adj. semitransparente.
sem·i·trop·i·cal (sĕm′ē-trŏp′ĭ-kəl) adj. subtropical (clima, país).
sem·i·week·ly (sĕm′ē-wēk′lē) I. adj. bisemanal II. s. [pl. **-lies**] publicación bisemanal *f* III. adv. dos veces por semana.
sem·i·year·ly (sĕm′ē-yîr′lē) I. adj. semestral II. s. [pl. **-lies**] publicación semestral *f* III. adv. dos veces al año.
sem·o·li·na (sĕm′ə-lē′nə) s. sémola.
sem·pi·ter·nal (sĕm′pī-tûr′nəl) adj. sempiterno, eterno.
sen·ate (sĕn′ĭt) s. HIST., POL. senado; EDUC. consejo ♦ **S.** Senado.
sen·a·tor (sĕn′ə-tər) s. HIST., POL. senador *m.*
sen·a·to·ri·al (sĕn′ə-tôr′ē-əl) adj. senatorial.
send (sĕnd) tr. **sent** (sĕnt), **send·ing** *(flowers, one's love)* mandar; *(letter, telegram)* enviar; *(into a state)* hacer <*the blow sent him staggering* el golpe le hizo tambalear>; JER. *(aesthetic experience)* chiflar, deleitar; RAD. transmitir ♦ **to s. as** DIPL. enviar de • **to s. away** echar, despedir • **to s. away for** escribir para que envíen, ordenar por correo • **to**

s. back (*person*) hacer regresar *o* volver; (*object*) devolver • **to s. chills down one's spine** darle a uno escalofríos • **to s. down** (*prices*) hacer bajar; G.B. (*student*) expulsar (de la universidad) • **to s. for** (*someone*) enviar a alguien a buscar; (*to place an order for*) escribir para que envíen, ordenar por correo • **to s. forth** (*a cry*) dar; (*roots, smoke*) echar • **to s. in** (*an entry*) mandar; (*a person*) hacer entrar *o* pasar <s. him in hágalo pasar> • **to s. into** lanzar • **to s. off** (*letter*) enviar, echar al buzón; (*person*) despedir, ir a despedir • **to s. on** reexpedir, mandar • **to s. out** (*invoices, invitations*) enviar; (*leaves, smell*) echar; (*light, heat*) emitir • **to s. out for** enviar a alguien a buscar • **to s. packing** FIG., FAM. despedir con cajas destempladas • **to s. to** (*jail, school*) mandar *o* enviar a; (*book, source*) remitir a • **to s. up** (*in jail*) meter en la cárcel; (*upstairs*) mandar arriba; (*prices*) hacer subir; (*spacecraft*) lanzar —intr. enviar.
send·er (sĕn'dər) s. (*one that sends*) remitente *mf*; RAD. transmisor *m*.
send-off (sĕnd'ôf') s. (*farewell*) despedida afectuosa.
send-up (sĕnd'ŭp') s. FAM. parodia, sátira.
Sen·e·gal (sĕn'ĭ-gôl') s. Senegal *m*.
Sen·e·gal·ese (sĕn'ĭ-gə-lēz') adj. & s. [pl. **Senegalese**] senegalés *m* ♦ **the S.** los senegaleses.
se·nes·cent (sĭ-nĕs'ənt) adj. senescente.
se·nile (sē'nīl', sĕn'īl') adj. senil.
se·nil·i·ty (sĭ-nĭl'ĭ-tē) s. senectud *f*.
sen·ior (sēn'yər) I. adj. (*father*) padre <*John Smith s. and John Smith junior* John Smith padre y John Smith hijo>; (*partner*) principal; (*senator*) más antiguo; (*officer*) superior; (*year in school*) del último año ♦ **s. citizen** anciano • **to be five years s. to someone** tener cinco años más que alguien, llevarle cinco años a alguien II. s. (*old person*) anciano; (*student*) estudiante del último año *mf* ♦ **to be someone's s.** ser mayor que alguien • **to be someone's s. by five years** llevarle cinco años a alguien, tener cinco años más que alguien.
senior high school s. instituto de segunda enseñanza.
sen·ior·i·ty (sēn-yôr'ĭ-tē) s. antigüedad *f*, precedencia.
sen·sa·tion (sĕn-sā'shən) s. sensación *f*.
sen·sa·tion·al (sĕn-sā'shə-nəl) adj. sensacional.
sen·sa·tion·al·ism (sĕn-sā'shə-nə-lĭz'əm) s. sensacionalismo.
sen·sa·tion·al·ize (sĕn-sā'shə-nə-līz') tr. -ized, -iz·ing exagerar.
sense (sĕns) I. s. (*function*) sentido <*the five senses* los cinco sentidos>; (*of humor, timing*) sentido; (*feeling*) sentimiento, sensación *f* <*a s. of security* una sensación de seguridad>; (*consciousness*) sentimiento <*a s. of guilt* un sentimiento de culpabilidad>; (*reason*) sentido <*there is no s. in waiting* no tiene sentido esperar>; (*meaning*) sentido; (*judgment*) juicio, sentido común <*to have no s.* no tener sentido común>; (*consensus*) parecer *m* ♦ **good s.** sentido común, sensatez • **in a s.** en cierto sentido • **in every s.** en todos los sentidos • **to be in one's right senses** estar uno en su sano juicio • **to come to one's senses** recobrar el juicio • **to have the s. to** tener la cordura de • **to make s.** tener sentido • **to make s. of something** comprender el sentido de algo • **to talk s.** hablar con sentido común II. tr. **sensed, sens·ing** (*to perceive*) darse cuenta de <*to s. the danger* darse cuenta del peligro>; (*to detect*) detectar.
sense·less (sĕns'lĭs) adj. (*meaningless*) sin sentido; (*foolish*) insensato; (*unconscious*) inconsciente, sin sentido.
sense organ s. FISIOL. órgano sensorio.
sen·si·bil·i·ty (sĕn'sə-bĭl'ĭ-tē) s. [pl. -ties] sensibilidad *f* ♦ **sensibilities** susceptibilidad.
sen·si·ble (sĕn'sə-bəl) adj. (*wise*) sensato; (*practical*) cómodo, práctico; (*perceptible*) sensible ♦ **to be s. of** darse cuenta de.
sen·si·bly (sĕn'sə-blē) adv. (*perceptibly*) perceptiblemente, sensiblemente; (*reasonably*) sensatamente, razonablemente.
sen·si·tive (sĕn'sĭ-tĭv) adj. (*person*) sensible; (*film, skin*) sensible; (*instrument*) sensible, delicado; (*information*) delicado ♦ **to be s. to** *o* **about** ser susceptible a.
sen·si·tive·ly (sĕn'sĭ-tĭv-lē) adv. sensiblemente.

sen·si·tive·ness (sĕn'sĭ-tĭv-nĭs) s. (*quality*) sensibilidad *f*; (*susceptibility*) susceptibilidad *f*.
sen·si·tiv·i·ty (sĕn'sĭ-tĭv'ĭ-tē) s. [pl. -ties] (*quality*) sensibilidad *f*; (*susceptibility*) susceptibilidad *f*.
sen·si·tize (sĕn'sĭ-tīz') tr. & intr. -tized, -tiz·ing sensibilizar(se).
sen·sor (sĕn'sər, -sôr') s. ELEC., ELECTRÓN. sensor *m*.
sen·so·ry (sĕn'sə-rē) adj. FISIOL. sensorio.
sen·su·al (sĕn'shoō-əl) adj. sensual.
sen·su·al·i·ty (sĕn'shoō-ăl'ĭ-tē) s. sensualidad *f*.
sen·su·ous (sĕn'shoō-əs) adj. sensual.
sent (sĕnt) pret. y part. p. de **send**.
sen·tence (sĕn'təns) I. s. GRAM. oración *f*, frase *f*; DER. sentencia, fallo ♦ **death s.** pena de muerte • **life s.** condena perpetua • **to be under s. of death** estar condenado a muerte • **to pass s. on** sentenciar • **to serve out one's s.** cumplir la sentencia II. tr. -tenced, -tenc·ing DER. sentenciar.
sen·ten·tious (sĕn-tĕn'shəs) adj. sentencioso.
sen·tience (sĕn'shəns) s. (*consciousness*) estado consciente; (*feeling*) capacidad de sentir *f*.
sen·tient (sĕn'shənt) adj. (*conscious*) consciente; (*experiencing feeling*) sensible.
sen·ti·ment (sĕn'tə-mənt) s. (*feeling*) sentimiento; (*sentimentality*) sentimentalismo; (*view, thought*) opinión *f*, parecer *m*.
sen·ti·men·tal (sĕn'tə-mĕn'tl) adj. sentimental.
sen·ti·men·tal·ism (sĕn'tə-mĕn'tl-ĭz'əm) s. sentimentalismo.
sen·ti·men·tal·i·ty (sĕn'tə-mĕn-tăl'ĭ-tē) s. [pl. -ties] sentimentalismo.
sen·ti·men·tal·ize (sĕn'tə-mĕn'tl-īz') tr. -ized, -iz·ing hablar con sentimentalismo de —intr. ponerse sentimental.
sen·ti·nel (sĕn'tə-nəl) s. centinela *m*.
sen·try (sĕn'trē) s. [pl. -tries] centinela *m*, guardia *m* ♦ **to be on s.** *o* **to stand s.** estar de guardia.
sentry box s. garita de centinela.
Seoul (sōl) s. Seúl.
se·pal (sē'pəl) s. BOT. sépalo.
sep·a·ra·ble (sĕp'ər-ə-bəl) adj. separable.
sep·a·rate I. tr. (sĕp'ə-rāt') -rat·ed, -rat·ing separar ♦ **to s. from** (*to divide*) separar de; (*to distinguish*) distinguir entre; (*service*) licenciar; (*employment*) despedir • **to s. into** dividir en —intr. separarse ♦ **to s. out** QUÍM. separarse II. adj. (sĕp'ər-ĭt) (*detached*) separado; (*loose*) suelto; (*different*) distinto; (*another*) otro <*write it on a s. sheet* escríbalo en otra hoja>; (*independent*) independiente III. s. (sĕp'ər-ĭt) ♦ **separates** prendas de vestir que se compran por separado.
sep·a·rate·ly (sĕp'ər-ĭt-lē) adv. separadamente, por separado.
sep·a·rate·ness (sĕp'ər-ĭt-nĭs) s. estado de separación.
sep·a·ra·tion (sĕp'ə-rā'shən) s. (*act*) separación *f*; (*of marriage*) separación, separación de cuerpos; (*from service*) licencia; (*from employment*) separación *f*.
sep·a·ra·tist (sĕp'ər-ə-tĭst) s. separatista *mf*.
Se·phar·di (sə-fär'dē) s. [pl. -dim (-dĭm)] sefardí *mf*, sefardita *mf*.
se·pi·a (sē'pē-ə) s. PINT. sepia.
se·poy (sē'poi') s. cipayo, soldado indio.
sep·sis (sĕp'sĭs) s. [pl. -ses (-sēz')] MED. septicemia.
sep·ta (sĕp'tə) pl. de **septum**.
Sep·tem·ber (sĕp-tĕm'bər) s. septiembre *m*, setiembre *m*.
sep·ten·ni·al (sĕp-tĕn'ē-əl) adj. septenal.
sep·tet *o* **sep·tette** (sĕp-tĕt') s. MÚS. septeto.
sep·tic (sĕp'tĭk) I. adj. séptico II. s. substancia séptica.
sep·ti·ce·mi·a (sĕp'tĭ-sē'mē-ə) s. MED. septicemia.
septic tank s. fosa séptica, pozo séptico.
sep·tu·a·ge·nar·i·an (sĕp'toō-ə-jə-nâr'ē-ən, -tyoō-) s. & adj. septuagenario.
sep·tum (sĕp'təm) s. [pl. -ta (-tə)] BIOL. septo, septum *m*.
sep·ul·cher (sĕp'əl-kər) I. s. sepulcro II. tr. sepultar.
se·pul·chral (sə-pŭl'krəl, -pool'-) adj. sepulcral.
sep·ul·ture (sĕp'əl-choōr', -chər) s. sepultura.
se·quel (sē'kwəl) s. (*continuation*) continuación; (*consequence*) consecuencia, resultado.

ā rey / ä año / b boca / ch chico / d dar / ě el / ē mil / g gato / h joya / hw juez / ī aire / k casa / kw cuan /

se·quence (sē'kwəns) **I.** s. *(succession)* sucesión *f*; *(arrangement)* orden *m*; *(series)* serie *f*; *(in cards)* escalera; CINEM., RELIG. secuencia **II.** tr. **-quenced, -quenc·ing** ordenar en serie.

se·quent (sē'kwənt) **I.** adj. *(subsequent)* subsiguiente, consecutivo; *(consequent)* consecuente, subsecuente **II.** s. consecuencia.

se·quen·tial (sĭ-kwĕn'shəl) adj. consecutivo.

se·ques·ter (sĭ-kwĕs'tər) tr. *(to hold apart)* secuestrar; *(from an individual)* embargar; *(from the enemy)* apoderarse de; *(jury)* aislar ♦ **to s. oneself** retirarse.

se·ques·trate (sē'kwĭ-strāt, sĕk'wĭ-, sĭ-kwĕs'trāt') tr. **-trat·ed, -trat·ing** confiscar, embargar.

se·ques·tra·tion (sē'kwĭ-strā'shən, sĕk'wĭ-) s. *(detention)* secuestro; *(seizure)* embargo; *(confiscation)* confiscación *f*.

se·quin (sē'kwĭn) s. *(spangle)* lentejuela; HIST. *(gold coin)* cequí *m*.

se·quoi·a (sĭ-kwoi'ə) s. BOT. secoya.

se·ra (sîr'ə) un pl. de serum.

se·ra·glio (sə-răl'yō) s. [pl. **-glios**] *(harem)* harén *m*; *(palace)* palacio de un sultán.

ser·aph (sĕr'əf) s. [pl. **-a·phim** (-ə-fĭm) o **-aphs**] serafín *m*.

Serb (sûrb) s. *(inhabitant, language)* servio; *(Serbo-Croatian)* servocroata *mf*.

Ser·bi·a (sûr'bē-ə) s. Serbia, Servia.

Ser·bi·an (sûr'bē-ən) **I.** s. *(inhabitant, language)* servio; *(Serbo-Croatian)* servocroata *mf* **II.** adj. servio.

Ser·bo-Cro·a·tian (sûr'bō-krō-ā'shən) s. & adj. servocroata *mf*.

sere (sîr) adj. marchito, seco.

ser·e·nade (sĕr'ə-nād') **I.** s. serenata **II.** tr. **-nad·ed, -nad·ing** dar una serenata a.

ser·e·nad·er (sĕr'ə-nā'dər) s. persona que da serenatas.

ser·en·dip·i·ty (sĕr'ən-dĭp'ĭ-tē) s. hallazgo debido a la fortuna.

se·rene (sə-rēn') adj. *(sky)* sereno, despejado; *(person)* sereno, apacible ♦ **His S. Highness** Su Alteza Serenísima.

se·ren·i·ty (sə-rĕn'ĭ-tē) s. serenidad *f*, calma.

serf (sûrf) s. siervo.

serf·dom (sûrf'dəm) s. servidumbre *f*.

serge (sûrj) s. TEJ. sarga.

ser·geant (sär'jənt) s. sargento.

sergeant at arms s. DER. ujier *m*, ofical de orden *m*.

sergeant major s. MIL. sargento mayor.

se·ri·al (sîr'ē-əl) **I.** adj. *(program)* seriado; *(novel, story)* por entregas; *(order)* consecutivo; *(number)* de serie; *(rights)* de publicación por entregas **II.** s. serial *m*.

se·ri·al·ize (sîr'ē-ə-līz') tr. **-ized, -iz·ing** publicar por entregas o como serial.

se·ri·al·ly (sîr'ē-ə-lē) adv. *(in a series)* en serie; *(novel)* por entregas, por fascículos; *(movie)* por episodios.

serial number s. número de serie.

ser·i·cul·ture (sĕr'ĭ-kŭl'chər) s. sericultura.

se·ries (sîr'ēz) s. [pl. **series**] serie *f*.

ser·if (sĕr'ĭf) s. IMPR. línea de pie, trazo de pie.

se·ri·o·com·ic (sîr'ē-ō-kŏm'ĭk) adj. tragicómico.

se·ri·ous (sîr'ē-əs) adj. *(grave, sincere)* serio; *(illness)* grave ♦ **are you s.?** ¿en serio?, ¿hablas en serio? • **to be s.** *(illness)* estar grave; *(book, crime)* ser serio; *(person)* hablar en serio • **to be s. about** tomar en serio.

se·ri·ous·ly (sîr'ē-əs-lē) adv. seriamente, en serio.

se·ri·ous-mind·ed (sîr'ē-əs-mīn'dĭd) adj. serio.

se·ri·ous·ness (sîr'ē-əs-nĭs) s. seriedad *f*.

ser·mon (sûr'mən) s. sermón *m*.

ser·mon·ize (sûr'mə-nīz') tr. & intr. **-ized, -iz·ing** sermonear.

se·rous (sîr'əs) adj. seroso.

ser·pent (sûr'pənt) s. *(snake)* serpiente *f*; FIG. *(person)* serpiente, víbora; *(firework)* buscapiés *m*.

ser·pen·tine (sûr'pən-tēn', -tīn') **I.** adj. serpentino, sinuoso **II.** s. MIN. serpentina.

ser·rate (sĕr'āt') o **ser·rat·ed** (-ā'tĭd) adj. serrado, dentado.

se·rum (sîr'əm) s. [pl. **se·rums** o **se·ra** (sîr'ə)] MED. suero.

ser·val (sûr'vəl, sər-văl') s. ZOOL. gato serval.

ser·vant (sûr'vənt) s. *(privately employed)* criado, sirviente *m*; *(publicly employed)* funcionario, empleado.

serve (sûrv) **I.** tr. **served, serv·ing** *(to work for)* servir; *(to be a servant to)* servir, estar al servicio de; *(to offer)* servir <*to s. tea* servir el té>; *(to wait on)* servir <*may I s. you?* ¿qué se va a servir?>; *(in a store)* despachar, atender <*are you being served?* ¿lo atienden?>; *(to supply)* abastecer, surtir; *(at Mass)* ayudar a; *(to aid)* servir, ser útil a <*to s. the national interest* ser útil a los intereses nacionales>; *(post, assignment)* ejercer, desempeñar; *(homage, obedience)* servir <*to s. God and the country* servir a Dios y a la patria>; ZOOL. cubrir, montar; DER. entregar; DEP. servir, sacar; TEC. manejar, hacer funcionar ♦ **if my memory serves me right** si la memoria no me falla, si mal no recuerdo • **it serves you right!** ¡lo tienes bien merecido! • **to s. a purpose** servir para un propósito • **to s. as** servir de • **to s. for** servir de • **to s. no purpose** no servir para nada • **to s. on** ser miembro de • **to s. the purpose** servir para el caso • **to s. time** cumplir una condena • **to s. up** servir —intr. *(to work as a servant)* servir, ser criado; *(to carry out duties)* desempeñar los deberes; *(to do service)* prestar servicio; *(to wait on table)* servir, atender; *(to satisfy)* bastar, ser suficiente; *(to be of service)* servir, ser útil; DEP. *(to start play)* efectuar el saque, servir **II.** s. DEP. saque *m*.

serv·er (sûr'vər) s. *(servant)* criado; *(waiter)* camarero; *(tray)* bandeja; *(at Mass)* acólito, monaguillo; *(player)* saque *m*.

serv·ice (sûr'vĭs) **I.** s. *(employment)* servicio, empleo; *(in the military)* servicio militar <*compulsory s.* servicio militar obligatorio>; *(work)* cargo, función *f*; *(maintenance)* servicio de mantenimiento; *(assistance)* favor, servicio <*they render a great s. to the community* le prestan un gran servicio a la comunidad>; *(benefit)* utilidad *f*, beneficio <*to be of great s.* ser de gran utilidad>; *(manner)* atención *f*, servicio <*a restaurant noted for its fine s.* un restaurant reconocido por su esmerada atención>; *(set)* juego, servicio <*a silver tea s.* un juego de té, de plata>; RELIG. *(devotional act)* oficio, servicio; *(rite)* rito, ceremonia; DEP. saque *m*, servicio; ZOOL. monta; DER. entrega ♦ **at your s.** a su disposición, a sus órdenes • **civil s.** administración pública • **diplomatic s.** cuerpo diplomático • **in s.** en funcionamiento, funcionando • **to be of s. (to)** servir (a), ser útil (a) • **to be on active s.** estar en servicio activo • **to be out of s.** no funcionar • **to bring into s.** poner en servicio • **to hold s.** RELIG. celebrar un servicio • **to go into s.** entrar a servir • **to take into one's s.** emplear **II.** adj. *(used by the help)* de servicio <*a s. entrance* una entrada de servicio>; *(military)* militar, de las fuerzas armadas <*a s. uniform* un uniforme militar> **III.** tr. **-iced, -ic·ing** *(to maintain)* mantener; *(to repair)* reparar; *(to check)* revisar; ZOOL. cubrir.

serv·ice·a·ble (sûr'vĭ-sə-bəl) adj. *(usable)* utilizable, servible; *(durable)* duradero.

service charge s. recargo por servicios.

serv·ice·man (sûr'vĭs-măn') s. [pl. **-men** (-mĕn')] *(soldier)* militar *m*; *(repairman)* mecánico.

service station s. estación de servicio *f*.

ser·vi·ette (sûr'vē-ĕt') s. servilleta.

ser·vile (sûr'vəl, -vīl') adj. servil.

ser·vil·i·ty (sûr-vĭl'ĭ-tē) s. servilismo.

serv·ing (sûr'vĭng) s. *(act)* servicio; CUL. porción *f*; DEP. saque *m*; ZOOL. monta.

ser·vi·tude (sûr'vĭ-tōōd', -tyōōd') s. servidumbre *f*.

ser·vo·mech·a·nism (sûr'vō-mĕk'-ə-nĭz'əm) s. TEC. servomecanismo.

ser·vo·mo·tor (sûr'vō-mō'tər) s. TEC. servomotor *m*.

ses·a·me (sĕs'ə-mē) s. BOT. sésamo, ajonjolí (planta y semilla) *m*.

ses·qui·cen·ten·ni·al (sĕs'kwĭ-sĕn-tĕn'ē-əl) adj. & s. sesquicentenario.

ses·sion (sĕsh'ən) s. *(meeting)* sesión *f*; *(of a legislature, council)* reunión *f*, período de sesiones <*the next s. of Congress* la próxima reunión del Congreso> ♦ **court of sessions** audiencia • **recording s.** MÚS. grabación • **summer s.** EDUC. curso(s) de verano • **to be in s.** estar en reunión.

ses·tet (sĕ-stĕt') s. POÉT. los dos últimos tercetos de un soneto.

set¹ (sĕt) **I.** tr. **set, set·ting** *(to place)* poner, colocar *<he s. the book on the table* puso el libro en la mesa>; *(to locate)* situar, ubicar *<the castle is s. on a hilltop* el castillo está situado en la cima de una colina>; *(into a specified state)* poner *<to s. in motion* poner en marcha>; *(a bone)* encajar; *(a saw)* triscar; *(a watch)* poner en hora; *(a dial, alarm)* poner; *(sails)* desplegar; *(to arrange)* poner, preparar *<to s. the table* poner la mesa>; *(to harden)* endurecer; *(to congeal)* cuajar; *(type)* componer; *(music, words)* poner *<to s. words to music* poner música a la letra>; *(stage, scenery)* montar; *(a precedent, rule)* sentar; *(date, amount)* fijar, señalar; *(to assign)* poner *<they s. him to cleaning windows* lo pusieron a limpiar ventanas>; *(a record)* establecer; *(an example)* dar; *(fashion)* imponer; *(a pearl, diamond)* montar, engastar; *(with jewels)* guarnecer, adornar; BOT. dar, echar (semilla, fruto); TEC. *(to adjust)* ajustar; *(to calibrate)* calibrar ♦ **to be s. back from** estar a cierta distancia de ♦ **to be s. for life** tener el porvenir asegurado ♦ **to be s. in** LIT., TEAT. desarrollarse en, tener lugar en ♦ **to s. about** ponerse a ♦ **to s. above** anteponer ♦ **to s. after** echarse tras ♦ **to s. against** *(to balance)* poner contra; *(to pit)* enemistar con, enfrentar con; *(to compare)* contraponer a ♦ **to s. a great deal** o **great store by** valorar en mucho ♦ **to s. apart** separar, poner a un lado ♦ **to s. aside** *(to separate)* apartar, hacer a un lado; *(for future use)* separar, guardar; *(claim)* rechazar; *(one's feelings)* dejar de lado; *(decision)* anular ♦ **to s. at** *(amount)* fijar en; *(liberty)* poner en ♦ **to s. at odds** enemistar ♦ **to s. a trap for** *(animals)* poner una trampa a o para; FIG. *(people)* tender una trampa a ♦ **to s. back** *(a clock, progress)* atrasar; FAM. *(to cost)* salir por, costar *<that coat s. me back $400* ese abrigo me costó $400> ♦ **to s. course for** poner rumbo a ♦ **to s. down** *(to lay down)* poner en el suelo, depositar; FAM. *(to seat)* poner, sentar; *(to record)* consignar, poner por escrito; *(to attribute)* atribuir, achacar *<they s. it down to inexperience* lo achacaron a la falta de experiencia>; *(to establish)* fijar ♦ **to s. eyes on** FIG. poner los ojos en ♦ **to s. fire to** prenderle fuego a ♦ **to s. foot in** entrar ♦ **to s. foot on** pisar ♦ **to s. forth** exponer, presentar ♦ **to s. free** liberar ♦ **to s. in** *(to insert)* encajar, insertar; *(sleeves)* montar ♦ **to s. limits to** poner límites a ♦ **to s. off** *(a reaction, war)* iniciar, desencadenar; *(anger)* enojar, enfadar; *(an explosion)* causar; *(a bomb)* hacer estallar; *(an alarm)* hacer sonar; *(to distinguish)* hacer sobresalir, distinguir; *(to accentuate)* hacer resaltar, realzar ♦ **to s. on** azuzar (un perro) contra ♦ **to s. on edge** *(a person)* sacar de quicio; *(nerves)* ponerle a uno los nervios de punta ♦ **to s. on fire** prender fuego ♦ **to s. oneself up as** dárselas de ♦ **to s. one's heart** o **mind on** estar resuelto a ♦ **to s. one's house in order** FIG. arreglar los asuntos de uno ♦ **to s. one's sights on** echar el ojo a ♦ **to s. one's teeth on edge** darle dentera a uno ♦ **to s. out** *(to lay out)* disponer, repartir; *(to display)* desplegar; *(opinions)* exponer; *(on a trip)* ponerse en camino, salir ♦ **to s. out to** proponerse ♦ **to s. sail** hacerse a la vela ♦ **to s. straight** *(to show the truth)* desengañar; *(to chastise)* corregir; *(to clarify)* poner en claro ♦ **to s. the stage for** crear las condiciones necesarias para ♦ **to s. to (work)** ponerse a (trabajar) ♦ **to s. (to) thinking** dar que pensar a ♦ **to s. up** *(upright)* levantar, parar; *(monument)* levantar; *(machine)* armar, montar; *(tent)* instalar; *(exhibit)* montar; *(office)* poner, abrir; *(in power)* instaurar; *(as an example)* poner; *(equipment, plans)* preparar; *(house)* poner; *(cry, protest)* levantar; *(a theory)* proponer; FAM. *(to stimulate)* levantar los ánimos ♦ **to s. up in** ayudar a establecerse en (un negocio) ♦ **to s. upon** acometer, atacar ♦ **to s. up shop** FAM. establecerse, instalarse —intr. *(sun, moon)* ponerse; *(power, influence)* menguar, decaer; *(fowl)* empollar; *(cement)* endurecerse; *(gelatin)* cuajar; *(dye, color)* fijarse; FAM. *(to sit)* sentarse; *(bone)* encajarse; *(a seed)* formarse; *(pregnant)* caer ♦ **to s. down** AVIA. aterrizar ♦ **to s. forth** salir, irse de viaje ♦ **to s. in** *(winter, night)* cerrar; *(rains)* llegar; *(wind)* levantarse; *(tide)* subir; *(discontent)* arraigar ♦ **to s. off** salir, partir ♦ **to s. out** salir, ponerse en camino ♦ **to s. to** *(to begin working)* poner manos a la obra; *(to start fighting)* venir a las manos ♦ **to s. up** establecerse **II.** adj. *(agreed upon)* seña-

lado, convenido *<at the s. time* a la hora señalada>; *(price, schedule)* fijo; *(customary)* establecido; *(procedure, hours)* reglamentario; *(phrase)* hecho; *(customs)* arraigado; *(ideas)* estricto; *(opinion)* firme; *(speech)* preparado; *(deliberate)* determinado; *(face)* inmóvil; *(gaze, frown)* fijo; *(smile)* forzado; *(determined)* resuelto, decidido; *(ready)* listo ♦ **ready, get s., go** preparados, listos, fuera ♦ **to be all s.** estar listo ♦ **to be dead s. against** estar resueltamente en contra de ♦ **to be s. in one's ways** tener costumbres muy arraigadas ♦ **to be s. on** *(doing something)* estar empeñado en, estar resuelto a; *(an idea)* estar aferrado a ♦ **to get s. to** o **for** prepararse a o para **III.** s. *(of the head, shoulders)* postura, porte m; *(of a garment)* caída; *(hardening)* endurecimiento; *(of gelatin)* cuajadura; *(of sun, moon)* puesta; *(of wind, current)* dirección f.

set² (sĕt) s. *(of things)* juego; *(of rules, conditions)* serie f, conjunto; *(of clothes)* muda; *(of animals)* tiro; *(of people)* grupo, círculo; *(gang)* cuadrilla; *(of volumes, works)* colección f *<a s. of plays* una colección de obras de teatro>; TEAT. decorado; CINEM. plató m; RAD., TELEV. aparato m; MAT. conjunto, serie; DEP. set m; TEC. tren m ♦ **generating s.** ELEC. grupo electrógeno ♦ **s. of dishes** vajilla ♦ **s. of teeth** FAM. dentadura ♦ **television s.** televisor ♦ **the smart s.** la gente elegante.

set·back (sĕt'băk') s. *(reverse)* revés m *<to suffer a s.* sufrir un revés>; ARG. retallo; MED. recaída.

set·off (sĕt'ôf') s. *(decoration)* realce m; *(of debt)* compensación f; *(counterbalance)* contrapeso; ARQ. saliente m.

set·screw (sĕt'skrōō') s. tornillo de fijación.

set·tee (sĕ-tē') s. sofá m.

set·ter (sĕt'ar) s. *(dog)* perro de muestra, setter m; JOY. engastador m.

set theory s. MAT. teoría de los conjuntos.

set·ting (sĕt'ĭng) s. *(place)* marco; *(of an action)* escenario; *(scenery)* decorado; MÚS. *(for text)* música; *(of a gem)* engastadura, engarce m; *(of the sun)* puesta; *(of cement)* fraguado; *(of type)* composición f.

set·tle (sĕt'l) tr. **-tled, -tling** *(affairs)* arreglar; *(a claim)* satisfacer; *(a debt, account)* saldar, liquidar; *(a dispute)* arreglar, resolver; *(a quarrel)* poner fin a; *(a problem)* resolver; *(doubts)* disipar; *(a date)* fijar; *(a plan)* decidir; *(a person)* instalar, acomodar *<she settled her family in Ohio* instaló a su familia en Ohio>; *(a territory)* colonizar, poblar; *(in business, a profession)* establecer, colocar; *(nerves)* calmar; *(stomach)* asentar; *(dust)* asentar, hacer caer; *(a liquid)* clarificar; *(situation, condition)* estabilizar, normalizar; DER. asignar ♦ **that settles it!** ¡no hay más que hablar! ♦ **to s. accounts** FIG. ajustar cuentas ♦ **to s. for** conformarse o contentarse con ♦ **to s. on** o **upon** *(to choose)* decidirse por; *(to agree on)* llegar a un acuerdo sobre ♦ **to s. up** saldar, ajustar —intr. *(bird, gaze)* posarse; *(stomach, nerves)* calmarse, tranquilizarse; *(conditions, weather)* estabilizarse, normalizarse; *(night)* caer; *(dust, sediment)* asentarse, depositarse; *(contents, building)* asentarse; *(liquid)* clarificarse, asentarse; *(in a house)* instalarse; *(in a country, city)* establecerse; *(in a job, situation)* acostumbrarse, adaptarse; *(disease)* localizarse; *(in a dispute)* arreglarse, llegar a un acuerdo ♦ **to s. down** *(in a place)* establecerse, quedarse a vivir; *(in one's ways)* sentar cabeza, formalizarse; *(a child, things)* calmarse; *(conditions)* normalizarse; *(in marriage)* casarse ♦ **to s. down (to write, work)** ponerse a (escribir, trabajar) ♦ **to s. out of court** arreglar amistosamente ♦ **to s. up** ajustar cuentas.

set·tled (sĕt'ld) adj. *(established)* arraigado; *(stabilized)* estable, firme; *(paid)* pagado.

set·tle·ment (sĕt'l-mənt) s. *(of a dispute)* arreglo; *(of a problem)* solución f; *(agreement)* acuerdo, convenio; *(of a people)* establecimiento; *(of territory)* población f, colonización; *(community)* población f, poblado; *(colony)* colonia; *(of account, debt)* liquidación f ♦ **to reach a s.** llegar a un acuerdo.

set·tler (sĕt'lər) s. *(arbiter)* árbitro; *(colonizer)* poblador m; colono.

set-to (sĕt'tōō') [pl. **-tos**] *(verbal)* disputa, debate m; *(physical)* lucha, refriega.

set·up (sĕt'ŭp') s. *(organization)* organización f; *(plan)* plan *m*; *(situation)* situación *f*; *(of body)* porte *m*; JER. *(fight)* combate amañado; *(fraud)* engaño.

sev·en (sĕv'ən) s. & adj.   siete *m* ♦ **s. o'clock** las siete.

sev·en·fold (sĕv'ən-fōld') **I.** adj. séptuplo **II.** adv. siete veces.

seven hundred s. & adj. setecientos.

sev·en·teen (sĕv'ən-tēn') s. & adj.   diecisiete *m*, diez y siete *m*.

sev·en·teenth (sĕv'ən-tēnth') **I.** s. *(place)* diecisiete *m*; *(part)* diecisieteavo *o* diecisieteava parte **II.** adj. *(place)* decimoséptimo; *(part)* diecisieteavo.

sev·enth (sĕv'ənth) s. & adj.   séptimo.

seventh heaven s.   séptimo cielo.

sev·en·ti·eth (sĕv'ən-tē-ĭth) **I.** s. *(place)* setenta *m*; *(part)* setentavo, septuagésima parte **II.** adj. *(place, part)* septuagésimo.

sev·en·ty (sĕv'ən-tē) s. [pl. **-ties**] & adj.   setenta *m*.

sev·en·ty-one (sĕv'ən-tē-wŭn') s. & adj.   setenta y uno.

sev·er (sĕv'ər) **I.** tr. *(to cut)* cortar; FIG. *(to break off)* romper (relaciones) ♦ **to s. from** separar de **II.** intr. romperse.

sev·er·a·ble (sĕv'ər-ə-bəl) adj. *(separable)* separable; DER. divisible.

sev·er·al (sĕv'ər-əl) **I.** adj. *(some)* algunos, varios <*s. miles* varias millas>; *(distinct)* distinto; *(respective)* respectivo; DER. individual ♦ **joint and s. bond** DER. obligación solidaria **II.** s. varios.

sev·er·ance (sĕv'ər-əns) s. *(separation)* separación *f*; *(breakup)* ruptura.

severance pay s.   indemnización por despido *f*.

se·vere (sə-vîr') adj. **-ver·er, -ver·est** *(strict)* severo <*a s. taskmaster* un supervisor severo>; *(exact)* estricto, exacto <*s. accuracy* precisión exacta>; *(harsh)* riguroso <*s. disciplinary measures* medidas disciplinarias rigurosas>; *(intense)* intenso, fuerte; *(extreme)* agudo <*s. pain* dolor agudo>; *(grave)* grave, serio.

se·vere·ly (sə-vîr'lē) adv. *(harshly)* severamente; *(gravely)* de gravedad.

se·ver·i·ty (sə-vĕr'ĭ-tē) s. *(of punishment, dress)* severidad *f*; *(of climate)* rigor *m*; *(of crime, illness)* seriedad *f*, gravedad *f*; *(of pain)* agudeza.

Se·ville (sə-vĭl') s.   Sevilla.

sew (sō) tr. **sewed, sewn** (sōn) *o* **sewed, sew·ing** CIR., COST. coser ♦ **to s. in** *o* **on** • **to s. up** *(a deal)* cerrar; *(the market)* monopolizar; CIR., COST. coser —intr. coser.

sew·age (sōō'ĭj) s.   aguas cloacales *o* residuales.

sew·er¹ (sōō'ər) s. *(conduit)* alcantarilla, cloaca.

sew·er² (sōō'ər) s.   HIST. *(servant)* sirviente *m*.

sew·er³ (sō'ər) s.   COST. costurera.

sew·er·age (sōō'ər-ĭj) s. *(system)* alcantarillado; *(sewage)* aguas cloacales *o* residuales.

sew·ing (sō'ĭng) s.   costura.

sewing basket s.   cesto de la costura.

sewing circle s.   grupo de costureras.

sewing machine s.   máquina de coser.

sewn (sōn) un part. p. de **sew.**

sex (sĕks) s.   sexo ♦ **s. life** vida sexual • **to have s. (with)** tener relaciones sexuales (con).

sex·a·ge·nar·i·an (sĕk'sə-jə-nâr'ē-ən) s. & adj. sexagenario.

sex appeal s.   atractivo sexual.

sex·en·ni·al (sĕk-sĕn'ē-əl) **I.** adj. *(duration)* que dura seis años; *(interval)* que ocurre cada seis años **II.** s. sexenio.

sex·ism (sĕk'sĭz'əm) s.   prejuicio sexual (esp. contra la mujer).

sex·ist (sĕk'sĭst) **I.** adj. que tiene prejuicios sexuales **II.** s. persona que tiene prejuicios sexuales.

sex·less (sĕks'lĭs) adj.   asexual, asexuado.

sex·tant (sĕks'tənt) s.   MARÍT. sextante *m*.

sex·tet *o* **sex·tette** (sĕk-stĕt') s.   MÚS. sexteto.

sex·ton (sĕk'stən) s.   RELIG. sacristán *m*.

sex·tu·ple (sĕk-stŭp'əl, sĕk'stə-pəl) **I.** tr. & intr. **-pled, -pling** sextuplicar(se) **II.** adj. & s. séxtuplo.

sex·tu·plet (sĕk-stŭp'lĭt) s.   séxtuplo.

si·ne di·e (sī'nē dī'ē, sĭn'ā dā'ā') adv. indefinidamente.

sex·u·al (sĕk'shōō-əl) adj.   sexual.

sexual intercourse s.   coito, relaciones sexuales *f*.

sex·u·al·i·ty (sĕk'shōō-ăl'ĭ-tē) s.   sexualidad *f*.

sex·y (sĕk'sē) adj. **-i·er, -i·est** *(person)* atractivo, excitante; *(film, book)* erótico.

sh! (sh) interj.   ¡chitón!, ¡silencio!

shab·bi·ness (shăb'ē-nĭs) s. *(of a person)* aspecto andrajoso; *(of house)* aspecto lastimoso.

shab·by (shăb'ē) adj. **-bi·er, -bi·est** *(clothing, upholstery)* raído; *(beggar)* andrajoso; *(house, neighborhood)* derruido, pobre; *(treatment)* malo, mezquino.

shack (shăk) s.   choza ♦ **to s. up with** JER. *(to stay)* quedarse con, alojarse con; *(to live)* vivir con, cohabitar con.

shack·le (shăk'əl) **I.** s. *(for prisoners)* grilletes *m*; *(for animals)* traba ♦ **shackles** FIG. trabas **II.** tr. **-led, -ling** *(a prisoner)* poner grilletes a; *(an animal)* poner trabas a; FIG. *(to hamper)* poner trabas a, trabar.

shad (shăd) s. [pl. **shad** *o* **shads**] ICT. sábalo.

shade (shād) **I.** s. *(from sun)* sombra <*I sat in the s.* me senté a la sombra>; *(for a lamp)* pantalla; *(for a window)* persiana; *(of color)* tono; *(of meaning)* matiz *m*; *(bit)* pizca, poquito; *(of a photograph)* sombra; *(ghost)* sombra, fantasma *m* ♦ **light and s.** PINT. claroscuro • **s. tree** árbol que da sombra • **shades** JER. *(sunglasses)* gafas *o* anteojos de sol; *(shadows)* sombras; *(echoes)* recuerdos **II.** tr. **shad·ed, shad·ing** *(from light, heat)* resguardar; *(to cause shade in)* dar sombra a; *(a picture)* sombrear; *(a meaning)* matizar; FAM. *(prices)* reducir ligeramente.

shad·i·ness (shā'dē-nĭs) s. *(shade)* sombra; FIG., FAM. *(aspect)* lo turbio (de un negocio, asunto).

shad·ing (shā'dĭng) s. *(from light, heat)* protección *f*; *(of meaning)* matizado; DIB., PINT. *(of darkness)* sombreado; *(of color)* degradación *f*.

shad·ow (shăd'ō) **I.** s. *(image)* sombra; *(ghost)* sombra, fantasma *m*; *(companion)* sombra; *(spy)* espía *mf*; *(detective)* policía *mf*; *(premonition)* presentimiento, presagio; *(vestige)* sombra <*a s. of his former self* una sombra de lo que fue>; PINT. sombra, sombreado; FOTOG., TELEV. sombra ♦ **beyond a s. of a doubt** sin lugar a dudas • **shadows** oscuridad • **to cast a s. (on)** hacer sombra (sobre) • **to cast a s. on** *o* **over** FIG. oscurecer, ensombrecer **II.** tr. *(to shade)* sombrear, dar sombra a; *(to cloud)* oscurecer; *(to trail)* seguir (la pista de); DIB., PINT. sombrear ♦ **to s. forth** *o* **out** presentir **III.** adj. POL. fantasma.

shad·ow·box (shăd'ō-bŏks') intr.   boxear con la sombra de uno.

shad·ow·y (shăd'ō-ē) adj. **-i·er, -i·est** *(dark)* obscuro; *(vague)* vago; *(shady)* turbio.

shad·y (shā'dē) adj. **-i·er, -i·est** *(place)* sombreado; *(person)* sospechoso; *(business)* turbio.

shaft (shăft) **I.** s. *(of a spear)* asta; *(of an arrow)* astil *m*; *(arrow)* flecha; FAM. *(remark)* dardo; *(of light)* rayo; *(of a feather)* cañón *m*; *(of a bone)* caña; *(of a broom)* palo; *(of a hammer)* mango; *(of a vehicle)* varal *m*; *(mine)* pozo; *(passage)* hueco, pozo <*elevator s.* hueco de ascensor>; MEC. eje *m*, árbol *m*; ARQ. *(column)* columna; *(of a column)* fuste *m*, caña ♦ **to get the s.** JER. salir perjudicado **II.** tr. JER. perjudicar ♦ **to get shafted** JER. salir perjudicado.

shag (shăg) s. *(hair)* greñas; *(nap)* pelusa; *(tobacco)* picadura.

shag·gy (shăg'ē) adj. **-gi·er, -gi·est** *(hairy)* peludo; *(woolly)* lanudo; *(unkempt)* desgreñado.

shah (shä) s.   chah *m*, sha *m* (soberano de Persia).

shake (shāk) **I.** tr. **shook** (shōōk), **shak·en** (shā'kən), **shak·ing** *(rug, cloth)* sacudir; *(house, ground)* hacer temblar; *(trees, bottle)* agitar; *(one's faith)* hacer vacilar; *(a habit, one's pursuers)* librarse de; *(dice)* mover; *(person)* sacudir ♦ **to s. a leg** darse prisa, apurarse • **to s. down** FAM. *(to extort)* sacar dinero a; *(to search)* registrar • **to s. hands** darse la mano • **to s. hands with** *o* **s. someone's hand** dar la mano a, estrechar la mano a • **to s. off** *(dust, snow)* sacudir; *(a cold, one's pursuers)* liberarse de • **to s. one's finger at** decir que no con el dedo a • **to s. one's head** negar con la cabeza • **to s. out** sacudir • **to s. up** *(bottle)* agitar; *(person)* sacudir; *(organization)* reorganizar —intr. *(house, ground)* temblar; *(person)* temblar; *(voice, hands)* temblar; MÚS. trinar ♦ **to s. with (fear, cold)** temblar de, estremecerse de (miedo, frío) **II.** s. *(shaking)* sacudida; *(tremble)* temblor *m*, estremecimiento; FAM. *(earthquake)* temblor de tierra; *(fissure)* grieta; JER. *(instant)* instante *m*, periquete *m*; *(beverage)* batido; MÚS. trino ♦ **to be no great shakes** JER. no valer gran cosa • **to give someone the s.** JER. liberarse de • **to have the shakes** FAM. tener escalofríos.

shake·down (shāk′doun′) I. s. *(trial)* prueba; FAM. *(extortion)* extorsión *f*; *(search)* registro II. adj. de prueba <*a s. flight* vuelo de prueba>.

shak·er (shā′kər) s. *(for cocktails)* coctelera; *(for salt)* salero; *(for pepper)* pimentero.

Shake·spear·e·an *o* **Shake·spear·i·an** (shāk-spîr′ē-ən) I. adj. shakesperiano, de Shakespeare II. s. especialista en la obra de Shakespeare *mf*.

shake·up (shāk′ŭp′) s. *(reorganization)* reorganización *f*; *(shake)* sacudida.

shak·ing (shā′kĭng) I. adj. *(shaky)* tembloroso; *(upsetting)* desconcertante II. s. sacudida.

shak·o (shăk′ō, shā′kō) s. [pl. **-os** *o* **-oes**] MIL. chacó.

shak·y (shā′kē) adj. **-i·er, -i·est** *(hands, voice)* tembloroso; *(table)* inestable; *(alliance)* poco sólido; *(principles)* discutibles ♦ **to feel s.** sentirse débil.

shale (shāl) s. MIN. esquisto.

shall §G4 (shăl) aux. [pret. **should** (shŏŏd)] [ú. para formar el futuro simple] <*I s. be 28 tomorrow* cumpliré 28 años mañana>; [ú. para indicar una intención, promesa] <*he s. answer for his misdeeds* pagará por sus delitos>; [ú. para expresar algo que se ha de cumplir] <*that day s. come* ese día llegará>; [ú. para expresar una orden] <*students s. report weekly to their tutors* los estudiantes deberán presentarse semanalmente a sus tutores>; [ú. para expresar una obligación, requisito] <*the penalty s. not exceed two years in prison* el castigo no excederá más de dos años de cárcel>; [ú. en preguntas que implican deber, mando u obligación] <*shall I call?* ¿quiere que llame por teléfono?>.

shal·lot (shə-lŏt′, shăl′ət) s. BOT. chalote *m*.

shal·low (shăl′ō) I. adj. **-er, -est** *(water, pool)* poco profundo; *(dish)* llano; FIG. *(superficial)* superficial II. s. ♦ **shallows** MARÍT. bajíos, bajos III. tr. & intr. hacer(se) menos profundo.

shal·low·ness (shăl′ō-nĭs) s. *(little depth)* poca profundidad; FIG. *(superficiality)* superficialidad *f*.

shalt (shălt) aux. ANT. segunda persona sing., tiempo pres., de **shall** ♦ **thou s. not kill** BÍBL. no matarás.

sham (shăm) I. s. *(fake)* falsificación *f*; *(fraud)* farsa; *(impostor)* impostor *m* II. adj. *(fake)* falso <*s. title* título falso>; *(feigned)* fingido <*a s. illness* una enfermedad fingida>; JOY. de imitación III. tr. & intr. **shammed, shamming** fingir.

sha·man (shā′mən, shā′-) s. RELIG. shamán *m*, chamán *m*.

sham·ble (shăm′bəl) intr. **-bled, -bling** andar arrastrando los pies.

sham·bles (shăm′bəlz) s.pl. [ú. con v. sing.] *(chaos)* confusión *f*, caos *m*; FIG. *(carnage)* carnicería, matanza; *(slaughterhouse)* matadero ♦ **to make a s. of** convertir en caos.

shame (shām) I. s. *(humiliation)* vergüenza <*filled with s.* lleno de vergüenza>; *(modesty)* vergüenza <*have you no s.?* ¿no te da vergüenza?>; *(pity)* pena, lástima <*it's a crying s.* es una verdadera lástima> ♦ **s. on you!** ¡qué vergüenza! • **to bring s. on** deshonrar a • **to put to shame** FIG. avergonzar II. tr. **shamed, sham·ing** *(to humiliate)* avergonzar; *(to dishonor)* deshonrar.

shame·faced (shām′fāst′) adj. *(ashamed)* avergonzado; *(shy)* tímido.

shame·ful (shām′fəl) adj. vergonzoso ♦ **how s.!** ¡qué vergüenza!

shame·ful·ness (shām′fəl-nĭs) s. vergüenza.

shame·less (shām′lĭs) adj. *(person)* descarado, sinvergüenza; *(behavior, lie)* vergonzoso.

sham·poo (shăm-pōō′) I. s. [pl. **-poos**] champú *m* II. tr. **-pooed, -poo·ing** dar un champú a —intr. lavarse la cabeza con champú.

sham·rock (shăm′rŏk′) s. BOT. trébol *m*.

shang·hai (shăng-hī′) tr. **-haied, -hai·ing** *(to kidnap)* embriagar (a alguien) para llevárselo como marinero; *(to force)* obligar a hacer algo por la fuerza.

Shan·gri·la (shăng′grī-lä′) s. lugar paradisíaco imaginario, tierra de Jauja.

shank (shăngk) s. *(lower leg)* espinilla; *(leg)* pierna; *(of a horse)* caña; *(cut of meat)* pierna; *(of a pin, key)* tija; *(of an anchor)* caña; *(of a shoe)* enfranque *m*; *(of a tool, spoon)* mango; *(of a plant)* tallo.

shan't *o* **sha'nt** (shănt, shänt) contr. de **shall not.**

shan·ty (shăn′tē) s. [pl. **-ties**] choza.

shan·ty·town (shăn′tē-toun′) s. villa miseria, barrio de las latas *o* de las chabolas.

shape (shāp) I. s. *(form)* forma <*to be in the s. of a bird* tener la forma de un pájaro>; *(body)* figura, cuerpo; *(guise)* aspecto, apariencia; *(figure)* figura; *(of garment)* hechura, corte *m*; *(for hats)* horma ♦ **to be in good s.** *(car)* estar en buen estado; *(athlete)* estar en buena forma; *(financially)* estar bien • **to be in no s. to** no estar en condiciones de *o* para • **to be in tip-top s.** *(car)* estar en excelente estado; *(athlete)* estar en plena forma • **to be out of s.** DEP. no estar en forma • **to get into s.** *(athlete)* ponerse en forma; *(book, team)* poner en condiciones • **to keep in s.** mantener en forma • **to knock out of s.** deformar • **to take s.** tomar forma, formarse II. tr. **shaped, shap·ing** *(one's character)* formar; *(object)* dar forma a; *(idea)* concebir; *(one's life)* adaptar ♦ **shaped** en forma de <*mushroom-shaped* en forma de hongo> • **to s. into** dar forma de • **to s. up** poner en buenas condiciones —intr. ♦ **to s. up** FAM. *(to come along)* desarrollarse; *(to improve)* ponerse en condiciones.

shape·less (shāp′lĭs) adj. *(formless)* amorfo, informe; *(not shapely)* deforme.

shape·ly (shāp′lē) adj. **-li·er, -li·est** bien proporcionado.

shap·er (shā′pər) s. TEC. moldeador *m*; METAL. embutidora.

shard (shärd) s. *(of pottery)* casco; *(of glass, metal)* fragmento; ENTOM. élitro.

share¹ (shâr) I. s. *(part)* parte *f*; *(of stock)* acción *f* ♦ **to go shares in** ir a partes iguales en II. tr. **shared, shar·ing** compartir <*to s. an apartment* compartir un apartamento> • **to s. out** repartir —intr. compartir ♦ **to s. and s. alike** compartir por partes iguales • **to s. in** participar en, tener parte en.

share² (shâr) s. AGR. reja de arado.

share·crop (shâr′krŏp′) tr. & intr. **-cropped, -crop·ping** AGR. trabajar como aparcero.

share·crop·per (shâr′krŏp′ər) s. AGR. aparcero.

share·hold·er (shâr′hōl′dər) s. FIN. accionista *mf*.

shar·er (shâr′ər) s. partícipe *mf*.

shark (shärk) s. ICT. tiburón *m*; JER. *(usurer)* usurero; *(expert)* experto.

shark·skin (shärk′skĭn′) s. piel de tiburón *f*.

sharp (shärp) I. adj. **-er, -est** *(cutting)* afilado <*a s. knife* un cuchillo afilado>; *(pointed)* puntiagudo; *(outline, image)* claro, nítido; *(feature)* anguloso; *(contrast)* marcado, profundo; *(abrupt)* brusco, repentino <*a s. increase* un aumento repentino>; *(incline)* empinado; *(curve)* cerrado; *(angle)* agudo; *(shrewd)* vivo, despierto; *(observation, mind)* agudo, penetrante; *(underhand)* fullero, tramposo; *(alert)* atento; *(eyesight)* agudo; *(sense of smell, hearing)* fino; *(eyes)* de lince; *(in movement)* vivo, rápido; *(criticism)* mordaz; *(tongue)* de víbora; *(tone, reply)* áspero; *(fierce)* feroz (lucha, ataque); *(strong)* fuerte (restricciones); *(pain, voice)* agudo; *(appetite)* voraz; *(wind)* penetrante; *(smell, taste)* acre; *(cheese)* fuerte; MÚS. *(raised in pitch)* sostenido; *(high)* agudo, alto; JER. *(stylish)* elegante ♦ **to be s. at** ser un hacha en (historia, matemáticas) • **to have a s. temper** enojarse fácilmente • **to keep a s. eye on** no perder de vista II. adv. *(abruptly)* repentinamente, de pronto; *(punctually)* en punto <*at three o'clock s.* a las tres en punto>; MÚS. *(high)* muy alto ♦ **to look s.** estar atento III. s. FAM. *(cheater)* fullero; MÚS. sostenido IV. tr. MÚS. marcar con un sostenido —intr. MÚS. dar un agudo.

sharp·en (shär′pən) tr. *(blade)* afilar; *(pencil)* sacar punta a; *(appetite)* aguzar, abrir; *(wits)* aguzar —intr. afilarse.

sharp·en·er (shär′pə-nər) s. *(for pencil)* sacapuntas *m*; *(machine)* afiladora.

ā rey / ä año / b boca / ch chico / d dar / ĕ el / ē mil / g gato / h joya / hw juez / ī aire / k casa / kw cuan /

sharp·er (shär'pər) s. *(cardsharper)* fullero; *(swindler)* estafador *m*.

sharp-eyed (shärp'īd') adj. *(having good sight)* que tiene ojos de lince; *(observant)* observador.

sharp·ie (shär'pē) s. *(boat)* barco de pesca de poco calado, con uno o dos mástiles y velas triangulares; *(person)* persona de ingenio agudo.

sharp·ly (shärp'lē) adv. *(abruptly)* repentinamente; *(brusquely)* severamente; *(clearly)* claramente; *(to criticize)* de modo incisivo; *(for answer)* con aspereza; *(to differ, contrast)* profundamente.

sharp·ness (shärp'nĭs). s. *(of knife)* lo afilado; *(of edge, cliff)* lo puntiagudo; *(of increase)* brusquedad *f*; *(of outline, image)* nitidez *f*, claridad *f*; *(of mind, eyesight)* agudeza; *(of senses)* finura; *(of reply, tone)* aspereza; *(of criticism)* mordacidad *f*; *(of voice, pain)* agudeza; *(of curve)* lo cerrado; *(of taste)* acritud *f*.

sharp·shoot·er (shärp'shoo'tər) s. tirador de primera *m*.

sharp-sight·ed (shärp'sī'tĭd) adj. *(having good sight)* que tiene ojos de lince; *(observant)* observador.

sharp-tongued (shärp'tŭngd') adj. de lengua viperina.

sharp-wit·ted (shärp'wĭt'ĭd) adj. *(witty)* agudo, ingenioso; *(shrewd)* perspicaz.

shat·ter (shăt'ər) I. tr. *(to break)* hacer añicos; FIG. *(to destroy)* baldar —intr. hacerse añicos II. s. ♦ **in shatters** hecho añicos.

shat·ter·proof (shăt'ər-prōōf') adj. inastillable, a prueba de fracturas (dic. del vidrio).

shave (shāv) I. tr. **shaved, shaved** *o* **shav·en** (shā'vən), **shav·ing** *(to cut beard)* afeitar; *(to cut hair)* rapar; *(wood)* cepillar; *(cheese)* cortar en tajadas finas ♦ **to s. off** afeitarse (el bigote, la barba) —intr. afeitarse II. s. afeitado ♦ **to get a s.** afeitarse • **to have a close s.** FIG. librarse por los pelos.

shav·er (shā'vər) s. *(barber)* barbero; *(device)* afeitadora; FAM. *(young boy)* chaval *m*, mozalbete *m*.

shav·ing (shā'vĭng) s. *(sliver)* viruta; *(act)* afeitado; TEC. cepillado ♦ **s. cream** crema de afeitar.

shawl (shôl) s. chal *m*.

she (shē) §G29 I. pron. ella <*s. didn't see anything* ella no vio nada> II. s. hembra <*is it a he or a s.?* ¿es macho o hembra?>.

sheaf (shēf) I. s. [pl. **sheaves** (shēvz)] AGR. gavilla; *(of arrows)* haz *m*; *(quiver)* aljaba; *(collection)* fajo II. tr. AGR. agavillar.

shear (shîr) I. tr. **sheared, sheared** *o* **shorn** (shôrn), **shear·ing** *(sheep)* esquilar, trasquilar; *(hair)* rapar; *(fabric)* tundir; *(metal)* cizallar; *(hedge)* cortar con tijeras ♦ **to s. of** privar *o* despojar de • **to s. off** cortar —intr. ♦ **to s. off** TEC. romperse por cizallamiento • **to s. through** abrirse paso II. s. *(act of shearing)* esquila, trasquila; *(pair of shears)* tijeras *f*.

shears (shîrz) s.pl. *(for trimming)* tijeras; TEC. *(for metal)* cizalla; *(for hoisting)* cabria.

sheath (shēth) I. s. [pl. **sheaths** (shēthz, shēths)] *(for sword)* vaina; *(dress)* vestido tubular; *(condom)* preservativo; BIOL., BOT. vaina II. tr. envainar.

sheathe (shēth) tr. **sheathed, sheath·ing** *(a knife)* enfundar; *(a sword)* envainar; *(claws)* retraer; *(a cable)* forrar.

sheath·ing (shē'thĭng) s. *(act)* enfundadura; CONSTR. cubierta; MARÍT. revestimiento (de la quilla).

sheath knife s. cuchillo de monte.

sheave¹ (shēv) tr. **sheaved, sheav·ing** AGR. agavillar.

sheave² (shēv, shĭv) s. MEC. roldana (de polea).

sheaves (shēvz) pl. de **sheaf**.

shed¹ (shěd) tr. **shed, shed·ding** *(tears)* derramar; *(water)* verter; *(skin)* mudar; *(clothes, leaves)* despojarse de; *(weight)* perder ♦ **to s. light on** iluminar; FIG. aclarar —intr. *(skin)* mudar; *(leaves)* caer.

shed² (shěd) s. *(for storage)* cobertizo; *(hangar)* hangar; *(for cattle)* establo.

she'd (shěd) contr. de **she had** *o* **she would**.

sheen (shēn) s. *(brightness)* brillo; *(of silk)* viso; *(attire)* atavío espléndido.

sheep (shēp) s. [pl. **sheep**] ZOOL. oveja; *(leather)* badana;

FIG. *(easily led person)* corderito; AGR. ganado lanar ♦ **a wolf in sheep's clothing** un lobo con piel de oveja.

sheep·cote (shēp'kōt') s. G.B. aprisco, majada.

sheep dog *o* **sheep·dog** (shēp'dôg') s. perro pastor.

sheep·fold (shēp'fōld') s. aprisco, redil *m*.

sheep·herd·er (shēp'hûr'dər) s. pastor *m*.

sheep·herd·ing (shēp'hûr'dĭng) I. adj. pastoril II. s. pastoreo.

sheep·ish (shē'pĭsh) adj. *(shy)* tímido; *(bashful)* vergonzoso.

sheep·shear·ing (shēp'shîr'ĭng) s. esquileo.

sheep·skin (shēp'skĭn') s. *(hide)* piel de carnero *o* de oveja *f*; *(leather)* badana; *(parchment)* pergamino; *(diploma)* diploma.

sheer¹ (shîr) I. intr. ♦ **to s. away from** AUTO., MARÍT. desviarse II. s. *(course)* desviación *f*; MARÍT. *(curve)* arrufadura, arrufo.

sheer² (shîr) I. adj. **-er, -est** *(fabric)* fino, transparente; *(drop)* vertical; *(cliff)* escarpado; *(total)* total; *(utter)* puro <*s. madness* pura locura> II. adv. perpendicularmente.

sheer·ness (shîr'nĭs) s. pureza, transparencia.

sheet¹ (shēt) I. s. *(for bed)* sábana; *(of paper)* hoja, lámina; *(of metal)* chapa; *(of glass)* lámina; *(of ice, snow)* capa; *(of smoke, rain)* cortina; *(tabloid)* periodicucho; *(of stamps)* pliego entero; GEOL. banco, capa ♦ **s. metal** metal en chapa II. tr. cubrir ♦ **sheeted with** cubierto de (hielo, nieve).

sheet² (shēt) MARÍT. s. escota ♦ **sheets** espacios en la proa y popa de un bote • **three sheets to the wind** FAM. ebrio, borracho.

sheet music s. música en impresos sueltos.

Sheet·rock (shēt'rŏk') s. CONSTR. sheetrock (marca registrada de una clase de cartón-yeso) *f*.

sheik *o* **sheikh** (shēk) s. *(Arab chieftain)* jeque *m*; FAM. *(seducer)* seductor *m*, conquistador *m*.

shek·el (shěk'əl) s. FIN. moneda de Israel; NUMIS. siclo (moneda hebrea); JER. *(coin)* moneda ♦ **shekels** JER. pasta, plata (dinero).

shelf (shělf) s. pl. **shelves** (shělvz) *(in closet)* tabla, anaquel *m*; *(in kitchen)* estante *m*, repisa; *(in store)* estante; GEOL. *(of continent)* plataforma; *(of rock)* arrecife *m*; *(of sand)* banco ♦ **on the s.** FIG. arrinconado, olvidado.

shell (shěl) I. s. *(of mollusks, turtles)* concha; *(of crustaceans)* caparazón *m*; *(of nuts, eggs)* cáscara; *(of peas)* vaina; *(of building)* armazón *f*, esqueleto; *(of person)* apariencia; MARÍT. *(hull)* casco; *(boat)* yola; ARM. *(for cannon)* proyectil *m*; *(for firearm)* casquillo; FÍS. *(of atom)* capa ♦ **to come out of one's s.** FIG. salir uno de su concha II. tr. *(peas)* pelar, desvainar; *(nuts)* descascarar; *(corn, wheat)* desgranar; MIL. bombardear ♦ **to s. out** FAM. soltar, aflojar.

she'll (shěl) contr. de **she shall** *o* **she will**.

shel·lac (shə-lăk') I. s. laca II. tr. **-lacked, -lack·ing** *(to varnish)* dar laca, laquear; JER. *(to defeat)* derrotar completamente; *(to batter)* dar una paliza.

shel·lack·ing (shə-lăk'ĭng) s. FAM. paliza.

shell·fire (shěl'fīr') s. MIL. cañoneo, bombardeo.

shell·fish (shěl'fĭsh') s. pl. **shellfish** *o* **-fish·es** ZOOL. *(mollusk)* molusco; *(crustacean)* crustáceo; CUL. mariscos.

shell game s. *(thimblerig)* juego de manos que se hace con tres cubiletes; *(swindle)* estafa.

shell shock s. MED. trauma psicológica causada por la guerra.

shel·ter (shěl'tər) I. s. *(from rain)* cobertizo; *(from attack)* refugio; *(for homeless)* asilo ♦ **to take s.** ponerse a cubierto, refugiarse II. tr. *(to protect)* proteger; *(to harbor)* acoger —intr. refugiarse.

shel·tered (shěl'tərd) adj. protegido.

shelve (shělv) tr. **shelved, shelv·ing** *(to place in)* poner en un estante; *(to put aside)* dar carpetazo a; *(to furnish with)* poner estantes en —intr. estar en declive.

shelves (shělvz) pl. de **shelf**.

shelv·ing (shěl'vĭng) s. *(shelves)* estantería; *(postponement)* aplazamiento indefinido; *(incline)* pendiente *f*.

---

she·nan·i·gan (shə-năn′ĭ-gən) s. FAM. engaño ♦ **shenani-gans** travesuras.

shep·herd (shĕp′ərd) I. s. pastor *m* ♦ **the Good S.** BÍBL. el Buen Pastor II. tr. cuidar.

shepherd dog s. perro pastor.

shep·herd·ess (shĕp′ər-dĭs) s. pastora.

shepherd's pie s. CUL. pàstel de carne y patatas *m*.

sher·bet (shûr′bĭt) s. sorbete *m*.

sherd (shûrd) s. var. de **shard**.

sher·iff (shĕr′ĭf) s. DER. sheriff *m*, alguacil de policía de un condado *m*.

sher·ry (shĕr′ē) s. [pl. **-ries**] jerez *m*, vino de Jerez.

she's (shēz) contr. de **she is** *o* **she has**.

shield (shēld) I. s. HER., MIL., ZOOL. *(plate)* escudo; *(protection)* escudo, protección *f*; *(of police)* placa; *(of garment)* sobaquera; FÍS. blindaje *m* II. tr. *(to protect)* escudar, proteger; *(to conceal)* tapar —intr. servir de escudo.

shift (shĭft) I. tr. *(load)* pasar <*s. a parcel from one arm to the other* pasar un paquete de un brazo al otro>; *(to switch)* cambiar de; *(the blame)* echar ♦ **to s. gears** AUTO. cambiar de velocidad —intr. *(to change)* cambiar; *(person)* moverse; AUTO. cambiar de velocidad ♦ **to s. for oneself** arreglárselas solo II. s. *(of workers)* turno <*night s.* turno de la noche>; *(change)* cambio; *(of players)* desplazamiento lateral; *(dodge)* escapatoria; *(trick)* artificio, subterfugio; *(dress)* traje recto; GEOL. falla; GRAM., MÚS. cambio ♦ **in shifts** por turnos.

shift·less (shĭft′lĭs) adj. *(lazy)* vago, perezoso; *(incapable)* incapaz, inútil.

shift·y (shĭf′tē) adj. **-i·er, -i·est** *(crafty)* astuto; *(furtive)* evasivo; *(resourceful)* ingenioso.

shill (shĭl) s. JER. cómplice *m*.

shil·ling (shĭl′ĭng) s. FIN. chelín *m*.

shil·ly-shal·ly (shĭl′ē-shăl′ē) I. intr. **-lied, -ly·ing** *(to hesitate)* titubear, vacilar; *(to dawdle)* perder el tiempo II. adj. titubeante, vacilante III. s. [pl. **-lies**] titubeo, vacilación *f*.

shim (shĭm) I. s. MEC. calce *m* II. tr. **shimmed, shim·ming** calzar.

shim·mer (shĭm′ər) I. intr. rielar, brillar II. s. luz trémula, resplandor débil *m*.

shim·mer·ing (shĭm′ər-ĭng) adj. *(light)* trémulo; *(glittering)* reluciente; *(tint)* tornasolado.

shim·my (shĭm′ē) I. s. [pl. **-mies**] *(dance)* shimmy *m*; AUTO. trepidación oscilante *f* II. intr. **-mied, -my·ing** AUTO. oscilar.

shin (shĭn) I. s. ANAT. *(of the leg)* espinilla; *(shinbone)* tibia; CUL. jarrete *m*, corva II. tr. **shinned, shin·ning** *(to climb)* trepar; *(to kick)* golpear en la espinilla —intr. ♦ **to s. up** trepar.

shin·bone (shĭn′bōn′) s. ANAT. tibia.

shin·dig (shĭn′dĭg′) s. JER. fiesta, guateque *m*.

shine (shīn) I. intr. **shone** (shōn) *o* **shined, shin·ing** *(to beam)* brillar, relucir; *(to excel)* brillar, sobresalir; *(to become apparent)* rebosar de ♦ **to s. on** *(to illuminate)* iluminar; *(to keep shining)* seguir brillando —tr. *(to polish)* sacar brillo a; *(a light)* dirigir II. s. *(brightness)* brillo, lustre *m*; *(shoeshine)* brillo de zapatos ♦ **rain or s.** llueva *o* truene • **to take a s. to** aficionarse a, coger cariño a.

shin·er (shī′nər) s. *(one that shines)* limpiabotas *m*; JER. *(black eye)* ojo a la funerala, ojo amoratado; ICT. carpa plateada.

shin·gle¹ (shĭng′gəl) I. s. CONSTR. tablilla ♦ **to hang out one's s.** FAM. establecerse II. tr. **-gled, -gling** cubrir con tablillas.

shin·gle² (shĭng′gəl) s. *(beach)* playa de guijarros; *(large gravel)* guijarro grande, cascajo.

shin·gler (shĭng′glər) s. tejador *m*.

shin·gles (shĭng′gəlz) s.pl. [ú. con v. sing. o pl.] MED. zona.

shin·i·ness (shī′nē-nĭs) s. brillo.

shin·ny (shĭn′ē) intr. **-nied, -ny·ing** trepar.

Shin·to (shĭn′tō) s. RELIG. sintoísmo.

shin·y (shī′nē) adj. **-i·er, -i·est** *(bright)* brillante; *(glossy)* radiante, lustroso.

ship (shĭp) I. s. *(vessel)* barco *m* *(boat)* buque *m* <*merchant s.* buque mercante>; *(crew)* tripulación *f*; *(airship)* aeronave *f* ♦ **when one's s. comes in** cuando lleguen las vacas gor-

das II. tr. **shipped, ship·ping** *(parcels, goods)* enviar; MA-RÍT. *(rudder)* montar; *(oars)* desarmar; *(sailors)* enrolar; *(water)* hacer agua ♦ **to s. off to** enviar, mandar (a la escuela) —intr. ♦ **to s. as** enrolarse de • **to s. well** COM. soportar bien el transporte.

ship·board (shĭp′bôrd′) s. MARÍT. bordo <*on s.* a bordo>.

ship·build·er (shĭp′bĭl′dər) s. constructor naval *m*.

ship·build·ing (shĭp′bĭl′dĭng) s. construcción naval *f*.

ship·load (shĭp′lōd′) s. MARÍT. carga, cargamento.

ship·mas·ter (shĭp′măs′tər) s. MARÍT. capitán de un barco mercante *m*.

ship·mate (shĭp′māt′) s. MARÍT. compañero de tripulación.

ship·ment (shĭp′mənt) s. *(act)* embarque *m*; *(cargo shipped)* cargamento.

ship·per (shĭp′ər) s. MARÍT., COM. expedidor *m*; AVIA. transportista *m*.

ship·ping (shĭp′ĭng) s. MARÍT. *(act)* embarque *m*; *(ships of a port)* barcos, buques *m*; *(fleet)* flota; *(passage)* pasaje en barco *m*.

shipping clerk s. MARÍT., COM. expedidor *m*.

ship·shape (shĭp′shāp′) adj. en orden, ordenado.

ship's papers s.pl. MARÍT. documentación del buque *f*.

ship·wreck (shĭp′rĕk′) I. s. naufragio II. tr. MARÍT. hacer naufragar; FIG. *(to ruin)* arruinar, hundir ♦ **to be ship-wrecked** naufragar.

ship·wright (shĭp′rīt′) s. MARÍT. carpintero de barcos.

ship·yard (shĭp′yärd′) s. MARÍT. astillero.

shire (shīr) s. G.B. condado.

shirk (shûrk) I. tr. eludir, esquivar II. intr. *(to evade)* esquivarse; MIL. escurrir el bulto.

shirk·er (shûr′kər) s. gandul *m*.

shirr (shûr) I. tr. COST. fruncir; CUL. cocer en el horno (huevos) II. s. COST. frunce *m*.

shirt (shûrt) s. *(for men)* camisa; *(for women)* blusa ♦ **in s. sleeves** en mangas de camisa • **stuffed s.** FAM. persona envarada *o* estirada • **to keep one's s. on** JER. no sulfurarse • **to lose one's s.** JER. perder hasta la camisa.

shirt·dress (shûrt′drĕs′) s. COST. camisola.

shirt-sleeve (shûrt′slēv′) adj. *(person)* en mangas de camisa; *(weather)* templado; *(biography)* franco.

shirt·tail (shûrt′tāl′) I. s. COST. faldón de camisa *m* II. adj. *(children)* jovencito, chaval; *(cousin)* lejano; *(cabin, ranch)* diminuto, insignificante.

shirt·waist (shûrt′wāst′) s. *(shirt)* camisa; *(dress)* vestido camisa *o* camisero.

shit (shĭt) VULG. I. tr. & intr. **shit** *o* **shat** (shăt), **shit·ting** cagar II. s. *(excrement)* mierda; *(nonsense)* tontería ♦ **not to give a s.** no importarle a uno un comino • **shit!** ¡mierda! • **to be full of s.** decir tonterías • **to take a s.** cagar.

shiv·er¹ (shĭv′ər) I. intr. *(with cold)* tiritar; *(with fear)* temblar, estremecerse —tr. MARÍT. hacer flamear II. s. *(of cold)* escalofrío; *(of fear)* estremecimiento, escalofrío.

shiv·er² (shĭv′ər) intr. & tr. *(to break)* hacer añicos *o* astillas.

shiv·er·y (shĭv′ə-rē) adj. *(trembling)* tembloroso; *(chilling)* estremecedor.

shoal¹ (shōl) I. s. *(sandbank)* banco de arena, bajío II. intr. *(to become shallow)* hacerse menos profundo, disminuir en profundidad III. adj. poco profundo.

shoal² (shōl) I. s. *(of people)* multitud *f*, muchedumbre *f*; *(of fish)* cardumen *m*, banco II. intr. *(people)* agruparse; *(fish)* ir en bancos.

shoat (shōt) s. ZOOL. cochinillo, lechón *m*.

shock¹ (shŏk) I. s. *(mental, emotional)* golpe *m*; *(of an explosion)* choque *m*; *(of an earthquake)* sacudida; *(of muscles)* choque *m*; MED. choque, conmoción *f* II. tr. chocar ♦ **to be shocked at** escandalizar por —intr. chocar.

shock² (shŏk) I. s. *(of hair)* melena, greñas; AGR. tresnal *m* II. tr. AGR. hacinar.

shock ab·sorb·er (əb-sôrb′ər) s. AUTO. amortiguador *m*.

shock·er (shŏk′ər) s. *(thing)* cosa horrible; FIG., FAM. *(person)* sinvergüenza *mf*.

shock·ing (shŏk′ĭng) adj. *(highly disturbing)* horroroso; *(highly offensive)* indecente; *(said of color)* chillón.

shock·proof (shŏk′prōōf′) adj. a prueba de choques.

shock therapy s. MED. tratamiento por electrochoques.

shock troops s.pl. MIL. tropas de choque.
shock wave s. FÍS. onda de choque.
shod (shŏd) pret. y part. p. de **shoe.**
shod·dy (shŏd'ē) I. s. [pl. **-dies**] *(cloth)* lana regenerada; *(goods)* mercancía de mala calidad II. adj. **-di·er, -di·est** *(cloth)* regenerado; *(goods)* de mala calidad; *(work)* mal hecho.
shoe (shōō) I. s. *(for people)* zapato <*a pair of shoes* un par de zapatos>; *(for horses)* herradura; *(of brake)* zapata; *(of pole)* regatón m; *(of sled)* patín m; *(of tire)* cubierta ♦ **like s. leather** FIG. como suela de zapato • **to be in another's shoes** estar en el lugar de otro • **to fill someone's shoes** ocupar el lugar de otro II. tr. **shod** (shŏd), **shod** o **shod·den** (shŏd'n), **shoe·ing** *(person)* calzar; *(horse)* herrar.
shoe·horn (shōō'hôrn') I. s. calzador m II. tr. *(to squeeze)* apretujar, apretar; *(to force)* forzar, obligar.
shoe·lace (shōō'lās') s. cordón m.
shoe·mak·er (shōō'mā'kər) s. zapatero.
shoe·mak·ing (shōō'mā'kĭng) s. zapatería.
shoe polish s. betún m, bola.
shoe·string (shōō'strĭng') I. s. *(shoelace)* cordón m ♦ **on a s.** con poco dinero II. adj. de poco dinero.
shoe·tree (shōō'trē') s. horma.
shone (shōn) un pret. y part. p. de **shine.**
shoo (shōō) I. interj. ¡fuera!, ¡zape! II. tr. **shooed, shoo·ing** oxear, ahuyentar.
shook (shŏŏk) pret. de **shake.**
shook-up (shŏŏk-ŭp') adj. JER. perturbado.
shoot (shōōt) I. tr. **shot** (shŏt), **shoot·ing** *(a weapon)* disparar; *(to wound)* herir; *(to kill)* matar a tiros; *(to hit)* pegar un tiro; *(to execute)* fusilar <*he was shot for treason* le fusilaron por traición>; *(to send)* lanzar; *(to film)* rodar, filmar; *(to photograph)* fotografiar; *(bolt)* correr; *(rapids)* salvar; *(retort)* lanzar, espetar; *(glance)* echar; DEP. *(to score)* marcar; *(to play)* jugar a <*to s. pool* jugar al billar>; *(marbles, ball)* tirar ♦ **to s. down** *(to kill)* matar a tiros; *(plane)* derribar; FIG., FAM. *(theory)* echar abajo • **to s. forth** BOT. echar • **to s. it out** resolverlo a tiros • **to s. off** disparar • **to s. the breeze** FAM. charlar, parlotear • **to s. the works** FAM. jugarse el todo por el todo • **to s. to death** o **s. dead** matar a tiros • **to s. up** FAM. *(to terrorize)* aterrorizar (pegando tiros); JER. *(to inject)* inyectar (narcóticos) —intr. *(to fire)* disparar; *(to hunt)* cazar; *(bolt)* correrse, echarse; *(to film)* rodar, filmar; DEP. *(ball, puck)* tirar ♦ **to s. across** o **through** pasar o cruzar rápidamente • **to s. ahead** tomar rápidamente la delantera • **to s. at** tirar a • **to s. for** tratar de lograr • **to s. forth** BOT. echar • **to s. from the hip** FIG. hablar a tontas y a locas • **to s. in** entrar como un torbellino • **to s. off** o **out** salir disparando • **to s. off one's mouth** hablar demasiado • **to s. out** *(sparks, water)* brotar; *(lava)* salir; *(projection)* sobresalir, proyectarse • **to s. past** o **by** pasar como un rayo • **to s. up** *(to grow)* espigar, crecer; *(prices)* subir de repente; *(flames)* salir; *(water, sparks)* brotar; *(plants)* crecer; JER. *(drugs)* inyectar drogas II. s. BOT. *(sprout)* brote m, retoño; *(rapid)* rápido; *(for trash)* vertedero; FAM. *(of rocket)* lanzamiento; *(of firearm)* alcance m; DEP. *(contest)* tiro <*skeet s.* tiro al plato> III. interj. *(darn!)* ¡rábanos!, ¡miércoles!; *(talk!)* ¡habla!, ¡larga!
shoot·er (shōō'tər) s. tirador m; DEP. goleador m; MIL. arma de fuego.
shoot·ing (shōō'tĭng) I. s. *(firing)* tiro, disparo; *(shoot-out)* tiroteo; *(execution)* fusilamiento; *(killing)* matanza; *(murder)* asesinato; CINEM. *(filming)* rodaje m, filmación f II. adj. ♦ **s. pain** dolor punzante • **s. script** CINEM. guión técnico.
shooting brake s. G.B., AUTO. furgoneta.
shooting gallery s. *(at the fair)* barraca de tiro al blanco; MIL. galería de tiro.
shooting iron s. arma de fuego.
shooting star s. ASTRON. estrella fugaz; BOT. primavera.
shoot-out o **shoot·out** (shōōt'out') s. tiroteo.
shop (shŏp) I. s. *(store)* tienda; *(workshop)* taller m; *(department)* departamento, sección f; EDUC. *(manual arts)* artes f y oficios ♦ **s. window** escaparate • **to set up s.** *(a*

store) abrir o poner una tienda; *(a business)* poner un negocio • **to talk s.** hablar del trabajo II. intr. **shopped, shop·ping** *(to look)* ir de compras; *(to buy)* hacer compras ♦ **to s. around (for)** buscar • **to s. for** ir a buscar, ir a comprar —tr. comprar.
shop·keep·er (shŏp'kē'pər) s. tendero.
shop·lift·er (shŏp'lĭf'tər) s. ratero de tiendas, mechero.
shoppe (shŏp) s. var. de **shop.**
shop·per (shŏp'ər) s. comprador m.
shop·ping (shŏp'ĭng) s. compras f ♦ **to go s.** ir de compras.
shopping bag s. bolsa de la compra.
shopping center s. centro comercial.
shopping mall s. galería comercial.
shop steward s. enlace sindical m.
shop·talk (shŏp'tôk') s. conversación sobre el trabajo f.
shop·worn (shŏp'wôrn') adj. estropeado; FIG. *(too familiar)* gastado.
shore[1] (shôr) s. *(coast)* orilla, costa; *(land)* tierra; *(beach)* playa ♦ **shores** tierra.
shore[2] (shôr) I. tr. **shored, shor·ing** ♦ **to s. up** apuntalar II. s. *(timber)* puntal m.
shore bird s. pájaro que habita costas o playas.
shore·line (shôr'līn') s. ribera.
shore·ward (shôr'wərd) o **shore·wards** (-wərdz) adv. hacia la costa.
shor·ing (shôr'ĭng) s. *(propping up)* apuntalamiento; *(shores)* puntales m.
shorn (shôrn) un part. p. de **shear.**
short (shôrt) I. adj. **-er, -est** *(in length)* corto <*she has s. hair* tiene el cabello corto>; *(in height)* bajo; *(in duration)* corto; *(in distance)* corto <*a s. trip* un viaje corto>; *(in amount)* poco; *(succinct)* conciso, breve; *(abrupt)* seco, brusco <*he was very s. with me* fue muy seco conmigo>; GRAM. breve; FIN. al descubierto; CUL. crujiente ♦ **a s. distance from** a poca distancia de • **a s. time ago** hace un momento • **a s. way off** a corta distancia • **a s. while ago** hace un momento • **in s. order** sin demora • **in s. supply** escaso • **in the s. run** a corto plazo • **on s. notice** en poco tiempo • **s. and sweet** FAM. corto y bueno • **s. and to the point** conciso, breve • **to be s.** faltarle a uno algo <*I am ten dollars s.* me faltan diez dólares> • **to be s. of** *(money)* andar escaso de; *(breath)* faltarle a uno • **to be s. on** tener poco • **to be too s.** tener de menos <*the skirt is two inches too s.* la falda tiene dos pulgadas de menos> • **to get the s. end of the stick** llevar la peor parte • **to have a s. memory** fallarle a uno la memoria • **to have a s. temper** o **fuse** enojarse fácilmente • **to make s. work of** despachar • **to run s.** agotarse • **to run s. of** o **on** agotársele (a uno), acabársele (a uno) II. adv. *(abruptly)* en seco <*to stop s.* pararse en seco>; *(near)* cerca ♦ **nothing s. of** nada menos que • **s. of** *(except)* excepto, menos; *(before)* antes de • **to catch s.** cogerle a uno desprevenido • **to come up s.** quedarse corto • **to cut s.** interrumpir bruscamente • **to fall s. of** *(target)* no alcanzar; *(expectations)* no corresponder a • **to sell s.** FIN. *(commodities)* vender al descubierto; FIG. *(person)* subestimar III. s. FONÉT. *(syllable)* sílaba breve; *(vowel)* vocal breve f; CINEM. cortometraje m; FIN. *(sale)* venta al descubierto; *(salesperson)* vendedor al descubierto m; ELEC. cortocircuito ♦ **for s.** de mote • **in s.** en resumen • **shorts** *(trousers)* pantalones cortos; *(underpants)* calzoncillos • **the long and s. of it** el todo IV. tr. engañar, estafar • **to s.** o **s. out** ELEC. poner en cortocircuito —intr. ♦ **to s. out** ELEC. ponerse en cortocircuito.
short·age (shôr'tĭj) s. *(deficit)* déficit m; *(lack)* falta; *(insufficiency)* insuficiencia.
short·bread (shôrt'brĕd') s. torta o galleta hecha de harina, azúcar y mantequilla.
short·cake (shôrt'kāk') s. CUL. torta de frutas.
short·change (shôrt'chānj') tr. **-changed, -chang·ing** FAM., COM. dar de menos en el cambio; *(to cheat)* estafar, engañar.
short circuit s. ELEC. cortocircuito.
short-cir·cuit (shôrt'sûr'kĭt) tr. ELEC. poner en cortocircuito; FAM. *(to impede)* frustrar —intr. ELEC. ponerse en cortocircuito.

short·com·ing (shôrt′kŭm′ĭng) s. *(defect)* defecto; *(shortage)* falta.

short·cut (shôrt′kŭt′) s. atajo.

short division s. MAT. división hecha mentalmente.

short·en (shôr′tn) tr. & intr. acortar(se).

short·en·ing (shôr′tn-ĭng) s. CUL. materia grasa; *(abbreviation)* abreviación *f*, acortamiento.

short·fall (shôrt′fôl′) s. déficit *m*.

short·hand (shôrt′hănd′) s. *(stenography)* taquigrafía; FIG. *(abbreviated language)* lenguaje abreviado.

short·hand·ed (shôrt′hăn′dĭd) adj. falto *o* escaso de mano de obra.

short·lived (shôrt′līvd′, -lĭvd′) adj. de breve duración, efímero.

short·ly (shôrt′lē) adv. *(soon)* en breve, dentro de poco; *(concisely)* brevemente, en pocas palabras; *(curtly)* bruscamente, secamente.

short·ness (shôrt′nĭs) s. *(in length)* cortedad *f*; *(in height)* pequeñez *f*; *(in duration)* brevedad *f*; *(of breath)* falta; *(of manner)* sequedad *f*.

short order s. plato de preparación rápida (en un restaurante) ♦ **in s.** pronto.

short-range (shôrt′rānj′) adj. de alcance *o* futuro reducido.

short·sight·ed (shôrt′sī′tĭd) adj. *(myopic)* miope, corto de vista; FIG. *(lacking foresight)* miope, corto de vista.

short story s. LIT. cuento.

short-tem·pered (shôrt′tĕm′pərd) adj. fácilmente enojado.

short-term (shôrt′tûrm′) adj. a corto plazo.

short ton s. tonelada corta (de 2000 libras o 907 kilogramos).

short wave s. RAD. onda corta.

short-wave (shôrt′wāv′) adj. *(having a short wavelength)* de onda corta; *(receiving or transmitting at short wavelengths)* en onda corta.

short-wind·ed (shôrt′wĭn′dĭd) adj. *(short of breath)* de respiración corta, corto de resuello; *(choppy)* inconexo.

shot[1] (shŏt) s. ARM. *(discharge)* tiro, disparo <*to hear shots in the distance* oír disparos a lo lejos>; *(person who shoots)* tirador *m*; *(range)* alcance *m*; *(launch)* lanzamiento <*moon s.* lanzamiento de un cohete hacia la luna>; *(drink)* trago; DEP. *(ball)* peso, pesa <*to put the s.* lanzar el peso>; *(in basketball, hockey)* tiro; *(in pool)* golpe *m*, jugada; CINEM. *(view)* plano general>; *(take)* toma; FOTOG. foto *f*; MED. *(injection)* inyección *f*; ARM. *(pellets)* perdigones *m* ♦ **big s.** pez gordo • **like a s.** como una bala • **not by a long s.** ni mucho menos • **s. in the arm** FIG. estímulo • **s. in the dark** conjetura al azar • **to call the shots** FIG. llevar la voz cantante • **to take a s. at** tratar de (hacer algo) • **without firing a s.** sin pegar un tiro.

shot[2] (shŏt) adj. *(fabric)* tornasolado; FAM. *(day)* perdido; *(clothes)* gastado ♦ **her nerves are s.** tiene los nervios destrozados.

shot[3] (shŏt) pret. y. part. p. de **shoot.**

shote (shŏt) s. var. de **shoat.**

shot·gun (shŏt′gŭn′) s. ARM. escopeta.

shotgun wedding s. matrimonio a la fuerza.

shot-put (shŏt′pŏŏt′) s. DEP. *(event)* lanzamiento de peso; *(ball)* peso, pesa.

should §G11 (shŏŏd) aux. [pret. de **shall**] [ú. para expresar obligación] tener que, deber <*you s. send her a note* deberías enviarle una nota>; [ú. para expresar expectación] deber de <*they s. arrive at noon* deben de llegar a mediodía>; [ú. para expresar condición] <*if he s. fall, so would I* si él se cayera, me caería yo también> ♦ **how s. I know?** ¿cómo iba yo a saber?

shoul·der (shŏl′dər) I. s. ANAT., COST., IMPR. hombro; *(of meat)* espaldilla, paletilla; FORT. saliente *m*; *(of road)* orilla; *(of hill)* rellano ♦ **s. to s.** hombro a hombro, hombro con hombro • **to give someone the cold s.** tratar con frialdad a alguien • **to shrug one's shoulders** encogerse de hombros II. tr. *(to carry)* llevar en hombros; *(to place)* echarse al hombro; *(to assume)* cargar con (responsabilidad); *(to push)* empujar con el hombro ♦ **to s. one's way through a crowd** abrirse paso a codazos entre la muchedumbre.

shoulder bag s. bolso de bandolera.

shoulder belt s. AUTO. cinturón de seguridad *m*.

shoulder blade s. ANAT. omóplato.

shoulder strap s. *(on underwear)* tirante *m*; MIL. dragona.

should·n't (shŏŏd′nt) contr. de **should not.**

shouldst (shŏŏdst) *o* **should·est** (shŏŏd′ĭst) ANT. segunda persona sing. del pret. de **shall.**

shout (shout) I. s. grito II. tr. & intr. gritar.

shout·er (shou′tər) s. gritador *m*.

shout·ing (shou′tĭng) I. s. gritos *m*, vocería II. adj. que grita.

shove (shŭv) I. tr. **shoved, shov·ing** empujar a —intr. dar empujones, dar un empujón ♦ **to s. off** FAM. largarse, marcharse II. s. empujón *m*.

shov·el (shŭv′əl) I. s. *(for scooping)* pala; *(shovelful)* paletada, pala II. tr. *(snow)* quitar con la pala; *(steps, road)* limpiar con la pala; FIG. *(to pile)* echar mucho ♦ **to s. food into one's mouth** zamparse la comida.

shov·el·er *o* **shov·el·ler** (shŭv′ə-lər) s. *(person)* paleador *m*; ORNIT. espátula común.

shov·el·ful (shŭv′əl-fŏŏl′) s. [pl. **-fuls**] pala, paletada.

show (shō) I. tr. **showed, shown** (shōn) *o* **showed, show·ing** *(to make visible)* mostrar, enseñar <*he showed me the pictures* me mostró las fotografías>; *(to guide)* llevar, conducir; *(to present)* presentar; *(to grant)* conceder; *(to make clear)* demostrar, probar <*that shows how little you know* eso demuestra lo poco que sabes>; *(to reveal)* dejar ver; *(to manifest)* manifestar; *(to indicate)* indicar, señalar <*could you s. me the way?* ¿puede indicarme el camino?>; *(slides)* proyectar, enseñar; *(courage)* mostrar; *(in an exhibit)* exponer; *(on an instrument)* indicar, marcar ♦ **to have nothing to show for something** no sacar ningún beneficio • **to s. off** *(to hightlight)* hacer resaltar; *(to display)* hacer alarde de, alardear • **to s. one's face** aparecer, dejarse ver • **to s. one's hand** poner las cartas boca arriba • **to s. oneself** dejarse ver • **to s. someone around** hacer visitar • **to s. someone how to** enseñar a alguien a (hacer algo) • **to s. someone in** hacer entrar a alguien • **to s. someone out** acompañar a la puerta a alguien • **to s. someone the door** IRÓN. echar de la casa • **to s. up** *(to embarrass)* poner en evidencia; *(to expose)* revelar, descubrir • **what can I s. you?** COM. ¿qué desea Ud.? —intr. *(to be visible)* verse, notarse; FAM. *(to come)* aparecer; CINEM. poner, dar <*what's showing tonight?* ¿qué ponen esta noche?>; DEP. llegar en tercer lugar ♦ **it just goes to s.!** ¡hay que ver! • **to s. off** farolear, alardear • **to s. up** aparecer • **to s. up against** destacarse *o* sobresalir II. s. *(display)* demostración *f* <*s. of strength* demostración de fuerza>; *(pretense)* alarde *m*; TELEV. programa *m*; TEAT. espectáculo; DEP. tercer lugar ♦ **by a s. of hands** a mano alzada • **fashion s.** desfile de modelos • **for s.** para impresionar a los demás • **horse s.** concurso hípico • **one-man s.** exposición individual • **to make** *o* **put on a s. of** hacer gala *o* alarde de • **to run the s.** llevar la voz cantante, ser el que manda • **to steal the s.** llevarse todos los aplausos, ser la sensación.

show bill s. cartel *m*.

show·boat (shō′bōt′) s. *(steamboat)* barco donde se dan espectáculos; *(person)* presumido.

show business s. espectáculos, mundo del espectáculo.

show·case (shō′kās′) I. s. escaparate *m*, vitrina II. tr. **-cased, -cas·ing** poner bien a la vista.

show·down (shō′doun′) s. *(moment)* momento decisivo; *(confrontation)* confrontación *f*.

show·er[1] (shou′ər) I. s. *(rain)* aguacero, chaparrón *m*; *(hail)* granizada; *(snow)* nevada; FIG. *(fall of objects)* lluvia; *(outpouring)* avalancha; *(party)* fiesta en la que todas traen regalos; *(shower bath)* ducha II. tr. *(to sprinkle)* regar, mojar; *(to pour)* derramar —intr. *(to pour down)* llover; *(to take a shower)* ducharse.

show·er[2] (shō′ər) s. *(exhibitor)* expositor *m*.

shower bath s. ducha.

show·girl (shō′gûrl′) s. TEAT. corista.

show·i·ly (shō′ə-lē) adv. ostentosamente, llamativamente.

show·ing (shō′ĭng) s. *(exhibition)* exposición *f*; *(performance)* actuación *f*; *(presentation)* presentación (de hechos, datos, etc.).

ã rey / ä año / b boca / ch chico / d dar / ĕ el / ē mil / g gato / h joya / hw juez / ī aire / k casa / kw cuan /

show·man (shō′mən) s. [pl. **-men**] TEAT. *(producer)* empresario de espectáculos.
show·man·ship (shō′mən-shĭp′) s. TEAT. talento para organizar espectáculos; FIG. *(theatricality)* teatralidad *f.*
shown (shōn) un part. p. de **show.**
show·off (shō′ôf′) s. *(ostentation)* ostentación *f,* alarde *m;* FAM. *(exhibitionist)* presumido.
show·piece (shō′pēs′) s. obra maestra.
show·room o **show room** (shō′rōōm′) s. sala de exposición.
show·stop·per (shō′stŏp′ər) s. artista cuya actuación suscita gran aplauso *mf.*
show·y (shō′ē) adj. **-i·er, -i·est** *(striking)* llamativo, vistoso; *(ostentatious)* ostentoso.
shrank (shrăngk) un pret. de **shrink.**
shrap·nel (shrăp′nəl) s. [pl. **shrapnel**] ARM. *(shell)* granada fragmentaria o de metralla; *(metal balls, fragments)* metralla.
shred (shrĕd) I. s. *(strip)* jirón *m,* tira; *(particle)* fragmento, pedazo ♦ **to tear to shreds** *(something)* hacer trizas; *(an argument)* echar abajo II. tr. **shred·ded, shred·ding** hacer trizas.
shred·der (shrĕd′ər) s. desfibradora.
shrew (shrōō) s. ZOOL. musaraña; FAM. *(woman)* mujer regañona.
shrewd (shrōōd) adj. **-er, -est** *(astute)* astuto; *(cunning)* perspicaz, sagaz; *(penetrating)* penetrante.
shrewd·ness (shrōōd′nĭs) s. astucia, sagacidad *f.*
shrew·ish (shrōō′ĭsh) adj. regañón, de mal genio.
shriek (shrēk) I. s. chillido, grito II. tr. gritar —intr. chillar, gritar ♦ **to s. with laughter** reírse a carcajadas.
shrift (shrĭft) s. ANT. *(confession)* confesión *f;* *(absolution)* absolución *f* ♦ **to give someone short s.** despachar a alguien.
shrill (shrĭl) I. adj. **-er, -est** chillón, agudo II. tr. & intr. chillar.
shrill·ness (shrĭl′nĭs) s. lo agudo.
shrimp (shrĭmp) I. s. [pl. **shrimp** o **shrimps**] ZOOL. camarón *m,* gamba; JER. *(small fry)* renacuajo, hombrecillo II. intr. pescar camarones.
shrine (shrīn) s. *(reliquary)* relicario; *(tomb)* mausoleo, sepulcro; *(site)* capilla, lugar santo.
shrink (shrĭngk) I. intr. **shrank** (shrăngk) o **shrunk** (shrŭngk), **shrunk** o **shrunk·en** (shrŭng′kən), **shrink·ing** *(to contract)* encoger, contraerse; *(to dwindle)* disminuir, mermar; *(to recoil)* retroceder; *(to be reluctant)* encogerse ♦ **to s. away** o **back** echarse atrás —tr. encoger, contraer II. s. encogimiento; JER. *(psychiatrist)* psiquiatra *mf.*
shrink·age (shrĭng′kĭj) s. *(process)* encogimiento, contracción *f;* *(reduction)* reducción *f,* disminución *f;* *(loss)* pérdida, merma.
shrinking violet s. FAM. persona tímida.
shrink wrap s. envoltura de plástico transparente para empaquetar productos.
shrive (shrīv) tr. **shrove** (shrōv) o **shrived, shriv·en** (shrĭv′ən) o **shrived, shriv·ing** *(to hear the confession of)* confesar a; *(to obtain absolution for)* obtener la absolución para —intr. *(to make confession)* confesarse; *(to hear confessions)* confesar.
shriv·el (shrĭv′əl) tr. & intr. *(to shrink)* encoger(se); *(to wrinkle)* arrugar(se); *(to lose vitality)* marchitar(se), secar(se); *(to waste away)* consumir(se).
shriv·en (shrĭv′ən) un part. p. de **shrive.**
shroud (shroud) I. s. *(winding sheet)* sudario, mortaja; FIG. *(something that veils)* velo; *(something that covers)* manto; MARÍT. obenque *m* ♦ **the Holy S.** el Santo Sudario II. tr. *(to wrap)* amortajar; *(to hide)* tapar, ocultar; ANT. *(to protect)* proteger.
shrove (shrōv) un pret. de **shrive.**
Shrove·tide (shrōv′tīd′) s. RELIG. carnestolendas.
shrub¹ (shrŭb) s. *(plant)* arbusto; *(bush)* matorral *m.*
shrub² (shrŭb) s. *(beverage)* zumo de frutas con licor.
shrub·ber·y (shrŭb′ə-rē) s. [pl. **-ies**] arbustos, matorrales *m.*
shrub·by (shrŭb′ē) adj. **-bi·er, -bi·est** *(full of shrubs)* lleno de arbustos; *(like a shrub)* parecido a un arbusto.
shrug (shrŭg) I. intr. **shrugged, shrug·ging** encogerse de

hombros —tr. encoger ♦ **to s. off** *(to minimize the importance of)* no hacer caso de; *(to get rid of)* echar de lado con una sacudida II. s. *(gesture)* encogimiento de hombros; *(jacket)* chaqueta de mujer.
shrunk (shrŭngk) un pret. y part. p. de **shrink.**
shrunk·en (shrŭng′kən) un part. p. de **shrink.**
shuck (shŭk) I. s. *(of nuts)* cáscara; *(of corn)* espata; *(of peas)* vaina; *(of oysters)* concha; JER. *(sham)* engaño, impostura II. tr. *(nuts)* pelar; *(corn)* quitar la espata de; *(peas)* desvainar; *(oysters)* desbullar; JER. *(to deceive)* engañar ♦ **shucks** ¡cáscaras!, ¡caramba!
shud·der (shŭd′ər) I. intr. temblar, estremecerse II. s. temblor *m,* estremecimiento.
shuf·fle (shŭf′əl) I. tr. **-fled, -fling** *(to drag feet)* arrastrar (los pies); *(to move)* cambiar de sitio; *(to stir)* revolver, mezclar; *(to mix)* barajar (cartas); *(to cover up)* encubrir —intr. *(to move)* arrastrar los pies; *(to dance)* bailar arrastrando los pies; *(to shift about)* moverse de un lado para otro; *(to equivocate)* andar con rodeos; *(to mix)* barajar cartas ♦ **to s. along** arrastrar los pies • **to s. off** irse, marcharse II. s. *(movement)* arrastramiento de los pies; *(evasion)* evasiva; *(of cards)* barajada; *(turn)* turno de barajar.
shun (shŭn) tr. **shunned, shun·ning** evitar, rehuir.
shunt (shŭnt) I. s. *(shift)* desviación *f;* F.C. *(of trains)* maniobras; *(railway points)* agujas; ELEC. derivación *f* II. tr. *(to move aside)* desviar; *(to evade)* desviar; F.C. cambiar de vía; ELEC. derivar —intr. *(to turn aside)* desviarse, apartarse; F.C. cambiar de vía; ELEC. derivarse.
shush (shŭsh, shōōsh) I. interj. ¡chitón! II. tr. hacer callar.
shut (shŭt) I. tr. **shut, shut·ting** cerrar ♦ **to s. away** *(to keep under lock and key)* guardar bajo llave; *(to imprison)* encerrar • **to s. down** *(to confine)* encerrar; *(to surround)* rodear, cercar • **to s. off** *(to isolate)* aislar; *(to prevent the passage of)* cortar (gas, electricidad); *(to turn off)* desconectar • **to s. out** *(not to admit)* no admitir, dejar fuera; *(to keep from coming in)* tapar, ocultar (de la vista) • **to s. up** *(to close)* cerrar; *(to confine)* encerrar; *(to silence)* hacer callar —intr. cerrarse ♦ **to s. up** callarse la boca II. s. MEC. juntura, costura de unión (en soldadura).
shut·down (shŭt′doun′) s. cierre *m.*
shut·eye (shŭt′ī′) s. JER. sueño ♦ **to get some s.** echar una siesta, dormirse.
shut·off (shŭt′ôf′) s. *(valve)* válvula; *(stoppage)* interrupción *f,* cierre *m.*
shut·out (shŭt′out′) s. *(lockout)* cierre patronal *m;* DEP. partido ganado sin que el adversario marque un tanto.
shut·ter (shŭt′ər) I. s. *(window)* persiana, contraventana; FOTOG. obturador *m* II. tr. *(to close)* cerrar los postigos de; *(to furnish with shutters)* poner postigos a.
shut·ter·bug (shŭt′ər-bŭg′) s. FAM. aficionado a la fotografía.
shut·tle (shŭt′l) I. s. *(in sewing and weaving)* lanzadera; *(travel, route)* trayecto corto entre dos puntos; *(vehicle)* vehículo que hace trayectos cortos entre dos puntos; *(space shuttle)* transbordador espacial *m* II. intr. **-tled, -tling** hacer trayectos cortos y regulares —tr. *(to move)* ir y venir con frecuencia (entre dos puntos); *(to transport)* transportar (en trayectos cortos y frecuentes).
shut·tle·cock (shŭt′l-kŏk′) s. DEP. volante *m.*
shy¹ (shī) I. adj. **shi·er** o **shy·er, shi·est** o **shy·est** *(timid)* tímido; *(bashful)* vergonzoso; *(said of an animal)* asustadizo; *(wary)* cauteloso; FAM. *(lacking)* escaso ♦ **s. of** falto de • **to be s. of** desconfiar de • **to be s. of doing something** no atreverse a hacer algo II. intr. **shied, shy·ing** *(to move suddenly)* asustarse, sobresaltarse; *(to draw back)* echarse atrás asustado ♦ **to s. away** espantarse • **to s. away from** huir II. s. [pl. **shies**] respingo, espantada.
shy² (shī) I. tr. & intr. **shied, shy·ing** lanzar, tirar II. s. [pl. **shies**] *(fling)* lanzamiento, tiro; FAM. *(sneer)* mofa, sarcasmo.
shy·lock (shī′lŏk′) s. usurero.
shy·ly (shī′lē) adv. tímidamente, con vergüenza.
shy·ness (shī′nĭs) s. *(bashfulness)* timidez *f;* *(caution)* cautela.
shy·ster (shī′stər) s. JER. picapleitos.

---

ng inglés / ŏ la / ō bou / ô corre / oi oigo / ōō uno / ou auto / yōō ciudad / w hueco / y yo / z mismo

si (sē) s. MÚS. si *m.*

Si·am (sī-ăm') s. Siam *m.*

Si·a·mese (sī'ə-mēz') adj. & s. [pl. **Siamese**] siamés *m* ♦ **the S.** los siameses • **s. twins** MED. hermanos siameses.

Si·be·ri·a (sī-bîr'ē-ə) s. Siberia.

Si·be·ri·an (sī-bîr'ē-ən) adj. & s. siberiano.

sib·i·lant (sĭb'ə-lənt) adj. & s. FONET. sibilante *f.*

sib·ling (sĭb'lĭng) s. *(brother)* hermano; *(sister)* hermana.

sib·yl (sĭb'əl) s. sibila.

sib·yl·line (sĭb'ə-līn') *o* **si·byl·ic** *o* **si·byl·lic** (sĭ-bĭl'ĭk) adj. sibilino.

sic¹ (sĭk) adv. LAT. sic.

sic² (sĭk) tr. **sicced, sic·cing** *(to urge to attack)* echar (un perro); *(to chase)* atacar.

Si·cil·i·an (sī-sĭl'yən) adj. & s. siciliano.

Sic·i·ly (sĭs'ə-lē) s. Sicilia.

sick¹ (sĭk) adj. **-er, -est** *(ailing)* enfermo; *(disturbed)* trastornado; *(morbid)* morboso; *(defective)* malo; *(upset)* preocupado; *(disgusted)* asqueado; *(tired)* cansado; *(longing)* anhelante; *(said of soil)* pobre, agotada (tierra) ♦ **the s.** los enfermos • **to be s.** *(to be ill)* estar enfermo; *(to vomit)* vomitar • **to be s. and tired of** estar harto de • **to feel s.** tener náuseas, estar mareado • **to feel s. at heart** estar desesperado • **to get s.** *(seasick)* marearse; *(to take sick)* ponerse enfermo • **to make s.** FIG. poner enfermo, dar asco.

sick² (sĭk) v. var. de **sic²**.

sick·bay (sĭk'bā') s. enfermería.

sick·bed (sĭk'bĕd') s. lecho de enfermo.

sick call s. MIL. *(daily line-up)* visita médica; *(announcing signal)* toque de visita médica *m.*

sick·en (sĭk'ən) tr. & intr. enfermar(se).

sick·en·ing (sĭk'ə-nĭng) adj. *(causing sickness)* nauseabundo, repugnante; *(distressing)* deprimente.

sick·ie (sĭk'ē) s. JER. enfermo, malo.

sick·le (sĭk'əl) I. s. hoz *f* II. tr. **-led, -ling** cortar con una hoz.

sick leave s. baja por enfermedad.

sick·ly (sĭk'lē) adj. **-li·er, -li·est** *(ailing)* enfermizo; *(weak)* enclenque; *(unhealthy)* malsano; *(pale)* pálido; *(nauseating)* nauseabundo.

sick·ness (sĭk'nĭs) s. *(illness)* enfermedad *f*; *(nausea)* náusea.

sick pay s. subsidio por enfermedad.

sick·room (sĭk'rōōm', -rōōm') s. cuarto de enfermo.

side (sīd) I. s. *(location)* lado <*on the right s.* en el lado derecho>; *(surface)* lado, costado; *(of a mountain, hill)* ladera, falda; *(of a boat)* costado; *(of flat objects)* lado, cara; *(of a solid)* cara; *(shore)* orilla, margen *f*; *(edge)* borde <*write your comments on the s. of the page* escriba sus comentarios en el borde de la página>; *(lineage)* lado, parte *f* <*my aunt on my mother's s.* mi tía por parte de mi madre>; *(aspect)* aspecto, lado <*the cruel s. of her nature* el lado cruel de su naturaleza>; DEP. *(team)* facción *f*, parte *f*; MAT. lado; MIL. flanco, lado ♦ **at** *o* **by the s. of** al lado de • **from all sides** de todos lados, de todas partes • **on all sides** por todos lados, por todas partes • **on both sides** por ambos lados, por ambas partes • **on either s.** de cada lado • **on every s.** por todos lados, por todas partes • **on one s.** a un lado, aparte • **on the left-hand s.** a la izquierda • **on the right-hand s.** a la derecha • **on the s.** aparte de la ocupación habitual, fuera del trabajo normal • **on this s.** por este lado • **s. by s.** juntos, uno al lado del otro • **the other s. of the picture** FIG. el reverso de la medalla • **the right s.** *(of cloth)* el derecho; *(the correct side)* el lado bueno; *(the right-hand side)* la derecha • **the under s.** la parte inferior • **to be on the safe s.** *(to eliminate risk)* ir sobre seguro, obrar sin riesgo; *(for safety's sake)* para estar tranquilo • **to change sides** cambiar de partido • **to get on the right s. of someone** granjearse la simpatía de alguien • **to have on one's s.** tener de parte de uno • **to keep on the good** *o* **right s. of someone** llevarse bien con alguien • **to keep on the right s. of the law** mantenerse dentro de la ley • **to move to one s.** apartarse, hacerse a un lado • **to sleep on one's s.** dormir de costado • **to take sides** tomar partido • **to take sides with** some-

one ponerse del lado *o* de parte de alguien • **to turn over on one's s.** *(person)* ponerse de costado; *(vehicle)* volcar • **wrong s. out** al revés, del revés II. adj. lateral <*a s. door* una puerta lateral>; *(indirect)* indirecto <*a s. remark* una observación indirecta>; *(supplementary)* adicional; *(secondary)* secundario <*s. effects* efectos secundarios> ♦ **s. view** vista de perfil III. tr. **sid·ed, sid·ing** poner lados a —intr. ♦ **to s. with** ponerse del lado de.

side arm s. arma de mano.

side·board (sīd'bôrd') s. aparador *m.*

side·burns (sīd'bûrnz') s.pl. patillas.

side·car (sīd'kär') s. *(car)* sidecar *m*; *(cocktail)* cóctel *m* de coñac, licor *m* de naranja y zumo de limón.

sid·ed (sī'dĭd) adj. con lados.

side effect s. efecto secundario.

side issue s. cuestión secundaria.

side·kick (sīd'kĭk') s. JER. amigo, compañero.

side·line *o* **side line** (sīd'līn') I. s. *(of business)* negocio suplementario; *(activity)* empleo suplementario, actividad suplementaria; DEP. línea de banda ♦ **sidelines** DEP. *(space)* banquillo; *(position)* barrera II. tr. **-lined, -lin·ing** poner fuera de juego.

side·long (sīd'lông') I. adj. *(lateral)* lateral; *(sideways)* de soslayo; *(slanting)* inclinado II. adv. *(sideways)* lateralmente; *(obliquely)* oblicuamente.

side·man (sīd'măn') s. [pl. **-men** (-měn')] músico de jazz.

si·de·re·al (sī-dîr'ē-əl) adj. ASTRON. sideral, sidéreo.

side·sad·dle (sīd'săd'l) I. s. silla de amazona II. adj. a la amazona, a mujeriegas.

side·show *o* **side show** (sīd'shō') s. *(small show)* atracción secundaria; *(diverting incident)* acontecimiento secundario.

side·slip (sīd'slĭp') intr. **-slipped, -slip·ping** *(to skid, slide)* resbalar, patinar (lateralmente); AER. resbalar; ESGR. deslizarse lateralmente.

side·split·ting (sīd'splĭt'ĭng) adj. divertidísimo.

side·step (sīd'stĕp') intr. **-stepped, -step·ping** *(to step aside)* dar un paso lateral; *(to dodge)* eludir —tr. *(to step out of the way of)* esquivar, evitar; *(to evade)* eludir (problema).

side step s. *(step to one side)* paso lateral; DEP. quiebro; MIL. paso de lado.

side·stroke *o* **side stroke** (sīd'strōk') s. DEP. brazada de costado (en natación).

side·swipe (sīd'swīp') I. tr. **-swiped, -swip·ing** chocar de refilón contra II. s. golpe de refilón *m.*

side·track (sīd'trăk') I. tr. F.C. *(train)* desviar; *(an issue)* dejar de lado —intr. apartarse, desviarse II. s. F.C. desvío, apartadero.

side·walk (sīd'wôk') s. acera.

side·ward (sīd'wərd) I. adj. lateral, de lado ♦ **a s. glance** una mirada de soslayo II. adv. *(to fall)* de lado, de costado; *(to step)* hacia un lado.

side·ways (sīd'wāz') I. adv. *(to fall)* de lado, de costado; *(to step)* hacia un lado II. adj. lateral, de lado.

side·wheel (sīd'hwēl') s. rueda de paleta (de un vapor).

side·whis·kers (sīd'hwĭs'kərz) s.pl. patillas.

side·wind·er (sīd'wīn'dər) s. ZOOL. especie de crótalo, serpiente de cascabel *f*; DEP. fuerte golpe lateral en el boxeo *m*; MIL. cohete supersónico.

side·wise (sīd'wīz') adv. & adj. var. de **sideways**.

sid·ing (sī'dĭng) s. F.C. desvío, apartadero; CONSTR., CARP. tablas de forro, tablas de chilla.

si·dle (sīd'l) I. tr. & intr. **-dled, -dling** mover(se) furtiva y lateralmente II. s. movimiento furtivo.

siege (sēj) I. s. MIL. sitio; *(exhausting period)* calvario II. tr. **sieged, sieg·ing** sitiar.

si·er·ra (sē-ĕr'ə) s. *(range)* sierra; *(fish)* pez sierra *m.*

Sierra Le·one (lē-ōn') s. República de Sierra Leona.

si·es·ta (sē-ĕs'tə) s. siesta.

sieve (sĭv) I. s. tamiz *m*, cedazo II. tr. **sieved, siev·ing** tamizar, cribar.

sift (sĭft) tr. *(to strain)* tamizar, cerner; FIG. *(to separate)* separar; *(to examine)* examinar, escudriñar —intr. *(to pass through a straining device)* pasar por un tamiz; *(to make an examination)* examinar.

sift·er (sĭf'tər) s. tamiz *m*, cedazo.

ă rey / ä año / b boca / ch chico / d dar / ĕ el / ē mil / g gato / h joya / hw juez / ī aire / k casa / kw cuan /

sift·ings (sĭf′tĭngz) s.pl. cerniduras.
sigh (sī) I. intr. *(to exhale)* suspirar; *(to emit a sound)* gemir, susurrar —tr. decir suspirando II. s. suspiro.
sight (sīt) I. s. *(eyesight)* vista; *(vision)* visión *f*; *(prospect)* perspectiva; *(thing worth seeing)* cosa digna de verse; *(something unsightly)* facha; *(of a device)* mira; *(examination)* examen *m*; FIG. *(large quantity)* gran cantidad *f*, montón *m* ♦ **a s. for sore eyes** FAM. persona grata (cuya vista le encanta a uno) • **at first s.** a primera vista • **on s.** a primera vista, nada más verlo • **out of s.** *(out of view)* fuera de la vista; JER. *(great)* maravilloso • **sights** meta, objetivo • **s. unseen** sin haberlo visto • **to be in s. of** estar a la vista de • **to catch s. of** avistar, divisar • **to come into s.** aparecer • **to know by s.** conocer de vista • **to lose s. of** perder de vista II. tr. *(to see)* ver, divisar; *(to observe)* observar; *(to adjust)* ajustar (mira); *(to aim)* apuntar, apuntar con (arma).
sight draft s. COM. letra a la vista.
sight·ed (sī′tĭd) adj. de vista normal, que ve.
sight·less (sīt′lĭs) adj. *(blind)* ciego; *(invisible)* invisible.
sight·li·ness (sīt′lē-nĭs) s. vistosidad *f*, hermosura.
sight·ly (sīt′lē) adj. **-li·er, -li·est** agradable a la vista, hermoso.
sight-read (sīt′rēd′) tr. & intr. **-read** (-rĕd′), **-read·ing** MÚS. ejecutar a primera vista, repentizar.
sight·see (sīt′sē′) intr. **-saw** (-sô′), **-seen** (-sēn′), **-see·ing** visitar lugares de interés.
sight·see·ing (sīt′sē′ĭng) I. s. visita a lugares de interés II. adj. que visita lugares de interés.
sight·se·er (sīt′sē′ər) s. turista *mf*.
sig·ma (sĭg′mə) s. sigma (letra griega).
sign (sīn) I. s. *(indication)* signo; *(gesture)* gesto, ademán *m*; *(notice)* anuncio; *(poster)* cartel *m*, letrero; *(symbol)* símbolo; *(trace)* rastro, huella; *(presage)* presagio; *(action)* señal *f*; *(of the zodiac)* signo; MED. síntoma *m* ♦ **the s. of the cross** la señal de la cruz • **to make no s.** no dar señales • **to show signs of** dar muestras de • **to use s. language** hablar por señas II. tr. *(to write)* firmar; *(to express)* indicar; *(to bless)* santiguar ♦ **to s. away** ceder • **to s. on** contratar • **to s. over** ceder • **to s. up** contratar —intr. *(to signal)* hacer señas; *(to write)* firmar ♦ **to s. in** inscribirse • **to s. on** *(to join)* alistarse; MARÍT. enrolarse • **to s. off** *(on the radio)* acabar el programa; *(to finish)* terminar • **to s. out** firmar y salir • **to s. up** *(to join)* alistarse; MARÍT. enrolarse.
sig·nal (sĭg′nəl) I. s. señal *f* ♦ **s. flare** bengala de señales II. adj. señalado, notable III. tr. *(to make a signal to)* dar la señal de o para; *(to make known)* indicar —intr. hacer señales, avisar.
sig·nal·ize (sĭg′nə-līz′) tr. **-ized, -iz·ing** señalar.
sig·nal·man (sĭg′nəl-măn′) s. [pl. **-men** (-mĕn′)] F.C. guardavía *m*.
sig·na·to·ry (sĭg′nə-tôr′ē) adj. & s. [pl. **-ries**] signatario, firmante *mf*.
sig·na·ture (sĭg′nə-chər) s. *(name, mark)* firma; *(act)* signatura; MÚS. armadura; IMPR. signatura.
sign·er (sī′nər) s. firmante *mf*, signatario.
sig·net (sĭg′nĭt) s. sello.
signet ring s. sortija de sello, sello.
sig·nif·i·cance (sĭg-nĭf′ĭ-kəns) o **sig·nif·i·can·cy** (-kən-sē) s. significación *f*, significado.
sig·nif·i·cant (sĭg-nĭf′ĭ-kənt) adj. significativo.
sig·ni·fi·ca·tion (sĭg′nə-fĭ-kā′shən) s. significación *f*.
sig·nif·i·ca·tive (sĭg-nĭf′ĭ-kā′tĭv) adj. significativo.
sig·ni·fy (sĭg′nə-fī′) tr. **-fied, -fy·ing** *(to mean)* significar; *(to intimate)* expresar —intr. *(to have meaning)* significar; *(to have importance)* tener importancia.
sign language s. lenguaje por señas *m*.
sign·post (sīn′pōst′) s. *(post with a sign)* poste indicador *m*; *(notice)* letrero.
si·lage (sī′lĭj) s. AGR. ensilaje *m*.
si·lence (sī′ləns) I. s. silencio II. tr. **-lenced, -lenc·ing** *(to make silent)* hacer callar; *(to suppress)* reprimir.
si·lenc·er (sī′lən-sər) s. TEC. silenciador *m*.
si·lent (sī′lənt) adj. *(quiet)* silencioso; *(mute)* mudo; *(tacit)*

tácito; *(inactive)* inactivo; CINEM., FONÉT. mudo ♦ **to be s.** callar.
silent butler s. recolector de colillas y migajas *m*.
si·lent·ly (sī′lənt-lē) adv. silenciosamente, calladamente.
silent partner s. COM. socio comanditario.
sil·hou·ette (sĭl′ōō-ĕt′) I. s. silueta II. tr. **-et·ted, -et·ting** siluetear.
sil·i·ca (sĭl′ĭ-kə) s. MIN. sílice *f*.
sil·i·cate (sĭl′ĭ-kāt′) s. QUÍM. silicato.
sil·i·con (sĭl′ĭ-kŏn′) s. QUÍM. silicio.
sil·i·cone (sĭl′ĭ-kōn′) s. QUÍM. silicona.
silk (sĭlk) I. s. *(fiber, fabric)* seda; *(corn)* estigma del maíz ♦ **silks** DEP. gorra y chaquetilla del jockey II. intr. madurar (maíz).
silk cotton s. TEJ. seda vegetal.
silk-cot·ton tree (sĭlk′kŏt′n) s. BOT. ceiba de lana, árbol de algodón *m*.
silk·en (sĭl′kən) adj. *(made of silk)* de seda; *(smooth)* sedoso; *(pleasing)* suave; *(luxurious)* lujoso.
silk hat s. sombrero de copa, chistera.
silk screen s. IMPR. serigrafía.
silk-stock·ing (sĭlk′stŏk′ĭng) s. aristócrata *mf*.
silk·worm (sĭlk′wûrm′) s. ENTOM. gusano de seda.
silk·y (sĭl′kē) adj. **-i·er, -i·est** *(lustrous)* sedoso; *(made of silk)* de seda; *(suave)* suave.
sill (sĭl) s. ARQ. solera; *(door)* umbral *m*; *(window)* alféizar *m*; GEOL. capa.
sil·li·ness (sĭl′ē-nĭs) s. tontería, bobada.
sil·ly (sĭl′ē) adj. **-li·er, -li·est** *(stupid)* tonto, bobo; *(ridiculous)* ridículo; *(absurd)* absurdo.
si·lo (sī′lō) s. [pl. **-los**] AGR., MIL. silo.
silt (sĭlt) I. s. cieno, légamo II. tr. *(port)* enarenar; *(canal)* encenagar —intr. *(port)* enarenarse; *(canal)* encenagarse.
sil·van (sĭl′vən) adj. & s. var. de **sylvan**.
sil·ver (sĭl′vər) I. s. QUÍM. plata; *(coins)* monedas de plata; *(color)* plateado; *(silverware)* plata II. adj. *(of silver)* de plata; *(like silver)* plateado; *(melodious)* argentino; *(of an anniversary)* de plata ♦ **s. tongue** pico de oro III. tr. *(to silver-plate)* platear; *(to coat)* azogar (un espejo).
silver age s. edad de plata *f*.
sil·ver·fish (sĭl′vər-fĭsh′) s. [pl. **silverfish** o **-fish·es**] ICT. pez plateado; ENTOM. lepisma.
silver fox s. ZOOL. zorro plateado (animal y piel).
silver plate s. vajilla de plata, platería.
silver screen s. CINEM. pantalla.
sil·ver·smith (sĭl′vər-smĭth′) s. platero.
silver spoon s. FIG. riqueza heredada.
sil·ver·ware (sĭl′vər-wâr′) s. vajilla de plata, plata.
sil·ver·y (sĭl′və-rē) adj. *(silver-plated)* plateado; FIG. *(clear sound)* argentino (voz, tono).
sim·i·an (sĭm′ē-ən) I. adj. símico II. s. simio.
sim·i·lar (sĭm′ə-lər) adj. similar, parecido; MAT. semejante.
sim·i·lar·i·ty (sĭm′ə-lăr′ĭ-tē) s. [pl. **-ties**] similitud *f*, semejanza.
sim·i·lar·ly (sĭm′ə-lər-lē) adv. del mismo modo.
sim·i·le (sĭm′ə-lē) s. RET. símil *m*.
si·mil·i·tude (sĭ-mĭl′ĭ-tōōd′, -tyōōd′) s. similitud *f*, semejanza.
sim·mer (sĭm′ər) intr. *(to boil)* hervir a fuego lento; *(to seethe)* fermentar, estar a punto de estallar ♦ **to s. down** calmarse, sosegarse —tr. hervir a fuego lento.
si·mon-pure (sī′mən-pyōōr′) adj. *(pure)* auténtico, puro; IRÓN. *(virtuous)* santurrón.
si·mon·y (sī′mə-nē, sĭm′ə-) s. [pl. **-ies**] simonía.
simp (sĭmp) s. JER. tonto, bobo.
sim·per (sĭm′pər) I. intr. sonreír tontamente o con afectación —tr. decir con una sonrisa tonta II. s. sonrisa tonta.
sim·ple (sĭm′pəl) I. adj. **-pler, -plest** *(easy)* simple; *(not elaborate)* simple, sencillo; *(sincere)* sincero; BIOL., MÚS. simple II. s. *(fool)* simple *mf*; *(person of humble condition)* persona de condición humilde; FARM. simple.
simple fraction s. MAT. fracción ordinaria.
simple interest s. FIN. interés simple *m*.
sim·ple-mind·ed (sĭm′pəl-mīn′dĭd) adj. *(artless)* ingenuo; *(silly)* tonto; *(stupid)* simple.
sim·ple·ton (sĭm′pəl-tn) s. simplón *m*, bobalicón *m*.

sim·plex (sĭm'plĕks') adj. TELEG. simplex, unidireccional.

sim·plic·i·ty (sĭm-plĭs'ĭ-tē) s. [pl. **-ties**] *(condition, plainness)* sencillez *f*; *(foolishness)* simpleza.

sim·pli·fi·ca·tion (sĭm'plə-fĭ-kā'shən) s. simplificación *f*.

sim·pli·fy (sĭm'plə-fī') tr. **-fied, -fy·ing** simplificar.

sim·ply (sĭm'plē) adv. *(plainly)* simplemente, sencillamente; *(really)* realmente, absolutamente <*the program was s. wonderful* el programa era absolutamente tremendo>; *(merely)* meramente, simplemente.

sim·u·la·crum (sĭm'yə-lā'krəm) s. [pl. **-la·cra** (-lā'krə)] simulacro.

sim·u·late (sĭm'yə-lāt') I. tr. **-lat·ed, -lat·ing** simular, fingir II. adj. simulado.

sim·u·la·tion (sĭm'yə-lā'shən) s. *(imitation)* imitación *f*; *(false appearance)* simulación *f*, fingimiento; *(simulacrum)* simulacro.

sim·u·la·tor (sĭm'yə-lā'tər) s. TEC. simulador *m*.

si·mul·cast (sī'məl-kăst', sĭm'əl-) I. tr. **-cast·ed, -cast·ing** transmitir simultáneamente por radio y televisión II. s. transmisión simultánea por radio y televisión.

si·mul·ta·ne·i·ty (sī'məl-tə-nē'ĭ-tē, -nā'-) o **si·mul·ta·ne·ous·ness** (sī'məl-tā'nē-əs-nĭs) s. simultaneidad *f*.

si·mul·ta·ne·ous (sī'məl-tā'nē-əs) adj. simultáneo.

sin (sĭn) I. s. pecado II. intr. **sinned, sin·ning** pecar.

since (sĭns) I. adv. desde entonces <*he left town and hasn't been here s.* se fue y no ha estado aquí desde entonces>; hace <*five days s.* hace cinco días> ♦ **a short time s.** hace poco • **ever s.** desde entonces • **how long s.?** ¿cuánto tiempo hace? • **long s.** hace tiempo, hace mucho tiempo • **not long s.** hace poco, no hace mucho tiempo • **s. when?** ¿desde cuándo? II. prep. desde <*I have been running s. ten o'clock* estoy corriendo desde las diez> ♦ **s. that time** desde entonces, a partir de entonces III. conj. desde que <*I have not seen you s. you got married* no te he visto desde que te casaste>; *(inasmuch as)* ya que, puesto que <*s. you are not interested, I won't tell you* ya que no estás interesado, no te diré nada> ♦ **ever s.** desde que.

sin·cere (sĭn-sîr') adj. **-cer·er, -cer·est** sincero.

sin·cere·ly (sĭn-sîr'lē) adv. sinceramente ♦ **s. yours** le saluda atentamente.

sin·cer·i·ty (sĭn-sĕr'ĭ-tē) s. sinceridad *f* ♦ **in all s.** con toda sinceridad.

sine (sīn) s. MAT. seno.

si·ne·cure (sī'nĭ-kyŏor', sĭn'ĭ-) s. canonjía, sinecura.

si·ne di·e (sī'nĭ dī'ē, sĭn'ā dē'ā') adv. indefinidamente.

si·ne qua non (sĭn'ĭ kwä nŏn') s. elemento *o* condición absolutamente necesaria.

sin·ew (sĭn'yōō) s. *(tendon)* tendón *m*; *(vigorous strength)* vigor *m*, nervio ♦ **sinews** FIG. recursos, elementos.

sin·ew·y (sĭn'yōō-ē) adj. *(muscular)* nervudo; *(strong)* fuerte.

sin·ful (sĭn'fəl) adj. *(deed)* pecaminoso; *(person)* pecador.

sing (sĭng) I. intr. **sang** (săng), **sung** (sŭng), **sing·ing** cantar ♦ **to s. a baby to sleep** arrullar a un niño • **to s. a different tune** cambiar de tono II. s. canto (de un grupo).

Sin·ga·pore (sĭng'ə-pôr', sĭng'gə-) s. Singapur *m*.

Sin·ga·por·e·an (sĭng'ə-pôr'ē-ən, sĭng'gə-) adj. & s. singapurense *mf*.

singe (sĭnj) I. tr. **singed, singe·ing** *(to scorch)* chamuscar, socarrar; *(to burn the ends of)* quemar las puntas de II. s. chamusquina.

sing·er (sĭng'ər) s. cantor *m*, cantante *mf*.

Sin·gha·lese (sĭng'gə-lēz', -lēs') o **Sin·ha·lese** (sĭng'hə-) I. adj. cingalés II. s. [pl. **Singhalese** o **Sinhalese**] *(inhabitant, language)* cingalés *m*.

sing·ing (sĭng'ĭng) s. MÚS. *(popular)* canción *f*; *(operatic)* canto.

sin·gle (sĭng'gəl) I. adj. *(sole)* solo; *(for one person)* individual; *(unmarried)* soltero; BOT. simple ♦ **every s. person** todos • **not a s. one** ni uno • **not a s. person** nadie • **not a s. thing** nada • **s. bed** cama para una persona II. s. *(person)* persona, individuo; *(thing)* cosa, objeto; *(accommodation)* alojamiento individual; *(unmarried person)* soltero; *(bill)* billete de un dólar *m*; DEP. *(in baseball)* primera base; *(in cricket)* golpe que marca un tanto *m*; *(in golf)* juego entre dos jugadores ♦ **singles** DEP. individual,

simple (tenis) III. tr. **-gled, -gling** ♦ **to s. out** *(to isolate)* separar; *(to choose)* escoger; *(to distinguish)* distinguir.

sin·gle-breast·ed (sĭng'gəl-brĕs'tĭd) adj. COST. recto, sin cruzar <*a s. jacket* una chaqueta recta>.

single combat s. combate singular *m*.

single entry s. TEN. partida simple.

single file s. hilera, fila india.

sin·gle-hand·ed (sĭng'gəl-hăn'dĭd) adj. *(unassisted)* solo, sin ayuda; *(used with one hand)* que se emplea con una sola mano; *(having only one hand)* manco.

sin·gle-mind·ed (sĭng'gəl-mīn'dĭd) adj. *(having one opinion)* sincero, franco; *(steadfast)* con un solo objetivo, resuelto.

sin·gles bar (sĭng'gəlz) s. bar para gente soltera *m*.

sin·gle-space (sĭng'gəl-spās') tr. & intr. **-spaced, -spac·ing** escribir a máquina a un solo espacio.

sin·gle·ton (sĭng'gəl-tən) s. *(card)* única carta de un palo; *(in bridge)* semifallo.

sin·gly (sĭng'glē) adv. *(alone)* solo; *(individually)* individualmente, separadamente.

sing·song (sĭng'sông') s. sonsonete *m*, tono monótono.

sin·gu·lar (sĭng'gyə-lər) I. adj. *(individual)* individual; *(rare)* raro, singular; *(peculiar)* extraño; *(unique)* único; GRAM. singular II. s. GRAM. singular *m* ♦ **in the s.** en singular.

sin·gu·lar·i·ty (sĭng'gyə-lăr'ĭ-tē) s. [pl. **-ties**] *(distinctiveness)* singularidad *f*; *(peculiarity)* peculiaridad *f*.

sin·gu·lar·ly (sĭng'gyə-lər-lē) adv. singularmente, particularmente.

sin·is·ter (sĭn'ĭ-stər) adj. siniestro.

sink (sĭngk) I. intr. **sank** (săngk) o **sunk** (sŭngk), **sunk, sink·ing** *(to descend)* descender, bajar; *(to drop)* dejarse caer <*she sank into a chair* se dejó caer en una silla>; *(to incline)* inclinarse; *(to submerge)* hundirse <*the ship sank* el barco se hundió>; *(to become weaker)* debilitarse, consumirse; *(to diminish)* disminuir, bajar; *(to penetrate)* penetrar, entrar; *(to set)* ponerse, ocultarse (sol) ♦ **his heart sank** se le cayó el alma a los pies • **to s. in** o **into** *(to go under)* hundirse; *(to penetrate)* penetrar; *(to go down)* caer en; *(to be understood)* ser comprendido; *(to make an impression)* causar impresión (palabras) • **to s. into a deep sleep** caer en un profundo sueño • **to s. or swim** triunfar o fracasar —tr. *(to make go under)* hundir <*to s. a ship* hundir un barco>; *(to cause to drop)* echar al fondo; *(to force into the ground)* echar abajo; *(to dig)* cavar, excavar; *(to make weaker)* debilitar; *(to make lower)* bajar; *(to degrade)* degradar; *(to hide)* ocultar; FAM. *(to defeat)* vencer, derrotar; COM. *(to invest)* invertir; *(to pay off)* pagar (deuda) ♦ **to be sunk in** estar sumido en II. s. *(in bathroom)* lavabo; *(in kitchen)* fregadero, pila; *(cesspool)* pozo negro; *(drain)* sumidero; FIG. *(place of vice)* antro, cloaca.

sink·er (sĭng'kər) s. *(excavator)* excavador *m*; *(fishing line weight)* plomo.

sink·hole (sĭngk'hōl') s. sumidero.

sink·ing (sĭng'kĭng) s. *(of ship, terrain)* hundimiento; *(of a well)* excavación *f*; *(of forces)* debilitación *f*, disminución *f*; *(of debt)* amortización *f*; *(feeling)* sensación de hundimiento *f*.

sinking fund s. FIN. fondo de amortización.

sin·less (sĭn'lĭs) adj. inmaculado, exento de pecado.

sin·ner (sĭn'ər) s. *(person who sins)* pecador *m*; *(scamp)* bribón *m*, pícaro.

Si·nol·o·gy (sī-nŏl'ə-jē) s. sinología.

sin·u·os·i·ty (sĭn'yōō-ŏs'ĭ-tē) s. [pl. **-ties**] sinuosidad *f*.

sin·u·ous (sĭn'yōō-əs) adj. sinuoso.

si·nus (sī'nəs) s. seno.

si·nus·i·tis (sī'nə-sī'tĭs) s. MED. sinusitis *f*.

Si·on (sī'ən) var. de Zion.

sip (sĭp) I. tr. & intr. **sipped, sip·ping** sorber, beber a sorbos II. s. sorbo.

si·phon (sī'fən) I. s. sifón *m* II. tr. sacar con sifón —intr. pasar a través de un sifón.

sir (sûr) s. señor *m*, caballero ♦ **Dear S.** muy señor mío • **S.** sir (título de caballero de orden y de barón).

sire (sīr) s. *(father)* padre *m*; *(stud animal)* semental *m*;

ANT. *(forefather)* progenitor *m*; *(title)* Majestad *f*, mi Señor.

si·ren (sī'rən) s. sirena.

siren song s. atracción engañosa.

Sir·i·us (sĭr'ē-əs) s. ASTRON. Sirio.

sir·loin (sûr'loin') s. CUL. solomillo, lomo.

sir·rah (sĭr'ə) s. ANT., DESPEC. señoritongo.

sir·up (sĭr'əp) s. var. de **syrup**.

sis (sĭs) s. FAM. hermana.

si·sal (sī'səl) s. sisal *m*, henequén *m*.

sis·si·fied (sĭs'ə-fīd') adj. afeminado.

sis·sy (sĭs'ē) I. s. [pl. **-sies**] *(milksop)* afeminado; *(coward)* gallina *m*; *(timid person)* persona tímida; FAM. *(sister)* hermana II. adj. afeminado.

sis·ter (sĭs'tər) s. *(relative)* hermana; *(kinswoman)* parienta; *(fellow member)* hermana; *(friend)* amiga; *(companion)* compañera; FAM. *(woman)* mujer; G.B. *(nurse)* enfermera jefe ◆ S. RELIG. hermana • s. ships buques gemelos.

sis·ter·hood (sĭs'tər-hŏŏd') s. *(relationship)* hermandad *f*; RELIG. comunidad de monjas *f*.

sis·ter·in·law (sĭs'tər-ĭn-lô') s. [pl. **sis·ters·in·law**] *(sister of one's spouse, wife of one's brother)* cuñada, hermana política; *(wife of the brother of one's spouse)* concuñada.

sis·ter·ly (sĭs'tər-lē) adj. de hermana, fraternal.

Sis·y·phus (sĭs'ĭ-fəs) s. MITOL. Sísifo.

sit (sĭt) intr. **sat** (săt), **sit·ting** *(to rest)* sentarse <*to s. in a chair* sentarse en una silla>; *(to be at rest)* estar sentado; *(to perch)* posarse (pájaro); *(to brood)* empollar; *(to lie)* estar situado <*a house that sits on a hill* una casa que está situada en una colina>; *(to pose)* posar <*she sat for a portrait* posó para un retrato>; *(to occupy a seat)* ocupar un escaño <*to s. in Congress* ocupar un escaño parlamentario>; *(to hold a session)* reunirse, celebrar sesión; *(to be inactive)* quedarse, permanecer; *(to weigh)* pesar; *(to fit)* sentar <*the jacket sits well on you* la chaqueta le sienta bien>; *(to please)* agradar <*the idea did not s. well with him* la idea no le agradó>; *(to baby-sit)* cuidar a niños ◆ **to be sitting pretty** FAM. estar en posición ventajosa • **to s. at home** quedarse en casa • **to s. back** sentarse cómodamente • **to s. down** sentarse • **to s. in** *(to attend)* asistir; *(to participate)* participar <*she sat in on the discussion* asistió a la discusión>; <*to s. in at a lecture* participar en una conferencia>; *(to take part in a sit-in)* tomar parte en una sentada • **to s. for an examination** G.B. presentarse a un examen • **to s. in for** reemplazar • **to s. on** *o* **upon** *(to deliberate on)* celebrar una reunión para tratar sobre (asunto, tema); *(to have a seat on)* ser miembro de (junta, comité); FAM. *(to suppress)* ocultar <*they sat on the evidence* ocultaron los hechos>; *(to repress)* reprimir; *(to rebuke)* reprender • **to s. on one's hands** no hacer nada • **to s. still** no moverse • **to s. tight** FAM. *(to keep the same position)* no arriesgarse; *(to refrain from action)* no moverse, no hacer nada • **to s. up** *(to raise the body)* incorporarse; *(to straighten one's back)* ponerse derecho; *(to stay up)* quedarse levantado, no acostarse; *(to become alert)* prestar atención —tr. *(to seat)* sentar <*the woman sat him in the chair* la mujer lo sentó en la silla>; *(to ride)* montar (un caballo) ◆ **to s. oneself** sentarse • **to s. out** *(to stay through)* quedarse hasta el final; *(to remain seated during)* quedarse sentado durante (baile); *(to stay later than)* quedarse más tiempo que (otros) • **to s. through** quedarse sentado durante.

sit·com *o* **sit-com** (sĭt'kŏm') s. FAM. comedia.

sit-down (sĭt'doun') I. s. huelga de brazos cruzados *o* de brazos caídos II. adj. que se hace sentado.

site (sĭt) I. s. *(place)* lugar, sitio; *(location)* ubicación *f*, emplazamiento II. tr. **sit·ed, sit·ing** situar.

sit-in (sĭt'ĭn') s. ocupación (de un establecimiento u oficina) *f*.

sit·ter (sĭt'ər) s. *(baby sitter)* persona que cuida niños; *(hen)* gallina clueca.

sit·ting (sĭt'ĭng) s. *(period of time)* sentada, asentada; *(session)* sesión *f*; *(incubation period)* incubación *f*; *(number of eggs)* nidada.

sitting duck s. FAM. *(easy target)* blanco muy fácil; *(easy victim)* víctima fácil.

sitting room s. cuarto de estar, sala de estar.

sit·u·ate (sĭch'ŏŏ-āt') tr. **-at·ed, -at·ing** situar, ubicar.

sit·u·a·tion (sĭch'ŏŏ-ā'shən) s. *(circumstance)* situación *f*; *(position)* puesto, empleo.

situation comedy s. RAD., TELEV. comedia a base de distintos episodios interpretados por los mismos personajes.

sit-up (sĭt'ŭp') s. ejercicio gimnástico en que se pone recto el tronco desde posición supina.

six (sĭks) s. & adj. seis *m* ◆ **at sixes and sevens** en desorden • **s. o'clock** las seis.

six-gun (sĭks'gŭn') s. revólver de seis tiros *m*.

six hundred s. & adj. seiscientos.

six-pack (sĭks'păk') s. caja de seis botellas *o* latas.

six·pence (sĭks'pəns) s. G.B. seis peniques *m*.

six·pen·ny (sĭks'pə-nē) adj. *(worth sixpence)* de seis peniques; FIG. *(paltry)* barato; *(of nails)* de dos pulgadas.

six-shoot·er (sĭks'shŏŏ'tər) s. FAM. revólver de seis tiros *m*.

six·teen (sĭk-stēn') s. & adj. dieciséis *m*, diez y seis *m*.

six·teenth (sĭk-stēnth') I. s. *(place)* dieciséis *m*; *(part)* dieciseisavo, decimosexta parte II. adj. *(place)* decimosexto; *(part)* dieciseisavo.

sixteenth note s. MÚS. semicorchea.

sixth (sĭksth) s. & adj. sexto.

sixth sense s. sexto sentido.

six·ti·eth (sĭk'stē-ĭth) I. s. *(place)* sesenta *m*; *(part)* sesentavo, sexagésima parte II. adj. *(place, part)* sexagésimo.

six·ty (sĭk'stē) s. [pl. **-ties**] & adj. sesenta *m*.

six·ty-one (sĭk'stē-wŭn') s. & adj. sesenta y uno.

siz·a·ble (sī'zə-bəl) adj. considerable, grande.

size¹ (sīz) I. s. *(dimensions)* tamaño <*the s. of the house* el tamaño de la casa>; *(of a person)* talla, estatura; *(of shoes, gloves)* número; *(of garments)* talla; *(magnitude)* magnitud *f*; FIG. *(capacity)* talla ◆ **that's about the s. of it** es más o menos eso • **to cut down to s.** FIG. bajarle los humos a alguien • **to cut to s.** cortar algo del tamaño que se necesita • **to try on for s.** probar • **what s. shoes do you take?** ¿qué número calza usted? II. tr. **sized, siz·ing** *(to classify)* clasificar según el tamaño; *(to make)* hacer de cierto tamaño ◆ **to s. up** *(to estimate)* evaluar; *(to compare)* comparar.

size² (sīz) I. s. *(paper, cloth)* apresto, cola II. tr. **sized, siz·ing** aprestar, encolar.

size·a·ble (sī'zə-bəl) adj. var. de **sizable**.

sized (sīzd) adj. de tamaño.

siz·ing (sī'zĭng) s. *(filler)* apresto, cola; *(treatment)* aparejo, aderezo.

siz·zle (sĭz'əl) I. intr. **-zled, -zling** *(to make a hissing sound)* chisporrotear; *(to be hot)* estar excesivamente caliente; FIG. *(to be furious)* hervir II. s. chisporroteo.

siz·zler (sĭz'lər) s. FAM. día de calor excesivo *m*.

skate¹ (skāt) I. s. *(ice skate)* patín (de hielo) *m*; *(roller skate)* patín (de ruedas) II. intr. **skat·ed, skat·ing** patinar.

skate² (skāt) s. ICT. raya.

skate·board (skāt'bôrd') s. tabla de patinar sobre ruedas.

skat·er (skā'tər) s. *(person)* patinador *m*; ENTOM. tejedor *m*, chinche de agua *m*.

skat·ing (skā'tĭng) s. patinaje *m*.

ske·dad·dle (skĭ-dăd'l) intr. **-dled, -dling** FAM. salir pitando.

skeet (skēt) s. tiro al plato.

skein (skān) s. *(wound thread)* madeja, FIG. *(tangle)* enredo, maraña; *(birds)* bandada.

skel·e·tal (skĕl'ĭ-tl) adj. esquelético.

skel·e·ton (skĕl'ĭ-tn) s. ANAT. esqueleto; TEC. armadura, armazón (de un edificio) *f*; *(of an organization)* estructura; *(outline)* bosquejo, esquema *m*; FAM. *(thin person)* esqueleto.

skeleton key s. llave maestra.

skep·tic (skĕp'tĭk) s. escéptico.

skep·ti·cal (skĕp'tĭ-kəl) adj. escéptico.

skep·ti·cism (skĕp'tĭ-sĭz'əm) s. escepticismo.

sketch (skĕch) I. s. *(drawing)* esbozo, bosquejo; *(outline)* bosquejo, esquema *m*; TEAT. *(person)* persona divertida; LIT. obra corta; MÚS. pieza corta; TEAT. obra corta II. tr. esbozar, bosquejar —intr. hacer un croquis.

---

ng inglés / ŏ la / ō bou / ô corre / oi oigo / ŏŏ uno / ou auto / yŏŏ ciudad / w hueco / y yo / z mismo

sketch·book (skĕch'bŏŏk') s. *(drawing pad)* bloc de dibujo *m*; *(book)* colección de obras cortas *f.*

sketch·y (skĕch'ē) adj. **-i·er, -i·est** *(not detailed)* sin detalles; *(incomplete)* incompleto; *(superficial)* superficial.

skew (skyōō) **I.** intr. *(to twist)* torcerse; *(to look obliquely)* torcer la vista, mirar de soslayo —tr. *(to cut slantingly)* sesgar; *(to distort)* tergiversar, desvirtuar **II.** adj. *(asymmetric)* asimétrico; *(slanting)* oblicuo; *(not straight)* sesgado; GEOM. alabeado **III.** s. oblicuidad *f*, sesgo.

skew·er (skyōō'ər) **I.** s. broqueta, espetón *m* **II.** tr. espetar, ensartar.

ski (skē) **I.** s. esquí *m* ♦ **ski run** *o* **slope** pista de esquí **II.** intr. & tr. **skied, ski·ing** esquiar.

skid (skĭd) **I.** s. *(slip)* patinazo, resbalón *m*; *(block of wood)* calzo; *(for unloading)* rampa de descarga; AVIA. patín *m* ♦ **skids** MARÍT. varadera • **to be on the skids** estar de capa caída • **to put the skids under** causar la ruina **II.** intr. **skid·ded, skid·ding** patinar, resbalar (rueda, automóvil) —tr. *(to slide down a ramp)* hacer deslizar; *(to block)* calzar; *(to cause to slide)* hacer patinar; MARÍT. poner varaderas a.

skid row s. JER. barrio bajo.

ski·er (skē'ər) s. esquiador *m.*

skiff (skĭf) s. MARÍT. esquife *m.*

ski·ing (skē'ĭng) s. esquí (deporte) *m.*

ski jump s. *(leap)* salto con esquís; *(course)* pista de salto con esquís.

skil·ful (skĭl'fəl) adj. var. de **skillful.**

ski lift s. telesquí *m.*

skill (skĭl) s. *(ability)* habilidad *f*, maña; *(art)* arte *m*, técnica; *(experience)* experiencia; *(trade)* oficio.

skilled (skĭld) adj. *(having ability)* hábil, mañoso; *(qualified)* cualificado, especializado.

skil·let (skĭl'ĭt) s. *(frying pan)* sartén *f*; G.B. *(saucepan)* cacerola *o* cazuela pequeña.

skill·ful (skĭl'fəl) adj. hábil, mañoso.

skill·ful·ly (skĭl'fə-lē) adv. hábilmente, mañosamente.

skill·ful·ness (skĭl'fəl-nĭs) s. habilidad *f*, maña *f.*

skim (skĭm) **I.** tr. **skimmed, skim·ming** *(a liquid)* espumar; *(milk)* desnatar; *(to hurl)* hacer cabrillas con; *(to brush)* rozar; *(to glance at)* echar una ojeada a; *(to read)* hojear (libro) ♦ **to s. along** AVIA. volar a ras de ♦ **to s. over** *(a surface)* pasar rozando; *(an airplane)* volar rozando, volar a ras de; *(a subject)* tratar superficialmente • **to s. through** *(to flick through)* hojear; *(to read quickly)* echar una ojeada a —intr. *(to glide)* deslizarse; *(to read)* hojear (libro); *(to become coated)* cubrirse con una capa fina **II.** s. *(act of skimming)* espumado; *(milk)* leche desnatada; *(thin layer)* capa fina.

skim·mer (skĭm'ər) s. *(for skimming liquids)* espumadera; *(for milk)* desnatadora; ORNIT. rayador *m*, picotijera *m.*

skim milk s. leche desnatada.

skim·ming (skĭm'ĭng) s. *(thing removed)* espuma; *(action)* despumación *f.*

skimp (skĭmp) **I.** tr. *(to do hastily)* chapucear; *(to scrimp)* escatimar —intr. economizar **II.** adj. escaso, limitado.

skimp·y (skĭm'pē) adj. **-i·er, -i·est** *(scanty)* escaso; *(thrifty)* tacaño; *(small)* pequeño.

skin (skĭn) **I.** s. *(integument, pelt)* piel *f*; *(of fruit)* piel *f*; MARÍT. *(of a ship)* forro; *(container)* pellejo, odre *m* ♦ **by the s. of one's teeth** por los pelos • **he is nothing but s. and bones** está hecho un esqueleto, está en los huesos • **it's no s. off my nose** esto no me va ni me viene, esto no es asunto mío • **soaked to the s.** calado hasta los huesos • **to get under one's s.** *(to irritate)* irritarle a uno, exasperarle a uno; *(to be an obsession)* ser una obsesión • **to have a thick s.** ser insensible, ser imperturbable • **to have a thin s.** ser muy susceptible • **to have someone under one's s.** tener a alguien en la masa de la sangre • **to jump out of one's s.** llevarse un susto tremendo • **to save one's s.** salvar el pellejo • **to strip to the s.** desnudarse completamente • **under the s.** en el fondo **II.** tr. **skinned, skin·ning** *(to remove)* despellejar, desollar <*he skinned the lamb* despellejó el cordero>; *(to peel)* pelar; *(to cover)* cubrir con piel; *(to peel off)* quitar; *(to scrape)* arañar, desollar <*she skinned her knee* se desolló la rodilla>; JER.

(to fleece) pelar, desplumar ♦ **to s. alive** *(to flay)* desollar vivo a; *(to scold)* escarmentar, regañar mucho; *(to punish)* castigar; *(to defeat)* vencer, derrotar —intr. *(to pass by)* pasar justo; *(to go hurriedly)* ir apresuradamente ♦ **to s. out** escaparse • **to s. over** MED. cicatrizarse <*the wound skinned over* la herida se cicatrizó>.

skin-deep (skĭn'dēp') **I.** adj. superficial **II.** adv. superficialmente.

skin-dive (skĭn'dīv') intr. **-dived, -div·ing** bucear.

skin diving s. buceo.

skin·flint (skĭn'flĭnt') s. tacaño.

skin·ner (skĭn'ər) s. *(person who strips skin)* desollador *m*; *(furrier)* peletero.

skin·ny (skĭn'ē) adj. **-ni·er, -ni·est** flaco.

skin·ny-dip (skĭn'ē-dĭp') intr. **-dipped, -dip·ping** FAM. nadar desnudo.

skin test s. MED. cutirreacción *f*, dermorreacción *f.*

skin·tight (skĭn'tīt') adj. ajustado, ceñido.

skip (skĭp) **I.** intr. **skipped, skip·ping** *(to hop)* saltar, brincar; *(to skim)* pasar rozando; *(to omit)* saltar, pasar (de una cosa a otra); *(to misfire)* fallar; *(to rebound)* rebotar; FAM. *(to abscond)* desaparecer; EDUC. *(to be promoted)* saltar un curso —tr. *(to hop)* saltar; *(to omit)* omitir, saltar; *(to cause to ricochet)* hacer rebotar; *(to fail to attend)* dejar de ir a; FAM. *(to leave)* desaparecer; EDUC. *(to be promoted)* saltarse un curso ♦ **s. it!** ¡olvídalo! • **to s. over** *(to jump)* saltar por encima de; *(to omit)* omitir, saltar • **to s. town** FAM. largarse **II.** s. *(hop)* salto, brinco; *(omission)* salto, omisión *f*; *(rebound)* rebote *m.*

skip·per[1] (skĭp'ər) s. MARÍT. capitán *m*, patrón *m.*

skip·per[2] (skĭp'ər) s. ENTOM. insecto saltador; ICT. pez saltador *m.*

skir·mish (skûr'mĭsh) MIL. **I.** s. escaramuza; *(dispute)* pelea **II.** intr. escaramuzar, escaramucear.

skir·mish·er (skûr'mĭ-shər) s. MIL. escaramuzador *m.*

skirt (skûrt) **I.** s. COST. falda; *(outer edge)* borde *m*; *(leather flap)* faldón *m*; JER. *(woman)* gachí *f* ♦ **skirts** afueras **II.** tr. & intr. *(to bound)* bordear; *(to pass around)* rodear; *(to elude)* eludir.

skit (skĭt) s. TEAT. escena satírica; *(writing)* sátira.

skit·ter (skĭt'ər) intr. pasar rozando el agua.

skit·tish (skĭt'ĭsh) adj. *(excitable)* asustadizo; *(timid)* tímido; *(frivolous)* frívolo; *(undependable)* caprichoso.

skit·tle (skĭt'l) DEP. s. bolo ♦ **skittles** bolos.

skiv·vy (skĭv'ē) JER. s. [pl. **-vies**] camiseta ♦ **skivvies** calzoncillo y camiseta • **to be in one's skivvies** estar en paños menores (hombre).

skul·dug·ger·y (skŭl-dŭg'ə-rē) s. var. de **skullduggery.**

skulk (skŭlk) **I.** intr. *(to lurk)* esconderse; *(to malinger)* zafarse, escurrir el bulto **II.** s. *(person)* remolón *m*; *(foxes)* manada de zorros.

skull (skŭl) s. ANAT. cráneo; FIG. *(head)* cabeza, mente *f* ♦ **to be out of one's s.** FAM. estar loco.

skull and crossbones s. calavera (de bandera de piratas).

skull·cap (skŭl'kăp') s. *(hat)* gorro; *(yarmulke)* gorro (usado por los judíos); BOT. escutelaria.

skull·dug·ger·y (skŭl-dŭg'ə-rē) s. [pl. **-ies**] FAM. engaños, trampas.

skunk (skŭngk) **I.** s. ZOOL. mofeta; JER. *(person)* canalla *m* **II.** tr. JER. *(to defeat)* ganar; *(to cheat)* estafar.

sky (skī) **I.** s. [pl. **skies**] cielo, firmamento ♦ **skies** METEOR. tiempo, cielo <*cloudy skies* cielo nublado> ♦ **out of the clear blue s.** en el momento menos pensado • **to praise someone to the skies** poner a alguien por las nubes **II.** tr. **skied, sky·ing** *(to throw)* bombear; *(to hang)* colgar muy alto.

sky·cap (skī'kăp') s. mozo de cuerda, changador de un aeropuerto *m.*

sky·dive (skī'dīv') intr. **-dived, -div·ing** DEP. lanzarse en paracaídas.

sky-high (skī'hī') **I.** adv. por las nubes **II.** adj. muy alto.

sky·jack (skī'jăk') tr. secuestrar (un avión) en vuelo.

sky·lark (skī'lärk') **I.** s. ORNIT. alondra **II.** intr. *(to have fun)* divertirse; *(to be mischievous)* hacer travesuras.

sky·light (skī'līt') s. claraboya, tragaluz *m.*

sky·line (skī′līn′) s. *(horizon)* horizonte *m*; *(outline)* silueta, perfil *m*; *(of a city)* perfil, contorno.

sky·rock·et (skī′rŏk′ĭt) I. s. cohete *m* II. tr. & intr. subir rápidamente.

sky·scrap·er (skī′skrā′pər) s. rascacielos.

sky·ward (skī′wərd) I. adj. dirigido hacia el cielo II. adv. hacia el cielo.

sky·way (skī′wā′) s. AVIA. *(air lane)* ruta aérea; *(highway)* autopista elevada.

sky·writ·ing (skī′rī′tĭng) s. escritura con humo echado al cielo por un avión.

slab (slăb) I. s. *(piece)* trozo; *(of cake)* porción *f*; *(of stone)* losa; *(of metal)* lámina, plancha; *(of wood)* costero II. tr. **slabbed, slab·bing** *(to cut from a log)* cortar los costeros de; *(to cover)* aplicar una capa espesa de; *(to pave)* enlosar.

slack[1] (slăk) I. adj. **-er, -est** *(sluggish)* lento; *(not busy)* de poco trabajo, de poca actividad <*a s. business season* una temporada de poco trabajo>; *(loose)* flojo <*a s. rope* una cuerda floja>; *(negligent)* negligente <*a s. worker* un trabajador negligente>; *(lazy)* perezoso; *(said of the wind)* que sopla lentamente; *(said of a tide)* que fluye lentamente II. tr. *(to slacken)* aflojar; *(to slake)* apagar —intr. *(to loosen)* aflojarse; *(to be remiss)* ser negligente ♦ **to s. off** disminuir • **to s. up** reducir la velocidad, aflojar el paso III. s. *(loose part)* parte floja (de una cuerda); *(looseness)* flojedad *f*, flojera; *(lull)* período de poca actividad; *(cessation of movement)* inactividad *f*, inercia; *(still water)* aguas muertas ♦ **slacks** pantalones ♦ **there is a lot of s. in the rope** la cuerda está muy floja • **to take up the s. in a rope** tensar una cuerda IV. adv. flojamente, de manera floja.

slack[2] (slăk) s. *(coal)* cisco.

slack·en (slăk′ən) tr. *(to slow down)* aminorar; *(to lessen)* disminuir, reducir; *(to loosen)* aflojar —intr. *(to slow down)* amainar (viento); *(to lessen)* disminuir; *(to loosen)* aflojarse.

slack·er (slăk′ər) s. haragán *m*; MIL. prófugo.

slack·ness (slăk′nĭs) s. *(looseness)* flojedad *f*; *(inactivity)* inactividad *f*; *(laziness)* pereza; *(carelessness)* negligencia; *(of business)* estancamiento; *(of discipline)* relajación *f*.

slag (slăg) s. escoria.

slain (slān) part. p. de **slay.**

slake (slāk) tr. **slaked, slak·ing** *(to quench)* aplacar; *(to satisfy)* saciar; *(lime)* apagar —intr. *(to disintegrate)* desintegrarse; *(lime)* apagarse.

sla·lom (slä′ləm) s. DEP. slalom *m*.

slam[1] (slăm) I. tr. **slammed, slam·ming** *(to shut)* cerrar de golpe; *(to move)* hacer golpear; *(to hit)* golpear con estrépito, pegar fuerte; FAM. *(to criticize harshly)* vapulear ♦ **to s. something down on a table** poner algo violentamente en la mesa • **to s. the door** dar un portazo • **to s. the door on** cerrar la puerta a —intr. *(to close)* cerrarse de golpe; *(to crash)* chocar II. s. *(blow)* golpe fuerte *m*; *(of a door)* portazo; FAM. vapuleo.

slam[2] (slăm) *(in bridge)* slam *m*.

slan·der (slăn′dər) I. s. *(libel)* calumnia; DER. difamación *f* II. tr. *(to libel)* calumniar; DER. difamar.

slan·der·er (slăn′dər-ər) s. *(libeler)* calumniador *m*; DER. difamador *m*.

slan·der·ous (slăn′dər-əs) adj. *(libelous)* calumnioso; DER. difamador.

slang (slăng) s. jerga.

slang·y (slăng′ē) adj. **-i·er, -i·est** vulgar (lengua).

slant (slănt) I. tr. *(to incline)* inclinar; *(a problem)* enfocar de modo parcial —intr. inclinarse II. s. *(incline)* inclinación *f*; *(slope)* pendiente *f*, declive *m*; *(point of view)* parecer *m*, punto de vista.

slap (slăp) I. s. *(blow with open hand)* palmada; *(on the face)* bofetada; *(on the head)* cachetada; FIG. *(insult)* insulto, desaire ♦ **a s. in the face** una afrenta, una bofetada • **a s. on the back** un espaldazo II. tr. **slapped, slap·ping** *(to strike)* dar una palmada; *(the face)* abofetear; *(the head)* dar una cachetada; *(to slam)* poner violentamente; FIG. *(to insult)* insultar ♦ **to s. down** prohibir —intr. dar una palmada III. adv. FAM. de lleno <*she ran s. into the wall* dio de lleno contra la pared>.

slap·dash (slăp′dăsh′) I. adj. chapucero, descuidado II. adv. descuidadamente.

slap·hap·py (slăp′hăp′ē) adj. **-pi·er, -pi·est** JER. *(dazed)* aturdido; *(happy-go-lucky)* despreocupado.

slap·stick (slăp′stĭk′) s. *(paddle)* palmeta de payaso; *(comedy)* payasada, bufonada.

slash (slăsh) I. tr. *(to cut, slit)* acuchillar; *(to lash)* azotar; *(with the edge of a sword)* dar un tajo a; *(to criticize)* vapulear, poner por los suelos; *(to reduce)* rebajar (precios) —intr. *(to make strokes)* tirar *o* dar tajos; *(to cut one's way)* abrirse paso dando tajos II. s. *(cut)* tajo, cuchillada; *(slit in clothing)* cuchillada; *(in a forest)* tala; IMPR. *(virgule)* vírgula ♦ **slashes** tierra pantanosa.

slash·er (slăsh′ər) s. *(person)* acuchillador *m*; *(machine)* cuchilla.

slash·ing (slăsh′ĭng) adj. *(critical)* mordaz, áspero; *(pelting)* fuerte <*a s. rain* una lluvia fuerte>.

slat (slăt) s. tablilla, listón *m*.

slate (slāt) I. s. *(rock, writing surface)* pizarra; *(record)* antecedentes *m*; *(list of candidates)* lista de candidatos elegibles ♦ **to clean the s.** borrar los antecedentes • **to have a clean s.** no tener antecedentes II. tr. **slat·ed, slat·ing** *(to cover)* empizarrar; *(to put on a list)* inscribir; *(to appoint)* designar.

slath·er (slăth′ər) I. tr. FAM. *(to lavish)* usar en gran cantidad; *(to spread with)* extender en gran cantidad II. s. JER. gran cantidad *f*.

slat·ing (slā′tĭng) s. *(action)* empizarrado; *(slates collectively)* pizarras.

slat·tern (slăt′ərn) s. mujer desaliñada.

slaugh·ter (slô′tər) I. s. *(killing of animals)* matanza, sacrificio; *(massacre)* matanza, carnicería II. tr. *(animals)* matar, sacrificar; *(to massacre)* exterminar; *(to kill brutally)* matar brutalmente.

slaugh·ter·house (slô′tər-hous′) s. matadero.

Slav (släv) adj. & s. eslavo.

slave (slāv) I. s. esclavo ♦ **s. labor** trabajo de esclavo II. intr. **slaved, slav·ing** trabajar como esclavo.

slave driver s. negrero, capataz de esclavos *m*.

slave·hold·er (slāv′hōl′dər) s. negrero.

slav·er[1] (slăv′ər) I. intr. babear II. s. *(drooling saliva)* baba; *(slobbering flattery)* halago.

slav·er[2] (slā′vər) s. *(ship)* barco negrero, buque traficante de esclavos *m*; *(person)* negrero, traficante de esclavos *m*.

slav·er·y (slā′və-rē, slāv′rē) s. [pl. **-ies**] esclavitud *f* ♦ **white s.** trata de blancas.

slave state s. dictadura ♦ **S. State** HIST. estado esclavista en EE. UU.

slave trade s. trata de esclavos.

Slav·ic (slä′vĭk) adj. & s. eslavo.

slav·ish (slā′vĭsh) adj. *(servile)* servil; *(oppressive)* tiránico, opresivo.

Sla·vo·ni·a (slə-vō′nē-ə) s. Eslavonia, Croacia.

Sla·vo·ni·an (slə-vō′nē-ən) adj. eslavonio, eslavón.

Sla·von·ic (slə-vŏn′ĭk) s. & adj. eslavo.

slaw (slô) s. CUL. ensalada de col.

slay (slā) tr. **slew** (slōō), **slain** (slān), **slay·ing** *(to kill)* matar; *(to amuse)* encantar, chiflar.

slay·er (slā′ər) s. asesino.

slea·zy (slē′zē) adj. **-zi·er, -zi·est** *(flimsy)* ligero; *(cheap)* de mala calidad; *(vulgar)* vulgar; *(of doubtful honesty)* de honradez sospechosa.

sled (slĕd) I. s. trineo II. tr. **sled·ded, sled·ding** llevar *o* transportar en trineo —intr. ir en trineo.

sled·ding (slĕd′ĭng) s. *(action)* transporte por trineo; FAM. *(progress)* progreso.

sledge (slĕj) s. trineo.

sledge·ham·mer (slĕj′hăm′ər) I. s. almádena, almádana II. tr. golpear con la almádena III. adj. aplastante.

sleek (slēk) adj. **-er, -est** *(smooth)* suave y brillante; *(well-groomed)* elegante; *(slick)* meloso.

sleek·ness (slēk′nĭs) s. *(smoothness)* suavidad *f*; *(elegance)* elegancia.

sleep (slēp) I. s. sueño ♦ **deep s.** sueño profundo • **in one's s.** durante el sueño • **overcome with s.** vencido por el sueño • **to drop off to s.** quedarse dormido • **to get to s.**

quedarse dormido • **to go to s.** dormirse • **to lose s.** perder el sueño • **to put to s.** *(child)* adormecer, hacer dormir; *(animal)* sacrificar • **to walk in one's s.** ser sonámbulo **II.** *intr.* **slept** (slĕpt), **sleep·ing** dormir ♦ **to s. around** FAM. acostarse con todos • **to s. in** *(to oversleep)* dormir demasiado; *(to sleep late)* dormir hasta tarde • **to s. like a log** dormir como un tronco —*tr.* *(to spend sleeping)* pasar durmiendo <*he slept the whole day* pasó el día entero durmiendo>; *(to provide with accommodations)* tener cabida para, poder alojar <*the hotel sleeps fifty people* el hotel tiene cabida para cincuenta personas> ♦ **not to s. a wink** no pegar ojo en toda la noche • **to s. off** dormir hasta que pase (dolor de cabeza, borrachera) • **to s. on it** consultar con la almohada • **to s. with** acostarse con.

sleep·er (slē′pər) s. *(person)* persona que duerme; *(sleeping car)* coche cama *m*; FAM. *(success)* éxito inesperado; G.B. *(crosstie)* traviesa, durmiente *m* ♦ **to be a heavy s.** tener el sueño pesado • **to be a light s.** tener el sueño ligero.

sleep-in (slēp′ĭn′) adj. ♦ **s. maid (nurse)** criada (enfermera) que duerme donde trabaja.

sleep·i·ness (slē′pē-nĭs) s. somnolencia.

sleep·ing (slē′pĭng) **I.** *adj.* durmiente, dormido **II.** *s.* sueño.

sleeping bag s. saco de dormir.

sleeping car s. F.C. coche cama *m*.

sleeping pill s. somnífero.

sleeping sickness s. MED. *(African disease)* enfermedad del sueño *f*, tripanosomiasis *f*; *(encephalitis lethargica)* encefalitis letárgica.

sleep·less (slēp′lĭs) adj. *(without sleep)* en blanco <*I passed a s. night* pasé la noche en blanco>; *(unable to sleep)* desvelado, insomne; *(never resting)* incansable.

sleep·walk·ing (slēp′wô′kĭng) s. sonambulismo.

sleep·y (slē′pē) adj. **-i·er, -i·est** *(drowsy)* soñoliento; *(lethargic)* letárgico; *(dull)* soporífero; *(quiet)* dormido.

sleep·y·head (slē′pē-hĕd′) s. FAM. dormilón *m*.

sleet (slēt) **I.** s. aguanieve *f* **II.** *intr.* cellisquear.

sleeve (slēv) **I.** s. *(of a garment)* manga; *(of a record)* funda; MEC. *(of a shaft)* manguito; *(of a cylinder)* camisa ♦ **up one's s.** en reserva —*tr.* **sleeved, sleev·ing** *(garment)* poner manga a; MEC. colocar un manguito *o* una camisa a.

sleeve·less (slēv′lĭs) adj. COST. sin mangas; MEC. sin camisa.

sleigh (slā) **I.** s. trineo **II.** *intr.* ir en trineo.

sleight (slīt) s. *(dexterity)* habilidad *f*; *(stratagem)* estratagema ♦ **s. of hand** prestidigitación *f*, juego de manos.

slen·der (slĕn′dər) adj. **-er, -est** *(slim)* delgado; *(thin and graceful)* esbelto; *(meager)* escaso; *(frail)* ligero.

slen·der·ize (slĕn′də-rīz′) intr. & tr. **-ized, -iz·ing** adelgazar.

slen·der·ness (slĕn′dər-nĭs) s. *(slimness)* delgadez *f*; *(gracefulness)* esbeltez *f*; *(meagerness)* escasez *f*.

slept (slĕpt) pret. y part. p. de **sleep.**

sleuth (slōōth) **I.** s. FAM. *(detective)* detective *m*; *(sleuthhound)* sabueso **II.** *tr.* investigar a, seguir la pista de —*intr.* hacer de detective.

sleuth·hound (slōōth′hound′) s. *(dog)* sabueso; FAM. *(detective)* detective *m*.

slew¹ (slōō) s. FAM. *(a lot)* montón *m*.

slew² (slōō) pret. de **slay.**

slice (slīs) **I.** s. *(of meat)* tajada; *(of bread)* rebanada; *(of ham)* loncha, lonja; *(of salami)* raja, rodaja; *(of melon)* tajada, raja; *(of fish)* raja; *(part)* parte *f* <*a s. of the profits* una parte de las ganancias>; *(knife)* paleta; DEP. *(stroke)* golpe que da efecto a la pelota *m* **II.** tr. **sliced, slic·ing** *(to divide)* cortar en rodajas; *(to cut)* cortar; *(to parcel out)* dividir; DEP. *(to hit)* golpear con efecto (la pelota) ♦ **to s. off** cortar —*intr.* DEP. dar efecto a la pelota.

slice-of-life (slīs′əv-līf′) adj. TEAT. realista.

slic·er (slī′sər) s. máquina de cortar.

slick (slĭk) **I.** adj. **-er, -est** *(slippery)* resbaladizo; *(adroit)* diestro; *(wily)* astuto; *(glib)* fácil **II.** s. *(slippery surface)* superficie resbaladiza; *(tool)* herramienta para alisar **III.** tr. *(to make smooth)* alisar; FAM. *(to make neat)* acicalar ♦ **to s. oneself up** acicalarse.

slick·er (slĭk′ər) s. *(raincoat)* impermeable *m*; FAM. *(swindler)* estafador *m*; *(dandy)* dandi *m*.

slide (slīd) **I.** *intr.* **slid** (slĭd), **slid·ing** *(to slip)* resbalar; *(to*

coast) deslizarse; *(to glide)* pasar suavemente; *(to move downward)* bajar ♦ **to let things s.** dejar pasar las cosas sin hacer nada • **to s. by** *o* **away** pasar (tiempo) • **to s. down** bajar deslizándose por • **to s. up to someone** acercarse furtivamente a alguien —*tr.* hacer resbalar, hacer deslizar ♦ **to s. over** pasar por alto (un tema) **II.** s. *(act of sliding)* deslizamiento, desliz *m*; *(smooth surface)* superficie resbaladiza; *(playground apparatus)* tobogán *m*; *(track)* resbaladero; *(glass plate)* portaobjeto (para microscopio); *(avalanche)* desprendimiento, avalancha; MÚS. vara corredera; FOTOG. diapositiva, transparencia.

slide rule s. regla de cálculo.

sliding scale s. escala móvil.

slight (slīt) **I.** adj. **-er, -est** *(meager)* escaso; *(trifling)* insignificante; *(slender)* delgado; *(frail)* ligero **II.** tr. *(to neglect)* menospreciar, despreciar; *(to shirk)* descuidar, desatender **III.** s. desaire *m*.

slight·ly (slīt′lē) adv. *(carelessly)* descuidadamente; *(somewhat)* un poco; *(lightly)* ligeramente.

slight·ness (slīt′nĭs) s. *(slenderness)* delgadez *f*; *(trifle)* insignificancia.

slim (slĭm) **I.** adj. **slim·mer, slim·mest** *(slender)* delgado; *(scant)* escaso; *(light)* ligero **II.** tr. & intr. **slimmed, slim·ming** adelgazar.

slime (slīm) **I.** s. *(mud)* limo, fango; *(animal substance)* baba, baba *II.* tr. **slimed, slim·ing** enfangar.

slim·i·ness (slī′mē-nĭs) s. *(muddiness)* fangosidad *f*; *(viscosity)* viscosidad *f*.

slim·y (slī′mē) adj. **-i·er, -i·est** *(muddy)* fangoso; *(viscous)* viscoso; *(mucous)* baboso.

sling (slĭng) **I.** s. *(weapon)* honda; *(slingshot)* tirador *m*; *(for a rifle)* portafusil *m*; MED. *(loop of cloth)* cabestrillo; MARÍT. eslinga **II.** tr. **slung** (slŭng), **sling·ing** *(to throw)* tirar con honda; *(to hang)* colgar; *(to fling)* tirar, arrojar; MED. poner en cabestrillo ♦ **to s. hash** JER. trabajar en un restaurante barato.

sling·shot (slĭng′shŏt′) s. tirador *m*.

slink (slĭngk) **I.** *intr.* **slunk** (slŭngk), **slink·ing** escabullirse —*tr.* VET. malparir **II.** s. VET. aborton *m* **III.** adj. prematuro.

slink·y (slĭng′kē) adj. **-i·er, -i·est** *(stealthy)* sigiloso; *(furtive)* furtivo; FAM. *(graceful)* elegante; *(provocative)* provocativo.

slip¹ (slĭp) **I.** *intr.* **slipped, slip·ping** *(to glide)* deslizarse; *(to move stealthily)* escurrirse, escabullirse; *(to pass gradually)* pasar <*time slips by* el tiempo pasa>; *(to lose one's balance)* resbalar <*he slipped and fell* resbaló y se cayó>; *(to shift position)* soltarse, desprenderse; *(to escape)* desatarse, soltarse <*the dog slipped out of its collar* el perro se soltó del collar>; *(to get away)* irse; *(to fall behind)* retrasarse; *(to make a mistake)* equivocarse; FAM. *(to decline)* debilitarse; *(to fall off)* empeorar <*his work is slipping* su trabajo está empeorando> ♦ **my foot slipped** se me fue el pie • **to let an opportunity slip by** perder *o* dejar pasar una oportunidad • **to let s.** decir sin querer <*she let his name slip* dijo sin querer el nombre de él> • **to s. away** *(to go stealthily)* escabullirse; *(to disappear)* desaparecer; *(time)* correr, pasar • **to s. back** volver sigilosamente • **to s. by** *(time)* pasar, correr; *(to pass unnoticed)* pasar inadvertido • **to s. down** dejarse caer • **to s. in** introducirse, meterse • **to s. off** *(to go stealthily)* escabullirse; *(to fall off)* caerse • **to s. out** *(to go)* salir inadvertido; *(to become known)* saberse • **to s. through** escabullirse por • **to s. through one's fingers** escapársele de las manos, caérsele • **to s. up** FAM. equivocarse, meter la pata —*tr.* *(to put)* poner, meter; *(to ease)* colocar suavemente; *(to get loose from)* librarse de; *(to unfasten)* deshacer, desatar <*to s. the knot* deshacer el nudo>; *(in knitting)* dejar sin hacer (un punto); *(to slide open)* descorrer; *(to slide shut)* correr; *(used of animals)* parir antes de tiempo; MED. dislocar ♦ **to s. anchor** MARÍT. levantar anclas • **to s. in** introducir • **to s. on** *(to don)* ponerse; *(to enter)* entrar • **to s. its skin** cambiar de piel (serpiente) • **to s. off** quitarse (ropa) • **to s. on** ponerse (ropa) • **to s. one over on** FAM. pegársela, hacer una mala pasada (a alguien) • **to s. one's mind** olvidársele a uno, írsele de la memoria a uno **II.** s. *(slipping)* resbalón *m* <*a* *s. on the ice* un resbalón en el hielo>; *(false step)* paso en falso; *(error)* error *m*, equivocación *f*; *(lapse)* desliz *m*, descuido; *(undergarment)* combinación *f*; *(pillowcase)* funda; MARÍT. *(pier)* muelle *m*, embarcadero; *(slipway)* grada; GEOL. *(crack)* grieta, hendidura; *(fault)* falla; AVIA. pérdida de velocidad teórica ♦ **s. of the tongue** lapsus linguae • **to give someone the s.** JER. dar esquinazo a alguien, eludir a alguien.

slip² (slĭp) **I.** s. *(cutting)* esqueje *m*; *(strip)* tira; *(slender person)* mozuelo esbelto, chiquillo *<a s. of a girl* una chiquilla>; *(piece of paper)* papeleta; *(narrow pew)* banco de iglesia angosto **II.** tr. **slipped, slip·ping** esquejar.

slip³ (slĭp) s. CERÁM. barbotina.

slip·case (slĭp′kās′) s. *(for books)* estuche *m*; *(for records)* funda.

slip·cov·er (slĭp′kŭv′ər) **I.** s. funda (de un mueble) **II.** tr. poner una funda a.

slip·knot (slĭp′nŏt′) s. nudo corredizo.

slip·on (slĭp′ŏn′) s. prenda de vestir de quitaipón.

slip·page (slĭp′ĭj) s. *(slipping)* resbalamiento; MEC. pérdida de fuerza de transmisión.

slip·per (slĭp′ər) s. zapatilla.

slip·per·y (slĭp′ə-rē) adj. **-i·er, -i·est** *(causing sliding)* resbaladizo; *(tending to slip from one's grasp)* escurridizo; *(evasive)* evasivo.

slip·shod (slĭp′shŏd′) adj. *(careless)* descuidado; *(shabby)* desaliñado, desaseado.

slip·stream (slĭp′strēm′) s. AVIA. estela.

slip·up (slĭp′ŭp′) s. FAM. error *m*.

slit (slĭt) **I.** s. *(cut)* corte *m*; *(opening)* abertura **II.** tr. **slit, slit·ting** hender, cortar ♦ **to s. someone's throat** degollar a alguien.

slith·er (slĭth′ər) **I.** intr. *(to slip)* resbalar; *(to crawl)* deslizarse, culebrear —tr. *(to cause to slip)* hacer resbalar; *(to cause to crawl)* hacer deslizar **II.** s. deslizamiento.

sliv·er (slĭv′ər) **I.** s. *(splinter)* astilla; TEJ. torzal *m* **II.** tr. & intr. astillar(se).

slob (slŏb) s. DESPEC., FAM. palurdo, patán *m*.

slob·ber (slŏb′ər) **I.** intr. *(to drool)* babear; FIG. *(to indulge in sentimentality)* decir sensiblerías —tr. babosear **II.** s. *(drool)* baba, baboseo; *(sentimentality)* sensiblería.

sloe (slō) s. *(blackthorn)* endrino; *(fruit)* endrina.

slog (slŏg) **I.** tr. **slogged, slog·ging** golpear —intr. *(to plod)* andar pesadamente; *(to work diligently)* trabajar como un burro **II.** s. *(hard blow)* golpetazo; *(hard work)* trabajo pesado; *(exhausting march)* caminata dura.

slo·gan (slō′gən) s. *(motto)* lema *m*; *(in advertising)* eslogan *m*, lema publicitario.

sloop (slōōp) s. MARÍT. balandro.

slop (slŏp) **I.** s. *(mud)* fango, barro; *(watery food)* aguachirle *f*; *(writing)* sensiblería(s) ♦ **slops** *(swill)* bazofia; *(excrement)* excremento, heces; *(mash)* lías, heces **II.** intr. **slopped, slop·ping** *(to splash)* salpicar; *(to spill)* derramarse, verterse; *(to gush)* ponerse muy sentimental; *(to plod)* chapotear, avanzar chapoteando ♦ **to s. over** derramarse —tr. *(to spill)* derramar, verter (un líquido); *(to splash)* salpicar; *(to serve clumsily)* servir con brusquedad; *(to feed)* cebar con pocilgadas.

slope (slōp) **I.** intr. **sloped, slop·ing** *(to incline)* inclinarse; *(to move)* ir oblicuamente ♦ **to s. down** bajar, descender • **to s. up** subir, ascender —tr. inclinar **II.** s. *(incline)* pendiente *f*, cuesta; *(of mountain)* falda, ladera; *(of roof)* vertiente *f*; *(inclination)* inclinación *f* ♦ **degree of s.** inclinación • **on a s.** en declive.

slop·pi·ness (slŏp′ē-nĭs) s. *(of food)* estado líquido; *(of the ground)* estado fangoso; *(carelessness)* descuido; *(dirtiness)* suciedad *f*; *(slovenliness)* desaliño, desgarbo; *(sentimental rubbish)* sensiblería.

slop·py (slŏp′ē) adj. **-pi·er, -pi·est** *(muddy)* fangoso *<s. ground* terreno fangoso>; *(wet)* mojado; *(watery)* aguado; FAM. *(messy)* desordenado *<a s. house* una casa desordenada>; *(careless)* descuidado, chapucero *<s. work* trabajo chapucero>; *(gushy)* sensiblero, sentimental.

slosh (slŏsh) **I.** tr. salpicar —intr. chapotear *<the water was sloshing around in the bottom of the boat* el agua chapoteaba en el fondo del barco> **II.** s. *(slush)* aguanieve *f*; *(mud)* lodo.

slot¹ (slŏt) **I.** s. *(groove)* ranura, muesca; *(place on a roster)* puesto en el escalafón; FAM. *(niche)* rincón *m* **II.** tr. **slot·ted, slot·ting** *(to make a slot)* hacer una ranura; FAM. *(to assign to a niche)* encajar.

slot² (slŏt) s. *(trail)* huella, rastro.

sloth (slôth, slōth) s. *(laziness)* pereza, indolencia; ZOOL. perezoso.

sloth·ful (slôth′fəl, slōth′-) adj. perezoso, indolente.

slot machine s. *(vending machine)* distribuidor automático; *(gambling machine)* máquina tragaperras.

slouch (slouch) **I.** intr. *(to walk)* andar con los hombros caídos; *(to sit)* repantigarse (en un asiento); *(to stand)* estar en postura desgarbada; *(to hang)* colgar fláccidamente ♦ **to s. around** gandulear, holgazanear —tr. *(to cause to droop)* bajar; *(to bend)* echar hacia adelante **II.** s. *(posture)* andar desgarbado; *(lazy person)* perezoso *<don't be a s.* no seas perezoso>; *(inept person)* inepto ♦ **to walk with a s.** andar con los hombros caídos.

slouch hat s. sombrero flexible.

slough¹ (slōō, slou) s. *(muddy place)* fangal *m*, cenagal *m*; *(state of despair)* estado de abatimiento, estado de desánimo; FIG. *(abyss)* abismo.

slough² (slŭf) **I.** s. ZOOL. camisa, piel *f*; MED. postilla, costra; *(covering)* capa **II.** intr. *(to come off)* caerse; *(to shed)* mudar de piel; MED. desprenderse (costra) —tr. deshacerse de, abandonar (hábito) ♦ **to s. off** deshacerse de • **to s. over** quitar importancia a.

Slo·vak (slō′väk′ -väk′) **I.** adj. eslovaco **II.** s. *(inhabitant, language)* eslovaco.

Slo·vak·i·a (slō-vä′kē-ə) s. Eslovaquia.

Slo·vak·i·an (slō-vä′kē-ən) adj. eslovaco.

slov·en (slŭv′ən) s. *(untidy person)* persona desaseada; *(idle person)* vago.

Slo·vene (slō′vēn′) **I.** adj. esloveno **II.** s. *(inhabitant, language)* esloveno.

slov·en·ly (slŭv′ən-lē) adj. *(untidy)* desaliñado, desaseado; *(idle)* vago; *(careless)* descuidado, dejado.

slow (slō) **I.** adj. **-er, -est** *(not fast)* lento *<a s. boat* un barco lento>; *(of a clock)* atrasado; *(tardy)* retrasado, atrasado; *(not precipitate)* lento *<s. to accept* lento en aceptar>; *(obtuse)* lento, torpe *<a s. student* un estudiante torpe>; FAM. *(boring)* aburrido *<a s. party* una fiesta aburrida>* ♦ **business is s.** hay poca actividad *o* poco negocio • **my watch is five minutes s.** mi reloj tiene cinco minutos de retraso • **s. fire** fuego lento • **to be s. to** tardar en **II.** adv. **-er, -est** lentamente, despacio **III.** tr. *(to make slow)* aminorar la velocidad de, reducir la marcha de; *(to retard)* retrasar, retardar —intr. ir más despacio, aminorar la velocidad ♦ **s. down!** ¡más despacio!

slow·down (slō′doun′) s. retraso.

slow·ly (slō′lē) adv. lentamente, despacio ♦ **s. but surely** despacio pero seguro.

slow motion s. CINEM., TELEV. cámara lenta.

slow·ness (slō′nĭs) s. *(sluggishness)* lentitud *f*; *(boredom)* aburrimiento, pesadez *f*; *(stupidity)* torpeza.

slow·poke (slō′pōk′) s. FAM. tortuga (persona).

slow·wit·ted (slō′wĭt′ĭd) adj. lento, torpe.

sludge (slŭj) s. *(mud)* cieno, fango; *(sewage)* fango de alcantarillado; *(sediment)* sedimento; *(ice)* capa de hielo flotante.

slue¹ (slōō) tr. **slued, slu·ing** *(to turn)* hacer girar; MARÍT. virar —intr. *(to turn)* girar; *(to twist)* torcer.

slue² (slōō) s. var. de **slew¹**.

slug¹ (slŭg) **I.** s. *(bullet)* posta; *(metal disk)* ficha; *(lump of metal)* trozo de metal; FAM. *(shot of liquor)* trago; IMPR. *(for spacing)* lingote *m*; *(line)* línea de linotipia; FÍS. unidad de masa *f* **II.** tr. **slugged, slug·ging** IMPR. añadir líneas a.

slug² (slŭg) s. ZOOL. babosa; FAM. *(sluggard)* holgazán *m*.

slug³ (slŭg) **I.** tr. **slugged, slug·ging** pegar un porrazo **II.** s. porrazo.

slug·fest (slŭg′fĕst′) s. JER. pelea ♦ **a verbal s.** una discusión acalorada.

slug·gard (slŭg′ərd) s. & adj. holgazán *m*.

---

ng inglés / ŏ la / ō bou / ô corre / oi oigo / ōō uno / ou auto / yōō ciudad / w hueco / y yo / z mismo

slug·ger (slŭg′ər) s. luchador *m*.
slug·gish (slŭg′ĭsh) adj. *(slow)* lento; *(inactive)* perezoso; COM., ECON. inactivo, flojo.
sluice (slōōs) I. s. *(channel)* canal *m*; *(gate)* compuerta, esclusa; *(body of water)* agua del canal; *(drainage channel)* canal de desagüe; *(mill)* saetín *m* II. tr. **sluiced, sluic·ing** *(to drench)* regar; *(to wash)* lavar; *(to send down)* transportar por un canal —intr. salir el agua.
sluice·way (slōōs′wā′) s. *(of reservoir)* aliviadero; *(channel)* canal *m*.
slum (slŭm) I. s. barrio bajo II. intr. **slummed, slum·ming** ♦ **to go slumming** visitar los barrios bajos.
slum·ber (slŭm′bər) I. intr. *(to sleep)* dormir; *(to be dormant)* dormitar, estar medio dormido —tr. pasar durmiendo II. s. *(sleep)* sueño; *(dormancy)* sopor *m* ♦ **s. party** reunión de niños amigos para pasar la noche durmiendo en la casa de uno de ellos.
slum·ber·er (slŭm′bər-ər) s. dormilón *m*.
slum·ber·ous (slŭm′bər-əs) *o* **slum·brous** (-brəs) adj. *(drowsy)* soñoliento; *(asleep)* dormido; *(quiet)* tranquilo; *(soporific)* adormecedor.
slum·lord (slŭm′lôrd′) s. FAM. dueño de viviendas pobres (esp. uno que permite su deterioración).
slump (slŭmp) I. intr. *(to fall suddenly)* desplomarse; *(to sink)* hundirse; *(to decline)* disminuir bruscamente; *(to slouch)* repantigarse II. s. *(decline)* disminución brusca; *(depression)* depresión *f*.
slung (slŭng) pret. y part. p. de **sling**.
slunk (slŭngk) pret. y part. p. de **slink**.
slur (slûr) I. tr. **slurred, slur·ring** *(to treat lightly)* hacer poco caso de; *(to pronounce indistinctly)* pronunciar mal; *(to disparage)* mancillar, manchar; *(to slander)* difamar, calumniar; MÚS. *(to glide over smoothly)* ligar; IMPR. macular II. s. *(affront)* afrenta; FIG. *(stain)* mancha; *(aspersion)* calumnia, difamación *f*; *(speech)* pronunciación incomprensible *f*; MÚS. ligado; IMPR. maculatura.
slurp (slûrp) tr. & intr. *(to eat)* comer haciendo ruido; *(to drink)* beber haciendo ruido.
slush (slŭsh) I. s. *(melted snow)* aguanieve *f*; *(mud)* fango, lodo; *(grease)* grasa; *(sentimental drivel)* sensiblería, sentimentalismo exagerado II. tr. *(to daub)* engrasar *(maquinaria)*; *(to wash)* lavar con agua *(piso)*; *(to splash)* enlodar, enfangar; CONSTR. rellenar con mortero —intr. *(to walk)* andar chapoteando; *(to make a splashing sound)* chapotear ♦ **to s. through** vadear.
slush fund s. *(fund)* fondos apartados para usos placenteros (y en entidades políticas, deshonestos); MARÍT. dinero obtenido de la venta de desechos.
slush·y (slŭsh′ē) adj. **-i·er, -i·est** *(muddy)* lodoso, fangoso; *(sentimental)* sensiblero, sentimentaloide; *(said of snow)* medio derretida.
slut (slŭt) s. DESPEC. *(slattern)* puerca; *(loose woman)* mujerzuela; *(prostitute)* prostituta, suripanta; *(dog)* perra.
sly (slī) adj. **sli·er, sli·est** *o* **sly·er, sly·est** *(cunning)* astuto; *(deceitful)* furtivo; *(roguish)* travieso.
sly·ly (slī′lē) adv. *(cunningly)* astutamente; *(deceitfully)* furtivamente.
sly·ness (slī′nĭs) s. *(cunning)* astucia; *(deceit)* disimulo.
smack¹ (smăk) I. tr. *(to make a sound with the lips)* hacer un chasquido con los labios; *(to kiss)* besar sonoramente; *(to strike)* dar un palmada —intr. *(to make a sound)* chasquear; *(to give a kiss)* dar un beso sonoro II. s. *(sound)* chasquido; *(kiss)* beso sonoro; *(blow)* golpe *m* III. adv. *(with a blow)* de golpe; *(directly)* de lleno <he ran *s. into a pole* dio de lleno contra un palo>.
smack² (smăk) I. s. *(flavor)* gusto, sabor *m*; *(trace)* indicio; *(small amount)* pizca II. intr. *(to have a distinctive flavor)* saber; FIG. *(to suggest)* oler a <this smacks of corruption esto huele a corrupción>.
smack³ (smăk) s. MARÍT. pequeño barco velero de pesca.
smack⁴ (smăk) s. JER. heroína.
smack-dab (smăk′dăb′) adv. JER. justo en medio.
smack·er (smăk′ər) s. *(kiss)* beso sonoro; *(blow)* bofetón *m*; JER. *(dollar)* dólar *m*.
smack·ing (smăk′ĭng) adj. fresco *(brisa, aire)*.
small (smôl) I. adj. **-er, -est** *(little)* pequeño <a *s. country*

un país pequeño>; *(minor)* sin importancia, insignificante <a *s. matter* un asunto sin importancia>; *(modest)* modesto, humilde <s. *people* gente humilde>; *(very young)* pequeño <s. *children* niños pequeños>; *(petty)* mezquino; *(humiliated)* humillado; *(weak)* flojo (licor, bebida); *(lacking strength)* débil <a *s. voice* una voz débil> ♦ **in a s. way** en pequeña escala • **in s. numbers** poco numerosos, pocos • **s. holding** pequeña propiedad • **s. letters** minúsculas • **s. print** letra pequeña • **to feel s.** sentir vergüenza • **to make oneself s.** achicarse • **to make someone look** *o* **feel s.** achicar a alguien • **when he was s.** cuando era pequeño II. adv. **-er, -est** *(in small pieces)* en trozos pequeños <cut it up *s.* córtalo en trozos pequeños>; *(softly)* débilmente III. s. *parte pequeña* ♦ **smalls** *(small things)* cosas pequeñas, artículos menudos; G.B. *(smallclothes)* ropa interior, paños menores • **the s. of the back** la región lumbar.
small arm s. arma portátil.
small change s. *(money)* cambio, dinero suelto; FIG. *(something insignificant)* cosa de poco valor.
small-claims court (smôl′klāmz′) s. juzgado de demandas menores.
small fry s. FAM. *(children)* gente menuda; *(persons)* gente sin importancia *f*; *(things)* cosas sin importancia.
small game s. caza menor.
small intestine s. ANAT. intestino delgado.
small-mind·ed (smôl′mīn′dĭd) adj. *(selfish)* mezquino; *(narrow-minded)* de miras estrechas.
small·ness (smôl′nĭs) s. *(in size)* pequeñez *f*; *(meannness)* mezquindad *f*; *(insignificance)* insignificancia.
small potatoes s.pl. FAM. *(person)* don nadie *m*; *(thing)* cosa de poca monta.
small·pox (smôl′pŏks′) s. MED. viruela.
small-scale (smôl′skāl′) adj. en pequeña escala.
small talk s. conversación ociosa, charloteo.
small-time (smôl′tīm′) adj. FAM. de poca monta.
smart (smärt) I. adj. **-er, -est** *(intelligent)* listo, inteligente; *(witty)* ingenioso <a *s. remark* un comentario ingenioso>; *(impertinent)* impertinente; *(quick)* rápido <a *s. pace* un paso rápido>; *(shrewd)* astuto; *(elegant)* elegante; *(fashionable)* de moda II. intr. *(to sting)* escocer, picar; *(to hurt)* dar punzadas; *(to suffer)* sufrir III. s. *(sharp pain)* punzada; *(sting)* escozor *m*; *(mental anguish)* resquemor *m* ♦ **smarts** FAM. inteligencia.
smart al·eck (ăl′ĭk′) s. FAM. sabihondo, sabelotodo.
smart bomb s. ARM., MIL. bomba teledirigida.
smart·en (smär′tn) tr. *(to spruce up)* arreglar; *(to make quicker)* aumentar la velocidad —intr. espabilarse.
smart·ly (smärt′lē) adv. *(intelligently)* inteligentemente; *(quickly)* rápidamente; *(shrewdly)* astutamente; *(wittily)* ingeniosamente; *(elegantly)* elegantemente; *(fashionably)* a la moda.
smart·ness (smärt′nĭs) s. *(intelligence)* inteligencia; *(elegance)* elegancia; *(shrewdness)* astucia; *(impertinence)* impertinencia, *(wit)* ingenio.
smash (smăsh) I. tr. *(to break)* romper; *(to shatter)* destrozar; *(to throw)* estrellar <he smashed the glass against the wall estrelló el vaso contra la pared>; *(to batter)* golpear violentamente; *(to crush)* aplastar (resistencia); *(in tennis)* dar un mate —intr. *(to break)* romperse; *(to crash)* estrellarse; *(to be crushed)* hacerse pedazos; *(to go bankrupt)* quebrar, arruinarse; *(in tennis)* dar un mate II. s. *(breakage)* rotura; *(sound)* estrépito; *(defeat)* ruina; *(bankruptcy)* quiebra; *(collision)* choque *m*; *(tennis stroke)* golpe violento; FAM. *(hit)* éxito <the film was a *s.* la película fue un éxito> III. adj. ♦ **s. hit** un gran éxito IV. *(violently)* violentamente; *(noisily)* estrepitosamente.
smash·er (smăsh′ər) s. *(blow)* golpe demoledor *m*; *(wonder)* maravilla.
smash·ing (smăsh′ĭng) adj. FAM. magnífico, extraordinario.
smash-up (smăsh′ŭp′) s. *(ruin)* ruina; *(crash)* choque *m*.
smat·ter (smăt′ər) I. tr. *(a language)* chapurrear (un idioma); *(to dabble in)* conocer superficialmente II. s. ligero conocimiento, noción superficial *f*.
smat·ter·ing (smăt′ər-ĭng) s. ligero conocimiento, noción superficial *f*.

smear (smîr) I. tr. *(to spread)* untar; *(to dirty)* embadurnar; *(to stain)* manchar; FIG. *(to vilify)* calumniar, difamar; JER. *(to smash)* aplastar —intr. *(to become dirtied)* embadurnarse; *(to become stained)* mancharse II. s. *(blot)* mancha; *(substance to be spread)* ungüento; *(vilification)* calumnia, difamación *f*; BACT., BIOQUÍM. frotis *m*.

smear·y (smîr′ē) adj. **-i·er, -i·est** grasiento.

smell (smĕl) I. tr. **smelled** *o* **smelt** (smĕlt), **smell·ing** *(to sniff)* oler; *(to detect)* olfatear ♦ **I s. a rat** hay gato encerrado • **to s. out** olfatear —intr. *(to sniff)* oler; *(to have an odor)* oler <*the flower smells good* la flor huele bien>; *(to stink)* apestar; FIG. *(to be suggestive)* oler <*it smells fishy* huele a chamusquina> II. s. *(act)* olfateo; *(sense)* olfato; *(odor)* olor *m*.

smelling salts s.pl. [ú. con v. sing. o pl.] sales aromáticas.

smell·y (smĕl′ē) adj. **-i·er, -i·est** FAM. maloliente.

smelt¹ (smĕlt) tr. & intr. fundir (metales).

smelt² (smĕlt) s. [pl. **smelts** *o* **smelt**] ICT. eperlano.

smelt³ (smĕlt) un pret. y part. p. de **smell**.

smelt·er (smĕl′tər) s. *(apparatus)* horno de fusión; *(plant)* fundición *f*; *(person)* fundidor *m*.

smid·gen *o* **smid·geon** *o* **smid·gin** (smĭj′ən) s. FAM. pizca.

smile (smīl) I. s. sonrisa II. intr. **smiled, smil·ing** sonreír, sonreírse —tr. *(to direct a smile of)* dirigir una sonrisa de; *(to express)* expresar con una sonrisa ♦ **to s. on** favorecer.

smil·ing (smī′lĭng) adj. risueño, sonriente.

smirch (smûrch) tr. *(to dirty)* ensuciar, manchar; *(to defame)* manchar, mancillar.

smirk (smûrk) I. intr. sonreír con afectación II. s. sonrisa afectada.

smite (smīt) tr. **smote** (smōt), **smit·ten** (smĭt′n) *o* **smote, smit·ing** *(to hit)* golpear, pegar; *(to punish)* castigar; *(to defeat)* aplastar; *(to destroy)* destruir ♦ **to be smitten with** *(fear)* estar lleno de; *(an illness)* estar aquejado de; *(a girl)* estar encaprichado por —intr. golpear con fuerza.

smith (smĭth) s. herrero.

smith·er·eens (smĭth′ə-rēnz′) s.pl. FAM. añicos.

smith·y (smĭth′ē, smĭth′ē) s. [pl. **-ies**] herrería.

smit·ten (smĭt′n) un part. p. de **smite**.

smock (smŏk) I. s. guardapolvo II. tr. *(to clothe)* llevar guardapolvo; COST. fruncir.

smock·ing (smŏk′ĭng) s. COST. fruncido.

smog (smŏg) s. smog *m*, niebla contaminada con humo.

smog·gy (smŏg′ē) adj. **-gi·er, -gi·est** lleno de humo y niebla.

smoke (smōk) I. s. *(vapor)* humo; *(cigarette smoking)* fumada; FAM. *(cigarette)* pitillo, cigarrillo ♦ **s. bomb** bomba de humo • **to go up in s.** quedar en nada, irse en humo • **where there's s. there's fire** cuando el río suena, agua lleva II. intr. **smoked, smok·ing** *(to emit)* humear; *(of tobacco)* fumar —tr. *(of tobacco)* fumar; *(to preserve)* ahumar; *(to fumigate)* fumigar ♦ **to s. out** *(to cause to move)* ahuyentar *o* desalojar con humo; *(to reveal)* descubrir.

smoked (smōkt) adj. ahumado <*s. glass* cristal ahumado>.

smoke detector s. ahumadero.

smoke·less (smōk′lĭs) adj. sin humo.

smok·er (smō′kər) s. *(person)* fumador *m*; *(social gathering)* tertulia de hombres (en la que se fuma), F.C. coche de fumadores *m*.

smoke screen s. MIL. cortina de humo; FIG. cortina *o* pantalla de humo.

smoke·stack (smōk′stăk′) s. *(chimney)* chimenea; *(pipe)* conducto de humos.

smok·ing (smō′kĭng) s. el fumar ♦ **cigarette s.** fumar cigarrillos • **to give up s.** dejar de fumar.

smoking jacket s. batín *m*.

smok·y (smō′kē) adj. **-i·er, -i·est** *(emitting smoke)* humeante; *(filled with smoke)* lleno de humo; *(discolored with smoke)* ahumado; *(tasting of smoke)* ahumado.

smol·der (smōl′dər) I. intr. *(to burn)* arder (sin llama); FIG. *(to exist in a suppressed state)* estar latente; *(to keep under control)* arder <*his eyes smoldered with rage* ardía la furia en sus ojos> II. s. humo espeso.

smooch (smōoch) JER. I. s. beso II. intr. besarse, besuquearse.

smooth (smōoth) I. adj. **-er, -est** *(even)* liso; *(fine-textured)* liso, suave; *(gentle)* suave (movimiento); *(calm)* tranquilo, sereno; *(fluid)* fluido <*a s. style* un estilo fluido>; *(uneventful)* sin novedad; *(ingratiating)* meloso; *(refined)* refinado; *(unwrinkled)* sin arrugas; *(beardless)* imberbe, barbilampiño; *(bland)* suave <*a s. wine* un vino suave>; GRAM. suave ♦ **s. talk** zalamerías II. tr. *(to level)* alisar; *(to polish)* pulir, esmerilar; *(to soothe)* aliviar ♦ **to s. the way for** preparar el terreno para • **to s. things over** limar asperezas —intr. alisarse III. s. *(evenness)* parte lisa; *(smoothing act)* alisado.

smooth·en (smōo′thən) tr. & intr. *(to polish)* pulir(se); *(to soften)* suavizar(se); *(to even)* emparejar(se).

smooth·ly (smōoth′lē) adv. *(gently)* suavemente; *(well)* bien <*everything went s.* todo salió bien>; *(quietly)* tranquilamente.

smooth·ness (smōoth′nĭs) s. *(softness)* suavidad *f*; *(quietness)* tranquilidad *f*; *(fluidity)* fluidez *f*; *(evenness)* uniformidad *f*.

smooth-spo·ken (smōoth′spō′kən) adj. bien hablado.

smooth-tongued (smōoth′tŭngd′) adj. zalamero.

smote (smōt) pret. y un part. p. de **smite**.

smoth·er (smŭth′ər) I. tr. *(to suffocate)* sofocar; *(to asphyxiate)* asfixiar; *(to put out)* sofocar, apagar (fuego, incendio); *(to conceal)* enterrar, echar tierra a (asunto); *(to contain)* contener (bostezo, ira); *(to cover)* cubrir <*he smothered her with kisses* la cubrió de besos>; *(to overwhelm)* abrumar, colmar (de atención, amor) —intr. *(to suffocate)* asfixiarse; *(to go out)* apagarse (fuego, pasión); *(to be concealed)* taparse, esconderse; *(to be surfeited)* colmarse II. s. *(asphyxia)* asfixia; *(smoke)* humareda; *(dust)* polvareda.

smoul·der (smōl′dər) v. & s. var. de **smolder**.

smudge (smŭj) I. tr. **smudged, smudg·ing** *(to dirty)* manchar; *(to blur)* emborronar; *(to fumigate)* fumigar —intr. manchar(se) II. s. *(stains)* mancha; *(used against insects)* humo para fumigar.

smudge pot s. recipiente para ahumar *m*.

smudg·y (smŭj′ē) adj. **-i·er, -i·est** *(dirty)* manchado; *(blurred)* emborronado.

smug (smŭg) adj. **smug·ger, smug·gest** presumido, pagado de sí mismo.

smug·gle (smŭg′əl) tr. **-gled, -gling** pasar de contrabando —intr. contrabandear.

smug·gler (smŭg′lər) s. contrabandista *mf*.

smug·gling (smŭg′lĭng) s. contrabando.

smug·ness (smŭg′nĭs) s. presunción *f*.

smut (smŭt) I. s. *(particle)* hollín *m*, carbonilla; *(smudge)* mancha de tizne; FIG. *(obscenity)* obscenidad *f*; BOT., AGR. tizón *m*, añublo II. tr. **smut·ted, smut·ting** *(to smudge)* manchar, tiznar; FIG. *(to make obscene)* mancillar; BOT., AGR. *(affect with the disease)* atizonar, añublar; *(to rid of the disease)* destizonar —intr. *(to emit dirt)* emitir hollín *o* carbonilla; *(to become smudged)* mancharse, tiznarse; BOT., AGR. atizonarse, añublarse.

smutch (smŭch) I. tr. manchar II. s. mancha.

smut·ti·ness (smŭt′ē-nĭs) s. *(dirt)* suciedad *f*; *(obscenity)* obscenidad *f*.

smut·ty (smŭt′ē) adj. **-ti·er, -ti·est** *(dirty)* manchado, tiznado; *(obscene)* obsceno; AGR., BOT. atizonado.

snack (snăk) I. s. bocado, tentempié *m* II. intr. tomar(se) un bocado.

snack bar s. cafetería, bar *m*.

sna·fu (snă-fōo′) JER. I. adj. embrollado II. tr. **-fued, -fu·ing** embrollar III. s. embrollo.

snag (snăg) I. s. *(protuberance)* protuberancia; *(of a branch)* gancho; *(of a tree)* tocón *m*; *(submerged tree)* tronco sumergido; *(snaggletooth)* raigón *m*; FIG. *(obstacle)* obstáculo, tropiezo; TEJ. *(tear)* rotura, rasgadura II. tr. **snagged, snag·ging** *(to tear)* rasgar; *(to free of obstacles)* librar de obstáculos; FAM. *(to catch unexpectedly)* agarrar (de repente) —intr. rasgarse.

snail (snāl) s. ZOOL. *(shell)* caracol *m*; *(slug)* babosa; FIG. *(person)* tortuga.

snake (snāk) I. s. ZOOL. serpiente *f*; FIG. *(person)* traidor *m*; *(wire)* alambre flexible *m* II. tr. & intr. **snaked, snak·ing** serpentear.

snake·bite (snāk′bīt′) s. mordedura de serpiente.
snake charmer s. encantador de serpientes *m.*
snake in the grass s. FIG., FAM. traidor *m.*
snake oil s. potingue *m.*
snake·skin (snāk′skĭn′) s. piel de serpiente *f.*
snak·y (snā′kē) adj. **-i·er, -i·est** *(winding)* serpentino; *(full of snakes)* lleno de serpientes; *(treacherous)* traidor.
snap (snăp) I. intr. **snapped, snap·ping** *(to click)* crujir, chasquear; *(to break)* romperse, quebrarse; *(to bite)* morder; *(to move)* ponerse <*to s. to attention* ponerse firme> ♦ **s. out of it!** ¡anímate! • **to s. at** *(to take)* agarrarse a; *(a dog)* intentar morder; *(to speak harshly to)* hablar con brusquedad a • **to s. off** desprenderse • **to s. open (shut)** abrirse (cerrarse) de golpe —tr. *(to bite)* morder, mordisquear; *(to break)* romper, quebrar <*he snapped the branch* rompió la rama>; *(to utter)* decir bruscamente; *(to crack)* chasquear <*to s. the whip* chasquear el látigo>; FOTOG. tomar una instantánea de ♦ **to s. one's fingers at** burlarse de • **to s. someone's head off** FIG. responderle a alguien tosca y bruscamente • **to s. up** llevarse II. s. *(sound)* chasquido, crujido; *(breaking)* rotura, quieba; *(of the fingers)* castañeteo; *(clasp)* broche de presión *m; (cookie)* galleta; *(brief spell)* ola (de frío o mal tiempo); FAM. *(energy)* energía <*he has a lot of s.* tiene mucha energía>; *(effortless task)* cosa fácil; DEP. *(pass)* pase inicial de la pelota *m;* FOTOG. foto instantánea ♦ **put some s. into it!** ¡venga! III. adj. *(quick)* instantáneo, rápido <*a s. decision* una decisión rápida>; FAM. *(simple)* fácil, tirado IV. adv. con un chasquido.
snap·drag·on (snăp′drăg′ən) s. BOT. dragón *m.*
snap·per (snăp′ər) s. [pl. **snapper** o **snappers**] *(fish)* cubera; *(turtle)* tortuga mordedora.
snapping turtle s. ZOOL. tortuga mordedora.
snap·pish (snăp′ĭsh) adj. *(liable to bite)* mordedor; *(irritable)* irritable.
snap·py (snăp′ē) adj. **-pi·er, -pi·est** FAM. *(brisk)* vivo, animado; *(smart)* elegante; *(liable to bite)* mordedor; *(irritable)* irritable.
snap·shot (snăp′shŏt′) s. FOTOG. instantánea.
snare¹ (snâr) I. s. trampa, lazo II. tr. **snared, snar·ing** *(to entrap)* tener trampas; *(to trap)* cazar con trampa.
snare² (snâr) s. MÚS. cuerda (de tambor).
snare drum s. tambor *m.*
snarl¹ (snärl) I. intr. *(to growl)* gruñir; *(to speak angrily)* refunfuñar —tr. decir gruñendo II. s. *(growl)* gruñido; *(hostile utterance)* refunfuño.
snarl² (snärl) I. s. *(tangled mass)* maraña, enredo; *(predicament)* enredo, lío II. tr. & intr. enmarañar(se), enredar(se).
snatch (snăch) I. tr. *(to grasp suddenly)* arrebatar, agarrar; *(to seize illicitly)* secuestrar —intr. tratar de arrebatar II. s. *(action)* arrebatamiento; *(moment)* momento, ratito; *(fragment)* pedacito, fragmento; JER. *(kidnaping)* secuestro; DEP. *(in weightlifting)* arrancada.
snatch·er (snăch′ər) s. arrebatador *m.*
snaz·zy (snăz′ē) adj. **-zi·er, -zi·est** JER. llamativo.
sneak (snēk) I. intr. *(to move in a stealthy way)* andar a hurtadillas; *(to betray)* traicionar —tr. hacer furtivamente II. s. *(cowardly person)* persona cobarde; *(exit)* salida disimulada.
sneak·er (snē′kər) s. *(person)* persona cobarde; *(shoe)* zapato de lona.
sneak·ing (snē′kĭng) adj. *(cowardly)* cobarde; *(furtive)* furtivo; *(secret)* secreto; *(persistent)* continuo; *(slight)* ligero.
sneak thief s. ratero.
sneak·y (snē′kē) adj. **-i·er, -i·est** *(furtive)* furtivo; *(surreptitious)* solapado.
sneer (snîr) I. s. *(facial expression)* gesto de desprecio; *(mockery)* mofa, escarnio II. tr. decir con desprecio —intr. *(to assume a scornful expression)* hacer un gesto de desprecio; *(to mock)* mofarse (de).
sneeze (snēz) I. intr. **sneezed, sneez·ing** estornudar II. s. estornudo.
sneez·ing (snē′zĭng) I. s. estornudo II. adj. estornutatorio.
snick·er (snĭk′ər) I. intr. reírse disimuladamente II. s. risita.

snide (snīd) adj. **snid·er, snid·est** *(derogatory)* deshonroso; *(sarcastic)* sarcástico.
sniff (snĭf) I. intr. *(to inhale)* aspirar por la nariz; *(to indicate contempt)* despreciar; *(to savor an odor)* oliscar —tr. olfatear, oler II. s. *(inhalation)* aspiración *f; (smelling)* olfateo.
snif·fle (snĭf′əl) I. intr. **-fled, -fling** *(to breathe audibly)* resollar; *(to whimper)* lloriquear II. s. *(breathing)* resuello; *(whimper)* lloriqueo ♦ **sniffles** FAM. resfriado.
sniff·y (snĭf′ē) adj. **-i·er, -i·est** FAM. desdeñoso.
snif·ter (snĭf′tər) s. *(goblet)* copa de licor; JER. *(portion of liquor)* trago.
snig·ger (snĭg′ər) I. s. risa disimulada II. intr. reir disimuladamente.
snip (snĭp) I. tr. & intr. **snipped, snip·ping** tijeretear II. s. *(action)* tijeretada, tijeretazo; *(piece)* recorte *m;* FAM. *(young person)* joven impertinente *mf;* JER. *(something easy)* ganga, cosa fácil ♦ **snips** tijeras de hojalatero.
snipe (snĭp) I. s. [pl. **snipe** o **snipes**] ORNIT. agachadiza; *(shot)* tiro de emboscada II. intr. **sniped, snip·ing** *(to shoot birds)* cazar agachadizas; *(to shoot)* tirar desde una posición emboscada; *(to make malicious remarks)* atacar solapadamente.
snip·er (snī′pər) s. francotirador *m.*
snip·pet (snĭp′ĭt) s. *(morsel)* recorte *m,* retazo; FAM. *(person)* persona insignificante.
snip·py (snĭp′ē) adj. **-pi·er, -pi·est** FAM. *(impertinent)* impertinente; *(fragmentary)* fragmentario.
snit (snĭt) JER. s. arranque de cólera *m* ♦ **to be in a s.** estar enfadado.
snitch (snĭch) JER. I. tr. birlar, robar —intr. soplar, chivarse II. s. *(thief)* ratero, ladrón; *(informer)* chivato, soplón *m.*
sniv·el (snĭv′əl) I. intr. *(to whine)* lloriquear, gimotear; *(to run at the nose)* moquear II. s. *(whining)* lloriqueo, gimoteo; *(mucus)* moco.
snob (snŏb) s. esnob *m.*
snob·ber·y (snŏb′ə-rē) s. [pl. **-ies**] esnobismo.
snob·bish (snŏb′ĭsh) adj. como un esnob.
snob·bism (snŏb′ĭz′əm) s. esnobismo.
snood (snōōd) s. redecilla.
snook·er (snōōk′ər) s. billar ruso.
snoop (snōōp) FAM. I. intr. entrometerse ♦ **to s. around** husmear II. s. curioso, entrometido.
snoop·er (snōō′pər) s. curioso.
snoop·y (snōō′pē) adj. **-i·er, -i·est** FAM. curioso, entrometido.
snoot (snōōt) s. JER. *(snout)* hocico, trompa; *(nose)* nariz *f; (snob)* esnob *m.*
snoot·y (snōō′tē) adj. **-i·er, -i·est** JER. altanero.
snooze (snōōz) FAM. I. intr. **snoozed, snooz·ing** dormitar II. s. cabezada, sueño ligero.
snore (snôr) I. intr. **snored, snor·ing** roncar II. s. ronquido.
snor·kel (snôr′kəl) I. s. *(of a submarine)* esnórquel *m; (of skin divers)* tubo de respiración II. intr. bucear con tubo de respiración.
snort (snôrt) I. s. *(sound)* bufido, resoplido; JER. *(a drink)* trago; *(of a drug)* inhalación *f* II. intr. *(to breath forcefully)* bufar, resoplar; JER. *(to inhale a drug)* inhalar una droga —tr. *(to utter)* decir con un bufido; JER. *(to inhale)* inhalar (una droga).
snot (snŏt) s. JER. *(mucus)* moco; *(person)* mocoso.
snot·ty (snŏt′ē) adj. **-ti·er, -ti·est** FAM. mocoso; JER. *(mean)* despreciable; *(angry)* irritable, de mal humor.
snout (snout) s. *(nose)* hocico; JER. *(human nose)* nariz *f.*
snow (snō) I. s. *(precipitation)* nieve *f; (snowstorm)* nevada; TELEV. nieve; JER. *(cocaine)* cocaína; *(heroin)* heroína II. intr. nevar —tr. *(to cover)* cubrir con nieve; *(to flatter)* adular; *(to deceive)* embaucar ♦ **to s. under** *(to overwhelm)* abrumar; *(to defeat)* derrotar abrumadoramente.
snow·ball (snō′bôl′) I. s. *(mass of snow)* bola de nieve; BOT. mundillo, bola de nieve II. intr. & tr. *(to throw)* tirar bolas de nieve; *(to grow)* aumentar rápidamente.

ā rey / ä año / b boca / ch chico / d dar / ĕ el / ē mil / g gato / h joya / hw juez / ī aire / k casa / kw cuan /

snow·bank (snō'băngk') s. montón de nieve *m*, banco de nieve.

snow blindness s. deslumbramiento causado por el reflejo de la nieve.

snow·bound (snō'bound') adj. bloqueado por la nieve.

snow·cap (snō'kăp') s. capa de nieve.

snow·drift (snō'drĭft') s. ventisquero.

snow·drop (snō'drŏp') s. BOT. campanilla de invierno.

snow·fall (snō'fôl') s. nevada.

snow·flake (snō'flāk') s. *(crystal of snow)* copo de nieve; BOT. campanilla.

snow job s. JER. embaucamiento.

snow line s. límite de las nieves perpetuas *m*.

snow·man (snō'măn') s. [pl. -men (-měn')] muñeco de nieve.

snow·mo·bile (snō'mō-bēl') s. vehículo automotor para ir por la nieve.

snow·plow (snō'plou') s. *(plow)* quitanieves *m*; *(ski)* cuña.

snow·shoe (snō'shōō') I. s. raqueta II. intr. -shoed, -shoe·ing caminar sobre la nieve con raquetas.

snow·slide (snō'slīd') s. alud de nieve *m*.

snow·storm (snō'stôrm') s. tormenta de nieve.

snow·suit (snō'sōōt') s. traje que usan los niños en la nieve *m*.

snow tire s. neumático para nieve.

snow-white (snō'hwīt') adj. blanco como la nieve.

snow·y (snō'ē) adj. -i·er, -i·est *(covered with snow)* nevado; *(subject to snow)* nevoso; FIG. *(white)* blanco como la nieve.

snub (snŭb) I. tr. **snubbed, snub·bing** *(to slight)* desairar; *(to scorn)* reprender; *(to turn down)* rechazar; *(to stop abruptly)* parar bruscamente II. s. *(slight)* desaire *m*; *(rejection)* rechazo; *(abrupt stop)* parada brusca.

snub-nosed (snŭb'nōzd') adj. de nariz chata.

snuff¹ (snŭf) I. tr. *(to inhale)* aspirar; *(to sniff)* olfatear, oler —intr. *(to inhale)* aspirar; *(to sniff)* oler II. s. *(inhalation)* inhalación *f*; *(sniff)* olfateo.

snuff² (snŭf) I. s. pabilo *(of a candle)* II. tr. *(to cut off the wick)* despabilar; *(to extinguish)* apagar ♦ **to s. out** destruir.

snuff³ (snŭf) I. s. *(tabacco)* rapé *m* ♦ **to be up to s.** FAM. *(in normal health)* tener buena salud; *(up to standard)* ser satisfactorio ♦ **to dip s.** tomar rapé II. intr. tomar rapé.

snuff·box (snŭf'bŏks') s. caja de rapé.

snuff·er¹ (snŭf'ər) s. adicto al rapé.

snuff·er² (snŭf'ər) apagavelas *m* ♦ **snuffers** despabiladeras.

snuf·fle (snŭf'əl) I. intr. -fled, -fling *(to breathe noisily)* resollar; *(to sniff)* husmear; *(to whine)* ganguear —tr. decir gangueando II. s. *(noise)* resuello; *(action)* ganguео ♦ **snuffles** FAM. resfrío, romadizo.

snug (snŭg) I. adj. **snug·ger, snug·gest** *(cozy)* cómodo, confortable; *(warm)* calentito; *(tight)* ajustado, ceñido; MARÍT. bien aparejado ♦ **to be as s. as a bug in a rug** estar muy cómodo II. tr. **snugged, snug·ging** ajustar *(vestido, prenda)* —intr. acurrucarse ♦ **to s. down** aparejar, preparar *(para mal tiempo, tormenta)*.

snug·gle (snŭg'əl) intr. -gled, -gling acurrucarse, arrimarse —tr. apretar, acurrucar.

snug·ly (snŭg'lē) adv. *(comfortably)* cómodamente; *(neatly)* ordenadamente; *(under shelter)* al abrigo ♦ **to fit s.** ajustarse *o* caber perfectamente.

so¹ (sō) I. adv. *(thus)* así, de esta manera <*why does he think so?* ¿por qué piensa él de esa manera?>; *(to such an extent)* de tal manera, tan <*he was so weary that he fell* estaba tan fatigado que se cayó>; *(consequently)* por eso, por consiguiente <*he was weary and so he fell* estaba fatigado y por eso se cayó>; *(approximately)* de este, así de <*the wound was so wide* la herida era así de ancha>; *(likewise)* igualmente, también <*you were on time and so was I* tú llegaste a tiempo y yo también>; *(so much)* así, tanto <*why do you cry so?* ¿por qué lloras tanto?>; *(then)* así que <*so you think you've got troubles?* ¿así que tú crees que tienes problemas?> ♦ **and so on and so forth** y así sucesivamente, etcétera ♦ **and so it was that** y así fue que ♦ **how so?** ¿cómo es eso? ♦ **if so** en ese caso, si es así ♦ **I hope so** eso espero, espero que sí ♦ **is that so?** ¿es verdad?, ¿ah, sí?

♦ **I think so** creo que sí ♦ **I told you so!** ¡ya te lo dije!, ¡ya te lo advertí! ♦ **it just so happens that** pues resulta que ♦ **just so** *o* **quite so** ni más ni menos, así es ♦ **not so** no es así, eso no es verdad ♦ **not so much as** ni siquiera ♦ **or so** más o menos <*the ticket costs ten dollars or so* la entrada cuesta diez dólares más o menos> ♦ **so as to** a fin de, para ♦ **so be it** así sea ♦ **so far** *(distance)* hasta aquí, hasta allí; *(time)* hasta ahora; *(point)* hasta cierto punto <*we can only push him so far* solamente podemos obligarle hasta cierto punto> ♦ **so far as** hasta donde ♦ **so far as I'm concerned** por lo que a mí respecta ♦ **so far as I know** que yo sepa ♦ **so far so good** por ahora, bien ♦ **so it is!** ¡es verdad!, ¡así es! ♦ **so it seems** así parece ♦ **so long** *(duration)* tanto *(tiempo)*; *(good-bye)* hasta luego, hasta pronto ♦ **so long as** mientras que, hasta que ♦ **so many** tantos ♦ **so much for** vaya <*so much for his generosity* ¡vaya generosidad!> ♦ **so much for that** ¿qué le vamos a hacer? ♦ **so so** más o menos, así, así ♦ **so that** de manera que ♦ **so that's that** así están las cosas ♦ **so then** así pues ♦ **so to speak** por decirlo así ♦ **so what?** ¿y qué? ♦ **to be so kind as to** tener la bondad de ♦ **very much so** mucho ♦ **you don't say so!** ¡no me diga! II. adj. así <*I wouldn't have told you this if it weren't so* yo no te hubiera dicho esto si no fuera así> III. conj. así que, por lo tanto <*he failed to appear, so we went on without him* no vino, así que decidimos continuar sin él> ♦ **so that** para que, a fin de que <*I have two jobs so that you can go to school* tengo dos empleos para que tú puedas ir a la universidad> IV. pron. lo mismo, igual <*he became my loyal friend and remained so* se hizo mi fiel amigo y quedó lo mismo>.

so² (sō) s. var. de **sol¹**.

soak (sōk) I. tr. *(to wet)* mojar, empapar; *(to immerse)* remojar; *(to absorb)* absorber *(líquido)*; FAM. *(to drink)* beber con exceso; *(to make drunk)* emborrachar; JER. *(to overcharge)* cobrar demasiado ♦ **to s. to the skin** calar hasta los huesos —intr. *(to be immersed)* remojarse; *(to penetrate)* infiltrarse; JER. *(to drink)* beber *(demasiado)* ♦ **to s. through** *(to penetrate)* penetrar; *(to drench)* calar <*the rain soaked through the raincoat* la lluvia le caló el impermeable> II. s. *(immersion)* remojo; *(of a person)* empapamiento, remojón *m*; *(liquid)* líquido *(para remojar)*; JER. *(drunkard)* borracho.

soak·ing (sō'kĭng) I. s. remojón *m* II. adj. empapado, calado ♦ **s. wet** calado hasta los huesos.

so-and-so (sō'ən-sō') s. Fulano de Tal.

soap (sōp) I. s. *(cleansing agent)* jabón *m*; JER. *(money)* dinero (esp. para sobornar); *(soap opera)* serial *m* II. tr. *(to wash)* enjabonar, jabonar; JER. *(to bribe)* untar, sobornar.

soap·box *o* **soap box** (sōp'bŏks') s. *(carton)* caja de jabón; FIG. *(speaking platform)* tribuna improvisada.

soap bubble s. pompa *o* burbuja de jabón.

soap flakes s.pl. jabón en escamas *pl*.

soap opera s. RAD., TELEV. serial *m*.

soap·stone (sōp'stōn') s. esteatita, jaboncillo de sastre.

soap·suds (sōp'sŭdz') s.pl. espuma (de jabón).

soap·y (sō'pē) adj. -i·er, -i·est *(sudsy)* jabonoso; JER. *(unctuous)* meloso, pegajoso.

soar (sôr) I. intr. *(to rise)* remontarse, elevarse; *(to skyrocket)* subir desmesuradamente; FIG. *(to ascend suddenly)* elevarse súbitamente; AER. planear II. s. *(flight)* vuelo; FIG. *(scope attained)* alcance *m*.

soar·ing (sôr'ĭng) s. vuelo.

sob (sŏb) I. intr. **sobbed, sob·bing** sollozar —tr. decir sollozando II. s. sollozo.

sob·bing (sŏb'ĭng) s. sollozos.

so·ber (sō'bər) I. adj. -er, -est *(temperate)* sobrio, moderado; *(not intoxicated)* sobrio; *(serious)* serio, grave; *(plain)* sobrio, discreto; *(devoid of exaggeration)* sereno, tranquilo; *(reasonable)* cuerdo, sensato II. tr. *(to calm)* calmar; *(a drunken person)* desembriagar —intr. ♦ **to s. up** pasársele a uno la embriaguez.

so·ber·sides (sō'bər-sīdz') s.pl. FAM. persona muy seria.

so·bri·e·ty (sō-brī'ĭ-tē) s. *(seriousness)* seriedad *f*; *(absence of intoxication)* sobriedad *f*.

so·bri·quet (sō'brĭ-kā') s. apodo, mote *m*.

sob story s. FAM. historia sentimental.

---

so-called (sō'kôld') adj. llamado, supuesto.
soc·cer (sŏk'ər) s. fútbol m.
so·cia·bil·i·ty (sō'shə-bĭl'ĭ-tē) s. [pl. -ties] sociabilidad f.
so·cia·ble (sō'shə-bəl) I. adj. (social) sociable; (friendly) amistoso II. s. reunión f.
so·cial (sō'shəl) I. adj. (societal) social; (sociable) sociable; (friendly) amistoso ♦ **s. climber** arribista • **s. column** PERIOD. ecos de sociedad • **s. disease** enfermedad venérea • **s. outcast** paria II. s. reunión f.
so·cial·ism (sō'shə-lĭz'əm) s. socialismo.
so·cial·ist (sō'shə-lĭst) s. & adj. socialista mf.
so·cial·is·tic (sō'shə-lĭs'tĭk) adj. socialista <s. policies política socialista>.
so·cial·ite (sō'shə-līt') s. persona de alta sociedad.
so·cial·ize (sō'shə-līz') tr. -ized, -iz·ing (to place under collective ownership) socializar; (to make sociable) volver sociable —intr. alternar.
socialized medicine s. medicina estatal.
so·cial·ly (sō'shə-lē) adv. (of society) socialmente; (to society) para la sociedad <s. acceptable aceptable para la sociedad>.
social science s. ciencias sociales.
social security s. seguridad social f.
social service s. asistencia social ♦ **social services** programa de asistencia social.
social studies s.pl. EDUC. curso de las escuelas secundarias que se dedica a la educación cívica, la sociología y otras materias.
social work s. asistencia social, auxilio social.
so·ci·e·tal (sə-sī'ĭ-tl) adj. social.
so·ci·e·ty (sə-sī'ĭ-tē) s. [pl. -ties] (public) sociedad f; (upper class) alta sociedad, aristocracia; (companionship) compañía <I enjoy her s. disfruto de su compañía>; (association) asociación f, gremio; (BIOL.) colonia, sociedad (de insectos, animales) ♦ **high s.** buena sociedad • **s. page** PERIOD. noticias de la sociedad • **to go into s.** ser presentada en sociedad.
so·ci·o·ec·o·nom·ic (sō'sē-ō-ĕk'ə-nŏm'ĭk) adj. socioeconómico.
so·ci·o·log·i·cal (sō'sē-ə-lŏj'ĭ-kəl) adj. sociológico.
so·ci·ol·o·gist (sō'sē-ŏl'ə-jĭst, -shē-) s. sociólogo.
so·ci·ol·o·gy (sō'sē-ŏl'ə-jē, -shē-) s. sociología.
so·ci·o·path (sō'sē-ə-păth', -shē-) s. persona antisocial.
so·ci·o·po·lit·i·cal (sō'sē-ō-pə-lĭt'ĭ-kəl, -shē-) adj. sociopolítico.
sock¹ (sŏk) I. s. [pl. socks o sox (sŏks)] (stocking) calcetín m; (windsock) manga para indicar la dirección del viento II. tr. poner calcetines ♦ **to s. away** FAM. guardar o esconder dinero • **to s. in** cerrar al tráfico aéreo a causa de niebla.
sock² (sŏk) JER. I. tr. golpear, pegar —intr. dar un golpe II. s. golpe fuerte m, puñetazo.
sock·et (sŏk'ĭt) I. s. (opening) hueco; ELEC. (of a bulb) casquillo; (connection) enchufe (hembra) m; ANAT. (of a tooth) alveolo; (of a bone) glena; (of the eye) cuenca II. tr. encajar o colocar en el hueco.
so·cle (sō'kəl) s. ARQ. zócalo.
Soc·ra·tes (sŏk'rə-tēz') s. Sócrates.
So·crat·ic (sə-krăt'ĭk) adj. & s. socrático.
sod¹ (sŏd) I. s. (surface) césped m; (piece) tepe m II. tr. **sod·ded, sod·ding** cubrir de césped.
sod² (sŏd) s. G.B., JER. cabrón m.
so·da (sō'də) s. QUÍM. carbonato de sodio; (sodium oxide) sosa, soda; (carbonated water) gaseosa; (refreshment) soda.
soda ash s. QUÍM. carbonato de sodio anhidro, sosa comercial.
soda cracker s. galleta salada.
soda fountain s. (siphon) sifón m; (counter) mostrador en el que se despachan bebidas gaseosas y heladas m.
soda jerk s. JER. dependiente de una heladería mf.
soda lime s. QUÍM. hidróxido sódico-cálcico o potásico-cálcico (mezcla absorbente).
so·dal·i·ty (sō-dăl'ĭ-tē) s. [pl. -ties] RELIG. cofradía, hermandad f; (fellowship) asociación f.
soda pop s. FAM. soda, gaseosa.

soda water s. soda, gaseosa.
sod·den (sŏd'n) I. adj. (soaked) empapado; (doughy) mal cocido; (bloated) embrutecido (por el alcohol); (unimaginative) apático II. tr. & intr. empapar(se).
so·di·um (sō'dē-əm) s. QUÍM. sodio.
sodium bicarbonate s. QUÍM. bicarbonato de sodio.
sodium chloride s. QUÍM. cloruro de sodio.
Sod·om (sŏd'əm) s. Sodoma.
sod·om·ite (sŏd'ə-mīt') s. (pederast) sodomita m.
sod·om·y (sŏd'ə-mē) s. sodomía.
so·fa (sō'fə) s. sofá m.
sof·fit (sŏf'ĭt) s. ARQ. sofito.
soft (sôft) I. adj. **-er, -est** (not hard) blando <a s. cushion un almohadón blando>; (not loud) bajo <a s. voice una voz dulce>; (gentle, smooth) suave; (subdued) suave <s. colors colores suaves>; (balmy) templado, suave; (tender) tierno; (lenient) indulgente, complaciente; (weak) débil; (nonalcoholic) no alcohólico; (said of diet) blando, suave; (said of water) blanda; (persuadable) fácil de persuadir; FAM. (easy) fácil <a s. job un trabajo fácil>; FÍS. poco penetrante; FOTOG. borroso, desenfocado; FONÉT. (consonante) suave ♦ **s. in the head** estúpido, tonto • **to be s. on** (to be lenient with) ser indulgente con; (to be fond of) estar enamorado de • **to go s.** (to lose consistency) ponerse blando; (to go crazy) perder la cabeza II. s. parte blanda III. adv. **-er, -est** (smoothly) blandamente, suavemente; (tenderly) tiernamente.
soft·ball (sôft'bôl') s. DEP. variedad de béisbol que se juega con una pelota blanda f; (ball) pelota blanda de béisbol.
soft-boiled (sôft'boild') adj. CUL. (egg) pasado por agua; FAM. (lenient) blando; (sentimental) sentimental, sensiblero.
soft coal s. hulla grasa, carbón bituminoso.
soft drink s. bebida no alcohólica, gaseosa.
soft·en (sô'fən) tr. & intr. ablandar(se).
soft·en·er (sô'fə-nər) s. ablandador m.
soft·en·ing (sô'fə-nĭng) I. adj. suavizador II. s. ablandamiento, reblandecimiento.
soft goods s.pl. mercería.
soft·head·ed (sôft'hĕd'ĭd) adj. tonto, bobo.
soft·heart·ed (sôft'här'tĭd) adj. compasivo, bondadoso.
soft landing s. ASTRONÁUT. aterrizaje suave (sin destrucción de la nave espacial) m.
soft·ly (sôft'lē) adv. (smoothly) blandamente, suavemente; (delicately) delicadamente.
soft·ness (sôft'nĭs) s. (smoothness) suavidad f, blandura; (weakness) debilidad f; (tenderness) dulzura, ternura; (lenience) indulgencia, tolerancia; (stupidity) estupidez f.
soft palate s. ANAT. velo del paladar.
soft-ped·al (sôft'pĕd'l) tr. MÚS. tocar con sordina (piano); FAM. (to play down) suavizar, moderar.
soft sell s. FAM. (selling) venta discreta; (advertising) publicidad discreta.
soft-shell (sôft'shĕl') o **soft-shelled** (-shĕld') adj. de concha blanda.
soft-shoe (sôft'shoō') s. zapateado ejecutado con zapatos sin chapas de metal.
soft shoulder s. borde de tierra blanda al costado de una carretera m.
soft soap s. (soap) jabón líquido; FAM. (flattery) pelotilla, adulación f.
soft-soap (sôft'sōp') tr. engatusar.
soft-spo·ken (sôft'spō'kən) adj. (with a gentle voice) de voz suave o baja; (smooth) suave, afable.
soft·ware (sôft'wâr') s. COMPUT. software m, logicial m.
soft·wood (sôft'wŏŏd') s. (wood) madera blanda; (tree) árbol de madera blanda m.
soft·y (sôf'tē) s. [pl. -ies] FAM. (sentimental person) sensiblero; (indulgent person) blando.
sog·gy (sŏg'ē) adj. **-gi·er, -gi·est** (soaked) empapado; (dull) pesado; (sultry) pastoso.
soil¹ (soil) s. (land) tierra.
soil² (soil) I. tr. (to dirty) ensuciar; (to disgrace) manchar, mancillar; (to corrupt) corromper; (with excrement) ensuciar con excremento —intr. ensuciarse, mancharse II. s.

(dirtiness) suciedad *f; (stain)* mancha; *(refuse)* basura; *(manure)* estiércol *m.*

soil·age (soi'lĭj) s. AGR. verdes *m,* alcacer *m.*

soiled (soiled) adj. sucio <*s. clothes* ropa sucia>.

so·journ (sō'jûrn') I. intr. residir temporalmente II. s. residencia temporal, estada.

sol¹ (sōl) s. MÚS. sol *m.*

sol² (sōl) s. FIN. sol (unidad monetaria del Perú) *m.*

sol·ace (sŏl'ĭs) I. s. consuelo II. tr. **-aced, -ac·ing** consolar.

sol·ace·ment (sŏl'ĭs-mənt) s. consuelo.

so·lar (sō'lər) adj. ASTRON. solar.

solar cell s. FÍS. pila solar.

solar collector s. TEC. colector de radiación solar *m.*

solar energy s. energía solar.

so·lar·i·um (sō-lâr'ē-əm) s. [pl. **-i·a** (-ē-ə) *o* **-i·ums**] solana, carasol *m.*

solar plexus s. ANAT. plexo solar.

solar system s. ASTRON. sistema solar *m.*

sold (sōld) pret. y part. p. de **sell.**

sol·der (sŏd'ər) I. s. soldadura II. tr. & intr. soldar(se).

sol·dier (sōl'jər) I. s. MIL. soldado; ENTOM. *(ant)* obrera II. intr. MIL. servir como soldado; *(to make a show of working)* fingir trabajar.

sol·dier·ly (sōl'jər-lē) adj. militar, marcial.

soldier of fortune s. *(mercenary)* mercenario; FIG. *(adventurer)* aventurero.

sol·dier·y (sōl'jə-rē) s. [pl. **-ies**] MIL. *(soldiers)* tropa, soldadesca; *(profession)* milicia.

sold-out (sōld'out') adj. COM. agotado.

sole¹ (sōl) I. s. *(of a foot)* planta; *(of a shoe)* suela; *(bottom part)* base *f* II. tr. **soled, sol·ing** poner suela a (zapato, bota).

sole² (sōl) adj. *(single)* único <*his s. purpose* su único propósito>; *(exclusive)* exclusivo (participación, derecho); DER. *(unmarried)* soltero.

sole³ (sōl) s. [pl. **sole** *o* **soles**] ICT. lenguado.

sole·ly (sōl'lē) adv. *(alone)* solamente, únicamente; *(exclusively)* exclusivamente.

sol·emn (sŏl'əm) adj. *(grave)* solemne; *(sacred)* sagrado; *(somber)* serio; *(pompous)* estirado.

so·lem·ni·ty (sə-lĕm'nĭ-tē) s. [pl. **-ties**] *(graveness)* solemnidad *f; (ceremony)* ceremonia; *(seriousness)* seriedad *f.*

sol·em·nize (sŏl'əm-nīz') tr. **-nized, -niz·ing** *(to perform with ceremony)* solemnizar; *(a marriage)* celebrar; *(to make serious)* solemnizar.

so·le·noid (sō'lə-noid') s. ELEC. solenoide *m.*

sol·fa (sōl-fä') s. MÚS. solfeo.

sol·feg·gio (sōl-fĕj'ē-ō', -fĕj'ō) s. MÚS. solfeo.

so·lic·it (sə-lĭs'ĭt) tr. *(to seek to obtain)* solicitar; *(to importune)* importunar; *(to incite)* incitar; *(to induce)* inducir; *(to offer sexual services)* abordar (prostituta) —intr. hacer una petición.

so·lic·i·ta·tion (sə-lĭs'ĭ-tā'shən) s. *(request)* solicitación *f; (incitation)* incitación *f.*

so·lic·i·tor (sə-lĭs'ĭ-tər) s. *(agent)* agente *m; (chief law officer)* procurador *m;* G.B. *(lawyer)* abogado.

solicitor general s. [pl. **solicitors general**] *(undersecretary)* subsecretario de justicia; *(law officer)* procurador general (de un estado) *m;* G.B. *(prosecutor)* procurador de la corona *m.*

so·lic·i·tous (sə-lĭs'ĭ-təs) adj. *(attentive)* solícito, atento; *(eager)* ansioso; *(worried)* preocupado.

so·lic·i·tude (sə-lĭs'ĭ-tōod', -tyōod') s. *(attention)* solicitud *f,* cuidado; *(worry)* preocupación *f; (eagerness)* ansiedad *f.*

sol·id (sŏl'ĭd) I. adj. *(of state, dimension)* sólido; *(not hollow)* macizo <*a s. gold bar* una barra de oro macizo>; *(continuous)* continuo <*a s. line* una línea continua>; *(well-made)* fuerte, resistente; *(substantial)* sustancioso; *(reliable)* fidedigno, seguro <*s. information* información segura>; *(upstanding)* modelo <*a s. citizen* un ciudadano modelo>; *(unanimous)* unánime; *(of color)* uniforme; *(full)* atestado, lleno <*the place was s. with people* el lugar estaba lleno de gente>; IMPR. sin interlíneas ♦ **s. as a rock** firme como una roca II. s. sólido.

sol·i·dar·i·ty (sŏl'ĭ-dăr'ĭ-tē) s. solidaridad *f.*

solid geometry s. geometría tridimensional, geometría del espacio.

so·lid·i·fi·ca·tion (sə-lĭd'ə-fĭ-kā'shən) s. solidificación *f.*

so·lid·i·fy (sə-lĭd'ə-fī') tr. & intr. **-fied, -fy·ing** solidificar(se), volver(se) sólido.

so·lid·i·ty (sə-lĭd'ĭ-tē) s. solidez *f.*

sol·id·ly (sŏl'ĭd-lē) adv. *(unanimously)* unánimemente <*they were s. for the new law* estaban unánimemente a favor de la nueva ley>; *(non-stop)* sin parar <*they drove s. for eight hours* manejaron sin parar durante ocho horas>; *(strongly)* sólidamente <*s. built* sólidamente construido>.

sol·id-state (sŏl'ĭd-stāt') adj. ELECTRÓN., FÍS. estado sólido.

so·lil·o·quize (sə-lĭl'ə-kwīz') intr. & tr. **-quized, -quiz·ing** soliloquiar, monologar.

so·lil·o·quy (sə-lĭl'ə-kwē) s. [pl. **-quies**] soliloquio, monólogo.

sol·ip·sism (sŏl'ĭp-sĭz'əm, sō'lĭp-) s. FILOS. solipsismo.

sol·i·taire (sŏl'ĭ-târ') s. *(gem)* solitario; *(card game)* solitario.

sol·i·tar·y (sŏl'ĭ-tĕr'ē) I. adj. *(alone)* solitario; *(remote)* solitario, alejado; *(single)* único, solo II. s. [pl. **-ies**] *(recluse)* solitario FAM.; *(confinement)* incomunicación *f.*

sol·i·tude (sŏl'ĭ-tōod') s. *(isolation)* aislamiento; *(loneliness)* soledad *f; (place)* lugar solitario, lugar desierto.

so·lo (sō'lō) I. s. [pl. **-los**] MÚS. solo; *(in cards)* solo II. adj. solo III. adv. a solas IV. intr. **-loed, -lo·ing** volar solo.

so·lo·ist (sō'lō-ĭst) s. MÚS. solista *mf.*

Sol·o·mon (sŏl'ə-mən) s. BÍBL., HIST. Salomón.

Solomon Islands s. Islas Salomón.

so long interj. FAM. hasta pronto, hasta luego.

sol·stice (sŏl'stĭs) s. ASTRON. solsticio.

sol·u·bil·i·ty (sŏl'yə-bĭl'ĭ-tē) s. [pl. **-ties**] solubilidad *f.*

sol·u·ble (sŏl'yə-bəl) adj. soluble.

sol·ute (sŏl'yōot) I. s. QUÍM. soluto, substancia disuelta II. adj. disuelto.

so·lu·tion (sə-lōo'shən) s. *(dissolution)* disolución *f; (answer)* solución *f;* QUÍM., FÍS., MAT. solución *f;* DER. resolución *f.*

solv·a·ble (sŏl'və-bəl) adj. soluble.

solve (sŏlv) tr. **solved, solv·ing** resolver, solucionar.

sol·ven·cy (sŏl'vən-sē) s. solvencia.

sol·vent (sŏl'vənt) I. adj. COM. solvente; QUÍM. *(to dissolve)* disolvente II. s. QUÍM. solvente *m,* disolvente *m.*

So·ma·li (sō-mä'lē) I. adj. somalí II. s. [pl. **Somali** *o* **Somalis**] somalí *mf* ♦ **the S.** los somalíes.

So·ma·li·a (sō-mä'lē-ə) s. Somalia.

So·ma·li·an (sō-mä'lē-ən) adj. & s. somalí *mf.*

so·mat·ic (sō-măt'ĭk) adj. somático.

so·ma·tol·o·gy (sō'mə-tŏl'ə-jē) s. somatología.

som·ber (sŏm'bər) adj. sombrío.

some (sŭm) §G18, 36 I. adj. *(several)* algunos <*s. people* algunas personas>; *(a little)* algo de, un poco de <*put s. sugar in it* échale un poco de azúcar>; cierto <*after s. time* después de cierto tiempo>; unos, varios <*s. days ago* hace varios días>; unos, unos cuantos <*it happened s. years back* sucedió hace unos cuantos años>; *(expressing irony)* menudo, valiente <*s. advice he gave me!* ¡menudo consejo que me dio!>; *(remarkable)* extraordinario <*it was s. show!* ¡fue un gran espectáculo!> ♦ **for s. reason or other** por una razón u otra, por alguna razón • **s. day** algún día, un día de éstos • **s. luck!** ¡vaya suerte! • **s. other time** *(day)* otro día; *(moment)* otro momento • **s. way or other** de una manera u otra II. pron. *(several)* algunos <*s. came and others did not* algunos vinieron y otros no>; *(a little)* un poco, algo <*have s. of this salad* sírvete un poco de esta ensalada> ♦ **and then s.** y luego un poco más, y más todavía III. adv. *(approximately)* unos <*some forty people* unas cuarenta personas>; FAM. *(somewhat)* un poco, algo <*it hurt s.* dolió un poco>.

some·bod·y (sŭm'bŏd'ē) I. pron. alguien, alguno <*s. told me so* me lo dijo alguien> ♦ **s. else** algún otro II. s. [pl. **-ies**] FAM. alguien *m,* personaje *m* <*he thinks he's s. now* ahora se cree alguien>.

some·day (sŭm'dā') adv. algún día, un día de éstos.

some·how (sŭm'hou') adv. *(in some way)* de algún modo, de alguna manera; *(for some reason)* por alguna razón.

some·one (sŭm'wŭn') pron. & s. consulte **somebody.**

---

ng inglés / ŏ la / ō bou / ô corre / oi oigo / ōo uno / ou auto / yōo ciudad / w hueco / y yo / z mismo

some·place (sŭm'plās') adv. en alguna parte.
som·er·sault (sŭm'ər-sôlt') **I.** s. *(acrobatic stunt)* salto mortal; FIG. *(reversal)* cambio total (de opinion o de ánimo) **II.** intr. dar un salto mortal.
some·thing (sŭm'thĭng) pron. & s. algo *<give me s. to read* dame algo para leer> ♦ **is s. the matter?** ¿pasa algo?, ¿le pasa algo? • **or s.** o algo por el estilo *<he broke his arm or s.* se rompió el brazo o algo por el estilo> • **s. else** *(another thing)* otra cosa, algo más; JER. *(exceptional thing)* algo extraordinario • **s. or other** *(choice)* una cosa u otra; *(name)* y no sé qué más *<his name is John s. or other* su nombre es Juan y no sé qué más> • **to be quite s.** ser algo extraordinario • **to be s.** ser de alguna importancia • **to be s. of a . . .** tener algo de . . . • **to have a certain s.** tener un no sé qué **III.** adv. *(somewhat)* algo, un poco *<she looks s. like her mother* ella se parece algo a su madre>; *(extremely)* sumamente.
some·time (sŭm'tīm') **I.** adv. *(at an indefinite time)* alguna vez, algún día; *(sometimes)* a veces, de vez en cuando ♦ **s. or other** tarde o temprano • **s. soon** pronto, algún día de éstos *<write to me s. soon* escríbeme pronto> **II.** adj. *(former)* ex, antiguo *<the s. mayor of New York* el ex alcalde de Nueva York>.
some·times (sŭm'tīmz') adv. de vez en cuando, a veces.
some·way (sŭm'wā') o **some·ways** (-wāz') adv. de alguna manera.
some·what (sŭm'hwŏt') adv. algo.
some·where (sŭm'hwâr') **I.** adv. *(at or in an unspecified place)* en alguna parte, en algún lugar *<s. in the city* en alguna parte de la ciudad>; *(to an unspecified place)* a alguna parte; *(approximately)* más o menos, entre *<s. between two and three months* entre dos y tres meses> ♦ **s. near here** cerca de aquí, por aquí ♦ **s. or other** en alguna parte, por ahí *<I left it s. or other* lo dejé por ahí> **II.** s. sitio, lugar m.
som·nam·bu·lant (sŏm-năm'byə-lənt) s. & adj. sonámbulo, somnámbulo.
som·nam·bu·lism (sŏm-năm'byə-lĭz'əm) s. sonambulismo, somnambulismo.
som·nif·er·ous (sŏm-nĭf'ər-əs) adj. somnífero.
som·no·lence (sŏm'nə-ləns) s. somnolencia.
som·no·lent (sŏm'nə-lənt) adj. *(sleepy)* soñoliento; *(soporific)* soporífico.
so much I. adv. tanto *<if he wins, so much the better for him* si gana, tanto mejor para él> **II.** adj. tanto **III.** pron. *(something)* tanto *<it costs so much a kilo* cuesta tanto por kilo>; *(everything)* todo.
so much as adv. siquiera *<he wouldn't so much as look at her* ni siquiera la miraría>.
son (sŭn) s. *(male offspring)* hijo; *(descendant)* hijo, descendiente m; *(adopted child)* hijo adoptivo; *(son-in-law)* hijo político, yerno; FAM. *(young man)* hijo, muchacho ♦ **the S.** RELIG. el Hijo.
so·nar (sō'när') s. sonar m.
so·na·ta (sə-nä'tə) s. MÚS. sonata.
song (sông) s. *(musical composition)* canción f; *(act)* canto, cantar; *(melodious utterance)* canto; *(poetry)* canto, poesía ♦ **for a s.** por poca cosa • **to give someone a s. and dance** FAM. contarle a alguien toda una historia • **to sing the same old s.** FAM. volver a la misma cantilena.
song·bird (sông'bûrd') s. ORNIT. ave canora, pájaro cantor.
Song of Solomon s. BÍBL. Cantar de los Cantares m.
Song of Songs s. BÍBL. Cantar de los Cantares m.
song·ster (sông'stər) s. MÚS. *(singer)* cantante mf; *(songwriter)* autor de canciones m.
song·writ·er (sông'rī'tər) s. *(composer)* compositor (de canciones) m; *(lyricist)* autor de la letra (de una canción) m.
son·ic (sŏn'ĭk) adj. sónico, acústico.
sonic barrier s. barrera del sonido.
sonic boom s. AER. estampido supersónico.
son-in-law (sŭn'ĭn-lô') s. [pl. **sons-in-law**] yerno, hijo político.
son·net (sŏn'ĭt) s. soneto.
son·net·eer (sŏn'ĭ-tîr') s. *(composer)* sonetista mf; *(inferior poet)* poetastro.
son·ny (sŭn'ē) s. [pl. **-nies**] FAM. hijito.

so·nor·i·ty (sə-nôr'ĭ-tē) s. [pl. **-ties**] sonoridad f.
so·no·rous (sə-nôr'əs) adj. sonoro.
soon (soon) adv. **-er, -est** *(shortly)* pronto, dentro de poco *<I'll come back s.* volveré pronto>; *(promptly)* pronto, rápidamente *<come as s. as possible* ven lo más pronto posible>; *(early)* pronto, temprano *<you are back so s.?* ¿tan temprano y ya habéis regresado?> ♦ **as s. as** en cuanto, tan pronto como • **had sooner** preferiría • **how s.?** ¿cuándo?, ¿cuándo a más tardar? • **no sooner said than done** dicho y hecho • **s. after** poco después • **the sooner the better** cuanto más pronto, mejor • **sooner or later** tarde o temprano.
soot (soot, soot) **I.** s. tizne m, hollín m **II.** tr. tiznar, cubrir de hollín.
soothe (sooth) tr. **soothed, sooth·ing** *(to calm)* calmar; *(to placate)* aplacar; *(to relieve from pain)* calmar, aliviar —intr. calmar, aliviar.
sooth·ing (soo'thĭng) adj. *(calming)* tranquilizador; MED. calmante, sedante.
sooth·say·er (sooth'sā'ər) s. adivino.
soot·y (soot'ē, soot'ē) adj. **-i·er, -i·est** *(with soot)* tiznado; *(producing soot)* tiznero; *(dark)* ennegrecido.
sop (sŏp) **I.** tr. **sopped, sop·ping** remojar ♦ **to s. up** absorber —intr. remojarse **II.** s. *(bread)* sopa de pan; *(compensation)* compensación f; *(bribe)* soborno.
soph·ism (sŏf'ĭz'əm) s. sofisma m.
soph·ist (sŏf'ĭst) s. filósofo, pensador m ♦ **S.** HIST. sofista.
so·phis·ti·cate (sə-fĭs'tĭ-kāt') **I.** tr. **-cat·ed, -cat·ing** *(to make complex)* sofisticar; *(a text)* falsificar; *(wine)* adulterar; *(method)* perfeccionar —intr. usar sofismas **II.** s. (sə-fĭs'tĭ-kĭt) persona sofisticada.
so·phis·ti·cat·ed (sə-fĭs'tĭ-kā'tĭd) adj. *(refined)* sofisticado; *(complicated)* complicado, complejo.
so·phis·ti·ca·tion (sə-fĭs'tĭ-kā'shən) s. *(sophistry)* sofistería; *(refinement)* sofisticación f.
soph·is·try (sŏf'ĭ-strē) s. [pl. **-tries**] *(argumentation)* sofistería; *(sophism)* sofisma m.
soph·o·more (sŏf'ə-môr') s. estudiante de segundo año mf.
soph·o·mor·ic (sŏf'ə-môr'ĭk) adj. *(of a sophomore)* de estudiante de segundo año; FIG. *(immature)* inmaduro; *(overconfident)* demasiado confiado.
sop·o·rif·ic (sŏp'ə-rĭf'ĭk, sō'pə-) adj. & s. soporífico.
sop·ping (sŏp'ĭng) **I.** adj. empapado **II.** adv. ♦ **s. wet** *(thing)* empapado; *(person)* calado hasta los huesos.
sop·py (sŏp'ē) adj. **-pi·er, -pi·est** *(soaked)* empapado; *(rainy)* lluvioso; JER. *(sentimental)* sensiblero.
so·pran·o (sə-prăn'ō, -prä'nō) s. [pl. **-os**] MÚS. soprano mf.
sor·bic acid (sôr'bĭk) s. QUÍM. ácido sórbico.
sor·cer·er (sôr'sər-ər) s. hechicero, brujo.
sor·cer·ess (sôr'sər-ĭs) s. hechicera, bruja.
sor·cer·y (sôr'sə-rē) s. hechicería, brujería.
sor·did (sôr'dĭd) adj. *(squalid)* sórdido; *(filthy)* sucio, inmundo; *(base)* sórdido.
sore (sôr) **I.** adj. **sor·er, sor·est** *(painful)* dolorido; *(grievous)* grande *<s. need* gran necesidad>; *(embarrassing)* delicado, espinoso *<a s. point* un asunto delicado>; *(sorrowful)* doloroso; FAM. *(offended)* molesto ♦ **to be s.** doler *<my throat is s.* me duele la garganta> • **to be s. at heart** tener el corazón dolorido • **to be s. at someone** FAM. estar enfadado con alguien • **to get s.** ofenderse, enfadarse **II.** s. *(wound)* herida; *(ulcer)* llaga, úlcera; *(pain)* dolor m.
sore·head (sôr'hĕd') s. JER. cascarrabias mf.
sore·ly (sôr'lē) adv. *(painfully)* dolorosamente; *(extremely)* extremadamente, sumamente; *(a lot)* mucho; *(very)* muy.
sore·ness (sôr'nĭs) s. *(pain)* dolor m; *(resentment)* resentimiento.
sore throat s. dolor de garganta m.
sor·ghum (sôr'gəm) s. BOT. sorgo, zahína; *(syrup)* melaza de sorgo.
so·ror·i·ty (sə-rôr'ĭ-tē) s. [pl. **-ties**] club femenino de estudiantes.
sorp·tion (sôrp'shən) s. absorción f, adsorción f.
sor·rel¹ (sôr'əl) s. BOT. acedera.
sor·rel² (sôr'əl) s. *(color)* alazán m; *(horse)* alazán.
sor·row (sŏr'ō) **I.** s. *(sadness)* pesar m, dolor m; *(misfor-*

tune) infortunio, desgracia; *(grieving)* duelo, lamento **II.** intr. sentir pesar *o* pena.

sor·row·ful (sŏr′ə-fəl) adj. *(person)* pesaroso; *(news)* doloroso.

sor·ry (sŏr′ē) **I.** adj. **-ri·er, -ri·est** *(sad)* triste <*a s. sight* un espectáculo triste>; *(paltry)* insignificante; *(grievous)* lamentable ♦ **a s. fellow** un infeliz • **I'm s.** lo siento • **to be s.** sentir <*I'm s. to be late* siento llegar tarde> • **to feel s. for** compadecer • **to feel s. for oneself** sentirse desgraciado • **you'll be s!** ¡te arrepentirás! **II.** interj. ¡perdón!, ¡lo siento!

sort (sôrt) **I.** s. *(class)* clase *f*, tipo; *(type)* especie *f*; *(manner)* modo, manera; *(person)* tipo <*he is a strange s.* es un tipo raro> ♦ **after a s.** de mala manera • **I'm s. of lost** estoy como perdido • **it's s. of big** es más bien grande • **it takes all sorts to make the world** de todo hay en el mundo • **nothing of the s.!** ¡nada de eso! • **of sorts** una especie de • **out of sorts** *(unwell)* pachucho; *(cross)* de mal humor • **something of the s.** algo por el estilo **II.** tr. *(to classify)* clasificar; *(to put in order)* ordenar ♦ **to s. out** *(to separate)* separar; *(to resolve)* resolver (problemas, conflictos).

sort·er (sôr′tər) s. *(person)* clasificador *m*; *(machine)* clasificadora.

sor·tie (sôr′tē) s. MIL. salida.

S O S (ĕs′ō-ĕs′) s. RAD. S O S *m*; FIG. *(call for help)* llamada de auxilio.

so-so (sō′sō′) adj. & adv. regular.

sot (sŏt) s. borracho.

sou·bri·quet (sōō′brĭ-kā′) s. var. de **sobriquet.**

sough (sŭf, sou) **I.** intr. susurrar **II.** s. susurro.

sought (sôt) pret. y part. p. de **seek.**

soul (sōl) s. *(spiritual essence)* alma; *(spirit)* espíritu *m*, alma; *(human being)* persona, alma <*not a s. in sight* no se veía un alma>; *(personification)* personificación *f* <*the s. of honor* la personificación del honor>; MÚS., TEAT. garra <*his acting has no s.* su actuación no tiene garra> ♦ **a good s.** un alma de Dios • **All Souls' Day** Día de Difuntos • **God rest his s.** que Dios le tenga en su gloria • **poor s.** pobre, pobrecito • **unable to call one's s. one's own** completamente esclavizado.

soul food s. comida tradicional de los negros del sur de EE. UU.

soul·ful (sōl′fəl) adj. sentimental.

soul·less (sōl′lĭs) adj. sin alma.

soul-search·ing (sōl′sûr′chĭng) s. examen de conciencia *m*.

sound¹ (sound) **I.** s. *(audible frequency)* sonido; *(auditory material)* sonido (de voz, película); *(noise)* ruido; *(implication)* implicación *f* ♦ **I don't like the s. of it** no me huele bien • **I like the s. of it** me parece bien • **to the s. of** al son de **II.** intr. *(to resonate)* sonar; *(to seem)* parecer <*it sounds wonderful* parece magnífico> ♦ **to s. off** MIL. marcar el paso; *(to express)* protestar a voz en grito —tr. *(to play)* tocar <*s. the trumpets* que toquen las trompetas>; *(to signal)* hacer sonar, dar <*to s. the alarm* dar la alarma>; *(to celebrate)* celebrar; *(to pronounce)* pronunciar; MED. auscultar.

sound² (sound) adj. **-er, -est** *(in good condition)* en buenas condiciones; *(healthy)* sano; *(firm)* firme; *(secure)* seguro <*a s. economy* una economía segura>; *(sensible)* bien fundado, válido; *(thorough)* completo; *(deep)* profundo <*a s. sleep* un sueño profundo>; *(trustworthy)* de confianza; *(levelheaded)* razonable; *(conservative)* conservador; DER. *(valid)* válido, legal ♦ **to be s. as a bell** *(solid)* ser muy seguro; *(healthy)* estar más sano que una manzana • **to be s. of mind** estar uno en su sano juicio.

sound³ (sound) s. MARÍT. *(channel)* estrecho; *(inlet)* brazo de mar; ICT. *(bladder)* vejiga natatoria.

sound⁴ (sound) **I.** tr. *(to fathom)* sondear, escandallar; *(to examine)* tantear, sondear; MED. sondar ♦ **to s. out** sondear —intr. *(to fathom)* sondear (profundidad); *(to dive)* sumergirse (ballena); *(to investigate)* sondear **II.** s. CIR. sonda.

sound barrier s. barrera del sonido.

sound camera s. CINEM. cámara con equipo de sonido.

sound effects s.pl. CINEM., RAD., TELEV. efectos sonoros.

sound·er (soun′dər) s. sonador *m*, resonador *m*.

sound·ing¹ (soun′dĭng) s. *(action)* sonido; GEOL., MARÍT. sondeo ♦ **soundings** aguas poco profundas.

sound·ing² (soun′dĭng) adj. *(resonant)* resonante; *(noisy)* sonoro; *(high-sounding)* altisonante.

sounding board s. MÚS. *(of a piano)* tabla de armonía; *(of an organ)* secreto; *(spokesman)* portavoz *m*.

sound·less (sound′lĭs) adj. *(noiseless)* silencioso; *(silent)* mudo.

sound·ly (sound′lē) adv. *(solidly)* sólidamente; *(deeply)* profundamente.

sound·ness (sound′nĭs) s. *(solidity)* solidez *f*; *(depth)* profundidad *f*; *(solvency)* solvencia; *(validity)* validez *f*; *(good sense)* sensatez *f*.

sound·proof (sound′prōōf′) **I.** adj. insonoro, a prueba de sonido **II.** tr. insonorizar.

sound stage s. CINEM. estudio para filmar con sonido.

sound·track (sound′trăk′) s. CINEM. pista *o* banda sonora.

soup (sōōp) s. *(food)* sopa; *(fog)* niebla espesa ♦ **from s. to nuts** de cabo a rabo • **to be in the s.** JER. estar en un apuro • **to s. up** AUTO. aumentar la potencia de.

soup kitchen s. comedor de beneficencia *m*.

soup·spoon (sōōp′spōōn′) s. cuchara de sopa, cuchara sopera.

soup·y (sōō′pē) adj. **-i·er, -i·est** *(of soup)* espeso; *(foggy)* con niebla espesa; FAM. *(sentimental)* muy sentimental.

sour (sour) **I.** adj. **-er, -est** *(acerbic)* agrio, ácido; *(rancid)* rancio; *(milk)* cortado; *(smell)* acre; FIG. *(peevish)* agrio <*a s. face* una cara agria>; *(bitter)* amargo ♦ **to turn** *o* **go s.** *(wine)* agriarse; *(character)* agriarse; *(milk)* cortarse **II.** tr. & intr. *(wine)* agriar(se); *(bread)* poner(se) rancio; *(milk)* cortar(se); FIG. *(person)* amargar(se) **III.** s. *(taste)* acidez *f*; *(drink)* cóctel (de whisky con limón) *m*.

source (sôrs) s. *(origin)* origen *m*, fuente *f*; *(of river)* manantial *m*, nacimiento; *(of supply, information)* fuente; MED. foco ♦ **reliable s.** fuente fidedigna.

sour·dough (sour′dō′) s. *(leaven)* levadura; JER. *(prospector)* explorador *m*, cateador *m*.

sour grapes s.pl. FIG. desprecio de algo que no puede conseguirse.

sour·ness (sour′nĭs) s. *(of taste)* acidez *f*; FIG. *(of character)* acritud *f*, desabrimiento.

sou·sa·phone (sōō′zə-fōn′, -sə-) s. instrumento similar a la tuba.

souse (sous) **I.** tr. **soused, sous·ing** *(to plunge)* sumergir; *(to drench)* empapar; JER. *(to make drunk)* emborrachar; CUL. conservar en vinagre **II.** s. *(pickled meat or fish)* conserva en vinagre; *(for meat)* adobo; *(for fish)* escabeche *m*; JER. *(drunkard)* borracho.

sou·tane (sōō-tän′, -tǎn′) s. sotana.

south (south) **I.** s. sur *m* ♦ **the S.** los estados del sur (de EE. UU.) **II.** adj. del sur, austral **III.** adv. hacia el sur.

South Africa s. África del Sur.

South African adj. & s. sudafricano.

South America s. América del Sur, Sudamérica.

South American adj. & s. sudamericano.

south·bound (south′bound′) adj. con rumbo al sur.

south·east (south-ēst′) **I.** s. sudeste *m* **II.** adj. del sudeste **III.** adv. hacia el sudeste.

south·east·er (south-ē′stər) s. viento del sudeste.

south·east·er·ly (south-ē′stər-lē) **I.** adj. del sudeste **II.** adv. hacia el sudeste.

south·east·ern (south-ē′stərn) adj. del sudeste.

south·east·ward (south-ēst′wərd) **I.** adv. & adj. *(toward the southwest)* hacia el sudeste; *(at the southwest)* en el sudeste **II.** s. *(direction)* dirección sudeste *f*; *(region)* región sudeste *f*.

south·er (sou′thər) s. sur *m*, austro (viento del sur).

south·er·ly (sŭth′ər-lē) **I.** adj. del sur **II.** s. [pl. **-lies**] sur *m*, viento del sur **III.** adv. hacia el sur.

south·ern (sŭth′ərn) adj. del sur.

Southern Cross s. ASTRON. Cruz del Sur *f*.

south·ern·er (sŭth′ər-nər) s. habitante del sur *m*, sureño; HIST. sudista *mf*.

Southern Hemisphere s. hemisferio austral.

southern lights s.pl. METEOR. aurora austral.

---

south·ern·most (sŭth'ərn-mōst') adj. del extremo sur.
South Korea s. Corea del Sur.
south·land (south'lănd') s. región austral *f.*
south·paw (south'pô') s. JER. zurdo.
South Pole s. GEOG. Polo Sur.
south-south·east (south'south-ēst') I. s. sudsudeste *m* II. adj. del sudsudeste III. adv. hacia el sudsudeste.
south-south·west (south'south-wĕst') I. s. sursudoeste *m* II. adj. del sursudoeste III. adv. hacia el sursudoeste.
south·ward (south'wərd) I. adv. hacia el sur II. adj. en el sur III. s. sur *m.*
south·west (south-wĕst') I. s. suroeste *m,* sudoeste *m* II. adj. del sudoeste III. adv. hacia el sudoeste.
south·west·er (south-wĕs'tər) s. *(wind)* viento del sudoeste; *(hat)* (sou-wĕs'tər) sueste *m.*
south·west·er·ly (south-wĕs'tər-lē) I. adj. del sudoeste II. adv. hacia el sudoeste.
south·west·ern (south-wĕs'tərn) adj. del sudoeste.
south·west·ward (south-wĕst'wərd) I. adj. del sudoeste II. adv. hacia el sudoeste.
sou·ve·nir (sōō'və-nîr') s. recuerdo.
sov·er·eign (sŏv'ər-ĭn) I. s. *(in a monarchy)* soberano; *(gold coin)* soberano II. adj. *(independent)* soberano (estado); FIG. *(absolute, supreme)* soberano, total.
sov·er·eign·ty (sŏv'ər-ĭn-tē) s. [pl. **-ties**] *(of a sovereign or state)* soberanía; *(independent state)* estado soberano.
so·vi·et (sō'vē-ĕt') I. s. soviet *m* ♦ **Soviets** soviéticos II. adj. soviético ♦ **S.** soviético.
so·vi·et·ize *o* **So·vi·et·ize** (sō'vē-ĭ-tīz') tr. **-ized, -iz·ing** sovietizar.
Soviet Socialist Republics, Union of s. Unión de Repúblicas Socialistas Soviéticas.
Soviet Union s. Unión Soviética.
sow¹ (sō) tr. **sowed, sown** (sōn) *o* **sowed, sow·ing** *(to scatter seed)* sembrar; FIG. *(to propagate)* sembrar, propagar.
sow² (sou) s. ZOOL. *(female hog)* cerda; METAL. galápago.
sow·er (sō'ər) s. *(person)* sembrador *m;* *(machine)* sembradora; *(person who propagates)* sembrador, propagador *m.*
sow·ing (sō'ĭng) s. siembra.
sown (sōn) un part. p. de **sow¹**.
sox (sŏks) un pl. de **sock¹**.
soy (soi) s. BOT. soja.
soy·a (soi'ə) s. soja (semilla).
soy·bean (soi'bēn') s. BOT. *(plant)* soja; *(seed)* semilla de soja.
soy sauce s. CUL. salsa de soja fermentada en salmuera.
spa (spä) s. *(mineral spring)* manantial de agua mineral *m;* *(resort)* balneario.
space (spās) I. s. *(expanse)* espacio; *(universe)* universo, espacio; *(empty area)* espacio; *(blank)* espacio en blanco; *(place)* sitio, lugar *m <it takes up too much s.* ocupa demasiado sitio>; *(interval of time)* período, espacio; FÍS., GEOM. espacio ♦ **outer s.** espacio exterior • **s. band** TIP. espaciador • **s. bar** espaciador (de la máquina de escribir) • **s. line** TIP. interlínea • **to leave a s. for** dejar un espacio para • **to stare into s.** tener la mirada perdida II. tr. **spaced, spac·ing** *(to arrange with spaces between)* espaciar, distanciar; *(to separate)* separar ♦ **to s. out** separar, distanciar *<well spaced out* bastante distanciados>.
space age s. era espacial.
space·craft (spās'krăft') s. [pl. **spacecraft**] nave espacial *f,* astronave *f.*
space·flight (spās'flīt') s. vuelo espacial.
space·man (spās'măn') s. [pl. **-men** (-mĕn')] *(person)* astronauta *mf,* cosmonauta *mf;* *(visitor from outer space)* visitante del espacio *mf,* visitante extraterrestre.
space·port (spās'pôrt') s. estación de lanzamiento de naves espaciales *f.*
spac·er (spā'sər) s. espaciador *m.*
space·ship *o* **space ship** (spās'shĭp') s. nave espacial *f.*
space shuttle s. transbordador espacial (vehículo espacial para transportar astronoautas entre la tierra y una estación espacial en órbita) *m.*
space station s. estación espacial *f.*
space suit s. traje espacial *m.*
spa·cial (spā'shəl) adj. var. de **spatial.**

spac·ing (spā'sĭng) s. *(arranging into spaces)* espaciamiento; *(space)* espacio.
spa·cious (spā'shəs) adj. espacioso, amplio.
spade¹ (spād) I. s. *(digging tool)* pala; MIL. espolón *m,* rejas ♦ **to call a s. a s.** llamar al pan pan y al vino vino II. tr. **spad·ed, spad·ing** remover con pala.
spade² (spād) s. *(cards)* espada, pico; DESPEC. *(black person)* negro ♦ **spades** espadas, picos.
spade·work (spād'wûrk') s. *(work requiring a spade)* trabajo con pala; FIG. *(preparatory work)* trabajo preparatorio.
spa·ghet·ti (spə-gĕt'ē) s. CUL. espagueti *m.*
Spain (spān) s. España.
span¹ (spăn) I. s. *(breadth)* anchura; *(of wings)* envergadura; CONSTR. *(distance between two supports of a bridge)* luz *f,* ojo; ARQ., CONSTR. *(part of a bridge)* arcada, tramo *<a bridge with seven spans* un puente de siete arcadas>; *(of hand, as measure)* palmo; *(period of time)* duración *f <the average life s.* la duración media de la vida> II. tr. **spanned, span·ning** *(to form a span over)* cruzar, atravesar *<the bridge spans the river* el puente cruza el río>; *(to build a bridge)* tender un puente sobre; *(to measure by hand)* medir en palmos; *(in time)* durar *<a career that spanned forty years* una carrera que duró cuarenta años>.
span² (spăn) I. tr. **spanned, span·ning** MARÍT. amarrar; *(to fetter)* ligar, atar II. s. MARÍT. eslinga; *(pair of animals)* pareja (de caballos o bueyes).
span·drel *o* **span·dril** (spăn'drəl) s. ARQ. enjuta.
span·gle (spăng'gəl) I. s. lentejuela II. tr. **-gled, -gling** adornar con lentejuelas —intr. brillar.
Span·iard (spăn'yərd) s. español *m.*
span·iel (spăn'yəl) s. ZOOL. perro de aguas; *(person)* adulador *m,* persona servil.
Span·ish (spăn'ĭsh) I. adj. español II. s. *(inhabitant)* español; *(language)* español, castellano ♦ **the S.** los españoles.
Spanish America s. Hispanoamérica.
Span·ish-A·mer·i·can (spăn'ĭsh-ə-mĕr'ĭ-kən) adj. & s. hispanoamericano.
Spanish Armada s. HIST. Armada Invencible.
Spanish Main s. HIST., GEOG. *(coast)* costa norte de América del Sur; *(Caribbean)* Caribe *m.*
Span·ish-speak·ing (spăn'ĭsh-spē'kĭng) adj. hispanoparlante, hispanohablante.
spank (spăngk) I. tr. dar una zurra a, zurrar —intr. ir de prisa II. s. zurra.
spank·ing (spăng'kĭng) I. adj. FAM. *(remarkable)* fenomenal; *(brisk)* fuerte; *(fresh)* fresco II. adv. extraordinariamente III. s. zurra, nalgada.
span·ner (spăn'ər) s. G.B. llave inglesa.
spar¹ (spär) I. s. MARÍT. palo; AVIA. larguero II. tr. **sparred, spar·ring** MARÍT. poner palos a; AVIA. poner largueros a.
spar² (spär) I. intr. **sparred, spar·ring** *(in boxing)* entrenarse; *(to dispute)* discutir; *(cocks)* pelear con espolones II. s. *(in boxing)* combate de entrenamiento *m;* *(cock fight)* pelea con espolones.
spar³ (spär) s. MIN. espato.
spare (spâr) I. tr. **spared, spar·ing** *(to be sparing with)* escatimar *<to s. expenses* escatimar gastos>; *(to conserve)* reservar (fuerzas, energías); *(to avoid)* evitar *<they spared him the trouble* le evitaron la molestia de hacerlo>; *(not to destroy)* perdonar *<the fire spared nothing* el incendio no perdonó nada>; *(to save somebody)* salvar; *(to save something)* ahorrar; *(to do without)* prescindir de *<we can't s. him* no podemos prescindir de él>; *(to afford)* dar, dedicar *<I can't s. the time* no puedo dedicar el tiempo>; *(to dispose)* disponer de, tener ♦ **and to s.** más que suficiente, de sobra • **to s.** de sobra *<we have two bottles to s.* tenemos dos botellas de sobra> • **to s. oneself** cuidarse, ahorrarse trabajos • **to s. someone's feelings** no herir los sentimientos de alguien —intr. *(to be frugal)* ser frugal; *(to be merciful)* tener piedad II. adj. **spar·er, spar·est** *(part)* de repuesto, de recambio; *(extra)* sobrante, de sobra *<s. cash* dinero sobrante>; *(unoccupied)* libre *<I'll do that in my s. time* lo haré en mis ratos libres>; *(mean)* mezquino; *(frugal)* parco (comida); *(thin)* delgado, enjuto ♦ **s. room** cuarto en desuso III. s. *(replacement)* pieza de recambio, repuesto.

ã rey / ä año / b boca / ch chico / d dar / ĕ el / ē mil / g gato / h joya / hw juez / ī aire / k casa / kw cuan /

spare·ribs (spâr′rĭbz′) s.pl. CUL. costillas de cerdo.
spar·ing (spâr′ĭng) adj. *(frugal)* frugal, económico; *(scarce)* escaso, parco; *(lenient)* indulgente, tolerante.
spar·ing·ly (spâr′ĭng-lē) adv. *(frugally)* frugalmente; *(scarcely)* escasamente.
spark¹ (spärk) **I.** s. chispa ♦ **bright s.** FIG., FAM. tipo muy listo • **sparks** FAM. telegrafista • **to give off sparks** echar chispas **II.** intr. echar chispas, chispear —tr. activar, provocar ♦ **to s. off** FIG. causar, provocar.
spark² (spärk) **I.** s. *(dandy)* petimetre m, pisaverde m; *(gallant)* galán m; *(lover)* enamorado **II.** tr. & intr. galantear.
sparking plug s. G.B. var. de **sparkplug**.
spar·kle (spär′kəl) **I.** intr. **-kled, -kling** *(to give off sparks)* chispear, echar chispas; *(to glitter)* centellear; *(to effervesce)* burbujear; FIG. *(to excel)* brillar (en algo) **II.** s. *(glitter)* centelleo, destello; *(vivacity)* vivacidad f, viveza; *(effervescence)* burbujeo.
spar·kler (spär′klər) s. *(firework)* cohete chispero; FAM. *(diamond)* diamante m.
sparkling wine s. vino espumoso.
spark·plug (spärk′plŭg′) s. AUTO. bujía; FAM. *(person)* persona emprendedora, persona con iniciativa.
spark·y (spär′kē) adj. **-i·er, -i·est** animado.
spar·row (spăr′ō) s. ORNIT. gorrión m.
sparrow hawk s. ORNIT. gavilán m.
sparse (spärs) adj. **spars·er, spars·est** disperso, infrecuente.
Spar·ta (spär′tə) s. Esparta.
Spar·tan (spär′tn) adj. & s. espartano.
spasm (spăz′əm) s. *(contraction)* espasmo; *(sudden attack)* arrebato (indignación).
spas·mod·ic (spăz-mŏd′ĭk) adj. espasmódico.
spas·tic (spăs′tĭk) adj. & s. espástico.
spat¹ (spăt) un pret. y part. p. de **spit¹**.
spat² (spăt) s. polaina ♦ **spats** polainas.
spat³ (spăt) **I.** s. *(quarrel)* riña, pelea; FAM. *(slap)* bofetada **II.** intr. **spat·ted, spat·ting** *(to quarrel)* reñir, pelear; *(to slap)* abofetear —tr. FAM. abofetear.
spate (spāt) s. *(outpouring)* torrente m; G.B. *(flood)* crecida, avenida.
spa·tial (spā′shəl) adj. espacial.
spat·ter (spăt′ər) **I.** tr. *(to splash)* salpicar, rociar; *(to soil)* manchar; FIG. *(to defame)* manchar —intr. salpicar **II.** s. salpicadura.
spat·u·la (spăch′ə-lə) s. espátula.
spav·in (spăv′ĭn) s. VET. esparaván m.
spawn (spôn) **I.** s. *(of fish)* freza, hueva; *(of a frog)* huevos; *(of mushroom)* micelio; FIG. *(outcome)* resultado; *(offspring)* engendro **II.** intr. *(fishes)* desovar, frezar; FIG. *(to produce offspring)* reproducirse, multiplicarse —tr. *(fishes)* depositar huevas; FIG. *(to engender)* engendrar, producir <*the tyranny spawned revolt* la tiranía engendró la rebelión>.
spawn·ing (spô′nĭng) s. freza, desove m.
spay (spā) tr. VET. quitar los ovarios.
speak (spēk) intr. **spoke** (spōk), **spo·ken** (spō′kən), **speak·ing** *(to talk)* hablar; *(to express oneself)* expresarse; *(in assembly)* tomar la palabra, intervenir; *(on good terms)* hablarse, tener buenas relaciones; *(to convey a message)* decir, expresar <*the facts s. more than words* los hechos dicen más que las palabras>; *(to produce a sound)* sonar, oírse ♦ **generally speaking** hablando en general • **roughly speaking** aproximadamente • **so to s.** por así decirlo • **to s. of** hablar de, mencionar <*there is nothing to s. of* no hay nada que mencionar> • **to s. out** hablar claro • **to s. to the point** ir al grano, dejarse de rodeos • **to s. up** hablar más fuerte —tr. *(to tell)* decir <*I s. the truth* digo la verdad>; *(a language)* hablar <*do you s. German?* ¿hablas alemán?>; FIG. *(to reveal)* revelar, expresar; MARÍT. comunicar con ♦ **to s. for** *(to recommend)* recomendar, hablar en favor de; *(on behalf of)* hablar en nombre de • **to s. for itself** hablar por sí mismo, ser evidente • **to s. one's mind** decir uno lo que piensa, hablar con franqueza • **to s. volumes for** decir muchísimo de • **to s. well (ill) of** hablar bien (mal) de.

speak·eas·y (spēk′ē′zē) s. [pl. **-ies**] taberna clandestina.
speak·er (spē′kər) s. *(person who speaks)* persona que habla; *(spokesperson)* portavoz m, vocero; *(orator)* orador m; *(lecturer)* conferenciante mf, conferencista mf; *(loudspeaker)* altoparlante m, altavoz m; POL. presidente de la asamblea legislativa m.
speak·er·ship (spē′kər-shĭp′) s. POL. presidencia de una asamblea legislativa.
speak·ing (spē′kĭng) adj. *(eloquent)* elocuente; *(striking)* fiel, vivo; *(who is speaking)* hablante ♦ **s. acquaintance** conocido • **to be on s. terms** hablarse.
spear (spîr) **I.** s. *(weapon)* lanza; *(harpoon)* arpón m; POÉT. *(person)* lancero; BOT. brizna **II.** tr. *(to pierce)* traspasar, atravesar (con una lanza); *(to harpoon)* arponear —intr. *(to stab)* clavar una lanza; BOT. brotar.
spear·head (spîr′hĕd′) **I.** s. *(point)* punta de lanza; *(leading forces)* vanguardia **II.** tr. encabezar.
spear·mint (spîr′mĭnt′) s. BOT. menta verde, hierbabuena.
spe·cial (spĕsh′əl) **I.** adj. *(exceptional)* especial <*a s. show* un espectáculo especial>; *(particular)* especial, particular <*nothing s.* nada de particular>; *(superior)* superior, de categoría; *(close)* íntimo (amigo); *(extra)* extraordinario (edición, vuelo) **II.** s. *(train)* tren especial m; *(edition)* número extraordinario; COM. *(offer)* oferta especial; TELEV. programa extraordinario, programa especial.
special delivery s. entrega inmediata (de correo).
spe·cial·ist (spĕsh′ə-lĭst) s. especialista mf.
spe·ci·al·i·ty (spĕsh′ē-ăl′ĭ-tē) s. [pl. **-ties**] especialidad.
spe·cial·i·za·tion (spĕsh′ə-lĭ-zā′shən) s. especialización f.
spe·cial·ize (spĕsh′ə-līz′) intr. **-ized, -iz·ing** *(to train in a specific area)* especializarse; BIOL. diferenciarse —tr. *(to particularize)* especializar; BIOL. adaptar.
spe·cial·ty (spĕsh′əl-tē) s. [pl. **-ties**] especialidad f.
spe·cie (spē′shē, -sē) s. metálico, efectivo ♦ **in s.** en metálico.
spe·cies (spē′shēz, -sēz) s. [pl. **species**] BIOL., LÓG. especie f; RELIG. especies sacramentales.
spe·cif·ic (spĭ-sĭf′ĭk) **I.** adj. específico **II.** s. *(attribute)* cualidad específica; MED. específico.
spec·i·fi·ca·tion (spĕs′ə-fĭ-kā′shən) s. especificación f ♦ **specifications** descripción detallada.
specific gravity s. FÍS. peso específico.
spec·i·fy (spĕs′ə-fī′) tr. **-fied, -fy·ing** especificar.
spec·i·men (spĕs′ə-mən) s. *(sample)* muestra; BIOL. espécimen m.
spe·cious (spē′shəs) adj. especioso.
speck (spĕk) **I.** s. *(small spot)* mancha, mota; *(particle)* partícula **II.** tr. salpicar de manchas, motear.
speck·le (spĕk′əl) **I.** s. *(small spot)* mancha, mota; *(freckle)* peca **II.** tr. **-led, -ling** motear, salpicar de manchas.
speck·led (spĕk′əld) adj. *(spotted)* moteado, salpicado de manchas; *(freckled)* pecoso; *(motley)* diverso, variado.
specs (spĕks) s.pl. FAM. *(eyeglasses)* anteojos, gafas; *(specifications)* especificaciones f.
spec·ta·cle (spĕk′tə-kəl) s. espectáculo ♦ **spectacles** gafas, lentes ♦ **to make a s. of oneself** ponerse en ridículo, dar el espectáculo.
spec·tac·u·lar (spĕk-tăk′yə-lər) **I.** adj. espectacular, grandioso **II.** s. TEAT. espectáculo grandioso.
spec·ta·tor (spĕk′tā′tər) s. espectador m.
spec·ter (spĕk′tər) s. espectro.
spec·tra (spĕk′trə) pl. de **spectrum**.
spec·tral (spĕk′trəl) adj. espectral.
spec·tro·gram (spĕk′trə-grăm′) s. espectrograma m.
spec·tro·graph (spĕk′trə-grăf′) s. espectrógrafo.
spec·trom·e·ter (spĕk-trŏm′ĭ-tər) s. FÍS. espectrómetro.
spec·tro·scope (spĕk′trə-skōp′) s. OPT. espectroscopio.
spec·tros·co·py (spĕk-trŏs′kə-pē) s. FÍS. espectroscopia.
spec·u·late (spĕk′yə-lāt′) intr. **-lat·ed, -lat·ing** especular.
spec·u·la·tion (spĕk′yə-lā′shən) s. especulación f.
spec·u·la·tive (spĕk′yə-lə-tĭv, -lā′-) adj. especulativo.
spec·u·la·tor (spĕk′yə-lā′tər) s. especulador m.
spec·u·lum (spĕk′yə-ləm) s. [pl. **-la** (-lə) o **-lums**] ÓPT. espejo; CIR. espéculo; ZOOL. espéculo, espejo.
sped (spĕd) un pret. y part. p. de **speed**.
speech (spēch) s. *(oral communication)* habla; *(pronunci-*

---

ation) pronunciación *f* <*he has a s. impediment* tiene un defecto de pronunciación>; *(conversation)* conversación *f*; *(address)* conferencia, discurso <*closing s.* discurso de clausura>; *(language)* lenguaje *m*; *(dialect)* habla <*regional s.* habla regional>; MÚS. sonoridad *f*; GRAM. oración *f* <*direct s.* oración directa> ♦ **figure of s.** tropo, figura • **free s.** libertad de expresión • **to deliver** *o* **make a s.** pronunciar un discurso • **to lose (recover) one's s.** perder (recobrar) el habla.

speech·i·fy (spē'chə-fī') intr. **-fied, -fy·ing** perorar.

speech·less (spēch'lĭs) adj. mudo, sin habla ♦ **to be** *o* **be left s.** quedarse mudo.

speech·mak·er (spēch'mā'kər) s. orador *m*.

speed (spēd) I. s. *(velocity)* velocidad *f*; TEC. *(transmission gear)* velocidad *f* <*a five-speed gearbox* una caja de cambios de cinco velocidades>; JER. *(drug)* metanfetamina ♦ **at full** *o* **top s.** a toda velocidad • **to make s.** llevar velocidad • **to pick up s.** coger velocidad, acelerar • **to put on s.** acelerar II. tr. **sped** (spēd) *o* **speed·ed, speed·ing** *(to accelerate)* acelerar (vehículo, producción); *(a motor vehicle)* conducir velozmente ♦ **to s. up** *(to accelerate)* acelerar; *(to hasten)* dar prisa a; *(to expedite)* acelerar, activar —intr. *(to go rapidly)* ir de prisa, ir corriendo; *(to hurry)* apresurarse; *(to drive fast)* conducir con exceso de velocidad • **to s. along** ir a gran velocidad • **to s. up** acelerar.

speed·boat (spēd'bōt') s. lancha motora.

speed·er (spē'dər) s. automovilista que va a gran velocidad *mf*.

speed·ing (spē'dĭng) I. adj. veloz, rápido II. s. AUTO. exceso de velocidad.

speed limit s. límite de velocidad *m*, velocidad máxima permitida.

speed·om·e·ter (spĭ-dŏm'ĭ-tər) s. *(speed indicator)* velocímetro, indicador de velocidad *m*; *(odometer)* odómetro.

speed·ster (spēd'stər) s. *(speeder)* automovilista que va a gran velocidad *mf*; *(car)* automóvil rápido.

speed·up (spēd'ŭp') s. ECON., COM. aumento de productividad (sin aumento de salarios o personal).

speed·way (spēd'wā') s. AUTO. *(racing course)* pista de carreras; *(expressway)* autopista.

speed·y (spē'dē) adj. **-i·er, -i·est** *(rapid)* rápido, veloz; *(prompt)* pronto.

spe·le·ol·o·gy (spē'lē-ŏl'ə-jē) s. espeleología.

spell¹ (spěl) tr. **spelled** *o* **spelt** (spělt), **spell·ing** *(to name letter by letter)* deletrear; *(to write)* escribir <*how do you s. his name?* ¿cómo se escribe su nombre?>; *(to mean)* significar <*it spells ruin* significa la ruina> ♦ **to s. out** *(letter by letter)* deletrear; *(to explain)* explicar —intr. escribir.

spell² (spěl) s. *(of an evil spirit)* sortilegio, maleficio; *(fascination)* fascinación *f*, encanto ♦ **to be under a s.** estar hechizado • **to cast** *o* **to put a s. on somebody** hechizar a alguien.

spell³ (spěl) I. s. *(of time)* temporada; *(of work)* turno; FAM. *(of weather)* racha, ola <*a cold s.* una racha de frío>; *(of bad temper)* acceso; *(of illness)* ataque *m* II. intr. tomarse un descanso —tr. *(to relieve)* relevar, reemplazar; *(to allow to rest)* dejar descansar.

spell·bind·ing (spěl'bīnd'-ĭng) adj. hechizante, cautivador.

spell·bound (spěl'bound') adj. *(fascinated)* fascinado; *(entranced)* hechizado.

spell·er (spěl'ər) s. *(person)* deletreador *m*; *(book)* abecedario, manual de ortografía *m* ♦ **to be a good (bad) s.** tener buena (mala) ortografía.

spell·ing (spěl'ĭng) s. *(orthography)* ortografía; *(action)* deletreo.

spelt¹ (spělt) s. BOT. espelta, escanda.

spelt² (spělt) un pret. y part. p. de **spell¹**.

spe·lunk·er (spĭ-lŭng'kər, spē'lŭng'-) s. espeleólogo (explorador y estudioso de cavernas).

spend (spěnd) tr. **spent** (spěnt), **spend·ing** *(money)* gastar; *(time)* pasar, dedicar; *(force, anger)* agotar, consumir; *(to use)* emplear, usar —intr. gastar dinero.

spend·a·ble (spěn'də-bəl) adj. gastable.

spend·er (spěn'dər) s. gastador *m*, derrochador *m*.

spend·ing (spěn'dĭng) I. s. gasto II. adj. para gastar.

spending money s. dinero para gastos menudos.

spend·thrift (spěnd'thrĭft') s. & adj. derrochador *m*, manirroto.

spent (spěnt) I. pret. y part. p. de **spend** II. adj. *(consumed)* gastado; *(passed)* acabado, terminado; *(exhausted)* agotado.

sperm¹ (spûrm) s. [pl. **sperm** *o* **sperms**] BIOL. esperma, semen *m*.

sperm² (spûrm) s. espermaceti *m*, esperma de ballena.

sper·ma·ce·ti (spûr'mə-sē'tē, -sět'ē) s. esperma de ballena.

sper·mat·o·phyte (spər-măt'ə-fīt') s. BOT. espermatofita.

sper·mat·o·zo·on (spər-măt'ə-zō'ŏn', spûr'mə-tə-) s. [pl. **-zo·a** (-zō'ə)] BIOL. espermatozoo, espermatozoide *m*.

sperm oil s. aceite de ballena *m*.

sperm whale s. ZOOL. cachalote *m*.

spew (spyoō) I. tr. & intr. *(to vomit)* vomitar; *(to eject)* arrojar II. s. vómito.

sphere (sfîr) s. GEOM. esfera; FIG. *(range)* esfera <*s. of influence* esfera de influencia>; ASTRON. planeta, astro ♦ **s. of activity** esfera de actividad.

spher·i·cal (sfîr'ĭ-kəl, sfěr'-) *o* **spher·ic** (sfîr'ĭk, sfěr'-) adj. esférico.

sphe·roid (sfîr'oid', sfěr'-) s. GEOM. esferoide *m*.

sphinc·ter (sfĭngk'tər) s. ANAT., ZOOL. esfínter *m*.

sphinx (sfĭngks) s. esfinge *f*.

spic (spĭk) s. DESPEC. persona de habla española.

spic-and-span (spĭk'ən-spăn') adj. var. de **spick-and-span**.

spi·cate (spī'kāt') adj. espigado.

spice (spīs) I. s. *(seasoning)* especia; FIG. *(something adding zest)* sabor *m*, interés *m*; *(perfume)* aroma, fragancia II. tr. **spiced, spic·ing** *(to season)* sazonar, condimentar; FIG. *(to add zest to)* sazonar, salpimentar.

spic·i·ness (spī'sē-nĭs) s. *(aroma)* sabor *m*, picante *m*; *(piquancy)* picante.

spick (spĭk) s. var. de **spic**.

spick-and-span (spĭk'ən-spăn') adj. *(spotless)* impecable; *(brand-new)* flamante.

spic·ule (spĭk'yoōl) s. espícula.

spic·y (spī'sē) adj. **-i·er, -i·est** *(piquant)* picante; FIG. *(risqué)* picante.

spi·der (spī'dər) s. ZOOL. araña; MEC., TEC. araña; *(trivet)* trébede *f*.

spider monkey s. ZOOL. mono araña.

spi·der·y (spī'də-rē) adj. *(like a spider)* que tiene forma de araña; *(like a spider's web)* que tiene forma de telaraña; *(infested with spiders)* lleno de telarañas ♦ **s. handwriting** patas de mosca, garabatos • **s. legs** patas de alambre.

spied (spīd) pret. y part. p. de **spy**.

spiel (spēl) JER. I. s. rollo, perorata II. intr. & tr. perorar.

spif·fy (spĭf'ē) adj. **-fi·er, -fi·est** JER. estupendo.

spig·ot (spĭg'ət) s. *(faucet)* grifo; *(barrel tap)* espita; *(plug)* espiche *m*.

spike¹ (spīk) I. s. *(sharp-pointed piece)* punta, púa; *(nail)* clavo, pincho; *(pointed rod)* estaca ♦ **spikes** *(athletic shoes)* zapatillas con clavos; *(for women)* zapatos de tacones altos y puntiagudos II. tr. **spiked, spik·ing** *(to impale)* empalar, perforar; *(to nail)* clavar; FIG. *(to block)* impedir, frustrar (intenciones, planes); *(to add liquor to)* echar licor a; MIL. *(a gun)* clavar.

spike² (spīk) s. *(ear of grain)* espiga.

spike·nard (spīk'närd') s. BOT. nardo.

spik·y (spī'kē) adj. **-i·er, -i·est** puntiagudo, erizado.

spill¹ (spĭl) I. tr. **spilled** *o* **spilt** (spĭlt), **spill·ing** *(liquid)* derramar, verter <*I spilled the soup on the table* he derramado la sopa en la mesa>; *(a container)* volcar; *(to cause to fall)* hacer caer (un caballo a su jinete); *(to divulge)* revelar ♦ **to s. the beans** FIG., FAM. revelar el secreto, descubrir el pastel • **to s. the blood of** derramar la sangre de —intr. *(liquid)* derramarse, verterse; *(to fall)* caerse ♦ **to s. out** salir, desbordar • **to s. over** salirse II. s. *(of liquid)* derrame *m*, derramamiento; *(fall)* caída ♦ **to have** *o* **take a s.** sufrir una caída, caerse.

spill² (spĭl) s. *(for fire)* pajuela; *(spile)* espita.

spill·age (spĭl'ĭj) s. *(act)* derramamiento; *(amount)* derrame *m*.

spill·way (spĭl'wā') s. derramadero, aliviadero.

spilt (spĭlt) un pret. y part. p. de **spill¹**.

spin (spĭn) **I.** tr. **spun** (spŭn), **spin·ning** *(fibers, thread)* hilar; *(web)* tejer; *(to twirl)* hacer girar, dar vueltas a; FIG. *(to relate)* contar <*to s. tales for the children* contar cuentos a los niños>; DEP. *(a ball)* dar efecto a ♦ **to s. a coin** echar a cara o cruz ♦ **to s. a yarn** FIG. contar algo increíble • **to s. off** derivar • **to s. out** alargar, prolongar —intr. *(to make a thread)* hilar; *(a spider)* tejer la tela; *(to whirl)* girar, dar vueltas; FIG. *(to reel)* tener vértigo; *(wheels)* patinar; *(plane)* entrar o descender en barrena ♦ **my head was spinning** me daba vueltas la cabeza • **to s. along** ir volando **II.** s. *(whirling motion)* giro, vuelta; *(mental confusion)* confusión *f*, aturdimiento; FAM. *(short drive)* vuelta, paseo (en coche); ELECTRÓN. espín *m*, spin *m* ♦ **to be in a s.** estar aturdido • **to go for a s.** dar una vueltecita (en coche) • **to go into a s.** AVIA. entrar en barrena; FIG. *(to become upset)* aturdirse.
spin·ach (spĭn'ĭch) s. BOT. espinaca.
spi·nal (spī'nəl) **I.** adj. espinal, vertebral **II.** s. MED. anestesia por conducto vertebral.
spinal column s. espina dorsal, columna vertebral.
spinal cord s. médula espinal.
spinal meningitis s. MED. meningitis.
spin·dle (spĭn'dl) **I.** s. TEJ. huso; MEC. eje *m*; *(of a lathe)* mandril *m* **II.** tr. **-dled, -dling** atravesar, perforar (con la punta de una aguja).
spin·dly (spĭnd'lē) adj. **-dli·er, -dli·est** *(elongated)* espigado; FAM. *(thin and weakly)* larguirucho.
spin·drift (spĭn'drĭft') s. rocío del mar.
spine (spīn) s. ANAT. espina dorsal; *(bookbinding)* lomo; FIG. *(will power)* temple *m*, espíritu *m*; ZOOL., BOT. espina, púa.
spine·less (spīn'lĭs) adj. *(invertebrate)* invertebrado; *(without spines)* sin espinas, sin púas; FIG. *(without will power)* blando, débil.
spin·et (spĭn'ĭt) s. MÚS. espineta.
spin·na·ker (spĭn'ə-kər) s. MARÍT. velón *m*, vela balón.
spin·ner (spĭn'ər) s. *(person)* hilador *m*, hilandero; *(machine)* hiladora, máquina de hilar; *(angler's lure)* cebo artificial de cuchara; *(device for a board game)* aguja giratoria; AVIA. ojiva, cono (de la hélice).
spin·ner·et (spĭn'ə-rĕt') s. ENTOM., TEC. hilera.
spin·ning (spĭn'ĭng) s. hilado.
spinning wheel s. rueca.
spin·off (spĭn'ôf') s. subproducto, derivado.
spi·nose (spī'nōs') adj. espinoso.
spin·ster (spĭn'stər) s. *(old maid)* solterona; *(woman who spins)* hilandera.
spin·y (spī'nē) adj. **-i·er, -i·est** espinoso.
spi·ral (spī'rəl) **I.** s. *(form)* espiral *f*; FIG. *(trend)* espiral <*the inflationary s.* la espiral inflacionista> **II.** adj. espiral ♦ **s. staircase** escalera de caracol **III.** intr. moverse en espiral, dar vueltas ♦ **to s. down (up)** descender (ascender) en espiral.
spiral galaxy s. ASTRON. galaxia espiral.
spire¹ (spīr) **I.** s. *(pinnacle)* cúspide *f*, cima; *(steeple)* aguja; BOT. brizna **II.** tr. & intr. **spired, spir·ing** rematar en punta.
spire² (spīr) s. *(whorl)* vuelta, rosca (de una espiral).
spir·it (spĭr'ĭt) **I.** s. *(soul)* espíritu *m*, alma; *(ghost)* espíritu, fantasma *m*; *(person)* persona, ser *m*; *(essential nature)* espíritu, carácter *m*; *(mood)* temple *m*, humor *m*; *(vigor)* vigor *m*, vitalidad *f*; *(energy)* energía; *(courage)* valor *m*, ánimo; *(of a period)* espíritu <*the s. of the age* el espíritu de la época>; *(real sense)* espíritu <*the s. of the law* el espíritu de la ley>; QUÍM. *(alcohol)* alcohol *m* ♦ **in a friendly s.** de manera amistosa • **in s.** para sus adentros • **spirits** *(mood)* humor; *(alcohol)* alcohol • **the S.** RELIG. el Espíritu Santo • **to be in high o good spirits** estar de buen humor, estar muy animado • **to be in poor o low spirits** estar desanimado • **to keep up one's spirits** no perder el ánimo • **to raise someone's spirits** animar o levantar el ánimo a alguien **II.** tr. alentar, animar ♦ **to s. away o off** FIG. llevarse, hacer desaparecer.
spir·it·ed (spĭr'ĭ-tĭd) adj. *(animated)* animado; *(vigorous)* vigoroso, enérgico; *(vehement)* fogoso, brioso.
spir·it·ism (spĭr'ĭ-tĭz'əm) s. espiritismo.

spirit lamp s. lámpara de alcohol.
spir·it·less (spĭr'ĭt-lĭs) adj. desanimado.
spir·i·tu·al (spĭr'ĭ-chōo-əl) **I.** adj. *(relating to the spirit)* espiritual; *(supernatural)* sobrenatural; *(religious)* religioso **II.** s. MÚS. canción religiosa de los negros de EE. UU.
spir·i·tu·al·ism (spĭr'ĭ-chōo-ə-lĭz'əm) s. *(practice)* espiritismo; *(doctrine)* espiritualismo.
spir·i·tu·al·ist (spĭr'ĭ-chōo-ə-lĭst) s. espiritista *mf*; FILOS., RELIG. espiritualista *mf*.
spir·i·tu·al·is·tic (spĭr'ĭ-chōo-ə-lĭs'tĭk) adj. espiritista; FILOS., RELIG. espiritualista.
spir·i·tu·al·i·ty (spĭr'ĭ-chōo-ăl'ĭ-tē) s. [pl. **-ties**] espiritualidad *f* ♦ **spiritualities** RELIG. bienes eclesiásticos.
spir·i·tu·al·ize (spĭr'ĭ-chōo-ə-līz') tr. **-ized, -iz·ing** espiritualizar.
spir·i·tu·al·ly (spĭr'ĭ-chōo-ə-lē) adv. espiritualmente.
spi·ro·chete (spī'rə-kēt') s. BACT. espiroqueta.
spirt (spûrt) s. & v. G.B. var. de **spurt**.
spit¹ (spĭt) **I.** s. *(saliva)* saliva; *(act of expectorating)* escupitajo, salivazo; *(sprinkling rain)* rocío; ENTOM. espuma **II.** tr. **spat** (spăt) o **spit**, **spit·ting** *(to expectorate)* escupir; *(to eject)* escupir, arrojar —intr. *(to expectorate)* escupir; *(to express contempt)* despreciar; *(to make a sputtering noise)* chisporrotear; *(to rain)* gotear, chispear.
spit² (spĭt) **I.** s. *(pointed rod)* espetón *m*; GEOG. punta; *(of sand)* banco *m* **II.** tr. **spit·ted, spit·ting** espetar, ensartar.
spit curl s. bucle pegado a la frente o a la mejilla *m*.
spite (spīt) **I.** s. rencor *m*, ojeriza ♦ **in s. of** a pesar de, no obstante • **to do something out of s.** hacer algo por despecho **II.** tr. **spit·ed, spit·ing** *(to show ill toward)* mostrar rencor; *(to annoy)* fastidiar, molestar.
spite·ful (spīt'fəl) adj. rencoroso.
spit·fire (spĭt'fīr') s. persona colérica.
spitting image s. vivo retrato.
spit·tle (spĭt'l) s. *(saliva)* saliva; ENTOM. espuma.
spit·toon (spĭ-tōon') s. escupidera.
splash (splăsh) **I.** tr. *(to spatter)* salpicar <*he splashed me with soup* me salpicó de sopa>; *(to swash)* chapotear; *(to spray)* rociar; *(to scatter)* salpicar —intr. *(to spatter)* salpicar; *(to move through liquid)* ir chapoteando ♦ **to s. down** amerizar **II.** s. *(flying mass of liquid)* salpicadura; *(sound)* chapoteo; *(of drink)* chorro <*a wine with a s. of soda* un vino con un chorro de soda>; FIG. *(of light, color)* mancha ♦ **to make a s.** causar sensación, impresionar.
splash·down (splăsh'doun') s. ASTRONÁUT. amerizaje *m*.
splash·ing (splăsh'ĭng) s. salpicadura.
splash·y (splăsh'ē) adj. **-i·er, -i·est** *(muddy)* fangoso; *(covered with splashes)* salpicado; FAM. *(showy)* llamativo.
splat (splăt) s. *(of a chair)* listón del espaldar *m*; *(sound)* ruido sordo.
splat·ter (splăt'ər) **I.** tr. & intr. salpicar, aplastar(se) **II.** s. salpicadura.
splay (splā) **I.** adj. *(spread out)* extendido; *(clumsy)* torpe, pesado **II.** s. *(expansion)* extensión *f*; ARQ. alféizar *m*, derrame *m* **III.** tr. *(to spread out)* extender; *(to bevel)* achaflanar; VET. dislocar —intr. *(to be spread out)* extenderse, ensancharse; *(to slant)* sesgarse, inclinarse.
splay·foot (splā'fōot') s. MED. pie plano y torcido.
spleen (splēn) s. ANAT., ZOOL. bazo; *(whim)* capricho, antojo; *(ill temper)* mal humor; FIG., ANT. *(melancholy)* melancolía.
splen·dent (splĕn'dənt) adj. brillante.
splen·did (splĕn'dĭd) adj. espléndido.
splen·dor (splĕn'dər) s. esplendor *m*.
splen·dor·ous (splĕn'dər-əs) o **splen·drous** (-drəs) adj. esplendoroso.
splice (splīs) **I.** tr. **spliced, splic·ing** *(to join)* empalmar; FAM. *(to unite)* unir, casar **II.** s. empalme *m*.
splic·er (splī'sər) s. encoladora.
spline (splīn) s. *(flexible piece)* tira; *(projection)* lengüeta; *(slot)* ranura; *(slat)* tablilla.
splint (splĭnt) **I.** s. *(splinter)* astilla; *(wood strip)* varilla; MED. tablilla; VET. sobrecaña **II.** tr. MED. entablillar.
splin·ter (splĭn'tər) **I.** s. *(of wood)* astilla; *(of bone)* esquirla; *(fragment)* fragmento; *(group)* grupo disidente **II.** tr. & intr. astillar.

splin·ter·y (splĭn'tə-rē) adj. astilloso.

split (splĭt) **I.** tr. **split, split·ting** *(to divide)* partir, dividir; *(to crack)* hender, agrietar; *(to rend)* desgarrar, rajar; *(to share)* repartir, compartir <*we s. the meal with you* compartimos la comida con vosotros>; FIG. *(to disunite)* dividir; QUÍM. descomponer; FÍS. desintegrar ♦ **to s. hairs** FIG. hilar muy fino • **to s. off** separar • **to s. one's sides laughing** FIG. partirse de risa • **to s. up** *(to divide)* dividir, repartir; *(to separate)* separar; *(friends, lovers)* romper las relaciones, separar —intr. *(piece of wood)* partirse; *(to crack)* henderse, agrietarse; *(to tear)* desgarrarse, rajarse; *(leather)* reventarse; *(wall)* resquebrajarse, cuartearse; *(boat)* estrellarse; FIG. *(group of persons)* separarse, fraccionarse; JER. *(to leave)* irse, largarse <*let's s.* larguémonos> ♦ **my head is splitting** tengo un terrible dolor de cabeza • **to s. off** separarse • **to s. up** separarse **II.** s. *(crack)* grieta, hendidura; *(tear)* raja, desgarrón m; *(in a group)* ruptura, escisión f; *(half bottle)* media botella ♦ **splits** despatarrada **III.** adj. *(wood)* partido; *(cracked)* agrietado; *(torn)* desgarrado; *(shoe)* reventado; *(group of persons)* separado, dividido; *(party)* escindido.

split-lev·el (splĭt'lĕv'əl) adj. de pisos construidos a desnivel.

split personality s. desdoblamiento de la personalidad.

split second s. fracción de segundo f.

split shift s. jornada de turnos (en el trabajo).

split·ter (splĭt'ər) s. ♦ **atom s.** ciclotrón m.

split·ting (splĭt'ĭng) adj. *(acute)* agudo; *(piercing)* penetrante ♦ **s. headache** dolor de cabeza fuertísimo.

splotch (splŏch) **I.** s. manchón m, borrón m **II.** tr. manchar.

splotch·y (splŏch'ē) adj. **-i·er, -i·est** manchado.

splurge (splûrj) **I.** intr. **splurged, splurg·ing** *(to indulge)* derrochar; *(to be ostentatious)* fachendear —tr. derrochar **II.** s. *(display)* fachenda; *(expenditure)* derroche m.

splut·ter (splŭt'ər) **I.** intr. & tr. farfullar **II.** s. farfulla.

spoil (spoil) **I.** tr. **spoiled** o **spoilt** (spoilt), **spoil·ing** *(to damage)* estropear, echar a perder; *(to impair)* dañar, deteriorar; *(to make ugly)* afear, estropear <*this makeup spoils her face* este maquillaje le afea la cara>; *(child)* mimar; *(to plunder)* saquear; *(to despoil)* despojar ♦ **to s. someone's fun** estropearle a alguien la fiesta —intr. estropearse, echarse a perder <*if you leave it here, it will s.* si lo dejas aquí, se estropeará> ♦ **to be spoiling for** tener ganas de **II.** s. *(prey)* presa; *(refuse material)* escombros ♦ **spoils** *(of war)* botín; *(of political party)* prebendas.

spoil·age (spoi'lĭj) s. *(result)* desechos, desperdicios; *(process)* putrefacción f.

spoil·er (spoi'lər) s. *(pillager)* saqueador m; AER. freno aerodinámico; POL. candidato que puede causar el triunfo o la derrota de otros.

spoil·sport (spoil'spôrt') s. aguafiestas mf.

spoils system s. acaparamiento de los cargos públicos por el partido triunfador.

spoilt (spoilt) un pret. y part p. de **spoil**.

spoke¹ (spōk) s. *(brace)* radio (de una rueda); *(rung)* peldaño; MARÍT. cabilla (del timón) **II.** tr. **spoked, spok·ing** enrayar.

spoke² (spōk) pret. de **speak**.

spo·ken (spō'kən) **I.** part. p. de **speak II.** adj. hablado.

spokes·man (spōks'mən) s. [pl. **-men**] portavoz m, vocero.

spokes·per·son (spōks'pûr'sən) s. vocero, portavoz mf.

spokes·wom·an (spōks'wŏŏm'ən) s. [pl. **-wom·en** (-wĭm'ĭn)] portavoz f.

spo·li·a·tion (spō'lē-ā'shən) s. *(pillage)* saqueo; *(alteration)* alteración de documentos f.

sponge (spŭnj) **I.** s. *(for domestic use)* esponja; *(cake)* bizcocho; FIG. *(sponger)* gorrón; ZOOL. esponja ♦ **to throw** o **toss in the s.** FAM. darse por vencido, abandonar la lucha **II.** tr. **sponged, spong·ing** *(to clean with a sponge)* limpiar con esponja; FIG. *(to obtain free)* conseguir de gorra, gorronear ♦ **to s. up** absorber —intr. *(to fish)* pescar esponjas; FIG. *(to borrow money)* sablear, dar sablazos ♦ **to s. off of someone** FIG. vivir a costa de alguien.

sponge bath s. lavado con paño o esponja sin inmersión.

sponge cake s. bizcocho.

spong·er (spŭn'jər) s. *(gatherer)* pescador de esponjas m; FIG. *(parasite)* gorrón m.

sponge rubber s. goma esponjosa.

spong·y (spŭn'jē) adj. **-i·er, -i·est** esponjoso.

spon·sor (spŏn'sər) **I.** s. *(backer)* patrocinador m; *(warrantor)* fiador m, garante m; *(godparent)* padrino, madrina; *(advertiser)* patrocinador m **II.** tr. *(to act as a sponsor)* patrocinar; *(to warrant)* garantizar, fiar; *(as godparent)* apadrinar, amadrinar.

spon·sor·ship (spŏn'sər-shĭp') s. patrocinio, fianza ♦ **under the s. of** patrocinado por, bajo los auspicios de.

spon·ta·ne·i·ty (spŏn'tə-nē'ĭ-tē, -nā'-) s. [pl. **-ties**] espontaneidad f.

spon·ta·ne·ous (spŏn-tā'nē-əs) adj. espontáneo.

spontaneous combustion s. combustión espontánea f.

spontaneous generation s. BIOL. abiogénesis f; generación espontánea.

spon·ta·ne·ous·ly (spŏn-tā'nē-əs-lē) adv. espontáneamente.

spoof (spŏŏf) **I.** s. *(nonsense)* tontería; *(hoax)* engaño; *(parody)* broma **II.** tr. *(to deceive)* engañar; *(to satirize)* bromear, satirizar.

spook (spŏŏk) FAM. **I.** s. *(specter)* espectro; *(spy)* espía mf **II.** tr. *(to haunt)* aparecer en; *(to scare)* asustar.

spook·y (spŏŏ'kē) adj. **-i·er, -i·est** FAM. *(ghostly)* fantasmal; *(eerie)* espectral; *(skittish)* asustadizo.

spool (spŏŏl) **I.** s. carrete m, bobina **II.** tr. encanillar, enrollar.

spoon (spŏŏn) **I.** s. *(utensil)* cuchara <*soup s.* cuchara sopera>; *(spoonful)* cucharada; DEP. *(in fishing)* cuchara; *(golf club)* spoon m, cuchara ♦ **to be born with a silver s. in one's mouth** FIG. criarse en buenos pañales **II.** tr. sacar con cuchara —intr. *(in fishing)* pescar con cuchara; FAM. *(to make love)* acariciarse, hacerse carantoñas.

spoon·e·rism (spŏŏ'nə-rĭz'əm) s. trastocamiento no intencionado de las sílabas de una o más palabras que resulta en una oración graciosa <*a well-boiled icicle* en lugar de *a well-oiled bicycle*>.

spoon-fed (spŏŏn'fĕd') adj. *(nourished with a spoon)* alimentado con cuchara; *(coddled)* mimado.

spoon·ful (spŏŏn'fŏŏl') s. [pl. **-fuls**] cucharada.

spoor (spŏŏr) **I.** s. rastro **II.** tr. rastrear —intr. seguir el rastro (de un animal).

spo·rad·ic (spə-răd'ĭk) o **spo·rad·i·cal** (-ĭ-kəl) adj. esporádico.

spore (spôr) **I.** s. espora **II.** intr. **spored, spor·ing** formar esporas.

spo·ro·phyte (spôr'ə-fīt') s. BOT. esporófito.

sport (spôrt) **I.** s. *(game)* deporte m; *(active pastime)* juego, diversión f; *(hunting)* caza; *(jest)* broma, burla; *(good loser)* buen perdedor; BIOL. mutación f ♦ **athletic sports** DEP. atletismo • **in s.** en broma • **to be a good s.** *(to be a gentleman)* portarse como un caballero; *(to be a good person)* ser buena persona, ser buen chico • **to make s. of** burlarse de **II.** intr. *(to play)* jugar, divertirse; *(to frolic)* juguetear; *(to joke)* bromear —tr. lucir <*she is sporting a new dress* luce un nuevo vestido> **III.** adj. de sport <*a s. shirt* una camisa de sport>.

sport·ing (spôr'tĭng) adj. *(sports-related)* deportivo; *(gambling-related)* jugador.

sporting chance s. buena posibilidad de éxito.

spor·tive (spôr'tĭv) adj. *(playful)* juguetón; *(sporting)* deportivo.

sports (spôrts) adj. deportivo, de sport <*s. jacket* chaqueta de sport>.

sports car s. AUTO. automóvil deportivo m.

sports·cast (spôrts'kăst') s. RAD., TELEV. programa deportivo.

sports·man (spôrts'mən) s. [pl. **-men**] *(participator)* deportista m; *(gentleman)* jugador que se conforma con las reglas m.

sports·man·ship (spôrts'mən-shĭp') s. deportividad f.

sports·wear (spôrts'wâr') s. ropa de sport.

sports·wom·an (spôrts'wŏŏm'ən) s. [pl. **-wom·en** (-wĭm'ĭn)] deportista f.

sports·writ·er (spôrts'rī'tər) s. cronista deportivo mf.

ã rey / ä año / b boca / ch chico / d dar / ĕ el / ē mil / g gato / h joya / hw juez / ī aire / k casa / kw cuan /

sport·y (spôr′tē) adj. -**i·er**, -**i·est** FAM. *(clothes)* de sport, casual; *(suitable for sport)* deportivo; *(carefree)* alegre.
spot (spŏt) I. s. *(place)* sitio, lugar *m* <*a pleasant s.* un lugar agradable>; *(stain)* mancha; *(fabric pattern)* lunar *m* <*a cloth with blue spots* un paño con lunares azules>; *(on the skin)* grano, espinilla; *(drop)* gota, gotita; *(commercial)* anuncio; FIG. *(on one's reputation)* mancha; FAM. *(spotlight)* proyector *m*, foco; G.B., FAM. *(small amount)* poco, poquito <*just a s., thanks* sólo un poquito, gracias> ♦ **beauty s.** lunar • **black s.** mancha (en la reputación) • **in a bad** *o* **tight s.** en apuros • **in spots** de vez en cuando • **night s.** sala de fiestas • **on the s.** *(immediately)* en el acto, inmediatamente; *(on the site)* allí mismo, en el lugar; *(in a pressed position)* en situación precaria • **tender** *o* **sore s.** FIG. punto débil, punto sensible • **to hit the s.** FAM. venirle muy bien a uno (esp. comida o bebida) • **to put someone on the s.** poner a uno en un aprieto • **to touch a sore s.** poner el dedo en la llaga II. tr. **spot·ted, spot·ting** *(to soil)* manchar; *(to speckle)* motear, salpicar <*the car spotted him with mud* el coche le salpicó de lodo>; *(to place)* emplazar, localizar; *(to detect)* detectar, notar; *(to recognize)* reconocer; *(to select)* elegir, escoger; DEP. *(to yield as a handicap)* dar como ventaja —intr. *(to become spotted)* mancharse; *(to make a stain)* manchar; MIL. observar el tiro III. adj. COM., FIN. *(paid immediately)* contante <*s. cash* dinero contante>; *(delivered immediately)* para entrega inmediata; RAD., TELEV. entre programas.
spot check s. inspección de control hecha al azar *f.*
spot-check (spŏt′chĕk′) tr. & intr. inspeccionar al azar.
spot·less (spŏt′lĭs) adj. *(clean)* inmaculado; *(irreproachable)* intachable (conducta).
spot·less·ness (spŏt′lĭs-nĭs) s. limpieza perfecta, falta absoluta de mancha.
spot·light (spŏt′līt′) I. s. *(beam of light)* foco; *(instrument)* foco, proyector *m*; FIG. *(center of attention)* centro de atención II. tr. -**light·ed** *o* -**lit** (-lĭt′), -**light·ing** *(to illuminate)* iluminar (con lámpara, foco); FIG. *(to focus attention on)* destacar.
spot price s. COM. precio actual en el mercado.
spot remover s. quitamanchas *m.*
spot·ted (spŏt′ĭd) adj. *(strained)* manchado; *(marked)* moteado.
spotted fever s. MED. *(typhus)* tifus *m*; *(meningitis)* meningitis cerebroespinal *f.*
spot·ter (spŏt′ər) s. MIL. *(person)* observador de tiro *m*; *(aircraft)* avión de observación *m.*
spot·ty (spŏt′ē) adj. -**ti·er**, -**ti·est** *(stained)* manchado; *(spotted)* moteado; *(not consistent)* irregular.
spou·sal (spou′zəl) I. adj. nupcial II. s. ♦ **spousals** desposorios.
spouse (spous, spouz) I. s. cónyuge *mf*, esposo II. tr. **spoused, spous·ing** ANT. desposar, casar.
spout (spout) I. intr. *(to gush)* chorrear; FAM. *(to speak)* perorar —tr. *(to gush)* echar, arrojar; *(to utter pompously)* soltar (tonterías); G.B., JER. *(to pawn)* empeñar (artículo) II. s. *(pouring end)* pico; *(tube)* caño; *(stream)* chorro; G.B., JER. *(pawn shop)* casa de empeños.
sprain (sprān) MED. I. s. torcedura II. tr. torcer (tobillo).
sprang (sprăng) pret. de **spring.**
sprawl (sprôl) I. intr. *(to sit)* repantigarse; *(to spread out)* extenderse —tr. extender II. s. *(posture)* postura desgarbada; *(disorderly growth)* extensión *f* ♦ **urban s.** urbanización desordenada.
spray¹ (sprā) I. s. *(of water)* rociada; *(atomizer)* pulverizador *m*, vaporizador *m*; MARÍT. espuma ♦ **s. paint** pintura para atomizador • **s. can** lata de atomizador II. tr. rociar —intr. vaporizarse.
spray² (sprā) s. *(bouquet)* ramo, ramillete *m.*
spray·er (sprā′ər) s. vaporizador *m*, pulverizador *m.*
spray gun s. pistola para pulverizar.
pray·ing (sprā′ĭng) s. pulverización *f.*
spread (sprĕd) I. tr. **spread, spread·ing** *(to stretch)* extender <*to s. the tablecloth* extender el mantel; *(to move further apart)* separar; *(to extend outward)* abrir (brazos, piernas); *(to apply)* extender (pintura); *(to cover with a layer)* untar <*to s. butter on bread* untar mantequilla en el

pan>; *(to propagate)* propagar <*to s. religion* propagar una religión>; *(to distribute)* sembrar (pánico, destrucción); *(to set)* poner <*to s. the table* poner la mesa>; *(to serve)* servir (la mesa) ♦ **to s. oneself thin** dedicarse a muchas actividades • **to s. out** esparcir, extender —intr. *(to expand)* esparcirse; *(to extend)* extenderse; *(to be distributed)* propagarse <*the disease s. rapidly* la enfermedad se propagó rápidamente>; *(to become known)* difundirse, propagarse (noticias, ideas); *(to move apart)* separarse; *(to be put on as a layer)* untarse (mantequilla, mermelada) ♦ **to s. out** *(to stretch)* extenderse; *(to develop)* desarrollarse; *(to get wider)* ensancharse II. s. *(diffusion)* difusión *f*, propagación (de enfermedad, ideas) *f*; *(expanse)* extensión (de terreno, zona) *f*; *(ranch)* rancho; *(range)* gama; *(bedspread)* colcha; *(tablecloth)* mantel *m*; *(food to be spread)* comida (para untar); FAM. *(meal)* comida (sobre la mesa); IMPR. *(facing pages)* página doble; *(story, advertisement)* artículo *o* anuncio a dos *o* más columnas; COM. *(difference)* diferencia (entre precios, cifras).
spread eagle s. figura de un águila con las alas extendidas.
spread·er (sprĕd′ər) s. *(spreading object)* untador (de manteca, grasa) *m*; *(farm implement)* esparcidora; *(separating device)* viga cepo, viga de separación.
spree (sprē) s. *(drinking bout)* borrachera; *(wild party)* parranda, jarana ♦ **to go on a shopping** *o* **a spending s.** hacer muchas compras.
sprig (sprĭg) I. s. BOT. *(twig)* ramito; *(brad)* puntilla, tachuela; *(immature person)* jovenzuelo II. tr. **sprigged, sprig·ging** *(to decorate)* adornar (con ramitos); *(to trim)* podar; *(to fasten)* clavar (con tachuelas).
spright (sprīt) s. var. de **sprite.**
spright·ly (sprīt′lē) I. adj. -**li·er**, -**li·est** vivo II. adv. con vivacidad.
spring (sprĭng) I. intr. **sprang** (sprăng) *o* **sprung** (sprŭng), **spring·ing** *(to jump)* saltar; *(to emerge)* brotar, salir; *(to arise)* surgir, derivarse; *(to warp)* alabearse; ARQ. *(arches, vaults)* arrancar ♦ **to s. back** volver a su posición original • **to s. forth** brotar • **to s. forward** saltar hacia adelante • **to s. open** abrirse de un golpe • **to s. shut** cerrarse de un golpe • **to s. to one's feet** levantarse de un salto • **to s. up** *(to gush)* surgir, brotar; *(building)* elevarse, levantarse; *(wind)* levantarse; *(to grow rapidly)* espigarse; *(to emerge)* surgir ♦ **to s. upon** abalanzarse sobre —tr. *(to put springs on)* poner muelles a; *(a trap)* hacer funcionar; *(to cause to come forth)* hacer salir *o* brotar; *(to jump over)* saltar <*the boy sprang the fence* el niño saltó la cerca>; *(to release)* soltar; *(to warp)* combar, torcer; JER. *(to free)* poner en libertad, soltar ♦ **to s. a leak** empezar a hacer agua • **to s. a surprise on someone** coger de sorpresa a alguien • **to s. at** abalanzarse *o* lanzarse sobre II. s. *(coil)* resorte *m*, muelle *m*; *(resilience)* elasticidad *f*; *(jump)* salto; *(fountain)* fuente *f*, manantial *m*; *(season)* primavera; *(source)* fuente, origen *m*; ARQ. arranque *m.*
spring·board (sprĭng′bôrd′) s. *(trampoline)* trampolín *m*; *(starting place)* punto de partida.
spring-clean·ing (sprĭng′klē′nĭng) s. limpieza general hecha en primavera.
spring fever s. desasosiego ocasionado por la llegada de la primavera.
spring lock s. cerradura de golpe.
spring tide s. MARÍT. *(tide)* marea viva, aguas vivas; FIG. *(flood)* torrente *m.*
spring·time (sprĭng′tīm′) s. primavera.
spring·y (sprĭng′ē) adj. -**i·er**, -**i·est** elástico.
sprin·kle (sprĭng′kəl) I. tr. -**kled**, -**kling** rociar —intr. *(to spray)* rociar; *(to drizzle)* lloviznar II. s. *(spraying)* rociada; *(drizzle)* llovizna; *(small amount)* pizca.
sprin·kler (sprĭng′klər) s. *(watering device)* regadera; *(fire extinguisher)* extintor *m.*
sprinkler system s. *(in agriculture)* sistema de aspersión *m*; *(fire precaution)* sistema de aspersión automática.
sprin·kling (sprĭng′klĭng) s. *(spray)* aspersión *f*; *(small amount)* pizca.
sprint (sprĭnt) DEP. I. s. sprint *m* II. intr. sprintar, esprintar.
sprint·er (sprĭn′tər) s. sprinter *m*; corredor de velocidad *m.*

---

sprit (sprīt) s. MARÍT. *(pole)* verga; *(bowsprit)* bauprés *m*.

sprite (sprīt) s. *(supernatural being)* duende *m*; *(specter)* espectro; ANT. *(soul)* alma.

sprock·et (sprŏk'ĭt) s. MEC. diente *m*.

sprocket wheel s. MEC. rueda catalina, rueda dentada.

sprout (sprout) I. intr. BOT. *(to grow)* brotar; *(to burgeon)* crecer rápidamente —tr. hacer crecer II. s. brote *m* ♦ **sprouts** coles de Bruselas.

spruce¹ (sprōōs) s. BOT. picea.

spruce² (sprōōs) I. adj. **spruc·er, spruc·est** *(neat)* ordenado; *(dapper)* elegante II. tr. **spruced, spruc·ing** vestir —intr. ♦ **to s. up** ataviarse, acicalarse.

sprung (sprŭng) un pret. y part. p. de **spring**.

spry (sprī) adj. **spri·er** *o* **spry·er, spri·est** *o* **spry·est** *(active)* activo; *(lively)* vivo.

spud (spŭd) I. s. *(digging tool)* escarda; JER. *(potato)* papa, patata II. tr. **spud·ded, spud·ding** escardar.

spume (spyōōm) I. s. espuma II. intr. **spumed, spum·ing** espumar, hacer espuma.

spun (spŭn) pret. y part. p. de **spin**.

spun glass s. lana de vidrio.

spunk (spŭngk) s. *(tinder)* yesca; FAM. *(pluck)* valor *m*.

spunk·y (spŭng'kē) adj. **-i·er, -i·est** valiente.

spur (spûr) I. s. *(spiked wheel)* espuela; *(incentive)* incentivo, estímulo; *(crampon)* garfio, trepador *m*; ORNIT. espolón *m*; BOT. cornezuelo; GEOG. estribación *f*; ARQ. puntal *m*, contrafuerte *m*; CARP. riostra; MARÍT. espolón, tajamar *m*; F.C. apartadero, vía muerta ♦ **on the s. of the moment** sin pensarlo II. tr. **spurred, spur·ring** *(to urge on)* espolear; *(to put spurs on)* poner espuelas en ♦ **to s. on** *(to prod)* espolear; *(to stir)* estimular, incitar —intr. hincar las espuelas.

spu·ri·ous (spyŏŏr'ē-əs) adj. *(false)* falso, espurio; *(forged)* falsificado; *(bastard)* bastardo, espurio.

spurn (spûrn) I. tr. *(to reject)* rechazar (con desdén); *(to scorn)* despreciar, desdeñar —intr. despreciar, desdeñar II. s. desdén *m*.

spurt (spûrt) I. s. *(gush)* chorro; *(outbreak)* arrebato II. intr. salir a chorros —tr. echar.

sput·ter (spŭt'ər) I. intr. *(to crackle)* chisporrotear; *(to mutter)* farfullar —tr. *(to spit out)* espurrear; *(to utter)* farfullar, balbucear II. s. *(muttering)* farfulla; *(of particles)* chisporroteo.

sput·ter·ing (spŭt'ər-ĭng) s. chisporroteo.

spu·tum (spyōō'təm) s. [pl. **-ta** (-tə)] esputo.

spy (spī) I. s. [pl. **spies**] espía *mf*, espionaje *m* II. tr. **spied, spy·ing** *(to watch)* espiar; *(to see)* divisar —intr. *(to watch)* espiar; *(to investigate)* escudriñar.

spy·glass (spī'glăs') s. catalejo ♦ **spyglasses** prismáticos, gemelos.

spy·ing (spī'ĭng) s. espionaje *m*.

squab (skwŏb) I. s. ORNIT. pichón implume *m*; *(plump person)* persona regordeta; *(cushion)* almohadón *m*; *(sofa)* sofá II. adj. *(squat)* regordete; *(unfledged)* sin plumas.

squab·ble (skwŏb'əl) I. intr. **-bled, -bling** pelearse II. s. pelea, riña.

squad (skwŏd) s. *(small group)* cuadrilla; *(team)* equipo; MIL. pelotón *m*.

squad car s. coche patrulla *m*.

squad·ron (skwŏd'rən) s. MARÍT. escuadra; MIL. escuadrón *m*; AER. escuadrilla.

squal·id (skwŏl'ĭd) adj. *(dirty)* escuálido; *(repulsive)* asqueroso; *(sordid)* sórdido.

squall¹ (skwôl) I. s. *(cry)* berrido, chillido II. tr. *(to cry harshly)* chillar, berrear.

squall² (skwôl) I. s. *(windstorm)* ráfaga, racha; *(sudden rain)* chubasco; FAM. *(commotion)* disturbio II. intr. soplar con fuerza.

squal·or (skwŏl'ər) s. escualidez *f*.

squan·der (skwŏn'dər) I. tr. *(money)* malgastar, derrochar; *(time)* desperdiciar II. s. derroche *m*.

square (skwâr) I. s. GEOM. cuadrado; *(design)* cuadro; *(tool)* escuadra; *(of a chessboard)* casilla, cuadro; *(in a town)* plaza; JER. *(fogy)* persona chapada a la antigua, carca *m*; MAT. cuadrado; MIL. cuadro II. adj. **squar·er, squar·est** *(having four equal sides)* cuadrado; *(in a right angle)* en ángulo recto, a escuadra; *(quadrate)* cuadrado *(casa, hombros)*; *(honest)* honrado; *(direct)* directo <*a s. answer* una respuesta directa>; *(just)* justo, equitativo; *(paid-up)* saldado; *(firm)* rotundo, terminante <*a s. negative* una negativa terminante>; FAM. *(abundant)* abundante, completo <*s. meal* comida completa>; JER. *(old-fashioned)* anticuado, chapado a la antigua; MAT. cuadrado <*s. feet* pies cuadrados>; MARÍT. cuadrado ♦ **to get s. with** FAM. ajustarle las cuentas a III. tr. **squared, squar·ing** *(to make square)* cuadrar; *(to adapt)* ajustar, adaptar; *(to settle)* saldar, liquidar; MAT. cuadrar, elevar al cuadrado ♦ **to s. accounts with** ajustarle las cuentas a • **to s. away** dejar en orden —intr. cuadrar ♦ **to s. off** ponerse de guardia (para pelear) IV. adv. *(at right angles)* en ángulo recto, a escuadra; *(in square shape)* en forma cuadrada; *(solidly)* firmemente, sólidamente; *(directly)* directamente; *(straightforwardly)* honradamente.

square dance s. baile de figuras *m*.

square deal s. FAM. trato justo.

square knot s. nudo de envergue *o* de rizo.

square·ly (skwâr'lē) adv. *(at right angles)* a escuadra, en ángulo recto; *(firmly)* firmemente; *(face to face)* cara a cara, de frente; *(honestly)* honradamente; *(exactly)* justo, exactamente.

square measure s. medida de superficie.

square·ness (skwâr'nĭs) s. *(form)* forma cuadrada; *(honesty)* honradez *f*.

square rig s. MARÍT. aparejo con velas cuadradas.

square-rig·ger (skwâr'rĭg'ər) s. MARÍT. buque de cruz *m*.

square root s. MAT. raíz cuadrada.

squash¹ (skwŏsh, skwôsh) s. BOT. calabaza.

squash² (skwŏsh, skwôsh) I. tr. *(to crush)* aplastar; *(to squeeze)* apretar; *(to suppress)* aplastar, sofocar <*to s. a revolt* sofocar una revuelta>; *(to silence)* callar, apabullar —intr. *(to crush)* aplastarse; *(to crowd)* apretarse, apiñarse II. s. *(crowd)* tropel *m*, gentío; G.B. *(soft drink)* gaseosa con limón; DEP. *(game)* juego de pelota que se juega contra una pared y con una raqueta.

squash·y (skwŏsh'ē, skwô'shē) adj. **-i·er, -i·est** *(soft)* blando; *(pulpy)* de pulpa blanda; *(boggy)* cenagoso.

squat (skwŏt) I. intr. **squat·ted, squat·ting** *(to hunker down)* ponerse en cuclillas; *(to settle)* ocupar ilegalmente un lugar —tr. *(to hunker down)* ponerse en cuclillas; *(to occupy)* ocupar ilegalmente II. adj. **squat·ter, squat·test** *(hunkered down)* en cuclillas; *(stocky)* regordete III. s. *(posture)* posición en cuclillas *f*; *(land)* lugar ocupado ilegalmente.

squat·ter (skwŏt'ər) s. persona que ocupa ilegalmente un lugar.

squaw (skwô) s. india norteamericana.

squawk (skwôk) I. intr. & tr. graznar, chillar; *(to complain)* quejar(se) II. s. *(screech)* graznido, chillido; *(protest)* protesta.

squeak (skwēk) I. intr. *(to squeal)* chirriar; FAM. *(to inform on)* chivatear —tr. ♦ **to s. through** *o* **by** pasar dificultosamente —tr. decir con voz aguda II. s. *(sound)* chirrido; FIG., FAM. *(escape)* escape (apenas) <*a narrow s.* un escape apenas>.

squeak·y (skwē'kē) adj. **-i·er, -i·est** chirriante.

squeal (skwēl) I. intr. *(to squeak)* chirriar; JER. *(to betray)* chivatear —tr. decir chillando II. s. chillido.

squeal·er (skwē'lər) s. *(squeaker)* chillón *m*; FAM. *(informer)* chivato, soplón *m*.

squea·mish (skwē'mĭsh) adj. *(easily offended)* delicado; *(prudish)* pudibundo; *(oversensitive)* remilgado ♦ **to feel s.** sentir náuseas, estar mareado.

squee·gee (skwē'jē') s. enjugador *m*, rodillo de goma.

squeeze (skwēz) I. tr. **squeezed, squeez·ing** *(to compress)* apretar, comprimir; *(to crush)* exprimir <*to s. an orange* exprimir una naranja>; *(to extract)* extraer <*to s. juice from a lemon* extraer jugo de un limón>; *(to extort)* sonsacar; *(to cram)* forzar, entrar a la fuerza; *(to oppress)* oprimir; *(to embrace)* abrazar ♦ **to s. into** meterse con dificultad en • **to s. out** *(to extract)* sacar; *(to exclude)* excluir • **to s. through** hacer pasar por —intr. *(to give way)* estrujarse <*sponges s. easily* las esponjas se estrujan fácilmente>; *(to exert pressure)* ejercer presión ♦ **to s. in**

meterse con dificultad • **to s. out** salir con dificultad • **to s. through** *o* **by** pasar a duras penas • **to s. together** apiñarse, apretujarse **II.** s. *(compression)* presión *f; (handclasp)* apretón *m; (embrace)* abrazo; *(crush)* gentío; *(difficult spot)* aprieto; *(shortage)* escasez *f.*

squelch (skwĕlch) **I.** tr. *(to crush)* aplastar; *(to squash)* despachurrar; FIG. *(to silence)* callar, apabullar —intr. chapotear **II.** s. *(sound)* chapoteo; *(answer)* réplica.

squib (skwĭb) s. *(firecracker)* buscapiés *m; (lampoon)* pasquín *m.*

squid (skwĭd) s. [pl. **squids** *o* **squid**] ICT. calamar *m.*

squig·gle (skwĭg'əl) **I.** s. garabato **II.** intr. **-gled, -gling** retorcerse.

squint (skwĭnt) **I.** intr. *(to screw up one's eyes)* entrecerrar los ojos; *(to look to the side)* mirar de reojo; *(to suffer strabismus)* bizquear; *(to have tendency)* tender a —tr. *(to cause to squint)* bizquear; *(to half-close)* entrecerrar (los ojos) **II.** s. *(look)* mirada bizca; *(side-glance)* mirada de reojo; *(inclination)* inclinación *f*, tendencia; *(strabismus)* estrabismo **III.** adj. *(looking obliquely)* que mira de reojo; *(strabismic)* bizco.

squire (skwīr) s. HIST. *(young nobleman)* escudero; G.B. *(country gentleman)* terrateniente *m; (judge)* juez *mf; (dignitary)* señor *m; (gallant)* galán *m* **II.** tr. **squired, squir·ing** acompañar.

squirm (skwûrm) **I.** intr. *(to writhe)* retorcerse; *(to feel humiliation)* avergonzarse **II.** s. retorcimiento.

squir·rel (skwûr'əl) s. ZOOL. ardilla (animal y piel).

squirt (skwûrt) **I.** intr. salir a chorros —tr. *(to spurt)* dejar salir a chorros; *(to wet)* echar agua a **II.** s. *(spurt)* chorro; *(device)* jeringa; FAM. *(child)* niño; *(brat)* mequetrefe *m.*

squish (skwĭsh) FAM. **I.** tr. & intr. chapotear **II.** s. chapoteo.

Sri Lan·ka (srē läng'kə) s. Sri Lanka.

Sri Lan·kan (läng'kən) adj. de Sri Lanka.

stab (stăb) **I.** tr. **stabbed, stab·bing** *(to knife)* apuñalar; *(to wound)* herir con un cuchillo • **to s. someone in the back** FIG. darle a alguien una puñalada por la espalda • **to s. to death** matar a puñaladas —intr. dar una puñalada **II.** s. *(knife thrust)* puñalada; *(wound)* herida; FIG. *(attempt)* intento • **to take a s. at** FIG. intentar.

stab·ber (stăb'ər) s. apuñalador *m.*

stab·bing (stăb'ĭng) **I.** s. *(piercing)* perforación *f; (criminal act)* puñalada, asesinato a puñaladas **II.** adj. punzante (dolor).

sta·bil·i·ty (stə-bĭl'ĭ-tē) s. [pl. **-ties**] *(steadiness)* estabilidad *f*; FIG. *(steadfastness)* firmeza; RELIG. voto.

sta·bi·li·za·tion (stā'bə-lĭ-zā'shən) s. estabilización *f.*

sta·bi·lize (stā'bə-līz') intr. **-lized, -liz·ing** estabilizar(se).

sta·bi·liz·er (stā'bə-lī'zər) s. estabilizador *m.*

sta·bi·liz·ing (stā'bə-lī'zĭng) adj. estabilizador.

sta·ble¹ (stā'bəl) adj. **-bler, -blest** *(steady)* estable; *(enduring)* duradero; *(balanced)* equilibrado, ecuánime; FÍS., QUÍM. estable.

sta·ble² (stā'bəl) **I.** s. *(building)* establo, cuadra; *(racehorses)* cuadra (de caballos); FIG. *(group)* grupo, equipo <*the manager has a fine s. of tenors* el empresario tiene un espléndido equipo de tenores> **II.** tr. **-bled, -bling** poner en un establo —intr. estar en una cuadra.

sta·bling (stā'blĭng) s. establos, cuadras.

stac·ca·to (stə-kä'tō) adj. & s. [pl. **-tos** *o* **-ti** (-tē)] staccato.

stack (stăk) **I.** s. *(pile)* montón *m*, pila; *(of chimney)* cañón *m; (smokestack)* chimenea; FAM. *(large quantity)* montón; AGR. hacina, almiar *m; MIL.* pabellón *m* **♦ stacks** biblioteca, estantes • **to blow one's s.** reventar de ira **II.** tr. *(to heap)* amontonar, apilar; *(to load)* xllenar, atiborrar; AGR. hacinar • **to s. the cards** *o* **the deck** hacer trampas • **to s. up** *(to pile)* amontonar, apilar; *(to compare)* comparar.

stacked (stăkt) adj. JER. de forma escultural, de cuerpo voluptuoso (díc. de una mujer).

sta·di·um (stā'dē-əm) s. [pl. **-di·a** (-dē-ə) *o* **-di·ums**] *(sports arena)* estadio; *(Greek arena)* estadio, coliseo; MED. fase *f.*

staff (stăf) **I.** s. [pl. **staffs** *o* **staves** (stāvz)] *(personnel)* personal *m*, plantilla; *(servants)* servidumbre *f; (aides)* cuerpo de administración *m; (walking stick)* bastón *m; (cudgel)* garrote *m*, cachiporra; *(stick)* palo; *(flagpole)* asta;

(yardstick) vara de medir; *(of shepherd)* cayado; *(of pilgrims)* bordón *m; (of command)* bastón de mando; RELIG. báculo; TOP. mira; MIL. plana mayor; MÚS. pentagrama **♦ editorial s.** redacción, redactores • **teaching s.** cuerpo docente, profesorado • **to be on the s.** estar en plantilla **II.** tr. proveer de personal.

staff·er (stăf'ər) s. FAM. empleado.

staff of life s. FIG. alimento básico.

stag (stăg) **I.** s. ZOOL. ciervo; *(castrated animal)* animal castrado; *(man)* hombre (sin compañera en una reunión) *m; (male reunion)* reunión de hombres solos *f* **II.** adj. para hombres **♦ s. party** reunión de hombres solos **III.** adv. solo (sin compañera) **IV.** intr. **stagged, stag·ging** ir sin compañera.

stage (stāj) **I.** s. *(platform)* estrado, plataforma; *(scaffold)* andamio; *(setting)* escenario, escena; *(resting place)* posta, parada; *(phase)* etapa, fase *f* <*a s. in a person's life* una etapa en la vida de una persona>; *(of a microscope)* platina, portaobjeto; *(stagecoach)* diligencia; TEAT. *(area)* escenario, escena; *(the boards)* tablas, teatro; MED. fase; ASTRONAUT. cuerpo; GEOL. piso; ELECTRON. elemento, unidad *f* **♦ by stages** progresivamente o por etapas • **to come on the s.** salir a escena • **to go on the s.** dedicarse al teatro **II.** tr. **staged, stag·ing** TEAT. representar, poner en escena; *(to arrange)* organizar <*to s. a boxing match* organizar una pelea> —intr. representarse.

stage·coach (stāj'kōch') s. diligencia.

stage·craft (stāj'krăft') s. TEAT. arte escénico.

stage direction s. TEAT. acotación *f.*

stage door s. TEAT. entrada de artistas.

stage effect s. TEAT. efecto teatral *o* escénico.

stage fright s. TEAT. miedo al público, nerviosismo frente al público.

stage·hand (stāj'hănd') s. TEAT. tramoyista *m.*

stage manager s. TEAT. regidor de escena *m.*

stage-struck (stāj'strŭk') adj. apasionado por el teatro.

stage whisper s. TEAT. aparte *m.*

stag·ey (stā'jē) adj. var. de **stagy.**

stag·fla·tion (stăg-flā'shən) s. ECON. inflación acompañada por el estancamiento de la economía.

stag·ger (stăg'ər) **I.** intr. *(to totter)* tambalearse; *(to vacillate)* vacilar, titubear —tr. *(to cause to totter)* hacer tambalearse; *(to overwhelm)* asombrar; *(to alternate)* escalonar **II.** s. tambaleo.

stag·ger·ing (stăg'ər-ĭng) adj. *(tottering)* tambaleante; *(overwhelming)* asombroso.

stag·ing (stā'jĭng) s. *(scaffold)* andamio; TEAT. *(play presentation)* puesta en escena, montaje *m; MIL.* estacionamiento.

staging area s. MIL. zona de estacionamiento (de tropas).

stag·nant (stăg'nənt) adj. *(not flowing)* estancado; *(foul)* rancio; *(sluggish)* inactivo.

stag·nate (stăg'nāt') intr. **-nat·ed, -nat·ing** estancarse.

stag·na·tion (stăg-nā'shən) s. estancamiento.

stag·y (stā'jē) adj. **-i·er, -i·est** teatral.

staid (stād) adj. serio.

stain (stān) **I.** tr. *(to spot)* manchar, ensuciar; *(to dye)* teñir; *(to color)* colorar; FIG. *(to taint)* mancillar (nombre, honor); *(to corrupt)* corromper —intr. mancharse, ensuciarse **II.** s. *(spot)* mancha; *(dye)* tinte *m*, tintura; *(marking solution)* colorante *m; FIG. (blemish)* mancha, estigma.

stained glass s. vidrio con dibujos coloreados.

stain·less (stān'lĭs) adj. *(clean)* limpio; *(corrosion-resistant)* inoxidable; FIG. *(unblemished)* inmaculado.

stainless steel s. acero inoxidable.

stair (stâr) s. escalón *m*, peldaño **♦ stairs** escalera.

stair·case (stâr'kās') s. escalera.

stair·way (stâr'wā') s. escalera.

stair·well (stâr'wĕl') s. caja de la escalera.

stake (stāk) **I.** s. *(stick)* estaca; *(post)* poste *m; (interest)* intereses *m* <*a s. in something* tener intereses en algo>; RELIG. división territorial *f* **♦ at s.** en juego • **stakes** *(bet)* apuesta; *(prize)* premio; *(race)* carrera • **the s.** *(place)* hoguera <*Joan of Arc was burned at the s.* Juana de Arco fue quemada en la hoguera>; *(death)* muerte en la hoguera • **to pull up stakes** irse **II.** tr. **staked, stak·ing** *(to* *secure)* estacar, sujetar con estacas; *(to delimit)* delimitar con estacas; *(to tether)* amarrar a un poste; *(to support)* rodrigar (una planta); *(to gamble)* apostar; *(to risk)* arriesgar, jugarse *<to s. one's life on something* jugarse la vida en algo>; *(to finance)* financiar, invertir en ♦ **to s. a claim** delimitar una propiedad con estacas.

stake·out (stāk'out') s. vigilancia.

sta·lac·tite (stə-lăk'tīt') s. estalactita.

sta·lag·mite (stə-lăg'mīt') s. estalagmita.

stale (stāl) I. adj. **stal·er, stal·est** *(food)* rancio; *(bread)* duro; *(wine)* picado; *(not new)* viejo *<s. news* noticias viejas>; *(trite)* trillado; *(run-down)* decaído; *(invalid)* caducado, vencido II. tr. & intr. **staled, stal·ing** echar(se) a perder.

stale·mate (stāl'māt') I. s. *(chess position)* ahogado; *(deadlock)* estancamiento, punto muerto II. tr. **-mat·ed, -mat·ing** *(to bring to a draw)* ahogar (en el ajedrez); *(to deadlock)* estancar.

stale·ness (stāl'nĭs) s. *(of food)* ranciedad *f*; *(invalidity)* vencimiento, caducidad *f*.

Sta·lin·ism (stä'lə-nĭz'əm) s. POL. stalinismo.

stalk¹ (stôk) s. BOT. *(plant stem)* tallo; *(flower stem)* pedúnculo; *(leaf stem)* peciolo.

stalk² (stôk) intr. caminar con paso impresionante —tr. *(to pursue)* acechar; *(to hunt)* cazar al acecho.

stalk·er (stô'kər) s. cazador *m*.

stalk·ing-horse (stô'kĭng-hôrs') s. *(screen)* buey de cabestrillo *m*; FIG. *(pretext)* tapadera, pantalla; POL. candidato falso.

stall (stôl) I. s. *(stable compartment)* pesebre *m*; *(booth)* caseta; *(selling post)* puesto; *(chancel seat)* sitial *m*, silla de coro; *(pew)* banco de iglesia; *(parking space)* lugar de estacionamiento *m*; *(finger sheath)* dedil *m*; *(delaying tactic)* evasiva, pretexto; G.B. *(seat)* butaca; AER. pérdida de velocidad II. tr. *(to put in stable)* poner en un pesebre; *(to detain)* detener; *(to delay)* demorar; AUTO. calar, parar (motor); AER. hacer perder velocidad ♦ **to s. off** evitar (acreedores, pago) —intr. *(to stick)* estar atascado; *(to delay)* andar con rodeos *<come on, don't s.* vamos, no andes con rodeos>; AUTO. calarse, pararse (motor); AER. perder velocidad.

stal·lion (stăl'yən) s. semental *m*.

stal·wart (stôl'wərt) I. adj. *(robust)* robusto; *(uncompromising)* firme II. s. *(strong person)* persona fuerte; *(supporter)* partidario fiel.

sta·men (stā'mən) s. [pl. **sta·mens** *o* **sta·mi·na** (stā'mə-nə, stăm'ə-)] BOT. estambre *m*.

stam·i·na (stăm'ə-nə) s. *(endurance)* aguante *m*; *(physical strength)* vigor *m*.

stam·i·nate (stăm'ə-nāt', stăm'ə-) adj. BOT. estaminífero.

stam·mer (stăm'ər) I. tr. & intr. tartamudear II. s. tartamudez *f*, tartamudeo.

stam·mer·ing (stăm'ər-ĭng) s. tartamudeo.

stamp (stămp) I. tr. *(to crush)* pisotear; *(to imprint)* estampar, imprimir; *(to affix an adhesive stamp)* poner un sello a; *(to identify)* señalar, catalogar; *(to impress forcibly)* marcar, impresionar ♦ **to s. on** pisar • **to s. one's feet** golpear el suelo con los pies, patear • **to s. out** *(a fire)* apagar con el pie; *(a rebellion)* acabar con, sofocar —intr. *(to thrust the foot downward)* golpear con los pies, patear; *(to walk)* caminar con pasos pesados II. s. *(device, mark)* sello; *(postage)* sello, estampilla; *(fiscal)* timbre *m*; *(of shares)* cupón *m*; TEC. *(for forging)* estampa; *(die)* cuño; *(for printing)* prensa de estampar; *(graver)* punzón *m* ♦ **trading s.** cupón.

stamp collector s. coleccionista de sellos *mf*, filatelista *mf*.

stam·pede (stăm-pēd') I. s. espantada, desbandada II. tr. **-ped·ed, -ped·ing** *(to cause flight)* espantar (animales); *(to frighten)* infundir terror a —intr. abalanzarse, precipitarse.

stance (stăns) s. postura.

stanch¹ (stônch, stŏnch) tr. restañar (sangre).

stanch² (stônch, stŏnch) adj. var. de **staunch¹.**

stan·chion (stăn'chən, -shən) I. s. *(post)* poste *m*, puntal *m* II. tr. apuntalar.

stand (stănd) I. intr. **stood** (stŏod), **stand·ing** *(to be on one's feet)* estar de pie *<I stood through the whole performance* estuve de pie durante toda la función>; *(in an erect position)* ponerse derecho *<s. straight* ponte derecho>; *(to rise)* ponerse de pie, levantarse *<everybody s.!* ¡pónganse de pie!>; *(to place oneself)* ponerse, colocarse *<I stood at her side* me coloqué a su lado>; *(to measure)* medir *<to s. five feet tall* medir cinco pies de altura>; *(to remain valid)* regir, tener vigencia *<the law still stands* la ley todavía tiene vigencia>; *(to be committed to)* mantenerse, permanecer; *(to be situated)* erguirse, levantarse; *(to rank)* ser *<she stands third in her class* es la tercera de la clase>; *(to stagnate)* estancarse; MARÍT. ir rumbo a, dirigirse ♦ **to s. alone** *(to be alone)* estar solo; *(to be the only one)* ser el único • **to s. aside** *(to move aside)* apartarse, hacerse a un lado; *(to retire)* retirarse • **to s. at attention** MIL. cuadrarse • **to s. back** retroceder • **to s. by** *(to be ready)* estar listo; *(to be an onlooker)* mirar y no hacer nada • **to s. down** retirarse del estrado • **to s. fast** no cejar, no ceder • **to s. in good stead** servir, ser útil • **to s. in line** hacer cola, ponerse en la fila • **to s. in the way** ser un impedimento, estorbar • **to s. off** *(at a distance)* apartarse, mantenerse a distancia; *(boat)* apartarse de la costa • **to s. on end** *(hair)* erizarse; *(thing)* ponerse de punta • **to s. on one's own feet** valerse de sí mismo • **to s. out** *(to be conspicuous)* resaltar, destacarse; *(to protrude)* sobresalir • **to s. out of the way** quitarse de en medio • **to s. still** estarse quieto, no moverse • **to s. to reason** ser lógico, ser justo • **to s. to (win, lose)** tener la probabilidad de (ganar, perder) • **to s. together** mantenerse unidos • **to s. up** ponerse de pie, levantarse • **to s. up to a test** salir bien de una prueba • **where do you s.?** ¿qué opinión tienes?, ¿cuál es tu punto de vista? —tr. *(to place upright)* poner derecho, poner de pie; *(to place)* colocar, poner; *(to withstand)* tolerar, aguantar *<I can't s. pain* no tolero el dolor>; *(to resist)* resistir, hacer frente a *<to s. siege* resistir un bloqueo>; *(to treat)* invitar, pagar ♦ **to s. a chance** tener una posibilidad • **to s. against** resistir, hacer frente a • **to s. by** *(to be true to)* ser fiel a, permanecer fiel a; *(to help)* ayudar • **to s. fire** MIL. aguantar el fuego del enemigo; QUÍM. resistir el calor • **to s. for** *(to represent)* representar; *(to mean)* significar, querer decir; *(to support)* abogar por, defender; *(to endure)* soportar, tolerar • **to s. in for** reemplazar • **to s. off** *(to avoid)* mantener a raya; *(to ward off)* repeler, rechazar • **to s. on** *(to be located)* estar en, estar colocado sobre; *(to rest on)* estar sostenido por; *(to insist on)* insistir en • **to s. (something) on end** poner (algo) derecho • **to s. one's ground** mantenerse firme, no ceder • **to s. someone in good stead** servir a alguien • **to s. the test** pasar por la prueba • **to s. up** FAM. dejar plantado, faltar a una cita con • **to s. up for** defender, sacar la cara por • **to s. up to** *(to confront)* enfrentar, confrontar; *(to resist)* hacer frente a; *(to last)* resistir, no gastarse II. s. *(halt)* parada, alto; *(standstill)* pausa, alto; *(opinion)* opinión *f*, actitud *f* *<to take a s.* adoptar una actitud>; *(dais)* estrado; *(platform)* plataforma; *(booth)* quiosco; *(counter)* mostrador *m*; *(pedestal)* pie *m*, pedestal *m*; *(music stand)* atril *m*; *(prop)* soporte *m*, sostén *m*; *(for taxis)* parada; *(for coats, hats)* percha, perchero; *(for umbrellas)* paragüero; *(table)* velador *m*; TEAT. *(performance)* representación *f*, función *f*; DER. *(witness stand)* barra de los testigos ♦ **stands** graderías, tribuna • **to make a s. against** oponerse a • **to take a s. for** declararse a favor de • **to take a firm s.** adoptar una actitud firme • **to take the s.** DER. subir a la barra de los testigos, comparecer ante un tribunal.

stand-a·lone (stănd'ə-lōn') adj. MEC. automático.

stan·dard (stăn'dərd) I. s. *(flag)* bandera, estandarte *m*; *(criterion)* criterio *<using that s. any poem is good* usando ese criterio cualquier poema es bueno>; *(model)* patrón *m*, modelo; *(level)* nivel *m*; G.B., EDUC. *(grade)* grado, clase *f*; JOY. *(proportion)* ley *f*; FIN. *(backing commodity)* patrón ♦ **standards** normas de conducta II. adj. *(of accepted value)* standard; *(commonly accepted)* normal, corriente *<of s. use* de uso corriente>; *(of recognized excellence)* clásico; *(correct)* correcto.

stan·dard-bear·er (stăn'dərd-bâr'ər) s. *(flag bearer)* abanderado; FIG. *(leader)* jefe *m*, abanderado.

ã rey / ä año / b boca / ch chico / d dar / ĕ el / ē mil / g gato / h joya / hw juez / ī aire / k casa / kw cuan /

standard deviation s. MAT. medida de dispersión en una distribución.
standard gauge s. F.C. *(railroad track)* vía o trocha normal.
stan·dard·ize (stăn'dər-dīz') tr. **-ized, -iz·ing** estandardizar.
standard of living s. nivel de vida *m.*
standard time s. hora civil.
stand·by (stănd'bī') s. [pl. **-bys**] *(dependable person)* persona de confianza; *(favorite choice)* persona o cosa preferida; *(substitute)* substituto ♦ **s. list** lista de espera (de pasajeros) • **s. passenger** pasajero que está en la lista de espera.
stand-in (stănd'ĭn') s. TEAT. suplente *mf;* CINEM. doble *m; (substitute)* substituto; DEP. *(reserve)* suplente.
stand·ing (stăn'dĭng) **I.** s. *(position)* posición vertical *f; (reputation)* reputación *f; (length of time)* antigüedad *<an employee of long* s. un empleado de mucha antigüedad> **II.** adj. *(upright)* de pie, parado *<the boxer remained* s. *after the blows* el boxeador permaneció parado después de los golpes>; *(permanent)* permanente, *(stationary)* fijo; *(stagnant)* estancado *<s. water* agua estancada>.
standing army s. MIL. ejército permanente.
standing room s. sitio donde la gente permanece de pie.
stand·off (stănd'ôf') s. empate *m.*
stand·off·ish (stănd-ô'fĭsh) adj. distante, reservado.
stand·out (stănd'out') s. persona que se destaca.
stand·pipe (stănd'pīp') s. depósito de agua elevado.
stand·point (stănd'point') s. punto de vista.
stand·still (stănd'stĭl') s. parada.
stank (stăngk) un pret. de **stink**.
stan·za (stăn'zə) s. POÉT. estrofa, estancia.
staph·y·lo·coc·cus (stăf'ə-lō-kŏk'əs) s. [pl. **-coc·ci** (-kŏk'sī', -kŏk'ī')] estafilococo.
sta·ple¹ (stā'pəl) **I.** s. *(commodity)* producto básico (de una región), *(trade item)* producto principal; *(feature)* elemento básico; *(raw material)* materia prima; *(fiber)* fibra **II.** tr. **-pled, -pling** clasificar según la longitud de las fibras.
sta·ple² (stā'pəl) **I.** s. grapa **II.** tr. **-pled, -pling** *(to fasten)* sujetar con una grapa.
sta·pler (stā'plər) s. grapador *m.*
star (stär) **I.** s. *(heavenly body)* estrella, astro; *(asterisk)* asterisco; *(performer)* estrella *<Marilyn Monroe was a great* s. Marilyn Monroe fue una gran estrella>; VET. estrella, lucero ♦ **pole s.** estrella polar • **shooting s.** estrella fugaz • **to see stars** FIG. ver las estrellas • **to thank one's lucky stars** dar las gracias a Dios • **stars** ASTROL. astros **II.** tr. **starred, star·ring** *(to adorn)* estrellar, sembrar de estrellas; *(to place an asterisk on)* poner un asterisco en; *(to feature)* presentar como protagonista —intr. *(to play the leading role)* protagonizar; *(to perform well)* destacarse (en juego, actividad) **III.** adj. *(of a star)* estelar; *(excellent)* excelente, estelar.
star·board (stär'bərd) **I.** s. MARÍT. estribor *m* **II.** adj. de estribor **III.** adv. a estribor.
starch (stärch) **I.** s. *(food-stuff)* fécula; *(stiffening substance)* almidón *m; (behavior)* rigidez *f; (vigor)* vigor *m* **II.** tr. almidonar.
starch·y (stär'chē) adj. **-i·er, -i·est** *(containing starch)* feculento; *(like starch)* almidonado; FAM. *(stiff)* tieso; *(formal)* rígido.
star·dom (stär'dəm) s. estrellato.
stare (stâr) **I.** intr. **stared, star·ing** *(to give a look)* mirar fijamente; *(to bristle)* erizarse; G.B., FIG. *(to stand out)* saltar a la vista, llamar la atención —tr. fijar la vista en, mirar fijamente a ♦ **to s. down** hacer bajar la vista a **II.** s. mirada fija.
star·fish (stär'fĭsh') s. [pl. **starfish** o **-fish·es**] ICT. estrella de mar.
star·gaze (stär'gāz') intr. **-gazed, -gaz·ing** *(to gaze at the stars)* mirar las estrellas; *(to daydream)* mirar a las musarañas.
star·gaz·er (stär'gā'zər) s. *(daydreamer)* soñador *m;* FAM. *(astronomer)* astrónomo; *(astrologer)* astrólogo.
stark (stärk) **I.** adj. **-er, -est** *(bleak)* desolado; FIG. *(blunt)* desnudo *<the* s. *truth* la verdad desnuda>; *(complete)* to-

tal, completo; *(extreme)* extremado **II.** adv. totalmente, completamente.
stark·ness (stärk'nĭs) s. *(bleakness)* desolación *f; (bareness)* austeridad.
star·let (stär'lĭt) s. TEAT., CINEM. actriz joven *f.*
star·light (stär'lĭt') s. luz de las estrellas *f.*
star·ling (stär'lĭng) s. ORNIT. estornino.
star·lit (stär'lĭt') adj. iluminado por las estrellas.
Star of Da·vid (dā'vĭd) s. estrella de David.
star·ry (stär'ē) adj. **-ri·er, –ri·est** *(marked with stars)* estrellado; *(shining)* brillante; *(star-shaped)* en forma de estrella; *(starlit)* iluminado por las estrellas; *(stellar)* estelar.
star·ry-eyed (stär'ē-īd') adj. soñador.
Stars and Stripes s. bandera de EE. UU.
star sapphire s. zafiro estrellado.
star shell s. MIL. bengala, cohete luminoso *m.*
Star-Span·gled Banner (stär'spăng'gəld) s. *(flag)* bandera de EE. UU.; *(anthem)* himno nacional de EE. UU.
start (stärt) **I.** intr. *(to begin)* empezar, comenzar; *(to set out)* salir *<the train started from the station* el tren salió de la estación>; *(to jerk)* sobresaltarse; *(to bulge)* salirse; *(to become loosened)* aflojarse ♦ **to s. back** emprender el regreso • **to s. in** empezar • **to s. off** o **out** empezar *<s. off by learning shorthand* empieza por aprender taquigrafía> • **to s. up** arrancar *<that motor starts up easily* ese motor arranca con facilidad> • **to s. with** para comenzar —tr. *(to commence)* comenzar, empezar; *(to set into motion)* poner en marcha *<s. the motor* pon el motor en marcha>; *(to initiate)* iniciar; DEP. *(to be in the line-up)* formar parte del equipo *<he starts for the local team* él forma parte del equipo primero local>; *(to motivate)* impulsar; *(to found)* establecer, fundar; *(to flush an animal)* levantar **II.** s. *(beginning)* principio, comienzo; *(startle)* sobresalto; *(loose part)* parte suelta; *(place)* salida, punto de partida; *(lead)* ventaja; *(opportunity)* oportunidad *f;* DEP. *(signal)* señal de salida *f* ♦ **at the s.** al principio • **by fits and starts a** trompicones, a rachas • **false s.** DEP. salida nula • **flying s.** salida lanzada • **from the s.** desde el principio • **to get off to a good s.** empezar bien • **to give someone a s.** *(to help)* ayudar a alguien; *(to startle)* dar un susto a alguien • **to make a fresh s.** empezar de nuevo • **with a s.** sobresaltando.
start·er (stär'tər) s. *(one that starts)* iniciador *m;* AUTO. arranque *m;* DEP. *(official)* juez de salida *m; (competitor)* competidor *m,* participante *mf.*
start·ing (stär'tĭng) s. *(beginning)* comienzo; *(ignition)* arranque *m,* puesta en marcha ♦ **s. point** punto de partida.
star·tle (stär'tl) **I.** tr. & intr. **-tled, -tling** sobresaltar(se), asustar(se) **II.** s. sobresalto.
start-up (stärt'ŭp') s. puesta en marcha.
star·va·tion (stär-vā'shən) s. *(hunger)* hambre *f;* MED. inanición *f* ♦ **s. wages** sueldos de hambre.
starve (stärv) intr. **starved, starv·ing** *(to be hungry)* pasar hambre; *(to die)* morirse de hambre —tr. *(not to feed)* no dar de comer; *(to kill)* matar de hambre ♦ **to s. for** *(to need)* carecer de; *(to desire)* anhelar.
starve·ling (stärv'lĭng) **I.** s. hambriento, muerto de hambre **II.** adj. *(starving)* hambriento, muerto de hambre; *(inadequate)* inadecuado.
starv·ing (stär'vĭng) **I.** adj. hambriento **II.** s. hambre *f.*
stash (stăsh) FAM. **I.** tr. esconder **II.** s. *(cache)* escondrijo; *(hidden thing)* cosa escondida.
sta·sis (stā'sĭs) s. [pl. **-ses** (-sēz')] MED. estasis *f.*
state (stāt) **I.** s. *(condition)* condición *f,* estado; *(stage)* fase *f; (disposition)* estado *<s. of mind* estado de ánimo>; *(social position)* rango; *(pomp)* pompa *<buried in s.* sepultado con pompa>; CIENT. estado *<ice is water in a solid s.* el hielo es agua en estado sólido>; POL. estado ♦ **s. of emergency** estado de emergencia • **s. of seige** estado de sitio • **the States** los Estados Unidos • **to be in a s.** ponerse nervioso, agitarse • **to lie in s.** estar en capilla ardiente **II.** tr. **stat·ed, stat·ing** *(to declare)* declarar; *(to say)* decir; *(to write down)* escribir **III.** adj. *(government controlled)* estatal, de estado; *(ceremonious)* solemne; *(official)* oficial.
state·craft (stāt'krăft') s. arte de gobernar *m.*

state·hood (stāt'hŏŏd') s. condición del ser estado (de EE. UU.) f.

state house o **State House** s. edificio de la cámara legislativa de un estado de EE. UU.

state·li·ness (stāt'lē-nĭs) s. majestuosidad f.

state·ly (stāt'lē) I. adj. **-li·er, -li·est** majestuoso II. adv. majestuosamente.

state·ment (stāt'mənt) s. (declaration) declaración f; DER. (formal pleading) alegato; COM. (bill) cuenta; (periodic report) estado de cuenta.

state of the art s. últimos adelantos.

state·room (stāt'rŏŏm', -rŏŏm') s. MARÍT. camarote m; F.C. compartimiento privado.

state's evidence o **State's evidence** s. DER. testimonio en contra del reo; (person) testigo en contra del reo ♦ **to turn s.** dar uno testimonio en contra de sus cómplices.

state·side (stāt'sīd') adj. FAM. hacia o en o de los Estados Unidos.

states·man (stāts'mən) s. [pl. **-men**] POL., DIPL. estadista m.

states·man·ship (stāts'mən-shĭp') s. arte de gobernar m.

states·wom·an (stāts'wŏŏm'ən) s. [pl. **-wom·en** (-wĭm'ĭn)] estadista f.

state university s. universidad de un estado de EE. UU. f.

state·wide (stāt'wīd') adj. en todo el estado, por todo el estado.

stat·ic (stăt'ĭk) I. adj. (at rest) estático II. s. RAD. parásitos; (interference) intromisión f; JER. (back talk) insolencias, cháchara alborotosa.

static electricity s. ELEC. electricidad estática.

stat·ics (stăt'ĭks) s.pl. [ú. con v. sing.] MEC. estática.

sta·tion (stā'shən) I. s. (post) puesto; (operations center) estación f; (social position) rango, posición social f; (depot) estación; RAD., TELEV. estación ♦ **military s.** guarnición • **naval s.** puerto militar • **police s.** comisaría • **service s.** estación de servicio II. tr. apostar, estacionar.

sta·tion·ar·y (stā'shə-nĕr'ē) adj. (not moving) estacionario; (fixed) fijo.

station break s. RAD., TELEV. interrupción de un programa (para identificación de emisora) f.

sta·tion·er (stā'shə-nər) s. (person) papelero; (store) papelería.

sta·tion·er·y (stā'shə-nĕr'ē) s. (writing paper) papel y sobres m; (office supplies) objetos de escritorio; (store) papelería.

station house s. (police station) comisaría; (fire station) cuartel de bomberos m.

sta·tion·mas·ter (stā'shən-măs'tər) s. jefe de estación m.

station wagon s. AUTO. camioneta.

sta·tis·tic (stə-tĭs'tĭk) s. estadística.

sta·tis·ti·cal (stə-tĭs'tĭ-kəl) adj. estadístico.

sta·tis·ti·cal·ly (stə-tĭs'tĭ-kə-lē) adv. según las estadísticas.

stat·is·ti·cian (stăt'ĭ-stĭsh'ən) s. estadístico.

sta·tis·tics (stə-tĭs'tĭks) s. {ú. con v. sing.] (science) estadística; (data group) estadísticas.

sta·tor (stā'tər) s. MEC. estator m.

stat·u·ar·y (stăch'ŏŏ-ĕr'ē) I. s. [pl. **-ies**] (statues) estatuas; (sculptor) escultor m, estatuario; (art) estatuaria II. adj. estatuario.

stat·ue (stăch'ŏŏ) s. estatua.

stat·u·esque (stăch'ŏŏ-ĕsk') adj. escultural.

stat·u·ette (stăch'ŏŏ-ĕt') s. estatuilla, figurina.

stat·ure (stăch'ər) s. (height) estatura; FIG. (importance) categoría.

sta·tus (stā'təs, stăt'əs) s. DER. (legal condition) estado; (stage) etapa; (position) posición social f; (standing) categoría; (situation) situación f.

sta·tus quo (stā'təs kwō', stăt'əs) s. statu quo m.

stat·ute (stăch'ŏŏt) s. DER., POL. (established rule) estatuto, decreto.

statute law s. derecho escrito.

statute mile s. milla terrestre.

statute of limitations s. DER. ley de prescripción f.

stat·u·to·ry (stăch'ə-tôr'ē) adj. estatuario, establecido por la ley.

statutory offense s. DER. crimen establecido por ley m.

statutory rape s. DER. corrupción de menores f.

staunch¹ (stônch, stŏnch) adj. **-er, -est** (steadfast) constante, firme; (true) fiel; (strong) fuerte.

staunch² (stônch, stŏnch) v. var. de **stanch¹**.

stave (stāv) I. s. (barrel strip) duela; (ladder rung) escalón m, peldaño; (chair rung) barrote m; (staff) bastón m; MÚS. pentagrama m; POET. estrofa II. tr. **staved** o **stove** (stōv), **sta·ving** (to break barrel strips) romper las duelas; (to break a hole) abrir un agujero; (to crush inward) desfondar; (to furnish) poner duelas a ♦ **to s. off** (to repel) rechazar; (to delay) demorar —intr. (to be crushed) desfondarse; (to break) romperse.

staves (stāvz) pl. de **staff¹**.

stay¹ (stā) I. intr. (to remain) quedarse, permanecer; (to sojourn) alojarse, hospedarse; (to stop) detenerse; (to wait) esperar; (to endure) aguantar, resistir; (to keep up) mantenerse, seguir ♦ **it is here to s.** se ha establecido • **to s. away** (to absent oneself) ausentarse; (not to come) no venir • **to s. in** quedarse en casa • **to s. in bed** guardar cama • **to s. on** quedarse • **to s. over** pasar la noche • **to s. out** (to remain outside) no entrar; (not to come home) no venir a casa • **to s. put** quedarse quieto, no moverse • **to s. up** no dormir, quedarse levantado • **to s. up late** acostarse tarde —tr. (to halt) detener; (to postpone) aplazar; (to appease) apaciguar, calmar ♦ **to s. away from** evitar • **to s. the course** FIG. continuar hasta el final II. s. (halt) parada, detención f; (visit) estancia, permanencia; DER. aplazamiento.

stay² (stā) I. tr. (to brace) afianzar; (to support) apoyar II. s. (support) apoyo; (stiffener) ballena.

stay³ (stā). MARÍT. I. s. estay m II. tr. (to brace) asegurar; (to change tack) cambiar de bordada —intr. virar.

staying power s. resistencia, aguante m.

stay·sail (stā'səl, -sāl') s. MARÍT. vela de estay.

stead (stĕd) s. lugar m ♦ **in someone's** o **something's s.** en lugar de alguien o de algo • **to stand someone in good s.** serle útil a alguien.

stead·fast (stĕd'făst', -fəst) adj. (fixed) fijo; (unchanging) constante, firme; (loyal) leal.

stead·i·ly (stĕd'l-ē) adv. (firmly) firmemente; (constantly) sin interrupción <he talked s. for an hour habló sin interrupción durante una hora>.

stead·i·ness (stĕd'ē-nĭs) s. (stability) estabilidad f; (firmness) firmeza <the s. of his aim la firmeza de su puntería>; (continuity) continuidad f.

stead·y (stĕd'ē) I. adj. **-i·er, -i·est** (firm) firme, fijo; (stable) estable; (sure) seguro; (continuous) continuo, constante <a s. wind un viento constante>; (uniform) uniforme; (calm) tranquilo, sereno; (reliable) seguro; (sober) sensato, equilibrado <he is a s. young man es un joven equilibrado> II. tr. & intr. **stead·ied, stead·y·ing** (to make stable) estabilizar(se); (to calm) calmar(se) III. interj. (calm down) ¡calma!, ¡tranquilo!; MARÍT. ¡mantengan el rumbo! IV. s. [pl. **-ies**] novio, novia.

steak (stāk) s. (beef) bistec m; (fish) filete m; (patty) hamburguesa.

steal (stēl) I. tr. **stole** (stōl), **sto·len** (stō'lən), **steal·ing** (to rob) robar —intr. robar ♦ **to s. away** escabullirse • **to s. in, out** entrar, salir furtivamente II. s. (theft) robo; JER. (bargain) ganga.

steal·er (stē'lər) s. ladrón m.

steal·ing (stē'lĭng) s. robo.

stealth (stĕlth) s. sigilo ♦ **by s.** furtivamente.

stealth·y (stĕl'thē) adj. **-i·er, -i·est** (person) cauteloso; (action) furtivo.

steam (stēm) I. s. (water vapor) vapor m; (heating) calefacción f; (energy) energía II. intr. (to emit) echar vapor; (to rise up) humear; (to fog up) empañarse; (to function) funcionar con vapor; MARÍT. hacer, avanzar; FAM. (to fume) echar humo —tr. CUL. cocer al vapor.

steam bath s. baño de vapor.

steam·boat (stēm'bōt') s. vapor m, buque a vapor m.

steam boiler s. caldera de vapor.

steam engine s. máquina a vapor.

steam·er (stē'mər) s. (ship) vapor m, buque de vapor m; CUL. olla de vapor.

steamer trunk s. baúl (de camarote) m.

ā rey / ä año / b boca / ch chico / d dar / ĕ el / ē mil / g gato / h joya / hw juez / ī aire / k casa / kw cuan /

steam·fit·ter (stĕm'fĭt'ər) s. montador de calderas de vapor *m.*

steam heating s. calefacción de vapor *f.*

steam iron s. plancha de vapor.

steam·roll·er *o* **steam roller** (stĕm'rō'lər) **I.** s. *(vehicle)* apisonadora; FIG. *(force)* fuerza irresistible **II.** tr. *(to level)* apisonar; *(to overwhelm)* arrollar, aplastar —intr. arrollar.

steam·ship (stĕm'shĭp') s. vapor *m,* buque de vapor *m.*

steam shovel s. pala mecánica.

steam turbine s. turbina de vapor.

steam·y (stĕ'mē) adj. **-i·er, -i·est** *(smokey)* vaporoso; JER. *(erotic)* erótico, apasionado.

ste·a·rate (stē'ə-rāt') s. QUÍM. estearato.

ste·a·rin (stē'ər-ĭn, stîr'ĭn) s. QUÍM. estearina.

steed (stēd) s. corcel *m.*

steel (stēl) **I.** s. *(metal)* acero; *(strength)* acero; *(sword)* acero; *(knife sharpener)* chaira, eslabón *m;* *(stiffener)* ballena **II.** adj. de acero ♦ **s. industry** la industria siderúrgica **III.** tr. *(to cover with steel)* acerar; *(to strengthen)* fortalecer ♦ **to s. one's heart** volverse insensible, endurecerse • **to s. oneself** *(to harden)* endurecerse, volverse insensible; *(to strengthen)* fortalecer.

steel engraving s. grabado en acero.

steel mill s. fábrica de acero, acería.

steel wool s. estropajo.

steel·work (stēl'wûrk') objeto de acero ♦ **steelworks** planta siderúrgica.

steel·work·er (stēl'wûr'kər) s. obrero de una fábrica de acero.

steel·y (stē'lē) adj. **-i·er, -i·est** *(made of steel)* de acero; *(like steel)* acerado ♦ **s. eyes** mirada penetrante.

steel·yard (stēl'yärd') s. romana (balanza).

steep¹ (stēp) adj. **-er, -est** *(inclined)* empinado; *(precipitous)* escarpado; *(sudden)* abrupto; *(excessive)* excesivo, alto *(precio)*; *(difficult)* difícil.

steep² (stēp) **I.** tr. *(to soak)* remojar; *(to wet thoroughly)* empapar —intr. *(to undergo soaking)* estar en remojo **II.** s. remojo.

steep·en (stē'pən) tr. & intr. volver(se) más empinado.

stee·ple (stē'pəl) s. ARQ. *(tower)* torrecilla, campanario; *(spire)* aguja.

stee·ple·chase (stē'pəl-chās') s. EQUIT. carrera de obstáculos.

stee·ple·jack (stē'pəl-jăk') s. reparador de campanarios *o* chimeneas *m.*

steep·ly (stēp'lē) adv. en pendiente.

steep·ness (stēp'nĭs) s. pendiente *f.*

steer¹ (stîr) **I.** tr. *(to operate rudder)* gobernar (el timón); *(to drive)* manejar, conducir; *(to direct)* dirigir; *(to maneuver)* guiar, orientar —intr. *(to guide vessel)* gobernar; *(to drive)* conducir, manejar; *(to follow set course)* encaminarse; *(to be capable of guidance)* conducirse <it steers easy se conduce fácilmente> **II.** s. JER. consejo <a bum s. un mal consejo>.

steer² (stîr) s. *(ox)* novillo.

steer·age (stîr'ĭj) s. MARÍT. *(ship guidance)* gobierno; *(apparatus)* timón *m;* *(accommodation)* tercera clase, entrepuente *m.*

steer·ing (stîr'ĭng) s. MARÍT. *(control)* gobierno; *(accomodation)* tercera clase, entrepuente *m.*

steering committee s. comité directivo *m.*

steering wheel s. MARÍT. rueda del timón; AUTO. volante *m.*

steers·man (stîrz'mən) s. [pl. **-men**] MARÍT. piloto, timonel *m.*

stein (stīn) s. jarra (de cerveza).

ste·le (stē'lē) s. [pl. **-les** *o* **-lae** (-lē)] ARQ. estela; BOT. estela.

stel·lar (stĕl'ər) adj. ASTRON. estelar; TEAT., CINEM. estelar; *(main)* estelar, principal.

stel·late (stĕl'āt') adj. estrellado, radiado.

stem¹ (stĕm) **I.** s. *(trunk)* tronco; *(stalk)* tallo; *(banana bunch)* racimo; *(pipe tube)* cañón *m;* *(goblet support)* pie *m;* *(shaft)* cañón *m;* *(lineage)* estirpe *f;* MEC. vástago; IMPR. grueso; MÚS. rabo; FILOL. radical *m;* MARÍT. *(prow beam)* roda, tajamar *m;* *(prow)* proa ♦ **from s. to stern** MARÍT.

(bow to aft) de proa a popa; FIG. *(end to end)* de punta a punta, de cabo a rabo **II.** tr. **stemmed, stem·ming** *(to remove stem)* despalillar; MARÍT. hacer frente a, mantenerse contra —intr. ♦ **to s. from** ser el resultado de.

stem² (stĕm) tr. **stemmed, stem·ming** *(to check)* contener, detener <to s. the tide contener la marea>; *(in skiing)* inclinar (el esquí) para disminuir la velocidad —intr. disminuir la velocidad volviendo los esquíes hacia adentro.

stem·ware (stĕm'wâr') s. copas (de pie).

stench (stĕnch) s. hedor *m,* peste *f.*

sten·cil (stĕn'səl) **I.** s. *(lettering)* estarcido; IMPR. plantilla **II.** tr. estarcir.

sten·o·graph (stĕn'ə-grăf') **I.** s. *(machine)* máquina de taquigrafía; *(shorthand character)* signo **II.** tr. estenografiar, taquigrafiar.

ste·nog·ra·pher (stə-nŏg'rə-fər) s. estenógrafo, taquígrafo.

ste·nog·ra·phy (stə-nŏg'rə-fē) s. estenografía, taquigrafía.

sten·o·type (stĕn'ə-tīp') s. estenotipo.

sten·to·ri·an (stĕn-tôr'ē-ən) adj. estentóreo.

step (stĕp) **I.** s. *(in walking)* paso <one s. forward un paso adelante>; *(sound)* paso, pisada <a heavy s. una pisada fuerte>; *(footprint)* huella; *(of stairs, ladder)* escalón *m,* peldaño; *(measure)* medida <to take steps to reduce a deficit tomar medidas para reducir un déficit>; *(stage)* paso, etapa; *(degree)* escalón; MÚS. intervalo; MARÍT. carlinga ♦ **in s. with** de acuerdo con • **out of s. with** en desacuerdo con • **s. by s.** paso a paso • **steps** *(course)* pasos; *(staircase)* escaleras; *(stepladder)* escalera de tijera • **to keep in s.** llevar el paso • **to retrace one's steps** volver uno sobre sus pasos, desandar lo andado • **to take a s.** dar un paso • **watch your step!** ¡vaya con cuidado! **II.** intr. **stepped, step·ping** *(to put the foot down)* poner el pie, pisar <you are stepping on my shoe me está pisando el zapato>; *(to take a step)* dar un paso; *(to go)* ir; *(to go in)* entrar; *(to humiliate)* rebajar, pisotear ♦ **s. this way!** ¡pase por aquí! • **to s. aside** hacerse a un lado, apartarse • **to s. back** retroceder, dar un paso atrás • **to s. down** *(to descend)* bajar, descender; *(to resign)* renunciar • **to s. forward** avanzar, dar un paso adelante • **to s. in** *(to go in)* entrar; *(to intervene)* intervenir, meterse • **to s. out** *(to go out)* salir; *(of a vehicle)* apearse; *(to walk fast)* apretar el paso • **to s. up** subir —tr. *(to put down)* poner (el pie); *(to measure)* medir a pasos; *(to furnish with steps)* escalonar; *(to dance)* bailar; COMPUT. ejecutar (una operación); MARÍT. plantar ♦ **s. it up!** *o* **s. on it!** ¡date prisa! • **to s. on** pisar • **to s. up** *(to accelerate)* acelerar; *(to increase)* aumentar.

step·broth·er (stĕp'brŭth'ər) s. hermanastro.

step·child (stĕp'chīld') s. [pl. **-chil·dren** (-chĭl'drən)] hijastro.

step·daugh·ter (stĕp'dô'tər) s. hijastra.

step-down (stĕp'doun') **I.** adj. reductor **II.** s. reducción *f.*

step·fa·ther (stĕp'fä'thər) s. padrastro.

step·lad·der (stĕp'lăd'ər) s. escalera de tijera.

step·moth·er (stĕp'mŭth'ər) s. madrastra.

step·par·ent (stĕp'pâr'ənt) s. *(father)* padrastro; *(mother)* madrastra.

steppe (stĕp) s. estepa.

stepped-up (stĕpt'ŭp') adj. *(accelerated)* acelerado; *(increased)* aumentado.

step·ping·stone (stĕp'ĭng-stōn') s. *(stone)* pasadera; FIG. *(rung)* trampolín *m.*

step·sis·ter (stĕp'sĭs'tər) s. hermanastra.

step·son (stĕp'sŭn') s. hijastro.

step-up (stĕp'ŭp') **I.** adj. *(accelerated)* acelerado; *(increased)* aumentado **II.** s. *(acceleration)* aceleración *f;* *(increase)* aumento.

step·wise (stĕp'wīz') **I.** adj. progresivo **II.** adv. paso a paso.

stere (stîr) s. estéreo, metro cúbico.

ster·e·o (stĕr'ē-ō', stîr'-) s. [pl. **-os**] *(sound equipment)* equipo estereofónico; *(sound)* sonido estereofónico; *(stereotype)* estereotipo; *(stereoscopy)* estereoscopia.

ster·e·og·ra·phy (stĕr'ē-ŏg'rə-fē, stîr'-) s. estereografía.

ster·e·o·phon·ic (stĕr'ē-ō-fŏn'ĭk, stîr'-) adj. estereofónico.

ster·e·op·ti·con (stĕr'ē-ŏp'tĭ-kŏn') s. estereóptico, linterna mágica.

ster·e·o·scope (stĕr'ē-ə-skōp', stîr'-) s. estereoscopio.

---

ng inglés / ŏ la / ō bou / ô corre / oi oigo / o͞o uno / ou auto / yo͞o ciudad / w hueco / y yo / z mismo

ster·e·o·scop·ic (stĕr'ē-ə-skŏp'ĭk) adj. estereoscópico.
ster·e·os·co·py (stĕr'ē-ŏs'kə-pē, stĭr'-) s. estereoscopia.
ster·e·o·type (stĕr'ē-ə-tīp', stĭr'-) I. s. estereotipo II. tr. **-typed, -typ·ing** estereotipar.
ster·e·o·ty·py (stĕr'ē-ə-tī'pē) s. estereotipia.
ster·ic (stĕr'ĭk, stĭr'-) adj. FÍS., QUÍM. espacial (apl. a los átomos en la molécula).
ster·ile (stĕr'əl, -īl') adj. estéril.
ster·il·i·ty (stə-rĭl'ĭ-tē) s. esterilidad f.
ster·il·i·za·tion (stĕr'ə-lĭ-zā'shən) s. esterilización f.
ster·il·ize (stĕr'ə-līz') tr. **-ized, -iz·ing** esterilizar.
ster·ling (stûr'lĭng) I. s. FIN. (pound) libra esterlina; (silver) plata de ley; (tableware) plata II. adj. FIN. de la libra esterlina; (silver-related) de plata de ley; FIG. (high-quality) de primera calidad.
sterling silver s. (alloy) plata de ley; (objects) artículos de plata de ley.
stern¹ (stûrn) adj. **-er, -est** (firm) firme; (severe) severo; (gloomy) sombrío; (relentless) implacable.
stern² (stûrn) s. MARÍT. popa; (rear part) parte trasera.
ster·most (stûrn'mōst') adj. MARÍT. popel.
ster·num (stûr'nəm) s. [pl. **-nums** o **-na** (-nə)] esternón m.
stern·ward (stûrn'wərd) I. adj. de popa II. adv. hacia la popa.
stern-wheel·er (stûrn'hwē'lər) s. barco de ruedas a popa.
ster·oid (stîr'oid', stĕr'-) s. QUÍM. esteroide m.
ster·ol (stîr'ŏl', stĕr'-) s. QUÍM. esterol m.
ster·to·rous (stûr'tər-əs) adj. estertoroso.
stet (stĕt) I. s. IMPR. vale (lo tachado) II. tr. **stet·ted, stet·ting** marcar como válido (lo tachado).
steth·o·scope (stĕth'ə-skōp') s. estetoscopio.
Stet·son (stĕt'sən) s. marca registrada de un sombrero.
ste·ve·dore (stē'və-dôr') MARÍT. I. s. estibador m II. tr. & intr. **-dored, -dor·ing** estibar.
stew (stōō, styōō) I. tr. CUL. guisar —intr. (to be cooked) cocerse; FAM. (to swelter) cocerse, ahogarse (de calor); (to worry) agitarse II. s. (dish) guiso; FAM. (agitation) agitación f ♦ **in a s.** agitado.
stew·ard (stōō'ərd, styōō'-) I. s. (manager) administrador m; (household manager) mayordomo; AVIA. auxiliar de vuelo m; MARÍT. (attendant) camarero; (officer) despensero ♦ **shop s.** enlace sindical II. tr. & intr. (to manage) administrar; (to serve) servir.
stew·ard·ess (stōō'ər-dĭs, styōō'-) s. AVIA. azafata.
stew·ard·ship (stōō'ərd-shĭp', styōō'-) s. gerencia, administración f.
stewed (stōōd, styōōd) adj. (cooked) guisado; JER. (drunk) borracho.
stick (stĭk) I. s. (piece of wood) vara, palo; (rod) vara, bastón m; (wand) varilla; (stake) estaca; (of dynamite) cartucho; (of chocolate) barra; (handle) palo, mango; (poke) hurgonazo; (stab) pinchazo, estocada; (adhesiveness) adhesión f; JER. (skinny person) persona flaca; MARÍT. mástil m; palo; MÚS. batuta; IMPR. componedor m, palanca de mando; DEP. palo ♦ **the sticks** región apartada II. tr. **stuck** (stŭk), **stick·ing** (to thrust into) clavar; (to push into) introducir, meter <to s. a stake in the ground meter una estaca en la tierra>; (to add) colocar, poner <s. a few examples in your composition pon algunos ejemplos en tu composición>; (to jab) pinchar; (to fasten) fijar, sujetar; (to pin) prender (con alfileres); (to glue) pegar, adherir; (to impale) clavar; (to delay) retrasar; FAM. (to baffle) desconcertar; (to burden) hacer pagar <they stuck him with the bill le hicieron pagar la cuenta>; JER. (to cheat) estafar, timar ♦ **s. it!** ¡te lo puedes quedar! • **to s. by (someone)** ser fiel a (alguien) • **to s. down** pegar • **to s. it out** JER. aguantarlo, soportarlo • **to s. one's neck out** arriesgarse • **to s. out** (tongue) mostrar, sacar; (head) asomar • **to s. up** (to rob) asaltar, atracar; (to affix) pegar • **to s. up for** defender —intr. (as a nail, pin) clavarse; (to cling) pegarse, adherirse; (to be at a standstill) quedarse parado, detenerse; (to hesitate) dudar, vacilar; (to persevere) perseverar, ser constante; (to stay) quedarse, permanecer; (to become obstructed) atascarse, bloquearse ♦ **to s. around** quedarse • **to s. at** vacilar en • **to s. at it** FAM. persistir • **s. at nothing** FAM. no reparar en nada • **to s. close** man-

tenerse juntos • **to s. out** sobresalir • **to s. to** (responsibilities) cumplir con; (word, promise) cumplir; (friend) ser fiel a; (truth, source) ceñirse a; (to become affixed) pegarse o adherirse fuertemente a; (to persevere) perseverar, persistir en • **to s. to business** dejarse de rodeos • **to s. to it** perseverar, no abandonar • **to s. to one's guns** mantenerse uno en sus trece • **to s. to the point** no divagar • **to s. together** mantenerse unidos, no separarse.
stick·er (stĭk'ər) s. (adhesive label) etiqueta adhesiva; (prickle) espina; (tiresome person) lapa, pelma mf; (tenacious person) persona tenaz.
stick·i·ness (stĭk'ē-nĭs) s. (adhesiveness) adhesividad f; (dampness) humedad f.
sticking plaster s. esparadrapo.
stick-in-the-mud (stĭk'ĭn-thə-mŭd') s. FAM. (spoilsport) aguafiestas mf; (unmotivated person) persona sin iniciativa.
stick·le (stĭk'əl) intr. **-led, -ling** ser rigorista.
stick·le·back (stĭk'əl-băk') s. ICT. picón m, pez espinoso.
stick·ler (stĭk'lər) s. (person) persona rigorista; (problem) problema peliagudo.
stick·pin (stĭk'pĭn') s. alfiler de corbata m.
stick shift s. AUTO. cambio manual.
stick·up (stĭk'ŭp') s. JER. robo, atraco.
stick·y (stĭk'ē) adj. **-i·er, -i·est** (adhesive) pegajoso; (humid) húmedo, pegajoso; FAM. (difficult) difícil.
stiff (stĭf) I. adj. **-er, -est** (rigid) rígido; (not limber) tieso, duro; (joint) anquilosado; (taut) tenso, tirante; (formal) formal, ceremonioso; (thick) espeso; (unyielding) firme, inflexible; (strong) fuerte, recio (corriente, viento); (drink) fuerte, cargado; (difficult) difícil, arduo; (said of punishment) severo, duro; (said of prices) excesivo, alto ♦ **to keep a s. upper lip** a mal tiempo buena cara II. adv. ♦ **to be bored s.** estar muy aburrido • **to be scared s.** estar muerto de miedo III. s. JER. (corpse) fiambre m; (priggish person) pedante mf; (drunk) borracho; (tramp) vagabundo; (miser) tacaño.
stiff·en (stĭf'ən) tr. & intr. ponerse rígido.
stiff-necked (stĭf'nĕkt') adj. terco, obstinado.
stiff·ness (stĭf'nĭs) s. (rigidity) rigidez f, inflexibilidad f; (toughness) dureza; (thickness) consistencia, espesor m; (of a drink) fuerza; (of a knee) anquilosamiento; (of a muscle) agarrotamiento, entumecimiento; FIG. (difficulty) dificultad f, lo difícil; (obstinacy) obstinación f, terquedad f.
sti·fle¹ (stī'fəl) tr. **-fled, -fling** (to suffocate) sofocar; (to cut off) amortiguar, sofocar; (to suppress) reprimir, sofocar —intr. sofocarse.
sti·fle² (stī'fəl) s. ZOOL. babilla.
stig·ma (stĭg'mə) s. [pl. **stig·ma·ta** (stĭg-mä'tə, stĭg'mə-tə) o **stig·mas**] (brand) estigma m; FIG. (stain) tacha, desdoro ♦ **stigmata** RELIG. estigmas.
stig·mat·ic (stĭg-măt'ĭk) adj. (stigmatized) infamante, estigmatizador; ÓPT. anastigmático.
stig·ma·tize (stĭg'mə-tīz') tr. **-tized, -tiz·ing** estigmatizar.
stile¹ (stīl) s. (steps) peldaños para pasar por encima de una cerca; (turnstile) torniquete m.
stile² (stīl) s. ARQ. montante m.
sti·let·to (stə-lĕt'ō) s. [pl. **-tos** o **-toes**] (dagger) estilete m; COST. (piercing tool) punzón m.
still¹ (stīl) I. adj. **-er, -est** (silent) silencioso; (hushed) suave; (at rest) inmóvil; (tranquil) sosegado, apacible; (free of current) mansa <the s. waters of the lake las aguas mansas del lago>; (not effervescent) no espumoso <s. wine vino no espumoso>; FOTOG. fija II. s. (silence) silencio; (stillness) quietud f; FOTOG. foto fija III. adv. (motionlessly) quieto <stand s.! ¡quédate quieto!>; (yet) todavía <he is s. awake todavía está despierto>; (even) aun <s. more complaints arrived llegaron aun más quejas; (nevertheless) a pesar de, sin embargo IV. conj. sin embargo, con todo V. tr. (to make tranquil) tranquilizar; (to silence) callar, hacer callar <he stilled the noisy students hizo callar a los alumnos bulliciosos>; (to stop) detener, parar <to s. all movement detener todo movimiento>; (to allay) aplacar, apaciguar; (to calm) calmar —intr. (to calm down)

calmarse; *(to become quiet)* callarse *<the class stilled as the teacher came in* la clase se calló al entrar el profesor>.

still² (stĭl) s. *(apparatus)* alambique *m*; *(distillery)* destilería.

still·birth (stĭl'bûrth') s. *(birth)* parto de un mortinato; *(fetus)* feto muerto al nacer.

still·born (stĭl'bôrn') adj. nacido muerto.

still life s. [pl. **still lifes**] ARTE. naturaleza muerta, bodegón *m*.

still·ness (stĭl'nĭs) s. *(quietness)* quietud *f*, calma; *(silence)* silencio.

stilt (stĭlt) I. s. *(walking pole)* zanco; *(support post)* pilote *m*; ORNIT. [pl. **stilts** o **stilt**] zancuda II. tr. *(to raise)* poner en zancos; *(to support)* poner sobre pilotes.

stilt·ed (stĭl'tĭd) adj. *(artificial)* afectado; ARQ. peraltado (arco).

stim·u·lant (stĭm'yə-lənt) s. FISIOL. *(accelerating agent)* estimulante *m*; *(stimulus)* estímulo; *(beverage)* bebida alcohólica.

stim·u·late (stĭm'yə-lāt') tr. **-lat·ed, -lat·ing** estimular —intr. *(to be a stimulant)* servir de estímulo; *(to act as a stimulus)* actuar como estimulante.

stim·u·la·tion (stĭm'yə-lā'shən) s. estímulo.

stim·u·la·tive (stĭm'yə-lā'tĭv) o **stim·u·la·to·ry** (-lə-tôr'ē) adj. estimulante.

stim·u·lus (stĭm'yə-ləs) s. [pl. **-li** (-lī')] FISIOL. estímulo; *(incentive)* incentivo.

sting (stĭng) I. tr. **stung** (stŭng), **sting·ing** *(to bite)* picar *<mosquitoes will s. you* los mosquitos te picarán>; *(to hurt)* escocer; FIG. *(to wound)* herir *<her words stung him deeply* sus palabras le hirieron profundamente>; JER. *(to cheat)* estafar, clavar —intr. *(to prick)* picar, pinchar; *(to cause pain)* hacer escocer II. s. *(bite)* picadura; *(pain)* escozor *m*; FIG. *(power)* vigor *m*, fuerza; *(stimulus)* estímulo; *(sarcasm)* mordacidad *f* *<he was offended by the s. of her words* le ofendió la mordacidad de sus palabras>; FIG. *(power)* vigor, fuerza *<his words lack s.* sus palabras carecen de fuerza>; FAM. *(swindle)* estafa; BOT., ZOOL. aguijón *m*.

sting·er (stĭng'ər) s. *(organ)* aguijón *m*; FIG. *(insult)* pulla; *(cocktail)* cóctel de crema de menta y coñac *m*.

stin·gi·ness (stĭn'jē-nĭs) s. mezquindad *f.*

sting·ray (stĭng'rā') s. ICT. pastinaca.

stin·gy (stĭn'jē) adj. **-gi·er, -gi·est** *(miserly)* tacaño, avariento; *(insufficient)* escaso.

stink (stĭngk) I. intr. **stank** (stăngk) o **stunk** (stŭngk), **stunk, stink·ing** *(to smell)* heder, apestar; *(to be in bad repute)* tener mala fama; JER. *(to reek)* oler *<the situation stinks of danger* la situación huele a peligro>; *(to be bad)* ser muy malo, estar fatal *<his performance stank* su actuación estuvo fatal> ♦ **to s. of money** estar podrido de dinero • **to s. up** dar mal olor II. s. hedor *m* ♦ **to make** o **raise a s.** armar un escándalo.

stink·er (stĭng'kər) s. *(smelly person)* persona que apesta; JER. *(contemptible person)* canalla *mf*, mala persona; *(difficult thing)* gran problema *m*.

stink·ing (stĭng'kĭng) I. adj. *(fetid)* apestoso; JER. *(drunk)* borracho II. adv. JER. enormemente, muy.

stint (stĭnt) I. tr. *(to restrict)* restringir, limitar; *(to be sparing with)* escatimar II. s. *(work)* trabajo, tarea; *(limitation)* limitación *f*, restricción *f.*

sti·pend (stī'pĕnd') s. estipendio.

stip·ple (stĭp'əl) I. tr. **-pled, -pling** puntear II. s. punteado.

stip·u·lar (stĭp'yə-lər) adj. BOT. estipular.

stip·u·late¹ (stĭp'yə-lāt') tr. & intr. **-lat·ed, -lat·ing** estipular.

stip·u·late² (stĭp'yə-lĭt) adj. BOT. estipulado.

stip·u·la·tion (stĭp'yə-lā'shən) s. estipulación *f.*

stip·ule (stĭp'yōōl) s. BOT. estípula.

stir¹ (stûr) I. tr. **stirred, stir·ring** *(to mix)* revolver, mezclar; *(to move)* mover, agitar *<the wind stirred the leaves* el viento agitaba las hojas>; *(to rouse)* despertar (del sueño, de la indiferencia); *(to incite)* incitar, provocar; *(to excite)* excitar, avivar; *(to affect)* conmover *<the music stirred him* la música le conmovió>; *(to evoke)* despertar *<her words stirred forgotten memories* sus palabras despertaron recuerdos olvidados>* ♦ **to s. up** *(to mix)* mezclar; *(to provoke)* provocar —intr. *(to change position)* cambiar de posición *<he stirred constantly while he slept* cambiaba de

posición constantemente al dormir>; *(to move)* moverse; *(to happen)* ocurrir *<something stirred inside him* algo ocurría en su interior>; *(to be easily mixed)* mezclarse II. s. *(movement)* movimiento; *(disturbance)* conmoción *f*, agitación *f*; *(flurry)* sensación *f* *<to create a s.* causar una sensación>.

stir² (stûr) s. JER. *(jail)* prisión *f*, chirona.

stir·rer (stûr'ər) s. agitador *m.*

stir·ring (stûr'ĭng) adj. *(rousing)* bullicioso, emocionante; *(active)* activo; *(lively)* animado.

stir·rup (stûr'əp, stĭr'-) s. EQUIT. estribo; MARÍT. estribo de marchapié.

stitch (stĭch) I. s. COST. *(needle stroke)* puntada; *(loop)* punto; *(arrangement)* punto; *(suture)* punto de sutura; FIG. *(bit)* puntada, pizca; MED. punzada ♦ **a s. in time saves nine** más vale prevenir que curar • **to be in stitches** estar muerto de risa • **without a s. on** en cueros II. tr. *(to sew)* coser; *(to ornament)* ribetear; *(to bind)* encuadernar —intr. coser.

stitch·er (stĭch'ər) s. COST. *(person)* costurero; *(machine)* máquina de coser.

sto·a (stō'ə) s. [pl. **sto·ae** (stō'ē') o **sto·as**] s. HIST. pórtico.

stoat (stōt) s. [pl. **stoats** o **stoat**] G.B. armiño.

stock (stŏk) I. s. *(inventory)* existencias, stock *m*; *(supply)* surtido; *(livestock)* ganado; *(capital)* capital social o comercial *m*; *(shares)* acciones *f*; *(paper)* papel *m*; *(ancestry)* familia *<to come from good s.* proceder de una buena familia>; *(lineage)* linaje *m*; *(race)* raza; *(raw material)* materia prima; *(broth)* extracto, caldo; *(supporting structure)* soporte *m*, base *f*; *(of a tree)* tronco; *(of a weapon)* culata; *(of a tool, whip)* mango; *(of an anchor)* cepo; *(of a lathe)* cabezal *m*; *(of a plow)* mancera; *(repertoire)* repertorio ♦ **in s.** en existencia, en depósito • **laughing s.** hazmerreír • **lock, s. and barrel** por completo • **out of s.** agotado • **surplus s.** excedentes • **to put s. in** darle importancia a • **to take s. of** evaluar II. tr. *(to supply)* surtir, abastecer; *(to store)* almacenar; *(to keep in supply)* tener existencias de ♦ **to s. up on** proveerse o abastecerse de —intr. brotar III. adj. *(kept in stock)* en existencia, de surtido; *(dealing with stock)* de las existencias; *(said of an animal)* reproductor; *(pertaining to livestock)* ganadero; *(said of repertoire)* de repertorio ♦ **a s. answer** una respuesta trillada o muy repetida.

stock·ade (stŏ-kād') I. s. *(barrier)* empalizada; *(prison)* prisión militar *f* II. tr. **-ad·ed, -ad·ing** empalizar, vallar.

stock·breed·ing (stŏk'brē'dĭng) s. ganadería.

stock·bro·ker (stŏk'brō'kər) s. FIN. corredor de bolsa *m*, agente de bolsa *m.*

stock·bro·king (stŏk'brō'kĭng) o **stock·bro·ker·age** (-brō'kər-ĭj) s. COM., FIN. correduría o corretaje de bolsa *m.*

stock car s. AUTO. automóvil corriente modificado para carreras; F.C. vagón para el ganado *m.*

stock certificate s. FIN. título de acciones.

stock company s. FIN. sociedad anónima.

stock exchange s. FIN. bolsa.

stock·hold·er (stŏk'hōl'dər) s. FIN. accionista *mf.*

Stock·holm (stŏk'hōm', -hōlm') s. Estocolmo.

stock·ing (stŏk'ĭng) s. *(hose)* media; *(sock)* calcetín *m.*

stocking cap s. gorro (en forma de cono y con borla).

stock-in-trade (stŏk'ĭn-trād') s. COM. *(of a store)* existencias *f*; FIG. *(of a person)* repertorio *<that joke is part of his s.* éste es un chiste de su repertorio>.

stock·job·ber (stŏk'jŏb'ər) s. G.B. *(broker's agent)* agente de corredores de bolsa *m*; *(broker)* corredor de bolsa *m.*

stock·man (stŏk'mən) s. [pl. **-men**] *(cattle raiser)* ganadero; *(warehouse worker)* almacenero.

stock market s. FIN. bolsa.

stock·pile o **stock pile** (stŏk'pīl') I. s. reservas II. tr. **-piled, -pil·ing** acumular.

stock·room o **stock room** (stŏk'rōōm', -rōōm') s. depósito (de mercancía).

stock-still (stŏk'stĭl') adj. completamente inmóvil *<he stood s.* se quedó completamente inmóvil>.

stock·tak·ing (stŏk'tā'kĭng) s. COM. inventario.

stock·y (stŏk'ē) adj. **-i·er, -i·est** *(solidly built)* fuerte, robusto; *(plump)* rechoncho.

stock·yard (stŏk′yärd′) s. corral de ganado m.
stodg·y (stŏj′ē) adj. **-i·er, -i·est** *(dull)* aburrido, pesado; *(heavy)* pesado; *(stocky)* robusto.
sto·gy *o* **sto·gie** (stō′gē) s. [pl. **-gies**] *(cigar)* tagarnina, cigarro puro barato; *(shoe)* zapato fuerte.
sto·ic (stō′ĭk) *o* **sto·i·cal** (-ĭ-kəl) adj. & s. estoico.
sto·i·cism (stō′ĭ-sĭz′əm) s. estoicismo.
stoke (stōk) tr. & intr. **stoked, stok·ing** alimentar, echar combustible a.
stoke·hold (stōk′hōld′) s. MARÍT. cuarto de calderas.
stoke·hole (stōk′hōl′) s. MARÍT. *(opening)* boca del horno; *(stokehold)* cuarto de calderas.
stok·er (stō′kər) s. *(person)* fogonero; *(feeding device)* cargador mecánico.
stole¹ (stōl) s. estola.
stole² (stōl) pret. de **steal**.
sto·len (stō′lən) part. p. de **steal**.
stol·id (stŏl′ĭd) adj. impasible.
sto·ma (stō′mə) s. [pl. **-ma·ta** (-mə-tə) *o* **-mas**] estoma m.
stom·ach (stŭm′ək) **I.** s. ANAT., ZOOL. estómago; *(abdomen)* abdomen m, vientre m; FIG. *(appetite)* apetito; *(desire)* deseo, gana **II.** tr. aguantar, soportar.
stom·ach·ache (stŭm′ək-āk′) s. dolor de estómago m.
stom·ach·ic (stə-măk′ĭk) adj. & s. estomacal.
stomach pump s. MED. bomba gástrica.
stomp (stŏmp, stômp) **I.** tr. & intr. pisotear **II.** s. *(dance)* baile con zapateo pesado m; *(music)* música de jazz (para baile con zapateo).
stone (stōn) **I.** s. *(rock)* piedra; *(pebble)* guijarro; *(tombstone)* lápida; *(millstone)* piedra, muela; *(milestone)* mojón m; *(gem)* piedra preciosa; *(hailstone)* granizo; G.B. *(weight unit)* peso que equivale a 6,350 kg; BOT. hueso; ANAT., MED. cálculo; IMPR. piedra ♦ **within a stone's throw** a dos pasos • **to cast the first s.** lanzar la primera piedra • **to leave no s. unturned** remover Roma con Santiago **II.** tr. **stoned, ston·ing** *(to throw)* apedrear, lapidar; *(to pit)* deshuesar, quitar el hueso; *(to cover)* empedrar; *(to polish)* pulir; *(to sharpen)* afilar.
Stone Age s. ARQUEOL. Edad de Piedra f.
stone-blind (stōn′blīnd′) adj. completamente ciego.
stone-broke (stōn′brōk′) adj. JER. sin un centavo.
stone-cut·ter (stōn′kŭt′ər) s. *(one who cuts)* cantero, picapedrero; *(machine)* máquina para labrar piedra.
stoned (stōnd) adj. JER. *(drunk)* borracho; *(drugged)* drogado, intoxicado.
stone-deaf (stōn′dĕf′) adj. sordo como una tapia.
stone·ma·son (stōn′mā′sən) s. albañil m.
stone·wall (stōn′wôl′) **I.** intr. FAM. *(to stall)* ganar tiempo; *(to refuse)* negarse a contestar *o* a cooperar; DEP. *(to defend only)* jugar a la defensiva (solamente) **II.** tr. FAM. negarse a contestar a *o* a cooperar con.
stone·ware (stōn′wâr′) s. gres m.
stone·work (stōn′wûrk′) s. *(technique)* construcción de piedra f; *(masonry)* cantería.
ston·y *o* **ston·ey** (stō′nē) adj. **-i·er, -i·est** *(stone-covered)* pedregoso; *(like stone)* pétreo; FIG. *(unemotional)* frío; *(impassive)* impasible; *(numbing)* paralizador.
stood (stŏod) pret. y part. p. de **stand**.
stooge (stōoj) s. *(follower)* secuaz mf; *(stool pigeon)* soplón m; TEAT. comparsa m.
stool (stōol) **I.** s. *(seat)* taburete m; *(footrest)* escabel m; *(privy)* retrete m, excusado; *(bowel movement)* evacuación del vientre f; *(fecal matter)* deposiciones f, heces fecales f; BOT. *(stump)* planta madre; *(shoot)* tallo **II.** intr. *(to sprout)* echar retoños; *(to defecate)* defecar; JER. *(to act as stool pigeon)* hacer el papel de soplón.
stool pigeon s. *(pigeon)* reclamo; JER. *(informer)* soplón m, delator m.
stoop¹ (stōop) **I.** intr. *(to bend)* agacharse, encorvarse; *(to walk)* caminar agachado *o* encorvado; *(to lower oneself)* rebajarse, humillarse; *(to condescend)* condescender; *(to swoop)* arrojarse (sobre presa) —tr. *(to bend)* encorvar; *(to debase)* rebajar, degradar **II.** s. *(habitual bending)* inclinación de hombros f.
stoop² (stōop) s. *(porch)* pórtico.
stoop³ (stōop) s. var. de **stoup**.

stop (stŏp) **I.** tr. **stopped, stop·ping** *(to halt)* parar, detener <*the policeman stopped the car* el policía detuvo el automóvil>; *(to cease)* dejar de <*the criminal stopped running* el criminal dejó de correr>; *(to end)* acabar; *(to prevent)* impedir, evitar; *(to interrupt)* interrumpir; *(to staunch)* restañar; *(to plug)* taponar, tapar <*we must s. the leak in the ceiling* tenemos que tapar la gotera en el techo>; *(to constrict)* estrechar (orificio, apertura); *(to obstruct)* obstruir, bloquear <*the crane was stopping traffic* la grúa bloqueaba el tráfico>; MÚS. *(to press a string)* pisar; *(to cease)* tapar (agujero) ♦ **s. it!** ¡basta! • **to s. a bullet** recibir un balazo • **to s. a check** anular *o* cancelar un cheque • **to s. one's ears** taparse las orejas, no escuchar • **to s. up** taponar —intr. *(to halt)* detenerse, pararse; *(to cease)* cesar <*the noise stopped* el ruido cesó>; *(to visit briefly)* hacer alto, hacer una parada; *(to stay)* quedarse, alojarse ♦ **to s. at nothing** no pararse en barras • **to s. by** *o* **in** hacer una visita corta • **to s. dead** *o* **short** pararse en seco • **to s. off** pararse, detenerse • **to s. over** quedarse, alojarse **II.** s. *(act)* detención f; *(cessation)* cesación f; *(finish)* fin m, término; *(stay)* estancia f; *(place)* parada, apeadero; AVIA., MARÍT. *(route stop)* escala <*the flight makes a s. in New York* el vuelo hace escala en Nueva York>; *(plug)* tapón m; COM., FIN. *(withholding order)* orden de suspensión de pago f; MÉC. tope m; FOTOG. *(diaphragm)* diafragma m; GRAM. punto <*put a s. at the end of the sentence* pon un punto al final de la oración>; MÚS. *(act of pressing)* pisada (de cuerdas); *(stoppage)* obturación; *(on a wind instrument)* agujero; *(fret)* traste m; *(key)* llave f; *(organ)* registro; MARÍT. *(line)* boza; FONÉT. consonante oclusiva ♦ **full s.** punto • **to be at a s.** estar parado *o* en calma • **to come to a s.** pararse • **to pull out all the stops** tocar todos los registros • **to put a s. to** poner fin a **III.** adj. de finalización, final.
stop·cock (stŏp′kŏk′) s. llave de paso f.
stop·gap (stŏp′găp′) s. substituto.
stop·light (stŏp′līt′) s. *(traffic signal)* semáforo; AUTO. *(brake light)* luz de frenado f.
stop·o·ver (stŏp′ō′vər) s. *(interruption)* escala; *(place)* lugar visitado.
stop·page (stŏp′ĭj) s. *(stop)* parada; *(work halt)* paro.
stop·per (stŏp′ər) **I.** *(cork, plug)* tapón m; MEC. obturador m **II.** tr. taponar.
stop sign s. señal de alto (para el tráfico) f.
stop·watch (stŏp′wŏch′) s. cronómetro.
stor·age (stôr′ĭj) s. *(action)* almacenamiento; *(space)* depósito, almacén m; *(fee)* almacenaje m; ELEC. acumulación f.
storage battery s. ELEC. acumulador m.
storage cell s. ELEC. acumulador m.
store (stôr) **I.** s. *(shop)* tienda, almacén m; *(supply)* provisión f, surtido <*a large s. of candy* un gran surtido de dulces>; *(warehouse)* almacén, depósito; *(abundance)* acopio, abundancia ♦ **department s.** gran almacén • **in s.** en depósito • **stores** MIL. *(equipment)* pertrechos; *(supplies)* provisiones, víveres • **to be in s. for one** esperarle a uno • **to have in s.** tener guardado, guardar • **to set s. by** dar importancia a **II.** tr. **stored, stor·ing** *(to supply)* abastecer, proveer; *(to deposit)* almacenar, poner en depósito ♦ **to s. away** guardar • **to s. up** almacenar, acumular —intr. *(to keep)* conservarse <*milk does not s. well* la leche no se conserva bien>.
store-bought (stôr′bôt′) adj. FAM. de tienda, de confección <*s. clothes* ropa de tienda>.
store·front (stôr′frŭnt′) s. local que da a la calle y está situado en la planta baja m.
store·house (stôr′hous′) s. depósito, almacén m.
store·keep·er (stôr′kē′pər) s. *(shopkeeper)* tendero; *(food-store keeper)* almacenero.
store·room (stôr′rōom′, -rōom′) s. despensa, bodega.
sto·rey (stôr′ē) s. var. de **story²**.
sto·ried (stôr′ēd) adj. *(celebrated)* celebrado por la historia; *(ornamented)* historiado <*s. tapestry* tapiz historiado>.
stork (stôrk) s. cigüeña.
storm (stôrm) **I.** s. *(atmospheric disturbance)* tormenta; *(wind)* vendaval m; *(shower)* bombardeo, lluvia <*a s. of protest* una lluvia de protestas>; *(outburst)* arrebato (de furia); *(upheaval)* conmoción f, tumulto; *(attack)* ataque

m, asalto ♦ **to ride out** *o* **weather a s.** capear el temporal • **to take by s.** tomar por asalto **II.** intr. *(to blow, rain)* haber tormenta; *(to rant)* vociferar; *(to shower)* bombardear <*they stormed him with questions* lo bombardearon con preguntas> ♦ **to s. in (out)** entrar (salir) violentamente —tr. tomar por asalto.

storm·bound (stôr′bound′) adj. detenido por la tormenta.

storm cellar s. refugio contra los ciclones.

storm center s. *(central area)* centro de la tormenta; FIG. *(center of trouble)* centro *o* foco de disturbios.

storm cloud s. nubarrón *m.*

storm door s. contrapuerta.

storm·i·ness (stôr′mē-nĭs) s. *(weather condition)* estado tempestuoso; *(atmosphere)* atmósfera caldeada (en discusión, reunión).

storm trooper s. HIST. miliciano nazi.

storm window s. contraventana, ventana suplementaria.

storm·y (stôr′mē) adj. **-i·er, -i·est** *(tempestuous)* tempestuoso; *(violent)* violento, turbulento.

sto·ry¹ (stôr′ē) **I.** s. [pl. **-ries**] *(narration)* narración *f;* *(narrative)* cuento, relato; *(plot)* trama, argumento <*the s. of the play is good* la trama de la obra de teatro es buena>; *(version)* versión *f;* *(article)* artículo <*write a s. for the paper* escribe un artículo para el periódico>; *(anecdote)* anécdota; *(lie)* embuste *m,* mentira; *(legend)* leyenda **II.** tr. **-ried, -ry·ing** ANT. narrar.

sto·ry² (stôr′ē) s. [pl. **-ries**] piso (de edificio).

sto·ry·book (stôr′ē-bŏŏk′) **I.** s. libro de cuentos **II.** adj. FIG. *(perfect)* perfecto; *(romantic)* romántico.

sto·ry·tell·er (stôr′ē-tĕl′ər) s. *(author)* cuentista *mf;* *(narrator)* narrador *m;* FAM. *(liar)* mentiroso.

stoup (stōōp) s. *(tankard)* jarra; RELIG. pila de agua bendita.

stout (stout) **I.** adj. **-er, -est** *(bulky)* corpulento; *(determined)* determinado, resuelto; *(brave)* valiente, bravo; *(sturdy)* fornido, vigoroso; *(substantial)* sólido; *(powerful)* enérgico; *(staunch)* firme **II.** s. *(person)* persona corpulenta; *(size)* tamaño grande (de prenda); *(beer)* cerveza de malta, cerveza negra.

stout·heart·ed (stout′här′tĭd) adj. valiente.

stove¹ (stōv) s. *(cooker)* cocina; *(kiln)* horno; *(heater)* estufa; *(hothouse)* invernadero.

stove² (stōv) un pret. y part. p. de **stave.**

stove·pipe (stōv′pīp′) s. *(pipe)* tubo (de chimenea, estufa); *(hat)* chistera.

stow (stō) tr. *(to store)* guardar; *(to fill)* llenar, atestar ♦ **s. it!** JER. ¡cierra el pico! • **to s. away** *(to put away)* guardar, almacenar; FIG., FAM. *(to gobble up)* tragar, zamparse; *(to be a stowaway)* viajar de polizón.

stow·age (stō′ĭj) s. *(storage)* almacenamiento; *(goods)* provisiones *f;* *(fee)* almacenaje *m.*

stow·a·way (stō′ə-wā′) s. polizón *m.*

stra·bis·mus (strə-bĭz′məs) s. MED. estrabismo.

strad·dle (străd′l) **I.** tr. **-dled, -dling** *(to sit)* sentarse a horcajadas sobre *o* en; *(to favor two sides)* no tomar ningún partido en; *(to shoot)* encuadrar (el blanco) ♦ **to s. the fence** nadar entre dos aguas —intr. *(to sit)* sentarse a horcajadas; *(to sprawl)* esparrancarse; *(to favor two sides)* nadar entre dos aguas **II.** s. *(posture)* posición a horcajadas *f;* FIG. *(noncommittal position)* posición ambigua; FIN. opción (de compra y venta) *f.*

strafe (străf) MIL. **I.** tr. **strafed, straf·ing** bombardear **II.** s. bombardeo.

strag·gle (străg′əl) intr. **-gled, -gling** *(to fall behind)* rezagarse; *(to spread out)* desparramarse.

strag·gly (străg′lē) adj. desordenado.

straight (strāt) **I.** adj. **-er, -est** *(not curved)* recto <*a s. road* un camino recto>; *(not bent)* derecho <*a s. piece of wire* un pedazo de alambre derecho>; *(erect)* erguido; *(frank)* sincero, franco <*give me a s. answer* dame una respuesta franca>; *(uninterrupted)* seguido, consecutivo <*he worked ten s. hours* trabajó diez horas seguidas>; *(in cards)* en escalera; *(orderly)* arreglado, en orden; *(undeviating)* auténtico <*a s. communist* un comunista auténtico>; *(in sequence)* en orden; *(undiluted)* puro <*a s. whisky, please*

un whiskey puro, por favor>; *(without discount)* fijo <*that is the s. price* ése es el precio fijo>; *(even)* parejo <*s. teeth* dientes parejos>; *(honorable)* honrado, honesto <*a s. man* un hombre honrado>; JER. *(conventional)* conservador, convencional <*she is too s. for my liking* es demasiado convencional paro mi gusto>; *(heterosexual)* heterosexual; *(sober)* sobrio <*she's still s. after five drinks* todavía está sobria después de cinco tragos>; MEC. con los cilindros en línea recta ♦ **s. hair** pelo lacio • **s. talk** lenguaje franco • **to keep a s. face** mantenerse impávido **II.** adv. **-er, -est** *(direct)* en línea recta; *(erect)* derecho <*stand s.* ponte derecho>; *(without delay)* directamente <*come s. home* ven directamente a casa>; *(candidly)* sinceramente, francamente; *(continuously)* continuamente; *(at a fixed price)* a precio fijo ♦ **s. ahead** *(in front)* en frente; *(forward)* todo seguido, para adelante • **s. away** *o* **off** *(at once)* inmediatamente; *(without interruption)* sin interrupción • **to go s.** enmendarse • **to look someone s. in the eye** mirar a alguien a los ojos • **to read s. through** leer de un tirón • **to set s.** *(to correct)* corregir; *(to fix)* arreglar; *(watch)* poner en hora; *(to put in order)* poner en orden, arreglar; *(to cure)* curar; *(to set right)* poner bien • **to tell someone something s.** decirle algo a alguien sin rodeos **III.** s. DEP. *(section)* recta <*he passed him on the final s.* le pasó en la recta final>; *(line)* línea recta; *(the straight part)* recta; *(card sequence)* escalera; JER. *(heterosexual person)* persona heterosexual; *(conventional person)* persona conservadora *o* convencional ♦ **the s. and narrow** el buen camino.

straight angle s. GEOM. ángulo plano *o* recto.

straight·a·way (strāt′ə-wā′) **I.** adj. recto, derecho **II.** s. recta **III.** adv. (strāt′ə-wā′) en seguida, inmediatamente.

straight·edge (strāt′ĕj′) s. regla (recta).

straight·en (strāt′n) tr. & intr. enderezar(se) ♦ **to s. out** *(to put in order)* ordenar; *(to solve)* resolver; *(to rectify)* rectificar; *(to improve)* mejorar.

straight face s. cara seria.

straight flush s. escalera de color (en naipes).

straight·for·ward (strāt-fôr′wərd) **I.** adj. *(direct)* directo; *(honest)* honesto, honrado; *(frank)* sincero **II.** adv. *(directly)* directamente; *(frankly)* sinceramente.

straight·jack·et (strāt′jăk′ĭt) s. & v. var. de **straitjacket.**

straight-line (strāt′līn′) adj. *(position)* en línea recta; MEC. de variación lineal; COM. a plazos.

straight man s. TEAT. actor que da pie a un cómico *m.*

straight razor s. navaja de afeitar.

straight·way (strāt′wā′) adv. en seguida, inmediatamente.

strain¹ (strān) **I.** tr. *(to stretch)* estirar, tensar; *(a point)* forzar; *(the nerves)* agotar; *(a limb)* torcer; *(shoulder)* dislocar; *(noodles, vegetables)* colar; *(to sieve)* tamizar; TEC. deformar ♦ **to s. one's eyes** cansar *o* agotar la vista —intr. *(to strive)* esforzarse; *(to stretch)* tenderse; *(to filter)* filtrarse ♦ **to s. under a burden** soportar un peso con gran esfuerzo **II.** s. *(effort)* esfuerzo; *(tension)* tensión *f;* *(exhaustion)* agotamiento; *(twisting)* torcedura; TEC. deformación *f.*

strain² (strān) s. *(race)* raza; *(descent)* cepa; *(tendency)* tendencia; *(kind)* clase *f;* *(tenor)* sentido; *(tone)* tono <*to speak in an angry s.* hablar con un tono de enojo>; *(in poetry)* acentos • **strains** *(sounds)* sonidos lejanos; *(tune)* acordes • **to bear the s. of** llevar el peso de.

strained (strānd) adj. *(through a strainer)* colado; *(forced)* forzado; FIG. *(tense)* tirante (relaciones, situación).

strain·er (strā′nər) s. *(filter)* filtro; *(colander)* colador *m;* *(sieve)* cedazo.

strait (strāt) **I.** s. *(water passage)* estrecho; *(difficult position)* apuro, aprieto ♦ **straits** *(passage)* estrecho; *(position)* aprieto, apuros **II.** adj. ANT. *(confined)* restringido; *(narrow)* angosto, apretado; *(strict)* estricto.

strait·en (strāt′n) tr. *(to make narrow)* estrechar; *(to limit)* limitar; *(to restrict)* restringir.

strait·jack·et (strāt′jăk′ĭt) **I.** s. camisa de fuerza **II.** tr. poner la camisa de fuerza.

strait-laced (strāt′lāst′) adj. puritano, gazmoño.

strand¹ (strănd) **I.** s. *(coastline)* costa; *(beach)* playa **II.** tr.

& intr. MARÍT. *(to run aground)* varar, encallar; *(to abandon)* dejar desamparado.

strand² (stränd) **I.** s. *(tuft)* mechón *m; (of rope)* ramal *m; (single thread)* hebra; *(filament)* filamento; *(of pearls)* sarta **II.** tr. trenzar.

strange (stränj) adj. **strang·er, strang·est** *(familiar)* desconocido; *(odd)* extraño, raro; *(peculiar)* peculiar; *(unexpected)* inesperado; *(exotic)* exótico; *(unacquainted)* desacostumbrado ♦ **strangest of all . . .** lo más extraño del caso es que . . . • **to feel s.** sentirse extraño.

strange·ly (stränj'lē) adv. extrañamente ♦ **s. enough** aunque parezca extraño.

strange·ness (stränj'nĭs) s. *(quality)* lo extraño, lo raro; FÍS. extrañeza, número cuántico.

strang·er (strän'jər) s. *(unknown person)* desconocido; *(foreigner)* extranjero; *(outsider)* forastero ♦ **to be no s.** ser muy conocido • **to be no s. to** conocer muy bien • **to make a s. of** tratar con frialdad a.

stran·gle (sträng'gəl) tr. **-gled, -gling** *(to kill)* estrangular; *(to smother)* sofocar; FIG. *(to suppress)* sofocar; *(to restrict)* limitar —intr. estrangularse.

strangle hold s. *(in wrestling)* collar de fuerza *m;* FIG. *(suppressing action)* dominio completo.

stran·gler (sträng'glər) s. estrangulador *m.*

stran·gling (sträng'glĭng) s. estrangulación *m.*

stran·gu·late (sträng'gyə-lāt') tr. & intr. **-lat·ed, -lat·ing** estrangular(se).

stran·gu·la·tion (sträng'gyə-lā'shən) s. estrangulación *f.*

strap (sträp) **I.** s. *(strip)* tira, correa; *(band)* banda; *(holding loop)* tirante *m; (razor strop)* suavizador (para navaja de afeitar) *m; (whip)* látigo **II.** tr. **strapped, strap·ping** *(to fasten)* atar; *(to whip)* azotar; *(to strop)* suavizar, asentar (una navaja).

strap·hang·er (sträp'häng'ər) s. pasajero de autobús o subterráneo.

strap·less (sträp'lĭs) **I.** adj. *(bandless)* sin tiras; *(dress, undergarment)* sin tirantes **II.** s. COST. vestido sin tirantes.

strapped (sträpt) adj. FAM. sin un centavo.

strap·ping (sträp'ĭng) adj. fornido.

stra·ta (strā'tə, strät'ə) un pl. de **stratum.**

strat·a·gem (strät'ə-jəm) s. estratagema, ardid *m.*

stra·te·gic (strə-tē'jĭk) o **stra·te·gi·cal** (-jĭ-kəl) adj. estratégico.

strat·e·gist (strät'ə-jĭst) s. estratega *m.*

strat·e·gy (strät'ə-jē) s. [pl. **-gies**] estratégia.

strat·i·fi·ca·tion (strät'ə-fĭ-kā'shən) s. estratificación *f.*

strat·i·fy (strät'ə-fī') tr. & intr. **-fied, -fy·ing** estratificar(se).

stra·to·cu·mu·lus (strä'tō-kyōōm'yə-ləs, strät'ō-) s. [pl. **-li** (-lī')] estratocúmulo.

strat·o·sphere (strät'ə-sfîr') s. estratósfera.

stra·tum (strā'təm) s. [pl. **-ta** (-tə) o **-tums**] estrato, capa.

stra·tus (strā'təs, strät'əs) s. [pl. **stra·ti** (strā'tī', strät'ī')] METEOR. estrato.

straw (strô) **I.** s. BOT. paja; *(trifle)* comino <*not to care a s.* (no) importarle un comino> ♦ **a s. in the wind** un indicio • **the last s.** el colmo, la última gota • **to grasp at a s.** o **at straws** agarrarse a un pelo, agarrarse a un clavo ardiendo • **to draw straws** echar suertes **II.** adj. *(made of straw)* de paja; *(color)* pajizo; *(unimportant)* insignificante.

straw·ber·ry (strô'bĕr'ē) s. [pl. **-ries**] frutilla, fresa (planta y fruta).

straw boss s. FAM. capataz interino.

straw man s. *(front man)* testaferro, títere *m; (scarecrow)* hombre de paja *m; (nonentity)* pelele *m,* don nadie *m.*

straw vote s. POL. encuesta preelectoral.

stray (strā) **I.** intr. *(to wander about)* desviarse, apartarse; *(to become lost)* extraviarse, perderse; *(to roam)* errar; *(to go astray)* descarriarse **II.** s. *(dog)* perro callejero; *(cat)* gato callejero; *(child)* niño abandonado **III.** adj. *(lost)* perdido; *(abandoned)* abandonado.

streak (strēk) **I.** s. *(stripe)* raya, línea; *(trait)* fondo, lado <*to have a mean s.* tener un fondo malo>; *(run)* racha <*a s. of good luck* una racha de buena suerte>; MIN. veta **II.** tr. rayar, vetear —intr. pasar con gran rapidez.

streak·ing (strē'kĭng) s. *(hair)* claritos; *(prank)* el correr desnudo por un lugar público.

streak·y (strē'kē) adj. **-i·er, -i·est** *(streaked)* rayado; *(veined)* veteado.

stream (strēm) **I.** s. *(river)* río; *(small river)* arroyo; *(current)* corriente *f; (of blood, water)* chorro; *(of insults)* sarta; *(of tears)* torrente *m; (of people)* oleada ♦ **against the s.** contra la corriente • **to go with the s.** seguir la corriente **II.** intr. *(to flow)* correr, fluir; *(to wave)* ondear, flotar ♦ **to s. in** entrar a raudales • **to s. out** *(people)* salir en tropel; *(liquid)* salir a torrentes.

stream·bed (strēm'bĕd') s. cauce *m,* lecho.

stream·er (strē'mər) s. *(pennant)* gallardete *m; (long strip)* serpentina; *(headline)* titular *m.*

stream·line (strēm'līn') **I.** s. FÍS., MEC. *(fluid line)* corriente natural *f; (contour)* forma aerodinámica **II.** tr. **-lined, -lining** *(to build)* construir en forma aerodinámica; FIG. *(to modernize)* modernizar.

stream·lined (strēm'līnd') s. *(shaped)* aerodinámico; FIG. *(modernized)* moderno, modernizado.

street (strēt) s. calle *f* ♦ **on the s.** FIG. *(unemployed)* en la calle sin trabajo; *(at liberty)* en libertad, en la calle.

street·car (strēt'kär') s. tranvía *m.*

street door s. puerta de la calle, puerta principal.

street·lamp (strēt'lämp') s. farola.

street·light (strēt'līt') s. farola.

street sweeper s. *(person)* barrendero; *(machine)* barredera.

street·walk·er (strēt'wô'kər) s. prostituta.

strength (strĕngkth) s. *(power)* fuerza; *(impregnability)* fortaleza, resistencia; *(solidity)* solidez *f; (intensity)* intensidad *f,* fuerza; *(validity)* validez *f; (efficacy)* eficacia; *(firmness)* firmeza; *(potency)* potencia, poder *m;* MIL., POL. fuerza numérica; COM. firmeza ♦ **by sheer s.** a fuerza viva • **on the s. of** teniendo como base, en virtud de • **s. of character** entereza, firmeza • **to be present in great s.** estar en gran número.

strength·en (strĕngk'thən) tr. *(to reinforce)* reforzar, consolidar; *(to intensify)* dar mayor intensidad a; *(ties)* estrechar; *(relations)* intensificar; MED. fortificar, fortalecer —intr. *(relations)* intensificarse; *(ties)* estrecharse.

strength·en·er (strĕngk'thə-nər) s. *(reinforcement)* refuerzo; *(support)* respaldo, apoyo.

stren·u·ous (strĕn'yōō-əs) adj. *(hard)* penoso; *(active)* vigoroso; *(energetic)* enérgico; *(intense)* intenso.

strep throat s. MED. inflamación de la garganta *f.*

strep·to·coc·cus (strĕp'tə-kŏk'əs) s. [pl. **-coc·ci** (-kŏk'sī', -kŏk'ī')] BACT. estreptococo.

strep·to·my·cin (strĕp'tə-mī'sĭn) s. FARM. estreptomicina.

stress (strĕs) **I.** s. *(significance)* hincapié *m; (compulsion)* presión *f;* GRAM. acento tónico, énfasis *m;* ING., MEC. fatiga ♦ **by s. of weather** a causa de un temporal • **to lay s. on** hacer hincapié en, insistir en **II.** tr. *(to emphasize)* hacer hincapié en, recalcar; ING., MEC. someter a un esfuerzo; GRAM. acentuar.

stres·sor (strĕs'ər) s. elemento de tensión.

stretch (strĕch) **I.** tr. *(to lengthen)* estirar, alargar; *(to reach)* extender, tender <*she stretched out her hand* extendió la mano>; *(muscle, tendon)* distender; *(wings)* desplegar, extender; *(budget, meal)* estirar; *(wire, banner)* tender; *(shoes)* ensanchar ♦ **to s. a point** excederse • **to s. it** exagerar, llevar al extremo • **to s. oneself** estirarse, desperezarse • **to s. the rules** hacer una excepción —intr. *(to become lengthened)* estirarse, alargarse; *(to reach over)* extenderse; *(shoes)* ensancharse ♦ **to s. out** *(the body)* estirarse, desperezarse; *(to lie down)* echarse, tumbarse **II.** s. *(lengthening)* alargamiento; *(elasticity)* elasticidad *f; (of a highway, railroad)* tramo, trecho; *(of a track)* recta; *(of time)* período, tiempo; *(of land)* extensión *f; (of imagination)* esfuerzo ♦ **at a s.** *(in one go)* de un tirón; *(continuously)* seguido • **home s.** última etapa.

stretch·er (strĕch'ər) s. *(litter)* camilla; *(for canvas)* bastidor *m; (for shoes)* horma; CARP. viga, tirante *m.*

stretch·er-bear·er (strĕch'ər-bâr'ər) s. camillero.

stretch·ing (strĕch'ĭng) s. estiramiento.

strew (strōō) tr. **strewn** (strōōn) o **strewed, strew·ing** *(to spread)* esparcir; *(scatter)* desparramar; salpicar.

stri·a (strī'ə) s. [pl. **stri·ae** (strī'ē')] estría.

---

stri·ate (strī′āt′) **I.** adj. estriado **II.** tr. **-at·ed, -at·ing** estriar.
stri·at·ed (strī′āt·ed) adj. estriado.
stri·a·tion (strī-ā′shən) s. *(state)* estriación *f,* estriado; *(stria)* estría.
strick·en (strĭk′ən) **I.** un part. p. de **strike II.** adj. *(wounded)* herido; *(afflicted)* afligido; *(leveled)* nivelado.
strict (strĭkt) adj. **-er, -est** *(exact)* estricto, exacto <a *s. interpretation* una interpretación estricta>; *(severe)* estricto, severo; *(stringent)* estricto, riguroso.
strict·ly (strĭkt′lē) adv. *(exactly)* estrictamente, exactamente; *(severely)* severamente, rigurosamente ♦ **s. speaking** en realidad <*s. speaking, he's right* en realidad tiene razón>.
strict·ness (strĭkt′nĭs) s. *(exactness)* exactitud *f;* *(severity)* severidad *f,* rigor *m.*
stric·ture (strĭk′chər) s. *(criticism)* crítica severa, censura; MED. estrechez *f.*
stride (strīd) **I.** intr. **strode** (strōd), **strid·den** (strĭd′n), **strid·ing** caminar a grandes pasos —tr. *(to stride through)* cruzar a zancadas; *(to straddle)* sentarse a horcajadas en **II.** s. zancada, tranco ♦ **strides** progreso, adelanto • **to make great strides** progresar a grandes pasos • **to take something in one's s.** tomarse las cosas con calma.
stri·dent (strīd′nt) adj. estridente.
strid·u·late (strĭj′ə-lāt′) intr. **-lat·ed, -lat·ing** chirriar.
strife (strīf) s. *(dissension)* disensión *f;* *(conflict)* lucha, conflicto; *(endeavor)* esfuerzo, empeño.
strike (strīk) **I.** tr. **struck** (strŭk), **struck** o **strick·en** (strĭk′ən), **strik·ing** *(to hit sharply)* golpear, pegar; *(to inflict)* asestar, dar <*to s. a blow* asestar un golpe>; *(to crash into)* chocar con, dar contra; *(to hit)* golpear, dar un golpe en <*she then struck the desk with her fist* luego ella dio un golpe en el escritorio con el puño>; *(to collide with)* chocar contra, dar contra; *(to wound)* herir; *(to bite)* morder; *(to attack)* atacar; *(coins, medals)* acuñar; *(an instrument)* tocar; *(lightning)* caer en; *(clock)* dar; *(target)* dar en; *(fish)* coger con el anzuelo; *(a match)* encender <*to s. a match* encender un fósforo>; *(sparks)* hacer saltar; *(to expunge)* tachar; *(to discover)* descubrir, hallar <*to s. gold* hallar oro>; *(to fall upon)* caer o dar en <*a bright light struck her face* una luz fuerte le dio en la cara>; *(to impress)* dar la impresión <*it strikes me as a good idea* me da la impresión de que es una idea muy buena>; *(to appear to)* ocurrírsele a uno <*the thought struck me from out of the blue* la idea se me ocurrió inesperadamente>; *(to cause)* infundir <*he struck terror into their hearts* infundió terror en sus corazones>; *(a pose)* adoptar, tomar; *(sails)* recoger; *(flags)* arriar; *(camp)* desmontar; *(to refuse to work)* declararse en huelga contra; *(to level)* allanar, nivelar; TEAT. desmontar ♦ **to s. a balance** COM. hacer balance; *(equilibrium)* encontrar el término medio o equilibrio • **to s. a bargain** cerrar un trato • **to s. against** o **upon** chocar con, estrellarse contra • **to s. against** atacar, acometer • **to s. a jury** elegir jurado • **to s. an average** encontrar el término medio • **to s. blind** cegar • **to s. down** *(to knock down)* derribar; *(disease)* abatir; MARÍT. arriar • **to s. for** dirigirse hacia • **to s. in with** intervenir con *(idea, sugerencia)* • **to s. into** empezar con ímpetu • **to s. off** *(to expunge)* sacar; *(to cross out)* tachar; *(to deduct)* deducir; IMPR. tirar, imprimir • **to s. oil** COM. encontrar petróleo; FIG., FAM. *(to become rich)* hacerse rico de repente • **to s. on** *(to hit)* dar contra; *(to occur)* ocurrírsele a uno • **to s. out** *(to cross out)* tachar; *(idea, plan)* forjar, idear • **to s. out for** ponerse en marcha hacia • **to s. roots** echar raíces • **to s. through** atravesar, traspasar • **to s. up** *(friendship)* trabar; *(music)* empezar a tocar; *(conversation)* entablar; *(song)* entonar, cantar • **to s. upon** ocurrírsele a uno • **to s. with admiration** llenar de admiración • **to s. with terror** sobrecoger de terror —intr. *(to deal blows)* golpear, dar golpes; *(to attack)* atacar; *(to collide)* chocar; *(to penetrate)* penetrar, atravesar; *(bell, hour)* sonar, dar <*the hour has struck* (el reloj) dio la hora, ha sonado la hora>; *(to become ignited)* encenderse; *(to come unexpectedly)* ocurrir; *(to set out)* dirigirse hacia; *(to engage in a strike)* declararse en huelga; *(fish)* morder la carnada; *(snakes)* morder ♦ **to s. back** devolver golpe por golpe, desquitarse • **to s. home** dar en

el blanco • **to s. out** *(to hit out)* pegar; *(to start out)* tomar una resolución; *(to be a failure)* fallar • **to s. up** MÚS. empezar a tocar **II.** s. *(act)* golpe *m;* *(attack)* ataque *m;* *(cessation of work)* huelga; *(discovery)* descubrimiento; *(by fish)* mordida, picada; *(minting)* acuñación *f;* *(strickle)* rasero; GEOG., MIN. rumbo, arrumbamiento ♦ **a lucky s.** FAM. un golpe de suerte • **to go on s.** declararse en huelga • **to have two strikes against oneself** FAM. estar uno en posición desventajosa.
strike·break·er (strīk′brā′kər) s. rompehuelgas *mf.*
strik·er (strī′kər) s. *(knocker)* golpeador *m;* *(employee)* huelguista *mf;* *(clapper)* badajo; *(of a gun)* percutor *m;* *(harpoon)* harpón *m;* *(harpooner)* harponero *m;* MIL. ordenanza.
strik·ing (strī′kĭng) adj. notable, sorprendente.
string (strĭng) **I.** s. *(cord)* cuerda, cordel *m;* *(things in a row)* hilera, fila; *(series)* sucesión *f,* serie *f* <a *s. of victories* una serie de triunfos>; *(of a violin, racket)* cuerda; *(in billiards)* línea de arranque ♦ **strings** MÚS. instrumentos de cuerda; *(conditions)* condiciones, estipulaciones • **s. of beads** *(rosary)* rosario; *(necklace)* collar • **s. orchestra** orquesta de cuerdas • **to have someone on a s.** tener a alguien en un puño **II.** tr. **strung** (strŭng), **string·ing** *(to fit with strings)* encordar; *(to thread)* enhebrar, ensartar; *(to fasten)* atar con una cuerda; *(to stretch out)* tender ♦ **high strung** muy nervioso, tenso • **to s. along with** acompañar a • **to s. someone along** *(to keep dangling)* dejar a alguien pendiente; *(to deceive)* engañar —intr. *(to form strings)* formar hilos; *(to stretch out)* extenderse.
string bean s. BOT., CUL. judía verde; JER. *(tall person)* persona larguirucha.
string·course (strĭng′kôrs′) s. ARQ. hilada volada, cordón saliente *m.*
stringed (strĭngd) adj. *(tied)* atado; MÚS. de cuerda.
strin·gen·cy (strĭn′jən-sē) s. *(severity)* severidad *f,* rigor *m;* *(scarcity)* escasez *f.*
strin·gent (strĭn′jənt) adj. *(measures)* severo, riguroso; *(time limit)* estricto; *(financial situation)* apurado, difícil; *(imperative)* imperioso.
string·er (strĭng′ər) s. *(one that strings)* ensartador *m;* ARQ. *(horizontal timber)* travesaño; *(stringboard)* riostra; F.C. durmiente *m;* *(free-lance correspondent)* corresponsal pagado por línea *m,* colaborador *m.*
string quartet s. MÚS. *(musicians)* cuarteto de cuerdas; *(composition)* composición para cuarteto de cuerdas.
string·y (strĭng′ē) adj. **-i·er, -i·est** *(fibrous)* fibroso, filamentoso; *(with strings)* lleno de fibras; *(slender)* enjuto.
strip¹ (strĭp) tr. **stripped, strip·ping** *(clothing)* quitar; *(to undress)* desnudar; *(a bed)* deshacer, quitar la ropa de; *(fruit)* pelar; *(tree)* descortezar; *(to dismantle)* desmantelar; *(a screw)* estropear • **to s. down** *(paint)* raspar; *(motor)* desmontar • **to s. of** despojar de • **to s. off** quitar —intr. *(to undress)* desvestirse, desnudarse; *(paint)* desprenderse; *(paper, wood)* despegarse ♦ **to s. off** desnudarse.
strip² (strĭp) **I.** s. *(long piece)* tira, faja; *(fringe)* franja; *(stripe)* lista, listón *m;* AER. pista de aterrizaje **II.** tr. **stripped, strip·ping** hacer tiras.
stripe¹ (strīp) **I.** s. *(long band)* lista, raya; *(fabric)* tela a rayas; MIL. *(chevron)* galón *m;* *(kind)* calaña, clase *f.* <*all politicians are of one s.* todos los políticos son de la misma calaña> ♦ **stripes** uniforme a rayas (de un presidiario) **II.** tr. **striped, strip·ing** rayar.
stripe² (strīp) s. azote, latigazo.
striped (strīpt, strī′pĭd) adj. a rayas, rayado.
strip·ling (strĭp′lĭng) s. mozalbete *m,* joven *m.*
strip mine s. MIN. mina a cielo abierto.
strip-mine (strĭp′mīn′) tr. **-mined, -min·ing** explotar una mina a cielo abierto.
strip·per (strĭp′ər) s. TEAT., JER. bailarina (de strip-tease); MEC. desmoldador *m,* separador *m.*
strip-tease o **strip tease** (strĭp′tēz′) s. strip-tease *m.*
strive (strīv) intr. **strove** (strōv), **striv·en** (strĭv′ən) o **strived, striv·ing** *(to try hard)* esforzarse, procurar <*s. to succeed* esforzarse por triunfar>; *(to struggle)* luchar.

strobe (strōb) s. FOTOG. *(instrument)* estroboscopio; *(light)* luz estroboscópica.
strobe light s. FOTOG. luz estroboscópica.
strob·o·scope (strō'bə-skōp') s. estroboscopio.
strode (strōd) pret. de **stride.**
stroke (strōk) **I.** s. *(strike)* golpe *m*; *(of a bell)* tañido, campanada; MED. *(apoplexy)* apoplejía; *(of the heart)* latido; *(in rowing)* palada, golpe de remo *m*; *(oarsman)* primer remero; *(in swimming)* brazada; *(in golf, tennis)* golpe; *(with a brush)* pincelada; *(with pencil, pen)* trazo ♦ **at the s. of . . .** al dar las . . . • **finishing s.** golpe de gracia • **finishing strokes** toques finales • **s. of luck** suerte • **s. of genius** idea genial • **with one s.** de un plumazo **II.** tr. **stroked, strok·ing** *(to caress)* acariciar; *(in rowing)* fijar el ritmo de la remada para.
stroll (strōl) **I.** intr. pasearse —tr. dar un paseo por **II.** s. paseo.
stroll·er (strō'lər) s. *(promenader)* paseante *mf*; *(actor)* cómico de la legua, cómico ambulante; *(vagabond)* vagabundo; *(for children)* cochecito de niño.
strong (strông) adj. **-er, -est** *(healthy)* fuerte, robusto; *(said of smells, tastes, colors)* fuerte, intenso; *(solid)* fuerte, resistente; *(said of memory, eyes)* bueno; *(proficient)* fuerte, competente; *(powerful)* poderoso; *(resolute)* fuerte, enérgico; *(convincing)* convincente; *(persuasive)* persuasivo; *(said of convictions, emotions, faith)* fuerte, profundo; *(said of accent)* fuerte, marcado; *(said of language)* subido de tono, subido de color ♦ **as s. as an ox** fuerte como un toro *o* un roble • **strong point** fuerte <*discretion is not her s. point* la discreción no es su fuerte> • **to be going s.** FAM. marchar bien • **to be s. in numbers** ser numerosos • **to have a s. character** tener mucho carácter • **to have a s. stomach** tener un buen estómago • **to have s. feelings about something** tener ideas muy firmes sobre algo.
strong-arm (strông'ärm') FAM. **I.** adj. de mano dura ♦ **s. tactics** fuerza **II.** tr. *(to beat)* pegar; *(to intimidate)* intimidar.
strong·box (strông'bŏks') s. caja fuerte, caja de caudales.
strong·hold (strông'hōld') s. MIL. fortaleza; FIG. *(of views, attitudes)* baluarte *m*.
strong·ly (strông'lē) adv. *(with strength)* fuertemente; *(with energy)* vigorosamente, enérgicamente.
strong-mind·ed (strông'mīn'dĭd) adj. determinado, resuelto.
stron·ti·um (strŏn'chē-əm, -tē-) s. QUÍM. estroncio.
strop (strŏp) **I.** s. suavizador (de navajas) *m* **II.** tr. **stropped, strop·ping** suavizar, asentar (una navaja).
stro·phe (strō'fē) s. LIT. estrofa.
strove (strōv) un pret. de **strive.**
struck (strŭk) **I.** pret. y un part. p. de **strike II.** adj. cerrado (por huelga).
struc·tur·al (strŭk'chər-əl) adj. estructural.
struc·tur·al·ism (strŭk'chər-ə-lĭz'əm) s. estructuralismo.
structural steel s. acero para la construcción.
struc·ture (strŭk'chər) **I.** s. *(framework)* estructura; *(construction)* construcción *f* **II.** tr. **-tured, -tur·ing** estructurar.
struc·tured (strŭk'chərd) adj. estructurado.
strug·gle (strŭg'əl) **I.** intr. **-gled, -gling** *(to grapple)* luchar, forcejear; *(to strive)* luchar, esforzarse <*he struggled to be the best* se esforzó por ser el mejor> **II.** s. *(act)* lucha; *(effort)* esfuerzo; *(combat)* lucha, combate *m*.
strug·gling (strŭg'lĭng) **I.** s. lucha **II.** adj. que lucha.
strum (strŭm) MÚS. **I.** tr. **strummed, strum·ming** —intr. rasguear **II.** s. rasgueo.
strum·pet (strŭm'pĭt) s. ramera, prostituta.
strung (strŭng) pret. y part. p. de **string.**
strut (strŭt) **I.** intr. **strut·ted, strut·ting** pavonearse —tr. apuntalar **II.** s. *(gait)* pavoneo; *(rod)* puntal *m*, riostra.
strych·nine (strĭk'nīn', -nĭn) s. QUÍM. estricnina.
stub (stŭb) **I.** s. *(short end)* tocón *m*, cabo; *(coupon)* talón *m*; *(voucher)* resguardo, comprobante de pago *m* **II.** tr. **stubbed, stub·bing** *(weeds)* arrancar; *(a field)* desherbar; *(toe, foot)* tropezar con; *(a cigarette)* apagar.
stub·ble (stŭb'əl) s. *(stalks)* rastrojo; *(beard)* barba incipiente ♦ **s. field** campo de rastrojos.

stub·born (stŭb'ərn) adj. *(obstinate)* obstinado, testarudo <*a s. child* un niño testarudo>; *(persistent)* tenaz; *(resistant)* duro.
stub·born·ness (stŭb'ərn-nĭs) s. obstinación *f*, testarudez *f*.
stub·by (stŭb'ē) adj. **-bi·er, -bi·est** *(person)* rechoncho; *(land)* lleno de cepas.
stuc·co (stŭk'ō) **I.** s. [pl. **-coes** *o* **-cos**] estuco **II.** tr. **-coed, -co·ing** estucar.
stuck (stŭk) pret. y part. p. de **stick.**
stuck-up (stŭk'ŭp') adj. FAM. *(snobbish)* presumido; *(conceited)* engreído.
stud¹ (stŭd) **I.** s. ARQ. *(support post)* montante *m*; *(ornament)* tachón *m*; *(brace)* travesaño; *(spindle)* espiga, husillo **II.** tr. **stud·ded, stud·ding** *(to provide with studs)* tachonar; FIG. *(to strew)* salpicar, llenar.
stud² (stŭd) s. *(breeding horses)* cuadra; *(stable)* caballeriza; *(stallion)* semental *m*; JER. *(man)* hombre viril *m* ♦ **at s.** de cría.
stu·dent (stōōd'nt, styōōd'-) s. *(of a college)* estudiante *mf*; *(pupil)* alumno; *(researcher)* investigador *m*; *(observer)* observador *m*.
student body s. estudiantado.
stud·ied (stŭd'ēd) adj. *(calculated)* premeditado, calculado; *(contrived)* artificioso, afectado; *(learned)* docto.
stu·di·o (stōō'dē-ō', styōō'-) s. [pl. **-os**] ARTE., FOTOG. estudio; CINEM., TELEV., RAD. estudios, estudio; *(of an artist)* taller *m* ♦ **s. apartment** departamento de una habitación, baño y cocina.
stu·di·ous (stōō'dē-əs, styōō'-) adj. *(given to study)* estudioso; *(diligent)* aplicado; *(heedful)* cuidadoso; *(deliberate)* pensado; *(for study)* propicio para el estudio.
stud·y (stŭd'ē) **I.** s. [pl. **-ies**] *(act)* estudio; *(investigation)* estudio, investigación *f*; *(state)* ensimismamiento, meditación *f*; *(room)* estudio, despacho; ARTE., LIT. estudio, bosquejo; MÚS. estudio ♦ **studies** estudios <*he abandoned his studies* abandonó los estudios> **II.** tr. **-ied, -y·ing** *(to attempt learning)* estudiar; *(to scrutinize)* estudiar, examinar ♦ **to s. a part** TEAT. aprender un papel —intr. *(to try to learn)* estudiar; *(to take a course)* cursar estudios, estudiar; *(to ponder)* meditar ♦ **to s. to be** estudiar para • **to s. under** ser alumno de, estudiar con.
stuff (stŭf) **I.** s. *(material, substance)* material *m*; FAM. *(belongings)* cosas <*put your s. over here* pon tus cosas aquí>; *(junk)* basura, disparate <*don't give me that s.* no me contestes con esos disparates>; *(that)* eso <*what is that s.?* ¿qué es eso?>; *(worthless objects)* porquería <*get that s. out of here* saquen esa porquería de aquí>; *(capability)* pasta, madera <*they showed their s. by winning* mostraron su pasta ganando el partido>; G.B. *(fabric)* género, tejido; JER. *(money)* dinero; *(drugs)* drogas ♦ **do your s.!** ¡muestra lo que sabes! • **same old s.** lo mismo de siempre • **to be hot s.** ser fenomenal • **to know one's s.** conocer el percal **II.** tr. *(to cram)* llenar, rellenar; *(to plug)* taponar, tapar; *(to fill)* rellenar; *(an animal skin)* disecar; *(to fill with food)* llenar, atiborrar; *(to place votes)* poner votos falsos en; *(to soften)* impregnar con aceite (cuero) ♦ **get stuffed** FAM. vete a paseo —intr. atiborrarse, hartarse.
stuffed (stŭft) adj. relleno.
stuffed shirt s. FAM. persona estirada.
stuff·ing (stŭf'ĭng) s. relleno.
stuff·y (stŭf'ē) adj. **-i·er, -i·est** *(suffocating)* sofocante, mal ventilado; *(congested)* congestionado, tupido; FAM. *(dull)* aburrido; *(formal)* pomposo.
stul·ti·fy (stŭl'tə-fī') tr. **-fied, -fy·ing** *(to dispirit)* desanimar; *(to disable)* anular; *(to ridicule)* ridiculizar, poner en ridículo; DER. alegar incapacidad mental.
stum·ble (stŭm'bəl) **I.** intr. **-bled, -bling** *(to trip)* tropezar; *(to flounder)* balbucear; *(to blunder)* cometer un desliz; *(to come upon)* encontrar de casualidad —tr. hacer tropezar ♦ **to s. across** *o* **on** *o* **upon** tropezar con **II.** s. *(act)* tropiezo, traspié *m*; *(mistake)* desliz *m*.
stumbling block s. tropiezo, escollo.
stump (stŭmp) **I.** s. *(trunk remains)* tocón *m*, toza; *(part)* fragmento; *(limb stub)* muñón *m*; *(tooth)* raigón *m*; *(footstep)* pisada; *(place)* tribuna política; DIB. *(pointed roll)*

483

difumino; G.B. *(in cricket)* estaca ♦ **stumps** FAM. *(legs)* piernas; *(artificial leg)* pierna artificial • **up a s.** perplejo **II.** tr. *(to clear)* arrancar los tocones; *(to shade)* esfumar, difuminar; FAM. *(to baffle)* dejar perplejo; POL. *(to tour)* hacer giras políticas.

stump·y (stŭm′pē) adj. **-i·er, -i·est** *(person)* rechoncho; *(land)* lleno de tocones.

stun (stŭn) **I.** tr. **stunned, stun·ning** *(to daze)* aturdir; *(to render senseless)* dejar sin sentido; *(to deafen)* ensordecer; *(to astound)* dejar estupefacto o pasmado **II.** s. choque m, sacudida.

stung (stŭng) pret. y part. p. de **sting**.

stunk (stŭngk) un pret. y part. p. de **stink**.

stun·ning (stŭn′ĭng) adj. *(shocking)* aturdidor; *(attractive)* imponente.

stunt¹ (stŭnt) **I.** tr. impedir el crecimiento de **II.** s. *(person)* persona falta de crecimiento; BOT. planta enana.

stunt² (stŭnt) **I.** s. *(feat)* proeza; *(publicity trick)* truco publicitario **II.** tr. hacer acrobacias.

stunt man s. CINE., TELEV. doble especial (para escenas peligrosas) m.

stu·pe·fac·tion (stōō′pə-făk′shən) s. estupefacción f.

stu·pe·fy (stōō′pə-fī′) tr. **-fied, -fy·ing** *(to dull)* atontar; *(to amaze)* dejar estupefacto.

stu·pen·dous (stōō-pĕn′dəs) adj. *(tremendous)* estupendo; *(amazing)* asombroso.

stu·pid (stōō′pĭd) **I.** adj. **-er, -est** *(dimwitted)* estúpido, tonto; *(stunned)* atontado **II.** s. estúpido, tonto.

stu·pid·i·ty (stōō-pĭd′ĭ-tē) s. [pl. **-ties**] estupidez f, tontería.

stu·por (stōō′pər) s. *(torpor)* estupor m; *(daze)* atontamiento.

stur·di·ness (stûr′dē-nĭs) s. *(firmness)* firmeza; *(strength)* fortaleza, robustez f.

stur·dy (stûr′dē) **I.** adj. **-di·er, -di·est** *(strong)* fuerte; *(robust)* robusto; *(energetic)* enérgico; *(firm)* firme **II.** s. VET. modorra.

stur·geon (stûr′jən) s. ICT. esturión m.

stut·ter (stŭt′ər) **I.** intr. & tr. tartamudear **II.** s. tartamudeo.

stut·ter·er (stŭt′ər-ər) s. tartamudo.

stut·ter·ing (stŭt′ər-ĭng) **I.** s. tartamudeo **II.** adj. tartamudo.

St. Vi·tus' dance (sānt vī′təs) s. MED. baile de San Vito m.

sty¹ (stī) **I.** s. [pl. **sties**] *(for swine)* pocilga, porqueriza; FIG. *(filthy place)* pocilga **II.** intr. **stied, sty·ing** vivir en una pocilga.

sty² o **stye** (stī) s. [pl. **sties** o **styes**] MED. orzuelo.

Styg·i·an (stĭj′ē-ən) adj. *(of Styx)* estigio; FIG. *(infernal)* estigio, infernal; *(dark)* oscuro, tenebroso.

style (stīl) **I.** s. *(manner)* estilo; *(vogue)* moda; *(cut of clothes)* hechura; *(elegance)* estilo, elegancia; *(type)* modelo, tipo; *(title)* título, tratamiento; *(of a phonograph)* aguja; ZOOL. púa, pincho; MED., TEC. estilete m ♦ **in s.** *(with class)* con estilo; *(in vogue)* de moda **II.** tr. **styled, styl·ing** *(to stylize)* estilizar; *(to design)* diseñar; *(to update)* poner a la moda; *(to coif)* peinar a la moda; *(to designate)* titular, nombrar.

styl·ing (stī′lĭng) s. estilización f.

styl·ish (stī′lĭsh) adj. *(fashionable)* a la moda; *(elegant)* elegante.

styl·ist (stī′lĭst) s. *(designer)* diseñador m; *(hairdresser)* peluquero; LIT. estilista mf.

sty·lis·tic (stī-lĭs′tĭk) adj. estilístico.

styl·ize (stī′līz′) tr. **-ized, -iz·ing** estilizar.

sty·lo·graph (stī′lə-grăf′) s. estilógrafo.

sty·lus (stī′ləs) s. [pl. **-lus·es** o **-li** (-lī′)] *(instrument)* estilo; *(needle)* aguja (de fonógrafo); *(tool)* punzón m.

sty·mie o **sty·my** (stī′mē) **I.** tr. **-mied, -mie·ing** o **-mied, -my·ing** obstaculizar, bloquear **II.** s. obstáculo.

styp·tic (stĭp′tĭk) MED. **I.** adj. *(astringent)* astringente; *(hemostatic)* hemostático **II.** s. astringente m.

styptic pencil s. lápiz hemostático.

sty·rene (stī′rēn′) s. QUÍM. estireno.

Sty·ro·foam (stī′rə-fōm′) s. QUÍM. marca registrada de un plástico esponjoso.

Styx (stĭks) s. MITOL. Laguna Estigia.

su·a·ble (sōō′ə-bəl) adj. DER. demandable.

sua·sion (swā′zhən) s. persuasión f.

suave (swäv) adj. afable.

sub (sŭb) FAM. **I.** s. *(boat)* submarino; *(substitute)* substituto; *(sandwich)* sandwich m o emparedado grande ♦ **to s. for** substituir a **II.** intr. **subbed, sub·bing** substituir.

sub·al·tern (sŭb-ôl′tərn) **I.** adj. *(of a lower rank)* subalterno; LÓG. particular **II.** s. *(subordinate)* subordinado; MIL., G.B. alférez; LÓG. proposición particular f.

sub·arc·tic (sŭb′ärk′tĭk, -är′tĭk) adj. subártico.

sub·a·tom·ic (sŭb′ə-tŏm′ĭk) adj. subatómico.

sub·class (sŭb′klăs′) s. *(subdivision)* subdivisión f; BIOL. subclase f.

sub·com·mit·tee (sŭb′kə-mĭt′ē) s. subcomité m.

sub·com·pact (sŭb-kŏm′păkt′) s. automóvil pequeño.

sub·con·scious (sŭb′kŏn′shəs) adj. & s. subconsciente m.

sub·con·ti·nent (sŭb′kŏn′tə-nənt) s. subcontinente m.

sub·con·tract (sŭb-kŏn′trăkt′) **I.** s. subcontrato **II.** tr. (sŭb′kən-trăkt′) subcontratar.

sub·con·trac·tor (sŭb-kŏn′trăk′tər, sŭb′kən-trăk′-) s. subcontratista mf.

sub·cul·ture (sŭb′kŭl′chər) s. BIOL. subcultivo.

sub·cu·ta·ne·ous (sŭb′kyōō-tā′nē-əs) adj. subcutáneo.

sub·di·vide (sŭb′dĭ-vīd′) tr. & intr. **-vid·ed, -vid·ing** subdividir(se).

sub·di·vi·sion (sŭb′dĭ-vĭzh′ən) subdivisión f.

sub·due (səb-dōō′, -dyōō′) tr. **-dued, -du·ing** *(to subjugate)* sojuzgar, subyugar; *(to make tractable)* amansar, serenar; *(to tone down)* suavizar, atenuar; *(to restrain)* dominar, reprimir; *(to plant)* cultivar, poner en cultivo.

sub·freez·ing (sŭb-frē′zĭng) adj. debajo del punto de congelación.

sub·ge·nus (sŭb′jē′nəs) s. [pl. **-gen·er·a** (-jĕn′ər-ə)] BIOL. subgénero.

sub·group (sŭb′grōōp′) s. subgrupo.

sub·hu·man (sŭb-hyōō′mən) adj. infrahumano.

sub·ja·cent (sŭb-jā′sənt) adj. subyacente.

sub·ject (sŭb′jĭkt) **I.** adj. sometido, dominado <*to hold s.* mantener dominado> ♦ **s. to** *(prone to)* propenso a; *(exposed to)* expuesto a; *(dependent on)* sujeto a, supeditado a **II.** s. *(of a country)* súbdito; *(individual)* sujeto; *(theme)* tema; *(course)* asignatura; *(cause)* motivo; *(of gossip, criticism)* objeto; GRAM., LÓG., FILOS. sujeto; MÚS. tema; PINT. motivo ♦ **on the s. of** a propósito de • **to keep off a s.** no tocar el tema **III.** tr. (səb-jĕkt′) someter, dominar ♦ **to s. to** *(to submit to)* someter a; *(to expose to)* exponer a; *(to make dependent on)* supeditar a.

sub·jec·tion (səb-jĕk′shən) s. sujeción f.

sub·jec·tive (səb-jĕk′tĭv) adj. subjetivo.

sub·jec·tive·ly (səb-jĕk′tĭv-lē) adv. subjetivamente.

sub·jec·tive·ness (səb-jĕk′tĭv-nĭs) s. subjetividad f.

sub·jec·tiv·ism (səb-jĕk′tə-vĭz′əm) s. FILOS. subjetivismo.

sub·jec·tiv·i·ty (sŭb′jĕk-tĭv′ĭ-tē) s. subjetividad f.

subject matter s. materia, tema m.

sub·join (səb-join′) tr. añadir, anexar.

sub·ju·gate (sŭb′jə-gāt′) tr. **-gat·ed, -gat·ing** subyugar, sojuzgar.

sub·ju·ga·tion (sŭb′jə-gā′shən) s. dominación f.

sub·ju·ga·tor (sŭb′jə-gā′tər) s. dominador m.

sub·junc·tive (səb-jŭngk′tĭv) adj. & s. GRAM. subjuntivo.

sub·lease (sŭb-lēs′) **I.** tr. **-leased, -leas·ing** subarrendar, subalquilar **II.** s. (sŭb′lēs′) subarrendamiento, subarriendo.

sub·let (sŭb-lĕt′) **I.** tr. **-let, -let·ting** subarrendar, subalquilar **II.** s. (sŭb′lĕt′) FAM. subarrendamiento.

sub·li·mate (sŭb′lə-māt′) tr. **-mat·ed, -mat·ing** sublimar.

sub·li·ma·tion (sŭb′lə-mā′shən) s. sublimación f.

sub·lime (sə-blīm′) **I.** adj. sublime **II.** s. ♦ **the s.** lo sublime **III.** tr. & intr. **-limed, -lim·ing** sublimar(se).

sub·lim·i·nal (sə-blĭm′ə-nəl) adj. subconsciente.

sub·lim·i·ty (sə-blĭm′ĭ-tē) s. sublimidad f.

sub·ma·chine gun (sŭb′mə-shēn′) s. pistola ametralladora, metralleta.

sub·ma·rine (sŭb′mə-rēn′) **I.** adj. submarino **II.** s. *(boat)* submarino; JER. *(sandwich)* sandwich m o emparedado grande.

sub·merge (səb-mûrj′) tr. **-merged, -merg·ing** *(to plunge)* sumergir; *(to inundate)* inundar; *(to obscure)* ocultar.

sub·merged (səb-mûrjd′) adj. *(living in misery)* sumido en la miseria; *(hidden)* oculto; BOT. sumergido.

sub·mer·gence (səb-mûr′jəns) s. sumersión *f.*

sub·merse (səb-mûrs′) tr. **-mersed, -mers·ing** sumergir, hundir.

sub·mers·i·ble (səb-mûr′sə-bəl) adj. & s. sumergible *m.*

sub·mis·sion (səb-mĭsh′ən) s. *(act)* sometimiento; *(meekness)* sumisión *f*; *(proposal)* proposición *f.*

sub·mis·sive (səb-mĭs′ĭv) adj. sumiso, dócil.

sub·mit (səb-mĭt′) tr. **-mit·ted, -mit·ting** *(to subject)* someter; *(to present)* presentar; *(to propose)* proponer; *(to suggest)* sugerir, indicar —intr. *(to give in)* someterse, rendirse; *(to acquiesce)* conformarse.

sub·mit·tal (səb-mĭt′l) s. sumisión *f.*

sub·nor·mal (sŭb-nôr′məl) adj. anormal, subnormal.

sub·or·bit·al (sŭb-ôr′bĭ-tl) adj. ASTRONÁUT. suborbital (vuelo, trayectoria).

sub·or·di·nate (sə-bôr′dn-ĭt) I. adj. *(under someone else's control)* subordinado; *(secondary)* secundario II. s. subordinado III. tr. (sə-bôr′dn-āt′) **-nat·ed, -nat·ing** *(to lower in rank)* subordinar; *(to subdue)* someter.

sub·or·di·na·tion (sə-bôr′dn-ā′shən) s. subordinación *f.*

sub·orn (sə-bôrn′) tr. sobornar.

sub·plot (sŭb′plŏt′) s. LIT. trama secundaria.

sub·poe·na (sə-pē′nə) DER. I. s. citación *f* II. tr. **-naed, -na·ing** citar.

sub·scribe (səb-skrīb′) tr. & intr. **-scribed, -scrib·ing** subscribir(se), abonarse.

sub·scrib·er (səb-skrī′bər) s. subscriptor *m.*

sub·script (sŭb′skrĭpt′) I. adj. subscrito II. s. signo debajo de una letra.

sub·scrip·tion (səb-skrĭp′shən) s. *(signature)* firma; *(purchase)* subscripción *f*, abono; *(adherence)* adhesión *f*; *(membership fees)* cuota, subscripción.

sub·se·quence (sŭb′sĭ-kwĕns′) s. *(sequel)* secuela, consecuencia; *(posteriority)* posterioridad *f.*

sub·se·quent (sŭb′sĭ-kwĕnt′) adj. *(following)* subsiguiente, consecutivo; *(later)* posterior.

sub·se·quent·ly (sŭb′sĭ-kwĕnt′lē) adv. posteriormente.

sub·serve (səb-sûrv′) tr. **-served, -serv·ing** ayudar, promover.

sub·ser·vi·ent (səb-sûr′vē-ənt) adj. *(subordinate)* subordinado; *(servile)* servil; *(submissive)* sumiso.

sub·set (sŭb′sĕt′) s. MAT. serie de cantidades contenida en otra *f.*

sub·side (səb-sīd′) intr. **-sid·ed, -sid·ing** *(to sink)* hundirse; *(to fall down)* dejarse caer, desplomarse; *(to settle)* asentarse, depositarse; *(to abate)* apaciguarse, calmarse.

sub·si·dence (səb-sīd′ns, sŭb′sĭ-dns) s. *(sinking)* hundimiento; *(descent)* descenso; *(settling)* asentamiento; *(appeasement)* apaciguamiento, calma.

sub·sid·i·ar·y (səb-sĭd′ē-ĕr′ē) I. adj. *(auxiliary)* auxiliar; *(secondary)* secundario; *(of a subsidy)* subsidiario II. s. [pl. **-ies**] *(helper)* ayudante *mf*, auxiliar *mf*; *(company)* sucursal *f*, filial *f.*

sub·si·di·za·tion (sŭb′sĭ-dĭ-zā′shən) s. otorgamiento de subvención o subsidio.

sub·si·dize (sŭb′sĭ-dīz′) tr. **-dized, -diz·ing** *(to support)* subvencionar; *(to assist)* dar subsidio a.

sub·si·dy (sŭb′sĭ-dē) s. [pl. **-dies**] COM. *(government assistance)* subsidio; *(monetary aid)* subvención *f.*

sub·sist (səb-sĭst′) intr. *(to exist)* existir; *(to remain)* perdurar, permanecer; *(to live)* subsistir —tr. mantener.

sub·sis·tence (səb-sĭs′təns) s. *(existence)* subsistencia; *(sustenance)* sustento.

sub·soil (sŭb′soil′) s. subsuelo.

sub·son·ic (sŭb-sŏn′ĭk) adj. subsónico.

sub·spe·cies (sŭb′spē′shēz, -sēz) s. [pl. **subspecies**] BIOL., BOT. subespecie *f.*

sub·stance (sŭb′stəns) s. *(matter)* sustancia, substancia; *(essence)* esencia, fondo; *(solidity)* solidez *f*; *(body)* cuerpo, consistencia; FIG. *(goods)* bienes *m*, caudal *m* ♦ **in s.** en sustancia, en lo esencial • **man of s.** FIG. hombre acaudalado.

sub·stan·dard (sŭb-stăn′dərd) adj. *(inferior)* inferior a lo normal; *(vulgar)* vulgar.

sub·stan·tial (səb-stăn′shəl) adj. *(material)* material; *(real)* real, verdadero; *(strong)* fuerte, sólido; *(sustaining)* sustancioso, nutritivo; *(important)* sustancial, importante; *(considerable)* considerable <a s. increase un aumento considerable>; *(well-to-do)* adinerado.

sub·stan·ti·ate (səb-stăn′shē-āt′) tr. **-at·ed, -at·ing** *(to justify)* justificar; *(to prove)* establecer, probar; *(to embody)* encarnar.

sub·stan·ti·a·tion (səb-stăn′shē-ā′shən) s. justificación *f.*

sub·stan·tive (sŭb′stən-tĭv) I. adj. *(substantial)* considerable, importante; *(independent)* independiente; *(real)* real; *(essential)* esencial; GRAM. sustantivo II. s. GRAM. sustantivo.

sub·sta·tion (sŭb′stā′shən) s. sucursal *f.*

sub·sti·tute (sŭb′stĭ-tōōt′, -tyōōt′) I. s. *(thing)* substituto; *(person)* substituto, suplente *mf* II. tr. & intr. **-tut·ed, -tut·ing** substituir, sustituir.

sub·sti·tu·tion (sŭb′stĭ-tōō′shən, -tyōō′-) s. substitución *f*, reemplazo.

sub·stra·tum (sŭb′strā′təm, -străt′əm) s. [pl. **-stra·ta** (-strā′tə, -străt′ə) o **-stra·tums**] *(layer)* substrato; *(subsoil)* subsuelo; *(groundwork)* fundamento; *(foundation)* base *f*; FILOS. substancia, sustancia; BIOL. medio.

sub·struc·ture (sŭb′strŭk′chər) s. infraestructura.

sub·sume (səb-sōōm′) tr. **-sumed, -sum·ing** incluir en una categoría.

sub·tem·per·ate (sŭb-tĕm′pər-ĭt) adj. semitemplado.

sub·ten·ant (sŭb-tĕn′ənt) s. subarrendatario.

sub·ter·fuge (sŭb′tər-fyōōj′) s. subterfugio.

sub·ter·ra·ne·an (sŭb′tə-rā′nē-ən) adj. subterráneo.

sub·ti·tle (sŭb′tīt′l) I. s. subtítulo II. tr. **-tled, -tling** subtitular.

sub·tle (sŭt′l) adj. **-tler, -tlest** *(elusive)* sutil; *(keen)* agudo; *(clever)* astuto; *(devious)* taimado; *(insidious)* insidioso.

sub·tle·ty (sŭt′l-tē) s. [pl. **-ties**] *(cleverness)* astucia; *(distinction)* sutileza, sutilidad *f.*

sub·tly (sŭt′lē) adv. sutilmente.

sub·top·ic (sŭb′tŏp′ĭk) s. subtema *m.*

sub·to·tal (sŭb′tōt′l) I. s. MAT. subtotal *m* II. tr. (sŭb′tōt′l) sumar parte de una serie de números.

sub·tract (səb-trăkt′) tr. MAT. sustraer, restar.

sub·trac·tion (səb-trăk′shən) s. MAT. sustracción *f*, resta.

sub·trac·tive (səb-trăk′tĭv) adj. que resta.

sub·tra·hend (sŭb′trə-hĕnd′) s. MAT. substraendo, sustraendo.

sub·trop·i·cal (sŭb-trŏp′ĭ-kəl) adj. subtropical.

sub·trop·ics (sŭb-trŏp′ĭks) s.pl. regiones subtropicales *f.*

sub·urb (sŭb′ûrb′) s. suburbio ♦ **suburbs** afueras, suburbios.

sub·ur·ban (sə-bûr′bən) adj. suburbano.

sub·ur·ban·ite (sə-bûr′bə-nīt′) s. habitante de un suburbio *mf.*

sub·ur·bi·a (sə-bûr′bē-ə) s. *(suburbs)* afueras, suburbios; *(group)* habitantes de los suburbios *m.*

sub·ven·tion (səb-vĕn′shən) s. *(aid)* ayuda, subsidio; *(grant)* subvención *f.*

sub·ver·sion (səb-vûr′zhən) s. subversión *f.*

sub·ver·sive (səb-vûr′sĭv) adj. subversivo.

sub·vert (səb-vûrt′) tr. *(to destroy)* destruir furtivamente; *(to corrupt)* corromper; *(to overthrow)* derribar, derrocar.

sub·way (sŭb′wā′) s. *(railroad)* subterráneo, metro; *(passage)* paso subterráneo; *(conduit)* conducto subterráneo.

suc·ceed (sək-sēd′) intr. *(to be successful)* triunfar, tener éxito; *(to turn out well)* salir bien; *(to accomplish)* conseguir <he succeeded in having the law repealed consiguió que hicieran revocar la ley>; *(to follow)* seguir, suceder; ANT. *(to devolve)* recaer por derecho de sucesión ♦ **to s. to the throne** heredar el trono —tr. *(to replace)* suceder a; *(to follow)* seguir.

suc·cess (sək-sĕs′) s. *(accomplishment)* éxito, triunfo; *(person)* persona que tiene éxito ♦ **box-office s.** éxito de taquilla.

suc·cess·ful (sək-sĕs′fəl) adj. *(good outcome)* de éxito, exitoso; *(lucky)* afortunado; *(prosperous)* próspero.

ă rey / ä año / b boca / ch chico / d dar / ĕ el / ē mil / g gato / h joya / hw juez / ī aire / k casa / kw cuan /

suc·cess·ful·ly (sək-sĕs'fə-lē) adv. con éxito.
suc·ces·sion (sək-sĕsh'ən) s. sucesión *f* ♦ **in s.** seguido, en serie • **in s. to** como sucesor de, como heredero de.
suc·ces·sive (sək-sĕs'ĭv) adj. *(sequential)* sucesivo; *(consecutive)* consecutivo.
suc·ces·sor (sak-sĕs'ər) s. sucesor *m.*
suc·cinct (sək-sĭngkt') adj. sucinto, conciso.
suc·cor (sŭk'ər) **I.** s. socorro, auxilio **II.** tr. socorrer.
suc·cu·bus (sŭk'yə-bəs) s. [pl. **-bus·es, -bi** (-bī', -bē')] súcubo (demonio femenino).
suc·cu·lence (sŭk'yə-ləns) s. suculencia.
suc·cu·lent (sŭk'yə-lənt) **I.** adj. *(juicy)* suculento; BOT. carnoso; *(interesting)* interesante **II.** s. BOT. planta carnosa.
suc·cumb (sə-kŭm') intr. *(to yield)* sucumbir; *(to die)* morir ♦ **to s. to** sucumbir a.
such (sŭch) **I.** adj. *(of this nature)* tal, semejante <*I never dreamed that they could do s. work* nunca me imaginé que podrían hacer semejante trabajo>; *(of this kind)* de esta índole, de este tipo <*s. people are never satisfied* la gente de este tipo nunca está satisfecha>; *(so extreme)* tanto, semejante <*I was embarrassed by s. praise* me sentí turbado frente a semejante elogio>; *(so big)* tan, tan grande <*he is s. a braggart!* ¡es un fanfarrón tan grande!>; *(so much)* tanto <*s. luck* tanta suerte> ♦ **one s.** un tal • **s. and s.** tal, tal o cual, tal y cual • **s. as it is** tal cual es **II.** adv. tan <*s. good work* tan buen trabajo> **III.** pron. *(someone implied)* los que <*s. as live here* los que viven aquí>; *(so great)* tal <*s. is his generosity* tal es su generosidad>; *(the like)* cosas similares, cosas por el estilo <*pins, needles and s.* alfileres, agujas y cosas por el estilo>; *(similar people)* gente similar <*there were senators, lawyers and s.* había senadores, abogados y gente similar> ♦ **as s.** *(of itself)* en sí, de por sí <*money as s. will seldom bring happiness* el dinero en sí raramente trae la felicidad>; *(as what one is)* como tal <*a diplomat must negotiate as s.* un diplomático debe negociar como tal> • **s. is life** así es la vida.
such·like (sŭch'līk') **I.** adj. de esta clase, de este tipo **II.** pron. cosas o personas semejantes.
suck (sŭk) **I.** tr. *(a thumb, blood)* chupar; *(a liquid)* sorber; *(air)* aspirar; JER., VULG. *(to perform fellatio on)* mamar —intr. *(to draw in)* dar chupadas; JER., VULG. *(to be disgusting)* ser asqueroso **II.** s. chupada.
suck·er (sŭk'ər) **I.** s. *(person that sucks)* chupador *m;* FAM. *(dupe)* primo, incauto; *(lollipop)* pirulí *m,* caramelo con palito; *(suction part)* ventosa; TEC. émbolo; BOT. chupón *m* **II.** tr. FAM. *(to dupe)* engañar, embaucar; BOT. podar chupones —intr. BOT. echar chupones.
suck·ing (sŭk'ĭng) adj. *(animal)* de leche, lechal; *(child)* de pecho; *(sound)* de succión.
suck·le (sŭk'əl) tr. **-led, -ling** *(to nurse)* amamantar, dar de mamar a; *(to rear)* criar —intr. tomar el pecho o la teta.
suck·ling (sŭk'lĭng) **I.** s. mamón *m* **II.** adj. *(animal)* de leche, lechal; *(child)* de pecho.
su·cre (sōō'krā) s. sucre (unidad monetaria del Ecuador) *m.*
su·crose (sōō'krōs') s. QUÍM. sucrosa.
suc·tion (sŭk'shən) **I.** s. *(process)* succión *f;* *(aspiration)* aspiración **II.** adj. de succión.
suction pump s. bomba aspirante.
Su·dan (sōō-dăn') s. Sudán *m.*
Su·da·nese (sōōd'n-ēz') adj. & s. sudanés *m* ♦ **the S.** los sudaneses.
sud·den (sŭd'n) adj. *(unforeseen)* imprevisto; *(abrupt)* brusco; *(swift)* súbito, repentino ♦ **all of a s.** de repente.
sud·den·ly (sŭd'n-lē) adv. de repente, de pronto.
sud·den·ness (sŭd'n-nĭs) s. lo súbito.
su·do·rif·ic (sōō'də-rĭf'ĭk) adj. & s. MED. sudorífero.
suds (sŭdz) s.pl. *(soapy water)* jabonaduras; *(lather)* espuma; JER. *(beer)* cerveza.
sue (sōō) tr. **sued, su·ing** *(to beseech)* suplicar; DER. *(to beg redress)* demandar; *(to accuse)* poner pleito a; *(to carry through)* entablar juicio; *(to woo)* cortejar ♦ **to s. for divorce** presentar demanda de divorcio —intr. *(to bring suit)* entablar acción judicial; *(to request)* solicitar, pedir; *(to woo)* hacer la corte, cortejar.
suede o **suède** (swād) s. gamuza, ante *m.*
su·et (sōō'ĭt) s. sebo.

suf·fer (sŭf'ər) **I.** intr. *(to feel pain)* sufrir; *(to be damaged)* ser dañado **II.** tr. *(to undergo)* sufrir; *(to stand)* aguantar, soportar <*she could not s. opposition* no podía soportar que no estuvieran de acuerdo con ella>; *(to allow)* permitir, tolerar ♦ **to s. from** adolecer de, padecer de.
suf·fer·a·ble (sŭf'ər-ə-bəl) adj. soportable.
suf·fer·ance (sŭf'ər-əns) s. *(tolerance)* tolerancia; *(tacit assent)* consentimiento tácito.
suf·fer·er (sŭf'ər-ər) s. *(victim)* víctima; *(patient)* paciente *mf.*
suf·fer·ing (sŭf'ər-ĭng) s. sufrimiento.
suf·fice (sə-fīs') intr. **-ficed, -fic·ing** *(to be sufficient)* ser suficiente; *(to be enough)* bastar —tr. ser suficiente, bastar ♦ **s. it to say** basta (con) decir
suf·fi·cien·cy (sə-fĭsh'ən-sē) s. *(state)* desahogo, holgura; *(quantity)* cantidad suficiente *f.*
suf·fi·cient (sə-fĭsh'ənt) adj. bastante, suficiente.
suf·fi·cient·ly (sə-fĭsh'ənt-lē) adv. bastante.
suf·fix (sŭf'ĭks') GRAM. **I.** s. sufijo **II.** tr. añadir como sufijo.
suf·fo·cate (sŭf'ə-kāt') tr. **-cat·ed, -cat·ing** *(to asphyxiate)* asfixiar; *(to choke)* ahogar; *(to cause discomfort)* sofocar; *(to stifle)* suprimir, reprimir —intr. *(to asphyxiate)* asfixiarse; *(to be stifled)* reprimirse.
suf·fo·ca·tion (sŭf'ə-kā'shən) s. asfixia, ahogo.
suf·frage (sŭf'rĭj) s. *(vote)* sufragio; *(right)* derecho al voto; RELIG. súplica.
suf·fra·gette (sŭf'rə-jĕt') s. sufragista (mujer).
suf·fra·gist (sŭf'rə-jĭst) s. sufragista *mf.*
suf·fuse (sə-fyōōz') tr. **-fused, -fus·ing** *(to cover)* cubrir; *(to spread over)* extenderse por.
suf·fu·sion (sə-fyōō'zhən) s. difusión *f.*
Su·fi (sōō'fē) s. RELIG. sufí *m.*
sug·ar (shŏŏg'ər) **I.** s. *(sweetener)* azúcar *mf;* *(cube)* terrón de azúcar *m;* JER. *(darling)* querido, amorcito **II.** tr. *(to sweeten)* azucarar, poner azúcar a; *(to coat)* confitar, garapiñar; FIG. *(to soften)* suavizar, endulzar —intr. granularse ♦ **to s. the pill** FIG. dorar la píldora.
sugar beet s. BOT. remolacha azucarera.
sugar bowl s. azucarero, azucarera.
sugar candy s. azúcar candi *m,* azúcar cande.
sugar cane s. caña de azúcar.
sug·ar·coat (shŏŏg'ər-kōt') tr. *(to coat)* cubrir con una capa de azúcar; *(to make more pleasant)* endulzar, suavizar ♦ **to s. the pill** FIG. dorar la píldora.
sug·ar·coat·ed (shŏŏg'ər-kō'tĭd) adj. cubierto con una capa de azúcar.
sugar daddy s. JER. viejo que mantiene a una querida joven.
sug·ared (shŏŏg'ərd) adj. *(sugary)* azucarado; FIG. *(made appealing)* suavizado, endulzado.
sugar loaf s. pan de azúcar *m.*
sugar maple s. arce azucarero.
sugar mill s. ingenio de azúcar, trapiche *m.*
sug·ar·plum (shŏŏg'ər-plŭm') s. confite *m.*
sug·ar·y (shŏŏg'ə-rē) adj. **-i·er, -i·est** *(having sugar)* azucarado; *(sweet)* dulce; FIG. *(tasting like sugar)* dulzón; FAM. *(cloyingly sweet)* meloso, empalagoso.
sug·gest (səg-jĕst') tr. *(to propose)* proponer, sugerir; *(to evoke)* hacer pensar en, evocar <*a cavern that suggests a tomb* una cueva que hace pensar en una tumba>; *(to demand)* requerir <*such behavior suggests immediate action* esa forma de conducta requiere una acción inmediata>; *(to advise)* aconsejar, sugerir; *(to imply)* insinuar.
sug·gest·i·ble (səg-jĕs'tə-bəl) adj. sugestionable.
sug·ges·tion (səg-jĕs'chən) s. *(act, thing suggested)* sugerencia; *(insinuation)* insinuación *f;* *(hint)* indicación *f;* *(idea)* idea; PSIC. sugestión *f.*
sug·ges·tive (səg-jĕs'tĭv) adj. *(that suggests)* sugestivo; *(indicative)* evocador; *(insinuating)* insinuante.
su·i·cid·al (sōō'ĭ-sīd'l) adj. suicida.
su·i·cide (sōō'ĭ-sīd') s. suicidio; *(detriment)* perjuicio; *(person)* suicida *mf* ♦ **to commit s.** suicidarse.
su·i ge·ne·ris (sōō'ī' jĕn'ər-ĭs, sōō'ē) adj. sui generis, único en su género.
suit (sōōt) **I.** s. *(garments)* traje *m;* *(set)* conjunto, juego;

(cards) palo; *(court proceedings)* pleito; *(courtship)* galanteo, cortejo ♦ **to follow s.** *(in cards)* jugar el mismo palo; *(as an example)* seguir el ejemplo **II.** tr. *(to accommodate)* ajustarse a, adaptarse a; *(to satisfy)* satisfacer; *(to dress)* vestir ♦ **to s. oneself** hacer lo que uno quiere • **to s. to** adaptar a —intr. convenir.

suit·a·bil·i·ty (sōō′tə-bĭl′ĭ-tē) s. *(appropriateness)* conveniencia; *(of two people)* compatibilidad.

suit·a·ble (sōō′tə-bəl) adj. *(appropriate)* conveniente; *(compatible)* compatible; *(capable)* apto.

suit·a·bly (sōō′tə-blē) adv. convenientemente.

suit·case (sōōt′kās) s. maleta, valija.

suite (swēt) s. *(retinue)* séquito; *(succession)* sucesión f; *(apartment)* apartamento, suite f; *(furniture set)* juego; MÚS. suite.

suit·ing (sōō′tĭng) s. TEJ. tela para trajes.

suit·or (sōō′tər) s. *(petitionary)* peticionario; *(plaintiff)* demandante mf; *(wooer)* pretendiente m.

sul·fa drug (sŭl′fə) s. FARM. sulfamida.

sul·fate (sŭl′fāt) **I.** s. QUÍM. sulfato **II.** tr. & intr. **-fat·ed, -fat·ing** ELEC., QUÍM. sulfatar(se).

sul·fide (sŭl′fīd) s. QUÍM. sulfuro.

sul·fite (sŭl′fīt) s. QUÍM. sulfito.

sulfur (sŭl′fər) **I.** s. azufre m **II.** tr. QUÍM. *(to combine)* sulfurar; *(to treat)* azufrar.

sulfur dioxide s. QUÍM. dióxido de azufre.

sul·fu·ric (sŭl-fyōor′ĭk) adj. QUÍM. sulfúrico.

sulfuric acid s. QUÍM. ácido sulfúrico.

sul·fur·ize (sŭl′fə-rīz′) tr. **-ized, -iz·ing** *(to impregnate)* azufrar; AGR., QUÍM. sulfurar.

sul·fur·ous (sŭl′fər-əs, sŭl-fyōor′-) adj. QUÍM. sulfuroso; *(from burning sulfur)* azufroso, sulfúreo; FIG. *(hellish)* infernal.

sulfurous acid s. QUÍM. ácido sulfuroso.

sulk (sŭlk) **I.** intr. estar de malhumor, enfurruñarse **II.** s. enfado, mal humor m.

sulk·y¹ (sŭl′kē) adj. **-i·er, -i·est** *(sullen)* malhumorado; *(gloomy)* triste.

sulk·y² (sŭl′kē) s. [pl. **-ies**] *(vehicle)* tilburí m, sulky m.

sul·len (sŭl′ən) adj. **-er, -est** *(sulky)* resentido, malhumorado; *(somber in color)* plomizo, sombrío; *(gloomy)* triste, sombrío; *(slow)* lento.

sul·ly (sŭl′ē) **I.** tr. **-lied, -ly·ing** manchar, mancillar **II.** s. [pl. **-lies**] ANT. mancha.

sul·phur¹ (sŭl′fər) s. mariposa anaranjada o amarilla.

sul·phur² (sŭl′fər) s. & v. var. de **sulfur.**

sul·tan (sŭl′tən) s. sultán m.

sul·tan·a (sŭl-tăn′ə, -tä′nə) s. *(sultan's female relative)* sultana; *(raisin)* pasa de Esmirna.

sul·tan·ate (sŭl′tə-nāt′) s. sultanato, sultanía.

sul·try (sŭl′trē) adj. **-tri·er, -tri·est** *(very hot)* bochornoso, caluroso; *(torrid)* tórrido, sofocante; *(sensual)* sensual; *(voluptuous)* voluptuoso.

sum (sŭm) **I.** s. MAT. *(addition)* suma; *(total)* total m, suma; *(amount of money)* cantidad f; *(arithmetic)* aritmética *<a child good at sums* un niño bueno en aritmética> ♦ **in s.** en resumen **II.** tr. **summed, sum·ming** sumar ♦ **to sum up** resumir, recapitular.

su·mac o **su·mach** (sōō′măk′, shōō′-) s. BOT. zumaque m.

Su·me·ri·an (sōō-mîr′ē-ən, -mĕr′-) adj. & s. sumerio.

sum·ma cum lau·de (sōōm′ə kōōm lou′də) adv. con el más alto encomio.

sum·ma·rize (sŭm′ə-rīz′) tr. **-rized, -riz·ing** resumir.

sum·ma·ry (sŭm′ə-rē) **I.** adj. *(concise)* sumario, breve; *(fast)* rápido **II.** s. [pl. **-ries**] resumen m, compendio.

sum·ma·tion (sə-mā′shən) s. *(addition)* adición f; suma; *(summary)* recapitulación f.

sum·mer¹ (sŭm′ər) **I.** s. *(season)* verano, estío; *(age)* abriles *<a girl of fifteen summers* una chica de quince abriles> ♦ **s. clothes** ropa de verano **II.** tr. pastar durante el verano (el ganado) —intr. ♦ **to s. at** o **in** veranear en.

sum·mer² (sŭm′ər) s. ARQ. *(beam)* viga maestra; *(lintel)* dintel m; *(heavy stone)* sotabanco.

sum·mer·house (sŭm′ər-hous′) s. pérgola, cenador en un jardín m.

summer house s. casa de verano.

sum·mer·sault (sŭm′ər-sôlt′) s. & v. var. de **somersault.**

summer squash s. BOT. calabaza.

sum·mer·time (sŭm′ər-tīm′) s. verano, estío.

sum·mer·y (sŭm′ə-rē) adj. veraniego.

sum·mit (sŭm′ĭt) s. *(highest point)* cima, cúspide f; *(height)* apogeo, cumbre f; POL. *(summit conference)* conferencia cumbre o de alto nivel.

summit conference s. POL. conferencia cumbre o de alto nivel.

sum·mon (sŭm′ən) tr. *(to convene)* convocar; *(to send for)* llamar; *(to order)* ordenar; *(to evoke)* evocar; DER. citar, emplazar ♦ **to s. up** reunir, armarse de (valor, fuerza).

sum·mons (sŭm′ənz) **I.** s. [pl. **-mons·es**] *(notice)* notificación f; DER. *(to a defendant)* citación judicial f; *(to a juror)* requerimiento judicial **II.** tr. **-monsed, -mons·ing** citar ante la justicia.

sump (sŭmp) s. *(low area)* sumidero; *(cesspool)* pozo negro, letrina; *(of an engine)* colector de aceite m ♦ **s. pump** bomba de desagüe.

sump·tu·ar·y (sŭmp′chōō-ĕr′ē) adj. suntuario.

sump·tu·ous (sŭmp′chōō-əs) adj. suntuoso.

sum total s. MAT. total m, suma total.

sun (sŭn) **I.** s. sol m ♦ **in the s.** al sol, en público • **to have a place in the s.** tener una buena situación • **under the s.** en el mundo **II.** tr. & intr. **sunned, sun·ning** solear(se), asolear(se).

sun·bath (sŭn′băth′, -băth) s. baño de sol.

sun·bathe (sŭn′bāth′) intr. **-bathed, -bath·ing** tomar el sol.

sun·bath·er (sŭn′bā′thər) s. persona que toma el sol.

sun·beam (sŭn′bēm′) s. rayo de sol.

sun·belt o **Sun·belt** (sŭn′bĕlt′) estados del sur y del suroeste de EE. UU.

sun·bon·net (sŭn′bŏn′ĭt) s. cofia, papalina.

sun·burn (sŭn′bûrn′) **I.** quemadura de sol **II.** tr. & intr. **-burned** o **-burnt** (-bûrnt′), **burn·ing** quemar(se) al sol.

sun·burst (sŭn′bûrst′) s. *(burst of sunlight)* rayo repentino de sol, sol resplandeciente m; *(brooch)* broche en forma de sol m.

sun·dae (sŭn′dē) s. helado con frutas, nueces y almíbar.

Sun·day (sŭn′dē) s. domingo.

Sunday school s. RELIG. escuela de catequesis, escuela dominical.

sun·der (sŭn′dər) tr. & intr. separar(se).

sun·di·al (sŭn′dī′əl) s. reloj de sol m.

sun·down (sŭn′doun′) s. puesta del sol, ocaso.

sun·dries (sŭn′drēz) s.pl. miscelánea, artículos diversos.

sun·dry (sŭn′drē) adj. misceláneos, diversos.

sun·fast (sŭn′făst′) adj. que no pierde el color al sol.

sun·fish (sŭn′fĭsh′) s. [pl. **sunfish** o **-fish·es**] pez luna m.

sun·flow·er (sŭn′flou′ər) s. girasol m.

sung (sŭng) un pret. y part. p. de **sing.**

sun·glass·es (sŭn′glăs′ĭz) s.pl. gafas o anteojos de sol.

sun god s. RELIG. dios del sol m.

sunk (sŭngk) un pret. y part. p. de **sink.**

sunk·en (sŭng′kən) **I.** part. p. de **sink II.** adj. hundido.

sun·lamp (sŭn′lămp′) s. *(lamp)* lámpara de rayos ultravioletas; FOTOG. foco.

sun·less (sŭn′lĭs) adj. *(dark)* sin sol, oscuro; FIG. *(gloomy)* sombrío.

sun·light (sŭn′līt′) s. luz del sol f, luz solar.

sun·lit (sŭn′lĭt′) adj. iluminado por el sol.

Sun·ni (sōōn′ē) s. RELIG. sunnita (musulmán) m.

sun·ny (sŭn′ē) adj. **-ni·er, -ni·est** *(with sun)* soleado; *(cheerful)* risueño, alegre.

sun·rise (sŭn′rīz′) s. amanecer m, salida del sol.

sun·roof (sŭn′rōof′, -rōof′) s. capota.

sun·screen (sŭn′skrēn′) s. crema protectora del sol.

sun·set (sŭn′sĕt′) s. *(time)* puesta del sol, ocaso; FIG. *(decline)* ocaso.

sun·shade (sŭn′shād′) s. *(umbrella)* quitasol m; *(awning)* toldo.

sun·shine (sŭn′shīn′) s. *(light)* sol m, luz del sol f; *(happiness)* alegría.

sun·spot (sŭn′spŏt′) s. mancha solar.

sun·stroke (sŭn′strōk′) s. MED. insolación f.

sun·tan (sŭn′tăn′) s. bronceado.

ā rey / ä año / b boca / ch chico / d dar / ĕ el / ē mil / g gato / h joya / hw juez / ī aire / k casa / kw cuan /

sun·up (sŭn'ŭp') s. salida del sol.
sup[1] (sŭp) I. tr. **supped, sup·ping** *(to sip)* sorber II. s. *(sip)* sorbo.
sup[2] (sŭp) intr. **supped, sup·ping** *(to have supper)* cenar.
su·per (sōō'pər) FAM. I. s. *(building superintendent)* portero, conserje *m; (actor)* extra *m; (superior quality)* calidad extrafina II. adj. estupendo, formidable.
su·per·a·ble (sōō'pər-ə-bəl) adj. superable.
su·per·a·bun·dance (sōō'pər-ə-bŭn'dəns) s. superabundancia.
su·per·a·bun·dant (sōō'pər-ə-bŭn'dənt) adj. superabundante.
su·per·an·nu·ate (sōō'pər-ăn'yōō-āt') tr. **-at·ed, -at·ing** *(to retire)* jubilar; *(to discard)* arrumbar, arrinconar.
su·per·an·nu·at·ed (sōō'pər-ăn'yōō-ā'tĭd) adj. *(retired)* jubilado; *(obsolete)* anticuado.
su·perb (sōō-pûrb') adj. *(excellent)* excelente; *(majestic)* majestuoso, magnífico; *(luxurious)* lujoso.
su·per·car·go (sōō'pər-kär'gō) s. [pl. **-goes** o **-go**] MARÍT. sobrecargo.
su·per·charge (sōō'pər-chärj') I. tr. **-charged, -charg·ing** *(to increase power)* sobrealimentar; *(to overload)* sobrecargar II. s. sobrecarga.
su·per·cil·i·ous (sōō'pər-sĭl'ē-əs) adj. presumido, desdeñoso.
su·per·con·duc·tiv·i·ty (sōō'pər-kŏn'dŭk-tĭv'ĭ-tē) s. [pl. **-ties**] ELEC. superconductividad *f,* supraconductividad *f.*
su·per·cool (sōō'pər-kōōl') tr. QUÍM. enfriar por debajo del punto de congelación sin solidificar —intr. enfriarse por debajo del punto de congelación sin solidificarse.
su·per·e·go (sōō'pər-ē'gō, -ĕg'ō) s. [pl. **-gos**] PSIC. superego.
su·per·er·o·ga·tion (sōō'pər-ĕr'ə-gā'shən) s. supererogación *f.*
su·per·fi·cial (sōō'pər-fĭsh'əl) adj. superficial.
su·per·fi·ci·al·i·ty (sōō'pər-fĭsh'ē-ăl'ĭ-tē) s. superficialidad *f.*
su·per·fi·cial·ly (sōō'pər-fĭsh'ə-lē) adv. superficialmente.
su·per·fine (sōō'pər-fīn') adj. *(extrafine)* superfino; *(refined)* refinado.
su·per·flu·i·ty (sōō'pər-flōō'ĭ-tē) s. [pl. **-ties**] *(superficiality)* superfluidad *f; (excess)* exceso, superabundancia.
su·per·flu·ous (sōō-pûr'flōō-əs) adj. superfluo.
su·per·heat (sōō'pər-hēt') I. tr. *(to overheat)* recalentar; *(to heat steam)* calentar por encima del punto de saturación; *(to heat a liquid)* calentar por encima del punto de ebullición sin que evapore II. s. (sōō'pər-hēt') *(temperature)* temperatura a la que se somete el vapor por encima del punto de saturación; *(heat)* calor despedido en el recalentamiento.
su·per·high frequency (sōō'pər-hī') s. RAD. frecuencia superalta.
su·per·high·way (sōō'pər-hī'wā') s. autopista.
su·per·hu·man (sōō'pər-hyōō'mən) adj. sobrehumano.
su·per·im·pose (sōō'pər-ĭm-pōz') tr. **-posed, -pos·ing** superponer, sobreponer.
su·per·in·tend (sōō'pər-ĭn-tĕnd') tr. *(to watch over)* vigilar; *(to supervise)* supervisar.
su·per·in·ten·dent (sōō'pər-ĭn-tĕn'dənt) s. *(supervisor)* superintendente *m; (of a building)* portero, conserje *m.*
su·pe·ri·or (sōō-pîr'ē-ər) adj. & s. superior *m.*
su·pe·ri·or·i·ty (sōō-pîr'ē-ôr'ĭ-tē) s. superioridad *f.*
su·per·la·tive (sōō-pûr'lə-tĭv) adj. & s. superlativo.
su·per·man (sōō'pər-măn') s. [pl. **-men** (-mĕn')] superhombre *m.*
su·per·mar·ket (sōō'pər-mär'kĭt) s. supermercado.
su·per·nal (sōō-pûr'nəl) adj. *(celestial)* celestial; *(from the sky)* celeste.
su·per·nat·u·ral (sōō'pər-năch'ər-əl) adj. sobrenatural ♦ **the s.** lo sobrenatural.
su·per·nat·u·ral·ism (sōō'pər-năch'ər-ə-lĭz'əm) s. sobrenaturalismo.
su·per·nu·mer·ar·y (sōō'pər-nōō'mə-rĕr'ē, -nyōō'-) I. adj. *(extra)* supernumerario; *(superfluous)* superfluo II. s. [pl. **-ies**] *(supernumerary person)* supernumerario; TEAT. figurante *m;* CINEM. extra *m.*
su·per·phos·phate (sōō'pər-fŏs'fāt') s. QUÍM. superfosfato.

su·per·pose (sōō'pər-pōz') tr. **-posed, -pos·ing** sobreponer, superponer.
su·per·pow·er (sōō'pər-pou'ər) s. POL. superpotencia, gran potencia.
su·per·sat·u·rate (sōō'pər-săch'ə-rāt') tr. **-rat·ed, -rat·ing** supersaturar, sobresaturar.
su·per·script (sōō'pər-skrĭpt') I. adj. sobrescrito II. s. MAT. signo *o* índice sobrescrito.
su·per·sede (sōō'pər-sēd') tr. **-sed·ed, -sed·ing** *(to replace)* suplantar, reemplazar; *(to invalidate)* invalidar, anular.
su·per·sen·si·tive (sōō'pər-sĕn'sĭ-tĭv) adj. hipersensible.
su·per·son·ic (sōō'pər-sŏn'ĭk) adj. supersónico.
su·per·star (sōō'pər-stär') s. gran estrella.
su·per·sti·tion (sōō'pər-stĭsh'ən) s. superstición *f.*
su·per·sti·tious (sōō'pər-stĭsh'əs) adj. supersticioso.
su·per·struc·ture (sōō'pər-strŭk'chər) s. superestructura.
su·per·tank·er (sōō'pər-tăng'kər) s. MARÍT. petrolero gigante.
su·per·vene (sōō'pər-vēn') intr. **-vened, -ven·ing** sobrevenir, seguir.
su·per·vise (sōō'pər-vīz') tr. **-vised, -vis·ing** supervisar.
su·per·vi·sion (sōō'pər-vĭzh'ən) s. supervisión *f.*
su·per·vi·sor (sōō'pər-vī'zər) s. *(inspector)* inspector *m,* supervisor *m; (officer)* superintendente *m.*
su·per·vi·so·ry (sōō'pər-vī'zə-rē) adj. de supervisión, de supervisor <*s. post* cargo de supervisor>.
su·pine (sōō-pīn') adj. *(on the back)* supino; *(passive)* indolente; *(inclined)* inclinado, pendiente.
sup·per (sŭp'ər) s. cena ♦ **to have s.** cenar.
sup·plant (sə-plănt') tr. suplantar, reemplazar.
sup·ple (sŭp'əl) I. adj. **-pler, -plest** *(flexible)* flexible; *(adaptable)* adaptable, flexible II. tr. **-pled, -pling** *(make flexible)* volver flexible; *(to make amiable)* volver amigable —intr. volverse flexible.
sup·ple·ment (sŭp'lə-mənt) I. s. suplemento II. tr. *(to provide)* suplir, completar; *(to add to)* aumentar.
sup·ple·men·ta·ry (sŭp'lə-mĕn'tə-rē) o **-men·tal** (mĕn'tl) adj. suplementario.
sup·ple·men·ta·tion (sŭp'lə-mĕn-tā'shən) s. suplemento.
sup·pli·cant (sŭp'lĭ-kənt) s. & adj. suplicante *m.*
sup·pli·cate (sŭp'lĭ-kāt') tr. & intr. **-cat·ed -cat·ing** suplicar, rogar.
sup·pli·ca·tion (sŭp'lĭ-kā'shən) s. súplica.
sup·pli·er (sə-plī'ər) s. suministrador *m,* abastecedor *m.*
sup·ply (sə-plī') I. tr. **-plied, -ply·ing** *(to provide, furnish with)* suministrar, proveer; *(to satisfy)* satisfacer; *(to substitute)* suplir, sustituir —intr. sustituir II. s. [pl. **-plies**] *(act)* suministro, abastecimiento; *(stock)* surtido; ECON. oferta <*the law of s. and demand* la ley de la oferta y la demanda>; RELIG. cura suplente ♦ **office supplies** artículos de oficina (lápices, borradores, sujetapapeles) • **supplies** *(provisions)* provisiones; MIL. pertrechos • **to be in short s.** escasear.
sup·port (sə-pôrt') I. tr. *(weight)* aguantar, sostener; *(strain, pressure)* soportar; *(suspicions, doubts)* confirmar, corroborar; *(a spouse, child)* mantener; *(a cause, theory)* sostener, respaldar; *(with money)* ayudar ♦ **to s. oneself** *(to earn one's living)* ganarse la vida; *(to learn)* apoyarse II. s. *(act)* apoyo; *(maintenance)* mantenimiento *f;* ARQ., TEC. soporte *m.*
sup·port·a·ble (sə-pôr'tə-bəl) adj. soportable.
sup·port·er (sə-pôr'tər) s. *(sustainer)* soporte *m; (advocate)* defensor *m,* partidario; DEP. aficionado.
sup·por·tive (sə-pôr'tĭv) adj. sustentador, que apoya.
sup·pose (sə-pōz') tr. **-posed, -pos·ing** *(to assume)* suponer <*let's s. that A equals Z* supongamos que A es igual a Z>; creer <*you don't s. that I did it, do you?* tú no creerás que yo lo hice, ¿verdad?>; *(to imagine)* imaginar; *(to presuppose)* presuponer, suponer ♦ **s. he doesn't come** suponer que él no venga *o* ¿qué pasaría si él no viniera? • **s. we dine together** ¿y si cenáramos juntos? *o* ¿qué tal si cenamos juntos? —intr. imaginarse, conjeturar.
sup·posed (sə-pōzd', -pō'zĭd) adj. *(presumed)* presunto; *(required)* supuesto.
sup·pos·ing (sə-pō'zĭng) conj. suponiendo que, en el supuesto de que.

---

sup·po·si·tion (sŭp'ə-zĭsh'ən) s. suposición f.

sup·pos·i·to·ry (sə-pŏz'ĭ-tôr'ē) s. [pl. **-ries**] supositorio.

sup·press (sə-prĕs') tr. *(to subdue)* suprimir; *(to prohibit)* prohibir; *(to conceal)* ocultar; *(to repress)* reprimir; *(to restrain)* contener; MED. detener, parar.

sup·pres·sion (sə-prĕsh'ən) s. *(act)* supresión f; *(repression)* represión f; PSIC. inhibición f.

sup·pres·sive (sə-prĕs'ĭv) adj. represivo.

sup·pu·rate (sŭp'yə-rāt') intr. **-rat·ed, -rat·ing** supurar.

sup·pu·ra·tion (sŭp'yə-rā'shən) s. MED. *(discharge)* supuración f; *(pus)* pus m.

su·pra·na·tion·al (sōō'prə-nãsh'ə-nəl) adj. supranacional.

su·prem·a·cist (sōō-prĕm'ə-sĭst) s. POL. defensor de la supremacía m.

su·prem·a·cy (sōō-prĕm'ə-sē) s. [pl. **-cies**] supremacía.

su·preme (sōō-prĕm') adj. *(paramount)* supremo; *(greatest)* sumo, máximo.

Supreme Being s. RELIG. Ser Supremo.

supreme court s. DER. corte suprema, tribunal supremo.

su·preme·ly (sōō-prĕm'lē) adv. sumamente.

Supreme Soviet s. POL. soviet supremo.

sur·cease (sûr'sēs', sər-sēs') ANT. I. tr. & intr. **-ceased, -ceas·ing** cesar II. s. cesación f.

sur·charge (sûr'chärj') I. s. *(additional sum)* sobrecarga; *(overcharge)* recargo II. tr. **-charged, -charg·ing** *(to overload, overcharge)* sobrecargar, recargar; *(to overfill)* sobrellenar.

sur·coat (sûr'kōt') s. sobretodo.

sure (shōōr) I. adj. **sur·er, sur·est** *(certain)* seguro; *(infallible)* infalible, certero <*a s. shot* un tiro certero>; *(said of a hand)* firme ♦ **s. thing!** ¡claro!, ¡por supuesto! • **to be s.** sin duda • **to make s.** asegurarse II. adv. *(surely)* seguramente; *(of course)* por supuesto, claro <*s. I will come claro que se vendré*> ♦ **for s.** con toda seguridad • **s. enough** efectivamente.

sure-fire (shōōr'fīr') adj. FAM. seguro, de éxito seguro.

sure-foot·ed (shōōr'fōōt'ĭd) adj. de pie firme, seguro.

sure·ly (shōōr'lē) adv. seguramente, ciertamente ♦ **s.!** ¡por supuesto!

sure·ness (shōōr'nĭs) s. seguridad f.

sur·e·ty (shōōr'ĭ-tē) s. [pl. **-ties**] *(sureness)* seguridad f; *(pledge)* garantía, fianza; *(person)* garante mf, fiador m.

surf (sûrf) I. s. *(waves)* resaca, oleaje m; *(foam)* espuma II. intr. hacer surfing, practicar el deporte de la tabla hawaiana.

sur·face (sûr'fəs) I. s. superficie f ♦ **on the s.** FIG. en apariencia, superficialmente II. adj. superficial, de la superficie III. tr. **-faced, -fac·ing** *(to smooth)* pulir; *(to level)* alisar, allanar; *(to coat)* revestir —intr. salir a la superficie.

surface tension s. FÍS. tensión superficial f.

sur·face-to-air missile (sûr'fəs-tōō-âr') s. MIL. proyectil superficie-aire m.

sur·fac·ing (sûr'fə-sĭng) s. *(finish)* acabado; *(coating)* revestimiento; *(of a road)* afirmado; F.C. nivelación f.

surf·fac·tant (sər-fãk'tənt) s. QUÍM. agente flotador m.

surf·board (sûrf'bôrd') s. DEP. tabla hawaiana.

sur·feit (sûr'fĭt) I. tr. saciar, hartar II. s. *(satiety)* saciedad f, hartura; *(indigestion)* empacho m; *(excess)* exceso m.

surf·er (sûr'fər) s. deportista que practica el deporte de la tabla hawaiana mf.

surf·ing (sûr'fĭng) s. DEP. deporte de la tabla hawaiana m.

surge (sûrj) I. intr. **surged, surg·ing** *(the sea)* encresparse, levantarse; *(energy, enthusiasm)* subir súbitamente; *(a rope)* lascarse, aflojarse —tr. lascar, aflojar II. s. *(of waves)* oleaje m, oleada; *(billow)* mar de fondo; *(onrush)* arranque m; ELEC. sobretensión f; MARÍT. mecha (del cabrestante).

sur·geon (sûr'jən) s. cirujano.

sur·ger·y (sûr'jə-rē) s. [pl. **-ies**] *(treatment)* intervención quirúrgica; *(operating room)* quirófano; *(surgeon's work)* cirugía; G.B. *(doctor's office)* consultorio médico, consulta.

sur·gi·cal (sûr'jĭ-kəl) adj. quirúrgico.

Su·ri·nam (sōōr'ə-nãm') o **Su·ri·na·me** (sōōr'ə-nã'mə) s. Suriname m.

Su·ri·na·mese (sōōr'ə-nə-mēz') s. [pl. **Surinamese**] surinamés m ♦ **the S.** los surinameses.

sur·ly (sûr'lē) adj. **-li·er, -li·est** *(ill-humored)* malhumorado; ANT. *(arrogant)* arrogante.

sur·mise (sər-mīz') tr. **-mised, -mis·ing** suponer, conjeturar II. s. suposición f, conjetura.

sur·mount (sər-mount') tr. *(to overcome)* vencer, superar (un obstáculo); *(to climb)* escalar; *(to place)* poner sobre; *(to surpass)* sobrepasar.

sur·name (sûr'nãm') I. s. *(family name)* apellido; *(nickname)* apodo II. tr. **-named, -nam·ing** apellidar.

sur·pass (sər-pãs') tr. *(to transcend)* sobrepasar, superar; *(to exceed)* superar, rebasar.

sur·pass·ing (sər-pãs'ĭng) adj. incomparable, sin igual.

sur·plice (sûr'plĭs) s. RELIG. sobrepelliz f.

sur·plus (sûr'pləs) I. adj. excedente II. s. *(excess)* excedente m; COM. superávit m.

sur·prise (sər-prīz') I. tr. **-prised, -pris·ing** *(to catch unawares)* sorprender; *(to astonish)* sorprender, asombrar ♦ **to be surprised at** sorprenderse de o con II. s. sorpresa ♦ **s. attack** MIL. ataque por sorpresa • **s. visit** visita inesperada • **to take by s.** coger desprevenido • **what a s.!** ¡qué sorpresa!, ¡vaya sorpresa!

sur·pris·ing (sər-prī'zĭng) adj. sorprendente, asombroso.

sur·prize (sər-prīz') v. & s. var. de **surprise**.

sur·re·al (sə-rē'əl) adj. surrealista.

sur·re·al·ism (sə-rē'ə-lĭz'əm) s. ARTE., LIT. surrealismo.

sur·re·al·is·tic (sə-rē'ə-lĭs'tĭk) adj. surrealista.

sur·ren·der (sə-rĕn'dər) I. tr. *(to hand over)* rendir, entregar; *(to give up)* ceder; *(to abandon)* abandonar ♦ **to s. oneself** entregarse a —intr. rendirse, entregarse II. s. *(submission)* rendición f; *(handing over)* entrega; *(abandonment)* abandono.

sur·rep·ti·tious (sûr'əp-tĭsh'əs) adj. subrepticio.

sur·ro·gate (sûr'ə-gĭt, -gāt') I. s. *(substitute)* substituto, sustituto; DER. juez de testamentarías m II. adj. substituto, sustituto III. tr. **-gat·ed, -gat·ing** substituir, sustituir.

sur·round (sə-round') tr. rodear, cercar.

sur·round·ings (sə-roun'dĭngz) s.pl. alrededores m.

sur·tax (sûr'tãks') ECON. I. s. sobretasa, recargo II. tr. poner un recargo a.

sur·veil·lance (sər-vā'ləns) s. vigilancia.

sur·vey (sər-vā') I. tr. *(to examine)* examinar; *(to inspect)* inspeccionar; *(to measure)* medir —intr. hacer una encuesta II. s. (sûr'vā') [pl. **-veys**] *(inspection)* inspección f; *(view)* vista, panorama m; *(measurement)* medición f; *(map)* mapa fotográfico.

sur·vey·ing (sər-vā'ĭng) s. agrimensura, topografía.

sur·vey·or (sər-vā'ər) s. *(of land)* agrimensor m, topógrafo; *(inspector)* inspector m; *(of customs)* inspector de aduanas.

sur·viv·al (sər-vī'vəl) s. supervivencia.

sur·vive (sər-vīv') tr. & intr. **-vived, -viv·ing** sobrevivir ♦ **to s. on** subsistir con.

sur·vi·vor (sər-vī'vər) s. superviviente mf, sobreviviente mf.

sur·vi·vor·ship (sər-vī'vər-shĭp') s. DER. supervivencia.

sus·cep·ti·bil·i·ty (sə-sĕp'tə-bĭl'ĭ-tē) s. [pl. **-ties**] *(condition)* susceptibilidad f; *(sensitivity)* sensibilidad f.

sus·cep·ti·ble (sə-sĕp'tə-bəl) adj. *(easily affected)* susceptible; *(vulnerable)* vulnerable; *(liable)* propenso; *(sensitive)* sensible; *(impressionable)* impresionable ♦ **to be s. of** permitir • **to be s. to** ser propenso a.

sus·cep·tive (sə-sĕp'tĭv) adj. *(susceptible)* susceptible; *(sensible)* sensible.

sus·pect (sə-spĕkt') I. tr. *(to imagine)* sospechar, tener la impresión de; *(to distrust)* sospechar de, recelar de; *(to believe to be guilty)* sospechar, tener la sospecha de —intr. *(to be suspicious)* sospechar, tener sospechas; *(to believe)* imaginarse, figurarse <*I suspected as much* ya me lo imaginaba> II. s. adj. (sûs'pĕkt') sospechoso.

sus·pend (sə-spĕnd') tr. *(to interrupt)* suspender, interrumpir <*to s. a trial* interrumpir un proceso>; *(to bar)* suspender; *(to hang)* suspender, colgar; DER. suspender —intr. suspender.

suspended animation s. MED. interrupción de las funciones vitales *f.*
sus·pend·er (sə-spĕn′dər) s. suspendedor *m* ♦ **suspenders** tirantes, tiradores.
sus·pense (sə-spĕns′) s. *(suspension)* suspensión *f; (doubt)* duda, incertidumbre *f;* CINEM. suspenso.
sus·pen·sion (sə-spĕn′shən) s. suspensión *f.*
suspension bridge s. puente colgante *m.*
sus·pen·sive (sə-spĕn′sĭv) adj. suspensivo.
sus·pen·so·ry (sə-spĕn′sə-rē) I. adj. *(supporter)* suspensorio; *(suspensive)* suspensivo II. s. [pl. **-ries**] MED. suspensorio.
sus·pi·cion (sə-spĭsh′ən) s. *(doubt)* sospecha; *(mistrust)* desconfianza; *(pinch)* pizca ♦ **above s.** fuera de toda sospecha • **on s.** como sospechoso • **to come under s. of** ser sospechado de • **under s.** bajo sospecha.
sus·pi·cious (sə-spĭsh′əs) adj. *(questionable)* sospechoso; *(distrustful)* desconfiado; *(malicious)* suspicaz.
sus·pi·cious·ly (sə-spĭsh′əs-lē) adv. sospechosamente.
sus·pi·cious·ness (sə-spĭsh′əs-nĭs) s. *(suspicion)* suspicacia; *(mistrust)* recelo, desconfianza.
sus·tain (sə-stān′) tr. *(to provide for)* sostener, mantener; *(to encourage)* animar <*the spectators sustained the players* los espectadores animaban a los jugadores>; *(weight)* sostener, aguantar; *(to maintain)* mantener <*s. a conversation* mantener una conversación>; *(an idea)* apoyar; *(loss, injury)* sufrir; *(hardships)* soportar, aguantar; MIL. sostener.
sus·tain·a·ble (sə-stā′nə-bəl) adj. sostenible.
sus·tain·ment (sə-stān′mənt) s. sostenimiento.
sus·te·nance (sŭs′tə-nəns) s. *(act)* sustento; *(maintenance)* mantenimiento; *(nourishment)* alimento; *(livelihood)* medios de subsistencia.
sus·ten·ta·tion (sŭs′tən-tā′shən, -tĕn-) s. *(support)* sostenimiento, apoyo; *(maintenance)* mantenimiento, sustentación *f.*
su·sur·ra·tion (sōō′sə-rā′shən) s. susurro, murmullo.
su·ture (sōō′chər) MED., CIR. I. s. sutura II. tr. -tured, -turing suturar.
su·ze·rain (sōō′zər-ən, -zə-rān′) s. POL. *(lord)* señor feudal *m; (nation)* estado protector.
su·ze·rain·ty (sōō′zər-ən-tē, -zə-rān′-) s. [pl. **-ties**] POL. *(power)* soberanía feudal, señorío feudal; *(domain)* soberanía.
svelte (svĕlt) adj. **svelt·er, svelt·est** esbelto.
swab (swŏb) I. s. MED. tapón *m; (mop)*′ estropajo; JER. *(sailor)* marinero; *(lout)* patán *m* II. tr. **swabbed, swab·bing** MED. limpiar con tapón; *(to mop)* fregar con estropajo.
swad·dle (swŏd′l) I. tr. **-dled, -dling** *(to wrap)* envolver; *(to diaper)* poner los pañales a; *(to restrain)* trabar II. s. *(band)* faja; *(diaper)* pañal *m.*
swaddling clothes s.pl. faja.
swag (swăg) I. s. *(ornament)* festón *m;* JER. *(loot)* botín *m; (bundle)* bulto II. intr. **swagged, swag·ging** G.B. tambalearse, bambolearse.
swage (swāj) I. s. tas de estampar *m* II. tr. **swaged, swag·ing** forjar, estampar.
swag·ger (swăg′ər) I. intr. *(to strut)* pavonearse, contonearse; *(to boast)* vanagloriarse II. s. *(movement)* pavoneo, contoneo; *(manner)* jactancia.
swagger stick s. MIL. bastón de mando *m.*
swain (swān) s. *(shepherd)* pastor *m; (suitor)* pretendiente *m.*
swal·low¹ (swŏl′ō) I. tr. *(food, drink)* tragar; *(to ingest)* ingerir, tomar; *(insults, pride)* tragarse; FAM. *(to believe)* creer, tragar(se) <*you s. all his lies* te tragas todas sus mentiras>; *(to suppress)* reprimir, contener (sentimientos) ♦ **to s. one's words** comerse sus palabras • **to s. up** *(to take in)* tragar; *(to engulf)* destruir —intr. tragar II. s. *(act)* deglución *f; (of drink)* trago; *(of food)* bocado ♦ **at** *o* **with one s.** de un trago.
swal·low² (swŏl′ō) s. ORNIT. golondrina.
swal·low-tailed (swŏl′ō-tāld′) adj. con cola como la de una golondrina.
swallow-tailed coat s. frac *m.*
swam (swăm) pret. de **swim.**

swamp (swŏmp, swômp) I. s. pantano II. tr. *(to inundate)* inundar, anegar; *(to sink)* hundir; FIG. *(to overwhelm)* —intr. irse a pique, hundirse.
swamp·land (swŏmp′lănd′, swômp′-) s. ciénaga.
swamp·y (swŏm′pē, swôm′-) adj. **-i·er, -i·est** pantanoso.
swan (swŏn) s. cisne *m.*
swan dive s. DEP. salto del ángel.
swank (swăngk) I. adj. **-er, -est** *(grand)* lujoso; *(ostentatious)* ostentoso II. s. *(elegance)* elegancia; *(swagger)* vanagloria, jactancia II. intr. darse humos, fanfarronear.
swank·y (swăng′kē) adj. **-i·er, -i·est** lujoso, elegante.
swan song s. canto del cisne.
swap (swŏp) FAM. I. tr. & intr. **swapped, swap·ping** trocar, canjear II. s. canje *m,* trueque *m.*
sward (swôrd) s. césped *m.*
swarm¹ (swôrm) I. s. *(of ants)* hormiguero; *(of bees)* enjambre *m; (of people)* muchedumbre II. intr. *(to move, emerge)* pulular, hormiguear; *(bees)* salir en enjambre —tr. invadir, inundar ♦ **to s. with** rebosar con, bullir de.
swarm² (swôrm) intr. & intr. ♦ **to s. up** trepar.
swarth (swôrth) s. var. de **sward.**
swar·thy (swôr′thē) adj. **-thi·er, -thi·est** moreno, prieto.
swash (swŏsh, swôsh) I. s. *(sound)* chapoteo; *(channel)* canalizo; *(sand bank)* banco de arena; *(swaggering person)* fanfarrón *m* II. intr. *(to strike)* chapotear; *(to swagger)* fanfarronear —tr. *(to splash)* chapotear; *(to splash against)* arrojar, echar sobre.
swash·buck·ler (swŏsh′bŭk′lər, swôsh′-) s. *(swordsman)* espadachín *m; (adventurer)* bravucón *m.*
swas·ti·ka (swŏs′tĭ-kə) s. esvástica, cruz gamada.
swat (swŏt) I. tr. **swat·ted, swat·ting** aplastar II. s. golpe repentino.
swatch (swŏch) s. muestra (de un tejido, color).
swath (swŏth, swôth) s. *(scythe stroke)* golpe de guadaña *m; (path)* ringlera ♦ **to cut a wide s.** FIG. hacer un gran papel.
swathe¹ (swŏth, swôth, swăth) I. tr. **swathed, swath·ing** *(to wrap)* vendar; *(to enfold)* envolver II. s. venda.
swathe² (swŏth, swôth) var. de **swath.**
swat·ter (swŏt′ər) s. matamoscas *m.*
sway (swā) I. tr. *(to move back and forth)* hacer oscilar; *(to cause to lean)* inclinar; *(to divert)* desviar, apartar; FIG. *(to influence)* ejercer influencia en <*his speech swayed the public* su discurso ejerció influencia en el público>; *(to convince)* persuadir, convencer; ANT. *(to govern)* gobernar, dirigir ♦ **to s. somebody from** apartar a alguien de • **to s. up** MARÍT. izar —intr. *(to move back and forth)* balancearse; *(to move unsteadily)* tambalearse; FIG. *(to incline)* inclinarse; *(to hesitate)* vacilar II. s. *(moving from side to side)* balanceo, oscilación *f;* FIG. *(power)* dominio ♦ **to be under the s. of** estar dominado por • **to hold s. over** dominar.
sway·back (swā′băk′) s. lomo hundido.
Swa·zi (swä′zē) I. adj. swazi II. s. [pl. **Swazi** *o* **-zis**] swazi *mf* ♦ **the S.** los swazis.
Swa·zi·land (swä′zē-lănd′) s. swazilandia.
swear (swâr) intr. **swore** (swôr), **sworn** (swôrn), **swear·ing** *(to vow)* jurar, prestar juramento; *(to declare)* jurar <*I s. to you I spoke the truth* les juro que dije la verdad>; DER. declarar bajo juramento ♦ **to s. up and down** FAM. jurar por todos los santos, jurar y perjurar —tr. *(to declare solemnly)* jurar <*I s. that it is true* juro que es verdad>; *(to pledge)* jurar, prometer <*to s. loyalty to* jurar lealtad a>; DER. tomar juramento a ♦ **to s. at** insultar, maldecir • **to s. by** jurar por • **to s. in** investir de un cargo bajo juramento • **to s. off** FAM. prometer renunciar a • **to s. someone to secrecy** hacer que alguien jure guardar un secreto • **to s. to** afirmar bajo juramento.
swear·er (swâr′ər) s. DER. el que presta juramento; *(blasphemous)* blasfemo.
swear-word (swâr′wûrd′) s. palabrota, taco.
sweat (swĕt) I. intr. **sweat·ed** *o* **sweat, sweat·ing** *(to perspire)* sudar; *(to exude)* rezumar; *(to ferment)* fermentar —tr. *(to excrete)* sudar; *(to cause to perspire)* hacer sudar; *(to make wet)* empapar de sudor; *(to overwork)* explotar (obreros), FAM. *(to interrogate)* someter a interrogatorio; *(to extract information from)* hacer cantar a ♦ **to s. it out**

JER. pasar un mal rato **II.** s. *(perspiration)* sudor *m*; *(moisture)* humedad *f*; *(drudgery)* trabajo pesado; *(exercise run)* ejercicio preparatorio (de un caballo) ♦ **no s.** no es ningún problema, fácil • **old s.** veterano • **to be in a s.** estar angustiado.

sweat·band (swĕt'bănd') s. bandana de sombrero.

sweat·box (swĕt'bŏks') s. *(box)* tina de apelambrar; *(room)* sudadero.

sweat·er (swĕt'ər) s. suéter *m*, jersey *m*.

sweat gland s. ANAT. glándula sudorípara.

sweat shirt s. jersey *m*.

sweat·shop (swĕt'shŏp') s. fábrica en la que se explota al obrero.

sweat suit s. chandal *m*.

sweat·y (swĕt'ē) adj. **-i·er, -i·est** *(sweating)* sudoroso; *(laborious)* agotador.

Swede (swēd) s. sueco.

Swe·den (swēd'n) s. Suecia.

Swed·ish (swē'dĭsh) adj. & s. sueco.

sweep (swēp) **I.** tr. **swept** (swĕpt), **sweep·ing** *(to brush)* barrer <*to s. the floor* barrer el piso>; *(to remove)* arrastrar, llevarse <*the wind swept tiles from the roof* el viento se llevó tejas del techo>; *(to destroy)* arrasar, asolar; *(to traverse)* recorrer; *(to drag for mines)* dragar ♦ **to s. a constituency** POL. llevarse la mayoría de los votos • **to s. away** *(to clean)* barrer; *(snow)* limpiar; *(to carry sway)* llevar, arrastrar • **to s. off one's feet** FIG., FAM. hacerle perder la cabeza a uno • **to s. the board** FIG., FAM. barrer con todos los premios, llevarse todo • **to s. up** *(a room)* barrer; *(dust, sawdust)* recoger —intr. *(to clean)* barrer; *(to flow)* pasar rápidamente; *(to trail)* arrastrarse; *(to extend)* extenderse ♦ **to s. along** andar rápidamente • **to s. by** pasar rápidamente **II.** s. *(sweeping)* barrido; *(motion)* movimiento amplio; *(reach)* alcance *m*; *(curve)* curva; *(chimney sweep)* deshollinador *m*; *(winnings)* ganancia; *(victory)* victoria aplastante; *(oar)* remo; *(pole)* cigoñal (de un pozo) *m*; *(of telescope, radar)* giro ♦ **at one s.** de una vez • **sweeps** barreduras, basuras • **to make a clean s. of** *(to get rid of)* hacer tabla rasa de; *(to get hold of)* acaparar, llevarse todo.

sweep·er (swē'pər) s. *(person)* barrendero; *(machine)* barredora, barredera.

sweep·ing (swē'pĭng) **I.** adj. *(extensive)* extenso, vasto; *(dramatic)* dramático; *(gesture)* amplio; *(car)* aerodinámico **II.** s. barrido • **sweepings** basura.

sweep·stakes (swēp'stāks') o **sweep·stake** (-stāk') s. [pl. **sweepstakes**] lotería.

sweet (swēt) **I.** adj. **-er, -est** *(sugary)* dulce; *(containing sugar)* azucarado; *(gratifying)* agradable, grato; *(lovable)* encantador, adorable; *(fresh)* fresco; *(potable)* potable ♦ **at one's own s. will** al antojo de uno • **how s.!** ¡qué encantador! • **s. oil** aceite de oliva • **s. one** querido • **s. pepper** pimiento morrón • **s. sixteen** quince abriles • **to be s. on** estar enamorado de • **to have a s. tooth** ser goloso • **to take one's own s. time** no darse prisa • **to taste s.** estar dulce **II.** s. *(sweetness)* dulzura; *(candy)* dulce *m*; *(toffee)* caramelo; *(beloved person)* amor *m*, cariño; G.B. *(dessert)* postre *m*.

sweet·bread (swēt'brĕd') s. mollejas.

sweet·en (swēt'n) tr. *(to make sweet)* endulzar, azucarar; *(to make pleasurable)* suavizar; *(to make bearable)* aplacar; FAM. *(in poker)* aumentar una apuesta —intr. endulzarse.

sweet·en·er (swēt'n-ər) s. dulcificante *m*, edulcorante *m*.

sweet·en·ing (swēt'n-ĭng) s. *(process)* endulzamiento; *(sweetener)* dulcificante *m*, edulcorante *m*.

sweet·heart (swēt'härt') s. *(lover)* enamorado, novio; *(lovable person)* persona adorable.

sweet·meat (swēt'mēt') s. dulce *m*, confitura.

sweet·ness (swēt'nĭs) s. dulzura.

sweet potato s. batata, boniato.

sweet·shop (swēt'shŏp') s. confitería.

sweet talk s. lisonja(s).

sweet tooth s. gusto por la confitura ♦ **to have a s.** ser goloso.

swell (swĕl) **I.** intr. **swelled, swelled** o **swol·len** (swō'lən), **swell·ing** *(to dilate)* hincharse, inflarse <*my eyes are swol-

len* tengo los ojos hinchados>; *(to increase)* crecer, aumentar <*membership swelled* el número de miembros aumentó>; *(to grow louder)* subir, aumentar; *(to rise)* subir, crecer; *(to be filled with emotion)* hincharse, engreírse ♦ **to s. out** hincharse, inflarse • **to s. up** *(eyes, joint)* hincharse; *(membership, numbers)* aumentar —tr. *(to dilate)* hinchar; *(to cause to increase)* hacer aumentar ♦ **to get a swollen head** FIG., FAM. engreírse **II.** s. *(act)* inflamiento; *(swollen part)* hinchazón *f*, abultamiento; *(wave)* oleada; *(rounded hill)* ondulación *f*; FAM. *(handsome person)* guapo; *(important person)* pez gordo, personaje *m*; **III.** adj. **-er, -est** FAM. *(stylish)* elegante; *(fine)* fenomenal, excelente.

swelled head s. FIG., FAM. engreído.

swell·ing (swĕl'ĭng) s. *(increase in size)* inflamiento; MED. *(protuberance)* abultamiento, hinchazón *f*; *(swollen part)* hinchazón; *(ganglion)* ganglio; *(bruise)* bulto, chichón *m*.

swel·ter (swĕl'tər) **I.** intr. sofocarse de calor —tr. *(to affect)* abrumar de calor **II.** s. calor sofocante *m*.

swel·ter·ing (swĕl'tər-ĭng) adj. *(hot)* abrasador; *(person)* sudando a mares.

swept (swĕpt) pret. y part. p. de **sweep.**

swept·back (swĕpt'băk') adj. en flecha.

swerve (swûrv) **I.** tr. & intr. **swerved, swerv·ing** desviar(se) **II.** s. desviación *f*.

swift (swĭft) **I.** adj. **-er, -est** *(fast)* veloz; *(quick)* rápido **II.** adv. rápido **III.** s. *(cylinder)* carrete *m*; *(reel)* devanadera; ORNIT. vencejo; ZOOL. lagartija.

swift·ness (swĭft'nĭs) s. rapidez *f*, velocidad *f*.

swig (swĭg) FAM. **I.** s. trago **II.** tr. & intr. **swigged, swig·ging** beber a tragos.

swill (swĭl) **I.** tr. *(to drink)* beber a tragos; *(to flood)* empapar —intr. emborracharse **II.** s. *(inedible food)* bazofia; *(refuse)* basura; *(liquor)* trago.

swim (swĭm) **I.** intr. **swam** (swăm), **swum** (swŭm), **swim·ming** *(to move in the water)* nadar; *(to glide)* deslizarse; *(to float)* flotar; *(to be immersed)* estar cubierto, estar lleno; *(to whirl)* dar vueltas ♦ **to s. across** atravesar a nado • **to s. against the stream** ir en contra de la corriente • **to s. for it** salvarse a nado • **to s. with the tide** seguir la corriente —tr. *(to go by swimming)* nadar; *(to cause to swim)* hacer nadar; *(to swim across)* atravesar a nado • **swimming in** cubierto de, lleno de • **to s. across** atravesar a nado **II.** s. *(swimming)* natación *f*; *(period of swimming)* baño; *(vertigo)* vértigo, mareo ♦ **to go for** o **to take a s.** ir a nadar.

swim bladder s. ICT. vejiga natatoria.

swim·ming (swĭm'ĭng) **I.** s. *(in water)* natación *f*; *(vertigo)* vértigo **II.** adj. *(in water)* nadador; *(in tears)* lleno de lágrimas (ojos).

swim·ming·ly (swĭm'ĭng-lē) adv. espléndidamente, a las mil maravillas.

swimming pool s. piscina, pileta.

swimming suit s. traje de baño *m*.

swim·suit (swĭm'sōōt') s. traje de baño *m*.

swin·dle (swĭn'dl) **I.** tr. & intr. **-dled, -dling** estafar; timar **II.** s. timo, estafa.

swin·dler (swĭnd'lər) s. estafador *m*, timador *m*.

swine (swīn) s. [pl. **swine**] cerdo.

swine·herd (swīn'hûrd') s. porquerizo.

swing (swĭng) **I.** intr. **swung** (swŭng), **swing·ing** *(to oscillate)* oscilar; *(on a swing)* columpiarse, balancearse; *(on hinges)* girar; *(to vacillate)* dar un giro, virar; JER. *(to be hanged)* colgar (un ahorcado); *(to be up to date)* estar al día; MÚS. tocar con ritmo ♦ **to s. clear** AUTO. dar un viraje para evitar un choque • **to s. to** cerrarse • **to s. to and fro** balancearse —tr. *(to cause to move)* hacer girar; *(on a swing)* hacer balancear; *(in the arms)* mecer; *(to move)* mover; *(to hang)* colgar; *(to cause to change)* hacer cambiar; JER. *(to manage)* lograr; MÚS. tocar (una canción) con ritmo ♦ **to s. a blow** pegar un golpe • **to s. an election** ganar una eleccion • **to s. around a corner** AUTO. doblar una esquina • **to s. at** dirigir un golpe a **II.** s. *(oscillation)* oscilacion *f*, balanceo; *(force)* impulso; *(swoop)* descenso rápido; *(for children)* columpio, balancín *m*; MÚS. ritmo ♦ **at full s.** a toda velocidad • **in full s.** en plena marcha • **to**

go with a s. ir sobre ruedas **III.** adj. giratorio, sobre goznes.

swing·er (swǐng′ər) s. *(one that swings)* oscilador *m*; JER. *(person)* persona a la última moda y sin inhibiciones.

swing·ing (swǐng′ǐng) JER. **I.** s. libertinaje *m* **II.** adj. *(up-to-date)* muy moderno; *(spirited)* alegre; MÚS. rítmico.

swin·ish (swī′nǐsh) adj. cochino.

swipe (swīp) **I.** s. *(blow)* golpetazo; *(lever)* cigüeñal *m* **II.** tr. **swiped, swip·ing** *(to hit)* dar un tortazo, golpear; JER. *(to steal)* robar, birlar —intr. barrer.

swirl (swûrl) **I.** intr. *(to rotate)* dar vueltas; *(to be dizzy)* marearse —tr. girar **II.** s. *(motion)* giro, vuelta; *(whirlpool)* remolino; *(whorl)* espiral *m*.

swish (swǐsh) s. **I.** intr. *(whips, canes)* silbar; *(fabrics)* crujir; JER. *(to move effeminately)* menearse —tr. *(a whip, cane)* sacudir, hacer chasquear; *(to brandish)* blandir; *(to hit)* azotar **II.** s. *(hissing sound)* silbido; *(rustle)* crujido; *(whip)* látigo; JER. *(swishing male)* afeminado, maricón *m* **III.** adj. G.B. elegante.

Swiss (swǐs) **I.** adj. suizo **II.** s. [pl. **Swiss**] suizo ♦ **the S.** los suizos.

switch (swǐch) **I.** s. ELEC. interruptor *m*; *(flexible rod)* látigo; *(lashing)* latigazo; FIG. *(shift)* cambio; *(bushy tip)* mechón *m*; *(false hair)* trenza postiza; F.C. *(switching)* cambio (de vías) **II.** tr. ELEC. *(to disconnect)* desconectar; *(to connect)* conectar; *(to whip)* azotar; FIG. *(to shift)* cambiar de (conversación, tema); *(to exchange)* cambiar, intercambiar; F.C. desviar ♦ **to s. off** ELEC. *(current)* desconectar; *(lights)* apagar; *(appliance, motor)* parar, apagar • **to s. on** ELEC. *(current)* conectar; *(lights)* encender; *(appliance, motor)* poner en marcha —intr. cambiar <*to s. from oil to gas* cambiar de aceite a gas>.

switch·back (swǐch′băk′) s. *(road)* carretera en zigzag; *(railway)* vía de tren en zigzag; *(trail)* camino o sendero en zigzag; G.B. *(roller coaster)* montaña rusa.

switch·blade knife (swǐch′blād′) s. navaja de muelle.

switch·board (swǐch′bôrd′) s. ELEC. tablero o cuadro de distribución; TEL. conmutador *m*, centralita de teléfonos ♦ **s. operator** telefonista *mf*.

switch·man (swǐch′mən) s. [pl. **-men**] F.C. guardagujas *m*.

switch·yard (swǐch′yärd′) s. F.C. patio de maniobras.

Swit·zer·land (swǐt′sər-lənd) s. Suiza.

swiv·el (swǐv′əl) **I.** s. *(link)* eslabón giratorio; *(pivot)* pivote *m* **II.** tr. hacer girar —intr. girar.

swivel chair s. silla giratoria.

swiz·zle stick (swǐz′əl) s. varilla de cóctel.

swob (swŏb) s. & v. var. de **swab**.

swol·len (swō′lən) un part. p. de **swell**.

swoon (swōōn) **I.** intr. desmayarse, desvanecerse **II.** s. desmayo, desvanecimiento.

swoop (swōōp) **I.** intr. abalanzarse —tr. arrebatar **II.** s. calada, descenso rápido ♦ **in one fell s.** de un solo golpe.

swoosh (swōōsh, swŏŏsh) intr. *(a whip, cane)* silbar; *(to flow)* salir a chorros.

swop (swŏp) v. & s. var. de **swap**.

sword (sôrd) s. *(weapon)* espada; *(instrument)* arma; *(power)* poder militar *m* ♦ **to be at sword's points** estar a punto de matarse • **to cross swords with** *(to fight)* cruzar la espada con; *(to argue)* habérselas con alguien • **to put to the s.** pasar a cuchillo.

sword·fish (sôrd′fǐsh′) s. [pl. **swordfish** o **-fish·es**] pez espada *m*.

sword·play (sôrd′plā′) s. DEP. esgrima.

swords·man (sôrdz′mən) s. [pl. **-men**] DEP. *(fencer)* esgrimista *m*; *(fighter)* espadachín *m*.

swords·man·ship (sôrdz′mən-shǐp′) s. DEP. arte de la esgrima *m*.

swore (swôr) pret. de **swear**.

sworn (swôrn) part. p. de **swear**.

swum (swŭm) part. p. de **swim**.

swung (swŭng) pret. y part. p. de **swing**.

syb·a·rite (sǐb′ə-rīt′) s. sibarita *mf*.

syc·a·more (sǐk′ə-môr′) s. BOT. sicomoro, sicómoro.

syc·o·phant (sǐk′ə-fənt) s. adulador *m*, adulón *m*.

syl·la·bi (sǐl′ə-bī′) un pl. de **syllabus**.

syl·lab·ic (sǐ-lăb′ǐk) adj. silábico.

syl·lab·i·cate (sǐ-lăb′ǐ-kāt′) tr. **-cat·ed, -cat·ing** silabear, dividir en sílabas.

syl·lab·i·ca·tion (sǐ-lăb′ǐ-kā′shən) s. silabeo.

syl·lab·i·fy (sǐ-lăb′ǐ-fī′) tr. **-fied, -fy·ing** silabear, dividir en sílabas.

syl·la·ble (sǐl′ə-bəl) **I.** s. GRAM. sílaba **II.** tr. **-bled, -bling** silabear.

syl·la·bus (sǐl′ə-bəs) s. [pl. **-bus·es** o **-bi** (-bī′)] *(course program)* programa de estudios *m*; *(summary)* resumen *m*.

syl·lo·gism (sǐl′ə-jǐz′əm) s. silogismo.

syl·lo·gis·tic (sǐl′ə-jǐs′tǐk) o **syl·lo·gis·ti·cal** (-tǐ-kəl) adj. silogístico.

sylph (sǐlf) s. sílfide *f*.

syl·van (sǐl′vən) **I.** adj. selvático, silvestre **II.** s. habitante de los bosques *mf*.

sym·bi·o·sis (sǐm′bē-ō′sǐs, -bī-) s. BIOL., PSIC. simbiosis.

sym·bi·ot·ic (sǐm′bē-ŏt′ǐk, -bī-) adj. simbiótico.

sym·bol (sǐm′bəl) **I.** s. símbolo, emblema *m* **II.** tr. simbolizar.

sym·bol·ic (sǐm-bŏl′ǐk) o **sym·bol·i·cal** (-ǐ-kəl) adj. simbólico.

symbolic language s. COMPUT. lenguaje simbólico.

symbolic logic s. MAT. cálculo simbólico.

sym·bol·ism (sǐm′bə-lǐz′əm) s. simbolismo.

sym·bol·ist (sǐm′bə-lǐst) s. simbolista *mf*.

sym·bol·ize (sǐm′bə-līz′) tr. **-ized, -iz·ing** simbolizar —intr. usar símbolos.

sym·met·ric (sǐ-mět′rǐk) o **sym·met·ri·cal** (-rǐ-kəl) adj. simétrico.

sym·me·try (sǐm′ǐ-trē) s. [pl. **-tries**] simetría.

sym·pa·thet·ic (sǐm′pə-thět′ǐk) adj. *(compassionate)* compasivo; *(understanding)* comprensivo; *(kind)* amable; *(favorable)* favorable; *(in accord)* afín; *(supporting)* simpatizante; ANAT. simpático.

sym·pa·thize (sǐm′pə-thīz′) intr. **-thized, -thiz·ing** *(to commiserate)* compadecerse; *(to understand)* comprender; *(to share)* compartir; ANT. *(to agree)* congeniar.

sym·pa·thiz·er (sǐm′pə-thī′zər) s. simpatizante *mf*.

sym·pa·thy (sǐm′pə-thē) s. [pl. **-thies**] *(affinity)* simpatía, afinidad *f*; *(compatibility)* compatibilidad *f*; *(understanding)* comprensión *f*; *(expression of sorrow)* pésame *m*, condolencias; *(compassion)* compasión *f* ♦ **her sympathies lie with the communists** simpatiza con los comunistas • **message of s.** pésame ♦ **to be in s. with** *(to favor)* estar a favor de; *(to identify oneself with)* estar de acuerdo con.

sym·phon·ic (sǐm-fŏn′ǐk) adj. MÚS. sinfónico.

sym·pho·ny (sǐm′fə-nē) s. [pl. **-nies**] MÚS. *(composition)* sinfonía; *(orchestra)* orquesta sinfónica; *(harmony)* armonía, consonancia.

symphony orchestra s. MÚS. orquesta sinfónica.

sym·po·si·um (sǐm-pō′zē-əm) s. [pl. **-si·ums** o **-si·a** (-zē-ə)] *(conference)* simposio; *(collection of writings)* colección *f*, recopilación *f*; ANT. *(convivial meeting)* banquete *m*.

symp·tom (sǐmp′təm) s. *(indication)* indicio *m*; MED. síntoma *m*.

symp·to·mat·ic (sǐmp′tə-mǎt′ǐk) adj. sintomático.

syn·a·gogue o **syn·a·gog** (sǐn′ə-gŏg′) s. RELIG. sinagoga.

syn·apse (sǐn′ăps′, sǐ-năps′) s. ANAT., BIOL. sinapsis (conexión) *f*.

syn·ap·tic (sǐ-năp′tǐk) adj. ANAT., BIOL. sináptico.

sync o **synch** (sǐngk) FAM. **I.** s. *(synchronization)* sincronización *f*; *(synchronism)* sincronismo ♦ **to be out of s.** no estar sincronizado **II.** intr. *(to be simultaneous)* coincidir, ocurrir simultáneamente; *(to operate in unison)* ser sincrónico, funcionar sincrónicamente —tr. sincronizar.

syn·chro·nism (sǐng′krə-nǐz′əm) s. sincronismo.

syn·chro·ni·za·tion (sǐng′krə-nǐ-zā′shən) s. sincronización *f*.

syn·chro·nize (sǐng′krə-nīz′) intr. **-nized, -niz·ing** *(to be simultaneous)* coincidir; *(to operate in unison)* ser sincrónico —tr. sincronizar.

syn·chro·niz·er (sǐng′krə-nī′zər) s. sincronizador *m*.

syn·chro·nous (sǐng′krə-nəs) adj. *(simultaneous)* sincrónico; ELEC., MEC. síncrono.

syn·cline (sǐn′klīn′) s. GEOL. sinclinal (pliegue hundido) *m*.

syn·co·pa·tion (sǐng′kə-pā′shən, sǐn′-) s. GRAM., MÚS. síncopa.

syn·cre·tism (sǐng′krǐ-tǐz′əm) s. RELIG. sincretismo.

syn·dic (sǐn′dǐk) s. síndico.

syn·di·cal·ism (sǐn′dǐ-kə-lǐz′əm) s. sindicalismo.

syn·di·cate (sǐn′dǐ-kǐt) I. s. (association) sindicato; (agency) agencia de prensa; (of newspapers) cadena de periódicos; (office) sindicado II. tr. (sǐn′dǐ-kāt′) -cat·ed, -cat·ing (to organize) sindicar; PERIOD. (to sell) vender a través de una agencia —intr. sindicarse.

syn·di·ca·tion (sǐn′dǐ-kā′shən) s. sindicalización f.

syn·drome (sǐn′drōm′) s. MED. síndrome m.

syn·er·gism (sǐn′ər-jǐz′əm) o **syn·er·gy** (-ər-jē) s. FISIOL., MED. sinergia.

syn·fu·el (sǐn′fyōō′əl) s. QUÍM. combustible sintético.

syn·od (sǐn′əd) s. RELIG. sínodo.

syn·od·i·cal (sǐ-nǒd′ǐ-kəl) o **syn·od·ic** (-nǒd′ǐk) adj. sinódico.

syn·o·nym (sǐn′ə-nǐm′) s. sinónimo.

syn·on·y·mous (sǐ-nǒn′ə-məs) adj. sinónimo.

syn·on·y·my (sǐ-nǒn′ə-mē) s. [pl. -mies] sinonimia.

syn·op·sis (sǐ-nǒp′sǐs) s. [pl. -ses (-sēz′)] sinopsis f.

syn·op·tic (sǐ-nǒp′tǐk) o **syn·op·ti·cal** (-tǐ-kəl) adj. sinóptico ♦ **S.** RELIG. evangelios sinópticos.

syn·tac·tic (sǐn-tǎk′tǐk) o **syn·tac·tic·al** (-tǐ-kəl) adj. GRAM. sintáctico.

syn·tax (sǐn′tǎks′) s. GRAM. sintaxis f.

syn·the·sis (sǐn′thǐ-sǐs) s. [pl. -ses (-sēz′)] síntesis f.

syn·the·size (sǐn′thǐ-sīz′) tr. -sized, -siz·ing sintetizar.

syn·the·siz·er (sǐn′thǐ-sī′zər) s. sintetizador m.

syn·thet·ic (sǐn-thět′ǐk) I. adj. sintético II. s. QUÍM. material sintético.

syph·i·lis (sǐf′ə-lǐs) s. MED. sífilis f.

syph·i·lit·ic (sǐf′ə-lǐt′ǐk) adj. & s. MED. sifilítico.

sy·phon (sī′fən) s. & v. var. de **siphon.**

Syr·a·cuse (sǐr′ə-kyōōs′) s. Siracusa.

Syr·i·a (sǐr′ē-ə) s. Siria.

Syr·i·an (sǐr′ē-ən) adj. & s. sirio.

Syrian Arab Republic s. República Árabe Siria.

sy·rin·ga (sə-rǐng′gə) BOT. jeringuilla, celinda.

sy·ringe (sə-rǐnj′, sǐr′ǐnj) s. jeringa, jeringuilla.

syr·up (sǐr′əp) s. MED. jarabe m; CUL. almíbar m.

sys·tal·tic (sǐ-stôl′tǐk, -stǎl′-) adj. FISIOL. sistáltico.

sys·tem (sǐs′təm) s. (arrangement, principles) sistema m; (network) red f; (human body) organismo.

sys·tem·at·ic (sǐs′tə-mǎt′ǐk) o **sys·tem·at·i·cal** (-ǐ-kəl) adj. sistemático.

sys·tem·a·tize (sǐs′tə-mə-tīz′) tr. -tized, -tiz·ing sistematizar.

sys·tem·ic (sǐ-stěm′ǐk) adj. (of a system) sistemático; (of the body) que afecta al organismo.

sys·tem·ize (sǐs′tə-mīz′) tr. -ized, -iz·ing sistematizar.

sys·to·le (sǐs′tə-lē) s. FISIOL. sístole f.

T

t, T (tē) s. [pl. **t's, T's**] vigésima letra del alfabeto inglés ♦ **to a T** a la perfección <she fits the role to a T se ajusta al rol a la perfección>.

tab (tǎb) I. s. (flap) lengüeta; (label) etiqueta; FAM. (at a restaurant) cuenta; (of a typewriter) tabulador m; AER. aleta ♦ **to keep tabs on** controlar, observar detalladamente II. tr. **tabbed, tab·bing** marcar (con tiras, etiquetas).

tab·by (tǎb′ē) I. s. [pl. -bies] (striped cat) gato atigrado; (female cat) gata; (old maid) solterona; (gossip) chismosa; (silk) seda (con aguas) II. adj. (striped) atigrado; (made of silk) de seda con aguas.

tab·er·na·cle (tǎb′ər-nǎk′əl) s. (place of worship) templo, santuario; MARÍT. carlinga; ARQ. templete ♦ **T.** RELIG. tabernáculo.

tab·la·ture (tǎb′lə-chōōr′, -chər) s. MÚS. notación cifrada, entabladura; (engraved surface) superficie con inscripciones f.

ta·ble (tā′bəl) I. s. (furniture) mesa <to set the t. poner la mesa>; (food) mesa, comida <to set a good t. servir una buena mesa>; (fellow diners) comensales m; (companions) mesa <a t. of remarkable persons una mesa de personas notables>; (data) tabla, cuadro; (tableland) meseta; JOY. (upper surface) mesa, faceta superior; (diamond) diamante m; ARQ. (panel) tablero; (molding) moldura ♦ **t. of contents** índice m, tabla de materias • **gambling t.** mesa de juego • **multiplication t.** tabla de multiplicar • **tables of the Law** BÍBL. tablas de la Ley • **to turn the tables on someone** FIG. volver las tornas a alguien, devolver la pelota a alguien • **under the t.** FIG. (covertly) bajo la mesa; (drunk) completamente borracho II. tr. **-bled, -bling** (to place) poner sobre una mesa; (to shelve) dar carpetazo a, postergar indefinidamente; (to tabulate) tabular; FIG. (to present) presentar, poner sobre el tapete.

tab·leau (tǎb′lō′, tǎ-blō′) s. [pl. **tab·leaux** o **tab·leaus** (tǎb′lōz′, tǎ-blōz′)] cuadro ♦ **t. vivant** TEAT. cuadro vivo.

ta·ble·cloth (tā′bəl-klôth′) s. mantel m.

ta·ble·land (tā′bəl-lǎnd′) s. (plateau) meseta; (elevated region) altiplano.

table linen s. mantelería.

table salt s. sal de mesa f.

ta·ble·spoon (tā′bəl-spōōn′) s. (utensil) cuchara de sopa; (quantity) cucharada.

ta·ble·spoon·ful (tā′bəl-spōōn′fōōl′) s. [pl. -fuls] cucharada.

tab·let (tǎb′lǐt) s. (slab) tableta, tablilla (para inscripciones); (writing pad) taco, bloc m; (pill) pastilla, tableta.

table talk s. conversación de sobremesa f.

table tennis s. tenis de mesa m, ping pong m.

ta·ble·ware (tā′bəl-wâr′) s. vajilla, servicio de mesa.

tab·loid (tǎb′loid′) s. periódico de formato reducido.

ta·boo (tǎ-bōō′) I. s. [pl. -boos] (prohibition) tabú m; (object) tabú; (ban) prohibición f II. adj. tabú, prohibido III. tr. **-booed, -boo·ing** declarar tabú, prohibir.

ta·bor o **ta·bour** (tā′bər) s. MÚS. tamboril m.

ta·bu (tǎ-bōō′) s., adj. & v. var. de **taboo.**

tab·u·lar (tǎb′yə-lər) adj. tabular.

tab·u·late (tǎb′yə-lāt′) I. tr. **-lat·ed, -lat·ing** (to arrange) tabular; (to list) listar; (to form) formar con superficie plana II. adj. plano.

tab·u·la·tion (tǎb′yə-lā′shən) s. tabulación f.

tab·u·la·tor (tǎb′yə-lā′tər) s. (person, key) tabulador m; (machine) tabuladora.

ta·chom·e·ter (tǎ-kǒm′ǐ-tər) s. AUTO. tacómetro.

tac·it (tǎs′ǐt) adj. (unspoken) tácito; (implicit) implícito.

tac·i·turn (tǎs′ǐ-tûrn′) adj. taciturno.

tack (tǎk) I. s. (nail) tachuela, puntilla; (stickiness) pegajosidad f, adherencia; FIG. (direction) dirección f, línea (de política, conducta); (tactics) táctica, maniobra; COST. hilvan m; MARÍT. (rope) amura; (of a sail) puño de la amura ♦ **to get down to brass tacks** concretar, ir al grano II. tr. (to nail) clavar o fijar con tachuelas; (to stitch) hilvanar; FIG. (to put together) unir, juntar; (to append) añadir, agregar <tacked the tip on to the bill agregó la propina en la cuenta>; MARÍT. virar por avante ♦ **to t. on** o **on to** fijar algo ligeramente en —intr. (to change) cambiar de política o conducta; MARÍT. cambiar de bordada.

tack·le (tǎk′əl) I. s. (gear) equipo, avíos m <fishing t. avíos de pescar>; (harness) arreos m; MARÍT. aparejo, jarcias II. tr. **-led, -ling** (situation, problem) atacar, abordar; (horse) enjaezar, poner arreos a; DEP. agarrar, atajar —intr. DEP. atajar al adversario.

tack·y¹ (tǎk′ē) adj. **-i·er, -i·est** pegajoso.

tack·y² (tǎk′ē) adj. **-i·er, -i·est** FAM. (shabby) descuidado; (lacking style) cursi; (vulgar) vulgar, de mal gusto; (dowdy) pasado de moda.

tact (tǎkt) s. tacto.

tact·ful (tǎkt′fəl) adj. (possessing tact) que tiene tacto, discreto; (considerate) considerado.

tac·tic (tǎk′tǐk) I. s. táctica, maniobra II. adj. táctico.

tac·ti·cal (tǎk′tǐ-kəl) adj. táctico.

tac·ti·cian (tǎk-tǐsh′ən) s. táctico.

tac·tics (tǎk′tǐks) s. [ú. con v. sing.] táctica.

tac·tile (tǎk′təl, -tīl′) adj. táctil, tangible.

tact·less (tăkt′lĭs) adj. *(without tact)* falto de tacto; *(inconsiderate)* falto de consideración.

tac·tu·al (tăk′chŏō-əl) adj. táctil, del tacto.

tad·pole (tăd′pōl′) s. renacuajo.

taff·rail (tăf′rāl′, -rəl) s. MARÍT. *(rail)* pasamano; *(stern upper part)* coronamiento.

taf·fy (tăf′ē) s. [pl. **-fies**] *(candy)* melcocha; FAM. *(flattery)* halago, lisonja.

tag¹ (tăg) **I.** s. *(label)* etiqueta; *(aglet)* herrete m; *(in fishing)* pedazo de papel brillante (usado con el anzuelo); *(wool)* vedija; *(tatter)* pingajo, arrapiezo; *(of a boot)* tirador m; *(on a signature)* rúbrica; *(quotation)* cita; *(cliché)* cliché m; *(refrain)* estribillo; *(characterization)* etiqueta, epíteto **II.** tr. **tagged, tag·ging** *(to attach a label to)* etiquetar, marcar con etiqueta; *(to identify)* identificar; *(to name)* denominar, llamar; *(to characterize)* denominar; *(to fine)* multar (a un automovilista); *(to follow)* seguir de cerca ♦ *(to add)* añadir, agregar; *(to follow)* seguir —intr. ♦ **to t. along** seguir, acompañar.

tag² (tăg) s. *(game)* mancha, pillarse m, la pega.

tag·a·long (tăg′ə-lông′) s. persona que sigue a otra persistentemente.

tag line s. TEAT. gracia, punto; COM., POL. slogan m.

Ta·hi·ti (tə-hē′tē) s. Tahití m.

Ta·hi·tian (tə-hē′shən) adj. & s. tahitiano.

tail (tāl) **I.** s. *(of an animal)* cola, rabo; *(backside)* trasero; *(rear)* parte trasera; *(of a shirt)* faldón m; *(of a comet)* cola, cabellera; *(of hair, people, kite)* cola; *(of a journey, storm)* final m; *(retinue)* comitiva, séquito; FAM. *(spy)* espía mf; IMPR. pie de página m; AER. *(of a fuselage)* cola; *(stabilizer)* plano de cola ♦ **from head to t.** de pies a cabeza • **tails** *(of a coin)* cruz, reverso (de una moneda); *(tailcoat)* frac, levita • **to be on someone's t.** *(to trail)* seguirle el rastro a alguien; FAM. *(to annoy)* fastidiar, irritar • **to turn t. and run** poner pies en polvorosa, huir • **with his t. between his legs** con el rabo entre las piernas **II.** tr. *(to furnish with a tail)* poner cola a; *(to dock)* descolar, desrabar; *(to be at the rear of)* cerrar, estar al final de *<to t. a parade* cerrar un desfile>; *(to connect)* juntar, unir; FAM. *(to follow)* seguir de cerca, espiar; ARQ. *(to fasten into a wall)* empotrar —intr. FAM. *(to follow)* seguir de cerca; ARQ. estar empotrado ♦ **to t. away** o **off** ir disminuyendo • **to t. out** extenderse, alargarse.

tail end s. *(rear)* parte trasera f; *(end)* fin m, final m.

tail·gate (tāl′gāt′) **I.** s. *(of a vehicle)* compuerta de cola; *(gate)* compuerta **II.** tr. & intr. **-gat·ed, -gat·ing** seguir demasiado cerca (a otro vehículo).

tail·ing (tā′lĭng) s. ARQ. entrega, cola ♦ **tailings** deshechos.

tail·light (tāl′līt′) s. AUTO. luz de cola f, luz trasera.

tai·lor (tā′lər) **I.** s. sastre m **II.** tr. hacer a la medida; *(to outfit)* vestir; FIG. *(to adapt)* adaptar, ajustar —intr. trabajar como sastre.

tai·lored (tā′lərd) adj. *(trim)* de corte prolijo; *(custom-made)* hecho a medida, hecho por un sastre.

tai·lor·ing (tā′lər-ĭng) s. COST. *(craft)* sastrería; *(act)* corte m, confección f.

tai·lor-made (tā′lər-mād′) **I.** adj. *(custom-made)* hecho por un sastre, hecho a medida **II.** s. prenda hecha por un sastre.

tail·piece (tāl′pēs′) s. *(end item)* pieza de cola; *(appendage)* apéndice m; IMPR. viñeta, colofón m; ARQ. viga de cabecero; MÚS. cordal m, cola.

tail pipe s. AUTO., MEC. tubo de escape.

tail·spin (tāl′spĭn′) s. FIG. *(collapse)* colapso emocional; AER. barrena.

tail wind s. viento de cola o trasero.

taint (tānt) **I.** tr. *(honor, reputation)* manchar; *(to infect)* infectar, contagiar; *(to spoil)* contaminar; *(to corrupt)* corromper —intr. *(to become discolored)* mancharse; *(to rot)* corromperse **II.** s. *(moral defect)* mácula, defecto; *(influence)* mala influencia.

Tai·wan (tī-wän′) s. Taiwán m.

Tai·wan·ese (tī′wə-nēz′) adj. & s. [pl. **Taiwanese**] taiwanés m ♦ **the T.** los taiwaneses.

take (tāk) **I.** tr. **took** (tŏŏk), **tak·en** (tā′kən), **tak·ing** *(to grasp)* tomar, agarrar *<t. these chairs and bring them inside*

toma estas sillas y llévalas adentro>; *(to seize)* tomar, capturar; *(to snatch)* quitar, hurtar; *(to confiscate, steal)* apoderarse de, apropiarse de; *(to arrest)* detener, capturar; *(to win)* ganar, llevarse *<to t. the first prize* ganar el primer premio>; *(to buy)* llevar, comprar; *(to rent)* alquilar, tomar; *(to cost)* costar *<it takes money to live in that town* vivir en esa ciudad cuesta dinero>; *(to swindle)* engañar, defraudar *<you were taken* te han engañado>; *(to choose)* tomar, escoger; *(to help oneself)* tomar, servirse *<t. more cake* sírvete más torta>; *(to ingest)* tomar *<t. two capsules a day* tome dos cápsulas por día>; *(to inhale)* tomar; *(to carry along)* llevarse *<t. your raincoat with you* llévate el impermeable>; *(to convey)* llevar *<this bus will take you to New York* este autobús te lleva a Nueva York>; *(to travel by)* tomar, coger *<to t. the train* tomar el tren>; *(chair, seat)* tomar *<t. a seat* tome asiento>; *(to startle)* coger, tomar *<it took me by surprise* me tomó de sorpresa>; *(to captivate)* cautivar, encantar *<he was completely taken by the puppy* estaba totalmente cautivado por el cachorrito>; *(to admit)* recibir *<to t. a new partner into the firm* recibir a un nuevo socio en la compañía>; *(to accept)* aceptar *<to t. a job* aceptar un trabajo>; *(to assume)* asumir, aceptar *<to t. responsibility* asumir responsabilidad>; *(to assume to be)* tomar *<who do you t. me for?* ¿por quién me tomas?>; *(to require)* tomar, requerir *<it takes a lot of work* requiere mucho trabajo>; *(as punishment, reward)* recibir *<to t. a beating* recibir una paliza>; *(to withstand)* aguantar, soportar; *(to operate with)* usar, admitir *<this camera takes 35 mm. film* esta cámara admite películas de 35 milímetros>; *(in time)* tomar, llevar *<how long does it t.?* ¿cuánto tiempo va a llevar?>; *(in clothing)* usar *<what size jacket do you t.?* ¿qué talla de chaqueta usa?>; *(in shoes)* calzar *<what size shoe do you t.?* ¿qué número de zapatos calza?>; *(to study)* estudiar *<I am taking biology* estudio la biología>; *(in chess, checkers)* comerse, capturar; *(to remove)* sacar; *(to subtract)* sustraer, restar ♦ **as I t. it** según creo, a mi entender • **t. it from me!** ¡créame! • **t. it or leave it** lo toma o lo deja • **t. that!** ¡toma! • **to be taken with** gustarle a uno • **to t. a back seat** asumir un rol pasivo • **to t. a bite** comer algo • **to t. a bow** *(actor)* agradecer el aplauso; *(to be acknowledged)* recibir reconocimiento • **to t. a chance on** o **with** arriesgarse, probar • **to t. action** actuar, tomar medidas • **to t. a dislike to someone** tomarle antipatía a alguien • **to t. advantage of** *(to benefit)* sacarle partido a, aprovecharse de; *(to abuse)* abusar de • **to t. a fancy to** prendarse de • **to t. a hint** hacer caso a una indirecta • **to t. aim at** tomar puntería, apuntar a • **to t. a joke** aguantar una broma • **to t. a leap** dar un salto • **to t. a liking to** tomar cariño a • **to t. along** llevar consigo, llevarse • **to t. a look at** echar una ojeada a, mirar • **to t. amiss** tomar mal, ofenderse • **to t. a nap** hacer o echarse una siesta • **to t. an examination** dar un examen • **to t. an oath** prestar juramento • **to t. an opportunity** aprovechar una oportunidad • **to t. apart** *(to disassemble)* desarmar, desmontar; *(to analize)* analizar; *(to wreck)* despedazar, hacer pedazos • **to t. a rest** descansar • **to t. a short cut** *(route)* ir por un atajo; *(method)* ahorrar tiempo y esfuerzo • **to t. a step** *(foot)* dar un paso; *(measure)* tomar una medida • **to t. a trip** hacer un viaje • **to t. a walk** dar un paseo • **to t. away** *(to remove)* quitar, sacar; *(to subtract)* restar; *(to carry away)* llevarse; *(to separate)* separar • **to t. a wife** casarse • **to t. back** *(to return)* devolver; *(to receive back)* recibir de vuelta, aceptar la devolución de; *(person)* volver a recibir; *(former employee)* volver a emplear; *(to retract)* retractar, desdecirse de; *(to bring back)* volver a llevar; *(to escort)* acompañar, llevar; *(to bring to mind)* hacer recordar, hacer pensar en • **to t. by storm** tomar por asalto • **to t. care** tener cuidado • **to t. care not to** tener cuidado de que no • **to t. care of** cuidar de, atender a • **to t. chances** *(to risk)* correr el riesgo, arriesgar; *(to leave to fate)* dejar a la suerte • **to t. charge of** encargarse de, hacerse cargo de • **to t. cover** abrigarse, buscar abrigo • **to t. cover** o **shelter** ponerse a cubierto • **to t. down** *(to write down)* tomar nota de, anotar; *(to remove)* quitar; *(to bring down)* bajar, poner más bajo; *(curtains, pictures)* bajar, descolgar; *(to disassemble)* desarmar, desmontar; *(to knock down)* derribar • **to t. effect** *(drug)* surtir efecto; *(law)* entrar en vigencia • **to t. exception to** oponerse a, no aceptar (aserción, punto de vista) • **to t. fire** *(coals, wood)* encenderse; *(building)* incendiarse • **to t. flight** huir, darse a la fuga • **to t. for a fool** tomar por un tonto • **to t. for granted** dar por sentado • **to t. from** *(to deprive)* quitar a, despojar a; *(to copy)* copiar de; *(to subtract)* restar de, substraer de • **to t. heart** animarse, cobrar aliento • **to t. heed** hacer caso • **to t. hold of** *(to grasp)* agarrar, asir; *(to take possession of)* tomar posesión, apoderarse • **to t. in** *(to accept)* tomar, aceptar; *(to lodge)* alojar, recibir; *(to understand)* comprender; *(to include)* abarcar, incluir; *(to realize)* darse cuenta de, percatarse de; *(to deceive)* engañar; *(to believe)* tragarse; *(to earn)* ganar; COST. *(a seam)* embeber, meter; *(a dress)* achicar; *(in knitting)* menguar • **to t. into account** o **consideration** tomar en cuenta • **to t. into one's head** metérsele a uno en la cabeza • **to t. issue with** oponerse a, no estar de acuerdo con • **to t. it easy** *(to relax)* descansar; *(to go easy)* ir despacio, no afanarse mucho • **to t. it out on** desquitarse a costa de, hacer pagar el pato a • **to t. it that** suponer que, inferir que • **to t. leave** despedirse, marcharse • **to t. no notice of** hacer caso omiso a o de • **to t. note of** *(to write down)* tomar nota, apuntar; *(to notice)* notar, advertir • **to t. notes** hacer apuntes • **to t. notice of** hacer caso de, prestar atención a • **to t. off** *(to remove)* quitar; *(clothes, hat)* quitarse; *(time)* tomarse; *(to amputate)* amputar; *(to deduct)* rebajar, hacer un descuento; *(to carry off)* llevarse; *(to make fun of)* imitar, remedar • **to t. offense** ofenderse • **to t. office** asumir el poder, entrar en funciones • **to t. on** *(characteristic, attitude)* asumir, tomar; *(responsibility)* emprender, encargarse de; *(employee)* contratar, tomar; *(passengers)* recibir a bordo; *(bet, challenge)* aceptar; *(adversary)* enfrentarse a, competir con; *(habit, accent)* adoptar; *(client, patient)* aceptar • **to t. out** *(to take outside)* llevar afuera, poner afuera; *(to remove)* sacar *‹she took out her glasses from her purse sacó las gafas de su cartera›*; *(license, policy)* sacar; *(stain, spot)* quitar, extraer; *(tooth)* sacar, extraer • **to t. (it) out on** desahogar con *‹he took his anger out on me desahogó la ira conmigo›* • **to t. over** *(to take charge of)* hacerse cargo de; *(responsibility)* asumir; *(to appropriate)* expropiar, tomar posesión de • **to t. part in** participar en, intervenir en • **to t. pity on** tener lástima de • **to t. place** tener lugar, ocurrir • **to t. precedence over** tener prioridad sobre • **to t. responsibility for** hacerse responsable de • **to t. root** arraigar, enraizar • **to t. shape** tomar forma, concretarse • **to t. sides with** ponerse de parte de • **to t. stock of** evaluar, examinar • **to t. the cake** ser el colmo • **to t. to heart** tomar a pecho • **to t. up** *(to raise)* llevar arriba; *(to pick up)* levantar, alzar; *(liquids)* absorber; *(time, space)* ocupar, llenar; *(position, post)* tomar posesión de; *(bill)* pagar; *(loan)* tomar; *(challenge, bet)* aceptar; *(career, profession)* dedicarse a; *(study)* empezar, comenzar; *(residence)* establecer; COST. *(to shorten)* acortar • **to t. upon oneself** tomar a cargo de uno, encargarse de • **to t. up with** asociarse con • **to t. warning** estar alerta, tener cuidado • **to t. water** MARÍT. hacer agua —intr. *(to stick)* pegar, adherirse; *(to succeed)* gustar, tener éxito; *(to set)* cuajar; *(plants)* prender, arraigar; *(vaccination)* prender, agarrar; *(fish)* picar; *(photos)* salir ♦ **to t. after** *(appearance)* salir a, parecerse a; *(behavior)* seguir el ejemplo de • **to t. ill** o **sick** caer enfermo • **to t. off** *(to leave)* irse, partir; *(aircraft)* despegar, levantar vuelo • **to t. over** *(responsibility)* asumir la autoridad, hacerse cargo; *(post)* entrar en funciones • **to t. to** empezar a • **to t. to someone** tomarle simpatía a alguien • **to t. to something** aficionarse a algo • **to t. up with someone** relacionarse con alguien **II.** s. *(receipts)* entrada, ingresos; *(in hunting)* presa; *(in fishing)* pesca; *(in chess, checkers)* captura, toma; CINEM. toma.

take·down (tāk′doun′) **I.** adj. desarmable, desmontable **II.** s. *(object)* objeto desarmable; *(mechanism)* mecanismo desarmable; FAM. *(humiliation)* humillación f.

take-home pay (tāk′hōm′) s. sueldo neto.

tak·en (tā′kən) part. p. de **take.**

take-off (tāk′ôf′) s. *(place)* lugar de despegue m; FAM. *(imitation)* imitación burlona, caricatura; AVIA. despegue m.

take·o·ver o **take-o·ver** (tāk′ō′vər) s. toma de poder.

tak·er (tā′kər) s. *(bettor)* apostador (que acepta una apuesta) m; *(buyer)* comprador m.

tak·ing (tā′kĭng) **I.** adj. *(fetching)* atractivo, encantador; *(contagious)* contagioso **II.** s. *(act)* toma; *(catch)* presa, pesca ♦ **takings** ingresos.

talc (tălk) **I.** s. talco **II.** tr. **talcked, talck·ing** o **talced, talc·ing** poner talco a.

tal·cum (tăl′kəm) s. MIN. talco; *(talcum powder)* polvos de talco.

talcum powder s. talco, polvos de talco.

tale (tāl) s. *(story)* cuento; *(lie)* mentira; *(gossip)* chisme m ♦ **old wives' tale** cuento de viejas, conseja • **to tell tales** contar chismes.

tale-bear·er (tāl′bâr′ər) s. chismoso, soplón m.

tal·ent (tăl′ənt) s. *(endowment)* talento; *(ability)* habilidad f; *(aptitude)* aptitud f, don m; *(persons)* talento *‹bring the t. in* hagan pasar al talento›*; HIST. *(money, weight)* talento.

tal·ent·ed (tăl′ən-tĭd) adj. talentoso, de talento.

talent scout s. persona encargada de descubrir gente con talento en las áreas de negocios, deportes o las artes.

tales·man (tālz′mən, tā′lēz-) s. [pl. **-men**] DER. jurado suplente.

tale-tell·er (tāl′tĕl′ər) s. *(storyteller)* narrador de historias m; *(talebearer)* chismoso.

ta·li (tā′lī′) pl. de **talus¹.**

tal·is·man (tăl′ĭs-mən) s. [pl. **-mans**] talismán m.

talk (tôk) **I.** tr. *(to speak)* expresar, decir *‹you are talking nonsense estás diciendo tonterías›*; *(to discuss)* hablar de *‹they were talking business estaban hablando de negocios›*; *(a language)* hablar (en) *‹to t. English hablar (en) inglés›* ♦ **to t. a blue streak** FAM. hablar por los codos • **to t. away** malgastar hablando *‹he talked the evening away malgastó la noche hablando›* • **to t. down** desmerecer, quitar mérito • **to t. sense** hablar sensatamente, hablar con sensatez • **to t. someone into doing something** persuadir a alguien para que haga algo • **to t. someone out of something** disuadir a alguien de que haga algo • **to t. turkey** no andarse con rodeos —intr. *(to converse)* hablar, conversar *‹we talked for hours hablamos durante horas›*; *(to utter words)* hablar *‹the baby can t. el bebé habla›*; *(to chatter)* charlar, parlotear *‹she did nothing but t. no hizo nada más que charlar›*; *(to gossip)* hablar *‹people will t. la gente hablará›* ♦ **look who's talking!** ¡mira quién habla! • **now you're talking!** o **now we're talking!** ¡así se habla!, ¡eso es hablar! • **to t. away** hablar sin parar • **to t. back** replicar, contestar con insolencia • **to t. behind someone's back** hablar (mal) de alguien a sus espaldas • **to t. down to** hablar con altivez a • **to t. for the sake of talking** hablar por hablar • **to t. through one's hat** JER. decir disparates **II.** s. *(conversation)* conversación f; *(speech)* discurso; *(conference)* conferencia; *(jargon)* habla; *(rumor)* rumor m, mención f *‹there is t. of war hay un rumor de guerra›*; *(subject of conversation)* chisme m, comidilla *‹the t. of the town la comidilla del pueblo›*; *(empty speech)* palabras, palabrería *‹much t. and no action mucha palabrería y nada de acción›* ♦ **talks** negociaciones • **to have a t. with** tener una conversación con.

talk·a·tive (tô′kə-tĭv) adj. hablador, locuaz.

talk·a·tive·ness (tô′kə-tĭv-nĭs) s. locuacidad f.

talk·er (tô′kər) s. hablador m.

talk·ie (tô′kē) s. CINEM., FAM. película sonora.

talk·ing (tô′kĭng) adj. *(that talks)* parlante, que habla; *(movie)* sonora.

talk·ing-to (tô′kĭng-tōō′) s. [pl. **-tos**] FAM. bronca, rapapolvo.

talk·y (tô′kē) adj. **-i·er, -i·est** *(person)* hablador, parlanchín; *(movie, play)* con demasiado diálogo.

tall (tôl) **I.** adj. **-er, -est** *(person)* alto, espigado; *(tree, building)* alto, elevado; *(of certain height)* de alto, de altura *‹a mast twelve feet t. un mástil de doce pies de altura›*; FIG., FAM. *(fanciful)* exagerado, increíble *‹a t. tale un cuento increíble›*; *(difficult)* difícil, enorme *‹that is a t. order ésa es una tarea enorme> ♦ **how t. are you?** ¿cuánto mide usted? **II.** adv. ♦ **to walk t.** caminar con porte altivo.

tall·boy (tôl′boi′) s. G.B. cómoda alta, ropero.

tall·ness (tôl′nĭs) s. *(of people)* estatura, altura; *(of trees, buildings)* altura.

tal·low (tăl′ō) **I.** s. sebo **II.** tr. ensebar.

tal·ly (tăl′ē) **I.** s. [pl. **-lies**] *(stick)* tarja, tara; *(score)* cómputo, cuenta <*to keep a t.* llevar la cuenta>; *(mark)* marca; *(label)* etiqueta, rótulo; *(receipt)* talón m; COM. lista **II.** tr. **-lied, -ly·ing** *(to record)* tarjar, marcar; *(to score)* llevar la cuenta; *(to label)* etiquetar; *(to cause to agree)* hacer cuadrar o concordar —intr. cuadrar, concordar <*the two stories t.* las dos historias concuerdan> ♦ **to t. with** corresponder con.

tal·ly·ho (tăl′ē-hō′) interj. ¡hala! (grito de caza).

Tal·mud (tăl′mŏŏd′, tăl′məd) s. RELIG. Talmud m.

tal·on (tăl′ən) s. *(claw)* garra; *(lock part)* saliente (de cerradura) f.

ta·lus¹ (tā′ləs) s. [pl. **-li** (-lī′)] ANAT. *(tarsal bone)* astrágalo; *(ankle)* tobillo.

ta·lus² (tā′ləs) s. [pl. **-lus·es**] GEOL. talud detrítico.

tam (tăm) s. boina escocesa.

tam·a·rind (tăm′ə-rĭnd′) s. BOT. tamarindo.

tam·a·risk (tăm′ə-rĭsk′) s. BOT. tamarisco.

tam·bour (tăm′bŏŏr′) s. *(drum)* tambor m; *(drummer)* tambor (músico); *(desk top)* tapa enrollable de escritorio; COST. *(hoop)* bastidor m; *(embroidery)* bordado.

tam·bou·rine (tăm′bə-rēn′) s. pandereta.

tame (tām) **I.** adj. **tam·er, tam·est** *(domesticated)* domesticado <*a t. horse* un caballo domesticado>; *(gentle)* manso; *(docile)* dócil; FAM. *(insipid)* insípido <*a t. story* un cuento insípido>; *(calm)* manso, calmo **II.** tr. **tamed, tam·ing** *(to domesticate)* domesticar; *(to break)* domar; FIG. *(to subdue)* dominar <*to t. anger* dominar el enfado>; *(to soften)* suavizar <*age tames the passions of youth* la edad suaviza las pasiones de la juventud>.

tam·o'-shan·ter (tăm′ə-shăn′tər) s. boina escocesa.

tamp (tămp) tr. apisonar, pisonear.

tam·per (tăm′pər) intr. ♦ **to t. with** *(to interfere)* interferir en; *(to meddle)* entrometerse en; *(to influence)* sobornar —tr. alterar.

tam·pon (tăm′pŏn′) **I.** s. tapón m, tampón m **II.** tr. taponar.

tan (tăn) **I.** tr. **tanned, tan·ning** *(leather)* curtir; *(the skin)* broncear, tostar; FAM. *(to beat)* zurrar ♦ **to t. someone's hide** dar una paliza a alguien —intr. broncearse, tostarse **II.** s. *(color)* color tostado, bronceado; *(tanbark)* casca; *(tannin)* tanino **III.** adj. **tan·ner, tan·nest** tostado, bronceado.

tan·dem (tăn′dəm) **I.** s. tándem m **II.** adv. uno tras otro, en tándem.

tang¹ (tăng) s. *(flavor)* gusto fuerte; *(odor)* olor m, aroma (penetrante) m; *(of a tool)* cola, espiga.

tang² (tăng) **I.** s. tañido **II.** tr. & intr. tañer, tocar.

Tan·gan·yi·ka (tăn′gən-yē′kə) s. Tanganica.

tan·ge·lo (tăn′jə-lō′) s. [pl. **-los**] cruza de mandarina y pomelo.

tan·gent (tăn′jənt) **I.** adj. *(touching)* tangente; *(irrelevant)* inaplicable **II.** s. tangente f ♦ **to go off on a t.** irse por la tangente.

tan·gen·tial (tăn-jĕn′shəl) adj. tangencial.

tan·ger·ine (tăn′jə-rēn′) s. *(color)* anaranjado rojizo; *(tree)* mandarino; *(fruit)* mandarina.

tan·gi·ble (tăn′jə-bəl) adj. *(palpable)* tangible, palpable; *(real)* real, concreto; DER. de valor monetario **II.** s. cosa concreta ♦ **tangibles** bienes materiales.

Tan·gier (tăn-jîr′) o **Tan·giers** (-jîrz′) s. Tánger.

tan·gle (tăng′gəl) **I.** tr. & intr. **-gled, -gling** *(to mix)* enredar(se); *(to snarl)* enmarañar(se); *(to entangle)* embrollar(se) ♦ **to t. with** meterse con **II.** s. *(state)* enredo, embrollo; *(confusion)* confusión f; *(argument)* discusión f, pelea.

tan·gled (tăng′gəld) adj. embrollado, enredado.

tan·go (tăng′gō) **I.** s. [pl. **-gos**] MÚS. tango **II.** intr. bailar el tango.

tang·y (tăng′ē) adj. **-i·er, -i·est** fuerte, penetrante (sabor, olor).

tank (tăngk) **I.** s. *(container, contents)* tanque m; *(reservoir)* estanque m; *(cistern)* cisterna; *(vehicle)* tanque; JER. *(jail)* cárcel f **II.** tr. almacenar en un tanque ♦ **to t. up** *(to drink)* beber mucho; *(to become drunk)* emborracharse.

tank·age (tăng′kĭj) s. *(capacity)* capacidad f; *(storage)* almacenamiento; *(fee)* tarifa; *(fertilizer)* fertilizante orgánico.

tank·ard (tăng′kərd) s. jarra de cerveza.

tank·er (tăng′kər) s. *(ship)* buque tanque m; *(truck)* camión tanque m; *(plane)* avión tanque m; MIL. tanquista.

tan·ner¹ (tăn′ər) s. curtidor m.

tan·ner² (tăn′ər) G.B., JER. moneda de seis peniques.

tan·ner·y (tăn′ə-rē) s. [pl. **-ies**] curtiduría, curtiembre f.

tan·nic (tăn′ĭk) adj. QUÍM. tánico.

tannic acid s. QUÍM. ácido tánico.

tan·nin (tăn′ĭn) s. QUÍM. tanino.

tan·ning (tăn′ĭng) s. *(leather processing)* curtimiento; *(skin bronzing)* bronceado; FAM. *(beating)* zurra, paliza.

tan·ta·lize (tăn′tl-īz′) tr. **-lized, -liz·ing** tentar.

tan·ta·liz·ing (tăn′tl-īz′ĭng) adj. tentador, atormentador.

tan·ta·lum (tăn′tl-əm) s. QUÍM. tantalio.

Tan·ta·lus (tăn′tl-əs) s. MITOL. Tántalo.

tan·ta·mount (tăn′tə-mount′) adj. ♦ **t. to** equivalente a.

tan·trum (tăn′trəm) s. rabieta, pataleta.

Tan·za·ni·a, United Republic of (tăn′zə-nē′ə) s. República Unida de Tanzanía.

Tan·za·ni·an (tăn′zə-nē′ən) adj. & s. tanzaniano.

Tao·ism (tou′ĭz′əm, dou′-) s. RELIG. taoísmo.

tap¹ (tăp) **I.** tr. **tapped, tap·ping** *(to strike gently)* golpear ligeramente, dar una palmadita <*t. him on the back* dále una palmadita en la espalda>; *(to rap)* dar golpecitos con; *(to repair)* poner tapas o tacones a (calzado) ♦ **to t. in** clavar dando golpes leves —intr. *(to strike)* tocar, dar golpes ligeros <*to t. at the door* tocar a la puerta>; *(with the fingers)* tamborilear; *(with the feet)* zapatear **II.** s. *(light blow)* golpe ligero, palmadita; *(sole)* media suela; *(metal tip)* chapa.

tap² (tăp) **I.** s. *(faucet)* grifo; *(spigot)* canilla, espita; *(plug)* tapón m, tarugo; *(beer)* cerveza de barril; MED. drenaje m; MEC. macho de roscar; ELEC. toma de corriente, derivación f ♦ **on t.** de barril <*beer on t.* cerveza de barril> **II.** tr. **tapped, tap·ping** *(to put a tap on)* espitar, poner una espita en; *(to pierce)* horadar; *(a tree)* sangrar; *(to draw)* sacar de un barril; *(to make use of)* aprovechar, utilizar; *(to connect)* hacer una conexión en (cañería); *(wiretap)* intervenir, interceptar (comunicaciones telefónicas); FAM. *(to sponge)* dar un sablazo a; ELEC. desviar; MEC. *(to thread)* roscar, aterrajar; MED. drenar.

tap dance s. zapateo americano.

tap-dance (tăp′dăns′) intr. **-danced, -danc·ing** zapatear.

tape (tāp) **I.** s. *(strip)* cinta; *(adhesive tape)* cinta adhesiva; *(magnetic tape)* cinta magnética; *(tape measure)* cinta métrica, metro; *(recording)* grabación f en cinta magnética; DEP. cinta de llegada ♦ **red t.** papeleo, burocracia **II.** tr. **taped, tap·ing** *(to fasten)* asegurar con cinta; *(to glue)* pegar con cinta adhesiva; *(to measure)* medir; *(to record)* grabar —intr. medir.

tape deck s. grabadora que es parte de un equipo estereofónico.

tape measure s. cinta métrica, metro.

tape player s. grabadora (para escuchar cintas magnetofónicas).

ta·per (tā′pər) **I.** s. *(candle)* cirio, vela delgada; *(wick)* cerilla; *(light source)* fuente débil de luz f; *(gradual decrease)* ahusamiento **II.** tr. & intr. ♦ **to t. off** *(to diminish)* disminuir; *(to become narrower)* estrechar(se) **III.** adj. ahusado.

tape-re·cord (tāp′rĭ-kôrd′) tr. grabar en cinta magnetofónica.

tape recorder s. grabadora magnetofónica.

tape recording s. *(tape)* cinta grabada; *(sound)* grabación f.

tap·es·try (tăp′ĭ-strē) s. [pl. **-tries**] tapiz m.

tape·worm (tāp′wûrm′) s. BIOL. tenia, solitaria.

tap·i·o·ca (tăp′ē-ō′kə) s. tapioca.

ta·pir (tā′pər) s. ZOOL. tapir m.

tap·pet (tăp′ĭt) s. MEC. brazo o palanca de levantamiento.

tap·ping (tăp′ĭng) s. (act) golpe leve m; (of a liquid) extracción f; (of trees) sangría; CIR. paracentesis f; ELEC. toma, derivación f.

tap·room (tăp′rōōm′, -rōōm′) s. bar m, taberna.

tap·root (tăp′rōōt′, -rōōt′) s. BOT. raíz primaria.

taps (tăps) s. [ú. con v. sing.] MIL. toque de queda m.

tap·ster (tăp′stər) s. mozo de taberna, barman m.

tar¹ (tär) I. s. (from oil) alquitrán m, brea; (coal tar) alquitrán mineral o de hulla II. tr. **tarred, tar·ring** alquitranar, embrear ♦ **to t. and feather** embrear y emplumar (como castigo); FAM. (to excoriate) criticar severamente, excoriar.

tar² (tär) s. FAM. marinero.

tar·an·tel·la (tär′ən-tĕl′ə) s. tarantela.

ta·ran·tu·la (tə-răn′chə-lə) s. tarántula.

tar·di·ness (tär′dē-nĭs) s. (delay) tardanza; (slowness) lentitud f.

tar·dy (tär′dē) adj. **-di·er, -di·est** (delayed) demorado; (late) tarde; (slow) lento, pesado.

tare¹ (târ) s. BOT. vicia, algarroba ♦ **tares** cizaña.

tare² (târ) COM. I. s. tara II. tr. destarar.

tar·get (tär′gĭt) I. s. (mark) blanco (de tiro); MIL. (object shot at) blanco, objetivo; (in an x-ray tube) anticátodo; FIG. (butt) blanco, objeto <to be the t. of scorn ser objeto de burlas>; (goal) meta, objetivo <to have realistic targets tener objetivos realistas>; F.C. disco, placa de señal; TOP. mirilla; HIST. (shield) rodela ♦ **t. practice** tiro al blanco • **to be on t.** (comment, remark) dar en el blanco; (budget, plan) estar en donde se había previsto estar II. tr. fijar como objetivo <the plan targeted a moderate growth el plan fijó como objetivo un crecimiento moderado>.

tar·iff (tăr′ĭf) I. s. (price schedule) tarifa; (duty) arancel m, tarifa II. tr. (to fix duty) fijar los aranceles de; (to fix price) tarifar.

tar·mac (tär′măk′) s. (substance) asfalto; (pavement) asfalto, pavimento; (runway) pista.

tar·mac·ad·am (tär′mə-kăd′əm) s. CONSTR. pavimento de piedras molidas y alquitrán.

tarn (tärn) s. lago pequeño de montaña.

tar·na·tion (tär-nā′shən) s. & interj. FAM. maldición f.

tar·nish (tär′nĭsh) I. tr. & intr. (to dull) empañar(se); (to discolor) descolorar(se); (to spoil) estropear(se); (to taint) manchar(se) II. s. (condition) empañamiento; (discolored luster) deslustre m; (besmirchment) mancha.

ta·ro (tär′ō, tăr′ō) s. [pl. **-ros**] BOT. (plant) taro, malangay mf; (rootstock) rizoma.

tar·ot (tăr′ō) s. naipe m de dibujos alegóricos que se usa en la adivinación.

tar·pa·per (tär′pā′pər) s. papel alquitranado m.

tar·pau·lin (tär-pô′lĭn, tär′pə-) s. encerado, alquitranado.

tar·pon (tär′pən) s. [pl. **tarpon** o **-pons**] ICT. tarpón m.

tar·ra·gon (tär′ə-gŏn′) s. BOT. estragón m.

tar·ry¹ (tär′ē) I. intr. **-ried, -ry·ing** (to delay) demorar; (to linger) rezagarse; (to wait) aguardar; (to remain) quedarse II. s. [pl. **-ries**] parada o residencia temporaria.

tar·ry² (tär′ē) adj. **-ri·er, -ri·est** alquitranado.

tar·sal (tär′səl) adj. ANAT. tarsal, tarsiano.

tar·sus (tär′səs) s. [pl. **-si** (-sī′)] ANAT., ZOOL. tarso; ORNIT. tarsometatarso.

tart¹ (tärt) adj. **-er, -est** (taste) acre; FIG. (voice) cáustico; (tone, meaning) hiriente.

tart² (tärt) s. (pie) pastelillo; (prostitute) prostituta.

tar·tan (tär′tn) s. (pattern, fabric) tartán m; (plaid fabric) tela escocesa.

tar·tar (tär′tər) s. QUÍM. tártaro; ODONT. sarro.

Tar·tar (tär′tər) s. (people) tártaro; (language) tártaro ♦ **t.** (savage) persona feroz.

tar·tar·ic acid (tär-tăr′ĭk) s. QUÍM. ácido tartárico.

tar·tar·ous (tär′tər-əs) adj. QUÍM. tartaroso, tartarado.

tartar sauce o **tar·tare sauce** (tär′tər) s. CUL. salsa tártara.

tar·trate (tär′trāt′) s. QUÍM. tartrato.

task (tăsk) I. s. (work) tarea; (duty) deber m; (difficult undertaking) faena; (function) misión f; (objective) objetivo ♦ **to take to t.** reprender II. tr. (to assign) dar una tarea; (to overburden) atarear, agobiar con tareas.

task force s. MIL. fuerza operante, ejército expedicionario.

task·mas·ter (tăsk′măs′tər) s. capataz m o supervisor exigente m.

tas·sel (tăs′əl) I. s. borla II. tr. decorar con borlas.

taste (tāst) I. tr. **tast·ed, tast·ing** (to discern flavors) notar un sabor a <to t. cinnamon in a dessert notar un sabor a canela en un postre>; (to try) probar <t. this pruebe esto>; (to sample) catar; (to experience) experimentar, conocer <to t. the bitterness of defeat conocer la amargura de la derrota>; ANT. (to enjoy) saborear, apreciar —intr. (to distinguish flavors) sentir sabor; (to have a flavor) saber, tener sabor o gusto <it tastes sweet tiene un sabor dulce> II. s. (sense) gusto; (flavor) gusto, sabor m; (act) degustación f; (small portion) pizca; (experience) experiencia, muestra <a t. of city life una muestra de lo que es la vida de ciudad>; (preference) gusto, inclinación f; (discernment) gusto, discernimiento <to have good t. in music tener buen gusto en música> ♦ **in good t.** de buen gusto • **to have a t. for** gustar de, gustarle a uno.

taste bud s. papila del gusto.

taste·ful (tāst′fəl) adj. de buen gusto.

taste·less (tāst′lĭs) adj. (flat) sin sabor; (insipid) insípido; (tacky) de mal gusto, cursi.

tast·er (tā′stər) s. (person) catador m; (wineglass) catavino.

tast·y (tā′stē) adj. **-i·er, -i·est** (savory) sabroso; (tasteful) de buen gusto.

tat (tăt) I. tr. **tat·ted, tat·ting** hacer encaje de frivolité —intr. tejer (encaje de frivolité).

Ta·tar (tä′tər) s. var. de **Tartar**.

tat·ter (tăt′ər) I. s. (cloth) andrajo; (shred) jirón m ♦ **tatters** harapos II. tr. convertir en harapos —intr. deshilacharse.

tat·tered (tăt′ərd) adj. (cloth) andrajoso, hecho jirones; (person) andrajoso.

tat·ting (tăt′ĭng) s. encaje de hilo m.

tat·tle (tăt′l) I. intr. **-tled, -tling** (to gossip) chismear, comadrear; (to prattle) charlar, cotorrear —tr. divulgar (secretos, planes) II. s. (gossip) chisme m; (prattle) charla, parloteo (tattletale) chismoso.

tat·tler (tăt′lər) s. (gossip) chismoso; (prattler) parlanchín m.

tat·tle·tale (tăt′l-tāl′) I. s. (gossip) chismoso; (informer) acusón m; (talebearer) cuentista mf II. adj. revelador.

tat·too¹ (tă-tōō′) I. s. [pl. **-toos**] MIL. (parade) desfile militar m; (retreat) retreta; (drumming) tamboreo II. intr. **-tooed, -too·ing** tamborilear.

tat·too² (tă-tōō′) I. s. [pl. **-toos**] tatuaje m II. tr. tatuar.

tau (tou, tô) s. tau (letra griega) f.

taught (tôt) pret. y part. p. de **teach**.

taunt (tônt) I. tr. (to deride) ridiculizar; (to jeer at) mofarse de, burlarse de; (to incite) incitar (con burlas) II. s. provocación f, burla.

taupe (tōp) s. gris pardo.

tau·rine (tôr′ĭn) adj. taurino.

Tau·rus (tôr′əs) s. ASTROL. Tauro.

taut (tôt) adj. **-er, -est** (tight) tirante; (strained) forzado, tenso; (trim) aseado, prolijo.

taut·en (tôt′n) tr. & intr. tensar(se).

tau·tol·o·gy (tô-tŏl′ə-jē) s. [pl. **-gies**] (redundancy) redundancia; LÓG. tautología.

tav·ern (tăv′ərn) s. (bar) taberna; (inn) posada f.

taw¹ (tô) tr. curtir en blanco.

taw² (tô) I. s. (marble) canica, bola; (line) línea de lanzamiento II. intr. jugar con canicas.

taw·dri·ness (tô′drē-nĭs) s. charrería.

taw·dry (tô′drē) adj. **-dri·er, -dri·est** charro.

taw·ny (tô′nē) adj. **-ni·er, -ni·est** pardo, leonado.

tax (tăks) I. s. (levy) impuesto, contribución f; (at customs) arancel m; (strain) carga ♦ **t. collector** recaudador de impuestos II. tr. (to charge) gravar; (to make demands upon) abrumar, agotar; DER. tasar, avaluar ♦ **to t. with** acusar de.

tax·a·ble (tăk′sə-bəl) adj. gravable.

taxable income s. renta gravable o imponible.

tax·a·tion (tăk-sā′shən) s. (tax imposition) fijación de impuestos f; (tax) impuesto.

---

tax·de·duct·i·ble (tăks′dĭ-dŭk′tə-bəl) adj. que se puede deducir como gasto.

tax·ex·empt (tăks′ĭg-zĕmpt′) adj. libre de impuestos.

tax-free (tăks′frē′) adj. libre de impuestos.

tax·i (tăk′sē) **I.** s. [pl. **-is** o **-ies**] taxi *m* **II.** intr. **tax·ied**, **taxi·ing** o **tax·y·ing** *(to take a taxi)* ir o viajar en taxi; *(airplane)* carretear, rodar de suelo —tr. hacer carretear (avión).

tax·i·cab (tăk′sē-kăb′) s. taxi *m*.

tax·i·der·my (tăk′sĭ-dûr′mē) s. taxidermia.

taxi driver s. taxista *mf.*

tax·i·me·ter (tăk′sē-mē′tər) s. taxímetro.

tax·ing (tăk′sĭng) adj. *(burdensome)* pesado; *(wearing)* desgastador, agotador.

tax·is (tăk′sĭs) s. BIOL. taxismo; MED. taxis *f.*

taxi stand s. parada de taxis.

tax·on·o·my (tăk-sŏn′ə-mē) s. taxonomía.

tax·pay·er (tăks′pā′ər) s. contribuyente *mf.*

tax rate s. tasa de impuestos.

tax shelter s. inversión que reduce el impuesto a pagar *f.*

tax system s. sistema de impuestos *m*, sistema impositivo.

T-bone (tē′bōn′) s. bistec grueso que se corta de la punta del lomo y que contiene un hueso en forma de T.

tea (tē) s. *(drink)* té *<mint t.* té de menta>; *(shrub)* té (planta y hojas) *m*; *(infusion)* infusión *f*; G.B. *(snack)* té, merienda; *(gathering)* reunión social (en la cual se sirve té) *f* ♦ **it's not my cup of t.** no es exactamente lo que me gusta a mí.

tea bag s. bolsita de té.

tea biscuit s. galletita de té.

tea·cart (tē′kärt′) s. carrito del té, mesa rodante.

teach (tēch) tr. **taught** (tôt), **teach·ing** *(to impart knowledge)* enseñar; *(students)* dar clases a; *(a subject matter)* dar clases de *<I t. Spanish* doy clases de español>; *(to advocate)* abogar, predicar —intr. ser maestro, dar clases.

teach·er (tē′chər) s. *(grade-school level)* maestro; *(highschool, college)* profesor *m*.

teachers college o **teachers' college** s. escuela normal.

teacher training s. formación pedagógica.

teach·in (tēch′ĭn′) s. EDUC. mitin de estudiantes para explorar un asunto difícil y controvertido *m*.

teach·ing (tē′chĭng) s. enseñanza ♦ **t. methods** métodos pedagógicos • **teachings** doctrina, enseñanzas • **t. staff** cuerpo docente.

tea·cup (tē′kŭp′) s. taza de té.

tea dance s. té danzante *m*.

tea·house (tē′hous′) s. salón de té *m*.

teak (tēk) s. *(color)* gris verdeoliva *m*, gris pardo; *(tree, wood)* teca (árbol y madera).

tea·ket·tle (tē′kĕt′l) s. caldero, hervidor (en forma de tetera) *m*.

teak·wood (tēk′wŏŏd′) s. madera de teca, teca.

teal (tēl) s. [pl. **teal** o **teals**] *(duck)* cerceta; *(color)* verde azuloso.

team (tēm) **I.** s. *(draft animals)* yunta, tiro; *(group)* grupo, equipo *<rescue t.* equipo de salvamento>; *(brood)* camada; *(flock)* cría; DEP. equipo, cuadra **II.** tr. *(to yoke)* uncir, enyugar; *(to haul)* acarrear con yunta, transportar ♦ **to t. up with** asociarse con, unir fuerzas con —intr. *(to form a team)* formar un equipo, asociarse; *(to drive a team)* guiar un tiro de caballos ♦ **to t. up** agruparse, asociarse.

team·mate (tēm′māt′) s. compañero de equipo.

team·ster (tēm′stər) s. *(cart driver)* carretero; *(truck driver)* camionero profesional.

team·work (tēm′wûrk′) s. trabajo de equipo.

tea·pot (tē′pŏt′) s. tetera.

tear¹ (târ) **I.** tr. **tore** (tôr), **torn** (tôrn), **tear·ing** *(to rend)* desgarrar, rasgar *<she tore her dress by catching her heel in it* rasgó su vestido con el taco de su zapato>; *(to rip)* romper, despedazar *<he tore up his application and threw it away* despedazó su solicitud y la tiró>; *(to pull)* arrancar *<they tore the announcement off the wall* arrancaron el aviso de la pared>; *(to wound)* herir, lacerar; *(to wrench)* distender, desgarrar *<to t. a ligament* desgarrar un ligamento>; FIG. *(to distress)* angustiar, atormentar *<torn between love and duty* atormentado entre el deber y el amor>

♦ **to t. apart** *(to rip)* romper; *(to disunite)* dividir *<the political tension will t. the party apart* la tensión política dividirá al partido>* • **to t. away, off** o **out** arrancar • **to t. down** *(to demolish)* demoler, derribar; *(to disassemble)* desmontar, desarmar; *(to denigrate)* denigrar • **to t. in** o **to pieces** despedazar, hacer añicos • **to t. oneself away** separarse o partir contra la voluntad de uno • **to t. up** *(to tear to pieces)* hacer pedazos, desbaratar; *(to make a hole in)* romper *<he tore up the sidewalk to add a drain* rompió la vereda para poner otro tubo de desagüe>; *(to uproot)* desarraigar, sacar de raíz —intr. desgarrarse, rasgarse ♦ **to t. around** *(to move in haste)* correr como un loco; *(to lead a wild life)* llevar una vida desordenada • **to t. away, off** o **out** irse precipitadamente • **to t. into** acometer **II.** s. *(rip)* desgarradura, rasgadura; *(rage)* rabia, furor *m*; *(haste)* prisa, precipitación *f*; JER. *(spree)* jarana.

tear² (tîr) **I.** s. *(teardrop)* lágrima; *(drop)* gota ♦ **in tears** llorando • **tears** lágrimas, llanto • **to be bored to tears** aburrirse como una ostra • **to move to tears** conmover, hacer llorar • **to shed tears** llorar, derramar lágrimas **II.** intr. llenarse de lágrimas *<his eyes teared* los ojos se le llenaron de lágrimas>.

tear·drop (tîr′drŏp′) s. lágrima.

tear·ful (tîr′fəl) adj. *(accompanied by tears)* lacrimoso; *(piteous)* conmovedor, lastimoso.

tear gas (tîr) s. gas lacrimógeno.

tear-jerk·er (tîr′jûr′kər) s. JER. drama sentimentaloide *m*.

tea·room (tē′rōōm′, -rŏŏm′) s. salón de té *m*.

tease (tēz) **I.** tr. **teased**, **teas·ing** *(to annoy)* fastidiar, molestar; *(to make fun of)* tomar el pelo a, reírse de; *(to tantalize)* provocar, tentar; *(wool)* cardar **II.** s. *(act)* fastidio, molestia; *(joke)* broma; *(joker)* bromista *mf.*

teas·er (tē′zər) s. *(joker)* bromista *mf*; FAM. *(coquette)* (mujer) provocadora; *(puzzle)* rompecabezas *m*.

tea service s. juego de té.

tea·spoon (tē′spōōn′) s. *(utensil)* cucharita de té; *(content)* cucharadita.

tea·spoon·ful (tē′spōōn′fŏŏl′) s. [pl. **-fuls**] cucharadita.

teat (tēt, tĭt) s. *(pap)* teta; *(nipple)* pezón *m*.

tea wagon s. carrito de servir té.

tech·ne·ti·um (tĕk-nē′shē-əm) s. QUÍM. tecnecio.

tech·nic (tĕk′nĭk) **I.** s. técnica ♦ **technics** [ú. con v. sing. o pl.] métodos técnicos **II.** adj. técnico.

tech·ni·cal (tĕk′nĭ-kəl) adj. *(of, from technique)* técnico, de la técnica; *(specialized)* especializado *<a t. school* una escuela especializada>; *(scientific)* científico *<a t. paper* un ensayo científico>; *(technological)* tecnológico; *(theoretical)* teórico, de forma *<t. point* cuestión de forma>.

tech·ni·cal·i·ty (tĕk′nĭ-kăl′ĭ-tē) s. [pl. **-ties**] *(condition)* tecnicidad *f*; *(expression)* expresión técnica, tecnicismo *<legal t.* tecnicismo legal>.

tech·ni·cal·ly (tĕk′nĭ-kə-lē) adv. *(in technical terms)* técnicamente, en términos técnicos *<expressed t.* expresado en términos técnicos>; *(theoretically)* en teoría.

tech·ni·cian (tĕk-nĭsh′ən) s. técnico, experto *<lab t.* experto en técnicas de laboratorios>.

Tech·ni·col·or (tĕk′nĭ-kŭl′ər) s. CINEM., FOTOG. tecnicolor (marca registrada) *m*.

tech·nique (tĕk-nēk′) s. técnica (sistema, habilidad) ♦ **t.** o **technic** técnica (grado de habilidad).

tech·noc·ra·cy (tĕk-nŏk′rə-sē) s. [pl. **-cies**] tecnocracia.

tech·no·crat (tĕk′nə-krăt′) s. tecnócrata *mf.*

tech·no·crat·ic (tĕk′nə-krăt′ĭk) adj. tecnócrata.

tech·no·log·i·cal (tĕk′nə-lŏj′ĭ-kəl) o **tech·no·log·ic** (-lŏj′ĭk) s. tecnológico, de la tecnología.

tech·nol·o·gist (tĕk-nŏl′ə-jĭst) s. tecnólogo.

tech·nol·o·gy (tĕk-nŏl′ə-jē) s. [pl. **-gies**] tecnología.

tec·ton·ic (tĕk-tŏn′ĭk) adj. *(architectural)* arquitectónico, arquitectural; GEOL. tectónico; CONSTR. tectónico, estructural ♦ **tectonics** [ú. con v. sing.] ARQ. arquitectura (esp. de edificios grandes); GEOL. tectónica.

ted·dy bear (tĕd′ē) s. osito de juguete o de felpa.

te·di·ous (tē′dē-əs) adj. *(boring)* tedioso, aburrido; *(wearisome)* cansador.

te·di·um (tē′dē-əm) s. tedio.

tee¹ (tē) **I.** s. DEP. *(peg)* tee *m*; *(area)* punto de partida (en el golf) **II**. tr. **teed, tee·ing** DEP. colocar sobre un tee (a la pelota de golf) ♦ **to t. off** DEP. *(to hit)* pegarle a la pelota desde el tee; FIG. *(to start)* comenzar (acción, actividad); JER. *(to make angry)* enojar <*he tees me off* me enoja>.

tee² (tē) s. meta (en un juego) ♦ **to a t.** a la perfección.

teem (tēm) intr. hervir, abundar —tr. ANT. parir.

teen (tēn) adj. & s. adolescente *mf*, joven *mf*.

teen-age (tēn′āj′) *o* **teen-aged** (-ājd′) adj. adolescente, de la adolescencia.

teen·ag·er (tēn′ā′jər) s. *(youth)* joven (entre los 13 y 19 años) *mf*; *(adolescent)* adolescente *mf*.

teens (tēnz) s.pl. *(numbers)* números entre 13 y 19; *(age)* adolescencia ♦ **to be in one's t.** tener entre 13 y 19 años, ser adolescente • **salary in the mid-teens** sueldo alrededor de quince mil dólares al año.

tee·ny (tē′nē) *o* **teen·sy** (tēn′sē) adj. **-ni·er, -ni·est** *o* **-si·er, -si·est** pequeñito.

tee·pee (tē′pē) s. var. de **tepee**.

tee shirt s. var. de **T-shirt**.

tee·ter (tē′tər) **I**. intr. *(to totter)* FAM. bambolearse, tambalearse; *(to vacillate)* vacilar, dudar **II**. s. *(seesaw)* sube y baja *m*, balanceo; *(motion)* tambaleo, bamboleo.

tee·ter·tot·ter (tē′tər-tŏt′ər) s. columpio, subibaja *m*.

teeth (tēth) pl. de **tooth**.

teethe (tēth) intr. **teethed, teeth·ing** echar los dientes.

tee·to·tal·er *o* **tee·to·tal·ler** (tē′tōt′l-ər) s. abstemio.

Tef·lon (tĕf′lŏn′) s. QUÍM. teflón (marca registrada de un plástico resistente al calor) *m*.

teg·u·ment (tĕg′yə-mənt) s. tegumento.

Te·he·ran (tē′ə-rän′) *o* **Teh·ran** (tē-rän′) s. Teherán.

tel·e·cast (tĕl′ĭ-kăst′) **I**. tr. & intr. **-cast** *o* **-cast·ed, -cast·ing** televisar, transmitir por televisión **II**. s. transmisión de televisión *f*.

tel·e·com·mu·ni·ca·tion (tĕl′ĭ-kə-myōō′nĭ-kā′shən) s. telecomunicación *f* ♦ **telecommunications** [ú. con v. sing.] CIENT. la ciencia de telecomunicaciones.

tel·e·gen·ic (tĕl′ə-jĕn′ĭk) adj. telegénico.

tel·e·gram (tĕl′ĭ-grăm′) s. telegrama *m*.

tel·e·graph (tĕl′ĭ-grăf′) **I**. s. *(system)* telégrafo; *(telegram)* telegrama *m* **II**. tr. telegrafiar —intr. mandar un telegrama.

te·leg·ra·pher (tə-lĕg′rə-fər) *o* **te·leg·ra·phist** (-fĭst′) s. telegrafista *mf*.

tel·e·graph·ic (tĕl′ĭ-grăf′ĭk) *o* **tel·e·graph·i·cal** (-ĭ-kəl) adj. telegráfico.

te·leg·ra·phy (tə-lĕg′rə-fē) s. telegrafía *f*.

tel·e·ki·ne·sis (tĕl′ĭ-kĭ-nē′sĭs, -kī-) s. telequinesis *f*.

tel·e·me·ter (tĕl′ə-mē′tər) s. telémetro.

te·lem·e·try (tə-lĕm′ĭ-trē) s. telemetría *f*.

tel·e·ol·o·gy (tĕl′ē-ŏl′ə-jē, tē′lē-) s. [pl. **-gies**] FILOS. teleología.

te·lep·a·thy (tə-lĕp′ə-thē) s. PSIC. telepatía.

tel·e·phone (tĕl′ə-fōn′) **I**. s. teléfono **II**. tr. **-phoned, -phon·ing** telefonear, llamar por teléfono —intr. comunicarse por teléfono.

telephone book s. guía de teléfonos, guía telefónica.

telephone booth s. cabina de teléfono o telefónica.

telephone directory s. guía de teléfonos, guía telefónica.

telephone message s. mensaje telefónico, telefonema *m*.

telephone operator s. telefonista *mf*.

tel·e·phon·ic (tĕl′ə-fŏn′ĭk) adj. telefónico.

tel·e·pho·to (tĕl′ə-fō′tō) adj. telefotográfico.

tel·e·pho·to·graph (tĕl′ə-fō′tə-grăf′) **I**. s. telefotografía **II**. tr. fotografiar con una lente telefotográfica.

telephoto lens s. teleobjetivo.

tel·e·play (tĕl′ə-plā′) s. obra teatral para televisión.

tel·e·print·er (tĕl′ə-prĭn′tər) s. TEL. teletipo, teleimpresor *m*.

tel·e·proc·ess·ing (tĕl′ə-prŏs′ĕs′ĭng, -prō′cĕs′-) s. COMPUT. teleproceso.

Tel·e·promp·ter (tĕl′ə-prŏmp′tər) s. TELEV. marca registrada de un dispositivo visual usado en televisión para recordar un texto.

tel·e·scope (tĕl′ĭ-skōp′) **I**. s. ASTRON. telescopio; *(spy glass)* catalejo; TOP. anteojo de teodolito; RAD. radiotelescopio **II**. tr. **-scoped, -scop·ing** *(to cause to telescope)* extender,

encajar (partes, unas entre otras); FIG. *(to compress)* comprimir, condensar —tr. extenderse, plegarse.

tel·e·scop·ic (tĕl′ĭ-skŏp′ĭk) adj. *(of a telescope)* del telescopio, telescópico; *(adjustable)* de secciones que se encastran unas entre otras ♦ **t. sight** mira telescópica.

tel·e·thon (tĕl′ə-thŏn′) s. TELEV. programa de televisión extenso destinado para recaudar fondos.

Tel·e·type (tĕl′ĭ-tīp′) s. teletipo (marca registrada) ♦ **t.** mensaje, despacho (transmitido por teletipo).

tel·e·type·writ·er (tĕl′ĭ-tīp′rī′tər) s. máquina de escribir telegráfica, teletipo.

tel·e·view·er (tĕl′ə-vyōō′ər) s. televidente *mf*.

tel·e·vise (tĕl′ə-vīz′) tr. & intr. **-vised, -vis·ing** TELEV. televisar, transmitir por televisión.

tel·e·vi·sion (tĕl′ə-vĭzh′ən) s. televisión *f* ♦ **color t.** televisión en color • **t. screen** pantalla del televisor • **t. set** televisor.

tel·ex (tĕl′ĕks′) **I**. s. télex *m* **II**. intr. enviar un télex.

tell (tĕl) tr. **told** (tōld), **tell·ing** *(to narrate)* decir, contar <*t. me what he said to you* cuéntame lo que él te dijo>; *(to express)* decir <*"when in doubt t. the truth", said Mark Twain* "cuando tengas dudas di la verdad", dijo Mark Twain>; *(to inform)* comunicar; *(to reveal)* revelar <*a smile that told her happiness* una sonrisa que revelaba su felicidad>; *(to command)* decir, mandar <*do what I told you* haz lo que te dije>; *(to discriminate)* distinguir <*to t. one thing from another* distinguir una cosa de otra>; *(to recognize)* reconocer, identificar; *(to assure)* asegurar <*I t. you, he's an honest man* él es un hombre honrado, te lo aseguro>; *(to know)* adivinar, saber <*one can't t. what will happen* no se puede saber qué pasará>; *(to count)* contar; *(to explain)* explicar <*I really cannot t. you how it happened* realmente no puedo explicarte cómo sucedió> ♦ **all told** *(in total)* contando todo, en total; *(all things considered)* mirándolo bien • **I t. you what** se me ocurre una idea • **I told you so!** ¡ya te lo dije!, ¡ya te lo advertí! • **to t. against** perjudicar, ser perjudicial para • **to t. of** dar un informe sobre, hablar de • **to t. off** FAM. *(to criticize)* poner en su lugar, cantar las cuarenta; *(to appoint)* designar • **to t. on** *(affect)* afectar a; *(to betray)* denunciar, delatar • **to t. you the truth** a decir la verdad • **you're telling me!** ¡mira a quién se lo cuentas!, ¿a mí me lo vas a decir? —intr. *(to give an account)* relatar, contar; *(to have an effect)* producir efecto <*efforts that are beginning to t.* esfuerzos que están comenzando a producir efecto>; *(to give evidence)* notarse ♦ **you never can t.** nunca se puede decir o saber, las apariencias engañan.

tell·er (tĕl′ər) s. *(narrator)* narrador *m*; *(bank employee)* cajero.

tell·ing (tĕl′ĭng) adj. *(effective)* efectivo, eficaz; *(revealing)* revelador; *(significant)* significante.

tell·tale (tĕl′tāl′) s. *(informer)* soplón *m*; *(gossip)* chismoso; *(sign)* señal *f*; *(device)* indicador *m*.

tel·lu·ri·an (tĕ-lŏŏr′ē-ən) **I**. adj. telúrico **II**. s. terrícola *mf*.

tel·lu·ric (tĕ-lŏŏr′ĭk) adj. QUÍM. telúrico.

tel·lu·ri·um (tĕ-lŏŏr′ē-əm) s. QUÍM. telurio.

tel·ly (tĕl′ē) s. [pl. **-lies**] G.B., FAM. televisión *f*, tele *f*.

Tel·star (tĕl′stär′) s. satélite para comunicaciones *m*.

tem·blor (tĕm′blər, -blôr′) s. temblor de tierra *m*.

te·mer·i·ty (tə-mĕr′ĭ-tē) s. temeridad *f*.

tem·per (tĕm′pər) **I**. tr. & intr. templar(se) **II**. s. *(disposition)* temperamento; *(composure)* compostura, serenidad *f*; *(tendency towards anger)* genio, mal genio; *(anger)* cólera, ira; TEC. *(of a metal)* temple *m*; *(substance)* substancia templadora ♦ **to keep one's t.** dominarse • **to lose one's t.** perder los estribos, enfadarse.

tem·pe·ra (tĕm′pər-ə) s. PINT. pintura al temple.

tem·per·a·ment (tĕm′prə-mənt) s. *(disposition)* temperamento; *(temper)* disposición de ánimo *f*; MÚS. temperamento.

tem·per·a·men·tal (tĕm′prə-mĕn′tl) adj. *(of the temperament)* temperamental; *(moody)* caprichoso, irritable; *(unpredictable)* impredecible, inconstante.

tem·per·ance (tĕm′pər-əns) s. *(self-restraint)* templanza; *(moderation)* moderación *f*; *(abstinence)* abstinencia.

ã rey / ä año / b boca / ch chico / d dar / ĕ el / ē mil / g gato / h joya / hw juez / ī aire / k casa / kw cuan /

tem·per·ate (tĕm'pər-ĭt) adj. *(moderate)* moderado; *(tempered)* templado; *(mild)* templado (clima, día).
Temperate Zone s. GEOG. zona templada.
tem·per·a·ture (tĕm'pər-ə-chŏŏr', -chər) s. FÍS. temperatura; MED. temperatura, fiebre *f.*
tem·pered (tĕm'pərd) adj. *(disposed)* dispuesto (mal, bien); *(moderated)* moderado; METAL. templado; MÚS. templado.
tem·pest (tĕm'pĭst) I. s. *(storm)* tempestad *f;* FIG. *(tumult)* tumulto, alboroto II. tr. agitar (violentamente).
tem·pes·tu·ous (tĕm-pĕs'chŏŏ-əs) adj. *(of a tempest)* tempestuoso, borrascoso; FIG. *(tumultuous)* turbulento.
tem·pi (tĕm'pē) un pl. de **tempo.**
Tem·plar (tĕm'plər) s. HIST. templario (caballero) ♦ **t.** G.B. *(lawyer)* abogado del Temple de Londres; *(student)* estudiante de derecho en el Temple de Londres.
tem·plate (tĕm'plĭt) s. *(pattern)* plantilla, patrón *m;* ARQ. solera; BIOL. molécula patrón.
tem·ple¹ (tĕm'pəl) s. *(house of worship)* templo; *(synagogue)* sinagoga; *(sanctuary)* templo, santuario ♦ **T.** G.B. sociedad de abogados en Londres.
tem·ple² (tĕm'pəl) s. ANAT. sien *f.*
tem·ple³ (tĕm'pəl) s. TEJ. *(stretching device)* templén *m.*
tem·plet (tĕm'plĭt) s. var. de **template.**
tem·po (tĕm'pō) s. [pl. **-pos** o **-pi** (-pē)] *(rhythm)* ritmo (de vida, actividad); MÚS. tempo.
tem·po·ral¹ (tĕm'pər-əl) adj. *(of time)* temporal; *(secular)* secular; *(temporary)* temporal; RELIG. laico; GRAM. de tiempo.
tem·po·ral² (tĕm'pər-əl) adj. ANAT. temporal.
temporal bone s. ANAT. hueso temporal.
tem·po·ral·i·ty (tĕm'pə-răl'ĭ-tē) s. [pl. **-ties**] temporalidad *f.*
tem·po·rar·y (tĕm'pə-rĕr'ē) I. adj. *(job, measures)* transitorio, provisional; *(worker)* temporero, temporario; *(position)* interino II. s. [pl. **-ies**] empleado temporario, temporero.
tem·po·rize (tĕm'pə-rīz') intr. **-rized, -riz·ing** contemporizar, temporizar.
tempt (tĕmpt) tr. *(entice)* tentar; *(to seduce)* seducir; *(to provoke)* provocar; *(to dispose)* inclinar <*she was tempted to resign* se sintió inclinada a renunciar>.
temp·ta·tion (tĕmp-tā'shən) s. tentación *f.*
tempt·er (tĕmp'tər) s. tentador *m* ♦ **the T.** el diablo.
tempt·ing (tĕmp'tĭng) adj. tentador, seductor.
tempt·ress (tĕmp'trĭs) s. mujer tentadora o seductora.
ten (tĕn) I. s. *(numeral)* diez *m;* *(ten-dollar bill)* billete de diez dólares *m* ♦ **t. o'clock** las diez II. adj. diez.
ten·a·ble (tĕn'ə-bəl) adj. *(sustainable)* sostenible, lógico (razón, idea); *(defensible)* defensible.
te·na·cious (tə-nā'shəs) adj. *(firm of purpose)* tenaz, persistente; *(cohesive)* firme; *(adhesive)* adhesivo; *(retentive)* retentivo <*a t. memory* una memoria retentiva>.
te·nac·i·ty (tə-năs'ĭ-tē) s. tenacidad *f.*
ten·an·cy (tĕn'ən-sē) s. [pl. **-cies**] *(possession)* tenencia legal; *(time period)* tiempo de posesión; *(habitation)* inquilinato, arrendamiento.
ten·ant (tĕn'ənt) I. s. *(renter)* inquilino, arrendatario; *(dweller)* ocupante *mf,* inquilino; *(legal holder)* arrendatario, inquilino II. tr. *(to rent)* arrendar, alquilar; *(to occupy)* ocupar —intr. ser inquilino o arrendatario.
tenant farmer s. agricultor arrendatario *m.*
ten·ant·ry (tĕn'ən-trē) s. [pl. **-ries**] *(tenants)* inquilinato; *(tenancy)* tenencia.
Ten Commandments s.pl. BÍBL. los diez mandamientos.
tend¹ (tĕnd) intr. *(to head)* dirigirse <*our course tended towards the north* nuestro rumbo se dirigía hacia el norte>; *(to be likely)* tener la tendencia, tender <*these things t. to happen* estas cosas tienden a ocurrir>; *(to be inclined)* propender a <*he tends toward violence* él propende a la violencia>.
tend² (tĕnd) tr. *(to look after)* cuidar, atender (enfermo, niño); *(to serve at)* servir, atender (mesas, bar) —intr. *(to serve)* atender; FAM. *(to pay attention)* prestar atención a.
ten·den·cy (tĕn'dən-sē) s. [pl. **-cies**] tendencia, propensión *f.*
ten·den·tious o **ten·den·cious** (tĕn-dĕn'shəs) adj. tendencioso.

ten·der¹ (tĕn'dər) I. adj. **-er, -est** *(fragile)* frágil; *(soft)* blando, tierno <*t. meat* carne tierna>; *(delicate)* delicado; *(young)* joven; *(sensitive)* sensible; *(painful)* que duele, dolorido <*a t. tooth* un diente dolorido>; *(affectionate)* cariñoso; *(cautious)* cauteloso II. tr. enternecer.
ten·der² (tĕn'dər) I. s. *(offer)* oferta de pago; *(bid)* propuesta ♦ **legal t.** dinero II. tr. presentar, ofrecer (renuncia, pago).
tend·er³ (tĕn'dər) s. *(one who tends)* vigilante (de equipo, máquina) *mf;* MARIT. buque nodriza *m.*
ten·der·foot (tĕn'dər-fŏŏt') s. [pl. **-foots** o **-feet** (-fēt')] *(greenhorn)* bisoño, novato; *(beginner)* principiante *mf.*
ten·der·heart·ed (tĕn'dər-här'tĭd) adj. susceptible al sufrimiento de otros, compasivo.
ten·der·ize (tĕn'də-rīz') tr. **-ized, -iz·ing** CUL. ablandar.
ten·der·iz·er (tĕn'də-rī'zər) s. CUL. condimento ablandador de carne.
ten·der·loin (tĕn'dər-loin') s. CUL. lomo, filete *m.*
ten·der·ly (tĕn'dər-lē) adv. tiernamente.
ten·der·ness (tĕn'dər-nĭs) s. ternura.
ten·don (tĕn'dən) s. tendón *m.*
ten·dril (tĕn'drəl) s. zarcillo.
ten·e·brous (tĕn'ə-brəs) adj. tenebroso.
ten·e·ment (tĕn'ə-mənt) s. *(building)* residencia con departamentos de alquiler; *(rundown building)* conventillo; G.B. *(apartment)* departamento, vivienda; DER. propiedad *f.*
ten·et (tĕn'ĭt) s. *(doctrine)* dogma *m;* *(principle)* principio.
ten·fold (tĕn'fōld') I. adj. décuplo II. adv. diez veces.
ten-gal·lon hat (tĕn'găl'ən) s. sombrero de copa alta y ala ancha, usado esp. por vaqueros tejanos.
ten·nis (tĕn'ĭs) s. DEP. tenis *m* ♦ **lawn t.** tenis sobre cesped.
tennis court s. cancha de tenis.
tennis player s. jugador de tenis *m.*
tennis shoes s.pl. zapatos de tenis.
ten·on (tĕn'ən) I. s. CARP. espiga barbilla II. tr. *(to provide with a tenon)* espigar; *(to join)* ensamblar.
ten·or (tĕn'ər) s. *(general sense)* sentido, tono; *(meaning)* sentido, significado; DER. *(exact meaning)* contenido literal; *(exact copy)* copia exacta; MÚS. tenor.
tenpenny nail s. clavo de tres pulgadas.
ten·pin (tĕn'pĭn') s. bolo ♦ **tenpins** [ú. con v. sing.] bolos, juego de bolos.
tense¹ (tĕns) I. adj. **tens·er, tens·est** *(stretched)* estirado; *(taut)* tirante; *(strained)* tenso II. tr. **tensed, tens·ing** *(to make tense)* poner tenso, tensar —intr. ponerse o volverse tenso.
tense² (tĕns) s. GRAM. tiempo.
tense·ness (tĕns'nĭs) s. *(tension)* tensión *f;* *(tautness)* tirantez *f.*
ten·sile (tĕn'səl, -sīl') adj. *(of tension)* de tensión, tensivo; *(extensible)* extensible, dúctil.
tensile strength s. FÍS. resistencia a la tensión.
ten·sion (tĕn'shən) s. tensión *f.*
ten·sor (tĕn'sər, -sôr') s. ANAT., MAT. tensor *m.*
tent (tĕnt) I. s. tienda, carpa II. intr. *(to camp)* acampar con carpas —tr. *(to cover)* cubrir con una carpa; *(to house)* alojar en carpas.
ten·ta·cle (tĕn'tə-kəl) s. tentáculo.
ten·tac·u·lar (tĕn-tăk'yə-lər) adj. tentacular.
ten·ta·tive (tĕn'tə-tĭv) I. adj. *(experimental)* experimental; *(provisional)* provisorio; *(uncertain)* indeciso II. s. tentativa.
ten·ter·hook (tĕn'tər-hŏŏk') s. escarpia, gancho de bastidor ♦ **to be on tenterhooks** estar sobre o en ascuas.
tenth (tĕnth) I. s. *(place)* décimo, decima parte II. adj. décimo.
te·nu·i·ty (tĕ-nŏŏ'ĭ-tē, -nyŏŏ'-) s. *(lack of firmness)* tenuidad *f;* *(fragility)* fragilidad *f.*
ten·u·ous (tĕn'yŏŏ-əs) adj. *(flimsy)* tenue; *(slender)* delgado; *(dilute)* diluido; *(weak)* débil (resplandor, luz).
ten·ure (tĕn'yər, -yŏŏr') s. *(occupation)* ocupación *f,* ejercicio; *(terms)* condiciones (de ejercitación) *f;* *(period)* período de ocupación, ejercicio; *(permanence)* permanencia (en un cargo, ejercicio).
te·pee (tē'pē) s. tienda o carpa de los indios norteamericanos.

---

tep·id (tĕp'ĭd) adj. tibio.
te·qui·la (tə-kē'lə) s. tequila *mf.*
ter·bi·um (tûr'bē-əm) s. QUÍM. terbio.
ter·cet (tûr'sĭt) s. terceto.
term (tûrm) I. s. *(time period)* período, plazo; *(school year)* período académico, curso; *(deadline)* término, fin *m* <*to come to its t.* llegar a su fin>; *(of a president, official)* mandato; DER. *(court session)* período de sesión; *(holding period)* término; *(estate)* tenencia, posesión *f*; *(obligation time)* período de obligación *o* validez; GRAM. voz *f*, vocablo; LÓG., MAT. término; ARQ. poste *o* marcador de límite *m* ✦ **born before t.** prematuro • **easy terms** facilidades de pago • **in no uncertain terms** muy claramente • **in set terms** en términos explícitos • **in terms of** en cuanto a, desde el punto de vista de • **in the long t.** a la larga, a largo plazo • **not on any terms** de ninguna manera, bajo ningún concepto • **terms** *(conditions)* condiciones; *(terminology)* términos; *(relations)* relaciones <*to be on good terms* tener buenas relaciones> • **to come to terms** *(to agree)* llegar a un arreglo; *(to accept)* aceptar <*he came to terms with his destiny* aceptó su destino> II. tr. calificar de, llamar <*he termed it a defeat* lo llamó una derrota>.
ter·ma·gant (tûr'mə-gənt) s. tarasca, arpía.
ter·mi·na·ble (tûr'mə-nə-bəl) adj. terminable.
ter·mi·nal (tûr'mə-nəl) I. adj. *(fatal)* fatal; *(final)* final; *(periodic)* periódico, recurrente; *(limiting)* limítrofe, de demarcación; BIOL. terminal II. s. *(end point)* extremo, término; *(station)* terminal *f*, estación terminal *f*; ELEC. terminal *m*, borne *m*; COMPUT. terminal.
terminal leave s. MIL. licencia *o* permiso final.
ter·mi·nate (tûr'mə-nāt') tr. **-nat·ed, -nat·ing** *(to end)* terminar, concluir; *(employment)* dejar cesante —intr. *(to end)* terminar; *(to result in)* tener como resultado <*the war terminated in the ruin of the city* la guerra tuvo como resultado la ruina de la ciudad>.
ter·mi·na·tion (tûr'mə-nā'shən) s. *(act)* terminación *f*; *(end)* final *m*, fin *m*; GRAM. terminación, desinencia.
ter·mi·na·tive (tûr'mə-nā'tĭv) adj. concluyente.
ter·mi·na·tor (tûr'mə-nā'tər) s. *(person)* persona que termina; ASTRON. línea divisoria.
ter·mi·ni (tûr'mə-nī') un pl. de **terminus.**
ter·mi·nol·o·gy (tûr'mə-nŏl'ə-jē) s. [pl. **-gies**] terminología.
term insurance s. seguro de plazo fijo.
ter·mi·nus (tûr'mə-nəs) s. [pl. **-nus·es** *o* **-ni** (-nī')] *(end)* fin *m*, final *m*; *(terminal)* estación terminal *f*; *(border)* límite *m.*
ter·mite (tûr'mīt') s. ENTOM. termita, comején *m.*
term paper s. EDUC. trabajo requerido en los liceos y universidades de los EE. UU.
tern (tûrn) s. golondrina de mar.
ter·na·ry (tûr'nə-rē) adj. ternario.
ter·race (tĕr'ĭs) I. s. *(veranda)* balcón *m*; *(roof)* azotea; *(court)* patio, terraza; *(embankment)* bancal *m*, terraplén *m*; *(of a street)* terraza, terraplén II. tr. **-raced, -rac·ing** terraplenar, abancalar.
ter·ra cot·ta (tĕr'ə kŏt'ə) s. terracota.
ter·rain (tə-rān') I. *(tract of land)* terreno, campo; *(topography)* topografía; GEOG. área, región *f*; GEOL. terreno.
ter·rar·i·um (tə-râr'ē-əm) s. [pl. **-iums** *o* **-i·a** (-ē-ə)] terrario.
ter·raz·zo (tə-rät'sō, -răz'ō) s. terrazo, piso veneciano (de mármol).
ter·res·tri·al (tə-rĕs'trē-əl) I. adj. *(of the earth)* terrestre; *(mundane)* mundano; BIOL. terrestre II. s. terrícola *mf.*
ter·ri·ble (tĕr'ə-bəl) adj. *(disease, catastrophe)* terrible, aterrador; *(guilt, responsibility)* tremenda, atroz; *(party, person)* desagradable; *(objectionable)* terrible <*a t. hypocrisy* una terrible hipocresía>.
ter·ri·bly (tĕr'ə-blē) adv. terriblemente.
ter·ri·er (tĕr'ē-ər) s. terrier *m.*
ter·ri·fic (tə-rĭf'ĭk) adj. *(terrifying)* terrorífico; *(frightful)* espantoso, atroz; *(extraordinary)* extraordinario <*a t. cook* un cocinero extraordinario>; *(awesome)* tremendo (poder, velocidad).
ter·ri·fy (tĕr'ə-fī') tr. **-fied, -fy·ing** *(to scare)* aterrorizar; *(to alarm)* alarmar; *(to threaten)* amenazar, amedrentar.
ter·ri·to·ri·al (tĕr'ĭ-tôr'ē-əl) I. adj. *(of a territory)* territorial;

(regional) regional; MIL. de defensa local II. s. ✦ **T.** HIST. soldado del ejército territorial.
ter·ri·to·ri·al·ism (tĕr'ĭ-tôr'ē-ə-lĭz'əm) s. supremacía de los terratenientes.
ter·ri·to·ri·al·i·ty (tĕr'ĭ-tôr'ē-ăl'ĭ-tē) s. [pl. **-ties**] territorialidad *f.*
ter·ri·to·ri·al·ize (tĕr'ĭ-tôr'ē-ə-līz') tr. **-ized, -iz·ing** *(to add territory to)* convertir en territorio federal; *(to change status)* organizar en forma territorial.
territorial waters s.pl. aguas territoriales *o* jurisdiccionales.
ter·ri·to·ry (tĕr'ĭ-tôr'ē) s. [pl. **-ries**] *(region)* zona, región *f*; *(jurisdiction)* territorio; *(sphere)* esfera, sector (de influencia, acción) *m*; DEP. terreno, campo ✦ **T.** *(region)* territorio de EE. UU. que no ha llegado a ser estado; *(colony)* colonia.
ter·ror (tĕr'ər) s. *(fear)* terror *m*; *(fearful thing)* terror, cosa terrorífica; *(violence)* violencia, terror ✦ **t.** *o* **holy t.** FAM. niño travieso • **the T.** HIST. el Terror.
ter·ror·ism (tĕr'ə-rĭz'əm) s. terrorismo.
ter·ror·ist (tĕr'ə-rĭst) s. terrorista *mf.*
ter·ror·is·tic (tĕr'ə-rĭs'tĭk) adj. terrorista.
ter·ror·ize (tĕr'ə-rīz') tr. **-ized, -iz·ing** *(to terrify)* aterrorizar, aterrar; *(to coerce)* amedrentar, coaccionar.
ter·ry (tĕr'ē) s. [pl. **-ries**] TEJ. tejido esponja ✦ **t. cloth** tela de toalla.
terse (tûrs) adj. **ters·er, ters·est** conciso.
ter·tian (tûr'shən) adj. & s. terciana.
ter·ti·ar·y (tûr'shē-ĕr'ē) adj. & s. [pl. **-ies**] *(third)* tercero; CIENT., ORNIT., RELIG. terciario ✦ **T.** GEOL. terciario.
ter·va·lent (tər-vā'lənt) adj. var. de **trivalent.**
tes·sel·lat·ed (tĕs'ə-lā'təd) adj. de mosaico.
test¹ (tĕst) I. s. *(examination)* examen *m*, prueba; *(criterion)* criterio; BIOQUÍM., QUÍM. *(analysis)* análisis *m*; *(reagent)* reactivo; *(cupel)* copela ✦ **to put to the t.** poner a prueba • **to stand the t. of time** resistir el paso del tiempo II. tr. *(to examine)* examinar; *(to subject to a test)* poner *o* someter a prueba; QUÍM. analizar —intr. *(to undergo a test)* tomar un examen, hacerse examinar <*I'm going to t. to determine my aptitude* voy a tomar un examen para determinar mi aptitud>; *(to achieve a result)* obtener resultados <*he tests well* obtiene buenos resultados en los exámenes>.
test² (tĕst) s. ZOOL. testa, concha.
tes·ta·cy (tĕs'tə-sē) s. DER. la condición de haber hecho testamento antes de morir.
tes·ta·ment (tĕs'tə-mənt) s. *(credo)* credo, creencia; DER. testamento; RELIG. convenio entre el hombre y Dios ✦ **T.** BÍBL. Testamento • **to be a t. to** ser testimonio de.
tes·ta·men·ta·ry (tĕs'tə-mĕn'tə-rē) adj. testamentario.
tes·tate (tĕs'tāt') adj. DER. testado.
tes·ta·tor (tĕs'tā'tər) s. DER. testador *m.*
tes·ta·trix (tĕ-stā'trĭks) s. DER. testadora.
test case s. DER. caso de prueba.
tes·ter¹ (tĕs'tər) s. *(over a bed)* dosel *m*, pabellón *m.*
tes·ter² (tĕs'tər) s. *(person)* probador *m*, ensayador *m.*
tes·tes (tĕs'tēz') pl. de **testis.**
test flight s. vuelo de prueba.
tes·ti·cle (tĕs'tĭ-kəl) s. ANAT. testículo.
tes·ti·fy (tĕs'tə-fī') intr. **-fied, -fy·ing** *(to declare)* declarar; *(to serve as witness)* ser testigo; DER. atestiguar bajo juramento —tr. *(to bear witness for)* testimoniar, revelar; *(to declare)* declarar; DER. atestiguar bajo juramento ✦ **to t. to** *(to declare)* declarar; *(to provide evidence for)* probar, evidenciar.
tes·ti·mo·ni·al (tĕs'tə-mō'nē-əl) I. s. *(testifying statement)* testimonio, atestación *f*; *(recommendation)* recomendación *f*, carta de recomendación; *(tribute)* tributo, homenaje *m* II. adj. testimonial.
tes·ti·mo·ny (tĕs'tə-mō'nē) s. [pl. **-nies**] *(proof)* evidencia, prueba; DER. testimonio, atestación *f*; RELIG. declaración *f*, testimonio ✦ **T.** RELIG. Tablas de la Ley.
tes·tis (tĕs'tĭs) s. [pl. **-tes** (-tēz')] ANAT. teste *m*, testículo.
tes·tos·ter·one (tĕ-stŏs'tə-rōn') s. BIOQUÍM. testosterona.
test paper s. *(examination)* examen *m*; QUÍM. papel reactivo *o* indicador.
test pilot s. AVIA. piloto de pruebas.
test tube s. tubo de ensayo, probeta.

ā rey / ä año / b boca / ch chico / d dar / ĕ el / ē mil / g gato / h joya / hw juez / ī aire / k casa / kw cuan /

tes·ty (tĕs′tē) adj. **-ti·er, -ti·est** *(irritable)* irritable; *(ill-humored)* malhumorado.

tet·a·nus (tĕt′n-əs) s. MED. tétanos *m*, tétano.

tetch·y (tĕch′ē) adj. **-i·er, -i·est** irritable, quisquilloso.

teth·er (tĕth′ər) **I.** s. traílla, correa ♦ **at the end of one's t.** *(financially)* en las últimas; *(patience)* harto **II.** tr. atar, estacar (con traílla, correa).

tet·ra·chlo·ride (tĕt′rə-klôr′īd′) s. QUÍM. tetracloruro.

tet·ra·cy·cline (tĕt′rə-sī′klēn′) s. FARM. tetraciclina.

tet·rad (tĕt′răd′) s. BIOL., BOT. tétrade *m*; QUÍM. elemento tetravalente; FÍS. átomo tetravalente.

tet·ra·gon (tĕt′rə-gŏn′) s. GEOM. tetrágono.

tet·ra·he·dral (tĕt′rə-hē′drəl) adj. GEOM. tetraédrico.

tet·ra·he·dron (tĕt′rə-hē′drən) s. [pl. **-drons** o **-dra** (-drə)] GEOM. tetraedro.

te·tral·o·gy (tĕ-trăl′ə-jē, -trŏl′-) s. [pl. **-gies**] tetralogía.

te·tram·e·ter (tĕ-trăm′ĭ-tər) s. POÉT. tetrámero.

tet·ra·pod (tĕt′rə-pŏd′) adj. tetrápode.

tet·ra·va·lent (tĕt′rə-vā′lənt) adj. QUÍM. tetravalente.

tet·rode (tĕt′rōd′) s. ELECTRÓN. tetrodo.

tet·ter (tĕt′ər) s. MED. herpes *mf* ♦ **scaly t.** psoriasis • **crusty t.** impétigo.

Teu·ton (tōōt′n, tyōōt′n) s. teutón *m*.

Teu·ton·ic (tōō-tŏn′ĭk, tyōō-) adj. & s. teutónico.

Tex·an (tĕk′sən) adj. & s. tejano.

tex·as (tĕk′səs) s. MARÍT. estructura, en un barco a vapor, que contiene la cabina del piloto y los cuartos de la oficialidad.

Tex·as (tĕk′səs) s. Tejas.

Texas Ranger s. policía montado del estado de Tejas.

text (tĕkst) s. *(words)* texto; *(main part)* texto; *(theme)* tema *m*; *(book)* libro de texto, texto.

text·book (tĕkst′bōōk′) s. libro de texto.

tex·tile (tĕk′stīl′, -stəl) s. & adj. textil.

tex·tu·al (tĕks′chōō-əl) adj. textual.

tex·tur·al (tĕks′chər-əl) adj. de textura.

tex·ture (tĕks′chər) s. *(appearance)* textura; *(structure)* estructura, textura.

tex·tured (tĕks′chərd) adj. de textura.

Thai (tī) adj. & s. [pl. **Thai** o **Thais**] tailandés *m*.

Thai·land (tī′lănd′) s. Tailandia.

thal·a·mus (thăl′ə-məs) s. [pl. **-mi** (-mī′)] ANAT., BOT. tálamo.

tha·lid·o·mide (thə-lĭd′ə-mīd′) s. FARM. talidomida.

thal·li·um (thăl′ē-əm) s. QUÍM. talio.

thal·lo·phyte (thăl′ə-fīt′) s. BOT. talofita.

Thames (tĕmz) s. Támesis.

than (thăn, thən) conj. [ú. en comparaciones desiguales] que <*she is a better athlete t. I* ella es mejor atleta que yo>; [ú. con números] de <*more t. half* más de la mitad>; [seguido por una oración] del que, de lo que <*more complex t. I had anticipated* más complejo de lo que había previsto ♦ **no other t.** nadie más que, nadie excepto • **other t.** aparte de, fuera de • **rather t.** antes que.

thane (thān) s. G.B., HIST. barón en Escocia *m*.

thank (thăngk) tr. agradecer, dar las gracias a ♦ **t. you** gracias • **t. you very much** muchas gracias.

thank·ful (thăngk′fəl) adj. agradecido.

thank·less (thăngk′lĭs) adj. *(ungrateful)* desagradecido; *(not appreciated)* ingrato <*t. task* tarea ingrata>.

thanks (thăngks) s.pl. *(acknowledgment)* reconocimiento; *(gratitude)* gratitud *f*; *(expression)* gracias <*to give t. to* dar las gracias a> ♦ **no t. to** a pesar de, no ser gracias a <*I did it, no t. to you* lo hice a pesar de ti> • **t. to** debido a <*we arrived late t. to the storm* llegamos tarde debido a la tormenta>.

thanks·giv·ing (thăngks-gĭv′ĭng) s. acción de gracias *f*.

Thanksgiving Day s. día de acción de gracias *m*.

that (thăt, thət) §G24, 33, 34 **I.** adj. dem. [pl. **those** (thōz)] *(relatively near)* ese, esa <*t. car is mine* ese automóvil es mío>; *(further removed)* aquel, aquella <*t. route is shorter than this one* aquel camino es más corto que éste> ♦ **t. one** *(near)* ése, ésa; *(distant)* aquél, aquélla • **t. way** *(direction)* por aquel camino; *(manner)* de ese modo • **those people who** la gente que, aquellos que **II.** pron. dem. [pl. **those**] *(relatively near)* ése, ésa <*what kind of soup is t.?* ¿qué tipo

de sopa es ésa?>; *(further removed)* aquél, aquélla <*t. is for sale; this is not* aquél está para la venta; éste no>; *(neuter, just referred to)* eso <*t. is true* eso es verdad>; *(neuter, remote reference)* aquello ♦ **and all t.** y cosas por el estilo • **and t.'s that!** ¡y eso es todo! • **for all t.** a pesar de eso • **how do you like t.?** ¿qué le parece? • **like t.** así • **t.'s it!** ¡eso es! • **those who** los que, aquellos que **III.** pron. rel. [pl. **that**] que <*the house t. I sold and the people t. bought it* la casa que vendí y la gente que la compró>; quien <*the person t. you've heard from* la persona de quien recibiste noticias>; el que, la que <*the closet t. you keep your clothes in* el armario en el que guardas tu ropa>; lo que <*all t. they knew* todo lo que ellos sabían>; el, la, lo <*t. of yesterday may not be good today* lo de ayer puede no servir hoy en día>; en que <*the day t. I was born* el día en que yo nací> ♦ **at t.** *(without further elaboration)* así, sin más; *(nevertheless)* sin embargo, a pesar de eso; *(furthermore)* todavía, más aún • **for all t.** a pesar de eso • **t. I know of** que yo sepa • **t. is how** así es como • **t. is** o **t. is to say** es decir • **t. may be so** es posible, es probable • **t. which** el que, lo cual • **the one t.** el que, quien **IV.** adv. tan <*is your problem t. complicated?* ¿es tan complicado su problema?>; así de <*the steps were t. high* los escalones eran así de alto> ♦ **t. many** tantos • **t. much** tanto **V.** conj. que <*he said t. he was poor* dijo que era pobre>; de que <*he was sure t. he was right* estaba seguro de que tenía razón>; para que <*we did it t. you may have more time for us* lo hicimos para que pudieras tener más tiempo para nosotros>; que, porque <*it is not t. I don't like it* no es porque no me guste> ♦ **in t.** por cuanto • **oh, t. . . .!** ¡ojalá (que) . . .! <*oh, t. I were rich!* ¡ojalá fuera rico!> • **save t.** salvo que • **so t.** para que, de modo que.

thatch (thăch) **I.** s. *(straw)* paja, barda; FIG., FAM. *(thick hair)* pelo tupido **II.** tr. *(to cover)* bardar, cubrir con paja.

thatch·er (thăch′ər) s. persona que trabaja con barda para hacer techos.

thau·ma·turge (thô′mə-tûrj′) o **thau·ma·tur·gist** (-tûr′-jĭst) s. taumaturgo.

thau·ma·tur·gy (thô′mə-tûr′jē) s. taumaturgia.

thaw (thô) **I.** intr. *(to melt)* derretirse; *(to soften)* ablandarse; *(to become warm)* ponerse tibio (el clima); *(to relax)* relajarse, ablandarse; *(to become less reserved)* cobrar confianza —tr. ♦ **to t. out** *(food)* descongelar; *(snow)* derretir **II.** s. *(melting)* derretimiento, deshielo; *(warm period)* tiempo tibio; *(relaxation)* ablandamiento.

thaw·ing (thô′ĭng) s. *(melting)* deshielo; FIG. *(warming)* mejora (de relaciones, amistad).

the[1] §G17, 21 *(thē* antes de vocablo; *thə* antes de consonante)* art. def. el, la, lo, las, los <*t. child* el niño>; [pronunciado con énfasis] *(the most popular)* el más popular <*it is t. show of the 80's* es el espectáculo más popular de los años ochenta>; *(the best)* el mejor <*it is t. art gallery in this city* es la mejor galería de arte de la ciudad>; *(the famous)* el famoso <*do you mean t. Vladimir Horowitz?* ¿te refieres al famoso Vladimir Horowitz?> ♦ **at t. time** en aquel entonces, entonces • **t. one** el, la.

the[2] *(thē* antes de vocablo; *thə* antes de consonante)* adv. ♦ **t. less . . . t. better** cuanto menos . . . mejor <*t. less we talk about it t. better* cuanto menos hablemos de esto, mejor> • **t. more . . . t. more** cuanto más . . . más <*t. more I get, t. more I want* cuanto más recibo más quiero> • **t. sooner t. better** cuanto antes mejor • **to be all t. better** es tanto mejor.

the·ar·chy (thē′är′kē) s. [pl. **-chies**] teocracia.

the·a·ter (thē′ə-tər) s. *(building)* teatro; *(auditorium)* auditorio; *(literature, performance)* teatro, arte dramático *m*; *(milieu)* ambiente de teatro *m*; *(audience)* público de un teatro; *(setting)* local *m*, lugar *m*; MIL. teatro ♦ **operating t.** quirófano.

the·a·ter·go·er (thē′ə-tər-gō′ər) s. el que va al teatro.

theater ticket s. entrada, boleto.

the·a·tre (thē′ə-tər) s. var. de **theater.**

the·at·ri·cal (thē-ăt′rĭ-kəl) o **the·at·ric** (-ăt′rĭk) **I.** adj. teatral **II.** s. ♦ **theatricals** funciones de teatro (por aficionados) *f*.

the·at·ri·cal·ism (thē-ăt′rĭ-kə-lĭz′əm) s. teatralidad *f*.

ng inglés / ŏ la / ō bou / ô corre / oi oigo / ōō uno / ou auto / yōō ciudad / w hueco / y yo / z mismo

the·at·rics (thē-ăt′rĭks) s. [ú. con v. sing.] *(art form)* arte escénico *m*; *(effects)* efectos teatrales.

Thebes (thēbz) *o* **The·bae** (thē′bē) s. Tebas.

the·ca (thē′kə) s. [pl. **-cae** (-sē′, -kē′)] ANAT., BOT. teca.

thee (thē) pron. ANT., POÉT. te, ti ♦ **with t.** contigo.

theft (thĕft) s. robo.

their §G23 (thâr) pron. pos. su, suyo, suya, de ellos, de ellas <*t. house* su casa, la casa de ellos>.

theirs §G32 (thârz) pron. pos. [ú. con v. sing. o pl.] (el) suyo, (la) suya, (los) suyos, (las) suyas, de ellos, de ellas <*this is our school and that one is t.* ésta es nuestra escuela y aquélla es (la) suya> ♦ **of t.** de ellos, suyo <*a friend of theirs* una amiga suya, una amiga de ellos>.

the·ism (thē′ĭz′əm) s. FILOS., RELIG. teísmo.

them §G29 (thĕm, thəm) pron. [como complemento directo de un verbo] los, las <*she accompanied t.* ella los acompañó>; [como complemento indirecto de un verbo] les <*he offered t. a new contract* les ofreció un nuevo contrato>; [como complemento de una preposición] ellos, ellas <*it was signed by t.* fue firmado por ellos>.

the·mat·ic (thĭ-măt′ĭk) adj. temático.

theme (thēm) s. *(topic)* tema *m*; *(idea)* idea central, tema; *(composition)* ensayo; MÚS. tema, motivo; FILOL. raíz (de vocablo) *f*.

theme song s. *(main song)* canción principal *f*; *(signature)* canción que identifica a un cantante *o* grupo.

them·selves §G37 (thĕm-sĕlvz′, thəm-) pron. [como objeto de un verbo] se <*they prepared t. for battle* ellos se prepararon para la batalla>; [como sujeto de un verbo] mismos, mismas <*they t. were affected* ellos mismos se sintieron afectados>; [como objeto de preposición] sí mismos, sí mismas <*they are always bragging about t.* están siempre haciendo alarde de sí mismos>; ellos, ellas <*they are always playing among t.* están siempre jugando entre ellos> ♦ **all by t.** ellos solos • **by t.** solos • **with t.** consigo mismos.

then (thĕn) I. adv. *(at that time)* entonces, en aquel tiempo <*I was younger t.* yo era más joven entonces>; *(afterward)* después, luego <*first you eat and t. you go to bed* primero comes y luego te vas a la cama>; *(in that case)* entonces <*if you're late, you'd better leave now* si es tarde para ti, entonces es mejor que te vayas ahora>; *(in addition)* además <*t. there are taxes to be paid* además hay impuestos que hay que pagar>; *(consequently)* por lo tanto, en consecuencia <*if x equals 3 and y equals 2, t. x plus y equals 5* si x es igual a 3 e y es igual a 2, en consecuencia x más y es igual a 5> ♦ **and what t.?** ¿y qué pasó?, ¿y qué más? • **but t.** si bien es cierto que <*they lost the election, but t. they never really expected to win* perdieron la elección si bien es cierto que ellos realmente nunca esperaron ganar> • **now and t.** de vez en cuando • **now . . . t.** unas veces . . . otras veces • **now t.** ahora bien, veamos <*now t., what did you want?* veamos ¿qué querías?> • **t. and there** ahí mismo, al momento II. s. entonces <*by t. they were gone* para entonces ellos ya se habían ido> ♦ **before t.** antes de eso • **every now and t.** de vez en cuando • **from t. on** a partir de entonces, desde entonces • **since t.** desde entonces, desde aquel tiempo • **until t.** hasta entonces III. adj. entonces, de entonces <*the t. mayor* el entonces alcalde>.

thence (thĕns) adv. *(from there)* de allí; *(thenceforth)* desde entonces; *(therefrom)* a partir de.

thence·forth (thĕns-fôrth′) adv. desde entonces.

thence·for·ward (thĕns-fôr′wərd) *o* **thence·for·wards** (-wərdz) adv. *(thenceforth)* desde entonces; *(from that place)* desde ese lugar; *(from that time)* desde entonces.

the·o·cen·tric (thē′ō-sĕn′trĭk) adj. TEO. teocéntrico.

the·oc·ra·cy (thē-ŏk′rə-sē) s. [pl. **-cies**] teocracia.

the·o·crat (thē′ə-krăt′) s. teócrata *mf*.

the·o·lo·gian (thē′ə-lō′jən) s. teólogo.

the·o·log·i·cal (thē′ə-lŏj′ĭ-kəl) *o* **the·o·log·ic** (-lŏj′ĭk) adj. teológico.

the·ol·o·gize (thē-ŏl′ə-jīz′) tr. **-gized, -giz·ing** dar carácter teológico a —intr. teologizar.

the·ol·o·gy (thē-ŏl′ə-jē) s. [pl. **-gies**] teología.

the·o·rem (thē′ər-əm) s. teorema *m*.

the·o·ret·i·cal (thē′ə-rĕt′ĭ-kəl) *o* **the·o·ret·ic** (-rĕt′ĭk) adj.

(theory-based) teórico; *(speculative)* teorizante, especulativo.

the·o·ret·i·cal·ly (thē′ə-rĕt′ĭ-kə-lē) adv. teóricamente.

the·o·re·ti·cian (thē′ər-ə-tĭsh′ən) s. teórico.

the·o·ret·ics (thē′ə-rĕt′ĭks) s. [ú. con v. sing.] teoría, principios.

the·o·rist (thē′ər-ĭst) s. teórico.

the·o·ri·za·tion (thē′ər-ĭ-zā′shən) s. teorización *f*.

the·o·rize (thē′ə-rīz′) intr. **-rized, -riz·ing** *(to formulate, analyze)* teorizar; *(to speculate)* especular.

the·o·ry (thē′ə-rē) s. [pl. **-ries**] *(systematic knowledge)* teoría; *(speculation)* especulación *f*; *(guess)* teoría.

the·os·o·phy (thē-ŏs′ə-fē) s. FILOS., RELIG. teosofía.

ther·a·peu·tic (thĕr′ə-pyōō′tĭk) *o* **ther·a·peu·ti·cal** (-tĭ-kəl) adj. terapéutico.

ther·a·peu·tics (thĕr′ə-pyōō′tĭks) s. [ú. con v. sing.] MED. terapéutica.

ther·a·pist (thĕr′ə-pĭst) s. terapeuta *mf*.

ther·a·py (thĕr′ə-pē) s. [pl. **-pies**] MED. terapia; PSIC. psicoterapia.

there §G12 (thâr) adv. allí, allá <*sit over t.* siéntate allá>; ahí <*it is t., near you* está ahí, cerca de ti>; *(in that matter)* en eso, en cuanto a eso <*I can't agree with you t.* no estoy de acuerdo contigo en eso> ♦ **here and t.** aquí y allá • **I have been t. before** FIG. ya sé lo que es eso, eso no es nada nuevo para mí • **not to be all t.** faltarle a alguien un tornillo • **t. and then** en seguida, inmediatamente • **you t.!** ¡usted!, ¡oiga! II. pron. ♦ **t. are** hay • **t. is** hay • **t. was** había, hubo • **t. were** habían, hubo • **t. will be** habrá III. s. ese lugar, aquel punto IV. interj. ¡vaya! <*t., now I can have some peace!* ¡vaya! ¡ahora puedo tener un poco de paz!> ♦ **t. now!** ¡ya está! • **there, there** ya, ya <*there, there, don't cry* ya, ya, no llores>.

there·a·bout (thâr′ə-bout′) *o* **there·a·bouts** (-bouts′) adv. más *o* menos, aproximadamente <*she was twenty-one or t.* ella tenía veintiún años aproximadamente>.

there·af·ter (thâr-ăf′tər) adv. de allí en adelante <*an apprentice for a year, an assistant t.* aprendiz por un año, de allí en adelante ayudante>.

there·at (thâr-ăt′) adv. *(there)* allí; *(at such a time)* en ese momento, en esa ocasión.

there·by (thâr-bī′) adv. *(by that means)* con lo cual, por medio de eso; *(in a specified connection)* por eso, debido a eso; *(around there)* por allí, alrededor.

there·fore (thâr′fôr′) adv. en consecuencia, por lo tanto.

there·from (thâr-frŭm′, -frŏm′) adv. de allí, de ahí.

there·in (thâr-ĭn′) adv. *(in that place)* allí dentro; *(in that circumstance)* en eso <*t. lies the fault* en eso está la falla>.

there·of (thâr-ŭv′, -ŏv′) adv. *(of this)* de eso; *(therefrom)* de eso, de allí <*those are the facts: t. one can deduce this* éstos son los datos: de allí se puede deducir esto>.

there·on (thâr-ŏn′) adv. *(on that)* sobre eso; *(thereupon)* inmediatamente después; *(therefore)* en consecuencia.

there·to (thâr-tōō′) adv. a eso, a ello.

there·to·fore (thâr′tə-fôr′) adv. hasta entonces, antes de eso.

there·un·der (thâr-ŭn′dər) adv. debajo, por debajo.

there·un·to (thâr′ŭn-tōō′) adv. a eso, a esto.

there·up·on (thâr′ə-pŏn′) adv. *(upon this)* sobre esto, sobre eso; *(directly following)* luego, inmediatamente después; *(therefore)* por lo tanto, en consecuencia.

there·with (thâr-wĭth′) adv. *(with that)* con eso; *(in addition to)* además <*he had a sword and a dagger t.* tenía una espada y un puñal además>; *(thereafter)* inmediatamente después.

there·with·al (thâr′wĭth-ôl′) adv. *(with all that)* con todo eso; *(besides)* además.

therm (thûrm) s. FÍS. termia.

ther·mal (thûr′məl) *o* **ther·mic** (-mĭk) I. adj. *(producing heat)* termal, térmico <*t. underwear* ropa interior térmica>; FÍS. calorífico, térmico <*t. radiation* radiación térmica>; GEOL. termal <*t. waters* aguas termales> II. s. corriente de aire caliente *f*.

therm·i·on (thûr′mī′ən) s. FÍS. termión *m*, termoelectrón *m*.

ther·mo·chem·is·try (thûr′mō-kĕm′ĭ-strē) s. QUÍM. termoquímica.

ã rey / ä año / b boca / ch chico / d dar / ĕ el / ē mil / g gato / h joya / hw juez / ī aire / k casa / kw cuan /

ther·mo·cou·ple (thûr′mə-kŭp′əl) s. ELEC. termopar *m*, par termoeléctrico *m*.

ther·mo·dy·nam·ic (thûr′mō-dī-năm′ĭk) adj. termodinámico.

ther·mo·dy·nam·ics (thûr′mō-dī-năm′ĭks) s. [ú. con v. sing.] termodinámica.

ther·mo·e·lec·tric (thûr′mō-ĭ-lĕk′trĭk) *o* **ther·mo·e·lec·tri·cal** (-trĭ-kəl) adj. termoeléctrico.

thermoelectric couple s. par termoeléctrico, termopar *m*.

ther·mo·e·lec·tric·i·ty (thûr′mō-ĭ-lĕk-trĭs′ĭ-tē) s. termoelectricidad *f*.

ther·mo·graph (thûr′mə-grăf′) s. termógrafo, termómetro registrador automático.

ther·mom·e·ter (thər-mŏm′ĭ-tər) s. termómetro.

ther·mom·e·try (thər-mŏm′ĭ-trē) s. termometría.

ther·mo·nu·cle·ar (thûr′mō-nōō′klē-ər, -nyōō′-) adj. termonuclear.

ther·mo·plas·tic (thûr′mə-plăs′tĭk) **I.** adj. termoplástico **II.** s. resina *o* producto termoplástico.

Ther·mos bottle (thûr′məs) s. termo (marca registrada de una botella aislante).

ther·mo·set·ting (thûr′mō-sĕt′ĭng) adj. FÍS., QUÍM. termofraguante, termoestable (díc. de los plásticos termoendurecibles).

ther·mo·sphere (thûr′mə-sfîr′) s. METEOR. termosfera.

ther·mo·stat (thûr′mə-stăt′) s. termostato.

ther·mo·ther·a·py (thûr′mō-thĕr′ə-pē) s. termoterapia.

the·sau·rus (thĭ-sôr′əs) s. [pl. **-sau·ri** (-sôr′ī′) *o* **-sau·rus·es**] *(dictionary)* diccionario; *(book of synonyms)* libro de sinónimos.

these (*thēz*) pl. de **this**.

the·sis (thē′sĭs′) s. [pl. **the·ses** (thē′sēz′)] tesis *f*.

Thes·pi·an *o* **thes·pi·an** (thĕs′pē-ən) **I.** adj. de Tespis ♦ **t.** dramático, trágico **II.** s. ♦ **t.** actor *m*, actriz *f*.

Thes·sa·lo·ni·ans (thĕs′ə-lō′nē-ənz) s. BÍBL. Tesalonicenses.

the·ta (thā′tə, thē′-) s. theta (letra griega).

the·ur·gy (thē′ûr-jē) s. [pl. **-gies**] HIST., RELIG. teurgia.

thew (thōō, thyōō) s. ANAT. músculo ♦ **thews** fuerza muscular, vigor.

they §G29 (thā) pron. ellos, ellas <*we had a cat and a dog, but* t. *fought all the time* teníamos un gato y un perro, pero ellos se peleaban todo el tiempo> ♦ **t. say** dicen, se dice <*t. say it will rain tonight* se dice que va a llover esta noche> • **t. who** los que, quienes.

they'd (*thād*) contr. de **they had** *o* **they would**.

they'll (*thāl*) contr. de **they will** *o* **they shall**.

they're (*thâr*) contr. de **they are**.

they've (*thāv*) contr. de **they have**.

thi·a·mine (thī′ə-mĭn, -mēn′) *o* **thi·a·min** (-mĭn) s. BIOQUÍM. tiamina.

thick (thĭk) **I.** adj. **-er, -est** *(not thin)* grueso; *(not watery)* espeso; *(in thickness)* de grosor <*it's twelve centimeters* t. tiene doce centímetros de grosor>; *(thickset)* grueso, gordo; *(sultry)* sofocante (aire, color); *(full of)* atestado de <*a room* t. *with flies* un cuarto atestado de moscas>; *(impenetrable)* impenetrable (neblina, oscuridad); *(indistinct)* poco claro, confuso <*the* t. *speech of a drunkard* el habla confusa de un borracho>; *(pronounced)* fuerte, marcado <*a* t. *accent* un acento marcado>; *(said of a crowd)* denso; *(stuffy)* cargado, viciado; *(said of a beard)* tupido; *(said of lips)* grueso; FAM. *(stupid)* bruto, duro (de entendimiento); *(intimate)* íntimos (amigos, compañeros) **II.** adv. *(not thinly)* grueso <*cut it* t. córtalo grueso>; *(densely)* densamente; *(indistinctly)* con voz poco clara; *(pronouncedly)* marcadamente ♦ **t. as thieves** inseparables • **to lay it on t.** FAM. exagerar al dar cumplidos, irse la mano **III.** s. *(thickness)* grosor *m*; *(most active part)* lo más reñido <*in the* t. *of the fighting* en lo más reñido de la pelea> ♦ **through t. and thin** contra viento y marea.

thick·en (thĭk′ən) tr. & intr. *(to make or become thicker)* espesar(se); *(to make or become complex)* embrollar(se), complicar(se).

thick·en·ing (thĭk′ə-nĭng) s. *(act)* espesamiento; *(material)* mezcla para espesar.

thick·et (thĭk′ĭt) s. *(bush)* matorral *m*; *(copse)* soto, bosquecillo.

thick·head·ed (thĭk′hĕd′əd) adj. estúpido, torpe.

thick·ness (thĭk′nĭs) s. grosor *m*, espesor *m*.

thick·set (thĭk′sĕt′) adj. *(stout)* corpulento, grueso; *(closely planted)* denso, muy poblado.

thick-skinned (thĭk′skĭnd′) adj. *(having a thick skin)* de piel gruesa; FIG. *(not easily offended)* de mucho estómago; *(insensitive)* insensible.

thick-wit·ted (thĭk′wĭt′ĭd) adj. estúpido, imbécil.

thief (thēf) s. [pl. **thieves** (thēvz)] ladrón *m*.

thieve (thēv) tr. & intr. thieved, thiev·ing robar, hurtar.

thiev·er·y (thē′və-rē) s. [pl. **-ies**] robo, hurto.

thieves (thēvz) pl. de **thief**.

thiev·ish (thē′vĭsh) adj. *(thieving)* ratero, ladrón; *(furtive)* furtivo.

thigh (thī) s. ANAT. muslo.

thigh·bone (thī′bōn′) s. ANAT. fémur *m*.

thim·ble (thĭm′bəl) s. COST. dedal *m*; MEC. abrazadera, manguito; MARÍT. guardacabo; ELEC. casquillo.

thim·ble·ful (thĭm′bəl-fōōl′) s. [pl. **-fuls**] dedada.

thin (thĭn) **I.** adj. **thin·ner, thin·nest** *(not thick)* fino, delgado <*a* t. *thread* un hilo fino>; *(narrow)* angosto; *(lean)* delgado, flaco; *(said of lips)* fino; *(said of fingers)* delgado; *(sparse)* escaso; *(thinning)* ralo <*t. hair* pelo ralo>; *(rarefied)* enrarecido; *(watery)* aguado (café, sopa); *(flimsy)* débil, flojo; *(tinny)* débil (sonido, voz); *(weak)* ténue (luz, fotografía) ♦ **to be as** t. **as a rail** estar en los huesos • **to disappear into** t. **air** esfumarse, hacerse humo • **to get thinner** adelgazar **II.** adv. débilmente, escasamente **III.** tr. **thinned, thin·ning** *(to make lean)* hacer adelgazar; *(to dilute)* diluir, aguar; *(to cut away)* entresacar; *(to reduce)* reducir ♦ **to** t. **out** hacer menos denso —intr. *(to get lean)* adelgazar; *(to diminish)* reducirse (población, multitud); *(to fade)* disiparse <*the fog is thinning* la niebla se está disipando>.

thine (*thīn*) pron. ANT. *(yours)* tuyo, tuya <*the victory is* t. la victoria es tuya>; *(used substantively)* el tuyo, la tuya <*my luck and* t. mi suerte y la tuya>.

thing (thĭng) s. *(single entity)* cosa; *(object)* objeto <*the table is a* t. la mesa es un objeto>; *(creature)* criatura <*the poor little* t. la pobre criatura>; *(commodity)* objeto, artículo <*things of little value* objetos poco valiosos>; *(unspecified object)* cosa <*how many of these things did you buy?* ¿cuántas cosas de éstas compraste?>; *(act, work)* cosa <*he is always building things* siempre está fabricando cosas>; *(notion, information)* cosa <*one should not say such things* no se deben decir cosas así>; *(matter, circumstance)* cosa <*don't think about those things* no piense en esas cosas>; *(obsession)* obsesión *f* <*he has a* t. *about guns* tiene obsesión por los revólveres>; *(situation)* asunto, cuestión *f* <*the* t. *is this* la cuestión es la siguiente>; *(dislike)* manía <*she has this* t. *about my mother* le tiene manía a mi madre> ♦ **above all things** por sobre todas las cosas • **a dumb** t. **to say** una estupidez • **a terrible** t. algo terrible • **a** t. **or two** unas cuantas cosas • **first** t. a primera hora • **first things first** cada cosa a su debido tiempo • **for another** t. por otro lado, además • **for one** t. en primer lugar • **how are things (with you, them)?** ¿cómo (te, les) van las cosas? • **it's a good** t. **that** menos mal que • **last** t. a última hora • **neither one** t. **nor the other** ni lo uno ni lo otro • **no such t.!** ¡nada de eso! • **not a** t. nada • **not to know the first t. about** no saber ni papa de • **of all things!** ¡lo que son las cosas! • **one of those things** cosas que pasan • **one** t. **or the other** una de dos • **poor (little) thing!** ¡pobrecito! • **sure t.!** ¡seguro! • **that** t. ese • **the (good, bad)** t. **is that** lo (bueno, malo) es que • **the latest** t. **in** *(fashions)* el último grito de; *(latest development)* la última palabra en • **the main** t. lo más importante • **the** t. **to (do, remember)** lo que hay que (hacer, recordar) • **the** t. **to wear** JER. el último grito de la moda • **things** *(belongings)* cosas; *(equipment)* trastos, equipo <*fishing things* trastos de pescar>; *(conditions)* cosas <*as things stand* tal y como están las cosas>; DER. bienes • **this** t. esto • **to be just the** t. **for** *o* **to** ser precisamente lo que hace falta para • **to be the real** t. *(product)* ser el de verdad; *(action)* ir en serio • **to do**

one's own t. JER. hacer lo que uno quiere • **to have many things on one's mind** tener muchas preocupaciones • **to know a t. or two about** saber uno su poco de • **to make a big t. out of** dar mucha importancia a • **to pack up one's things** hacer las maletas • **to see things** ver visiones.

thing·a·ma·jig (thĭng′ə-mə-jĭg′) o **thing·a·ma·bob** (-bŏb′) s. FAM. cómo se llama *m*, cosa.

think (thĭngk) tr. **thought** (thôt), **think·ing** *(to conceive)* pensar; *(to ponder)* pensar en, considerar <*t. how complex language is* consideren lo complejo que es el lenguaje>; *(to decide)* pensar, determinar; *(to regard)* creer, parecerle a uno <*he thought the verdict was fair* le pareció que el veredicto era justo>; *(to believe)* pensar, parecerle a uno <*I always thought he was right* siempre pensaba que tenía razón>; *(to expect)* pensar, creer <*he thought he'd arrive early* pensaba que llegaría temprano>; *(to intend)* pensar, tener la intención (de); *(to remember)* recordar, acordarse <*I can't t. what his name was* no recuerdo cómo se llamaba>; *(to imagine)* imaginarse <*t. what would happen* imagínese lo que pasaría>; *(to concentrate on)* pensar en <*to t. of nothing but profits* pensar solamente en las ganancias> • **after thinking it over** después de haberlo pensado bien • **come to t. of it** pensándolo bien • **to be thought to be (smart, rich)** tener fama de (listo, rico) • **to be well thought of** *(person)* ser tenido en mucho; *(actions)* ser visto con buenos ojos • **to t. about** *(to examine)* pensar <*t. about it* piénselo>; *(to reflect upon)* pensar en <*he thought about them* pensó en ellos> • **to t. it only fair to** creer que lo menos que se puede hacer es • **to t. nothing of** no molestarle nada a uno • **to t. of** *(to consider)* pensar (hacer algo); *(to recall)* recordar, acordarse de; *(to have regard for)* pensar en <*we thought of our family first* pensamos primero en la familia> • **to t. of oneself as** o **t. oneself to be** creerse, dárselas de (experto, patriota) • **to t. out** *(to consider)* pensar bien <*to t. things out* pensar bien las cosas>; *(a theory, plan)* elaborar; *(a problem)* resolver; *(a solution)* encontrar • **to t. over** pensar bien • **to t. somebody (a fool, mad)** tener a alguien por (tonto, loco) • **to t. through** pensar bien • **to t. up** *(a plan, excuse)* inventar; *(an idea)* ocurrírsele a uno —intr. *(to reason)* pensar <*I was not able to t. clearly* no pude pensar con claridad>; *(to consider)* pensar, reflexionar <*t. before making a decision* piense antes de decidir>; *(to believe)* creer, parecerle a uno <*I t. so* creo que sí>; *(to expect)* pensar, creer <*more than you thought* más de lo que usted pensaba> • **just t.!** ¡imagínese!, ¡figúrese! • **not to know what to t.** no saber a qué atenerse • **not to t. much of** *(a dress, car)* no parecerle a uno gran cosa; *(a person)* no tener un gran concepto de • **to make one t.** dar que pensar a uno • **to t. again** o **twice** pensarlo bien, reconsiderar • **to t. back** recordar, acordarse • **to t. better of it** cambiar de parecer • **to t. of** *(to conceive of)* ocurrírsele a uno <*the only solution I can t. of* la única solución que se me ocurre>; *(to believe)* pensar de, parecerle a uno; *(to imagine)* imaginarse, figurarse.

think·a·ble (thĭng′kə-bəl) adj. concebible.

think·er (thĭng′kər) s. pensador *m*.

think·ing (thĭng′kĭng) I. s. *(thought)* pensamiento; *(judgment)* juicio, opinión *f* II. adj. pensante, racional <*man is a t. animal* el hombre es un animal racional>.

thinking cap s. FIG. • **to put on one's t.** sumirse en la reflexión.

think tank s. grupo cuya función es buscar soluciones.

thin·ly (thĭn′lē) adv. apenas, poco.

thin·ner (thĭn′ər) s. PINT. diluyente *m*, adelgazador (esp. de pintura) *m*.

thin·ness (thĭn′nĭs) s. *(leanness)* delgadez *f*; *(weakness)* debilidad *f*; *(scarcity)* escasez *f*; *(of soup, argument)* poca consistencia, flojedad *f*.

thin-skinned (thĭn′skĭnd′) adj. *(having thin skin)* de piel fina o delgada; FIG. *(oversensitive)* delicado, suceptible.

third (thûrd) I. s. *(ordinal number)* tercero; *(part)* tercio, tercera parte <*I want a half, not a t.* quiero la mitad, no un tercio>; MÚS. tercera; AUTO. tercera; ASTRON., GEOM. tercero • **two thirds** dos tercios, dos terceras partes II. adj. tercero • **every t. day** cada tres días.

third class s. *(mail)* tercera clase *f*; *(accommodations)* tercera, tercera clase (alojamiento, servicios).

third-class (thûrd′klăs′) I. adj. de tercera clase, de tercera II. adv. en tercera clase, en tercera.

third degree s. interrogatorio severo (esp. con tortura).

third-de·gree burn (thûrd′dĭ-grē′) s. MED. quemadura de tercer grado.

third dimension s. tercera dimensión.

third·ly (thûrd′lē) adv. en tercer lugar.

third party s. DER. tercera persona; POL. tercer partido.

third person s. GRAM. tercera persona; DER. tercero.

Third World o **third world** s. POL. el Tercer Mundo.

thirst (thûrst) I. s. *(desire to drink)* sed *f*; FIG. *(craving)* deseo ardiente, ansia II. intr. tener sed • **to t. after** o **for** ansiar, anhelar.

thirst·y (thûr′stē) adj. -i·er, -i·est *(desiring to drink)* sediento; *(arid)* árido, seco; *(causing thirst)* que da o provoca sed • **to be t. for** tener sed de • **to make t.** dar sed.

thir·teen (thûr-tēn′) s. & adj. trece *m*.

thir·teenth (thûr-tēnth′) I. s. *(place)* trece *m*; *(part)* trezavo, decimotercera parte II. adj. *(place)* decimotercero; *(part)* trezavo.

thir·ti·eth (thûr′tē-ĭth) I. s. *(place)* treinta *m*; *(part)* treintavo, trigésima parte II. adj. *(place)* trigésimo; *(part)* treintavo.

thir·ty (thûr′tē) adj. & s. [pl. **-ties**] treinta *m*.

thir·ty-one (thûr′tē-wŭn′) s. & adj. treinta y uno.

this §G24, 33 (thĭs) I. pron. [pl. **these** (thēz)] éste, ésta, esto <*t. is my cat* éste es mi gato> II. adj. [pl. **these**] este, esta <*she left early t. morning* partió temprano esta mañana> • **t. way** *(direction)* por aquí, por acá; *(manner)* de este modo, así III. adv. tan <*I have never stayed up t. late* nunca me he quedado levantado tan tarde>; así de <*it was t. long* era así de largo> • **t. much** esta cantidad, tanto <*they did not know it would cost t. much* ellos no sabían que costaría tanto>.

this·tle (thĭs′əl) s. cardo.

this·tle-down (thĭs′əl-doun′) s. vilano del cardo.

thith·er (thĭth′ər) I. adv. hacia allá, más allá II. adj. lejano.

tho (thō) FAM. var. de **though**.

Tho·mism (tō′mĭz′əm) s. FILOS., TEOL. tomismo.

thong (thông) s. *(strip)* tira de cuero, correa; *(whiplash)* tralla; *(sandal)* sandalia de tiras.

tho·ra·ces (thôr′ə-sēz′) un pl. de **thorax**.

tho·rac·ic (thə-răs′ĭk) adj. ANAT. torácico.

tho·rax (thôr′ăks′) s. [pl. **tho·rax·es** o **tho·ra·ces** (thôr′ə-sēz′)] ANAT. tórax *m*, pecho; ENTOM. región media.

tho·ri·um (thôr′ē-əm) s. QUÍM. torio.

thorn (thôrn) s. BOT. *(woody spine)* espina; *(plant)* espino, endrino; *(prickle)* espina, púa; FIG. *(pain)* espina <*to have a t. in one's side* tener una espina clavada en el costado>.

thorn·y (thôr′nē) adj. -i·er, -i·est *(full of thorns)* espinoso; *(thornlike)* parecido a una espina; FIG., FAM. *(difficult)* espinoso, peliagudo.

thor·ough (thûr′ō) adj. *(complete)* completo; *(detailed)* detallado, minucioso; *(total)* total.

thor·ough·bred (thûr′ə-brĕd′) I. s. *(animal)* pura sangre *mf*; *(person)* persona bien nacida • **T.** caballo de carrera de pura sangre II. adj. *(animal)* de pura sangre, de buena raza; *(person)* bien nacido.

thor·ough·fare (thûr′ə-fâr′) s. *(highway)* carretera, camino principal; *(of a town)* calle *f*, vía publica; *(passage)* pasaje *m*, paso; *(heavily traveled passage)* vía o canal muy transitado • **no t.** *(no entry)* prohibido el paso; *(no exit)* calle sin salida.

thor·ough·go·ing (thûr′ə-gō′ĭng) adj. *(complete)* cabal, completo; FIG. *(unmitigated)* rematado <*a t. liar* un mentiroso rematado>.

thor·ough·ly (thûr′ə-lē) adv. *(completely)* completamente; *(totally)* totalmente.

thor·ough·ness (thûr′ə-nĭs) s. minuciosidad *f*.

those (thōz) pl. de **that**.

thou¹ (thou) pron. ANT., POÉT. tú.

thou² (thou) s. JER. mil (dólares) *m*.

though (thō) I. conj. *(although)* aunque, a pesar de que <*t. it was raining* aunque llovía>; *(even if)* aunque <*t. they* *may not succeed, they will be happier* aunque no tengan éxito, estarán más contentos> ◊ **as t.** como si • **even t.** aunque <*even t. he doesn't want to do that* aunque él no quiere hacerlo> **II.** adv. sin embargo, no obstante <*it is not so easy, t.* sin embargo, no es tan fácil>.

thought (thôt) **I.** pret. y part. p. de **think II.** s. *(act)* pensamiento; *(idea)* idea <*a happy t.* una idea feliz>; *(philosophy)* filosofía, pensamiento <*the t. of Kant* la filosofía de Kant>; *(consideration)* consideración *f* <*he has no t. for his friends* no tiene consideración con sus amigos>; *(intention, purpose)* intención *f*, propósito <*I had no t. of offending you* no tenía la intención de ofenderle>; *(opinion)* opinión *f*, punto de vista <*she keeps her thoughts to herself* ella no revela sus opiniones> ◊ **a t.** FIG., FAM. *(a bit)* un poquito • **at the t. of** al pensar en • **on second t.** pensándolo bien • **that's a t.!** ¡buena idea! • **the mere t. of it** sólo en pensarlo • **to be lost in t.** estar absorto en meditación • **to collect one's thoughts** pensar, concentrarse <*let me collect my thoughts* déjame pensar> • **to fall into deep t.** ensimismarse • **to give t. to something** pensar en, considerar algo • **to have thoughts of doing something** tener la intención de hacer algo • **to read somebody's thoughts** adivinar los pensamientos de alguien.

thought·ful (thôt'fəl) adj. *(contemplative)* pensativo, meditabundo; *(well thought out)* bien pensado, serio <*a t. essay* un ensayo serio>; *(considerate)* atento, solícito <*he is very t. of others* es muy solícito con los demás> ◊ **how t. of you!** ¡es usted muy amable!

thought·ful·ly (thôt'fə-lē) adv. *(pensively)* pensativamente, con aire pensativo; *(with consideration)* atentamente, con consideración.

thought·ful·ness (thôt'fəl-nĭs) s. *(meditation)* meditación *f*; *(seriousness)* seriedad *f*; *(solicitude)* solicitud *f*, cuidado.

thought·less (thôt'lĭs) adj. *(unthinking)* irreflexivo, imprudente; *(careless)* descuidado; *(inconsiderate)* falto de consideración, desatento.

thou·sand (thou'zənd) **I.** s. *(numeral)* mil *m*; *(bulk)* millar *m* <*bricks are sold by the t.* los ladrillos se venden por millar> ◊ **in** o **by the thousands** a millares **II.** adj. mil <*a t. voices* mil voces>.

thou·sandth (thou'zəndth) **I.** s. *(place)* mil *m*; *(part)* milésimo, milésima parte **II.** adj. *(place, part)* milésimo.

Thrace (thrās) s. Tracia.

thrall (thrôl) **I.** s. *(slave)* esclavo, siervo; *(slavery)* esclavitud *f*, servidumbre **II.** tr. ANT. esclavizar.

thrash (thrăsh) **I.** tr. *(to flog)* azotar, zurrar; *(to flail)* sacudir, agitar; *(to vanquish)* derrotar, aplastar; AGR. trillar, desgranar; MARÍT. navegar contra el viento ◊ **to t. out** discutir a fondo —intr. sacudirse, agitarse; MARÍT. navegar contra viento o marea **II.** s. *(flogging)* azotaina; *(swimming kick)* patada, patada.

thrash·er (thrăsh'ər) s. ORNIT. sinsonte *m*, cenzontle *m*.

thrash·ing (thrăsh'ĭng) s. *(flogging)* azotaina, zurra; AGR. trilla.

thread (thrĕd) **I.** s. *(for sewing, weaving)* hilo; *(fiber)* fibra; *(strand)* hebra; *(of light)* rayo; FIG. *(continuity)* hilo, continuidad *f* <*the t. of a story* el hilo de una historia>; MEC. filete *m*, rosca; MIN. filón *m*, veta ◊ **threads** JER. ropa, trapos • **to be hanging by a t.** FIG. estar pendiente de un hilo • **to lose the t.** FIG. perder el hilo • **to pick up the t. again** FIG. coger el hilo, reanudar **II.** tr. *(a needle)* ensartar, enhebrar; *(beads)* ensartar; *(film, tape)* cargar con; *(screw, nut)* filetear, roscar ◊ **to t. one's way through** FIG. abrirse paso por —intr. ◊ **to t. through** colarse o deslizarse por.

thread·bare (thrĕd'bâr') adj. *(cloth)* raído, gastado; *(person)* andrajoso; FIG. *(trite)* trillado.

thread·y (thrĕd'ē) adj. **-i·er, -i·est** *(filamentous)* fibroso, filamentoso; *(viscid)* viscoso; *(weak)* débil.

threat (thrĕt) **I.** s. amenaza **II.** tr. ANT. amenazar.

threat·en (thrĕt'n) tr. & intr. amenazar.

threat·en·ing·ly (thrĕt'n-ĭng-lē) adv. de modo amenazador, amenazantemente.

three (thrē) s. & adj. tres *m* ◊ **t. o'clock** las tres.

three-D o **3-D** (thrē'dē') **I.** adj. tridimensional **II.** s. representación tridimensional *f*.

three-deck·er (thrē'dĕk'ər) s. *(ship)* barco de tres cubiertas; *(sandwich)* emparedado de tres pisos de pan.

three-di·men·sion·al (thrē'dĭ-mĕn'shə-nəl, -dī-) adj. tridimensional.

three·fold (thrē'fōld') **I.** adj. triple **II.** adv. tres veces.

three hundred s. & adj. trescientos.

three·pen·ny (thrĭp'ə-nē, thrŭp'-) adj. G.B. *(worth)* de tres peniques; FIG. *(trifling)* de poco valor, barato.

three-piece (thrē'pēs') adj. de tres piezas <*a t. suit* traje de tres piezas>.

three-point landing (thrē'point') s. AVIA. aterrizaje en tres puntos *m*.

three-quar·ter (thrē'kwôr'tər) adj. de tres cuartos.

three-ring circus (thrē'rĭng') s. *(circus)* circo de tres arenas; FIG. *(confusion)* confusión *f*, caos *m*.

three R's s.pl. EDUC., FAM. lectura, escritura y aritmética.

three-score (thrē'skôr') s. sesenta.

three·some (thrē'səm) **I.** adj. triple **II.** s. grupo de tres, trío.

thresh (thrĕsh) tr. *(grain, cereal)* trillar, desgranar; *(issue, idea)* machacar; *(to thrash)* azotar —intr. *(grain, cereal)* trillar granos; *(to toss)* revolverse, agitarse.

thresh·er (thrĕsh'ər) s. *(person)* trillador *m*; *(machine)* trilladora; *(shark)* zorra marina.

threshing machine s. trilladora.

thresh·old (thrĕsh'ōld', -hōld') s. umbral *m*.

threw (thrōō) pret. de **throw.**

thrice (thrīs) adv. tres veces.

thrift (thrĭft) s. *(economy)* economía, ahorro; BIOL. crecimiento.

thrift·i·ness (thrĭf'tē-nĭs) s. economía, ahorro.

thrift·less (thrĭft'lĭs) adj. *(lacking value)* de poco valor; *(wasteful)* despilfarrador, derrochador.

thrift shop s. tienda de gangas.

thrift·y (thrĭf'tē) adj. **-i·er, -i·est** *(frugal)* económico, ahorrativo; *(prosperous)* progresista; *(thriving)* floreciente.

thrill (thrĭl) **I.** tr. *(to excite)* excitar, emocionar; *(to mesmerize)* hacer vibrar, electrizar; *(to delight)* encantar, deleitar —intr. estremecerse, temblar **II.** s. *(quiver)* temblor *m*, estremecimiento; *(excitement)* emoción *f*; MED. tremor *m*, vibración *f*.

thrill·er (thrĭl'ər) s. FAM. *(book)* novela de aventuras excitantes; *(movie)* película de aventuras excitantes.

thrive (thrīv) intr. **throve** (thrōv) o **thrived, thrived** o **thriv·en** (thrĭv'ən), **thriv·ing** *(to prosper)* prosperar, medrar; *(to flourish)* crecer; *(to develop)* desarrollarse con fuerza.

throat (thrōt) **I.** s. *(neck)* cuello; ANAT. garganta; GEOG. paso, garganta; TEC. tragante o boca de horno) *m* ◊ **to clear one's t.** aclararse la voz • **to cut one's own t.** FIG. arruinarse a sí mismo • **to jump down someone's t.** regañar, saltarle encima a alguien • **to ram down someone's t.** meterle a alguien por las narices **II.** tr. decir con voz áspera o gutural.

throat·y (thrō'tē) adj. **-i·er, -i·est** gutural, ronco.

throb (thrŏb) **I.** intr. **throbbed, throb·bing** *(to beat)* latir, palpitar; *(with pain)* dar punzadas; *(motors)* vibrar; *(engines)* zumbar **II.** s. *(beat)* latido, palpitación *f*; *(of pain)* punzada; *(of engines)* zumbido; *(vibration)* vibración *f*.

throe (thrō) s. espasmo, punzada ◊ **in the throes of** en medio de, en los dolores o suplicio de • **throes** *(of death)* ansias, agonía; *(of childbirth)* dolores.

throm·bin (thrŏm'bĭn) s. BIOQUÍM. trombina.

throm·bo·sis (thrŏm-bō'sĭs) s. MED. trombosis *f*.

throm·bus (thrŏm'bəs) s. [pl. **-bi** (-bī')] MED. trombo.

throne (thrōn) **I.** s. trono ◊ **thrones** RELIG. ángeles **II.** tr. **throned, thron·ing** entronizar, poner en el trono —intr. ocupar el trono.

throng (thrông) **I.** s. *(crowd)* gentío, muchedumbre *f*; *(host)* montón *m*, multitud *f* **II.** tr. *(to crowd into)* atestar, llenar <*the customers were thronging the showroom* los clientes llenaban la sala de exposición>; *(to press in on)* apretar, aplastar —intr. *(to gather)* amontonarse, apiñarse; *(to flock)* afluir.

throt·tle[1] (thrŏt'l) s. FAM. *(throat)* gaznate *m*, garguero *m*; *(windpipe)* tráquea; TEC. válvula de admisión o de estrangulación.

---

throt·tle² (thrŏt'l) tr. **-tled, -tling** FAM. *(to choke)* estrangular, ahogar; FIG. *(to suppress)* suprimir; TEC. estrangular, obturar (gases, vapores) ♦ **to t. back** *o* **down** reducir la velocidad de.

through (thrōō) I. prep. por <*we went t. the tunnel* fuimos por el túnel>; *(among)* a través de <*a walk t. the wheat fields* una caminata a través de los trigales>; *(by way of)* por <*I climbed in t. the window* entré por la ventana>; *(by the agency of)* por medio de, a través de <*we got this antique t. a friend* conseguimos esta antigüedad a través de un amigo>; *(during)* durante <*I've applied this principle all t. my life* he aplicado este principio durante toda mi vida>; entre <*I found it as I was going t. her papers* lo encontré mientras buscaba entre sus papeles>; *(from beginning to end of)* durante, del principio al fin de <*t. the summer* del principio al fin del verano>; *(because of)* por <*it was done t. error* se hizo por error>; de . . . a, desde . . . hasta <*open Monday t. Friday* abierto de lunes a viernes>; *(thanks to)* gracias a, a causa de <*I have succeeded t. hard work* he triunfado gracias al gran esfuerzo que realicé> ♦ **to have been t. it all** haberlas pasado, haber pasado por momentos muy malos II. adv. *(from one end to another)* de un lado al otro; *(from beginning to end)* hasta el final, desde el principio hasta el fin <*I stayed right t.* me quedé hasta el final>; *(completely)* completamente <*to be soaked t.* estar completamente empapado> ♦ **t. and t.** *(completely)* completamente; *(throughout)* hasta los tuétanos <*to be soaked t. and t.* estar empapado hasta los tuétanos> • **to carry something t.** llevar algo a cabo • **to fall t.** fracasar III. adj. *(direct)* directo <*a t. bus* un autobús directo>; de paso libre, de vía libre <*a t. street* una calle de vía libre>; *(washed-up)* acabado <*she is t. as a pianist* está acabada como pianista> ♦ **to be t.** *(to have finished)* haber terminado; *(not to be able to take it)* no poder más • **to be t. with** *(to have finished)* haber terminado con <*he is t. with the project* ha terminado con el proyecto>; *(to be fed up with)* haber terminado con, no querer ver más a.

through·out (thrōō-out') I. prep. *(all through)* por todo, en todo <*t. the world* en todo el mundo>; *(during every part of)* durante todo, a lo largo de <*t. the season* durante toda la temporada> II. adv. *(everywhere)* por todas partes <*she cleaned the house t.* ha limpiado la casa por todas partes>; *(completely)* completamente; *(during the entire time)* desde el principio hasta el final, todo el tiempo.

through·way (thrōō'wā') s. var. de **thruway.**

throve (thrōv') un pret. de **thrive.**

throw (thrō) I. tr. **threw** (thrōō), **thrown** (thrōn), **throw·ing** *(to cast)* tirar, arrojar <*to t. a stone* arrojar una piedra>; *(punches, jabs)* dar, asestar; *(into the air)* disparar (a), lanzar (a) <*a cannon that throws a shell ten miles* un cañón que dispara proyectiles a diez millas>; *(to the ground, floor)* desmontar, echar por tierra <*the horse threw its rider* el caballo echó por tierra al jinete>; *(an opponent)* derribar, tumbar; *(pottery)* modelar; *(fibers)* torcer; *(dice)* tirar, echar; *(to roll with dice)* sacar <*t. a six* sacar un seis>; *(a scene)* hacer; *(a glance)* echar, dirigir; *(a party)* dar; *(a lever)* echar, conectar; FAM. *(to lose a contest)* perder adrede *o* intencionalmente ♦ **to t. a bridge** tender un puente • **to t. a fit** enfurecerse • **to t. aside** echar a un lado, desechar • **to t. away** *(to hurl)* tirar, arrojar; *(to waste)* desperdiciar, malgastar; *(to squander)* despilfarrar, malgastar; *(to miss)* desaprovechar, desperdiciar; *(to discard)* deshacerse de, desechar • **to t. back** *(to hinder progress)* retrasar <*this situation will t. the schedule back one month* esta situación retrasará el programa un mes>; *(to reflect)* reflejar; *(to return)* devolver; *(to push back)* echar hacia atrás • **to t. down** echar por tierra, derribar • **to t. in** *(to add)* añadir, dar de más; *(to interject)* intercalar, insertar • **to t. in the clutch** embragar • **to t. in the sponge** *o* **towel** tirar la esponja *o* la toalla • **to t. light on a subject** aclarar un asunto, esclarecer algo • **to t. off** *(to reject)* desechar, deshacerse de; *(to emit)* despedir; *(to give up)* renunciar • **to t. on** echarse encima, ponerse rápidamente • **to t. oneself at** lanzarse sobre • **to t. oneself away** sacrificarse tontamente • **to t. oneself into** lanzarse en • **to t. out** *(to reject)* rechazar <*the committee threw out her proposal* el

comité rechazó su propuesta>; *(to throw away)* tirar • **to t. over** *(to abandon)* abandonar; *(to overturn)* derrocar • **to t. overboard** tirar por la borda, echar al agua • **to t. someone in jail** meter a alguien en la cárcel • **to t. up** *(to abandon)* dejar, abandonar; *(to relinquish)* renunciar a; *(to raise)* levantar, alzar; *(into the air)* lanzar al aire; *(to construct hurriedly)* construir rápidamente —intr. arrojar, lanzar ♦ **to t. up** vomitar, devolver II. s. *(act)* lanzamiento, tiro; *(of dice)* lance *m*; *(coverlet)* colcha, cobertor *m*; *(rug)* alfombra pequeña; GEOL. dislocación *f*, falla; MIN. desviación *f*.

throw·a·way (thrō'ə-wā') I. s. volante *m* II. adj. *(disposable)* desechable, para tirar; FIG. *(offhand)* casual.

throw·back (thrō'băk') s. retroceso.

throw·er (thrō'ər) s. *(of dice)* jugador de dados *m*; DEP. lanzador *m*.

thrown (thrōn) part. p. de **throw.**

throw rug s. alfombra pequeña.

thru (thrōō) FAM. consulte **through.**

thrum¹ (thrŭm) I. intr. **thrummed, thrum·ming** sonar monótonamente II. s. sonido monótono.

thrum² (thrŭm) I. s. *(on a loom)* cabo de la urdimbre; *(fringe)* fleco, cairel *m* ♦ **thrums** MARÍT. cabos cortos para hacer palletes II. tr. **thrummed, thrum·ming** *(to fringe)* guarnecer con flecos *o* caireles; MARÍT. hacer palletes.

thrush (thrŭsh) s. ORNIT. tordo, zorzal *m*.

thrust (thrŭst) I. tr. **thrust, thrust·ing** *(to push)* meter con fuerza; *(to stab)* clavar <*to t. a knife into someone's chest* clavarle un puñal en el pecho a alguien>; *(to put in)* meter <*to t. the hand into a pocket* meter la mano en un bolsillo>; FIG. *(to force oneself into)* meterse en ♦ **to t. at** asestar un golpe a • **to t. through** atravesar • **to t. upon** imponer —intr. *(to push)* empujar, dar un empujón; *(to stab)* dar una puñalada; *(to force one's way)* abrirse paso (por la fuerza); FIG. *(to butt in)* entrometerse II. s. *(push)* empujón *m*, embestida; *(stab)* puñalada, estocada; FIG. *(direction)* dirección *f*; *(impetus)* ímpetu, energía; FÍS., ASTRONÁUT. empuje *m*, fuerza propulsora; ARQ. empuje.

thru·way (thrōō'wā') s. autopista, carretera directa.

thud (thŭd) I. s. *(sound)* ruido sordo; *(blow)* batacazo, golpe seco II. intr. **thud·ded, thud·ding** dar un batacazo, hacer un ruido sordo.

thug (thŭg) s. *(hoodlum)* maleante *m*, matón *m*; HIST. asesino fanático de una secta de la India.

thu·li·um (thōō'lē-əm, thyōō'-) s. QUÍM. tulio.

thumb (thŭm) I. s. ANAT. pulgar *m*; ARQ. óvalo, cuarto bocel *m* ♦ **thumbs up!** FAM. ¡buena suerte! • **to be all thumbs** ser torpe *o* desmañado • **to be thumbs down on** estar en contra de II. tr. *(to finger)* manosear; FAM. *(a ride)* hacer dedo a —intr. *(to hitchhike)* hacer dedo *o* autostop ♦ **to t. one's nose** hacer un palmo de narices • **to t. through** hojear.

thumb index s. uñeros, índice alfabético al borde de las páginas de un libro de consulta.

thumb·nail (thŭm'nāl') I. s. uña del pulgar II. adj. *(small)* pequeño, minúsculo; *(brief)* breve, conciso ♦ **t. sketch** cuadro conciso.

thumb·screw (thŭm'skrōō') s. MEC. tornillo de mariposa *o* de orejas.

thumb·tack (thŭm'tăk') I. s. chinche *f*, chincheta II. tr. sujetar con una chinche *o* chincheta.

thump (thŭmp) I. s. *(heavy blow)* puñetazo, porrazo; *(noise)* ruido sordo, baque *m* II. tr. *(to beat)* golpear, aporrear; FIG. *(to drub)* derrotar completamente —intr. *(to pound)* golpear, aporrear; *(to stump)* caminar pesadamente; *(to throb)* latir violentamente.

thump·ing (thŭm'pĭng) adj. FAM. enorme, colosal.

thun·der (thŭn'dər) I. s. METEOR. trueno; FIG. *(roar)* estruendo, estrépito II. intr. *(to produce thunder)* tronar, hacer sonar como trueno; *(to vociferate)* vociferar, tronar (encolerizado) —tr. vociferar.

thun·der·bolt (thŭn'dər-bōlt') s. METEOR. rayo; FIG. *(bomb)* rayo, bomba <*the news hit us like a t.* la noticia nos cayó como una bomba>.

thun·der·clap (thŭn'dər-klăp') s. METEOR. trueno; FIG. *(bomb)* bomba.

ã rey / ä año / b boca / ch chico / d dar / ĕ el / ē mil / g gato / h joya / hw juez / ī aire / k casa / kw cuan /

thun·der·cloud (thŭn'dər-kloud') s. METEOR. nubarrón *m*; FIG. *(menace)* nubarrón <*thunderclouds of impending war* nubarrones de guerra inminente>.

thun·der·head (thŭn'dər-hĕd') s. METEOR. masa de nubes.

thun·der·ous (thŭn'dər-əs) adj. *(producing thunder)* que truena; *(loud)* estruendoso, atronador; *(deafening)* ensordecedor <*a t. ovation* una ovación ensordecedora>.

thun·der·show·er (thŭn'dər-shou'ər) s. METEOR. borrasca con truenos y lluvia.

thun·der·storm (thŭn'dər-stôrm') s. METEOR. tormenta.

thun·der·struck (thŭn'dər-strŭk') adj. atónito, asombrado.

thu·ri·ble (thŏŏr'ə-bəl) s. RELIG. incensario.

thu·ri·fer (thŏŏr'ə-fər) s. RELIG. turiferario.

Thurs·day (thûrz'dē) s. jueves *m*.

thus (thŭs) adv. *(in this manner)* así, de esta manera; *(therefore)* así que, por eso ♦ **t. far** hasta aquí, hasta ahora.

thus·ly (thŭs'lē) adv. *(in this manner)* así, de esta manera; *(therefore)* así que, por eso.

thwack (thwăk) I. tr. golpear, aporrear (esp. con tabla) II. s. golpe fuerte y sonoro (con algo plano).

thwart (thwôrt) I. tr. *(plan, idea)* frustrar, desbaratar; *(person)* contrariar, frustrar II. s. banco, bancada (de un bote).

thy (thī) adj. pos. ANT. tu, tus.

thyme (tīm) s. BOT. tomillo.

thy·mus (thī'məs) s. ANAT. timo.

thy·roid (thī'roid') I. adj. tiroideo, de la tiroides II. s. ANAT. tiroides *f*; FARM. tiroidina.

thyroid gland s. ANAT. glándula tiroides.

thy·rox·in (thī-rŏk'sĭn) o **thy·rox·ine** (-sēn', -sĭn) s. BIOQUÍM. tiroxina.

thy·self (thī-sĕlf') pron. reflex. ANT. *(yourself)* te <*dress t. quickly* vístete pronto>; *(emphatic)* tú mismo, ti mismo <*love thy neighbor as t.* ama a tu prójimo como a ti mismo>.

ti (tē) s. MÚS. si *m*.

ti·ar·a (tē-ăr'ə, -ä'rə) s. *(papal crown)* tiara; *(headpiece)* diadema.

Ti·bet (tĭ-bĕt') s. Tíbet *m*.

Ti·bet·an (tĭ-bĕt'n) adj. & s. tibetano.

tib·i·a (tĭb'ē-ə) s. [pl. **-i·ae** (-ē-ē') o **-i·as**] ANAT. tibia; ENTOM. cuarta articulación en la pata de los insectos.

tic (tĭk) s. MED. tic *m*.

tick¹ (tĭk) I. s. *(of a clock)* tictac *m*; *(mark)* marca, señal *f*; G.B. *(moment)* momento, instante *m* II. intr. hacer tictac ♦ **to t. away** pasar, transcurrir —tr. contar, registrar (por medio de tictacs); *(to mark off)* marcar con una señal ♦ **to t. off** JER. *(to make angry)* enojar, irritar.

tick² (tĭk) ENTOM. s. garrapata.

tick³ (tĭk) s. *(case)* funda (de colchón, almohada); *(ticking)* cotí (tela fuerte de algodón) *m*.

tick·er (tĭk'ər) s. TELEG. teletipo, teleimpresor (usado en la bolsa) *m*; FAM. *(watch)* reloj *m*; JER. *(heart)* corazón *m*.

ticker tape s. TELEG. cinta de teleimpresor.

tick·et (tĭk'ĭt) s. *(for transport)* billete *m*, boleto; *(for movies, theater)* entrada, boleto; *(permit)* pase *m*; *(label)* etiqueta (de precio); *(summons)* boleta <*speeding t.* boleta por exceso de velocidad>; *(license)* título <*captain's t.* título de capitán>; *(of ration book)* cupón *m* ♦ **coatroom t.** número de guardarropa • **complimentary t.** entrada de favor • **one-way t.** boleto de ida • **round-trip t.** boleto de ida y vuelta • **that's the t.!** ¡eso es!, ¡muy bien! II. tr. *(to sell ticket to)* vender billete a; *(to label)* etiquetar; *(a motorist)* darle una boleta a.

ticket agent s. *(travel agent)* agente de viajes *mf*; *(seller)* vendedor de billetes *m*, taquillero.

ticket office s. taquilla, boletería.

ticket window s. taquilla, boletería.

tick·ing (tĭk'ĭng) s. cotí (tela fuerte de algodón) *m*.

tick·le (tĭk'əl) I. tr. **-led, -ling** *(to touch the body lightly)* hacer cosquillas, cosquillear; *(to titillate)* excitar agradablemente; *(to delight)* halagar, deleitar ♦ **tickled to death** contentísimo • **to t. pink** FAM. encantar, halagar —intr. sentir cosquillas o hormiguear II. s. cosquilleo, hormigueo.

tick·ler (tĭk'lər) s. *(thing)* algo que cosquillea o pica; *(memory aid)* aviso en la agenda o diario.

tick·lish (tĭk'lĭsh) adj. *(sensitive to tickling)* cosquilloso; FIG. *(touchy)* quisquilloso, susceptible; *(problem, situation)* delicado, espinoso.

tick·tack·toe o **tick-tack-toe** (tĭk'tăk'tō') s. tres en raya (juego) *m*.

tick·tock (tĭk'tŏk') s. tictac (de un reloj de péndulo) *m*.

tid·al (tīd'l) adj. *(having tides)* de marea; *(dependent upon the tide)* regulado por la marea.

tidal wave s. MARÍT. marejada, oleada (causada por tormenta, terremoto); FIG. *(manifestation)* marejada, oleada <*a t. of public anger* una oleada de indignación pública>.

tid·bit (tĭd'bĭt') s. *(choice morsel)* bocado; FIG. *(gossip)* chisme *m*.

tide (tīd) I. s. *(of the oceans)* marea, flujo y reflujo; *(current)* corriente *f*, flujo; FIG. *(wave)* ola, corriente <*t. of opinion* corriente de opinión>; *(season)* temporada, estación *f* <*Christmastide* estación navideña>; ANT. *(opportunity)* oportunidad *f*, ocasión favorable *f* II. intr. **tid·ed, tid·ing** navegar con la marea ♦ **to t. in** o **out** entrar o salir con la marea —tr. hacer llevar o arrastrar con la marea ♦ **to t. one over** bastarle a uno <*ten dollars will t. me over till Monday* con diez dólares me bastará hasta el lunes>.

tide·land (tīd'lănd') s. marisma, terreno inundable por la marea.

tide·wa·ter (tīd'wô'tər) s. *(water)* agua de marea; *(land)* tierras bajas del litoral.

tid·ings (tī'dĭngz) s.pl. nuevas, noticias.

ti·dy (tī'dē) I. adj. **-di·er, -di·est** *(neat)* ordenado, arreglado; *(clean)* limpio, pulcro <*a t. apartment* un apartamento pulcro>; FAM. *(adequate)* adecuado, satisfactorio; *(substantial)* substancial, considerable <*a t. sum* una cantidad considerable> II. tr. **-died, -dy·ing** ♦ **to t. up** *(to put in order)* ordenar, arreglar; *(to clean)* limpiar —intr. ♦ **to t. up** *(to put in order)* sentar orden, ordenar; *(to clean)* limpiar III. s. [pl. **-dies**] cobertura para los brazos o respaldo de un sillón.

tie (tī) I. tr. **tied, ty·ing** *(to fasten)* atar, liar; *(to knot)* hacer un nudo a, anudar; FIG. *(to restrict)* atar, limitar <*tied to his job* atado a su trabajo>; *(to link)* ligar, vincular <*tied by common interests* ligados por intereses comunes> ♦ **to be tied hand and foot** FIG. estar pies y manos ♦ **to t. down** atar, sujetar • **to t. in** *(to bring together)* conectar, relacionar • **to t. the knot** FIG. casarse • **to t. up** *(to fasten)* atar, envolver; *(to confine)* restringir, limitar <*she's tied up with her family* se limita a su vida de familia>; *(traffic)* obstruir, bloquear; *(boat)* amarrar, atracar; *(capital)* invertir, inmovilizar —intr. *(to be fastened)* atarse; *(to draw)* empatar <*the two candidates tied* los dos candidatos empataron> ♦ **to t. in (with)** relacionarse (con) II. s. *(cord)* cuerda, atadura; *(necktie)* corbata; *(rail support)* traviesa; *(draw)* empate *m*; *(tie beam)* tirante *m*; FIG. *(bond)* lazo, vínculo <*the ties of blood* los lazos del parentesco>; *(attachment)* atadura <*marital ties* ataduras del matrimonio>.

tie-in (tī'ĭn') s. relación *f*, conexión *f*.

tie line s. TEL., ELEC. línea de enlace o unión.

tie-pin (tī'pĭn') s. alfiler de corbata *m*.

tier¹ (tîr) I. s. *(row)* fila, hilera <*t. of guns* hilera de cañones>; *(in an amphitheater)* grada; *(at a theater)* fila de palcos; *(of a cake)* piso II. tr. disponer en gradas o en filas —intr. estar dispuesto en gradas o en filas.

ti·er² (tī'ər) s. persona que ata.

tierce (tîrs) s. RELIG. tercia; *(capacity)* 42 galones; *(in cards)* tercia; *(in fencing)* tercera (en esgrima).

tie-up (tī'ŭp') s. paralización *f*, interrupción *f*.

tiff (tĭf) I. s. *(irritation)* pique *m*, disgusto; *(quarrel)* riña, pelea II. intr. reñir, pelear.

ti·ger (tī'gər) s. ZOOL. tigre *m*; FAM. *(person)* tigre, fiera.

tiger lily s. lirio de tigre, azucena atigrada.

tight (tīt) I. adj. **-er, -est** *(screw, knot)* apretado; *(sealed)* hermético; *(faucet, lid)* bien cerrado; *(clothes, shoes)* ajustado; *(opening)* estrecho; *(rope, situation)* tenso, tirante; FIG. *(strict)* estricto, severo <*t. control* control estricto>; *(stingy)* tacaño; *(with words)* callado, reservado; *(money, credit)* escaso; *(closely contested)* reñido, disputado <*a very t. match* un partido muy reñido> ♦ **as t. as a drum**

muy tirante • **to be in a t. corner** *o* **spot** FIG. estar en un aprieto • **to be t.** JER. estar borracho • **to get t.** JER. emborracharse **II.** adv. *(firmly)* bien, fuertemente <**to hold something t.** agarrar algo fuertemente>; *(soundly)* profundamente ♦ **hold t.!** ¡agárrense bien! • **to sit t.** *(to wait)* cruzarse de brazos; *(to be quiet)* estarse quieto.

tight·en (tīt'n) tr. *(a knot, screw)* apretar; *(a cord)* tensar; *(bonds)* estrechar ♦ **to t. one's belt** FIG. apretarse el cinturón —intr. *(knot, screw)* apretarse; *(control, situation)* volverse más estricto.

tight·fist·ed (tīt'fĭs'tĭd) adj. FAM. tacaño, avaro.

tight·lipped (tīt'lĭpt') adj. *(having the lips pressed)* con los labios apretados; *(reticent)* reservado, callado.

tight·ly (tīt'lē) adv. *(firmly)* bien, fuertemente; *(soundly)* profundamente.

tight·ness (tīt'nĭs) s. *(quality)* estrechez *f*; *(of screws, nuts)* lo apretado; *(tension)* tensión *f*, tirantez *f*; FIG. *(stinginess)* tacañería.

tight·rope (tīt'rōp') s. cuerda floja.

tights (tīts) s.pl. malla (esp. de bailarines, acróbatas).

tight·wad (tīt'wŏd') s. JER. tacaño, avaro.

ti·gress (tī'grĭs) s. ZOOL. tigresa; *(woman)* fiera, tigresa.

tike (tīk) s. var. de **tyke.**

til·de (tĭl'də) s. tilde *f*.

tile (tīl) **I.** s. *(of a roof)* teja; *(of a floor)* losa, baldosa; *(of a wall)* azulejo; *(drainpipe)* tubo de desagüe; *(tiling)* enlosado; *(of a game)* pieza **II.** tr. **tiled, til·ing** *(a roof)* tejar; *(a floor)* embaldosar; *(a wall)* azulejar.

til·ing (tī'lĭng) s. *(laying of tiles)* colocación de tejas *o* baldosas *f*; *(of a floor)* embaldosado; *(floor tiles)* baldosas; *(wall tiles)* azulejos.

till[1] (tĭl) tr. AGR. labrar, cultivar.

till[2] (tĭl) **I.** prep. hasta, hasta donde **II.** conj. hasta que.

till[3] (tĭl) s. *(container for money)* caja, cajón *m*.

till·age (tĭl'ĭj) s. AGR. labranza, cultivo.

till·er[1] (tĭl'ər) s. AGR. labrador *m*, agricultor *m*.

til·ler[2] (tĭl'ər) s. MARÍT. caña del timón.

tilt (tĭlt) **I.** tr. *(to incline)* inclinar, ladear; HIST. *(to aim)* apuntar (una lanza); *(to charge)* arremeter a ♦ **to t. at windmills** FIG. arremeter contra molinos de viento —intr. *(to slope)* inclinarse, ladearse; HIST. *(to joust)* participar en una justa *o* en un torneo; *(to quarrel)* pelearse, reñir ♦ **to t. over** *(to lean)* inclinarse; *(to fall)* volcarse, caer **II.** s. *(slant)* inclinación *f*; *(joust)* torneo, justa; *(lance thrust)* lanzada ♦ **(at) full t.** a toda velocidad • **to be on a t.** estar inclinado.

tilth (tĭlth) AGR. s. *(cultivation)* cultivo, labranza; *(land)* tierra cultivada.

tim·bal (tĭm'bəl) s. MÚS. timbal *m*.

tim·ber (tĭm'bər) **I.** s. *(trees)* árboles maderables *o* para madera *m*; *(lumber)* maderamen *m*, madera para construcción; *(beam)* viga; MARÍT. cuaderna; FIG. *(material)* material *m*, madera <*he is executive t.* tiene madera de ejecutivo> **II.** tr. *(to provide with timbers)* enmaderar; *(a mine)* entibar; MARÍT. enramar.

tim·bered (tĭm'bərd) adj. *(constructed, covered)* enmaderado; *(a mine)* entibado; *(wooded)* arbolado, boscoso.

tim·ber·land (tĭm'bər-lănd') s. bosque maderable *m*.

tim·ber·line *o* **timber line** (tĭm'bər-līn') s. altitud límite de la vegetación arbórea *f*.

timber wolf s. lobo gris.

tim·bre (tăm'bər, tĭm'-) s. FONÉT., MÚS. timbre *m*.

time (tīm) **I.** s. *(continuum)* tiempo <*a long period of t.* un período largo de tiempo>; *(moment)* momento *m*, *(instant)* instante *m*; *(period)* período, lapso, *(season)* estación *f*, temporada; *(era)* era, época; *(a specified time)* hora <*it is t. to get up* es la hora de levantarse>; *(occasion)* ocasión *f*, momento <*is this a good t. to talk to you?* ¿es éste un buen momento para hablar contigo?> *(instance)* vez *f* <*I've told you so many times already* te lo he dicho tantas veces ya>; *(lifetime)* vida; *(prison sentence)* condena <*he is doing t. for robbery* está cumpliendo una condena por robo>; MÚS. *(rhythm)* tiempo <*waltz t.* tiempo de vals>; *(tempo)* compás *m* <*you have to learn to keep t.* tienes que aprender a llevar el compás>; *(duration)* duración *f*; GRAM. tiempo ♦ **against t.** contra el reloj • **all in good t.** todo a su tiempo

• **all the t.** *(every moment)* todo el tiempo; *(always)* siempre • **a long t.** mucho tiempo • **a long t. ago** hace mucho tiempo • **(at) any t.** a cualquier hora, en cualquier momento • **a short t.** *(formal)* poco tiempo; *(informal)* un rato • **at all times** en todo momento • **at a t.** a la vez • **at no t.** en ningún momento, nunca • **at one t.** en cierta época, en un tiempo • **at some t.** en una *u* otra ocasión, en un momento *o* en otro • **at the present t.** al presente, en la actualidad • **at the same t.** a la vez, al mismo tiempo • **at the wrong t.** en un mal momento • **at times** a veces, a ratos • **behind the times** *(out-of-date)* atrasado; *(old-fashioned)* anticuado • **by that t.** para entonces • **each** *o* **every t.** cada vez • **for all t.** para siempre • **for some t.** durante algún tiempo • **for the t. being** por ahora, por el momento • **from this t.** desde hoy, a partir de ahora • **from this t. on** desde ahora en adelante • **from t. to t.** de cuando en cuando, de vez en cuando • **hard** *o* **bad t.** mal rato • **hard** *o* **bad times** tiempos difíciles • **have a good t.!** ¡que lo pasen bien!, ¡diviértanse! • **in a short t.** en breve, dentro de poco • **in due t.** en su día • **in no t. (at all)** en un abrir y cerrar de ojos • **in t.** *(on time)* a tiempo <*were you in t. for your bus?* ¿llegaste a tiempo para tomar tu autobús?>; *(with time)* con el tiempo <*I shall make it in t.* con el tiempo lograré lo que deseo>; MÚS. al compás • **many a time** *o* **many times** muchas veces • **on t.** a tiempo, puntual(mente) • **t. after t.** *o* **t. and t. again** muchas veces, repetidas veces • **t. is money** el tiempo es oro • **t. off** horas libres, tiempo libre • **time's up!** ¡es la hora! • **t. will tell** el tiempo dirá • **to be behind t.** estar retrasado • **to bide one's t.** esperar el momento propicio • **to keep good t.** andar bien (un reloj) • **to keep up with** *o* **abreast of the times** estar al tanto de las cosas, mantenerse informado • **to make t.** ganar tiempo • **to pass the t.** pasar el tiempo *o* el rato • **to pass** *o* **while the t. away** matar el tiempo • **to serve t.** cumplir una condena • **to take one's t.** tomarse tiempo • **to waste t.** perder el tiempo • **what is the t.?** ¿qué hora es? • **what t. is it?** ¿qué hora es? • **within the required t.** dentro del plazo fijado **II.** adj. *(relating to time)* del tiempo; de tiempo <*a t. bomb* una bomba de tiempo>; *(on installment)* a plazos **III.** tr. **timed, tim·ing** *(to set the time for)* fijar la hora *o* el tiempo de; *(to regulate)* regular, poner a la hora <*to t. one's watch with another's* poner el reloj de uno a la hora con el del otro>; *(to record)* cronometrar.

time bill s. COM. letra de cambio pagadera a tiempo determinado.

time bomb s. bomba de tiempo.

time capsule s. cápsula en la que se preserva información actual para las futuras generaciones.

time·card (tīm'kärd') s. tarjeta de marcar (de un trabajador).

time clock s. reloj registrador *m*.

timed (tīmd) adj. *(test, answer)* de duración limitada; DEP. *(car race)* cronometrado.

time deposit s. COM., FIN. depósito a término fijo.

time draft s. COM., FIN. orden de pago a plazo *f*, giro a plazo.

time exposure s. FOTOG. *(exposure)* exposición *f*; *(image)* pose de tiempo *f*.

time-hon·ored (tīm'ŏn'ərd) adj. tradicional, consagrado por el tiempo.

time immemorial s. tiempo inmemorial.

time·keep·er (tīm'kē'pər) s. *(timepiece)* cronómetro, reloj *m*; MÚS. marcador de tiempo *m*; DEP. cronometrador *m*.

time-lapse (tīm'lăps') adj. FOTOG. a intervalos.

time·less (tīm'lĭs) adj. *(eternal)* eterno, infinito; *(ageless)* sin limitación de tiempo; ANT. *(untimely)* prematuro.

time limit s. límite de tiempo *m*, plazo.

time·li·ness (tīm'lē-nĭs) s. *(punctuality)* puntualidad *f*; *(fitness of time)* oportunidad *f*.

time loan s. COM. préstamo a plazo fijo.

time lock s. cerradura que se abre a un determinado tiempo.

time·ly (tīm'lē) **I.** adj. **-li·er, -li·est** *(opportune)* oportuno; *(punctual)* puntual; ANT. *(early)* temprano, prematuro

---

ã rey / ä año / b boca / ch chico / d dar / ĕ el / ē mil / g gato / h joya / hw juez / ī aire / k casa / kw cuan

II. adv. *(opportunely)* oportunamente, a tiempo; ANT. *(early)* temprano, bien pronto.

time-out *o* **time out** (tīm'out') s. DEP. interrupción temporal (de un partido) *f*; FIG. *(break)* descanso, pausa.

time-piece (tīm'pēs') s. reloj *m*, cronómetro.

tim-er (tī'mər) s. *(timekeeper)* cronometrador *m*; *(timepiece)* cronómetro, cronógrafo; TEC., ELEC. regulador eléctrico; AUTO. distribuidor del encendido.

times (tīmz) prep. multiplicado por, por.

time-sav-ing (tīm'sā'vĭng) adj. que ahorra tiempo.

time-serv-er (tīm'sûr'vər) s. oportunista *mf*.

time-shar-ing (tīm'shâr'ĭng) s. COMPUT. tiempo compartido, red de comunicación electrónica *f*; *(joint ownership)* posesión *o* propiedad compartida.

time signature s. MÚS. compás *m*.

times sign s. MAT. el símbolo x (por).

time-ta-ble (tīm'tā'bəl) s. *(of classes, events)* horario; *(of trains, planes)* horario, guía.

time-work (tīm'wûrk') s. trabajo por hora.

time-worn (tīm'wôrn') adj. *(used)* usado, gastado; FIG. *(trite)* trillado, gastado.

time zone s. huso horario.

tim-id (tĭm'ĭd) adj. **-er, -est** *(hesitant)* temeroso; *(shy)* tímido.

ti-mid-i-ty (tĭ-mĭd'ĭ-tē) s. timidez *f*, temor *m*.

tim-ing (tī'mĭng) s. *(timeliness)* oportunidad *f*; MÚS. compás *m*, cadencia; DEP. ritmo, coordinación *f*; TEC., AUTO. regulación de tiempo (en el encendido).

tim-or-ous (tĭm'ər-əs) adj. timorato, miedoso.

tim-o-thy (tĭm'ə-thē) s. BOT. fleo.

Tim-o-thy (tĭm'ə-thē) s. BÍBL. Timoteo.

tim-pa-ni (tĭm'pə-nē) s.pl. MÚS. tímpanos, timbales *m*.

tim-pa-num (tĭm'pə-nəm) s. var. de **tympanum**.

tin (tĭn) **I.** s. *(metal)* estaño *m*; *(tin plate)* hojalata; *(container)* lata, bote *m; (for baking)* molde *m* **II.** tr. **tinned, tin-ning** *(to coat with tin)* estañar; G.B. *(to can)* enlatar, envasar.

tin can s. *(container)* lata, bote *m*; MARÍT., JER. *(destroyer)* destructor *m*.

tinc-ture (tĭngk'chər) **I.** s. *(dyeing substance)* colorante *m*, pigmento; *(hue)* color *m*, tinte *m*; *(trace)* traza, vestigio; QUÍM., FARM. tintura; HER. esmalte **II.** tr. **-tured, -tur-ing** *(to dye)* teñir; FIG. *(to imbue)* imbuir, impregnar.

tin-der (tĭn'dər) s. yesca, mecha.

tin-der-box (tĭn'dər-bŏks') s. *(box)* yesquero; FIG. *(place ready to blow up)* polvorín *m*.

tine (tīn) s. *(of a pitchfork)* punta, púa; *(of a fork)* diente *m*.

tin-foil *o* **tin foil** (tĭn'foil') s. papel de estaño *m*.

ting (tĭng) **I.** s. tintín, tintineo **II.** intr. tintinear, tintinar.

tinge (tĭnj) **I.** tr. **tinged, tinge-ing** *o* **ting-ing** *(to tint)* matizar, teñir; FIG. *(to affect slightly)* afectar ligeramente, matizar <happiness tinged with sadness una alegría matizada con tristeza> **II.** s. *(hue)* matiz *m*, tinte *m*; *(trace)* pizca, vestigio.

tin-gle (tĭng'gəl) **I.** intr. **-gled, -gling** *(with excitement, cold)* sentir picazón u hormigueo; *(with feelings)* estremecerse —tr. picar, causar picazón a **II.** s. *(a prickly sensation)* picazón *f*, hormigueo; *(quiver)* estremecimiento.

tin-horn (tĭn'hôrn') s. JER. fanfarrón de poca monta (esp. un jugador) *m*.

tin-ker (tĭng'kər) **I.** s. *(tinsmith)* calderero *o* hojalatero remendón; *(gypsy)* gitano; *(bungler)* chapucero **II.** intr. *(to work)* trabajar *o* remendar como calderero; *(to play)* entretenerse —tr. arreglar, componer ♦ **to t. with** *(to play with)* entretenerse con; *(to fiddle with)* toquetear.

tinker's damn *o* **tinker's dam** s. JER. bagatela, nadería ♦ **it's not worth a t.** no vale un comino.

tin-kle (tĭng'kəl) **I.** intr. **-kled, -kling** tintinear, tintinar —tr. hacer tintinear **II.** s. tintineo.

tin-kling (tĭng'klĭng) s. tintineo.

tin-ny (tĭn'ē) adj. **-ni-er, -ni-est** *(of tin)* de estaño, de hojalata; *(containing tin)* estañoso; *(sound)* metálico; *(flimsy)* falto de buen metal, frágil.

Tin Pan Alley *o* **tin-pan alley** (tĭn'păn') s. *(place)* distrito en Nueva York frecuentado por compositores de música popular; *(group)* compositores de música popular.

tin plate s. hojalata.

tin-plate (tĭn'plāt') tr. **-plat-ed, -plat-ing** estañar.

tin-sel (tĭn'səl) **I.** s. oropel *m* **II.** adj. de oropel **III.** tr. adornar con oropel.

tin-smith (tĭn'smĭth') s. hojalatero, estañero.

tint (tĭnt) **I.** s. *(color)* tinte *m*, color *m*; *(hair dye)* tinte para el cabello; *(hue)* matiz *m*, tono; *(trace)* traza, huella; ARTE. media tinta; IMPR. fondo **II.** tr. matizar, colorear.

tin-tin-nab-u-la-tion (tĭn'tĭ-năb'yə-lā'shən) s. tintineo.

tin-type (tĭn'tīp') s. FOTOG. ferrotipo.

tin-ware (tĭn'wâr') s. quincalla, artículos de hojalata.

tin-work (tĭn'wûrk') s. trabajo *o* artículo de estaño ♦ **tin-works** [ú. con v. sing. o pl.] *(factory)* fábrica de estaño.

ti-ny (tī'nē) adj. **-ni-er, -ni-est** diminuto, minúsculo.

tip¹ (tĭp) s. *(end)* punta, cabo; *(extremity)* extremidad *f*, extremo; *(apex)* ápice *m*, cúspide *f*; *(ferrule)* casquillo, virola; *(of a cigarrette)* filtro ♦ **from t. to toe** de pies a cabeza • **to have it on the t. of one's tongue** tenerlo en la punta de la lengua.

tip² (tĭp) **I.** tr. **tipped, tip-ping** *(to topple)* volcar, derribar; *(to tilt)* inclinar, ladear • **to t. one's hat to** saludar (con el sombrero) a • **to t. over** volcar, derribar —intr. *(to topple over)* volcar, derribar; *(to lean)* inclinarse, ladearse; G.B. *(to dump)* volcarse de golpe, descargarse ♦ **to t. off** caerse • **to t. over** volcarse **II.** s. *(slant)* inclinación *f*; G.B. *(slag heap)* escorial *m*, vertedero.

tip³ (tĭp) **I.** tr. **tipped, tip-ping** golpear ligeramente **II.** s. golpe ligero, golpecito.

tip⁴ (tĭp) **I.** s. *(gratuity)* propina; *(information)* información *f*; *(hint, advice)* consejo; DEP. dato **II.** tr. **tipped, tip-ping** *(with money)* dar una propina; *(with information)* dar una información a; DEP. pronosticar ♦ **to t. off** dar una pista *o* información a —intr. *(money)* dar propinas; *(information)* dar informes • **to t. one's hand** revelar uno sus verdaderas intenciones *o* recursos.

tip-cart (tĭp'kärt') s. AUTO. volquete *m*.

ti-pi (tē'pē) s. var. de **tepee**.

tip-off (tĭp'ôf') s. FAM. información *f*, soplo.

tip-pet (tĭp'ĭt) s. *(short cape)* palatina, esclavina; RELIG. estola larga usada por el clero anglicano.

tip-ple¹ (tĭp'əl) **I.** intr. **-pled, -pling** FAM. empinar el codo —tr. FAM. beber mucho y habitualmente **II.** s. FAM. bebida alcohólica, trago.

tip-ple² (tĭp'əl) s. mecanismo de vuelco para descarga.

tip-pler (tĭp'lər) s. FAM. borrachín *m*.

tip-ster (tĭp'stər) s. FAM. persona que vende pronósticos.

tip-sy (tĭp'sē) adj. **-si-er, -si-est** *(slightly drunk)* achispado, algo borracho; *(unsteady)* vacilante, tambaleante.

tip-toe (tĭp'tō') **I.** intr. **-toed, -toe-ing** *(to walk on the toes)* andar de puntillas; *(to walk stealthily)* andar sigilosamente **II.** s. punta del pie **III.** adj. *(on tiptoe)* de puntillas; *(stealthily)* sigiloso, cauteloso **IV.** adv. de puntillas.

tip-top (tĭp'tŏp') **I.** s. *(summit)* cumbre *f*, cima; *(highest quality)* calidad superior *f*, excelencia **II.** adj. de calidad superior, excelente **III.** adv. perfectamente.

ti-rade (tī'rād') s. perorata.

tire¹ (tīr) intr. **tired, tir-ing** *(to grow fatigued)* cansarse; *(to grow bored)* aburrirse <I tired of reading me aburrí de leer> —tr. *(to make weary)* cansar; *(to bore)* aburrir, cansar ♦ **to t. somebody out** cansar, agotar a alguien.

tire² (tīr) s. *(of rubber)* llanta, neumático; *(of metal)* calce *m*, llanta.

tired (tīrd) adj. *(fatigued)* cansado, fatigado; *(bored)* aburrido; *(hackneyed)* trillado, cansado.

tire-less (tīr'lĭs) adj. incansable, infatigable.

tire-some (tīr'səm) adj. *(tiring)* cansado, aburrido; *(tedious)* tedioso, pesado.

Ti-rol (tī'rōl, tīr'əl) s. Tirol *m*.

'tis (tĭz) contr. de **it is**.

tis-sue (tĭsh'ōō) s. BIOL. *(cellular matter)* tejido <muscle t. tejido muscular>; *(fine cloth)* tisú *m*; *(fine paper)* papel de seda *m*; *(handkerchief)* pañuelo de papel; FIG. *(web)* red *f*, sarta.

tit¹ (tĭt) s. ORNIT. paro.

tit² (tĭt) s. *(teat)* teta; *(nipple)* pezón *m*; JER. teta, pecho.

Ti-tan (tīt'n) s. MITOL. Titán *m* ♦ **t.** FIG. gigante, coloso.

ti·tan·ic (tī-tăn′ĭk) adj. *(colossal)* gigantesco, colosal; *(powerful)* poderoso, inmenso ♦ **T.** MITOL. titánico.

ti·ta·ni·um (tī-tā′nē-əm) s. QUÍM. titanio.

tit·bit (tĭt′bĭt′) s. var. de **tidbit.**

ti·ter (tī′tər) s. MED., QUÍM. títulos, valor (de una solución) *m.*

tit for tat s. ♦ **to give t.** FIG. devolver golpe por golpe, pagar con la misma moneda.

tithe (tīth) **I.** s. RELIG. diezmo; *(tenth part)* décima parte; *(small part)* minucia, menudencia **II.** tr. tithed, tith·ing diezmar —intr. pagar el diezmo.

tith·ing (tī′thĭng) s. cobro *o* pago del diezmo.

tit·il·late (tĭt′l-āt′) tr. **-lat·ed, -lat·ing** *(to tickle)* cosquillear; *(to stimulate)* estimular, excitar.

tit·i·vate (tĭt′ə-vāt′) tr. **-vat·ed, -vat·ing** acicalar, emperifollar.

ti·tle (tīt′l) **I.** s. *(of a book, work of art)* título; CINEM. subtítulo; DER. *(of a legal document)* título; *(legal right)* derecho, título <t. of property título de propiedad>; *(formal appellation)* título de nobleza; DEP. campeonato **II.** tr. **-tled, -tling** *(to give a title to)* conferir título a; *(to confer a name upon)* titular.

ti·tled (tīt′ld) adj. *(book)* titulado, intitulado; *(person)* con título (esp. de nobleza).

title deed s. título de propiedad.

ti·tle·hold·er (tīt′l-hōl′dər) s. *(titulary)* poseedor del título *m*; titular *mf*; *(champion)* campeón *m.*

title page s. IMPR. portada.

title role s. CINEM., TEAT. papel principal *m.*

tit·mouse (tĭt′mous′) s. [pl. **-mice** (-mīs′)] ORNIT. paro, herrerillo.

ti·trate (tī′trāt′) QUÍM. tr. **-trat·ed, -trat·ing** titular —intr. efectuar una titulación.

ti·tra·tion (tī-trā′shən) s. QUÍM. titulación *f*, análisis volumétrico.

ti·tre (tī′tər) s. var. de **titer.**

tit·ter (tĭt′ər) **I.** intr. reír entre dientes **II.** s. risa entre dientes.

tit·tle (tĭt′l) s. *(accent)* acento; *(dot)* punto; *(bit)* pizca, ápice *m.*

tit·tle-tat·tle (tĭt′l-tăt′l) **I.** s. chismorreo, chismes *m* **II.** intr. **-tled, -tling** chismear, comadrear.

tit·u·lar (tĭch′ə-lər) **I.** adj. *(of a title)* titular; *(nominal)* nominal **II.** s. titular *mf.*

tit·u·lar·y (tĭch′ə-lĕr′ē) s. [pl. **-ies**] titular *mf.*

Ti·tus (tī′təs) s. BÍBL. Tito.

tiz·zy (tĭz′ē) s. [pl. **-zies**] JER. *(confusion)* confusión *f*, aturdimiento; *(dither)* agitación *f.*

TNT (tē′ĕn-tē′) s. QUÍM. T.N.T. (abrev. de trinitrotolueno).

to §G1 (tōō, tə) **I.** prep. *(direction)* a, hacia, en dirección a <I went to the city fui a la ciudad>; *(as far as)* hasta <rotten to the core podrido hasta la médula>; *(toward a given state)* a <the Nazi rise to power la subida al poder de los nazis>; *(against)* contra <their faces pressed to the windows sus caras apretadas contra las ventanas>; *(in front of)* a <face to face cara a cara>; *(of, for)* de, para <do you have the belt to this dress ¿tienes el cinturón de este vestido?>; *(concerning, regarding)* a <deaf to my pleas sordo a mis súplicas>; *(in relationship with)* a <parallel to the road paralelo a la carretera>; *(in respect of)* de <the secret to her success el secreto de su éxito>; *(constituting)* por <two cups to a pint dos tazas por pinta>; *(in accord with)* según, de acuerdo con <to my way of thinking según mi modo de pensar>; *(as compared with)* comparado con *o* a <a book superior to his others un libro superior, comparado con sus otros>; *(before)* menos, para <the time is ten to five son las cinco menos diez *o* faltan diez minutos para las cinco>; *(until)* a, hasta <I work from nine to five trabajo de nueve a cinco *o* nueve hasta las cinco>; *(for the purpose of)* a, para, en <she went out to lunch salió a almorzar>; *(in honor of)* por, en honor a *o* de <a toast to the queen un brindis en honor a la reina>; *(with the result)* para, ante <to his amazement para su asombro>; *(toward)* con <to be kind to someone ser amable con alguien>; [no se traduce cuando representa infinitivo] <tell him if you want to díselo si quieres> ♦ **down to** hasta • **to be or not to be** ser *o* no ser • **to one's face** en la misma

cara • **up to** hasta **II.** adv. *(to consciousness)* en sí <the patient was in his room when he came to el paciente estaba en su cuarto cuando volvió en sí>; *(at hand)* cerca ♦ **to and fro** de acá para allá, de un lado a otro.

toad (tōd) s. ZOOL. sapo; FIG., FAM. *(person)* persona desagradable *o* repulsiva.

toad·stool (tōd′stōōl′) s. BOT. hongo venenoso.

toad·y (tō′dē) **I.** s. [pl. **-ies**] *(adulator)* adulador, cobista *mf* **II.** tr. **-ied, -y·ing** adular a, dar coba —intr. adular.

to and fro adv. de un lado a otro, de acá para allá.

to-and-fro (tōō′ən-frō′) adj. alternativo, de vaivén.

toast[1] (tōst) **I.** tr. *(bread)* tostar; FIG. *(body, hands)* calentar, hacer entrar en calor —intr. tostarse **II.** s. tostada.

toast[2] (tōst) **I.** s. *(drink)* brindis *m*; FIG. *(hero)* héroe *m* ♦ **the t. of the town** el héroe de la ciudad • **to drink a t. to** brindar por **II.** tr. brindar a, beber por —intr. brindar.

toast·er (tō′stər) s. tostadora.

toast·mas·ter (tōst′măs′tər) s. maestro de ceremonias en un banquete.

to·bac·co (tə-băk′ō) s. [pl. **-cos** *o* **-coes**] BOT. tabaco; *(habit)* hábito de fumar <I gave up t. dejé el hábito de fumar>.

to·bac·co·nist (tə-băk′ə-nĭst) s. estanquero, tabaquero.

to-be (tōō-bē′) adj. [ú. en palabras compuestas] futuro <bride-to-be la futura novia>.

to·bog·gan (tə-bŏg′ən) s. tobogán *m.*

toc·ca·ta (tə-kä′tə) s. MÚS. tocata.

toc·sin (tŏk′sĭn) s. *(on a bell)* campanada de alarma, rebato; *(warning)* señal *f.*

to·day *o* **to-day** (tə-dā′) **I.** adv. *(on the present day)* hoy, en el presente día; *(at the present time)* en el tiempo presente, actualmente ♦ **a week ago t.** hace una semana • **a week from t.** dentro de una semana **II.** s. *(the present day)* hoy; *(the present time)* hoy (en) día, actualidad *f* ♦ **the t. generation** la generación actual.

tod·dle (tŏd′l) **I.** intr. **-dled, -dling** hacer pinitos, andar con paso incierto **II.** s. pino, pinito.

tod·dler (tŏd′lər) s. *(child)* niño que empieza a andar; *(size)* tamaño de ropa para niño.

tod·dy (tŏd′ē) s. [pl. **-dies**] *(drink)* ponche *m*; *(sap, liquor)* savia de palma.

to-do (tə-dōō′) s. [pl. **-dos** (-dōōz′)] FAM. alboroto, jaleo.

toe (tō) **I.** s. *(of the foot)* dedo del pie; *(of a shoe, sock)* puntera ♦ **from top** *o* **head to t.** de pies a cabeza • **to be on one's toes** FIG. estar alerta, estar despierto • **to dance on toes** ARTE. bailar en puntas • **to step on someone's toes** FIG. herir los sentimientos de alguien • **to turn up one's toes** FIG., FAM. estirar la pata **II.** tr. **toed, toe·ing** *(to touch)* tocar con la punta del pie; *(to put a toe to)* poner puntera a; *(a ball)* tirar con la punta del pie; *(a nail, spike)* clavar oblicuamente ♦ **to t. the line** *o* **mark** FIG. conformarse, someterse a las reglas —intr. ♦ **to t. in** *o* **out** andar con los pies hacia adentro *o* hacia afuera.

toed (tōd) adj. ZOOL. de ... dedos en el pie <a two-toed sloth un perezoso de dos dedos en el pie>; CARP. metido oblicuamente <a t. nail un clavo metido oblicuamente>.

toe dance s. baile en punta de pies *m.*

toe·hold (tō′hōld′) s. *(in climbing)* hendidura para apoyar la punta del pie; FIG. *(advantage)* asidero, punto de apoyo para comenzar una empresa.

toe·nail (tō′nāl′) **I.** s. ANAT. uña del dedo del pie; CARP. *(nail)* clavo oblicuo **II.** tr. CARP. clavar oblicuamente.

tof·fee (tôf′ē) s. melcocha, arropía.

tog (tŏg) FAM. **I.** s. *(jacket)* chaqueta; *(cloak)* capa ♦ **togs** ropa **II.** tr. **togged, tog·ging** vestir.

to·ga (tō′gə) s. toga.

to·geth·er (tə-gĕth′ər) adv. *(in a single group)* juntos <they live t. viven juntos>; *(in concert)* juntos, a la vez <all t. now! ¡todos a la vez!>; *(in total)* en total, todos (juntos) <she's worth more than all of us t. tiene más dinero que todos nosotros juntos> ♦ **getting along t.** llevándose bien • **to bring t.** reunir • **to come** *o* **to get t.** juntarse, reunirse • **to go t.** *(to go out)* salir juntos, ir juntos; *(colors, flavors)* armonizar, ir juntos • **we are gathered t. here** nos encontramos reunidos aquí.

ã rey / ä año / b boca / ch chico / d dar / ĕ el / ē mil / g gato / h joya / hw juez / ī aire / k casa / kw cuan /

to·geth·er·ness (tə-gĕth′ər-nĭs) s. *(solidarity)* solidaridad *f*, unión *f*; *(spirit)* espíritu de grupo *m*.

tog·gle (tŏg′əl) I. s. MARÍT. cabilla; MEC. *(pin)* fiador atravesado; *(lever)* palanca acodada; *(for wire, rope)* tensor *m*; *(joint)* junta de codillo, rótula; *(button)* alamar *m* II. tr. **-gled, -gling** sujetar.

toggle joint s. junta de codillo, articulación *f*.

toggle switch s. ELEC. interruptor eléctrico.

To·go (tō′gō) s. Togo.

To·go·lese (tō′gə-lēz′) adj. & s. [pl. **Togolese**] togolés *m* ♦ **the T.** los togoleses.

toil¹ (toil) I. intr. *(to work)* trabajar duro; *(to move)* moverse con dificultad II. s. *(effort)* esfuerzo, trabajo; ANT. *(strife)* lucha, conflicto.

toil² (toil) s. *(net)* red (para cazar) *f* ♦ **toils** FIG. red, trampa.

toi·let (toi′lĭt) s. *(lavatory)* retrete *m*, lavabo; *(toilette)* arreglo, aseo; *(clothes)* traje *m*, vestido; ANT. *(dressing table)* tocador *m*.

toilet paper s. papel higiénico.

toi·let·ry (toi′lĭ-trē) s. [pl. **-ries**] artículo de tocador.

toi·lette (twä-lĕt′) s. *(grooming)* arreglo; aseo; *(clothes)* traje *m*, vestido; *(costume)* disfraz *m*.

toilet water s. agua de tocador, agua de Colonia.

toil·some (toil′səm) adj. trabajoso, laborioso.

to·ken (tō′kən) I. s. *(sign)* señal *f*, prueba <*in t. of* en señal de, como prueba de>; *(symbol)* símbolo <*the scepter is a t. of kingship* el cetro es un símbolo de la realeza>; *(souvenir)* recuerdo; *(substitute for currency)* ficha ♦ **by the same t.** igualmente, por el mismo modo de razonar II. adj. simbólico <*a t. gesture* un gesto simbólico> ♦ **t. payment** pago parcial.

to·ken·ism (tō′kə-nĭz′əm) s. política de aparente integración racial *o* religiosa.

To·kyo (tō′kē-ō′) s. Tokio.

told (tōld) pret. y part. p. de **tell.**

tol·er·a·ble (tŏl′ər-ə-bəl) adj. *(bearable)* tolerable, sufrible; *(passable)* mediano, pasable.

tol·er·ance (tŏl′ər-əns) s. *(acceptance)* tolerancia, indulgencia; *(patience)* paciencia; MED., METAL., TEC. tolerancia.

tol·er·ant (tŏl′ər-ənt) adj. tolerante.

tol·er·ate (tŏl′ə-rāt′) tr. **-at·ed, -at·ing** *(behavior, situation)* tolerar, permitir; *(opinions, beliefs)* tolerar, admitir; *(suffering, pain)* sufrir, aguantar; MED. tolerar.

tol·er·a·tion (tŏl′ə-rā′shən) s. tolerancia.

toll¹ (tōl) I. s. *(at a bridge, tunnel)* peaje *m*; *(on a phone call)* tasa, recargo; *(loss)* bajas, número de víctimas ♦ **to take a t. of** *(loss)* infligir una pérdida a; *(repercussion)* repercutir en II. tr. cobrar peaje.

toll² (tōl) I. tr. & intr. *(to ring)* tañer, tocar II. s. tañido.

toll·booth (tōl′bōōth′) s. caseta *o* garita de peaje.

toll call s. TEL. llamada de larga distancia.

toll collector s. peajero.

toll·gate (tōl′gāt′) s. barrera de peaje.

toll·house (tōl′hous′) s. *(house)* casa del peajero; *(tollbooth)* garita de peaje.

Tol·tec (tŏl′tĕk′, tōl′-) s. tolteca *mf*.

tol·u·ene (tŏl′yōō-ēn′) s. QUÍM. tolueno.

tom (tŏm) s. macho (de algunos animales como el gato y el pavo).

tom·a·hawk (tŏm′ə-hôk′) I. s. hacha de guerra de los indios norteamericanos ♦ **to bury the t.** FIG. hacer la paz II. tr. herir *o* matar con hacha de guerra.

to·ma·to (tə-mā′tō, -mä′-) s. [pl. **-toes**] BOT. *(plant)* tomatera, tomate *m*; *(fruit)* tomate; JER. *(girl)* joven atractiva, bombón *m*.

tomb (tōōm) s. *(grave)* tumba, sepulcro; *(place)* sepultura; *(monument)* tumba.

tom·boy (tŏm′boi′) s. FAM. niña *o* jovencita que se conduce como un muchacho, marimacho.

tomb·stone (tōōm′stōn′) s. lápida.

tom·cat (tŏm′kăt′) s. gato macho.

Tom, Dick and Harry (tŏm′ dĭk′ ən hăr′ē) s. Fulano, Mengano y Zutano ♦ **every T.** cualquiera.

tome (tōm) s. *(volume)* tomo, volumen *m*; *(huge book)* libraco.

tom·fool (tŏm′fōōl′) s. necio, tonto.

tom·fool·er·y (tŏm-fōō′lə-rē) s. [pl. **-ies**] *(foolish behavior)* tonterías; *(nonsense)* disparate *m*, desatino.

tom·my (tŏm′ē) s. [pl. **-mies**] G.B., FAM. *(bread)* pan; *(provisions)* comestibles *m* ♦ **T.** MIL. soldado raso inglés.

Tommy gun s. MIL., FAM. pistola ametralladora, metralleta.

tom·my·rot (tŏm′ē-rŏt′) s. JER. tontería, disparate *m*.

to·mor·row (tə-môr′ō) I. s. *(day following today)* mañana; FIG. *(the near future)* mañana <*the world of t.* el mundo de mañana> ♦ **the day after t.** pasado mañana II. adv. mañana <*see you tomorrow* hasta mañana>.

Tom Thumb s. *(character)* Pulgarcito; *(midget)* enano.

tom-tom (tŏm′tŏm′) s. tantán *m*, tam-tam *m*.

ton (tŭn) s. tonelada ♦ **tons** FIG., FAM. montones <*he makes tons of money* gana montones de dinero>.

to·nal (tō′nəl) adj. tonal.

to·nal·i·ty (tō-năl′ĭ-tē) s. [pl. **-ties**] MÚS., PINT. tonalidad *f*.

tone (tōn) I. s. *(of sound, color)* tono; *(of voice)* tono, timbre *m* <*an angry t.* un tono enfadado>; *(of a word, phrase)* entonación *f*, inflexión; *(style)* estilo, carácter *m*; *(of muscles)* tono ♦ **to change one's t.** mudar el tono • **to lower one's t.** bajar el tono II. tr. **toned, ton·ing** *(a word, phrase)* dar tono a, modificar el tono de; *(colors)* matizar ♦ **to t. down** bajar, suavizar (sonido, color) • **to t. in with** combinarse armoniosamente con • **to t. up** *(color)* intensificar; *(muscle)* tonificar —intr. armonizarse (sonidos, colores).

tone arm s. brazo de tocadiscos.

tone·less (tōn′lĭs) adj. *(lacking tone)* apagado; *(listless)* inexpresivo, apagado.

tone poem s. MÚS. poema sinfónico.

tongs (tôngz) s.pl. [ú. con v. sing. o pl.] *(for sugar)* tenacillas; TEC. alicate *m*, tenazas.

tongue (tŭng) I. s. ANAT. lengua; *(language)* lengua, idioma *m* <*mother t.* lengua materna>; *(of a shoe)* lengüeta; *(of a bell)* badajo; *(of a flame)* lengua; *(of land)* lengua, punta de tierra; *(of railway line)* aguja ♦ **to have an evil t.** tener una mala lengua • **to have it on the tip of one's t.** tenerlo en la punta de la lengua • **to hold** *o* **bite one's t.** morderse la lengua, callarse • **to stick out one's t.** sacar la lengua • **watch your t.!** ¡ten cuidado con lo que dices! • **with t. in cheek** irónicamente, burlonamente II. tr. **tongued, tongu·ing** *(to touch with the tongue)* lamer; CARP. ensamblar, machihembrar; MÚS. usar la lengua para articular notas, esp. en los metales.

tongue and groove s. CARP. ensambladura de lengüeta y ranura, machihembrado.

tongue-in-cheek (tŭng′ĭn-chĕk′) adj. irónicamente, burlonamente.

tongue-lash·ing (tŭng′lăsh′ĭng) s. FAM. reprimenda, regaño.

tongue-tied (tŭng′tīd′) adj. FIG. con la lengua atada, mudo.

tongue twister s. trabalenguas *m*.

ton·ic (tŏn′ĭk) I. s. MED. tónico; MÚS., FONÉT. tónica; *(quinine water)* agua tónica II. adj. tónico.

to·nic·i·ty (tō-nĭs′ĭ-tē) s. FISIOL. tonicidad *f*.

to·night (tə-nīt′) adv. & s. esta noche.

ton·ka bean (tŏng′kə) s. BOT. sarapia, haba tonca.

ton·nage (tŭn′ĭj) s. *(weight capacity)* tonelaje *m*; *(duty)* impuesto cobrado por tonelada a los buques de carga.

ton·sil (tŏn′səl) s. ANAT. amígdala.

ton·sil·lec·to·my (tŏn′sə-lĕk′tə-mē) s. [pl. **-mies**] CIR. tonsilectomía, amigdalectomía.

ton·sil·li·tis (tŏn′sə-lī′tĭs) s. MED. amigdalitis *f*.

ton·so·ri·al (tŏn-sôr′ē-əl) adj. barberil, propio de los barberos.

ton·sure (tŏn′shər) s. RELIG. tonsura.

ton·tine (tŏn′tēn′, tŏn-tēn′) s. COM. tontina (asociación mutua).

to·nus (tō′nəs) s. tono muscular, tonicidad *f*.

too (tōō) adv. *(also)* también <*she's coming t.* ella también viene>; *(as well as)* además <*and it's broken t.* y además está roto>; *(excessively)* demasiado <*it's t. hard* es demasiado duro>; *(very)* muy <*it's t. late for that* es muy tarde para eso> ♦ **not t.** FAM. no muy, nada <*he's not t. intelligent* no es muy inteligente, no es nada inteligente> • **to be t. much** ser demasiado <*this is t. much for me* esto es

---

demasiado para mí> • **t. bad!** ¡qué pena! • **t. little** *(amount)* demasiado poco; *(size)* muy pequeño • **t. many** demasiados <*there are t. many heads in this office* hay demasiados jefes en esta oficina>.

took (tŏok) pret. de **take.**

tool (tōol) **I.** s. *(hammer, drill)* herramienta; *(machine)* máquina herramienta; *(utensil)* utensilo, útil *m*; FIG. *(instrument)* instrumento <*words are the tools of his work* las palabras son el instrumento de su trabajo>; *(dupe)* instrumento <*she was only a t. of his designs* ella ha sido sólo un instrumento para sus designios> **II.** tr. *(to form with a tool)* labrar; *(to equip with tools)* equipar con herramientas; *(a book, designs)* estampar; FAM. *(a car)* conducir ♦ **to t. up** equipar con maquinaria (una planta) —intr. trabajar utilizando herramientas.

tool·box (tōol′bŏks′) s. caja de herramientas.

tool·ing (tōo′lĭng) s. *(ornamentation)* trabajo ornamental; *(of a factory)* montaje de maquinaria *m*.

toot (tōot) **I.** intr. sonar, emitir sonidos (pito, bocina) —tr. tocar, hacer sonar (pito, bocina) ♦ **to t. one's own horn** FAM. echarse flores **II.** s. pitazo, bocinazo.

tooth (tōoth) **I.** s. [pl. **teeth** (tēth)] *(of a person, animal)* diente *m*; *(molar)* muela; *(of a saw)* diente; *(of a comb)* púa ♦ **an eye for an eye, a t. for a t.** ojo por ojo, diente por diente • **armed to the teeth** FIG. armado hasta los dientes • **by the skin of one's teeth** por poco, por un pelo • **to cut one's teeth** echar los dientes • **to fight t. and nail** luchar a brazo partido • **to get one's teeth into** FIG. meterse bien en (tarea, estudio) • **to have a sweet t.** ser goloso • **to say between the teeth** decir entre dientes • **to put teeth into** fortalecer • **to show one's teeth** FIG. mostrar los dientes • **wisdom t.** muela del juicio **II.** tr. (tōoth, tōoth) dentar (una herramienta) —intr. engranar.

tooth·ache (tōoth′āk′) s. dolor de muelas *m*.

tooth and nail adv. a brazo partido, encarnizadamente.

tooth·brush (tōoth′brŭsh′) s. cepillo de dientes.

toothed (tōotht, tōothd) adj. *(having teeth)* dentado, que tiene dientes; *(having certain kind of teeth)* de dientes . . . <*saw-toothed* de dientes aserrados>.

tooth·less (tōoth′lĭs) adj. *(lacking teeth)* sin dientes, desdentado; FIG. *(ineffectual)* ineficaz, ineficiente.

tooth·paste (tōoth′pāst′) s. pasta dentífrica, dentífrico.

tooth·pick (tōoth′pĭk′) s. mondadientes *m*, palillo de dientes.

tooth·pow·der (tōoth′pou′dər) s. polvo dentífrico.

tooth·some (tōoth′səm) adj. *(delicious)* sabroso, apetitoso; FIG. *(attractive)* atractivo <*a t. offer* una oferta atractiva>.

tooth·y (tōo′thē) adj. **-i·er, -i·est** *(having large teeth)* dentudo; *(showing teeth)* mostrando los dientes.

top¹ (tŏp) **I.** s. *(the uppermost part)* parte superior *m*, parte de arriba <*the t. of a cabinet* la parte de arriba de un armario>; *(of the head)* coronilla; *(of a container)* tope *m*, borde *m* <*fill it to the t.* llénelo hasta el borde>; *(of a mountain)* cumbre *f*, cima; *(of a house)* techo; *(of a car)* capota; *(of a tree, hat)* copa; *(of a bottle, pan)* tapa; *(of a page)* principio, cabeza; *(of shoes, desks)* la parte de arriba; *(of liquids)* superficie *f*; *(of carrots, beets)* tallo, hojas; *(blouse)* blusa; *(jacket, upper part)* chaqueta; *(of a bikini)* sostén *m*, corpiño; *(peak)* cumbre *f* <*he reached the t. of his art* llegó a la cumbre de su arte>; MARÍT. cofa ♦ **at the t. of** a la cabeza de, al primero • **at the t. of one's form** en plena forma • **at the t. of one's voice** a voz en cuello • **from t. to bottom** de arriba abajo • **from t. to toe** de pies a cabeza • **on t.** encima • **on t.** de además de, encima de <*and on t. of it, they gave me a bonus* y encima de esto, me dieron una gratificación> • **on t. of it all** por si fuera poco, para colmo de males • **to come out on t.** salir ganando • **to blow one's t.** FIG., FAM. salirse de sus casillas **II.** adj. *(of the uppermost part)* de arriba <*the t. shelf* el estante de arriba>; *(topmost)* último <*the t. floor* el último piso>; *(highest)* más alto; *(great)* muy bueno, de categoría <*a t. driver* un conductor de categoría>; *(best)* mejor <*the t. singing group* el mejor grupo musical>; *(maximum)* máximo, extremo <*t. speed* velocidad máxima>; *(the most important)* más importante **III.** tr. **topped, top·ping** *(to form a top of)* coronar, rematar <*an aerial tops the building*

una antena remata el edificio>; *(to reach a top)* llegar a la cumbre de (montaña, profesión); *(to cover)* cubrir; *(to surpass)* superar; *(to be at the head of)* estar a la cabeza de <*he topped his class* estaba a la cabeza de su clase>; *(to be bigger than)* medir más que, ser más alto que <*she tops me* es más alta que yo>; *(trees)* desmochar, descabezar; *(a ball)* golpear en la parte superior ♦ **to t. it all off** por si fuera poco, para colmo de males • **to t. off** o **out** rematar, coronar (efificio, carrera) • **to t. up** llenar hasta el tope.

top² (tŏp) s. *(toy)* peonza, trompo.

to·paz (tō′păz′) s. topacio.

top·coat (tŏp′kōt′) s. abrigo, sobretodo.

top dog s. FIG., FAM. persona que tiene máximo prestigio o autoridad.

top-drawer (tŏp′drôr′) FAM. adj. *(first-class)* de la más alta categoría; *(of people)* de la alta sociedad, aristocrático.

tope (tŏp) tr. & intr. **toped, top·ing** beber con exceso.

top·er (tō′pər) s. bebedor *m*.

top·flight (tŏp′flīt′) adj. de primera categoría, superior.

top·gal·lant (tə-găl′ənt, tŏp-) adj. MARÍT. de juanete.

top hat s. sombrero de copa.

top-heav·y (tŏp′hĕv′ē) adj. **-i·er, -i·est** *(with weights)* más pesado arriba que abajo, inestable; FIG. *(with executives)* con demasiados directores.

to·pi·ar·y (tō′pē-ĕr′ē) **I.** adj. de la jardinería (ornamental o artística) **II.** s. [pl. **-ies**] *(art)* jardinería; *(garden)* jardín ornamental o artístico.

top·ic (tŏp′ĭk) s. tópico, tema *m*.

top·i·cal (tŏp′ĭ-kəl) adj. *(local)* tópico, local; *(contemporary)* corriente, actual; *(thematic)* temático; MED. tópico.

top·knot (tŏp′nŏt′) s. *(of hair)* moño alto; *(of feathers, bows)* copete *m*.

top·less (tŏp′lĭs) adj. *(having no top)* sin la parte superior; *(woman)* con el busto desnudo.

top·loft·y (tŏp′lôf′tē) adj. **-i·er, -i·est** vanidoso, pomposo.

top·mast (tŏp′məst, -măst′) s. MARÍT. mastelero.

top·most (tŏp′mōst′) adj. *(highest)* más alto, más elevado; *(uppermost)* máximo.

top·notch (tŏp′nŏch′) adj. FAM. de primera clase, excelente.

to·pog·ra·pher (tə-pŏg′rə-fər) s. topógrafo.

to·pog·ra·phy (tə-pŏg′rə-fē) s. topografía.

to·pol·o·gy (tə-pŏl′ə-jē) s. ANAT., GEOM., TOP. topología.

top·per (tŏp′ər) s. JER. *(person)* persona extraordinaria; *(top hat)* sombrero de copa.

top·ping (tŏp′ĭng) **I.** s. CUL. *(sauce)* salsa; *(frosting)* cobertura, garapiña; *(garnish)* aderezo, adorno; TEC. acabado ♦ **toppings** desmoche, copete (de planta o árbol) **II.** adj. *(outstanding)* distinguido, eminente; G.B. *(first-rate)* de primera clase, excelente.

top·ple (tŏp′əl) tr. **-pled, -pling** *(to push over)* hacer caer, derribar; *(to overturn)* volcar; FIG. *(to cause to fall)* derribar —intr. *(to fall)* caerse, volcarse; *(to totter)* tambalearse, bambolearse.

tops (tŏps) adj. JER. fantástico, buenísimo <*he is t. in his work* él es buenísimo en su trabajo>.

top·sail (tŏp′səl, -sāl′) s. MARÍT. gavia.

top-se·cret (tŏp′sē′krĭt) adj. estrictamente confidencial, absolutamente secreto.

top·side (tŏp′sīd′) **I.** s. FIG. autoridad máxima ♦ **topsides** MARÍT. borda **II.** adv. *(with authority)* en autoridad; MARÍT. en cubierta.

top·soil (tŏp′soil′) **I.** s. tierra, capa superficial del suelo **II.** tr. sacar la capa superior del suelo de o a.

top·sy-tur·vy (tŏp′sē-tûr′vē) **I.** adv. *(upside-down)* patas arriba, al revés; *(in disorder)* en desorden **II.** adj. desordenado, revuelto **III.** s. caos *m*, desorden *m*.

toque (tōk) s. toca (gorra de mujer).

tor (tôr) s. peñasco, tormo.

to·rah o **To·rah** (tôr′ə) s. RELIG. tora.

torch (tôrch) s. *(flambeau)* antorcha; *(for welding)* soplete *m*; G.B. *(flashlight)* linterna; FIG. *(guide, enlightenment)* antorcha ♦ **to carry a t. for someone** estar enamorado de alguien sin ser correspondido.

torch·bear·er (tôrch′bâr′ər) s. *(torch carrier)* hachero, el que alumbra con hacha; FIG. *(leader)* abanderado, el que porta la antorcha (de la luz, el conocimiento).

ā rey / ä año / b boca / ch chico / d dar / ĕ el / ē mil / g gato / h joya / hw juez / ī aire / k casa / kw cuan /

torch song s. canción de amor correspondido *f.*
tore (tôr) pret. de **tear**[1].
tor·e·a·dor (tôr′ē-ə-dôr′) s. toreador *m.*
tor·ment I. s. (tôr′měnt′) *(physical, mental)* tormento; *(torture)* tortura, suplicio II. tr. (tôr-měnt′) *(physically, mentally)* atormentar; *(to torture)* torturar; *(to pester)* molestar, fastidiar.
tor·men·tor *o* **tor·ment·er** (tôr-měn′tər) s. *(one that torments)* atormentador *m*, torturador *m*; TEAT. bastidor *m*; CINEM. pantalla amortiguadora de sonido.
torn (tôrn) part. p. de **tear**[1].
tor·na·do (tôr-nā′dō) s. [pl. **-does** *o* **-dos**] tornado.
tor·pe·do (tôr-pē′dō) I. s. [pl. **-does**] *(underwater projectile)* torpedo; *(used in railroads)* petardo; *(for oil or gas wells)* detonador *m*; *(firecracker)* petardo; *(fish)* torpedo II. tr. **-doed, -do·ing** torpedear.
torpedo boat s. lancha torpedera, torpedero.
tor·pid (tôr′pĭd) adj. *(benumbed)* tórpido, entumecido; *(lethargic)* letárgico, aletargado; *(apathetic)* apático.
tor·por (tôr′pər) s. *(dullness)* torpor *m*, entorpecimiento; *(apathy)* apatía, indiferencia.
torque (tôrk) FÍS., MEC. I. s. momento *o* fuerza de torsión, par de torsión *m* II. tr. **torqued, torqu·ing** torcer, impartir forma helicoidal a.
tor·rent (tôr′ənt) s. torrente *m.*
tor·ren·tial (tô-rěn′shəl) adj. torrencial, torrentoso.
tor·rid (tôr′ĭd) adj. *(parched by heat)* tórrido, quemado; *(scorching)* abrasado, ardiente; FIG. *(ardent)* ardiente, ardoroso.
Torrid Zone s. GEOG. zona tórrida.
tor·sion (tôr′shən) s. torsión *f.*
tor·so (tôr′sō) s. [pl. **-sos** *o* **-si** (-sē′)] torso.
tort (tôrt) s. DER. agravio, daño indemnizable en juicio civil.
tor·ti·lla (tôr-tē′yə) s. tortilla (de maíz).
tor·toise (tôr′tĭs) s. ZOOL. tortuga de tierra.
tor·toise·shell *o* **tor·toise-shell** *o* **tortoise shell** (tôr′tĭs-shěl′) s. concha de carey, carey m.
tor·tu·ous (tôr′chōō-əs) adj. *(winding)* tortuoso, sinuoso *<a t. trail* un camino sinuoso>; *(devious)* tortuoso, torcido *<t. mind* mente torcida>; *(complex)* complicado.
tor·ture (tôr′chər) I. s. *(physical, mental)* tortura, tormento II. tr. **-tured, -tur·ing** *(physically)* torturar; *(mentally)* atormentar; FIG. *(to distort)* torcer, tergiversar.
tor·tur·er (tôr′chər-ər) s. torturador *m.*
tor·tur·ous (tôr′chər-əs) adj. atormentador.
To·ry (tôr′ē) s. [pl. **-ries**] G.B., POL. conservador *m*; HIST. realista ♦ t. miembro del Partido Conservador (en Canadá, Inglaterra).
toss (tôs) I. tr. *(a ball, frisbee)* tirar, lanzar; *(one's head, hair)* echar para atrás; *(to jerk)* sacudir, mover a tirones; *(to drop)* dejar caer, tirar *<the horse tossed its rider* el caballo tiró al jinete>; *(in a blanket)* mantear; *(salads, spaghetti)* revolver, dar vueltas a; *(coin)* echar ♦ **to t. aside** apartar, echar a un lado • **to t. off** *o* **down** *(to drink up)* beber de un trago *<he tossed down one glass of beer after another* se bebió un vaso tras otro de cerveza>; *(to accomplish easily)* hacer fácilmente • **to t. up** *(a coin)* lanzar al aire; *(a meal)* preparar rápidamente —intr. *(to be flung to and fro)* ser agitado, revolverse; *(to flip a coin)* echar una moneda a cara o cruz; *(in bed)* dar vueltas en la cama ♦ **to t. and turn** dar vueltas en la cama II. s. *(act)* lanzamiento, tiro; *(rapid movement)* movimiento rápido, sacudida; *(fall)* caída; *(even chance)* sorteo a cara o cruz ♦ **to take a t.** ser lanzado del caballo • **to win the t.** ganar a cara o cruz, ganar la apuesta.
toss·up (tôs′ŭp′) FAM. s. *(act)* lanzamiento de una moneda a cara o cruz; *(equal probability)* probabilidad pareja ♦ **it's a t.** las probabilidades son iguales.
tot[1] (tŏt) s. *(child)* nene *m*, niño de corta edad; *(drop)* trago (de licor).
tot[2] (tŏt) tr. **tot·ted, tot·ting** ♦ **to t. up** sumar, totalizar.
to·tal (tōt′l) I. s. *(sum)* total *m*, suma; *(entirety)* totalidad *f*, todo II. adj. *(entire)* entero, total; *(complete)* completo, total III. tr. & intr. totalizar, sumar ♦ **to t. up to** totalizar, ascender a.

to·tal·i·tar·i·an (tō-tăl′ĭ-târ′ē-ən) adj. totalitario.
to·tal·i·tar·i·an·ism (tō-tăl′ĭ-târ′ē-ə-nĭz′əm) s. totalitarismo.
to·tal·i·ty (tō-tăl′ĭ-tē) s. [pl. **-ties**] totalidad *f.*
to·tal·ly (tōt′l-ē) adv. totalmente, completamente.
tote[1] (tōt) I. tr. **tot·ed, tot·ing** *(to carry)* llevar, cargar; *(to pack)* llevar, portar *<toting guns* llevando armas> II. s. carga, peso.
tote[2] (tōt) s. totalizador *m.*
tote bag s. bolso grande.
to·tem (tō′təm) s. tótem *m.*
totem pole s. poste *m o* talla de un tótem.
tot·ter (tŏt′ər) intr. *(to shake)* bambolearse, tambalearse; *(to stagger)* caminar con paso vacilante, tambalearse ♦ **to t. on the brink of** estar al borde de.
tot·ter·ing (tŏt′ər-ĭng) I. adj. *(about to fall)* a punto de derrumbarse; *(staggering)* tambaleante, bamboleante II. s. bamboleo.
tou·can (tōō′kăn′, tōō-kän′) s. ORNIT. tucán *m.*
touch (tŭch) I. tr. *(with hand, fingers)* tocar *<t. it and feel how soft it is* tócalo y siente qué suave es>; *(to taste)* probar, tocar *<she didn't t. her dinner* no tocó su cena>; *(to disturb)* toquetear, manosear *<just don't t. anything in my room!* ¡no toquetees nada en mi cuarto!>; *(to border)* lindar con; *(to equal)* compararse con, igualarse a *<his work couldn't t. his master's* su trabajo no podía compararse con el de su maestro>; *(to mention)* aludir a, referirse a; *(to treat of)* aludir a, referirse a; *(to concern)* concernir a, afectar a *<a problem that touches many people* un problema que afecta a mucha gente>; *(to move emotionally)* conmover *<her crying touched him deeply* su llanto lo conmovió profundamente>; *(to lay hands on)* tocar, poner las manos encima a *<I never touched him!* ¡no llegué a ponerle las manos encima!>; *(to spoil)* estropear, dañar *<frost touched the plants* la helada dañó las plantas>; *(to hurt the feelings of)* herir; *(to obtain a loan from)* dar un sablazo, pedir prestado; ARTE. delinear, esbozar; MÚS. tocar; GEOM. ser tangente con ♦ **to t. bottom** tocar fondo • **t. off** *(a drawing)* esbozar; *(a firearm)* descargar, disparar; *(to set off)* desencadenar, provocar • **t. on** *o* **upon** *(to refer to)* referirse a, concernir a; *(to treat lightly)* tratar ligeramente *o* superficialmente; *(to border on)* rayar en, acercarse a • **t. up** *(to add touches to)* corregir, retocar; *(to finish off)* dar los últimos toques a • **t.** *(to come into contact)* tocarse, rozarse *<we stood and our shoulders touched* nos paramos y nuestros hombros se rozaron>; *(to be in contact)* estar en contacto ♦ **to t. down** AVIA. aterrizar II. s. *(act)* toque *m*, tacto; *(sense)* tacto; *(tap)* toque; *(subtle effect)* nota, toque *<candlelight provided just the right t.* la luz de las velas proporcionaba el toque justo>; *(tinge)* poquitín *m*, toque *<a t. of jealousy* un poquitín de celos>; *(mild attack)* ataque ligero *<a t. of flu* un ataque ligero de gripe>; *(dash)* pizca, poquito; *(of a typist)* toque, pulsación *f*; *(of a pianist)* tecleo; *(style)* sello, estilo; *(facility)* mano *<to lose one's t.* perder la mano>; *(contact)* contacto, comunicación *f <let's keep in t.* mantengámonos en contacto>; JER. *(approach for a loan)* sablazo ♦ **by t.** al tacto • **final** *o* **finishing t.** último toque • **to be in t. with something** estar al corriente *o* al tanto de algo • **to be out of t. with** *(people)* haber perdido el contacto con; *(things)* no estar al corriente *o* al tanto de.
touch-and-go (tŭch′ən-gō′) adj. FIG. arriesgado, precario *<a t. situation* una situación arriesgada>.
touch·down (tŭch′doun′) s. AER. aterrizaje *m*; DEP. tanto, gol (en fútbol americano) m.
touched (tŭcht) adj. *(emotionally moved)* conmovido, enternecido; FAM. *(mentally unbalanced)* chiflado, tocado de la cabeza.
touch·ing (tŭch′ĭng) I. adj. conmovedor, enternecedor II. prep. ANT. tocante a, en cuanto a.
touch·stone (tŭch′stōn′) s. MIN. piedra de toque, jaspe negro; FIG. *(criterion)* criterio de prueba, standard *m.*
touch-type (tŭch′tīp′) intr. **-typed, -typ·ing** mecanografiar al tacto.
touch·up (tŭch′ŭp′) s. retocar, corregir.
touch·y (tŭch′ē) adj. **-i·er, -i·est** *(oversensitive)* susceptible,

quisquilloso; *(requiring tact)* delicado <*a t. affair* un asunto delicado>; *(easily ignited)* inflamable.
tough (tŭf) **I.** adj. **-er, -est** *(hard to break, cut, chew)* duro; *(physically hardy)* fuerte, robusto <*a t. gymnast* un gimnasta fuerte>; FIG. *(harsh)* severo, áspero <*a t. winter* un invierno áspero>; *(aggressive)* agresivo, violento; *(difficult)* difícil <*a t. duty* una obligación difícil>; *(resolute)* decidido; *(rough)* tosco, bruto; *(unyielding)* inflexible ♦ **t.!** *o* **t. luck!** FAM. ¡mala suerte! **II.** s. matón *m.*
tough·en (tŭf′ən) tr. & intr. endurecer(se).
tough-mind·ed (tŭf′mīn′dĭd) adj. decidido, duro (de carácter).
tough·ness (tŭf′nĭs) s. *(of a body)* dureza, resistencia; *(of meat)* lo correoso, lo duro; *(of an action)* dificultad *f*, lo penoso; *(of character)* inflexibilidad *f*, firmeza.
tou·pee (tōō-pā′) s. *(hairpiece)* peluquín *m*; *(a curl)* tupé *m*, mechón *m.*
tour (tōōr) **I.** s. *(organized trip)* excursión *f*, viaje *m* <*a t. of the country* un viaje por el país>; *(visit)* visita <*a guided t. of a museum* una visita guiada a un museo>; *(of a theater company)* gira ♦ **circular t.** circuito • **package t.** viaje con todo comprendido • **to make a t. of** hacer un viaje, recorrer **II.** tr. *(to make a tour of)* recorrer, hacer un viaje por; *(a theatre company)* presentar en gira —intr. ir de viaje *o* excursión.
tour·ing (tōōr′ĭng) **I.** s. turismo **II.** adj. *(involved in tourism)* de turismo, que se dedica a hacer excursiones; *(theatrical company)* que está de gira.
touring car s. coche abierto de cuatro puertas.
tour·ism (tōōr′ĭz′əm) s. turismo.
tour·ist (tōōr′ĭst) **I.** s. turista *mf* **II.** adj. de turista <*t. hotel* hotel de turistas> ♦ **t. attraction** atracción turística.
tourist class s. clase turista.
tourist trade s. turismo, industria del turismo.
tour·ma·line (tōōr′mə-lēn′) s. MIN. turmalina.
tour·na·ment (tōōr′nə-mənt, tûr′-) s. *(competition)* torneo, competencia; ANT. *(joust)* justa, torneo.
tour·ney (tōōr′nē, tûr′-) **I.** intr. tornear, participar en un torneo **II.** s. [pl. **-neys**] torneo, competencia.
tour·ni·quet (tōōr′nĭ-kĭt, tûr′-) s. MED. torniquete *m.*
tou·sle (tou′zəl) **I.** tr. **-sled, -sling** *(hair)* desordenar, alborotar; *(clothes)* arrugar, desarreglar **II.** s. maraña, cabello revuelto *o* desgreñado.
tout (tout) FAM. **I.** s. *(brazen solicitor)* gancho; *(in racehorses)* vendedor de informaciones sobre caballos de carrera *m*; *(of tickets)* revendedor *m* **II.** tr. *(to puff)* dar gran importancia a, recomendar; *(to solicit)* solicitar (clientes, votos); *(to importune)* importunar, molestar.
tow¹ (tō) **I.** tr. remolcar **II.** s. *(towed vehicle)* remolque *m*, vehículo remolcado; *(tow truck)* camión remolcador *m*; *(tugboat)* remolcador *m*; *(rope, cable)* remolque, sirga ♦ **to have** *o* **take in t.** *(car, boat)* remolcar; FIG. llevar a cuestas <*he has his children in t.* lleva a sus niños a cuestas>.
tow² (tō) s. *(fiber)* estopa.
tow·age (tō′ĭj) s. *(act)* remolque *m*; *(tow fee)* derechos de remolque.
to·ward (tôrd, tə-wôrd′) *o* **to·wards** (tôrdz, tə-wôrdz′) prep. *(in the direction of)* hacia <*he is driving t. home* está conduciendo hacia su casa>; *(facing)* próximo a, cercano a; *(for)* para <*we're saving t. our vacation* estamos ahorrando dinero para las vacaciones>; *(with)* con, para con <*his relationship t. the family* sus relaciones con la familia>; *(near in time)* hacia, alrededor de <*t. noon* hacia el mediodía>.
tow·boat (tō′bōt′) s. remolcador *m.*
tow·el (tou′əl) **I.** s. toalla, paño ♦ **to throw in the t.** DEP. tirar la esponja (en boxeo); FIG. darse por vencido **II.** tr. & intr. secar(se) *o* frotar(se) con una toalla.
tow·er (tou′ər) **I.** s. *(tall building)* torre *f*; *(fortress)* torreón *m*, fortaleza; *(watch tower)* atalaya *f*; AER. *(control tower)* torre de control *o* de mando **II.** intr. encumbrarse, elevarse ♦ **to t. over** *o* **above** dominar, destacarse de *o* sobre.
tow·er·ing (tou′ər-ĭng) adj. *(very high)* altísimo, grande; FIG. *(outstanding)* sobresaliente, destacado; *(intense)* extremado, intenso <*a t. rage* una rabia intensa>.

tow·head (tō′hĕd′) s. persona rubia (de cabellos casi blancos).
tow·line (tō′līn′) s. remolque *m*, sirga.
town (toun) **I.** s. *(city)* ciudad *f*; *(small city, village)* pueblo, población *f*; *(commercial center)* centro, ciudad <*she's going into t. for shopping* se va de compras al centro>; *(residents)* gente *f*, pueblo <*the talk of the t.* la comidilla del pueblo> ♦ **to be out of t.** estar fuera, estar de viaje • **to go out on the t.** FAM. salir a divertirse • **to go to t. on something** FAM. hacer algo con toda el alma • **to paint the t. red** JER. ir de juerga, ir de parranda **II.** adj. de la ciudad, urbano.
town clerk s. secretario de ayuntamiento.
town crier s. ANT. pregonero.
town hall s. ayuntamiento, municipalidad *f.*
town house s. *(in the city)* casa particular en la ciudad; *(connected building)* casa unida a otra por paredes medianeras.
town meeting s. concejo municipal.
towns·folk (tounz′fōk′) s.pl. *(citizens)* habitantes de una ciudad *mf*; *(neighbors)* vecinos de un pueblo.
town·ship (toun′shĭp′) s. municipio, municipalidad *f.*
towns·man (tounz′mən) s. [pl. **-men**] *(resident)* habitante de la ciudad *m*; *(a fellow resident)* conciudadano.
towns·peo·ple (tounz′pē′pəl) s.pl. *(citizens)* habitantes de una ciudad *mf*; *(neighbors)* vecinos de un pueblo.
tow·rope (tō′rōp′) s. remolque *m*, sirga.
tow truck s. camión *m* *o* grúa de remolque.
tox·e·mi·a (tŏk-sē′mē-ə) s. MED. toxemia.
tox·ic (tŏk′sĭk) s. *(of a toxin)* tóxico; FIG. *(deadly)* destructivo, mortal.
tox·i·cant (tŏk′sĭ-kənt) s. & adj. tóxico.
tox·ic·i·ty (tŏk-sĭs′ĭ-tē) s. [pl. **-ties**] toxicidad *f.*
tox·i·col·o·gist (tŏk′sĭ-kŏl′ə-jĭst) s. toxicólogo.
tox·i·col·o·gy (tŏk′sĭ-kŏl′ə-jē) s. toxicología.
tox·in (tŏk′sĭn) s. toxina.
tox·oid (tŏk′soid′) s. MED., QUÍM. toxoide *m.*
toy (toi) **I.** s. *(for children)* juguete *m*; *(trifle)* nadería, futilidad *f*; *(bauble)* chuchería, baratija **II.** adj. *(for playing)* de juguete <*a t. gun* una pistola de juguete>; *(diminutive)* diminuto ♦ **t. dog** perro faldero, perrito • **t. poodle** perro de lanas enano • **t. soldier** soldadito de plomo **III.** intr. jugar, juguetear ♦ **to t. with** *(to play with)* jugar *o* juguetear con; FIG. *(an idea)* acariciar, dar vueltas a; *(someone's love, affection)* jugar con.
trace¹ (trās) **I.** s. *(mark)* pista; *(footprint)* huella, rastro; *(sign)* señal *f*, indicio <*without leaving a t.* sin dejar el menor indicio>; *(small amount)* pizca <*not a t. of irony* ni pizca de ironía>; *(vestige)* vestigio; MED., QUÍM. indicio; FÍS., MAT. traza **II.** tr. **traced, trac·ing** *(to sketch)* dibujar, trazar; *(to follow a trail)* seguir (pista, huellas); *(to locate)* localizar, encontrar <*she was finally traced* por fin la encontraron> ♦ **to t. (back) to** *(to derive from)* derivar de; *(to find out)* descubrir • **to t. out** *(a plan)* trazar; *(an origin)* determinar, descubrir.
trace² (trās) s. *(strap)* tirante *m*, tiradera; MEC. brazo transmisor de movimiento.
trace·a·ble (trā′sə-bəl) adj. fácil de seguir *o* encontrar.
trace element s. QUÍM. oligoelemento, microelemento.
trac·er (trā′sər) s. *(investigator)* investigador *m*; *(instrument)* tiralíneas *m*; COST. patrón *m*; MIL. bala trazadora; QUÍM. indicador *m.*
tracer bullet s. MIL. bala trazadora.
trac·er·y (trā′sə-rē) s. [pl. **-ies**] ARQ. tracería.
tra·che·a (trā′kē-ə) s. [pl. **-che·ae** (-kē-ē′) *o* **-che·as**] ANAT. tráquea.
tra·che·ot·o·my (trā′kē-ŏt′ə-mē) s. [pl. **-mies**] CIR. traqueotomía.
tra·cho·ma (trə-kō′mə) s. MED. tracoma.
trac·ing (trā′sĭng) s. *(of an original)* calco, calcado; *(of a line)* trazado; *(graph)* gráfico ♦ **t. paper** papel de calcar.
track (trăk) **I.** s. *(path)* camino, senda; *(footprint)* huella, rastro; *(of a person)* pista; *(of an animal)* huella; *(of things)* vestigio, rastro; *(of a wheel)* rodada, carril *m*; *(of a tape recorder)* pista; *(of a boat)* estela; *(of a bullet)* trayectoria, recorrido; *(railway)* vía (férrea); DEP. *(for running)*

pista; *(athletic competition)* atletismo en pista ♦ **in one's tracks** allí mismo • **to be off the t.** *(train)* estar descarrillado; FIG. *(person)* estar despistado • **to be on the right t.** ir por buen camino • **to be on somebody's t.** estar sobre la pista de alguien • **to jump the tracks** descarrillar • **to cover up one's tracks** no dejar rastro • **to keep t.** of *(to stay informed about)* seguir con atención, estar al día con; *(to follow)* vigilar de cerca, controlar • **to lose t.** of *(people)* perder de vista; *(time)* perder la noción de; *(thought, conversation)* perder el hilo de • **to make tracks** JER. irse, marcharse II. tr. *(to trail)* seguir, rastrear (pista, indicio); *(to observe)* observar, seguir <*to t. an aircraft by radar* seguir un avión con el radar> ♦ **to t. down** *(a thief)* perseguir y atrapar; *(to locate)* localizar; *(source, origin)* averiguar el origen de —intr. *(wheels)* estar alineadas; *(to pursue)* seguir una huella.

track·age (trăk'ĭj) s. F.C. *(tracks)* carriles *m*, rieles *m*; *(right)* derecho a utilizar vías de otra compañía.

track and field s. DEP. atletismo de campo y pista.

track·er (trăk'ər) s. *(person)* perseguidor *m*; *(dog)* rastrero, rastreador *m*.

track·ing¹ (trăk'ĭng) s. EDUC. agrupamiento de estudiantes según sus habilidades.

track·ing² (trăk'ĭng) s. *(by radar, radio)* seguimiento, localización *f*; RAD. lectura de una grabación; MIL. persecución *f*.

tracking station s. *(radar, radio)* estación de seguimiento *f*.

track·less (trăk'lĭs) adj. *(without tracks)* sin rieles; *(without a path)* sin caminos o senderos; *(without traces)* sin huellas o rastros.

track meet s. DEP. concurso o encuentro de atletismo.

track·suit (trăk'so͞ot') s. chandal *m*.

tract¹ (trăkt) s. *(land)* tracto, trecho (de terreno); ANAT. sistema <*the digestive t.* el sistema digestivo>; POÉT., ANT. período, espacio (de tiempo).

tract² (trăkt) s. *(pamphlet)* folleto, opúsculo.

trac·ta·ble (trăk'tə-bəl) adj. *(governable)* tratable, dócil; *(malleable)* maleable, dúctil.

trac·tile (trăk'təl, -tīl') adj. dúctil, maleable.

trac·tion (trăk'shən) s. tracción *f*.

trac·tor (trăk'tər) s. *(for farming)* tractor *m*; *(truck)* tractor, máquina de arrastre.

trad·a·ble (trā'də-bəl) adj. que puede ser negociado.

trade (trād) I. s. *(occupation)* oficio, ocupación *f*; *(craft)* artesanía; *(commerce)* comercio, negocio; *(industry)* industria <*the tourist t.* la industria del turismo>; *(transaction)* transacción *f*; *(exchange)* cambio, tráfico (de mercancías); *(businessmen)* comerciantes *m*, negociantes *m*; *(people in the same business)* gremio; *(customers)* clientela ♦ **by t.** de profesión <*he's a lawyer by t.* es abogado de profesión> • **to be in t.** ser comerciante, tener un negocio • **trades** METEOR. vientos alisios II. intr. **trad·ed, trad·ing** *(to engage in business)* comerciar, negociar; *(to be a customer)* ser cliente • **to t. on** aprovecharse de, abusar de (una ventaja, situación) —tr. cambiar, trocar ♦ **to t. in** dar un artículo usado como pago inicial por otro nuevo • **to t. off** trocar.

trade·a·ble (trā'də-bəl) adj. var. de **tradable**.

trade acceptance s. COM. letra de cambio.

trade discount s. COM. descuento usual del ramo.

trade-in (trād'ĭn') s. COM. s. *(merchandise)* artículo entregado como pago parcial de una compra; *(act)* trueque *m*.

trade·mark (trād'märk') I. s. *(name)* marca de fábrica, marca registrada; FIG. *(sign)* marca, sello distintivo II. tr. *(to give a trademark to)* poner la marca de fábrica a; *(to register)* registrar.

trade name s. COM. *(of a commodity, service)* nombre comercial; *(business name)* razón social *f*.

trade-off o **trade-off** (trād'ôf') s. trueque *m*.

trad·er (trā'dər) s. *(dealer)* comerciante *mf*, negociante *mf*; *(ship)* buque mercante *m*; FIN. bolsista *mf*.

trade route s. COM. vía marítima.

trade school s. EDUC. escuela vocacional, escuela de artes y oficios.

trades·man (trādz'mən) s. [pl. **-men**] *(shopkeeper)* tendero, comerciante *mf*; *(craftsman)* artesano.

trade union s. sindicato, gremio de obreros.

trade unionist s. sindicalista *mf*.

trade winds s. METEOR. vientos alisios.

trad·ing (trā'dĭng) I. s. comercio, trato II. adj. comercial, mercantil.

trading account s. cuenta comercial.

trading post s. tienda rural de ramos generales.

tra·di·tion (trə-dĭsh'ən) s. tradición *f*.

tra·di·tion·al (trə-dĭsh'ə-nəl) adj. tradicional.

tra·di·tion·al·ism (trə-dĭsh'ə-nə-lĭz'əm) s. tradicionalismo.

tra·di·tion·al·ist (trə-dĭsh'ə-nə-lĭst) s. & adj. tradicionalista *mf*.

tra·duce (trə-do͞os') tr. **-duced, -duc·ing** calumniar, difamar.

tra·duc·er (trə-do͞o'sər) s. calumniador *m*, difamador *m*.

traf·fic (trăf'ĭk) I. s. *(of vehicles, pedestrians)* tráfico, tránsito; *(of boats, planes)* tráfico; COM. *(trade)* comercio, negocio; *(illegal trade)* tráfico (de narcóticos, armas); *(exchange)* cambio; FIG. *(of ideas)* intercambio II. intr. **-ficked, -fick·ing** traficar, negociar.

traffic circle s. círculo de tráfico, glorieta de tráfico.

traffic island s. refugio, isleta para peatones.

traffic jam s. embotellamiento, atasco de vehículos.

traf·fick·er (trăf'ĭ-kər) s. *(dealer)* negociante *mf*; *(of drugs)* traficante *mf*.

traffic light s. luz *f* o disco de tráfico, semáforo.

traffic sign s. señal de tránsito *f*.

traffic signal s. señal de tráfico *f*.

tra·ge·di·an (trə-jē'dē-ən) s. TEAT. trágico (dramaturgo o actor).

tra·ge·di·enne (trə-jē'dē-ĕn') s. TEAT. trágica (actriz).

trag·e·dy (trăj'ĭ-dē) s. [pl. **-dies**] tragedia.

trag·ic (trăj'ĭk) o **trag·i·cal** (trăj'ĭ-kəl) adj. trágico.

trag·i·com·e·dy (trăj'ĭ-kŏm'ĭ-dē) s. [pl. **-dies**] LIT., TEAT. tragicomedia.

trag·i·com·ic (trăj'ĭ-kŏm'ĭk) o **trag·i·com·i·cal** (-kŏm'ĭ-kəl) adj. tragicómico.

trail (trāl) I. tr. *(to drag)* arrastrar; *(to track)* rastrear, seguir las huellas de (animal, ladrón); *(to follow)* seguir; *(to lag behind)* rezagar ♦ **to t. arms** MIL. bajar o suspender el arma —intr. *(to be dragged along)* arrastrarse; *(a plant)* colgar, trepar ♦ **to t. along** avanzar penosamente • **to t. behind** quedarse a la zaga • **to t. off** apagarse, desvanecerse II. s. *(trace)* huella, rastro; *(of a person)* pista; *(of smoke)* estela; *(of a comet)* cola; *(path)* camino, sendero; FIG. *(train)* serie *f*, estela <*a t. of bitter recriminations* una estela de amargas recriminaciones> ♦ **to be on the t.** of seguir la pista de • **to lose** o **to pick up the t.** perder o encontrar la pista.

trail·blaz·er (trāl'blā'zər) s. pionero.

trail·er (trā'lər) I. s. *(one who trails)* rastreador *m*; *(vehicle)* remolque *m*, casa-remolque *m*, caravana; CINEM. *(advance)* avance publicitario (de una película); *(blank film)* película en blanco al final del rollo ♦ **t. truck** camión de remolque II. tr. remolcar.

trailer camp s. campamento para casas-remolques.

trailing edge s. AVIA. borde de salida *m*.

train (trān) I. s. *(rail)* tren *m* <*is it a passenger or a freight t.?* ¿es un tren de pasajeros o de carga?>; *(succession)* sucesión *f*, serie *f* <*a t. of cars* una serie de coches>; *(of persons)* séquito, cortejo <*persons in the king's t.* personas del cortejo real>; *(of a dress)* cola; *(of a comet)* cola; *(of ships)* convoy *m*; MIL. tren de campaña *m*; TEC. tren <*t. of gears* tren de engranajes> ♦ **to go by t.** viajar en tren • **to lose one's t. of thought** perder el hilo de lo que uno iba a decir II. tr. *(a person)* enseñar, preparar; *(a child)* disciplinar, educar; *(an animal)* domar, amaestrar; *(an athlete)* entrenar; *(a plant)* guiar ♦ **to t. in** *(to practice)* ejercitarse en; *(to study)* estudiar • **to t. on** *(a gun)* apuntar a; *(a camera)* enfocar a o hacia • **to t. someone** formar a alguien —intr. *(to instruct oneself)* prepararse, formarse; *(an athlete)* entrenarse; MIL. hacer la instrucción; FAM. ir en tren <*then we trained to Paris* luego fuimos en tren a París>.

trained (trānd) adj. *(educated)* entrenado, especializado;

(physically) preparado; *(said of animals)* amaestrado, domado ♦ **to have a t. eye** tener un ojo experto.

train·ee (trā-nē′) s. *(person being trained)* persona que se entrena *o* adiestra; *(apprentice)* aprendiz *mf.*

train·er (trā′nər) s. *(of athletes)* entrenador *m; (of horses)* preparador *m; (of animals)* amaestrador *m; (apparatus)* aparato para entrenamiento; MIL. *(gun operator)* operador de cañón *m; (instructor)* instructor *m.*

train·ing (trā′nĭng) s. *(teaching)* instrucción *f,* enseñanza; *(apprenticeship)* aprendizaje; *(of animals)* amaestramiento; DEP. entrenamiento, preparación *f.*

train·load (trān′lōd′) s. capacidad total de un tren *f* ♦ **a t. of** un tren lleno de.

train·man (trān′mən) s. [pl. **-men**] F.C. ferroviario, operador del ferrocarril *m.*

traipse (trāps) intr. **traipsed, traips·ing** FAM. andar.

trait (trāt) s. rasgo distintivo, característica.

trai·tor (trā′tər) s. traidor.

trai·tor·ous (trā′tər-əs) adj. traidor, traicionero.

tra·jec·to·ry (trə-jĕk′tə-rē) s. [pl. **-ries**] trayectoria.

tram (trăm) s. G.B. *(streetcar)* tranvía; *(tramway)* rieles *m,* carriles (de tranvía) *m; (cable car)* teleférico; *(small wagon)* vagoneta.

tram·car (trăm′kär′) s. G.B. *(streetcar)* tranvía (de pasajeros); *(coal car)* vagoneta (en una mina).

tram·mel (trăm′əl) I. s. *(for horses)* traba; *(net)* trasmallo ♦ **trammels** FIG. trabas, obstáculos II. tr. *(to hinder)* poner trabas a, obstaculizar; *(to catch)* pescar con trasmallo.

tramp (trămp) I. intr. *(to trudge)* andar con pasos pesados; *(to walk)* caminar, ir a pie; *(to wander)* vagar, errar —tr. *(to trample)* pisotear con fuerza; *(to walk across)* recorrer a pie II. s. *(sound of a footfall)* ruido (de pasos) <*the t. of soldiers' boots* el ruido de las botas de los soldados>; *(walking trip)* caminata, paseo largo; *(vagrant)* vagabundo; JER. *(prostitute)* fulana, ramera.

tram·ple (trăm′pəl) I. tr. **-pled, -pling** pisotear, pisar repetidamente ♦ **to t. on** hollar, pisotear <*to t. on someone's rights* pisotear los derechos de alguien> —intr. pisar rudamente II. s. *(act)* pisoteo; *(sound)* ruido de pisadas.

tram·po·line (trăm′pə-lēn′, -lĭn) s. DEP. trampolín *m,* cama elástica (para saltos acrobáticos).

tram·way (trăm′wā′) s. G.B. *(street track)* carriles *m,* rieles de tranvía *m; (streetcar line)* vía de tranvía; *(of a cablecar)* cable *m,* sistema de cables *m.*

trance (trăns) I. s. *(hypnotic state)* trance *m,* estado hipnótico; *(catalepsy)* catalepsia; *(stupor)* estupor *m;* POÉT. éxtasis *m,* arrobamiento II. tr. **tranced, tranc·ing** POÉT. extasiar, arrobar.

tran·quil (trăng′kwəl) adj. *(serene)* tranquilo, sereno; *(steady)* quieto, calmo.

tran·quil·ize *o* **tran·quil·lize** (trăng′kwə-līz′) tr. & intr. **-ized, -iz·ing** *o* **-lized, -liz·ing** tranquilizar(se), calmar(se).

tran·quil·iz·er (trăng′kwə-līz′ər) s. FARM. tranquilizante *m,* calmante *m.*

tran·quil·li·ty *o* **tran·quil·i·ty** (trăng-kwĭl′ĭ-tē) s. tranquilidad *f,* calma.

trans·act (trăn-săkt′) tr. llevar a cabo, ejecutar —intr. negociar, comerciar.

trans·ac·tion (trăn-săk′shən) s. *(act)* negociación *f,* tramitación *f; (deal)* transacción *f,* negocio ♦ **transactions** actas, memorias.

trans·ac·tion·al (trăn-săk′shən-əl, -zăk′-) adj. de transacción.

trans·ac·tor (trăn-săk′tər) s. negociante *mf,* comerciante *mf.*

trans·at·lan·tic (trăns′ət-lăn′tĭk) adj. transatlántico, trasatlántico.

trans·ceiv·er (trăn-sē′vər) s. RAD. aparato transmisor-receptor, transceptor *m.*

tran·scend (trăn-sĕnd′) tr. *(to rise above)* trascender; *(to surpass)* superar, sobrepasar; *(to go beyond)* ir más allá de —intr. trascender.

tran·scen·dence (trăn-sĕn′dəns) *o* **tran·scen·den·cy** (-dən-sē) s. transcendencia, trascendencia.

tran·scen·dent (trăn-sĕn′dənt) adj. trascendente.

tran·scen·den·tal (trăn′sĕn-dĕn′tl) adj. trascendental.

tran·scen·den·tal·ism (trăn′sĕn-dĕn′tl-ĭz′əm) s. FILOS. trascendentalismo.

trans·con·ti·nen·tal (trăns′kŏn-tə-nĕn′tl) adj. transcontinental.

tran·scribe (trăn-skrīb′) tr. **-scribed, -scrib·ing** *(to copy)* transcribir, copiar; COMPUT. transcribir datos de un soporte a otro; MÚS. adaptar, arreglar; RAD. grabar para difundir posteriormente; FONÉT. representar con signos.

tran·scrib·er (trăn-skrī′bər) s. transcriptor *m.*

tran·script (trăn′skrĭpt′) s. transcripción *f.*

tran·scrip·tion (trăn-skrĭp′shən) s. *(act)* transcripción *f; (recording)* grabación *f;* MÚS. transcripción; RAD., TELEV. emisión diferida.

trans·duc·er (trăns-dōō′sər, -dyōō′-) s. ELEC., ELECTRÓN., FÍS. transductor *m.*

tran·sect (trăn-sĕkt′) tr. cortar transversalmente.

tran·sept (trăn′sĕpt′) s. ARQ. crucero, nave transversal *f.*

trans·fer (trăns-fûr′) I. tr. **-ferred, -fer·ring** *(to convey)* trasladar; *(to shift)* transferir —intr. *(to move)* trasladarse; *(to change carrier)* transbordar II. s. (trăns′fər) *(ticket)* boleto de transbordo; *(place)* lugar de transbordo *m; (of money)* transferencia; *(of power)* transmisión *f; (of a design)* calcomanía.

trans·fer·a·ble (trăns-fûr′ə-bəl) adj. transferible.

trans·fer·al (trăns-fûr′əl) s. *(conveyance)* transferencia; *(removal)* traslado; *(design)* calcomanía; DER. transferencia; PSIC. transferencia (mecanismo psicoanalítico).

trans·fer·ee (trăns′fə-rē′) s. DER. cesionario.

trans·fer·ence (trăns-fûr′əns, trăns′fər-) s. transferencia.

trans·fer·or (trăns′fə-rôr′) s. DER. cesionista *mf.*

trans·fer·ral (trăns-fûr′əl) s. var. de **transferal**.

trans·fer·rer (trăns-fûr′ər) s. transferidor *m.*

transfer RNA s. BIOL. transferidor ARN *m.*

trans·fig·u·ra·tion (trăns-fĭg′yə-rā′shən) s. transfiguración *f,* transformación *f* ♦ **T.** RELIG. transfiguración de Jesucristo.

trans·fig·ure (trăns-fĭg′yər) tr. **-ured, -ur·ing** *(to alter radically)* transfigurar, transformar; *(to exalt)* exaltar, glorificar.

trans·fix (trăns-fĭks′) tr. *(to pierce through)* traspasar, atravesar; FIG. *(to render motionless)* paralizar, inmovilizar <*he was transfixed with fear* estaba paralizado por el miedo>.

trans·form (trăns-fôrm′) tr. transformar.

trans·for·ma·tion (trăns′fər-mā′shən) s. transformación *f.*

trans·form·er (trăns-fôr′mər) s. transformador *m.*

trans·fuse (trăns-fyōōz′) tr. **-fused, -fus·ing** *(to transfer)* transvasar, trasegar (líquidos); *(to permeate)* impregnar; MED. hacer una transfusión de *o* a.

trans·fu·sion (trăns-fyōō′zhən) s. *(of liquids)* trasiego; MED. transfusión *f.*

trans·gress (trăns-grĕs′) tr. *(a limit, boundary)* traspasar; *(a rule)* transgredir; *(the law)* infringir, violar —intr. *(to sin)* pecar; *(to break the law)* cometer una infracción.

trans·gres·sion (trăns-grĕsh′ən) s. *(of a law)* infracción *f; (of a rule)* transgresión *f; (of limits)* traspaso; *(sin)* pecado.

trans·gres·sor (trăns-grĕs′sər) s. *(offender)* transgresor *m,* infractor *m; (sinner)* pecador *m.*

tran·ship (trăn-shĭp′, trăns-) v. var. de **transship**.

tran·sience (trăn′shəns) *o* **tran·sien·cy** (-shən-sē) s. transitoriedad *f.*

tran·sient (trăn′shənt) I. adj. *(transitory)* transitorio; *(passing through)* transeúnte II. s. *(passing guest)* transeúnte *mf;* ELEC. oscilación momentánea.

tran·sis·tor (trăn-zĭs′tər) s. ELECTRÓN. transistor *m.*

tran·sis·tor·ize (trăn-zĭs′tə-rīz′) tr. **-ized, -iz·ing** ELECTRÓN. equipar con transistores a.

transistor radio s. radio a transistores, transistor *m.*

tran·sit (trăn′sĭt) I. s. *(passage)* tránsito; *(transport)* transporte *m; (transition)* transición *f;* ASTRON. culminación *f* II. tr. & intr. *(to pass)* transitar (por); ASTRON. culminar (por).

tran·si·tion (trăn-zĭsh′ən) s. transición *f.*

tran·si·tion·al (trăn-zĭsh′ə-nəl) adj. de transición.

tran·si·tive (trăn′sĭ-tĭv) GRAM. **I.** adj. transitivo **II.** s. verbo transitivo.

tran·si·to·ry (trăn′sĭ-tôr′ē) adj. transitorio.

trans·lat·a·ble (trăns-lā′tə-bəl) adj. traducible.

trans·late (trăns-lāt′, trăns′lāt′) tr. **-lat·ed, -lat·ing** *(language)* traducir; *(to explain)* explicar; *(to convert)* convertir; RELIG. trasladar; TELEG. *(to retransmit)* retransmitir; FÍS. trasladar —intr. *(to make a translation)* traducir; *(to admit of translation)* traducirse.

trans·la·tion (trăns-lā′shən) s. *(language change)* traducción *f*; FÍS. traslación *f*; TELEG. retransmisión *f*.

trans·la·tor (trăns-lā′tər) s. traductor *m*.

trans·lit·er·ate (trăns-lĭt′ə-rāt′) tr. **-at·ed, -at·ing** transcribir, traducir de un alfabeto a otro.

trans·lo·cate (trăns′lō-kāt′) tr. **-cat·ed, -cat·ing** desplazar.

trans·lo·ca·tion (trăns′lō-kā′shən) s. desplazamiento.

trans·lu·cent (trăns-lōō′sənt) adj. translúcido.

trans·lu·cid (trăns-lōō′sĭd) adj. translúcido.

trans·mi·grant (trăns-mī′grənt) s. inmigrante de paso, en dirección al país adonde va a establecerse.

trans·mi·grate (trăns-mī′grāt′) intr. **-grat·ed, -grat·ing** *(people)* emigrar; *(the soul)* transmigrar.

trans·mi·gra·tion (trăns′mī-grā′shən) s. *(of people)* emigración *f*; *(of souls)* transmigración *f*.

trans·mis·si·ble (trăns-mĭs′ə-bəl) adj. transmisible.

trans·mis·sion (trăns-mĭsh′ən) s. transmisión *f* ♦ **automatic t.** AUTO. cambio automático (de velocidad).

trans·mis·sive (trăns-mĭs′ĭv, trănz-) adj. transmisor, transmisible.

trans·mit (trăns-mĭt′) tr. & intr. **-mit·ted, -mit·ting** transmitir.

trans·mit·tal (trăns-mĭt′l) s. transmisión *f*.

trans·mit·tance (trăns-mĭt′ns) s. transmisión *f*.

trans·mit·ter (trăns-mĭt′ər) s. *(apparatus)* transmisor *m*; *(station)* emisora.

trans·mog·ri·fy (trăns-mŏg′rə-fī′) tr. **-fied, -fy·ing** transformar.

trans·mu·ta·tion (trăns′myōō-tā′shən) s. transmutación *f*.

trans·mute (trăns-myōōt′) tr. **-mut·ed, -mut·ing** transmutar.

trans·na·tion·al (trăns-năsh′ə-nəl) adj. transnacional.

trans·o·ce·an·ic (trăns′ō-shē-ăn′ĭk) adj. transoceánico.

tran·som (trăn′səm) s. *(window)* montante *m*, listón *m*; *(crosspiece)* travesaño; MARÍT. yugo.

tran·son·ic (trăn-sŏn′ĭk) adj. transónico.

trans·par·ence (trăns-pâr′əns) s. transparencia.

trans·par·en·cy (trăns-pâr′ən-sē) s. [pl. **-cies**] *(quality, state)* transparencia; *(slide)* diapositiva.

trans·par·ent (trăns-pâr′ənt) adj. transparente.

tran·spi·ra·tion (trăn′spə-rā′shən) adj. transpiración *f*.

tran·spire (trăn-spīr′) tr. **-spired, -spir·ing** transpirar —intr. *(to exude)* transpirar; FIG. *(to reveal)* revelarse; *(to happen)* acontecer, suceder.

trans·plant **I.** tr. (trăns-plănt′) trasplantar **II.** s. (trăns′plănt′) trasplante *m*.

trans·plan·ta·tion (trăns′plăn-tā′shən) s. trasplante *m*.

trans·po·lar (trăns-pō′lər) adj. transpolar, que atraviesa el polo.

tran·spond·er (trăn-spŏn′dər) s. radiofaro de respuesta.

trans·port **I.** tr. (trăns-pôrt′) *(to convey)* transportar; *(to enrapture)* arrebatar, embelesar; *(to deport)* deportar **II.** s. (trăns′pôrt′) *(conveyance)* transporte *m*; *(rapture)* arrebato, embeleso; *(ship)* buque de transporte *m*; *(aircraft)* avión de transporte *m*.

trans·port·a·ble (trăns-pôr′tə-bəl) adj. transportable.

trans·por·ta·tion (trăns′pər-tā′shən) s. *(act)* transportación *f*; *(state)* transporte *m*; *(means)* medio de transporte; *(business)* servicio de transporte; *(fare)* tarifa *o* costo de transporte; *(deportation)* deportación *f*.

trans·port·er (trăns-pôr′tər) s. transportador *m*.

trans·port·ing (trăns-pôr′tĭng) adj. *(transporter)* transportador *m*; *(captivating)* arrebatador.

trans·pose (trăns-pōz′) tr. **-posed, -pos·ing** *(to interchange)* intercambiar; *(place, order)* trasponer, transponer; *(to transform)* transformar; MAT. transponer; MÚS. transportar.

trans·po·si·tion (trăns′pə-zĭsh′ən) s. *(act)* transposición *f*; MÚS. transporte *m*.

trans·ship (trăns-shĭp′) tr. **-shipped, -ship·ping** transbordar.

tran·sub·stan·ti·ate (trăn′səb-stăn′shē-āt′) tr. **-at·ed, -at·ing** transubstanciar.

tran·sub·stan·ti·a·tion (trăn′səb-stăn-shē-ā′shən) s. transubstanciación *f*.

trans·u·ran·ic (trăns′yōō-răn′ĭk, -rā′nĭk) *o* **trans·u·ra·ni·um** (-rā′nē-əm) adj. QUÍM. transuránico.

trans·ver·sal (trăns-vûr′səl) adj. & s. transversal *f*.

trans·verse (trăns-vûrs′) adj. & s. transversal *f*, trasversal *f*.

transverse colon s. ANAT. colon transverso.

Tran·syl·va·nia (trăn′sal-vān′yə) s. Transilvania.

trap¹ (trăp) **I.** s. *(device)* trampa; *(stratagem)* celada, trampa; TEC. *(sealing device)* sifón *m*, bombillo; DEP. *(hurling device)* lanzaplatos (para tiro al blanco); *(in golf)* hoyo de arena; TEAT. escotillón *m*; JER. boca ♦ **shut your t.!** JER. ¡cierra el pico! • **traps** MÚS. instrumentos de percusión **II.** tr. **trapped, trap·ping** *(to ensnare)* coger en una trampa; *(to catch)* atrapar; *(to seal off)* retener, detener (gas, líquido); *(a pipe)* poner un sifón a —intr. poner trampas.

trap² (trăp) s. FAM. ♦ **traps** *(things)* cosas, trastos.

trap³ (trăp) s. *(rock)* basalto.

trap door s. *(window)* ventana de ventilación; *(on the floor)* trampa, escotillón *m*.

tra·peze (tră-pēz′) s. trapecio.

trapeze artist s. trapecista *mf*.

tra·pe·zi·um (trə-pē′zē-əm) s. [pl. **-zi·ums** *o* **-zi·a** (-zē-ə)] GEOM. trapezoide *m*; ANAT. trapecio; G.B. *(trapezoid)* trapecio.

tra·pe·zi·us (trə-pē′zē-əs) s. ANAT. trapecio.

trap·e·zoid (trăp′ĭ-zoid′) **I.** s. ANAT. trapezoide *m*; MAT. trapecio **II.** adj. MAT. trapecial.

trap·per (trăp′ər) s. trampero.

trap·ping (trăp′ĭng) s. ♦ **trappings** *(ornamentation)* adornos, atavíos; *(for a horse)* jaeces, arreos.

Trap·pist (trăp′ĭst) s. & adj. RELIG. trapense *m*.

trap·rock (trăp′rŏk′) s. roca trapeana.

trap·shoot·ing (trăp′shōō′tĭng) s. tiro al plato.

trash (trăsh) **I.** s. *(refuse)* desechos, desperdicios; *(foolish talk)* tonterías; *(tree cuttings)* escamondadura; *(insignificant people)* gentuza; LIT., ARTE. basura **II.** tr. *(to trim)* podar; *(to discard)* desechar; JER. *(to smash)* destrozar.

trash can s. cubo de la basura.

trash·y (trăsh′ē) adj. **-i·er, -i·est** malo, de baja calidad.

trau·ma (trou′mə, trô′-) s. [pl. **-mas** *o* **-ma·ta** (-mə-tə)] MED., PSIC. trauma *m*.

trau·mat·ic (trou-măt′ĭk, trô-) adj. MED., PSIC. traumático.

trau·ma·tize (trou′mə-tīz′, trô′-) tr. **-tized, -tiz·ing** MED., PSIC. traumatizar.

tra·vail (trə-vāl′) **I.** s. *(weariness)* fatiga, cansancio; *(anguish)* congoja; MED. *(childbirth)* dolores de parto *m* **II.** intr. *(to toil)* afanarse; MED. estar de parto.

trave (trāv) s. ARQ. travesaño.

trav·el (trăv′əl) **I.** intr. *(to journey)* viajar; *(to be a salesman)* ser viajante <*he travels for his company* es viajante de su compañía>; *(light, sound)* propagarse; *(cars)* circular; *(pain)* extenderse; frecuentar; *(to transport)* transportarse; FAM. *(to move)* moverse velozmente ♦ **to t. light** viajar con poco equipaje —tr. viajar por **II.** s. *(traffic)* tráfico <*t. is heavy on this street* hay mucho tráfico en esta calle> ♦ **travels** viajes.

travel agency s. agencia de viajes.

travel agent s. agente de viajes *mf*.

travel bureau s. agencia de viajes.

trav·eled *o* **trav·elled** (trăv′əld) adj. *(journeyed)* que ha viajado mucho; *(frequented)* frecuentado.

trav·el·er *o* **trav·el·ler** (trăv′ə-lər) s. *(person)* viajero; G.B. *(salesman)* viajante *m*; MARÍT. *(metal ring)* racamenta, racamento; *(rope)* corredera.

traveler's check s. cheque de viajero.

traveling salesman s. viajante de comercio *m*.

trav·e·logue *o* **trav·e·log** (trăv′ə-lôg′) s. *(film)* documental

---

ng inglés / ŏ la / ō bou / ô corre / oi oigo / ōō uno / ou auto / yōō ciudad / w hueco / y yo / z mismo

sobre un viaje *m*; *(lecture)* conferencia ilustrada sobre un viaje.

tra·vers·a·ble (trə-vûr′sə-bəl) adj. atravesable.

tra·vers·al (trə-vûr′səl) s. travesía.

tra·verse (trə-vûrs′) I. tr. **-versed, -vers·ing** *(to cross)* atravesar, cruzar; *(to move along)* recorrer; *(to swivel)* hacer girar (sobre un eje); *(to examine)* examinar; DEP. *(to zigzag)* recorrer en diagonal; DER. *(to deny)* negar —intr. *(to cross)* cruzar; *(to swivel)* girar sobre un eje; *(in skiing)* descender en diagonal II. s. (trăv′ərs) *(crossing)* travesía; *(route)* ruta sinuosa; *(crosspiece)* travesaño; *(in surveying)* línea quebrada; DEP. *(zigzag descent)* descenso en zigzag; MEC. *(lateral movement)* traslación *f*; DER. *(denial)* negación *f* III. adj. **trav·erse** (trăv′ərs, trə-vûrs′) transversal.

tra·vers·er (trə-vûr′sər) s. transbordador *m*.

trav·es·ty (trăv′ĭ-stē) I. s. [pl. **-ties**] *(parody)* parodia, caricatura; *(imitation)* imitación grotesca II. tr. **-tied, -ty·ing** parodiar.

trawl (trôl) MARÍT. I. s. *(net)* red barredera; *(setline)* palangre *m* II. tr. & intr. pescar con red barredera.

trawl·er (trô′lər) s. *(boat)* jábega; *(fisherman)* jabeguero.

tray (trā) s. bandeja.

treach·er·ous (trĕch′ər-əs) adj. *(traitorous)* traicionero; *(unreliable)* de poca confianza; *(dangerous)* peligroso.

treach·er·y (trĕch′ə-rē) s. [pl. **-ies**] traición *f*.

trea·cle (trē′kəl) s. *(syrup)* melaza; ANT., MED. triaca.

tread (trĕd) I. tr. **trod** (trŏd), **trod·den** (trŏd′n) o **trod, tread·ing** *(to walk on)* pisar; *(to trample)* pisotear; *(to crush)* aplastar; ORNIT. *(to copulate)* pisar ♦ **to t. dry land** pisar tierra firme • **to t. the boards** TEAT. pisar las tablas • **to t. water** pedalear en el agua • **well-trodden path** camino trillado —intr. *(to step on)* pisar; *(to walk)* andar, caminar <*he's treading along the path* está caminando por el sendero> ♦ **to t. lightly** andar con tiento • **to t. on someone's heels** pisarle los talones a alguien II. s. *(step)* pisada; *(gait)* andar *m*; *(sole)* suela; *(horizontal step)* huella (de un escalón); F.C. *(of rails)* ancho; *(of a tire)* banda de rodadura.

tread·le (trĕd′l) I. s. pedal *m* II. intr. **-led, -ling** pedalear.

tread·mill (trĕd′mĭl′) s. *(device)* rueda de andar; FIG. *(routine)* rutina.

trea·son (trē′zən) s. traición *f*.

trea·son·a·ble (trē′zə-nə-bəl) adj. traicionero.

trea·son·ous (trē′zə-nəs) adj. traicionero.

treas·ure (trĕzh′ər) I. s. tesoro II. tr. **-ured, -ur·ing** *(to accumulate)* atesorar; *(to appreciate)* estimar, apreciar.

treas·ur·er (trĕzh′ər-ər) s. tesorero.

treas·ure-trove (trĕzh′ər-trōv′) s. *(hidden wealth)* tesoro hallado; *(discovery)* descubrimiento de valor, hallazgo.

treas·ur·y (trĕzh′ə-rē) s. [pl. **-ies**] *(office)* tesorería; *(public funds)* erario público; *(values)* tesoro ♦ **T.** Ministerio de Hacienda.

treasury note s. bono del tesoro.

treat (trēt) I. tr. *(to act toward)* tratar <*please, t. them nicely* por favor, trátalos bien>; *(subject matter, theme)* tratar; *(to invite)* convidar, invitar <*I'll t. you to the theater* te invito al teatro>; *(to consider)* tomar <*he treats it as a joke* lo toma a broma>; MED., QUÍM. tratar ♦ **to t. of** tratar sobre • **to t. oneself to** darse el lujo o el placer de —intr. *(to pay)* invitar, convidar; *(to negotiate)* negociar II. s. *(present)* regalo; *(invitation)* invitación *f*; *(delight)* placer *m*; *(feast)* banquete *m* ♦ **to go Dutch t.** pagar a escote o a medias.

treat·a·ble (trē′tə-bəl) adj. MED. tratable, curable.

trea·tise (trē′tĭs) s. tratado.

treat·ment (trēt′mənt) s. *(handling)* trato, tratamiento; MED. tratamiento.

trea·ty (trē′tē) s. [pl. **-ties**] *(agreement)* convenio; *(between states)* tratado.

tre·ble (trĕb′əl) I. adj. MAT. triple; MÚS. *(highest voice)* de soprano, de tiple II. s. MÚS. soprano, tiple *m* III. tr. & intr. **-led, -ling** triplicar(se).

treble clef s. MÚS. clave de sol *f*.

tree (trē) I. s. *(plant)* árbol *m*; *(for shoes)* horma; *(post)* poste *m* ♦ **Christmas t.** árbol de Navidad • **family t.** árbol genealógico • **to bark up the wrong t.** FIG. equivocarse • **to**

be up a t. FIG. estar en un aprieto II. tr. **treed, tree·ing** *(to force to climb a tree)* hacer refugiarse en un árbol; FIG. *(to corner)* poner en un aprieto.

tree frog o **tree toad** s. ZOOL. rana de zarzal.

tree·top (trē′tŏp′) s. copa (de un árbol).

tre·foil (trē′foil′, trĕf′oil) s. BOT. trébol *m*; ARQ. trébol, trifolio.

trek (trĕk) I. intr. **trekked, trek·king** *(to travel)* hacer un viaje largo; *(to journey)* viajar en carreta II. s. *(difficult journey)* viaje largo y difícil; *(migration)* migración *f*; *(journey)* viaje en carreta.

trel·lis (trĕl′ĭs) I. s. *(frame)* enrejado; *(arbor)* parra II. tr. *(a wall, plant)* poner un enrejado a; *(grapes)* emparrar.

trem·ble (trĕm′bəl) I. intr. **-bled, -bling** temblar II. s. temblor *m* ♦ **trembles** [ú. con v. sing.] VET. tembladera.

trem·bly (trĕm′blē) adj. trémulo, tembloroso.

tre·men·dous (trĭ-mĕn′dəs) adj. *(terrible)* terrible; *(enormous)* tremendo, enorme; FAM. *(marvelous)* extraordinario.

trem·o·lo (trĕm′ə-lō′) s. [pl. **-los**] MÚS. trémolo.

trem·or (trĕm′ər, trē′mər) s. temblor *m*.

trem·u·lous (trĕm′yə-ləs) adj. *(trembling)* trémulo, tembloroso; *(timid)* tímido.

trench (trĕnch) I. s. *(furrow)* zanja; *(ditch)* cuneta, foso; MIL. trinchera II. tr. *(to dig)* abrir zanjas en; *(to protect)* atrincherar; *(to cut)* cortar; *(to slash)* tallar —intr. *(to dig)* abrir zanjas o trincheras; *(to cut)* cortar ♦ **to t. on** lindar con, rayar en • **to t. on** o **upon** invadir.

trench·ant (trĕn′chənt) adj. *(vigorous)* vigoroso; *(incisive)* mordaz; *(caustic)* cáustico; *(clear-cut)* nítido.

trench coat s. trinchera, impermeable.

trench·er¹ (trĕn′chər) s. *(cutting board)* picador *m*; ANT. *(person)* trinchante.

trench·er² (trĕn′chər) s. *(digger)* persona que hace zanjas o acequias.

trench mouth s. MED. inflamación de las encías *f*.

trend (trĕnd) I. s. *(direction)* dirección *f*; *(tendency)* tendencia; *(custom, habits)* moda II. intr. *(to move)* dirigirse; *(to tend)* tender a, inclinarse a.

trend·set·ter (trĕnd′sĕt′ər) s. persona que dicta una moda.

trend·y (trĕn′dē) adj. **-i·er, -i·est** FAM. que sigue la última moda.

tre·pan (trĭ-păn′) MED., MIN. I. s. trépano II. tr. **-panned, -pan·ning** trepanar.

trep·a·na·tion (trĭ-pă-nā′shən) s. MED. trepanación *f*.

tre·phine (trĭ-fēn′) CIR. I. s. trépano II. tr. **-phined, -phin·ing** trepanar.

trep·i·da·tion (trĕp′ĭ-dā′shən) s. *(apprehension)* aprensión *f*, temor *m*; *(vibration)* trepidación *f*.

tres·pass (trĕs′pəs, -păs′) I. intr. *(to infringe upon)* infringir; DER. *(to enter)* entrar ilegalmente; RELIG. *(to transgress)* pecar II. s. *(transgression)* violación *f*; *(offense)* ofensa; DER. *(trespassing)* transgresión *f* ♦ **no trespassing** prohibido el paso • **trespasses** RELIG. *(in the Lord's Prayer)* deudas, pecados.

tres·pass·er (trĕs′pə-sər) s. *(intruder)* intruso; DER. delincuente *m*, infractor *m*; RELIG. pecador *m*, deudor *m*.

tress (trĕs) s. *(lock of hair)* mechón *f*; *(braid)* trenza ♦ **tresses** cabellera.

tres·tle (trĕs′əl) s. caballete *m*.

trey (trā) s. tres (en cartas, dados o dominós) *m*.

tri·a·ble (trī′ə-bəl) adj. *(capable of being tested)* que se puede someter a examen; DER. enjuiciable.

tri·ac·id (trī-ăs′ĭd) adj. & s. QUÍM. triácido.

tri·ad (trī′ăd) s. *(group)* tríada, trío; MÚS. acorde perfecto.

tri·al (trī′əl) I. s. *(testing)* prueba, ensayo; *(experiment)* experimento; *(attempt)* tentativa; *(hardship)* dificultad *f*; *(test)* prueba; *(suffering)* sufrimiento; *(nuisance)* molestia, tormento; DER. proceso, juicio; DEP. *(game)* partido de preselección; *(competition)* concurso ♦ **on t.** *(being judged)* enjuiciado, procesado; *(being tested)* a título de prueba • **to bring** o **to put to t.** encausar, enjuiciar • **to do something by t. and error** hacer algo por un método de tanteos • **to give someone a t.** poner a alguien a prueba • **to give something a t.** probar algo • **to go on t.** ser procesado • **take on t.** tomar a prueba II. adj. DER. *(pertaining to a*

trial) procesal; *(testing)* de prueba, de ensayo <*t. flight* vuelo de prueba>.
trial and error s. método de tanteos, experimento.
trial balance s. COM. balance de comprobación *m.*
trial balloon s. globo sonda *o* de ensayo.
trial jury s. DER. jurado.
trial run s. experimento, prueba.
tri·an·gle (trī′ăng′gǝl) s. *(shape)* triángulo; DIB. escuadra, cartabón *m;* MÚS. triángulo.
tri·an·gu·lar (trī-ăng′gyǝ-lǝr) adj. triangular.
tri·an·gu·late (trī-ăng′gyǝ-lāt′) I. tr. **-lat·ed, -lat·ing** triangular II. adj. triangulado.
tri·an·gu·la·tion (trī-ăng′gyǝ-lā′shǝn) s. MARÍT., TOP. triangulación *f.*
tri·a·tom·ic (trī′ǝ-tŏm′ĭk) adj. QUÍM. triatómico.
trib·al (trī′bǝl) adj. tribal.
trib·al·ism (trī′bǝ-lĭz′ǝm) s. sistema tribal *m.*
tribe (trīb) s. *(organization)* tribu *f;* FAM., FIG. *(large family)* familia numerosa.
tribes·man (trībz′mǝn) s. [pl. **-men**] miembro de una tribu.
trib·u·la·tion (trĭb′yǝ-lā′shǝn) s. tribulación *f.*
trib·u·nal (trī-byōō′nǝl, trĭ-) s. tribunal *m.*
trib·une[1] (trĭb′yōōn) s. HIST. tribuno (en la antigua Roma); *(protector)* defensor de los derechos *m.*
trib·une[2] (trĭb′yōōn) s. *(platform)* tribuna.
trib·u·tar·y (trĭb′yǝ-tĕr′ē) I. adj. tributario II. s. [pl. **-ies**] *(river)* afluente *m;* *(person)* tributario.
trib·ute (trĭb′yōōt) s. *(payment, acknowledgment)* tributo; *(gift)* ofrenda.
trice (trīs) I. s. instante *m* ◆ **in a t.** en un abrir y cerrar de ojos, en un dos por tres II. tr. **triced, tric·ing** MARÍT. ◆ **to t. up** izar (las velas).
tri·cen·ten·ni·al (trī′sĕn-tĕn′ē-ǝl) I. adj. de trescientos años II. s. tricentenario.
tri·ceps (trī′sĕps) s. [pl. **-ceps·es** *o* **triceps**] ANAT. tríceps *m.*
tri·cer·a·tops (trī-sĕr′ǝ-tŏps′) s. tricerátopo (dinosaurio tricorne).
tri·chi·na (trī-kī′nǝ) s. [pl. **-nae** (-nē) *o* **-nas**] triquina (parásito).
trich·i·no·sis (trĭk′ǝ-nō′sĭs) s. MED. triquinosis *f.*
tri·chlo·ride (trī-klôr′īd′) *o* **tri·chlo·rid** (-ĭd) s. QUÍM. tricloruro.
tri·chot·o·my (trī-kŏt′ǝ-mē) s. [pl. **-mies**] tricotomía.
tri·chro·mat·ic (trī′krō-măt′ĭk) *o* **tri·chrome** (trī′krōm′) adj. tricromático.
trick (trĭk) I. s. *(deceit)* ardid *m,* truco; *(swindle)* estafa; *(joke)* broma; *(prank)* travesura; *(special skill)* maña, habilidad *f;* *(knack)* tranquillo, truco <*I've got the t. of it* le cogí el truco>; *(mannerism)* manía, tic *m* <*it's just a t. he has* es una manía suya>; *(legerdemain)* juego de manos, truco; *(of cards)* baza <*he takes all the tricks* gana todas las bazas>; *(turn of duty)* turno ◆ **a dirty t.** una mala jugada, una trastada • **not to miss a t.** no perder una • **to be up to one's tricks** estar haciendo de las suyas • **to do the t.** resolver el problema, surtir efecto • **to go back to one's old tricks** volver a las andadas • **to play a dirty t. on (somebody)** hacer una mala jugada a (alguien) • **to resort to tricks** andar con triquiñuelas • **to turn tricks** JER. practicar la prostitución II. tr. *(to deceive)* engañar, burlar; *(to swindle)* estafar, timar ◆ **to t. into** obligar con engaño III. adj. de truco • **t. photography** FOTOG. trucaje • **t. question** pega, pregunta de pega.
trick·er·y (trĭk′ǝ-rē) s. [pl. **-ies**] *(deceit)* engaño; *(cunning)* astucia.
trick·le (trĭk′ǝl) I. intr. **-led, -ling** gotear ◆ **to t. in** *(things)* llegar en pequeñas cantidades; *(people)* llegar en pequeños grupos —tr. echar, verter poco a poco II. s. *(dripping)* goteo; *(small amount)* gota.
trick·ster (trĭk′stǝr) s. burlador *m,* timador *m.*
trick·y (trĭk′ē) adj. **-i·er, -i·est** *(wily)* astuto; *(situation, problem)* difícil, delicado.
tri·col·or (trī′kŭl′ǝr) s. bandera tricolor ◆ **T.** bandera francesa.
tri·corn *o* **tri·corne** (trī′kôrn′) s. tricornio.
tri·cot (trē′kō) s. tejido de punto, tricot *m.*
tri·cus·pid (trī-kŭs′pĭd) adj. & s. ANAT. tricúspide *f.*

tri·cy·cle (trī′sĭ-kǝl) s. triciclo.
tri·dent (trīd′nt) s. tridente *m.*
tried (trīd) I. adj. *(tested)* probado; *(reliable)* seguro; *(experienced)* experimentado II. pret. y part. p. de **try.**
tried-and-true (trīd′n-trōō′) adj. *(tested)* probado; *(reliable)* seguro.
tri·en·ni·al (trī-ĕn′ē-ǝl) I. adj. trienal II. s. *(anniversary)* tercer aniversario; *(event)* acontecimiento trienal.
tries (trīz) I. tercera persona sing. del pres. indic. de **try** II. pl. de **try.**
tri·fle (trī′fǝl) I. s. *(unimportant thing)* nadería; *(small amount)* pizca, poquito; *(dessert)* bizcocho borracho ◆ **a t.** un poquito, algo <*he's a t. stingy* es algo tacaño> • **to stop at trifles** pararse a pelillos II. intr. **-fled, -fling** *(to jest)* bromear; FIG. *(to play with something)* jugar con (palabras, sentimientos) —tr. ◆ **to t. away** *(time)* perder; *(money)* malgastar.
tri·fler (trī′flǝr) s. persona frívola.
tri·fling (trī′flĭng) adj. *(insignificant)* insignificante; *(frivolous)* frívolo.
tri·fo·cal (trī-fō′kǝl) adj. trifocal ◆ **trifocals** lentes trifocales.
tri·fo·li·ate (trī-fō′lē-āt′) adj. BOT. trifoliado.
trig[1] (trĭg) I. adj. *(trim)* acicalado; *(healthy)* sano, vigoroso II. tr. **trigged, trig·ging** ataviar, acicalar.
trig[2] (trĭg) I. tr. **trigged, trig·ging** *(to wedge)* calzar (una rueda); *(to support)* apoyar II. s. calce *m,* calzo.
trig[3] (trĭg) s. FAM. trigonometría.
trig·ger (trĭg′ǝr) I. s. *(of a firearm)* gatillo; *(of a mechanism)* disparador *m;* *(provocation)* provocación *f* II. tr. poner en funcionamiento ◆ **to t. off** provocar, desencadenar.
trig·ger-hap·py (trĭg′ǝr-hăp′ē) adj. *(quick to shoot)* pronto a disparar; JER. impulsivo.
tri·glyc·er·ide (trī-glĭs′ǝ-rīd′) s. QUÍM. triglicérido (lípido).
tri·glyph (trī′glĭf′) s. ARQ. triglifo.
trig·o·no·met·ric (trĭg′ǝ-nǝ-mĕt′rĭk) *o* **trig·o·no·met·ri·cal** (-rĭ-kǝl) adj. trigonométrico.
trig·o·nom·e·try (trĭg′ǝ-nŏm′ĭ-trē) s. MAT. trigonometría.
tri·he·dral (trī-hē′drǝl) s. MAT. triedro.
trike (trīk) s. FAM. triciclo.
tri·lat·er·al (trī-lăt′ǝr-ǝl) s. trilátero.
trill (trĭl) s. *(warble)* gorjeo; MÚS. trino; FONÉT. vibración *f.*
tril·lion (trĭl′yǝn) s. billón *m;* G.B. trillón *m.*
tril·li·um (trĭl′ē-ǝm) s. BOT. lirio del bosque.
tri·lo·bate (trī-lō′bāt′) *o* **tri·lo·bat·ed** (-lō′bā′tĭd) *o* **tri·lobed** (trī′lōbd′) adj. BOT. trilobulado.
tri·lo·bite (trī′lǝ-bīt′) s. PALEON. trilobite (artrópodo) *m.*
tril·o·gy (trĭl′ǝ-jē) s. [pl. **-gies**] LIT. trilogía.
trim (trĭm) I. tr. **trimmed, trim·ming** *(to make tidy)* arreglar, ordenar; *(hair)* entresacar, recortar; *(nails)* recortar; *(branches)* podar; *(wood)* desbastar, alisar; *(candle, lamp)* despabilar; *(to ornament)* decorar, adornar <*to t. a Christmas tree* adornar un árbol de Navidad>; *(in bookbinding)* guillotinar; *(to reduce)* reducir <*to t. a budget* reducir un presupuesto>; *(to equip)* equipar; MARÍT. *(sails)* orientar; AVIA., MARÍT. *(to balance)* equilibrar ◆ **to t. down** reducir • **to t. off** *o* **away** recortar, podar • **to t. one's sails** FIG. adaptarse, amoldarse • **to t. up** arreglar, acicalar —intr. MARÍT. *(a ship)* estar equilibrado; FIG. *(to be neutral)* nadar entre dos aguas II. s. *(condition)* condición *f,* estado; *(ornamentation)* adorno, decoración *f;* *(cuttings)* recorte *m;* MARÍT. *(of a ship)* asiento; *(of sails)* orientación *f;* AVIA. equilibrio ◆ **in good t.** en forma • **out of t.** *(person)* en baja forma; *(boat)* mal estibado III. adj. **trim·mer, trim·mest** *(in good order)* aseado, arreglado; *(elegant)* elegante; *(looking well)* apuesto, bien parecido IV. adv. en orden, en regla.
tri·mes·ter (trī-mĕs′tǝr) s. trimestre *m.*
trim·mer (trĭm′ǝr) s. *(person)* desbastador *m;* *(machine)* máquina desbastadora; FIG. *(opportunist)* oportunista *mf.*
trim·ming (trĭm′ĭng) s. *(of an ornament)* adorno; FAM. *(beating)* paliza, zurra ◆ **trimmings** *(accesories)* accesorios *m;* CUL. guarnición; *(scraps)* recortes.
trim·ness (trĭm′nĭs) s. aspecto ordenado, orden *m.*
tri·mo·lec·u·lar (trī′mǝ-lĕk′yǝ-lǝr) adj. QUÍM. trimolecular, de tres moléculas.

---

tri·month·ly (trī-mŭnth'lē) adj. trimestral.

tri·na·ry (trī'nə-rē) adj. ternario.

trine (trīn) I. adj. *(triple)* triple; ASTROL. en trigono II. s. *(group of three)* tríada; ASTROL. trígono.

Trin·i·dad and To·ba·go (trĭn'ĭ-dăd'; tə-bā'gō) s. Trinidad y Tobago.

Trin·i·tar·i·an (trĭn'ĭ-târ'ē-ən) I. adj. RELIG. trinitario ♦ t. triple II. s. RELIG. *(believer)* creyente· de la Trinidad *mf*; *(member of an order)* trinitario.

trin·i·ty (trĭn'ĭ-tē) s. [pl. **-ties**] trío ♦ T. RELIG. Trinidad; *(Sunday)* domingo de la Santísima Trinidad.

trin·ket (trĭng'kĭt) s. *(ornament)* dije *m*; *(trifle)* chuchería.

tri·no·mi·al (trī-nō'mē-əl) I. adj. BIOL. trinomial; MAT. de trinomio II. s. MAT. trinomio; BIOL. nombre trinomial *m*.

tri·o (trē'ō) s. [pl. **-os**] trío.

tri·ode (trī'ōd') s. ELECTRÓN. tríodo.

tri·ox·ide (trī-ŏk'sīd') o **tri·ox·id** (-sĭd) s. QUÍM. trióxido.

trip (trĭp) I. s. *(journey)* viaje *m* <business t. viaje de negocios>; *(excursion)* excursión *f*; *(tread)* paso (ligero); *(stumble)* tropezón *m*, traspié *m*; *(trick)* zancadilla; FIG. *(mistake)* desliz *m*, error *m*; JER. *(drugs' effect)* viaje *m*; TEC. *(of a watch)* trinquete *m*; *(of a mechanism)* disparador *m* ♦ **round t.** viaje de ida y vuelta II. intr. **tripped, trip·ping** *(to make a trip)* viajar; *(to stumble)* dar un traspié; *(to move nimbly)* andar con paso ligero; *(an alarm)* sonar; *(a catch, spring)* soltarse; FIG. *(to make a mistake)* equivocarse —tr. *(to cause to stumble)* hacer tropezar o caer, hacer una zancadilla; *(an alarm)* hacer sonar; *(a catch, spring)* soltar, disparar; FIG. *(to catch in an error)* coger en una falta; *(to confuse)* hacer confundir <he tripped me up me hizo confundir>; MARÍT. *(the anchor)* levar; *(a mast)* izar.

tri·par·tite (trī-pär'tīt') adj. tripartito.

tripe (trīp) s. CUL. callos, mondongo; FAM. *(rubbish)* tonterías.

trip hammer o **trip·ham·mer** o **trip-ham·mer** (trĭp'hăm'ər) s. MAQ., MEC. martinete *m*.

tri·phos·phate (trī-fŏs'fāt') s. QUÍM. trifosfato.

triph·thong (trĭf'thông', trĭp'-) s. FONÉT. triptongo.

tri·ple (trĭp'əl) I. adj. *(threefold)* triple; MÚS. ternario II. s. triple *m* III. tr. & intr. **-pled, -pling** triplicar(se).

tri·ple-space (trĭp'əl-spās') tr. & intr. **-spaced, -spac·ing** escribir a máquina dejando dos líneas en blanco.

tri·plet (trĭp'lĭt) s. *(set)* trío; *(baby)* trillizo; POÉT. terceto; MÚS. tresillo.

triple time s. MÚS. compás ternario.

tri·plex (trĭp'lĕks', trī'plĕks') adj. triple.

trip·li·cate (trĭp'lĭ-kĭt) I. s. triplicado ♦ **in t.** por triplicado II. tr. (-kāt') **-cat·ed, -cat·ing** *(to multiply)* triplicar; *(to copy)* hacer por triplicado.

tri·pod (trī'pŏd') s. trípode *m*.

trip·tych (trĭp'tĭk) s. tríptico.

tri·sect (trī'sĕkt') tr. MAT. trisecar.

tri·sec·tion (trī-sĕk'shən) s. MAT. trisección *f*.

tris·mus (trĭz'məs) s. MED. trismo.

tri·sul·fide (trī-sŭl'fīd') s. QUÍM. trisulfuro.

trite (trīt) adj. **trit·er, trit·est** trillado.

trit·i·um (trĭt'ē-əm, trĭsh'ē-) s. QUÍM. tritio.

tri·ton[1] (trīt'n) s. ICT. tritón *m* ♦ T. MITOL. tritón.

tri·ton[2] (trī'tŏn') s. FÍS. tritón (núcleo) *m*.

trit·u·rate (trĭch'ə-rāt') I. tr. **-rat·ed, -rat·ing** triturar II. s. (-ər-ĭt) substancia triturada.

tri·umph (trī'əmf) I. intr. *(to win)* triunfar, vencer; *(to exult)* alegrarse, regocijarse ♦ **to t. over** triunfar sobre, vencer II. s. *(success)* triunfo, éxito; *(exultation)* regocijo, júbilo.

tri·um·phal (trī-ŭm'fəl) adj. triunfal.

tri·um·phant (trī-ŭm'fənt) adj. triunfante, victorioso.

tri·um·vir (trī-ŭm'vər) s. [pl. **-virs** o **-vi·ri** (-və-rī')] triumviro.

tri·um·vi·rate (trī-ŭm'vər-ĭt) s. triunvirato.

tri·une (trī'yōōn') s. tríada ♦ T. RELIG. Trinidad.

tri·va·lent (trī-vā'lənt) adj. QUÍM. trivalente.

triv·et (trĭv'ĭt) s. *(for cooking)* trébedes *m*; *(for the table)* salvamantel *m*.

triv·i·a (trĭv'ē-ə) s.pl. trivialidades *f*.

triv·i·al (trĭv'ē-əl) adj. *(insignificant)* insignificante; *(superficial)* trivial.

triv·i·al·i·ty (trĭv'ē-ăl'ĭ-tē) s. [pl. **-ties**] *(quality)* trivialidad *f*; *(insignificance)* insignificancia.

triv·i·um (trĭv'ē-əm) s. [pl. **-i·a** (-ē-ə)] trivio.

tri·week·ly (trī-wēk'lē) I. adj. *(three times a week)* trisemanal; *(every three weeks)* de cada tres semanas II. adv. *(three times a week)* tres veces por semana; *(every three weeks)* cada tres semanas III. s. publicación trisemanal *f*.

tro·che (trō'kē) s. FARM. pastilla.

trod (trŏd) pret. y un part. p. de **tread.**

trod·den (trŏd'n) un part. p. de **tread.**

trog·lo·dyte (trŏg'lə-dīt') s. troglodita *mf*.

troi·ka (troi'kə) s. troica.

Tro·jan (trō'jən) s. & adj. HIST. troyano.

Trojan horse s. HIST. caballo de Troya.

troll[1] (trōl) I. tr. *(to fish)* pescar con cebo de cuchara; *(to sing)* cantar en canon; *(to roll)* revolver II. s. *(lure)* cebo de cuchara; MÚS. canon *m*.

troll[2] (trōl) s. duende *m*, gnomo.

trol·ley (trŏl'ē) s. [pl. **-leys**] *(streetcar)* tranvía *m*; *(carriage)* carretilla; *(electric device)* colector de corriente *m*; MIN. vagoneta; G.B. carreta.

trolley bus s. trolebús *m*.

trolley car s. tranvía *m*.

trol·lop (trŏl'əp) s. *(slattern)* puerca, mujer sucia; *(prostitute)* prostituta.

trom·bone (trŏm-bōn') s. MÚS. trombón *m*.

trom·bon·ist (trŏm-bō'nĭst) s. MÚS. trombón *m*.

trom·mel (trŏm'əl) s. TEC. tambor *m*.

troop (trōōp) I. s. *(group)* grupo; *(of animals)* manada; *(of soldiers)* escuadrón *m*; *(scouts)* grupo; *(a great many)* tropel *m* ♦ **troops** tropas II. intr. *(to move)* ir en grupo; *(to assemble)* agruparse.

troop·er (trōō'pər) s. MIL. *(cavalryman)* soldado de caballería; *(horse)* caballo; *(mounted policeman)* policía montado; *(state police)* patrullero ♦ **to be a t.** FIG., FAM. ser un profesional.

troop·ship (trōōp'shĭp') s. MIL. buque de transporte *m*.

trope (trōp) s. LIT. tropo.

tro·phy (trō'fē) s. [pl. **-phies**] trofeo.

trop·ic (trŏp'ĭk) I. s. ASTRON., GEOG. trópico II. adj. GEOG. tropical.

trop·i·cal (trŏp'ĭ-kəl) adj. tropical.

tropical year s. ASTRON. año trópico.

tropic of Cancer s. ASTRON. trópico de Cáncer.

tropic of Capricorn s. ASTRON. trópico de Capricornio.

tro·pism (trō'pĭz'əm) s. BIOL. tropismo.

tro·po·sphere (trō'pə-sfîr', trŏp'ə-) s. troposfera.

trot (trŏt) I. s. *(gait)* trote *m*; *(jog)* paso corto; FAM. *(translation)* traducción literal; *(toddler)* infante *m*; *(crone)* vieja arpía II. intr. **trot·ted, trot·ting** *(to move)* trotar; *(to hurry)* apurarse —tr. hacer trotar ♦ **to t. out** FAM. *(to bring out)* sacar a relucir; *(to show off)* hacer alarde de.

troth (trôth, trŏth) I. s. *(fidelity)* fidelidad *f*; *(betrothal)* compromiso ♦ **to plight one's t.** dar palabra de matrimonio II. tr. prometer.

trot·ter (trŏt'ər) s. *(horse)* trotón *m*; CUL. pata de cerdo.

trou·ba·dour (trōō'bə-dôr', -dōōr') s. trovador *m*.

trou·ble (trŭb'əl) I. s. *(affliction)* pena; *(misfortune)* desgracia; *(distress)* apuro, aprieto; *(worry)* inquietud *f*, preocupación *f*; *(annoyance)* disgusto; *(difficulty)* dificultad *f*, problema *m* <did you have any t.? ¿tuviste algún problema?>; *(hindrance)* estorbo, inconveniente *m* <their parents are a big t. to them sus padres son un gran estorbo para ellos>; *(bother)* molestia <it's no t. no es molestia>; *(effort)* esfuerzo; *(dispute)* conflicto; *(disturbance)* disturbios; MED. *(disease)* enfermedad *f*, trastorno <mental troubles trastornos mentales>; *(malfunction)* avería, fallo ♦ **may I t. you?** ¿me hace usted el favor? • **no t. at all** con mucho gusto • **that's the t.** ése es el inconveniente • **to ask for t.** FAM. buscarse líos • **to be in t.** estar en un aprieto • **to be looking for t.** buscar camorra • **to be worth the t.** valer la pena • **to get into t.** meterse en líos • **to start t.** dar problemas • **to have t. with** tener dificultades con • **to stay out of t.** no meterse en líos • **to stir up t.** armar un lío • **to take the t. to (do)** tomarse la molestia de (hacer) • **what's the t.?** ¿cuál es el problema?, ¿qué pasa? II. tr. **-bled,**

-bling *(to disturb)* agitar, turbar; *(to affect)* afligir, afectar <*the news troubled him* la noticia le afligió>; *(to worry)* inquietar, preocupar; *(to afflict)* afligir, aquejar; *(to bother)* molestar, incomodar <*I'm sorry to t. you* lamento molestarle> —intr. *(to be worried)* preocuparse, inquietarse <*don't t. to return it* no se preocupe por devolverlo>; *(to take pains)* molestarse, tomarse la molestia <*he didn't t. to shut the door* no se tomó la molestia de cerrar la puerta>.

trou·ble·mak·er (trŭb′əl-mā′kər) s. perturbador *m*, camorrista *mf*.

trou·ble·shoot·er (trŭb′əl-shōō′tər) s. *(worker)* reparador de averías *m*; *(mediator)* mediador *m*, experto en resolver problemas tecnológicos *o* administrativos.

trou·ble·some (trŭb′əl-səm) adj. *(worrisome)* inquietante; *(difficult)* penoso, dificultoso.

trough (trôf) s. *(for drinking)* abrevadero; *(for feeding)* pesebre *m*; *(gutter)* canalón *m*; *(depression)* depresión *f*; *(low point)* mínimo; METEOR. zona de presiones bajas.

trounce (trouns) tr. **trounced, trounc·ing** *(to hit)* zurrar; DEP. *(to defeat)* derrotar rotundamente.

troupe (trōōp) s. TEAT. compañía.

troup·er (trōō′pər) s. TEAT. actor *m*.

trou·sers (trou′zərz) s.pl. pantalones *m*.

trous·seau (trōō′sō) s. [pl. **-seaux** (-sōz) *o* **-seaus**] ajuar *m*.

trout (trout) s. [pl. **trout** *o* **trouts**] ICT. trucha.

trove (trōv) s. descubrimiento, hallazgo.

trow·el (trou′əl) I. s. *(for leveling)* palustre *m*; *(for digging)* desplantador *m* II. tr. extender con el palustre.

trow·sers (trou′zərz) s.pl. var. de **trousers**.

troy (troi) adj. troy, del peso troy.

Troy (troi) s. Troya.

troy weight s. peso troy (sistema de pesos cuya unidad es la libra de 12 onzas).

tru·an·cy (trōō′ən-sē) s. [pl. **-cies**] falta a clase, rabona.

tru·ant (trōō′ənt) I. s. *(from school)* persona que hace novillos *o* la rabona; *(lazy person)* haragán *m* ♦ **to play t.** hacer novillos, hacerse la rabona II. adj. *(from school)* que hace novillos *o* la rabona; *(lazy)* perezoso.

truce (trōōs) s. *(cessation)* tregua; *(respite)* pausa, respiro.

truck¹ (trŭk) I. s. *(heavy vehicle)* camión *m*; *(barrow)* carretilla; *(bogie)* carretón *m*; G.B., F.C. *(wagon)* vagón raso II. tr. transportar en camión —intr. conducir un camión.

truck² (trŭk) I. tr. *(to barter)* trocar; *(to peddle)* vender de puerta en puerta —intr. comerciar II. s. *(trade goods)* artículos de comercio; *(garden produce)* hortalizas (para el mercado); *(exchange)* trueque *m*; FAM. *(rubbish)* baratijas; *(business)* comercio.

truck·age (trŭk′ĭj) s. transporte por camión *m*, acarreo.

truck driver s. camionero.

truck·er (trŭk′ər) s. *(driver)* camionero; *(company)* compañía de transporte.

truck farm s. huerto, huerta.

truck·ing (trŭk′ĭng) s. transporte por camión *m*, acarreo.

truck·le (trŭk′əl) I. s. *(wheel)* ruedecilla; *(trundle bed)* carriola, cama con ruedas II. intr. **-led, -ling** ♦ **to t. to** ser servil para con.

truck·load (trŭk′lōd′) s. camión (carga).

truc·u·lent (trŭk′yə-lənt) adj. *(fierce)* feroz, cruel; *(pugnacious)* belicoso, agresivo.

trudge (trŭj) I. intr. **trudged, trudg·ing** caminar con dificultad II. s. caminata larga y penosa.

true (trōō) I. adj. **tru·er, tru·est** *(not false)* verdadero, verídico <*a t. story* una historia verdadera>; *(factual)* cierto, verdadero <*that is t.* eso es cierto>; *(genuine)* verdadero, auténtico <*t. value* valor auténtico>; *(loyal)* leal, fiel; *(legitimate)* legítimo <*a t. heir* un heredero legítimo>; *(accurate, standard)* exacto; *(essential)* esencial, fundamental <*the t. motive* el motivo esencial>; MÚS. afinado; MEC. centrado; CONSTR. a plomo ♦ **it's too good to be t.** es demasiado bueno para ser cierto • **to be t. to one's word** ser fiel a su palabra • **to come t.** realizarse, cumplirse • **t. to life** conforme a la realidad II. adv. *(rightly)* verdaderamente; *(exactly)* exactamente III. s. verdad *f* ♦ **to be out of t.** *(lacking alignment)* estar desalineado; *(a wheel)* estar des-

centrado IV. tr. **trued, tru·ing** MEC. *(a mechanism)* rectificar, corregir; *(a wheel)* centrar.

true bill s. DER. acta de acusación.

true-blue (trōō′blōō′) I. s. persona leal II. adj. leal.

true-born (trōō′bôrn′) adj. auténtico.

true-false test (trōō′fôls′) s. prueba de cierto o falso.

true-life (trōō′līf′) adj. de la vida real.

true·love (trōō′lŭv′) s. amor *m*.

true·ness (trōō′nĭs) s. *(faithfulness)* fidelidad *f*, lealtad *f*; *(sincerity)* sinceridad *f*; *(truth)* verdad *f*.

truf·fle (trŭf′əl) s. trufa.

tru·ism (trōō′ĭz′əm) s. perogrullada.

tru·ly (trōō′lē) adv. *(sincerely)* sinceramente; *(truthfully)* verdaderamente; *(indeed)* realmente, verdaderamente <*t. ugly* realmente feo>; *(properly)* propiamente ♦ **we are t. sorry** lo sentimos de verdad • **yours t.** suyo atentamente, su seguro servidor.

trump¹ (trŭmp) I. s. *(in cards)* triunfo; *(key resource)* recurso clave; FAM. *(good person)* buen sujeto ♦ **to hold all the trumps** tener todos los triunfos en la mano II. tr. matar con un triunfo —intr. jugar un triunfo ♦ **to t. up** inventar, falsificar.

trump² (trŭmp) s. MÚS. trompeta.

trum·per·y (trŭm′pə-rē) s. [pl. **-ies**] *(bric-a-brac)* baratija; *(nonsense)* tonterías; *(fraud)* engaño.

trum·pet (trŭm′pĭt) I. s. MÚS. trompeta; *(sound)* trompetilla; *(organ)* trompetilla acústica; *(animal call)* bramido II. intr. *(to play)* tocar la trompeta; *(to call)* bramar —tr. pregonar, anunciar a son de trompeta.

trum·pet·er (trŭm′pĭ-tər) s. *(player)* trompetista *mf*; *(herald)* pregonero, portavoz *m*; ORNIT. agamí *m*.

trun·cate (trŭng′kāt′) I. tr. **-cat·ed, -cat·ing** truncar II. adj. truncado.

trun·cat·ed (trŭng′kā′tĭd) adj. GEOM. truncado.

trun·cheon (trŭn′chən) I. s. *(baton)* bastón de mando *m*; *(billy)* cachiporra, porra; ANT. *(cudgel)* matraca II. tr. ANT. zurrar, golpear.

trun·dle (trŭn′dl) I. s. *(roller)* rueda pequeña; *(bed)* carriola; *(dolly)* carretilla de mano II. tr. *(to push)* empujar; *(a hoop)* hacer rodar —intr. rodar.

trun·dle bed (trŭn′dl) s. carriola.

trunk (trŭngk) s. *(of a human body, a tree)* tronco; *(of an insect)* tórax *m*; *(of an elephant)* trompa; *(luggage)* baúl *m*; *(of a car)* portaequipaje *m*, maletera; TEL. línea interurbana; F.C. línea principal; TEC. conducto, tubería; ARQ. fuste *m* ♦ **trunks** *(for swimming)* bañador, pantaloncitos; *(shorts)* pantalón corto.

trunk line s. TEL. línea interurbana; F.C. línea principal.

truss (trŭs) I. s. MED. braguero; *(framework)* armazón *mf*; MARÍT. troza; *(cluster)* racimo II. tr. *(to tie up)* atar; *(to support)* apuntalar; CUL. sujetar con una brocheta.

trust (trŭst) I. s. *(confidence)* confianza <*breach of t.* abuso de confianza>; *(charge)* custodia, responsabilidad *f*; *(duty)* deber *m*, obligación *f*; *(hope)* fe *m*, esperanza <*to have t. in the future* tener fe en el futuro>; *(credit)* crédito, fiado <*to sell on t.* vender a crédito>; DER. *(of property)* fideicomiso; COM., FIN. *(associated firms)* trust *m*, consorcio ♦ **in t.** DER. en depósito • **to take on t.** FIG. creer *o* aceptar a ojos cerrados II. intr. *(to depend)* depender; *(to hope)* esperar, confiar; *(to sell)* vender a crédito —tr. *(to have confidence in)* tener confianza en, fiarse de <*don't you t. me?* ¿no te fías de mí?>; *(to believe)* creer; *(to hope)* esperar <*I t. he'll be on time* espero que venga a tiempo>; *(to entrust)* confiar, encomendar; COM., FIN. dar crédito a.

trust·bust·er (trŭst′bŭs′tər) s. FAM. funcionario encargado de disolver monopolios.

trust company s. FIN. *(corporation)* empresa fideicomisaria; *(bank)* banco de depósito.

trus·tee (trŭ-stē′) I. s. *(administrator)* fideicomisario; *(member of a board)* síndico; *(country)* país fideicomisario ♦ **board of trustees** consejo de administración II. tr. **-teed, -tee·ing** encomendar a un síndico —intr. ser síndico.

trus·tee·ship (trŭ-stē′shĭp′) s. *(position)* cargo de síndico; *(territory)* fideicomiso.

trust·ful (trŭst′fəl) adj. confiado.

trust fund s. ECON. fondo fiduciario.
trust·ing (trŭs'tĭng) adj. confiado.
trust territory s. territorio bajo fideicomiso.
trust·wor·thy (trŭst'wûr'thē) adj. -thi·er, -thi·est de confianza.
trust·y (trŭs'tē) I. adj. -i·er, -i·est de confianza II. s. [pl. -ies] *(trusted person)* persona digna de confianza; *(convict)* preso a quien conceden ciertos privilegios por su buena conducta.
truth (trōōth) s. [pl. **truths** (trōōthz, trōōths)] *(conformity to fact)* verdad *f; (exactitude)* exactitud *f; (reality)* realidad *f; (veracity)* veracidad *f; (sincerity)* sinceridad *f* ♦ **in t.** en verdad • **T.** RELIG. Dios • **the moment of t.** la hora de la verdad • **to tell the t.** a decir verdad, la verdad sea dicha.
truth·ful (trōōth'fəl) adj. *(honest)* sincero; *(true)* verídico.
truth·ful·ly (trōōth'fə-lē) adv. verazmente.
truth·ful·ness (trōōth'fəl-nĭs) s. veracidad *f.*
truth serum s. CRIMIN., PSIC. suero de la verdad.
truth-val·ue (trōōth'văl'yōō) s. LÓG. veracidad o falsedad de una proposición.
try (trī) I. tr. **tried, try·ing** *(to make a trial of)* probar <*now, t. steering with one hand* prueba conducir con una sola mano ahora>; *(to make an effort at)* tratar de, procurar <*t. to keep your eyes open* trata de mantener los ojos abiertos>; *(to attempt)* intentar, tratar de <*she tried to learn French* intentó aprender francés>; *(to taste)* probar; *(to test)* poner a prueba; DER. *(a case)* ver, someter a juicio; *(a person)* juzgar, procesar; FIG. *(to tire)* cansar, fatigar <*to t. one's eyes by reading too much* cansarse los ojos leyendo demasiado> ♦ **to t. for** intentar conseguir • **to t. on** *(a garment)* probarse; *(to test)* probar • **to t. one's best** hacer todo lo posible • **to t. one's hand at** *(something)* probar uno su habilidad en; *(game)* probar uno su suerte a *o* en • **to t. out** *(to give it a try)* probar; *(lard)* derretir; *(metal)* refinar —intr. *(to make an effort)* esforzarse ♦ **to t. and do something** tratar de hacer algo • **to t. hard** esforzarse mucho II. s. [pl. **tries**] *(attempt)* tentativa, intento; DEP. ensayo ♦ **to have a t. at doing something** intentar hacer algo.
try·ing (trī'ĭng) adj. irritante, molesto.
try·out (trī'out') s. *(test)* prueba de aptitud; *(audition)* audición *f.*
tryp·sin (trĭp'sĭn) s. BIOQUÍM. tripsina.
try·sail (trī'səl, -sāl') s. MARÍT. vela cangreja.
try square s. CARP. escuadra de comprobación.
tryst (trĭst) I. s. *(date)* cita (entre amantes); *(place)* lugar de cita II. intr. cumplir con una cita.
tsar (tsär) s. var. de **czar.**
tset·se fly (tsĕt'sē, tsĕt'-) s. ENTOM. mosca tse-tsé.
T-shirt (tē'shûrt') s. camiseta.
T-square (tē'skwâr') s. escuadra en T, regla T.
tub (tŭb) I. s. *(vessel)* tonel (recipiente y contenido) *m; (bathtub)* baño; FAM. *(bath)* baño; *(ship)* carraca; MIN. cubo II. tr. **tubbed, tub·bing** *(to store)* encubar; *(to bathe)* bañar —intr. bañarse.
tu·ba (tōō'bə, tyōō'-) s. MÚS. tuba.
tu·bal (tōō'bəl, tyōō'-) adj. MED. tubárico, tubario.
tub·by (tŭb'ē) adj. -bi·er, -bi·est rechoncho.
tube (tōōb, tyōōb) I. s. *(hollow cylinder)* tubo; ANAT. *(duct)* trompa <*Eustachian t.* trompa de Eustaquio>; ANAT., BOT. tubo <*capillary t.* tubo capilar>; ELECTRÓN. tubo, lámpara; AUTO. *(of a tire)* cámara de aire; *(tunnel)* túnel *m;* FAM. *(television)* tele *f;* G.B. *(subway)* metro, subterráneo II. tr. **tubed, tub·ing** entubar.
tube·less tire (tōōb'lĭs, tyōōb'-) s. neumático *o* llanta sin cámara.
tu·ber (tōō'bər, tyōō'-) s. BOT., MED. tubérculo; ANAT. tuberosidad *f.*
tu·ber·cle (tōō'bər-kəl, tyōō'-) s. tubérculo.
tubercle bacillus s. MED. bacilo de Koch.
tu·ber·cu·lar (tōō-bûr'kyə-lər, tyōō-) adj. & s. tuberculoso.
tu·ber·cu·lin (tōō-bûr'kyə-lĭn, tyōō-) s. BACT. tuberculina.
tu·ber·cu·lo·sis (tōō-bûr'kyə-lō'sĭs, tyōō-) s. MED. tuberculosis *f.*
tu·ber·cu·lous (tōō-bûr'kyə-ləs, tyōō-) adj. tuberculoso.
tube·rose (tōōb'rōz') s. BOT. tuberosa, nardo.

tu·ber·ous (tōō'bər-əs, tyōō'-) adj. BOT. tuberoso.
tub·ing (tōō'bĭng, tyōō'-) s. *(piping)* tubería; MED., TEC. entubado.
tu·bu·lar (tōō'byə-lər, tyōō'-) adj. tubular.
tu·bule (tōō'byōōl, tyōō'-) s. *(small tube)* tubo pequeño; ANAT. túbulo.
tuck¹ (tŭk) I. tr. *(to make folds in)* plegar, alforzar; *(to introduce)* meter; *(to put in a snug place)* esconder <*a village tucked among the woods* una aldea escondida en el bosque> ♦ **to t. away** *(to hide)* ocultar, esconder <*you t. it away in your pocket* lo ocultas en el bolsillo>; *(to swallow)* tragar • **to t. in** arropar (en la cama) • **to t. up** *(sleeves)* arremangar; *(child)* arropar —intr. hacer pliegues ♦ **to t. in** comer con buen apetito II. s. *(fold)* pliegue *m,* alforza; G.B., FAM. *(food)* comida; *(sweets)* dulces *m,* golosinas.
tuck² (tŭk) s. *(on a drum)* toque de tambor *m.*
tuck·er¹ (tŭk'ər) s. *(device)* alforzador *m; (ornament)* escote *m.*
tuck·er² (tŭk'ər) tr. FAM. *(to exhaust)* agotar ♦ **to be all tuckered out** FAM. estar agotado.
Tues·day (tōōz'dē, tyōōz'-) s. martes *m.*
tu·fa (tōō'fə, tyōō'-) s. MIN. toba.
tuft (tŭft) I. s. *(cluster)* mechón *m; (bush)* mata; *(goatee)* perilla II. tr. *(to decorate)* poner una borla a; *(to secure)* fijar (con hilos, botones).
tug (tŭg) I. tr. **tugged, tug·ging** *(to pull)* tirar de; *(to drag)* arrastrar; *(to tow)* remolcar —intr. *(to pull)* tirar fuerte; *(to strain)* esforzarse; *(to contend)* luchar II. s. *(pull)* tirón *m; (struggle)* lucha; *(tugboat)* remolcador *m; (strap)* tirante *m.*
tug·boat (tŭg'bōt') s. remolcador *m.*
tug of war s. DEP. juego de la cuerda; FIG. *(struggle)* lucha.
tu·i·tion (tōō-ĭsh'ən, tyōō-) s. *(fee)* matrícula; *(instruction)* enseñanza; ANT. *(guardianship)* tutela.
tu·lip (tōō'lĭp, tyōō'-) s. tulipán *m.*
tulle (tōōl) s. tul *m.*
tum·ble (tŭm'bəl) I. intr. **-bled, -bling** *(to roll)* rodar, dar tumbos *o* volteretas; *(to fall)* caerse; *(in bed)* agitarse, revolverse; *(to collapse)* derrumbarse, venirse abajo; *(to drop)* caerse (precios) ♦ **to t. down** derrumbarse, desplomarse • **to t. out** salir a montones, salir en desorden —tr. *(to knock down)* derribar, tumbar; *(to disarrange)* desarreglar, desordenar; FIG. *(a government)* derrocar ♦ **to t. into** *o* **upon** tropezar con • **to t. on** dar con, encontrar <*we tumbled on a first-rate restaurant* dimos con un restaurante de primera categoría> • **to t. to** JER. caer en (la cuenta de), comprender II. s. *(fall)* caída; *(somersault)* voltereta ♦ **in a t.** en desorden • **to have** *o* **take a t.** dar un tumbo, caerse.
tum·ble-down (tŭm'bəl-doun') adj. destartalado.
tum·bler (tŭm'blər) s. *(acrobat, gymnast)* volatinero; *(glass)* vaso; *(of a lock)* seguro, guarda; TEC. balancín *m;* ORNIT. pichón volteador.
tum·ble·weed (tŭm'bəl-wēd') s. BOT. planta rodadora.
tum·bling (tŭm'blĭng) s. DEP. acrobacia.
tum·brel *o* **tum·bril** (tŭm'brəl) s. *(cart)* volquete *m;* HIST. carreta (para transportar prisioneros).
tu·me·fac·tion (tōō'mə-făk'shən, tyōō'-) s. tumefacción *f.*
tu·mes·cence (tōō-mĕs'əns, tyōō-) s. tumescencia.
tu·mid (tōō'mĭd, tyōō'-) adj. MED. túmido, hinchado; FIG. *(said of style)* ampuloso, inchado.
tum·my (tŭm'ē) s. [pl. -mies] FAM. barriga.
tum·my·ache (tŭm'ē-āk') s. FAM. dolor de estómago *m.*
tu·mor (tōō'mər, tyōō'-) s. MED. tumor *m.*
tu·mult (tōō'mŭlt', tyōō'-) s. *(crowd)* tumulto; FIG. *(agitation)* agitación *f; (riot)* motín *m.*
tu·mul·tu·ous (tōō-mŭl'chōō-əs, tyōō-) adj. tumultuoso.
tu·na¹ (tōō'nə, tyōō'-) s. [pl. **tuna** *o* **-nas**] CUL., ICT. atún *m.*
tu·na² (tōō'nə, tyōō'-) s. *(plant)* tuna; *(fruit)* higo chumbo.
tun·dra (tŭn'drə) s. GEOG. tundra.
tune (tōōn, tyōōn) s. MÚS. *(melody)* melodía; *(pitch)* tono; FIG. *(harmony)* armonía; ELECTRÓN. sintonización *f* ♦ **in t.** MÚS. afinado • **in t. with** FIG. en armonía con, de acuerdo con • **out of t.** MÚS. desafinado • **to be out of t. with** FIG. desentonar con • **to change one's t.** FIG. cam-

---

ã rey / ä año / b boca / ch chico / d dar / ĕ el / ē mil / g gato / h joya / hw juez / ī aire / k casa / kw cuan /

biar de tono, cambiar de razonamiento • **to the t. of** FIG. por la cantidad *o* la suma de **II.** tr. **tuned, tun·ing** MÚS. afinar; MEC. poner a punto; FIG. *(to adapt)* adaptar • **to t. in** RAD., TELEV. sintonizar • **to t. out** JER. *(to dissociate oneself from)* desprenderse de; *(to ignore)* desatender, no prestar atención a <*he tunes out the noises of the street* no presta atención a los ruidos de la calle> • **to t. up** MÚS. afinar; MED. poner a punto —intr. • **to t. up** MÚS. afinar los instrumentos.

tune·ful (tōōn'fəl, tyōōn'-) adj. melodioso, armonioso.

tun·er (tōō'nər, tyōō'-) s. MÚS. *(person)* afinador *m*; RAD. *(device)* sintonizador *m*.

tune-up (tōōn'ŭp', tyōōn'-) s. MEC. reglaje *m*, puesta a punto (de un motor).

tung oil s. aceite de palo *m*.

tung·sten (tŭng'stən) s. QUÍM. tungsteno.

tung tree s. BOT. copayero.

tu·nic (tōō'nĭk, tyōō'-) s. *(garment)* túnica; MIL. *(jacket)* guerrera; *(blouse)* blusa; ANAT., BOT. túnica; RELIG. *(tunicle)* tunicela.

tun·ing (tōō'nĭng, tyōō'-) s. MÚS. afinamiento, afinación *f*; RAD. sintonización *f*; TEC. reglaje *m*.

tuning fork s. MÚS. diapasón *m*.

Tu·ni·sia (tōō-nē'zhə) s. Túnez *m*.

Tu·ni·sian (tōō-nē'zhən) adj. & s. tunecino.

tun·nel (tŭn'əl) **I.** s. *(underground passage)* túnel *m*; MIN. galería **II.** tr. *(to construct)* construir un túnel en; *(to dig)* cavar —intr. hacer un túnel.

tun·ny (tŭn'ē) s. [pl. **tun·nies** *o* **tunny**] ICT. atún *m*.

tup (tŭp) s. ZOOL. carnero, morueco; MEC. martinete *m*.

tup·pence (tŭp'əns) G.B. var. de **twopence**.

tur·ban (tûr'bən) s. turbante *m*.

tur·bid (tûr'bĭd) adj. *(muddy)* turbio; *(dense)* espeso; *(confused)* confuso.

tur·bi·nate (tûr'bə-nĭt, -nāt') *o* **tur·bi·nat·ed** (-nā'tĭd) adj. turbinado.

tur·bine (tûr'bĭn') s. turbina.

tur·bo·charg·er (tûr'bō-chär'jər) s. TEC. turbocompresor *m*.

tur·bo·jet (tûr'bō-jĕt') s. AER. turborreactor *m*.

tur·bo·prop (tûr'bō-prŏp') s. AER. turbopropulsor *m*, turbohélice *m*.

tur·bot (tûr'bət) s. [pl. **turbot** *o* **-bots**] ICT. rodaballo.

tur·bu·lence (tûr'byə-ləns) s. turbulencia.

tur·bu·lent (tûr'byə-lənt) adj. turbulento.

turd (tûrd) s. JER. sorete *m*, mierda.

tu·reen (tōō-rēn', tyōō-) s. sopera.

turf (tûrf) s. *(sod)* césped *m*; *(piece of earth)* tepe *m*; *(peat)* turba; JER. *(territory)* territorio; DEP. *(track)* hipódromo; *(sport)* hipismo.

tur·ges·cence (tûr-jĕs'əns) s. MED. turgencia, hinchazón *f*; FIG. *(pomposity)* ampulosidad *f*.

tur·gid (tûr'jĭd) adj. MED. hinchado; FIG. *(grandiloquent)* ampuloso.

Turk (tûrk) s. *(inhabitant)* turco; *(Moslem)* musulmán *m*; *(brute)* tirano.

tur·key (tûr'kē) s. [pl. **-keys**] CUL., ORNIT. pavo; JER., TEAT. fiasco, fracaso; *(person)* fracasado.

Tur·key (tûr'kē) s. Turquía.

turkey buzzard s. ORNIT. zopilote *m*, aura.

turkey cock s. ORNIT. pavo.

Turk·ish (tûr'kĭsh) adj. & s. turco.

Turkish bath s. baño turco.

Turkish coffee s. café a la turca *m*.

Turkish delight s. golosina de gelatina cubierta con azúcar impalpable.

Turkish towel s. toalla de felpa.

Tur·ko·man (tûr'kə-mən) s. [pl. **-mans**] turcomano.

tur·ma·line (tōōr'mə-lēn') s. var. de **tourmaline**.

tur·mer·ic (tûr'mər-ĭk) s. BOT. cúrcuma.

tur·moil (tûr'moil') s. *(confusion)* confusión *f*; *(agitation)* agitación *f*; *(tumult)* tumulto.

turn (tûrn) **I.** tr. *(to revolve)* hacer girar, dar vueltas a <*to t. a crank* dar vueltas a una manivela>; *(to flip)* pasar, volver <*to t. a page* pasar una página>; *(to rotate)* girar, volver <*don't t. your head yet* no vuelvas la cabeza todavía>; *(to go around)* dar la vuelta a, doblar <*to t. a corner*

dar la vuelta a la esquina>; *(to perform, execute)* dar <*to t. a somersault* dar una voltereta>; *(to shape)* modelar, tornear; *(a phrase)* construir; *(to twist)* torcer <*to t. an ankle* torcerse un tobillo>; *(to upset)* revolver <*that turns my stomach* eso me revuelve el estómago>; *(to influence)* hacer cambiar <*his speech turned my thinking* su discurso hizo cambiar mi modo de pensar>; *(to deflect)* desviar; *(to point)* apuntar; *(to devote)* entregarse, dedicarse <*he turned himself to music* se entregó a la música>; *(to direct)* dirigir <*t. your eyes to the sky* dirija su vista al cielo>; *(to surpass)* superar, sobrepasar; *(to become)* cumplir <*she just turned sixteen* acaba de cumplir dieciséis años>; *(to curdle)* cortar; *(to change color)* cambiar el color de; *(to transform)* convertir, transformar <*they turned a run-down house into a showplace* convirtieron una casa en ruina en algo digno de verse>; *(to curve)* doblar; *(to blunt)* embotar; COM. vender <*we turned a great deal of merchandise during the holidays* vendimos mucha mercadería durante las fiestas> • **to t. about** dar la vuelta a • **to t. a deaf ear to** hacer oídos sordos a • **to t. against** volver en contra de, enemistar con • **to t. a profit** ganar, producir una ganancia • **to t. around** *(words)* tergiversar, desvirtuar; *(to turn over)* dar vuelta a • **to t. aside** *(to move over)* hacerse a un lado; *(to deflect)* desviar; *(eyes)* apartar • **to t. away** *(to send away)* no admitir, negar la entrada a; *(to deflect)* rechazar; *(head)* volver; *(eyes)* desviar • **to t. back** *(to send back)* devolver; *(to drive back)* hacer retroceder; *(the clock)* retrasar • **to t. down** *(to diminish)* bajar; FAM. *(to reject)* rechazar, rehusar; *(to fold)* doblar, plegar; *(card)* poner boca abajo • **to t. from** apartar(se) de, alejar de • **to t. in** *(to give over)* presentar, entregar; *(to betray)* entregar a la policía; *(to produce)* hacer <*he turns in good work* hace un buen trabajo>; *(to bend inward)* doblar hacia adentro • **to t. inside out** poner al revés • **to t. into** *(to change)* transformar en, convertir en; *(to make a turn into)* entrar en; *(to become)* volverse • **to t. loose** soltar, dejar libre • **to t. off** *(radio, light)* apagar; *(tap, gas)* cerrar; *(electricity, water)* cortar; *(to dismiss)* despedir, echar; *(an engine)* parar; JER. *(to disgust)* disgustar • **to t. on** *(water, gas)* abrir la llave; *(radio)* poner; *(light)* encender; *(an engine)* poner en marcha; *(a tap)* abrir; *(stove, fire)* encender, prender; *(electrical current)* conectar; *(to become hostile)* volverse en contra de; JER. *(to excite)* excitar • **to t. one's attention to** fijar la atención en • **to t. one's back on** volver la espalda a • **to t. one's coat** FIG., FAM. cambiar de opinión • **to t. out** *(light)* apagar; *(to shut off)* cerrar; *(to manufacture)* producir, fabricar; *(to evict)* expulsar, echar <*he turned his tenants out* echó a sus inquilinos> • **to t. over** *(to reverse in position)* invertir, volcar; *(to think about)* considerar, dar vueltas a; *(to transfer)* entregar; *(a page)* pasar; *(in business)* sacar, tener un volumen de negocios de <*to t. over a million dollars a year* sacar un millón de dólares al año>; *(to fold)* doblar • **to t. over a new leaf** FIG. enmendarse, comenzar de nuevo • **to t. over in one's mind** pensar con detenimiento, meditar sobre • **to t. over to** *(to transfer)* traspasar a; *(to entrust)* dejar a cargo de, dejar al cuidado de • **to t. the cold shoulder to** desairar, tratar con desprecio • **to t. the scales** cambiar el orden de las cosas • **to t. the stomach** causar asco • **to t. the tables** cambiar la suerte • **to t. the tide of** cambiar el curro *o* el rumbo de • **to t. the trick** llevar a cabo • **to t. thumbs down on** condenar a • **to t. to advantage** *o* **profit** sacar partido de, aprovechar • **to t. up** *(to find)* encontrar <*he turned up the missing papers under his blotter* encontró los papeles que le faltaban debajo de su carpeta>; *(to fold)* doblar hacia arriba; *(sleeves)* arremangar; *(radio, television)* subir, poner más fuerte; *(light)* aumentar; *(the collar)* alzar, levantar; *(a hem)* subir, meter; *(to place face up)* poner boca arriba; *(to shorten)* acortar; *(to bring to light)* desenterrar • **to t. up one's nose at** desdeñar, mirar con desprecio • **to t. upside down** poner patas arriba —intr. *(to rotate)* girar <*wheels turning at a rapid rate* ruedas girando a gran velocidad>; *(to change direction)* dar la vuelta; *(to turn around)* volverse, darse vuelta <*they are still looking; don't t. yet* ellos nos están mirando todavía; no te des vuelta aún>; *(to switch one's* *loyalty*) cambiar (de opinión, posición); *(to devote oneself)* dedicarse; *(to become transformed)* transformarse, convertirse en; *(to change color)* cambiar de color <*the leaves have turned* las hojas han cambiado de color>; *(to run a lathe)* tornear; *(wood)* tornearse; *(to become bent)* curvarse; *(weather, luck)* cambiar; *(to become)* ponerse, volverse <*to t. bitter with age* volverse amargo con los años>; *(to curdle)* cortarse; *(to ferment)* avinagrarse; *(to sour)* ponerse rancio ♦ **to t. around** dar la vuelta, darse vuelta • **to t. aside** desviarse, torcer • **to t. away** *(to begin to leave)* alejarse; *(to turn one's back)* volver la cara *o* la espalda • **to t. back** *(in a reverse direction)* retroceder; *(to go back)* volverse • **to t. down a street** doblar por una calle • **to t. in** FAM. *(to go to bed)* acostarse; *(to point inward)* estar vuelto hacia adentro • **to t. off** *(to make a turn into)* desviarse, torcer • **to t. out** *(to be found to be)* resultar; *(assemble)* acudir, asistir; *(to point outward)* estar vuelto hacia afuera • **to t. out to be** resultar, salir • **to t. over** *(car, truck)* volcar; *(airplane)* capotar; *(to shift position)* voltearse; *(to face the other way)* cambiar de frente, voltearse; *(to change opinion)* cambiar de opinión • **to t. round and round** dar vueltas • **to t. short** dar media vuelta • **to t. to** recurrir a <*who can I t. to?* ¿a quién puedo recurrir?>; *(to begin to work on)* empezar • **to t. up** *(to be found)* aparecer <*the papers will t. up sooner or later* los papeles aparecerán tarde o temprano>; *(to come up)* salir <*his name turns up in gossip columns* su nombre sale en las gacetillas>; *(to happen)* ocurrir **II.** s. *(rotation)* rotación *f*; *(revolution)* revolución *f*, vuelta; *(change of direction)* vuelta; *(change)* cambio; *(opportunity)* oportunidad *f*, ocasión *f*; *(opportunity, time)* turno, vez *f*; *(adeptness)* aptitud *f*; *(inclination)* inclinación *f*, propensión *f*; *(deed)* proceder *m*; *(action)* acción *f*; *(advantage)* provecho, utilidad *f*; *(short tour)* vuelta, paseo corto <*a t. in the park* un paseo corto por el parque>; *(twist in shape)* torcimiento, torcedura; *(curve)* curva; *(a single wind)* vuelta; *(spell)* ataque *m*; *(shock)* susto, sobresalto; TEAT. número ♦ **at every t.** a cada instante, a cada momento • **at the t. of the century** al final del siglo pasado • **by turns** por turnos • **in t.** a su vez • **to take another t.** cambiar de aspecto, tomar otro cariz • **to take a t. for the better (worse)** mejorarse (empeorarse) • **to take turns at** turnarse, alternarse en.

turn·a·bout (tûrn'ə-bout') s. *(turn)* vuelta; *(shift)* cambio radical.

turn·a·round (tûrn'ə-round') s. *(space)* área de viraje; *(turn)* vuelta.

turn·buck·le (tûrn'bŭk'əl) s. tensor *m*.

turn·coat (tûrn'kōt') s. renegado, traidor *m*.

turn·down (tûrn'doun') s. rechazo.

turned-up (tûrnd'ŭp') adj. *(said of a nose)* respingada; *(folded up)* doblado hacia arriba; *(said of a collar)* alto.

turn·er¹ (tûr'nər) s. tornero.

tur·ner² (tûr'nər) s. gimnasta *mf*, volatinero.

turn·ing (tûr'nĭng) s. *(deviation)* viraje *m*; *(shaping)* tornada.

turning point s. momento crucial.

tur·nip (tûr'nĭp) s. BOT., CUL. nabo; *(watch)* especie de reloj de bolsillo.

turn·key (tûrn'kē') s. [pl. **-keys**] carcelero.

turn·off (tûrn'ôf') s. *(on a road)* desvío; JER. *(disappointment)* desilusión *f*, decepción *f*.

turn·out (tûrn'out') s. *(attendance)* concurrencia; *(spectators)* público, entrada <*there was a poor t.* no había mucho público>; *(output)* producción *f*; *(outfit)* atuendo; *(carriage)* carroza (de lujo); F.C. vía muerta, apartadero; G.B. *(strike)* huelga; *(striker)* huelguista *mf*.

turn·o·ver (tûrn'ō'vər) **I.** s. *(upset)* vuelco; *(turn-up)* vuelta; *(reversal)* cambio brusco; *(pastry)* empanada; COM. *(of stock)* movimiento de mercancías; *(of business)* volumen de negocios *m*; *(of sales)* volumen de ventas; *(of staff)* cambio de personal **II.** adj. vuelto.

turn·pike (tûrn'pīk') s. *(highway)* autopista de peaje; *(tollgate)* barrera de portazgo.

turn·screw (tûrn'skrōō') s. destornillador *m*.

turn·spit (tûrn'spĭt') s. asador *m*.

turn·stile (tûrn'stīl') s. torniquete *m*, molinete *m*.

turn·ta·ble (tûrn'tā'bəl) s. *(platform)* plataforma giratoria; *(of a phonograph)* plato; *(disk)* placa giratoria.

tur·pen·tine (tûr'pən-tīn') **I.** s. QUÍM. trementina **II.** tr. **-tined, -tin·ing** *(to apply to)* aplicar trementina a; *(to extract from)* extraer trementina.

tur·pi·tude (tûr'pĭ-tōōd', -tyōōd') s. bajeza.

tur·quoise (tûr'kwoiz', -koiz') adj. & s. turquesa.

tur·ret (tûr'ĭt) s. *(tower)* torreón *m*; MIL. *(enclosure)* torre blindada.

tur·ret·ed (tûr'ĭ-tĭd) adj. *(ship)* con torres; *(having turrets)* con torreones.

tur·tle¹ (tûr'tl) **I.** s. ZOOL. tortuga **II.** intr. **-tled, -tling** cazar tortugas.

tur·tle² (tûr'tl) s. ANT. tórtola.

tur·tle·dove (tûr'tl-dŭv') s. ORNIT. tórtola.

tur·tle·neck (tûr'tl-nĕk') s. *(collar)* cuello vuelto *o* alto; *(sweater)* suéter con cuello vuelto *o* alto.

Tus·can (tŭs'kən) adj. & s. toscano.

Tus·ca·ny (tŭs'kə-nē) s. Toscana.

tush¹ (tŭsh) inter. ¡bah!

tush² (tōōsh) s. JER. *(buttocks)* nalgas.

tusk (tŭsk) **I.** s. ZOOL. colmillo; *(tooth)* diente grande *m* **II.** tr. excavar con el colmillo.

tus·sle (tŭs'əl) **I.** intr. **-sled, -sling** forcejear, pelearse **II.** s. forcejeo, pelea.

tus·sock (tŭs'ək) s. *(of grass)* mata de hierba; *(tuft)* penacho.

tut (tŭt) interj. ¡vaya!, ¡basta!

tu·te·lage (tōōt'l-ĭj, tyōōt'-) s. tutela.

tu·te·lar·y (tōōt'l-ĕr'ē, tyōōt'-) *o* **tu·te·lar** (tōōt'l-ər, tyōōt'-) **I.** adj. tutelar **II.** s. [pl. **-lar·ies** *o* **-lars**] entidad tutelar *f*.

tu·tor (tōō'tər, tyōō'-) **I.** s. *(private instructor)* profesor particular *m*; *(in a family)* preceptor *m*, ayo; *(in colleges, universities)* tutor *m*; DER. tutor **II.** tr. *(to teach privately)* dar clases particulares a; DER. ser tutor de —intr. ser tutor.

tu·to·ri·al (tōō-tôr'ē-əl, tyōō-) **I.** adj. *(of a tutor)* de tutor; DER. tutelar **II.** s. clase particular *f*.

tu·tor·ship (tōō'tər-shĭp', tyōō'-) s. *(post)* cargo de tutor; DER. tutela.

tut·ti-frut·ti (tōō'tē-frōō'tē) s. & adj. tutti frutti *m*.

tu·tu (tōō'tōō) s. tutú *m*.

Tu·va·lu (tōō-vä'lōō) s. Tuvalu.

tu·xe·do (tŭk-sē'dō) s. [pl. **-dos** *o* **-does**] smoking *m*, esmoquin.

TV (tē'vē') s. [pl. **TVs** *o* **TV's**] televisión *f*.

twad·dle (twŏd'l) **I.** intr. **-dled, -dling** decir tonterías **II.** s. tonterías.

twain (twān) adj. & s. ANT. dos *m*.

twang (twăng) **I.** intr. *(string)* vibrar; *(voice)* ganguear —tr. *(to vibrate)* hacer vibrar; *(to utter)* hablar ganguean do **II.** s. *(vibrating sound)* sonido vibrante; *(of guitar)* tañido; *(nasal sound)* gangueo.

twang·y (twăng'ē) adj. *(said of the voice)* gangoso.

'twas (twŏz, twŭz) contr. de **it was.**

tweak (twēk) s. **I.** tr. pellizcar **II.** s. pellizco.

tweed (twēd) s. tejido de lana ♦ **tweeds** traje de lana.

twee·dle·dum and twee·dle·dee (twēd'l-dŭm' ən twēd'-l-dē') s. dos personas *o* grupos que se parecen mucho.

tweed·y (twē'dē) adj. **-i·er, -i·est** *(similar to tweed)* parecido a la lana; *(wearing tweeds)* que viste con traje de lana.

'tween (twēn) contr. de **between.**

tweet (twēt) **I.** intr. piar **II.** s. pío pío.

tweet·er (twē'tər) s. RAD. altavoz (de altas frecuencias) *m*.

tweeze (twēz) tr. **tweezed, tweez·ing** sacar con pinzas.

tweez·ers (twē'zərz) s.pl. pinzas.

twelfth (twĕlfth) **I.** s. *(place)* doce *m*; *(part)* doceavo, doceava parte *f* **II.** adj. *(place)* duodécimo; *(part)* doceava.

Twelfth-day (twĕlfth'dā') s. Día de Reyes *m*, Epifanía.

Twelfth-night (twĕlfth'nīt') s. Vigilia de Reyes.

twelve (twĕlv) s. & adj. doce *m* ♦ **t. o'clock** las doce.

twelve-month (twĕlv'mŭnth') s. año.

twelve-tone (twĕlv'tōn') adj. MÚS. dodecafónico.

twen·ti·eth (twĕn'tē-ĭth) **I.** s. *(place)* veinte *m*; *(part)* vigésimo, vigésima parte *f* **II.** adj. *(place, part)* vigésimo.

twen·ty (twĕn'tē) adj. & s. [pl. **-ties**] veinte *m*.

twen·ty-one (twĕn'tē-wŭn') **I.** s. *(number)* veintiuno;

(game) veintiuno (juego de naipes) **II.** adj. veintiún, veintiuno.

twen·ty-twen·ty *o* **20/20** (twĕn'tē-twĕn'tē) adj. MED. que tiene visión normal.

twerp (twûrp) s. JER. imbécil *mf*, idiota *mf.*

twice (twīs) adv. dos veces, el doble ♦ **t. as** *o* **t. as many** *o* **t. as much** dos veces más • **t. over** dos veces • **t. the amount** *o* **the sum** el doble.

twice-told (twīs'tōld') adj. conocido, repetido.

twid·dle (twĭd'l) **I.** tr. **-dled, -dling** hacer girar —intr. ♦ **to t. one's thumbs** matar el tiempo • **to t. with** jugar con **II.** s. vuelta.

twig[1] (twĭg) s. BOT. ramita.

twig[2] (twĭg) tr. **twigged, twig·ging** G.B. *(to notice)* fijarse en; *(to understand)* comprender —intr. caer en la cuenta.

twig[3] (twĭg) s. G.B. *(fashion)* moda.

twig·gy (twĭg'ē) adj. **-gi·er, -gi·est** *(slender)* delgado; *(full of twigs)* ramoso, lleno de ramas.

twi·light (twī'līt') **I.** s. *(time)* crepúsculo; *(light)* media luz; *(decline)* ocaso **II.** adj. crepuscular.

twill (twĭl) TEJ. **I.** s. tela cruzado *o* asargada **II.** tr. cruzar.

'twill (twĭl) contr. de **it will.**

twin (twĭn) **I.** s. *(baby)* gemelo, mellizo; FIG. *(counterpart)* doble *m* ♦ **Siamese twins** hermanos siameses • **Twins** ASTRON. Géminis **II.** adj. *(sibling)* gemelo, mellizo; FIG. *(identical)* idéntico, gemelo **III.** intr. **twinned, twin·ning** *(a woman)* dar a luz a gemelos; *(an animal)* parir dos crías al mismo tiempo; *(to be paired)* hacer pareja —tr. ligar, hermanar.

twin bed s. cama separada *o* gemela.

twin bill s. programa doble *m.*

twin brother s. hermano gemelo.

twine (twīn) **I.** s. *(cord)* cordel *m*, bramante *m*; *(twist)* retorcedura; *(knot)* nudo **II.** tr. **twined, twin·ing** *(to intertwine)* trenzar, entretejer; *(to encircle)* ceñir, rodear —intr. enroscarse.

twinge (twĭnj) **I.** s. *(pain)* punzada; *(remorse)* remordimiento **II.** tr. & intr. **twinged, twing·ing** dar punzadas.

twin·kle (twĭng'kəl) **I.** intr. **-kled, -kling** *(to glimmer)* centellear; *(to shine)* brillar; *(to blink)* parpadear; *(to wink)* guiñar **II.** s. *(glimmer)* centelleo; *(brightness)* brillo; *(instant)* instante *m.*

twin·kling (twĭng'klĭng) s. *(blinking)* parpadeo, pestañeo; *(winking)* guiño; *(instant)* instante *m.*

twin-screw (twĭn'skrōō') adj. MARÍT. de dos hélices.

twin sister s. hermana gemela.

twin-size (twĭn'sīz') adj. tamaño de cama gemela.

twirl (twûrl) **I.** tr. *(to spin)* girar; *(to wind)* retorcer; *(in baseball)* lanzar (la pelota) —intr. *(to spin around)* dar vueltas; *(to whirl)* girar en redondo **II.** s. *(twisting)* vuelta; *(twist)* enroscadura; *(of dancers)* pirueta.

twirp (twûrp) s. var. de **twerp.**

twist (twĭst) **I.** tr. *(threads, strands)* torcer, retorcer; *(vines, rope)* enrollar, arrollar; *(hair)* trenzar; *(washing)* estrujar, escurrir; *(a cork, jar top)* dar vueltas a; *(an arm, ankle)* torcer; *(the face, mouth)* deformar, torcer; *(a ball)* dar efecto a; FIG. *(meanings)* tergiversar, desvirtuar ♦ **to t. in** *o* **into** entretejer en, trenzar en • **to t. off** romper retorciendo —intr. *(to become twisted)* torcerse, retorcerse; *(to coil)* enrollarse, enroscarse; *(to meander)* serpentear, dar vueltas (río, camino) ♦ **to t. and turn** *(road)* serpentear; *(in bed)* dar vueltas • **to t. around** dar una vuelta repentina **II.** s. *(act)* torsión *f*, torcimiento; *(of hair)* trenza; *(of tobacco leaves)* andullo, rollo; *(of bread)* rosca de pan; *(of wire)* vuelta; *(of a road, river)* vuelta, recodo; *(of a muscle, face)* contorsión *f*; *(of an ankle)* esguince *m*, torcedura; FIG. *(unexpected change)* giro imprevisto; *(of the character)* rasgo, peculiaridad *f*; *(inclination)* inclinación *f*, tendencia; *(dance)* twist *m* ♦ **to give a t. to** *(something)* retorcer; *(a ball)* dar efecto a; *(words, facts)* tergiversar, desvirtuar.

twist drill s. TEC. broca helicoidal.

twist·er (twĭs'tər) s. *(person)* torcedor *m*; DEP. pelota lanzada con efecto; FAM. *(tornado)* ciclón *m*, tornado.

twit (twĭt) **I.** tr. **twit·ted, twit·ting** mofarse *o* burlarse de **II.** s. *(mockery)* burla; *(reproach)* censura; G.B., JER. *(an idiot)* imbécil *mf.*

twitch (twĭch) **I.** tr. *(to pull)* tirar bruscamente de —intr. crisparse **II.** s. *(twinge)* punzada; *(spasmodic movement)* tic *m*; *(tug)* tirón *m*; *(restraining cord)* acial *m.*

twit·ter (twĭt'ər) **I.** intr. *(to chirp)* gorjear; *(to tremble)* temblar —tr. decir a media voz **II.** s. *(chirp)* gorjeo; *(flutter)* agitación *f.*

twixt *o* **'twixt** (twĭkst) contr. de **betwixt.**

two (tōō) s. & adj. dos *m* ♦ **by** *o* **in twos** de dos en dos • **in t.** en dos • **to be t. of a kind** ser tal para cual • **to put t. and t. together** FIG. atar cabos • **t. by t.** de dos en dos • **t. o'clock** las dos.

two-bit (tōō'bĭt') adj. JER. de poca monta.

two bits s.pl. FAM. *(twenty-five cents)* veinticinco centavos; *(petty amount)* cantidad insignificante *f.*

two-by-four (tōō'bī-fôr') **I.** adj. de dos por cuatro **II.** s. madera de dos por cuatro.

two cents worth s. FAM. opinión *f.*

two-di·men·sion·al (tōō'dĭ-mĕn'shə-nəl, -dī-) adj. de dos dimensiones.

two-edged (tōō'ĕjd') adj. de dos filos, de doble filo.

two-faced (tōō'fāst') adj. *(with two surfaces)* de dos caras; *(false)* falso.

two-fist·ed (tōō'fĭs'tĭd) adj. FAM. viril, vigoroso.

two·fold (tōō'fōld') **I.** adj. doble **II.** adv. dos veces.

two-hand·ed (tōō'hăn'dĭd) adj. *(with both hands)* de dos manos; *(tool)* para dos manos; *(for people)* para dos personas; *(ambidextrous)* ambidextro; *(having two hands)* con *o* de dos manos.

two hundred s. & adj. doscientos *m.*

two·pence (tŭp'əns) s. [pl. **twopence** *o* **-penc·es**] G.B., FIN. dos peniques *m*; FIG. *(whit)* comino *<he doesn't care t. (no) le importa un comino>.*

two·pen·ny (tŭp'ə-nē, tōō'pĕn'ē) adj. *(worth)* de dos peniques; *(cheap)* barato, de cuatro perras.

two-phase (tōō'fāz') adj. ELEC. bifásico, difásico.

two-piece (tōō'pēs') **I.** adj. de dos piezas **II.** s. conjunto de dos piezas.

two-ply (tōō'plī') adj. *(of two layers)* de dos capas; *(of two strands)* de dos tramas.

two·some (tōō'səm) s. *(couple)* pareja; DEP. simple *m.*

two-step (tōō'stĕp') s. baile de salón en 2/4 *m.*

two-time (tōō'tīm') tr. **-timed, -tim·ing** JER. engañar, poner los cuernos a.

two-tim·er (tōō'tī'mər) s. JER. traidor (en asuntos amorosos) *m.*

two-way (tōō'wā') adj. *(street, traffic)* de doble dirección; TEL. emisor y receptor *<t. radio* aparato emisor y receptor>; *(mutual)* mutuo; *(bilateral)* bilateral; TECH. *(valve)* de doble paso.

ty·coon (tī-kōōn') s. magnate.

ty·ing (tī'ĭng) s. atadura, ligadura.

tyke (tīk) s. FAM. *(child)* chiquillo travieso, mocoso; *(dog)* perro que no es de raza; *(boor)* tunante *m.*

tym·bal (tĭm'bəl) s. var. de **timbal.**

tym·pan (tĭm'pən) s. tímpano.

tym·pa·na (tĭm'pə-nə) un pl. de **tympanum.**

tym·pa·ni (tĭm'pə-nē) s.pl. var. de **timpani.**

tym·pan·ic (tĭm-păn'ĭk) adj. timpánico.

tym·pa·nist (tĭm'pə-nĭst) s. MÚS. timbalero.

tym·pa·num (tĭm'pə-nəm) s. [pl. **-na** (-nə) *o* **-nums**] ANAT., ARQ., ZOOL. tímpano; TEL. diafragma (del teléfono) *m.*

tym·pa·ny (tĭm'pə-nē) s. [pl. **-nies**] MÚS. tímpanos.

type (tīp) **I.** s. *(characteristic specimen)* tipo; *(kind)* tipo, género *<people of that t.* gente de ese tipo>; FAM. *(person)* tipo, tío *<he's an odd t.* es un tipo raro>; *(model)* modelo, tipo *<a new t. of car* un nuevo modelo de automóvil>; TIP. tipo, carácter *m* ♦ **bold t.** TIP. negrita **II.** tr. **typed, typ·ing** *(with a typewriter)* escribir a máquina, mecanografiar; MED. *(to determine the type of)* determinar el grupo sanguíneo del; *(to classify)* clasificar; *(to represent)* respresentar, tipificar —intr. escribir a máquina.

type·cast (tīp'kăst') tr. **-cast, -cast·ing** TEAT. *(to cast)* asignar un papel de acuerdo con la personalidad del actor; *(to assign repeatedly)* encasillar (a un actor).

type·face (tīp'fās') s. IMPR. *(typography)* tipografía; *(character)* carácter *m*, tipo.

---

ng inglés / ŏ la / ō bou / ô corre / oi oigo / ōō uno / ou auto / yōō ciudad / w hueco / y yo / z mismo

type genus s. BIOL. género tipo.
type metal s. IMPR. metal tipográfico o de imprenta.
type-script (tīp'skrĭpt') s. texto mecanografiado.
type-set (tīp'sĕt') tr. **-set, -set-ting** IMPR. componer.
type-set-ter (tīp'sĕt'ər) s. IMPR. tipógrafo.
type-set-ting (tīp'sĕt'ĭng) s. IMPR. composición f.
type species s. BIOL. especie de tipo f.
type-write (tīp'rīt') tr. **-wrote** (-rōt'), **-writ-ten** (-rĭt'n), **-writ-ing** mecanografiar —intr. escribir a máquina.
type-writ-er (tīp'rī'tər) s. *(machine)* máquina de escribir; ANT. *(person)* mecanógrafo.
type-writ-ing (tīp'rī'tĭng) s. mecanografía, dactilografía.
type-writ-ten (tīp'rĭt'n) adj. mecanografiado.
ty-phoid (tī'foid') **I.** s. MED. fiebre tifoidea **II.** adj. tifoideo.
typhoid fever s. MED. fiebre tifoidea.
ty-phoon (tī-fōōn') s. tifón m.
ty-phus (tī'fəs) s. MED. tifus m.
typ-i-cal (tĭp'ĭ-kəl) o **typ-ic** (-ĭk) adj. típico, característico.
typ-i-cal-ly (tĭp'ĭ-kə-lē) adv. típicamente.
typ-i-fy (tĭp'ə-fī') tr. **-fied, -fy-ing** *(to embody)* representar el tipo de; *(to symbolize)* simbolizar.
typ-ing (tī'pĭng) s. mecanografía, dactilografía.
typ-ist (tī'pĭst) s. mecanógrafo, dactilógrafo.
ty-po (tī'pō) s. [pl. **-pos**] FAM. error tipográfico o de imprenta, errata.
ty-pog-ra-pher (tī-pŏg'rə-fər) s. tipógrafo.
ty-po-graph-i-cal error (tī'pə-grăf'ĭ-kəl) s. IMPR. error tipográfico o de imprenta, errata.
ty-pog-ra-phy (tī-pŏg'rə-fē) s. [pl. **-phies**] tipografía.
ty-pol-o-gy (tī-pŏl'ə-jē) s. [pl. **-gies**] tipología.
ty-ran-ni-cal (tĭ-răn'ĭ-kəl, tī-) o **ty-ran-nic** (-răn'ĭk) adj. tiránico, despótico.
tyr-an-nize (tĭr'ə-nīz') intr. **-nized, -niz-ing** ser un tirano ♦ **to t. over** tiranizar —tr. tiranizar.
ty-ran-no-saur (tĭ-răn'ə-sôr', tī-) o **ty-ran-no-saur-us** (tĭ-răn'ə-sôr'əs, tī-) s. PALEON. tiranosauro.
tyr-an-nous (tĭr'ə-nəs) adj. tiránico.
tyr-an-ny (tĭr'ə-nē) s. [pl. **-nies**] tiranía.
ty-rant (tī'rənt) s. tirano.
tyre (tīr) s. G.B. var. de **tire²**.
ty-ro (tī'rō) s. [pl. **-ros**] aprendiz m, principiante m.
Ty-rol (tī'rōl, tīr'əl) s. Tirol m.
Ty-ro-le-an (tĭ-rō'lē-ən, tī-) s. & adj. tirolés m.
tzar (tsär) s. var. de **czar**.
tza-ri-na (tsä-rē'nə) s. var. de **czarina**.
tzet-ze fly (tsĕt'sē, tsēt'sē) s. var. de **tsetse fly**.

U

u, U (yōō) s. [pl. **u's, U's**] vigésima primera letra del alfabeto inglés.
u-biq-ui-tous (yōō-bĭk'wĭ-təs) adj. ubicuo.
u-biq-ui-ty (yōō-bĭk'wĭ-tē) s. ubicuidad f.
U-boat (yōō'bōt') s. submarino alemán.
ud-der (ŭd'ər) s. ZOOL. ubre f.
UFO (yōō'ĕf-ō') s. [pl. **UFOs** o **UFO's**] AER. OVNI (abr. de objeto volador no identificado).
U-gan-da (yōō-găn'də, -gän'-) s. Uganda.
U-gan-dan (yōō-găn'dən, -gän'-) adj. & s. ugandés m.
ugh (ŭg, ŭk) interj. ¡uf!
ug-li-ness (ŭg'lē-nĭs) s. fealdad f.
ug-ly (ŭg'lē) adj. **-li-er, li-est** *(unsightly)* feo; *(unpleasant)* desagradable; *(bad)* malo; *(ominous)* peligroso, amenazante; FAM. *(disagreeable)* desagradable, mal <he has a *ery* u. *temper* él tiene muy mal genio> ♦ **to turn u.** *(person)* ponerse furioso; *(situation)* ponerse feo.
uh-huh (ə-hŭ') interj. FAM. sí, ajá.
u-kase (yōō-kās', -kāz') s. ucase (decreto, orden).
U-kraine (yōō-krān', yōō'krān') s. Ucrania.
U-krain-i-an (yōō-krā'nē-ən) adj. & s. ucranio, ucraniano.
Ukrainian Soviet Socialist Republic s. República Socialista Soviética de Ucrania.
u-ku-le-le (yōō'kə-lā'lē) s. MÚS. ukelele m.

ul-cer (ŭl'sər) s. MED. úlcera; FIG. *(corruption)* cáncer m.
ul-cer-ate (ŭl'sə-rāt') tr. & intr. **-at-ed, -at-ing** MED. ulcerar(se).
ul-cer-a-tion (ŭl'sə-rā'shən) s. MED. ulceración f.
ul-cer-ous (ŭl'sər-əs) adj. MED. ulceroso.
ul-na (ŭl'nə) s. [pl. **-nae** (-nē) o **-nas**] ANAT. cúbito.
ul-ster (ŭl'stər) s. abrigo amplio y largo.
ul-te-ri-or (ŭl-tîr'ē-ər) adj. *(distant)* ulterior; *(subsequent)* subsecuente, subsiguiente ♦ **u. motive** motivo oculto, segunda intención.
ul-ti-mate (ŭl'tə-mĭt) **I.** adj. *(farthest)* último; *(final)* final (objetivo, logro); *(eventual)* eventual (suceso, victoria); *(fundamental)* fundamental, FÍS. *(elemental)* elemental (división, partícula); *(maximum)* máximo **II.** s. *(fact)* hecho fundamental; *(conclusion)* conclusión f; *(the absolute)* lo absoluto, lo último <the u. *in space technology* lo último en tecnología espacial>.
ul-ti-mate-ly (ŭl'tə-mĭt-lē) adv. *(finally)* finalmente, al fin; *(basically)* en el fondo, básicamente.
ul-ti-ma-tum (ŭl'tə-mā'təm) s. [pl. **-tums** o **-ta** (-tə)] ultimátum m.
ul-ti-mo (ŭl'tə-mō') adv. del mes pasado o último.
ul-tra (ŭl'trə) **I.** adj. excesivo, extremado **II.** s. ultra mf, extremista mf.
ul-tra-con-ser-va-tive (ŭl'trə-kən-sûr'və-tĭv) adj. & s. ultraconservador m.
ultra-high frequency (ŭl'trə-hī') s. ELECTRÓN., RAD. frecuencia ultraalta.
ul-tra-ma-rine (ŭl'trə-mə-rēn') **I.** s. azul ultramarino **II.** adj. *(said of color)* de color azul ultramarino; *(beyond the sea)* ultramarino.
ul-tra-mod-ern (ŭl'trə-mŏd'ərn) adj. ultramoderno.
ul-tra-son-ic (ŭl'trə-sŏn'ĭk) adj. *(said of sound)* ACÚS. ultrasonoro, ultrasónico; AVIA. *(said of speed)* supersónico.
ul-tra-sound (ŭl'trə-sound') s. ACÚS. ultrasonido.
ul-tra-vi-o-let (ŭl'trə-vī'ə-lĭt) FÍS. **I.** adj. ultravioleta **II.** s. luz ultravioleta.
ultraviolet lamp s. FÍS. lámpara de luz ultravioleta.
ul-u-late (ŭl'yə-lāt') intr. **-lat-ed, -lat-ing** ulular, aullar.
U-lys-ses (yōō-lĭs'ēz') s. MITOL. Ulises.
um-bel (ŭm'bəl) s. BOT. umbela.
um-ber (ŭm'bər) PINT. **I.** s. *(pigment)* tierra de sombra; *(color)* pardo oscuro **II.** adj. de la tierra de sombra; *(brown)* de color pardo oscuro **III.** tr. oscurecer.
um-bil-i-cal (ŭm-bĭl'ĭ-kəl) **I.** adj. ANAT. umbilical **II.** s. ASTRONÁUT. línea de abastecimiento.
umbilical cord s. ANAT. cordón umbilical m; ASTRONÁUT. línea de abastecimiento.
um-bil-i-cus (ŭm-bĭl'ĭ-kəs, ŭm'bə-lī'-) s. [pl. **-ci** (-sī')] ANAT., BOT. ombligo.
um-brage (ŭm'brĭj) s. *(offense)* ofensa; *(resentment)* resentimiento; ANT. *(shade)* sombra, umbría ♦ **to take u. at** ofenderse o resentirse por.
um-brel-la (ŭm-brĕl'ə) s. *(for the rain)* paraguas m; *(for the shade)* sombrilla, parasol m; MIL. *(air cover)* cobertura aérea; ICT. *(of jellyfishes)* umbrela ♦ **u. group** o **organization** POL. cuerpo coordinador • **u. stand** paragüero.
um-laut (ŭm'lout') **I.** s. FONÉT. metafonía; GRAM. diéresis f **II.** tr. FONÉT. modificar por metafonía; GRAM. poner una diéresis sobre.
um-pire (ŭm'pīr') **I.** s. DEP., DER. árbitro; *(judge)* juez mf **II.** tr. **-pired, -pir-ing** arbitrar —intr. ser arbitro.
ump-teen (ŭmp'tēn') adj. FAM. muchísimos, innumerables <u. *reasons* innumerables razones>.
ump-teenth (ŭmp-tēnth') adj. enésimo.
un-a-bashed (ŭn'ə-băsht') adj. *(uninhibited)* desenvuelto; *(poised)* imperturbable, sereno; *(undisguised)* sin disimulo.
un-a-bat-ed (ŭn'ə-bā'tĭd) adj. *(undiminished)* no disminuido; *(constant)* constante <u. *interest* interés constante>.
un-a-ble (ŭn-ā'bəl) adj. *(physically)* impotente, imposibilitado; *(intellectually)* incapaz, incompetente.
un-a-bridged (ŭn'ə-brĭjd') adj. no abreviado, completo (libro, documento).

ā rey / ä año / b boca / ch chico / d dar / ĕ el / ē mil / g gato / h joya / hw juez / ī aire / k casa / kw cuan /

un·ac·cent·ed (ŭn-ăk′sĕn-tĭd) adj. inacentuado, sin acento.
un·ac·cept·a·ble (ŭn′ăk-sĕp′tə-bəl) adj. inaceptable.
un·ac·com·pa·nied (ŭn′ə-kŭm′pə-nēd) adj. *(alone)* solo, sin compañía; MÚS. solo, sin acompañamiento.
un·ac·com·plished (ŭn′ə-kŏm′plĭsht) adj. *(unfinished)* incompleto, no acabado; *(untalented)* falto de aptitudes o cualidades.
un·ac·count·a·ble (ŭn′ə-koun′tə-bəl) adj. *(inexplicable)* inexplicable; *(strange)* extraño; *(not responsible)* no responsable.
un·ac·count·ed (ŭn′ə-koun′tĭd) adj. ♦ **u. for** *(missing)* desaparecido, no encontrado <*two soldiers are u. for* han desaparecido dos soldados>; *(unexplained)* inexplicado.
un·ac·cus·tomed (ŭn′ə-kŭs′təmd) adj. *(not used to)* no acostumbrado; *(unusual)* insólito, desacostumbrado; *(unfamiliar)* extraño <*u. surroundings* un medio extraño>.
un·ac·knowl·edged (ŭn′ăk-nŏl′ĭjd) adj. *(ignored)* no reconocido; *(omitted)* no declarado; *(unanswered)* por contestar, no contestado.
un·ac·quaint·ed (ŭn′ə-kwān′tĭd) adj. ♦ **u. with** ignorante de, no versado en.
un·a·dorned (ŭn′ə-dôrnd′) adj. *(plain)* llano, sin adorno; *(simple)* simple.
un·a·dul·ter·at·ed (ŭn′ə-dŭl′tə-rā′tĭd) adj. no adulterado, puro.
un·ad·vised (ŭn′əd-vīzd′) adj. *(not informed)* sin informar, no informado; *(imprudent)* imprudente, irreflexivo.
un·af·fect·ed (ŭn′ə-fĕk′tĭd) adj. *(not affected)* no afectado; *(natural)* sin afectación; *(genuine)* genuino.
un·a·fraid (ŭn′ə-frād′) adj. sin temor, sin miedo.
un·aid·ed (ŭn-ā′dĭd) adj. sin ayuda, solo.
un·al·ien·a·ble (ŭn-āl′yə-nə-bəl) adj. inalienable.
un·al·lo·cat·ed (ŭn-ăl′ə-kā′tĭd) adj. no asignado.
un·al·low·a·ble (ŭn′ə-lou′ə-bəl) adj. *(not permissible)* no permisible, no tolerable; *(inadmissible)* inadmisible.
un·al·loyed (ŭn′ə-loid′) adj. METAL. *(pure)* no mezclado, puro; FIG. *(complete)* completo, entero <*u. approval* completa aprobación>.
un·al·ter·a·ble (ŭn-ôl′tər-ə-bəl) adj. inalterable.
un·am·big·u·ous (ŭn′ăm-bĭg′yōō-əs) adj. sin ambigüedad, inequívoco.
un-A·mer·i·can (ŭn′ə-mĕr′ĭ-kən) adj. *(anti-American)* antiamericano, antinorteamericano; *(unlike an American)* poco americano, no americano.
u·na·nim·i·ty (yōō′nə-nĭm′ĭ-tē) s. unanimidad f.
u·nan·i·mous (yōō-năn′ə-məs) adj. unánime.
un·an·nounced (ŭn′ə-nounst′) adj. sin ser anunciado.
un·an·swer·a·ble (ŭn-ăn′sər-ə-bəl) adj. *(irrefutable)* incontestable, irrefutable; *(incontrovertible)* incontrovertible.
un·ap·peal·a·ble (ŭn′ə-pē′lə-bəl) adj. DER. inapelable.
un·ap·pe·tiz·ing (ŭn-ăp′ĭ-tī′zĭng) adj. *(not tasty)* poco apetitoso; FIG. *(not interesting)* poco apetecible (idea, proposición).
un·ap·proach·a·ble (ŭn′ə-prō′chə-bəl) adj. *(not friendly)* inaccesible, esquivo; *(unreachable)* inaccesible, inalcanzable.
un·ap·pro·pri·at·ed (ŭn′ə-prō′prē-ā′tĭd) adj. *(not designated)* no asignado o concedido (partida, fondo); *(not assigned to)* libre, realengo.
un·ap·proved (ŭn′ə-prōōvd′) adj. no aprobado.
un·armed (ŭn-ärmd′) adj. *(without weapons)* desarmado, sin armas; *(defenseless)* indefenso; BOT., ZOOL. inerme, sin púas o espinas.
un·asked (ŭn-ăskt′) adj. *(opinion, advice)* sin solicitar, no solicitado; *(question)* sin formular; *(guest)* no invitado o convidado.
un·as·sail·a·ble (ŭn′ə-sā′lə-bəl) adj. inexpugnable, inatacable.
un·as·sign·a·ble (ŭn′ə-sī′nə-bəl) adj. intransferible.
un·as·sist·ed (ŭn′ə-sĭs′tĭd) adj. sin ayuda, solo.
un·as·sum·ing (ŭn′ə-sōō′mĭng) adj. modesto.
un·at·tached (ŭn′ə-tăcht′) adj. *(loose)* suelto, separado; *(independent)* independiente, libre; *(not married)* soltero; DER. *(not seized)* no embargado.
un·at·tain·a·ble (ŭn′ə-tā′nə-bəl) adj. inalcanzable, inaccesible.

un·at·tend·ed (ŭn′ə-tĕn′dĭd) adj. *(unstaffed)* desatendido; *(without assistance)* solo; *(neglected)* descuidado.
un·at·test·ed (ŭn′ə-tĕs′tĭd) adj. no atestiguado.
un·at·trac·tive (ŭn′ə-trăk′tĭv) adj. inatractivo.
un·au·thor·ized (ŭn-ô′thə-rīzd′) adj. desautorizado, sin autorización.
un·a·vail·a·ble (ŭn′ə-vā′lə-bəl) adj. *(not available)* no disponible, agotado; *(not accessible)* inaccesible, inalcanzable; *(busy)* ocupado.
un·a·vail·ing (ŭn′ə-vā′lĭng) adj. *(useless)* inútil, vano; *(unsuccessful)* infructuoso, ineficaz.
un·a·void·a·ble (ŭn′ə-voi′də-bəl) adj. inevitable, ineludible.
un·a·ware (ŭn′ə-wâr′) **I.** adj. ignorante, inconsciente **II.** adv. *(unexpectedly)* de improviso, repentinamente; *(unintentionally)* sin pensar, inadvertidamente ♦ **to be u. of** no tener conocimiento de, ignorar.
un·a·wares (ŭn′ə-wârz′) adv. *(unexpectedly)* de improviso, repentinamente; *(unintentionally)* sin pensar, inadvertidamente ♦ **to take** o **catch u.** coger o tomar desprevenido.
un·backed (ŭn-băkt′) adj. *(lacking support)* sin apoyo, sin ayuda; *(without a backrest)* sin respaldo (silla, taburete).
un·bal·ance (ŭn-băl′əns) **I.** tr. **-anced, -anc·ing** *(to cause imbalance)* desequilibrar; *(to derange)* trastornar, enloquecer **II.** s. desequilibrio.
un·bal·anced (ŭn-băl′ənst) adj. *(not in balance)* desequilibrado; *(mentally deranged)* desequilibrado, trastornado; COM. no balanceado.
un·bap·tized (ŭn′băp-tīzd′) adj. no bautizado, sin bautizar.
un·bar (ŭn-bär′) tr. **-barred, -bar·ring** *(to unlock)* desatrancar (una puerta); FIG. *(to open)* abrir.
un·bear·a·ble (ŭn-bâr′ə-bəl) adj. insoportable, intolerable.
un·beat·a·ble (ŭn-bē′tə-bəl) adj. *(undefeatable)* invencible; *(insurmountable)* insuperable.
un·beat·en (ŭn-bēt′n) adj. *(not defeated)* invicto; *(unexplored)* inexplorado, virgen.
un·be·com·ing (ŭn′bĭ-kŭm′ĭng) adj. *(unattractive)* que sienta o cae mal; *(improper)* impropio, indecoroso.
un·be·known (ŭn′bĭ-nōn′) adj. desconocido.
un·be·knownst (ŭn′bĭ-nōnst′) adv. ♦ **u. to me** sin saberlo yo.
un·be·lief (ŭn′bĭ-lēf′) s. *(disbelief)* incredulidad f; *(skepticism)* escepticismo.
un·be·liev·a·ble (ŭn′bĭ-lē′və-bəl) adj. increíble.
un·be·liev·er (ŭn′bĭ-lē′vər) s. *(in a religion)* ateo, no creyente mf; *(doubter)* incrédulo, descreído.
un·be·liev·ing (ŭn′bĭ-lē′vĭng) adj. *(incredulous)* incrédulo; *(skeptical)* escéptico.
un·bend (ŭn-bĕnd′) tr. **-bent** (-bĕnt′), **-bend·ing** *(to straighten)* enderezar, desencorvar; *(a bow, rope)* aflojar, soltar; MARÍT. *(sails)* desenvergar; *(the mind)* relajar —intr. *(to become straight)* enderezarse, desencorvarse; *(to relax)* aflojarse, relajarse.
un·bend·ing (ŭn-bĕn′dĭng) adj. *(inflexible)* inflexible; *(firm)* firme.
un·bi·ased o **un·bi·assed** (ŭn-bī′əst) adj. imparcial, neutral.
un·bid·den (ŭn-bĭd′n) o **un·bid** (-bĭd′) adj. *(not invited)* no invitado; *(unasked)* no pedido o solicitado.
un·bind (ŭn-bīnd′) tr. **-bound** (-bound′), **-bind·ing** *(to untie)* desatar, desamarrar; MED. *(a wound)* desvendar; *(to free)* liberar.
un·blessed o **un·blest** (ŭn-blĕst′) adj. RELIG. *(not consecrated)* no bendito, sin bendecir; FIG., FAM. *(unfortunate)* desafortunado; *(evil)* maligno.
un·blink·ing (ŭn-blĭng′kĭng) adj. *(said of the eyes)* sin pestañear; FIG. *(unmoved)* impasible; *(rigorous)* riguroso.
un·blush·ing (ŭn-blŭsh′ĭng) adj. *(not blushing)* que no se ruboriza; *(shameless)* desvergonzado.
un·bolt (ŭn-bōlt′) tr. *(to unbar)* desatrancar; *(to unlock)* abrir.
un·bolt·ed (ŭn-bōl′tĭd) adj. *(unbarred)* desatrancado; *(not sifted)* sin cerner (harina).
un·born (ŭn-bôrn′) adj. *(not yet born)* no nacido aún; *(future)* futuro, venidero.
un·bos·om (ŭn-bōōz′əm) tr. revelar, descubrir —intr. desahogarse, abrir el corazón.

---

un·bound (ŭn-bound') adj. *(said of a book)* sin encuadernar, en rústica; *(released)* suelto; *(untied)* desatado.

un·bound·ed (ŭn-boun'dĭd) adj. ilimitado, sin límites.

un·bowed (ŭn-boud') adj. *(head up)* recto, erguido; FIG. *(not subdued)* no subyugado, no sometido.

un·break·a·ble (ŭn-brā'kə-bəl) adj. *(not breakable)* irrompible; *(said of a horse)* indomable.

un·breath·a·ble (ŭn-brē'thə-bəl) adj. irrespirable.

un·bri·dled (ŭn-brīd'ld) adj. *(without a bridle)* desembridado; FIG. *(unrestrained)* desenfrenado.

un·bro·ken (ŭn-brō'kən) *o* **un·broke** (-brōk') adj. *(not broken)* sin romper, entero; *(intact)* intacto; *(not violated)* inviolado; *(uninterrupted)* ininterrumpido, continuo; *(untamed)* no domado, cerril; DEP. *(said of record)* no superado *o* batido.

un·buck·le (ŭn-bŭk'əl) tr. **-led, -ling** desabrochar, deshebillar.

un·bur·den (ŭn-bûr'dn) tr. *(to unload)* descargar, quitar la carga de; FIG. *(to relieve)* aliviar, desahogar.

un·busi·ness·like (ŭn-bĭz'nĭs-līk') adj. *(unmethodical)* poco metódico; *(informal)* informal; *(unethical)* falto de ética; *(inappropriate)* incorrecto; *(ineffective)* ineficaz.

un·but·ton (ŭn-bŭt'n) tr. & intr. desabotonar(se), desabrochar(se).

un·caged (ŭn-kājd') adj. libre, suelto.

un·called-for (ŭn-kôld'fôr') adj. *(unrequested)* no reclamado *o* requerido; *(out of place)* inapropiado, fuera de lugar; *(unnecessary)* innecesario.

un·can·ny (ŭn-kăn'ē) adj. **-ni·er, -ni·est** *(inexplicable)* inexplicable, misterioso; *(keen)* agudo.

un·cap (ŭn-kăp') tr. **-capped, -cap·ping** destapar, quitar la tapa *o* cubierta a.

un·ceas·ing (ŭn-sē'sĭng) adj. incesante, continuo.

un·cel·e·brat·ed (ŭn-sĕl'ə-brā'tĭd) adj. *(not celebrated)* no celebrado *u* honrado; FIG. *(obscure)* poco conocido, obscuro.

un·cer·e·mo·ni·ous (ŭn-sĕr'ə-mō'nē-əs) adj. *(informal)* informal, poco ceremonioso; *(lacking courtesy)* descortés; *(abrupt)* brusco.

un·cer·tain (ŭn-sûr'tn) adj. *(doubtful)* incierto, dudoso <from an u. source de procedencia dudosa>; *(undecided)* indeciso <u. plans planes indecisos>; *(variable)* variable, cambiable <u. weather tiempo cambiable>; *(unsteady)* inestable <u. support apoyo inestable>; **♦ to be u. of** no estar seguro de.

un·cer·tain·ty (ŭn-sûr'tn-tē) s. [pl. **-ties**] *(doubt)* incertidumbre *f*, duda; *(something uncertain)* lo incierto, cosa dudosa.

un·chain (ŭn-chān') tr. desencadenar.

un·chal·lenged (ŭn-chăl'ənjd) adj. *(not challenged)* no retado, no puesto en duda; *(indisputable)* indiscutido, indisputable; DER. no recusado.

un·change·a·ble (ŭn-chān'jə-bəl) adj. invariable, inalterable.

un·changed (ŭn-chānjd') adj. invariado, inalterado.

un·chang·ing (ŭn-chān'jĭng) adj. invariable, inalterable.

un·charged (ŭn-chärjd') adj. ARM. *(not loaded)* no cargado, descargado; DER. *(not formally accused)* no acusado; ELEC. *(lacking a charge)* sin carga, descargado.

un·char·i·ta·ble (ŭn-chăr'ĭ-tə-bəl) adj. *(not charitable)* poco caritativo; *(unkind)* severo, duro.

un·chart·ed (ŭn-chär'tĭd) adj. *(not on a map)* que no figura en el mapa; *(unexplored)* inexplorado; *(unknown)* desconocido.

un·chaste (ŭn-chāst') adj. *(not chaste)* incontinente; *(lewd)* impúdico, lascivo.

un·chris·tian (ŭn-krĭs'chən) adj. *(not christian)* poco cristiano; *(pagan)* pagano, infiel; *(dreadful)* indecente.

un·cir·cum·cised (ŭn-sûr'kəm-sīzd') adj. *(not circumcised)* no circuncidado; FIG. *(not Jewish)* no judío.

un·civ·il (ŭn-sĭv'əl) adj. *(impolite)* incivil, descortés; *(uncivilized)* incivilizado, salvaje.

un·civ·i·lized (ŭn-sĭv'ə-līzd') adj. incivilizado.

un·clad (ŭn-klăd') adj. desvestido, desnudo.

un·claimed (ŭn-klāmd') adj. no reclamado, sin reclamar.

un·clasp (ŭn-klăsp') tr. & intr. *(buckle, brooch)* desabrochar(se); *(hands, embrace)* separar(se).

un·clas·si·fied (ŭn-klăs'ə-fīd') adj. *(not classified)* sin clasificar; *(not secret)* no clasificado como secreto.

un·cle (ŭng'kəl) **I.** s. tío **II.** interj. **♦ cry u.!** ¡ríndete!

un·clean (ŭn-klēn') adj. **-er, -est** *(dirty)* sucio; FIG. *(dishonest)* deshonesto; *(obscene)* obsceno; *(impure)* impuro.

un·clean·li·ness (ŭn-klĕn'lē-nĭs) s. *(dirtiness)* suciedad *f*; FIG. *(impurity)* impureza.

un·clean·ly (ŭn-klĕn'lē) adj. **-li·er, -li·est** *(dirty)* sucio; FIG. *(dishonest)* deshonesto; *(impure)* impuro.

un·clear (ŭn-klîr') adj. **-er, -est** *(not clear)* poco claro; *(confused)* confuso, no explícito.

un·clench (ŭn-klĕnch') tr. & intr. relajar(se), aflojar(se).

Uncle Sam (săm) s. FAM. el tío Sam (representación gráfica del gobierno de EE. UU.).

Uncle Tom (tŏm) s. tío Tom (término despreciativo aplicado al negro sumiso a un blanco).

un·cloak (ŭn-klōk') tr. *(to remove a cloak)* desencapotar; FIG. *(to expose)* desenmascarar.

un·clog (ŭn-klŏg') tr. **-clogged, -clog·ging** desatancar, desatascar.

un·close (ŭn-klōz') tr. & intr. **-closed, -clos·ing** *(to open)* abrir(se); *(to disclose)* revelar(se), descubrir(se).

un·clothe (ŭn-klōth') tr. **-clothed, -cloth·ing** desvestir, desnudar.

un·coil (ŭn-koil') tr. & intr. desenrollar(se).

un·col·lect·a·ble (ŭn'kə-lĕk'tə-bəl) adj. COM. incobrable.

un·col·lect·ed (ŭn'kə-lĕk'tĭd) adj. COM. *(not collected)* sin cobrar, no cobrado; *(scattered)* no recogido, disperso; *(lacking aplomb)* sin aplomo.

un·com·fort·a·ble (ŭn-kŭm'fər-tə-bəl) adj. *(not comfortable)* incómodo, poco confortable; *(awkward)* incómodo, molesto; intranquilo; *(disquieting)* inquietante.

un·com·mer·cial (ŭn'kə-mûr'shəl) adj. COM. *(not engaged in trade)* poco comercial; *(improper)* contrario a los métodos comerciales.

un·com·mit·ted (ŭn'kə-mĭt'ĭd) adj. no comprometido.

un·com·mon (ŭn-kŏm'ən) adj. **-er, -est** *(not common)* poco común *o* frecuente, raro; *(remarkable)* excepcional, extraordinario.

un·com·mu·ni·ca·tive (ŭn'kə-myōō'nĭ-kā'tĭv, -kə-tĭv) adj. *(not communicative)* poco comunicativo, callado; *(taciturn)* taciturno, reservado.

un·com·plain·ing (ŭn'kəm-plā'nĭng) adj. que no protesta, resignado.

un·com·pli·cat·ed (ŭn-kŏm'plĭ-kā'tĭd) adj. *(simple)* sencillo, simple; MED. *(without complications)* sin complicaciones.

un·com·pli·men·ta·ry (ŭn-kŏm'plə-mĕn'tə-rē) adj. *(not complimentary)* poco halagüeño; *(derogatory)* despectivo, peyorativo.

un·com·pro·mis·ing (ŭn-kŏm'prə-mī'zĭng) adj. *(intransigent)* intransigente; *(inflexible)* inflexible.

un·con·cern (ŭn'kən-sûrn') s. *(indifference)* indiferencia; *(lack of worry)* despreocupación *f*.

un·con·cerned (ŭn'kən-sûrnd') adj. *(indifferent)* indiferente; *(unworried)* despreocupado.

un·con·di·tion·al (ŭn'kən-dĭsh'ə-nəl) adj. incondicional, total.

un·con·di·tioned (ŭn'kən-dĭsh'ənd) adj. *(unconditional)* incondicional; *(unrestricted)* no restringido, ilimitado; PSIC. *(natural)* natural, no condicionado.

un·con·fined (ŭn'kən-fīnd') adj. *(limitless)* ilimitado; *(free)* libre, sin trabas *u* obstáculos.

un·con·firmed (ŭn'kən-fûrmd') adj. no confirmado, sin confirmar.

un·con·gen·ial (ŭn'kən-jēn'yəl) adj. *(not compatible)* incompatible, que no congenia; *(inappropriate)* impropio, inadecuado; *(not agreeable)* desagradable.

un·con·nect·ed (ŭn'kə-nĕk'tĭd) adj. *(not joined)* no relacionado, inconexo; *(incoherent)* incoherente.

un·con·quer·a·ble (ŭn-kŏng'kər-ə-bəl) adj. *(impregnable)* inconquistable; *(invincible)* invencible; *(insurmountable)* insuperable.

un·con·scion·a·ble (ŭn-kŏn'shə-nə-bəl) adj. *(beyond reason)* sin consciencia; *(unscrupulous)* inescrupuloso; *(excessive)* desmesurado, exorbitante.

ã rey / ä año / b boca / ch chico / d dar / ĕ el / ē mil / g gato / h joya / hw juez / ī aire / k casa / kw cuan /

un·con·scious (ŭn-kŏn′shəs) **I.** adj. PSIC. *(without awareness)* inconsciente; MED. *(not conscious)* desmayado, sin conocimiento; *(involuntary)* involuntario **II.** s. PSIC. inconsciente *m.*

un·con·sid·ered (ŭn′kən-sĭd′ərd) adj. *(without consideration)* inconsiderado, desconsiderado; *(rash)* irreflexivo.

un·con·sti·tu·tion·al (ŭn-kŏn′stĭ-tōō′shə-nəl, -tyōō′-) adj. inconstitucional.

un·con·trol·la·ble (ŭn′kən-trō′lə-bəl) adj. incontrolable.

un·con·trolled (ŭn′kən-trōld′) adj. *(not controlled)* no controlado; *(unrestrained)* desenfrenado.

un·con·ven·tion·al (ŭn′kən-vĕn′shə-nəl) adj. poco convencional, desacostumbrado.

un·con·vinc·ing (ŭn′kən-vĭn′sĭng) adj. poco convincente.

un·cooked (ŭn-kŏŏkt′) adj. *(raw)* crudo; *(not fully cooked)* sin cocer.

un·cork (ŭn-kôrk′) tr. *(a bottle)* descorchar; FIG. *(to uncover)* destapar; *(to let out)* dar rienda suelta a.

un·cor·rect·ed (ŭn′kə-rĕk′tĭd) adj. no corregido, sin corregir.

un·cor·rupt·ed (ŭn′kə-rŭp′tĭd) adj. incorrupto.

un·count·ed (ŭn-koun′tĭd) adj. *(not counted)* sin contar; *(innumerable)* innumerable, incalculable.

un·cou·ple (ŭn-kŭp′əl) tr. **-pled, -pling** *(to disconnect)* desconectar; *(to unfasten)* desenganchar, desacoplar; *(a pair)* desparejar, deshacer —intr. desconectarse, separarse.

un·couth (ŭn-kōōth′) adj. *(crude)* tosco, rústico; *(awkward)* desgarbado, torpe.

un·cov·er (ŭn-kŭv′ər) tr. *(to lay bare)* destapar; *(the head)* quitarse el sombrero de; FIG. *(to reveal)* revelar —intr. descubrirse, quitarse el sombrero.

un·cov·ered (ŭn-kŭv′ərd) adj. *(exposed)* destapado; COM. *(said of a check)* al descubierto, sin fondo; *(bareheaded)* sin sombrero.

un·crit·i·cal (ŭn-krĭt′ĭ-kəl) adj. desprovisto de sentido crítico.

un·cross (ŭn-krôs′) tr. descruzar.

unc·tion (ŭngk′shən) s. *(act)* unción *f*, ungimiento; *(ointment)* ungüento, untura; *(balm)* bálsamo; FIG. *(syrupiness)* untuosidad *f.*

unc·tu·ous (ŭngk′chōō-əs) adj. *(greasy)* untuoso, aceitoso; *(said of soil)* ubérrimo; *(moldable)* plástico, moldeable; FIG. *(syrupy)* meloso.

un·cul·ti·vat·ed (ŭn-kŭl′tə-vā′tĭd) adj. AGR. *(land)* sin cultivar; *(person)* inculto, rústico.

un·cut (ŭn-kŭt′) adj. *(not cut)* sin cortar; *(said of stones)* sin tallar, en bruto; *(book pages)* intonso; *(unabridged)* entero, sin cortes.

un·dam·aged (ŭn-dăm′ĭjd) adj. *(not damaged)* libre de daño, en buen estado; *(unhurt)* ileso; *(intact)* intacto.

un·daunt·ed (ŭn-dôn′tĭd) adj. *(resolute)* resoluto; *(dauntless)* impávido, imperturbable.

un·de·ceive (ŭn′dĭ-sēv′) tr. **-ceived, -ceiv·ing** desengañar, desilusionar.

un·de·cid·ed (ŭn′dĭ-sī′dĭd) adj. *(not settled)* no resuelto *o* determinado; *(irresolute)* irresoluto, indeciso; *(uncommitted)* no comprometido.

un·de·feat·ed (ŭn′dĭ-fē′tĭd) adj. invicto.

un·de·fin·a·ble (ŭn′dĭ-fī′nə-bəl) adj. indefinible.

un·de·mon·stra·tive (ŭn′dĭ-mŏn′strə-tĭv) adj. poco expresivo, reservado.

un·de·ni·a·ble (ŭn′dĭ-nī′ə-bəl) adj. *(irrefutable)* irrefutable, innegable; *(outstanding)* muy bueno, excelente <*u. quality* excelente calidad>.

un·de·pend·a·ble (ŭn′dĭ-pĕn′də-bəl) adj. que no es de fiar.

un·der (ŭn′dər) **I.** prep. *(below)* (por) debajo de <*u. the bed* debajo de la cama>; *(beneath)* bajo <*u. the sky* bajo el cielo>; *(a surface)* debajo <*put it u. here* ponlo aquí de­bajo>; *(less than)* menos de <*in u. two hours* en menos de dos horas>; *(lower in rank)* por debajo de; *(subject to)* bajo <*u. a dictatorship* bajo una dictadura>; *(during)* durante el reinado de <*u. Elizabeth II* durante el reinado de Isabel II>; *(receiving the effects of)* bajo <*u. treatment* bajo tratamiento>; *(receiving the care of)* a <*he is u. the care of his father* está al cuidado de su padre>; *(according to)* según, conforme a <*his rights u. the contract* sus dere

chos según el contrato>; *(in the process of)* en <*u. discus­sion* en discusión>; *(because of)* en, a causa de <*u. these conditions* a causa de estas condiciones>; *(with)* con <*to study u. a great master* estudiar con un gran maestro> ♦ **right u. one's nose** FIG. delante de las narices de uno • **u. age** menor de edad • **u. cover** FIG. al abrigo, a cubierto • **u. full sail** MARÍT. a toda vela • **u. lock and key** bajo llave, encerrado • **u. oath** bajo juramento • **u. one's breath** susurrando • **u. one's wing** FIG. bajo el ala de uno • **u. repair** en reparación • **u. sentence of** DER. condenado a, bajo sentencia de • **u. separate cover** por separado • **u. the circumstances** dadas las circunstancias **II.** adv. *(below)* bajo, debajo; *(less)* menos <*two hours or u.* dos ho­ras o menos> ♦ **to bring u.** FIG. someter, subyugar • **to go u.** COM., MARÍT. fracasar, hundirse • **to keep u.** FIG. oprimir, mantener sometido **III.** adj. *(on a lower level)* bajo, inferior; *(subordinate)* subalterno; *(insufficient)* insuficiente <*an u. dose of medication* una dosis insuficiente de medi­cación>.

un·der·a·chieve (ŭn′dər-ə-chēv′) intr. **-chieved, -chiev·ing** rendir *o* lograr menos de lo que se espera de uno.

un·der·age (ŭn′dər-āj′) adj. menor de edad.

un·der·arm (ŭn′dər-ärm′) **I.** s. ANAT. axila, sobaco **II.** adj. *(under the arm)* bajo el brazo, por debajo del brazo; DEP. a un nivel más bajo que el hombro, por lo bajo **III.** adv. DEP. con la mano por debajo del hombro.

un·der·bel·ly (ŭn′dər-bĕl′ē) s. [pl. **-lies**] *(of animals)* bajo vientre; FIG. *(weakest part)* parte más débil *o* vulnerable *f.*

un·der·bid (ŭn′dər-bĭd′) tr. **-bid, -bid·ding** COM. ofrecer menos que, rebajar (precios) —intr. rebajar innecesariamente (oferta).

un·der·brush (ŭn′dər-brŭsh′) s. maleza.

un·der·car·riage (ŭn′dər-kăr′ĭj) s. AUTO. chasis *m*; AVIA. tren de aterrizaje *m.*

un·der·charge I. tr. (ŭn′dər-chärj′) **-charged, -charg·ing** COM. cobrar menos de lo debido; ARM. cargar insuficientemente (armas) **II.** s. (ŭn′dər-chärj′) COM. cobro insuficiente; ARM. carga insuficiente.

un·der·class (ŭn′dər-klăs′) s. SOCIOL. clase baja *o* inferior.

un·der·class·man (ŭn′dər-klăs′mən) s. [pl. **-men**] EDUC. estudiante universitario de primer *o* segundo año.

un·der·clothes (ŭn′dər-klōthz′) s.pl. ropa interior.

un·der·cloth·ing (ŭn′dər-klō′thĭng) s. ropa interior.

un·der·coat (ŭn′dər-kōt′) **I.** s. *(jacket)* chaqueta interior; *(fur)* pelo corto cubierto por el pelaje; PINT. *(paint)* primera capa *o* mano; AUTO. *(undercoating)* capa anticorrosiva **II.** tr. aplicar una primera capa a.

un·der·cov·er (ŭn′dər-kŭv′ər) adj. *(secret)* secreto, oculto; *(clandestine)* clandestino.

un·der·cur·rent (ŭn′dər-kûr′ənt) s. MARÍT. corriente submarina; FIG. *(tendency)* fondo.

un·der·cut I. tr. (ŭn′dər-kŭt′) **-cut, -cut·ting** *(to undermine)* socavar; *(to carve)* tallar en relieve; *(to sell)* vender más barato que; *(to work for less)* trabajar más barato que; DEP. *(in tennis, golf)* cortar —intr. *(to sell)* vender a menor precio; *(to work)* trabajar más barato **II.** s. (ŭn′dər-kŭt′) *(cut)* corte *m*; G.B. *(tenderloin)* solomillo; DEP. *(slice)* corte.

un·der·de·vel·oped (ŭn′dər-dĭ-vĕl′əpt) adj. *(muscle, body)* insuficientemente desarrollado; *(country, area)* subdesarrollado; FOTOG. *(picture)* insuficientemente revelada.

un·der·de·vel·op·ment (ŭn′dər-dĭ-vĕl′əp-mənt) s. *(of a muscle)* desarrollo insuficiente; *(of a country)* subdesarrollo; FOTOG. *(of a picture)* revelado insuficiente.

un·der·dog (ŭn′dər-dôg′) s. *(in a contest, struggle)* el que no es favorito; *(helpless person)* desvalido, desamparado.

un·der·done (ŭn′dər-dŭn′) adj. CUL. soasado, poco hecho.

un·der·draw·ers (ŭn′dər-drôrz′) s.pl. calzoncillos.

un·der·dressed (ŭn′dər-drĕst′) adj. vestido de forma inapropiada.

un·der·em·ployed (ŭn′dər-ĕm-ploid′) adj. que no utiliza toda la capacidad *o* preparación obrera.

un·der·em·ploy·ment (ŭn′dər-ĕm-ploi′mənt) s. empleo limitado de la mano de obra disponible.

un·der·es·ti·mate (ŭn′dər-ĕs′tə-māt′) **I.** tr. **-mat·ed, -mat·ing** subestimar **II.** s. (-mĭt) subestimación *f.*

un·der·es·ti·ma·tion (ŭn'dər-ĕs'tə-mā'-shən) s. subestimación *f.*

un·der·ex·pose (ŭn'dər-ĭk-spōz') tr. **-posed, -pos·ing** FOTOG. subexponer.

un·der·ex·po·sure (ŭn'dər-ĭk-spō'zhər) s. FOTOG. subexposición *f.*

un·der·feed (ŭn'dər-fēd') tr. **-fed** (-fĕd'), **-feed·ing** *(to undernourish)* alimentar insuficientemente; TEC. *(to fuel)* alimentar con combustible por la parte inferior.

un·der·foot (ŭn'dər-fŏŏt') adv. *(directly below)* bajo los pies; *(in the way)* en el camino, estorbando.

un·der·fund (ŭn'dər-fŭnd') tr. proveer con fondos insuficientes a.

un·der·gar·ment (ŭn'dər-gär'mənt) s. prenda interior.

un·der·gird (ŭn'dər-gûrd') tr. **-gird·ed** *o* **-girt** (-gûrt'), **-gird·ing** ceñir *o* reforzar desde abajo.

un·der·go (ŭn'dər-gō') tr. **-went** (-wĕnt'), **-gone** (-gôn'), **-go·ing** *(to experience)* experimentar, pasar por; *(to endure)* sufrir, padecer.

un·der·grad·u·ate (ŭn'dər-grăj'ŏŏ-ĭt) I. s. estudiante universitario aún no graduado II. adj. de *o* para estudiante universitario no graduado.

un·der·ground (ŭn'dər-ground') I. adj. *(below ground)* subterráneo; *(clandestine)* clandestino; *(illegal)* ilegal, secreto; *(avant-garde)* de vanguardia II. s. *(clandestine movement)* movimiento clandestino; G.B. *(subway)* metro, subterráneo; MIL. *(resistance)* resistencia III. adv. *(under the ground)* bajo tierra; *(secretly)* secretamente.
Underground Railroad s. EE. UU., HIST. organización secreta que ayudaba a los esclavos a escapar a los estados libres.

un·der·grown (ŭn'dər-grōn') adj. *(not fully grown)* de desarrollo incompleto; *(puny)* pequeño, diminuto.

un·der·growth (ŭn'dər-grōth') s. *(brushwood)* maleza; *(incomplete growth)* crecimiento *o* desarrollo incompleto.

un·der·hand (ŭn'dər-hănd') I. adj. *(sneaky)* solapado, bajo mano; DEP. a un nivel más bajo que el hombro II. adv. *(sneakily)* solapadamente, bajo mano *o* cuerda; DEP. con la mano por debajo del hombro, por lo bajo.

un·der·hand·ed (ŭn'dər-hăn'dĭd) adj. *(underhand)* solapado, furtivo; *(short-handed)* falto *o* escaso de mano de obra.

un·der·lay I. tr. (ŭn'dər-lā') **-laid** (-lād'), **-lay·ing** *(to put under)* poner debajo de; *(to provide with a base)* sostener; IMPR. calzar II. s. (ŭn'dər-lā') *(support)* soporte *m;* IMPR. alza.

un·der·let (ŭn'dər-lĕt') tr. **-let, -let·ting** *(to lease for less)* alquilar por debajo del precio real; *(to sublet)* subarrendar, realquilar.

un·der·lie (ŭn'dər-lī') tr. **-lay** (-lā'), **-lain** (-lān'), **-ly·ing** *(to lie under)* estar *o* extenderse debajo de; FIG. *(to be the basis of)* ser la base de; FIN. *(to have priority over)* tener prioridad sobre.

un·der·line (ŭn'dər-līn') I. tr. **-lined, -lin·ing** *(to underscore)* subrayar; FIG. *(to emphasize)* acentuar, recalcar II. s. raya.

un·der·ling (ŭn'dər-lĭng) s. *(subordinate)* subalterno; *(follower)* secuaz *m.*

un·der·ly·ing (ŭn'dər-lī'ĭng) adj. *(lying underneath)* subyacente; FIG. *(basic)* fundamental, esencial.

un·der·mine (ŭn'dər-mīn') tr. **-mined, -min·ing** *(to dig)* socavar, minar; FIG. *(to sap gradually)* subvertir, minar.

un·der·most (ŭn'dər-mōst') adj. más bajo, último.

un·der·neath (ŭn'dər-nēth') I. adv. *(in a place beneath)* debajo, por debajo; *(on the lower part)* en la cara *o* parte inferior *<an anticorrosive layer u.* una capa anticorrosiva en la parte inferior*>* II. prep. bajo, debajo de III. adj. inferior, de abajo IV. s. fondo, parte inferior *f.*

un·der·nour·ish (ŭn'dər-nûr'ĭsh) tr. alimentar de modo deficiente, desnutrir.

un·der·nour·ish·ment (ŭn'dər-nûr'ĭsh-mĭnt) s. desnutrición *f,* alimentación deficiente *f.*

un·der·paid (ŭn'dər-pād') s. insuficientemente retribuido, mal pagado.

un·der·pants (ŭn'dər-pănts') s.pl. calzoncillos.

un·der·pass (ŭn'dər-păs') s. paso por debajo, paso subterráneo.

un·der·pay (ŭn'dər-pā') tr. **-paid** (-pād'), **-pay·ing** pagar poco *o* insuficientemente por.

un·der·pin (ŭn'dər-pĭn') tr. **-pinned, -pin·ning** *(to support from below)* apuntalar, sostener; FIG. *(to corroborate)* corroborar.

un·der·pin·ning (ŭn'dər-pĭn'ĭng) s. CONSTR. apuntalamiento ♦ **underpinnings** *(foundation)* base, estructura; FAM. *(the legs)* las piernas.

un·der·play (ŭn'dər-plā') tr. CINEM., TEAT. interpretar flojamente —intr. interpretar flojamente un papel.

un·der·pop·u·lat·ed (ŭn'dər-pŏp'yə-lā'tĭd) adj. poco poblado, con baja densidad de población.

un·der·price (ŭn'dər-prīs') tr. **-priced, -pric·ing** *(to price lower)* poner un precio más bajo de lo que corresponde; *(to undercut)* vender a menor precio que.

un·der·priv·i·leged (ŭn'dər-prĭv'ə-lĭjd) adj. desamparado, desvalido.

un·der·pro·duc·tion (ŭn'dər-prə-dŭk'shən) s. producción baja *o* insuficiente.

un·der·prop (ŭn'dər-prŏp') tr. **-propped, -prop·ping** apuntalar.

un·der·rate (ŭn'dər-rāt') tr. **-rat·ed, -rat·ing** subestimar, menospreciar.

un·der·score (ŭn'dər-skôr') I. tr. **-scored, -scor·ing** *(to underline)* subrayar; FIG. *(to emphasize)* acentuar, recalcar II. s. subrayado.

un·der·sea (ŭn'dər-sē') I. adj. submarino II. adv. bajo la superficie del mar.

un·der·sec·re·tar·y (ŭn'dər-sĕk'rĭ-tĕr'ē) s. [pl. **-ies**] s. subsecretario.

un·der·sell (ŭn'dər-sĕl') tr. **-sold** (-sōld'), **-sell·ing** *(the competition)* vender más barato que; *(the real value)* malbaratar, malvender.

un·der·shirt (ŭn'dər-shûrt') s. camiseta.

un·der·shorts (ŭn'dər-shôrts') s.pl. calzoncillos.

un·der·shot (ŭn'dər-shŏt') adj. TEC. *(driven from below)* de impulsión por abajo; *(said of the jaw)* sobresaliente, saliente.

un·der·side (ŭn'dər-sīd') s. parte de abajo *f,* lado inferior.

un·der·sign (ŭn'dər-sīn') tr. subscribir, firmar.

un·der·signed (ŭn'dər-sīnd') s. [pl. **undersigned**] ♦ **the u.** el suscrito, el abajo firmante *m.*

un·der·sized (ŭn'dər-sīzd') *o* **un·der·size** (-sīz') adj. *(said of a person)* de talla baja, achaparrado; *(small)* pequeño.

un·der·skirt (ŭn'dər-skûrt') s. COST. enagua.

un·der·slung (ŭn'dər-slŭng') adj. AUTO. colgante, suspendido de las ballestas.

un·der·sold (ŭn'dər-sōld') pret. y. part. p. de **undersell.**

un·der·staffed (ŭn'dər-stăft') adj. con poco personal ♦ **to be u.** tener poco personal.

un·der·stand (ŭn'dər-stănd') tr. **-stood** (-stŏŏd'), **-stand·ing** *(to comprehend)* comprender, entender; *(to assume)* tener entendido que *<I u. they left yesterday* tengo entendido que se marcharon ayer*>; (to infer)* entender *<am I to u. that you are not coming?* ¿debo entender que tú no vienes?*>; (to grasp the nature of)* entender de, ser entendido en *<to u. politics* entender de política*>* —intr. entender, comprender.

un·der·stand·a·ble (ŭn'dər-stăn'də-bəl) adj. comprensible.

un·der·stand·ing (ŭn'dər-stăn'dĭng) I. s. *(comprehension)* comprensión *f; (intelligence)* inteligencia, entendimiento; *(opinion)* opinión *f; (agreement)* acuerdo *<they reached an u.* llegaron a un acuerdo*>* ♦ **on the u. that** con tal que, a condición de que II. adj. comprensivo.

un·der·state (ŭn'dər-stāt') tr. **-stat·ed, -stat·ing** *(to state inadequately)* exponer insuficientemente; *(to underestimate)* subestimar; *(to express with restraint)* expresar con reticencia ♦ **to u. one's age** declarar menos edad que la que uno tiene —intr. dar una exposición inadecuada.

un·der·state·ment (ŭn'dər-stāt'mənt) s. *(incomplete statement)* exposición exageradamente modesta; *(euphemism)* eufemismo.

un·der·stood (ŭn'dər-stŏŏd') adj. *(agreed upon)* entendido, acordado; *(implied)* sobreentendido, implícito ♦ **it is u.**

ã **rey** / ä **año** / b **boca** / ch **chico** / d **dar** / ĕ **el** / ē **mil** / g **gato** / h **joya** / hw **juez** / ī **aire** / k **casa** / kw **cuan** /

that se supone que, se sobreentiende que • **I wish it to be u. that** que quede bien claro que, que conste que • **that's u.** se sobreentiende, por supuesto • **to make oneself u.** hacerse comprender • **understood?** ¿entendido?, ¿comprendido?

un·der·stud·y (ŭn'dər-stŭd'ē) TEAT. **I.** tr. **-ied, -y·ing** *(to learn a role)* aprender un papel para reemplazar a; *(to act)* actuar como sobresaliente de —intr. estudiar un papel **II.** s. [pl. **-ies**] suplente *mf*, sobresaliente *m*.

un·der·take (ŭn'dər-tāk') tr. **-took** (-tŏŏk'), **-tak·en** (-tā'kən), **-tak·ing** *(task, journey)* emprender, acometer; *(responsibility, duty)* encargarse de, tomar a su cargo; *(to promise)* prometer, comprometerse a.

un·der·tak·er (ŭn'dər-tā'kər) s. *(entrepreneur)* empresario, contratista *mf*; *(mortician)* agente funerario, empresario de pompas fúnebres.

un·der·tak·ing (ŭn'dər-tā'kĭng) s. *(task)* empresa, tarea; *(promise)* promesa, compromiso; *(trade)* pompas fúnebres.

un·der-the-count·er (ŭn'dər-*th*ə-koun'tər) adj. FIG. bajo mano, ilegal.

un·der·tone (ŭn'dər-tōn') s. *(low voice)* voz baja; *(color)* color apagado de fondo; FIG. *(underlying meaning)* fondo.

un·der·took (ŭn'dər-tŏŏk') pret. de **undertake**.

un·der·tow (ŭn'dər-tō') s. MARÍT. resaca, contracorriente *f*.

un·der·val·u·a·tion (ŭn'dər-văl'yŏŏ-ā'shən) s. infravaloración *f*, subestimación *f*.

un·der·val·ue (ŭn'dər-văl'yŏŏ) tr. **-ued, -u·ing** *(to underestimate)* apreciar en menos; *(to underrate)* desapreciar, subestimar.

un·der·wa·ter (ŭn'dər-wô'tər) adj. submarino, subacuático.

under way adv. *(being put in motion)* andando, principiando; *(already commenced)* en camino, en marcha.

un·der·wear (ŭn'dər-wâr') s. ropa interior.

un·der·weight (ŭn'dər-wāt') **I.** adj. de peso insuficiente, de peso menor que el normal **II.** s. peso insuficiente.

un·der·went (ŭn'dər-wĕnt') pret. de **undergo**.

un·der·world (ŭn'dər-wûrld') s. *(realm, region)* el otro mundo; *(hell)* infierno; *(antipodes)* antípoda; *(criminal world)* hampa *m*; ANT. la tierra.

un·der·write (ŭn'dər-rīt') tr. **-wrote** (-rōt'), **-writ·ten** (-rīt'n), **-writ·ing** *(to subscribe)* subscribir; *(to sign)* firmar, endorsar; *(to finance)* financiar, respaldar; *(to insure)* asegurar; FIN. *(bonds)* subscribir —intr. COM. trabajar en seguros.

un·der·writ·er (ŭn'dər-rī'tər) s. COM. *(insurer)* asegurador *m*; FIN. *(of bonds)* subscritor *m*.

un·de·served (ŭn'dĭ-zûrvd') adj. inmerecido.

un·de·sir·a·ble (ŭn'dĭ-zīr'ə-bəl) **I.** adj. indeseable, poco deseable **II.** s. persona indeseable.

un·de·ter·mined (ŭn'dĭ-tûr'mĭnd) adj. *(undecided)* indeciso; *(uncertain)* incierto, indeterminado.

un·did (ŭn-dĭd') pret. de **undo**.

un·dies (ŭn'dēz) s. FAM. ropa interior.

un·dig·ni·fied (ŭn-dĭg'nə-fīd') adj. indecoroso, sin dignidad.

un·dip·lo·mat·ic (ŭn-dĭp'lə-măt'ĭk) adj. poco diplomático.

un·di·rect·ed (ŭn'dĭ-rĕk'tĭd, -dī-) adj. *(not guided)* no dirigido, no gobernado; *(without address)* sin dirección, sin señas.

un·dis·cern·a·ble (ŭn'dĭ-sûr'nə-bəl, -zûr'-) adj. indiscernible, imperceptible.

un·dis·ci·plined (ŭn-dĭs'ə-plĭnd) adj. indisciplinado.

un·dis·cov·ered (ŭn'dĭ-skŭv'ərd) adj. *(not discovered)* no descubierto, sin descubrir; *(unknown)* desconocido.

un·dis·crim·i·nat·ing (ŭn'dĭ-skrĭm'ə-nā'tĭng) adj. *(indiscriminate)* indistinto; *(without discernment)* sin criterio, falto de sentido crítico.

un·dis·guised (ŭn'dĭs-gīzd') adj. *(not disguised)* sin disfraz; FIG. *(sincere)* sincero, franco.

un·dis·posed (ŭn'dĭ-spōzd') adj. *(unwilling)* poco dispuesto; *(unsold)* no vendido • **u. of** *(unused)* sin utilizar; *(unsold)* sin vender; *(not invested)* sin invertir.

un·dis·put·ed (ŭn'dĭ-spyŏŏ'tĭd) adj. incontestable, indisputable.

un·dis·tin·guish·a·ble (ŭn'dĭ-stĭng'gwĭ-shə-bəl) adj. indistinguible.

un·dis·tin·guished (ŭn'dī-stĭng'gwĭsht) adj. poco distinguido, ordinario.

un·dis·turbed (ŭn'dĭ-stûrbd') adj. *(not disturbed)* no perturbado; *(calm)* tranquilo, sereno; *(untouched)* sin tocar.

un·do (ŭn-dŏŏ') tr. **-did** (-dĭd'), **-done** (-dŭn'), **-do·ing** *(to annul)* contrarrestar, reparar *<to u. the suffering caused by the war* reparar el dolor producido por la guerra>; *(shoelace, tie)* desatar, aflojar; *(package, parcel)* abrir, desenvolver; *(zipper)* bajar; *(clasp, button)* desabrochar, desabotonar; *(to destroy)* destruir, arruinar; *(to take apart)* deshacer; *(to unsettle)* perturbar, trastornar —intr. desatarse, abrirse.

un·dock (ŭn-dŏk') tr. desenganchar, desacoplar.

un·do·ing (ŭn-dŏŏ'ĭng) s. *(of a damage)* reparación *f*; *(loosening)* aflojamiento, desatadura; *(downfall)* ruina, perdición *f*.

un·done (ŭn-dŭn') **I.** part. p. de **undo II.** adj. *(not done)* no hecho, sin hacer; *(unfinished)* inacabado, sin acabar; *(untied)* desatado; *(emotionally exhausted)* deshecho; *(button)* desabrochado ♦ **to come u.** desatarse, soltarse • **to leave u.** dejar sin hacer.

un·doubt·ed (ŭn-dou'tĭd) adj. indudable, cierto.

un·dress (ŭn-drĕs') **I.** tr. *(to disrobe)* desvestir, desnudar; MED. *(to remove bandages)* desvendar, quitar el vendaje de —intr. desvestirse, desnudarse **II.** s. *(informal attire)* ropa de casa; *(nakedness)* desnudez *f*.

un·dressed (ŭn-drĕst') adj. *(naked)* desnudo; *(not fully dressed)* en bata; *(said of leather)* sin adobar; *(said of stone)* sin labrar; *(unseasoned)* sin aderezar; *(timber)* sin desbastar.

un·due (ŭn-dŏŏ', -dyŏŏ') adj. *(excessive)* excesivo, indebido; *(improper)* impropio; *(undeserved)* inmerecido; DER. *(unlawful)* ilegítimo, ilegal; COM. *(debt)* no vencido.

un·du·lant (ŭn'jə-lənt) adj. ondulante.

undulant fever s. MED. fiebre ondulante *f*, fiebre de Malta.

un·du·late (ŭn'jə-lāt') **I.** tr. **-lat·ed, -lat·ing** *(to cause to move)* hacer ondear; *(to give a wavelike appearance)* ondular —intr. *(to move in waves)* ondular, ondear; *(to have a wavelike form)* ser ondulado **II.** adj. (-lĭt, -lāt') ondulado.

un·du·la·tion (ŭn'jə-lā'shən) s. *(motion, form)* ondulación *f*; *(wave)* onda; ACÚS. pulsación *f*.

un·du·ly (ŭn-dŏŏ'lē, -dyŏŏ'-) adv. *(excessively)* excesivamente, indebidamente; *(improperly)* impropiamente.

un·dy·ing (ŭn-dī'ĭng) adj. *(everlasting)* eterno, perpetuo; *(immortal)* inmortal, imperecedero.

un·earned (ŭn-ûrnd') adj. *(not gained)* no ganado; *(undeserved)* inmerecido; COM. *(not yet earned)* no devengado.

unearned increment s. plusvalía.

un·earth (ŭn-ûrth') tr. *(to dig up)* desenterrar, excavar; FIG. *(to uncover)* descubrir, revelar.

un·earth·ly (ŭn-ûrth'lē) adj. **-li·er, -li·est** *(supernatural)* sobrenatural, extraterreno; *(terrifying)* aterrador, espantoso; *(absurd)* absurdo.

un·eas·i·ly (ŭn-ē'zə-lē) adv. inquietamente, ansiosamente.

un·eas·i·ness (ŭn-ē'zē-nĭs) s. *(restlessness)* inquietud *f*, intranquilidad *f*; *(worry)* preocupación *f*; *(uncomfortableness)* incomodidad *f*.

un·eas·y (ŭn-ē'zē) adj. **-i·er, -i·est** *(disturbed)* inquieto, intranquilo; *(worried)* preocupado, ansioso *<an u. wait* una ansiosa espera>; *(awkward)* embarazoso, incómodo *<he feels u. with strangers* se siente incómodo con extraños>.

un·ed·u·cat·ed (ŭn-ĕj'ə-kā'tĭd) adj. ineducado, inculto.

un·em·ploy·a·ble (ŭn'ĕm-ploi'ə-bəl) **I.** adj. que no puede tener un empleo **II.** s. persona incapacitada para tener un empleo.

un·em·ployed (ŭn'ĕm-ploid') **I.** adj. *(out of work)* desempleado, parado; *(idle)* sin utilizar, no usado **II.** s. desempleado, parado ♦ **the u.** los desempleados, los parados.

un·em·ploy·ment (ŭn'ĕm-ploi'mənt) s. desempleo, paro.

unemployment compensation s. beneficio del seguro contra el desempleo.

un·en·cum·bered (ŭn'ĕn-kŭm'bərd) adj. DER. libre de gravámenes ♦ **u. by** sin las trabas de, sin las limitaciones de.

un·end·ing (ŭn-ĕn'dĭng) adj. interminable, sin fin.

un·e·qual (ŭn-ē'kwəl) adj. *(unlike)* desigual, distinto; *(not matched)* desigual, desparejo; *(asymmetric)* asimétrico;

(fluctuating) fluctuante; *(inadequate)* inadecuado, no a la altura de.

un·e·qualed *o* **un·e·qualled** (ŭn-ē′kwəld) adj. sin igual, sin par.

un·e·quiv·o·cal (ŭn′ĭ-kwĭv′ə-kəl) adj. *(without doubt)* inequívoco, indudable; *(clear)* claro.

un·err·ing (ŭn-ûr′ĭng) adj. infalible.

un·es·sen·tial (ŭn′ĭ-sĕn′shəl) I. adj. innecesario, no esencial II. s. algo innecesario.

un·e·ven (ŭn-ē′vən) adj. **-er, -est** *(not equal)* desigual; *(said of a color, shade)* desparejo; *(said of a surface)* desigual, accidentado; MAT. *(odd)* impar.

un·e·ven·ness (ŭn-ē′vən-nĭs) s. desigualdad *f*, irregularidad *f*.

un·e·vent·ful (ŭn′ĭ-vĕnt′fəl) adj. sin acontecimientos, sin novedad.

un·ex·cep·tion·a·ble (ŭn′ĭk-sĕp′shə-nə-bəl) adj. irreprochable, intachable.

un·ex·cep·tion·al (ŭn′ĭk-sĕp′shə-nəl) adj. *(usual)* usual, corriente; *(without exceptions)* sin excepción, absoluto.

un·ex·pect·ed (ŭn′ĭk-spĕk′tĭd) adj. inesperado, imprevisto.

un·ex·ploit·ed (ŭn′ĭk-sploi′tĭd) adj. *(not exploited)* inexplotado; *(not developed)* no desarrollado.

un·ex·plored (ŭn′ĭk-splôrd′) adj. inexplorado, no conocido.

un·ex·posed (ŭn′ĭk-spōzd′) adj. FOTOG. no expuesto; FIG. *(not revealed)* no descubierto.

un·ex·pres·sive (ŭn′ĭk-sprĕs′ĭv) adj. inexpresivo.

un·fail·ing (ŭn-fā′lĭng) adj. *(inexhaustible)* inagotable; *(constant)* constante, persistente; *(certain)* seguro, cierto; *(infallible)* infalible, indefectible.

un·fair (ŭn-fâr′) adj. **-er, -est** *(not just)* injusto; *(unethical)* poco ético, inmoral; COM. *(said of competition)* desleal; *(said of wages)* no equitativo.

un·fair·ness (ŭn-fâr′nĭs) s. *(injustice)* injusticia, falta de equidad; COM. *(in competition)* deslealtad *f*, mala fe.

un·faith·ful (ŭn-fāth′fəl) adj. *(disloyal)* infiel, desleal; *(adulterous)* adúltero, infiel; *(inaccurate)* inexacto; ANT., RELIG. infiel, incrédulo.

un·faith·ful·ness (ŭn-fāth′fəl-nĭs) s. infidelidad *f*, deslealtad *f*.

un·fa·mil·iar (ŭn′fə-mĭl′yər) adj. *(strange)* extraño, desconocido; *(not conversant)* no familiarizado, no versado ♦ **u. with** no familiarizado con, no versado en.

un·fa·mil·iar·i·ty (ŭn′fə-mĭl-yăr′ĭ-tē) s. falta de familiaridad.

un·fash·ion·a·ble (ŭn-făsh′ə-nə-bəl) adj. *(out of date)* fuera de moda, pasado de moda; *(not elegant)* poco elegante.

un·fas·ten (ŭn-făs′ən) tr. & intr. desatar(se), desabrochar(se).

un·fa·thered (ŭn-fä′thərd) adj. *(bastard)* sin padre, ilegítimo; *(of uncertain origin)* de origen desconocido.

un·fath·om·a·ble (ŭn-făth′ə-mə-bəl) adj. MARÍT. *(incapable of being known)* insondable, impenetrable; FIG. *(difficult to understand)* insondable.

un·fa·vor·a·ble (ŭn-fā′vər-ə-bəl) adj. *(not propitious)* desfavorable; *(negative)* negativo; *(not pleasing)* desagradable.

un·feel·ing (ŭn-fē′lĭng) adj. *(insentient)* insensible, inconsciente; *(callous)* duro de corazón, cruel.

un·feigned (ŭn-fānd′) adj. sincero, no fingido.

un·fet·ter (ŭn-fĕt′ər) tr. *(from fetters)* destrabar, desencadenar; FIG. *(from restraints)* libertar.

un·fin·ished (ŭn-fĭn′ĭsht) adj. *(not finished)* inconcluso, no acabado; *(incomplete)* incompleto; TEC. *(not processed)* natural, bruto.

un·fit (ŭn-fĭt′) adj. *(not suitable)* inadecuado; *(unqualified)* incompetente, inepto; *(physically)* en malas condiciones físicas.

un·fit·ness (ŭn-fĭt′nĭs) s. *(incompetence)* incompetencia, ineptitud *f*; *(inappropriateness)* impropiedad *f*; *(physical condition)* mala condición física.

un·fix (ŭn-fĭks′) tr. *(unfasten)* soltar, aflojar; *(to unsettle)* desequilibrar, perturbar.

un·flag·ging (ŭn-flăg′ĭng) adj. *(untiring)* incansable, infatigable; *(constant)* constante, persistente.

un·flap·pa·ble (ŭn-flăp′ə-bəl) adj. impasible, imperturbable.

un·flat·ter·ing (ŭn-flăt′ər-ĭng) adj. poco halagüeño, desfavorable.

un·fledged (ŭn-flĕjd′) adj. ORNIT. sin plumas; FIG. *(immature)* inmaduro.

un·flinch·ing (ŭn-flĭn′chĭng) adj. resuelto, decidido.

un·fo·cused *o* **un·fo·cussed** (ŭn-fō′kəst) adj. fuera de foco, sin enfocar.

un·fold (ŭn-fōld′) tr. *(papers)* desdoblar, desplegar; *(sheets)* extender; FIG. *(plot)* descubrir, revelar; *(theory)* exponer, desarrollar —intr. *(to become spread out)* desdoblarse, desplegarse; FIG. *(story, plot)* desarrollarse; *(to open out)* abrirse, extenderse.

un·fore·seen (ŭn′fər-sēn′) adj. imprevisto, inesperado.

un·for·get·ta·ble (ŭn′fər-gĕt′ə-bəl) adj. inolvidable.

un·for·giv·a·ble (ŭn′fər-gĭv′ə-bəl) adj. imperdonable, inexcusable.

un·formed (ŭn-fôrmd′) adj. *(shapeless)* informe, sin forma; *(uncreated)* no formado aún.

un·for·tu·nate (ŭn-fôr′chə-nĭt) I. adj. *(unlucky)* desgraciado, desafortunado; *(disastrous)* desastroso; *(regrettable)* lamentable, deplorable II. s. desgraciado, desafortunado.

un·found·ed (ŭn-foun′dĭd) adj. *(not yet established)* no fundado, no establecido; *(groundless)* infundado, sin fundamento.

un·fre·quent·ed (ŭn′frē-kwĕn′tĭd) adj. poco frecuentado.

un·friend·li·ness (ŭn-frĕnd′lē-nĭs) s. hostilidad *f*.

un·friend·ly (ŭn-frĕnd′lē) adj. **-li·er, -li·est** *(not friendly)* poco amistoso, seco; *(hostile)* hostil, enemigo; *(unfavorable)* desfavorable, poco propicio.

un·frock (ŭn-frŏk′) tr. RELIG. despojar de los privilegios eclesiásticos.

un·fruit·ful (ŭn-frōōt′fəl) adj. *(barren)* estéril, infértil; *(useless)* infructuoso, inútil.

un·fund·ed (ŭn-fŭn′dĭd) adj. *(said of a debt)* flotante, no consolidado; *(without funds)* sin fondos.

un·furl (ŭn-fûrl′) tr. & intr. desplegar(se), desdoblar(se).

un·fur·nished (ŭn-fûr′nĭsht) adj. desamueblado, sin muebles.

un·gain·ly (ŭn-gān′lē) adj. **-li·er, -li·est** *(clumsy)* torpe, desmañado; *(unwieldy)* pesado, difícil de mover.

un·glued (ŭn-glōōd′) adj. *(separated)* despegado; JER. *(upset)* trastornado.

un·god·ly (ŭn-gŏd′lē) adj. **-li·er, -li·est** *(impious)* impío, profano; *(wicked)* perverso, malvado; FAM. *(outrageous)* atroz, inoportuno.

un·gov·ern·a·ble (ŭn-gŭv′ər-nə-bəl) adj. ingobernable, incontrolable.

un·gra·cious (ŭn-grā′shəs) adj. *(rude)* poco amable, brusco; *(unattractive)* desagradable.

un·gram·mat·i·cal (ŭn′grə-măt′ĭ-kəl) adj. GRAM. incorrecto, antigramatical.

un·grate·ful (ŭn-grāt′fəl) adj. ingrato, desagradecido.

un·ground·ed (ŭn-groun′dĭd) adj. infundado, sin fundamento.

un·guard·ed (ŭn-gär′dĭd) adj. *(defenseless)* desguarnecido, sin defensa; *(careless)* desprevenido, descuidado; *(incautious)* incauto.

un·guent (ŭng′gwənt) s. FARM., MED. ungüento.

un·gu·late (ŭng′gyə-lĭt, -lāt′) adj. & s. ZOOL. ungulado.

un·hal·lowed (ŭn-hăl′ōd) adj. *(unconsecrated)* no consagrado; *(impious)* impío, profano; *(immoral)* inmoral.

un·hand (ŭn-hănd′) tr. desasir, soltar.

un·hand·y (ŭn-hăn′dē) adj. **-i·er, -i·est** *(unwieldy)* incómodo, difícil de manejar; *(clumsy)* desmañado, torpe.

un·hap·pi·ness (ŭn-hăp′ē-nĭs) s. desgracia, infortunio.

un·hap·py (ŭn-hăp′ē) adj. **-pi·er, -pi·est** *(not happy)* infeliz, desgraciado; *(unlucky)* desafortunado, desventurado; *(inappropriate)* impropio, inoportuno.

un·har·ness (ŭn-här′nĭs) tr. *(horses, oxen)* desenjaezar; FIG. *(to release)* soltar, liberar.

un·health·y (ŭn-hĕl′thē) adj. **-i·er, -i·est** *(sick)* enfermo, indispuesto; *(sickly)* enfermizo, achacoso; *(unwholesome)* insalubre; *(corruptive)* malsano; *(dangerous)* peligroso.

un·heard (ŭn-hûrd′) adj. *(not heard)* no oído; *(not considered)* desatendido.

ā rey / ä año / b boca / ch chico / d dar / ĕ el / ē mil / g gato / h joya / hw juez / ī aire / k casa / kw cuan /

un·heard-of (ŭn-hûrd′ŭv′, -ŏv′) adj. *(unprecedented)* inaudito, sin precedente; *(unknown)* desconocido.

un·hes·i·tat·ing (ŭn-hĕz′ĭ-tā′tĭng) adj. *(ready)* pronto, listo; *(unfaltering)* sin titubear, resuelto.

un·hes·i·tat·ing·ly (ŭn-hĕz′ĭ-tā-tĭng-lē) adv. sin titubear, resueltamente.

un·hinge (ŭn-hĭnj′) tr. **-hinged, -hing·ing** *(a door, window)* desgoznar; *(the mind)* trastornar, desquiciar.

un·hitch (ŭn-hĭch′) tr. desenganchar, desprender.

un·ho·ly (ŭn-hō′lē) adj. **-li·er, -li·est** *(profane)* profano; *(impious)* impío; FAM. *(outrageous)* tremendo, infernal.

un·hook (ŭn-hŏŏk′) tr. desenganchar, descolgar.

un·hoped-for (ŭn-hōpt′fôr′) adj. inesperado, nunca soñado.

u·ni·cel·lu·lar (yōō′nĭ-sĕl′yə-lər) adj. BIOL. unicelular.

u·ni·corn (yōō′nĭ-kôrn′) s. MITOL. unicornio.

u·ni·cy·cle (yōō′nĭ-sī′kəl) s. monociclo.

u·ni·den·ti·fied flying object (ŭn′ī-dĕn′tə-fīd′) s. AER. objeto volador no identificado (OVNI).

u·ni·fi·ca·tion (yōō′nə-fĭ-kā′shən) s. unificación *f.*

u·ni·fied (yōō′nə-fīd′) pret. y part. p. de **unify.**

u·ni·fi·er (yōō′nə-fī′ər) s. unificador *m.*

u·ni·form (yōō′nə-fôrm′) **I.** adj. *(unvarying)* uniforme, parejo; *(consistent)* de consistencia invariable; *(identical)* idéntico **II.** s. uniforme *m* **III.** tr. *(to make uniform)* uniformizar; *(to dress)* poner un uniforme, uniformar.

u·ni·for·mi·ty (yōō′nə-fôr′mĭ-tē) s. uniformidad *f.*

u·ni·form·ly (yōō′nə-fôrm′lē) adv. uniformemente.

u·ni·fy (yōō′nə-fī′) tr. & intr. **-fied, -fy·ing** unificar(se), unir(se).

u·ni·lat·er·al (yōō′nə-lăt′ər-əl) adj. unilateral.

un·i·mag·i·na·ble (ŭn′ĭ-măj′ə-nə-bəl) adj. inimaginable.

un·im·peach·a·ble (ŭn′ĭm-pē′chə-bəl) adv. *(beyond reproach)* irreprochable, irreprensible; *(unquestionable)* irrecusable.

un·im·por·tant (ŭn′ĭm-pôr′tnt) adj. poco importante, insignificante.

un·im·proved (ŭn′ĭm-prōōvd′) adj. *(not bettered)* no mejorado; *(not put to advantage)* no aprovechado; *(not cultivated)* sin cultivar; *(undeveloped)* sin urbanizar.

un·in·form·a·tive (ŭn′ĭn-fôr′mə-tĭv) adj. nada informativo.

un·in·formed (ŭn′ĭn-fôrmd′) adj. *(badly informed)* mal informado; *(uneducated)* ignorante.

un·in·hab·it·a·ble (ŭn′ĭn-hăb′ĭ-tə-bəl) adj. inhabitable.

un·in·hab·it·ed (ŭn′ĭn-hăb′ĭ-tĭd) adj. *(not inhabited)* inhabitado, deshabitado; *(deserted)* despoblado.

un·in·hib·it·ed (ŭn′ĭn-hĭb′ĭ-tĭd) adj. *(open)* franco, desenfadado; *(free)* sin inhibiciones.

un·in·jured (ŭn-ĭn′jərd) adj. indemne, ileso.

un·in·spired (ŭn′ĭn-spīrd′) adj. falto de inspiración, sin inspiración.

un·in·sured (ŭn′ĭn-shŏŏrd′) adj. no asegurado, sin asegurar.

un·in·tel·li·gent (ŭn′ĭn-tĕl′ə-jənt) adj. falto de inteligencia, poco inteligente.

un·in·tel·li·gi·ble (ŭn′ĭn-tĕl′ə-jə-bəl) adj. ininteligible.

un·in·ter·est·ed (ŭn-ĭn′trĭs-tĭd) adj. *(not interested)* desinteresado; *(indifferent)* indiferente, apático.

un·in·ter·est·ing (ŭn-ĭn′trĭ-stĭng) adj. falto de interés, que no interesa.

un·in·ter·rupt·ed (ŭn-ĭn′tə-rŭp′tĭd) adj. ininterrumpido, continuo.

un·ion (yōōn′yən) s. *(act, state)* unión *f;* *(alliance)* alianza; *(marriage)* enlace *m;* *(intercourse)* relación sexual *f;* *(labor confederation)* gremio, sindicato; MAT. unión ♦ **the u. movement** el movimiento sindical • **U.** *(student center)* centro estudiantil; POL. los Estados Unidos.

union card s. tarjeta de sindicato.

un·ion·ism (yōōn′yə-nĭz′əm) s. sindicalismo.

un·ion·ist (yōōn′yə-nĭst) s. *(trade unionist)* sindicalista *mf;* EE. UU., HIST. unionista *mf,* persona leal a la Unión en la guerra civil.

un·ion·ize (yōōn′yə-nīz′) tr. & intr. **-ized, -iz·ing** sindicar(se), sindicalizar(se).

union Jack s. bandera ♦ **U.** bandera nacional de Gran Bretaña.

Union of Soviet Socialist Republics s. Unión de Repúblicas Socialistas Soviéticas.

union shop s. empresa que sólo emplea a trabajadores sindicados.

u·ni·po·lar (yōō′nĭ-pō′lər) adj. FÍS. unipolar.

u·nique (yōō-nēk′) adj. *(sole)* único en su género; *(unparalleled)* sin igual, sin paralelo.

u·nique·ness (yōō-nēk′nĭs) s. singularidad *m,* originalidad *f.*

u·ni·sex (yōō′nĭ-sĕks′) adj. unisexo.

u·ni·sex·u·al (yōō′nĭ-sĕk′shōō-əl) adj. BOT., ZOOL. unisexual, de un solo sexo; *(unisex)* unisexo.

u·ni·son (yōō′nĭ-sən) s. MÚS. *(pitch)* unisonancia; *(speaking together)* unísono; *(agreement)* acuerdo, armonía.

u·nit (yōō′nĭt) s. *(elementary constituent)* unidad *f;* *(group)* grupo, equipo; *(part)* parte *f* <*the lens u. of a camera*>; *(device)* aparato, máquina; *(standard)* unidad; *(set)* conjunto; *(center)* centro <*research u.* centro de investigaciones>; MAT. unidad.

U·ni·tar·i·an (yōō′nĭ-târ′ē-ən) s. & adj. RELIG. unitario.

u·ni·tar·y (yōō′nĭ-tĕr′ē) adj. *(of a unit)* unitario; *(whole)* entero, íntegro; FÍS., MAT. unitario.

u·nite (yōō-nīt′) tr. & intr. **-nit·ed, -nit·ing** *(to bring together)* unir(se); *(to combine)* combinar(se); *(to adhere)* pegar(se).

United Arab Emirates s. Emiratos Árabes Unidos.

United Kingdom s. Reino Unido.

United Kingdom of Great Britain and Northern Ireland s. Reino Unido de Gran Bretaña e Irlanda del Norte.

United Nations s.pl. [ú. con v. sing. o pl.] Naciones Unidas.

United States of America s. Estados Unidos de América.

u·ni·ty (yōō′nĭ-tē) s. [pl. **-ties**] *(singleness)* unidad *f;* *(concord)* acuerdo armonía; *(unification)* unificación *f;* *(continuity)* continuidad *f;* MAT. unidad; LIT., TEAT. unidad.

u·ni·va·lent (yōō′nĭ-vā′lənt) **I.** adj. QUÍM. univalente **II.** s. BIOL. cromosoma impar.

u·ni·valve (yōō′nĭ-vălv′) adj. BOT., ZOOL. univalvo.

u·ni·ver·sal (yōō′nə-vûr′səl) **I.** adj. *(cosmic)* universal; *(worldwide)* mundial, universal; MEC. *(adaptable)* universal **II.** s. FILOS. universal *m.*

U·ni·ver·sal·ist (yōō′nə-vûr′sə-lĭst) s. & adj. TEOL. universalista *mf.*

u·ni·ver·sal·i·ty (yōō′nə-vər-săl′ĭ-tē) s. [pl. **-ties**] universalidad *f.*

universal joint s. MEC. junta universal *o* de cardán.

universal time s. hora de Greenwich.

u·ni·verse (yōō′nə-vûrs′) s. *(cosmos)* universo, cosmos *m;* *(world)* mundo; *(mankind)* humanidad *f;* FILOS. *(system)* sistema completo.

u·ni·ver·si·ty (yōō′nə-vûr′sĭ-tē) s. [pl. **-ties**] EDUC. universidad *f.*

un·just (ŭn-jŭst′) adj. *(not just)* injusto, inicuo; ANT. *(dishonest)* deshonesto, falso.

un·jus·ti·fi·a·ble (ŭn-jŭs′tə-fī′ə-bəl) adj. injustificable, inexcusable.

un·kempt (ŭn-kĕmpt′) adj. *(uncombed)* despeinado, desgreñado; *(messy)* desarreglado, descuidado.

un·kind (ŭn-kīnd′) adj. **-er, -est** *(lacking kindness)* poco amable, duro; *(harsh)* severo.

un·know·ing (ŭn-nō′ĭng) adj. *(ignorant)* que no sabe, ignorante; *(unaware)* inconsciente.

un·known (ŭn-nōn′) **I.** adj. *(not known)* desconocido; *(not identified)* no identificado, incógnito; *(not verified)* no establecido *o* verificado **II.** s. *(person)* desconocido; MAT. incógnita.

un·lace (ŭn-lās′) tr. **-laced, -lac·ing** *(ribbon, lace)* desatar, desenlazar; *(clothing)* aflojar, desabrochar.

un·lade (ŭn-lād′) tr. & intr. **-lad·ed, -lad·ing** descargar.

un·la·dy·like (ŭn′lā′dē-līk′) adj. impropio de una dama.

un·lash (ŭn-lăsh′) tr. desamarrar, desatar.

un·latch (ŭn-lăch′) tr. abrir levantando el picaporte —intr. abrirse.

un·law·ful (ŭn-lô′fəl) adj. *(illegal)* ilegal, ilícito; *(illegitimate)* ilegítimo.

un·lead·ed (ŭn-lĕd′ĭd) adj. *(without lead)* sin plomo; IMPR. *(not spaced)* desinterlineado.

---

un·learn·ed (ŭn-lûr'nĭd) adj. *(not educated)* ignorante, inculto; *(unskilled)* no especializado, lego.
un·leash (ŭn-lēsh') tr. *(to release)* soltar; FIG. *(to free)* liberar, desencadenar.
un·leav·ened (ŭn-lĕv'ənd) adj. ázimo, sin levadura.
un·less (ŭn-lĕs') I. conj. a menos que, a no ser que II. prep. salvo, excepto.
un·let·tered (ŭn-lĕt'ərd) adj. *(illiterate)* analfabeto, ignorante; *(devoid of lettering)* desprovisto de letras.
un·li·censed (ŭn-lī'sənst) adj. *(having no license)* sin licencia, sin permiso; *(not authorized)* no autorizado, sin autorización.
un·like (ŭn'līk') I. adj. *(not alike)* nada parecido, distinto; *(dissimilar)* disímil; *(not equal)* desigual, diferente II. prep. *(different from)* diferente de, no como; *(not typical of)* no característico de, impropio de.
un·like·li·hood (ŭn-līk'lē-hōŏd') s. improbabilidad *f.*
un·like·ly (ŭn-līk'lē) adj. -li·er, -li·est *(improbable)* improbable, remoto; *(unexpected)* inverosímil; *(likely to fail)* poco prometedor.
un·lim·ber (ŭn-lĭm'bər) tr. ARM. *(a gun)* quitar el avantrén (de un cañón); FIG. *(to make ready)* alistar para la acción —intr. alistarse para la acción.
un·lim·it·ed (ŭn-lĭm'ĭ-tĭd) adj. *(having no limits)* ilimitado, infinito; *(unrestrained)* sin restricciones.
un·link (ŭn-lĭngk') tr. *(to disconnect)* separar los eslabones de; *(to unfasten)* desatar, soltar.
un·list·ed (ŭn-lĭs'tĭd) adj. *(not on a list)* que no figura en la lista; FIN. *(stock)* no cotizado.
un·load (ŭn-lōd') tr. *(to remove)* descargar; FIG. *(to unburden)* desahogar; *(to dispose of)* deshacerse de —intr. descargar.
un·load·er (ŭn-lō'dər) s. descargador *m.*
un·load·ing (ŭn-lō'dĭng) s. descarga.
un·lock (ŭn-lŏk') tr. *(with a key)* abrir; FIG. *(to open)* abrir; *(to release)* liberar, dejar salir; *(to reveal)* revelar, descubrir —intr. abrirse.
un·looked-for (ŭn-lōōkt'fôr') adj. inesperado, imprevisto.
un·loos·en (ŭn-lōō'sən) tr. soltar, desatar.
un·love·ly (ŭn-lŭv'lē) adj. -li·er, -li·est desagradable, sin gracia.
un·luck·i·ness (ŭn-lŭk'ē-nĭs) s. infortunio, mala suerte.
un·luck·y (ŭn-lŭk'ē) adj. -i·er, -i·est *(unfortunate)* desgraciado, desafortunado; *(inauspicious)* aciago, de mal agüero ♦ **to be u.** tener mala suerte.
un·make (ŭn-māk') tr. -made (-mād'), -mak·ing *(to depose)* deponer, destituir; *(to destroy)* destruir, aniquilar.
un·man (ŭn-măn') tr. -manned, -man·ning *(to deprive of courage)* acobardar; *(to castrate)* castrar.
un·man·age·a·ble (ŭn-măn'ĭ-jə-bəl) adj. inmanejable, poco manejable.
un·man·ly (ŭn-măn'lē) adj. -li·er, -li·est *(dishonorable)* deshonroso, impropio de un hombre; *(cowardly)* cobarde; *(effeminate)* afeminado, poco viril.
un·manned (ŭn-mănd') adj. sin tripulación.
un·man·nered (ŭn-măn'ərd) adj. descortés, mal educado.
un·man·ner·ly (ŭn-măn'ər-lē) adj. descortés, grosero.
un·marked (ŭn-märkt') adj. *(without a mark)* sin marcar; *(without a gravestone)* sin lápida; *(unnoticed)* desapercibido.
un·mar·ket·a·ble (ŭn-mär'kĭ-tə-bəl) adj. invendible, no comerciable.
un·mar·ried (ŭn-măr'ēd) adj. soltero.
un·mask (ŭn-măsk') tr. *(to remove)* quitar la máscara, desenmascarar; FIG. *(to expose)* descubrir —intr. quitarse la máscara, desenmascararse.
un·matched (ŭn-măcht') adj. *(unique)* único, sin par; *(not paired)* no emparejado, sin pareja.
un·meant (ŭn-mĕnt') adj. involuntario, sin intención.
un·men·tion·a·ble (ŭn-mĕn'shə-nə-bəl) I. adj. *(unfit to mention)* impropio, que no se debe mencionar; *(unspeakable)* indecible II. s. algo que no se debe mencionarse ♦ **un·mentionables** FAM. ropa interior.
un·mer·ci·ful (ŭn-mûr'sĭ-fəl) adj. *(merciless)* despiadado; *(excessive)* excesivo.

un·mind·ful (ŭn-mīnd'fəl) adj. negligente, olvidadizo ♦ **u. of** descuidando, sin pensar en.
un·mis·tak·a·ble (ŭn'mĭ-stā'kə-bəl) adj. *(obvious)* obvio, evidente; *(unequivocal)* inequívoco, inconfundible.
un·mit·i·gat·ed (ŭn-mĭt'ĭ-gā'tĭd) adj. *(unrelieved)* implacable, sin tregua; *(absolute)* absoluto.
un·mor·al (ŭn-môr'əl) adj. amoral.
un·moved (ŭn-mōōvd') adj. *(in its place)* en su sitio, inmóvil; *(indifferent)* impasible, indiferente; *(unflinching)* impávido; *(insensitive)* insensible.
un·named (ŭn-nāmd') adj. *(having no name)* sin nombre; *(anonymous)* anónimo.
un·nat·u·ral (ŭn-năch'ər-əl) adj. *(not natural)* no natural; *(affected)* artificial, afectado; *(against nature)* contranatural, contra natura; *(inhuman)* inhumano.
un·nec·es·sar·y (ŭn-nĕs'ĭ-sĕr'ē) adj. innecesario, superfluo.
un·nerve (ŭn-nûrv') tr. -nerved, -nerv·ing amilanar, turbar.
un·no·tice·a·ble (ŭn-nō'tĭ-sə-bəl) adj. imperceptible.
un·no·ticed (ŭn-nō'tĭst) adj. inadvertido, desapercibido.
un·num·bered (ŭn-nŭm'bərd) adj. *(countless)* innumerable; *(lacking a number)* no numerado, sin número.
un·ob·served (ŭn'əb-zûrvd') adj. desapercibido, inadvertido.
un·ob·tain·a·ble (ŭn'əb-tā'nə-bəl) adj. inasequible, inalcanzable.
un·ob·tru·sive (ŭn'əb-trōō'sĭv) adj. discreto.
un·oc·cu·pied (ŭn-ŏk'yə-pīd') adj. *(vacant)* desocupado, vacante; *(idle)* desempleado, ocioso; MIL. *(not occupied)* no ocupado.
un·of·fi·cial (ŭn'ə-fĭsh'əl) adj. extraoficial, no oficial.
un·or·gan·ized (ŭn-ôr'gə-nīzd') adj. *(lacking order)* no organizado; BIOL. *(inorganic)* sin estructura orgánica; *(not unionized)* sin sindicar.
un·o·rig·i·nal (ŭn'ə-rĭj'ə-nəl) adj. *(lacking originality)* poco original, sin originalidad; *(trite)* trillado.
un·or·tho·dox (ŭn-ôr'thə-dŏks') adj. poco ortodoxo.
un·pack (ŭn-păk') tr. *(to remove contents of)* desempacar, desembalar; *(to unload)* descargar —intr. deshacer las maletas.
un·paid (ŭn-pād') adj. *(not yet paid)* impago, sin pagar; *(unsalaried)* no remunerado.
un·pal·at·a·ble (ŭn-păl'ə-tə-bəl) adj. *(bad tasting)* desabrido, desagradable al paladar; FIG. *(unpleasant)* desagradable, difícil de aceptar.
un·par·al·leled (ŭn-păr'ə-lĕld') adj. sin paralelo, sin igual.
un·par·don·a·ble (ŭn-pär'dn-ə-bəl) adj. imperdonable, inexcusable.
un·par·lia·men·ta·ry (ŭn-pär'lə-mĕn'tə-rē) adj. contrario a las reglas parlamentarias.
un·pa·tri·ot·ic (ŭn-pā'trē-ŏt'ĭk) adj. antipatriótico, poco patriótico.
un·peo·pled (ŭn-pē'pəld) adj. despoblado, deshabitado.
un·pin (ŭn-pĭn') tr. -pinned, -pin·ning COST. *(to remove pins from)* quitar alfileres a; *(to take off)* desprender.
un·pleas·ant (ŭn-plĕz'ənt) adj. *(disagreeable)* desagradable, molesto; *(unfriendly)* antipático.
un·pleas·ant·ness (ŭn-plĕz'ənt-nĭs) s. *(displeasure)* desagrado, disgusto; *(unfriendliness)* antipatía.
un·plug (ŭn-plŭg') tr. -plugged, -plug·ging *(to remove the plug from)* destapar; ELEC. desconectar, desenchufar.
un·plumbed (ŭn-plŭmd') adj. MARÍT. *(depth)* sin sondear; FIG. *(meaning)* insondable.
un·pol·ished (ŭn-pŏl'ĭsht) adj. *(not polished)* sin pulir, deslustrado; *(said of shoes)* sin lustrar; FIG. *(crude)* rudo, grosero.
un·pol·lut·ed (ŭn'pə-lōō'tĭd) adj. no contaminado, incontaminado.
un·pop·u·lar (ŭn-pŏp'yə-lər) adj. impopular.
un·pop·u·lar·i·ty (ŭn-pŏp'yə-lăr'ĭ-tē) s. impopularidad *f.*
un·prac·ticed (ŭn-prăk'tĭst) adj. falto de práctica, inexperto.
un·prec·e·dent·ed (ŭn-prĕs'ĭ-dĕn'tĭd) adj. *(without precedent)* sin precedente; *(unheard-of)* inaudito, nunca oído.
un·pre·dict·a·ble (ŭn'prĭ-dĭk'tə-bəl) adj. *(event)* que no se puede predecir *o* pronosticar; *(person)* caprichoso, imprevisible.

---

un·prej·u·diced (ŭn-prĕj′ə-dĭst) adj. sin prejuicios, imparcial.

un·pre·med·i·tat·ed (ŭn′prē-mĕd′ĭ-tā′tĭd) adj. impremeditado, irreflexivo.

un·pre·pared (ŭn′prĭ-pârd′) adj. *(not prepared)* no preparado, desprevenido; *(off-the-cuff)* improvisado.

un·pre·pos·sess·ing (ŭn-prē′pə-zĕs′ĭng) adj. poco impresionante.

un·pre·tend·ing (ŭn′prĭ-tĕn′dĭng) adj. modesto, sin pretenciones.

un·pre·ten·tious (ŭn′prĭ-tĕn′shəs) adj. modesto, sin pretenciones.

un·priced (ŭn-prīst′) adj. sin precio asignado *o* marcado.

un·prin·ci·pled (ŭn-prĭn′sə-pəld) adj. falto de principios, sin escrúpulos.

un·print·a·ble (ŭn-prĭn′tə-bəl) adj. impublicable.

un·pro·duc·tive (ŭn′prə-dŭk′tĭv) adj. *(soil)* improductivo; *(attempt)* infructuoso; *(business)* improductivo, poco lucrativo.

un·pro·fes·sion·al (ŭn′prə-fĕsh′ə-nəl) adj. *(not qualified)* no profesional, sin título; *(said of ethics)* contrario a la ética profesional; *(incompetent)* incompetente; DEP. *(amateurish)* de diletante.

un·prof·it·a·ble (ŭn-prŏf′ĭ-tə-bəl) adj. ECON. *(not profitable)* improductivo, poco lucrativo; *(useless)* inútil, infructuoso.

un·pro·nounce·a·ble (ŭn′prə-noun′sə-bəl) adj. *(difficult to pronounce)* impronunciable, imposible de pronunciar; *(unmentionable)* que no debe mencionarse.

un·proved (ŭn-prōovd′) *o* **un·prov·en** (-prōō′vən) adj. *(not proved)* no probado, no demostrado; *(not verified)* no comprobado, no verificado.

un·pro·voked (ŭn′prə-vōkt′) adj. no provocado, sin provocar.

un·qual·i·fied (ŭn-kwŏl′ə-fīd′) adj. *(incompetent)* incompetente; *(lacking qualifications)* sin título, sin licencia; *(without reservations)* sin reserva, incondicional <*an u. approval* una aprobación incondicional>.

un·ques·tion·a·ble (ŭn-kwĕs′chə-nə-bəl) adj. indiscutible, incuestionable.

un·ques·tioned (ŭn-kwĕs′chənd) adj. *(not interrogated)* no interrogado, no examinado; *(indisputable)* incuestionable; *(not doubted)* indiscutido.

un·qui·et (ŭn-kwī′ĭt) adj. **-er, -est** *(uneasy)* inquieto, agitado; *(turbulent)* turbulento; *(noisy)* ruidoso.

un·quote (ŭn-kwōt′) interj. fin de la cita.

un·rav·el (ŭn-răv′əl) tr. *(to untangle)* desenredar, desenmarañar; *(to knit knitting)* deshacer, deshilachar; FIG. *(to solve)* desenmarañar, desembrollar —intr. desenredarse, desenmarañarse.

un·read (ŭn-rĕd′) adj. *(not read)* no leído, sin leer; *(ignorant)* poco leído, inculto.

un·read·a·ble (ŭn-rē′də-bəl) adj. *(illegible)* ilegible; *(not worth reading)* que no vale la pena leer; *(incomprehensible)* incomprensible, obscuro.

un·read·i·ness (ŭn-rĕd′ē-nĭs) s. falta de preparación.

un·read·y (ŭn-rĕd′ē) adj. **-i·er, -i·est** no listo, no preparado.

un·re·al (ŭn-rēl′) adj. *(not real)* irreal, imaginario; JER. *(excellent)* excelente, fantástico.

un·re·al·is·tic (ŭn-rē′ə-lĭs′tĭk) adj. no realista, poco práctico.

un·re·al·i·ty (ŭn′rē-ăl′ĭ-tē) s. [pl. **-ties**] *(quality, state)* irrealidad *f*; *(something imaginary)* ficción *f*.

un·rea·son·a·ble (ŭn-rē′zə-nə-bəl) adj. *(not reasonable)* irrazonable; *(excessive)* excesivo, exorbitante.

un·rea·son·ing (ŭn-rē′zə-nĭng) adj. irracional, irreflexivo.

un·rec·og·niz·a·ble (ŭn-rĕk′əg-nī′zə-bəl) adj. irreconocible, que no puede reconocerse.

un·re·cov·er·a·ble (ŭn′rĭ-kŭv′ər-ə-bəl) adj. *(not recoverable)* irrecuperable; *(incurable)* incurable.

un·reel (ŭn-rēl′) tr. & intr. desenrollar(se).

un·re·gen·er·ate (ŭn′rĭ-jĕn′ər-ĭt) adj. incorregible.

un·re·hearsed (ŭn′rĭ-hûrst′) adj. improvisado, sin ensayar.

un·re·lat·ed (ŭn′rĭ-lā′tĭd) adj. inconexo, no relacionado ♦ **to be u.** no ser de la misma familia.

un·re·lent·ing (ŭn′rĭ-lĕn′tĭng) adj. inexorable, implacable.

un·re·li·a·ble (ŭn′rĭ-lī′ə-bəl) adj. que no es de fiar.

un·re·mark·a·ble (ŭn′rĭ-mär′kə-bəl) adj. ordinario, que no llama la atención.

un·re·mit·ting (ŭn′rĭ-mĭt′ĭng) adj. incesante, persistente.

un·re·served (ŭn′rĭ-zûrvd′) adj. *(not reserved)* libre, sin reservar; *(unqualified)* sin reservas; *(candid)* franco.

un·re·spon·sive (ŭn′rĭ-spŏn′sĭv) adj. insensible, indiferente.

un·rest (ŭn-rĕst′) s. desasosiego, inquietud *f*.

un·re·strained (ŭn′rĭ-strānd′) adj. *(unchecked)* libre; *(unruly)* desenfrenado; *(natural)* natural, suelto.

un·re·strict·ed (ŭn′rĭ-strĭk′tĭd) adj. sin restricciones, libre.

un·right·eous (ŭn-rī′chəs) adj. *(wicked)* malo, perverso; *(unjust)* injusto.

un·ripe (ŭn-rīp′) adj. **-rip·er, -rip·est** *(immature)* inmaduro; BOT. *(green)* verde.

un·ri·valed (ŭn-rī′vəld) adj. *(peerless)* sin rival, sin igual; *(unequaled)* sin par, incomparable.

un·roll (ŭn-rōl′) tr. *(to unwind)* desenrollar; *(to reveal)* desplegar, exhibir —intr. desenrollarse.

un·ruf·fled (ŭn-rŭf′əld) adj. tranquilo, sereno.

un·ru·ly (ŭn-rōō′lē) adj. **-li·er, -li·est** indócil, revoltoso.

un·sad·dle (ŭn-săd′l) tr. **-dled, -dling** *(to remove)* desensillar; *(to throw)* derribar.

un·safe (ŭn-sāf′) adj. peligroso.

un·said (ŭn-sĕd′) adj. sin decir, callado.

un·sal·a·ble *o* **un·sale·a·ble** (ŭn-sā′lə-bəl) adj. COM. invendible.

un·san·i·tar·y (ŭn-săn′ĭ-tĕr′ē) adj. antihigiénico.

un·sat·is·fac·to·ry (ŭn-săt′ĭs-făk′tə-rē) adj. insatisfactorio.

un·sat·u·rat·ed (ŭn-săch′ə-rā′tĭd) adj. sin grasas saturadas, no saturado.

un·saved (ŭn-sāvd′) adj. sin salvación.

un·sa·vor·y (ŭn-sā′və-rē) adj. *(insipid)* insípido, soso; *(distasteful)* desabrido; FIG. *(offensive)* ofensivo.

un·scathed (ŭn-skā*th*d′) adj. ileso, sano y salvo.

un·schooled (ŭn-skōold′) adj. *(uninstructed)* sin instrucción; *(natural)* natural, innato.

un·sci·en·tif·ic (ŭn-sī′ən-tĭf′ĭk) adj. poco científico.

un·scram·ble (ŭn-skrăm′bəl) tr. **-bled, -bling** *(to straighten out)* arreglar; *(to decipher)* descifrar.

un·screw (ŭn-skrōō′) tr. *(to take out)* destornillar; *(to loosen)* desenroscar —intr. destornillarse.

un·scru·pu·lous (ŭn-skrōō′pyə-ləs) adj. sin escrúpulos, inescrupuloso.

un·seal (ŭn-sēl′) tr. romper el sello de, abrir.

un·sea·son·a·ble (ŭn-sē′zə-nə-bəl) adj. *(out of season)* fuera de temporada; *(uncommon)* fuera de tiempo, fuera de lo normal; *(inopportune)* inoportuno, fuera de lugar.

un·sea·soned (ŭn-sē′zənd) adj. *(unsavory)* desabrido, soso; *(unripe)* verde; FIG. *(inexperienced)* sin experiencia.

un·seat (ŭn-sēt′) tr. *(to unsaddle)* desarzonar, derribar; *(a government official)* destituir; *(from a job)* quitar el puesto.

un·sea·wor·thy (ŭn-sē′wûr′*th*ē) adj. **-thi·er, -thi·est** MARÍT. innavegable.

un·seem·ly (ŭn-sēm′lē) **I.** adj. **-li·er, -li·est** de mal gusto, indecoroso **II.** adv. indecorosamente.

un·seen (ŭn-sēn′) adj. *(not evident)* inadvertido; *(invisible)* invisible; *(hidden)* oculto.

un·seg·re·gat·ed (ŭn-sĕg′rĭ-gā′tĭd) adj. libre de segregación.

un·sel·fish (ŭn-sĕl′fĭsh) adj. generoso.

un·set (ŭn-sĕt′) adj. *(not solidified)* sin cuajar; *(unmounted)* sin montar; *(said of concrete)* no fraguado.

un·set·tle (ŭn-sĕt′l) tr. **-tled, -tling** *(to disrupt)* trastornar; *(to disturb)* perturbar —intr. perturbarse.

un·set·tled (ŭn-sĕt′ld) adj. *(unstable)* inestable; *(variable)* variable; *(not resolved)* pendiente; *(not paid)* sin liquidar; *(unpopulated)* despoblado; *(not fixed)* errante, inconstante; *(said of weather)* inseguro, incierto.

un·shack·le (ŭn-shăk′əl) tr. **-led, -ling** quitar los grillos, liberar.

un·shak·a·ble *o* **un·shake·a·ble** (ŭn-shā′kə-bəl) adj. inquebrantable, firme.

un·shak·en (ŭn-shā′kən) adj. firme, inconmovible.

---

ng inglés / ŏ la / ō bou / ô corre / oi oigo / ōō uno / ou auto / yōō ciudad / w hueco / y yo / z mismo

un·shaped (ŭn-shāpt′) adj. *(not shaped)* informe, sin forma; *(imperfect)* mal formado.

un·shape·ly (ŭn-shāp′lē) adj. **-li·er, -li·est** desproporcionado.

un·shav·en (ŭn-shā′vən) adj. sin afeitar.

un·sheathe (ŭn-shē*th*′) tr. **-sheathed, -sheath·ing** desenvainar.

un·shell (ŭn-shĕl′) tr. descascarar.

un·shod (ŭn-shŏd′) adj. descalzo.

un·sight·ly (ŭn-sīt′lē) adj. **-li·er, -li·est** *(ugly)* feo; *(unpleasant)* desagradable.

un·skilled (ŭn-skĭld′) adj. *(lacking skills)* sin entrenamiento; *(not specialized)* no especializado; *(crude)* sin pulir.

un·skill·ful (ŭn-skĭl′fəl) adj. *(inexpert)* inexperto; ANT. *(ignorant)* ignorante.

un·sling (ŭn-slĭng′) tr. **-slung** (-slŭng′), **-sling·ing** *(to remove)* descolgar; MARÍT. quitar de la eslinga.

un·snap (ŭn-snăp′) tr. **-snapped, -snap·ping** desabrochar.

un·snarl (ŭn-snärl′) tr. desenredar.

un·so·cia·ble (ŭn-sō′shə-bəl) adj. *(reserved)* reservado; *(solitary)* solitario, insociable.

un·sold (ŭn-sōld′) adj. sin vender.

un·so·lic·it·ed (ŭn′sə-lĭs′ĭ-tĭd) adj. sin solicitar.

un·solved (ŭn-sŏlvd′) adj. sin resolver.

un·so·phis·ti·cat·ed (ŭn′sə-fĭs′tĭ-kā′tĭd) adj. sencillo, ingenuo.

un·sought (ŭn-sôt′) adj. gratuito, sin solicitar.

un·sound (ŭn-sound′) adj. **-er, -est** *(not solid)* poco firme; *(defective)* defectuoso; *(diseased)* enfermizo; *(mentally imbalanced)* demente; *(false)* falso.

un·spar·ing (ŭn-spâr′ĭng) adj. *(generous)* generoso, pródigo; *(cruel)* cruel, despiadado.

un·speak·a·ble (ŭn-spē′kə-bəl) adj. *(indescribable)* indescriptible, inenarrable; *(atrocious)* atroz, abominable; *(not spoken)* indecible.

un·spe·cial·ized (ŭn-spĕsh′ə-līzd′) adj. *(general)* general, no específico; *(without specialty)* sin especializar.

un·spent (ŭn-spĕnt′) adj. sin gastar, inexhausto.

un·spo·ken (ŭn-spō′kən) adj. *(tacit)* tácito; *(understood)* sobreentendido.

un·spot·ted (ŭn-spŏt′ĭd) adj. sin mancha, inmaculado.

un·sta·ble (ŭn-stā′bəl) adj. **-bler, -blest** *(unsteady)* inestable; *(erratic)* errático; *(fluctuating)* fluctuante; PSIC. *(maladjusted)* inadaptado; QUÍM. *(decomposing)* inestable.

un·stead·i·ness (ŭn-stĕd′ē-nĭs) s. *(unstableness)* inestabilidad *f*; *(of footing)* inseguridad *f*; *(tremor)* temblor *m*; *(inconstancy)* inconstancia.

un·stead·y (ŭn-stĕd′ē) adj. **-i·er, -i·est** *(said of hands)* temblorosa; *(said of footing)* vacilante; *(unstable)* inestable; *(inconstant)* inconstante; *(uneven)* desigual; *(variable)* variable.

un·stick (ŭn-stĭk′) tr. **-stuck** (-stŭk′), **-stick·ing** desprender, despegar.

un·stint·ing (ŭn-stĭn′tĭng) adj. generoso, pródigo.

un·stop (ŭn-stŏp′) tr. **-stopped, -stop·ping** *(to remove the stopper from)* destapar; *(to open)* abrir, dar paso a.

un·stop·pa·ble (ŭn-stŏp′ə-bəl) adj. incontenible, irrefrenable.

un·strap (ŭn-străp′) tr. **-strapped, -strap·ping** quitar *o* aflojar las correas a.

un·stressed (ŭn-strĕst′) adj. *(not stressed)* sin acento, inacentuado; *(not emphasized)* sin énfasis.

un·string (ŭn-strĭng′) tr. **-strung** (-strŭng′), **-string·ing** *(to undo)* desensartar; *(to unfasten)* desatar; *(to unnerve)* trastornar (los nervios).

un·struc·tured (ŭn-strŭk′chərd) adj. falto de estructura.

un·strung (ŭn-strŭng′) adj. *(unfastened)* desatado; *(unnerved)* trastornado.

un·stuck (ŭn-stŭk′) pret. y part. p. de **unstick**.

un·stud·ied (ŭn-stŭd′ēd) adj. sin afectación, natural ♦ **u. in** no versado en, sin conocimientos de.

un·sub·stan·tial (ŭn′səb-stăn′shəl) adj. *(insubstantial)* insubstancial; *(flimsy)* ligero; *(lacking basis)* sin fundamento.

un·suc·cess·ful (ŭn′sək-sĕs′fəl) adj. *(without success)* sin éxito, fracasado; *(futile)* vano, infructuoso <*an u. search*

una búsqueda infructuosa> ♦ **to be u.** fracasar, no tener éxito.

un·suit·a·ble (ŭn-soo′tə-bəl) adj. *(not suitable)* inadecuado; *(incompetent)* incompetente; *(inconvenient)* inconveniente, inoportuno; *(unbecoming)* inapropiado.

un·sung (ŭn-sŭng′) adj. *(not sung)* no cantado; *(uncelebrated)* no alabado, no celebrado ♦ **an u. hero** un héroe olvidado.

un·sus·pect·ed (ŭn′sə-spĕk′tĭd) adj. insospechado.

un·sus·pect·ing (ŭn′sə-spĕk′tĭng) adj. confiado, sin sospechar.

un·sym·met·ri·cal (ŭn′sĭ-mĕt′rĭ-kəl) adj. asimétrico.

un·sym·pa·thet·ic (ŭn-sĭm′pə-thĕt′ĭk) adj. *(indifferent)* indiferente, sin compasión; *(hostile)* antagónico, hostil.

un·sys·tem·at·ic (ŭn-sĭs′tə-măt′ĭk) adj. poco metódico, sin sistema.

un·tamed (ŭn-tāmd′) adj. indomado.

un·tan·gle (ŭn-tăng′gəl) tr. **-gled, -gling** *(to disentangle)* desenredar; *(to resolve)* resolver.

un·tapped (ŭn-tăpt′) adj. *(barrels, casks)* sin abrir; *(not utilized)* sin utilizar, sin explotar.

un·taught (ŭn-tôt′) adj. *(ignorant)* ignorante, sin instrucción; *(natural)* natural.

un·ten·a·ble (ŭn-tĕn′ə-bəl) adj. *(that cannot be defended)* indefensible; *(that cannot be sustained)* insostenible; *(uninhabitable)* inhabitable.

un·thank·ful (ŭn-thăngk′fəl) adj. *(ungrateful)* ingrato; *(unwelcome)* malagradecido.

un·think·a·ble (ŭn-thĭng′kə-bəl) adj. *(inconceivable)* inconcebible, inimaginable; *(out of the question)* impensable.

un·think·ing (ŭn-thĭng′kĭng) adj. *(heedless)* desatento; *(inadvertent)* inadvertido; *(impulsive)* irreflexivo.

un·thought-of (ŭn-thôt′ŭv′, -ŏv′) adj. inconcebible.

un·thread (ŭn-thrĕd′) tr. *(to unstring)* desensartar; *(to exit)* encontrar la salida; *(to solve)* desenmarañar.

un·ti·di·ness (ŭn-tī′dē-nĭs) s. *(sloppiness)* desaliño, desaseo; *(lack of order)* desorden *m*.

un·ti·dy (ŭn-tī′dē) adj. **-di·er, -di·est** *(sloppy)* desaliñado, desaseado; *(disorderly)* desordenado.

un·tie (ŭn-tī′) tr. **-tied, -ty·ing** *(to undo)* desatar; *(to free)* soltar; *(to resolve)* resolver —intr. desatarse.

un·til (ŭn-tĭl′) **I.** prep. hasta <*we danced u. dawn* bailamos hasta el amanecer> **II.** conj. hasta que <*you cannot leave u. your work is finished* tú no puedes irte hasta que tu trabajo esté terminado>.

un·time·ly (ŭn-tīm′lē) **I.** adj. **-li·er, -li·est** *(inopportune)* inoportuno; *(premature)* prematuro **II.** adv. *(inopportunely)* inoportunamente; *(prematurely)* prematuramente.

un·tir·ing (ŭn-tīr′ĭng) adj. *(not tiring)* incansable, infatigable; *(constant)* constante.

un·to (ŭn′too) prep. *(until)* hasta; *(to)* a.

un·told (ŭn-tōld′) adj. *(not revealed)* nunca antes dicho; *(beyond description)* indescriptible, sin igual; *(beyond measure)* incalculable.

un·touch·a·ble (ŭn-tŭch′ə-bəl) **I.** adj. *(not to be touched)* intocable; *(beyond criticism)* libre de toda crítica, invulnerable **II.** s. ♦ **U.** intocable (casta inferior hindú) *m*.

un·to·ward (ŭn-tôrd′, ŭn′tə-wôrd′) adj. *(unfavorable)* desfavorable; *(obstinate)* obstinado.

un·trans·fer·a·ble (ŭn′trăns-fûr′ə-bəl) adj. intransferible.

un·trav·eled (ŭn-trăv′əld) adj. *(road)* poco frecuentado; *(person)* que no ha viajado.

un·tried (ŭn-trīd′) adj. *(experimental)* experimental, no probado; *(inexperienced)* inexperto; DER. sin procesar.

un·trod·den (ŭn-trŏd′n) adj. no hollado, virgen.

un·true (ŭn-troo′) adj. **-tru·er, -tru·est** *(false)* falso; *(inaccurate)* inexacto; *(unfaithful)* desleal.

un·trust·wor·thy (ŭn-trŭst′wûr′*th*ē) adj. **-thi·er, -thi·est** indigno de confianza, que no es de confiar.

un·truth (ŭn-trooth′) s. *(lie)* mentira; *(lack of truth)* falsedad *f*.

un·truth·ful (ŭn-trooth′fəl) adj. *(false)* falso; *(mendacious)* mendaz, mentiroso.

un·tu·tored (ŭn-too′tərd, -tyoo′-) adj. *(uneducated)* sin instrucción; *(simple)* sencillo.

un·twine (ŭn-twīn′) tr. & intr. **-twined, -twin·ing** *(to separate)* destorcer(se), desenrollar(se); *(to untangle)* desenredar(se).

un·twist (ŭn-twĭst′) tr. & intr. desenrollar(se), desenredar(se).

un·used (ŭn-yōōzd′) adj. *(not in use)* sin usar; *(new)* nuevo ♦ **to be u. to** (ŭn-yōōst′) no estar acostumbrado a.

un·u·su·al (ŭn-yōō′zhōō-əl) adj. *(strange)* fuera de lo común, raro; *(exceptional)* extraordinario, excepcional; *(unique)* original; *(uncommon)* desacostumbrado, poco común.

un·ut·ter·a·ble (ŭn-ŭt′ər-ə-bəl) adj. inexpresable, indecible.

un·val·ued (ŭn-văl′yōōd) adj. *(unappreciated)* despreciado, sin valorar; *(not appraised)* sin valorar; ANT. *(inestimable)* inestimable.

un·var·nished (ŭn-vär′nĭsht) adj. *(not varnished)* sin barnizar; FIG. *(plain)* liso y llano, puro <*the u. truth* la pura verdad>.

un·veil (ŭn-vāl′) tr. *(to remove)* quitar el velo; *(to reveal)* revelar, descubrir —intr. descubrirse.

un·voiced (ŭn-voist′) adj. *(not expressed)* no expresado; FO-NÉT. sordo.

un·want·ed (ŭn-wŏn′tĭd) adj. *(not wanted)* no deseado; *(unsolicited)* no solicitado, no pedido; *(superfluous)* superfluo.

un·war·rant·ed (ŭn-wôr′ən-tĭd) adj. injustificado.

un·war·y (ŭn-wâr′ē) adj. **-i·er, -i·est** incauto, desprevenido.

un·washed (ŭn-wŏsht′) adj. *(unclean)* sin lavar, desaseado; *(plebeian)* plebeyo.

un·wea·ried (ŭn-wîr′ēd) adj. *(fresh)* fresco; *(tireless)* incansable.

un·wed (ŭn-wĕd′) adj. & s. soltero.

un·wel·come (ŭn-wĕl′kəm) adj. *(guest, visit)* inoportuno, molesto; *(visitor, customer)* mal recibido, mal acogido; *(news)* desagradable; *(unwanted)* no deseado, incómodo.

un·well (ŭn-wĕl′) adj. enfermo, indispuesto.

un·wept (ŭn-wĕpt′) adj. *(not mourned)* no lamentado; *(not shed)* no vertidas <*u. tears* lágrimas no vertidas>.

un·whole·some (ŭn-hōl′səm) adj. *(not healthy)* insalubre, malsano; *(harmful)* nocivo; *(loathsome)* repulsivo.

un·wield·y (ŭn-wēl′dē) adj. **-i·er, -i·est** *(unmanageable)* difícil de manejar; *(clumsy)* torpe.

un·will·ing (ŭn-wĭl′ĭng) adj. *(not willing)* no dispuesto, maldispuesto; *(reluctant)* renuente, reacio.

un·will·ing·ly (ŭn-wĭl′ĭng-lē) adv. de mala gana, a disgusto.

un·will·ing·ness (ŭn-wĭl′ĭng-nĭs) s. desgana, resistencia.

un·wind (ŭn-wīnd′) tr. **-wound** (-wound′), **-wind·ing** *(to undo)* desenrollar; *(to disentangle)* desenredar —intr. *(to become unwound)* desenrollarse; *(to relax)* relajarse.

un·wise (ŭn-wīz′) adj. **-wis·er, -wis·est** poco inteligente, desaconsejado.

un·wit·ting (ŭn-wĭt′ĭng) adj. *(unaware)* inconsciente; *(unintentional)* sin intención.

un·wont·ed (ŭn-wŏn′tĭd, -wōn′-) adj. fuera de lo común, inusitado.

un·world·ly (ŭn-wûrld′lē) adj. **-li·er, -li·est** *(unearthly)* poco mundano; *(spiritual)* espiritual; *(naive)* ingenuo.

un·wor·thi·ness (ŭn-wûr′thē-nĭs) s. falta de mérito.

un·wor·thy (ŭn-wûr′thē) adj. **-thi·er, -thi·est** *(undeserving)* indigno, que no merece <*plans u. of consideration* planes que no merecen consideración alguna>; *(not befitting)* no digno de; *(worthless)* sin valor; *(despicable)* despreciable, desdeñable.

un·wound (ŭn-wound′) pret. y part. p. de **unwind.**

un·wound·ed (ŭn-wōōn′dĭd) adj. ileso.

un·wrap (ŭn-răp′) tr. & intr. **-wrapped, -wrap·ping** desenvolver(se).

un·writ·ten (ŭn-rĭt′n) adj. *(not written)* no escrito; *(oral)* oral; *(traditional)* tradicional; *(blank)* en blanco.

unwritten law s. DER. derecho consuetudinario.

un·yield·ing (ŭn-yēl′dĭng) adj. *(inflexible)* inflexible, rígido; *(obstinate)* obstinado.

un·yoke (ŭn-yōk′) tr. **-yoked, -yok·ing** *(draft animals)* desuncir; *(to separate)* separar.

un·zip (ŭn-zĭp′) tr. **-zipped, -zip·ping** bajar la cremallera *o* cierre relámpago de —intr. abrirse *o* bajarse la cremallera.

up (ŭp) **I.** adv. hacia arriba, en lo alto <*looking up* mirando hacia arriba>; arriba <*I put it up there* lo puse allí arriba>; para arriba <*from ten dollars up* de diez dólares para arriba> ♦ **close up** cerca • **face up** boca arriba • **high up** muy arriba • **to be up all night** no acostarse en toda la noche • **to come** *o* **go up to** acercarse a, acudir a • **to feel up to** sentirse capaz de, estar en condiciones de • **to get up** levantarse • **to go up** subir • **up!** *o* **get up!** ¡levántate!, ¡arriba! • **up above** arriba • **up against** al lado de, junto a • **up and down** de arriba abajo • **up north** hacia *o* en el norte • **up to** hasta • **up to date** al día, al corriente • **up to now** hasta ahora **II.** adj. *(moving upward)* que va hacia arriba, de subida <*an up elevator* un ascensor que va hacia arriba>; *(erect)* de pie, en pie; *(out of bed)* levantado; *(said of tide, river)* alto, crecido; *(well-informed)* bien enterado, informado <*to be up on sports* estar bien informado sobre deportes>; *(ahead)* con . . . de ventaja <*to be up two holes in a golf match* estar con dos hoyos de ventaja en un encuentro de golf> ♦ **it is up to you** decídelo tú, eres tú quien tiene que decidir • **time is up** es la hora (de cerrar, concluir) • **to be up against** tener que hacer frente a, tener que luchar con • **to be up against it** estar en apuros • **to be up and around** estar haciendo vida normal, de nuevo en pie • **to be up to standard** estar conforme a la norma, satisfacer los requisitos • **to be up to something** estar tramando algo • **up for** *(approval)* presentarse para; *(at court)* ser procesado por; *(to be a candidate)* ser candidato a; *(to feel like)* tener ganas de <*is anyone up for a game of tennis?* ¿tiene alguien ganas de jugar un partido de tenis?> • **up for trial** ante el tribunal • **up in arms** MIL. en armas, alzado; *(furious)* enojado, furioso • **up to** *(height, time)* hasta; *(prepared to)* con voluntad de <*I am not up to talking about his death yet* no estoy con voluntad de hablar sobre su muerte todavía>; *(capable of)* capacitado <*he is not up to the task* él no está capacitado para esa tarea> • **what are you up to?** ¿en qué andas?, ¿qué estás por hacer? • **what's up?** ¿qué pasa? **III.** prep. arriba <*up the road* camino arriba>; *(against)* contra <*up the wind* contra el viento>; *(on the top of)* en lo alto de, arriba de **IV.** s. tierra elevada, subida ♦ **on the up and up** honesto, legal • **to be on an up** FAM. estar eufórico • **to be on the up** COM. estar en subida *o* subiendo **V.** tr. **upped, up·ping** *(to increase)* aumentar; *(to raise)* elevar —intr. levantarse, subir.

▲ En algunos casos, *up* sigue a un verbo para reforzar su sentido pero no se traduce al español <*to warm up* calentar> <*to hurry up* apurarse>. En otros casos, *up* sigue a un verbo para indicar que la acción ha de realizarse por completo o totalmente. Su traducción al español es optativa <*to finish up* terminar (completamente)> <*to burn up* quemar algo (por completo)>; a veces *up* se expresa en español haciendo el verbo reflexivo <*to eat up* comerse> <*to drink up* beberse>. Aún en otros casos, *up* modifica totalmente el sentido del verbo <*to bring up* traer a colación> <*to look up* consultar, buscar>. En dichos casos consulte los verbos correspondientes.

up-and-com·ing (ŭp′ən-kŭm′ĭng) adj. prometedor.

up-and-down (ŭp′ən-doun′) adj. *(variable)* variante; *(vertical)* vertical.

up·beat (ŭp′bēt) **I.** s. MÚS. nota inmediatamente anterior a la primera de un compás **II.** adj. FAM. *(optimistic)* optimista; *(happy)* alegre.

up·braid (ŭp-brād′) tr. reprochar.

up·bring·ing (ŭp′brĭng′ĭng) s. crianza.

up·cast (ŭp′kăst′) **I.** adj. dirigido hacia arriba **II.** s. pozo de ventilación.

up·chuck (ŭp′chŭk′) intr. & tr. JER. vomitar, devolver.

up·com·ing (ŭp′kŭm′ĭng) adj. próximo, futuro.

up·coun·try (ŭp′kŭn′trē) **I.** s. interior *m* **II.** adj. del interior **III.** adv. en *o* hacia el interior.

up·date (ŭp-dāt′) **I.** tr. **-dat·ed, -dat·ing** poner al día **II.** s. (ŭp′dāt′) *(information)* información actualizada; *(act)* actualización *f*.

up·draft (ŭp′drăft′) s. corriente ascendente *f*.

up·end (ŭp-ĕnd′) tr. *(to turn up)* poner de punta; *(to overturn)* derribar —intr. levantarse.

---

ng inglés / ŏ la / ō bou / ô corre / oi oigo / ōō uno / ou auto / yōō ciudad / w hueco / y yo / z mismo

up·front (ŭp'frŭnt') adj. *(frank)* franco; *(in advance)* por adelantado.
up·grade (ŭp'grād') **I.** tr. **-grad·ed, -grad·ing** *(to improve)* mejorar la calidad de; *(to promote)* ascender **II.** s. rampa, cuesta ◆ **on the u.** FIG. prosperando **III.** adj. ascendente **IV.** adv. hacia arriba.
up·heave (ŭp-hēv') tr. & intr. **-heaved, -heav·ing** levantar(se).
up·heav·al (ŭp-hē'vəl) s. *(rising)* levantamiento; *(disruption)* trastorno; GEOL. *(uplift)* solevantamiento.
up·held (ŭp-hĕld') pret. y part. p. de **uphold.**
up·hill (ŭp'hĭl') **I.** adj. *(up a hill)* ascendente; FIG. *(difficult)* arduo **II.** s. cuesta **III.** adv. cuesta arriba.
up·hold (ŭp-hōld') tr. **-held** (-hĕld'), **-hold·ing** *(to raise)* levantar; *(to support)* sostener; FIG. *(to sustain)* sustentar, defender.
up·hol·ster (ŭp-hōl'stər) tr. tapizar.
up·hol·ster·er (ŭp-hōl'stər-ər) s. tapicero.
up·hol·ster·y (ŭp-hōl'stə-rē) s. [pl. **-ies**] tapicería.
up·keep (ŭp'kēp') s. *(maintenance)* mantenimiento; *(cost)* gastos de mantenimiento.
up·land (ŭp'lənd) **I.** s. meseta, altiplanicie *f* **II.** adj. elevado, alto.
up·lift I. tr. (ŭp-lĭft') *(to raise up)* alzar; FIG. *(to elevate)* elevar; *(to exalt)* exaltar **II.** adj. (ŭp'lĭft') elevado **III.** s. (ŭp'lĭft') *(act)* alzamiento; FIG. *(improvement)* mejoramiento; *(influence)* influencia edificante; GEOL. solevantamiento.
up·most (ŭp'mōst') **I.** adj. más alto, supremo **II.** adv. en primer lugar.
up·on (ə-pŏn') prep. sobre, por.
up·per (ŭp'ər) **I.** adj. *(superior)* superior; *(inland)* interior; *(northern)* del norte, norteño ◆ **U.** superior, alto **II.** s. *(of a shoe)* pala; JER. *(drug)* pepa (anfetamina); *(euphoria)* euforia ◆ **uppers** FAM. dentadura superior.
upper atmosphere s. atmósfera superior.
upper case s. FAM. la flor y nata.
up·per-case (ŭp'ər-kās') adj. IMPR. en mayúsculas.
up·per-class (ŭp'ər-klăs') adj. de la clase alta.
up·per-class·man (ŭp'ər-klăs'mən) s. [pl. **-men**] estudiante del tercer o cuarto año (de la escuela superior o la universidad) *mf.*
upper crust s. FAM. la flor y nata.
up·per·cut (ŭp'ər-kŭt') s. DEP. gancho (en boxeo).
upper hand s. dominio ◆ **to have the u.** llevar ventaja, dominar.
Upper House o **upper house** s. POL. cámara alta.
up·per·most (ŭp'ər-mōst') **I.** adj. más alto, supremo **II.** adv. en primer lugar.
Upper Vol·ta (vŏl'tə, vōl'-) s. Alto Volta.
up·pish (ŭp'ĭsh) adj. FAM. presumido, altanero.
up·pi·ty (ŭp'ĭ-tē) adj. FAM. presumido, altanero.
up·raise (ŭp-rāz') tr. **-raised, -rais·ing** levantar, elevar.
up·right (ŭp'rīt') **I.** adj. *(vertical)* vertical, perpendicular; *(straight)* derecho, erguido; *(honorable)* recto, respetable **II.** adv. verticalmente **III.** s. *(verticality)* verticalidad *f*; *(beam)* montante *m*, listón *m*; MÚS. *(piano)* piano vertical.
up·rise (ŭp-rīz') **I.** intr. **-rose** (-rōz'), **-ris·en** (-rĭz'ən), **-ris·ing** *(to stand up)* levantarse; *(to ascend)* ascender; *(to rise)* alzarse; *(to swell)* hincharse **II.** s. (ŭp'rīz') *(act)* levantamiento; *(slope)* pendiente *f.*
up·ris·ing (ŭp'rī'zĭng) s. *(act)* levantamiento; *(insurrection)* insurrección *f*; *(slope)* pendiente ascendente *f.*
up·riv·er (ŭp'rĭv'ər) adj. & adv. río arriba.
up·roar (ŭp'rôr') s. *(tumult)* tumulto, alboroto; *(controversy)* discusión acalorada.
up·roar·i·ous (ŭp-rôr'ē-əs) adj. *(tumultous)* tumultuoso; *(boisterous)* ruidoso; *(hilarious)* hilarante, cómico.
up·root (ŭp-rōot', -rŏot') tr. *(a plant)* arrancar; FIG. *(to eradicate)* erradicar; *(to force out)* desarraigar.
up·rose (ŭp-rōz') pret. de **uprise.**
ups and downs s.pl. altibajos, vicisitudes *f.*
up·set I. tr. (ŭp-sĕt') **-set, -set·ting** *(to tip over)* volcar, tumbar; *(to throw into disorder)* desbaratar, desordenar; *(to displease)* disgustar, afectar <*the bad news u. me a lot* la mala noticia me afectó mucho>; *(to worry)* preocupar, en-

fadar <*don't u. yourself* no te enfades>; *(physically, mentally)* trastornar, perturbar; *(food, drinks)* sentar mal, caer mal a <*white wine upsets my stomach* el vino blanco me cae mal al estómago>; *(a government)* derrocar; *(an opponent)* vencer inesperadamente —intr. volcarse **II.** s. (ŭp'sĕt') *(a tipping over)* vuelco; *(difficulty)* dificultad *f*, contratiempo; *(a minor ailment)* indisposición *f*, malestar *m*; *(trouble)* molestia; *(defeat)* derrota o resultado inesperado **III.** adj. (ŭp-sĕt') *(disordered)* desbaratado, desordenado; *(worried)* preocupado, enfadado; *(indisposed)* indispuesto ◆ **don't be u.** *(worried)* no te preocupes; *(angry)* no te enojes; *(displeased)* no te disgustes • **to have an u. stomach** estar descompuesto del estómago, sentirse mal del estómago.
upset price s. COM. precio inicial, precio mínimo.
up·shot (ŭp'shŏt') s. conclusión *f*, resultado.
up·side-down (ŭp'sīd-doun') **I.** adj. *(overturned)* al revés, boca abajo; *(topsy-turvy)* patas arriba **II.** adv. patas arriba.
up·si·lon (ŭp'sə-lŏn', yōōp'-) s. ypsilon *f*, ipsilon (letra griega) *f.*
up·stage (ŭp'stāj') **I.** adj. *(of a stage)* del fondo del escenario; *(haughty)* presumido **II.** adv. o hacia el fondo del escenario **III.** tr. **-staged, -stag·ing** TEAT. robar la escena; FIG., FAM. *(to eclipse)* eclipsar; *(to treat haughtily)* desairar, tratar con altanería.
up·stairs (ŭp'stârz') **I.** adv. *(at a higher level)* arriba; *(on an upper floor)* en el piso superior **II.** adj. de arriba, del piso superior <*the u. window* la ventana del piso superior> **III.** s. [ú. con v. sing. o pl.] piso de arriba, piso superior.
up·stand·ing (ŭp-stăn'dĭng) adj. *(straight)* erguido; *(honest)* recto.
up·start (ŭp'stärt') **I.** s. & adj. *(parvenu)* arribista *mf*, advenedizo; *(self-important)* presuntuoso **II.** intr. saltar, sobresaltar.
up·state (ŭp'stāt') adv. hacia la parte norte del estado.
up·stream (ŭp'strēm') adv. aguas arriba.
up·surge (ŭp-sûrj') **I.** intr. **-surged, -surg·ing** subir repentinamente **II.** s. (ŭp'sûrj') subida o ascenso repentino.
up·sweep (ŭp'swēp') s. *(rise)* subida; *(hairdo)* peinado alto.
up·swing (ŭp'swĭng') s. *(movement)* movimiento pendular hacia arriba; *(increase)* alza.
up·take (ŭp'tāk') s. canal de salida de la chimenea *m* ◆ **very quick on the u.** que comprende muy rápidamente.
up·tight o **up tight** (ŭp'tīt') adj. JER. adj. *(tense)* tenso, nervioso; *(financially pressed)* apretado, necesitado; *(conventional)* convencional.
up-to-date (ŭp'tə-dāt') adj. *(modern)* actual, moderno; *(current)* al día; *(keeping up)* al tanto, al corriente.
up-to-the-min·ute (ŭp'tə-thə-mĭn'ĭt) adj. de última hora.
up·town (ŭp'toun') **I.** adv. hacia la parte residencial, hacia la parte alta de una ciudad **II.** s. parte alta de la ciudad, zona residencial.
up·turn I. tr. (ŭp-tûrn') *(to turn over)* volcar, virar; *(to upset)* trastornar; *(to turn up)* volver hacia arriba —intr. *(to turn over)* virarse; *(to turn up)* volverse hacia arriba **II.** s. (ŭp'tûrn') *(turn)* vuelta; COM. *(trend)* alza.
up·ward (ŭp'wərd) o **up·wards** (-wərdz) adv. & adj. hacia arriba, para arriba <*tickets cost ten dollars and u.* las entradas cuestan de diez dólares para arriba> ◆ **u. of** en exceso de, más de.
▲ Como adverbio, las formas *upward* y *upwards* son intercambiables. Como adjetivo, úsese solamente *upward.*
up·wind (ŭp'wĭnd') adj. contra el viento.
u·rae·mi·a (yōō-rē'mē-ə) s. var. de **uremia.**
U·ral Mountains (yōōr'əl) s. Montes Urales *m.*
u·ran·ic (yōō-răn'ĭk, -rā'nĭk) adj. QUÍM. uránico.
u·ra·nin·ite (yōō-rā'nə-nīt') s. QUÍM. uraninita.
u·ra·ni·um (yōō-rā'nē-əm) s. QUÍM. uranio.
U·ra·nus (yōōr'ə-nəs, yōō'rā'-) s. ASTRON., MITOL. Urano.
u·rate (yōōr'āt') s. QUÍM. urato.
ur·ban (ûr'bən) adj. urbano.
ur·bane (ûr-bān') adj. urbano, cortés.
ur·ban·ite (ûr'bə-nīt') s. habitante de una ciudad *mf.*
ur·ban·i·ty (ûr-băn'ĭ-tē) s. [pl. **-ties**] cortesía, finura ◆ **urbanities** buenos modales.

ur·ban·ize (ûr′bə-nīz′) tr. **-ized, -iz·ing** urbanizar.
urban renewal s. renovación urbana.
ur·chin (ûr′chĭn) s. *(boy)* golfillo, chiquillo; ICT. *(sea urchin)* erizo de mar.
u·re·a (yŏo-rē′ə) s. BIOQUÍM. urea.
u·re·mi·a (yŏo-rē′mē-ə) s. MED. uremia.
u·re·ter (yŏor′ĭ-tər) s. ANAT. uréter *m.*
u·re·thane (yŏor′ə-thān′) s. QUÍM. uretano.
u·re·thra (yŏo-rē′thrə) s. [pl. **-thras** o **-thrae** (-thrē)] ANAT. uretra.
urge (ûrj) I. tr. **urged, urg·ing** *(to impel)* incitar; *(to exhort)* exhortar; *(to advocate)* pedir con insistencia, propugnar <*to u. passage of a bill* propugnar la adopción de un proyecto de ley>; *(to excite)* excitar, estimular; *(to persuade)* instar —intr. *(to advocate)* abogar por; *(to push)* instar, incitar ♦ **to u. against** argüir contra, hacer objeciones contra II. s. *(impulse)* impulso; *(desire)* deseo.
ur·gen·cy (ûr′jən-sē) s. [pl. **-cies**] urgencia.
ur·gent (ûr′jənt) adj. *(pressing)* urgente, apremiante; *(insistent)* insistente.
u·ric (yŏor′ĭk) adj. MED., QUÍM. úrico.
u·ri·nal (yŏor′ə-nəl) s. *(fixture, place)* urinal *m,* urinario; *(receptacle)* orinal *m.*
u·ri·nal·y·sis (yŏor′ə-năl′ĭ-sĭs) s. [pl. **-ses** (-sēz′)] MED. análisis de la orina *m.*
u·ri·nar·y (yŏor′ə-nĕr′ē) adj. urinario, de la orina.
u·ri·nate (yŏor′ə-nāt′) intr. **-nat·ed, -nat·ing** orinar.
u·rine (yŏor′ĭn) s. orina.
u·ri·no·gen·i·tal (yŏor′ə-nō-jĕn′ĭ-tl) adj. var. de **urogenital**.
urn (ûrn) s. *(vase)* urna; *(tea or coffee container)* recipiente grande (usado para servir té o café) *m.*
u·ro·gen·i·tal (yŏor′ō-jĕn′ĭ-tl) adj. ANAT. urogenital, urinogenital.
u·rol·o·gy (yŏo-rŏl′ə-jē) s. MED. urología.
Ur·sa Major (ûr′sə) s. ASTRON. Osa Mayor.
Ursa Minor s. ASTRON. Osa Menor.
U·ru·guay (yŏor′ə-gwā′, -gwī′) s. Uruguay *m.*
U·ru·guay·an (yŏor′ə-gwā′ən, -gwī′-) adj. & s. uruguayo.
us §G29 (ŭs) pron. [ú. como complemento directo o indirecto de verbo] nos <*the movie impressed us* la película nos impresionó>; [ú. como el complemento de una preposición] nosotros, nosotras <*his father gave money to us* su padre nos dio dinero a nosotros>.
U.S. (yŏo′ĕs′) o **U.S.A.** (yŏo′ĕs-ā′) s. EE. UU. *m.*
us·a·ble (yŏo′zə-bəl) adj. utilizable, usable.
us·age (yŏo′sĭj) s. *(use)* uso; *(customary practice)* usanza; *(parlance)* lenguaje *m.*
use (yŏoz) I. tr. **used** (yŏozd), **us·ing** *(to employ)* usar, emplear <*u. soap for washing* use jabón para lavar>; *(to exercise)* usar, valerse de <*u. your own judgment* use su propio criterio>; *(to treat)* tratar, portarse con, <*to u. a friend badly* tratar mal a un amigo>; FAM. *(to exploit)* usar, utilizar; *(drugs, alcohol)* tomar ♦ **to be used as** servir de, ser utilizado como • **to be used for** servir para • **to u. up** *(to finish)* acabar totalmente, terminar; *(to consume)* agotar, consumir —intr. [ú. solamente en la forma imperfecta **used** (yŏost)] soler, acostumbrar <*I used to go to Florida every winter* yo solía ir a la Florida todos los inviernos> ♦ **to be used to** estar acostumbrado a • **to get used to** acostumbrarse a II. s. (yŏos) *(act)* uso, empleo <*the u. of a pencil for writing* el uso de un lápiz para escribir>; *(employment)* uso, manejo <*the proper u. of power tools* el manejo correcto de herramientas mecánicas>; *(usefulness)* utilidad *f,* servicio; *(habitual practice)* uso, hábito; DER. uso, usufructo; RELIG. rito ♦ **for emergency u. only** utilícese sólo en caso de emergencia • **for external u.** para uso externo • **in u.** en uso, usándose • **it's no u.** es inútil • **out of u.** fuera de uso • **to be of no u.** no servir para nada • **to be of u.** servir • **to come into u.** empezar a utilizarse • **to have no u. for** *(to have no need of)* no tener necesidad de, no necesitar; *(to dislike)* no gustarle a uno • **to have the u. of** poder usar, tener uno a su disposición • **to make good u. of** hacer buen uso de • **to put to good u.** sacar partido de • **what's the use!** ¡no vale la pena!, ¡para qué!
use·a·ble (yŏo′zə-bəl) adj. var. de **usable**.
used (yŏozd) adj. usado.

use·ful (yŏos′fəl) adj. útil, provechoso.
use·ful·ness (yŏos′fəl-nĭs) s. utilidad *f,* provecho.
use·less (yŏos′lĭs) adj. *(worthless)* ineficaz; *(futile)* inútil.
use·less·ness (yŏos′lĭs-nĭs) s. inutilidad *f.*
us·er (yŏo′zər) s. *(person)* usuario; *(drug addict)* adicto.
ush·er (ŭsh′ər) I. s. *(in a theatre)* acomodador *m;* DER. *(doorkeeper)* ujier *mf* II. tr. *(in a theatre)* acomodar; *(to escort)* acompañar; FIG. *(to introduce)* anunciar (la primavera, huésped).
ush·er·ette (ŭsh′ə-rĕt′) s. acomodadora.
U.S.S.R. (yŏo′ĕs′ĕs-är′) s. U.R.S.S. *f.*
u·su·al (yŏo′zhŏo-əl) adj. *(habitual)* usual; *(ordinary)* usual, corriente; *(customary)* acostumbrado ♦ **as u.** como de costumbre • **the u. thing** lo de siempre.
u·su·al·ly (yŏo′zhŏo-ə-lē) adv. usualmente, por lo general.
u·su·fruct (yŏo′zə-frŭkt′, -sə-) s. DER. usufructo.
u·su·rer (yŏo′zhər-ər) s. usurero.
u·su·ri·ous (yŏo-zhŏor′ē-əs) adj. usurario, de usurero.
u·surp (yŏo-sûrp′, -zûrp′) tr. & intr. usurpar.
u·sur·pa·tion (yŏo′sûr-pā′shən) s. usurpación *f.*
u·surp·er (yŏo-sûr′pər, -zûr′-) s. usurpador *m.*
u·su·ry (yŏo′zhə-rē) s. [pl. **-ries**] usura.
u·ten·sil (yŏo-tĕn′səl) s. utensilio.
u·ter·ine (yŏo′tər-ĭn) adj. uterino.
u·ter·us (yŏo′tər-əs) s. [pl. **u·ter·i** (yŏo′tə-rī′) o **-us·es**] ANAT., BIOL. útero.
u·til·i·tar·i·an (yŏo-tĭl′ĭ-târ′ē-ən) I. adj. *(useful)* utilitario; FILOS. *(advocate)* utilitarista II. s. utilitarista *mf.*
u·til·i·tar·i·an·ism (yŏo-tĭl′ĭ-târ′ē-ə-nĭz′əm) s. FILOS., POL. utilitarismo.
u·til·i·ty (yŏo-tĭl′ĭ-tē) s. [pl. **-ties**] *(usefulness)* utilidad *f; (article)* artículo de gran utilidad; *(public service)* servicio público ♦ **public u.** empresa de servicio público.
u·til·iz·a·ble (yŏot′l-ī′zə-bəl) adj. utilizable, usable.
u·til·i·za·tion (yŏot′l-ĭ-zā′shən) s. utilización *f,* uso.
u·til·ize (yŏot′l-īz′) tr. **-ized, -iz·ing** utilizar, usar.
u·til·iz·er (yŏot′l-ī′zər) s. utilizador *m.*
ut·most (ŭt′mōst′) I. adj. *(of highest degree)* máximo, mayor <*a matter of u. importance* un asunto de máxima importancia>; *(farthest)* más lejano II. s. máximo ♦ **to do one's u.** hacer todo lo posible • **to the u.** hasta más no poder.
u·to·pi·a (yŏo-tō′pē-ə) s. utopía ♦ **U.** utopía.
u·to·pi·an (yŏo-tō′pē-ən) I. adj. utópico ♦ **U.** utópico II. s. utopista *mf.*
u·to·pi·an·ism (yŏo-tō′pē-ə-nĭz′əm) s. utopía, idea utópica.
ut·ter[1] (ŭt′ər) tr. *(to say)* decir; *(to pronounce)* pronunciar; *(to express)* expresar; *(sigh, cry)* dar, emitir; *(to put into circulation)* emitir (dinero, cheque falso).
ut·ter[2] (ŭt′ər) adj. total, absoluto.
ut·ter·a·ble (ŭt′ər-ə-bəl) adj. decible.
ut·ter·ance (ŭt′ər-əns) s. *(pronunciation)* pronunciación *f; (elocution)* elocución *f; (expression)* expresión *f; (of a sound)* emisión *f; (word)* palabra.
ut·ter·er (ŭt′ər-ər) s. pronunciador *m.*
ut·ter·ly (ŭt′ər-lē) adv. absolutamente, totalmente.
ut·ter·most (ŭt′ər-mōst′) adj. *(utmost)* extremo; *(outermost)* último.
U-turn (yŏo′tûrn′) s. AUTO. media vuelta, giro de 180°.
u·vu·la (yŏo′vyə-lə) s. ANAT. úvula, campanilla.
ux·o·ri·ous (ŭk-sôr′ē-əs, ŭg-zôr′-) adj. perdidamente enamorado de la esposa.

V

v, V (vē) s. [pl. **v's, V's**] vigésima segunda letra del alfabeto inglés.
va·can·cy (vā′kən-sē) s. [pl. **-cies**] *(state)* vacío, vacuidad *f; (empty space)* vacío; *(gap)* hueco; *(unfilled position)* vacante *f; (in a hotel)* habitación libre *f; (inanity)* vaciedad *f.*
va·cant (vā′kənt) adj. *(empty)* vacío; *(not occupied)* libre, desocupado; *(expressionless)* inexpresivo; *(lost)* perdido, vago <*a v. stare* una mirada perdida>; *(free)* libre, dis-

ponible (habitación, silla); *(not active)* libre, de ocio <*v. hours* horas de ocio>.

va·cate (vă′kāt′) tr. **-cat·ed, -cat·ing** *(to cease to occupy)* dejar vacante; *(to empty)* desocupar; *(to annul)* anular —intr. irse, marcharse.

va·ca·tion (vā-kā′shən) **I.** s. vacaciones *f* <*to be on v.* estar de vacaciones> **II.** intr. tomar las vacaciones.

vac·ci·nate (văk′sə-nāt′) tr. & intr. MED. **-nat·ed, -nat·ing** vacunar.

vac·ci·na·tion (văk′sə-nā′shən) s. MED. *(inoculation)* vacunación *f*, inoculación *f*; *(scar)* cicatriz de vacuna *f.*

vac·cine (văk-sēn′, văk′sēn′) s. MED. vacuna.

vac·il·late (văs′ə-lāt′) intr. **-lat·ed, -lat·ing** *(to waver)* vacilar, titubear; *(to oscillate)* oscilar.

vac·il·la·tion (văs′ə-lā′shən) s. *(wavering)* vacilación *f*; titubeo; *(oscillation)* oscilación *f.*

va·cu·i·ty (vă-kyōō′ĭ-tē) s. [pl. **-ties**] *(emptiness)* vacuidad *f*; *(vacuum)* vacío; *(lack)* falta <*a v. of taste* una falta de gusto>; *(remark)* vaciedad *f.*

vac·u·ole (văk′yōō-ōl′) s. BIOL. vacuola.

vac·u·ous (văk′yōō-əs) adj. *(empty)* vacío; *(stupid)* necio, alelado; *(inane)* vacuo; *(look)* vago, perdido.

vac·u·um (văk′yōō-əm, -yōōm) **I.** s. [pl. **-u·ums** *o* **-u·a** (-yōō-ə)] FÍS. *(void)* vacío; *(emptiness)* vacío; *(isolation)* aislamiento ♦ **vacuums** aspiradora **II.** tr. & intr. limpiar con aspiradora, pasar la aspiradora (por).

vacuum bottle s. termo.

vacuum cleaner s. aspiradora.

vacuum gauge s. manómetro al vacío.

vac·u·um-packed (văk′yōōm-păkt′) adj. envasado al vacío.

vacuum pump s. bomba neumática, bomba de vacío.

vacuum tube s. tubo de vacío.

va·de me·cum (vā′dē mē′kəm) s. [pl. **vade mecums**] vademécum *m*, libro de consulta.

vag·a·bond (văg′ə-bŏnd′) **I.** s. & adj. vagabundo **II.** intr. vagar, vagabundear.

va·ga·ry (vā′gə-rē, və-gâr′ē) s. [pl. **-ries**] *(caprice)* capricho; *(eccentricity)* extravagancia.

va·gi·na (və-jī′nə) s. [pl. **-nas** *o* **-nae** (-nē)] ANAT. vagina; BOT. vaina.

vag·i·nal (văj′ə-nəl) adj. ANAT. vaginal.

vag·i·ni·tis (văj′ə-nī′tĭs) s. MED. vaginitis *f.*

va·gran·cy (vā′grən-sē) s. [pl. **-cies**] vagancia.

va·grant (vā′grənt) **I.** s. *(wanderer)* vagabundo; *(bum)* vago, linyera *mf* **II.** adj. *(wandering)* vagabundo; *(wayward)* errabundo.

vague (vāg) adj. **vagu·er, vagu·est** *(not clear)* vago; *(ambiguous)* ambiguo; *(undefined)* impreciso; *(uncertain)* dudoso, indeciso; *(indistinct)* borroso, vago.

vague·ly (vāg′lē) adv. *(not defined)* vagamente; *(not certain)* dudosamente; *(hardly)* apenas <*I v. remember him* apenas me acuerdo de él>.

vague·ness (vāg′nĭs) s. *(lack of clarity)* vaguedad *f*; *(imprecision)* imprecisión *f.*

vail (vāl) tr. & intr. ANT. *(to lower)* bajar (bandera, pendón); *(to doff)* quitar(se) (sombrero).

vain (vān) adj. **-er, -est** *(fruitless)* vano, inútil; *(conceited)* vanidoso ♦ **in v.** en vano, vanamente.

vain·glo·ri·ous (vān-glôr′ē-əs) adj. vanaglorioso.

vain·glo·ry (vān-glôr′ē) s. [pl. **-ries**] vanagloria.

vain·ly (vān′lē) adv. *(in vain)* vanamente; *(conceitedly)* vanidosamente.

val·ance (văl′əns, vā′ləns) **I.** s. *(ornamental drapery)* doselera; *(short drapery)* guardamalleta **II.** tr. **-anced, -anc·ing** colocar una doselera *o* guardamalleta.

vale (vāl) s. valle *m.*

val·e·dic·tion (văl′ĭ-dĭk′shən) s. *(leave-taking)* despedida; *(speech)* discurso de despedida.

val·e·dic·to·ri·an (văl′ĭ-dĭk-tôr′ē-ən) s. alumno que da el discurso de fin de curso.

val·e·dic·to·ry (văl′ĭ-dĭk′tə-rē) **I.** adj. de despedida **II.** s. [pl. **-ries**] discurso de despedida.

Va·len·ci·a (və-lĕn′shē-ə, vä-lĕn′syä) s. Valencia.

va·lence (vā′ləns) *o* **va·len·cy** (-lən-sē) s. [pl. **-lenc·es** *o* **-len·cies**] QUÍM. valencia.

val·en·tine (văl′ən-tīn′) s. *(card)* tarjeta que se manda para

el día de los enamorados; *(gift)* regalo; *(sweetheart)* novio, novia.

Valentine's Day *o* **Valentines Day** s. día de San Valentín *m*, día de los enamorados.

va·le·ri·an (və-lîr′ē-ən) s. BOT. valeriana (planta y raíz).

val·et (văl′ĭt, vă-lā′) **I.** s. *(assistant)* ayuda de cámara *m*; *(hotel attendant)* camarero **II.** tr. & intr. servir de ayuda de cámara.

val·e·tu·di·nar·i·an (văl′ĭ-tōōd′n-âr′ē-ən, -tyōōd′-) s. valetudinario, enfermizo.

Val·hal·la (văl-hăl′ə) s. MITOL. walhala.

val·iance (văl′yəns) *o* **val·ian·cy** (-yən-sē) s. valentía, bravura.

val·iant (văl′yənt) adj. & s. valiente *mf.*

val·id (văl′ĭd) adj. *(sound)* válido; *(efficacious)* eficaz; DER. *(in effect)* vigente; *(incontestable)* válido ♦ **no longer v.** caducado.

val·i·date (văl′ĭ-dāt) tr. **-dat·ed, -dat·ing** *(to sanction)* validar; *(to verify)* verificar, comprobar la exactitud de.

val·i·da·tion (văl′ĭ-dā′shən) s. *(sanction)* validación *f*; *(verification)* verificación *f.*

va·lid·i·ty (və-lĭd′ĭ-tē) s. validez *f.*

va·lise (və-lēs′) s. maleta, valija.

Val·kyr·ie (văl-kîr′ē) s. MITOL. walkiria.

val·ley (văl′ē) s. [pl. **-leys**] *(lowland)* valle *m*; ARQ. *(roof trough)* lima hoya.

val·or (văl′ər) s. valor *m*, valentía.

val·or·i·za·tion (văl′ər-ĭ-zā′shən) s. valorización *f.*

val·or·ize (văl′ə-rīz′) tr. **-ized, -iz·ing** valorizar.

val·or·ous (văl′ər-əs) adj. valeroso, valiente.

val·our (văl′ər) s. G.B. var. de **valor.**

val·u·a·ble (văl′yōō-ə-bəl) **I.** adj. *(having value)* valioso, de valor; *(important)* importante, de valor (información, ayuda) ♦ **to be v.** valer mucho **II.** s. ♦ **valuables** objetos de valor.

val·u·ate (văl′yōō-āt′) tr. **-at·ed, -at·ing** valorar, tasar.

val·u·a·tion (văl′yōō-ā′shən) s. *(appraisal)* valoración *f*, tasación *f*; *(estimation)* estimación *f*, valuación *f*; *(estimated value)* valor estimado.

val·ue (văl′yōō) **I.** s. *(fair return)* valor *m* <*v. in gold* valor en oro>; *(price)* precio; *(worth)* valor, importancia <*a person of great v.* una persona de gran importancia>; *(meaning)* significado, sentido <*the right v. of a word* el significado justo de una palabra>; FONÉT., MAT., MÚS. valor ♦ **market** *o* **commercial v.** COM. valor comercial • **to attach little v. to** (something) dar poco valor a (algo) • **to be of (no) v.** (no) ser valioso, (no) tener valor • **to lose v.** desvalorizarse • **to set a v. on** estimar, valuar **II.** tr. **-ued, -u·ing** *(to appraise)* valorizar, tasar; *(to rate)* estimar, valorar <*to v. health above money* valorar la salud sobre el dinero>; *(to esteem)* estimar, apreciar <*I v. her highly for her sincerity* la estimo mucho por su sinceridad>.

val·ue-ad·ded tax (văl′yōō-ăd′ĭd) s. COM., FIN. impuesto al valor añadido.

val·ued (văl′yōōd) adj. estimado, apreciado.

val·ue·less (văl′yōō-lĭs) adj. sin valor.

valve (văl′v) **I.** s. ANAT., TEC. válvula; MÚS. llave *f*; BIOL., BOT. valva; G.B., ELECTRÓN. tubo electrónico **II.** tr. **valved, valv·ing** *(to provide with)* poner una válvula a; *(to control with)* controlar con una válvula.

val·vu·lar (văl′vyə-lər) adj. valvular.

va·moose (vă-mōōs′) intr. **-moosed, -moos·ing** JER. irse apuradamente, largarse.

vamp¹ (vămp) **I.** s. *(shoe part)* empeine *m*; MÚS. acompañamiento improvisado **II.** tr. *(to put a vamp on)* poner un empeine a (zapato, bota); *(to patch)* remendar; MÚS. improvisar (un acompañamiento) —intr. MÚS. improvisar.

vamp² (vămp) **I.** s. vampiresa, seductora **II.** tr. seducir —intr. hacer la parte de vampiresa.

vam·pire (văm′pīr′) s. *(corpse)* vampiro; *(bat)* murciélago; FIG. *(exploiter)* explotador *m*; *(woman)* vampiresa.

vam·pir·ism (văm′pīr′ĭz′əm) s. vampirismo.

van¹ (văn) s. *(truck)* camioneta, furgoneta; G.B., F.C. vagón de carga *m.*

van² (văn) s. vanguardia.

va·na·di·um (və-nā′dē-əm) s. QUÍM. vanadio.

ã rey / ä año / b boca / ch chico / d dar / ĕ el / ē mil / g gato / h joya / hw juez / ī aire / k casa / kw cuan /

Van·dal (văn′dl) s. HIST. vándalo ♦ **v.** vándalo.
van·dal·ism (văn′dl-ĭz′əm) s. vandalismo.
van·dal·ize (văn′dl-īz′) tr. **-ized, -iz·ing** destrozar, destruir.
Van·dyke (văn-dīk′) s. *(beard)* barba puntiaguda, perilla; *(collar)* valona.
vane (văn) s. *(weathercock)* veleta; *(of a propeller)* paleta; *(of a waterwheel)* álabe m; *(of a windmill)* aspa; *(of a feather)* barbas; *(of an arrow)* pluma estabilizadora.
van·guard (văn′gärd′) s. vanguardia.
va·nil·la (və-nĭl′ə) s. *(plant)* vainilla; *(extract)* (extracto de) vainilla.
va·nil·lin (văn′ə-lĭn) s. CUL., QUÍM. vainillina.
van·ish (văn′ĭsh) intr. *(to disappear)* desaparecer; *(to fade)* desvanecerse ♦ **to v. into thin air** esfumarse, desaparecer.
vanishing cream s. crema de belleza.
vanishing point s. DIB. punto de fuga.
van·i·ty (văn′ĭ-tē) s. [pl. **-ties**] *(vainness)* vanidad f; *(conceit)* engreimiento, presunción f; *(worthlessness)* inutilidad f; *(pride)* orgullo, vanagloria; *(case)* neceser m; *(table)* tocador m.
vanity case s. *(compact)* polvera; *(case)* neceser m.
Vanity Fair o **vanity fair** s. feria de vanidades.
van·quish (văng′kwĭsh) tr. *(to defeat)* derrotar, vencer; *(to overcome)* dominar.
van·quish·ment (văng′kwĭsh-mənt) s. derrota.
van·tage (văn′tĭj) s. *(advantage)* ventaja; *(position)* posición de ventaja f.
vantage point s. lugar ventajoso, posición ventajosa.
vap·id (văp′ĭd, vā′pĭd) adj. insípido, soso.
va·por (vā′pər) I. s. *(diffused matter)* vapor m; *(mist)* niebla, bruma; *(fumes)* humo, vapor ♦ **vapors** MED. vapores II. tr. vaporar, vaporizar —intr. *(to evaporate)* evaporarse, vaporizarse; FIG. *(to boast)* alardear, fanfarronear.
va·por·i·za·tion (vā′pər-ĭ-zā′shən) s. FÍS. vaporización f.
va·por·ize (vā′pə-rīz′) tr. & intr. **-ized, -iz·ing** vaporizar(se).
va·por·iz·er (vā′pə-rī′zər) s. MED. vaporizador m; FÍS. *(spray)* pulverizador m.
va·por·ous (vā′pər-əs) adj. *(of vapor)* vaporoso; *(misty)* nebuloso, brumoso; FIG. *(ethereal)* etéreo, nebuloso.
va·pour (vā′pər) s. G.B. var. de **vapor**.
var·i·a·bil·i·ty (vâr′ē-ə-bĭl′ĭ-tē) s. variabilidad f.
var·i·a·ble (vâr′ē-ə-bəl) I. adj. *(changeable)* variable, cambiable; *(inconstant)* inconstante, inestable; BIOL., MAT. variable II. s. MAT. variable f.
var·i·ance (vâr′ē-əns) s. *(act)* variación f; *(disagreement)* desacuerdo, disensión f; DER. *(discrepancy)* discrepancia, discordancia; *(deviation)* desviación f, diferencia; MAT., QUÍM. variancia ♦ **at v.** en desacuerdo.
var·i·ant (vâr′ē-ənt) I. adj. *(differing)* variante, diferente; *(variable)* variable, cambiable II. s. variante f.
var·i·ate (vâr′ē-ĭt, -āt′) s. *(a variable)* cosa variable; MAT. variable.
var·i·a·tion (vâr′ē-ā′shən) s. variación f.
var·i·col·ored (vâr′ĭ-kŭl′ərd) adj. *(multicolored)* multicolor, de muchos colores; *(variegated)* abigarrado.
var·i·cose (văr′ĭ-kōs′) adj. MED. varicoso.
var·ied (vâr′ēd) adj. variado, diverso.
var·i·e·gate (vâr′ē-ĭ-gāt′) tr. **-gat·ed, -gat·ing** *(to streak)* vetear, jaspear; *(to make varied)* variar.
var·i·e·gat·ed (vâr′ē-ĭ-gā′tĭd) adj. *(varicolored)* abigarrado, jaspeado; *(diversified)* diversificado, variado.
va·ri·e·ty (və-rī′ĭ-tē) s. [pl. **-ties**] *(diversity)* variedad f, diversidad f; *(assortment)* variedad, surtido; BIOL. variedad (de una especie) ♦ **in a v. of** en varios (modelos, colores) • **v. show** TEAT. espectáculo de variedades.
var·i·form (vâr′ə-fôrm′) adj. diversiforme.
var·i·ous (vâr′ē-əs) adj. *(of diverse kinds)* vario, diverso; *(different)* diferente; *(several)* varios, múltiples.
var·let (vär′lĭt) s. ANT. *(attendant)* lacayo; *(page)* paje m; *(rascal)* bribón m.
var·mint (vär′mĭnt) s. FAM. *(troublesome animal)* sabandija; FIG. *(person)* canalla, sabandija.
var·nish (vär′nĭsh) I. s. *(paint)* barniz m; *(coating)* capa de barniz; *(ceramic gloss)* mogate m, vidriado; FIG. *(show)* barniz, apariencia <*his joy is only v.* su alegría es sólo una

apariencia> ♦ **v. remover** quitaesmalte II. tr. *(to cover)* barnizar; *(to finish with gloss)* vidriar; FIG. *(to gloss over)* disimular, embellecer.
var·si·ty (vär′sĭ-tē) s. [pl. **-ties**] *(team)* equipo universitario; G.B. *(university)* universidad f.
var·y (vâr′ē) tr. **-ied, -y·ing** *(to make varied)* variar, diversificar; *(to modify)* cambiar, variar; MÚS. variar —intr. *(to change)* variar, cambiar <*the temperature varies rapidly* la temperatura cambia rápidamente>; *(to be different)* diferir, ser diferente <*ideas v. from one person to another* las ideas difieren de una persona a otra>; *(to deviate)* desviarse.
var·y·ing (vâr′ē-ĭng) adj. variante, variable.
vas (văs) s. [pl. **va·sa** (vā′zə)] ANAT. vaso, conducto ♦ **v. deferens** conducto deferente.
vas·cu·lar (văs′kyə-lər) adj. vascular.
vase (vās, vāz, väz) s. *(container)* jarrón m; *(flower holder)* florero.
va·sec·to·my (və-sĕk′tə-mē, vä-zĕk′-) s. [pl. **-mies**] CIR. vasectomía.
Vas·e·line (văs′ə-lēn′) s. vaselina (marca registrada).
va·so·con·stric·tion (vā′zō-kən-strĭk′shən) s. FISIOL. vasoconstricción f.
va·so·dil·a·ta·tion (vā′zō-dĭl′ə-tā′shən) o **va·so·di·la·tion** (-dī-lā′shən) s. FISIOL. vasodilatación f.
vas·sal (văs′əl) s. HIST. *(land holder)* vasallo; FIG. *(slave)* siervo.
vas·sal·age (văs′ə-lĭj) s. *(condition)* vasallaje m; FIG. *(servitude)* servidumbre f.
vast (văst) adj. **-er, -est** *(large)* vasto, enorme; *(immense)* inmenso ♦ **to win by a v. majority of votes** vencer por una abrumadora mayoría de votos.
vast·ly (văst′lē) adv. vastamente, muchísimo.
vast·ness (văst′nĭs) s. vastedad f, inmensidad f.
vat (văt) I. s. cuba II. tr. **vat·ted, vat·ting** poner en cuba.
V.A.T. (vē′ā-tē′) s. COM., FIN. *(Value Added Tax)* I.V.A. m, impuesto al valor añadido.
Vat·i·can (văt′ĭ-kən) s. RELIG. Vaticano.
Vatican City State s. Estado de la Ciudad del Vaticano.
va·tic·i·na·tion (və-tĭs′ə-nā′shən) s. vaticinio, pronóstico.
vaude·ville (vôd′vĭl′, vôd′-) s. TEAT. *(show)* vodevil m (espectáculo de variedades); *(song)* canción satírica.
vault¹ (vôlt) I. s. ARQ. *(arched structure)* bóveda; *(cellar)* sótano; *(of a bank)* cámara acorazada; *(burial chamber)* cripta, tumba subterránea; ANAT. bóveda (palatina) II. tr. ARQ. abovedar, voltear.
vault² (vôlt) I. tr. *(to jump)* saltar; DEP. *(to pole vault)* saltar con garrocha —intr. DEP. *(to pole vault)* saltar con garrocha II. s. *(jump)* salto; *(pole vault)* salto con garrocha.
vault·ing¹ (vôl′tĭng) s. ARQ. bóveda.
vault·ing² (vôl′tĭng) adj. *(leaping)* saltador; FIG. *(exaggerated)* desmesurado <*v. ambition* ambición desmesurada>; *(used in leaping)* para salto.
vaunt (vônt) I. tr. jactarse de —intr. jactarse, alardear II. s. alarde m, jactancia.
veal (vēl) s. carne de ternera f, ternera.
vec·tor (vĕk′tər) s. MAT. vector m; MED. portador m, vector; FIG. *(force)* fuerza.
veep (vēp) s. FAM. vicepresidente m ♦ **V.** POL. el Vicepresidente de EE. UU.
veer¹ (vîr) I. intr. *(to swerve)* virar, desviarse <*the car veered to the left* el auto se desvió hacia la izquierda>; METEOR. *(the wind)* variar, cambiar; MARÍT. *(a boat)* virar —tr. *(to alter the course of)* cambiar el rumbo; MARÍT. *(a boat)* virar II. s. *(course change)* cambio; *(swerve)* desvío, viraje m.
veer² (vîr) tr. MARÍT. largar (ancla, cabo).
veg·e·ta·ble (vĕj′tə-bəl) I. s. CUL. *(edible plant)* verdura, legumbre f; BOT. *(plant)* vegetal m; FIG. *(person)* persona inactiva, vegetal II. adj. vegetal.
vegetable garden s. huerto, huerta.
vegetable kingdom s. reino vegetal.
vegetable market s. *(store)* verdulería, frutería; *(market)* mercado de verduras.
vegetable oil s. CUL. aceite vegetal m.

veg·e·tal (vĕj'ĭ-tl) adj. *(of a plant)* vegetal; *(vegetative)* vegetativo.

veg·e·tar·i·an (vĕj'ĭ-târ'ē-ən) I. s. *(person)* vegetariano; *(herbivore)* herbívoro II. adj. vegetariano.

veg·e·tar·i·an·ism (vĕj'ĭ-târ'ē-ə-nĭz'əm) s. vegetarianismo.

veg·e·tate (vĕj'ĭ-tāt') intr. **-tat·ed, -tat·ing** vegetar.

veg·e·ta·tion (vĕj'ĭ-tā'shən) s. vegetación f.

veg·e·ta·tive (vĕj'ĭ-tā'tĭv) o **veg·e·tive** (vĕj'ĭ-tĭv) adj. vegetativo.

ve·he·mence (vē'ə-məns) s. vehemencia.

ve·he·ment (vē'ə-mənt) adj. *(forceful)* vehemente; *(strong)* vigoroso <*a v. denial* una negación vigorosa>.

ve·hi·cle (vē'ĭ-kəl) s. *(transportation device)* vehículo; FIG. *(medium)* vehículo, medio; FARM. *(excipient)* excipiente m; *(mixing base)* base f.

ve·hic·u·lar (vē-hĭk'yə-lər) adj. de o para vehículos.

veil (vāl) I. s. *(of a bride, nun)* velo; FIG. *(façade)* velo, capa; BIOL. velo ♦ **to take the v.** tomar los hábitos, hacerse monja • **under a v. of secrecy** en secreto II. tr. *(to cover)* cubrir con un velo, velar; *(clouds, mist)* velar <*the mist veiled the town* la niebla velaba el pueblo>; FIG. *(to disguise)* velar, disimular.

vein (vān) I. s. ANAT. vena; BOT. vena, nervio; ENTOM. nervio; GEOL., MIN. veta, filón m; *(in wood, marble)* vena, veta; *(fissure)* grieta, hendidura; FIG. *(streak)* vena, rasgo (de carácter); *(style)* estilo; *(mood)* humor m, disposición f ♦ **in the same v.** del mismo estilo II. tr. vetear, marcar con venas.

veined (vānd) adj. ANAT. *(having veins)* que tiene venas, venoso; *(streaked)* veteado, jaspeado.

vein·ing (vā'nĭng) s. ANAT. *(venation)* red venal f; *(speckling)* jaspeado.

ve·lar (vē'lər) I. adj. ANAT., FONÉT. velar II. s. FONÉT. sonido velar m.

vel·lum (vĕl'əm) s. *(parchment)* vitela, pergamino; *(paper)* papel pergamino.

ve·loc·i·pede (və-lŏs'ə-pēd') s. [pl. **-des**] velocípedo.

ve·loc·i·ty (və-lŏs'ĭ-tē) s. [pl. **-ties**] velocidad f.

ve·lour o **ve·lours** (və-lŏŏr') s. [pl. **-lours** (-lŏŏrz')] TEJ. veludillo, terciopelo.

ve·lum (vē'ləm) s. [pl. **-la** (-lə)] BIOL. velo; ANAT. velo del paladar.

vel·vet (vĕl'vĭt) I. s. *(fabric)* terciopelo; FIG. *(smoothness)* suavidad f; ZOOL. *(on antlers)* vello (de las astas de los ciervos) II. adj. *(made of velvet)* de terciopelo; *(like velvet)* aterciopelado.

vel·vet·een (vĕl'vĭ-tēn') s. TEJ. pana.

vel·vet·y (vĕl'vĭ-tē) adj. aterciopelado.

ve·nal (vē'nəl) adj. *(purchasable)* venal; *(corruptible)* corruptible; *(bribable)* sobornable.

ve·nal·i·ty (vē-năl'ĭ-tē) s. [pl. **-ties**] venalidad f.

ve·na·tion (vē-nā'shən) s. ANAT. nervadura, disposición de las venas f.

vend (vĕnd) tr. *(to sell)* vender; FIG. *(to publish)* divulgar —intr. vender(se).

vend·a·ble (vĕn'də-bəl) adj. & s. var. de **vendible.**

vend·ee (vĕn-dē') s. DER. comprador m.

vend·er (vĕn'dər) s. *(seller)* vendedor m; *(vending machine)* máquina vendedora.

ven·det·ta (vĕn-dĕt'ə) s. vendetta, venganza.

vend·i·ble (vĕn'də-bəl) I. adj. *(salable)* vendible; *(venal)* venal II. s. artículo vendible.

vending machine s. máquina vendedora.

ven·dor (vĕn'dər) s. var. de **vender.**

ve·neer (və-nîr') I. s. *(covering)* chapa, hoja de chapear; *(of plywood)* capa de madera terciada; FIG. *(appearance)* apariencia, barniz m II. tr. *(to cover)* chapear, enchapar; *(to glue)* pegar (hojas de madera) para hacer madera terciada; FIG. *(to conceal)* encubrir, disfrazar.

ve·neer·ing (və-nîr'ĭng) s. chapeado, enchapado.

ven·er·a·ble (vĕn'ər-ə-bəl) adj. venerable, respetable.

ven·er·ate (vĕn'ə-rāt') tr. **-at·ed, -at·ing** venerar, reverenciar.

ven·er·a·tion (vĕn'ə-rā'shən) s. veneración f, respeto.

ve·ne·re·al (və-nîr'ē-əl) adj. venéreo.

venereal disease s. MED. enfermedad venérea.

ven·er·y¹ (vĕn'ə-rē) s. ANAT. *(sexual pleasure)* deleite sexual m; *(sexual intercourse)* acto carnal.

ven·er·y² (vĕn'ə-rē) s. ANT. montería, caza mayor.

Ve·ne·tian (və-nē'shən) adj. & s. veneciano.

Venetian blind o **venetian blind** s. persiana veneciana, celosías.

Ven·e·zue·la (vĕn'ĭz-wā'lə, -wē'-) s. Venezuela.

Ven·e·zue·lan (vĕn'ĭz-wā'lən, -wē'-) adj. & s. venezolano.

ven·geance (vĕn'jəns) s. venganza, vindicta ♦ **to take v. on someone** vengarse de alguien • **with a v.** *(furiously)* con violencia, con toda el alma; *(excessively)* extremadamente.

venge·ful (vĕnj'fəl) adj. vengativo.

V-en·gine (vē'ĕn'jən) s. AUTO., MEC. motor de cilindros en V m, motor en V m.

ve·ni·al (vē'nē-əl) adj. venial, leve ♦ **v. sin** RELIG. pecado venial.

Ven·ice (vĕn'ĭs) s. Venecia.

ve·ni·re (və-nī'rē) s. DER. mesa de jurador ♦ **v. facias** acto de convocación del jurado.

ve·ni·re·man (və-nī'rē-mən) s. [pl. **-men**] DER. persona citada para actuar como jurado.

ven·i·son (vĕn'ĭ-sən) s. CUL. carne de venado f.

ven·om (vĕn'əm) s. *(secretion)* veneno, ponzoña; FIG. *(spite)* veneno, rencor m.

ven·om·ous (vĕn'ə-məs) adj. venenoso.

ve·nose (vē'nōs') adj. venoso <*a v. leaf* una hoja venosa>.

ve·nous (vē'nəs) adj. ANAT. venoso <*v. blood* sangre venosa>.

vent (vĕnt) I. s. *(for air)* respiradero, agujero de ventilación; *(hole)* agujero, abertura; ARM. *(of a gun)* fogón m; MÚS. *(of wind instruments)* agujero; TEC. *(valve)* válvula; ZOOL. *(excretory opening)* ano, abertura anal ♦ **to give v. to (grief, anger)** FIG. desahogarse, dar rienda suelta a (congoja, cólera) II. tr. *(to make an opening in)* hacer o abrir un agujero en; TEC. *(to discharge)* dar salida a, descargar; FIG. *(feelings, words)* desahogar, dar rienda suelta a <*he vented his indignation* dio rienda suelta a su indignación>.

ven·ter (vĕn'tər) s. ANAT. vientre m, abdomen m; *(cavity)* cavidad f, concavidad f; DER. *(womb)* matriz f.

ven·ti·late (vĕn'tl-āt') tr. **-lat·ed, -lat·ing** *(to air)* ventilar, airear; *(to put a vent in)* proveer con un respiradero a; MED. *(blood)* oxigenar; FIG. *(to discuss)* ventilar, discutir.

ven·ti·la·tion (vĕn'tl-ā'shən) s. *(system)* ventilación f; *(ventilating)* aeración f; MED. *(of blood)* oxigenación f; FIG. *(discussion)* discusión f.

ven·ti·la·tor (vĕn'tl-ā'tər) s. ventilador m.

ven·tral (vĕn'trəl) adj. ANAT., BOT. ventral, abdominal.

ven·tri·cle (vĕn'trĭ-kəl) s. ANAT. ventrículo.

ven·tric·u·lar (vĕn-trĭk'yə-lər) adj. ANAT. ventricular.

ven·tril·o·quism (vĕn-trĭl'ə-kwĭz'əm) s. ventriloquia.

ven·tril·o·quist (vĕn-trĭl'ə-kwĭst) s. ventrílocuo.

ven·tril·o·quy (vĕn-trĭl'ə-kwē) s. var. de **ventriloquism.**

ven·ture (vĕn'chər) I. s. *(undertaking)* aventura; *(stake)* riesgo; COM. *(proposition)* empresa o negocio arriesgado ♦ **at a v.** a la ventura, al azar II. tr. **-tured, -tur·ing** *(to risk)* aventurar, arriesgar; *(to dare)* atreverse a, desafiar; *(to hazard)* atreverse, osar; *(an opinion)* aventurar; *(to gamble)* jugar ♦ **nothing ventured nothing gained** el que no arriesga no gana —intr. *(to dare)* atreverse, osar; *(to go)* ir ♦ **to v. forth** irse, salir.

venture capital s. ECON., FIN. capital de inversión m.

ven·ture·some (vĕn'chər-səm) adj. *(adventurous)* aventurado, arriesgado; *(enterprising)* emprendedor; *(hazardous)* peligroso, riesgoso.

ven·tur·ous (vĕn'chər-əs) adj. *(courageous)* valiente, arrojado; *(hazardous)* peligroso, riesgoso.

ven·ue (vĕn'yōō) s. *(of a crime)* lugar (de un crimen) m; DER. *(jurisdiction)* jurisdicción f.

Ve·nus (vē'nəs) s. ASTRON., MITOL. Venus f.

Ve·nu·sian (vĭ-nōō'zhən) adj. & s. venusino.

ve·ra·cious (və-rā'shəs) adj. veraz, verídico.

ve·rac·i·ty (və-răs'ĭ-tē) s. [pl. **-ties**] *(truthfulness)* veracidad f; *(accuracy)* exactitud f; *(truth)* verdad f.

ve·ran·dah o **ve·ran·da** (və-răn'də) s. terraza, mirador m.

verb (vûrb) s. GRAM. verbo.

---

ver·bal (vûr′bəl) adj. *(oral)* oral, verbal; *(literal)* literal; GRAM. verbal.

ver·bal·ism (vûr′bə-lĭz′əm) s. expresión verbal *f.*

ver·bal·ist (vûr′bə-lĭst) s. verbalista *mf.*

ver·bal·ize (vûr′bə-līz′) tr. **-ized, -iz·ing** *(to put in words)* expresar con palabras; GRAM. convertir en verbo —intr. expresarse con verbosidad.

ver·ba·tim (vər-bā′tĭm) **I.** adj. literal **II.** adv. palabra por palabra, literalmente.

ver·be·na (vər-bē′nə) s. verbena.

ver·bi·age (vûr′bē-ĭj) s. *(wordiness)* palabrería, verborrea; *(diction)* dicción *f*, lenguaje *m.*

ver·bose (vər-bōs′) adj. verboso.

ver·bos·i·ty (vər-bōs′ĭ-tē) s. verbosidad *f*, verborrea.

ver·dant (vûr′dnt) adj. *(green)* verde; FIG. *(inexperienced)* verde, inexperto.

ver·dict (vûr′dĭkt) s. DER. *(of a jury)* veredicto, dictamen *m*; *(judgment)* fallo, sentencia.

ver·di·gris (vûr′dĭ-grēs′) s. QUÍM. verdín *m*, cardenillo.

ver·dure (vûr′jər) s. LIT. *(verdancy)* verdor *m*; FIG. *(freshness)* frescura.

verge¹ (vûrj) **I.** s. *(edge, rim)* borde *m*, margen *m*; *(boundary)* límite *m*; *(staff)* vara, cetro; ARQ. *(of a column)* fuste *m* ♦ **to be on the v. of** estar al borde de, estar a punto de <*she was on the v. of crying* estaba a punto de llorar> **II.** intr. **verged, verg·ing** ♦ **to v. on** *o* **upon** *(to come near)* rayar en; *(to tend towards)* tirar a, estar al borde de.

verge² (vûrj) intr. **verged, verg·ing** ♦ **to v. into** *o* **on** *(to lean)* orientarse *o* inclinarse hacia; *(to pass into)* rayar, acercarse a <*dawn verging into day* la aurora que raya en el día>.

verg·er (vûr′jər) s. *(mace bearer)* macero *m*; G.B. *(sexton)* sacristán *m.*

ver·i·fi·ca·tion (vĕr′ə-fĭ-kā′shən) s. *(act)* verificación *f*, comprobación *f*; DER. *(oath)* confirmación *f.*

ver·i·fi·er (vĕr′ə-fī′ər) s. verificador *m.*

ver·i·fy (vĕr′ə-fī′) tr. **-fied, -fy·ing** *(to prove)* verificar, comprobar; *(to substantiate)* establecer, determinar; DER. *(to affirm)* afirmar bajo juramento, autenticar.

ver·i·ly (vĕr′ə-lē) adv. LIT. *(in truth)* en verdad; *(assuredly)* verdaderamente.

ver·i·sim·i·lar (vĕr′ə-sĭm′ə-lər) adj. verosímil.

ver·i·si·mil·i·tude (vĕr′ə-sĭ-mĭl′ĭ-tŏŏd′, -tyŏŏd′) s. verosimilitud *f.*

ver·i·ta·ble (vĕr′ĭ-tə-bəl) adj. verdadero.

ver·i·ty (vĕr′ĭ-tē) s. [pl. **-ties**] LIT. verdad *f.*

ver·meil (vûr′məl, -māl′) **I.** s. *(color)* bermellón *m*; *(gilded metal)* metal sobredorado **II.** adj. bermejo.

ver·mi·cel·li (vûr′mə-chĕl′ē, -sĕl′ē) s. CUL. fideos delgados.

ver·mi·cide (vûr′mĭ-sīd′) s. vermicida *m.*

ver·mic·u·late (vər-mĭk′yə-lāt′) **I.** tr. **-lat·ed, -lat·ing** *(to adorn)* poner adornos vermiformes **II.** adj. (-lĭt, -lāt′) *(said of shape, motion)* vermiforme, vermicular; *(having worms)* vermicular.

ver·mi·form (vûr′mə-fôrm′) adj. vermiforme.

vermiform appendix s. ANAT. apéndice vermiforme.

ver·mi·fuge (vûr′mə-fyŏŏj′) s. & adj. FARM. vermífugo.

ver·mil·ion *o* **ver·mil·lion** (vər-mĭl′yən) **I.** s. MIN. bermellón *m* **II.** adj. bermejo **III.** tr. enrojar.

ver·min (vûr′mĭn) s. [pl. **vermin**] *(pest)* bicho, sabandija; FIG. *(contemptible person)* canalla *m*, bribón *m*; *(rabble)* chusma.

ver·mouth (vər-mŏŏth′) s. vermut *m.*

ver·nac·u·lar (vər-năk′yə-lər) **I.** s. *(language)* lengua vernácula, habla local; *(popular speech)* lenguaje popular *m*; *(jargon)* jerga <*the medical v.* la jerga médica> ♦ **to put in the v.** expresar en lenguaje popular **II.** adj. *(language)* vernáculo, local; *(speech)* popular, vulgar.

ver·nal (vûr′nəl) adj. *(in spring)* vernal, primaveral; FIG. *(youthful)* juvenil.

vernal equinox s. ASTRON. equinoccio de primavera.

ver·ni·er (vûr′nē-ər) **I.** s. FÍS., MEC. nonio, vernier *m* **II.** adj. del nonio.

vernier caliper s. TEC. calibrador micrométrico.

ver·sa·tile (vûr′sə-tl, -tīl′) adj. *(person)* de talentos variados, polifacético; *(mind)* flexible, ágil; *(object)* de muchos usos; *(changeable)* que cambia, versátil.

ver·sa·til·i·ty (vûr′sə-tĭl′ĭ-tē) s. *(of an object)* versatilidad *f*, varios usos; *(of a person)* varios talentos, aptitudes diversas; *(of the mind)* flexibilidad *f*, agilidad *f.*

verse¹ (vûrs) **I.** s. *(poetry)* verso; *(stanza)* estrofa; *(of a song)* cuplé *m*; *(of the Bible)* versículo **II.** tr. & intr. **versed, vers·ing** versificar.

verse² (vûrs) tr. **versed, vers·ing** familiarizarse con, hacerse práctico en ♦ **to be versed in** estar familiarizado con.

versed (vûrst) adj. versado.

ver·si·fi·ca·tion (vûr′sə-fĭ-kā′shən) s. versificación.

ver·si·fi·er (vûr′sə-fī′ər) s. versificador *m.*

ver·si·fy (vûr′sə-fī′) tr. & intr. **-fied, -fy·ing** POÉT. versificar.

ver·sion (vûr′zhən) s. *(of an event, story)* versión *f*; *(translation)* versión, traducción *f*; *(adaptation)* adaptación *f*; *(interpretation)* versión, interpretación *f*; *(of a fetus)* versión.

ver·so (vûr′sō) s. [pl. **-sos**] IMPR. *(of a page)* verso, página par; *(of a coin)* reverso.

ver·sus (vûr′səs) prep. contra <*conjecture v. evidence* la conjetura contra la evidencia>.

ver·te·bra (vûr′tə-brə) s. [pl. **-brae** (-brē) *o* **-bras**] ANAT., ZOOL. vértebra.

ver·te·bral (vûr′tə-brəl) adj. vertebral, de las vértebras.

vertebral column s. columna vertebral, espina dorsal.

ver·te·brate (vûr′tə-brāt′) adj. & s. ANAT., ZOOL. vertebrado.

ver·tex (vûr′tĕks′) s. [pl. **-tex·es** *o* **-ti·ces** (-tĭ-sēz′)] *(apex)* ápice *m*, cúspide *f*; ANAT., GEOM. vértice *m*; ASTRON. cenit, zenit *m.*

ver·ti·cal (vûr′tĭ-kəl) **I.** adj. ECON., GEOM. vertical; *(at the vertex)* situado en el vértice *o* ápice; ANAT. del vértice **II.** s. GEOM. vertical *f.*

ver·ti·ces (vûr′tĭ-sēz′) un pl. de **vertex**.

ver·tig·i·nous (vər-tĭj′ə-nəs) adj. vertiginoso.

ver·ti·go (vûr′tĭ-gō′) s. [pl. **-goes** *o* **-gos**] MED. vértigo, vahido.

ver·vain (vûr′vān′) s. BOT. verbena.

verve (vûrv) s. POÉT., ARTE. *(inspiration)* ardor *m*, inspiración *f*; *(vitality)* vitalidad *f*, vivacidad *f.*

ver·y (vĕr′ē) **I.** adv. *(extremely)* muy <*I'm very happy* estoy muy contento>; *(truly)* de veras, en efecto <*it's the v. best cheese* éste es de veras el mejor queso>; *(indeed)* mucho <*are you tired? v.* ¿estás cansado? mucho>; *(precisely)* precisamente, exactamente <*the v. same one* exactamente el mismo>; *(used as an intensive)* muy, tan <*he is so v. poor* es tan pobre> ♦ **at the v. latest** a más tardar • **at the v. least** como mínimo, por lo menos • **at the v. most** a lo más, a lo sumo • **not v.** poco <*it was not v. interesting* fue poco interesante> • **that's v. kind of you** es usted muy amable • **the v. best** el mejor (de todos), lo mejor • **to do one's v. best** hacer uno todo lo posible, hacer todo lo que uno puede • **v. good** *(extremely good)* muy bueno; *(extremely well)* muy bien • **v. much (so)** muchísimo • **v., v. good (bad)** buenísimo (malísimo) **II.** adj. **-i·er, -i·est** *(absolute)* absoluto, puro <*the v. truth* la verdad absoluta>; *(selfsame, exact)* mismo <*at that v. moment* en ese mismo momento>; *(mere)* mero, simple <*the v. thought frightens us* el mero pensamiento nos espanta>; *(used as an intensive)* mismo, mismísimo <*the v. President himself was there* el mismísimo presidente estaba allí> ♦ **at the v. end (beginning)** al final (principio) de todo • **the v. idea!** ¡vaya idea! • **to be the v. image of** ser el vivo retrato de, ser la viva imagen de • **to shudder at the v. thought of it** temblar con sólo pensarlo.

very high frequency s. RAD. frecuencia muy alta.

very low frequency s. RAD. frecuencia muy baja.

ves·i·cant (vĕs′ĭ-kənt) s. & adj. MED. vesicante *m.*

ves·i·cate (vĕs′ĭ-kāt′) tr. & intr. **-cat·ed, -cat·ing** ampollar(se).

ves·i·cle (vĕs′ĭ-kəl) s. vesícula.

ve·sic·u·lar (vĕ-sĭk′yə-lər) adj. vesicular.

ves·per (vĕs′pər) s. POÉT. *(evening)* anochecer *m* ♦ **V.** estrella vespertina • **Vespers** RELIG. vísperas.

ves·per·al (vĕs′pər-əl) RELIG. **I.** s. *(book)* vesperal *m*; *(covering)* funda protectora **II.** adj. vespertino.

ves·per·tine (vĕs′pər-tīn′) *o* **ves·per·ti·nal** (vĕs′pər-tī′nəl) adj. vespertino.

ves·sel (vĕs′əl) s. *(container)* vaso, vasija; MARÍT. nave *f*, embarcación *f*; *(airship)* aeroplano, avión *m*; ANAT., BOT. vaso.

vest (vĕst) **I.** s. *(waistcoat)* chaleco; G.B. *(underwear)* camiseta **II.** tr. RELIG. revestirse ♦ **to v. in** *(rights, property)* conceder, conferir; *(authority, power)* investir, dotar —intr. RELIG. revestirse.

ves·tal (vĕs′təl) adj. & s. vestal *f*.

vest·ed (vĕs′tĭd) adj. DER. *(settled)* concedido, establecido; RELIG. *(dressed)* revestido.

vested interest s. DER. intereses creados, derecho adquirido; *(personal involvement)* interés personal *m*.

ves·ti·bule (vĕs′tə-byōōl′) **I.** s. ARQ. *(lobby)* vestíbulo; *(entrance)* pórtico, zaguán *m*; F.C. pasillo flexible, fuelle (entre vagones) *m*; ANAT. vestíbulo **II.** tr. **-buled, -bul·ing** proveer con un vestíbulo a.

ves·tige (vĕs′tĭj) s. vestigio, rastro.

ves·tig·i·al (vĕ-stĭj′ē-əl) adj. BIOL. *(rudimentary)* rudimentario; *(atrophied)* atrofiado.

vest·ment (vĕst′mənt) s. *(robe)* toga; RELIG. vestidura, vestimenta.

vest-pock·et (vĕst′pŏk′ĭt) adj. *(for a pocket)* de bolsillo; *(diminutive)* diminuto.

ves·try (vĕs′trē) s. [pl. **-tries**] RELIG. *(sacristy)* sacristía, vestuario; *(meeting room)* salón parroquial *m*; *(committee)* junta parroquial anglicana.

ves·ture (vĕs′chər) s. *(clothing)* vestidura; *(covering)* cobertura, cubierta.

Ve·su·vi·us (və-sōō′vē-əs) s. Vesuvio.

vet (vĕt) **I.** s. FAM. *(veterinarian)* veterinario; *(veteran)* veterano **II.** tr. **vet·ted, vet·ting** VET. *(to examine)* examinar a un animal enfermo; *(article, manuscript)* revisar, corregir.

vetch (vĕch) s. BOT. arveja.

vet·er·an (vĕt′ər-ən) s. *(experienced person)* veterano, persona experimentada; MIL. veterano, excombatiente *m* ♦ **a v. actor** un actor veterano.

Veterans Day s. día de los veteranos (EE. UU.).

vet·er·i·nar·i·an (vĕt′ər-ə-nâr′ē-ən) s. veterinario.

vet·er·i·nar·y (vĕt′ər-ə-nĕr′ē) adj. & s. [pl. **-ies**] veterinario.

ve·to (vē′tō) **I.** s. [pl. **-toes**] veto **II.** tr. **-toed, -to·ing** *(to exercise one's veto)* vetar; *(to prohibit)* prohibir.

vex (vĕks) tr. *(to bother)* fastidiar, molestar; *(to afflict)* afligir, incomodar <*my toothache vexed me all night long* el dolor de muela me incomodó toda la noche>; *(to baffle)* confundir; *(to debate)* discutir, debatir; *(to shake up)* agitar, sacudir.

vex·a·tion (vĕk-sā′shən) s. *(act)* fastidio, molestia; *(discomfort)* incomodidad *f*, indisposición *f*; *(affliction)* aflicción *f*, dolor *m*.

vex·a·tious (vĕk-sā′shəs) adj. *(annoying)* fastidioso, molesto; *(annoyed)* fastidiado, disgustado.

vexed (vĕkst) adj. *(person)* enfadado, irritado; *(question, matter)* controvertido.

vi·a (vī′ə, vē′ə) prep. *(by way of)* vía <*Rome-New York, v. Madrid* Roma-Nueva York, vía Madrid>; *(by means of)* vía, por <*v. air mail* por vía aérea>.

vi·a·bil·i·ty (vī′ə-bĭl′ĭ-tē) s. viabilidad *f*.

vi·a·ble (vī′ə-bəl) adj. viable.

vi·a·duct (vī′ə-dŭkt′) s. viaducto.

vi·al (vī′əl) s. frasco.

vi·and (vī′ənd) s. vianda ♦ **viands** provisiones, manjares.

vi·at·i·cum (vī-ăt′ĭ-kəm) s. [pl. **-ca** (-kə) o **-cums**] RELIG. viático; *(supplies)* provisiones de viaje.

vibes (vībz) s. MÚS. *(vibraphone)* vibráfono; FAM. *(vibrations)* vibraciones *f*.

vi·bran·cy (vī′brən-sē) s. vibración *f*.

vi·brant (vī′brənt) adj. *(vibrating)* vibrante; FIG. *(energetic)* enérgico, vigoroso.

vi·bra·phone (vī′brə-fōn′) s. MÚS. vibráfono.

vi·brate (vī′brāt′) intr. **-brat·ed, -brat·ing** *(to shake)* vibrar; *(to resonate)* resonar, repercutir; FIG. *(to thrill)* conmoverse, estremecerse; *(to vacillate)* vacilar, titubear —tr. vibrar.

vi·bra·tion (vī-brā′shən) s. *(act)* vibración *f*; *(quiver)* temblor *m*, estremecimiento ♦ **vibrations** FAM. vibraciones <*good vibrations* buenas vibraciones>.

vi·bra·tor (vī′brā′tər) s. *(for massage)* vibrador *m*; ELEC. vibrador, interruptor intermitente *m*; RAD. oscilador *m*.

vi·bra·to·ry (vī′brə-tôr′ē) adj. vibratorio.

vi·bur·num (vī-bûr′nəm) s. BOT. viburno, mundillo.

vic·ar (vĭk′ər) s. RELIG. vicario.

vic·ar·age (vĭk′ər-ĭj) s. RELIG. vicaría.

vi·car·i·ous (vī-kâr′ē-əs) adj. *(punishment)* sufrido por otro; *(act)* hecho por otro; *(pleasure)* indirecto.

vice¹ (vīs) s. *(depravity)* vicio, depravación *f*; *(immorality)* inmoralidad *f*; *(corruption)* corrupción *f*; *(defect)* defecto, imperfección *f*.

vice² (vīs) s. & v. var. de **vise**.

vice³ (vīs) **I.** s. *(used as a prefix)* vice **II.** prep. en lugar de, sustituyendo a.

vice admiral s. vicealmirante *m*.

vice chancellor s. DER. canciller ayudante *m*; *(of a university)* rector *m*; *(of a country)* vicecanciller *m*.

vice consul s. vicecónsul *m*.

vice president s. vicepresidente *m*.

vice·re·gal (vīs-rē′gəl) adj. de virrey, virreinal.

vice regent s. vicerregente *m*.

vice·roy (vīs′roi′) s. virrey *m*.

vice·roy·al·ty (vīs-roi′əl-tē) s. [pl. **-ties**] virreinato.

vice squad s. dependencia policial que combate el vicio y la adicción.

vi·ce ver·sa (vī′sə vûr′sə) adv. viceversa.

vi·cin·i·ty (vī-sĭn′ĭ-tē) s. [pl. **-ties**] *(nearness)* proximidad *f*; *(neighborhood)* vecindad, vecindario ♦ **in the v. of** aproximadamente, alrededor de.

vi·cious (vĭsh′əs) adj. *(addicted to vice)* vicioso; *(perverse)* perverso, corrompido; *(depraved)* depravado, inmoral; *(harmful)* malsano, nocivo; *(malicious)* malicioso, rencoroso <*a v. gossip* un comadreo malicioso>; *(violent)* violento, fuerte <*a v. storm* una tempestad violenta>; *(savage)* salvaje, atroz (animal, crimen).

vicious circle s. círculo vicioso.

vi·cis·si·tude (vī-sĭs′ĭ-tōōd′, -tyōōd′) s. vicisitud *f* ♦ **vicissitudes** vicisitudes, altibajos.

vic·tim (vĭk′tĭm) s. víctima ♦ **to fall (a) v. to** sucumbir a.

vic·tim·ize (vĭk′tə-mīz′) tr. **-ized, -iz·ing** *(to make a victim of)* hacer víctima; *(to swindle)* estafar, embaucar.

vic·tor (vĭk′tər) s. vencedor *m*, triunfador *m*.

vic·to·ri·a (vĭk-tôr′ē-ə) s. *(carriage)* victoria; BOT. victoria regia.

Vic·to·ri·an (vĭk-tôr′ē-ən) **I.** adj. HIST. victoriano, de la época victoriana; *(prudish)* mojigato; *(conservative)* conservador **II.** s. HIST. victoriano.

vic·to·ri·ous (vĭk-tôr′ē-əs) adj. triunfante, vencedor.

vic·to·ry (vĭk′tə-rē) s. [pl. **-ries**] victoria, triunfo.

vict·ual·er o **vict·ual·ler** (vĭt′l-ər) s. *(supplier)* abastecedor *m*, proveedor *m*; *(supply ship)* buque abastecedor *m*; G.B. *(innkeeper)* mesonero, hostelero.

vic·tuals (vĭt′lz) s.pl. *(food)* vituallas; *(provisions)* provisiones *f*, víveres *m*.

vi·de (vī′dē, vē′dā′) LAT. véase ♦ **v. supra** LAT. véase más arriba.

vi·del·i·cet (vī-dĕl′ĭ-sĕt′) adv. LAT. a saber, es decir.

vid·e·o (vĭd′ē-ō′) TELEV. **I.** adj. vídeo, de la televisión **II.** s. *(visual portion)* vídeo; *(television)* televisión *f*.

vid·e·o·cas·sette (vĭd′ē-ō-kə-sĕt′) s. videocasete *mf*.

vid·e·o·con·fer·ence (vĭd′ē-ō-kŏn′fər-əns) s. TELEV. teleconferencia, conferencia en la cual los participantes reciben imágenes televisadas de los demás conferenciantes.

vid·e·o·disc o **vid·e·o·disk** (vĭd′ē-ō-dĭsk′) s. TELEV. videodisco.

video game s. juego electrónico.

vid·e·o·tape (vĭd′ē-ō-tāp′) TELEV. **I.** s. videocinta **II.** tr. **-taped, -tap·ing** grabar en videocinta.

videotape recorder s. vídeo *m*.

video terminal s. vídeo *m*, pantalla de computadora.

vie (vī) intr. **vied, vy·ing** competir, contender —tr. ANT. *(to match)* cotejar; *(to bet)* apostar.

Vi·en·na (vē-ĕn′ə) s. Viena.

Vi·en·nese (vē′ə-nēz′) adj. & s. [pl. **Viennese**] vienés *m* ♦ **the V.** los vieneses.

Viet·nam (vē-ĕt′näm′, -năm′) s. Viet Nam, Vietnam *m*.

ã rey / ä año / b boca / ch chico / d dar / ĕ el / ē mil / g gato / h joya / hw juez / ī aire / k casa / kw cuan /

Viet·nam·ese (vĕ-ĕt′nə-mēz′) adj. & s. [pl. **Vietnamese**] *(inhabitant, language)* vietnamita *m* ♦ **the V.** los vietnamitas.
view (vyōō) **I.** s. *(sight)* vista <*the plane disappeared from v.* el avión desapareció de la vista>; *(vista)* vista, panorama *m* <*it's a fine v. from the tower* es un bello panorama desde la torre>; *(examination)* examinación *f*, inspección *f* <*a v. of the matter* una examinación del asunto>; *(systematic survey)* panorama *m*, visión de conjunto *f* <*a v. of modern poetry* un panorama de la poesía moderna>; *(opinion)* opinión *f*, parecer *m* <*his views on art* sus opiniones sobre el arte>; *(approach)* enfoque *m* <*our v. of the problem* nuestro enfoque del problema>; *(intention)* intención *f*, propósito <*with a v. to doing something* con el propósito de hacer algo>; *(chance)* posibilidad *f*, perspectiva <*there is no v. of success* no existe posibilidad de éxito>; PINT. vista, paisaje *m* ♦ **at first v.** a primera vista • **in v. of** en vista de, considerando • **point of v.** punto de vista <*from my point of v.* desde mi punto de vista> • **to be in v.** estar a la vista (de) • **to be on v.** estar a la vista, estar expuesto • **to come into v.** aparecer • **to go out of v.** desaparecer • **to have in v.** *(a project)* tener a la vista; *(to keep in mind)* tener en la mente, tener presente • **to keep in v.** no perder de vista • **to take a closer v. (of)** examinar más de cerca • **to take a dim v. of** ver con malos ojos • **to take the v. that** pensar que, tener la impresión de que • **with a v. to** con miras a, con el propósito de • **with this in v.** con este fin **II.** tr. *(to see)* ver, mirar; *(to examine)* examinar, inspeccionar; *(to consider)* considerar, enfocar <*the problem may be viewed in different ways* el problema puede ser enfocado de diferentes maneras>.
view·er (vyōō′ər) s. *(onlooker)* espectador *m*; *(television viewer)* telespectador *m*, televidente *mf*; FOTOG. visor *m*.
view finder s. FOTOG. visor *m*.
view·point (vyōō′point′) s. punto de vista.
vig·il (vĭj′əl) s. *(sleeplessness)* vigilia, vela; *(watch)* vigilia, vigilancia; RELIG. vigilia ♦ **vigils** RELIG. vísperas.
vig·i·lance (vĭj′ə-ləns) s. vigilancia.
vig·i·lant (vĭj′ə-lənt) adj. vigilante, alerto.
vig·i·lan·te (vĭj′ə-lăn′tē) s. vigilante *mf*, miembro de una junta vigilante que actúa como policía.
vi·gnette (vĭn-yĕt′) **I.** s. IMPR. viñeta; FOTOG. retrato con bordes esfumados; LIT. bosquejo corto; CINEM. escena corta **II.** tr. **-gnett·ed, -gnett·ing** FOTOG. esfumar (retrato, ilustración); *(to describe)* describir brevemente.
vig·or (vĭg′ər) s. *(energy)* vigor *m*, energía física; *(intensity)* vigor, fuerza; DER. *(validity)* validez *f*, vigencia.
vig·or·ous (vĭg′ər-əs) adj. *(strong)* vigoroso, fuerte; *(energetic)* enérgico.
vig·our (vĭg′ər) s. G.B. var. de **vigor**.
Vi·king (vī′kĭng) s. HIST. vikingo.
vile (vīl) adj. **vil·er, vil·est** *(abject)* vil, ruin; *(loathsome)* repulsivo, odioso; *(unpalatable)* desagradable; *(poor)* miserable; *(said of weather)* pésimo, horrible.
vile·ness (vīl′nĭs) s. *(abjection)* vileza, ruindad *f*; *(baseness)* infamia, bajeza.
vil·i·fy (vĭl′ə-fī′) tr. **-fied, -fy·ing** difamar, denigrar.
vil·la (vĭl′ə) s. *(country house)* villa, casa de campo, quinta; *(estate)* finca, hacienda; G.B. *(residence)* chalet *m*.
vil·lage (vĭl′ĭj) s. *(hamlet)* aldea; *(town)* pueblo; *(inhabitants)* población *f*.
vil·lag·er (vĭl′ĭ-jər) s. aldeano.
vil·lain (vĭl′ən) s. *(scoundrel)* villano, canalla *m*; CINEM., TEAT. villano; FIG. *(cause)* causa <*poverty is the v. in the rise of crime* la pobreza es la causa del incremento del crimen>; HIST. var. de **villein**.
vil·lain·ous (vĭl′ə-nəs) adj. *(vile)* vil, infame; *(wicked)* villano, malvado; *(obnoxious)* repugnante, odioso.
vil·lain·y (vĭl′ə-nē) s. [pl. **-ies**] villanía, vileza.
vil·lein (vĭl′ən) s. HIST. villano, siervo de la gleba.
vim (vĭm) s. energía, brío.
vin·ai·grette (vĭn′ī-grĕt′) s. *(container)* vinagrera; CUL. *(sauce)* vinagreta.
vin·ci·ble (vĭn′sə-bəl) adj. vencible, que puede vencerse.
vin·di·cate (vĭn′dĭ-kāt′) tr. **-cat·ed, -cat·ing** *(to clear)* vindicar, exculpar; *(to justify)* justificar; *(to prove the worth of)* reivindicar.

vin·di·ca·tion (vĭn′dĭ-kā′shən) s. vindicación *f*, reivindicación *f*.
vin·dic·tive (vĭn-dĭk′tĭv) adj. vengativo.
vine (vīn) s. BOT. *(creeper)* enredadera; *(grapevine)* parra, vid *f* ♦ **clinging v.** FIG. mujer pegajosa.
vin·e·gar (vĭn′ĭ-gər) s. CUL. vinagre *m*.
vin·e·gar·y (vĭn′ĭ-gə-rē) *o* **vin·e·gar·ish** (-gər-ĭsh, -grĭsh) adj. avinagrado.
vine grower s. viticultor *m*, vitícola *mf*.
vine·stock (vīn′stŏk′) s. BOT. cepa (de la vid).
vine·yard (vĭn′yərd) s. *(growing area)* viñedo, viña; FIG. *(field)* campo.
vin·i·cul·ture (vĭn′ĭ-kŭl′chər, vī′nĭ-) s. vinicultura.
vi·nous (vī′nəs) adj. *(of wine)* vinoso; *(said of color)* de color vino.
vin·tage (vĭn′tĭj) **I.** s. *(season)* vendimia; *(crop)* cosecha **II.** adj. *(relating to the vintage)* de vendimia; *(wine)* añejo, de calidad; *(classic)* clásico; *(old)* antiguo; *(of the best)* de lo mejor, excelente <*it was a v. year for us* ha sido un año excelente para nosotros>.
vin·tag·er (vĭn′tĭ-jər) s. vendimiador *m*.
vint·ner (vĭnt′nər) s. vinatero.
vi·nyl (vī′nəl) s. QUÍM. vinilo.
vi·ol (vī′əl) s. MÚS. viola.
vi·o·la¹ (vē-ō′lə) s. MÚS. viola.
vi·o·la² (vī-ō′lə, vī′ə-lə) s. BOT. viola, violeta.
vi·o·la·ble (vī′ə-lə-bəl) adj. que se puede violar.
vi·o·late (vī′ə-lāt′) tr. **-lat·ed, -lat·ing** *(to breach)* violar, infringir; *(to rape)* violar; *(to desecrate)* profanar; *(to disturb)* perturbar.
vi·o·la·tion (vī′ə-lā′shən) s. violación *f*.
vi·o·la·tor (vī′ə-lā′tər) s. violador *m*.
vi·o·lence (vī′ə-ləns) s. violencia ♦ **to do v. to** *(physically)* violentar (a alguien); FIG. violar, ir en contra de.
vi·o·lent (vī′ə-lənt) adj. *(person, act)* violento; *(pain)* intenso, acerbo; *(feeling)* profundo; *(color)* chillón ♦ **to become v.** mostrarse violento.
vi·o·let (vī′ə-lĭt) s. *(plant)* violeta; *(color)* violeta *m*.
vi·o·lin (vī′ə-lĭn′) s. MÚS. violín *m*.
vi·o·lin·ist (vī′ə-lĭn′ĭst) s. MÚS. violinista *mf*.
vi·ol·ist (vē-ō′lĭst) s. MÚS. intérprete de la viola *mf*.
vi·o·lon·cel·lo (vē′ə-lən-chĕl′ō) [pl. **-los**] MÚS. violoncelo.
VIP (vē′ī-pē′) s. [pl. **VIPs**] FAM. persona muy importante, personalidad *f*.
vi·per (vī′pər) s. *(snake)* víbora; FIG. *(person)* víbora.
vi·per·ous (vī′pər-əs) adj. *(snake-like)* viperino; FIG. *(malicious)* malicioso.
vi·ra·go (və-rä′gō, -rä′-) s. [pl. **-goes** *o* **-gos**] virago *f*, mujer varonil *f*.
vi·ral (vī′rəl) adj. BACT., MED. causado por un virus, virulento.
vir·gin (vûr′jĭn) **I.** s. virgen *f* ♦ **The V.** la Virgen María **II.** adj. *(chaste)* virgen; FIG. *(unexplored)* virgen; *(initial)* inicial, primero; *(unsullied)* puro, intacto.
vir·gin·al¹ (vûr′jə-nəl) adj. virginal.
vir·gin·al² (vûr′jə-nəl) s. MÚS. espineta (clavicordio).
virgin birth s. RELIG. parto virginal (de María).
Vir·gin·ia creeper (vər-jĭn′yə) s. enredadera de Virginia.
Virgin Islands s.pl. Islas Vírgenes.
vir·gin·i·ty (vər-jĭn′ī-tē) s. [pl. **-ties**] *(chastity)* virginidad *f*; *(purity)* pureza.
Virgin Mar·y (mâr′ē) s. RELIG. la Virgen María.
Vir·go (vûr′gō, vîr′-) s. ASTROL. Virgo.
vir·gule (vûr′gyōōl) s. TIP. vírgula, virgulilla.
vir·ile (vîr′əl, -īl′) adj. *(masculine)* viril, varonil; *(vigorous)* vigoroso; *(potent)* viril.
vi·ril·i·ty (və-rĭl′ī-tē) s. virilidad *f*.
vi·rol·o·gy (vī-rŏl′ə-jē) s. MED. virología.
vir·tu (vər-tōō′) s. *(love, taste)* afición a los objetos de arte *f*; *(curios, antiques)* objetos de arte, antigüedades *f*.
vir·tu·al (vûr′chōō-əl) adj. virtual.
virtual focus s. FÍS., OPT. foco virtual.
vir·tu·al·ly (vûr′chōō-ə-lē) adv. prácticamente, casi <*it is v. impossible* es casi imposible>.
virtual machine s. COMPUT. máquina virtual.
vir·tue (vûr′chōō) s. *(moral excellence)* virtud *f*; *(chastity)*

---

castidad *f*, honra; *(advantage)* virtud, ventaja <*it has the v. of being practical* tiene la ventaja de ser práctico> ♦ **by** *o* **in v. of** en virtud de • **of easy v.** fácil • **virtues** RELIG. virtudes.

vir·tu·o·si (vûr'chōō-ō'sē) un pl. de **virtuoso.**

vir·tu·os·i·ty (vûr'chōō-ŏs'ĭ-tē) s. [pl. **-ties**] virtuosismo.

vir·tu·o·so (vûr'chōō-ō'sō, -zō) s. [pl. **-sos** *o* **-si** (-sē)] *(master performer)* virtuoso; *(amateur)* aficionado a objetos de arte.

vir·tu·ous (vûr'chōō-əs) adj. *(righteous)* virtuoso; *(chaste)* casto, puro.

vir·tu·ous·ness (vûr'chōō-əs-nĭs) s. virtud *f.*

vir·u·lence (vîr'yə-ləns, vîr'ə-) s. virulencia.

vir·u·lent (vîr'yə-lənt, vîr'ə-) adj. MED. virulento; FIG. *(harsh)* cruel, duro.

vi·rus (vī'rəs) s. BACT., MED. virus *m.*

vi·sa (vē'zə) I. s. visa, visado II. tr. **-saed, -sa·ing** *(to endorse)* visar; *(to give a visa to)* otorgar una visa a.

vis·age (vĭz'ĭj) s. *(face)* cara, rostro; *(countenance)* semblante *m*; *(aspect)* aspecto.

vis-à-vis (vē'zə-vē') I. s. [pl. **vis-à-vis** (-vēz', -vē')] persona colocada enfrente de otra II. adv. frente a frente, cara a cara III. prep. *(opposite to)* frente a, enfrente de; *(compared with)* comparado con, con relación a <*your situation is better v. mine* tu situación comparada con la mía, es mejor>; *(in relation to)* con respecto a, acerca de <*his ideas v. the situation* sus ideas acerca de la situación>.

vis·cer·a (vĭs'ər-ə) s.pl. ANAT. vísceras.

vis·cer·al (vĭs'ər-əl) adj. ANAT. visceral, de las vísceras; FIG. *(profound)* profundo, íntimo; *(instinctive)* instintivo <*a v. reaction* una reacción instintiva>.

vis·cid (vĭs'ĭd) adj. *(thick)* viscoso, espeso; *(sticky)* pegajoso.

vis·cose (vĭs'kōs') I. s. viscosa II. adj. viscoso.

vis·cos·i·ty (vĭ-skŏs'ĭ-tē) s. [pl. **-ties**] FÍS. viscosidad *f.*

vis·count (vī'kount') s. vizconde *m.*

vis·count·cy (vī'kount'sē) s. [pl. **-cies**] vizcondado.

vis·count·ess (vī'koun'tĭs) s. vizcondesa.

vis·cous (vĭs'kəs) adj. FÍS. viscoso.

vise (vīs) MEC. I. s. tornillo de banco II. tr. **vised, vis·ing** apretar con tornillo de banco.

vis·i·ble (vĭz'ə-bəl) adj. *(to the eye)* visible; *(apparent)* manifiesto; *(evident)* evidente; *(on hand)* a la vista.

vis·i·bil·i·ty (vĭz'ə-bĭl'ĭ-tē) s. [pl. **-ties**] visibilidad *f.*

Vis·i·goth (vĭz'ĭ-gŏth') s. HIST. visigodo.

vi·sion (vĭzh'ən) I. s. *(sight)* vista, visión *f* <*good v.* visión buena>; *(foresight)* clarividencia, previsión *f*; *(mental image)* visión, fantasía; *(beauty)* belleza, maravilla <*she's a v.* es una belleza> ♦ **a person of v.** una persona clarividente II. tr. imaginar, evocar en una visión.

vi·sion·ar·y (vĭzh'ə-nĕr'ē) I. adj. *(foresighted)* visionario; *(dreamy)* de ensueño; *(prophetic)* profético; *(utopian)* utópico II. s. [pl. **-ies**] *(seer)* visionario; *(dreamer)* soñador *m.*

vis·it (vĭz'ĭt) I. tr. *(to go to see)* visitar, ir a ver; *(as a guest)* pasar una temporada en; *(as an official)* inspeccionar; FIG. *(to assail)* asaltar <*a plague visited the village* una plaga asaltó el pueblo>; *(to inflict)* infligir, enviar (castigo, desgracia) —intr. *(to make a visit)* hacer una visita, ir de visita; FAM. *(to chat)* charlar, platicar <*v. with me for a while* charla conmigo un ratito> II. s. *(act)* visita; *(stay)* estadía (como invitado); *(inspection)* inspección *f* ♦ **to be on a v.** to estar de visita en • **to pay a v. to someone** visitar a alguien.

vis·i·tant (vĭz'ĭ-tnt) s. *(guest)* invitado, huésped *mf*; *(ghost)* fantasma *m*, aparecido.

vis·i·ta·tion (vĭz'ĭ-tā'shən) s. *(visit)* visita; *(inspection)* inspección *f*; DER. *(visiting right)* derecho de visita (a hijos después de divorcio); *(calamity)* desgracia, calamidad *f*; *(appearance)* visitación *f*, aparición *f*; RELIG. disposición divina ♦ V. RELIG. Fiesta de la Visitación.

vis·it·ing (vĭz'ĭ-tĭng) adj. *(card, hours)* de visita; *(person)* visitante.

visiting card s. tarjeta de visita.

vis·i·tor (vĭz'ĭ-tər) s. visita, visitante *mf.*

vi·sor (vī'zər) I. s. *(of a cap)* visera; *(of a helmet)* visera,

máscara II. tr. *(to protect)* proteger con visera; *(to mask)* enmascarar.

vis·ta (vĭs'tə) s. *(view)* vista, perspectiva; FIG. *(total view)* panorama *m.*

vi·su·al (vĭzh'ōō-əl) adj. *(of sight)* visual; *(visible)* visible; *(optical)* óptico; *(by sight)* ocular <*a v. inspection* una inspección ocular>.

visual aid s. EDUC. medio visual.

visual field s. campo visual.

vi·su·al·i·za·tion (vĭzh'ōō-ə-lĭ-zā'shən) s. visualización *f.*

vi·su·al·ize (vĭzh'ōō-ə-līz') tr. & intr. **-ized, -iz·ing** visualizar.

vi·tal (vīt'l) adj. *(of life)* vital <*v. functions* funciones vitales>; *(animated)* vivaz, animado; *(essential)* vital, fundamental <*of v. importance* de importancia fundamental>; *(fatal)* mortal, fatal.

vi·tal·ism (vīt'l-ĭz'əm) s. BIOL., FILOS. vitalismo.

vi·tal·i·ty (vī-tăl'ĭ-tē) s. [pl. **-ties**] vitalidad *f.*

vi·tal·ize (vīt'l-īz') tr. **-ized, -iz·ing** vitalizar.

vi·tals (vīt'lz) s.pl. BIOL. órganos vitales; MEC. *(essential parts)* partes esenciales *f.*

vital signs s.pl. MED. signos vitales.

vital statistics s.pl. estadística demográfica.

vi·ta·min (vī'tə-mĭn) s. vitamina.

vi·tel·lus (vī-tĕl'əs) s. yema de huevo.

vi·ti·ate (vĭsh'ē-āt') tr. **-at·ed, -at·ing** *(to impair)* viciar; *(to corrupt)* corromper; *(to invalidate)* invalidar.

vit·i·cul·ture (vĭt'ĭ-kŭl'chər, vī'tĭ-) s. viticultura.

vit·re·ous (vĭt'rē-əs) adj. FIS. vítreo.

vitreous humor s. ANAT. humor vítreo (del ojo).

vit·ri·fi·ca·tion (vĭt'rə-fĭ-kā'shən) s. vitrificación *f.*

vit·ri·fy (vĭt'rə-fī') tr. & intr. **-fied, -fy·ing** vitrificar(se).

vit·ri·ol (vĭt'rē-əl) I. s. QUÍM. *(sulphur compound)* vitriolo; FIG. *(vituperative expression)* virulencia, veneno II. tr. vitriolar.

vit·ri·ol·ic (vĭt'rē-ŏl'ĭk) adj. *(of vitriol)* vitriólico; FIG. *(vituperative)* virulento; *(biting)* mordaz.

vi·tu·per·ate (vī-tōō'pə-rāt') tr. **-at·ed, -at·ing** vituperar.

vi·tu·per·a·tion (vī-tōō'pə-rā'shən, -tyōō'-) s. vituperación *f.*

vi·tu·per·a·tive (vī-tōō'pər-ə-tĭv, -tyōō'-) adj. vituperante.

vi·va·cious (vĭ-vā'shəs, vī-) adj. vivaz.

vi·vac·i·ty (vĭ-văs'ĭ-tē, vī-) s. vivacidad *f.*

vi·var·i·um (vī-vâr'ē-əm) s. [pl. **-i·ums** *o* **-i·a** (-ē-ə)] vivero.

viv·id (vĭv'ĭd) adj. *(bright)* vívido; *(fresh)* vivo <*a v. memory* un recuerdo vivo>; *(intense)* intenso, claro; *(active)* vívido, vivo <*a v. imagination* una imaginación vívida>.

viv·id·ly (vĭv'ĭd-lē) adv. vívidamente.

viv·id·ness (vĭv'ĭd-nĭs) s. *(brightness)* viveza, brillo; *(intensity)* intensidad *f.*

viv·i·fy (vĭv'ə-fī') tr. **-fied, -fy·ing** *(to enliven)* vivificar; *(to animate)* animar, avivar.

vi·vip·a·rous (vī-vĭp'ər-əs) s. ZOOL. vivíparo.

viv·i·sect (vĭv'ĭ-sĕkt') tr. ZOOL. hacer la vivisección de —intr. practicar la vivisección.

viv·i·sec·tion (vĭv'ĭ-sĕk'shən) s. ZOOL. vivisección *f.*

vix·en (vĭk'sən) s. *(female fox)* zorra; FIG. *(woman)* arpía.

vi·zier *o* **vi·zir** (vĭ-zîr') s. HIST. visir *m.*

vi·zor (vī'zər) s. & v. var. de **visor.**

vo·ca·ble (vō'kə-bəl) s. vocablo, voz *f.*

vo·cab·u·lar·y (vō-kăb'yə-lĕr'ē) s. [pl. **-ies**] vocabulario.

vo·cal (vō'kəl) I. adj. *(of the voice)* vocal; *(oral)* oral, verbal; *(resounding)* resonante, ruidoso; *(outspoken)* que dice lo que piensa; *(vocalic)* vocálico; *(voiced)* sonoro II. s. FONÉT. vocal *f.*

vocal cords s.pl. ANAT. cuerdas vocales.

vo·cal·ism (vō'kə-lĭz'əm) s. *(vocalization)* vocalización *f*; *(singing)* canto; FONÉT. *(vowel)* vocal *f*; *(vowel system)* vocalismo.

vo·cal·ist (vō'kə-lĭst) s. MÚS. cantante *mf*, vocalista *mf.*

vo·cal·ize (vō'kə-līz') tr. **-ized, -iz·ing** *(to produce with the voice)* producir con la voz; *(to articulate)* articular —intr. vocalizar.

vo·ca·tion (vō-kā'shən) s. vocación *f.*

vo·ca·tion·al (vō-kā'shə-nəl) adj. *(professional)* profesional; *(of a vocation)* vocacional.

vocational school s. EDUC. escuela vocacional, escuela de oficios.

voc·a·tive (vŏk′ə-tĭv) adj. & s. GRAM. vocativo.

vo·cif·er·ate (vō-sĭf′ə-rāt′) tr. & intr. **-at·ed, -at·ing** vociferar.

vo·cif·er·ous (vō-sĭf′ər-əs) adj. vociferador, vociferante.

vod·ka (vŏd′kə) s. vodka.

vogue (vōg) s. moda, boga ♦ **in v.** en boga.

voice (vois) I. s. *(vocal sound)* voz *f* <*a clear v.* una voz clara>; *(timbre)* tono <*a gentle v.* un tono dulce>; GRAM., MÚS. voz ♦ **at the top of one's v.** a voz en cuello, a voz en grito • **in a loud v.** en voz alta • **in a low v.** en voz baja • **to be in good v.** MÚS. estar en buena voz • **to give v. to** expresar <*he gave v. to his feelings* expresó sus sentimientos> • **to have a v. in (a matter)** tener voz en (un asunto) • **to lose one's v.** perder la voz • **to raise one's v.** alzar la voz, levantar el tono • **with one v.** a una voz, al unísono II. tr. **voiced, voic·ing** *(to utter)* expresar; FONÉT. sonorizar (consonantes); MÚS. afinar, modular el sonido.

voice box s. ANAT. laringe *f.*

voiced (voist) adj. *(having a specific voice)* de voz <*harsh-v.* de voz áspera>; FONÉT. *(said of consonants)* sonoro.

voice·less (vois′lĭs) adj. *(mute)* mudo; FONÉT. *(said of consonants)* sordo.

voice-o·ver (vois′ō′vər) s. CINEM., TELEV. voz del comentador o narrador que no aparece en la imagen *f.*

void (void) I. adj. *(empty)* vacío; *(vacant)* vacante (puesto); *(lacking)* falto, desprovisto <*v. of intelligence* desprovisto de inteligencia>; DER. *(null)* nulo, inválido ♦ **null and v.** DER. nulo y sin valor II. s. *(empty space, emptiness)* vacío; *(in cards)* fallo III. tr. *(to invalidate)* invalidar, anular; *(to empty)* vaciar; FISIOL. *(to evacuate)* evacuar; *(to vacate)* dejar libre o vacante —intr. FISIOL. evacuar.

void·a·ble (voi′də-bəl) adj. anulable.

voile (voil) s. COST., TEJ. gasa.

vo·lant (vō′lənt) adj. *(flying)* volador; *(agile)* ágil; HER. *(with extended wings)* volante.

vol·a·tile (vŏl′ə-tl, -tīl′) adj. *(that evaporates)* volátil, evaporable; *(explosive)* volátil, explosivo; *(changeable)* cambiable, inconstante.

vol·a·til·i·ty (vŏl′ə-tĭl′ĭ-tē) s. volatilidad *f.*

vol·can·ic (vŏl-kăn′ĭk) adj. GEOL. volcánico; FIG. *(explosivo)* explosivo, volcánico.

vol·ca·nism (vŏl′kə-nĭz′əm) s. GEOL. volcanismo, vulcanismo.

vol·ca·no (vŏl-kā′nō) s. [pl. **-noes** o **-nos**] GEOL. volcán *m.*

vole (vōl) s. ZOOL. campañol *m.*

vo·li·tion (və-lĭsh′ən) s. volición *f*, voluntad *f.*

vol·ley (vŏl′ē) s. [pl. **-leys**] *(of missiles, bullets)* descarga, andanada; *(of stones)* lluvia; *(of oaths, insults)* torrente *m*, estallido; *(in tennis)* voleo II. tr. **-leyed, -ley·ing** MIL. lanzar —intr. DEP. volear, lanzar de voleo.

vol·ley·ball (vŏl′ē-bôl′) s. DEP. *(game)* balonvolea, voleibol *m*; *(ball)* balón *m*, pelota de voleibol.

volt¹ (vōlt) s. ELEC. voltio.

volt² (vōlt) s. EQUIT. *(turn)* vuelta (trotando de lado); ESGR. *(avoidance move)* esquiva.

volt·age (vōl′tĭj) s. ELEC. voltaje *m*, tensión *f.*

vol·ta·ic (vŏl-tā′ĭk) adj. ELEC. voltaico; *(galvanic)* galvánico.

voltaic battery s. ELEC. pila voltaica.

vol·tam·e·ter (vōl-tăm′ə-tər) s. ELEC. voltámetro.

volt·am·me·ter (vōlt′ăm′mē′tər) s. ELEC. voltamperímetro.

volt-am·pere (vōlt′ăm′pîr′) s. ELEC. voltamperio.

volt·me·ter (vōlt′mē′tər) s. ELEC. voltímetro.

vol·u·ble (vŏl′yə-bəl) adj. *(talkative)* locuaz; *(rotating)* voluble; BOT. voluble.

vol·ume (vŏl′yōōm) s. volumen *m* ♦ **v. control** botón del volumen • **volumes** gran cantidad, montones.

vol·u·met·ric (vŏl′yōō-mĕt′rĭk) adj. volumétrico.

vo·lu·mi·nous (və-lōō′mə-nəs) adj. *(bulky)* voluminoso; FIG. *(information, data)* abundante; *(prolific)* prolífico.

vol·un·tar·y (vŏl′ən-tĕr′ē) I. adj. *(uncompelled)* voluntario; *(benevolent)* benévolo; *(spontaneous)* espontáneo II. s. [pl. **-ies**] *(volunteer)* voluntario; MÚS. música de órgano.

vol·un·teer (vŏl′ən-tîr′) I. s. voluntario II. adj. *(voluntary)*

voluntario; *(police, army)* de voluntarios III. tr. & intr. *(to offer)* ofrecer(se) o contribuir voluntariamente; MIL. alistar(se) como voluntario.

vo·lup·tu·ar·y (və-lŭp′chōō-ĕr′ē) s. [pl. **-ies**] voluptuoso.

vo·lup·tu·ous (və-lŭp′chōō-əs) adj. voluptuoso, sensual.

vo·lute (və-lōōt′) s. ARQ. *(ornament)* voluta; ZOOL. *(shell whorl)* espira (de una concha) *f*; *(mollusk)* voluta.

vo·lu·tion (və-lōō′shən) s. *(spiral)* espiral *f*; ZOOL. *(whorl)* espira (de una concha).

vom·it (vŏm′ĭt) I. tr. & intr. vomitar II. s. *(act, substance)* vómito; *(emetic)* vomitivo, emético.

voo·doo (vōō′dōō) I. s. [pl. **-doos**] vodú, vudú *f* II. tr. **-dooed, -doo·ing** hechizar, embrujar.

voo·doo·ism (vōō′dōō-ĭz′əm) s. voduismo.

vo·ra·cious (vô-rā′shəs) adj. *(ravenous)* voraz; *(greedy)* glotón.

vor·tex (vôr′tĕks′) s. [pl. **-tex·es** o **-ti·ces** (-tĭ-sēz′)] *(water mass)* vórtice, remolino; FIG. *(whirlpool)* torbellino, vorágine *f.*

vo·ta·ry (vō′tə-rē) s. [pl. **-ries**] *(devotee)* devoto; *(fan)* aficionado.

vote (vōt) I. s. *(ballot, approval)* voto; *(act, result)* votación *f*; *(right)* derecho de voto <*to have the v.* tener el derecho de voto>; *(group of voters)* votos <*the labor v.* los votos de los obreros> ♦ **by a majority v.** por una mayoría de votos • **inconclusive v.** votación nula • **popular v.** votación popular • **secret v.** votación secreta • **to give one's v. to** dar uno su voto a, votar por • **to have** o **to take a v. on something** poner o someter algo a votación • **to put to the v.** poner o someter a votación • **unanimous v.** votación por unanimidad • **v. of censure** voto de censura • **v. of confidence** voto de confianza II. intr. **vot·ed, vot·ing** votar <*to v. for or against* votar por o en contra de> —tr. *(to choose by vote)* votar; *(to approve)* votar, aprobar <*to v. new funds for defense* votar nuevos fondos para la defensa>; *(to elect)* elegir <*it was voted the best movie* fue elegida como la mejor película>; *(to declare)* declarar, proclamar; FAM. *(to suggest)* sugerir, proponer ♦ **to v. down** votar en contra de, rechazar • **to v. in** elegir (por votación) • **to v. out** derrotar en las elecciones (apoyando a la oposición).

vote·less (vōt′lĭs) adj. sin voto.

vot·er (vō′tər) s. votante *mf*, elector *m.*

vot·ing (vō′tĭng) I. s. *(act)* votación *f* II. adj. *(person, public)* votante; *(campaign)* electoral.

voting machine s. máquina de votar, máquina registradora de votos.

vo·tive (vō′tĭv) adj. votivo.

vouch (vouch) tr. *(to verify)* verificar, comprobar; DER. *(to summon)* citar, emplazar (a un testigo); ANT. *(to cite)* citar; *(to assert)* sostener —intr. ♦ **to v. for** avalar, responder por.

vouch·er (vou′chər) s. *(person)* fiador *m*, garante *mf*; *(document)* comprobante *m*, vale *m.*

vouch·safe (vouch-sāf′) tr. **-safed, -saf·ing** dignarse a dar.

vow (vou) I. s. *(promise)* promesa *f*; RELIG. *(pledge)* voto ♦ **to take vows** RELIG. hacer votos monásticos II. tr. *(to pledge)* jurar; *(to promise)* prometer —intr. prometer.

vow·el (vou′əl) s. FONÉT., GRAM. vocal *f.*

voy·age (voi′ĭj) I. s. viaje *m*, travesía II. intr. **-aged, -ag·ing** hacer un viaje, viajar —tr. cruzar, atravesar.

vo·yeur (voi-yûr′) s. mirón (el que goza mirando actos u órganos sexuales) *m.*

vo·yeur·ism (voi-yûr′ĭz′əm) s. goce que se obtiene al mirar actos u órganos sexuales *m.*

Vul·can (vŭl′kən) s. MITOL. Vulcano.

vul·ca·nism (vŭl′kə-nĭz′əm) s. var. de **volcanism**.

vul·ca·nize (vŭl′kə-nīz′) tr. **-nized, -niz·ing** TÉC. vulcanizar.

vul·gar (vŭl′gər) adj. *(common)* común, corriente <*a v. face* una cara común>; *(vernacular)* vulgar, popular; *(indecent)* indecente, verde <*a v. joke* un chiste verde>; *(coarse)* vulgar, ordinario; *(rude)* grosero, vulgar <*don't be v.!* ¡no seas grosero!>.

vul·gar·i·an (vŭl-gâr′ē-ən) s. persona vulgar adinerada.

vul·gar·ism (vŭl′gə-rĭz′əm) s. *(vulgarity)* vulgaridad *f*; FILOL. vulgarismo.

vul·gar·i·ty (vŭl-găr'ĭ-tē) s. [pl. **-ties**] *(condition)* vulgaridad *f; (act)* vulgaridad, grosería.

vul·gar·ize (vŭl'gə-rīz') tr. **-ized, -iz·ing** vulgarizar.

vul·gate (vŭl'gāt', -gĭt) s. *(vernacular)* lenguaje popular *m; (accepted text)* texto comúnmente aceptado ♦ **V.** BÍBL. Vulgata.

vul·ner·a·bil·i·ty (vŭl'nər-ə-bĭl'ĭ-tē) s. [pl. **-ties**] vulnerabilidad *f.*

vul·ner·a·ble (vŭl'nər-ə-bəl) adj. vulnerable ♦ **to be v. to** *(susceptible)* ser susceptible a; *(unprotected)* sentirse indefenso contra.

vul·ture (vŭl'chər) s. *(bird)* buitre *m;* FIG. *(person)* persona rapaz.

vul·va (vŭl'və) s. [pl. **-vae** (-vē')] ANAT. vulva.

vul·vi·tis (vŭl-vī'tĭs) s. MED. vulvitis *f.*

W

w, W (dŭb'əl-yōō) s. [pl. **w's, W's**] vigésima tercera letra del alfabeto inglés.

Wac (wăk) s. miembro del Cuerpo Militar femenino de los EE. UU.

wack·y (wăk'ē) adj. **-i·er, -i·est** JER. loco, chiflado.

wad (wŏd) I. s. *(for stuffing, padding)* taco, tapón *m; (of cotton, money)* rollo, fajo; *(of papers)* lío; *(of straw)* manojo; FIG., FAM. *(large amount)* dineral *m,* montón de dinero *m;* ARM. taco II. tr. **wad·ded, wad·ding** *(to stuff)* rellenar; *(to pad)* forrar; *(a wall, coat)* acolchar; *(an aperture)* tapar; ARM. atacar.

wad·ding (wŏd'ĭng) s. *(stuffing)* taco, tapón *m; (lining)* entretela, forro; *(wad)* fajo; ARM. taco.

wad·dle (wŏd'l) I. intr. **-dled, -dling** *(like a duck)* caminar como pato; *(to sway)* contonearse II. s. *(gait)* contoneo; *(of ducks)* manera de caminar los patos.

wade (wād) I. intr. **wad·ed, wad·ing** *(to walk in, through)* caminar en, cruzar por (nieve, agua); FIG. *(to struggle through)* avanzar con dificultad —tr. vadear ♦ **to w. in** *o* **into** FIG. arremeter con II. s. vadeo.

wad·er (wā'dər) s. *(person)* vadeador *m;* ORNIT. ave zancuda. ♦ **waders** botas altas de vadeo.

wading bird s. ORNIT. ave zancuda.

wa·fer (wā'fər) I. s. *(crisp cake)* barquillo, galletita fina dulce *o* salada; *(seal)* sello de lacre, oblea; RELIG. hostia II. tr. cerrar con un sello de lacre.

waf·fle¹ (wŏf'əl) s. panqueque al estilo de barquillo *m.*

waf·fle² (wŏf'əl) FAM. I. intr. **-fled, -fling** *(to speak)* perorar sin decir ni que sí ni que no; *(to mislead)* engañar II. s. discurso vago y evasivo (escrito u oral).

waffle iron s. molde para hacer barquillos *m.*

waft (wăft, wăft) I. tr. llevar por el aire *o* sobre el agua —intr. flotar II. s. *(of odor, breeze)* soplo, ráfaga; MARÍT. bandera de señales.

wag¹ (wăg) I. intr. **wagged, wag·ging** *(to shake)* agitarse; *(to be active)* moverse; *(to waddle)* contonearse —tr. menear II. s. *(movement)* meneo; *(tail whipping)* coleo.

wag² (wăg) s. *(joker)* bromista *mf.*

wage (wāj) I. s. pago, sueldo *m* ♦ **wages** *(pay)* salarios; FIG. *(recompense)* frutos (de trabajo, esfuerzo) II. tr. **waged, wag·ing** *(war)* hacer; *(a fight)* librar; *(a campaign)* emprender.

wage earner s. *(salaried worker)* asalariado; *(hourly worker)* jornalero; *(household supporter)* persona que mantiene una familia.

wa·ger (wā'jər) I. s. apuesta II. tr. & intr. apostar.

wage scale s. COM., FIN. escala de sueldos.

wag·ger·y (wăg'ə-rē) s. [pl. **-ies**] broma, travesura.

wag·gish (wăg'ĭsh) adj. bromista.

wag·gle (wăg'əl) I. tr. **-gled, -gling** *(to wiggle)* menear rápidamente —intr. *(to move shakily)* agitarse; *(to wobble)* tambalearse II. s. meneo.

wag·on (wăg'ən) I. s. *(horse-drawn vehicle)* carro; *(railway car)* vagón *m; (station wagon)* furgoneta, camioneta; *(table)* carrito (para servir bebidas) ♦ **to be** *o* **to go on the w.**

JER. no beber, dejar de beber II. tr. transportar en vagón —intr. viajar en vagón.

wag·on·load (wăg'ən-lōd') s. vagón (carga) *m.*

wagon train s. *(train)* tren de carga *m; (wagon convoy)* convoy de carretas (en la conquista del oeste) *m.*

waif (wāf) s. *(stray child)* expósito, niño abandonado; *(animal)* animal abandonado; *(object)* bien mostrenco.

wail (wāl) I. intr. *(to grieve audibly)* gemir, lamentarse; *(to howl)* aullar —tr. lamentar II. s. *(cry)* lamento; *(howl)* aullido.

wail·ful (wāl'fəl) adj. *(mournful)* triste; *(sobbing)* sollozante.

wain (wān) s. carro, carreta.

wain·scot (wān'skət, -skŏt', -skŏt') I. s. revestimiento de madera II. tr. revestir con madera.

wain·scot·ing *o* **wain·scot·ting** (wān'skə-tĭng, -skŏt'ĭng) s. *(wall)* zócalo; *(material)* revestimiento para paredes; *(paneling)* entablado.

wain·wright (wān'rīt') s. carretero.

waist (wāst) s. ANAT. *(middle)* cintura; COST. *(garment section)* talle *m; (blouse)* blusa.

waist·band (wāst'bănd') s. COST. *(belt)* cinturón *m; (sash)* pretina.

waist·cloth (wāst'klôth') s. taparrabo.

waist·coat (wĕs'kĭt, wāst'kōt') s. G.B. chaleco.

waist·line (wāst'līn') s. cintura, talle *m.*

wait (wāt) I. intr. *(to remain)* esperar <*w. a moment!* ¡espera un momento!>; *(to work as a waiter)* ser camarero ♦ **to w. up** esperar sin acostarse —tr. *(to await)* esperar <*I'm waiting my turn* estoy esperando mi turno>; *(to delay)* retrasar, aplazar <*to w. lunch* retrasar el almuerzo> ♦ **to w. for** esperar • **to w. on** *o* **upon** *(to serve)* servir, atender; *(to visit)* hacer una visita (de cortesía), presentar los respetos; *(to depend upon)* ser consecuencia de • **to w. on tables** servir, atender • **to w. out** aguardar, esperar a que se termine II. s. espera ♦ **to lie in w.** estar al acecho, acechar.

wait·er (wā'tər) s. *(person)* camarero, mozo; *(tray)* bandeja.

wait·ing (wā'tĭng) s. espera ♦ **in w.** de compañía.

waiting game s. ♦ **to play the w.** dejar pasar el tiempo para sacar una ventaja.

waiting list s. lista de espera.

waiting room s. sala de espera.

wait·ress (wā'trĭs) s. camarera.

waive (wāv) tr. **waived, waiv·ing** *(to relinquish)* renunciar a; *(to refrain)* desistir de; *(to dispense with)* descartar, suspender; *(to put off)* postergar.

waiv·er (wā'vər) s. DER. *(relinquishment)* renuncia; *(document)* documento de renuncia.

wake¹ (wāk) I. intr. **woke** (wōk) *o* **waked** (wākt), **waked** *o* **wo·ken** (wō'kən), **wak·ing** *(to cease to sleep)* despertarse; *(to be awake)* estar despierto ♦ **to w. up** *(after sleep)* despertarse; FIG. *(to be alert)* despabilarse • **to w. up to** FIG. darse cuenta de, llegar a comprender —tr. *(to awaken)* despertar; FIG. *(to alert)* alertar, llamar la atención; *(to revive)* resucitar, despertar <*to w. old animosities* resucitar enemistades antiguas>; *(a corpse)* velar ♦ **to w. up** *(from sleep)* despertar; FIG. *(memories)* despertar; *(somebody)* despabilar II. s. *(vigil)* vigilia, vela; *(over a corpse)* velatorio.

wake² (wāk) s. *(track)* huella; *(of a ship)* estela ♦ **in the w. of** *(after)* inmediatamente después de; *(as a result of)* a raíz de.

wake·ful (wāk'fəl) adj. *(awake)* despierto; *(alert)* alerta, vigilante; *(sleepless)* desvelado, insomne ♦ **to have a w. night** pasar la noche en blanco *o* desvelado.

wak·en (wā'kən) tr. & intr. despertar(se) ♦ **to w. to the point** *o* **fact** FIG. caer en la cuenta.

wale (wāl) I. s. *(welt)* verdugón *m,* cardenal *m;* MARÍT. riostra II. tr. **waled, wal·ing** marcar con verdugones.

Wales (wālz) s. Gales *m.*

walk (wôk) I. intr. *(to move on foot)* caminar, andar <*can't you w. faster?* ¿no puedes caminar más rápido?>; *(to go on foot)* ir caminando, ir a pie <*they had to w. to school today* hoy tuvieron que ir a la escuela a pie>; *(to stroll)* pasear, dar un paseo; *(horse)* ir al paso; *(ghost)* salir, aparecer ♦ **to be out walking** estar dando un paseo • **to w. about** *o*

around pasear(se) • **to w. along** caminar • **to w. away** irse, màrcharse • **to w. in** entrar • **to w. in on** aparecérsele inesperadamente a • **to w. in one's sleep** ser sonámbulo • **to w. off** irse • **to w. on** *(to proceed)* seguir el camino de uno; TEAT. salir a escena • **to w. out** *(to go on strike)* declararse en huelga; *(to leave)* irse • **to w. right in** pasar adelante —tr. *(to traverse)* caminar por, recorrer a pie; *(a distance)* caminar, andar; *(a horse)* llevar al paso; *(to escort)* acompañar, ir caminando con <*he walked her home* fue caminando con ella hasta su casa> ♦ **to w. along** caminar por • **to w. away from** *(a person)* alejarse de; *(problems)* evitar, dar la espalda a; *(a competitor)* dejar atrás; *(an accident)* salir ileso de • **to w. away o off with** llevarse (premio, dinero) • **to w. into** *(a room, building)* entrar en; *(a wall, tree)* chocar contra; *(a trap)* caer en • **to w. on** pisar • **to w. out of** salir de • **to w. out on** FAM. dejar abandonado • **to w. out with** salir con • **to w. over** FAM. *(a person)* tratar como a un perro; *(a person's rights)* pisotear; *(to win)* ganar fácilmente • **to w. the streets** FIG. buscar hombres (una mujer) • **to w. through** TEAT. ensayar rápidamente **II.** s. *(stroll)* paseo; *(hike)* caminata; *(pace)* paso <*at a slow w.* a paso lento>; *(gait)* modo de andar; *(route)* recorrido, ronda; *(promenade)* paseo; *(sidewalk)* acera; *(between trees)* alameda ♦ **people from all walks of life** todo tipo de gente • **to go for o to take a w.** dar un paseo • **to take for a w.** sacar a pasear • **w. of life** *(social class)* condición, esfera; *(occupation)* profesión.

walk·a·way (wô′kə-wā′) s. victoria fácil.

walk·er (wô′kər) s. *(pedestrian)* peatón m; *(stroller)* paseante mf; *(for infants)* andador m, tacataca m; *(shoe)* zapato para caminar.

walk·ie-talk·ie (wô′kē-tô′kē) s. [pl. **-ies**] RAD. receptor-transmisor portátil m, radioteléfono portátil.

walk-in (wôk′ĭn′) adj. *(closet)* tan grande que uno puede entrar en él; *(apartment)* con puerta a la calle; *(services)* que no requiere cita previa.

walk·ing (wô′kĭng) **I.** s. *(act)* andar m; *(walk)* caminata, paseo **II.** adj. *(moving)* ambulante; *(tour)* a pie; *(shoes)* de o para andar.

walking papers s.pl. FAM. nota de despido.

walking stick s. *(cane)* bastón m; ENTOM. caballo de palo.

walk-on (wôk′ŏn′) TEAT. *(role)* papel de figurante m; *(person)* figurante m.

walk·out (wôk′out′) s. *(strike)* huelga; *(quitting)* renuncia (en signo de protesta).

walk·o·ver (wôk′ō′vər) s. FAM. *(easy victory)* victoria fácil; *(pushover)* pan comido.

walk·up o walk-up (wôk′ŭp′) s. *(building)* edificio sin ascensor; *(apartment)* departamento en un edificio sin ascensor.

walk·way (wôk′wā′) s. pasarela, pasillo.

walk·y-talk·y (wô′kē-tô′kē) s. var. de **walkie-talkie.**

wall (wôl) **I.** s. *(of a room)* tabique m, pared f; *(around a house)* muro; *(of city)* muralla; *(of garden)* tapia; FIG. *(obstacle)* barrera <*a w. of fog* una barrera de niebla>; ANAT. pared <*the abdominal w.* la pared abdominal> ♦ **the walls have ears** las paredes oyen • **to drive o push someone to the w.** poner a alguien entre la espada y la pared • **to drive somebody up the w.** volver loco a alguien • **to hit one's head against the w.** FAM. darse uno contra la pared • **with one's back to the w.** acorralado, entre la espada y la pared **II.** tr. poner un muro o una pared a **to w. in o up** *(house, town)* amurallar; *(garden)* tapiar, encerrar con muro; *(person)* emparedar • **to w. off** separar con una pared **III.** adj. de pared, mural <*a w. map* un mapa de pared>.

wall·board (wôl′bôrd′) s. madera prensada, panel m.

wall·et (wôl′ĭt) s. billetera, cartera.

wall·eye (wôl′ī′) s. OFTAL. *(an eye)* ojo albino; *(leukoma)* leucoma m.

wall·eyed (wôl′īd′) adj. *(of whitish eyes)* de ojos albinos; *(having leukoma)* leucomático; *(having strabismus)* estrábico; *(bulging)* de ojos protuberantes.

wall·flow·er (wôl′flou′ər) s. *(flower)* alhelí m; FIG. *(person)* persona que no participa (en bailes, reuniones).

Wal·loon (wŏ-lōōn′) s. & adj. valón m.

wal·lop (wôl′əp) **I.** tr. *(to thrash)* azotar, zurrar; *(to strike)*

pegar con fuerza; *(to defeat)* derrotar —intr. *(to waddle)* contonearse; *(to boil)* hervir (ruidosamente) **II.** s. *(blow)* golpe fuerte m; *(force)* fuerza, impacto <*his punch packs a w.* su golpe tiene mucha fuerza>.

wal·lop·ing (wôl′ə-pĭng) FAM. **I.** adj. *(very large)* muy grande, enorme; *(truly smashing)* verdaderamente grande, impresionante **II.** s. paliza.

wal·low (wôl′ō) **I.** intr. *(in mud, water)* revolcarse; *(in vices, drugs)* sumirse; *(in money)* nadar; *(to move clumsily)* moverse pesadamente **II.** s. *(act)* revuelco; *(of animals)* bañadero.

wall·pa·per (wôl′pā′pər) **I.** s. papel de empapelar m **II.** tr. & intr. empapelar.

wall plug s. ELEC. enchufe m.

wall-to-wall (wôl′tə-wôl′) **I.** adj. *(covering completely)* de pared a pared, completamente cubierto; *(all-inclusive)* total <*w. luxury* lujo total> **II.** s. alfombra de pared a pared.

wal·nut (wôl′nŭt) s. BOT. *(nut)* nuez f; *(tree, wood)* nogal m.

wal·rus (wôl′rəs) s. [pl. **walrus** o **-rus·es**] ZOOL. morsa.

waltz (wôlts) **I.** s. vals m **II.** intr. bailar el vals, valsar —tr. bailar el vals con ♦ **to w. through** FIG., FAM. hacer o pasar como si tal cosa <*she waltzed through the exam* ella pasó el examen como si tal cosa>.

wam·pum (wŏm′pəm) s. *(beads)* cuentas hechas de conchas (usadas como dinero por los indios norteamericanos); JER. *(money)* dinero.

wan (wŏn) **I.** adj. **wan·ner, wan·nest** *(pale)* pálido, macilento; *(weary)* pesaroso; *(melancholy)* melancólico **II.** intr. **wanned, wan·ning** empalidecer.

wand (wŏnd) s. *(magician's rod)* varita mágica; *(musician's baton)* batuta; *(twig)* varilla; *(rod)* vara; DEP. *(archery target)* blanco.

wan·der (wŏn′dər) intr. *(to roam)* errar, vagar; *(to go astray)* desviarse; *(to be incoherent)* desvariar ♦ **to w. off** alejarse —tr. *(to roam through)* vagar o errar por ♦ **to w. away from** apartarse de • **to w. off the point** salirse del tema, irse por las ramas.

wan·der·er (wŏn′dər-ər) s. *(vagabond)* vagabundo, trotamundos mf; *(undecided person)* persona indecisa.

wan·der·ing (wŏn′dər-ĭng) **I.** adj. *(nomadic)* nómada; *(not attentive)* distraído; *(said of the mind)* que desvaría ♦ **the W. Jew** el Judío Errante **II.** s. *(roaming)* vagabundeo; *(delirium)* desvarío; *(rambling digression)* divagación f.

wan·der·lust (wŏn′dər-lŭst′) s. pasión por los viajes f, deseos de viajar.

wane (wān) **I.** intr. **waned, wan·ing** *(to decrease)* disminuir; *(to decline)* declinar; *(to end)* finalizar; ASTRON. menguar (luna) **II.** s. *(diminishing)* disminución f; *(ending)* ocaso; ASTRON. cuarto menguante ♦ **on the w.** en declinación.

wan·gle (wăng′gəl) FAM. **I.** tr. **-gled, -gling** conseguir mañosa o tramposamente —intr. *(to manipulate)* hacer trampa; FIG. *(to extricate)* desenredarse **II.** s. engaño.

wan·ing (wā′nĭng) s. mengua, disminución f.

wan·ness (wŏn′nĭs) s. *(paleness)* palidez f; *(melancholy)* melancolía.

want (wŏnt, wônt) **I.** tr. *(to wish for)* querer <*I w. a glass of milk* quiero un vaso de leche>; *(to desire)* desear, anhelar <*I w. to travel a lot* deseo viajar mucho>; *(to lack)* carecer de, faltar <*he wants talent* carece de talento>; *(to need)* necesitar, hacer falta <*all I w. is sleep* todo lo que necesito es dormir>; *(to request the presence of)* querer ver, querer hablar con <*the boss wants you* el patrón quiere hablar contigo>; *(to seek)* buscar <*he is wanted by the police* lo busca la policía>; *(to ask)* pedir <*how much do you w. for this?* ¿cuánto pide por esto?> ♦ **it wants some doing** exige mucho esfuerzo / hacerlo, no es nada fácil • **to be wanted** *(to be needed)* hacer falta; *(in a place)* ser reclamado <*you are wanted in the office* te reclaman en el despacho> • **not to be wanted** estar de más <*he is not wanted here* él está de más aquí> • **to w. in** FAM. querer ser parte (de), querer participar (en) • **to w. out** FAM. querer irse, no querer saber nada • **wanted** *(by the police)* se busca (asesino, delincuente); *(by an employer)* necesítase <*wanted: waiter* necesítase camarero> —intr. querer <*call me if you w.*

llámame si quieres> ♦ **to w. for** carecer de, hacer falta <*we w. for nothing* no carecemos de nada, no nos hace falta nada> **II.** s. *(lack)* falta, ausencia <*w. of judgment* falta de juicio>; *(need)* necesidad *f; (poverty)* miseria, pobreza; *(wish)* deseo, anhelo ♦ **to be in w. of** *(to need)* necesitar, hacer falta; *(to lack)* carecer de, estar desprovisto de.

want ad s. FAM. aviso, anuncio (en periódico, revista).

want·ing (wŏn′tĭng, wôn′-) **I.** adj. *(absent)* ausente; *(lacking)* falto; *(deficient)* deficiente (calidad, esfuerzo) **II.** prep. *(without)* sin; *(minus)* menos.

wan·ton (wŏn′tən) **I.** adj. *(lewd)* sensual, lascivo; *(unjust)* sin sentido, sin piedad <*w. cruelty* crueldad sin piedad>; *(unrestrained)* desenfrenado; *(luxuriant)* lujuriante, exuberante; *(excessive)* excesivo, extravagante; *(playful)* juguetón; *(undisciplined)* indisciplinado **II.** intr. jugar, juguetear **III.** s. *(libertine)* libertino; *(child)* niño juguetón.

wan·ton·ly (wŏn′tən-lē) adv. *(lasciviously)* lascivamente; *(lacking moderation)* desenfrenadamente, exuberantemente; *(without motive)* sin motivo, gratuitamente.

wan·ton·ness (wŏn′tən-nĭs) s. *(licentiousness)* libertinaje *m; (lack of moderation)* desenfreno; *(exuberance)* exuberancia; *(extravagance)* extravagancia; *(cruelty)* crueldad *f.*

war (wôr) **I.** s. guerra ♦ **the Great W.** o **First World W.** la Primera Guerra Mundial • **the Second World W.** la Segunda Guerra Mundial • **to be at w. with** estar en guerra con • **to declare w. on** o **upon** declarar la guerra a o contra • **to go to w.** declarar la guerra, entrar en guerra • **to make** o **wage w. (on)** hacer la guerra (a) • **w. of nerves** guerra de nervios **II.** adj. guerrero, de guerra ♦ **to be on a w. footing** FIG. estar en pie de guerra • **w. council** consejo de guerra • **w. crime** crimen de guerra • **W. Department** Ministerio de Guerra **III.** intr. **warred, war·ring** estar en guerra, guerrear.

war·ble (wôr′bəl) **I.** tr. **-bled, -bling** cantar trinando —intr. trinar, gorjear **II.** s. *(sound)* gorjeo, trino; *(song)* canto.

war·bler (wôr′blər) s. ORNIT. *(European bird)* curruca; *(American bird)* silvido.

war bonnet s. vincha con cola de plumas (de los indios norteamericanos).

war club s. garrote de guerra (de los indios norteamericanos) *m.*

war cry s. grito de guerra.

ward (wôrd) **I.** s. *(district)* distrito, barrio; *(of hospital)* sala <*maternity w.* sala de maternidad>; *(of jail)* pabellón *m;* DER. *(minor)* pupilo; *(custody)* custodia, tutela; MEC. *(of a lock)* guarda; *(of a key)* muesca **II.** tr. proteger ♦ **to w. off** *(to parry)* parar, desviar; *(to avert)* prevenir, evitar; *(attack)* rechazar.

war dance s. danza de guerra.

war·den (wôr′dn) s. *(prison official)* director *m; (custodian)* guardián *m,* guarda *m;* G.B. *(superintendent)* director.

ward·er (wôr′dər) s. *(guard)* guardia; *(watchman)* centinela *mf;* G.B. *(prison guard)* carcelero.

ward heel·er (hē′lər) s. secuaz de un político de un distrito de la ciudad *mf.*

ward·robe (wôr′drōb′) s. *(closet, cabinet)* armario, guardarropa; *(garments)* vestuario; TEAT. *(costumes)* vestuario; *(storage)* guardarropa.

ward·room (wôrd′rōōm′, -rŏŏm′) s. MARÍT. *(recreation area)* comedor de oficiales *m; (officers)* oficiales *m.*

ward·ship (wôrd′shĭp′) s. *(guardianship)* tutela; *(custody)* custodia.

ware¹ (wâr) s. *(articles)* artículos (de vidrio, plata); *(ceramics)* cerámica, loza ♦ **wares** mercaderías, mercancías.

ware² (wâr) tr. **wared, war·ing** tener cuidado con.

ware·house **I.** s. (wâr′hous′) *(storehouse)* depósito, almacén *m;* G.B. *(shop)* tienda mayorista **II.** tr. (-hous′, -houz′) **-housed, -hous·ing** almacenar, guardar en depósito.

ware·hous·ing (wâr′hou′sĭng, -zĭng) s. almacenamiento.

war·fare (wôr′fâr′) s. *(war)* guerra; *(conflict)* contienda, lucha.

war game s. MIL. maniobras de guerra simuladas.

war·head (wôr′hĕd′) s. MIL. ojiva de proyectil.

war·horse o **war horse** (wôr′hôrs′) s. *(combat horse)* caba-

llo de guerra; FAM. *(veteran)* veterano; MÚS., TEAT. *(hackneyed work)* caballito de batalla.

war·like (wôr′līk′) adj. *(belligerent)* belicoso; *(hostile)* hostil; *(of war)* guerrero; *(martial)* marcial.

war·lock (wôr′lŏk′) s. *(male witch)* brujo; *(sorcerer)* mago.

war·lord (wôr′lôrd′) s. jefe militar *m.*

warm (wôrm) **I.** adj. **-er, -est** *(moderately hot)* tibio, caliente; *(weather)* cálido; *(day, summer)* caluroso, de calor; *(clothing, blanket)* que mantiene abrigado; FIG. *(enthusiastic)* entusiasta, ardiente; *(debate)* acalorado; *(cordial)* caluroso, cordial; *(loving)* afectuoso, cariñoso; *(color)* cálido <*a w. yellow* un amarillo cálido>; *(fresh)* fresco, reciente; *(in finding games)* caliente (en juegos de adivinanzas); FIG., FAM. *(dangerous)* peligroso <*the situation is getting w.* la situación se está poniendo peligrosa> ♦ **toasty w.** FAM. calentito • **to be w.** *(weather)* hacer calor; *(person)* tener calor; *(thing)* estar caliente • **to get w.** *(weather)* empezar a hacer calor; *(person)* entrar en calor; *(thing)* calentarse • **to keep w.** *(thing)* conservar caliente; *(person)* calentar(se), abrigar(se) **II.** tr. *(to make warm)* calentar; FIG. *(one's heart)* alegrar, regocijar; *(one's blood)* calentar ♦ **to w. over** recalentar • **to w. up** *(food)* calentar, recalentar; *(body)* hacer entrar en calor; *(atmosphere, debate)* avivar, animar —intr. calentarse ♦ **to w. to someone** tomarle simpatía a alguien, volverse amistoso con alguien • **to w. up** *(to get warm)* entrar en calor; *(to become animated)* animarse; *(to become enthusiastic)* entusiasmarse **III.** s. FAM. calentamiento.

warm-blood·ed (wôrm′blŭd′ĭd) adj. ZOOL. de sangre caliente; FIG. *(ardent)* ardiente, apasionado.

warm-heart·ed (wôrm′här′tĭd) adj. afectuoso, cariñoso.

warming pan s. calentador de cama *m.*

war·mon·ger (wôr′mŭng′gər) s. belicista *mf,* fomentador de la guerra *m.*

warmth (wôrmth) s. *(heat)* calor *m;* FIG. *(affection)* afecto, amor *m; (friendliness)* calor humano; *(ardor)* ardor *m;* ARTE. *(glow)* calidez (en los colores) *f.*

warm-up (wôrm′ŭp′) s. DEP. calentamiento.

warn (wôrn) tr. *(to caution)* advertir, prevenir; *(to admonish)* amonestar; *(to notify)* poner sobre aviso; *(to apprise)* apercibir —intr. poner sobre aviso, advertir.

warn·ing (wôr′nĭng) **I.** s. *(intimation)* advertencia; *(signal)* señal *f; (advice)* aviso; *(example)* ejemplo, lección *f* ♦ **without w.** *(without notice)* sin aviso; *(suddenly)* de repente **II.** adj. *(cautionary)* de advertencia; *(serving to warn)* de alarma <*a w. device* un dispositivo de alarma>.

warp (wôrp) **I.** tr. *(wood)* alabear, deformar; *(character, behavior)* pervertir; *(yarn, thread)* urdir; FIG. *(meaning)* tergiversar, torcer —intr. *(to become twisted)* alabearse, torcerse; *(to deviate)* pervertirse **II.** s. *(distortion)* alabeo, deformación *f; (in weaving)* urdimbre *f; (mental deviation)* perversión *f.*

war paint s. *(paint)* pintura que ciertas tribus se aplicaban en el cuerpo para ir a la guerra; FAM. *(cosmetics)* maquillaje *m,* cosméticos; *(regalia)* adornos, atavíos.

warp and woof s. TEJ. urdimbre *f* y trama; FIG. estructura, base *f.*

war·path (wôr′păth′, -päth′) s. camino de guerra (de los indios norteamericanos) ♦ **to be on the w.** estar buscando pendencia, estar propenso a pelear.

war·plane (wôr′plān′) s. AER., MIL. avión de guerra *m.*

war·rant (wôr′ənt) **I.** s. *(authorization)* autorización *f; (guarantee)* garantía, comprobante *m; (grounds)* justificación *f;* COM. *(of payment)* mandamiento de pago; *(receipt of deposit)* recibo de depósito; DER. *(of search, arrest)* orden judicial *f* **II.** tr. *(to guarantee)* garantizar; *(to justify)* justificar <*the facts don't w. it* los hechos no lo justifican>; *(to authorize)* autorizar.

war·rant·a·ble (wôr′ən-tə-bəl) adj. *(that can be warranted)* garantizable; *(justifiable)* justificable.

war·ran·tee (wôr′ən-tē′) s. DER. persona que recibe una garantía, persona garantizada.

warrant officer s. MIL. suboficial *m,* oficial asimilado.

war·ran·tor (wôr′ən-tər, -tôr′) s. DER. garante *mf,* fiador *m.*

war·ran·ty (wôr′ən-tē) s. [pl. **-ties**] COM., DER. *(guarantee)*

ã **rey** / ä **año** / b **boca** / ch **chico** / d **dar** / ĕ **el** / ē **mil** / g **gato** / h **joya** / hw **juez** / ī **aire** / k **casa** / kw **cuan** /

garantía; *(grounds)* justificación *f*; *(authorization)* autorización *f*.

war·ren (wôr'ən) s. *(burrow)* madriguera de conejos, conejera; FIG. *(overcrowded place)* colmena, conejera.

war·ri·or (wôr'ē-ər) s. guerrero.

War·saw (wôr'sô') s. Varsovia.

war·ship (wôr'shĭp') s. MARÍT., MIL. buque de guerra *m*.

wart (wôrt) s. verruga.

wart hog s. ZOOL. jabalí verrugoso.

war·time (wôr'tīm') s. época *o* tiempo de guerra.

war·y (wâr'ē) adj. **-i·er, -i·est** *(guarded)* precavido, cauteloso; *(watchful)* cuidadoso.

was (wŏz, wŭz, wəz) pret. de **be**.

wash (wŏsh) **I.** tr. *(to clean)* lavar <*to w. a sweater* lavar un suéter>; *(grease, stains)* quitar; *(dishes)* lavar, fregar; *(to moisten)* mojar, humedecer; *(to lap)* bañar <*waves washing the shores* olas que bañan las playas>; *(river, lake)* regar; *(wound, eyes)* bañar; *(soul)* purificar, limpiar; *(metals)* dar un baño a, dar una capa de metal a; *(gases)* depurar; *(walls)* dar una mano *o* capa de color a; *(to erode)* erosionar ♦ **to w. away** *(grease, stains)* quitar (lavando); *(to carry away)* llevarse, arrastrar ♦ **to w. down** *(to clean)* baldear, limpiar; *(to gulp down)* tragar; *(with wine, beer)* rociar ♦ **to w. off** quitar (lavando) ● **to w. one's hands** FIG. lavarse las manos ● **to w. oneself** lavarse ● **to w. out** *(grease, stains)* quitar (lavando); *(clothes)* lavar; *(to carry away)* llevarse, arrastrar; *(an event)* suspender ● **to w. up** *(dishes)* lavar, fregar; *(to throw)* arrojar —intr. *(oneself)* lavarse; *(clothes)* lavar, lavar ropa; *(without fading)* no perder el color, no desteñir <*this fabric will w.* esta tela no perderá el color> ♦ **to w. along** ser llevado *o* flotar (por el agua) ● **to w. away** derrumbarse ● **to w. off** salir en el lavado ● **to w. out** *(colors)* desteñirse; *(to fail)* fracasar ● **to w. up** *(oneself)* lavarse; *(the dishes)* lavar los platos **II.** s. *(act)* lavado; *(clothes to be washed)* ropa para lavar; *(laundered clothes)* ropa lavada; *(waste liquid)* desperdicio; *(swill)* bazofia; *(fermented liquid)* aguachirle *f*, bebida aguada; *(coating)* baño; *(of paint)* mano, capa; *(erosion)* erosión *f*; *(debris)* depósito, aluvión *m*; *(rush of water, waves)* golpe de agua *m*; *(sound of water, waves)* rumor *m*, murmullo ♦ **it will all come out in the w.** al final todo se arreglará **III.** adj. *(used for washing)* de *o* para lavar; *(washable)* lavable.

wash·a·ble (wŏsh'ə-bəl) adj. lavable.

wash-and-wear (wŏsh'ən-wâr') adj. que no se plancha.

wash·ba·sin (wŏsh'bā'sĭn) s. lavabo.

wash·board (wŏsh'bôrd') s. *(laundry aid)* tabla de lavar; CARP. rodapié *m*.

wash·bowl (wŏsh'bōl') s. lavabo.

wash·cloth (wŏsh'klôth') s. toallita para lavarse el cuerpo *o* la cara.

wash·day (wŏsh'dā') s. día para lavar (ropa) *m*.

washed-out (wŏsht'out') adj. *(lacking color)* descolorido, desteñido; FIG. *(exhausted)* extenuado, agotado.

washed-up (wŏsht'ŭp') adj. FIG. *(unsuccessful)* fracasado; *(finished)* acabado; *(ready to quit)* listo para abandonar.

wash·er (wŏsh'ər) s. *(person)* lavador *m*; MEC. *(disc)* arandela; *(machine)* máquina de lavar (ropa, platos).

wash·er·wom·an (wŏsh'ər-wŏŏm'ən) s. [pl. **-wom·en** (-wĭm'ĭn)] lavandera.

wash·ing (wŏsh'ĭng) s. *(act, process)* lavado; *(clothes to be done)* ropa para lavar; *(laundered clothes)* ropa lavada; *(residue)* residuo ♦ **to do the w.** lavar la ropa ● **washings** lavazas.

washing machine s. máquina de lavar ropa, lavadora.

washing soda s. sosa para lavar.

Wash·ing·ton (wŏsh'ĭng-tən) s. Washington.

wash·out (wŏsh'out') s. *(erosion)* derrubio; FIG. *(failure)* fracaso.

wash·room (wŏsh'rōōm', -rŏŏm') s. baño, servicios.

wash sale s. FIN. venta ficticia de acciones.

wash·stand (wŏsh'stănd') s. lavabo.

wash·tub (wŏsh'tŭb') s. tina de lavar.

wash·wom·an (wŏsh'wŏŏm'ən) s. var. de **washerwoman**.

was·n't (wŏz'ənt, wŭz'-) contr. de **was not**.

wasp (wŏsp) s. ENTOM. avispa.

Wasp *o* **WASP** (wŏsp) s. blanco de religión protestante y ascendencia anglosajona.

wasp·ish (wŏs'pĭsh) adj. FIG. *(slender)* esbelto; *(snappish)* irritable, irascible.

was·sail (wŏs'əl) **I.** s. *(toast)* brindis *m*; *(drink)* bebida hecha con cerveza o vino, manzanas asadas y azúcar; *(festivity)* fiesta, juerga **II.** tr. brindar por.

wast (wăst, wŭst) ANT. pret. de **be**.

wast·age (wā'stĭj) s. *(wear)* desgaste *m*; *(deterioration)* deterioro; *(waste)* desperdicio.

waste (wāst) **I.** tr. **wast·ed, wast·ing** *(money, fortune)* despilfarrar, derrochar; *(time)* perder; *(chance, opportunity)* perder, desaprovechar; *(life, talent)* desperdiciar; *(to exhaust)* agotar, consumir <*the fever wasted him* la fiebre le consumía>; *(to enfeeble)* debilitar; *(to destroy)* destruir, devastar; JER. *(to kill)* matar ♦ **to w. one's breath** FIG. gastar saliva en balde —intr. *(goods)* desperdiciarse, desgastarse; *(time)* perderse; *(strength, vigor)* debilitarse, enflaquecer ♦ **to w. away** disminuir, consumirse **II.** s. *(act, result)* despilfarro, derroche *m*; *(wastage)* pérdidas, desperdicios; *(of time, energy)* pérdida <*it's a w. of time* es una pérdida de tiempo>; *(from an industrial process)* residuos, desechos; *(garbage)* basura; *(uncultivated region)* erial *m*; *(wilderness)* desierto, yermo ♦ **to go to w.** desperdiciarse, no utilizarse **III.** adj. *(useless)* inútil; *(not used)* desperdiciado; *(rejected)* de desecho; *(left over)* sobrante, superfluo; *(residual)* residual; *(land)* baldío, yermo ♦ **to lay w.** devastar, arrasar ● **to lie w.** AGR. quedar sin cultivar.

waste·bas·ket (wāst'băs'kĭt) s. cesto de papeles.

wast·ed (wā'stĭd) adj. *(badly used)* desperdiciado; *(superfluous)* superfluo, innecesario; *(deteriorated)* deteriorado; *(ravaged)* devastado; *(haggard)* demacrado; JER. *(stoned)* drogado.

waste·ful (wāst'fəl) adj. *(given to waste)* despilfarrador; *(extravagant)* derrochador.

waste·land (wāst'lănd') s. *(land)* yermo, páramo; FIG. *(unproductive endeavor)* páramo (artístico, intelectual).

wast·ing (wā'stĭng) adj. *(deteriorating)* en deterioro, en declinación; *(debilitating)* debilitante.

wast·rel (wā'strəl) s. *(waster)* derrochador *m*; *(idler)* vagabundo.

watch (wŏch) **I.** intr. *(to look)* mirar, observar <*first, you have to w.* primero hay que observar>; *(to stay awake)* velar; *(to keep vigil)* vigilar ♦ **to w. out** estar atento, tener cuidado ● **w. out!** ¡ten cuidado! —tr. *(to look at)* mirar, observar; *(to see)* ver <*did you w. the parade?* ¿viste el desfile?>; *(to pay attention to)* fijarse en <*w. him!* ¡fíjate en él!>; *(to guard)* vigilar (a un preso); *(to take care of)* cuidar (niño, animal); *(to stand vigil over)* velar (a un enfermo, muerto); *(to be careful with)* tener cuidado con; *(to observe)* seguir, observar <*to w. the elections* seguir las elecciones> ♦ **to w. for** esperar <*he's watching for a good opportunity* está esperando una buena oportunidad> ● **to w. one's chance** esperar el momento oportuno ● **to w. one's step** FIG. tener cuidado (con lo que uno hace) ● **to w. out for** estar atento a, tener cuidado con ● **to w. over** vigilar, velar **II.** s. *(timepiece)* reloj (de pulsera o bolsillo) *m*; *(act)* vigilia, vela; *(vigilance)* vigilancia; *(watchman)* guarda *m*, vigilante *m*; *(group of persons)* ronda, guardia; MIL. centinela *m*; MARÍT. *(period of time)* guardia; *(crew on duty)* brigada de guardia; *(lookout)* vigía *m*, marinero de guardia ♦ **to be on the w.** estar en alerta o en guardia ● **to keep w.** estar de guardia ● **to keep w. on** *o* **over** vigilar, velar.

watch·dog (wŏch'dôg') s. *(dog)* perro guardián; FIG. guardián *m*, vigilante *m*.

watch·ful (wŏch'fəl) adj. *(observant)* observador; *(alert)* alerta, vigilante.

watch·ing (wŏch'ĭng) s. *(vigilance)* vigilancia; *(observation)* observación *f*.

watch·mak·er (wŏch'mā'kər) s. relojero.

watch·man (wŏch'mən) s. [pl. **-men**] sereno.

watch night s. nochevieja.

watch·tow·er (wŏch'tou'ər) s. atalaya, garita.

watch·word (wŏch'wûrd') s. *(password)* contraseña; *(slogan)* lema *m.*

wa·ter (wô'tər) **I.** s. agua <*a glass of* w. un vaso de agua>; QUÍM. óxido de hidrógeno, agua; FISIOL. *(urine)* orina; *(amniotic fluid)* agua de la placenta; TEJ. *(of a fabric)* aguas (de telas); MARÍT. marea <*high* w. marea alta>; FIN. *(stock)* acciones diluídas; *(assets)* capital inflado; JOY. *(of a diamond)* agua ◆ **drinking w.** agua potable • **like w.** FIG. en gran abundancia • **running w.** agua corriente • **salt w.** agua salada • **to be above w.** estar fuera de peligro • **to be in deep** *o* **hot w.** estar en un gran aprieto *o* estar en apuros • **to hold w.** FIG. ser lógico, tener fundamento • **to keep one's head above w.** FIG. mantenerse a flote • **to pass w.** orinar • **to throw cold w. on** FIG. echar un jarro de agua fría sobre **II.** tr. *(a garden)* regar; *(animals)* dar de beber a, abrevar; *(to pour)* echar agua a; *(to make wet)* mojar, humedecer; *(to dilute)* diluir, aguar; *(to give a sheen to)* tornasolar; FIN. *(to dilute shares)* diluir; *(to inflate assets)* inflar ◆ **to w. down** FIG. suavizar, moderar —intr. *(to shed tears)* llorar; *(to salivate)* hacerse agua, aguarse; *(an animal)* beber agua; MARÍT. suplirse ◆ **to make one's mouth w.** hacérsele agua la boca a uno.

water bed s. cama con colchón de agua.

water bird s. ORNIT. ave acuática.

wa·ter·borne (wô'tər-bôrn') adj. *(floating)* flotante; *(said of freight)* transportado por barco; *(said of a germ)* propagado por agua.

water boy s. aguatero, aguador *m.*

water buffalo s. ZOOL. búfalo de la India.

water clock s. reloj de agua *m.*

water closet s. inodoro, retrete *m*, water *m.*

water color *o* **wa·ter·col·or** (wô'tər-kŭl'ər) s. ARTE. acuarela.

water-color *o* **watercolor** adj. ARTE. de acuarela.

water col·or·ist (kŭl'ər-ĭst) s. ARTE. acuarelista *mf.*

water cooler s. refrigerador de agua *m.*

wa·ter·course (wô'tər-kôrs') s. *(waterway)* vía navegable; *(bed of a waterway)* lecho, cauce *m*; *(channel)* canal *m.*

wa·ter·craft (wô'tər-krăft') s. *(skill)* habilidad *f*; *(boat)* embarcación *f*, barco.

wa·ter·cress (wô'tər-krĕs') s. berro, mastuerzo.

water cure s. hidroterapia, cura de aguas.

wa·ter·fall (wô'tər-fôl') s. catarata, cascada.

wa·ter·fowl (wô'tər-foul') s. [pl. **waterfowl** *o* **-fowls**] ORNIT. ave acuática.

wa·ter·front (wô'tər-frŭnt') s. *(land)* ribera, costanera; *(dock zone)* puerto, muelles *m.*

water gate s. compuerta, esclusa.

water glass s. *(drinking glass)* vaso; *(viewing artifact)* caja con fondo de vidrio; *(gauge)* indicador de nivel *m*; *(clepsydra)* clepsidra, reloj de agua *m*; QUÍM. silicato de sodio.

water heater s. calentador de agua *m.*

water hole s. charco, aguadero.

wa·ter·ing (wô'tər-ĭng) **I.** s. *(of gardens)* riego; *(of fields)* irrigación *f*; *(of wine, spirits)* aguado **II.** adj. *(used in pouring)* de riego; *(said of the eyes)* lloroso.

watering can s. regadera.

watering hole s. *(water hole)* charco, aguadero; FIG. bar *m.*

watering place s. *(water hole)* charco, aguadero; FIG. bar *m.*

watering pot s. regadera.

wa·ter·less (wô'tər-lĭs) adj. *(without water)* sin agua; *(dry)* seco; *(not needing water)* que no necesita agua.

water level s. *(surface level)* nivel de agua *m*; GEOL. nivel hidrostático; MARÍT. línea de flotación.

water lily s. BOT. ninfea, nenúfar *m.*

water line s. MARÍT. *(flotation line)* línea de flotación; *(level mark)* nivel de agua *m.*

wa·ter·logged (wô'tər-lôgd') adj. MARÍT. *(sluggish)* pesado (barco); *(saturated)* saturado de agua.

wa·ter·loo (wô'tər-lōō') s. [pl. **-loos**] ◆ **to meet one's w.** sufrir una derrota terminante.

water main s. cañería principal de agua.

wa·ter·man (wô'tər-mən, wŏt'ər-) s. remero, botero.

wa·ter·mark (wô'tər-märk') **I.** s. *(level indicator)* marca de nivel de agua; *(in paper)* filigrana, marca de agua **II.** tr. imprimir con filigrana.

wa·ter·mel·on (wô'tər-mĕl'ən) s. sandía.

water meter s. medidor *o* contador de agua *m.*

water mill s. molino de agua.

water pipe s. *(conduit)* cañería de agua; *(hookah)* narguile *m*, pipa.

water pitcher s. jarra.

water polo s. water-polo *m.*

wa·ter·pow·er (wô'tər-pou'ər) s. *(energy)* energía hidráulica; *(waterfall)* cascada, salto de agua.

wa·ter·proof (wô'tər-prōōf') **I.** adj. impermeable, resistente al agua **II.** s. *(material)* material impermeable *m*; G.B. *(raincoat)* impermeable *m* **III.** tr. impermeabilizar.

wa·ter·re·pel·lent (wô'tər-rĭ-pĕl'ənt) adj. que repele el agua.

wa·ter·re·sis·tant (wô'tər-rĭ-zĭs'tənt) adj. resistente al agua, hidrófugo.

water right s. *(for irrigation)* derecho de agua; *(for navigation)* derecho ribereño.

wa·ter·shed (wô'tər-shĕd') s. GEOL. línea divisoria (de cauces); *(drainage region)* cuenca; FIG. *(critical point)* momento crítico.

wa·ter·side (wô'tər-sīd') **I.** s. costa, ribera **II.** adj. costero, ribereño.

wa·ter·ski (wô'tər-skē') DEP. **I.** intr. **-skied, -ski·ing** hacer esquí acuático **II.** s. [pl. **-skis** *o* **-ski**] esquí acuático.

water snake s. ZOOL. serpiente de agua *f.*

water softener s. ablandador de agua *m.*

wa·ter·spout (wô'tər-spout') s. *(tornado)* tromba marina; *(pipe)* boquilla (de surtidor).

water supply s. *(available water)* provisión *f o* reserva de agua; *(system)* abastecimiento de agua.

water system s. *(river system)* sistema fluvial *m*; *(water supply)* abastecimiento de agua.

water table s. ARQ. *(ledge)* retallo de derrame; GEOF. *(saturation level)* nivel hidrostático.

wa·ter·tight (wô'tər-tīt') adj. *(impenetrable)* a prueba de agua; *(waterproof)* impermeable; FIG. *(irrefutable)* irrefutable; *(flawless)* perfecto.

water tower s. *(tank)* tanque de agua elevado; *(lifting apparatus)* torre de elevación (usada por bomberos) *f.*

water vapor s. vapor de agua *m.*

wa·ter·way (wô'tər-wā') s. vía fluvial.

water wheel s. rueda hidráulica.

water wings s.pl. salvavidas de natación en forma de alas *m.*

wa·ter·works (wô'tər-wûrks') s.pl. [ú. con v. sing. o pl.] *(system)* sistema de abastecimiento de agua *m*; *(pumping station)* planta de agua potable; *(exhibition)* juegos de agua (fuentes artificiales); JER. *(tears)* lágrimas.

wa·ter·y (wô'tə-rē) adj. **-i·er, -i·est** *(very moist)* acuoso, aguachento; *(liquid)* líquido; *(diluted)* aguado; MED. que secreta agua; FIG. *(without force)* sin fuerza; *(said of colors)* pálido, desteñido; *(insipid)* insípido.

watt (wŏt) s. ELEC., FÍS. vatio, watt *m.*

watt·age (wŏt'ĭj) s. ELEC., FÍS. potencia en vatios.

watt-hour (wŏt'our') s. ELEC., FÍS. vatio-hora *f.*

wat·tle (wŏt'l) **I.** s. *(intertwined branches)* zarzo, estera; ZOOL. carnosidad *f*, barba; ICT. barbilla **II.** tr. **-tled, -tling** *(to construct)* construir con zarzos; *(to weave)* entretejer con zarzos.

watt·me·ter (wŏt'mē'tər) s. ELEC. watímetro, vatímetro.

wave (wāv) **I.** intr. **waved, wav·ing** *(to flutter)* ondear; *(with the hand)* hacer señales con la mano, agitar la mano <*they waved in salute* saludaron agitando las manos>; *(hair)* ondularse —tr. *(to cause to flutter)* agitar, hacer ondear (bandera, abanico); *(a sword)* agitar, blandir; *(a hand)* agitar, hacer señales con; *(hair)* ondular <*to* w. *one's hair* ondularse el pelo> ◆ **to w. aside** *o* **away** echar a un lado, apartar con la mano • **to w. good-bye** decir adiós (agitando el brazo, pañuelo) • **to w. one's fist** amenazar con el puño **II.** s. *(of water)* ola; *(on a surface, hair)* ondulación *f*; *(of a hand)* movimiento; *(gesture)* gesto, ademán *m*; METEOR. *(of cold, hot weather)* ola; FIG. *(of indignation, enthusiasm)* ola, oleada; *(series)* serie *f*, racha <*a* w. *of* *protests throughout the country* una racha de protestas por todo el país>; *(of people)* oleadas <*the immigrants came in waves* los inmigrantes vinieron en oleadas>; FIG., RAD. onda ♦ **the waves** POÉT. el mar, el océano.

wave·band (wāv'bănd') s. RAD. banda de ondas, gama de frecuencias.

wave·length (wāv'lĕngth') s. FÍS. longitud de onda *f* ♦ **to be on the same w.** FIG. estar en la misma onda.

wa·ver (wā'vər) I. intr. *(to sway)* oscilar, balancearse; *(to vacillate)* vacilar, titubear; *(to yield)* ceder <*they wavered under the pressure* cedieron ante la presión>; *(to flicker)* fluctuar, oscilar (llama, luz) II. s. *(oscillation)* oscilación *f,* fluctuación *f; (vacillation)* vacilación *f,* titubeo.

wav·y (wā'vē) adj. **-i·er, -i·est** *(having waves)* ondulante; *(sinuous)* sinuoso, onduloso; *(curly)* ondulado, ondeado <*w. hair* cabello ondulado>.

wax[1] (wăks) I. s. *(substance)* cera; *(cerumen)* cerumen *m,* cerilla (de los oídos) II. tr. encerar.

wax[2] (wăks) intr. *(to enlarge)* crecer <*the enthusiasm waxed among the public* el entusiasmo creció entre el público>; *(the moon)* crecer, aparecer gradualmente ♦ **to w. angry** enojarse ♦ **to w. old** envejecer.

wax·en (wăk'sən) adj. *(of wax)* céreo; *(covered with wax)* encerado; *(like wax)* ceroso, pálido <*w. skin* piel pálida>.

wax·er (wăk'sər) s. encerador *m.*

wax·ing (wăk'sĭng) s. *(polishing)* enceramiento; *(growing)* crecimiento (de la luna).

wax paper s. papel encerado, papel parafinado.

wax·work (wăks'wûrk') s. figura de cera ♦ **waxworks** [ú. con v. sing. o pl.] museo de cera.

wax·y (wăk'sē) adj. **-i·er, -i·est** *(resembling wax)* ceroso; *(covered by wax)* encerado; *(made of wax)* céreo.

way (wā) I. s. *(road, street)* camino, ruta; *(highway)* carretera; *(passage)* pasaje *m,* acceso <*this door is the only w. into the attic* esta puerta es el único acceso a la buhardilla>; *(route)* vía <*the public w.* la vía pública>; *(space)* espacio, camino <*to clear the w. for the parade* despejar el camino para el desfile>; *(direction)* dirección *f* <*he glanced my w.* miró en dirección hacia mí>; *(course)* rumbo, dirección; *(method)* manera, modo <*do it this w.* hazlo de este modo>; *(means)* método, procedimiento <*a w. to cut costs* un método para bajar los costos>; *(mode)* estilo <*the American w. of life* el estilo de vida norteamericano>; *(aspect)* aspecto, respecto <*he resembles his father in many ways* se parece a su padre en muchos aspectos>; *(talent)* facilidad *f* <*she has a w. with words* tiene facilidad de palabra>; FAM. *(condition)* situación *f,* estado <*in a bad w. financially* en mala situación financiera>; *(habit)* hábito, costumbre *f* <*to fall in evil ways* caer en hábitos malos>; *(behavior)* manera de ser, modo de obrar <*to learn the ways of other people* aprender el modo de obrar de otra gente>; *(manner)* modales *m* <*to have a pleasant w.* tener modales agradables>; *(respect)* aspecto, punto <*she's right in some ways* ella tiene razón en algunos aspectos>; *(experience)* experiencia, esfera de acción ♦ **across the w.** enfrente, al otro lado • **a good w. off** a una buena distancia *o* trecho • **a little w. off** cerca de, no muy lejos • **all the w.** *(distance)* por *o* durante todo el camino; *(effort)* hasta el final, hasta el fin; *(completely)* en todo • **a long w. from** lejos de • **a long w. off** muy lejos, lejísimos • **both ways** *(sides)* ambos lados; *(manner)* de las dos maneras • **by the w.** *(on the way)* en el camino, por el camino; *(by the by)* entre paréntesis, a propósito <*by the w., who else is coming?* a propósito ¿quién más viene?> • **by w. of** *(through)* pasando por; *(as a means of)* a título de, a manera de • **each w.** *(side)* de cada lado; *(manner)* en cualquier forma • **in a big w.** en gran escala • **in a small w.** en pequeña escala • **in a w.** en cierto modo, hasta cierto punto • **in every w.** en todos los aspectos, desde todo punto de vista • **in my own w.** a mi modo, a mi manera • **in no w.** de ninguna manera, de ningún modo • **in the w.** de por medio, que obstruye • **no w.** de ninguna manera, de ningún modo • **on the w.** en camino <*your check is on the w.* su cheque está en camino> • **on the w. to** camino de, con rumbo a • **out of my w.!** FAM. ¡quítate de en medio!, ¡fuera de aquí! • **out of the w.** *(out of one's course)* fuera de camino; *(remote)*

lejano, remoto; *(hidden)* escondido; *(disposed of)* hecho, despachado; *(remarkable)* extraordinario, original • **parting of the ways** terminación de una relación • **right of w.** derecho de paso • **that's the w.!** ¡así se hace!, ¡eso es! • **that w.** *(direction)* por allí, por ahí; *(manner)* así, de ese modo • **the other w. around** al contrario, al revés • **there's no w. out** no hay ninguna salida • **the w. of the world** las costumbres de moda • **the w. things are** como están *o* son las cosas • **this w.** *(direction)* por aquí, por acá; *(thus)* así, de este modo • **this w. and that** en todas direcciones • **this w. out!** ¡salgan por aquí! • **to be in the w.** estar en el camino, estorbar • **to be set in one's ways** estar acostumbrado a la forma de uno • **to be under w.** *(ship)* estar navegando; *(to make progress)* estar progresando • **to block the w.** cerrar el paso • **to clear the w.** quitar los obstáculos, despejar el camino • **to come one's w.** presentársele a uno • **to feel one's w.** tantear el camino, proceder con tiento • **to find a w.** encontrar la manera *o* forma de <*we have to find the w. to solve this* tenemos que encontrar la manera de solucionar esto>; *(solution)* encontrar una solución • **to force one's w.** abrirse paso por la fuerza • **to get in the w.** ponerse en medio, obstaculizar • **to get** *o* **have one's w.** salirse con la suya • **to get out of the w.** quitar(se) de en medio • **to get under w.** *(to progress)* avanzar, progresar; *(to set out)* ponerse en camino; *(to weigh anchor)* zarpar • **to give w.** *(to allow to go)* dejar pasar, ceder el paso; *(to retire)* retroceder, ceder • **to give w. to** *(to be replaced by)* ceder el paso a; *(to give in to)* ceder ante; *(to despair)* dejarse llevar por, entregarse a • **to go a long w. towards** contribuir mucho a • **to go one's w.** seguir su camino • **to go out of one's w.** tomarse la molestia de, hacer todo lo posible por • **to have a w. with** tener don de • **to lead the w.** *(to show the way)* enseñar el camino; *(to be first)* ser el primero • **to look the other w.** *(to look away)* mirar al otro lado, desviar la vista; *(to overlook)* hacer la vista gorda, hacerse el que no ve • **to make one's w.** abrirse paso, avanzar • **to make w. for** dar paso a, hacer lugar para • **to mend one's ways** enmendarse, cambiar de vida • **to pave the w. for** preparar el terreno para • **to stand in the w. of** *(to hinder)* obstaculizar; *(to be a hindrance)* ser un obstáculo • **to take the easy w. out** tomar el camino más fácil, optar por la solución más cómoda • **w. down** bajada • **w. in** entrada • **w. out** salida • **ways** MEC. guía, resbaladera • **w. up** subida • **which w.?** ¿por dónde?, ¿en qué dirección? II. adv. allá <*w. over there* allá a lo lejos>.

way·bill (wā'bĭl') s. COM. itinerario, hoja de ruta.

way·far·er (wā'fâr'ər) s. caminante *m,* viajero (que viaja a pie).

way·far·ing (wā'fâr'ĭng) adj. que camina.

way·lay (wā'lā') tr. **-laid** (-lād') **, -lay·ing** *(to lie in wait)* acechar; *(to accost)* abordar; *(to delay)* demorar, detener.

ways and means s.pl. FIN. medios y arbitrios.

way·side (wā'sīd') I. s. orilla *o* borde *m* del camino II. adj. al borde del camino.

way station FIG. estación intermedia, apeadero.

way·ward (wā'wərd) adj. *(naughty)* desobediente, díscolo; *(unpredictable)* caprichoso.

we §G29 (wē) pron. nosotros, nosotras.

weak (wēk) adj. **-er, -est** *(lacking strength)* débil, flojo; *(lacking firmness)* poco sólido, frágil; *(lacking leadership)* poco enérgico; *(lacking skill)* flojo <*a student w. in math* un alumno flojo en matemáticas>; *(faint)* débil, tenue; *(said of health)* débil; *(unconvincing)* poco convincente, flojo; FONÉT. débil ♦ **someone's w. side** el punto débil de alguien • **the weaker sex** el sexo débil, las mujeres • **to grow w.** debilitarse • **to have a w. stomach** FIG. ser cobarde.

weak·en (wē'kən) tr. & intr. debilitar(se), enflaquecer(se).

weak·en·ing (wē'kə-nĭng) I. s. debilitamiento II. adj. debilitante.

weak-kneed (wēk'nēd') adj. tímido, sin carácter.

weak·ling (wēk'lĭng) s. *(weak person)* alfeñique *m,* enclenque *m*; FIG. *(timid person)* tímido, apocado.

weak·ly (wēk'lē) adj. **-li·er, -li·est** enfermizo, enclenque.

weak-mind·ed (wēk'mīn'dĭd) adj. *(irresolute)* irresoluto, indeciso; *(foolish)* tonto, mentecato; *(feeble-minded)* falto de inteligencia.

weak·ness (wĕk'nĭs) s. MED. debilidad *f,* debilitamiento; *(failing)* punto flaco o débil; *(fondness)* debilidad <*a w. for cookies* debilidad por las galletitas>.

weal¹ (wĕl) s. *(prosperity)* prosperidad *f,* felicidad *f; (general good)* bienestar general o público.

weal² (wĕl) s. *(welt)* cardenal *f,* roncha.

wealth (wĕlth) s. *(riches)* riqueza; *(affluence)* opulencia; *(profusion)* profusión *f,* abundancia <*a w. of information* una abundancia de información>; ECON. caudal *m.*

wealth·i·ness (wĕl'thē-nĭs) s. riqueza, opulencia.

wealth·y (wĕl'thē) adj. **-i·er, -i·est** rico, adinerado.

wean (wēn) tr. *(a child, animal)* destetar; *(to give up)* desacostumbrar, dejar <*to w. oneself from cigarettes* dejar de fumar>.

wean·ling (wēn'lĭng) s. animal destetado.

weap·on (wĕp'ən) I. s. *(instrument, means)* arma; MIL. arma, proyectil *m;* BOT., ZOOL. defensa II. tr. armar, suplir con armas.

weap·on·ry (wĕp'ən-rē) s. armamento, armas.

wear¹ (wâr) I. tr. **wore** (wôr), **worn** (wôrn), **wear·ing** *(clothes)* llevar, tener puesto <*to w. a dress* llevar un vestido>; *(to put on)* ponerse; *(shoes)* calzar; *(objects)* llevar, tener <*he always wears a gun* siempre lleva arma>; *(smile, look)* tener; *(hair, nails)* llevar, tener <*she wears her hair long* lleva el pelo largo>; FIG. *(to damage)* deteriorar, desgastar; *(to exhaust)* agotar <*his stubbornness wore my patience* su terquedad me agotó la paciencia> ♦ **to w. away** *(to damage)* desgastar; *(time)* pasar lentamente • **to w. black** estar vestido de negro • **to w. down** *(to damage)* gastar, desgastar; *(to exhaust)* agotar • **to w. off** raer, gastar • **to w. out** *(to consume)* gastar, consumir; *(to tire)* cansar, agotar • **to w. one's age well** conservarse bien, no representar la edad que uno tiene —intr. *(to last)* durar, conservarse; *(to break down through use)* gastarse, desgastarse ♦ **to w. away** *(pain)* atenuarse, disminuir; *(time)* pasar lentamente • **to w. down** *(to become worn)* gastarse, desgastarse; *(to exhaust)* agotarse • **to w. off** *(to diminish)* disminuir, disiparse; *(to disappear)* desaparecer • **to w. thin** disminuir, estar acabándose • **to w. on** pasar lentamente • **to w. out** raerse, gastarse II. s. *(use)* uso <*for everyday w.* para uso diario>; *(clothing)* ropa <*children's w.* ropa para niños>; *(damage or diminution)* desgaste *m,* deterioro <*engine w.* desgaste del motor>; *(durability)* resistencia, durabilidad *f.*

wear² (wâr) tr. **wore** (wôr), **worn** (wôrn), **wear·ing** MARÍT. hacer virar a sotavento —intr. virar a sotavento.

wear·a·ble (wâr'ə-bəl) adj. *(for wear)* que se puede usar; *(capable of being worn)* desgastable ♦ **wearables** ropas, vestidos.

wear and tear s. desgaste *m,* deterioro.

wear·er (wâr'ər) s. persona que lleva o usa.

wea·ried (wîr'ēd) adj. *(tired)* cansado, fatigado; *(annoyed)* enfadado, fastidiado.

wear·ing (wâr'ĭng) adj. *(of clothing)* para vestir <*w. apparel* ropa para vestir>; *(tiring)* fatigoso, agotador.

wea·ri·some (wîr'ē-səm) adj. *(fatiguing)* fatigoso; *(tedious)* tedioso, aburridor.

wea·ry (wîr'ē) I. adj. **-ri·er, -ri·est** *(tired)* cansado, fatigado; *(annoyed)* fastidiado; *(wearisome)* fatigoso II. tr. **-ried, -ry·ing** *(to tire)* cansar, fatigar; *(to bore)* aburrir; *(to annoy)* fastidiar —intr. *(to become tired)* cansarse, fatigarse; *(to become annoyed)* aburrirse, aburrirse.

wea·sel (wē'zəl) I. s. ZOOL. comadreja; JER. *(sneak)* chivato, soplón *m* II. intr. ser evasivo, emplear subterfugios.

weath·er (wĕth'ər) I. s. METEOR. *(atmosphere)* tiempo <*bad w.* mal tiempo>; *(storm)* tormenta, mal tiempo ♦ **to be under the w.** FAM. *(indisposed)* estar indispuesto; *(drunk)* estar borracho II. tr. *(to expose to the weather)* exponer a la intemperie; *(to outride)* aguantar, hacer frente a *(tormenta, dificultad)*; MARÍT. *(ship)* pasar a barlovento —intr. *(to deteriorate)* deteriorarse; *(the skin)* curtirse; *(wood)* curarse; *(to resist)* resistir <*some paints w. better* ciertas pinturas resisten mejor> ♦ **to w. through** FIG., FAM. salir de apuros III. adj. METEOR. meteorológico, del

tiempo; MARÍT. de barlovento • **w. forecast** boletín meteorológico, pronóstico del tiempo;

weather balloon s. METEOR. globo, sonda *m.*

weath·er·beat·en (wĕth'ər-bēt'n) adj. *(worn by exposure)* deteriorado por la intemperie; *(leathery)* curtido por el viento.

weath·er·board (wĕth'ər-bôrd') s. CARP., CONSTR. tabla de chilla, tabla solapada; MARÍT. lado del viento.

weath·er·bound (wĕth'ər-bound') adj. cancelado o detenido por mal tiempo.

weather bureau s. servicio meteorológico.

weath·er·cock (wĕth'ər-kŏk') s. *(weather vane)* veleta, giraldilla; FIG. *(person)* veleta, persona inconstante.

weath·ered (wĕth'ərd) adj. *(seasoned)* curtido por la intemperie; ARQ. inclinado.

weath·er·ing (wĕth'ər-ĭng) s. GEOL. desgaste de las rocas por acción atmosférica *m.*

weath·er·man (wĕth'ər-măn') s. [pl. **-men** (-mĕn')] FAM. meteorólogo.

weather map s. METEOR. mapa meteorológico.

weath·er·proof (wĕth'ər-prōōf') I. adj. a prueba de la intemperie, que resiste a la intemperie II. tr. hacer a prueba de la intemperie, hacer resistente a la intemperie.

weather report s. boletín meteorológico.

weather station s. METEOR. estación meteorológica.

weath·er·strip (wĕth'ər-strĭp') tr. **-stripped, -strip·ping** proveer de burletes a (ventana, puerta).

weather stripping s. *(material)* burlete *m; (work)* acondicionamiento con burletes.

weather vane s. veleta.

weave (wēv) I. tr. **wove** (wōv), **wo·ven** (wō'vən), **weav·ing** *(yarns, threads)* tejer; *(to interlace)* entrelazar, entretejer; *(to spin)* hilar; FIG. *(to scheme)* tejer, urdir ♦ **to w. one's way** *(through a crowd)* abrirse paso; *(through traffic)* zigzaguear para avanzar —intr. *(at a loom)* tejer; *(to become interlaced)* entrelazarse; *(through traffic)* zigzaguear II. s. tejido.

weav·er (wē'vər) s. *(person)* tejedor *m;* ORNIT. tejedor.

weav·ing (wē'vĭng) I. s. *(weave)* tejido; *(art)* tejeduría II. adj. de tejer, para tejer.

web (wĕb) s. *(fabric)* tejido, tela; *(of a spider)* telaraña; *(network)* red *f; (of lies)* sarta; ANAT., ZOOL. membrana; *(of a feather)* barba; *(of a saw)* hoja, cuchilla; TIP. *(roll of paper)* bobina de papel.

webbed (wĕbd) adj. *(having a web)* tejido; ORNIT. palmeado.

web·bing (wĕb'ĭng) s. *(strip)* cincha, correa tejida; *(weave)* tejedura, tejido.

we·ber (wĕb'ər) s. FÍS. wéber *m,* unidad de flujo magnético *f.*

web-foot·ed (wĕb'fŏŏt'ĭd) adj. ORNIT. palmeado, palmípedo.

wed (wĕd) tr. **wed·ded, wed** o **wed·ded, wed·ding** *(to take spouse)* casarse con, tomar por esposo o esposa; *(to join in matrimony)* casar, unir en matrimonio; FIG. *(to unite)* unir, aunar —intr. casarse, contraer matrimonio.

we'd (wēd) contr. de **we had, we should,** o **we would.**

wed·ding (wĕd'ĭng) I. s. *(act)* boda, casamiento; *(anniversary)* bodas <*a silver w.* bodas de plata>; FIG. *(bond)* enlace *m,* unión *f* II. adj. de boda, nupcial <*w. dress* traje nupcial>.

wedding ring s. anillo de boda, sortija de matrimonio.

wedge (wĕj) I. s. *(for splitting)* cuña; *(slice)* trozo, pedazo; *(for securing)* calce *m,* calzo; *(for shoes)* cuña; TIP. cuña de fijación; DEP., MIL. *(arrangement)* formación en cuña *f* ♦ **to drive a w. between** o **into** FIG. separar, desunir II. tr. *(to split)* partir (con cuña); *(to fix in place)* poner cuñas a, calzar; FIG. *(to crowd)* apretar.

wed·lock (wĕd'lŏk') s. matrimonio, casamiento ♦ **out of w.** bastardo, ilegítimo.

Wednes·day (wĕnz'dē) s. miércoles *m.*

wee (wē) adj. **we·er, we·est** pequeñito, diminuto ♦ **the w. hours of the morning** las primeras horas de la mañana, el amanecer.

weed¹ (wĕd) I. s. BOT. *(undesired plant)* mala hierba, maleza; *(seaweed)* alga; FIG., FAM. *(tobacco)* tabaco; *(ciga-*

rette) pitillo; JER. *(marijuana)* marihuana **II.** tr. desherbar, escardar ♦ **to w. out** *(a plant)* arrancar; FIG. *(something unwanted)* extirpar, eliminar —intr. arrancar la maleza.

weed² (wēd) s. brazalete negro, franja de luto ♦ **weeds** ropa de luto de una viuda.

weed·er (wē′dər) s. escardador *m.*

weed·y (wē′dē) adj. **-i·er, -i·est** *(full of weeds)* lleno de malas hierbas, cubierto de maleza; FIG. *(spindly)* larguirucho; *(gawky)* desgarbado.

week (wēk) s. semana <*last w.* la semana pasada> ♦ **a w. per semana** <*I see him twice a w.* le veo dos veces por semana> • **a w. from today** dentro de una semana, de hoy en ocho días • **Holy W.** Semana Santa • **two weeks from today** de hoy en quince días • **w. by w.** todas las semanas, cada semana • **w. in w. out** *o* **w. after w.** semana tras semana.

week·day (wēk′dā′) s. día de trabajo *m*, día laborable.

week·end (wēk′ĕnd′) **I.** s. fin de semana *m* **II.** intr. pasar el fin de semana.

week·ly (wēk′lē) **I.** adv. semanalmente, por semana **II.** adj. semanal **III.** s. [pl. **-lies**] semanario, publicación semanal *f.*

weep (wēp) **I.** tr. **wept** (wĕpt), **weep·ing** *(to mourn)* llorar, llorar por; *(to lament)* lamentar, deplorar; *(tears)* derramar, verter; MED. *(to discharge)* supurar; FIG. *(a wall)* rezumar ♦ **to w. one's eyes out** llorar a lágrima viva —intr. *(to cry)* llorar; *(to grieve)* apenarse, dolerse; FIG. *(to drip)* gotear, sudar **II.** s. ♦ **weeps** llanto, lágrimas.

weep·er (wē′pər) s. *(one that weeps)* llorador *m*, llorón *m*; *(hired mourner)* plañidera; *(mourning badge)* brazalete *m.*

weep·ing (wē′pĭng) adj. *(tearful)* lloroso, plañidero; *(dropping rain)* lluvioso, que trae lluvia; BOT. llorón.

weeping willow s. BOT. sauce llorón *m.*

wee·vil (wē′vəl) s. ENTOM. gorgojo, mordihuí *m.*

weft (wĕft) s. TEJ. *(woof)* trama; *(woven fabric)* tela tejida.

weigh¹ (wā) tr. *(with a scale)* pesar; *(with the hand)* sopesar; FIG. *(in one's mind)* medir, pesar; MARÍT. levar (anclas) ♦ **to w. down** *(to overburden)* sobrecargar; FIG. *(to oppress)* abrumar, oprimir • **to w. out** *o* **up** pesar —intr. *(to have a weight)* pesar <*it weighs two kilos* pesa dos kilos>; FIG. *(to have influence)* pesar, influir ♦ **to w. in** *(jockey, boxer)* pesarse *o* ser pesado; *(with an argument, comment)* intervenir • **to w. with** importar a, tener importancia para.

weigh² (wā) s. ♦ **under w.** MARÍT. en camino, en marcha.

weigh·er (wā′ər) s. pesador *m.*

weigh·ing (wā′ĭng) **I.** s. peso, pesada **II.** adj. de pesar, para pesar.

weight (wāt) **I.** s. *(heaviness)* peso; *(unit measure)* peso <*a system of weights and measures* un sistema de pesos y medidas>; *(measured heaviness)* pesa <*put a two-pound w. on the scale* pon una pesa de dos libras en la balanza>; *(of clock)* pesa; DEP. peso; FIG. *(burden)* peso, carga <*the w. of responsibilities* la carga de las responsabilidades>; *(preponderance)* preponderancia, peso <*the w. of evidence* el peso de la evidencia>; *(importance)* importancia, peso <*a person of no w.* una persona de poca importancia>; *(authority)* autoridad *f* <*he carries no w.* no tiene autoridad>; *(force)* fuerza, peso (de golpe, palabras, decisión) ♦ **by w.** por peso • **gross w.** peso bruto • **net w.** peso neto • **to lift a w. off one's mind** FIG. quitarle a uno un peso de encima • **to lose w.** adelgazar • **to pull one's w.** FIG. hacer su parte • **to put on w.** engordar • **to throw one's w. around** FIG. darse importancia **II.** tr. *(to add heaviness to)* añadir peso a; *(to hold down)* sujetar con un peso; FIG. *(to burden)* cargar (con responsabilidades); *(statistically)* ponderar, dar valor a.

weight·i·ness (wā′tē-nĭs) s. *(heaviness)* pesadez *f*, ponderosidad *f*; *(importance)* importancia, peso.

weight·less (wāt′lĭs) adj. sin peso, ingrávido.

weight lifter s. DEP. levantador de pesas *m.*

weight·lift·ing (wāt′lĭf′tĭng) s. DEP. levantamiento de pesas.

weight·y (wā′tē) adj. **-i·er, -i·est** *(heavy)* pesado; FIG. *(burdensome)* gravoso, opresivo; *(momentous)* trascendental, de suma importancia; *(influential)* de peso, influyente.

weir (wîr) s. presa.

weird (wîrd) **I.** adj. **-er, -est** *(unearthly)* sobrenatural; *(eerie)* misterioso; FAM. *(strange)* raro, extraño **II.** s. destino, sino.

weird·o (wîr′dō) s. [pl. **-oes**] JER. persona estrafalaria.

welch (wĕlch) v. var. de **welsh.**

wel·come (wĕl′kəm) **I.** adj. *(gladly received)* bienvenido, recibido con agrado; *(agreeable)* grato, agradable ♦ **you're w.!** ¡no hay de qué!, ¡de nada! • **you are w. to it** está a su disposición **II.** s. *(greeting)* saludo de bienvenida; *(act)* bienvenida, buena acogida **III.** tr. *(to greet)* dar la bienvenida a; *(to accept)* acoger *o* aceptar con beneplácito **IV.** interj. ¡bienvenido!

weld (wĕld) **I.** tr. METAL. soldar; FIG. *(to bring together)* unir, juntar —intr. soldarse **II.** s. METAL. soldadura.

weld·er (wĕl′dər) s. soldador *m.*

weld·ing (wĕl′dĭng) **I.** s. soldadura **II.** adj. de soldar, para soldar.

wel·fare (wĕl′fâr′) s. *(health)* salud *f*, bienestar *m*; *(happiness)* felicidad *f*; *(prosperity)* prosperidad *f*; *(work)* trabajo social *o* de beneficencia; *(benefits)* asistencia social ♦ **to be on w.** recibir asistencia social.

welfare state s. SOCIOL. estado de asistencia y seguridad social; POL. estado benefactor.

well¹ (wĕl) **I.** s. *(of water, oil)* pozo <*to drill a w.* perforar un pozo>; *(spring)* fuente *f*, manantial *m*; *(for holding a liquid)* depósito; CONSTR. *(for stairs, elevator)* caja; FIG. *(source)* fuente *f.* **II.** intr. *(tears)* fluir, manar; *(feelings)* brotar —tr. verter, derramar.

well² §G28 (wĕl) **I.** adv. **better** (bĕt′ər), **best** (bĕst) *(in a good manner)* bien <*they behaved w.* se portaron bien>; *(satisfactorily, sufficiently)* adecuadamente, bien <*I slept w.* dormí bien>; *(reasonably)* razonablemente, honestamente <*I can't very w. say no* honestamente, no puedo decir que no>; *(perfectly)* perfectamente, claramente <*they w. understood her meaning* entendieron perfectamente lo que ella quería decir>; *(to a considerable extent)* muy <*I am w. pleased* estoy muy satisfecho>; *(with careful attention)* atentamente, cuidadosamente <*listen w.* escuchen atentamente> ♦ **as w.** también, y además • **as w. as** *(additionally)* así como también, además de; *(just as)* así como • **that is just as w.** es mejor así • **to do w.** prosperar, progresar • **w. ahead** muy adelante • **w. done!** ¡bravo!, ¡bien hecho! • **w. over** *(quantity)* mucho más; *(in age)* mayor de **II.** adj. *(in good health)* bien <*she is quite w.* se siente bastante bien>; *(prudent)* prudente <*it would be w. not to ask* mejor sería no preguntar> ♦ **to get w.** mejorar, reponerse • **very w.** muy bien • **w. and good** tanto mejor, muy bien **III.** interj. ¡vaya!, ¡bueno!

we'll (wēl) contr. de **we shall** *o* **we will.**

well-aged (wĕl′ājd′) adj. añejo.

well-ap·point·ed (wĕl′ə-poin′tĭd) adj. bien amueblado, bien equipado.

well-bal·anced (wĕl′băl′ənst) adj. *(proportioned)* bien equilibrado; FIG. *(round)* equilibrado, sensato.

well-be·haved (wĕl′bĭ-hāvd′) adj. bien educado, de buena conducta.

well-be·ing (wĕl′bē′ĭng) s. bienestar *m*, comodidad *f.*

well-born (wĕl′bôrn′) adj. bien nacido, de buena familia.

well-bred (wĕl′brĕd′) adj. *(person)* bien criado, bien educado; *(animal)* de buena raza.

well-de·fined (wĕl′dĭ-fīnd′) adj. *(said of features)* bien definido; *(accurate)* preciso, bien definido.

well digger s. pocero.

well-dis·posed (wĕl′dĭ-spōzd′) adj. bien dispuesto, bien intencionado.

well-done (wĕl′dŭn′) adj. CUL. *(meat)* bien cocido, bien asado; *(properly accomplished)* bien hecho.

well-fed (wĕl′fĕd′) adj. *(properly nourished)* bien alimentado, bien nutrido; *(overfed)* regordete, rollizo.

well-fixed (wĕl′fĭkst′) adj. FAM. acomodado, adinerado.

well-found·ed (wĕl′foun′dĭd) adj. bien fundado, bien fundamentado.

well-groomed (wĕl′grōōmd′, -grōōmd′) adj. *(person)* bien arreglado, acicalado; *(animal, lawn)* bien cuidado.

well-ground·ed (wĕl′groun′dĭd) adj. *(well-founded)* bien fundado, bien fundamentado; *(properly versed)* bien versado.

well·head (wĕl′hĕd′) s. *(spring)* manantial *m;* FIG. *(source)* fuente *f.*

well-heeled (wĕl′hēld′) adj. JER. pudiente, rico.

well-in·ten·tioned (wĕl′ĭn-tĕn′shənd) adj. bien intencionado.

well-known (wĕl′nōn′) adj. *(famous)* bien conocido, famoso; *(widely known)* notorio, sabido.

well-man·nered (wĕl′măn′ərd) adj. de buenos modales, cortés.

well-mean·ing (wĕl′mē′nĭng) adj. bien intencionado.

well-meant (wĕl′mĕnt′) adj. honesto, bien intencionado.

well-nigh (wĕl′nī′) adv. ANT., POÉT. casi.

well-off (wĕl′ôf′) adj. próspero, acomodado.

well-read (wĕl′rĕd′) adj. leído, ilustrado.

well-round·ed (wĕl′roun′dĭd) adj. acabado, completo.

well-spo·ken (wĕl′spō′kən) adj. *(speech)* bien dicho, acertado; *(person)* bienhablado, que se expresa bien.

well·spring (wĕl′sprĭng′) s. *(fountainhead)* manantial *m,* fuente *f;* FIG. *(source)* fuente, origen *m.*

well-thought-of (wĕl-thôt′ŭv′, -ŏv′) adj. bien considerado, de buena reputación.

well-timed (wĕl′tīmd′) adj. oportuno.

well-to-do (wĕl′tə-dōō′) adj. próspero, acomodado.

well-turned (wĕl′tûrnd′) adj. MEC. bien torneado, redondeado *(pieza)*, FIG. *(ankle)* bien torneado; *(sentence)* bien construido, elegante.

well-wish·er (wĕl′wĭsh′ər) s. persona que desea el bien de otra.

well-worn (wĕl′wôrn′) adj. *(worn-out)* desgastado, raído; *(hackneyed)* trillado; *(properly worn)* usado con propiedad.

welsh (wĕlsh, wĕlch) intr. ♦ **to w. on** JER. estafar.

Welsh (wĕlsh) adj. & s. [pl. **Welsh**] galés *m* ♦ **the W.** los galeses.

Welsh·man (wĕlsh′mən) s. [pl. **-men**] galés *m.*

Welsh rabbit *o* **Welsh rare·bit** (râr′bĭt′) s. CUL. pan tostado con queso derretido.

Welsh·wom·an (wĕlsh′wŏŏm′ən) s. [pl. **-wom·en** (-wĭm′ĭn)] galesa.

welt (wĕlt) I. s. *(of a shoe)* vira; COST. *(welting)* vivo, ribete *m;* *(injury to skin)* verdugón *m,* roncha; FAM. *(beating)* latigazo *o* azotazo que causa un verdugón II. tr. *(raise a weal on)* levantar un verdugón; COST. *(to trim)* rivetear.

wel·ter (wĕl′tər) I. intr. *(to wallow)* revolcarse; *(the sea)* elevarse, hincharse II. s. confusión *f,* revoltijo.

wel·ter·weight (wĕl′tər-wāt′) s. DEP. pugilista peso welter *m,* welter *m.*

wen (wĕn) s. MED. lobanillo, quiste cebáceo.

wench (wĕnch) I. s. *(girl)* moza, muchacha; *(servant)* criada, sirvienta; ANT. *(prostitute)* ramera, prostituta II. intr. andar con prostitutas.

wend (wĕnd) tr. ♦ **to w. one's way** dirigirse a —intr. seguir uno su camino, ir.

went (wĕnt) pret. de **go.**

wept (wĕpt) pret. y part. p. de **weep.**

were (wîr) pret. de **be.**

we're contr. de **we are.**

were·n't (wûrnt, wûr′ənt) contr. de **were not.**

were·wolf (wîr′wŏŏlf′, wûr′-, wâr′-) s. [pl. **-wolves** (-wŏŏlvz′)] hombre lobo, licántropo.

west (wĕst) I. s. oeste *m,* occidente *m* ♦ **the W.** *(of the world)* el Occidente; *(in U.S.)* el Oeste II. adj. del oeste, occidental III. adv. al oeste, hacia el oeste ♦ **w. of** al oeste de.

West Berlin s. Berlín Occidental *m.*

west·bound (wĕst′bound′) adj. con rumbo al oeste.

west by north I. s. oeste cuarta al noroeste *m* II. adj. del oeste cuarta al noroeste III. adv. a *o* hacia el oeste cuarta al noroeste.

west by south I. s. oeste cuarta al sudoeste *m* II. adj. del oeste cuarta al sudoeste III. adv. a *o* hacia el oeste cuarta al sudoeste.

west·er·ly (wĕs′tər-lē) I. adj. & adv. *(in or toward the west)*

en *o* hacia el oeste; *(from the west)* del oeste II. s. [pl. **-lies**] viento *o* tormenta del oeste.

west·ern (wĕs′tərn) I. adj. occidental, del oeste ♦ **W.** *(occidental)* occidental; RELIG. *(said of the church)* latina, católica romana II. s. habitante del oeste *m* ♦ **W.** CINEM. película del oeste.

west·ern·er (wĕs′tər-nər) s. *(inhabitant)* habitante del oeste *m,* occidental *m;* *(of the western United States)* norteamericano del oeste.

Western Hemisphere s. hemisferio occidental.

west·ern·ize (wĕs′tər-nīz′) tr. **-ized, -iz·ing** occidentalizar.

west·ern·most (wĕs′tərn-mōst′) adj. el más occidental.

West Germany s. Alemania Occidental.

West Indian adj. & s. antillano.

West Indies s.pl. Indias Occidentales, las Antillas.

west-north-west (wĕst′nôrth-wĕst′) I. s. oesnoroeste *m* II. adj. del oesnoroeste III. adv. a *o* hacia el oesnoroeste.

west-south-west (wĕst′south-wĕst′) I. s. oessudoeste *m* II. adj. del oessudoeste III. adv. a *o* hacia el oessudoeste.

west·ward (wĕst′wərd) I. adv. hacia el oeste II. adj. occidental, del oeste III. s. región occidental *f.*

wet (wĕt) I. adj. **wet·ter, wet·test** *(soaked)* mojado, empapado; *(humid)* húmedo; *(rainy)* lluvioso; *(paint, ink)* fresco ♦ **all w.** JER. totalmente equivocado • **to be soaking w.** estar calado hasta los huesos, estar hecho una sopa • **to be w. behind the ears** FIG. ser un imberbe II. s. *(moisture)* mojadura, humedad *f;* *(rainy weather)* tiempo lluvioso *o* húmedo; FIG., FAM. *(one opposed to Prohibition)* antiprohibicionista (en EE. UU.) *mf* III. tr. **wet** *o* **wet·ted, wet·ting** *(to dampen)* mojar, humedecer; *(by urination)* mojar, orinar ♦ **to w. one's whistle** FIG., FAM. beber un trago, mojar el gaznate —intr. mojarse, empaparse.

wet·back (wĕt′băk′) s. DESPEC., JER. bracero mejicano que entra ilegalmente a EE. UU.

wet blanket s. FIG., FAM. aguafiestas *mf.*

wet cell s. ELEC. pila húmeda.

weth·er (wĕth′ər) s. ZOOL. carnero castrado.

wet·land (wĕt′lănd′) s. tierra húmeda, tierra pantanosa.

wet nurse s. ama de leche *o* de cría, nodriza.

wet suit s. DEP. traje húmedo (usado para retener el calor del cuerpo).

we've (wēv) contr. de **we have.**

whack (hwăk) I. tr. FAM. *(to hit)* pegar, golpear —intr. dar golpes, dar una paliza ♦ **to have** *o* **take a w. at** intentar, probar II. s. *(blow)* golpe fuerte *m,* bofetón *m;* *(attempt)* intento, prueba ♦ **out of w.** fuera de servicio, averiado.

whack·y (hwăk′ē) adj. var. de **wacky.**

whale¹ (hwāl) I. s. ZOOL. ballena ♦ **a w. of a sale** una gran venta, gran liquidación II. intr. **whaled, whal·ing** cazar ballenas.

whale² (hwāl) tr. **whaled, whal·ing** zurrar, dar una tunda —intr. atacar con vehemencia, vapulear.

whale·boat (hwāl′bōt′) s. MARÍT. bote ballenero.

whale·bone (hwāl′bōn′) s. barba de ballena, ballena.

whal·er (hwā′lər) s. ballenero (pescador, buque).

whal·ing (hwā′lĭng) s. pesca de la ballena.

wham (hwăm) I. s. *(blow)* golpe fuerte *m;* *(thud)* ruido sordo II. tr. **whammed, wham·ming** golpear con fuerza resonante —intr. chocar *o* romper ruidosamente.

wham·my (hwăm′ē) s. [pl. **-mies**] FAM. hechizo.

whang (hwăng) I. s. *(whip)* látigo, fusta; *(blow)* golpe resonante *m,* golpazo II. tr. FAM. *(to whip)* azotar, zurrar; *(to hit)* golpear con fuerza —intr. golpear con resonancia.

wharf (hwôrf) I. s. [pl. **wharves** *o* **wharfs**] *(pier)* muelle *m,* desembarcadero *o* muelle II. tr. *(to store)* almacenar en un muelle; *(to furnish)* proveer con un muelle —intr. atracar en un muelle.

wharf·age (hwôr′fĭj) s. MARÍT. *(use of a wharf)* muellaje *m;* *(wharves)* muelles *m.*

wharves (hwôrvz) un pl. de **wharf.**

what §G25, 34, 40 (hwŏt, hwŭt, hwət) I. pron. interrog. qué, qué cosa <w. did you say? ¿qué dijiste?>; cómo <w. is this called? ¿cómo se llama esto?>; cuál <w. is the reason? ¿cuál es el motivo?> ♦ **so w.?** ¿y qué? • **w. about?** ¿qué te parece? • **w. about it?** ¿y qué?, ¿y eso qué importa? • **w. does it matter?** ¿qué importa?, ¿qué importancia tiene? •

ã rey / ä año / b boca / ch chico / d dar / ĕ el / ē mil / g gato / h joya / hw juez / ī aire / k casa / kw cuan /

w. else? ¿qué más? • **w. for?** ¿para qué? • **w. if?** ¿y si? <*w. if she doesn't like it?* ¿y si a ella no le gusta?>; ¿y qué importa si? <*w. if they don't speak English?* ¿y qué importa si ellos no hablan inglés?> • **w. is it all about?** ¿de qué se trata? • **w. is that?** ¿qué es eso? • **w. is the matter?** ¿qué pasa?, ¿qué problema hay? • **w. is this all about?** ¿a qué viene todo esto? • **w. next?** y ahora ¿qué?, entonces ¿qué? • **w. of it?** ¿y qué?, ¿y eso qué importa? **II.** pron. rel. el que, la que, lo que, aquello que <*listen to w. I tell you* presta atención a lo que te digo>; JER. los que <*it's the poor w. gets the blame* son los pobres los que reciben la culpa> ♦ **and w. not** y yo qué sé qué más • **come w. may** o **will** pase lo que pase, suceda lo que suceda • **say w. they will** digan lo que digan • **to know what's w.** estar bien enterado, conocer bien el asunto • **w. is more** más aún • **w. it takes** lo que es necesario • **w. with . . . and** entre . . . y <*w. with her health and the trip* entre su salud y el viaje> **III.** adj. interrog. qué <*w. time is it?* ¿qué hora es?>; cuál <*w. sweater do you want?* ¿cuál suéter quieres?>; qué, de qué <*w. material is that dress made of?* ¿de qué genero está hecho ese vestido?> ♦ **w. good is it?** ¿de qué sirve? **IV.** adj. rel. que <*get w. magazine you like* compra la revista que quieras> **V.** adv. cuánto, cómo <*w. I've cried!* ¡cuánto he llorado!> **VI.** interj. ¡cómo! <*w.! no dinner!* ¡cómo, no hay cena!> ♦ **w. a man!** ¡qué hombre! • **w. a pity!** ¡qué lástima! • **w. nonsense!** ¡qué tontería!

what·ev·er (hwŏt-ĕv'ər, hwŭt-) **I.** pron. (*anything that*) lo que, todo lo que <*do w. you want* haz lo que quieras>; (*the whole of what*) todo lo que <*w. we have is yours* todo lo que tenemos es vuestro>; (*no matter what*) cualquier cosa, lo que <*w. happens, we'll meet here tonight* pase lo que pase, nos veremos aquí esta noche>; FAM. (*what*) qué <*w. does he mean?* ¿qué quiere decir?> ♦ **w. it may be** sea lo que sea **II.** adj. (*any*) cualquiera que (sea) <*w. book you choose* cualquier libro que elija>; (*of any kind at all*) nada en absoluto <*it's of no use w.* no sirve para nada en absoluto> ♦ **nothing w.** absolutamente nada.

what·not (hwŏt'nŏt', hwŭt'-) s. (*object*) cualquier cosa (esp. pequeña); CARP. rinconera.

what·so·ev·er (hwŏt'sō-ĕv'ər, hwŭt'-) pron. & adj. var. de **whatever.**

wheat (hwēt) s. trigo.

wheat germ s. BOT. germen de trigo *m.*

whee·dle (hwēd'l) tr. **-dled, -dling** (*to cajole*) engatusar, persuadir; (*to get by cunning*) sonsacar —intr. hacer zalamerías, lisonjear.

wheel (hwēl) **I.** s. (*of vehicle, mechanism*) rueda; (*steering device*) volante *m*; (*of a ship*) timón *m*; (*of a potter*) torno; (*for torture*) rueda; FAM. (*bicycle*) bicicleta; (*act of turning*) vuelta, rotación *f*; JER. (*important person*) personaje *m* <*he thinks he's a big w.* se cree un gran personaje>; MIL. vuelta, giro ♦ **fifth w.** FIG. objeto o persona superflua • **to be behind** o **at the w.** (*to drive*) conducir, manejar el coche; FIG. (*in charge*) dirigir, controlar • **to grease the wheels** FIG., FAM. aceitar los engranajes, dar coimas • **wheels** TÉC. engranaje; JER. (*car*) automóvil; FIG. (*forces*) mecanismos <*the wheels of commerce* los mecanismos del comercio> **II.** tr. (*to carry on wheels*) llevar o transportar sobre ruedas; (*to cause to rotate*) hacer girar o rodar —intr. (*to rotate*) girar, dar vueltas; (*to roll on wheels*) rodar; (*birds, butterflies*) revolotear ♦ **to w. about** o **around** (*to pivot*) dar una vuelta, girar sobre los talones; FIG. (*one's mind*) cambiar de opinión.

wheel·bar·row (hwēl'băr'ō) s. carretilla.

wheel·base (hwēl'bās') s. AUTO. distancia entre los dos ejes de las ruedas.

wheel·chair o **wheel chair** (hwēl'chār') s. silla de ruedas.

wheeled (hwēld) adj. que tiene ruedas, de ruedas <*a three-wheeled vehicle* vehículo de tres ruedas>.

wheel·er (hwē'lər) s. vehículo (de cierto número) de ruedas <*a four-wheeler* un vehículo de cuatro ruedas>; (*wheel horse*) caballo de tronco.

wheel·er-deal·er (hwē'lər-dē'lər) s. FAM. persona que anda en tramoyas.

wheel house s. MARÍT. caseta del timón, timonera.

wheel·wright (hwēl'rīt') s. carretero, ruedero.

wheeze (hwēz) **I.** intr. **wheezed, wheez·ing** (*to breathe*) respirar con dificultad; (*to pant*) jadear; FAM. (*to talk hoarsely*) gañir —tr. ♦ **to w. out** decir resollando **II.** s. (*sound*) resuello ronco; FAM. (*old joke*) cuento o chiste viejo.

wheez·y (hwē'zē) adj. **-i·er, -i·est** jadeante, que respira con dificultad.

whelk¹ (hwĕlk, wĕlk) s. ICT. buccino.

whelk² (hwĕlk, wĕlk) s. MED. pústula.

whelm (hwĕlm) tr. (*to submerge*) sumergir, anegar; (*to overwhelm*) abrumar, agobiar.

whelp (hwĕlp) **I.** s. ZOOL. (*young animal*) cachorro; FIG. (*urchin*) granuja **II.** tr. & intr. parir (animales).

when §G40 (hwĕn) **I.** adv. (*at what time*) cuándo, a qué hora <*w. will we leave?* ¿a qué hora partiremos?>; (*at which time*) cuando <*I know w. to leave* sé cuando debo irme> **II.** conj. (*at the time that*) cuando <*in the spring, when the snow melts* en la primavera, cuando se derrite la nieve>; (*as soon as*) al, en cuanto <*I'll call you w. I get there* te llamaré en cuanto llegue>; (*whenever*) cuando, cada vez <*w. the wind blows all the doors rattle* cada vez que hay viento todas las puertas se sacuden>; (*while*) cuando, de <*w. I was younger* cuando yo era más joven>; (*considering that*) si <*how can he succeed w. he won't work?* ¿cómo puede triunfar si no quiere trabajar?> **III.** pron. cuándo <*since w. has this been going on?* ¿desde cuándo está ocurriendo esto?> **IV.** s. fecha, momento.

whence (hwĕns) **I.** adv. de dónde <*w. comes this man?* ¿de dónde viene este hombre?> **II.** conj. de donde, de lo cual <*w. I conclude that . . .* de lo cual concluyo que . . .>.

when·ev·er (hwĕn-ĕv'ər) adv. & conj. (*at whatever time*) en cualquier momento (que), cuando quiera (que) <*come w. you like* ven cuando quieras>; (*when*) cuando <*w. you see it, stop* cuando lo veas, para>; (*every time that*) siempre que, cada vez que <*I smile w. I see him* siempre que le veo, sonrío>.

where §G40 (hwâr) **I.** adv. dónde <*w. is the telephone?* ¿dónde está el teléfono?>; dónde, en dónde <*w. would we be without your help?* ¿en dónde estaríamos sin tu ayuda?>; de dónde <*w. did you get this idea?* ¿de dónde sacaste esa idea?>; adónde, a dónde <*w. is this argument leading?* ¿a dónde nos lleva esta discusión?>; por dónde <*w. should I start?* ¿por dónde debo comenzar?> **II.** conj. donde, en donde <*I am fine w. I am* estoy bien en donde estoy>; donde, en donde, en el cual, en la cual, en los cuales, en las cuales <*cities w. the air is polluted* ciudades en las cuales el aire está contaminado>; adonde, a donde <*we should go w. it is quieter* deberíamos de ir a donde es más tranquilo>; donde, a donde, al que, al cual, a la cual, a los cuales, a las cuales <*the city w. I will move to* la ciudad a la cual me mudaré> **III.** s. lugar *m*, sitio.

where·a·bouts (hwâr'ə-bouts') **I.** adv. dónde, por dónde <*w. do you live?* ¿por dónde vives?> **II.** s. [ú. con v. sing. o pl.] paradero, ubicación *f* <*his present w. is unknown* se desconoce su paradero actual>.

where·as (hwâr-ăz') **I.** conj. (*it being the fact that*) visto que, considerando que; (*while*) mientras (que), en tanto (que) **II.** s. DER. considerando.

where·at (hwâr-ăt') conj. a lo cual, con lo cual.

where·by (hwâr-bī') conj. por o según el cual <*the sign w. he shall be known* el signo por el cual lo conoceremos>.

where·fore (hwâr'fôr') **I.** adv. (*why*) por qué; (*for which*) por lo que, por lo cual **II.** s. porqué *m*, motivo ♦ **the whys and wherefores** las causas y los motivos, el cómo y el porqué.

where·from (hwâr'frŏm', -frŭm') conj. de donde, de lo cual.

where·in (hwâr-ĭn') **I.** adv. en dónde, en qué respecto **II.** conj. donde, en que <*the country w. you live* el país en que vives>.

where·of (hwâr-ŏv', -ŭv') conj. (*of what*) de que, de lo que <*he knows w. he speaks* él sabe de lo que habla>; (*of which, of whom*) del que, de la que.

where·to (hwâr'tōō') **I.** adv. (*to what place*) adónde; (*toward what end*) para qué **II.** conj. a lo cual, con lo cual.

where·up·on (hwâr'ə-pŏn') conj. después de o con lo cual.

wher·ev·er (hwâr-ĕv'ər) **I.** adv. (*to whatever place*) dondequiera que, a dondequiera que <*w. you go, I'll go too* dondequiera que vayas, te acompañaré>; FAM. *(where)* dónde, dónde diablos II. conj. dondequiera que <*she makes enemies w. she goes* ella hace enemigos dondequiera que va>.

where·with (hwâr′wĭth′, -wĭth′, wâr′-) I. adv. con el que, con lo cual II. pron. aquello con lo que, lo necesario para III. conj. con que, con lo cual.

where·with·al (hwâr′wĭth-ôl′) I. conj. con que, con (el, la, lo) cual II. s. medios, recursos.

whet (hwĕt) I. tr. **whet·ted, whet·ting** *(to sharpen)* afilar; FIG. *(appetite)* abrir; *(curiosity)* despertar, estimular II. s. *(act)* estimulación *f*; FIG. *(appetizer)* aperitivo.

wheth·er (hwĕth′ər) conj. *(if)* si <*I don't know w. the museum is open* no sé si el museo está abierto>; *(for alternative possibilities)* sea . . . o <*w. he wins or loses I will still love him* sea que él gane o pierda yo lo querré igual> ♦ **w. or not** de todos modos, en todo caso.

whet·stone (hwĕt′stōn′) s. TEC. piedra de afilar, piedra de amolar.

whew (hwōō, hyōō) interj. ¡vaya!

whey (hwā) s. suero de la leche.

which §G25, 34, 40 (hwĭch) I. pron. interrog. cuál <*w. of these is yours?* ¿cuál de éstos es el tuyo?>; quién <*w. of you did it?* ¿quién de ustedes lo hizo?> ♦ **w. is w.?** ¿cuál es cuál? • **w. of them?** ¿cuál de ellos? II. pron. rel. que <*take those w. are yours* toma aquellos que son tuyos>; el cual, la cual, los cuales, las cuales <*my house, w. is small and old* mi casa, la cual es pequeña y vieja>; lo cual, lo que <*he acted very rudely, w. did not surprise me* se portó muy groseramente, lo que no me sorprendió>; el que, la que, el cual, la cual, lo cual <*the subject on w. he spoke* el tema sobre el cual él habló> ♦ **all (of) w.** todo lo que III. adj. interrog. ¿qué?, ¿cuál?, ¿cuáles? <*w. color do you prefer?* ¿qué color prefieres?> ♦ **w. one?** ¿cuál? • **w. ones?** ¿cuáles? • **w. way?** ¿por dónde? IV. adj. rel. cuyo, cuya <*for w. reason* por cuya razón>; cualquier, cualquiera <*use w. door you please* use cualquier puerta que usted quiera>.

which·ev·er (hwĭch′-ĕv′ər) I. pron. *(whatever one)* cualquiera <*w. of the methods you choose* cualquiera de los métodos que elijas>; *(the one who, the one that)* el que, lo que <*buy w. you want* compra el que quieras> II. adj. cualquier, cualquiera que sea <*w. route you take, you'll get there* cualquiera sea la ruta que tomes, llegarás bien>.

whiff (hwĭf) I. s. *(waft)* soplo; *(of odor)* olor *m*; *(of smoke)* bocanada II. intr. soplar —tr. exhalar.

while (hwīl) I. s. rato, tiempo <*stay for a little w.* quédate un rato> ♦ **after a w.** poco tiempo después • **a (little) w. ago** hace poco tiempo, no hace mucho • **a w. after** poco después, a poco • **for a w.** por o durante algún tiempo • **little w.** ratito • **once in a w.** de vez en cuando • **the w.** mientras tanto, entre tanto • **to be worth (one's) w.** merecer *o* valer la pena II. conj. *(as long as)* mientras (que) <*it was lovely w. it lasted* fue encantador mientras duró>; *(although)* aunque, si bien <*w. he loves his children, he is strict with them* aunque ama a sus hijos, él es estricto con ellos>; *(whereas)* mientras que <*the walls are gray, w. the ceiling is white* las paredes son grises mientras que el techo es blanco> III. tr. **whiled, whil·ing** pasar <*to w. the hours away* pasar el tiempo>.

whilst (hwīlst) conj. G.B. var. de **while**.

whim (hwĭm) s. *(fancy)* fantasía; *(caprice)* capricho, antojo.

whim·per (hwĭm′pər) I. intr. *(to sob)* lloriquear; *(to complain)* quejarse —tr. decir gimiendo II. s. gemido, quejido.

whim·sey (hwĭm′zē) s. var. de **whimsy**.

whim·si·cal (hwĭm′zĭ-kəl) adj. *(capricious)* caprichoso; *(fanciful)* extravagante.

whim·sy (hwĭm′zē) s. [pl. **-sies**] *(fancy)* capricho; *(fanciful thing)* extravagancia.

whine (hwīn) I. intr. **whined, whin·ing** *(to whimper)* gimotear; *(to complain)* quejarse; *(to buzz)* zumbar —tr. decir gimoteando II. s. *(act, sound)* gimoteo, quejido; *(complaint)* queja, quejido.

whin·ny (hwĭn′ē) I. intr. **-nied, -ny·ing** relinchar II. s. [pl. **-nies**] relincho.

whip (hwĭp) I. tr. **whipped** *o* **whipt** (hwĭpt), **whip·ping** *(to lash)* azotar, dar latigazos a; *(to flog)* flagelar; FIG. *(to reprove)* fustigar, censurar duramente; *(to strike)* azotar, golpear <*the snow whipped his face* la nieve le azotaba la cara>; *(cream, eggs)* batir; *(in sewing)* sobrecoser, rebatir; FAM. *(to outdo)* dar una paliza a; MARÍT. izar con candaliza, elevar con el aparejo ♦ **to w. away** arrebatar, llevarse de un golpe • **to w. off** quitarse rápidamente • **to w. on** *(a horse)* dar latigazos a; *(clothes)* ponerse rápidamente • **to w. out** sacar de repente • **to w. up** *(to excite)* estimular, excitar <*to w. up the mob* excitar a la muchedumbre>; FAM. *(to prepare quickly)* preparar rápidamente —intr. *(to dart)* precipitarse, lanzarse; *(to snap about)* restallar <*flags whipping in a high wind* las banderas restallando al viento> ♦ **to w. about** moverse rápidamente • **to w. around** volverse de repente, darse vuelta rápidamente • **to w. off** **away** irse rápido, marcharse de prisa II. s. *(lash)* látigo, azote *m*; *(for horses)* fusta; *(blow)* latigazo, azote; *(windmill arm)* asta; *(hoist)* aparejo; *(antenna)* antena flexible; CUL. *(whisk)* batidor *m*; *(dessert)* batido; POL. miembro de un cuerpo legislativo encargado de hacer observar las consignas del partido.

whip hand s. *(hand)* mano del látigo; *(advantage)* ventaja.

whip·lash (hwĭp′lăsh′) s. *(cord)* tralla; *(blow)* latigazo.

whip·per·snap·per (hwĭp′ər-snăp′ər) s. mequetrefe *m*.

whip·pet (hwĭp′ĭt) s. lebrel *m*.

whip·ping (hwĭp′ĭng) s. *(act)* azotamiento; *(thrashing)* paliza; *(stitching)* rebatido; CUL. batido.

whip·poor·will *o* **whip-poor-will** (hwĭp′ər-wĭl′) s. ORNIT. chotacabras *m*, dormilón *m*.

whip·saw (hwĭp′sô′) I. s. sierra abrazadera, sierra cabrilla II. tr. **-sawed** *o* **-sawn** (-sôn′), **-saw·ing** *(to saw)* aserrar; *(to win)* ganar dos apuestas; *(to defeat)* hacer perder.

whip·stitch (hwĭp′stĭch′) COST. I. tr. sobrehilar II. s. sobrehilo.

whip·stock (hwĭp′stŏk′, wĭp′-) s. puño *o* mango del látigo.

whipt (hwĭpt) un pret. y part. p. de **whip**.

whir (hwûr) I. intr. **whirred, whir·ring** zumbar —tr. hacer zumbar II. s. zumbido.

whirl (hwûrl) I. intr. *(to spin)* dar vueltas, girar rápidamente; *(to turn)* dar una vuelta <*she whirled around to face him* dió una vuelta para verle de cara>; *(to reel)* dar vueltas, tener vértigo <*my head is whirling* mi cabeza está dando vueltas>; *(dust, water)* arremolinarse ♦ **to w. along** pasar a toda velocidad —tr. *(to spin)* hacer girar, hacer dar vueltas; *(leaves, debris)* levantar en remolinos; *(to hurl)* lanzar con honda II. s. *(act)* giro, rotación *f*; *(of dust, water)* remolino, torbellino; *(tumult)* tumulto, agitación *f*; FIG. *(of events)* serie *f*, torbellino <*the w. of social life* el torbellino de la vida social>; *(dizziness)* mareo, vértigo ♦ **to give it a w.** FAM. tratar, intentar hacer.

whirl·i·gig (hwûr′lĭ-gĭg′) s. *(toy)* molinete *m*; *(carousel)* tiovivo, calesita; *(spinning thing)* torbellino.

whirl·pool (hwûrl′pōōl′) s. *(eddy)* remolino, vórtice *m*; *(whirl)* torbellino; FIG. *(force)* vorágine *f*.

whirl·wind (hwûrl′wĭnd′) I. s. torbellino, remolino II. adj. intenso *y* rápido.

whirl·y·bird (hwûr′lē-bûrd′) s. JER. helicóptero.

whisk (hwĭsk) I. tr. *(to move)* mover (rápidamente), sacudir; CUL. batir ♦ **to w. away** *(insects)* espantar, ahuyentar; *(a tear)* secarse, enjugar; *(to take away)* llevarse de golpe *o* rápidamente —intr. moverse rápidamente ♦ **to w. away** *o* **off** irse, marcharse a toda velocidad • **to w. past** pasar a toda velocidad II. s. *(motion)* movimiento rápido; *(whiskbroom)* cepillo de ropa; CUL. *(utensil)* batidor *m*.

whisk·broom (hwĭsk′brōōm′, -brŏŏm′) s. cepillo de ropa.

whisk·er (hwĭs′kər) s. pelo (de la barba o del bigote) ♦ **whiskers** *(of man)* barbas; *(sideburns)* patillas; *(of animal)* bigotes.

whisk·ered (hwĭs′kərd) adj. *(with mustache)* bigotudo; *(bearded)* barbudo.

whis·key *o* **whis·ky** (hwĭs′kē) s. [pl. **-keys** *o* **-kies**] whisky *m*.

whis·per (hwĭs′pər) I. s. *(soft speech)* murmullo, cuchicheo; *(soft utterance)* susurro; *(rumor)* rumor *m*; *(rustling sound)* susurro, murmullo II. intr. *(to speak softly)* susurrar; *(to* *gossip)* hacer correr la voz <*it is whispered that she is pregnant* se corre la voz de que está embarazada>; *(to rustle)* susurrar, murmurar —tr. *(to utter)* decir en voz baja, susurrar; *(to tell secretly)* decir en secreto.

whis·per·ing (hwĭs′pər-ĭng) **I.** s. *(soft talk)* murmullo, cuchicheo; *(sound)* susurro, murmullo; *(rumor)* murmuración *f* **II.** adj. susurrante, murmurador.

whis·tle (hwĭs′əl) **I.** intr. **-tled, -tling** *(with the mouth)* silbar; *(with a device)* pitar; *(birds)* piar ♦ **to w. in the dark** FIG. intentar cobrar ánimo • **to w. past** pasar silbando (bala, viento) —tr. silbar ♦ **to w. for** llamar con un silbido **II.** s. *(instrument)* pito, silbato; *(act, sound)* silbido, pitido ♦ **to wet one's w.** FIG., FAM. mojarse el gaznate.

whis·tler (hwĭs′lər) s. *(one that whistles)* silbador *m*; ZOOL. marmota norteamericana; ORNIT. pato que silba.

whistle stop s. F.C. *(station)* apeadero; POL. visita corta.

whit (hwĭt) s. pizca <*there's not a w. of truth in it* no hay ni una pizca de verdad en ello>.

white (hwīt) **I.** s. *(color)* blanco; *(of an egg)* clara; *(of an eyeball, target)* blanco; *(person)* blanco ♦ **whites** vestido *o* equipo blanco **II.** adj. **whit·er, whit·est** *(color)* blanco <*a w. shirt* una camisa blanca>; *(pale)* *(said of hair, beard)* cano, blanco; *(colorless)* transparente, incoloro; *(pure)* puro, inocente ♦ **as w. as a sheet** *o* **ghost** blanco como el papel • **to go** *o* **turn w.** ponerse pálido, palidecer.

white blood cell s. glóbulo blanco, leucocito.

white coal s. energía hidráulica.

white-col·lar (hwīt′kŏl′ər) adj. de oficina.

white corpuscle s. glóbulo blanco, leucocito.

white elephant s. elefante blanco.

white·fish (hwīt′fĭsh′) s. [pl. **whitefish** *o* **-fish·es**] pescado blanco.

white flag s. bandera blanca.

white heat s. *(frenzy)* frenesí *m*, excitación *f*; FÍS. calor blanco, rojo blanco; ELEC. incandescencia.

white-hot (hwīt′hŏt′) adj. *(fervid)* al rojo vivo, candente; FÍS. al rojo blanco; ELEC. incandescente.

White House s. EE. UU. *(house)* la Casa Blanca; *(government branch)* poder ejecutivo.

white lie s. mentirilla.

white-liv·ered (hwīt′lĭv′ərd) adj. cobarde.

white magic s. magia blanca.

white matter s. ANAT. substancia blanca del cerebro y médula.

white meat s. CUL. carne de ave *f.*

whit·en (hwīt′n) tr. & intr. blanquear(se).

white·ness (hwīt′nĭs) s. *(of snow)* blancura; *(of skin)* palidez *f*; FIG. *(pureness)* pureza, inocencia.

white paper s. *(paper)* libro blanco, informe oficial *m*; TELEV. programa investigativo sobre un tema.

white pine s. pino blanco (árbol y madera).

white poplar s. álamo blanco.

white potato s. patata blanca.

white sauce s. salsa blanca *o* bechamel.

white slave s. esclava blanca.

white sugar s. azúcar blanca, azúcar refinada.

white-tailed deer (hwīt′tāld′) s. ciervo de Virginia.

white tie s. *(bow tie)* corbatín blanco *m*; *(formal attire)* frac *m*, ropa de gala masculina.

white-wall tire *o* **white-wall** (hwīt′wôl′) s. AUTO. neumático de banda blanca.

white·wash (hwīt′wŏsh′) **I.** s. *(for walls, fences)* cal *f*, lechada de cal; FIG. *(concealing)* encubrimiento; *(excuse)* perdón *m*; *(total defeat)* derrota absoluta **II.** tr. *(wall, fence)* blanquear, enjalbegar; FIG. *(failure)* encubrir; *(to gloss over)* perdonar.

white water s. agua espumosa (de catarata, rápido).

whit·ey (hwī′tē) s. [pl. **-eys**] JER. *(blond)* rubio; DESPEC. *(white person)* blanco.

whith·er (hwĭ*th*′ər) adv. *(where)* adónde, a dónde <*w. are we going?* ¿adónde vamos?>; *(to which)* hacia donde, adonde; *(wherever)* dondequiera.

whit·ing¹ (hwī′tĭng) s. blanco de España, albayalde *m.*

whit·ing² (hwī′tĭng) s. ICT. merluza, pescadilla.

whit·ish (hwī′tĭsh) adj. blancuzco, blanquecino.

whit·low (hwĭt′lō, wĭt′-) s. MED. panadizo.

Whit·sun (hwĭt′sən) adj. de Pentecostés.

Whit·sun·day (hwĭt′sən-dē) s. domingo de Pentecostés.

Whit·sun·tide (hwĭt′sən-tīd′) s. semana de Pentecostés.

whit·tle (hwĭt′l) tr. **-tled, -tling** *(to carve)* tallar; *(to reduce)* reducir —intr. *(to carve)* tallar; *(to wear out)* cansarse, desgastarse.

whiz *o* **whizz** (hwĭz) **I.** intr. **whizzed, whiz·zing** zumbar ♦ **to w. by** *o* **past** pasar velozmente *o* como un rayo —tr. arrojar velozmente **II.** s. [pl. **whiz·zes**] zumbido ♦ **to be a w.** FAM. ser un as.

who §G34, 35, 40 (hōō) **I.** pron. interrog. quién, quiénes <*w. did it?* ¿quién lo hizo?> ♦ **w. is it?** ¿quién es? **II.** pron. rel. quien, quienes, el que, la que, los que, las que <*it was my parents w. built this business* fueron mis padres quienes establecieron este negocio>; que, el cual, los cuales, las cuales <*my parents, w. built this business* mis padres, los cuales establecieron este negocio> ♦ **those w.** los que, los que.

whoa (hwō) interj. ¡so!, ¡jo!, ¡cho!

who'd (hōōd) contr. de **who would** *o* **who had.**

who·dun·it (hōō-dŭn′ĭt) s. FAM. *(book)* novela policial; *(film)* película policial.

who·ev·er (hōō-ĕv′ər) pron. *(no matter who)* quienquiera que, cualquiera que <*w. finds it can keep it* quienquiera que lo encuentre puede quedárselo>; *(who)* el que, quien <*w. said that is an idiot* el que dijo esto es un imbécil>; FAM. *(who the heck)* ¿quién diablos? <*w. did that?* ¿quién diablos hizo eso?>.

whole (hōl) **I.** adj. *(entire)* entero, todo <*the w. world* el mundo entero>; *(total)* completo, total <*the w. volume* el volumen total>; *(healthy)* sano <*a w. organism* un organismo sano>; *(healed)* curado <*he is a w. man again* es un hombre completamente curado>; *(undamaged)* intacto, ileso <*not a cup was left w.* no quedó taza intacta>; *(brother, sister)* carnal <*w. sister* hermana carnal>; MAT. entero ♦ **a w. lot of** muchísimo, una gran cantidad de **II.** s. *(totality)* todo, totalidad *f* <*the w. and its parts* el todo y sus partes>; *(complete entity)* suma, conjunto <*the w. of his works* el conjunto de sus obras> ♦ **as a w.** en conjunto • **on the w.** *(in general)* en general; *(considering everything)* considerándolo todo **III.** adv. FAM. completamente, enteramente <*a w. new idea* una idea completamente nueva>.

whole·heart·ed (hōl′här′tĭd) adj. *(sincere)* sincero, franco; *(unconditional)* incondicional, completo.

whole hog s. ♦ **to go w.** JER. hacerlo por completo, no quedarse a medias.

whole milk s. leche sin desnatar *f.*

whole·ness (hōl′nĭs) s. integridad *f.*

whole note s. MÚS. redonda.

whole number s. MAT. entero, número entero.

whole·sale (hōl′sāl′) **I.** s. venta al por mayor **II.** adj. *(in large quantities)* al por mayor; *(general)* general <*w. destruction* destrucción general> **III.** adv. *(in large quantities)* al por mayor; *(extensively)* en general, en masa **IV.** tr. & intr. **-saled, -sal·ing** vender(se) al por mayor.

whole·sal·er (hōl′sā′lər) s. mayorista *mf.*

whole·some (hōl′səm) adj. *(healthy)* sano; *(salutary)* saludable.

whole-wheat (hōl′hwēt′) adj. ♦ **w. bread** pan integral.

who'll (hōōl) contr. de **who will** *o* **who shall.**

whol·ly (hō′lē, hōl′lē) adv. totalmente, completamente.

whom §G34, 35 (hōōm) **I.** pron. interrog. a quién, a quiénes <*w. did you see?* ¿a quién viste?>; de quién, de quiénes <*from w. did you get it?* ¿de quién lo recibiste?> **II.** pron. rel. que, quien, quienes, a quien, a quienes <*the man with w. I was talking* el hombre con quien yo estaba hablando> ♦ **both of w.** ambos, ambas • **of w.** del cual, de quien.

whom·ev·er (hōōm-ĕv′ər) pron. a quienquiera, a cualquiera.

whom·so·ev·er (hōōm′sō-ĕv′ər) pron. var. de **whomever.**

whoop (hōōp, hwōōp) **I.** s. *(shout)* grito, chillido; *(bird's cry)* graznido, chillido; *(gasp)* estertor de la tos ferina *m* **II.** intr. *(to shout)* gritar; *(to hoot)* chillar, graznar; *(to gasp)* toser ahogándose —tr. *(to shout)* gritar; *(to drive)* llevar, conducir dando gritos ♦ **to w. it up** armar jaleo, jaranear.

whoop·ee (hwŏŏp'ē, hwŏŏ'pē) JER. interj. ¡viva!, ¡hurra! ♦ **to make w.** *(to celebrate)* celebrar, jaranear; *(to make love)* hacer el amor.

whooping cough s. tos ferina, tos convulsa.

whooping crane s. grulla blanca (norteamericana).

whoops (hwŏŏps, hwŏŏps) interj. ¡epa!

whoosh (hwŏŏsh, hwŏŏsh) **I.** intr. pasar como un silbido **II.** s. silbido.

whop (hwŏp) **I.** tr. **whopped, whop·ping** derrotar, dar una paliza **II.** s. golpe m **III.** adv. con un golpe.

whop·per (hwŏp'ər) s. *(large thing)* cosa enorme; *(lie)* mentira colosal.

whop·ping (hwŏp'ĭng) adj. FAM. colosal, enorme.

whore (hôr) **I.** s. prostituta, puta **II.** intr. **whored, whor·ing** *(to frequent whores)* irse de putas; *(to act)* prostituirse.

whore·house (hôr'hous') s. prostíbulo, casa de putas, burdel m.

whorl (hwôrl, hwûrl) s. BOT. verticillo; *(coil, curl)* espiral f; ZOOL. espira.

who's (hŏŏz) contr. de **who is** o **who has.**

whose §G25, 34, 35 (hŏŏz) **I.** pron interrog. de quién, de quiénes <*w. are these magazines?* ¿de quién son estas revistas?> **II.** adj. interrog. de quién, de quiénes, a quién, a quiénes <*w. magazines are these?* ¿de quién son estas revistas?, ¿a quién pertenecen estas revistas?> **III.** pron. rel. cuyo, cuya, cuyos, cuyas <*people w. faces I don't remember* gente cuyas caras no recuerdo, gente de cuyas caras no me acuerdo> ♦ **for w.** en cuyo, por cuyo • **from w.** de cuyo.

who·so·ev·er (hŏŏ'sō-ĕv'ər) pron. var. de **whoever.**

why §G40 (hwī) **I.** adv. por qué, para qué, con qué objeto <*w. did you have to leave?* ¿por qué te tuviste que ir?> **II.** conj. por que, por lo que, por el cual, por la cual, por los cuales, por las cuales <*I know w. you left* sé por que te fuiste> **III.** s. [pl. **whys**] *(cause)* (la) causa, (el) porqué m; *(problem)* problema m, enigma m **IV.** interj. ¡vaya!, ¡toma! <*w., it's you!* ¡vaya, eres tú!>; si <*w., I just saw him* si recién lo acabo de ver> ♦ **w., certainly** por supuesto, desde luego • **w. yes** pues, sí.

wick (wĭk) s. mecha.

wick·ed (wĭk'ĭd) adj. *(vicious)* malvado; *(depraved)* perverso; *(mischievous)* travieso; *(fierce)* feroz; *(pernicious)* espantoso <*a w. cough* una tos espantosa>; *(offensive)* desagradable; *(formidable)* formidable, tremendo <*a w. tennis player* un formidable jugador de tenis>.

wick·ed·ness (wĭk'ĭd-nĭs) s. *(evil)* maldad f; *(perversity)* perversidad f.

wick·er (wĭk'ər) **I.** s. *(shoot)* mimbre m; *(wickerwork)* artículos de mimbre **II.** adj. de mimbre.

wick·er·work (wĭk'ər-wûrk') s. *(items)* artículos de mimbre; *(craft)* cestería.

wick·et (wĭk'ĭt) s. *(small gate)* portillo; *(small window)* ventanilla; *(sluice gate)* compuerta; DEP. *(in soccer)* puerta, portería; *(in croquet)* argolla.

wide (wīd) **I.** adj. **wid·er, wid·est** *(broad)* ancho <*a w. bed* una cama ancha>; *(in width)* de ancho <*a ribbon two inches w.* una cinta de dos pulgadas de ancho>; *(extensive)* extenso <*a w. plain* una llanura extensa>; *(large)* grande, amplio <*a w. selection* una amplia selección>; *(ample)* ancho, holgado <*the legs on these jeans are too w.* las piernas de estos vaqueros son muy anchas>; *(open)* dilatado, muy abierto <*to look with w. eyes* mirar con ojos muy abiertos>; FONÉT. relajado ♦ **how w. is it?** ¿qué ancho tiene?, ¿cuál es el ancho? • **in a wider sense** en un sentido más amplio • **to make wider** ensanchar • **w. of the mark** lejos del blanco **II.** adv. *(completely)* de par en par <*the door was open w.* la puerta estaba abierta de par en par>; *(to the full extent)* bien abierto, bien grande <*open your mouth w.* abra la boca bien grande> ♦ **far and w.** por todas partes • **to go w.** *(observation, criticism)* no hacer efecto; *(blow, shot)* errar el blanco • **w. apart** muy separados, muy alejados • **w. open** de par en par.

wide-an·gle lens s. FOTOG. objetivo gran angular.

wide-a·wake (wīd'ə-wāk') adj. *(awake)* despierto; *(alert)* alerta.

wide-eyed (wīd'īd') adj. *(with open eyes)* con los ojos muy abiertos; *(innocent)* inocente, crédulo.

wide·ly (wīd'lē) adv. *(very)* muy <*a w. read book* un libro muy leído>; *(much)* mucho; *(extensively)* extensamente, generalmente <*a w. known writer* un escritor generalmente conocido>.

wide-mouthed (wīd'mouthd', -moutht') adj. *(big-mouthed)* bocón; *(agape)* boquiabierto.

wid·en (wīd'n) tr. & intr. ensanchar(se).

wide·ness (wīd'nĭs) s. *(width)* anchura, ancho; *(extent)* extensión f, amplitud f.

wide-o·pen (wīd'ō'pən) adj. *(open)* abierto de par en par; *(lawless)* sin ley.

wide·spread o **wide-spread** (wīd'sprĕd') adj. *(spread)* extendido; *(occurring widely)* difundido, general.

wid·ow (wĭd'ō) **I.** s. *(woman)* viuda; *(card hand)* baceta; IMPR. línea corta sobrante **II.** tr. dejar viuda ♦ **to be widowed** enviudar, quedar viuda.

wid·ow·er (wĭd'ō-ər) s. viudo.

wid·ow·hood (wĭd'ō-hŏŏd') s. viudez f.

widow's mite (wĭd'ōz) s. BÍBL. el óbolo de la viuda.

widow's walk s. balcón de una casa que da al mar m.

width (wĭdth) s. *(wideness)* anchura, ancho; *(of fabrics)* ancho; *(distance)* distancia; *(wingspan)* envergadura; FIG. *(extent)* amplitud f.

wield (wēld) tr. *(weapon)* esgrimir, blandir; *(tool)* manejar; *(power, influence)* ejercer.

wie·ner (wē'nər) s. salchicha de Viena.

wife (wīf) s. [pl. **wives** (wīvz)] esposa, mujer f.

wig (wĭg) **I.** s. peluca **II.** tr. **wigged, wig·ging** retar.

wig·an (wĭg'ən) s. COST. entretela tiesa.

wig·gle (wĭg'əl) **I.** intr. & tr. **-gled, -gling** menear(se) **II.** s. meneo.

wig·wag (wĭg'wăg') **I.** tr. & intr. **-wagged, -wag·ging** comunicar por señales **II.** s. mensaje de señales m.

wig·wam (wĭg'wŏm') s. tienda de los indios norteamericanos.

wild (wīld) **I.** adj. **-er, -est** *(animal, man)* salvaje; *(plant)* silvestre; *(field)* no cultivado; *(country)* salvaje, agreste; *(savage)* feroz, cruel; *(character)* violento; *(lacking discipline)* desordenado, desmandado <*a w. child* un niño desmandado>; *(unruly)* desenfrenado; *(reckless)* imprudente; *(laughter, look)* loco, extraviado; *(frenzied)* frenético, insensato; *(incoherent)* delirante, disparatado; *(extravagant)* extravagante, estrafalario; *(fantastic)* fantástico; *(weather)* tormentoso; *(wind)* furioso, violento; *(sea)* enfurecido, bravo; *(torrent)* impetuoso; *(period of time)* turbulento; *(at random)* al azar <*to make a w. guess* adivinar al azar> ♦ **to be w. about something** FAM. estar loco por algo • **to be w. with** *(anger, joy)* estar loco de (cólera, alegría) • **to drive w.** volver loco • **to have a w. time** pasarlo en grande • **to run** o **grow w.** *(plants)* crecer en estado salvaje; FIG. *(to spread)* propagarse desmesuradamente • **w. beast** fiera salvaje • **w. man** FIG. extremista **II.** s. *(uninhabited region)* tierra virgen, región salvaje f; *(uncultivated region)* región sin cultivar ♦ **in the w.** en estado natural • **the w.** la naturaleza <*the call of the w.* la llamada de la naturaleza> • **the wilds** *(desert)* desierto; *(unexplored region)* región inexplorada **III.** adv. *(in an unruly manner)* alocadamente; *(without being planted)* sin cultivo; *(violently)* violentamente.

wild boar s. jabalí m.

wild·cat (wīld'kăt') **I.** s. *(fierce person)* fiera; ZOOL. gato montés; TEC. sondeo de exploración **II.** adj. arriesgado, descabellado ♦ **w. strike** huelga no aprobada por el sindicato.

wil·de·beest (wĭl'də-bēst', vĭl'-) s. ZOOL. ñú m.

wil·der·ness (wĭl'dər-nĭs) s. *(uncultivated region)* región sin cultivar f; *(desert)* desierto; *(lonely place)* soledad f, yermo; *(extensive area)* infinidad f.

wild-eyed (wīld'īd') adj. *(with wild look)* de mirada furiosa; *(extremist)* extremista <*w. leftist* izquierdista extremista>.

wild·fire (wīld'fīr') s. *(fire)* incendio descontrolado; *(light-*

ning) relámpago ♦ **to spread like w.** propagarse como un reguero de pólvora.

wild·flow·er *o* **wild flower** (wīld'flou'ər) s. flor silvestre *f.*

wild·fowl (wīld'foul') s. [pl. **wildfowl** *o* **-fowls**] ave silvestre *f,* ave de caza.

wild-goose chase (wīld'gōōs') s. FIG. búsqueda inútil.

wild·life (wīld'līf') s. fauna.

wild·ly (wīld'lē) adv. *(violently)* violentamente, furiosamente; *(frenziedly)* frenéticamente, locamente; *(disorderly)* desordenadamente; *(without thinking)* insensatamente, sin reflexión; *(not cultivated)* en estado salvaje; *(at random)* al azar <*to talk w.*> hablar al azar, hablar sin ton ni son> ♦ **to be w. happy** estar loco de alegría • **to rush w.** correr como un loco.

wild·ness (wīld'nĭs) s. *(of animals, region)* estado salvaje; *(of plants)* estado silvestre *o* campestre; *(violence)* violencia, furia; *(ferocity)* ferocidad *f*; *(of character, behavior)* desenfreno; *(frenzy)* frenesí *m,* locura; *(foolishness)* insensatez *f*; *(extravagance)* extravagancia.

wild oat s. avena silvestre ♦ **to sow one's wild oats** correr sus mocedades • **wild oats** excesos de la juventud.

Wild West s. el Oeste (de EE. UU. en época de su colonización).

wild·wood (wīld'wŏŏd') s. bosque virgen *m.*

wile (wīl) **I.** s. *(trick)* ardid *m,* treta; *(cunning)* astucia **II.** tr. **wiled, wil·ing** *(to influence)* seducir (con engaños); *(to entice)* atraer ♦ **to w. away the time** pasar el tiempo.

wil·ful (wīl'fəl) adj. var. de **willful.**

will¹ (wĭl) **I.** s. *(volition)* voluntad *f* <*this is the king's w.* ésta es la voluntad del rey>; *(wish, desire)* voluntad, deseo <*the w. of the people* la voluntad del pueblo>; DER. testamento <*she made her w.* hizo el testamento> ♦ **against one's w.** contra la voluntad de uno • **at w.** a voluntad • **free w.** libre albedrío • **good** *o* **ill w.** buena *o* mala voluntad • **last w. and testament** última voluntad • **of one's own free w.** por voluntad propia • **to have one's w.** salirse con la suya **II.** tr. *(to desire)* desear, querer <*if you w.* si usted quiere>; *(to dispose)* disponer; *(to order)* ordenar; *(to urge by will power)* lograr a fuerza de voluntad; DER. legar.

will² §G4, 11, 13 (wĭl) **I.** aux. [pret. **would** (wŏŏd)] *(simple futurity)* <*they w. come later* vendrán más tarde>; *(likelihood, certainty)* ir a <*you w. regret this* lo vas a lamentar>; *(willingness)* querer <*w. you help me with this package?* ¿quieres ayudarme con este paquete?>; *(requirement, command)* deber <*you w. report to me afterward* deberás venir a verme luego>; *(wish)* querer <*let them do what they w.* déjelos hacer lo que quieran>; *(habitual action)* soler, acostumbrar <*she would spend hours in the kitchen* solía pasar horas en la cocina>; *(probability, expectation)* deber <*that w. be the postman ringing* debe de ser el cartero el que está tocando el timbre>; *(emphasis)* <*I w. do it!* ¡sí, lo haré!>; *(stubbornness)* empeñarse en, insistir en <*she w. drink although she knows she shouldn't* ella insiste en beber, a pesar de que sabe que no debería hacerlo> **II.** tr. & intr. querer <*do what you w.* haz lo que quieras>.

willed (wĭld) adj. *(having will)* de voluntad, que tiene voluntad; *(determined)* decidido.

will·ful (wĭl'fəl) adj. *(deliberate)* deliberado, intencionado; *(obstinate)* obstinado, terco.

wil·lies (wĭl'ēz) s.pl. escalofrío, pelos de punta <*this place gives me the w.* este lugar me pone los pelos de punta>.

will·ing (wĭl'ĭng) adj. *(voluntary)* de buena gana, de buena voluntad; *(acquiescent)* condescendiente; *(compliant)* complaciente, servicial; *(spontaneous)* espontáneo, de buena gana ♦ **God w.** si Dios quiere • **w. or not** quiera o no quiera, de grado o por fuerza.

will·ing·ly (wĭl'ĭng-lē) adv. *(not obliged)* de buena gana; *(gladly)* gustosamente.

will·ing·ness (wĭl'ĭng-nĭs) s. *(good will)* buena voluntad; *(consent)* consentimiento.

will-o'-the-wisp (wĭl'ə-thə-wĭsp') s. *(wildfire)* fuego fatuo; *(delusive goal)* quimera.

wil·low (wĭl'ō) s. BOT. sauce (árbol y madera) *m*; DEP. bate (de cricket) *m.*

wil·low·y (wĭl'ō-ē) adj. **-i·er, -i·est** *(terrain)* poblado de sauces; FIG. *(person)* esbelto, gracioso.

will power s. fuerza de voluntad.

wil·ly-nil·ly (wĭl'ē-nĭl'ē) adv. quieras o no quieras, de grado o por fuerza.

wilt¹ (wĭlt) **I.** intr. & tr. *(to droop)* marchitar(se); *(to weaken)* debilitar(se) **II.** s. marchitamiento.

wilt² (wĭlt) ANT. segunda persona sing. del pres. indic. de **will².**

wil·y (wī'lē) adj. **-i·er, -i·est** astuto, artero.

wimp (wĭmp) s. JER. mentecato, persona inútil *o* pusilánime.

wim·ple (wĭm'pəl) **I.** s. *(headdress)* griñón *m*; *(pleat)* pliegue (en tela) *m*; *(ripple)* onda (de agua); *(curve)* recodo, curva **II.** tr. **-pled, -pling** *(to cover)* vestir con griñón; *(to fold)* plegar; *(to ripple)* hacer ondear —intr. *(to fold)* caer en pliegues; *(to ripple)* ondearse, rizarse.

win (wĭn) **I.** intr. **won** (wŭn), **win·ning** *(to be victorious)* ganar, triunfar, vencer ♦ **to succeed)** tener éxito ♦ **to be w. out,** salir victorioso —tr. *(race, bet)* ganar; *(prize, victory)* ganar, llevarse; *(fame, glory)* ganar, hacerse; *(to obtain)* obtener, conseguir; *(favor, support)* alcanzar, lograr obtener; *(affection, sympathy)* conquistar, granjearse; *(attention)* captar, atraer; MIN. extraer, sacar ♦ **to w. at** ganar en • **to w. glory** cosechar laureles • **to w. someone over** ganarse la amistad, el apoyo de alguien • **to w. the favor of** caer en gracia a **II.** s. *(victory)* victoria, triunfo <*another w. for the President* una nueva victoria del presidente>; *(amount earned)* ganancia.

wince (wĭns) **I.** intr. **winced, winc·ing** respingar, sobresaltarse (de dolor, miedo) **II.** s. respingo, sobresalto.

winch (wĭnch) **I.** s. *(hoisting machine)* torno, cabrestante *m*; *(crank)* manivela, cigüeña **II.** tr. levantar, izar con un cabrestante.

wind¹ (wĭnd) **I.** s. *(air)* viento <*west w.* viento del oeste>; *(artificially produced)* aire *m*; FIG. *(verbiage)* palabrería, aire; MARÍT. viento; FISIOL. *(breath)* respiración *f,* aliento; *(flatulence)* gases *m,* flatulencia ♦ **against w. and tide** FIG. contra viento y marea • **before the w.** MARÍT. con el viento en popa • **fair w.** viento favorable • **from the four winds** FIG. de los cuatro vientos, de todas partes • **gone with the w.** FIG. lo que el viento se llevó • **head w.** viento en contra • **into** *o* **up the w.** MARÍT. contra el viento • **off the w.** MARÍT. con viento en popa • **there's something in the w.** FIG. algo flota en el aire • **to break w.** FAM. ventosear, tirar gases • **to get w. of** FIG. descubrir, enterarse de • **to go like the w.** ir como el viento • **to have the w. knocked out of one** quedar sin aliento • **to recover one's w.** recobrar el aliento • **to see which way the w. blows** FIG. ver de qué lado sopla el viento • **w. ahead** MARÍT. viento de proa • **winds** MÚS. instrumentos de viento **II.** tr. *(to expose to the wind)* airear; *(to ventilate)* ventilar; *(to scent)* olfatear; *(to leave breathless)* dejar sin aliento, quitar el aliento <*they were winded after the race* la carrera les dejó sin aliento>; *(to afford a rest)* dejar recobrar el aliento.

wind² (wīnd) **I.** tr. **wound** (wound), **wind·ing** *(to wrap around)* envolver; *(to entwine)* enrollar; *(wool, cotton)* devanar; *(to bend)* torcer, curvar; *(a watch)* dar cuerda a; *(to lift)* levantar con cabrestante ♦ **to be wound up** estar muy nervioso • **to w. down** disminuir, bajar • **to w. off** desenrollar, desenvolver • **to w. somebody around one's little finger** FIG. tener a alguien bajo la influencia de uno, manejar a alguien • **to w. up** *(thread, wire)* enrollar; *(to hoist)* levantar con torno; *(clock)* dar cuerda a; FIG., FAM. *(to end)* concluir, terminar; *(affairs)* resolver; *(business)* liquidar —intr. *(river, road)* serpentear; *(thread, rope)* enrollarse; *(snake)* enroscarse; *(to twist)* torcerse; *(to bend)* encorvar ♦ **to w. around** enroscarse • **to w. up** FIG. *(to conclude)* terminar, acabar <*how does the novel w. up?* ¿cómo termina la novela?>; *(company, business)* liquidarse **II.** s. vuelta.

wind³ (wĭnd, wīnd) tr. **wind·ed** *o* **wound** (wound), **wind·ing** *(to blow)* soplar (trompeta, clarín); *(to make sound)* hacer sonar (trompeta, clarín).

wind·bag (wĭnd'băg') s. JER. charlatán *m.*

wind-borne (wĭnd'bôrn') adj. acarreado por el viento.

wind-break (wĭnd'brāk') s. protección contra el viento *f.*

Wind·break·er (wĭnd′brā′kər) s. marca registrada de una chaqueta abrigada para actividades al aire libre.

wind·ed (wĭn′dĭd) adj. jadeante, falto de aliento.

wind·er (wĭn′dər) s. *(person)* devanador m; *(spool)* devanadera; *(winding key)* llave de cuerda f; *(step)* escalón de abanico m.

wind·fall (wĭnd′fôl′) s. *(fruit)* fruta caída; *(luck)* suerte inesperada, algo caído del cielo.

wind·flow·er (wĭnd′flou′ər) s. anémona.

wind·i·ness (wĭn′dē-nĭs) s. *(gust)* ventolera; *(flatulence)* flatulencia; *(verbosity)* verbosidad f.

wind·ing (wĭn′dĭng) I. s. *(act)* enrollamiento; *(spiral)* espiral f; *(of a road)* vuelta, serpenteo; *(of a river)* serpenteo; *(of a reel)* devanado; *(of a clock)* cuerda; ELEC. bobinado, devanado II. adj. *(sinuous)* sinuoso, tortuoso; *(spiral)* en espiral, de caracol <w. staircase escalera de caracol>.

wind·ing-sheet (wĭn′dĭng-shēt′) s. mortaja.

wind instrument (wĭnd) s. instrumento de viento.

wind·jam·mer (wĭnd′jăm′ər) s. MARÍT. *(ship)* velero; *(sailor)* marinero, tripulante mf.

wind·lass (wĭnd′ləs) s. MEC. torno, molinete m.

wind·mill (wĭnd′mĭl′) s. *(mill)* molino de viento; *(toy)* molinete m; FIG. *(enemy)* molino de viento <tilting at windmills luchando contra molinos de viento>.

win·dow (wĭn′dō) s. *(of a building)* ventana; *(of a vehicle, ticket office)* ventanilla; *(pane of glass)* cristal m; *(of a shop)* escaparate m, vidriera; *(of an envelope)* ventana ♦ to lean out of the w. asomarse a la ventana • to look out the w. mirar por la ventana.

window box s. jardinera, macetero.

win·dow-dress·ing o **window dressing** (wĭn′dō-drĕs′ĭng) s. *(occupation)* decoración de vidrieras f; FIG. *(appearance)* engaño, oropel m.

window frame s. marco de la ventana.

win·dow·pane (wĭn′dō-pān′) s. cristal de ventana m.

window shade s. persiana, cortinilla.

win·dow-shop (wĭn′dō-shŏp′) intr. **-shopped, -shop·ping** mirar los escaparates de las tiendas, comprar con los ojos.

win·dow·sill (wĭn′dō-sĭl′) s. antepecho de la ventana, alféizar m.

wind·pipe (wĭnd′pīp′) s. ANAT. tráquea.

wind·row (wĭnd′rō′) I. s. *(row)* hilera, montón (creado por el viento); AGR. hilera de trigo o heno puesto a secar II. tr. poner en hileras.

wind·screen (wĭnd′skrēn′) s. G.B. parabrisas m.

wind·shield (wĭnd′shēld′) s. parabrisas m ♦ w. wiper limpiaparabrisas m.

wind·sock (wĭnd′sŏk′) s. METEOR. manga de aire.

wind·storm (wĭnd′stôrm′) s. vendaval m, ventarrón m.

wind·swept (wĭnd′swĕpt′) adj. barrido por el viento.

wind tee (wĭnd) s. AER. T indicadora del viento.

wind tunnel (wĭnd) s. AER., MEC. túnel aerodinámico.

wind-up (wĭnd′ŭp′) I. s. conclusión f, final m II. adj. de cuerda.

wind·ward (wĭnd′wərd) I. s. barlovento II. adj. de barlovento III. adv. hacia barlovento, a barlovento.

wind·y (wĭn′dē) adj. **-i·er, -i·est** *(windswept)* ventoso, de mucho viento; *(unsheltered)* abierto, expuesto al viento; *(resembling the wind)* parecido al viento, de viento; *(empty)* frívolo, fútil; *(verbose)* verboso; *(flatulent)* flatulento.

wine (wīn) I. s. vino ♦ red w. vino tinto • sparkling w. vino espumoso II. tr. **wined, win·ing** ♦ to w. and dine someone agasajar a alguien —intr. beber vino.

wine cellar s. bodega.

wine·glass (wīn′glăs′) s. copa para vino.

wine·grow·er (wīn′grō′ər) s. vinicultor m.

wine·press (wīn′prĕs′) s. trujal m, lagar m.

win·er·y (wī′nə-rē) s. [pl. **-ies**] vinería, lagar m.

wine·skin (wīn′skĭn′) s. odre m, pellejo de vino.

wing (wĭng) I. s. *(of a bird, plane)* ala; *(of a building)* ala, sector m; *(of a door, partition)* hoja; *(of a windmill)* asta; *(of a chair)* oreja; *(vane)* ala, paleta; *(air force unit)* escuadrilla, brigada aérea; FAM. *(arm)* brazo; POL. ala, facción f; AUTO. aleta; ANAT., BOT. ala, aleta; MIL. ala, flanco; DEP. ala, extremo ♦ on the w. al vuelo, volando • to clip someone's wings cortarle las alas a alguien • to

take under one's w. tomar bajo el ala de uno • to take w. alzar el vuelo, echar a volar • wings TEAT. bastidores, bambalinas; MIL. alas II. intr. volar —tr. *(to empower)* dar alas a; *(an arrow)* emplumar; *(to speed along)* atravesar volando, transportar sobre las alas; *(to wound)* herir en el ala o brazo; ARQ. añadir alas a ♦ to w. it FAM. improvisar.

wing chair s. sillón de orejas m.

wing-ding (wĭng′dĭng′) s. FAM. fiesta animada.

winged (wĭngd, wĭng′ĭd) adj. *(having wings)* alado; *(flying)* volador; *(sublime)* sublime; *(swift)* veloz; *(wounded)* herido en el ala <a w. bird un pájaro herido en el ala>.

wing nut s. tuerca de mariposa, palometa.

wing·span (wĭng′spăn′) s. AVIA., ORNIT. envergadura.

wing·spread (wĭng′sprĕd′) s. AVIA., ORNIT. envergadura.

wink (wĭngk) I. intr. *(to blink)* pestañear; *(lights)* parpadear, titilar; *(stars)* centellear ♦ to w. at *(someone)* guiñar el ojo a alguien; *(something)* FIG. hacer la vista gorda a —tr. guiñar II. s. *(blink)* pestañeo; *(hint)* guiño; *(of light)* parpadeo; FAM. *(short time)* momento, instante m ♦ in a w. FIG. en un abrir y cerrar de ojos • not to sleep a w. no pegar los ojos, pasar la noche en blanco • to get forty winks FIG., FAM. echarse un sueñecito.

win·ner (wĭn′ər) s. *(victor)* ganador m, triunfador m; IRÓN. *(loser)* perdedor m <that guy is a real w. ese tipo es un perdedor>.

win·ning (wĭn′ĭng) I. adj. *(victorious)* vencedor, victorioso; *(book, ticket)* premiado; *(charming)* encantador, atractivo II. s. *(victory)* victoria; MIN. pozo de extracción ♦ winnings ganancias.

win·now (wĭn′ō) tr. *(grain)* aventar; FIG. *(to examine closely)* examinar, escudriñar; *(to separate)* separar; *(to select)* seleccionar, pasar por la criba.

win·some (wĭn′səm) adj. simpático, encantador.

win·ter (wĭn′tər) I. s. invierno ♦ w. clothing ropa de invierno II. intr. invernar, pasar el invierno —tr. hacer pasar el invierno, hacer invernar.

win·ter·green (wĭn′tər-grēn′) s. BOT. *(plant)* gaulteria; *(oil)* aceite de gaulteria m.

win·ter·ize (wĭn′tə-rīz′) tr. **-ized, -iz·ing** preparar para el invierno.

winter solstice s. ASTRON. solsticio de invierno.

win·ter·time (wĭn′tər-tīm′) s. invierno, temporada de invierno.

winter wheat s. trigo de invierno.

win·try (wĭn′trē) o **win·ter·y** (wĭn′tə-rē) adj. **-tri·er, -tri·est** o **-i·er, -i·est** *(of winter)* invernal; FIG. *(cold)* helado <a w. smile una sonrisa helada>.

wipe (wīp) I. tr. **wiped, wip·ing** *(to clean)* limpiar; *(to dry)* secar; *(eyes, forehead)* enjugar; *(nose)* sonar ♦ to w. away *(dirt)* quitar frotando; *(tears)* enjugar • to w. off *(a smile)* borrar; *(dirt)* quitar frotando • to w. the slate clean FIG. hacer borrón y cuenta nueva • to w. out *(to clean)* limpiar; FIG. *(to destroy)* destruir; *(to annihilate)* aniquilar; *(to erase)* borrar; *(a debt)* cancelar; FAM. *(to murder)* asesinar, matar • to w. the floor with FIG. humillar, derrotar por completo • to w. up *(to clean)* limpiar, secar; *(to dry)* secar; *(to destroy)* destruir, aniquilar II. s. *(act)* limpieza; FAM. *(blow)* mamporro; *(swipe)* bofetada.

wipe·out (wīp′out′) s. *(cleaning)* limpieza; FIG. *(destruction)* destrucción f, derrota.

wip·er (wī′pər) s. *(person)* limpiador m; *(duster)* trapo, paño; *(windshield wiper)* limpiaparabrisas m; MEC. leva.

wire (wīr) I. s. *(metallic strand)* alambre m, hilo; *(of a racetrack)* línea de llegada; ELEC. cordón m, cable m; TELEG. *(system)* telegrafía, telégrafo; *(telegram)* telegrama m ♦ to send a w. enviar o poner un telegrama • under the w. FIG. al último momento II. tr. **wired, wir·ing** ELEC. *(to equip)* alambrar; *(a house)* instalar el alambrado de; TELEG. telegrafiar —intr. TELEG. poner un telegrama, telegrafiar.

wire brush s. cepillo metálico.

wire coil s. bobina de alambre.

wired (wīrd) adj. ELEC. con instalación de alambres; JER. *(hyper)* sobreexcitado, nervioso; ELECTRÓN. que tiene dispositivos de espionaje.

ā rey / ă año / b boca / ch chico / d dar / ĕ el / ē mil / g gato / h joya / hw juez / ī aire / k casa / kw cuan /

wire-draw (wīr'drô') tr. **-drew** (-drōō'), **-drawn** (-drôn') *(metal)* trefilar; *(a subject)* debatir hasta el cansancio.

wire gauge s. *(gauge)* calibrador de alambres *m*; *(standard)* sistema tipo de calibración de alambres *m*.

wire·less (wīr'lĭs) I. adj. sin alambres II. s. *(system)* radio *mf*; *(message)* mensaje (telefónico, telegráfico) *m*; G.B. *(radio set, system)* radio.

wireless telephone s. radioteléfono.

Wire·pho·to (wīr'fō'tō) s. telefotografía (marca registrada).

wire·pull·er (wīr'pōōl'ər) s. FIG. maquinador *m*, manipulador *m*.

wire·tap (wīr'tăp') I. s. *(device)* dispositivo interceptor; *(act)* interceptación de líneas telefónicas *f* II. tr. & intr. **-tapped, -tap·ping** *(to monitor)* interceptar (una línea telefónica); *(to place a wiretap)* colocar (un dispositivo interceptor) en una línea telefónica.

wir·ing (wīr'ĭng) s. *(act)* conexión de cables *f*; *(system)* instalación eléctrica.

wir·y (wīr'ē) adj. **-i·er, -i·est** *(of wire)* de alambre; *(kinky)* ensortijado, crespo; *(lean)* enjuto y fuerte.

wis·dom (wĭz'dəm) s. *(knowledge)* sabiduría; *(common sense)* cordura; *(learning)* conocimientos, erudición *f*.

wisdom tooth s. muela del juicio.

wise¹ (wīz) I. adj. **wis·er, wis·est** *(knowing)* sabio; *(judicious)* juicioso; *(having common sense)* sensato, prudente; *(erudite)* sabio, erudito; *(informed)* informado ♦ **the Three W. Men** BÍBL. los Reyes Magos • **to get w.** JER. *(to understand)* caer en el chiste; *(to become insolent)* ponerse impertinente • **to put someone w. to** JER. poner a alguien al tanto de, abrir los ojos a alguien (con respecto a) II. tr. & intr. **wised, wis·ing** ♦ **to w. up** JER. caer en el chiste, poner(se) al tanto.

wise² (wīz) s. manera, modo ♦ **in any w.** de cualquier modo • **in no w.** de ninguna manera • **in some w.** en cierta manera.

wise·a·cre (wīz'ā'kər) s. FAM. sabelotodo *mf*; sabihondo.

wise·crack (wīz'krăk') I. s. JER. salida, ocurrencia II. intr. tener salidas graciosas.

wise guy s. JER. sabihondo, sabelotodo *mf*.

wise·ly (wīz'lē) adv. *(with wisdom)* sabiamente; *(prudently)* prudentemente, con prudencia.

wish (wĭsh) I. s. *(desire)* deseo <*his last w.* su último deseo>; *(petition)* ruego ♦ **to give best wishes** dar recuerdos <*give her my best wishes* dale recuerdos de mi parte> • **to make a w.** expresar un deseo • **wishes** votos <*my best wishes* mis mejores votos> • **your w. is my command** sus deseos son órdenes para mí II. tr. *(to want)* querer <*I don't w. to do it* no lo quiero hacer>; *(to desire)* desear <*we w. you a Merry Christmas* le deseamos una Feliz Navidad>; *(to like to)* gustar <*we w. we had a baby* nos gustaría tener un niño>; *(to bid)* dar <*he wished her good night* le dio las buenas noches> ♦ **I w. I knew!** ¡ojalá lo supiera! • **to w. on** forzar, imponer • **to w. someone good luck** desearle a alguien mucha suerte • **to w. someone well** *o* **ill** desear a alguien buena *o* mala suerte —intr. ♦ **to w. for** desear, anhelar <*what more could I w. for?* ¿qué más puedo desear?>.

wish·bone (wĭsh'bōn') s. ORNIT. espoleta.

wish·ful (wĭsh'fəl) adj. deseoso.

wishful thinking s. ilusiones *f*.

wish·y-wash·y (wĭsh'ē-wŏsh'ē) adj. FAM. **-i·er, -i·est** *(watery)* aguado; *(feeble)* débil; *(insipid)* soso, insulso; *(lacking character)* ni fu ni fa.

wisp (wĭsp) I. s. *(small bunch)* manojo, hacecillo; *(hair)* mechón *m*; *(trace)* vestigio; *(flock)* vuelo; *(ignis fatuus)* fuego fatuo ♦ **a w. of a woman** una mujer menuda II. tr. hacer manojos de.

wist (wĭst) pret. y part. p. de **wit²**.

wis·ter·i·a (wĭ-stîr'ē-ə) *o* **wis·tar·i·a** (wĭ-stâr'ē-ə) s. BOT. glicina.

wist·ful (wĭst'fəl) adj. nostálgico, melancólico.

wit¹ (wĭt) s. *(intelligence)* inteligencia *f*; *(good sense)* talento, juicio; *(imagination)* imaginación *f*, inventiva; *(cleverness)* agudeza, ingenio; *(sanity)* juicio, cordura; *(person)* persona aguda *o* ingeniosa ♦ **to be at wits' end** no saber qué hacer • **to collect one's wits** serenarse • **to have** *o* **to keep**

one's wits about one estar uno en sus cinco sentidos, no perder la cabeza • **to live by one's wits** vivir uno de su ingenio • **to use one's wits** valerse de su propio ingenio • **wits** *(sound judgment)* juicio, razón; *(ingenuity)* ingenio.

wit² (wĭt) tr. & intr. **wist** (wĭst), **wit·ting** ANT. saber ♦ **to w.** es decir, a saber.

witch (wĭch) I. s. *(sorceress)* bruja, hechicera; *(hag)* bruja; FAM. *(young woman)* mujer encantadora, hechicera II. tr. hechizar.

witch·craft (wĭch'krăft') s. *(sorcery)* brujería, hechicería; *(charm)* embrujo.

witch doctor s. hechicero.

witch·er·y (wĭch'ə-rē) s. [pl. **-ies**] *(sorcery)* brujería, hechicería; *(charm)* embrujo.

witch grass s. BOT. gramilla colorada, pata de perdiz.

witch hazel s. *(solution)* agua de hamamelis; BOT. hamamelis *m*.

witch-hunt (wĭch'hŭnt') s. HIST. *(religious trial)* persecución de brujas *f*; FIG. *(mendacious politics)* investigación falsa para sacar ventaja política.

witch·ing (wĭch'ĭng) I. adj. hechicero, mágico II. s. *(sorcery)* brujería, hechicería; *(charm)* embrujo.

with (wĭth) prep. con <*who went w. him?* ¿quién fue con él?>; *(next to)* junto a <*stand w. her* párate junto a ella>; con, de <*a man w. a mustache* un hombre con bigote>; *(in the keeping of)* a, en manos de <*he left the letter w. the doorman* dejó la carta en manos del portero>; *(in the employ of)* en, para <*he is w. a publishing company* trabaja para una compañía editorial>; *(in spite of)* con, a pesar de <*w. all his talent he could not get a job* a pesar de su capacidad no podía conseguir empleo>; *(according to)* de acuerdo con, según <*it varies w. the light* varía según la luz>; *(in comparison)* a <*a dress identical w. the one she has just bought* un vestido idéntico al que ella acaba de comprar>; de <*a trunk crammed w. old shoes* un baúl lleno de zapatos viejos>; *(against)* contra <*wrestling w. an opponent* luchando contra un adversario>; *(because of)* de <*trembling w. fear* temblando de miedo>; *(added to)* junto con <*those, w. the ones we have, will be enough* ésos, junto con los que tenemos, serán suficientes>; *(among)* entre <*he is at ease w. his peers* él se siente cómodo entre sus compañeros> ♦ **to abound w.** abundar en • **to be good w.** saber manejar bien • **to begin w.** en primer término • **to be ill w.** tener • **to be w. child** estar embarazada • **to be w. it** FAM. estar al corriente, estar al tanto • **to part w.** separarse de • **w. her** *o* **him** consigo • **w. me** conmigo • **w. no** sin • **w. that** con eso, dicho eso • **w. time** con (el) tiempo • **w. you** contigo, con usted, con ustedes.

with·al (wĭth-ôl') ANT. I. adv. *(in addition)* además, también II. prep. *(with)* con.

with·draw (wĭth-drô') tr. **-drew** (-drōō'), **-drawn** (-drôn'), **-draw·ing** *(to take away)* sacar, quitar; *(to retract)* retractar —intr. *(to draw back)* retraerse; *(to draw away)* apartarse.

with·draw·al (wĭth-drô'əl) s. *(retreat)* retiro; *(detachment)* separación *f*; *(removal)* retiro, retirada; *(termination)* abandono (de acción, hábito); FISIOL. síntomas de reajuste (por falta de droga, alcohol) *m*.

with·drawn (wĭth-drôn') adj. *(unapproachable)* remoto, reservado; *(shy)* tímido; *(unresponsive)* indiferente.

with·er (wĭth'ər) intr. *(to dry up)* secarse; *(to droop)* marchitarse —tr. *(to fade)* marchitar; FIG. *(to stun)* helar, fulminar <*he withered her with a glance* la fulminó con una mirada>.

with·hold (wĭth-hōld') tr. **-held** (-hĕld'), **-hold·ing** *(to restrain)* retener, contener; *(to refuse)* negarse a conceder, rehusar; COM. deducir (impuestos del salario) —intr. ♦ **to w. from** abstenerse de.

withholding tax s. COM. impuesto retenido.

with·in (wĭth-ĭn') I. adv. *(inside)* dentro <*w. and without* dentro y fuera>; *(at home)* en casa, adentro; *(inwardly)* internamente, en el espíritu <*to make pure w.* purificarse internamente> II. prep. *(inside)* dentro de; *(distance)* a menos de <*the village is w. a mile of the river* el pueblo está a menos de una milla del río>; *(time)* en (un plazo de), antes de <*you have to pay it w. two weeks* tienes que pagarlo en (un plazo de) dos semanas>; *(not beyond)* dentro de los límites de <*I live w. my income* vivo dentro de los límites de mis ingresos> ♦ **to keep w. bounds** mantener a raya • **w. an inch (of)** FIG. a dos dedos (de) • **w. call** al alcance de la voz • **w. reach** a tiro, al alcance de la mano • **w. walking distance** a corta distancia III. s. adentro <*a revolution from w.* una revolución desde adentro>.

with-it (wĭth'ĭt) adj. FAM. moderno, al día.

with-out (wĭth-out') I. adv. fuera II. prep. *(lacking)* sin <*three days w. food* tres días sin comer>; *(at, on, to the outside of)* (a)fuera de (casa, ciudad) ♦ **it goes w. saying** se sobreentiende • **to do** *o* **go w.** pasar(se) sin • **w. doubt** sin duda, ciertamente • **w. end** sin fin, infinito.

with-stand (wĭth-stănd') tr. **-stood** (-stŏŏd'), **-stand-ing** resistir a —intr. resistirse.

with-y (wĭth'ē, wĭth'ē) I. adj. **-i-er, -i-est** *(flexible)* flexible, ágil; *(made of withes)* de mimbre *o* junco II. s. [pl. **-ies**] mimbre *m*, junco.

wit-less (wĭt'lĭs) adj. estúpido, tonto.

wit-ness (wĭt'nĭs) I. s. *(person)* testigo; *(act)* testimonio; *(evidence)* prueba ♦ **to bear false w.** perjurarse • **w. for the defense** testigo de descargo • **w. for the prosecution** testigo de cargo II. tr. *(to be present at)* atestiguar; *(to provide evidence of)* dar prueba de, demostrar; *(to attest to)* atestiguar firmando —intr. *(to testify)* atestiguar, dar prueba ♦ **to w. to** atestiguar.

witness box s. G.B. barra de los testigos.

witness stand s. DER. barra de los testigos.

wit-ti-cism (wĭt'ĭ-sĭz'əm) s. dicho *o* salida graciosa.

wit-ty (wĭt'ē) adj. **-ti-er, -ti-est** *(clever)* agudo, ingenioso; *(humorous)* gracioso, chistoso.

wives (wīvz) pl. de **wife**.

wiz (wĭz) s. FAM. as *m*, genio.

wiz-ard (wĭz'ərd) I. s. *(sorcerer)* mago, hechicero; FIG. *(expert)* genio, as *m* <*he is a w. at math* es un as de las matemáticas>; ANT. *(sage)* sabio II. adj. *(of wizardry)* mágico, de hechicería; G.B. *(excellent)* excelente.

wiz-ard-ry (wĭz'ər-drē) s. magia, hechicería.

wiz-en (wĭz'ən) I. tr. & intr. marchitar(se) II. adj. marchito.

wiz-ened (wĭz'ənd) adj. *(shriveled)* arrugado, *(wizen)* marchito.

wob-ble (wŏb'əl) I. intr. **-bled, -bling** *(to sway)* bambolearse, tambalearse; *(to waver)* vacilar —tr. hacer tambalear(se) II. s. *(unsteady motion)* tambaleo, bamboleo; *(sound)* temblor *m*, fluctuación (de sonido, voz) *f*.

wob-bly (wŏb'lē) adj. **-bli-er, -bli-est** *(shaky)* tambaleante, bamboleante; *(unsteady)* fluctuante, temblorosa (voz); *(uncertain)* vacilante.

woe (wō) I. s. *(sorrow)* tristeza, pesar *m*; *(misfortune)* infortunio; *(calamity)* calamidad *f* II. interj. ¡ay! ♦ **w. is me** ¡ay de mí!

woe-be-gone (wō'bĭ-gôn') adj. *(sorrowful)* triste, melancólico; *(run-down)* en mal estado, decrépito.

woe-ful *o* **wo-ful** (wō'fəl) adj. *(mournful)* apenado; *(causing woe)* que causa pena; *(pitiful)* lamentable.

woke (wōk) un pret. de **wake¹**.

wo-ken (wō'kən) un part. p. de **wake¹**.

wold (wōld) s. llanura ondulada.

wolf (wŏŏlf) I. s. [pl. **wolves** (wŏŏlvz)] ZOOL. lobo (animal y piel); FIG. *(person)* persona rapaz y feroz; JER. *(woman chaser)* don Juan *m*, tenorio; MÚS. sonido discordante, disonancia ♦ **lone w.** FIG. persona solitaria • **to cry w.** dar la alarma sin causa • **w. in sheep's clothing** lobo con piel de oveja, hipócrita II. tr. comer vorazmente.

wolf-hound (wŏŏlf'hound') s. galgo ruso, perro lobo.

wolf pack s. *(animals)* manada de lobos; MIL. flotilla de submarinos de ataque simultáneo.

wolf-ram-ite (wŏŏl'frə-mīt') s. MIN., QUÍM. volframita.

wolfs-bane (wŏŏlfs'bān') s. BOT. luparia, uva lupina.

wol-ver-ine (wŏŏl'və-rēn') s. ZOOL. glotón *m*.

wolves (wŏŏlvz) pl. de **wolf**.

wom-an (wŏŏm'ən) s. [pl. **wom-en** (wĭm'ĭn)] *(female)* mujer *f*; *(servant)* criada; FAM. *(wife)* esposa.

wom-an-hood (wŏŏm'ən-hŏŏd') s. *(womanliness)* feminidad *f*; *(womankind)* mujeres *f*, sexo femenino ♦ **to reach w.** hacerse mujer.

wom-an-ish (wŏŏm'ə-nĭsh) adj. *(womanlike)* femenino, de mujer; *(effeminate)* afeminado.

wom-an-ize (wŏŏm'ə-nīz') tr. **-ized, -iz-ing** afeminar —intr. ser mujeriego.

wom-an-kind (wŏŏm'ən-kīnd') s. las mujeres, la mujer.

wom-an-ly (wŏŏm'ən-lē) adj. **-li-er, -li-est** femenino.

womb (wŏŏm) s. ANAT. útero, matriz *f*; FIG. *(birthplace)* origen *m*, cuna.

wom-bat (wŏm'băt') s. oso australiano.

wom-en (wĭm'ĭn) pl. de **woman**.

wom-en-folk (wĭm'ĭn-fōk') *o* **wom-en-folks** (-fōks') s.pl. las mujeres.

won¹ (wŏn) s. [pl. **won**] FIN. hwan (unidad monetaria coreana).

won² (wŭn) pret. y part. p. de **win**.

won-der (wŭn'dər) I. s. *(marvel)* maravilla <*the wonders of the city* las maravillas de la ciudad>; *(portent)* milagro, prodigio <*the wonders of technology* los milagros de la tecnología>; *(miracle)* milagro <*it is a w. that they did survive* es un milagro que hayan sobrevivido>; *(astonishment)* asombro, admiración *f* <*he looked at us with w.* nos miró con asombro> ♦ **no** *o* **small w.** no es de extrañar • **the w. of it** lo asombroso (de algo) • **to do** *o* **to work wonders** obrar *o* hacer milagros • **w. boy** *o* **child** niño prodigio • **w. drug** medicamento milagroso • **Wonders of the World** maravillas del mundo II. intr. *(to ponder)* pensar <*his answer set us wondering* su respuesta nos dio que pensar>; *(to be doubtful)* no saber, dudar ♦ **to w. at** asombrarse de, admirarse de • **to w. about** *(to speculate about)* estar pensando sobre; *(to have doubts about)* pensar con incertidumbre en • tr. *(to be curious about)* preguntarse <*I w. whether they will do it* me pregunto si lo harán>; *(to consider)* pensar <*we were wondering what would be best* estábamos pensando qué sería lo mejor>.

won-der-ful (wŭn'dər-fəl) adj. *(astonishing)* asombroso, admirable; *(excellent)* maravilloso, fantástico; *(person)* encantador ♦ **w.!** ¡fantástico!, ¡estupendo!

won-der-land (wŭn'dər-lănd') s. *(imaginary realm)* país de las maravillas *m* <*Alice in W.* Alicia en el País de las Maravillas>; *(real place)* lugar bellísimo <*Switzerland is a w.* Suiza es un lugar bellísimo>.

won-der-ment (wŭn'dər-mənt) s. *(astonishment)* asombro, admiración *f*; *(marvel)* maravilla; *(curiosity)* curiosidad *f*.

won-drous (wŭn'drəs) I. adj. maravilloso II. adv. ANT. extraordinariamente.

wont (wônt, wōnt) I. adj. *(accustomed)* acostumbrado <*he is w. to complain* está acostumbrado a quejarse>; *(apt)* propenso <*she is w. to cry* es propensa al llanto> II. s. costumbre *f* III. tr. & intr. acostumbrar(se).

won't (wônt) contr. de **will not**.

wont-ed (wôn'tĭd, wōn'-) adj. *(accustomed)* acostumbrado; *(usual)* habitual, usual.

woo (wŏŏ) tr. *(to court)* cortejar, galantear; *(to seek)* buscar <*he is wooing fame* está buscando la fama>; *(to invite)* tentar, invitar; *(to solicit)* solicitar —intr. cortejar.

wood (wŏŏd) I. s. *(stick)* palo; *(firewood)* leña; *(in golf)* palo con cabeza de madera; BOT., CONSTR. madera • **woods** *(forest)* bosque, monte; MÚS. instrumentos de viento de madera II. tr. *(to fuel)* alimentar con leña; *(to forest)* poblar con árboles —intr. recoger leña.

wood alcohol s. QUÍM. alcohol metílico.

wood-bin (wŏŏd'bĭn') s. leñera.

wood-bine (wŏŏd'bĭn') s. BOT. madreselva.

wood-block (wŏŏd'blŏk') s. *(in paving)* tarugo, adoquín de madera *m*; *(woodcut)* grabado en madera.

wood-carv-ing (wŏŏd'kär'vĭng) s. *(craft)* tallado en madera; *(object)* talla de madera.

wood-chuck (wŏŏd'chŭk') s. ZOOL. marmota de Norteamérica.

wood coal s. *(charcoal)* carbón vegetal *m*; *(lignite)* lignito.

wood-cock (wŏŏd'kŏk') s. [pl. **woodcock** *o* **-cocks**] ORNIT. coalla, becada.

wood-craft (wŏŏd'kräft') s. *(craft)* artesanía en madera; *(outdoors experience)* conocimiento de la vida del bosque.

ã rey / ä año / b boca / ch chico / d dar / ĕ el / ē mil / g gato / h joya / hw juez / ī aire / k casa / kw cuan /

wood·cut (wŏŏd′kŭt′) s. grabado en madera.
wood·cut·ter (wŏŏd′kŭt′ər)·s. leñador *m.*
wood·ed (wŏŏd′ĭd) adj. arbolado, boscoso.
wood·en (wŏŏd′n) adj. *(made of wood)* de madera; *(leg)* de palo; *(stiff)* tieso (actuación); *(expressionless)* sin expresión ♦ **to take w. nickels** FAM. aceptar gato por liebre.
wood engraving s. grabado en madera.
wood·land (wŏŏd′lənd, -lănd′) s. bosque *m*, región arbolada.
wood·peck·er (wŏŏd′pĕk′ər) s. ORNIT. pájaro carpintero, picamaderos *m.*
wood·pile (wŏŏd′pīl′) s. montón de leña *m.*
wood pulp s. pasta de madera, pulpa de madera.
wood·shed (wŏŏd′shĕd′) s. leñera.
woods·man (wŏŏdz′mən) s. [pl. **-men**] habitante de los bosques *m.*
woods·y (wŏŏd′zē) adj. **-i·er, -i·est** boscoso, poblado de árboles.
wood·turn·ing (wŏŏd′tûr′nĭng) s. CARP. torneado de madera.
wood·wind (wŏŏd′wĭnd′) s. MÚS. instrumento de viento de madera ♦ **woodwinds** instrumentos de madera.
wood·work (wŏŏd′wûrk′) s. *(craft)* carpintería; CARP., CONSTR. maderaje *m*, enmaderado.
wood·worm (wŏŏd′wûrm′) s. ENTOM. carcoma.
wood·y (wŏŏd′ē) adj. **-i·er, -i·est** *(plant, tissue)* leñoso; *(smell, taste)* a madera; *(land)* arbolado, poblado de árboles.
woof¹ (wŏŏf, wŏŏf) s. TEJ. *(threads)* trama; *(texture)* textura, tejido; FIG. *(essential element)* elemento esencial.
woof² (wŏŏf) s. *(bark)* ladrido.
woof·er (wŏŏf′ər) s. amplificador para sonidos graves *m.*
wool (wŏŏl) s. *(hair, material)* lana;·*(garment)* prenda de lana ♦ **knitting w.** lana de hacer punto • **steel w.** lana de acero • **w. socks** calcetines de lana.
wool·en (wŏŏl′ən) I. adj. de lana II. s. ♦ **woolens** *(fabric)* lana; *(garments)* prendas de lana.
wool·gath·er·ing (wŏŏl′găth′ər-ĭng) I. s. distracción *f* II. adj. distraído.
wool·grow·er (wŏŏl′grō′ər) s. criador de ganado lanar *m.*
wool·len (wŏŏl′ən) adj. & s. var. de **woolen.**
wool·ly (wŏŏl′ē) I. adj. **-li·er, -li·est** *(consisting of wool)* de lana; *(fleecy)* lanoso, lanudo <*w. sheep* ovejas lanudas>; *(hair)* ensortijado, rizado; *(leaf)* aterciopelado; *(in thought)* enmarañado, impreciso; *(in outline)* borroso II. s. [pl. **-lies**] prenda interior de lana.
wool·pack (wŏŏl′păk′) s. *(for wool)* fardo de lana; METEOR. *(cumulus)* cúmulo.
wool·y (wŏŏl′ē) adj. & s. var. de **woolly.**
woo·zy (wŏŏ′zē, wŏŏz′ē) adj. **-zi·er, -zi·est** *(dazed)* aturdido; *(queasy)* indispuesto; *(dizzy)* mareado.
word (wûrd) s. *(sound, representation)* palabra <*the spoken w.* la palabra hablada>; *(sworn intention)* palabra, promesa <*she kept her w.* cumplió su promesa>; *(order)* orden *f*; *(password)* santo y seña; *(news)* noticia, información *f* <*the latest w.* la última noticia>; *(rumor)* rumor *m* <*w. has it that she is married* según los rumores, ella está casada> • **a man of his w.** hombre de palabra • **a w. of advice** un consejo • **beyond words** hasta lo indecible • **by w. of mouth** verbalmente, de palabra • **in a w.** en una palabra • **in every sense of the w.** en toda la extensión de la palabra • **in other words** en otras palabras • **in so many words** *(precisely)* palabra por palabra, textualmente; *(clearly)* claramente, sin ambages • **in the words of** según las palabras de, según dice • **mark my words** tome nota de lo que digo, advierta mis palabras • **my w.!** ¡válgame Dios!, ¡Dios mío! • **on my w.** bajo mi palabra • **play on words** juego de palabras • **take my w. for it** se lo aseguro, le doy mi palabra • **The W.** RELIG. el Verbo • **to eat one's words** tragarse las palabras, retractarse • **to have the last w.** decir la última palabra • **to have words with someone** tener algunas palabras con alguien, reñir de palabra con alguien • **to leave w. that** dejar dicho que • **to put in a good w. for someone** decir unas palabras en favor de (alguien) • **to take someone's w. for it** creer en

la palabra de alguien • **to take the words out of someone's mouth** quitarle a alguien la palabra de la boca • **to twist someone's words** tergiversar las palabras de alguien • **to waste one's words** hablar en vano • **upon my w.** bajo mi palabra • **without a w.** sin decir palabra • **with these words** dichas *o* con estas palabras • **w. for w.** palabra por palabra, literalmente • **words** *(speech)* discurso; *(talk)* charla; *(quarrel)* disputa, discusión; MÚS. letra.
word blindness s. MED. alexia (pérdida de la capacidad de leer).
word·book (wûrd′bŏŏk′) s. vocabulario, lexicón *m.*
word·ing (wûr′dĭng) s. *(phraseology)* redacción *f*; *(diction)* dicción *f.*
word·less (wûrd′lĭs) adj. mudo, sin palabras.
word play s. juego de palabras.
word processing s. COMPUT. procesador de palabras (sistema) *m.*
word processor s. COMPUT. procesador de palabras (aparato) *m.*
word·y (wûr′dē) adj. **-i·er, -i·est** *(verbal)* verbal; *(redundant)* verboso.
wore (wôr) pret. de **wear¹·².**
work (wûrk) I. s. *(toil)* trabajo, labor *f*; *(employment)* trabajo, empleo <*to look for w.* buscar trabajo>; *(occupation)* ocupación *f*, empleo; *(task)* trabajo, labor <*to begin the day's w.* comenzar la labor del día>; *(office)* trabajo, empleo <*he called her at w.* la llamó a su empleo>; MEC., TEC. pieza ♦ **a good day's w.** una buena labor • **at w.** trabajando • **down to w.!** ¡manos a la obra! • **keep up the good w.!** ¡siga haciendo tan buen trabajo! • **let's get to w.!** ¡manos a la obra! • **the works** JER. todo, de todo • **to be out of w.** estar sin empleo, no tener trabajo • **to make short w. of** *(to finish)* terminar rápidamente; *(to eat)* comer rápidamente; *(to rid of)* deshacerse rápidamente de • **to put someone out of w.** despedir a alguien • **works** *(output)* obra <*the works of Verdi* las obras de Verdi>; *(needlework)* labor, costura; *(embroidery)* bordado; *(factory)* fábrica, taller; *(mechanism)* mecanismo, maquinaria <*the works of a watch* el mecanismo de un reloj>; RELIG. obras II. intr. **worked** *o* **wrought** (rôt), **work·ing** *(to toil)* trabajar; *(to be employed)* tener trabajo, estar empleado; *(to operate)* operar, funcionar <*the machine does not w.* la máquina no funciona>; *(to be effectual)* tener éxito, surtir efecto <*the combination worked* la combinación surtió efecto>; *(to contort)* torcerse <*her mouth worked with fear* su boca se torcía de miedo>; *(to ferment)* fermentar ♦ **to w. away** trabajar, seguir trabajando • **to w. down** descender poco a poco • **to w. free** soltarse, desatarse • **to w. loose** aflojarse • **to w. out** salir bien <*my plan did not w. out* mi plan no salió bien>; *(to do exercises)* hacer gimnasia • **to w. through** penetrar poco a poco —tr. *(to bring about)* producir, hacer <*to w. miracles* hacer milagros>; *(to handle)* accionar, manejar <*to w. a power mower* manejar un cortacésped a motor>; *(to forge)* forjar, moldear; *(to solve)* resolver; *(to embroider)* bordar; *(to arrange)* disponer, arreglárselas <*he worked it so that* se las arregló de tal forma que>; *(to cultivate)* cultivar; *(to drive)* hacer trabajar <*he works his laborers hard* hace trabajar duro a sus obreros>; *(to persuade)* influir en, inducir; *(to be in charge of)* tener a su cargo; *(to ferment)* hacer fermentar; CUL. mezclar, combinar ♦ **to w. at** trabajar en, ocuparse de • **to w. down** hacer bajar • **to w. in** introducir, meter <*to w. a few jokes during a speech* meter algunos chistes en un discurso> • **to w. into** meter en, intercalar en • **to w. off** *(weight)* quitarse; *(anger)* desahogar • **to w. on** *o* **upon** *(to continue working)* seguir trabajando en; *(to work)* trabajar en; *(to affect)* afectar, obrar sobre; *(to persuade)* influir en, persuadir; *(to study)* estudiar • **to w. one's head off** trabajar hasta más no poder • **to w. one's way through** abrirse camino por • **to w. one's will upon** imponer la voluntad de uno a • **to w. out** *(to solve)* resolver, solucionar; *(blame)* expiar, borrar; *(calculation)* calcular; *(addition)* sumar; *(to develop)* desarrollar, elaborar; *(mine, soil)* agotar • **to w. over** alterar, rehacer • **to w. up** *(to excite)* estimular, excitar; *(to develop)* desarrollar, preparar.

work·a·ble (wûr′kə-bəl) adj. *(exploitable)* que se puede trabajar, explotable; *(feasible)* factible.

work·a·day (wûr′kə-dā′) adj. *(of working days)* laborable; *(everyday)* cotidiano, ordinario.

work·a·hol·ic (wûr′kə-hô′lĭk, -hŏl′ĭk) s. trabajador compulsivo.

work·bench (wûrk′bĕnch′) s. mesa de trabajo, banco de taller.

work·book (wûrk′bŏok′) s. *(exercise booklet)* cuaderno de ejercicios; *(manual)* manual de instrucciones m; *(work record)* libro de trabajo.

work·box (wûrk′bŏks′) s. COST. costurero; MEC. caja de herramientas.

work·day (wûrk′dā′) I. s. *(day)* día laborable m; *(hours)* horas de trabajo II. adj. *(of working days)* laborable; *(everyday)* cotidiano; *(commonplace)* ordinario.

work·er (wûr′kər) s. *(person)* trabajador m, obrero; *(ant, bee)* obrera.

work force s. trabajadores m, mano de obra f.

work·horse (wûrk′hôrs′) s. *(horse)* caballo de tiro; *(person)* persona muy trabajadora.

work·house (wûrk′hous′) s. *(prison)* correccional m; G.B. *(poorhouse)* asilo para pobres.

work·ing (wûr′kĭng) I. adj. *(employed)* que trabaja <the w. woman la mujer que trabaja>; *(population, class)* obrero; *(clothes, hours)* de trabajo; *(expenses)* de explotación; *(day)* laborable, de trabajo; *(knowledge)* básico, pasable; *(majority)* suficiente; *(hypothesis, draft)* de trabajo; *(model)* operativo; MEC. móvil, mecánico ♦ **to be in w. order** *o* **condition** estar funcionando • **w. drawing** TEC. plano adecuado (de construcción) • **w. speed** velocidad de funcionamiento; *(handling)* manejo; *(performing)* realización f; *(of metals, cloths)* labrado; *(of the soil)* labrado, cultivo; *(of a mine)* explotación f; *(of a drug)* efecto ♦ **workings** funcionamiento.

working capital s. COM. capital activo, fondo de operaciones.

working class s. clase obrera, proletariado.

work·ing·man (wûr′kĭng-măn′) s. [pl. **-men** (-mĕn′)] trabajador m, obrero.

working papers s.pl. permiso de trabajo.

work·less (wûrk′lĭs) adj. desocupado, sin trabajo.

work·load (wûrk′lōd′) s. *(amount)* carga de trabajo; MEC. capacidad de trabajo f.

work·man (wûrk′mən) s. [pl. **-men**] trabajador m, obrero.

work·man·like (wûrk′mən-līk′) *o* **work·man·ly** (-lē) adj. bien hecho, hecho a conciencia.

work·man·ship (wûrk′mən-shĭp′) s. *(skill)* destreza; *(product)* producto, fabricación f.

work·out (wûrk′out′) s. *(exercise)* ejercicio; *(task)* tarea difícil; DEP. entrenamiento.

work·peo·ple (wûrk′pē′pəl) s.pl. G.B. obreros, jornaleros.

work plan s. plan de trabajo m, plan de acción.

work·room (wûrk′rōom′, -rōom′) s. taller m, sala de trabajo.

work·shop (wûrk′shŏp′) s. *(location)* taller m; *(group)* grupo (de trabajo, estudio), taller.

work stoppage s. paro, suspensión de trabajo f.

work·ta·ble (wûrk′tā′bəl) s. mesa de trabajo.

work·up (wûrk′ŭp′) s. examen médico detallado.

work·week (wûrk′wēk′) s. total de horas de trabajo en una semana m.

world (wûrld) s. mundo ♦ **all over the w.** *o* **the w. over** en el mundo entero, en todas partes • **all the w.** el mundo entero • **a w. away** lejos, lejísimo • **a w. of (difference)** la mar de (diferencias) • **for all the w.** exactamente, ni más ni menos • **it's a small w.** ¡qué pequeño es el mundo! • **man of the w.** hombre de mundo • **not for all the w.** por nada del mundo • **not to be long for this w.** quedarle poco a uno • **on top of the w.** FAM. en el séptimo cielo • **out of this w.** FIG., FAM. increíble, extraordinario • **the other** *o* **the next w.** el otro mundo • **to be all the w. to someone** ser todo para alguien • **to bring into the w.** traer al mundo • **to come down in the w.** venir a menos • **to have the best**

of both worlds tenerlo todo al mismo tiempo • **to live in a w. of one's own** vivir en un mundo aparte • **to make a w. of difference** ser muy distinto • **to move up in the w.** prosperar • **to see the w.** ver *o* correr mundo • **to think the w. of** poner por las nubes a • **(where, what) in the w. . . . ?** (¿dónde, qué) diablos . . . ? • **w. champion** campeón mundial • **w. history** historia universal • **worlds of** cantidad de • **w. without end** RELIG. por los siglos de los siglos.

world·li·ness (wûrld′lē-nĭs) s. espíritu mundano.

world·ling (wûrld′lĭng) s. persona de mundo.

world·ly (wûrld′lē) I. adj. **-li·er, -li·est** *(secular)* secular; *(worldly-wise)* sofisticado; *(material)* material II. adv. de forma mundana.

world·ly-wise (wûrld′lē-wīz′) adj. sofisticado, con experiencia de la vida.

world power s. potencia mundial.

World War I s. la Primera Guerra Mundial.

World War II s. la Segunda Guerra Mundial.

world-wea·ry (wûrld′wîr′ē) adj. **-ri·er, -ri·est** hastiado del mundo.

world-wide (wûrld′wīd′) adj. mundial.

worm (wûrm) I. s. ZOOL. *(invertebrate)* gusano, lombriz f; *(larva)* gusano; *(parasite)* helminto, solitaria; FIG. *(tormenting force)* gusanillo (de la conciencia); *(vile person)* canalla m, granuja m; *(insignificant person)* gusano; TEC. *(thread)* rosca, filete m; *(worm screw)* tornillo sin fin; *(coil)* serpentín (de alambique) m ♦ **worms** MED. helmintiasis, lombrices II. tr. *(to make way)* colarse, introducirse en (como un gusano); *(to elicit)* sacar, sonsacar <to w. a secret out of somebody sonsacarle un secreto a alguien>; *(to cure)* curar de lombrices, librar de gusanos; MARÍT. reforzar con cuerda —intr. arrastrarse, deslizarse.

worm-eat·en (wûrm′ēt′n) adj. *(eaten)* carcomido, agusanado; *(decayed)* podrido; *(antiquated)* anticuado, decrépito.

worm gear s. MEC. *(gear)* engranaje de tornillo sin fin m; *(wheel)* rueda helicoidal.

worm·hole (wûrm′hōl′) s. agujero hecho por un gusano.

worm wheel s. MEC. rueda dentada de tornillo sin fin.

worm·wood (wûrm′wŏod′) s. *(bitterness)* amargura; BOT. absintio, ajenjo (planta y bebida).

worm·y (wûr′mē) adj. **-i·er, -i·est** *(infested with worms)* agusanado, gusaniento; *(worm-eaten)* carcomido; *(motheaten)* apolillado; FIG. *(devious)* tortuoso, rastrero.

worn (wôrn) I. part. p. de **wear**[1,2] II. adj. *(used)* gastado, desgastado; *(exhausted)* agotado; *(trite)* gastado, trillado.

worn-out (wôrn′out′) adj. *(used)* gastado; *(exhausted)* agotado.

wor·ri·er (wûr′ē-ər) s. aprensivo.

wor·ri·ment (wûr′ē-mənt) s. preocupación f, inquietud f.

wor·ri·some (wûr′ē-səm) adj. *(causing worry)* inquietante; *(anxious)* aprensivo.

wor·ry (wûr′ē) I. intr. **-ried, -ry·ing** preocupar <he worries about everything se preocupa por todo> —tr. *(to distress)* preocupar <that did not w. me eso no me preocupaba>; *(to bother)* atormentar, molestar <don't w. us with your complaints no nos molestes con tus quejas>; *(to toy with)* jugar con ♦ **to w. away at** luchar con • **to w. one's head about** FAM. preocuparse por II. s. [pl. **-ries**] *(anxiety)* preocupación f, inquietud f; *(trouble)* preocupación, problema m ♦ **to be a w. to** preocupar a.

wor·ry·wart (wûr′ē-wôrt′) s. persona aprensiva (sin razón).

worse (wûrs) I. adj. [comp. de **bad**; comp. de **ill**] *(more severe)* más fuerte <the rain was w. yesterday la lluvia fue más fuerte ayer>; *(in quality, effect)* peor ♦ **to get w. and w.** *(patient)* ponerse cada vez peor; *(situation)* ir de mal en peor • **to get** *o* **to grow w.** empeorar, ponerse peor • **to go from bad to w.** ir de mal en peor • **to make things** *o* **matters w.** para empeorar las cosas II. s. ♦ **and w.** y cosas peores <he is a thief and w. es un ladrón y cosas peores> • **to change** *o* **take a turn for the w.** empeorar • **so much the w.** tanto peor • **to be none the w. for it** no perjudicarle a uno • **to think none the w. of** no tener en menos III. adv. *(in a worse way)* peor <I felt w. today hoy me sentí peor>; *(more severely)* más <it snowed w. than ever nevó más que nunca> ♦ **to be w. off** estar peor.

ã rey / ä año / b boca / ch chico / d dar / ĕ el / ē mil / g gato / h joya / hw juez / ī aire / k casa / kw cuan /

wors·en (wûr′sən) tr. & intr. empeorar(se).

wor·ship (wûr′shĭp) I. s. *(adoration)* adoración *f*, reverencia; *(ritual)* culto; *(devotion)* devoción *f* ♦ **Your W.** G.B. Señoría, Vuestra Merced II. tr. RELIG. venerar; FIG. *(to adore)* idolatrar, adorar —intr. RELIG. venerar.

wor·ship·er *o* **wor·ship·per** (wûr′shĭ-pər) s. *(devotee)* devoto; *(admirer)* adorador *m*; *(participant in a religious service)* fiel *mf*.

wor·ship·ful (wûr′shĭp-fəl) adj. *(reverent)* reverente; *(adoring)* adorador; G.B. *(honorable)* honorable.

worst (wûrst) I. adj. [superl. de **bad**; superl. de **ill**] *(in quality, effect)* peor *<the w. movie I ever saw* la peor película que he visto>; *(most severe)* más fuerte ♦ **in the w. way** FAM. de mala manera, mucho II. adv. *(in the worst manner)* peor *<he writes w. when he stops to think* cuando se detiene a pensar es cuando peor escribe>; *(most severely)* más *<where does your injury hurt w.?* ¿en dónde te duele más la herida?> ♦ **w. of all** peor aún III. tr. derrotar, vencer IV. s. ♦ **at w.** en el peor de los casos • **if (the) w. comes to (the) w.** en el peor de los casos • **the w. of it is that** lo peor del caso es que • **to be at its w.** *(in quality)* estar peor que nunca; *(situation)* estar en el peor momento • **to be the w. of it** llevar la peor parte, salir perdiendo • **to turn out for the w.** salir de la peor forma posible.

wor·sted (wŏos′tĭd, wûr′stĭd) TEJ. I. s. *(yarn)* estambre *m*; *(fabric)* tela de estambre II. adj. de estambre.

wort (wûrt, wôrt) s. *(malt infusion)* mosto de cerveza; BOT. *(liverwort)* hepática; *(madwort)* raspilla.

worth (wûrth) I. s. *(value)* valor *m* *<a jewel of considerable w.* una joya de gran valor>; *(wealth)* fortuna *<her w. is estimated at over two million* se calcula que su fortuna es de más de dos millones>; *(moral value)* valor, valía; *(merit)* mérito ♦ **to be of great w.** ser muy valioso para • **to get one's money's w.** sacar provecho de lo pagado • **to get one's money's w. out of** sacarle el dinero a • **(two, four) dollars' w. of change** (dos, cuatro) dólares en menudo II. adj. *(monetarily)* que vale *<a pen w. five dollars* una pluma que vale cinco dólares>; *(deserving of)* digno de, que merece *<a proposal w. considering* una idea digna de consideración> ♦ **for all one is w.** con todas las fuerzas de uno • **for what it is w.** por si sirve de algo • **to be w.** *(in price)* valer *<the house is w. much more* la casa vale mucho más>; *(in value)* tener un valor de *<a coupon that is w. fifty cents* un cupón que tiene un valor de cincuenta centavos>; *(to be the equivalent of)* valer por *<he is w. the whole lot* vale por todos ellos>; *(financially)* tener un capital de • **to be w. it** *o* **the trouble** valer la pena • **to be w. one's salt** valer mucho • **to be w. one's weight in gold** valer uno su peso en oro.

wor·thi·ness (wûr′thē-nĭs) s. mérito.

worth·less (wûrth′lĭs) adj. *(useless)* sin valor, inútil; *(contemptible)* despreciable.

worth·while (wûrth′hwīl′) adj. que vale la pena.

wor·thy (wûr′thē) I. adj. **-thi·er, -thi·est** *(having merit)* meritorio; *(useful)* útil; *(just)* justo; *(honorable)* noble, digno; *(admirable)* admirable; *(deserving)* digno *<w. of fame* digno de fama> II. s. [pl. **-thies**] persona ilustre, clero varón.

would §G5, 11 (wŏod) pret. de **will²**.

would-be (wŏod′bē′) adj. *(supposedly)* supuesto; *(aspiring)* aspirante.

wouldn't (wŏod′nt) contr. de **would not.**

wouldst (wŏodst) *o* **would·est** (wŏod′ĭst) ANT. segunda persona sing., tiempo pret., de **will²**.

wound¹ (wŏond) I. s. herida II. tr. & intr. herir.

wound² (wound) pret. y part. p. de **wind²,³**.

wove (wōv) pret. y part. p. de **weave**.

wo·ven (wō′vən) part. p. de **weave**.

wow (wou) FAM. I. interj. ¡increíble!, ¡cáspita! II. s. gran éxito III. tr. asombrar *<the singer wowed the audience* el cantante asombró al público>.

wrack (răk) s. despojo, ruina ♦ **to go to w. and ruin** echarse a perder, arruinarse.

wraith (rāth) s. fantasma *m*, espectro.

wran·gle (răng′gəl) I. intr. **-gled, -gling** *(to dispute)* disputar; *(to quarrel)* pelear —tr. *(to get)* obtener arguyendo; *(to herd)* rodear (ganado, caballos) II. s. *(argument)* discusión *f*, pelea; *(roundup)* rodeo (de ganado, caballos).

wran·gler (răng′glər) s. *(quarreler)* pendenciero, discutidor *m*; *(cowboy)* vaquero.

wrap (răp) I. tr. **wrapped** *o* **wrapt** (răpt), **wrap·ping** *(a child, package)* envolver; *(rope, chain)* enrollar; *(one's arms)* cubrir, pasar; *(in fog, secrecy)* envolver ♦ **to be wrapped up in** FIG. estar absorto en • **to w. up** FIG. *(a deal)* cerrar; *(a game, meeting)* poner punto final a; *(to summarize)* resumir —intr. enrollarse ♦ **to w. up** abrigarse II. s. *(robe)* bata; *(cloak, shawl)* manto; *(coat)* abrigo; *(wrapping)* envoltura ♦ **to keep under wraps** FIG. tener guardado en secreto.

wrap·a·round (răp′ə-round′) s. *(coat)* capa, manto; IMPR. pliego de cuatro páginas encuadernado en un libro *o* revista.

wrap·per (răp′ər) s. *(person)* empaquetador *m*; *(wrap)* envoltura; *(book jacket)* sobrecubierta; *(tobacco leaf)* capa, hoja de tabaco; *(robe)* bata.

wrap·ping (răp′ĭng) s. envoltura.

wrapt (răpt) un pret. y part. p. de **wrap**.

wrap-up (răp′ŭp′) s. resumen *m*.

wrath (răth, räth) I. s. *(anger)* ira; *(fury)* furia; *(divine retribution)* castigo de Dios II. adj. ANT. furioso.

wrath·ful (răth′fəl, räth′-) adj. furioso, iracundo.

wreak (rēk) tr. *(vengeance, punishment)* infligir; *(anger, resentment)* descargar ♦ **to w. havoc** hacer estragos.

wreath (rēth) s. [pl. **wreaths** (rēthz)] *(circle)* guirnalda, corona; *(spiral)* espiral (de humo, vapor) *m*.

wreathe (rēth) tr. **wreathed, wreath·ing** *(to entwine)* trenzar, hacer una guirnalda de; *(to crown)* coronar con guirnalda; *(to decorate)* enguirnaldar; *(to curl)* enrollar; *(to surround)* rodear —intr. *(to curl)* enroscarse; *(to writhe)* retorcerse; *(smoke)* subir en espirales.

wreck (rĕk) I. s. *(destruction)* destrucción *f*; *(shipwreck)* naufragio; *(ship's remains)* restos de un naufragio; *(collision remains)* restos, destrozos; *(broken-down thing)* cascajo *<this car is a w.* este carro es un cascajo> II. tr. *(to destroy)* destrozar; *(a ship)* hacer naufragar, hundir; *(a train)* hacer descarrilar; *(to tear down)* derrumbar; *(to ruin)* arruinar —intr. *(to suffer destruction)* destruirse, destrozarse; *(to tear down)* destrozarse, derrumbarse.

wreck·age (rĕk′ĭj) s. *(act)* destrozo; *(remains)* restos, despojos.

wreck·er (rĕk′ər) s. *(destroyer)* destructor *m*; *(demolition crew member)* demoledor *m*; *(recovery truck)* grúa; *(salvager)* persona que rescata restos de naufragios; *(plunderer)* saqueador *m*.

wrecking bar s. barra sacaclavos.

wren (rĕn) s. ORNIT. reyezuelo, abadejo.

wrench (rĕnch) I. s. *(injury)* torcedura; *(grief)* dolor *m*, angustia; *(distortion)* tergiversación *f*; MEC. llave *f* *<adjustable w.* llave inglesa> II. tr. *(to twist)* torcer; *(to grieve)* doler, angustiar *<it wrenched her to say good-by* le dolió decir adiós>; *(a statement)* torcer, tergiversar ♦ **to w. off** *o* **out** arrancar • **to w. open** abrir de un tirón.

wrest (rĕst) I. tr. *(to obtain)* arrebatar, arrancar *<I wrested the book from his hands* le arranqué el libro de las manos>; *(to usurp)* tomar a la fuerza, arrebatar; *(to extract)* arrancar; *(to distort)* distorcionar, deformar II. s. *(action)* torción violenta; MÚS. llave de afinación *f*.

wres·tle (rĕs′əl) I. intr. **-tled, -tling** luchar —tr. *(to contend)* luchar con *o* contra; *(to throw)* derribar (a un ternero para marcarlo) II. s. lucha.

wres·tler (rĕs′lər) s. DEP. luchador *m*.

wres·tling (rĕs′lĭng) s. DEP. lucha.

wrest pin s. MÚS. clavija.

wretch (rĕch) s. *(unhappy person)* desgraciado, infeliz *mf*; *(base person)* canalla *mf*, miserable *mf* ♦ **little w.** pillín.

wretch·ed (rĕch′ĭd) adj. *(miserable)* desgraciado, desdichado; *(shabby)* horrible, miserable; *(despicable)* misera-

---

ble, vil; *(in quality)* horrible, espantoso; *(luck, weather)* malo, pésimo; *(damned)* desgraciado, condenado <*this w. idiot* este condenado idiota> ◆ **to feel w.** sentirse terriblemente mal.

wretch·ed·ness (rĕch´ĭd-nĭs) s. *(misery)* miseria, pobreza; *(unfortunateness)* desdicha, desgracia; *(depression)* depresión *f*, abatimiento; *(vileness)* vileza, infamia; *(of situation, action)* lo horrible.

wrig·gle (rĭg´əl) I. intr. **-gled, -gling** *(to squirm)* retorcerse, menearse; *(to proceed)* culebrear <*wriggling he crossed the rocks* culebreando cruzó las rocas>; *(to get out)* escabullirse <*he wriggled out of the situation* se escabulló de la situación>; *(to get into)* insinuarse <*he wriggled into the conversation* se insinuó en la conversación> —tr. menear, contonear II. s. meneo, culebreo.

wring (rĭng) I. tr. **wrung** (rŭng), **wring·ing** *(a towel, clothes)* escurrir; *(to wrench)* torcer, retorcer <*to w. someone's neck* retorcerle el pescuezo a alguien> ◆ **to w. money from** sacarle dinero a • **to w. out** *(clothes, water)* escurrir; *(truth, money)* sacar • **to w. someone's heart** partirle el corazón a alguien —intr. retorcerse II. s. torcedura.

wring·er (rĭng´ər) s. escurridor *m*.

wrin·kle (rĭng´kəl) I. s. *(crease)* arruga; FAM. *(innovation)* método nuevo II. tr. **-kled, -kling** *(to crease)* arrugar; *(to draw up)* fruncir (cejas, ceño) —intr. arrugarse.

wrist (rĭst) s. *(of a shirt, glove)* puño; ANAT. muñeca.

wrist·band (rĭst´bănd´) s. *(band)* muñequera; *(sleeve section)* bocamanga.

wrist·lock (rĭst´lŏk´) s. DEP. llave (en lucha) *f*.

wrist pin s. MEC. pasador de pistón *m*.

wrist watch s. reloj de pulsera *m*.

writ (rĭt) s. DER. mandato, orden *f* ◆ **W.** RELIG. Escritura <*Holy W.* la Sagrada Escritura>.

write (rīt) tr. **wrote** (rōt), **writ·ten** (rĭt´n), **writ·ing** *(an address, words)* escribir <*he wrote his name on the card* escribió su nombre en la tarjeta>; *(to author, compose)* escribir, componer; *(a will, contract)* redactar; *(a check)* extender, hacer; *(an insurance policy)* preparar (una póliza); *(to ordain)* escribir <*it was written that they would lose* estaba escrito que perderían>; COMPUT. escribir, guardar en la memoria ◆ **to be written on one's face** tener escrito *o* vérsele a uno en la cara • **to w. down** *(to put in writing)* poner por escrito; *(to make a note of)* anotar, apuntar; *(to depreciate)* rebajar; *(to disparage)* calumniar, denigrar • **to w. in** intercalar *o* insertar en • **to w. in (pencil, ink)** escribir con (lápiz, tinta) • **to w. in** *o* **off for** solicitar por escrito • **to w. in for more details** escribir para pedir mayor información • **to w. off** *(a person)* dar por perdido; COM. *(to depreciate)* amortizar; *(a debt)* cancelar; *(to declare)* declarar (como pérdida) • **to w. out** *(to put in writing)* poner por escrito; *(a check)* extender, hacer; *(to write in full)* escribir con todas las letras • **to w. someone off as** clasificar a alguien como • **to w. up** *(a note, news)* redactar; *(events)* hacer un reportaje sobre; *(a journal)* poner al día; TEN. *(assets)* sobrestimar; FAM. *(to fine)* poner una multa a; *(to praise)* poner por las nubes —intr. escribir ◆ **as I w.** mientras escribo estas letras • **to be nothing to w. home about** no ser nada del otro mundo • **to w. back** contestar • **to w. in** escribir.

write-down (rīt´doun´) s. COM., FIN. rebaja de valor.

write-in (rīt´ĭn´) s. POL. voto para un candidato no oficial.

write-off (rīt´ôf´) s. COM. *(cancellation)* cancelación *f*; *(depreciation)* amortización *f*.

writ·er (rī´tər) s. escritor *m*.

write-up (rīt´ŭp´) s. *(review)* crítica, nota; COM. valorización excesiva del activo.

writhe (rīth) I. intr. **writhed, writh·ing** *(to twist)* retorcerse; *(to move)* serpentear; *(to suffer)* retorcerse de dolor —tr. hacer retorcer II. s. contorsión *f*, retorcimiento.

writ·ing (rī´tĭng) s. *(language, symbols)* escritura; *(inscription)* inscripción *f*; *(handwriting)* letra; *(written work)* escrito; *(literary composition)* escrito, obra <*the writings of Emerson* las obras de Emerson>; *(style)* estilo; *(act)* escritura ◆ **at the time of w.** al escribir estas letras • **in one's own w.** del propio puño y letra de uno • **in w.** por escrito • **the w. on the wall** los signos del destino • **the w. profession** la profesión de escritor.

writing desk s. escritorio.

writing pad s. bloc *m*.

writing paper s. papel de escribir *m*.

writ·ten (rĭt´n) part. p. de **write**.

wrong (rông) I. adj. *(immoral)* malo <*cheating is w.* es malo hacer trampas>; *(unfair)* injusto <*such severe punishment is w.* un castigo tan fuerte es injusto>; *(incorrect)* erróneo, equivocado; *(false)* falso; *(mistaken)* equivocado <*a w. telephone number* un número de teléfono equivocado>; *(not suitable)* inadecuado; *(inopportune)* malo, inoportuno; *(improper)* indebido ◆ **in the w. place** en el lugar equivocado, mal colocado • **in the w. sense** en sentido equivocado • **is anything w.?** ¿pasa algo? • **that is the w. way of doing it** eso no se hace así • **there is something w. with** *(physical condition, functioning)* no andar bien; *(mood)* pasarle algo a • **the w. side of (a sock, sweater)** el revés de (una media, suéter) • **the w. one** el que no es <*he read the w. one* leyó el que no era> • **to be the w. (person, tool) for** no ser (la persona, herramienta) adecuada para • **to be w.** *(to be immoral)* ser malo, estar mal; *(to act improperly)* hacer mal <*they were w. to tell him* hicieron mal en decírselo>; *(to be false)* no ser cierto; *(to be mistaken)* equivocarse, no tener razón; *(to be amiss)* andar mal, pasar <*something was w.* algo pasaba>; *(in operation)* no estar bien (reloj, termómetro) • **to get on the w. side of someone** ponerse a malas con alguien • **to get up on the w. side of the bed** levantarse con el pie izquierdo • **to go the w. way** tomar el camino equivocado • **to have** *o* **get the w. number** TEL. equivocarse de número • **what is w. with . . . ?** *(doing something)* ¿qué tiene de malo . . . ?; *(a person)* ¿qué le pasa a . . . ? • **w. move** FIG. paso en falso II. adv. *(immorally)* mal <*to behave w.* conducirse mal>; *(unfairly)* mal, injustamente; *(incorrectly)* mal <*he told it w.* lo contó mal> ◆ **to do someone w.** *(to be unjust to)* ser injusto con; FAM. *(to be unfaithful to)* serle infiel a • **to do w.** hacer mal • **to get w.** *(an answer)* tener mal; *(a statement, person)* no entender bien • **to go w.** *(morally)* ir por mal camino, descarriarse; *(to act mistakenly)* equivocarse, fallar <*where did we go w?* ¿en qué fallamos?>; *(to go amiss)* salir mal • **to have it all w.** *(in doing)* haberlo hecho todo mal; *(in understanding)* estar totalmente equivocado • **you can't go w.** FAM. no hay forma de equivocarse III. s. *(evil)* mal *m* <*to tell right from w.* distinguir entre el bien y el mal>; *(unjust act)* injusticia; *(bad deed)* mala acción, maldad *f*; *(fault)* error *m*; DER. agravio indemnizable ◆ **to be in the w.** no tener razón • **to right a w.** deshacer un entuerto IV. tr. *(to treat unjustly)* ser injusto con; *(to treat dishonorably)* agraviar, injuriar <*to w. the nation* injuriar al país>; *(to malign)* calumniar, afrentar.

wrong·do·er (rông´dōō´ər) s. delincuente *mf*, maleante *mf*.

wrong·do·ing (rông´dōō´ĭng) s. *(wrong)* mal *m*; DER. delito.

wrong·ful (rông´fəl) adj. *(unjust)* injusto; *(unlawful)* ilegal.

wrong·ful·ly (rông´fə-lē) adv. *(unjustly)* injustamente; *(unlawfully)* ilegalmente.

wrong·ful·ness (rông´fəl-nĭs) s. *(injustice)* injusticia; *(illegality)* ilegalidad *f*.

wrong·head·ed (rông´hĕd´ĭd) adj. obstinado.

wrong·ly (rông´lē) adv. *(unjustly)* injustamente; *(incorrectly)* erróneamente.

wrote (rōt) pret. de **write**.

wroth (rôth) adj. *(wrathful)* furioso; *(angry)* airado.

wrought (rôt) I. un pret. y part. p. de **work** II. adj. *(put together)* armado <*carefully w.* cuidadosamente armado>; *(shaped)* formado, forjado; *(elaborately made)* labrado ◆ **w. up** agitado.

wrought iron s. hierro forjado.

wrung (rŭng) pret. y part. p. de **wring**.

wry (rī) adj. **wri·er, wri·est** *o* **wry·er, wry·est** *(crooked)* torcido <*w. neck* cuello torcido>; *(twisted)* forzado <*a w. smile* una sonrisa forzada>; *(ironical)* irónico; *(not quite right)* en desajuste con lo correcto ◆ **to make a w. face** poner mala cara.

wurst (wûrst, wōōrst) s. salchicha, embutido.

wy·vern (wī´vərn) s. HER. dragón alado.

X

x, X (ĕks) s. [pl. **x's, X's**] vigésima cuarta letra del alfabeto inglés; MAT. incógnita ♦ **an x amount of money** una cantidad equis de dinero • **to x out** tachar.
xan·than gum (zăn'thən) s. QUÍM. goma xantánica.
xan·thate (zăn'thāt') s. QUÍM. xantato.
xan·thene (zăn'thēn') s. QUÍM. xanteno.
xan·thic acid (zăn'thĭk) adj. QUÍM. xántico; *(yellowish)* amarillento.
xan·thine (zăn'thēn') s. BIOQUÍM. xantina.
xan·thous (zăn'thəs) adj. *(yellow)* amarillo; MED. xantodermo, xantoso.
x-ax·is (ĕks'ăk'sĭs) s. [pl. **x-ax·es** (ĕks'ăk'sēz)] MAT. abscisa, eje horizontal *m.*
X-chro·mo·some (ĕks'krō'mə-sōm') s. BIOL. cromosoma X.
xe·bec (zē'bĕk') s. MARÍT. jabeque *m.*
xen·o·cur·ren·cy (zĕn'ō-kûr'ən-sē, zē'nō-) s. FIN. moneda de un país que circula en el exterior.
xen·o·gen·e·sis (zĕn'ə-jĕn'ĭ-sĭs, zē'nə-) s. BIOL. xenogénesis *f*, xenogenia.
xe·non (zē'nŏn') s. QUÍM. xenón *m.*
xen·o·phile (zĕn'ə-fīl') s. xenófilo (amigo de lo extranjero).
xen·o·phil·i·a (zĕn'ə-fīl'ē-ə) s. afición a lo extranjero *f.*
xen·o·phobe (zĕn'ə-fōb', zē'nə-) s. xenófobo.
xen·o·pho·bi·a (zĕn'ə-fō'bē-ə, zē'nə-) s. xenofobia.
xen·o·pho·bic (zĕn'ə-fō'bĭk, zē'nə) adj. xenófobo.
xe·ric (zĕr'ĭk, zîr'-) adj. BOT. xerofítico.
xe·ro·graph·ic (zîr'ə-grăf'ĭk) adj. xerográfico, de xerografía.
xe·rog·ra·phy (zĭ-rŏg'rə-fē) s. xerografía.
xe·roph·i·lous (zĭ-rŏf'ə-ləs) adj. BOT. xerófilo.
xe·ro·phyte (zîr'ə-fīt') s. BOT. xerofita.
xe·ro·sis (zĭ-rō'sĭs) s. MED. xerosis *f.*
Xe·rox (zîr'ŏks') I. s. *(process)* marca registrada de un proceso rápido de reproducción; *(copy)* xerocopia, xerografía II. tr. xerografiar, hacer una copia de.
xi (zī, sī) xi (letra griega) *f.*
xiph·oid (zĭf'oid') ANAT. I. adj. xifoideo II. s. xifoides *m.*
X·mas (krĭs'məs, ĕks'məs) s. FAM. Navidad *f*, Navidades *f.*
x-ra·di·a·tion (ĕks'rā'dē-ā'shən) s. MED. tratamiento con rayos X, radioterapia; FÍS. radiación de rayos X *f.*
X-rat·ed (ĕks'rā'tĭd) adj. CINEM. no apto para menores de 16 años.
x-ray, X-ray o **x ray, X ray** (ĕks'rā') I. s. *(image)* radiografía; FÍS. rayo X ♦ **x-rays** MED. rayos X II. tr. *(to examine)* examinar con rayos X; *(to radiograph)* radiografiar.
x-ray tube s. tubo de rayos X.
xy·lem (zī'ləm) s. BOT. xilema.
xy·lene (zī'lēn') s. QUÍM. xileno, dimetilbenceno.
xy·lo·graph (zī'lə-grăf') s. xilografía.
xy·log·ra·phy (zī-lŏg'rə-fē) s. *(engraving)* grabado en madera; *(process)* xilografía.
xy·loid (zī'loid') adj. xiloide, de madera.
xy·lo·phone (zī'lə-fōn') s. MÚS. xilófono, xilofón *m.*
xys·ter (zĭs'tər) s. CIR. xister *m*, legra.

Y

y, Y (wī) s. [pl. **y's, Y's**] vigésima quinta letra del alfabeto inglés.
yacht (yät) I. s. yate *m* II. intr. *(to sail)* andar en yate; *(to race)* participar en una regata.
yacht club s. club náutico.
yacht·ing (yä'tĭng) s. navegación (en yate) *f.*
yachts·man (yäts'mən) s. [pl. **-men**] navegante *m.*
yack (yăk) v. var. de **yak²**.
ya·hoo (yä'hōō, yä'-) s. [pl. **-hoos**] FAM. bruto, bestia.
yak¹ (yăk) s. ZOOL. yac *m.*
yak² (yăk) JER. I. intr. **yakked, yak·king** parlotear, cotorrear II. s. cotorreo, charla.
y'all (yôl) pron. var. de **you-all**.

yam (yăm) s. *(root)* ñame *f*; *(sweet potato)* batata.
yam·mer (yăm'ər) I. intr. *(to whimper)* lloriquear; *(to whine)* plañir; *(to talk)* parlotear II. s. *(whimper)* lloriqueo; *(talk)* parloteo.
yang o **Yang** (yăng) s. FILOS. yang (principio masculino) *m.*
yank (yăngk) I. tr. & intr. tironear (de), dar un tirón (a) II. s. tirón *m.*
Yank (yăngk) s. FAM. yanqui *mf.*
Yan·kee (yăng'kē) s. yanqui *mf.*
Yan·kee·ism (yăng'kē-ĭz'əm) s. yanquismo.
yap (yăp) I. intr. **yapped, yap·ping** *(to yelp)* gañir; *(to bark)* ladrar; JER. *(to jabber)* cotorrear; *(to scold)* retar II. s. *(yelp)* gañido; *(bark)* ladrido; JER. *(jabber)* cotorreo, cháchara; *(person)* patán *m*; *(mouth)* boca, hocico.
yard¹ (yärd) s. *(measure)* yarda; MARÍT. verga.
yard² (yärd) I. s. *(enclosed grounds)* patio; *(surrounding grounds)* jardín *m*; *(work area)* depósito, taller *m*; *(winter pasture)* apacentadero; *(corral)* corral; F.C. estación de depósito *f* II. tr. meter en el corral.
yard·age¹ (yär'dĭj) s. *(measurement)* medida en yardas; *(cloth)* tela.
yard·age² (yär'dĭj) s. *(cattle enclosure)* encierro, acorralamiento de ganado junto a una estación de ferrocarril; *(fee)* tarifa, costo de encierro.
yard·arm (yärd'ärm') s. MARÍT. penol *m.*
yard goods s.pl. tela vendida por yardas, géneros.
yard·mas·ter (yärd'măs'tər) s. jefe de estación de depósito *m.*
yard·stick (yärd'stĭk') s. *(measuring stick)* vara de una yarda de largo; FIG. *(standard)* patrón *m*, norma.
yar·mul·ke o **yar·mel·ke** (yär'məl-kə) s. casquete que usan en la cabeza los judíos *m.*
yarn (yärn) I. s. *(thread)* hilo; FAM. *(story)* cuento, historia II. intr. contar cuentos o historias.
yar·row (yăr'ō) s. BOT. milenrama.
yaup (yôp) v. & s. var. de **yawp**.
yaw (yô) I. intr. *(a ship)* guiñar; AER. desviarse II. s. *(act)* guiñada; *(deviation)* desvío.
yawl (yôl) s. *(sailing vessel)* yola; *(boat)* bote a remos *m.*
yawn (yôn) I. intr. *(to open the mouth)* bostezar; *(to gape)* abrirse (un agujero, caverna) —tr. decir bostezando II. s. bostezo.
yawn·ing (yô'nĭng) adj. *(gaping)* abierto (agujero, precipicio); *(cavernous)* cavernoso.
yawp (yôp) I. intr. *(to cry)* gritar; *(to yelp)* gañir; JER. *(to talk)* parlotear II. s. *(bark)* ladrido; *(yelp)* gañido; *(talk)* parloteo.
yaws (yôz) s. [ú. con v. sing. o pl.] MED. frambesia, pián *m.*
y-ax·is (wī'ăk'sĭs) s. [pl. **y-ax·es** (wī'ăk'sēz)] MAT. ordenada, eje vertical *m.*
y-chro·mo·some (wī'krō'mə-sōm') s. BIOL. cromosoma Y.
ye¹ (thē) art. def. ANT. el, la <**ye** *tavern* la taberna>.
ye² (yē) pron. pers. ANT. vosotros, ustedes.
yea (yā) I. adv. *(yes)* sí; *(indeed)* incluso, aún <*they have spoken, y., shouted their reply* han dicho, aún gritado, su respuesta> II. s. *(affirmative statement)* sí *m*; *(person)* persona que vota a favor.
yeah (yĕ'ə, yă'ə) adv. FAM. sí.
year (yîr) s. año <*last y.* el año pasado> ♦ **a y.** por año, anualmente • **all y. round** durante todo el año • **by the y.** por año • **every y.** cada año • **every other y.** cada dos años • **financial y.** año económico • **from y. to y.** año tras año, cada año • **in the y. of our Lord** en el año del Señor • **in years to come** en los años venideros • **leap y.** año bisiesto • **New Y.** Año Nuevo • **once a y.** una vez al año • **school y.** año escolar • **to be thirty years old** tener treinta años • **y. by y.** año tras año, cada año • **y. in, y. out** año tras año • **years** *(age)* edad <*she feels her years* ya siente su edad>; *(long period)* mucho tiempo, una eternidad <*I waited years* he esperado una eternidad>.
year·book (yîr'bŏŏk') s. anuario (de información, estudiantil).
year-end o **year·end** (yîr'ĕnd') I. s. COM., FIN. fin de año fiscal II. adj. de fin de año.
year·ling (yîr'lĭng) I. s. animal de un año de edad *m* II. adj. anual, añal.

---

year·long (yîr'lông') adj. de un año de duración, que dura un año.

year·ly (yîr'lē) I. adj. anual II. adv. anualmente III. s. [pl. **-lies**] anuario (revista, libro).

yearn (yûrn) intr. *(to desire)* desear; *(to long)* añorar, anhelar; *(to feel compassion)* sentir compasión o ternura ♦ **to y. for** añorar, anhelar.

yearn·ing (yûr'nĭng) I. s. anhelo, añoranza II. adj. *(longing)* anheloso; *(tender)* tierno.

year-round (yîr'round') adj. *(establishment)* abierto durante todo el año; *(sports, activities)* que se practica durante todo el año; *(clothes)* de todo tiempo.

yeast (yēst) I. s. *(leaven)* levadura, fermento; *(froth)* espuma; FIG. *(ferment)* fermento, germen *m* II. intr. *(to ferment)* fermentar; *(to froth)* espumar.

yeast·y (yē'stē) adj. **-i-er**, **-i-est** *(of yeast)* de levadura; *(frothy)* espumoso; FIG. *(unsettled)* turbulento, inquieto; *(frivolous)* frívolo.

yeh (yĕ'ə, yä'ə) adv. var. de **yeah.**

yell (yĕl) I. tr. & intr. gritar ♦ **to y. for help** pedir auxilio a gritos II. s. grito.

yel·low (yĕl'ō) I. s. *(color)* amarillo; *(yolk)* yema ♦ **yellows** ictericia II. adj. *(color)* amarillo; *(hair)* rubio; JER. *(cowardly)* cobarde ♦ **to go** o **turn y.** amarillear, ponerse amarillo III. tr. & intr. volver(se) amarillo, amarillear(se).

yel·low-bel·lied (yĕl'ō-bĕl'ēd) adj. *(said of birds)* de panza amarilla; FIG., JER. *(cowardly)* cobarde.

yellow fever s. MED. fiebre amarilla.

yel·low·ish (yĕl'ō-ĭsh) adj. amarillento.

yellow jack s. *(fever)* fiebre amarilla *f*; MARÍT. bandera amarilla; ICT. jurel *m*.

yellow jacket s. avispa.

yellow journalism s. periodismo sensacionalista, exagerado y distorsionado.

yel·low·y (yĕl'ō-ē) adj. amarillento.

yelp (yĕlp) I. intr. *(to yap)* gañir; *(to yell)* gritar II. s. gañido.

Yem·en (yĕm'ən) s. Yemen *m*.

Yem·e·ni (yĕm'ə-nē) adj. & s. yemení *m*.

Yem·en·ite (yĕm'ə-nīt') adj. & s. yemenita *mf*.

yen¹ (yĕn) I. intr. **yenned, yen·ning** desear, anhelar II. s. deseo, anhelo ♦ **to have a y. for** desear • **to have a y. to** tener ganas de.

yen² (yĕn) s. [pl. **yen**] FIN. yen (unidad monetaria japonesa) *m*.

yen·ta (yĕn'tə) s. mujer entrometida.

yeo·man (yō'mən) I. s. [pl. **-men**] *(assistant)* ayudante *mf*; *(diligent worker)* trabajador eficaz *m*; MARÍT. oficial oficinista *m*; G.B. *(landholder)* pequeño terrateniente; *(guard)* alabardero, soldado; *(attendant)* criado II. adj. *(of yeoman rank)* de rango de guardia real; *(workmanlike)* sólido, de buena categoría.

yeo·man·ry (yō'mən-rē) s. *(farmers)* terratenientes pequeños; G.B. *(volunteer cavalry)* cuerpo de caballería voluntaria.

yep (yĕp) adv. FAM. sí.

yes (yĕs) I. adv. sí <*y. or no?* ¿sí o no?> ♦ **to say y.** dar el sí, asentir a casarse • **y.?** *(hello?)* ¿sí?; *(come in!)* ¡adelante!; *(expressing surprise)* ¿sí?, ¿ah, sí?; *(expressing doubt)* ¿de veras?, ¿es cierto esto? • **y. indeed** sí, por cierto, claro que sí • **y. of course!** ¡claro que sí!, ¡por supuesto! II. s. [pl. **yes·es**] sí *m* III. tr. **yessed, yes·sing** asentir.

yes man s. FAM. subordinado servil.

yes·ter·day (yĕs'tər-dā') I. adv. ayer <*y. morning* ayer por la mañana> ♦ **I wasn't born y.** FIG. no he nacido ayer, no soy tan ingenuo • **late y.** ayer a última hora II. s. (el día de) ayer *m* ♦ **the day before y.** anteayer, antes de ayer • **yesterdays** pasado, antaño <*all our yesterdays* todo nuestro pasado>.

yes·ter·year (yĕs'tər-yîr') s. *(last year)* el año pasado; *(yore)* antaño.

yet §G41 (yĕt) I. adv. *(at this time)* todavía, aún <*don't speak y.* no hables aún>; *(thus far)* ya <*has the doctor arrived y.?* ¿llegó ya el doctor?>; *(still)* todavía, aún <*there is y. a solution to be found* todavía se puede encon-

trar una solución>; *(in addition)* todavía <*I have y. to visit the cathedral* todavía tengo que visitar la catedral>; *(still more)* aún más <*a y. sadder story* una historia aún más triste>; *(eventually)* eventualmente, probablemente <*he may y. see the truth* probablemente entienda la verdad> ♦ **as (of) y.** hasta ahora <*no one has as y. been here* nadie ha estado aquí hasta ahora> • **y. again** otra vez, una vez más • **y. more** aún más II. conj. *(nevertheless)* sin embargo, no obstante <*and y. she loves him* y sin embargo lo quiere>; *(but)* pero <*he's young y. wise* es joven pero sensato>.

ye·ti (yĕt'ē) s. el abominable hombre de las nieves.

yew (yōō) s. BOT. tejo.

yid (yĭd) s. DESPEC. judío.

Yid·dish (yĭd'ĭsh) s. yiddish *m*.

yield (yēld) I. tr. *(field, crop)* dar, producir; *(investment, profit)* rendir, proporcionar <*an investment that yields six per cent* una inversión que rinde el seis por ciento>; *(to give up)* ceder, renunciar <*they yielded the field to the enemy* han cedido el campo al enemigo>; *(town)* entregar; *(to concede)* conceder, dar ♦ **to y. to** ceder o consentir a, dar preferencia a <*to y. to temptation* ceder a la tentación> • **to y. up** *(to give up)* rendir, entregar <*to y. up the ghost* entregar el alma>; *(secret)* descubrir, revelar —intr. *(to be productive)* ser productivo, producir; *(to submit)* rendirse, someterse <*we'll never y.* no nos rendiremos nunca>; *(to give way)* ceder; *(in traffic)* ceder el paso II. s. INDUS. producción *m*, rendimiento; AGR. cosecha; COM., FIN. *(profit)* beneficio; *(interest)* interés *m*.

yield·ing (yēl'dĭng) adj. *(flexible)* flexible; *(docile)* dócil.

yin (yĭn) s. FILOS. yin (principio femenino) *m*.

yip (yĭp) I. s. *(bark)* ladrido agudo; *(yelp)* gañido II. intr. **yipped, yip·ping** *(to bark)* ladrar; *(to yelp)* gañir.

yip·pee (yĭp'ē) interj. ¡hurra!, ¡yupi!, ¡huija!

yo·del (yōd'l) I. tr. & intr. cantar a la tirolesa II. s. canto tirolés.

yo·ga (yō'gə) s. yoga *m*.

yo·ghurt o **yo·ghourt** (yō'gərt) s. var. de **yogurt.**

yo·gi (yō'gē) s. [pl. **-gis**] yoghi, yogui *m*.

yo·gurt (yō'gərt) s. yogur *m*, yogurt *m*.

yoke (yōk) I. s. *(for oxen)* yugo; *(pair of oxen)* yunta; *(carried by a person)* balancín *m*, percha; *(on a ship)* barra; *(clamp)* brida, horquilla; *(of a garment)* canesú *m*; *(subjugation)* yugo, opresión *f* <*under the y. of the Nazis* bajo el yugo de los nazis>; ELECTRÓN. culata ♦ **to throw off the y.** FIG. sacudir el yugo, liberarse II. tr. & intr. **yoked, yok·ing** *(to join)* uncir, atar; FIG. *(to bind)* unir; *(to oppress)* oprimir.

yo·kel (yō'kəl) s. paleto, patán *m*.

yolk (yōk) s. yema.

yolk sac s. ZOOL. membrana o saco vitelino.

yon (yŏn) adj. & adv. var. de **yonder.**

yon·der (yŏn'dər) I. adj. aquel, ese <*y. tree* el árbol aquel> II. adv. allí, allá <*walk y.* camina allá> III. pron. aquél, ése.

yoo-hoo (yōō'hōō) interj. ¡eh!, ¡hola!

yore (yôr) s. antaño.

York·shire pudding (yôrk'shər) s. masa de harina, huevos y mantequilla que se hornea en la salsa natural de la carne asada.

you §G6, 29 (yōō) pron. pers. [familiar, singular] tú <*how are y.?* ¿cómo estás tú?>; [formal, singular] usted <*how are you?* ¿cómo está usted?>; [familiar, plural] vosotros <*how are you?* ¿cómo estáis vosotros?>; [formal, plural] ustedes <*how are you?* ¿cómo están ustedes?>; [direct or indirect object, singular] te <*I told y.* te lo dije> <*I handed it to y.* te lo di>; [indirect object, singular and plural] se <*I handed it to y.* se lo di>; [direct or indirect object, plural] os, a vosotros, a ustedes <*I'm giving it to y. straight* os lo digo sin rodeos, se lo digo a ustedes sin rodeos>; [after a preposition, informal, singular] ti <*this is for y.* esto es para ti>; [after a preposition, formal, singular] usted <*this is for y.* esto es para usted>; [after a preposition, plural] ustedes, vosotros <*this is for y.* esto es para ustedes>; [direct object] os, la, lo, los, las <*I saw y., sir* lo vi, señor> [indirect object] le, les <*I told y. all I know* les dije todo lo que sé>

ă rey / ä año / b boca / ch chico / d dar / ĕ el / ē mil / g gato / h joya / hw juez / ī aire / k casa / kw cuan /

♦ **all of** y. todos vosotros, todas vosotras, todos ustedes • **between y. and me** entre tú y yo, entre nosotros • **if I were y.** yo que tú, yo en tu lugar • **with y.** contigo, con usted, con ustedes, con vosotros, con vosotras • **y. can't do that** eso no se debe hacer, eso no se permite • **y. never know** uno nunca sabe.

you-all (yōō-ôl′) pron. FAM. ustedes, vosotros.

you'd (yōōd) contr. de **you had** o **you would.**

you'll (yōōl, yŏol) contr. de **you will** o **you shall.**

young (yŭng) I. adj. **-er, -est** *(not old)* joven; *(pertaining to early life)* de juventud <*a y. love* un amor de juventud>; *(newly begun)* joven, nuevo <*the evening is still y.* la noche es joven todavía> ♦ **in my younger days** en mi juventud • **my y. man** o **woman** mi novio o mi novia • **the y. people** la gente joven, la juventud • **to look younger** parecer más joven • **y. lady** señorita • **y. man** joven • **y. woman** joven II. s. *(youth)* juventud *f; (the young people)* gente joven *f,* jóvenes *mf; (offspring)* cría (de animal) ♦ **with y.** preñada.

young·ish (yŭng′ĭsh) adj. bastante joven, más bien joven.

young·ling (yŭng′lĭng) s. *(person)* joven *mf; (animal)* cría.

young·ster (yŭng′stər) s. *(child)* niño; *(youth)* jovencito, joven *mf.*

Young Turk s. POL. rebelde *mf.*

your §G23 (yōor, yər) adj. pos. [familiar, singular] tu, tus <*y. house* tu casa>; [formal, singular] su, sus, de usted <*y. eyes* sus ojos>; [familiar, plural] vuestro, vuestra, vuestros, vuestras <*y. school* vuestra escuela>; [formal, plural] sus, de ustedes <*y. contributions have not been received* sus contribuciones no han sido recibidas> ♦ **Y. Majesty** Majestad.

you're (yōor, yər) contr. de **you are.**

yours §G32 (yōorz) pron. pers. [familiar, singular] (el) tuyo, (la) tuya <*this scarf is y.* esta bufanda es la tuya>; [formal, singular] (el) de usted, (la) de usted, el suyo <*these books are y.* estos libros son de ustedes>; [familiar, plural] (el) vuestro, (la) vuestra <*these are our toys and those are y.* estos son nuestros juguetes y aquéllos son los vuestros>; [formal, plural] (el) de usted, (la) de usted, (el) suyo, (la) suya <*these gloves are y., madam* estos guantes son suyos, señora>.

your·self §G37 (yōor-sĕlf′, yər-) I. pron. pers. [familiar] tú (mismo), tú (misma) <*write it down y.* escríbelo tú mismo>; [formal] usted (mismo), usted (misma) <*you said it y.* usted mismo lo dijo> II. pron. reflex. [familiar] te <*please, don't hurt y.* por favor, no te hagas daño>; [formal] se <*dry y. before you come out of the shower* séquese antes de salir de la ducha>.

your·selves §G37 (yōor-sĕlvz′, yər-) I. pron. pers. [familiar] vosotros (mismos), vosotras (mismas) <*you y. wanted it* vosotros mismos lo quisisteis>; [formal] ustedes (mismos), ustedes (mismas) <*you did it to y.* se lo buscaron ustedes mismos> II. pron. reflex. [familiar] os <*have you dressed y. yet?* ¿os habéis vestido ya?>; [formal] se <*give y. plenty of time* dense suficiente tiempo>.

youth (yōōth) s. [pl. **youths** (yōōths, yōōthz)] *(condition, epoch)* juventud *f; (young people)* juventud; *(young person)* joven *mf.*

youth·ful (yōōth′fəl) adj. *(young)* joven, juvenil; *(of youth)* juvenil; *(new)* nuevo.

youth hostel s. albergue para jóvenes *m.*

you've (yōōv) contr. de **you have.**

yowl (youl) I. intr. dar aullidos, aullar II. s. aullido.

yo-yo (yō′yō′) I. s. [pl. **-yos**] *(toy)* yoyó; FAM. *(vacillator)* persona que vacila; JER. *(dope)* tonto, patán *m* II. intr. **-yoed, -yo·ing** vacilar.

yt·ter·bi·um (ĭ-tûr′bē-əm) s. QUÍM. iterbio.

yt·tri·um (ĭt′rē-əm) s. QUÍM. itrio.

yuc·ca (yŭk′ə) s. yuca.

Yu·go·slav (yōō′gō-släv′) o **Yu·go·sla·vi·an** (yōō′gō-slä′vē-ən) adj. & s. yugoslavo, yugoeslavo.

Yu·go·sla·vi·a (yōō′gō-slä′vē-ə) s. Yugoslavia.

Yule (yōōl) s. Navidad *f.*

yule log s. tronco que se quema durante la Navidad.

Yule·tide (yōōl′tīd′) s. Navidad *f,* Navidades *f.*

yum·my (yŭm′ē) adj. **-mi·er, -mi·est** FAM. delicioso, rico.

Z

z, Z (zē) s. [pl. **z's, Z's**] vigésima sexta letra del alfabeto inglés.

zaf·fer o **zaf·fre** (zăf′ər) s. MIN. zafre *m,* safre *m.*

Zaire (zīr, zä-îr′) s. Zaire *m.*

Zair·i·an (zī′rē-ən, zä-îr′ē-ən) adj. & s. zairense *mf.*

Zam·be·zi (zăm-bē′zē) s. Zambeze.

Zam·bi·a (zăm′bē-ə) s. Zambia.

Zam·bi·an (zăm′bē-ən) adj. & s. zambiano.

za·ny (zā′nē) I. s. [pl. **-nies**] *(outlandish person)* persona cómica y estrafalaria; TEAT. bufón *m* II. adj. **-ni·er, -ni·est** *(comical)* cómico, estrafalario; *(clownish)* bufo; *(bizarre)* grotesco.

zap (zăp) JER. I. tr. **zapped, zap·ping** *(to kill)* matar; *(to destroy)* destruir; *(to defeat)* vencer, derrotar; *(to jolt)* impresionar, sobresaltar —intr. ir como una bala II. s. vigor *m,* brío III. interj. ¡zas!

zeal (zēl) s. celo, ahínco, fervor *m.*

zeal·ot (zĕl′ət) s. HIST., RELIG. zelote *m* ♦ **z.** fanático.

zeal·ot·ry (zĕl′ə-trē) s. celo excesivo, fanatismo.

zeal·ous (zĕl′əs) adj. celoso, fervoroso.

ze·bra (zē′brə) s. cebra.

ze·bu (zē′bōō, -byōō) s. cebú *m.*

Zech·a·ri·ah (zĕk′ə-rī′ə) s. BÍBL. Zacarías.

zed (zĕd) s. G.B. zeta, zeda.

ze·in (zē′ĭn) s. BIOQUÍM. zeína, ceína.

Zeit·geist (tsīt′gīst′) s. gustos y perspectiva de una época.

Zen Buddhism (zĕn) s. FILOS., RELIG. Budismo Zen.

ze·nith (zē′nĭth) s. *(region)* región cenital *f;* FIG. *(peak)* cenit *m,* apogeo; ASTRON. cenit.

ze·o·lite (zē′ə-līt′) s. MIN. zeolita, ceolita.

zeph·yr (zĕf′ər) s. *(west wind)* céfiro; *(breeze)* brisa; TEJ. céfiro.

zep·pe·lin (zĕp′ə-lĭn) s. AER. zepelín *m,* dirigible *m.*

ze·ro (zîr′ō) I. s. [pl. **-ros** o **-roes**] *(cipher)* cero; *(nothing)* nada <*today we accomplished z.* hoy no hemos hecho nada>; FÍS., METEOR. cero grado; MIL. mira de un arma; JER. *(person)* cero (a la izquierda) II. adj. nulo <*z. visibility* visibilidad nula> III. tr. **-roed, -ro·ing** poner en el cero ♦ **to z. in on** *(to aim)* afinar la puntería hacia; *(to close in)* apuntar hacia, dirigir la atención hacia.

ze·ro-base (zîr′ō-bās′) o **ze·ro-based** (-bāst′) adj. ECON. que justifica los gastos en términos de necesidad o costo.

zero gravity s. ASTRONÁUT., FÍS. gravedad cero *f,* gravedad nula.

zero hour s. hora cero.

zest (zĕst) I. s. *(flavor)* gusto, sabor *m; (enjoyment)* brío; *(rind)* cáscara II. tr. dar bríos a (reunión, fiesta).

zest·ful (zĕst′fəl) adj. *(tasty)* sabroso; *(spirited)* animado, lleno de vida.

ze·ta (zā′tə, zē′-) s. zeta, sexta letra del alfabeto griego.

Zeus (zōōs) s. MITOL. Zeus.

zib·e·line o **zib·el·line** (zĭb′ə-lēn′, -lĭn′) s. *(fabric)* cebellina; *(sable)* marta cebellina (animal y piel).

zig·gu·rat (zĭg′ə-răt′) s. ARQ., HIST. zigurat (pirámide) *m.*

zig·zag (zĭg′zăg′) I. s. zigzag *m* II. adj. zigzagueante, en zigzag III. adv. ♦ **to go z.** ir zigzagueando IV. intr. **-zagged, -zag·ging** ir zigzagueando —tr. poner en zigzag.

zilch (zĭlch) s. JER. *(nothing)* nada, cero; *(person)* don nadie *m,* nulidad *f.*

zil·lion (zĭl′yən) s. FAM. número astronómico.

Zim·ba·bwe (zĭm-bäb′wē, -wä) s. Zimbabwe.

Zim·bab·we·an (zĭm-bäb′wē-ən) adj. & s. simbabwense *mf.*

zinc (zĭngk) s. QUÍM. cinc *m,* zinc *m.*

zinc·og·ra·phy (zĭng-kŏg′rə-fē) s. IMPR. cincografía.

zinc ointment s. ungüento de cinc.

zinc oxide s. QUÍM. óxido de cinc.

zin·fan·del o **Zin·fan·del** (zĭn′fən-dĕl′) s. vino tinto de California.

zing (zĭng) I. s. zumbido II. intr. FAM. zumbar.

zing·er (zĭng′ər) s. FAM. *(remark)* observación mordaz *f; (surprise)* sorpresa; *(revelation)* revelación *f.*

zin·ni·a (zĭn′ē-ə) s. BOT. cinnia.

Zi·on (zī′ən) s. *(Israel)* Israel *m*; *(Jewish homeland)* Sión *m*.
Zi·on·ism (zī′ə-nĭz′əm) s. RELIG. sionismo.
Zi·on·ist (zī′ə-nĭst) s. sionista *mf*.
zip (zĭp) **I.** s. *(sound)* silbido; *(energy)* energía, vigor *m* **II.** intr. **zipped, zip·ping** zumbar ♦ **to z. by** ir *o* pasar como una bala —tr. dar vigor ♦ **to z. shut** cerrar con cremallera, cerrar la cremallera de • **to z. up** subir *o* cerrar la cremallera de.
Zip Code *o* **zip code** s. código postal.
zip·per (zĭp′ər) s. cierre relámpago *m*, cremallera.
zip·py (zĭp′ē) adj. **-pi·er, -pi·est** *(lively)* vivaz, enérgico; *(fast)* rápido, veloz.
zir·con (zûr′kŏn′) s. MIN. zircón *m*, circón *m*.
zir·co·ni·um (zûr-kō′nē-əm) s. QUÍM. circonio.
zirconium oxide s. MIN., QUÍM. óxido de ziroconio, zirconia.
zith·er (zĭth′ər, zĭth′-) s. MÚS. cítara.
zo·di·ac (zō′dē-ăk′) s. ASTRON. zodíaco.
zoi·site (zoi′sīt′) s. MIN. zoisita, tulita.
zom·bie *o* **zom·bi** (zŏm′bē) s. *(snake god)* dios serpiente (en el vudú) *m*; *(corpse)* cadáver resucitado por magia vudú; FIG. *(automaton)* autómata *m*.
zo·nal (zō′nəl) adj. zonal, en zonas.
zone (zōn) **I.** s. zona **II.** tr. **zoned, zon·ing** dividir en zonas.
zone·time (zōn′tīm′) s. MARÍT. hora *o* horario zonal.
zon·ing (zō′nĭng) s. restricciones para edificar en un barrio de una ciudad *f*.
zonked (zŏngkt) adj. JER. *(drunk)* mamado, borracho; *(drugged)* intoxicado.
zoo (zōō) s. [pl. **zoos**] *(park)* zoo, jardín zoológico *m*; FIG. *(disorder)* confusión *f*, desorden *m*.
zo·o·ge·og·ra·phy (zō′ə-jē-ŏg′rə-fē) s. zoogeografía.
zo·og·ra·phy (zō-ŏg′rə-fē) s. zoografía.
zo·oid (zō′oid′) s. BIOL., ZOOL. zooide *m*.
zo·o·log·i·cal (zō′ə-lŏj′ĭ-kəl) *o* **zo·o·log·ic** (-lŏj′ĭk) adj. zoológico.
zoological garden s. jardín zoológico, parque zoológico.

zo·ol·o·gist (zō-ŏl′ə-jĭst) s. zoólogo.
zo·ol·o·gy (zō-ŏl′ə-jē) s. zoología.
zoom (zōōm) **I.** intr. *(to buzz)* zumbar; AVIA. subir verticalmente; FOTOG. *(in)* acercarse; *(out)* alejarse ♦ **to z. away** salir zumbando —tr. AVIA. hacer subir verticalmente **II.** s. *(sound)* zumbido; AVIA. subida vertical.
zoom lens s. objetivo de distancia focal regulable, objetivo "zoom."
zo·o·phile (zō′ə-fīl′) s. persona que ama a los animales.
zo·o·phyte (zō′ə-fīt′) s. zoófito.
zo·o·plank·ton (zō′ə-plăngk′tən) s. zooplancton *m*.
zo·o·spore (zō′ə-spôr′) s. BOT., ZOOL. zoospora.
zo·o·tech·ny (zō′ə-tĕk′nē) s. zootecnia.
zo·ot·o·my (zō-ŏt′ə-mē) s. zootomía.
zo·ri (zôr′ē) s. [pl. **zori**] sandalia de paja *o* cuero.
Zo·ro·as·tri·an·ism (zôr′ō-ăs′trē-ə-nĭz′əm) s. FILOS., RELIG. zoroastrismo.
zos·ter (zŏs′tər) s. *(belt)* cinturón (en Grecia antigua) *m*; MED. herpe zoster *m*, zona.
Zou·ave (zōō-äv′) s. MIL. zuavo (antiguo soldado argelino).
zounds (zoundz) interj. ANT. ¡cáspita!
zuc·chet·to (zōō-kĕt′ō, tsōō-) s. [pl. **-tos**] solideo.
zuc·chi·ni (zōō-kē′nē) s. [pl. **zucchini**] calabacín *m*, calabacita, zapallito italiano.
Zu·lu (zōō′lōō) s. [pl. **Zulu** *o* **-lus**] zulú *mf*.
zwie·back (swē′băk′, swī′-) s. tostada de pan ligeramente azucarada.
zy·go·ma (zī-gō′mə) s. [pl. **-ma·ta** (-mə-tə) *o* **-mas**] ANAT. zigoma, cigoma *m*.
zy·go·mat·ic (zī′gə-măt′ĭk) adj. zigomático, cigomático.
zygomatic arch s. ANAT. arco cigomático *o* zigomático.
zy·go·spore (zī′gə-spôr′) s. BOT. cigospora, zigospora.
zy·gote (zī′gōt′) s. BIOL. zigoto, cigoto.
zy·mase (zī′mās′) s. BIOQUÍM. zimasa, cimasa.
zy·mol·o·gy (zī-mŏl′ə-jē) s. MED. zimología, cimología.
zy·mo·sis (zī-mō′sĭs) s. zimosis *f*, cimosis (infección) *f*.
zy·mur·gy (zī′mûr′jē) s. QUÍM. zimurgia, cimurgia.
zyz·zy·va (zĭz′ə-və) s. ENTOM. insecto del género zyzyva.

ā rey / ă año / b boca / ch chico / d dar / ĕ el / ē mil / g gato / h joya / hw juez / ī aire / k casa / kw cuan /

RÓTULOS Y ABREVIATURAS

abr.	abreviatura	DEP.	deportes
ACÚS.	acústica	DER.	derecho
adj.	adjetivo	DESPEC.	despectivo
adv.	adverbio	DIAL.	dialecto
AER.	aeronáutica	DIB.	dibujo
AGR.	agricultura	díc.	dícese
ANAT.	anatomía	DIPL.	diplomacia
ANT.	antiguo, arcaico		
ANTROP.	antropología	ECOL.	ecología
apl.	aplícase	ECON.	economía
apr.	aproximadamente	ECON. POL.	economía política
ARM.	armadura, armas	EDUC.	educación
ARQ.	arquitectura	EE. UU.	Estados Unidos
ARQUEOL.	arqueología	ELEC.	electricidad
art.	artículo	ELECTRÓN.	electrónica
ARTE.	bellas artes	ENTOM.	entomología
ASTROL.	astrología	EQUIT.	equitación
ASTRON.	astronomía	ESCULT.	escultura
ASTRONÁUT.	astronáutica	ESGR.	esgrima
AUTO.	automovilismo	esp.	especialmente
aux.	auxiliar	EUFEM.	eufemismo
AVIA.	aviación		
		f.	femenino
BACT.	bacteriología	FAM.	familiar
BÍBL.	bíblico	FARM.	farmacia
BIOL.	biología	F.C.	ferrocarril
BIOQUÍM.	bioquímica	FIG.	figurado
BOT.	botánica	FILAT.	filatelia
		FILOL.	filología
CARP.	carpintería	FILOS.	filosofía
CERÁM.	cerámica	FIN.	finanzas
CIENC. FIC.	ciencia ficción	FÍS.	física
CIENT.	científico	FISIOL.	fisiología
CINEM.	cinematografía	FONÉT.	fonética
CIR.	cirugía	FOR.	forense
COM.	comercio	FORT.	fortificación
comp.	comparativo	FOTOG.	fotografía
COMPUT.	computadoras		
conj.	conjunción	g.	generalmente
CONSTR.	construcción	G.B.	Gran Bretaña
contr.	contracción	GEOF.	geofísica
COST.	costura	GEOG.	geografía
CRIMIN.	criminología	GEOL.	geología
CUL.	culinario	GEOM.	geometría
		ger.	gerundio
def.	definido	GRAM.	gramática
dem.	demostrativo		